The National Hockey League

Official Guide & Record Book

2008

THE NATIONAL HOCKEY LEAGUE
Official Guide & Record Book/2008

TERMS & CONDITIONS FOR USING THE DATA CONTAINED IN THIS BOOK

ATTENTION: PLEASE READ THIS DOCUMENT CAREFULLY BEFORE USING THIS BOOK (THE "BOOK") AND/OR THE DATA IT CONTAINS (THE "DATA"). INDIVIDUALS OR ENTITIES USING THE DATA ("END USERS") AGREE TO BE BOUND BY THE TERMS OF THIS LICENSE. IF YOU DO NOT AGREE TO THE TERMS OF THIS LICENSE, DO NOT USE THE DATA AND PROMPTLY RETURN THE UNUSED BOOK AND PROOF OF PAYMENT TO THE FOLLOWING ADDRESS FOR A REFUND:

Dan Diamond & Associates, Inc.
194 Dovercourt Road, Toronto, Ontario, M6J 3C8
dda.nhl@sympatico.ca.

Dan Diamond & Associates, Inc. (the "Publisher") owns, and retains ownership of, the Data. The Publisher reserves any right not expressly granted to End Users.

1. License. End-Users are granted a limited, non-exclusive license to do only the following, subject to the restrictions set out in Section 2 below:
(a) End-Users may use the Data for personal, non-commercial purposes.
(b) End-Users may reproduce individual player records, tables and data panels in connection with bona fide private study and research.
(c) End-Users who are journalists may reproduce individual player records, tables and data panels for use by the broadcast and print media.
2. Restrictions. End-Users may NOT reproduce the Data, in whole or in part, in any form or by any means, electronic or mechanical, including photocopying, recording, or by any information storage and retrieval system now known or hereafter invented, without written permission from the Publisher. End-Users may NOT sublicense, assign, or distribute (via the World Wide Web or otherwise) copies of the Data, in whole or in part, to others. END-USERS MAY NOT MODIFY, ADAPT, TRANSLATE, RENT, LEASE, LOAN, RESELL FOR PROFIT, DISTRIBUTE, OR OTHERWISE ASSIGN OR TRANSFER THE DATA, OR CREATE DERIVATIVE WORKS BASED UPON THE DATA OR ANY PART THEREOF, EXCEPT AS PROVIDED ABOVE.
3. Commercial Users. Commercial users (such as sports reference and sports gaming websites) may obtain a license to use customized Data upon payment of a reasonable fee. Please contact the Publisher at the address provided above.
4. Termination. This License is effective until terminated. This License will terminate immediately without notice from the Publisher if the End User fails to comply with any of its provisions. Upon termination End Users must destroy the Data and all copies thereof.
5. General. This License will be governed by and construed in accordance with the laws of the province of Ontario and the laws of Canada applicable therein, and shall inure to the benefit of the Publisher and End-Users and their successors, assigns and legal representatives. If any provision of this License is held by a court of competent jurisdiction to be invalid or unenforceable to any extent under applicable law, that provision will be enforced to the maximum extent permissible and the remaining provisions of this License will remain in full force and effect. Any notices or other communications to be sent to the Publishers must be mailed first class, postage prepaid, to the address provided above. This Agreement constitutes the entire agreement between the parties with respect to the subject matter hereof, and all prior proposals, agreements, representations, statements and undertakings are hereby expressly cancelled and superseded. This Agreement may not be changed or amended except by a written instrument executed by a duly authorized officer of the Publisher.
6. Acknowledgment. BY USING THE DATA, THE END-USER ACKNOWLEDGES THAT IT HAS READ THIS LICENSE, UNDERSTANDS IT, AND AGREES TO BE BOUND BY ITS TERMS AND CONDITIONS. Should you have any questions concerning this License, contact the Publisher at the address provided above.

Compiled by the NHL Public Relations Department and the 30 NHL Club Public Relations Directors.

Published in Canada by: Dan Diamond and Associates, Inc., 194 Dovercourt Road, Toronto, Ontario M6J 3C8 Canada
ISBN in Canada 978-1-894801-11-9

Published in the United States by: Triumph Books, 542 South Dearborn Street, Chicago, Illinois 60605
ISBN in USA 978-1-60078-037-0

Staff

For the NHL: Dave McCarthy; Supervising Editor: Greg Inglis; Statistician: Benny Ercolani;
Editorial Staff: David Keon, Dave Baker, Mark Fischel, Jackie Rinaldi, Kelley Rosset, Julie Young.

Senior Managing Editor: Ralph Dinger
Production Editors: John Pasternak, Alex Dubiel
Publisher: Dan Diamond
Associate Managing Editor: Paul Bontje
Assistant Editor: Rachel Carr
Photo Editor: Eric Zweig

Data Management and Typesetting: Caledon Data Management, Eden, Ontario
Film Output and Scanning: Embassy Graphics, Toronto, Ontario
Printing: Sunrise Consulting Inc., Port Perry, Ontario; Webcom Limited, Toronto, Ontario
Production Management: Dan Diamond and Associates, Inc., Toronto, Ontario
Contributors and Photo Credits: see page 655

Distribution

Trade sales and distribution in Canada by:
North 49 Books, 35 Prince Andrew Drive, Toronto, Ontario M3C 2H2 416/449-4000; Fax 416/449-9924
Dan Diamond and Associates, Inc., Toronto 416/531-6535; Fax 416/531-3939 dda.nhl@sympatico.ca www.nhlofficialguide.com

Trade sales and distribution in the United States by:
Triumph Books, 542 South Dearborn Street, Chicago, Illinois 60605 312/939-3330; Fax 312/663-3557

International representatives:
Barkers Worldwide Publications, Unit 6/7 The Elms Centre, Glaziers Lane, Normandy, Guildford, Surrey GU3 2DF England
Tel 011/441/483/811-971; Fax 011/441/483/811-972 sales@bwpu.demon.co.uk www.bwpu.demon.co.uk

The National Hockey League
1185 Avenue of the Americas, New York, New York 10036
1800 McGill College Ave., Suite 2600, Montreal, Quebec H3A 3J6
50 Bay Street, 11th Floor, Toronto, Ontario M5J 2X8

Table of Contents

Table of Contents *continued*

Introduction

WELCOME TO THE 76TH EDITION OF *THE NATIONAL HOCKEY LEAGUE OFFICIAL GUIDE & RECORD BOOK*, the definitive statistical record of the NHL. If it has happened in this League, or if it's about to happen, it's in the Guide, from ten U.S.-born players selected in the first round at the 2007 Entry Draft (page 212) to superb rookies who made their mark in 2006-07 (137), today's superstars (page 136), the League's all-time top scorers (page 176) and inductees to three different Hockey Halls of Fame (231). In fact every one of the almost 6,000 players who have appeared in an NHL game, plus more than 1,000 prospects who have yet to do so, are in this book, either in the regular-season or playoff Record Books (pages 164 and 238), Hall of Fame section, Award Winners (207), All-Star Teams (224), Prospect Register (271), Active Player Register (343), Goaltender Register (581) or Retired Players Index (606). A special tribute to nine players who were honored by having their jersey numbers retired in 2006-07 is found on page 649.

The 2006-07 season was the National Hockey League's second played under modified rules. As in 2005-06, seven players recorded 100-point seasons whereas in 2003-04, the last season before the rules were changed to emphasize skill and speed, no player reached this milestone. (An all-time list of 50-goal and 100-point seasons begins on page 194.) Detailed statistics for 2006-07 begin on page 135.

This was also the second season of the shootout in the NHL, the result of which is that games can no longer end with the score tied. The shootout again proved popular with fans and created some surprising category leaders. Erik Christensen of the Pittsburgh Penguins and Mikko Koivu of the Minnesota Wild led the NHL with eight shootout goals, while the Tampa Bay Lightning had the top winning percentage at .833, winning 10 of 12 games that went into a shootout. Complete team and individual shootout statistics are found on page 143.

In addition, with two years of shootout statistics, we have created a series of single-season and all-time shootout records in the Regular-Season Record Book. Team shootout records are found on page 163. Individual shootout scoring records are on page 167; goaltending shootout records are on page 174.

Eliminating tie games has required some modification in the presentation of team and individual statistics. On the first page of each club's section (e.g. Anaheim Ducks, page 15), the club's previous season's results are listed with separate numbers for overtime losses (OTL) and shootout losses (SOL). In the year-by-year club results on that same page, overtime and shootout losses are combined into one "OL" column that includes all games in which the club earned one point. Because an NHL game can no longer end in with a tie score, the Ties column is left blank ("....") beginning with 2005-06.

In the Goaltender Register (beginning on page 581), the tie game column has been renamed "O/T". Recorded in this column are combined overtime losses and shootout losses beginning with 2005-06. In previous seasons, this column lists tie games. This combined O/T column serves a similar function in coach's data panels that appear in each club's section and in the All-Time Regular-Season NHL Coaching Register that begins on page 186.

A teenaged Sidney Crosby won the Art Ross Trophy and Hart Trophy as the NHL's scoring champion and most valuable player in 2006-07, becoming the youngest winner of a major-league scoring championship in any sport. Despite being in his second full season in the NHL, Crosby was the sixth-youngest player in the NHL last season as a member of a talented and young Penguins team. A new feature on the second page of each club's section in the *NHL Guide* is designed to provide an overview of the age of each club's roster. Birthdates for each player, which are available in each player's panel in the Registers, have been replaced with the player's age on the opening day of the 2007-08 NHL season. Crosby, instead of being listed as "8/7/87," is listed as "20" on page 108.

Also new in each club's section is a listing of key off-season signings and acquisitions. It is found in the top left corner of the first page of each club. (Clubs, listed alphabetically, begin on page 15.)

Two additional tables have been added to coverage of the 2007 Entry Draft on page 214. These break down U.S. and Canadian-born draftees by state or province of birth. Players from 14 states and nine provinces were drafted in 2007. Massachusetts and Minnesota each provided 14 drafted players to lead U.S. states, but three players from California and one from Texas are indicators of the growth of youth hockey programs that have flourished in new NHL markets.

An addition to the list of league abbreviations found on page 654 provides a way to describe some of these youth hockey programs and mirrors the standardization we applied to high school and prep school hockey by using "High-XX" in the League column of player and goaltender panels. Beginning with the 2008 edition of the Guide many youth leagues are now referred to as "Minor-XX." ("XX" refers to the standard two-letter abbreviation for state or province.)

A Free Agent Signing Register has been added to the NHL Guide and is found on page 650 of this edition. It is a companion to the Trade Register which follows on 652. All free agents who either signed with a new club or re-signed with the team that previously held their rights are listed here.

A key to the abbreviations and symbols used in individual player and goaltender data panels, along with useful information on how to use the Registers, is found on page 270. Late additions are found on page 605 and each NHL club's minor-pro affiliates are found on page 14. Referees and linesmen are listed on page 8.

As always, our thanks to readers, correspondents and members of the media who take the time to comment on the *Guide & Record Book*. Thanks as well to the people working in the communications departments of the NHL's member clubs and to their counterparts in minor pro, junior, college and European hockey. Your help has been appreciated since 1932-33!

Best wishes for an enjoyable 2007-08 season.

ACCURACY REMAINS THE *GUIDE & RECORD BOOK*'S TOP PRIORITY.

We appreciate comments and clarification from our readers. Please direct these to:

- Ralph Dinger — Senior Managing Editor, 194 Dovercourt Road, Toronto, Ontario M6J 3C8. e-mail: ralph.dda@sympatico.ca.
- Greg Inglis — 1185 Avenue of the Americas, New York, New York 10036 . . . or . . .
- David Keon — 50 Bay Street, 11th Floor, Toronto, Ontario, M5J 2X8

Your involvement makes a better book.

NATIONAL HOCKEY LEAGUE

New York, 1185 Avenue of the Americas, New York, NY 10036, 212/789-2000, Fax: 212/789-2020, PR Fax: 212/789-2080
Montréal, 1800 McGill College Avenue, Suite 2600, Montréal, Québec, H3A 3J6, 514/841-9220, Fax: 514/841-1070
Toronto, 50 Bay Street, 11th Floor, Toronto, Ontario, M5J 2X8, 416/981-2777, Fax: 416/981-2779
NHL Enterprises, L.P. — 1251 Avenue of the Americas, 47th Floor, New York, NY 10020-1198, 212/789-2000, Fax: 212/789-2020
NHL Enterprises Canada, L.P. — 50 Bay Street, 11th Floor, Toronto, Ontario, M5J 2X8, 416/981-2777, Fax: 416/981-2779
NHL Productions/NHL Images — 240 Pegasus Avenue, Northvale, NJ 07647, 201/750-5800, Fax: 201/750-5850

LEAGUE OPERATIONS

Executive

Commissioner....Gary B. Bettman
Deputy Commissioner....William Daly
Senior Executive Vice President & Director of Hockey Operations....Colin Campbell
Senior Executive Vice President & Chief Financial Officer....Craig Harnett
V.P., Administration, Human Resources & Executive Assistant to the Commissioner....Debbie Jordan

Administration

Vice President, Administration & Human Resources....Debbie Jordan
Vice President, Offices & Facilities....Andrew Crawford
Director, Human Resources....Patrice Distler
Manager, Employee Benefits....Josie Russell

Finance

Senior Executive Vice President & Chief Financial Officer....Craig Harnett
Executive Vice President, Finance....Joseph DeSousa
Group Vice President, Finance....Mary McCarthy
Vice President, Finance -New Media....Frank Dowling
Senior Director of Financial Reporting....Robert Dixon
Director, Finance (Montreal)....Marie-Josee Ashby
Director, Finance....Roberto Pasquini

Hockey Operations

Senior Executive Vice President of Hockey Operations....Colin Campbell
Senior Vice President, Hockey Operations (Toronto)....Jim Gregory
Senior Vice President & Director of Officiating (Toronto)....Stephen Walkom
Senior Vice President, Hockey Operations (Toronto)....Mike Murphy
Vice President & Managing Director, Central Registry (Toronto)....Sean MacLeod
Video Director (Toronto)....Damian Echevarrieta
Director of Alumni Relations (Toronto)....Patrick Flatley
Director, Central Scouting (Toronto)....E.J. McGuire
Director of Systems, Central Registry (Montreal)....Madeleine Supino
Senior Manager, Hockey Operations (Toronto)....Kris King
Senior Manager, Central Registry....Brandon Pridham
Managers, Officiating (Toronto)....Dave Baker, Randy Hall
Facilities Operations Manager....Dan Craig
Office Manager / Senior Assistant....Kelley Rosset
Consultant, Goaltender Equipment....Kay Whitmore

Information Technology

Executive Vice President, Chief Technology Officer....Peter DelGiacco
Senior Director, Network Services....Patrick Powers
Assistant Director (Montreal)....Luc Coulombe
Senior Manager, Technical Support....Dan O'Neill

NHL Legal

Executive Vice President, General Counsel....David Zimmerman
Senior Vice President, Deputy General Counsel....Julie Grand
Associate Counsel....Daniel Ages
Associate Counsel....Jessica Berman

Pension

Vice President and Managing Director, Pension (Montreal)....Yvon Chamberland
Senior Director & Controller, Pension (Montreal)....Mary Skiadopoulos
Manager, Pension (Montreal)....Lise de Jocas

Security

Senior Vice President, Security....Dennis Cunningham
Senior Director, Security....Joseph Caporicci
Manager, Security....Al Young

BUSINESS AND MEDIA

Senior Executive Vice President, Business and Media....John Collins

Broadcasting and Production

Senior Vice President, Broadcasting....John Shannon
Group Vice President, Video Production and Programming....Ken Rosen
Group Vice President, Media Operations & Planning....Patti Fallick
Vice President, Broadcasting & Programming....Adam Acone
Senior Director, Operations/Footage....Peg Walsh
Director, Broadcast Operations (Toronto)....Jim Wilkes
Director, NHL Radio....Gregg Baldinger
Senior Manager, Broadcasting....Phyllis DeCongilio
Senior Manager, Regional Television....Eric Haugen
Senior Manager, Network Television....Emily Nasits
Executive Producer....Darryl Lepik
Manager, Video Services....Chris Cesa
Manager, Broadcasting Operations....Lisa Litvack

Broadcast Business and Scheduling

Senior Vice President, Scheduling and Strategic Planning (Montreal)....Steve Hatze Petros
Senior Director, Research....Mark Erlichson

Corporate Sales

Senior Vice President (New York)....Keith Wachtel
Vice President (New York)....David Lehanski
Managing Director (Toronto)....Doug Brooks
Directors (Toronto)....Kyle McMann, Laurel Walzak
Senior Manager (New York)....Pete Helfer
Manager (New York)....Evin Dobson

International

Senior Vice President, NHL International and Business Affairs....Ken Yaffe
Sr. Director, International Licensing & Special Projects....Lynn White

Marketing

Executive Vice President, Marketing....Brian Jennings
Senior Vice President, Events & Entertainment....Ken Yaffe
Vice President, Sales & Partnership Marketing....Perry Cooper
Vice President, Consumer Products Marketing....James Haskins
Vice President, Events & Entertainment....Bill Miller
Vice President, Fan Development....Alysse Soll
Senior Director, Events & Entertainment....Dean Matsuzaki
Senior Director, Retail Sales & Marketing, Canada (Toronto)....Barry Monaghan
Senior Director, Entertainment Products....Dave McCarthy
Design Director....Paul Conway
Director, Events & Entertainment....Chie Chie Sakuma
Senior Manager, Consumer Products Marketing, Canada (Toronto)....Angie Andreou
Senior Manager, Apparel and Headwear....John Gulla
Senior Manager, Marketing/Fan Development....Suzanne Sherman
Senior Manager, Center Ice & Sporting Goods....Richard Villani
Manager, Retail Sales & Marketing....Dan Near
Manager, Entertainment Products....Bobbi Wilson

NHL Images

Group Vice President, Media Operations & Planning....Patti Fallick
Manager....Jessica Tomao

NHLE Legal and Business Affairs

Executive Vice President, General Counsel....Richard Zahnd
Group Vice President, Legal and Business Affairs....Tom Prochnow
Vice President, Legal and Business Affairs....Matthew Kline
Senior Counsel....Michael Gold
Director, Intellectual Property....Alison Nunez
Managers, Contracts Administration....Sara Cox, Linda Tomm

NHL Media

Group Vice President, Center Ice and NHL Network....Jody Shapiro
Vice President, Media....John Tortora
Senior Manager, NHL Center Ice Operations....Jennifer Wisniewski

NHL Interactive CyberEnterprises (NHL ICE)

President, NHL ICE and Senior Vice President, New Business Development....Keith Ritter
Vice President, Editorial & Production....Richard Libero
Vice President, Web Operations....Grant Nodine
Director, New Media Business Development....Troy Ewanchyna

NHL Media - Legal

Group Vice President, General Counsel....Robert Hawkins
Associate Counsel....Alexandre Simon

Quality Control

Vice President, Licensing and Trademark Compliance....Ruth Gruhin
Managers, Quality Control....Erin Versaggi, Cesare Desantis, Charlotte Villamil

COMMUNICATIONS, BRANDING & CLUB CONSULTING & SERVICES

Senior Executive Vice President, Communications, Branding & Club Consulting & Services....Ed Horne

Club Consulting and Services

Senior Vice President, Club Consulting and Services....Susan Cohig
Vice President, Club Consulting and Services (Toronto)....Laurie Kepron
Director, Club Services....Nicole Allison

Communications

Executive Vice President, Communications and Brand Strategy....Karen Durkin
Senior Vice President, Communications....Bernadette Mansur
Senior Vice President, Public Relations & Media Services (Toronto)....Gary Meagher
Group Vice President, Media Relations....Frank Brown
Vice President, Public Relations & Player Development....Jamey Horan
Vice President, Community and Diversity Programming....Ken Martin
Statistician and Information Officer (Toronto)....Benny Ercolani
Senior Director, News Services....Greg Inglis
Director, Entertainment Publicity....Nirva Milord
Director, Youth Development, NHL Diversity....Willie O'Ree
Senior Manager, Public Relations (Toronto)....David Keon
Senior Manager, Public Relations (Toronto)....Julie Young
Manager, Public Relations....Schuyler Baehman
Manager, Community Relations....Ann Marie Lynch
Publicist....Kerry McGovern
Manager, NHL Diversity....Robert Wooley
Manager, Community and Diversity Publicity....Mary Kay Wright

BOARD OF GOVERNORS

CHAIRMAN OF THE BOARD – JEREMY M. JACOBS
VICE CHAIR – TOM HICKS

Anaheim Ducks
Henry Samueli....Governor
Michael Schulman....Alternate Governor
Brian Burke....Alternate Governor
Tim Ryan....Alternate Governor
Susan Samueli....Alternate Governor

Atlanta Thrashers
Bruce Levenson....Governor
Don Waddell....Alternate Governor
Bernie Mullin....Alternate Governor
J. Rutherford Seydel, II....Alternate Governor
Ed Peskowitz....Alternate Governor

Boston Bruins
Jeremy M. Jacobs....Governor
Charles Jacobs....Alternate Governor
Jeremy Jacobs, Jr....Alternate Governor
Louis Jacobs....Alternate Governor
Harry J. Sinden....Alternate Governor
Peter Chiarelli....Alternate Governor

Buffalo Sabres
B. Thomas Golisano....Governor
Lawrence Quinn....Alternate Governor
Daniel J. DiPofi....Alternate Governor
Darcy Regier....Alternate Governor

Calgary Flames
Harley N. Hotchkiss....Governor
N. Murray Edwards....Alternate Governor
Ken King....Alternate Governor
Alvin Libin....Alternate Governor
Darryl Sutter....Alternate Governor

Carolina Hurricanes
Peter Karmanos, Jr....Governor
Jason Karmanos....Alternate Governor
Jim Rutherford....Alternate Governor
Michael Amendola....Alternate Governor

Chicago Blackhawks
William W. Wirtz....Governor
Robert J. Pulford....Alternate Governor
Peter R. Wirtz....Alternate Governor
John A. Ziegler, Jr....Alternate Governor

Colorado Avalanche
Stan Kroenke....Governor
Pierre Lacroix....Alternate Governor
Paul Andrews....Alternate Governor
Francois Giguere....Alternate Governor

Columbus Blue Jackets
John H. McConnell....Governor
John P. McConnell....Alternate Governor
Mike Priest....Alternate Governor
Scott Howson....Alternate Governor

Dallas Stars
Tom Hicks....Governor
Doug Armstrong....Alternate Governor
Jim Lites....Alternate Governor
Tom Hicks, Jr....Alternate Governor

Detroit Red Wings
Michael Ilitch....Governor
Jim Devellano....Alternate Governor
Ken Holland....Alternate Governor
Christopher Ilitch....Alternate Governor
Steve Yzerman....Alternate Governor

Edmonton Oilers
Cal Nichols....Governor
William K. Butler....Alternate Governor
Patrick LaForge....Alternate Governor
Kevin Lowe....Alternate Governor

Florida Panthers
Alan Cohen....Governor
Jordan Zimmerman....Alternate Governor
Steven Cohen....Alternate Governor
William A. Torrey....Alternate Governor
Richard Lehman....Alternate Governor
Michael Yormark....Alternate Governor
Jacques Martin....Alternate Governor
Cliff Viner....Alternate Governor

Los Angeles Kings
Timothy J. Leiweke....Governor
Philip F. Anschutz....Alternate Governor
Christian Anschutz....Alternate Governor
Shawn Hunter....Alternate Governor
Luc Robitaille....Alternate Governor

Minnesota Wild
Robert O. Naegele, Jr....Governor
Doug Risebrough....Alternate Governor
Jac Sperling....Alternate Governor

Montréal Canadiens
George Gillett, Jr....Governor
Pierre Boivin....Alternate Governor
Jeff Joyce....Alternate Governor
Fred Steer....Alternate Governor
Foster Gillett....Alternate Governor
Bob Gainey....Alternate Governor

Nashville Predators
Craig Leipold....Governor
Steve Violetta....Alternate Governor
Ed Lang....Alternate Governor
David Poile....Alternate Governor

New Jersey Devils
Lou Lamoriello....Governor
Jeff Vanderbeek....Alternate Governor
Michael Gilfillan....Alternate Governor

New York Islanders
Charles Wang....Governor
Roy Reichbach....Alternate Governor
Arthur J. McCarthy....Alternate Governor
Michael J. Picker....Alternate Governor
Garth Snow....Alternate Governor
Chris Dey....Alternate Governor

New York Rangers
James L. Dolan....Governor
Steve Mills....Alternate Governor
Glen Sather....Alternate Governor
Hank Ratner....Alternate Governor

Ottawa Senators
Eugene Melnyk....Governor
Roy Mlakar....Alternate Governor
Sheldon Plener....Alternate Governor

Philadelphia Flyers
Edward M. Snider....Governor
Philip I. Weinberg....Alternate Governor
Peter Luukko....Alternate Governor
Paul Holmgren....Alternate Governor

Phoenix Coyotes
Jeff Shumway....Governor
Wayne Gretzky....Alternate Governor
Doug Moss....Alternate Governor
Don Maloney....Alternate Governor

Pittsburgh Penguins
Ken Sawyer....Governor
Ronald Burkle....Alternate Governor
Anthony Liberati....Alternate Governor
Ray Shero....Alternate Governor
David Morehouse....Alternate Governor

St. Louis Blues
Dave Checketts....Governor
Kenneth Munoz....Alternate Governor
John Davidson....Alternate Governor
Larry Pleau....Alternate Governor
Michael McCarthy....Alternate Governor

San Jose Sharks
Greg Jamison....Governor
Kevin Compton....Alternate Governor
Doug Wilson....Alternate Governor

Tampa Bay Lightning
Thomas S. Wilson....Governor
Ronald J. Campbell....Alternate Governor
Jay H. Feaster....Alternate Governor

Toronto Maple Leafs
Larry Tanenbaum....Governor
Richard A. Peddie....Alternate Governor
Dale Lastman....Alternate Governor
Dean Metcalf....Alternate Governor
John Ferguson....Alternate Governor

Vancouver Canucks
Francesco Aquilini....Governor
David M. Nonis....Alternate Governor
Chris Zimmerman....Alternate Governor
Paolo Aquilini....Alternate Governor
Roberto Aquilini....Alternate Governor

Washington Capitals
Richard M. Patrick....Governor
Ted Leonsis....Alternate Governor
George McPhee....Alternate Governor

Commissioner and League Presidents

Gary B. Bettman

Gary B. Bettman took office as the NHL's first Commissioner on February 1, 1993. Since the League was formed in 1917, there have been five League Presidents.

NHL President	Years in Office
Frank Calder	1917-1943
Mervyn "Red" Dutton	1943-1946
Clarence Campbell	1946-1977
John A. Ziegler, Jr.	1977-1992
Gil Stein	1992-1993

Hockey Hall of Fame

Brookfield Place
30 Yonge Street
Toronto, Ontario M5E 1X8
Phone: 416/360-7735
Executive Fax: 416/360-1501
Resource Centre Fax: 416/360-1316
www.hhof.com

William C. Hay – Chairman and Chief Executive Officer
Jeff Denomme – President, C.O.O. and Treasurer
Craig Baines – Vice President, Operations
Peter Jagla – Vice President, Marketing
Phil Pritchard – Vice President, Resource Centre and Curator
Ron Ellis – Director, Public Affairs and Assistant to the President
Craig Campbell – Manager, Photography, Archives and Sales
Kelly Massé – Manager, Corporate & Media Relations
Steve Ozimec – Manager, Special Events & Hospitality
Jackie Schwartz – Manager, Marketing & Promotions
Matt Manor and Dave Sanford – Photographers

National Hockey League Players' Association

20 Bay Street, Suite 1700
Toronto, Ontario M5J 2N8
Phone: 416/313-2300
Fax: 416/313-2301
www.nhlpa.com

Ian Penny – Associate Counsel, Labour
Roland Lee – Associate Counsel, Labour
Stu Grimson – Associate Counsel, Labour
Adam Larry – Associate Counsel, Licensing
Mike Gartner – Director, Hockey Affairs
Kim Murdoch – Manager, Player Insurance and Pensions
Richard Smit – Controller
Devin Smith – Director, Club Marketing and Community Relations
Jonathan Weatherdon – Director, Communications

NHL On-Ice Officials

Total NHL Games and 2006-07 Games columns count regular-season games only.

Referees

#	Name	Birthplace	Birthdate	First NHL Game	Total NHL Games	2006-07 Games
15	Stephane Auger	Montreal, Que.	12/9/70	4/1/2000	384	74
44	David Banfield	Halifax, N.S.	4/30/79	…	…	…
41	Chris Ciamaga	Cheektowaga, N.Y.	9/13/77	…	…	…
10	Paul Devorski	Guelph, Ont.	8/18/58	10/14/89	1041	74
39	Gord Dwyer	Halifax, N.S.	5/18/77	11/19/05	96	75
2	Kerry Fraser	Sarnia, Ont.	5/30/52	4/6/75	1682	59
27	Eric Furlatt	Cap de la Madelaine, Que	12/2/71	10/8/01	313	74
30	Mike Hasenfratz	Regina, Sask.	7/19/66	10/21/00	396	75
8	Dave Jackson	Montreal, Que.	11/28/64	12/23/90	900	74
25	Marc Joannette	Verdun, Que.	11/3/68	10/27/99	435	74
18	Greg Kimmerly	Toronto, Ont.	12/8/64	11/30/96	523	75
12	Don Koharski	Halifax, N.S.	12/2/55	10/14/77	[1]1580	74
32	Tom Kowal	Vernon, B.C.	11/2/67	10/29/99	321	74
40	Steve Kozari	Penticton, B.C.	6/20/73	10/15/05	46	26
14	Dennis LaRue	Savannah, GA	7/14/59	3/26/91	715	67
48	Frederick L'Ecuyer	Trois-Rivieres, Que.	7/28/77	…	…	…
28	Chris Lee	Saint John, N.B.	7/7/70	4/2/00	294	75
3	Mike Leggo	North Bay, Ont.	10/7/64	3/3/98	514	74
6	Dan Marouelli	Edmonton, Alta.	7/16/55	11/2/84	1411	73
26	Rob Martell	Winnipeg, Man.	10/21/63	3/14/84	[2]409	48
4	Wes McCauley	Georgetown, Ont.	1/11/72	1/20/03	170	75
7	Bill McCreary	Guelph, Ont.	11/17/55	11/3/84	1451	74
19	Mick McGeough	Regina, Sask.	6/20/57	1/19/89	1023	74
34	Brad Meier	Dayton, OH	4/11/67	10/23/99	437	74
36	Dean Morton	Peterborough, Ont.	2/27/68	11/11/00	54	16
13	Dan O'Halloran	Essex, Ont.	3/25/64	10/14/95	593	74
42	Dan O'Rourke	Calgary, Alta.	8/31/72	10/2/99	[3]171	74
20	Tim Peel	Toronto, Ont.	4/27/66	10/21/99	446	75
43	Brian Pochmara	Detroit, MI	11/27/76	12/23/05	32	21
33	Kevin Pollock	Kincardine, Ont.	2/7/70	3/28/00	442	75
37	Kyle Rehman	Stettler, Alta.	9/15/78	…	…	…
5	Chris Rooney	Boston, MA	5/26/74	11/22/00	339	75
38	Francois St. Laurent	Greenfield Park, Que.	6/26/77	11/10/05	28	16
45	Justin St. Pierre	Dolbeau, Que.	2/17/72	11/9/05	99	73
16	Rob Shick	Port Alberni, B.C.	12/4/57	4/6/86	1212	68
11	Kelly Sutherland	Victoria, B.C.	4/18/71	12/19/00	379	75
21	Don Van Massenhoven	Parkhill, Ont.	7/17/60	11/11/93	815	60
29	Ian Walsh	Philadelphia, PA	5/9/72	10/14/00	280	74
35	Dean Warren	Toronto, Ont.	7/22/63	10/8/99	440	75
23	Brad Watson	Regina, Sask.	10/4/61	2/5/94	542	74

[1] plus 163 games as a linesman. [2] plus 1 game as a linesman. [3] plus 120 games as a linesman.

Linesmen

#	Name	Birthplace	Birthdate	First NHL Game	Total NHL Games	2006-07 Games
75	Derek Amell	Port Colborne, Ont.	9/16/68	10/13/97	580	74
59	Steve Barton	Ottawa, Ont.	12/27/71	11/1/00	358	75
96	David Brisebois	Sudbury, Ont.	4/14/76	10/11/99	314	75
74	Lonnie Cameron	Victoria, B.C.	7/15/64	10/5/96	697	73
67	Pierre Champoux	Ville St-Pierre, Que.	4/18/63	10/8/88	1151	73
50	Scott Cherrey	Drayton, Ont.	5/27/76	…	…	…
76	Michel Cormier	Trois-Rivieres, Que.	5/28/74	10/10/03	219	75
88	Mike Cvik	Calgary, Alta.	7/6/62	10/8/87	1279	73
60	Pat Dapuzzo	Hoboken, NJ	12/29/58	12/5/84	1512	70
54	Greg Devorski	Guelph, Ont.	8/3/69	10/9/93	858	73
68	Scott Driscoll	Seaforth, Ont.	5/2/68	10/10/92	930	74
66	Darren Gibbs	Edmonton, Alta.	9/30/66	10/1/97	547	72
82	Ryan Galloway	Winnipeg, Man.	7/12/72	10/17/02	243	72
91	Don Henderson	Calgary, Alta.	9/23/68	3/10/95	682	72
55	Shane Heyer	Summerland, B.C.	2/7/64	10/1/99	[4]859	74
71	Brad Kovachik	Woodstock, Ont.	3/7/71	10/10/96	662	67
86	Brad Lazarowich	Vancouver, B.C.	8/4/62	10/9/86	1374	72
78	Brian Mach	Little Falls, MN	4/15/74	10/7/00	422	74
90	Andy McElman	Chicago Heights, IL	8/4/61	10/7/93	865	74
89	Steve Miller	Stratford, Ont.	6/22/72	10/11/00	410	75
97	Jean Morin	Sorel, Que.	8/10/63	10/5/91	973	73
93	Brian Murphy	Dover, NH	12/13/64	10/7/88	[5]1074	74
95	Jonny Murray	Beauport, Que.	8/10/74	10/7/00	424	74
70	Derek Nansen	Ottawa, Ont.	12/6/71	10/11/02	281	72
80	Thor Nelson	Westminister, CA	1/6/68	2/16/95	580	71
77	Tim Nowak	Buffalo, NY	9/6/67	10/8/93	864	66
79	Mark Paré	Windsor, Ont.	7/26/57	10/11/79	1961	74
65	Pierre Racicot	Verdun, Que.	2/15/67	10/12/93	893	73
73	Vaughan Rody	Winnipeg, Man.	12/13/68	10/8/00	397	58
52	Dan Schachte	Madison, WI	7/13/58	10/6/82	1682	72
61	Lyle Seitz	Brooks, Alta.	1/22/69	10/6/92	[6]527	72
84	Anthony Sericolo	Troy, NY	7/17/68	10/21/98	516	73
57	Jay Sharrers	Jamaica, West Indies	7/3/67	10/6/90	[7]788	73
92	Mark Shewchyk	Hamilton, Ont.	6/1/75	10/9/03	217	75
56	Mark Wheler	North Battleford, Sask.	9/20/65	10/10/92	960	72

[4] plus 386 games as a referee. [5] plus 88 games as a referee. [6] plus 10 games as a referee. [7] plus 136 games as a referee.

NHL History

1917 — National Hockey League organized November 26 in Montreal following suspension of operations by the National Hockey Association of Canada Limited (NHA). Montreal Canadiens, Montreal Wanderers, Ottawa Senators and Quebec Bulldogs attended founding meeting. Delegates decided to use NHA rules.

Toronto Arenas were later admitted as fifth team; Quebec decided not to operate during the first season. Quebec players allocated to remaining four teams.

Frank Calder elected president and secretary-treasurer.

First NHL games played December 19, with Toronto only arena with artificial ice. Clubs played 22-game split schedule.

1918 — Emergency meeting held January 3 due to destruction by fire of Montreal Arena which was home ice for both Canadiens and Wanderers.

Wanderers withdrew, reducing the NHL to three teams; Canadiens played remaining home games at 3,250-seat Jubilee rink.

Quebec franchise sold to P.J. Quinn of Toronto on October 18 on the condition that the team operate in Quebec City for 1918-19 season. Quinn did not attend the November League meeting and Quebec did not play in 1918-19.

1919-20 — NHL reactivated Quebec Bulldogs franchise. Former Quebec players returned to the club. New Mount Royal Arena became home of Canadiens. Toronto Arenas changed name to St. Patricks. Clubs played 24-game split schedule.

1920-21 — H.P. Thompson of Hamilton, Ontario made application for the purchase of an NHL franchise. Quebec franchise shifted to Hamilton with other NHL teams providing players to strengthen the club.

1921-22 — Split schedule abandoned. First and second place teams at the end of full schedule to play for championship.

1922-23 — Clubs agreed that players could not be sold or traded to clubs in any other league without first being offered to all other clubs in the NHL. In March, Foster Hewitt broadcasts radio's first hockey game.

1923-24 — Ottawa's new 10,000-seat arena opened. First U.S. franchise granted to Boston for following season.

Dr. Cecil Hart Trophy donated to NHL to be awarded to the player judged most useful to his team.

1924-25 — Canadian Arena Company of Montreal granted a franchise to operate Montreal Maroons. NHL now six team league with two clubs in Montreal. Inaugural game in new Montreal Forum played November 29, 1924 as Canadiens defeated Toronto 7-1. Forum was home rink for the Maroons, but no ice was available in the Canadiens arena November 29, resulting in a shift to the Forum.

Hamilton finished first in the standings, receiving a bye into the finals. But Hamilton players, demanding $200 each for additional games in the playoffs, went on strike. The NHL suspended all players, fining them $200 each. Stanley Cup finalist to be the winner of NHL semi-final between Toronto and Canadiens.

Prince of Wales and Lady Byng trophies donated to NHL.

Clubs played 30-game schedule.

1925-26 — Hamilton club dropped from NHL. Players signed by new New York Americans franchise. Pittsburgh Pirates granted franchise.

Clubs played 36-game schedule.

1926-27 — New York Rangers granted franchise May 15, 1926. Chicago Black Hawks and Detroit Cougars granted franchises September 25, 1926. NHL now ten-team league with an American and a Canadian Division.

Stanley Cup came under the control of NHL. In previous seasons, winners of the now-defunct Western or Pacific Coast leagues would play NHL champion in Cup finals.

Toronto franchise sold to a new company controlled by Hugh Aird and Conn Smythe. Name changed from St. Patricks to Maple Leafs.

Clubs played 44-game schedule.

The Montreal Canadiens donated the Vezina Trophy to be awarded to the team allowing the fewest goals-against in regular season play. The winning team would, in turn, present the trophy to the goaltender playing in the greatest number of games during the season.

1930-31 — Detroit franchise changed name from Cougars to Falcons. Pittsburgh transferred to Philadelphia for one season. Pirates changed name to Philadelphia Quakers. Trading deadline for teams set at February 15 of each year. NHL approved operation of farm teams by Rangers, Americans, Falcons and Bruins. Four-sided electric arena clock first demonstrated.

1931-32 — Philadelphia dropped out. Ottawa withdrew for one season. New Maple Leaf Gardens completed.

Clubs played 48-game schedule.

1932-33 — Detroit franchise changed name from Falcons to Red Wings. Franchise application received from St. Louis but refused because of additional travel costs. Ottawa team resumed play.

1933-34 — First All-Star Game played as a benefit for injured player Ace Bailey. Leafs defeated All-Stars 7-3 in Toronto.

1934-35 — Ottawa franchise transferred to St. Louis. Team called St. Louis Eagles and consisted largely of Ottawa's players.

1935-36 — Ottawa-St. Louis franchise terminated. Montreal Canadiens finished season with very poor record. To strengthen the club, NHL gave Canadiens first call on the services of all French-Canadian players for three seasons.

1937-38 — Second benefit All-Star game staged November 2 in Montreal in aid of the family of the late Canadiens star Howie Morenz.

Montreal Maroons withdrew from the NHL on June 22, 1938, leaving seven clubs in the League.

1938-39 — Expenses for each club regulated at $5 per man per day for meals and $2.50 per man per day for accommodation.

1939-40 — Benefit All-Star Game played October 29, 1939 in Montreal for the children of the late Albert (Babe) Siebert.

1940-41 — Ross-Tyer puck adopted as the official puck of the NHL. Early in the season it was apparent that this puck was too soft. The Spalding puck was adopted in its place.

On May 16, 1941, Arthur Ross, NHL governor from Boston, donated a perpetual trophy to be awarded annually to the player voted outstanding in the league. Due to wartime restrictions, the trophy was never awarded.

1941-42 — New York Americans changed name to Brooklyn Americans.

1942-43 — Brooklyn Americans withdrew from NHL, leaving six teams: Boston, Chicago, Detroit, Montreal, New York and Toronto. Playoff format saw first-place team play third-place team and second play fourth.

Clubs played 50-game schedule.

Frank Calder, president of the NHL since its inception, died in Montreal. Meryn "Red" Dutton, former manager of the New York Americans, became president. The NHL commissioned the Calder Memorial Trophy to be awarded to the League's outstanding rookie each year.

1945-46 — Philadelphia, Los Angeles and San Francisco applied for NHL franchises.

The Philadelphia Arena Company of the American Hockey League applied for an injunction to prevent the possible operation of an NHL franchise in that city.

1946-47 — Mervyn Dutton retired as president of the NHL prior to the start of the season. He was succeeded by Clarence S. Campbell.

Individual trophy winners and all-star team members to receive $1,000 awards.

Playoff guarantees for players introduced.

Clubs played 60-game schedule.

1947-48 — The first annual All-Star Game for the benefit of the players' pension fund was played when the All-Stars defeated the Stanley Cup Champion Toronto Maple Leafs 4-3 in Toronto on October 13, 1947.

Criteria for awarding Art Ross Trophy changed. Now awarded to top scorer. Elmer Lach was its first winner.

Philadelphia and Los Angeles franchise applications refused.

National Hockey League Pension Society formed.

1949-50 — Clubs played 70-game schedule.

First intra-league draft held April 30, 1950. Clubs allowed to protect 30 players. Remaining players available for $25,000 each.

1951-52 — Referees included in the League's pension plan.

1952-53 — In May of 1952, City of Cleveland applied for NHL franchise. Application denied. In March of 1953, the Cleveland Barons of the AHL challenged the NHL champions for the Stanley Cup. The NHL governors did not accept this challenge.

1953-54 — The James Norris Memorial Trophy presented to the NHL for annual presentation to the League's best defenseman.

Intra-league draft rules amended to allow teams to protect 18 skaters and two goaltenders, claiming price reduced to $15,000.

1954-55 — Each arena to operate an "out-of-town" scoreboard.

1956-57 — Referees and linesmen to wear shirts of black and white vertical stripes. Standardized signals for referees and linesmen introduced.

1960-61 — Canadian National Exhibition, City of Toronto and NHL reach agreement for the construction of a Hockey Hall of Fame on the CNE grounds. Hall opens on August 26, 1961.

1963-64 — Player development league established with clubs operated by NHL franchises located in Minneapolis, St. Paul, Indianapolis, Omaha and, beginning in 1964-65, Tulsa. First universal amateur draft took place. All players of qualifying age (17) unaffected by sponsorship of junior teams available to be drafted.

1964-65 — Conn Smythe Trophy presented to the NHL to be awarded annually to the outstanding player in the Stanley Cup playoffs.

Minimum age of players subject to amateur draft changed to 18.

1965-66 — NHL announced expansion plans for a second six-team division to begin play in 1967-68.

1966-67 — Fourteen applications for NHL franchises received.

Lester Patrick Trophy presented to the NHL to be awarded annually for outstanding service to hockey in the United States.

NHL sponsorship of junior teams ceased, making all players of qualifying age not already on NHL-sponsored lists eligible for the amateur draft.

1967-68 — Six new teams added: California Seals, Los Angeles Kings, Minnesota North Stars, Philadelphia Flyers, Pittsburgh Penguins, St. Louis Blues. New teams to play in West Division. Remaining six teams to play in East Division.

Minimum age of players subject to amateur draft changed to 20.

Clubs played 74-game schedule.

Clarence S. Campbell Trophy awarded to team finishing the regular season in first place in West Division.

California Seals change name to Oakland Seals on December 8, 1967.

1968-69 — Clubs played 76-game schedule.

Amateur draft expanded to cover any amateur player of qualifying age throughout the world.

1970-71 — Two new teams added: Buffalo Sabres and Vancouver Canucks. These teams joined East Division: Chicago switched to West Division. Oakland Seals change name to California Golden Seals prior to season.

Clubs played 78-game schedule.

1971-72 — Playoff format amended. In each division, first to play fourth; second to play third.

1972-73 — Soviet Nationals and Canadian NHL stars play eight-game pre-season series. Canadians win 4-3-1.

Two new teams added. Atlanta Flames join West Division; New York Islanders join East Division.

1974-75 — Two new teams added: Kansas City Scouts and Washington Capitals. Teams realigned into two nine-team conferences, the Prince of Wales made up of the Norris and Adams Divisions, and the Clarence Campbell made up of the Smythe and Patrick Divisions.

Clubs played 80-game schedule.

1976-77 — California franchise transferred to Cleveland. Team named Cleveland Barons. Kansas City franchise transferred to Denver. Team named Colorado Rockies.

1977-78 — Clarence S. Campbell retires as NHL president. Succeeded by John A. Ziegler, Jr.

1978-79 — Cleveland and Minnesota franchises merge, leaving NHL with 17 teams. Merged team placed in Adams Division, playing home games in Minnesota.

Minimum age of players subject to amateur draft changed to 19.

1979-80 — Four new teams added: Edmonton Oilers, Hartford Whalers, Quebec Nordiques and Winnipeg Jets.

Minimum age of players subject to entry draft changed to 18.

1980-81 — Atlanta franchise shifted to Calgary, retaining "Flames" name.

1981-82 — Teams realigned within existing divisions. New groupings based on geographical areas. Unbalanced schedule adopted.

1982-83 — Colorado Rockies franchise shifted to East Rutherford, New Jersey. Team named New Jersey Devils. Franchise moved to Patrick Division from Smythe; Winnipeg moved to Smythe Division from Norris.

NHL History — *continued*

1991-92 — San Jose Sharks added, making the NHL a 22-team league. NHL celebrates 75th Anniversary Season. The 1991-92 regular season suspended due to a players' strike on April 1, 1992. Play resumed April 12, 1992.

1992-93 — Gil Stein named NHL president (October, 1992). Gary Bettman named first NHL Commissioner (February, 1993). Ottawa Senators and Tampa Bay Lightning added, making the NHL a 24-team league. NHL celebrates Stanley Cup Centennial. Clubs played 84-game schedule.

1993-94 — Mighty Ducks of Anaheim and Florida Panthers added, making the NHL a 26-team league. Minnesota franchise shifted to Dallas, team named Dallas Stars. Prince of Wales and Clarence Campbell Conferences renamed Eastern and Western. Adams, Patrick, Norris and Smythe Divisions renamed Northeast, Atlantic, Central and Pacific. Winnipeg moved to Central Division from Pacific; Tampa Bay moved to Atlantic Division from Central; Pittsburgh moved to Northeast Division from Atlantic.

1994-95 — A lockout resulted in the cancellation of 468 games from October 1, 1994 to January 19, 1995. Clubs played a 48-game schedule that began January 20, 1995 and ended May 3, 1995. No inter-conference games were played.

1995-96 — Quebec franchise transferred to Denver. Team named Colorado Avalanche and placed in Pacific Division of Western Conference. Clubs to play 82-game schedule.

1996-97 — Winnipeg franchise transferred to Phoenix. Team named Phoenix Coyotes and placed in Central Division of Western Conference.

1997-98 — Hartford franchise transferred to Raleigh. Team named Carolina Hurricanes and remains in Northeast Division of Eastern Conference.

1998-99 — The addition of the Nashville Predators made the NHL a 27-team league and brought about the creation of two new divisions and a League-wide realignment in preparation for further expansion to 30 teams by 2000-2001. Nashville was added to the Central Division of the Western Conference, while Toronto moved into the Northeast Division of the Eastern Conference. Pittsburgh was shifted from the Northeast to the Atlantic, while Carolina left the Northeast for the newly created Southeast Division of the Eastern Conference. Florida, Tampa Bay and Washington also joined the Southeast. In the Western Conference, Calgary, Colorado, Edmonton and Vancouver make up the new Northwest Division. Dallas and Phoenix moved from the Central to the Pacific Division.

The NHL retired uniform number 99 in honor of all-time scoring leader Wayne Gretzky who retired at the end of the season.

1999-2000 — Atlanta Thrashers added, making the NHL a 28-team league.

2000-01 — Columbus Blue Jackets and Minnesota Wild added, making the NHL a 30-team league.

2003-04 — First outdoor NHL game and largest crowd in League history as 57,167 attend Heritage Classic at Edmonton's Commonwealth Stadium. Montreal defeated Edmonton 4-3, November 22, 2003.

2004-05 — A lockout resulted in the cancellation of the season.

NHL Attendance

Season	Regular Season Games	Regular Season Attendance	Playoffs Games	Playoffs Attendance	Total Attendance
1960-61	210	2,317,142	17	242,000	2,559,142
1961-62	210	2,435,424	18	277,000	2,712,424
1962-63	210	2,590,574	16	220,906	2,811,480
1963-64	210	2,732,642	21	309,149	3,041,791
1964-65	210	2,822,635	20	303,859	3,126,494
1965-66	210	2,941,164	16	249,000	3,190,184
1966-67	210	3,084,759	16	248,336	3,333,095
1967-68	444	4,938,043	40	495,089	5,433,132
1968-69	456	5,550,613	33	431,739	5,982,352
1969-70	456	5,992,065	34	461,694	6,453,759
1970-71	546	7,257,677	43	707,633	7,965,310
1971-72	546	7,609,368	36	582,666	8,192,034
1972-73	624	8,575,651	38	624,637	9,200,288
1973-74	624	8,640,978	38	600,442	9,241,420
1974-75	720	9,521,536	51	784,181	10,305,717
1975-76	720	9,103,761	48	726,279	9,830,040
1976-77	720	8,563,890	44	646,279	9,210,169
1977-78	720	8,526,564	45	686,634	9,213,198
1978-79	680	7,758,053	45	694,521	8,452,574
1979-80	840	10,533,623	63	976,699	11,510,322
1980-81	840	10,726,198	68	966,390	11,692,588
1981-82	840	10,710,894	71	1,058,948	11,769,842
1982-83	840	11,020,610	66	1,088,222	12,028,832
1983-84	840	11,359,386	70	1,107,400	12,466,786
1984-85	840	11,633,730	70	1,107,500	12,741,230
1985-86	840	11,621,000	72	1,152,503	12,773,503
1986-87	840	11,855,880	87	1,383,967	13,239,847
1987-88	840	12,117,512	83	1,336,901	13,454,413
1988-89	840	12,417,969	83	1,327,214	13,745,183
1989-90	840	12,579,651	85	1,355,593	13,935,244
1990-91	840	12,343,897	92	1,442,203	13,786,100
1991-92	880	12,769,676	86	1,327,920	14,097,596
1992-93	1,008	14,158,177[1]	83	1,346,034	15,504,211
1993-94	1,092	16,105,604[2]	90	1,440,095	17,545,699
1994-95	624[3]	9,233,884	81	1,329,130	10,563,014
1995-96	1,066	17,041,614	86	1,540,140	18,581,754
1996-97	1,066	17,640,529	82	1,494,878	19,135,407
1997-98	1,066	17,264,678	82	1,507,416	18,772,094
1998-99	1,107	18,001,741	86	1,509,411	19,511,152
1999-2000	1,148	18,800,139	83	1,524,629	20,324,768
2000-01	1,230	20,373,379	86	1,584,011	21,957,390
2001-02	1,230	20,614,613	90	1,691,174	22,305,787
2002-03	1,230	20,408,704	89	1,636,120	22,044,824
2003-04	1,230	20,356,199	89	1,708,691	22,064,890
2004-05	....	....	....	....	....
2005-06	1,230	20,854,169	83	1,530,405	22,384,574
2006-07	1,230	20,861,787	81	1,496,501	22,358,288

NHL Expansion: the NHL operated as a six-team league from 1942-43 to 1966-67. Six teams were added in1967-68: California (later to move to Cleveland), Los Angeles, Minnesota (later to move to Dallas), Philadelphia, Pittsburgh and St. Louis. In 1970-71: Buffalo and Vancouver. In 1972-73: Atlanta (later to move to Calgary) and NY Islanders. In 1974-75: Kansas City (later to move to Colorado and then to New Jersey) and Washington. In 1979-80, Hartford (later tomove to Carolina), Edmonton, Quebec (later to move to Colorado) and Winnipeg (later to move to Phoenix). In 1991-92, San Jose. In 1992-93, Ottawa and Tampa Bay. In 1993-94, Anaheim and Florida. In 1998-99, Nashville. In 1999-2000, Atlanta. In 2000-01, Columbus and Minnesota.

[1] Includes 24 neutral site games • [2] Includes 26 neutral site games
[3] Lockout resulted in the cancellation of 468 regular-season games.

Major Rule Changes

1910-11 — Game changed from two 30-minute periods to three 20-minute periods.

1911-12 — National Hockey Association (forerunner of the NHL) originated six-man hockey, replacing seven-man game.

1917-18 — Goalies permitted to fall to the ice to make saves. Previously a goaltender was penalized for dropping to the ice.

1918-19 — Penalty rules amended. For minor fouls, substitutes not allowed until penalized player had served three minutes. For major fouls, no substitutes for five minutes. For match fouls, no substitutes allowed for the remainder of the game.

With the addition of two lines painted on the ice twenty feet from center, three playing zones were created, producing a forty-foot neutral center ice area in which forward passing was permitted. Kicking the puck was permitted in this neutral zone.

Tabulation of assists began.

1921-22 — Goaltenders allowed to pass the puck forward up to their own blue line.

Overtime limited to twenty minutes.

Minor penalties changed from three minutes to two minutes.

1923-24 — Match foul defined as actions deliberately injuring or disabling an opponent. For such actions, a player was fined not less than $50 and ruled off the ice for the balance of the game. A player assessed a match penalty may be replaced by a substitute at the end of 20 minutes. Match penalty recipients must meet with the League president who can assess additional punishment.

1925-26 — Delayed penalty rules introduced. Each team must have a minimum of four players on the ice at all times.

Two rules were amended to encourage offense: No more than two defensemen permitted to remain inside a team's own blue line when the puck has left the defensive zone. A faceoff to be called for ragging the puck unless short-handed.

Team captains only players allowed to talk to referees.

Goaltender's leg pads limited to 12-inch width.

Timekeeper's gong to mark end of periods rather than referee's whistle. Teams to dress a maximum of 12 players for each game from a roster of no more than 14 players.

1926-27 — Blue lines repositioned to sixty feet from each goal-line, thereby enlarging the neutral zone and standardizing distance from blue line to goal.

Uniform goal nets adopted throughout NHL with goal posts securely fastened to the ice.

1927-28 — To further encourage offense, forward passes allowed in defending and neutral zones and goaltender's pads reduced in width from 12 to 10 inches.

Game standardized at three twenty-minute periods of stop-time separated by ten-minute intermissions.

Teams to change ends after each period.

Ten minutes of sudden-death overtime to be played if the score is tied after regulation time.

Minor penalty to be assessed to any player other than a goaltender for deliberately picking up the puck while it is in play. Minor penalty to be assessed for deliberately shooting the puck out of play.

The Art Ross goal net adopted as the official net of the NHL.

Maximum length of hockey sticks limited to 53 inches measured from heel of blade to end of handle. No minimum length stipulated.

Home teams given choice of end to defend at start of game.

1928-29 — Forward passing permitted in defensive and neutral zones and into attacking zone if pass receiver is in neutral zone when pass is made. No forward passing allowed inside attacking zone.

Minor penalty to be assessed to any player who delays the game by passing the puck back into his defensive zone.

Ten-minute overtime without sudden-death provision to be played in games tied after regulation time. Games tied after this overtime period declared a draw.

Exclusive of goaltenders, team to dress at least 8 and no more than 12 skaters.

Major Rule Changes — *continued*

1929-30 — Forward passing permitted inside all three zones but not permitted across either blue line.

Kicking the puck allowed, but a goal cannot be scored by kicking the puck in.

No more than three players including the goaltender may remain in their defensive zone when the puck has gone up ice. Minor penalties to be assessed for the first two violations of this rule in a game; major penalties thereafter.

Goaltenders forbidden to hold the puck. Pucks caught must be cleared immediately. For infringement of this rule, a faceoff to be taken ten feet in front of the goal with no player except the goaltender standing between the faceoff spot and the goal-line.

Highsticking penalties introduced.

Maximum number of players in uniform increased from 12 to 15.

December 21, 1929 — Forward passing rules instituted at the beginning of the 1929-30 season more than doubled number of goals scored. Partway through the season, these rules were further amended to read, "No attacking player allowed to precede the play when entering the opposing defensive zone." This is similar to modern offside rule.

1930-31 — A player without a complete stick ruled out of play and forbidden from taking part in further action until a new stick is obtained. A player who has broken his stick must obtain a replacement at his bench.

A further refinement of the offside rule stated that the puck must first be propelled into the attacking zone before any player of the attacking side can enter that zone; for infringement of this rule a faceoff to take place at the spot where the infraction took place.

1931-32 — Though there is no record of a team attempting to play with two goaltenders on the ice, a rule was instituted which stated that each team was allowed only one goaltender on the ice at one time.

Attacking players forbidden to impede the movement or obstruct the vision of opposing goaltenders.

Defending players with the exception of the goaltender forbidden from falling on the puck within 10 feet of the net.

1932-33 — Each team to have captain on the ice at all times.

If the goaltender is removed from the ice to serve a penalty, the manager of the club to appoint a substitute.

Match penalty with substitution after five minutes instituted for kicking another player.

1933-34 — Number of players permitted to stand in defensive zone restricted to three including goaltender.

Visible time clocks required in each rink.

Two referees replace one referee and one linesman.

1934-35 — Penalty shot awarded when a player is tripped and thus prevented from having a clear shot on goal, having no player to pass to other than the offending player. Shot taken from inside a 10-foot circle located 38 feet from the goal. The goaltender must not advance more than one foot from his goal-line when the shot is taken.

1937-38 — Rules introduced governing icing the puck.

Penalty shot awarded when a player other than a goaltender falls on the puck within 10 feet of the goal.

1938-39 — Penalty shot modified to allow puck carrier to skate in before shooting.

One referee and one linesman replace two referee system.

Blue line widened to 12 inches.

Maximum number of players in uniform increased from 14 to 15.

1939-40 — A substitute replacing a goaltender removed from ice to serve a penalty may use a goaltender's stick and gloves but no other goaltending equipment.

1940-41 — Flooding ice surface between periods made obligatory.

1941-42 — Penalty shots classified as minor and major. Minor shot to be taken from a line 28 feet from the goal. Major shot, awarded when a player is tripped with only the goaltender to beat, permits the player taking the penalty shot to skate right into the goalkeeper and shoot from point-blank range.

One referee and two linesmen employed to officiate games.

For playoffs, standby minor league goaltenders employed by NHL as emergency substitutes.

1942-43 — Because of wartime restrictions on train scheduling, regular-season overtime was discontinued on November 21, 1942.

Player limit reduced from 15 to 14. Minimum of 12 men in uniform abolished.

1943-44 — Red line at center ice introduced to speed up the game and reduce offside calls. This rule is considered to mark the beginning of the modern era in the NHL.

1945-46 — Goal indicator lights synchronized with official time clock required at all rinks.

1946-47 — System of signals by officials to indicate infractions introduced.

Linesmen from neutral cities employed for all games.

1947-48 — Goal awarded when a player with the puck has an open net to shoot at and a thrown stick prevents the shot on goal. Major penalty to any player who throws his stick in any zone other than defending zone. If a stick is thrown by a player in his defending zone but the thrown stick is not considered to have prevented a goal, a penalty shot is awarded.

All playoff games played until a winner determined, with 20-minute sudden-death overtime periods separated by 10-minute intermissions.

1949-50 — Ice surface painted white.

Clubs allowed to dress 17 players exclusive of goaltenders.

Major penalties incurred by goaltenders served by a member of the goaltender's team instead of resulting in a penalty shot.

1950-51 — Each team required to provide an emergency goaltender in attendance with full equipment at each game for use by either team in the event of illness or injury to a regular goaltender.

1951-52 — Home teams to wear basic white uniforms; visiting teams basic colored uniforms.

Goal crease enlarged from 3 × 7 feet to 4 × 8 feet.

Number of players in uniform reduced to 15 plus goaltenders.

Faceoff circles enlarged from 10-foot to 15-foot radius.

1952-53 — Teams permitted to dress 15 skaters on the road and 16 at home.

1953-54 — Number of players in uniform set at 16 plus goaltenders.

1954-55 — Number of players in uniform set at 18 plus goaltenders up to December 1 and 16 plus goaltenders thereafter. Teams agree to wear colored uniforms at home and white uniforms on the road.

1956-57 — Player serving a minor penalty allowed to return to ice when a goal is scored by opposing team.

1959-60 — Players prevented from leaving their benches to enter into an altercation. Substitutions permitted providing substitutes do not enter into altercation.

1960-61 — Number of players in uniform set at 16 plus goaltenders.

1961-62 — Penalty shots to be taken by the player against whom the foul was committed. In the event of a penalty shot called in a situation where a particular player hasn't been fouled, the penalty shot to be taken by any player on the ice when the foul was committed.

1964-65 — No body contact on faceoffs.

In playoff games, each team to have its substitute goaltender dressed in his regular uniform except for leg pads and body protector. All previous rules governing standby goaltenders terminated.

1965-66 — Teams required to dress two goaltenders for each regular-season game. Maximum stick length increased to 55 inches.

1966-67 — Substitution allowed on coincidental major penalties.

Between-periods intermissions fixed at 15 minutes.

1967-68 — If a penalty incurred by a goaltender is a co-incident major, the penalty to be served by a player of the goaltender's team on the ice at the time the penalty was called. Limit of curvature of hockey stick blade set at $1^1/_2$ inches.

1969-70 — Limit of curvature of hockey stick blade set at 1 inch.

1970-71 — Home teams to wear basic white uniforms; visiting teams to wear basic colored uniforms.

Limit of curvature of hockey stick blade set at $^1/_2$ inch.

Minor penalty for deliberately shooting the puck out of the playing area.

1971-72 — Number of players in uniform set at 17 plus 2 goaltenders.

Third man to enter an altercation assessed an automatic game misconduct penalty.

1972-73 — Minimum width of stick blade reduced to 2 inches from $2^1/_2$ inches.

1974-75 — Bench minor penalty imposed if a penalized player does not proceed directly and immediately to the penalty box.

1976-77 — Rule dealing with fighting amended to provide a major and game misconduct penalty for any player who is clearly the instigator of a fight.

1977-78 — Teams requesting a stick measurement to be assessed a minor penalty in the event that the measured stick does not violate the rules.

1979-80 — Wearing of helmets made mandatory for players entering the NHL.

1980-81 — Maximum stick length increased to 58 inches.

1981-82 — If both of a team's listed goaltenders are incapacitated, the team can dress and play any eligible goaltender who is available.

1982-83 — Number of players in uniform set at 18 plus 2 goaltenders.

1983-84 — Five-minute sudden-death overtime to be played in regular-season games that are tied at the end of regulation time.

1985-86 — Substitutions allowed in the event of co-incidental minor penalties. Maximum stick length increased to 60 inches.

1986-87 — Delayed off-side is no longer in effect once the players of the offending team have cleared the opponents' defensive zone.

1990-91 — The goal lines, blue lines, defensive zone face-off circles and markings all moved one foot out from the end boards, creating 11 feet of room behind the nets and shrinking the neutral zone from 60 to 58 feet.

1991-92 — Video replays employed to assist referees in goal/no goal situations. Size of goal crease increased. Crease changed to semi-circular configuration. Time clock to record tenths of a second in last minute of each period and overtime. Major and game misconduct penalty for checking from behind into boards. Penalties added for crease infringement and unnecessary contact with goaltender. Goal disallowed if puck enters net while a player of the attacking team is standing on the goal crease line, is in the goal crease or places his stick in the goal crease.

1992-93 — No substitutions allowed in the event of coincidental minor penalties called when both teams are at full strength. Minor penalty for attempting to draw a penalty ("diving"). Major and game misconduct penalty for checking from behind into goal frame. Game misconduct penalty for instigating a fight. High sticking redefined to include any use of the stick above waist-height. Previous rule stipulated shoulder-height.

1993-94 — High sticking redefined to allow goals scored with a high stick below the height of the crossbar of the goal frame.

1996-97 — Maximum stick length increased to 63 inches. All players must be clear of the attacking zone prior to the puck being shot into that zone. The opportunity to "tag-up" and return into the zone has been removed.

1998-99 — The league instituted a two-referee system with each team to play 20 regular-season games with two referees and a pair of linesmen. Goal line moved to 13 feet from end boards. Goal crease altered to extend one foot beyond each goal post (eight feet across in total. Sides of crease squared off, extending 4'6". Only the top of the crease remains rounded. Only the top of the crease remains rounded.

1999-2000 — Each team to play 25 home and 25 road games using the two-referee system. Crease rule revised to implement a "no harm, no foul, no video review" standard. Teams to play with four skaters and a goaltender in regular-season overtime. If a goal is scored in regular-season overtime, the winner is awarded two points and the loser one point. In no goal is scored in overtime, both teams are awarded one point.

2000-01 — All games to be played using the two-referee system.

2002-03 — "Hurry-up" faceoff and line-change rules implemented.

2003-04 — Home teams to wear basic colored uniforms; visiting teams to wear basic white uniforms. Maximum length of goaltender's pads set at 38 inches.

2005-06 — The NHL adopted a comprehensive package of rule changes that included the following:

Goal line moved to 11 feet from end boards; blue lines moved to 75 feet from end boards, reducing neutral zone from 54 feet to 50 feet. Center red line eliminated for two-line passes. "Tag-up" off-side rule reinstituted. This rule was previously used from 1986-87 through 1995-96. Goaltender not permitted to play the puck outside a designated trapezoid-shaped area behind the net. A team that ices the puck will not be permitted to make any player substitutions prior to the ensuing faceoff. A player who instigates a fight in the final five minutes of regulation time or at any time of overtime will receive a minor, a major, a misconduct and an automatic one-game suspension. The size of goaltender equipment has been reduced by approximately 11 percent. If a game remains tied after five minutes of overtime, a shootout will be conducted to determine a winner.

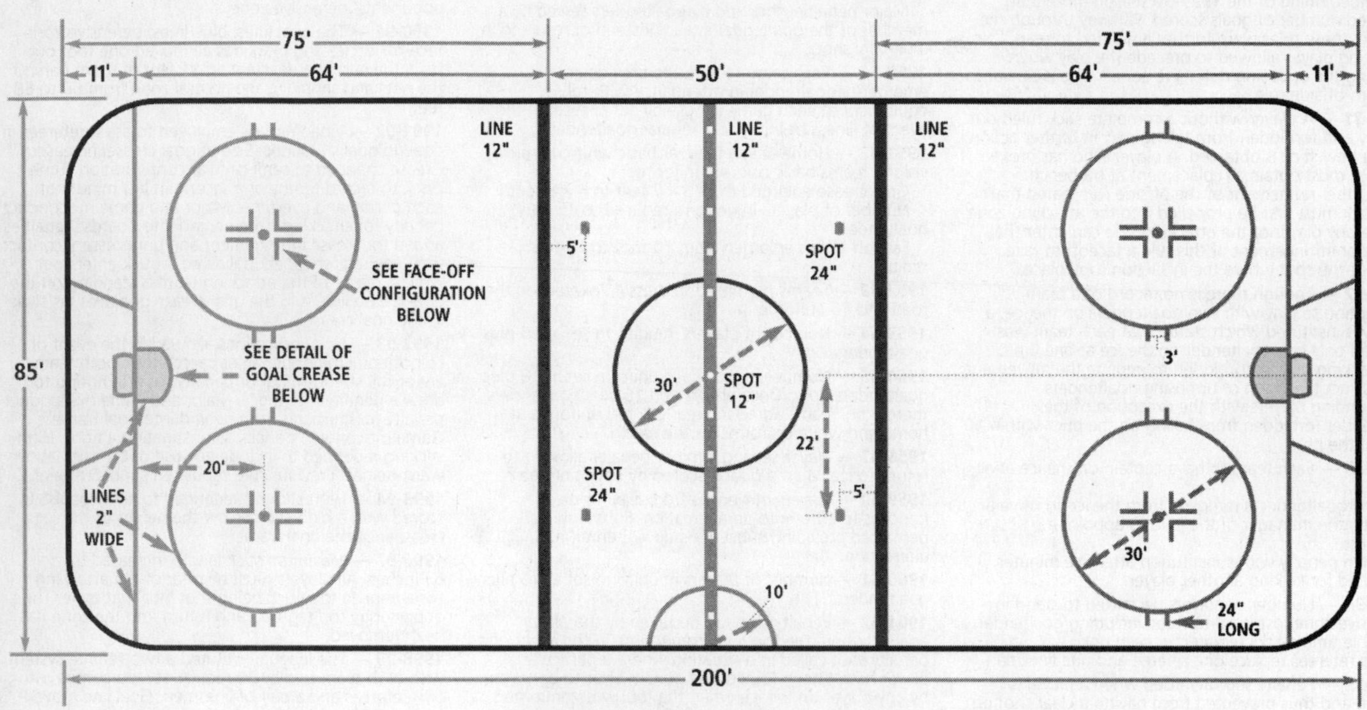

NHL RINK DIMENSIONS

FACEOFF CONFIGURATION

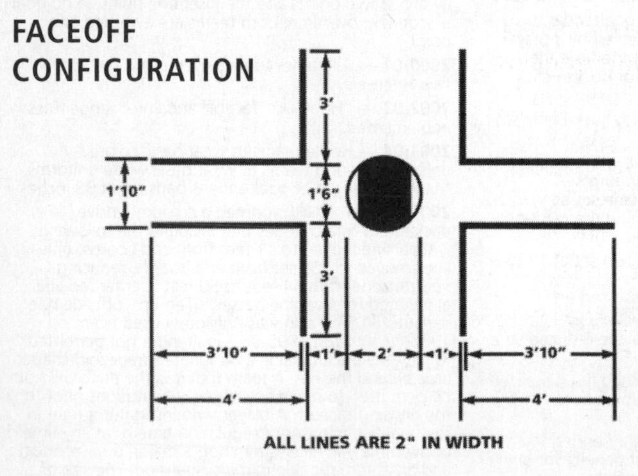

CREASE DIMENSIONS

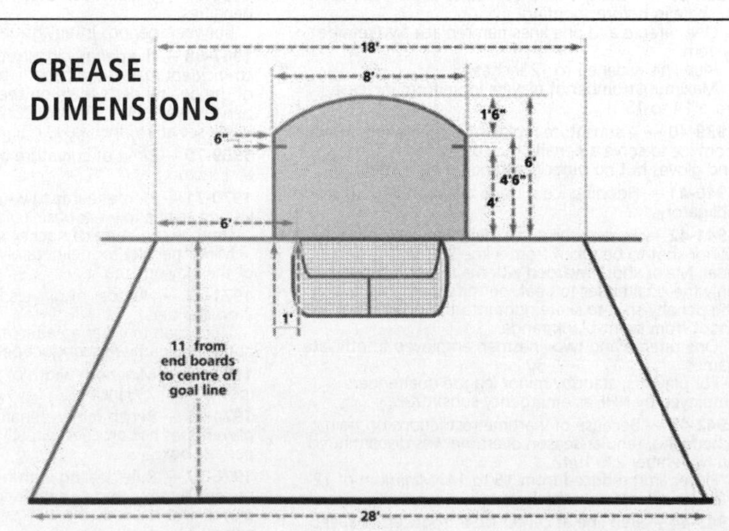

NHL League and Team Websites

National Hockey League......www.nhl.com
NHL Site for Kids................www.nhl.com/kids
NHL Merchandise Shop ....shop.nhl.com
NHL Job Postings.................hockeyjobs.nhl.com
Hockey Fights Cancer..........www.nhl.com/nhlhq/hockeyfightscancer/index.html

Official NHL Team Websites:

Anaheim..........................www.anaheimducks.com
Atlanta ....www.atlantathrashers.com
Boston ....www.bostonbruins.com
Buffalo............................www.sabres.com
Calgary ....www.calgaryflames.com
Carolina..........................www.carolinahurricanes.com
Chicago ....www.chicagoblackhawks.com
Colorado ....www.coloradoavalanche.com
Columbus ....www.bluejackets.com
Dallas ....www.dallasstars.com
Detroit............................www.detroitredwings.com
Edmonton ....www.edmontonoilers.com
Florida ....www.floridapanthers.com
Los Angeles ....www.lakings.com
Minnesota ....www.wild.com
Montreal.........................www.canadiens.com
Nashville ....www.nashvillepredators.com
New Jersey ....www.newjerseydevils.com
NY Islanders....................www.newyorkislanders.com
NY Rangers.....................www.newyorkrangers.com
Ottawa ....www.ottawasenators.com
Philadelphia ....www.philadelphiaflyers.com
Phoenix ....www.phoenixcoyotes.com
Pittsburgh ....www.pittsburghpenguins.com
St. Louis.........................www.stlouisblues.com
San Jose ....www.sjsharks.com
Tampa Bay ....www.tampabaylightning.com
Toronto..........................www.mapleleafs.com
Vancouver ....www.canucks.com
Washington ....www.washingtoncaps.com

To order the *NHL Official Guide & Record Book* and other books about hockey:

www.nhlofficialguide.com

NHL Clubs' Minor-League Affiliations, 2007-08

NHL Club	Minor-League Affiliates
Anaheim	Portland Pirates (AHL) Augusta Lynx (ECHL)
Atlanta	Chicago Wolves (AHL) Gwinnett Gladiators (ECHL)
Boston	Providence Bruins (AHL)
Buffalo	Rochester Americans (AHL)
Calgary	Quad Cities Flames (AHL) Las Vegas Wranglers (ECHL)
Carolina	Albany River Rats (AHL) Florida Everblades (ECHL)
Chicago	Rockford IceHogs (AHL) Pensacola Ice Pilots (ECHL)
Colorado	Lake Erie Monsters (AHL)
Columbus	Syracuse Crunch (AHL) Dayton Bombers (ECHL) Youngstown Steelhounds (CHL)
Dallas	Iowa Stars (AHL) Idaho Steelheads (ECHL)
Detroit	Grand Rapids Griffins (AHL)
Edmonton	Springfield Falcons (AHL) Stockton Thunder (ECHL)
Florida	Rochester Americans (AHL) Florida Everblades (ECHL)
Los Angeles	Manchester Monarchs (AHL) Reading Royals (ECHL)
Minnesota	Houston Aeros (AHL) Texas Wildcatters (ECHL) Austin Ice Bats (CHL)

NHL Club	Minor-League Affiliates
Montreal	Hamilton Bulldogs (AHL) Cincinnati Cyclones (ECHL)
Nashville	Milwaukee Admirals (AHL) Cincinnati Cyclones (ECHL)
New Jersey	Lowell Devils (AHL) Trenton Devils (ECHL)
NY Islanders	Bridgeport Sound Tigers (AHL) Utah Grizzlies (ECHL)
NY Rangers	Hartford Wolf Pack (AHL) Charlotte Checkers (ECHL)
Ottawa	Binghamton Senators (AHL)
Philadelphia	Philadelphia Phantoms (AHL) Wheeling Nailers (ECHL)
Phoenix	San Antonio Rampage (AHL) Phoenix RoadRunners (ECHL) Laredo Bucks (CHL)
Pittsburgh	Wilkes-Barre/Scranton Penguins (AHL) Wheeling Nailers (ECHL)
St. Louis	Peoria Rivermen (AHL) Alaska Aces (ECHL)
San Jose	Worcester Sharks (AHL) Fresno Falcons (ECHL)
Tampa Bay	Norfolk Admirals (AHL) Mississippi Sea Wolves (ECHL)
Toronto	Toronto Marlies (AHL) Columbia Inferno (ECHL)
Vancouver	Manitoba Moose (AHL) Victoria Salmon Kings (ECHL)
Washington	Hershey Bears (AHL) South Carolina Stingrays (ECHL)

Key Off-Season Signings/Acquisitions

2007

June 21 • Re-signed G **J.S. Giguere**.
23 • Acquired LW **Jason King** and a conditional pick in the 2009 Entry Draft from Vancouver for RW **Ryan Shannon**.
23 • Re-signed D **Sean O'Donnell** and D **Kent Huskins**.
July 1 • Signed D **Mathieu Schneider**.
2 • Signed RW **Todd Bertuzzi**.
5 • Re-signed LW **Brad May**.
6 • Signed D **Shane Hnidy**.

Anaheim Ducks

2006-07 Results: 48W-20L-4OTL-10SOL 110PTS.
First, Pacific Division

Year-by-Year Record

		Home				Road				Overall								
Season	GP	W	L	T	OL	W	L	T	OL	W	L	T	OL	GF	GA	Pts.	Finished	Playoff Result
2006-07	**82**	**26**	**6**	....	**9**	**22**	**14**	....	**5**	**48**	**20**	....	**14**	**258**	**208**	**110**	**1st, Pacific Div.**	**Won Stanley Cup**
2005-06	82	26	10	....	5	17	17	....	7	43	27	....	12	254	229	98	3rd, Pacific Div.	Lost Conf. Championship
2004-05	....	....	....	....	....	....	....	....	....	....	....	....	....	....	....	....		
2003-04	82	19	11	7	4	10	24	3	4	29	35	10	8	184	213	76	4th, Pacific Div.	Out of Playoffs
2002-03	82	22	10	7	2	18	17	2	4	40	27	9	6	203	193	95	2nd, Pacific Div.	Lost Final
2001-02	82	15	19	5	2	14	23	3	1	29	42	8	3	175	198	69	5th, Pacific Div.	Out of Playoffs
2000-01	82	15	20	4	2	10	21	7	3	25	41	11	5	188	245	66	5th, Pacific Div.	Out of Playoffs
1999-2000	82	19	13	7	2	15	20	5	1	34	33	12	3	217	227	83	5th, Pacific Div.	Out of Playoffs
1998-99	82	21	14	6	....	14	20	7	....	35	34	13	....	215	206	83	3rd, Pacific Div.	Lost Conf. Quarter-Final
1997-98	82	12	23	6	....	14	20	7	....	26	43	13	....	205	261	65	6th, Pacific Div.	Out of Playoffs
1996-97	82	23	12	6	....	13	21	7	....	36	33	13	....	245	233	85	2nd, Pacific Div.	Lost Conf. Semi-Final
1995-96	82	22	15	4	....	13	24	4	....	35	39	8	....	234	247	78	4th, Pacific Div.	Out of Playoffs
1994-95	48	11	9	4	....	5	18	1	....	16	27	5	....	125	164	37	6th, Pacific Div.	Out of Playoffs
1993-94	84	14	26	2	....	19	20	3	....	33	46	5	....	229	251	71	4th, Pacific Div.	Out of Playoffs

2007-08 Schedule

Month	Day	Date	Opponent
Sep.	Sat.	29	at Los Angeles*†
	Sun.	30	Los Angeles*†
Oct.	Wed.	3	at Detroit
	Fri.	5	at Columbus
	Sat.	6	at Pittsburgh
	Wed.	10	Boston
	Sun.	14	Minnesota*
	Mon.	15	Detroit
	Wed.	17	Nashville
	Sat.	20	at Dallas
	Tue.	23	at St. Louis
	Thu.	25	Phoenix
	Sun.	28	Edmonton*
Nov.	Thu.	1	Columbus
	Sat.	3	at Phoenix
	Mon.	5	Dallas
	Wed.	7	Phoenix
	Fri.	9	San Jose
	Tue.	13	Los Angeles
	Thu.	15	at Los Angeles
	Sat.	17	at San Jose
	Wed.	21	at Dallas
	Fri.	23	Phoenix*
	Sun.	25	Los Angeles*
	Tue.	27	at Vancouver
	Thu.	29	at Calgary
	Fri.	30	at Edmonton
Dec.	Sun.	2	Edmonton*
	Wed.	5	Buffalo
	Fri.	7	at Chicago
	Sat.	8	at Nashville
	Mon.	10	at Columbus
	Wed.	12	Vancouver
	Fri.	14	Minnesota
	Sun.	16	San Jose*
	Tue.	18	at San Jose
	Wed.	19	Colorado
	Sat.	22	at San Jose
	Thu.	27	at Edmonton
	Sat.	29	at Calgary
	Sun.	30	at Vancouver*
Jan.	Wed.	2	Columbus
	Fri.	4	Chicago
	Sat.	5	at Phoenix
	Mon.	7	Nashville
	Wed.	9	Toronto
	Sun.	13	San Jose*
	Tue.	15	Dallas
	Thu.	17	at Nashville
	Fri.	18	at Minnesota
	Sun.	20	at Dallas*
	Wed.	23	Detroit
	Thu.	24	at Los Angeles
	Wed.	30	at Minnesota
Feb.	Fri.	1	at St. Louis
	Sat.	2	at Philadelphia
	Tue.	5	at NY Islanders
	Thu.	7	at NY Rangers
	Fri.	8	at New Jersey
	Sun.	10	at Detroit*
	Tue.	12	at Colorado
	Fri.	15	Dallas
	Sun.	17	Calgary*
	Wed.	20	Colorado
	Fri.	22	St. Louis
	Sun.	24	Chicago*
	Fri.	29	Calgary
Mar.	Mon.	3	Ottawa
	Wed.	5	at Chicago
	Thu.	6	at Colorado
	Sun.	9	Montreal*
	Tue.	11	at Phoenix
	Wed.	12	Vancouver
	Sat.	15	St. Louis
	Wed.	19	at Dallas
	Fri.	21	at San Jose
	Sat.	22	at Phoenix
	Wed.	26	Los Angeles
	Fri.	28	San Jose
	Sun.	30	Dallas*
Apr.	Sat.	5	at Los Angeles*
	Sun.	6	Phoenix*

* Denotes afternoon game. † Games played in London, England.

François Beauchemin was a workhorse on the Ducks star-studded defense. He averaged 25:28 of ice time during 71 games in the regular season and a team-leading 30:33 during 21 playoff games en route to the Stanley Cup.

PACIFIC DIVISION
15th NHL Season

Franchise date: June 15, 1993

2007-08 Player Personnel

FORWARDS	HT	WT	S	Place of Birth	*Age	2006-07 Club
BERTUZZI, Todd	6-3	242	L	Sudbury, Ont.	32	Florida-Detroit
BOLT, Bobby	6-4	226	L	Thunder Bay, Ont.	20	Kingston-Portland (AHL)
CARTER, Ryan	6-1	205	L	White Bear Lake, MN	24	Portland (AHL)-Anaheim
DINGLE, Ryan	5-10	190	L	Steamboat Springs, CO	23	U. of Denver-Portland (AHL)
DIXON, Stephen	5-11	188	L	Halifax, N.S.	22	Wilkes-Barre
EBBETT, Andrew	5-10	174	L	Vernon, B.C.	24	Binghamton
GETZLAF, Ryan	6-3	211	R	Regina, Sask.	22	Anaheim
HYNES, Shane	6-3	210	R	Montreal, Que.	23	Portland (AHL)-Augusta
KEITH, Matt	6-2	200	R	Edmonton, Alta.	24	Chi-Norfolk-Port (AHL)
KING, Jason	6-1	195	L	Corner Brook, Nfld.	26	Skelleftea
KUNITZ, Chris	5-11	198	L	Regina, Sask.	28	Anaheim
LaCOUTURE, Dan	6-2	215	L	Hyannis, MA	30	New Jersey-Lowell
MARCHANT, Todd	5-10	180	L	Buffalo, NY	34	Anaheim
MAY, Brad	6-1	220	L	Toronto, Ont.	35	Colorado-Anaheim
McDONALD, Andy	5-11	185	L	Strathroy, Ont.	30	Anaheim
MILLER, Drew	6-2	174	L	Dover, NJ	23	Portland (AHL)-Anaheim
MOEN, Travis	6-2	216	L	Stewart Valley, Sask.	25	Anaheim
NIEDERMAYER, Rob	6-2	204	L	Cassiar, B.C.	32	Anaheim
PAHLSSON, Samuel	6-0	205	L	Ornskoldsvik, Sweden	29	Anaheim
PARROS, George	6-5	232	R	Washington, PA	27	Colorado-Anaheim
PERRY, Corey	6-3	202	R	Peterborough, Ont.	22	Anaheim
PETERS, Geoff	6-1	205	L	Hamilton, Ont.	29	Portland (AHL)
RYAN, Bobby	6-1	213	R	Cherry Hill, NJ	20	Owen Sound-Portland (AHL)
SEGAL, Brandon	6-3	213	R	Richmond, B.C.	24	Milwaukee
WIRTANEN, Petteri	6-1	202	L	Hyvinkaa, Finland	21	Portland (AHL)
DEFENSEMEN						
BEAUCHEMIN, Francois	6-0	210	L	Sorel, Que.	27	Anaheim
CALLAHAN, Joe	6-3	221	R	Brockton, MA	24	San Antonio
FESTERLING, Brett	6-1	208	L	Quesnel, B.C.	21	Vancouver (WHL)
HNIDY, Shane	6-2	210	R	Neepawa, Man.	31	Atlanta
HUSKINS, Kent	6-3	217	L	Ottawa, Ont.	28	Anaheim-Portland (AHL)
KONDRATIEV, Maxim	6-1	194	L	Togliatti, USSR	24	Togliatti
MIKKELSON, Brendan	6-2	202	L	Regina, Sask.	20	Vancouver (WHL)
NIEDERMAYER, Scott	6-1	200	L	Edmonton, Alta.	34	Anaheim
O'DONNELL, Sean	6-3	231	L	Ottawa, Ont.	35	Anaheim
PRONGER, Chris	6-6	220	L	Dryden, Ont.	32	Anaheim
ROME, Aaron	6-1	230	L	Nesbitt, Man.	24	Anaheim-Portland (AHL)
SALCIDO, Brian	6-2	198	L	Los Angeles, CA	22	Portland (AHL)
SAUNDERS, Nathan	6-4	220	R	Charlottetown, PEI	22	Portland (AHL)-Augusta
SCHNEIDER, Mathieu	5-11	191	L	New York, NY	38	Detroit
SKINNER, Brett	6-1	195	L	Brandon, Man.	24	Port (AHL)-Aug-Omaha
WILSON, Clay	6-0	195	L	Sturgeon Lake, MN	24	Portland (AHL)

GOALTENDERS	HT	WT	C	Place of Birth	*Age	2006-07 Club
BRYZGALOV, Ilya	6-3	208	L	Togliatti, USSR	27	Anaheim
COLEMAN, Gerald	6-4	214	L	Romeoville, IL	22	Sprfld-Jhnstn-Port (AHL)
GIGUERE, Jean-Sebastien	6-1	200	L	Montreal, Que.	30	Anaheim
HILLER, Jonas	6-2	181	R	Felben Wellhausen, Switz.	25	Davos
LEVASSEUR, Jean-Philippe	6-1	200	R	Victoriaville, Que.	20	Rouyn-Noranda

* – Age at start of 2007-08 season

Coach

RANDY CARLYLE

Coach, Anaheim Ducks. Born in Sudbury, Ont., April 19, 1956.

Randy Carlyle was hired as the head coach in Anaheim on August 1, 2005. In his first season behind the bench in 2005-06, he led the Ducks to the Western Conference Final. He led Anaheim to its first Stanley Cup championship in 2007.

Prior to joining the Ducks, Carlyle had served as the head coach of the Manitoba Moose, the Vancouver Canucks' primary development team. In all, Carlyle spent six seasons between 1996 and 2005 as head coach in Manitoba (both in the International and American Hockey Leagues) with his team posting an overall record of 222-159-52-7. He had the additional duties of general manager of the Moose from 1996 to 2000, and served as club president for the 2001-02 season. The Sudbury, Ontario, native helped the Moose to a 47-21-14 record for 108 points in 1998-99, for which he was named the IHL's general manager of the year.

Following the 2001-02 season, Carlyle joined the coaching staff of the Washington Capitals. He served as an assistant coach with Washington for two seasons (2002 to 2004), before rejoining Manitoba in 2004–05.

Carlyle played 17 seasons in the NHL with Toronto, Pittsburgh and Winnipeg. He appeared in 1,055 games and had 148 goals and 499 assists for 647 points. Known as a fiery, tough-nosed defenseman, he was selected to play in four NHL All-Star Games, winning the Norris Trophy as the league's top defenseman in 1981. At the conclusion of his playing career in 1993, Carlyle remained with the Winnipeg organization's hockey operations staff, eventually becoming an assistant coach for the 1995-96 season.

Coaching Record

		Regular Season				Playoffs		
Season	Team	Games	W	L	O/T	Games	W	L
1996-97	Manitoba (IHL)	32	16	14	2	....	....	....
1997-98	Manitoba (IHL	82	39	36	7	3	0	3
1998-99	Manitoba (IHL)	82	47	21	14	5	2	3
99-2000	Manitoba (IHL)	82	37	31	14	2	0	2
2000-01	Manitoba (IHL)	82	39	31	12	13	6	7
2004-05	Manitoba (AHL)	80	44	33	3	14	6	8
2005-06	**Anaheim (NHL)**	**82**	**43**	**27**	**12**	**16**	**9**	**7**
2006-07*	**Anaheim (NHL)**	**82**	**48**	**20**	**14**	**21**	**16**	**5**
	NHL Totals	**164**	**91**	**47**	**26**	**37**	**25**	**12**

* Stanley Cup win.

2006-07 Scoring

* – rookie

Regular Season

Pos	#	Player	Team	GP	G	A	Pts	+/–	PIM	PP	SH	GW	S	%
R	8	Teemu Selanne	ANA	82	48	46	94	26	82	25	0	10	257	18.7
C	19	Andy McDonald	ANA	82	27	51	78	16	46	8	0	3	252	10.7
D	27	Scott Niedermayer	ANA	79	15	54	69	6	86	9	0	3	172	8.7
L	14	Chris Kunitz	ANA	81	25	35	60	23	81	11	0	5	180	13.9
D	25	Chris Pronger	ANA	66	13	46	59	27	69	8	0	2	166	7.8
C	15	Ryan Getzlaf	ANA	82	25	33	58	17	66	11	1	6	203	12.3
R	17 *	Dustin Penner	ANA	82	29	16	45	–2	58	9	0	5	204	14.2
R	10	Corey Perry	ANA	82	17	27	44	12	55	4	0	3	194	8.8
D	23	Francois Beauchemin	ANA	71	7	21	28	7	49	2	0	0	128	5.5
C	26	Samuel Pahlsson	ANA	82	8	18	26	–4	42	0	0	1	111	7.2
C	22	Todd Marchant	ANA	56	8	15	23	7	44	0	3	2	115	7.0
L	32	Travis Moen	ANA	82	11	10	21	–4	101	0	0	0	124	8.9
D	21	Sean O'Donnell	ANA	79	2	15	17	9	92	0	0	1	47	4.3
C	44	Rob Niedermayer	ANA	82	5	11	16	–8	77	0	0	0	106	4.7
D	5	Ric Jackman	FLA	7	1	0	1	–3	10	0	0	1	13	7.7
			ANA	24	1	10	11	3	10	1	0	0	23	4.3
			TOTAL	31	2	10	12	0	20	1	0	1	36	5.6
R	38 *	Ryan Shannon	ANA	53	2	9	11	–2	10	0	0	0	77	2.6
L	45	Shawn Thornton	ANA	48	2	7	9	3	88	0	0	0	60	3.3
D	33	Joe Dipenta	ANA	76	2	6	8	1	48	0	0	1	33	6.1
L	24	Brad May	COL	10	0	3	3	0	8	0	0	0	11	0.0
			ANA	14	0	1	1	–1	13	0	0	0	11	0.0
			TOTAL	24	0	4	4	–1	21	0	0	0	22	0.0
C	13	Mark Hartigan	CBJ	6	1	2	3	2	2	1	0	0	11	9.1
			ANA	6	0	0	0	–1	4	0	0	0	4	0.0
			TOTAL	12	1	2	3	1	6	1	0	0	15	6.7
D	40	Kent Huskins	ANA	33	0	3	3	–3	14	0	0	0	16	0.0
R	43 *	Bjorn Melin	ANA	3	1	0	1	–1	0	0	0	0	1	100.0
C	47 *	Tim Brent	ANA	15	1	0	1	–5	6	0	0	0	14	7.1
R	16	George Parros	COL	2	0	0	0	–1	0	0	0	0	1	0.0
			ANA	32	1	0	1	–2	102	0	0	0	18	5.6
			TOTAL	34	1	0	1	–3	102	0	0	0	19	5.3
D	18	Ian Moran	ANA	1	0	0	0	–1	0	0	0	0	0	0.0
D	34 *	Aaron Rome	ANA	1	0	0	0	–1	0	0	0	0	1	0.0

Goaltending

No.	Goaltender	GPI	Mins	Avg	W	L	OT	EN	SO	GA	SA	S%	G	A	PIM
29	Sebastien Caron	1	28	2.14	0	0	0	1	0	1	6	.833	0	0	0
35	J-S Giguere	56	3245	2.26	36	10	8	1	4	122	1490	.918	0	2	0
30	Ilja Bryzgalov	27	1509	2.47	10	8	6	0	1	62	668	.907	0	0	0
31	* Michael Wall	4	202	2.97	2	2	0	1	0	10	81	.877	0	1	0
	Totals	**82**	**5010**	**2.37**	**48**	**20**	**14**	**3**	**5**	**198**	**2248**	**.912**			

Playoffs

Pos	#	Player	Team	GP	G	A	Pts	+/–	PIM	PP	SH	GW	OT	S	%
C	15	Ryan Getzlaf	ANA	21	7	10	17	1	32	3	1	3	0	57	12.3
R	10	Corey Perry	ANA	21	6	9	15	5	37	1	0	1	0	58	10.3
R	8	Teemu Selanne	ANA	21	5	10	15	1	10	0	0	2	1	60	8.3
D	25	Chris Pronger	ANA	19	3	12	15	10	26	1	0	0	0	58	5.2
C	19	Andy McDonald	ANA	21	10	4	14	6	10	5	0	0	0	64	15.6
L	32	Travis Moen	ANA	21	7	5	12	5	22	0	0	3	1	34	20.6
C	26	Samuel Pahlsson	ANA	21	3	9	12	10	20	0	0	2	0	30	10.0
D	27	Scott Niedermayer	ANA	21	3	8	11	2	26	1	0	2	2	42	7.1
C	44	Rob Niedermayer	ANA	21	5	5	10	9	39	0	1	1	0	42	11.9
D	23	Francois Beauchemin	ANA	20	4	4	8	2	16	4	0	0	0	58	6.9
R	17 *	Dustin Penner	ANA	21	3	5	8	4	2	0	0	2	0	37	8.1
L	14	Chris Kunitz	ANA	13	1	5	6	1	19	0	0	0	0	28	3.6
C	22	Todd Marchant	ANA	11	0	3	3	–1	12	0	0	0	0	19	0.0
D	5	Ric Jackman	ANA	7	1	1	2	2	2	1	0	0	0	2	50.0
D	21	Sean O'Donnell	ANA	21	0	2	2	8	10	0	0	0	0	13	0.0
L	24	Brad May	ANA	18	0	1	1	–1	28	0	0	0	0	14	0.0
D	40	Kent Huskins	ANA	21	0	1	1	4	11	0	0	0	0	5	0.0
C	13	Mark Hartigan	ANA	1	0	0	0	0	0	0	0	0	0	0	0.0
D	34 *	Aaron Rome	ANA	1	0	0	0	–2	0	0	0	0	0	0	0.0
R	46	Joe Motzko	ANA	3	0	0	0	0	2	0	0	0	0	2	0.0
L	18 *	Andrew Miller	ANA	3	0	0	0	1	2	0	0	0	0	3	0.0
C	52 *	Ryan Carter	ANA	4	0	0	0	–1	0	0	0	0	0	0	0.0
R	16	George Parros	ANA	5	0	0	0	0	10	0	0	0	0	1	0.0
R	38 *	Ryan Shannon	ANA	11	0	0	0	0	6	0	0	0	0	5	0.0
L	45	Shawn Thornton	ANA	15	0	0	0	–3	19	0	0	0	0	5	0.0
D	33	Joe Dipenta	ANA	16	0	0	0	0	4	0	0	0	0	3	0.0

Goaltending

No.	Goaltender	GPI	Mins	Avg	W	L	EN	SO	GA	SA	S%	G	A	PIM
35	J-S Giguere	18	1067	1.97	13	4	0	1	35	451	.922	0	0	0
30	Ilja Bryzgalov	5	267	2.25	3	1	0	0	10	128	.922	0	0	0
	Totals	**21**	**1341**	**2.01**	**16**	**5**	**0**	**1**	**45**	**579**	**.922**			

Club Records

Team

(Figures in brackets for season records are games played; records for fewest points, wins, ties, losses, goals, goals against are for 70 or more games)

Most Points	110	2006-07 (82)
Most Wins	48	2006-07 (82)
Most Ties	13	1996-97 (82), 1997-98 (82), 1998-99 (82)
Most Losses	46	1993-94 (84)
Most Goals	258	2006-07 (82)
Most Goals Against	261	1997-98 (82)
Fewest Points	65	1997-98 (82)
Fewest Wins	25	2000-01 (82)
Fewest Ties	5	1993-94 (84)
Fewest Losses	20	2006-07 (82)
Fewest Goals	175	2001-02 (82)
Fewest Goals Against	193	2002-03 (82)
Longest Winning Streak		
Overall	7	Feb. 20-Mar. 7/99
Home	7	Mar. 7-Apr. 4/06
Away	7	Nov. 28-Dec. 13/06
Longest Undefeated Streak		
Overall	12	Feb. 22-Mar. 19/97 (7 wins, 5 ties)
Home	14	Feb. 12-Apr. 9/97 (10 wins, 4 ties)
Away	7	Nov. 28-Dec. 13/06 (7 wins)
Longest Losing Streak		
Overall	8	Oct. 12-30/96, Nov. 3-20/05
Home	8	Jan. 10-Feb. 9/01
Away	7	Oct. 8-Nov. 12/05
Longest Winless Streak		
Overall	9	Three times
Home	11	Jan. 5-Feb. 14/01 (8 losses, 3 ties)
Away	13	Nov. 1-Dec. 27/03 (11 losses, 2 ties)
Most Shutouts, Season	9	2002-03 (82)
Most PIM, Season	1,843	1997-98 (82)
Most Goals, Game	8	Three times

Individual

Most Seasons	10	Steve Rucchin
Most Games	616	Steve Rucchin
Most Goals, Career	313	Teemu Selanne
Most Assists, Career	369	Paul Kariya
Most Points, Career	669	Paul Kariya (300G, 369A)
Most PIM, Career	788	Dave Karpa
Most Shutouts, Career	27	Guy Hebert
Longest Consecutive Games Streak	275	Samuel Pahlsson (Feb. 7/03-to date)
Most Goals, Season	52	Teemu Selanne (1997-98)
Most Assists, Season	62	Paul Kariya (1998-99)
Most Points, Season	109	Teemu Selanne (1996-97; 51G, 58A)
Most PIM, Season	285	Todd Ewen (1995-96)
Most Points, Defenseman, Season	69	Scott Niedermayer (2006-07; 15G, 54A)
Most Points, Center, Season	85	Andy McDonald (2005-06; 34G, 51A)
Most Points, Right Wing, Season	109	Teemu Selanne (1996-97; 51G, 58A)
Most Points, Left Wing, Season	108	Paul Kariya (1995-96; 50G, 58A)
Most Points, Rookie, Season	45	Dustin Penner (2006-07; 29G, 16A)
Most Shutouts, Season	8	Jean-Sebastien Giguere (2002-03)
Most Goals, Game	3	Twenty-four times
Most Assists, Game	5	Dmitri Mironov (Dec. 12/97), Teemu Selanne (Nov. 19/06)
Most Points, Game	5	Nine times

General Managers' History

Jack Ferreira, 1993-94 to 1997-98; Pierre Gauthier, 1998-99 to 2001-02; Bryan Murray, 2002-03, 2003-04; Al Coates, 2004-05; Brian Burke, 2005-06 to date.

Coaching History

Ron Wilson, 1993-94 to 1996-97; Pierre Page, 1997-98; Craig Hartsburg, 1998-99, 1999-2000; Craig Hartsburg and Guy Charron, 2000-01; Bryan Murray, 2001-02; Mike Babcock, 2002-03 to 2004-05; Randy Carlyle, 2005-06 to date.

Captains' History

Troy Loney, 1993-94; Randy Ladouceur, 1994-95, 1995-96; Paul Kariya, 1996-97; Paul Kariya and Teemu Selanne, 1997-98; Paul Kariya, 1998-99 to 2002-03; Steve Rucchin, 2003-04; Scott Niedermayer, 2005-06 to date.

All-time Record vs. Other Clubs

Regular Season

	At Home								On Road								Total							
	GP	W	L	T	OL	GF	GA	PTS	GP	W	L	T	OL	GF	GA	PTS	GP	W	L	T	OL	GF	GA	PTS
Atlanta	5	3	2	0	0	14	10	6	5	4	1	0	0	18	11	8	10	7	3	0	0	32	21	14
Boston	9	2	3	2	2	18	24	8	9	4	4	0	1	27	27	9	18	6	7	2	3	45	51	17
Buffalo	9	2	7	0	0	15	30	4	10	2	4	3	1	22	28	8	19	4	11	3	1	37	58	12
Calgary	30	16	8	6	0	97	77	38	29	9	19	1	0	64	84	19	59	25	27	7	0	161	161	57
Carolina	10	5	4	1	0	31	32	11	10	3	6	1	0	21	27	7	20	8	10	2	0	52	59	18
Chicago	26	15	7	3	1	73	55	34	28	14	12	2	0	71	72	30	54	29	19	5	1	144	127	64
Colorado	25	9	11	3	2	62	66	23	25	6	13	4	2	61	78	18	50	15	24	7	4	123	144	41
Columbus	12	6	3	1	2	37	31	15	12	5	7	0	0	28	32	10	24	11	10	1	2	65	63	25
Dallas	35	15	16	3	1	86	90	34	35	7	23	2	3	66	119	19	70	22	39	5	4	152	209	53
Detroit	26	10	12	4	0	63	71	24	26	2	19	3	2	53	92	9	52	12	31	7	2	116	163	33
Edmonton	30	17	11	2	0	87	77	36	29	9	17	0	3	60	71	21	59	26	28	2	3	147	148	57
Florida	10	4	5	1	0	28	30	9	9	3	3	2	1	22	27	9	19	7	8	3	1	50	57	18
Los Angeles	38	17	8	7	6	131	106	47	38	14	18	4	2	98	110	34	76	31	26	11	8	229	216	81
Minnesota	12	8	2	0	2	31	26	18	12	3	6	2	1	21	28	9	24	11	8	2	3	52	54	27
Montreal	8	3	5	0	0	25	27	6	9	3	4	2	0	24	27	8	17	6	9	2	0	49	54	14
Nashville	16	13	1	0	2	50	26	28	16	6	6	2	2	38	37	16	32	19	7	2	4	88	63	44
New Jersey	11	5	5	1	0	30	28	11	8	1	6	0	1	14	31	3	19	6	11	1	1	44	59	14
NY Islanders	10	2	4	3	1	22	29	8	8	3	4	1	0	23	24	7	18	5	8	4	1	45	53	15
NY Rangers	9	6	1	0	2	35	29	14	9	5	2	1	1	26	23	12	18	11	3	1	3	61	52	26
Ottawa	9	4	3	2	0	21	18	10	9	4	4	1	0	23	27	9	18	8	7	3	0	44	45	19
Philadelphia	10	4	4	2	0	34	35	10	8	2	3	3	0	17	22	7	18	6	7	5	0	51	57	17
Phoenix	35	23	9	3	0	109	83	49	34	18	12	2	2	98	92	40	69	41	21	5	2	207	175	89
Pittsburgh	9	6	3	0	0	32	26	12	9	2	5	2	0	27	29	6	18	8	8	2	0	59	55	18
St. Louis	26	10	14	2	0	70	78	22	26	10	11	3	2	72	81	25	52	20	25	5	2	142	159	47
San Jose	38	15	19	2	2	104	121	34	38	19	16	2	1	106	107	41	76	34	35	4	3	210	228	75
Tampa Bay	9	5	3	1	0	28	22	11	10	6	4	0	0	27	20	12	19	11	7	1	0	55	42	23
Toronto	11	5	5	1	0	34	28	11	16	2	10	4	0	32	53	8	27	7	15	5	0	66	81	19
Vancouver	29	9	11	7	2	73	84	27	30	12	16	2	0	74	95	26	59	21	27	9	2	147	179	53
Washington	10	6	2	1	1	31	25	14	10	6	4	0	0	28	17	12	20	12	6	1	1	59	42	26
Totals	**517**	**245**	**188**	**58**	**26**	**1471**	**1384**	**574**	**517**	**184**	**259**	**49**	**25**	**1261**	**1491**	**442**	**1034**	**429**	**447**	**107**	**51**	**2732**	**2875**	**1016**

Playoffs

	Series	W	L	GP	W	L	T	GF	GA	Last Mtg.	Rnd.	Result
Calgary	1	1	0	7	4	3	0	17	16	2006	CQF	W 4-3
Colorado	1	1	0	4	4	0	0	16	4	2006	CSF	W 4-0
Dallas	1	1	0	6	4	2	0	14	14	2003	CSF	W 4-2
Detroit	4	2	2	18	8	10	0	40	53	2007	CF	W 4-2
Edmonton	1	0	1	5	1	4	0	13	16	2006	CF	L 1-4
Minnesota	2	2	0	9	8	1	0	21	10	2007	CQF	W 4-1
New Jersey	1	0	1	7	3	4	0	12	19	2003	F	L 3-4
Ottawa	1	1	0	5	4	1	0	16	11	2007	F	W 4-1
Phoenix	1	1	0	7	4	3	0	17	17	1997	CQF	W 4-3
Vancouver	1	1	0	5	4	1	0	14	8	2007	CSF	W 4-1
Totals	**14**	**10**	**4**	**73**	**44**	**29**	**0**	**180**	**168**			

Carolina totals include Hartford, 1993-94 to 1996-97.
Colorado totals include Quebec, 1993-94 to 1994-95.
Phoenix totals include Winnipeg, 1993-94 to 1995-96.

Playoff Results 2007-2002

Year	Round	Opponent	Result	GF	GA
2007	**F**	**Ottawa**	**W 4-1**	**16**	**11**
	CF	Detroit	W 4-2	16	17
	CSF	Vancouver	W 4-1	14	8
	CQF	Minnesota	W 4-1	12	9
2006	CF	Edmonton	L 1-4	13	16
	CSF	Colorado	W 4-0	16	4
	CQF	Calgary	W 4-3	17	16
2003	F	New Jersey	L 3-4	12	19
	CF	Minnesota	W 4-0	9	1
	CSF	Dallas	W 4-2	14	14
	CQF	Detroit	W 4-0	10	6

Abbreviations: Round: F - Final; **CF** – conference final; **CSF** – conference semi-final; **CQF** – conference quarter-final

2006-07 Results

Month	Day	Opponent	Score	Month	Day	Opponent	Score
Oct.	6	Los Angeles	4-3	**Jan.**	2	at Detroit	1-2
	7	at Phoenix	2-1		5	Columbus	3-4
	9	St. Louis	2-0		7	Detroit	4-2
	11	NY Islanders	4-5†		9	at Nashville	4-5*
	15	Dallas	3-4†		11	at Dallas	5-1
	18	Detroit	4-1		13	Colorado	2-3†
	20	Minnesota	2-1		16	St. Louis	2-6
	22	at Los Angeles	3-2†		18	at Edmonton	1-4
	25	Edmonton	6-2		19	at Calgary	2-3
	27	at Minnesota	2-3†		28	Dallas	4-1
	28	at Chicago	3-0		31	Phoenix	2-1
	30	at St. Louis	6-5†	**Feb.**	3	at Nashville	0-3
Nov.	1	NY Rangers	3-4*		6	at San Jose	7-4
	3	Phoenix	6-2		7	San Jose	2-3
	6	Pittsburgh	3-2*		10	at Dallas	0-1
	9	at Vancouver	6-0		13	at Colorado	0-2
	10	at Calgary	0-3		15	at Phoenix	5-4*
	12	Minnesota	3-2		17	at Los Angeles	3-2†
	15	Philadelphia	4-7		18	Los Angeles	3-4†
	17	Chicago	3-4†		20	Vancouver	2-3*
	19	Phoenix	6-4		23	at Dallas	1-4
	21	San Jose	5-0		25	Colorado	5-3
	22	at Colorado	2-3†		26	at San Jose	3-2
	24	New Jersey	4-2	**Mar.**	1	at Los Angeles	3-4*
	26	Calgary	5-3		2	San Jose	3-1
	28	at Edmonton	3-2*		4	Nashville	3-2†
	30	at Vancouver	2-1		7	Phoenix	2-1
Dec.	2	at Los Angeles	4-3		9	Edmonton	5-1
	3	Los Angeles	2-3		11	Vancouver	4-2
	6	Nashville	4-0		14	Columbus	4-5†
	8	at Washington	6-1		16	Chicago	5-2
	9	at Tampa Bay	4-3		18	Los Angeles	3-5
	12	at Florida	5-4		22	at Phoenix	1-2
	13	at Atlanta	2-1		23	Dallas	3-2*
	16	at San Jose	3-4		26	at Detroit	0-1
	18	Calgary	4-1		28	at Chicago	3-1
	20	Dallas	4-1		29	at Columbus	5-2
	23	at Phoenix	0-2		31	at St. Louis	3-2*
	26	at San Jose	4-3	**Apr.**	4	San Jose	2-3†
	29	at Carolina	2-4		6	at Dallas	1-2†
	31	at Minnesota	3-4		7	at Columbus	4-3

* – Overtime † – Shootout

Entry Draft Selections 2007-1993

2007

Pick	
19	Logan MacMillan
42	Eric Tangradi
63	Maxime Macenauer
92	Justin Vaive
93	Steven Kampfer
98	Sebastian Stefaniszin
121	Mattias Modig
151	Brett Morrison

2006

Pick	
19	Mark Mitera
38	Bryce Swan
83	John Degray
112	Matt Beleskey
172	Petteri Wirtanen

2005

Pick	
2	Bobby Ryan
31	Brendan Mikkelson
63	Jason Bailey
127	Bobby Bolt
141	Brian Salcido
197	Jean-Philippe Levasseur

2004

Pick	
9	Ladislav Smid
39	Jordan Smith
74	Kyle Klubertanz
75	Tim Brent
172	Matt Auffrey
203	Gabriel Bouthillette
236	Matt Christie
269	Janne Pesonen

2003

Pick	
19	Ryan Getzlaf
28	Corey Perry
86	Shane Hynes
90	Juha Alen
119	Nathan Saunders
186	Drew Miller
218	Dirk Southern
250	Shane O'Brien
280	Ville Mantymaa

2002

Pick	
7	Joffrey Lupul
37	Tim Brent
71	Brian Lee
103	Joonas Vihko
140	George Davis
173	Luke Fritshaw
261	Francois Caron
267	Chris Petrow

2001

Pick	
5	Stanislav Chistov
35	Mark Popovic
69	Joel Stepp
102	Timo Parssinen
105	Vladimir Korsunov
118	Brandon Rogers
137	Joel Perreault
170	Jan Tabacek
224	Tony Martensson
232	Martin Gerber
264	Pierre Parenteau

2000

Pick	
12	Alexei Smirnov
44	Ilya Bryzgalov
98	Jonas Ronnqvist
134	Peter Podhradsky
153	Bill Cass

1999

Pick	
44	Jordan Leopold
83	Niclas Havelid
105	Alexandr Chagodayev
141	Maxim Rybin
173	Jan Sandstrom
230	Petr Tenkrat
258	Brian Gornick

1998

Pick	
5	Vitaly Vishnevski
32	Stephen Peat
112	Viktor Wallin
150	Trent Hunter
178	Jesse Fibiger
205	David Bernier
233	Pelle Prestberg
245	Andreas Andersson

1997

Pick	
18	Michael Holmqvist
45	Maxim Balmochnykh
72	Jay Legault
125	Luc Vaillancourt
178	Tony Mohagen
181	Mat Snesrud
209	Rene Stussi
235	Tommi Degerman

1996

Pick	
9	Ruslan Salei
35	Matt Cullen
117	Brendan Buckley
149	Blaine Russell
172	Timo Ahmaoja
198	Kevin Kellett
224	Tobias Johwelin

1995

Pick	
4	Chad Kilger
29	Brian Wesenberg
55	Mike Leclerc
107	Igor Nikulin
133	Peter LeBoutillier
159	Mike LaPlante
185	Igor Karpenko

1994

Pick	
2	Oleg Tverdovsky
28	Johan Davidsson
67	Craig Reichert
80	Byron Briske
106	Pavel Trnka
132	Bates Battaglia
158	Rocky Welsing
184	Brad Englehart
236	Tommi Miettinen
262	Jeremy Stevenson

1993

Pick	
4	Paul Kariya
30	Nikolai Tsulygin
56	Valeri Karpov
82	Joel Gagnon
108	Mikhail Shtalenkov
134	Antti Aalto
160	Matt Peterson
186	Tom Askey
212	Vitali Kozel
238	Anatoli Fedotov
264	David Penney

Vice President and General Manager

BRIAN BURKE
Executive Vice President/General Manager, Anaheim Ducks.
Born in Providence, RI, June 30, 1955.

Brian Burke, former president and general manager of the Vancouver Canucks, was named Anaheim's new executive vice president and general manager on June 20, 2005. In his first year on the job in 2005-06, the Ducks reached the Western Conference Final. In 2007, Anaheim won the Stanley Cup.

Burke had served as the president and general manager of the Vancouver Canucks from 1998 to 2004. Under his leadership, the team increased its point total four consecutive years from 1999 to 2003. With 104 and 101 points respectively the last two NHL seasons (2002 to 2004), the Canucks joined only Detroit, Ottawa and Philadelphia to record consecutive seasons with at least 100 points. The 2003–04 Canucks finished with a record of 43-24-10-5 for 101 points, winning the Northwest Division. Over his last four seasons with the team, Burke engineered four consecutive seasons of at least 90 points. In 2001, he was named NHL executive of the year by *The Sporting News*.

One of the most respected and experienced executives in the NHL, Burke originally joined the Canucks in June, 1987 as vice president and director of hockey operations. He left the Canucks in 1992 to become general manager of the Hartford Whalers, before being named NHL senior vice president and director of hockey operations (1993 to 1998). While working at the NHL league office, Burke worked closely with commissioner Gary Bettman on a wide variety of league issues and policies and was the NHL's chief disciplinarian.

Burke was born in New England and raised in Minnesota. He signed with the Philadelphia Flyers in 1977 as a player and was a member of the 1978 Calder Cup champion Maine Mariners. Burke then returned to Harvard Law School, where he graduated in 1981 before practicing law for six years in Boston. During his two stints in Vancouver, Burke was a valued and active member of the community, including his serving on the board of directors for Canuck Place.

Club Directory

Honda Center

Anaheim Ducks
Honda Center
2695 Katella Ave.
Anaheim, CA 92806
Phone **714/940-2900**
FAX 714/940-2953
Ticket Information 877/WILDWING
www.anaheimducks.com
Capacity: 17,174

Executive Management
Owners. . . . . Henry and Susan Samueli
Chief Executive Officer . . . . Michael Schulman
Executive Vice President/General Manager . . . . Brian P. Burke
Executive Vice President/COO . . . . Tim Ryan
Senior Vice President/G.M., Honda Center . . . . Mike O'Donnell
Senior Vice President, Hockey Operations . . . . Bob Murray
Senior Vice President/Chief Marketing Officer . . . . . Bob Wagner
Assistant General Manager . . . . David McNab
Vice President of Sales & Marketing . . . . Steve Obert
Senior Advisor to the General Manager. . . . . Al Coates
Executive Assistant to the Exec. V.P./G.M. . . . . Maureen Nyeholt
Executive Assistant to the Exec. V.P./COO . . . . Cheryl Gorman
Executive Assistant to the Sr. V.P./CMO. . . . . Janet Conley
Executive Assistant . . . . Robin Schuette
Administrative Assistant, Hockey Operations . . . . . . Christina Morrow

Coaching Staff
Head Coach . . . . Randy Carlyle
Assistant Coaches. . . . . Dave Farrish, Newell Brown
Goaltending Consultant . . . . Francois Allaire
Video Coordinator . . . . Joe Trotta
Strength & Conditioning Coach . . . . Sean Skahan

Hockey Club Operations
Director of Professional Scouting. . . . . Rick Paterson
Director of Amateur Scouting . . . . Alain Chainey
Scouting Staff . . . Scott Carter, Jeff Crisp, Jan-Åke Danielson, Todd Hearty, Pavel Routa, John McMorrow, Trent Yawney, Casey Hankinson, Konstantin Krylov, Donald Marier, Daryl Stanley
Head Trainer. . . . . Tim Clark
Massage Therapist . . . . James Partida
Equipment Manager . . . . Doug Shearer
Assistant Equipment Manager. . . . . John Allaway
Visiting Team Equipment Attendant . . . . Chris Kincaid
Manager of Hockey Operations. . . . . Ryan Lichtenfels
Portland Pirates (AHL) Head Coach . . . . Kevin Dineen
Portland Assistant Coaches. . . . . Gord Dineen, Matt Laatsch
Portland Trainer/Equipment Manager . . . . Rick Burrill/Chris Aldridge
Team Physicians . . . . Dr. Ronald Glousman, Dr. Craig Milhouse
Oral Surgeon . . . . Dr. Jeff Pulver

Broadcasting
Director of Broadcasting . . . . Aaron Teats
Associate Producer . . . . Bob Sipowich
TV, Fox Sports Prime Ticket (Cable), KDOC-TV. . . . . John Ahlers, Brian Hayward
Radio, KLAA AM 830 & Ducks Radio Network . . . . Steve Carroll, Brent Severyn

Communications
Director of Media & Communications . . . . Alex Gilchrist
Media & Communications Coordinator. . . . . Lauren O'Gorman
Game Night Communications Staff. . . . Lisa Parris, Grant Young, Courtney Strayer, Larry Woodard

Community Relations
Director of Community Relations & Public Affairs . . Wendy Yamagishi
Community Relations Managers . . . . Jesse Tyler, Jennifer Walker

Entertainment
Director of Entertainment/Multi-Media . . . . Rod Murray
Production Manager . . . . Kent French
Entertainment Manager . . . . Chris Brown
Editor/Producer. . . . . Rich Cooley
Arena Vision Editor/Producer. . . . . Davin Maske

Fan Development
Director of Fan Development . . . . Matt Savant
Manager, School/Youth Hockey Programs. . . . . Joseph Hwang/Lynsie Estes

Finance and Administration
Vice President of Human Resources. . . . . Kim Kutcher
Vice President of Finance . . . . Doug Heller
Controller. . . . . Melody Martin
IT Manager. . . . . Mike Wing
Human Resources Manager . . . . Wendy Mulhall

Corporate Partnerships
Director of Corporate Partnerships . . . . Wendy Grover
Director of Media Sales. . . . . Tanya Mitchell
Director of Corporate Relations & Research. . . . . . . Alex Evezich
Senior Manager of Media Sales. . . . . Jamal Spears
Senior Sales Managers . . . . Bonner Paddock, Aimee Perrin
Sales Managers. . . . . Matt Wiech, Bret Gerber
Media Sales Manager . . . . Guy Tomcheck
Naming and Title Rights Manager. . . . . Rachel Kaizoji

Marketing
Director of Marketing . . . . Tracie Jones
Sr. Manager, Signature Programs & Events . . . . Kris Loomis
Sr. Manager, Marketing . . . . Allison Wright
Signature Programs & Events Manager . . . . Jamie Minkler
Premium Marketing Manager . . . . Melissa Goldstein
Manager of Graphic Design . . . . Seth Cable
Media Buying Manager. . . . . Adam Mendelsohn
Marketing Manager . . . . Shannon O'Maley

Publications and New Media
Director of Publications & New Media . . . . Adam Brady

Premium Sales and Customer Service
Director of Premium Sales & Service . . . . Jim Panetta
Premium Account Executives. . . . . Geoff Matthews, Timothy Thompson
Premium Services Manager . . . . Jana Cannavo

Ticketing
Manager of Ticket Operations. . . . . James Bakken
Assistant Ticketing Manager . . . . Jonas Calicdan
Assistant Manager, Premium Ticketing . . . . Gina Bulgheroni

Ticket Sales and Customer Service
Director of Ticket Sales & Service. . . . . Lisa Johnson
Senior Manager of Season & Group Sales . . . . Mike Morrow
Inside Sales Manager . . . . Zach Hollins

Atlanta Thrashers

2006-07 Results: 43W-28L-7OTL-4SOL 97PTS.
First, Southeast Division

Key Off-Season Signings/Acquisitions

2007

- **Apr. 20** • Signed 2006 1st-round pick (12th overall), C **Bryan Little**.
- **June 22** • Re-signed LW **Brad Larsen** and D **Steve McCarthy**.
- **22** • Acquired C **Chris Thorburn** from Pittsburgh for a 3rd-round pick in the 2007 Entry Draft.
- **July 1** • Re-signed LW **Pascal Dupuis**.
- **1** • Signed C **Eric Perrin**.
- **2** • Signed D **Ken Klee**.
- **4** • Re-signed LW **Vyacheslav Kozlov**.
- **17** • Re-signed D **Garnet Exelby**.

Year-by-Year Record

		Home				Road				Overall								
Season	**GP**	**W**	**L**	**T**	**OL**	**W**	**L**	**T**	**OL**	**W**	**L**	**T**	**OL**	**GF**	**GA**	**Pts.**	**Finished**	**Playoff Result**
2006-07	82	23	12	....	6	20	16	....	5	43	28	....	11	246	245	97	1st, Southeast Div.	Lost Conf. Quarter-Final
2005-06	82	24	13	....	4	17	20	....	4	41	33	....	8	281	275	90	3rd, Southeast Div.	Out of Playoffs
2004-05	....	....	....	....	....	....	....	....	....	....	....	....	....	....	....	....		
2003-04	82	18	17	4	2	15	20	4	2	33	37	8	4	214	243	78	2nd, Southeast Div.	Out of Playoffs
2002-03	82	15	19	4	3	16	20	3	2	31	39	7	5	226	284	74	3rd, Southeast Div.	Out of Playoffs
2001-02	82	11	21	9	0	8	26	2	5	19	47	11	5	187	288	54	5th, Southeast Div.	Out of Playoffs
2000-01	82	10	23	6	2	13	22	6	0	23	45	12	2	211	289	60	4th, Southeast Div.	Out of Playoffs
1999-2000	82	9	26	3	3	5	31	4	1	14	57	7	4	170	313	39	5th, Southeast Div.	Out of Playoffs

2007-08 Schedule

Month	Day	Date	Opponent
Oct.	Fri.	5	Washington
	Sat.	6	at Tampa Bay
	Wed.	10	Ottawa
	Thu.	11	at Buffalo
	Sat.	13	New Jersey
	Tue.	16	at Philadelphia
	Thu.	18	NY Rangers
	Sat.	20	at Tampa Bay
	Tue.	23	at Toronto
	Thu.	25	at Nashville
	Sat.	27	at Chicago
	Tue.	30	at Montreal
Nov.	Thu.	1	at Ottawa
	Sat.	3	at Tampa Bay
	Tue.	6	Washington
	Fri.	9	at Florida
	Sat.	10	Carolina
	Tue.	13	Florida
	Fri.	16	at Carolina
	Mon.	19	Tampa Bay
	Wed.	21	at Washington
	Fri.	23	New Jersey
	Sat.	24	at Pittsburgh
	Thu.	29	Toronto
Dec.	Sat.	1	at NY Islanders
	Sun.	2	at New Jersey*
	Wed.	5	NY Islanders
	Fri.	7	NY Rangers
	Sat.	8	at Washington
	Wed.	12	Boston
	Fri.	14	Toronto
	Sat.	15	at Ottawa
	Tue.	18	Tampa Bay
	Thu.	20	Ottawa
	Sat.	22	Montreal
	Sun.	23	at St. Louis*
	Wed.	26	at Columbus
	Thu.	27	Florida
	Sat.	29	Boston
	Mon.	31	at Boston*
Jan.	Wed.	2	at Carolina
	Fri.	4	Carolina
	Sun.	6	Buffalo*
	Tue.	8	Philadelphia
	Thu.	10	Florida
	Sat.	12	Pittsburgh
	Tue.	15	at Detroit
	Thu.	17	Montreal
	Fri.	18	at Buffalo
	Sun.	20	Edmonton*
	Tue.	22	at NY Rangers
	Thu.	24	at NY Rangers
	Wed.	30	Pittsburgh
Feb.	Fri.	1	Buffalo
	Sat.	2	at Washington
	Tue.	5	Philadelphia
	Thu.	7	Vancouver
	Sat.	9	Tampa Bay
	Wed.	13	Washington
	Fri.	15	at New Jersey
	Sat.	16	at NY Islanders
	Thu.	21	at Carolina
	Sat.	23	at Toronto
	Tue.	26	at Montreal
	Thu.	28	NY Islanders
Mar.	Sat.	1	at Boston*
	Sun.	2	at Pittsburgh*
	Wed.	5	Carolina
	Fri.	7	Minnesota
	Sat.	8	at Florida
	Tue.	11	Colorado
	Thu.	13	Calgary
	Fri.	14	at Washington
	Sun.	16	at Florida*
	Tue.	18	at Philadelphia
	Wed.	19	Carolina
	Fri.	21	Washington
	Thu.	27	at Florida
	Fri.	28	at Carolina
	Mon.	31	at Tampa Bay
Apr.	Tue.	1	Florida
	Sat.	5	Tampa Bay

* Denotes afternoon game.

Atlanta was Alexei Zhitnik's third, final and most successful stop in 2006-07. In 18 games with the Thrashers, he averaged 25:49 of ice time and had 14 points (two goals, 12 assists). Overall, Zhitnik had seven goals and 31 assists for 38 points in 79 games, more than any other Atlanta blueliner.

SOUTHEAST DIVISION
9th NHL Season

Franchise date: June 25, 1997

2007-08 Player Personnel

FORWARDS	HT	WT	S	Place of Birth	*Age	2006-07 Club
BARTOVIC, Milan	5-11	200	L	Trencin, Czech.	26	Malmo-Zurich
CRABB, Joey	6-1	190	R	Anchorage, AK	24	Chicago (AHL)
DESBIENS, Guillaume	6-2	210	R	Alma, Que.	22	Chicago (AHL)
DUPUIS, Pascal	6-0	200	L	Laval, Que.	28	Min-NYR-Atl
GIROUX, Alexandre	6-3	190	L	Quebec City, Que.	26	Washington-Hershey
HAYDAR, Darren	5-9	170	R	Toronto, Ont.	27	Atlanta-Chicago (AHL)
HOLIK, Bobby	6-4	230	R	Jihlava, Czech.	36	Atlanta
HOSSA, Marian	6-1	210	L	Stara Lubovna, Czech.	28	Atlanta
KOVALCHUK, Ilya	6-1	225	R	Tver, USSR	24	Atlanta
KOZLOV, Vyacheslav	5-10	190	L	Voskresensk, USSR	35	Atlanta
KROG, Jason	5-11	185	R	Fernie, B.C.	31	Atl-Chi (AHL)-NYR
LARSEN, Brad	6-0	210	L	Nakusp, B.C.	30	Atlanta
LaVALLEE, Jordan	6-3	220	L	Corvallis, OR	21	Chicago (AHL)
LITTLE, Bryan	5-11	200	R	Edmonton, Alta.	19	Barrie-Chicago (AHL)
PAINCHAUD, Chad	6-1	185	L	Mississauga, Ont.	21	Gwinnett
PERRIN, Eric	5-9	180	L	Laval, Que.	31	Tampa Bay
POSPISIL, Tomas	6-0	185	R	Sumperk, Czech.	20	Sarnia
RUCCHIN, Steve	6-2	215	L	Thunder Bay, Ont.	36	Atlanta
SCHULTZ, Jesse	6-1	195	R	Strasbourg, Sask.	25	Vancouver-Manitoba
SLATER, Jim	6-0	190	L	Petoskey, MI	24	Atlanta
STERLING, Brett	5-8	180	L	Los Angeles, CA	23	Chicago (AHL)
STOESZ, Myles	6-2	215	R	Steinbach, Man.	20	Chilliwack-Regina
STUART, Colin	6-2	205	L	Rochester, MN	25	Chicago (AHL)
THORBURN, Chris	6-3	220	R	Sault Ste. Marie, Ont.	24	Pittsburgh-Wilkes-Barre
WHITE, Todd	5-10	195	L	Kanata, Ont.	32	Minnesota
DEFENSEMEN						
DENNY, Chad	6-3	220	L	Sydney, N.S.	20	Lewiston
ENSTROM, Tobias	5-10	175	L	Nordingra, Sweden	22	MODO
EXELBY, Garnet	6-1	215	L	Ste. Anne, Man.	26	Atlanta
HAVELID, Niclas	6-0	200	L	Stockholm, Sweden	34	Atlanta
KLEE, Ken	6-0	215	R	Indianapolis, IN	36	Colorado
LEHMAN, Scott	6-2	200	L	Fort McMurray, Alta.	21	Chicago (AHL)-Gwinnett
LEWIS, Grant	6-3	200	R	Pittsburgh, PA	22	Dartmouth
McCARTHY, Steve	6-1	205	L	Trail, B.C.	26	Atlanta
OYSTRICK, Nathan	6-0	215	L	Regina, Sask.	24	Chicago (AHL)
PILAR, Karel	6-3	210	R	Prague, Czech.	29	Toronto (AHL)-Sparta
POPOVIC, Mark	6-1	210	L	Stoney Creek, Ont.	24	Atlanta-Chicago (AHL)
VALABIK, Boris	6-7	230	L	Nitra, Czech.	21	Chicago (AHL)
ZHITNIK, Alexei	5-11	215	L	Kiev, USSR	34	NYI-Phi-Atl

GOALTENDERS	HT	WT	C	Place of Birth	*Age	2006-07 Club
BRATHWAITE, Fred	5-7	185	L	Ottawa, Ont.	34	Chicago (AHL)
HEDBERG, Johan	6-0	185	L	Leksand, Sweden	34	Atlanta
LEHTONEN, Kari	6-4	200	L	Helsinki, Finland	23	Atlanta
PAVELEC, Ondrej	6-2	200	L	Kladno, Czech.	20	Cape Breton
TURPLE, Dan	6-6	210	L	Oakville, Ont.	22	Gwinnett

* – Age at start of 2007-08 season

Vice President and General Manager

DON WADDELL
Vice President/General Manager, Atlanta Thrashers.
Born in Detroit, MI, August 19, 1958.

As the only general manager in the history of the Atlanta Thrashers, Don Waddell has established a foundation for long-term success in Atlanta by infusing the club with solid veterans to support a talented young line-up.

Waddell has built a team that set club records in wins (43) and points (97) in 2006-07, winning the Southeast Division and reaching the playoffs for the first time. The team's first step toward achieving this success came during the 2002-03 season when it made a very dramatic second-half turnaround which was keyed by Waddell's decision to hire proven Stanley Cup winner Bob Hartley as coach. Prior to hiring Hartley, Waddell made his own successful NHL coaching debut with a win at Carolina on December 27, 2002. (He served as interim head coach until January 13, 2003.)

Waddell came to the franchise on June 23, 1998 – almost a year to the day after the NHL granted Atlanta a team. He has built the core of the franchise through the NHL Entry Draft and by stockpiling impressive prospects. He made Ilya Kovalchuk the first Russian player selected first overall in the history of the Entry Draft. In the 2002 Entry Draft, Waddell made Kari Lehtonen of Finland the highest-selected European goaltender in NHL draft history.

Waddell has a long-standing relationship with USA Hockey as a player and in management, and served as assistant general manager for the 2004 World Championship and World Cup teams. He was general manager of the 2005 World Championship team and the 2006 Olympic team. His extensive organizational experience also includes having previously built two professional hockey franchises: the San Diego Gulls and the Orlando Solar Bears of the now-defunct International Hockey League. He's also no stranger to winning through his role as assistant general manager for the Stanley Cup champion Detroit Red Wings during the 1997-98 season.

Waddell's playing experience includes more than nine seasons of professional hockey, mostly in the IHL. He was drafted by the NHL's Los Angeles Kings in 1978 and spent three years with the organization from 1980 to 1983. During a successful amateur career, Waddell helped the U.S. national team win the gold medal at the 1983 B-Pool World Championships. He played Division I hockey at Northern Michigan University from 1976 to 1980, where he majored in business management.

NHL Coaching Record

		Regular Season				Playoffs		
Season	Team	Games	W	L	T	Games	W	L
2002-03	Atlanta	10	4	5	1	....	....	....
	NHL Totals	**10**	**4**	**5**	**1**	....	....	....

2006-07 Scoring

* – rookie

Regular Season

Pos	#	Player	Team	GP	G	A	Pts	+/–	PIM	PP	SH	GW	S	%
R	18	Marian Hossa	ATL	82	43	57	100	18	49	17	3	5	340	12.6
L	13	Vyacheslav Kozlov	ATL	81	28	52	80	9	36	8	0	8	190	14.7
L	17	Ilya Kovalchuk	ATL	82	42	34	76	–2	66	18	0	7	336	12.5
L	8	Keith Tkachuk	STL	61	20	23	43	3	92	8	0	1	160	12.5
			ATL	18	7	8	15	8	34	2	0	3	36	19.4
			TOTAL	79	27	31	58	11	126	10	0	4	196	13.8
D	77	Alexei Zhitnik	NYI	30	2	9	11	13	40	0	0	1	49	4.1
			PHI	31	3	10	13	–16	38	1	0	0	61	4.9
			ATL	18	2	12	14	4	14	2	0	1	22	9.1
			TOTAL	79	7	31	38	1	92	3	0	2	132	5.3
R	19	Scott Mellanby	ATL	69	12	24	36	–9	63	5	0	2	103	11.7
C	22	Eric Belanger	CAR	56	8	12	20	–2	14	3	0	1	100	8.0
			ATL	24	9	6	15	0	12	1	0	0	49	18.4
			TOTAL	80	17	18	35	–2	26	4	0	1	149	11.4
R	14	Jonathan Sim	ATL	77	17	12	29	–1	60	2	0	1	141	12.1
C	16	Bobby Holik	ATL	82	11	18	29	–3	86	2	1	1	190	5.8
D	7	Greg de Vries	ATL	82	3	21	24	–3	66	0	0	0	102	2.9
C	20	Steve Rucchin	ATL	47	5	16	21	–4	14	1	0	1	56	8.9
D	28	Niclas Havelid	ATL	77	3	18	21	–2	52	1	0	1	82	3.7
L	9	Pascal Dupuis	MIN	48	10	3	13	–7	38	2	2	0	106	9.4
			NYR	6	1	0	1	–4	0	0	0	0	10	10.0
			ATL	17	3	2	5	–6	4	0	0	1	40	7.5
			TOTAL	71	14	5	19	–17	42	2	2	1	156	9.0
C	23	Jim Slater	ATL	74	5	14	19	8	62	0	0	2	90	5.6
D	5	Steve McCarthy	ATL	46	4	12	16	4	24	3	0	0	51	7.8
D	25	Andy Sutton	ATL	55	2	14	16	6	76	0	1	0	51	3.9
L	29	Brad Larsen	ATL	72	7	6	13	–11	39	0	2	0	61	11.5
R	11	Jean-Pierre Vigier	ATL	72	5	8	13	0	27	0	0	0	83	6.0
D	34	Shane Hnidy	ATL	72	5	7	12	15	63	0	1	1	86	5.8
D	2	Garnet Exelby	ATL	58	2	8	10	2	56	0	1	0	57	3.5
L	36	Eric Boulton	ATL	45	3	4	7	2	49	0	0	0	42	7.1
D	6 *	Mark Popovic	ATL	3	0	1	1	1	0	0	0	0	1	0.0
C	21	Derek MacKenzie	ATL	4	0	0	0	1	0	0	0	0	3	0.0
R	38	Darren Haydar	ATL	4	0	0	0	0	0	0	0	0	4	0.0

Goaltending

No.	Goaltender	GPI	Mins	Avg	W	L	OT	EN	SO	GA	SA	S%	G	A	PIM
32	Kari Lehtonen	68	3934	2.79	34	24	9	5	4	183	2075	.912	0	1	6
1	Johan Hedberg	21	1057	2.89	9	4	2	2	0	51	500	.898	0	1	6
	Totals	**82**	**5015**	**2.88**	**43**	**28**	**11**	**7**	**4**	**241**	**2582**	**.907**			

Playoffs

Pos	#	Player	Team	GP	G	A	Pts	+/–	PIM	PP	SH	GW	OT	S	%
L	8	Keith Tkachuk	ATL	4	1	2	3	2	12	0	0	0	0	11	9.1
L	9	Pascal Dupuis	ATL	4	1	2	3	2	4	0	0	0	0	7	14.3
L	17	Ilya Kovalchuk	ATL	4	1	1	2	–1	19	0	0	0	0	12	8.3
L	29	Brad Larsen	ATL	4	0	2	2	1	0	0	0	0	0	4	0.0
D	28	Niclas Havelid	ATL	4	0	2	2	–5	0	0	0	0	0	4	0.0
D	7	Greg de Vries	ATL	4	1	0	1	–2	4	0	0	0	0	5	20.0
D	34	Shane Hnidy	ATL	4	1	0	1	–1	0	0	0	0	0	4	25.0
C	22	Eric Belanger	ATL	4	1	0	1	–6	12	1	0	0	0	3	33.3
C	16	Bobby Holik	ATL	4	0	1	1	0	0	0	0	0	0	12	0.0
R	18	Marian Hossa	ATL	4	0	1	1	–6	6	0	0	0	0	10	0.0
R	19	Scott Mellanby	ATL	4	0	0	0	–2	4	0	0	0	0	4	0.0
L	13	Vyacheslav Kozlov	ATL	4	0	0	0	–6	6	0	0	0	0	7	0.0
D	77	Alexei Zhitnik	ATL	4	0	0	0	–4	4	0	0	0	0	5	0.0
L	36	Eric Boulton	ATL	4	0	0	0	–1	24	0	0	0	0	1	0.0
R	14	Jonathan Sim	ATL	4	0	0	0	–1	0	0	0	0	0	2	0.0
D	25	Andy Sutton	ATL	4	0	0	0	–2	10	0	0	0	0	4	0.0
D	2	Garnet Exelby	ATL	4	0	0	0	–1	6	0	0	0	0	3	0.0
C	23	Jim Slater	ATL	4	0	0	0	–2	2	0	0	0	0	1	0.0

Goaltending

No.	Goaltender	GPI	Mins	Avg	W	L	EN	SO	GA	SA	S%	G	A	PIM
1	Johan Hedberg	2	117	2.56	0	2	1	0	5	69	.928	0	0	0
32	Kari Lehtonen	2	118	5.59	0	2	0	0	11	73	.849	0	0	0
	Totals	**4**	**240**	**4.25**	**0**	**4**	**1**	**0**	**17**	**143**	**.881**			

General Managers' History

Don Waddell, 1999-2000 to date.

Captains' History

Kelly Buchberger, 1999-2000; Steve Staios, 2000-01; Ray Ferraro, 2001-02; no captain, 2002-03; Shawn McEachern, 2003-04; Scott Mellanby, 2005-06, 2006-07.

Coaching History

Curt Fraser, 1999-2000 to 2001-02; Curt Fraser, Don Waddell and Bob Hartley, 2002-03; Bob Hartley, 2003-04 to date.

Club Records

Team

(Figures in brackets for season records are games played.)

Record		
Most Points	97	2006-07 (82)
Most Wins	43	2006-07 (82)
Most Ties	12	2000-01 (82)
Most Losses	57	1999-2000 (82)
Most Goals	281	2005-06 (82)
Most Goals Against	313	1999-2000 (82)
Fewest Points	39	1999-2000 (82)
Fewest Wins	14	1999-2000 (82)
Fewest Ties	7	1999-2000 (82), 2002-03 (82)
Fewest Losses	33	2005-06 (82)
Fewest Goals	170	1999-2000 (82)
Fewest Goals Against	243	2003-04 (82)
Longest Winning Streak		
Overall	5	Three times
Home	7	Mar. 2-18/07
Away	4	Jan. 13-Feb. 7/03
Longest Undefeated Streak		
Overall	5	Four times
Home	6	Mar. 20-Apr. 15/06 (6 wins)
Away	7	Oct. 21-Nov. 13/00 (3 wins, 4 ties)
Longest Losing Streak		
Overall	12	Jan. 24-Feb. 20/00
Home	*11	Jan. 24-Mar. 16/00
Away	10	Oct. 6-Nov. 18/01
Longest Winless Streak		
Overall	16	Jan. 16-Feb. 20/00 (2 ties, 14 losses)
Home	*17	Jan. 19-Mar. 29/00 (2 ties, 15 losses)
Away	10	Oct. 6-Nov. 18/01 (10 losses)
Most Shutouts, Season	5	2005-06 (82)
Most PIM, Season	1,505	2003-04 (82)
Most Goals, Game	9	Nov. 12/05 (Atl. 9 at Car. 0)

Individual

Record		
Most Seasons	6	Patrik Stefan
Most Games	414	Patrik Stefan
Most Goals, Career	202	Ilya Kovalchuk
Most Assists, Career	179	Vyacheslav Kozlov
Most Points, Career	379	Ilya Kovalchuk (202G, 177A)
Most PIM, Career	532	Jeff Odgers
Most Shutouts, Career	7	Kari Lehtonen
Longest Consecutive Games Streak	164	Greg de Vries (Oct. 5/05-Apr. 7/07)
Most Goals, Season	52	Ilya Kovalchuk (2005-06)
Most Assists, Season	69	Marc Savard (2005-06)
Most Points, Season	100	Marian Hossa (2006-07; 43G, 57A)
Most PIM, Season	226	Jeff Odgers (2000-01)
Most Points, Defenseman, Season	38	Jaroslav Modry (2005-06; 7G, 31A), Alexei Zhitnik (2006-07; 7G, 31A)
Most Points, Center, Season	97	Marc Savard (2005-06; 28G, 69A)
Most Points, Right Wing, Season	100	Marian Hossa (2006-07; 43G, 57A)
Most Points, Left Wing, Season	98	Ilya Kovalchuk (2005-06; 52G, 46A)
Most Points, Rookie, Season	67	Dany Heatley (2001-02; 26G, 41A)
Most Shutouts, Season	4	Kari Lehtonen (2006-07)
Most Goals, Game	4	Pascal Rheaume (Jan. 19/02), Ilya Kovalchuk (Nov. 11/05)
Most Assists, Game	4	Five times
Most Points, Game	5	Six times

* NHL Record.

Vyacheslav Kozlov had a career-high 80 points with 28 goals and 52 assists in 2006-07.

All-time Record vs. Other Clubs

Regular Season

	At Home								On Road								Total							
	GP	W	L	T	OL	GF	GA	PTS	GP	W	L	T	OL	GF	GA	PTS	GP	W	L	T	OL	GF	GA	PTS
Anaheim	5	1	4	0	0	11	18	2	5	2	3	0	0	10	14	4	10	3	7	0	0	21	32	6
Boston	14	7	7	0	0	43	40	14	14	6	4	2	2	51	47	16	28	13	11	2	2	94	87	30
Buffalo	14	8	3	1	2	45	43	19	14	6	8	0	0	40	57	12	28	14	11	1	2	85	100	31
Calgary	4	3	0	1	0	8	5	7	4	0	4	0	0	7	18	0	8	3	4	1	0	15	23	7
Carolina	21	5	10	3	3	53	65	16	21	7	10	1	3	64	67	18	42	12	20	4	6	117	132	34
Chicago	5	2	2	0	1	18	15	5	2	0	2	0	0	0	6	0	7	2	4	0	1	18	21	5
Colorado	4	1	1	1	1	7	8	4	5	3	2	0	0	16	20	6	9	4	3	1	1	23	28	10
Columbus	4	3	1	0	0	10	8	6	4	2	1	0	1	11	12	5	8	5	2	0	1	21	20	11
Dallas	5	0	4	0	1	12	21	1	5	1	4	0	0	9	11	2	10	1	8	0	1	21	32	3
Detroit	4	1	3	0	0	14	25	2	4	0	2	0	2	8	17	2	8	1	5	0	2	22	42	4
Edmonton	3	1	2	0	0	3	8	2	5	1	3	1	0	12	19	3	8	2	5	1	0	15	27	5
Florida	21	13	3	4	1	74	56	31	21	11	7	1	2	65	52	25	42	24	10	5	3	139	108	56
Los Angeles	5	2	3	0	0	13	18	4	5	1	4	0	0	15	26	2	10	3	7	0	0	28	44	6
Minnesota	2	0	2	0	0	6	10	0	4	0	3	1	0	6	13	1	6	0	5	1	0	12	23	1
Montreal	14	3	9	2	0	23	39	8	14	4	9	0	1	31	45	9	28	7	18	2	1	54	84	17
Nashville	5	3	0	1	1	16	13	8	3	1	2	0	0	6	12	2	8	4	2	1	1	22	25	10
New Jersey	14	5	7	2	0	33	50	12	14	6	7	1	0	29	40	13	28	11	14	3	0	62	90	25
NY Islanders	14	4	8	2	0	41	55	10	14	6	8	0	0	33	52	12	28	10	16	2	0	74	107	22
NY Rangers	14	5	9	0	0	38	48	10	14	9	4	1	0	46	40	19	28	14	13	1	0	84	88	29
Ottawa	14	5	8	1	0	49	57	11	14	5	8	1	0	38	61	11	28	10	16	2	0	87	118	22
Philadelphia	14	2	9	1	2	32	49	7	14	2	9	2	1	41	61	7	28	4	18	3	3	73	110	14
Phoenix	5	1	3	0	1	10	17	3	6	0	5	1	0	9	21	1	11	1	8	1	1	19	38	4
Pittsburgh	14	4	8	0	2	42	50	10	14	4	9	0	1	39	53	9	28	8	17	0	3	81	103	19
St. Louis	5	2	2	1	0	16	16	5	3	0	3	0	0	1	11	0	8	2	5	1	0	17	27	5
San Jose	5	1	3	1	0	8	16	3	5	0	4	1	0	10	21	1	10	1	7	2	0	18	37	4
Tampa Bay	21	11	5	3	2	66	58	27	21	6	11	1	3	52	78	16	42	17	16	4	5	118	136	43
Toronto	13	5	7	0	1	25	46	11	13	4	8	1	0	30	48	9	26	9	15	1	1	55	94	20
Vancouver	3	1	2	0	0	11	12	2	4	1	2	1	0	7	13	3	7	2	4	1	0	18	25	5
Washington	21	11	6	2	2	61	61	26	21	6	9	3	3	61	75	18	42	17	15	5	5	122	136	44
Totals	**287**	**110**	**131**	**26**	**20**	**788**	**927**	**266**	**287**	**94**	**155**	**19**	**19**	**747**	**1010**	**226**	**574**	**204**	**286**	**45**	**39**	**1535**	**1937**	**492**

Playoffs

	Series	W	L	GP	W	L	T	GF	GA	Last Mtg.	Rnd.	Result
NY Rangers	1	0	1	4	0	4	0	6	17	2007	CQF	L 0-4
Totals	**1**	**0**	**1**	**4**	**0**	**4**	**0**	**6**	**17**			

Playoff Results 2007-2002

Year	Round	Opponent	Result	GF	GA
2007	CQF	NY Rangers	L 0-4	6	17

Abbreviations: Round: CQF – conference quarter-final.

2006-07 Results

Month	Date	Opponent	Score
Oct.	5	Tampa Bay	2-3†
	7	Florida	6-0
	9	at Tampa Bay	1-0
	11	Boston	4-1
	13	Carolina	3-4
	14	at Washington	4-3*
	19	Washington	4-3†
	21	Florida	4-2
	23	at Florida	6-3
	25	at Carolina	4-5*
	26	at Philadelphia	2-3†
	28	at Buffalo	5-4†
	30	at Toronto	2-4
Nov.	1	Carolina	2-5
	3	at Washington	4-3
	4	at NY Islanders	4-1
	6	Boston	5-3
	8	Ottawa	5-4
	10	NY Rangers	2-5
	11	at Tampa Bay	3-5
	17	Dallas	3-5
	18	at Montreal	1-3
	22	at Washington	4-2
	24	at Tampa Bay	2-3*
	25	Florida	1-0
	28	at NY Rangers	5-4*
	30	Toronto	5-0
Dec.	2	at Florida	3-1
	5	at Toronto	5-2
	7	at Tampa Bay	0-8
	9	Pittsburgh	3-4*
	13	Anaheim	1-2
	15	Washington	2-3*
	16	at NY Islanders	0-6
	19	at New Jersey	4-3†
	21	Pittsburgh	4-3†
	23	New Jersey	5-2
	26	Tampa Bay	2-1
	27	at Pittsburgh	4-2
	30	at Buffalo	1-4
Jan.	1	at Ottawa	3-2*
	2	at Minnesota	1-5
	5	Phoenix	4-5*
	6	at Washington	2-3*
	9	at Montreal	2-4
	12	at New Jersey	1-2
	13	at Carolina	4-3†
	16	Los Angeles	6-2
	18	Montreal	1-4
	20	at NY Rangers	3-1
	26	NY Islanders	5-4*
	28	Philadelphia	1-2
	30	New Jersey	5-4†
Feb.	1	NY Islanders	2-5
	3	Philadelphia	2-5
	6	Buffalo	3-4†
	8	at Colorado	6-3
	10	at Vancouver	2-3
	11	at Edmonton	1-5
	13	at Calgary	1-4
	17	at Ottawa	3-5
	20	at Carolina	3-1
	22	Tampa Bay	4-5*
	24	Carolina	1-4
	26	at Boston	3-2
Mar.	2	Ottawa	4-2
	4	Carolina	3-1
	6	Florida	4-2
	8	Montreal	6-2
	10	at Florida	2-3
	12	Washington	4-2
	15	at Philadelphia	2-3
	16	NY Rangers	2-1*
	18	Buffalo	4-3*
	22	San Jose	1-5
	24	at Pittsburgh	1-2
	28	at Florida	2-3†
	29	Toronto	3-2*
	31	at Boston	3-2
Apr.	4	Washington	2-3
	6	at Carolina	4-1
	7	Tampa Bay	3-2†

* – Overtime † – Shootout

Entry Draft Selections 2007-1999

2007

Pick	
67	Spencer Machacek
115	Niclas Lucenius
175	John Albert
205	Paul Postma

2006

Pick	
12	Bryan Little
43	Riley Holzapfel
80	Michael Forney
135	Alex Kangas
165	Jonas Enlund
195	Jesse Martin
200	Arturs Kulda
210	Will O'Neill

2005

Pick	
16	Alex Bourret
41	Ondrej Pavelec
49	Chad Denny
53	Andrew Kozek
116	Jordan LaVallee
135	Tomas Pospisil
187	Andrei Zubarev
207	Myles Stoesz

2004

Pick	
10	Boris Valabik
40	Grant Lewis
76	Scott Lehman
106	Chad Painchaud
142	Juraj Gracik
186	Dan Turple
204	Miikka Tuomainen
237	Mitch Carefoot
270	Matt Siddall

2003

Pick	
8	Braydon Coburn
110	Jim Sharrow
116	Guillaume Desbiens
136	Michael Vannelli
145	Brett Sterling
175	Mike Hamilton
203	Denis Loginov
239	Tobias Enstrom
269	Rylan Kaip

2002

Pick	
2	Kari Lehtonen
30	Jim Slater
116	Patrick Dwyer
124	Lane Manson
144	Paul Flache
167	Brad Schell
198	Nathan Oystrick
230	Colton Fretter
236	Tyler Boldt
257	Pauli Levokari

2001

Pick	
1	Ilya Kovalchuk
80	Michael Garnett
100	Brian Sipotz
112	Milan Gajic
135	Colin Stuart
189	Pasi Nurminen
199	Matt Suderman
201	Colin FitzRandolph
262	Mario Cartelli

2000

Pick	
2	Dany Heatley
31	Ilja Nikulin
42	Libor Ustrnul
107	Carl Mallette
108	Blake Robson
147	Matt McRae
168	Zdenek Smid
178	Jeff Dwyer
180	Darcy Hordichuk
230	Samu Isosalo
242	Evan Nielsen
244	Eric Bowen
288	Mark McRae
290	Simon Gamache

1999

Pick	
1	Patrik Stefan
30	Luke Sellars
68	Zdenek Blatny
98	David Kaczowka
99	Rob Zepp
128	Derek MacKenzie
159	Yuri Dobryshkin
188	Stephen Baby
217	Garnet Exelby
245	Tommi Santala
246	Raymond DiLauro

Picked second overall in 2002, Kari Lehtonen has quickly become number one in the Thrashers net.

Coach

BOB HARTLEY
Coach, Atlanta Thrashers. Born in Hawkesbury, Ont., September 7, 1960.

Bob Hartley, the second head coach in Thrashers history, has used his experience as a Stanley Cup champion in Colorado to develop the young talent in the organization. In 2006-07, Hartley's team set club records in wins (43) and points (97), winning the Southeast Division and reaching the playoffs for the first time.

Prior to joining the Thrashers, Hartley guided the Colorado Avalanche to the 2001 Stanley Cup championship. In the 2002 playoffs, he became the first NHL coach to lead his team to the Conference Final in each of his first four seasons with the same club. His Avalanche teams won at least 42 games in four consecutive seasons from 1998 to 2002.

Hartley became the second head coach of the Avalanche, and the 11th in franchise history, when he was named to the position on June 30, 1998. He served there until December 18, 2002 and is Colorado's all-time coaching victory leader (193), having guided the Avalanche to four consecutive Northwest Division titles and four straight trips to the Western Conference Final. Hartley guided the 2000-01 Avalanche to its most successful season in franchise history. Colorado established team records for points (118), wins (52) and goals against (192).

Hartley has been a proven winner at every level he has coached. Prior to joining Colorado, Hartley coached four seasons in the American Hockey League from 1994 to 1998, posting a 151-136-33 regular-season record and making four consecutive trips to the playoffs with Cornwall (1994 to 1996) and Hershey (1996 to 1998). He guided Hershey to the 1997 Calder Cup championship. After serving as an assistant coach for Cornwall in 1993-94, Hartley guided the Aces to the Southern Division title in 1994-95, and a trip to the Southern Division Final again in 1995-96. He led Laval to the Quebec Major Junior Hockey League championship and the Memorial Cup in 1993, and compiled an 81-52-7 record in two seasons with Laval from 1991 to 1993.

From 1987 to 1991, Hartley served as head coach for Hawkesbury of the Canadian Junior Hockey League. After enduring an 18-point season in his rookie term behind the Hawks' bench, he guided the club to an impressive 117-45-5 mark during the next three seasons, including CJHL championships in 1990 and 1991. His teams dropped just three postseason games in 1990 and 1991, going 24-3 in that span. Overall, his teams in Hawkesbury advanced to the playoffs four consecutive seasons and finished 31-13 in the postseason during that span.

Throughout his coaching career, Hartley has shared a strong sense of dedication with his community. He was honored in his hometown of Hawkesbury, where the local ice arena was renamed Complex Bob Hartley in August 1998 in recognition of his service to the community where he grew up and coached. He has been involved in hockey camps and charitable endeavors throughout his career.

Club Directory

Philips Arena

Atlanta Thrashers
Centennial Tower
101 Marietta St.
Suite 1900
Atlanta, GA 30303
Phone **404/878-3800**
FAX 404/878-3712
www.atlantathrashers.com
Capacity: 18,545

Ownership – Atlanta Spirit, LLC

Owners	Bruce Levenson, Michael Gearon, Steve Belkin, Ed Peskowitz, Rutherford Seydel, Todd Foreman, Felix Riccio, Michael Gearon, Sr., Beau Turner

Executive Management

President and Chief Executive Officer	Bernard J. Mullin
Executive V.P. and G.M., Atlanta Thrashers	Don Waddell
President of Philips Arena	Bob Williams
Executive V.P. and G.M., Atlanta Hawks	Billy Knight
Executive V.P./Chief Marketing Officer	Lou DePaoli
Executive V.P./Chief Financial Officer	Bill Duffy
Sr. V.P. of Philips Arena	Trey Feazell
Sr. V.P. of Communications	Tom Hughes
Sr. V.P. of Broadcast and Corporate Partnerships	Tracy White
V.P. of Ticket Sales and Service	Brendan Donohue
V.P. of Community Development	LaVerne Henderson
V.P. of Building and Event Operations, Philips Arena	Barry Henson
V.P. of Finance	Phil Ebinger
V.P. and Assistant G.M., Hawks	Gary Fitzsimmons
V.P. of Operations, Philips Arena	Patrick Lane
V.P. of Business Development	David Lee
V.P. of Leisure Services, Philips Arena	Lenny McNally
V.P. of Strategic Planning	Ailey Penningroth
V.P. of Marketing, Advertising and Branding	Jim Pfeifer
V.P. of Human Resources	Ginni Siler
V.P. and Assistant G.M., Thrashers	Larry Simmons
V.P. of Public Relations, Hawks	Arthur Triche
V.P. and Chief Legal Officer/Assistant G.M., Hawks	Scott Wilkinson
V.P. of Basketball	Dominique Wilkins

Hockey Operations

Executive V.P. and General Manager	Don Waddell
Vice President and Assistant General Manager	Larry Simmons
Director of Amateur Scouting and Player Development	Dan Marr
Director of Player Personnel	Mark Dobson
Senior Director of Team Services	Michele Zarzaca
Executive Assistant to Don Waddell, Practice Facility Office Manager	Leisa Ludwin

Coaching Staff

Head Coach	Bob Hartley
Assistant Coaches	Brad McCrimmon, Steve Weeks
Video Coach	Tony Borgford

Scouting Staff

Head Scout	Marcel Comeau
Full-Time Scouts	Evgeny Bogdanovich, Bernd Freimuller, Mark Hillier, Travis MacMillan, Peter Mahovlich, Bob Owen, John Perpich, Normand Poisson
Part-Time Scouts	Terry Brennan, Pat Carmichael, Shin Larsson

Training Staff

Strength and Conditioning Coach	Ray Bear
Head Athletic Trainer	Craig Brewer
Assistant Athletic Trainer	Step Roberts
Massage Therapist	Inar Treiguts

Equipment Staff

Head Equipment Manager	Bobby Stewart
Assistant Equipment Managers	Joe Guilmet, Jim Guilmet

Medical Staff

Head Team Physician and Orthopaedic Surgeon	Dr. Scott Gillogly
Assistant Team Physician and Internist	Dr. William Whaley
Oral and Maxillofacial Surgeon	Dr. Glenn Maron
Team Dentists	Dr. Lawrence Saltzman, Dr. Brett Silverman

Public Relations

Senior Director of Public Relations	Rob Koch
Assistant Director of Media Relations	Brian Potter
Media Relations Assistant	Rob Tillotson

Miscellaneous

Television	SportSouth
Television Broadcasters	JP Dellacamera, Darren Eliot
Radio	680 The Fan
Radio Broadcasters	Dan Kamal, Jeff Odgers

Coaching Record

		Regular Season				Playoffs		
Season	Team	Games	W	L	O/T	Games	W	L
1991-92	Laval (QMJHL)	70	38	27	5	10	4	6
1992-93	Laval (QMJHL)	70	43	25	2	13	12	1
1994-95	Cornwall (AHL)	80	38	33	9	15	8	7
1995-96	Cornwall (AHL)	80	34	39	7	8	3	5
1996-97	Hershey (AHL)	80	43	27	10	23	15	8
1997-98	Hershey (AHL)	80	36	37	7	7	3	4
1998-99	**Colorado (NHL)**	**82**	**44**	**28**	**10**	**19**	**11**	**8**
1999-2000	**Colorado (NHL)**	**82**	**42**	**29**	**11**	**17**	**11**	**6**
2000-01*	**Colorado (NHL)**	**82**	**52**	**20**	**10**	**23**	**16**	**7**
2001-02	**Colorado (NHL)**	**82**	**45**	**29**	**8**	**21**	**11**	**10**
2002-03	**Colorado (NHL)**	**31**	**10**	**12**	**9**	....	....	....
	Atlanta (NHL)	**39**	**19**	**15**	**5**	....	....	....
2003-04	**Atlanta (NHL)**	**82**	**33**	**41**	**8**	....	....	....
2004-05	**Atlanta (NHL)**			Season Cancelled				
2005-06	**Atlanta (NHL)**	**82**	**41**	**33**	**8**	....	....	....
2006-07	**Atlanta (NHL)**	**82**	**43**	**28**	**11**	**4**	**0**	**4**
	NHL Totals	**644**	**329**	**235**	**80**	**84**	**49**	**35**

* Stanley Cup win.

Boston Bruins

Key Off-Season Signings/Acquisitions

2007

May 5 • Signed G **Tuukka Rask**.

June 12 • Re-signed D **Andrew Alberts**.

18 • Re-signed RW **Brandon Bochenski**.

21 • Named **Claude Julien** head coach.

July 1 • Acquired G **Manny Fernandez** from Minnesota for RW **Petr Kalus** and a 4th-round pick in the 2009 Entry Draft.

1 • Signed RW **Shawn Thornton**.

6 • Re-signed D **Bobby Allen**.

11 • Re-signed D **Dennis Wideman**.

17 • Acquired LW **Peter Schaefer** from Ottawa for RW **Shean Donovan**.

23 • Acquired C **Carl Soderberg** from St. Louis for G **Hannu Toivonen**.

Aug. 1 • Named **Craig Ramsay** and **Geoff Ward** assistant coaches.

2007-08 Schedule

Oct.	Fri.	5	at Dallas
	Sat.	6	at Phoenix
	Wed.	10	at Anaheim
	Fri.	12	at Los Angeles
	Sat.	13	at San Jose
	Thu.	18	Tampa Bay
	Sat.	20	NY Rangers
	Mon.	22	at Montreal
	Thu.	25	Chicago
	Sat.	27	Philadelphia
Nov.	Thu.	1	Buffalo
	Sat.	3	at Ottawa
	Sun.	4	Ottawa
	Wed.	7	at Buffalo
	Thu.	8	Montreal
	Sat.	10	Buffalo
	Thu.	15	Toronto
	Sat.	17	at Montreal
	Tue.	20	at Toronto
	Fri.	23	NY Islanders*
	Sat.	24	at NY Islanders
	Mon.	26	at Philadelphia
	Thu.	29	at Florida
Dec.	Sat.	1	at Tampa Bay
	Mon.	3	at NY Islanders
	Wed.	5	at New Jersey
	Thu.	6	Montreal
	Sat.	8	at Toronto
	Mon.	10	at Buffalo
	Wed.	12	at Atlanta
	Thu.	13	New Jersey
	Sat.	15	Columbus
	Tue.	18	Ottawa
	Thu.	20	Pittsburgh
	Sat.	22	St. Louis*
	Sun.	23	at Pittsburgh*
	Fri.	28	at Carolina
	Sat.	29	at Atlanta
	Mon.	31	Atlanta*
Jan.	Thu.	3	Washington
	Sat.	5	New Jersey
	Tue.	8	Carolina
	Thu.	10	Montreal
	Sat.	12	at Philadelphia*
	Thu.	17	Toronto
	Sat.	19	NY Rangers*
	Sun.	20	at NY Rangers*
	Tue.	22	at Montreal
	Thu.	24	NY Islanders
	Tue.	29	Nashville
	Thu.	31	at Ottawa
Feb.	Sat.	2	Detroit
	Tue.	5	Buffalo
	Fri.	8	at Buffalo
	Sat.	9	Florida
	Tue.	12	Carolina
	Wed.	13	at Pittsburgh
	Sat.	16	at Toronto
	Tue.	19	at Carolina
	Thu.	21	at Florida
	Sat.	23	at Tampa Bay
	Tue.	26	Ottawa
	Thu.	28	Pittsburgh
Mar.	Sat.	1	Atlanta*
	Mon.	3	at Washington
	Tue.	4	Florida
	Thu.	6	Toronto
	Sat.	8	Washington*
	Sun.	9	at NY Rangers*
	Tue.	11	at Ottawa
	Thu.	13	Tampa Bay
	Sat.	15	Philadelphia*
	Sun.	16	at Washington*
	Thu.	20	Montreal
	Sat.	22	at Montreal
	Tue.	25	at Toronto
	Thu.	27	Toronto
	Sat.	29	Ottawa*
	Sun.	30	at Buffalo*
Apr.	Wed.	2	at New Jersey
	Fri.	4	at Ottawa
	Sat.	5	Buffalo

* Denotes afternoon game.

NORTHEAST DIVISION
84th NHL Season

Franchise date: November 1, 1924

2006-07 Results: 35W-41L-2OTL-4SOL 76PTS.
Fifth, Northeast Division

Year-by-Year Record

		Home				Road				Overall								
Season	**GP**	**W**	**L**	**T**	**OL**	**W**	**L**	**T**	**OL**	**W**	**L**	**T**	**OL**	**GF**	**GA**	**Pts.**	**Finished**	**Playoff Result**
2006-07	82	18	19	....	4	17	22	....	2	35	41	....	6	219	289	76	5th, Northeast Div.	Out of Playoffs
2005-06	82	16	15	....	10	13	22	....	6	29	37	....	16	230	266	74	5th, Northeast Div.	Out of Playoffs
2004-05	....	....	....	....	....	....	....	....	....	....	....	....	....	....	....	....		
2003-04	82	18	12	9	2	23	7	6	5	41	19	15	7	209	188	104	1st, Northeast Div.	Lost Conf. Quarter-Final
2002-03	82	23	11	5	2	13	20	6	2	36	31	11	4	245	237	87	3rd, Northeast Div.	Lost Conf. Quarter-Final
2001-02	82	23	11	2	5	20	13	4	4	43	24	6	9	236	201	101	1st, Northeast Div.	Lost Conf. Quarter-Final
2000-01	82	21	12	5	3	15	18	3	5	36	30	8	8	227	249	88	4th, Northeast Div.	Out of Playoffs
1999-2000	82	12	17	11	1	12	16	8	5	24	33	19	6	210	248	73	5th, Northeast Div.	Out of Playoffs
1998-99	82	22	10	9	....	17	20	4	....	39	30	13	....	214	181	91	3rd, Northeast Div.	Lost Conf. Semi-Final
1997-98	82	19	16	6	....	20	14	7	....	39	30	13	....	221	194	91	2nd, Northeast Div.	Lost Conf. Quarter-Final
1996-97	82	14	20	7	....	12	27	2	....	26	47	9	....	234	300	61	6th, Northeast Div.	Out of Playoffs
1995-96	82	22	14	5	....	18	17	6	....	40	31	11	....	282	269	91	2nd, Northeast Div.	Lost Conf. Quarter-Final
1994-95	48	15	7	2	....	12	11	1	....	27	18	3	....	150	127	57	3rd, Northeast Div.	Lost Conf. Quarter-Final
1993-94	84	20	14	8	....	22	15	5	....	42	29	13	....	289	252	97	2nd, Northeast Div.	Lost Conf. Semi-Final
1992-93	84	29	10	3	....	22	16	4	....	51	26	7	....	332	268	109	1st, Adams Div.	Lost Div. Semi-Final
1991-92	80	23	11	6	....	13	21	6	....	36	32	12	....	270	275	84	2nd, Adams Div.	Lost Conf. Championship
1990-91	80	26	9	5	....	18	15	7	....	44	24	12	....	299	264	100	1st, Adams Div.	Lost Conf. Championship
1989-90	80	23	13	4	....	23	12	5	....	46	25	9	....	289	232	101	1st, Adams Div.	Lost Final
1988-89	80	17	15	8	....	20	14	6	....	37	29	14	....	289	256	88	2nd, Adams Div.	Lost Div. Final
1987-88	80	24	13	3	....	20	17	3	....	44	30	6	....	300	251	94	2nd, Adams Div.	Lost Final
1986-87	80	25	11	4	....	14	23	3	....	39	34	7	....	301	276	85	3rd, Adams Div.	Lost Div. Semi-Final
1985-86	80	24	9	7	....	13	22	5	....	37	31	12	....	311	288	86	3rd, Adams Div.	Lost Div. Semi-Final
1984-85	80	21	15	4	....	15	19	6	....	36	34	10	....	303	287	82	4th, Adams Div.	Lost Div. Semi-Final
1983-84	80	25	12	3	....	24	13	3	....	49	25	6	....	336	261	104	1st, Adams Div.	Lost Div. Semi-Final
1982-83	80	28	6	6	....	22	14	4	....	50	20	10	....	327	228	110	1st, Adams Div.	Lost Conf. Championship
1981-82	80	24	12	4	....	19	15	6	....	43	27	10	....	323	285	96	2nd, Adams Div.	Lost Div. Final
1980-81	80	26	10	4	....	11	20	9	....	37	30	13	....	316	272	87	2nd, Adams Div.	Lost Prelim. Round
1979-80	80	27	9	4	....	19	12	9	....	46	21	13	....	310	234	105	2nd, Adams Div.	Lost Quarter-Final
1978-79	80	25	10	5	....	18	13	9	....	43	23	14	....	316	270	100	1st, Adams Div.	Lost Semi-Final
1977-78	80	29	6	5	....	22	12	6	....	51	18	11	....	333	218	113	1st, Adams Div.	Lost Final
1976-77	80	27	7	6	....	22	16	2	....	49	23	8	....	312	240	106	1st, Adams Div.	Lost Final
1975-76	80	27	5	8	....	21	10	9	....	48	15	17	....	313	237	113	1st, Adams Div.	Lost Semi-Final
1974-75	80	29	5	6	....	11	21	8	....	40	26	14	....	345	245	94	2nd, Adams Div.	Lost Prelim. Round
1973-74	78	33	4	2	....	19	13	7	....	52	17	9	....	349	221	113	1st, East Div.	Lost Final
1972-73	78	27	10	2	....	24	12	3	....	51	22	5	....	330	235	107	2nd, East Div.	Lost Quarter-Final
1971-72	**78**	**28**	**4**	**7**	....	**26**	**9**	**4**	....	**54**	**13**	**11**	....	**330**	**204**	**119**	**1st, East Div.**	**Won Stanley Cup**
1970-71	78	33	4	2	....	24	10	5	....	57	14	7	....	399	207	121	1st, East Div.	Lost Quarter-Final
1969-70	**76**	**27**	**3**	**8**	....	**13**	**14**	**11**	....	**40**	**17**	**19**	....	**277**	**216**	**99**	**2nd, East Div.**	**Won Stanley Cup**
1968-69	76	29	3	6	....	13	15	10	....	42	18	16	....	303	221	100	2nd, East Div.	Lost Semi-Final
1967-68	74	22	9	6	....	15	18	4	....	37	27	10	....	259	216	84	3rd, East Div.	Lost Quarter-Final
1966-67	70	10	21	4	....	7	22	6	....	17	43	10	....	182	253	44	6th,	Out of Playoffs
1965-66	70	15	17	3	....	6	26	3	....	21	43	6	....	174	275	48	5th,	Out of Playoffs
1964-65	70	12	17	6	....	9	26	0	....	21	43	6	....	166	253	48	6th,	Out of Playoffs
1963-64	70	13	15	7	....	5	25	5	....	18	40	12	....	170	212	48	6th,	Out of Playoffs
1962-63	70	7	18	10	....	7	21	7	....	14	39	17	....	198	281	45	6th,	Out of Playoffs
1961-62	70	9	22	4	....	6	25	4	....	15	47	8	....	177	306	38	6th,	Out of Playoffs
1960-61	70	13	17	5	....	2	25	8	....	15	42	13	....	176	254	43	6th,	Out of Playoffs
1959-60	70	21	11	3	....	7	23	5	....	28	34	8	....	220	241	64	5th,	Out of Playoffs
1958-59	70	21	11	3	....	11	18	6	....	32	29	9	....	205	215	73	2nd,	Lost Semi-Final
1957-58	70	15	14	6	....	12	14	9	....	27	28	15	....	199	194	69	4th,	Lost Final
1956-57	70	20	9	6	....	14	15	6	....	34	24	12	....	195	174	80	3rd,	Lost Final
1955-56	70	14	14	7	....	9	20	6	....	23	34	13	....	147	185	59	5th,	Out of Playoffs
1954-55	70	16	10	9	....	7	16	12	....	23	26	21	....	169	188	67	4th,	Lost Semi-Final
1953-54	70	22	8	5	....	10	20	5	....	32	28	10	....	177	181	74	4th,	Lost Semi-Final
1952-53	70	19	10	6	....	9	19	7	....	28	29	13	....	152	172	69	3rd,	Lost Final
1951-52	70	15	12	8	....	10	17	8	....	25	29	16	....	162	176	66	4th,	Lost Semi-Final
1950-51	70	13	12	10	....	9	18	8	....	22	30	18	....	178	197	62	4th,	Lost Semi-Final
1949-50	70	15	12	8	....	7	20	8	....	22	32	16	....	198	228	60	5th,	Out of Playoffs
1948-49	60	18	10	2	....	11	13	6	....	29	23	8	....	178	163	66	2nd,	Lost Semi-Final
1947-48	60	12	8	10	....	11	16	3	....	23	24	13	....	167	168	59	3rd,	Lost Semi-Final
1946-47	60	18	7	5	....	8	16	6	....	26	23	11	....	190	175	63	3rd,	Lost Semi-Final
1945-46	50	11	5	4	....	13	13	4	....	24	18	8	....	167	156	56	2nd,	Lost Final
1944-45	50	11	12	2	....	5	18	2	....	16	30	4	....	179	219	36	4th,	Lost Semi-Final
1943-44	50	15	8	2	....	4	18	3	....	19	26	5	....	223	268	43	5th,	Out of Playoffs
1942-43	50	17	3	5	....	7	14	4	....	24	17	9	....	195	176	57	2nd,	Lost Final
1941-42	48	17	4	3	....	8	13	3	....	25	17	6	....	160	118	56	3rd,	Lost Semi-Final
1940-41	**48**	**15**	**4**	**5**	....	**12**	**4**	**8**	....	**27**	**8**	**13**	....	**168**	**102**	**67**	**1st,**	**Won Stanley Cup**
1939-40	48	20	3	1	....	11	9	4	....	31	12	5	....	170	98	67	1st,	Lost Semi-Final
1938-39	**48**	**20**	**2**	**2**	....	**16**	**8**	**0**	....	**36**	**10**	**2**	....	**156**	**76**	**74**	**1st,**	**Won Stanley Cup**
1937-38	48	18	3	3	....	12	8	4	....	30	11	7	....	142	89	67	1st, Amn. Div.	Lost Semi-Final
1936-37	48	9	11	4	....	14	7	3	....	23	18	7	....	120	110	53	2nd, Amn. Div.	Lost Quarter-Final
1935-36	48	15	8	1	....	7	12	5	....	22	20	6	....	92	83	50	2nd, Amn. Div.	Lost Quarter-Final
1934-35	48	17	7	0	....	9	9	6	....	26	16	6	....	129	112	58	1st, Amn. Div.	Lost Semi-Final
1933-34	48	11	11	2	....	7	14	3	....	18	25	5	....	111	130	41	4th, Amn. Div.	Out of Playoffs
1932-33	48	19	2	3	....	6	13	5	....	25	15	8	....	124	88	58	1st, Amn. Div.	Lost Semi-Final
1931-32	48	11	10	3	....	4	11	9	....	15	21	12	....	122	117	42	4th, Amn. Div.	Out of Playoffs
1930-31	44	16	1	5	....	12	9	1	....	28	10	6	....	143	90	62	1st, Amn. Div.	Lost Semi-Final
1929-30	44	21	1	0	....	17	4	1	....	38	5	1	....	179	98	77	1st, Amn. Div.	Lost Final
1928-29	**44**	**15**	**6**	**1**	....	**11**	**7**	**4**	....	**26**	**13**	**5**	....	**89**	**52**	**57**	**1st, Amn. Div.**	**Won Stanley Cup**
1927-28	44	13	4	5	....	7	9	6	....	20	13	11	....	77	70	51	1st, Amn. Div.	Lost Semi-Final
1926-27	44	15	7	0	....	6	13	3	....	21	20	3	....	97	89	45	2nd, Amn. Div.	Lost Final
1925-26	36	10	7	1	....	7	8	3	....	17	15	4	....	92	85	38	4th,	Out of Playoffs
1924-25	30	3	12	0	....	3	12	0	....	6	24	0	....	49	119	12	6th,	Out of Playoffs

2007-08 Player Personnel

FORWARDS	HT	WT	S	Place of Birth	*Age	2006-07 Club
AXELSSON, P.J.	6-1	175	L	Kungalv, Sweden	32	Boston
BERGERON, Patrice	6-0	186	R	Ancienne-Lorette, Que.	22	Boston
BOCHENSKI, Brandon	6-1	187	R	Blaine, MN	25	Chicago-Norfolk-Boston
COLLINS, Chris	5-10	181	R	Fairport, NY	23	Providence (AHL)-Long Beach
DiCASMIRRO, Nate	5-11	205	L	Atikokan, Ont.	29	Providence (AHL)
HAMILL, Zach	6-0	175	R	Vancouver, B.C.	19	Everett
HENDRICKS, Matt	6-0	215	L	Blaine, MN	26	Hershey
HOGGAN, Jeff	6-1	188	L	Hope, B.C.	29	Boston-Providence (AHL)
KARSUMS, Martins	5-10	198	R	Riga, USSR	21	Providence (AHL)
KESSEL, Phil	6-0	193	R	Madison, WI	19	Boston-Providence (AHL)
KOBASEW, Chuck	6-0	193	L	Vancouver, B.C.	25	Calgary-Boston
KREJCI, David	6-0	178	R	Sternberk, Czech.	21	Boston-Providence (AHL)
LEHTONEN, Mikko	6-5	203	R	Espoo, Finland	20	Suomi U20-Blues
MOWERS, Mark	5-11	174	R	Decatur, GA	33	Boston
MURRAY, Glen	6-3	215	R	Halifax, N.S.	34	Boston
PELLETIER, Pascal	5-11	197	R	Labrador City, Nfld.	24	Providence (AHL)
RABBIT, Wacey	5-10	171	L	Lethbridge, Alta.	20	Prov (AHL)-Van (WHL)
REICH, Jeremy	6-1	200	L	Craik, Sask.	28	Boston-Providence (AHL)
SAVARD, Marc	5-10	196	L	Ottawa, Ont.	30	Boston
SCHAEFER, Peter	5-11	195	L	Yellow Grass, Sask.	30	Ottawa
SODERBERG, Carl	6-3	198	L	Malmo, Sweden	21	Malmo
STURM, Marco	6-0	198	L	Dingolfing, West Germany	29	Boston
THOMPSON, Nate	6-0	206	L	Anchorage, AK	22	Boston-Providence (AHL)
THORNTON, Shawn	6-1	209	R	Oshawa, Ont.	30	Anaheim-Portland (AHL)
TREVELYAN, T.J.	5-10	187	L	Mississauga, Ont.	23	Providence (AHL)-Long Beach
WALTER, Ben	6-1	195	L	Beaconsfield, Que.	23	Boston-Providence (AHL)
DEFENSEMEN						
ALBERTS, Andrew	6-4	216	L	Minneapolis, MN	26	Boston
ALLEN, Bobby	6-1	215	L	Weymouth, MA	28	Boston-Providence (AHL)
CHARA, Zdeno	6-9	251	L	Trencin, Czech.	30	Boston
CURRY, Sean	6-4	230	R	Burnsville, MN	25	Providence (AHL)
FERENCE, Andrew	5-10	191	L	Edmonton, Alta.	28	Calgary-Boston
HUNWICK, Matt	5-11	190	L	Warren, MI	22	U. of Michigan
LASHOFF, Matt	6-2	204	L	East Greenbush, NY	21	Boston-Providence (AHL)
McQUAID, Adam	6-4	209	R	Charlottetown, PEI	20	Sudbury
SIGALET, Jonathan	6-1	185	L	Vancouver, B.C.	21	Boston-Providence (AHL)
STUART, Mark	6-1	219	L	Rochester, MN	23	Boston-Providence (AHL)
WARD, Aaron	6-2	215	R	Windsor, Ont.	34	NY Rangers-Boston
WIDEMAN, Dennis	6-0	208	R	Kitchener, Ont.	24	St. Louis-Boston

GOALTENDERS	HT	WT	C	Place of Birth	*Age	2006-07 Club
BROWN, Mike	6-0	203	L	Syracuse, NY	22	Providence (AHL)-Long Beach
FERNANDEZ, Manny	6-0	207	L	Etobicoke, Ont.	33	Minnesota
RASK, Tuukka	6-3	169	L	Savonlinna, Finland	20	Suomi U20-Ilves
SIGALET, Jordan	6-1	180	L	New Westminster, B.C.	26	Providence (AHL)
THOMAS, Tim	5-11	201	L	Flint, MI	33	Boston

* – Age at start of 2007-08 season

2006-07 Scoring

* – rookie

Regular Season

Pos	#	Player	Team	GP	G	A	Pts	+/–	PIM	PP	SH	GW	S	%
C	91	Marc Savard	BOS	82	22	74	96	–19	96	10	1	3	221	10.0
C	37	Patrice Bergeron	BOS	77	22	48	70	–28	26	14	0	6	224	9.8
R	27	Glen Murray	BOS	59	28	17	45	–12	44	12	0	4	201	13.9
L	16	Marco Sturm	BOS	76	27	17	44	–24	46	10	2	1	224	12.1
D	33	Zdeno Chara	BOS	80	11	32	43	–21	100	9	0	3	204	5.4
C	81	* Phil Kessel	BOS	70	11	18	29	–12	12	1	0	0	170	6.5
L	11	P.J. Axelsson	BOS	55	11	16	27	–10	52	3	2	0	81	13.6
D	6	Dennis Wideman	STL	55	5	17	22	–7	44	4	0	1	94	5.3
			BOS	20	1	2	3	–3	27	0	0	0	28	3.6
			TOTAL	75	6	19	25	–10	71	4	0	1	122	4.9
R	10	Brandon Bochenski	CHI	10	2	0	2	–2	2	0	0	0	20	10.0
			BOS	31	11	11	22	3	14	3	0	2	72	15.3
			TOTAL	41	13	11	24	1	16	3	0	2	92	14.1
R	12	Chuck Kobasew	CGY	40	4	13	17	7	37	1	0	1	69	5.8
			BOS	10	1	1	2	–6	25	1	0	0	24	4.2
			TOTAL	50	5	14	19	1	62	2	0	1	93	5.4
R	22	Shean Donovan	BOS	76	6	11	17	–13	56	0	0	0	108	5.6
R	18	Mark Mowers	BOS	78	5	12	17	–10	26	0	1	0	60	8.3
D	44	Aaron Ward	NYR	60	3	10	13	–3	57	0	0	0	45	6.7
			BOS	20	1	2	3	–8	18	0	0	0	17	5.9
			TOTAL	80	4	12	16	–11	75	0	0	0	62	6.5
D	21	Andrew Ference	CGY	54	2	10	12	7	66	1	0	0	51	3.9
			BOS	26	1	2	3	–2	31	0	0	0	29	3.4
			TOTAL	80	3	12	15	5	97	1	0	0	80	3.8
R	17	Petr Tenkrat	BOS	64	9	5	14	–16	34	2	0	1	82	11.0
L	13	Stanislav Chistov	ANA	1	0	0	0	0	0	0	0	0	0	0.0
			BOS	60	5	8	13	–8	36	1	0	1	49	10.2
			TOTAL	61	5	8	13	–8	36	1	0	1	49	10.2
D	41	Andrew Alberts	BOS	76	0	10	10	–15	124	0	0	0	41	0.0
D	25	Jason York	BOS	49	1	7	8	–14	32	0	0	0	27	3.7
C	47	* Petr Kalus	BOS	9	4	1	5	0	6	1	0	0	8	50.0
D	38	Bobby Allen	BOS	31	0	3	3	–1	10	0	0	0	14	0.0
D	49	* Matt Lashoff	BOS	12	0	2	2	–6	12	0	0	0	8	0.0
C	43	* Yan Stastny	BOS	21	0	2	2	–3	19	0	0	0	7	0.0
R	32	Jeff Hoggan	BOS	46	0	2	2	–8	33	0	0	0	53	0.0
D	28	Wade Brookbank	BOS	7	1	0	1	–1	15	0	0	0	1	100.0
D	45	* Mark Stuart	BOS	15	0	1	1	7	14	0	0	0	4	0.0
D	21	Nathan Dempsey	BOS	17	0	1	1	–2	6	0	0	0	4	0.0
L	53	Jeremy Reich	BOS	32	0	1	1	–10	63	0	0	0	27	0.0
D	50	* Jonathan Sigalet	BOS	1	0	0	0	–2	4	0	0	0	1	0.0
C	52	* Nate Thompson	BOS	4	0	0	0	0	0	0	0	0	5	0.0
C	56	* Ben Walter	BOS	4	0	0	0	0	0	0	0	0	0	0.0
C	46	* David Krejci	BOS	6	0	0	0	–3	2	0	0	0	2	0.0

Goaltending

No.	Goaltender	GPI	Mins	Avg	W	L	OT	EN	SO	GA	SA	S%	G	A	PIM
31	Joey MacDonald	7	358	2.68	2	2	1	1	0	16	195	.918	0	0	0
60	* Brian Finley	2	59	3.05	0	1	0	1	0	3	33	.909	0	0	0
30	Tim Thomas	66	3619	3.13	30	29	4	7	3	189	1985	.905	0	0	6
54	* Hannu Toivonen	18	894	4.23	3	9	1	1	0	63	502	.875	0	0	2
35	Philippe Sauve	2	41	5.85	0	0	0	0	0	4	23	.826	0	0	0
	Totals	**82**	**4998**	**3.42**	**35**	**41**	**6**	**10**	**3**	**285**	**2748**	**.896**			

Coach

CLAUDE JULIEN

Coach, Boston Bruins. Born in Orleans, Ont., April 23, 1960.

The Boston Bruins named Claude Julien the 28th head coach in club history on June 21, 2007. Julien joined the Bruins with four years of NHL head coaching experience, most recently with the New Jersey Devils. In his lone season with New Jersey, he held a record of 47-24-8 before being replaced on April 2, 2007 with three games remaining in the 2006-07 regular season. At the time he was replaced by the Devils, Julien's club was in first place in the Atlantic Division.

Prior to being named head coach of the Devils, Julien spent three seasons as the head coach of the Montreal Canadiens, serving from January 2003 until January of 2006. During his tenure with Montreal, Julien led the Canadiens to a record of 72-71-16 in 159 games.

Before joining the NHL coaching ranks, Julien spent four seasons with Hull of the Quebec Major Junior Hockey League and three campaigns with Hamilton of the American Hockey League. While with Hamilton, Julien was co-awarded the Louis A. R. Pieri Award as the league's outstanding coach during the 2002-03 season.

Julien has also coached at the international level, having served as an assistant coach to Team Canada at the 2006 World Championship after he led Team Canada to a bronze medal as a head coach at the 2000 World Junior Championship.

A defenseman, Julien's professional playing career spanned 12 seasons from 1981 to 1992, highlighted by stints with the Quebec Nordiques between 1984 and 1986.

Coaching Record

		Regular Season				Playoffs		
Season	Team	Games	W	L	O/T	Games	W	L
1996-97	Hull (QMJHL)	70	48	19	3	14	12	2
1997-98	Hull (QMJHL)	70	32	37	1	11	6	5
1998-99	Hull (QMJHL)	70	23	38	9	23	15	8
1999-00	Hull (QMJHL)	72	42	24	6	15	9	6
2000-01	Hamilton (AHL)	80	28	46	6	....	....	....
2001-02	Hamilton (AHL)	80	37	33	10	15	10	5
2002-03	Hamilton (AHL)	45	33	9	3	....	....	....
2002-03	**Montreal (NHL)**	**36**	**12**	**21**	**3**	....	....	....
2003-04	**Montreal (NHL)**	**82**	**41**	**34**	**7**	**11**	**4**	**7**
2004-05	**Montreal (NHL)**			Season Cancelled				
2005-06	**Montreal (NHL)**	**41**	**19**	**16**	**6**	....	....	....
2006-07	**New Jersey (NHL)**	**79**	**47**	**24**	**8**	....	....	....
	NHL Totals	**238**	**119**	**95**	**24**	**11**	**4**	**7**

Captains' History

No captain, 1924-25 to 1926-27; Lionel Hitchman, 1927-28 to 1930-31; George Owen, 1931-32; Dit Clapper, 1932-33 to 1937-38; Cooney Weiland, 1938-39; Dit Clapper, 1939-40 to 1945-46; Dit Clapper and John Crawford, 1946-47; John Crawford 1947-48 to 1949-50; Milt Schmidt, 1950-51 to 1953-54; Milt Schmidt, Ed Sanford, 1954-55; Fern Flaman, 1955-56 to 1960-61; Don McKenney, 1961-62, 1962-63; Leo Boivin, 1963-64 to 1965-66; John Bucyk, 1966-67; no captain, 1967-68 to 1972-73; John Bucyk, 1973-74 to 1976-77; Wayne Cashman, 1977-78 to 1982-83; Terry O'Reilly, 1983-84, 1984-85; Raymond Bourque, Rick Middleton (co-captains) 1985-86 to 1987-88; Raymond Bourque, 1988-89 to 1999-2000; Jason Allison, 2000-01; no captain, 2001-02; Joe Thornton, 2002-03, 2003-04; Joe Thornton and no captain, 2005-06; Zdeno Chara, 2006-07 to date.

Coaching History

Art Ross, 1924-25 to 1927-28; Cy Denneny, 1928-29; Art Ross, 1929-30 to 1933-34; Frank Patrick, 1934-35, 1935-36; Art Ross, 1936-37 to 1938-39; Cooney Weiland, 1939-40, 1940-41; Art Ross, 1941-42 to 1944-45; Dit Clapper, 1945-46 to 1948-49; Georges Boucher, 1949-50; Lynn Patrick, 1950-51 to 1953-54; Lynn Patrick and Milt Schmidt, 1954-55; Milt Schmidt, 1955-56 to 1960-61; Phil Watson, 1961-62; Phil Watson and Milt Schmidt, 1962-63; Milt Schmidt, 1963-64 to 1965-66; Harry Sinden, 1966-67 to 1969-70; Tom Johnson, 1970-71, 1971-72; Tom Johnson and Bep Guidolin, 1972-73; Bep Guidolin, 1973-74; Don Cherry, 1974-75 to 1978-79; Fred Creighton and Harry Sinden, 1979-80; Gerry Cheevers, 1980-81 to 1983-84; Gerry Cheevers and Harry Sinden, 1984-85; Butch Goring, 1985-86; Butch Goring and Terry O'Reilly, 1986-87; Terry O'Reilly, 1987-88, 1988-89; Mike Milbury, 1989-90, 1990-91; Rick Bowness, 1991-92; Brian Sutter, 1992-93 to 1994-95; Steve Kasper, 1995-96, 1996-97; Pat Burns, 1997-98 to 1999-2000; Pat Burns and Mike Keenan, 2000-01; Robbie Ftorek, 2001-02; Robbie Ftorek and Mike O'Connell, 2002-03; Mike Sullivan, 2003-04 to 2005-06; Dave Lewis, 2006-07; Claude Julien, 2007-08.

Club Records

Team

(Figures in brackets for season records are games played; records for fewest points, wins, ties, losses, goals, goals against are for 70 or more games)

Most Points **121** 1970-71 (78)
Most Wins **57** 1970-71 (78)
Most Ties **21** 1954-55 (70)
Most Losses **47** 1961-62 (70), 1996-97 (82)
Most Goals **399** 1970-71 (78)
Most Goals Against **306** 1961-62 (70)
Fewest Points **38** 1961-62 (70)
Fewest Wins **14** 1962-63 (70)
Fewest Ties **5** 1972-73 (78)
Fewest Losses **13** 1971-72 (78)
Fewest Goals **147** 1955-56 (70)
Fewest Goals Against **172** 1952-53 (70)

Longest Winning Streak
Overall .... **14** Dec. 3/29-Jan. 9/30
Home .... ***20** Dec. 3/29-Mar. 18/30
Away .... **8** Feb. 17-Mar. 8/72, Mar. 15-Apr. 14/93

Longest Undefeated Streak
Overall .... **23** Dec. 22/40-Feb. 23/41 (15 wins, 8 ties)
Home .... **27** Nov. 22/70-Mar. 20/71 (26 wins, 1 tie)
Away .... **15** Dec. 22/40-Mar. 16/41 (9 wins, 6 ties)

Longest Losing Streak
Overall .... **11** Dec. 3/24-Jan. 5/25
Home .... ***11** Dec. 8/24-Feb. 17/25
Away .... **14** Dec. 27/64-Feb. 21/65

Longest Winless Streak
Overall .... **20** Jan. 28-Mar. 11/62 (16 losses, 4 ties)
Home .... **11** Dec. 8/24-Feb. 17/25 (11 losses)
Away .... **14** Three times
Most Shutouts, Season **15** 1927-28 (44)
Most PIM, Season **2,443** 1987-88 (80)
Most Goals, Game .... **14** Jan. 21/45 (NYR 3 at Bos. 14)

Individual

Most Seasons .... **21** John Bucyk, Raymond Bourque
Most Games .... **1,518** Raymond Bourque
Most Goals, Career .... **545** John Bucyk
Most Assists, Career ...... **1,111** Raymond Bourque
Most Points, Career .... **1,506** Raymond Bourque (395G, 1,111A)
Most PIM, Career .... **2,095** Terry O'Reilly
Most Shutouts, Career .... **74** Tiny Thompson
Longest Consecutive Games Streak .... **418** John Bucyk (Jan. 23/69-Mar. 2/75)
Most Goals, Season .... **76** Phil Esposito (1970-71)
Most Assists, Season .... **102** Bobby Orr (1970-71)
Most Points, Season .... **152** Phil Esposito (1970-71; 76G, 76A)
Most PIM, Season .... **302** Jay Miller (1987-88)
Most Points, Defenseman, Season .... ***139** Bobby Orr (1970-71; 37G, 102A)
Most Points, Center, Season .... **152** Phil Esposito (1970-71; 76G, 76A)
Most Points, Right Wing, Season .... **105** Ken Hodge (1970-71; 43G, 62A), (1973-74; 50G, 55A), Rick Middleton (1983-84; 47G, 58A)
Most Points, Left Wing, Season .... **116** John Bucyk (1970-71; 51G, 65A)
Most Points, Rookie, Season .... **102** Joe Juneau (1992-93; 32G, 70A)
Most Shutouts, Season .... **15** Hal Winkler (1927-28)
Most Goals, Game .... **4** Twenty times
Most Assists, Game .... **6** Ken Hodge (Feb. 9/71), Bobby Orr (Jan. 1/73)
Most Points, Game .... **7** Bobby Orr (Nov. 15/73; 3G, 4A), Phil Esposito (Dec. 19/74; 3G, 4A), Barry Pederson (Apr. 4/82; 3G, 4A), Cam Neely (Oct. 16/88; 3G, 4A)

* NHL Record.

Retired Numbers

2	Eddie Shore	1926-1940
3	Lionel Hitchman	1925-1934
4	Bobby Orr	1966-1976
5	Dit Clapper	1927-1947
7	Phil Esposito	1967-1975
8	Cam Neely	1986-1996
9	John Bucyk	1957-1978
15	Milt Schmidt	1936-1955
24	Terry O'Reilly	1971-1985
77	Raymond Bourque	1979-2000

All-time Record vs. Other Clubs

Regular Season

	At Home								On Road								Total							
	GP	W	L	T	OL	GF	GA	PTS	GP	W	L	T	OL	GF	GA	PTS	GP	W	L	T	OL	GF	GA	PTS
Anaheim	9	5	4	0	0	27	27	10	9	5	2	2	0	24	18	12	18	10	6	2	0	51	45	22
Atlanta	14	6	4	2	2	47	51	16	14	7	6	0	1	40	43	15	28	13	10	2	3	87	94	31
Buffalo	115	63	37	14	1	422	341	141	116	41	59	15	1	340	423	98	231	104	96	29	2	762	764	239
Calgary	48	29	12	6	1	168	132	65	45	22	19	4	0	154	163	48	93	51	31	10	1	322	295	113
Carolina	82	47	27	7	1	284	223	102	80	37	33	9	1	275	268	84	162	84	60	16	2	559	491	186
Chicago	284	161	89	34	0	1023	808	356	287	95	145	45	2	772	929	237	571	256	234	79	2	1795	1737	593
Colorado	63	31	22	9	1	240	194	72	67	36	25	6	0	272	238	78	130	67	47	15	1	512	432	150
Columbus	2	1	1	0	0	8	7	2	4	2	0	0	2	18	8	6	6	3	1	0	2	26	15	8
Dallas	61	41	9	10	1	259	148	93	61	30	17	13	1	220	175	74	122	71	26	23	2	479	323	167
Detroit	287	154	89	43	1	1007	761	352	286	80	153	52	1	726	955	213	573	234	242	95	2	1733	1716	565
Edmonton	31	22	6	3	0	129	80	47	30	16	11	3	0	102	102	35	61	38	17	6	0	231	182	82
Florida	26	9	12	4	1	68	71	23	25	11	11	2	1	72	80	25	51	20	23	6	2	140	151	48
Los Angeles	62	44	12	6	0	287	175	94	61	33	21	7	0	224	210	73	123	77	33	13	0	511	385	167
Minnesota	4	0	4	0	0	5	15	0	3	1	2	0	0	5	9	2	7	1	6	0	0	10	24	2
Montreal	343	158	127	56	2	1009	926	374	342	99	196	47	0	805	1145	245	685	257	323	103	2	1814	2071	619
Nashville	5	2	2	1	0	14	9	5	7	4	2	0	1	16	18	9	12	6	4	1	1	30	27	14
New Jersey	60	32	16	8	4	230	187	76	57	28	16	11	2	181	150	69	117	60	32	19	6	411	337	145
NY Islanders	63	33	17	11	2	232	179	79	65	27	27	10	1	206	219	65	128	60	44	21	3	438	398	144
NY Rangers	302	160	96	42	4	1083	849	366	306	116	135	55	0	858	939	287	608	276	231	97	4	1941	1788	653
Ottawa	41	24	12	5	0	144	114	53	39	18	12	3	6	117	103	45	80	42	24	8	6	261	217	98
Philadelphia	80	47	20	11	2	293	224	107	77	33	33	10	1	226	254	77	157	80	53	21	3	519	478	184
Phoenix	31	22	4	4	1	137	94	49	30	14	13	3	0	102	101	31	61	36	17	7	1	239	195	80
Pittsburgh	82	59	17	6	0	362	232	124	84	36	32	15	1	300	288	88	166	95	49	21	1	662	520	212
St. Louis	59	35	14	9	1	247	161	80	60	23	24	9	4	200	191	59	119	58	38	18	5	447	352	139
San Jose	11	7	1	3	0	41	32	17	11	5	4	2	0	38	30	12	22	12	5	5	0	79	62	29
Tampa Bay	27	19	2	6	0	105	66	44	27	14	10	3	0	81	77	31	54	33	12	9	0	186	143	75
Toronto	306	166	92	47	1	988	812	380	307	96	158	51	2	794	1025	245	613	262	250	98	3	1782	1837	625
Vancouver	53	39	7	7	0	219	124	85	52	27	17	8	0	211	171	62	105	66	24	15	0	430	295	147
Washington	60	35	15	9	1	220	160	80	59	30	16	12	1	204	164	73	119	65	31	21	2	424	324	153
Defunct Clubs	164	112	39	13	0	525	306	237	164	79	67	18	0	496	440	176	328	191	106	31	0	1021	746	413
Totals	**2775**	**1563**	**809**	**376**	**27**	**9823**	**7508**	**3529**	**2775**	**1065**	**1266**	**415**	**29**	**8079**	**8936**	**2574**	**5550**	**2628**	**2075**	**791**	**56**	**17902**	**16444**	**6103**

Playoffs

	Series	W	L	GP	W	L	T	GF	GA	Last Mtg.	Rnd.	Result
Buffalo	7	5	2	39	21	18	0	139	130	1999	CSF	L 2-4
Carolina	3	3	0	19	12	7	0	63	48	1999	CQF	W 4-2
Chicago	6	5	1	22	16	5	1	97	63	1978	QF	W 4-0
Colorado	2	1	1	11	6	5	0	37	36	1983	DSF	W 3-1
Dallas	1	0	1	3	0	3	0	13	20	1981	PRE	L 0-3
Detroit	7	4	3	33	19	14	0	96	98	1957	SF	W 4-1
Edmonton	2	0	2	9	1	8	0	20	41	1990	F	L 1-4
Florida	1	0	1	5	1	4	0	16	22	1996	CQF	L 1-4
Los Angeles	2	2	0	13	8	5	0	56	38	1977	QF	W 4-2
Montreal	30	7	23	152	57	95	0	371	469	2004	CQF	L 3-4
New Jersey	4	1	3	23	8	15	0	60	68	2003	CQF	L 1-4
NY Islanders	2	0	2	11	3	8	0	35	49	1983	CF	L 2-4
NY Rangers	9	6	3	42	22	18	2	114	104	1973	QF	L 1-4
Philadelphia	4	2	2	20	11	9	0	60	57	1978	SF	W 4-1
Pittsburgh	4	2	2	19	9	10	0	62	67	1992	CF	L 0-4
St. Louis	2	2	0	8	8	0	0	48	15	1972	SF	W 4-0
Toronto	13	5	8	62	30	31	1	153	150	1974	QF	W 4-0
Washington	2	1	1	10	6	4	0	28	21	1998	CQF	L 2-4
Defunct Clubs	3	1	2	11	4	5	2	20	20			
Totals	**104**	**47**	**57**	**512**	**242**	**264**	**6**	**1488**	**1516**			

Calgary totals include Atlanta Flames, 1972-73 to 1979-80. Carolina totals include Hartford, 1979-80 to 1996-97.
Colorado totals include Quebec, 1979-80 to 1994-95. Dallas totals include Minnesota North Stars, 1967-68 to 1992-93.
New Jersey totals include Kansas City, 1974-75, 1975-76, and Colorado Rockies, 1976-77 to 1981-82.
Phoenix totals include Winnipeg, 1979-80 to 1995-96.

Playoff Results 2007-2002

Year	Round	Opponent	Result	GF	GA
2004	CQF	Montreal	L 3-4	14	19
2003	CQF	New Jersey	L 1-4	8	13
2002	CQF	Montreal	L 2-4	18	20

Abbreviations: Round: F - Final; **CF** - conference final; **CSF** - conference semi-final; **CQF** - conference quarter-final; **DSF** - division semi-final; **SF** - semi-final; **QF** - quarter-final; **PRE** - preliminary round.

2006-07 Results

Month	Date	Opponent	Score
Oct.	6	at Florida	3-8
	7	at Tampa Bay	3-2
	11	at Atlanta	1-4
	12	at St. Louis	2-3†
	14	at NY Islanders	1-4
	19	Calgary	3-2
	21	Buffalo	2-6
	26	Montreal	2-3
	28	Ottawa	2-1
Nov.	2	Buffalo	4-5†
	4	Tampa Bay	6-5*
	6	at Atlanta	3-5
	9	Toronto	4-6
	11	Ottawa	4-3
	15	at Washington	3-2†
	16	Toronto	2-1*
	18	Washington	3-2*
	20	Florida	2-3
	22	at Pittsburgh	4-3†
	24	Carolina	1-5
	25	at Toronto	3-1
	28	at Toronto	4-1
	30	Tampa Bay	4-3†
Dec.	2	at Carolina	2-5
	4	at Montreal	6-5
	7	Toronto	3-1
	9	New Jersey	1-5
	12	at Montreal	3-4
	14	New Jersey	5-3
	16	Florida	3-6
	19	at Ottawa	7-2
	21	Vancouver	2-0
	23	Montreal	4-2
	26	at Columbus	4-5*
	29	at Chicago	5-3
	30	at Nashville	0-5
Jan.	1	at Toronto	1-5
	4	Toronto	2-10
	6	Philadelphia	4-3
	9	at Ottawa	2-5
	11	NY Islanders	4-5†
	13	at NY Rangers	1-3
	15	Buffalo	3-2†
	17	at Buffalo	3-6
	18	Pittsburgh	5-4†
	20	Ottawa	0-3
	27	at Ottawa	1-3
	29	NY Rangers	1-6
	30	at Buffalo	1-7
Feb.	1	Buffalo	1-3
	3	at Carolina	4-3*
	6	at Washington	3-2†
	8	Carolina	2-5
	10	NY Islanders	4-3†
	13	Edmonton	3-0
	15	at NY Islanders	1-4
	17	at Buffalo	4-3†
	19	at Philadelphia	6-3
	20	at Toronto	3-0
	23	at Tampa Bay	6-2
	24	at Florida	2-7
	26	Atlanta	2-3
Mar.	1	Philadelphia	3-4*
	3	Montreal	3-1
	4	at New Jersey	4-1
	6	Colorado	0-2
	8	Minnesota	1-2
	10	at Philadelphia	1-4
	11	at Detroit	6-3
	15	Washington	4-3†
	17	at NY Rangers	0-7
	20	at Montreal	0-1
	22	Montreal	3-6
	24	NY Rangers	1-2†
	25	at Pittsburgh	0-5
	27	at Ottawa	3-2
	29	Pittsburgh	2-4
	31	Atlanta	2-3
Apr.	1	at New Jersey	1-3
	3	at Montreal	0-2
	5	at Buffalo	2-4
	7	Ottawa	3-6

* – Overtime † – Shootout

Entry Draft Selections 2007-1993

2007

Pick	
8	Zach Hamill
35	Tommy Cross
130	Denis Reul
159	Alain Goulet
169	Radim Ostrcil
189	Jordan Knackstedt

2006

Pick	
5	Phil Kessel
37	Yuri Alexandrov
50	Milan Lucic
71	Brad Marchand
128	Andrew Bodnarchuk
158	Levi Nelson

2005

Pick	
22	Matt Lashoff
39	Petr Kalus
83	Mikko Lehtonen
100	Jonathan Sigalet
106	Vladimir Sobotka
154	Wacey Rabbit
172	Lukas Vantuch
217	Brock Bradford

2004

Pick	
63	Dave Krejci
64	Martins Karsums
108	Ashton Rome
134	Kris Versteeg
160	Ben Walter
224	Matt Hunwick
255	Anton Hedman

2003

Pick	
21	Mark Stuart
45	Patrice Bergeron
66	Masi Marjamaki
107	Byron Bitz
118	Frank Rediker
129	Patrik Valcak
153	Mike Brown
183	Nate Thompson
247	Benoit Mondou
277	Kevin Regan

2002

Pick	
29	Hannu Toivonen
56	Vladislav Evseev
130	Jan Kubista
153	Peter Hamerlik
228	Dmitri Utkin
259	Yan Stastny
290	Pavel Frolov

2001

Pick	
19	Shaone Morrisonn
77	Darren McLachlan
111	Matti Kaltiainen
147	Jiri Jakes
179	Andrew Alberts
209	Jordan Sigalet
241	Milan Jurcina
282	Marcel Rodman

2000

Pick	
7	Lars Jonsson
27	Martin Samuelsson
37	Andy Hilbert
59	Ivan Huml
66	Tuukka Makela
73	Sergei Zinovjev
102	Brett Nowak
174	Jarno Kultanen
204	Chris Berti
237	Zdenek Kutlak
268	Pavel Kolarik
279	Andreas Lindstrom

1999

Pick	
21	Nick Boynton
56	Matt Zultek
89	Kyle Wanvig
118	Jaakko Harikkala
147	Seamus Kotyk
179	Donald Choukalos
207	Greg Barber
236	John Cronin
247	Mikko Eloranta
264	Georgy Pujacs

1998

Pick	
48	Jonathan Girard
52	Bobby Allen
78	Peter Nordstrom
135	Andrew Raycroft
165	Ryan Milanovic

1997

Pick	
1	Joe Thornton
8	Sergei Samsonov
27	Ben Clymer
54	Mattias Karlin
63	Lee Goren
81	Karol Bartanus
135	Denis Timofeev
162	Joel Trottier
180	Jim Baxter
191	Antti Laaksonen
218	Eric Van Acker
246	Jay Henderson

1996

Pick	
8	Johnathan Aitken
45	Henry Kuster
53	Eric Naud
80	Jason Doyle
100	Trent Whitfield
132	Elias Abrahamsson
155	Chris Lane
182	Thomas Brown
208	Bob Prier
234	Anders Soderberg

1995

Pick	
9	Kyle McLaren
21	Sean Brown
47	Paxton Schafer
73	Bill McCauley
99	Cameron Mann
151	Yevgeny Shaldybin
177	P.J. Axelsson
203	Sergei Zhukov
229	Jonathon Murphy

1994

Pick	
21	Evgeni Ryabchikov
47	Daniel Goneau
99	Eric Nickulas
125	Darren Wright
151	Andre Roy
177	Jeremy Schaefer
229	John Grahame
255	Neil Savary
281	Andrei Yakhanov

1993

Pick	
25	Kevyn Adams
51	Matt Alvey
88	Charles Paquette
103	Shawn Bates
129	Andrei Sapozhnikov
155	Milt Mastad
181	Ryan Golden
207	Hal Gill
233	Joel Prpic
259	Joakim Persson

Zdeno Chara averaged 27:57 of ice time per game in 80 games in 2006-07.

General Manager

PETER CHIARELLI

General Manager, Boston Bruins. Born in Nepean, Ont., August 5, 1964.

Peter Chiarelli became just the seventh man in club history to hold the position of general manager when he was named to the post on May 26, 2006. He is in charge of every aspect of the team's hockey operations. He officially began his position in Boston on July 10, 2006 as a result of a league-arbitrated compensation agreement that saw the Bruins surrender a third-round draft pick in the 2006 NHL Entry Draft (Eric Gryba, 68th overall) to the Ottawa Senators.

Chiarelli came to the Bruins after seven seasons with the Ottawa Senators, five as the director of legal relations and the last two as assistant general manager. He was involved in all aspects of that team's hockey operations, including contract research and negotiations, salary arbitration and all player personnel matters. He was also involved in overseeing Ottawa's top developmental affiliate, the Binghamtom Senators of the American Hockey League. The Senators had four 100+ point seasons during his tenure and never finished below 94 points, finished with the NHL's top record in 2002-03 (113 points) and the best record in the Eastern Conference in 2005-06 (113 points).

A native of the Ottawa area, Chiarelli played four seasons of college hockey at Harvard University where he served the team as captain and was a teammate of former Bruin Don Sweeney. He had 21 goals and 28 assists for 49 points with 70 penalty minutes in 109 career college games and earned his degree in Economics in 1987. He played professionally in Europe for one year before returning to school and obtaining his law degree from the University of Ottawa. He was admitted to the Ontario bar in 1993 and spent six years as a lawyer and player agent prior to joining the Senators front office in 1999.

Club Directory

TD Banknorth Garden

Boston Bruins
TD Banknorth Garden
100 Legends Way
Boston, MA 02114
Phone **617/624-2327**
FAX 617/523-7184
www.bostonbruins.com
Capacity: 17,565

Executive

Owner & Governor . . . . Jeremy M. Jacobs
Alternate Governors . . . . Charles Jacobs, Jeremy Jacobs Jr., Louis Jacobs, Harry Sinden, Peter Chiarelli
Senior Advisor to the Owner . . . . Harry Sinden
Executive Vice President . . . . Charlie Jacobs
Vice President, Business Operations . . . . Dan Zimmer
Senior Vice President, Sales and Marketing . . . . Amy Latimer
Director of Administration . . . . Dale Hamilton-Powers
Executive Assistant . . . . Rita Brandano
Administrative Assistant and Receptionist . . . . Karen Ondo

Hockey Operations

General Manager . . . . Peter Chiarelli
Assistant General Manager . . . . Jim Benning
Dir. of Hockey Operations and Player Development . . Don Sweeney
Director of Amateur Scouting . . . . Scott Bradley
Scouting Staff . . . . Adam Creighton, Alexei Dementiev, Scott Fitzgerald, Don Matheson, Mike McGraw, Tom McVie, Wayne Smith, Grant Sonier, Tom Songin, Svenake Svensson, John Weisbrod
Manager of Hockey Administration . . . . Ryan Nadeau
Team Road Services Coordinator . . . . John Bucyk

Coaching

Head Coach . . . . Claude Julien
Assistant Coaches . . . . Doug Houda, Craig Ramsay, Geoff Ward
Goaltending Coach . . . . Bob Essensa
Skating Coach . . . . Paul Vincent
Video Coordinator . . . . Brant Berglund
Coach, Providence Bruins . . . . Scott Gordon
Assistant Coach, Providence Bruins . . . . Rob Murray

Medical & Training

Strength & Conditioning Coach . . . . John Whitesides
Athletic Trainer . . . . Don DelNegro
Physical Therapist . . . . Scott Waugh
Massage Therapist . . . . Derek Repucci
Equipment Manager . . . . Mark Dumas
Assistant Equipment Managers . . . . Keith Robinson, TBA
Head Team Physician/Orthopedist . . . . Dr. Bertram Zarins
Team Psychologist . . . . Dr. Frank Lodato

Communications & Community Relations

Director of Communications . . . . Matthew Chmura
Director of Publications and Information . . . . Heidi Holland
Director of Community Relations and Promotions . . Kerry Collins
Director of Development, Boston Bruins Foundation . . Bob Sweeney
Content Manager, BostonBruins.com . . . . John Bishop
Fan Relations Manager . . . . John Hughes
Community Relations Coordinator . . . . Eryn Gallagher
Fan Relations Coordinator . . . . Courtney McNeice
Coordinator, Boston Bruins Foundation . . . . Jay Southwood
Administrative Assistant, Alumni Office . . . . Mal Viola

Sales & Marketing

Senior Vice President of Sales and Marketing . . . . . Amy Latimer
Director of Marketing . . . . Dave Turk
Director of Ticket Sales . . . . Leigh Castergine
Ticket Sales Manager . . . . Mark Rodrigues
Promotions Manager . . . . Brian Hayes
Advertising Coordinator . . . . Liz d'Entremont
Promotions Coordinator . . . . Dave Mello

Finance, Legal & Box Office

Vice President of Business Operations . . . . Dan Zimmer
Chief Legal Officer . . . . Michael Wall
Controller . . . . Rick McGlinchey
Receipts and Disbursements Administrator . . . . Linda Bartlett
Payroll and Benefits Manager . . . . Botin Bou
Director of Ticket Operations . . . . Matthew Whelan
Assistant Director of Ticket Operations . . . . Jim Foley
Ticket Office Receptionist . . . . Jo-Ann Connolly-White

Television & Radio

Television . . . . New England Sports Network (NESN) Jack Edwards (play-by-play); Andy Brickley (color)
Radio . . . . WBZ (1030 AM) & Bruins Radio Network Dave Goucher (play-by-play); Bob Beers (color)

Miscellaneous

Home Start Times:
All Nights . . . . 7:00 p.m.
Matinees . . . . 1:00 p.m.
Exceptions . . . . November 23 – 12:00 noon
Nov. 10, Jan. 10, Feb. 26 – 7:30 p.m.

General Managers' History

Art Ross, 1924-25 to 1953-54; Lynn Patrick, 1954-55 to 1964-65; Hap Emms, 1965-66, 1966-67; Milt Schmidt, 1967-68 to 1971-72; Harry Sinden, 1972-73 to 1999-2000; Harry Sinden and Mike O'Connell, 2000-01; Mike O'Connell, 2001-02 to 2005-06; Peter Chiarelli, 2006-07 to date.

Key Off-Season Signings/Acquisitions

2007

June 30 • Re-signed C **Adam Mair**.
July 4 • Re-signed D **Teppo Numminen**.
5 • Signed G **Jocelyn Thibault**.
5 • Re-signed LW **Andrew Peters** and C **Michael Ryan**.
19 • Re-signed LW **Daniel Paille**.
27 • Re-signed C **Derek Roy**.
31 • Re-signed D **Nathan Paetsch**.

Buffalo Sabres

2006-07 Results: 53W-22L-3OTL-4SOL 113PTS.
First, Northeast Division

With a record of 40-16-6 in 2006-07, Ryan Miller established a new Sabres record for wins in a season. He broke the previous mark of 38 set by Don Edwards in 1977-78.

2007-08 Schedule

Oct.	Fri.	5	NY Islanders
	Sat.	6	at NY Islanders
	Thu.	11	Atlanta
	Sat.	13	Washington
	Mon.	15	Toronto
	Fri.	19	Columbus
	Sat.	20	at Montreal
	Wed.	24	at Carolina
	Fri.	26	at Florida
	Sat.	27	at Tampa Bay
Nov.	Thu.	1	at Boston
	Fri.	2	Florida
	Mon.	5	at Montreal
	Wed.	7	Boston
	Fri.	9	Toronto
	Sat.	10	at Boston
	Thu.	15	at Ottawa
	Fri.	16	Montreal
	Wed.	21	Ottawa
	Fri.	23	Montreal
	Sat.	24	at Montreal
	Mon.	26	at Washington
	Wed.	28	St. Louis
Dec.	Sat.	1	Carolina
	Wed.	5	at Anaheim
	Thu.	6	at Los Angeles
	Sat.	8	at San Jose
	Mon.	10	Boston
	Wed.	12	NY Islanders
	Fri.	14	at Washington
	Sat.	15	Chicago
	Wed.	19	at NY Islanders
	Fri.	21	Philadelphia
	Sat.	22	at Philadelphia
	Wed.	26	Ottawa
	Fri.	28	at New Jersey
	Sat.	29	at Pittsburgh
Jan.	Tue.	1	Pittsburgh*
	Fri.	4	Ottawa
	Sun.	6	at Atlanta*
	Tue.	8	at New Jersey
	Thu.	10	at Ottawa
	Sat.	12	New Jersey
	Wed.	16	at NY Rangers
	Fri.	18	Atlanta
	Sat.	19	at Toronto
	Mon.	21	at Phoenix*
	Thu.	24	at Dallas
	Tue.	29	at Tampa Bay
	Wed.	30	at Florida
Feb.	Fri.	1	at Atlanta
	Tue.	5	at Boston
	Wed.	6	New Jersey
	Fri.	8	Boston
	Sun.	10	Florida
	Tue.	12	at Ottawa
	Wed.	13	Toronto
	Sat.	16	at NY Rangers*
	Sun.	17	Pittsburgh*
	Wed.	20	Tampa Bay
	Thu.	21	at Toronto
	Sat.	23	NY Rangers
	Mon.	25	Philadelphia
	Wed.	27	Nashville
	Fri.	29	Montreal
Mar.	Sun.	2	Detroit*
	Tue.	4	at Philadelphia
	Wed.	5	Washington
	Sat.	8	at Carolina
	Mon.	10	NY Rangers
	Wed.	12	at Pittsburgh
	Fri.	14	Carolina
	Sat.	15	at Toronto
	Wed.	19	Tampa Bay
	Fri.	21	Toronto
	Tue.	25	Ottawa
	Thu.	27	at Ottawa
	Fri.	28	Montreal
	Sun.	30	Boston*
Apr.	Tue.	1	at Toronto
	Thu.	3	at Montreal
	Sat.	5	at Boston

* Denotes afternoon game.

Year-by-Year Record

		Home				Road				Overall								
Season	GP	W	L	T	OL	W	L	T	OL	W	L	T	OL	GF	GA	Pts.	Finished	Playoff Result
2006-07	82	28	10	....	3	25	12	....	4	53	22	....	7	308	242	113	1st, Northeast Div.	Lost Conf. Championship
2005-06	82	27	11	....	3	25	13	....	3	52	24	....	6	281	239	110	2nd, Northeast Div.	Lost Conf. Championship
2004-05	....	....	....	....	....	....	....	....	....	....	....	....	....	....	....	....		
2003-04	82	21	13	4	3	16	21	3	1	37	34	7	4	220	221	85	5th, Northeast Div.	Out of Playoffs
2002-03	82	18	16	5	2	9	21	5	6	27	37	10	8	190	219	72	5th, Northeast Div.	Out of Playoffs
2001-02	82	20	16	5	0	15	19	6	1	35	35	11	1	213	200	82	5th, Northeast Div.	Out of Playoffs
2000-01	82	26	12	3	0	20	18	2	1	46	30	5	1	218	184	98	2nd, Northeast Div.	Lost Conf. Semi-Final
1999-2000	82	21	14	5	1	14	18	6	3	35	32	11	4	213	204	85	3rd, Northeast Div.	Lost Conf. Quarter-Final
1998-99	82	23	12	6	....	14	16	11	....	37	28	17	....	207	175	91	4th, Northeast Div.	Lost Final
1997-98	82	20	13	8	....	16	16	9	....	36	29	17	....	211	187	89	3rd, Northeast Div.	Lost Conf. Championship
1996-97	82	24	11	6	....	16	19	6	....	40	30	12	....	237	208	92	1st, Northeast Div.	Lost Conf. Semi-Final
1995-96	82	19	17	5	....	14	25	2	....	33	42	7	....	247	262	73	5th, Northeast Div.	Out of Playoffs
1994-95	48	15	8	1	....	7	11	6	....	22	19	7	....	130	119	51	4th, Northeast Div.	Lost Conf. Quarter-Final
1993-94	84	22	17	3	....	21	15	6	....	43	32	9	....	282	218	95	4th, Northeast Div.	Lost Conf. Quarter-Final
1992-93	84	25	15	2	....	13	21	8	....	38	36	10	....	335	297	86	4th, Adams Div.	Lost Div. Final
1991-92	80	22	13	5	....	9	24	7	....	31	37	12	....	289	299	74	3rd, Adams Div.	Lost Div. Semi-Final
1990-91	80	15	13	12	....	16	17	7	....	31	30	19	....	292	278	81	3rd, Adams Div.	Lost Div. Semi-Final
1989-90	80	27	11	2	....	18	16	6	....	45	27	8	....	286	248	98	2nd, Adams Div.	Lost Div. Semi-Final
1988-89	80	25	12	3	....	13	23	4	....	38	35	7	....	291	299	83	3rd, Adams Div.	Lost Div. Semi-Final
1987-88	80	19	14	7	....	18	18	4	....	37	32	11	....	283	305	85	3rd, Adams Div.	Lost Div. Semi-Final
1986-87	80	18	18	4	....	10	26	4	....	28	44	8	....	280	308	64	5th, Adams Div.	Out of Playoffs
1985-86	80	23	16	1	....	14	21	5	....	37	37	6	....	296	291	80	5th, Adams Div.	Out of Playoffs
1984-85	80	23	10	7	....	15	18	7	....	38	28	14	....	290	237	90	3rd, Adams Div.	Lost Div. Semi-Final
1983-84	80	25	9	6	....	23	16	1	....	48	25	7	....	315	257	103	2nd, Adams Div.	Lost Div. Semi-Final
1982-83	80	25	7	8	....	13	22	5	....	38	29	13	....	318	285	89	3rd, Adams Div.	Lost Div. Final
1981-82	80	23	8	9	....	16	18	6	....	39	26	15	....	307	273	93	3rd, Adams Div.	Lost Div. Semi-Final
1980-81	80	21	7	12	....	18	13	9	....	39	20	21	....	327	250	99	1st, Adams Div.	Lost Quarter-Final
1979-80	80	27	5	8	....	20	12	8	....	47	17	16	....	318	201	110	1st, Adams Div.	Lost Semi-Final
1978-79	80	19	13	8	....	17	15	8	....	36	28	16	....	280	263	88	2nd, Adams Div.	Lost Prelim. Round
1977-78	80	25	7	8	....	19	12	9	....	44	19	17	....	288	215	105	2nd, Adams Div.	Lost Quarter-Final
1976-77	80	27	8	5	....	21	16	3	....	48	24	8	....	301	220	104	2nd, Adams Div.	Lost Quarter-Final
1975-76	80	28	7	5	....	18	14	8	....	46	21	13	....	339	240	105	2nd, Adams Div.	Lost Quarter-Final
1974-75	80	28	6	6	....	21	10	9	....	49	16	15	....	354	240	113	1st, Adams Div.	Lost Final
1973-74	78	23	10	6	....	9	24	6	....	32	34	12	....	242	250	76	5th, East Div.	Out of Playoffs
1972-73	78	30	6	3	....	7	21	11	....	37	27	14	....	257	219	88	4th, East Div.	Lost Quarter-Final
1971-72	78	11	19	9	....	5	24	10	....	16	43	19	....	203	289	51	6th, East Div.	Out of Playoffs
1970-71	78	16	13	10	....	8	26	5	....	24	39	15	....	217	291	63	5th, East Div.	Out of Playoffs

NORTHEAST DIVISION
38th NHL Season

Franchise date: May 22, 1970

2007-08 Player Personnel

FORWARDS	HT	WT	S	Place of Birth	*Age	2006-07 Club
AFINOGENOV, Maxim	6-0	191	L	Moscow, USSR	28	Buffalo
CONNOLLY, Tim	6-1	195	R	Syracuse, NY	26	Buffalo
GAUSTAD, Paul	6-4	222	L	Fargo, ND	25	Buffalo
HECHT, Jochen	6-1	195	L	Mannheim, West Germany	30	Buffalo
HUNTER, Dylan	5-11	204	L	Quebec City, Que.	22	Rochester
KALETA, Patrick	5-11	202	R	Buffalo, NY	21	Buffalo-Rochester
KOTALIK, Ales	6-1	227	R	Jindrichuv Hradec, Czech.	28	Buffalo
MacARTHUR, Clarke	6-0	190	L	Lloydminster, Alta.	22	Buffalo-Rochester
MAIR, Adam	6-1	208	R	Hamilton, Ont.	28	Buffalo
MANCARI, Mark	6-3	220	R	London, Ont.	22	Buffalo-Rochester
PAILLE, Dan	6-0	197	L	Welland, Ont.	23	Buffalo-Rochester
PETERS, Andrew	6-4	228	L	St. Catharines, Ont.	27	Buffalo
POMINVILLE, Jason	6-0	186	R	Repentigny, Que.	24	Buffalo
ROY, Derek	5-9	186	L	Ottawa, Ont.	24	Buffalo
RYAN, Michael	6-1	186	L	Boston, MA	27	Buffalo-Rochester
STAFFORD, Drew	6-2	213	R	Milwaukee, WI	21	Buffalo-Rochester
VANEK, Thomas	6-2	203	R	Vienna, Austria	23	Buffalo
ZAGRAPAN, Marek	6-1	198	L	Presov, Czech.	20	Rochester
DEFENSEMEN						
CAMPBELL, Brian	6-0	190	L	Strathroy, Ont.	28	Buffalo
CARD, Mike	6-0	189	R	Kitchener, Ont.	21	Buf-Roch-Fla (ECHL)
FUNK, Michael	6-4	213	L	Abbotsford, B.C.	21	Buffalo-Rochester
KALININ, Dmitri	6-3	212	L	Chelyabinsk, USSR	27	Buffalo
LYDMAN, Toni	6-1	210	L	Lahti, Finland	30	Buffalo
NUMMINEN, Teppo	6-2	198	R	Tampere, Finland	39	Buffalo
PAETSCH, Nathan	6-0	198	L	Humboldt, Sask.	24	Buffalo
SEKERA, Andrej	6-0	201	L	Bojnice, Czech.	21	Buffalo-Rochester
SPACEK, Jaroslav	5-11	204	L	Rokycany, Czech.	33	Buffalo
TALLINDER, Henrik	6-3	214	L	Stockholm, Sweden	28	Buffalo

GOALTENDERS	HT	WT	C	Place of Birth	*Age	2006-07 Club
DENNIS, Adam	5-11	185	L	Toronto, Ont.	22	Rochester
MILLER, Ryan	6-2	172	L	East Lansing, MI	27	Buffalo
THIBAULT, Jocelyn	5-11	169	L	Montreal, Que.	32	Pittsburgh

* – Age at start of 2007-08 season

Captains' History

Floyd Smith, 1970-71; Gerry Meehan, 1971-72 to 1973-74; Gerry Meehan and Jim Schoenfeld, 1974-75; Jim Schoenfeld, 1975-76, 1976-77; Danny Gare, 1977-78 to 1980-81; Danny Gare and Gilbert Perreault, 1981-82; Gilbert Perreault, 1982-83 to 1985-86; Gilbert Perreault and Lindy Ruff, 1986-87; Lindy Ruff, 1987-88; Lindy Ruff and Mike Foligno, 1988-89; Mike Foligno, 1989-90; Mike Foligno and Mike Ramsey, 1990-91; Mike Ramsey, 1991-92; Mike Ramsey and Pat LaFontaine, 1992-93; Pat LaFontaine and Alexander Mogilny, 1993-94; Pat LaFontaine, 1994-95 to 1996-97; Donald Audette and Michael Peca, 1997-98; Michael Peca, 1998-99, 1999-2000; no captain, 2000-01; Stu Barnes. 2001-02, 2002-03; Miroslav Satan, Chris Drury, James Patrick, J.P. Dumont, Daniel Briere, 2003-04; Daniel Briere and Chris Drury, 2005-06, 2006-07.

Coaching History

Punch Imlach, 1970-71; Punch Imlach, Floyd Smith and Joe Crozier, 1971-72; Joe Crozier, 1972-73, 1973-74; Floyd Smith, 1974-75 to 1976-77; Marcel Pronovost, 1977-78; Marcel Pronovost and Billy Inglis, 1978-79; Scotty Bowman, 1979-80; Roger Neilson, 1980-81; Jim Roberts and Scotty Bowman, 1981-82; Scotty Bowman 1982-83 to 1984-85; Jim Schoenfeld and Scotty Bowman, 1985-86; Scotty Bowman, Craig Ramsay and Ted Sator, 1986-87; Ted Sator, 1987-88, 1988-89; Rick Dudley, 1989-90, 1990-91; Rick Dudley and John Muckler, 1991-92; John Muckler, 1992-93 to 1994-95; Ted Nolan, 1995-96, 1996-97; Lindy Ruff, 1997-98 to date.

Coach

LINDY RUFF

Coach, Buffalo Sabres. Born in Warburg, Alta., February, 17, 1960.

A former captain of the Sabres, Lindy Ruff was appointed as the club's 15th head coach on July 21, 1997. In 1999, he led the Sabres to the Stanley Cup Finals for just the second time in club history and in 2006 he guided the Sabres to the Eastern Conference Final and was rewarded with the Jack Adams Award as coach of the year. The Sabres won the Presidents' Trophy for finishing first overall in the NHL standings in 2006-07, recording 113 points and a franchise-record 53 wins. Ruff is the winningest coach in club history. As a player, Ruff was drafted 32nd overall by the Sabres in the 1979 Entry Draft. He played both defense and left wing in an NHL career that spanned 12 seasons including 608 regular-season games with Buffalo. He became a playing assistant coach with Rochester of the AHL in 1991-92 and San Diego of the IHL in 1992-93. Ruff's San Diego club set a pro hockey record with 62 wins. In 1993-94 he became an NHL assistant coach with the Florida Panthers.

Coaching Record

		Regular Season				Playoffs		
Season	**Team**	**Games**	**W**	**L**	**O/T**	**Games**	**W**	**L**
1997-98	**Buffalo (NHL)**	82	36	29	17	15	10	5
1998-99	**Buffalo (NHL)**	82	37	28	17	21	14	7
1999-2000	**Buffalo (NHL)**	82	35	36	11	5	1	4
2000-01	**Buffalo (NHL)**	82	46	31	5	13	7	6
2001-02	**Buffalo (NHL)**	82	35	36	11	....	....	....
2002-03	**Buffalo (NHL)**	82	27	45	10	....	....	....
2003-04	**Buffalo (NHL)**	82	37	38	7	....	....	....
2004-05	**Buffalo (NHL)**	Season Cancelled						
2005-06	**Buffalo (NHL)**	82	52	24	6	18	11	7
2006-07	**Buffalo (NHL)**	82	53	22	7	16	9	7
	NHL Totals	738	358	289	91	88	52	36

Assistant coaches Brian McCutheon and Scott Arniel shared an 0-1 record as replacement coach when Ruff was sidelined due to a family illness, March 20, 2006. Loss is credited to Ruff's coaching record.

2006-07 Scoring

* – rookie

Regular Season

Pos	#	Player	Team	GP	G	A	Pts	+/-	PIM	PP	SH	GW	S	%
C	48	Daniel Briere	BUF	81	32	63	95	17	89	9	0	6	234	13.7
L	26	Thomas Vanek	BUF	82	43	41	84	47	40	15	0	5	237	18.1
C	23	Chris Drury	BUF	77	37	32	69	1	30	17	3	9	199	18.6
R	29	Jason Pominville	BUF	82	34	34	68	25	30	2	2	5	212	16.0
C	9	Derek Roy	BUF	75	21	42	63	37	60	6	1	3	130	16.2
R	61	Maxim Afinogenov	BUF	56	23	38	61	19	66	7	0	3	151	15.2
R	15	Dainius Zubrus	WSH	60	20	32	52	–16	50	9	0	4	127	15.7
			BUF	19	4	4	8	–3	12	1	0	0	31	12.9
			TOTAL	79	24	36	60	–19	62	10	0	4	158	15.2
L	55	Jochen Hecht	BUF	76	19	37	56	19	39	3	0	1	197	9.6
D	51	Brian Campbell	BUF	82	6	42	48	28	35	1	0	1	92	6.5
R	12	Ales Kotalik	BUF	66	16	22	38	–5	46	3	0	4	162	9.9
D	45	Dmitri Kalinin	BUF	82	7	22	29	19	36	0	1	0	86	8.1
D	27	Teppo Numminen	BUF	79	2	27	29	17	32	0	0	0	69	2.9
R	21 *	Drew Stafford	BUF	41	13	14	27	5	33	3	0	3	67	19.4
D	38 *	Nathan Paetsch	BUF	63	2	22	24	10	50	0	0	0	62	3.2
C	28	Paul Gaustad	BUF	54	9	13	22	11	74	3	0	0	75	12.0
D	6	Jaroslav Spacek	BUF	65	5	16	21	20	62	1	0	2	78	6.4
D	5	Toni Lydman	BUF	67	2	17	19	10	55	0	0	1	44	4.5
D	10	Henrik Tallinder	BUF	47	4	10	14	19	34	0	0	0	34	11.8
L	20 *	Daniel Paille	BUF	29	3	8	11	5	18	0	0	0	45	6.7
C	22	Adam Mair	BUF	82	2	9	11	–1	128	0	0	0	73	2.7
L	41 *	Clarke MacArthur	BUF	19	3	4	7	4	4	0	0	0	16	18.8
C	37	Michael Ryan	BUF	19	3	2	5	–8	2	0	1	0	34	8.8
L	76	Andrew Peters	BUF	58	1	1	2	–1	125	0	0	0	19	5.3
D	3 *	Michael Funk	BUF	5	0	2	2	2	0	0	0	0	1	0.0
R	36 *	Patrick Kaleta	BUF	7	0	2	2	3	21	0	0	0	6	0.0
C	19	Tim Connolly	BUF	2	1	0	1	1	2	0	0	0	2	50.0
R	25 *	Mark Mancari	BUF	3	0	1	1	–1	2	0	0	0	1	0.0
D	44 *	Andrej Sekera	BUF	2	0	0	0	1	2	0	0	0	0	0.0
D	33 *	Mike Card	BUF	4	0	0	0	0	0	0	0	0	0	0.0

Goaltending

No.	Goaltender	GPI	Mins	Avg	W	L	OT	EN	SO	GA	SA	S%	G	A	PIM
30	Ryan Miller	63	3692	2.73	40	16	6	1	2	168	1886	.911	0	2	2
43	Martin Biron	19	1066	3.04	12	4	1	2	0	54	533	.899	0	0	25
35	Ty Conklin	5	227	3.44	1	2	0	0	0	13	120	.892	0	0	2
	Totals	**82**	**5008**	**2.85**	**53**	**22**	**7**	**3**	**2**	**238**	**2542**	**.906**			

Playoffs

Pos	#	Player	Team	GP	G	A	Pts	+/-	PIM	PP	SH	GW	OT	S	%
C	48	Daniel Briere	BUF	16	3	12	15	3	16	2	0	1	0	49	6.1
C	23	Chris Drury	BUF	16	8	5	13	3	2	3	0	3	0	43	18.6
L	26	Thomas Vanek	BUF	16	6	4	10	2	10	1	0	2	0	36	16.7
R	29	Jason Pominville	BUF	16	4	6	10	2	0	0	0	0	0	40	10.0
R	61	Maxim Afinogenov	BUF	15	5	4	9	3	6	3	0	2	1	36	13.9
C	19	Tim Connolly	BUF	16	0	9	9	6	4	0	0	0	0	25	0.0
R	15	Dainius Zubrus	BUF	15	0	8	8	1	8	0	0	0	0	25	0.0
D	51	Brian Campbell	BUF	16	3	4	7	0	14	2	0	0	0	29	10.3
C	9	Derek Roy	BUF	16	2	5	7	3	14	0	0	0	0	19	10.5
L	55	Jochen Hecht	BUF	16	4	1	5	2	10	0	0	1	0	45	8.9
D	45	Dmitri Kalinin	BUF	16	2	3	5	9	14	0	0	0	0	16	12.5
C	22	Adam Mair	BUF	16	1	4	5	5	10	0	0	0	0	10	10.0
R	21 *	Drew Stafford	BUF	10	2	2	4	3	4	0	0	0	0	16	12.5
D	5	Toni Lydman	BUF	16	2	2	4	–5	14	0	0	0	0	14	14.3
R	12	Ales Kotalik	BUF	16	2	2	4	–3	8	0	0	0	0	34	5.9
D	27	Teppo Numminen	BUF	16	0	4	4	10	4	0	0	0	0	9	0.0
D	10	Henrik Tallinder	BUF	16	0	2	2	–4	10	0	0	0	0	12	0.0
C	28	Paul Gaustad	BUF	7	0	1	1	–1	2	0	0	0	0	4	0.0
L	20 *	Daniel Paille	BUF	1	0	0	0	0	0	0	0	0	0	1	0.0
D	6	Jaroslav Spacek	BUF	16	0	0	0	3	10	0	0	0	0	15	0.0

Goaltending

No.	Goaltender	GPI	Mins	Avg	W	L	EN	SO	GA	SA	S%	G	A	PIM
30	Ryan Miller	16	1029	2.22	9	7	1	0	38	489	.922	0	0	2
	Totals	**16**	**1036**	**2.26**	**9**	**7**	**1**	**0**	**39**	**490**	**.920**			

Club Records

Team

(Figures in brackets for season records are games played; records for fewest points, wins, ties, losses, goals, goals against are for 70 or more games)

Record		
Most Points	113	1974-75 (80), 2006-07 (82)
Most Wins	53	2006-07 (82)
Most Ties	21	1980-81 (80)
Most Losses	44	1986-87 (80)
Most Goals	354	1974-75 (80)
Most Goals Against	308	1986-87 (80)
Fewest Points	51	1971-72 (78)
Fewest Wins	16	1971-72 (78)
Fewest Ties	5	2000-01 (82)
Fewest Losses	16	1974-75 (80)
Fewest Goals	190	2002-03 (82)
Fewest Goals Against	175	1998-99 (82)
Longest Winning Streak		
Overall	10	Jan. 4-23/84, Oct. 4-26/06
Home	12	Nov. 12/72-Jan. 7/73, Oct. 13-Dec. 10/89
Away	*10	Dec. 10/83-Jan. 23/84, Oct. 4-Nov. 13/06
Longest Undefeated Streak		
Overall	14	Mar. 6-Apr. 6/80 (8 wins, 6 ties)
Home	21	Oct. 8/72-Jan. 7/73 (18 wins, 3 ties)
Away	10	Dec. 10/83-Jan. 23/84 (10 wins), Oct. 4-Nov. 13/06 (10 wins)
Longest Losing Streak		
Overall	7	Four times
Home	6	Oct. 10-Nov. 10/93, Mar. 3-Apr. 3/96
Away	7	Oct. 14-Nov. 7/70, Feb. 6-27/71, Jan. 10-Feb. 3/96
Longest Winless Streak		
Overall	12	Nov. 23-Dec. 20/91 (8 losses, 4 ties)
Home	12	Jan. 27-Mar. 10/91 (7 losses, 5 ties)
Away	23	Oct. 30/71-Feb. 19/72 (15 losses, 8 ties)
Most Shutouts, Season	13	1997-98 (82)
Most PIM, Season	*2,713	1991-92 (80)
Most Goals, Game	14	Jan. 21/75 (Wsh. 2 at Buf. 14), Mar. 19/81 (Tor. 4 at Buf. 14)

Individual

Record		
Most Seasons	17	Gilbert Perreault
Most Games	1,191	Gilbert Perreault
Most Goals, Career	512	Gilbert Perreault
Most Assists, Career	814	Gilbert Perreault
Most Points, Career	1,326	Gilbert Perreault (512G, 814A)
Most PIM, Career	3,189	Rob Ray
Most Shutouts, Career	55	Dominik Hasek
Longest Consecutive Games Streak	776	Craig Ramsay (Mar. 27/73-Feb. 10/83)
Most Goals, Season	76	Alexander Mogilny (1992-93)
Most Assists, Season	95	Pat LaFontaine (1992-93)
Most Points, Season	148	Pat LaFontaine (1992-93; 53G, 95A)
Most PIM, Season	354	Rob Ray (1991-92)
Most Points, Defenseman, Season	81	Phil Housley (1989-90; 21G, 60A)
Most Points, Center, Season	148	Pat LaFontaine (1992-93; 53G, 95A)
Most Points, Right Wing, Season	127	Alexander Mogilny (1992-93; 76G, 51A)
Most Points, Left Wing, Season	95	Rick Martin (1974-75; 52G, 43A)
Most Points, Rookie, Season	74	Rick Martin (1971-72; 44G, 30A)
Most Shutouts, Season	13	Dominik Hasek (1997-98)
Most Goals, Game	5	Dave Andreychuk (Feb. 6/86)
Most Assists, Game	5	Gilbert Perreault (Feb. 1/76, Mar. 9/80, Jan. 4/84), Dale Hawerchuk (Jan. 15/92), Pat LaFontaine (Dec. 31/92, Feb. 10/93)
Most Points, Game	7	Gilbert Perreault (Feb. 1/76; 2G, 5A)

* NHL Record.

Retired Numbers

No.	Player	Years
2	Tim Horton	1972-1974
7	Rick Martin	1971-1981
11	Gilbert Perreault	1970-1987
14	Rene Robert	1971-1979
16	Pat Lafontaine	1991-1996
18	Danny Gare	1974-1981

All-time Record vs. Other Clubs

Regular Season

	At Home								On Road								Total							
	GP	W	L	T	OL	GF	GA	PTS	GP	W	L	T	OL	GF	GA	PTS	GP	W	L	T	OL	GF	GA	PTS
Anaheim	10	5	2	3	0	28	22	13	9	7	2	0	0	30	15	14	19	12	4	3	0	58	37	27
Atlanta	14	8	5	0	1	57	40	17	14	5	6	1	2	43	45	13	28	13	11	1	3	100	85	30
Boston	116	60	39	15	2	423	340	137	115	38	61	14	2	341	422	92	231	98	100	29	4	764	762	229
Calgary	46	28	13	5	0	192	133	61	47	18	18	11	0	147	156	47	93	46	31	16	0	339	289	108
Carolina	81	48	25	7	1	324	240	104	82	38	32	11	1	247	237	88	163	86	57	18	2	571	477	192
Chicago	53	32	14	7	0	199	138	71	52	19	27	6	0	141	165	44	105	51	41	13	0	340	303	115
Colorado	64	36	19	9	0	249	207	81	65	23	31	11	0	203	231	57	129	59	50	20	0	452	438	138
Columbus	4	2	2	0	0	13	9	4	3	0	2	1	0	6	8	1	7	2	4	1	0	19	17	5
Dallas	53	29	13	11	0	192	142	69	54	21	27	6	0	156	173	48	107	50	40	17	0	348	315	117
Detroit	52	33	11	8	0	226	153	74	56	19	31	5	1	162	205	44	108	52	42	13	1	388	358	118
Edmonton	31	11	13	7	0	111	113	29	30	6	21	3	0	77	121	15	61	17	34	10	0	188	234	44
Florida	27	18	6	3	0	77	47	39	25	11	13	1	0	72	72	23	52	29	19	4	0	149	119	62
Los Angeles	54	29	16	9	0	227	158	67	54	23	22	9	0	187	185	55	108	52	38	18	0	414	343	122
Minnesota	4	1	3	0	0	8	13	2	4	3	1	0	0	10	6	6	8	4	4	0	0	18	19	8
Montreal	110	58	31	19	2	343	292	137	111	39	60	12	0	331	412	90	221	97	91	31	2	674	704	227
Nashville	4	0	3	1	0	9	16	1	6	4	2	0	0	16	12	8	10	4	5	1	0	25	28	9
New Jersey	58	33	17	8	0	225	175	74	58	27	21	9	1	185	173	64	116	60	38	17	1	410	348	138
NY Islanders	65	36	19	9	1	218	176	82	65	28	27	9	1	182	184	66	130	64	46	18	2	400	360	148
NY Rangers	72	42	19	10	1	295	223	95	70	26	27	15	2	193	225	69	142	68	46	25	3	488	448	164
Ottawa	39	25	11	3	0	123	80	53	41	18	15	7	1	108	112	44	80	43	26	10	1	231	192	97
Philadelphia	67	35	24	8	0	230	186	78	71	18	40	12	1	178	242	49	138	53	64	20	1	408	428	127
Phoenix	32	20	6	5	1	128	82	46	29	14	13	2	0	92	87	30	61	34	19	7	1	220	169	76
Pittsburgh	75	37	19	17	2	287	201	93	75	20	36	18	1	232	277	59	150	57	55	35	3	519	478	152
St. Louis	52	29	17	6	0	200	164	64	51	14	28	7	2	127	183	37	103	43	45	13	2	327	347	101
San Jose	12	11	1	0	0	52	32	22	10	1	4	4	1	33	36	7	22	12	5	4	1	85	68	29
Tampa Bay	27	16	9	2	0	83	74	34	27	18	6	3	0	85	56	39	54	34	15	5	0	168	130	73
Toronto	77	49	21	6	1	314	205	105	75	32	28	12	3	256	229	79	152	81	49	18	4	570	434	184
Vancouver	53	27	18	8	0	190	155	62	53	16	26	11	0	163	197	43	106	43	44	19	0	353	352	105
Washington	60	38	16	6	0	237	159	82	60	35	16	9	0	211	153	79	120	73	32	15	0	448	312	161
Defunct Clubs	23	13	5	5	0	94	63	31	23	12	8	3	0	97	76	27	46	25	13	8	0	191	139	58
Totals	**1435**	**809**	**417**	**197**	**12**	**5354**	**4038**	**1827**	**1435**	**553**	**651**	**212**	**19**	**4311**	**4695**	**1337**	**2870**	**1362**	**1068**	**409**	**31**	**9665**	**8733**	**3164**

Playoffs

	Series	W	L	GP	W	L	T	GF	GA	Last Mtg.	Rnd.	Result
Boston	7	2	5	39	18	21	0	130	139	1999	CSF	W 4-2
Carolina	1	0	1	7	3	4	0	17	22	2006	CF	L 3-4
Chicago	2	2	0	9	8	1	0	36	17	1980	QF	W 4-0
Colorado	2	0	2	8	2	6	0	27	35	1985	DSF	L 2-3
Dallas	3	1	2	13	5	8	0	37	39	1999	F	L 2-4
Montreal	7	3	4	35	17	18	0	111	124	1998	CSF	W 4-0
New Jersey	1	0	1	7	3	4	0	14	14	1994	CQF	L 3-4
NY Islanders	4	1	3	21	8	13	0	62	70	2007	CQF	W 4-1
NY Rangers	2	2	0	9	6	3	0	28	19	2007	CSF	W 4-2
Ottawa	4	3	1	21	13	8	0	52	47	2007	CF	L 1-4
Philadelphia	8	3	5	43	18	25	0	123	124	2006	CQF	W 4-2
Pittsburgh	2	0	2	10	4	6	0	26	26	2001	CSF	L 3-4
St. Louis	1	1	0	3	2	1	0	7	8	1976	PRE	W 2-1
Toronto	1	1	0	5	4	1	0	21	16	1999	CF	W 4-1
Vancouver	2	2	0	7	6	1	0	28	14	1981	PRE	W 3-0
Washington	1	0	1	6	2	4	0	11	13	1998	CF	L 2-4
Totals	**48**	**21**	**27**	**243**	**119**	**124**	**0**	**730**	**727**			

Calgary totals include Atlanta Flames, 1972-73 to 1979-80. Carolina totals include Hartford, 1979-80 to 1996-97.
Colorado totals include Quebec, 1979-80 to 1994-95. Dallas totals include Minnesota North Stars, 1970-71 to 1992-93.
New Jersey totals include Kansas City, 1974-75, 1975-76, and Colorado Rockies, 1976-77 to 1981-82.
Phoenix totals include Winnipeg, 1979-80 to 1995-96.

Playoff Results 2007-2002

Year	Round	Opponent	Result	GF	GA
2007	CF	Ottawa	L 1-4	10	15
	CSF	NY Rangers	W 4-2	17	13
	CQF	NY Islanders	W 4-1	17	11
2006	CF	Carolina	L 3-4	17	22
	CSF	Ottawa	W 4-1	16	13
	CQF	Philadelphia	W 4-2	27	14

Abbreviations: Round: F - Final; **CF** - conference final; **CSF** - conference semi-final; **CQF** - conference quarter-final; **DSF** - division semi-final; **SF** - semi-final; **QF** - quarter-final; **PRE** - preliminary round.

2006-07 Results

Month	Date	Opponent	Score
Oct.	4	at Carolina	3-2†
	6	Montreal	5-4†
	7	at Ottawa	4-3
	13	at Detroit	3-2†
	14	NY Rangers	7-4
	17	Philadelphia	9-1
	20	Carolina	5-4
	21	at Boston	6-2
	23	at Montreal	4-1
	26	at NY Islanders	3-0
	28	Atlanta	4-5†
Nov.	2	at Boston	5-4†
	4	Toronto	1-4
	5	at NY Rangers	4-3*
	10	Florida	5-4*
	11	at Philadelphia	5-4*
	13	at Carolina	7-4
	15	Ottawa	2-4
	17	Pittsburgh	4-2
	18	at Ottawa	1-4
	20	Tampa Bay	7-2
	22	Toronto	7-4
	24	Montreal	1-2*
	26	at NY Rangers	3-2*
Dec.	1	NY Rangers	4-3†
	2	at Washington	4-7
	5	at Tampa Bay	4-1
	7	at Florida	1-3
	9	at Montreal	3-2†
	12	at New Jersey	3-2
	14	Florida	2-1
	16	Ottawa	1-3
	19	Montreal	2-5
	21	at Nashville	7-2
	23	at St. Louis	2-3*
	26	Washington	6-3
	28	Carolina	4-1
	30	Atlanta	4-1
Jan.	1	NY Islanders	3-1
	3	at Ottawa	3-6
	5	Pittsburgh	2-4
	6	at Toronto	4-3
	10	at Chicago	2-1
	11	Toronto	2-4
	13	Tampa Bay	2-3
	15	at Boston	2-3†
	17	Boston	6-3
	19	Vancouver	4-3†
	20	at Montreal	3-4
	26	at Columbus	2-3
	27	at NY Islanders	3-5
	30	Boston	7-1
Feb.	1	at Boston	3-1
	3	at New Jersey	2-3
	6	at Atlanta	4-3†
	7	Ottawa	3-2
	10	Calgary	3-2†
	15	Edmonton	2-1*
	17	Boston	3-4†
	20	Philadelphia	6-3
	22	Ottawa	6-5†
	24	at Ottawa	5-6
	27	at Toronto	6-1
Mar.	2	Montreal	8-5
	3	at Toronto	3-1
	7	Colorado	2-3
	9	Minnesota	1-5
	10	New Jersey	2-3
	13	at Pittsburgh	4-5†
	15	at Florida	5-3
	16	at Tampa Bay	3-2
	18	at Atlanta	3-4*
	21	Washington	5-2
	23	Toronto	5-4
	24	at Toronto	1-4
	28	New Jersey	4-3
	30	NY Islanders	6-4
	31	at Montreal	3-4
Apr.	3	at Pittsburgh	4-1
	5	Boston	4-2
	7	at Washington	2-0
	8	at Philadelphia	3-4

* – Overtime † – Shootout

Entry Draft Selections 2007-1993

2007

Pick	
31	TJ Brennan
59	Drew Schiestel
89	Corey Tropp
139	Bradley Eidsness
147	Jean-Simon Allard
179	Paul Byron
187	Nick Eno
209	Drew Mackenzie

2006

Pick	
24	Dennis Persson
46	Jhonas Enroth
57	Mike Weber
117	Felix Schutz
147	Alex Biega
207	Benjamin Breault

2005

Pick	
13	Marek Zagrapan
48	Philip Gogulla
87	Marc-Andre Gragnani
96	Chris Butler
142	Nathan Gerbe
182	Adam Dennis
191	Vyacheslav Buravchikov
208	Matt Generous
227	Andrew Orpik

2004

Pick	
13	Drew Stafford
43	Michael Funk
71	Andrej Sekera
145	Michal Valent
176	Patrick Kaleta
207	Mark Mancari
241	Mike Card
273	Dylan Hunter

2003

Pick	
5	Thomas Vanek
65	Branislav Fabry
74	Clarke MacArthur
106	Jan Hejda
114	Denis Ezhov
150	Thomas Morrow
172	Pavel Voroshnin
202	Nathan Paetsch
235	Jeff Weber
266	Louis-Philippe Martin

2002

Pick	
11	Keith Ballard
20	Dan Paille
76	Michael Tessier
82	John Adams
108	Jakub Hulva
121	Marty Magers
178	Maxim Schevjev
208	Radoslav Hecl
241	Dennis Wideman
271	Martin Cizek

2001

Pick	
22	Jiri Novotny
32	Derek Roy
50	Chris Thorburn
55	Jason Pominville
155	Michal Vondrka
234	Calle Aslund
247	Marek Dubec
279	Ryan Jorde

2000

Pick	
15	Artem Kryukov
48	Gerard Dicaire
111	Ghyslain Rousseau
149	Denis Denisov
213	Vasili Bizyayev
220	Paul Gaustad
258	Sean McMorrow
277	Ryan Courtney

1999

Pick	
20	Barrett Heisten
35	Milan Bartovic
55	Doug Janik
64	Mike Zigomanis
73	Tim Preston
117	Karel Mosovsky
138	Ryan Miller
146	Matt Kinch
178	Seneque Hyacinthe
206	Bret DeCecco
235	Brad Self
263	Craig Brunel

1998

Pick	
18	Dmitri Kalinin
34	Andrew Peters
47	Norm Milley
50	Jaroslav Kristek
77	Mike Pandolfo
137	Aaron Goldade
164	Ales Kotalik
191	Brad Moran
218	David Moravec
249	Edo Terglav

1997

Pick	
21	Mika Noronen
48	Henrik Tallinder
69	Maxim Afinogenov
75	Jeff Martin
101	Luc Theoret
128	Torrey DiRoberto
156	Brian Campbell
184	Jeremy Adduono
212	Kamil Piros
238	Dylan Kemp

1996

Pick	
7	Erik Rasmussen
27	Cory Sarich
33	Darren Van Oene
54	Francois Methot
87	Kurt Walsh
106	Mike Martone
115	Alexei Tezikov
142	Ryan Davis
161	Darren Mortier
222	Scott Buhler

1995

Pick	
14	Jay McKee
16	Martin Biron
42	Mark Dutiaume
68	Mathieu Sunderland
94	Matt Davidson
111	Marian Menhart
119	Kevin Popp
123	Daniel Bienvenue
172	Brian Scott
198	Mike Zanutto
224	Rob Skrlac

1994

Pick	
17	Wayne Primeau
43	Curtis Brown
69	Rumun Ndur
121	Sergei Klimentiev
147	Cal Benazic
168	Steve Plouffe
173	Shane Hnidy
176	Steve Webb
199	Bob Westerby
225	Craig Millar
251	Mark Polak
277	Shayne Wright

1993

Pick	
38	Denis Tsygurov
64	Ethan Philpott
116	Richard Safarik
142	Kevin Pozzo
168	Sergei Petrenko
194	Mike Barrie
220	Barrie Moore
246	Chris Davis
272	Scott Nichol

General Managers' History

Punch Imlach, 1970-71 to 1977-78; John Anderson, 1978-79; Scotty Bowman, 1979-80 to 1985-86; Scotty Bowman and Gerry Meehan, 1986-87; Gerry Meehan, 1987-88 to 1992-93; John Muckler, 1993-94 to 1996-97; Darcy Regier, 1997-98 to date.

General Manager

DARCY REGIER

General Manager, Buffalo Sabres. Born in Swift Current, Sask., Nov. 27, 1957.

Darcy Regier became the sixth general manager of the Buffalo Sabres on June 11, 1997 after a lengthy management apprenticeship in the New York Islanders organization. As a player, Regier played eight pro seasons, including part of the 1977-78 season with the Cleveland Barons and parts of the 1982-83 and 1983-84 campaigns with the New York Islanders.

He began his career as an administrator with the Islanders in 1984-85 and went on to serve in a variety of capacities including director of administration, assistant director of hockey operations, assistant coach and assistant general manager. He also served as an assistant coach with Hartford in 1991-92.

While with the Islanders, Regier benefited from working with talented managers and coaches including Bill Torrey and Al Arbour. As a minor pro player with Indianapolis of the CHL he became associated with another important influence on his hockey career, current Detroit Red Wing executive Jim Devellano.

Club Directory

HSBC Arena

Buffalo Sabres
HSBC Arena
One Seymour H. Knox III Plaza
Buffalo, NY 14203
Phone **716/855-4100**
Fax 716/855-4110
Tickets, U.S.: 888/GO-SABRES
Canada: 888/669-GOAL
www.sabres.com
Capacity: 18,690

Executive
Owner . . . . . B. Thomas Golisano
Managing Partner . . . . . Lawrence Quinn
Chief Operating Officer . . . . . Daniel DiPofi

Hockey Department
General Manager . . . . . Darcy Regier
Director of Amateur Scouting . . . . . Kevin Devine
Pro Scout . . . . . Jon Christiano
Amateur Scouts . . . . . Bo Berglund, Iouri Khmylev, Al MacAdam, Paul Merritt, Craig Benning, Kim Gellert
Director of Amateur Scouting Operations . . . . . Scott Schranz
Hockey Department Analyst . . . . . Mark Jakubowski
Amateur Video Scout . . . . . Nick Fattey
Pro Video Scout . . . . . Bryan Stewart
Coordinator of Hockey Operations . . . . . Michael Bermingham
Amateur Video Scouting Coordinator . . . . . Eric Weissman

Coaching Staff
Head Coach . . . . . Lindy Ruff
Associate Coach . . . . . Brian McCutcheon
Assistant Coach . . . . . James Patrick
Strength & Conditioning Coach . . . . . Doug McKenney
Asst. Strength & Conditioning Coach . . . . . Kevin Collins
Goaltender Coach . . . . . Jim Corsi
Administrative Assistant Coach . . . . . Corey Smith
Athletic Trainer . . . . . Tim Macre
Equipment Managers . . . . . Rip Simonick, Dave Williams
Assistant Equipment Manager . . . . . George Babcock
Massage Therapist . . . . . Chuck Garlow

Medical
Medical Director . . . . . Les Bisson, M.D.
Team Physicians . . . . . Nicholas Aquino, M.D., William Hartrich, M.D.
Oral Surgeon . . . . . Steven Jenson, DDS
Team Dentist . . . . . Daniel Yustin, DDS, M.S.
Team Doctor Emeritus . . . . . John L. Butsch, M.D.

Legal
Director of Legal Affairs & Human Resources . . . . . Richard Mugel

Finance and Administration
Director of Finance & Administration . . . . . Chuck LaMattina
Accounting Manager . . . . . Christine Ivansitz
Payroll & Human Resource Manager . . . . . Birgid Haensel
Accounts Payable Clerk . . . . . Kim Binkley
Executive Assistant . . . . . Nadine Lawicki
IT Systems Engineer . . . . . Justin Elze

Broadcast
Executive Producer . . . . . Matt Gould
Staff Producer . . . . . Joe Pinter
Broadcast Director . . . . . Eric Grossman
Director of Broadcast Services . . . . . Chrisanne Bellas
Feature Producer/Editor . . . . . Jeff Hill
Broadcast Team . . . . . Rick Jeanneret (Play-by-Play), Jim Lorentz (Commentator), Kevin Sylvester (Studio Host), Mike Robitaille, Rob Ray (Analysts)

Merchandise
Director of Merchandise . . . . . Mike Kaminska
Merchandise Manager – Inventory Control . . . . . Glenn Barker
Merchandise Manager – Event Sales . . . . . Jeff Smith
Store Manager . . . . . Alec Moslow

Marketing
Director of Marketing . . . . . Rob Kopacz
Director of Game Presentation . . . . . Martin McCreary
Promotions Manager . . . . . Rich Wall
Database Marketing Manager . . . . . Tom Matheny
Website Manager . . . . . Brian Wheeler
Director of Creative Services . . . . . Frank Cravotta

Public and Community Relations
Director of Public Relations . . . . . Michael Gilbert
Manager of Publications & Hockey Information . . . . . Kevin Snow
Manager of Community Development . . . . . Rich Jureller
Coordinator of Media Relations . . . . . Chris Bandura
Community Relations Coordinator . . . . . Teresa Belbas
Mascot Coordinator . . . . . Ed Grudzinski
Team Photographer . . . . . Bill Wippert
Director of Alumni Relations . . . . . Larry Playfair
Corporate & Community Relations Liaison . . . . . Gilbert Perreault

Sales and Business Development
V.P. Sales & Business Development . . . . . John Livsey
Senior Account Managers . . . . . Joe Foy, Chris Luterek
Account Manager . . . . . Joe Shaw
Director of Sales/Marketing – Rochester . . . . . Gary Muxworthy

Ticket Sales and Operations
Director of Ticket Operations & Services . . . . . John Sinclair
Account Services Manager . . . . . Michael Tout
Box Office Manager . . . . . Christopher Makowski
Assistant Box Office Manager . . . . . Marty Maloney
Account Services Representatives . . . Roxanne Anderson, Andrea Keane, Lisa Wells, Melissa Rugg
Account Executives . . . . . Sarah Kretz, Scott Loffler
Special Consultant . . . . . Joe Crozier

HSBC Arena
Director of Arena Operations . . . . . Stan Makowski, Jr.
Director of Event Booking . . . . . Jennifer Van Rysdam
Arena Marketing Manager . . . . . Christine Adamczyk
Director of Amateur Athletics . . . . . Kevin Sylvester
Event Managers . . . . . Matt Rabinowitz, Beth Guiliani Gatto
Manager of Technical Communications . . . . . Mike Queeno
Chief Engineer . . . . . Barry Becker

Calgary Flames

Key Off-Season Signings/Acquisitions

2007

June 1 • Re-signed C **Matthew Lombardi** and LW **Marcus Nilson**.

14 • Named **Mike Keenan** head coach.

20 • Re-signed LW **David Moss**.

22 • Acquired D **Adrian Aucoin** and a 7th-round pick in the 2007 Entry Draft from Chicago for D **Andrei Zyuzin** and D **Steve Marr**.

28 • Re-signed C **Wayne Primeau** and D **David Hale**.

July 1 • Signed D **Cory Sarich**.

3 • Signed RW **Owen Nolan**.

4 • Re-signed RW **Jarome Iginla** and D **Robyn Regehr**.

5 • Signed D **Anders Eriksson**.

2006-07 Results: 43W-29L-5OTL-5SOL 96PTS.
Third, Northwest Division

Alex Tanguay established career highs with 59 assists and 81 points in 2006-07. His assists led the team while his points ranked him second behind Jarome Iginla.

2007-08 Schedule

Oct.	Thu.	4	Philadelphia
	Sat.	6	Vancouver
	Wed.	10	at Detroit
	Fri.	12	at Dallas
	Sat.	13	at Nashville
	Tue.	16	at Colorado
	Thu.	18	Los Angeles
	Sat.	20	Edmonton
	Mon.	22	San Jose
	Wed.	24	Minnesota
	Fri.	26	Colorado
	Tue.	30	Nashville
Nov.	Thu.	1	Detroit
	Sat.	3	at Minnesota
	Mon.	5	at Colorado
	Thu.	8	Vancouver
	Sat.	10	Edmonton
	Tue.	13	Minnesota
	Sat.	17	at Edmonton
	Sun.	18	at Vancouver*
	Tue.	20	Colorado
	Thu.	22	Chicago
	Sat.	24	at Colorado
	Sun.	25	at St. Louis*
	Tue.	27	at Detroit
	Thu.	29	Anaheim
Dec.	Sat.	1	Columbus
	Tue.	4	St. Louis
	Thu.	6	Pittsburgh
	Sun.	9	at Chicago
	Tue.	11	at Florida
	Thu.	13	at Tampa Bay
	Fri.	14	at Carolina
	Sun.	16	at St. Louis*
	Tue.	18	at Columbus
	Fri.	21	Dallas
	Sun.	23	New Jersey
	Thu.	27	at Vancouver
	Sat.	29	Anaheim
	Mon.	31	Vancouver
Jan.	Wed.	2	NY Rangers
	Thu.	3	at San Jose
	Sat.	5	at Los Angeles
	Tue.	8	Phoenix
	Fri.	11	NY Islanders
	Sun.	13	at Edmonton
	Tue.	15	at Nashville
	Wed.	16	at Minnesota
	Fri.	18	Los Angeles
	Tue.	22	Minnesota
	Wed.	30	San Jose
Feb.	Sat.	2	Dallas
	Mon.	4	at Edmonton
	Tue.	5	Phoenix
	Thu.	7	Chicago
	Sat.	9	Edmonton*
	Tue.	12	at San Jose
	Fri.	15	at Los Angeles
	Sun.	17	at Anaheim*
	Tue.	19	at Phoenix
	Wed.	20	at Dallas
	Fri.	22	Detroit
	Sun.	24	at Minnesota*
	Tue.	26	Colorado
	Fri.	29	at Anaheim
Mar.	Sat.	1	at Phoenix
	Tue.	4	Columbus
	Fri.	7	Nashville
	Mon.	10	St. Louis
	Wed.	12	at Washington
	Thu.	13	at Atlanta
	Sun.	16	at Chicago*
	Tue.	18	at Columbus
	Thu.	20	Colorado
	Sat.	22	Minnesota
	Mon.	24	at Colorado
	Tue.	25	Vancouver
	Sat.	29	Edmonton
	Sun.	30	at Vancouver
Apr.	Tue.	1	at Edmonton
	Thu.	3	at Minnesota
	Sat.	5	at Vancouver

* Denotes afternoon game.

NORTHWEST DIVISION
36th NHL Season

Franchise date: June 6, 1972

Transferred from Atlanta to Calgary, June 24, 1980.

Year-by-Year Record

Season	GP	Home W	Home L	Home T	Home OL	Road W	Road L	Road T	Road OL	Overall W	Overall L	Overall T	Overall OL	GF	GA	Pts.	Finished	Playoff Result
2006-07	82	30	9	....	2	13	20	....	8	43	29	....	10	258	226	96	3rd, Northwest Div.	Lost Conf. Quarter-Final
2005-06	82	30	7	....	4	16	18	....	7	46	25	....	11	218	200	103	1st, Northwest Div.	Lost Conf. Quarter-Final
2004-05	....	....	....	....	....	....	....	....	....	....	....	....	....	....	....	....		
2003-04	82	21	14	5	1	21	16	2	2	42	30	7	3	200	176	94	3rd, Northwest Div.	Lost Final
2002-03	82	14	16	10	1	15	20	3	3	29	36	13	4	186	228	75	5th, Northwest Div.	Out of Playoffs
2001-02	82	20	14	5	2	12	21	7	1	32	35	12	3	201	220	79	4th, Northwest Div.	Out of Playoffs
2000-01	82	12	18	9	2	15	18	6	2	27	36	15	4	197	236	73	4th, Northwest Div.	Out of Playoffs
1999-2000	82	20	14	6	1	11	22	4	4	31	36	10	5	211	256	77	4th, Northwest Div.	Out of Playoffs
1998-99	82	15	20	6	....	15	20	6	....	30	40	12	....	211	234	72	3rd, Northwest Div.	Out of Playoffs
1997-98	82	18	17	6	....	8	24	9	....	26	41	15	....	217	252	67	5th, Pacific Div.	Out of Playoffs
1996-97	82	21	18	2	....	11	23	7	....	32	41	9	....	214	239	73	5th, Pacific Div.	Out of Playoffs
1995-96	82	18	18	5	....	16	19	6	....	34	37	11	....	241	240	79	2nd, Pacific Div.	Lost Conf. Quarter-Final
1994-95	48	15	7	2	....	9	10	5	....	24	17	7	....	163	135	55	1st, Pacific Div.	Lost Conf. Quarter-Final
1993-94	84	25	12	5	....	17	17	8	....	42	29	13	....	302	256	97	1st, Pacific Div.	Lost Conf. Quarter-Final
1992-93	84	23	14	5	....	20	16	6	....	43	30	11	....	322	282	97	2nd, Smythe Div.	Lost Div. Semi-Final
1991-92	80	19	14	7	....	12	23	5	....	31	37	12	....	296	305	74	5th, Smythe Div.	Out of Playoffs
1990-91	80	29	8	3	....	17	18	5	....	46	26	8	....	344	263	100	2nd, Smythe Div.	Lost Div. Semi-Final
1989-90	80	28	7	5	....	14	16	10	....	42	23	15	....	348	265	99	1st, Smythe Div.	Lost Div. Semi-Final
1988-89	**80**	**32**	**4**	**4**	....	**22**	**13**	**5**	....	**54**	**17**	**9**	....	**354**	**226**	**117**	**1st, Smythe Div.**	**Won Stanley Cup**
1987-88	80	26	11	3	....	22	12	6	....	48	23	9	....	397	305	105	1st, Smythe Div.	Lost Div. Final
1986-87	80	25	13	2	....	21	18	1	....	46	31	3	....	318	289	95	2nd, Smythe Div.	Lost Div. Semi-Final
1985-86	80	23	11	6	....	17	20	3	....	40	31	9	....	354	315	89	2nd, Smythe Div.	Lost Final
1984-85	80	23	11	6	....	18	16	6	....	41	27	12	....	363	302	94	3rd, Smythe Div.	Lost Div. Semi-Final
1983-84	80	22	11	7	....	12	21	7	....	34	32	14	....	311	314	82	2nd, Smythe Div.	Lost Div. Final
1982-83	80	21	12	7	....	11	22	7	....	32	34	14	....	321	317	78	2nd, Smythe Div.	Lost Div. Final
1981-82	80	20	11	9	....	9	23	8	....	29	34	17	....	334	345	75	3rd, Smythe Div.	Lost Div. Semi-Final
1980-81	80	25	5	10	....	14	22	4	....	39	27	14	....	329	298	92	3rd, Patrick Div.	Lost Semi-Final
1979-80*	80	18	15	7	....	17	17	6	....	35	32	13	....	282	269	83	4th, Patrick Div.	Lost Prelim. Round
1978-79*	80	25	11	4	....	16	20	4	....	41	31	8	....	327	280	90	4th, Patrick Div.	Lost Prelim. Round
1977-78*	80	20	13	7	....	14	14	12	....	34	27	19	....	274	252	87	3rd, Patrick Div.	Lost Prelim. Round
1976-77*	80	22	11	7	....	12	23	5	....	34	34	12	....	264	265	80	3rd, Patrick Div.	Lost Prelim. Round
1975-76*	80	19	14	7	....	16	19	5	....	35	33	12	....	262	237	82	3rd, Patrick Div.	Lost Prelim. Round
1974-75*	80	24	9	7	....	10	22	8	....	34	31	15	....	243	233	83	4th, Patrick Div.	Out of Playoffs
1973-74*	78	17	15	7	....	13	19	7	....	30	34	14	....	214	238	74	4th, West Div.	Lost Quarter-Final
1972-73*	78	16	16	7	....	9	22	8	....	25	38	15	....	191	239	65	7th, West Div.	Out of Playoffs

* Atlanta Flames

2007-08 Player Personnel

FORWARDS	HT	WT	S	Place of Birth	*Age	2006-07 Club
BOYD, Dustin	6-0	192	L	Winnipeg, Man.	21	Calgary-Omaha
CHUCKO, Kris	6-2	211	R	Burnaby, B.C.	21	Omaha
CONROY, Craig	6-2	197	R	Potsdam, NY	36	Los Angeles-Calgary
COUTURE, Derek	6-2	206	R	Calgary, Alta.	23	Omaha
CRACKNELL, Adam	6-3	214	R	Prince Albert, Sask.	22	Las Vegas
CUNNING, Cam	6-1	215	L	Powell River, B.C.	22	Omaha
DONALLY, Ryan	6-5	224	L	Tecumseh, Ont.	22	Omaha-Las Vegas
GERMYN, Carsen	5-10	185	R	Campbell River, B.C.	25	Calgary-Omaha
GODARD, Eric	6-4	220	R	Vernon, B.C.	27	Calgary-Omaha
HUSELIUS, Kristian	6-1	184	L	Osterhaninge, Sweden	28	Calgary
IGINLA, Jarome	6-1	204	R	Edmonton, Alta.	30	Calgary
LANGKOW, Daymond	5-10	179	L	Edmonton, Alta.	31	Calgary
LOMBARDI, Matthew	6-0	193	L	Montreal, Que.	25	Calgary
MAKI, Tomi	5-11	187	L	Helsinki, Finland	24	Calgary-Omaha
MOSS, Dave	6-3	203	L	Dearborn, MI	25	Calgary-Omaha
NILSON, Marcus	6-2	193	R	Balsta, Sweden	29	Calgary
NOLAN, Owen	6-1	215	R	Belfast, N.Ireland	35	Phoenix
NYSTROM, Eric	6-1	205	L	Syosset, NY	24	Omaha
PETERS, Warren	6-0	200	L	Saskatoon, Sask.	25	Omaha
PRIMEAU, Wayne	6-4	231	L	Scarborough, Ont.	31	Boston-Calgary
PRUST, Brandon	5-11	195	L	London, Ont.	23	Calgary-Omaha
RYDER, Dan	5-11	191	R	Bonavista, Nfld.	20	Peterborough-Plymouth
SEITSONEN, Aki	6-3	203	R	Riihimaki, Finland	21	Omaha-Las Vegas
STEVENSON, Grant	5-11	170	R	Spruce Grove, Alta.	25	Worcester
SUTTER, Brett	6-0	191	L	Viking, Alta.	20	Red Deer
TANGUAY, Alex	6-1	191	L	Ste-Justine, Que.	27	Calgary
TARATUKHIN, Andrei	6-0	211	L	Omsk, USSR	24	Omaha
VAN DER GULIK, David	5-11	183	L	Abbotsford, B.C.	24	Omaha
WATT, J.D.	6-2	203	R	Calgary, Alta.	20	Vancouver (WHL)
YELLE, Stephane	6-2	186	L	Ottawa, Ont.	33	Calgary
DEFENSEMEN						
AUCOIN, Adrian	6-2	215	R	Ottawa, Ont.	34	Chicago
BALDWIN, Gord	6-5	211	L	Winnipeg, Man.	20	Medicine Hat
COLE, Brad	6-3	185	L	Miniota, Man.	20	Saskatoon
ERIKSSON, Anders	6-2	220	L	Bollnas, Sweden	32	Columbus
GIORDANO, Mark	6-0	203	L	Toronto, Ont.	23	Calgary-Omaha
HALE, David	6-2	215	L	Colorado Springs, CO	26	N.J.-Lowell (AHL)-Cgy
PALIN, Brett	6-2	200	R	Nanaimo, B.C.	23	Omaha
PARDY, Adam	6-4	220	L	Bonavista, Nfld.	23	Omaha
PELECH, Matt	6-4	224	R	Toronto, Ont.	20	Belleville
PHANEUF, Dion	6-3	210	L	Edmonton, Alta.	22	Calgary
RAMHOLT, Tim	6-2	193	L	Zurich, Switz.	22	Omaha
REGEHR, Robyn	6-3	225	L	Recife, Brazil	27	Calgary
SARICH, Cory	6-3	210	R	Saskatoon, Sask.	29	Tampa Bay
WARRENER, Rhett	6-1	208	R	Shaunavon, Sask.	31	Calgary

GOALTENDERS	HT	WT	C	Place of Birth	*Age	2006-07 Club
IRVING, Leland	6-0	176	L	Barrhead, Alta.	19	Everett
KEETLEY, Matt	6-1	187	R	Medicine Hat, Alta.	21	Medicine Hat
KIPRUSOFF, Miikka	6-1	186	L	Turku, Finland	30	Calgary
LALANDE, Kevin	6-0	182	L	Kingston, Ont.	20	Belleville
McELHINNEY, Curtis	6-3	207	L	London, Ont.	24	Omaha

* – Age at start of 2007-08 season

Coach

MIKE KEENAN

Coach, Calgary Flames. Born in Bowmanville, Ont., October 21, 1949.

Mike Keenan became the 13th head coach of the Calgary Flames on June 14, 2007, bringing an impressive coaching resume. He is sixth all-time in coaching wins with 584 and has reached the Stanley Cup Final on four occasions, winning in 1994 with the New York Rangers. He also coached teams to championships with Peterborough (OHL-1980), Rochester (AHL-1983) and the University of Toronto (CIAU-1984). He first coached in the NHL with Philadelphia and went on to coach seven NHL clubs: the Flyers, Blackhawks, Rangers, Blues, Canucks, Bruins and Panthers. He also served as general manager in Florida and coached Team Canada at the IIHF World Junior Championship in 1980 and the World Championship in 1993.

Coaching Record

		Regular Season				Playoffs		
Season	Team	Games	W	L	O/T	Games	W	L
1979-80	Peterborough (OHL)	68	47	20	1	18	15	3
1980-81	Rochester (AHL)	80	30	42	8	....	....	....
1981-82	Rochester (AHL)	80	40	31	9	9	4	5
1982-83	Rochester (AHL)	80	46	25	9	16	12	4
1983-84	U. of Toronto (CIAU)	49	41	5	3	....	....	....
1984-85	**Philadelphia (NHL)**	**80**	**53**	**20**	**7**	**19**	**12**	**7**
1985-86	**Philadelphia (NHL)**	**80**	**53**	**23**	**4**	**5**	**2**	**3**
1986-87	**Philadelphia (NHL)**	**80**	**46**	**26**	**8**	**26**	**15**	**11**
1987-88	**Philadelphia (NHL)**	**80**	**38**	**33**	**9**	**7**	**3**	**4**
1988-89	**Chicago (NHL)**	**80**	**27**	**41**	**12**	**16**	**9**	**7**
1989-90	**Chicago (NHL)**	**80**	**41**	**33**	**6**	**20**	**10**	**10**
1990-91	**Chicago (NHL)**	**80**	**49**	**23**	**8**	**6**	**2**	**4**
1991-92	**Chicago (NHL)**	**80**	**36**	**29**	**15**	**18**	**12**	**6**
1993-94*	**NY Rangers (NHL)**	**84**	**52**	**24**	**8**	**23**	**16**	**7**
1994-95	**St. Louis (NHL)**	**48**	**28**	**15**	**5**	**7**	**3**	**4**
1995-96	**St. Louis (NHL)**	**82**	**32**	**34**	**16**	**13**	**7**	**6**
1996-97	**St. Louis (NHL)**	**33**	**15**	**17**	**1**	....	....	....
1997-98	**Vancouver (NHL)**	**63**	**21**	**30**	**12**	....	....	....
1998-99	**Vancouver (NHL)**	**45**	**15**	**24**	**6**	....	....	....
2000-01	**Boston (NHL)**	**74**	**33**	**34**	**7**	....	....	....
2001-02	**Florida (NHL)**	**56**	**16**	**32**	**8**	....	....	....
2002-03	**Florida (NHL)**	**82**	**24**	**45**	**13**	....	....	....
2003-04	**Florida (NHL)**	**15**	**5**	**8**	**2**	....	....	....
	NHL Totals	**1222**	**584**	**491**	**147**	**160**	**91**	**69**

* Stanley Cup win.

2006-07 Scoring

* – rookie

Regular Season

Pos	#	Player	Team	GP	G	A	Pts	+/–	PIM	PP	SH	GW	S	%
R	12	Jarome Iginla	CGY	70	39	55	94	12	40	13	1	7	264	14.8
L	40	Alex Tanguay	CGY	81	22	59	81	12	44	5	0	0	107	20.6
R	20	Kristian Huselius	CGY	81	34	43	77	21	26	14	2	6	173	19.7
C	22	Daymond Langkow	CGY	81	33	44	77	23	44	10	1	6	247	13.4
D	3	Dion Phaneuf	CGY	79	17	33	50	10	98	13	0	4	230	7.4
C	18	Matthew Lombardi	CGY	81	20	26	46	10	48	5	4	5	176	11.4
D	4	Roman Hamrlik	CGY	75	7	31	38	22	88	1	0	1	125	5.6
C	24	Craig Conroy	L.A.	52	5	11	16	–13	38	4	0	2	73	6.8
			CGY	28	8	13	21	10	18	0	1	0	39	20.5
			TOTAL	80	13	24	37	–3	56	4	1	2	112	11.6
R	10	Tony Amonte	CGY	81	10	20	30	–4	40	1	1	1	139	7.2
C	11	Stephane Yelle	CGY	56	10	14	24	5	32	1	1	1	55	18.2
C	19	Wayne Primeau	BOS	51	7	8	15	–15	75	2	1	1	72	9.7
			CGY	27	3	4	7	–2	36	0	1	2	35	8.6
			TOTAL	78	10	12	22	–17	111	2	2	3	107	9.3
D	6	Brad Stuart	BOS	48	7	10	17	–22	26	1	0	2	74	9.5
			CGY	27	0	5	5	12	18	0	0	0	35	0.0
			TOTAL	75	7	15	22	–10	44	1	0	2	109	6.4
D	28	Robyn Regehr	CGY	78	2	19	21	27	75	0	0	0	66	3.0
L	58 *	David Moss	CGY	41	10	8	18	5	12	3	0	1	70	14.3
D	5 *	Mark Giordano	CGY	48	7	8	15	7	36	3	0	2	49	14.3
L	26	Marcus Nilson	CGY	63	5	10	15	7	27	0	0	1	69	7.2
C	15	Byron Ritchie	CGY	64	8	6	14	3	68	0	1	0	46	17.4
L	16	Jeff Friesen	CGY	72	6	6	12	–2	34	0	1	0	55	10.9
D	44	Rhett Warrener	CGY	62	4	6	10	6	67	1	1	1	31	12.9
D	7	Andrei Zyuzin	CGY	49	1	5	6	–2	30	0	0	0	36	2.8
C	41 *	Dustin Boyd	CGY	13	2	2	4	5	4	0	0	1	8	25.0
D	49 *	Richie Regehr	CGY	6	1	1	2	–1	0	1	0	0	4	25.0
R	17	Eric Godard	CGY	19	0	1	1	0	50	0	0	0	3	0.0
D	21	David Hale	N.J.	43	0	1	1	2	26	0	0	0	21	0.0
			CGY	11	0	0	0	–2	10	0	0	0	12	0.0
			TOTAL	54	0	1	1	0	36	0	0	0	33	0.0
R	57 *	Tomi Maki	CGY	1	0	0	0	0	0	0	0	0	0	0.0
C	39 *	Carsen Germyn	CGY	2	0	0	0	0	0	0	0	0	3	0.0
D	8	Brad Ference	CGY	5	0	0	0	–1	2	0	0	0	1	0.0
C	37 *	Brandon Prust	CGY	10	0	0	0	1	25	0	0	0	1	0.0
R	25	Darren McCarty	CGY	32	0	0	0	–3	58	0	0	0	15	0.0

Goaltending

No.	Goaltender	GPI	Mins	Avg	W	L	OT	EN	SO	GA	SA	S%	G	A	PIM
34	Miikka Kiprusoff	74	4419	2.46	40	24	9	6	7	181	2190	.917	0	0	2
29	Jamie McLennan	9	533	3.60	3	5	1	2	0	32	304	.895	0	0	16
	Totals	**82**	**4976**	**2.66**	**43**	**29**	**10**	**8**	**7**	**221**	**2502**	**.912**			

Playoffs

Pos	#	Player	Team	GP	G	A	Pts	+/–	PIM	PP	SH	GW	OT	S	%
C	22	Daymond Langkow	CGY	6	2	2	4	–3	4	2	0	1	0	15	13.3
R	12	Jarome Iginla	CGY	6	2	2	4	–2	12	0	0	1	0	13	15.4
L	40	Alex Tanguay	CGY	6	1	3	4	–2	8	1	0	0	0	9	11.1
C	24	Craig Conroy	CGY	6	1	1	2	–1	8	0	0	0	0	11	9.1
C	18	Matthew Lombardi	CGY	6	1	1	2	–1	0	1	0	0	0	6	16.7
C	19	Wayne Primeau	CGY	6	0	2	2	–1	14	0	0	0	0	3	0.0
R	20	Kristian Huselius	CGY	6	0	2	2	–4	4	0	0	0	0	7	0.0
D	5 *	Mark Giordano	CGY	4	1	0	1	–1	0	1	0	0	0	3	33.3
D	7	Andrei Zyuzin	CGY	5	1	0	1	0	2	0	1	0	0	5	20.0
D	3	Dion Phaneuf	CGY	6	1	0	1	–4	7	1	0	0	0	13	7.7
R	10	Tony Amonte	CGY	6	0	1	1	–1	0	0	0	0	0	5	0.0
D	4	Roman Hamrlik	CGY	6	0	1	1	–3	8	0	0	0	0	9	0.0
D	6	Brad Stuart	CGY	6	0	1	1	–3	6	0	0	0	0	7	0.0
L	58 *	David Moss	CGY	6	0	1	1	–3	0	0	0	0	0	5	0.0
C	15	Byron Ritchie	CGY	1	0	0	0	0	10	0	0	0	0	0	0.0
D	28	Robyn Regehr	CGY	1	0	0	0	–1	0	0	0	0	0	0	0.0
D	21	David Hale	CGY	2	0	0	0	–1	6	0	0	0	0	0	0.0
L	16	Jeff Friesen	CGY	5	0	0	0	–1	2	0	0	0	0	1	0.0
C	11	Stephane Yelle	CGY	6	0	0	0	–3	2	0	0	0	0	8	0.0
D	44	Rhett Warrener	CGY	6	0	0	0	–3	10	0	0	0	0	2	0.0
L	26	Marcus Nilson	CGY	6	0	0	0	–3	2	0	0	0	0	7	0.0

Goaltending

No.	Goaltender	GPI	Mins	Avg	W	L	EN	SO	GA	SA	S%	G	A	PIM
29	Jamie McLennan	1	0	.00	0	0	0	0	0	0	.000	0	0	12
34	Miikka Kiprusoff	6	384	2.81	2	4	0	0	18	255	.929	0	0	0
	Totals	**6**	**384**	**2.81**	**2**	**4**	**0**	**0**	**18**	**255**	**.929**			

Coaching History

Bernie Geoffrion, 1972-73, 1973-74; Bernie Geoffrion and Fred Creighton, 1974-75; Fred Creighton, 1975-76 to 1978-79; Al MacNeil, 1979-80 to 1981-82; Bob Johnson, 1982-83 to 1986-87; Terry Crisp, 1987-88 to 1989-90; Doug Risebrough, 1990-91; Doug Risebrough and Guy Charron, 1991-92; Dave King, 1992-93 to 1994-95; Pierre Page, 1995-96, 1996-97; Brian Sutter, 1997-98 to 1999-2000; Don Hay and Greg Gilbert, 2000-01; Greg Gilbert, 2001-02; Greg Gilbert, Al MacNeil and Darryl Sutter, 2002-03; Darryl Sutter, 2003-04 to 2005-06; Jim Playfair, 2006-07; Mike Keenan, 2007-08.

Captains' History

Keith McCreary, 1972-73 to 1974-75; Pat Quinn, 1975-76, 1976-77; Tom Lysiak, 1977-78, 1978-79; Jean Pronovost, 1979-80; Brad Marsh, 1980-81; Phil Russell, 1981-82, 1982-83; Lanny McDonald, Doug Risebrough, 1983-84; Lanny McDonald, Doug Risebrough, Jim Peplinski, 1984-85 to 1986-87; Lanny McDonald, Jim Peplinski, 1987-88; Lanny McDonald, Jim Peplinski, Tim Hunter, 1988-89; Brad McCrimmon, 1989-90; alternating captains, 1990-91; Joe Nieuwendyk, 1991-92 to 1994-95; Theoren Fleury, 1995-96, 1996-97; Todd Simpson, 1997-98, 1998-99; Steve Smith, 1999-2000; Steve Smith and Dave Lowry, 2000-01; Dave Lowry; Bob Boughner and Craig Conroy, 2001-02; Bob Boughner and Craig Conroy, 2002-03; Jarome Iginla, 2003-04 to date.

Club Records

Team

(Figures in brackets for season records are games played; records for fewest points, wins, ties, losses, goals, goals against are for 70 or more games)

Record		
Most Points	**117**	1988-89 (80)
Most Wins	**54**	1988-89 (80)
Most Ties	**19**	1977-78 (80)
Most Losses	**41**	1996-97 (82), 1997-98 (82), 1999-2000 (82)
Most Goals	**397**	1987-88 (80)
Most Goals Against	**345**	1981-82 (80)
Fewest Points	**65**	1972-73 (78)
Fewest Wins	**25**	1972-73 (78)
Fewest Ties	**3**	1986-87 (80)
Fewest Losses	**17**	1988-89 (80)
Fewest Goals	**186**	2002-03 (82)
Fewest Goals Against	**176**	2003-04 (82)
Longest Winning Streak		
Overall	**10**	Oct. 14-Nov. 3/78
Home	**10**	Nov. 7-Dec. 12/06
Away	**7**	Nov. 10-Dec. 4/88
Longest Undefeated Streak		
Overall	**13**	Nov. 10-Dec. 8/88 (12 wins, 1 tie)
Home	**18**	Dec. 29/90-Mar. 14/91 (17 wins, 1 tie)
Away	**9**	Feb. 20-Mar. 21/88 (6 wins, 3 ties), Nov. 11-Dec. 16/90 (6 wins, 3 ties)
Longest Losing Streak		
Overall	**11**	Dec. 14/85-Jan. 7/86
Home	**6**	Dec. 5-31/98
Away	**9**	Dec. 1/85-Jan. 12/86
Longest Winless Streak		
Overall	**11**	Dec. 14/85-Jan. 7/86 (11 losses), Jan. 5-26/93 (9 losses, 2 ties)
Home	**10**	Oct. 21-Dec. 4/00 (6 losses, 4 ties)
Away	**13**	Feb. 3-Mar. 29/73 (10 losses, 3 ties)
Most Shutouts, Season	**11**	2003-04 (82)
Most PIM, Season	**2,643**	1991-92 (80)
Most Goals, Game	**13**	Feb. 10/93 (S.J. 1 at Cgy. 13)

Individual

Record		
Most Seasons	**13**	Al MacInnis
Most Games	**803**	Al MacInnis
Most Goals, Career	**364**	Theoren Fleury
Most Assists, Career	**609**	Al MacInnis
Most Points, Career	**830**	Theoren Fleury (364G, 466A)
Most PIM, Career	**2,405**	Tim Hunter
Most Shutouts, Career	**21**	Miikka Kiprusoff
Longest Consecutive Games Streak	**257**	Brad Marsh (Oct. 11/78-Nov. 10/81)
Most Goals, Season	**66**	Lanny McDonald (1982-83)
Most Assists, Season	**82**	Kent Nilsson (1980-81)
Most Points, Season	**131**	Kent Nilsson (1980-81; 49G, 82A)
Most PIM, Season	**375**	Tim Hunter (1988-89)
Most Points, Defenseman, Season	**103**	Al MacInnis (1990-91; 28G, 75A)
Most Points, Center, Season	**131**	Kent Nilsson (1980-81; 49G, 82A)
Most Points, Right Wing, Season	**110**	Joe Mullen (1988-89; 51G, 59A)
Most Points, Left Wing, Season	**90**	Gary Roberts (1991-92; 53G, 37A)
Most Points, Rookie, Season	**92**	Joe Nieuwendyk (1987-88; 51G, 41A)
Most Shutouts, Season	**10**	Miikka Kiprusoff (2005-06)
Most Goals, Game	**5**	Joe Nieuwendyk (Jan. 11/89)
Most Assists, Game	**6**	Guy Chouinard (Feb. 25/81), Gary Suter (Apr. 4/86)
Most Points, Game	**7**	Sergei Makarov (Feb. 25/90; 2G, 5A)

Records include Atlanta Flames, 1972-73 through 1979-80.

Retired Numbers

9	Lanny McDonald	1981-1989
30	Mike Vernon	1982-1994; 2000-02

All-time Record vs. Other Clubs

Regular Season

	At Home								On Road								Total							
	GP	W	L	T	OL	GF	GA	PTS	GP	W	L	T	OL	GF	GA	PTS	GP	W	L	T	OL	GF	GA	PTS
Anaheim	29	19	9	1	0	84	64	39	30	8	14	6	2	77	97	24	59	27	23	7	2	161	161	63
Atlanta	4	4	0	0	0	18	7	8	4	0	3	1	0	5	8	1	8	4	3	1	0	23	15	9
Boston	45	19	22	4	0	163	154	42	48	13	29	6	0	132	168	32	93	32	51	10	0	295	322	74
Buffalo	47	18	18	11	0	156	147	47	46	13	26	5	2	133	192	33	93	31	44	16	2	289	339	80
Carolina	30	22	6	2	0	143	92	46	28	13	10	5	0	103	91	31	58	35	16	7	0	246	183	77
Chicago	67	31	22	13	1	212	199	76	65	24	27	13	1	190	207	62	132	55	49	26	2	402	406	138
Colorado	55	26	19	9	1	195	165	62	55	20	23	11	1	179	200	52	110	46	42	20	2	374	365	114
Columbus	12	8	3	0	1	35	24	17	12	3	8	0	1	26	37	7	24	11	11	0	2	61	61	24
Dallas	66	36	15	14	1	218	161	87	66	21	33	11	1	203	241	54	132	57	48	25	2	421	402	141
Detroit	64	37	20	6	1	238	184	81	63	19	34	10	0	186	233	48	127	56	54	16	1	424	417	129
Edmonton	89	49	30	9	1	348	290	108	89	33	44	10	2	288	323	78	178	82	74	19	3	636	613	186
Florida	9	5	3	1	0	26	24	11	9	4	3	2	0	22	21	10	18	9	6	3	0	48	45	21
Los Angeles	98	58	28	12	0	427	321	128	95	38	46	9	2	326	348	87	193	96	74	21	2	753	669	215
Minnesota	18	12	2	3	1	47	33	28	19	9	6	1	3	39	43	22	37	21	8	4	4	86	76	50
Montreal	50	17	26	7	0	149	166	41	47	12	27	8	0	116	168	32	97	29	53	15	0	265	334	73
Nashville	16	7	5	3	1	45	38	18	17	4	12	1	0	35	61	9	33	11	17	4	1	80	99	27
New Jersey	42	28	6	8	0	184	111	64	46	28	15	3	0	166	129	59	88	56	21	11	0	350	240	123
NY Islanders	49	24	14	11	0	172	145	59	52	17	26	9	0	145	194	43	101	41	40	20	0	317	339	102
NY Rangers	49	27	11	10	1	216	148	65	53	23	23	5	2	186	182	53	102	50	34	15	3	402	330	118
Ottawa	12	7	4	1	0	40	26	15	11	3	5	3	0	25	27	9	23	10	9	4	0	65	53	24
Philadelphia	52	25	18	9	0	208	172	59	52	15	33	3	1	137	200	34	104	40	51	12	1	345	372	93
Phoenix	75	42	23	9	1	311	234	94	74	27	34	11	2	252	276	67	149	69	57	20	3	563	510	161
Pittsburgh	46	27	11	8	0	204	140	62	45	11	24	10	0	136	169	32	91	38	35	18	0	340	309	94
St. Louis	66	33	26	5	2	215	187	73	68	27	31	9	1	211	238	64	134	60	57	14	3	426	425	137
San Jose	36	21	11	4	0	129	97	46	38	18	15	4	1	112	114	41	74	39	26	8	1	241	211	87
Tampa Bay	11	6	4	0	1	34	27	13	10	4	5	1	0	32	31	9	21	10	9	1	1	66	58	22
Toronto	62	35	22	5	0	240	195	75	54	18	28	7	1	193	207	44	116	53	50	12	1	433	402	119
Vancouver	106	61	30	15	0	411	303	137	107	49	36	18	4	352	361	120	213	110	66	33	4	763	664	257
Washington	39	24	8	7	0	159	97	55	41	14	21	6	0	139	153	34	80	38	29	13	0	298	250	89
Defunct Clubs	13	8	4	1	0	51	34	17	13	7	3	3	0	43	33	17	26	15	7	4	0	94	67	34
Totals	**1357**	**736**	**420**	**188**	**13**	**5078**	**3985**	**1673**	**1357**	**495**	**644**	**191**	**27**	**4189**	**4752**	**1208**	**2714**	**1231**	**1064**	**379**	**40**	**9267**	**8737**	**2881**

Playoffs

	Series	W	L	GP	W	L	T	GF	GA	Last Mtg.	Rnd.	Result
Anaheim	1	0	1	7	3	4	0	16	17	2006	CQF	L 3-4
Chicago	3	2	1	12	7	5	0	37	33	1996	CQF	L 0-4
Dallas	1	0	1	6	2	4	0	18	25	1981	SF	L 2-4
Detroit	3	1	2	14	6	8	0	26	38	2007	CQF	L 2-4
Edmonton	5	1	4	30	11	19	0	96	132	1991	DSF	L 3-4
Los Angeles	6	2	4	26	13	13	0	112	105	1993	DSF	L 2-4
Montreal	2	1	1	11	5	6	0	32	31	1989	F	W 4-2
NY Rangers	1	0	1	4	1	3	0	8	14	1980	PRE	L 1-3
Philadelphia	2	1	1	11	4	7	0	28	43	1981	QF	W 4-3
Phoenix	3	1	2	13	6	7	0	43	45	1987	DSF	L 2-4
St. Louis	1	1	0	7	4	3	0	28	22	1986	CF	W 4-3
San Jose	2	1	1	13	7	6	0	51	38	2004	CF	W 4-2
Tampa Bay	1	0	1	7	3	4	0	14	13	2004	F	L 3-4
Toronto	1	0	1	2	0	2	0	5	9	1979	PRE	L 0-2
Vancouver	6	4	2	32	17	15	0	101	96	2004	CQF	W 4-3
Totals	**38**	**15**	**23**	**195**	**89**	**106**	**0**	**615**	**661**			

Playoff Results 2007-2002

Year	Round	Opponent	Result	GF	GA
2007	CQF	Detroit	L 2-4	10	18
2006	CQF	Anaheim	L 3-4	16	17
2004	F	Tampa Bay	L 3-4	14	13
	CF	San Jose	W 4-2	16	12
	CSF	Detroit	W 4-2	11	12
	CQF	Vancouver	W 4-3	19	16

Abbreviations: Round: F - Final; **CF** - conference final; **CSF** - conference semi-final; **CQF** - conference quarter-final; **DSF** - division semi-final; **SF** - semi-final; **QF** - quarter-final; **PRE** - preliminary round.

Carolina totals include Hartford, 1979-80 to 1996-97.
Colorado totals include Quebec, 1979-80 to 1994-95.
Dallas totals include Minnesota North Stars, 1972-73 to 1992-93.
New Jersey totals include Kansas City, 1974-75, 1975-76, and Colorado Rockies, 1976-77 to 1981-82.
Phoenix totals include Winnipeg, 1979-80 to 1995-96.

2006-07 Results

Month	Day	Opponent	Score
Oct.	5	at Edmonton	1-3
	7	Edmonton	2-1
	9	San Jose	1-4
	12	at Ottawa	1-0
	14	at Toronto	4-5*
	17	at Montreal	4-5
	19	at Boston	2-3
	24	Phoenix	6-1
	28	Nashville	2-3
	30	Washington	2-4
Nov.	1	at Detroit	2-3
	3	at Columbus	4-5†
	4	at St. Louis	3-2
	7	Dallas	3-1
	10	Anaheim	3-0
	11	at Vancouver	3-2
	14	St. Louis	3-0
	17	Detroit	4-1
	21	at Edmonton	1-2
	22	Chicago	4-1
	25	at Los Angeles	1-3
	26	at Anaheim	3-5
	28	Colorado	5-2
Dec.	1	Columbus	2-1
	5	Carolina	3-0
	7	at Minnesota	2-3†
	9	Vancouver	5-3
	12	Minnesota	5-2
	14	at Vancouver	1-3
	16	at Phoenix	6-3
	18	at Anaheim	1-4
	19	at Los Angeles	5-3
	23	at San Jose	1-4
	26	Vancouver	1-3
	27	at Vancouver	5-6*
	29	Los Angeles	6-4
	31	Edmonton	4-2
Jan.	2	Vancouver	2-3
	4	Florida	5-4*
	6	Dallas	4-2
	9	Minnesota	3-0
	11	at Colorado	7-3
	13	Edmonton	3-1
	15	at Nashville	3-5
	17	at Dallas	2-4
	19	Anaheim	3-2
	20	at Edmonton	4-0
	26	at Minnesota	1-2†
	28	at Chicago	3-4*
	30	Los Angeles	4-1
Feb.	2	Columbus	6-2
	3	Vancouver	4-3
	6	Chicago	2-3†
	8	at Columbus	1-2
	10	at Buffalo	2-3†
	11	at Detroit	4-7
	13	Atlanta	4-1
	15	Colorado	5-7
	17	Colorado	5-2
	20	at Colorado	3-4
	22	at Phoenix	2-3*
	24	San Jose	7-4
	26	Phoenix	5-2
	28	Minnesota	2-1†
Mar.	3	at Edmonton	4-2
	6	at St. Louis	4-2
	8	at Nashville	3-6
	10	Tampa Bay	2-3*
	12	St. Louis	5-4†
	14	at Colorado	2-3
	15	at Dallas	2-4
	17	Minnesota	2-4
	20	Detroit	2-1
	22	Nashville	3-2*
	25	at Chicago	3-2
	27	at Minnesota	1-0†
	29	at Minnesota	4-2
	31	at Vancouver	3-2
Apr.	3	Colorado	3-4
	5	at San Jose	3-4
	7	Edmonton	2-3
	8	at Colorado	3-6

* – Overtime † – Shootout

Entry Draft Selections 2007-1993

2007
Pick
24 Mikael Backlund
70 John Negrin
116 Keith Aulie
143 Mickey Renaud
186 C.J. Severyn

2006
Pick
26 Leland Irving
87 John Armstrong
89 Aaron Marvin
118 Hugo Carpentier
149 Juuso Puustinen
179 Jordan Fulton
187 Devin Didiomete
209 Per Jonsson

2005
Pick
26 Matt Pelech
69 Gord Baldwin
74 Dan Ryder
111 J.D. Watt
128 Kevin Lalande
158 Matt Keetley
179 Brett Sutter
221 Myles Rumsey

2004
Pick
24 Kris Chucko
70 Brandon Prust
98 Dustin Boyd
118 Aki Seitsonen
121 Kris Hogg
173 Adam Pardy
182 Fred Wikner
200 Matt Schneider
213 James Spratt
279 Adam Cracknell

2003
Pick
9 Dion Phaneuf
39 Tim Ramholt
97 Ryan Donally
112 Jamie Tardif
143 Greg Moore
173 Tyler Johnson
206 Thomas Bellemare
240 Cam Cunning
270 Kevin Harvey

2002
Pick
10 Eric Nystrom
39 Brian McConnell
90 Matthew Lombardi
112 Yuri Artemenkov
141 Jiri Cetkovsky
142 Emanuel Peter
146 Viktor Bobrov
159 Kristofer Persson
176 Curtis McElhinney
206 David Van Der Gulik
207 Pierre Johnsson
238 Jyri Marttinen

2001
Pick
14 Chuck Kobasew
41 Andrei Taratukhin
56 Andrei Medvedev
108 Tomi Maki
124 Yegor Shastin
145 James Hakewill
164 Yuri Trubachev
207 Garrett Bembridge
220 Dave Moss
233 Joe Campbell
251 Ville Hamalainen

2000
Pick
9 Brent Krahn
40 Kurtis Foster
46 Jarret Stoll
116 Levente Szuper
141 Wade Davis
155 Travis Moen
176 Jukka Hentunen
239 David Hajek
270 Micki DuPont

1999
Pick
11 Oleg Saprykin
38 Dan Cavanaugh
77 Craig Anderson
106 Roman Rozakov
135 Matt Doman
153 Jesse Cook
166 Cory Pecker
170 Matt Underhill
190 Blair Stayzer
252 Dmitri Kirilenko

1998
Pick
6 Rico Fata
33 Blair Betts
62 Paul Manning
102 Shaun Sutter
108 Dany Sabourin
120 Brent Gauvreau
192 Radek Duda
206 Jonas Frogren
234 Kevin Mitchell

1997
Pick
6 Daniel Tkaczuk
32 Evan Lindsay
42 John Tripp
51 Dmitri Kokorev
60 Derek Schutz
70 Erik Andersson
92 Chris St. Croix
100 Ryan Ready
113 Martin Moise
140 Ilja Demidov
167 Jeremy Rondeau
223 Dustin Paul

1996
Pick
13 Derek Morris
39 Travis Brigley
40 Steve Begin
73 Dmitri Vlasenkov
89 Toni Lydman
94 Christian Lefebvre
122 Josef Straka
202 Ryan Wade
228 Ronald Petrovicky

1995
Pick
20 Denis Gauthier
46 Pavel Smirnov
72 Rocky Thompson
98 Jan Labraaten
150 Clarke Wilm
176 Ryan Gillis
233 Steve Shirreffs

1994
Pick
19 Chris Dingman
45 Dmitri Ryabykin
77 Chris Clark
91 Ryan Duthie
97 Johan Finnstrom
107 Nils Ekman
123 Frank Appel
149 Patrick Haltia
175 Ladislav Kohn
201 Keith McCambridge
227 Jorgen Jonsson
253 Mike Peluso
279 Pavel Torgaev

1993
Pick
18 Jesper Mattsson
44 Jamie Allison
70 Dan Tompkins
95 Jason Smith
96 Marty Murray
121 Darryl Lafrance
122 John Emmons
148 Andreas Karlsson
200 Derek Sylvester
252 German Titov
278 Burke Murphy

General Manager

DARRYL SUTTER
General Manager, Calgary Flames. Born in Viking, Alta., August 19, 1958.

Darryl Sutter was named general manager of the Calgary Flames on April 11, 2003 after having joined the club as coach on December 28, 2002. In 2003-04, he led the team back to the playoffs after a seven-year absence and guided the club on a thrilling run to the seventh game of the Stanley Cup Finals.

Before joining the Flames, Sutter was the San Jose Sharks franchise leader in regular-season games coached (434) and wins (192). Prior to San Jose, Sutter coached Chicago for three years (1992 to 1995) and spent two seasons (1995 to 1997) with the Blackhawks as a consultant for special assignments. He spent the 1987-88 campaign as a Blackhawks assistant coach to Bob Murdoch and served as an associate coach for Mike Keenan during the 1990-91 and 1991-92 seasons. During his final season as associate coach, the Blackhawks advanced to the Stanley Cup Finals. Sutter spent two seasons coaching the Blackhawks' top development affiliate in the IHL, which played in Saginaw (1988-89) and in Indianapolis (1989-90). Under his leadership, the Indianapolis Ice won the Turner Cup championship. He was named IHL coach of the year.

As a player, Sutter was selected by Chicago in the ninth round, 179th overall, in the 1978 NHL Entry Draft. During his eight-year career with the Blackhawks from 1979 to 1987, he scored 279 points (161 goals, 118 assists) with 288 penalty minutes in 406 NHL career games. Sutter served as team captain with the Blackhawks for five seasons before he was forced to retire prematurely due to a series of injuries.

Darryl is a member of the famous Sutter hockey family that had six brothers who played in the NHL. Along with his brothers, Darryl is very involved in the Sutter Foundation, which raises money for non-profit organizations in Alberta.

NHL Coaching Record

		Regular Season				Playoffs		
Season	Team	Games	W	L	O/T	Games	W	L
1992-93	Chicago	84	47	25	12	4	0	4
1993-94	Chicago	84	39	36	9	6	2	4
1994-95	Chicago	48	24	19	5	16	9	7
1997-98	San Jose	82	34	38	10	6	2	4
1998-99	San Jose	82	31	33	18	6	2	4
1999-2000	San Jose	82	35	37	10	12	5	7
2000-01	San Jose	82	40	30	12	6	2	4
2001-02	San Jose	82	44	30	8	12	7	5
2002-03	San Jose	24	8	14	2	....	....	....
	Calgary	46	19	19	8	....	....	....
2003-04	Calgary	82	42	33	7	26	15	11
2005-06	Calgary	82	46	25	11	7	3	4
	NHL Totals	**860**	**409**	**339**	**112**	**101**	**47**	**54**

Club Directory

Pengrowth Saddledome

Calgary Flames
Pengrowth Saddledome
P.O. Box 1540 Station M
Calgary, Alberta T2P 3B9
Phone **403/777-2177**
FAX 403/777-2195
www.calgaryflames.com
Capacity: 19,289

Owners: N. Murray Edwards (Chairman & Alt. Gov.), Harley N. Hotchkiss (Governor), Alvin G. Libin (Alt. Gov.), Allan P. Markin, Jeff McCaig, Clayton H. Riddell, Byron J. Seaman, Daryl K. Seaman

Executive
President, CEO & Alt. Gov. .... Ken King
General Manager & Alt. Gov. .... Darryl Sutter
V.P., Hockey Administration/CFO .... Michael Holditch
V.P., Building Operations .... Libby Raines
V.P., Advertising, Sponsorship & Marketing....... Jim Bagshaw
V.P., Sales.................................. Rollie Cyr
V.P., Communications .... Peter Hanlon
V.P., Business Development .... Jim Peplinski
V.P., Food and Beverage .... Mark Valliant

Hockey Club Personnel
Head Coach .... Mike Keenan
V.P., Hockey Administration/CFO .... Michael Holditch
Director, Hockey Administration .... Mike Burke
Associate Coach .... Jim Playfair
Assistant Coaches............................. Rich Preston, Rob Cookson
Assistant Coach, Development .... Wayne Fleming
Goaltending Coach............................. David Marcoux
Team Services Manager .... Sean O'Brien
Exec. Asst. to GM and Hockey Operations........ Brenda Koyich
Director of Scouting .... Tod Button
Director of Amateur Scouting .... Mike Sands
Western Pro Scout .... Ron Sutter
Eastern Pro Scout .... Tom Webster
Scouts .... Fred Devereaux, Tomas Jelinek, Bob MacMillan, Greg Rajanen, Sergei Samoilov, Anders Steen, Rich Thibeau, Al Tuer

Medical/Training Staff
Strength & Conditioning Coach .... Rich Hesketh
Athletic Therapist .... Morris Boyer
Assistant Athletic Therapist.................... Gerry Kurylowich
Equipment Manager............................ Gus Thorson
Assistant Equipment Manager................... Mark De Pasquale
Team Physician .... Dr. Kelly Brett
Team Physician .... Dr. Jim Thorne
Team Dentist .... Dr. Bill Blair
Dressing Room Attendant........................ Jules Carriere

Quad City Flames
President, GM, Quad Cities..................... Tim Taylor
Head Coach, Quad Cities .... Ryan McGill
Assistant Coach, Quad Cities .... Scott Allen
Director of Broadcasting & Media Relations....... Aaron Roof

Communications
V.P., Communications .... Peter Hanlon
Manager, Media Relations .... Sean Kelso
Administrative Assistant, Communications .... Bernie Hargrave

Administration
V.P., Hockey Administration/CFO .... Michael Holditch
Director of Financial Reporting .... Lisa Gutierrez
Controller.................................... Scott Budau
Exec. Asst. to President/CEO .... Judy O'Brien
Exec. Asst. to VP Hockey Admin./CFO .... Jill Stang

Marketing/Ticketing
V.P., Advertising, Sponsorship & Marketing....... Jim Bagshaw
V.P., Sales.................................. Rollie Cyr
V.P., Business Development .... Jim Peplinski
Senior Director, Advertising.................... Pat Halls
Director, Corporate Sponsorship................. Kevin Gross
Corporate, Key Account Manager................. Mark Stiles
Advertising/Promotions Manager .... Cheryl Sundell
Executive Assistant Marketing................... Yvette Mutcheson
Director, Executive Suites .... Bob White
Sales Manager .... Mike Franco
Customer Service Manager .... Marc Leost
Director/Producer, Enmax Energy Board .... Carlo Petrini
Entertainment Director .... Steve Johnston
Director, Retail/FanAttic .... Kevin Lawton
Publishing Manager .... Laurie Wheeler
Website Manager .... Mike Board

Pengrowth Saddledome
V.P., Building Operations .... Libby Raines
V.P., Food and Beverage .... Mark Vaillant
Operations Manager............................ George Greenwood
Director, Food Services .... Art Hernandez
Concessions Manager........................... Sheila Parisien
Security/Parking Manager .... Bob Godun

Miscellaneous Data
Radio Affiliate................................ The FAN 960 (960 AM)
TV Affiliate.................................. Rogers Sportsnet, CBC-TV, Flames PPV, TSN

General Managers' History

Cliff Fletcher, 1972-73 to 1990-91; Doug Risebrough, 1991-92 to 1994-95; Doug Risebrough and Al Coates, 1995-96; Al Coates, 1996-97 to 1999-2000; Craig Button, 2000-01 to 2002-03; Darryl Sutter, 2003-04 to date.

Carolina Hurricanes

2006-07 Results: 40W-34L-3OTL-5SOL 88PTS.
Third, Southeast Division

Key Off-Season Signings/Acquisitions

2007

Apr. 13 • Re-signed LW **Ray Whitney**.
17 • Re-signed GM **Jim Rutherford**.
May 31 • Re-signed G **Cam Ward**.
June 1 • Re-signed D **Glen Wesley**.
20 • Re-signed RW **Scott Walker**.
July 1 • Signed C **Jeff Hamilton**.
17 • Acquired C **Matt Cullen** from NY Rangers for D **Andrew Hutchinson**, C **Joe Barnes** and a 3rd-round pick in the 2008 Entry Draft.

With 56 assists and 82 points in 2006-07, Rod Brind'Amour enjoyed his most productive offensive season in those categories since the mid 1990s. He also reached the 1,000-point plateau.

2007-08 Schedule

Oct.	Wed.	3	Montreal	**Jan.**	Wed.	2	Atlanta
	Fri.	5	Pittsburgh		Fri.	4	at Atlanta
	Sat.	6	at Washington		Sat.	5	at St. Louis
	Tue.	9	at Toronto		Tue.	8	at Boston
	Thu.	11	at Ottawa		Thu.	10	New Jersey
	Sat.	13	at Montreal		Sat.	12	Colorado
	Fri.	19	at Pittsburgh		Tue.	15	at Toronto
	Sat.	20	at Philadelphia		Thu.	17	at Ottawa
	Mon.	22	Vancouver		Fri.	18	Edmonton
	Wed.	24	Buffalo		Mon.	21	at NY Islanders*
	Fri.	26	Montreal		Tue.	22	NY Islanders
	Sat.	27	at NY Islanders		Tue.	29	NY Rangers
	Wed.	31	at Florida		Thu.	31	Toronto
Nov.	Sat.	3	Florida	**Feb.**	Sat.	2	at Pittsburgh
	Mon.	5	Washington		Tue.	5	at Nashville
	Thu.	8	Tampa Bay		Fri.	8	at Washington
	Sat.	10	at Atlanta		Sat.	9	at New Jersey
	Mon.	12	at Florida		Tue.	12	at Boston
	Wed.	14	at Tampa Bay		Thu.	14	Pittsburgh
	Fri.	16	Atlanta		Sat.	16	Florida
	Sat.	17	Florida		Mon.	18	at New Jersey*
	Wed.	21	Philadelphia		Tue.	19	Boston
	Fri.	23	Tampa Bay		Thu.	21	Atlanta
	Sat.	24	at Washington		Sat.	23	Washington*
	Wed.	28	Philadelphia		Tue.	26	New Jersey
	Fri.	30	Washington		Thu.	28	NY Rangers
Dec.	Sat.	1	at Buffalo	**Mar.**	Sat.	1	Tampa Bay
	Mon.	3	at NY Rangers		Wed.	5	at Atlanta
	Thu.	6	at Tampa Bay		Thu.	6	Minnesota
	Sat.	8	at Montreal		Sat.	8	Buffalo
	Sun.	9	at Detroit*		Wed.	12	at Chicago
	Wed.	12	Ottawa		Fri.	14	at Buffalo
	Fri.	14	Calgary		Sun.	16	Ottawa*
	Sat.	15	at Philadelphia		Wed.	19	at Atlanta
	Tue.	18	Toronto		Thu.	20	at Florida
	Thu.	20	at Florida		Tue.	25	Washington
	Sat.	22	at Tampa Bay		Fri.	28	Atlanta
	Wed.	26	at NY Rangers		Sat.	29	at Tampa Bay
	Fri.	28	Boston	**Apr.**	Tue.	1	at Washington
	Sat.	29	at Columbus		Wed.	2	Tampa Bay
	Mon.	31	NY Islanders		Fri.	4	Florida

* Denotes afternoon game.

SOUTHEAST DIVISION
29th NHL Season

Franchise date: June 22, 1979

Transferred from Hartford to Carolina, June 25, 1997.

Year-by-Year Record

		Home				Road				Overall								
Season	**GP**	**W**	**L**	**T**	**OL**	**W**	**L**	**T**	**OL**	**W**	**L**	**T**	**OL**	**GF**	**GA**	**Pts.**	**Finished**	**Playoff Result**
2006-07	82	21	16	....	4	19	18	....	4	40	34	....	8	241	253	88	3rd, Southeast Div.	Out of Playoffs
2005-06	**82**	**31**	**8**	....	**2**	**21**	**14**	....	**6**	**52**	**22**	....	**8**	**294**	**260**	**112**	**1st, Southeast Div.**	**Won Stanley Cup**
2004-05	....	....	....	....	....	....	....	....	....	....	....	....	....	....	....	....		
2003-04	82	13	18	8	2	15	16	6	4	28	34	14	6	172	209	76	3rd, Southeast Div.	Out of Playoffs
2002-03	82	12	17	9	3	10	26	2	3	22	43	11	6	171	240	61	5th, Southeast Div.	Out of Playoffs
2001-02	82	15	13	11	2	20	13	5	3	35	26	16	5	217	217	91	1st, Southeast Div.	Lost Final
2000-01	82	23	15	3	0	15	17	6	3	38	32	9	3	212	225	88	2nd, Southeast Div.	Lost Conf. Quarter-Final
1999-2000	82	20	16	5	0	17	19	5	0	37	35	10	0	217	216	84	3rd, Southeast Div.	Out of Playoffs
1998-99	82	20	12	9	....	14	18	9	....	34	30	18	....	210	202	86	1st, Southeast Div.	Lost Conf. Quarter-Final
1997-98	82	16	18	7	....	17	23	1	....	33	41	8	....	200	219	74	6th, Northeast Div.	Out of Playoffs
1996-97*	82	23	15	3	....	9	24	8	....	32	39	11	....	226	256	75	5th, Northeast Div.	Out of Playoffs
1995-96*	82	22	15	4	....	12	24	5	....	34	39	9	....	237	259	77	4th, Northeast Div.	Out of Playoffs
1994-95*	48	12	10	2	....	7	14	3	....	19	24	5	....	127	141	43	5th, Northeast Div.	Out of Playoffs
1993-94*	84	14	22	6	....	13	26	3	....	27	48	9	....	227	288	63	6th, Northeast Div.	Out of Playoffs
1992-93*	84	12	25	5	....	14	27	1	....	26	52	6	....	284	369	58	5th, Adams Div.	Out of Playoffs
1991-92*	80	13	17	10	....	13	24	3	....	26	41	13	....	247	283	65	4th, Adams Div.	Lost Div. Semi-Final
1990-91*	80	18	16	6	....	13	22	5	....	31	38	11	....	238	276	73	4th, Adams Div.	Lost Div. Semi-Final
1989-90*	80	17	18	5	....	21	15	4	....	38	33	9	....	275	268	85	4th, Adams Div.	Lost Div. Semi-Final
1988-89*	80	21	17	2	....	16	21	3	....	37	38	5	....	299	290	79	4th, Adams Div.	Lost Div. Semi-Final
1987-88*	80	21	14	5	....	14	24	2	....	35	38	7	....	249	267	77	4th, Adams Div.	Lost Div. Semi-Final
1986-87*	80	26	9	5	....	17	21	2	....	43	30	7	....	287	270	93	1st, Adams Div.	Lost Div. Semi-Final
1985-86*	80	21	17	2	....	19	19	2	....	40	36	4	....	332	302	84	4th, Adams Div.	Lost Div. Final
1984-85*	80	17	18	5	....	13	23	4	....	30	41	9	....	268	318	69	5th, Adams Div.	Out of Playoffs
1983-84*	80	19	16	5	....	9	26	5	....	28	42	10	....	288	320	66	5th, Adams Div.	Out of Playoffs
1982-83*	80	13	22	5	....	6	32	2	....	19	54	7	....	261	403	45	5th, Adams Div.	Out of Playoffs
1981-82*	80	13	17	10	....	8	24	8	....	21	41	18	....	264	351	60	5th, Adams Div.	Out of Playoffs
1980-81*	80	14	17	9	....	7	24	9	....	21	41	18	....	292	372	60	4th, Norris Div.	Out of Playoffs
1979-80*	80	22	12	6	....	5	22	13	....	27	34	19	....	303	312	73	4th, Norris Div.	Lost Prelim. Round

* Hartford Whalers

2007-08 Player Personnel

FORWARDS	HT	WT	S	Place of Birth	*Age	2006-07 Club
ADAMS, Craig	6-0	200	R	Seria, Brunei	30	Carolina
ANGELIDIS, Mike	6-1	210	L	Woodbridge, Ont.	22	Albany-Florida (ECHL)
AUCOIN, Keith	5-9	187	R	Waltham, MA	28	Carolina-Albany
BAYDA, Ryan	5-11	185	L	Saskatoon, Sask.	26	Carolina-Albany
BLANCHARD, Nicolas	6-3	200	L	Granby, Que.	20	Chicoutimi-Albany
BRIND'AMOUR, Rod	6-1	205	L	Ottawa, Ont.	37	Carolina
COLE, Erik	6-2	205	L	Oswego, NY	28	Carolina
CULLEN, Matt	6-1	205	L	Virginia, MN	30	NY Rangers
DWYER, Patrick	5-11	175	R	Great Falls, MT	24	Albany
GILLIES, Trevor	6-3	215	L	Cambridge, Ont.	28	Portland (AHL)-Augusta
GOVE, David	5-9	190	L	Centerville, MA	29	Carolina-Albany
HAMILTON, Jeff	5-10	185	R	Englewood, OH	30	Chicago
HUGHES, Bobby	5-10	180	L	Richmond Hill, Ont.	19	Kingston-Albany
LADD, Andrew	6-2	201	L	Maple Ridge, B.C.	21	Carolina
LaROSE, Chad	5-10	181	R	Fraser, MI	25	Carolina
LETOWSKI, Trevor	5-10	180	R	Thunder Bay, Ont.	30	Carolina
NOLAN, Brandon	5-10	185	L	Sault Ste. Marie, Ont.	24	Bridgeport-Vaxjo
PETRUZALEK, Jakub	5-10	176	R	Most, Czech.	22	Hart-Char-Alb
SAMSON, Jerome	5-11	175	R	Greenfield Park, Que.	20	Moncton-Val-d'Or
STAAL, Eric	6-4	205	L	Thunder Bay, Ont.	22	Carolina
STILLMAN, Cory	6-0	200	L	Peterborough, Ont.	33	Carolina
WALKER, Scott	5-10	196	R	Cambridge, Ont.	34	Carolina
WHITNEY, Ray	5-10	180	R	Fort Saskatchewan, Alta.	35	Carolina
WILLIAMS, Justin	6-1	195	R	Cobourg, Ont.	25	Carolina
DEFENSEMEN						
BABIN, Noah	6-0	200	R	Palm Beach Gardens, FL	23	U. of Notre Dame-Albany
BORER, Casey	6-2	205	L	Minneapolis, MN	22	St. Cloud State-Albany
BROOKBANK, Wade	6-4	227	L	Lanigan, Sask.	30	Bos-Prov (AHL)-Wilkes-Barre
CARSON, Brett	6-5	220	R	Regina, Sask.	21	Albany-Florida (ECHL)
COMMODORE, Mike	6-5	228	R	Fort Saskatchewan, Alta.	27	Carolina
CONBOY, Tim	6-2	210	R	Farmington, MN	25	Albany
FLOOD, Mark	6-1	190	R	Charlottetown, PEI	23	Syracuse-Albany
FORREST, J.D.	5-9	185	L	Auburn, NY	26	Albany
GLEASON, Tim	6-0	217	L	Clawson, MI	24	Carolina
HEDICAN, Bret	6-2	210	L	St. Paul, MN	37	Carolina
KABERLE, Frantisek	6-0	190	L	Kladno, Czech.	33	Carolina
MORMINA, Joey	6-6	220	L	Montreal, Que.	25	Manchester
SEIDENBERG, Dennis	6-1	210	L	Schwenningen, W. Ger.	26	Phoenix-Carolina
WALLIN, Niclas	6-3	220	L	Boden, Sweden	32	Carolina
WESLEY, Glen	6-1	207	L	Red Deer, Alta.	38	Carolina

GOALTENDERS	HT	WT	C	Place of Birth	*Age	2006-07 Club
GRAHAME, John	6-3	220	L	Denver, CO	32	Carolina
LEIGHTON, Michael	6-3	186	L	Petrolia, Ont.	26	Port (AHL)-Nsh-Phi-Phi (AHL)
MANZATO, Daniel	6-0	178	L	Fribourg, Switz.	23	Basel
NASTIUK, Kevin	6-1	180	L	Edmonton, Alta.	22	Las Vegas
PETERS, Justin	6-1	209	L	Blyth, Ont.	21	Albany-Florida (ECHL)
WARD, Cam	6-1	200	L	Saskatoon, Sask.	23	Carolina

* – Age at start of 2007-08 season

2006-07 Scoring

* – rookie

Regular Season

Pos	#	Player	Team	GP	G	A	Pts	+/–	PIM	PP	SH	GW	S	%
L	13	Ray Whitney	CAR	81	32	51	83	–5	46	6	0	6	215	14.9
C	17	Rod Brind'Amour	CAR	78	26	56	82	7	46	9	2	5	181	14.4
C	12	Eric Staal	CAR	82	30	40	70	–6	68	12	1	1	288	10.4
R	11	Justin Williams	CAR	82	33	34	67	–11	73	12	2	8	258	12.8
L	26	Erik Cole	CAR	71	29	32	61	2	76	9	0	4	166	17.5
R	24	Scott Walker	CAR	81	21	30	51	–10	45	6	0	6	183	11.5
D	22	Mike Commodore	CAR	82	7	22	29	0	113	0	2	1	136	5.1
R	77	Anson Carter	CBJ	54	10	17	27	–1	16	3	0	1	62	16.1
			CAR	10	1	0	1	–3	2	1	0	0	8	12.5
			TOTAL	64	11	17	28	–4	18	4	0	1	70	15.7
L	61	Cory Stillman	CAR	43	5	22	27	–8	24	1	0	0	85	5.9
C	63	Josef Vasicek	NSH	38	4	9	13	1	29	0	0	0	47	8.5
			CAR	25	2	7	9	–6	22	0	0	0	30	6.7
			TOTAL	63	6	16	22	–5	51	0	0	0	77	7.8
L	16	Andrew Ladd	CAR	65	11	10	21	1	46	2	0	3	109	10.1
R	59	Chad LaRose	CAR	80	6	12	18	–2	10	0	2	0	94	6.4
D	45	David Tanabe	CAR	60	5	12	17	5	44	2	0	0	83	6.0
R	27	Craig Adams	CAR	82	7	7	14	–9	54	0	1	1	71	9.9
D	28	Andrew Hutchinson	CAR	41	3	11	14	0	30	2	0	0	45	6.7
D	48	Anton Babchuk	CAR	52	2	12	14	–6	30	0	0	2	63	3.2
D	2	Glen Wesley	CAR	68	1	12	13	11	56	0	1	1	51	2.0
D	7	Niclas Wallin	CAR	67	2	8	10	–2	48	0	0	0	76	2.6
D	6	Bret Hedican	CAR	50	0	10	10	–8	36	0	0	0	44	0.0
D	5	Frantisek Kaberle	CAR	27	2	6	8	8	20	1	0	1	33	6.1
D	4	Dennis Seidenberg	PHX	32	1	1	2	–4	16	0	0	0	36	2.8
			CAR	20	1	5	6	–12	2	0	0	0	47	2.1
			TOTAL	52	2	6	8	–16	18	0	0	0	83	2.4
R	19	Trevor Letowski	CAR	61	2	6	8	–8	18	0	0	0	69	2.9
D	8	Tim Gleason	CAR	57	2	4	6	–10	57	1	0	0	72	2.8
L	18	Ryan Bayda	CAR	9	1	1	2	–1	2	0	0	0	10	10.0
R	37	Keith Aucoin	CAR	8	0	1	1	1	0	0	0	0	6	0.0
L	34	David Gove	CAR	1	0	0	0	0	0	0	0	0	0	0.0

Goaltending

No.	Goaltender	GPI	Mins	Avg	W	L	OT	EN	SO	GA	SA	S%	G	A	PIM
47	John Grahame	28	1515	2.85	10	13	2	6	0	72	702	.897	0	3	2
30	Cam Ward	60	3422	2.93	30	21	6	3	2	167	1625	.897	0	1	6
	Totals	**82**	**4962**	**3.00**	**40**	**34**	**8**	**9**	**2**	**248**	**2336**	**.894**			

Justin Williams led the Hurricanes with a career-high 33 goals in 2006-07.

Coach

PETER LAVIOLETTE

Coach, Carolina Hurricanes. Born in Norwood, MA, December 7, 1964

On December 15, 2003 the Carolina Hurricanes made Peter Laviolette the 11th head coach in team history. Laviolette most recently coached the New York Islanders during the 2001-02 and 2002-03 seasons, and led the Islanders to the playoffs both seasons after the team missed the postseason seven straight times between 1994 and 2001. In 2006, he led Carolina to the first Stanley Cup victory in franchise history.

Prior to joining the Islanders, Laviolette served as an assistant coach with the Boston Bruins after two years of guiding Boston's AHL affiliate, Providence. In 1998-99, Laviolette led the Providence Bruins to a 56-16-8 regular-season record, and a 15-4 playoff record that culminated with Providence hoisting the Calder Cup and Laviolette being named AHL coach of the year.

Laviolette played 11 seasons of professional hockey, mostly in the AHL and IHL, but did play 12 games with the New York Rangers during the 1988-89 season. He was a member of the 1988 and 1994 U.S. Olympic hockey teams, and captained the 1994 Olympic squad.

In the spring of 2004, Laviolette helped assure the United States a spot in the 2006 Olympic Games in Torino, Italy, when he guided Team USA to a bronze medal at the 2004 World Championship in the Czech Republic. He also served as an assistant to San Jose Sharks head coach Ron Wilson behind the bench for Team USA in the 2004 World Cup of Hockey and was head coach again at the 2005 World Championship and 2006 Olympics.

Coaching Record

		Regular Season				Playoffs		
Season	Team	Games	W	L	O/T	Games	W	L
1997-98	Wheeling (ECHL)	70	37	24	9	15	8	7
1998-99	Providence (AHL)	80	56	16	8	19	15	4
1999-00	Providence (AHL)	80	33	38	9	14	10	4
2001-02	**NY Islanders (NHL)**	**82**	**42**	**32**	**8**	**7**	**3**	**4**
2002-03	**NY Islanders (NHL)**	**82**	**35**	**36**	**11**	**5**	**1**	**4**
2003-04	**Carolina (NHL)**	**52**	**20**	**26**	**6**	....	....	....
2004-05	**Carolina (NHL)**				Season Cancelled			
2005-06*	**Carolina (NHL)**	**82**	**52**	**22**	**8**	**25**	**16**	**9**
2006-07	**Carolina (NHL)**	**82**	**40**	**34**	**8**	....	....	....
	NHL Totals	**380**	**189**	**150**	**41**	**37**	**20**	**17**

* Stanley Cup win.

Coaching History

Don Blackburn, 1979-80; Don Blackburn and Larry Pleau, 1980-81; Larry Pleau, 1981-82; Larry Kish, Larry Pleau and John Cuniff, 1982- 83; Jack Evans, 1983-84 to 1986-87; Jack Evans and Larry Pleau, 1987-88; Larry Pleau, 1988-89; Rick Ley, 1989-90, 1990-91; Jim Roberts, 1991-92; Paul Holmgren, 1992-93; Paul Holmgren and Pierre Maguire, 1993-94; Paul Holmgren, 1994-95; Paul Holmgren and Paul Maurice, 1995-96; Paul Maurice, 1996-97 to 2002-03; Paul Maurice and Peter Laviolette, 2003-04; Peter Laviolette, 2004-05 to date.

Captains' History

Rick Ley, 1979-80; Rick Ley and Mike Rogers, 1980-81; Dave Keon, 1981-82; Russ Anderson, 1982-83; Mark Johnson, 1983-84; Mark Johnson and Ron Francis, 1984-85; Ron Francis, 1985-86 to 1990-91; Randy Ladouceur, 1991-92; Pat Verbeek, 1992-93 to 1994-95; Brendan Shanahan, 1995-96; Kevin Dineen, 1996-97, 1997-98; Keith Primeau, 1998-99; Keith Primeau and Ron Francis, 1999-2000; Ron Francis, 2000-01 to 2003-04; Rod Brind'Amour, 2005-06 to date.

Club Records

Team

(Figures in brackets for season records are games played; records for fewest points, wins, ties, losses, goals, goals against are for 70 or more games)

Most Points **112** 2005-06 (82)
Most Wins **52** 2005-06 (82)
Most Ties **19** 1979-80 (80)
Most Losses **54** 1982-83 (80)
Most Goals **332** 1985-86 (80)
Most Goals Against **403** 1982-83 (80)
Fewest Points **45** 1982-83 (80)
Fewest Wins **19** 1982-83 (80)
Fewest Ties **4** 1985-86 (80)
Fewest Losses **22** 2005-06 (82)
Fewest Goals **171** 2002-03 (82)
Fewest Goals Against **202** 1998-99 (82)

Longest Winning Streak
Overall .... **9** Oct. 22-Nov. 11/05, Dec. 31/05-Jan. 19/06
Home .... **9** Dec. 31/05-Jan. 28/06
Away .... **6** Nov. 10-Dec. 7/90

Longest Undefeated Streak
Overall .... **10** Jan. 20-Feb. 10/82 (6 wins, 4 ties)
Home .... **9** Dec. 15/00-Jan. 18/01 (8 wins, 1 tie), Dec. 31/05-Jan. 28/06 (9 wins)
Away .... **8** Nov. 11-Dec. 5/96 (4 wins, 4 ties)

Longest Losing Streak
Overall .... **9** Feb. 19-Mar. 8/83
Home .... **7** Dec. 27/02-Jan. 20/03
Away .... **13** Dec. 18/82-Feb. 5/83

Longest Winless Streak
Overall .... **14** Jan. 4-Feb. 9/92 (8 losses, 6 ties)
Home .... **13** Jan. 15-Mar. 10/85 (11 losses, 2 ties)
Away .... **15** Nov. 11/79-Jan. 9/80 (11 losses, 4 ties), Jan. 7-Mar. 2/03 (13 losses, 2 ties)

Most Shutouts, Season **8** 1998-99 (82)
Most PIM, Season **2,354** 1992-93 (84)
Most Goals, Game .... **11** Feb. 12/84 (Edm. 0 at Hfd. 11), Oct. 19/85 (Mtl. 6 at Hfd. 11), Jan. 17/86 (Que. 6 at Hfd. 11), Mar. 15/86 (Chi. 4 at Hfd. 11)

Individual

Most Seasons .... **16** Ron Francis
Most Games .... **1,186** Ron Francis
Most Goals, Career .... **382** Ron Francis
Most Assists, Career .... **793** Ron Francis
Most Points, Career .... **1,175** Ron Francis (382G, 793A)
Most PIM, Career .... **1,439** Kevin Dineen
Most Shutouts, Career .... **20** Arturs Irbe
Longest Consecutive Games Streak .... **419** Dave Tippett (Mar. 3/84-Oct. 7/89)
Most Goals, Season .... **56** Blaine Stoughton (1979-80)
Most Assists, Season .... **69** Ron Francis (1989-90)
Most Points, Season .... **105** Mike Rogers (1979-80; 44G, 61A), (1980-81; 40G, 65A)
Most PIM, Season .... **358** Torrie Robertson (1985-86)
Most Points, Defenseman, Season .... **69** Dave Babych (1985-86; 14G, 55A)
Most Points, Center, Season .... **105** Mike Rogers (1979-80; 44G, 61A), (1980-81; 40G, 65A)
Most Points, Right Wing, Season .... **100** Blaine Stoughton (1979-80; 56G, 44A)
Most Points, Left Wing, Season .... **89** Geoff Sanderson (1992-93; 46G, 43A)
Most Points, Rookie, Season .... **72** Sylvain Turgeon (1983-84; 40G, 32A)
Most Shutouts, Season .... **6** Arturs Irbe (1998-99, 2000-01), Kevin Weekes (2003-04)
Most Goals, Game .... **4** Jordy Douglas (Feb. 3/80), Ron Francis (Feb. 12/84)
Most Assists, Game .... **6** Ron Francis (Mar. 5/87)
Most Points, Game .... **6** Paul Lawless (Jan. 4/87; 2G, 4A), Ron Francis (Mar. 5/87; 6A) (Oct. 8/89; 3G, 3A)

Records include Hartford Whalers, 1979-80 through 1996-97.

All-time Record vs. Other Clubs

Regular Season

	At Home								On Road								Total							
	GP	W	L	T	OL	GF	GA	PTS	GP	W	L	T	OL	GF	GA	PTS	GP	W	L	T	OL	GF	GA	PTS
Anaheim	10	6	3	1	0	27	21	13	10	4	5	1	0	32	31	9	20	10	8	2	0	59	52	22
Atlanta	21	13	6	1	1	67	64	28	21	13	4	3	1	65	53	30	42	26	10	4	2	132	117	58
Boston	80	34	36	9	1	268	275	78	82	28	47	7	0	223	284	63	162	62	83	16	1	491	559	141
Buffalo	82	33	37	11	1	237	247	78	81	26	47	7	1	240	324	60	163	59	84	18	2	477	571	138
Calgary	28	10	13	5	0	91	103	25	30	6	22	2	0	92	143	14	58	16	35	7	0	183	246	39
Chicago	31	15	12	4	0	102	96	34	29	10	16	3	0	83	117	23	60	25	28	7	0	185	213	57
Colorado	62	24	25	12	1	203	214	61	66	17	40	9	0	193	279	43	128	41	65	21	1	396	493	104
Columbus	5	4	1	0	0	15	12	8	3	2	1	0	0	9	6	4	8	6	2	0	0	24	18	12
Dallas	33	14	15	4	0	106	114	32	30	10	16	2	2	90	120	24	63	24	31	6	2	196	234	56
Detroit	31	18	12	1	0	107	88	37	31	7	16	7	1	86	119	22	62	25	28	8	1	193	207	59
Edmonton	29	11	11	7	0	112	98	29	32	7	20	5	0	93	124	19	61	18	31	12	0	205	222	48
Florida	33	21	9	3	0	105	81	45	34	12	12	8	2	79	99	34	67	33	21	11	2	184	180	79
Los Angeles	32	16	11	5	0	116	116	37	31	11	17	3	0	116	131	25	63	27	28	8	0	232	247	62
Minnesota	2	2	0	0	0	3	0	4	5	1	2	2	0	16	14	4	7	3	2	2	0	19	14	8
Montreal	82	32	37	13	0	240	280	77	79	22	49	7	1	233	316	52	161	54	86	20	1	473	596	129
Nashville	6	3	1	1	1	19	17	8	4	1	3	0	0	7	9	2	10	4	4	1	1	26	26	10
New Jersey	48	19	20	8	1	146	144	47	49	18	25	4	2	155	167	42	97	37	45	12	3	301	311	89
NY Islanders	49	25	18	5	1	169	155	56	48	21	21	4	2	131	143	48	97	46	39	9	3	300	298	104
NY Rangers	47	27	17	3	0	158	146	57	49	15	29	4	1	121	183	35	96	42	46	7	1	279	329	92
Ottawa	31	17	10	4	0	90	80	38	33	15	14	4	0	85	92	34	64	32	24	8	0	175	172	72
Philadelphia	48	15	22	9	2	156	175	41	47	11	28	5	3	116	174	30	95	26	50	14	5	272	349	71
Phoenix	31	14	11	6	0	103	91	34	32	15	15	2	0	116	118	32	63	29	26	8	0	219	209	66
Pittsburgh	52	25	22	5	0	193	187	55	50	20	23	6	1	187	197	47	102	45	45	11	1	380	384	102
St. Louis	32	13	17	2	0	96	99	28	31	9	18	3	1	94	119	22	63	22	35	5	1	190	218	50
San Jose	12	7	5	0	0	40	27	14	12	4	8	0	0	34	54	8	24	11	13	0	0	74	81	22
Tampa Bay	35	19	7	7	2	109	97	47	34	11	18	3	2	89	102	27	69	30	25	10	4	198	199	74
Toronto	41	20	14	6	1	156	133	47	40	19	15	5	1	137	135	44	81	39	29	11	2	293	268	91
Vancouver	29	12	12	5	0	94	100	29	31	10	13	6	2	84	109	28	60	22	25	11	2	178	209	57
Washington	57	20	26	10	1	160	177	51	55	19	32	4	0	144	187	42	112	39	58	14	1	304	364	93
Totals	**1079**	**489**	**430**	**147**	**13**	**3488**	**3437**	**1138**	**1079**	**364**	**576**	**116**	**23**	**3150**	**3949**	**867**	**2158**	**853**	**1006**	**263**	**36**	**6638**	**7386**	**2005**

Playoffs

	Series	W	L	GP	W	L	T	GF	GA	Last Mtg.	Rnd.	Result
Boston	3	0	3	19	7	12	0	48	63	1999	CQF	L 2-4
Buffalo	1	1	0	7	4	3	0	22	17	2006	CF	W 4-3
Colorado	2	1	1	9	5	4	0	35	34	1987	DSF	L 2-4
Detroit	1	0	1	5	1	4	0	7	14	2002	F	L 1-4
Edmonton	1	1	0	7	4	3	0	19	16	2006	F	W 4-3
Montreal	7	2	5	39	16	23	0	106	125	2006	CQF	W 4-2
New Jersey	3	2	1	17	10	7	0	34	41	2006	CSF	W 4-1
Toronto	1	1	0	6	4	2	0	10	6	2002	CF	W 4-2
Totals	**19**	**8**	**11**	**109**	**51**	**58**	**0**	**281**	**316**			

Playoff Results 2007-2002

Year	Round	Opponent	Result	GF	GA
2006	**F**	**Edmonton**	**W 4-3**	**19**	**16**
	CF	Buffalo	W 4-3	22	17
	CSF	New Jersey	W 4-1	17	10
	CQF	Montreal	W 4-2	15	17
2002	F	Detroit	L 1-4	7	14
	CF	Toronto	W 4-2	10	6
	CSF	Montreal	W 4-2	21	12
	CQF	New Jersey	W 4-2	9	11

Abbreviations: Round: F - Final; **CF** - conference final; **CSF** - conference semi-final; **CQF** - conference quarter-final; **DSF** - division semi-final.

Calgary totals include Atlanta Flames, 1979-80.
Dallas totals include Minnesota North Stars, 1979-80 to 1992-93.
Phoenix totals include Winnipeg, 1979-80 to 1995-96.

Colorado totals include Quebec, 1979-80 to 1994-95.
New Jersey totals include Colorado Rockies, 1979-80 to 1981-82.

2006-07 Results

Oct.	4	Buffalo	2-3†	**Jan.**	2	at Pittsburgh	0-3
	6	New Jersey	0-4		4	Phoenix	0-2
	7	at Washington	2-5		6	NY Islanders	4-2
	11	at Florida	3-6		9	at Toronto	4-1
	13	at Atlanta	4-3		11	Florida	6-4
	14	at Pittsburgh	5-1		13	Atlanta	3-4†
	16	at Tampa Bay	5-1		16	at Florida	3-2*
	20	at Buffalo	4-5		18	Washington	2-5
	21	at NY Islanders	3-4*		20	Tampa Bay	5-6†
	25	Atlanta	5-4*		26	Washington	6-2
	26	at Tampa Bay	1-5		27	at Washington	3-7
	28	Tampa Bay	6-4		30	Toronto	1-4
Nov.	1	at Atlanta	5-2	**Feb.**	1	Tampa Bay	0-4
	2	Montreal	0-4		3	Boston	3-4*
	4	at Ottawa	3-2		6	at Montreal	2-1
	7	at New Jersey	2-3†		8	at Boston	5-2
	9	Washington	5-0		10	at Minnesota	4-5
	11	Pittsburgh	6-2		13	Los Angeles	2-1
	13	Buffalo	4-7		15	NY Rangers	1-4
	15	NY Rangers	2-1		17	at Montreal	5-3
	17	at Washington	4-1		20	Atlanta	1-3
	18	Dallas	5-4		22	Philadelphia	3-2*
	21	at NY Rangers	0-4		24	at Atlanta	4-1
	22	at NY Islanders	2-4		27	Ottawa	2-4
	24	at Boston	5-1		28	at Ottawa	0-2
	28	Ottawa	1-4	**Mar.**	2	Pittsburgh	3-2
	30	Montreal	4-2		4	at Atlanta	1-3
Dec.	2	Boston	5-2		9	at Washington	3-0
	5	at Calgary	0-3		11	at NY Rangers	1-2†
	6	at Edmonton	1-3		13	Florida	3-1
	8	at Vancouver	3-4*		15	New Jersey	2-3
	11	at Colorado	2-5		17	at New Jersey	7-2
	15	Toronto	3-4		22	Washington	4-3
	16	at Tampa Bay	3-2		24	San Jose	6-4
	19	at Philadelphia	2-1		27	at Toronto	1-6
	22	NY Islanders	5-1		28	at Philadelphia	1-5
	23	at Florida	3-2*		30	Tampa Bay	2-4
	26	Florida	4-2	**Apr.**	1	at Florida	4-3*
	28	at Buffalo	1-4		3	at Tampa Bay	2-3
	29	Anaheim	4-2		6	Atlanta	1-4
	31	Philadelphia	2-5		7	Florida	5-4*

* – Overtime † – Shootout

Entry Draft Selections 2007-1993

2007

Pick	
11	Brandon Sutter
72	Drayson Bowman
102	Justin McCrae
132	Chris Terry
162	Brett Bellemore

2006

Pick	
63	Jamie McBain
93	Harrison Reed
123	Bobby Hughes
153	Stefan Chaput
183	Nick Dodge
213	Justin Krueger

2005

Pick	
3	Jack Johnson
58	Nate Hagemo
64	Joe Barnes
94	Jakub Vojta
123	Ondrej Otcenas
145	Tim Kunes
159	Risto Korhonen
192	Nicolas Blanchard
198	Kyle Lawson

2004

Pick	
4	Andrew Ladd
38	Justin Peters
69	Casey Borer
109	Brett Carson
137	Magnus Akerlund
202	Ryan Pottruff
235	Jonas Fiedler
268	Martin Vagner

2003

Pick	
2	Eric Staal
31	Danny Richmond
102	Aaron Dawson
126	Kevin Nastiuk
130	Matej Trojovsky
137	Tyson Strachan
198	Shay Stephenson
230	Jamie Hoffmann
262	Ryan Rorabeck

2002

Pick	
25	Cam Ward
91	Jesse Lane
160	Daniel Manzato
224	Adam Taylor

2001

Pick	
15	Igor Knyazev
46	Mike Zigomanis
91	Kevin Estrada
110	Rob Zepp
181	Daniel Boisclair
211	Sean Curry
244	Carter Trevisani
274	Peter Reynolds

2000

Pick	
32	Tomas Kurka
80	Ryan Bayda
97	Niclas Wallin
110	Jared Newman
181	J.D. Forrest
212	Magnus Kahnberg
235	Craig Kowalski
276	Troy Ferguson

1999

Pick	
16	David Tanabe
49	Brett Lysak
84	Brad Fast
113	Ryan Murphy
174	Damian Surma
202	Jim Baxter
231	David Evans
237	Antti Jokela
259	Yevgeny Kurilin

1998

Pick	
11	Jeff Heerema
70	Kevin Holdridge
71	Erik Cole
91	Josef Vasicek
93	Tommy Westlund
97	Chris Madden
184	Don Smith
208	Jaroslav Svoboda
211	Mark Kosick
239	Brent McDonald

1997

Pick	
22	Nikos Tselios
28	Brad DeFauw
80	Francis Lessard
88	Shane Willis
142	Kyle Dafoe
169	Andrew Merrick
195	Niklas Nordgren
199	Randy Fitzgerald
225	Kent McDonell

1996

Pick	
34	Trevor Wasyluk
61	Andrei Petrunin
88	Craig MacDonald
104	Steve Wasylko
116	Mark McMahon
143	Aaron Baker
171	Greg Kuznik
197	Kevin Marsh
223	Craig Adams
231	Ashkat Rakhmatullin

1995

Pick	
13	Jean-Sebastien Giguere
35	Sergei Fedotov
85	Ian MacNeil
87	Sami Kapanen
113	Hugh Hamilton
165	Byron Ritchie
191	Milan Kostolny
217	Mike Rucinski

1994

Pick	
5	Jeff O'Neill
83	Hnat Domenichelli
109	Ryan Risidore
187	Tom Buckley
213	Ashlin Halfnight
230	Matt Ball
239	Brian Regan
265	Steve Nimigon

1993

Pick	
2	Chris Pronger
72	Marek Malik
84	Trevor Roenick
115	Nolan Pratt
188	Manny Legace
214	Dmitri Gorenko
240	Wes Swinson
266	Igor Chibirev

General Managers' History

Jack Kelley, 1979-80, 1980-81; Larry Pleau, 1981-82, 1982-83; Emile Francis, 1983-84 to 1988-89; Eddie Johnston, 1989-90 to 1991-92; Brian Burke, 1992-93; Paul Holmgren, 1993-94; Jim Rutherford, 1994-95 to date.

President and General Manager

JIM RUTHERFORD
President/General Manager, Carolina Hurricanes.
Born in Beeton, Ont., February 17, 1949.

Jim Rutherford, a former NHL goaltender, is the franchise's seventh general manager and the only general manager of the Carolina Hurricanes. Named to his position on June 28, 1994, Rutherford has always taken an aggressive approach towards improving the fortunes of the franchise through trades and the NHL entry draft. In 2002, the team reached the Stanley Cup Finals for the first time in history. The Hurricanes won the Cup in 2006.

A veteran of 13 NHL seasons, Rutherford began his professional goaltending career in 1969 as a first-round selection of the Detroit Red Wings. While playing for Detroit, Pittsburgh, Toronto and Los Angeles, Rutherford collected 14 career shutouts. For five seasons he also served as the Red Wings' player representative. Rutherford also played for Team Canada at the World Championships in Vienna in 1977 and Moscow in 1979.

After his playing days with the Red Wings, Rutherford joined Compuware to serve as the director of hockey operations for Compuware Sports Corporation. Rutherford gained a wealth of experience in youth hockey and junior programs. As a former player, coach, and general manager, his ability to develop players and produce winning programs is widely respected throughout the hockey community.

He started his management career by guiding Compuware Sports Corporation's purchase of the Windsor Spitfires of the Ontario Hockey League in April of 1984. During the next four years, Rutherford acted as general manager of the Spitfires. After the Spitfires advanced to the 1988 Memorial Cup finals, Rutherford led Compuware's efforts to bring the first American-based OHL franchise to Detroit on December 11, 1989. Rutherford was voted the 1987 executive of the year in both the OHL and the Canadian Hockey League and won the OHL executive of the year award again in 1988.

Club Directory

RBC Center

Carolina Hurricanes
1400 Edwards Mill Rd.
Raleigh, NC 27607
Phone **919/467-7825**
FAX 919/462-0123
Tickets 1.866.NHL.CANES
www.carolinahurricanes.com
Capacity: 18,639

Executive Management
Chief Executive Officer/Owner/Governor . . . . Peter Karmanos, Jr.
President/General Manager. . . . . Jim Rutherford
General Partner . . . . Thomas Thewes
Vice President/Assistant General Manager. . . . . Jason Karmanos
Chief Financial Officer. . . . . Mike Amendola
Vice President and G.M., RBC Center . . . . Davin Olsen

Hockey Operations
Head Coach . . . . Peter Laviolette
Associate Head Coach . . . . Kevin McCarthy
Assistant Coach . . . . Jeff Daniels
Assistant Coach/Goaltending Coach . . . . Greg Stefan
Director of Player Development. . . . . Ron Francis
Director of Amateur Scouting . . . . Tony MacDonald
Amateur Scouts . . . . Phil Horner, Bob Luccini, Martin Madden, Bert Marshall
Director of Pro Scouting . . . . Marshall Johnston
Pro Scouts . . . . Claude Larose, Ron Smith
Video Coach. . . . . Chris Huffine
Head Athletic Trainer/Strength Conditioning Coach . . Peter Friesen
Assistant Athletic Trainer. Jason Bailey
Equipment Managers . . . . Wally Tatomir, Skip Cunningham, Bob Gorman
Albany River Rats Head Coach/General Manager. . . Tom Rowe
Albany River Rats Assistant Coach. . . . . Geordie Kinnear
Director of Team Operations. . . . . Brian Tatum
Executive Assistant to the President & G.M.. . . . . . . Kelly Kirwin
Motivational Consultant/Community Development . . Doris E. Barksdale

Administration
Receptionists . . . . Mary Lou Ruetz, Janet Davis
General Office Assistant . . . . Angela Dennis

Arena Operations
Assistant General Manager, RBC Center . . . . Larry Perkins
Marketing Coordinator . . . . Crystal Pace
Guest Services Coordinator/Executive Assistant . . . . April Keeley
Security Manager . . . . Clinton Peterson
Parking Manager . . . . Mike Alexander
Event Services Manager . . . . Steve Congress
Premium Services Manager . . . . Suzanne Golden
Operations Manager. . . . . Dan McGowan
Assistant Operations Manager . . . . Brett Shaw
Facility Systems Manager . . . . Rick Dunning
Director of Ticket Operations . . . . Bill Nowicki
Box Office Manager . . . . Joe Sousa
Assistant Box Office Manager . . . . Erin Wallace
Arena Office Manager . . . . Hilman Huskey

Broadcasters
Television Play-by-Play. . . . . John Forslund
Television Analyst . . . . Tripp Tracy
Radio Play-by-Play. . . . . Chuck Kaiton

Communications
Director of Media Relations. . . . . Mike Sundheim
Manager of Media Relations/Broadcast Coordinator . . Kyle Hanlin
Community Relations Manager. . . . . Doug Warf
Community Relations Senior Coordinator . . . . Anne Clinard Nelson
Community Relations Coordinator . . . . Mike King
Team Photographers. . . . . Gregg Forwerck, Stan Gilliland

Finance/Information Technology
Director of Arena Finance and Legal Affairs. . . . . . . William Traurig
Accounts Payable/Receivable. . . . . Michael Arrington/Patty Hilliard, Temika Smith-Harris
Director of Information Technology. . . . . Glenn Johnson

Food and Beverage
Director of Food and Beverage . . . . Chris Diamond
Concessions Manager. . . . . Rick Rhodes
Assistant Concessions Mgr./Group Coordinator . . . Barbara Couch
Chefs . . . . Dennis Atkinson, Michael Flood, Andrew Booger, Lecan Huynh, James Williamson, Kevin Heintz
Catering Manager . . . . Mary Williams
Restaurant/Club Manager. Skip Roach
Restaurant/Club Banquet Captain . . . . Scott Myers
Commissary Manager. . . . . Gary Berry
Suites Food and Beverage Manager . . . . Lori Holtz
Senior Assistant Manager of Concessions . . . . Jim O'Brien

Marketing
Director of Marketing. . . . . Curt Johnson
Director of New Media and Creative Services . . . . . Ben Aycock
Website Producer . . . . Paul Branecky
Graphic Designer . . . . Kara Kelly
Junior Graphic Designer . . . . Lauren Baxter
Manager of Promotions and Fan Development . . . . Jon Chase
Youth and Amateur Hockey Coordinator . . . . Paul Strand
Promotions Coordinator . . . . Mari Jeter

Gale Force Media, CanesVision and Wolfpack TV
Director . . . . Pete Soto
Producers . . . . Charles Graham, Don Sill
Graphics Producer . . . . Stephen Rutherford

Merchandise
Retail Operations Manager . . . . James Blitch

Sales
Director of Corporate Sales. . . . . Mike Hurley
Senior Sales Executive, Corporate Suites . . . . Kristin Ryan
Senior Account Executives, Corporate Sales. . . . . . . Rick Francis, Timothy Kuhl, Julia Zeigler
Director of Ticket Sales . . . . Kyle Prairie
Hurricanes Group Sales Manager . . . . Brian Kapusta
RBC Center Group Sales Manager. . . . . Brian Slais

Team Information
Cable Television Rightsholder . . . . FSN South
Radio Flagship . . . . WCMC 99.9 FM

Key Off-Season Signings/Acquisitions

2007

Apr. 18 • Re-signed G **Patrick Lalime**.

May 15 • Named **John Torchetti** assistant coach.

16 • Signed 2006 1st-round pick (3rd overall), C **Jonathan Toews**.

June 16 • Acquired LW **Sergei Samsonov** from Montreal for D **Jassen Cullimore** and LW **Tony Salmelainen**.

22 • Acquired D **Andrei Zyuzin** and D **Steve Marr** from Calgary for D **Adrian Aucoin** and a 7th-round pick in the 2007 Entry Draft.

July 2 • Signed C **Yanic Perreault** and C **Robert Lang**.

18 • Re-signed D **Jim Vandermeer**.

25 • Signed 2007 1st-round pick (1st overall), C **Patrick Kane**.

Chicago Blackhawks

2006-07 Results: 31W-42L-2OTL-7SOL 71PTS.
Fifth, Central Division

Year-by-Year Record

		Home				Road				Overall								
Season	GP	W	L	T	OL	W	L	T	OL	W	L	T	OL	GF	GA	Pts.	Finished	Playoff Result
2006-07	82	17	20	....	4	14	22	....	5	31	42	....	9	201	258	71	5th, Central Div.	Out of Playoffs
2005-06	82	16	19	....	6	10	24	....	7	26	43	....	13	211	285	65	4th, Central Div.	Out of Playoffs
2004-05	....	....	....	....	....	....	....	....	....	....	....	....	....	....	....	....		
2003-04	82	13	17	6	5	7	26	5	3	20	43	11	8	188	259	59	5th, Central Div.	Out of Playoffs
2002-03	82	17	15	7	2	13	18	6	4	30	33	13	6	207	226	79	3rd, Central Div.	Out of Playoffs
2001-02	82	28	7	5	1	13	20	8	0	41	27	13	1	216	207	96	3rd, Central Div.	Lost Conf. Quarter-Final
2000-01	82	14	21	4	2	15	19	4	3	29	40	8	5	210	246	71	4th, Central Div.	Out of Playoffs
1999-2000	82	16	19	5	1	17	18	5	1	33	37	10	2	242	245	78	3rd, Central Div.	Out of Playoffs
1998-99	82	20	17	4	....	9	24	8	....	29	41	12	....	202	248	70	3rd, Central Div.	Out of Playoffs
1997-98	82	14	19	8	....	16	20	5	....	30	39	13	....	192	199	73	5th, Central Div.	Out of Playoffs
1996-97	82	16	21	4	....	18	14	9	....	34	35	13	....	223	210	81	5th, Central Div.	Lost Conf. Quarter-Final
1995-96	82	22	13	6	....	18	15	8	....	40	28	14	....	273	220	94	2nd, Central Div.	Lost Conf. Semi-Final
1994-95	48	11	10	3	....	13	9	2	....	24	19	5	....	156	115	53	3rd, Central Div.	Lost Conf. Championship
1993-94	84	21	16	5	....	18	20	4	....	39	36	9	....	254	240	87	5th, Central Div.	Lost Conf. Quarter-Final
1992-93	84	25	11	6	....	22	14	6	....	47	25	12	....	279	230	106	1st, Norris Div.	Lost Div. Semi-Final
1991-92	80	23	9	8	....	13	20	7	....	36	29	15	....	257	236	87	2nd, Norris Div.	Lost Final
1990-91	80	28	8	4	....	21	15	4	....	49	23	8	....	284	211	106	1st, Norris Div.	Lost Div. Semi-Final
1989-90	80	25	13	2	....	16	20	4	....	41	33	6	....	316	294	88	1st, Norris Div.	Lost Conf. Championship
1988-89	80	16	14	10	....	11	27	2	....	27	41	12	....	297	335	66	4th, Norris Div.	Lost Conf. Championship
1987-88	80	21	17	2	....	9	24	7	....	30	41	9	....	284	328	69	3rd, Norris Div.	Lost Div. Semi-Final
1986-87	80	18	13	9	....	11	24	5	....	29	37	14	....	290	310	72	3rd, Norris Div.	Lost Div. Semi-Final
1985-86	80	23	12	5	....	16	21	3	....	39	33	8	....	351	349	86	1st, Norris Div.	Lost Div. Semi-Final
1984-85	80	22	16	2	....	16	19	5	....	38	35	7	....	309	299	83	2nd, Norris Div.	Lost Conf. Championship
1983-84	80	25	13	2	....	5	29	6	....	30	42	8	....	277	311	68	4th, Norris Div.	Lost Div. Semi-Final
1982-83	80	29	8	3	....	18	15	7	....	47	23	10	....	338	268	104	1st, Norris Div.	Lost Conf. Championship
1981-82	80	20	13	7	....	10	25	5	....	30	38	12	....	332	363	72	4th, Norris Div.	Lost Conf. Championship
1980-81	80	21	11	8	....	10	22	8	....	31	33	16	....	304	315	78	2nd, Smythe Div.	Lost Prelim. Round
1979-80	80	21	12	7	....	13	15	12	....	34	27	19	....	241	250	87	1st, Smythe Div.	Lost Quarter-Final
1978-79	80	18	12	10	....	11	24	5	....	29	36	15	....	244	277	73	1st, Smythe Div.	Lost Quarter-Final
1977-78	80	20	9	11	....	12	20	8	....	32	29	19	....	230	220	83	1st, Smythe Div.	Lost Quarter-Final
1976-77	80	19	16	5	....	7	27	6	....	26	43	11	....	240	298	63	3rd, Smythe Div.	Lost Prelim. Round
1975-76	80	17	15	8	....	15	15	10	....	32	30	18	....	254	261	82	1st, Smythe Div.	Lost Quarter-Final
1974-75	80	24	12	4	....	13	23	4	....	37	35	8	....	268	241	82	3rd, Smythe Div.	Lost Quarter-Final
1973-74	78	20	6	13	....	21	8	10	....	41	14	23	....	272	164	105	2nd, West Div.	Lost Semi-Final
1972-73	78	26	9	4	....	16	18	5	....	42	27	9	....	284	225	93	1st, West Div.	Lost Final
1971-72	78	28	3	8	....	18	14	7	....	46	17	15	....	256	166	107	1st, West Div.	Lost Semi-Final
1970-71	78	30	6	3	....	19	14	6	....	49	20	9	....	277	184	107	1st, West Div.	Lost Final
1969-70	76	26	7	5	....	19	15	4	....	45	22	9	....	250	170	99	1st, East Div.	Lost Semi-Final
1968-69	76	20	14	4	....	14	19	5	....	34	33	9	....	280	246	77	6th, East Div.	Out of Playoffs
1967-68	74	20	13	4	....	12	13	12	....	32	26	16	....	212	222	80	4th, East Div.	Lost Semi-Final
1966-67	70	24	5	6	....	17	12	6	....	41	17	12	....	264	170	94	1st,	Lost Semi-Final
1965-66	70	21	8	6	....	16	17	2	....	37	25	8	....	240	187	82	2nd,	Lost Semi-Final
1964-65	70	20	13	2	....	14	15	6	....	34	28	8	....	224	176	76	3rd,	Lost Final
1963-64	70	26	4	5	....	10	18	7	....	36	22	12	....	218	169	84	2nd,	Lost Semi-Final
1962-63	70	17	9	9	....	15	12	8	....	32	21	17	....	194	178	81	2nd,	Lost Semi-Final
1961-62	70	20	10	5	....	11	16	8	....	31	26	13	....	217	186	75	3rd,	Lost Final
1960-61	**70**	**20**	**6**	**9**	....	**9**	**18**	**8**	....	**29**	**24**	**17**	....	**198**	**180**	**75**	**3rd,**	**Won Stanley Cup**
1959-60	70	18	11	6	....	10	18	7	....	28	29	13	....	191	180	69	3rd,	Lost Semi-Final
1958-59	70	14	12	9	....	14	17	4	....	28	29	13	....	197	208	69	3rd,	Lost Semi-Final
1957-58	70	15	17	3	....	9	22	4	....	24	39	7	....	163	202	55	5th,	Out of Playoffs
1956-57	70	12	15	8	....	4	24	7	....	16	39	15	....	169	225	47	6th,	Out of Playoffs
1955-56	70	9	19	7	....	10	20	5	....	19	39	12	....	155	216	50	6th,	Out of Playoffs
1954-55	70	6	21	8	....	7	19	9	....	13	40	17	....	161	235	43	6th,	Out of Playoffs
1953-54	70	8	21	6	....	4	30	1	....	12	51	7	....	133	242	31	6th,	Out of Playoffs
1952-53	70	14	11	10	....	13	17	5	....	27	28	15	....	169	175	69	4th,	Lost Semi-Final
1951-52	70	9	19	7	....	8	25	2	....	17	44	9	....	158	241	43	6th,	Out of Playoffs
1950-51	70	8	22	5	....	5	25	5	....	13	47	10	....	171	280	36	6th,	Out of Playoffs
1949-50	70	13	18	4	....	9	20	6	....	22	38	10	....	203	244	54	6th,	Out of Playoffs
1948-49	60	13	12	5	....	8	19	3	....	21	31	8	....	173	211	50	5th,	Out of Playoffs
1947-48	60	10	17	3	....	10	17	3	....	20	34	6	....	195	225	46	6th,	Out of Playoffs
1946-47	60	10	17	3	....	9	20	1	....	19	37	4	....	193	274	42	6th,	Out of Playoffs
1945-46	50	15	5	5	....	8	15	2	....	23	20	7	....	200	178	53	3rd,	Lost Semi-Final
1944-45	50	9	14	2	....	4	16	5	....	13	30	7	....	141	194	33	5th,	Out of Playoffs
1943-44	50	15	6	4	....	7	17	1	....	22	23	5	....	178	187	49	4th,	Lost Final
1942-43	50	14	3	8	....	3	15	7	....	17	18	15	....	179	180	49	5th,	Out of Playoffs
1941-42	48	15	8	1	....	7	15	2	....	22	23	3	....	145	155	47	4th,	Lost Quarter-Final
1940-41	48	11	10	3	....	5	15	4	....	16	25	7	....	112	139	39	5th,	Lost Semi-Final
1939-40	48	15	7	2	....	8	12	4	....	23	19	6	....	112	120	52	4th,	Lost Quarter-Final
1938-39	48	5	13	6	....	7	15	2	....	12	28	8	....	91	132	32	7th,	Out of Playoffs
1937-38	**48**	**10**	**10**	**4**	....	**4**	**15**	**5**	....	**14**	**25**	**9**	....	**97**	**139**	**37**	**3rd, Amn. Div.**	**Won Stanley Cup**
1936-37	48	8	13	3	....	6	14	4	....	14	27	7	....	99	131	35	4th, Amn. Div.	Out of Playoffs
1935-36	48	15	7	2	....	6	12	6	....	21	19	8	....	93	92	50	3rd, Amn. Div.	Lost Quarter-Final
1934-35	48	12	9	3	....	14	8	2	....	26	17	5	....	118	88	57	2nd, Amn. Div.	Lost Quarter-Final
1933-34	**48**	**13**	**4**	**7**	....	**7**	**13**	**4**	....	**20**	**17**	**11**	....	**88**	**83**	**51**	**2nd, Amn. Div.**	**Won Stanley Cup**
1932-33	48	12	7	5	....	4	13	7	....	16	20	12	....	88	101	44	4th, Amn. Div.	Out of Playoffs
1931-32	48	13	5	6	....	5	14	5	....	18	19	11	....	86	101	47	2nd, Amn. Div.	Lost Quarter-Final
1930-31	44	13	8	1	....	11	9	2	....	24	17	3	....	108	78	51	2nd, Amn. Div.	Lost Final
1929-30	44	12	9	1	....	9	9	4	....	21	18	5	....	117	111	47	2nd, Amn. Div.	Lost Quarter-Final
1928-29	44	3	13	6	....	4	16	2	....	7	29	8	....	33	85	22	5th, Amn. Div.	Out of Playoffs
1927-28	44	2	18	2	....	5	16	1	....	7	34	3	....	68	134	17	5th, Amn. Div.	Out of Playoffs
1926-27	44	12	8	2	....	7	14	1	....	19	22	3	....	115	116	41	3rd, Amn. Div.	Lost Quarter-Final

2007-08 Schedule

Month	Day	Date	Opponent	Month	Day	Date	Opponent
Oct.	Thu.	4	at Minnesota		Tue.	8	at Montreal
	Sat.	6	Detroit		Wed.	9	Dallas
	Wed.	10	San Jose		Fri.	11	Minnesota
	Fri.	12	at Detroit		Sun.	13	at Nashville
	Sat.	13	Dallas		Wed.	16	St. Louis
	Wed.	17	St. Louis		Fri.	18	at Colorado
	Fri.	19	Colorado		Sat.	19	at Phoenix
	Sat.	20	at Toronto		Tue.	22	at San Jose
	Tue.	23	Columbus		Thu.	24	Columbus
	Thu.	25	at Boston		Wed.	30	at Colorado
	Sat.	27	Atlanta	Feb.	Sat.	2	at San Jose*
	Wed.	31	at Dallas		Wed.	6	at Edmonton
Nov.	Sat.	3	at St. Louis		Thu.	7	at Calgary
	Sun.	4	Nashville		Sun.	10	at Vancouver
	Wed.	7	Columbus		Wed.	13	at Columbus
	Fri.	9	St. Louis		Thu.	14	at Nashville
	Sun.	11	Detroit		Sun.	17	Colorado*
	Wed.	14	at Columbus		Tue.	19	at St. Louis
	Thu.	15	at Nashville		Wed.	20	Minnesota
	Sat.	17	at Detroit		Sat.	23	at Los Angeles*
	Thu.	22	at Calgary		Sun.	24	at Anaheim*
	Sat.	24	at Edmonton		Wed.	27	Phoenix
	Sun.	25	at Vancouver		Thu.	28	at Dallas
	Wed.	28	Tampa Bay	Mar.	Sun.	2	Vancouver*
	Fri.	30	Phoenix		Tue.	4	at Minnesota
Dec.	Sat.	1	at St. Louis		Wed.	5	Anaheim
	Wed.	5	Vancouver		Fri.	7	San Jose
	Fri.	7	Anaheim		Sun.	9	Edmonton*
	Sun.	9	Calgary		Tue.	11	at Detroit
	Wed.	12	Los Angeles		Wed.	12	Carolina
	Sat.	15	at Buffalo		Fri.	14	at Columbus
	Sun.	16	Florida		Sun.	16	Calgary*
	Wed.	19	Nashville		Wed.	19	Washington
	Sat.	22	at Ottawa		Sat.	22	at Nashville*
	Sun.	23	Edmonton		Sun.	23	St. Louis*
	Wed.	26	Nashville		Wed.	26	at Columbus
	Sun.	30	Los Angeles		Sat.	29	at St. Louis
Jan.	Tue.	1	at Los Angeles		Sun.	30	Columbus
	Thu.	3	at Phoenix	Apr.	Wed.	2	Detroit
	Fri.	4	at Anaheim		Fri.	4	Nashville
	Sun.	6	Detroit		Sun.	6	at Detroit*

* Denotes afternoon game.

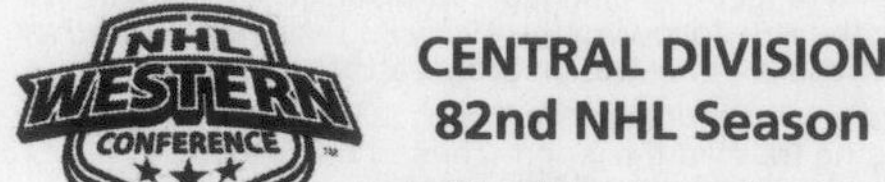

CENTRAL DIVISION
82nd NHL Season

Franchise date: September 25, 1926

2007-08 Player Personnel

FORWARDS	HT	WT	S	Place of Birth	*Age	2006-07 Club
ADAMS, Kevyn	6-1	200	R	Washington, DC	32	Carolina-Phoenix
BERTI, Adam	6-3	198	L	Scarborough, Ont.	21	Norfolk
BICKELL, Bryan	6-4	223	L	Bowmanville, Ont.	21	Chicago-Norfolk
BLUNDEN, Michael	6-3	207	R	Toronto, Ont.	20	Chicago-Norfolk
BOLLAND, Dave	6-0	176	R	Toronto, Ont.	21	Chicago-Norfolk
BOURQUE, Rene	6-2	213	L	Lac La Biche, Alta.	25	Chicago-Norfolk
BROPHEY, Evan	6-1	203	L	Kitchener, Ont.	20	Plymouth
BROUWER, Troy	6-3	220	R	Vancouver, B.C.	22	Chicago-Norfolk
BURISH, Adam	6-1	189	R	Madison, WI	24	Chicago-Norfolk
DOWELL, Jake	6-0	202	L	Eau Claire, WI	22	U. of Wisconsin-Norfolk
FRASER, Colin	6-1	190	L	Surrey, B.C.	22	Chicago-Norfolk
HAVLAT, Martin	6-1	204	L	Mlada Boleslav, Czech.	26	Chicago
KANE, Patrick	5-10	163	L	Buffalo, NY	18	London
KOCI, David	6-6	238	L	Prague, Czech.	26	Chicago-Norfolk
KONTIOLA, Petri	6-0	197	R	Seinajoki, Finland	22	Tappara
LANG, Robert	6-3	216	R	Teplice, Czech.	36	Detroit
LAPOINTE, Martin	5-11	215	R	Ville St-Pierre, Que.	34	Chicago
PARENTEAU, Pierre	5-11	194	R	Hull, Que.	24	Port (AHL)-Chi-Norfolk
PERREAULT, Yanic	5-11	185	L	Sherbrooke, Que.	36	Phoenix-Toronto
RUUTU, Tuomo	6-0	200	L	Vantaa, Finland	24	Chicago
SAMSONOV, Sergei	5-8	188	R	Moscow, USSR	28	Montreal
SHARP, Patrick	6-1	197	R	Thunder Bay, Ont.	25	Chicago
SKILLE, Jack	6-1	198	R	Madison, WI	20	U. of Wisconsin-Norfolk
TOEWS, Jonathan	6-1	203	L	Winnipeg, Man.	19	North Dakota
VERSTEEG, Kris	5-10	179	R	Lethbridge, Alta.	21	Providence (AHL)-Norfolk
WILLIAMS, Jason	5-11	194	R	London, Ont.	27	Detroit-Chicago
DEFENSEMEN						
BARKER, Cam	6-3	222	L	Winnipeg, Man.	21	Chicago-Norfolk
BYFUGLIEN, Dustin	6-3	246	R	Minneapolis, MN	22	Chicago-Norfolk
FAHEY, Jim	6-0	205	R	Boston, MA	28	New Jersey-Lowell
HJALMARSSON, Niklas	6-3	196	L	Eksjo, Sweden	20	HV 71 Jr.-HV 71-Oskarshamn
JOHANSSON, Magnus	5-11	180	L	Linkoping, Sweden	34	Linkoping
KEITH, Duncan	6-0	187	L	Winnipeg, Man.	24	Chicago
RICHMOND, Danny	6-0	192	L	Chicago, IL	23	Chicago-Norfolk
RYAN, Prestin	6-0	190	L	Arcola, Sask.	27	Manitoba
ST. JACQUES, Bruno	6-2	216	L	Montreal, Que.	27	Portland (AHL)-Norfolk
SAWYER, Jean-Claude	6-3	194	L	Saint John, N.B.	21	Cape Breton
SEABROOK, Brent	6-3	220	R	Richmond, B.C.	22	Chicago
VANDERMEER, Jim	6-1	208	L	Caroline, Alta.	27	Chicago
WISNIEWSKI, James	6-0	207	R	Canton, MI	23	Chicago-Norfolk
ZYUZIN, Andrei	6-1	208	L	Ufa, USSR	29	Calgary

GOALTENDERS	HT	WT	C	Place of Birth	*Age	2006-07 Club
BRODEUR, Mike	6-2	171	L	Calgary, Alta.	24	Norfolk-Augusta-Toledo
CRAWFORD, Corey	6-2	183	L	Montreal, Que.	22	Norfolk
FLAHERTY, Wade	6-0	171	L	Terrace, B.C.	39	Manitoba
KHABIBULIN, Nikolai	6-1	208	L	Sverdlovsk, USSR	34	Chicago
LALIME, Patrick	6-3	189	L	St-Bonaventure, Que.	33	Chicago-Norfolk

* – Age at start of 2007-08 season

2006-07 Scoring

* – rookie

Regular Season

Pos	#	Player	Team	GP	G	A	Pts	+/–	PIM	PP	SH	GW	S	%
R	24	Martin Havlat	CHI	56	25	32	57	15	28	5	0	1	176	14.2
R	16	Radim Vrbata	CHI	77	14	27	41	–4	26	5	0	2	215	6.5
L	51	Jeff Hamilton	CHI	70	18	21	39	–4	22	3	0	4	138	13.0
C	15	Tuomo Ruutu	CHI	71	17	21	38	4	95	1	0	1	115	14.8
R	10	Patrick Sharp	CHI	80	20	15	35	–15	74	5	3	1	160	12.5
C	29	Jason Williams	DET	58	11	15	26	7	24	3	0	2	111	9.9
			CHI	20	4	2	6	–6	20	2	1	0	38	10.5
			TOTAL	78	15	17	32	1	44	5	1	2	149	10.1
D	2	Duncan Keith	CHI	82	2	29	31	0	76	0	0	0	122	1.6
C	19	Denis Arkhipov	CHI	79	10	17	27	–13	54	2	1	1	112	8.9
R	22	Martin Lapointe	CHI	82	13	11	24	–14	98	5	1	2	102	12.7
D	7	Brent Seabrook	CHI	81	4	20	24	–6	104	0	0	0	144	2.8
R	34	Nikita Alexeev	T.B.	63	10	11	21	10	12	2	0	2	102	9.8
			CHI	15	2	0	2	–3	0	0	0	0	15	13.3
			TOTAL	78	12	11	23	7	12	2	0	2	117	10.3
L	14	Rene Bourque	CHI	44	7	10	17	–4	38	2	1	1	82	8.5
L	8	* Tony Salmelainen	CHI	57	6	11	17	–3	26	0	0	1	54	11.1
D	33	Adrian Aucoin	CHI	59	4	12	16	–22	50	2	0	3	96	4.2
R	12	Peter Bondra	CHI	37	5	9	14	2	26	2	0	3	46	10.9
C	17	Mikael Holmqvist	CHI	63	6	7	13	–5	31	1	0	0	80	7.5
D	43	* James Wisniewski	CHI	50	2	8	10	3	39	0	0	0	55	3.6
C	26	Michal Handzus	CHI	8	3	5	8	4	6	1	0	0	9	33.3
D	25	* Cam Barker	CHI	35	1	7	8	–12	44	1	0	0	38	2.6
D	23	Jim Vandermeer	CHI	46	1	6	7	–3	53	0	0	0	50	2.0
D	5	Jassen Cullimore	CHI	65	1	6	7	–6	64	0	0	0	17	5.9
C	27	Craig MacDonald	CHI	25	3	2	5	–2	14	0	1	0	30	10.0
C	47	* Martin St. Pierre	CHI	14	1	3	4	–3	8	1	0	0	13	7.7
D	52	* Dustin Byfuglien	CHI	9	1	2	3	–2	10	0	0	0	18	5.6
L	38	* Bryan Bickell	CHI	3	2	0	2	1	0	0	0	0	10	20.0
C	32	* Jonas Nordqvist	CHI	3	0	2	2	1	2	0	0	0	2	0.0
D	44	* Danny Richmond	CHI	22	0	2	2	–1	48	0	0	0	13	0.0
L	58	* Pierre Parenteau	CHI	5	0	1	1	–1	2	0	0	0	7	0.0
C	49	Carl Corazzini	CHI	7	0	1	1	0	2	0	0	0	5	0.0
C	46	* Colin Fraser	CHI	1	0	0	0	–1	2	0	0	0	0	0.0
C	36	* Dave Bolland	CHI	1	0	0	0	–1	0	0	0	0	1	0.0
R	12	* Matt Keith	CHI	2	0	0	0	–2	4	0	0	0	0	0.0
R	34	Reed Low	CHI	6	0	0	0	–1	31	0	0	0	0	0.0
L	48	* David Koci	CHI	9	0	0	0	–3	88	0	0	0	3	0.0
R	37	* Adam Burish	CHI	9	0	0	0	–4	2	0	0	0	12	0.0
R	28	* Michael Blunden	CHI	9	0	0	0	–5	10	0	0	0	10	0.0
R	29	* Troy Brouwer	CHI	10	0	0	0	–7	7	0	0	0	7	0.0

Goaltending

No.	Goaltender	GPI	Mins	Avg	W	L	OT	EN	SO	GA	SA	S%	G	A	PIM
29	Sebastien Caron	1	60	1.00	1	0	0	0	0	1	25	.960	0	0	0
39	Nikolai Khabibulin	60	3425	2.86	25	26	5	7	1	163	1668	.902	0	0	8
40	Patrick Lalime	12	645	3.07	4	6	1	0	1	33	317	.896	0	0	0
35	Brian Boucher	15	827	3.26	1	10	3	2	1	45	389	.884	0	0	0
	Totals	**82**	**4996**	**3.01**	**31**	**42**	**9**	**9**	**3**	**251**	**2408**	**.896**			

Coach

DENIS SAVARD
Coach, Chicago Blackhawks. Born in Pointe Gatineau, Que., February 4, 1961.

Denis Savard was named the 36th head coach in Chicago Blackhawks history on November 27, 2006. Savard first joined the Blackhawks coaching staff as an assistant coach on December 3, 1997 after beginning the 1997-98 season as the Blackhawks' developmental coach. He entered coaching after announcing his retirement from the National Hockey League in June of 1997.

A 17-year NHL veteran with Chicago, Montreal and Tampa Bay, Savard scored 473 goals and 865 assists (1,338 points) in 1,196 games played. As a Blackhawk, Savard recorded 377 goals and 719 assists (1,096 points) in 881 games played. In playoff competition, Savard scored 66 goals and 109 assists (175 points) in 169 games. As a Blackhawk, he tallied 61 goals and added 84 assists (145 points) in 131 playoff games.

Savard was originally the Blackhawks' first-round pick (third overall) in the 1980 NHL Entry Draft and recorded 75 points (28 goals, 47 assists) during his rookie season in 1980-81. He recorded 32 goals and 87 assists for 119 points the following season to become the second Blackhawk in history to record 100+ points in a single season. Savard was named to the NHL All-Star Second Team for the 1982-83 season when he compiled 35 goals and 86 assists for 121 points in 78 games. He appeared in seven NHL All-Star Games during his career (1982-84, 1986, 1988, 1991 and 1996). Savard tallied a career-high 47 goals during the 1985-86 campaign. He tallied career-highs in assists (87) and points (131) during the 1987-88 season. His 131-point season in 1987-88 is a Blackhawk record and his 87-assist seasons in 1981-82 and 1987-88 are also Blackhawk highs.

After 10 seasons with the Blackhawks, Savard was traded to the Montreal Canadiens in exchange for Chris Chelios and a second-round draft pick (Mike Pomichter) on June 29, 1990. Savard played three seasons for the Canadiens and won the Stanley Cup in 1993. He then played parts of two seasons with the Tampa Bay Lightning before being traded back to the Blackhawks on April 6, 1995.

Savard is one of only five players in Blackhawk history to have his number retired. His #18 was raised to the United Center rafters in a special pregame ceremony on March 19, 1998. He joined Blackhawk legends Glenn Hall (1), Bobby Hull (9), Stan Mikita (21) and Tony Esposito (35) as the only Blackhawks to be so honored. He was inducted into the Hockey Hall of Fame in 2000.

Coaching Record

		Regular Season				Playoffs		
Season	Team	Games	W	L	O/T	Games	W	L
2006-07	Chicago (NHL)	61	24	30	7	....	....	....
	NHL Totals	61	24	30	7	....	....	....

General Managers' History

Major Frederic McLaughlin, 1926-27 to 1941-42; Bill Tobin, 1942-43 to 1953-54; Tommy Ivan, 1954-55 to 1976-77; Bob Pulford, 1977-78 to 1989-90; Mike Keenan, 1990-91, 1991-92; Mike Keenan and Bob Pulford, 1992-93; Bob Pulford, 1993-94 to 1996-97; Bob Murray, 1997-98, 1998-99; Bob Murray and Bob Pulford, 1999-2000; Mike Smith, 2000-01 to 2002-03; Mike Smith and Bob Pulford, 2003-04; Bob Pulford, 2004-05; Dale Tallon, 2005-06 to date.

Vice President and General Manager

DALE TALLON
General Manager, Chicago Blackhawks.
Born in Noranda, Que., October 19, 1950.

The Chicago Blackhawks announced on June 21, 2005 that Dale Tallon had been named the eighth general manager in the team's storied history. Tallon, in his second stint with the Blackhawks front office, was named assistant general manager on November 5, 2003. He served four years (1998 to 2002) as the Blackhawks' director of player personnel before he returned to the radio and television booth prior to the 2002-03 season as color analyst for Blackhawk hockey.

Tallon was the Vancouver Canucks' first-round selection and the second player chosen overall (behind Gilbert Perreault, Buffalo) in the 1970 NHL Entry Draft. A defenseman, he immediately jumped into the NHL with the Canucks in the 1970–71 season. Tallon recorded a career-high 17 goals in 69 games with Vancouver during the 1971–72 season and appeared in the 1971 and 1972 NHL All-Star Games.

Tallon was traded to the Blackhawks for Jerry Korab and Gary Smith on May 14,1973. He had his best season as a professional with Chicago in 1975–76 with a career-high 47 assists and 62 points in 80 games. During his five-year Blackhawk career (1973 to 1978), Tallon scored 44 goals and added 112 assists for 156 points with 296 penalty minutes. He was dealt to Pittsburgh on October 9, 1978 and finished his playing career by playing two seasons with the Penguins. During his 10-year NHL career, Tallon scored 98 goals and added 238 assists for 336 points in 642 games. After retiring from the NHL following the 1979–80 season, he served as the Blackhawks color analyst for radio and television broadcasts for 16 seasons.

At the start of the 1998-99 season, Tallon joined the Blackhawk front office as director of player personnel. As he traveled the world scouting hockey, Tallon's knowledge and expertise of the game were honed while aiding in selecting and developing the Blackhawks' young prospects.

Club Records

Team

(Figures in brackets for season records are games played; records for fewest points, wins, ties, losses, goals, goals against are for 70 or more games)

Record		
Most Points	**107**	1970-71 (78), 1971-72 (78)
Most Wins	**49**	1970-71 (78), 1990-91 (80)
Most Ties	**23**	1973-74 (78)
Most Losses	**56**	2005-06 (82)
Most Goals	**351**	1985-86 (80)
Most Goals Against	**363**	1981-82 (80)
Fewest Points	**31**	1953-54 (70)
Fewest Wins	**12**	1953-54 (70)
Fewest Ties	**6**	1989-90 (80)
Fewest Losses	**14**	1973-74 (78)
Fewest Goals	***133**	1953-54 (70)
Fewest Goals Against	**164**	1973-74 (78)
Longest Winning Streak		
Overall	**8**	Dec. 9-26/71, Jan. 4-21/81
Home	**13**	Nov. 11-Dec. 20/70
Away	**7**	Dec. 9-29/64
Longest Undefeated Streak		
Overall	**15**	Jan. 14-Feb. 16/67 (12 wins, 3 ties), Oct. 29-Dec. 3/75 (6 wins, 9 ties)
Home	**18**	Oct. 11-Dec. 20/70 (16 wins, 2 ties)
Away	**12**	Nov. 2-Dec. 16/67 (6 wins, 6 ties)
Longest Losing Streak		
Overall	**12**	Feb. 25-Mar. 25/51
Home	**10**	Jan. 29-Mar. 21/28
Away	**19**	Nov. 10/03-Jan. 29/04
Longest Winless Streak		
Overall	**21**	Dec. 17/50-Jan. 28/51 (18 losses, 3 ties)
Home	**15**	Dec. 16/28-Feb. 28/29 (11 losses, 4 ties)
Away	**22**	Dec. 19/50-Mar. 25/51 (20 losses, 2 ties)
Most Shutouts, Season	**15**	1969-70 (76)
Most PIM, Season	**2,663**	1991-92 (80)
Most Goals, Game	**12**	Jan. 30/69 (Chi. 12 at Phi. 0)

Individual

Record		
Most Seasons	**22**	Stan Mikita
Most Games	**1,394**	Stan Mikita
Most Goals, Career	**604**	Bobby Hull
Most Assists, Career	**926**	Stan Mikita
Most Points, Career	**1,467**	Stan Mikita (541G, 926A)
Most PIM, Career	**1,495**	Chris Chelios
Most Shutouts, Career	**74**	Tony Esposito
Longest Consecutive Games Streak	**884**	Steve Larmer (Oct. 6/82-Apr. 15/93)
Most Goals, Season	**58**	Bobby Hull (1968-69)
Most Assists, Season	**87**	Denis Savard (1981-82, 1987-88)
Most Points, Season	**131**	Denis Savard (1987-88; 44G, 87A)
Most PIM, Season	**408**	Mike Peluso (1991-92)
Most Points, Defenseman, Season	**85**	Doug Wilson (1981-82; 39G, 46A)
Most Points, Center, Season	**131**	Denis Savard (1987-88; 44G, 87A)
Most Points, Right Wing, Season	**101**	Steve Larmer (1990-91; 44G, 57A)
Most Points, Left Wing, Season	**107**	Bobby Hull (1968-69; 58G, 49A)
Most Points, Rookie, Season	**90**	Steve Larmer (1982-83; 43G, 47A)
Most Shutouts, Season	**15**	Tony Esposito (1969-70)
Most Goals, Game	**5**	Grant Mulvey (Feb. 3/82)
Most Assists, Game	**6**	Pat Stapleton (Mar. 30/69)
Most Points, Game	**7**	Max Bentley (Jan. 28/43; 4G, 3A), Grant Mulvey (Feb. 3/82; 5G, 2A)

* NHL Record.

Retired Numbers

1	Glenn Hall	1957-1967
9	Bobby Hull	1957-1972
18	Denis Savard	1980-1990, 1995-1997
21	Stan Mikita	1958-1980
35	Tony Esposito	1969-1984

All-time Record vs. Other Clubs

Regular Season

	At Home								On Road								Total							
	GP	W	L	T	OL	GF	GA	PTS	GP	W	L	T	OL	GF	GA	PTS	GP	W	L	T	OL	GF	GA	PTS
Anaheim	28	12	14	2	0	72	71	26	26	8	15	3	0	55	73	19	54	20	29	5	0	127	144	45
Atlanta	2	2	0	0	0	6	0	4	5	3	2	0	0	15	18	6	7	5	2	0	0	21	18	10
Boston	287	147	95	45	0	929	772	339	284	89	161	34	0	808	1023	212	571	236	256	79	0	1737	1795	551
Buffalo	52	27	18	6	1	165	141	61	53	14	32	7	0	138	199	35	105	41	50	13	1	303	340	96
Calgary	65	28	24	13	0	207	190	69	67	23	30	13	1	199	212	60	132	51	54	26	1	406	402	129
Carolina	29	16	9	3	1	117	83	36	31	12	15	4	0	96	102	28	60	28	24	7	1	213	185	64
Colorado	45	23	16	3	3	152	141	52	43	14	23	6	0	137	170	34	88	37	39	9	3	289	311	86
Columbus	18	11	5	1	1	53	37	24	19	7	9	1	2	58	63	17	37	18	14	2	3	111	100	41
Dallas	114	66	33	15	0	421	303	147	116	44	54	16	2	349	397	106	230	110	87	31	2	770	700	253
Detroit	346	156	136	51	3	1032	981	366	343	100	209	33	1	852	1184	234	689	256	345	84	4	1884	2165	600
Edmonton	48	24	15	7	2	179	159	57	49	19	25	5	0	153	180	43	97	43	40	12	2	332	339	100
Florida	10	5	3	2	0	34	30	12	9	5	2	1	1	33	22	12	19	10	5	3	1	67	52	24
Los Angeles	79	37	33	9	0	270	229	83	78	35	34	8	1	259	258	79	157	72	67	17	1	529	487	162
Minnesota	12	4	6	1	1	26	37	10	12	2	7	0	3	27	42	7	24	6	13	1	4	53	79	17
Montreal	274	94	125	55	0	733	762	243	276	54	173	48	1	653	1067	157	550	148	298	103	1	1386	1829	400
Nashville	25	13	10	1	1	66	67	28	24	9	10	3	2	68	83	23	49	22	20	4	3	134	150	51
New Jersey	47	24	12	10	1	178	130	59	48	16	20	11	1	143	149	44	95	40	32	21	2	321	279	103
NY Islanders	49	26	17	5	1	163	164	58	48	14	19	15	0	143	168	43	97	40	36	20	1	306	332	101
NY Rangers	287	129	115	43	0	872	793	301	286	113	118	55	0	808	843	281	573	242	233	98	0	1680	1636	582
Ottawa	9	5	2	2	0	22	21	12	10	6	4	0	0	30	31	12	19	11	6	2	0	52	52	24
Philadelphia	61	26	16	19	0	207	175	71	63	16	36	11	0	162	207	43	124	42	52	30	0	369	382	114
Phoenix	52	27	14	10	1	191	138	65	54	20	27	5	2	169	177	47	106	47	41	15	3	360	315	112
Pittsburgh	61	40	11	10	0	240	158	90	60	23	29	7	1	194	215	54	121	63	40	17	1	434	373	144
St. Louis	126	71	37	18	0	461	363	160	123	45	59	17	2	382	414	109	249	116	96	35	2	843	777	269
San Jose	29	14	11	2	2	87	91	32	30	10	16	3	1	77	89	24	59	24	27	5	3	164	180	56
Tampa Bay	14	8	4	2	0	45	35	18	12	4	4	3	1	30	29	12	26	12	8	5	1	75	64	30
Toronto	319	157	120	42	0	971	832	356	315	97	164	54	0	821	1071	248	634	254	284	96	0	1792	1903	604
Vancouver	75	47	18	7	3	274	179	104	76	23	37	15	1	217	229	62	151	70	55	22	4	491	408	166
Washington	40	22	12	6	0	151	120	50	42	16	21	5	0	131	148	37	82	38	33	11	0	282	268	87
Defunct Clubs	139	79	40	20	0	408	268	178	140	52	67	21	0	316	346	125	279	131	107	41	0	724	614	303
Totals	**2742**	**1340**	**971**	**410**	**21**	**8732**	**7470**	**3111**	**2742**	**893**	**1422**	**404**	**23**	**7523**	**9209**	**2213**	**5484**	**2233**	**2393**	**814**	**44**	**16255**	**16679**	**5324**

Playoffs

	Series	W	L	GP	W	L	T	GF	GA	Last Mtg.	Rnd.	Result
Boston	6	1	5	22	5	16	1	63	97	1978	QF	L 0-4
Buffalo	2	0	2	9	1	8	0	17	36	1980	QF	L 0-4
Calgary	3	1	2	12	5	7	0	33	37	1996	CQF	W 4-0
Colorado	2	0	2	12	4	8	0	28	49	1997	CQF	L 2-4
Dallas	6	4	2	33	19	14	0	120	118	1991	DSF	L 2-4
Detroit	14	8	6	69	38	31	0	210	190	1995	CF	L 1-4
Edmonton	4	1	3	20	8	12	0	77	102	1992	CF	W 4-0
Los Angeles	1	1	0	5	4	1	0	10	7	1974	QF	W 4-1
Montreal	17	5	12	81	29	50	2	185	261	1976	QF	L 0-4
NY Islanders	2	0	2	6	0	6	0	6	21	1979	QF	L 0-4
NY Rangers	5	4	1	24	14	10	0	66	54	1973	SF	W 4-1
Philadelphia	1	1	0	4	4	0	0	20	8	1971	QF	W 4-0
Pittsburgh	2	1	1	8	4	4	0	24	23	1992	F	L 0-4
St. Louis	10	7	3	50	28	22	0	171	142	2002	CQF	L 1-4
Toronto	9	3	6	38	15	22	1	89	111	1995	CQF	W 4-3
Vancouver	2	1	1	9	5	4	0	24	24	1995	CSF	W 4-0
Defunct Clubs	4	2	2	9	5	3	1	16	15			
Totals	**90**	**40**	**50**	**411**	**188**	**218**	**5**	**1159**	**1295**			

Calgary totals include Atlanta Flames, 1972-73 to 1979-80. Carolina totals include Hartford, 1979-80 to 1996-97.
Colorado totals include Quebec, 1979-80 to 1994-95. Dallas totals include Minnesota North Stars, 1967-68 to 1992-93.
New Jersey totals include Kansas City, 1974-75, 1975-76, and Colorado Rockies, 1976-77 to 1981-82.
Phoenix totals include Winnipeg, 1979-80 to 1995-96.

Playoff Results 2007-2002

Year	Round	Opponent	Result	GF	GA
2002	CQF	St. Louis	L 1-4	5	13

Abbreviations: Round: F - Final; **CF** - conference final; **CSF** - conference semi-final; **CQF** - conference quarter-final; **DSF** - division semi-final; **SF** - semi-final; **QF** - quarter-final.

2006-07 Results

Month	Date	Opponent	Score
Oct.	5	at Nashville	8-6
	7	Columbus	4-5
	12	Nashville	3-1
	14	at St. Louis	3-4
	16	at Colorado	5-3
	18	Montreal	2-1
	20	at Dallas	4-5
	21	St. Louis	3-4
	25	Vancouver	0-5
	28	Anaheim	0-3
	30	at Philadelphia	0-3
	31	at NY Islanders	2-5
Nov.	2	Detroit	1-2
	9	at New Jersey	1-2†
	10	St. Louis	3-1
	12	Columbus	1-0
	16	at Phoenix	2-3†
	17	at Anaheim	4-3†
	19	at Vancouver	1-2
	22	at Calgary	1-4
	24	at Edmonton	1-5
	29	Dallas	2-1
Dec.	1	St. Louis	5-2
	2	at Nashville	4-3*
	5	at Minnesota	2-3†
	7	Phoenix	1-2†
	9	at Minnesota	4-5*
	10	Edmonton	4-1
	12	at St. Louis	3-2
	14	Detroit	2-3
	16	at Columbus	6-4
	17	Colorado	2-1
	20	Nashville	1-2
	22	Toronto	3-1
	23	at Colorado	2-3
	26	Dallas	2-1
	29	Boston	3-5
	31	at Columbus	1-3
Jan.	2	at St. Louis	4-1
	4	at St. Louis	0-2
	5	Nashville	3-8
	7	Phoenix	2-4
	10	Buffalo	1-2
	13	at Detroit	3-6
	14	Minnesota	3-4†
	16	Columbus	4-5*
	19	Minnesota	0-3
	20	at Nashville	3-6
	26	Nashville	1-3
	28	Calgary	4-3*
Feb.	1	at Los Angeles	3-2*
	3	at San Jose	2-4
	6	at Calgary	3-2†
	7	at Vancouver	3-0
	9	at Edmonton	1-2
	11	at Columbus	5-4
	14	at Pittsburgh	4-5†
	16	Vancouver	1-2†
	18	at NY Rangers	1-2
	21	at Detroit	2-4
	22	San Jose	0-2
	25	St. Louis	5-1
	27	Detroit	1-4
Mar.	1	Colorado	1-6
	2	at Detroit	2-6
	4	Ottawa	4-3†
	6	Los Angeles	3-0
	10	at Phoenix	7-5
	13	at San Jose	1-7
	15	at Los Angeles	4-3†
	16	at Anaheim	2-5
	20	at Columbus	2-5
	21	San Jose	1-4
	23	Los Angeles	1-2
	25	Calgary	2-3
	28	Anaheim	1-3
	30	Columbus	3-1
Apr.	1	Edmonton	2-1
	3	at Nashville	3-2†
	5	Detroit	3-2†
	7	at Detroit	2-7
	8	at Dallas	2-3

* – Overtime † – Shootout

Entry Draft Selections 2007-1993

2007

Pick	
1	Patrick Kane
38	William Sweatt
56	Akim Aliu
69	Maxime Tanguay
86	Josh Unice
126	Joseph Lavin
156	Richard Greenop

2006

Pick	
3	Jonathan Toews
33	Igor Makarov
61	Simon Danis-Pepin
76	Tony Lagerstrom
95	Ben Shutron
96	Joe Palmer
156	Jan-Mikael Juutilainen
169	Chris Auger
186	Peter Leblanc

2005

Pick	
7	Jack Skille
43	Michael Blunden
54	Dan Bertram
68	Evan Brophey
108	Niklas Hjalmarsson
113	Nathan Davis
117	Denis Istomin
134	Brennan Turner
167	Joseph Fallon
188	Joe Charlebois
202	David Kuchejda
203	Adam Hobson

2004

Pick	
3	Cam Barker
32	Dave Bolland
41	Bryan Bickell
45	Ryan Garlock
54	Jakub Sindel
68	Adam Berti
120	Mitch Maunu
123	Karel Hromas
131	Trevor Kell
140	Jake Dowell
165	Scott McCulloch
196	Petri Kontiola
214	Troy Brouwer
223	Jared Walker
229	Eric Hunter
256	Matthew Ford
260	Marko Anttila

2003

Pick	
14	Brent Seabrook
52	Corey Crawford
59	Michal Barinka
151	Lasse Kukkonen
156	Alexei Ivanov
181	Johan Andersson
211	Mike Brodeur
245	Dustin Byfuglien
275	Michael Grenzy
282	Chris Porter

2002

Pick	
21	Anton Babchuk
54	Duncan Keith
93	Alexander Kojevnikov
128	Matt Ellison
156	James Wisniewski
188	Kevin Kantee
219	Tyson Kellerman
251	Jason Kostadine
282	Adam Burish

2001

Pick	
9	Tuomo Ruutu
29	Adam Munro
59	Matt Keith
73	Craig Anderson
104	Brent MacLellan
115	Vladimir Gusev
119	Alexei Zotkin
142	Tommi Jaminki
174	Alexander Golovin
186	Petr Puncochar
205	Teemu Jaaskelainen
216	Oleg Minakov
268	Jeff Miles

2000

Pick	
10	Mikhail Yakubov
11	Pavel Vorobiev
49	Jonas Nordqvist
74	Igor Radulov
106	Scott Balan
117	Olli Malmivaara
151	Alexander Barkunov
177	Michael Ayers
193	Joey Martin
207	Cliff Loya
225	Vladislav Luchkin
240	Adam Berkhoel
262	Peter Flache
271	Reto Von Arx
291	Arne Ramholt

1999

Pick	
23	Steve McCarthy
46	Dimitri Levinski
63	Stepan Mokhov
134	Michael Jacobsen
165	Michael Leighton
194	Mattias Wennerberg
195	Yorick Treille
223	Andrew Carver

1998

Pick	
8	Mark Bell
94	Matthias Trattnig
156	Kent Huskins
158	Jari Viuhkola
166	Jonathan Pelletier
183	Tyler Arnason
210	Sean Griffin
238	Alexandre Couture
240	Andrei Yershov

1997

Pick	
13	Daniel Cleary
16	Ty Jones
39	Jeremy Reich
67	Mike Souza
110	Ben Simon
120	Peter Gardiner
130	Kyle Calder
147	Heath Gordon
174	Jerad Smith
204	Sergei Shikhanov
230	Chris Feil

1996

Pick	
31	Remi Royer
42	Jeff Paul
46	Geoff Peters
130	Andy Johnson
184	Mike Vellinga
210	Chris Twerdun
236	Andrei Kozyrev

1995

Pick	
19	Dmitri Nabokov
45	Christian Laflamme
71	Kevin McKay
82	Chris Van Dyk
97	Pavel Kriz
146	Marc Magliarditi
149	Marty Wilford
175	Steve Tardif
201	Casey Hankinson
227	Mike Pittman

1994

Pick	
14	Ethan Moreau
40	Jean-Yves Leroux
85	Steve McLaren
118	Marc Dupuis
144	Jim Enson
170	Tyler Prosofsky
196	Mike Josephson
222	Lubomir Jandera
248	Lars Weibel
263	Rob Mara

1993

Pick	
24	Eric Lecompte
50	Eric Manlow
54	Bogdan Savenko
76	Ryan Huska
90	Eric Daze
102	Patrik Pysz
128	Jonni Vauhkonen
180	Tom White
206	Sergei Petrov
232	Mike Rusk
258	Mike McGhan
284	Tom Noble

Coaching History

Pete Muldoon, 1926-27; Barney Stanley and Hugh Lehman, 1927-28; Herb Gardiner and Dick Irvin, 1928-29; Tom Shaughnessy and Bill Tobin, 1929-30; Dick Irvin, 1930-31; Bill Tobin, 1931-32; Emil Iverson, Godfrey Matheson and Tommy Gorman, 1932-33; Tommy Gorman, 1933-34; Clem Loughlin, 1934-35 to 1936-37; Bill Stewart, 1937-38; Bill Stewart and Paul Thompson, 1938-39; Paul Thompson, 1939-40 to 1943-44; Paul Thompson and Johnny Gottselig, 1944-45; Johnny Gottselig, 1945-46, 1946-47; Johnny Gottselig and Charlie Conacher, 1947-48; Charlie Conacher, 1948-49, 1949-50; Ebbie Goodfellow, 1950-51, 1951-52; Sid Abel, 1952-53, 1953-54; Frank Eddolls, 1954-55; Dick Irvin, 1955-56; Tommy Ivan, 1956-57; Tommy Ivan and Rudy Pilous, 1957-58; Rudy Pilous, 1958-59 to 1962-63; Billy Reay, 1963-64 to 1975-76; Billy Reay and Bill White, 1976-77; Bob Pulford, 1977-78, 1978-79; Eddie Johnston, 1979-80; Keith Magnuson, 1980-81; Keith Magnuson and Bob Pulford, 1981-82; Orval Tessier, 1982-83, 1983-84; Orval Tessier and Bob Pulford, 1984-85; Bob Pulford, 1985-86, 1986-87; Bob Murdoch, 1987-88; Mike Keenan, 1988-89 to 1991-92; Darryl Sutter, 1992-93 to 1994-95; Craig Hartsburg, 1995-96 to 1997-98; Dirk Graham and Lorne Molleken, 1998-99; Lorne Molleken and Bob Pulford, 1999-2000; Alpo Suhonen, 2000-01; Brian Sutter, 2001-02 to 2003-04; Trent Yawney, 2005-06; Trent Yawney and Denis Savard, 2006-07; Denis Savard, 2007-08.

Captains' History

Dick Irvin, 1926-27 to 1928-29; Duke Dukowski, 1929-30; Ty Arbour, 1930-31; Cy Wentworth, 1931-32; Helge Bostrom, 1932-33; Charlie Gardiner, 1933-34; no captain, 1934-35; Johnny Gottselig, 1935-36 to 1939-40; Earl Seibert, 1940-41, 1941-42; Doug Bentley, 1942-43, 1943-44; Clint Smith 1944-45; John Mariucci, 1945-46; Red Hamill, 1946-47; John Mariucci, 1947-48; Gaye Stewart, 1948-49; Doug Bentley, 1949-50; Jack Stewart, 1950-51, 1951-52; Bill Gadsby, 1952-53, 1953-54; Gus Mortson, 1954-55 to 1956-57; no captain, 1957-58; Ed Litzenberger, 1958-59 to 1960-61; Pierre Pilote, 1961-62 to 1967-68, no captain, 1968-69; Pat Stapleton, 1969-70; no captain, 1970-71 to 1974-75; Stan Mikita and Pit Martin, 1975-76; Stan Mikita, Pit Martin and Keith Magnuson, 1976-77; Keith Magnuson, 1977-78, 1978-79; Keith Magnuson and Terry Ruskowski, 1979-80; Terry Ruskowski, 1980-81, 1981-82; Darryl Sutter, 1982-83 to 1984-85; Darryl Sutter and Bob Murray, 1985-86; Darryl Sutter, 1986-87; no captain, 1987-88; Denis Savard and Dirk Graham, 1988-89; Dirk Graham, 1989-90 to 1994-95; Chris Chelios, 1995-96 to 1998-99; Doug Gilmour, 1999-2000; Tony Amonte, 2000-01, 2001-02; Alex Zhamnov, 2002-03, 2003-04; Adrian Aucoin and Martin Lapointe, 2005-06, 2006-07.

Club Directory

United Center

Chicago Blackhawks
United Center
1901 W. Madison Street
Chicago, IL 60612
Phone **312/455-7000**
FAX 312/455-7041
www.chicagoblackhawks.com
Capacity: 20,500

President	William W. Wirtz
Senior Vice President	Robert J. Pulford
Vice President	Jack Davison
Vice President	Peter R. Wirtz
General Manager	Dale Tallon
Assistant G.M.	Rick Dudley
Assistant G.M., Hockey Operations	Stan Bowman
Rockford G.M., Hockey Operations & Director of Player Evaluations	Al MacIssac
Head Coach	Denis Savard
Assistant Coach	Mark Hardy
Assistant Coach	John Torchetti
Skating Coach	Dan Jansen
Strength & Conditioning Coach	Phil Walker
Goaltending Coach	Stephane Waite
Video Coach	Ryan Stewart
Director of Pro Scouting	Marc Bergevin
Chief Amateur Scout	Michel Dumas
Amateur Scouts	Ron Anderson, Bruce Franklin, Mark Kelley, Tim Keon, Rob Pulford
European Amateur Scouts	Karl Pavlik, Ruslan Shabanov
European Pro Scout	Mats Hallin
Executive Assistant	Cindy Brueck
Training/Equipment Staff	
Head Athletic Trainer	Michael Gapski
Assistant Atheltic Trainer	Jeff Thomas
Massage Therapist	Pawel Prylinski
Equipment Manager	Troy Parchman
Asst. Equipment Manager	Russ Holden
Equipment Assistant	Clinton Reif
Medical Staff	
Head Team Physician, Orthopedics	Michael Terry
Team Physician, Orthopedics	Sherwin Ho
Team Physicians, Internal Medicine	William Harper, Carl Meyer, Todd Stern
Team Dentists	Russ Baer, Anthony LaVacca, Martin Marcus
Eye Doctors	William Mieler, Louise Sclafani
Public Relations/Marketing	
Exec. Dir., Communications, Broadcasting & Comm. Outreach	Jim De Maria
Director, Team Services & Publications	Tony Ommen
Dir., Public Relations & Community Outreach	Jim Blaney
Manager of Community Outreach	Angela Armbruster
Website Producer	Adam Kempenaar
Exec. Dir., Sales & Marketing	Jim Sofranko
Director, Corporate Sponsorships	Steve Waight
Director, Advertising & Promotions	Pete Hassen
Manager, Client Services	Kelly Smith
Account Exec., Corporate Sponsorships	Sara Bailey
Manager, Game Operations	Ben Broder
Executive Assistant	Alison Finley
Finance	
Executive Director of Finance	John Kerr
Ticketing	
Exec. Director, Ticket Operations	James K. Bare
Director of Ticket Sales	Doug Ryan
Sr. Customer Service Representative	Kathie Raimondi
Manager of Customer Service	Trisha Ithal
Customer Service Representative	Jordan Horst
Inside Sales Manager	Ildegardo Esparza
Senior Account Executives	Brad Bober, Steve McNelley, Rich Sommers, Matthew Powers, Chris Terwood, Allison Ardolino
Broadcasting	
Radio Station	WSCR (AM 670)
Television Station	Comcast Sports Net Chicago
TV Play-By-Play	Dan Kelly
TV Color Analyst	Eddie Olczyk
Radio Play-By-Play	John Wiedeman
Radio Color Analyst	Troy Murray
Miscellaneous	
Team Photographer	Bill Smith
Assistant Photographer	Rudy Ayasse
Organist	Frank Pellico
Public Address Announcer	Gene Honda
Website Contributor	Harvey Wittenberg

Colorado Avalanche

2006-07 Results: 44W-31L-3OTL-4SOL 95PTS.
Fourth, Northwest Division

Key Off-Season Signings/Acquisitions

2007

Apr. 9 • Re-signed C **Joe Sakic**.
May 21 • Re-signed D **Jordan Leopold**, D **Kurt Sauer** and D **Jeff Finger**.
June 13 • Re-signed RW **Scott Parker**.
15 • Re-signed RW **Ben Guite** and C **Cody McCormick**.
25 • Re-signed C **Tyler Arnason**.
July 1 • Signed LW **Ryan Smyth** and D **Scott Hannan**.
5 • Re-signed RW **Marek Svatos**.
17 • Re-signed RW **Mark Rycroft**.
17 • Signed D **Jeff Jillson** and D **Dale Purinton**.

Joe Sakic had another big year for Colorado in 2006-07. His first 100-point season since 2000-01 gave him six for his career. He reached the 1,500-point plateau on October 25, 2006 and scored his 600th goal on February 15, 2007.

2007-08 Schedule

Oct.	Wed.	3	Dallas		Tue.	8	at Detroit
	Thu.	4	at Nashville		Wed.	9	at Washington
	Sun.	7	San Jose		Sat.	12	at Carolina
	Fri.	12	at St. Louis		Sun.	13	at Florida*
	Sat.	13	Columbus		Tue.	15	at Tampa Bay
	Tue.	16	Calgary		Fri.	18	Chicago
	Fri.	19	at Chicago		Sun.	20	Columbus
	Sun.	21	at Minnesota*		Tue.	22	Nashville
	Tue.	23	at Edmonton		Thu.	24	Minnesota
	Fri.	26	at Calgary		Wed.	30	Chicago
	Sun.	28	Minnesota	**Feb.**	Fri.	1	at Detroit
Nov.	Thu.	1	Pittsburgh		Sat.	2	at St. Louis
	Sat.	3	Vancouver		Mon.	4	Phoenix
	Mon.	5	Calgary		Wed.	6	at San Jose
	Wed.	7	Edmonton		Sat.	9	at Vancouver
	Fri.	9	at Vancouver		Tue.	12	Anaheim
	Sun.	11	Minnesota		Thu.	14	St. Louis
	Fri.	16	at Dallas		Sun.	17	at Chicago*
	Sun.	18	at Minnesota*		Mon.	18	Detroit
	Tue.	20	at Calgary		Wed.	20	at Anaheim
	Thu.	22	at Edmonton		Fri.	22	at Phoenix
	Sat.	24	Calgary		Sun.	24	at Edmonton
	Wed.	28	Edmonton		Tue.	26	at Calgary
	Fri.	30	at San Jose		Wed.	27	at Vancouver
Dec.	Sat.	1	at Los Angeles	**Mar.**	Sat.	1	Los Angeles
	Mon.	3	San Jose		Tue.	4	Vancouver
	Wed.	5	at Columbus		Thu.	6	Anaheim
	Fri.	7	Philadelphia		Sat.	8	Dallas
	Sun.	9	St. Louis		Sun.	9	at Dallas
	Wed.	12	at Columbus		Tue.	11	at Atlanta
	Thu.	13	at Nashville		Thu.	13	Edmonton
	Sat.	15	Nashville		Sat.	15	New Jersey*
	Mon.	17	at Los Angeles		Mon.	17	at Minnesota
	Wed.	19	at Anaheim		Thu.	20	at Calgary
	Fri.	21	NY Rangers		Sat.	22	at Edmonton*
	Sun.	23	Vancouver		Mon.	24	Calgary
	Thu.	27	Detroit		Wed.	26	Vancouver
	Sat.	29	Los Angeles*		Fri.	28	Edmonton
	Mon.	31	at Phoenix		Sun.	30	at Minnesota*
Jan.	Wed.	2	Phoenix	**Apr.**	Tue.	1	at Vancouver
	Sat.	5	NY Islanders		Sun.	6	Minnesota*

* Denotes afternoon game.

Year-by-Year Record

		Home				Road				Overall								
Season	**GP**	**W**	**L**	**T**	**OL**	**W**	**L**	**T**	**OL**	**W**	**L**	**T**	**OL**	**GF**	**GA**	**Pts.**	**Finished**	**Playoff Result**
2006-07	82	22	16	....	3	22	15	....	4	44	31	....	7	272	251	95	4th, Northwest Div.	Out of Playoffs
2005-06	82	25	10	....	6	18	20	....	3	43	30	....	9	283	257	95	2nd, Northwest Div.	Lost Conf. Semi-Final
2004-05	....	....	....	....	....	....	....	....	....	....	....	....	....	....	....	....		
2003-04	82	19	14	6	2	21	8	7	5	40	22	13	7	236	198	100	2nd, Northwest Div.	Lost Conf. Semi-Final
2002-03	82	21	9	8	3	21	10	5	5	42	19	13	8	251	194	105	1st, Northwest Div.	Lost Conf. Quarter-Final
2001-02	82	24	12	4	1	21	16	4	0	45	28	8	1	212	169	99	1st, Northwest Div.	Lost Conf. Championship
2000-01	**82**	**28**	**6**	**5**	**2**	**24**	**10**	**5**	**2**	**52**	**16**	**10**	**4**	**270**	**192**	**118**	**1st, Northwest Div.**	**Won Stanley Cup**
1999-2000	82	25	12	4	0	17	16	7	1	42	28	11	1	233	201	96	1st, Northwest Div.	Lost Conf. Championship
1998-99	82	21	14	6	....	23	14	4	....	44	28	10	....	239	205	98	1st, Northwest Div.	Lost Conf. Championship
1997-98	82	21	10	10	....	18	16	7	....	39	26	17	....	231	205	95	1st, Pacific Div.	Lost Conf. Quarter-Final
1996-97	82	26	10	5	....	23	14	4	....	49	24	9	....	277	205	107	1st, Pacific Div.	Lost Conf. Championship
1995-96	**82**	**24**	**10**	**7**	....	**23**	**15**	**3**	....	**47**	**25**	**10**	....	**326**	**240**	**104**	**1st, Pacific Div.**	**Won Stanley Cup**
1994-95*	48	19	1	4	....	11	12	1	....	30	13	5	....	185	134	65	1st, Northeast Div.	Lost Conf. Quarter-Final
1993-94*	84	19	17	6	....	15	25	2	....	34	42	8	....	277	292	76	5th, Northeast Div.	Out of Playoffs
1992-93*	84	23	17	2	....	24	10	8	....	47	27	10	....	351	300	104	2nd, Adams Div.	Lost Div. Semi-Final
1991-92*	80	18	19	3	....	2	29	9	....	20	48	12	....	255	318	52	5th, Adams Div.	Out of Playoffs
1990-91*	80	9	23	8	....	7	27	6	....	16	50	14	....	236	354	46	5th, Adams Div.	Out of Playoffs
1989-90*	80	8	26	6	....	4	35	1	....	12	61	7	....	240	407	31	5th, Adams Div.	Out of Playoffs
1988-89*	80	16	20	4	....	11	26	3	....	27	46	7	....	269	342	61	5th, Adams Div.	Out of Playoffs
1987-88*	80	15	23	2	....	17	20	3	....	32	43	5	....	271	306	69	5th, Adams Div.	Out of Playoffs
1986-87*	80	20	13	7	....	11	26	3	....	31	39	10	....	267	276	72	4th, Adams Div.	Lost Div. Final
1985-86*	80	23	13	4	....	20	18	2	....	43	31	6	....	330	289	92	1st, Adams Div.	Lost Div. Semi-Final
1984-85*	80	24	12	4	....	17	18	5	....	41	30	9	....	323	275	91	2nd, Adams Div.	Lost Conf. Championship
1983-84*	80	24	11	5	....	18	17	5	....	42	28	10	....	360	278	94	3th, Adams Div.	Lost Div. Final
1982-83*	80	23	10	7	....	11	24	5	....	34	34	12	....	343	336	80	4th, Adams Div.	Lost Div. Semi-Final
1981-82*	80	24	13	3	....	9	18	13	....	33	31	16	....	356	345	82	4th, Adams Div.	Lost Conf. Championship
1980-81*	80	18	11	11	....	12	21	7	....	30	32	18	....	314	318	78	4th, Adams Div.	Lost Prelim. Round
1979-80*	80	17	16	7	....	8	28	4	....	25	44	11	....	248	313	61	5th, Adams Div.	Out of Playoffs

* Quebec Nordiques

NHL WESTERN CONFERENCE

NORTHWEST DIVISION
29th NHL Season

Franchise date: June 22, 1979

Transferred from Quebec to Denver, June 21, 1995.

2007-08 Player Personnel

FORWARDS	HT	WT	S	Place of Birth	*Age	2006-07 Club
ARNASON, Tyler	5-11	204	L	Oklahoma City, OK	28	Colorado
BRUNETTE, Andrew	6-1	212	L	Sudbury, Ont.	34	Colorado
BURKI, Codey	6-0	190	L	Winnipeg, Man.	19	Brandon
DASILVA, Dan	6-1	195	R	Saskatoon, Sask.	22	Albany-Arizona
GUITE, Ben	6-1	211	R	Montreal, Que.	29	Colorado-Albany
HEALEY, Eric	5-11	201	L	Hull, MA	32	Springfield
HEJDUK, Milan	6-0	190	R	Usti nad Labem, Czech.	31	Colorado
HENSICK, T.J.	5-10	185	R	Lansing, MI	21	U. of Michigan
HLINKA, Jaroslav	5-10	185	L	Prague, Czech.	30	Sparta
HUSSEY, Matt	6-2	212	L	New Haven, CT	28	Detroit-Grand Rapids
JONES, David	6-2	220	R	Guelph, Ont.	23	Dartmouth
LAPERRIERE, Ian	6-1	200	R	Montreal, Que.	33	Colorado
McCORMICK, Cody	6-3	215	R	London, Ont.	24	Colorado-Albany
McLEOD, Cody	6-2	210	L	Binscarth, Man.	23	Albany
ORESKOVICH, Victor	6-3	215	R	Whitby, Ont.	21	Kitchener
PARKER, Scott	6-5	240	R	Hanford, CA	29	San Jose-Colorado
RICHARDSON, Brad	5-11	185	L	Belleville, Ont.	22	Colorado-Albany
RYCROFT, Mark	6-0	192	R	Penticton, B.C.	29	Colorado
SAKIC, Joe	5-11	195	L	Burnaby, B.C.	38	Colorado
SMYTH, Ryan	6-1	190	L	Banff, Alta.	31	Edmonton-NY Islanders
STASTNY, Paul	6-0	205	L	Quebec City, Que.	21	Colorado
STEWART, Chris	6-2	228	R	Toronto, Ont.	19	Kingston-Albany
SVATOS, Marek	5-10	185	R	Kosice, Czech.	25	Colorado
WOLSKI, Wojtek	6-3	200	L	Zabrze, Poland	21	Colorado
DEFENSEMEN						
BOYCHUK, Johnny	6-2	225	R	Edmonton, Alta.	23	Albany
CLARK, Brett	6-0	195	L	Wapella, Sask.	30	Colorado
CUMISKEY, Kyle	5-10	185	L	Abbotsford, B.C.	20	Colorado-Albany
FINGER, Jeff	6-1	205	R	Hancock, MI	27	Colorado-Albany
HANNAN, Scott	6-1	225	L	Richmond, B.C.	28	San Jose
JILLSON, Jeff	6-3	215	R	North Smithfield, RI	27	Eisbaren Berlin
LEOPOLD, Jordan	6-1	200	L	Golden Valley, MN	27	Colorado
LILES, John-Michael	5-10	185	L	Zionsville, IN	26	Colorado
LOVE, Mitch	6-0	200	L	Quesnel, B.C.	23	Albany
MACIAS, Raymond	6-2	195	R	Long Beach, CA	21	Kamloops
PURINTON, Dale	6-3	228	L	Fort Wayne, IN	30	Hartford
SAUER, Kurt	6-4	220	L	St. Cloud, MN	26	Colorado
SKRASTINS, Karlis	6-1	210	L	Riga, USSR	33	Colorado
VERNACE, Michael	6-2	200	L	Toronto, Ont.	21	Albany-Arizona

GOALTENDERS	HT	WT	C	Place of Birth	*Age	2006-07 Club
BUDAJ, Peter	6-1	200	L	Banska Bystrica, Czech.	25	Colorado
THEODORE, Jose	5-11	182	R	Laval, Que.	31	Colorado
WALL, Michael	6-2	209	L	Telkwa, B.C.	22	Ana-Port (AHL)-Arizona
WEIMAN, Tyler	5-11	180	L	Saskatoon, Sask.	23	Albany

* – Age at start of 2007-08 season

2006-07 Scoring

* – rookie

Regular Season

Pos	#	Player	Team	GP	G	A	Pts	+/–	PIM	PP	SH	GW	S	%
C	19	Joe Sakic	COL	82	36	64	100	2	46	16	0	4	258	14.0
L	15	Andrew Brunette	COL	82	27	56	83	–8	36	9	0	2	173	15.6
C	26 *	Paul Stastny	COL	82	28	50	78	4	42	11	0	6	185	15.1
R	23	Milan Hejduk	COL	80	35	35	70	10	44	12	1	6	257	13.6
L	8 *	Wojtek Wolski	COL	76	22	28	50	2	14	7	0	2	165	13.3
C	39	Tyler Arnason	COL	82	16	33	49	–8	26	1	0	3	211	7.6
D	4	John-Michael Liles	COL	71	14	30	44	0	24	8	0	3	128	10.9
D	5	Brett Clark	COL	82	10	29	39	5	50	4	0	1	140	7.1
C	53	Brett McLean	COL	78	15	20	35	8	36	0	0	3	134	11.2
R	40	Marek Svatos	COL	66	15	15	30	1	46	8	0	2	179	8.4
R	14	Ian Laperriere	COL	81	8	21	29	5	133	0	0	0	118	6.8
C	12	Brad Richardson	COL	73	14	8	22	4	28	0	3	3	129	10.9
D	2	Ken Klee	COL	81	3	16	19	18	68	0	0	0	90	3.3
R	20	Mark Rycroft	COL	66	6	6	12	3	31	0	0	2	74	8.1
R	28	Ben Guite	COL	39	3	8	11	–4	16	0	1	1	63	4.8
D	71	Patrice Brisebois	COL	33	1	10	11	–5	22	1	0	0	36	2.8
D	3	Karlis Skrastins	COL	68	0	11	11	0	30	0	0	0	65	0.0
D	27	Ossi Vaananen	COL	74	2	6	8	6	69	0	0	1	32	6.3
C	87	Pierre Turgeon	COL	17	4	3	7	–1	10	1	0	0	31	12.9
D	34	Kurt Sauer	COL	48	0	6	6	–3	24	0	0	0	29	0.0
D	44	Jordan Leopold	COL	15	2	3	5	–4	14	1	1	0	19	10.5
D	6	Jeff Finger	COL	22	1	4	5	10	11	0	0	0	16	6.3
L	24	Antti Laaksonen	COL	41	3	1	4	–3	16	0	1	0	43	7.0
D	48 *	Kyle Cumiskey	COL	9	1	1	2	0	2	0	0	0	8	12.5
R	29	Scott Parker	S.J.	11	0	0	0	0	22	0	0	0	3	0.0
			COL	10	1	1	2	0	6	0	0	0	2	50.0
			TOTAL	21	1	1	2	0	28	0	0	0	5	20.0
C	11	Cody McCormick	COL	6	0	1	1	1	6	0	0	0	6	0.0

Goaltending

No.	Goaltender	GPI	Mins	Avg	W	L	OT	EN	SO	GA	SA	S%	G	A	PIM
31	Peter Budaj	57	3199	2.68	31	16	6	6	3	143	1499	.905	0	2	0
60	Jose Theodore	33	1748	3.26	13	15	1	3	0	95	870	.891	0	1	6
	Totals	**82**	**4976**	**2.98**	**44**	**31**	**7**	**9**	**3**	**247**	**2378**	**.896**			

Peter Budaj joined Patrick Roy and David Aebischer as the only goalies in franchise history to win 30 games in a single season.

Coach

JOEL QUENNEVILLE
Coach, Colorado Avalanche. Born in Windsor, Ont., September 15, 1958.

Joel Quenneville returned to the franchise where he began his NHL coaching career, as an assistant coach, in 1994-95 when he was named the fourth head coach in Colorado Avalanche, and the 12th in franchise history on July 7, 2004.

The former Colorado Rockies defenseman was the winningest coach in St. Louis Blues history, compiling a 307-209-77 record while spending 593 regular-season games behind the St. Louis bench, the most of any Blues coach. He reached the personal milestone of 500 career games coached on January 23, 2003 versus Chicago.

Under his guidance, the Blues reached the Western Conference Finals in 2001, the first time the team had done so since 1986, and won the Presidents' Trophy in 1999-2000 with a league-leading and franchise-high 114 points. He served as head coach of the North American All-Stars at the 2001 All-Star Game in Denver, and was named the NHL's coach of the year for 1999-00, capturing the Jack Adams Award.

The former NHL defenseman spent two-and-a-half seasons with the Colorado Avalanche/Quebec Nordiques as an assistant coach prior to being named the Blues' head coach on January 6, 1997. He was instrumental in the Avs' drive for their first Stanley Cup in 1996. He retired as an active player after the 1991-92 season, when he served as a player-coach for the St. John's Maple Leafs (AHL). Quenneville played 13 seasons in the NHL, closing out his career with 54 goals and 136 assists for 190 points adding 705 penalty minutes in 803 games played with Hartford, Washington, New Jersey, Toronto, and the Colorado Rockies. A short time later, he received his first coaching opportunity with the Springfield Indians (AHL) in 1993-94.

Coaching Record

		Regular Season				Playoffs		
Season	Team	Games	W	L	O/T	Games	W	L
1993-94	Springfield (AHL)	80	29	38	13	6	2	4
1996-97	**St. Louis (NHL)**	**40**	**18**	**15**	**7**	**6**	**2**	**4**
1997-98	**St. Louis (NHL)**	**82**	**45**	**29**	**8**	**10**	**6**	**4**
1998-99	**St. Louis (NHL)**	**82**	**37**	**32**	**13**	**13**	**6**	**7**
1999-2000	**St. Louis (NHL)**	**82**	**51**	**20**	**11**	**7**	**3**	**4**
2000-01	**St. Louis (NHL)**	**82**	**43**	**27**	**12**	**15**	**9**	**6**
2001-02	**St. Louis (NHL)**	**82**	**43**	**31**	**8**	**10**	**5**	**5**
2002-03	**St. Louis (NHL)**	**82**	**41**	**30**	**11**	**7**	**3**	**4**
2003-04	**St. Louis (NHL)**	**61**	**29**	**25**	**7**	....	....	....
2004-05	**Colorado (NHL)**			Season Cancelled				
2005-06	**Colorado (NHL)**	**82**	**43**	**30**	**9**	**9**	**4**	**5**
2006-07	**Colorado (NHL)**	**82**	**44**	**31**	**7**	....	....	....
	NHL Totals	**757**	**394**	**270**	**93**	**77**	**38**	**39**

Coaching History

Jacques Demers, 1979-80; Maurice Filion and Michel Bergeron, 1980-81; Michel Bergeron, 1981-82 to 1986-87; Andre Savard and Ron Lapointe, 1987-88; Ron Lapointe and Jean Perron, 1988-89; Michel Bergeron, 1989-90; Dave Chambers, 1990-91; Dave Chambers and Pierre Page, 1991-92; Pierre Page, 1992-93, 1993-94; Marc Crawford, 1994-95 to 1997-98; Bob Hartley, 1998-99 to 2001-02; Bob Hartley and Tony Granato, 2002-03; Tony Granato, 2003-04; Joel Quenneville, 2004-05 to date.

Captains' History

Marc Tardif, 1979-80, 1980-81; Robbie Ftorek and Andre Dupont, 1981-82; Mario Marois, 1982-83 to 1984-85; Mario Marois and Peter Stastny, 1985-86; Peter Stastny, 1986-87 to 1989-90; Joe Sakic and Steven Finn, 1990-91; Mike Hough, 1991-92; Joe Sakic, 1992-93 to date.

Club Records

Team

(Figures in brackets for season records are games played; records for fewest points, wins, ties, losses, goals, goals against are for 70 or more games)

Record		
Most Points	118	2000-01 (82)
Most Wins	52	2000-01 (82)
Most Ties	18	1980-81 (80)
Most Losses	61	1989-90 (80)
Most Goals	360	1983-84 (80)
Most Goals Against	407	1989-90 (80)
Fewest Points	31	1989-90 (80)
Fewest Wins	12	1989-90 (80)
Fewest Ties	5	1987-88 (80)
Fewest Losses	16	2000-01 (82)
Fewest Goals	212	2001-02 (82)
Fewest Goals Against	169	2001-02 (82)
Longest Winning Streak		
Overall	12	Jan. 10-Feb. 7/99
Home	10	Nov. 26/83-Jan. 10/84, Mar. 6-Apr. 16/95
Away	7	Jan. 10-Feb. 7/99
Longest Undefeated Streak		
Overall	12	Dec. 23/96-Jan. 20/97 (9 wins, 3 ties), Jan. 10-Feb. 7/99 (12 wins)
Home	14	Nov. 19/83-Jan. 21/84 (11 wins, 3 ties)
Away	10	Jan. 10-Mar. 3/99 (8 wins, 2 ties)
Longest Losing Streak		
Overall	14	Oct. 21-Nov. 19/90
Home	8	Oct. 21-Nov. 24/90
Away	18	Jan. 18-Apr. 1/90
Longest Winless Streak		
Overall	17	Oct. 21-Nov. 25/90 (15 losses, 2 ties)
Home	11	Nov. 14-Dec. 26/89 (7 losses, 4 ties)
Away	33	Oct. 8/91-Feb. 27/92 (25 losses, 8 ties)
Most Shutouts, Season	11	2001-02 (82)
Most PIM, Season	2,104	1989-90 (80)
Most Goals, Game	12	Three times

Individual

Record		
Most Seasons	18	Joe Sakic
Most Games	1,319	Joe Sakic
Most Goals, Career	610	Joe Sakic
Most Assists, Career	979	Joe Sakic
Most Points, Career	1,589	Joe Sakic (610G, 979A)
Most PIM, Career	1,562	Dale Hunter
Most Shutouts, Career	37	Patrick Roy
Longest Consecutive Games Streak	312	Dale Hunter (Oct. 9/80-Mar. 13/84)
Most Goals, Season	57	Michel Goulet (1982-83)
Most Assists, Season	93	Peter Stastny (1981-82)
Most Points, Season	139	Peter Stastny (1981-82; 46G, 93A)
Most PIM, Season	301	Gord Donnelly (1987-88)
Most Points, Defenseman, Season	82	Steve Duchesne (1992-93; 20G, 62A)
Most Points, Center, Season	139	Peter Stastny (1981-82; 46G, 93A)
Most Points, Right Wing, Season	103	Jacques Richard (1980-81; 52G, 51A)
Most Points, Left Wing, Season	121	Michel Goulet (1983-84; 56G, 65A)
Most Points, Rookie, Season	109	Peter Stastny (1980-81; 39G, 70A)
Most Shutouts, Season	9	Patrick Roy (2001-02)
Most Goals, Game	5	Mats Sundin (Mar. 5/92), Mike Ricci (Feb. 17/94)
Most Assists, Game	5	Eight times
Most Points, Game	8	Peter Stastny (Feb. 22/81; 4G, 4A), Anton Stastny (Feb. 22/81; 3G, 5A)

Records include Quebec Nordiques, 1979-80 through 1994-95.

Retired Numbers

3	J.C. Tremblay*	1972-1979
8	Marc Tardif*	1979-1983
16	Michel Goulet*	1979-1990
26	Peter Stastny*	1980-1990
33	Patrick Roy	1995-2003
77	Raymond Bourque	2000-2001

* Quebec Nordiques

All-time Record vs. Other Clubs

Regular Season

	At Home								On Road								Total							
	GP	W	L	T	OL	GF	GA	PTS	GP	W	L	T	OL	GF	GA	PTS	GP	W	L	T	OL	GF	GA	PTS
Anaheim	25	15	5	4	1	78	61	35	25	13	6	3	3	66	62	32	50	28	11	7	4	144	123	67
Atlanta	5	2	2	0	1	20	16	5	4	2	1	1	0	8	7	5	9	4	3	1	1	28	23	10
Boston	67	25	36	6	0	238	272	56	63	23	31	9	0	194	240	55	130	48	67	15	0	432	512	111
Buffalo	65	31	22	11	1	231	203	74	64	19	35	9	1	207	249	48	129	50	57	20	2	438	452	122
Calgary	55	24	19	11	1	200	179	60	55	20	26	9	0	165	195	49	110	44	45	20	1	365	374	109
Carolina	66	40	17	9	0	279	193	89	62	26	24	12	0	214	203	64	128	66	41	21	0	493	396	153
Chicago	43	23	13	6	1	170	137	53	45	19	23	3	0	141	152	41	88	42	36	9	1	311	289	94
Columbus	12	11	1	0	0	45	17	22	12	10	0	1	1	48	17	22	24	21	1	1	1	93	34	44
Dallas	45	23	12	7	3	160	117	56	45	16	23	5	1	130	150	38	90	39	35	12	4	290	267	94
Detroit	46	21	19	4	2	157	154	48	44	16	26	1	1	131	161	34	90	37	45	5	3	288	315	82
Edmonton	55	27	23	4	1	204	193	59	54	22	26	4	2	174	211	50	109	49	49	8	3	378	404	109
Florida	12	5	4	3	0	35	31	13	11	10	1	0	0	48	30	20	23	15	5	3	0	83	61	33
Los Angeles	46	24	19	3	0	187	157	51	47	14	27	5	1	154	191	34	93	38	46	8	1	341	348	85
Minnesota	19	13	4	2	0	61	45	28	18	10	3	1	4	56	42	25	37	23	7	3	4	117	87	53
Montreal	64	33	26	5	0	218	223	71	65	16	39	10	0	203	269	42	129	49	65	15	0	421	492	113
Nashville	16	8	5	2	1	45	36	19	16	7	4	3	2	55	47	19	32	15	9	5	3	100	83	38
New Jersey	35	18	13	4	0	124	98	40	37	14	19	4	0	125	150	32	72	32	32	8	0	249	248	72
NY Islanders	34	20	11	3	0	123	97	43	33	13	19	1	0	113	134	27	67	33	30	4	0	236	231	70
NY Rangers	35	19	13	3	0	143	130	41	35	12	19	4	0	101	135	28	70	31	32	7	0	244	265	69
Ottawa	16	12	3	1	0	72	47	25	19	8	8	3	0	66	54	19	35	20	11	4	0	138	101	44
Philadelphia	35	12	10	12	1	124	122	37	35	11	21	2	1	95	125	25	70	23	31	14	2	219	247	62
Phoenix	45	24	15	5	1	163	149	54	44	21	15	7	1	160	153	50	89	45	30	12	2	323	302	104
Pittsburgh	32	17	13	2	0	142	122	36	38	17	16	5	0	155	149	39	70	34	29	7	0	297	271	75
St. Louis	45	23	14	7	1	154	119	54	44	16	24	4	0	130	157	36	89	39	38	11	1	284	276	90
San Jose	27	16	6	4	1	95	53	37	28	17	10	1	0	102	81	35	55	33	16	5	1	197	134	72
Tampa Bay	14	9	3	2	0	54	30	20	12	3	8	1	0	32	39	7	26	12	11	3	0	86	69	27
Toronto	30	18	7	5	0	116	90	41	36	16	16	4	0	137	119	36	66	34	23	9	0	253	209	77
Vancouver	55	28	18	8	1	186	152	65	55	26	20	7	2	208	183	61	110	54	38	15	3	394	335	126
Washington	35	15	15	5	0	108	121	35	33	11	18	4	0	105	131	26	68	26	33	9	0	213	252	61
Totals	**1079**	**556**	**368**	**138**	**17**	**3932**	**3364**	**1267**	**1079**	**428**	**508**	**123**	**20**	**3523**	**3836**	**999**	**2158**	**984**	**876**	**261**	**37**	**7455**	**7200**	**2266**

Playoffs

	Series	W	L	GP	W	L	T	GF	GA	Last Mtg.	Rnd.	Result
Anaheim	1	0	1	4	0	4	0	4	16	2006	CSF	L 0-4
Boston	2	1	1	11	5	6	0	36	37	1983	DSF	L 1-3
Buffalo	2	2	0	8	6	2	0	35	27	1985	DSF	W 3-2
Carolina	2	1	1	9	4	5	0	34	35	1987	DSF	W 4-2
Chicago	2	2	0	12	8	4	0	49	28	1997	CQF	W 4-2
Dallas	4	2	2	24	14	10	0	66	62	2006	CQF	W 4-1
Detroit	5	3	2	30	17	13	0	79	76	2002	CF	L 3-4
Edmonton	2	1	1	12	7	5	0	35	30	1998	CQF	L 3-4
Florida	1	1	0	4	4	0	0	15	4	1996	F	W 4-0
Los Angeles	2	2	0	14	8	6	0	33	23	2002	CQF	W 4-3
Minnesota	1	0	1	7	3	4	0	17	16	2003	CQF	L 3-4
Montreal	5	2	3	31	14	17	0	85	105	1993	DSF	L 2-4
New Jersey	1	1	0	7	4	3	0	19	11	2001	F	W 4-3
NY Islanders	1	0	1	4	0	4	0	9	18	1982	CF	L 0-4
NY Rangers	1	0	1	6	2	4	0	19	25	1995	CQF	L 2-4
Philadelphia	2	0	2	11	4	7	0	29	39	1985	CF	L 2-4
Phoenix	1	1	0	5	4	1	0	17	10	2000	CQF	W 4-1
St. Louis	1	1	0	5	4	1	0	17	11	2001	CF	W 4-1
San Jose	3	2	1	19	10	9	0	51	52	2004	CSF	L 2-4
Vancouver	2	2	0	10	8	2	0	40	26	2001	CQF	W 4-0
Totals	**41**	**24**	**17**	**233**	**126**	**107**	**0**	**689**	**651**			

Calgary totals include Atlanta Flames, 1979-80.
Dallas totals include Minnesota North Stars, 1979-80 to 1992-93.
Phoenix totals include Winnipeg, 1979-80 to 1995-96.

Playoff Results 2007-2002

Year	Round	Opponent	Result	GF	GA
2006	CSF	Anaheim	L 0-4	4	16
	CQF	Dallas	W 4-1	18	15
2004	CSF	San Jose	L 2-4	7	14
	CQF	Dallas	W 4-1	19	10
2003	CQF	Minnesota	L 3-4	17	16
2002	CF	Detroit	L 3-4	13	22
	CSF	San Jose	W 4-3	25	21
	CQF	Los Angeles	W 4-3	16	13

Abbreviations: Round: F - Final; **CF** - conference final; **CSF** - conference semi-final; **CQF** - conference quarter-final; **DSF** - division semi-final.

Carolina totals include Hartford, 1979-80 to 1996-97.
New Jersey totals include Colorado Rockies, 1979-80 to 1981-82.

2006-07 Results

Month	Day	Opponent	Score
Oct.	4	Dallas	2-3*
	5	at Minnesota	2-3*
	8	Vancouver	3-2
	14	Edmonton	3-4
	16	Chicago	3-5
	18	at Toronto	4-1
	19	at Ottawa	2-1
	21	at Montreal	5-8
	23	Los Angeles	6-1
	25	Washington	3-5
	29	Minnesota	4-1
Nov.	1	at Columbus	5-3
	2	at St. Louis	1-4
	4	Vancouver	3-2
	7	Los Angeles	5-6
	11	at Nashville	0-1
	13	Edmonton	1-2
	15	San Jose	3-4
	17	at Columbus	3-0
	18	at Minnesota	2-1†
	20	at Dallas	4-5
	22	Anaheim	3-2†
	25	Vancouver	4-1
	28	at Calgary	2-5
	30	at Edmonton	7-3
Dec.	2	at Vancouver	1-2
	5	Columbus	0-3
	7	at San Jose	5-2
	9	at Los Angeles	4-5
	11	Carolina	5-2
	13	St. Louis	4-1
	15	Edmonton	4-1
	17	at Chicago	1-2
	19	at Edmonton	7-6
	23	Chicago	3-2
	27	Dallas	4-5
	29	St. Louis	2-4
	30	at St. Louis	0-2
Jan.	1	at Nashville	5-3
	5	Tampa Bay	4-2
	6	at Minnesota	2-1†
	9	Detroit	3-4†
	11	Calgary	3-7
	13	at Anaheim	3-2†
	15	at San Jose	1-3
	17	Phoenix	4-3
	20	Detroit	3-1
	26	Phoenix	4-5†
	28	at Detroit	1-3
	30	Nashville	4-3
Feb.	1	Minnesota	3-5
	3	Edmonton	2-3
	6	Florida	5-4*
	8	Atlanta	3-6
	11	at Dallas	5-7
	13	Anaheim	2-0
	15	at Calgary	7-5
	17	at Calgary	2-5
	18	at Vancouver	4-5
	20	Calgary	4-3
	22	Minnesota	3-4
	24	at Los Angeles	5-6†
	25	at Anaheim	3-5
	27	Columbus	3-2
Mar.	1	at Chicago	6-1
	4	at Detroit	4-3*
	6	at Boston	2-0
	7	at Buffalo	3-2
	11	at Minnesota	2-3*
	14	Calgary	3-2
	17	at Phoenix	6-3
	18	San Jose	4-3*
	21	at Edmonton	5-1
	23	at Edmonton	3-4†
	25	at Vancouver	5-4†
	27	Vancouver	0-3
	29	at Phoenix	4-3
	31	Minnesota	2-1
Apr.	3	at Calgary	4-3
	5	at Vancouver	3-1
	7	Nashville	2-4
	8	Calgary	6-3

* – Overtime † – Shootout

Entry Draft Selections 2007-1993

2007

Pick	
14	Kevin Shattenkirk
45	Colby Cohen
49	Trevor Cann
55	T.J. Galiardi
105	Brad Malone
113	Kent Patterson
135	Paul Carey
155	Jens Hellgren
195	Johan Alcen

2006

Pick	
18	Chris Stewart
51	Nigel Williams
59	Codey Burki
81	Michael Carman
110	Kevin Montgomery
201	Billy Sauer

2005

Pick	
34	Ryan Stoa
44	Paul Stastny
47	Tom Fritsche
52	Chris Durand
88	T.J. Hensick
124	Raymond Macias
166	Jason Lynch
168	Justin Mercier
222	Kyle Cumiskey

2004

Pick	
21	Wojtek Wolski
55	Victor Oreskovich
72	Denis Parshin
154	Richard Demen-Willaume
184	Derek Peltier
215	Ian Keserich
239	Brandon Yip
249	J.D. Corbin
281	Steve McClellan

2003

Pick	
63	David Liffiton
131	David Svagrovsky
146	Mark McCutcheon
163	Brad Richardson
204	Linus Videll
225	Brett Hemingway
257	Darryl Yacboski
288	David Jones

2002

Pick	
28	Jonas Johansson
61	Johnny Boychuk
94	Eric Lundberg
107	Mikko Kalteva
129	Tom Gilbert
164	Tyler Weiman
195	Taylor Christie
227	Ryan Steeves
258	Sergei Shemetov
289	Sean Collins

2001

Pick	
63	Peter Budaj
97	Danny Bois
130	Colt King
143	Frantisek Skladany
144	Cody McCormick
149	Mikko Viitanen
165	Pierre-Luc Emond
184	Scott Horvath
196	Charlie Stephens
227	Marek Svatos

2000

Pick	
14	Vaclav Nedorost
47	Jared Aulin
50	Sergei Soin
63	Agris Saviels
88	Kurt Sauer
92	Sergei Klyazmin
119	Brian Fahey
159	John-Michael Liles
189	Chris Bahen
221	Aaron Molnar
252	Darryl Bootland
266	Sean Kotary
285	Blake Ward

1999

Pick	
25	Mikhail Kuleshov
45	Martin Grenier
93	Branko Radivojevic
112	Sanny Lindstrom
122	Kristian Kovac
142	Will Magnuson
152	Jordan Krestanovich
158	Anders Lovdahl
183	Riku Hahl
212	Radim Vrbata
240	Jeff Finger

1998

Pick	
12	Alex Tanguay
17	Martin Skoula
19	Robyn Regehr
20	Scott Parker
28	Ramzi Abid
38	Philippe Sauve
53	Steve Moore
79	Evgeny Lazarev
141	K.C. Timmons
167	Alexander Riazantsev

1997

Pick	
26	Kevin Grimes
53	Graham Belak
55	Rick Berry
78	Ville Nieminen
87	Brad Larsen
133	Aaron Miskovich
161	David Aebischer
217	Doug Schmidt
243	Kyle Kidney
245	Stephen Lafleur

1996

Pick	
25	Peter Ratchuk
51	Yuri Babenko
79	Mark Parrish
98	Ben Storey
107	Randy Petruk
134	Luke Curtin
146	Brian Willsie
160	Kai Fischer
167	Dan Hinote
176	Samuel Pahlsson
188	Roman Pylner
214	Matt Scorsune
240	Justin Clark

1995

Pick	
25	Marc Denis
51	Nic Beaudoin
77	John Tripp
81	Tomi Kallio
129	Brent Johnson
155	John Cirjak
181	Dan Smith
207	Tomi Hirvonen
228	Chris George

1994

Pick	
12	Wade Belak
22	Jeffrey Kealty
35	Josef Marha
61	Sebastien Bety
72	Chris Drury
87	Milan Hejduk
113	Tony Tuzzolino
139	Nicholas Windsor
165	Calvin Elfring
191	Jay Bertsch
217	Tim Thomas
243	Chris Pittman
285	Steven Low

1993

Pick	
10	Jocelyn Thibault
14	Adam Deadmarsh
49	Ashley Buckberger
75	Bill Pierce
101	Ryan Tocher
127	Anders Myrvold
137	Nicholas Checco
153	Christian Matte
179	David Ling
205	Petr Franek
231	Vincent Auger
257	Mark Pivetz
283	John Hillman

Club Directory

Pepsi Center

Colorado Avalanche
Pepsi Center
1000 Chopper Circle
Denver, CO 80204
Phone **303/405-1100**
FAX 303/893-0614
Press Box 303/575-1926
http://avalanche.nhl.com
Capacity: 18,007

Owner & Governor	E. Stanley Kroenke
President & Alternate Governor	Pierre Lacroix
Exec. V.P., G.M. & Alternate Governor	Francois Giguere
Head Coach	Joel Quenneville
Assistant Coaches	Jacques Cloutier, Tony Granato
Goaltending Coach	Jeff Hackett
Assistant General Manager	Greg Sherman
Assistant to the Exec. V.P./General Manager	Michel Goulet
Director of Player Personnel	Brad Smith
Director of Player Development	Craig Billington
Player Development Coordinator	Steve Konowalchuk
Chief Scout	Ted Hampson
Executive Director of Hockey Administration	Charlotte Grahame
Video Coordinator	Bryan Vines
Team Services Coordinator	Erin DeGraff
Pro Scouts	Garth Joy, Terry Martin
Scouts	Anders Carlsson, Luc Gauthier, Gary Harker, Alan Hepple, Michal Krupa, Kirill Ladygin, Joni Lehto, Don Paarup, Richard Pracey, Neil Shea
Strength and Conditioning Coach	Paul Goldberg
Head Athletic Trainer	Matthew Sokolowski
Assistant Athletic Trainer	Scott Woodward
Massage Therapist	Gregorio Pradera
Head Equipment Manager	Mark Miller
Inventory Manager	Wayne Flemming
Assistant Equipment Managers	Kurt Harvey, Cliff Halstead
Communications Department	
Sr. V.P., Communications & Business Operations	Jean Martineau
Director of Communications	Damen Zier
Director of Media Services/Internet	Brendan McNicholas
Website Coordinator	Craig Stancher
Lake Erie Monsters (AHL affiliate)	
General Manager	David Oliver
Head Coach	Joe Sacco
Assistant Coach	Sylvain Lefebvre
Head Athletic Trainer	Glenn Burke
Head Equipment Manager	Terry Geer
Team Information	
Practice Facility	South Suburban Family Sports Center
Television Outlet	Altitude Sports & Entertainment Network
Radio	Altitude Radio Network (flagship: KKFN AM-950)

General Managers' History

Maurice Filion, 1979-80 to 1987-88; Martin Madden, 1988-89; Martin Madden and Maurice Filion, 1989-90; Pierre Page, 1990-91 to 1993-94; Pierre Lacroix, 1994-95 to 2005-06; Francois Giguere, 2006-07 to date.

Executive Vice President/ General Manager

FRANCOIS GIGUERE
Executive Vice President/General Manager, Colorado Avalanche.
Born in Ste-Foy, Que., June 24, 1963.

On May 24, 2006, the Colorado Avalanche announced the appointment of Francois Giguere as the club's executive vice president and general manager to lead the day-to-day operations of the club. Giguere returned to the franchise where he began his hockey tutelage over 16 years before. During that time, Giguere was involved with nearly every facet of an NHL hockey operation. Before spending five years with the Dallas Stars as assistant general manager, Giguere served as vice president of hockey operations for the Colorado Avalanche during the 2000-01 season. His roots with the organization date back to 1990 when he served as controller in the finance department with the Quebec Nordiques. In addition, he's held hockey administration (1992 to 1995), assistant GM (1995 to 2000) and VP hockey operations (2000-01) posts within the organization.

During his tenure with the Avalanche, Giguere was instrumental in developing and managing the hockey operations budget, and worked closely with Pierre Lacroix on contract negotiations, arbitration cases, player transactions and matters involving player personnel. He was also responsible for overseeing player development and player personnel staff and was the club's central liaison with its minor league hockey affiliates.

A 1985 graduate of Laval University where he obtained a degree in Administration, a license in accounting and a law certificate, Giguere worked for three years with a prominent Quebec accounting firm Caron Belanger Ernst and Young before being hired by the Nordiques as controller in 1990. His role with the Nordiques was expanded in 1992 to include hockey administration responsibilities by then general manager Pierre Page who needed additional support after Page assumed the head coaching role with the Nordiques in 1991. Pierre Lacroix named Giguere as assistant GM before the shortened 1994-95 season and he accompanied the franchise in its move to Colorado in May 1995.

Colorado's first choice in the 2004 Entry Draft, Wojtek Wolski spent his first full season in the NHL in 2006-07 and had 22 goals and 28 assists.

Key Off-Season Signings/Acquisitions

2007

June 15 • Named **Scott Howson** general manager.
28 • Named **Claude Noel** assistant coach.
July 2 • Re-signed C **Alexander Svitov** and C **Ole-Kristian Tollefsen**.
3 • Signed C **Jiri Novotny**.
5 • Signed D **Jan Hejda**.
Aug. 7 • Signed C **Kris Beech**.

Columbus Blue Jackets

2006-07 Results: 33W-42L-2OTL-5SOL 73PTS.
Fourth, Central Division

Year-by-Year Record

		Home				Road				Overall								
Season	GP	W	L	T	OL	W	L	T	OL	W	L	T	OL	GF	GA	Pts.	Finished	Playoff Result
2006-07	82	18	19	....	4	15	23	....	3	33	42	....	7	201	249	73	4th, Central Div.	Out of Playoffs
2005-06	82	23	18	....	0	12	25	....	4	35	43	....	4	223	279	74	3rd, Central Div.	Out of Playoffs
2004-05	....	....	....	....	....	....	....	....	....	....	....	....	....	....	....	....		
2003-04	82	17	18	4	2	8	27	4	2	25	45	8	4	177	238	62	4th, Central Div.	Out of Playoffs
2002-03	82	20	14	5	2	9	28	3	1	29	42	8	3	213	263	69	5th, Central Div.	Out of Playoffs
2001-02	82	14	18	5	4	8	29	3	1	22	47	8	5	164	255	57	5th, Central Div.	Out of Playoffs
2000-01	82	19	15	4	3	9	24	5	3	28	39	9	6	190	233	71	5th, Central Div.	Out of Playoffs

2007-08 Schedule

Oct.	Fri.	5	Anaheim		Sat.	5	at San Jose
	Sat.	6	at Minnesota		Tue.	8	at St. Louis
	Wed.	10	Phoenix		Fri.	11	St. Louis
	Sat.	13	at Colorado		Sat.	12	Nashville
	Wed.	17	Dallas		Tue.	15	Vancouver
	Fri.	19	at Buffalo		Thu.	17	at Phoenix
	Sun.	21	Vancouver*		Sat.	19	at Dallas*
	Tue.	23	at Chicago		Sun.	20	at Colorado
	Thu.	25	St. Louis		Tue.	22	at Dallas
	Sat.	27	San Jose*		Thu.	24	at Chicago
	Wed.	31	at Los Angeles		Tue.	29	Phoenix
Nov.	Thu.	1	at Anaheim		Thu.	31	at Nashville
	Sun.	4	St. Louis*	**Feb.**	Sat.	2	Minnesota
	Wed.	7	at Chicago		Tue.	5	Washington
	Fri.	9	at Detroit		Thu.	7	at Phoenix
	Sat.	10	at Nashville		Fri.	8	at San Jose
	Mon.	12	Nashville		Sun.	10	Los Angeles
	Wed.	14	Chicago		Wed.	13	Chicago
	Fri.	16	at St. Louis		Fri.	15	at Detroit
	Sun.	18	Detroit*		Sun.	17	at St. Louis*
	Wed.	21	Florida		Tue.	19	at Toronto
	Fri.	23	at Minnesota*		Thu.	21	at Ottawa
	Sat.	24	Detroit		Sat.	23	at Montreal
	Mon.	26	at Edmonton		Wed.	27	San Jose
	Thu.	29	at Vancouver		Fri.	29	at Vancouver
Dec.	Sat.	1	at Calgary	**Mar.**	Sun.	2	at Edmonton
	Mon.	3	Dallas		Tue.	4	at Calgary
	Wed.	5	Colorado		Fri.	7	Edmonton
	Sat.	8	Minnesota		Sun.	9	Tampa Bay*
	Mon.	10	Anaheim		Fri.	14	Chicago
	Wed.	12	Colorado		Sun.	16	Detroit*
	Sat.	15	at Boston		Tue.	18	Calgary
	Tue.	18	Calgary		Wed.	19	at Detroit
	Fri.	21	Los Angeles		Sat.	22	Detroit
	Sun.	23	Nashville*		Tue.	25	at Nashville
	Wed.	26	Atlanta		Wed.	26	Chicago
	Thu.	27	at Nashville		Fri.	28	Nashville
	Sat.	29	Carolina		Sun.	30	at Chicago
	Mon.	31	Edmonton	**Apr.**	Thu.	3	at Detroit
Jan.	Wed.	2	at Anaheim		Sat.	5	at St. Louis*
	Thu.	3	at Los Angeles		Sun.	6	St. Louis*

* Denotes afternoon game.

Fredrik Modin scored 22 goals for the Blue Jackets during his first season in Columbus. Only Rick Nash scored more.

CENTRAL DIVISION
8th NHL Season

Franchise date: June 25, 1997

2007-08 Player Personnel

FORWARDS	HT	WT	S	Place of Birth	*Age	2006-07 Club
BEECH, Kris	6-3	211	L	Salmon Arm, B.C.	26	Washington
BRASSARD, Derick	6-1	180	L	Hull, Que.	20	Drummondville
BRULE, Gilbert	5-10	180	R	Edmonton, Alta.	20	Columbus
CHIMERA, Jason	6-2	206	L	Edmonton, Alta.	28	Columbus
FEDOROV, Sergei	6-2	205	L	Pskov, USSR	37	Columbus
FRITSCHE, Dan	6-1	202	R	Parma, OH	22	Columbus
GLENCROSS, Curtis	6-1	195	L	Kindersley, Sask.	24	Ana-Port (AHL)-CBJ-Syr
GOERTZEN, Steven	6-2	216	R	Stony Plain, Alta.	23	Columbus-Syracuse
KONOPKA, Zenon	6-1	213	L	Niagara Falls, Ont.	26	Togliatti-Port (AHL)-CBJ-Syr
LINDSTROM, Joakim	6-0	187	L	Skelleftea, Sweden	23	Columbus-Syracuse
MacKENZIE, Derek	5-11	185	L	Sudbury, Ont.	26	Atlanta-Chicago (AHL)
MALHOTRA, Manny	6-2	215	L	Mississauga, Ont.	27	Columbus
MODIN, Fredrik	6-4	220	L	Sundsvall, Sweden	32	Columbus
NASH, Rick	6-4	215	L	Brampton, Ont.	23	Columbus
NOVOTNY, Jiri	6-4	194	R	Pelhrimov, Czech.	24	Buffalo-Washington
PICARD, Alexandre	6-2	190	L	Les Saules, Que.	21	Columbus-Syracuse
PLATT, Geoff	5-9	175	L	Toronto, Ont.	22	Columbus-Syracuse
SHELLEY, Jody	6-4	230	L	Thompson, Man.	31	Columbus
SVITOV, Alexander	6-3	228	L	Omsk, USSR	24	Columbus
VYBORNY, David	5-10	189	L	Jihlava, Czech.	32	Columbus
ZHERDEV, Nikolai	6-2	197	R	Kiev, USSR	22	Mytischi-Columbus
DEFENSEMEN						
BROOKBANK, Sheldon	6-2	215	R	Lanigan, Sask.	26	Nashville-Milwaukee
CAMPBELL, Darcy	6-1	180	L	Airdrie, Alta.	23	Alaska-Columbus
FOOTE, Adam	6-2	224	R	Toronto, Ont.	36	Columbus
HAINSEY, Ron	6-3	211	L	Bolton, CT	26	Columbus
HEJDA, Jan	6-3	209	L	Prague, Czech.	29	Edmonton-Hamilton
KLESLA, Rostislav	6-3	216	L	Novy Jicin, Czech.	25	Columbus
METHOT, Marc	6-3	224	L	Ottawa, Ont.	22	Columbus-Syracuse
RUSSELL, Kris	5-10	167	L	Caroline, Alta.	20	Medicine Hat
SMITH, Dan	6-2	200	L	Fernie, B.C.	30	Grand Rapids
TOLLEFSEN, Ole-Kristian	6-2	211	L	Oslo, Norway	23	Columbus
WESTCOTT, Duvie	5-11	197	R	Winnipeg, Man.	29	Columbus

GOALTENDERS	HT	WT	C	Place of Birth	*Age	2006-07 Club
LECLAIRE, Pascal	6-2	200	L	Repentigny, Que.	24	Columbus
NORRENA, Fredrik	6-0	189	L	Pietarsaari, Finland	33	Columbus
POPPERLE, Tomas	6-1	187	L	Broumov, Czech.	22	Columbus-Syracuse

* – Age at start of 2007-08 season

2006-07 Scoring

* – rookie

Regular Season

Pos	#	Player	Team	GP	G	A	Pts	+/-	PIM	PP	SH	GW	S	%
R	9	David Vyborny	CBJ	82	16	48	64	6	60	6	0	2	158	10.1
L	61	Rick Nash	CBJ	75	27	30	57	–8	73	9	1	5	228	11.8
L	33	Fredrik Modin	CBJ	79	22	20	42	–3	50	6	0	4	220	10.0
C	91	Sergei Fedorov	CBJ	73	18	24	42	–7	56	7	2	2	163	11.0
L	25	Jason Chimera	CBJ	82	15	21	36	2	91	2	2	2	151	9.9
D	6	Ron Hainsey	CBJ	80	9	25	34	–19	69	7	0	0	136	6.6
R	13	Nikolai Zherdev	CBJ	71	10	22	32	–19	26	3	0	2	164	6.1
C	49	Dan Fritsche	CBJ	59	12	15	27	3	35	5	1	4	81	14.8
C	27	Manny Malhotra	CBJ	82	9	16	25	–8	76	2	0	3	109	8.3
D	2	Anders Eriksson	CBJ	79	0	23	23	12	46	0	0	0	78	0.0
D	97	Rostislav Klesla	CBJ	75	9	13	22	–13	105	2	0	0	159	5.7
C	17	* Gilbert Brule	CBJ	78	9	10	19	–21	28	3	0	0	98	9.2
C	16	Alexander Svitov	CBJ	76	7	11	18	–10	145	1	0	2	83	8.4
D	52	Adam Foote	CBJ	59	3	9	12	–17	71	2	0	0	78	3.8
D	10	Duvie Westcott	CBJ	23	4	6	10	–13	18	2	0	1	34	11.8
D	44	Aaron Johnson	CBJ	61	3	7	10	–9	38	0	0	0	52	5.8
C	47	* Geoff Platt	CBJ	26	4	5	9	1	10	0	0	0	40	10.0
D	55	* Ole-Kristian Tollefs	CBJ	70	2	3	5	2	123	1	0	0	39	5.1
D	48	* Marc Methot	CBJ	20	0	4	4	5	12	0	0	0	11	0.0
D	4	Bryan Berard	CBJ	11	0	3	3	–4	8	0	0	0	22	0.0
D	23	Derrick Walser	CBJ	9	2	0	2	–1	0	2	0	0	10	20.0
L	40	Jaroslav Balastik	CBJ	8	1	1	2	–3	4	1	0	0	6	16.7
L	45	Jody Shelley	CBJ	72	1	1	2	–6	125	0	0	0	32	3.1
R	37	Joe Motzko	CBJ	7	1	0	1	0	0	0	0	0	10	10.0
C	38	* Joakim Lindstrom	CBJ	9	1	0	1	–3	4	0	0	0	9	11.1
L	20	* Curtis Glencross	ANA	2	1	0	1	–1	2	0	0	0	5	20.0
			CBJ	7	0	0	0	–4	0	0	0	0	3	0.0
			TOTAL	9	1	0	1	–5	2	0	0	0	8	12.5
L	19	* Alexandre Picard	CBJ	23	0	1	1	–3	6	0	0	0	20	0.0
D	37	* Darcy Campbell	CBJ	1	0	0	0	0	0	0	0	0	0	0.0
D	46	* Filip Novak	CBJ	6	0	0	0	1	2	0	0	0	3	0.0
C	28	Zenon Konopka	CBJ	6	0	0	0	–2	20	0	0	0	2	0.0
R	39	Steven Goertzen	CBJ	7	0	0	0	0	10	0	0	0	1	0.0

Goaltending

No.	Goaltender	GPI	Mins	Avg	W	L	OT	EN	SO	GA	SA	S%	G	A	PIM
1	* Tomas Popperle	2	45	1.33	0	0	0	0	0	1	14	.929	0	0	0
30	Fredrik Norrena	55	2952	2.78	24	23	3	4	3	137	1420	.904	0	0	6
31	Pascal Leclaire	24	1315	2.97	6	15	2	1	1	65	629	.897	0	0	2
35	Ty Conklin	11	491	3.30	2	3	2	0	0	27	210	.871	0	0	0
35	Brian Boucher	3	142	3.80	1	1	0	0	0	9	67	.866	0	0	0
	Totals	**82**	**4983**	**2.94**	**33**	**42**	**7**	**5**	**4**	**244**	**2345**	**.896**			

Coach

KEN HITCHCOCK

Coach, Columbus Blue Jackets. Born in Edmonton, Alta., December 17, 1951.

Ken Hitchcock was named head coach of the Columbus Blue Jackets on November 22, 2006. In eight full seasons behind the bench before arriving in Columbus, Hitchcock led his teams to six division titles (Dallas, Central Division: 1996 to 2001; Philadelphia, Atlantic Division: 2003-04) and had a pair of second place finishes while recording at least 40 wins and 100 points in each of those campaigns. He also led his teams to a 66-51 record in the Stanley Cup playoffs, including a 16-7 mark in 1998-99 when he guided the Dallas Stars to the Stanley Cup championship.

Hitchcock began his professional coaching career as an assistant coach with the Flyers from 1990 to 1993 before spending two-plus seasons as the head coach of the Kalamazoo Wings/Michigan K-Wings, International Hockey League affiliate of the Dallas Stars. He took over as head coach of the Stars midway through the 1995-96 season and in his first full season at the helm led them to the Central Division title. That year, Dallas became just the ninth team in NHL history to go from last place to first place in one season. The club's 38-point improvement from 66 to 104 was tied for the fifth-best in league history. He holds Stars franchise records for career wins (277), playoff wins (47), regular-season winning percentage (.610) and playoff winning percentage (.588) and in 1998-99 led the club to franchise single season records for wins, points and highest winning percentage with a 51-19-12 record.

On May 14, 2002, Hitchcock was named Flyers head coach and led the club to three-straight 100-point seasons, capturing the Atlantic Division title in 2003-04 and also advanced to the Eastern Conference Finals that year. On March 21, 2006, Hitchcock guided the Flyers to a 2-1 win over New Jersey, becoming the fifth-fastest coach in NHL history to record 400 wins (736 games). The Edmonton, Alberta native has represented Canada at numerous international competitions, winning gold medals as an assistant/associate coach at the 2002 Salt Lake City Olympics, the 2004 World Cup of Hockey, the 2002 World Championship and the 1987 World Junior Championship. Prior to joining the professional ranks, Hitchcock was one of the winningest coaches in the history of the Western Hockey League with the Kamloops Blazers.

Coaching History

Dave King, 2000-01, 2001-02; Dave King and Doug MacLean, 2002-03; Doug MacLean and Gerard Gallant, 2003-04; Gerard Gallant, 2004-05, 2005-06; Gerard Gallant, Gary Agnew and Ken Hitchcock, 2006-07; Ken Hitchcock, 2007-08.

Coaching Record

		Regular Season				Playoffs		
Season	Team	Games	W	L	O/T	Games	W	L
1984-85	Kamloops (WHL)	71	52	17	2	15	10	5
1985-86	Kamloops (WHL)	72	49	19	4	16	14	2
1986-87	Kamloops (WHL)	72	55	14	3	13	8	5
1987-88	Kamloops (WHL)	72	45	26	1	18	12	6
1988-89	Kamloops (WHL)	72	34	33	5	16	8	8
1989-90	Kamloops (WHL)	72	56	16	0	17	14	3
1993-94	Kalamazoo (IHL)	81	48	26	7	5	1	4
1994-95	Kalamazoo (IHL)	81	43	24	14	16	10	6
1995-96	Michigan (IHL)	40	19	10	11	....	....	....
	Dallas (NHL)	**43**	**15**	**23**	**5**	....	....	....
1996-97	**Dallas (NHL)**	**82**	**48**	**26**	**8**	**7**	**3**	**4**
1997-98	**Dallas (NHL)**	**82**	**49**	**22**	**11**	**17**	**10**	**7**
1998-99*	**Dallas (NHL)**	**82**	**51**	**19**	**12**	**23**	**16**	**7**
1999-2000	**Dallas (NHL)**	**82**	**43**	**29**	**10**	**23**	**14**	**9**
2000-01	**Dallas (NHL)**	**82**	**48**	**26**	**8**	**10**	**4**	**6**
2001-02	**Dallas (NHL)**	**50**	**23**	**21**	**6**	....	....	....
2002-03	**Philadelphia (NHL)**	**82**	**45**	**24**	**13**	**13**	**6**	**7**
2003-04	**Philadelphia (NHL)**	**82**	**40**	**27**	**15**	**18**	**11**	**7**
2004-05	**Philadelphia (NHL)**				Season Cancelled			
2005-06	**Philadelphia (NHL)**	**82**	**45**	**26**	**11**	**6**	**2**	**4**
2006-07	**Philadelphia (NHL)**	**8**	**1**	**6**	**1**	....	....	....
	Columbus (NHL)	**62**	**28**	**29**	**5**	....	....	....
	NHL Totals	**749**	**407**	**243**	**99**	**117**	**66**	**51**

* Stanley Cup win.

Club Records

Team

(Figures in brackets for season records are games played.)

Most Points .... 74 — 2005-06 (82)
Most Wins .... 35 — 2005-06 (82)
Most Ties .... 9 — 2000-01 (82)
Most Losses .... 47 — 2001-02 (82)
Most Goals .... 223 — 2005-06 (82)
Most Goals Against .... 279 — 2005-06 (82)
Fewest Points .... 57 — 2001-02 (82)
Fewest Wins .... 22 — 2001-02 (82)
Fewest Ties .... 8 — 2001-02 (82), 2002-03 (82), 2003-04 (82)
Fewest Losses .... 39 — 2000-01 (82)
Fewest Goals .... 164 — 2001-02 (82)
Fewest Goals Against .... 233 — 2000-01 (82)
Longest Winning Streak
Overall .... 6 — Mar. 24-Apr. 3/06
Home .... 5 — Jan. 20-Feb. 8/06
Away .... 4 — Dec. 2-12/06
Longest Undefeated Streak
Overall .... 6 — Mar. 24-Apr. 3/06 (6 wins)
Home .... 6 — Jan. 20-Feb. 12/03 (4 wins, 2 ties)
Away .... 4 — Jan. 3-11/03 (3 wins, 1 tie), Dec. 2-12/06 (4 wins)
Longest Losing Streak
Overall .... 8 — Nov. 17-Dec. 3/00, Mar. 3-18/04
Home .... 6 — Oct. 12-Nov. 9/01
Away .... 11 — Mar. 25-Oct. 29/02
Longest Winless Streak
Overall .... 9 — Dec. 4-23/03 (8 losses, 1 tie)
Home .... 8 — Oct. 4-Nov. 9/01 (6 losses, 2 ties), Dec. 4-31/03 (7 losses, 1 tie)
Away .... 14 — Oct. 9-Dec. 23/03 (13 losses, 1 tie)
Most Shutouts, Season .... 5 — 2002-03 (82), 2003-04 (82)
Most PIM, Season .... 1,505 — 2002-03 (82)
Most Goals, Game .... 7 — Three times

Individual

Most Seasons .... 6 — Rostislav Klesla, Jody Shelley, David Vyborny
Most Games .... 477 — David Vyborny
Most Goals, Career .... 116 — Rick Nash
Most Assists, Career .... 185 — David Vyborny
Most Points, Career .... 291 — David Vyborny (106G, 185A)
Most PIM, Career .... 981 — Jody Shelley
Most Shutouts, Career .... 12 — Marc Denis
Longest Consecutive Games Streak .... 194 — David Vyborny (Oct. 17/02 to Dec. 20/05)
Most Goals, Season .... 41 — Rick Nash (2003-04)
Most Assists, Season .... 52 — Ray Whitney (2002-03)
Most Points, Season .... 76 — Ray Whitney (2002-03; 24G, 52A)
Most PIM, Season .... 249 — Jody Shelley (2002-03)
Most Points, Defenseman, Season .... 45 — Jaroslav Spacek (2002-03; 9G, 36A)
Most Points, Center, Season .... 68 — Andrew Cassels (2002-03; 20G, 48A)
Most Points, Right Wing, Season .... 65 — David Vyborny (2005-06; 22G, 43A)
Most Points, Left Wing, Season .... 76 — Ray Whitney (2002-03; 24G, 52A)
Most Points, Rookie, Season .... 39 — Rick Nash (2002-03; 17G, 22A)
Most Shutouts, Season .... 5 — Marc Denis (2002-03, 2003-04)
Most Goals, Game .... 4 — Geoff Sanderson (Jan. 11/03)
Most Assists, Game .... 5 — Espen Knutsen (Mar. 24/01)
Most Points, Game .... 5 — Espen Knutsen (Mar. 24/01; 5A), Geoff Sanderson (Jan. 11/03; 4G, 1A), Andrew Cassels (Jan. 11/03; 1G, 4A), David Vyborny (Feb. 28/04; 1G, 4A)

Gilbert Brule celebrates a goal with David Vyborny and Rick Nash. Brule was picked sixth overall in the 2005 NHL Entry Draft and spent his first full season in the NHL in 2006-07.

Captains' History

Lyle Odelein, 2000-01, 2001-02; Ray Whitney, 2002-03; Luke Richardson, 2003-04; Luke Richardson and Adam Foote, 2005-06; Adam Foote, 2006-07 to date.

2006-07 Results

Oct.	6	Vancouver	2-3*		6	at San Jose	2-5
	7	at Chicago	5-4		9	St. Louis	3-4†
	9	Phoenix	5-1		12	at Nashville	0-2
	14	at Minnesota	0-5		13	Nashville	1-4
	20	Toronto	2-4		16	at Chicago	5-4*
	21	at Pittsburgh	3-5		18	at Nashville	0-4
	23	San Jose	0-3		19	Detroit	3-1
	27	Los Angeles	2-0		26	Buffalo	3-2
	28	at New Jersey	0-1		27	Minnesota	3-2
Nov.	1	Colorado	3-5		30	at Vancouver	3-2†
	3	Calgary	5-4†		31	at Edmonton	2-5
	4	at Detroit	1-4	Feb.	2	at Calgary	2-6
	9	at St. Louis	4-2		6	Phoenix	0-3
	10	Edmonton	1-4		8	Calgary	2-1
	12	at Chicago	0-1		11	Chicago	4-5
	15	Nashville	4-5		14	St. Louis	2-4
	17	Colorado	0-3		16	San Jose	3-0
	18	at Nashville	2-4		18	Montreal	2-3
	20	Nashville	1-3		20	at St. Louis	4-5†
	22	St. Louis	3-4†		22	Edmonton	0-4
	24	at Philadelphia	2-3		24	at NY Rangers	3-2
	25	Minnesota	5-3		25	Nashville	3-4†
	28	at Vancouver	0-1		27	at Colorado	2-3
Dec.	1	at Calgary	1-2	Mar.	2	at Dallas	3-2†
	2	at Edmonton	4-0		3	at Phoenix	4-3
	5	at Colorado	3-0		7	Los Angeles	3-2*
	9	at St. Louis	5-1		9	Dallas	0-3
	10	Ottawa	6-2		10	at Nashville	1-2
	12	at Dallas	3-1		14	at Anaheim	5-4†
	14	at Phoenix	4-5†		16	at San Jose	0-3
	16	Chicago	4-6		17	at Los Angeles	3-5
	18	Detroit	4-3		20	Chicago	5-2
	20	at Detroit	0-5		22	at Detroit	2-1†
	22	Vancouver	3-2		25	St. Louis	4-1
	23	at NY Islanders	0-4		27	at St. Louis	4-1
	26	Boston	5-4*		29	Anaheim	2-5
	28	Detroit	4-7		30	at Chicago	1-3
	29	at Minnesota	3-4*	Apr.	1	Detroit	1-4
	31	Chicago	3-1		3	at Detroit	0-3
Jan.	3	at Los Angeles	0-3		5	Dallas	2-1*
	5	at Anaheim	4-3		7	Anaheim	3-4

* – Overtime † – Shootout

All-time Record vs. Other Clubs

Regular Season

	At Home								On Road								Total							
	GP	W	L	T	OL	GF	GA	PTS	GP	W	L	T	OL	GF	GA	PTS	GP	W	L	T	OL	GF	GA	PTS
Anaheim	12	7	5	0	0	32	28	14	12	5	5	1	1	31	37	12	24	12	10	1	1	63	65	26
Atlanta	4	2	2	0	0	12	11	4	4	1	3	0	0	8	10	2	8	3	5	0	0	20	21	6
Boston	4	2	2	0	0	8	18	4	2	1	1	0	0	7	8	2	6	3	3	0	0	15	26	6
Buffalo	3	2	0	1	0	8	6	5	4	2	2	0	0	9	13	4	7	4	2	1	0	17	19	9
Calgary	12	9	2	0	1	37	26	19	12	4	8	0	0	24	35	8	24	13	10	0	1	61	61	27
Carolina	3	1	2	0	0	6	9	2	5	1	4	0	0	12	15	2	8	2	6	0	0	18	24	4
Chicago	19	11	7	1	0	63	58	23	18	6	11	1	0	37	53	13	37	17	18	2	0	100	111	36
Colorado	12	1	10	1	0	17	48	3	12	1	10	0	1	17	45	3	24	2	20	1	1	34	93	6
Dallas	12	4	8	0	0	29	39	8	12	2	9	0	1	20	38	5	24	6	17	0	1	49	77	13
Detroit	19	4	10	1	4	37	61	13	18	4	12	0	2	40	71	10	37	8	22	1	6	77	132	23
Edmonton	12	2	7	3	0	26	41	7	12	3	8	0	1	26	42	7	24	5	15	3	1	52	83	14
Florida	2	1	1	0	0	4	4	2	4	2	2	0	0	12	13	4	6	3	3	0	0	16	17	6
Los Angeles	12	8	4	0	0	35	40	16	12	3	8	1	0	22	32	7	24	11	12	1	0	57	72	23
Minnesota	11	9	1	1	0	33	16	19	12	3	7	0	2	23	39	8	23	12	8	1	2	56	55	27
Montreal	2	0	2	0	0	3	6	0	4	2	1	1	0	6	6	5	6	2	3	1	0	9	12	5
Nashville	18	7	9	0	2	45	57	16	19	4	14	1	0	37	61	9	37	11	23	1	2	82	118	25
New Jersey	5	3	2	0	0	16	15	6	3	0	2	1	0	4	6	1	8	3	4	1	0	20	21	7
NY Islanders	5	4	0	1	0	17	10	9	3	2	1	0	0	11	11	4	8	6	1	1	0	28	21	13
NY Rangers	5	4	1	0	0	20	10	8	3	1	1	1	0	8	9	3	8	5	2	1	0	28	19	11
Ottawa	3	1	1	1	0	13	11	3	3	0	2	1	0	6	12	1	6	1	3	2	0	19	23	4
Philadelphia	4	0	2	2	0	7	10	2	3	0	2	1	0	5	10	1	7	0	4	3	0	12	20	3
Phoenix	12	6	5	1	0	31	27	13	12	2	6	3	1	29	39	8	24	8	11	4	1	60	66	21
Pittsburgh	4	2	0	0	2	16	10	6	4	1	3	0	0	12	17	2	8	3	3	0	2	28	27	8
St. Louis	18	8	5	2	3	45	46	21	19	6	9	1	3	51	66	16	37	14	14	3	6	96	112	37
San Jose	12	6	5	0	1	32	25	13	12	1	10	0	1	18	50	3	24	7	15	0	2	50	75	16
Tampa Bay	3	1	1	1	0	5	4	3	4	1	3	0	0	5	9	2	7	2	4	1	0	10	13	5
Toronto	2	1	1	0	0	6	7	2	3	0	2	1	0	4	10	1	5	1	3	1	0	10	17	3
Vancouver	12	4	5	2	1	30	42	11	12	3	8	0	1	33	49	7	24	7	13	2	2	63	91	18
Washington	4	1	2	0	1	11	15	3	3	0	2	1	0	7	11	1	7	1	4	1	1	18	26	4
Totals	**246**	**111**	**102**	**18**	**15**	**644**	**700**	**255**	**246**	**61**	**156**	**15**	**14**	**524**	**817**	**151**	**492**	**172**	**258**	**33**	**29**	**1168**	**1517**	**406**

Entry Draft Selections 2007-2000

2007

Pick	
7	Jakub Voracek
37	Stefan Legein
53	Will Weber
68	Jake Hansen
94	Maxim Mayorov
158	Allen York
211	Trent Vogelhuber

2006

Pick	
6	Derick Brassard
69	Steve Mason
85	Tommy Sestito
113	Ben Wright
129	Robert Nyholm
136	Nick Sucharski
142	Maxime Frechette
159	Jesse Dudas
189	Derek Dorsett
194	Matt Marquardt

2005

Pick	
6	Gilbert Brule
55	Adam McQuaid
67	Kris Russell
101	Jared Boll
131	Tomas Popperle
177	Derek Reinhart
189	Kirill Starkov
201	Trevor Hendrikx

2004

Pick	
8	Alexandre Picard
46	Adam Pineault
59	Kyle Wharton
93	Dan Lacosta
96	Andrey Plekhanov
133	Petr Pohl
167	Rob Page
190	Lennart Petrell
198	Justin Vienneau
231	Brian Mcguirk
233	Matt Greer
271	Grant Clitsome

2003

Pick	
4	Nikolai Zherdev
46	Dan Fritsche
71	Dmitry Kosmachev
103	Kevin Jarman
104	Philippe Dupuis
138	Arsi Piispanen
168	Marc Methot
200	Alexander Guskov
233	Mathieu Gravel
283	Trevor Hendrikx

2002

Pick	
1	Rick Nash
41	Joakim Lindstrom
65	Ole-Kristian Tollefsen
96	Jeff Genovy
98	Ivan Tkachenko
119	Jekabs Redlihs
133	Lasse Pirjeta
168	Tim Konsorada
184	Jaroslav Balastik
199	Greg Mauldin
225	Steven Goertzen
231	Jaroslav Kracik
263	Sergei Mozyakin

2001

Pick	
8	Pascal Leclaire
38	Tim Jackman
53	Kiel McLeod
85	Aaron Johnson
87	Per Mars
141	Cole Jarrett
173	Justin Aikins
187	Artem Vostrikov
204	Raffaele Sannitz
236	Ryan Bowness
242	Andrew Murray

2000

Pick	
4	Rostislav Klesla
69	Ben Knopp
133	Petteri Nummelin
138	Scott Heffernan
150	Tyler Kolarik
169	Shane Bendera
200	Janne Jokila
231	Peter Zingoni
278	Martin Paroulek
286	Andrej Nedorost
292	Louis Mandeville

General Managers' History

Doug MacLean, 2000-01 to 2006-07; Scott Howson, 2007-08.

General Manager

SCOTT HOWSON
General Manager, Columbus Blue Jackets.
Born in Toronto, Ont., April 9, 1960.

The Columbus Blue Jackets announced the signing of Scott Howson as the second general manager in franchise history on June 15, 2007. Howson joins the Blue Jackets after spending seven years with the Edmonton Oilers. He joined the Oilers in June 2000 as assistant to the general manager and was named assistant general manager a year later. In that role, he was responsible for all aspects of the club's hockey administration, including player contracts, personnel decisions, the collective bargaining agreement, its American Hockey League affiliates and the salary cap.

During his six seasons with the Oilers, the club posted five-straight winning campaigns from 2000 to 2006, averaged 37 wins and 89 points per season, topped 90 points four times and advanced to the 2006 Stanley Cup Finals, where they were defeated in seven games by the Carolina Hurricanes.

Prior to his arrival in Edmonton, Howson spent six years with the club's AHL affiliates. As general manager of the Cape Breton Oilers from 1994 1o 1996, he oversaw the franchise's move to Hamilton in 1996 and was the Bulldogs' general manager from 1996 to 2000. During that time, he led Hamilton to a pair of berths in the Calder Cup Finals (1997, 2003) and a conference semifinals appearance in 2002.

Howson played three seasons in the Ontario Hockey League as a forward with the Kingston Canadiens from 1978 to 1981, serving as team captain and earning OHL All-Star honors. Following his junior career, he signed a free agent contract with the New York Islanders and spent the next five years playing at various levels throughout the organization.

During his rookie season in 1981-82, he was named the International Hockey League's rookie of the year after registering 55 goals and 65 assists for 120 points in 71 games with the Toledo Goaldiggers. He was the league's second-leading scorer that year and helped Toledo capture the league championship. Howson also won a Central Hockey League title with the Indianapolis Checkers in 1982-83. He made his NHL debut with the Islanders during the 1984-85 season and tallied 4 goals and one assist in eight games. He added a goal and two assists in 10 games the following season before retiring as a player at the end of the 1985-86 season. Howson received his bachelor's degree in 1987 from York University in Toronto and is a 1990 graduate of the university's Osgoode Hall Law School.

Club Directory

Nationwide Arena

Columbus Blue Jackets
Nationwide Arena
200 W. Nationwide Blvd.
Columbus, Ohio 43215
Phone **614/246-4625**
FAX 614/246-4007
www.BlueJackets.com
Capacity: 18,144

Ownership
Majority Owner/Governor . . . . . John H. McConnell
Alternate Governor . . . . . John P. McConnell

Executive Staff
President/Alternate Governor . . . . . Mike Priest
Sr. Vice President of Business Operations . . . . . Larry Hoepfner
Vice President of Ticketing . . . . . David Paitson
Vice President of Corporate Development . . . . . Paul D'Aiuto
Vice President of Marketing . . . . . Marc Gregory
Vice President of Public Relations . . . . . Todd Sharrock
General Counsel . . . . . Greg Kirstein
Chief Financial Officer . . . . . T.J. LaMendola

Hockey Operations
General Manager . . . . . Scott Howson
Assistant General Manager . . . . . Jim Clark
Assistant to the General Manager . . . . . Chris MacFarland
Director of Player Personnel . . . . . Don Boyd
Head Coach . . . . . Ken Hitchcock
Assistant Coaches . . . . . Gary Agnew, Gord Murphy, Claude Noel
Goaltending Coach . . . . . Clint Malarchuk
Development Coach . . . . . Tyler Wright
Video Coordinator . . . . . Dan Singleton
Director of Pro Scouting . . . . . Bob Strumm
Director of Amateur Scouting . . . . . Paul Castron
Amateur Scouts . . . . . Brian Bates, Sam McMaster, John Williams
Pro Scout . . . . . Peter Dineen
European Scout . . . . . Kjell Larsson
Regional Scouts . . . . . John McNamara, Bryan Raymond, Rob Riley, Andrew Shaw, Artem Telepin, Milan Tichy
Manager of Team Services . . . . . Jim Rankin
Hockey Operations Coordinator . . . . . Julie Uhler
Head Athletic Trainer . . . . . Chris Mizer
Strength & Conditioning Coach . . . . . Barry Brennan
Massage Therapist . . . . . Chris Hannan
Equipment Manager . . . . . Tim LeRoy
Assistant Equipment Manager . . . . . Jamie Healy
Equipment Assistant . . . . . Jason Stypinski

Business Operations
Director of Partnership Marketing . . . . . Cheri Wiles
Director of Communications . . . . . Karen Davis
Director of Event Presentation/Production . . . . . Kimberly Kershaw
Director of Marketing & Fan Development . . . . . J.D. Kershaw
Director of Community Development . . . . . Wendy Bradshaw
Director of Creative Services . . . . . Jason Rothwell
Director of Human Resources . . . . . Kelley Walton
Director of Retail Operations . . . . . Chris Weller
Asst. Dir., Strategic Partnership Marketing . . . . . Angela Yock
Senior Graphic Designer . . . . . Will Bennett
Graphic Designer . . . . . James Korte
Manager of Communications . . . . . Ryan Holtmann
Manager of Multimedia . . . . . Ryan Mulcrone
Communications Coordinator . . . . . Brian Dancel
Manager of Partnership Marketing . . . . . Michelle Fogle
Business Development Analyst . . . . . Craig Smith
Corporate Development Sr. Account Executive . . . . Steve Sefner
Corporate Development Account Executives . . . . . Jerry Angel, Brian Laurent, A.J. Poole
Premium Sales Manager . . . . . Joe Jerele
Premium Seating Manager . . . . . Amanda Horning
Managers of Production . . . . . David Bakalik, David Traube
Manager of Event Presentation . . . . . Lynn Truitt
Payroll Coordinator . . . . . Christine Parthemore
Manager of Human Resources . . . . . Jennifer Holtmann
Manager of Fan Development . . . . . Joel Siegman
Manager of Marketing . . . . . Nate Ferrall
Manager of Marketing, Youth & Amateur Hockey . . Gordy Haggard
Marketing Coordinator . . . . . Joe DiPietro
Manager of Community Development . . . . . Kate Furman
Mascot Coordinator . . . . . Jason Zumpano
Retail Operations Warehouse Manager . . . . . Rick Matteo
Retail Manager . . . . . Mark Karr
Retail Manager, Mall at Tuttle Crossing . . . . . Lisa Fricker
Retail Manager, Chiller locations . . . . . Pam Morlan
Retail Associates . . . . . Matt Baker, Nate Gabay, Brent Heinisch, Stephen Pawlak
Administrative Asst., Marketing/Ticketing . . . . . Laurie Sanders
Administrative Asst., Legal . . . . . Rachel Phillips
Paralegal . . . . . Ken Erney

Finance
Controller . . . . . Jeff Abbot
Assistant Controller . . . . . Jeremy Manly
Staff Accountant . . . . . Nora Ludwig
Accounts Payable Coordinator . . . . . Beth Carpenter
Accounts Payable Coordinator . . . . . Lindsay Wohlheter
Director of Information Technology . . . . . Jim Connolly
Executive Assistant . . . . . Rachel Mayfield
Receptionist . . . . . Beth Trexler

Ticket Operations
Director of Ticket Operations . . . . . Mark Morris
Director of Season Ticket Sales . . . . . Joseph Cote
Director of Group Sales . . . . . Joe Ondrejko
Inside Sales Manager . . . . . Cory Rowe
Group Sales Account Executives . . . . Clint Heiber, Andy Hire, Matt McKay, Fabyan Saxe, Ray Strain, Heather Sweeney, Jennifer Watts
Season Ticket Account Executives . . . Kevin Dunigan, Zach Guerrieri, Genevieve Schrier, Joe Streck

Broadcasting
Director of Broadcasting . . . . . Russ Mollohan
FSN Ohio Play-by-Play/Color . . . . . Jeff Rimer/Danny Gare
Radio Play-by-Play/Color . . . . . George Matthews, Bill Davidge

Key Off-Season Signings/Acquisitions

2007

July 1 • Re-signed D **Sergei Zubov**.
6 • Signed LW **Brad Winchester**.
9 • Signed LW **Todd Fedoruk**.
12 • Re-signed C **Mike Ribeiro** and C **Joel Lundqvist**.
18 • Signed 2006 1st-round pick (27th overall), D **Ivan Vishnevskiy**.
30 • RW **Antti Miettinen** awarded one-year contract in arbitration.

Dallas Stars

2006-07 Results: 50W-25L-3OTL-4SOL 107PTS.
Third, Pacific Division

The Stars named Brenden Morrow their new captain prior to the start of the 2006-07 season. A wrist injury limited him to just 40 games, but he still managed 16 goals and 15 assists.

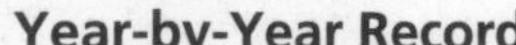

2007-08 Schedule

Oct.	Wed.	3	at Colorado
	Fri.	5	Boston
	Sat.	6	at Nashville
	Wed.	10	Los Angeles
	Fri.	12	Calgary
	Sat.	13	at Chicago
	Wed.	17	at Columbus
	Sat.	20	Anaheim
	Thu.	25	at Los Angeles
	Sat.	27	at Phoenix
	Mon.	29	San Jose
	Wed.	31	Chicago
Nov.	Fri.	2	Phoenix
	Mon.	5	at Anaheim
	Wed.	7	at San Jose
	Thu.	8	at Phoenix
	Sat.	10	at Los Angeles
	Wed.	14	San Jose
	Fri.	16	Colorado
	Mon.	19	Los Angeles
	Wed.	21	Anaheim
	Fri.	23	Toronto
	Sun.	25	at NY Rangers*
	Mon.	26	at NY Islanders
	Wed.	28	at New Jersey
	Fri.	30	at Pittsburgh
Dec.	Sat.	1	at Philadelphia
	Mon.	3	at Columbus
	Wed.	5	San Jose
	Fri.	7	Ottawa
	Mon.	10	Edmonton
	Thu.	13	Los Angeles
	Sat.	15	at San Jose*
	Tue.	18	at Edmonton
	Thu.	20	at Vancouver
	Fri.	21	at Calgary
	Sun.	23	Montreal
	Wed.	26	Minnesota
	Sat.	29	St. Louis
	Mon.	31	Nashville
Jan.	Wed.	2	at Detroit
	Thu.	3	at Minnesota
	Sat.	5	Detroit*
	Mon.	7	Minnesota
	Wed.	9	at Chicago
	Thu.	10	at St. Louis
	Sat.	12	at Los Angeles*
	Tue.	15	at Anaheim
	Thu.	17	at San Jose
	Sat.	19	Columbus*
	Sun.	20	Anaheim*
	Tue.	22	Columbus
	Thu.	24	Buffalo
	Tue.	29	at Vancouver
Feb.	Fri.	1	at Edmonton
	Sat.	2	at Calgary
	Tue.	5	Vancouver
	Thu.	7	at Minnesota
	Sat.	9	St. Louis
	Mon.	11	Phoenix
	Thu.	14	at Phoenix
	Fri.	15	at Anaheim
	Sun.	17	Detroit*
	Wed.	20	Calgary
	Fri.	22	Edmonton
	Sat.	23	at Nashville
	Tue.	26	at St. Louis
	Thu.	28	Chicago
Mar.	Sat.	1	Nashville
	Wed.	5	Phoenix
	Sat.	8	at Colorado
	Sun.	9	Colorado
	Thu.	13	at Detroit
	Sat.	15	Vancouver
	Wed.	19	Anaheim
	Sat.	22	Los Angeles*
	Thu.	27	at San Jose
	Sat.	29	at Los Angeles*
	Sun.	30	at Anaheim*
Apr.	Thu.	3	at Phoenix
	Fri.	4	Phoenix
	Sun.	6	San Jose*

* Denotes afternoon game.

Year-by-Year Record

		Home				Road				Overall								
Season	GP	W	L	T	OL	W	L	T	OL	W	L	T	OL	GF	GA	Pts.	Finished	Playoff Result
2006-07	82	28	11	....	2	22	14	....	5	50	25	....	7	226	197	107	3rd, Pacific Div.	Lost Conf. Quarter-Final
2005-06	82	28	11	....	2	25	12	....	4	53	23	....	6	265	218	112	1st, Pacific Div.	Lost Conf. Quarter-Final
2004-05	....	....	....	....	....	....	....	....	....	....	....	....	....	....	....	....		
2003-04	82	26	7	8	0	15	19	5	2	41	26	13	2	194	175	97	2nd, Pacific Div.	Lost Conf. Quarter-Final
2002-03	82	28	5	6	2	18	12	9	2	46	17	15	4	245	169	111	1st, Pacific Div.	Lost Conf. Semi-Final
2001-02	82	18	13	6	4	18	15	7	1	36	28	13	5	215	213	90	4th, Pacific Div.	Out of Playoffs
2000-01	82	26	10	5	0	22	14	3	2	48	24	8	2	241	187	106	1st, Pacific Div.	Lost Conf. Semi-Final
1999-2000	82	21	11	5	4	22	12	5	2	43	23	10	6	211	184	102	1st, Pacific Div.	Lost Final
1998-99	**82**	**29**	**8**	**4**	....	**22**	**11**	**8**	....	**51**	**19**	**12**	....	**236**	**168**	**114**	**1st, Pacific Div.**	**Won Stanley Cup**
1997-98	82	26	8	7	....	23	14	4	....	49	22	11	....	242	167	109	1st, Central Div.	Lost Conf. Championship
1996-97	82	25	13	3	....	23	13	5	....	48	26	8	....	252	198	104	1st, Central Div.	Lost Conf. Quarter-Final
1995-96	82	14	18	9	....	12	24	5	....	26	42	14	....	227	280	66	6th, Central Div.	Out of Playoffs
1994-95	48	9	10	5	....	8	13	3	....	17	23	8	....	136	135	42	5th, Central Div.	Lost Conf. Quarter-Final
1993-94	84	23	12	7	....	19	17	6	....	42	29	13	....	286	265	97	3rd, Central Div.	Lost Conf. Semi-Final
1992-93*	84	18	17	7	....	18	21	3	....	36	38	10	....	272	293	82	5th, Norris Div.	Out of Playoffs
1991-92*	80	20	16	4	....	12	26	2	....	32	42	6	....	246	278	70	4th, Norris Div.	Lost Div. Semi-Final
1990-91*	80	19	15	6	....	8	24	8	....	27	39	14	....	256	266	68	4th, Norris Div.	Lost Final
1989-90*	80	26	12	2	....	10	28	2	....	36	40	4	....	284	291	76	4th, Norris Div.	Lost Div. Semi-Final
1988-89*	80	17	15	8	....	10	22	8	....	27	37	16	....	258	278	70	3rd, Norris Div.	Lost Div. Semi-Final
1987-88*	80	10	24	6	....	9	24	7	....	19	48	13	....	242	349	51	5th, Norris Div.	Out of Playoffs
1986-87*	80	17	20	3	....	13	20	7	....	30	40	10	....	296	314	70	5th, Norris Div.	Out of Playoffs
1985-86*	80	21	15	4	....	17	18	5	....	38	33	9	....	327	305	85	2nd, Norris Div.	Lost Div. Semi-Final
1984-85*	80	14	19	7	....	11	24	5	....	25	43	12	....	268	321	62	4th, Norris Div.	Lost Div. Final
1983-84*	80	22	14	4	....	17	17	6	....	39	31	10	....	345	344	88	1st, Norris Div.	Lost Conf. Championship
1982-83*	80	23	6	11	....	17	18	5	....	40	24	16	....	321	290	96	2nd, Norris Div.	Lost Div. Final
1981-82*	80	21	7	12	....	16	16	8	....	37	23	20	....	346	288	94	1st, Norris Div.	Lost Div. Semi-Final
1980-81*	80	23	10	7	....	12	18	10	....	35	28	17	....	291	263	87	3rd, Adams Div.	Lost Final
1979-80*	80	25	8	7	....	11	20	9	....	36	28	16	....	311	253	88	3rd, Adams Div.	Lost Semi-Final
1978-79*	80	19	15	6	....	9	25	6	....	28	40	12	....	257	289	68	4th, Adams Div.	Out Of Playoffs
1977-78*	80	12	24	4	....	6	29	5	....	18	53	9	....	218	325	45	5th, Smythe Div.	Out of Playoffs
1976-77*	80	17	14	9	....	6	25	9	....	23	39	18	....	240	310	64	2nd, Smythe Div.	Lost Prelim. Round
1975-76*	80	15	22	3	....	5	31	4	....	20	53	7	....	195	303	47	4th, Smythe Div.	Out of Playoffs
1974-75*	80	17	20	3	....	6	30	4	....	23	50	7	....	221	341	53	4th, Smythe Div.	Out of Playoffs
1973-74*	78	18	15	6	....	5	23	11	....	23	38	17	....	235	275	63	7th, West Div.	Out of Playoffs
1972-73*	78	26	8	5	....	11	22	6	....	37	30	11	....	254	230	85	3rd, West Div.	Lost Quarter-Final
1971-72*	78	22	11	6	....	15	18	6	....	37	29	12	....	212	191	86	2nd, West Div.	Lost Quarter-Final
1970-71*	78	16	15	8	....	12	19	8	....	28	34	16	....	191	223	72	4th, West Div.	Lost Semi-Final
1969-70*	76	11	16	11	....	8	19	11	....	19	35	22	....	224	257	60	3rd, West Div.	Lost Quarter-Final
1968-69*	76	11	21	6	....	7	22	9	....	18	43	15	....	189	270	51	6th, West Div.	Out of Playoffs
1967-68*	74	17	12	8	....	10	20	7	....	27	32	15	....	191	226	69	4th, West Div.	Lost Semi-Final

* Minnesota North Stars

PACIFIC DIVISION
41st NHL Season

Franchise date: June 5, 1967

Transferred from Minnesota to Dallas, June 9, 1993.

2007-08 Player Personnel

FORWARDS	HT	WT	S	Place of Birth	*Age	2006-07 Club
BARCH, Krys	6-2	200	L	Hamilton, Ont.	27	Dallas-Iowa
BARNES, Stu	5-11	180	R	Spruce Grove, Alta.	36	Dallas
CONNER, Chris	5-7	180	L	Westland, MI	23	Dallas-Iowa
ERIKSSON, Loui	6-1	183	L	Goteborg, Sweden	22	Dallas-Iowa
FEDORUK, Todd	6-2	235	L	Redwater, Alta.	28	Anaheim-Philadelphia
HAGMAN, Niklas	6-0	205	L	Espoo, Finland	27	Dallas
HALPERN, Jeff	6-0	203	R	Potomac, MD	31	Dallas
JOKINEN, Jussi	5-11	190	L	Kalajoki, Finland	24	Dallas
LEHTINEN, Jere	6-0	200	R	Espoo, Finland	34	Dallas
LESSARD, Junior	6-0	195	R	St-Joseph-de-Beauce, Que.	27	Dallas-Iowa
LINDGREN, Perttu	6-0	185	L	Tampere, Finland	20	Suomi U20-Ilves
LUNDQVIST, Joel	6-1	194	L	Are, Sweden	25	Dallas-Iowa
MIETTINEN, Antti	6-0	190	R	Hameenlinna, Finland	27	Dallas
MODANO, Mike	6-3	205	L	Livonia, MI	37	Dallas
MORROW, Brenden	5-11	210	L	Carlyle, Sask.	28	Dallas
OTT, Steve	6-0	195	L	Summerside, P.E.I.	25	Dallas-Iowa
PETERSEN, Toby	5-10	197	L	Minneapolis, MN	28	Edmonton-Iowa
RIBEIRO, Mike	6-0	175	L	Montreal, Que.	27	Dallas
WINCHESTER, Brad	6-5	230	L	Madison, WI	26	Edmonton
DEFENSEMEN						
BAUMGARTNER, Nolan	6-2	205	R	Calgary, Alta.	31	Phi-Phi (AHL)-Dal
BOUCHER, Philippe	6-3	221	R	Ste-Apollinaire, Que.	34	Dallas
DALEY, Trevor	5-11	207	L	Toronto, Ont.	23	Dallas
FISTRIC, Mark	6-2	232	L	Edmonton, Alta.	21	Iowa
GROSSMAN, Nicklas	6-3	206	L	Stockholm, Sweden	22	Dallas-Iowa
KHOMITSKI, Vadim	6-1	185	L	Voskresensk, USSR	25	Iowa-Mytischi
NISKANEN, Matt	6-0	194	R	Virginia, MN	20	U. Minn-Duluth-Iowa
NORSTROM, Mattias	6-2	210	L	Stockholm, Sweden	35	Los Angeles-Dallas
ROBIDAS, Stephane	5-11	189	R	Sherbrooke, Que.	30	Dallas
ZUBOV, Sergei	6-1	200	R	Moscow, USSR	37	Dallas
GOALTENDERS	**HT**	**WT**	**C**	**Place of Birth**	***Age**	**2006-07 Club**
SMITH, Mike	6-3	211	L	Kingston, Ont.	25	Dallas
TURCO, Marty	5-11	183	L	Sault Ste. Marie, Ont.	32	Dallas

* – Age at start of 2007-08 season

Coach

DAVE TIPPETT
Coach, Dallas Stars. Born in Moosomin, Sask., August 25, 1961.

Dallas Stars general manager Doug Armstrong announced the hiring of Dave Tippett as the club's head coach on May 16, 2002. In his first season behind the bench in 2002-03, he led the Stars to the best record in the Western Conference and the second best in the NHL. The Stars have topped 100 points in three of the last four seasons.

Before joining the Stars, Tippett had spent the previous three seasons as an assistant coach with the Los Angeles Kings. He served a five-game stint as interim head coach in 2002 while head coach Andy Murray recovered from an auto accident. In all three seasons Tippett was in Los Angeles the Kings qualified for the playoffs. They had reached the postseason just once out of the previous six seasons.

Under Tippett's direction, the Kings power-play led the NHL in 2001-02 with a 20.7 percent success rate. In 1998-99, the year before Tippett came aboard, the Kings power-play unit ranked 24th in the league. As a highly regarded minor league coach with tremendous work ethic, Tippett posted two 50-win seasons at Houston (International Hockey League) and led the Aeros to the 1999 Turner Cup championship while serving as general manager/head coach. He was also named IHL coach of the year.

Prior to becoming a coach, Tippett played 11 years as a forward in the National Hockey League with the Hartford Whalers, Washington Capitals, Pittsburgh Penguins and Philadelphia Flyers. He ended his playing career in 1995 as a player-assistant coach with the Houston Aeros (IHL). Internationally, he captained the 1984 Canadian Olympic team in Sarajevo, Yugoslavia, and he earned a silver medal as a member of the Canadian Olympic team in Albertville, France, in 1992. He was a member of the 1982 NCAA Division I championship squad at the University of North Dakota with former Stars defenseman Craig Ludwig.

Coaching Record

		Regular Season				Playoffs		
Season	Team	Games	W	L	O/T	Games	W	L
1995-96	Houston (IHL)	42	17	18	7	....	....	....
1996-97	Houston (IHL)	82	44	30	8	13	8	5
1997-98	Houston (IHL)	82	50	22	10	4	1	3
1998-99	Houston (IHL)	82	54	15	13	19	11	8
2002-03	**Dallas (NHL)**	**82**	**46**	**21**	**15**	**12**	**6**	**6**
2003-04	**Dallas (NHL)**	**82**	**41**	**28**	**13**	**5**	**1**	**4**
2004-05	**Dallas (NHL)**			Season Cancelled				
2005-06	**Dallas (NHL)**	**82**	**53**	**23**	**6**	**5**	**1**	**4**
2006-07	**Dallas (NHL)**	**82**	**50**	**25**	**7**	**7**	**3**	**4**
	NHL Totals	**328**	**190**	**97**	**41**	**29**	**11**	**18**

2006-07 Scoring

* – rookie

Regular Season

Pos	#	Player	Team	GP	G	A	Pts	+/–	PIM	PP	SH	GW	S	%
C	63	Mike Ribeiro	DAL	81	18	41	59	3	22	6	0	3	111	16.2
L	17	Ladislav Nagy	PHX	55	8	33	41	–2	48	2	0	0	113	7.1
			DAL	25	4	10	14	–3	6	2	0	1	33	12.1
			TOTAL	80	12	43	55	–5	54	4	0	1	146	8.2
D	56	Sergei Zubov	DAL	78	12	42	54	0	26	9	0	3	156	7.7
D	43	Philippe Boucher	DAL	76	19	32	51	2	104	12	0	4	222	8.6
L	36	Jussi Jokinen	DAL	82	14	34	48	8	18	6	0	1	121	11.6
R	26	Jere Lehtinen	DAL	73	26	17	43	5	16	11	1	5	194	13.4
C	9	Mike Modano	DAL	59	22	21	43	9	34	9	0	7	141	15.6
L	10	Brenden Morrow	DAL	40	16	15	31	–2	33	8	0	3	101	15.8
L	15	Niklas Hagman	DAL	82	17	12	29	3	34	2	1	2	152	11.2
C	88	Eric Lindros	DAL	49	5	21	26	–1	70	1	0	0	95	5.3
C	14	Stu Barnes	DAL	82	13	12	25	–2	40	1	0	2	118	11.0
R	20	Antti Miettinen	DAL	74	11	14	25	–5	38	6	0	1	141	7.8
C	11	Jeff Halpern	DAL	76	8	17	25	–7	78	1	0	4	106	7.5
D	5	Darryl Sydor	DAL	74	5	16	21	–4	36	2	0	1	75	6.7
L	21 *	Loui Eriksson	DAL	59	6	13	19	–3	18	2	0	0	78	7.7
D	3	Stephane Robidas	DAL	75	0	17	17	–1	86	0	0	0	106	0.0
D	6	Trevor Daley	DAL	74	4	8	12	2	63	0	0	1	68	5.9
C	27	Patrik Stefan	DAL	41	5	6	11	5	10	0	1	1	41	12.2
D	4	Mattias Norstrom	L.A.	62	2	7	9	–20	40	0	0	0	44	4.5
			DAL	14	0	2	2	2	8	0	0	0	16	0.0
			TOTAL	76	2	9	11	–18	48	0	0	0	60	3.3
R	77	Matthew Barnaby	DAL	39	1	6	7	5	127	0	0	0	22	4.5
C	39 *	Joel Lundqvist	DAL	36	3	3	6	–5	14	0	0	0	36	8.3
R	50	Krys Barch	DAL	26	3	2	5	2	107	0	0	2	12	25.0
C	29	Steve Ott	DAL	19	0	4	4	–4	35	0	0	0	17	0.0
R	65 *	Chris Conner	DAL	11	1	2	3	–3	4	0	0	0	18	5.6
D	42	Jon Klemm	DAL	38	1	2	3	0	24	0	0	0	25	4.0
D	25	Nolan Baumgartner	PHI	6	0	1	1	0	21	0	0	0	4	0.0
			DAL	7	0	2	2	0	0	0	0	0	4	0.0
			TOTAL	13	0	3	3	0	21	0	0	0	8	0.0
R	22	Junior Lessard	DAL	1	1	0	1	1	0	1	0	0	3	33.3
L	24 *	Vojtech Polak	DAL	2	0	0	0	–1	0	0	0	0	2	0.0
D	2 *	Niklas Grossman	DAL	8	0	0	0	–1	4	0	0	0	8	0.0

Goaltending

No.	Goaltender	GPI	Mins	Avg	W	L	OT	EN	SO	GA	SA	S%	G	A	PIM
41	* Mike Smith	23	1213	2.23	12	5	2	3	3	45	511	.912	0	0	2
35	Marty Turco	67	3764	2.23	38	20	5	5	6	140	1564	.910	0	4	18
	Totals	**82**	**5009**	**2.31**	**50**	**25**	**7**	**8**	**9**	**193**	**2083**	**.907**			

Playoffs

Pos	#	Player	Team	GP	G	A	Pts	+/–	PIM	PP	SH	GW	OT	S	%
C	14	Stu Barnes	DAL	7	1	3	4	1	4	1	0	0	0	14	7.1
D	56	Sergei Zubov	DAL	6	0	4	4	3	2	0	0	0	0	18	0.0
L	10	Brenden Morrow	DAL	7	2	1	3	–1	18	2	0	1	1	17	11.8
C	11	Jeff Halpern	DAL	7	2	1	3	–1	4	0	0	1	0	9	22.2
C	63	Mike Ribeiro	DAL	7	0	3	3	–3	4	0	0	0	0	8	0.0
C	39 *	Joel Lundqvist	DAL	7	2	0	2	1	6	0	0	0	0	8	25.0
R	20	Antti Miettinen	DAL	4	1	1	2	0	2	0	0	0	0	11	9.1
C	9	Mike Modano	DAL	7	1	1	2	0	4	1	0	1	0	19	5.3
D	5	Darryl Sydor	DAL	7	1	1	2	2	4	0	0	0	0	16	6.3
L	17	Ladislav Nagy	DAL	7	1	1	2	1	2	0	0	0	0	15	6.7
D	6	Trevor Daley	DAL	7	1	0	1	–3	4	0	0	0	0	12	8.3
L	36	Jussi Jokinen	DAL	4	0	1	1	–1	0	0	0	0	0	3	0.0
L	21 *	Loui Eriksson	DAL	4	0	1	1	0	0	0	0	0	0	7	0.0
D	43	Philippe Boucher	DAL	7	0	1	1	–5	6	0	0	0	0	15	0.0
D	3	Stephane Robidas	DAL	7	0	1	1	–1	2	0	0	0	0	17	0.0
L	15	Niklas Hagman	DAL	7	0	1	1	–1	10	0	0	0	0	20	0.0
D	42	Jon Klemm	DAL	1	0	0	0	0	2	0	0	0	0	0	0.0
C	88	Eric Lindros	DAL	3	0	0	0	–2	4	0	0	0	0	3	0.0
C	29	Steve Ott	DAL	6	0	0	0	0	8	0	0	0	0	5	0.0
D	4	Mattias Norstrom	DAL	7	0	0	0	0	8	0	0	0	0	7	0.0
R	26	Jere Lehtinen	DAL	7	0	0	0	–2	2	0	0	0	0	16	0.0

Goaltending

No.	Goaltender	GPI	Mins	Avg	W	L	EN	SO	GA	SA	S%	G	A	PIM
35	Marty Turco	7	509	1.30	3	4	2	3	11	229	.952	0	0	4
	Totals	**7**	**512**	**1.52**	**3**	**4**	**2**	**3**	**13**	**231**	**.944**			

Coaching History

Wren Blair, 1967-68; Wren Blair and John Muckler, 1968-69; Wren Blair and Charlie Burns, 1969-70; Jack Gordon, 1970-71 to 1972-73; Jack Gordon and Parker MacDonald, 1973-74; Jack Gordon and Charlie Burns, 1974-75; Ted Harris, 1975-76, 1976-77; Ted Harris, André Beaulieu and Lou Nanne, 1977-78; Harry Howell and Glen Sonmor, 1978-79; Glen Sonmor, 1979-80 to 1981-82; Glen Sonmor and Murray Oliver, 1982-83; Bill Mahoney, 1983-84, 1984-85; Lorne Henning, 1985-86; Lorne Henning and Glen Sonmor, 1986-87; Herb Brooks, 1987-88; Pierre Page, 1988-89, 1989-90; Bob Gainey, 1990-91 to 1994-95; Bob Gainey and Ken Hitchcock, 1995-96; Ken Hitchcock, 1996-97 to 2000-01; Ken Hitchcock and Rick Wilson, 2001-02; Dave Tippett, 2002-03 to date.

Club Records

Team

(Figures in brackets for season records are games played; records for fewest points, wins, ties, losses, goals, goals against are for 70 or more games)

Most Points **114** 1998-99 (82)
Most Wins **53** 2005-06 (82)
Most Ties **22** 1969-70 (76)
Most Losses **53** 1975-76 (80), 1977-78 (80)
Most Goals **346** 1981-82 (80)
Most Goals Against **349** 1987-88 (80)
Fewest Points **45** 1977-78 (80)
Fewest Wins **18** 1968-69 (76), 1977-78 (80)
Fewest Ties **4** 1989-90 (80)
Fewest Losses **17** 2002-03 (82)
Fewest Goals **189** 1968-69 (76)
Fewest Goals Against **167** 1997-98 (82)

Longest Winning Streak
Overall .... **7** Mar. 16-28/80, Mar. 16-Apr. 2/97, Nov. 22-Dec. 5/97
Home .... **11** Nov. 4-Dec. 27/72
Away .... **7** Four times

Longest Undefeated Streak
Overall .... **15** Dec. 6/98-Jan. 6/99 (12 wins, 3 ties)
Home .... **17** Jan. 23-Mar. 20/04 (13 wins, 4 ties)
Away .... **10** Jan. 12-Mar. 4/99 (8 wins, 2 ties), Dec. 27/02-Feb. 25/03 (7 wins, 3 ties)

Longest Losing Streak
Overall .... **10** Feb. 1-20/76
Home .... **6** Jan. 17-Feb. 4/70
Away .... **8** Oct. 19-Nov. 13/75, Jan. 28-Mar. 3/88

Longest Winless Streak
Overall .... **20** Jan. 15-Feb. 28/70 (15 losses, 5 ties)
Home .... **12** Jan. 17-Feb. 25/70 (8 losses, 4 ties)
Away .... **23** Oct. 25/74-Jan. 28/75 (19 losses, 4 ties)

Most Shutouts, Season **11** 2000-01 (82), 2002-03 (82)
Most PIM, Season **2,313** 1987-88 (80)
Most Goals, Game .... **15** Nov. 11/81 (Wpg. 2 at Min. 15)

Individual

Most Seasons .... **18** Mike Modano
Most Games .... **1,238** Mike Modano
Most Goals, Career .... **507** Mike Modano
Most Assists, Career .... **719** Mike Modano
Most Points, Career .... **1,226** Mike Modano (507G, 719A)
Most PIM, Career .... **1,883** Shane Churla
Most Shutouts, Career .... **30** Marty Turco
Longest Consecutive Games Streak .... **442** Danny Grant (Dec. 4/68-Apr. 7/74)
Most Goals, Season .... **55** Dino Ciccarelli (1981-82), Brian Bellows (1989-90)
Most Assists, Season .... **76** Neal Broten (1985-86)
Most Points, Season .... **114** Bobby Smith (1981-82; 43G, 71A)
Most PIM, Season .... **382** Basil McRae (1987-88)
Most Points, Defenseman, Season .... **77** Craig Hartsburg (1981-82; 17G, 60A)
Most Points, Center, Season .... **114** Bobby Smith (1981-82; 43G, 71A)
Most Points, Right Wing, Season .... **106** Dino Ciccarelli (1981-82; 55G, 51A)
Most Points, Left Wing, Season .... **99** Brian Bellows (1989-90; 55G, 44A)
Most Points, Rookie, Season .... **98** Neal Broten (1981-82; 38G, 60A)
Most Shutouts, Season .... **9** Ed Belfour (1997-98)
Most Goals, Game .... **5** Tim Young (Jan. 15/79)
Most Assists, Game .... **5** Murray Oliver (Oct. 24/71), Larry Murphy (Oct. 17/89)
Most Points, Game .... **7** Bobby Smith (Nov. 11/81; 4G, 3A)

Records include Minnesota North Stars, 1967-68 through 1992-93.

Retired Numbers

7	Neal Broten	1980-1995, 1996-1997
8	Bill Goldsworthy*	1967-1976
19	Bill Masterton*	1967-1968

* Minnesota North Stars

All-time Record vs. Other Clubs

Regular Season

	At Home								On Road								Total							
	GP	W	L	T	OL	GF	GA	PTS	GP	W	L	T	OL	GF	GA	PTS	GP	W	L	T	OL	GF	GA	PTS
Anaheim	35	26	7	2	0	119	66	54	35	17	13	3	2	90	86	39	70	43	20	5	2	209	152	93
Atlanta	5	4	1	0	0	11	9	8	5	5	0	0	0	21	12	10	10	9	1	0	0	32	21	18
Boston	61	18	30	13	0	175	220	49	61	10	41	10	0	148	259	30	122	28	71	23	0	323	479	79
Buffalo	54	27	21	6	0	173	156	60	53	13	29	11	0	142	192	37	107	40	50	17	0	315	348	97
Calgary	66	34	20	11	1	241	203	80	66	16	34	14	2	161	218	48	132	50	54	25	3	402	421	128
Carolina	30	18	10	2	0	120	90	38	33	15	14	4	0	114	106	34	63	33	24	6	0	234	196	72
Chicago	116	56	43	16	1	397	349	129	114	33	66	15	0	303	421	81	230	89	109	31	1	700	770	210
Colorado	45	24	14	5	2	150	130	55	45	15	22	7	1	117	160	38	90	39	36	12	3	267	290	93
Columbus	12	10	1	0	1	38	20	21	12	8	2	0	2	39	29	18	24	18	3	0	3	77	49	39
Detroit	110	52	39	18	1	377	331	123	110	39	55	16	0	349	417	94	220	91	94	34	1	726	748	217
Edmonton	49	26	16	7	0	173	135	59	48	19	20	8	1	161	188	47	97	45	36	15	1	334	323	106
Florida	9	4	2	2	1	29	25	11	11	5	4	1	1	29	24	12	20	9	6	3	2	58	49	23
Los Angeles	92	57	22	13	0	350	247	127	90	33	37	19	1	261	295	86	182	90	59	32	1	611	542	213
Minnesota	12	8	2	1	1	43	28	18	12	6	5	0	1	25	29	13	24	14	7	1	2	68	57	31
Montreal	59	17	30	12	0	153	203	46	59	12	38	9	0	146	254	33	118	29	68	21	0	299	457	79
Nashville	16	14	2	0	0	47	18	28	16	7	8	1	0	35	39	15	32	21	10	1	0	82	57	43
New Jersey	46	27	13	6	0	167	118	60	43	19	21	3	0	132	146	41	89	46	34	9	0	299	264	101
NY Islanders	48	18	21	8	1	139	173	45	48	14	25	8	1	134	176	37	96	32	46	16	2	273	349	82
NY Rangers	62	20	31	11	0	189	226	51	62	15	36	11	0	165	213	41	124	35	67	22	0	354	439	92
Ottawa	11	7	4	0	0	44	28	14	10	6	3	0	1	26	22	13	21	13	7	0	1	70	50	27
Philadelphia	67	28	23	16	0	219	214	72	67	9	42	16	0	150	255	34	134	37	65	32	0	369	469	106
Phoenix	63	32	22	9	0	225	185	73	62	34	24	4	0	210	188	72	125	66	46	13	0	435	373	145
Pittsburgh	65	37	21	6	1	249	217	81	63	19	38	6	0	178	236	44	128	56	59	12	1	427	453	125
St. Louis	119	56	40	22	1	396	342	135	121	33	65	21	2	342	436	89	240	89	105	43	3	738	778	224
San Jose	37	19	12	4	2	102	85	44	38	23	13	1	1	106	89	48	75	42	25	5	3	208	174	92
Tampa Bay	12	7	4	1	0	42	33	15	14	11	1	2	0	39	21	24	26	18	5	3	0	81	54	39
Toronto	97	50	36	11	0	365	306	111	102	36	49	17	0	321	357	89	199	86	85	28	0	686	663	200
Vancouver	75	41	22	12	0	270	216	94	75	31	32	10	2	224	262	74	150	72	54	22	2	494	478	168
Washington	42	22	11	8	1	156	111	53	41	17	16	8	0	132	124	42	83	39	27	16	1	288	235	95
Defunct Clubs	33	19	8	6	0	123	86	44	32	10	16	6	0	84	105	26	65	29	24	12	0	207	191	70
Totals	**1548**	**778**	**528**	**228**	**14**	**5282**	**4570**	**1798**	**1548**	**530**	**769**	**231**	**18**	**4384**	**5359**	**1309**	**3096**	**1308**	**1297**	**459**	**32**	**9666**	**9929**	**3107**

Playoffs

	Series	W	L	GP	W	L	T	GF	GA	Last Mtg.	Rnd.	Result
Anaheim	1	0	1	6	2	4	0	14	14	2003	CSF	L 2-4
Boston	1	1	0	3	3	0	0	20	13	1981	PRE	W 3-0
Buffalo	3	2	1	13	8	5	0	39	37	1999	F	W 4-2
Calgary	1	1	0	6	4	2	0	25	18	1981	SF	W 4-2
Chicago	6	2	4	33	14	19	0	118	120	1991	DSF	W 4-2
Colorado	4	2	2	24	10	14	0	62	66	2006	CQF	L 1-4
Detroit	3	0	3	18	6	12	0	40	55	1998	CF	L 2-4
Edmonton	8	6	2	42	27	15	0	118	104	2003	CQF	W 4-2
Los Angeles	1	1	0	7	4	3	0	26	21	1968	QF	W 4-3
Montreal	2	1	1	13	6	7	0	37	48	1980	QF	W 4-3
New Jersey	1	0	1	6	2	4	0	9	15	2000	F	L 2-4
NY Islanders	1	0	1	5	1	4	0	16	26	1981	F	L 1-4
Philadelphia	2	0	2	11	3	8	0	26	41	1980	SF	L 1-4
Pittsburgh	1	0	1	6	2	4	0	16	28	1991	F	L 2-4
St. Louis	12	6	6	66	34	32	0	197	187	2001	CSF	L 0-4
San Jose	2	2	0	11	8	3	0	31	19	2000	CSF	W 4-1
Toronto	2	2	0	7	6	1	0	35	26	1983	DSF	W 3-1
Vancouver	2	0	2	12	4	8	0	23	31	2007	CQF	L 3-4
Totals	**53**	**26**	**27**	**289**	**144**	**145**	**0**	**852**	**869**			

Calgary totals include Atlanta Flames, 1972-73 to 1979-80. Carolina totals include Hartford, 1979-80 to 1996-97.
Colorado totals include Quebec, 1979-80 to 1994-95.
New Jersey totals include Kansas City, 1974-75, 1975-76, and Colorado Rockies, 1976-77 to 1981-82.
Phoenix totals include Winnipeg, 1979-80 to 1995-96.

Playoff Results 2007-2002

Year	Round	Opponent	Result	GF	GA
2007	CQF	Vancouver	L 3-4	12	13
2006	CQF	Colorado	L 1-4	15	18
2004	CQF	Colorado	L 1-4	10	19
2003	CSF	Anaheim	L 2-4	14	14
	CQF	Edmonton	W 4-2	20	11

Abbreviations: Round: F - Final; **CF** - conference final; **CSF** - conference semi-final; **CQF** - conference quarter-final; **DSF** - division semi-final; **SF** - semi-final; **QF** - quarter-final; **PRE** - preliminary round.

2006-07 Results

Oct.	4	at Colorado	3-2*
	7	New Jersey	3-1
	12	at Los Angeles	4-1
	14	at Los Angeles	4-1
	15	at Anaheim	4-3†
	17	at San Jose	0-2
	20	Chicago	5-4
	21	at Phoenix	4-0
	23	Vancouver	2-1
	27	Detroit	3-4
	28	Los Angeles	3-2
Nov.	1	St. Louis	4-1
	3	at Edmonton	3-2
	6	at Vancouver	1-2
	7	at Calgary	1-3
	9	at Phoenix	1-0
	15	NY Islanders	0-3
	17	at Atlanta	5-3
	18	at Carolina	4-5
	20	Colorado	5-4
	22	Nashville	1-0
	24	Los Angeles	5-3
	27	at Detroit	1-2
	29	at Chicago	1-2
	30	at Washington	3-4
Dec.	2	Minnesota	4-3†
	4	San Jose	1-0
	6	Phoenix	3-0
	8	Edmonton	0-2
	9	at Phoenix	4-3*
	12	Columbus	1-3
	14	NY Rangers	2-5
	16	at Los Angeles	4-3†
	20	at Anaheim	1-4
	21	at San Jose	3-0
	23	Edmonton	3-2
	26	at Chicago	1-2
	27	at Colorado	5-4
	29	Nashville	4-1
	31	San Jose	2-4
Jan.	3	at Vancouver	1-2†
	4	at Edmonton	6-5†
	6	at Calgary	2-4
	9	Phoenix	2-5
	11	Anaheim	1-5
	15	Los Angeles	3-1
	17	Calgary	4-2
	20	at Minnesota	2-1†
	26	Pittsburgh	3-4†
	28	at Anaheim	1-4
	30	at San Jose	3-2†
Feb.	1	at San Jose	4-2
	3	at St. Louis	0-2
	6	Minnesota	4-2
	10	Anaheim	1-0
	11	Colorado	7-5
	14	Detroit	1-3
	18	San Jose	5-2
	20	at Minnesota	1-2†
	23	Anaheim	4-1
	25	Vancouver	2-1*
	27	at Tampa Bay	2-1*
Mar.	1	at Florida	1-2*
	2	Columbus	2-3†
	4	San Jose	0-4
	8	at St. Louis	3-5
	9	at Columbus	3-0
	11	Los Angeles	4-3*
	13	Philadelphia	3-2
	15	Calgary	4-2
	17	at Nashville	2-3
	18	Phoenix	5-4*
	21	at Los Angeles	4-2
	23	at Anaheim	2-3*
	24	at Phoenix	4-3†
	27	Phoenix	6-0
	30	at Detroit	4-3†
	31	at Nashville	4-2
Apr.	2	St. Louis	2-4
	5	at Columbus	1-2*
	6	Anaheim	2-1†
	8	Chicago	3-2

* – Overtime † – Shootout

Entry Draft Selections 2007-1993

2007

Pick	
50	Nico Sacchetti
64	Sergei Korostin
112	Colton Sceviour
128	Austin Smith
129	Jamie Benn
136	Ondrej Roman
149	Michael Neal
172	Luke Gazdic

2006

Pick	
27	Ivan Vishnevskiy
90	Aaron Snow
120	Richard Bachman
138	David McIntyre
150	Max Warn

2005

Pick	
28	Matt Niskanen
33	James Neal
71	Richard Clune
75	Perttu Lindgren
146	Tom Wandell
160	Matt Watkins
223	Pat McGann

2004

Pick	
28	Mark Fistric
34	Johan Fransson
52	Raymond Sawada
56	Nicklas Grossman
86	John Lammers
104	Fredrik Naslund
183	Trevor Ludwig
218	Sergei Kukushkin
248	Lukas Vomela
280	Matt McKnight

2003

Pick	
33	Loui Eriksson
36	Vojtech Polak
54	B.J. Crombeen
99	Matt Nickerson
134	Alexander Naurov
144	Eero Kilpelainen
165	Gino Guyer
185	Francis Wathier
195	Drew Bagnall
196	Elias Granath
259	Niko Vainio

2002

Pick	
26	Martin Vagner
32	Janos Vas
34	Tobias Stephan
42	Marius Holtet
43	Trevor Daley
78	Geoff Waugh
110	Jarkko A. Immonen
147	David Bararuk
180	Kirill Sidorenko
210	Bryan Hamm
243	Tuomas Mikkonen
273	Ned Havern

2001

Pick	
26	Jason Bacashihua
70	Yared Hagos
92	Anthony Aquino
126	Daniel Volrab
161	Mike Smith
167	Michal Blazek
192	Jussi Jokinen
255	Marco Rosa
265	Dale Sullivan
285	Marek Tomica

2000

Pick	
25	Steve Ott
60	Dan Ellis
68	Joel Lundqvist
91	Alexei Tereschenko
123	Vadim Khomitsky
139	Ruslan Bernikov
162	Artem Chernov
192	Ladislav Vlcek
219	Marco Tuokko
224	Antti Miettinen

1999

Pick	
32	Michael Ryan
66	Dan Jancevski
96	Mathias Tjarnqvist
126	Jeff Bateman
156	Gregor Baumgartner
184	Justin Cox
186	Brett Draney
215	Jeff MacMillan
243	Brian Sullivan
265	Jamie Chamberlain
272	Mikhail Donika

1998

Pick	
39	John Erskine
57	Tyler Bouck
86	Gabriel Karlsson
153	Pavel Patera
173	Niko Kapanen
200	Scott Perry

1997

Pick	
25	Brenden Morrow
52	Roman Lyashenko
77	Steve Gainey
105	Marcus Kristoffersson
132	Teemu Elomo
160	Alexei Timkin
189	Jeff McKercher
216	Alexei Komarov
242	Brett McLean

1996

Pick	
5	Ric Jackman
70	Jon Sim
90	Mike Hurley
112	Ryan Christie
113	Yevgeny Tsybuk
166	Eoin McInerney
194	Joel Kwiatkowski
220	Nick Bootland

1995

Pick	
11	Jarome Iginla
37	Patrick Cote
63	Petr Buzek
69	Sergey Gusev
115	Wade Strand
141	Dominic Marleau
173	Jeff Dewar
193	Anatoli Koveshnikov
202	Sergei Luchinkin
219	Stephen Lowe

1994

Pick	
20	Jason Botterill
46	Lee Jinman
98	Jamie Wright
124	Marty Turco
150	Evgeny Petrochinin
228	Marty Flichel
254	Jimmy Roy
280	Chris Szysky

1993

Pick	
9	Todd Harvey
35	Jamie Langenbrunner
87	Chad Lang
136	Rick Mrozik
139	Per Svartvadet
165	Jeremy Stasiuk
191	Rob Lurtsema
243	Jordan Willis
249	Bill Lang
269	Cory Peterson

Club Directory

American Airlines Center

Dallas Stars
Office Address:
2601 Ave. of the Stars
Frisco, TX 75034
Phone **214/387-5500**
FAX 214/387-5564
Ticket Information 214/GO STARS
www.dallasstars.com
Capacity: 18,532

Chairman of the Board & Owner	Thomas O. Hicks
President	James R. Lites
General Manager	Doug Armstrong
Assistant General Manager	Les Jackson
Assistant General Manager	Frank Provenzano
Director, Player Personnel	Dave Taylor
Special Advisor, Hockey Operations	Brett Hull
Head Coach	Dave Tippett
Associate Coach	Rick Wilson
Assistant Coaches	Mark Lamb, Ulf Dahlen
Director, Player Development	Andy Moog
Video Coach	Derek MacKinnon
Director, Hockey Administration & Team Services	Lesa Moake
Director, Amateur Scouting	Tim Bernhardt
Director, Professional Scouting	Doug Overton
Director, European Scouting	Kari Takko
Scout	Bob Gernander
Professional Scouts	Kevin Maxwell, Paul McIntosh, Scott White
Regional Scouts	Shane Churla, Jack Foley, Dennis Holland, Jiri Hrdina, Jim Johnston, Matti Kautto, Butch Ott, Jim Pederson, Borys Protsenko, Brad Robson
Head Athletic Trainer	Dave Surprenant
Head Equipment Manager	Steve Sumner
Strength and Conditioning Coach	J.J. McQueen
Assistant Strength and Conditioning Coach	Manny Hernando
Assistant Athletic Trainer	David Zeis
Assistant Equipment Manager	Chris Davidson-Adams
Equipment Assistant	Dennis Soetaert
Massage Therapist	Cleo Bates
Administrative Assistant, Hockey Operations	Pam Wenzel
Senior Director, Communications	Rob Scichili
Director, Public Relations	Mark Janko
Manager, Media and Team Services	Jason Rademan
Television Networks	FSN Southwest, My 27
Radio Flagship	WBAP 820-AM
Play-By-Play Announcer (TV/Radio Simulcast)	Ralph Strangis
Color Analyst (TV/Radio Simulcast)	Daryl Reaugh
Director of Broadcasting	Jason Walsh

Captains' History

Bob Woytowich, 1967-68; Moose Vasko, 1968-69; Claude Larose, 1969-70; Ted Harris, 1970-71 to 1973-74; Bill Goldsworthy, 1974-75, 1975-76; Bill Hogaboam, 1976-77; Nick Beverley, 1977-78; J.P. Parise, 1978-79; Paul Shmyr, 1979-80, 1980-81; Tim Young, 1981-82; Craig Hartsburg, 1982-83; Craig Hartsburg and Brian Bellows, 1983-84; Craig Hartsburg, 1984-85 to 1987-88; Curt Fraser, Bob Rouse and Curt Giles, 1988-89; Curt Giles, 1989-90, 1990-91; Mark Tinordi, 1991-92 to 1993-94; Neal Broten and Derian Hatcher, 1994-95; Derian Hatcher, 1995-96 to 2002-03; Mike Modano, 2003-04 to 2005-06; Brenden Morrow, 2006-07 to date.

General Managers' History

Wren Blair, 1967-68 to 1973-74; Jack Gordon, 1974-75 to 1976-77; Lou Nanne, 1977-78 to 1987-88; Jack Ferreira, 1988-89, 1989-90; Bob Clarke 1990-91, 1991-92; Bob Gainey, 1992-93 to 2000-01; Bob Gainey and Doug Armstrong, 2001-02; Doug Armstrong, 2002-03 to date.

General Manager

DOUG ARMSTRONG
General Manager, Dallas Stars. Born in Sarnia, Ont., September 24, 1964.

Doug Armstrong was in his ninth season as an assistant to Bob Gainey when he was elevated to the position of general manager on January 25, 2002. In his first full season on the job in 2002-03, the Stars had the best record in the Western Conference and the second best in the NHL. The Stars have topped 100 points in three of the last four seasons.

Armstrong originally joined the club in 1991. As Gainey's assistant, he worked on contract information and season scheduling and handled the day-to-day operations of the hockey department. In five seasons from 1996 to 2001, he helped Gainey build a team that won five straight division championships, as well as the Presidents' Trophy for the best regular-season record in the NHL twice, and the 1999 Stanley Cup. At the international level, Armstrong served as Team Canada's assistant general manger at the 2002 World Championships in Sweden.

A native of Sarnia, Ontario, Armstrong attended Western Michigan University for two years before transferring to Florida State University in Tallahassee, where he earned his B.S. in Business Administration with a major in marketing.

Selected 124th overall by Dallas back in 1994, Marty Turco has posted stellar numbers for the Stars since reaching the NHL in 2000-01.

Key Off-Season Signings/Acquisitions

2007

June **12** • Re-signed D **Chris Chelios**.
July **2** • Signed D **Brian Rafalski**.
5 • Re-signed C **Jiri Hudler**.
6 • Re-signed G **Dominik Hasek**.
9 • Signed RW **Dallas Drake**.

Detroit Red Wings

2006-07 Results: 50W-19L-5OTL-8SOL 113PTS.
First, Central Division

Year-by-Year Record

		Home				Road				Overall								
Season	GP	W	L	T	OL	W	L	T	OL	W	L	T	OL	GF	GA	Pts.	Finished	Playoff Result
2006-07	82	29	4	....	8	21	15	....	5	50	19	....	13	254	199	113	1st, Central Div.	Lost Conf. Championship
2005-06	82	27	9	....	5	31	7	....	3	58	16	....	8	305	209	124	1st, Central Div.	Lost Conf. Quarter-Final
2004-05	....	....	....	....	....	....	....	....	....	....	....	....	....	....	....	....	....	....
2003-04	82	30	7	4	0	18	14	7	2	48	21	11	2	255	189	109	1st, Central Div.	Lost Conf. Semi-Final
2002-03	82	28	6	5	2	20	14	5	2	48	20	10	4	269	203	110	1st, Central Div.	Lost Conf. Quarter-Final
2001-02	**82**	**28**	**7**	**5**	**1**	**23**	**10**	**5**	**3**	**51**	**17**	**10**	**4**	**251**	**187**	**116**	**1st, Central Div.**	**Won Stanley Cup**
2000-01	82	27	9	3	2	22	11	6	2	49	20	9	4	253	202	111	1st, Central Div.	Lost Conf. Quarter-Final
1999-2000	82	28	9	3	1	20	13	7	1	48	22	10	2	278	210	108	2nd, Central Div.	Lost Conf. Semi-Final
1998-99	82	27	12	2	....	16	20	5	....	43	32	7	....	245	202	93	1st, Central Div.	Lost Conf. Semi-Final
1997-98	**82**	**25**	**8**	**8**	....	**19**	**15**	**7**	....	**44**	**23**	**15**	....	**250**	**196**	**103**	**2nd, Central Div.**	**Won Stanley Cup**
1996-97	**82**	**20**	**12**	**9**	....	**18**	**14**	**9**	....	**38**	**26**	**18**	....	**253**	**197**	**94**	**2nd, Central Div.**	**Won Stanley Cup**
1995-96	82	36	3	2	....	26	10	5	....	62	13	7	....	325	181	131	1st, Central Div.	Lost Conf. Championship
1994-95	48	17	4	3	....	16	7	1	....	33	11	4	....	180	117	70	1st, Central Div.	Lost Final
1993-94	84	23	13	6	....	23	17	2	....	46	30	8	....	356	275	100	1st, Central Div.	Lost Conf. Quarter-Final
1992-93	84	25	14	3	....	22	14	6	....	47	28	9	....	369	280	103	2nd, Norris Div.	Lost Div. Semi-Final
1991-92	80	24	12	4	....	19	13	8	....	43	25	12	....	320	256	98	1st, Norris Div.	Lost Div. Final
1990-91	80	26	14	0	....	8	24	8	....	34	38	8	....	273	298	76	3rd, Norris Div.	Lost Div. Semi-Final
1989-90	80	20	14	6	....	8	24	8	....	28	38	14	....	288	323	70	5th, Norris Div.	Out of Playoffs
1988-89	80	20	14	6	....	14	20	6	....	34	34	12	....	313	316	80	1st, Norris Div.	Lost Div. Semi-Final
1987-88	80	24	10	6	....	17	18	5	....	41	28	11	....	322	269	93	1st, Norris Div.	Lost Conf. Championship
1986-87	80	20	14	6	....	14	22	4	....	34	36	10	....	260	274	78	2nd, Norris Div.	Lost Conf. Championship
1985-86	80	10	26	4	....	7	31	2	....	17	57	6	....	266	415	40	5th, Norris Div.	Out of Playoffs
1984-85	80	19	14	7	....	8	27	5	....	27	41	12	....	313	357	66	3rd, Norris Div.	Lost Div. Semi-Final
1983-84	80	18	20	2	....	13	22	5	....	31	42	7	....	298	323	69	3rd, Norris Div.	Lost Div. Semi-Final
1982-83	80	14	19	7	....	7	25	8	....	21	44	15	....	263	344	57	5th, Norris Div.	Out of Playoffs
1981-82	80	15	19	6	....	6	28	6	....	21	47	12	....	270	351	54	6th, Norris Div.	Out of Playoffs
1980-81	80	16	15	9	....	3	28	9	....	19	43	18	....	252	339	56	5th, Norris Div.	Out of Playoffs
1979-80	80	14	21	5	....	12	22	6	....	26	43	11	....	268	306	63	5th, Norris Div.	Out of Playoffs
1978-79	80	15	17	8	....	8	24	8	....	23	41	16	....	252	295	62	5th, Norris Div.	Out of Playoffs
1977-78	80	22	11	7	....	10	23	7	....	32	34	14	....	252	266	78	2nd, Norris Div.	Lost Quarter-Final
1976-77	80	12	22	6	....	4	33	3	....	16	55	9	....	183	309	41	5th, Norris Div.	Out of Playoffs
1975-76	80	17	15	8	....	9	29	2	....	26	44	10	....	226	300	62	4th, Norris Div.	Out of Playoffs
1974-75	80	17	17	6	....	6	28	6	....	23	45	12	....	259	335	58	4th, Norris Div.	Out of Playoffs
1973-74	78	21	12	6	....	8	27	4	....	29	39	10	....	255	319	68	6th, East Div.	Out of Playoffs
1972-73	78	22	12	5	....	15	17	7	....	37	29	12	....	265	243	86	5th, East Div.	Out of Playoffs
1971-72	78	25	11	3	....	8	24	7	....	33	35	10	....	261	262	76	5th, East Div.	Out of Playoffs
1970-71	78	17	15	7	....	5	30	4	....	22	45	11	....	209	308	55	7th, East Div.	Out of Playoffs
1969-70	76	20	11	7	....	20	10	8	....	40	21	15	....	246	199	95	3rd, East Div.	Lost Quarter-Final
1968-69	76	23	8	7	....	10	23	5	....	33	31	12	....	239	221	78	5th, East Div.	Out of Playoffs
1967-68	74	18	15	4	....	9	20	8	....	27	35	12	....	245	257	66	6th, East Div.	Out of Playoffs
1966-67	70	21	11	3	....	6	28	1	....	27	39	4	....	212	241	58	5th,	Out of Playoffs
1965-66	70	20	8	7	....	11	19	5	....	31	27	12	....	221	194	74	4th,	Lost Final
1964-65	70	25	7	3	....	15	16	4	....	40	23	7	....	224	175	87	1st,	Lost Semi-Final
1963-64	70	23	9	3	....	7	20	8	....	30	29	11	....	191	204	71	4th,	Lost Final
1962-63	70	19	10	6	....	13	15	7	....	32	25	13	....	200	194	77	4th,	Lost Final
1961-62	70	17	11	7	....	6	22	7	....	23	33	14	....	184	219	60	5th,	Out of Playoffs
1960-61	70	15	13	7	....	10	16	9	....	25	29	16	....	195	215	66	4th,	Lost Final
1959-60	70	18	14	3	....	8	15	12	....	26	29	15	....	186	197	67	4th,	Lost Semi-Final
1958-59	70	13	17	5	....	12	20	3	....	25	37	8	....	167	218	58	6th,	Out of Playoffs
1957-58	70	16	11	8	....	13	18	4	....	29	29	12	....	176	207	70	3rd,	Lost Semi-Final
1956-57	70	23	7	5	....	15	13	7	....	38	20	12	....	198	157	88	1st,	Lost Semi-Final
1955-56	70	21	6	8	....	9	18	8	....	30	24	16	....	183	148	76	2nd,	Lost Final
1954-55	**70**	**25**	**5**	**5**	....	**17**	**12**	**6**	....	**42**	**17**	**11**	....	**204**	**134**	**95**	**1st,**	**Won Stanley Cup**
1953-54	**70**	**24**	**4**	**7**	....	**13**	**15**	**7**	....	**37**	**19**	**14**	....	**191**	**132**	**88**	**1st,**	**Won Stanley Cup**
1952-53	70	20	5	10	....	16	11	8	....	36	16	18	....	222	133	90	1st,	Lost Semi-Final
1951-52	**70**	**24**	**7**	**4**	....	**20**	**7**	**8**	....	**44**	**14**	**12**	....	**215**	**133**	**100**	**1st,**	**Won Stanley Cup**
1950-51	70	25	3	7	....	19	10	6	....	44	13	13	....	236	139	101	1st,	Lost Semi-Final
1949-50	**70**	**19**	**9**	**7**	....	**18**	**10**	**7**	....	**37**	**19**	**14**	....	**229**	**164**	**88**	**1st,**	**Won Stanley Cup**
1948-49	60	21	6	3	....	13	13	4	....	34	19	7	....	195	145	75	1st,	Lost Final
1947-48	60	16	9	5	....	14	9	7	....	30	18	12	....	187	148	72	2nd,	Lost Final
1946-47	60	14	10	6	....	8	17	5	....	22	27	11	....	190	193	55	4th,	Lost Semi-Final
1945-46	50	16	5	4	....	4	15	6	....	20	20	10	....	146	159	50	4th,	Lost Semi-Final
1944-45	50	19	5	1	....	12	9	4	....	31	14	5	....	218	161	67	2nd,	Lost Final
1943-44	50	18	5	2	....	8	13	4	....	26	18	6	....	214	177	58	2nd,	Lost Semi-Final
1942-43	**50**	**16**	**4**	**5**	....	**9**	**10**	**6**	....	**25**	**14**	**11**	....	**169**	**124**	**61**	**1st,**	**Won Stanley Cup**
1941-42	48	14	7	3	....	5	18	1	....	19	25	4	....	140	147	42	5th,	Lost Final
1940-41	48	14	5	5	....	7	11	6	....	21	16	11	....	112	102	53	3rd,	Lost Final
1939-40	48	11	10	3	....	5	16	3	....	16	26	6	....	91	126	38	5th,	Lost Semi-Final
1938-39	48	14	8	2	....	4	16	4	....	18	24	6	....	107	128	42	5th,	Lost Semi-Final
1937-38	48	8	10	6	....	4	15	5	....	12	25	11	....	99	133	35	4th, Amn. Div.	Out of Playoffs
1936-37	**48**	**14**	**5**	**5**	....	**11**	**9**	**4**	....	**25**	**14**	**9**	....	**128**	**102**	**59**	**1st, Amn. Div.**	**Won Stanley Cup**
1935-36	**48**	**14**	**5**	**5**	....	**10**	**11**	**3**	....	**24**	**16**	**8**	....	**124**	**103**	**56**	**1st, Amn. Div.**	**Won Stanley Cup**
1934-35	48	11	8	5	....	8	14	2	....	19	22	7	....	127	114	45	4th, Amn. Div.	Out of Playoffs
1933-34	48	15	5	4	....	9	9	6	....	24	14	10	....	113	98	58	1st, Amn. Div.	Lost Final
1932-33*	48	17	3	4	....	8	12	4	....	25	15	8	....	111	93	58	2nd, Amn. Div.	Lost Semi-Final
1931-32	48	15	3	6	....	3	17	4	....	18	20	10	....	95	108	46	3rd, Amn. Div.	Lost Quarter-Final
1930-31**	44	10	7	5	....	6	14	2	....	16	21	7	....	102	105	39	4th, Amn. Div.	Out of Playoffs
1929-30	44	9	10	3	....	5	14	3	....	14	24	6	....	117	133	34	4th, Amn. Div.	Out of Playoffs
1928-29	44	11	6	5	....	8	10	4	....	19	16	9	....	72	63	47	3rd, Amn. Div.	Lost Quarter-Final
1927-28	44	9	10	3	....	10	9	3	....	19	19	6	....	88	79	44	4th, Amn. Div.	Out of Playoffs
1926-27***	44	5	16	0	....	7	12	4	....	12	28	4	....	76	105	28	5th, Amn. Div.	Out of Playoffs

* Team name changed to Red Wings. ** Team name changed to Falcons. *** Team named Cougars.

2007-08 Schedule

Oct.	Wed.	3	Anaheim		Sat.	5	at Dallas*
	Sat.	6	at Chicago		Sun.	6	at Chicago
	Mon.	8	Edmonton		Tue.	8	Colorado
	Wed.	10	Calgary		Thu.	10	Minnesota
	Fri.	12	Chicago		Sat.	12	at Ottawa
	Sun.	14	at Los Angeles*		Tue.	15	Atlanta
	Mon.	15	at Anaheim		Thu.	17	Vancouver
	Thu.	18	at San Jose		Sat.	19	at San Jose
	Sat.	20	at Phoenix		Tue.	22	at Los Angeles
	Wed.	24	Vancouver		Wed.	23	at Anaheim
	Fri.	26	San Jose		Wed.	30	Phoenix
	Sun.	28	at Vancouver	**Feb.**	Fri.	1	Colorado
	Tue.	30	at Edmonton		Sat.	2	at Boston
Nov.	Thu.	1	at Calgary		Tue.	5	at Minnesota
	Wed.	7	Nashville		Thu.	7	Los Angeles
	Fri.	9	Columbus		Sat.	9	at Toronto*
	Sun.	11	at Chicago		Sun.	10	Anaheim*
	Tue.	13	at St. Louis		Tue.	12	at Nashville
	Sat.	17	Chicago		Fri.	15	Columbus
	Sun.	18	at Columbus*		Sun.	17	at Dallas*
	Wed.	21	St. Louis		Mon.	18	at Colorado
	Thu.	22	at Nashville		Fri.	22	at Calgary
	Sat.	24	at Columbus		Sat.	23	at Vancouver
	Tue.	27	Calgary		Tue.	26	at Edmonton
	Thu.	29	Tampa Bay		Fri.	29	San Jose
Dec.	Sat.	1	Phoenix	**Mar.**	Sun.	2	at Buffalo*
	Tue.	4	at Montreal		Wed.	5	St. Louis
	Fri.	7	Minnesota		Sun.	9	Nashville*
	Sun.	9	Carolina*		Tue.	11	Chicago
	Mon.	10	at Nashville		Thu.	13	Dallas
	Thu.	13	Edmonton		Sat.	15	Nashville*
	Sat.	15	Florida		Sun.	16	at Columbus*
	Mon.	17	Washington		Wed.	19	Columbus
	Wed.	19	Los Angeles		Thu.	20	at Nashville
	Thu.	20	at St. Louis		Sat.	22	at Columbus
	Sat.	22	at Minnesota		Tue.	25	at St. Louis
	Wed.	26	at St. Louis		Fri.	28	St. Louis
	Thu.	27	at Colorado		Sun.	30	Nashville*
	Sat.	29	at Phoenix	**Apr.**	Wed.	2	at Chicago
	Mon.	31	St. Louis		Thu.	3	Columbus
Jan.	Wed.	2	Dallas		Sun.	6	Chicago*

* Denotes afternoon game.

NHL WESTERN CONFERENCE

CENTRAL DIVISION
82nd NHL Season

Franchise date: September 25, 1926

2007-08 Player Personnel

FORWARDS	HT	WT	S	Place of Birth	*Age	2006-07 Club
CLEARY, Daniel	6-0	210	L	Carbonear, Nfld.	28	Detroit
CORAZZINI, Carl	5-10	182	R	Framingham, MA	28	Chicago-Norfolk
CULLEN, Mark	5-11	190	L	Moorhead, MN	28	Phi-Phi (AHL)
DATSYUK, Pavel	5-11	197	L	Sverdlovsk, USSR	29	Detroit
DRAKE, Dallas	6-1	195	L	Trail, B.C.	38	St. Louis
DRAPER, Kris	5-10	188	L	Toronto, Ont.	36	Detroit
ELLIS, Matt	6-0	188	L	Welland, Ont.	26	Detroit-Grand Rapids
FILPPULA, Valtteri	6-0	189	L	Vantaa, Finland	23	Detroit-Grand Rapids
FRANZEN, Johan	6-3	218	L	Landsbro, Sweden	27	Detroit
GELECH, Randall	6-3	220	R	Wynard, Sask.	23	San Antonio
HARTIGAN, Mark	6-0	200	L	Fort St. John, B.C.	29	CBJ-Syr-Ana-Port (AHL)
HOLMSTROM, Tomas	6-0	202	L	Pitea, Sweden	34	Detroit
HUDLER, Jiri	5-9	178	L	Olomouc, Czech.	23	Detroit
KOPECKY, Tomas	6-3	199	L	Ilava, Czech.	25	Detroit
MALTBY, Kirk	5-11	196	R	Guelph, Ont.	34	Detroit
SAMUELSSON, Mikael	6-2	210	L	Mariefred, Sweden	30	Detroit
ZETTERBERG, Henrik	5-11	195	L	Njurunda, Sweden	26	Detroit
DEFENSEMEN						
CHELIOS, Chris	5-11	191	R	Chicago, IL	45	Detroit
FERENCE, Brad	6-3	218	R	Calgary, Alta.	28	Calgary-Omaha
KRONWALL, Niklas	6-0	189	L	Stockholm, Sweden	26	Detroit
LEBDA, Brett	5-9	194	L	Buffalo Grove, IL	25	Detroit
LIDSTROM, Nicklas	6-1	193	L	Vasteras, Sweden	37	Detroit
LILJA, Andreas	6-3	230	L	Helsingborg, Sweden	32	Detroit
MEECH, Derek	5-11	197	L	Winnipeg, Man.	23	Detroit-Grand Rapids
QUINCEY, Kyle	6-1	207	L	Kitchener, Ont.	22	Detroit-Grand Rapids
RAFALSKI, Brian	5-10	195	R	Dearborn, MI	34	New Jersey
STAFFORD, Garrett	6-0	200	R	Los Angeles, CA	27	Worcester

GOALTENDERS	HT	WT	C	Place of Birth	*Age	2006-07 Club
HASEK, Dominik	6-1	166	L	Pardubice, Czech.	42	Detroit
HOWARD, James	6-0	218	L	Syracuse, NY	23	Grand Rapids
OSGOOD, Chris	5-10	176	L	Peace River, Alta.	34	Detroit

* – Age at start of 2007-08 season

Tomas Holmstrom set a career high with 30 goals in 2006-07.

Coach

MIKE BABCOCK

Coach, Detroit Red Wings. Born in Manitouwadge, Ont., April 29, 1963.

Mike Babcock became the 26th coach in Detroit Red Wings history on July 14, 2005, bringing a winning track record at all levels of play including college and junior hockey, the American Hockey League, the National Hockey League and the highest level of international competition. He is the only man to coach Team Canada to victories at both the World Junior Championship (1997) and senior World Championship (2004).

In his first season in Detroit, Babcock led the Red Wings to the NHL's best record. In 2006–07, the Red Wings topped the Western Conference standings and reached the Western Conference Final in the playoffs. Previously, he had spent two seasons with Anaheim, leading the team to the Stanley Cup finals in his first season behind the bench in 2002–03. He became the first rookie coach to reach the Finals since Florida's Doug MacLean in 1996. With a four-game sweep over Detroit in the first round of the playoffs, the Ducks became the first team since the 1952 Red Wings (over Toronto) to sweep a defending Stanley Cup champion. Babcock led the team to the best regular season in the club's history with 40 wins and 95 points in 2002–03.

Before joining Anaheim, Babcock spent two seasons as head coach of the Cincinnati Mighty Ducks (2000 to 2002), the primary development affiliate for both Detroit and Anaheim in the American Hockey League. He led the club to a franchise-best 41 wins and 95 points in 2000-01. Babcock moved to Cincinnati after a successful six-year run as the head coach of the Spokane Chiefs of the Western Hockey League (1994 through 2000). He was twice named WHL coach of the year (1996 and 2000) after taking the Chiefs to the league finals in both seasons. He began his WHL coaching career with the Moose Jaw Warriors in 1991–92. In Canadian university play, Babcock won a national championship and was named the coach of the year with the Lethbridge Pronghorns in 1993-94. In 1988, he was named head coach at Red Deer College in Red Deer, Alberta. He spent three seasons at the school, winning the Alberta college championship and coach of the year award in 1989.

Babcock played in the WHL for Saskatoon (1980-81) and Kelowna (1982-83), where he was team captain. In between, he spent a year at the University of Saskatoon. Babcock also played four years at McGill University (1983 to 1987), twice being named an All-Star defenseman and team captain. He earned his bachelor's degree in physical education and attended graduate school in sports psychology at McGill.

2006-07 Scoring

* – rookie

Regular Season

Pos	#	Player	Team	GP	G	A	Pts	+/–	PIM	PP	SH	GW	S	%
C	13	Pavel Datsyuk	DET	79	27	60	87	36	20	5	2	5	207	13.0
L	40	Henrik Zetterberg	DET	63	33	35	68	26	36	11	1	10	224	14.7
D	5	Nicklas Lidstrom	DET	80	13	49	62	40	46	10	0	1	224	5.8
L	96	Tomas Holmstrom	DET	77	30	22	52	13	58	13	0	5	176	17.0
C	20	Robert Lang	DET	81	19	33	52	12	66	6	0	4	166	11.4
D	23	Mathieu Schneider	DET	68	11	41	52	12	66	2	1	2	184	6.0
R	11	Daniel Cleary	DET	71	20	20	40	6	24	6	2	5	135	14.8
L	17	Kyle Calder	PHI	59	9	12	21	–31	36	2	2	0	88	10.2
			DET	19	5	9	14	6	22	1	0	2	42	11.9
			TOTAL	78	14	21	35	–25	58	3	2	2	130	10.8
R	37	Mikael Samuelsson	DET	53	14	20	34	1	28	6	0	2	189	7.4
C	93	Johan Franzen	DET	69	10	20	30	20	37	0	1	2	151	6.6
C	33	Kris Draper	DET	81	14	15	29	7	58	0	5	1	157	8.9
C	26 *	Jiri Hudler	DET	76	15	10	25	16	36	3	0	4	107	14.0
D	55	Niklas Kronvall	DET	68	1	21	22	0	54	1	0	0	104	1.0
D	22	Brett Lebda	DET	74	5	13	18	16	61	1	0	2	107	4.7
C	51 *	Valtteri Filppula	DET	73	10	7	17	8	20	0	0	1	76	13.2
D	95	Danny Markov	DET	66	4	12	16	25	59	0	0	0	66	6.1
L	18	Kirk Maltby	DET	82	6	5	11	–9	50	0	0	0	113	5.3
R	44	Todd Bertuzzi	FLA	7	1	6	7	–4	13	1	0	0	8	12.5
			DET	8	2	2	4	3	6	0	0	0	15	13.3
			TOTAL	15	3	8	11	–1	19	1	0	0	23	13.0
D	24	Chris Chelios	DET	71	0	11	11	11	34	0	0	0	72	0.0
D	3	Andreas Lilja	DET	57	0	5	5	6	54	0	0	0	37	0.0
L	15	Josh Langfeld	DET	33	0	2	2	2	12	0	0	0	37	0.0
D	45 *	Kyle Quincey	DET	6	1	0	1	0	0	0	0	0	7	14.3
R	28 *	Tomas Kopecky	DET	26	1	0	1	–2	22	0	0	0	27	3.7
D	17	Brad Norton	DET	6	0	1	1	2	20	0	0	0	2	0.0
D	36 *	Derek Meech	DET	4	0	0	0	1	2	0	0	0	3	0.0
C	43	Matt Hussey	DET	5	0	0	0	0	2	0	0	0	6	0.0
R	27 *	Darryl Bootland	DET	6	0	0	0	0	9	0	0	0	4	0.0
L	8 *	Matt Ellis	DET	16	0	0	0	–1	6	0	0	0	22	0.0

Goaltending

No.	Goaltender	GPI	Mins	Avg	W	L	OT	EN	SO	GA	SA	S%	G	A	PIM
39	Dominik Hasek	56	3341	2.05	38	11	6	2	8	114	1309	.913	0	2	20
30	Chris Osgood	21	1161	2.38	11	3	6	1	0	46	496	.907	0	1	6
31	Joey MacDonald	8	468	3.46	1	5	1	1	0	27	211	.872	0	0	0
	Totals	**82**	**4990**	**2.30**	**50**	**19**	**13**	**4**	**8**	**191**	**2020**	**.905**			

Playoffs

Pos	#	Player	Team	GP	G	A	Pts	+/–	PIM	PP	SH	GW	OT	S	%
D	5	Nicklas Lidstrom	DET	18	4	14	18	0	6	4	0	2	0	39	10.3
C	13	Pavel Datsyuk	DET	18	8	8	16	2	8	4	0	2	0	66	12.1
L	40	Henrik Zetterberg	DET	18	6	8	14	1	12	3	0	1	0	78	7.7
R	11	Daniel Cleary	DET	18	4	8	12	2	30	1	2	0	0	53	7.5
R	37	Mikael Samuelsson	DET	18	3	8	11	2	14	1	0	1	0	45	6.7
L	96	Tomas Holmstrom	DET	15	5	3	8	2	14	4	0	1	0	26	19.2
C	20	Robert Lang	DET	18	2	6	8	5	8	0	0	0	0	28	7.1
R	44	Todd Bertuzzi	DET	16	3	4	7	–2	15	1	0	0	0	24	12.5
C	93	Johan Franzen	DET	18	3	4	7	8	10	0	0	2	1	47	6.4
D	24	Chris Chelios	DET	18	1	6	7	7	12	0	1	0	0	27	3.7
D	23	Mathieu Schneider	DET	11	2	4	6	4	16	1	0	1	1	38	5.3
C	51 *	Valtteri Filppula	DET	18	3	2	5	–2	2	0	0	0	0	22	13.6
C	33	Kris Draper	DET	18	2	0	2	–5	24	0	0	0	0	26	7.7
L	18	Kirk Maltby	DET	18	1	1	2	0	10	0	1	0	0	20	5.0
C	26 *	Jiri Hudler	DET	6	0	2	2	2	4	0	0	0	0	6	0.0
D	22	Brett Lebda	DET	12	0	2	2	4	8	0	0	0	0	19	0.0
D	3	Andreas Lilja	DET	18	1	0	1	–4	10	0	0	0	0	12	8.3
L	17	Kyle Calder	DET	13	0	1	1	1	8	0	0	0	0	13	0.0
R	28 *	Tomas Kopecky	DET	4	0	0	0	–1	6	0	0	0	0	2	0.0
D	45 *	Kyle Quincey	DET	13	0	0	0	0	2	0	0	0	0	6	0.0
D	95	Danny Markov	DET	18	0	0	0	–2	13	0	0	0	0	27	0.0

Goaltending

No.	Goaltender	GPI	Mins	Avg	W	L	EN	SO	GA	SA	S%	G	A	PIM
39	Dominik Hasek	18	1140	1.79	10	8	1	2	34	444	.923	0	0	2
	Totals	**18**	**1147**	**1.83**	**10**	**8**	**1**	**2**	**35**	**445**	**.921**			

Coaching Record

		Regular Season				Playoffs		
Season	Team	Games	W	L	O/T	Games	W	L
1991-92	Moose Jaw (WHL)	72	33	36	3	4	0	4
1992-93	Moose Jaw (WHL)	72	27	42	3	....	....	....
1993-94	U. of Lethbridge (CIAU)	28	19	7	2	....	....	....
1994-95	Spokane (WHL)	72	32	36	4	11	6	5
1995-96	Spokane (WHL)	72	50	18	4	9	3	6
1996-97	Spokane (WHL)	65	31	30	4	9	4	5
1997-98	Spokane (WHL)	72	45	23	4	18	10	8
1998-99	Spokane (WHL)	72	19	44	9	....	....	....
1999-2000	Spokane (WHL)	72	47	21	4	20	15	5
2000-01	Cincinnati (WHL)	80	41	26	13	4	1	3
2001-02	Cincinnati (WHL)	80	33	33	14	3	1	2
2002-03	**Anaheim (NHL)**	**82**	**40**	**33**	**9**	**21**	**15**	**6**
2003-04	**Anaheim (NHL)**	**82**	**29**	**43**	**10**	....	....	....
2004-05	**Anaheim (NHL)**			Season Cancelled				
2005-06	**Detroit (NHL)**	**82**	**58**	**16**	**8**	**6**	**2**	**4**
2006-07	**Detroit (NHL)**	**82**	**50**	**19**	**13**	**18**	**10**	**8**
	NHL Totals	**328**	**177**	**111**	**40**	**45**	**27**	**18**

Club Records

Team

(Figures in brackets for season records are games played; records for fewest points, wins, ties, losses, goals, goals against are for 70 or more games)

Record		
Most Points	**131**	1995-96 (82)
Most Wins	***62**	1995-96 (82)
Most Ties	**18**	1952-53 (70), 1980-81 (80), 1996-97 (82)
Most Losses	**57**	1985-86 (80)
Most Goals	**369**	1992-93 (84)
Most Goals Against	**415**	1985-86 (80)
Fewest Points	**40**	1985-86 (80)
Fewest Wins	**16**	1976-77 (80)
Fewest Ties	**4**	1966-67 (70)
Fewest Losses	**13**	1950-51 (70), 1995-96 (82)
Fewest Goals	**167**	1958-59 (70)
Fewest Goals Against	**132**	1953-54 (70)
Longest Winning Streak		
Overall	**9**	Six times
Home	**14**	Jan. 21-Mar. 25/65
Away	**12**	Mar. 1-Apr. 15/06
Longest Undefeated Streak		
Overall	**15**	Nov. 27-Dec. 28/52 (8 wins, 7 ties)
Home	**19**	Dec. 31/00-Apr.7/01 (17 wins, 2 ties)
Away	**15**	Oct. 18-Dec. 20/51 (10 wins, 5 ties)
Longest Losing Streak		
Overall	**14**	Feb. 24-Mar. 25/82
Home	**7**	Feb. 20-Mar. 25/82
Away	**14**	Oct. 19-Dec. 21/66
Longest Winless Streak		
Overall	**19**	Feb. 26-Apr. 3/77 (18 losses, 1 tie)
Home	**10**	Dec. 11/85-Jan. 18/86 (9 losses, 1 tie)
Away	**26**	Dec. 15/76-Apr. 3/77 (23 losses, 3 ties)
Most Shutouts, Season	**13**	1953-54 (70)
Most. PIM, Season	**2,393**	1985-86 (80)
Most Goals, Game	**15**	Jan. 23/44 (NYR 0 at Det. 15)

Individual

Record		
Most Seasons	**25**	Gordie Howe
Most Games	**1,687**	Gordie Howe
Most Goals, Career	**786**	Gordie Howe
Most Assists, Career	**1,063**	Steve Yzerman
Most Points, Career	**1,809**	Gordie Howe (786G, 1,023A)
Most PIM, Career	**2,090**	Bob Probert
Most Shutouts, Career	**85**	Terry Sawchuk
Longest Consecutive Games Streak	**548**	Alex Delvecchio (Dec. 13/56-Nov. 11/64)
Most Goals, Season	**65**	Steve Yzerman (1988-89)
Most Assists, Season	**90**	Steve Yzerman (1988-89)
Most Points, Season	**155**	Steve Yzerman (1988-89; 65G, 90A)
Most PIM, Season	**398**	Bob Probert (1987-88)
Most Points, Defenseman, Season	**80**	Nicklas Lidstrom (2005-06; 16G, 64A)
Most Points, Center, Season	**155**	Steve Yzerman (1988-89; 65G, 90A)
Most Points, Right Wing, Season	**103**	Gordie Howe (1968-69; 44G, 59A)
Most Points, Left Wing, Season	**105**	John Ogrodnick (1984-85; 55G, 50A)
Most Points, Rookie, Season	**87**	Steve Yzerman (1983-84; 39G, 48A)
Most Shutouts, Season	**12**	Terry Sawchuk (1951-52, 1953-54, 1954-55), Glenn Hall (1955-56)
Most Goals, Game	**6**	Syd Howe (Feb. 3/44)
Most Assists, Game	***7**	Billy Taylor (Mar. 16/47)
Most Points, Game	**7**	Carl Liscombe (Nov. 5/42; 3G, 4A), Don Grosso (Feb. 3/44; 1G, 6A), Billy Taylor (Mar. 16/47; 7A)

* NHL Record.

Retired Numbers

No.	Player	Years
1	Terry Sawchuk	1949-55, 57-64, 68-69
7	Ted Lindsay	1944-57, 64-65
9	Gordie Howe	1946-1971
10	Alex Delvecchio	1951-1973
12	Sid Abel	1938-43, 45-52
19	Steve Yzerman	1983-2006

All-time Record vs. Other Clubs

Regular Season

	At Home								On Road								Total							
	GP	W	L	T	OL	GF	GA	PTS	GP	W	L	T	OL	GF	GA	PTS	GP	W	L	T	OL	GF	GA	PTS
Anaheim	26	21	2	3	0	92	53	45	26	12	10	4	0	71	63	28	52	33	12	7	0	163	116	73
Atlanta	4	4	0	0	0	17	8	8	4	3	1	0	0	25	14	6	8	7	1	0	0	42	22	14
Boston	286	154	80	52	0	955	726	360	287	90	153	43	1	761	1007	224	573	244	233	95	1	1716	1733	584
Buffalo	56	32	18	5	1	205	162	70	52	11	33	8	0	153	226	30	108	43	51	13	1	358	388	100
Calgary	63	34	19	10	0	233	186	78	64	21	37	6	0	184	238	48	127	55	56	16	0	417	424	126
Carolina	31	17	7	7	0	119	86	41	31	12	18	1	0	88	107	25	62	29	25	8	0	207	193	66
Chicago	343	210	98	33	2	1184	852	455	346	139	152	51	4	981	1032	333	689	349	250	84	6	2165	1884	788
Colorado	44	27	15	1	1	161	131	56	46	21	21	4	0	154	157	46	90	48	36	5	1	315	288	102
Columbus	18	14	2	0	2	71	40	30	19	14	4	1	0	61	37	29	37	28	6	1	2	132	77	59
Dallas	110	55	38	16	1	417	349	127	110	40	51	18	1	331	377	99	220	95	89	34	2	748	726	226
Edmonton	48	27	15	3	3	183	154	60	48	15	20	10	3	168	184	43	96	42	35	13	6	351	338	103
Florida	8	4	1	3	0	30	21	11	10	6	1	2	1	29	20	15	18	10	2	5	1	59	41	26
Los Angeles	83	40	30	13	0	321	282	93	84	27	42	14	1	261	330	69	167	67	72	27	1	582	612	162
Minnesota	12	8	3	1	0	43	27	17	12	7	1	2	2	34	27	18	24	15	4	3	2	77	54	35
Montreal	281	131	97	53	0	807	717	315	282	67	172	43	0	636	994	177	563	198	269	96	0	1443	1711	492
Nashville	25	18	2	2	3	96	54	41	24	12	8	2	2	70	64	28	49	30	10	4	5	166	118	69
New Jersey	41	26	13	2	0	169	131	54	41	11	21	9	0	105	139	31	82	37	34	11	0	274	270	85
NY Islanders	46	26	18	2	0	166	137	54	47	20	23	4	0	141	167	44	93	46	41	6	0	307	304	98
NY Rangers	286	165	76	45	0	1008	702	375	285	93	134	58	0	742	871	244	571	258	210	103	0	1750	1573	619
Ottawa	10	6	4	0	0	35	22	12	10	6	3	1	0	29	28	13	20	12	7	1	0	64	50	25
Philadelphia	60	32	18	10	0	216	185	74	59	13	35	11	0	169	236	37	119	45	53	21	0	385	421	111
Phoenix	55	27	20	8	0	216	183	62	53	22	17	14	0	171	154	58	108	49	37	22	0	387	337	120
Pittsburgh	66	41	13	12	0	256	179	94	66	18	44	4	0	197	281	40	132	59	57	16	0	453	460	134
St. Louis	118	57	42	17	2	430	354	133	118	40	55	20	3	332	388	103	236	97	97	37	5	762	742	236
San Jose	29	25	3	1	0	115	51	51	30	15	12	3	0	113	108	33	59	40	15	4	0	228	159	84
Tampa Bay	12	10	1	1	0	47	21	21	15	10	4	1	0	67	46	21	27	20	5	2	0	114	67	42
Toronto	323	169	106	46	2	973	793	386	316	105	164	47	0	846	1045	257	639	274	270	93	2	1819	1838	643
Vancouver	70	42	18	8	2	283	200	94	69	28	31	10	0	222	248	66	139	70	49	18	2	505	448	160
Washington	47	21	15	11	0	161	135	53	47	21	21	5	0	151	171	47	94	42	36	16	0	312	306	100
Defunct Clubs	141	76	40	25	0	430	307	177	141	49	63	29	0	364	375	127	282	125	103	54	0	794	682	304
Totals	**2742**	**1519**	**814**	**390**	**19**	**9439**	**7248**	**3447**	**2742**	**948**	**1351**	**425**	**18**	**7656**	**9134**	**2339**	**5484**	**2467**	**2165**	**815**	**37**	**17095**	**16382**	**5786**

Playoffs

	Series	W	L	GP	W	L	T	GF	GA	Last Mtg.	Rnd.	Result
Anaheim	4	2	2	18	10	8	0	53	40	2007	CF	L 2-4
Boston	7	3	4	33	14	19	0	98	96	1957	SF	L 1-4
Calgary	3	2	1	14	8	6	0	38	26	2007	CQF	W 4-2
Carolina	1	1	0	5	4	1	0	14	7	2002	F	W 4-1
Chicago	14	6	8	69	31	38	0	190	210	1995	CF	W 4-1
Colorado	5	2	3	30	13	17	0	76	79	2002	CF	W 4-3
Dallas	3	3	0	18	12	6	0	55	40	1998	CF	W 4-2
Edmonton	3	0	3	16	4	12	0	43	58	2006	CQF	L 2-4
Los Angeles	2	1	1	10	6	4	0	32	21	2001	CQF	L 2-4
Montreal	12	7	5	62	29	33	0	149	161	1978	QF	L 1-4
Nashville	1	1	0	6	4	2	0	12	9	2004	CQF	W 4-2
New Jersey	1	0	1	4	0	4	0	7	16	1995	F	L 0-4
NY Rangers	5	4	1	23	13	10	0	57	49	1950	F	W 4-3
Philadelphia	1	1	0	4	4	0	0	16	6	1997	F	W 4-0
Phoenix	2	2	0	12	8	4	0	44	28	1998	CQF	W 4-2
St. Louis	7	5	2	40	24	16	0	125	103	2002	CSF	W 4-1
San Jose	3	2	1	17	11	6	0	64	36	2007	CSF	W 4-2
Toronto	23	11	12	117	59	58	0	321	311	1993	DSF	L 3-4
Vancouver	1	1	0	6	4	2	0	22	16	2002	CQF	W 4-2
Washington	1	1	0	4	4	0	0	13	7	1998	F	W 4-0
Defunct Clubs	4	3	1	10	7	2	1	21	13			
Totals	**103**	**58**	**45**	**518**	**269**	**248**	**1**	**1450**	**1332**			

Calgary totals include Atlanta Flames, 1972-73 to 1979-80.
Carolina totals include Hartford, 1979-80 to 1996-97.
Colorado totals include Quebec, 1979-80 to 1994-95.
Dallas totals include Minnesota North Stars, 1967-68 to 1992-93.
New Jersey totals include Kansas City, 1974-75, 1975-76, and Colorado Rockies, 1976-77 to 1981-82.
Phoenix totals include Winnipeg, 1979-80 to 1995-96.

Playoff Results 2007-2002

Year	Round	Opponent	Result	GF	GA
2007	CF	Anaheim	L 2-4	17	16
	CSF	San Jose	W 4-2	13	9
	CQF	Calgary	W 4-2	18	10
2006	CQF	Edmonton	L 2-4	17	19
2004	CSF	Calgary	L 2-4	12	11
	CQF	Nashville	W 4-2	12	9
2003	CQF	Anaheim	L 0-4	6	10
2002	**F**	**Carolina**	**W 4-1**	**14**	**7**
	CF	Colorado	W 4-3	22	13
	CSF	St. Louis	W 4-1	14	11
	CQF	Vancouver	W 4-2	22	16

Abbreviations: Round: F - Final; **CF** - conference final; **CSF** - conference semi-final; **CQF** - conference quarter-final; **DSF** - division semi-final; **SF** - semi-final; **QF** - quarter-final.

2006-07 Results

Month	Day	Opponent	Score
Oct.	5	Vancouver	1-3
	7	at Pittsburgh	2-0
	11	Phoenix	9-2
	13	Buffalo	2-3†
	16	at Los Angeles	3-1
	18	at Anaheim	1-4
	19	at San Jose	1-5
	21	at Edmonton	1-3
	25	San Jose	2-1
	27	at Dallas	4-3
	28	at St. Louis	3-2
Nov.	1	Calgary	3-2
	2	at Chicago	2-1
	4	Columbus	4-1
	8	Edmonton	3-0
	10	Nashville	3-0
	14	at Vancouver	3-2
	17	at Calgary	1-4
	18	at Edmonton	3-4†
	22	Vancouver	3-4*
	24	St. Louis	2-3†
	25	at Nashville	2-6
	27	Dallas	2-1
Dec.	1	at Minnesota	3-0
	2	San Jose	2-3
	5	at St. Louis	5-1
	7	St. Louis	4-3*
	9	Toronto	5-1
	12	Ottawa	2-3
	14	at Chicago	3-2
	16	at New Jersey	2-1
	18	at Columbus	3-4
	20	Columbus	5-0
	22	Minnesota	3-1
	23	at Minnesota	2-3*
	27	Minnesota	3-1
	28	at Columbus	7-4
	31	Los Angeles	6-2
Jan.	2	Anaheim	2-1
	4	at San Jose	4-9
	6	at Los Angeles	2-4
	7	at Anaheim	2-4
	9	at Colorado	4-3†
	11	at Phoenix	5-1
	13	Chicago	6-3
	15	Montreal	2-0
	17	Nashville	5-3
	19	at Columbus	1-3
	20	at Colorado	1-3
	26	at St. Louis	1-2*
	28	Colorado	3-1
	30	at NY Islanders	4-3*
Feb.	2	St. Louis	5-3
	5	at NY Rangers	4-3
	7	Phoenix	4-2
	8	at St. Louis	0-1
	11	Calgary	7-4
	12	at Philadelphia	1-6
	14	at Dallas	3-1
	17	at Phoenix	4-1
	21	Chicago	4-2
	23	Edmonton	3-4†
	24	at Nashville	3-4*
	27	at Chicago	4-1
Mar.	2	Chicago	6-2
	4	Colorado	3-4*
	6	Nashville	4-3†
	9	Los Angeles	3-2*
	11	Boston	3-6
	13	at Nashville	5-2
	14	Nashville	4-2
	17	at Vancouver	1-4
	20	at Calgary	1-2
	22	Columbus	1-2†
	24	St. Louis	2-3†
	26	Anaheim	1-0
	29	at Nashville	2-1
	30	Dallas	3-4†
Apr.	1	at Columbus	4-1
	3	Columbus	3-0
	5	at Chicago	2-3†
	7	Chicago	7-2

* – Overtime † – Shootout

Entry Draft Selections 2007-1993

2007
Pick
27 Brendan Smith
88 Joakim Andersson
148 Randy Cameron
178 Zack Torquato
208 Bryan Rufenach

2006
Pick
41 Cory Emmerton
47 Shawn Matthias
62 Dick Axelsson
92 Daniel Larsson
182 Jan Mursak
191 Nick Oslund
212 Logan Pyett

2005
Pick
19 Jakub Kindl
42 Justin Abdelkader
80 Christofer Lofberg
103 Mattias Ritola
132 Darren Helm
137 Johan Ryno
151 Jeff May
175 Juho Mielonen
214 Bretton Stamler

2004
Pick
97 Johan Franzen
128 Evan McGrath
151 Sergei Kolesov
162 Tyler Haskins
192 Anton Axelsson
226 Steven Covington
257 Gennady Stolyarov
290 Nils Backstrom

2003
Pick
64 James Howard
132 Kyle Quincey
164 Ryan Oulahen
170 Andreas Sundin
194 Stefan Blom
226 Tomas Kollar
258 Vladimir Kutny
289 Mikael Johansson

2002
Pick
58 Jiri Hudler
63 Tomas Fleischmann
95 Valtteri Filppula
131 Johan Berggren
166 Logan Koopmans
197 Jimmy Cuddihy
229 Derek Meech
260 Pierre-Olivier Beaulieu
262 Christian Soderstrom
291 Jonathan Ericsson

2001
Pick
62 Igor Grigorenko
121 Drew MacIntyre
129 Miroslav Blatak
157 Andreas Jamtin
195 Nick Pannoni
258 Dmitri Bykov
288 Francois Senez

2000
Pick
29 Niklas Kronwall
38 Tomas Kopecky
102 Stefan Liv
127 Dmitri Semenov
128 Alexander Seluyanov
130 Aaron Van Leusen
187 Per Backer
196 Paul Ballantyne
228 Jimmie Svensson
251 Todd Jackson
260 Yevgeny Bumagin

1999
Pick
120 Jari Tolsa
149 Andrei Maximenko
181 Kent McDonell
210 Henrik Zetterberg
238 Anton Borodkin
266 Ken Davis

1998
Pick
25 Jiri Fischer
55 Ryan Barnes
56 Tomek Valtonen
84 Jake McCracken
111 Brent Hobday
142 Calle Steen
151 Adam DeLeeuw
171 Pavel Datsyuk
198 Jeremy Goetzinger
226 David Petrasek
256 Petja Pietilainen

1997
Pick
49 Yuri Butsayev
76 Petr Sykora
102 Quintin Laing
129 John Wikstrom
157 B.J. Young
186 Mike Laceby
213 Steve Willejto
239 Greg Willers

1996
Pick
26 Jesse Wallin
52 Aren Miller
108 Johan Forsander
135 Michal Podolka
144 Magnus Nilsson
162 Alexandre Jacques
189 Colin Beardsmore
215 Craig Stahl
241 Eugeny Afanasiev

1995
Pick
26 Maxim Kuznetsov
52 Philippe Audet
58 Darryl Laplante
104 Anatoli Ustyugov
125 Chad Wilchynski
126 David Arsenault
156 Tyler Perry
182 Per Eklund
208 Andrei Samokhvalov
234 David Engblom

1994
Pick
23 Yan Golubovsky
49 Mathieu Dandenault
75 Sean Gillam
114 Frederic Deschenes
127 Doug Battaglia
153 Pavel Agarkov
205 Jason Elliot
231 Jeff Mikesch
257 Tomas Holmstrom
283 Toivo Suursoo

1993
Pick
22 Anders Eriksson
48 Jon Coleman
74 Kevin Hilton
97 John Jakopin
100 Benoit Larose
126 Norm Maracle
152 Tim Spitzig
178 Yuri Yeresko
204 Vitezslav Skuta
230 Ryan Shanahan
256 James Kosecki
282 Gordon Hunt

General Manager

KEN HOLLAND
General Manager, Detroit Red Wings. Born in Vernon, B.C., Nov. 10, 1955.

Ken Holland has served in the Red Wings front office since 1985, and has been the club's general manager since July 18, 1997. He has established himself as one of the most innovative and aggressive GMs in the National Hockey League. Detroit's Stanley Cup victory in 2002 marked the team's second championship under his leadership. Holland began his tenure as the club's general manager after serving as assistant general manager for the previous three seasons.

Holland oversees all aspects of hockey operations including all matters relating to player personnel, development, contract negotiations and player movements, though he now takes a less prominent role in the NHL draft than he did during his seven years as the club's director of amateur scouting.

At the conclusion of his playing days as a goaltender, spending most of his pro career at the American Hockey League level, Holland began his off-ice career in 1985 as a western Canada scout followed by five years as an amateur scouting director before promotions led to his current position as general manager.

A native of Vernon, BC, Holland played in the junior ranks for Medicine Hat (WHL) in 1974-75. He was Toronto's 13th pick (188th overall) in the 1975 draft but never saw action with the Maple Leafs. Holland twice signed with NHL teams as a free agent — in 1980 with Hartford and 1983 with Detroit. He spent most of his pro career with AHL clubs in Binghamton and Springfield, along with Adirondack, but did appear in four NHL games, making his debut with Hartford in 1980-81 and playing three contests for Detroit in 1983-84.

Club Directory

Joe Louis Arena

Detroit Red Wings
Joe Louis Arena
600 Civic Center Drive
Detroit, MI 48226
Phone **313/396-7535**
FAX PR: 313/567-0296
Media Hotline: 313/396-7599
www.detroitredwings.com
Capacity: 20,066

Owner/Governor . . . . . Mike Ilitch
Owner/Secretary-Treasurer . . . . . Marian Ilitch
President and CEO Ilitch Holdings/ Alternate Governor Red Wings . . . . . Christopher Ilitch
Vice-President Olympia Entertainment/ General Counsel Red Wings . . . . . Robert E. Carr
Senior Vice President. . . . . Jim Devellano
Vice President/General Manager . . . . . Ken Holland
Vice President. . . . . Steve Yzerman
Assistant General Manager . . . . . Jim Nill
Director of Hockey Administration . . . . . Ryan Martin
Consultant . . . . . Scotty Bowman
Head Coach . . . . . Mike Babcock
Assistant Coaches. . . . . Paul MacLean, Todd McLellan
Video Coach. . . . . Jay Woodcroft
Goaltending Coach. . . . . Jim Bedard
Director of Pro Scouting . . . . . Mark Howe
Pro Scouts . . . . . Bob McCammon, Pat Verbeek, Glenn Merkosky
Director of Amateur Scouting . . . . . Joe McDonnell
Amateur Scouts . . . . . Bruce Haralson, Mark Leach, Dave Kolb
Director of European Scouting . . . . . Hakan Andersson
European Scouts. . . . . Vladimir Havluj, Evgeni Erfilov
Part-Time Scout . . . . . Marty Stein
Vice-President of Finance . . . . . Paul MacDonald
Executive Assistant . . . . . Kathi Wyatt
Accounting Assistant . . . . . Bridget Merritt
Athletic Therapist . . . . . Piet Van Zant
Equipment Manager. . . . . Paul Boyer
Assistant Athletic Therapist. . . . . Russ Baumann
Assistant Equipment Manager. . . . . Chris Scoppetto
Team Masseur . . . . . Sergei Tchekmarev
Senior Director of Communications. . . . . John Hahn
Media Relations Manager . . . . . Mike Brinich
Community Relations Manager. . . . . AnneMarie Krappmann
Public Relations Coordinator . . . . . Lisa Hickok
Medical Director . . . . . Dr. Donald Weaver
Team Physicians . . . . . Dr. Anthony Colucci, Dr. Doug Plagens
Team Dentist . . . . . Dr. C.J. Regula
Team Photographer . . . . . Dave Reginek
Radio Announcers, AM 1270 WXYT . . . . . Ken Kal, Paul Woods
Television Announcers, Fox Sports Net Detroit. . . . . Ken Daniels, Mickey Redmond

Coaching History

Art Duncan, 1926-27; Jack Adams, 1927-28 to 1946-47; Tommy Ivan, 1947-48 to 1953-54; Jimmy Skinner, 1954-55 to 1956-57; Jimmy Skinner and Sid Abel, 1957-58; Sid Abel, 1958-59 to 1967-68; Bill Gadsby, 1968-69; Bill Gadsby and Sid Abel, 1969-70; Ned Harkness and Doug Barkley, 1970-71; Doug Barkley and Johnny Wilson, 1971-72; Johnny Wilson, 1972-73; Ted Garvin and Alex Delvecchio, 1973-74; Alex Delvecchio, 1974-75; Doug Barkley and Alex Delvecchio, 1975-76; Alex Delvecchio and Larry Wilson, 1976-77; Bobby Kromm, 1977-78, 1978-79; Bobby Kromm and Ted Lindsay, 1979-80; Ted Lindsay and Wayne Maxner, 1980-81; Wayne Maxner and Billy Dea, 1981-82; Nick Polano, 1982-83 to 1984-85; Harry Neale and Brad Park, 1985-86; Jacques Demers, 1986-87 to 1989-90; Bryan Murray, 1990-91 to 1992-93; Scotty Bowman, 1993-94 to 1997-98; Dave Lewis, Barry Smith (co-coaches) and Scotty Bowman, 1998-99; Scotty Bowman, 1999-2000 to 2001-02; Dave Lewis, 2002-03, 2003-04; Mike Babcock, 2005-06 to date.

General Managers' History

Art Duncan and Duke Keats, 1926-27; Jack Adams, 1927-28 to 1961-62; Sid Abel, 1962-63 to 1969-70; Sid Abel and Ned Harkness, 1970-71; Ned Harkness, 1971-72 to 1973-74; Alex Delvecchio, 1974-75, 1975-76; Alex Delvecchio and Ted Lindsay, 1976-77; Ted Lindsay, 1977-78 to 1979-80; Jimmy Skinner, 1980-81, 1981-82; Jim Devellano, 1982-83 to 1989-90; Bryan Murray, 1990-91 to 1993-94; Jim Devellano (Senior Vice President), 1994-95 to 1996-97; Ken Holland, 1997-98 to date.

Captains' History

Art Duncan, 1926-27; Reg Noble, 1927-28 to 1929-30; George Hay, 1930-31; Carson Cooper, 1931-32; Larry Aurie, 1932-33; Herbie Lewis, 1933-34; Ebbie Goodfellow, 1934-35; Doug Young, 1935-36 to 1937-38; Ebbie Goodfellow, 1938-39 to 1940-41; Ebbie Goodfellow and Syd Howe, 1941-42; Sid Abel, 1942-43; Mud Bruneteau, Flash Hollett, 1943-44; Flash Hollett, 1944-45; Flash Hollett and Sid Abel, 1945-46; Sid Abel, 1946-47 to 1951-52; Ted Lindsay, 1952-53 to 1955-56; Red Kelly, 1956-57, 1957-58; Gordie Howe, 1958-59 to 1961-62; Alex Delvecchio, 1962-63 to 1972-73; Alex Delvecchio, Nick Libett, Red Berenson, Gary Bergman, Ted Harris, Mickey Redmond and Larry Johnston, 1973-74; Marcel Dionne, 1974-75; Danny Grant and Terry Harper, 1975-76; Danny Grant and Dennis Polonich, 1976-77; Dan Maloney and Dennis Hextall, 1977-78; Dennis Hextall, Nick Libett and Paul Woods, 1978-79; Dale McCourt, 1979-80; Errol Thompson and Reed Larson, 1980-81; Reed Larson, 1981-82; Danny Gare, 1982-83 to 1985-86; Steve Yzerman, 1986-87 to 2005-06; Nicklas Lidstrom, 2006-07 to date.

Key Off-Season Signings/Acquisitions

2007

May 2 • Signed 2005 1st-round pick (25th overall), C **Andrew Cogliano**.

July 1 • Signed D **Dick Tarnstrom**.

1 • Acquired D **Joni Pitkanen**, LW **Geoff Sanderson** and a 3rd-round pick in the 2009 Entry Draft from Philadelphia for D **Jason Smith** and RW **Joffrey Lupul**.

July 3 • Signed G **Mathieu Garon**.

3 • Re-signed LW **Raffi Torres**.

4 • Re-signed D **Matt Greene**.

Aug. 2 • Signed RW **Dustin Penner**.

Edmonton Oilers

2006-07 Results: 32W-43L-4OTL-3SOL 71PTS.
Fifth, Northwest Division

Year-by-Year Record

Season	GP	Home W	Home L	Home T	Home OL	Road W	Road L	Road T	Road OL	Overall W	Overall L	Overall T	Overall OL	GF	GA	Pts.	Finished	Playoff Result
2006-07	82	19	19	....	3	13	24	....	4	32	43	....	7	195	248	71	5th, Northwest Div.	Out of Playoffs
2005-06	82	20	15	....	6	21	13	....	7	41	28	....	13	256	251	95	3rd, Northwest Div.	Lost Final
2004-05	....	....	....	....	....	....	....	....	....	....	....	....	....	....	....	....		
2003-04	82	22	12	4	3	14	17	8	2	36	29	12	5	221	208	89	4th, Northwest Div.	Out of Playoffs
2002-03	82	20	12	5	4	16	14	6	5	36	26	11	9	231	230	92	4th, Northwest Div.	Lost Conf. Quarter-Final
2001-02	82	23	14	4	0	15	14	8	4	38	28	12	4	205	182	92	3rd, Northwest Div.	Out of Playoffs
2000-01	82	23	9	7	2	16	19	5	1	39	28	12	3	243	222	93	2nd, Northwest Div.	Lost Conf. Quarter-Final
1999-2000	82	18	11	9	3	14	15	7	5	32	26	16	8	226	212	88	2nd, Northwest Div.	Lost Conf. Quarter-Final
1998-99	82	17	19	5	....	16	18	7	....	33	37	12	....	230	226	78	2nd, Northwest Div.	Lost Conf. Quarter-Final
1997-98	82	20	16	5	....	15	21	5	....	35	37	10	....	215	224	80	3rd, Pacific Div.	Lost Conf. Semi-Final
1996-97	82	21	16	4	....	15	21	5	....	36	37	9	....	252	247	81	3rd, Pacific Div.	Lost Conf. Semi-Final
1995-96	82	15	21	5	....	15	23	3	....	30	44	8	....	240	304	68	5th, Pacific Div.	Out of Playoffs
1994-95	48	11	12	1	....	6	15	3	....	17	27	4	....	136	183	38	5th, Pacific Div.	Out of Playoffs
1993-94	84	17	22	3	....	8	23	11	....	25	45	14	....	261	305	64	6th, Pacific Div.	Out of Playoffs
1992-93	84	16	21	5	....	10	29	3	....	26	50	8	....	242	337	60	5th, Smythe Div.	Out of Playoffs
1991-92	80	22	13	5	....	14	21	5	....	36	34	10	....	295	297	82	3rd, Smythe Div.	Lost Conf. Championship
1990-91	80	22	15	3	....	15	22	3	....	37	37	6	....	272	272	80	3rd, Smythe Div.	Lost Conf. Championship
1989-90	**80**	**23**	**11**	**6**	....	**15**	**17**	**8**	....	**38**	**28**	**14**	....	**315**	**283**	**90**	**2nd, Smythe Div.**	**Won Stanley Cup**
1988-89	80	21	16	3	....	17	18	5	....	38	34	8	....	325	306	84	3rd, Smythe Div.	Lost Div. Semi-Final
1987-88	**80**	**28**	**8**	**4**	....	**16**	**17**	**7**	....	**44**	**25**	**11**	....	**363**	**288**	**99**	**2nd, Smythe Div.**	**Won Stanley Cup**
1986-87	**80**	**29**	**6**	**5**	....	**21**	**18**	**1**	....	**50**	**24**	**6**	....	**372**	**284**	**106**	**1st, Smythe Div.**	**Won Stanley Cup**
1985-86	80	32	6	2	....	24	11	5	....	56	17	7	....	426	310	119	1st, Smythe Div.	Lost Div. Final
1984-85	**80**	**26**	**7**	**7**	....	**23**	**13**	**4**	....	**49**	**20**	**11**	....	**401**	**298**	**109**	**1st, Smythe Div.**	**Won Stanley Cup**
1983-84	**80**	**31**	**5**	**4**	....	**26**	**13**	**1**	....	**57**	**18**	**5**	....	**446**	**314**	**119**	**1st, Smythe Div.**	**Won Stanley Cup**
1982-83	80	25	9	6	....	22	12	6	....	47	21	12	....	424	315	106	1st, Smythe Div.	Lost Final
1981-82	80	31	5	4	....	17	12	11	....	48	17	15	....	417	295	111	1st, Smythe Div.	Lost Div. Semi-Final
1980-81	80	17	13	10	....	12	22	6	....	29	35	16	....	328	327	74	4th, Smythe Div.	Lost Quarter-Final
1979-80	80	17	14	9	....	11	25	4	....	28	39	13	....	301	322	69	4th, Smythe Div.	Lost Prelim. Round

2007-08 Schedule

Month	Day	Date	Opponent	Month	Day	Date	Opponent
Oct.	Thu.	4	San Jose		Thu.	3	at Nashville
	Sat.	6	Philadelphia*		Sat.	5	NY Rangers
	Mon.	8	at Detroit		Mon.	7	NY Islanders
	Wed.	10	at Minnesota		Thu.	10	Phoenix
	Fri.	12	Vancouver		Sun.	13	Calgary
	Sat.	13	at Vancouver		Tue.	15	Los Angeles
	Thu.	18	at Phoenix		Thu.	17	at Washington
	Sat.	20	at Calgary		Fri.	18	at Carolina
	Tue.	23	Colorado		Sun.	20	at Atlanta*
	Thu.	25	Minnesota		Tue.	22	at Tampa Bay
	Sat.	27	at Los Angeles		Thu.	24	at Florida
	Sun.	28	at Anaheim*		Tue.	29	San Jose
	Tue.	30	Detroit	**Feb.**	Fri.	1	Dallas
Nov.	Fri.	2	Nashville		Mon.	4	Calgary
	Mon.	5	at Minnesota		Wed.	6	Chicago
	Wed.	7	at Colorado		Sat.	9	at Calgary*
	Sat.	10	at Calgary		Tue.	12	Minnesota
	Wed.	14	at Vancouver		Thu.	14	at San Jose
	Thu.	15	Minnesota		Sat.	16	at Vancouver
	Sat.	17	Calgary		Tue.	19	at Nashville
	Tue.	20	Vancouver		Fri.	22	at Dallas
	Thu.	22	Colorado		Sun.	24	Colorado
	Sat.	24	Chicago		Tue.	26	Detroit
	Mon.	26	Columbus		Thu.	28	Los Angeles
	Wed.	28	at Colorado	**Mar.**	Sun.	2	Columbus
	Fri.	30	Anaheim		Tue.	4	Nashville
Dec.	Sun.	2	at Anaheim*		Fri.	7	at Columbus
	Mon.	3	at Los Angeles		Sun.	9	at Chicago*
	Wed.	5	Pittsburgh		Tue.	11	St. Louis
	Fri.	7	St. Louis		Thu.	13	at Colorado
	Mon.	10	at Dallas		Sat.	15	at Phoenix
	Tue.	11	at St. Louis		Sun.	16	at San Jose*
	Thu.	13	at Detroit		Tue.	18	Phoenix
	Sat.	15	Vancouver		Thu.	20	Vancouver
	Tue.	18	Dallas		Sat.	22	Colorado*
	Fri.	21	New Jersey		Mon.	24	Minnesota
	Sun.	23	at Chicago		Wed.	26	at Minnesota
	Thu.	27	Anaheim		Fri.	28	at Colorado
	Sat.	29	at Minnesota		Sat.	29	at Calgary
	Mon.	31	at Columbus	**Apr.**	Tue.	1	Calgary
Jan.	Wed.	2	at St. Louis		Thu.	3	at Vancouver

* Denotes afternoon game.

Ales Hemsky played just 60 games in 2006-07, but led the team with 40 assists and tied for the lead with 53 points.

NORTHWEST DIVISION
29th NHL Season

Franchise date: June 22, 1979

2007-08 Player Personnel

FORWARDS	HT	WT	S	Place of Birth	*Age	2006-07 Club
ALMTORP, Jonas	6-1	189	L	Uppsala, Sweden	23	Brynas
BODIE, Troy	6-4	196	R	Portage La Prairie, Man.	22	Hamilton-Stockton
BRODZIAK, Kyle	6-2	198	R	St. Paul, Alta.	23	Edmonton-Wilkes-Barre
COGLIANO, Andrew	5-10	178	L	Toronto, Ont.	20	U. of Michigan
FLINN, Ryan	6-5	248	L	Halifax, N.S.	27	San Antonio
GOULET, Stephane	6-3	185	L	Levis, Que.	21	Grand Rapids-Stockton
HEMSKY, Ales	6-0	192	R	Pardubice, Czech.	24	Edmonton
HORCOFF, Shawn	6-1	204	L	Trail, B.C.	29	Edmonton
JACQUES, Jean-Francois	6-4	217	L	Montreal, Que.	22	Edmonton-Wilkes-Barre
JOHANSSON, Fredrik	5-11	178	L	Goteburg, Sweden	23	Frolunda-Frolunda Jr.
McDONALD, Colin	6-3	205	R	New Haven, CT	22	Providence College
MOREAU, Ethan	6-2	220	L	Huntsville, Ont.	32	Edmonton
NILSSON, Robert	5-11	185	L	Calgary, Alta.	22	Bridgeport-Edm-Wilkes-Barre
O'MARRA, Ryan	6-2	193	R	Tokyo, Japan	20	Erie (OHL)-Saginaw
PAUKOVICH, Geoff	6-4	208	L	Englewood, CO	21	U. of Denver
PENNER, Dustin	6-4	245	L	Winkler, Man.	25	Anaheim
PISANI, Fernando	6-1	205	L	Edmonton, Alta.	30	Edmonton
POULIOT, Marc-Antoine	6-1	195	R	Quebec City, Que.	22	Edmonton-Wilkes-Barre
REASONER, Marty	6-1	200	L	Honeoye Falls, NY	30	Edmonton
REDDOX, Liam	5-10	177	L	East York, Ont.	21	Stockton
ROHLFS, David	6-3	219	R	Ann Arbor, MI	23	U. of Michigan
SANDERSON, Geoff	6-0	190	L	Hay River, N.W.T.	35	Philadelphia
SCHREMP, Rob	5-11	200	L	Syracuse, NY	21	Edmonton-Wilkes-Barre
SESTITO, Tim	5-11	195	L	Rome, NY	23	Wilkes-Barre-Stockton
SPURGEON, Tyler	5-10	188	L	Edmonton, Alta.	21	Wilkes-Barre-Stockton
STOLL, Jarret	6-1	201	R	Melville, Sask.	25	Edmonton
STORTINI, Zachery	6-3	228	R	Elliot Lake, Ont.	22	Edmonton-Hamilton
THORESEN, Patrick	5-11	188	L	Oslo, Norway	19	Edmonton-Wilkes-Barre
TORRES, Raffi	6-0	216	L	Toronto, Ont.	25	Edmonton
TRUKHNO, Vyacheslav	6-1	197	L	Khimki, USSR	20	Gatineau
DEFENSEMEN						
BISAILLON, Sebastien	6-0	205	R	Mont-Laurier, Que.	20	Edmonton-Val-d'Or
GILBERT, Tom	6-3	210	R	Minneapolis, MN	24	Edmonton-Wilkes-Barre
GREBESHKOV, Denis	6-0	190	L	Yaroslavl, USSR	23	Yaroslavl
GREENE, Matt	6-3	223	R	Grand Ledge, MI	24	Edmonton
KEMP, T.J.	5-11	197	L	Pickering, Ont.	26	Manchester
PECKHAM, Theo	6-2	216	L	Richmond Hill, Ont.	19	Owen Sound
PITKANEN, Joni	6-3	210	L	Oulu, Finland	24	Philadelphia
REYNOLDS, T.J.	6-2	225	R	Kitchener, Ont.	26	Milwaukee-Rockford
ROURKE, Allan	6-2	215	L	Mississauga, Ont.	27	NY Islanders-Bridgeport
ROY, Mathieu	6-2	214	R	St-Georges, Que.	24	Edmonton-Hamilton
SMID, Ladislav	6-3	204	L	Frydlant V Cechach, Czech.	21	Edmonton
SOURAY, Sheldon	6-4	227	L	Elk Point, Alta.	31	Montreal
STAIOS, Steve	6-1	200	R	Hamilton, Ont.	34	Edmonton
SYVRET, Danny	5-11	203	L	Millgrove, Ont.	22	Edmonton-Grand Rapids
TARNSTROM, Dick	6-1	205	L	Sundbyberg, Sweden	32	Lugano
YOUNG, Bryan	6-1	191	L	Kitchener, Ont.	21	Edm-Milwaukee-Stockton-Wilkes-Barre

GOALTENDERS	HT	WT	C	Place of Birth	*Age	2006-07 Club
DROUIN-DESLAURIERS, Jeff	6-4	189	R	St-Jean-Richelieu, Que.	23	Wilkes-Barre
DUBNYK, Devan	6-6	194	L	Regina, Sask.	21	Wilkes-Barre-Stockton
FISHER, Glenn	6-1	160	L	Edmonton, Alta.	24	U. of Denver
GARON, Mathieu	6-2	192	R	Chandler, Que.	29	Los Angeles
ROLOSON, Dwayne	6-1	178	L	Simcoe, Ont.	37	Edmonton

* – Age at start of 2007-08 season

Coach

CRAIG MacTAVISH

Coach, Edmonton Oilers. Born in London, Ont., August 15, 1958.

The Edmonton Oilers named Craig MacTavish as their head coach on June 22, 2000. He became the eighth person in the club's NHL history to hold the position. MacTavish joined Kevin Lowe and Glen Sather as head coaches who were former captains of the Oilers. In 2006, he led the Oilers to game seven of the Stanley Cup Final.

MacTavish played for 18 seasons in the NHL, including eight-and-three-quarter campaigns with the Oilers. He was instrumental in helping his teams win four Stanley Cup titles; three with Edmonton and one with the New York Rangers. Although he was the last player in the NHL to play without a helmet, MacTavish was known for his aggressive style, combined with above average skills.

MacTavish retired as a player in 1997 and was immediately named an assistant coach with the New York Rangers. He was with the Rangers for two seasons prior to joining the Oilers' coaching staff as an assistant under Kevin Lowe in 1999-2000. He also served as an assistant coach for Team Canada at the 2005 World Championship.

Coaching Record

		Regular Season				Playoffs		
Season	Team	Games	W	L	O/T	Games	W	L
2000-01	Edmonton (NHL)	82	39	31	12	6	2	4
2001-02	Edmonton (NHL)	82	38	32	12	....	....	....
2002-03	Edmonton (NHL)	82	36	35	11	6	2	4
2003-04	Edmonton (NHL)	82	36	34	12	....	....	....
2004-05	Edmonton (NHL)			Season Cancelled				
2005-06	Edmonton (NHL)	82	41	28	13	24	15	9
2006-07	Edmonton (NHL)	82	32	43	7	....	....	....
	NHL Totals	492	222	203	67	36	19	17

2006-07 Scoring

* – rookie

Regular Season

Pos	#	Player	Team	GP	G	A	Pts	+/–	PIM	PP	SH	GW	S	%
R	71	Petr Sykora	EDM	82	22	31	53	–20	40	6	0	6	206	10.7
R	83	Ales Hemsky	EDM	64	13	40	53	–7	40	5	0	1	122	10.7
C	10	Shawn Horcoff	EDM	80	16	35	51	–22	56	5	0	5	168	9.5
C	16	Jarret Stoll	EDM	51	13	26	39	2	48	6	1	2	115	11.3
L	14	Raffi Torres	EDM	82	15	19	34	–7	88	1	0	0	154	9.7
R	15	Joffrey Lupul	EDM	81	16	12	28	–29	45	5	0	1	172	9.3
R	34	Fernando Pisani	EDM	77	14	14	28	–1	40	2	1	0	142	9.9
C	19	Marty Reasoner	EDM	72	6	14	20	–15	60	0	0	1	84	7.1
D	24	Steve Staios	EDM	58	2	15	17	–5	97	0	0	0	71	2.8
L	28 *	Patrick Thoresen	EDM	68	4	12	16	–1	52	0	1	2	73	5.5
C	20	Toby Petersen	EDM	64	6	9	15	–18	4	0	2	1	92	6.5
D	29	Daniel Tjarnqvist	EDM	37	3	12	15	3	30	2	0	0	33	9.1
C	93	Petr Nedved	PHI	21	1	6	7	–20	18	0	0	0	18	5.6
			EDM	19	1	4	5	–5	10	1	0	0	21	4.8
			TOTAL	40	2	10	12	–25	28	1	0	0	39	5.1
C	78 *	Marc-Antoine Pouliot	EDM	46	4	7	11	–2	18	0	0	0	73	5.5
D	21	Jason Smith	EDM	82	2	9	11	–13	103	0	0	1	61	3.3
D	5 *	Ladislav Smid	EDM	77	3	7	10	–16	37	0	0	0	53	5.7
D	2	Matt Greene	EDM	78	1	9	10	–22	109	0	0	0	52	1.9
L	26 *	Brad Winchester	EDM	59	4	5	9	–10	86	0	0	0	66	6.1
D	25	Jan Hejda	EDM	39	1	8	9	–6	20	0	0	1	33	3.0
D	77 *	Tom Gilbert	EDM	12	1	5	6	–1	0	0	0	0	13	7.7
D	36 *	Mathieu Roy	EDM	16	2	0	2	–7	30	0	0	0	18	11.1
C	12	Robert Nilsson	EDM	4	1	0	1	–1	4	0	0	0	8	12.5
C	23 *	Kyle Brodziak	EDM	6	1	0	1	0	2	0	0	0	11	9.1
L	18	Ethan Moreau	EDM	7	1	0	1	–4	12	0	0	0	18	5.6
R	46 *	Zachery Stortini	EDM	29	1	0	1	–7	105	0	0	0	17	5.9
D	40 *	Danny Syvret	EDM	16	0	1	1	–10	6	0	0	0	15	0.0
C	44 *	Rob Schremp	EDM	1	0	0	0	0	0	0	0	0	2	0.0
L	8 *	Alexei Mikhnov	EDM	2	0	0	0	0	0	0	0	0	0	0.0
D	60 *	Sebastien Bisaillon	EDM	2	0	0	0	–1	0	0	0	0	3	0.0
D	76 *	Bryan Young	EDM	15	0	0	0	–8	10	0	0	0	2	0.0
L	22 *	Jean-Francois Jacques	EDM	37	0	0	0	–11	33	0	0	0	23	0.0

Goaltending

No.	Goaltender	GPI	Mins	Avg	W	L	OT	EN	SO	GA	SA	S%	G	A	PIM
35	Dwayne Roloson	68	3932	2.75	27	34	6	9	4	180	1969	.909	0	3	12
30	Jussi Markkanen	22	992	3.15	5	9	1	4	0	52	457	.886	0	0	0
	Totals	**82**	**4958**	**2.96**	**32**	**43**	**7**	**13**	**4**	**245**	**2439**	**.900**			

Dustin Penner (above) and Joni Pitkanen are new additions to the Edmonton roster for 2007-08. Penner joins the Oilers as a free agent from Anaheim, while Pitkanen came aboard in a multi-player deal with Philadelphia.

Coaching History

Glen Sather, 1979-80; Bryan Watson and Glen Sather, 1980-81; Glen Sather, 1981-82 to 1988-89; John Muckler, 1989-90, 1990-91; Ted Green, 1991-92, 1992-93; Ted Green and Glen Sather, 1993-94; George Burnett and Ron Low, 1994-95; Ron Low, 1995-96 to 1998-99; Kevin Lowe, 1999-2000; Craig MacTavish, 2000-01 to date.

Club Records

Team

(Figures in brackets for season records are games played; records for fewest points, wins, ties, losses, goals, goals against are for 70 or more games)

Record		
Most Points	119	1983-84 (80), 1985-86 (80)
Most Wins	57	1983-84 (80)
Most Ties	16	1980-81 (80), 1999-2000 (82)
Most Losses	50	1992-93 (84)
Most Goals	*446	1983-84 (80)
Most Goals Against	337	1992-93 (84)
Fewest Points	60	1992-93 (84)
Fewest Wins	25	1993-94 (84)
Fewest Ties	5	1983-84 (80)
Fewest Losses	17	1981-82 (80), 1985-86 (80)
Fewest Goals	195	2006-07 (82)
Fewest Goals Against	182	2001-02 (82)
Longest Winning Streak		
Overall	9	Feb. 20-Mar. 13/01
Home	8	Jan. 19-Feb. 22/85, Feb. 24-Apr. 2/86
Away	8	Dec. 9/86-Jan. 17/87
Longest Undefeated Streak		
Overall	15	Oct. 11-Nov. 9/84 (12 wins, 3 ties)
Home	14	Nov. 15/89-Jan. 6/90 (11 wins, 3 ties)
Away	9	Jan. 17-Mar. 2/82 (6 wins, 3 ties), Nov. 23/82-Jan. 18/83 (7 wins, 2 ties)
Longest Losing Streak		
Overall	11	Oct. 16-Nov. 7/93
Home	9	Oct. 16-Nov. 24/93
Away	9	Nov. 25-Dec. 30/80, Feb. 25-Apr. 5/07
Longest Winless Streak		
Overall	14	Oct. 11-Nov. 7/93 (13 losses, 1 tie)
Home	9	Oct. 16-Nov. 24/93 (9 losses)
Away	11	Dec. 18/01-Feb. 8/02 (7 losses, 4 ties)
Most Shutouts, Season	8	1997-98 (82); 2000-01 (82); 2001-02 (82)
Most PIM, Season	2,173	1987-88 (80)
Most Goals, Game	13	Nov. 19/83 (N.J. 4 at Edm. 13), Nov. 8/85 (Van. 0 at Edm. 13)

Individual

Record		
Most Seasons	15	Kevin Lowe
Most Games	1,037	Kevin Lowe
Most Goals, Career	583	Wayne Gretzky
Most Assists, Career	1,086	Wayne Gretzky
Most Points, Career	1,669	Wayne Gretzky (583G, 1,086A)
Most PIM, Career	1,747	Kelly Buchberger
Most Shutouts, Career	23	Tommy Salo
Longest Consecutive Games Streak	519	Craig MacTavish (Oct. 11/86-Jan. 2/93)
Most Goals, Season	*92	Wayne Gretzky (1981-82)
Most Assists, Season	*163	Wayne Gretzky (1985-86)
Most Points, Season	*215	Wayne Gretzky (1985-86; 52G, 163A)
Most PIM, Season	286	Steve Smith (1987-88)
Most Points, Defenseman, Season	138	Paul Coffey (1985-86; 48G, 90A)
Most Points, Center, Season	*215	Wayne Gretzky (1985-86; 52G, 163A)
Most Points, Right Wing, Season	135	Jari Kurri (1984-85; 71G, 64A)
Most Points, Left Wing, Season	106	Mark Messier (1982-83; 48G, 58A)
Most Points, Rookie, Season	75	Jari Kurri (1980-81; 32G, 43A)
Most Shutouts, Season	8	Curtis Joseph (1997-98), Tommy Salo (2000-01)
Most Goals, Game	5	Wayne Gretzky (Feb. 18/81, Dec. 30/81, Dec. 15/84, Dec. 6/87), Jari Kurri (Nov. 19/83), Pat Hughes (Feb. 3/84)
Most Assists, Game	*7	Wayne Gretzky (Feb. 15/80, Dec. 11/85, Feb. 14/86)
Most Points, Game	8	Wayne Gretzky (Nov. 19/83; 3G, 5A), (Jan. 4/84; 4G, 4A), Paul Coffey (Mar. 14/86; 2G, 6A)

* NHL Record.

Retired Numbers

3	Al Hamilton	1972-1980
7	Paul Coffey	1980-1987
11	Mark Messier	1980-1991
17	Jari Kurri	1980-1990
31	Grant Fuhr	1981-1991
99	Wayne Gretzky	1979-1988

Captains' History

Ron Chipperfield, 1979-80; Blair MacDonald and Lee Fogolin, Jr., 1980-81; Lee Fogolin, Jr., 1981-82, 1982-83; Wayne Gretzky, 1983-84 to 1987-88; Mark Messier, 1988-89 to 1990-91; Kevin Lowe, 1991-92; Craig MacTavish, 1992-93, 1993-94; Shayne Corson, 1994-95; Kelly Buchberger, 1995-96 to 1998-99; Doug Weight, 1999-2000, 2000-01; Jason Smith, 2001-02 to 2006-07.

All-time Record vs. Other Clubs

Regular Season

	At Home								On Road								Total							
	GP	W	L	T	OL	GF	GA	PTS	GP	W	L	T	OL	GF	GA	PTS	GP	W	L	T	OL	GF	GA	PTS
Anaheim	29	20	8	0	1	71	60	41	30	11	17	2	0	77	87	24	59	31	25	2	1	148	147	65
Atlanta	5	3	1	1	0	19	12	7	3	2	1	0	0	8	3	4	8	5	2	1	0	27	15	11
Boston	30	11	15	3	1	102	102	26	31	6	21	3	1	80	129	16	61	17	36	6	2	182	231	42
Buffalo	30	21	6	3	0	121	77	45	31	13	10	7	1	113	111	34	61	34	16	10	1	234	188	79
Calgary	89	46	32	10	1	323	288	103	89	31	49	9	0	290	348	71	178	77	81	19	1	613	636	174
Carolina	32	20	7	5	0	124	93	45	29	11	11	7	0	98	112	29	61	31	18	12	0	222	205	74
Chicago	49	25	19	5	0	180	153	55	48	17	24	7	0	159	179	41	97	42	43	12	0	339	332	96
Colorado	54	28	21	4	1	211	174	61	55	24	27	4	0	193	204	52	109	52	48	8	1	404	378	113
Columbus	12	9	2	0	1	42	26	19	12	7	1	3	1	41	26	18	24	16	3	3	2	83	52	37
Dallas	48	21	15	8	4	188	161	54	49	16	25	7	1	135	173	40	97	37	40	15	5	323	334	94
Detroit	48	23	14	10	1	184	168	57	48	18	25	3	2	154	183	41	96	41	39	13	3	338	351	98
Florida	8	5	2	1	0	28	17	11	9	2	5	2	0	24	24	6	17	7	7	3	0	52	41	17
Los Angeles	81	42	24	15	0	364	288	99	81	36	29	15	1	327	310	88	162	78	53	30	1	691	598	187
Minnesota	19	7	8	3	1	38	43	18	18	10	5	1	2	42	43	23	37	17	13	4	3	80	86	41
Montreal	36	19	17	0	0	122	116	38	31	10	16	4	1	97	108	25	67	29	33	4	1	219	224	63
Nashville	16	8	6	0	2	46	47	18	17	7	7	3	0	49	43	17	33	15	13	3	2	95	90	35
New Jersey	31	14	10	6	1	136	114	35	34	16	13	3	2	113	113	37	65	30	23	9	3	249	227	72
NY Islanders	29	16	8	5	0	107	87	37	32	7	15	9	1	112	131	24	61	23	23	14	1	219	218	61
NY Rangers	28	12	13	3	0	101	94	27	31	14	9	6	2	117	117	36	59	26	22	9	2	218	211	63
Ottawa	12	7	3	2	0	42	30	16	11	5	3	2	1	29	23	13	23	12	6	4	1	71	53	29
Philadelphia	28	14	8	6	0	98	83	34	32	10	20	2	0	88	130	22	60	24	28	8	0	186	213	56
Phoenix	76	48	21	6	1	328	244	103	75	39	27	5	4	326	299	87	151	87	48	11	5	654	543	190
Pittsburgh	30	22	7	1	0	148	98	45	31	13	14	3	1	130	118	30	61	35	21	4	1	278	216	75
St. Louis	48	24	18	4	2	175	158	54	48	17	23	7	1	166	171	42	96	41	41	11	3	341	329	96
San Jose	37	22	8	7	0	124	83	51	36	13	16	5	2	108	124	33	73	35	24	12	2	232	207	84
Tampa Bay	11	7	4	0	0	27	24	14	11	6	3	2	0	35	31	14	22	13	7	2	0	62	55	28
Toronto	44	23	14	6	1	180	141	53	38	15	21	2	0	157	158	32	82	38	35	8	1	337	299	85
Vancouver	89	53	26	7	3	376	281	116	90	42	32	12	4	348	321	100	179	95	58	19	7	724	602	216
Washington	30	16	10	4	0	124	91	36	29	9	18	2	0	93	118	20	59	25	28	6	0	217	209	56
Totals	**1079**	**586**	**347**	**125**	**21**	**4129**	**3353**	**1318**	**1079**	**427**	**487**	**137**	**28**	**3709**	**3937**	**1019**	**2158**	**1013**	**834**	**262**	**49**	**7838**	**7290**	**2337**

Playoffs

	Series	W	L	GP	W	L	T	GF	GA	Last Mtg.	Rnd.	Result
Anaheim	1	1	0	5	4	1	0	16	13	2006	CF	W 4-1
Boston	2	2	0	9	8	1	0	41	20	1990	F	W 4-1
Calgary	5	4	1	30	19	11	0	132	96	1991	DSF	W 4-3
Carolina	1	0	1	7	3	4	0	16	19	2006	F	L 3-4
Chicago	4	3	1	20	12	8	0	102	77	1992	CF	L 0-4
Colorado	2	1	1	12	5	7	0	30	35	1998	CQF	W 4-3
Dallas	8	2	6	42	15	27	0	104	118	2003	CQF	L 2-4
Detroit	3	3	0	16	12	4	0	58	43	2006	CQF	W 4-2
Los Angeles	7	5	2	36	24	12	0	154	127	1992	DSF	W 4-2
Montreal	1	1	0	3	3	0	0	15	6	1981	PRE	W 3-0
NY Islanders	3	1	2	15	6	9	0	47	58	1984	F	W 4-1
Philadelphia	3	2	1	15	8	7	0	49	44	1987	F	W 4-3
Phoenix	6	6	0	26	22	4	0	120	75	1990	DSF	W 4-3
San Jose	1	1	0	6	4	2	0	19	12	2006	CSF	W 4-2
Vancouver	2	2	0	9	7	2	0	35	20	1992	DF	W 4-2
Totals	**49**	**34**	**15**	**251**	**152**	**99**	**0**	**938**	**763**			

Calgary totals include Atlanta Flames, 1979-80.
Colorado totals include Quebec, 1979-80 to 1994-95.
New Jersey totals include Colorado Rockies, 1979-80 to 1981-82.

Playoff Results 2007-2002

Year	Round	Opponent	Result	GF	GA
2006	F	Carolina	L 3-4	16	19
	CF	Anaheim	W 4-1	16	13
	CSF	San Jose	W 4-2	19	12
	CQF	Detroit	W 4-2	19	17
2003	CQF	Dallas	L 2-4	11	20

Abbreviations: Round: F - Final; **CF** - conference final; **CQF** - conference quarter-final; **DF** - division final;**DSF** - division semi-final; **PRE** - preliminary round.

Carolina totals include Hartford, 1979-80 to 1996-97.
Dallas totals include Minnesota North Stars, 1979-80 to 1992-93.
Phoenix totals include Winnipeg, 1979-80 to 1995-96.

2006-07 Results

Oct.	5	Calgary	3-1
	7	at Calgary	1-2
	12	San Jose	6-4
	14	at Colorado	4-3
	16	at Vancouver	1-2
	17	Vancouver	2-1
	21	Detroit	3-1
	23	Phoenix	5-2
	25	at Anaheim	2-6
	26	at Phoenix	2-6
	28	Washington	4-0
Nov.	1	Nashville	3-5
	3	Dallas	2-3
	7	at Montreal	2-3†
	8	at Detroit	0-3
	10	at Columbus	4-1
	12	at St. Louis	3-5
	13	at Colorado	2-1
	16	St. Louis	6-2
	18	Detroit	4-3†
	21	Calgary	2-1
	24	Chicago	5-1
	28	Anaheim	2-3*
	30	Colorado	3-7
Dec.	2	Columbus	0-4
	4	at Vancouver	4-0
	6	Carolina	3-1
	8	at Dallas	2-0
	10	at Chicago	1-4
	12	at Nashville	2-3
	14	Minnesota	3-1
	15	at Colorado	1-4
	19	Colorado	6-7
	21	at Phoenix	3-2
	23	at Dallas	2-3
	28	Los Angeles	4-7
	30	Vancouver	2-6
	31	at Calgary	2-4
Jan.	2	Florida	4-1
	4	Dallas	5-6†
	5	at Vancouver	2-3*
	8	at Los Angeles	2-1*
	10	at San Jose	3-2
	12	Minnesota	2-4
	13	at Calgary	1-3
	16	at Minnesota	2-1
	18	Anaheim	4-1
	20	Calgary	0-4
	26	San Jose	1-5
	27	Los Angeles	4-3
	31	Columbus	5-2
Feb.	1	at Vancouver	3-5
	3	at Colorado	3-2
	6	Vancouver	2-5
	9	Chicago	2-1
	11	Atlanta	5-1
	13	at Boston	0-3
	15	at Buffalo	1-2*
	17	at Toronto	3-4
	20	at Ottawa	3-4†
	22	at Columbus	4-0
	23	at Detroit	4-3†
	25	at Minnesota	1-4
	27	Phoenix	0-3
Mar.	1	Minnesota	0-5
	3	Calgary	2-4
	7	Tampa Bay	1-3
	9	at Anaheim	1-5
	11	at San Jose	0-3
	12	at Los Angeles	1-5
	15	Minnesota	1-2
	17	St. Louis	2-3*
	19	Vancouver	1-2
	21	Colorado	1-5
	23	Colorado	4-3†
	24	Nashville	0-4
	27	at Nashville	3-4
	29	at St. Louis	2-5
Apr.	1	at Chicago	1-2
	3	at Minnesota	0-3
	5	at Minnesota	0-3
	7	at Calgary	3-2

* – Overtime † – Shootout

Entry Draft Selections 2007-1993

2007

Pick	
6	Sam Gagner
15	Alex Plante
21	Riley Nash
97	Linus Omark
127	Milan Kytnar
157	William Quist

2006

Pick	
45	Jeff Petry
75	Theo Peckham
133	Bryan Pitton
140	Cody Wild
170	Alexander Bumagin

2005

Pick	
25	Andrew Cogliano
36	Taylor Chorney
81	Danny Syvret
86	Robby Dee
97	Chris Vande Velde
120	Vyacheslav Trukhno
157	Fredrik Pettersson
220	Matthew Glasser

2004

Pick	
14	Devan Dubnyk
25	Rob Schremp
44	Roman Tesliuk
57	Geoff Paukovich
112	Liam Reddox
146	Bryan Young
177	Max Gordichuk
208	Stephane Goulet
242	Tyler Spurgeon
274	Bjorn Bjurling

2003

Pick	
22	Marc-Antoine Pouliot
51	Colin McDonald
68	Jean-Francois Jacques
72	Mishail Joukov
94	Zachery Stortini
147	Kalle Olsson
154	David Rohlfs
184	Dragan Umicevic
214	Kyle Brodziak
215	Mathieu Roy
248	Josef Hrabal
278	Troy Bodie

2002

Pick	
15	Jesse Niinimaki
31	Jeff Drouin-Deslauriers
36	Jarret Stoll
44	Matt Greene
79	Brock Radunske
106	Ivan Koltsov
111	Jonas Almtorp
123	invalid pick
148	Glenn Fisher
181	Mikko Luoma
205	J.F. Dufort
211	Patrick Murphy
244	Dwight Helminen
245	Tomas Micka
274	Fredrik Johansson

2001

Pick	
13	Ales Hemsky
43	Doug Lynch
52	Ed Caron
84	Kenny Smith
133	Jussi Markkanen
154	Jake Brenk
185	Mikael Svensk
215	Dan Baum
248	Kari Haakana
272	Ales Pisa
278	Shay Stephenson

2000

Pick	
17	Alexei Mikhnov
35	Brad Winchester
83	Alexander Liubimov
113	Lou Dickenson
152	Paul Flache
184	Shaun Norrie
211	Joe Cullen
215	Matthew Lombardi
247	Jason Platt
274	Yevgeny Muratov

1999

Pick	
13	Jani Rita
36	Alexei Semenov
41	Tony Salmelainen
81	Adam Hauser
91	Mike Comrie
139	Jonathan Fauteux
171	Chris Legg
199	Christian Chartier
256	Tamas Groschl

1998

Pick	
13	Michael Henrich
67	Alex Henry
99	Shawn Horcoff
113	Kristian Antila
128	Paul Elliott
144	Oleg Smirnov
159	Trevor Ettinger
186	Mike Morrison
213	Christian Lefebvre
241	Maxim Spiridonov

1997

Pick	
14	Michel Riesen
41	Patrick Dovigi
68	Sergei Yerkovich
94	Jonas Elofsson
121	Jason Chimera
141	Peter Sarno
176	Kevin Bolibruck
187	Chad Hinz
205	Chris Kerr
231	Alexander Fomichev

1996

Pick	
6	Boyd Devereaux
19	Matthieu Descoteaux
32	Chris Hajt
59	Tom Poti
114	Brian Urick
141	Bryan Randall
168	David Bernier
170	Brandon Lafrance
195	Fernando Pisani
221	John Hultberg

1995

Pick	
6	Steve Kelly
31	Georges Laraque
57	Lukas Zib
83	Mike Minard
109	Jan Snopek
161	Martin Cerven
187	Stephen Douglas
213	Jiri Antonin

1994

Pick	
4	Jason Bonsignore
6	Ryan Smyth
32	Mike Watt
53	Corey Neilson
60	Brad Symes
79	Adam Copeland
95	Jussi Tarvainen
110	Jon Gaskins
136	Terry Marchant
160	Curtis Sheptak
162	Dmitri Shulga
179	Chris Wickenheiser
185	Rob Guinn
188	Jason Reid
214	Jeremy Jablonski
266	Ladislav Benysek

1993

Pick	
7	Jason Arnott
16	Nick Stajduhar
33	David Vyborny
59	Kevin Paden
60	Alexander Kerch
111	Miroslav Satan
163	Alexander Zhurik
189	Martin Bakula
215	Brad Norton
241	Oleg Maltsev
267	Ilja Byakin

General Managers' History

Larry Gordon, 1979-80; Glen Sather, 1980-81 to 1999-2000; Kevin Lowe, 2000-01 to date.

Vice President and General Manager

KEVIN LOWE
Executive Vice President/General Manager, Edmonton Oilers.
Born in Lachute, Que., April 15, 1959.

The Edmonton Oilers named Kevin Lowe as their general manager on June 9, 2000, filling the position left vacant when Glen Sather resigned on May 19th. Lowe moved into the front office after spending the 1999-2000 season as coach of the Oilers. In his role as Oilers' g.m., Lowe has worked with Wayne Gretzky as assistant executive director of Canada's gold medal-winning team at the 2002 Winter Olympics and at the 2004 World Cup of Hockey. His Oilers reached the Stanley Cup Final in 2006.

After a brilliant 19-year playing career with the Edmonton Oilers and New York Rangers, Lowe announced his retirement on July 30, 1998 and joined the Edmonton Oilers coaching staff. He replaced Ron Low as head coach on June 18, 1999.

Lowe was the Oilers' first-ever draft pick when he was selected 21st overall in the 1979 NHL Entry Draft. He went on to play in 1,254 regular-season games and 214 playoff games, winning six Stanley Cup championships; the first five with Edmonton (1984, 1985, 1987, 1988, 1990) followed by a sixth title with the Rangers in 1994.

Besides being the first draft choice in Oilers history, Lowe also scored the first goal in team history on October 10, 1979. He holds the Oilers' record for most games played in both the regular season (1,037) and playoffs (172), and became the sixth captain in team history in 1990-91. He was no less a leader off the ice, becoming the only player to win the King Clancy Memorial Trophy and the Budweiser/NHL Man of the Year Award in the same season (1989-90). Both awards are presented for leadership qualities and humanitarian contributions. His work with the Edmonton Christmas Bureau has set the standard for the Oilers' commitment to community involvement.

NHL Coaching Record

		Regular Season				Playoffs		
Season	Team	Games	W	L	T	Games	W	L
1999-2000	Edmonton	82	32	34	16	5	1	4
	NHL Totals	**82**	**32**	**34**	**16**	**5**	**1**	**4**

Club Directory

Rexall Place

Edmonton Oilers
11230 – 110 Street
Edmonton, Alberta T5G 3H7
Phone **780/414-4000**
Press Box 780/409-3780
Ticketing 780/414-4625
Media Lounge 780/409-3778
FAX 780/409-5848
www.edmontonoilers.com
Capacity: 16,839

Owner	Edmonton Investors Group Ltd.
Governor	Cal Nichols
Alternate Governors	Patrick R. LaForge, Kevin Lowe, William Butler
President & Chief Executive Officer	Patrick R. LaForge
Exec. Vice-President & General Manager	Kevin Lowe
Exec. Vice President, Commercial Operations	Stew MacDonald
Vice-President of Finance and CFO	Darryl Boessenkool
Exec. Assistant to the President	Connie Stoddard
Exec. Assistant to the General Manager	James McGregor
Office Mgr. & Exec. Asst. to the CFO	Sherry Smith
Security	Gary Goulet
Hockey Operations	
Vice-President, Hockey Operations	Kevin Prendergast
Director, Hockey Administration	Rick Olczyk
Head Coach	Craig MacTavish
Assistant Coaches	Rob Daum, Charlie Huddy, Bill Moores
Goaltending Coach	Pete Peeters
Video Coach	Brian Ross
Development Coach	Bob Mancini
Skating & Skills Coach	Steve Serdachny
Strength & Conditioning Consultant	Chad Moreau
Dir., Research, Analysis & Software Development	Sean Draper
Scouting Staff	Michael Abbamont, Bob Brown, Bill Dandy, Brad Davis, Lorne Davis, Morey Gare, Kent Hawley, Stu MacGregor, Chris McCarthy, Frank Musil, Kent Nilsson, Dave Semenko
Medical and Training Staff	
Head Medical Trainer	Ken Lowe
Head Equipment Manager	Barrie Stafford
Assistant Medical Trainer/Fitness Coordinator	Scott Hoyer
Equipment Manager	Lyle Kulchisky
Assistant Equipment Manager	Jeff Lang
Massage Therapist	Steve Lines
Team Medical Chief of Staff/Director of Glen Sather Sports Medicine Clinic	Dr. David C. Reid
Team Physicians	Dr. John Clarke, Dr. Dhiren Naidu
Team Dermatologist	Dr. Don Groot
Team Dentists	Dr. Ben Eastwood, Dr. Tony Sneazwell
Fitness Consultants	Dr. Art Quinney, Dr. Gordon Bell
Physical Therapy Consultant	Dr. Dave Magee
Team Optometrist	Dr. Brent Saik
Finance & Administration	
Controller	Jason Quilley
Assistant Controller	Zeina Charara
Human Resource Manager	Tandy Kustiak
Legal Counsel	Keely Brown
Director, Operations	Craig Tkachuk
Payroll Manager	Shawna Quigley
Intermediate Accountant	Christine Marceau
Accounting Coordinators	Yvonne Weleschuk, Jaimie Hui
Director of IT	Alfred Ng
IT Manager	Rod Pruden
Senior Business Analyst	Sharon Lyseng
Business Analyst	Jason Lee
Facilities Coordinator	Gilbert da Silva
Receptionists	Cheryl Thomas, Sandy Langley
Communications & Broadcast	
Vice President, Communications & Broadcast	Allan Watt
Manager, Communications & Media Relations	J.J. Hebert
Manager, Corporate Communications	Darren Krill
Information Coordinator	Steve Knowles
Team Services Coordinator	Patrick Garland
Director of Broadcast	Don Metz
Corporate Sales	
Vice President, Corporate Sales	Brad MacGregor
Corporate Sales Managers	Lisa Munro, Scott Murray, Daryl Zelinski
Executive Suites Manager	Bob Haromy
Corporate Sales Coordinators	Laurie Block, Bryce Crittenden, Abe Hajar, Stefan Kalenchuk, Jessica Kosta, Angela Thompson
Manager, Events	Carmen Day
Events Coordinators	Ryan Dubyk, Kathy Mendes
Ticket Sales & Service	
Vice President, Ticket Sales and Customer Relationships	Eric Upton
Sales Administrative Assistant	Lesli Rentz
Client Service Representatives	Tabitha Lidgett, Jody Young, Shannon Hopkins
Box Office Manager	Ian Weiss
Ticket Operations Manager	Corrine Carey
Ticket Inventory Manager	Jamie Schenknecht
Ticketing Coordinator	Kendra Morton
Marketing & Fan Development	
Director, Marketing	Sean Price
Director, Fan Development	Natalie Minckler
Manager, E-Marketing & Research	Christine Dmytryshyn
Manager, Merchandising & Licensing	Joyce LaBriola
Manager, New Media Production	Andreas Schwabe
New Media Production Coordinator	Marc Ciampa
Fan Development Coordinator	Sara Ripko
Edmonton Oilers Community Foundation	
Executive Director	Darryl Lindenbach
Community Partnership Coordinator	Jill Metz
Grant & Fund Development Coordinator	Erin Barrett
ICE School Program Coordinator	Sandy VanRiper
Team Information	
Television Outlets	Sportsnet , CBXT TV & TSN
Radio Flagship Station	630 CHED (AM); Rod Phillips (Play-by-play) & Morley Scott (Colour)

Florida Panthers

2006-07 Results: 35W-31L-8OTL-8SOL 86PTS.
Fourth, Southeast Division

Key Off-Season Signings/Acquisitions

2007

- **Apr. 25** • Re-signed LW **Ville Peltonen**.
- **June 13** • Re-signed D **Bryan Allen**.
- **21** • Re-signed RW **Nathan Horton**.
- **22** • Acquired G **Tomas Vokoun** from Nashville for a 1st-round pick in the 2008 Entry Draft and a 2nd-round pick in 2007.
- **25** • Re-signed G **Craig Anderson**.
- **29** • Re-signed C **Jozef Stumpel**.
- **July 1** • Signed C **Brett McLean**.
- **2** • Signed RW **Richard Zednik** and RW **Radek Dvorak**.
- **Aug. 6** • D **Steve Montador** awarded one-year contract in arbitration.

Year-by-Year Record

		Home				Road				Overall								
Season	**GP**	**W**	**L**	**T**	**OL**	**W**	**L**	**T**	**OL**	**W**	**L**	**T**	**OL**	**GF**	**GA**	**Pts.**	**Finished**	**Playoff Result**
2006-07	82	23	12	....	6	12	19	....	10	35	31	....	16	247	257	86	4th, Southeast Div.	Out of Playoffs
2005-06	82	25	11	....	5	12	23	....	6	37	34	....	11	240	257	85	4th, Southeast Div.	Out of Playoffs
2004-05	....	....	....	....	....	....	....	....	....	....	....	....	....	....	....	....		
2003-04	82	16	15	7	3	12	20	8	1	28	35	15	4	188	221	75	4th, Southeast Div.	Out of Playoffs
2002-03	82	8	21	7	5	16	15	6	4	24	36	13	9	176	237	70	4th, Southeast Div.	Out of Playoffs
2001-02	82	11	23	3	4	11	21	7	2	22	44	10	6	180	250	60	4th, Southeast Div.	Out of Playoffs
2000-01	82	12	18	7	4	10	20	6	5	22	38	13	9	200	246	66	3rd, Southeast Div.	Out of Playoffs
1999-2000	82	26	9	4	2	17	18	2	4	43	27	6	6	244	209	98	2nd, Southeast Div.	Lost Conf. Quarter-Final
1998-99	82	17	17	7	....	13	17	11	....	30	34	18	....	210	228	78	2nd, Southeast Div.	Out of Playoffs
1997-98	82	11	24	6	....	13	19	9	....	24	43	15	....	203	256	63	6th, Atlantic Div.	Out of Playoffs
1996-97	82	21	12	8	....	14	16	11	....	35	28	19	....	221	201	89	3rd, Atlantic Div.	Lost Conf. Quarter-Final
1995-96	82	25	12	4	....	16	19	6	....	41	31	10	....	254	234	92	3rd, Atlantic Div.	Lost Final
1994-95	48	9	12	3	....	11	10	3	....	20	22	6	....	115	127	46	5th, Atlantic Div.	Out of Playoffs
1993-94	84	15	18	9	....	18	16	8	....	33	34	17	....	233	233	83	5th, Atlantic Div.	Out of Playoffs

2007-08 Schedule

Oct.	Thu.	4	at NY Rangers		Sat.	5	at Pittsburgh
	Sat.	6	New Jersey		Tue.	8	Pittsburgh
	Wed.	10	at Tampa Bay		Thu.	10	at Atlanta
	Thu.	11	New Jersey		Sat.	12	Tampa Bay
	Sat.	13	Tampa Bay		Sun.	13	Colorado*
	Tue.	16	at Montreal		Wed.	16	at Philadelphia
	Thu.	18	at Toronto		Fri.	18	at New Jersey
	Sat.	20	at Ottawa		Sat.	19	at Washington
	Wed.	24	Philadelphia		Tue.	22	Ottawa
	Fri.	26	Buffalo		Thu.	24	Edmonton
	Sat.	27	at Nashville		Wed.	30	Buffalo
	Wed.	31	Carolina	**Feb.**	Fri.	1	Vancouver
Nov.	Fri.	2	at Buffalo		Sat.	2	at Tampa Bay
	Sat.	3	at Carolina		Tue.	5	at Toronto
	Mon.	5	Tampa Bay		Thu.	7	at Ottawa
	Wed.	7	at Tampa Bay		Sat.	9	at Boston
	Fri.	9	Atlanta		Sun.	10	at Buffalo
	Mon.	12	Carolina		Wed.	13	Montreal
	Tue.	13	at Atlanta		Fri.	15	Washington
	Thu.	15	Washington		Sat.	16	at Carolina
	Sat.	17	at Carolina		Tue.	19	at Pittsburgh
	Mon.	19	at Washington		Thu.	21	Boston
	Wed.	21	at Columbus		Sat.	23	at Philadelphia
	Fri.	23	NY Rangers		Sun.	24	at NY Rangers
	Wed.	28	at Washington		Wed.	27	Toronto
	Thu.	29	Boston		Fri.	29	Minnesota
Dec.	Sat.	1	Washington	**Mar.**	Sun.	2	at NY Islanders*
	Wed.	5	Ottawa		Tue.	4	at Boston
	Fri.	7	NY Islanders		Thu.	6	Pittsburgh
	Tue.	11	Calgary		Sat.	8	Atlanta
	Thu.	13	at St. Louis		Wed.	12	NY Islanders
	Sat.	15	at Detroit		Fri.	14	NY Rangers
	Sun.	16	at Chicago		Sun.	16	Atlanta*
	Tue.	18	at Montreal		Thu.	20	Carolina
	Thu.	20	Carolina		Sat.	22	Tampa Bay
	Sat.	22	Toronto		Tue.	25	at Tampa Bay
	Thu.	27	at Atlanta		Thu.	27	Atlanta
	Fri.	28	Montreal		Sat.	29	Washington
	Sun.	30	Philadelphia*	**Apr.**	Tue.	1	at Atlanta
Jan.	Wed.	2	at New Jersey		Fri.	4	at Carolina
	Thu.	3	at NY Islanders		Sat.	5	at Washington

* Denotes afternoon game.

Olli Jokinen topped the 30-goal plateau for the fourth time in his last five NHL seasons. He established new career highs in goals (38), assists (51), points (89) and plus/minus (+18).

SOUTHEAST DIVISION
15th NHL Season

Franchise date: June 14, 1993

2007-08 Player Personnel

FORWARDS	HT	WT	S	Place of Birth	*Age	2006-07 Club
BOOTH, David	6-0	212	L	Detroit, MI	22	Florida-Rochester
CAMPBELL, Gregory	6-0	194	L	London, Ont.	23	Florida
DVORAK, Radek	6-2	200	R	Tabor, Czech.	30	St. Louis
GLOBKE, Rob	6-2	208	R	Farmington, MI	24	Florida-Rochester
HORTON, Nathan	6-2	229	R	Welland, Ont.	22	Florida
JOKINEN, Olli	6-3	218	L	Kuopio, Finland	28	Florida
KREPS, Kamil	6-2	194	R	Litomerice, Czech.	22	Florida-Rochester
McLEAN, Brett	5-11	185	L	Comox, B.C.	29	Colorado
OLESZ, Rostislav	6-1	214	L	Bilovec, Czech.	21	Florida-Rochester
PELTONEN, Ville	5-11	182	L	Vantaa, Finland	34	Florida
STEWART, Anthony	6-2	239	R	LaSalle, Que.	22	Florida-Rochester
STUMPEL, Jozef	6-3	222	R	Nitra, Czech.	35	Florida
WEISS, Stephen	5-11	185	L	Toronto, Ont.	24	Florida
ZEDNIK, Richard	6-0	200	L	Banska Bystrica, Czech.	31	Washington-NY Islanders
DEFENSEMEN						
ALLEN, Bryan	6-4	220	L	Kingston, Ont.	27	Florida
BOUWMEESTER, Jay	6-4	212	L	Edmonton, Alta.	24	Florida
ELLERBY, Keaton	6-4	186	L	Strathmore, Alta.	18	Kamloops
LOJEK, Martin	6-4	220	R	Brno, Czech.	22	Florida-Rochester
MEZEI, Branislav	6-4	235	L	Nitra, Czech.	26	Florida
MONTADOR, Steve	6-0	205	R	Vancouver, B.C.	27	Florida
MURPHY, Cory	5-10	185	L	Kanata, Ont.	29	HIFK
SALEI, Ruslan	6-1	212	L	Minsk, USSR	32	Florida
VAN RYN, Mike	6-1	198	R	London, Ont.	28	Florida
WELCH, Noah	6-4	218	L	Brighton, MA	25	Pit-Wilkes-Barre-Fla-Roch

GOALTENDERS	HT	WT	C	Place of Birth	*Age	2006-07 Club
ANDERSON, Craig	6-2	180	L	Park Ridge, IL	26	Florida-Rochester
VOKOUN, Tomas	6-0	195	R	Karlovy Vary, Czech.	31	Nashville

* – Age at start of 2007-08 season

2006-07 Scoring

* – rookie

Regular Season

Pos	#	Player	Team	GP	G	A	Pts	+/–	PIM	PP	SH	GW	S	%
C	12	Olli Jokinen	FLA	82	39	52	91	18	78	9	1	8	351	11.1
R	16	Nathan Horton	FLA	82	31	31	62	15	61	7	1	3	217	14.3
C	15	Jozef Stumpel	FLA	73	23	34	57	2	22	9	2	4	131	17.6
C	9	Stephen Weiss	FLA	74	20	28	48	–1	28	10	0	1	176	11.4
L	23	Martin Gelinas	FLA	82	14	30	44	7	36	7	0	1	171	8.2
D	4	Jay Bouwmeester	FLA	82	12	30	42	23	66	3	0	3	174	6.9
L	18	Ville Peltonen	FLA	72	17	20	37	7	28	4	0	0	145	11.7
C	77	Chris Gratton	FLA	81	13	22	35	1	94	1	0	1	131	9.9
D	24	Ruslan Salei	FLA	82	6	26	32	–13	102	2	0	0	148	4.1
L	85	Rostislav Olesz	FLA	75	11	19	30	2	28	2	0	2	164	6.7
D	26	Mike Van Ryn	FLA	78	4	25	29	–5	64	1	0	0	121	3.3
R	13	Juraj Kolnik	FLA	64	11	14	25	2	18	0	0	1	113	9.7
D	5	Bryan Allen	FLA	82	4	21	25	7	112	0	0	0	99	4.0
L	46 *	David Booth	FLA	48	3	7	10	0	12	0	0	1	86	3.5
C	11	Gregory Campbell	FLA	79	6	3	9	–10	66	0	1	0	103	5.8
D	7	Steve Montador	FLA	72	1	8	9	1	119	0	0	0	88	1.1
C	25	Joe Nieuwendyk	FLA	15	5	3	8	–4	4	2	0	2	30	16.7
D	21	Alexei Semenov	FLA	23	0	5	5	9	28	0	0	0	23	0.0
D	6 *	Noah Welch	PIT	22	1	1	2	1	22	0	0	0	14	7.1
			FLA	2	1	0	1	3	2	0	0	0	4	25.0
			TOTAL	24	2	1	3	4	24	0	0	0	18	11.1
C	38 *	Janis Sprukts	FLA	13	1	2	3	1	2	0	0	0	10	10.0
D	2	Branislav Mezei	FLA	45	0	3	3	5	55	0	0	0	24	0.0
C	50 *	Drew Larman	FLA	16	2	0	2	–3	2	0	0	0	15	13.3
C	54 *	Kamil Kreps	FLA	14	1	1	2	–1	6	0	0	0	20	5.0
D	47 *	Martin Lojek	FLA	3	0	1	1	2	0	0	0	0	0	0.0
C	57 *	Anthony Stewart	FLA	10	0	1	1	1	2	0	0	0	8	0.0
C	51 *	Rob Globke	FLA	19	0	1	1	–3	0	0	0	0	15	0.0
C	40 *	Greg Jacina	FLA	3	0	0	0	–1	2	0	0	0	2	0.0

Goaltending

No.	Goaltender	GPI	Mins	Avg	W	L	OT	EN	SO	GA	SA	S%	G	A	PIM
31	Craig Anderson	5	217	2.21	1	1	1	0	0	8	116	.931	0	0	0
20	Ed Belfour	58	3289	2.77	27	17	10	2	1	152	1550	.902	0	2	10
35	Alexander Auld	27	1471	3.34	7	13	5	5	1	82	729	.888	0	1	2
	Totals	**82**	**4992**	**2.99**	**35**	**31**	**16**	**7**	**2**	**249**	**2402**	**.896**			

General Managers' History

Bob Clarke, 1993-94; Bryan Murray, 1994-95 to 1999-2000; Bryan Murray and Bill Torrey, 2000-01; Bill Torrey and Chuck Fletcher, 2001-02; Rick Dudley, 2002-03, 2003-04; Mike Keenan, 2004-05, 2005-06; Jacques Martin, 2006-07 to date.

Coach and General Manager

JACQUES MARTIN
Coach/General Manager, Florida Panthers.
Born in St. Pascal, Ont., October 1, 1952.

Jacques Martin was hired as coach of the Florida Panthers on May 26, 2004, joining the team after eight-and-a-half seasons with the Ottawa Senators. For his career with the Senators, he posted a 341-255-96 regular-season record and stands as the franchise's all-time leader in games coached (692), regular-season wins (341), playoff wins (31) and playoff games coached (69). He is the ninth coach in Panthers history. He took over the role of general manager as well on September 3, 2006.

Under Martin's guidance, the Senators earned their first Presidents' Trophy and Eastern Conference title, posting a 52-22-8 mark in 2002-03. Martin has been nominated for the Jack Adams Award as coach of the year four times. He won the award in 1998-99 and was nominated in 1996-97, 2000-01 and 2002-03. Martin was named as an associate coach for Team Canada's men's hockey team that won gold at the 2002 Olympic Winter Games in Salt Lake City and served in the same capacity with Team Canada at the World Cup of Hockey in 2004 and at the Olympics again in 2006.

Martin joined Ottawa after spending the first half of the 1995-96 season with the Stanley Cup champion Colorado Avalanche, where he served as an assistant coach. Martin entered the NHL as head coach of the St. Louis Blues in 1986-87 and 1987-88, leading the Blues to the Norris Division championship in his rookie season. He joined the Blues after guiding the Ontario Hockey League's Guelph Platers to the 1986 Memorial Cup championship and winning OHL coach of the year honors.

Coaching Record

		Regular Season				Playoffs		
Season	**Team**	**Games**	**W**	**L**	**O/T**	**Games**	**W**	**L**
1983-84	Peterborough (OHL)	70	43	23	4	....	....	....
1984-85	Peterborough (OHL)	66	42	20	4	....	....	....
1985-86	Guelph (OHL)	66	41	23	2	....	....	....
1986-87	**St. Louis (NHL)**	**80**	**32**	**33**	**15**	**6**	**2**	**4**
1987-88	**St. Louis (NHL)**	**80**	**34**	**38**	**8**	**10**	**5**	**5**
1993-94	Cornwall (AHL)	80	33	36	11	13	8	5
1995-96	**Ottawa (NHL)**	**38**	**10**	**24**	**4**	....	....	....
1996-97	**Ottawa (NHL)**	**82**	**31**	**36**	**15**	**7**	**3**	**4**
1997-98	**Ottawa (NHL)**	**82**	**34**	**33**	**15**	**11**	**5**	**6**
1998-99	**Ottawa (NHL)**	**82**	**44**	**23**	**15**	**4**	**0**	**4**
1999-2000	**Ottawa (NHL)**	**82**	**41**	**30**	**11**	**6**	**2**	**4**
2000-01	**Ottawa (NHL)**	**82**	**48**	**25**	**9**	**4**	**0**	**4**
2001-02	**Ottawa (NHL)**	**80**	**38**	**33**	**9**	**12**	**7**	**5**
2002-03	**Ottawa (NHL)**	**82**	**52**	**22**	**8**	**18**	**11**	**7**
2003-04	**Ottawa (NHL)**	**82**	**43**	**29**	**10**	**7**	**3**	**4**
2004-05	**Florida (NHL)**			Season Cancelled				
2005-06	**Florida (NHL)**	**82**	**37**	**34**	**11**	....	....	....
2006-07	**Florida (NHL)**	**82**	**35**	**31**	**16**	....	....	....
	NHL Totals	**1016**	**479**	**391**	**146**	**85**	**38**	**47**

Martin stepped aside (with NHL permission) during the final two games of the 2001-02 season in order to allow assistant coach Roger Neilson to reach the 1,000-game plateau, April 11 and 13, 2002.

Picked third overall in the 2003 Entry Draft, Nathan Horton has become a 30-goal scorer in his third NHL season.

Club Records

Team

(Figures in brackets for season records are games played; records for fewest points, wins, ties, losses, goals, goals against are for 70 or more games)

Most Points **98** 1999-2000 (82)
Most Wins **43** 1999-2000 (82)
Most Ties **19** 1996-97 (82)
Most Losses **44** 2001-02 (82)
Most Goals **254** 1995-96 (82)
Most Goals Against **257** 2005-06 (82), 2006-07 (82)
Fewest Points **60** 2001-02 (82)
Fewest Wins **22** 2000-01 (82), 2001-02 (82)
Fewest Ties **6** 1999-2000 (82)
Fewest Losses **27** 1999-2000 (82)
Fewest Goals **176** 2002-03 (82)
Fewest Goals Against **201** 1996-97 (82)

Longest Winning Streak
Overall .... **7** Nov. 2-14/95, Mar. 17-29/06
Home .... **5** Nov. 5-14/95, Mar. 17-Apr. 1/06
Away .... **4** Four times

Longest Undefeated Streak
Overall .... **12** Oct. 5-30/96 (8 wins, 4 ties)
Home .... **8** Nov. 5-26/95 (7 wins, 1 tie)
Away .... **7** Dec. 7-29/93 (5 wins, 2 ties), Oct. 5-29/96 (4 wins, 3 ties)

Longest Losing Streak
Overall .... **13** Feb. 7-Mar. 23/98
Home .... **6** Feb. 25-Mar. 23/98
Away .... **13** Oct. 27-Dec. 17/05

Longest Winless Streak
Overall .... **15** Feb. 1-Mar. 23/98 (14 losses, 1 tie)
Home .... **13** Feb. 5-Mar. 24/03 (11 losses, 2 ties)
Away .... **16** Jan. 2-Mar. 21/98 (12 losses, 4 ties)

Most Shutouts, Season **7** 2002-03 (82)
Most PIM, Season **1,994** 2001-02 (82)
Most Goals, Game .... **10** Nov. 26/97 (Bos. 5 at Fla. 10)

Individual

Most Seasons .... **9** Paul Laus
Most Games .... **573** Robert Svehla
Most Goals, Career .... **157** Scott Mellanby
Most Assists, Career .... **229** Robert Svehla
Most Points, Career .... **354** Scott Mellanby (157G, 197A)
Most PIM, Career .... **1,702** Paul Laus
Most Shutouts, Career .... **22** Roberto Luongo
Longest Consecutive Games Streak .... **300** Robert Svehla (Dec. 23/98-Apr. 14/02)
Most Goals, Season .... **59** Pavel Bure (2000-01)
Most Assists, Season .... **53** Viktor Kozlov (1999-2000)
Most Points, Season .... **94** Pavel Bure (1999-2000; 58G, 36A)
Most PIM, Season .... **354** Peter Worrell (2001-02)
Most Points, Defenseman, Season .... **57** Robert Svehla (1995-96; 8G, 49A)
Most Points, Center, Season .... **91** Olli Jokinen (2006-07; 39G, 52A)
Most Points, Right Wing, Season .... **94** Pavel Bure (1999-2000; 58G, 36A)
Most Points, Left Wing, Season .... **71** Ray Whitney (1999-2000; 29G, 42A)
Most Points, Rookie, Season .... **50** Jesse Belanger (1993-94; 17G, 33A)
Most Shutouts, Season .... **7** Roberto Luongo (2003-04)
Most Goals, Game .... **4** Mark Parrish (Oct. 30/98); Pavel Bure (Jan. 1/00, Feb. 10/01)
Most Assists, Game .... **4** Four times
Most Points, Game .... **6** Olli Jokinen (Feb. 17/07; 2G, 4A)

Coaching History

Roger Neilson, 1993-94, 1994-95; Doug MacLean, 1995-96, 1996-97; Doug MacLean and Bryan Murray, 1997-98; Terry Murray, 1998-99, 1999-2000; Terry Murray and Duane Sutter, 2000-01; Duane Sutter and Mike Keenan, 2001-02; Mike Keenan, 2002-03; Mike Keenan, Rick Dudley and John Torchetti, 2003-04; Jacques Martin, 2004-05 to date.

Captains' History

Brian Skrudland, 1993-94 to 1996-97; Scott Mellanby, 1997-98 to 2000-01; Pavel Bure, 2001-02; no captain, 2002-03; Olli Jokinen, 2003-04 to date.

All-time Record vs. Other Clubs

Regular Season

	At Home								On Road								Total							
	GP	W	L	T	OL	GF	GA	PTS	GP	W	L	T	OL	GF	GA	PTS	GP	W	L	T	OL	GF	GA	PTS
Anaheim	9	4	3	2	0	27	22	10	10	5	3	1	1	30	28	12	19	9	6	3	1	57	50	22
Atlanta	21	9	10	1	1	52	65	20	21	4	10	4	3	56	74	15	42	13	20	5	4	108	139	35
Boston	25	12	10	2	1	80	72	27	26	13	9	4	0	71	68	30	51	25	19	6	1	151	140	57
Buffalo	25	13	11	1	0	72	72	27	27	6	16	3	2	47	77	17	52	19	27	4	2	119	149	44
Calgary	9	3	3	2	1	21	22	9	9	3	4	1	1	24	26	8	18	6	7	3	2	45	48	17
Carolina	34	14	6	8	6	99	79	42	33	9	19	3	2	81	105	23	67	23	25	11	8	180	184	65
Chicago	9	3	5	1	0	22	33	7	10	3	5	2	0	30	34	8	19	6	10	3	0	52	67	15
Colorado	11	1	10	0	0	30	48	2	12	4	4	3	1	31	35	12	23	5	14	3	1	61	83	14
Columbus	4	2	0	0	2	13	12	6	2	1	1	0	0	4	4	2	6	3	1	0	2	17	16	8
Dallas	11	5	5	1	0	24	29	11	9	3	4	2	0	25	29	8	20	8	9	3	0	49	58	19
Detroit	10	2	4	2	2	20	29	8	8	1	4	3	0	21	30	5	18	3	8	5	2	41	59	13
Edmonton	9	5	2	2	0	24	24	12	8	2	5	1	0	17	28	5	17	7	7	3	0	41	52	17
Los Angeles	9	4	2	3	0	23	21	11	10	4	6	0	0	30	30	8	19	8	8	3	0	53	51	19
Minnesota	3	1	2	0	0	6	8	2	4	0	3	1	0	3	14	1	7	1	5	1	0	9	22	3
Montreal	26	14	9	3	0	78	65	31	25	11	7	3	4	57	64	29	51	25	16	6	4	135	129	60
Nashville	5	3	0	1	1	18	11	8	5	2	1	2	0	10	8	6	10	5	1	3	1	28	19	14
New Jersey	29	9	14	4	2	65	77	24	28	7	16	3	2	54	85	19	57	16	30	7	4	119	162	43
NY Islanders	29	13	10	6	0	92	90	32	29	12	11	2	4	78	78	30	58	25	21	8	4	170	168	62
NY Rangers	29	12	12	2	3	76	81	29	28	9	15	4	0	64	86	22	57	21	27	6	3	140	167	51
Ottawa	26	10	14	1	1	79	85	22	26	11	11	2	2	66	79	26	52	21	25	3	3	145	164	48
Philadelphia	28	7	18	1	2	65	98	17	29	11	11	6	1	74	77	29	57	18	29	7	3	139	175	46
Phoenix	9	4	5	0	0	28	23	8	11	4	3	3	1	34	31	12	20	8	8	3	1	62	54	20
Pittsburgh	26	15	9	1	1	77	62	32	27	11	11	3	2	80	83	27	53	26	20	4	3	157	145	59
St. Louis	10	3	4	2	1	20	21	9	9	1	7	1	0	12	25	3	19	4	11	3	1	32	46	12
San Jose	10	2	3	5	0	26	29	9	10	2	6	2	0	19	32	6	20	4	9	7	0	45	61	15
Tampa Bay	36	23	7	4	2	117	86	52	36	16	13	6	1	105	81	39	72	39	20	10	3	222	167	91
Toronto	21	6	10	5	0	57	62	17	19	5	10	2	2	48	66	14	40	11	20	7	2	105	128	31
Vancouver	8	3	3	1	1	21	27	8	10	1	3	5	1	22	29	8	18	4	6	6	2	43	56	16
Washington	36	17	13	4	2	97	91	40	36	14	15	5	2	89	106	35	72	31	28	9	4	186	197	75
Totals	**517**	**219**	**204**	**65**	**29**	**1429**	**1444**	**532**	**517**	**175**	**233**	**77**	**32**	**1282**	**1512**	**459**	**1034**	**394**	**437**	**142**	**61**	**2711**	**2956**	**991**

Playoffs

	Series	W	L	GP	W	L	T	GF	GA	Last Mtg.	Rnd.	Result
Boston	1	1	0	5	4	1	0	22	16	1996	CQF	W 4-1
Colorado	1	0	1	4	0	4	0	4	15	1996	F	L 0-4
New Jersey	1	0	1	4	0	4	0	6	12	2000	CQF	L 0-4
NY Rangers	1	0	1	5	1	4	0	10	13	1997	CQF	L 1-4
Philadelphia	1	1	0	6	4	2	0	15	11	1996	CSF	W 4-2
Pittsburgh	1	1	0	7	4	3	0	20	15	1996	CF	W 4-3
Totals	**6**	**3**	**3**	**31**	**13**	**18**	**0**	**77**	**82**			

Colorado totals include Quebec, 1993-94 to 1994-95.
Phoenix totals include Winnipeg, 1993-94 to 1995-96.

Carolina totals include Hartford, 1993-94 to 1996-97.

Playoff Results 2007-2002

(Last playoff appearance: 2000)

Abbreviations: Round: F - Final;
CF - conference final; **CSF** - conference semi-final;
CQF - conference quarter-final.

2006-07 Results

Month	Date	Opponent	Score
Oct.	6	Boston	8-3
	7	at Atlanta	0-6
	9	at Toronto	1-2†
	11	Carolina	6-3
	13	Tampa Bay	3-2
	14	at Tampa Bay	1-4
	18	at Washington	2-5
	20	Philadelphia	3-2
	21	at Atlanta	2-4
	23	Atlanta	3-6
	25	at NY Rangers	4-2
	26	at New Jersey	0-2
	28	at NY Islanders	3-4†
	31	San Jose	1-2
Nov.	2	Toronto	4-2
	8	NY Rangers	3-4†
	10	at Buffalo	4-5*
	11	at New Jersey	2-4
	13	Washington	1-4
	16	Montreal	5-1
	18	NY Islanders	1-4
	20	at Boston	3-2
	22	Tampa Bay	4-6
	24	Ottawa	4-6
	25	at Atlanta	0-1
	28	at Montreal	0-1†
	30	at Ottawa	0-6
Dec.	2	Atlanta	1-3
	5	at Pittsburgh	3-2
	7	Buffalo	3-1
	9	at NY Islanders	4-5†
	10	at NY Rangers	1-2
	12	Anaheim	4-5
	14	at Buffalo	1-2
	16	at Boston	6-3
	19	at Toronto	7-3
	21	NY Rangers	3-2
	23	Carolina	2-3*
	26	at Carolina	2-4
	27	Philadelphia	3-1
	29	Montreal	3-1
Jan.	2	at Edmonton	1-4
	4	at Calgary	4-5*
	7	at Vancouver	3-4†
	10	Pittsburgh	5-2
	11	at Carolina	4-6
	13	Washington	7-3
	16	Carolina	2-3*
	18	Toronto	2-3
	20	at Washington	4-1
	27	New Jersey	4-2
	30	at Pittsburgh	0-3
Feb.	1	Washington	6-3
	3	Los Angeles	0-7
	6	at Colorado	4-5*
	8	at Minnesota	2-4
	10	Phoenix	5-2
	13	at Montreal	1-0
	14	at Ottawa	0-4
	17	Tampa Bay	5-4*
	20	at Tampa Bay	2-3†
	22	Pittsburgh	1-2*
	24	Boston	7-2
	27	at Washington	6-5†
Mar.	1	Dallas	2-1*
	3	Tampa Bay	6-2
	6	at Atlanta	2-4
	8	at Philadelphia	2-1
	10	Atlanta	3-2
	13	at Carolina	1-3
	15	Buffalo	3-5
	17	NY Islanders	8-5
	20	at Philadelphia	4-1
	22	Ottawa	2-4
	24	New Jersey	3-4†
	27	at Tampa Bay	5-2
	28	Atlanta	3-2†
	30	Washington	3-2*
Apr.	1	Carolina	3-4*
	3	at Washington	0-1
	6	at Tampa Bay	7-2
	7	at Carolina	4-5*

* – Overtime † – Shootout

Entry Draft Selections 2007-1993

2007
Pick
10 Keaton Ellerby
40 Michal Repik
71 Evgeni Dadonov
101 Matt Rust
131 John Lee
181 Corey Syvret
191 Ryan Watson
202 Sergei Gayduchenko

2006
Pick
10 Michael Frolik
73 Brady Calla
103 Michael Caruso
116 Derrick Lapoint
155 Peter Aston
193 Marc Cheverie

2005
Pick
20 Kenndal McArdle
32 Tyler Plante
90 Dan Collins
93 Olivier Legault
104 Matt Duffy
161 Brian Foster
164 Roman Derlyuk
224 Zach Bearson

2004
Pick
7 Rostislav Olesz
37 David Shantz
53 David Booth
105 Evan Schafer
152 Bret Nasby
267 Spencer Dillon
283 Luke Beaverson

2003
Pick
3 Nathan Horton
25 Anthony Stewart
38 Kamil Kreps
55 Stefan Meyer
105 Martin Lojek
124 James Pemberton
141 Dan Travis
162 Martin Tuma
171 Denis Stasyuk
223 Dany Roussin
234 Petr Kadlec
264 John Hecimovic
265 Tanner Glass

2002
Pick
3 Jay Bouwmeester
9 Petr Taticek
40 Rob Globke
67 Gregory Campbell
134 Topi Jaakola
158 Vince Bellissimo
169 Jeremy Swanson
196 Mikael Vuorio
200 Denis Yachmenev
232 Peter Hafner

2001
Pick
4 Stephen Weiss
24 Lukas Krajicek
34 Greg Watson
64 Tomas Malec
68 Grant McNeill
117 Mike Woodford
136 Billy Thompson
169 Dustin Johner
200 Toni Koivisto
231 Kyle Bruce
263 Jan Blanar
267 Ivan Majesky

2000
Pick
58 Vladimir Sapozhnikov
77 Robert Fried
82 Sean O'Connor
115 Chris Eade
120 Davis Parley
190 Josh Olson
234 Janis Sprukts
253 Mathew Sommerfeld

1999
Pick
12 Denis Shvidki
40 Alex Auld
70 Niklas Hagman
80 Jean-Francois Laniel
103 Morgan McCormick
109 Rod Sarich
169 Brad Woods
198 Travis Eagles
227 Jonathon Charron

1998
Pick
30 Kyle Rossiter
61 Joe DiPenta
63 Lance Ward
89 Ryan Jardine
117 Jaroslav Spacek
148 Chris Ovington
176 B.J. Ketcheson
203 Ian Jacobs
231 Adrian Wichser

1997
Pick
20 Mike Brown
47 Kristian Huselius
56 Vratislav Cech
74 Nick Smith
95 Ivan Novoseltsev
127 Pat Parthenais
155 Keith Delaney
183 Tyler Palmer
211 Doug Schueller
237 Benoit Cote

1996
Pick
20 Marcus Nilson
60 Chris Allen
65 Oleg Kvasha
82 Joey Tetarenko
129 Andrew Long
156 Gaetan Poirier
183 Alexandre Couture
209 Denis Khloptonov
235 Russell Smith

1995
Pick
10 Radek Dvorak
36 Aaron MacDonald
62 Mike O'Grady
80 Dave Duerden
88 Daniel Tjarnqvist
114 Francois Cloutier
166 Peter Worrell
192 Filip Kuba
218 David Lemanowicz

1994
Pick
1 Ed Jovanovski
27 Rhett Warrener
31 Jason Podollan
36 Ryan Johnson
84 David Nemirovsky
105 Dave Geris
157 Matt O'Dette
183 Jason Boudrias
235 Tero Lehtera
261 Per Gustafsson

1993
Pick
5 Rob Niedermayer
41 Kevin Weekes
57 Chris Armstrong
67 Mikael Tjallden
78 Steve Washburn
83 Bill McCauley
109 Todd MacDonald
135 Alain Nasreddine
161 Trevor Doyle
187 Briane Thompson
213 Chad Cabana
239 John Demarco
265 Eric Montreuil

Top draft picks Jay Bouwmeester (third overall in 2002) and Stephen Weiss (fourth in 2001) celebrate a Panthers goal. Weiss scored 20 goals last season while Bouwmeester had a career-high 12 from the blue line.

Club Directory

BankAtlantic Center

Florida Panthers
BankAtlantic Center
One Panther Parkway
Sunrise, FL 33323
Phone **954/835-7000**
FAX 954/835-7700
www.floridapanthers.com
Capacity: 19,250

Executive
General Partner/Chairman of the Board/ Chief Executive Officer/Governor . . . . . Alan Cohen
Vice Chairman/Governor . . . . . Cliff Viner
Limited Partners . . . . . Steve Cohen, David Epstein, Dr. Elliott Hahn (LABE Partners, LLC), H. Wayne Huizenga (HHI, LLC), Bernie Kosar (KHOC, LLC), Richard C. Lehman M.D., Al E. Maroone, Michael E. Maroone, Jordan Zimmerman (JRB Pelican Point, LLC)
President/Chief Operating Officer . . . . . Michael R. Yormark
Alternate Governor . . . . . William A. Torrey
Sr. V.P., Corporate Marketing and New Business Development . . . . . Pedro Goncalves
Sr. V.P., Sales & Marketing . . . . . Chad Johnson
Chief Financial Officer, V.P. Finance . . . . . Evelyn Lopez
G.M., BankAtlantic Center/V.P., Operations . . . . . Brett Stefansson
Exec. Asst. to the President . . . . . Janine Shea
Exec. Asst. to Chief Financial Officer . . . . . Cathy Stevenson

Hockey Operations
General Manager/Head Coach . . . . . Jacques Martin
Assistant General Manager . . . . . Randy Sexton
Special Consultant to the G.M. . . . . . Joe Nieuwendyk
Executive Assistant to the G.M. . . . . . Giselle Seaone
Assistant Coaches . . . . . Guy Charron, Mike Kitchen
Goaltending Coach/Assistant Coach . . . . . Pierre Groulx
Strength & Conditioning Coach . . . . . Andrew O'Brien
Director of Amateur Scouting . . . . . Scott Luce
Director of Professional Scouting . . . . . Bill O'Flaherty
Director, Player Development . . . . . Duane Sutter
Manager, Hockey Administration . . . . . Murray Cawker
Manager, Team Services . . . . . Mike Dixon
Amateur Scouts . . . . . Fred Bandel, Paul Gallagher, Erin Ginnell, Luke Williams, Mike Yandle
Pro Scouts . . . . . Jack Birch, Phil Myre
European Scouts . . . . . Niklas Blomgren, Jari Kekalainen, Vadim Podrezov
Head Athletic Trainer . . . . . Curtis Bell
Assistant Athletic Trainers . . . . . Dave Zenobi, Kevin Elliott
Head Equipment Manager . . . . . Robert McLean
Assistant Equipment Manager . . . . . Chris Moody

Communications
Manager, Communications . . . . . Justin Copertino
Manager, Public Relations . . . . . Matthew F. Sacco
Coordinator, Communications . . . . . Brian Goldman
Coordinator, Publications & Photography . . . . . Tenille Lively
Editor . . . . . John Hett

Community Development, Youth Hockey & Broadcasting
VP, Broadcasting & Panthers Alumni . . . . . Randy Moller
Exec. Director, Foundation & Community Dev. . . . . . Alaina Miller
Director, Game Presentation . . . . . Denis Docil
Producer, Game Presentation . . . . . Richard McLelland
Editor, Game Presentation . . . . . Brian Lenihan

Corporate Partnerships & Brand Activation
V.P., New Business Development . . . . . Ted Major
V.P., Corporate Sales . . . . . Jarrett Nasca
V.P., Integrated Sales . . . . . Dan Parisi
Sr. Director, Brand Activation . . . . . Steve Ziff
Sr. Manager, Brand Activation . . . . . Lindsay Harris
Manager, SSE Publication Sales . . . . . David Krakower

Sales, Service & Marketing
V.P., Corporate Development . . . . . RJ Martino
V.P. Client Services & Retention . . . . . Carrie Rubin
Director, Ticket Sales . . . . . Ryan Bringger
Director, Premium Seating . . . . . Ryan McCoy
Director, Ticket Operations . . . . . Sammy Wallace
Assistant Director, Ticket Operations . . . . . Orvandis Almonte
Director, Internet & Publication Content . . . . . Dave Joseph
Director, Marketing . . . . . Nadia Abich
Coordinator, Website . . . . . Glen Odebralski

Finance and Business Support
V.P., Business Affairs . . . . . Ed Wildermuth
V.P., Human Resources/Payroll . . . . . Carol Duncanson
V.P., Information Technology . . . . . Kelly Moyer
Director, Human Resources & Immigration . . . . . Mary Lou Veroline
Controller/Senior Director, Accounting . . . . . Phillip Reitz
Director, Purchasing . . . . . Laura Barrera
Director, Merchandise . . . . . Jennifer Simmons
Sr. Manager, Accounting . . . . . Fayon Bryce

BankAtlantic Center Building Operations
Director, Security & Safety . . . . . Bram Bottfeld
Director, Event Services . . . . . Erik Waldman
Director, Event Programming . . . . . Sid Greenfeig

Radio/Television Broadcasting
Television . . . . . FSN Florida
TV Play-by-Play Announcer . . . . . Steve Goldstein
TV Analyst . . . . . Denis Potvin
TV Host . . . . . Craig Minervini
Radio Flagship . . . . . Sports Talk 790 AM The Ticket
Radio Play-by-Play . . . . . TBA
Radio Analyst . . . . . Randy Moller

Key Off-Season Signings/Acquisitions

2007

July 2 • Signed LW **Kyle Calder**, C **Michal Handzus**, LW **Ladislav Nagy** and D **Tom Preissing**.
3 • Re-signed G **Jason LaBarbera**.
3 • Signed D **Brad Stuart**.
11 • Re-signed D **Lubomir Visnovsky**.
17 • Signed 2007 1st-round pick (4th overall), D **Thomas Hickey**.
Aug. 6 • LW **Mike Cammalleri** awarded two-year contract in arbitration.

Los Angeles Kings

2006-07 Results: 27W-41L-8OTL-6SOL 68PTS.
Fourth, Pacific Division

Alexander Frolov, a first-round choice by the Kings in 2000, led the club in goals with 35 and was second in points with 71 last season. Each of the Kings' top five scorers in 2006-07 (Michael Cammalleri, Frolov, Anze Kopitar, Lubomir Visnovsky and Dustin Brown) was originally drafted by the team.

2007-08 Schedule

Month	Day	Date	Opponent
Sep.	Sat.	29	Anaheim*†
	Sun.	30	at Anaheim*†
Oct.	Sat.	6	St. Louis
	Wed.	10	at Dallas
	Fri.	12	Boston
	Sun.	14	Detroit*
	Tue.	16	Minnesota
	Thu.	18	at Calgary
	Fri.	19	at Vancouver
	Tue.	23	Nashville
	Thu.	25	Dallas
	Sat.	27	Edmonton
	Wed.	31	Columbus
Nov.	Fri.	2	at San Jose
	Sat.	3	San Jose
	Sat.	10	Dallas
	Tue.	13	at Anaheim
	Thu.	15	Anaheim
	Sat.	17	Phoenix*
	Mon.	19	at Dallas
	Wed.	21	at Phoenix
	Sat.	24	at San Jose
	Sun.	25	at Anaheim*
	Wed.	28	at San Jose
Dec.	Sat.	1	Colorado
	Mon.	3	Edmonton
	Wed.	5	at Phoenix
	Thu.	6	Buffalo
	Sat.	8	Phoenix
	Mon.	10	Vancouver
	Wed.	12	at Chicago
	Thu.	13	at Dallas
	Sat.	15	Minnesota
	Mon.	17	Colorado
	Wed.	19	at Detroit
	Fri.	21	at Columbus
	Sat.	22	at Nashville
	Wed.	26	San Jose
	Sat.	29	at Colorado*
	Sun.	30	at Chicago
Jan.	Tue.	1	Chicago
	Thu.	3	Columbus
	Sat.	5	Calgary
	Tue.	8	Nashville
	Thu.	10	Toronto
	Sat.	12	Dallas*
	Tue.	15	at Edmonton
	Fri.	18	at Calgary
	Sat.	19	at Vancouver
	Tue.	22	Detroit
	Thu.	24	Anaheim
	Tue.	29	at Philadelphia
	Thu.	31	at NY Islanders
Feb.	Sat.	2	at New Jersey
	Tue.	5	at NY Rangers
	Thu.	7	at Detroit
	Sat.	9	at Pittsburgh*
	Sun.	10	at Columbus
	Tue.	12	at St. Louis
	Fri.	15	Calgary
	Sat.	16	at Phoenix
	Mon.	18	Phoenix
	Thu.	21	St. Louis
	Sat.	23	Chicago*
	Thu.	28	at Edmonton
Mar.	Sat.	1	at Colorado
	Sun.	2	at Minnesota*
	Tue.	4	at St. Louis
	Thu.	6	Ottawa
	Sat.	8	Montreal*
	Mon.	10	Vancouver
	Thu.	13	at Nashville
	Sat.	15	at Minnesota
	Tue.	18	San Jose
	Thu.	20	at Phoenix
	Sat.	22	at Dallas*
	Wed.	26	at Anaheim
	Thu.	27	Phoenix
	Sat.	29	Dallas*
Apr.	Tue.	1	at San Jose
	Thu.	3	San Jose
	Sat.	5	Anaheim*

* Denotes afternoon game. † Games played in London, England.

Year-by-Year Record

Season	GP	Home W	Home L	Home T	Home OL	Road W	Road L	Road T	Road OL	Overall W	Overall L	Overall T	Overall OL	GF	GA	Pts.	Finished	Playoff Result
2006-07	82	16	16	....	9	11	25	....	5	27	41	....	14	227	283	68	4th, Pacific Div.	Out of Playoffs
2005-06	82	26	14	....	1	16	21	....	4	42	35	....	5	249	270	89	4th, Pacific Div.	Out of Playoffs
2004-05	....	....	....	....	....	....	....	....	....	....	....	....	....	....	....	....		
2003-04	82	15	16	9	1	13	13	7	8	28	29	16	9	205	217	81	3rd, Pacific Div.	Out of Playoffs
2002-03	82	19	19	2	1	14	18	4	5	33	37	6	6	203	221	78	3rd, Pacific Div.	Out of Playoffs
2001-02	82	22	12	6	1	18	15	5	3	40	27	11	4	214	190	95	3rd, Pacific Div.	Lost Conf. Quarter-Final
2000-01	82	20	12	8	1	18	16	5	2	38	28	13	3	252	228	92	3rd, Pacific Div.	Lost Conf. Semi-Final
1999-2000	82	21	13	5	2	18	14	7	2	39	27	12	4	245	228	94	2nd, Pacific Div.	Lost Conf. Quater-Final
1998-99	82	18	20	3	....	14	25	2	....	32	45	5	....	189	222	69	5th, Pacific Div.	Out of Playoffs
1997-98	82	22	16	3	....	16	17	8	....	38	33	11	....	227	225	87	2nd, Pacific Div.	Lost Conf. Quater-Final
1996-97	82	18	16	7	....	10	27	4	....	28	43	11	....	214	268	67	6th, Pacific Div.	Out of Playoffs
1995-96	82	16	16	9	....	8	24	9	....	24	40	18	....	256	302	66	6th, Pacific Div.	Out of Playoffs
1994-95	48	7	11	6	....	9	12	3	....	16	23	9	....	142	174	41	4th, Pacific Div.	Out of Playoffs
1993-94	84	18	19	5	....	9	26	7	....	27	45	12	....	294	322	66	5th, Pacific Div.	Out of Playoffs
1992-93	84	22	15	5	....	17	20	5	....	39	35	10	....	338	340	88	3rd, Smythe Div.	Lost Final
1991-92	80	20	11	9	....	15	20	5	....	35	31	14	....	287	296	84	2nd, Smythe Div.	Lost Div. Semi-Final
1990-91	80	26	9	5	....	20	15	5	....	46	24	10	....	340	254	102	1st, Smythe Div.	Lost Div. Final
1989-90	80	21	16	3	....	13	23	4	....	34	39	7	....	338	337	75	4th, Smythe Div.	Lost Div. Final
1988-89	80	25	12	3	....	17	19	4	....	42	31	7	....	376	335	91	2nd, Smythe Div.	Lost Div. Final
1987-88	80	19	18	3	....	11	24	5	....	30	42	8	....	318	359	68	4th, Smythe Div.	Lost Div. Semi-Final
1986-87	80	20	17	3	....	11	24	5	....	31	41	8	....	318	341	70	4th, Smythe Div.	Lost Div. Semi-Final
1985-86	80	9	27	4	....	14	22	4	....	23	49	8	....	284	389	54	5th, Smythe Div.	Out of Playoffs
1984-85	80	20	14	6	....	14	18	8	....	34	32	14	....	339	326	82	4th, Smythe Div.	Lost Div. Semi-Final
1983-84	80	13	19	8	....	10	25	5	....	23	44	13	....	309	376	59	5th, Smythe Div.	Out of Playoffs
1982-83	80	20	13	7	....	7	28	5	....	27	41	12	....	308	365	66	5th, Smythe Div.	Out of Playoffs
1981-82	80	19	15	6	....	5	26	9	....	24	41	15	....	314	369	63	4th, Smythe Div.	Lost Div. Final
1980-81	80	22	11	7	....	21	13	6	....	43	24	13	....	337	290	99	2nd, Norris Div.	Lost Prelim. Round
1979-80	80	18	13	9	....	12	23	5	....	30	36	14	....	290	313	74	2nd, Norris Div.	Lost Prelim. Round
1978-79	80	20	13	7	....	14	21	5	....	34	34	12	....	292	286	80	3rd, Norris Div.	Lost Prelim. Round
1977-78	80	18	16	6	....	13	18	9	....	31	34	15	....	243	245	77	3rd, Norris Div.	Lost Prelim. Round
1976-77	80	20	13	7	....	14	18	8	....	34	31	15	....	271	241	83	2nd, Norris Div.	Lost Quarter-Final
1975-76	80	22	13	5	....	16	20	4	....	38	33	9	....	263	265	85	2nd, Norris Div.	Lost Quarter-Final
1974-75	80	22	7	11	....	20	10	10	....	42	17	21	....	269	185	105	2nd, Norris Div.	Lost Prelim. Round
1973-74	78	22	13	4	....	11	20	8	....	33	33	12	....	233	231	78	3rd, West Div.	Lost Quarter-Final
1972-73	78	21	11	7	....	10	25	4	....	31	36	11	....	232	245	73	6th, West Div.	Out of Playoffs
1971-72	78	14	23	2	....	6	26	7	....	20	49	9	....	206	305	49	7th, West Div.	Out of Playoffs
1970-71	78	17	14	8	....	8	26	5	....	25	40	13	....	239	303	63	5th, West Div.	Out of Playoffs
1969-70	76	12	22	4	....	2	30	6	....	14	52	10	....	168	290	38	6th, West Div.	Out of Playoffs
1968-69	76	19	14	5	....	5	28	5	....	24	42	10	....	185	260	58	4th, West Div.	Lost Semi-Final
1967-68	74	20	13	4	....	11	20	6	....	31	33	10	....	200	224	72	2nd, West Div.	Lost Quarter-Final

NHL WESTERN CONFERENCE

PACIFIC DIVISION
41st NHL Season

Franchise date: June 5, 1967

2007-08 Player Personnel

FORWARDS	HT	WT	S	Place of Birth	*Age	2006-07 Club
ARMSTRONG, Derek	6-0	190	R	Ottawa, Ont.	34	Los Angeles
BOYLE, Brian	6-6	222	L	Dorchester, MA	22	Boston College-Manchester
BROWN, Dustin	6-0	200	R	Ithaca, NY	22	Los Angeles
CALDER, Kyle	5-11	180	L	Mannville, Alta.	28	Philadelphia-Detroit
CAMMALLERI, Michael	5-9	185	L	Richmond Hill, Ont.	25	Los Angeles
FROLOV, Alexander	6-2	210	R	Moscow, USSR	25	Los Angeles
GIULIANO, Jeff	5-9	205	L	Nashua, NH	28	Manchester
HANDZUS, Michal	6-5	217	L	Banska Bystrica, Czech.	30	Chicago
IVANANS, Raitis	6-3	263	L	Riga, USSR	28	Los Angeles
KOPITAR, Anze	6-4	220	L	Jesenice, Yugoslavia	20	Los Angeles
MOULSON, Matt	6-1	195	L	North York, Ont.	23	Manchester
MURRAY, Brady	5-9	180	L	Brandon, Man.	23	Rapperswil
NAGY, Ladislav	5-11	192	L	Saca, Czech.	28	Phoenix-Dallas
O'SULLIVAN, Patrick	5-11	190	L	Winston Salem, NC	22	Los Angeles-Manchester
PARSE, Scott	6-1	185	R	Kalamazoo, MI	23	Nebraska-Omaha-Grand Rapids
THORNTON, Scott	6-3	220	L	London, Ont.	36	Los Angeles
TUKONEN, Lauri	6-2	200	R	Hyvinkaa, Finland	21	Los Angeles-Manchester
WILLSIE, Brian	6-1	202	R	London, Ont.	29	Los Angeles
ZEILER, John	6-0	193	R	Jefferson Hills, PA	24	Manchester-Los Angeles
DEFENSEMEN						
BLAKE, Rob	6-4	225	R	Simcoe, Ont.	37	Los Angeles
DALLMAN, Kevin	5-11	195	R	Niagara Falls, Ont.	26	Los Angeles-Manchester
HARROLD, Peter	5-11	195	R	Kirtland Hills, OH	24	Los Angeles-Manchester
JOHNSON, Jack	6-1	201	L	Indianapolis, IN	20	U. of Michigan-Los Angeles
MODRY, Jaroslav	6-2	220	L	Ceske Budejovice, Czech.	36	Dallas-Los Angeles
PETIOT, Richard	6-2	190	L	Daysland, Alta.	25	Manchester
PISKULA, Joe	6-3	214	L	Antigo, WI	23	U. of Wisconsin-Los Angeles
PREISSING, Tom	6-0	198	R	Arlington Heights, IL	28	Ottawa
STUART, Brad	6-2	213	L	Rocky Mountain House, Alta.	27	Boston-Calgary
TVERDOVSKY, Oleg	6-1	211	L	Donetsk, USSR	31	Los Angeles-Manchester
VISNOVSKY, Lubomir	5-10	188	L	Topolcany, Czech.	31	Los Angeles

GOALTENDERS	HT	WT	C	Place of Birth	*Age	2006-07 Club
CLOUTIER, Dan	6-1	195	L	Mont-Laurier, Que.	31	Los Angeles
ERSBERG, Erik	5-11	182	L	Sala, Sweden	25	HV 71
LABARBERA, Jason	6-3	230	L	Burnaby, B.C.	27	Manchester
QUICK, Jonathan	6-0	180	L	Milford, CT	21	Massachusetts

* – Age at start of 2007-08 season

Sensational Slovenian Anze Kopitar finished third among all NHL rookies with 41 assists and 61 points in 2006-07.

General Managers' History

Larry Regan, 1967-68 to 1972-73; Larry Regan and Jake Milford, 1973-74; Jake Milford, 1974-75 to 1976-77; George Maguire, 1977-78 to 1982-83; George Maguire and Rogie Vachon, 1983-84; Rogie Vachon, 1984-85 to 1991-92; Nick Beverley, 1992-93, 1993-94; Sam McMaster, 1994-95 to 1996-97; Dave Taylor, 1997-98 to 2005-06; Dean Lombardi, 2006-07 to date.

Captains' History

Bob Wall, 1967-68, 1968-69; Larry Cahan, 1969-70, 1970-71; Bob Pulford, 1971-72, 1972-73; Terry Harper, 1973-74, 1974-75; Mike Murphy, 1975-76 to 1980-81; Dave Lewis, 1981-82, 1982-83; Terry Ruskowski, 1983-84, 1984-85; Dave Taylor, 1985-86 to 1988-89; Wayne Gretzky, 1989-90 to 1991-92; Wayne Gretzky and Luc Robitaille, 1992-93; Wayne Gretzky, 1993-94, 1994-95; Wayne Gretzky and Rob Blake, 1995-96; Rob Blake, 1996-97 to 2000-01; Mattias Norstrom, 2001-02 to 2006-07.

2006-07 Scoring

* – rookie

Regular Season

Pos	#	Player	Team	GP	G	A	Pts	+/–	PIM	PP	SH	GW	S	%
C	13	Michael Cammalleri	L.A.	81	34	46	80	5	48	16	0	5	299	11.4
L	24	Alexander Frolov	L.A.	82	35	36	71	–8	34	10	1	6	195	17.9
C	11	* Anze Kopitar	L.A.	72	20	41	61	–12	24	7	2	1	193	10.4
D	17	Lubomir Visnovsky	L.A.	69	18	40	58	1	26	8	0	0	159	11.3
L	23	Dustin Brown	L.A.	81	17	29	46	–21	54	13	0	1	195	8.7
C	7	Derek Armstrong	L.A.	67	11	33	44	13	62	3	0	0	109	10.1
D	4	Rob Blake	L.A.	72	14	20	34	–26	82	11	0	1	208	6.7
D	6	Jamie Heward	WSH	52	4	12	16	4	27	2	0	1	50	8.0
			L.A.	19	2	6	8	–2	20	1	0	0	25	8.0
			TOTAL	71	6	18	24	2	47	3	0	1	75	8.0
R	29	Tom Kostopoulos	L.A.	76	7	15	22	–2	73	0	0	0	90	7.8
R	21	Brian Willsie	L.A.	81	11	10	21	–20	49	2	0	1	131	8.4
C	12	* Patrick O'Sullivan	L.A.	44	5	14	19	–6	14	2	0	1	92	5.4
D	44	Jaroslav Modry	DAL	57	1	9	10	10	32	0	0	0	60	1.7
			L.A.	19	0	8	8	1	22	0	0	0	29	0.0
			TOTAL	76	1	17	18	11	54	0	0	0	89	1.1
L	27	Scott Thornton	L.A.	58	7	6	13	–15	85	0	1	0	65	10.8
C	15	Jamie Lundmark	CGY	39	0	4	4	–4	31	0	0	0	28	0.0
			L.A.	29	7	2	9	–8	25	0	0	0	53	13.2
			TOTAL	68	7	6	13	–12	56	0	0	0	81	8.6
D	38	Kevin Dallman	L.A.	53	1	9	10	–13	12	0	0	0	76	1.3
D	8	Mike Weaver	L.A.	39	3	6	9	–4	16	1	0	1	22	13.6
L	41	Raitis Ivanans	L.A.	66	4	4	8	–12	140	0	0	0	37	10.8
D	3	Aaron Miller	L.A.	82	0	8	8	–14	60	0	0	0	56	0.0
R	9	* Konstantin Pushkarev	L.A.	16	2	2	4	–2	8	0	0	0	10	20.0
D	28	Oleg Tverdovsky	L.A.	26	0	4	4	–10	10	0	0	0	26	0.0
R	73	* John Zeiler	L.A.	23	1	2	3	–2	22	0	0	0	12	8.3
L	25	Noah Clarke	L.A.	13	2	0	2	–6	4	0	1	0	11	18.2
D	49	* Peter Harrold	L.A.	12	0	2	2	0	8	0	0	0	11	0.0
C	26	Marty Murray	L.A.	19	0	2	2	–5	4	0	0	0	4	0.0
C	10	Alyn McCauley	L.A.	10	1	0	1	0	2	0	0	0	4	25.0
L	22	* Shay Stephenson	L.A.	2	0	0	0	0	0	0	0	0	0	0.0
R	34	* Lauri Tukonen	L.A.	4	0	0	0	–2	0	0	0	0	1	0.0
R	43	Tim Jackman	L.A.	5	0	0	0	–1	10	0	0	0	3	0.0
D	33	* Jack Johnson	L.A.	5	0	0	0	–5	18	0	0	0	5	0.0
L	37	* Gabe Gauthier	L.A.	5	0	0	0	–1	2	0	0	0	6	0.0
D	22	* Joe Piskula	L.A.	5	0	0	0	–3	6	0	0	0	4	0.0

Goaltending

No.	Goaltender	GPI	Mins	Avg	W	L	OT	EN	SO	GA	SA	S%	G	A	PIM
31	Mathieu Garon	32	1779	2.66	13	10	6	3	2	79	849	.907	0	1	6
1	Sean Burke	23	1310	3.11	6	10	5	2	1	68	687	.901	0	1	4
32	* Barry Brust	11	486	3.70	2	4	1	2	0	30	245	.878	0	0	0
39	Dan Cloutier	24	1281	3.98	6	14	2	1	0	85	608	.860	0	1	21
33	* Yutaka Fukufuji	4	96	4.38	0	3	0	0	0	7	43	.837	0	0	0
	Totals	**82**	**4992**	**3.33**	**27**	**41**	**14**	**8**	**3**	**277**	**2440**	**.886**			

President and General Manager

DEAN LOMBARDI
President and General Manager, Los Angeles Kings.
Born in Holyoke, MA, March 5, 1958.

The Los Angeles Kings named Dean Lombardi president and general manager on April 21, 2006. Lombardi, formerly a member of the San Jose Sharks front office for 13 years, including seven seasons as general manager, followed by three years as a pro scout for the Philadelphia Flyers from 2003 to 2006, is the eighth general manager in Kings history.

An executive in the San Jose front office since 1990, Lombardi first served as assistant general manager (a post he held the previous two seasons with the Minnesota North Stars) for the expansion Sharks before being elevated to vice president, director of hockey operations in 1992. Four years later, he was promoted to executive vice president and general manager and given the responsibility of turning around the young franchise. During his tenure as general manager in San Jose from 1996 to 2003, Lombardi helped build the Sharks into one of the premier teams in the NHL. Under Lombardi, San Jose reached the playoffs five times – highlighted by two trips to the Western Conference Semifinals – and one Pacific Division title in 2002. The Lombardi-led Sharks in 2002 also tied an NHL-record with six consecutive seasons of improved point totals under one g.m. (Bill Torrey/New York Islanders) while building a roster that became progressively younger in age each season.

During his time as general manager in San Jose, Lombardi made many key personnel and player moves, stocking the Sharks organization with a good mix of veteran stars and up-and-coming youngsters that helped make the Sharks legitimate Stanley Cup contenders.

From the NHL Entry Draft, Lombardi brought to San Jose players like Patrick Marleau, Vesa Toskala, Jonathan Cheechoo, Brad Stuart, Scott Hannan, Marco Sturm, Marcel Goc and Christian Ehroff. *The Hockey News* ranked the Sharks' prospects (age 22 and under) as the best in the NHL in 1999-2000 and second best in 2000-01. Lombardi's history in San Jose as it relates to trades and free agency is impressive as well, having brought in such players as Owen Nolan, Teemu Selanne, Adam Graves, Vincent Damphousse, Mike Ricci, Kyle McClaren, Mike Vernon, Todd Harvey, Bryan Marchment and Scott Thornton.

Prior to joining the North Stars, Lombardi spent three seasons as a player representative, including the representation of five members of the 1988 United States Olympic team, and at the time he joined Minnesota's front office Lombardi was only the second former player agent to be employed in an NHL front office (Brian Burke/Vancouver Canucks was the other).

Born in Holyoke, Massachusetts, and raised in nearby Ludlow, Lombardi received his undergraduate degree from the University of New Haven where he finished third in his class. On the ice he was the hockey team's captain his final two seasons, and he received a full athletic scholarship and the school's student-athlete of the year award. In 1985, Lombardi earned his Law degree (with honors) from Tulane Law School where he specialized in Labor Law.

Club Records

Team

(Figures in brackets for season records are games played; records for fewest points, wins, ties, losses, goals, goals against are for 70 or more games)

Record		
Most Points	105	1974-75 (80)
Most Wins	46	1990-91 (80)
Most Ties	21	1974-75 (80)
Most Losses	52	1969-70 (76)
Most Goals	376	1988-89 (80)
Most Goals Against	389	1985-86 (80)
Fewest Points	38	1969-70 (76)
Fewest Wins	14	1969-70 (76)
Fewest Ties	5	1998-99 (82)
Fewest Losses	17	1974-75 (80)
Fewest Goals	168	1969-70 (76)
Fewest Goals Against	185	1974-75 (80)
Longest Winning Streak		
Overall	8	Oct. 21-Nov. 7/72, Feb. 23-Mar. 9/92
Home	12	Oct. 10-Dec. 5/92
Away	8	Dec. 18/74-Jan. 16/75
Longest Undefeated Streak		
Overall	11	Feb. 28-Mar. 24/74 (9 wins, 2 ties)
Home	13	Oct. 10-Dec. 8/92 (12 wins, 1 tie)
Away	11	Oct. 10-Dec. 11/74 (6 wins, 5 ties)
Longest Losing Streak		
Overall	11	Mar. 16-Apr. 4/04
Home	9	Feb. 8-Mar. 12/86
Away	11	Jan. 11-Feb. 15/70
Longest Winless Streak		
Overall	17	Jan. 29-Mar. 5/70 (13 losses, 4 ties)
Home	9	Jan. 29-Mar. 5/70 (8 losses, 1 tie), Feb. 8-Mar. 12/86 (9 losses)
Away	20	Jan. 11-Apr. 3/70 (16 losses, 4 ties)
Most Shutouts, Season	10	2000-01 (82)
Most PIM, Season	2,247	1992-93 (84)
Most Goals, Game	12	Nov. 29/84 (Van. 1 at L.A. 12)

Individual

Record		
Most Seasons	17	Dave Taylor
Most Games	1,111	Dave Taylor
Most Goals, Career	557	Luc Robitaille
Most Assists, Career	757	Marcel Dionne
Most Points Career	1,307	Marcel Dionne (550G, 757A)
Most PIM, Career	1,846	Marty McSorley
Most Shutouts, Career	32	Rogie Vachon
Longest Consecutive Games Streak	324	Marcel Dionne (Jan. 7/78-Jan. 9/82)
Most Goals, Season	70	Bernie Nicholls (1988-89)
Most Assists, Season	122	Wayne Gretzky (1990-91)
Most Points, Season	168	Wayne Gretzky (1988-89; 54G, 114A)
Most PIM, Season	399	Marty McSorley (1992-93)
Most Points, Defenseman, Season	76	Larry Murphy (1980-81; 16G, 60A)
Most Points, Center, Season	168	Wayne Gretzky (1988-89; 54G, 114A)
Most Points, Right Wing, Season	112	Dave Taylor (1980-81; 47G, 65A)
Most Points, Left Wing, Season	*125	Luc Robitaille (1992-93; 63G, 62A)
Most Points, Rookie, Season	84	Luc Robitaille (1986-87; 45G, 39A)
Most Shutouts, Season	8	Rogie Vachon (1976-77)
Most Goals, Game	4	Seventeen times
Most Assists, Game	6	Bernie Nicholls (Dec. 1/88), Tomas Sandstrom (Oct. 9/93)
Most Points, Game	8	Bernie Nicholls (Dec. 1/88; 2G, 6A)

* NHL Record.

Coaching History

Red Kelly, 1967-68, 1968-69; Hal Laycoe and Johnny Wilson, 1969-70; Larry Regan, 1970-71; Larry Regan and Fred Glover, 1971-72; Bob Pulford, 1972-73 to 1976-77; Ron Stewart, 1977-78; Bob Berry, 1978-79 to 1980-81; Parker MacDonald and Don Perry, 1981-82; Don Perry, 1982-83; Don Perry, Rogie Vachon and Roger Neilson, 1983-84; Pat Quinn, 1984-85, 1985-86; Pat Quinn and Mike Murphy 1986-87; Mike Murphy, Rogie Vachon and Robbie Ftorek, 1987-88; Robbie Ftorek, 1988-89; Tom Webster, 1989-90 to 1991-92; Barry Melrose, 1992-93, 1993-94; Barry Melrose and Rogie Vachon, 1994-95; Larry Robinson, 1995-96 to 1998-99; Andy Murray, 1999-2000 to 2003-04; Andy Murray and John Torchetti, 2005-06; Marc Crawford, 2006-07 to date.

Retired Numbers

16	Marcel Dionne	1975-1987
18	Dave Taylor	1977-1994
20	Luc Robitaille	1986-94, 97-01, 03-06
30	Rogie Vachon	1971-1978
99	Wayne Gretzky	1988-1996

All-time Record vs. Other Clubs

Regular Season

	At Home								On Road								Total							
	GP	W	L	T	OL	GF	GA	PTS	GP	W	L	T	OL	GF	GA	PTS	GP	W	L	T	OL	GF	GA	PTS
Anaheim	38	20	12	4	2	110	98	46	38	14	16	7	1	106	131	36	76	34	28	11	3	216	229	82
Atlanta	5	4	0	0	1	26	15	9	5	3	1	0	1	18	13	7	10	7	1	0	2	44	28	16
Boston	61	21	32	7	1	210	224	50	62	12	44	6	0	175	287	30	123	33	76	13	1	385	511	80
Buffalo	54	22	23	9	0	185	187	53	54	16	29	9	0	158	227	41	108	38	52	18	0	343	414	94
Calgary	95	48	38	9	0	348	326	105	98	28	55	12	3	321	427	71	193	76	93	21	3	669	753	176
Carolina	31	17	11	3	0	131	116	37	32	11	14	5	2	116	116	29	63	28	25	8	2	247	232	66
Chicago	78	35	33	8	2	258	259	80	79	33	36	9	1	229	270	76	157	68	69	17	3	487	529	156
Colorado	47	28	14	5	0	191	154	61	46	19	24	3	0	157	187	41	93	47	38	8	0	348	341	102
Columbus	12	8	3	1	0	32	22	17	12	4	5	0	3	40	35	11	24	12	8	1	3	72	57	28
Dallas	90	38	32	19	1	295	261	96	92	22	54	13	3	247	350	60	182	60	86	32	4	542	611	156
Detroit	84	43	27	14	0	330	261	100	83	30	37	13	3	282	321	76	167	73	64	27	3	612	582	176
Edmonton	81	30	35	15	1	310	327	76	81	24	42	15	0	288	364	63	162	54	77	30	1	598	691	139
Florida	10	6	4	0	0	30	30	12	9	2	4	3	0	21	23	7	19	8	8	3	0	51	53	19
Minnesota	12	4	4	2	2	25	29	12	12	5	4	3	0	27	27	13	24	9	8	5	2	52	56	25
Montreal	65	19	37	9	0	199	256	47	65	8	46	11	0	162	292	27	130	27	83	20	0	361	548	74
Nashville	16	9	6	0	1	49	44	19	16	9	4	3	0	40	31	21	32	18	10	3	1	89	75	40
New Jersey	43	29	8	6	0	204	132	64	43	19	18	5	1	148	142	44	86	48	26	11	1	352	274	108
NY Islanders	46	22	17	7	0	167	145	51	44	15	24	5	0	123	156	35	90	37	41	12	0	290	301	86
NY Rangers	61	24	26	10	1	203	217	59	58	17	35	6	0	172	233	40	119	41	61	16	1	375	450	99
Ottawa	10	8	1	1	0	46	21	17	10	4	5	1	0	29	35	9	20	12	6	2	0	75	56	26
Philadelphia	67	21	38	8	0	196	227	50	63	16	40	7	0	156	244	39	130	37	78	15	0	352	471	89
Phoenix	82	34	33	14	1	321	308	83	84	28	42	11	3	270	332	70	166	62	75	25	4	591	640	153
Pittsburgh	70	44	17	8	1	268	187	97	73	25	38	10	0	233	265	60	143	69	55	18	1	501	452	157
St. Louis	82	38	32	12	0	274	233	88	82	20	51	10	1	210	308	51	164	58	83	22	1	484	541	139
San Jose	45	25	15	4	1	137	122	55	45	14	25	3	3	122	156	34	90	39	40	7	4	259	278	89
Tampa Bay	12	1	9	2	0	25	40	4	11	5	5	0	1	24	26	11	23	6	14	2	1	49	66	15
Toronto	65	34	21	10	0	234	191	78	69	23	34	11	1	225	267	58	134	57	55	21	1	459	458	136
Vancouver	103	53	34	16	0	403	321	122	101	33	51	16	1	313	381	83	204	86	85	32	1	716	702	205
Washington	48	27	14	6	1	189	147	61	47	21	18	7	1	174	189	50	95	48	32	13	2	363	336	111
Defunct Clubs	35	27	6	2	0	141	76	56	34	11	14	9	0	91	109	31	69	38	20	11	0	232	185	87
Totals	**1548**	**739**	**582**	**211**	**16**	**5537**	**4976**	**1705**	**1548**	**491**	**815**	**213**	**29**	**4677**	**5944**	**1224**	**3096**	**1230**	**1397**	**424**	**45**	**10214**	**10920**	**2929**

Playoffs

	Series	W	L	GP	W	L	T	GF	GA	Last Mtg.	Rnd.	Result
Boston	2	0	2	13	5	8	0	38	56	1977	QF	L 2-4
Calgary	6	4	2	26	13	13	0	105	112	1993	DSF	W 4-2
Chicago	1	0	1	5	1	4	0	7	10	1974	QF	L 1-4
Colorado	2	0	2	14	6	8	0	23	33	2002	CQF	L 3-4
Dallas	1	0	1	7	3	4	0	21	26	1968	QF	L 3-4
Detroit	2	1	1	10	4	6	0	21	32	2001	CQF	W 4-2
Edmonton	7	2	5	36	12	24	0	127	154	1992	DSF	L 2-4
Montreal	1	0	1	5	1	4	0	12	15	1993	F	L 1-4
NY Islanders	1	0	1	4	1	3	0	10	21	1980	PRE	L 1-3
NY Rangers	2	0	2	6	1	5	0	14	32	1981	PRE	L 1-3
St. Louis	2	0	2	8	0	8	0	13	32	1998	CQF	L 0-4
Toronto	3	1	2	12	5	7	0	31	41	1993	CF	W 4-3
Vancouver	3	2	1	17	9	8	0	66	60	1993	DF	W 4-2
Defunct Clubs	1	1	0	7	4	3	0	23	25			
Totals	**34**	**11**	**23**	**170**	**65**	**105**	**0**	**511**	**649**			

Calgary totals include Atlanta Flames, 1972-73 to 1979-80. Carolina totals include Hartford, 1979-80 to 1996-97.
Colorado totals include Quebec, 1979-80 to 1994-95. Dallas totals include Minnesota North Stars, 1967-68 to 1992-93.
New Jersey totals include Kansas City, 1974-75, 1975-76, and Colorado Rockies, 1976-77 to 1981-82.
Phoenix totals include Winnipeg, 1979-80 to 1995-96.

Playoff Results 2007-2002

Year	Round	Opponent	Result	GF	GA
2002	CQF	Colorado	L 3-4	13	16

Abbreviations: Round: F - Final; **CF** - conference final; **CSF** - conference semi-final; **CQF** - conference quarter-final; **DF** - division final; **DSF** - division semi-final; **QF** - quarter-final; **PRE** - preliminary round.

2006-07 Results

Oct.	6	at Anaheim	3-4
	7	St. Louis	4-1
	10	NY Islanders	4-2
	12	Dallas	1-4
	14	Dallas	1-4
	16	Detroit	1-3
	18	Minnesota	1-2*
	19	at Phoenix	4-0
	22	Anaheim	2-3†
	23	at Colorado	1-6
	25	at Minnesota	1-3
	27	at Columbus	0-2
	28	at Dallas	2-3
	30	NY Rangers	4-1
Nov.	1	Pittsburgh	3-4*
	4	at Phoenix	4-6
	7	at Colorado	6-5
	9	San Jose	3-7
	11	Minnesota	2-3†
	13	San Jose	4-2
	16	Philadelphia	3-4
	18	Phoenix	5-3
	22	at San Jose	3-6
	24	at Dallas	3-5
	25	Calgary	3-1
	27	New Jersey	3-2†
	30	at Phoenix	4-7
Dec.	2	Anaheim	3-4
	3	at Anaheim	3-2
	7	Nashville	1-4
	9	Colorado	5-4
	12	San Jose	1-3
	14	at San Jose	4-2
	16	Dallas	3-4†
	19	Calgary	3-5
	21	at St. Louis	2-5
	23	at Nashville	0-7
	26	Phoenix	4-3†
	28	at Edmonton	7-4
	29	at Calgary	4-6
	31	at Detroit	2-6
Jan.	3	Columbus	3-0
	6	Detroit	4-2
	8	Edmonton	1-2*
	11	San Jose	2-5
	13	at St. Louis	5-6
	15	at Dallas	1-3
	16	at Atlanta	2-6
	18	St. Louis	1-3
	20	Phoenix	2-3
	26	at Vancouver	3-2*
	27	at Edmonton	3-4
	30	at Calgary	1-4
Feb.	1	Chicago	2-3*
	3	at Florida	7-0
	6	at Tampa Bay	2-3†
	8	at Washington	3-4*
	10	at Nashville	4-1
	13	at Carolina	1-2
	17	Anaheim	2-3†
	18	at Anaheim	4-3†
	22	Vancouver	2-3
	24	Colorado	6-5†
Mar.	1	Anaheim	4-3*
	3	Nashville	3-6
	6	at Chicago	0-3
	7	at Columbus	2-3*
	9	at Detroit	2-3*
	11	at Dallas	3-4*
	12	Edmonton	5-1
	15	Chicago	3-4†
	17	Columbus	5-3
	18	at Anaheim	5-3
	21	Dallas	2-4
	23	at Chicago	2-1
	24	at Minnesota	1-4
	27	at San Jose	1-3
	29	Vancouver	2-4
Apr.	1	at San Jose	2-6
	3	at Vancouver	2-4
	5	at Phoenix	2-3
	7	Phoenix	3-2

* – Overtime † – Shootout

Entry Draft Selections 2007-1993

2007

Pick	
4	Thomas Hickey
52	Oscar Moller
61	Wayne Simmonds
82	Bryan Cameron
95	Alec Martinez
109	Dwight King
124	Linden Rowat
137	Joshua Turnbull
184	Josh Kidd
188	Matt Fillier

2006

Pick	
11	Jonathan Bernier
17	Trevor Lewis
48	Joe Ryan
74	Jeff Zatkoff
86	Bud Holloway
114	Niclas Andersen
134	David Meckler
144	Martin Nolet
164	Constantin Braun

2005

Pick	
11	Anze Kopitar
50	Dany Roussin
60	T.J. Fast
72	Jonathan Quick
139	Patrik Hersley
184	Ryan McGinnis
206	Josh Meyers
226	John Seymour

2004

Pick	
11	Lauri Tukonen
95	Paul Baier
110	Ned Lukacevic
143	Eric Neilson
174	Scott Parse
205	Mike Curry
221	Daniel Taylor
238	Yutaka Fukufuji
264	Valtteri Tenkanen

2003

Pick	
13	Dustin Brown
26	Brian Boyle
27	Jeff Tambellini
44	Konstantin Pushkarev
82	Ryan Munce
152	Brady Murray
174	Esa Pirnes
231	Matt Zaba
244	Mike Sullivan
274	Marty Guerin

2002

Pick	
18	Denis Grebeshkov
50	Sergei Anshakov
66	Petr Kanko
104	Aaron Rome
115	Mark Rooneem
152	Greg Hogeboom
157	Joel Andresen
185	Ryan Murphy
215	Mikhail Lyubushin
248	Tuukka Pulliainen
279	Connor James

2001

Pick	
18	Jens Karlsson
30	Dave Steckel
49	Michael Cammalleri
51	Jaroslav Bednar
83	Henrik Juntunen
116	Richard Petiot
152	Terry Denike
153	Tuukka Mantyla
214	Cristobal Huet
237	Mike Gabinet
277	Sebastien Laplante

2000

Pick	
20	Alexander Frolov
54	Andreas Lilja
86	Yanick Lehoux
118	Lubomir Visnovsky
165	Nathan Marsters
201	Yevgeny Fedorov
206	Tim Eriksson
218	Craig Olynick
245	Dan Welch
250	Flavien Conne
282	Carl Grahn

1999

Pick	
43	Andrei Shefer
74	Jason Crain
76	Frantisek Kaberle
92	Cory Campbell
104	Brian McGrattan
125	Daniel Johansson
133	Jean-Francois Nogues
193	Kevin Baker
222	George Parros
250	Noah Clarke

1998

Pick	
21	Mathieu Biron
46	Justin Papineau
76	Alexei Volkov
103	Kip Brennan
133	Joe Rullier
163	Tomas Zizka
190	Tommi Hannus
217	Jim Henkel
248	Matthew Yeats

1997

Pick	
3	Olli Jokinen
15	Matt Zultek
29	Scott Barney
83	Joe Corvo
99	Sean Blanchard
137	Richard Seeley
150	Jeff Katcher
193	Jay Kopischke
220	Konrad Brand

1996

Pick	
30	Josh Green
37	Marian Cisar
57	Greg Phillips
84	Mikael Simons
96	Eric Belanger
120	Jesse Black
123	Peter Hogan
190	Stephen Valiquette
193	Kai Nurminen
219	Sebastien Simard

1995

Pick	
3	Aki Berg
33	Don MacLean
50	Pavel Rosa
59	Vladimir Tsyplakov
118	Jason Morgan
137	Igor Melyakov
157	Benoit Larose
163	Juha Vuorivirta
215	Brian Stewart

1994

Pick	
7	Jamie Storr
33	Matt Johnson
59	Vitali Yachmenev
111	Chris Schmidt
163	Luc Gagne
189	Andrew Dale
215	Jan Nemecek
241	Sergei Shalomai

1993

Pick	
42	Shayne Toporowski
68	Jeff Mitchell
94	Bob Wren
105	Frederick Beaubien
117	Jason Saal
120	Tomas Vlasak
146	Jere Karalahti
172	Justin Martin
198	John-Tra Dillabough
224	Martin Strbak
250	Kimmo Timonen
276	Patrick Howald

Coach

MARC CRAWFORD
Coach, Los Angeles Kings. Born in Belleville, Ont., February 13, 1961.

The Kings hired Marc Crawford as the club's head coach on May 22, 2006. The 21st head coach in Kings history, Crawford formerly was the head coach of the Vancouver Canucks and Colorado Avalanche/Quebec Nordiques, where he won a Stanley Cup in 1996 with the Avalanche. He is the only coach in Kings history to have a Stanley Cup win on his resume.

In his first season with the Kings in 2006-07, Crawford helped lead the team to a power play success rate of 18.3 percent, which was the highest for the club since the 2001-02 season, and he also earned his 1,000th career regular-season point behind the bench. Overall, he currently is the 16th winningest coach in NHL history with 438 career regular season wins and he is the all-time leader in regular season wins for Vancouver with 246.

Crawford began his NHL coaching career with Quebec in 1994 and in his first season he became the youngest coach to win the Jack Adams Award. After the Nordiques relocated to Denver he won the Stanley Cup in 1996 and with the win became the third-youngest coach in NHL history to raise Lord Stanley. Crawford's four seasons with Colorado/Quebec were marked by incredible success. In addition to the Stanley Cup, the franchise's first, Crawford helped lead the Avalanche to the Western Conference Finals the following year. He coached the Avalanche for three seasons, then spent time providing analysis for CBC's Hockey Night in Canada before being hired as the 15th head coach of the Canucks, the club he played every game of his nine-year professional career with.

As a left winger, Crawford recorded 50 points (19 goals, 31 assists) and 229 penalty minutes in 176 regular season NHL games from 1981 to 1987. He was a rookie on the Canucks team that reached the Stanley Cup Finals in 1982 and had previously been a member of two Memorial Cup championship teams with Cornwall in 1980 and 1981. He was also named to the Memorial Cup All-Star Team in 1981.

Crawford's coaching accomplishments also include stints behind the bench for Team Canada. He served as the head coach in the 1998 Winter Olympic Games in Nagano where his squad finished first in its pool and advanced to the semifinals before losing to the eventual champions, the Czech Republic, 2-1 in a shootout. Crawford also served as an assistant coach for Team Canada for the silver medal-winning squad at the 1996 World Cup of Hockey. Prior to beginning his NHL coaching career with the Nordiques, Crawford spent three seasons as the head coach of St. John's in the American Hockey League and two seasons with Cornwall of the Ontario Hockey League.

Club Directory

STAPLES Center

Los Angeles Kings
STAPLES Center
1111 South Figueroa Street
Los Angeles, CA 90015
Phone **213/742-7100**
GM FAX 310/535-4525
www.lakings.com
Capacity: 18,118

Executive

Owner . . . . Philip F. Anschutz
Owner . . . . Edward P. Roski, Jr.
Governor . . . . Timothy J. Leiweke
President, Business Operations . . . . Luc Robitaille

Hockey Operations – Executive

President/General Manager . . . . Dean Lombardi
Assistant General Manager . . . . Ron Hextall
Special Assistant to the G.M. . . . . Jack Ferreira
Director of Hockey Ops & Legal Affairs . . . . Jeff Solomon
Director of Pro Development . . . . Mike O'Connell
Director of Operations . . . . Marshall Dickerson
Royal Ambassador . . . . Rogie Vachon

Coaches

Head Coach . . . . Marc Crawford
Associate Coach . . . . Mike Johnston
Assistant Coach & Dir. of Amateur Dev. . . . . Jamie Kompon
Assistant Coach . . . . Nelson Emerson
Goaltending Coach . . . . Bill Ranford
Strength and Conditioning Coach . . . . Chad Smith

Trainers – Medical

Head Athletic Trainer . . . . Chris Kingsley
Assistant Athletic Trainer . . . . Joe Caligiuri
Rehabilitation Trainer . . . . Bobby Walls
Massage Therapist . . . . Mario Serban

Trainers – Equipment

Head Equipment Manager . . . . Darren Granger
Assistant Equipment Manager . . . . Corey Osmak
Assistant Equipment Manager . . . . Dana Bryson

Scouts/Hockey Operations

Co-Director of Amateur Scouting . . . . Mark Yannetti
Co-Director of Amateur Scouting . . . . Michael Futa
Amateur Scouts . . . . Brent McEwen, Tony Gasparini, Pertti Hasanen, Bob Crocker, Mike Donnelly, Steve Greeley, Sergei Bobrov
Pro Scout . . . . Rob Laird, Nickolai Bobrov, Bob Berry, Oto Hascak
Scouting Coordinator . . . . Lee Callans
Video Coordinator . . . . Bob Friedlander
Video Technician . . . . Bill Gurney
Assistant Goaltending Consultant . . . . Kim Dillabaugh
Executive Assistant, President/G.M. . . . . Kely Lyon

Communications/Broadcasting

Vice President, Communications & Broadcasting . . . Michael Altieri
Communications Director . . . . Jeff Moeller
Communications Manager . . . . Mike Kalinowski
Communications & Broadcasting Supervisor . . . . . . Stephanie Krauss

Broadcasters

TV Play-by-Play Announcer . . . . Bob Miller
Radio Play-by-Play Announcer . . . . Nick Nickson
TV Color Commentator . . . . Jim Fox
Radio Color Commentator . . . . Daryl Evans

Medical

Team Physician . . . . Dr. Ronald Kvitne
Internist . . . . Dr. Michael Mellman
Dentist . . . . Dr. Jeffrey Hoy
Opthamologist . . . . Dr. Howard Lazerson

Miscellaneous

Training Center . . . . Toyota Sports Center
Television . . . . FSN West
Radio Flagship . . . . KTLK AM 1150

Coaching Record

		Regular Season				Playoffs		
Season	Team	Games	W	L	O/T	Games	W	L
1989-90	Cornwall (OHL)	66	24	38	4	6	2	4
1990-91	Cornwall (OHL)	66	23	42	1	....	....	....
1991-92	St. John's (AHL)	80	39	29	12	16	11	5
1992-93	St. John's (AHL)	80	41	26	13	9	4	5
1993-94	St. John's (AHL)	80	45	23	12	11	6	5
1994-95	**Quebec (NHL)**	**48**	**30**	**13**	**5**	**6**	**2**	**4**
1995-96*	**Colorado (NHL)**	**82**	**47**	**25**	**10**	**22**	**16**	**6**
1996-97	**Colorado (NHL)**	**82**	**49**	**24**	**9**	**17**	**10**	**7**
1997-98	**Colorado (NHL)**	**82**	**39**	**26**	**17**	**7**	**3**	**4**
1998-99	**Vancouver (NHL)**	**37**	**8**	**23**	**6**	....	....	....
1999-2000	**Vancouver (NHL)**	**82**	**30**	**37**	**15**	....	....	....
2000-01	**Vancouver (NHL)**	**82**	**36**	**35**	**11**	**4**	**0**	**4**
2001-02	**Vancouver (NHL)**	**82**	**42**	**33**	**7**	**6**	**2**	**4**
2002-03	**Vancouver (NHL)**	**82**	**45**	**24**	**13**	**14**	**7**	**7**
2003-04	**Vancouver (NHL)**	**82**	**43**	**29**	**10**	**7**	**3**	**4**
2004-05	**Vancouver (NHL)**			Season Cancelled				
2005-06	**Vancouver (NHL)**	**82**	**42**	**32**	**8**	....	....	....
2006-07	**Los Angeles (NHL)**	**82**	**27**	**41**	**14**	....	....	....
	NHL Totals	**905**	**438**	**342**	**125**	**83**	**43**	**40**

* Stanley Cup win.

Minnesota Wild

2006-07 Results: 48W-26L-1OTL-7SOL 104PTS.
Second, Northwest Division

Key Off-Season Signings/Acquisitions

2007

June 12 • Re-signed G **Niklas Backstrom**.
30 • Re-signed C **Mikko Koivu** and D **Martin Skoula**.
July 1 • Acquired RW **Petr Kalus** and a 4th-round pick in the 2009 Entry Draft from Boston for G **Manny Fernandez**.
2 • Signed D **Sean Hill**.
3 • Signed C **Eric Belanger**.
3 • Re-signed C **Wes Walz**.
5 • Re-signed RW **Pierre-Marc Bouchard**.
11 • Re-signed G **Josh Harding**.
17 • Re-signed D **Kurtis Foster**.
18 • Re-signed LW **Derek Boogaard**.
23 • Re-signed D **Nick Schultz**.

Year-by-Year Record

		Home				Road				Overall								
Season	**GP**	**W**	**L**	**T**	**OL**	**W**	**L**	**T**	**OL**	**W**	**L**	**T**	**OL**	**GF**	**GA**	**Pts.**	**Finished**	**Playoff Result**
2006-07	82	29	7	....	5	19	19	....	3	48	26	....	8	235	191	104	2nd, Northwest Div.	Lost Conf. Quarter-Final
2005-06	82	23	16	....	2	15	20	....	6	38	36	....	8	231	215	84	5th, Northwest Div.	Out of Playoffs
2004-05	....	....	....	....	....	....	....	....	....	....	....	....	....	....	....	....		
2003-04	82	19	13	7	2	11	16	13	1	30	29	20	3	188	183	83	5th, Northwest Div.	Out of Playoffs
2002-03	82	25	13	3	0	17	16	7	1	42	29	10	1	198	178	95	3rd, Northwest Div.	Lost Conf. Championship
2001-02	82	14	14	8	5	12	21	4	4	26	35	12	9	195	238	73	5th, Northwest Div.	Out of Playoffs
2000-01	82	14	13	10	4	11	26	3	1	25	39	13	5	168	210	68	5th, Northwest Div.	Out of Playoffs

2007-08 Schedule

Month	Day	Date	Opponent
Oct.	Thu.	4	Chicago
	Sat.	6	Columbus
	Wed.	10	Edmonton
	Sat.	13	at Phoenix
	Sun.	14	at Anaheim*
	Tue.	16	at Los Angeles
	Sat.	20	at St. Louis
	Sun.	21	Colorado*
	Wed.	24	at Calgary
	Thu.	25	at Edmonton
	Sun.	28	at Colorado
	Tue.	30	Pittsburgh
Nov.	Thu.	1	St. Louis
	Sat.	3	Calgary
	Mon.	5	Edmonton
	Sun.	11	at Colorado
	Tue.	13	at Calgary
	Thu.	15	at Edmonton
	Fri.	16	at Vancouver
	Sun.	18	Colorado*
	Wed.	21	Vancouver
	Fri.	23	Columbus*
	Sat.	24	at Nashville
	Wed.	28	Phoenix
	Fri.	30	St. Louis
Dec.	Sun.	2	Vancouver*
	Wed.	5	Philadelphia
	Fri.	7	at Detroit
	Sat.	8	at Columbus
	Tue.	11	at San Jose
	Fri.	14	at Anaheim
	Sat.	15	at Los Angeles
	Tue.	18	Nashville
	Thu.	20	NY Rangers
	Sat.	22	Detroit
	Wed.	26	at Dallas
	Thu.	27	at Phoenix
	Sat.	29	Edmonton
	Mon.	31	San Jose
Jan.	Thu.	3	Dallas
	Sat.	5	at Nashville
	Mon.	7	at Dallas
	Thu.	10	at Detroit
	Fri.	11	at Chicago
	Sun.	13	Phoenix*
	Wed.	16	Calgary
	Fri.	18	Anaheim
	Mon.	21	at Vancouver
	Tue.	22	at Calgary
	Thu.	24	at Colorado
	Wed.	30	Anaheim
Feb.	Sat.	2	at Columbus
	Tue.	5	Detroit
	Thu.	7	Dallas
	Sat.	9	NY Islanders*
	Sun.	10	at St. Louis*
	Tue.	12	at Edmonton
	Thu.	14	at Vancouver
	Sun.	17	Nashville
	Tue.	19	Vancouver
	Wed.	20	at Chicago
	Sun.	24	Calgary*
	Tue.	26	at Washington
	Wed.	27	at Tampa Bay
	Fri.	29	at Florida
Mar.	Sun.	2	Los Angeles*
	Tue.	4	Chicago
	Thu.	6	at Carolina
	Fri.	7	at Atlanta
	Sun.	9	San Jose*
	Thu.	13	New Jersey
	Sat.	15	Los Angeles
	Mon.	17	Colorado
	Wed.	19	at San Jose
	Fri.	21	at Vancouver
	Sat.	22	at Calgary
	Mon.	24	at Edmonton
	Wed.	26	Edmonton
	Fri.	28	Vancouver
	Sun.	30	Colorado*
Apr.	Thu.	3	Calgary
	Sun.	6	at Colorado*

* Denotes afternoon game.

Signed as a free agent after several stellar seasons in his native Finland, Niklas Backstrom led the NHL in with a 1.97 goals-against average and .929 save percentage in 2006-07 as the Wild allowed the fewest goals in the NHL.

NORTHWEST DIVISION
8th NHL Season

Franchise date: June 25, 1997

2007-08 Player Personnel

FORWARDS	HT	WT	S	Place of Birth	*Age	2006-07 Club
BELANGER, Eric	6-0	188	L	Sherbrooke, Que.	29	Carolina-Atlanta
BOOGAARD, Derek	6-7	254	R	Saskatoon, Sask.	25	Minnesota
BOUCHARD, Pierre-Marc	5-10	172	L	Sherbrooke, Que.	23	Minnesota
DEMITRA, Pavol	6-0	202	L	Dubnica, Czech.	32	Minnesota
FOY, Matt	6-2	219	R	Oakville, Ont.	24	Minnesota-Houston
GABORIK, Marian	6-1	193	L	Trencin, Czech.	25	Minnesota
IRMEN, Danny	6-0	190	R	Fargo, ND	23	Houston
KALUS, Petr	6-1	201	L	Ostrava, Czech.	20	Boston-Providence (AHL)
KELLY, Steve	6-2	205	L	Vancouver, B.C.	30	Frankfurt
KOIVU, Mikko	6-3	207	L	Turku, Finland	24	Minnesota
MOORE, Dominic	6-0	193	L	Thornhill, Ont.	27	Pittsburgh-Minnesota
PARRISH, Mark	5-11	205	R	Bloomington, MN	30	Minnesota
POULIOT, Benoit	6-3	199	L	Alfred, Ont.	21	Minnesota-Houston
RADIVOJEVIC, Branko	6-2	210	R	Piestany, Czech.	26	Minnesota
ROLSTON, Brian	6-2	211	L	Flint, MI	34	Minnesota
VEILLEUX, Stephane	6-1	193	L	Beauceville, Que.	25	Minnesota
VOROS, Aaron	6-3	178	L	Vancouver, B.C.	26	Lowell-Houston
WALZ, Wes	5-10	189	R	Calgary, Alta.	37	Minnesota
WARD, Joel	6-2	205	R	Toronto, Ont.	26	Minnesota-Houston
DEFENSEMEN						
BELLE, Shawn	6-1	232	L	Edmonton, Alta.	22	Minnesota-Houston
BURNS, Brent	6-4	207	R	Ajax, Ont.	22	Minnesota
CARNEY, Keith	6-2	204	L	Providence, RI	37	Minnesota
FOSTER, Kurtis	6-5	218	R	Carp, Ont.	25	Minnesota
HILL, Sean	6-0	211	R	Duluth, MN	37	NY Islanders
JOHNSSON, Kim	6-1	200	L	Malmo, Sweden	31	Minnesota
LAKOS, Andre	6-6	230	R	Vienna, Austria	28	Salzburg
NUMMELIN, Petteri	5-10	191	L	Turku, Finland	34	Minnesota
REITZ, Erik	6-1	210	R	Detroit, MI	25	Minnesota-Houston
SCHULTZ, Nick	6-1	201	L	Strasbourg, Sask.	25	Minnesota
SCOTT, John	6-8	247	L	St. Catharines, Ont.	25	Houston
SKOULA, Martin	6-3	215	L	Litomerice, Czech.	27	Minnesota

GOALTENDERS	HT	WT	C	Place of Birth	*Age	2006-07 Club
BACKSTROM, Niklas	6-2	196	L	Helsinki, Finland	25	Minnesota
HARDING, Josh	6-1	193	R	Regina, Sask.	23	Minnesota-Houston
SCHAEFER, Nolan	6-2	200	R	Yellow Grass, Sask.	27	Worcester-Hershey-Wilkes-Barre

* – Age at start of 2007-08 season

Coach

JACQUES LEMAIRE
Coach, Minnesota Wild. Born in LaSalle, Que., September 7, 1945.

The Minnesota Wild announced the signing of Jacques Lemaire as the club's first head coach on June 19, 2000. In 2002-03, he led Minnesota into the playoffs after just three seasons and went all the way to the Western Conference Final. He also won the Jack Adams Award as coach of the year. The Wild reached the playoffs again in 2006-07. Prior to joining the Wild, Lemaire had spent parts of the previous two seasons as a senior consultant to the general manager for the Montreal Canadiens, the franchise with which he captured eight Stanley Cup championships as a player.

Lemaire spent five seasons behind the New Jersey Devils bench and compiled a 199-122-57 mark. In 1994-95, he coached the Devils to their first Stanley Cup championship. In his first season with the team (1993-94), he was awarded the Jack Adams Award for the first time.

Lemaire began his NHL coaching career with the Montreal Canadiens in 1983-84. He stepped aside as head coach following the 1984-85 campaign and moved to the front office where he held the position of assistant to the managing director. In that role, Lemaire played a part in Montreal's Stanley Cup championships of 1986 and 1993.

Lemaire spent his entire NHL playing career with Montreal from 1967 to 1979 winning the Stanley Cup eight times. He then began his coaching career in Switzerland where he served as player/coach of the Sierre club. He returned to North America in 1981 and was named the first head coach of the Quebec Major Junior Hockey League's expansion Longueuil Chevaliers. In his only season at the helm (1982-83), Lemaire guided the team to the QMJHL finals.

Coaching Record

		Regular Season				Playoffs		
Season	Team	Games	W	L	O/T	Games	W	L
1979-80	Sierre (Switzerland)	STATISTICS NOT AVAILABLE						
1980-81	Sierre (Switzerland)	STATISTICS NOT AVAILABLE						
1982-83	Longueuil (QMJHL)	70	37	29	4	15	9	6
1983-84	**Montreal (NHL)**	**17**	**7**	**10**	**0**	**15**	**9**	**6**
1984-85	**Montreal (NHL)**	**80**	**41**	**27**	**12**	**12**	**6**	**6**
1993-94	**New Jersey (NHL)**	**84**	**47**	**25**	**12**	**20**	**11**	**9**
1994-95*	**New Jersey (NHL)**	**48**	**22**	**18**	**8**	**20**	**16**	**4**
1995-96	**New Jersey (NHL)**	**82**	**37**	**33**	**12**	....	....	....
1996-97	**New Jersey (NHL)**	**82**	**45**	**23**	**14**	**10**	**5**	**5**
1997-98	**New Jersey (NHL)**	**82**	**48**	**23**	**11**	**6**	**2**	**4**
2000-01	**Minnesota (NHL)**	**82**	**25**	**44**	**13**	....	....	....
2001-02	**Minnesota (NHL)**	**82**	**26**	**44**	**12**	....	....	....
2002-03	**Minnesota (NHL)**	**82**	**42**	**30**	**10**	**18**	**8**	**10**
2003-04	**Minnesota (NHL)**	**82**	**30**	**32**	**20**	....	....	....
2004-05	**Minnesota (NHL)**	Season Cancelled						
2005-06	**Minnesota (NHL)**	**82**	**42**	**35**	**5**	....	....	....
2006-07	**Minnesota (NHL)**	**82**	**48**	**26**	**8**	**5**	**1**	**4**
	NHL Totals	**967**	**460**	**370**	**137**	**196**	**58**	**48**

* Stanley Cup win.

2006-07 Scoring

* – rookie

Regular Season

Pos	#	Player	Team	GP	G	A	Pts	+/–	PIM	PP	SH	GW	S	%
R	12	Brian Rolston	MIN	78	31	33	64	6	46	13	1	6	305	10.2
R	38	Pavol Demitra	MIN	71	25	39	64	0	28	9	1	4	175	14.3
R	10	Marian Gaborik	MIN	48	30	27	57	12	40	12	1	7	196	15.3
R	96	Pierre-Marc Bouchard	MIN	82	20	37	57	13	14	5	0	3	173	11.6
C	9	Mikko Koivu	MIN	82	20	34	54	6	58	9	2	2	162	12.3
C	28	Todd White	MIN	77	13	31	44	8	24	6	1	1	162	8.0
R	21	Mark Parrish	MIN	76	19	20	39	9	18	5	0	4	141	13.5
D	8	Brent Burns	MIN	77	7	18	25	16	26	3	0	3	108	6.5
R	92	Branko Radivojevic	MIN	82	11	13	24	–9	21	4	0	3	116	9.5
C	37	Wes Walz	MIN	62	9	15	24	3	30	0	1	1	77	11.7
D	26	Kurtis Foster	MIN	57	3	20	23	–3	52	0	0	0	135	2.2
D	5	Kim Johnsson	MIN	76	3	19	22	–4	64	3	0	0	98	3.1
D	33	Petteri Nummelin	MIN	51	3	17	20	–15	22	0	0	0	69	4.3
L	19	Stephane Veilleux	MIN	75	7	11	18	3	47	0	0	1	84	8.3
C	11	Dominic Moore	PIT	59	6	9	15	1	46	0	0	0	100	6.0
			MIN	10	2	0	2	3	10	0	0	1	11	18.2
			TOTAL	69	8	9	17	4	56	0	0	1	111	7.2
R	18	Adam Hall	NYR	49	4	8	12	–13	18	3	0	0	61	6.6
			MIN	23	2	3	5	2	8	0	0	0	42	4.8
			TOTAL	72	6	11	17	–11	26	3	0	0	103	5.8
D	3	Keith Carney	MIN	80	4	13	17	22	58	0	0	1	31	12.9
D	41	Martin Skoula	MIN	81	0	15	15	9	36	0	0	0	91	0.0
D	55	Nick Schultz	MIN	82	2	10	12	0	42	0	0	1	69	2.9
C	17	Wyatt Smith	MIN	61	3	3	6	–8	16	1	0	0	44	6.8
R	18	Mattias Weinhandl	MIN	12	1	1	2	–2	10	0	0	0	3	33.3
D	4 *	Shawn Belle	MIN	9	0	1	1	4	0	0	0	0	3	0.0
R	27 *	Joel Ward	MIN	11	0	1	1	0	0	0	0	0	12	0.0
L	24	Derek Boogaard	MIN	48	0	1	1	0	120	0	0	0	11	0.0
D	6 *	Erik Reitz	MIN	1	0	0	0	1	0	0	0	0	0	0.0
L	67 *	Benoit Pouliot	MIN	3	0	0	0	–1	0	0	0	0	1	0.0
C	23	Jason Morgan	MIN	4	0	0	0	–1	4	0	0	0	0	0.0
R	83 *	Matt Foy	MIN	9	0	0	0	–1	4	0	0	0	6	0.0

Goaltending

No.	Goaltender	GPI	Mins	Avg	W	L	OT	EN	SO	GA	SA	S%	G	A	PIM
29	* Josh Harding	7	361	1.16	3	2	1	0	1	7	174	.960	0	0	0
32	Niklas Backstrom	41	2227	1.97	23	8	6	1	5	73	1028	.929	0	1	2
35	Manny Fernandez	44	2422	2.55	22	16	1	0	2	103	1158	.911	0	0	12
	Totals	**82**	**5025**	**2.20**	**48**	**26**	**8**	**1**	**8**	**184**	**2361**	**.922**			

Playoffs

Pos	#	Player	Team	GP	G	A	Pts	+/–	PIM	PP	SH	GW	OT	S	%
R	10	Marian Gaborik	MIN	5	3	1	4	3	8	1	1	1	0	18	16.7
C	38	Pavol Demitra	MIN	5	1	3	4	–1	0	0	0	0	0	9	11.1
D	33	Petteri Nummelin	MIN	3	1	1	2	1	0	1	0	0	0	5	20.0
L	12	Brian Rolston	MIN	5	1	1	2	–2	4	0	0	0	0	23	4.3
R	96	Pierre-Marc Bouchard	MIN	5	1	1	2	–3	0	0	0	0	0	2	50.0
D	26	Kurtis Foster	MIN	3	0	2	2	0	0	0	0	0	0	5	0.0
R	21	Mark Parrish	MIN	5	1	0	1	2	0	0	0	0	0	13	7.7
C	9	Mikko Koivu	MIN	5	1	0	1	–1	4	0	0	0	0	8	12.5
L	24	Derek Boogaard	MIN	4	0	1	1	0	20	0	0	0	0	1	0.0
C	37	Wes Walz	MIN	5	0	1	1	1	4	0	0	0	0	9	0.0
D	55	Nick Schultz	MIN	5	0	1	1	–3	0	0	0	0	0	4	0.0
D	8	Brent Burns	MIN	5	0	1	1	1	14	0	0	0	0	12	0.0
R	18	Adam Hall	MIN	3	0	0	0	0	7	0	0	0	0	2	0.0
D	5	Kim Johnsson	MIN	4	0	0	0	–1	2	0	0	0	0	4	0.0
C	17	Wyatt Smith	MIN	4	0	0	0	0	0	0	0	0	0	2	0.0
C	28	Todd White	MIN	4	0	0	0	–1	0	0	0	0	0	6	0.0
D	3	Keith Carney	MIN	5	0	0	0	1	4	0	0	0	0	1	0.0
D	41	Martin Skoula	MIN	5	0	0	0	2	4	0	0	0	0	5	0.0
R	92	Branko Radivojevic	MIN	5	0	0	0	–1	2	0	0	0	0	9	0.0
L	19	Stephane Veilleux	MIN	5	0	0	0	0	4	0	0	0	0	6	0.0

Goaltending

No.	Goaltender	GPI	Mins	Avg	W	L	EN	SO	GA	SA	S%	G	A	PIM
32	Niklas Backstrom	5	297	2.22	1	4	1	0	11	145	.924	0	1	2
	Totals	**5**	**300**	**2.40**	**1**	**4**	**1**	**0**	**12**	**146**	**.918**			

In addition to his 20 goals in 2006-07, Mikko Koivu scored eight in the shootout to share the NHL lead.

Club Records

Team

(Figures in brackets for season records are games played.)

Most Points 104 2006-07 (82)
Most Wins 48 2006-07 (82)
Most Ties 20 2003-04 (82)
Most Losses 39 2000-01 (82)
Most Goals 235 2006-07 (82)
Most Goals Against 238 2001-02 (82)
Fewest Points 68 2000-01 (82)
Fewest Wins 25 2000-01 (82)
Fewest Ties 10 2002-03 (82)
Fewest Losses 29 2002-03 (82), 2003-04 (82)
Fewest Goals 168 2000-01 (82)
Fewest Goals Against 178 2002-03 (82)
Longest Winning Streak
  Overall .... 9 Mar. 8-24/07
  Home .... 8 Oct. 5-Nov. 2/06
  Away .... 5 Mar. 8-17/07
Longest Undefeated Streak
  Overall .... 9 Dec. 13-30/03 (4 wins, 5 ties) Mar. 8-24/07 (9 wins)
  Home .... 9 Dec. 13/00-Jan. 10/01 (5 wins, 4 ties)
  Away .... 7 Dec. 6-30/03 (2 wins, 5 ties)
Longest Losing Streak
  Overall .... 5 Mar. 11-19/01, Jan. 28-Feb. 8/02, Mar. 29-Apr. 5/02
  Home .... 4 Oct. 29-Nov. 15/00
  Away .... 6 Feb. 12-Mar. 22/06
Longest Winless Streak
  Overall .... 12 Mar. 11-Apr. 4/01 (9 losses, 3 ties)
  Home .... 8 Feb. 26-Mar. 28/01 (5 losses, 3 ties)
  Away .... 12 Dec. 18/03-Jan. 31/04 (5 losses, 7 ties)
Most Shutouts, Season 8 2006-07 (82)
Most PIM, Season 1,209 2001-02 (82), 2005-06 (82)
Most Goals, Game .... 8 Mar. 25/04 (Min. 8 at Chi. 2)

Individual

Most Seasons .... 6 Pascal Dupuis, Manny Fernandez, Marian Gaborik, Wes Walz
Most Games .... 427 Wes Walz
Most Goals, Career .... 164 Marian Gaborik
Most Assists, Career ...... 167 Marian Gaborik
Most Points, Career .... 331 Marian Gaborik (164G, 167A)
Most PIM, Career .... 698 Matt Johnson
Most Shutouts, Career ..... 15 Dwayne Roloson
Longest Consecutive Games Streak ... 288 Antti Laaksonen (Oct. 6/00-Dec. 29/03)
Most Goals, Season .... 38 Marian Gaborik (2005-06)
Most Assists, Season ...... 48 Andrew Brunette (2001-02)
Most Points, Season .... 79 Brian Rolston (2005-06; 34G, 45A)
Most PIM, Season .... 201 Matt Johnson (2002-03)
Most Points, Defenseman, Season ... 34 Lubomir Sekeras (2000-01; 11G, 23A)
Most Points, Center, Season ... 79 Brian Rolston (2005-06; 34G, 45A)
Most Points, Right Wing, Season ... 67 Marian Gaborik (2001-02; 30G, 37A)
Most Points, Left Wing, Season ... 69 Andrew Brunette (2001-02; 21G, 48A)
Most Points, Rookie, Season ... 36 Marian Gaborik (2000-01; 18G, 18A)
Most Shutouts, Season ..... 5 Dwayne Roloson (2001-02, 2003-04), Nicklas Backstrom (2006-07)
Most Goals, Game .... 3 Antti Laaksonen (Nov. 26/00), Marian Gaborik (Eight times), Marc Chouinard (Oct. 5/05), Brian Rolston (Nov. 5/05), Mark Parrish (Dec. 9/06)
Most Assists, Game .... 4 Andrew Brunette (Mar. 10/02), Marian Gaborik (Oct. 26/02) Pascal Dupuis (Mar. 25/04)
Most Points, Game .... 6 Marian Gaborik (Oct. 26/02; 2G, 4A)

General Managers' History

Doug Risebrough, 2000-01 to date.

Coaching History

Jacques Lemaire, 2000-01 to date.

Captains' History

Sean O'Donnell, Scott Pellerin, Wes Walz, Brad Bombardir, Darby Hendrickson, 2000-01; Jim Dowd, Filip Kuba, Brad Brown, Andrew Brunette, 2001-02; Brad Bombardir, Matt Johnson, Sergei Zholtok, 2002-03; Brad Brown, Andrew Brunette, Richard Park, Brad Bombardir, Jim Dowd, 2003-04; Alex Henry, Filip Kuba, Willie Mitchell, Brian Rolston, Wes Walz, 2005-06; Brian Rolston, Keith Carney, Mark Parrish, 2006-07.

2006-07 Results

Oct.	5	Colorado	3-2*
	7	Nashville	6-5
	10	Vancouver	2-1†
	12	Washington	3-2†
	14	Columbus	5-0
	18	at Los Angeles	2-1*
	20	at Anaheim	1-2
	21	at San Jose	4-1
	25	Los Angeles	3-1
	27	Anaheim	3-2†
	29	at Colorado	1-4
Nov.	2	Vancouver	5-2
	4	Nashville	3-4
	7	at San Jose	1-3
	11	at Los Angeles	3-2†
	12	at Anaheim	2-3
	14	at Phoenix	3-4
	16	at Nashville	7-6†
	18	Colorado	1-2†
	20	at Ottawa	3-5
	22	at Montreal	2-4
	24	Phoenix	4-0
	25	at Columbus	3-5
	29	San Jose	1-2
Dec.	1	Detroit	0-3
	2	at Dallas	3-4†
	5	Chicago	3-2†
	7	Calgary	3-2†
	9	Chicago	5-4*
	12	at Calgary	2-5
	14	at Edmonton	1-3
	16	at Vancouver	1-2
	19	Vancouver	5-2
	22	at Detroit	1-3
	23	Detroit	3-2*
	26	at Toronto	3-4
	27	at Detroit	1-3
	29	Columbus	4-3*
	31	Anaheim	4-3
Jan.	2	Atlanta	5-1
	4	Tampa Bay	2-3
	6	Colorado	1-2†
	9	at Calgary	0-3
	11	at Vancouver	5-2
	12	at Edmonton	4-2
	14	at Chicago	4-3†
	16	Edmonton	1-2
	19	at Chicago	3-0
	20	Dallas	1-2†
	26	Calgary	2-1†
	27	at Columbus	2-3
	30	at St. Louis	5-2
Feb.	1	at Colorado	5-3
	3	at Phoenix	1-0
	6	at Dallas	2-4
	8	Florida	4-2
	10	Carolina	5-4
	14	Vancouver	2-3*
	17	at Nashville	4-1
	18	at St. Louis	3-5
	20	Dallas	2-1†
	22	at Colorado	4-3
	25	Edmonton	4-1
	28	at Calgary	1-2†
Mar.	1	at Edmonton	5-0
	4	at Vancouver	3-4†
	6	San Jose	0-3
	8	at Boston	2-1
	9	at Buffalo	5-1
	11	Colorado	3-2*
	13	at Vancouver	3-2*
	15	at Edmonton	2-1
	17	at Calgary	4-2
	20	Phoenix	3-2
	22	St. Louis	5-1
	24	Los Angeles	4-1
	27	Calgary	0-1†
	29	Calgary	2-4
	31	at Colorado	1-2
Apr.	3	Edmonton	3-0
	5	Edmonton	3-0
	7	St. Louis	5-1

* – Overtime † – Shootout

All-time Record vs. Other Clubs

Regular Season

	At Home								On Road								Total							
	GP	W	L	T	OL	GF	GA	PTS	GP	W	L	T	OL	GF	GA	PTS	GP	W	L	T	OL	GF	GA	PTS
Anaheim	12	7	2	2	1	28	21	17	12	4	7	0	1	26	31	9	24	11	9	2	2	54	52	26
Atlanta	4	3	0	1	0	13	6	7	2	2	0	0	0	10	6	4	6	5	0	1	0	23	12	11
Boston	3	2	1	0	0	9	5	4	4	4	0	0	0	15	5	8	7	6	1	0	0	24	10	12
Buffalo	4	1	3	0	0	6	10	2	4	3	1	0	0	13	8	6	8	4	4	0	0	19	18	8
Calgary	19	9	7	1	2	43	39	21	18	3	11	3	1	33	47	10	37	12	18	4	3	76	86	31
Carolina	5	2	1	2	0	14	16	6	2	0	2	0	0	0	3	0	7	2	3	2	0	14	19	6
Chicago	12	10	2	0	0	42	27	20	12	7	4	1	0	37	26	15	24	17	6	1	0	79	53	35
Colorado	18	7	7	1	3	42	56	18	19	4	13	2	0	45	61	10	37	11	20	3	3	87	117	28
Columbus	12	9	2	0	1	39	23	19	11	1	7	1	2	16	33	5	23	10	9	1	3	55	56	24
Dallas	12	6	5	0	1	29	25	13	12	3	6	1	2	28	43	9	24	9	11	1	3	57	68	22
Detroit	12	3	6	2	1	27	34	9	12	3	8	1	0	27	43	7	24	6	14	3	1	54	77	16
Edmonton	18	7	9	1	1	43	42	16	19	9	5	3	2	43	38	23	37	16	14	4	3	86	80	39
Florida	4	3	0	1	0	14	3	7	3	2	1	0	0	8	6	4	7	5	1	1	0	22	9	11
Los Angeles	12	4	4	3	1	27	27	12	12	6	3	2	1	29	25	15	24	10	7	5	2	56	52	27
Montreal	3	2	0	0	1	10	8	5	4	1	2	1	0	10	13	3	7	3	2	1	1	20	21	8
Nashville	12	6	3	3	0	38	30	15	12	3	7	2	0	25	34	8	24	9	10	5	0	63	64	23
New Jersey	3	1	1	1	0	7	8	3	4	0	2	1	1	10	16	2	7	1	3	2	1	17	24	5
NY Islanders	3	2	1	0	0	9	9	4	4	2	2	0	0	10	9	4	7	4	3	0	0	19	18	8
NY Rangers	4	1	2	0	1	11	13	3	4	1	3	0	0	8	13	2	8	2	5	0	1	19	26	5
Ottawa	4	1	1	1	1	11	14	4	3	1	2	0	0	7	9	2	7	2	3	1	1	18	23	6
Philadelphia	2	1	0	1	0	5	3	3	5	1	4	0	0	5	14	2	7	2	4	1	0	10	17	5
Phoenix	12	5	4	2	1	27	25	13	12	4	6	1	1	27	33	10	24	9	10	3	2	54	58	23
Pittsburgh	3	2	0	1	0	9	5	5	4	3	1	0	0	17	6	6	7	5	1	1	0	26	11	11
St. Louis	12	7	1	2	2	39	22	18	12	4	4	3	1	23	26	12	24	11	5	5	3	62	48	30
San Jose	12	5	6	1	0	27	28	11	12	6	5	1	0	25	28	13	24	11	11	2	0	52	56	24
Tampa Bay	4	3	1	0	0	15	11	6	3	1	1	1	0	9	8	3	7	4	2	1	0	24	19	9
Toronto	2	1	1	0	0	5	4	2	4	0	4	0	0	6	15	0	6	1	5	0	0	11	19	2
Vancouver	19	10	6	2	1	55	46	23	18	6	5	3	4	44	46	19	37	16	11	5	5	99	92	42
Washington	4	4	0	0	0	9	3	8	3	1	2	0	0	6	7	2	7	5	2	0	0	15	10	10
Totals	**246**	**124**	**76**	**28**	**18**	**653**	**563**	**294**	**246**	**85**	**118**	**27**	**16**	**562**	**652**	**213**	**492**	**209**	**194**	**55**	**34**	**1215**	**1215**	**507**

Playoffs

	Series	W	L	GP	W	L	T	GF	GA	Last Mtg.	Rnd.	Result
Anaheim	2	0	2	9	1	8	0	10	21	2007	CQF	L 1-4
Colorado	1	1	0	7	4	3	0	16	17	2003	CQF	W 4-3
Vancouver	1	1	0	7	4	3	0	26	17	2003	CSF	W 4-3
Totals	**4**	**2**	**2**	**23**	**9**	**14**	**0**	**52**	**55**			

Playoff Results 2007-2002

Year	Round	Opponent	Result	GF	GA
2007	CQF	Anaheim	L 1-4	9	12
2003	CF	Anaheim	L 0-4	1	9
	CSF	Vancouver	W 4-3	26	17
	CQF	Colorado	W 4-3	16	17

Abbreviations: Round: CF – conference final; **CSF** – conference semi-final; **CQF** – conference quarter-final.

Entry Draft Selections 2007-2000

2007

Pick	
16	Colton Gillies
110	Justin Falk
140	Cody Almond
170	Harri Ilvonen
200	Carson McMillan

2006

Pick	
9	James Sheppard
40	Ondrej Fiala
72	Cal Clutterbuck
102	Kyle Medvec
132	Niko Hovinen
162	Julian Walker
192	Chris Hickey

2005

Pick	
4	Benoit Pouliot
57	Matt Kassian
65	Kristofer Westblom
110	Kyle Bailey
122	Morten Madsen
129	Anthony Aiello
199	Riley Emmerson

2004

Pick	
12	A.J. Thelen
42	Roman Voloshenko
78	Peter Olvecky
79	Clayton Stoner
111	Ryan Jones
114	Patrick Bordeleau
117	Julien Sprunger
161	Jean-Claude Sawyer
175	Aaron Boogaard
195	Jean-Michel Rizk
206	Anton Khudobin
272	Kyle Wilson

2003

Pick	
20	Brent Burns
56	Patrick O'Sullivan
78	Danny Irmen
157	Marcin Kolusz
187	Miroslav Kopriva
207	Georgy Misharin
219	Adam Courchaine
251	Mathieu Melanson
281	Jean-Michel Bolduc

2002

Pick	
8	Pierre-Marc Bouchard
38	Josh Harding
72	Mike Erickson
73	Barry Brust
155	Armands Berzins
175	Matt Foy
204	Niklas Eckerblom
237	Christoph Brandner
268	Mikhail Tyulyapkin
269	Mika Hannula

2001

Pick	
6	Mikko Koivu
36	Kyle Wanvig
74	Chris Heid
93	Stephane Veilleux
103	Tony Virta
202	Derek Boogaard
239	Jake Riddle

2000

Pick	
3	Marian Gaborik
33	Nick Schultz
99	Marc Cavosie
132	Maxim Sushinsky
170	Erik Reitz
199	Brian Passmore
214	Peter Bartos
232	Lubomir Sekeras
255	Eric Johansson

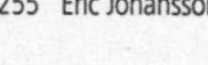

The team's first-ever draft pick in 2000, Marian Gaborik had 30 goals and 27 assists in just 48 games played in 2006-07.

President and General Manager

DOUG RISEBROUGH
President/General Manager, Minnesota Wild.
Born in Guelph, Ont., January 29, 1954.

Doug Risebrough was hired as the first executive vice president and general manager of the Minnesota Wild on September 2, 1999. He is responsible for the club's overall hockey operations. His efforts to build a winner through the draft has been exemplified by the success of Marian Gaborik, the club's first-round choice in 2000. The Wild qualified for the playoffs after just three seasons, going all the way to the 2003 Western Conference Final. They reached the playoffs again in 2006-07.

After ending his 13-year NHL playing career with the Flames in 1987, Risebrough was named as assistant coach with Calgary and joined Terry Crisp behind the bench. Risebrough was appointed head coach of the Flames on May 18, 1990 and on May 16, 1991, he also assumed the role of general manager. Late in the 1991-92 campaign he directed his energies full-time to general manager duties, handing the coaching responsibilities over to Guy Charron for the balance of the season. Risebrough served as g.m. in Calgary through the start of the 1995-96 season. He was vice president of hockey operations for the Edmonton Oilers from 1996 to 1999.

Risebrough was Montreal's first selection, seventh overall, in the 1974 Amateur Draft. During his nine years with the Canadiens, he helped his club to four consecutive Stanley Cup championships between 1976 and 1979. He joined the Flames prior to the start of the club's 1982 training camp. During his NHL career, his clubs have won five Stanley Cup titles (1976-1979 as a player and 1989 as an assistant coach with Calgary) and two Presidents' Trophies (1987-88 and 1988-89 as an assistant coach).

NHL Coaching Record

		Regular Season				Playoffs		
Season	Team	Games	W	L	T	Games	W	L
1990-91	Calgary	80	46	26	8	7	3	4
1991-92	Calgary	64	25	30	9	....	....	....
	NHL Totals	**144**	**71**	**56**	**17**	**7**	**3**	**4**

Club Directory

Xcel Energy Center

Minnesota Wild
317 Washington Street
St. Paul, MN 55102
Phone **651/602-6000**
FAX 651/222-1055
Tickets 651/222-9453
www.wild.com
Capacity: 18,064

Naegele Sports, LLC
Board Members . . . . . Bob Naegele, Jr., Jac Sperling, John Thomas, Rick Pepin
Investors in MSE include (listed in alphabetical order)
Investors Gage Hockey Ventures, LLC (Edwin Gage, Barbara Gage, Geoffrey Gage, Scott Gage, Rick Gage), Trisha and Greg Hoyt, Hubbard Broadcasting, Inc., Horace Irvine III, Bob Naegele, Jr., Bob Naegele III, Glen Nelson, Dick Nicholson, Ford Nicholson, Todd Nicholson, Vance Opperman, Mike Reilly, Jac Sperling, John Thomas, Jill and John Trautz

Executive Management
Chairman . . . . . Bob Naegele, Jr.
Vice Chairman . . . . . Jac Sperling
President/General Manager . . . . . Doug Risebrough
Exec. Vice President, Chief Financial Officer . . . . . Pamela Wheelock
Exec. Vice President . . . . . Matt Majka
Vice President, Sales and Service . . . . . Steve Griggs
Vice President/G.M., RiverCentre . . . . . Jim Ibister
Vice President/G.M., Xcel Energy Center . . . . . Jack Larson
Vice President, Communications and Broadcasting . Bill Robertson
Vice President, Minor League Sports Properties . . . . Tom Garrity
Executive Assistant . . . . . Stephanie Huseby
Executive Assistant, Hockey Operations . . . . . Laura Kinzel
Administrative Assistant, Sales and Service . . . . . Tawnya Vidnovic
Administrative Assistant, Communications and Broadcasting, Marketing, Human Resources . . . . Deb Hanson

Hockey Operations
Assistant General Manager/Hockey Operations . . . . Tom Lynn
Assistant General Manager/Player Personnel . . . . . Tom Thompson
Head Coach . . . . . Jacques Lemaire
Assistant Coaches . . . . . Mike Ramsey, Mario Tremblay
Goaltending Coach . . . . . Bob Mason
Strength and Conditioning Coach . . . . . Kirk Olson
Coordinator of Amateur Scoutin . . . . . Guy Lapointe
Director of Player Development . . . . . Barry MacKenzie
Director of Professional Scouting . . . . . Blair Mackasey
Amateur Scouts . . . . . Brian Hunter, Christopher Hamel, Doug Mosher, Ernie Vargas, Glen Sonmor, Marc Chamard, Paul Charles
European Scouts . . . . . Branislav Gaborik, Jiri Koluch, Ken Hoodikoff, Matti Vaisanen
Professional Scout . . . . . Jamie Hislop
Athletic Therapist . . . . . Don Fuller
Equipment Manager . . . . . Tony DaCosta
Assistant Trainer . . . . . Mike Vogt
Assistant Equipment Managers . . . . . Brent Proulx, Matt Benz
Video Coordinator . . . . . Matt Shaw
Director of Hockey Operations . . . . . Chris Snow
Hockey Operations Administrator . . . . . Cindy Sweiger
Medical Director . . . . . Dr. Sheldon Burns
Orthopedic Surgeon . . . . . Dr. Joel Boyd
Nutritionist . . . . . Carrie Peterson
Team Dentists . . . . . Kyle Edlund, Mike Nanne, Mike Pelke

Sales & Service
Senior Director, Customer Sales and Service . . . . . Jamie Spencer
Manager, Ticket Operations . . . . . Chris Turns
Manager, New Business Development . . . . . Michael Brinkman
Account Manager, Group and Event Suites . . . . . Cory Effertz
Senior Manager, Customer Service . . . . . Maria Troje
Account Service Executives . . . . . Anna Johnson, Joshua Simonson, Natalie Kaess

Retail Operation
Director, Retail Operations . . . . . Nikki Braxmeier
Manager, Retail Operations . . . . . Scott Sarkis

Corporate Partnerships
Senior Director, Corporate Sales and Service . . . . . Carin Anderson
Director, Corporate Sales . . . . . Mike Snee
Senior Account Executive . . . . . Chris Poitras
Account Executives . . . . . Carl Levi, Travis Hoban
Senior Manager, Corporate Services . . . . . Kathleen Borschke

Communications & Broadcasting
Manager, Media Relations and Team Services . . . . . Aaron Sickman
Manager, Media Relations, Xcel Energy Center . . . . Kathy Ross
Coordinator, Media Relations and Team Services . . . Wayne Carlson
Manager of Broadcasting . . . . . Maggie Kukar
Website Content . . . . . Glen Andresen
Radio Play-By-Play/Analyst . . . . . Bob Kurtz/Tom Reid
Television Play-By-Play/Analyst . . . . . Dan Terhaar/Mike Greenlay

Marketing
Senior Director, Marketing . . . . . John Maher
Director, Events and Promotions . . . . . Wayne Petersen
Manager, Game Presentation . . . . . Paul Loomis
Manager, Production Services . . . . . Hank Dolan
Manager, Marketing . . . . . Emily Gausman
Team Curator . . . . . Roger Godin

Community Giving
Director, Community Partnerships . . . . . Brad Bombardir
Manager, Community Giving . . . . . Amy Woog-Patnode

Finance & Accounting
Controller . . . . . Danette Kleinprintz
Senior Financial Analyst . . . . . Mitch Helgerson

Human Resources
Director, Human Resources . . . . . Delores Murphy

Information Technology
Director, Information Technology . . . . . David Weisbrod
Website Manager . . . . . Holly Doyle

Miscellaneous
Radio Network Flagship . . . . . WCCO (830 AM)
Television Networks . . . . . KSTC.TV Channel 45 (Over-the-Air),Fox Sports Net North (Cable)
Team Photographer . . . . . Bruce Kluckhohn
Public Address Announcer . . . . . Adam Abrams
Head of Off-Ice Officials . . . . . Barry Fritz

Key Off-Season Signings/Acquisitions

2007

May 28 • Re-signed D **Andrei Markov**.
June 15 • Re-signed LW **Christopher Higgins** and D **Mike Komisarek**.
July 2 • Signed D **Roman Hamrlik** and C **Bryan Smolinski**.
4 • Signed RW **Tom Kostopoulos**.
5 • Re-signed C **Tomas Plekanec**.
5 • Signed D **Mathieu Biron** and D **Jamie Rivers**.
17 • Re-signed D **Josh Gorges**.
29 • Re-signed RW **Michael Ryder**.
Aug. 3 • Signed D **Patrice Brisebois**.

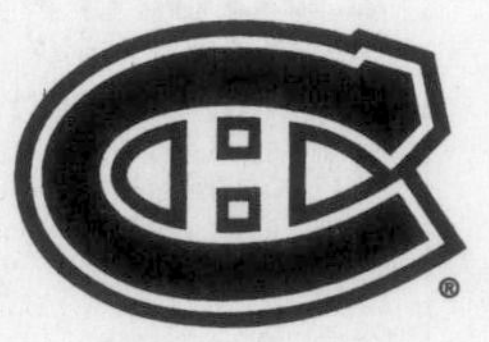

Montreal Canadiens

2006-07 Results: 42W-34L-1OTL-5SOL 90PTS.
Fourth, Northeast Division

Year-by-Year Record

		Home				Road				Overall								
Season	GP	W	L	T	OL	W	L	T	OL	W	L	T	OL	GF	GA	Pts.	Finished	Playoff Result
2006-07	82	26	12	....	3	16	22	....	3	42	34	....	6	245	256	90	4th, Northeast Div.	Out of Playoffs
2005-06	82	24	13	....	4	18	18	....	5	42	31	....	9	243	247	93	3rd, Northeast Div.	Lost Conf. Quarter-Final
2004-05	....	....	....	....	....	....	....	....	....	....	....	....	....	....	....	....		
2003-04	82	23	13	4	1	18	17	3	3	41	30	7	4	208	192	93	4th, Northeast Div.	Lost Conf. Semi-Final
2002-03	82	16	16	5	4	14	19	3	5	30	35	8	9	206	234	77	4th, Northeast Div.	Out of Playoffs
2001-02	82	21	13	6	1	15	18	6	2	36	31	12	3	207	209	87	4th, Northeast Div.	Lost Conf. Semi-Final
2000-01	82	15	20	4	2	13	20	4	4	28	40	8	6	206	232	70	5th, Northeast Div.	Out of Playoffs
1999-2000	82	18	17	5	1	17	17	4	3	35	34	9	4	196	194	83	4th, Northeast Div.	Out of Playoffs
1998-99	82	21	15	5	....	11	24	6	....	32	39	11	....	184	209	75	5th, Northeast Div.	Out of Playoffs
1997-98	82	15	17	9	....	22	15	4	....	37	32	13	....	235	208	87	4th, Northeast Div.	Lost Conf. Semi-Final
1996-97	82	17	17	7	....	14	19	8	....	31	36	15	....	249	276	77	4th, Northeast Div.	Lost Conf. Quarter-Final
1995-96	82	23	12	6	....	17	20	4	....	40	32	10	....	265	248	90	3rd, Northeast Div.	Lost Conf. Quarter-Final
1994-95	48	15	5	4	....	3	18	3	....	18	23	7	....	125	148	43	6th, Northeast Div.	Out of Playoffs
1993-94	84	26	12	4	....	15	17	10	....	41	29	14	....	283	248	96	3rd, Northeast Div.	Lost Conf. Quarter-Final
1992-93	**84**	**27**	**13**	**2**	....	**21**	**17**	**4**	....	**48**	**30**	**6**	....	**326**	**280**	**102**	**3rd, Adams Div.**	**Won Stanley Cup**
1991-92	80	27	8	5	....	14	20	6	....	41	28	11	....	267	207	93	1st, Adams Div.	Lost Div. Final
1990-91	80	23	12	5	....	16	18	6	....	39	30	11	....	273	249	89	2nd, Adams Div.	Lost Div. Final
1989-90	80	26	8	6	....	15	20	5	....	41	28	11	....	288	234	93	3rd, Adams Div.	Lost Div. Final
1988-89	80	30	6	4	....	23	12	5	....	53	18	9	....	315	218	115	1st, Adams Div.	Lost Final
1987-88	80	26	8	6	....	19	14	7	....	45	22	13	....	298	238	103	1st, Adams Div.	Lost Div. Final
1986-87	80	27	9	4	....	14	20	6	....	41	29	10	....	277	241	92	2nd, Adams Div.	Lost Conf. Championship
1985-86	**80**	**25**	**11**	**4**	....	**15**	**22**	**3**	....	**40**	**33**	**7**	....	**330**	**280**	**87**	**2nd, Adams Div.**	**Won Stanley Cup**
1984-85	80	24	10	6	....	17	17	6	....	41	27	12	....	309	262	94	1st, Adams Div.	Lost Div. Final
1983-84	80	19	19	2	....	16	21	3	....	35	40	5	....	286	295	75	4th, Adams Div.	Lost Conf. Championship
1982-83	80	25	6	9	....	17	18	5	....	42	24	14	....	350	286	98	2nd, Adams Div.	Lost Div. Semi-Final
1981-82	80	25	6	9	....	21	11	8	....	46	17	17	....	360	223	109	1st, Adams Div.	Lost Div. Semi-Final
1980-81	80	31	7	2	....	14	15	11	....	45	22	13	....	332	232	103	1st, Norris Div.	Lost Prelim. Round
1979-80	80	30	7	3	....	17	13	10	....	47	20	13	....	328	240	107	1st, Norris Div.	Lost Quarter-Final
1978-79	**80**	**29**	**6**	**5**	....	**23**	**11**	**6**	....	**52**	**17**	**11**	....	**337**	**204**	**115**	**1st, Norris Div.**	**Won Stanley Cup**
1977-78	**80**	**32**	**4**	**4**	....	**27**	**6**	**7**	....	**59**	**10**	**11**	....	**359**	**183**	**129**	**1st, Norris Div.**	**Won Stanley Cup**
1976-77	**80**	**33**	**1**	**6**	....	**27**	**7**	**6**	....	**60**	**8**	**12**	....	**387**	**171**	**132**	**1st, Norris Div.**	**Won Stanley Cup**
1975-76	**80**	**32**	**3**	**5**	....	**26**	**8**	**6**	....	**58**	**11**	**11**	....	**337**	**174**	**127**	**1st, Norris Div.**	**Won Stanley Cup**
1974-75	80	27	8	5	....	20	6	14	....	47	14	19	....	374	225	113	1st, Norris Div.	Lost Semi-Final
1973-74	78	24	12	3	....	21	12	6	....	45	24	9	....	293	240	99	2nd, East Div.	Lost Quarter-inal
1972-73	**78**	**29**	**4**	**6**	....	**23**	**6**	**10**	....	**52**	**10**	**16**	....	**329**	**184**	**120**	**1st, East Div.**	**Won Stanley Cup**
1971-72	78	29	3	7	....	17	13	9	....	46	16	16	....	307	205	108	3rd, East Div.	Lost Quarter-Final
1970-71	**78**	**29**	**7**	**3**	....	**13**	**16**	**10**	....	**42**	**23**	**13**	....	**291**	**216**	**97**	**3rd, East Div.**	**Won Stanley Cup**
1969-70	76	21	9	8	....	17	13	8	....	38	22	16	....	244	201	92	5th, East Div.	Out of Playoffs
1968-69	**76**	**26**	**7**	**5**	....	**20**	**12**	**6**	....	**46**	**19**	**11**	....	**271**	**202**	**103**	**1st, East Div.**	**Won Stanley Cup**
1967-68	**74**	**26**	**5**	**6**	....	**16**	**17**	**4**	....	**42**	**22**	**10**	....	**236**	**167**	**94**	**1st, East Div.**	**Won Stanley Cup**
1966-67	70	19	9	7	....	13	16	6	....	32	25	13	....	202	188	77	2nd,	Lost Final
1965-66	**70**	**23**	**11**	**1**	....	**18**	**10**	**7**	....	**41**	**21**	**8**	....	**239**	**173**	**90**	**1st,**	**Won Stanley Cup**
1964-65	**70**	**20**	**8**	**7**	....	**16**	**15**	**4**	....	**36**	**23**	**11**	....	**211**	**185**	**83**	**2nd,**	**Won Stanley Cup**
1963-64	70	22	7	6	....	14	14	7	....	36	21	13	....	209	167	85	1st,	Lost Semi-Final
1962-63	70	15	10	10	....	13	9	13	....	28	19	23	....	225	183	79	3rd,	Lost Semi-Final
1961-62	70	26	2	7	....	16	12	7	....	42	14	14	....	259	166	98	1st,	Lost Semi-Final
1960-61	70	24	6	5	....	17	13	5	....	41	19	10	....	254	188	92	1st,	Lost Semi-Final
1959-60	**70**	**23**	**4**	**8**	....	**17**	**14**	**4**	....	**40**	**18**	**12**	....	**255**	**178**	**92**	**1st,**	**Won Stanley Cup**
1958-59	**70**	**21**	**8**	**6**	....	**18**	**10**	**7**	....	**39**	**18**	**13**	....	**258**	**158**	**91**	**1st,**	**Won Stanley Cup**
1957-58	**70**	**23**	**8**	**4**	....	**20**	**9**	**6**	....	**43**	**17**	**10**	....	**250**	**158**	**96**	**1st,**	**Won Stanley Cup**
1956-57	**70**	**23**	**6**	**6**	....	**12**	**17**	**6**	....	**35**	**23**	**12**	....	**210**	**155**	**82**	**2nd,**	**Won Stanley Cup**
1955-56	**70**	**29**	**5**	**1**	....	**16**	**10**	**9**	....	**45**	**15**	**10**	....	**222**	**131**	**100**	**1st,**	**Won Stanley Cup**
1954-55	70	26	5	4	....	15	13	7	....	41	18	11	....	228	157	93	2nd,	Lost Final
1953-54	70	27	5	3	....	8	19	8	....	35	24	11	....	195	141	81	2nd,	Lost Final
1952-53	**70**	**18**	**12**	**5**	....	**10**	**11**	**14**	....	**28**	**23**	**19**	....	**155**	**148**	**75**	**2nd,**	**Won Stanley Cup**
1951-52	70	22	8	5	....	12	18	5	....	34	26	10	....	195	164	78	2nd,	Lost Final
1950-51	70	17	10	8	....	8	20	7	....	25	30	15	....	173	184	65	3rd,	Lost Final
1949-50	70	17	8	10	....	12	14	9	....	29	22	19	....	172	150	77	2nd,	Lost Semi-Final
1948-49	60	19	8	3	....	9	15	6	....	28	23	9	....	152	126	65	3rd,	Lost Semi-Final
1947-48	60	13	13	4	....	7	16	7	....	20	29	11	....	147	169	51	5th,	Out of Playoffs
1946-47	60	19	6	5	....	15	10	5	....	34	16	10	....	189	138	78	1st,	Lost Final
1945-46	**50**	**16**	**6**	**3**	....	**12**	**11**	**2**	....	**28**	**17**	**5**	....	**172**	**134**	**61**	**1st,**	**Won Stanley Cup**
1944-45	50	21	2	2	....	17	6	2	....	38	8	4	....	228	121	80	1st,	Lost Semi-Final
1943-44	**50**	**22**	**0**	**3**	....	**16**	**5**	**4**	....	**38**	**5**	**7**	....	**234**	**109**	**83**	**1st,**	**Won Stanley Cup**
1942-43	50	14	4	7	....	5	15	5	....	19	19	12	....	181	191	50	4th,	Lost Semi-Final
1941-42	48	12	10	2	....	6	17	1	....	18	27	3	....	134	173	39	6th,	Lost Quarter-Final
1940-41	48	11	9	4	....	5	17	2	....	16	26	6	....	121	147	38	6th,	Lost Quarter-Final
1939-40	48	5	14	5	....	5	19	0	....	10	33	5	....	90	167	25	7th,	Out of Playoffs
1938-39	48	8	11	5	....	7	13	4	....	15	24	9	....	115	146	39	6th,	Lost Quarter-Final
1937-38	48	13	4	7	....	5	13	6	....	18	17	13	....	123	128	49	3rd, Cdn. Div.	Lost Quarter-Final
1936-37	48	16	8	0	....	8	10	6	....	24	18	6	....	115	111	54	1st, Cdn. Div.	Lost Semi-Final
1935-36	48	5	11	8	....	6	15	3	....	11	26	11	....	82	123	33	4th, Cdn. Div.	Out of Playoffs
1934-35	48	11	11	2	....	8	12	4	....	19	23	6	....	110	145	44	3rd, Cdn. Div.	Lost Quarter-Final
1933-34	48	16	6	2	....	6	14	4	....	22	20	6	....	99	101	50	2nd, Cdn. Div.	Lost Quarter-Final
1932-33	48	15	5	4	....	3	20	1	....	18	25	5	....	92	115	41	3rd, Cdn. Div.	Lost Quarter-Final
1931-32	48	18	3	3	....	7	13	4	....	25	16	7	....	128	111	57	1st, Cdn. Div.	Lost Semi-Final
1930-31	**44**	**15**	**3**	**4**	....	**11**	**7**	**4**	....	**26**	**10**	**8**	....	**129**	**89**	**60**	**1st, Cdn. Div.**	**Won Stanley Cup**
1929-30	**44**	**13**	**5**	**4**	....	**8**	**9**	**5**	....	**21**	**14**	**9**	....	**142**	**114**	**51**	**2nd, Cdn. Div.**	**Won Stanley Cup**
1928-29	44	12	4	6	....	10	3	9	....	22	7	15	....	71	43	59	1st, Cdn. Div.	Lost Semi-Final
1927-28	44	12	7	3	....	14	4	4	....	26	11	7	....	116	48	59	1st, Cdn. Div.	Lost Semi-Final
1926-27	44	15	5	2	....	13	9	0	....	28	14	2	....	99	67	58	2nd, Cdn. Div.	Lost Semi-Final
1925-26	36	5	12	1	....	6	12	0	....	11	24	1	....	79	108	23	7th,	Out of Playoffs
1924-25	30	10	5	0	....	7	6	2	....	17	11	2	....	93	56	36	3rd,	Lost Final
1923-24	**24**	**10**	**2**	**0**	....	**3**	**9**	**0**	....	**13**	**11**	**0**	....	**59**	**48**	**26**	**2nd,**	**Won Stanley Cup**
1922-23	24	10	2	0	....	3	7	2	....	13	9	2	....	73	61	28	2nd,	Lost NHL Final
1921-22	24	8	3	1	....	4	8	0	....	12	11	1	....	88	94	25	3rd,	Out of Playoffs
1920-21	24	9	3	0	....	4	8	0	....	13	11	0	....	112	99	26	3rd and 2nd*	Out of Playoffs
1919-20	24	8	4	0	....	5	7	0	....	13	11	0	....	129	113	26	2nd and 3rd*	Out of Playoffs
1918-19	18	7	2	0	....	3	6	0	....	10	8	0	....	88	78	20	1st and 2nd*	Cup Final but no Decision
1917-18	22	8	3	0	....	5	6	0	....	13	9	0	....	115	84	26	1st and 3rd*	Lost NHL Final

* Season played in two halves with no combined standing at end.
From 1917-18 through 1925-26, NHL champions played against PCHA/WCHL champions for Stanley Cup.

2007-08 Schedule

Month	Day	Date	Opponent
Oct.	Wed.	3	at Carolina
	Sat.	6	at Toronto
	Wed.	10	at Pittsburgh
	Sat.	13	Carolina
	Tue.	16	Florida
	Thu.	18	at Ottawa
	Sat.	20	Buffalo
	Mon.	22	Boston
	Fri.	26	at Carolina
	Sat.	27	at Pittsburgh
	Tue.	30	Atlanta
Nov.	Thu.	1	Philadelphia
	Sat.	3	Toronto
	Mon.	5	Buffalo
	Thu.	8	at Boston
	Sat.	10	at Ottawa*
	Tue.	13	at Toronto
	Fri.	16	at Buffalo
	Sat.	17	Boston
	Mon.	19	Ottawa
	Wed.	21	at NY Islanders
	Fri.	23	at Buffalo
	Sat.	24	Buffalo
	Tue.	27	at Toronto
	Fri.	30	at New Jersey
Dec.	Sat.	1	Nashville
	Tue.	4	Detroit
	Thu.	6	at Boston
	Sat.	8	Carolina
	Tue.	11	Tampa Bay
	Thu.	13	at Philadelphia
	Sat.	15	Toronto
	Tue.	18	Florida
	Thu.	20	at Washington
	Sat.	22	at Atlanta
	Sun.	23	at Dallas
	Thu.	27	at Tampa Bay
	Fri.	28	at Florida
	Sun.	30	at NY Rangers
Jan.	Thu.	3	Tampa Bay
	Sat.	5	Washington*
	Tue.	8	Chicago
	Thu.	10	at Boston
	Sat.	12	at NY Rangers
	Tue.	15	at NY Islanders
	Thu.	17	at Atlanta
	Sat.	19	Pittsburgh
	Tue.	22	Boston
	Thu.	24	at New Jersey
	Tue.	29	Washington
	Thu.	31	at Washington
Feb.	Sat.	2	NY Islanders*
	Sun.	3	NY Rangers*
	Tue.	5	Ottawa
	Thu.	7	Toronto
	Sat.	9	at Ottawa
	Tue.	12	at Tampa Bay
	Wed.	13	at Florida
	Sat.	16	Philadelphia
	Sun.	17	at Philadelphia
	Tue.	19	NY Rangers
	Thu.	21	Pittsburgh
	Sat.	23	Columbus
	Tue.	26	Atlanta
	Fri.	29	at Buffalo
Mar.	Sat.	1	New Jersey
	Mon.	3	at San Jose
	Thu.	6	at Phoenix
	Sat.	8	at Los Angeles*
	Sun.	9	at Anaheim*
	Tue.	11	New Jersey
	Thu.	13	Ottawa
	Sat.	15	NY Islanders
	Tue.	18	St. Louis
	Thu.	20	at Boston
	Sat.	22	Boston
	Mon.	24	Ottawa
	Fri.	28	at Buffalo
	Sat.	29	at Toronto
Apr.	Tue.	1	at Ottawa
	Thu.	3	Buffalo
	Sat.	5	Toronto

* Denotes afternoon game.

NORTHEAST DIVISION
91st NHL Season

Franchise date: November 22, 1917

2007-08 Player Personnel

FORWARDS	HT	WT	S	Place of Birth	*Age	2006-07 Club
BEGIN, Steve	6-0	193	L	Trois-Rivieres, Que.	29	Montreal
CHIPCHURA, Kyle	6-2	205	L	Westlock, Alta.	21	Hamilton
FERLAND, Jonathan	6-2	212	R	Ste-Marie-de-Beauce, Que.	24	Hamilton
GRABOVSKI, Mikhail	5-9	172	L	Potsdam, East Germany	23	Montreal-Hamilton
HIGGINS, Christopher	6-0	202	L	Smithtown, NY	24	Montreal
KOIVU, Saku	5-10	187	L	Turku, Finland	32	Montreal
KOSTITSYN, Andrei	6-0	200	L	Novopolotsk, USSR	22	Montreal-Hamilton
KOSTOPOULOS, Tom	6-0	205	R	Mississauga, Ont.	28	Los Angeles
KOVALEV, Alex	6-1	222	L	Togliatti, USSR	34	Montreal
LAHTI, Janne	6-0	200	L	Riihimaki, Finland	25	HPK
LAPIERRE, Maxim	6-2	196	R	St. Leonard, Que.	22	Montreal-Hamilton
LATENDRESSE, Guillaume	6-2	229	L	Ste-Catherine, Que.	20	Montreal
MURRAY, Garth	6-2	208	L	Regina, Sask.	25	Montreal
PLEKANEC, Tomas	5-10	196	L	Kladno, Czech.	24	Montreal
RYDER, Michael	6-0	192	R	Bonavista, Nfld.	27	Montreal
SMOLINSKI, Bryan	6-1	215	R	Toledo, OH	35	Chicago-Vancouver
DEFENSEMEN						
BIRON, Mathieu	6-6	230	R	Lac-St-Charles, Que.	27	Worcester-Hamilton
BOUILLON, Francis	5-8	201	L	New York, NY	31	Montreal
BRISEBOIS, Patrice	6-2	203	R	Montreal, Que.	36	Colorado
COTE, Jean-Philippe	6-3	213	L	Charlesbourg, Que.	25	Hamilton
DANDENAULT, Mathieu	6-0	215	R	Sherbrooke, Que.	31	Montreal
GORGES, Josh	6-1	195	L	Kelowna, B.C.	23	S.J.-Worcester-Mtl
HAMRLIK, Roman	6-2	208	L	Gottwaldov/Zlin, Czech.	33	Calgary
KOMISAREK, Mike	6-4	242	R	West Islip, NY	25	Montreal
MARKOV, Andrei	6-0	203	L	Voskresensk, USSR	28	Montreal
O'BYRNE, Ryan	6-5	234	R	Victoria, B.C.	23	Hamilton
RIVERS, Jamie	6-1	206	L	Ottawa, Ont.	32	St. Louis-Peoria
STREIT, Mark	6-0	196	L	Englisberg, Switz.	29	Montreal
VALENTENKO, Pavel	6-2	214	L	Nizhnekamsk, USSR	19	Nizhnekamsk

GOALTENDERS	HT	WT	C	Place of Birth	*Age	2006-07 Club
HALAK, Jaroslav	5-11	180	L	Bratislava, Czech.	22	Montreal-Hamilton
HUET, Cristobal	6-0	204	L	St. Martin d'Heres, France	32	Montreal
PRICE, Carey	6-3	212	L	Vancouver, B.C.	20	Tri-City-Hamilton

* – Age at start of 2007-08 season

2006-07 Scoring

* – rookie

Regular Season

Pos	#	Player	Team	GP	G	A	Pts	+/–	PIM	PP	SH	GW	S	%
C	11	Saku Koivu	MTL	81	22	53	75	–21	74	11	1	4	154	14.3
D	44	Sheldon Souray	MTL	81	26	38	64	–28	135	19	1	6	224	11.6
R	73	Michael Ryder	MTL	82	30	28	58	–25	60	17	2	3	221	13.6
D	79	Andrei Markov	MTL	77	6	43	49	2	56	5	0	2	128	4.7
C	35	Tomas Plekanec	MTL	81	20	27	47	10	36	5	2	1	150	13.3
R	27	Alex Kovalev	MTL	73	18	29	47	–19	78	8	0	5	197	9.1
L	21	Christopher Higgins	MTL	61	22	16	38	–11	26	8	3	3	159	13.8
D	32	Mark Streit	MTL	76	10	26	36	–5	14	2	1	1	102	9.8
R	20	Mike Johnson	MTL	80	11	20	31	6	40	1	2	1	131	8.4
L	84	* G. Latendresse	MTL	80	16	13	29	–20	47	5	0	3	121	13.2
L	15	Sergei Samsonov	MTL	63	9	17	26	–4	10	0	0	0	114	7.9
C	14	Radek Bonk	MTL	74	13	10	23	0	54	1	2	1	111	11.7
D	8	Mike Komisarek	MTL	82	4	15	19	7	96	0	2	1	78	5.1
L	42	Alexander Perezhogin	MTL	61	6	9	15	11	48	1	0	1	103	5.8
D	51	Francis Bouillon	MTL	62	3	11	14	–10	52	1	0	1	56	5.4
C	40	* Maxim Lapierre	MTL	46	6	6	12	–7	24	0	1	2	82	7.3
R	46	* Andrei Kostitsyn	MTL	22	1	10	11	3	6	0	0	0	38	2.6
C	22	Steve Begin	MTL	52	5	5	10	–6	46	0	0	0	64	7.8
D	25	Mathieu Dandenault	MTL	68	2	6	8	–8	40	0	0	0	54	3.7
D	26	Josh Gorges	S.J.	47	1	3	4	–3	26	0	0	0	37	2.7
			MTL	7	0	0	0	–1	0	0	0	0	3	0.0
			TOTAL	54	1	3	4	–4	26	0	0	0	40	2.5
L	57	Garth Murray	MTL	43	2	1	3	–10	32	0	0	0	28	7.1
D	6	Janne Niinimaa	MTL	41	0	3	3	–13	36	0	0	0	29	0.0
R	47	Aaron Downey	MTL	21	1	0	1	–6	48	0	0	1	10	10.0
R	62	* Duncan Milroy	MTL	5	0	1	1	–2	0	0	0	0	6	0.0
C	59	* Mikhail Grabovski	MTL	3	0	0	0	–2	0	0	0	0	5	0.0

Goaltending

No.	Goaltender	GPI	Mins	Avg	W	L	OT	EN	SO	GA	SA	S%	G	A	PIM
39	Cristobal Huet	42	2286	2.81	19	16	3	1	2	107	1280	.916	0	1	0
41	* Jaroslav Halak	16	912	2.89	10	6	0	2	2	44	469	.906	0	1	2
30	David Aebischer	32	1760	3.17	13	12	3	4	0	93	929	.900	0	0	2
	Totals	**82**	**4987**	**3.02**	**42**	**34**	**6**	**7**	**4**	**251**	**2685**	**.907**			

Coaching History

Jack Laviolette, 1909-10; Adolphe Lecours, 1910-11; Napoleon Dorval, 1911-12, 1912-13; Jimmy Gardner, 1913-14, 1914-15; Newsy Lalonde, 1915-16 to 1920-21; Newsy Lalonde and Léo Dandurand, 1921-22; Léo Dandurand, 1922-23 to 1925-26; Cecil Hart, 1926-27 to 1931-32; Newsy Lalonde, 1932-33, 1933-34; Newsy Lalonde and Léo Dandurand, 1934-35; Sylvio Mantha, 1935-36; Cecil Hart, 1936-37, 1937-38; Cecil Hart and Jules Dugal, 1938-39; Babe Siebert, 1939*; Pit Lepine, 1939-40; Dick Irvin 1940-41 to 1954-55; Toe Blake, 1955-56 to 1967-68; Claude Ruel, 1968-69, 1969-70; Claude Ruel and Al MacNeil, 1970-71; Scotty Bowman, 1971-72 to 1978-79; Bernie Geoffrion and Claude Ruel, 1979-80; Claude Ruel, 1980-81; Bob Berry, 1981-82, 1982-83; Bob Berry and Jacques Lemaire, 1983-84; Jacques Lemaire, 1984-85; Jean Perron, 1985-86 to 1987-88; Pat Burns, 1988-89 to 1991-92; Jacques Demers, 1992-93 to 1994-95; Jacques Demers, Jacques Laperriere, Mario Tremblay, 1995-96; Mario Tremblay, 1996-97; Alain Vigneault, 1997-98 to 1999-2000; Alain Vigneault and Michel Therrien, 2000-01; Michel Therrien, 2001-02; Michel Therrien and Claude Julien, 2002-03; Claude Julien, 2003-04, 2004-05; Claude Julien and Bob Gainey, 2005-06; Guy Carbonneau, 2006-07 to date.

* Named coach in summer but died before 1939-40 season began.

Vice President and General Manager

BOB GAINEY
Executive Vice President/General Manager, Montreal Canadiens.
Born in Peterborough, Ont., December 13, 1953.

On June 2, 2003, the Montreal Canadiens announced the appointment of Bob Gainey as executive vice president and general manager, effective July 1, 2003. During the 2005-06 season, he also took over behind the bench and coached the Canadiens into the playoffs.

As a player in Montreal, Gainey brought many elements to the Canadiens over his 16-year career. Described as the world's best all-around player by legendary Soviet national team coach Viktor Tikhonov, Gainey was a tenacious competitor, relentless checker and a respected team leader. His presence helped the Canadiens win the Stanley Cup five times in the decade between 1976 and 1986. He won the Conn Smythe Trophy as playoff MVP in 1979 and was a four-time winner of the Selke Trophy as the NHL's best defensive forward. Gainey was captain of the Canadiens from 1981 until his retirement in 1989. He was elected to the Hockey Hall of Fame in 1992.

Gainey spent a year as a player-coach of the Epinal franchise in France before becoming head coach of the Minnesota North Stars in 1990-91. He was given the g.m.'s job in 1992 and was in the dual role when the Stars relocated to Dallas in 1993. Gainey stepped down as coach on January 8, 1996 to focus solely on the duties of general manager and built a powerhouse club that won five straight division titles from 1996-97 to 2000-01, the Presidents' Trophy in 1998 and 1999, and the Stanley Cup in 1999.

NHL Coaching Record

		Regular Season				Playoffs		
Season	Team	Games	W	L	O/T	Games	W	L
1990-91	Minnesota	80	27	39	14	23	14	9
1991-92	Minnesota	80	32	42	6	7	3	4
1992-93	Minnesota	84	36	38	10	....	....	....
1993-94	Dallas	84	42	29	13	9	5	4
1994-95	Dallas	48	17	23	8	5	1	4
1995-96	Dallas	39	11	19	9	....	....	....
2005-06	Montreal	41	23	15	3	6	2	4
	NHL Totals	**456**	**188**	**205**	**63**	**50**	**25**	**25**

Christopher Higgins scored 22 goals in just 61games in 2006-07, nearly matching the 23 goals he scored in 80 games in the previous season.

General Managers' History

Jack Laviolette and Joseph Cattarinich, 1909-1910; George Kennedy, 1910-11 to 1920-21; Leo Dandurand, 1921-22 to 1934-35; Ernest Savard, 1935-36; Cecil Hart, 1936-37 to 1938-39; Jules Dugal, 1939-40; Tom P. Gorman, 1940-41 to 1945-46; Frank J. Selke, 1946-47 to 1963-64; Sam Pollock, 1964-65 to 1977-78; Irving Grundman, 1978-79 to 1982-83; Serge Savard, 1983-84 to 1994-95; Serge Savard and Réjean Houle, 1995-96; Réjean Houle, 1996-97 to 1999-2000; Réjean Houle and Andre Savard, 2000-01; Andre Savard, 2001-02, 2002-03; Bob Gainey, 2003-04 to date.

Captains' History

Jack Laviolette, 1909-10; Newsy Lalonde, 1910-11; Jack Laviolette, 1911-12; Newsy Lalonde, 1912-13; Jimmy Gardner, 1913-14, 1914-15; Howard McNamara, 1915-16; Newsy Lalonde, 1916-17 to 1921-22; Sprague Cleghorn, 1922-23 to 1924-25; Bill Coutu, 1925-26; Sylvio Mantha, 1926-27 to 1931-32; George Hainsworth, 1932-33; Sylvio Mantha, 1933-34 to 1935-36; Babe Siebert, 1936-37 to 1938-39; Walt Buswell, 1939-40; Toe Blake, 1940-41 to 1946-47; Toe Blake and Bill Durnan, 1947-48; Butch Bouchard, 1948-49 to 1955-56; Maurice Richard, 1956-57 to 1959-60; Doug Harvey, 1960-61; Jean Béliveau, 1961-62 to 1970-71; Henri Richard, 1971-72 to 1974-75; Yvan Cournoyer, 1975-76 to 1978-79; Serge Savard, 1979-80, 1980-81; Bob Gainey, 1981-82 to 1988-89; Guy Carbonneau and Chris Chelios, 1989-90; Guy Carbonneau, 1990-91 to 1993-94; Kirk Muller and Mike Keane, 1994-95; Mike Keane and Pierre Turgeon, 1995-96; Pierre Turgeon and Vincent Damphousse, 1996-97; Vincent Damphousse, 1997-98, 1998-99; Saku Koivu, 1999-2000 to date.

Club Records

Team

(Figures in brackets for season records are games played; records for fewest points, wins, ties, losses, goals, goals against are for 70 or more games)

Record		
Most Points	***132**	1976-77 (80)
Most Wins	**60**	1976-77 (80)
Most Ties	**23**	1962-63 (70)
Most Losses	**40**	1983-84 (80), 2000-01 (82)
Most Goals	**387**	1976-77 (80)
Most Goals Against	**295**	1983-84 (80)
Fewest Points	**65**	1950-51 (70)
Fewest Wins	**25**	1950-51 (70)
Fewest Ties	**5**	1983-84 (80)
Fewest Losses	***8**	1976-77 (80)
Fewest Goals	**155**	1952-53 (70)
Fewest Goals Against	***131**	1955-56 (70)
Longest Winning Streak		
Overall	**12**	Jan. 6-Feb. 3/68
Home	**13**	Nov. 2/43-Jan. 8/44, Jan. 30-Mar. 26/77
Away	**8**	Dec. 18/77-Jan. 18/78, Jan. 21-Feb. 21/82
Longest Undefeated Streak		
Overall	**28**	Dec. 18/77-Feb. 23/78 (23 wins, 5 ties)
Home	***34**	Nov. 1/76-Apr. 2/77 (28 wins, 6 ties)
Away	***23**	Nov. 27/74-Mar. 12/75 (14 wins, 9 ties)
Longest Losing Streak		
Overall	**12**	Feb. 13-Mar. 13/26
Home	**7**	Dec. 16/39-Jan. 18/40, Oct. 28-Nov. 25/00
Away	**10**	Jan. 16-Mar. 13/26
Longest Winless Streak		
Overall	**12**	Feb. 13-Mar. 13/26 (12 losses), Nov. 28-Dec. 29/35 (8 losses, 4 ties)
Home	**15**	Dec. 16/39-Mar. 7/40 (12 losses, 3 ties)
Away	**12**	Nov. 26/33-Jan. 28/34 (8 losses, 4 ties), Oct. 20-Dec. 13/51 (8 losses, 4 ties)
Most Shutouts, Season	***22**	1928-29 (44)
Most PIM, Season	**1,847**	1995-96 (82)
Most Goals, Game	***16**	Mar. 3/20 (Mtl. 16 at Que. 3)

Individual

Record		
Most Seasons	**20**	Henri Richard, Jean Béliveau
Most Games	**1,256**	Henri Richard
Most Goals, Career	**544**	Maurice Richard
Most Assists, Career	**728**	Guy Lafleur
Most Points, Career	**1,246**	Guy Lafleur (518G, 728A)
Most PIM, Career	**2,248**	Chris Nilan
Most Shutouts, Career	**75**	George Hainsworth
Longest Consecutive Games Streak	**560**	Doug Jarvis (Oct. 8/75-Apr. 4/82)
Most Goals, Season	**60**	Steve Shutt (1976-77), Guy Lafleur (1977-78)
Most Assists, Season	**82**	Pete Mahovlich (1974-75)
Most Points, Season	**136**	Guy Lafleur (1976-77; 56G, 80A)
Most PIM, Season	**358**	Chris Nilan (1984-85)
Most Points, Defenseman, Season	**85**	Larry Robinson (1976-77; 19G, 66A)
Most Points, Center, Season	**117**	Pete Mahovlich (1974-75; 35G, 82A)
Most Points, Right Wing, Season	**136**	Guy Lafleur (1976-77; 56G, 80A)
Most Points, Left Wing, Season	**110**	Mats Naslund (1985-86; 43G, 67A)
Most Points, Rookie, Season	**71**	Mats Naslund (1982-83; 26G, 45A), Kjell Dahlin (1985-86; 32G, 39A)
Most Shutouts, Season	***22**	George Hainsworth (1928-29)
Most Goals, Game	**6**	Newsy Lalonde (Jan. 10/20)
Most Assists, Game	**6**	Elmer Lach (Feb. 6/43)
Most Points, Game	**8**	Maurice Richard (Dec. 28/44; 5G, 3A), Bert Olmstead (Jan. 9/54; 4G, 4A)

* NHL Record.

Retired Numbers

1	Jacques Plante	1952-1963
2	Doug Harvey	1947-1961
4	Jean Béliveau	1950-1971
5	Bernard Geoffrion	1950-1964
7	Howie Morenz	1923-1937
9	Maurice Richard	1942-1960
10	Guy Lafleur	1971-1984
12	Dickie Moore	1951-1963
	Yvan Cournoyer	1963-1979
16	Henri Richard	1955-1975
18	Serge Savard	1966-1981
29	Ken Dryden	1970-1979

All-time Record vs. Other Clubs

Regular Season

	At Home								On Road								Total							
	GP	W	L	T	OL	GF	GA	PTS	GP	W	L	T	OL	GF	GA	PTS	GP	W	L	T	OL	GF	GA	PTS
Anaheim	9	4	3	2	0	27	24	10	8	5	3	0	0	27	25	10	17	9	6	2	0	54	49	20
Atlanta	14	10	3	0	1	45	31	21	14	9	3	2	0	39	23	20	28	19	6	2	1	84	54	41
Boston	342	196	98	47	1	1145	805	440	343	129	155	56	3	926	1009	317	685	325	253	103	4	2071	1814	757
Buffalo	111	60	36	12	3	412	331	135	110	33	56	19	2	292	343	87	221	93	92	31	5	704	674	222
Calgary	47	27	12	8	0	168	116	62	50	26	16	7	1	166	149	60	97	53	28	15	1	334	265	122
Carolina	79	50	21	7	1	316	233	108	82	37	30	13	2	280	240	89	161	87	51	20	3	596	473	197
Chicago	276	174	54	48	0	1067	653	396	274	125	94	55	0	762	733	305	550	299	148	103	0	1829	1386	701
Colorado	65	39	15	10	1	269	203	89	64	26	32	5	1	223	218	58	129	65	47	15	2	492	421	147
Columbus	4	1	1	1	1	6	6	4	2	2	0	0	0	6	3	4	6	3	1	1	1	12	9	8
Dallas	59	38	12	9	0	254	146	85	59	30	17	12	0	203	153	72	118	68	29	21	0	457	299	157
Detroit	282	172	67	43	0	994	636	387	281	97	130	53	1	717	807	248	563	269	197	96	1	1711	1443	635
Edmonton	31	17	9	4	1	108	97	39	36	17	17	0	2	116	122	36	67	34	26	4	3	224	219	75
Florida	25	11	10	3	1	64	57	26	26	9	14	3	0	65	78	21	51	20	24	6	1	129	135	47
Los Angeles	65	46	8	11	0	292	162	103	65	37	19	9	0	256	199	83	130	83	27	20	0	548	361	186
Minnesota	4	2	1	1	0	13	10	5	3	1	1	0	1	8	10	3	7	3	2	1	1	21	20	8
Nashville	4	4	0	0	0	15	9	8	5	2	2	1	0	13	19	5	9	6	2	1	0	28	28	13
New Jersey	58	33	19	6	0	188	146	72	58	25	28	4	1	200	177	55	116	58	47	10	1	388	323	127
NY Islanders	64	39	16	9	0	230	178	87	64	26	30	6	2	179	198	60	128	65	46	15	2	409	376	147
NY Rangers	294	192	62	40	0	1137	682	424	294	120	119	54	1	853	846	295	588	312	181	94	1	1990	1528	719
Ottawa	41	22	14	4	1	122	116	49	39	17	19	1	2	107	124	37	80	39	33	5	3	229	240	86
Philadelphia	78	37	26	14	1	268	237	89	77	31	29	16	1	231	234	79	155	68	55	30	2	499	471	168
Phoenix	30	25	3	2	0	147	68	52	29	13	9	7	0	112	94	33	59	38	12	9	0	259	162	85
Pittsburgh	86	64	12	10	0	401	220	138	86	42	29	13	2	305	257	99	172	106	41	23	2	706	477	237
St. Louis	59	41	11	7	0	255	161	89	58	29	14	15	0	199	150	73	117	70	25	22	0	454	311	162
San Jose	12	8	2	2	0	42	22	18	11	4	4	2	1	28	33	11	23	12	6	4	1	70	55	29
Tampa Bay	26	14	11	1	0	72	61	29	27	12	10	5	0	75	64	29	53	26	21	6	0	147	125	58
Toronto	341	203	92	43	3	1195	852	452	341	119	176	45	1	890	1040	284	682	322	268	88	4	2085	1892	736
Vancouver	54	38	11	5	0	244	139	81	56	33	14	8	1	204	152	75	110	71	25	13	1	448	291	156
Washington	64	38	17	8	1	242	138	85	63	26	28	9	0	188	175	61	127	64	45	17	1	430	313	146
Defunct Clubs	231	148	58	25	0	779	469	321	230	98	97	35	0	586	606	231	461	246	155	60	0	1365	1075	552
Totals	**2855**	**1753**	**704**	**382**	**16**	**10517**	**7008**	**3904**	**2855**	**1180**	**1195**	**455**	**25**	**8256**	**8281**	**2840**	**5710**	**2933**	**1899**	**837**	**41**	**18773**	**15289**	**6744**

Playoffs

	Series	W	L	GP	W	L	T	GF	GA	Last Mtg.	Rnd.	Result
Boston	30	23	7	152	95	57	0	469	371	2004	CQF	W 4-3
Buffalo	7	4	3	35	18	17	0	124	111	1998	CSF	L 0-4
Calgary	2	1	1	11	6	5	0	31	32	1989	F	L 2-4
Carolina	7	5	2	39	23	16	0	125	106	2006	CQF	L 2-4
Chicago	17	12	5	81	50	29	2	261	185	1976	QF	W 4-0
Colorado	5	3	2	31	17	14	0	105	85	1993	DSF	W 4-2
Dallas	2	1	1	13	7	6	0	48	37	1980	QF	L 3-4
Detroit	12	5	7	62	33	29	0	161	149	1978	QF	W 4-1
Edmonton	1	0	1	3	0	3	0	6	15	1981	PRE	L 0-3
Los Angeles	1	1	0	5	4	1	0	15	12	1993	F	W 4-1
New Jersey	1	0	1	5	1	4	0	11	22	1997	CQF	L 1-4
NY Islanders	4	3	1	22	14	8	0	64	55	1993	CF	W 4-1
NY Rangers	14	7	7	61	34	25	2	188	158	1996	CQF	L 2-4
Philadelphia	4	3	1	21	14	7	0	72	52	1989	CF	W 4-2
Pittsburgh	1	1	0	6	4	2	0	18	15	1998	CQF	W 4-2
St. Louis	3	3	0	12	12	0	0	42	14	1977	QF	W 4-0
Tampa Bay	1	0	1	4	0	4	0	5	14	2004	CSF	L 0-4
Toronto	15	8	7	71	42	29	0	215	160	1979	QF	W 4-0
Vancouver	1	1	0	5	4	1	0	20	9	1975	QF	W 4-1
Defunct Clubs	11*	6	4	28	15	9	4	70	71			
Totals	**139***	**87**	**51**	**667**	**393**	**266**	**8**	**2050**	**1673**			

* 1919 Final incomplete due to influenza epidemic.

Playoff Results 2007-2002

Year	Round	Opponent	Result	GF	GA
2006	CQF	Carolina	L 2-4	17	15
2004	CSF	Tampa Bay	L 0-4	5	14
	CQF	Boston	W 4-3	19	14
2002	CSF	Carolina	L 2-4	12	21
	CQF	Boston	W 4-2	20	18

Abbreviations: Round: F - Final; **CF** - conference final; **CSF** - conference semi-final; **CQF** - conference quarter-final; **DSF** - division semi-final; **QF** - quarter-final; **PRE** - preliminary round.

Calgary totals include Atlanta Flames, 1972-73 to 1979-80.
Colorado totals include Quebec, 1979-80 to 1994-95.
Carolina totals include Hartford, 1979-80 to 1996-97.
Dallas totals include Minnesota North Stars, 1967-68 to 1992-93.
New Jersey totals include Kansas City, 1974-75, 1975-76, and Colorado Rockies, 1976-77 to 1981-82.
Phoenix totals include Winnipeg, 1979-80 to 1995-96.

2006-07 Results

Month	Day	Opponent	Score
Oct.	6	at Buffalo	4-5†
	7	at Toronto	3-2†
	11	at Philadelphia	3-1
	14	Ottawa	2-3†
	17	Calgary	5-4
	18	at Chicago	1-2
	21	Colorado	8-5
	23	Buffalo	1-4
	26	at Boston	3-2
	28	Toronto	4-5†
	31	Ottawa	4-2
Nov.	2	at Carolina	4-0
	4	New Jersey	1-2
	7	Edmonton	3-2†
	11	at Toronto	1-5
	13	at Ottawa	6-3
	15	at Tampa Bay	3-1
	16	at Florida	1-5
	18	Atlanta	3-1
	22	Minnesota	4-2
	24	at Buffalo	2-1*
	25	Philadelphia	2-4
	28	Florida	1-0†
	30	at Carolina	2-4
Dec.	2	Toronto	4-3†
	4	Boston	5-6
	6	at New Jersey	1-2*
	7	at NY Islanders	4-2
	9	Buffalo	2-3†
	12	Boston	4-3
	14	Tampa Bay	4-2
	16	Pittsburgh	6-3
	19	at Buffalo	5-2
	21	Philadelphia	4-2
	23	at Boston	2-4
	27	at Washington	4-1
	29	at Florida	1-3
	30	at Tampa Bay	1-3
Jan.	2	Tampa Bay	5-2
	4	at Washington	1-5
	6	NY Rangers	3-4
	7	New Jersey	0-3
	9	Atlanta	4-2
	11	at Philadelphia	4-2
	13	at Ottawa	3-8
	15	at Detroit	0-2
	16	Vancouver	0-4
	18	at Atlanta	4-1
	20	Buffalo	4-3
	27	at Toronto	1-4
	29	Ottawa	3-1
Feb.	1	at Pittsburgh	4-5†
	3	NY Islanders	2-4
	4	Pittsburgh	4-3*
	6	Carolina	1-2
	8	at Ottawa	1-4
	10	Ottawa	3-5
	13	Florida	0-1
	14	at New Jersey	2-5
	17	Carolina	3-5
	18	at Columbus	3-2
	20	Washington	5-3
	22	at Nashville	6-5†
	24	at NY Islanders	2-3
	26	Toronto	5-4
	27	at NY Rangers	0-4
Mar.	2	at Buffalo	5-8
	3	at Boston	1-3
	8	at Atlanta	2-6
	10	at St. Louis	4-3
	13	NY Islanders	5-3
	16	at Pittsburgh	3-6
	17	Toronto	3-2†
	20	Boston	1-0
	22	at Boston	6-3
	24	Washington	4-1
	27	NY Rangers	6-4
	30	at Ottawa	2-5
	31	Buffalo	4-3
Apr.	3	Boston	2-0
	5	at NY Rangers	1-3
	7	at Toronto	5-6

* – Overtime † – Shootout

Entry Draft Selections 2007-1993

2007

Pick	
12	Ryan McDonagh
22	Max Pacioretty
43	P.K. Subban
65	Olivier Fortier
73	Yannick Weber
133	Joe Stejskal
142	Andrew Conboy
163	Nichlas Torp
192	Scott Kishel

2006

Pick	
20	David Fischer
49	Ben Maxwell
53	Mathieu Carle
66	Ryan White
139	Pavel Valentenko
199	Cameron Cepek

2005

Pick	
5	Carey Price
45	Guillaume Latendresse
121	Juraj Mikus
130	Mathieu Aubin
190	Matt D'Agostini
200	Sergei Kostitsyn
229	Philippe Paquet

2004

Pick	
18	Kyle Chipchura
84	Alexei Yemelin
100	James Wyman
150	Mikhail Grabovski
181	Loic Lacasse
212	Jon Gleed
246	Greg Stewart
262	Mark Streit
278	Alex Dulac-Lemelin

2003

Pick	
10	Andrei Kostitsyn
40	Cory Urquhart
61	Maxim Lapierre
79	Ryan O'Byrne
113	Corey Locke
123	Danny Stewart
177	Chris Heino-Lindberg
188	Mark Flood
217	Oskari Korpikari
241	Jimmy Bonneau
271	Jaroslav Halak

2002

Pick	
14	Chris Higgins
45	Tomas Linhart
99	Michael Lambert
182	Andre Deveaux
212	Jonathan Ferland
275	Konstantin Korneev

2001

Pick	
7	Mike Komisarek
25	Alexander Perezhogin
37	Duncan Milroy
71	Tomas Plekanec
109	Martti Jarventie
171	Eric Himelfarb
203	Andrew Archer
266	Viktor Ujcik

2000

Pick	
13	Ron Hainsey
16	Marcel Hossa
78	Jozef Balej
79	Tyler Hanchuck
109	Johan Eneqvist
114	Christian Larrivee
145	Ryan Glenn
172	Scott Selig
182	Petr Chvojka
243	Joni Puurula
275	Jonathan Gauthier

1999

Pick	
39	Alexander Buturlin
58	Matt Carkner
97	Chris Dyment
107	Evan Lindsay
136	Dusty Jamieson
145	Marc-Andre Thinel
150	Matt Shasby
167	Sean Dixon
196	Vadim Tarasov
225	Mikko Hyytia
253	Jerome Marois

1998

Pick	
16	Eric Chouinard
45	Mike Ribeiro
75	Francois Beauchemin
132	Andrei Bashkirov
152	Gordie Dwyer
162	Andrei Markov
189	Andrei Kruchinin
201	Craig Murray
216	Michael Ryder
247	Darcy Harris

1997

Pick	
11	Jason Ward
37	Gregor Baumgartner
65	Ilkka Mikkola
91	Daniel Tetrault
118	Konstantin Sidulov
122	Gennady Razin
145	Jonathan Desroches
172	Ben Guite
197	Petr Kubos
202	Andrei Sidyakin
228	Jarl Espen Ygranes

1996

Pick	
18	Matt Higgins
44	Mathieu Garon
71	Arron Asham
92	Kim Staal
99	Etienne Drapeau
127	Daniel Archambault
154	Brett Clark
181	Timo Vertala
207	Mattia Baldi
233	Michel Tremblay

1995

Pick	
8	Terry Ryan
60	Miloslav Guren
74	Martin Hohenberger
86	Jonathan Delisle
112	Niklas Anger
138	Boyd Olson
164	Stephane Robidas
190	Greg Hart
216	Eric Houde

1994

Pick	
18	Brad Brown
44	Jose Theodore
54	Chris Murray
70	Marko Kiprusoff
74	Martin Belanger
96	Arto Kuki
122	Jimmy Drolet
148	Joel Irving
174	Jessie Rezansoff
200	Peter Strom
226	Tomas Vokoun
252	Chris Aldous
278	Ross Parsons

1993

Pick	
21	Saku Koivu
47	Rory Fitzpatrick
73	Sebastien Bordeleau
85	Adam Wiesel
99	Jean-Francois Houle
113	Jeff Lank
125	Dion Darling
151	Darcy Tucker
177	David Ruhly
203	Alan Letang
229	Alexandre Duchesne
255	Brian Larochelle
281	Russell Guzior

Coach

GUY CARBONNEAU
Coach, Montreal Canadiens. Born in Sept-Iles, Que., March 18, 1960.

Guy Carbonneau was hired as an associate coach to Bob Gainey on January 14, 2006 and worked the last 41 games of the 2005-06 regular season. Almost five months later, on May 5, 2006, Carbonneau officially took over head coaching duties from Gainey. When going behind the bench himself and hiring Carbonneau as his assistant, Gainey had announced that Carbonneau would be the Canadiens' new head coach beginning with the 2006-07 season.

Carbonneau began his coaching career as an assistant coach with the Canadiens from November 2000 until the end of the 2001-02 season (144 regular-season games and 12 playoff games). He held the position of supervisor of prospect development from August to November 2000. The 18-year NHL veteran had announced his retirement as a player in July 2000, following a brilliant career that saw him win three Stanley Cup championships and three Frank Selke trophies as the NHL's top defensive forward (1988, 1989 and 1992).

Carbonneau was a Canadiens' third round selection, 44th overall in 1979. He spent the first 12 seasons of his career in Montreal, winning the Stanley Cup in 1986 and 1993. Captain of the Canadiens for five seasons (1989 to 1994), he also donned a St. Louis Blues jersey in 1994-95, before joining the Dallas Stars where he played from 1995 to 2000 winning a third Stanley Cup in 1998-99. He made the Stanley Cup playoffs 17 out of 18 NHL seasons. Carbonneau also served as an assistant general manager in Dallas from 2002-03 until returning to Montreal during the 2005-06 season.

Coaching Record

		Regular Season				Playoffs		
Season	**Team**	**Games**	**W**	**L**	**O/T**	**Games**	**W**	**L**
2006-07	Montreal (NHL)	82	42	34	6	....	....	....
	NHL Totals	82	42	34	6	....	....	....

Club Directory

Bell Centre

Club de Hockey Canadien
1260 de La Gauchetière Street W.
Montréal, QC H3B 5E8
Phone: **514/932-2582**
Media Hotline: 514/989-2835
Fax Lines (all area code 514):
Communications 932-8285
Hockey 989-2717
Press Lounge 932-5258
Marketing 925-2145
Community Relations 925-2144
www.canadiens.com
Capacity: 21,273

Executive Management
Chairman and Governor .... George N. Gillett Jr.
Vice Chairman .... Jeff Joyce
President, Canadiens, Bell Centre & Alt. Gov. .... Pierre Boivin
Managing Partner & Alternate Governor .... Foster Gillett
Assistant to the President .... Marie-Claude Pinel
Exec. V.P., Hockey, G.M. & Alt. Gov. .... Bob Gainey
Chief Financial Officer & Alt. Gov. .... Fred Steer
V.P., Marketing and Sales .... Ray Lalonde
V.P., Communications and Community Relations .. Donald Beauchamp
V.P., Building Operations .... Alain Gauthier
V.P. & G.M., Gillett Entertainment Group .... Jacques Aubé
President, Effix – Advertising & Sponsorship Sales .... François Seigneur
President, Canadiens Alumni .... Réjean Houle

Hockey
Assistant General Manager .... Pierre Gauthier
V.P., Hockey Operations .... Julien BriseBois
Director of Player Recruitment and Development... Trevor Timmins
Head Coach .... Guy Carbonneau
Associate Coach .... Doug Jarvis
Assistant Coaches .... Roland Melanson, Kirk Muller
Professional Scouts .... Gordie Roberts, Doug Gibson
Scouting Staff .... Elmer Benning, Bill Berglund, Michel Boucher, Pelle Eklund, Vaughn Karpan, Hannu Laine, Dave Mayville, Mike McCann, Denis Morel, Antonin Routa, Nikolai Vakourov, Pat Westrum
Team Services & Hockey Administration Manager .. Claudine Crépin
Administrative Assistant to the General Manager .. Suzanne Charlebois
Team Services Coordinator .... Alain Gagnon

Medical and Training Staff
Club Physician and Chief Surgeon .... Dr. David Mulder
Consultant, Orthopedic Surgeon .... Dr. Eric Lenczner
Dentist .... Dr. Jean-François Desjardins
Consultant, Ophthalmologist .... Dr. John Little
Consultant, Sports Medicine .... Dr. Vincent Lacroix
Head Athletic Therapist .... Graham Rynbend
Athletic Therapist .... Nick Addey-Jibb
Strength & Conditioning Coordinator .... Scott Livingston
Video Supervisor .... Mario Leblanc
Equipment Manager .... Pierre Gervais
Assistants to the Equipment Manager .... Patrick Langlois, Pierre Ouellette
Visiting team Coordinator .... Richard Généreux

Communications
Director of Media Relations .... Dominick Saillant
Administrative Assistant to the V.P. Communications .. Sylvie Lambert
Manager, History and Archives .... Carl Lavigne
Communications Coordinator .... Jasmin Pilon

Community Relations
CEO, Canadiens Children's Foundation .... Robert Sirois
Director, Community Relations .... Geneviève Paquette
Coordinator, Canadiens Children's Foundation .... Marie-Christine Boucher
Community Relations Coordinator .... Anne-Marie Bégin
Assistant, Community Relations .... Sylvie Nadeau

Marketing and Sales
Director, Group Sales and Administration .... Pierre Constant
Executive Director, Luxury Suites and Services .... Richard Primeau
Director, Ticket Sales .... Vincent Lucier
Director, Marketing, Media and Broadcast .... Jon Trzcienski
Group Manager, Events, Programs and Promotions . Patrick Boivin
Director, Consumer Products .... Matt Zalkowitz
Group Manager, Broadcast and Advertising .... Jonathan Prunier
Group Manager, Creative Services and Publications .. Jean Simard

Building Operations
Director of Ticket Office .... Cathy D'Ascoli
Assistant Director of Ticket Office .... Lucie Masse
Director of Building Operations .... Xavier Luydlin
Director of Concessions .... Alec Beaudry
Director of Customer Satisfaction .... Caroline Hamel
Administrative Assistant to the V.P. Operations .... Maryse Cartwright

Finance
Executive Director, Information & Communication Technology .... Pierre-Éric Belzile
Controller .... Dennis McKinley
Assistant Controller .... Raymond Lamarche
Administrative Assistant, Chief Financial Officer.... Christine Ouellette

Broadcasting
Play-by-play – Radio/TV .... Pierre Houde (RDS & SRC), Martin McGuire (CKAC), Rick Moffat (CJAD)
Colormen – Radio/TV .... Yvon Pedneault (RDS & SRC), Dany Dubé (CKAC), Murray Wilson (CJAD)
Radio/television Flagship Stations .... RDS (Cable 33), CKAC (730 AM), CJAD (800 AM)

Nashville Predators

Key Off-Season Signings/Acquisitions

2007

June 19 • Re-signed C **Jarred Smithson**.
30 • Re-signed C **Scott Nichol**.
July 1 • Signed RW **Jed Ortmeyer**.
2 • Signed C **Radek Bonk** and D **Greg de Vries**.
3 • Re-signed G **Chris Mason**.
16 • Re-signed LW **Darcy Hordichuk** and D **Greg Zanon**.
18 • Re-signed C **Vernon Fiddler**.
26 • Signed LW **Martin Gelinas**.

2006-07 Results: 51W-23L-3OTL-5SOL 110PTS.
Second, Central Division

Year-by-Year Record

		Home				Road				Overall								
Season	GP	W	L	T	OL	W	L	T	OL	W	L	T	OL	GF	GA	Pts.	Finished	Playoff Result
2006-07	82	28	8	....	5	23	15	....	3	51	23	....	8	272	212	110	2nd, Central Div.	Lost Conf. Quarter-Final
2005-06	82	32	8	....	1	17	17	....	7	49	25	....	8	259	227	106	2nd, Central Div.	Lost Conf. Quarter-Final
2004-05	....	....	....	....	....	....	....	....	....	....	....	....	....	....	....	....		
2003-04	82	22	10	7	2	16	19	4	2	38	29	11	4	216	217	91	3rd, Central Div.	Lost Conf. Quarter-Final
2002-03	82	18	17	5	1	9	18	8	6	27	35	13	7	183	206	74	4th, Central Div.	Out of Playoffs
2001-02	82	17	16	8	0	11	25	5	0	28	41	13	0	196	230	69	4th, Central Div.	Out of Playoffs
2000-01	82	16	18	7	0	18	18	2	3	34	36	9	3	186	200	80	3rd, Central Div.	Out of Playoffs
1999-2000	82	15	21	3	2	13	19	4	5	28	40	7	7	199	240	70	4th, Central Div.	Out of Playoffs
1998-99	82	15	22	4	....	13	25	3	....	28	47	7	....	190	261	63	4th, Central Div.	Out of Playoffs

2007-08 Schedule

Month	Day	Date	Opponent
Oct.	Thu.	4	Colorado
	Sat.	6	Dallas
	Wed.	10	at St. Louis
	Thu.	11	Phoenix
	Sat.	13	Calgary
	Wed.	17	at Anaheim
	Sat.	20	at San Jose
	Tue.	23	at Los Angeles
	Thu.	25	Atlanta
	Sat.	27	Florida
	Tue.	30	at Calgary
Nov.	Thu.	1	at Vancouver
	Fri.	2	at Edmonton
	Sun.	4	at Chicago
	Wed.	7	at Detroit
	Sat.	10	Columbus
	Mon.	12	at Columbus
	Thu.	15	Chicago
	Sat.	17	St. Louis
	Mon.	19	at St. Louis
	Thu.	22	Detroit
	Sat.	24	Minnesota
	Thu.	29	at Ottawa
Dec.	Sat.	1	at Montreal
	Tue.	4	at Toronto
	Thu.	6	Vancouver
	Sat.	8	Anaheim
	Mon.	10	Detroit
	Thu.	13	Colorado
	Sat.	15	at Colorado
	Tue.	18	at Minnesota
	Wed.	19	at Chicago
	Sat.	22	Los Angeles
	Sun.	23	at Columbus*
	Wed.	26	at Chicago
	Thu.	27	Columbus
	Sat.	29	San Jose
	Mon.	31	at Dallas
Jan.	Thu.	3	Edmonton
	Sat.	5	Minnesota
	Mon.	7	at Anaheim
	Tue.	8	at Los Angeles
	Sat.	12	at Columbus
	Sun.	13	Chicago
	Tue.	15	Calgary
	Thu.	17	Anaheim
	Sat.	19	at St. Louis
	Mon.	21	St. Louis*
	Tue.	22	at Colorado
	Thu.	24	at Phoenix
	Tue.	29	at Boston
	Thu.	31	Columbus
Feb.	Sat.	2	Phoenix
	Tue.	5	Carolina
	Thu.	7	Tampa Bay
	Sat.	9	at San Jose
	Sun.	10	at Phoenix
	Tue.	12	Detroit
	Thu.	14	Chicago
	Sat.	16	St. Louis
	Sun.	17	at Minnesota
	Tue.	19	Edmonton
	Thu.	21	Vancouver
	Sat.	23	Dallas
	Wed.	27	at Buffalo
Mar.	Sat.	1	at Dallas
	Tue.	4	at Edmonton
	Thu.	6	at Vancouver
	Fri.	7	at Calgary
	Sun.	9	at Detroit*
	Tue.	11	San Jose
	Thu.	13	Los Angeles
	Sat.	15	at Detroit*
	Tue.	18	Washington
	Thu.	20	Detroit
	Sat.	22	Chicago*
	Tue.	25	Columbus
	Fri.	28	at Columbus
	Sun.	30	at Detroit*
Apr.	Tue.	1	at St. Louis
	Thu.	3	St. Louis
	Fri.	4	at Chicago

* Denotes afternoon game.

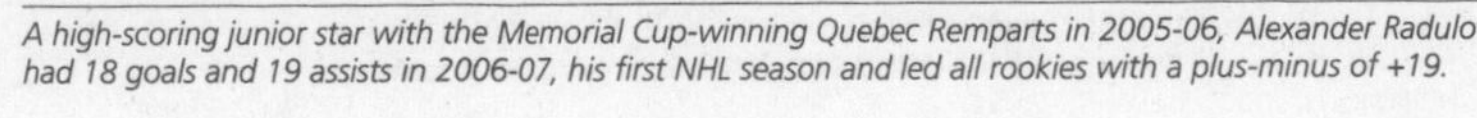

A high-scoring junior star with the Memorial Cup-winning Quebec Remparts in 2005-06, Alexander Radulov had 18 goals and 19 assists in 2006-07, his first NHL season and led all rookies with a plus-minus of +19.

CENTRAL DIVISION
10th NHL Season

Franchise date: June 25, 1997

2007-08 Player Personnel

FORWARDS	HT	WT	S	Place of Birth	*Age	2006-07 Club
ARNOTT, Jason	6-4	220	R	Collingwood, Ont.	32	Nashville
BONK, Radek	6-3	213	L	Krnov, Czech.	31	Montreal
DUMONT, J.P.	6-1	205	L	Montreal, Que.	29	Nashville
ELLISON, Matt	6-0	192	R	Duncan, B.C.	23	Phi-Phi (AHL)
ERAT, Martin	6-0	195	L	Trebic, Czech.	26	Nashville
FIDDLER, Vern	5-11	204	L	Edmonton, Alta.	27	Nashville
GELINAS, Martin	5-11	195	L	Shawinigan, Que.	37	Florida
HORDICHUK, Darcy	6-1	215	L	Kamsack, Sask.	27	Nashville
LEGWAND, David	6-2	190	L	Detroit, MI	27	Nashville
NICHOL, Scott	5-9	175	R	Edmonton, Alta.	32	Nashville
O'REILLY, Cal	6-0	187	L	Toronto, Ont.	20	Milwaukee
ORTMEYER, Jed	6-0	197	R	Omaha, NE	29	NY Rangers-Hartford
PEVERLEY, Rich	6-0	185	R	Guelph, Ont.	25	Nashville-Milwaukee
RADULOV, Alexander	6-1	188	L	Nizhny Tagil, USSR	21	Nashville-Milwaukee
SMITHSON, Jerred	6-3	194	R	Vernon, B.C.	28	Nashville
SULLIVAN, Steve	5-8	165	R	Timmins, Ont.	33	Nashville
TOOTOO, Jordin	5-9	194	R	Churchill, Man.	24	Nashville
VIGILANTE, John	6-0	190	L	Dearborn, MI	22	Milwaukee
WILLIS, Shane	6-1	195	R	Edmonton, Alta.	30	Albany
DEFENSEMEN						
BLUM, Jonathon	6-0	168	R	Long Beach, CA	18	Vancouver (WHL)
de VRIES, Greg	6-2	215	L	Sundridge, Ont.	34	Atlanta
HAMHUIS, Dan	6-1	200	L	Smithers, B.C.	24	Nashville
HENRY, Alex	6-5	220	L	Elliot Lake, Ont.	27	Milwaukee
KLEIN, Kevin	6-1	195	R	Kitchener, Ont.	22	Nashville-Milwaukee
SUTER, Ryan	6-1	196	L	Madison, WI	22	Nashville
WEBER, Shea	6-3	213	R	Sicamous, B.C.	22	Nashville
YONKMAN, Nolan	6-6	245	R	Punnichy, Sask.	26	Milwaukee
ZANON, Greg	5-11	211	L	Burnaby, B.C.	27	Nashville-Milwaukee
ZIDLICKY, Marek	5-11	190	R	Most, Czech.	30	Nashville

GOALTENDERS	HT	WT	C	Place of Birth	*Age	2006-07 Club
ELLIS, Dan	6-0	185	L	Orangeville, Ont.	27	Iowa
MASON, Chris	6-0	195	L	Red Deer, Alta.	31	Nashville
RINNE, Pekka	6-5	207	L	Kempele, Finland	24	Milwaukee

* – Age at start of 2007-08 season

Captains' History

Tom Fitzgerald, 1998-99 to 2001-02; Greg Johnson, 2002-03 to 2005-06; Kimmo Timonen, 2006-07.

General Managers' History

David Poile, 1998-99 to date.

Vice President and General Manager

DAVID POILE
Executive Vice President/General Manager, Nashville Predators.
Born in Toronto, Ont., February 14, 1949.

Since joining the Predators as general manager on July 9, 1997, David Poile has made a commitment to building for the future, surrounding himself with one of the youngest and most talented staffs in the National Hockey League. In 2003-04, Nashville reached the playoffs for the first time in franchise history and qualified again in 2005-06. During the 2006-07 season, Nashville was in contention for first overall in the NHL, setting club records with 51 wins and 110 points. Poile has an impressive reputation as an NHL leader and in 2001 he received the Lester Patrick Trophy for his contributions to hockey in the United States. His father, Norman "Bud" Poile, had won the honor in 1989.

Prior to joining Nashville, Poile spent 15 seasons as vice president/general manager of the Washington Capitals. During his tenure in Washington, the Capitals made 14 postseason appearances, winning their only Patrick Division title in 1989 and advancing to the Conference Finals in 1990. During Poile's 15 years in Washington, the Capitals compiled a record of 594-454-132, finished second in the Patrick Division seven times and recorded 90-or-more points seven different seasons.

Poile started his professional hockey career as an administrative assistant for the Atlanta Flames in 1972, shortly after graduating from Northeastern University in Boston. At Northeastern, he was hockey team captain, leading scorer and most valuable player for two years.

In 1977, he was named assistant general manager of the Atlanta Flames (who moved to Calgary in 1980), serving as the manager and coordinator of the Flames farm club.

Poile is a member of the NHL's general managers committee and was instrumental in the NHL's adoption of the instant replay rule in 1991. He was awarded *Inside Hockey*'s man of the year for his leadership on the issue. He was also twice honored as *The Sporting News* NHL executive of the year following the 1982-83 and 1983-84 seasons. Poile served as general manager of the 1998 and 1999 U.S. national teams for the World Championships.

2006-07 Scoring

* – rookie

Regular Season

Pos	#	Player	Team	GP	G	A	Pts	+/–	PIM	PP	SH	GW	S	%
L	9	Paul Kariya	NSH	82	24	52	76	6	36	5	0	2	224	10.7
R	71	Jean-Pierre Dumont	NSH	82	21	45	66	14	28	5	0	3	143	14.7
C	11	David Legwand	NSH	78	27	36	63	23	44	3	1	7	153	17.6
R	26	Steve Sullivan	NSH	57	22	38	60	16	20	6	3	4	122	18.0
L	10	Martin Erat	NSH	68	16	41	57	13	50	5	1	3	132	12.1
C	21	Peter Forsberg	PHI	40	11	29	40	2	72	5	0	2	63	17.5
			NSH	17	2	13	15	5	16	1	0	1	36	5.6
			TOTAL	57	13	42	55	7	88	6	0	3	99	13.1
D	44	Kimmo Timonen	NSH	80	13	42	55	20	42	8	0	2	121	10.7
C	19	Jason Arnott	NSH	68	27	27	54	15	48	12	0	6	190	14.2
D	6	Shea Weber	NSH	79	17	23	40	13	60	6	0	2	152	11.2
L	17	Scott Hartnell	NSH	64	22	17	39	19	96	10	0	2	150	14.7
R	47 *	Alexander Radulov	NSH	64	18	19	37	19	26	5	0	4	96	18.8
D	3	Marek Zidlicky	NSH	79	4	26	30	8	72	2	0	1	114	3.5
C	38	Vernon Fiddler	NSH	72	11	15	26	11	40	0	1	1	90	12.2
D	20	Ryan Suter	NSH	82	8	16	24	10	54	1	0	0	87	9.2
D	2	Dan Hamhuis	NSH	81	6	14	20	8	66	0	0	1	84	7.1
C	12	Scott Nichol	NSH	59	7	6	13	7	79	1	1	2	58	12.1
D	4	Vitaly Vishnevski	ATL	52	3	9	12	–5	31	0	0	0	41	7.3
			NSH	15	0	1	1	1	10	0	0	0	6	0.0
			TOTAL	67	3	10	13	–4	41	0	0	0	47	6.4
C	25	Jerred Smithson	NSH	64	5	7	12	–8	42	1	1	2	47	10.6
R	22	Jordin Tootoo	NSH	65	3	6	9	–11	116	0	0	0	77	3.9
D	5	Greg Zanon	NSH	66	3	5	8	16	32	0	0	0	43	7.0
L	14	Ramzi Abid	NSH	13	1	4	5	–3	13	0	0	0	12	8.3
L	16	Darcy Hordichuk	NSH	53	1	3	4	–2	90	0	0	0	22	4.5
D	42	Mikko Lehtonen	NSH	15	1	2	3	0	8	0	0	0	14	7.1
D	8 *	Kevin Klein	NSH	3	1	0	1	3	0	0	0	0	2	50.0
D	34 *	Sheldon Brookbank	NSH	3	0	1	1	0	12	0	0	0	3	0.0
C	37 *	Rich Peverley	NSH	13	0	1	1	–1	0	0	0	0	9	0.0
R	28	Patrick Leahy	NSH	1	0	0	0	0	0	0	0	0	0	0.0

Goaltending

No.	Goaltender	GPI	Mins	Avg	W	L	OT	EN	SO	GA	SA	S%	G	A	PIM
30	Chris Mason	40	2342	2.38	24	11	4	5	5	93	1244	.925	0	1	4
29	Tomas Vokoun	44	2601	2.40	27	12	4	3	5	104	1299	.920	0	2	4
49	Michael Leighton	1	20	6.00	0	0	0	0	0	2	10	.800	0	0	0
	Totals	**82**	**4989**	**2.49**	**51**	**23**	**8**	**8**	**11**	**207**	**2561**	**.919**			

Tomas Vokoun and Chris Mason shared a shutout vs. Vancouver on Nov 23, 2006.

Playoffs

Pos	#	Player	Team	GP	G	A	Pts	+/–	PIM	PP	SH	GW	OT	S	%
R	71	Jean-Pierre Dumont	NSH	5	4	2	6	4	0	1	1	1	0	8	50.0
R	47 *	Alexander Radulov	NSH	4	3	1	4	1	19	0	0	0	0	13	23.1
C	21	Peter Forsberg	NSH	5	2	2	4	2	12	0	0	0	0	7	28.6
C	19	Jason Arnott	NSH	5	2	1	3	0	2	1	0	0	0	11	18.2
C	11	David Legwand	NSH	5	0	3	3	–2	2	0	0	0	0	14	0.0
D	6	Shea Weber	NSH	5	0	3	3	0	2	0	0	0	0	14	0.0
L	17	Scott Hartnell	NSH	5	1	1	2	–1	28	1	0	0	0	5	20.0
C	38	Vernon Fiddler	NSH	5	1	1	2	–3	4	0	0	0	0	2	50.0
L	9	Paul Kariya	NSH	5	0	2	2	–4	2	0	0	0	0	10	0.0
D	44	Kimmo Timonen	NSH	5	0	2	2	–1	4	0	0	0	0	7	0.0
D	5	Greg Zanon	NSH	5	0	2	2	–2	2	0	0	0	0	7	0.0
D	3	Marek Zidlicky	NSH	5	0	2	2	–1	4	0	0	0	0	8	0.0
D	20	Ryan Suter	NSH	5	1	0	1	0	8	0	0	0	0	9	11.1
L	10	Martin Erat	NSH	3	0	1	1	–1	0	0	0	0	0	3	0.0
R	22	Jordin Tootoo	NSH	4	0	1	1	–2	21	0	0	0	0	6	0.0
D	2	Dan Hamhuis	NSH	5	0	1	1	–3	2	0	0	0	0	7	0.0
L	14	Ramzi Abid	NSH	2	0	0	0	–1	0	0	0	0	0	0	0.0
L	16	Darcy Hordichuk	NSH	2	0	0	0	0	0	0	0	0	0	0	0.0
C	12	Scott Nichol	NSH	5	0	0	0	1	17	0	0	0	0	3	0.0
C	25	Jerred Smithson	NSH	5	0	0	0	–2	17	0	0	0	0	0	0.0

Goaltending

No.	Goaltender	GPI	Mins	Avg	W	L	EN	SO	GA	SA	S%	G	A	PIM
29	Tomas Vokoun	5	324	2.96	1	4	0	0	16	163	.902	0	0	2
	Totals	**5**	**328**	**2.93**	**1**	**4**	**0**	**0**	**16**	**163**	**.902**			

Now the number-one goalie in Nashville, Chris Mason ranked second in the NHL with a .925 save percentage in 2006-07.

Club Records

Team

(Figures in brackets for season records are games played; records for fewest points, wins, ties, losses, goals, goals against are for 70 or more games)

Most Points **110** 2006-07 (82)
Most Wins **51** 2006-07 (82)
Most Ties **13** 2001-02 (82), 2002-03 (82)
Most Losses **47** 1998-99 (82)
Most Goals **272** 2006-07 (82)
Most Goals Against **261** 1998-99 (82)
Fewest Points **63** 1998-99 (82)
Fewest Wins **27** 2002-03 (82)
Fewest Ties **7** 1998-99 (82), 1999-2000 (82)
Fewest Losses **23** 2006-07 (82)
Fewest Goals **183** 2002-03 (82)
Fewest Goals Against **200** 2000-01 (82)
Longest Winning Streak
Overall .... **8** Oct. 5-25/05
Home .... **8** Jan. 6-Feb. 8/07
Away .... **7** Oct. 16-Nov. 4/06
Longest Undefeated Streak
Overall .... **8** Dec. 18/99-Jan. 1/00 (5 wins, 3 ties), Oct. 5-25/05 (8 wins)
Home .... **11** Dec. 20/03-Jan. 31/04 (9 wins, 2 ties), Nov. 3-Dec. 23/01 (8 wins, 3 ties)
Away .... **7** Oct. 16-Nov. 4/06 (7 wins)
Longest Losing Streak
Overall .... **7** Nov. 20-Dec. 2/99
Home .... **6** Jan. 21-Feb. 15/99, Feb. 26-Mar. 21/02
Away .... **7** Jan. 26-Mar. 5/06
Longest Winless Streak
Overall .... **15** Mar. 10-Apr. 6/03 (12 losses (2 in OT), 3 ties)
Home .... **9** Jan. 21-Mar. 2/99 (8 losses, 1 tie)
Away .... **9** Three times
Most Shutouts, Season **11** 2006-07 (82)
Most PIM, Season **1,517** 2005-06 (82)
Most Goals, Game .... **9** Mar. 4/04 (Nsh. 9 at Pit. 4), Mar. 18/06 (Cgy. 4 at Nsh. 9)

Individual

Most Seasons .... **8** David Legwand, Kimmo Timonen, Tomas Vokoun
Most Games .... **573** Kimmo Timonen
Most Goals, Career .... **106** David Legwand
Most Assists, Career .... **222** Kimmo Timonen
Most Points, Career .... **301** Kimmo Timonen (79G, 222A)
Most PIM, Career .... **544** Scott Hartnell
Most Shutouts, Career .... **21** Tomas Vokoun
Longest Consecutive Games Streak .... **269** Karlis Skrastins (Feb. 21/00-Apr. 6/03)
Most Goals, Season .... **31** Paul Kariya (2005-06), Steve Sullivan (2005-06)
Most Assists, Season .... **54** Paul Kariya (2005-06)
Most Points, Season .... **85** Paul Kariya (2005-06; 31G, 54A)
Most PIM, Season .... **242** Patrick Cote (1999-2000)
Most Points, Defenseman, Season .... **55** Kimmo Timonen (2006-07; 13G, 42A)
Most Points, Center, Season .... **63** David Legwand (2006-07; 27G, 36A)
Most Points, Right Wing, Season .... **67** Scott Walker (2003-04; 25G, 42A)
Most Points, Left Wing, Season .... **85** Paul Kariya (2005-06; 31G, 54A)
Most Points, Rookie, Season .... **37** Alexander Radulov (2006-07; 18G, 19A)
Most Shutouts, Season .... **5** Tomas Vokoun (2006-07), Chris Mason (2006-07)
Most Goals, Game .... **3** Twelve times
Most Assists, Game .... **5** Mark Zidlicky (Feb. 18/04)
Most Points, Game .... **5** Mark Zidlicky (Feb. 18/04; 5A), Dan Hamhuis (Mar. 4/04; 1G-4A)

2006-07 Results

Oct.	5	Chicago	6-8		6	St. Louis	3-2
	7	at Minnesota	5-6		9	Anaheim	5-4*
	12	at Chicago	1-3		12	Columbus	2-0
	14	Phoenix	4-1		13	at Columbus	4-1
	16	at NY Islanders	2-1†		15	Calgary	5-3
	18	at NY Rangers	3-0		17	at Detroit	3-5
	19	at New Jersey	4-3†		18	Columbus	4-0
	21	Vancouver	3-4*		20	Chicago	6-3
	26	San Jose	4-3		26	at Chicago	3-1
	28	at Calgary	3-2		27	at St. Louis	6-3
	31	at Vancouver	3-2		30	at Colorado	3-4
Nov.	1	at Edmonton	5-3	**Feb.**	1	at Phoenix	2-3
	4	at Minnesota	4-3		3	Anaheim	3-0
	10	at Detroit	0-3		6	at Pittsburgh	1-4
	11	Colorado	1-0		8	Toronto	4-2
	15	at Columbus	5-4		10	Los Angeles	1-4
	16	Minnesota	6-7†		14	San Jose	5-0
	18	Columbus	4-2		16	at St. Louis	0-1
	20	at Columbus	3-1		17	Minnesota	1-4
	22	at Dallas	0-1		19	Phoenix	4-1
	23	Vancouver	6-0		22	Montreal	5-6†
	25	Detroit	6-2		24	Detroit	4-3*
	29	at Philadelphia	3-2		25	at Columbus	4-3†
	30	at St. Louis	5-4		28	at San Jose	4-3†
Dec.	2	Chicago	3-4*	**Mar.**	3	at Los Angeles	6-3
	4	at Phoenix	2-3		4	at Anaheim	2-3†
	6	at Anaheim	0-4		6	at Detroit	3-4†
	7	at Los Angeles	4-1		8	Calgary	6-3
	9	at San Jose	1-3		10	Columbus	2-1
	12	Edmonton	3-2		13	Detroit	2-5
	14	Ottawa	6-0		14	at Detroit	2-4
	16	St. Louis	3-2†		17	Dallas	3-2
	17	at St. Louis	2-1*		21	at Vancouver	0-2
	20	at Chicago	2-1		22	at Calgary	2-3*
	21	Buffalo	2-7		24	at Edmonton	4-0
	23	Los Angeles	7-0		27	Edmonton	4-3
	26	St. Louis	3-2†		29	Detroit	1-2
	29	at Dallas	1-4		31	Dallas	2-4
	30	Boston	5-0	**Apr.**	3	Chicago	2-3†
Jan.	1	Colorado	3-5		5	St. Louis	4-1
	5	at Chicago	8-3		7	at Colorado	4-2

* – Overtime † – Shootout

All-time Record vs. Other Clubs

Regular Season

	At Home								On Road								Total							
	GP	W	L	T	OL	GF	GA	PTS	GP	W	L	T	OL	GF	GA	PTS	GP	W	L	T	OL	GF	GA	PTS
Anaheim	16	8	5	2	1	37	38	19	16	3	11	0	2	26	50	8	32	11	16	2	3	63	88	27
Atlanta	3	2	1	0	0	12	6	4	5	1	2	1	1	13	16	4	8	3	3	1	1	25	22	8
Boston	7	3	4	0	0	18	16	6	5	2	2	1	0	9	14	5	12	5	6	1	0	27	30	11
Buffalo	6	2	3	0	1	12	16	5	4	3	0	1	0	16	9	7	10	5	3	1	1	28	25	12
Calgary	17	12	4	1	0	61	35	25	16	6	4	3	3	38	45	18	33	18	8	4	3	99	80	43
Carolina	4	3	1	0	0	9	7	6	6	2	2	1	1	17	19	6	10	5	3	1	1	26	26	12
Chicago	24	12	7	3	2	83	68	29	25	11	13	1	0	67	66	23	49	23	20	4	2	150	134	52
Colorado	16	6	7	3	0	47	55	15	16	6	7	2	1	36	45	15	32	12	14	5	1	83	100	30
Columbus	19	14	3	1	1	61	37	30	18	11	6	0	1	57	45	23	37	25	9	1	2	118	82	53
Dallas	16	8	7	1	0	39	35	17	16	2	13	0	1	18	47	5	32	10	20	1	1	57	82	22
Detroit	24	10	12	2	0	64	70	22	25	5	15	2	3	54	96	15	49	15	27	4	3	118	166	37
Edmonton	17	7	7	3	0	43	49	17	16	8	6	0	2	47	46	18	33	15	13	3	2	90	95	35
Florida	5	1	2	2	0	8	10	4	5	1	3	1	0	11	18	3	10	2	5	3	0	19	28	7
Los Angeles	16	4	9	3	0	31	40	11	16	7	6	0	3	44	49	17	32	11	15	3	3	75	89	28
Minnesota	12	7	2	2	1	34	25	17	12	3	6	3	0	30	38	9	24	10	8	5	1	64	63	26
Montreal	5	2	1	1	1	19	13	6	4	0	3	0	1	9	15	1	9	2	4	1	2	28	28	7
New Jersey	6	1	4	0	1	12	18	3	6	4	1	0	1	18	18	9	12	5	5	0	2	30	36	12
NY Islanders	6	4	2	0	0	16	17	8	5	3	1	0	1	14	12	7	11	7	3	0	1	30	29	15
NY Rangers	5	2	3	0	0	14	19	4	7	4	2	1	0	18	18	9	12	6	5	1	0	32	37	13
Ottawa	5	3	2	0	0	14	11	6	5	1	4	0	0	7	15	2	10	4	6	0	0	21	26	8
Philadelphia	5	1	2	2	0	8	10	4	6	3	2	1	0	12	19	7	11	4	4	3	0	20	29	11
Phoenix	16	9	5	2	0	47	37	20	16	6	9	0	1	47	48	13	32	15	14	2	1	94	85	33
Pittsburgh	7	5	2	0	0	26	14	10	6	2	2	2	0	18	18	6	13	7	4	2	0	44	32	16
St. Louis	25	13	9	3	0	60	59	29	24	10	11	1	2	49	66	23	49	23	20	4	2	109	125	52
San Jose	16	9	6	1	0	43	40	19	16	6	7	1	2	40	42	15	32	15	13	2	2	83	82	34
Tampa Bay	6	2	4	0	0	12	16	4	5	1	2	2	0	13	15	4	11	3	6	2	0	25	31	8
Toronto	2	2	0	0	0	7	4	4	6	3	2	1	0	18	13	7	8	5	2	1	0	25	17	11
Vancouver	17	8	5	1	3	52	45	20	16	4	11	1	0	37	58	9	33	12	16	2	3	89	103	29
Washington	5	3	1	1	0	16	11	7	5	2	3	0	0	13	12	4	10	5	4	1	0	29	23	11
Totals	**328**	**163**	**120**	**34**	**11**	**905**	**821**	**371**	**328**	**120**	**156**	**26**	**26**	**796**	**972**	**292**	**656**	**283**	**276**	**60**	**37**	**1701**	**1793**	**663**

Playoffs

	Series	W	L	GP	W	L	T	GF	GA	Last Mtg.	Rnd.	Result
Detroit	1	0	1	6	2	4	0	9	12	2004	CQF	L 2-4
San Jose	2	0	2	10	2	8	0	24	33	2007	CQF	L 1-4
Totals	**3**	**0**	**3**	**16**	**4**	**12**	**0**	**33**	**45**			

Playoff Results 2007-2002

Year	Round	Opponent	Result	GF	GA
2007	CQF	San Jose	L 1-4	14	16
2006	CQF	San Jose	L 1-4	10	17
2004	CQF	Detroit	L 2-4	9	12

Abbreviations: Round: CQF - conference quarter-final.

Entry Draft Selections 2007-1998

2007

Pick	
23	Jonathon Blum
54	Jeremy Smith
58	Nick Spaling
81	Ryan Thang
114	Ben Ryan
119	Mark Santorelli
144	Andreas Thuresson
174	Robert Dietrich
204	Atte Engren

2006

Pick	
56	Blake Geoffrion
105	Niko Snellman
146	Mark Dekanich
176	Ryan Flynn
206	Viktor Sjodin

2005

Pick	
18	Ryan Parent
78	Teemu Laakso
79	Cody Franson
150	Cal O'Reilly
176	Ryan Maki
213	Scott Todd
230	Patric Hornqvist

2004

Pick	
15	Alexander Radulov
81	Vaclav Meidl
107	Nick Fugere
139	Kyle Moir
147	Janne Niskala
178	Mike Santorelli
193	Kevin Schaeffer
209	Stanislav Balan
243	Denis Kulyash
258	Pekka Rinne
275	Craig Switzer

2003

Pick	
7	Ryan Suter
35	Konstantin Glazachev
37	Kevin Klein
49	Shea Weber
76	Richard Stehlik
89	Paul Brown
92	Alexander Sulzer
98	Grigory Shafigulin
117	Teemu Lassila
133	Rustam Sidikov
210	Andrei Mukhachev
213	Miroslav Hanuljak
268	Lauris Darzins

2002

Pick	
6	Scottie Upshall
102	Brandon Segal
138	Patrick Jarrett
172	Mike McKenna
203	Josh Morrow
235	Kaleb Betts
264	Matt Davis
266	Steven Spencer

2001

Pick	
12	Dan Hamhuis
33	Timofei Shishkanov
42	Tomas Slovak
75	Denis Platonov
76	Oliver Setzinger
98	Jordin Tootoo
178	Anton Lavrentiev
240	Gustav Grasberg
271	Mikko Lehtonen

2000

Pick	
6	Scott Hartnell
36	Daniel Widing
72	Mattias Nilsson
89	Libor Pivko
131	Matt Hendricks
137	Mike Stuart
154	Matt Koalska
173	Tomas Harant
197	Zbynek Irgl
203	Jure Penko
236	Mats Christeen
284	Martin Hohener

1999

Pick	
6	Brian Finley
33	Jonas Andersson
52	Adam Hall
54	Andrew Hutchinson
61	Ed Hill
65	Jan Lasak
72	Brett Angel
121	Yevgeny Pavlov
124	Alexandre Krevsun
131	Konstantin Panov
162	Timo Helbling
191	Martin Erat
205	Kyle Kettles
220	Miroslav Durak
248	Darren Haydar

1998

Pick	
2	David Legwand
60	Denis Arkhipov
85	Geoff Koch
88	Kent Sauer
138	Martin Beauchesne
147	Craig Brunel
202	Martin Bartek
230	Karlis Skrastins

Coaching History

Barry Trotz, 1998-99 to date.

Coach

BARRY TROTZ

Coach, Nashville Predators. Born in Winnipeg, Man., July 15, 1962.

Barry Trotz realized his dream of becoming an NHL head coach on August 6, 1997, after serving four seasons as head coach and director of hockey operations for the American Hockey League's Portland Pirates. He and assistant Paul Gardner spent the 1997-98 season scouting in preparation for the inaugural season of the Predators. In his sixth season behind the bench in 2003-04, Trotz led Nashville into the playoffs for the first time. They reached the playoffs again in 2005-06. During the 2006-07 season, Nashville was in contention for first overall in the NHL, setting club records with 51 wins and 110 points.

Trotz began his coaching career in 1984 as assistant coach with the University of Manitoba for one season, before serving two seasons as the head coach and general manager of the Dauphin Kings Junior Hockey Club from 1985 to 1987. He became head coach of the University of Manitoba during the 1987 season and also served as a scout for the Spokane Chiefs of the Western Hockey League that season. Trotz joined the Washington Capitals organization as their chief western scout during the 1988 season. The Winnipeg, Manitoba native was appointed an assistant coach of the Capitals' American Hockey League affiliate in Baltimore prior to the 1991 season before being named head coach prior to the 1992 season. When the franchise relocated to Portland, he guided the Pirates to two AHL Calder Cup Final appearances in the club's first four seasons. He led the Pirates to a league-best 43-27-10 record, captured the Calder Cup championship and was named the American Hockey League coach of the year following the 1994-95 season.

In 1995, Trotz guided Portland to a new North American professional hockey league record 17-game unbeaten streak (14-0-3) to start the season. He was named head coach for the U.S. team at the American Hockey League All-Star Game in 1996.

Prior to his coaching career, Trotz played junior hockey for the Western Hockey League's Regina Pats from 1979-83. During that time, he recorded 39 goals, 121 assists for 160 points, along with 490 penalty minutes in 204 games.

Coaching Record

		Regular Season				Playoffs		
Season	Team	Games	W	L	O/T	Games	W	L
1992-93	Baltimore (AHL)	80	28	40	12	7	3	4
1993-94	Portland (AHL)	80	43	27	10	8	6	2
1994-95	Portland (AHL)	80	46	22	12	7	3	4
1995-96	Portland (AHL)	80	32	38	10	24	14	10
1996-97	Portland (AHL)	80	37	33	10	5	2	3
1998-99	**Nashville (NHL)**	**82**	**28**	**47**	**7**	....	....	....
1999-2000	**Nashville (NHL)**	**82**	**28**	**47**	**7**	....	....	....
2000-01	**Nashville (NHL)**	**82**	**34**	**39**	**9**	....	....	....
2001-02	**Nashville (NHL)**	**82**	**28**	**41**	**13**	....	....	....
2002-03	**Nashville (NHL)**	**82**	**27**	**42**	**13**	....	....	....
2003-04	**Nashville (NHL)**	**82**	**38**	**33**	**11**	**6**	**2**	**4**
2004-05	**Nashville (NHL)**			Season Cancelled				
2005-06	**Nashville (NHL)**	**82**	**49**	**25**	**8**	**5**	**1**	**4**
2006-07	**Nashville (NHL)**	**82**	**51**	**23**	**8**	**5**	**1**	**4**
	NHL Totals	**656**	**283**	**297**	**76**	**16**	**4**	**12**

Club Directory

Sommet Center

Nashville Predators
Sommet Center
501 Broadway
Nashville, TN 37203
Phone **615/770-2300**
FAX 615/770-2309
Ticket Information 615/770-PUCK
www.nashvillepredators.com
Capacity: 17,113

Owner, Chairman and Governor . . . . . Craig Leipold
General Partner . . . . . Nashville Predators, LLC
Exec. V.P./G.M. and Alternate Governor . . . . . David Poile
Exec. V.P., Finance & Admin./CFO & Alt. Gov. . . . . . Ed Lang
Exec. V.P., Business Affairs & Alt. Gov. . . . . . Steve Violetta
Sr. V.P. Communications & Development . . . . . Gerry Helper

Hockey Operations
Assistant General Manager . . . . . Paul Fenton
Director of Hockey Operations . . . . . Mike Santos
Head Coach . . . . . Barry Trotz
Associate Coach . . . . . Brent Peterson
Assistant Coach . . . . . Peter Horachek
Goaltending Coach . . . . . Mitch Korn
Video Coach . . . . . Robert Bouchard
Strength and Conditioning Coach . . . . . David Good
Chief Amateur Scout . . . . . Jeff Kealty
Professional Scouts . . . . . Nick Beverley, Shawn Dineen
North American Amateur Scouts . . . . . Jason Bukala, Gord Donnelly, Rick Knickle, Gary Knickle, Glen Sanders, David Westby
European Scouts . . . . . Lucas Bergman, Janne Kekalainen, Martin Bakula
Head Athletic Trainer . . . . . Dan Redmond
Assistant Athletic Trainer . . . . . Andy Hosler
Equipment Manager . . . . . Pete Rogers
Assistant Equipment Manager . . . . . Jeff Camelio
Locker Room Attendant . . . . . Craig "Partner" Baugh
Director of Team Services . . . . . Gregory Harvey
Hockey Operations Manager . . . . . Brandon Walker
Executive Assistant . . . . . Caitlin Nierenberg

Medical
Richard W. Garman MD, Blake Garside MD, Donald Griffin MD, Carl Hampf MD, David Moore MD, Bryan D. Oslin MD, Gary S. Solomon PhD, Cristin Wallace DDS, Daniel Weikert MD

Communiucations/Development
Director of Communications . . . . . Ken Anderson
Communications Manager . . . . . Tim Darling
Internet Development Manager . . . . . Doug Brumley
Communications/Website Coordinator . . . . . Kevin Wilson
Director of Community Relations . . . . . Rebecca Ward
Youth/Amateur Hockey Coordinator . . . . . Andee Boiman
Community Relations Coordinator . . . . . Erich Wilhelm
Team Photographer . . . . . John Russell

Corporate Sales
Vice President of Corporate Development . . . . . Jason Bitsoff
Director of Corporate Development . . . . . Delmar Smith
Account Executives – Corporate Partnerships . . . . . Shad Adams, John McMillin
Senior Account Manager Corporate Development . . . . . Kristy Estes-Adoff
Corporate Partnerships Account Managers . . . . . Emily Cutler, Kat Cloud
Executive Assistant . . . . . Gerry Pring

Marketing
Vice President of Marketing . . . . . Randy Campbell
Entertainment Manager . . . . . Adam DeVault
Advertising Manager . . . . . Melissa Hindman
Database Marketing Manager . . . . . Jason Koettel
Game Operations Coordinator . . . . . Brian Campbell
Marketing Coordinators . . . . . Shannon Lake, Kelly Sparks
Art Director . . . . . Jennifer Sheets
Graphic Artist . . . . . Chuck Stephens

Premium Seating
Vice President of Premium Seating Service . . . . . Susie Masotti
Director of Premium Seating . . . . . Britt Kincheloe

Finance/Administration/Human Resources
Vice President of Finance . . . . . Beth Snider
Director of Human Resources . . . . . Allison Winters
Payroll Manager . . . . . Susan Charnley
Accountants . . . . . Melanie Ainsworth, Michael Kruspe
Human Resources Coordinator . . . . . Erin Grosvenor
Accounts Payable . . . . . Jamie France
Executive Assistant . . . . . Elaine Lewis

Technical Operations
Director of Technical Operations . . . . . Blake Grant
Technical Operations Coordinator . . . . . Patrick Abell

Broadcast
Director of Broadcasting . . . . . Bob Kohl
Play-by-Play Announcer . . . . . Pete Weber
Color Analyst . . . . . Terry Crisp
Manager, Video Production . . . . . Mitch Jordan
Videographer/Editor . . . . . David White

Ticket Operations
Vice President of Ticket Sales . . . . . Scott Wampold
Director of Season Ticket Sales . . . . . Nat Harden
Director of Suite and Group Sales . . . . . Chris Junghans
Senior Account Executive of Group Sales . . . . . Tim Wilson
Account Executives . . . . . Chris Burton, Brad Gillispie, Todd McNamara, Jenny Moss, Jason Mott, Thomas Tilney, Dan Shaefer, Tiffany Vanek
Ticket Operations/Fan Relations Manager . . . . . Brad MacLachlan
Ticket Operations Coordinators . . . . . Sara Endwright, Mary Jane Rodgers
Fan Relations Coordinators . . . . . Paige Belew, Courtney Gray, Chris Harrington, Mac Maddox
Ticket Sales Coordinator . . . . . Mollie Roach

Miscellaneous
Radio Flagship . . . . . WGFX 104.5-FM, WNSR 560-AM
TV Flagship . . . . . FSN South

New Jersey Devils

2006-07 Results: 49W-24L-1OTL-8SOL 107PTS.
First, Atlantic Division

Key Off-Season Signings/Acquisitions

2007

- **June** 13 • Re-signed D **Andy Greene**.
- **July** 3 • Signed D **Karel Rachunek** and RW **Dainius Zubrus**.
- 5 • Signed G **Kevin Weekes**.
- 10 • Signed D **Vitaly Vishnevski**.
- 13 • Named **Brent Sutter** head coach.
- **Aug.** 1 • Re-signed LW **Zach Parise**.
- 7 • Signed RW **Arron Asham**.

Martin Brodeur led the league with a career-high 12 shutouts in 2006-07 and set a new NHL record with 48 wins, surpassing Bernie Parent's previous mark of 47 from 1973-74. Brodeur has won 40 or more games a record six times.

2007-08 Schedule

Month	Day	Date	Opponent
Oct.	Thu.	4	at Tampa Bay
	Sat.	6	at Florida
	Mon.	8	at Ottawa*
	Thu.	11	at Florida
	Sat.	13	at Atlanta
	Wed.	17	at Pittsburgh
	Thu.	18	at Philadelphia
	Sat.	20	at NY Islanders
	Thu.	25	at NY Rangers
	Sat.	27	Ottawa
	Wed.	31	Tampa Bay
Nov.	Fri.	2	Toronto
	Sat.	3	at NY Rangers
	Mon.	5	Pittsburgh
	Thu.	8	Philadelphia
	Sat.	10	at NY Islanders
	Mon.	12	at Pittsburgh
	Wed.	14	NY Rangers
	Fri.	16	NY Islanders
	Sat.	17	at Philadelphia
	Wed.	21	at Pittsburgh
	Fri.	23	at Atlanta
	Sat.	24	at Tampa Bay
	Wed.	28	Dallas
	Fri.	30	Montreal
Dec.	Sun.	2	Atlanta*
	Wed.	5	Boston
	Fri.	7	Washington
	Sun.	9	at NY Rangers*
	Mon.	10	at Washington
	Thu.	13	at Boston
	Sat.	15	Phoenix*
	Sun.	16	Philadelphia*
	Tue.	18	at Vancouver
	Fri.	21	at Edmonton
	Sun.	23	at Calgary
	Fri.	28	Buffalo
	Sat.	29	at NY Islanders
Jan.	Wed.	2	Florida
	Fri.	4	Philadelphia
	Sat.	5	at Boston
	Tue.	8	Buffalo
	Thu.	10	at Carolina
	Sat.	12	at Buffalo
	Wed.	16	NY Islanders
	Fri.	18	Florida
	Sun.	20	Toronto*
	Tue.	22	at Philadelphia
	Thu.	24	Montreal
	Tue.	29	Pittsburgh
Feb.	Fri.	1	NY Rangers
	Sat.	2	Los Angeles
	Mon.	4	Pittsburgh
	Wed.	6	at Buffalo
	Fri.	8	Anaheim
	Sat.	9	Carolina
	Wed.	13	Ottawa
	Fri.	15	Atlanta
	Sat.	16	at Ottawa
	Mon.	18	Carolina*
	Wed.	20	San Jose
	Sat.	23	NY Islanders*
	Sun.	24	at Washington*
	Tue.	26	at Carolina
	Fri.	29	Washington
Mar.	Sat.	1	at Montreal
	Tue.	4	at Toronto
	Fri.	7	Tampa Bay
	Sat.	8	at Toronto
	Tue.	11	at Montreal
	Thu.	13	at Minnesota
	Sat.	15	at Colorado*
	Wed.	19	NY Rangers
	Fri.	21	NY Islanders
	Sat.	22	at Pittsburgh
	Tue.	25	Pittsburgh
	Thu.	27	at NY Rangers
	Fri.	28	Philadelphia
Apr.	Tue.	1	at NY Islanders
	Wed.	2	Boston
	Fri.	4	at Philadelphia
	Sun.	6	NY Rangers*

* Denotes afternoon game.

Year-by-Year Record

		Home				Road				Overall								
Season	GP	W	L	T	OL	W	L	T	OL	W	L	T	OL	GF	GA	Pts.	Finished	Playoff Result
2006-07	82	25	10	....	6	24	14	....	3	49	24	....	9	216	201	107	1st, Atlantic Div.	Lost Conf. Semi-Final
2005-06	82	27	11	....	3	19	16	....	6	46	27	....	9	242	229	101	1st, Atlantic Div.	Lost Conf. Semi-Final
2004-05	....	....	....	....	....	....	....	....	....	....	....	....	....	....	....	....		
2003-04	82	22	13	5	1	21	12	7	1	43	25	12	2	213	164	100	2nd, Atlantic Div.	Lost Conf. Quarter-Final
2002-03	**82**	**25**	**11**	**3**	**2**	**21**	**9**	**7**	**4**	**46**	**20**	**10**	**6**	**216**	**166**	**108**	**1st, Atlantic Div.**	**Won Stanley Cup**
2001-02	82	22	13	4	2	19	15	5	2	41	28	9	4	205	187	95	3rd, Atlantic Div.	Lost Conf. Quarter-Final
2000-01	82	24	11	6	0	24	8	6	3	48	19	12	3	295	195	111	1st, Atlantic Div.	Lost Final
1999-2000	**82**	**28**	**9**	**3**	**1**	**17**	**15**	**5**	**4**	**45**	**24**	**8**	**5**	**251**	**203**	**103**	**2nd, Atlantic Div.**	**Won Stanley Cup**
1998-99	82	19	14	8	....	28	10	3	....	47	24	11	....	248	196	105	1st, Atlantic Div.	Lost Conf. Quarter-Final
1997-98	82	29	10	2	....	19	13	9	....	48	23	11	....	225	166	107	1st, Atlantic Div.	Lost Conf. Quarter-Final
1996-97	82	23	9	9	....	22	14	5	....	45	23	14	....	231	182	104	1st, Atlantic Div.	Lost Conf. Semi-Final
1995-96	82	22	17	2	....	15	16	10	....	37	33	12	....	215	202	86	6th, Atlantic Div.	Out of Playoffs
1994-95	**48**	**14**	**4**	**6**	....	**8**	**14**	**2**	....	**22**	**18**	**8**	....	**136**	**121**	**52**	**2nd, Atlantic Div.**	**Won Stanley Cup**
1993-94	84	29	11	2	....	18	14	10	....	47	25	12	....	306	220	106	2nd, Atlantic Div.	Lost Conf. Championship
1992-93	84	24	14	4	....	16	23	3	....	40	37	7	....	308	299	87	4th, Patrick Div.	Lost Div. Semi-Final
1991-92	80	24	12	4	....	14	19	3	....	38	31	11	....	289	259	87	4th, Patrick Div.	Lost Div. Semi-Final
1990-91	80	23	10	7	....	9	23	8	....	32	33	15	....	272	264	79	4th, Patrick Div.	Lost Div. Semi-Final
1989-90	80	22	15	3	....	15	19	6	....	37	34	9	....	295	288	83	2nd, Patrick Div.	Lost Div. Semi-Final
1988-89	80	17	18	5	....	10	23	7	....	27	41	12	....	281	325	66	5th, Patrick Div.	Out of Playoffs
1987-88	80	23	16	1	....	15	20	5	....	38	36	6	....	295	296	82	4th, Patrick Div.	Lost Conf. Championship
1986-87	80	20	17	3	....	9	28	3	....	29	45	6	....	293	368	64	6th, Patrick Div.	Out of Playoffs
1985-86	80	17	21	2	....	11	28	1	....	28	49	3	....	300	374	59	6th, Patrick Div.	Out of Playoffs
1984-85	80	13	21	6	....	9	27	4	....	22	48	10	....	264	346	54	5th, Patrick Div.	Out of Playoffs
1983-84	80	10	28	2	....	7	28	5	....	17	56	7	....	231	350	41	5th, Patrick Div.	Out of Playoffs
1982-83	80	11	20	9	....	6	29	5	....	17	49	14	....	230	338	48	5th, Patrick Div.	Out of Playoffs
1981-82**	80	14	21	5	....	4	28	8	....	18	49	13	....	241	362	49	5th, Smythe Div.	Out of Playoffs
1980-81**	80	15	16	9	....	7	29	4	....	22	45	13	....	258	344	57	5th, Smythe Div.	Out of Playoffs
1979-80**	80	12	20	8	....	7	28	5	....	19	48	13	....	234	308	51	6th, Smythe Div.	Out of Playoffs
1978-79**	80	8	24	8	....	7	29	4	....	15	53	12	....	210	331	42	4th, Smythe Div.	Out of Playoffs
1977-78**	80	17	14	9	....	2	26	12	....	19	40	21	....	257	305	59	2nd, Smythe Div.	Lost Prelim. Round
1976-77**	80	12	20	8	....	8	26	6	....	20	46	14	....	226	307	54	5th, Smythe Div.	Out of Playoffs
1975-76*	80	8	24	8	....	4	32	4	....	12	56	12	....	190	351	36	5th, Smythe Div.	Out of Playoffs
1974-75*	80	12	20	8	....	3	34	3	....	15	54	11	....	184	328	41	5th, Smythe Div.	Out of Playoffs

* Kansas City Scouts. ** Colorado Rockies.

NHL EASTERN CONFERENCE

ATLANTIC DIVISION
34th NHL Season

Franchise date: June 11, 1974

Transferred from Denver to New Jersey, June 30, 1982.
Transferred from Kansas City to Denver, August 25, 1976.

2007-08 Player Personnel

FORWARDS	HT	WT	S	Place of Birth	*Age	2006-07 Club
ASHAM, Arron	5-11	210	R	Portage La Prairie, Man.	29	NY Islanders
BERGFORS, Nicklas	5-11	190	R	Sodertalje, Sweden	20	Lowell
BRYLIN, Sergei	5-10	190	L	Moscow, USSR	33	New Jersey
CLARKE, Noah	5-9	190	L	La Verne, CA	28	Los Angeles-Manchester
CLARKSON, David	6-1	205	R	Toronto, Ont.	23	New Jersey-Lowell
DAVIS, Patrick	6-3	205	R	Sterling, MI	20	Lowell
ELIAS, Patrik	6-1	195	L	Trebic, Czech.	31	New Jersey
GIONTA, Brian	5-7	175	R	Rochester, NY	28	New Jersey
GIONTA, Stephen	5-7	185	R	Rochester, NY	23	Lowell
HALISCHUK, Matt	5-11	175	R	Toronto, Ont.	19	Kitchener
JANSSEN, Cam	6-0	210	R	St. Louis, MO	23	New Jersey-Lowell
KHOMUTOV, Ivan	6-3	210	L	Saratov, USSR	22	Lowell-Trenton
LANGENBRUNNER, Jamie	6-1	200	R	Cloquet, MN	32	New Jersey
LETOURNEAU-LEBLOND, Pierre-Luc	6-2	215	L	Levis, Que.	22	Trenton
MADDEN, John	5-11	190	L	Barrie, Ont.	34	New Jersey
MARSHALL, Grant	6-1	200	R	Mississauga, Ont.	34	Lowell
MONDOU, Benoit	5-9	175	L	Sorel, Que.	22	Trenton
MURPHY, Ryan	6-1	205	L	Van Nuys, CA	28	Lowell
PALMIERI, Nick	6-3	215	R	Utica, NY	18	Erie (OHL)
PANDOLFO, Jay	6-1	190	L	Winchester, MA	32	New Jersey
PANDOLFO, Mike	6-3	225	L	Winchester, MA	28	Lowell-Trenton
PARISE, Zach	5-11	190	L	Minneapolis, MN	23	New Jersey
PELLEY, Rod	6-0	200	L	Kitimat, B.C.	23	New Jersey-Lowell
ROMANO, Tony	5-11	185	R	Smithtown, NY	19	Cornell
ROONEY, Joe	5-10	170	L	Canton, MA	22	Boston College
RUPP, Mike	6-5	230	L	Cleveland, OH	27	New Jersey
RYZNAR, Jason	6-4	205	L	Anchorage, AK	24	Lowell
TALLACKSON, Barry	6-5	210	R	Grafton, ND	24	New Jersey-Lowell
VIUHKOLA, Jari	6-0	200	L	Oulu, Finland	27	Karpat
VRANA, Petr	5-10	190	L	Sternberk, Czech.	22	Lowell
ZAJAC, Travis	6-2	200	R	Winnipeg, Man.	22	New Jersey
ZUBRUS, Dainius	6-5	225	L	Elektrenai, USSR	29	Washington-Buffalo

DEFENSEMEN	HT	WT	S	Place of Birth	*Age	2006-07 Club
CORRENTE, Matthew	6-0	195	R	Mississauga, Ont.	19	Saginaw-Mississauga
FRASER, Mark	6-4	210	L	Ottawa, Ont.	21	New Jersey-Lowell
GRAND-PIERRE, Jean-Luc	6-3	225	R	Montreal, Que.	30	Dusseldorf
GREENE, Andy	5-11	195	L	Trenton, MI	24	New Jersey-Lowell
MAGNAN-GRENIER, Olivier	6-2	200	L	Sherbrooke, Que.	21	Lowell-Trenton
MALMIVAARA, Olli	6-7	220	L	Kajaani, Finland	25	Lowell
MARTIN, Paul	6-1	190	L	Minneapolis, MN	26	New Jersey
MATVICHUK, Richard	6-3	215	L	Edmonton, Alta.	34	New Jersey
MOLLE, Ryan	6-3	195	R	Winnipeg, Man.	18	Swift Current
MORAN, Ian	6-0	205	R	Cleveland, OH	35	Ana-Port (AHL)-Eisbaren Berlin
MOTTAU, Mike	6-0	190	L	Quincy, MA	29	Lowell
ODUYA, Johnny	6-0	200	L	Stockholm, Sweden	26	New Jersey
RACHUNEK, Karel	6-2	220	R	Gottwaldov/Zlin, Czech.	28	NY Rangers
TARKIR, Zach	6-0	185	R	Fresno, CA	23	Northern Mich.-Lowell
TULUPOV, Kirill	6-3	210	R	Moscow, USSR	19	Chicoutimi
VISHNEVSKI, Vitaly	6-2	215	L	Kharkov, USSR	27	Atlanta-Nashville
WHITE, Colin	6-4	215	L	New Glasgow, N.S.	29	New Jersey
ZIMMERMAN, Sean	6-3	205	R	Denver, CO	20	Spokane-Lowell

GOALTENDERS	HT	WT	C	Place of Birth	*Age	2006-07 Club
BRODEUR, Martin	6-2	215	L	Montreal, Que.	35	New Jersey
CARUSO, David	6-1	215	L	Roswell, GA	25	Chicago (AHL)-Gwinnett
DOYLE, Frank	6-1	185	L	Guelph, Ont.	27	Lowell
PARISE, Jordan	5-11	195	L	Faribault, MN	25	Lowell
SMITH, Jason	6-1	170	L	St-Lambert, Que.	22	Sacred Heart
WEEKES, Kevin	6-1	215	L	Toronto, Ont.	32	NY Rangers

* – Age at start of 2007-08 season

President and General Manager

LOU LAMORIELLO
CEO/President/General Manager, New Jersey Devils.
Born in Providence, RI, October 21, 1942.

Lou Lamoriello has been president and general manager of the Devils since 1987-88 following more than 20 years with Providence College as a player, coach and administrator. His trades, signings and draft choices helped lead the Devils to their first Stanley Cup Championship in 1995 and were followed by victories again in 2000 and 2003. During his tenure, the club's record was 776-545-197 (.583) during the regular-season and 117-94 (.555) in the post-season, which includes ten 100-point seasons, four Eastern Conference and seven Atlantic Division regular-season championships over the past 13 seasons. In 2005-06, Lamoriello took over behind the bench and coached the Devils to first place in the Atlantic Division.

While at Providence, Lamoriello served as hockey coach for 15 seasons, compiling an impressive .578 winning percentage (248-179-13), while guiding the Friars to 12 post-season tournaments in a row. During his last five seasons (1978-83) of coaching, the school compiled a record of 107-58-4 and had more players drafted by the National Hockey League after entering college than any other college team during those years. Lamoriello helped propel numerous players and administrators toward NHL careers during his tenure at Providence. He was hired as president of the Devils on April 30, 1987, and assumed the responsibility of general manager on September 10, 1987. Lamoriello was G.M. of Team USA for the first World Cup of Hockey in 1996 as the U.S. captured the championship. He was also the G.M. for the 1998 U.S. Olympic Team.

NHL Coaching Record

		Regular Season				Playoffs		
Season	Team	Games	W	L	O/T	Games	W	L
2005-06	New Jersey	50	32	14	4	9	5	4
2006-07	New Jersey	3	2	0	1	11	5	6
	NHL Totals	**53**	**34**	**14**	**5**	**20**	**10**	**10**

Posted an 0-1 playoff record as replacement coach when Jim Schoenfeld was suspended, May 10, 1988. Loss is credited to Schoenfeld's coaching record.

2006-07 Scoring

* – rookie

Regular Season

Pos	#	Player	Team	GP	G	A	Pts	+/–	PIM	PP	SH	GW	S	%
L	26	Patrik Elias	N.J.	75	21	48	69	1	38	8	0	5	267	7.9
L	9	Zach Parise	N.J.	82	31	31	62	–3	30	9	0	7	247	12.6
R	15	Jamie Langenbrunner	N.J.	82	23	37	60	–9	64	12	0	7	243	9.5
C	23	Scott Gomez	N.J.	72	13	47	60	7	42	4	0	1	248	5.2
D	28	Brian Rafalski	N.J.	82	8	47	55	4	34	3	1	4	148	5.4
R	14	Brian Gionta	N.J.	62	25	20	45	–3	36	11	0	4	194	12.9
C	19 *	Travis Zajac	N.J.	80	17	25	42	1	16	6	0	2	134	12.7
L	18	Sergei Brylin	N.J.	82	16	24	40	–5	35	8	0	2	97	16.5
C	11	John Madden	N.J.	74	12	20	32	–7	14	0	0	1	153	7.8
L	20	Jay Pandolfo	N.J.	82	13	14	27	–5	8	0	1	1	109	11.9
D	7	Paul Martin	N.J.	82	3	23	26	–9	18	1	0	0	84	3.6
D	21	Brad Lukowich	N.J.	75	4	8	12	1	36	0	1	2	50	8.0
D	29 *	John Oduya	N.J.	76	2	9	11	–5	61	0	0	0	55	3.6
C	10	Erik Rasmussen	N.J.	71	3	7	10	–3	25	0	0	0	80	3.8
C	17	Mike Rupp	N.J.	76	6	3	9	–10	92	0	0	1	60	10.0
C	12	Jim Dowd	N.J.	66	4	4	8	–5	20	0	1	1	44	9.1
D	5	Colin White	N.J.	69	0	8	8	–8	69	0	0	0	47	0.0
D	6 *	Andy Greene	N.J.	23	1	5	6	–1	6	1	0	0	23	4.3
R	27 *	David Clarkson	N.J.	7	3	1	4	–1	6	2	0	1	18	16.7
R	25	Cam Janssen	N.J.	48	1	0	1	–2	114	0	0	0	9	11.1
D	6	Jim Fahey	N.J.	13	0	1	1	0	2	0	0	0	7	0.0
D	8	Alexander Brooks	N.J.	19	0	1	1	–1	4	0	0	0	4	0.0
D	24	Richard Matvichuk	N.J.	1	0	0	0	–1	0	0	0	0	0	0.0
L	16 *	Thomas Pihlman	N.J.	2	0	0	0	0	0	0	0	0	0	0.0
R	27 *	Barry Tallackson	N.J.	3	0	0	0	–1	0	0	0	0	3	0.0
L	22	Dan LaCouture	N.J.	6	0	0	0	0	7	0	0	0	0	0.0
D	6 *	Mark Fraser	N.J.	7	0	0	0	–1	7	0	0	0	1	0.0
C	22 *	Rodney Pelley	N.J.	9	0	0	0	–3	0	0	0	0	8	0.0

Goaltending

No.	Goaltender	GPI	Mins	Avg	W	L	OT	EN	SO	GA	SA	S%	G	A	PIM
30	Martin Brodeur	78	4697	2.18	48	23	7	5	12	171	2182	.922	0	1	12
40	Scott Clemmensen	6	305	3.15	1	1	2	1	0	16	144	.889	0	0	0
	Totals	**82**	**5024**	**2.30**	**49**	**24**	**9**	**6**	**12**	**193**	**2332**	**.917**			

Playoffs

Pos	#	Player	Team	GP	G	A	Pts	+/–	PIM	PP	SH	GW	OT	S	%
C	23	Scott Gomez	N.J.	11	4	10	14	6	14	0	0	1	1	37	10.8
L	9	Zach Parise	N.J.	11	7	3	10	4	8	2	0	1	0	45	15.6
L	26	Patrik Elias	N.J.	10	1	9	10	3	4	1	0	0	0	48	2.1
R	14	Brian Gionta	N.J.	11	8	1	9	5	4	3	0	1	0	37	21.6
R	15	Jamie Langenbrunner	N.J.	11	2	6	8	3	7	1	0	1	1	38	5.3
D	28	Brian Rafalski	N.J.	11	2	6	8	–1	8	2	0	0	0	11	18.2
C	19 *	Travis Zajac	N.J.	11	1	4	5	4	4	0	0	0	0	18	5.6
D	7	Paul Martin	N.J.	11	0	4	4	–4	6	0	0	0	0	6	0.0
D	6 *	Andy Greene	N.J.	11	2	1	3	6	2	0	0	1	0	10	20.0
L	18	Sergei Brylin	N.J.	11	1	2	3	–8	6	1	0	0	0	13	7.7
C	11	John Madden	N.J.	11	1	1	2	–6	2	0	0	0	0	24	4.2
L	20	Jay Pandolfo	N.J.	11	1	0	1	–8	4	0	0	0	0	10	10.0
D	29 *	John Oduya	N.J.	6	0	1	1	2	6	0	0	0	0	4	0.0
R	17	Mike Rupp	N.J.	9	0	1	1	1	7	0	0	0	0	0	0.0
D	21	Brad Lukowich	N.J.	11	0	1	1	2	2	0	0	0	0	4	0.0
R	27 *	David Clarkson	N.J.	3	0	0	0	–1	2	0	0	0	0	2	0.0
D	5	Colin White	N.J.	7	0	0	0	–4	6	0	0	0	0	2	0.0
D	24	Richard Matvichuk	N.J.	9	0	0	0	–4	10	0	0	0	0	0	0.0
C	12	Jim Dowd	N.J.	11	0	0	0	–2	4	0	0	0	0	4	0.0
C	10	Erik Rasmussen	N.J.	11	0	0	0	–1	14	0	0	0	0	4	0.0

Goaltending

No.	Goaltender	GPI	Mins	Avg	W	L	EN	SO	GA	SA	S%	G	A	PIM
30	Martin Brodeur	11	688	2.44	5	6	1	1	28	332	.916	0	1	2
	Totals	**11**	**695**	**2.50**	**5**	**6**	**1**	**1**	**29**	**333**	**.913**			

Captains' History

Simon Nolet, 1974-75 to 1976-77; Wilf Paiement, 1977-78; Gary Croteau, 1978-79; Mike Christie, Rene Robert and Lanny McDonald, 1979-80; Lanny McDonald, 1980-81; Lanny McDonald and Rob Ramage, 1981-82; Don Lever, 1982-83; Don Lever and Mel Bridgman, 1983-84; Mel Bridgman, 1984-85 to 1986-87; Kirk Muller, 1987-88 to 1990-91; Bruce Driver, 1991-92; Scott Stevens, 1992-93 to 2002-03; Scott Stevens and Scott Neidermayer, 2003-04; no captain, 2005-06; Patrik Elias, 2006-07 to date.

Coaching History

Bep Guidolin, 1974-75; Bep Guidolin, Sid Abel and Eddie Bush, 1975-76; Johnny Wilson, 1976-77; Pat Kelly, 1977-78; Pat Kelly and Aldo Guidolin, 1978-79; Don Cherry, 1979-80; Bill MacMillan, 1980-81; Bert Marshall and Marshall Johnston, 1981-82; Bill MacMillan, 1982-83; Bill MacMillan and Tom McVie, 1983-84; Doug Carpenter, 1984-85 to 1986-87; Doug Carpenter and Jim Schoenfeld, 1987-88; Jim Schoenfeld, 1988-89; Jim Schoenfeld and John Cunniff, 1989-90; John Cunniff and Tom McVie, 1990-91; Tom McVie, 1991-92; Herb Brooks, 1992-93; Jacques Lemaire, 1993-94 to 1997-98; Robbie Ftorek, 1998-99; Robbie Ftorek and Larry Robinson, 1999-2000; Larry Robinson, 2000-01; Larry Robinson and Kevin Constantine, 2001-02; Pat Burns, 2002-03 to 2004-05; Larry Robinson and Lou Lamoriello, 2005-06; Claude Julien and Lou Lamoriello, 2006-07; Brent Sutter, 2007-08.

Club Records

Team

(Figures in brackets for season records are games played; records for fewest points, wins, ties, losses, goals, goals against are for 70 or more games)

Record		
Most Points	**111**	2000-01 (82)
Most Wins	**49**	2006-07 (82)
Most Ties	**21**	1977-78 (80)
Most Losses	**56**	1975-76 (80), 1983-84 (80)
Most Goals	**308**	1992-93 (84)
Most Goals Against	**374**	1985-86 (80)
Fewest Points	***36**	1975-76 (80)
	41	1983-84 (80)
Fewest Wins	***12**	1975-76 (80)
	17	1982-83 (80), 1983-84 (80)
Fewest Ties	**3**	1985-86 (80)
Fewest Losses	**19**	2000-01 (82)
Fewest Goals	***184**	1974-75 (80)
	205	2001-02 (82)
Fewest Goals Against	**164**	2003-04 (82)
Longest Winning Streak		
Overall	**13**	Feb. 26-Mar. 23/01
Home	**8**	Oct. 9-Nov. 7/87, Jan. 3-Feb. 4/03, Jan. 3-Feb. 7/06
Away	****10**	Feb. 27-Apr. 7/01
Longest Undefeated Streak		
Overall	**13**	Four times
Home	**15**	Jan. 8-Mar. 15/97 (9 wins, 6 ties)
Away	**10**	Feb. 27-Apr. 7/01 (10 wins)
Longest Losing Streak		
Overall	***14**	Dec. 30/75-Jan. 29/76
	10	Oct. 14-Nov. 4/83
Home	**9**	Dec. 22/85-Feb. 6/86
Away	**12**	Oct. 19-Dec. 1/83
Longest Winless Streak		
Overall	***27**	Feb. 12-Apr. 4/76 (21 losses, 6 ties)
	18	Oct. 20-Nov. 26/82 (14 losses 4 ties)
Home	***14**	Feb. 12-Mar. 30/76 (10 losses, 4 ties), Feb. 4-Mar. 31/79 (12 losses, 2 ties)
	9	Dec. 22/85-Feb. 6/86 (9 losses)
Away	***32**	Nov. 12/77-Mar. 15/78 (22 losses, 10 ties)
	14	Dec. 26/82-Mar. 5/83 (13 losses, 1 tie)
Most Shutouts, Season	**14**	2003-04 (82)
Most PIM, Season	**2,494**	1988-89 (80)
Most Goals, Game	**9**	Nine times

Individual

Record		
Most Seasons	**20**	Ken Daneyko
Most Games	**1,283**	Ken Daneyko
Most Goals, Career	**347**	John MacLean
Most Assists, Career	**364**	Scott Niedermayer
Most Points, Career	**701**	John MacLean (347G, 354A)
Most PIM, Career	**2,519**	Ken Daneyko
Most Shutouts, Career	**92**	Martin Brodeur
Longest Consecutive Games Streak	**388**	Ken Daneyko (Nov. 4/89-Mar. 29/94)
Most Goals, Season	**48**	Brian Gionta (2005-06)
Most Assists, Season	**60**	Scott Stevens (1993-94)
Most Points, Season	**96**	Patrik Elias (2000-01; 40G, 56A)
Most PIM, Season	**295**	Krzysztof Oliwa (1997-98)
Most Points, Defenseman, Season	**78**	Scott Stevens (1993-94; 18G, 60A)
Most Points, Center, Season	**94**	Kirk Muller (1987-88; 37G, 57A)
Most Points, Right Wing, Season	**89**	Brian Gionta (2005-06; 48G, 41A)
Most Points, Left Wing, Season	**96**	Patrik Elias (2000-01; 40G, 56A)
Most Points, Rookie, Season	**70**	Scott Gomez (1999-2000; 19G, 51A)
Most Shutouts, Season	**12**	Martin Brodeur (2006-07)
Most Goals, Game	**4**	Five times
Most Assists, Game	**5**	Greg Adams (Oct. 10/85), Kirk Muller (Mar. 25/87), Tom Kurvers (Feb. 13/89), Scott Gomez (Mar. 30/03)
Most Points, Game	**6**	Kirk Muller (Nov. 29/86; 3G, 3A)

* Records include Kansas City Scouts and Colorado Rockies, 1974-75 through 1981-82.

** NHL Record.

General Managers' History

Sid Abel, 1974-75, 1975-76; Ray Miron, 1976-77 to 1980-81; Bill MacMillan, 1981-82, 1982-83; Bill MacMillan and Max McNab, 1983-84; Max McNab 1984-85 to 1986-87; Lou Lamoriello, 1987-88 to date.

Retired Numbers

3	Ken Daneyko	1982-2003
4	Scott Stevens	1991-2005

All-time Record vs. Other Clubs

Regular Season

	At Home								On Road								Total							
	GP	W	L	T	OL	GF	GA	PTS	GP	W	L	T	OL	GF	GA	PTS	GP	W	L	T	OL	GF	GA	PTS
Anaheim	8	7	1	0	0	31	14	14	11	5	5	1	0	28	30	11	19	12	6	1	0	59	44	25
Atlanta	14	7	4	1	2	40	29	17	14	7	3	2	2	50	33	18	28	14	7	3	4	90	62	35
Boston	57	18	28	11	0	150	181	47	60	20	30	8	2	187	230	50	117	38	58	19	2	337	411	97
Buffalo	58	22	27	9	0	173	185	53	58	17	33	8	0	175	225	42	116	39	60	17	0	348	410	95
Calgary	46	15	28	3	0	129	166	33	42	6	27	8	1	111	184	21	88	21	55	11	1	240	350	54
Carolina	49	27	18	4	0	167	155	58	48	21	18	8	1	144	146	51	97	48	36	12	1	311	301	109
Chicago	48	21	16	11	0	149	143	53	47	13	24	10	0	130	178	36	95	34	40	21	0	279	321	89
Colorado	37	19	13	4	1	150	125	43	35	13	18	4	0	98	124	30	72	32	31	8	1	248	249	73
Columbus	3	2	0	1	0	6	4	5	5	2	2	0	1	15	16	5	8	4	2	1	1	21	20	10
Dallas	43	21	19	3	0	146	132	45	46	13	26	6	1	118	167	33	89	34	45	9	1	264	299	78
Detroit	41	21	11	9	0	139	105	51	41	13	25	2	1	131	169	29	82	34	36	11	1	270	274	80
Edmonton	34	15	16	3	0	113	113	33	31	11	14	6	0	114	136	28	65	26	30	9	0	227	249	61
Florida	28	18	7	3	0	85	54	39	29	16	9	4	0	77	65	36	57	34	16	7	0	162	119	75
Los Angeles	43	19	19	5	0	142	148	43	43	8	27	6	2	132	204	24	86	27	46	11	2	274	352	67
Minnesota	4	3	0	1	0	16	10	7	3	1	1	1	0	8	7	3	7	4	1	2	0	24	17	10
Montreal	58	29	25	4	0	177	200	62	58	19	32	6	1	146	188	45	116	48	57	10	1	323	388	107
Nashville	6	2	3	0	1	18	18	5	6	5	1	0	0	18	12	10	12	7	4	0	1	36	30	15
NY Islanders	92	39	40	11	2	297	314	91	93	24	56	11	2	265	367	61	185	63	96	22	4	562	681	152
NY Rangers	94	51	35	7	1	319	295	110	92	27	43	20	2	275	344	76	186	78	78	27	3	594	639	186
Ottawa	27	16	9	2	0	76	64	34	28	17	7	3	1	71	64	38	55	33	16	5	1	147	128	72
Philadelphia	91	50	33	8	0	309	294	108	93	28	54	10	1	239	347	67	184	78	87	18	1	548	641	175
Phoenix	29	12	11	6	0	95	87	30	32	7	22	3	0	82	117	17	61	19	33	9	0	177	204	47
Pittsburgh	89	44	31	13	1	323	289	102	87	40	42	4	1	292	314	85	176	84	73	17	2	615	603	187
St. Louis	47	22	18	7	0	148	131	51	47	13	26	7	1	148	195	34	94	35	44	14	1	296	326	85
San Jose	12	7	4	1	0	44	24	15	11	6	3	1	1	32	26	14	23	13	7	2	1	76	50	29
Tampa Bay	30	19	7	2	2	106	61	42	29	14	8	5	2	86	65	35	59	33	15	7	4	192	126	77
Toronto	50	18	15	15	2	171	156	53	52	13	34	5	0	144	191	31	102	31	49	20	2	315	347	84
Vancouver	50	21	21	6	2	154	159	50	47	9	27	11	0	130	175	29	97	30	48	17	2	284	334	79
Washington	83	42	33	7	1	256	237	92	83	28	49	6	0	238	317	62	166	70	82	13	1	494	554	154
Defunct Clubs	8	4	2	2	0	25	19	10	8	2	3	3	0	19	27	7	16	6	5	5	0	44	46	17
Totals	**1279**	**611**	**494**	**159**	**15**	**4154**	**3912**	**1396**	**1279**	**418**	**669**	**169**	**23**	**3703**	**4663**	**1028**	**2558**	**1029**	**1163**	**328**	**38**	**7857**	**8575**	**2424**

Playoffs

	Series	W	L	GP	W	L	T	GF	GA	Last Mtg.	Rnd.	Result
Anaheim	1	1	0	7	4	3	0	19	12	2003	F	W 4-3
Boston	4	3	1	23	15	8	0	68	60	2003	CQF	W 4-1
Buffalo	1	1	0	7	4	3	0	14	14	1994	CQF	W 4-3
Carolina	3	1	2	17	7	10	0	41	34	2006	CSF	L 1-4
Colorado	1	0	1	7	3	4	0	11	19	2001	F	L 3-4
Dallas	1	1	0	6	4	2	0	15	9	2000	F	W 4-2
Detroit	1	1	0	4	4	0	0	16	7	1995	F	W 4-0
Florida	1	1	0	4	4	0	0	12	6	2000	CQF	W 4-0
Montreal	1	1	0	5	4	1	0	22	11	1997	CQF	W 4-1
NY Islanders	1	1	0	6	4	2	0	23	18	1988	DSF	W 4-2
NY Rangers	4	1	3	23	11	12	0	63	60	2006	CQF	W 4-0
Ottawa	3	1	2	18	7	11	0	40	41	2007	CSF	L 1-4
Philadelphia	4	2	2	20	9	11	0	50	49	2004	CQF	L 1-4
Pittsburgh	5	2	3	29	15	14	0	86	80	2001	CF	W 4-1
Tampa Bay	2	2	0	11	8	3	0	33	22	2007	CQF	W 4-2
Toronto	2	2	0	13	8	5	0	37	27	2001	CSF	W 4-3
Washington	2	1	1	13	6	7	0	43	44	1990	DSF	L 2-4
Totals	**37**	**22**	**15**	**213**	**117**	**96**	**0**	**593**	**513**			

Calgary totals include Atlanta Flames, 1974-75 to 1979-80.
Colorado totals include Quebec, 1979-80 to 1994-95.
Phoenix totals include Winnipeg, 1979-80 to 1995-96.
Carolina totals include Hartford, 1979-80 to 1996-97.
Dallas totals include Minnesota North Stars, 1974-75 to 1992-93.

Playoff Results 2007-2002

Year	Round	Opponent	Result	GF	GA
2007	CSF	Ottawa	L 1-4	11	15
	CQF	Tampa Bay	W 4-2	19	14
2006	CSF	Carolina	L 1-4	10	17
	CQF	NY Rangers	W 4-0	17	4
2004	CQF	Philadelphia	L 1-4	9	14
2003	**F**	**Anaheim**	**W 4-3**	**19**	**12**
	CF	Ottawa	W 4-3	17	13
	CSF	Tampa Bay	W 4-1	14	8
	CQF	Boston	W 4-1	13	8
2002	CQF	Carolina	L 2-4	11	9

Abbreviations: Round: F – Final; **CF** – conference final; **CSF** – conference semi-final; **CQF** – conference quarter-final; **DSF** – division semi-final.

2006-07 Results

Month	Day	Opponent	Score	Month	Day	Opponent	Score
Oct.	6	at Carolina	4-0		7	at Montreal	3-0
	7	at Dallas	1-3		10	St. Louis	2-3
	12	Toronto	7-6†		12	Atlanta	2-1
	14	Philadelphia	3-2		13	at NY Islanders	2-1*
	16	at NY Rangers	2-4		16	NY Rangers	1-0
	18	at Pittsburgh	2-1		18	Tampa Bay	2-3†
	19	Nashville	3-4†		20	Philadelphia	4-3†
	21	at Ottawa	1-8		26	at Tampa Bay	2-0
	24	at Pittsburgh	2-4		27	at Florida	2-4
	26	Florida	2-0		30	at Atlanta	4-5†
	28	Columbus	1-0	**Feb.**	1	at Philadelphia	6-5*
Nov.	2	NY Islanders	2-5		3	Buffalo	3-2
	4	at Montreal	2-1		6	NY Rangers	3-2†
	7	Carolina	3-2†		8	NY Islanders	2-0
	9	Chicago	2-1†		11	Tampa Bay	1-4
	11	Florida	4-2		14	Montreal	5-2
	14	at NY Rangers	2-3		16	Pittsburgh	4-5
	17	Ottawa	3-2		17	at NY Islanders	2-0
	18	at Toronto	2-1		20	NY Rangers	2-1
	22	at Phoenix	1-3		22	at NY Rangers	3-2†
	24	at Anaheim	2-4		24	Washington	2-4
	25	at San Jose	0-2		25	at Washington	3-2
	27	at Los Angeles	2-3†		27	at Pittsburgh	1-0
Dec.	1	Pittsburgh	5-2	**Mar.**	2	Toronto	3-4†
	2	at Philadelphia	4-3†		4	Boston	1-4
	6	Montreal	2-1*		6	at Philadelphia	4-5*
	8	Philadelphia	2-0		8	at Pittsburgh	4-3†
	9	at Boston	5-1		10	at Buffalo	3-2
	12	Buffalo	2-3		14	Pittsburgh	0-3
	14	at Boston	3-5		15	at Carolina	3-2
	16	Detroit	1-2		17	Carolina	2-7
	17	at NY Rangers	6-1		20	at Toronto	1-2
	19	Atlanta	3-4†		22	at Tampa Bay	1-3
	22	at Washington	4-1		24	at Florida	4-3†
	23	at Atlanta	2-5		27	at NY Islanders	3-2
	26	Pittsburgh	3-0		28	at Buffalo	3-4
	29	Washington	4-3		30	Philadelphia	3-1
	30	at NY Islanders	2-0	**Apr.**	1	Boston	3-1
Jan.	2	NY Rangers	2-3†		3	Ottawa	2-1†
	4	NY Islanders	4-3		5	at Philadelphia	3-2
	6	at Ottawa	3-2		8	NY Islanders	2-3†

* – Overtime † – Shootout

Entry Draft Selections 2007-1993

2007
Pick
57 Mike Hoeffel
79 Nick Palmieri
87 Corbin McPherson
117 Matt Halischuk
177 Vili Sopanen
207 Ryan Molle

2006
Pick
30 Matthew Corrente
58 Alexander Vasyunov
67 Kirill Tulupov
77 Vladimir Zharkov
107 T.J. Miller
148 Olivier Magnan
178 Tony Romano
208 Kyell Henegan

2005
Pick
23 Nicklas Bergfors
38 Jeff Frazee
84 Mark Fraser
99 Patrick Davis
155 Mark Fayne
170 Sean Zimmerman
218 Alexander Sundstrom

2004
Pick
20 Travis Zajac
155 Alexander Mikhailishin
185 Josh Disher
216 Pierre-Luc Letourneau-Leblond
217 Tyler Eckford
250 Nathan Perkovich
282 Valeri Klimov

2003
Pick
17 Zach Parise
42 Petr Vrana
93 Ivan Khomutov
167 Zach Tarkir
197 Jason Smith
261 Joey Tenute
292 Arseny Bondarev

2002
Pick
51 Anton Kadeykin
53 Barry Tallackson
64 Jason Ryznar
84 Marek Chvatal
85 Ahren Nittel
117 Cam Janssen
154 Krisjanis Redlihs
187 Eric Johansson
218 Ilkka Pikkarainen
250 Dan Glover
281 Bill Kinkel

2001
Pick
28 Adrian Foster
44 Igor Pohanka
48 Tuomas Pihlman
60 Victor Uchevatov
67 Robin Leblanc
72 Brandon Nolan
128 Andrei Posnov
163 Andreas Salomonsson
194 James Massen
229 Aaron Voros
257 Yevgeny Gamalei

2000
Pick
22 David Hale
39 Teemu Laine
56 Alexander Suglobov
57 Matt DeMarchi
62 Paul Martin
67 Max Birbraer
76 Mike Rupp
125 Phil Cole
135 Mike Danton
164 Matus Kostur
194 Deryk Engelland
198 Ken Magowan
257 Warren McCutcheon

1999
Pick
27 Ari Ahonen
42 Mike Commodore
50 Brett Clouthier
95 Andre Lakos
100 Teemu Kesa
185 Scott Cameron
214 Chris Hartsburg
242 Justin Dziama

1998
Pick
26 Mike Van Ryn
27 Scott Gomez
37 Christian Berglund
82 Brian Gionta
96 Mikko Jokela
105 Pierre Dagenais
119 Anton But
143 Ryan Flinn
172 Jacques Lariviere
199 Erik Jensen
227 Marko Ahosilta
257 Ryan Held

1997
Pick
24 Jean-Francois Damphousse
38 Stanislav Gron
104 Lucas Nehrling
131 Jiri Bicek
159 Sascha Goc
188 Mathieu Benoit
215 Scott Clemmensen
241 Jan Srdinko

1996
Pick
10 Lance Ward
38 Wes Mason
41 Josh DeWolf
47 Pierre Dagenais
49 Colin White
63 Scott Parker
91 Josef Boumedienne
101 Josh MacNevin
118 Glenn Crawford
145 Sean Ritchlin
173 Daryl Andrews
199 Willie Mitchell
205 Jay Bertsch
225 Pasi Petrilainen

1995
Pick
18 Petr Sykora
44 Nathan Perrott
70 Sergei Vyshedkevich
78 David Gosselin
79 Alyn McCauley
96 Henrik Rehnberg
122 Chris Mason
148 Adam Young
174 Richard Rochefort
200 Frederic Henry
226 Colin O'Hara

1994
Pick
25 Vadim Sharifijanov
51 Patrik Elias
71 Sheldon Souray
103 Zdenek Skorepa
129 Christian Gosselin
134 Ryan Smart
155 Luciano Caravaggio
181 Jeff Williams
207 Eric Bertrand
233 Steve Sullivan
259 Scott Swanjord
269 Mike Hanson

1993
Pick
13 Denis Pederson
32 Jay Pandolfo
39 Brendan Morrison
65 Krzysztof Oliwa
110 John Guirestante
143 Steve Brule
169 Nikolai Zavarukhin
195 Thomas Cullen
221 Judd Lambert
247 Jimmy Provencher
273 Mike Legg

Coach

BRENT SUTTER

Coach, New Jersey Devils. Born in Viking, Alta., June 10, 1962.

The New Jersey Devils named Brent Sutter to the position of head coach on July 13, 2007. He is the 14th coach since the club moved to New Jersey in 1982, but became the third new coach in as many seasons.

Sutter joined the Devils after spending the previous eight seasons as owner, president, general manager and coach of Red Deer of the Western Hockey League. Sutter guided Red Deer to its first league title and the Memorial Cup championship in 2001, and three consecutive WHL Eastern Conference championships from 2001 to 2003. He was the recipient of the 2001 Dunc McCallum Memorial Trophy as the league's top coach. Sutter has also coached internationally, guiding the Canadian national junior team to consecutive 6-0-0 marks and gold medals in 2005 and 2006, becoming the only individual to accomplish that feat.

Brent Sutter is the third youngest of seven Sutter brothers, six of whom played in the NHL. (His son Brandon was Carolina's first choice, 11th overall, in the 2007 NHL Entry Draft.) Brent's NHL playing career spanned 18 seasons with the New York Islanders and Chicago Blackhawks. A center, he recorded 363 goals and 466 assists for 829 points and 1,054 penalty minutes in 1,111 career regular-season games. Sutter added 30 goals and 44 assists for 74 points and 164 penalty minutes in 144 career playoff games.

Along with his brother Duane, he was a member of the Islanders' 1982 and 1983 Stanley Cup championship teams, and served as captain from 1987 through 1991. Sutter was traded to Chicago on October 25, 1991 and played seven more seasons, including three years for his brother Darryl. Sutter retired as a player on April 18, 1998. He was originally the Islanders' first choice, 17th overall, in the 1980 NHL Entry Draft.

Coaching Record

		Regular Season				Playoffs		
Season	Team	Games	W	L	O/T	Games	W	L
1999-00	Red Deer (WHL)	72	32	31	9	4	0	4
2000-01	Red Deer (WHL)	72	54	12	6	22	16	6
2001-02	Red Deer (WHL)	72	46	18	8	23	14	9
2002-03	Red Deer (WHL)	72	50	17	5	23	14	9
2003-04	Red Deer (WHL)	72	35	22	15	19	10	9
2004-05	Red Deer (WHL)	72	36	26	10	7	3	4
2005-06	Red Deer (WHL)	72	26	40	6	....	....	....
2006-07	Red Deer (WHL)	72	35	28	9	7	3	4

Club Directory

Prudential Center

New Jersey Devils
Prudential Center
165 Mulberry Street
Newark, NJ 07102
Phone **973/757-6100**
FAX 973/757-6399
www.newjerseydevils.com
Capacity: 17,625

Chairman/Managing Partner ... Jeff Vanderbeek
CEO/President/General Manager ... Louis A. Lamoriello
Sr. Executive Vice President/Chief Operating Officer ... Chris Modrzynski
Executive Vice President, Operations ... Peter S. McMullen
Executive Vice President/Chief Financial Officer ... Scott Struble
Executive Vice President, Administration ... Gordon Lavalette
Senior Vice President, General Counsel ... Joseph C. Benedetti
Senior Vice President, Ticket Operations ... Terry Farmer
Senior Vice President, Corporate Partnerships ... Kenneth F. Ferriter
Senior Vice President, Facilities ... Mark Gheduzzi
Senior Vice President, Communications ... Mike Levine
Vice President, Ticket Sales/Customer Service ... David Beck
Vice President, Marketing/Community Development ... Sandra van Meek

Hockey Club Personnel
Exec. V.P., Hockey Operations/Director, Scouting ... David Conte
Sr. V.P., Hockey Ops./G.M., Lowell/Trenton & Scout ... Chris Lamoriello
Vice President, Hockey Operations ... Steve Pellegrini
Head Coach ... Brent Sutter
Assistant Coaches ... Larry Robinson, John MacLean, Tommy Albelin
Goaltending Coach ... Jacques Caron
Consulting Coach ... Scott Stevens
Assistant Director, Scouting ... Claude Carrier
Scouting Staff ... Glen Dirk, Milt Fisher, Ferny Flaman, Dan Labraaten, Pierre Mondou, Larry Perris, Marcel Pronovost, Lou Reycroft, Vaclav Slansky, Jr., Steve Smith, Geoff Stevens, Tim Taylor, Ed Thomlinson, Les Widdifield
Pro Scouting Staff ... Bob Hoffmeyer, Jan Ludvig, Andre Boudrias, Gates Orlando
Special Assignments ... Pat Burns, Jacques Laperriere
Hockey Operations Video Coordinator ... Taran Singleton
Hockey Operations Video Assistant ... Mike Ford
Scouting Staff Assistant ... Callie A. Smith
Head Trainer ... Brent Smith
Assistant Trainer ... Richard Stinziano
Equipment Manager ... Rich Matthews
Assistant Equipment Managers ... Alex Abasto, Matt Mitchell
Strength/Conditioning Coordinator ... Michael Vasalani
Massage Therapist ... Tommy Plasko
Team Orthopedists ... Dr. Barry Fisher, Dr. Len Jaffe
Team Cardiologist ... Dr. Joseph Niznik
Team Dentist ... Dr. H. Hugh Gardy
Team Optometrist ... Dr. Paul Berman
Fitness Consultant ... Vladimir Bure
Exercise Physiologist ... Dr. Garret Caffrey
Physical Therapist ... David Feniger
Video Consultant ... Mitch Kaufman
Head Coach, Lowell ... Kurt Kleinendorst
Assistant Coach, Lowell ... Kevin Dean
Goaltending Coach, Lowell ... Chris Terreri
Video Coordinator, Lowell ... Lawrence Feloney
Assistant Equipment Manager, Lowell ... Mike Thibault

President's Office
Hockey Ops. Exec. Asst. to CEO/Pres./G.M. ... Marie Carnevale
Corporate Exec. Asst. to CEO/Pres./G.M. and Director, Human Resources ... Mary K. Morrison
Administrative Assistant ... Christine DellaBarca
Assistant General Counsel ... Daniel Pupel
Legal Assistant ... Lourdes Garcia

Operations
Receptionist ... Jelsa Belotta
Staff Assistants ... Pat Maione, Amanda Brown

Ticket Operations
Director/Manager, Ticket Operations ... Tom Bates/Andrea Marchesani, Frank Calandrillo
Director/Manager, Group Sales ... Neil Desormeaux/John Tierney

Sales
Assistant Director, Ticket Sales ... Brooke Alper
Account Managers ... Kelly Baron, Richard Bello, Mark Gennarelli, Kevin Levy, Colleen McClellan, Kris Rinaldi, Aaron Sanders, Glenn Sperber, Thomas Stocky
Receptionist, Sales ... Jessica Leschen

Corporate Partnerships
Director, Corporate Partnerships ... Michael DeMartino
Director, Corporate Partner Services ... Matt Dugan
Account Manager, Corporate Partnerships ... Greg Parassio

Marketing/Community Development
Director, Merchandising ... David Perricone
Manager, Merchandising ... Adam Manger
Director, Grassroots Programs ... Michael Merolla
Coordinator, Grassroots Programs ... Jason Romano
Director, Game Entertainment ... John Bochiaro
Manager, Game Entertainment ... David Schwinger
Coordinator, Game Entertainment ... Carley Simpson
Coordinator, Web Operations/Creative Services ... Greg Orlando
Administrative Assistant ... Heather Hall

Communications
Director, Communications ... Jeff Altstadter
Assistant Director, Communications ... Pete Albietz
Staff Assistant ... Daniel Beam
Copywriter ... Eric Marin

Finance
Controller ... Marc Weiss
Staff Accountants ... Mario Deludicibus, Kristin Farina, Joe Pannia, Daria Rodrigues, Michael Tonjes
Administrative Assistant ... Kristen Gore

Computer Operations
Director, Programming/Computer Operations ... Jack Skelley
Programmer/Analyst ... Joseph Wyks
Systems Administrator ... Mike Tukes
Technical Assistant ... Antonio da Silva

Alumni Representatives ... Ken Daneyko, Bruce Driver, Rob Skrlac

Devils Renaissance Development
Senior Vice President, Development ... Jim Cima
Dir., Security & Head, Govt. Relations ... Les Wiser
Business Coordinator ... Kim Rossi
Financial Analyst ... David Steinfeld
Staff Attorney ... Tim Lamoriello

Television/Radio
Television ... FOX Sports Net New York – Mike Emrick, Play-by-Play; Glenn Resch, Color
Radio ... Sports Radio 66 WFAN – Matt Loughlin, Play-by-Play; TBA, Color

Key Off-Season Signings/Acquisitions

2007

May 8 • Re-signed G **Wade Dubielewicz**.
July 1 • Signed RW **Jon Sim**.
4 • Signed LW **Ruslan Fedotenko**.
5 • Signed RW **Bill Guerin** and RW **Mike Comrie**.
12 • Signed D **Aaron Johnson**.
13 • Named **Gerard Gallant** and **John Chabot** assistant coaches.
16 • Re-signed D **Chris Campoli**.
23 • Re-signed LW **Chris Simon**.
Aug. 3 • RW **Trent Hunter** awarded one-year contract in arbitration.
10 • Signed D **Andy Sutton**.

New York Islanders

2006-07 Results: 40W-30L-7OTL-5SOL 92PTS.
Fourth, Atlantic Division

With a career-high 32 wins in 2006-07, Rick DiPietro became the first goalie in Islanders history with two 30-win seasons. He also set a franchise record with 56 saves in a game against the Rangers on March 5, 2007.

2007-08 Schedule

Month	Day	Date	Opponent
Oct.	Fri.	5	at Buffalo
	Sat.	6	Buffalo
	Mon.	8	Washington*
	Wed.	10	NY Rangers
	Thu.	11	at Toronto
	Sat.	13	at Philadelphia
	Thu.	18	at Washington
	Sat.	20	New Jersey
	Sat.	27	Carolina
Nov.	Thu.	1	Tampa Bay
	Sat.	3	Pittsburgh
	Tue.	6	NY Rangers
	Sat.	10	New Jersey
	Mon.	12	at Philadelphia
	Thu.	15	at Pittsburgh
	Fri.	16	at New Jersey
	Mon.	19	at NY Rangers
	Wed.	21	Montreal
	Fri.	23	at Boston*
	Sat.	24	Boston
	Mon.	26	Dallas
	Wed.	28	Ottawa
	Thu.	29	at NY Rangers
Dec.	Sat.	1	Atlanta
	Mon.	3	Boston
	Wed.	5	at Atlanta
	Fri.	7	at Florida
	Sat.	8	at Tampa Bay
	Wed.	12	at Buffalo
	Thu.	13	Phoenix
	Sat.	15	Pittsburgh
	Wed.	19	Buffalo
	Fri.	21	at Pittsburgh
	Sat.	22	Washington
	Wed.	26	Toronto
	Thu.	27	at Ottawa
	Sat.	29	New Jersey
	Mon.	31	at Carolina
Jan.	Thu.	3	Florida
	Sat.	5	at Colorado
	Mon.	7	at Edmonton
	Tue.	8	at Vancouver
	Fri.	11	at Calgary
	Sun.	13	at Ottawa
	Tue.	15	Montreal
	Wed.	16	at New Jersey
	Sat.	19	Philadelphia
	Mon.	21	Carolina*
	Tue.	22	at Carolina
	Thu.	24	at Boston
	Tue.	29	Ottawa
	Thu.	31	Los Angeles
Feb.	Sat.	2	at Montreal*
	Tue.	5	Anaheim
	Thu.	7	at Pittsburgh
	Sat.	9	at Minnesota*
	Tue.	12	Philadelphia
	Thu.	14	at Toronto
	Sat.	16	Atlanta
	Mon.	18	San Jose*
	Wed.	20	at Washington
	Thu.	21	Tampa Bay
	Sat.	23	at New Jersey*
	Tue.	26	Pittsburgh
	Thu.	28	at Atlanta
Mar.	Sat.	1	Philadelphia*
	Sun.	2	Florida*
	Tue.	4	at NY Rangers
	Thu.	6	NY Rangers
	Sat.	8	at Philadelphia
	Tue.	11	at Tampa Bay
	Wed.	12	at Florida
	Sat.	15	at Montreal
	Tue.	18	Toronto
	Fri.	21	at New Jersey
	Sun.	23	at Philadelphia
	Mon.	24	Pittsburgh
	Thu.	27	at Pittsburgh
	Sat.	29	Philadelphia
Apr.	Tue.	1	New Jersey
	Thu.	3	NY Rangers
	Fri.	4	at NY Rangers

* Denotes afternoon game.

Year-by-Year Record

		Home				Road				Overall								
Season	**GP**	**W**	**L**	**T**	**OL**	**W**	**L**	**T**	**OL**	**W**	**L**	**T**	**OL**	**GF**	**GA**	**Pts.**	**Finished**	**Playoff Result**
2006-07	82	22	13	....	6	18	17	....	6	40	30	....	12	248	240	92	4th, Atlantic Div.	Lost Conf. Quarter-Final
2005-06	82	20	18	....	3	16	22	....	3	36	40	....	6	230	278	78	4th, Atlantic Div.	Out of Playoffs
2004-05	....	....	....	....	....	....	....	....	....	....	....	....	....	....	....	....		
2003-04	82	25	11	4	1	13	18	7	3	38	29	11	4	237	210	91	3rd, Atlantic Div.	Lost Conf. Quarter-Final
2002-03	82	18	18	5	0	17	16	6	2	35	34	11	2	224	231	83	3rd, Atlantic Div.	Lost Conf. Quarter-Final
2001-02	82	21	13	5	2	21	15	3	2	42	28	8	4	239	220	96	2nd, Atlantic Div.	Lost Conf. Quarter-Final
2000-01	82	12	27	1	1	9	24	6	2	21	51	7	3	185	268	52	5th, Atlantic Div.	Out of Playoffs
1999-2000	82	10	25	5	1	14	23	4	0	24	48	9	1	194	275	58	5th, Atlantic Div.	Out of Playoffs
1998-99	82	11	23	7	....	13	25	3	....	24	48	10	....	194	244	58	5th, Atlantic Div.	Out of Playoffs
1997-98	82	17	20	4	....	13	21	7	....	30	41	11	....	212	225	71	4th, Atlantic Div.	Out of Playoffs
1996-97	82	19	18	4	....	10	23	8	....	29	41	12	....	240	250	70	7th, Atlantic Div.	Out of Playoffs
1995-96	82	14	21	6	....	8	29	4	....	22	50	10	....	229	315	54	7th, Atlantic Div.	Out of Playoffs
1994-95	48	10	11	3	....	5	17	2	....	15	28	5	....	126	158	35	7th, Atlantic Div.	Out of Playoffs
1993-94	84	23	15	4	....	13	21	8	....	36	36	12	....	282	264	84	4th, Atlantic Div.	Lost Conf. Quarter-Final
1992-93	84	20	19	3	....	20	18	4	....	40	37	7	....	335	297	87	3rd, Patrick Div.	Lost Conf. Championship
1991-92	80	20	15	5	....	14	20	6	....	34	35	11	....	291	299	79	5th, Patrick Div.	Out of Playoffs
1990-91	80	15	19	6	....	10	26	4	....	25	45	10	....	223	290	60	6th, Patrick Div.	Out of Playoffs
1989-90	80	15	17	8	....	16	21	3	....	31	38	11	....	281	288	73	4th, Patrick Div.	Lost Div. Semi-Final
1988-89	80	19	18	3	....	9	29	2	....	28	47	5	....	265	325	61	6th, Patrick Div.	Out of Playoffs
1987-88	80	24	10	6	....	15	21	4	....	39	31	10	....	308	267	88	1st, Patrick Div.	Lost Div. Semi-Final
1986-87	80	20	15	5	....	15	18	7	....	35	33	12	....	279	281	82	3rd, Patrick Div.	Lost Div. Final
1985-86	80	22	11	7	....	17	18	5	....	39	29	12	....	327	284	90	3rd, Patrick Div.	Lost Div. Semi-Final
1984-85	80	26	11	3	....	14	23	3	....	40	34	6	....	345	312	86	3rd, Patrick Div.	Lost Div. Final
1983-84	80	28	11	1	....	22	15	3	....	50	26	4	....	357	269	104	1st, Patrick Div.	Lost Final
1982-83	**80**	**26**	**11**	**3**	....	**16**	**15**	**9**	....	**42**	**26**	**12**	....	**302**	**226**	**96**	**2nd, Patrick Div.**	**Won Stanley Cup**
1981-82	**80**	**33**	**3**	**4**	....	**21**	**13**	**6**	....	**54**	**16**	**10**	....	**385**	**250**	**118**	**1st, Patrick Div.**	**Won Stanley Cup**
1980-81	**80**	**23**	**6**	**11**	....	**25**	**12**	**3**	....	**48**	**18**	**14**	....	**355**	**260**	**110**	**1st, Patrick Div.**	**Won Stanley Cup**
1979-80	**80**	**26**	**9**	**5**	....	**13**	**19**	**8**	....	**39**	**28**	**13**	....	**281**	**247**	**91**	**2nd, Patrick Div.**	**Won Stanley Cup**
1978-79	80	31	3	6	....	20	12	8	....	51	15	14	....	358	214	116	1st, Patrick Div.	Lost Semi-Final
1977-78	80	29	3	8	....	19	14	7	....	48	17	15	....	334	210	111	1st, Patrick Div.	Lost Quarter-Final
1976-77	80	24	11	5	....	23	10	7	....	47	21	12	....	288	193	106	2nd, Patrick Div.	Lost Semi-Final
1975-76	80	24	8	8	....	18	13	9	....	42	21	17	....	297	190	101	2nd, Patrick Div.	Lost Semi-Final
1974-75	80	22	6	12	....	11	19	10	....	33	25	22	....	264	221	88	3rd, Patrick Div.	Lost Semi-Final
1973-74	78	13	17	9	....	6	24	9	....	19	41	18	....	182	247	56	8th, East Div.	Out of Playoffs
1972-73	78	10	25	4	....	2	35	2	....	12	60	6	....	170	347	30	8th, East Div.	Out of Playoffs

ATLANTIC DIVISION
36th NHL Season

Franchise date: June 6, 1972

2007-08 Player Personnel

FORWARDS	HT	WT	S	Place of Birth	*Age	2006-07 Club
BATES, Shawn	6-0	210	R	Melrose, MA	32	NY Islanders
BERGENHEIM, Sean	5-10	194	L	Helsinki, Finland	23	Yaroslavl-Frolunda
BOOTLAND, Darryl	6-1	197	R	Toronto, Ont.	25	Detroit-Grand Rapids
BRENNAN, Kip	6-4	230	L	Kingston, Ont.	27	Her-Tor (AHL)-Long Beach
COMEAU, Blake	6-1	207	R	Meadow Lake, Sask.	21	NY Islanders-Bridgeport
COMRIE, Mike	5-10	185	L	Edmonton, Alta.	27	Phoenix-Ottawa
FEDOTENKO, Ruslan	6-2	195	L	Kiev, USSR	28	Tampa Bay
GUERIN, Bill	6-2	220	R	Worcester, MA	36	St. Louis-San Jose
HILBERT, Andy	5-11	194	L	Lansing, MI	26	NY Islanders
HUNTER, Trent	6-3	210	R	Red Deer, Alta.	27	NY Islanders
JACKMAN, Tim	6-4	210	R	Minot, ND	25	Los Angeles-Manchester
NIELSEN, Frans	5-11	172	L	Herning, Denmark	23	NY Islanders-Bridgeport
PARK, Richard	5-11	190	R	Seoul, South Korea	31	NY Islanders
SATAN, Miroslav	6-3	191	L	Topolcany, Czech.	32	NY Islanders
SILLINGER, Mike	5-11	198	R	Regina, Sask.	36	NY Islanders
SIM, Jon	5-10	195	L	New Glasgow, N.S.	30	Atlanta
SIMON, Chris	6-4	235	L	Wawa, Ont.	35	NY Islanders
TAMBELLINI, Jeff	5-11	186	L	Calgary, Alta.	23	NY Islanders-Bridgeport
DEFENSEMEN						
BERGERON, Marc-Andre	5-10	197	L	St-Louis-de-France, Que.	26	Edmonton-NY Islanders
CAMPOLI, Chris	5-11	190	L	North York, Ont.	23	NY Islanders-Bridgeport
FATA, Drew	6-1	211	L	Sault Ste. Marie, Ont.	24	NY Islanders-Bridgeport
GERVAIS, Bruno	6-0	188	R	Longueuil, Que.	22	NY Islanders-Bridgeport
JOHNSON, Aaron	6-2	211	L	Port Hawkesbury, N.S.	24	Columbus
MARTINEK, Radek	5-11	200	R	Havlickuv Brod, Czech.	31	NY Islanders
MEYER, Freddy	5-10	192	L	Sanbornville, NH	26	Philadelphia-NY Islanders
SUTTON, Andy	6-6	245	L	Kingston, Ont.	32	Atlanta
WITT, Brendan	6-2	223	L	Humboldt, Sask.	32	NY Islanders
GOALTENDERS	**HT**	**WT**	**C**	**Place of Birth**	***Age**	**2006-07 Club**
DiPIETRO, Rick	6-1	210	R	Winthrop, MA	26	NY Islanders
DUBIELEWICZ, Wade	5-10	185	L	Invermere, B.C.	29	NY Islanders-Bridgeport
MacDONALD, Joey	6-0	197	L	Pictou, N.S.	27	Detroit-Grand Rapids-Boston

* – Age at start of 2007-08 season

Coach

TED NOLAN

Coach, New York Islanders. Born in Sault Ste. Marie, Ont., April 7, 1958.

Hired as head coach by the New York Islanders on June 8, 2006, Ted Nolan has been a coaching success at every level of professional and amateur hockey, having reached the pinnacle when he was awarded the Jack Adams Award as NHL coach of the year for his work with the Buffalo Sabres in 1996-97. Nolan is noted for his ability to motivate and teach and he has a knack for drawing the most from the talent available on his teams. In 2006-07, Nolan guided the Islanders back into the playoffs after having failed to qualify the year before.

After an eight-year absence from competitive coaching, Nolan returned with a sterling debut as head coach and director of hockey operations for the Moncton Wildcats of the Quebec Major Junior Hockey League in 2005-06. He introduced 14 new players to the team, and led Moncton to its first President Cup as QMJHL champion, finishing first overall in the regular season at 52-15-3. The Wildcats advanced to the finals of the Memorial Cup (Canadian Junior championship) where they finished runner-up to Patrick Roy's Quebec Remparts.

Born on the Garden River First Nation Reserve just outside of Sault Ste. Marie, Ontario, Nolan is a member of the First Nations Ojibway tribe. Following his time in Buffalo, Nolan devoted himself to First Nations causes, including teaching hockey to First Nations children. His work in this area earned him the National Aboriginal Achievement Award, the Sault Ste. Marie Medal of Merit and the Order of Ontario.

As a player, Nolan skated for the Ontario Hockey Association's Sault Ste. Marie Greyhounds, the Kansas City Red Wings of the Central Hockey League, and the Adirondack Red Wings, Rochester Americans and Baltimore Skipjacks of the American Hockey League. He also played for the Pittsburgh Penguins and the Detroit Red Wings of the National Hockey League between 1981-82 and 1985-86. He became head coach of the Sault Ste. Marie Greyhounds in 1988, as a midseason replacement and coached there until the end of the 1994 season. Nolan led the Greyhounds to three consecutive Memorial Cup tournament berths, winning the Canadian national junior championship in 1993.

The Hartford Whalers hired Nolan before the 1994 regular season as an assistant coach for one season before accepting the position of head coach of the Buffalo Sabres where he had his best success. In his second season in Buffalo, he led the team to a strong regular season, culminating in the Northeast Division title. He was rewarded with the Jack Adams Award as the league's top coach.

Coaching Record

		Regular Season				Playoffs		
Season	Team	Games	W	L	O/T	Games	W	L
1988-89	S.S. Marie (OHL)	38	12	25	1	....	....	....
1989-90	S.S. Marie (OHL)	66	18	42	6	....	....	....
1990-91	S.S. Marie (OHL)	66	42	21	3	14	12	2
1991-92	S.S. Marie (OHL)	66	41	19	6	19	12	7
1992-93	S.S. Marie (OHL)	66	38	23	5	18	13	5
1993-94	S.S. Marie (OHL)	66	35	24	7	14	10	4
1995-96	**Buffalo (NHL)**	**82**	**33**	**42**	**7**	....	....	....
1996-97	**Buffalo (NHL)**	**82**	**40**	**30**	**12**	**12**	**5**	**7**
2005-06	Moncton (QMJHL)	70	52	15	3	21	16	5
2006-07	**NY Islanders (NHL)**	**82**	**40**	**30**	**12**	**5**	**1**	**4**
	NHL Totals	**246**	**113**	**102**	**31**	**17**	**6**	**11**

2006-07 Scoring

* – rookie

Regular Season

Pos	#	Player	Team	GP	G	A	Pts	+/–	PIM	PP	SH	GW	S	%
L	55	Jason Blake	NYI	82	40	29	69	1	34	14	0	7	305	13.1
L	94	Ryan Smyth	EDM	53	31	22	53	2	38	14	1	5	161	19.3
			NYI	18	5	10	15	0	14	1	0	0	49	10.2
			TOTAL	71	36	32	68	2	52	15	1	5	210	17.1
R	81	Miroslav Satan	NYI	81	27	32	59	–12	46	7	1	2	216	12.5
C	18	Mike Sillinger	NYI	82	26	33	59	5	46	11	2	3	152	17.1
C	25	Viktor Kozlov	NYI	81	25	26	51	12	28	5	0	4	165	15.2
C	79	Alexei Yashin	NYI	58	18	32	50	6	44	5	0	3	203	8.9
D	47	Marc-Andre Bergeron	EDM	55	8	17	25	–9	28	6	0	3	111	7.2
			NYI	23	6	15	21	5	10	4	0	1	55	10.9
			TOTAL	78	14	32	46	–4	38	10	0	4	166	8.4
D	3	Tom Poti	NYI	78	6	38	44	–1	74	6	0	1	134	4.5
C	27	Randy Robitaille	PHI	28	5	12	17	–4	22	2	0	0	46	10.9
			NYI	50	6	17	23	–2	22	1	0	1	74	8.1
			TOTAL	78	11	29	40	–6	44	3	0	1	120	9.2
R	7	Trent Hunter	NYI	77	20	15	35	5	22	5	1	2	168	11.9
C	11	Andy Hilbert	NYI	81	8	20	28	10	34	0	0	1	164	4.9
L	12	Chris Simon	NYI	67	10	17	27	17	75	2	0	0	82	12.2
C	10	Richard Park	NYI	82	10	16	26	4	33	0	2	2	93	10.8
D	6	Sean Hill	NYI	81	1	24	25	6	110	0	0	0	88	1.1
R	45	Arron Asham	NYI	80	11	12	23	3	63	0	0	2	85	12.9
R	20	Richard Zednik	WSH	32	6	12	18	–4	16	1	0	1	68	8.8
			NYI	10	1	2	3	–2	2	0	0	0	15	6.7
			TOTAL	42	7	14	21	–6	18	1	0	1	83	8.4
D	24	Radek Martinek	NYI	43	2	15	17	19	40	0	0	0	44	4.5
D	14	Chris Campoli	NYI	51	1	13	14	–3	23	0	0	0	41	2.4
D	32	Brendan Witt	NYI	81	1	13	14	14	131	0	0	0	75	1.3
C	17	Shawn Bates	NYI	48	4	6	10	13	34	0	1	0	50	8.0
L	15 *	Jeff Tambellini	NYI	23	2	7	9	6	6	0	0	0	20	10.0
D	44	Freddy Meyer	PHI	25	2	3	5	–4	14	1	0	0	27	7.4
			NYI	35	0	3	3	0	24	0	0	0	14	0.0
			TOTAL	60	2	6	8	–4	38	1	0	0	41	4.9
D	8	Bruno Gervais	NYI	51	0	6	6	–10	28	0	0	0	47	0.0
C	51 *	Frans Nielsen	NYI	15	1	1	2	–2	0	0	0	1	16	6.3
D	49 *	Drew Fata	NYI	3	1	0	1	–2	5	0	0	0	1	100.0
D	38	Allan Rourke	NYI	11	0	1	1	0	4	0	0	0	1	0.0
C	27 *	Jeremy Colliton	NYI	1	0	0	0	–1	0	0	0	0	0	0.0
L	48 *	Steve Regier	NYI	1	0	0	0	0	0	0	0	0	0	0.0
R	57 *	Blake Comeau	NYI	3	0	0	0	0	0	0	0	0	1	0.0
D	21	Deron Quint	NYI	5	0	0	0	0	0	0	0	0	2	0.0
R	33	Eric Boguniecki	NYI	11	0	0	0	0	8	0	0	0	2	0.0

Goaltending

No.	Goaltender	GPI	Mins	Avg	W	L	OT	EN	SO	GA	SA	S%	G	A	PIM
34	Wade Dubielewicz	8	379	2.06	4	1	0	1	0	13	198	.934	0	0	0
39	Rick DiPietro	62	3627	2.58	32	19	9	2	5	156	1917	.919	0	2	24
1	Mike Dunham	19	979	3.74	4	10	3	2	0	61	552	.889	0	1	0
	Totals	**82**	**5009**	**2.81**	**40**	**30**	**12**	**5**	**5**	**235**	**2672**	**.912**			

Playoffs

Pos	#	Player	Team	GP	G	A	Pts	+/–	PIM	PP	SH	GW	OT	S	%
L	94	Ryan Smyth	NYI	5	1	3	4	1	4	0	0	0	0	9	11.1
R	7	Trent Hunter	NYI	5	3	0	3	1	0	0	0	0	0	10	30.0
R	81	Miroslav Satan	NYI	5	1	2	3	0	0	0	0	0	0	10	10.0
L	55	Jason Blake	NYI	5	1	2	3	–2	2	0	0	0	0	14	7.1
D	3	Tom Poti	NYI	5	0	3	3	0	6	0	0	0	0	4	0.0
C	18	Mike Sillinger	NYI	5	1	1	2	–1	2	1	0	0	0	10	10.0
D	47	Marc-Andre Bergeron	NYI	5	1	1	2	1	6	1	0	1	0	13	7.7
D	14	Chris Campoli	NYI	5	1	1	2	–1	2	0	0	0	0	2	50.0
D	8	Bruno Gervais	NYI	5	1	1	2	–2	2	0	0	0	0	9	11.1
C	25	Viktor Kozlov	NYI	5	0	2	2	–2	2	0	0	0	0	11	0.0
C	27	Randy Robitaille	NYI	5	0	2	2	–5	8	0	0	0	0	8	0.0
R	45	Arron Asham	NYI	5	1	0	1	–3	0	0	0	0	0	5	20.0
D	32	Brendan Witt	NYI	5	0	1	1	–3	6	0	0	0	0	2	0.0
C	10	Richard Park	NYI	5	0	1	1	0	2	0	0	0	0	6	0.0
D	49 *	Drew Fata	NYI	1	0	0	0	–2	0	0	0	0	0	0	0.0
D	6	Sean Hill	NYI	4	0	0	0	–1	0	0	0	0	0	3	0.0
C	79	Alexei Yashin	NYI	5	0	0	0	0	0	0	0	0	0	7	0.0
R	20	Richard Zednik	NYI	5	0	0	0	–1	8	0	0	0	0	3	0.0
C	11	Andy Hilbert	NYI	5	0	0	0	–1	2	0	0	0	0	8	0.0

Goaltending

No.	Goaltender	GPI	Mins	Avg	W	L	EN	SO	GA	SA	S%	G	A	PIM
39	Rick DiPietro	4	236	3.31	1	3	0	0	13	127	.898	0	0	0
34	Wade Dubielewicz	1	59	4.07	0	1	0	0	4	35	.886	0	0	0
	Totals	**5**	**300**	**3.40**	**1**	**4**	**0**	**0**	**17**	**162**	**.895**			

Coaching History

Phil Goyette and Earl Ingarfield, 1972-73; Al Arbour, 1973-74 to 1985-86; Terry Simpson, 1986-87, 1987-88; Terry Simpson and Al Arbour, 1988-89; Al Arbour, 1989-90 to 1993-94; Lorne Henning, 1994-95; Mike Milbury, 1995-96; Mike Milbury and Rick Bowness, 1996-97; Rick Bowness and Mike Milbury, 1997-98; Mike Milbury and Bill Stewart, 1998-99; Butch Goring, 1999-2000; Butch Goring and Lorne Henning, 2000-01; Peter Laviolette, 2001-02, 2002-03; Steve Stirling, 2003-04, 2004-05; Steve Stirling and Brad Shaw, 2005-06; Ted Nolan, 2006-07 to date.

Club Records

Team

(Figures in brackets for season records are games played; records for fewest points, wins, ties, losses, goals, goals against are for 70 or more games)

Most Points **118** 1981-82 (80)
Most Wins **54** 1981-82 (80)
Most Ties **22** 1974-75 (80)
Most Losses **60** 1972-73 (78)
Most Goals **385** 1981-82 (80)
Most Goals Against **347** 1972-73 (78)
Fewest Points **30** 1972-73 (78)
Fewest Wins **12** 1972-73 (78)
Fewest Ties **4** 1983-84 (80)
Fewest Losses **15** 1978-79 (80)
Fewest Goals **170** 1972-73 (78)
Fewest Goals Against **190** 1975-76 (80)
Longest Winning Streak
Overall .... **15** Jan. 21-Feb. 20/82
Home .... **14** Jan. 2-Feb. 25/82
Away .... **8** Feb. 27-Mar. 29/81
Longest Undefeated Streak
Overall .... **15** Three times
Home .... **23** Oct. 17/78-Jan. 20/79 (19 wins, 4 ties), Jan. 2-Apr. 3/82 (21 wins, 2 ties)
Away .... **8** Three times
Longest Losing Streak
Overall .... **12** Dec. 27/72-Jan. 16/73, Nov. 22-Dec. 15/88
Home .... **7** Nov. 13-Dec. 14/99
Away .... **15** Jan. 20-Mar. 31/73
Longest Winless Streak
Overall .... **15** Nov. 22-Dec. 21/72 (12 losses, 3 ties)
Home .... **9** Mar. 2-Apr. 6/99 (7 losses, 2 ties)
Away .... **20** Nov. 3/72-Jan. 13/73 (19 losses, 1 tie)
Most Shutouts, Season **10** 1975-76 (80)
Most PIM, Season **1,857** 1986-87 (80)
Most Goals, Game .... **11** Dec. 20/83 (Pit. 3 at NYI 11), Mar. 3/84 (NYI 11 at Tor. 6)

Individual

Most Seasons .... **17** Billy Smith
Most Games .... **1,123** Bryan Trottier
Most Goals, Career .... **573** Mike Bossy
Most Assists, Career .... **853** Bryan Trottier
Most Points, Career .... **1,353** Bryan Trottier (500G, 853A)
Most PIM, Career .... **1,879** Mick Vukota
Most Shutouts, Career .... **25** Glenn Resch
Longest Consecutive Games Streak .... **576** Billy Harris (Oct. 7/72-Nov. 30/79)
Most Goals, Season .... **69** Mike Bossy (1978-79)
Most Assists, Season .... **87** Bryan Trottier (1978-79)
Most Points, Season .... **147** Mike Bossy (1981-82; 64G, 83A)
Most PIM, Season .... **356** Brian Curran (1986-87)
Most Points, Defenseman, Season .... **101** Denis Potvin (1978-79; 31G, 70A)
Most Points, Center, Season .... **134** Bryan Trottier (1978-79; 47G, 87A)
Most Points, Right Wing, Season .... **147** Mike Bossy (1981-82; 64G, 83A)
Most Points, Left Wing, Season .... **100** John Tonelli (1984-85; 42G, 58A)
Most Points, Rookie, Season .... **95** Bryan Trottier (1975-76; 32G, 63A)
Most Shutouts, Season .... **7** Glenn Resch (1975-76)
Most Goals, Game .... **5** Bryan Trottier (Dec. 23/78, Feb. 13/82), John Tonelli (Jan. 6/81)
Most Assists, Game .... **6** Mike Bossy (Jan. 6/81)
Most Points, Game .... **8** Bryan Trottier (Dec. 23/78; 5G, 3A)

Captains' History

Ed Westfall, 1972-73 to 1975-76; Ed Westfall and Clark Gillies, 1976-77; Clark Gillies, 1977-78, 1978-79; Denis Potvin, 1979-80 to 1986-87; Brent Sutter, 1987-88 to 1990-91; Brent Sutter and Pat Flatley, 1991-92; Pat Flatley, 1992-93 to 1995-96; no captain, 1996-97; Bryan McCabe and Trevor Linden, 1997-98; Trevor Linden, 1998-99; Kenny Jonsson, 1999-2000, 2000-01; Michael Peca, 2001-02 to 2003-04; Alexei Yashin, 2005-06, 2006-07; Bill Guerin, 2007-08.

Retired Numbers

5	Denis Potvin	1973-1988
9	Clark Gillies	1974-1986
19	Bryan Trottier	1975-1990
22	Mike Bossy	1977-1987
23	Bob Nystrom	1972-1986
31	Billy Smith	1972-1989

All-time Record vs. Other Clubs

Regular Season

	At Home								On Road								Total							
	GP	W	L	T	OL	GF	GA	PTS	GP	W	L	T	OL	GF	GA	PTS	GP	W	L	T	OL	GF	GA	PTS
Anaheim	8	4	3	1	0	24	23	9	10	5	2	3	0	29	22	13	18	9	5	4	0	53	45	22
Atlanta	14	8	6	0	0	52	33	16	14	8	3	2	1	55	41	19	28	16	9	2	1	107	74	35
Boston	65	28	27	10	0	219	206	66	63	19	31	11	2	179	232	51	128	47	58	21	2	398	438	117
Buffalo	65	28	27	9	1	184	182	66	65	20	35	9	1	176	218	50	130	48	62	18	2	360	400	116
Calgary	52	26	17	9	0	194	145	61	49	14	24	11	0	145	172	39	101	40	41	20	0	339	317	100
Carolina	48	23	21	4	0	143	131	50	49	19	25	5	0	155	169	43	97	42	46	9	0	298	300	93
Chicago	48	19	14	15	0	168	143	53	49	18	26	5	0	164	163	41	97	37	40	20	0	332	306	94
Colorado	33	19	13	1	0	134	113	39	34	11	20	3	0	97	123	25	67	30	33	4	0	231	236	64
Columbus	3	1	2	0	0	11	11	2	5	0	3	1	1	10	17	2	8	1	5	1	1	21	28	4
Dallas	48	26	14	8	0	176	134	60	48	22	18	8	0	173	139	52	96	48	32	16	0	349	273	112
Detroit	47	23	18	4	2	167	141	52	46	18	26	2	0	137	166	38	93	41	44	6	2	304	307	90
Edmonton	32	16	7	9	0	131	112	41	29	8	16	5	0	87	107	21	61	24	23	14	0	218	219	62
Florida	29	15	12	2	0	78	78	32	29	10	13	6	0	90	92	26	58	25	25	8	0	168	170	58
Los Angeles	44	24	15	5	0	156	123	53	46	17	22	7	0	145	167	41	90	41	37	12	0	301	290	94
Minnesota	4	2	2	0	0	9	10	4	3	1	2	0	0	9	9	2	7	3	4	0	0	18	19	6
Montreal	64	32	26	6	0	198	179	70	64	16	39	9	0	178	230	41	128	48	65	15	0	376	409	111
Nashville	5	2	2	0	1	12	14	5	6	2	4	0	0	17	16	4	11	4	6	0	1	29	30	9
New Jersey	93	58	23	11	1	367	265	128	92	42	36	11	3	314	297	98	185	100	59	22	4	681	562	226
NY Rangers	104	57	37	8	2	388	332	124	104	35	57	11	1	309	380	82	208	92	94	19	3	697	712	206
Ottawa	28	5	16	6	1	86	108	17	27	5	17	5	0	67	95	15	55	10	33	11	1	153	203	32
Philadelphia	106	53	38	15	0	377	314	121	103	34	58	11	0	292	363	79	209	87	96	26	0	669	677	200
Phoenix	30	13	9	8	0	113	91	34	31	15	12	4	0	108	102	34	61	28	21	12	0	221	193	68
Pittsburgh	94	51	32	8	3	373	312	113	96	37	43	14	2	335	363	90	190	88	75	22	5	708	675	203
St. Louis	50	25	13	11	1	185	134	62	48	21	17	9	1	159	169	52	98	46	30	20	2	344	303	114
San Jose	11	5	4	2	0	40	35	12	13	6	6	1	0	40	32	13	24	11	10	3	0	80	67	25
Tampa Bay	29	13	14	1	1	85	83	28	30	12	13	2	3	89	82	29	59	25	27	3	4	174	165	57
Toronto	57	33	20	3	1	221	164	70	59	24	30	4	1	197	207	53	116	57	50	7	2	418	371	123
Vancouver	48	26	12	10	0	175	137	62	47	21	23	3	0	153	155	45	95	47	35	13	0	328	292	107
Washington	85	46	37	2	0	317	261	94	85	32	40	11	2	265	279	77	170	78	77	13	2	582	540	171
Defunct Clubs	13	11	0	2	0	75	33	24	13	4	5	4	0	35	41	12	26	15	5	6	0	110	74	36
Totals	**1357**	**692**	**481**	**170**	**14**	**4858**	**4047**	**1568**	**1357**	**496**	**666**	**177**	**18**	**4209**	**4648**	**1187**	**2714**	**1188**	**1147**	**347**	**32**	**9067**	**8695**	**2755**

Playoffs

	Series	W	L	GP	W	L	T	GF	GA	Last Mtg.	Rnd.	Result
Boston	2	2	0	11	8	3	0	49	35	1983	CF	W 4-2
Buffalo	4	3	1	21	13	8	0	70	62	2007	CQF	L 1-4
Chicago	2	2	0	6	6	0	0	21	6	1979	QF	W 4-0
Colorado	1	1	0	4	4	0	0	18	9	1982	CF	W 4-0
Dallas	1	1	0	5	4	1	0	26	16	1981	F	W 4-1
Edmonton	3	2	1	15	9	6	0	58	47	1984	F	L 1-4
Los Angeles	1	1	0	4	3	1	0	21	10	1980	PRE	W 3-1
Montreal	4	1	3	22	8	14	0	55	64	1993	CF	L 1-4
New Jersey	1	0	1	6	2	4	0	18	23	1988	DSF	L 2-4
NY Rangers	8	5	3	39	20	19	0	129	132	1994	CQF	L 0-4
Ottawa	1	0	1	5	1	4	0	7	13	2003	CQF	L 1-4
Philadelphia	4	1	3	25	11	14	0	69	83	1987	DF	L 3-4
Pittsburgh	3	3	0	19	11	8	0	67	58	1993	DF	W 4-3
Tampa Bay	1	0	1	5	1	4	0	5	12	2004	CQF	L 1-4
Toronto	3	1	2	17	9	8	0	54	42	2002	CQF	L 3-4
Vancouver	2	2	0	6	6	0	0	26	14	1982	F	W 4-0
Washington	6	5	1	30	18	12	0	99	88	1993	DSF	W 4-2
Totals	**47**	**30**	**17**	**240**	**134**	**106**	**0**	**792**	**714**			

Calgary totals include Atlanta Flames, 1972-73 to 1979-80.
Carolina totals include Hartford, 1979-80 to 1996-97.
Colorado totals include Quebec, 1979-80 to 1994-95.
Dallas totals include Minnesota North Stars, 1972-73 to 1992-93.
New Jersey totals include Kansas City, 1974-75, 1975-76, and Colorado Rockies, 1976-77 to 1981-82.
Phoenix totals include Winnipeg, 1979-80 to 1995-96.

Playoff Results 2007-2002

Year	Round	Opponent	Result	GF	GA
2007	CQF	Buffalo	L 1-4	11	17
2004	CQF	Tampa Bay	L 1-4	5	12
2003	CQF	Ottawa	L 1-4	7	13
2002	CQF	Toronto	L 3-4	21	22

Abbreviations: Round: F – Final; **CF** – conference final; **CQF** – conference quarter-final; **DF** – division final; **DSF** – division semi-final; **QF** – quarter-final; **PRE** – preliminary round.

2006-07 Results

Oct.	5	at Phoenix	3-6
	7	at San Jose	0-2
	10	at Los Angeles	2-4
	11	at Anaheim	5-4†
	14	Boston	4-1
	16	Nashville	1-2†
	19	Pittsburgh	3-4*
	21	Carolina	4-3*
	26	Buffalo	0-3
	28	Florida	4-3†
	31	Chicago	5-2
Nov.	2	at New Jersey	5-2
	4	Atlanta	1-4
	6	Tampa Bay	1-5
	9	at Philadelphia	3-1
	15	at Dallas	3-0
	17	at Tampa Bay	2-3†
	18	at Florida	4-1
	20	at Toronto	2-4
	22	Carolina	4-2
	24	Pittsburgh	3-1
	25	Washington	4-1
	28	at Pittsburgh	2-3
	30	Philadelphia	2-3
Dec.	2	at Pittsburgh	5-3
	3	at NY Rangers	7-4
	5	Ottawa	2-4
	7	Montreal	2-4
	9	Florida	5-4†
	15	at Pittsburgh	4-7
	16	Atlanta	6-0
	19	at NY Rangers	4-3
	22	at Carolina	1-5
	23	Columbus	4-0
	26	NY Rangers	2-0
	27	at Ottawa	0-2
	30	New Jersey	0-2
Jan.	1	at Buffalo	1-3
	2	Philadelphia	2-3
	4	at New Jersey	3-4
	6	at Carolina	2-4
	9	at NY Rangers	5-3
	11	at Boston	5-4†
	13	New Jersey	1-2*
	15	Tampa Bay	3-4
	16	at Pittsburgh	2-5
	18	at Philadelphia	4-2
	26	at Atlanta	4-5*
	27	Buffalo	5-3
	30	Detroit	3-4*
Feb.	1	at Atlanta	5-2
	3	at Montreal	4-2
	4	at Washington	1-2†
	7	Philadelphia	2-0
	8	at New Jersey	0-2
	10	at Boston	3-4†
	13	at Toronto	3-2†
	15	Boston	4-1
	17	New Jersey	0-2
	19	Pittsburgh	6-5
	22	Toronto	3-2†
	24	Montreal	3-2
	27	Philadelphia	6-5*
Mar.	1	St. Louis	2-3*
	3	at Washington	6-2
	5	at NY Rangers	1-2†
	8	NY Rangers	1-2
	10	Washington	5-2
	13	at Montreal	3-5
	15	at Ottawa	2-5
	17	at Florida	5-8
	20	at Tampa Bay	3-4*
	22	Pittsburgh	3-1
	24	at Philadelphia	4-3
	25	NY Rangers	1-2*
	27	New Jersey	2-3
	30	at Buffalo	4-6
	31	Ottawa	2-5
Apr.	3	NY Rangers	3-2†
	5	Toronto	5-2
	7	at Philadelphia	4-2
	8	at New Jersey	3-2†

* – Overtime † – Shootout

Entry Draft Selections 2007-1993

2007

Pick	
62	Mark Katic
76	Jason Gregoire
106	Maxim Gratchev
166	Blake Kessel
196	Simon Lacroix

2006

Pick	
7	Kyle Okposo
60	Jesse Joensuu
70	Robin Figren
100	Rhett Rakhshani
108	Jase Weslosky
115	Tomas Marcinko
119	Doug Rogers
126	Shane Sims
141	Kim Johansson
160	Andrew Macdonald
171	Brian Day
173	Stefan Ridderwall
190	Troy Mattila

2005

Pick	
15	Ryan O'Marra
46	Dustin Kohn
76	Shea Guthrie
144	Masi Marjamaki
180	Tyrell Mason
196	Nicholas Tuzzolino
210	Luciano Aquino

2004

Pick	
16	Petteri Nokelainen
47	Blake Comeau
82	Sergei Ogorodnikov
115	Wes O'Neill
148	Steve Regier
179	Jaroslav Mrazek
210	Emil Axelsson
227	Chris Campoli
244	Jason Pitton
276	Sylvain Michaud

2003

Pick	
15	Robert Nilsson
48	Dmitri Chernykh
53	Evgeny Tunik
58	Jeremy Colliton
120	Stefan Blaho
182	Bruno Gervais
212	Denis Rehak
238	Cody Blanshan
246	Igor Volkov

2002

Pick	
22	Sean Bergenheim
87	Frans Nielsen
149	Marcus Paulsson
189	Alexei Stonkus
220	Brad Topping
252	Martin Chabada
283	Per Braxenholm

2001

Pick	
101	Cory Stillman
132	Dusan Salficky
166	Andy Chiodo
197	Jan Holub
228	Mike Bray
260	Bryan Perez
280	Roman Kuhtinov
287	Juha-Pekka Ketola

2000

Pick	
1	Rick DiPietro
5	Raffi Torres
101	Arto Tukio
105	Vladimir Gorbunov
136	Dmitri Upper
148	Kristofer Ottosson
202	Ryan Caldwell
264	Dmitri Altarev
267	Tomi Pettinen

1999

Pick	
5	Tim Connolly
8	Taylor Pyatt
10	Branislav Mezei
28	Kristian Kudroc
78	Mattias Weinhandl
87	Brian Collins
101	Juraj Kolnik
102	Johan Halvardsson
130	Justin Mapletoft
140	Adam Johnson
163	Bjorn Melin
228	Radek Martinek
255	Brett Henning
268	Tyler Scott

1998

Pick	
9	Mike Rupp
36	Chris Nielsen
95	Andy Burnham
123	Jiri Dopita
155	Kevin Clauson
182	Evgeny Korolev
209	Frederik Brindamour
237	Ben Blais
242	Jason Doyle
250	Radek Matejovsky

1997

Pick	
4	Roberto Luongo
5	Eric Brewer
31	Jeff Zehr
59	Jarrett Smith
79	Robert Schnabel
85	Petr Mika
115	Adam Edinger
139	Bobby Leavins
166	Kris Knoblauch
196	Jeremy Symington
222	Ryan Clark

1996

Pick	
3	J.P. Dumont
29	Dan LaCouture
56	Zdeno Chara
83	Tyrone Garner
109	Bubba Berenzweig
128	Petr Sachl
138	Todd Miller
165	J.R. Prestifilippo
192	Evgeny Korolev
218	Mike Muzechka

1995

Pick	
2	Wade Redden
28	Jan Hlavac
41	D.J. Smith
106	Vladimir Orszagh
158	Andrew Taylor
210	David MacDonald
211	Mike Broda

1994

Pick	
9	Brett Lindros
38	Jason Holland
63	Jason Strudwick
90	Brad Lukowich
112	Mark McArthur
116	Albert O'Connell
142	Jason Stewart
194	Mike Loach
203	Peter Hogardh
220	Gord Walsh
246	Kirk Dewaele
272	Dick Tarnstrom

1993

Pick	
23	Todd Bertuzzi
40	Bryan McCabe
66	Vladimir Chebaturkin
92	Warren Luhning
118	Tommy Salo
144	Peter LeBoutillier
170	Darren Van Impe
196	Rod Hinks
222	Daniel Johansson
248	Stephane Larocque
274	Carl Charland

General Managers' History

Bill Torrey, 1972-73 to 1991-92; Don Maloney, 1992-93 to 1994-95; Don Maloney and Mike Milbury, 1995-96; Mike Milbury, 1996-97 to 2005-06; Neil Smith and Garth Snow, 2006-07; Garth Snow, 2007-08.

General Manager

GARTH SNOW
General Manager, New York Islanders. Born in Wrentham, MA, July 28, 1969.

Former Islanders' goaltender Garth Snow retired as a player on July 18, 2006 to become the fifth general manager of the New York Islanders. In his first season as general manager, Snow successfully bolstered the lineup with several key additions, the most notable being his deal with Edmonton for Ryan Smyth just minutes before the trade deadline. The moves helped to propel the Islanders into the postseason for the first time since the 2003–04 season and earned Snow the title of NHL Executive of the Year from *Sports Illustrated*.

Snow spent four seasons with the Islanders and 12 in the NHL. The goaltender was 135-147-44 with a 2.80 goals-against average and .901 save percentage over 368 games with Quebec, Philadelphia, Vancouver, Pittsburgh and the Islanders. Originally selected in the sixth round by Quebec in the 1987 NHL Entry Draft, the native of Wrentham, Mass. signed with the Islanders as a free agent on July 1, 2001.

Club Directory

Nassau Veterans' Memorial Coliseum

New York Islanders
Executive Office
1535 Old Country Rd.
Plainview, NY 11803
Phone **516/501-6700**
FAX 516/501-6850
www.newyorkislanders.com
Arena
Nassau Veterans' Memorial Coliseum
Uniondale, NY 11553
Capacity: 16,234

Owner & Governor . . . Charles B. Wang

Operations
Sr. V.P./Chief Financial Officer and Alt. Gov. . . . Art McCarthy
Sr. V.P., Sales, Marketing & Operations & Alt. Gov. . . Chris Dey
General Manager & Alt. Gov. . . . Garth Snow
Sr. V.P., Public Relations and Special Projects . . . Paul Lancey

Hockey Operations
Executive Director of Player Development . . . Bryan Trottier
Assistant G.M./Director of Amateur Scouting . . . Ryan Jankowski
Director of Pro Scouting . . . Ken Morrow
Manager, Hockey Administration . . . Joanne Holewa
Assistant to the General Manager . . . Kerry Gwydir
Head Coach . . . Ted Nolan
Assistant Coaches . . . Gerard Gallant, John Chabot, Dan Lacroix
Equipment Manager . . . Scott Boggs
Assistant Equipment Manager . . . Richard Krouse
Equipment Assistant . . . Tom Kitz
Head Athletic Trainer . . . Garrett Timms
Assistant Athletic Trainer . . . Nates Goto
Strength & Conditioning Coach . . . Graham Black
Chief European Scout . . . Vellu-Pekka Kautonen
Pro Scouts . . . Anders Kallur, Rob Cowie, Tim Maclean, Chris O'Sullivan, Mario Saraceno, Jad Ramsey
Video Coordinator . . . Mike LaZazzera

Administration
General Counsel & Alternate Governor . . . Roy Reichbach
Assistant General Counsel . . . Jaimie Wolf
Staff Attorney . . . Ivy Shen
Human Resources Manager . . . Mary Molloy
Office Manager . . . John Lyons
Internship Coordinator . . . Michele Calabrese
IT Manager . . . Pawel Tauter
Receptionist . . . Bonnie Dreher

Sales and Marketing
Vice President of Corporate Partnerships . . . Dave Decina
Exec. Director of Corporate Relations . . . Mike Bossy
Sr. Director of Sales, Corporate Partnerships . . . Sean Argaman
Directors of Sales, Corporate Partnerships . . . Chris Lombardo, Bob Moran
Director of Corporate Partnerships . . . Larry Goldman
Assistant to Sr. V.P, Sales, Mktg. & Ops. . . . Eileen Brett
Assistant to V.P., Sales, Corp. Partnerships . . . Lori Ogden
Business Dev. & Corporate Suites Manager . . . Catie Bennett
Corporate Partnership Manager . . . Michelle Winter
Sales Executive, Corporate Partnerships . . . Kevin Waters
Corporate Partnerships Coordinator . . . Mike Matranga
Director of Marketing . . . Jackie Bronfeld
Marketing Coordinator/Assistant . . . Gabrielle Raymond, Adam Sherlip
Director of Retail Operations . . . Terry Goldstein
Merchandise Assistant . . . Colleen Carolan
Manager, Islanders Team Store . . . Monica Mantello
Sales Managers, Group Tickets . . . Adam Jacobs, Cliff Gault
Sales Executives, Group Tickets . . . Christine Myers, J.J. Molesso
Senior Sales Executives, Tickets . . . Steve Beisel, Bryan Davis, Marc Gerstein, Jeff Guida
Sales Executives, Tickets . . . Mike Surrey, Eddie Fisher, T.J. Carpenter, Keith Mitchell, Rich Pascullo, Matt Lazarus, Ariel Greenberg, Theresa Coscia, Larry Fitzpatrick, Stan Pesner, Bob Barra, Joseph Cirillo
Director of Customer Service . . . Kerry Cornils
Customer Service Representatives . . . Sara Pesserillo, Nicholas Tullo
Director of Operations, Events, Promotions . . . Ken Zore
Events & Promotions Manager . . . Dana Cipriano
Events & Promotions Coordinator . . . Ann Rina
Operations Coordinator . . . Andy Jacklin
Alumni Coordinator/Operations Asst. . . . Steve Webb

Media Relations/Communications
Vice President, Media Relations . . . Chris Botta
Media Relations Coordinator . . . Corey Witt
Website/Publications Coordinator . . . Jason Lockhart
Office Assistant . . . Todd Aronovich

Game Operations
V.P., Game Operations and Events . . . Tim Beach
Game Operations Manager . . . Mike Sciortino
Avid Editor . . . Brian Jones

Finance
Controller . . . Ralph Sellitti
Assistant Controllers . . . Marina Pi, Thomas Earvolino
Payroll Manager/Assistant . . . Christine Bowler, Michelle Finkelstein
Accounts Payable . . . Janet Nelson
Staff Accountants . . . Laura Ferritti, Chris Vardaro, Michelle Tubens, Jennifer Penning
Ticket Manager/Asst. Manager . . . Adam Ortiz, Karen Stepnowski

Marketing Services
Director of Marketing Services . . . Jessica Sousa-Tuttle
Creative Services Manager . . . Thomas Rakoczy
Marketing Account Manager . . . Suzanne Keller
Copywriter . . . Andrew Miller
Video Production Manager . . . Susan Schopp
Graphic Designer . . . John Tomaselli

Islanders TV
Vice President, Communications . . . Josh Bernstein
Producers . . . Victor Francois, Matt Holota, Steve Tronzano, Laura Marciano
Associate Producer . . . Matthew Riccardi

New York Rangers

2006-07 Results: 42W-30L-5OTL-5SOL 94PTS.
Third, Atlantic Division

Key Off-Season Signings/Acquisitions

2007

July 1 • Signed C **Chris Drury** and C **Scott Gomez**.
2 • Re-signed D **Jason Strudwick**.
5 • Re-signed RW **Petr Prucha**.
10 • Re-signed LW **Brendan Shanahan**.
11 • Re-signed G **Henrik Lundqvist**.
17 • Acquired D **Andrew Hutchinson**, C **Joe Barnes** and a 3rd-round pick in the 2008 Entry Draft from Carolina for C **Matt Cullen**.
31 • Re-signed LW **Marcel Hossa**.
Aug. 1 • LW **Sean Avery** awarded one-year contract in arbitration.

2007-08 Schedule

Month	Day	Date	Opponent	Month	Day	Date	Opponent
Oct.	Thu.	4	Florida		Sat.	5	at Edmonton
	Sat.	6	at Ottawa		Tue.	8	Tampa Bay
	Wed.	10	at NY Islanders		Thu.	10	Philadelphia
	Fri.	12	Washington		Sat.	12	Montreal
	Sat.	13	Ottawa		Mon.	14	at Pittsburgh
	Thu.	18	at Atlanta		Wed.	16	Buffalo
	Sat.	20	at Boston		Sat.	19	at Boston*
	Tue.	23	at Pittsburgh		Sun.	20	Boston*
	Thu.	25	New Jersey		Tue.	22	Atlanta
	Sat.	27	Toronto		Thu.	24	Atlanta
	Mon.	29	Tampa Bay		Tue.	29	at Carolina
Nov.	Thu.	1	Washington		Thu.	31	at Philadelphia
	Sat.	3	New Jersey	**Feb.**	Fri.	1	at New Jersey
	Mon.	5	Philadelphia		Sun.	3	at Montreal*
	Tue.	6	at NY Islanders		Tue.	5	Los Angeles
	Thu.	8	Pittsburgh		Thu.	7	Anaheim
	Sat.	10	at Toronto†		Sat.	9	at Philadelphia*
	Wed.	14	at New Jersey		Sun.	10	at Washington*
	Thu.	15	at Philadelphia		Sat.	16	Buffalo*
	Sat.	17	at Pittsburgh		Sun.	17	San Jose*
	Mon.	19	NY Islanders		Tue.	19	at Montreal
	Wed.	21	at Tampa Bay		Sat.	23	at Buffalo
	Fri.	23	at Florida		Sun.	24	Florida
	Sun.	25	Dallas*		Thu.	28	at Carolina
	Thu.	29	NY Islanders	**Mar.**	Sun.	2	Philadelphia*
Dec.	Sat.	1	at Ottawa*		Tue.	4	NY Islanders
	Mon.	3	Carolina		Thu.	6	at NY Islanders
	Thu.	6	Toronto		Sun.	9	Boston*
	Fri.	7	at Atlanta		Mon.	10	at Buffalo
	Sun.	9	New Jersey*		Fri.	14	at Florida
	Wed.	12	at Washington		Sat.	15	at Tampa Bay
	Sun.	16	Phoenix*		Tue.	18	Pittsburgh
	Tue.	18	Pittsburgh		Wed.	19	at New Jersey
	Thu.	20	at Minnesota		Fri.	21	at Philadelphia
	Fri.	21	at Colorado		Tue.	25	Philadelphia
	Sun.	23	Ottawa		Thu.	27	New Jersey
	Wed.	26	Carolina		Sun.	30	at Pittsburgh*
	Sat.	29	at Toronto		Mon.	31	Pittsburgh
	Sun.	30	Montreal	**Apr.**	Thu.	3	at NY Islanders
Jan.	Wed.	2	at Calgary		Fri.	4	NY Islanders
	Thu.	3	at Vancouver		Sun.	6	at New Jersey*

* Denotes afternoon game. † Hall of Fame Game.

Year-by-Year Record

		Home				Road				Overall								
Season	GP	W	L	T	OL	W	L	T	OL	W	L	T	OL	GF	GA	Pts.	Finished	Playoff Result
2006-07	82	21	15	....	5	21	15	....	5	42	30	....	10	242	216	94	3rd, Atlantic Div.	Lost Conf. Semi-Final
2005-06	82	25	10	....	6	19	16	....	6	44	26	....	12	257	215	100	3rd, Atlantic Div.	Lost Conf. Quarter-Final
2004-05	....	....	....	....	....	....	....	....	....	....	....	....	....	....	....	....		
2003-04	82	13	21	3	4	14	19	4	4	27	40	7	8	206	250	69	4th, Atlantic Div.	Out of Playoffs
2002-03	82	17	18	4	2	15	18	6	2	32	36	10	4	210	231	78	4th, Atlantic Div.	Out of Playoffs
2001-02	82	19	19	2	1	17	19	2	3	36	38	4	4	227	258	80	4th, Atlantic Div.	Out of Playoffs
2000-01	82	17	20	3	1	16	23	2	0	33	43	5	1	250	290	72	4th, Atlantic Div.	Out of Playoffs
1999-2000	82	15	20	5	1	14	18	7	2	29	38	12	3	218	246	73	4th, Atlantic Div.	Out of Playoffs
1998-99	82	17	19	5	....	16	19	6	....	33	38	11	....	217	227	77	4th, Atlantic Div.	Out of Playoffs
1997-98	82	14	18	9	....	11	21	9	....	25	39	18	....	197	231	68	5th, Atlantic Div.	Out of Playoffs
1996-97	82	21	14	6	....	17	20	4	....	38	34	10	....	258	231	86	4th, Atlantic Div.	Lost Conf. Championship
1995-96	82	22	10	9	....	19	17	5	....	41	27	14	....	272	237	96	2nd, Atlantic Div.	Lost Conf. Semi-Final
1994-95	48	11	10	3	....	11	13	0	....	22	23	3	....	139	134	47	4th, Atlantic Div.	Lost Conf. Semi-Final
1993-94	**84**	**28**	**8**	**6**	....	**24**	**16**	**2**	....	**52**	**24**	**8**	....	**299**	**231**	**112**	**1st, Atlantic Div.**	**Won Stanley Cup**
1992-93	84	20	17	5	....	14	22	6	....	34	39	11	....	304	308	79	6th, Patrick Div.	Out of Playoffs
1991-92	80	28	8	4	....	22	17	1	....	50	25	5	....	321	246	105	1st, Patrick Div.	Lost Div. Final
1990-91	80	22	11	7	....	14	20	6	....	36	31	13	....	297	265	85	2nd, Patrick Div.	Lost Div. Semi-Final
1989-90	80	20	11	9	....	16	20	4	....	36	31	13	....	279	267	85	1st, Patrick Div.	Lost Div. Final
1988-89	80	21	17	2	....	16	18	6	....	37	35	8	....	310	307	82	3rd, Patrick Div.	Lost Div. Semi-Final
1987-88	80	22	13	5	....	14	21	5	....	36	34	10	....	300	283	82	5th, Patrick Div.	Out of Playoffs
1986-87	80	18	18	4	....	16	20	4	....	34	38	8	....	307	323	76	4th, Patrick Div.	Lost Div. Semi-Final
1985-86	80	20	18	2	....	16	20	4	....	36	38	6	....	280	276	78	4th, Patick Div.	Lost Conf. Championship
1984-85	80	16	18	6	....	10	26	4	....	26	44	10	....	295	345	62	4th, Patrick Div.	Lost Div. Semi-Final
1983-84	80	27	12	1	....	15	17	8	....	42	29	9	....	314	304	93	4th, Patrick Div.	Lost Div. Semi-Final
1982-83	80	24	13	3	....	11	22	7	....	35	35	10	....	306	287	80	4th, Patrick Div.	Lost Div. Final
1981-82	80	19	15	6	....	20	12	8	....	39	27	14	....	316	306	92	2nd, Patrick Div.	Lost Div. Final
1980-81	80	17	13	10	....	13	23	4	....	30	36	14	....	312	317	74	4th, Patrick Div.	Lost Semi-Final
1979-80	80	22	10	8	....	16	22	2	....	38	32	10	....	308	284	86	3rd, Patrick Div.	Lost Quarter-Final
1978-79	80	19	13	8	....	21	16	3	....	40	29	11	....	316	292	91	3rd, Patrick Div.	Lost Final
1977-78	80	18	15	7	....	12	22	6	....	30	37	13	....	279	280	73	4th, Patrick Div.	Lost Prelim. Round
1976-77	80	17	18	5	....	12	19	9	....	29	37	14	....	272	310	72	4th, Patrick Div.	Out of Playoffs
1975-76	80	16	16	8	....	13	26	1	....	29	42	9	....	262	333	67	4th, Patrick Div.	Out of Playoffs
1974-75	80	21	11	8	....	16	18	6	....	37	29	14	....	319	276	88	2nd, Patrick Div.	Lost Prelim. Round
1973-74	78	26	7	6	....	14	17	8	....	40	24	14	....	300	251	94	3rd, East Div.	Lost Semi-Final
1972-73	78	26	8	5	....	21	15	3	....	47	23	8	....	297	208	102	3rd, East Div.	Lost Semi-Final
1971-72	78	26	6	7	....	22	11	6	....	48	17	13	....	317	192	109	2nd, East Div.	Lost Final
1970-71	78	30	2	7	....	19	16	4	....	49	18	11	....	259	177	109	2nd, East Div.	Lost Semi-Final
1969-70	76	22	8	8	....	16	14	8	....	38	22	16	....	246	189	92	4th, East Div.	Lost Quarter-Final
1968-69	76	27	7	4	....	14	19	5	....	41	26	9	....	231	196	91	3rd, East Div.	Lost Quarter-Final
1967-68	74	22	8	7	....	17	15	5	....	39	23	12	....	226	183	90	2nd, East Div.	Lost Quarter-Final
1966-67	70	18	12	5	....	12	16	7	....	30	28	12	....	188	189	72	4th,	Lost Semi-Final
1965-66	70	12	16	7	....	6	25	4	....	18	41	11	....	195	261	47	6th,	Out of Playoffs
1964-65	70	8	19	8	....	12	19	4	....	20	38	12	....	179	246	52	5th,	Out of Playoffs
1963-64	70	14	13	8	....	8	25	2	....	22	38	10	....	186	242	54	5th,	Out of Playoffs
1962-63	70	12	17	6	....	10	19	6	....	22	36	12	....	211	233	56	5th,	Out of Playoffs
1961-62	70	16	11	8	....	10	21	4	....	26	32	12	....	195	207	64	4th,	Lost Semi-Final
1960-61	70	15	15	5	....	7	23	5	....	22	38	10	....	204	248	54	5th,	Out of Playoffs
1959-60	70	10	15	10	....	7	23	5	....	17	38	15	....	187	247	49	6th,	Out of Playoffs
1958-59	70	14	16	5	....	12	16	7	....	26	32	12	....	201	217	64	5th,	Out of Playoffs
1957-58	70	14	15	6	....	18	10	7	....	32	25	13	....	195	188	77	2nd,	Lost Semi-Final
1956-57	70	15	12	8	....	11	18	6	....	26	30	14	....	184	227	66	4th,	Lost Semi-Final
1955-56	70	20	7	8	....	12	21	2	....	32	28	10	....	204	203	74	3rd,	Lost Semi-Final
1954-55	70	10	12	13	....	7	23	5	....	17	35	18	....	150	210	52	5th,	Out of Playoffs
1953-54	70	18	12	5	....	11	19	5	....	29	31	10	....	161	182	68	5th,	Out of Playoffs
1952-53	70	11	14	10	....	6	23	6	....	17	37	16	....	152	211	50	6th,	Out of Playoffs
1951-52	70	16	13	6	....	7	21	7	....	23	34	13	....	192	219	59	5th,	Out of Playoffs
1950-51	70	14	11	10	....	6	18	11	....	20	29	21	....	169	201	61	5th,	Out of Playoffs
1949-50	70	19	12	4	....	9	19	7	....	28	31	11	....	170	189	67	4th,	Lost Final
1948-49	60	13	12	5	....	5	19	6	....	18	31	11	....	133	172	47	6th,	Out of Playoffs
1947-48	60	11	12	7	....	10	14	6	....	21	26	13	....	176	201	55	4th,	Lost Semi-Final
1946-47	60	11	14	5	....	11	18	1	....	22	32	6	....	167	186	50	5th,	Out of Playoffs
1945-46	50	8	12	5	....	5	16	4	....	13	28	9	....	144	191	35	6th,	Out of Playoffs
1944-45	50	7	11	7	....	4	18	3	....	11	29	10	....	154	247	32	6th,	Out of Playoffs
1943-44	50	4	17	4	....	2	22	1	....	6	39	5	....	162	310	17	6th,	Out of Playoffs
1942-43	50	7	13	5	....	4	18	3	....	11	31	8	....	161	253	30	6th,	Out of Playoffs
1941-42	48	15	8	1	....	14	9	1	....	29	17	2	....	177	143	60	1st,	Lost Semi-Final
1940-41	48	13	7	4	....	8	12	4	....	21	19	8	....	143	125	50	4th,	Lost Quarter-Final
1939-40	**48**	**17**	**4**	**3**	....	**10**	**7**	**7**	....	**27**	**11**	**10**	....	**136**	**77**	**64**	**2nd,**	**Won Stanley Cup**
1938-39	48	13	8	3	....	13	8	3	....	26	16	6	....	149	105	58	2nd,	Lost Semi-Final
1937-38	48	15	5	4	....	12	10	2	....	27	15	6	....	149	96	60	2nd, Amn. Div.	Lost Quarter-Final
1936-37	48	9	7	8	....	10	13	1	....	19	20	9	....	117	106	47	3rd, Amn. Div.	Lost Final
1935-36	48	11	6	7	....	8	11	5	....	19	17	12	....	91	96	50	4th, Amn. Div.	Out of Playoffs
1934-35	48	11	8	5	....	11	12	1	....	22	20	6	....	137	139	50	3rd, Amn. Div.	Lost Semi-Final
1933-34	48	11	7	6	....	10	12	2	....	21	19	8	....	120	113	50	3rd, Amn. Div.	Lost Quarter-Final
1932-33	**48**	**12**	**7**	**5**	....	**11**	**10**	**3**	....	**23**	**17**	**8**	....	**135**	**107**	**54**	**3rd, Amn. Div.**	**Won Stanley Cup**
1931-32	48	13	7	4	....	10	10	4	....	23	17	8	....	134	112	54	1st, Amn. Div.	Lost Final
1930-31	44	10	9	3	....	9	7	6	....	19	16	9	....	106	87	47	3rd, Amn. Div.	Lost Semi-Final
1929-30	44	11	5	6	....	6	12	4	....	17	17	10	....	136	143	44	3rd, Amn. Div.	Lost Semi-Final
1928-29	44	12	6	4	....	9	7	6	....	21	13	10	....	72	65	52	2nd, Amn. Div.	Lost Final
1927-28	**44**	**10**	**8**	**4**	....	**9**	**8**	**5**	....	**19**	**16**	**9**	....	**94**	**79**	**47**	**2nd, Amn. Div.**	**Won Stanley Cup**
1926-27	44	13	5	4	....	12	8	2	....	25	13	6	....	95	72	56	1st, Amn. Div.	Lost Quarter-Final

ATLANTIC DIVISION
82nd NHL Season

Franchise date: May 15, 1926

2007-08 Player Personnel

FORWARDS	HT	WT	S	Place of Birth	*Age	2006-07 Club
ANISIMOV, Artem	6-3	187	L	Yaroslavl, USSR	19	Yaroslavl 2-Yaroslavl
AVERY, Sean	5-10	195	L	Pickering, Ont.	27	Los Angeles-NY Rangers
BARNES, Joe	6-3	212	L	Winnipeg, Man.	21	Albany
BETTS, Blair	6-3	210	L	Edmonton, Alta.	27	NY Rangers
BOURRET, Alex	5-11	205	L	Drummondville, Que.	20	Chicago (AHL)-Hartford
BYERS, Dane	6-3	190	L	Nipawin, Sask.	21	Hartford
CALLAHAN, Ryan	5-11	185	R	Rochester, NY	22	NY Rangers-Hartford
DAWES, Nigel	5-8	190	L	Winnipeg, Man.	22	NY Rangers-Hartford
DRURY, Chris	5-10	200	R	Trumbull, CT	31	Buffalo
DUBINSKY, Brandon	6-1	210	L	Anchorage, AK	21	NY Rangers-Hartford
DUPONT, Brodie	6-2	210	L	Russell, Man.	20	Calgary (WHL)
FRITZ, Mitch	6-8	258	L	Osoyoos, B.C.	26	Springfield
GOMEZ, Scott	5-11	200	L	Anchorage, AK	27	New Jersey
GRAHAM, Bruce	6-6	230	L	Moncton, N.B.	21	Hartford-Charlotte
HOLLWEG, Ryan	5-11	210	L	Downey, CA	24	NY Rangers
HOSSA, Marcel	6-3	220	L	Ilava, Czech.	25	NY Rangers
JAGR, Jaromir	6-3	240	L	Kladno, Czech.	35	NY Rangers
JESSIMAN, Hugh	6-6	231	R	New York, NY	23	Hartford-Charlotte
KORPIKOSKI, Lauri	6-1	190	L	Turku, Finland	21	Hartford
KOZAK, Rick	6-3	225	R	Norway House, Man.	22	Charlotte-Memphis
MOORE, Greg	6-1	225	R	Lisbon, ME	23	Hartford
ORR, Colton	6-3	220	R	Winnipeg, Man.	25	NY Rangers
PRUCHA, Petr	6-0	175	R	Chrudim, Czech.	25	NY Rangers
PYATT, Tom	6-0	185	L	Thunder Bay, Ont.	20	Saginaw-Hartford
SHANAHAN, Brendan	6-3	220	R	Mimico, Ont.	38	NY Rangers
STRAKA, Martin	5-9	180	L	Plzen, Czech.	35	NY Rangers
DEFENSEMEN						
BARANKA, Ivan	6-3	205	L	Ilava, Czech.	22	Hartford
BUSTO, Michael	6-2	210	R	Burnaby, B.C.	21	Kootenay
GIRARDI, Dan	6-2	205	R	Welland, Ont.	23	NY Rangers-Hartford
HUTCHINSON, Andrew	6-2	206	R	Evanston, IL	27	Carolina
KASPARAITIS, Darius	5-11	215	L	Elektrenai, USSR	34	NY Rangers-Hartford
LIFFITON, David	6-2	210	L	Windsor, Ont.	22	NY Rangers-Hartford
MALIK, Marek	6-6	240	L	Ostrava, Czech.	32	NY Rangers
MARA, Paul	6-4	219	L	Ridgewood, NJ	28	Boston-NY Rangers
POCK, Thomas	6-1	210	L	Klagenfurt, Austria	25	NY Rangers-Hartford
ROZSIVAL, Michal	6-2	210	R	Vlasim, Czech.	29	NY Rangers
SAUER, Michael	6-3	206	R	St. Cloud, MN	20	Portland (WHL)-Medicine Hat
STAAL, Marc	6-4	205	L	Thunder Bay, Ont.	20	Sudbury
STRUDWICK, Jason	6-4	225	L	Edmonton, Alta.	32	NY Rangers-Lugano
TYUTIN, Fedor	6-3	210	L	Izhevsk, USSR	24	NY Rangers

GOALTENDERS	HT	WT	C	Place of Birth	*Age	2006-07 Club
HOLT, Chris	6-3	221	L	Vancouver, B.C.	22	Hartford-Charlotte
LUNDQVIST, Henrik	6-1	195	L	Are, Sweden	25	NY Rangers
MONTOYA, Al	6-2	193	L	Chicago, IL	22	Hartford
VALIQUETTE, Steve	6-6	220	L	Etobicoke, Ont.	30	NY Rangers-Hartford

* – Age at start of 2007-08 season

Coach

TOM RENNEY

Coach, New York Rangers. Born in Cranbrook, B.C., March 1, 1955.

Tom Renney took over as interim coach of the New York Rangers on February 25, 2004. He was officially named the 33rd head coach in franchise history on July 6. In 2005-06, Renney guided the Rangers to their first playoff berth since 1996-97. In the 2007 playoffs, the Rangers won a series for the first time since 1997.

Renney joined the Rangers on July 31, 2000 as director of player personnel and was promoted to vice president, player development on June 21, 2002. In that position, he oversaw all facets of the team's amateur scouting operations, while also assisting with the professional scouting process and player development within the organization. Renney joined the Rangers coaching staff as an assistant coach on July 21, 2003.

From June of 1996 through November, 1997, Renney served as head coach of the Vancouver Canucks. Prior to his return to the National Hockey League in New York, Renney held the position of vice president and head coach of the Canadian national team. Renney rejoined the Canadian Hockey Association in May, 1998. He began his affiliation with the Canadian national team in 1992 and coached Canada's Olympic hockey team to a silver medal at the 1994 Winter Games in Lillehammer, Norway. Later that year, he served as an assistant coach on Team Canada's gold medal-winning team at the World Championships. He won silver again as an assistant coach at the 2005 World Championship. Previously, he won the Memorial Cup with the Kamloops Blazers in 1992.

Coaching Record

		Regular Season				Playoffs, Olympics or World Championships			
Year	Team	Games	W	L	O/T	Games	W	L	T
1990-91	Kamloops (WHL)	72	50	20	2	12	5	7	
1991-92	Kamloops (WHL)	72	51	17	4	16	11	5	
1993-94*	Canadian National	63	33	26	4	8	5	2	1
1994-95**	Canadian National	57	37	17	3	8	4	2	2
1995-96***	Canadian National	53	33	12	8	8	4	2	2
1996-97	**Vancouver (NHL)**	**82**	**35**	**40**	**7**	....	....	....	
1997-98	**Vancouver (NHL)**	**19**	**4**	**13**	**2**	....	....	....	
1999-00	Canadian National	56	27	23	6	....	....	....	....
2003-04	**NY Rangers (NHL)**	**20**	**5**	**15**	**0**	....	....	....	
2004-05	**NY Rangers (NHL)**			Season Cancelled					
2005-06	**NY Rangers (NHL)**	**82**	**44**	**26**	**12**	**4**	**0**	**4**	
2006-07	**NY Rangers (NHL)**	**82**	**42**	**30**	**10**	**10**	**6**	**4**	
	NHL Totals	**285**	**130**	**124**	**31**	**14**	**6**	**8**	

* Olympics (silver medal)
** World Championships (bronze)
*** World Championships (silver)

2006-07 Scoring

* – rookie

Regular Season

Pos	#	Player	Team	GP	G	A	Pts	+/–	PIM	PP	SH	GW	S	%
R	68	Jaromir Jagr	NYR	82	30	66	96	26	78	7	0	5	324	9.3
C	92	Michael Nylander	NYR	79	26	57	83	12	42	14	0	4	193	13.5
L	82	Martin Straka	NYR	77	29	41	70	16	24	8	0	6	165	17.6
L	14	Brendan Shanahan	NYR	67	29	33	62	2	47	14	3	3	295	9.8
L	16	Sean Avery	L.A.	55	10	18	28	–10	116	1	1	2	160	6.3
			NYR	29	8	12	20	11	58	1	0	0	89	9.0
			TOTAL	84	18	30	48	1	174	2	1	2	249	7.2
C	5	Matt Cullen	NYR	80	16	25	41	0	52	2	3	2	217	7.4
R	25	Petr Prucha	NYR	79	22	18	40	–7	30	8	0	2	136	16.2
D	3	Michal Rozsival	NYR	80	10	30	40	10	52	7	0	3	104	9.6
D	23	Karel Rachunek	NYR	66	6	20	26	–9	38	4	1	1	99	6.1
D	27	Paul Mara	BOS	59	3	15	18	–22	95	0	0	0	60	5.0
			NYR	19	2	3	5	6	18	1	0	0	40	5.0
			TOTAL	78	5	18	23	–16	113	1	0	0	100	5.0
D	8	Marek Malik	NYR	69	2	19	21	32	70	0	0	0	57	3.5
L	81	Marcel Hossa	NYR	64	10	8	18	–4	26	3	0	2	83	12.0
D	51	Fedor Tyutin	NYR	66	2	12	14	–8	44	1	1	0	75	2.7
C	19	Blair Betts	NYR	82	9	4	13	–4	24	1	1	0	120	7.5
R	41	Jed Ortmeyer	NYR	41	2	9	11	7	22	0	1	0	67	3.0
D	22	Thomas Pock	NYR	44	4	4	8	–4	16	0	0	0	76	5.3
R	43 *	Ryan Callahan	NYR	14	4	2	6	5	9	0	0	1	40	10.0
C	20	Jason Krog	ATL	14	1	3	4	3	6	0	0	0	14	7.1
			NYR	9	2	0	2	2	4	0	0	1	8	25.0
			TOTAL	23	3	3	6	5	10	0	0	1	22	13.6
C	38 *	Jarkko Immonen	NYR	14	1	5	6	–2	4	0	0	1	14	7.1
D	46 *	Daniel Girardi	NYR	34	0	6	6	7	8	0	0	0	33	0.0
L	15	Brad Isbister	NYR	19	1	4	5	5	14	1	0	0	36	2.8
D	6	Darius Kasparaitis	NYR	24	2	2	4	–1	30	0	0	0	9	22.2
R	28	Colton Orr	NYR	53	2	1	3	–2	126	0	0	1	23	8.7
L	44	Ryan Hollweg	NYR	78	1	2	3	–11	131	0	0	0	63	1.6
D	24	Sandis Ozolinsh	NYR	21	0	3	3	–8	8	0	0	0	15	0.0
L	10 *	Nigel Dawes	NYR	8	1	0	1	–4	0	0	0	0	7	14.3
D	26 *	Bryce Lampman	NYR	1	0	0	0	0	0	0	0	0	0	0.0
D	55 *	David Liffiton	NYR	2	0	0	0	1	7	0	0	0	2	0.0
C	54 *	Brandon Dubinsky	NYR	6	0	0	0	0	2	0	0	0	9	0.0
D	34	Jason Strudwick	NYR	8	0	0	0	0	2	0	0	0	3	0.0

Goaltending

No.	Goaltender	GPI	Mins	Avg	W	L	OT	EN	SO	GA	SA	S%	G	A	PIM
30	Henrik Lundqvist	70	4109	2.34	37	22	8	2	5	160	1927	.917	0	0	0
40	Stephen Valiquette	3	115	3.13	1	2	0	0	0	6	45	.867	0	0	0
80	Kevin Weekes	14	761	3.39	4	6	2	0	0	43	355	.879	0	0	0
	Totals	**82**	**5014**	**2.52**	**42**	**30**	**10**	**2**	**5**	**211**	**2329**	**.909**			

Playoffs

Pos	#	Player	Team	GP	G	A	Pts	+/–	PIM	PP	SH	GW	OT	S	%
C	92	Michael Nylander	NYR	10	6	7	13	9	0	2	0	2	0	23	26.1
R	68	Jaromir Jagr	NYR	10	5	6	11	6	12	2	0	0	0	48	10.4
L	82	Martin Straka	NYR	10	2	8	10	0	2	1	0	0	0	15	13.3
L	14	Brendan Shanahan	NYR	10	5	2	7	–5	12	3	0	2	0	41	12.2
D	3	Michal Rozsival	NYR	10	3	4	7	6	10	2	0	1	1	18	16.7
L	16	Sean Avery	NYR	10	1	4	5	–3	27	0	0	0	0	42	2.4
D	51	Fedor Tyutin	NYR	10	0	5	5	–3	8	0	0	0	0	9	0.0
D	27	Paul Mara	NYR	10	2	2	4	–4	18	2	0	0	0	11	18.2
L	81	Marcel Hossa	NYR	10	2	2	4	5	4	0	0	0	0	16	12.5
D	8	Marek Malik	NYR	10	1	3	4	6	10	0	0	0	0	4	25.0
C	5	Matt Cullen	NYR	10	1	3	4	–2	6	0	0	1	0	23	4.3
D	23	Karel Rachunek	NYR	6	0	4	4	–1	2	0	0	0	0	8	0.0
R	43 *	Ryan Callahan	NYR	10	2	1	3	1	6	1	0	0	0	26	7.7
D	22	Thomas Pock	NYR	4	0	3	3	0	4	0	0	0	0	4	0.0
R	25	Petr Prucha	NYR	10	0	1	1	0	4	0	0	0	0	22	0.0
L	10 *	Nigel Dawes	NYR	1	0	0	0	–2	0	0	0	0	0	2	0.0
C	44	Ryan Hollweg	NYR	2	0	0	0	–1	2	0	0	0	0	4	0.0
L	15	Brad Isbister	NYR	4	0	0	0	–3	2	0	0	0	0	2	0.0
R	28	Colton Orr	NYR	4	0	0	0	–1	12	0	0	0	0	1	0.0
R	41	Jed Ortmeyer	NYR	9	0	0	0	–1	2	0	0	0	0	8	0.0
C	19	Blair Betts	NYR	10	0	0	0	–5	4	0	0	0	0	9	0.0
D	46 *	Daniel Girardi	NYR	10	0	0	0	–4	4	0	0	0	0	7	0.0

Goaltending

No.	Goaltender	GPI	Mins	Avg	W	L	EN	SO	GA	SA	S%	G	A	PIM
30	Henrik Lundqvist	10	637	2.07	6	4	1	1	22	291	.924	0	0	0
	Totals	**10**	**641**	**2.15**	**6**	**4**	**1**	**1**	**23**	**292**	**.921**			

Coaching History

Lester Patrick, 1926-27 to 1938-39; Frank Boucher, 1939-40 to 1947-48; Frank Boucher and Lynn Patrick, 1948-49; Lynn Patrick, 1949-50; Neil Colville, 1950-51; Neil Colville and Bill Cook, 1951-52; Bill Cook, 1952-53; Frank Boucher and Muzz Patrick, 1953-54; Muzz Patrick, 1954-55; Phil Watson, 1955-56 to 1958-59; Phil Watson and Alf Pike, 1959-60; Alf Pike, 1960-61; Doug Harvey, 1961-62; Muzz Patrick and Red Sullivan, 1962-63; Red Sullivan, 1963-64, 1964-65; Red Sullivan and Emile Francis, 1965-66; Emile Francis, 1966-67, 1967-68; Bernie Geoffrion and Emile Francis, 1968-69; Emile Francis, 1969-70 to 1972-73; Larry Popein and Emile Francis, 1973-74; Emile Francis, 1974-75; Ron Stewart and John Ferguson, 1975-76; John Ferguson, 1976-77; Jean-Guy Talbot, 1977-78; Fred Shero, 1978-79, 1979-80; Fred Shero and Craig Patrick, 1980-81; Herb Brooks, 1981-82 to 1983-84; Herb Brooks and Craig Patrick, 1984-85; Ted Sator, 1985-86; Ted Sator, Tom Webster and Phil Esposito, 1986-87; Michel Bergeron, 1987-88; Michel Bergeron and Phil Esposito, 1988-89; Roger Neilson, 1989-90 to 1991-92; Roger Neilson and Ron Smith, 1992-93; Mike Keenan, 1993-94; Colin Campbell, 1994-95 to 1996-97; Colin Campbell and John Muckler, 1997-98; John Muckler, 1998-99; John Muckler and John Tortorella, 1999-2000; Ron Low, 2000-01, 2001-02; Bryan Trottier and Glen Sather, 2002-03; Glen Sather and Tom Renney, 2003-04; Tom Renney, 2004-05 to date.

Club Records

Team

(Figures in brackets for season records are games played; records for fewest points, wins, ties, losses, goals, goals against are for 70 or more games)

Record		
Most Points	112	1993-94 (84)
Most Wins	52	1993-94 (84)
Most Ties	21	1950-51 (70)
Most Losses	44	1984-85 (80)
Most Goals	321	1991-92 (80)
Most Goals Against	345	1984-85 (80)
Fewest Points	47	1965-66 (70)
Fewest Wins	17	1952-53 (70), 1954-55 (70), 1959-60 (70)
Fewest Ties	4	2001-02 (82)
Fewest Losses	17	1971-72 (78)
Fewest Goals	150	1954-55 (70)
Fewest Goals Against	177	1970-71 (78)
Longest Winning Streak		
Overall	10	Dec. 19/39-Jan. 13/40, Jan. 19-Feb. 10/73
Home	14	Dec. 19/39-Feb. 25/40
Away	7	Jan. 12-Feb. 12/35, Oct. 28-Nov. 29/78
Longest Undefeated Streak		
Overall	19	Nov. 23/39-Jan. 13/40 (14 wins, 5 ties)
Home	26	Mar. 29/70-Jan. 31/71 (19 wins, 7 ties)
Away	11	Nov. 5/39-Jan. 13/40 (6 wins, 5 ties)
Longest Losing Streak		
Overall	11	Oct. 30-Nov. 27/43
Home	7	Oct. 20-Nov. 14/76, Mar. 24-Apr. 14/93
Away	10	Oct. 30-Dec. 23/43, Feb. 8-Mar. 15/61
Longest Winless Streak		
Overall	21	Jan. 23-Mar. 19/44 (17 losses, 4 ties)
Home	10	Jan. 30-Mar. 19/44 (7 losses, 3 ties)
Away	16	Oct. 9-Dec. 20/52 (12 losses, 4 ties)
Most Shutouts, Season	13	1928-29 (44)
Most PIM, Season	2,018	1989-90 (80)
Most Goals, Game	12	Nov. 21/71 (Cal. 1 at NYR 12)

Individual

Record		
Most Seasons	18	Rod Gilbert
Most Games	1,160	Harry Howell
Most Goals, Career	406	Rod Gilbert
Most Assists, Career	741	Brian Leetch
Most Points, Career	1,021	Rod Gilbert (406G, 615A)
Most PIM, Career	1,226	Ron Greschner
Most Shutouts, Career	49	Ed Giacomin
Longest Consecutive Games Streak	560	Andy Hebenton (Oct. 7/55-Mar. 24/63)
Most Goals, Season	54	Jaromir Jagr (2005-06)
Most Assists, Season	80	Brian Leetch (1991-92)
Most Points, Season	123	Jaromir Jagr (2005-06; 54G, 69A)
Most PIM, Season	305	Troy Mallette (1989-90)
Most Points, Defenseman, Season	102	Brian Leetch (1991-92; 22G, 80A)
Most Points, Center, Season	109	Jean Ratelle (1971-72; 46G, 63A)
Most Points, Right Wing, Season	123	Jaromir Jagr (2005-06; 54G, 69A)
Most Points, Left Wing, Season	106	Vic Hadfield (1971-72; 50G, 56A)
Most Points, Rookie, Season	76	Mark Pavelich (1981-82; 33G, 43A)
Most Shutouts, Season	13	John Ross Roach (1928-29)
Most Goals, Game	5	Don Murdoch (Oct. 12/76), Mark Pavelich (Feb. 23/83)
Most Assists, Game	5	Walt Tkaczuk (Feb. 12/72), Rod Gilbert (Mar. 2/75, Mar. 30/75, Oct. 8/76), Don Maloney (Jan. 3/87), Brian Leetch (Apr. 18/95), Wayne Gretzky (Feb. 15/99)
Most Points, Game	7	Steve Vickers (Feb. 18/76; 3G, 4A)

Retired Numbers

1	Ed Giacomin	1965-1975
7	Rod Gilbert	1960-1977
11	Mark Messier	1991-97; 2000-04
35	Mike Richter	1989-2003

All-time Record vs. Other Clubs

Regular Season

	At Home								On Road								Total							
	GP	W	L	T	OL	GF	GA	PTS	GP	W	L	T	OL	GF	GA	PTS	GP	W	L	T	OL	GF	GA	PTS
Anaheim	9	3	5	1	0	23	26	7	9	3	6	0	0	29	35	6	18	6	11	1	0	52	61	13
Atlanta	14	4	6	1	3	40	46	12	14	9	3	0	2	48	38	20	28	13	9	1	5	88	84	32
Boston	306	135	116	55	0	939	858	325	302	100	160	42	0	849	1083	242	608	235	276	97	0	1788	1941	567
Buffalo	70	29	24	15	2	225	193	75	72	20	41	10	1	223	295	51	142	49	65	25	3	448	488	126
Calgary	53	25	23	5	0	182	186	55	49	12	27	10	0	148	216	34	102	37	50	15	0	330	402	89
Carolina	49	30	14	4	1	183	121	65	47	17	27	3	0	146	158	37	96	47	41	7	1	329	279	102
Chicago	286	118	113	55	0	843	808	291	287	115	128	43	1	793	872	274	573	233	241	98	1	1636	1680	565
Colorado	35	19	10	4	2	135	101	44	35	13	18	3	1	130	143	30	70	32	28	7	3	265	244	74
Columbus	3	1	1	1	0	9	8	3	5	1	4	0	0	10	20	2	8	2	5	1	0	19	28	5
Dallas	62	36	15	11	0	213	165	83	62	31	19	11	1	226	189	74	124	67	34	22	1	439	354	157
Detroit	285	134	93	58	0	871	742	326	286	76	165	45	0	702	1008	197	571	210	258	103	0	1573	1750	523
Edmonton	31	11	14	6	0	117	117	28	28	13	12	3	0	94	101	29	59	24	26	9	0	211	218	57
Florida	28	15	9	4	0	86	64	34	29	15	10	2	2	81	76	34	57	30	19	6	2	167	140	68
Los Angeles	58	35	17	6	0	233	172	76	61	27	24	10	0	217	203	64	119	62	41	16	0	450	375	140
Minnesota	4	3	1	0	0	13	8	6	4	3	1	0	0	13	11	6	8	6	2	0	0	26	19	12
Montreal	294	120	119	54	1	846	853	295	294	62	192	40	0	682	1137	164	588	182	311	94	1	1528	1990	459
Nashville	7	2	3	1	1	18	18	6	5	3	1	0	1	19	14	7	12	5	4	1	2	37	32	13
New Jersey	92	45	26	20	1	344	275	111	94	36	49	7	2	295	319	81	186	81	75	27	3	639	594	192
NY Islanders	104	58	34	11	1	380	309	128	104	39	56	8	1	332	388	87	208	97	90	19	2	712	697	215
Ottawa	27	12	15	0	0	86	85	24	27	12	11	3	1	71	81	28	54	24	26	3	1	157	166	52
Philadelphia	118	50	42	23	3	377	347	126	117	46	56	14	1	329	376	107	235	96	98	37	4	706	723	233
Phoenix	29	18	9	2	0	128	102	38	32	15	13	4	0	108	110	34	61	33	22	6	0	236	212	72
Pittsburgh	109	56	43	9	1	420	365	122	108	46	43	14	5	387	380	111	217	102	86	23	6	807	745	233
St. Louis	61	45	10	6	0	248	145	96	64	29	25	10	0	207	192	68	125	74	35	16	0	455	337	164
San Jose	10	7	2	1	0	40	29	15	14	10	2	2	0	52	32	22	24	17	4	3	0	92	61	37
Tampa Bay	31	16	11	2	2	100	89	36	29	12	13	3	1	96	99	28	60	28	24	5	3	196	188	64
Toronto	287	123	107	56	1	890	844	303	286	86	160	39	1	753	991	212	573	209	267	95	2	1643	1835	515
Vancouver	55	38	12	5	0	239	142	81	51	33	15	3	0	204	163	69	106	71	27	8	0	443	305	150
Washington	86	42	34	9	1	321	290	94	88	34	44	9	1	282	328	78	174	76	78	18	2	603	618	172
Defunct Clubs	139	87	30	22	0	460	290	196	139	82	34	23	0	441	291	187	278	169	64	45	0	901	581	383
Totals	**2742**	**1317**	**958**	**447**	**20**	**9009**	**7798**	**3101**	**2742**	**1000**	**1359**	**361**	**22**	**7967**	**9349**	**2383**	**5484**	**2317**	**2317**	**808**	**42**	**16976**	**17147**	**5484**

Playoffs

	Series	W	L	GP	W	L	T	GF	GA	Last Mtg.	Rnd.	Result
Atlanta	1	1	0	4	4	0	0	17	6	2007	CQF	W 4-0
Boston	9	3	6	42	18	22	2	104	114	1973	QF	W 4-1
Buffalo	2	0	2	9	3	6	0	19	28	2007	CSF	L 2-4
Calgary	1	1	0	4	3	1	0	14	8	1980	PRE	W 3-1
Chicago	5	1	4	24	10	14	0	54	66	1973	SF	L 1-4
Colorado	1	1	0	6	4	2	0	25	19	1995	CQF	W 4-2
Detroit	5	1	4	23	10	13	0	49	57	1950	F	L 3-4
Florida	1	1	0	5	4	1	0	13	10	1997	CQF	W 4-1
Los Angeles	2	2	0	6	5	1	0	32	14	1981	PRE	W 3-1
Montreal	14	7	7	61	25	34	2	158	188	1996	CQF	W 4-2
New Jersey	4	3	1	23	12	11	0	60	63	2006	CQF	L 0-4
NY Islanders	8	3	5	39	19	20	0	132	129	1994	CQF	W 4-0
Philadelphia	10	4	6	47	20	27	0	153	157	1997	CF	L 1-4
Pittsburgh	3	0	3	15	3	12	0	45	64	1996	CSF	L 1-4
St. Louis	1	1	0	6	4	2	0	29	22	1981	QF	W 4-2
Toronto	8	5	3	35	19	16	0	86	86	1971	QF	W 4-2
Vancouver	1	1	0	7	4	3	0	21	19	1994	F	W 4-3
Washington	4	2	2	22	11	11	0	71	75	1994	CSF	W 4-1
Defunct Clubs	9	6	3	22	11	7	4	43	29			
Totals	**89**	**43**	**46**	**400**	**189**	**203**	**8**	**1125**	**1154**			

Calgary totals include Atlanta Flames, 1972-73 to 1979-80.
Colorado totals include Quebec, 1979-80 to 1994-95.
Carolina totals include Hartford, 1979-80 to 1996-97.
Dallas totals include Minnesota North Stars, 1967-68 to 1992-93.
New Jersey totals include Kansas City, 1974-75, 1975-76, and Colorado Rockies, 1976-77 to 1981-82.
Phoenix totals include Winnipeg, 1979-80 to 1995-96.

Playoff Results 2007-2002

Year	Round	Opponent	Result	GF	GA
2007	CSF	Buffalo	L 2-4	13	17
	CQF	Atlanta	W 4-0	17	6
2006	CQF	New Jersey	L 0-4	4	17

Abbreviations: Round: F – Final; **CF** – conference final; **CSF** – conference semi-final; **CQF** – conference quarter-final; **SF** – semi-final; **QF** – quarter-final; **PRE** – preliminary round.

2006-07 Results

Oct.	5	Washington	5-2		4	Philadelphia	3-2
	7	at Philadelphia	5-4†		6	at Montreal	4-3
	10	Philadelphia	2-4		9	NY Islanders	3-5
	12	Pittsburgh	5-6		11	Ottawa	4-6
	14	at Buffalo	4-7		13	Boston	3-1
	16	New Jersey	4-2		16	at New Jersey	0-1
	18	Nashville	0-3		20	Atlanta	1-3
	21	at Toronto	5-4†		27	at Philadelphia	2-1
	25	Florida	2-4		29	at Boston	6-1
	28	at Phoenix	7-3		31	Toronto	1-2
	30	at Los Angeles	1-4	**Feb.**	3	at Tampa Bay	2-3
Nov.	1	at Anaheim	4-3*		5	Detroit	3-4
	2	at San Jose	3-1		6	at New Jersey	2-3†
	5	Buffalo	3-4*		9	Tampa Bay	5-0
	8	at Florida	4-3†		10	at Washington	5-2
	10	at Atlanta	5-2		15	at Carolina	4-1
	11	at Washington	1-3		17	Philadelphia	3-5
	14	New Jersey	3-2		18	Chicago	2-1
	15	at Carolina	1-2		20	at New Jersey	1-2
	18	at Pittsburgh	1-3		22	New Jersey	2-3†
	19	Tampa Bay	4-1		24	Columbus	2-3
	21	Carolina	4-0		27	Montreal	4-0
	25	at Pittsburgh	2-1*	**Mar.**	1	Pittsburgh	3-4†
	26	Buffalo	2-3*		3	St. Louis	3-2†
	28	Atlanta	4-5*		5	NY Islanders	2-1†
Dec.	1	at Buffalo	3-4†		8	at NY Islanders	2-1
	3	NY Islanders	4-7		10	at Pittsburgh	2-3*
	7	Pittsburgh	3-2†		11	Carolina	2-1†
	9	at Ottawa	3-1		13	Ottawa	2-3
	10	Florida	2-1		16	at Atlanta	1-2*
	12	at Philadelphia	3-1		17	Boston	7-0
	14	at Dallas	5-2		19	Pittsburgh	2-1
	16	at Toronto	2-9		21	Philadelphia	5-0
	17	New Jersey	1-6		24	at Boston	2-1†
	19	NY Islanders	3-4		25	at NY Islanders	2-1*
	21	at Florida	2-3		27	at Montreal	4-6
	23	at Tampa Bay	3-4		31	at Philadelphia	6-4
	26	at NY Islanders	0-2	**Apr.**	1	Toronto	7-2
	29	at Ottawa	0-1		3	at NY Islanders	2-3†
	30	Washington	4-1		5	Montreal	3-1
Jan.	2	at New Jersey	3-2†		7	at Pittsburgh	1-2

* – Overtime † – Shootout

Entry Draft Selections 2007-1993

2007
Pick
17 Alexei Cherepanov
48 Antoine Lafleur
138 Max Campbell
168 Carl Hagelin
193 David Skokan
198 Danny Hobbs

2006
Pick
21 Bobby Sanguinetti
54 Artem Anisimov
84 Ryan Hillier
104 David Kveton
137 Tomas Zaborsky
174 Eric Hunter
204 Lukas Zeliska

2005
Pick
12 Marc Staal
40 Michael Sauer
56 Marc-Andre Cliche
66 Brodie Dupont
77 Dalyn Flatt
107 Tom Pyatt
147 Trevor Koverko
178 Greg Beller
211 Ryan Russell

2004
Pick
6 Al Montoya
19 Lauri Korpikoski
36 Darin Olver
48 Dane Byers
51 Bruce Graham
60 Brandon Dubinsky
73 Zdenek Bahensky
80 Billy Ryan
127 Ryan Callahan
135 Roman Psurny
169 Jordan Foote
247 Jonathan Paiement
266 Jakub Petruzalek

2003
Pick
12 Hugh Jessiman
50 Ivan Baranka
75 Ken Roche
122 Corey Potter
149 Nigel Dawes
176 Ivan Dornic
179 Philippe Furrer
180 Chris Holt
209 Dylan Reese
243 Jan Marek

2002
Pick
33 Lee Falardeau
81 Marcus Jonasen
127 Nate Guenin
143 Mike Walsh
177 Jake Taylor
194 Kim Hirschovits
226 Joey Crabb
240 Petr Prucha
270 Rob Flynn

2001
Pick
10 Dan Blackburn
40 Fedor Tyutin
79 Garth Murray
113 Bryce Lampman
139 Shawn Collymore
176 Marek Zidlicky
206 Petr Preucil
226 Pontus Petterstrom
226 Pontus Petterstrom
230 Leonid Zhvachkin
238 Ryan Hollweg
269 Juris Stals

2000
Pick
64 Filip Novak
95 Dominic Moore
112 Premysl Duben
140 Nathan Martz
143 Brandon Snee
175 Sven Helfenstein
205 Henrik Lundqvist
238 Danny Eberly
269 Martin Richter

1999
Pick
4 Pavel Brendl
9 Jamie Lundmark
59 David Inman
79 Johan Asplund
90 Patrick Aufiero
137 Garrett Bembridge
177 Jay Dardis
197 Arto Laatikainen
226 Yevgeny Gusakov
251 Petter Henning
254 Alexei Bulatov

1998
Pick
7 Manny Malhotra
40 Randy Copley
66 Jason Labarbera
114 Boyd Kane
122 Patrick Leahy
131 Tomas Kloucek
180 Stefan Lundqvist
207 Johan Witehall
235 Jan Mertzig

1997
Pick
19 Stefan Cherneski
46 Wes Jarvis
73 Burke Henry
93 Tomi Kallarsson
126 Jason McLean
134 Johan Lindbom
136 Mike York
154 Shawn Degagne
175 Johan Holmqvist
182 Mike Mottau
210 Andrew Proskurnicki
236 Richard Miller

1996
Pick
22 Jeff Brown
48 Daniel Goneau
76 Dmitri Subbotin
131 Colin Pepperall
158 Ola Sandberg
185 Jeff Dessner
211 Ryan McKie
237 Ronnie Sundin

1995
Pick
39 Christian Dube
65 Mike Martin
91 Marc Savard
110 Alexei Vasiliev
117 Dale Purinton
143 Peter Slamiar
169 Jeff Heil
195 Ilya Gorokhov
221 Bob Maudie

1994
Pick
26 Dan Cloutier
52 Rudolf Vercik
78 Adam Smith
100 Alexander Korobolin
104 Sylvain Blouin
130 Martin Ethier
135 Yuri Litvinov
156 David Brosseau
182 Alexei Lazarenko
208 Craig Anderson
209 Vitali Yeremeyev
234 Eric Boulton
260 Radoslav Kropac
267 Jamie Butt
286 Kim Johnsson

1993
Pick
8 Niklas Sundstrom
34 Lee Sorochan
61 Maxim Galanov
86 Sergei Olimpiyev
112 Gary Roach
138 Dave Trofimenkoff
162 Sergei Kondrashkin
164 Todd Marchant
190 Ed Campbell
216 Ken Shepard
242 Andrei Kudinov
261 Pavel Komarov
268 Maxim Smelnitsky

President and General Manager

GLEN SATHER
President/General Manager, New York Rangers.
Born in High River, Alta., September 2, 1943.

Glen Sather, who spent parts of four seasons with the New York Rangers as a player from 1970 to 1974, became the franchise's 12th president and tenth general manager on June 2, 2000. He also served as coach of the team from January 30, 2003, to February 25, 2004.

Sather joined the Rangers following a 24-year career with the Edmonton Oilers, where he was the architect of five Stanley Cup championships between 1984 and 1990. One of the most respected executives in the National Hockey League, Sather was honored for his tremendous achievements in 1997 by becoming the first member of the Oilers organization to be selected to the Hockey Hall of Fame.

Named coach and vice president of hockey operations for the Oilers when the franchise joined the NHL in June of 1979, Sather became general manager and club president in May of 1980. He coached through the 1988-89 season and also returned for 60 games behind the bench in 1993-94. Sather-coached teams won the Stanley Cup four times in the 1980s. As general manager, Sather was instrumental in the Oilers' fifth Cup triumph in 1990.

He played for six different teams during a 10-year NHL career. He scored 80 goals in 658 games.

NHL Coaching Record

		Regular Season				Playoffs		
Season	Team	Games	W	L	T	Games	W	L
1979-80	Edmonton	80	28	39	13	3	0	3
1980-81	Edmonton	62	25	26	11	9	5	4
1981-82	Edmonton	80	48	17	15	5	2	3
1982-83	Edmonton	80	47	21	12	16	11	5
1983-84*	Edmonton	80	57	18	5	19	15	4
1984-85*	Edmonton	80	49	20	11	18	15	3
1985-86	Edmonton	80	56	17	7	10	6	4
1986-87*	Edmonton	80	50	24	6	21	16	5
1987-88*	Edmonton	80	44	25	11	18	16	2
1988-89	Edmonton	80	38	34	8	7	3	4
1993-94	Edmonton	60	22	27	11	....	....	....
2002-03	NY Rangers	28	11	13	4	....	....	....
2003-04	NY Rangers	62	22	33	7	....	....	....
	NHL Totals	**932**	**497**	**314**	**121**	**126**	**89**	**37**

* Stanley Cup win.

Club Directory

Madison Square Garden

New York Rangers
14th Floor
2 Pennsylvania Plaza
New York, New York 10121
Phone **212/465-6486**
PR FAX 212/465-6494
www.newyorkrangers.com
Capacity: 18,200

Team Executive Management
Chairman, Madison Square Garden .... James L. Dolan
Vice Chairman, Madison Square Garden .... Hank J. Ratner
President and COO, MSG Sports .... Steve Mills
President and General Manager .... Glen Sather
Senior V.P., Finance and Controller .... John Cudmore
Senior V.P., Sports Team Operations .... Mark Piazza
Senior V.P., Legal Affairs .... Marc Schoenfeld
V.P., Marketing .... Jeanie Baumgartner
V.P., Marketing Services .... Janet Duch
V.P., Sports Team Publicity .... Sandra Carreon-John
V.P., Public Relations & Player Recruitment .... John Rosasco
V.P., Team Sponsorships .... Robert Scolaro
V.P., Community Relations & Fan Development .... Kerryann Tomlinson
V.P., Sports Team Operations .... Jason Vogel

Hockey Club Personnel
Head Coach .... Tom Renney
Assistant G.M., Player Personnel and G.M., Hartford Wolf Pack .... Jim Schoenfeld
Assistant G.M., Hockey Administration .... Cameron Hope
Assistant Coaches .... Benoit Allaire, Perry Pearn, Mike Pelino
Director, Player Personnel .... Gordie Clark
Head Amateur Scout .... Jim Hammett
Director, Player Personnel – Europe .... Christer Rockstrom
Amateur Scouting Staff .... Andre Beaulieu, Rich Brown, Ray Clearwater, Jan Gajdosik, Ernie Gare, Vladimir Lutchenko, Shanon Sather
Professional Scouting Staff .... Frank Effinger, Rick Kehoe, Gilles Leger, Peter Stephan
Prospect Development .... Adam Graves
Head Athletic Trainer .... Jim Ramsay
Equipment Manager .... Acacio Marques
Assistant Equipment Manager .... James "Beets" Johnson
Massage Therapist/Assistant Trainer .... Bruce Lifrieri
Strength and Conditioning Coach .... Reg Grant
Strength and Conditioning Advisor .... Daniel Hedin
Video Analyst .... Jerry Dineen
Manager, MSG Training Center .... Pat Boller
Assistant, MSG Training Center .... Myles Fee

Operations
Director, Accounting .... Jeanine McGrory
Executive Assistant to the President and G.M. .... Sara Adamson
Manager of Scouting .... Victor Saljanin
Administrator .... Tim Criscitelli
Administrative Assistant .... Caroline Giglio

Public Relations
Director, Public Relations .... Sammy Steinlight
Manager, Public Relations .... Jody Sowa

Marketing
Director, Event Presentation .... Ryan Halkett
Manager, Internet Marketing and Development .... Dan David
Music Director, MSG Sports .... Ray Castoldi
Design Director .... Joanecy Kagalingan
Art Director .... Anthony Spera
Coordinator, Marketing .... Leigh Anne Berte
Administrative Assistant, Marketing .... Keely Respass

Sponsorship
Manager, Team Sponsorships .... Kelly Jutras
Coordinator, Team Sponsorships .... Nathan Finkel

Community Relations and Fan Development
Dir., Special Projects and Community Relations Rep. .... Rod Gilbert
Community Relations Development .... Adam Graves
Director, Fan Development .... Leon Friedrich
Manager, Community Relations .... David Martella
Coordinator, Community Relations .... Anthony Zucconi
Field Marketing Coordinator .... Bryan Girsch

Medical
Team Physician and Orthopedic Surgeon .... Dr. Andrew Feldman
Assistant Team Physician .... Dr. Anthony Maddalo
Medical Consultant .... Dr. Ronald Weissman
Team Dentists .... Dr. Joe Esposito, Dr. Don Salomon, Dr. Jeff Shapiro

Miscellaneous
Television Network .... MSG Network
Radio Network .... MSG Radio

General Managers' History

Lester Patrick, 1926-27 to 1945-46; Frank Boucher, 1946-47 to 1954-55; Muzz Patrick, 1955-56 to 1963-64; Emile Francis, 1964-65 to 1974-75; Emile Francis and John Ferguson, 1975-76; John Ferguson, 1976-77, 1977-78; John Ferguson and Fred Shero, 1978-79; Fred Shero, 1979-80; Fred Shero and Craig Patrick, 1980-81; Craig Patrick, 1981-82 to 1985-86; Phil Esposito, 1986-87 to 1988-89; Neil Smith, 1989-90 to 1999-2000; Glen Sather, 2000-01 to date.

Captains' History

Bill Cook, 1926-27 to 1936-37; Art Coulter, 1937-38 to 1941-42; Ott Heller, 1942-43 to 1944-45; Neil Colville 1945-46 to 1948-49; Buddy O'Connor, 1949-50; Frank Eddolls, 1950-51; Frank Eddolls and Allan Stanley, 1951-52; Allan Stanley, 1952-53; Allan Stanley and Don Raleigh, 1953-54; Don Raleigh, 1954-55; Harry Howell, 1955-56, 1956-57; Red Sullivan, 1957-58 to 1960-61; Andy Bathgate, 1961-62, 1962-63; Andy Bathgate and Camille Henry, 1963-64; Camille Henry and Bob Nevin, 1964-65; Bob Nevin 1965-66 to 1970-71; Vic Hadfield, 1971-72 to 1973-74; Brad Park, 1974-75; Brad Park and Phil Esposito, 1975-76; Phil Esposito, 1976-77, 1977-78; Dave Maloney, 1978-79, 1979-80; Dave Maloney, Walt Tkaczuk and Barry Beck, 1980-81; Barry Beck, 1981-82 to 1985-86; Ron Greschner, 1986-87; Ron Greschner and Kelly Kisio, 1987-88; Kelly Kisio, 1988-89 to 1990-91; Mark Messier, 1991-92 to 1996-97; Brian Leetch, 1997-98 to 1999-2000; Mark Messier, 2000-01 to 2003-04; no captain, 2005-06; Jaromir Jagr, 2006-07 to date.

Ottawa Senators

2006-07 Results: 48W-25L-3OTL-6SOL 105PTS.
Second, Northeast Division

Year-by-Year Record

Season	GP	Home W	Home L	Home T	Home OL	Road W	Road L	Road T	Road OL	Overall W	Overall L	Overall T	Overall OL	GF	GA	Pts.	Finished	Playoff Result
2006-07	82	25	13	....	3	23	12	....	6	48	25	....	9	288	222	105	2nd, Northeast Div.	Lost Final
2005-06	82	29	9	....	3	23	12	....	6	52	21	....	9	314	211	113	1st, Northeast Div.	Lost Conf. Semi-Final
2004-05	....	....	....	....	....	....	....	....	....	....	....	....	....	....	....	....		
2003-04	82	23	8	5	5	20	15	5	1	43	23	10	6	262	189	102	3rd, Northeast Div.	Lost Conf. Quarter-Final
2002-03	82	28	9	3	1	24	12	5	0	52	21	8	1	263	182	113	1st, Northeast Div.	Lost Conf. Championship
2001-02	82	21	13	3	4	18	14	6	3	39	27	9	7	243	208	94	3rd, Northeast Div.	Lost Conf. Semi-Final
2000-01	82	26	7	5	3	22	14	4	1	48	21	9	4	274	205	109	1st, Northeast Div.	Lost Conf. Quarter-Final
1999-2000	82	24	10	5	2	17	18	6	0	41	28	11	2	244	210	95	2nd, Northeast Div.	Lost Conf. Quarter-Final
1998-99	82	22	11	8	....	22	12	7	....	44	23	15	....	239	179	103	1st, Northeast Div.	Lost Conf. Quarter-Final
1997-98	82	18	16	7	....	16	17	8	....	34	33	15	....	193	200	83	5th, Northeast Div.	Lost Conf. Semi-Final
1996-97	82	16	17	8	....	15	19	7	....	31	36	15	....	226	234	77	3rd, Northeast Div.	Lost Conf. Quarter-Final
1995-96	82	8	28	5	....	10	31	0	....	18	59	5	....	191	291	41	6th, Northeast Div.	Out of Playoffs
1994-95	48	5	16	3	....	4	18	2	....	9	34	5	....	117	174	23	7th, Northeast Div.	Out of Playoffs
1993-94	84	8	30	4	....	6	31	5	....	14	61	9	....	201	397	37	7th, Northeast Div.	Out of Playoffs
1992-93	84	9	29	4	....	1	41	0	....	10	70	4	....	202	395	24	6th, Adams Div.	Out of Playoffs

Key Off-Season Signings/Acquisitions

2007

June 18 • Named **Bryan Murray** general manager.
22 • Re-signed C **Dean McAmmond**.
July 3 • Signed 2005 1st-round pick (9th overall), D **Brian Lee**.
6 • Named **John Paddock** head coach.
13 • Signed RW **Niko Dimitrakos**.
13 • Re-signed D **Lawrence Nycholat**.
17 • Acquired RW **Shean Donovan** from Boston for LW **Peter Schaefer**.
24 • Re-signed G **Ray Emery**.
31 • Re-signed C **Chris Kelly**.
Aug. 8 • Signed D **Luke Richardson**.

2007-08 Schedule

Oct.	Wed.	3	at Toronto
	Thu.	4	Toronto
	Sat.	6	NY Rangers
	Mon.	8	New Jersey*
	Wed.	10	at Atlanta
	Thu.	11	Carolina
	Sat.	13	at NY Rangers
	Thu.	18	Montreal
	Sat.	20	Florida
	Sat.	27	at New Jersey
Nov.	Thu.	1	Atlanta
	Sat.	3	Boston
	Sun.	4	at Boston
	Tue.	6	Toronto
	Thu.	8	Washington
	Sat.	10	Montreal*
	Thu.	15	Buffalo
	Sat.	17	at Toronto
	Mon.	19	at Montreal
	Wed.	21	at Buffalo
	Thu.	22	Pittsburgh
	Sat.	24	Philadelphia
	Wed.	28	at NY Islanders
	Thu.	29	Nashville
Dec.	Sat.	1	NY Rangers*
	Tue.	4	at Tampa Bay
	Wed.	5	at Florida
	Fri.	7	at Dallas
	Wed.	12	at Carolina
	Thu.	13	at Pittsburgh
	Sat.	15	Atlanta
	Tue.	18	at Boston
	Thu.	20	at Atlanta
	Sat.	22	Chicago
	Sun.	23	at NY Rangers
	Wed.	26	at Buffalo
	Thu.	27	NY Islanders
	Sat.	29	Washington*
Jan.	Tue.	1	at Washington*
	Fri.	4	at Buffalo
	Sat.	5	Tampa Bay
	Thu.	10	Buffalo
	Sat.	12	Detroit
	Sun.	13	NY Islanders
	Tue.	15	at Washington
	Thu.	17	Carolina
	Sat.	19	Tampa Bay
	Sun.	20	at Philadelphia
	Tue.	22	at Florida
	Thu.	24	at Tampa Bay
	Tue.	29	at NY Islanders
	Thu.	31	Boston
Feb.	Sat.	2	at Toronto
	Tue.	5	at Montreal
	Thu.	7	Florida
	Sat.	9	Montreal
	Tue.	12	Buffalo
	Wed.	13	at New Jersey
	Sat.	16	New Jersey
	Tue.	19	Philadelphia
	Thu.	21	Columbus
	Sat.	23	at Pittsburgh*
	Mon.	25	Toronto
	Tue.	26	at Boston
	Thu.	28	at Philadelphia
Mar.	Sat.	1	Pittsburgh*
	Mon.	3	at Anaheim
	Wed.	5	at San Jose
	Thu.	6	at Los Angeles
	Sat.	8	at Phoenix
	Tue.	11	Boston
	Thu.	13	at Montreal
	Sun.	16	at Carolina*
	Thu.	20	St. Louis
	Sat.	22	Toronto
	Mon.	24	at Montreal
	Tue.	25	at Buffalo
	Thu.	27	Buffalo
	Sat.	29	at Boston*
Apr.	Tue.	1	Montreal
	Thu.	3	at Toronto
	Fri.	4	Boston

* Denotes afternoon game.

NORTHEAST DIVISION
16th NHL Season

Franchise date: December 16, 1991

Dany Heatley had eight goals in his last eight games of the season to reach 50 on the year and become the first NHL player with back-to-back 50-goal seasons since Pavel Bure in 1999-2000 and 2000-01.

2007-08 Player Personnel

FORWARDS	HT	WT	S	Place of Birth	*Age	2006-07 Club
ALFREDSSON, Daniel	5-11	207	R	Goteborg, Sweden	34	Ottawa
BOIS, Danny	6-1	197	R	Thunder Bay, Ont.	24	Ottawa-Binghamton
DIMITRAKOS, Niko	5-11	205	R	Somerville, MA	28	Phi-Phi (AHL)-Chi (AHL)
DONOVAN, Shean	6-2	209	R	Timmins, Ont.	32	Boston
EAVES, Patrick	6-0	188	R	Calgary, Alta.	23	Ottawa
FISHER, Mike	6-1	213	R	Peterborough, Ont.	27	Ottawa
HEATLEY, Dany	6-3	216	L	Freiburg, West Germany	26	Ottawa
HENNESSY, Josh	6-0	198	L	Brockton, MA	22	Ottawa-Binghamton
KELLY, Chris	6-0	199	L	Toronto, Ont.	26	Ottawa
MAPLETOFT, Justin	6-1	202	L	Lloydminster, Sask.	26	Nurnberg
McAMMOND, Dean	5-11	189	L	Grand Cache, Alta.	34	Ottawa
McGRATTAN, Brian	6-4	231	R	Hamilton, Ont.	26	Ottawa
NEIL, Chris	6-1	209	R	Markdale, Ont.	28	Ottawa
SPEZZA, Jason	6-3	213	R	Mississauga, Ont.	24	Ottawa
VERMETTE, Antoine	6-0	199	L	St-Agapit, Que.	25	Ottawa

DEFENSEMEN	HT	WT	S	Place of Birth	*Age	2006-07 Club
CARKNER, Matt	6-4	230	R	Winchester, Ont.	26	Wilkes-Barre
CORVO, Joe	6-0	205	R	Oak Park, IL	30	Ottawa
KINCH, Matt	5-11	185	L	Red Deer, Alta.	27	Straubing
MESZAROS, Andrej	6-1	220	L	Povazska Bystrica, Czech.	21	Ottawa
NYCHOLAT, Lawrence	5-11	197	L	Calgary, Alta.	28	Wsh-Hershey-Ott
PHILLIPS, Chris	6-3	216	L	Calgary, Alta.	29	Ottawa
REDDEN, Wade	6-2	208	L	Lloydminster, Sask.	30	Ottawa
RICHARDSON, Luke	6-4	215	L	Ottawa, Ont.	38	Tampa Bay
SCHUBERT, Christoph	6-3	237	L	Munich, West Germany	25	Ottawa
VOLCHENKOV, Anton	6-1	226	L	Moscow, USSR	25	Ottawa

GOALTENDERS	HT	WT	C	Place of Birth	*Age	2006-07 Club
EMERY, Ray	6-2	202	L	Cayuga, Ont.	25	Ottawa
GERBER, Martin	5-11	201	L	Burgdorf, Switz.	33	Ottawa

* – Age at start of 2007-08 season

Coach

JOHN PADDOCK
Coach, Ottawa Senators. Born in Brandon, Man., June 9, 1954.

John Paddock was named the sixth head coach in Ottawa Senators history on July 6, 2007. Paddock joined the Senators in July 2002 as head coach of the club's American Hockey League affiliate in Binghamton. He was then named assistant coach by Bryan Murray on July 9, 2004, and served as co-coach with Dave Cameron for the 2004-05 Binghamton Senators during the NHL lockout.

Paddock began his pro coaching career during the 1981-82 season and led the NHL's Winnipeg Jets from 1991-92 to 1994-95. He was also general manager with the Jets/Phoenix Coyotes between 1993-94 and 1996-97. He is one of the most successful head coaches in AHL history, guiding three different franchises to Calder Cup wins (Maine in 1984, Hershey in 1988 and Hartford in 2000). In 14 AHL seasons as head coach with the Maine Mariners, Hershey Bears, Binghamton Rangers, Hartford Wolf Pack and Binghamton Senators, Paddock compiled a record of 542-382-103 (.578), ranking as one the league's best in all-time victories. He was the co-winner of the Louis A.R. Pieri Award as the AHL's coach of the year in 1988 (sharing the award with Mike Milbury), and is a two-time recipient of *The Hockey News* minor pro coach of the year honor (1986, 2000). The Ottawa Senators team that reached the Stanley Cup Final in 2007 featured nine players who had played under Paddock in Binghamton: Ray Emery, Chris Kelly, Denis Hamel, Brian McGrattan, Chris Neil, Christoph Schubert, Jason Spezza, Antoine Vermette and Anton Volchenkov.

A third-round draft choice of the Washington Capitals in 1974, Paddock appeared in 87 regular-season games over five seasons between 1975 and 1983, tallying eight goals and 14 assists with Washington, Philadelphia and Quebec. In addition to playing in the 1980 Stanley Cup Final with the Flyers, the right winger also skated in 445 career AHL matches from 1974 to 1984, winning back-to-back Calder Cups with Maine in 1978 and 1979.

Coaching Record

		Regular Season				Playoffs		
Season	Team	Games	W	L	O/T	Games	W	L
1981-82	Maine (AHL)	5	2	2	1	....	....	....
1983-84	Maine (AHL)	62	23	30	9	17	12	5
1984-85	Maine (AHL)	80	38	32	10	11	5	6
1985-86	Hershey (AHL)	80	48	29	3	18	10	8
1986-87	Hershey (AHL)	80	43	36	1	5	1	4
1987-88	Hershey (AHL)	80	50	27	3	12	12	0
1988-89	Hershey (AHL)	80	40	30	10	12	7	5
1990-91	Binghamton (AHL)	80	44	30	6	10	4	6
1991-92	**Winnipeg (NHL)**	**80**	**33**	**32**	**15**	**7**	**3**	**4**
1992-93	**Winnipeg (NHL)**	**84**	**40**	**37**	**7**	**6**	**2**	**4**
1993-94	**Winnipeg (NHL)**	**84**	**24**	**51**	**9**	....	....	....
1994-95	**Winnipeg (NHL)**	**33**	**9**	**18**	**6**	....	....	....
1999-2000	Hartford (AHL)	80	49	24	7	23	15	8
2000-01	Hartford (AHL)	80	40	32	8	5	2	3
2001-02	Hartford (AHL)	80	41	29	10	10	4	6
2002-03	Binghamton (AHL)	80	43	26	11	14	8	6
2003-04	Binghamton (AHL)	80	34	34	12	2	0	2
2004-05	Binghamton (AHL)	80	47	21	12	6	2	4
	NHL Totals	**281**	**106**	**138**	**37**	**13**	**5**	**8**

2006-07 Scoring

* – rookie

Regular Season

Pos	#	Player	Team	GP	G	A	Pts	+/–	PIM	PP	SH	GW	S	%
L	15	Dany Heatley	OTT	82	50	55	105	31	74	17	3	10	310	16.1
C	19	Jason Spezza	OTT	67	34	53	87	19	45	13	1	5	162	21.0
R	11	Daniel Alfredsson	OTT	77	29	58	87	42	42	7	2	7	240	12.1
C	12	Mike Fisher	OTT	68	22	26	48	15	41	7	2	3	193	11.4
L	27	Peter Schaefer	OTT	77	12	34	46	7	32	5	0	2	132	9.1
R	89	Mike Comrie	PHX	24	7	13	20	1	20	4	0	1	38	18.4
			OTT	41	13	12	25	–1	24	3	0	2	87	14.9
			TOTAL	65	20	25	45	0	44	7	0	3	125	16.0
L	20	Antoine Vermette	OTT	77	19	20	39	–2	52	2	3	2	151	12.6
C	22	Chris Kelly	OTT	82	15	23	38	28	40	1	2	0	131	11.5
D	42	Tom Preissing	OTT	80	7	31	38	40	18	3	0	0	94	7.4
D	7	Joe Corvo	OTT	76	8	29	37	8	42	3	0	2	160	5.0
L	61	Oleg Saprykin	PHX	59	14	20	34	8	54	2	0	2	135	10.4
			OTT	12	1	1	2	–3	4	0	0	0	15	6.7
			TOTAL	71	15	21	36	5	58	2	0	2	150	10.0
D	6	Wade Redden	OTT	64	7	29	36	1	50	4	0	3	122	5.7
D	14	Andrej Meszaros	OTT	82	7	28	35	–15	102	0	0	1	147	4.8
R	44	Patrick Eaves	OTT	73	14	18	32	1	36	3	1	1	130	10.8
C	37	Dean McAmmond	OTT	81	14	15	29	11	28	0	2	1	86	16.3
R	25	Chris Neil	OTT	82	12	16	28	6	177	3	0	3	139	8.6
D	4	Chris Phillips	OTT	82	8	18	26	36	80	0	1	3	94	8.5
D	5	Christoph Schubert	OTT	80	8	17	25	30	56	1	0	1	97	8.2
D	24	Anton Volchenkov	OTT	78	1	18	19	37	67	0	0	0	85	1.2
D	2	Lawrence Nycholat	WSH	18	2	6	8	–3	12	0	0	0	22	9.1
			OTT	1	0	0	0	0	0	0	0	0	3	0.0
			TOTAL	19	2	6	8	–3	12	0	0	0	25	8.0
R	16	Brian McGrattan	OTT	45	0	2	2	–1	100	0	0	0	22	0.0
C	36 *	Josh Hennessy	OTT	10	1	0	1	0	4	0	0	0	6	16.7
C	55 *	Alexei Kaigorodov	OTT	6	0	1	1	1	0	0	0	0	3	0.0
D	41	Tomas Malec	OTT	1	0	0	0	0	0	0	0	0	1	0.0
R	49 *	Danny Bois	OTT	1	0	0	0	0	7	0	0	0	1	0.0
C	43	Serge Payer	OTT	5	0	0	0	–1	0	0	0	0	4	0.0

Goaltending

No.	Goaltender	GPI	Mins	Avg	W	L	OT	EN	SO	GA	SA	S%	G	A	PIM
1	Ray Emery	58	3351	2.47	33	16	6	3	5	138	1691	.918	0	1	30
29	Martin Gerber	29	1599	2.78	15	9	3	1	1	74	784	.906	0	0	0
	Totals	**82**	**4974**	**2.61**	**48**	**25**	**9**	**4**	**6**	**216**	**2479**	**.913**			

Playoffs

Pos	#	Player	Team	GP	G	A	Pts	+/–	PIM	PP	SH	GW	OT	S	%
R	11	Daniel Alfredsson	OTT	20	14	8	22	4	10	6	1	4	1	66	21.2
L	15	Dany Heatley	OTT	20	7	15	22	4	14	2	0	2	0	59	11.9
C	19	Jason Spezza	OTT	20	7	15	22	5	10	3	0	0	0	49	14.3
C	12	Mike Fisher	OTT	20	5	5	10	–2	24	2	1	1	0	54	9.3
D	6	Wade Redden	OTT	20	3	7	10	6	10	3	0	1	0	23	13.0
D	7	Joe Corvo	OTT	20	2	7	9	4	6	1	0	1	1	49	4.1
L	37	Dean McAmmond	OTT	18	5	3	8	5	11	0	1	1	0	15	33.3
C	22	Chris Kelly	OTT	20	3	4	7	0	4	0	0	0	0	27	11.1
D	42	Tom Preissing	OTT	20	2	5	7	3	10	1	0	1	0	21	9.5
D	14	Andrej Meszaros	OTT	20	1	6	7	5	12	0	0	0	0	26	3.8
R	89	Mike Comrie	OTT	20	2	4	6	–1	17	0	0	0	0	25	8.0
D	24	Anton Volchenkov	OTT	20	2	4	6	–2	24	0	0	1	0	18	11.1
L	27	Peter Schaefer	OTT	20	1	5	6	1	10	0	0	0	0	33	3.0
L	20	Antoine Vermette	OTT	20	2	3	5	2	6	0	0	0	0	28	7.1
R	25	Chris Neil	OTT	20	2	2	4	0	20	0	0	0	0	31	6.5
L	61	Oleg Saprykin	OTT	15	1	1	2	0	4	0	0	1	0	19	5.3
R	44	Patrick Eaves	OTT	7	0	2	2	0	2	0	0	0	0	7	0.0
D	5	Christoph Schubert	OTT	20	0	1	1	–5	22	0	0	0	0	16	0.0
D	4	Chris Phillips	OTT	20	0	0	0	–2	24	0	0	0	0	7	0.0

Goaltending

No.	Goaltender	GPI	Mins	Avg	W	L	EN	SO	GA	SA	S%	G	A	PIM
1	Ray Emery	20	1249	2.26	13	7	0	3	47	505	.907	0	2	0
	Totals	**20**	**1256**	**2.25**	**13**	**7**	**0**	**3**	**47**	**505**	**.907**			

General Managers' History

Mel Bridgman, 1992-93; Randy Sexton, 1993-94, 1994-95; Randy Sexton and Pierre Gauthier, 1995-96; Pierre Gauthier, 1996-97, 1997-98; Rick Dudley, 1998-99; Marshall Johnston, 1999-2000 to 2001-02; John Muckler, 2002-03 to 2006-07; Bryan Murray, 2007-08.

Club Records

Team

(Figures in brackets for season records are games played; records for fewest points, wins, ties, losses, goals, goals against are for 70 or more games)

Most Points .... 113 — 2002-03 (82), 2005-06 (82)
Most Wins .... 52 — 2002-03 (82), 2005-06 (82)
Most Ties .... 15 — 1996-97 (82), 1997-98 (82), 1998-99 (82)
Most Losses .... 70 — 1992-93 (84)
Most Goals .... 312 — 2005-06 (82)
Most Goals Against .... 397 — 1993-94 (84)
Fewest Points .... 24 — 1992-93 (84)
Fewest Wins .... 10 — 1992-93 (84)
Fewest Ties .... 4 — 1992-93 (84)
Fewest Losses .... 21 — 2000-01 (82), 2002-03 (82), 2005-06 (82)
Fewest Goals .... 191 — 1995-96 (82)
Fewest Goals Against .... 179 — 1998-99 (82)
Longest Winning Streak
Overall .... 7 — Oct. 25-Nov. 13/01
Home .... 8 — Nov. 14-Dec. 14/02
Away .... 6 — Mar. 18-Apr. 5/03
Longest Undefeated Streak
Overall .... 11 — Three times
Home .... 12 — Dec. 18/03-Jan. 24/04 (10 wins, 2 ties)
Away .... 7 — Three times

** NHL records do not include neutral site games

Longest Losing Streak
Overall .... 14 — Mar. 2-Apr. 7/93
Home .... *11 — Oct. 27-Dec. 8/93
Away .... *38 — Oct. 10/92-Apr. 3/93**
Longest Winless Streak
Overall .... 21 — Oct. 10-Nov. 23/92 (20 losses, 1 tie)
Home .... *17 — Oct. 28/95-Jan. 27/96 (15 losses, 2 ties)
Away .... *38 — Oct. 10/92-Apr. 3/93 (38 losses)
Most Shutouts, Season .... 10 — 2001-02 (82)
Most PIM, Season .... 1,716 — 1992-93 (84)
Most Goals, Game .... 11 — Nov. 13/01 (Ott. 11 at Wsh. 5)

Individual

Most Seasons .... 11 — Daniel Alfredsson
Most Games, Career .... 783 — Daniel Alfredsson
Most Goals, Career .... 291 — Daniel Alfredsson
Most Assists, Career .... 467 — Daniel Alfredsson
Most Points, Career .... 758 — Daniel Alfredsson (291G, 467A)
Most PIM, Career .... 953 — Chris Neil
Most Shutouts, Career .... 30 — Patrick Lalime
Longest Consecutive Games Streak .... 292 — Alexei Yashin (Dec. 31/95-Apr. 17/99)
Most Goals, Season .... 50 — Dany Heatley (2005-06; 2006-07)
Most Assists, Season .... 71 — Jason Spezza (2005-06)
Most Points, Season .... 105 — Dany Heatley (2006-07; 50G, 55A)
Most PIM, Season .... 318 — Mike Peluso (1992-93)
Most Points, Defenseman, Season .... 63 — Norm Maciver (1992-93; 17G, 46A)
Most Points, Center, Season .... 94 — Alexei Yashin (1998-99; 44G, 50A)
Most Points, Right Wing, Season .... 103 — Daniel Alfredsson (2005-06; 43G, 60A)
Most Points, Left Wing, Season .... 105 — Dany Heatley (2006-07; 50G, 55A)
Most Points, Rookie, Season .... 79 — Alexei Yashin (1993-94; 30G, 49A)
Most Shutouts, Season .... 8 — Patrick Lalime (2002-03)
Most Goals, Game .... 4 — Three times
Most Assists, Game .... 5 — Marian Hossa (Jan. 4/01)
Most Points, Game .... 6 — Dan Quinn (Oct. 15/95; 3G, 3A), Radek Bonk (Jan. 4/01; 3G, 3A), Daniel Alfredsson (Nov. 2/05; 4G, 2A)

* NHL Record.

Coaching History

Rick Bowness, 1992-93 to 1994-95; Rick Bowness, Dave Allison and Jacques Martin, 1995-96; Jacques Martin, 1996-97 to 2000-01; Jacques Martin and Roger Neilson, 2001-02; Jacques Martin, 2002-03, 2003-04; Bryan Murray, 2004-05 to 2006-07; John Paddock, 2007-08.

Captains' History

Laurie Boschman, 1992-93; Brad Shaw, Mark Lamb and Gord Dineen, 1993-94; Randy Cunneyworth, 1994-95 to 1997-98; Alexei Yashin, 1998-99; Daniel Alfredsson, 1999-2000 to date.

Retired Numbers

8 Frank Finnigan 1924-1934

All-time Record vs. Other Clubs

Regular Season

	At Home								On Road								Total							
	GP	W	L	T	OL	GF	GA	PTS	GP	W	L	T	OL	GF	GA	PTS	GP	W	L	T	OL	GF	GA	PTS
Anaheim	9	4	3	1	1	27	23	10	9	3	4	2	0	18	21	8	18	7	7	3	1	45	44	18
Atlanta	14	8	2	1	3	61	38	20	14	8	4	1	1	57	49	18	28	16	6	2	4	118	87	38
Boston	39	18	18	3	0	103	117	39	41	12	23	5	1	114	144	30	80	30	41	8	1	217	261	69
Buffalo	41	16	15	7	3	112	108	42	39	11	21	3	4	80	123	29	80	27	36	10	7	192	231	71
Calgary	11	5	2	3	1	27	25	14	12	4	6	1	1	26	40	10	23	9	8	4	2	53	65	24
Carolina	33	14	13	4	2	92	85	34	31	10	17	4	0	80	90	24	64	24	30	8	2	172	175	58
Chicago	10	4	5	0	1	31	30	9	9	2	4	2	1	21	22	7	19	6	9	2	2	52	52	16
Colorado	19	8	8	3	0	54	66	19	16	3	12	1	0	47	72	7	35	11	20	4	0	101	138	26
Columbus	3	2	0	1	0	12	6	5	3	1	1	1	0	11	13	3	6	3	1	2	0	23	19	8
Dallas	10	4	6	0	0	22	26	8	11	4	7	0	0	28	44	8	21	8	13	0	0	50	70	16
Detroit	10	3	5	1	1	28	29	8	10	4	5	0	1	22	35	9	20	7	10	1	2	50	64	17
Edmonton	11	4	5	2	0	23	29	10	12	3	7	2	0	30	42	8	23	7	12	4	0	53	71	18
Florida	26	13	10	2	1	79	66	29	26	15	10	1	0	85	79	31	52	28	20	3	1	164	145	60
Los Angeles	10	5	3	1	1	35	29	12	10	1	8	1	0	21	46	3	20	6	11	2	1	56	75	15
Minnesota	3	2	1	0	0	9	7	4	4	2	1	1	0	14	11	5	7	4	2	1	0	23	18	9
Montreal	39	21	17	1	0	124	107	43	41	15	21	4	1	116	122	35	80	36	38	5	1	240	229	78
Nashville	5	4	1	0	0	15	7	8	5	2	3	0	0	11	14	4	10	6	4	0	0	26	21	12
New Jersey	28	8	15	3	2	64	71	21	27	9	14	2	2	64	76	22	55	17	29	5	4	128	147	43
NY Islanders	27	17	5	5	0	95	67	39	28	17	5	6	0	108	86	40	55	34	10	11	0	203	153	79
NY Rangers	27	12	12	3	0	81	71	27	27	15	12	0	0	85	86	30	54	27	24	3	0	166	157	57
Philadelphia	28	11	11	6	0	80	82	28	27	10	15	2	0	78	88	22	55	21	26	8	0	158	170	50
Phoenix	12	5	6	1	0	36	36	11	10	5	4	1	0	38	34	11	22	10	10	2	0	74	70	22
Pittsburgh	31	10	15	5	1	86	99	26	31	9	16	4	2	84	109	24	62	19	31	9	3	170	208	50
St. Louis	10	4	6	0	0	23	36	8	10	4	4	2	0	29	29	10	20	8	10	2	0	52	65	18
San Jose	10	4	2	4	0	36	28	12	9	4	5	0	0	16	18	8	19	8	7	4	0	52	46	20
Tampa Bay	27	18	9	0	0	103	61	36	27	16	9	2	0	96	76	34	54	34	18	2	0	199	137	70
Toronto	28	18	7	1	2	95	75	39	30	16	11	2	1	92	77	35	58	34	18	3	3	187	152	74
Vancouver	11	5	4	1	1	25	26	12	12	5	5	1	1	28	36	12	23	10	9	2	2	53	62	24
Washington	27	15	10	1	1	99	76	32	28	11	12	4	1	81	89	27	55	26	22	5	2	180	165	59
Totals	**559**	**262**	**216**	**60**	**21**	**1677**	**1526**	**605**	**559**	**221**	**266**	**55**	**17**	**1580**	**1771**	**514**	**1118**	**483**	**482**	**115**	**38**	**3257**	**3297**	**1119**

Playoffs

	Series	W	L	GP	W	L	T	GF	GA	Last Mtg.	Rnd.	Result
Anaheim	1	0	1	5	1	4	0	11	16	2007	F	L 1-4
Buffalo	4	1	3	21	8	13	0	47	52	2007	CF	W 4-1
New Jersey	3	2	1	18	11	7	0	41	40	2007	CSF	W 4-1
NY Islanders	1	1	0	5	4	1	0	13	7	2003	CQF	W 4-1
Philadelphia	2	2	0	11	8	3	0	28	12	2003	CSF	W 4-2
Pittsburgh	1	1	0	5	4	1	0	18	10	2007	CQF	W 4-1
Tampa Bay	1	1	0	5	4	1	0	23	13	2006	CQF	W 4-1
Toronto	4	0	4	24	8	16	0	42	57	2004	CQF	L 3-4
Washington	1	0	1	5	1	4	0	7	18	1998	CSF	L 1-4
Totals	**18**	**8**	**10**	**99**	**49**	**50**	**0**	**230**	**225**			

Playoff Results 2007-2002

Year	Round	Opponent	Result	GF	GA
2007	F	Anaheim	L 1-4	11	16
	CF	Buffalo	W 4-1	15	10
	CSF	New Jersey	W 4-1	15	11
	CQF	Pittsburgh	W 4-1	18	10
2006	CSF	Buffalo	L 1-4	13	16
	CQF	Tampa Bay	W 4-1	23	13
2004	CQF	Toronto	L 3-4	11	14
2003	CF	New Jersey	L 3-4	13	17
	CSF	Philadelphia	W 4-2	17	10
	CQF	NY Islanders	W 4-1	13	7
2002	CSF	Toronto	L 3-4	18	16
	CQF	Philadelphia	W 4-1	11	2

Abbreviations: Round: F - Final; **CF** – conference final; **CSF** – conference semi-final; **CQF** – conference quarter-final.

Colorado totals include Quebec, 1992-93 to 1994-95.
Dallas totals include Minnesota North Stars, 1992-93.

Carolina totals include Hartford, 1992-93 to 1996-97.
Phoenix totals include Winnipeg, 1992-93 to 1995-96.

2006-07 Results

Oct.	4	at Toronto	4-1		3	Buffalo	6-3
	5	Toronto	0-6		6	New Jersey	2-3
	7	Buffalo	3-4		7	Philadelphia	6-1
	12	Calgary	0-1		9	Boston	5-2
	14	at Montreal	3-2†		11	at NY Rangers	6-4
	19	Colorado	1-2		13	Montreal	8-3
	21	New Jersey	8-1		16	Washington	5-2
	24	at Toronto	6-2		18	Vancouver	1-2
	26	Toronto	7-2		20	at Boston	3-0
	28	at Boston	1-2		27	Boston	3-1
	31	at Montreal	2-4		29	at Montreal	1-3
Nov.	4	Carolina	2-3		30	Washington	3-2
	6	at Washington	3-4*	**Feb.**	3	Toronto	2-3†
	8	at Atlanta	4-5		7	at Buffalo	2-3
	10	at Pittsburgh	6-3		8	Montreal	4-1
	11	at Boston	3-4		10	at Montreal	5-3
	13	Montreal	3-6		14	Florida	4-0
	15	at Buffalo	4-2		17	Atlanta	5-3
	17	at New Jersey	2-3		20	Edmonton	4-3†
	18	Buffalo	4-1		22	at Buffalo	5-6†
	20	Minnesota	5-3		24	Buffalo	6-5
	22	at Philadelphia	3-2*		27	at Carolina	4-2
	24	at Florida	6-4		28	Carolina	2-0
	26	at Tampa Bay	1-3	**Mar.**	2	at Atlanta	2-4
	28	at Carolina	4-1		4	at Chicago	3-4†
	30	Florida	6-0		6	Pittsburgh	4-5†
Dec.	2	Tampa Bay	5-2		8	Toronto	5-1
	5	at NY Islanders	4-2		10	at Toronto	3-4*
	6	at Washington	2-6		13	at NY Rangers	3-2
	9	NY Rangers	1-3		15	NY Islanders	5-2
	10	at Columbus	2-6		17	Philadelphia	3-2
	12	at Detroit	3-2		18	at Pittsburgh	3-4†
	14	at Nashville	0-6		20	at St. Louis	4-2
	16	at Buffalo	3-1		22	at Florida	4-2
	19	Boston	2-7		24	at Tampa Bay	7-2
	21	Tampa Bay	2-4		27	Boston	2-3
	23	at Philadelphia	6-3		30	Montreal	5-2
	27	NY Islanders	2-0		31	at NY Islanders	5-2
	29	NY Rangers	1-0	**Apr.**	3	at New Jersey	1-2†
	30	at Toronto	3-2*		5	Pittsburgh	2-3
Jan.	1	Atlanta	2-3*		7	at Boston	6-3

* – Overtime † – Shootout

Entry Draft Selections 2007-1993

2007

Pick	
29	James O'Brien
60	Ruslan Bashkirov
90	Louie Caporusso
120	Ben Blood

2006

Pick	
28	Nick Foligno
68	Eric Gryba
91	Kaspars Daugavins
121	Pierre-Luc Lessard
151	Ryan Daniels
181	Kevin Koopman
211	Erik Condra

2005

Pick	
9	Brian Lee
70	Vitali Anikeyenko
95	Cody Bass
98	Ilja Zubov
115	Janne Kolehmainen
136	Tomas Kudelka
186	Dmitri Megalinsky
204	Colin Greening

2004

Pick	
23	Andrej Meszaros
58	Kirill Lyamin
77	Shawn Weller
87	Peter Regin
89	Jeff Glass
122	Alexander Nikulin
141	Jim McKenzie
156	Roman Wick
219	Joe Cooper
251	Matthew McIlvane
284	John Wikner

2003

Pick	
29	Patrick Eaves
67	Igor Mirnov
100	Philippe Seydoux
135	Mattias Karlsson
142	Tim Cook
166	Sergei Gimaev
228	Will Colbert
260	Ossi Louhivaara
291	Brian Elliott

2002

Pick	
16	Jakub Klepis
47	Alexei Kaigorodov
75	Arttu Luttinen
113	Scott Dobben
125	Johan Bjork
150	Brock Hooton
246	Josef Vavra
276	Vitali Atyushov

2001

Pick	
2	Jason Spezza
23	Tim Gleason
81	Neil Komadoski
99	Ray Emery
127	Christoph Schubert
162	Stefan Schauer
193	Brooks Laich
218	Jan Platil
223	Brandon Bochenski
235	Neil Petruic
256	Gregg Johnson
286	Toni Dahlman

2000

Pick	
21	Anton Volchenkov
45	Mathieu Chouinard
55	Antoine Vermette
87	Jan Bohac
122	Derrick Byfuglien
156	Greg Zanon
157	Grant Potulny
158	Sean Connolly
188	Jason Maleyko
283	James Demone

1999

Pick	
26	Martin Havlat
48	Simon Lajeunesse
62	Teemu Sainomaa
94	Chris Kelly
154	Andrew Ianiero
164	Martin Prusek
201	Mikko Ruutu
209	Layne Ulmer
213	Alexandre Giroux
269	Konstantin Gorovikov

1998

Pick	
15	Mathieu Chouinard
44	Mike Fisher
58	Chris Bala
74	Julien Vauclair
101	Petr Schastlivy
130	Gavin McLeod
161	Chris Neil
188	Michel Periard
223	Sergei Verenikin
246	Rastislav Pavlikovsky

1997

Pick	
12	Marian Hossa
58	Jani Hurme
66	Josh Langfeld
119	Magnus Arvedson
146	Jeff Sullivan
173	Robin Bacul
203	Nick Gillis
229	Karel Rachunek

1996

Pick	
1	Chris Phillips
81	Antti-Jussi Niemi
136	Andreas Dackell
163	Francois Hardy
212	Erich Goldmann
216	Ivan Ciernik
239	Sami Salo

1995

Pick	
1	Bryan Berard
27	Marc Moro
53	Brad Larsen
89	Kevin Bolibruck
103	Kevin Boyd
131	David Hruska
183	Kaj Linna
184	Ray Schultz
231	Erik Kaminski

1994

Pick	
3	Radek Bonk
29	Stan Neckar
81	Bryan Masotta
131	Mike Gaffney
133	Daniel Alfredsson
159	Doug Sproule
210	Frederic Cassivi
211	Danny Dupont
237	Stephen MacKinnon
274	Antti Tormanen

1993

Pick	
1	Alexandre Daigle
27	Radim Bicanek
53	Patrick Charbonneau
91	Cosmo Dupaul
131	Rick Bodkin
157	Sergei Poleschuk
183	Jason Disher
209	Toby Kvalevog
227	Pavol Demitra
235	Rick Schuwerk

General Manager

BRYAN MURRAY
General Manager, Ottawa Senators.
Born in Shawville, Que., December 5, 1942.

On June 18, 2007, Bryan Murray was appointed as the seventh general manager of the Ottawa Senators. Murray had joined the organization on June 8, 2004, when he was named the club's head coach. Murray resigned as senior vice president and general manager of Anaheim to take the coaching position in Ottawa. As coach in Ottawa in 2006–07, Murray led the Senators to the Stanley Cup Finals for the first time in franchise history, only to lose to his former Anaheim team. He also has previous front office experience as vice president and general manager of the Florida Panthers from 1994 to 2001, assembling a team that reached the Stanley Cup Finals in just its third year of existence in 1996.

Murray's NHL career began as head coach of the Washington Capials in 1981. He has served 16 years behind the bench, coaching more than 1,300 regular-season and playoff games, including 665 wins. He earned the Jack Adams Award as coach of the year in 1983-84. Murray's regular-season coaching record in Ottawa is 100-46-18 and includes winning the 2007 Prince of Wales Trophy as the NHL's Eastern Conference champions.

NHL Coaching Record

		Regular Season				Playoffs		
Season	Team	Games	W	L	O/T	Games	W	L
1981-82	Washington	66	25	28	13	....	....	....
1982-83	Washington	80	39	25	16	4	1	3
1983-84	Washington	80	48	27	5	8	4	4
1984-85	Washington	80	46	25	9	5	2	3
1985-86	Washington	80	50	23	7	9	5	4
1986-87	Washington	80	38	32	10	7	3	4
1987-88	Washington	80	38	33	9	14	7	7
1988-89	Washington	80	41	29	10	6	2	4
1989-90	Washington	46	18	24	4	....	....	....
1990-91	Detroit	80	34	38	8	7	3	4
1991-92	Detroit	80	43	25	12	11	4	7
1992-93	Detroit	84	47	28	9	7	3	4
1997-98	Florida	59	17	31	11	....	....	....
2001-02	Anaheim	82	29	45	8	....	....	....
2004-05	Ottawa				Season Cancelled			
2005-06	Ottawa	82	52	21	9	10	5	5
2006-07	Ottawa	82	48	25	9	20	13	7
	NHL Totals	**1221**	**613**	**459**	**149**	**108**	**52**	**56**

Club Directory

Scotiabank Place

Ottawa Senators
Scotiabank Place
1000 Palladium Drive
Ottawa, Ontario
K2V 1A5
Phone **613/599-0250**
FAX 613/599-0358
www.ottawasenators.com
Capacity: 19,153

Executive

Owner, Governor and Chairman	Eugene Melnyk
President, CEO and Alternate Governor	Roy Mlakar
Chief Operating Officer	Cyril Leeder
General Manager	Bryan Murray
V.P. and Executive Director, Scotiabank Place	Tom Conroy
Executive Assistant to the President and CEO	Cheryl Blake
Executive Assistant to the COO	Gail Martineau

Hockey Operations

Assistant General Manager	Tim Murray
Director of Hockey Operations	Brent Flahr
Director of Amateur Scouting	Frank Jay
Head Coach	John Paddock
Assistant Coaches	TBA, Greg Carvel
Strength and Conditioning Coach	Randy Lee
Video Coach	Tim Pattyson
Assistant to the General Manager	Allison Vaughan
Director of Player Services	Chad Schella
Head Athletic Therapist	Gerry Townend
Assistant Athletic Therapist	Andy Playter
Equipment Manager	Scott Allegrino
Assistant Equipment Manager	Chris Cook
Hockey Administrator	Kevin Billet

Scouts

Scout, Slovakia and Czech Republic	Vaclav Burda
Scouts	Wayne Daniels, Pierre Dorion, George Fargher, Bob Janecyk, Bob Lowes, Bill McCarthy, Lewis Mongelluzzo, Patrick Savard
Pro Scouts	Gord Pell, Nick Polano
Scout, Finland	Mikko Ruutu
Scout, Russia	Boris Shagas

Legal

General Counsel	Rhonda Wing
Law Clerk	Heather Havelock

Communications and Publications

Vice-President, Communications	Phil Legault
Director, Communications	Steve Keogh
Director, Publications	Karen Ruttan
Communications & Publications Co-ordinator	Brian Morris
Translator	Eric Tremblay
Communications & Publications Assistant	Deborah Wilson

Broadcasting

Vice-President, Broadcast	Jim Steel

Corporate & Ticket Sales and Service

Senior Vice-President, Corporate & Ticketing Sales	Mark Bonneau
Exec. Ass't. To Sr. V.P., Corporate & Ticketing Sales	Brooke Girard
Director, Corporate Sales	Bill Courchaine
Senior Corporate Account Managers	Steve Chestnut, Mark Clatney, Francois Robert
Director, Business Development	Gina Hillcoat
Director, Ticket Sales	Jim Orban
Manager, Inside Sales	Chris Atack
Manager, Group Sales	Devon Wingate
Senior Account Manager, Group Sales	Jim Armstrong
Director, Premium Services	Christine Clancy
Manager, Premium Client Services	Tracey Bonner

Finance

Chief Financial officer	Erin Crowe
Controller	Derek Winch
Accounting Manager, Ottawa Senators	Morgan Cranley

Information Technology

Director, Information Technology	Sean Shrubsole
Systems Administrator, Information Technology	Robin Zanichkowsky
Information Technology Support Specialist	Don Morin
Web Developer	Stéphane Bourbonnais

Marketing

Vice-President, Marketing	Jeff Kyle
Executive Assistant, Marketing	Kathy Downs
Director, Game Entertainment	Glen Gower
Art Director	Wendy Moenig
Director, E-Marketing	Isabelle Perrault-Lachapelle
Director Scotiabank Place Marketing	Krista Pogue
Director, Fan and Community Development	Aaron Robinson

Operations and Events

Assistant to the V.P. & Executive Director	Linda Julian
Director, Engineering & Operations	Ed Healy

Ottawa Senators Foundation

President	Dave Ready
Director, Corporate & Community Relations	Danielle Robinson

People Department

Director, People Department	Sandi Horner

Miscellaneous

Radio	Team 1200 (English), CJRC 1150 (French)
Television	Rogers Sportsnet, A-Channel and RDS
Team Photographer	Freestyle Photography (André Ringuette)
Anthem singer	Lyndon Slewidge
Mascot	Spartacat

Philadelphia Flyers

2006-07 Results: 22W-48L-6OTL-6SOL 56PTS.
Fifth, Atlantic Division

Key Off-Season Signings/Acquisitions

2007

- **May 11** • Re-signed RW **Scottie Upshall**.
- **14** • Re-signed LW **Ben Eager**.
- **17** • Re-signed D **Lasse Kukkonen**.
- **June 6** • Named **Joe Mullen** and **Jack McIlhargey** assistant coaches.
- **14** • Re-signed G **Antero Niittymaki**.
- **18** • Acquired D **Kimmo Timonen** and LW **Scott Hartnell** from Nashville for a 1st-round pick in the 2007 Entry Draft.
- **July 1** • Signed C **Daniel Briere**.
- **1** • Acquired D **Jason Smith** and RW **Joffrey Lupul** from Edmonton for D **Joni Pitkanen**, LW **Geoff Sanderson** and a 3rd-round pick in the 2009 Entry Draft.

Year-by-Year Record

Season	GP	Home W	Home L	Home T	Home OL	Road W	Road L	Road T	Road OL	Overall W	Overall L	Overall T	Overall OL	GF	GA	Pts.	Finished	Playoff Result
2006-07	82	10	24	....	7	12	24	....	5	22	48	....	12	214	303	56	5th, Atlantic Div.	Out of Playoffs
2005-06	82	22	13	....	6	23	13	....	5	45	26	....	11	267	259	101	2nd, Atlantic Div.	Lost Conf. Quarter-Final
2004-05	....	....	....	....	....	....	....	....	....	....	....	....	....	....	....	....		
2003-04	82	24	11	3	3	16	10	12	3	40	21	15	6	229	186	101	1st, Atlantic Div.	Lost Conf. Championship
2002-03	82	21	10	8	2	24	10	5	2	45	20	13	4	211	166	107	2nd, Atlantic Div.	Lost Conf. Semi-Final
2001-02	82	20	13	5	3	22	14	5	0	42	27	10	3	234	192	97	1st, Atlantic Div.	Lost Conf. Quarter-Final
2000-01	82	26	11	4	0	17	14	7	3	43	25	11	3	240	207	100	2nd, Atlantic Div.	Lost Conf. Quarter-Final
1999-2000	82	25	6	7	3	20	16	5	0	45	22	12	3	237	179	105	1st, Atlantic Div.	Lost Conf. Championship
1998-99	82	21	9	11	....	16	17	8	....	37	26	19	....	231	196	93	2nd, Atlantic Div.	Lost Conf. Quarter-Final
1997-98	82	24	11	6	....	18	18	5	....	42	29	11	....	242	193	95	2nd, Atlantic Div.	Lost Conf. Quarter-Final
1996-97	82	23	12	6	....	22	12	7	....	45	24	13	....	274	217	103	2nd, Atlantic Div.	Lost Final
1995-96	82	27	9	5	....	18	15	8	....	45	24	13	....	282	208	103	1st, Atlantic Div.	Lost Conf. Semi-Final
1994-95	48	16	7	1	....	12	9	3	....	28	16	4	....	150	132	60	1st, Atlantic Div.	Lost Conf. Championship
1993-94	84	19	20	3	....	16	19	7	....	35	39	10	....	294	314	80	6th, Atlantic Div.	Out of Playoffs
1992-93	84	23	14	5	....	13	23	6	....	36	37	11	....	319	319	83	5th, Patrick Div.	Out of Playoffs
1991-92	80	22	11	7	....	10	26	4	....	32	37	11	....	252	273	75	6th, Patrick Div.	Out of Playoffs
1990-91	80	18	16	6	....	15	21	4	....	33	37	10	....	252	267	76	5th, Patrick Div.	Out of Playoffs
1989-90	80	17	19	4	....	13	20	7	....	30	39	11	....	290	297	71	6th, Patrick Div.	Out of Playoffs
1988-89	80	22	15	3	....	14	21	5	....	36	36	8	....	307	285	80	4th, Patrick Div.	Lost Conf. Championship
1987-88	80	20	14	6	....	18	19	3	....	38	33	9	....	292	292	85	3rd, Patrick Div.	Lost Div. Semi-Final
1986-87	80	29	9	2	....	17	17	6	....	46	26	8	....	310	245	100	1st, Patrick Div.	Lost Final
1985-86	80	33	6	1	....	20	17	3	....	53	23	4	....	335	241	110	1st, Patrick Div.	Lost Div. Semi-Final
1984-85	80	32	4	4	....	21	16	3	....	53	20	7	....	348	241	113	1st, Patrick Div.	Lost Final
1983-84	80	25	10	5	....	19	16	5	....	44	26	10	....	350	290	98	3rd, Patrick Div.	Lost Div. Semi-Final
1982-83	80	29	8	3	....	20	15	5	....	49	23	8	....	326	240	106	1st, Patrick Div.	Lost Div. Semi-Final
1981-82	80	25	10	5	....	13	21	6	....	38	31	11	....	325	313	87	3rd. Patrick Div.	Lost Div. Semi-Final
1980-81	80	23	9	8	....	18	15	7	....	41	24	15	....	313	249	97	2nd, Patrick Div.	Lost Quarter-Final
1979-80	80	27	5	8	....	21	7	12	....	48	12	20	....	327	254	116	1st, Patrick Div.	Lost Final
1978-79	80	26	10	4	....	14	15	11	....	40	25	15	....	281	248	95	2nd, Patrick Div.	Lost Quarter-Final
1977-78	80	29	6	5	....	16	14	10	....	45	20	15	....	296	200	105	2nd, Patrick Div.	Lost Semi-Final
1976-77	80	33	6	1	....	15	10	15	....	48	16	16	....	323	213	112	1st, Patrick Div.	Lost Semi-Final
1975-76	80	36	2	2	....	15	11	14	....	51	13	16	....	348	209	118	1st, Patrick Div.	Lost Final
1974-75	**80**	**32**	**6**	**2**	....	**19**	**12**	**9**	....	**51**	**18**	**11**	....	**293**	**181**	**113**	**1st, Patrick Div.**	**Won Stanley Cup**
1973-74	**78**	**28**	**6**	**5**	....	**22**	**10**	**7**	....	**50**	**16**	**12**	....	**273**	**164**	**112**	**1st, West Div.**	**Won Stanley Cup**
1972-73	78	27	8	4	....	10	22	7	....	37	30	11	....	296	256	85	2nd, West Div.	Lost Semi-Final
1971-72	78	19	13	7	....	7	25	7	....	26	38	14	....	200	236	66	5th, West Div.	Out of Playoffs
1970-71	78	20	10	9	....	8	23	8	....	28	33	17	....	207	225	73	3rd, West Div.	Lost Quarter-Final
1969-70	76	11	14	13	....	6	21	11	....	17	35	24	....	197	225	58	5th, West Div.	Out of Playoffs
1968-69	76	14	16	8	....	6	19	13	....	20	35	21	....	174	225	61	3rd, West Div.	Lost Quarter-Final
1967-68	74	17	13	7	....	14	19	4	....	31	32	11	....	173	179	73	1st, West Div.	Lost Quarter-Final

2007-08 Schedule

Oct.	Thu.	4	at Calgary
	Sat.	6	at Edmonton*
	Wed.	10	at Vancouver
	Sat.	13	NY Islanders
	Tue.	16	Atlanta
	Thu.	18	New Jersey
	Sat.	20	Carolina
	Wed.	24	at Florida
	Thu.	25	at Tampa Bay
	Sat.	27	at Boston
Nov.	Thu.	1	at Montreal
	Fri.	2	at Washington
	Mon.	5	at NY Rangers
	Wed.	7	at Pittsburgh
	Thu.	8	at New Jersey
	Sat.	10	Pittsburgh
	Mon.	12	NY Islanders
	Thu.	15	NY Rangers
	Sat.	17	New Jersey
	Wed.	21	at Carolina
	Fri.	23	Washington*
	Sat.	24	at Ottawa
	Mon.	26	Boston
	Wed.	28	at Carolina
Dec.	Sat.	1	Dallas
	Wed.	5	at Minnesota
	Fri.	7	at Colorado
	Tue.	11	Pittsburgh
	Thu.	13	Montreal
	Sat.	15	Carolina
	Sun.	16	at New Jersey*
	Tue.	18	Phoenix
	Fri.	21	at Buffalo
	Sat.	22	Buffalo
	Thu.	27	Toronto
	Sat.	29	at Tampa Bay*
	Sun.	30	at Florida*
Jan.	Fri.	4	at New Jersey
	Sat.	5	at Toronto
	Tue.	8	at Atlanta
	Thu.	10	at NY Rangers
	Sat.	12	Boston*
	Sun.	13	at Washington*
	Wed.	16	Florida
	Sat.	19	at NY Islanders
	Sun.	20	Ottawa
	Tue.	22	New Jersey
	Thu.	24	Pittsburgh
	Tue.	29	Los Angeles
	Thu.	31	NY Rangers
Feb.	Sat.	2	Anaheim
	Tue.	5	at Atlanta
	Wed.	6	Washington
	Sat.	9	NY Rangers*
	Sun.	10	at Pittsburgh*
	Tue.	12	at NY Islanders
	Thu.	14	Tampa Bay
	Sat.	16	at Montreal
	Sun.	17	Montreal
	Tue.	19	at Ottawa
	Thu.	21	San Jose
	Sat.	23	Florida
	Mon.	25	at Buffalo
	Thu.	28	Ottawa
Mar.	Sat.	1	at NY Islanders*
	Sun.	2	at NY Rangers*
	Tue.	4	Buffalo
	Thu.	6	Tampa Bay
	Sat.	8	NY Islanders
	Tue.	11	at Toronto
	Wed.	12	Toronto
	Sat.	15	at Boston*
	Sun.	16	at Pittsburgh*
	Tue.	18	Atlanta
	Fri.	21	NY Rangers
	Sun.	23	NY Islanders
	Tue.	25	at NY Rangers
	Fri.	28	at New Jersey
	Sat.	29	at NY Islanders
Apr.	Wed.	2	at Pittsburgh
	Fri.	4	New Jersey
	Sun.	6	Pittsburgh*

* Denotes afternoon game.

Derian Hatcher and Mike Richards lead the Flyers off the ice after an overtime victory.

ATLANTIC DIVISION
41st NHL Season

Franchise date: June 5, 1967

2007-08 Player Personnel

FORWARDS	HT	WT	S	Place of Birth	*Age	2006-07 Club
BRIERE, Daniel	5-10	179	R	Gatineau, Que.	29	Buffalo
CARTER, Jeff	6-3	200	R	London, Ont.	22	Philadelphia
COTE, Riley	6-1	210	L	Winnipeg, Man.	25	Phi-Phi (AHL)
DOWNIE, Steve	5-11	200	R	Newmarket, Ont.	20	Ptrboro-Kitch-Phi (AHL)
EAGER, Ben	6-3	225	L	Ottawa, Ont.	23	Phi-Phi (AHL)
GAGNE, Simon	6-0	195	L	Ste-Foy, Que.	27	Philadelphia
GRANT, Triston	6-1	215	L	Brandon, Man.	23	Phi-Phi (AHL)
HARTNELL, Scott	6-2	210	L	Regina, Sask.	25	Nashville
KANE, Boyd	6-2	220	L	Swift Current, Sask.	29	Phi-Phi (AHL)
KAPANEN, Sami	5-10	185	L	Vantaa, Finland	34	Philadelphia
KNUBLE, Mike	6-3	230	R	Toronto, Ont.	35	Philadelphia
LUPUL, Joffrey	6-1	205	R	Fort Saskatchewan, Alta.	24	Edmonton
POTULNY, Ryan	6-0	190	L	Grand Forks, ND	23	Phi-Phi (AHL)
REID, Darren	6-2	205	R	Lac La Biche, Alta.	24	Sprfld-Phi-Phi (AHL)
RICHARDS, Mike	5-11	195	L	Kenora, Ont.	22	Philadelphia
RUZICKA, Stefan	6-0	205	R	Nitra, Czech.	22	Phi-Phi (AHL)
UMBERGER, R.J.	6-2	210	L	Pittsburgh, PA	25	Philadelphia
UPSHALL, Scottie	6-0	197	L	Fort McMurray, Alta.	23	Nsh-Milwaukee-Phi
DEFENSEMEN						
COBURN, Braydon	6-5	220	L	Calgary, Alta.	22	Atl-Chi (AHL)-Phi
GAUTHIER, Denis	6-3	224	L	Montreal, Que.	30	Philadelphia
GUENIN, Nate	6-2	210	R	Sewickley, PA	24	Phi-Phi (AHL)
HATCHER, Derian	6-5	235	L	Sterling Hts., MI	35	Philadelphia
JONES, Randy	6-2	200	L	Quispamsis, N.B.	26	Philadelphia
JONSSON, Lars	6-1	205	L	Borlange, Sweden	25	Phi-Phi (AHL)
KUKKONEN, Lasse	6-1	190	L	Oulu, Finland	26	Chicago-Philadelphia
PARENT, Ryan	6-2	200	L	Prince Albert, Sask.	20	Phi-Phi (AHL)-Guelph
PICARD, Alexandre	6-2	220	L	Gatineau, Que.	22	Phi-Phi (AHL)
RATHJE, Mike	6-5	235	L	Mannville, Alta.	33	Philadelphia
SMITH, Jason	6-3	215	R	Calgary, Alta.	33	Edmonton
TIMONEN, Jussi	6-0	200	L	Kuopio, Finland	24	Phi-Phi (AHL)
TIMONEN, Kimmo	5-10	194	L	Kuopio, Finland	32	Nashville

GOALTENDERS	HT	WT	C	Place of Birth	*Age	2006-07 Club
BEAUCHEMIN, Rejean	6-1	202	L	Winnipeg, Man.	22	Philadelphia (AHL)-Bakersfield
BIRON, Martin	6-3	163	L	Lac-St-Charles, Que.	30	Buffalo-Philadelphia
BOUCHER, Brian	6-2	198	L	Woonsocket, RI	30	Chicago-Columbus
HOULE, Martin	5-11	185	L	Montreal, Que.	22	Phi-Phi (AHL)
MUNROE, Scott	6-2	210	L	Moose Jaw, Sask.	25	Philadelphia (AHL)
NIITTYMAKI, Antero	6-1	195	L	Turku, Finland	27	Philadelphia

* – Age at start of 2007-08 season

Coaching History

Keith Allen, 1967-68, 1968-69; Vic Stasiuk, 1969-70, 1970-71; Fred Shero, 1971-72 to 1977-78; Bob McCammon and Pat Quinn, 1978-79; Pat Quinn, 1979-80, 1980-81; Pat Quinn and Bob McCammon, 1981-82; Bob McCammon, 1982-83, 1983-84; Mike Keenan, 1984-85 to 1987-88; Paul Holmgren, 1988-89 to 1990-91; Paul Holmgren and Bill Dineen, 1991-92; Bill Dineen, 1992-93; Terry Simpson, 1993-94; Terry Murray, 1994-95 to 1996-97; Wayne Cashman and Roger Neilson, 1997-98; Roger Neilson, 1998-99, 1999-2000; Craig Ramsay and Bill Barber, 2000-01; Bill Barber, 2001-02; Ken Hitchcock, 2002-03 to 2005-06; Ken Hitchcock and John Stevens, 2006-07; John Stevens, 2007-08.

Coach

JOHN STEVENS
Coach, Philadelphia Flyers. Born in Campbellton, N.B., December 30, 1965.

John Stevens took over as head coach of the Philadelphia Flyers on October 22, 2006. Stevens had been the head coach of the Flyers' American Hockey League affiliate, the Philadelphia Phantoms, for six seasons (2000-01 through 2005-06) and led the team to the Calder Cup championship in 2005. He was named assistant coach of the Flyers on June 5, 2006. Stevens joined the Phantoms coaching staff as an assistant on February 10, 1999 after announcing his retirement from hockey due to an eye injury. He became the second head coach in Phantoms history on June 8, 2000.

Stevens played 15 seasons of professional hockey as a defenseman (1984-85 to 1998-99), including 53 career NHL games with the Flyers and Hartford Whalers. Over parts of five seasons (1986-87 and 1987-88 with the Flyers and 1990-91, 1991-92 and 1993-94 with Hartford), Stevens recorded 10 assists and 48 penalty minutes in 53 games. He was a member of three Calder Cup championship teams as a player (Hershey,1988; Springfield, 1991; and Philadelphia, 1998) and won the Barry Ashbee Award as the Phantoms' top defenseman for the 1996-97 season. He was named the Phantoms' first captain on October 1, 1996. Stevens was originally drafted by the Flyers in the third round (47th overall) of the 1984 NHL Entry Draft.

Coaching Record

		Regular Season				Playoffs		
Season	Team	Games	W	L	O/T	Games	W	L
2000-01	Philadelphia (AHL)	80	36	34	10	10	5	5
2001-02	Philadelphia (AHL)	80	33	27	20	5	2	3
2002-03	Philadelphia (AHL)	80	33	33	14	....	....	....
2003-04	Philadelphia (AHL)	80	46	25	9	12	6	6
2004-05	Philadelphia (AHL)	80	48	25	7	21	16	5
2006-07	**Philadelphia (NHL)**	**74**	**21**	**42**	**11**	....	....	....
	NHL Totals	**74**	**21**	**42**	**11**	....	....	....

2006-07 Scoring

* – rookie

Regular Season

Pos	#	Player	Team	GP	G	A	Pts	+/–	PIM	PP	SH	GW	S	%
L	12	Simon Gagne	PHI	76	41	27	68	2	30	13	2	4	291	14.1
R	22	Mike Knuble	PHI	64	24	30	54	2	56	10	0	1	160	15.0
D	44	Joni Pitkanen	PHI	77	4	39	43	–25	88	1	0	0	137	2.9
C	17	Jeff Carter	PHI	62	14	23	37	–17	48	3	2	1	215	6.5
C	18	Mike Richards	PHI	59	10	22	32	–12	52	1	4	3	130	7.7
L	8	Geoff Sanderson	PHI	58	11	18	29	–16	44	3	0	2	143	7.7
C	20	R.J. Umberger	PHI	81	16	12	28	–32	41	2	2	1	134	11.9
R	24	Sami Kapanen	PHI	77	11	14	25	–21	22	1	2	1	129	8.5
D	6	Randy Jones	PHI	66	4	18	22	–14	38	0	0	0	67	6.0
D	45	* Alexandre Picard	PHI	62	3	19	22	–19	17	1	0	0	56	5.4
L	27	Dimitry Afanasenkov	T.B.	33	3	3	6	–6	8	0	0	0	31	9.7
			PHI	41	8	7	15	–19	12	0	0	0	65	12.3
			TOTAL	74	11	10	21	–25	20	0	0	0	96	11.5
L	61	Mike York	NYI	32	6	7	13	–9	14	2	0	1	46	13.0
			PHI	34	4	4	8	–9	8	0	0	1	41	9.8
			TOTAL	66	10	11	21	–18	22	2	0	2	87	11.5
R	9	Scottie Upshall	NSH	14	2	1	3	–1	18	0	0	2	27	7.4
			PHI	18	6	7	13	4	8	1	1	2	60	10.0
			TOTAL	32	8	8	16	3	26	1	1	4	87	9.2
D	28	* Lasse Kukkonen	CHI	54	5	9	14	5	30	1	0	2	45	11.1
			PHI	20	0	0	0	–1	8	0	0	0	9	0.0
			TOTAL	74	5	9	14	4	38	1	0	2	54	9.3
L	29	Todd Fedoruk	ANA	10	0	3	3	2	36	0	0	0	2	0.0
			PHI	48	3	8	11	–11	84	0	0	0	28	10.7
			TOTAL	58	3	11	14	–9	120	0	0	0	30	10.0
R	15	* Stefan Ruzicka	PHI	40	3	10	13	–6	18	1	0	0	75	4.0
C	11	* Ryan Potulny	PHI	35	7	5	12	1	22	0	0	2	56	12.5
L	55	* Ben Eager	PHI	63	6	5	11	–13	233	0	0	0	48	12.5
D	5	* Braydon Coburn	ATL	29	0	4	4	1	30	0	0	0	21	0.0
			PHI	20	3	4	7	–2	16	1	0	0	33	9.1
			TOTAL	49	3	8	11	–1	46	1	0	0	54	5.6
D	2	Derian Hatcher	PHI	82	3	6	9	–24	67	3	0	1	81	3.7
L	14	Denis Hamel	OTT	43	4	3	7	4	10	0	0	0	36	11.1
			ATL	3	1	0	1	0	0	0	0	0	3	33.3
			PHI	7	0	0	0	–4	0	0	0	0	3	0.0
			TOTAL	53	5	3	8	0	10	0	0	0	42	11.9
D	46	* Jussi Timonen	PHI	14	0	4	4	–10	6	0	0	0	8	0.0
D	23	Denis Gauthier	PHI	43	0	4	4	–11	45	0	0	0	23	0.0
R	40	Eric Meloche	PHI	13	1	2	3	–6	4	1	0	0	12	8.3
D	43	* Lars Jonsson	PHI	8	0	2	2	–4	6	0	0	0	4	0.0
D	65	* Nathan Guenin	PHI	9	0	2	2	0	4	0	0	0	0	0.0
L	28	Boyd Kane	PHI	15	0	2	2	–4	28	0	0	0	7	0.0
L	52	* Triston Grant	PHI	8	0	1	1	–1	10	0	0	0	3	0.0
D	3	Mike Rathje	PHI	18	0	1	1	–7	6	0	0	0	13	0.0
D	77	* Ryan Parent	PHI	1	0	0	0	0	0	0	0	0	1	0.0
R	36	Matt Ellison	PHI	2	0	0	0	0	0	0	0	0	1	0.0
D	32	* Martin Grenier	PHI	3	0	0	0	–3	0	0	0	0	0	0.0
C	14	Mark Cullen	PHI	3	0	0	0	–3	0	0	0	0	4	0.0
R	15	Niko Dimitrakos	PHI	5	0	0	0	–4	6	0	0	0	4	0.0
L	33	* Riley Cote	PHI	8	0	0	0	0	11	0	0	0	3	0.0
D	54	David Printz	PHI	12	0	0	0	–3	4	0	0	0	1	0.0
R	26	* Darren Reid	PHI	14	0	0	0	–7	18	0	0	0	8	0.0

Goaltending

No.	Goaltender	GPI	Mins	Avg	W	L	OT	EN	SO	GA	SA	S%	G	A	PIM
43	Martin Biron	16	935	3.02	6	8	2	1	0	47	509	.908	0	0	0
30	Antero Niittymaki	52	2943	3.38	9	29	9	8	0	166	1567	.894	0	0	2
49	Michael Leighton	4	195	3.69	2	2	0	0	0	12	102	.882	0	0	0
42	Robert Esche	18	860	4.33	5	9	1	0	1	62	483	.872	0	2	2
35	* Martin Houle	1	2	30.00	0	0	0	0	0	1	3	.667	0	0	0
	Totals	**82**	**4978**	**3.58**	**22**	**48**	**12**	**9**	**1**	**297**	**2673**	**.889**			

Captains' History

Lou Angotti, 1967-68; Ed Van Impe, 1968-69 to 1971-72; Ed Van Impe and Bobby Clarke, 1972-73; Bobby Clarke, 1973-74 to 1978-79; Mel Bridgman, 1979-80, 1980-81; Bill Barber, 1981-82; Bill Barber and Bobby Clarke, 1982-83; Bobby Clarke, 1983-84; Dave Poulin, 1984-85 to 1988-89; Dave Poulin and Ron Sutter, 1989-90; Ron Sutter, 1990-91; Rick Tocchet, 1991-92; no captain, 1992-93; Kevin Dineen, 1993-94; Eric Lindros, 1994-95 to 1998-99; Eric Lindros and Eric Desjardins, 1999-2000; Eric Desjardins, 2000-01; Eric Desjardins and Keith Primeau, 2001-02; Keith Primeau, 2002-03, 2003-04; Keith Primeau and Derian Hatcher, 2005-06; Peter Forsberg, 2006-07.

Club Records

Team

(Figures in brackets for season records are games played; records for fewest points, wins, ties, losses, goals, goals against are for 70 or more games)

Most Points	**118**	1975-76 (80)
Most Wins	**53**	1984-85 (80), 1985-86 (80)
Most Ties	***24**	1969-70 (76)
Most Losses	**48**	2006-07 (82)
Most Goals	**350**	1983-84 (80)
Most Goals Against	**319**	1992-93 (84)
Fewest Points	**56**	2006-07 (82)
Fewest Wins	**17**	1969-70 (76)
Fewest Ties	**4**	1985-86 (80)
Fewest Losses	**12**	1979-80 (80)
Fewest Goals	**173**	1967-68 (74)
Fewest Goals Against	**164**	1973-74 (78)
Longest Winning Streak		
Overall	**13**	Oct. 19-Nov. 17/85
Home	***20**	Jan. 4-Apr. 3/76
Away	**8**	Dec. 22/82-Jan. 16/83
Longest Undefeated Streak		
Overall	***35**	Oct. 14/79-Jan. 6/80 (25 wins, 10 ties)
Home	**26**	Oct. 11/79-Feb. 3/80 (19 wins, 7 ties)
Away	**16**	Oct. 20/79-Jan. 6/80 (11 wins, 5 ties)
Longest Losing Streak		
Overall	**9**	Dec. 8-27/06
Home	**13**	Nov. 29/06-Feb. 8/07
Away	**8**	Oct. 25-Nov. 26/72, Mar. 3-29/88
Longest Winless Streak		
Overall	**12**	Feb. 24-Mar. 16/99 (8 losses, 4 ties)
Home	**13**	Nov. 29/06-Feb. 8/07 (13 losses)
Away	**19**	Oct. 23/71-Jan. 27/72 (15 losses, 4 ties)
Most Shutouts, Season	**13**	1974-75 (80)
Most PIM, Season	**2,621**	1980-81 (80)
Most Goals, Game	**13**	Mar. 22/84 (Pit. 4 at Phi. 13), Oct. 18/84 (Van. 2 at Phi. 13)

Individual

Most Seasons	**15**	Bobby Clarke
Most Games	**1,144**	Bobby Clarke
Most Goals, Career	**420**	Bill Barber
Most Assists, Career	**852**	Bobby Clarke
Most Points, Career	**1,210**	Bobby Clarke (358G, 852A)
Most PIM, Career	**1,817**	Rick Tocchet
Most Shutouts, Career	**50**	Bernie Parent
Longest Consecutive Game Streak	**484**	Rod Brind'Amour (Feb. 24/93-Apr. 18/99)
Most Goals, Season	**61**	Reggie Leach (1975-76)
Most Assists, Season	**89**	Bobby Clarke (1974-75, 1975-76)
Most Points, Season	**123**	Mark Recchi (1992-93; 53G, 70A)
Most PIM, Season	***472**	Dave Schultz (1974-75)
Most Points, Defenseman, Season	**82**	Mark Howe (1985-86; 24G, 58A)
Most Points, Center, Season	**119**	Bobby Clarke (1975-76; 30G, 89A)
Most Points, Right Wing, Season	**123**	Mark Recchi (1992-93; 53G, 70A)
Most Points, Left Wing, Season	**112**	Bill Barber (1975-76; 50G, 62A)
Most Points, Rookie, Season	**82**	Mikael Renberg (1993-94; 38G, 44A)
Most Shutouts, Season	**12**	Bernie Parent (1973-74, 1974-75)
Most Goals, Game	**4**	Sixteen times
Most Assists, Game	**6**	Eric Lindros (Feb. 26/97)
Most Points, Game	**8**	Tom Bladon (Dec. 11/77; 4G, 4A)

* NHL Record.

Retired Numbers

1	Bernie Parent	1967-1971, 1973-1979
4	Barry Ashbee	1970-1974
7	Bill Barber	1972-1985
16	Bobby Clarke	1969-1984

All-time Record vs. Other Clubs

Regular Season

	At Home								On Road								Total							
	GP	W	L	T	OL	GF	GA	PTS	GP	W	L	T	OL	GF	GA	PTS	GP	W	L	T	OL	GF	GA	PTS
Anaheim	8	3	2	3	0	22	17	9	10	4	3	2	1	35	34	11	18	7	5	5	1	57	51	20
Atlanta	14	10	1	2	1	61	41	23	14	11	2	1	0	49	32	23	28	21	3	3	1	110	73	46
Boston	77	34	32	10	1	254	226	79	80	22	45	11	2	224	293	57	157	56	77	21	3	478	519	136
Buffalo	71	41	16	12	2	242	178	96	67	24	35	8	0	186	230	56	138	65	51	20	2	428	408	152
Calgary	52	34	14	3	1	200	137	72	52	18	25	9	0	172	208	45	104	52	39	12	1	372	345	117
Carolina	47	31	10	5	1	174	116	68	48	24	14	9	1	175	156	58	95	55	24	14	2	349	272	126
Chicago	63	36	16	11	0	207	162	83	61	16	26	19	0	175	207	51	124	52	42	30	0	382	369	134
Colorado	35	22	9	2	2	125	95	48	35	11	11	12	1	122	124	35	70	33	20	14	3	247	219	83
Columbus	3	2	0	1	0	10	5	5	4	2	0	2	0	10	7	6	7	4	0	3	0	20	12	11
Dallas	67	42	9	16	0	255	150	100	67	23	28	16	0	214	219	62	134	65	37	32	0	469	369	162
Detroit	59	35	13	11	0	236	169	81	60	18	32	10	0	185	216	46	119	53	45	21	0	421	385	127
Edmonton	32	20	10	2	0	130	88	42	28	8	14	6	0	83	98	22	60	28	24	8	0	213	186	64
Florida	29	12	10	6	1	77	74	31	28	20	7	1	0	98	65	41	57	32	17	7	1	175	139	72
Los Angeles	63	40	15	7	1	244	156	88	67	38	21	8	0	227	196	84	130	78	36	15	1	471	352	172
Minnesota	5	4	1	0	0	14	5	8	2	0	1	1	0	3	5	1	7	4	2	1	0	17	10	9
Montreal	77	30	30	16	1	234	231	77	78	27	35	14	2	237	268	70	155	57	65	30	3	471	499	147
Nashville	6	2	2	1	1	19	12	6	5	2	0	2	1	10	8	7	11	4	2	3	2	29	20	13
New Jersey	93	55	25	10	3	347	239	123	91	33	48	8	2	294	309	76	184	88	73	18	5	641	548	199
NY Islanders	103	58	32	11	2	363	292	129	106	38	51	15	2	314	377	93	209	96	83	26	4	677	669	222
NY Rangers	117	57	44	14	2	376	329	130	118	45	48	23	2	347	377	115	235	102	92	37	4	723	706	245
Ottawa	27	15	9	2	1	88	78	33	28	11	11	6	0	82	80	28	55	26	20	8	1	170	158	61
Phoenix	31	23	8	0	0	134	83	46	32	16	14	2	0	106	103	34	63	39	22	2	0	240	186	80
Pittsburgh	114	84	20	8	2	474	293	178	114	41	50	22	1	368	402	105	228	125	70	30	3	842	695	283
St. Louis	68	46	12	10	0	268	156	102	69	36	26	7	0	224	196	79	137	82	38	17	0	492	352	181
San Jose	11	6	3	2	0	36	27	14	13	7	4	2	0	32	28	16	24	13	7	4	0	68	55	30
Tampa Bay	29	14	6	7	2	86	65	37	30	17	12	1	0	88	89	35	59	31	18	8	2	174	154	72
Toronto	71	43	20	8	0	262	171	94	71	31	25	14	1	235	223	77	142	74	45	22	1	497	394	171
Vancouver	55	37	17	1	0	238	164	75	51	29	10	12	0	203	144	70	106	66	27	13	0	441	308	145
Washington	87	55	26	6	0	331	234	116	84	35	34	13	2	268	276	85	171	90	60	19	2	599	510	201
Defunct Clubs	34	24	4	6	0	137	67	54	35	13	14	8	0	102	89	34	69	37	18	14	0	239	156	88
Totals	**1548**	**915**	**416**	**193**	**24**	**5644**	**4060**	**2047**	**1548**	**620**	**646**	**264**	**18**	**4868**	**5059**	**1522**	**3096**	**1535**	**1062**	**457**	**42**	**10512**	**9119**	**3569**

Playoffs

	Series	W	L	GP	W	L	T	GF	GA	Last Mtg.	Rnd.	Result
Boston	4	2	2	20	9	11	0	57	60	1978	SF	L 1-4
Buffalo	8	5	3	43	25	18	0	124	123	2006	CQF	L 2-4
Calgary	2	1	1	11	7	4	0	43	28	1981	QF	L 3-4
Chicago	1	0	1	4	0	4	0	8	20	1971	QF	L 0-4
Colorado	2	2	0	11	7	4	0	39	29	1985	CF	W 4-2
Dallas	2	2	0	11	8	3	0	41	26	1980	SF	W 4-1
Detroit	1	0	1	4	0	4	0	6	16	1997	F	L 0-4
Edmonton	3	1	2	15	7	8	0	44	49	1987	F	L 3-4
Florida	1	0	1	6	2	4	0	11	15	1996	CSF	L 2-4
Montreal	4	1	3	21	7	14	0	52	72	1989	CF	L 2-4
New Jersey	4	2	2	20	11	9	0	49	50	2004	CQF	W 4-1
NY Islanders	4	3	1	25	14	11	0	83	69	1987	DF	W 4-3
NY Rangers	10	6	4	47	27	20	0	157	153	1997	CF	W 4-1
Ottawa	2	0	2	11	3	8	0	12	28	2003	CSF	L 2-4
Pittsburgh	3	3	0	18	12	6	0	66	51	2000	CSF	W 4-2
St. Louis	2	0	2	11	3	8	0	20	34	1969	QF	L 0-4
Tampa Bay	2	1	1	13	7	6	0	45	34	2004	CF	L 3-4
Toronto	6	5	1	36	22	14	0	119	85	2004	CSF	W 4-2
Vancouver	1	1	0	3	2	1	0	15	9	1979	PRE	W 2-1
Washington	3	1	2	16	7	9	0	55	65	1989	DSF	W 4-2
Totals	**65**	**36**	**29**	**346**	**180**	**166**	**0**	**1046**	**1016**			

Calgary totals include Atlanta Flames, 1972-73 to 1979-80. Carolina totals include Hartford, 1979-80 to 1996-97.
Colorado totals include Quebec, 1979-80 to 1994-95. Dallas totals include Minnesota North Stars, 1967-68 to 1992-93.
New Jersey totals include Kansas City, 1974-75, 1975-76, and Colorado Rockies, 1976-77 to 1981-82.
Phoenix totals include Winnipeg, 1979-80 to 1995-96.

Playoff Results 2007-2002

Year	Round	Opponent	Result	GF	GA
2006	CQF	Buffalo	L 2-4	14	27
2004	CF	Tampa Bay	L 3-4	19	21
	CSF	Toronto	W 4-2	17	13
	CQF	New Jersey	W 4-1	14	9
2003	CSF	Ottawa	L 2-4	10	17
	CQF	Toronto	W 4-3	24	16
2002	CQF	Ottawa	L 1-4	2	11

Abbreviations: Round: F – Final; **CF** – conference final; **CSF** – conference semi-final; **CQF** – conference quarter-final; **DF** – division final; **DSF** – division semi-final; **SF** – semi-final; **QF** – quarter-final; **PRE** – preliminary round.

2006-07 Results

Oct.	5	at Pittsburgh	0-4		7	at Ottawa	1-6
	7	NY Rangers	4-5†		9	at Washington	2-6
	10	at NY Rangers	4-2		11	Montreal	2-4
	11	Montreal	1-3		13	Pittsburgh	3-5
	14	at New Jersey	2-3		18	NY Islanders	2-4
	17	at Buffalo	1-9		20	at New Jersey	3-4†
	19	at Tampa Bay	1-4		27	NY Rangers	1-2
	20	at Florida	2-3		28	at Atlanta	2-1
	26	Atlanta	3-2†		30	Tampa Bay	3-4†
	28	Pittsburgh	2-8	**Feb.**	1	New Jersey	5-6*
	30	Chicago	3-0		3	at Atlanta	5-2
Nov.	2	Tampa Bay	2-5		7	at NY Islanders	0-2
	4	Washington	3-5		8	Pittsburgh	4-5†
	6	at Toronto	1-4		10	St. Louis	4-3*
	9	NY Islanders	1-3		12	Detroit	6-1
	11	Buffalo	4-5*		15	Toronto	2-4
	13	at Pittsburgh	2-3		17	at NY Rangers	5-3
	15	at Anaheim	7-4		19	Boston	3-6
	16	at Los Angeles	4-3		20	at Buffalo	3-6
	18	at San Jose	1-6		22	at Carolina	2-3*
	20	Pittsburgh	3-5		24	Toronto	2-5
	22	Ottawa	2-3*		27	at NY Islanders	5-6*
	24	Columbus	3-2	**Mar.**	1	at Boston	4-3*
	25	at Montreal	4-2		4	at Pittsburgh	3-4†
	29	Nashville	2-3		6	New Jersey	5-4*
	30	at NY Islanders	3-2		8	Florida	1-2
Dec.	2	New Jersey	3-4†		10	Boston	4-1
	8	at New Jersey	0-2		12	at Phoenix	0-4
	9	Washington	3-5		13	at Dallas	2-3
	12	NY Rangers	1-3		15	Atlanta	3-2
	13	at Pittsburgh	4-8		17	at Ottawa	2-3
	16	at Washington	1-4		20	Florida	1-4
	19	Carolina	1-2		21	at NY Rangers	0-5
	21	at Montreal	2-4		24	NY Islanders	3-4
	23	Ottawa	3-6		28	Carolina	5-1
	27	at Florida	1-3		30	at New Jersey	1-3
	28	at Tampa Bay	4-3		31	NY Rangers	4-6
	31	at Carolina	5-2	**Apr.**	3	at Toronto	2-3*
Jan.	2	at NY Islanders	3-2		5	New Jersey	2-3
	4	at NY Rangers	2-3		7	NY Islanders	2-4
	6	at Boston	3-4		8	Buffalo	4-3

* – Overtime † – Shootout

Entry Draft Selections 2007-1993

2007
Pick
2 James vanRiemsdyk
41 Kevin Marshall
66 Garrett Klotz
122 Mario Kempe
152 Jonathon Kalinski
161 Patrick Maroon
182 Brad Phillips

2006
Pick
22 Claude Giroux
39 Andreas Nodl
42 Michael Ratchuk
55 Denis Bodrov
79 Jonathan Matsumoto
101 Joonas Lehtivuori
109 Jakub Kovar
145 Jonathan Rheault
175 Michael Dupont
205 Andrei Popov

2005
Pick
29 Steve Downie
91 Oskars Bartulis
119 Jeremy Duchesne
152 Josh Beaulieu
174 John Flatters
215 Matt Clackson

2004
Pick
92 Rob Bellamy
101 R.J. Anderson
124 David Laliberte
144 Chris Zarb
149 Gino Pisellini
170 Ladislav Scurko
171 Frederik Cabana
232 Martin Houle
253 Travis Gawryletz
286 Triston Grant
291 John Carter

2003
Pick
11 Jeff Carter
24 Mike Richards
69 Colin Fraser
81 Stefan Ruzicka
85 Alexandre Picard
87 Ryan Potulny
95 Rick Kozak
108 Kevin Romy
140 David Tremblay
191 Rejean Beauchemin
193 Ville Hostikka

2002
Pick
4 Joni Pitkanen
105 Rosario Ruggeri
126 Konstantin Baranov
161 Dov Grumet-Morris
192 Nikita Korovkin
193 Joey Mormina
201 Mathieu Brunelle

2001
Pick
27 Jeff Woywitka
95 Patrick Sharp
146 Jussi Timonen
150 Bernd Bruckler
158 Roman Malek
172 Dennis Seidenberg
177 Andrei Razin
208 Thierry Douville
225 David Printz

2000
Pick
28 Justin Williams
94 Alexander Drozdetsky
171 Roman Cechmanek
195 Colin Shields
210 John Eichelberger
227 Guillaume Lefebvre
259 Regan Kelly
287 Milan Kopecky

1999
Pick
22 Maxime Ouellet
119 Jeff Feniak
160 Konstantin Rudenko
200 Pavel Kasparik
208 Vaclav Pletka
224 David Nystrom

1998
Pick
22 Simon Gagne
42 Jason Beckett
51 Ian Forbes
109 Jean-Philippe Morin
124 Francis Belanger
139 Garrett Prosofsky
168 Antero Niittymaki
175 Cam Ondrik
195 Tomas Divisek
222 Lubomir Pistek
243 Petr Hubacek
253 Bruno St. Jacques
258 Sergei Skrobot

1997
Pick
30 Jean-Marc Pelletier
50 Pat Kavanagh
62 Kris Mallette
103 Mikhail Chernov
158 Jordon Flodell
164 Todd Fedoruk
214 Marko Kauppinen
240 Par Styf

1996
Pick
15 Dainius Zubrus
64 Chester Gallant
124 Per-Ragna Bergqvist
133 Jesse Boulerice
187 Roman Malov
213 Jeff Milleker

1995
Pick
22 Brian Boucher
48 Shane Kenny
100 Radovan Somik
132 Dmitri Tertyshny
135 Jamie Sokolsky
152 Martin Spanhel
178 Martin Streit
204 Ruslan Shafikov
230 Jeff Lank

1994
Pick
62 Artem Anisimov
88 Adam Magarrell
101 Sebastien Vallee
140 Alex Selivanov
166 Colin Forbes
192 Derek Diener
202 Raymond Giroux
218 Johan Hedberg
244 Andre Payette
270 Jan Lipiansky

1993
Pick
36 Janne Niinimaa
71 Vaclav Prospal
77 Milos Holan
114 Vladimir Krechin
140 Mike Crowley
166 Aaron Israel
192 Paul Healey
218 Tripp Tracy
226 E.J. Bradley
244 Jeff Staples
270 Ken Hemenway

General Managers' History

Bud Poile, 1967-68, 1968-69; Bud Poile and Keith Allen, 1969-70; Keith Allen, 1970-71 to 1982-83; Bob McCammon, 1983-84; Bob Clarke, 1984-85 to 1989-90; Russ Farwell, 1990-91 to 1993-94; Bob Clarke, 1994-95 to 2005-06; Bob Clarke and Paul Holmgren, 2006-07; Paul Holmgren, 2007-08.

General Manager

PAUL HOLMGREN
General Manager, Philadelphia Flyers.
Born in St. Paul, MN, December 2, 1955.

Paul Holmgren was named interim general manager of the Philadelphia Flyers on November 11, 2006, replacing Bob Clarke who resigned on October 22. On March 14, 2007, Holmgren was officially announced as the club's new g.m. Prior to his promotion, Holmgren had served the previous seven seasons as the team's assistant general manager. He rejoined the Flyers organization as a scout after being replaced as the Hartford Whalers' head coach on November 6, 1995. He had served as a head coach with both the Whalers and the Flyers and also served as general manager in Hartford during the 1993–94 season.

Holmgren retired from playing after the 1984-85 season, having recorded 144 goals and 179 assists for 323 points and 1,684 penalty minutes in 527 career regular season NHL games with the Flyers and the Minnesota North Stars. He recorded 138 goals and 171 assists for 309 points and 1,600 penalty minutes in 500 games over parts of nine seasons with the Flyers (1975-76 to 1983-84). His 1,600 penalty minutes with the Flyers are second all-time in club history. Holmgren was drafted from the University of Minnesota by the Flyers in the sixth round (108th overall) of the 1975 NHL Entry Draft.

NHL Coaching Record

		Regular Season				Playoffs		
Season	**Team**	**Games**	**W**	**L**	**O/T**	**Games**	**W**	**L**
1988-89	Philadelphia	80	36	36	8	19	10	9
1989-90	Philadelphia	80	30	39	11	....	....	....
1990-91	Philadelphia	80	33	37	10	....	....	....
1991-92	Philadelphia	24	8	14	2	....	....	....
1992-93	Hartford	84	26	52	6	....	....	....
1993-94	Hartford	17	4	11	6	....	....	....
1994-95	Hartford	48	19	24	5	....	....	....
1995-96	Hartford	12	5	6	1	....	....	....
	NHL Totals	**425**	**161**	**219**	**45**	**19**	**10**	**9**

Club Directory

Wachovia Center

Philadelphia Flyers
Wachovia Center
3601 South Broad Street
Philadelphia, PA 19148-5290
Phone **215/465-4500**
PR FAX 215/389-9403
www.philadelphiaflyers.com
Capacity: 19,536

Executive Management
Chairman . . . . Ed Snider
President and COO, Comcast-Spectacor . . . . Peter Luukko
General Manager . . . . Paul Holmgren
Senior Vice President . . . . Bob Clarke
Executive Vice President . . . . Keith Allen
Governor . . . . Ed Snider
Alternate Governors . . . . Peter Luukko, Phil Weinberg
Vice President, Marketing and Communications . . . Shawn Tilger

Hockey Club Personnel
Assistant General Manager . . . . Barry Hanrahan
Head Coach . . . . John Stevens
Assistant Coaches . . . . Jack McIlhargey, Joe Mullen, Terry Murray
Goaltending Coach . . . . Reggie Lemelin
Director of Hockey Operations . . . . Chris Pryor
Director of Player Development . . . . Don Luce
Director of Player Personnel . . . . Dave Brown
Scouting Staff . . . . Patrick Burke, Wade Clarke, Mark Greig, Inge Hammarstrom, Simon Nolet, Dennis Patterson, Ilkka Sinisalo, Vaclav Slansky, Evgeny Zimin
Pro Scouts . . . . John Chapman, Ross Fitzpatrick, Al Hill
Video Coordinator . . . . Adam Patterson
Director of Team Services . . . . Bryan Hardenbergh
Executive Assistant . . . . Dianna Taylor
Administrative Assistant . . . . Jody Clarke

Medical/Training Staff
Team Physicians . . . . Bill DeLong, M.D.; Gary Dorshimer, M.D.; Tom Graham, M.D.; Guy Lanzi, D.M.D.; Emanuel Sanfilippo, D.C.
Athletic Trainer/Strength and Conditioning Coach . . Jim McCrossin
Assistant Athletic Trainer . . . . Sal Raffa
Massage Therapist . . . . Brad Smith
Head Equipment Manager . . . . Derek Settlemyre
Equipment Managers . . . . Harry Bricker, Anthony Oratorio, Luke Clarke
Training Center Maintenance . . . . Mike Craytor

Communications
Senior Director of Communications . . . . Zack Hill
Director of Media Services and Publications . . . . . . Joe Klueg
Manager, Communications and New Media . . . . . . Kevin Kurz
Communications Office Manager . . . . Jill Lipson
Media Services and Publications Coordinator . . . . . . Joe Siville

Community Relations
Manager of Community Relations . . . . Jeremy Bland
Ambassador of Hockey . . . . Bob Kelly
Fan Relations Assistant . . . . Jerry Callahan
Ambassadors . . . . Gary Dornhoefer, Joe Kadlec, Bernie Parent

Customer Service
Senior Director of Customer Service . . . . Cindy Stutman
Customer Service Manager . . . . Missy Keeler
Senior Customer Service Account Manager . . . . Emily Zoltowski
Customer Service Account Managers . . . . Lauren Cochran, Kyle Hilbert
Customer Service Assistant . . . . Debbie Brown

Finance
Director of Finance . . . . Dave Jablonski
Controller . . . . Justine Kostka
Staff Accountant . . . . Doreen Holmgren
Payroll Accountant . . . . Renee Eiler

Game Presentation
Director of Game Presentation . . . . Anthony Gioia
Game Presentation & Fan Development Coord. . . . . Mya Gupta
Producer/Director . . . . Artie Halstead
Public Address Announcer . . . . Lou Nolan
Anthem Singer . . . . Lauren Hart

Marketing
Director of Marketing . . . . Lindsey Domers
New Media Manager . . . . Jessica Palmer
Marketing Coordinator . . . . Eddie Hawkins

Special Events
Director of Special Events . . . . Linda Mantai

Ticket Sales
Vice President of Sales . . . . Jim Willits
Director of Ticket Sales . . . . Shawn Anderson
Ticket Sales Coordinator . . . . Angela Prendergast
Account Executives . . . . Bryan Anton, Erin Dunn, Chris Engart, Doug Gesele, Tim Gobs, Lindsay Heck, Travis Kraus, Scott Riese, Tom Quaile, J.T. Stewart
Sales Associates . . . . Warren Avart, P.J. Chipman, James Darlington

Ticketing
Vice President, Ticket Operations . . . . Cecilia Baker
Ticket Office Manager . . . . Linda Fleischer
Assistant Ticket Office Manager . . . . Lisa Albertson
Ticket Office Administration . . . . Joan Kadlec
Team Consultant . . . . Ron Ryan
Executive Assistants . . . . Sharon Allison, Cheri Arnao, Ann Marie Nasuti
Receptionists . . . . Ann Bachich, Debbie Brown

Key Off-Season Signings/Acquisitions

2007

May 30 • Named **Don Maloney** general manager.
31 • Signed 2005 1st-round pick (17th overall), C **Martin Hanzal**.
July 9 • Signed LW **Mike York**.
9 • Re-signed LW **Josh Gratton**.
12 • Signed 2006 1st-round pick (8th overall), C **Peter Mueller**.
12 • Re-signed D **Brendan Bell**.
13 • Re-signed RW **Bill Thomas** and G **David LeNeveu**.
13 • Signed LW **Tomas Surovy**.
19 • Signed G **David Aebischer**.
Aug. 13 • Signed G **Alex Auld**.

Phoenix Coyotes

2006-07 Results: 31W-46L-3OTL-2SOL 67PTS.
Fifth, Pacific Division

Year-by-Year Record

		Home				Road				Overall								
Season	GP	W	L	T	OL	W	L	T	OL	W	L	T	OL	GF	GA	Pts.	Finished	Playoff Result
2006-07	82	18	20	....	3	13	26	....	2	31	46	....	5	216	284	67	5th, Pacific Div.	Out of Playoffs
2005-06	82	19	18	....	4	19	21	....	1	38	39	....	5	246	271	81	5th, Pacific Div.	Out of Playoffs
2004-05	....	....	....	....	....	....	....	....	....	....	....	....	....	....	....	....		
2003-04	82	11	19	7	4	11	17	11	2	22	36	18	6	188	245	68	5th, Pacific Div.	Out of Playoffs
2002-03	82	17	16	6	2	14	19	5	3	31	35	11	5	204	230	78	4th, Pacific Div.	Out of Playoffs
2001-02	82	27	8	3	3	13	19	6	3	40	27	9	6	228	210	95	2nd, Pacific Div.	Lost Conf. Quarter-Final
2000-01	82	21	11	7	2	14	16	10	1	35	27	17	3	214	212	90	4th, Pacific Div.	Out of Playoffs
1999-2000	82	22	16	2	1	17	15	6	3	39	31	8	4	232	228	90	3rd, Pacific Div.	Lost Conf. Quarter-Final
1998-99	82	23	13	5	....	16	18	7	....	39	31	12	....	205	197	90	2nd, Pacific Div.	Lost Conf. Quarter-Final
1997-98	82	19	16	6	....	16	19	6	....	35	35	12	....	224	227	82	4th, Central Div.	Lost Conf. Quarter-Final
1996-97	82	15	19	7	....	23	18	0	....	38	37	7	....	240	243	83	3rd, Central Div.	Lost Conf. Quarter-Final
1995-96*	82	22	16	3	....	14	24	3	....	36	40	6	....	275	291	78	5th, Central Div.	Lost Conf. Quarter-Final
1994-95*	48	10	10	4	....	6	15	3	....	16	25	7	....	157	177	39	6th, Central Div.	Out of Playoffs
1993-94*	84	15	23	4	....	9	28	5	....	24	51	9	....	245	344	57	6th, Central Div.	Out of Playoffs
1992-93*	84	23	16	3	....	17	21	4	....	40	37	7	....	322	320	87	4th, Smythe Div.	Lost Div. Semi-Final
1991-92*	80	20	14	6	....	13	18	9	....	33	32	15	....	251	244	81	4th, Smythe Div.	Lost Div. Semi-Final
1990-91*	80	17	18	5	....	9	25	6	....	26	43	11	....	260	288	63	5th, Smythe Div.	Out of Playoffs
1989-90*	80	22	13	5	....	15	19	6	....	37	32	11	....	298	290	85	3rd, Smythe Div.	Lost Div. Semi-Final
1988-89*	80	17	18	5	....	9	24	7	....	26	42	12	....	300	355	64	5th, Smythe Div.	Out of Playoffs
1987-88*	80	20	14	6	....	13	22	5	....	33	36	11	....	292	310	77	3rd, Smythe Div.	Lost Div. Semi-Final
1986-87*	80	25	12	3	....	15	20	5	....	40	32	8	....	279	271	88	3rd, Smythe Div.	Lost Div. Final
1985-86*	80	18	19	3	....	8	28	4	....	26	47	7	....	295	372	59	3rd, Smythe Div.	Lost Div. Semi-Final
1984-85*	80	21	13	6	....	22	14	4	....	43	27	10	....	358	332	96	2nd, Smythe Div.	Lost Div. Final
1983-84*	80	17	15	8	....	14	23	3	....	31	38	11	....	340	374	73	4th, Smythe Div.	Lost Div. Semi-Final
1982-83*	80	22	16	2	....	11	23	6	....	33	39	8	....	311	333	74	4th, Smythe Div.	Lost Div. Semi-Final
1981-82*	80	18	13	9	....	15	20	5	....	33	33	14	....	319	332	80	2nd, Norris Div.	Lost Div. Semi-Final
1980-81*	80	7	25	8	....	2	32	6	....	9	57	14	....	246	400	32	6th, Smythe Div.	Out of Playoffs
1979-80*	80	13	19	8	....	7	30	3	....	20	49	11	....	214	314	51	5th, Smythe Div.	Out of Playoffs

* Winnipeg Jets

2007-08 Schedule

Month	Day	Date	Opponent
Oct.	Thu.	4	St. Louis
	Sat.	6	Boston
	Wed.	10	at Columbus
	Thu.	11	at Nashville
	Sat.	13	Minnesota
	Thu.	18	Edmonton
	Sat.	20	Detroit
	Thu.	25	at Anaheim
	Sat.	27	Dallas
	Tue.	30	at St. Louis
Nov.	Fri.	2	at Dallas
	Sat.	3	Anaheim
	Wed.	7	at Anaheim
	Thu.	8	Dallas
	Sat.	10	at San Jose
	Mon.	12	at San Jose
	Thu.	15	San Jose
	Sat.	17	at Los Angeles*
	Wed.	21	Los Angeles
	Fri.	23	at Anaheim*
	Sat.	24	Toronto*
	Wed.	28	at Minnesota
	Fri.	30	at Chicago
Dec.	Sat.	1	at Detroit
	Mon.	3	at Pittsburgh
	Wed.	5	Los Angeles
	Fri.	7	San Jose
	Sat.	8	at Los Angeles
	Thu.	13	at NY Islanders
	Sat.	15	at New Jersey*
	Sun.	16	at NY Rangers*
	Tue.	18	at Philadelphia
	Thu.	20	at San Jose
	Sat.	22	Vancouver
	Thu.	27	Minnesota
	Sat.	29	Detroit
	Mon.	31	Colorado
Jan.	Wed.	2	at Colorado
	Thu.	3	Chicago
	Sat.	5	Anaheim
	Tue.	8	at Calgary
	Thu.	10	at Edmonton
	Fri.	11	at Vancouver
	Sun.	13	at Minnesota*
	Tue.	15	San Jose
	Thu.	17	Columbus
	Sat.	19	Chicago
	Mon.	21	Buffalo*
	Thu.	24	Nashville
	Tue.	29	at Columbus
	Wed.	30	at Detroit
Feb.	Sat.	2	at Nashville
	Mon.	4	at Colorado
	Tue.	5	at Calgary
	Thu.	7	Columbus
	Sun.	10	Nashville
	Mon.	11	at Dallas
	Thu.	14	Dallas
	Sat.	16	Los Angeles
	Mon.	18	at Los Angeles
	Tue.	19	Calgary
	Fri.	22	Colorado
	Sun.	24	St. Louis
	Wed.	27	at Chicago
	Thu.	28	at St. Louis
Mar.	Sat.	1	Calgary
	Wed.	5	at Dallas
	Thu.	6	Montreal
	Sat.	8	Ottawa
	Tue.	11	Anaheim
	Thu.	13	Vancouver
	Sat.	15	Edmonton
	Mon.	17	at Vancouver
	Tue.	18	at Edmonton
	Thu.	20	Los Angeles
	Sat.	22	Anaheim
	Tue.	25	San Jose
	Thu.	27	at Los Angeles
	Sun.	30	at San Jose*
Apr.	Thu.	3	Dallas
	Fri.	4	at Dallas
	Sun.	6	at Anaheim*

* Denotes afternoon game.

Shane Doan topped the 20-goal plateau for the seventh straight season in 2006-07. His 27 goals, 28 assists and 55 points all led the Coyotes.

PACIFIC DIVISION
29th NHL Season

Franchise date: June 22, 1979

Transferred from Winnipeg to Phoenix, July 1, 1996.

2007-08 Player Personnel

FORWARDS	HT	WT	S	Place of Birth	*Age	2006-07 Club
CARCILLO, Daniel	5-11	202	L	King City, Ont.	22	Wilkes-Barre-Phoenix
DISALVATORE, Jon	6-1	200	R	Bangor, ME	26	Peoria
DOAN, Shane	6-2	216	R	Halkirk, Alta.	30	Phoenix
FISCHER, Patrick	5-11	194	L	Zug, Switz.	32	Phx-San Antonio-Rapperswil
GRATTON, Josh	6-2	214	L	Brantford, Ont.	25	Phoenix-San Antonio
HANZAL, Martin	6-5	208	L	Pisek, Czech.	20	Red Deer
KAIGORODOV, Alexei	6-1	183	L	Chelyabinsk, USSR	24	Ottawa-Magnitogorsk
KAPANEN, Niko	5-9	180	L	Hameenlinna, Finland	29	Atlanta-Phoenix
LEHOUX, Yanick	6-1	200	R	Montreal, Que.	25	Phoenix-San Antonio
MUELLER, Peter	6-2	205	R	Bloomington, MN	19	Everett
MURLEY, Matt	6-1	206	L	Troy, NY	27	Albany
PERRAULT, Joel	6-1	197	R	Montreal, Que.	24	Phx-StL-Peoria-San Antonio
REINPRECHT, Steve	6-0	195	L	Edmonton, Alta.	31	Phoenix
SJOSTROM, Fredrik	6-1	217	L	Fargelanda, Sweden	24	Phoenix
SUROVY, Tomas	6-1	205	L	Banska Bystrica, Czech.	26	Lulea
TENUTE, Joey	5-9	188	L	Hamilton, Ont.	24	Hershey
THOMAS, Bill	6-1	191	R	Pittsburgh, PA	24	Phoenix-San Antonio
TJARNQVIST, Mathias	6-1	183	L	Umea, Sweden	28	Dallas-Iowa-Phoenix
VRBATA, Radim	6-1	190	R	Mlada Boleslav, Czech.	26	Chicago
WELLER, Craig	6-3	195	R	Calgary, Alta.	26	Hartford
YORK, Mike	5-10	185	R	Waterford, MI	29	NY Islanders-Philadelphia
ZIGOMANIS, Mike	6-1	200	R	North York, Ont.	26	Phoenix
DEFENSEMEN						
BALLARD, Keith	5-11	208	L	Baudette, MN	24	Phoenix
BELL, Brendan	6-1	205	L	Ottawa, Ont.	24	Toronto-Phoenix
BOYNTON, Nick	6-2	211	R	Nobleton, Ont.	28	Phoenix
CALDWELL, Ryan	6-2	174	L	Deloraine, Man.	26	Syracuse
JONES, Matt	6-0	215	L	Downers Grove, IL	24	Phoenix-San Antonio
JOVANOVSKI, Ed	6-2	210	L	Windsor, Ont.	31	Phoenix
MICHALEK, Zbynek	6-1	200	R	Jindrichuv Hradec, Czech.	24	Phoenix
MORRIS, Derek	6-0	220	R	Edmonton, Alta.	29	Phoenix
ROCHE, Travis	6-1	200	R	Grand Cache, Alta.	29	Phoenix-San Antonio
YANDLE, Keith	6-2	195	L	Boston, MA	21	Phoenix-San Antonio

GOALTENDERS	HT	WT	C	Place of Birth	*Age	2006-07 Club
AEBISCHER, David	6-1	185	L	Fribourg, Switz.	29	Montreal
AULD, Alex	6-4	200	L	Cold Lake, Alta.	26	Florida
LeNEVEU, David	6-1	187	L	Fernie, B.C.	24	Phoenix-San Antonio
TELLQVIST, Mikael	5-11	185	L	Sundbyberg, Sweden	28	Toronto-Toronto (AHL)-Phoenix

* – Age at start of 2007-08 season

2006-07 Scoring

* – rookie

Regular Season

Pos	#	Player	Team	GP	G	A	Pts	+/-	PIM	PP	SH	GW	S	%
R	19	Shane Doan	PHX	73	27	28	55	–14	73	11	0	7	209	12.9
R	11	Owen Nolan	PHX	76	16	24	40	–2	56	2	3	1	154	10.4
C	28	Steve Reinprecht	PHX	49	9	24	33	–3	28	2	0	1	71	12.7
D	55	Ed Jovanovski	PHX	54	11	18	29	–6	63	6	0	1	135	8.1
C	97	Jeremy Roenick	PHX	70	11	17	28	–18	32	4	0	1	89	12.4
D	4	Zbynek Michalek	PHX	82	4	24	28	–20	34	3	0	0	144	2.8
D	2	Keith Ballard	PHX	69	5	22	27	–7	59	2	0	0	79	6.3
D	53	Derek Morris	PHX	82	6	19	25	–18	115	2	0	1	129	4.7
C	15	Mike Zigomanis	PHX	75	14	9	23	–8	46	2	1	0	142	9.9
C	8	Niko Kapanen	ATL	60	4	9	13	–12	20	1	0	0	51	7.8
			PHX	19	2	7	9	–11	8	1	0	1	28	7.1
			TOTAL	79	6	16	22	–23	28	2	0	1	79	7.6
D	77	Travis Roche	PHX	50	6	13	19	2	22	2	0	1	32	18.8
R	20	Fredrik Sjostrom	PHX	78	9	9	18	–11	48	2	0	1	125	7.2
R	21	* Bill Thomas	PHX	24	8	6	14	–6	2	4	0	1	60	13.3
L	22	Mathias Tjarnqvist	DAL	18	1	3	4	–3	4	0	0	0	13	7.7
			PHX	26	5	4	9	–2	2	0	1	0	31	16.1
			TOTAL	44	6	7	13	–5	6	0	1	0	44	13.6
C	14	Kevyn Adams	CAR	35	2	2	4	–10	17	0	1	0	36	5.6
			PHX	33	1	7	8	–10	8	0	0	0	51	2.0
			TOTAL	68	3	9	12	–20	25	0	1	0	87	3.4
D	44	Nick Boynton	PHX	59	2	9	11	–13	138	1	0	0	53	3.8
C	12	Patrick Fischer	PHX	27	4	6	10	0	24	0	0	1	32	12.5
C	38	Dave Scatchard	PHX	46	3	5	8	–18	72	0	0	1	77	3.9
L	13	* Daniel Carcillo	PHX	18	4	3	7	–7	74	3	0	0	32	12.5
D	6	* Brendan Bell	TOR	31	1	4	5	–3	19	1	0	0	29	3.4
			PHX	14	0	2	2	–8	8	0	0	0	18	0.0
			TOTAL	45	1	6	7	–11	27	1	0	0	47	2.1
D	5	* Matt Jones	PHX	45	1	6	7	–12	39	0	0	0	20	5.0
L	23	Jeff Taffe	PHX	17	4	2	6	–7	2	1	0	0	34	11.8
C	29	* Yanick Lehoux	PHX	7	1	2	3	–1	4	1	0	0	10	10.0
C	26	* Joel Perrault	PHX	9	1	1	2	–2	8	0	0	0	11	9.1
			STL	11	0	0	0	–4	0	0	0	0	13	0.0
			PHX	6	0	1	1	–1	6	0	0	0	7	0.0
			TOTAL	26	1	2	3	–7	14	0	0	0	31	3.2
C	23	Don MacLean	PHX	9	1	1	2	–4	0	0	0	0	12	8.3
R	90	* Enver Lisin	PHX	17	1	1	2	–18	16	1	0	0	35	2.9
L	24	* Josh Gratton	PHX	52	1	1	2	–9	188	0	0	0	29	3.4
D	3	* Keith Yandle	PHX	7	0	2	2	0	8	0	0	0	10	0.0
C	40	Mike Ricci	PHX	7	0	1	1	–1	4	0	0	0	4	0.0

Goaltending

No.	Goaltender	GPI	Mins	Avg	W	L	OT	EN	SO	GA	SA	S%	G	A	PIM
31	Curtis Joseph	55	2993	3.19	18	31	2	2	4	159	1481	.893	0	0	10
32	Mikael Tellqvist	30	1591	3.39	11	11	3	3	2	90	780	.885	0	1	0
30	* David LeNeveu	6	233	3.86	2	1	0	0	0	15	142	.894	0	0	0
1	Michael Morrison	4	127	6.14	0	3	0	0	0	13	62	.790	0	0	0
	Totals	**82**	**4970**	**3.40**	**31**	**46**	**5**	**5**	**6**	**282**	**2470**	**.886**			

Coach

WAYNE GRETZKY
Coach, Phoenix Coyotes. Born in Brantford, Ont., January 26, 1961.

Phoenix Coyotes chairman and governor Steve Ellman announced on August 8, 2005 that Wayne Gretzky had agreed to a multiyear contract to serve as head coach of the Phoenix Coyotes. In addition to serving as the Coyotes' head coach, Gretzky also continues as managing partner and alternate governor for the Coyotes, a role that he had performed for the previous four seasons. Gretzky officially joined the franchise on February 15, 2001, when the Ellman and Moyes ownership group completed the purchase of the Coyotes.

Gretzky played 20 seasons in the National Hockey League with Edmonton, Los Angeles, St. Louis and the New York Rangers, dominating the game unlike any player in history. Gretzky helped win four Stanley Cup championships and three Canada Cup tournament titles during his illustrious playing career. He became the NHL's all-time leading goal, assist and point producer for a single season and career (both regular season and playoffs). Gretzky won the Art Ross Trophy as the NHL's leading scorer 10 times, the Hart Trophy as the League's MVP nine times (including eight consecutive seasons) and the Conn Smythe Trophies as playoff MVP twice. He earned the Lady Byng Trophy as the NHL's most gentlemanly player five times and made 18 consecutive All-Star Game appearances, securing three All-Star MVP Awards. Gretzky is an eight-time First All-Star Team member and seven-time Second All-Star Team member. He holds virtually every offensive record in the NHL and his tireless support of the game has contributed significantly to the popularity it enjoys today.

On November 22, 1999 – seven months after his retirement – Gretzky was inducted into the Hockey Hall of Fame in Toronto, becoming the tenth and final player in Hockey Hall of Fame history to have the mandatory three-year waiting period for enshrinement waived by the Hall's board of directors.

Gretzky's incredible success in hockey has continued past his playing career. In a managerial role with Team Canada, Gretzky served as executive director for Team Canada, responsible for assembling Canada's best hockey players at the 2002 Olympic Winter Games in Salt Lake City and again in 2004 at the World Cup of Hockey. Under Gretzky's leadership, Team Canada won the gold medal for the first time in 50 years at the 2002 Olympics. Two years later, Team Canada repeated the feat by winning the 2004 World Cup of Hockey championship. Gretzky also served as executive director again at the 2006 Olympics.

Coaching Record

		Regular Season				Playoffs		
Season	**Team**	**Games**	**W**	**L**	**O/T**	**Games**	**W**	**L**
2005-06	**Phoenix (NHL)**	82	38	39	5	....	....	....
2006-07	**Phoenix (NHL)**	82	31	46	5	....	....	....
	NHL Totals	164	69	85	10	....	....	....

Assistant coach Rick Tocchet posted a 2-3 record as replacement coach when Gretzky was sidelined due to the death of his mother, December 17 to 28, 2005. All games are credited to Gretzky's coaching record.

In his ninth NHL season, defenseman Derek Morris played in all 82 games for the first time since his rookie campaign with Calgary in 1997-98.

Coaching History

Tom McVie and Bill Sutherland, 1979-80; Tom McVie, Bill Sutherland and Mike Smith, 1980-81; Tom Watt, 1981-82, 1982-83; Tom Watt and Barry Long, 1983-84; Barry Long, 1984-85; Barry Long and John Ferguson, 1985-86; Dan Maloney, 1986-87, 1987-88; Dan Maloney and Rick Bowness, 1988-89; Bob Murdoch, 1989-90, 1990-91; John Paddock, 1991-92 to 1993-94; John Paddock and Terry Simpson, 1994-95; Terry Simpson, 1995-96; Don Hay, 1996-97; Jim Schoenfeld, 1997-98, 1998-99; Bob Francis, 1999-2000 to 2002-03; Bob Francis and Rick Bowness, 2003-04; Rick Bowness, 2004-05; Wayne Gretzky, 2005-06 to date.

Club Records

Team

(Figures in brackets for season records are games played; records for fewest points, wins, ties, losses, goals, goals against are for 70 or more games)

Most Points ... **96** 1984-85 (80)
Most Wins ... **43** 1984-85 (80)
Most Ties ... **18** 2003-04 (82)
Most Losses ... **57** 1980-81 (80)
Most Goals ... **358** 1984-85 (80)
Most Goals Against ... **400** 1980-81 (80)
Fewest Points ... **32** 1980-81 (80)
Fewest Wins ... **9** 1980-81 (80)
Fewest Ties ... **6** 1995-96 (82)
Fewest Losses ... **27** 1984-85 (80), 2000-01 (82), 2001-02 (82)
Fewest Goals ... **188** 2003-04 (82)
Fewest Goals Against ... **197** 1998-99 (82)

Longest Winning Streak
Overall ... **9** Mar. 8-27/85
Home ... **9** Dec. 27/92-Jan. 23/93
Away ... **8** Feb. 25-Apr. 6/85

Longest Undefeated Streak
Overall ... **14** Oct. 25-Nov. 28/98 (12 wins, 2 ties)
Home ... **11** Dec. 23/83-Feb. 5/84 (6 wins, 5 ties), Oct. 15-Dec. 20/98 (10 wins, 1 tie)
Away ... **9** Feb. 25-Apr. 7/85 (8 wins, 1 tie), Dec. 7/03-Jan. 9/04 (5 wins, 4 ties)

Longest Losing Streak
Overall ... **10** Nov. 30-Dec. 20/80, Feb. 6-25/94
Home ... **5** Oct. 29-Nov. 13/93 Mar. 13-23/00
Away ... **13** Jan. 26-Apr. 14/94

Longest Winless Streak
Overall ... ***30** Oct. 19-Dec. 20/80 (23 losses, 7 ties)
Home ... **14** Oct. 19-Dec. 14/80 (9 losses, 5 ties)
Away ... **18** Oct. 10-Dec. 20/80 (16 losses, 2 ties)

Most Shutouts, Season ... **9** 1998-99 (82)
Most PIM, Season ... **2,278** 1987-88 (80)
Most Goals, Game ... **12** Feb. 25/85 (Wpg. 12 at NYR 5)

Individual

Most Seasons ... **15** Teppo Numminen
Most Games ... **1,098** Teppo Numminen
Most Goals, Career ... **379** Dale Hawerchuk
Most Assists, Career ... **553** Thomas Steen
Most Points, Career ... **929** Dale Hawerchuk (379G, 550A)
Most PIM, Career ... **1,508** Keith Tkachuk
Most Shutouts, Career ... **21** Nikolai Khabibulin
Longest Consecutive Games Streak ... **475** Dale Hawerchuk (Dec. 19/82-Dec. 10/88)
Most Goals, Season ... **76** Teemu Selanne (1992-93)
Most Assists, Season ... **79** Phil Housley (1992-93)
Most Points, Season ... **132** Teemu Selanne (1992-93; 76G, 56A)
Most PIM, Season ... **347** Tie Domi (1993-94)
Most Points, Defenseman, Season ... **97** Phil Housley (1992-93; 18G, 79A)
Most Points, Center, Season ... **130** Dale Hawerchuk (1984-85; 53G, 77A)
Most Points, Right Wing, Season ... **132** Teemu Selanne (1992-93; 76G, 56A)
Most Points, Left Wing, Season ... **98** Keith Tkachuk (1995-96; 50G, 48A)
Most Points, Rookie, Season ... ***132** Teemu Selanne (1992-93; 76G, 56A)
Most Shutouts, Season ... **8** Nikolai Khabibulin (1998-99)
Most Goals, Game ... **5** Willy Lindstrom (Mar. 2/82), Alexei Zhamnov (Apr. 1/95)
Most Assists, Game ... **5** Dale Hawerchuk (Mar. 6/84, Mar. 18/89, Mar. 4/90), Phil Housley (Jan. 18/93), Keith Tkachuk (Feb. 23/01)
Most Points, Game ... **6** Willy Lindstrom (Mar. 2/82; 5G, 1A), Dale Hawerchuk (Dec. 14/83; 3G, 3A, Mar. 5/88; 2G, 4A, Mar. 18/89; 1G, 5A), Thomas Steen (Oct. 24/84; 2G, 4A), Ed Olczyk (Dec. 21/91; 2G, 4A)

* NHL Record.
Records include Winnipeg Jets, 1979-80 through 1995-96.

Winnipeg Jets Retired Numbers

9	Bobby Hull	1972-1980
10	Dale Hawerchuk	1981-1990
25	Thomas Steen	1981-1995

Captains' History

Lars-Erik Sjoberg, 1979-80; Morris Lukowich, 1980-81; Dave Christian, 1981-82; Dave Christian and Lucien DeBlois, 1982-83; Lucien DeBlois, 1983-84; Dale Hawerchuk, 1984-85 to 1988-89; Randy Carlyle, Dale Hawerchuk and Thomas Steen (tri-captains), 1989-90; Randy Carlyle and Thomas Steen (co-captains), 1990-91; Troy Murray, 1991-92; Troy Murray and Dean Kennedy, 1992-93; Dean Kennedy and Keith Tkachuk, 1993-94; Keith Tkachuk, 1994-95; Kris King, 1995-96; Keith Tkachuk, 1996-97 to 2000-01; Teppo Numminen, 2001-02, 2002-03; Shane Doan, 2003-04 to date.

All-time Record vs. Other Clubs

Regular Season

	At Home								On Road								Total							
	GP	W	L	T	OL	GF	GA	PTS	GP	W	L	T	OL	GF	GA	PTS	GP	W	L	T	OL	GF	GA	PTS
Anaheim	34	14	14	2	4	92	98	34	35	9	21	3	2	83	109	23	69	23	35	5	6	175	207	57
Atlanta	6	5	0	1	0	21	9	11	5	4	1	0	0	17	10	8	11	9	1	1	0	38	19	19
Boston	30	13	14	3	0	101	102	29	31	5	22	4	0	94	137	14	61	18	36	7	0	195	239	43
Buffalo	29	13	14	2	0	87	92	28	32	7	20	5	0	82	128	19	61	20	34	7	0	169	220	47
Calgary	74	36	27	11	0	276	252	83	75	24	42	9	0	234	311	57	149	60	69	20	0	510	563	140
Carolina	32	15	14	2	1	118	116	33	31	11	13	6	1	91	103	29	63	26	27	8	2	209	219	62
Chicago	54	29	20	5	0	177	169	63	52	15	26	10	1	138	191	41	106	44	46	15	1	315	360	104
Colorado	44	16	21	7	0	153	160	39	45	16	22	5	2	149	163	39	89	32	43	12	2	302	323	78
Columbus	12	7	2	3	0	39	29	17	12	5	6	1	0	27	31	11	24	12	8	4	0	66	60	28
Dallas	62	24	31	4	3	188	210	55	63	22	31	9	1	185	225	54	125	46	62	13	4	373	435	109
Detroit	53	17	22	14	0	154	171	48	55	20	27	8	0	183	216	48	108	37	49	22	0	337	387	96
Edmonton	75	31	37	5	2	299	326	69	76	22	46	6	2	244	328	52	151	53	83	11	4	543	654	121
Florida	11	4	3	3	1	31	34	12	9	5	4	0	0	23	28	10	20	9	7	3	1	54	62	22
Los Angeles	84	45	27	11	1	332	270	102	82	34	32	14	2	308	321	84	166	79	59	25	3	640	591	186
Minnesota	12	7	4	1	0	33	27	15	12	5	5	2	0	25	27	12	24	12	9	3	0	58	54	27
Montreal	29	9	13	7	0	94	112	25	30	3	25	2	0	68	147	8	59	12	38	9	0	162	259	33
Nashville	16	10	4	0	2	48	47	22	16	5	7	2	2	37	47	14	32	15	11	2	4	85	94	36
New Jersey	32	22	7	3	0	117	82	47	29	11	12	6	0	87	95	28	61	33	19	9	0	204	177	75
NY Islanders	31	12	15	4	0	102	108	28	30	9	13	8	0	91	113	26	61	21	28	12	0	193	221	54
NY Rangers	32	13	14	4	1	110	108	31	29	9	17	2	1	102	128	21	61	22	31	6	2	212	236	52
Ottawa	10	4	5	1	0	34	38	9	12	6	5	1	0	36	36	13	22	10	10	2	0	70	74	22
Philadelphia	32	14	16	2	0	103	106	30	31	8	23	0	0	83	134	16	63	22	39	2	0	186	240	46
Pittsburgh	32	14	14	3	1	118	114	32	30	10	20	0	0	86	120	20	62	24	34	3	1	204	234	52
St. Louis	55	28	20	7	0	182	174	63	54	17	26	11	0	151	188	45	109	45	46	18	0	333	362	108
San Jose	43	21	16	3	3	133	121	48	40	18	18	4	0	124	137	40	83	39	34	7	3	257	258	88
Tampa Bay	12	6	6	0	0	29	29	12	11	5	6	0	0	36	38	10	23	11	12	0	0	65	67	22
Toronto	39	20	13	6	0	161	142	46	44	22	20	2	0	165	160	46	83	42	33	8	0	326	302	92
Vancouver	73	35	28	10	0	267	258	80	76	19	47	10	0	210	287	48	149	54	75	20	0	477	545	128
Washington	31	15	9	7	0	113	111	37	32	9	17	5	1	88	121	24	63	24	26	12	1	201	232	61
Totals	**1079**	**499**	**430**	**131**	**19**	**3712**	**3615**	**1148**	**1079**	**355**	**574**	**135**	**15**	**3247**	**4079**	**860**	**2158**	**854**	**1004**	**266**	**34**	**6959**	**7694**	**2008**

Playoffs

	Series	W	L	GP	W	L	T	GF	GA	Last Mtg.	Rnd.	Result
Anaheim	1	0	1	7	3	4	0	17	17	1997	CQF	L 3-4
Calgary	3	2	1	13	7	6	0	45	43	1987	DSF	W 4-2
Colorado	1	0	1	5	1	4	0	10	17	2000	CQF	L 1-4
Detroit	2	0	2	12	4	8	0	28	44	1998	CQF	L 2-4
Edmonton	6	0	6	26	4	22	0	75	120	1990	DSF	L 3-4
St. Louis	2	0	2	11	4	7	0	29	39	1999	CQF	L 3-4
San Jose	1	0	1	5	1	4	0	7	13	2002	CQF	L 1-4
Vancouver	2	0	2	13	5	8	0	34	50	1993	DSF	L 2-4
Totals	**18**	**2**	**16**	**92**	**29**	**63**	**0**	**245**	**343**			

Playoff Results 2007-2002

Year	Round	Opponent	Result	GF	GA
2002	CQF	San Jose	L 1-4	7	13

Abbreviations: Round: CQF – conference quarter-final; **DSF** – division semi-final.

Calgary totals include Atlanta Flames, 1979-80.
Colorado totals include Quebec, 1979-80 to 1994-95.
New Jersey totals include Colorado Rockies, 1979-80 to 1981-82.
Carolina totals include Hartford, 1979-80 to 1996-97.
Dallas totals include Minnesota North Stars, 1979-80 to 1992-93.

2006-07 Results

Month	Date	Opponent	Score
Oct.	5	NY Islanders	6-3
	7	Anaheim	1-2
	9	at Columbus	1-5
	11	at Detroit	2-9
	14	at Nashville	1-4
	17	at St. Louis	5-2
	19	Los Angeles	0-4
	21	Dallas	0-4
	23	at Edmonton	2-5
	24	at Calgary	1-6
	26	Edmonton	6-2
	28	NY Rangers	3-7
Nov.	3	at Anaheim	2-6
	4	Los Angeles	6-4
	9	Dallas	0-1
	11	San Jose	1-2
	14	Minnesota	4-3
	16	Chicago	3-2†
	18	at Los Angeles	3-5
	19	at Anaheim	4-6
	22	New Jersey	3-1
	24	at Minnesota	0-4
	25	at St. Louis	2-1
	30	Los Angeles	7-4
Dec.	4	Nashville	3-2
	6	at Dallas	0-3
	7	at Chicago	2-1†
	9	Dallas	3-4*
	11	at San Jose	0-4
	12	at Vancouver	2-5
	14	Columbus	5-4†
	16	Calgary	3-6
	21	Edmonton	2-3
	23	Anaheim	2-0
	26	at Los Angeles	3-4†
	28	at San Jose	3-2
	30	San Jose	8-0
Jan.	1	at Washington	3-2
	4	at Carolina	2-0
	5	at Atlanta	5-4*
	7	at Chicago	4-2
	9	at Dallas	5-2
	11	Detroit	1-5
	13	San Jose	1-4
	15	St. Louis	5-4†
	17	at Colorado	3-4
	18	at San Jose	2-5
	20	at Los Angeles	3-2
	26	at Colorado	5-4†
	27	Pittsburgh	2-7
	31	at Anaheim	1-2
Feb.	1	Nashville	3-2
	3	Minnesota	0-1
	6	at Columbus	3-0
	7	at Detroit	2-4
	10	at Florida	2-5
	13	at Tampa Bay	3-5
	15	Anaheim	4-5*
	17	Detroit	1-4
	19	at Nashville	1-4
	22	Calgary	3-2*
	26	at Calgary	2-5
	27	at Edmonton	3-0
Mar.	1	at Vancouver	3-4
	3	Columbus	3-4
	7	at Anaheim	1-2
	8	Vancouver	2-4
	10	Chicago	5-7
	12	Philadelphia	4-0
	15	San Jose	1-5
	17	Colorado	3-6
	18	at Dallas	4-5*
	20	at Minnesota	2-3
	22	Anaheim	2-1
	24	Dallas	3-4†
	27	at Dallas	0-6
	29	Colorado	3-4
	30	at San Jose	2-4
Apr.	3	St. Louis	2-5
	5	Los Angeles	3-2
	7	at Los Angeles	2-3
	8	Vancouver	3-1

* – Overtime † – Shootout

Entry Draft Selections 2007-1993

2007

Pick	
3	Kyle Turris
30	Nick Ross
32	Brett Maclean
36	Joel Gistedt
103	Vladimir Ruzicka
123	Maxim Goncharov
153	Scott Darling

2006

Pick	
8	Peter Mueller
29	Chris Summers
88	Jonas Ahnelov
130	Brett Bennett
131	Martin Latal
152	Jordan Bendfeld
188	Chris Frank
196	Benn Ferriero

2005

Pick	
17	Martin Hanzal
59	Pier-Olivier Pelletier
105	Keith Yandle
148	Anton Krysanov
212	Pat Brosnihan

2004

Pick	
5	Blake Wheeler
35	Logan Stephenson
50	Enver Lisin
103	Roman Tomanek
119	Kevin Porter
168	Kevin Cormier
199	Chad Kolarik
240	Aaron Gagnon
261	Will Engasser
265	Daniel Winnik

2003

Pick	
77	Tyler Redenbach
80	Dmitri Pestunov
115	Liam Lindstrom
178	Ryan Gibbons
208	Randall Gelech
242	Eduard Lewandowski
272	Sean Sullivan
290	Loic Burkhalter

2002

Pick	
19	Jakub Koreis
23	Ben Eager
46	David Leneveu
70	Joe Callahan
80	Matt Jones
97	Lance Monych
132	John Zeiler
186	Jeff Pietrasiak
216	Ladislav Kouba
249	Marcus Smith
280	Russell Spence

2001

Pick	
11	Fredrik Sjostrom
31	Matthew Spiller
45	Martin Podlesak
78	Beat Forster
148	David Klema
180	Scott Polaski
210	Steve Belanger
243	Frantisek Lukes
273	Severin Blindenbacher

2000

Pick	
19	Krys Kolanos
53	Alexander Tatarinov
85	Ramzi Abid
160	Nate Kiser
186	Brent Gauvreau
217	Igor Samoilov
249	Sami Venalainen
281	Peter Fabus

1999

Pick	
15	Scott Kelman
19	Kirill Safronov
53	Brad Ralph
71	Jason Jaspers
116	Ryan Lauzon
123	Preston Mizzi
168	Erik Lewerstrom
234	Goran Bezina
262	Alexei Litvinenko

1998

Pick	
14	Patrick DesRochers
43	Ossi Vaananen
73	Pat O'Leary
100	Ryan Vanbuskirk
115	Jay Leach
116	Josh Blackburn
129	Robert Schnabel
160	Rickard Wallin
187	Erik Westrum
214	Justin Hansen

1997

Pick	
43	Juha Gustafsson
96	Scott McCallum
123	Curtis Suter
151	Robert Francz
207	Alexander Andreyev
233	Wyatt Smith

1996

Pick	
11	Dan Focht
24	Daniel Briere
62	Per-Anton Lundstrom
119	Richard Lintner
139	Robert Esche
174	Trevor Letowski
200	Nicholas Lent
226	Marc-Etienne Hubert

1995

Pick	
7	Shane Doan
32	Marc Chouinard
34	Jason Doig
67	Brad Isbister
84	Justin Kurtz
121	Brian Elder
136	Sylvain Daigle
162	Paul Traynor
188	Jaroslav Obsut
189	Fredrik Loven
214	Rob Deciantis

1994

Pick	
30	Deron Quint
56	Dorian Anneck
58	Tavis Hansen
82	Steve Cheredaryk
108	Craig Mills
143	Steve Vezina
146	Chris Kibermanis
186	Ramil Saifullin
212	Henrik Smangs
238	Mike Mader
264	Jason Issel

1993

Pick	
15	Mats Lindgren
31	Scott Langkow
43	Alexei Budayev
79	Ruslan Batyrshin
93	Ravil Gusmanov
119	Larry Courville
145	Michal Grosek
171	Martin Woods
197	Adrian Murray
217	Vladimir Potapov
223	Ilja Stashenkov
228	Harijs Vitolinsh
285	Russ Hewson

General Managers' History

John Ferguson, 1979-80 to 1987-88; John Ferguson and Mike Smith, 1988-89; Mike Smith, 1989-90 to 1992-93; Mike Smith and John Paddock, 1993-94; John Paddock, 1994-95, 1995-96; John Paddock and Bobby Smith, 1996-97; Bobby Smith, 1997-98 to 1999-2000; Bobby Smith and Cliff Fletcher, 2000-01; Cliff Fletcher and Michael Barnett, 2001-02; Michael Barnett, 2002-03 to 2006-07; Don Maloney, 2007-08.

General Manager

DON MALONEY
General Manager, Phoenix Coyotes.
Born in Lindsay, Ont., September 5, 1958.

Don Maloney was signed as the new general manager of the Phoenix Coyotes on May 30, 2007, joining the team from the New York Rangers for whom he served as vice president of player personnel and assistant general manager. He assisted Rangers' president and g.m. Glen Sather in all player transactions and contract negotiations and was involved with the team's professional and amateur scouting operations. Maloney spent 10 seasons in the Rangers' front office. He played a key role in the Rangers' development of several prospects into productive NHL players, including Henrik Lundqvist and Peter Prucha. Maloney also served as assistant general manager for Team Canada squads that won gold medals at the 2003 and 2004 World Championships.

Maloney's first front office position in the NHL was as assistant general manager of the New York Islanders following his retirement as a player with the club on January 17, 1991. Maloney later served as Islanders' general manager from August 17, 1992 to December 2, 1995. Among the players drafted by the Islanders during Maloney's tenure with the club were Todd Bertuzzi, Bryan McCabe, Ziggy Palffy, Tommy Salo and Darius Kasparaitis. Maloney then served as Eastern professional scout for the San Jose Sharks during the 1996-97 season prior to joining the Rangers' front office.

As a player, Maloney registered 214 goals, 350 assists, and 564 points as well as 815 penalty minutes in 765 regular-season games over 13 NHL campaigns with the Rangers, Hartford Whalers and Islanders. He also collected 22 goals, 35 assists, and 57 points in 94 career playoff games. Maloney spent 11 seasons with the Rangers after being selected by the club in the second round (26th overall) of the 1978 NHL Entry Draft. He helped lead the Rangers to the 1980 Stanley Cup Final by posting 20 points (7 goals, 13 assists) that postseason, a playoff record for rookies at the time. Maloney played in the NHL All-Star Game in 1983 and 1984. He was named MVP of the 1984 game.

Club Directory

Jobing.com Arena

Phoenix Coyotes
6751 N. White Out Way #200
Glendale, AZ 85305
Phone **623/772-3200**
FAX 623/872-2000
Tickets 480/563-PUCK

Jobing.com Arena
9400 W. Maryland Avenue
Glendale, AZ 85305
Phone 623/772-3200
FAX 623/772-3201
Capacity: 17,799
www.PhoenixCoyotes.com

Club Officers and Executives

Majority Investor	Jerry Moyes
Chief Executive Officer & Governor	Jeff A. Shumway
Managing Partner, Alt. Gov. & Head Coach	Wayne Gretzky
President, Chief Operating Officer & Alt. Gov.	Douglas Moss
General Manager	Don Maloney
Assistant General Manager	Brad Treliving
Exec. Vice President of Business Development	John Browne
Exec. Vice President & Chief Marketing Officer	Michael Bucek
Sr. Vice President, Chief Financial Officer	Mike Nealy
Sr. Vice President of Corporate Communications	Jeff Holbrook
Executive Assistant to the CEO	Elly Penrod
Executive Assistant to the President	Cheryl Taylor
Administrative Assistant to the CMO	Pamela Mann
Administrative Assistant to the CFO	Melissa Rezvani
Hockey Operations	
Head Coach	Wayne Gretzky
Associate Coach	Ulf Samuelsson
Goaltending Coach	Grant Fuhr
Director of Player Personnel	Tom Kurvers
Director of Player Development	Eddie Mio
Director of Hockey Administration	Jay Neal
Strength & Conditioning Coordinator	Mike Bahn
Head Athletic Therapist	Chris Broadhurst
Massage Therapist	Jukka Nieminen
Head Equipment Manager	Stan Wilson
Equipment Manager	Tony Silva
Assistant Equipment Manager	Jason Rudee
Video Coordinator	Steve Peters
Power Skating Coach	Mark Ciaccio
Team Travel Coordinator	Rick Braunstein
Manager of Team Services	Lesa Guth
Team Internist	Robert Luberto, D.O.
Team Orthopedic Surgeons	Dr. Lawrence Emmott, Dr. Doug Freedberg, Dr. Gary Waslewski
Team Dentists	Dr. Ron Foeldi
San Antonio (AHL) Head Coach	TBD
San Antonio (AHL) Assistant Coach	TBD
Professional Scouts	Greg Malone, Rich Sutter
Director of Amateur Scouting	Keith Gretzky
European & Amateur Scouts	Patrik Augusta, Steve Lyons, Rob Murphy, Greg Royce, Christian Ruuttu, Barry Trapp
Director of Team Security	Jim O'Neal
Broadcasting	
TV Play-by-Play/Analyst	Dave Strader/Darren Pang
TV/Radio Host	Todd Walsh
Radio Play-by-Play/Analyst	Bob Heethuis/Louie DeBrusk
Director of Broadcasting	Doug Cannon
Communications	
Director of Media Relations & Publications	Kevin Crawley
Manager of Media Relations	Sergey Kocharov
Communications Assistant	Rob Crean
Community Relations	
Dir. of Comm. Relations & Fan Development	Sarah Finecey
Manager of Hockey Development	Scott Storkan
Marketing	
Director of Promotions	Stacey Cohen
Director of Advertising & Media	Ted Santiago
Director of New Media	Heath Price-Khan
Director of Event Presentation	Matt Coy
Creative Director of Event Presentation	David Rickles
Corporate Sales & Service	
Vice President of Corporate Partnerships	Joe Hickey
Sr. Director of Corporate Partner & Suite Services	Thea Crum
Senior Director of Corporate Partnerships	Judd Norris
Corporate Partnerships Directors	Bret Fishkind, Michael Whalen
Suite Sales	
Vice President of Suite Sales	Ron Campbell
Director of Suite Sales	Mike Briody
Ticket Operations	
Director of Ticket Operations	Douglas Vanderheyden
Ticket Sales & Services	
Senior Directors of Ticket Sales & Services	Al Guido, Flavil Hampsten
Director of Group Sales	Scott Schiff
Finance & Accounting	
Vice President of Finance and Controller	Joe Leibfried
Executive Director of Finance	Larry Silver
Assistant Controller	Burlenti Shaban
Legal	
General Counsel	Steve Weinreich
Human Resources	
Executive Director of Human Resources	Julie Atherton
Team Information	
Broadcast Television Station	KAZT-TV
Regional Sports Network	FSN Arizona
Radio Station	The FAN 1060 AM
Team Photographer	Norm Hall

Pittsburgh Penguins

2006-07 Results: 47W-24L-5OTL-6SOL 105PTS.
Second, Atlantic Division

Key Off-Season Signings/Acquisitions

2007

June 22 • Re-signed RW **Mark Recchi** and LW **Gary Roberts**.

July 2 • Signed D **Darryl Sydor**, RW **Petr Sykora** and G **Dany Sabourin**.

2 • Re-signed D **Ryan Whitney** and D **Rob Scuderi**.

5 • Re-signed C **Maxime Talbot** and C **Erik Christensen**.

10 • Re-signed C **Sidney Crosby**.

12 • Re-signed RW **Colby Armstrong**.

16 • Re-signed head coach **Michel Therrien**.

19 • Signed G **Ty Conklin**.

Sidney Crosby celebrates a goal. He had 36 goals and 84 assists for 120 points last season, making the 19-year-old the first teenager to win a scoring title in any major professional sport.

2007-08 Schedule

Oct.	Fri.	5	at Carolina		Tue.	8	at Florida
	Sat.	6	Anaheim		Thu.	10	at Tampa Bay
	Wed.	10	Montreal		Sat.	12	at Atlanta
	Sat.	13	at Toronto		Mon.	14	NY Rangers
	Wed.	17	New Jersey		Fri.	18	Tampa Bay
	Fri.	19	Carolina		Sat.	19	at Montreal
	Sat.	20	at Washington		Mon.	21	Washington
	Tue.	23	NY Rangers		Thu.	24	at Philadelphia
	Thu.	25	Toronto		Tue.	29	at New Jersey
	Sat.	27	Montreal		Wed.	30	at Atlanta
	Tue.	30	at Minnesota	**Feb.**	Sat.	2	Carolina
Nov.	Thu.	1	at Colorado		Mon.	4	at New Jersey
	Sat.	3	at NY Islanders		Thu.	7	NY Islanders
	Mon.	5	at New Jersey		Sat.	9	Los Angeles*
	Wed.	7	Philadelphia		Sun.	10	Philadelphia*
	Thu.	8	at NY Rangers		Wed.	13	Boston
	Sat.	10	at Philadelphia		Thu.	14	at Carolina
	Mon.	12	New Jersey		Sun.	17	at Buffalo*
	Thu.	15	NY Islanders		Tue.	19	Florida
	Sat.	17	NY Rangers		Thu.	21	at Montreal
	Wed.	21	New Jersey		Sat.	23	Ottawa*
	Thu.	22	at Ottawa		Sun.	24	San Jose*
	Sat.	24	Atlanta		Tue.	26	at NY Islanders
	Fri.	30	Dallas		Thu.	28	at Boston
Dec.	Sat.	1	at Toronto	**Mar.**	Sat.	1	at Ottawa*
	Mon.	3	Phoenix		Sun.	2	Atlanta*
	Wed.	5	at Edmonton		Tue.	4	at Tampa Bay
	Thu.	6	at Calgary		Thu.	6	at Florida
	Sat.	8	at Vancouver		Sun.	9	at Washington*
	Tue.	11	at Philadelphia		Wed.	12	Buffalo
	Thu.	13	Ottawa		Sun.	16	Philadelphia*
	Sat.	15	at NY Islanders		Tue.	18	at NY Rangers
	Tue.	18	at NY Rangers		Thu.	20	Tampa Bay
	Thu.	20	at Boston		Sat.	22	New Jersey
	Fri.	21	NY Islanders		Mon.	24	at NY Islanders
	Sun.	23	Boston*		Tue.	25	at New Jersey
	Thu.	27	Washington		Thu.	27	NY Islanders
	Sat.	29	Buffalo		Sun.	30	NY Rangers*
Jan.	Tue.	1	at Buffalo*		Mon.	31	at NY Rangers
	Thu.	3	Toronto	**Apr.**	Wed.	2	Philadelphia
	Sat.	5	Florida		Sun.	6	at Philadelphia*

* Denotes afternoon game.

Year-by-Year Record

		Home				Road				Overall								
Season	**GP**	**W**	**L**	**T**	**OL**	**W**	**L**	**T**	**OL**	**W**	**L**	**T**	**OL**	**GF**	**GA**	**Pts.**	**Finished**	**Playoff Result**
2006-07	82	26	10	....	5	21	14	....	6	47	24	....	11	277	246	105	2nd, Atlantic Div.	Lost Conf. Quarter-Final
2005-06	82	12	21	....	8	10	25	....	6	22	46	....	14	244	316	58	5th, Atlantic Div.	Out of Playoffs
2004-05	....	....	....	....	....	....	....	....	....	....	....	....	....	....	....	....		
2003-04	82	13	22	6	0	10	25	2	4	23	47	8	4	190	303	58	5th, Atlantic Div.	Out of Playoffs
2002-03	82	15	22	2	2	12	22	4	3	27	44	6	5	189	255	65	5th, Atlantic Div.	Out of Playoffs
2001-02	82	16	20	4	1	12	21	4	4	28	41	8	5	198	249	69	5th, Atlantic Div.	Out of Playoffs
2000-01	82	24	15	2	0	18	13	7	3	42	28	9	3	281	256	96	3rd, Atlantic Div.	Lost Conf. Championship
1999-2000	82	23	11	7	0	14	20	1	6	37	31	8	6	241	236	88	3rd, Atlantic Div.	Lost Conf. Semi-Final
1998-99	82	21	10	10	....	17	20	4	....	38	30	14	....	242	225	90	3rd, Atlantic Div.	Lost Conf. Semi-Final
1997-98	82	21	10	10	....	19	14	8	....	40	24	18	....	228	188	98	1st, Northeast Div.	Lost Conf. Quarter-Final
1996-97	82	25	11	5	....	13	25	3	....	38	36	8	....	285	280	84	2nd, Northeast Div.	Lost Conf. Quarter-Final
1995-96	82	32	9	0	....	17	20	4	....	49	29	4	....	362	284	102	1st, Northeast Div.	Lost Conf. Championship
1994-95	48	18	5	1	....	11	11	2	....	29	16	3	....	181	158	61	2nd, Northeast Div.	Lost Conf. Semi-Final
1993-94	84	25	9	8	....	19	18	5	....	44	27	13	....	299	285	101	1st, Northeast Div.	Lost Conf. Quarter-Final
1992-93	84	32	6	4	....	24	15	3	....	56	21	7	....	367	268	119	1st, Patrick Div.	Lost Div. Final
1991-92	**80**	**21**	**13**	**6**	....	**18**	**19**	**3**	....	**39**	**32**	**9**	....	**343**	**308**	**87**	**3rd, Patrick Div.**	**Won Stanley Cup**
1990-91	**80**	**25**	**12**	**3**	....	**16**	**21**	**3**	....	**41**	**33**	**6**	....	**342**	**305**	**88**	**1st, Patrick Div.**	**Won Stanley Cup**
1989-90	80	22	15	3	....	10	25	5	....	32	40	8	....	318	359	72	5th, Patrick Div.	Out of Playoffs
1988-89	80	24	13	3	....	16	20	4	....	40	33	7	....	347	349	87	2nd, Patrick Div.	Lost Div. Final
1987-88	80	22	12	6	....	14	23	3	....	36	35	9	....	319	316	81	6th, Patrick Div.	Out of Playoffs
1986-87	80	19	15	6	....	11	23	6	....	30	38	12	....	297	290	72	5th, Patrick Div.	Out of Playoffs
1985-86	80	20	15	5	....	14	23	3	....	34	38	8	....	313	305	76	5th, Patrick Div.	Out of Playoffs
1984-85	80	17	20	3	....	7	31	2	....	24	51	5	....	276	385	53	6th, Patrick Div.	Out of Playoffs
1983-84	80	7	29	4	....	9	29	2	....	16	58	6	....	254	390	38	6th, Patrick Div.	Out of Playoffs
1982-83	80	14	22	4	....	4	31	5	....	18	53	9	....	257	394	45	6th, Patrick Div.	Out of Playoffs
1981-82	80	21	11	8	....	10	25	5	....	31	36	13	....	310	337	75	4th, Patrick Div.	Lost Div. Semi-Final
1980-81	80	21	16	3	....	9	21	10	....	30	37	13	....	302	345	73	3rd, Norris Div.	Lost Prelim. Round
1979-80	80	20	13	7	....	10	24	6	....	30	37	13	....	251	303	73	3rd, Norris Div.	Lost Prelim. Round
1978-79	80	23	12	5	....	13	19	8	....	36	31	13	....	281	279	85	2nd, Norris Div.	Lost Quarter-Final
1977-78	80	16	15	9	....	9	22	9	....	25	37	18	....	254	321	68	4th, Norris Div.	Out of Playoffs
1976-77	80	22	12	6	....	12	21	7	....	34	33	13	....	240	252	81	3rd, Norris Div.	Lost Prelim. Round
1975-76	80	23	11	6	....	12	22	6	....	35	33	12	....	339	303	82	3rd, Norris Div.	Lost Prelim. Round
1974-75	80	25	5	10	....	12	23	5	....	37	28	15	....	326	289	89	3rd, Norris Div.	Lost Quarter-Final
1973-74	78	15	18	6	....	13	23	3	....	28	41	9	....	242	273	65	5th, West Div.	Out of Playoffs
1972-73	78	24	11	4	....	8	26	5	....	32	37	9	....	257	265	73	5th, West Div.	Out of Playoffs
1971-72	78	18	15	6	....	8	23	8	....	26	38	14	....	220	258	66	4th, West Div.	Lost Quarter-Final
1970-71	78	18	12	9	....	3	25	11	....	21	37	20	....	221	240	62	6th, West Div.	Out of Playoffs
1969-70	76	17	13	8	....	9	25	4	....	26	38	12	....	182	238	64	2nd, West Div.	Lost Semi-Final
1968-69	76	12	20	6	....	8	25	5	....	20	45	11	....	189	252	51	5th, West Div.	Out of Playoffs
1967-68	74	15	12	10	....	12	22	3	....	27	34	13	....	195	216	67	5th, West Div.	Out of Playoffs

NHL EASTERN CONFERENCE

ATLANTIC DIVISION
41st NHL Season

Franchise date: June 5, 1967

2007-08 Player Personnel

FORWARDS	HT	WT	S	Place of Birth	*Age	2006-07 Club
ARMSTRONG, Colby	6-2	188	R	Lloydminster, Sask.	24	Pittsburgh
BOOGAARD, Aaron	6-3	220	R	Newmarket, Ont.	21	Tri-City
BRENT, Tim	6-0	188	R	Cambridge, Ont.	23	Anaheim-Portland (AHL)
CHRISTENSEN, Erik	6-1	208	L	Edmonton, Alta.	23	Pittsburgh-Wilkes-Barre
CROSBY, Sidney	5-11	200	L	Cole Harbour, N.S.	20	Pittsburgh
ESPOSITO, Angelo	6-1	180	L	Montreal, Que.	18	Quebec (QMJHL)
FILEWICH, Jonathan	6-2	208	R	Kelowna, B.C.	22	Wilkes-Barre
JAMES, Connor	5-10	180	R	Calgary, Alta.	25	Wilkes-Barre
JENSEN, Joe	5-11	180	L	Maple Grove, MN	24	Wilkes-Barre-Wheeling
KENNEDY, Tyler	5-11	183	R	Sault Ste. Marie, Ont.	21	Wilkes-Barre
LARAQUE, Georges	6-3	243	R	Montreal, Que.	30	Phoenix-Pittsburgh
MALKIN, Evgeni	6-3	195	L	Magnitogorsk, USSR	21	Pittsburgh
MALONE, Ryan	6-4	224	L	Pittsburgh, PA	27	Pittsburgh
MINARD, Chris	6-1	190	L	Thompson, Man.	25	Lowell
RECCHI, Mark	5-10	195	L	Kamloops, B.C.	39	Pittsburgh
ROBERTS, Gary	6-2	209	L	North York, Ont.	41	Florida-Pittsburgh
RUUTU, Jarkko	6-0	200	L	Vantaa, Finland	32	Pittsburgh
SMITH, Nathan	6-2	206	L	Edmonton, Alta.	25	Vancouver-Manitoba
STAAL, Jordan	6-4	220	L	Thunder Bay, Ont.	19	Pittsburgh
STONE, Ryan	6-2	207	L	Calgary, Alta.	22	Wilkes-Barre
SYKORA, Petr	6-0	190	L	Plzen, Czech.	30	Edmonton
TAFFE, Jeff	6-3	207	L	Hastings, MN	26	Phoenix-San Antonio
TALBOT, Maxime	5-11	190	L	Lemoyne, Que.	23	Pittsburgh-Wilkes-Barre
DEFENSEMEN						
ARDELAN, Mark	5-11	202	L	Regina, Sask.	24	Iowa
BISSONNETTE, Paul	6-2	211	L	Welland, Ont.	22	Wilkes-Barre-Wheeling
EATON, Mark	6-2	204	L	Wilmington, DE	30	Pittsburgh
ENGELLAND, Deryk	6-2	202	R	Edmonton, Alta.	25	Hershey-Reading
FERNHOLM, Daniel	6-4	218	L	Stockholm, Sweden	23	Wheeling-Djurgarden
GOLIGOSKI, Alex	5-11	180	R	Grand Rapids, MN	22	U. of Minnesota
GONCHAR, Sergei	6-2	211	L	Chelyabinsk, USSR	33	Pittsburgh
LANNON, Ryan	6-1	198	L	Worcester, MA	24	Wilkes-Barre
LETANG, Kris	6-0	201	R	Montreal, Que.	20	Val-d'Or-Pit-Wilkes-Barre
NASREDDINE, Alain	6-1	204	L	Montreal, Que.	32	Pittsburgh-Wilkes-Barre
ORPIK, Brooks	6-2	219	L	San Francisco, CA	27	Pittsburgh
SCUDERI, Rob	6-0	213	L	Syosset, NY	28	Pittsburgh
SYDOR, Darryl	6-1	211	L	Edmonton, Alta.	35	Dallas
WEAVER, Mike	5-9	182	R	Bramalea, Ont.	29	Los Angeles-Manchester
WHITNEY, Ryan	6-4	219	L	Boston, MA	24	Pittsburgh
GOALTENDERS	**HT**	**WT**	**C**	**Place of Birth**	***Age**	**2006-07 Club**
BROWN, David	6-0	185	L	Stoney Creek, Ont.	22	U. of Notre Dame
CONKLIN, Ty	6-0	184	L	Anchorage, AK	31	Columbus-Syracuse-Buffalo
CURRY, John	5-11	185	L	Shorewood, MN	23	Boston University
FLEURY, Marc-Andre	6-2	180	L	Sorel, Que.	22	Pittsburgh
SABOURIN, Dany	6-4	200	L	Val-d'Or, Que.	27	Vancouver-Manitoba

* – Age at start of 2007-08 season

Coach

MICHEL THERRIEN

Coach, Pittsburgh Penguins. Born in Montreal, Que., November 4, 1963.

Michel Therrien took over as head coach of the Pittsburgh Penguins from Ed Olczyk on December 15, 2005. Therrien was promoted from Pittsburgh's top minor-league affiliate in Wilkes-Barre/Scranton, where he guided the Baby Penguins for two and a half seasons after he became the team's second head coach on July 15, 2003. In 2006-07, he guided Pittsburgh back into the playoffs for the first time since 2000-01.

Therrien was in the midst of the Baby Penguins' most successful season when he was promoted to Pittsburgh. He guided the team to a 21-1-2-1 start and 45 points in the team's first 25 games in the American Hockey League. Wilkes-Barre/Scranton won its first nine games of the season and did not lose a game in regulation time until its 24th game. The Baby Penguins also established an AHL road winning streak of 15 games, dating back to April 10 of last season. In his first season behind the bench, Therrien led the Penguins to the Calder Cup Finals. He followed the 2003-04 season by setting a new team mark for points in a season (88) in 2004-05.

Prior to joining the Penguins, Therrien spent six seasons in the Montreal Canadiens organization, including a stint as the team's head coach over parts of three seasons. In 2001-02, Therrien led the Canadiens to their first postseason appearance in four seasons. He spent four seasons as a head coach in the American Hockey League with the Canadiens' AHL affiliates, the Fredericton Canadiens and Quebec Citadelles, winning a division championship with the Citadelles in 1999-00.

Prior to joining the Canadiens, Therrien coached Laval and Granby in the Quebec Major Junior Hockey League. He posted a .720 winning percentage in four seasons as a head coach in the QMJHL, reaching the finals three times and was the head coach of the Memorial Cup winning team in Granby in 1995-96. Beginning in 1993-94, Therrien's teams led the QMJHL in points for three straight seasons. Therrien also played three seasons in the AHL (1983 to 1985 and 1986-87) for Nova Scotia, Sherbrooke and Baltimore, recording 89 points (16 goals, 73 assists).

Coaching Record

		Regular Season				Playoffs		
Season	Team	Games	W	L	O/T	Games	W	L
1993-94	Laval (QMJHL)	72	49	22	1	21	14	7
1994-95	Laval (QMJHL)	72	48	22	2	20	14	6
1995-96	Granby (QMJHL)	70	56	12	2	21	17	4
1996-97	Granby (QMJHL)	70	44	20	6	5	1	4
1997-98	Fredericton (AHL)	80	33	32	15	4	1	3
1998-99	Fredericton (AHL)	80	33	36	11	15	9	6
1999-2000	Quebec (AHL)	80	37	34	9	3	0	3
2000-01	Quebec (AHL)	19	12	6	1	....	....	....
	Montreal (NHL)	**62**	**23**	**33**	**6**	....	....	....
2001-02	**Montreal (NHL)**	**82**	**36**	**34**	**12**	**12**	**6**	**6**
2002-03	**Montreal (NHL)**	**46**	**18**	**23**	**5**	....	....	....
2003-04	Wilkes-Barre (AHL)	80	34	36	10	24	12	12
2004-05	Wilkes-Barre (AHL)	80	39	34	7	11	5	6
2005-06	Wilkes-Barre (AHL)	25	21	1	3	....	....	....
2005-06	**Pittsburgh (NHL)**	**51**	**14**	**29**	**8**	....	....	....
2006-07	**Pittsburgh (NHL)**	**82**	**47**	**24**	**8**	**5**	**1**	**4**
	NHL Totals	**323**	**138**	**143**	**42**	**17**	**7**	**10**

2006-07 Scoring

* – rookie

Regular Season

Pos	#	Player	Team	GP	G	A	Pts	+/–	PIM	PP	SH	GW	S	%
C	87	Sidney Crosby	PIT	79	36	84	120	10	60	13	0	4	250	14.4
C	71 *	Evgeni Malkin	PIT	78	33	52	85	2	80	16	0	6	242	13.6
R	8	Mark Recchi	PIT	82	24	44	68	1	62	14	0	3	190	12.6
D	55	Sergei Gonchar	PIT	82	13	54	67	–5	72	10	1	3	191	6.8
D	19	Ryan Whitney	PIT	81	14	45	59	9	77	9	0	2	129	10.9
R	7	Michel Ouellet	PIT	73	19	29	48	–3	30	11	0	2	148	12.8
C	11 *	Jordan Staal	PIT	81	29	13	42	16	24	4	7	4	131	22.1
L	10	Gary Roberts	FLA	50	13	16	29	5	71	2	0	3	94	13.8
			PIT	19	7	6	13	–5	26	4	0	1	31	22.6
			TOTAL	69	20	22	42	0	97	6	0	4	125	16.0
R	20	Colby Armstrong	PIT	80	12	22	34	2	67	1	1	3	145	8.3
C	16	Erik Christensen	PIT	61	18	15	33	–3	26	6	0	1	133	13.5
L	12	Ryan Malone	PIT	64	16	15	31	4	71	1	1	0	125	12.8
C	25	Maxime Talbot	PIT	75	13	11	24	–2	53	0	4	4	88	14.8
R	27	Georges Laraque	PHX	56	5	17	22	7	52	1	0	0	34	14.7
			PIT	17	0	2	2	–3	18	0	0	0	10	0.0
			TOTAL	73	5	19	24	4	70	1	0	0	44	11.4
L	37	Jarkko Ruutu	PIT	81	7	9	16	0	125	0	0	2	63	11.1
R	28	Nils Ekman	PIT	34	6	9	15	–14	24	2	0	0	69	8.7
D	2	Josef Melichar	PIT	70	1	11	12	1	44	0	0	0	57	1.8
D	5	Robert Scuderi	PIT	78	1	10	11	3	28	0	0	0	31	3.2
D	6	Joel Kwiatkowski	FLA	41	5	5	10	–5	20	1	0	2	46	10.9
			PIT	1	0	0	0	–1	0	0	0	0	0	0.0
			TOTAL	42	5	5	10	–6	20	1	0	2	46	10.9
L	10	John LeClair	PIT	21	2	5	7	–2	12	1	0	0	27	7.4
R	26	Ronald Petrovicky	PIT	31	3	3	6	4	28	0	0	1	27	11.1
D	44	Brooks Orpik	PIT	70	0	6	6	4	82	0	0	0	59	0.0
C	22 *	Chris Thorburn	PIT	39	3	2	5	1	69	0	0	1	40	7.5
D	32	Alain Nasreddine	PIT	44	1	4	5	12	18	0	0	0	29	3.4
D	3	Mark Eaton	PIT	35	0	3	3	–6	16	0	0	0	22	0.0
D	58 *	Kristopher Letang	PIT	7	2	0	2	–3	4	2	0	0	8	25.0
D	47	Micki Dupont	PIT	3	0	1	1	–3	4	0	0	0	6	0.0
D	33	Eric Cairns	PIT	1	0	0	0	0	5	0	0	0	0	0.0

Goaltending

No.	Goaltender	GPI	Mins	Avg	W	L	OT	EN	SO	GA	SA	S%	G	A	PIM
41	Jocelyn Thibault	22	1101	2.83	7	8	2	2	1	52	572	.909	0	0	0
29	Marc-Andre Fleury	67	3905	2.83	40	16	9	2	5	184	1954	.906	0	3	4
	Totals	**82**	**5032**	**2.86**	**47**	**24**	**11**	**4**	**6**	**240**	**2530**	**.905**			

Playoffs

Pos	#	Player	Team	GP	G	A	Pts	+/–	PIM	PP	SH	GW	OT	S	%
C	87	Sidney Crosby	PIT	5	3	2	5	0	4	1	0	1	0	20	15.0
L	10	Gary Roberts	PIT	5	2	2	4	0	2	1	0	0	0	4	50.0
D	55	Sergei Gonchar	PIT	5	1	3	4	–3	2	1	0	0	0	14	7.1
R	8	Mark Recchi	PIT	5	0	4	4	–3	0	0	0	0	0	11	0.0
C	71 *	Evgeni Malkin	PIT	5	0	4	4	–1	8	0	0	0	0	10	0.0
C	11 *	Jordan Staal	PIT	5	3	0	3	–1	2	0	0	0	0	8	37.5
D	19	Ryan Whitney	PIT	5	1	1	2	–4	6	1	0	0	0	4	25.0
R	7	Michel Ouellet	PIT	5	0	2	2	–1	6	0	0	0	0	7	0.0
R	20	Colby Armstrong	PIT	5	0	1	1	–2	11	0	0	0	0	6	0.0
C	25	Maxime Talbot	PIT	5	0	1	1	–2	7	0	0	0	0	5	0.0
R	28	Nils Ekman	PIT	1	0	0	0	0	0	0	0	0	0	2	0.0
R	27	Georges Laraque	PIT	2	0	0	0	–1	0	0	0	0	0	0	0.0
R	26	Ronald Petrovicky	PIT	3	0	0	0	0	2	0	0	0	0	1	0.0
C	16	Erik Christensen	PIT	4	0	0	0	–1	6	0	0	0	0	6	0.0
D	2	Josef Melichar	PIT	5	0	0	0	–1	2	0	0	0	0	1	0.0
L	37	Jarkko Ruutu	PIT	5	0	0	0	–1	10	0	0	0	0	1	0.0
D	5	Robert Scuderi	PIT	5	0	0	0	–1	2	0	0	0	0	0	0.0
D	3	Mark Eaton	PIT	5	0	0	0	–1	0	0	0	0	0	3	0.0
L	12	Ryan Malone	PIT	5	0	0	0	–4	0	0	0	0	0	7	0.0
D	44	Brooks Orpik	PIT	5	0	0	0	–2	8	0	0	0	0	0	0.0

Goaltending

No.	Goaltender	GPI	Mins	Avg	W	L	EN	SO	GA	SA	S%	G	A	PIM
41	Jocelyn Thibault	1	8	0.00	0	0	0	0	0	1	1.000	0	0	0
29	Marc-Andre Fleury	5	287	3.76	1	4	0	0	18	150	.880	0	0	0
	Totals	**5**	**300**	**3.60**	**1**	**4**	**0**	**0**	**18**	**151**	**.881**			

General Managers' History

Jack Riley, 1967-68 to 1969-70; Red Kelly, 1970-71; Red Kelly and Jack Riley, 1971-72; Jack Riley, 1972-73; Jack Riley and Jack Button, 1973-74; Jack Button, 1974-75; Wren Blair, 1975-76; Wren Blair and Baz Bastien, 1976-77; Baz Bastien, 1977-78 to 1982-83; Eddie Johnston, 1983-84 to 1987-88; Tony Esposito, 1988-89; Tony Esposito and Craig Patrick, 1989-90; Craig Patrick, 1990-91 to 2005-06; Ray Shero, 2006-07 to date.

Coaching History

Red Sullivan, 1967-68, 1968-69; Red Kelly, 1969-70 to 1971-72; Red Kelly and Ken Schinkel, 1972-73; Ken Schinkel and Marc Boileau, 1973-74; Marc Boileau, 1974-75; Marc Boileau and Ken Schinkel, 1975-76; Ken Schinkel, 1976-77; Johnny Wilson, 1977-78 to 1979-80; Eddie Johnston, 1980-81 to 1982-83; Lou Angotti, 1983-84; Bob Berry, 1984-85 to 1986-87; Pierre Creamer, 1987-88; Gene Ubriaco, 1988-89; Gene Ubriaco and Craig Patrick, 1989-90; Bob Johnson, 1990-91, 1991-92; Scotty Bowman, 1991-92, 1992-93; Eddie Johnston, 1993-94 to 1995-96; Eddie Johnston and Craig Patrick, 1996-97; Kevin Constantine, 1997-98, 1998-99; Kevin Constantine and Herb Brooks, 1999-2000; Ivan Hlinka, 2000-01; Ivan Hlinka and Rick Kehoe, 2001-02; Rick Kehoe, 2002-03; Ed Olczyk, 2003-04; Ed Olczyk and Michel Therrien, 2005-06; Michel Therrien, 2006-07 to date.

Club Records

Team

(Figures in brackets for season records are games played; records for fewest points, wins, ties, losses, goals, goals against are for 70 or more games)

Record		
Most Points	**119**	1992-93 (84)
Most Wins	**56**	1992-93 (84)
Most Ties	**20**	1970-71 (78)
Most Losses	**58**	1983-84 (80)
Most Goals	**367**	1992-93 (84)
Most Goals Against	**394**	1982-83 (80)
Fewest Points	**38**	1983-84 (80)
Fewest Wins	**16**	1983-84 (80)
Fewest Ties	**4**	1995-96 (82)
Fewest Losses	**21**	1992-93 (84)
Fewest Goals	**182**	1969-70 (76)
Fewest Goals Against	**188**	1997-98 (82)
Longest Winning Streak		
Overall	***17**	Mar. 9-Apr. 10/93
Home	**11**	Jan. 5-Mar. 7/91
Away	**7**	Mar. 14-Apr. 9/93
Longest Undefeated Streak		
Overall	**18**	Mar. 9-Apr. 14/93 (17 wins, 1 tie)
Home	**20**	Nov. 30/74-Feb. 22/75 (12 wins, 8 ties)
Away	**8**	Mar. 14-Apr. 14/93 (7 wins, 1 tie)
Longest Losing Streak		
Overall	**18**	Jan. 13-Feb. 22/04
Home	**14**	Dec. 31/03-Feb. 22/04
Away	**18**	Dec. 23/82-Mar. 4/83
Longest Winless Streak		
Overall	**18**	Jan. 2-Feb. 10/83 (17 losses, 1 tie), Jan. 13-Feb. 22/04 (18 losses)
Home	**16**	Dec. 31/03-Mar. 4/04 (15 losses, 1 tie)
Away	**18**	Oct. 25/70-Jan. 14/71 (11 losses, 7 ties), Dec. 23/82-Mar. 4/83 (18 losses)
Most Shutouts, Season	**9**	1998-99 (82)
Most PIM, Season	**2,670**	1988-89 (80)
Most Goals, Game	**12**	Mar. 15/75 (Wsh. 1 at Pit. 12), Dec. 26/91 (Tor. 1 at Pit. 12)

Individual

Record		
Most Seasons	**17**	Mario Lemieux
Most Games	**915**	Mario Lemieux
Most Goals, Career	**690**	Mario Lemieux
Most Assists, Career	**1,033**	Mario Lemieux
Most Points, Career	**1,723**	Mario Lemieux (690G, 1,033A)
Most PIM, Career	**1,048**	Kevin Stevens
Most Shutouts, Career	**22**	Tom Barrasso
Longest Consecutive Games Streak	**320**	Ron Schock (Oct. 24/73-Apr. 3/77)
Most Goals, Season	**85**	Mario Lemieux (1988-89)
Most Assists, Season	**114**	Mario Lemieux (1988-89)
Most Points, Season	**199**	Mario Lemieux (1988-89; 85G, 114A)
Most PIM, Season	**409**	Paul Baxter (1981-82)
Most Points, Defenseman, Season	**113**	Paul Coffey (1988-89; 30G, 83A)
Most Points, Center, Season	**199**	Mario Lemieux (1988-89; 85G, 114A)
Most Points, Right Wing, Season	***149**	Jaromir Jagr (1995-96; 62G, 87A)
Most Points, Left Wing, Season	**123**	Kevin Stevens (1991-92; 54G, 69A)
Most Points, Rookie, Season	**102**	Sidney Crosby (2005-06; 39G, 63A)
Most Shutouts, Season	**7**	Tom Barrasso (1997-98)
Most Goals, Game	**5**	Mario Lemieux (Three times)
Most Assists, Game	**6**	Ron Stackhouse (Mar. 8/75), Greg Malone (Nov. 28/79), Mario Lemieux (Three times)
Most Points, Game	**8**	Mario Lemieux (Oct. 15/88; 2G, 6A, Dec. 31/88; 5G, 3A)

* NHL Record.

Captains' History

Ab McDonald, 1967-68; Earl Ingarfield, 1968-69; no captain, 1968-69 to 1972-73; Ron Schock, 1973-74 to 1976-77; Jean Pronovost, 1977-78; Orest Kindrachuk, 1978-79 to 1980-81; Randy Carlyle, 1981-82 to 1983-84; Mike Bullard, 1984-85, 1985-86; Mike Bullard and Terry Ruskowski, 1986-87; Dan Frawley and Mario Lemieux, 1987-88; Mario Lemieux, 1988-89 to 1993-94; Ron Francis, 1994-95; Mario Lemieux, 1995-96, 1996-97; Ron Francis, 1997-98; Jaromir Jagr, 1998-99 to 2000-01; Mario Lemieux, 2001-02 to 2003-04; Mario Lemieux and no captain, 2005-06; no captain, 2006-07; Sidney Crosby, 2007-08.

Retired Numbers

21	Michel Brière	1969-1970
66	Mario Lemieux	1984-2006

All-time Record vs. Other Clubs

Regular Season

	At Home								On Road								Total							
	GP	W	L	T	OL	GF	GA	PTS	GP	W	L	T	OL	GF	GA	PTS	GP	W	L	T	OL	GF	GA	PTS
Anaheim	9	5	2	2	0	29	27	12	9	3	4	0	2	26	32	8	18	8	6	2	2	55	59	20
Atlanta	14	10	3	0	1	53	39	21	14	10	3	0	1	50	42	21	28	20	6	0	2	103	81	42
Boston	84	33	34	15	2	288	300	83	82	17	58	6	1	232	362	41	166	50	92	21	3	520	662	124
Buffalo	75	37	19	18	1	277	232	93	75	21	36	17	1	201	287	60	150	58	55	35	2	478	519	153
Calgary	45	24	11	10	0	169	136	58	46	11	27	8	0	140	204	30	91	35	38	18	0	309	340	88
Carolina	50	24	20	6	0	197	187	54	52	22	23	5	2	187	193	51	102	46	43	11	2	384	380	105
Chicago	60	30	23	7	0	215	194	67	61	11	40	10	0	158	240	32	121	41	63	17	0	373	434	99
Colorado	38	16	17	5	0	149	155	37	32	13	16	2	1	122	142	29	70	29	33	7	1	271	297	66
Columbus	4	3	1	0	0	17	12	6	4	2	2	0	0	10	16	4	8	5	3	0	0	27	28	10
Dallas	63	38	19	6	0	236	178	82	65	22	36	6	1	217	249	51	128	60	55	12	1	453	427	133
Detroit	66	44	18	4	0	281	197	92	66	13	40	12	1	179	256	39	132	57	58	16	1	460	453	131
Edmonton	31	15	13	3	0	118	130	33	30	7	22	1	0	98	148	15	61	22	35	4	0	216	278	48
Florida	27	13	10	3	1	83	80	30	26	10	13	1	2	62	77	23	53	23	23	4	3	145	157	53
Los Angeles	73	38	25	10	0	265	233	86	70	18	43	8	1	187	268	45	143	56	68	18	1	452	501	131
Minnesota	4	1	3	0	0	6	17	2	3	0	2	1	0	5	9	1	7	1	5	1	0	11	26	3
Montreal	86	31	41	13	1	257	305	76	86	12	61	10	3	220	401	37	172	43	102	23	4	477	706	113
Nashville	6	2	2	2	0	18	18	6	7	2	5	0	0	14	26	4	13	4	7	2	0	32	44	10
New Jersey	87	43	37	4	3	314	292	93	89	32	43	13	1	289	323	78	176	75	80	17	4	603	615	171
NY Islanders	96	45	35	14	2	363	335	106	94	35	49	8	2	312	373	80	190	80	84	22	4	675	708	186
NY Rangers	108	48	45	14	1	380	387	111	109	44	55	9	1	365	420	98	217	92	100	23	2	745	807	209
Ottawa	31	18	9	4	0	109	84	40	31	16	10	5	0	99	86	37	62	34	19	9	0	208	170	77
Philadelphia	114	51	41	22	0	402	368	124	114	22	80	8	4	293	474	56	228	73	121	30	4	695	842	180
Phoenix	30	20	10	0	0	120	86	40	32	15	14	3	0	114	118	33	62	35	24	3	0	234	204	73
St. Louis	65	32	21	12	0	239	194	76	65	15	42	6	2	171	250	38	130	47	63	18	2	410	444	114
San Jose	9	4	4	1	0	41	32	9	14	6	6	2	0	56	37	14	23	10	10	3	0	97	69	23
Tampa Bay	27	15	6	3	3	100	74	36	27	9	15	2	1	64	88	21	54	24	21	5	4	164	162	57
Toronto	73	38	28	6	1	292	235	83	71	25	32	11	3	228	282	64	144	63	60	17	4	520	517	147
Vancouver	51	33	11	7	0	229	175	73	50	23	22	4	1	187	180	51	101	56	33	11	1	416	355	124
Washington	87	51	29	7	0	340	268	109	90	35	45	9	1	330	374	80	177	86	74	16	1	670	642	189
Defunct Clubs	35	22	6	7	0	148	93	51	34	13	10	11	0	108	101	37	69	35	16	18	0	256	194	88
Totals	**1548**	**784**	**543**	**205**	**16**	**5735**	**5063**	**1789**	**1548**	**484**	**854**	**178**	**32**	**4724**	**6058**	**1178**	**3096**	**1268**	**1397**	**383**	**48**	**10459**	**11121**	**2967**

Playoffs

	Series	W	L	GP	W	L	T	GF	GA	Last Mtg.	Rnd.	Result
Boston	4	2	2	19	10	9	0	67	62	1992	CF	W 4-0
Buffalo	2	2	0	10	6	4	0	26	26	2001	CSF	W 4-3
Chicago	2	1	1	8	4	4	0	23	24	1992	F	W 4-0
Dallas	1	1	0	6	4	2	0	28	16	1991	F	W 4-2
Florida	1	0	1	7	3	4	0	15	20	1996	CF	L 3-4
Montreal	1	0	1	6	2	4	0	15	18	1998	CQF	L 2-4
New Jersey	5	3	2	29	14	15	0	80	86	2001	CF	L 1-4
NY Islanders	3	0	3	19	8	11	0	58	67	1993	DF	L 3-4
NY Rangers	3	3	0	15	12	3	0	64	45	1996	CSF	W 4-1
Ottawa	1	0	1	5	1	4	0	10	18	2007	CQF	L 1-4
Philadelphia	3	0	3	18	6	12	0	51	66	2000	CSF	L 2-4
St. Louis	3	1	2	13	6	7	0	40	45	1981	PRE	L 2-3
Toronto	3	0	3	12	4	8	0	27	39	1999	CSF	L 2-4
Washington	7	6	1	42	26	16	0	137	121	2001	CQF	W 4-2
Defunct Clubs	1	1	0	4	4	0	0	13	6			
Totals	**40**	**20**	**20**	**213**	**110**	**103**	**0**	**654**	**659**			

Calgary totals include Atlanta Flames, 1972-73 to 1979-80.
Colorado totals include Quebec, 1979-80 to 1994-95.
New Jersey totals include Kansas City, 1974-75, 1975-76, and Colorado Rockies, 1976-77 to 1981-82.
Phoenix totals include Winnipeg, 1979-80 to 1995-96.
Carolina totals include Hartford, 1979-80 to 1996-97.
Dallas totals include Minnesota North Stars, 1967-68 to 1992-93.

Playoff Results 2007-2002

Year	Round	Opponent	Result	GF	GA
2007	CQF	Ottawa	L 1-4	10	18

Abbreviations: Round: F – Final; **CF** – conference final; **CSF** – conference semi-final; **CQF** – conference quarter-final; **DF** – division final; **PRE** – preliminary round.

2006-07 Results

Month	Day	Opponent	Score
Oct.	5	Philadelphia	4-0
	7	Detroit	0-2
	12	at NY Rangers	6-5
	14	Carolina	1-5
	18	New Jersey	1-2
	19	at NY Islanders	4-3*
	21	Columbus	5-3
	24	New Jersey	4-2
	28	at Philadelphia	8-2
Nov.	1	at Los Angeles	4-3*
	4	at San Jose	2-3
	6	at Anaheim	2-3*
	8	Tampa Bay	3-4*
	10	Ottawa	3-6
	11	at Carolina	2-6
	13	Philadelphia	3-2
	17	at Buffalo	2-4
	18	NY Rangers	3-1
	20	at Philadelphia	5-3
	22	Boston	3-4†
	24	at NY Islanders	1-3
	25	NY Rangers	1-2*
	28	NY Islanders	3-2
Dec.	1	at New Jersey	2-5
	2	NY Islanders	3-5
	5	Florida	2-3
	7	at NY Rangers	2-3†
	9	at Atlanta	4-3*
	11	at Washington	5-4†
	13	Philadelphia	8-4
	15	NY Islanders	7-4
	16	at Montreal	3-6
	19	St. Louis	1-4
	21	at Atlanta	3-4†
	26	at New Jersey	0-3
	27	Atlanta	2-4
	29	Toronto	4-1
Jan.	2	Carolina	3-0
	5	at Buffalo	4-2
	7	Tampa Bay	2-3†
	9	at Tampa Bay	2-3
	10	at Florida	2-5
	13	at Philadelphia	5-3
	16	NY Islanders	5-2
	18	at Boston	4-5†
	20	Toronto	8-2
	26	at Dallas	4-3†
	27	at Phoenix	7-2
	30	Florida	3-0
Feb.	1	Montreal	5-4†
	3	Washington	2-0
	4	at Montreal	3-4*
	6	Nashville	4-1
	8	at Philadelphia	5-4†
	10	at Toronto	6-5*
	14	Chicago	5-4†
	16	at New Jersey	5-4
	18	Washington	3-2
	19	at NY Islanders	5-6
	22	at Florida	2-1*
	25	at Tampa Bay	1-5
	27	New Jersey	0-1
Mar.	1	at NY Rangers	4-3†
	2	at Carolina	2-3
	4	Philadelphia	4-3†
	6	at Ottawa	5-4†
	8	New Jersey	3-4†
	10	NY Rangers	3-2*
	13	Buffalo	5-4†
	14	at New Jersey	3-0
	16	Montreal	6-3
	18	Ottawa	4-3†
	19	at NY Rangers	1-2
	22	at NY Islanders	1-3
	24	Atlanta	2-1
	25	Boston	5-0
	27	at Washington	4-3
	29	at Boston	4-2
	31	at Toronto	4-5*
Apr.	3	Buffalo	1-4
	5	at Ottawa	3-2
	7	NY Rangers	2-1

* – Overtime † – Shootout

Entry Draft Selections 2007-1993

2007
Pick
20 Angelo Esposito
51 Keven Veilleux
78 Robert Bortuzzo
80 Casey Pierro-Zabotel
111 Luca Caputi
118 Alex Grant
141 Jake Muzzin
171 Dustin Jeffrey

2006
Pick
2 Jordan Staal
32 Carl Sneep
65 Brian Strait
125 Chad Johnson
185 Timo Seppanen

2005
Pick
1 Sidney Crosby
61 Michael Gergen
62 Kristopher Letang
125 Tommi Leinonen
126 Tim Crowder
194 Jean-Philippe Paquet
195 Joe Vitale

2004
Pick
2 Evgeni Malkin
31 Johannes Salmonsson
61 Alex Goligoski
67 Nick Johnson
85 Brian Gifford
99 Tyler Kennedy
130 Michal Sersen
164 Moises Gutierrez
194 Chris Peluso
222 Jordan Morrison
228 David Brown
259 Brian Ihnacak

2003
Pick
1 Marc-Andre Fleury
32 Ryan Stone
70 Jonathan Filewich
73 Daniel Carcillo
121 Paul Bissonnette
161 Evgeni Isakov
169 Lukas Bolf
199 Andy Chiodo
229 Stephen Dixon
232 Joe Jensen
263 Matt Moulson

2002
Pick
5 Ryan Whitney
35 Ondrej Nemec
69 Erik Christensen
101 Daniel Fernholm
136 Andrew Sertich
137 Cam Paddock
171 Robert Goepfert
202 Patrik Bartschi
234 Maxime Talbot
239 Ryan Lannon
265 Dwight Labrosse

2001
Pick
21 Colby Armstrong
54 Noah Welch
86 Drew Fata
96 Alexandre Rouleau
120 Tomas Surovy
131 Ben Eaves
156 Andy Schneider
217 Tomas Duba
250 Brandon Crawford-West

2000
Pick
18 Brooks Orpik
52 Shane Endicott
84 Peter Hamerlik
124 Michel Ouellet
146 David Koci
185 Patrick Foley
216 Jim Abbott
248 Steve Crampton
273 Roman Simicek
280 Nick Boucher

1999
Pick
18 Konstantin Koltsov
51 Matt Murley
57 Jeremy Van Hoof
86 Sebastien Caron
115 Ryan Malone
144 Tomas Skvaridlo
157 Vladimir Malenkykh
176 Doug Meyer
204 Tom Kostopoulos
233 Darcy Robinson
261 Andrew McPherson

1998
Pick
23 Milan Kraft
54 Alexander Zevakhin
80 David Cameron
110 Scott Myers
134 Rob Scuderi
169 Jan Fadrny
196 Joel Scherban
224 Mika Lehto
244 Toby Petersen
254 Matt Hussey

1997
Pick
17 Robert Dome
44 Brian Gaffaney
71 Josef Melichar
97 Alexandre Mathieu
124 Harlan Pratt
152 Petr Havelka
179 Mark Moore
208 Andrew Ference
234 Eric Lind

1996
Pick
23 Craig Hillier
28 Pavel Skrbek
72 Boyd Kane
77 Boris Protsenko
105 Michal Rozsival
150 Peter Bergman
186 Eric Meloche
238 Timo Seikkula

1995
Pick
24 Aleksey Morozov
76 Jean-Sebastien Aubin
102 Oleg Belov
128 Jan Hrdina
154 Alexei Kolkunov
180 Derrick Pyke
206 Sergei Voronov
232 Frank Ivankovic

1994
Pick
24 Chris Wells
50 Richard Park
57 Sven Butenschon
73 Greg Crozier
76 Alexei Krivchenkov
102 Tom O'Connor
128 Clint Johnson
154 Valentin Morozov
161 Serge Aubin
180 Drew Palmer
206 Boris Zelenko
232 Jason Godbout
258 Mikhail Kazakevich
284 Brian Leitza

1993
Pick
26 Stefan Bergkvist
52 Domenic Pittis
62 Dave Roche
104 Jonas Andersson-Junkka
130 Chris Kelleher
156 Patrick Lalime
182 Sean Selmser
208 Larry McMorran
234 Timothy Harberts
260 Leonid Toropchenko
286 Hans Jonsson

General Manager

RAY SHERO

General Manager, Pittsburgh Penguins. Born in Hartsdale, NY, July 28, 1962.

The Pittsburgh Penguins signed Ray Shero to a five-year contract as their new general manager on May 25, 2006. He is the son of the late Fred Shero, who coached the Philadelphia Flyers for seven years and led them to back-to-back Stanley Cup championships in 1973-74 and 1974-75. Fred Shero also was g.m. and coach of the New York Rangers from 1978 to 1980. Ray Shero played college hockey at St. Lawrence University, serving twice as team captain, and was drafted by the Los Angeles Kings in 1982. He worked as a player agent for seven years before entering NHL management.

Before joining the Penguins, Shero had been assistant general manager of the Nashville Predators for eight seasons, working closely with Predators g.m. David Poile on all aspects of the club's hockey operations. His specific responsibilities included scouting at the amateur and professional levels, contract negotiations, and personnel matters such as arbitration, in addition to overseeing operations of the Predators top minor-league affiliate, the Milwaukee Admirals of the American Hockey League. Before joining the Predators organization, Shero spent six seasons as assistant general manager of the Ottawa Senators – joining the club in its second year of existence as an expansion team.

Both Ottawa and Nashville made significant improvement during Shero's tenure as assistant g.m., building with youth while adhering to a budget and business plan. The Predators went 49-25-8 and established a club record with 106 points in 2005-06, qualifying for the Stanley Cup playoffs for the second straight season. They had the third-best record in the Western Conference and fifth-best in the NHL.

Shero also played an important role in the success of the Milwaukee Admirals, Nashville's top affiliate in the American Hockey League. In 2003-04, the Admirals led the AHL in wins (43) and points (102) and won the Calder Cup by defeating the Wilkes-Barre/Scranton Penguins in the league final. Milwaukee reached the Calder Cup Final again in 2005-06.

Club Directory

Mellon Arena

Pittsburgh Penguins
Mellon Arena
66 Mario Lemieux Place
Pittsburgh, PA 15219
Phone **412/642-1300**
FAX 412/642-1859
Media Relations FAX 412/642-1322
www.pittsburghpenguins.com
Capacity: 16,940

Ownership . . . . . Lemieux Group LP

Executive Operations
Chairman . . . . . Mario Lemieux
CEO . . . . . Ken Sawyer
President . . . . . David Morehouse
Executive VP/General Manager . . . . . Ray Shero
Vice President, Business & Legal Affairs . . . . . Ted Black
Vice President & Controller . . . . . Kevin Hart
Vice President, Sales & Marketing . . . . . David Soltesz
Vice President, Communications . . . . . Tom McMillan
Senior Consultant . . . . . Ron Porter
Executive Assistants . . . . . Fay McNamara, Kim Wood
Receptionist . . . . . Kelly Hart
Mailroom Supervisor . . . . . Brett Hart

Hockey Operations
Assistant General Manager . . . . . Chuck Fletcher
Senior Advisor/Hockey Operations . . . . . Ed Johnston
Director of Player Development . . . . . Tom Fitzgerald
Director of Hockey Administration . . . . . Jason Botterill
Head Coach . . . . . Michel Therrien
Assistant Coaches . . . . . Andre Savard, Mike Yeo
Goaltending Coach . . . . . Gilles Meloche
Strength & Conditioning Coach . . . . . TBA
Director of Amateur Scouting . . . . . Jay Heinbuck
Director of Pro Scouting . . . . . Dan MacKinnon
Pro Scouts . . . . . Derek Clancey, Kevin Stevens
Amateur Scouts . . . . . Brian Fitzgerald, Chuck Grillo, Jim Madigan, David McNamara, Wayne Meier, Darryl Plandowski, Matt Recchi
European Scouts . . . . . Patrik Allvin, Robert Neuhauser
Head Coach, Wilkes-Barre/Scranton (AHL) . . . . . Todd Richards
Assistant Coach, Wilkes-Barre/Scranton (AHL) . . . . . Dan Bylsma
Equipment Manager . . . . . Dana Heinze
Assistant Equipment Managers . . . . . Paul DeFazio, Danny Kroll
Team Physician . . . . . Dr. Charles Burke
Head Athletic Trainer . . . . . Chris Stewart
Assistant Athletic Trainer . . . . . Scott Adams
Physical Therapist . . . . . Mark Mortland
Snr. Dir. of Team Services and Media Relations . . . . . Frank Buonomo
Executive Assistant . . . . . Kristen Yunn
Video Coordinator . . . . . Travis Ramsay

Communications/Marketing
Assistant Director of Media Relations . . . . . Brian Werger
Manager of Media Relations . . . . . Jennifer Bullano
Director of Content/Publications . . . . . Joe Sager
Director of Marketing . . . . . Ross Miller
Director of Game Operations/Video Production . . . . . Chris DeVivo
Creative Director . . . . . Barb Pilarski
Director of Amateur Hockey . . . . . Mark Shuttleworth
Director of Community/Alumni Relations . . . . . Cindy Himes
Exec. Producer, Penguins Radio Network . . . . . Ray Walker
Radio Broadcasters . . . . . Mike Lange, Phil Bourque
Director of New Media . . . . . Jeremy Zimmer
Game Night Producer . . . . . TBA
Game Night Manager . . . . . James Archer
Manager of Arts & Graphics . . . . . Dori Minnis
Editors . . . . . Steve Finerty, Billy Wareham

Corporate Sales
Senior Director of Corporate Sales . . . . . Kimberly Bogesdorfer
Director of Corporate Sales . . . . . TBA
Managers of Corporate Sales . . . . . David Schleter, Danny Smith
Senior Account Service Manager . . . . . Lori Wineland
Account Service Manager . . . . . Jamie Greenwald
Account Service Coordinator . . . . . Ronald Hay
Corporate Sales Liason . . . . . Pierre Larouche

Finance
Assistant Controller . . . . . Mark R. Kuczinski
Senior Accountant . . . . . Troy Ussack
Payroll Manager . . . . . Andrea Winschel
Accounts Payable . . . . . Tawni Love

Ticketing
Senior Director of Ticketing . . . . . James Santilli
Director of Premium Seating/Group Sales . . . . . Mike Guiffre
Manager of Premium Sales . . . . . Brian Magness
Coordinator of Premium Services . . . . . Lydia Tobiasz
Group Sales Account Executive . . . . . Mike Zatchey
Director of Ticket Sales and Services . . . . . Chad Slencak
Ticket Sales Account Executives . . . . . George Birman, Bonnie Golinski, George Murphy, Chuck Pukansky
Inside Sales Representatives . . . . . Jeff Blizman, Beth Folcik, Robbie Hofmann, Nicole Kyslinger, Sarah Swartz
Box Office Manager . . . . . Carol Coulson
Manager of Box Office Operations . . . . . Jason Onufer
Box Office Assistant . . . . . Kelly Gabany
Manager of Customer Service . . . . . Kathy Davis
Customer Service Representatives . . . . . Cori Shrader, Amanda Rameas, Kathleen Unger
Director of Database Marketing . . . . . Jill Shipley
Database Manager . . . . . Erin Exley

General Information
TV Station . . . . . Fox Sports Net Pittsburgh
TV Announcers . . . . . Paul Steigerwald, Bob Errey
Radio Announcers . . . . . Mike Lange, Phil Bourque
Flagship Radio Station . . . . . The X (105.9 FM)
Minor League Affiliates . . . . . Wilkes-Barre/Scranton Penguins (AHL), Wheeling Nailers (ECHL)

Key Off-Season Signings/Acquisitions

2007

Apr. 19 • Signed 2006 1st-round pick (1st overall), D **Erik Johnson**.

June 26 • Acquired C **Keith Tkachuk** and a conditional draft pick from Atlanta for a 1st-round draft pick.

July 1 • Re-signed D **Barret Jackman**.

1 • Signed LW **Paul Kariya**.

23 • Acquired G **Hannu Toivonen** from Boston for C **Carl Soderberg**.

25 • Re-signed RW **Lee Stempniak**.

St. Louis Blues

2006-07 Results: 34W-35L-7OTL-6SOL 81PTS.
Third, Central Division

In his first full NHL season, Lee Stempniak led the Blues with 27 goals and was second on the team behind Doug Weight with 52 points.

2007-08 Schedule

Oct.	Thu.	4	at Phoenix
	Sat.	6	at Los Angeles
	Wed.	10	Nashville
	Fri.	12	Colorado
	Wed.	17	at Chicago
	Sat.	20	Minnesota
	Tue.	23	Anaheim
	Thu.	25	at Columbus
	Sat.	27	Washington
	Tue.	30	Phoenix
Nov.	Thu.	1	at Minnesota
	Sat.	3	Chicago
	Sun.	4	at Columbus*
	Fri.	9	at Chicago
	Tue.	13	Detroit
	Fri.	16	Columbus
	Sat.	17	at Nashville
	Mon.	19	Nashville
	Wed.	21	at Detroit
	Fri.	23	Vancouver
	Sun.	25	Calgary*
	Wed.	28	at Buffalo
	Fri.	30	at Minnesota
Dec.	Sat.	1	Chicago
	Tue.	4	at Calgary
	Fri.	7	at Edmonton
	Sun.	9	at Colorado
	Tue.	11	Edmonton
	Thu.	13	Florida
	Sun.	16	Calgary*
	Thu.	20	Detroit
	Sat.	22	at Boston*
	Sun.	23	Atlanta*
	Wed.	26	Detroit
	Fri.	28	San Jose
	Sat.	29	at Dallas
	Mon.	31	at Detroit
Jan.	Wed.	2	Edmonton
	Sat.	5	Carolina
	Tue.	8	Columbus
	Thu.	10	Dallas
	Fri.	11	at Columbus
	Sun.	13	Vancouver*
	Wed.	16	at Chicago
	Sat.	19	Nashville
	Mon.	21	at Nashville*
	Wed.	23	at Vancouver
	Thu.	24	at San Jose
	Tue.	29	at Toronto
Feb.	Fri.	1	Anaheim
	Sat.	2	Colorado
	Tue.	5	Tampa Bay
	Sat.	9	at Dallas
	Sun.	10	Minnesota*
	Tue.	12	Los Angeles
	Thu.	14	at Colorado
	Sat.	16	at Nashville
	Sun.	17	Columbus*
	Tue.	19	Chicago
	Thu.	21	at Los Angeles
	Fri.	22	at Anaheim
	Sun.	24	at Phoenix
	Tue.	26	Dallas
	Thu.	28	Phoenix
Mar.	Sat.	1	San Jose
	Tue.	4	Los Angeles
	Wed.	5	at Detroit
	Sat.	8	at Vancouver
	Mon.	10	at Calgary
	Tue.	11	at Edmonton
	Fri.	14	at San Jose
	Sat.	15	at Anaheim
	Tue.	18	at Montreal
	Thu.	20	at Ottawa
	Sun.	23	at Chicago*
	Tue.	25	Detroit
	Fri.	28	at Detroit
	Sat.	29	Chicago
Apr.	Tue.	1	Nashville
	Thu.	3	at Nashville
	Sat.	5	Columbus*
	Sun.	6	at Columbus*

* Denotes afternoon game.

Year-by-Year Record

		Home				Road				Overall								
Season	GP	W	L	T	OL	W	L	T	OL	W	L	T	OL	GF	GA	Pts.	Finished	Playoff Result
2006-07	82	18	19	....	4	16	16	....	9	34	35	....	13	214	254	81	3rd, Central Div.	Out of Playoffs
2005-06	82	12	23	....	6	9	23	....	9	21	46	....	15	197	292	57	5th, Central Div.	Out of Playoffs
2004-05	....	....	....	....	....	....	....	....	....	....	....	....	....	....	....	....		
2003-04	82	23	11	7	0	16	19	4	2	39	30	11	2	191	198	91	2nd, Central Div.	Lost Conf. Quarter-Final
2002-03	82	23	11	4	3	18	13	7	3	41	24	11	6	253	222	99	2nd, Central Div.	Lost Conf. Quarter-Final
2001-02	82	27	12	1	1	16	15	7	3	43	27	8	4	227	188	98	2nd, Central Div.	Lost Conf. Semi-Final
2000-01	82	28	5	5	3	15	17	7	2	43	22	12	5	249	195	103	2nd, Central Div.	Lost Conf. Championship
1999-2000	82	24	9	7	1	27	10	4	0	51	19	11	1	248	165	114	1st, Central Div.	Lost Conf. Quarter-Final
1998-99	82	18	17	6	....	19	15	7	....	37	32	13	....	237	209	87	2nd, Central Div.	Lost Conf. Semi-Final
1997-98	82	26	10	5	....	19	19	3	....	45	29	8	....	256	204	98	3rd, Central Div.	Lost Conf. Semi-Final
1996-97	82	17	20	4	....	19	15	7	....	36	35	11	....	236	239	83	4th, Central Div.	Lost Conf. Quarter-Final
1995-96	82	15	17	9	....	17	17	7	....	32	34	16	....	219	248	80	4th, Central Div.	Lost Conf. Semi-Final
1994-95	48	16	6	2	....	12	9	3	....	28	15	5	....	178	135	61	2nd, Central Div.	Lost Conf. Quarter-Final
1993-94	84	23	11	8	....	17	22	3	....	40	33	11	....	270	283	91	4th, Central Div.	Lost Conf. Quarter-Final
1992-93	84	22	13	7	....	15	23	4	....	37	36	11	....	282	278	85	4th, Norris Div.	Lost Div. Final
1991-92	80	25	12	3	....	11	21	8	....	36	33	11	....	279	266	83	3rd, Norris Div.	Lost Div. Semi-Final
1990-91	80	24	9	7	....	23	13	4	....	47	22	11	....	310	250	105	2nd, Norris Div.	Lost Div. Final
1989-90	80	20	15	5	....	17	19	4	....	37	34	9	....	295	279	83	2nd, Norris Div.	Lost Div. Final
1988-89	80	22	11	7	....	11	24	5	....	33	35	12	....	275	285	78	2nd, Norris Div.	Lost Div. Final
1987-88	80	18	17	5	....	16	21	3	....	34	38	8	....	278	294	76	2nd, Norris Div.	Lost Div. Final
1986-87	80	21	12	7	....	11	21	8	....	32	33	15	....	281	293	79	1st, Norris Div.	Lost Div. Semi-Final
1985-86	80	23	11	6	....	14	23	3	....	37	34	9	....	302	291	83	3rd, Norris Div.	Lost Conf. Championship
1984-85	80	21	12	7	....	16	19	5	....	37	31	12	....	299	288	86	1st, Norris Div.	Lost Div. Semi-Final
1983-84	80	23	14	3	....	9	27	4	....	32	41	7	....	293	316	71	2nd, Norris Div.	Lost Div. Final
1982-83	80	16	16	8	....	9	24	7	....	25	40	15	....	285	316	65	4th, Norris Div.	Lost Div. Semi-Final
1981-82	80	22	14	4	....	10	26	4	....	32	40	8	....	315	349	72	3rd Norris Div.	Lost Div. Final
1980-81	80	29	7	4	....	16	11	13	....	45	18	17	....	352	281	107	1st, Smythe Div.	Lost Quarter-Final
1979-80	80	20	13	7	....	14	21	5	....	34	34	12	....	266	278	80	2nd, Smythe Div.	Lost Prelim. Round
1978-79	80	14	20	6	....	4	30	6	....	18	50	12	....	249	348	48	3rd, Smythe Div.	Out of Playoffs
1977-78	80	12	20	8	....	8	27	5	....	20	47	13	....	195	304	53	4th, Smythe Div.	Out of Playoffs
1976-77	80	22	13	5	....	10	26	4	....	32	39	9	....	239	276	73	1st, Smythe Div.	Lost Quarter-Final
1975-76	80	20	12	8	....	9	25	6	....	29	37	14	....	249	290	72	3rd, Smythe Div.	Lost Prelim. Round
1974-75	80	23	13	4	....	12	18	10	....	35	31	14	....	269	267	84	2nd, Smythe Div.	Lost Prelim. Round
1973-74	78	16	16	7	....	10	24	5	....	26	40	12	....	206	248	64	6th, West Div.	Out of Playoffs
1972-73	78	21	11	7	....	11	23	5	....	32	34	12	....	233	251	76	4th, West Div.	Lost Quarter-Final
1971-72	78	17	17	5	....	11	22	6	....	28	39	11	....	208	247	67	3rd, West Div.	Lost Semi-Final
1970-71	78	23	7	9	....	11	18	10	....	34	25	19	....	223	208	87	2nd, West Div.	Lost Quarter-Final
1969-70	76	24	9	5	....	13	18	7	....	37	27	12	....	224	179	86	1st, West Div.	Lost Final
1968-69	76	21	8	9	....	16	17	5	....	37	25	14	....	204	157	88	1st, West Div.	Lost Final
1967-68	74	18	12	7	....	9	19	9	....	27	31	16	....	177	191	70	3rd, West Div.	Lost Final

CENTRAL DIVISION
41st NHL Season

Franchise date: June 5, 1967

2007-08 Player Personnel

FORWARDS	HT	WT	S	Place of Birth	*Age	2006-07 Club
BACKES, David	6-3	200	R	Blaine, MN	23	St. Louis-Peoria
BERGLUND, Patrik	6-4	187	L	Vasteras, Sweden	19	Vasteras-Vasteras Jr.
BIRNER, Michal	6-0	183	L	Litomerice, Czech.	21	Peoria
BOYES, Brad	6-1	197	R	Mississauga, Ont.	25	Boston-St. Louis
CAJANEK, Petr	5-11	193	L	Gottwaldov/Zlin, Czech.	32	St. Louis
DRAZENOVIC, Nicholas	6-0	172	L	Prince George, B.C.	20	Prince George
GLUMAC, Mike	6-2	200	R	Niagara Falls, Ont.	27	St. Louis-Peoria
GUENETTE, Francois-Pierre	6-0	184	R	Laval, Que.	23	Victoria
HINOTE, Dan	6-0	190	R	Leesburg, FL	30	St. Louis
JOHNSON, Ryan	6-1	211	L	Thunder Bay, Ont.	31	St. Louis
KANA, Tomas	6-0	202	R	Opava, Czech.	19	Vitkovice-Ml. Boleslav
KARIYA, Martin	5-9	175	R	Vancouver, B.C.	25	Blues
KARIYA, Paul	5-10	176	L	Vancouver, B.C.	32	Nashville
KING, D.J.	6-3	225	L	Meadow Lake, Sask.	23	St. Louis-Peoria
LEMTYUGOV, Nikolai	6-0	183	L	Miass, USSR	21	Cherepovets
LINGLET, Charles	6-2	205	L	Montreal, Que.	25	Peoria
MAYERS, Jamal	6-2	220	R	Toronto, Ont.	32	St. Louis
McCLEMENT, Jay	6-1	199	L	Kingston, Ont.	24	St. Louis
REAVES, Ryan	6-1	193	R	Winnipeg, Man.	20	Brandon
RUCINSKY, Martin	6-1	207	L	Most, Czech.	36	St. Louis
STASTNY, Yan	5-11	175	L	Quebec City, Que.	24	Bos-Prov (AHL)-Peoria
STEMPNIAK, Lee	6-0	190	R	Buffalo, NY	24	St. Louis
TKACHUK, Keith	6-2	225	L	Melrose, MA	35	St. Louis-Atlanta
TRUDEL, Jean-Guy	5-11	202	L	Sudbury, Ont.	31	Ambri
WEIGHT, Doug	5-11	201	L	Warren, MI	36	St. Louis
WHITFIELD, Trent	5-11	209	L	Estevan, Sask.	30	Peoria
DEFENSEMEN						
BACKMAN, Christian	6-4	206	L	Alingsas, Sweden	27	St. Louis
BREWER, Eric	6-4	229	L	Vernon, B.C.	28	St. Louis
BROOKS, Alex	6-1	195	R	Madison, WI	31	New Jersey-Lowell
DuPONT, Micki	5-10	186	R	Calgary, Alta.	27	Pittsburgh-Wilkes-Barre
HELLSTROM, Alexander	6-2	207	L	Falun, Sweden	20	Bjorkloven Jr.-Bjorkloven
JACKMAN, Barret	6-0	213	L	Trail, B.C.	26	St. Louis-Peoria
JOHNSON, Erik	6-4	222	R	Bloomington, MN	19	U. of Minnesota
JUNLAND, Jonas	6-2	198	L	Linkoping, Sweden	19	Linkoping Jr.-Oskarshamn-Linkoping
McKEE, Jay	6-3	199	L	Kingston, Ont.	30	St. Louis
POLAK, Roman	6-1	198	R	Ostrava, Czech.	21	St. Louis-Peoria
SALVADOR, Bryce	6-2	222	L	Brandon, Man.	31	St. Louis
WAGNER, Steve	6-2	190	L	Grand Rapids, MN	23	Minnesota State-Peoria
WALKER, Matt	6-3	229	R	Beaverlodge, Alta.	27	St. Louis-Peoria
WOYWITKA, Jeff	6-2	209	L	Vermilion, Alta.	24	St. Louis-Peoria

GOALTENDERS	HT	WT	C	Place of Birth	*Age	2006-07 Club
BACASHIHUA, Jason	5-11	177	L	Garden City, MI	25	St. Louis-Peoria
LEGACE, Manny	5-9	204	L	Toronto, Ont.	34	St. Louis
RIKSMAN, Juuso	6-1	174	L	Helsinki, Finland	30	Jokerit
SCHWARZ, Marek	6-0	180	R	Mlada Boleslav, Czech.	21	St. Louis-Peoria
TOIVONEN, Hannu	6-2	200	L	Kalvola, Finland	23	Boston-Providence (AHL)

* – Age at start of 2007-08 season

2006-07 Scoring

* – rookie

Regular Season

Pos	#	Player	Team	GP	G	A	Pts	+/–	PIM	PP	SH	GW	S	%
C	39	Doug Weight	STL	82	16	43	59	10	56	5	0	3	123	13.0
R	12	Lee Stempniak	STL	82	27	25	52	–2	33	8	0	4	166	16.3
C	26	Petr Cajanek	STL	77	15	33	48	9	54	1	0	1	167	9.0
C	38	Brad Boyes	BOS	62	13	21	34	–17	25	1	1	1	139	9.4
			STL	19	4	8	12	0	4	0	0	1	43	9.3
			TOTAL	81	17	29	46	–17	29	1	1	2	182	9.3
R	18	Radek Dvorak	STL	82	10	27	37	–6	48	1	1	1	139	7.2
C	9	Jay McClement	STL	81	8	28	36	3	55	0	0	0	104	7.7
C	22	Glen Metropolit	ATL	57	12	16	28	9	20	4	0	2	92	13.0
			STL	20	2	3	5	0	14	1	0	0	31	6.5
			TOTAL	77	14	19	33	9	34	5	0	2	123	11.4
L	62	Martin Rucinsky	STL	52	12	21	33	–3	48	4	0	3	96	12.5
D	4	Eric Brewer	STL	82	6	23	29	–10	69	2	0	1	111	5.4
D	5	Barret Jackman	STL	70	3	24	27	20	82	1	0	1	86	3.5
C	42	* David Backes	STL	49	10	13	23	6	37	2	0	2	89	11.2
R	21	Jamal Mayers	STL	80	8	14	22	–19	89	0	2	0	129	6.2
D	55	Christian Backman	STL	61	7	11	18	13	36	1	0	0	80	8.8
R	10	Dallas Drake	STL	60	6	6	12	–14	38	0	2	2	74	8.1
C	17	Ryan Johnson	STL	59	7	4	11	–7	47	0	2	0	50	14.0
R	58	Dan Hinote	STL	41	5	5	10	–8	23	0	0	1	37	13.5
D	27	Bryce Salvador	STL	64	2	5	7	–5	55	0	0	0	40	5.0
D	29	Jeff Woywitka	STL	34	1	6	7	4	12	0	0	0	28	3.6
D	28	Matt Walker	STL	48	0	5	5	7	72	0	0	0	34	0.0
L	15	Peter Sejna	STL	22	3	1	4	2	4	0	0	0	34	8.8
D	20	Jamie Rivers	STL	31	1	3	4	–7	36	1	0	0	17	5.9
L	19	* D.J. King	STL	27	1	1	2	–3	52	0	0	0	12	8.3
L	32	Ville Nieminen	S.J.	30	1	1	2	–7	14	0	0	0	30	3.3
			STL	14	0	0	0	–1	29	0	0	0	13	0.0
			TOTAL	44	1	1	2	–8	43	0	0	0	43	2.3
D	54	* Tomas Mojzis	STL	6	1	0	1	0	0	0	0	0	7	14.3
C	37	Mike Glumac	STL	3	0	1	1	1	0	0	0	0	4	0.0
D	46	* Roman Polak	STL	19	0	0	0	–3	6	0	0	0	13	0.0
D	74	Jay McKee	STL	23	0	0	0	–9	12	0	0	0	19	0.0

Goaltending

No.	Goaltender	GPI	Mins	Avg	W	L	OT	EN	SO	GA	SA	S%	G	A	PIM
34	Manny Legace	45	2522	2.59	23	15	5	6	5	109	1177	.907	0	0	2
40	* Marek Schwarz	2	60	3.00	0	1	0	0	0	3	25	.880	0	0	0
30	* Jason Bacashihua	19	894	3.15	3	7	3	1	0	47	450	.896	0	0	2
1	Curtis Sanford	31	1492	3.18	8	12	5	3	0	79	707	.888	0	0	0
	Totals	**82**	**5001**	**2.98**	**34**	**35**	**13**	**10**	**6**	**248**	**2369**	**.895**			

Manny Legace and Curtis Sanford shared a shutout vs. Detroit on Feb 8, 2007.

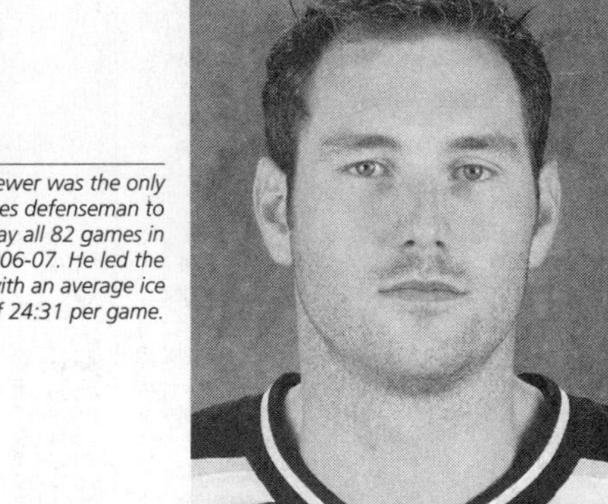

Eric Brewer was the only Blues defenseman to play all 82 games in 2006-07. He led the team with an average ice time of 24:31 per game.

Coach

ANDY MURRAY

Coach, St. Louis Blues. Born in Gladstone, Man., March 3, 1951.

Andy Murray was named the head coach of the St. Louis Blues on December 11, 2006. Previously, Murray coached the Los Angeles Kings from 1999 to 2006 and is the all-time franchise leader in wins (215) and games coached (480). Prior to joining the Kings, Murray was the head coach of the Canadian national team from 1996 to 1998. During the 1998-99 season, Murray coached Shattuck-St. Mary's in Faribault, Minnesota, where he led the prep school to a 70-9-2 record and the Midget Triple A USA Hockey national championship.

Murray's coaching career began in 1976 with the Brandon Travelers of the Manitoba Junior A Hockey League. He moved on to become head coach for Brandon University from 1978 to 1981 and led the Bobcats to a league championship and the number-one ranking in Canadian University hockey during his final year. His lengthy coaching experience also includes seven seasons as an NHL assistant or associate coach with the Winnipeg Jets (1993 to 1995), Minnesota North Stars (1990 to 1992) and Philadelphia Flyers (1988 to 1990). He has also coached in Europe and guided Canada to gold medals at the World Championship in 1997, 2003 and 2007.

Coaching Record

		Regular Season				Playoffs		
Season	**Team**	**Games**	**W**	**L**	**O/T**	**Games**	**W**	**L**
1999-2000	**Los Angeles (NHL)**	**82**	**39**	**31**	**12**	**4**	**0**	**4**
2000-01	**Los Angeles (NHL)**	**82**	**38**	**31**	**13**	**13**	**7**	**6**
2001-02	**Los Angeles (NHL)**	**82**	**40**	**31**	**11**	**7**	**3**	**4**
2002-03	**Los Angeles (NHL)**	**82**	**33**	**43**	**6**	....	....	....
2003-04	**Los Angeles (NHL)**	**82**	**28**	**38**	**16**	....	....	....
2004-05	**Los Angeles (NHL)**			Season Cancelled				
2005-06	**Los Angeles (NHL)**	**70**	**37**	**28**	**5**	....	....	....
2006-07	**St. Louis (NHL)**	**56**	**27**	**18**	**11**	....	....	....
	NHL Totals	**536**	**242**	**220**	**74**	**24**	**10**	**14**

Assistant coach Dave Tippett posted a 2-2-1 record as replacement coach when Murray was sidelined following a car accident, February 26 to March 6, 2002. All games are credited to Murray's coaching record.

Coaching History

Lynn Patrick and Scotty Bowman, 1967-68; Scotty Bowman, 1968-69, 1969-70; Al Arbour and Scotty Bowman, 1970-71; Sid Abel, Bill McCreary and Al Arbour, 1971-72; Al Arbour and Jean-Guy Talbot, 1972-73; Jean-Guy Talbot and Lou Angotti, 1973-74; Lou Angotti, Lynn Patrick and Garry Young, 1974-75; Garry Young, Lynn Patrick and Leo Boivin, 1975-76; Emile Francis, 1976-77; Leo Boivin and Barclay Plager, 1977-78; Barclay Plager, 1978-79; Barclay Plager and Red Berenson, 1979-80; Red Berenson, 1980-81; Red Berenson and Emile Francis, 1981-82; Emile Francis and Barclay Plager, 1982-83; Jacques Demers, 1983-84 to 1985-86; Jacques Martin, 1986-87, 1987-88; Brian Sutter, 1988-89 to 1991-92; Bob Plager and Bob Berry, 1992-93; Bob Berry, 1993-94; Mike Keenan, 1994-95, 1995-96; Mike Keenan, Jim Roberts and Joel Quenneville, 1996-97; Joel Quenneville, 1997-98 to 2002-03; Joel Quenneville and Mike Kitchen, 2003-04; Mike Kitchen, 2004-05, 2005-06; Mike Kitchen and Andy Murray, 2006-07; Andy Murray, 2007-08.

Captains' History

Al Arbour, 1967-68 to 1969-70; Red Berenson and Barclay Plager, 1970-71; Barclay Plager, 1971-72 to 1975-76; no captain, 1976-77; Red Berenson, 1977-78; Barry Gibbs, 1978-79; Brian Sutter, 1979-80 to 1987-88; Bernie Federko, 1988-89; Rick Meagher, 1989-90; Scott Stevens, 1990-91; Garth Butcher, 1991-92; Brett Hull, 1992-93 to 1994-95; Brett Hull, Shayne Corson and Wayne Gretzky, 1995-96; no captain, 1996-97; Chris Pronger, 1997-98 to 2001-02; Al MacInnis, 2002-03, 2003-04; Dallas Drake, 2005-06, 2006-07.

Club Records

Team

(Figures in brackets for season records are games played; records for fewest points, wins, ties, losses, goals, goals against are for 70 or more games)

Most Points 114 1999-2000 (82)
Most Wins 51 1999-2000 (82)
Most Ties 19 1970-71 (78)
Most Losses 50 1978-79 (80)
Most Goals 352 1980-81 (80)
Most Goals Against 349 1981-82 (80)
Fewest Points 48 1978-79 (80)
Fewest Wins 18 1978-79 (80)
Fewest Ties 7 1983-84 (80)
Fewest Losses 18 1980-81 (80)
Fewest Goals 177 1967-68 (74)
Fewest Goals Against 157 1968-69 (76)
Longest Winning Streak
Overall .... 10 Jan. 3-23/02
Home .... 9 Jan. 26-Feb. 26/91
Away .... *10 Jan. 21-Mar. 2/00
Longest Undefeated Streak
Overall .... 12 Nov. 10-Dec. 8/68 (5 wins, 7 ties), Nov. 24-Dec. 26/00 (11 wins, 1 tie)
Home .... 11 Four times
Away .... 11 Jan. 21-Mar. 4/00 (10 wins, 1 tie)
Longest Losing Streak
Overall .... 13 Mar. 16-Apr. 8/06
Home .... 7 Oct. 22-Nov. 26/05, Nov. 25-Dec. 17/06
Away .... 10 Jan. 20-Mar. 8/82, Dec. 29/05-Feb. 1/06
Longest Winless Streak
Overall .... 13 Mar. 16-Apr. 8/06 (10 losses, 3 OT losses)
Home .... 7 Dec. 28/82-Jan. 25/83 (5 losses, 2 ties), Oct. 22-Nov. 26/05 (6 losses, 1 OT loss)
Away .... 17 Jan. 23-Apr. 7/74 (14 losses, 3 ties)
Most Shutouts, Season 13 1968-69 (76)
Most PIM, Season 2,041 1990-91 (80)
Most Goals, Game .... 11 Feb. 26/94 (St.L. 11 at Ott. 1)

Individual

Most Seasons .... 13 Bernie Federko
Most Games .... 927 Bernie Federko
Most Goals, Career .... 527 Brett Hull
Most Assists, Career .... 721 Bernie Federko
Most Points, Career .... 1,073 Bernie Federko (352G, 721A)
Most PIM, Career .... 1,786 Brian Sutter
Most Shutouts, Career .... 16 Glenn Hall
Longest Consecutive Games Streak .... 662 Garry Unger (Feb. 7/71-Apr. 8/79)
Most Goals, Season .... 86 Brett Hull (1990-91)
Most Assists, Season .... 90 Adam Oates (1990-91)
Most Points, Season .... 131 Brett Hull (1990-91) (86G, 45A)
Most PIM, Season .... 306 Bob Gassoff (1975-76)
Most Points, Defenseman, Season .... 78 Jeff Brown (1992-93; 25G, 53A)
Most Points, Center, Season .... 115 Adam Oates (1990-91; 25G, 90A)
Most Points, Right Wing, Season .... 131 Brett Hull (1990-91; 86G, 45A)
Most Points, Left Wing, Season .... 102 Brendan Shanahan (1993-94; 52G, 50A)
Most Points, Rookie, Season .... 73 Jorgen Pettersson (1980-81; 37G, 36A)
Most Shutouts, Season .... 8 Glenn Hall (1968-69)
Most Goals, Game .... 6 Red Berenson (Nov. 7/68)
Most Assists, Game .... 5 Brian Sutter (Nov. 22/83), Bernie Federko (Feb. 27/88), Adam Oates (Jan. 26/91), Dallas Drake (Oct. 29/03)
Most Points, Game .... 7 Red Berenson (Nov. 7/68; 6G, 1A), Garry Unger (Mar. 13/71; 3G, 4A)

* NHL Record.

Retired Numbers

2	Al MacInnis	1994-2004
3	Bob Gassoff	1973-1977
8	Barclay Plager	1967-1977
11	Brian Sutter	1976-1988
16	Brett Hull	1987-1998
24	Bernie Federko	1976-1989

All-time Record vs. Other Clubs

Regular Season

	At Home								On Road								Total							
	GP	W	L	T	OL	GF	GA	PTS	GP	W	L	T	OL	GF	GA	PTS	GP	W	L	T	OL	GF	GA	PTS
Anaheim	26	13	7	3	3	81	72	32	26	14	10	2	0	78	70	30	52	27	17	5	3	159	142	62
Atlanta	3	3	0	0	0	11	1	6	5	2	2	1	0	16	16	5	8	5	2	1	0	27	17	11
Boston	60	28	23	9	0	191	200	65	59	15	35	9	0	161	247	39	119	43	58	18	0	352	447	104
Buffalo	51	30	14	7	0	183	127	67	52	17	29	6	0	164	200	40	103	47	43	13	0	347	327	107
Calgary	68	32	27	9	0	238	211	73	66	28	30	5	3	187	215	64	134	60	57	14	3	425	426	137
Carolina	31	19	9	3	0	119	94	41	32	17	13	2	0	99	96	36	63	36	22	5	0	218	190	77
Chicago	123	61	43	17	2	414	382	141	126	37	67	18	4	363	461	96	249	98	110	35	6	777	843	237
Colorado	44	24	14	4	2	157	130	54	45	15	23	7	0	119	154	37	89	39	37	11	2	276	284	91
Columbus	19	12	6	1	0	66	51	25	18	8	6	2	2	46	45	20	37	20	12	3	2	112	96	45
Dallas	121	67	33	21	0	436	342	155	119	41	55	22	1	342	396	105	240	108	88	43	1	778	738	260
Detroit	118	58	40	20	0	388	332	136	118	44	55	17	2	354	430	107	236	102	95	37	2	742	762	243
Edmonton	48	24	17	7	0	171	166	55	48	20	24	4	0	158	175	44	96	44	41	11	0	329	341	99
Florida	9	7	1	1	0	25	12	15	10	5	3	2	0	21	20	12	19	12	4	3	0	46	32	27
Los Angeles	82	52	19	10	1	308	210	115	82	32	38	12	0	233	274	76	164	84	57	22	1	541	484	191
Minnesota	12	5	4	3	0	26	23	13	12	3	6	2	1	22	39	9	24	8	10	5	1	48	62	22
Montreal	58	14	29	15	0	150	199	43	59	11	41	7	0	161	255	29	117	25	70	22	0	311	454	72
Nashville	24	13	9	1	1	66	49	28	25	9	9	3	4	59	60	25	49	22	18	4	5	125	109	53
New Jersey	47	27	12	7	1	195	148	62	47	18	22	7	0	131	148	43	94	45	34	14	1	326	296	105
NY Islanders	48	18	19	9	2	169	159	47	50	14	25	11	0	134	185	39	98	32	44	20	2	303	344	86
NY Rangers	64	25	28	10	1	192	207	61	61	10	44	6	1	145	248	27	125	35	72	16	2	337	455	88
Ottawa	10	4	4	2	0	29	29	10	10	6	4	0	0	36	23	12	20	10	8	2	0	65	52	22
Philadelphia	69	26	34	7	2	196	224	61	68	12	45	10	1	156	268	35	137	38	79	17	3	352	492	96
Phoenix	54	26	17	11	0	188	151	63	55	20	25	7	3	174	182	50	109	46	42	18	3	362	333	113
Pittsburgh	65	44	15	6	0	250	171	94	65	21	31	12	1	194	239	55	130	65	46	18	1	444	410	149
San Jose	32	18	12	1	1	104	86	38	28	21	5	1	1	94	62	44	60	39	17	2	2	198	148	82
Tampa Bay	11	10	1	0	0	44	24	20	14	5	5	3	1	46	43	14	25	15	6	3	1	90	67	34
Toronto	103	58	30	14	1	349	285	131	99	30	58	11	0	292	369	71	202	88	88	25	1	641	654	202
Vancouver	75	44	21	9	1	278	210	98	76	35	30	9	2	242	224	81	151	79	51	18	3	520	434	179
Washington	41	20	13	8	0	165	127	48	40	15	20	4	1	121	141	35	81	35	33	12	1	286	268	83
Defunct Clubs	32	25	4	3	0	131	55	53	33	11	10	12	0	95	100	34	65	36	14	15	0	226	155	87
Totals	**1548**	**807**	**505**	**218**	**18**	**5320**	**4477**	**1850**	**1548**	**536**	**770**	**214**	**28**	**4443**	**5385**	**1314**	**3096**	**1343**	**1275**	**432**	**46**	**9763**	**9862**	**3164**

2006-07 Results

Oct.	5	at San Jose	4-5*		9	at Columbus	4-3†
	7	at Los Angeles	1-4		10	at New Jersey	3-2
	9	at Anaheim	0-2		13	Los Angeles	6-5
	12	Boston	3-2†		15	at Phoenix	4-5†
	14	Chicago	4-3		16	at Anaheim	6-2
	17	Phoenix	2-5		18	at Los Angeles	3-1
	20	Vancouver	2-3*		20	at San Jose	1-0
	21	at Chicago	4-3		26	Detroit	2-1*
	28	Detroit	2-3		27	Nashville	3-6
	30	Anaheim	5-6†		30	Minnesota	2-5
Nov.	1	at Dallas	1-4	**Feb.**	2	at Detroit	3-5
	2	Colorado	4-1		3	Dallas	2-0
	4	Calgary	2-3		6	Toronto	1-2
	9	Columbus	2-4		8	Detroit	1-0
	10	at Chicago	1-3		10	at Philadelphia	3-4*
	12	Edmonton	5-3		13	San Jose	5-6
	14	at Calgary	0-3		14	at Columbus	4-2
	16	at Edmonton	2-6		16	Nashville	1-0
	17	at Vancouver	2-4		18	Minnesota	5-3
	22	at Columbus	4-3†		20	Columbus	5-4†
	24	at Detroit	3-2†		25	at Chicago	1-5
	25	Phoenix	1-2		27	Vancouver	3-1
	28	San Jose	0-2	**Mar.**	1	at NY Islanders	3-2*
	30	Nashville	4-5		3	at NY Rangers	2-3†
Dec.	1	at Chicago	2-5		6	Calgary	2-4
	5	Detroit	1-5		8	Dallas	5-3
	7	at Detroit	3-4*		10	Montreal	3-4
	9	Columbus	1-5		12	at Calgary	4-5†
	12	Chicago	2-3		15	at Vancouver	2-3*
	13	at Colorado	1-4		17	at Edmonton	3-2*
	16	at Nashville	2-3†		20	Ottawa	2-4
	17	Nashville	1-2*		22	at Minnesota	1-5
	19	at Pittsburgh	4-1		24	at Detroit	3-2†
	21	Los Angeles	5-2		25	at Columbus	1-4
	23	Buffalo	3-2*		27	Columbus	1-4
	26	at Nashville	2-3†		29	Edmonton	5-2
	29	at Colorado	4-2		31	Anaheim	2-3*
	30	Colorado	2-0	**Apr.**	2	at Dallas	4-2
Jan.	2	Chicago	1-4		3	at Phoenix	5-2
	4	Chicago	2-0		5	at Nashville	1-4
	6	at Nashville	2-3		7	at Minnesota	1-5

* – Overtime † – Shootout

Playoffs

	Series	W	L	GP	W	L	T	GF	GA	Last Mtg.	Rnd.	Result
Boston	2	0	2	8	0	8	0	15	48	1972	SF	L 0-4
Buffalo	1	0	1	3	1	2	0	8	7	1976	PRE	L 1-2
Calgary	1	0	1	7	3	4	0	22	28	1986	CF	L 3-4
Chicago	10	3	7	50	22	28	0	142	171	2002	CQF	W 4-1
Colorado	1	0	1	5	1	4	0	11	17	2001	CF	L 1-4
Dallas	12	6	6	66	32	34	0	187	197	2001	CSF	W 4-0
Detroit	7	2	5	40	16	24	0	103	125	2002	CSF	L 1-4
Los Angeles	2	2	0	8	8	0	0	32	13	1998	CQF	W 4-0
Montreal	3	0	3	12	0	12	0	14	42	1977	QF	L 0-4
NY Rangers	1	0	1	6	2	4	0	22	29	1981	QF	L 2-4
Philadelphia	2	2	0	11	8	3	0	34	20	1969	QF	W 4-0
Phoenix	2	2	0	11	7	4	0	39	29	1999	CQF	W 4-3
Pittsburgh	3	2	1	13	7	6	0	45	40	1981	PRE	W 3-2
San Jose	3	1	2	18	8	10	0	47	43	2004	CQF	L 1-4
Toronto	5	3	2	31	17	14	0	88	90	1996	CQF	W 4-2
Vancouver	2	0	2	14	6	8	0	48	44	2003	CQF	L 3-4
Totals	**57**	**23**	**34**	**303**	**138**	**165**	**0**	**857**	**943**			

Playoff Results 2007-2002

Year	Round	Opponent	Result	GF	GA
2004	CQF	San Jose	L 1-4	9	12
2003	CQF	Vancouver	L 3-4	21	17
2002	CSF	Detroit	L 1-4	11	14
	CQF	Chicago	W 4-1	13	5

Abbreviations: Round: CF – conference final; **CSF** – conference semi-final; **CQF** – conference quarter-final; **SF** – semi-final; **QF** – quarter-final; **PRE** – preliminary round.

Calgary totals include Atlanta Flames, 1972-73 to 1979-80. Carolina totals include Hartford, 1979-80 to 1996-97.
Colorado totals include Quebec, 1979-80 to 1994-95. Dallas totals include Minnesota North Stars, 1967-68 to 1992-93.
New Jersey totals include Kansas City, 1974-75, 1975-76, and Colorado Rockies, 1976-77 to 1981-82.
Phoenix totals include Winnipeg, 1979-80 to 1995-96.

Entry Draft Selections 2007-1993

2007
Pick
13 Lars Eller
18 Ian Cole
26 David Perron
39 Simon Hjalmarsson
44 Aaron Palushaj
85 Brett Sonne
96 Cade Fairchild
100 Travis Erstad
160 Anthony Peluso
190 Trevor Nill

2006
Pick
1 Erik Johnson
25 Patrik Berglund
31 Tomas Kana
64 Jonas Junland
94 Ryan Turek
106 Reto Berra
124 Andy Sackrison
154 Matthew McCollem
184 Alexander Hellstrom

2005
Pick
24 T.J. Oshie
37 Scott Jackson
85 Ben Bishop
156 Ryan Reaves
169 Mike Gauthier
171 Nicholas Drazenovic
219 Nikolai Lemtyugov

2004
Pick
17 Marek Schwarz
49 Carl Soderberg
83 Viktor Alexandrov
116 Michal Birner
136 Nikita Nikitin
180 Roman Polak
211 David Fredriksson
277 Jonathan Michel Boutin

2003
Pick
30 Shawn Belle
62 David Backes
84 Konstantin Barulin
88 Zack Fitzgerald
101 Konstantin Zakharov
127 Alexandre Bolduc
148 Lee Stempniak
159 Chris Beckford-Tseu
189 Jonathan Lehun
221 Yevgeny Skachkov
253 Andrei Pervyshin
284 Juhamatti Aaltonen

2002
Pick
48 Alexei Shkotov
62 Andrei Mikhnov
89 Tomas Troliga
120 Robin Jonsson
165 Justin Maiser
191 D.J. King
221 Jonas Johnson
253 Tom Koivisto
284 Ryan MacMurchy

2001
Pick
57 Jay McClement
89 Tuomas Nissinen
122 Igor Valeev
159 Dmitri Semin
190 Brett Scheffelmaier
253 Petr Cajanek
270 Grant Jacobsen
283 Simon Skoog

2000
Pick
30 Jeff Taffe
65 Dave Morisset
75 Justin Papineau
96 Antoine Bergeron
129 Troy Riddle
167 Craig Weller
229 Brett Lutes
261 Reinhard Divis
293 Lauri Kinos

1999
Pick
17 Barret Jackman
85 Peter Smrek
114 Chad Starling
143 Trevor Byrne
180 Tore Vikingstad
203 Phil Osaer
221 Colin Hemingway
232 Alexander Khavanov
260 Brian McMeekin
270 James Desmarais

1998
Pick
24 Christian Backman
41 Maxim Linnik
83 Matt Walker
157 Brad Voth
170 Andrei Troschinsky
197 Brad Twordik
225 Yevgeny Pastukh
255 John Pohl

1997
Pick
40 Tyler Rennette
86 Didier Tremblay
98 Jan Horacek
106 Jame Pollock
149 Nicholas Bilotto
177 Ladislav Nagy
206 Bobby Haglund
232 Dmitri Plekhanov
244 Marek Ivan

1996
Pick
14 Marty Reasoner
67 Gordie Dwyer
95 Jonathan Zukiwsky
97 Andrei Petrakov
159 Stephen Wagner
169 Daniel Corso
177 Reed Low
196 Andrej Podkonicky
203 Tony Hutchins
229 Konstantin Shafranov

1995
Pick
49 Jochen Hecht
75 Scott Roche
101 Michal Handzus
127 Jeff Ambrosio
153 Denis Hamel
179 Jean-Luc Grand-Pierre
205 Derek Bekar
209 Libor Zabransky

1994
Pick
68 Stephane Roy
94 Tyler Harlton
120 Edvin Frylen
172 Roman Vopat
198 Steve Noble
224 Marc Stephan
250 Kevin Harper
276 Scott Fankhouser

1993
Pick
37 Maxim Bets
63 Jamie Rivers
89 Jamal Mayers
141 Todd Kelman
167 Mike Buzak
193 Eric Boguniecki
219 Mike Grier
245 Libor Prochazka
271 Alexander Vasilevski
275 Christer Olsson

General Managers' History

Lynn Patrick, 1967-68; Scotty Bowman, 1968-69 to 1970-71; Lynn Patrick, 1971-72; Sid Abel, 1972-73; Charles Catto, 1973-74; Gerry Ehman, 1974-75; Dennis Ball, 1975-76; Emile Francis, 1976-77 to 1982-83; Ron Caron, 1983-84 to 1993-94; Mike Keenan, 1994-95, 1995-96; Mike Keenan and Ron Caron, 1996-97; Larry Pleau, 1997-98 to date.

Senior V.P. and General Manager

LARRY PLEAU
Senior Vice President/General Manager, St. Louis Blues.
Born in Lynn, MA, June 29, 1947.

Larry Pleau was named general manager on June 9, 1997, becoming the tenth person to hold that position in team history. Under his leadership the Blues won the President's Trophy in 1999-2000 and reached the Western Conference Finals in 2000-01. In international hockey, he served as associate general manager of the silver medal-winning 2002 U.S. Olympic team and as general manager of Team USA at the World Championships in 2003 and 2004 (bronze medal) and at the 2004 World Cup.

Pleau joined the Blues after spending eight seasons with the New York Rangers organization, reaching the position of vice president of player personnel. He joined the Rangers in 1989 as assistant general manager of player development. During Pleau's tenure in New York, the Rangers drafted NHL stars Sergei Zubov, Doug Weight, Alex Kovalev and Niklas Sundstrom. Prior to joining the Rangers, Pleau spent 17 seasons with the Hartford Whalers organization as a player, assistant coach, head coach, general manager and minor league general manager and head coach. He was also instrumental in drafting Ray Ferraro, Ron Francis, Kevin Dineen and Ulf Samuelsson while a member of the Whalers organization.

Pleau played three seasons with the Montreal Canadiens (1969-1972) in the National Hockey League before being the first player signed by the Hartford Whalers of the World Hockey Association. He was a center/left wing for the Whalers from 1972 until his retirement in 1979. He played in 468 regular season games for Hartford, accumulating 157 goals and 215 assists for 372 points. He also played for the 1968 United States Olympic team, the 1969 U.S. national team and went to training camp with Team USA for the 1976 Canada Cup tournament.

NHL Coaching Record

		Regular Season				Playoffs		
Season	Team	Games	W	L	T	Games	W	L
1980-81	Hartford	20	6	12	2	....	....	....
1981-82	Hartford	80	21	41	18	....	....	....
1982-83	Hartford	18	4	13	1	....	....	....
1987-88	Hartford	26	13	13	0	6	2	4
1988-89	Hartford	80	37	38	5	4	0	4
	NHL Totals	**224**	**81**	**117**	**26**	**10**	**2**	**8**

Club Directory

Scottrade Center

St. Louis Blues
Scottrade Center
1401 Clark Avenue
St. Louis, MO 63103
Phone **314/622-2500**
FAX 314/622-2582
www.stlouisblues.com
Capacity: 19,022

SCP Worldwide
Chairman/Governor . . . . . David W. Checketts
Partner/Alternate Governor . . . . . Kenneth W. Munoz
Partner/Alternate Governor . . . . . Michael McCarthy

Executive
President of Hockey Operations/Alt. Gov. . . . . . John Davidson
CEO of St. Louis Blues Enterprises/Alt. Gov. . . . . . Peter McLoughlin
Sr. V.P. and General Manager . . . . . Larry Pleau
Sr. V.P. and G.M., Scottrade Center . . . . . Dennis Petrullo
Sr. V.P., Sales and Marketing . . . . . Eric Stisser
Sr. V.P., Corporate and Sponsorship Sales . . . . . Mark Toffolo
Sr. V.P., Consumer Sales and Marketing . . . . . Dave Bullock
Vice President of Hockey Operations . . . . . Al MacInnis
Vice President, Building Operations . . . . . Fred Corsi
Vice President, Public Relations . . . . . Mike Caruso
Vice President, Sponsorship Sales . . . . . Jim Goessling
Vice President, Sales and Marketing Partnerships. . . Karrie Yager
Exec. Asst. to the President and G.M. . . . . . Donna Lembke
Exec. Asst. to the CEO, St. Louis Blues Ent. . . . . . Sheila Lattin
Exec. Asst. to the G.M., Scottrade Center . . . . . Cherri Haynes

Hockey Operations
Asst. G.M./Dir. of Amateur Scouting . . . . . Jarmo Kekalainen
Dir. of Pro Scouting and Peoria G.M. . . . . . Kevin McDonald
Head Coach . . . . . Andy Murray
Assistant Coach/Goaltending Coach . . . . . Rick Wamsley
Assistant Coaches . . . . . Ray Bennett, Brad Shaw
Strength and Conditioning Coach . . . . . Nelson Ayotte
Video Coach . . . . . Scott Masters
Asst. Dirs. of Public Relations/Team Services . . . . . Scott Bonanni, Rich Jankowski

Training
Athletic Trainer . . . . . Ray Barile
Equipment Manager . . . . . Bert Godin
Assistant Equipment Manager . . . . . Steve Wissman
Equipment Assistant . . . . . Ray Halle
Massage Therapist . . . . . Jeff Wright

Scouting
Professional Scouts . . . . . Wayne Mundey, Tony Feltrin, Jan Vopat
Amateur Scouts . . . . . Mike Antonovich, Bill Armstrong, Craig Channell, Dan Ginnell, Ville Siren
Part-Time Amateur Scouts . . . . . Rick Meagher, Thomas Carlsson, Vladimir Havluj, Jr., Barclay Parneta, Georgi Zhuravlev, Basil McRae

Medical
Orthopedic Surgeons . . . . . Drs. Rick Wright, Matt Matava, Jerome Gilden
Internists . . . . . Drs. William Birenbaum, Aaron Birenbaum
Neurosurgeon . . . . . Dr. Ralph Dacey
General Surgery . . . . . Dr. Michael Brunt
Plastic Surgery . . . . . Dr. Tom Francel
Dentist . . . . . Dr. Glenn Edwards
Ophthalmologist . . . . . Dr. Gill Grand
Optometrist . . . . . Dr. Rex Ghormley
Oral Surgeon . . . . . Dr. Ken Kram

Marketing
Exec. Director, Broadcasting & Blues Alumni . . . . . Bruce Affleck
Director of Corporate Sales . . . . . Bryan Lucas
Director of Corporate Sponsorship Services . . . . . Deni Allen
Director of Advertising and Promotions . . . . . Lisa Kampeter
Director of Digital Media . . . . . Beth Schwartz
Sponsorship Services Manager . . . . . Julie Drochelman
Sponsorship Services Coordinator . . . . . Rachel Morris
Sales and Marketing Coordinator/Webmaster . . . . . Lisa Cwiklowski
Event Presentation Director . . . . . Chris Frome
Community Relations Manager . . . . . Renah Jones
Community Relations Assistant . . . . . Ashley Green
Marketing Programs Manager . . . . . Josh Hardin
Web Site Manager . . . . . Chris Brauss
Webmaster/Content Developer . . . . . Chris Pinkert
KMOX Radio/Community Relations . . . . . Bob Plager
Marketing/Public Relations Assistant . . . . . Donna Ferguson
Team Photographer . . . . . Mark Buckner

Sales
Director of Ticket Sales and Service . . . . . Rob Fasoldt
Manager of Ticket Sales and Service . . . . . Theo Hodges
Premium Sales Executives . . . Dennis Dolan, Randy Walker, Nick Wierciak, Scott Witte, Yancey Jones
Sales Data Manager . . . . . Jason Penning
Ticket Sales Administrator . . . . . Paula Munder
Ticket Sales Representatives . . . . . Alec Gleason, Greg Rapini, Jennifer Lohrman, Neil Linders, Tony Patrico, Chase Ernst, Jason Berra, James Fox, Rob Mansis, Alvin Newsome, Matthew Olinik
Inside Sales Representatives . . . . . Charles Omelson, Julie Anderson, Lisa Zundel, Thomas Schmidt

Group Sales
Director of Group Ticket Sales . . . . . Jennifer Nevins
Group Ticket Executives . . . . . Renee Orr, Kari Takmajian, Jennifer Hyland
Sales Coordinator . . . . . Brenda Wilbur

Finance
Director of MIS/Accounting . . . . . Phil Siddle
Managers of Accounting . . . . . Craig Bryant, Toby Miller
Payroll Supervisor . . . . . Pam Di Rie
Payroll Assistant . . . . . Crystal Strasburg
Accountants . . . . . Deann Cromer, Chantay Kane, Carrin Stelmach, Mindy Wallace

Team Broadcasters
Radio Station . . . . . KMOX 1120 AM
Radio Broadcasters . . . . . Chris Kerber, Kelly Chase
Television Station . . . . . KPLR-TV, CW11
Regional Sports Network . . . . . FSN Midwest
Television Broadcasters . . . . . John Kelly, Bernie Federko, Dan McLaughlin

San Jose Sharks

Key Off-Season Signings/Acquisitions

2007

June 22 • Re-signed D **Craig Rivet**.
July 1 • Re-signed C **Joe Thornton**.
16 • Re-signed D **Rob Davison**.
27 • Signed D **Alexei Semenov**.

2006-07 Results: 51W-26L-3OTL-2SOL 107PTS.
Second, Pacific Division

Year-by-Year Record

		Home				Road				Overall								
Season	GP	W	L	T	OL	W	L	T	OL	W	L	T	OL	GF	GA	Pts.	Finished	Playoff Result
2006-07	82	25	12	....	4	26	14	....	1	51	26	....	5	258	199	107	2nd, Pacific Div.	Lost Conf. Semi-Final
2005-06	82	25	9	....	7	19	18	....	4	44	27	....	11	266	242	99	2nd, Pacific Div.	Lost Conf. Semi-Final
2004-05	....	....	....	....	....	....	....	....	....	....	....	....	....	....	....	....		
2003-04	82	24	8	7	2	19	13	5	4	43	21	12	6	219	183	104	1st, Pacific Div.	Lost Conf. Championship
2002-03	82	17	16	5	3	11	21	4	5	28	37	9	8	214	239	73	5th, Pacific Div.	Out of Playoffs
2001-02	82	25	11	3	2	19	16	5	1	44	27	8	3	248	199	99	1st, Pacific Div.	Lost Conf. Semi-Final
2000-01	82	22	14	4	1	18	13	8	2	40	27	12	3	217	192	95	2nd, Pacific Div.	Lost Conf. Quarter-Final
1999-2000	82	21	14	3	3	14	16	7	4	35	30	10	7	225	214	87	4th, Pacific Div.	Lost Conf. Semi-Final
1998-99	82	17	15	9	....	14	18	9	....	31	33	18	....	196	191	80	4th, Pacific Div.	Lost Conf. Quarter-Final
1997-98	82	17	19	5	....	17	19	5	....	34	38	10	....	210	216	78	4th, Pacific Div.	Lost Conf. Quarter-Final
1996-97	82	14	23	4	....	13	24	4	....	27	47	8	....	211	278	62	7th, Pacific Div.	Out of Playoffs
1995-96	82	12	26	3	....	8	29	4	....	20	55	7	....	252	357	47	7th, Pacific Div.	Out of Playoffs
1994-95	48	10	13	1	....	9	12	3	....	19	25	4	....	129	161	42	3rd, Pacific Div.	Lost Conf. Semi-Final
1993-94	84	19	13	10	....	14	22	6	....	33	35	16	....	252	265	82	3rd, Pacific Div.	Lost Conf. Semi-Final
1992-93	84	8	33	1	....	3	38	1	....	11	71	2	....	218	414	24	6th, Smythe Div.	Out of Playoffs
1991-92	80	14	23	3	....	3	35	2	....	17	58	5	....	219	359	39	6th, Smythe Div.	Out of Playoffs

2007-08 Schedule

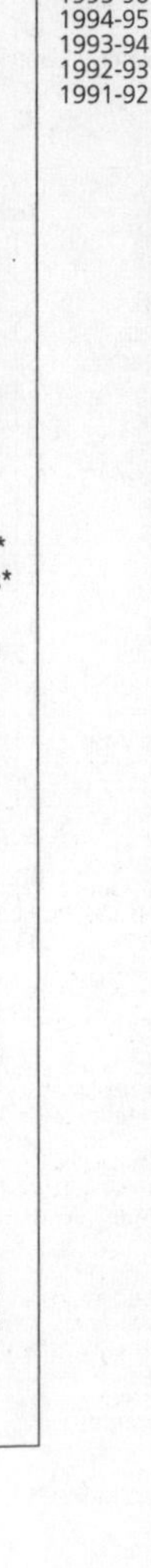

Oct.	Thu.	4	at Edmonton
	Fri.	5	at Vancouver
	Sun.	7	at Colorado
	Wed.	10	at Chicago
	Sat.	13	Boston
	Mon.	15	at Vancouver
	Thu.	18	Detroit
	Sat.	20	Nashville
	Mon.	22	at Calgary
	Fri.	26	at Detroit
	Sat.	27	at Columbus*
	Mon.	29	at Dallas
Nov.	Fri.	2	Los Angeles
	Sat.	3	at Los Angeles
	Wed.	7	Dallas
	Fri.	9	at Anaheim
	Sat.	10	Phoenix
	Mon.	12	Phoenix
	Wed.	14	at Dallas
	Thu.	15	at Phoenix
	Sat.	17	Anaheim
	Sat.	24	Los Angeles
	Wed.	28	Los Angeles
	Fri.	30	Colorado
Dec.	Mon.	3	at Colorado
	Wed.	5	at Dallas
	Fri.	7	at Phoenix
	Sat.	8	Buffalo
	Tue.	11	Minnesota
	Thu.	13	Vancouver
	Sat.	15	Dallas*
	Sun.	16	at Anaheim*
	Tue.	18	Anaheim
	Thu.	20	Phoenix
	Sat.	22	Anaheim
	Wed.	26	at Los Angeles
	Fri.	28	at St. Louis
	Sat.	29	at Nashville
	Mon.	31	at Minnesota
Jan.	Thu.	3	Calgary
	Sat.	5	Columbus
	Thu.	10	Vancouver
	Sat.	12	Toronto
	Sun.	13	at Anaheim*
	Tue.	15	at Phoenix
	Thu.	17	Dallas
	Sat.	19	Detroit
	Tue.	22	Chicago
	Thu.	24	St. Louis
	Tue.	29	at Edmonton
	Wed.	30	at Calgary
Feb.	Sat.	2	Chicago*
	Wed.	6	Colorado
	Fri.	8	Columbus
	Sat.	9	Nashville
	Tue.	12	Calgary
	Thu.	14	Edmonton
	Sun.	17	at NY Rangers*
	Mon.	18	at NY Islanders*
	Wed.	20	at New Jersey
	Thu.	21	at Philadelphia
	Sun.	24	at Pittsburgh*
	Wed.	27	at Columbus
	Fri.	29	at Detroit
Mar.	Sat.	1	at St. Louis
	Mon.	3	Montreal
	Wed.	5	Ottawa
	Fri.	7	at Chicago
	Sun.	9	at Minnesota*
	Tue.	11	at Nashville
	Fri.	14	St. Louis
	Sun.	16	Edmonton*
	Tue.	18	at Los Angeles
	Wed.	19	Minnesota
	Fri.	21	Anaheim
	Tue.	25	at Phoenix
	Thu.	27	Dallas
	Fri.	28	at Anaheim
	Sun.	30	Phoenix*
Apr.	Tue.	1	Los Angeles
	Thu.	3	at Los Angeles
	Sun.	6	at Dallas*

* Denotes afternoon game.

After winning the Art Ross Trophy with 125 points in 2005-06, Joe Thornton finished second in the scoring race with 114 points in 2006-07. He did lead the league in assists for the second straight season with 92.

PACIFIC DIVISION
17th NHL Season

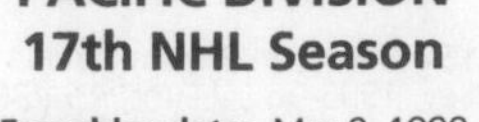

Franchise date: May 9, 1990

2007-08 Player Personnel

FORWARDS	HT	WT	S	Place of Birth	*Age	2006-07 Club
ARMSTRONG, Riley	5-11	185	R	Saskatoon, Sask.	22	Worcester
BERNIER, Steve	6-2	235	R	Quebec City, Que.	22	San Jose-Worcester
BROWN, Curtis	6-0	195	L	Unity, Sask.	31	San Jose
CAVANAGH, Tom	6-0	200	L	Warwick, RI	25	Worcester
CHEECHOO, Jonathan	6-1	200	R	Moose Factory, Ont.	27	San Jose
CLOWE, Ryane	6-2	225	R	St. John's, Nfld.	24	San Jose
COUTURE, Logan	6-0	195	L	Guelph, Ont.	18	Ottawa (OHL)
GOC, Marcel	6-1	195	L	Calw, West Germany	24	San Jose
GRIER, Mike	6-1	225	R	Detroit, MI	32	San Jose
IGGULDEN, Mike	6-3	215	R	St. Catherines, Ont.	24	Worcester
KASPAR, Lukas	6-2	210	L	Most, Czech.	22	Worcester
MARLEAU, Patrick	6-2	220	L	Aneroid, Sask.	28	San Jose
MICHALEK, Milan	6-2	225	L	Jindrichuv Hradec, Czech.	22	San Jose
MINK, Graham	6-3	220	R	Stowe, VT	28	Worcester
MITCHELL, Torrey	5-11	175	R	Montreal, Que.	22	U. of Vermont-Worcester
MORRIS, Mike	6-1	185	R	Dorchester, MA	24	Northeastern
PAVELSKI, Joe	5-11	195	L	Plover, WI	23	San Jose-Worcester
PLIHAL, Tomas	6-1	190	L	Frydlant v Cechach, Czech.	24	San Jose-Worcester
RISSMILLER, Patrick	6-4	215	L	Belmont, MA	28	San Jose
ROME, Ashton	6-1	205	R	Nesbitt, Man.	21	Worcester
SETOGUCHI, Devin	6-0	200	R	Taber, Alta.	20	Prince George
THORNTON, Joe	6-4	235	L	London, Ont.	28	San Jose
TREMBLAY, Jonathan	6-3	240	R	Fauquier, Ont.	23	Worcester-Fresno
VALETTE, Craig	6-0	200	L	Shellbrook, Sask.	24	Worcester
DEFENSEMEN						
CARLE, Matt	6-0	205	L	Anchorage, AK	23	San Jose-Worcester
DAVISON, Rob	6-3	220	L	St. Catharines, Ont.	27	San Jose
EHRHOFF, Christian	6-2	200	L	Moers, West Germany	25	San Jose
EVANS, Brennan	6-3	220	L	North Battleford, Sask.	25	Worcester
McLAREN, Kyle	6-5	230	L	Humboldt, Sask.	30	San Jose
MURRAY, Douglas	6-3	240	L	Bromma, Sweden	27	San Jose-Worcester
NORTON, Brad	6-6	235	L	Cambridge, MA	32	Detroit-Grand Rapids
PETRECKI, Nicholas	6-3	215	L	Schenectady, NY	18	Omaha
RIVET, Craig	6-2	210	R	North Bay, Ont.	33	Montreal-San Jose
SEMENOV, Alexei	6-6	235	L	Murmansk, USSR	26	Florida-Rochester-Ufa
SPANG, Dan	6-0	205	L	Winchester, MA	24	Worcester
STAUBITZ, Brad	6-1	215	R	Bright's Grove, Ont.	23	Worcester
VLASIC, Marc-Edouard	6-1	195	L	Montreal, Que.	20	San Jose
WISHART, Ty	6-4	205	L	Belleville, Ont.	19	Prince George

GOALTENDERS	HT	WT	C	Place of Birth	*Age	2006-07 Club
DAKERS, Taylor	6-1	175	L	Richmond, B.C.	21	Kootenay
GREISS, Thomas	6-1	200	L	Straubing, West Germany	21	Worcester-Fresno
NABOKOV, Evgeni	6-0	200	L	Ust-Kamenogorsk, USSR	32	San Jose
PATZOLD, Dimitri	6-0	195	L	Ust-Kamenogorsk, USSR	24	Worcester-Fresno

* – Age at start of 2007-08 season

2006-07 Scoring

* – rookie

Regular Season

Pos	#	Player	Team	GP	G	A	Pts	+/–	PIM	PP	SH	GW	S	%
C	19	Joe Thornton	S.J.	82	22	92	114	24	44	10	0	5	213	10.3
C	12	Patrick Marleau	S.J.	77	32	46	78	9	33	14	0	9	180	17.8
R	14	Jonathan Cheechoo	S.J.	76	37	32	69	11	69	15	0	5	250	14.8
R	9	Milan Michalek	S.J.	78	26	40	66	17	36	11	0	9	191	13.6
R	13	Bill Guerin	STL	61	28	19	47	8	52	7	0	6	189	14.8
			S.J.	16	8	1	9	2	14	2	0	1	36	22.2
			TOTAL	77	36	20	56	10	66	9	0	7	225	16.0
D	18	* Matthew Carle	S.J.	77	11	31	42	9	30	8	0	1	111	9.9
L	29	* Ryane Clowe	S.J.	58	16	18	34	4	78	4	0	3	93	17.2
R	25	Mike Grier	S.J.	81	16	17	33	–5	43	2	3	1	125	12.8
D	10	Christian Ehrhoff	S.J.	82	10	23	33	8	63	6	0	2	164	6.1
R	26	Steve Bernier	S.J.	62	15	16	31	5	29	6	0	4	104	14.4
C	8	* Joe Pavelski	S.J.	46	14	14	28	4	18	5	0	3	111	12.6
D	44	* Marc-Edouard Vlasic	S.J.	81	3	23	26	13	18	2	0	0	66	4.5
D	52	Craig Rivet	MTL	54	6	10	16	–7	57	2	0	0	58	10.3
			S.J.	17	1	7	8	8	12	0	0	0	31	3.2
			TOTAL	71	7	17	24	1	69	2	0	0	89	7.9
D	22	Scott Hannan	S.J.	79	4	20	24	1	38	0	1	1	79	5.1
C	34	Patrick Rissmiller	S.J.	79	7	15	22	1	22	1	0	0	100	7.0
L	7	Mark Bell	S.J.	71	11	10	21	–9	83	3	0	2	116	9.5
C	37	Curtis Brown	S.J.	78	8	12	20	–2	56	0	2	3	84	9.5
D	4	Kyle McLaren	S.J.	67	5	12	17	10	61	1	0	0	43	11.6
C	11	Marcel Goc	S.J.	78	5	8	13	–2	24	0	1	0	96	5.2
C	16	Mark Smith	S.J.	41	3	10	13	–4	42	2	0	0	38	7.9
D	3	Doug Murray	S.J.	35	0	3	3	0	31	0	0	0	18	0.0
D	5	Rob Davison	S.J.	22	0	2	2	–2	27	0	0	0	14	0.0
L	49	Mathieu Darche	S.J.	2	0	0	0	0	0	0	0	0	3	0.0
C	39	* Tomas Plihal	S.J.	3	0	0	0	0	0	0	0	0	10	0.0

Goaltending

No.	Goaltender	GPI	Mins	Avg	W	L	OT	EN	SO	GA	SA	S%	G	A	PIM
20	Evgeni Nabokov	50	2778	2.29	25	16	4	4	7	106	1227	.914	0	0	6
35	Vesa Toskala	38	2142	2.35	26	10	1	3	4	84	915	.908	0	3	0
	Totals	**82**	**4947**	**2.39**	**51**	**26**	**5**	**7**	**11**	**197**	**2149**	**.908**			

Playoffs

Pos	#	Player	Team	GP	G	A	Pts	+/–	PIM	PP	SH	GW	OT	S	%
C	19	Joe Thornton	S.J.	11	1	10	11	2	10	0	0	0	0	23	4.3
L	29	* Ryane Clowe	S.J.	11	4	2	6	–2	17	0	0	1	0	14	28.6
R	9	Milan Michalek	S.J.	11	4	2	6	3	4	0	0	1	0	27	14.8
C	12	Patrick Marleau	S.J.	11	3	3	6	–5	2	1	0	1	0	28	10.7
R	14	Jonathan Cheechoo	S.J.	11	3	3	6	1	6	1	0	1	0	27	11.1
D	52	Craig Rivet	S.J.	11	2	3	5	–5	18	1	0	0	0	21	9.5
D	18	* Matthew Carle	S.J.	11	2	3	5	3	0	1	0	1	0	12	16.7
R	25	Mike Grier	S.J.	11	2	2	4	1	27	0	0	0	0	31	6.5
C	34	Patrick Rissmiller	S.J.	11	1	3	4	1	0	0	0	1	1	18	5.6
D	4	Kyle McLaren	S.J.	11	0	4	4	–2	10	0	0	0	0	7	0.0
C	11	Marcel Goc	S.J.	11	2	1	3	3	4	0	0	0	0	16	12.5
R	13	Bill Guerin	S.J.	9	0	2	2	–3	12	0	0	0	0	22	0.0
C	37	Curtis Brown	S.J.	11	0	2	2	1	2	0	0	0	0	10	0.0
D	22	Scott Hannan	S.J.	11	0	2	2	4	33	0	0	0	0	6	0.0
D	10	Christian Ehrhoff	S.J.	11	0	2	2	1	6	0	0	0	0	12	0.0
C	8	* Joe Pavelski	S.J.	6	1	0	1	2	0	0	0	0	0	6	16.7
R	26	Steve Bernier	S.J.	11	0	1	1	2	2	0	0	0	0	15	0.0
D	44	* Marc-Edouard Vlasic	S.J.	11	0	1	1	5	2	0	0	0	0	3	0.0
C	16	Mark Smith	S.J.	3	0	0	0	0	4	0	0	0	0	7	0.0
L	7	Mark Bell	S.J.	4	0	0	0	–2	2	0	0	0	0	2	0.0

Goaltending

No.	Goaltender	GPI	Mins	Avg	W	L	EN	SO	GA	SA	S%	G	A	PIM
20	Evgeni Nabokov	11	701	2.23	6	5	1	1	26	323	.920	0	0	0
	Totals	**11**	**704**	**2.30**	**6**	**5**	**1**	**1**	**27**	**324**	**.917**			

Vice President and General Manager

DOUG WILSON
Executive Vice President/General Manager, San Jose Sharks.
Born in Ottawa, Ont., July 5, 1957.

Doug Wilson is the architect of the current San Jose Sharks team. After missing the playoffs in 2002-03, the Sharks rebounded to capture the Pacific Division title in 2003-04, setting a franchise record with 104 points, earning the second seed in the Western Conference playoffs and reaching the Western Conference Finals for the first time. The Sharks' record of 43-21-12-8 was the third-best mark in the NHL and the team's 31-point improvement over the previous season was the largest turnaround in the NHL. In 2006-07, the Sharks set new franchise records with 51 wins and 107 points.

Doug Wilson officially took over as the Sharks' executive vice president and general manager on May 13, 2003. In his current role, he has overall authority regarding all hockey-related operations. He oversees all player personnel decisions, negotiates player contracts, coordinates the efforts of the team's scouting department, leads the team in its draft-day preparations and administers the club's player evaluation process at all professional, minor and junior levels.

In his previous role as the team's director of pro development (1997 to 2003), the 16-year NHL veteran's primary responsibilities included evaluating talent at all professional and minor league levels and continuous assessment of the Sharks roster and reserve list. In addition, he provided valuable input assisting the club's player development programs and consulting with the hockey department on all major personnel issues, special assignments and contract negotiations.

A first-round choice (sixth overall) of the Blackhawks in 1977 after a stellar junior career with the Ottawa 67s, Wilson played 14 seasons in Chicago and still ranks as the club's highest scoring defenseman in goals (225), assists (554) and points (779). In addition, he led all Blackhawks defensemen in scoring for 10 consecutive seasons (1980-81 through 1990-91) and captured the 1982 Norris Trophy, symbolic of the NHL's top defenseman, when he tallied 39 goals and 85 points – still Blackhawks single-season records for goals and points by a defenseman.

General Managers' History

Jack Ferreira, 1991-92; Chuck Grillo (V.P. Director of Player Personnel), 1992-93 to 1995-96; Dean Lombardi, 1996-97 to 2002-03; Doug Wilson, 2003-04 to date.

Coaching History

George Kingston, 1991-92, 1992-93; Kevin Constantine, 1993-94, 1994-95; Kevin Constantine and Jim Wiley, 1995-96; Al Sims, 1996-97; Darryl Sutter, 1997-98 to 2001-02; Darryl Sutter and Ron Wilson, 2002-03; Ron Wilson, 2003-04 to date.

Club Records

Team

(Figures in brackets for season records are games played; records for fewest points, wins, ties, losses, goals, goals against are for 70 or more games)

Most Points **107** 2006-07 (82)
Most Wins **51** 2006-07 (82)
Most Ties **18** 1998-99 (82)
Most Losses ***71** 1992-93 (84)
Most Goals **266** 2005-06 (82)
Most Goals Against **414** 1992-93 (84)
Fewest Points **24** 1992-93 (84)
Fewest Wins **11** 1992-93 (84)
Fewest Ties ***2** 1992-93 (84)
Fewest Losses **26** 2006-07 (82)
Fewest Goals **196** 1998-99 (82)
Fewest Goals Against **183** 2003-04 (82)
Longest Winning Streak
  Overall .... **8** Apr. 3-15/06
  Home .... **8** Jan. 24-Mar. 3/04
  Away .... **6** Nov. 30-Dec. 19/01
Longest Undefeated Streak
  Overall .... **10** Nov. 27-Dec. 19/01 (9 wins, 1 tie)
  Home .... **11** Nov. 15-Dec. 29/03 (8 wins, 3 ties)
  Away .... **10** Dec. 26/00-Feb. 16/01 (6 wins, 4 ties)
Longest Losing Streak
  Overall .... ***17** Jan. 4-Feb. 12/93
  Home .... **9** Nov. 19-Dec. 19/92
  Away .... **19** Nov. 27/92-Feb. 12/93
Longest Winless Streak
  Overall .... **20** Dec. 29/92-Feb. 12/93 (19 losses, 1 tie)
  Home .... **9** Nov. 19-Dec. 19/92 (9 losses)
  Away .... **19** Nov. 27/92-Feb. 12/93 (19 losses)
Most Shutouts, Season **11** 2003-04 (82), 2006-07 (82)
Most PIM, Season **2,134** 1992-93 (84)
Most Goals, Game .... **10** Jan. 13/96 (S.J. 10 at Pit. 8), Mar. 30/02 (CBJ 2 at S.J. 10)

Individual

Most Seasons .... **11** Mike Rathje
Most Games, Career .... **717** Patrick Marleau
Most Goals, Career .... **219** Patrick Marleau
Most Assists, Career .... **272** Patrick Marleau
Most Points, Career .... **491** Patrick Marleau (219G, 272A)
Most PIM, Career .... **1,001** Jeff Odgers
Most Shutouts, Career .... **34** Evgeni Nabokov
Longest Consecutive Games Streak .... **228** Mike Ricci (Nov. 22/97-Oct. 20/00)
Most Goals, Season .... **56** Jonathan Cheechoo (2005-06)
Most Assists, Season .... **92** Joe Thornton (2006-07)
Most Points, Season .... **114** Joe Thornton (2006-07; 22G, 92A)
Most PIM, Season .... **326** Link Gaetz (1991-92)
Most Points, Defenseman, Season .... **64** Sandis Ozolinsh (1993-94; 26G, 38A)
Most Points, Center, Season .... **114** Joe Thornton (2006-07; 22G, 92A)
Most Points, Right Wing, Season .... **93** Jonathan Cheechoo (2005-06; 56G, 37A)
Most Points, Left Wing, Season .... **66** Johan Garpenlov (1992-93; 22G, 44A); Milan Michalek (2006-07; 26G, 40A)
Most Points, Rookie, Season .... **59** Pat Falloon (1991-92; 25G, 34A)
Most Shutouts, Season .... **9** Evgeni Nabokov (2003-04)
Most Goals, Game .... **4** Owen Nolan (Dec. 19/95)
Most Assists, Game .... **4** Thirteen times
Most Points, Game .... **6** Owen Nolan (Oct. 4/99; 3G, 3A)

* NHL Record.

Captains' History

Doug Wilson, 1991-92, 1992-93; Bob Errey, 1993-94; Bob Errey and Jeff Odgers, 1994-95; Jeff Odgers, 1995-96; Todd Gill, 1996-97, 1997-98; Owen Nolan, 1998-99 to 2002-03; Mike Ricci, Vincent Damphousse, Alyn McCauley, Patrick Marleau, 2003-04; Patrick Marleau, 2005-06 to date.

All-time Record vs. Other Clubs

Regular Season

	At Home								On Road								Total							
	GP	W	L	T	OL	GF	GA	PTS	GP	W	L	T	OL	GF	GA	PTS	GP	W	L	T	OL	GF	GA	PTS
Anaheim	38	17	18	2	1	107	106	37	38	21	13	2	2	121	104	46	76	38	31	4	3	228	210	83
Atlanta	5	4	0	1	0	21	10	9	5	3	0	1	1	16	8	8	10	7	0	2	1	37	18	17
Boston	11	4	5	2	0	30	38	10	11	1	7	3	0	32	41	5	22	5	12	5	0	62	79	15
Buffalo	10	5	1	4	0	36	33	14	12	1	11	0	0	32	52	2	22	6	12	4	0	68	85	16
Calgary	38	16	18	4	0	114	112	36	36	11	20	4	1	97	129	27	74	27	38	8	1	211	241	63
Carolina	12	8	4	0	0	54	34	16	12	5	7	0	0	27	40	10	24	13	11	0	0	81	74	26
Chicago	30	17	9	3	1	89	77	38	29	13	12	2	2	91	87	30	59	30	21	5	3	180	164	68
Colorado	28	10	17	1	0	81	102	21	27	7	15	4	1	53	95	19	55	17	32	5	1	134	197	40
Columbus	12	11	0	0	1	50	18	23	12	6	6	0	0	25	32	12	24	17	6	0	1	75	50	35
Dallas	38	14	18	1	5	89	106	34	37	14	18	4	1	85	102	33	75	28	36	5	6	174	208	67
Detroit	30	12	14	3	1	108	113	28	29	3	23	1	2	51	115	9	59	15	37	4	3	159	228	37
Edmonton	36	18	12	5	1	124	108	42	37	8	21	7	1	83	124	24	73	26	33	12	2	207	232	66
Florida	10	6	2	2	0	32	19	14	10	3	2	5	0	29	26	11	20	9	4	7	0	61	45	25
Los Angeles	45	28	14	3	0	156	122	59	45	16	23	4	2	122	137	38	90	44	37	7	2	278	259	97
Minnesota	12	5	5	1	1	28	25	12	12	6	4	1	1	28	27	14	24	11	9	2	2	56	52	26
Montreal	11	5	3	2	1	33	28	13	12	2	8	2	0	22	42	6	23	7	11	4	1	55	70	19
Nashville	16	9	5	1	1	42	40	20	16	6	8	1	1	40	43	14	32	15	13	2	2	82	83	34
New Jersey	11	4	5	1	1	26	32	10	12	4	6	1	1	24	44	10	23	8	11	2	2	50	76	20
NY Islanders	13	6	5	1	1	32	40	14	11	4	5	2	0	35	40	10	24	10	10	3	1	67	80	24
NY Rangers	14	2	10	2	0	32	52	6	10	2	6	1	1	29	40	6	24	4	16	3	1	61	92	12
Ottawa	9	5	4	0	0	18	16	10	10	2	4	4	0	28	36	8	19	7	8	4	0	46	52	18
Philadelphia	13	4	7	2	0	28	32	10	11	3	6	2	0	27	36	8	24	7	13	4	0	55	68	18
Phoenix	40	18	15	4	3	137	124	43	43	19	20	3	1	121	133	42	83	37	35	7	4	258	257	85
Pittsburgh	14	6	6	2	0	37	56	14	9	4	4	1	0	32	41	9	23	10	10	3	0	69	97	23
St. Louis	28	6	19	1	2	62	94	15	32	13	17	1	1	86	104	28	60	19	36	2	3	148	198	43
Tampa Bay	11	4	6	1	0	35	37	9	13	5	6	1	1	35	34	12	24	9	12	2	1	70	71	21
Toronto	15	5	7	3	0	32	40	13	19	5	12	2	0	52	73	12	34	10	19	5	0	84	113	25
Vancouver	38	14	17	5	2	108	118	35	36	12	19	4	1	98	129	29	74	26	36	9	3	206	247	64
Washington	11	7	3	1	0	33	27	15	13	8	5	0	0	39	36	16	24	15	8	1	0	72	63	31
Totals	**599**	**270**	**249**	**58**	**22**	**1774**	**1759**	**620**	**599**	**207**	**308**	**63**	**21**	**1560**	**1950**	**498**	**1198**	**477**	**557**	**121**	**43**	**3334**	**3709**	**1118**

Playoffs

	Series	W	L	GP	W	L	T	GF	GA	Last Mtg.	Rnd.	Result
Calgary	2	1	1	13	6	7	0	38	51	2004	CF	L 2-4
Colorado	3	1	2	19	9	10	0	52	51	2004	CSF	W 4-2
Dallas	2	0	2	11	3	8	0	19	31	2000	CSF	L 1-4
Detroit	3	1	2	17	6	11	0	36	64	2007	CSF	L 2-4
Edmonton	1	0	1	6	2	4	0	12	19	2006	CSF	L 2-4
Nashville	2	2	0	10	8	2	0	33	24	2007	CQF	W 4-1
Phoenix	1	1	0	5	4	1	0	13	7	2002	CQF	W 4-1
St. Louis	3	2	1	18	10	8	0	43	47	2004	CQF	W 4-1
Toronto	1	0	1	7	3	4	0	21	26	1994	CSF	L 3-4
Totals	**18**	**8**	**10**	**106**	**51**	**55**	**0**	**267**	**320**			

Carolina totals include Hartford, 1991-92 to 1996-97.
Dallas totals include Minnesota North Stars, 1991-92 to 1992-93.

Playoff Results 2007-2002

Year	Round	Opponent	Result	GF	GA
2007	CSF	Detroit	L 2-4	9	13
	CQF	Nashville	W 4-1	16	14
2006	CSF	Edmonton	L 2-4	12	19
	CQF	Nashville	W 4-1	17	10
2004	CF	Calgary	L 2-4	12	16
	CSF	Colorado	W 4-2	14	7
	CQF	St. Louis	W 4-1	12	9
2002	CSF	Colorado	L 3-4	21	25
	CQF	Phoenix	W 4-1	13	7

Abbreviations: Round: CF – conference final; **CSF** – conference semi-final; **CQF** – conference quarter-final.

Colorado totals include Quebec, 1991-92 to 1994-95.
Phoenix totals include Winnipeg, 1991-92 to 1995-96.

2006-07 Results

Oct.	5	St. Louis	5-4*		6	Columbus	5-2
	7	NY Islanders	2-0		10	Edmonton	2-3
	9	at Calgary	4-1		11	at Los Angeles	5-2
	12	at Edmonton	4-6		13	at Phoenix	4-1
	13	at Vancouver	6-4		15	Colorado	3-1
	17	Dallas	2-0		18	Phoenix	5-2
	19	Detroit	5-1		20	St. Louis	0-1
	21	Minnesota	1-4		26	at Edmonton	5-1
	23	at Columbus	3-0		28	at Vancouver	1-3
	25	at Detroit	1-2		30	Dallas	2-3†
	26	at Nashville	3-4	**Feb.**	1	Dallas	2-4
	29	at Tampa Bay	4-2		3	Chicago	4-2
	31	at Florida	2-1		6	Anaheim	4-7
Nov.	2	NY Rangers	1-3		7	at Anaheim	3-2
	4	Pittsburgh	3-2		13	at St. Louis	6-5
	7	Minnesota	3-1		14	at Nashville	0-5
	9	at Los Angeles	7-3		16	at Columbus	0-3
	11	at Phoenix	2-1		18	at Dallas	2-5
	13	at Los Angeles	2-4		21	at Washington	3-2†
	15	at Colorado	4-3		22	at Chicago	2-0
	18	Philadelphia	6-1		24	at Calgary	4-7
	21	at Anaheim	0-5		26	Anaheim	2-3
	22	Los Angeles	6-3		28	Nashville	3-4†
	25	New Jersey	2-0	**Mar.**	2	at Anaheim	1-3
	28	at St. Louis	2-0		4	at Dallas	4-0
	29	at Minnesota	2-1		6	at Minnesota	3-0
Dec.	2	at Detroit	3-2		9	Vancouver	1-2*
	4	at Dallas	0-1		11	Edmonton	3-0
	7	Colorado	2-5		13	Chicago	7-1
	9	Nashville	3-1		15	at Phoenix	5-1
	11	Phoenix	4-0		16	Columbus	3-0
	12	at Los Angeles	3-1		18	at Colorado	3-4*
	14	Los Angeles	2-4		21	at Chicago	4-1
	16	Anaheim	4-3		22	at Atlanta	5-1
	21	Dallas	0-3		24	at Carolina	4-6
	23	Calgary	4-1		27	Los Angeles	3-1
	26	Anaheim	3-4		30	Phoenix	4-2
	28	Phoenix	2-3	**Apr.**	1	Los Angeles	6-2
	30	at Phoenix	0-8		4	at Anaheim	3-2†
	31	at Dallas	4-2		5	Calgary	4-3
Jan.	4	Detroit	9-4		7	Vancouver	3-4*

* – Overtime † – Shootout

Entry Draft Selections 2007-1993

2007
Pick
9 Logan Couture
28 Nicholas Petrecki
83 Timo Pielmeier
91 Tyson Sexsmith
165 Patrik Zackrisson
173 Nick Bonino
201 Justin Braun
203 Frazer McLaren

2006
Pick
16 Ty Wishart
36 Jamie McGinn
98 James Delory
143 Ashton Rome
202 John McCarthy
203 Jay Barriball

2005
Pick
8 Devin Setoguchi
35 Marc-Edouard Vlasic
112 Alex Stalock
140 Taylor Dakers
149 Derek Joslin
162 P.J. Fenton
183 Will Colbert
193 Tony Lucia

2004
Pick
22 Lukas Kaspar
94 Thomas Greiss
126 Torrey Mitchell
129 Jason Churchill
153 Steven Zalewski
201 Michael Vernace
225 David MacDonald
234 Derek MacIntyre
288 Brian Mahoney-Wilson
289 Christian Jensen

2003
Pick
6 Milan Michalek
16 Steve Bernier
43 Josh Hennessy
47 Matt Carle
139 Patrick Ehelechner
201 Jonathan Tremblay
205 Joe Pavelski
216 Kai Hospelt
236 Alexander Hult
267 Brian O'Hanley
276 Carter Lee

2002
Pick
27 Mike Morris
52 Dan Spang
86 Jonas Fiedler
139 Kris Newbury
163 Tom Walsh
217 Tim Conboy
288 Michael Hutchins

2001
Pick
20 Marcel Goc
106 Christian Ehrhoff
107 Dimitri Patzold
140 Tomas Plihal
175 Ryane Clowe
182 Tom Cavanagh

2000
Pick
41 Tero Maatta
104 Jon Disalvatore
142 Michal Pinc
166 Nolan Schaefer
183 Michal Macho
246 Chad Wiseman
256 Pasi Saarinen

1999
Pick
14 Jeff Jillson
82 Mark Concannon
111 Willie Levesque
155 Niko Dimitrakos
229 Eric Betournay
241 Doug Murray
257 Hannes Hyvonen

1998
Pick
3 Brad Stuart
29 Jonathan Cheechoo
65 Eric Laplante
98 Rob Davison
104 Miroslav Zalesak
127 Brandon Coalter
145 Mikael Samuelsson
185 Robert Mulick
212 Jim Fahey

1997
Pick
2 Patrick Marleau
23 Scott Hannan
82 Adam Colagiacomo
107 Adam Nittel
163 Joe Dusbabek
192 Cam Severson
219 Mark Smith

1996
Pick
2 Andrei Zyuzin
21 Marco Sturm
55 Terry Friesen
102 Matt Bradley
137 Michel Larocque
164 Jake Deadmarsh
191 Cory Cyrenne
217 David Thibeault

1995
Pick
12 Teemu Riihijarvi
38 Peter Roed
64 Marko Makinen
90 Vesa Toskala
116 Miikka Kiprusoff
130 Michal Bros
140 Timo Hakanen
142 Jaroslav Kudrna
167 Brad Mehalko
168 Robert Jindrich
194 Ryan Kraft
220 Mikko Markkanen

1994
Pick
11 Jeff Friesen
37 Angel Nikolov
66 Alexei Yegorov
89 Vaclav Varada
115 Brian Swanson
141 Alexander Korolyuk
167 Sergei Gorbachev
193 Eric Landry
219 Evgeni Nabokov
240 Tomas Pisa
245 Aniket Dhadphale
271 David Beauregard

1993
Pick
6 Viktor Kozlov
28 Shean Donovan
45 Vlastimil Kroupa
58 Ville Peltonen
80 Alexander Osadchy
106 Andrei Buschan
132 Petri Varis
154 Fredrik Oduya
158 Anatoli Filatov
184 Todd Holt
210 Jonas Forsberg
236 Jeff Salajko
262 Jamie Matthews

Coach

RON WILSON
Coach, San Jose Sharks. Born in Windsor, Ont., May 28, 1955.

Named head coach of the Sharks on December 4, 2002, Ron Wilson's first full season behind the San Jose bench saw the team rebound from a disappointing 2002-03 campaign in which they finished last in the Pacific Division and 14th in the Western Conference to capture its second Pacific Division title with a franchise-best 104 points. The Sharks finished second overall in the Western Conference and reached the Western Conference Final for the first time. In 2006-07, the Sharks set new franchise records with 51 wins and 107 points.

Prior to spending five seasons with the Washington Capitals, Wilson had served as the first head coach of the expansion Mighty Ducks of Anaheim in 1993 and led the team to its first trip to the Stanley Cup playoffs in 1996-97. In four seasons behind the Anaheim bench, he posted a record of 120-145-31.

Throughout his professional and amateur career, Wilson has enjoyed a long-standing relationship with USA Hockey. In 1996, he led Team USA to the gold medal at the inaugural World Cup of Hockey. He coached the team again at the 2004 tournament. Wilson also coached the U.S. national team at the 1994 and 1996 World Championships, where his teams finished fourth and third respectively. Wilson also served as head coach for Team USA at the 1998 Nagano Winter Olympics.

Born in Windsor, Ontario, but raised in Riverside, Rhode Island, Wilson was selected by the Toronto Maple Leafs in the seventh round (132nd overall) of the 1975 NHL Entry Draft. He began his professional career with the Dallas Blackhawks (Central Hockey League) in the spring of 1977 and joined the Maple Leafs for the 1977-78 season. In 177 career games with Toronto and the Minnesota North Stars, Wilson posted 93 points (26 goals, 67 assists). He also played for the U.S. national team in 1975, 1981, 1983 and 1987.

Coaching Record

		Regular Season				Playoffs		
Season	**Team**	**Games**	**W**	**L**	**O/T**	**Games**	**W**	**L**
1993-94	Anaheim (NHL)	84	33	46	5	....	....	....
1994-95	Anaheim (NHL)	48	16	27	5	....	....	....
1995-96	Anaheim (NHL)	82	35	39	8	....	....	....
1996-97	Anaheim (NHL)	82	36	33	13	11	4	7
1997-98	Washington (NHL)	82	40	30	12	21	12	9
1998-99	Washington (NHL)	82	31	45	6	....	....	....
1999-2000	Washington (NHL)	82	44	26	12	5	1	4
2000-01	Washington (NHL)	82	41	31	10	6	2	4
2001-02	Washington (NHL)	82	36	35	11	....	....	....
2002-03	San Jose (NHL)	57	19	31	7	....	....	....
2003-04	San Jose (NHL)	82	43	27	12	17	10	7
2004-05	San Jose (NHL)			Season Cancelled				
2005-06	San Jose (NHL)	82	44	27	11	11	6	5
2006-07	San Jose (NHL)	82	51	26	5	11	6	5
	NHL Totals	**1009**	**469**	**423**	**117**	**82**	**41**	**41**

Club Directory

HP Pavilion at San Jose

San Jose Sharks
HP Pavilion at San Jose
525 West Santa Clara Street
San Jose, CA 95113
Phone **408/287-7070**
FAX 408/999-5797
www.sjsharks.com
Capacity: 17,496

San Jose Sports & Entertainment Enterprises
Board Members: Kevin Compton, Greg Reyes, Greg Jamison, Tom McEnery, Brent Jones

Investors in SJSEE include
Blue Line Associates (Kevin Compton, Greg Reyes, Hasso Plattner, Stratton Sclavos, Gary Valenzuela, Harvey Armstrong), William DelBiaggio, George Gund III, Greg Jamison, Floyd Kvamme, Tom McEnery, Gordon Russell, Rudy Staedler

Executive Staff
President & Chief Executive Officer . . . . Greg Jamison
Executive V.P. of Business Operations . . . . Malcolm Bordelon
Executive V.P. & G.M. (HP Pavilion at San Jose) . . . . Jim Goddard
Executive V.P. & General Counsel . . . . Don Gralnek
Executive V.P. & G.M. (Sharks) . . . . Doug Wilson
Executive V.P. & Chief Financial Officer . . . . Charlie Faas
Vice President of Finance . . . . Ken Caveney
Vice President of Sales & Marketing . . . . Kent Russell
Vice President of Building Operations . . . . Rich Sotelo
Vice President and Assistant G.M. (Sharks) . . . . Wayne Thomas
Executive Assistants . . . . Tricia Sullivan, Michelle Simmons, Niki Hartley

Hockey Operations
Head Coach . . . . Ron Wilson
Assistant Coaches. . . . . Tim Hunter, Rob Zettler
Director of Hockey Operations . . . . Joe Will
Director of Scouting . . . . Tim Burke
Director of Professional Scouting. . . . . Sean Coady
Scouts . . . . Gilles Cote, Pat Funk, Jack Gardiner, Rob Grillo, Brian Gross, Karel Masopust, Cap Raeder, Graeme Townshend
Director of Hockey Administration . . . . Rosemary Tebaldi
Head Athletic Trainer . . . . Ray Tufts, A.T.,C
Assistant Athletic Trainer and Massage Therapist. . . Wes Howard, A.T.C., CMT
Strength & Conditioning Coordinator . . . . Mike Potenza
Equipment Manager. . . . . Mike Aldrich
Assistant Equipment Manager. . . . . Rick Bronwell
Equipment Assistant & Equipment Transportation . . Roy Sneesby
Manager of Hockey Technology . . . . Paul Fink
Cleaning Specialist . . . . Norma Hernandez
Equipment Manager, Worcester Sharks (AHL) . . . . . Vinny Ferraiuolo
Asst. Equipment Manager, Worcester Sharks (AHL). . Kevin Sychowski
Team Physician . . . . Arthur J. Ting, M.D.
Team Internists . . . . John Chiu, M.D., Greg Whitley M.D.
Team Dentists. . . . . Robert Bonahoom, D.D.S., Don Goudy, D.D.S.
Team Vision Specialists . . . . Vincent S. Zuccaro, O.D., F.A.A.O.
Medical Staff . . . . Steve Franzino, M.D., Robert Millard, M.D., Mark Sontag, M.D.

SVS&E/Business Operations
Senior Director of Communications. . . . . Ken Arnold
Director of Broadcasting . . . . Frank Albin
Director of Ticket Sales . . . . John Castro
Director of Advertising & Promotions . . . . Andrew Ebel
Director of Media Relations. . . . . Scott Emmert
Director of Fan Development/The Sharks Foundation . Rob Jaynes
Director of Event Presentation. . . . . Steve Maroni
Director, Corporate Partnerships. . . . . Bryan Deierling
Director of Suite Sales & Service . . . . Bruce Ross
Director of Communications & Internet Services . . . Roger Ross
Director of Public Relations . . . . Jim Sparaco
Senior Sales Manager, Corporate Partnerships. . . . . Jennifer Birmingham
Senior Ticket Operations Manager . . . . Scott Fitzsimmons
Senior Service Manager, Corporate Partnerships . . . Heather Hunter
Managers, Corporate Partnerships . . . . Shawn Adelsberg, Spencer Jamison, Justin Piper
Event Account Rep., Corporate Partnerships . . . . . . Tarrah Pollaro
Account Sales Managers . . . . Ted Chuba, Patrick Frost, Adam King, Adam Requarth
Account Service Managers . . . . Sharon Holman, Sarah Bauerle, Julie Kennedy
Marketing Manager . . . . Doug Bentz
HP Pavilion Group Sales Manager . . . . TBD
Media Relations Manager . . . . Tom Holy
Suite Sales Manager . . . . Chris Hutchins
Creative Services Manager . . . . Michelle Kracht
Sharks Foundation Manager . . . . Laura Johnston
Mascot Operations Manager. . . . . Tim Patnode
Suite Service Manager. . . . . Kathy Payne-Tovar
Service Managers, Corporate Partnerships. . . . . Ryan Hilgers, Allison Lucia
Media Relations and Team Services Coordinator . . . Ryan Stenn
Executive Assistant . . . . Mary Grace Miller

Finance
Director of Human Resources . . . . Cathy Chandler
Manager of Information Technology. . . . . Uy Ut
Controller. . . . . Stephanie Reitz

Building Operations
Director of Ticket Operations . . . . Daniel DeBoer
Director of Booking & Events . . . . Steve Kirsner, James Hamnett
Director of Guest Services. . . . . David Cahill
Director of Building Services . . . . Monte Chavez
Facilities Technical Director . . . . Greg Carrolan

Miscellaneous
Television Station . . . . FSN Bay Area
Radio Network Flagship . . . . 98.5 K-FOX (KUFX FM)
Television Play-By-Play/Color . . . . Randy Hahn/Drew Remenda
Radio Play-By-Play/Color . . . . Dan Rusanowsky/Jamie Baker
Radio Reporter . . . . Dave Maley
In Game TV Host . . . . John Shrader
Production Associate . . . . Elisabeth Farkas
Team Photographers. . . . . Don Smith, Rocky Widner
P.A. Announcer . . . . Joe Ike
In Game Host . . . . Danny Miller
Mascot. . . . . S.J. Sharkie

Tampa Bay Lightning

2006-07 Results: 44W-33L-3OTL-2SOL 93PTS. Second, Southeast Division

Key Off-Season Signings/Acquisitions

2007

May 9 • Re-signed RW **Jason Ward**.

16 • Re-signed C **Andreas Karlsson**.

19 • Re-signed G **Johan Holmqvist**.

31 • Named **Mike Sullivan** assistant coach.

31 • Signed 2006 1st-round pick (15th overall), G **Riku Helenius**.

June 13 • Acquired C **Chris Gratton** from Florida for a 2nd-round pick in the 2007 Entry Draft.

14 • Signed LW **Jan Hlavac**.

21 • Re-signed D **Shane O'Brien**.

July 1 • Signed RW **Michel Ouellet**.

3 • Signed D **Brad Lukowich**.

13 • Re-signed D **Paul Ranger**.

Aug. 6 • C **Ryan Craig** awarded one-year contract in arbitration.

Year-by-Year Record

		Home				Road				Overall								
Season	**GP**	**W**	**L**	**T**	**OL**	**W**	**L**	**T**	**OL**	**W**	**L**	**T**	**OL**	**GF**	**GA**	**Pts.**	**Finished**	**Playoff Result**
2006-07	82	22	18	....	1	22	15	....	4	44	33	....	5	253	261	93	2nd, Southeast Div.	Lost Conf. Quarter-Final
2005-06	82	25	14	....	2	18	19	....	4	43	33	....	6	252	260	92	2nd, Southeast Div.	Lost Conf. Quarter-Final
2004-05	....	....	....	....	....	....	....	....	....	....	....	....	....	....	....	....		
2003-04	**82**	**24**	**10**	**4**	**3**	**22**	**12**	**4**	**3**	**46**	**22**	**8**	**6**	**245**	**192**	**106**	**1st, Southeast Div.**	**Won Stanley Cup**
2002-03	82	22	9	7	3	14	16	9	2	36	25	16	5	219	210	93	1st, Southeast Div.	Lost Conf. Semi-Final
2001-02	82	16	17	5	3	11	23	6	1	27	40	11	4	178	219	69	3rd, Southeast Div.	Out of Playoffs
2000-01	82	17	19	3	2	7	28	3	3	24	47	6	5	201	280	59	5th, Southeast Div.	Out of Playoffs
1999-2000	82	13	20	4	4	6	27	5	3	19	47	9	7	204	310	54	4th, Southeast Div.	Out of Playoffs
1998-99	82	12	25	4	....	7	29	5	....	19	54	9	....	179	292	47	4th, Southeast Div.	Out of Playoffs
1997-98	82	11	23	7	....	6	32	3	....	17	55	10	....	151	269	44	7th, Atlantic Div.	Out of Playoffs
1996-97	82	15	18	8	....	17	22	2	....	32	40	10	....	217	247	74	6th, Atlantic Div.	Out of Playoffs
1995-96	82	22	14	5	....	16	18	7	....	38	32	12	....	238	248	88	5th, Atlantic Div.	Lost Conf. Quarter-Final
1994-95	48	10	14	0	....	7	14	3	....	17	28	3	....	120	144	37	6th, Atlantic Div.	Out of Playoffs
1993-94	84	14	22	6	....	16	21	5	....	30	43	11	....	224	251	71	7th, Atlantic Div.	Out of Playoffs
1992-93	84	12	27	3	....	11	27	4	....	23	54	7	....	245	332	53	6th, Norris Div.	Out of Playoffs

2007-08 Schedule

Oct.	Thu.	4	New Jersey
	Sat.	6	Atlanta
	Wed.	10	Florida
	Sat.	13	at Florida
	Thu.	18	at Boston
	Sat.	20	Atlanta
	Wed.	24	at Washington
	Thu.	25	Philadelphia
	Sat.	27	Buffalo
	Mon.	29	at NY Rangers
	Wed.	31	at New Jersey
Nov.	Thu.	1	at NY Islanders
	Sat.	3	Atlanta
	Mon.	5	at Florida
	Wed.	7	Florida
	Thu.	8	at Carolina
	Sat.	10	at Washington
	Wed.	14	Carolina
	Fri.	16	Washington
	Mon.	19	at Atlanta
	Wed.	21	NY Rangers
	Fri.	23	at Carolina
	Sat.	24	New Jersey
	Wed.	28	at Chicago
	Thu.	29	at Detroit
Dec.	Sat.	1	Boston
	Tue.	4	Ottawa
	Thu.	6	Carolina
	Sat.	8	NY Islanders
	Mon.	10	at Toronto
	Tue.	11	at Montreal
	Thu.	13	Calgary
	Sat.	15	Washington
	Tue.	18	at Atlanta
	Thu.	20	Toronto
	Sat.	22	Carolina
	Wed.	26	at Washington
	Thu.	27	Montreal
	Sat.	29	Philadelphia*
Jan.	Tue.	1	at Toronto
	Thu.	3	at Montreal
	Sat.	5	at Ottawa
	Tue.	8	at NY Rangers
	Thu.	10	Pittsburgh
	Sat.	12	at Florida
	Tue.	15	Colorado
	Fri.	18	at Pittsburgh
	Sat.	19	at Ottawa
	Tue.	22	Edmonton
	Thu.	24	Ottawa
	Tue.	29	Buffalo
	Thu.	31	Vancouver
Feb.	Sat.	2	Florida
	Tue.	5	at St. Louis
	Thu.	7	at Nashville
	Sat.	9	at Atlanta
	Tue.	12	Montreal
	Thu.	14	at Philadelphia
	Sat.	16	Washington
	Wed.	20	at Buffalo
	Thu.	21	at NY Islanders
	Sat.	23	Boston
	Wed.	27	Minnesota
	Fri.	29	Toronto
Mar.	Sat.	1	at Carolina
	Tue.	4	Pittsburgh
	Thu.	6	at Philadelphia
	Fri.	7	at New Jersey
	Sun.	9	at Columbus*
	Tue.	11	NY Islanders
	Thu.	13	at Boston
	Sat.	15	NY Rangers
	Wed.	19	at Buffalo
	Thu.	20	at Pittsburgh
	Sat.	22	at Florida
	Tue.	25	Florida
	Thu.	27	Washington
	Sat.	29	Carolina
	Mon.	31	Atlanta
Apr.	Wed.	2	at Carolina
	Thu.	3	at Washington
	Sat.	5	at Atlanta

* Denotes afternoon game.

Martin St. Louis and Vincent Lecavalier make an odd couple, but they're a dynamic duo. Lecavalier led the NHL with 52 goals in 2006-07 and led the Lightning with 108 points. St. Louis topped the team with 59 assists and had 102 points.

SOUTHEAST DIVISION
16th NHL Season

Franchise date: December 16, 1991

2007-08 Player Personnel

FORWARDS	HT	WT	S	Place of Birth	*Age	2006-07 Club
CRAIG, Ryan	6-2	220	L	Abbotsford, B.C.	25	Tampa Bay
DARCHE, Mathieu	6-1	220	L	St. Laurent, Que.	30	San Jose-Worcester
GRATTON, Chris	6-4	231	L	Brantford, Ont.	32	Florida
HLAVAC, Jan	6-0	185	L	Prague, Czech.	31	Sparta
JONES, Blair	6-3	210	R	Central Butte, Sask.	21	Tampa Bay-Springfield
KARLSSON, Andreas	6-4	205	L	Ludvika, Sweden	32	Tampa Bay
LECAVALIER, Vincent	6-4	223	L	Ile Bizard, Que.	27	Tampa Bay
MacDONALD, Craig	6-1	195	L	Antigonish, N.S.	30	Chicago-Norfolk
MILLEY, Norm	6-0	211	R	Toronto, Ont.	27	Springfield
OUELLET, Michel	6-0	203	R	Rimouski, Que.	25	Pittsburgh
PROSPAL, Vaclav	6-1	194	L	Ceske Budejovice, Czech.	32	Tampa Bay
RICHARDS, Brad	6-0	198	L	Murray Harbour, P.E.I.	27	Tampa Bay
ROY, Andre	6-4	225	L	Port Chester, NY	32	Pittsburgh-Tampa Bay
ST. LOUIS, Martin	5-9	185	L	Laval, Que.	32	Tampa Bay
STEWART, Karl	5-11	185	L	Aurora, Ont.	24	Pit-Chi-T.B.
TARNASKY, Nick	6-2	233	L	Rocky Mtn. House, Alta.	22	Tampa Bay
TAYLOR, Tim	6-1	190	L	Stratford, Ont.	38	Tampa Bay
WANVIG, Kyle	6-2	210	R	Calgary, Alta.	26	Chi (AHL)-T.B.-Sprfld
WARD, Jason	6-2	205	R	Chapleau, Ont.	28	NYR-L.A.-T.B.
DEFENSEMEN						
BOYLE, Dan	5-11	190	R	Ottawa, Ont.	31	Tampa Bay
JANCEVSKI, Dan	6-3	220	L	Windsor, Ont.	26	Hamilton
JANIK, Doug	6-2	209	L	Agawam, MA	27	Tampa Bay
KUBA, Filip	6-3	205	L	Ostrava, Czech.	30	Tampa Bay
LAMPMAN, Bryce	6-1	199	L	Rochester, MN	25	NY Rangers-Hartford
LEACH, Jay	6-4	220	L	Syracuse, NY	28	Providence (AHL)
LUKOWICH, Brad	6-1	205	L	Cranbrook, B.C.	31	New Jersey
O'BRIEN, Shane	6-2	228	L	Port Hope, Ont.	24	Anaheim-Tampa Bay
RANGER, Paul	6-2	215	L	Whitby, Ont.	23	Tampa Bay
ROGERS, Andy	6-5	206	L	Calgary, Alta.	21	Springfield
SCHNEIDER, David	5-9	190	L	Melrose Park, IL	28	HPK
SMABY, Matt	6-6	239	L	Minneapolis, MN	22	Springfield

GOALTENDERS	HT	WT	C	Place of Birth	*Age	2006-07 Club
DENIS, Marc	6-1	193	L	Montreal, Que.	30	Tampa Bay
HOLMQVIST, Johan	6-3	195	L	Tolfta, Sweden	29	Tampa Bay
RAMO, Karri	6-2	192	L	Asikkala, Finland	21	Tampa Bay-Springfield

* – Age at start of 2007-08 season

Coaching History

Terry Crisp, 1992-93 to 1996-97; Terry Crisp, Rick Paterson and Jacques Demers, 1997-98; Jacques Demers, 1998-99; Steve Ludzik, 1999-2000; Steve Ludzik and John Tortorella, 2000-01; John Tortorella, 2001-02 to date.

Coach

JOHN TORTORELLA
Coach, Tampa Bay Lightning. Born in Boston, MA, June 24, 1958.

John Tortorella took over as head coach in Tampa Bay on January 6, 2001. He led the team to its first Eastern Conference and Stanley Cup championships, as well as its second consecutive Southeast Division championship in 2003-04. He was the winner of the Jack Adams Award as the National Hockey League's top coach after leading the Lightning to franchise records with 46 wins and 106 points before embarking on the successful playoff campaign. He is the winningest coach in franchise history.

A 14-year NHL coaching veteran, Tortorella became the fourth head coach in team history when he was named to that position on January 6, 2001. Recognized as one of the top teaching coaches in the game, the Boston native joined the Lightning organization when he was hired on as an associate coach prior to the 2000-01 season.

Tortorella began his playing career at Salem State College before transferring to the University of Maine. He spent three seasons with the Black Bears and was twice named an ECAC All-Star. After playing in Sweden, Tortorella played in the Atlantic Coast Hockey League with Virginia, Hampton Roads, and Erie. He spent two seasons as general manager and head coach of the Virginia Lancers (ACHL) from 1986 to 1988, where he garnered coach of the year honors both years while leading his 1986-87 team to the league championship. He was hired as an assistant coach with the New Haven Nighthawks of the American Hockey League in 1988-89 and became an assistant coach with the Buffalo Sabres the following season. Tortorella remained with the Sabres organization through the 1996-97 season, including two years as coach of their AHL affiliate in Rochester.

Tortorella returned to the NHL in 1997 as an assistant with the Phoenix Coyotes, where he spent two seasons before joining the Rangers for 1999-2000. He served as the Rangers' interim head coach for the final four games of the '99-00 season before joining the Lightning staff.

Coaching Record

		Regular Season				Playoffs		
Season	Team	Games	W	L	O/T	Games	W	L
1995-96	Rochester (AHL)	80	37	38	5	19	15	4
1996-97	Rochester (AHL)	80	40	30	9	10	6	4
1999-2000	**NY Rangers (NHL)**	**4**	**0**	**3**	**1**	....	....	....
2000-01	**Tampa Bay (NHL)**	**43**	**12**	**30**	**1**	....	....	....
2001-02	**Tampa Bay (NHL)**	**82**	**27**	**44**	**11**	....	....	....
2002-03	**Tampa Bay (NHL)**	**82**	**36**	**30**	**16**	**11**	**5**	**6**
2003-04*	**Tampa Bay (NHL)**	**82**	**46**	**28**	**8**	**23**	**16**	**7**
2004-05	**Tampa Bay (NHL)**				Season Cancelled			
2005-06	**Tampa Bay (NHL)**	**82**	**43**	**33**	**6**	**5**	**1**	**4**
2006-07	**Tampa Bay (NHL)**	**82**	**44**	**33**	**5**	**6**	**2**	**4**
	NHL Totals	**457**	**208**	**201**	**48**	**45**	**24**	**21**

* Stanley Cup win.

2006-07 Scoring

* – rookie

Regular Season

Pos	#	Player	Team	GP	G	A	Pts	+/-	PIM	PP	SH	GW	S	%
C	4	Vincent Lecavalier	T.B.	82	52	56	108	2	44	16	5	7	339	15.3
R	26	Martin St. Louis	T.B.	82	43	59	102	7	28	14	5	7	273	15.8
C	19	Brad Richards	T.B.	82	25	45	70	–19	23	12	1	3	272	9.2
D	22	Dan Boyle	T.B.	82	20	43	63	–5	62	10	1	4	203	9.9
L	20	Vaclav Prospal	T.B.	82	14	41	55	–24	36	2	0	1	219	6.4
D	71	Filip Kuba	T.B.	81	15	22	37	–9	36	5	1	2	106	14.2
C	9	Eric Perrin	T.B.	82	13	23	36	–7	30	2	1	0	151	8.6
R	17	Ruslan Fedotenko	T.B.	80	12	20	32	–3	52	2	0	1	154	7.8
D	54	Paul Ranger	T.B.	72	4	24	28	5	42	0	0	2	90	4.4
C	34	Ryan Craig	T.B.	72	14	13	27	–11	55	4	0	2	130	10.8
R	16	Jason Ward	NYR	46	4	6	10	–3	26	0	1	1	68	5.9
			L.A.	7	0	1	1	–1	4	0	0	0	2	0.0
			T.B.	17	4	4	8	–11	10	0	0	0	38	10.5
			TOTAL	70	8	11	19	–15	40	0	1	1	108	7.4
D	55	* Shane O'Brien	ANA	62	2	12	14	5	140	1	0	2	55	3.6
			T.B.	18	0	2	2	–8	36	0	0	0	17	0.0
			TOTAL	80	2	14	16	–3	176	1	0	2	72	2.8
D	21	Cory Sarich	T.B.	82	0	15	15	–6	70	0	0	0	64	0.0
D	3	Doug Janik	T.B.	75	2	9	11	–11	53	0	0	0	49	4.1
C	74	* Nick Tarnasky	T.B.	77	5	4	9	–6	80	0	0	1	41	12.2
C	24	Andreas Karlsson	T.B.	53	3	6	9	–4	12	0	0	1	25	12.0
D	44	Nolan Pratt	T.B.	81	1	7	8	0	44	0	0	0	30	3.3
C	27	Tim Taylor	T.B.	71	1	5	6	–5	16	0	0	1	59	1.7
L	61	* Karl Stewart	PIT	3	0	0	0	–1	2	0	0	0	0	0.0
			CHI	37	2	3	5	–2	43	0	1	0	19	10.5
			T.B.	7	0	0	0	–2	2	0	0	0	2	0.0
			TOTAL	47	2	3	5	–5	47	0	1	0	21	9.5
C	49	* Blair Jones	T.B.	20	1	2	3	0	2	0	0	0	6	16.7
L	36	Andre Roy	PIT	5	0	0	0	–1	12	0	0	0	1	0.0
			T.B.	51	1	2	3	–3	116	0	0	0	14	7.1
			TOTAL	56	1	2	3	–4	128	0	0	0	15	6.7
D	7	Luke Richardson	T.B.	27	0	3	3	3	16	0	0	0	3	0.0
R	56	Kyle Wanvig	T.B.	4	0	0	0	0	0	0	0	0	0	0.0

Goaltending

No.	Goaltender	GPI	Mins	Avg	W	L	OT	EN	SO	GA	SA	S%	G	A	PIM
40	Johan Holmqvist	48	2548	2.85	27	15	3	4	1	121	1134	.893	0	3	4
30	Marc Denis	44	2353	3.19	17	18	2	5	1	125	1068	.883	0	0	2
31	* Karri Ramo	2	70	3.43	0	0	0	0	0	4	23	.826	0	0	0
	Totals	**82**	**4995**	**3.11**	**44**	**33**	**5**	**9**	**2**	**259**	**2234**	**.884**			

Playoffs

Pos	#	Player	Team	GP	G	A	Pts	+/-	PIM	PP	SH	GW	OT	S	%
R	26	Martin St. Louis	T.B.	6	3	5	8	6	8	1	0	0	0	17	17.6
C	19	Brad Richards	T.B.	6	3	5	8	–4	6	2	0	0	0	26	11.5
C	4	Vincent Lecavalier	T.B.	6	5	2	7	4	10	1	0	1	0	30	16.7
L	20	Vaclav Prospal	T.B.	6	1	4	5	2	4	0	0	1	0	15	6.7
D	71	Filip Kuba	T.B.	6	1	4	5	–1	4	0	1	0	0	13	7.7
C	9	Eric Perrin	T.B.	6	1	1	2	–4	2	0	0	0	0	8	12.5
R	16	Jason Ward	T.B.	6	0	1	1	–6	6	0	0	0	0	9	0.0
D	22	Dan Boyle	T.B.	6	0	1	1	0	2	0	0	0	0	14	0.0
D	54	Paul Ranger	T.B.	6	0	1	1	3	4	0	0	0	0	6	0.0
D	3	Doug Janik	T.B.	1	0	0	0	0	0	0	0	0	0	0	0.0
R	17	Ruslan Fedotenko	T.B.	4	0	0	0	–4	4	0	0	0	0	1	0.0
C	27	Tim Taylor	T.B.	6	0	0	0	0	0	0	0	0	0	9	0.0
D	44	Nolan Pratt	T.B.	6	0	0	0	–2	5	0	0	0	0	1	0.0
C	24	Andreas Karlsson	T.B.	6	0	0	0	–1	0	0	0	0	0	5	0.0
L	36	Andre Roy	T.B.	6	0	0	0	0	17	0	0	0	0	1	0.0
D	21	Cory Sarich	T.B.	6	0	0	0	0	2	0	0	0	0	2	0.0
C	34	Ryan Craig	T.B.	6	0	0	0	–1	12	0	0	0	0	5	0.0
D	55	* Shane O'Brien	T.B.	6	0	0	0	–4	12	0	0	0	0	3	0.0
C	74	* Nick Tarnasky	T.B.	6	0	0	0	–1	10	0	0	0	0	3	0.0

Goaltending

No.	Goaltender	GPI	Mins	Avg	W	L	EN	SO	GA	SA	S%	G	A	PIM
40	Johan Holmqvist	6	370	2.92	2	4	1	0	18	168	.893	0	0	0
	Totals	**6**	**373**	**3.06**	**2**	**4**	**1**	**0**	**19**	**169**	**.888**			

General Managers' History

Phil Esposito, 1992-93 to 1997-98; Jacques Demers, 1998-99; Rick Dudley, 1999-2000, 2000-01; Rick Dudley and Jay Feaster, 2001-02; Jay Feaster, 2002-03 to date.

Club Records

Team

(Figures in brackets for season records are games played; records for fewest points, wins, ties, losses, goals, goals against are for 70 or more games)

Most Points **106** 2003-04 (82)
Most Wins **46** 2003-04 (82)
Most Ties **16** 2002-03 (82)
Most Losses **55** 1997-98 (82)
Most Goals **253** 2006-07 (82)
Most Goals Against **332** 1992-93 (84)
Fewest Points **44** 1997-98 (82)
Fewest Wins **17** 1997-98 (82)
Fewest Ties **6** 2000-01 (82)
Fewest Losses **22** 2003-04 (82)
Fewest Goals **151** 1997-98 (82)
Fewest Goals Against **192** 2003-04 (82)
Longest Winning Streak
Overall .... **8** Feb. 23-Mar. 6/04
Home .... **8** Mar. 17-Apr. 8/06
Away .... **5** Feb. 23-Mar. 6/04
Longest Undefeated Streak
Overall .... **13** Mar. 7-Apr. 2/03 (7 wins, 6 ties)
Home .... **10** Jan. 29-Mar. 12/03 (9 wins, 1 tie)
Away .... **7** Feb. 23-Mar. 10/04 (6 wins, 1 tie)
Longest Losing Streak
Overall .... **13** Jan. 3-Feb. 2/98
Home .... **10** Jan. 3-Feb. 26/98
Away .... **11** Oct. 24-Dec. 10/97
Longest Winless Streak
Overall .... **16** Oct. 10-Nov. 17/97 (15 losses, 1 tie), Jan. 2-Feb. 5/98 (14 losses, 2 ties)
Home .... **11** Jan. 2-Feb. 26/98 (10 losses, 1 tie)
Away .... **17** Dec. 2/99-Feb. 19/00 (14 losses, 3 ties)
Most Shutouts, Season **9** 2001-02 (82)
Most PIM, Season **1,823** 1997-98 (82)
Most Goals, Game .... **9** Nov. 8/03 (Pit. 0 at T.B. 9)

Individual

Most Seasons .... **8** Pavel Kubina, Vincent Lecavalier
Most Games, Career .... **629** Vincent Lecavalier
Most Goals, Career .... **233** Vincent Lecavalier
Most Assists, Career .... **306** Brad Richards
Most Points, Career .... **510** Vincent Lecavalier (233G, 277A)
Most PIM, Career .... **782** Chris Gratton
Most Shutouts, Career .... **14** Nikolai Khabibulin
Longest Consecutive Games Streak .... **388** Cory Sarich (Nov. 27/01 to date)
Most Goals, Season .... **52** Vincent Lecavalier (2006-07)
Most Assists, Season .... **68** Brad Richards (2005-06)
Most Points, Season .... **108** Vincent Lecavalier (2006-07; 52G, 56A)
Most PIM, Season .... **258** Enrico Ciccone (1995-96)
Most Points, Defenseman, Season .... **65** Roman Hamrlik (1995-96; 16G, 49A)
Most Points, Center, Season .... **91** Brad Richards (2005-06; 23G, 68A)
Most Points, Right Wing, Season .... **102** Martin St. Louis (2006-07; 43G, 59A)
Most Points, Left Wing, Season .... **80** Cory Stillman (2003-04; 25G, 55A), Vaclav Prospal (2005-06; 25G, 55A)
Most Points, Rookie, Season .... **62** Brad Richards (2000-01; 21G, 41A)
Most Shutouts, Season .... **7** Nikolai Khabibulin (2001-02)
Most Goals, Game .... **4** Chris Kontos (Oct. 7/92)
Most Assists, Game .... **4** Four times
Most Points, Game .... **6** Doug Crossman (Nov. 7/92; 3G, 3A)

Captains' History

No captain, 1992-93 to 1994-95; Paul Ysebaert, 1995-96, 1996-97; Paul Ysebaert and Mikael Renberg, 1997-98; Rob Zamuner, 1998-99; Bill Houlder, Chris Gratton and Vincent Lecavalier, 1999-2000; Vincent Lecavalier, 2000-01; no captain, 2001-02; Dave Andreychuk, 2002-03, 2003-04; Dave Andreychuk and no captain, 2005-06; Tim Taylor, 2006-07.

All-time Record vs. Other Clubs

Regular Season

	At Home								On Road								Total							
	GP	W	L	T	OL	GF	GA	PTS	GP	W	L	T	OL	GF	GA	PTS	GP	W	L	T	OL	GF	GA	PTS
Anaheim	10	4	6	0	0	20	27	8	9	3	5	1	0	22	28	7	19	7	11	1	0	42	55	15
Atlanta	21	14	5	1	1	78	52	30	21	7	10	3	1	58	66	18	42	21	15	4	2	136	118	48
Boston	27	10	12	3	2	77	81	25	27	2	16	6	3	66	105	13	54	12	28	9	5	143	186	38
Buffalo	27	6	16	3	2	56	85	17	27	9	15	2	1	74	83	21	54	15	31	5	3	130	168	38
Calgary	10	5	4	1	0	31	32	11	11	5	5	0	1	27	34	11	21	10	9	1	1	58	66	22
Carolina	34	20	11	3	0	102	89	43	35	9	17	7	2	97	109	27	69	29	28	10	2	199	198	70
Chicago	12	5	3	3	1	29	30	14	14	4	8	2	0	35	45	10	26	9	11	5	1	64	75	24
Colorado	12	8	2	1	1	39	32	18	14	3	9	2	0	30	54	8	26	11	11	3	1	69	86	26
Columbus	4	3	1	0	0	9	5	6	3	1	1	1	0	4	5	3	7	4	2	1	0	13	10	9
Dallas	14	1	10	2	1	21	39	5	12	4	7	1	0	33	42	9	26	5	17	3	1	54	81	14
Detroit	15	4	9	1	1	46	67	10	12	1	10	1	0	21	47	3	27	5	19	2	1	67	114	13
Edmonton	11	3	5	2	1	31	35	9	11	4	7	0	0	24	27	8	22	7	12	2	1	55	62	17
Florida	36	14	15	6	1	81	105	35	36	9	19	4	4	86	117	26	72	23	34	10	5	167	222	61
Los Angeles	11	6	4	0	1	26	24	13	12	9	1	2	0	40	25	20	23	15	5	2	1	66	49	33
Minnesota	3	1	1	1	0	8	9	3	4	1	3	0	0	11	15	2	7	2	4	1	0	19	24	5
Montreal	27	10	11	5	1	64	75	26	26	11	14	1	0	61	72	23	53	21	25	6	1	125	147	49
Nashville	5	2	1	2	0	15	13	6	6	4	2	0	0	16	12	8	11	6	3	2	0	31	25	14
New Jersey	29	10	14	5	0	65	86	25	30	9	19	2	0	61	106	20	59	19	33	7	0	126	192	45
NY Islanders	30	16	12	2	0	82	89	34	29	15	12	1	1	83	85	32	59	31	24	3	1	165	174	66
NY Rangers	29	14	11	3	1	99	96	32	31	13	15	2	1	89	100	29	60	27	26	5	2	188	196	61
Ottawa	27	9	15	2	1	76	96	21	27	9	18	0	0	61	103	18	54	18	33	2	1	137	199	39
Philadelphia	30	12	16	1	1	89	88	26	29	8	14	7	0	65	86	23	59	20	30	8	1	154	174	49
Phoenix	11	6	5	0	0	38	36	12	12	6	6	0	0	29	29	12	23	12	11	0	0	67	65	24
Pittsburgh	27	16	9	2	0	88	64	34	27	9	14	3	1	74	100	22	54	25	23	5	1	162	164	56
St. Louis	14	6	5	3	0	43	46	15	11	1	9	0	1	24	44	3	25	7	14	3	1	67	90	18
San Jose	13	7	5	1	0	34	35	15	11	6	4	1	0	37	35	13	24	13	9	2	0	71	70	28
Toronto	24	5	17	1	1	51	82	12	25	7	16	1	1	65	94	16	49	12	33	2	2	116	176	28
Vancouver	9	3	5	0	1	31	37	7	10	0	7	2	1	18	45	3	19	3	12	2	2	49	82	10
Washington	37	15	20	2	0	94	115	32	37	11	20	4	2	92	132	28	74	26	40	6	2	186	247	60
Totals	**559**	**235**	**250**	**56**	**18**	**1523**	**1670**	**544**	**559**	**180**	**303**	**56**	**20**	**1403**	**1845**	**436**	**1118**	**415**	**553**	**112**	**38**	**2926**	**3515**	**980**

Playoffs

	Series	W	L	GP	W	L	T	GF	GA	Last Mtg.	Rnd.	Result
Calgary	1	1	0	7	4	3	0	13	14	2004	F	W 4-3
Montreal	1	1	0	4	4	0	0	14	5	2004	CSF	W 4-0
New Jersey	2	0	2	11	3	8	0	22	33	2007	CQF	L 2-4
NY Islanders	1	1	0	5	4	1	0	12	5	2004	CQF	W 4-1
Ottawa	1	0	1	5	1	4	0	13	23	2006	CQF	L 1-4
Philadelphia	2	1	1	13	6	7	0	34	45	2004	CF	W 4-3
Washington	1	1	0	6	4	2	0	14	15	2003	CQF	W 4-2
Totals	**9**	**5**	**4**	**51**	**26**	**25**	**0**	**122**	**140**			

Playoff Results 2007-2002

Year	Round	Opponent	Result	GF	GA
2007	CQF	New Jersey	L 2-4	14	19
2006	CQF	Ottawa	L 1-4	13	23
2004	**F**	**Calgary**	**W 4-3**	**13**	**14**
	CF	Philadelphia	W 4-3	21	19
	CSF	Montreal	W 4-0	14	5
	CQF	NY Islanders	W 4-1	12	5
2003	CSF	New Jersey	L 1-4	8	14
	CQF	Washington	W 4-2	14	15

Abbreviations: Round: F – Final; **CF** – conference final; **CSF** – conference semi-final; **CQF** – conference quarter-final.

Carolina totals include Hartford, 1992-93 to 1996-97.
Dallas totals include Minnesota North Stars, 1992-93.

Colorado totals include Quebec, 1992-93 to 1994-95.
Phoenix totals include Winnipeg, 1992-93 to 1995-96.

2006-07 Results

Month	Date	Opponent	Score
Oct.	5	at Atlanta	3-2†
	7	Boston	2-3
	9	Atlanta	0-1
	13	at Florida	2-3
	14	Florida	4-1
	16	Carolina	1-5
	19	Philadelphia	4-1
	21	at Washington	6-4
	26	Carolina	5-1
	28	at Carolina	4-6
	29	San Jose	2-4
Nov.	1	Toronto	2-4
	2	at Philadelphia	5-2
	4	at Boston	5-6*
	6	at NY Islanders	5-1
	8	at Pittsburgh	4-3*
	11	Atlanta	5-3
	15	Montreal	1-3
	17	NY Islanders	3-2†
	19	at NY Rangers	1-4
	20	at Buffalo	2-7
	22	at Florida	6-4
	24	Atlanta	3-2*
	26	Ottawa	3-1
	28	Washington	2-5
	30	at Boston	3-4†
Dec.	2	at Ottawa	2-5
	5	Buffalo	1-4
	7	Atlanta	8-0
	9	Anaheim	3-4
	12	at Toronto	4-5
	14	at Montreal	2-4
	16	Carolina	2-3
	19	at Washington	5-4
	21	at Ottawa	4-2
	23	NY Rangers	4-3
	26	at Atlanta	1-2
	28	Philadelphia	3-4
	30	Montreal	3-1
Jan.	2	at Montreal	2-5
	4	at Minnesota	3-2
	5	at Colorado	2-4
	7	at Pittsburgh	3-2†
	9	Pittsburgh	3-2
	11	Washington	5-4
	13	at Buffalo	3-2
	15	at NY Islanders	4-3
	16	Toronto	2-4
	18	at New Jersey	3-2†
	20	at Carolina	6-5†
	26	New Jersey	0-2
	30	at Philadelphia	4-3†
Feb.	1	at Carolina	4-0
	3	NY Rangers	3-2
	6	Los Angeles	3-2†
	9	at NY Rangers	0-5
	11	at New Jersey	4-1
	13	Phoenix	5-3
	15	Washington	3-2†
	17	at Florida	4-5*
	20	Florida	3-2†
	22	at Atlanta	5-4*
	23	Boston	2-6
	25	Pittsburgh	5-1
	27	Dallas	1-2*
Mar.	1	at Washington	5-4†
	3	at Florida	2-6
	6	at Vancouver	1-5
	7	at Edmonton	3-1
	10	at Calgary	3-2*
	13	at Toronto	2-3
	16	Buffalo	2-3
	18	at Washington	1-7
	20	NY Islanders	4-3*
	22	New Jersey	3-1
	24	Ottawa	2-7
	27	Florida	2-5
	30	at Carolina	4-2
	31	Washington	5-2
Apr.	3	Carolina	3-2
	6	Florida	2-7
	7	at Atlanta	2-3†

* – Overtime † – Shootout

Entry Draft Selections 2007-1993

2007
Pick
47 Dana Tyrell
75 Luca Cunti
77 Alexander Killorn
107 Mitch Fadden
150 Matt Marshall
167 Johan Harju
183 Torrie Jung
197 Michael Ward
210 Justin Courtnall

2006
Pick
15 Riku Helenius
78 Kevin Quick
168 Dane Crowley
198 Denis Kazionov

2005
Pick
30 Vladimir Mihalik
73 Radek Smolenak
89 Chris Lawrence
92 Marek Bartanus
102 Blair Jones
133 Stanislav Lascek
163 Marek Kvapil
165 Kevin Beech
225 John Wessbecker

2004
Pick
30 Andy Rogers
65 Mark Tobin
102 Mike Lundin
158 Brandon Elliott
163 Dusty Collins
188 Jan Zapletal
191 Karri Ramo
245 Justin Keller

2003
Pick
34 Mike Egener
41 Matt Smaby
96 Jonathan Boutin
192 Doug O'Brien
224 Gerald Coleman
227 Jay Rosehill
255 Raimonds Danilics
256 Brady Greco
273 Albert Vishnyakov
286 Zbynek Hrdel
287 Nick Tarnasky

2002
Pick
60 Adam Henrich
100 Dmitri Kazionov
135 Joseph Pearce
162 Gerard Dicaire
170 P.J. Atherton
174 Karri Akkanen
183 Paul Ranger
213 Fredrik Norrena
233 Vasily Koshechkin
255 Ryan Craig
256 Darren Reid
286 Alexei Glukhov
287 John Toffey

2001
Pick
3 Alexander Svitov
47 Alexander Polushin
61 Andreas Holmqvist
94 Evgeny Artyukhin
123 Aaron Lobb
138 Paul Lynch
188 Art Femenella
219 Dennis Packard
222 Jeremy Van Hoof
252 J.F. Soucy
259 Dmitri Bezrukov
261 Vitali Smolyaninov
281 Ilja Solarev
289 Henrik Bergfors

2000
Pick
8 Nikita Alexeev
34 Ruslan Zainullin
81 Alexander Kharitonov
126 Johan Hagglund
161 Pavel Sedov
191 Aaron Gionet
222 Marek Priechodsky
226 Brian Eklund
233 Alexander Polukeyev
263 Thomas Ziegler

1999
Pick
47 Sheldon Keefe
67 Evgeny Konstantinov
75 Brett Scheffelmaier
88 Jimmie Olvestad
127 Kaspars Astashenko
148 Michal Lanicek
182 Fedor Fedorov
187 Ivan Rachunek
216 Erkki Rajamaki
244 Mikko Kuparinen

1998
Pick
1 Vincent Lecavalier
64 Brad Richards
72 Dmitry Afanasenkov
92 Eric Beaudoin
121 Curtis Rich
146 Sergei Kuznetsov
174 Brett Allan
194 Oak Hewer
221 Daniel Hulak
229 Chris Lyness
252 Martin Cibak

1997
Pick
7 Paul Mara
33 Kyle Kos
61 Matt Elich
108 Mark Thompson
109 Jan Sulc
112 Karel Betik
153 Andrei Skopintsev
168 Justin Jack
170 Eero Somervuori
185 Samuel St-Pierre
198 Shawn Skolney
224 Paul Comrie

1996
Pick
16 Mario Larocque
69 Curtis Tipler
125 Jason Robinson
152 Nikolai Ignatov
157 Xavier Delisle
179 Pavel Kubina

1995
Pick
5 Daymond Langkow
30 Mike McBain
56 Shane Willis
108 Konstantin Golokhvastov
134 Eduard Pershin
160 Cory Murphy
186 Joe Cardarelli
212 Zac Bierk

1994
Pick
8 Jason Wiemer
34 Colin Cloutier
55 Vadim Epanchintsev
86 Dmitri Klevakin
137 Daniel Juden
138 Bryce Salvador
164 Chris Maillet
190 Alexei Baranov
216 Yuri Smirnov
242 Shawn Gervais
268 Brian White

1993
Pick
3 Chris Gratton
29 Tyler Moss
55 Allan Egeland
81 Marian Kacir
107 Ryan Brown
133 Kiley Hill
159 Matthieu Raby
185 Ryan Nauss
211 Alexandre Laporte
237 Brett Duncan
263 Mark Szoke

Vice President and General Manager

JAY FEASTER
Executive Vice President/General Manager, Tampa Bay Lightning.
Born in Williamstown, PA, July 30, 1962.

Jay Feaster joined the Lightning on October 20, 1998 and was named general manager on February 10, 2002. He led Tampa Bay to the Stanley Cup in 2003-04 and was named NHL executive of the year by *The Sporting News*. The Lightning enjoyed a storybook season under Feaster's direction in 2003-04, winning a second consecutive Southeast Division title, capturing the top seed in the Eastern Conference and skating off with Lord Stanley's Cup after a hard-fought seven game series against the Calgary Flames. He has been widely praised for bringing continuity and stability to the Lightning franchise.

Feaster, named the fourth general manager in franchise history on February 10, 2002, joined the Lightning on October 20, 1998, from the Hershey Bears of the American Hockey League. He spent three-plus seasons as Tampa Bay's assistant general manager, overseeing all contractual, collective bargaining and NHL legal issues, as well as the organization's scouting department and its minor league affiliates. As general manager, Feaster has developed the Lightning into one of the most competitive and entertaining teams in the NHL. He also served as co-general manager of Team USA for the 2003 World Championships along with Larry Pleau of St. Louis.

To join the Lightning, Feaster resigned his post as president of the Hershey Bears and vice president of Hershey Sports and Entertainment. In that capacity, Feaster oversaw the operations of the Bears, the Hershey Wildcats professional soccer team and HersheyPark Arena/Stadium. In his nine years with the Bears, he led the team to a division title (1993-94) and a Calder Cup Championship (1997), while establishing three consecutive single-season attendance records (1991-92 to 1993-94) and entering into a five-year affiliation agreement with the NHL's Colorado Avalanche.

While in Hershey, Feaster spent time on the advisory boards of the Big 33 Scholarship Foundation, the Four Diamonds Fund at the Pennsylvania State University Milton S. Hershey Medical Center, and the Central PA Chapter of the National Multiple Sclerosis Society. He also taught business law and hotel law as a visiting faculty member at the Lebanon Valley College in Annville, Pennsylvania. Prior to joining the Hershey Company, Feaster practiced law with the firm of McNees, Wallace & Nurick in Harrisburg, Pennsylvania. He is a Summa Cum Laude graduate of Susquehanna University and a Cum Laude graduate of The Georgetown Law Center in Washington, D.C.

Club Directory

St. Pete Times Forum

Tampa Bay Lightning
St. Pete Times Forum
401 Channelside Drive
Tampa, FL 33602
Phone **813/301-6500**
FAX 813/301-1480
Ticket Info. 813/301-6600
www.tampabaylightning.com
Capacity: 19,758

Executive
Owner, Palace Sports & Entertainment .... Bill Davidson
Pres. of Palace Sports & Entertainment/Governor. . . Tom Wilson
Pres. of Tampa Bay Lightning/Alternate Governor . . Ron Campbell
Executive Vice President/Chief Operating Officer . . . Sean Henry
Executive VP of Corporate Sales & Marketing ..... Harry Hutt
Sr. Vice President of Sponsorship Sales .... Steve Grecsek
Director of Govt. Relations/Community Affairs .... Ron Pierce
Vice President of Sponsorship Sales............. Rob Keith
Vice President of Ticket Sales .... Todd Lambert
Vice President of Corporate Sales .... Kyle Draper
Executive Assistants .... Michele Rooney, Julie Stein
Executive Vice President, G.M. & Alt/Gov......... Jay Feaster
Hockey Ops Executive Assistant................ Elizabeth Sylvia
Executive Vice President Communications........ Bill Wickett
Vice President, Legal Affairs/Legal Counsel .... Paul Davis
Executive Vice President of Finance/CFO .... Joe Fada
Executive Director of Lightning Foundation .... Nancy Crane
Sr. Vice President of Administration .... David Everett

Hockey Operations
Executive Vice President, G.M. & Alt. Gov. .... Jay Feaster
Assistant General Manager.................... Claude Loiselle
Hockey Ops Executive Assistant................ Liz Sylvia
Director of Player Personnel .... Bill Barber
Assistant to the General Manager .... Ryan Belec
Head Coach .... John Tortorella
Assistant Coaches............................ Mike Sullivan, Jeff Reese
Strength & Conditioning Coach .... Eric Lawson
Video Coach................................ Nigel Kirwan
Chief Scout................................. Jake Goertzen
Associate Goaltending Coach & Scout .... Cory Schwab
Scouting Staff.............. Angelo Bumbacco, Charlie Hodge, Gerry O'Flaherty, Mikael Andersson, Stephen Baker, Larry Bernard, Dirk Graham, Dave Heitz, Kari Kettunen, Miroslav Prihoda, Darrell Young, Glen Zacharias, Cory Schwab, Yuri Yanchenkov
Director of Team Services .... Phil Thibodeau
Medical Director............................ Dr. Ira Guttentag
Head Medical Trainer .... Thomas Mulligan
Assistant Medical Trainer .... Jason Serbus
Massage Therapist .... Mike Griebel
Equipment Manager.......................... Ray Thill
Assistant Equipment Managers................. Jim Pickard, Rob Kennedy
Head Coach, Norfolk Admirals .... Steve Stirling
Assistant Coach, Norfolk Admirals .... Darren Rumble
Head Athletic Trainer, Norfolk Admirals.......... Rodney Bogart
Head Equipment Mgr, Norfolk Admirals .... Peter Henderson
Team Physician............................. Dr. Ira Guttentag

Premium Services
Director of Premium Services.................. Amanda Graul
Premium Services Ticket Manager.............. Missy Davis
Premium Services Suite Manager............... Lakisha Sharpe

Finance
Directors of Accounting .... Doug Riefler, Dave Weber
Accounts Payable .... Donna Clark
Staff Accountants........................... Jane Sheill, Debbie Myers, Krystal Mihopoulos

Internal Support Staff
Sr Vice President of Administration .... David Everett
Assistant Information Services Managers......... Rosie Chhuor, Jon Therrien
Manager of Web Services...................... Nick Gesacion

Box Office
Sr. Director of Ticket Operations .... Jim Mannino
Box Office Supervisors........................ Helen Junker, Clark Brooks, Bobby Lowman, Chad Therrien

Ticket Sales
Vice President of Ticket Sales .... Todd Lambert
Sr. Director of Group Sales .... Brad Lott
Director of Sales .... Patrick Duffy
Director of Suite Sales....................... Chris Diiorio

Sponsorship Sales and Marketing
Director of Promotions .... Mark Gullett
Sr Director of Corporate Partnerships .... Arden Robbins
Director of Corporate Partnerships .... Giles Dowden
Sr Director of Marketing .... Holly Brown
Director of Broadcast Production & Game Ops .... Jim Ciotoli
In Game Entertainment Coordinator .... Hope Reep
Director of Fan Development .... David Cole

Communications
Director of Public Relations .... Jay Preble
Media Relations Manager...................... Brian Breseman
Public Relations Coordinator, Tampa Bay Storm ... Jim Robinson
Executive Director of Lightning Foundation .... Nancy Crane
Community Relations/Lightning Foundation Mngr. . Arlynn Haarer

Broadcast Information
Director of Broadcasting & Programming .... Jason Dixon
Television .... Sun Sports Network
Television Broadcasters .... Rick Peckham, Bobby "the Chief" Taylor, Paul Kennedy
Radio .... WDAE 620 AM, WHOO 1080 AM (Orlando), WIXC 1060 AM (Melbourne), WDGF 1350 AM (Dade City)
Radio Broadcasters .... David Mishkin, Phil Esposito, Matt Sammon

Key Off-Season Signings/Acquisitions

2007

Apr. 26 • Re-signed C **Boyd Devereaux**.
May 8 • Re-signed D **Ian White**.
June 6 • Re-signed C **Nik Antropov**.
12 • Re-signed C **Mats Sundin**.
21 • Re-signed D **Carlo Colaiacovo**.
22 • Acquired G **Vesa Toskala** and C **Mark Bell** from San Jose for 1st-and 2nd-round picks in the 2007 Entry Draft and a 4th-round pick in 2009.
July 1 • Signed LW **Jason Blake**.
6 • Signed G **Scott Clemmensen**.

Toronto Maple Leafs

2006-07 Results: 40W-31L-4OTL-7SOL 91PTS.
Third, Northeast Division

Year-by-Year Record

Season	GP	Home W	Home L	Home T	Home OL	Road W	Road L	Road T	Road OL	Overall W	Overall L	Overall T	Overall OL	GF	GA	Pts.	Finished	Playoff Result
2006-07	82	21	15	....	5	19	16	....	6	40	31	....	11	258	269	91	3rd, Northeast Div.	Out of Playoffs
2005-06	82	26	12	....	3	15	21	....	5	41	33	....	8	257	270	90	4th, Northeast Div.	Out of Playoffs
2004-05	....	....	....	....	....	....	....	....	....	....	....	....	....	....	....	....		
2003-04	82	22	14	3	2	23	10	7	1	45	24	10	3	242	204	103	2nd, Northeast Div.	Lost Conf. Semi-Final
2002-03	82	24	13	4	0	20	15	3	3	44	28	7	3	236	208	98	2nd, Northeast Div.	Lost Conf. Quarter-Final
2001-02	82	24	11	6	0	19	14	4	4	43	25	10	4	249	207	100	2nd, Northeast Div.	Lost Conf. Championship
2000-01	82	19	11	7	4	18	18	4	1	37	29	11	5	232	207	90	3rd, Northeast Div.	Lost Conf. Semi-Final
1999-2000	82	24	12	5	0	21	15	2	3	45	27	7	3	246	222	100	1st, Northeast Div.	Lost Conf. Semi-Final
1998-99	82	23	13	5	....	22	17	2	....	45	30	7	....	268	231	97	2nd, Northeast Div.	Lost Conf. Championship
1997-98	82	16	20	5	....	14	23	4	....	30	43	9	....	194	237	69	6th, Central Div.	Out of Playoffs
1996-97	82	18	20	3	....	12	24	5	....	30	44	8	....	230	273	68	6th, Central Div.	Out of Playoffs
1995-96	82	19	15	7	....	15	21	5	....	34	36	12	....	247	252	80	3rd, Central Div.	Lost Conf. Quarter-Final
1994-95	48	15	7	2	....	6	12	6	....	21	19	8	....	135	146	50	4th, Central Div.	Lost Conf. Quarter-Final
1993-94	84	23	15	4	....	20	14	8	....	43	29	12	....	280	243	98	2nd, Central Div.	Lost Conf. Championship
1992-93	84	25	11	6	....	19	18	5	....	44	29	11	....	288	241	99	3rd, Norris Div.	Lost Conf. Championship
1991-92	80	21	16	3	....	9	27	4	....	30	43	7	....	234	294	67	5th, Norris Div.	Out of Playoffs
1990-91	80	15	21	4	....	8	25	7	....	23	46	11	....	241	318	57	5th, Norris Div.	Out of Playoffs
1989-90	80	24	14	2	....	14	24	2	....	38	38	4	....	337	358	80	3rd, Norris Div.	Lost Div. Semi-Final
1988-89	80	15	20	5	....	13	26	1	....	28	46	6	....	259	342	62	5th, Norris Div.	Out of Playoffs
1987-88	80	14	20	6	....	7	29	4	....	21	49	10	....	273	345	52	4th, Norris Div.	Lost Div. Semi-Final
1986-87	80	22	14	4	....	10	28	2	....	32	42	6	....	286	319	70	4th, Norris Div.	Lost Div. Final
1985-86	80	16	21	3	....	9	27	4	....	25	48	7	....	311	386	57	4th, Norris Div.	Lost Div. Final
1984-85	80	10	28	2	....	10	24	6	....	20	52	8	....	253	358	48	5th, Norris Div.	Out of Playoffs
1983-84	80	17	16	7	....	9	29	2	....	26	45	9	....	303	387	61	5th, Norris Div.	Out of Playoffs
1982-83	80	20	15	5	....	8	25	7	....	28	40	12	....	293	330	68	3rd, Norris Div.	Lost Div. Semi-Final
1981-82	80	12	20	8	....	8	24	8	....	20	44	16	....	298	380	56	5th, Norris Div.	Out of Playoffs
1980-81	80	14	21	5	....	14	16	10	....	28	37	15	....	322	367	71	5th, Adams Div.	Lost Prelim. Round
1979-80	80	17	19	4	....	18	21	1	....	35	40	5	....	304	327	75	4th, Adams Div.	Lost Prelim. Round
1978-79	80	20	12	8	....	14	21	5	....	34	33	13	....	267	252	81	3rd, Adams Div.	Lost Quarter-Final
1977-78	80	21	13	6	....	20	16	4	....	41	29	10	....	271	237	92	3rd, Adams Div.	Lost Semi-Final
1976-77	80	18	13	9	....	15	19	6	....	33	32	15	....	301	285	81	3rd, Adams Div.	Lost Quarter-Final
1975-76	80	23	12	5	....	11	19	10	....	34	31	15	....	294	276	83	3rd, Adams Div.	Lost Quarter-Final
1974-75	80	19	12	9	....	12	21	7	....	31	33	16	....	280	309	78	3rd, Adams Div.	Lost Quarter-Final
1973-74	78	21	11	7	....	14	16	9	....	35	27	16	....	274	230	86	4th, East Div.	Lost Quarter-Final
1972-73	78	20	12	7	....	7	29	3	....	27	41	10	....	247	279	64	6th, East Div.	Out of Playoffs
1971-72	78	21	11	7	....	12	20	7	....	33	31	14	....	209	208	80	4th, East Div.	Lost Quarter-Final
1970-71	78	24	9	6	....	13	24	2	....	37	33	8	....	248	211	82	4th, East Div.	Lost Quarter-Final
1969-70	76	18	13	7	....	11	21	6	....	29	34	13	....	222	242	71	6th, East Div.	Out of Playoffs
1968-69	76	20	8	10	....	15	18	5	....	35	26	15	....	234	217	85	4th, East Div.	Lost Quarter-Final
1967-68	74	24	9	4	....	9	22	6	....	33	31	10	....	209	176	76	5th, East Div.	Out of Playoffs
1966-67	**70**	**21**	**8**	**6**	....	**11**	**19**	**5**	....	**32**	**27**	**11**	....	**204**	**211**	**75**	**3rd,**	**Won Stanley Cup**
1965-66	70	22	9	4	....	12	16	7	....	34	25	11	....	208	187	79	3rd,	Lost Semi-Final
1964-65	70	17	15	3	....	13	11	11	....	30	26	14	....	204	173	74	4th,	Lost Semi-Final
1963-64	**70**	**22**	**7**	**6**	....	**11**	**18**	**6**	....	**33**	**25**	**12**	....	**192**	**172**	**78**	**3rd,**	**Won Stanley Cup**
1962-63	**70**	**21**	**8**	**6**	....	**14**	**15**	**6**	....	**35**	**23**	**12**	....	**221**	**180**	**82**	**1st,**	**Won Stanley Cup**
1961-62	**70**	**25**	**5**	**5**	....	**12**	**17**	**6**	....	**37**	**22**	**11**	....	**232**	**180**	**85**	**2nd,**	**Won Stanley Cup**
1960-61	70	21	6	8	....	18	13	4	....	39	19	12	....	234	176	90	2nd,	Lost Semi-Final
1959-60	70	20	9	6	....	15	17	3	....	35	26	9	....	199	195	79	2nd,	Lost Final
1958-59	70	17	13	5	....	10	19	6	....	27	32	11	....	189	201	65	4th,	Lost Final
1957-58	70	12	16	7	....	9	22	4	....	21	38	11	....	192	226	53	6th,	Out of Playoffs
1956-57	70	12	16	7	....	9	18	8	....	21	34	15	....	174	192	57	5th,	Out of Playoffs
1955-56	70	19	10	6	....	5	23	7	....	24	33	13	....	153	181	61	4th,	Lost Semi-Final
1954-55	70	14	10	11	....	10	14	11	....	24	24	22	....	147	135	70	3rd,	Lost Semi-Final
1953-54	70	22	6	7	....	10	18	7	....	32	24	14	....	152	131	78	3rd,	Lost Semi-Final
1952-53	70	17	12	6	....	10	18	7	....	27	30	13	....	156	167	67	5th,	Out of Playoffs
1951-52	70	17	10	8	....	12	15	8	....	29	25	16	....	168	157	74	3rd,	Lost Semi-Final
1950-51	**70**	**22**	**8**	**5**	....	**19**	**8**	**8**	....	**41**	**16**	**13**	....	**212**	**138**	**95**	**2nd,**	**Won Stanley Cup**
1949-50	70	18	9	8	....	13	18	4	....	31	27	12	....	176	173	74	3rd,	Lost Semi-Final
1948-49	**60**	**12**	**8**	**10**	....	**10**	**17**	**3**	....	**22**	**25**	**13**	....	**147**	**161**	**57**	**4th,**	**Won Stanley Cup**
1947-48	**60**	**22**	**3**	**5**	....	**10**	**12**	**8**	....	**32**	**15**	**13**	....	**182**	**143**	**77**	**1st,**	**Won Stanley Cup**
1946-47	**60**	**20**	**8**	**2**	....	**11**	**11**	**8**	....	**31**	**19**	**10**	....	**209**	**172**	**72**	**2nd,**	**Won Stanley Cup**
1945-46	50	10	13	2	....	9	11	5	....	19	24	7	....	174	185	45	5th,	Out of Playoffs
1944-45	**50**	**13**	**9**	**3**	....	**11**	**13**	**1**	....	**24**	**22**	**4**	....	**183**	**161**	**52**	**3rd,**	**Won Stanley Cup**
1943-44	50	13	11	1	....	10	12	3	....	23	23	4	....	214	174	50	3rd,	Lost Semi-Final
1942-43	50	17	6	2	....	5	13	7	....	22	19	9	....	198	159	53	3rd,	Lost Semi-Final
1941-42	**48**	**18**	**6**	**0**	....	**9**	**12**	**3**	....	**27**	**18**	**3**	....	**158**	**136**	**57**	**2nd,**	**Won Stanley Cup**
1940-41	48	16	5	3	....	12	9	3	....	28	14	6	....	145	99	62	2nd,	Lost Semi-Final
1939-40	48	15	3	6	....	10	14	0	....	25	17	6	....	134	110	56	3rd,	Lost Final
1938-39	48	13	8	3	....	6	12	6	....	19	20	9	....	114	107	47	3rd,	Lost Final
1937-38	48	13	6	5	....	11	9	4	....	24	15	9	....	151	127	57	1st, Cdn. Div.	Lost Final
1936-37	48	14	9	1	....	8	12	4	....	22	21	5	....	119	115	49	3rd, Cdn. Div.	Lost Quarter-Final
1935-36	48	15	4	5	....	8	15	1	....	23	19	6	....	126	106	52	2nd, Cdn. Div.	Lost Final
1934-35	48	16	6	2	....	14	8	2	....	30	14	4	....	157	111	64	1st, Cdn. Div.	Lost Final
1933-34	48	19	2	3	....	7	11	6	....	26	13	9	....	174	119	61	1st, Cdn. Div.	Lost Semi-Final
1932-33	48	16	4	4	....	8	14	2	....	24	18	6	....	119	111	54	1st, Cdn. Div.	Lost Final
1931-32	**48**	**17**	**4**	**3**	....	**6**	**14**	**4**	....	**23**	**18**	**7**	....	**155**	**127**	**53**	**2nd, Cdn. Div.**	**Won Stanley Cup**
1930-31	44	15	4	3	....	7	9	6	....	22	13	9	....	118	99	53	2nd, Cdn. Div.	Lost Quarter-Final
1929-30	44	10	8	4	....	7	13	2	....	17	21	6	....	116	124	40	4th, Cdn. Div.	Out of Playoffs
1928-29	44	15	5	2	....	6	13	3	....	21	18	5	....	85	69	47	3rd, Cdn. Div.	Lost Semi-Final
1927-28	44	9	8	5	....	9	10	3	....	18	18	8	....	89	88	44	4th, Cdn. Div.	Out of Playoffs
1926-27*	44	10	10	2	....	5	14	3	....	15	24	5	....	79	94	35	5th, Cdn. Div.	Out of Playoffs
1925-26	36	11	5	2	....	1	16	1	....	12	21	3	....	92	114	27	6th,	Out of Playoffs
1924-25	30	10	5	0	....	9	6	0	....	19	11	0	....	90	84	38	2nd,	Lost NHL S-Final
1923-24	24	7	5	0	....	3	9	0	....	10	14	0	....	59	85	20	3rd,	Out of Playoffs
1922-23	24	10	1	1	....	3	9	0	....	13	10	1	....	82	88	27	3rd,	Out of Playoffs
1921-22	**24**	**8**	**4**	**0**	....	**5**	**6**	**1**	....	**13**	**10**	**1**	....	**98**	**97**	**27**	**2nd,**	**Won Stanley Cup**
1920-21	24	9	3	0	....	6	6	0	....	15	9	0	....	105	100	30	2nd and 1st***	Lost NHL Final
1919-20**	24	8	4	0	....	4	8	0	....	12	12	0	....	119	106	24	3rd and 2nd***	Out of Playoffs
1918-19	18	5	4	0	....	0	9	0	....	5	13	0	....	64	92	10	3rd and 3rd***	Out of Playoffs
1917-18	**22**	**10**	**1**	**0**	....	**3**	**8**	**0**	....	**13**	**9**	**0**	....	**108**	**109**	**26**	**2nd and 1st*** **	**Won Stanley Cup**

* Name changed from St. Patricks to Maple Leafs (February, 1927). ** Name changed from Arenas to St. Patricks.
*** Season played in two halves with no combined standing at end.
From 1917-18 through 1925-26, NHL champions played against PCHA/WCHL champions for Stanley Cup.

2007-08 Schedule

Oct.	Wed.	3	Ottawa
	Thu.	4	at Ottawa
	Sat.	6	Montreal
	Tue.	9	Carolina
	Thu.	11	NY Islanders
	Sat.	13	Pittsburgh
	Mon.	15	at Buffalo
	Thu.	18	Florida
	Sat.	20	Chicago
	Tue.	23	Atlanta
	Thu.	25	at Pittsburgh
	Sat.	27	at NY Rangers
	Mon.	29	Washington
Nov.	Fri.	2	at New Jersey
	Sat.	3	at Montreal
	Tue.	6	at Ottawa
	Fri.	9	at Buffalo
	Sat.	10	NY Rangers†
	Tue.	13	Montreal
	Thu.	15	at Boston
	Sat.	17	Ottawa
	Tue.	20	Boston
	Fri.	23	at Dallas
	Sat.	24	at Phoenix*
	Tue.	27	Montreal
	Thu.	29	at Atlanta
Dec.	Sat.	1	Pittsburgh
	Tue.	4	Nashville
	Thu.	6	at NY Rangers
	Sat.	8	Boston
	Mon.	10	Tampa Bay
	Fri.	14	at Atlanta
	Sat.	15	at Montreal
	Tue.	18	at Carolina
	Thu.	20	at Tampa Bay
	Sat.	22	at Florida
	Wed.	26	at NY Islanders
	Thu.	27	at Philadelphia
	Sat.	29	NY Rangers
Jan.	Tue.	1	Tampa Bay
	Thu.	3	at Pittsburgh
	Sat.	5	Philadelphia
	Wed.	9	at Anaheim
	Thu.	10	at Los Angeles
	Sat.	12	at San Jose
	Tue.	15	Carolina
	Thu.	17	at Boston
	Sat.	19	Buffalo
	Sun.	20	at New Jersey*
	Wed.	23	Washington
	Thu.	24	at Washington
	Tue.	29	St. Louis
	Thu.	31	at Carolina
Feb.	Sat.	2	Ottawa
	Tue.	5	Florida
	Thu.	7	at Montreal
	Sat.	9	Detroit*
	Wed.	13	at Buffalo
	Thu.	14	NY Islanders
	Sat.	16	Boston
	Tue.	19	Columbus
	Thu.	21	Buffalo
	Sat.	23	Atlanta
	Mon.	25	at Ottawa
	Wed.	27	at Florida
	Fri.	29	at Tampa Bay
Mar.	Sat.	1	at Washington
	Tue.	4	New Jersey
	Thu.	6	at Boston
	Sat.	8	New Jersey
	Tue.	11	Philadelphia
	Wed.	12	at Philadelphia
	Sat.	15	Buffalo
	Tue.	18	at NY Islanders
	Fri.	21	at Buffalo
	Sat.	22	at Ottawa
	Tue.	25	Boston
	Thu.	27	at Boston
	Sat.	29	Montreal
Apr.	Tue.	1	Buffalo
	Thu.	3	Ottawa
	Sat.	5	at Montreal

* Denotes afternoon game. † Hall of Fame Game.

NHL EASTERN CONFERENCE

NORTHEAST DIVISION
91st NHL Season

Franchise date: November 22, 1917

2007-08 Player Personnel

FORWARDS	HT	WT	S	Place of Birth	*Age	2006-07 Club
ANTROPOV, Nik	6-6	230	L	Ust-Kamenogorsk, USSR	27	Toronto
BATTAGLIA, Bates	6-2	205	L	Chicago, IL	31	Toronto
BELL, Mark	6-4	220	L	St. Paul's, Ont.	27	San Jose
BLAKE, Jason	5-10	180	L	Moorhead, MN	34	NY Islanders
DEVEREAUX, Boyd	6-2	195	L	Seaforth, Ont.	29	Toronto-Toronto (AHL)
EARL, Robbie	6-0	195	L	Chicago, IL	22	Toronto (AHL)
FOSTER, Alex	6-1	200	L	Canton, MI	23	Toronto (AHL)-Columbia
GAMACHE, Simon	5-10	186	L	Thetford Mines, Que.	26	Bern
KILGER, Chad	6-4	224	L	Cornwall, Ont.	30	Toronto
MITCHELL, John	6-1	205	L	Waterloo, Ont.	22	Toronto (AHL)
NEWBURY, Kris	5-10	205	L	Brampton, Ont.	25	Toronto-Toronto (AHL)
ONDRUS, Ben	6-0	194	R	Sherwood Park, Alta.	25	Toronto-Toronto (AHL)
POHL, John	6-0	196	R	Rochester, MN	28	Toronto
PONIKAROVSKY, Alexei	6-4	220	L	Kiev, USSR	27	Toronto
STAJAN, Matt	6-1	200	L	Mississauga, Ont.	23	Toronto
STEEN, Alex	6-1	205	L	Winnipeg, Man.	23	Toronto
SUNDIN, Mats	6-5	231	R	Bromma, Sweden	36	Toronto
TLUSTY, Jiri	6-0	209	L	Slany, Czech.	19	Sault Ste. Marie-Tor (AHL)
TUCKER, Darcy	5-10	178	L	Castor, Alta.	32	Toronto
WELLWOOD, Kyle	5-10	180	R	Windsor, Ont.	24	Toronto
WILLIAMS, Jeremy	5-11	188	R	Regina, Sask.	23	Toronto-Toronto (AHL)
DEFENSEMEN						
BELAK, Wade	6-5	221	R	Saskatoon, Sask.	31	Toronto
CASHMAN, Reid	6-2	210	L	Red Wing, MN	24	Quinnipiac-Toronto (AHL)
COLAIACOVO, Carlo	6-1	200	L	Toronto, Ont.	24	Toronto-Toronto (AHL)
GILL, Hal	6-7	250	L	Concord, MA	32	Toronto
HARRISON, Jay	6-4	211	L	Oshawa, Ont.	24	Toronto-Toronto (AHL)
KABERLE, Tomas	6-1	198	L	Rakovnik, Czech.	29	Toronto
KRONWALL, Staffan	6-3	209	L	Jarfalla, Sweden	25	Toronto (AHL)
KUBINA, Pavel	6-4	244	R	Celadna, Czech.	30	Toronto
McCABE, Bryan	6-2	220	L	St. Catharines, Ont.	32	Toronto
WALSER, Derrick	5-10	190	L	New Glasgow, N.S.	29	Albany-Columbus-Syracuse
WHITE, Ian	5-10	185	R	Steinbach, Man.	23	Toronto
WOZNIEWSKI, Andy	6-5	225	L	Buffalo Grove, IL	27	Toronto-Toronto (AHL)

GOALTENDERS	HT	WT	C	Place of Birth	*Age	2006-07 Club
CLEMMENSEN, Scott	6-3	205	L	Des Moines, IA	30	New Jersey-Lowell
POGGE, Justin	6-3	204	L	Ft. McMurray, Alta.	21	Toronto (AHL)
RAYCROFT, Andrew	6-0	185	L	Belleville, Ont.	27	Toronto
TOSKALA, Vesa	5-10	195	L	Tampere, Finland	30	San Jose

* – Age at start of 2007-08 season

2006-07 Scoring

* – rookie

Regular Season

Pos	#	Player	Team	GP	G	A	Pts	+/–	PIM	PP	SH	GW	S	%
C	13	Mats Sundin	TOR	75	27	49	76	–2	62	6	1	3	321	8.4
D	15	Tomas Kaberle	TOR	74	11	47	58	3	20	2	0	1	128	8.6
D	24	Bryan McCabe	TOR	82	15	42	57	3	115	11	0	1	207	7.2
L	23	Alexei Ponikarovsky	TOR	71	21	24	45	8	63	6	0	1	198	10.6
R	16	Darcy Tucker	TOR	56	24	19	43	–11	81	15	0	6	143	16.8
C	92	Jeff O'Neill	TOR	74	20	22	42	1	54	6	0	3	165	12.1
C	42	Kyle Wellwood	TOR	48	12	30	42	3	0	7	0	2	99	12.1
C	14	Matt Stajan	TOR	82	10	29	39	3	44	1	1	1	132	7.6
C	94	Yanic Perreault	PHX	49	19	14	33	–2	30	7	0	5	101	18.8
			TOR	17	2	3	5	1	4	0	0	0	24	8.3
			TOTAL	66	21	17	38	–1	34	7	0	5	125	16.8
C	10	Alex Steen	TOR	82	15	20	35	5	26	4	0	5	192	7.8
C	80	Nik Antropov	TOR	54	18	15	33	8	44	4	0	4	125	14.4
L	33	Bates Battaglia	TOR	82	12	19	31	9	45	0	0	0	94	12.8
C	21	John Pohl	TOR	74	13	16	29	–4	10	3	0	1	105	12.4
L	18	Chad Kilger	TOR	82	14	14	28	–5	58	0	1	2	141	9.9
D	7 *	Ian White	TOR	76	3	23	26	8	40	1	0	1	138	2.2
D	31	Pavel Kubina	TOR	61	7	14	21	7	48	4	0	1	97	7.2
D	25	Hal Gill	TOR	82	6	14	20	11	91	0	0	1	79	7.6
C	22	Boyd Devereaux	TOR	33	8	11	19	4	12	0	0	0	57	14.0
D	8 *	Carlo Colaiacovo	TOR	48	8	9	17	5	22	0	0	1	60	13.3
C	27	Michael Peca	TOR	35	4	11	15	2	60	0	0	2	42	9.5
C	54 *	Kris Newbury	TOR	15	2	2	4	4	26	0	0	0	30	6.7
D	3	Wade Belak	TOR	65	0	3	3	–8	110	0	0	0	16	0.0
C	39	Travis Green	ANA	7	1	1	2	3	6	0	0	0	3	33.3
			TOR	24	0	0	0	1	21	0	0	0	19	0.0
			TOTAL	31	1	1	2	4	27	0	0	0	22	4.5
D	56	Andy Wozniewski	TOR	15	0	2	2	–1	14	0	0	0	10	0.0
R	26 *	Ben Ondrus	TOR	16	0	2	2	–5	20	0	0	0	7	0.0
R	48 *	Jeremy Williams	TOR	1	1	0	1	1	0	0	0	0	3	33.3
C	39	Erik Westrum	TOR	2	0	0	0	0	0	0	0	0	0	0.0
D	43 *	Jay Harrison	TOR	5	0	0	0	–5	6	0	0	0	3	0.0
R	9 *	Aleksander Suglobov	TOR	14	0	0	0	–6	4	0	0	0	17	0.0

Goaltending

No.	Goaltender	GPI	Mins	Avg	W	L	OT	EN	SO	GA	SA	S%	G	A	PIM
32	Mikael Tellqvist	1	59	2.03	0	1	0	0	0	2	19	.895	0	0	0
1	Andrew Raycroft	72	4108	2.99	37	25	9	8	2	205	1931	.894	0	1	8
30	J-Sebastien Aubin	20	804	3.43	3	5	2	1	0	46	371	.876	0	0	0
	Totals	**82**	**4997**	**3.15**	**40**	**31**	**11**	**9**	**2**	**262**	**2330**	**.888**			

Though injuries limited him to 56 games for Toronto in 2006-07, Darcy Tucker was still second on the team with 24 goals.

Coach

PAUL MAURICE

Coach, Toronto Maple Leafs. Born in Sault Ste. Marie, Ont., January 30, 1967.

The Toronto Maple Leafs named Paul Maurice as the team's new head coach on May 12, 2006. Maurice, who spent eight seasons as head coach of the Hartford Whalers and Carolina Hurricanes, first joined the Maple Leafs organization in 2005-06 as head coach of the team's American Hockey League club, the Toronto Marlies.

Maurice, the 26th head coach in Maple Leafs history, became the NHL's youngest head coach at only 28 years of age when he was elevated from assistant coach with the Whalers on November 6, 1995. He followed the club to Carolina where he went on to rank first in franchise history in regular season wins (268), games coached (674), playoff wins (17) and playoff games coached (35). Maurice guided the Hurricanes to four consecutive winning seasons from 1998 to 2002, where they captured Southeast Division titles in 1998-99 and 2001-02. His club eliminated the Leafs in six games during the Eastern Conference Final in 2002 to reach the Stanley Cup Final for the first time. He became the sixth-youngest coach in league history to reach the Final.

Maurice played junior hockey with the OHL's Windsor Compuware Spitfires (1984 to 88). He had his career cut short due to an eye injury and began coaching as an assistant with the Detroit Junior Red Wings shortly thereafter. He served six seasons in that capacity before taking over as head coach of the club in the 1993-94 season. Maurice led the team to the 1995 OHL championship and an appearance in the Memorial Cup in Kamloops, British Columbia. That season he finished second in voting to Guelph's Craig Hartsburg for the Matt Leyden Trophy, which is given annually to the OHL's coach of the year.

Coaching Record

		Regular Season				Playoffs		
Season	Team	Games	W	L	O/T	Games	W	L
1993-94	Detroit (OHL)	66	42	20	4	17	11	6
1994-95	Detroit (OHL)	66	44	18	4	21	16	5
1995-96	**Hartford (NHL)**	**70**	**29**	**33**	**8**	....	....	....
1996-97	**Hartford (NHL)**	**82**	**32**	**39**	**11**	....	....	....
1997-98	**Carolina (NHL)**	**82**	**33**	**41**	**8**	....	....	....
1998-99	**Carolina (NHL)**	**82**	**34**	**30**	**18**	**6**	**2**	**4**
1999-2000	**Carolina (NHL)**	**82**	**37**	**35**	**10**	....	....	....
2000-01	**Carolina (NHL)**	**82**	**38**	**35**	**9**	**6**	**2**	**4**
2001-02	**Carolina (NHL)**	**82**	**35**	**31**	**16**	**23**	**13**	**10**
2002-03	**Carolina (NHL)**	**82**	**22**	**49**	**11**	....	....	....
2003-04	**Carolina (NHL)**	**30**	**8**	**14**	**8**	....	....	....
2005-06	Toronto (AHL)	80	41	29	10	5	1	4
2006-07	**Toronto (NHL)**	**82**	**40**	**31**	**11**	....	....	....
	NHL Totals	**756**	**308**	**338**	**110**	**35**	**17**	**18**

Coaching History

Dick Carroll, 1917-18, 1918-19; Frank Heffernan and Harry Sproule, 1919-20; Frank Carroll, 1920-21; George O'Donohue, 1921-22; George O'Donohue and Charles Querrie, 1922-23; Charles Querrie, 1923-24; Eddie Powers, 1924-25, 1925-26; Charles Querrie, Mike Rodden and Alex Romeril, 1926-27; Conn Smythe, 1927-28 to 1929-30; Conn Smythe and Art Duncan, 1930-31; Art Duncan and Dick Irvin, 1931-32; Dick Irvin, 1932-33 to 1939-40; Hap Day, 1940-41 to 1949-50; Joe Primeau, 1950-51 to 1952-53; King Clancy, 1953-54 to 1955-56; Howie Meeker, 1956-57; Billy Reay, 1957-58; Billy Reay and Punch Imlach, 1958-59; Punch Imlach, 1959-60 to 1968-69; John McLellan, 1969-70 to 1972-73; Red Kelly, 1973-74 to 1976-77; Roger Neilson, 1977-78, 1978-79; Floyd Smith, Dick Duff and Punch Imlach, 1979-80; Punch Imlach, Joe Crozier and Mike Nykoluk, 1980-81; Mike Nykoluk, 1981-82 to 1983-84; Dan Maloney, 1984-85, 1985-86; John Brophy, 1986-87, 1987-88; John Brophy and George Armstrong, 1988-89; Doug Carpenter, 1989-90; Doug Carpenter and Tom Watt, 1990-91; Tom Watt, 1991-92; Pat Burns, 1992-93 to 1994-95; Pat Burns and Nick Beverley, 1995-96; Mike Murphy, 1996-97, 1997-98; Pat Quinn, 1998-99 to 2005-06; Paul Maurice, 2006-07 to date.

Captains' History

Hap Day, 1927-28 to 1936-37; Charlie Conacher, 1937-38; Red Horner, 1938-39, 1939-40; Syl Apps, 1940-41 to 1942-43; Bob Davidson, 1943-44, 1944-45; Syl Apps, 1945-46 to 1947-48; Ted Kennedy, 1948-49 to 1954-55; Sid Smith, 1955-56; Jimmy Thomson, Ted Kennedy, 1956-57; George Armstrong, 1957-58 to 1968-69; Dave Keon, 1969-70 to 1974-75; Darryl Sittler, 1975-76 to 1980-81; Rick Vaive, 1981-82 to 1985-86; no captain, 1986-87 to 1988-89; Rob Ramage, 1989-90, 1990-91; Wendel Clark, 1991-92 to 1993-94; Doug Gilmour, 1994-95 to 1996-97; Mats Sundin, 1997-98 to date.

Club Records

Team

(Figures in brackets for season records are games played; records for fewest points, wins, ties, losses, goals, goals against are for 70 or more games)

Most Points **103** 2003-04 (82)
Most Wins **45** 1998-99 (82), 1999-2000 (82), 2003-04 (82)
Most Ties **22** 1954-55 (70)
Most Losses **52** 1984-85 (80)
Most Goals **337** 1989-90 (80)
Most Goals Against **387** 1983-84 (80)
Fewest Points **48** 1984-85 (80)
Fewest Wins **20** 1981-82 (80), 1984-85 (80)
Fewest Ties **4** 1989-90 (80)
Fewest Losses **16** 1950-51 (70)
Fewest Goals **147** 1954-55 (70)
Fewest Goals Against ***131** 1953-54 (70)
Longest Winning Streak
Overall .... **10** Oct. 7-28/93
Home .... **9** Nov. 11-Dec. 26/53
Away .... **7** Three times
Longest Undefeated Streak
Overall .... **11** Oct. 15-Nov. 8/50 (8 wins, 3 ties), Jan. 6-Feb. 1/94 (7 wins, 4 ties)
Home .... **18** Nov. 28/33-Mar. 10/34 (15 wins, 3 ties), Oct. 31/53-Jan. 23/54 (16 wins, 2 ties)
Away .... **9** Nov. 30/47-Jan. 11/48 (4 wins, 5 ties)
Longest Losing Streak
Overall .... **10** Jan. 15-Feb. 8/67
Home .... **7** Nov. 11-Dec. 5/84
Away .... **11** Feb. 20-Apr. 1/88
Longest Winless Streak
Overall .... **15** Dec. 26/87-Jan. 25/88 (11 losses, 4 ties)
Home .... **11** Dec. 19/87-Jan. 25/88 (7 losses, 4 ties)
Away .... **18** Oct. 6/82-Jan. 5/83 (13 losses, 5 ties)
Most Shutouts, Season **13** 1953-54 (70)
Most PIM, Season **2,419** 1989-90 (80)
Most Goals, Game .... **14** Mar. 16/57 (NYR 1 at Tor. 14)

Individual

Most Seasons .... **21** George Armstrong
Most Games .... **1,187** George Armstrong
Most Goals, Career .... **389** Darryl Sittler
Most Assists, Career .... **620** Borje Salming
Most Points, Career .... **916** Darryl Sittler (389G, 527A)
Most PIM, Career .... **2,265** Tie Domi
Most Shutouts, Career .... **62** Turk Broda
Longest Consecutive Games Streak .... **486** Tim Horton (Feb. 11/61-Feb. 4/68)
Most Goals, Season .... **54** Rick Vaive (1981-82)
Most Assists, Season .... **95** Doug Gilmour (1992-93)
Most Points, Season .... **127** Doug Gilmour (1992-93; 32G, 95A)
Most PIM, Season .... **365** Tie Domi (1997-98)
Most Points, Defenseman, Season .... **79** Ian Turnbull (1976-77; 22G, 57A)
Most Points, Center, Season .... **127** Doug Gilmour (1992-93; 32G, 95A)
Most Points, Right Wing, Season .... **97** Wilf Paiement (1980-81; 40G, 57A)
Most Points, Left Wing, Season .... **99** Dave Andreychuk (1993-94; 53G, 46A)
Most Points, Rookie, Season .... **66** Peter Ihnacak (1982-83; 28G, 38A)
Most Shutouts, Season .... **13** Harry Lumley (1953-54)
Most Goals, Game .... **6** Corb Denneny (Jan. 26/21), Darryl Sittler (Feb. 7/76)
Most Assists, Game .... **6** Babe Pratt (Jan. 8/44), Doug Gilmour (Feb. 13/93)
Most Points, Game .... ***10** Darryl Sittler (Feb. 7/76; 6G, 4A)

* NHL Record.

Retired Numbers

5	Bill Barilko	1946-1951
6	Ace Bailey	1926-1934

Honored Numbers

1	Turk Broda	1936-43, 45-52
	Johnny Bower	1958-1970
4	Hap Day	1926-1937
	Red Kelly	1959-1967
7	King Clancy	1930-1937
	Tim Horton	1949-50, 51-70
9	Charlie Conacher	1929-1938
	Ted Kennedy	1942-55, 56-57
10	Syl Apps	1936-43, 45-48
	George Armstrong	1949-50, 51-71
21	Borje Salming	1973-1989
27	Frank Mahovlich	1956-1968
	Darryl Sittler	1970-1982

All-time Record vs. Other Clubs

Regular Season

	At Home								On Road								Total							
	GP	W	L	T	OL	GF	GA	PTS	GP	W	L	T	OL	GF	GA	PTS	GP	W	L	T	OL	GF	GA	PTS
Anaheim	16	10	2	4	0	53	32	24	11	5	5	1	0	28	34	11	27	15	7	5	0	81	66	35
Atlanta	13	8	3	1	1	48	30	18	13	8	4	0	1	46	25	17	26	16	7	1	2	94	55	35
Boston	307	160	96	51	0	1025	794	371	306	93	162	47	4	812	988	237	613	253	258	98	4	1837	1782	608
Buffalo	75	31	31	12	1	229	256	75	77	22	49	6	0	205	314	50	152	53	80	18	1	434	570	125
Calgary	54	29	17	7	1	207	193	66	62	22	33	5	2	195	240	51	116	51	50	12	3	402	433	117
Carolina	40	16	19	5	0	135	137	37	41	15	19	6	1	133	156	37	81	31	38	11	1	268	293	74
Chicago	315	164	97	54	0	1071	821	382	319	120	157	42	0	832	971	282	634	284	254	96	0	1903	1792	664
Colorado	36	16	16	4	0	119	137	36	30	7	18	5	0	90	116	19	66	23	34	9	0	209	253	55
Columbus	3	2	0	1	0	10	4	5	2	1	0	0	1	7	6	3	5	3	0	1	1	17	10	8
Dallas	102	49	36	17	0	357	321	115	97	36	50	11	0	306	365	83	199	85	86	28	0	663	686	198
Detroit	316	164	105	47	0	1045	846	375	323	108	169	46	0	793	973	262	639	272	274	93	0	1838	1819	637
Edmonton	38	21	15	2	0	158	157	44	44	15	22	6	1	141	180	37	82	36	37	8	1	299	337	81
Florida	19	12	5	2	0	66	48	26	21	10	6	5	0	62	57	25	40	22	11	7	0	128	105	51
Los Angeles	69	35	23	11	0	267	225	81	65	21	34	10	0	191	234	52	134	56	57	21	0	458	459	133
Minnesota	4	4	0	0	0	15	6	8	2	1	1	0	0	4	5	2	6	5	1	0	0	19	11	10
Montreal	341	177	117	45	2	1040	890	401	341	95	201	43	2	852	1195	235	682	272	318	88	4	1892	2085	636
Nashville	6	2	3	1	0	13	18	5	2	0	1	0	1	4	7	1	8	2	4	1	1	17	25	6
New Jersey	52	34	13	5	0	191	144	73	50	17	16	15	2	156	171	51	102	51	29	20	2	347	315	124
NY Islanders	59	31	23	4	1	207	197	67	57	21	31	3	2	164	221	47	116	52	54	7	3	371	418	114
NY Rangers	286	161	85	39	1	991	753	362	287	108	121	56	2	844	890	274	573	269	206	95	3	1835	1643	636
Ottawa	30	12	13	2	3	77	92	29	28	9	16	1	2	75	95	21	58	21	29	3	5	152	187	50
Philadelphia	71	26	30	14	1	223	235	67	71	20	42	8	1	171	262	49	142	46	72	22	2	394	497	116
Phoenix	44	20	22	2	0	160	165	42	39	13	20	6	0	142	161	32	83	33	42	8	0	302	326	74
Pittsburgh	71	35	24	11	1	282	228	82	73	29	38	6	0	235	292	64	144	64	62	17	1	517	520	146
St. Louis	99	58	28	11	2	369	292	129	103	31	58	14	0	285	349	76	202	89	86	25	2	654	641	205
San Jose	19	12	5	2	0	73	52	26	15	7	5	3	0	40	32	17	34	19	10	5	0	113	84	43
Tampa Bay	25	17	7	1	0	94	65	35	24	18	4	1	1	82	51	38	49	35	11	2	1	176	116	73
Vancouver	61	28	22	11	0	220	201	67	65	24	30	11	0	219	229	59	126	52	52	22	0	439	430	126
Washington	52	28	18	6	0	225	175	62	54	19	31	4	0	157	197	42	106	47	49	10	0	382	372	104
Defunct Clubs	232	158	53	21	0	860	515	337	233	84	120	29	0	607	745	197	465	242	173	50	0	1467	1260	534
Totals	**2855**	**1520**	**928**	**393**	**14**	**9830**	**8029**	**3447**	**2855**	**979**	**1463**	**390**	**23**	**7878**	**9561**	**2371**	**5710**	**2499**	**2391**	**783**	**37**	**17708**	**17590**	**5818**

Playoffs

	Series	W	L	GP	W	L	T	GF	GA	Last Mtg.	Rnd.	Result
Boston	13	8	5	62	31	30	1	150	153	1974	QF	L 0-4
Buffalo	1	0	1	5	1	4	0	16	21	1999	CF	L 1-4
Calgary	1	1	0	2	2	0	0	9	5	1979	PRE	W 2-0
Carolina	1	0	1	6	2	4	0	6	10	2002	CF	L 2-4
Chicago	9	6	3	38	22	15	1	111	89	1995	CQF	L 3-4
Dallas	2	0	2	7	1	6	0	26	35	1983	DSF	L 1-3
Detroit	23	12	11	117	58	59	0	311	321	1993	DSF	W 4-3
Los Angeles	3	2	1	12	7	5	0	41	31	1993	CF	L 3-4
Montreal	15	7	8	71	29	42	0	160	215	1979	QF	L 0-4
New Jersey	2	0	2	13	5	8	0	27	37	2001	CSF	L 3-4
NY Islanders	3	2	1	17	8	9	0	42	54	2002	CQF	W 4-3
NY Rangers	8	3	5	35	16	19	0	86	86	1971	QF	L 2-4
Ottawa	4	4	0	24	16	8	0	57	42	2004	CQF	W 4-3
Philadelphia	6	1	5	36	14	22	0	85	119	2004	CSF	L 2-4
Pittsburgh	3	3	0	12	8	4	0	39	27	1999	CSF	W 4-2
St. Louis	5	2	3	31	14	17	0	90	88	1996	CQF	L 2-4
San Jose	1	1	0	7	4	3	0	26	21	1994	CSF	W 4-3
Vancouver	1	0	1	5	1	4	0	9	16	1994	CF	L 1-4
Defunct Clubs	8	6	2	24	12	10	2	59	57			
Totals	**109**	**58**	**51**	**524**	**251**	**269**	**4**	**1350**	**1427**			

Calgary totals include Atlanta Flames, 1972-73 to 1979-80.
Colorado totals include Quebec, 1979-80 to 1994-95.
New Jersey totals include Kansas City, 1974-75, 1975-76, and Colorado Rockies, 1976-77 to 1981-82.
Phoenix totals include Winnipeg, 1979-80 to 1995-96.
Carolina totals include Hartford, 1979-80 to 1996-97.
Dallas totals include Minnesota North Stars, 1967-68 to 1992-93.

Playoff Results 2007-2002

Year	Round	Opponent	Result	GF	GA
2004	CSF	Philadelphia	L 2-4	13	17
	CQF	Ottawa	W 4-3	14	11
2003	CQF	Philadelphia	L 3-4	16	24
2002	CF	Carolina	L 2-4	6	10
	CSF	Ottawa	W 4-3	16	18
	CQF	NY Islanders	W 4-3	22	21

Abbreviations: Round: CF – conference final; **CSF** – conference semi-final; **CQF** – conference quarter-final; **DSF** – division semi-final; **QF** – quarter-final; **PRE** – preliminary round.

2006-07 Results

Oct.	4	Ottawa	1-4
	5	at Ottawa	6-0
	7	Montreal	2-3†
	9	Florida	2-1†
	12	at New Jersey	6-7†
	14	Calgary	5-4*
	18	Colorado	1-4
	20	at Columbus	4-2
	21	NY Rangers	4-5†
	24	Ottawa	2-6
	26	at Ottawa	2-7
	28	at Montreal	5-4†
	30	Atlanta	4-2
Nov.	1	at Tampa Bay	4-2
	2	at Florida	2-4
	4	at Buffalo	4-1
	6	Philadelphia	4-1
	9	at Boston	6-4
	11	Montreal	5-1
	16	at Boston	1-2*
	18	New Jersey	1-2
	20	NY Islanders	4-2
	22	at Buffalo	4-7
	24	at Washington	7-1
	25	Boston	1-3
	28	Boston	1-4
	30	at Atlanta	0-5
Dec.	2	at Montreal	3-4†
	5	Atlanta	2-5
	7	at Boston	1-3
	9	at Detroit	1-5
	12	Tampa Bay	5-4
	15	at Carolina	4-3
	16	NY Rangers	9-2
	19	Florida	3-7
	22	at Chicago	1-3
	23	Washington	2-3
	26	Minnesota	4-3
	29	at Pittsburgh	1-4
	30	Ottawa	2-3*
Jan.	1	Boston	5-1
	4	at Boston	10-2
	6	Buffalo	3-4
	9	Carolina	1-4
	11	at Buffalo	4-2
	13	Vancouver	1-6
	16	at Tampa Bay	4-2
	18	at Florida	3-2
	20	at Pittsburgh	2-8
	27	Montreal	4-1
	30	at Carolina	4-1
	31	at NY Rangers	2-1
Feb.	3	at Ottawa	3-2†
	6	at St. Louis	2-1
	8	at Nashville	2-4
	10	Pittsburgh	5-6*
	13	NY Islanders	2-3†
	15	at Philadelphia	4-2
	17	Edmonton	4-3
	20	Boston	0-3
	22	at NY Islanders	2-3†
	24	at Philadelphia	5-2
	26	at Montreal	4-5
	27	Buffalo	1-6
Mar.	2	at New Jersey	4-3†
	3	Buffalo	1-3
	6	Washington	3-0
	8	at Ottawa	1-5
	10	Ottawa	4-3*
	13	Tampa Bay	3-2
	16	at Washington	1-5
	17	at Montreal	2-3†
	20	New Jersey	2-1
	23	at Buffalo	4-5
	24	Buffalo	4-1
	27	Carolina	6-1
	29	at Atlanta	2-3*
	31	Pittsburgh	5-4*
Apr.	1	at NY Rangers	2-7
	3	Philadelphia	3-2*
	5	at NY Islanders	2-5
	7	Montreal	6-5

* – Overtime † – Shootout

Entry Draft Selections 2007-1993

2007

Pick	
74	Dale Mitchell
99	Matt Frattin
104	Ben Winnett
134	Juraj Mikus
164	Christopher Didomenico
194	Carl Gunnarsson

2006

Pick	
13	Jiri Tlusty
44	Nikolai Kulemin
99	James Reimer
111	Korbinian Holzer
161	Viktor Stalberg
166	Tyler Ruegsegger
180	Leo Komarov

2005

Pick	
21	Tuukka Rask
82	Phil Oreskovic
153	Alex Berry
173	Johan Dahlberg
216	Anton Stralman
228	Chad Rau

2004

Pick	
90	Justin Pogge
113	Roman Kukumberg
157	Dmitri Vorobiev
187	Robbie Earl
220	Maxim Semenov
252	Jan Steber
285	Pierce Norton

2003

Pick	
57	John Doherty
91	Martin Sagat
125	Konstantin Volkov
158	John Mitchell
220	Jeremy Williams
237	Shaun Landolt

2002

Pick	
24	Alex Steen
57	Matt Stajan
74	Todd Ford
88	Dominic D'Amour
122	David Turon
191	Ian White
222	Scott May
254	Jarkko Immonen
285	Staffan Kronwall

2001

Pick	
17	Carlo Colaiacovo
39	Karel Pilar
65	Brendan Bell
82	Jay Harrison
88	Nicolas Corbeil
134	Kyle Wellwood
168	Maxim Kondratiev
183	Jaroslav Sklenar
198	Ivan Kolozvary
213	Jan Chovan
246	Tomas Mojzis
276	Mike Knoepfli

2000

Pick	
24	Brad Boyes
51	Kris Vernarsky
70	Mikael Tellqvist
90	Jean-Francois Racine
100	Miguel Delisle
179	Vadim Sozinov
209	Markus Seikola
223	Lubos Velebny
254	Alexander Shinkar
265	Jean-Philippe Cote

1999

Pick	
24	Luca Cereda
60	Peter Reynolds
108	Mirko Murovic
110	Jon Zion
151	Vaclav Zavoral
161	Jan Sochor
211	Vladimir Kulikov
239	Pierre Hedin
267	Peter Metcalf

1998

Pick	
10	Nik Antropov
35	Petr Svoboda
69	Jamie Hodson
87	Alexei Ponikarovsky
126	Morgan Warren
154	Allan Rourke
181	Jonathan Gagnon
215	Dwight Wolfe
228	Michal Travnicek
236	Sergei Rostov

1997

Pick	
57	Jeff Farkas
84	Adam Mair
111	Frantisek Mrazek
138	Eric Gooldy
165	Hugo Marchand
190	Shawn Thornton
194	Russ Bartlett
221	Jonathan Hedstrom

1996

Pick	
36	Marek Posmyk
50	Francis Larivee
66	Mike Lankshear
68	Konstantin Kalmikov
86	Jason Sessa
103	Vladimir Antipov
110	Peter Cava
111	Brandon Sugden
140	Dmitri Yakushin
148	Chris Bogas
151	Lucio DeMartinis
178	Reggie Berg
204	Tomas Kaberle
230	Jared Hope

1995

Pick	
15	Jeff Ware
54	Ryan Pepperall
139	Doug Bonner
145	Yannick Tremblay
171	Marek Melenovsky
197	Mark Murphy
223	Danny Markov

1994

Pick	
16	Eric Fichaud
48	Sean Haggerty
64	Fredrik Modin
126	Mark Deyell
152	Kam White
178	Tommi Rajamaki
204	Rob Butler
256	Sergei Berezin
282	Doug Nolan

1993

Pick	
12	Kenny Jonsson
19	Landon Wilson
123	Zdenek Nedved
149	Paul Vincent
175	Jeff Andrews
201	David Brumby
253	Kyle Ferguson
279	Mikhail Lapin

General Managers' History

Charles Querrie, 1917-18 to 1926-27; Conn Smythe, 1927-28 to 1956-57; Hap Day, 1957-58; Punch Imlach, 1958-59 to 1968-69; Jim Gregory, 1969-70 to 1978-79; Punch Imlach, 1979-80, 1980-81; Punch Imlach and Gerry McNamara, 1981-82; Gerry McNamara, 1982-83 to 1987-88; Gord Stellick, 1988-89; Floyd Smith, 1989-90, 1990-91; Cliff Fletcher, 1991-92 to 1996-97; Ken Dryden, 1997-98, 1998-99; Pat Quinn, 1999-2000 to 2002-03; John Ferguson, 2003-04 to date.

General Manager

JOHN FERGUSON

General Manager, Toronto Maple Leafs. Born in Montreal, Que., July 7, 1967.

John Ferguson became the 12th person to hold the role of general manager of the Toronto Maple Leafs on August 29, 2003. Prior to his arrival in Toronto, Ferguson had served as vice-president and director of hockey operations for the St. Louis Blues since February 26, 2001. Prior to that he spent five seasons as assistant general manager with the club. Ferguson was also the president and general manager of the Worcester IceCats, the Blues' top minor league affiliate. He is a former chairman of the American Hockey League's Competition Committee and also served on the league's Legal Affairs Committee.

The son of former Montreal Canadiens great John Ferguson, John Jr. played hockey at Providence College and spent four professional seasons at the American Hockey League level with the Montreal Canadiens and Ottawa Senators organizations from 1989 to 1993. From 1993 to 1996 he was a member of the Ottawa Senators scouting staff as an amateur and professional scout. Before joining the Blues, he served as a player agent.

Club Directory

Air Canada Centre

Toronto Maple Leafs
Air Canada Centre
40 Bay St., Suite 400
Toronto, Ontario M5J 2X2
Phone **416/815-5700**
FAX 416/359-9331
www.mapleleafs.com
Capacity: 18,819

Board of Directors

Lawrence M. Tanenbaum (Chairman of the Board), Robert G. Bertram, James W. Leech, Dean Metcalf, Ivan Fecan, Robert MacLellan, Dale H. Lastman, Richard Peddie

Maple Leaf Sports & Entertainment

Chairman, NHL Governor . . . . . Lawrence M. Tanenbaum
President, CEO and Alternate NHL Governor . . . . . Richard Peddie
Alternate NHL Governors . . . . . John Ferguson, Dale H. Lastman, Dean Metcalf
Executive V.P., Chief Operating Officer . . . . . Tom Anselmi
Executive V.P., CFO and Business Development . . . . . Ian Clarke
Executive V.P., Venues & Entertainment . . . . . Bob Hunter
Senior V.P., General Counsel & Corporate Secretary . Robin Brudner
Senior V.P., Communications . . . . . John Lashway
Senior V.P., People . . . . . Mardi Walker
Senior V.P., Broadcast . . . . . Chris Hebb
Vice-President, Corporate Sales & Service . . . . . Dave Hopkinson
Vice-President, Finance . . . . . Kevin Nonomura
Vice-President, Marketing . . . . . Beth Robertson
Vice-President, Operations . . . . . Diego Roccasalva
President & General Manager, Toronto Raptors . . . . . Bryan Colangelo

Hockey Operations

Vice-President & General Manager . . . . . John Ferguson
Assistant G.M. & Director of Player Personnel . . . . . Mike Penny
Head Coach . . . . . Paul Maurice
Assistant Coaches . . . . . Keith Acton, Dallas Eakins, Randy Ladouceur
Director of Hockey Administration . . . . . Jeff Jackson
Player Development Coach . . . . . Paul Dennis
Player Development Advisor . . . . . Doug Gilmour
Manager, Hockey Admin. & Scouting Coord. . . . . . Reid Mitchell
Goaltending Coach . . . . . Stephen McKichan
Strength & Conditioning Coordinator . . . . . Matt Nichol
Manager, Team Services . . . . . Dave Griffiths
Coordinator, Team Services . . . . . Brad Lynn
Video Analyst . . . . . Chris Dennis
Community Representatives . . . . . Wendel Clark, Darryl Sittler, Rick Vaive
Director, Amateur Scouting . . . . . Dave Morrison
Professional Scouts . . . . . Don Granato, Shawn Simpson
Amateur Scouts . . . . . John Lilley, Garth Malarchuk, Mike Palmateer, Clint McConnachie, Allan Power, George Armstrong, Fred Bandel
European Scouts . . . . . Thommie Bergman, Peter Ihnacak, Jan Kovac, Nikolai Ladygin, Jari Gronstrand
Travel Coordinator . . . . . Mary Speck
Executive Assistant . . . . . Ann Clark

Communications and Community Development

Senior Vice-President, Communications . . . . . John Lashway
Director, Media Relations . . . . . Pat Park
Coordinators, Media Relations . . . . . Craig Downey, James Lamont
Manager, Corporate Communications . . . . . Rajani Kamath
Mgr., Leafs Fund, Comm. Relations & Game Ops. . . Nancy Gilks
Manager, Youth Hockey Development . . . . . Dave De Freitas

Medical and Training Staff

Head Athletic Therapist . . . . . Rudy Cantu
Assistant Athletic Therapist . . . . . Chris Davie
Equipment Manager . . . . . Brian Papineau
Assistant Equipment Managers . . . . . Tom Blatchford, Bobby Hastings
Team Doctor . . . . . Dr. Noah Forman
Orthopedic Consultant . . . . . Dr. John Theodoropoulos
Team Dentists . . . . . Dr. Marvin Lean, Dr. Charles Goldberg

Air Canada Centre

Director, Project Development . . . . . Dan Arts
Director, Media Sales . . . . . Anthony Attard
Director, Business Operations, MLS . . . . . Paul Beirne
Director, Retail Finance . . . . . Alldrick Britto
Director, Event Personnel . . . . . Brendan Costigan
Director, Corporate Sales . . . . . Jeff Deline
Director, Media Sales . . . . . Bob Doherty
Director, Food and Beverage . . . . . Michael Doyle
Director, Sales, Service/Business Ops., Marlies . . . . . Jim Edmands
Director, Labour Relations and Health & Safety . . . . Les Fisher
Director, Executive Suite Services . . . . . Kristy Fletcher
Director, Ticketing . . . . . Donna Henderson
Director, Marketing . . . . . Shannon Hosford
Director, Accounting . . . . . Bob Karabatsos
Director, Building Operations . . . . . Bryan Leslie
Director, Restaurant Ops., Executive Chef . . . . . Brad Long
Director, Corporate Sales . . . . . Tom Pistore
Director, Information Technology . . . . . Sasha Puric
Director, Corporate Partner Service & Activation . . . Lori Radke
Director, Finance . . . . . Suzanne Scott
Director, Live Entertainment . . . . . Patti-Anne Tarlton
Director, Consumer Products . . . . . Caroline Wright
Associate General Counsel . . . . . Peter Miller

Television and Radio Broadcast Information

Senior Vice-President, Broadcast . . . . . Chris Hebb
Director, Programming and Production, Leafs TV . . . Frank Hayward
Senior Broadcast Producer, Leafs TV . . . . . Mark Askin
Game Director, Leafs TV . . . . . Jacques Primeau
Director, Broadcast & Live Game Prod., Leafs TV . . . Liana Bristol
Senior Producer, Leafs TV . . . . . Chris Clarke
Producers, Leafs TV . . . . . Brian Bileski, Mike Brock
Jr. Producers, Leafs TV . . . . . Jamie Arnold, Filomena Lowry
Talent, Leafs TV . . . . . Joe Bowen, Paul Hendrick, Greg Millen, Harry Neale, Andi Petrillo, Rick Vaive, Jody Vance
AM 640 Toronto Radio, Play-By-Play . . . . . Joe Bowen, Dennis Beyak (mid-weeks)
AM 640 Toronto Radio, Analyst . . . . . Jim Ralph
Television Play-By-Play . . . . . Joe Bowen (mid-weeks)
Television Analyst . . . . . Harry Neale
Website . . . . . John McCauley, Mike Ball, Matthew Iaboni, Latham Bromwich

Key Off-Season Signings/Acquisitions

2007

- **June 4** • Re-signed LW **Taylor Pyatt**.
- **23** • Acquired RW **Ryan Shannon** from Anaheim for LW **Jason King** and a conditional pick in the 2009 Entry Draft.
- **28** • Re-signed LW **Jeff Cowan**.
- **July 3** • Re-signed D **Lukas Krajicek**.
- **3** • Signed G **Curtis Sanford**, C **Byron Ritchie** and LW **Brad Isbister**.
- **9** • Re-signed D **Kevin Bieksa**.
- **9** • Signed D **Aaron Miller**.

Vancouver Canucks

2006-07 Results: 49W-26L-3OTL-4SOL 105PTS.
First, Northwest Division

Roberto Luongo gave the Vancouver Canucks everything they had hoped for in goal. His 47 wins were one behind Martin Brodeur's record-breaking total of 48, while his 2.29 goals-against average and .921 save percentage also ranked among the league leaders.

2007-08 Schedule

Oct.	Fri.	5	San Jose
	Sat.	6	at Calgary
	Wed.	10	Philadelphia
	Fri.	12	at Edmonton
	Sat.	13	Edmonton
	Mon.	15	San Jose
	Fri.	19	Los Angeles
	Sun.	21	at Columbus*
	Mon.	22	at Carolina
	Wed.	24	at Detroit
	Fri.	26	at Washington
	Sun.	28	Detroit
Nov.	Thu.	1	Nashville
	Sat.	3	at Colorado
	Thu.	8	at Calgary
	Fri.	9	Colorado
	Wed.	14	Edmonton
	Fri.	16	Minnesota
	Sun.	18	Calgary*
	Tue.	20	at Edmonton
	Wed.	21	at Minnesota
	Fri.	23	at St. Louis
	Sun.	25	Chicago
	Tue.	27	Anaheim
	Thu.	29	Columbus
Dec.	Sun.	2	at Minnesota*
	Wed.	5	at Chicago
	Thu.	6	at Nashville
	Sat.	8	Pittsburgh
	Mon.	10	at Los Angeles
	Wed.	12	at Anaheim
	Thu.	13	at San Jose
	Sat.	15	at Edmonton
	Tue.	18	New Jersey
	Thu.	20	Dallas
	Sat.	22	at Phoenix
	Sun.	23	at Colorado
	Thu.	27	Calgary
	Sun.	30	Anaheim*
	Mon.	31	at Calgary
Jan.	Thu.	3	NY Rangers
	Tue.	8	NY Islanders
	Thu.	10	at San Jose
	Fri.	11	Phoenix
	Sun.	13	at St. Louis*
	Tue.	15	at Columbus
	Thu.	17	at Detroit
	Sat.	19	Los Angeles
	Mon.	21	Minnesota
	Wed.	23	St. Louis
	Tue.	29	Dallas
	Thu.	31	at Tampa Bay
Feb.	Fri.	1	at Florida
	Tue.	5	at Dallas
	Thu.	7	at Atlanta
	Sat.	9	Colorado
	Sun.	10	Chicago
	Thu.	14	Minnesota
	Sat.	16	Edmonton
	Tue.	19	at Minnesota
	Thu.	21	at Nashville
	Sat.	23	Detroit
	Wed.	27	Colorado
	Fri.	29	Columbus
Mar.	Sun.	2	at Chicago*
	Tue.	4	at Colorado
	Thu.	6	Nashville
	Sat.	8	St. Louis
	Mon.	10	at Los Angeles
	Wed.	12	at Anaheim
	Thu.	13	at Phoenix
	Sat.	15	at Dallas
	Mon.	17	Phoenix
	Thu.	20	at Edmonton
	Fri.	21	Minnesota
	Tue.	25	at Calgary
	Wed.	26	at Colorado
	Fri.	28	at Minnesota
	Sun.	30	Calgary
Apr.	Tue.	1	Colorado
	Thu.	3	Edmonton
	Sat.	5	Calgary

* Denotes afternoon game.

Year-by-Year Record

Season	GP	Home W	L	T	OL	Road W	L	T	OL	Overall W	L	T	OL	GF	GA	Pts.	Finished	Playoff Result
2006-07	82	26	11	....	4	23	15	....	3	49	26	....	7	222	201	105	1st, Northwest Div.	Lost Conf. Semi-Final
2005-06	82	25	10	....	6	17	22	....	2	42	32	....	8	256	255	92	4th, Northwest Div.	Out of Playoffs
2004-05	....	....	....	....	....	....	....	....	....	....	....	....	....	....	....	....		
2003-04	82	21	13	7	0	22	11	3	5	43	24	10	5	235	194	101	1st, Northwest Div.	Lost Conf. Quarter-Final
2002-03	82	22	13	6	0	23	10	7	1	45	23	13	1	264	208	104	2nd, Northwest Div.	Lost Conf. Semi-Final
2001-02	82	23	11	5	2	19	19	2	1	42	30	7	3	254	211	94	2nd, Northwest Div.	Lost Conf. Quarter-Final
2000-01	82	21	12	5	3	15	16	6	4	36	28	11	7	239	238	90	3rd, Northwest Div.	Lost Conf. Quarter-Final
1999-2000	82	16	14	5	6	14	15	10	2	30	29	15	8	227	237	83	3rd, Northwest Div.	Out of Playoffs
1998-99	82	14	21	6	....	9	26	6	....	23	47	12	....	192	258	58	4th, Northwest Div.	Out of Playoffs
1997-98	82	15	22	4	....	10	21	10	....	25	43	14	....	224	273	64	7th, Pacific Div.	Out of Playoffs
1996-97	82	20	17	4	....	15	23	3	....	35	40	7	....	257	273	77	4th, Pacific Div.	Out of Playoffs
1995-96	82	15	19	7	....	17	16	8	....	32	35	15	....	278	278	79	3rd, Pacific Div.	Lost Conf. Quarter-Final
1994-95	48	10	8	6	....	8	10	6	....	18	18	12	....	153	148	48	2nd, Pacific Div.	Lost Conf. Semi-Final
1993-94	84	20	19	3	....	21	21	0	....	41	40	3	....	279	276	85	2nd, Pacific Div.	Lost Final
1992-93	84	27	11	4	....	19	18	5	....	46	29	9	....	346	278	101	1st, Smythe Div.	Lost Div. Final
1991-92	80	23	10	7	....	19	16	5	....	42	26	12	....	285	250	96	1st, Smythe Div.	Lost Div. Final
1990-91	80	18	17	5	....	10	26	4	....	28	43	9	....	243	315	65	4th, Smythe Div.	Lost Div. Semi-Final
1989-90	80	13	16	11	....	12	25	3	....	25	41	14	....	245	306	64	5th, Smythe Div.	Out of Playoffs
1988-89	80	19	15	6	....	14	24	2	....	33	39	8	....	251	253	74	4th, Smythe Div.	Lost Div. Semi-Final
1987-88	80	15	20	5	....	10	26	4	....	25	46	9	....	272	320	59	5th, Smythe Div.	Out of Playoffs
1986-87	80	17	19	4	....	12	24	4	....	29	43	8	....	282	314	66	5th, Smythe Div.	Out of Playoffs
1985-86	80	17	18	5	....	6	26	8	....	23	44	13	....	282	333	59	4th, Smythe Div.	Lost Div. Semi-Final
1984-85	80	15	21	4	....	10	25	5	....	25	46	9	....	284	401	59	5th, Smythe Div.	Out of Playoffs
1983-84	80	20	16	4	....	12	23	5	....	32	39	9	....	306	328	73	3rd, Smythe Div.	Lost Div. Semi-Final
1982-83	80	20	12	8	....	10	23	7	....	30	35	15	....	303	309	75	3rd, Smythe Div.	Lost Div. Semi-Final
1981-82	80	20	8	12	....	10	25	5	....	30	33	17	....	290	286	77	2nd, Smythe Div.	Lost Final
1980-81	80	17	12	11	....	11	20	9	....	28	32	20	....	289	301	76	3rd, Smythe Div.	Lost Prelim. Round
1979-80	80	14	17	9	....	13	20	7	....	27	37	16	....	256	281	70	3rd, Smythe Div.	Lost Prelim. Round
1978-79	80	15	18	7	....	10	24	6	....	25	42	13	....	217	291	63	2nd, Smythe Div.	Lost Prelim. Round
1977-78	80	13	15	12	....	7	28	5	....	20	43	17	....	239	320	57	3rd, Smythe Div.	Out of Playoffs
1976-77	80	13	21	6	....	12	21	7	....	25	42	13	....	235	294	63	4th, Smythe Div.	Out of Playoffs
1975-76	80	22	11	7	....	11	21	8	....	33	32	15	....	271	272	81	2nd, Smythe Div.	Lost Prelim. Round
1974-75	80	23	12	5	....	15	20	5	....	38	32	10	....	271	254	86	1st, Smythe Div.	Lost Quarter-Final
1973-74	78	14	18	7	....	10	25	4	....	24	43	11	....	224	296	59	7th, East Div.	Out of Playoffs
1972-73	78	17	18	4	....	5	29	5	....	22	47	9	....	233	339	53	7th, East Div.	Out of Playoffs
1971-72	78	14	20	5	....	6	30	3	....	20	50	8	....	203	297	48	7th, East Div.	Out of Playoffs
1970-71	78	17	18	4	....	7	28	4	....	24	46	8	....	229	296	56	6th, East Div.	Out of Playoffs

NORTHWEST DIVISION
38th NHL Season

Franchise date: May 22, 1970

2007-08 Player Personnel

FORWARDS	HT	WT	S	Place of Birth	*Age	2006-07 Club
BALEJ, Jozef	6-1	195	R	Myjava, Czech.	25	Fribourg
BROWN, Mike	6-0	210	R	Northbrook, IL	22	Manitoba
BURROWS, Alexandre	6-1	190	L	Pincourt, Que.	26	Vancouver
CLASSEN, Greg	6-1	200	L	Aylsham, Sask.	30	Hamburg
COOKE, Matt	5-11	205	L	Belleville, Ont.	29	Vancouver
COWAN, Jeff	6-2	205	L	Scarborough, Ont.	31	Los Angeles-Vancouver
GENOWAY, Colby	6-1	201	R	Morden, Man.	23	Portland (AHL)-Manitoba
GRABNER, Michael	6-0	177	L	Villach, Austria	19	Spokane-Manitoba
HANSEN, Jannik	6-1	201	R	Herlev, Denmark	21	Manitoba-Vancouver
ISBISTER, Brad	6-4	231	R	Edmonton, Alta.	30	Alb-NYR-Hart
JAFFRAY, Jason	6-1	205	L	Rimbey, Alta.	26	Manitoba
KESLER, Ryan	6-2	205	R	Livonia, MI	23	Vancouver
MORAN, Brad	5-11	187	L	Abbotsford, B.C.	28	Vancouver-Manitoba
MORRISON, Brendan	5-11	181	L	Pitt Meadows, B.C.	32	Vancouver
NASLUND, Markus	5-11	195	L	Ornskoldsvik, Sweden	34	Vancouver
PYATT, Taylor	6-4	220	L	Thunder Bay, Ont.	26	Vancouver
RAYMOND, Mason	6-0	165	L	Cochrane, Alta.	22	U. Minn-Duluth-Manitoba
RITCHIE, Byron	5-10	190	L	Burnaby, B.C.	30	Calgary
RYPIEN, Rick	5-11	181	R	Coleman, Alta	23	Vancouver-Manitoba
SEDIN, Daniel	6-1	185	L	Ornskoldsvik, Sweden	27	Vancouver
SEDIN, Henrik	6-2	190	L	Ornskoldsvik, Sweden	27	Vancouver
SHANNON, Ryan	5-9	173	R	Darien, CT	24	Anaheim-Portland (AHL)
SIMEK, Juraj	6-1	189	L	Presov, Czech.	20	Brandon
DEFENSEMEN						
BIEKSA, Kevin	6-1	205	R	Grimsby, Ont.	26	Vancouver
BOURDON, Luc	6-3	211	L	Shippagan, N.B.	20	Van-Monc-Cape Breton-Manitoba
COULOMBE, Patrick	5-11	185	L	St-Fabien, Que.	22	Van-Manitoba-Victoria
EDLER, Alexander	6-3	220	L	Ostersund, Sweden	21	Vancouver-Manitoba
HESHKA, Shaun	6-1	209	R	Melville, Sask.	22	Manitoba-Victoria
KRAJICEK, Lukas	6-2	196	L	Prostejov, Czech.	24	Vancouver
McIVER, Nathan	6-2	206	L	Summerside, P.E.I.	22	Vancouver-Manitoba
MILLER, Aaron	6-3	218	R	Buffalo, NY	36	Los Angeles
MITCHELL, Willie	6-3	205	L	Port McNeill, B.C.	30	Vancouver
OHLUND, Mattias	6-2	220	L	Pitea, Sweden	31	Vancouver
RAHIMI, Daniel	6-3	221	L	Umea, Sweden	20	Bjorkloven Jr.-Manitoba-Bjorkloven
SALO, Sami	6-3	215	R	Turku, Finland	33	Vancouver
SHARROW, Jim	6-2	198	R	Framingham, MA	22	Chicago (AHL)

GOALTENDERS	HT	WT	C	Place of Birth	*Age	2006-07 Club
LUONGO, Roberto	6-3	205	L	Montreal, Que.	28	Vancouver
MacINTYRE, Drew	6-2	185	L	Charlottetown, PEI	24	Manitoba
SANFORD, Curtis	5-10	187	L	Owen Sound, Ont.	27	St. Louis-Peoria
SCHNEIDER, Cory	6-2	195	L	Marblehead, MA	21	Boston College

* – Age at start of 2007-08 season

Coach

ALAIN VIGNEAULT

Coach, Vancouver Canucks. Born in Quebec City, Que., May 14, 1961.

On June 20, 2006, Alain Vigneault became the 16th head coach in Vancouver Canucks history. He previously served in the NHL as head coach of the Montreal Canadiens from 1997 to 2001, becoming the organization's second youngest coach in club history at the age of 36. Vigneault was nominated for the Jack Adams Award as NHL coach of the year following the 1999-2000 season. In 2006-07, he led the Canucks to first place in the Northwest Division by setting new club records with 49 wins and 105 points after the club had missed the playoffs the previous season. Vigneault was rewarded with the Jack Adams Award as NHL coach of the year.

Vigneault joined the Canucks from the club's AHL affiliate, the Manitoba Moose, where he led the team to within one game of the conference finals in 2005-06. Prior to joining the Moose, Vigneault spent many years as a head coach in the QMJHL with Trois-Rivieres, Hull, Beauport and PEI. In 1988, Vigneault led the Hull Olympiques into the Memorial Cup and was subsequently named CHL coach of the year. He has also been honoured as coach of the QMJHL's Second All-Star team on three separate occasions. Vigneault has also achieved success on the international stage. He served as an assistant coach with Canada's national junior team in 1989 and 1991, winning a gold medal at the 1991 World Junior Championships in Saskatoon.

As a player, Vigneault was a member of the St. Louis Blues from 1981 to 1983. Drafted by the Blues in the eighth round, 167th overall, in the 1981 Entry Draft, the defenceman recorded two goals, five assists and 82 penalty minutes in his NHL career. Vigneault went on to serve as a scout for the Blues for two seasons and as an assistant coach for the Ottawa Senators from 1992 to 1996.

Coaching Record

		Regular Season				Playoffs		
Season	Team	Games	W	L	O/T	Games	W	L
1986-87	Trois-Rivières (QMJHL)	65	26	37	2	....	....	....
1987-88	Hull (QMJHL)	70	43	23	4	19	12	7
1988-89	Hull (QMJHL)	66	36	25	5	9	5	4
1989-90	Hull (QMJHL)	70	36	29	5	11	4	7
1990-91	Hull (QMJHL)	65	33	25	7	6	2	4
1991-92	Hull (QMJHL)	68	40	23	5	6	2	4
1995-96	Beauport (QMJHL)	31	19	7	5	20	13	7
1996-97	Beauport (QMJHL)	70	24	44	2	4	1	3
1997-98	**Montreal (NHL)**	**82**	**37**	**32**	**13**	**10**	**4**	**6**
1998-99	**Montreal (NHL)**	**82**	**32**	**39**	**11**	....	....	....
1999-2000	**Montreal (NHL)**	**82**	**35**	**38**	**9**	....	....	....
2000-01	**Montreal (NHL)**	**20**	**5**	**13**	**2**	....	....	....
2003-04	PEI (QMJHL)	70	40	25	5	11	6	5
2004-05	PEI (QMJHL)	70	24	39	7	....	....	
2005-06	Manitoba (AHL)	80	44	24	12	13	7	6
2006-07	**Vancouver (NHL)**	**82**	**49**	**26**	**7**	**12**	**5**	**7**
	NHL Totals	**348**	**158**	**148**	**42**	**22**	**9**	**13**

2006-07 Scoring

* – rookie

Regular Season

Pos	#	Player	Team	GP	G	A	Pts	+/–	PIM	PP	SH	GW	S	%
L	22	Daniel Sedin	VAN	81	36	48	84	19	36	16	0	8	236	15.3
C	33	Henrik Sedin	VAN	82	10	71	81	19	66	1	0	2	134	7.5
L	19	Markus Naslund	VAN	82	24	36	60	3	54	9	0	5	222	10.8
C	7	Brendan Morrison	VAN	82	20	31	51	–9	60	6	2	3	139	14.4
C	21	Bryan Smolinski	CHI	62	14	23	37	10	29	4	3	3	122	11.5
			VAN	20	4	3	7	–3	8	2	1	0	41	9.8
			TOTAL	82	18	26	44	7	37	6	4	3	163	11.0
D	3	Kevin Bieksa	VAN	81	12	30	42	1	134	6	0	2	203	5.9
L	9	Taylor Pyatt	VAN	76	23	14	37	5	42	9	0	4	150	15.3
D	6	Sami Salo	VAN	67	14	23	37	21	26	5	0	6	143	9.8
D	2	Mattias Ohlund	VAN	77	11	20	31	–3	80	6	0	2	170	6.5
L	24	Matt Cooke	VAN	81	10	20	30	0	64	1	0	3	133	7.5
D	4	Brent Sopel	L.A.	44	4	19	23	2	14	2	0	2	104	3.8
			VAN	20	1	4	5	0	10	0	0	0	27	3.7
			TOTAL	64	5	23	28	2	24	2	0	2	131	3.8
C	16	Trevor Linden	VAN	80	12	13	25	–6	34	5	0	1	92	13.0
C	38	Jan Bulis	VAN	79	12	11	23	–8	70	1	1	2	122	9.8
C	17	Ryan Kesler	VAN	48	6	10	16	1	40	0	0	0	88	6.8
D	5	Lukas Krajicek	VAN	78	3	13	16	–4	64	1	0	2	105	2.9
L	20	Jeff Cowan	L.A.	21	0	2	2	–1	32	0	0	0	28	0.0
			VAN	42	7	3	10	4	93	0	1	0	46	15.2
			TOTAL	63	7	5	12	3	125	0	1	0	74	9.5
D	8	Willie Mitchell	VAN	62	1	10	11	1	45	0	0	0	54	1.9
L	14	Alexandre Burrows	VAN	81	3	6	9	–7	93	0	0	1	70	4.3
C	25	Josh Green	VAN	57	2	5	7	0	25	0	0	2	74	2.7
D	18	Rory Fitzpatrick	VAN	58	1	6	7	12	46	0	0	1	41	2.4
C	26	Tommi Santala	VAN	30	1	5	6	0	24	0	0	0	20	5.0
C	32	Marc Chouinard	VAN	42	2	2	4	–2	10	1	0	0	15	13.3
D	28	Yannick Tremblay	VAN	12	1	2	3	–6	12	1	0	0	30	3.3
D	23 *	Alexander Edler	VAN	22	1	2	3	3	6	0	0	0	10	10.0
C	39	Brad Moran	VAN	3	0	1	1	0	2	0	0	0	3	0.0
D	29 *	Patrick Coulombe	VAN	7	0	1	1	–6	4	0	0	0	11	0.0
C	29 *	Nathan Smith	VAN	1	0	0	0	0	0	0	0	0	0	0.0
D	45 *	Nathan McIver	VAN	1	0	0	0	–3	7	0	0	0	0	0.0
R	27	Lee Goren	VAN	2	0	0	0	–1	0	0	0	0	2	0.0
R	20 *	Jesse Schultz	VAN	2	0	0	0	0	0	0	0	0	6	0.0
C	15 *	Rick Rypien	VAN	2	0	0	0	0	5	0	0	0	0	0.0
C	37 *	Brandon Reid	VAN	3	0	0	0	–1	0	0	0	0	8	0.0
L	21	Tyler Bouck	VAN	6	0	0	0	–1	16	0	0	0	7	0.0
D	4 *	Luc Bourdon	VAN	9	0	0	0	–1	4	0	0	0	3	0.0

Goaltending

No.	Goaltender	GPI	Mins	Avg	W	L	OT	EN	SO	GA	SA	S%	G	A	PIM
1	Roberto Luongo	76	4490	2.29	47	22	6	3	5	171	2169	.921	0	2	10
35	Dany Sabourin	9	480	2.63	2	4	1	2	0	21	224	.906	0	0	0
	Totals	**82**	**5006**	**2.36**	**49**	**26**	**7**	**5**	**5**	**197**	**2398**	**.918**			

Playoffs

Pos	#	Player	Team	GP	G	A	Pts	+/–	PIM	PP	SH	GW	OT	S	%
C	16	Trevor Linden	VAN	12	2	5	7	4	6	1	0	2	0	19	10.5
D	2	Mattias Ohlund	VAN	12	2	5	7	3	12	1	0	0	0	29	6.9
L	9	Taylor Pyatt	VAN	12	2	4	6	–2	6	0	0	1	1	30	6.7
L	19	Markus Naslund	VAN	12	4	1	5	–1	16	1	0	0	0	41	9.8
L	22	Daniel Sedin	VAN	12	2	3	5	–5	4	0	0	0	0	49	4.1
C	21	Bryan Smolinski	VAN	12	2	2	4	2	8	0	0	0	0	16	12.5
C	33	Henrik Sedin	VAN	12	2	2	4	–8	14	1	0	1	1	24	8.3
C	7	Brendan Morrison	VAN	12	1	3	4	4	6	0	0	0	0	21	4.8
L	20	Jeff Cowan	VAN	10	2	0	2	1	22	0	0	1	1	10	20.0
C	38	Jan Bulis	VAN	12	1	1	2	0	2	0	0	0	0	20	5.0
D	5	Lukas Krajicek	VAN	12	0	2	2	–2	12	0	0	0	0	11	0.0
L	14	Alexandre Burrows	VAN	11	1	0	1	0	14	0	0	0	0	12	8.3
C	37 *	Brandon Reid	VAN	1	0	1	1	1	0	0	0	0	0	2	0.0
C	25	Josh Green	VAN	9	0	1	1	1	12	0	0	0	0	9	0.0
D	6	Sami Salo	VAN	10	0	1	1	0	4	0	0	0	0	27	0.0
L	36 *	Jannik Hansen	VAN	10	0	1	1	0	4	0	0	0	0	17	0.0
D	8	Willie Mitchell	VAN	12	0	1	1	–2	12	0	0	0	0	10	0.0
L	24	Matt Cooke	VAN	1	0	0	0	0	2	0	0	0	0	1	0.0
C	26	Tommi Santala	VAN	1	0	0	0	0	0	0	0	0	0	0	0.0
C	17	Ryan Kesler	VAN	1	0	0	0	0	0	0	0	0	0	2	0.0
D	18	Rory Fitzpatrick	VAN	3	0	0	0	–1	6	0	0	0	0	0	0.0
C	29 *	Nathan Smith	VAN	4	0	0	0	0	0	0	0	0	0	0	0.0
D	3	Kevin Bieksa	VAN	9	0	0	0	–1	20	0	0	0	0	13	0.0
D	4	Brent Sopel	VAN	11	0	0	0	1	2	0	0	0	0	21	0.0

Goaltending

No.	Goaltender	GPI	Mins	Avg	W	L	EN	SO	GA	SA	S%	G	A	PIM
1	Roberto Luongo	12	847	1.77	5	7	0	0	25	427	.941	0	0	0
35	Dany Sabourin	2	14	4.29	0	0	0	0	1	11	.909	0	0	0
	Totals	**12**	**867**	**1.80**	**5**	**7**	**0**	**0**	**26**	**438**	**.941**			

Coaching History

Hal Laycoe, 1970-71, 1971-72; Vic Stasiuk, 1972-73; Bill McCreary and Phil Maloney, 1973-74; Phil Maloney, 1974-75, 1975-76; Phil Maloney and Orland Kurtenbach, 1976-77; Orland Kurtenbach, 1977-78; Harry Neale, 1978-79 to 1980-81; Harry Neale and Roger Neilson, 1981-82; Roger Neilson, 1982-83; Roger Neilson and Harry Neale, 1983-84; Bill Laforge and Harry Neale, 1984-85; Tom Watt, 1985-86, 1986-87; Bob McCammon, 1987-88 to 1989-90; Bob McCammon and Pat Quinn, 1990-91; Pat Quinn, 1991-92 to 1993-94; Rick Ley, 1994-95; Rick Ley and Pat Quinn, 1995-96; Tom Renney, 1996-97; Tom Renney and Mike Keenan, 1997-98; Mike Keenan and Marc Crawford, 1998-99; Marc Crawford, 1999-2000 to 2005-06; Alain Vigneault, 2006-07 to date.

Club Records

Team

(Figures in brackets for season records are games played; records for fewest points, wins, ties, losses, goals, goals against are for 70 or more games)

Record		
Most Points	**105**	2006-07 (82)
Most Wins	**49**	2006-07 (82)
Most Ties	**20**	1980-81 (80)
Most Losses	**50**	1971-72 (78)
Most Goals	**346**	1992-93 (84)
Most Goals Against	**401**	1984-85 (80)
Fewest Points	**48**	1971-72 (78)
Fewest Wins	**20**	1971-72 (78), 1977-78 (80)
Fewest Ties	**3**	1993-94 (84)
Fewest Losses	**24**	2002-03 (82)
Fewest Goals	**192**	1998-99 (82)
Fewest Goals Against	**194**	2003-04 (82)
Longest Winning Streak		
Overall	**10**	Nov. 9-30/02
Home	**9**	Nov. 6-Dec. 9/92
Away	**8**	Dec. 20/03-Jan. 13/04
Longest Undefeated Streak		
Overall	**14**	Jan.26-Feb. 25/03 (10 wins, 4 ties)
Home	**18**	Nov. 4/92-Jan. 16/93 (16 wins, 2 ties)
Away	**9**	Feb. 4-Mar. 3/03 (6 wins, 3 ties)
Longest Losing Streak		
Overall	**10**	Oct. 23-Nov. 11/97
Home	**6**	Dec. 18/70-Jan. 20/71
Away	**12**	Nov. 28/81-Feb. 6/82
Longest Winless Streak		
Overall	**13**	Nov. 9-Dec. 7/73 (10 losses, 3 ties)
Home	**11**	Dec. 18/70-Feb. 6/71 (10 losses, 1 tie)
Away	**20**	Jan. 2-Apr. 2/86 (14 losses, 6 ties)
Most Shutouts, Season	**8**	1974-75 (80), 2001-02 (82)
Most PIM, Season	**2,326**	1992-93 (84)
Most Goals, Game	**11**	Mar. 28/71 (Cal. 5 at Van. 11), Nov. 25/86 (L.A. 5 at Van. 11), Mar. 1/92 (Cgy. 0 at Van. 11)

Individual

Record		
Most Seasons	**15**	Trevor Linden
Most Games	**1,081**	Trevor Linden
Most Goals, Career	**321**	Markus Naslund
Most Assists, Career	**411**	Stan Smyl
Most Points, Career	**721**	Trevor Linden (311G, 410A)
Most PIM, Career	**2,127**	Gino Odjick
Most Shutouts, Career	**20**	Kirk McLean
Longest Consecutive Games Streak	**504**	Brendan Morrison (Mar. 16/00-Apr. 8/07)
Most Goals, Season	**60**	Pavel Bure (1992-93, 1993-94)
Most Assists, Season	**71**	Henrik Sedin (2006-07)
Most Points, Season	**110**	Pavel Bure (1992-93; 60G, 50A)
Most PIM, Season	**372**	Donald Brashear (1997-98)
Most Points, Defenseman, Season	**63**	Doug Lidster (1986-87; 12G, 51A)
Most Points, Center, Season	**91**	Patrik Sundstrom (1983-84; 38G, 53A)
Most Points, Right Wing, Season	**110**	Pavel Bure (1992-93; 60G, 50A)
Most Points, Left Wing, Season	**104**	Markus Naslund (2002-03; 48G, 56A)
Most Points, Rookie, Season	**60**	Ivan Hlinka (1981-82; 23G, 37A), Pavel Bure (1991-92; 34G, 26A)
Most Shutouts, Season	**7**	Dan Cloutier (2001-02)
Most Goals, Game	**4**	Twelve times
Most Assists, Game	**6**	Patrik Sundstrom (Feb. 29/84)
Most Points, Game	**7**	Patrik Sundstrom (Feb. 29/84; 1G, 6A)

Retired Numbers

12	Stan Smyl	1978-1991

General Managers' History

Bud Poile, 1970-71 to 1972-73; Hal Laycoe, 1973-74; Phil Maloney, 1974-75 to 1976-77; Jake Milford, 1977-78 to 1981-82; Harry Neale, 1982-83 to 1984-85; Jack Gordon, 1985-86, 1986-87; Pat Quinn, 1987-88 to 1997-98; Brian Burke, 1998-99 to 2003-04; David Nonis, 2004-05 to date.

Captains' History

Orland Kurtenbach, 1970-71 to 1973-74; no captain, 1974-75; Andre Boudrias, 1975-76; Chris Oddleifson, 1976-77; Don Lever, 1977-78; Don Lever and Kevin McCarthy, 1978-79; Kevin McCarthy, 1979-80 to 1981-82; Stan Smyl, 1982-83 to 1989-90; Dan Quinn, Doug Lidster and Trevor Linden, 1990-91; Trevor Linden, 1991-92 to 1996-97; Mark Messier, 1997-98 to 1999-2000; Markus Naslund, 2000-01 to date.

All-time Record vs. Other Clubs

Regular Season

	At Home								On Road								Total							
	GP	W	L	T	OL	GF	GA	PTS	GP	W	L	T	OL	GF	GA	PTS	GP	W	L	T	OL	GF	GA	PTS
Anaheim	30	16	12	2	0	95	74	34	29	13	9	7	0	84	73	33	59	29	21	9	0	179	147	67
Atlanta	4	2	1	1	0	13	7	5	3	2	1	0	0	12	11	4	7	4	2	1	0	25	18	9
Boston	52	17	26	8	1	171	211	43	53	7	38	7	1	124	219	22	105	24	64	15	2	295	430	65
Buffalo	53	26	16	11	0	197	163	63	53	18	26	8	1	155	190	45	106	44	42	19	1	352	353	108
Calgary	107	40	47	18	2	361	352	100	106	30	61	15	0	303	411	75	213	70	108	33	2	664	763	175
Carolina	31	15	10	6	0	109	84	36	29	12	12	5	0	100	94	29	60	27	22	11	0	209	178	65
Chicago	76	38	23	15	0	229	217	91	75	21	45	7	2	179	274	51	151	59	68	22	2	408	491	142
Colorado	55	22	24	7	2	183	208	53	55	19	26	8	2	152	186	48	110	41	50	15	4	335	394	101
Columbus	12	9	2	0	1	49	33	19	12	6	3	2	1	42	30	15	24	15	5	2	2	91	63	34
Dallas	75	34	30	10	1	262	224	79	75	22	40	12	1	216	270	57	150	56	70	22	2	478	494	136
Detroit	69	31	28	10	0	248	222	72	70	20	41	8	1	200	283	49	139	51	69	18	1	448	505	121
Edmonton	90	36	40	12	2	321	348	86	89	29	50	7	3	281	376	68	179	65	90	19	5	602	724	154
Florida	10	4	1	5	0	29	22	13	8	4	3	1	0	27	21	9	18	8	4	6	0	56	43	22
Los Angeles	101	52	31	16	2	381	313	122	103	34	52	16	1	321	403	85	204	86	83	32	3	702	716	207
Minnesota	18	9	3	3	3	46	44	24	19	7	9	2	1	46	55	17	37	16	12	5	4	92	99	41
Montreal	56	15	33	8	0	152	204	38	54	11	38	5	0	139	244	27	110	26	71	13	0	291	448	65
Nashville	16	11	3	1	1	58	37	24	17	8	8	1	0	45	52	17	33	19	11	2	1	103	89	41
New Jersey	47	27	9	11	0	175	130	65	50	23	21	6	0	159	154	52	97	50	30	17	0	334	284	117
NY Islanders	47	23	21	3	0	155	153	49	48	12	25	10	1	137	175	35	95	35	46	13	1	292	328	84
NY Rangers	51	15	33	3	0	163	204	33	55	12	38	5	0	142	239	29	106	27	71	8	0	305	443	62
Ottawa	12	6	5	1	0	36	28	13	11	5	5	1	0	26	25	11	23	11	10	2	0	62	53	24
Philadelphia	51	10	28	12	1	144	203	33	55	17	36	1	1	164	238	36	106	27	64	13	2	308	441	69
Phoenix	76	47	18	10	1	287	210	105	73	28	34	10	1	258	267	67	149	75	52	20	2	545	477	172
Pittsburgh	50	23	23	4	0	180	187	50	51	11	33	7	0	175	229	29	101	34	56	11	0	355	416	79
St. Louis	76	32	35	9	0	224	242	73	75	22	44	9	0	210	278	53	151	54	79	18	0	434	520	126
San Jose	36	20	11	4	1	129	98	45	38	19	14	5	0	118	108	43	74	39	25	9	1	247	206	88
Tampa Bay	10	8	0	2	0	45	18	18	9	6	3	0	0	37	31	12	19	14	3	2	0	82	49	30
Toronto	65	30	22	11	2	229	219	73	61	22	28	11	0	201	220	55	126	52	50	22	2	430	439	128
Washington	40	19	15	5	1	139	125	44	40	14	21	4	1	120	132	33	80	33	36	9	2	259	257	77
Defunct Clubs	19	14	3	2	0	82	48	30	19	10	8	1	0	71	68	21	38	24	11	3	0	153	116	51
Totals	**1435**	**651**	**553**	**210**	**21**	**4892**	**4628**	**1533**	**1435**	**464**	**772**	**181**	**18**	**4244**	**5356**	**1127**	**2870**	**1115**	**1325**	**391**	**39**	**9136**	**9984**	**2660**

Playoffs

	Series	W	L	GP	W	L	T	GF	GA	Last Mtg.	Rnd.	Result
Anaheim	1	0	1	5	1	4	0	8	14	2007	CSF	L 1-4
Buffalo	2	0	2	7	1	6	0	14	28	1981	PRE	L 0-3
Calgary	6	2	4	32	15	17	0	96	101	2004	CQF	L 3-4
Chicago	2	1	1	9	4	5	0	24	24	1995	CSF	L 0-4
Colorado	2	0	2	10	2	8	0	26	40	2001	CQF	L 0-4
Dallas	2	2	0	12	8	4	0	31	23	2007	CQF	W 4-3
Detroit	1	0	1	6	2	4	0	16	22	2002	CQF	L 2-4
Edmonton	2	0	2	9	2	7	0	20	35	1992	DF	L 2-4
Los Angeles	3	1	2	17	8	9	0	60	66	1993	DF	L 2-4
Minnesota	1	0	1	7	3	4	0	17	26	2003	CSF	L 3-4
Montreal	1	0	1	5	1	4	0	9	20	1975	QF	L 1-4
NY Islanders	2	0	2	6	0	6	0	14	26	1982	F	L 0-4
NY Rangers	1	0	1	7	3	4	0	19	21	1994	F	L 3-4
Philadelphia	1	0	1	3	1	2	0	9	15	1979	PRE	L 1-2
Phoenix	2	2	0	13	8	5	0	50	34	1993	DSF	W 4-2
St. Louis	2	2	0	14	8	6	0	44	48	2003	CQF	W 4-3
Toronto	1	1	0	5	4	1	0	16	9	1994	CF	W 4-1
Totals	**32**	**11**	**21**	**167**	**71**	**96**	**0**	**473**	**552**			

Calgary totals include Atlanta Flames, 1972-73 to 1979-80. Carolina totals include Hartford, 1979-80 to 1996-97.
Colorado totals include Quebec, 1979-80 to 1994-95. Dallas totals include Minnesota North Stars, 1970-71 to 1992-93.
New Jersey totals include Kansas City, 1974-75, 1975-76, and Colorado Rockies, 1976-77 to 1981-82.
Phoenix totals include Winnipeg, 1979-80 to 1995-96.

Playoff Results 2007-2002

Year	Round	Opponent	Result	GF	GA
2007	CSF	Anaheim	L 1-4	8	14
	CQF	Dallas	W 4-3	13	12
2004	CQF	Calgary	L 3-4	16	19
2003	CSF	Minnesota	L 3-4	17	26
	CQF	St. Louis	W 4-3	17	21
2002	CQF	Detroit	L 2-4	16	22

Abbreviations: Round: F – Final;
CF – conference final; **CSF** – conference semi-final;
CQF – conference quarter-final; **DF** – division final;
DSF – division semi-final; **QF** – quarter-final;
PRE – preliminary round.

2006-07 Results

Oct.	5	at Detroit	3-1
	6	at Columbus	3-2*
	8	at Colorado	2-3
	10	at Minnesota	1-2†
	13	San Jose	4-6
	16	Edmonton	2-1
	17	at Edmonton	1-2
	20	at St. Louis	3-2*
	21	at Nashville	4-3*
	23	at Dallas	1-2
	25	at Chicago	5-0
	27	Washington	3-2†
	31	Nashville	2-3
Nov.	2	at Minnesota	2-5
	4	at Colorado	2-3
	6	Dallas	2-1
	9	Anaheim	0-6
	11	Calgary	2-3
	14	Detroit	2-3
	17	St. Louis	4-2
	19	Chicago	2-1
	22	at Detroit	4-3*
	23	at Nashville	0-6
	25	at Colorado	1-4
	28	Columbus	1-0
	30	Anaheim	1-2
Dec.	2	Colorado	2-1
	4	Edmonton	0-4
	8	Carolina	4-3*
	9	at Calgary	3-5
	12	Phoenix	5-2
	14	Calgary	3-1
	16	Minnesota	2-1
	19	at Minnesota	2-5
	21	at Boston	0-2
	22	at Columbus	2-3
	26	at Calgary	3-1
	27	Calgary	6-5*
	30	at Edmonton	6-2
Jan.	2	at Calgary	3-2
	3	Dallas	2-1†
	5	Edmonton	3-2*
	7	Florida	4-3†
	11	Minnesota	2-5
	13	at Toronto	6-1
	16	at Montreal	4-0
	18	at Ottawa	2-1
	19	at Buffalo	3-4†
	26	Los Angeles	2-3*
	28	San Jose	3-1
	30	Columbus	2-3†
Feb.	1	Edmonton	5-3
	3	at Calgary	3-4
	6	at Edmonton	5-2
	7	Chicago	0-3
	10	Atlanta	3-2
	14	at Minnesota	3-2*
	16	at Chicago	2-1†
	18	Colorado	5-4
	20	at Anaheim	3-2*
	22	at Los Angeles	3-2
	25	at Dallas	1-2*
	27	at St. Louis	1-3
Mar.	1	Phoenix	4-3
	4	Minnesota	4-3†
	6	Tampa Bay	5-1
	8	at Phoenix	4-2
	9	at San Jose	2-1*
	11	at Anaheim	2-4
	13	Minnesota	2-3*
	15	St. Louis	3-2*
	17	Detroit	4-1
	19	at Edmonton	2-1
	21	Nashville	2-0
	25	Colorado	4-5†
	27	at Colorado	3-0
	29	at Los Angeles	4-2
	31	Calgary	2-3
Apr.	3	Los Angeles	4-2
	5	Colorado	1-3
	7	at San Jose	4-3*
	8	at Phoenix	1-3

* – Overtime † – Shootout

Entry Draft Selections 2007-1993

2007
Pick	
25	Patrick White
33	Taylor Ellington
145	Charles-Antoine Messier
146	Ilja Kablukov
176	Taylor Matson
206	Dan Gendur

2006
Pick	
14	Michael Grabner
82	Daniel Rahimi
163	Sergei Shirokov
167	Juraj Simek
197	Evan Fuller

2005
Pick	
10	Luc Bourdon
51	Mason Raymond
114	Alexandre Vincent
138	Matt Butcher
185	Kris Fredheim
205	Mario Bliznak

2004
Pick	
26	Cory Schneider
91	Alexander Edler
125	Andrew Sarauer
159	Mike Brown
189	Julien Ellis
254	David Schulz
287	Jannik Hansen

2003
Pick	
23	Ryan Kesler
60	Marc-Andre Bernier
111	Brandon Nolan
128	Ty Morris
160	Nicklas Danielsson
190	Chad Brownlee
222	Francois-Pierre Guenette
252	Sergei Topol
254	Nathan McIver
285	Matthew Hansen

2002
Pick	
49	Kirill Koltsov
55	Denis Grot
68	Brett Skinner
83	Lukas Mensator
114	John Laliberte
151	Rob McVicar
214	Marc-Andre Roy
223	Ilya Krikunov
247	Matt Violin
277	Thomas Nussli
278	Matt Gens

2001
Pick	
16	R.J. Umberger
66	Fedor Fedorov
114	Evgeny Gladskikh
151	Kevin Bieksa
212	Jason King
245	Konstantin Mikhailov

2000
Pick	
23	Nathan Smith
71	Thatcher Bell
93	Tim Branham
144	Pavel Duma
208	Brandon Reid
241	Nathan Barrett
272	Tim Smith

1999
Pick	
2	Daniel Sedin
3	Henrik Sedin
69	Rene Vydareny
129	Ryan Thorpe
172	Josh Reed
189	Kevin Swanson
218	Markus Kankaanpera
271	Darrell Hay

1998
Pick	
4	Bryan Allen
31	Artem Chubarov
68	Jarkko Ruutu
81	Justin Morrison
90	Regan Darby
136	David Ytfeldt
140	Rick Bertran
149	Paul Cabana
177	Vincent Malts
204	Greg Mischler
219	Curtis Valentine
232	Jason Metcalfe

1997
Pick	
10	Brad Ference
34	Ryan Bonni
36	Harold Druken
64	Kyle Freadrich
90	Chris Stanley
114	David Darguzas
117	Matt Cockell
144	Matt Cooke
148	Larry Shapley
171	Rod Leroux
201	Denis Martynyuk
227	Peter Brady

1996
Pick	
12	Josh Holden
75	Zenith Komarniski
93	Jonas Soling
121	Tyler Prosofsky
147	Nolan McDonald
175	Clint Cabana
201	Jeff Scissons
227	Lubomir Vaic

1995
Pick	
40	Chris McAllister
61	Larry Courville
66	Peter Schaefer
92	Lloyd Shaw
120	Todd Norman
144	Brent Sopel
170	Stewart Bodtker
196	Tyler Willis
222	Jason Cugnet

1994
Pick	
13	Mattias Ohlund
39	Robb Gordon
42	Dave Scatchard
65	Chad Allan
92	Mike Dubinsky
117	Yanick Dube
169	Yuri Kuznetsov
195	Rob Trumbley
221	Bill Muckalt
247	Tyson Nash
273	Robert Longpre

1993
Pick	
20	Mike Wilson
46	Rick Girard
98	Dieter Kochan
124	Scott Walker
150	Troy Creurer
176	Yevgeni Babariko
202	Sean Tallaire
254	Bert Robertsson
280	Sergei Tkachenko

Vice President and General Manager

DAVID NONIS
Senior Vice President/General Manager, Vancouver Canucks.
Born in Burnaby, B.C., May 25, 1966.

David Nonis was given his first assignment as general manager of an NHL hockey club when he was named to the position by the Vancouver Canucks on May 6, 2004. Nonis had spent the previous six seasons as senior vice president, director of hockey operations and was the Canucks' chief negotiator of player contracts. In his first act as general manager, Nonis appointed Steve Tambellini assistant general manager.

A native of Vancouver, Nonis broke into the NHL with the Canucks in 1990. In his first years he was primarily responsible for corporate contracts, computer scouting and team services. Prior to being named senior vice president in 1998, Nonis served as the National Hockey League's manager of hockey operations for four seasons. In his role with the NHL, Nonis gained a vast knowledge of the collective bargaining agreement and helped finalize sections of the document when the previous edition was drafted during the 1994-95 season. He also worked with the league's arbitration team, which included helping teams prepare for arbitration, researching salaries and interpreting contract language.

Nonis played for the Burnaby Blackhawks of the British Columbia Junior Hockey League from 1982 to 1984. He then played for the University of Maine where he served as captain for two seasons and graduated with a B.A. in 1988. Nonis played one season professionally in Denmark, then returned to Maine in 1989 to serve as graduate assistant under head coach Shawn Walsh. Nonis earned an MBA from the University of Maine in 1990.

Club Directory

General Motors Place

Vancouver Canucks
General Motors Place
800 Griffiths Way
Vancouver, B.C. V6B 6G1
Phone **604/899-4600**
FAX 604/899-4640
www.canucks.com
Capacity: 18,630

Executive
Chairman, VCLP & Governor, NHL . . . . . Francesco Aquilini
Alternate Governors . . . . . Roberto Aquilini, Paolo Aquilini
President, CEO & Alt. Gov., NHL . . . . . Chris Zimmerman
Senior Vice President, G.M. & Alt. Gov., NHL . . . . . David M. Nonis
Chief Operating Officer . . . . . Victor de Bonis
Corporate Counsel . . . . . TBD
Executive Vice President, Business . . . . . Jon Festinger
Vice President, People Development . . . . . Susanne Haine
Vice President & G.M., Arena Operations . . . . . Harvey Jones
Vice President, Business Development . . . . . Gord Forbes
Vice President, Finance . . . . . Todd Kobus
Vice President & Assistant G.M. . . . . . Steve Tambellini
Executive Assistant to President & CEO . . . . . Erin Lewyk

Hockey Operations
Senior Vice President, G.M. & Alt. Gov., NHL . . . . . David M. Nonis
Executive Assistant . . . . . Michelle J. Davies
Vice President & Assistant G.M. . . . . . Steve Tambellini
Executive Assistant . . . . . Lori Meehan
Head Coach . . . . . Alain Vigneault
Assistant Coaches . . . . . Rick Bowness, Barry Smith, Mike Kelly
Goaltending Consultant . . . . . Ian Clark
Strength & Conditioning Coach . . . . . Roger Takahashi
Director, Player Development . . . . . Stan Smyl
Director, Player Personnel . . . . . Lorne Henning
Sr. V.P. & G.M., Manitoba Moose . . . . . Craig Heisinger
Head Coach, Manitoba Moose . . . . . Scott Arniel
Assistant Coach, Manitoba Moose . . . . . Brad Berry
Director, Media Relations . . . . . T.C. Carling
Manager, Media Relations . . . . . Ben Brown
Coordinator, Media Relations . . . . . Stephanie Maniago
Director, Community Relations . . . . . Debbie Butt
Manager, Community Relations . . . . . Karen Christiansen
Coordinator, Community Relations . . . . . Jessica Danylchuk
Coordinator, Community Relations . . . . . Tara Clarke
Manager, Hockey Dev. & Alumni Liaison . . . . . Rod Brathwaite

Scouting Staff
Chief Amateur Scout . . . . . Ron Delorme
Amateur Scouts . . . Brian Chapman, Sergei Chibisov, Barry Dean, Thomas Gradin, Mario Marois, Harold Snepsts, Jim Eagle, Frank Kollar, Tim Lenardon, Branislav Pulis
Professional Scouts . . . . . Lucien DeBlois, Eric Crawford
Manager, Scouting & Player Information . . . . . Jonathan Wall

Medical and Training Staff
Medical Trainer . . . . . Mike Burnstein
Assistant Medical Trainers . . . . . Jon Sanderson, Marty Dudgeon
Equipment Manager . . . . . Pat O'Neill
Assistant Equipment Manager . . . . . Jamie Hendricks
Assistant Equipment Trainer . . . . . Brian Hamilton
Game Dressing Room Attendants . . . . . John Jukitch, Ron Shute, Brian Brumwell
Team Doctors . . . . . Dr. Rui Avelar, Dr. Bill Regan, Dr. Mike Wilkinson
Team Dentist . . . . . Dr. Jeffrey Norden
Team Chiropractor . . . . . Dr. Sid Sheard
Team Optometrist . . . . . Dr. Alan R. Boyco

Marketing and Creative Services
Director, Brand Management . . . . . Paul Dal Monte
Manager, Marketing . . . . . Jennifer Murtagh
Marketing Coordinator . . . . . Michelle Davies
Website Manager . . . . . Kevin Kinghorn
Manager, Creative Services . . . . . Ken Jones
Graphic Designers . . . . . Jenny McCleery, Andi Mortenson

Broadcast
Director, Facilities & In-house Productions . . . . . Paul Brettell
Director, Production Services . . . . . Mike Hall
Senior Broadcast Technician . . . . . Greg Story
Director, Technical Services . . . . . Vic Araujo
Senior Multimedia Producer . . . . . Jason Steensma
Multimedia Editor . . . . . TBD
Broadcast Business Manager . . . . . Shannon Baker
Production Assistant & Editor . . . . . Rory McGarry

Business Development
Directors, Business Development . . . . . David Altman, Sharon Butler, Jordan Thorsteinson
Director, Sponsorship Services . . . . . Darren Moscovitch
Director, Premium Sales & Services . . . . . Deborah Boren
Account Executives . . . . . Simon Louca, Lucas Spata, Theresa Jantzen
Administrative Assistant . . . . . Antonia Nassopoulos

Customer Sales and Service
Director, Customer Sales & Service . . . . . Mary Nagy
Manager, Customer Accounts. . Josh Bender, Martha Vassos, Aysha Wilkes, David Pan, Chris Wallace

Game Entertainment & Events
Manager, Game Entertainment & Events . . . . . Jamie Levchuk
Coordinators . . . . . Cam Goudreau, Art Green, Paul Buckley

Finance and Central Services
Controller, Hockey . . . . . Patricia Bigonzi
Corporate Controller . . . . . Aaron Wilson
Senior Accountant . . . . . Melissa Billesberger
Arena Accounting Manager . . . . . Lauri Shortyk
Accountant, Hockey & Canucks for Kids . . . . . Sara Klassen
Accountant . . . . . Wendy Jovanov

Canucks Team Store
Senior Manager, Retail . . . . . TBD
Retail Operations Manager . . . . . Jeff Winslade
Retail Operations Coordinator . . . . . Danielle Libonati

Radio and Television
Radio Affiliation . . . . . Team 1040
Television Affiliation . . . . . Rogers Sportsnet (Channel 22)

Washington Capitals

2006-07 Results: 28W-40L-3OTL-11SOL 70PTS.
Fifth, Southeast Division

Key Off-Season Signings/Acquisitions

2007

- **May 21** • Signed 2006 1st-round pick (4th overall), C **Nicklas Backstrom**.
- **July 1** • Signed D **Tom Poti** and C **Viktor Kozlov**.
- **2** • Signed C **Michael Nylander**.
- **10** • Signed RW **Joe Motzko**.
- **17** • Re-signed D **Steve Eminger**, C **Brian Sutherby**.
- **18** • Re-signed RW **Chris Clark**.
- **27** • Re-signed D **Milan Jurcina**.

A pair of Russians led the way in Washington. Alex Ovechkin had 46 goals and 46 assists for the Capitals in 2006-07 while Alexander Semin had 38 goals and 35 helpers.

2007-08 Schedule

Oct.	Fri.	5	at Atlanta
	Sat.	6	Carolina
	Mon.	8	at NY Islanders*
	Fri.	12	at NY Rangers
	Sat.	13	at Buffalo
	Thu.	18	NY Islanders
	Sat.	20	Pittsburgh
	Wed.	24	Tampa Bay
	Fri.	26	Vancouver
	Sat.	27	at St. Louis
	Mon.	29	at Toronto
Nov.	Thu.	1	at NY Rangers
	Fri.	2	Philadelphia
	Mon.	5	at Carolina
	Tue.	6	at Atlanta
	Thu.	8	at Ottawa
	Sat.	10	Tampa Bay
	Thu.	15	at Florida
	Fri.	16	at Tampa Bay
	Mon.	19	Florida
	Wed.	21	Atlanta
	Fri.	23	at Philadelphia*
	Sat.	24	Carolina
	Mon.	26	Buffalo
	Wed.	28	Florida
	Fri.	30	at Carolina
Dec.	Sat.	1	at Florida
	Fri.	7	at New Jersey
	Sat.	8	Atlanta
	Mon.	10	New Jersey
	Wed.	12	NY Rangers
	Fri.	14	Buffalo
	Sat.	15	at Tampa Bay
	Mon.	17	at Detroit
	Thu.	20	Montreal
	Sat.	22	at NY Islanders
	Wed.	26	Tampa Bay
	Thu.	27	at Pittsburgh
	Sat.	29	at Ottawa*
Jan.	Tue.	1	Ottawa*
	Thu.	3	at Boston
	Sat.	5	at Montreal*
	Wed.	9	Colorado
	Sun.	13	Philadelphia*
	Tue.	15	Ottawa
	Thu.	17	Edmonton
	Sat.	19	Florida
	Mon.	21	at Pittsburgh
	Wed.	23	at Toronto
	Thu.	24	Toronto
	Tue.	29	at Montreal
	Thu.	31	Montreal
Feb.	Sat.	2	Atlanta
	Tue.	5	at Columbus
	Wed.	6	at Philadelphia
	Fri.	8	Carolina
	Sun.	10	NY Rangers*
	Wed.	13	at Atlanta
	Fri.	15	at Florida
	Sat.	16	at Tampa Bay
	Wed.	20	NY Islanders
	Sat.	23	at Carolina*
	Sun.	24	New Jersey*
	Tue.	26	Minnesota
	Fri.	29	at New Jersey
Mar.	Sat.	1	Toronto
	Mon.	3	Boston
	Wed.	5	at Buffalo
	Sat.	8	at Boston*
	Sun.	9	Pittsburgh*
	Wed.	12	Calgary
	Fri.	14	Atlanta
	Sun.	16	Boston*
	Tue.	18	at Nashville
	Wed.	19	at Chicago
	Fri.	21	at Atlanta
	Tue.	25	at Carolina
	Thu.	27	at Tampa Bay
	Sat.	29	at Florida
Apr.	Tue.	1	Carolina
	Thu.	3	Tampa Bay
	Sat.	5	Florida

* Denotes afternoon game.

Year-by-Year Record

Season	GP	Home W	Home L	Home T	Home OL	Road W	Road L	Road T	Road OL	Overall W	Overall L	Overall T	Overall OL	GF	GA	Pts.	Finished	Playoff Result
2006-07	82	17	17	....	7	11	23	....	7	28	40	....	14	235	286	70	5th, Southeast Div.	Out of Playoffs
2005-06	82	16	18	....	7	13	23	....	5	29	41	....	12	237	306	70	5th, Southeast Div.	Out of Playoffs
2004-05	....	....	....	....	....	....	....	....	....	....	....	....	....	....	....	....		
2003-04	82	13	20	6	2	10	26	4	1	23	46	10	3	186	253	59	5th, Southeast Div.	Out of Playoffs
2002-03	82	24	13	2	2	15	16	6	4	39	29	8	6	224	220	92	2nd, Southeast Div.	Lost Conf. Quarter-Final
2001-02	82	21	12	6	2	15	21	5	0	36	33	11	2	228	240	85	2nd, Southeast Div.	Out of Playoffs
2000-01	82	24	9	6	2	17	18	4	2	41	27	10	4	233	211	96	1st, Southeast Div.	Lost Conf. Quarter-Final
1999-2000	82	26	5	8	2	18	19	4	0	44	24	12	2	227	194	102	1st, Southeast Div.	Lost Conf. Quarter-Final
1998-99	82	16	23	2	....	15	22	4	....	31	45	6	....	200	218	68	3rd, Southeast Div.	Out of Playoffs
1997-98	82	23	12	6	....	17	18	6	....	40	30	12	....	219	202	92	3rd, Atlantic Div.	Lost Final
1996-97	82	19	17	5	....	14	23	4	....	33	40	9	....	214	231	75	5th, Atlantic Div.	Out of Playoffs
1995-96	82	21	15	5	....	18	17	6	....	39	32	11	....	234	204	89	4th, Atlantic Div.	Lost Conf. Quarter-Final
1994-95	48	15	6	3	....	7	12	5	....	22	18	8	....	136	120	52	3rd, Atlantic Div.	Lost Conf. Quarter-Final
1993-94	84	17	16	9	....	22	19	1	....	39	35	10	....	277	263	88	3rd, Atlantic Div.	Lost Conf. Semi-Final
1992-93	84	21	15	6	....	22	19	1	....	43	34	7	....	325	286	93	2nd, Patrick Div.	Lost Div. Semi-Final
1991-92	80	25	12	3	....	20	15	5	....	45	27	8	....	330	275	98	2nd, Patrick Div.	Lost Div. Semi-Final
1990-91	80	21	14	5	....	16	22	2	....	37	36	7	....	258	258	81	3rd, Patrick Div.	Lost Div. Final
1989-90	80	19	18	3	....	17	20	3	....	36	38	6	....	284	275	78	3rd, Patrick Div.	Lost Conf. Championship
1988-89	80	25	12	3	....	16	17	7	....	41	29	10	....	305	259	92	1st, Patrick Div.	Lost Div. Semi-Final
1987-88	80	22	14	4	....	16	19	5	....	38	33	9	....	281	249	85	2nd, Patrick Div.	Lost Div. Final
1986-87	80	22	15	3	....	16	17	7	....	38	32	10	....	285	278	86	2nd, Patrick Div.	Lost Div. Semi-Final
1985-86	80	30	8	2	....	20	15	5	....	50	23	7	....	315	272	107	2nd, Patrick Div.	Lost Div. Final
1984-85	80	27	11	2	....	19	14	7	....	46	25	9	....	322	240	101	2nd, Patrick Div.	Lost Div. Semi-Final
1983-84	80	26	11	3	....	22	16	2	....	48	27	5	....	308	226	101	2nd, Patrick Div.	Lost Div. Final
1982-83	80	22	12	6	....	17	13	10	....	39	25	16	....	306	283	94	3rd, Patrick Div.	Lost Div. Semi-Final
1981-82	80	16	16	8	....	10	25	5	....	26	41	13	....	319	338	65	5th, Patrick Div.	Out of Playoffs
1980-81	80	16	17	7	....	10	19	11	....	26	36	18	....	286	317	70	5th, Patrick Div.	Out of Playoffs
1979-80	80	20	14	6	....	7	26	7	....	27	40	13	....	261	293	67	5th, Patrick Div.	Out of Playoffs
1978-79	80	15	19	6	....	9	22	9	....	24	41	15	....	273	338	63	4th, Norris Div.	Out of Playoffs
1977-78	80	10	23	7	....	7	26	7	....	17	49	14	....	195	321	48	5th, Norris Div.	Out of Playoffs
1976-77	80	17	15	8	....	7	27	6	....	24	42	14	....	221	307	62	4th, Norris Div.	Out of Playoffs
1975-76	80	6	26	8	....	5	33	2	....	11	59	10	....	224	394	32	5th, Norris Div.	Out of Playoffs
1974-75	80	7	28	5	....	1	39	0	....	8	67	5	....	181	446	21	5th, Norris Div.	Out of Playoffs

SOUTHEAST DIVISION
34th NHL Season

Franchise date: June 11, 1974

2007-08 Player Personnel

FORWARDS	HT	WT	S	Place of Birth	*Age	2006-07 Club
BACKSTROM, Nicklas	6-0	183	L	Gavle, Sweden	19	Brynas
BOUCHARD, Francois	6-0	180	L	Sherbrooke, Que.	19	Baie-Comeau
BOURQUE, Chris	5-8	181	L	Boston, MA	21	Hershey
BRADLEY, Matt	6-3	201	R	Stittsville, Ont.	29	Washington
BRASHEAR, Donald	6-2	235	L	Bedford, IN	35	Washington
CLARK, Chris	6-0	196	R	South Windsor, CT	31	Washington
CLYMER, Ben	6-1	200	R	Bloomington, MN	29	Washington
FEHR, Eric	6-4	212	R	Winkler, Man.	22	Washington-Hershey
FLEISCHMANN, Tomas	6-1	190	L	Koprivnice, Czech.	23	Washington-Hershey
GORDON, Andrew	5-11	180	R	Halifax, N.S.	21	St. Cloud State
GORDON, Boyd	6-1	201	R	Unity, Sask.	23	Washington
JOUDREY, Andrew	5-11	191	L	Halifax, N.S.	23	U. of Wisconsin-Hershey
KLEPIS, Jakub	6-1	198	R	Prague, Czech.	23	Washington-Hershey
KOZLOV, Viktor	6-5	235	R	Togliatti, USSR	32	NY Islanders
LAICH, Brooks	6-2	210	L	Wawota, Sask.	24	Washington
MORGAN, Jason	6-1	200	L	St. John's, Nfld.	30	Minnesota-Houston
MORIN, Travis	6-2	175	L	Minneapolis, MN	23	Minnesota State-South Carolina
MOTZKO, Joe	6-0	184	R	Bemidji, MN	27	CBJ-Syr-Port (AHL)-Ana
NYLANDER, Michael	6-1	195	L	Stockholm, Sweden	34	NY Rangers
OVECHKIN, Alex	6-2	220	R	Moscow, USSR	22	Washington
PETTINGER, Matt	6-1	210	L	Edmonton, Alta.	26	Washington
PINIZZOTTO, Steve	6-2	0	R	Mississauga, Ont.	23	RIT Tigers-Hershey
SEMIN, Alexander	6-2	200	L	Krasnoyarsk, USSR	23	Washington
STECKEL, David	6-5	222	L	Westbend, WI	25	Washington-Hershey
SUTHERBY, Brian	6-3	215	L	Edmonton, Alta.	25	Washington
WERNER, Steve	6-1	200	R	Washington, DC	23	Hershey-South Carolina
WILSON, Kyle	6-0	200	R	Oakville, Ont.	22	San Antonio-South Carolina-Her
DEFENSEMEN						
ALZNER, Karl	6-2	206	L	Burnaby, B.C.	19	Calgary (WHL)
COLLINS, Sean	6-1	212	R	Troy, MI	23	Ohio State-Hershey
DOVGAN, Viktor	6-2	205	L	Moscow, USSR	20	Hershey-South Carolina
EMINGER, Steve	6-2	211	R	Woodbridge, Ont.	23	Washington
ERSKINE, John	6-4	216	L	Kingston, Ont.	27	Washington-Hershey
GREEN, Mike	6-1	208	R	Calgary, Alta.	21	Washington
HUNT, Jamie	6-2	200	L	Calgary, Alta.	23	Washington-Hershey
JURCINA, Milan	6-4	233	R	Liptovsky Mikulas, Czech.	24	Boston-Washington
MORRISONN, Shaone	6-4	210	L	Vancouver, B.C.	24	Washington
POKULOK, Sasha	6-5	220	L	Montreal, Que.	21	Hershey-South Carolina
POLLOCK, Jame	6-1	210	R	Quebec City, Que.	28	Nurnberg
POTHIER, Brian	6-0	198	R	New Bedford, MA	30	Washington
POTI, Tom	6-3	202	L	Worcester, MA	30	NY Islanders
SCHULTZ, Jeff	6-6	224	L	Calgary, Alta.	21	Washington-Hershey

GOALTENDERS	HT	WT	C	Place of Birth	*Age	2006-07 Club
CASSIVI, Frederic	6-4	220	L	Sorel, Que.	32	Washington-Hershey
JOHNSON, Brent	6-3	199	L	Farmington, MI	30	Washington
KOLZIG, Olaf	6-3	221	L	Johannesburg, South Africa	37	Washington
MACHESNEY, Daren	6-0	182	L	Hamilton, Ont.	20	Hershey-South Carolina
NEUVIRTH, Michal	6-0	174	L	Usti nad Labem, Czech.	19	Plymouth

* – Age at start of 2007-08 season

2006-07 Scoring

* – rookie

Regular Season

Pos	#	Player	Team	GP	G	A	Pts	+/–	PIM	PP	SH	GW	S	%
L	8	Alex Ovechkin	WSH	82	46	46	92	–19	52	16	0	8	392	11.7
L	28	Alexander Semin	WSH	77	38	35	73	–7	90	17	0	6	243	15.6
R	17	Chris Clark	WSH	74	30	24	54	–10	66	9	4	2	164	18.3
L	18	Matt Pettinger	WSH	64	16	16	32	–13	22	4	3	2	111	14.4
C	15	Boyd Gordon	WSH	71	7	22	29	10	14	0	2	0	104	6.7
D	2	Brian Pothier	WSH	72	3	25	28	–11	44	2	0	0	118	2.5
C	24	Kris Beech	WSH	64	8	18	26	–11	46	3	0	0	77	10.4
D	27	Ben Clymer	WSH	66	7	13	20	–17	44	0	0	0	78	9.0
C	13 *	Jiri Novotny	BUF	50	6	7	13	–2	26	0	0	0	60	10.0
			WSH	18	0	6	6	–2	2	0	0	0	19	0.0
			TOTAL	68	6	13	19	–4	28	0	0	0	79	7.6
C	21	Brooks Laich	WSH	73	8	10	18	–2	29	2	3	0	119	6.7
C	16	Brian Sutherby	WSH	69	7	10	17	–9	78	1	0	0	87	8.0
D	44	Steve Eminger	WSH	68	1	16	17	–14	63	0	0	0	27	3.7
R	10	Matt Bradley	WSH	57	4	9	13	–5	47	0	0	0	77	5.2
L	87	Donald Brashear	WSH	77	4	9	13	1	156	0	0	0	47	8.5
D	26	Shaone Morrisonn	WSH	78	3	10	13	3	106	0	0	0	46	6.5
D	23	Milan Jurcina	BOS	40	2	1	3	–5	20	0	0	1	29	6.9
			WSH	30	2	7	9	5	24	0	0	0	42	4.8
			TOTAL	70	4	8	12	0	44	0	0	1	71	5.6
D	52 *	Mike Green	WSH	70	2	10	12	–10	36	0	0	0	68	2.9
C	38 *	Jakub Klepis	WSH	41	3	7	10	–2	28	0	0	0	38	7.9
L	43 *	Tomas Fleischmann	WSH	29	4	4	8	–6	8	1	0	1	52	7.7
D	47	Bryan Muir	WSH	26	3	4	7	3	42	0	0	1	28	10.7
D	4	John Erskine	WSH	29	1	6	7	–13	69	0	0	0	14	7.1
C	39 *	Alexandre Giroux	WSH	9	2	2	4	–4	2	0	0	0	11	18.2
R	14 *	Eric Fehr	WSH	14	2	1	3	3	8	0	0	1	25	8.0
D	55 *	Jeff Schultz	WSH	38	0	3	3	5	16	0	0	0	22	0.0
L	22	Rico Fata	WSH	10	1	1	2	3	2	0	0	0	15	6.7
D	29 *	Jameson Hunt	WSH	1	0	0	0	–1	0	0	0	0	0	0.0
D	51 *	Timo Helbling	WSH	2	0	0	0	–1	2	0	0	0	0	0.0
C	25 *	David Steckel	WSH	5	0	0	0	–2	2	0	0	0	4	0.0

Goaltending

No.	Goaltender	GPI	Mins	Avg	W	L	OT	EN	SO	GA	SA	S%	G	A	PIM
35	Frederic Cassivi	4	139	2.59	0	1	1	0	0	6	58	.897	0	0	0
37	Olaf Kolzig	54	3184	3.00	22	24	6	7	1	159	1771	.910	0	3	10
1	Brent Johnson	30	1644	3.61	6	15	7	4	0	99	894	.889	0	1	4
	Totals	**82**	**4996**	**3.30**	**28**	**40**	**14**	**11**	**1**	**275**	**2734**	**.899**			

Coach

GLEN HANLON

Coach, Washington Capitals. Born in Brandon, Man., February 20, 1957.

Glen Hanlon was in his second season as an assistant coach when he was promoted to the position of head coach on December 10, 2003. Previously, Hanlon had served as head coach for Washington's minor-league affiliate, the Portland Pirates, for three seasons.

During his first season at the helm of the Pirates in 1999-2000, Hanlon was named the American Hockey League's coach of the year after guiding Portland to a 46-24-10 record and a league-best 48-point turnaround. The Pirates finished with 103 points overall, second best in the AHL's New England Division.

In three seasons leading the Pirates, Hanlon guided the club to two Calder Cup playoff appearances. He finished his tenure posting the second-highest win total (110) in Pirates history.

Before arriving in Portland, Hanlon served eight seasons with the Vancouver Canucks as an assistant coach (1994 to 1999) and goaltending coach (1991 to 1994). He helped lead the Canucks to their first 40-win season in franchise history in 1991-92, and the team advanced to the Stanley Cup Finals in 1994. He also served as an assistant coach with the Canadian national team at the 1998 World Championships in Zurich, Switzerland.

Hanlon appeared in 477 NHL games in 14 seasons as a goaltender between 1977 and 1991, playing with the Vancouver Canucks, St. Louis Blues, New York Rangers and Detroit Red Wings. He posted a career record of 167-202-61, a 3.60 goals-against average and 13 shutouts. He also played 35 career NHL playoff games, compiling an 11-15-0 record, a 3.14 goals-against average and four shutouts.

Coaching Record

		Regular Season				Playoffs		
Season	**Team**	**Games**	**W**	**L**	**O/T**	**Games**	**W**	**L**
1999-00	Portland (AHL)	80	46	24	10	4	1	3
2000-01	Portland (AHL)	80	34	42	4	3	0	3
2001-02	Portland (AHL)	80	30	35	15	....	....	....
2003-04	**Washington (NHL)**	**54**	**15**	**30**	**9**	....	....	....
2004-05	**Washington (NHL)**	Season Cancelled						
2005-06	**Washington (NHL)**	**82**	**29**	**41**	**12**	....	....	....
2006-07	**Washington (NHL)**	**82**	**28**	**40**	**14**	....	....	....
	NHL Totals	**218**	**81**	**109**	**28**	....	....	....

Washington's new logo and uniform for 2007-08 mark a return to the patriotic colors Caps players wore when the franchise joined the NHL in 1974-75.

Coaching History

Jim Anderson, Red Sullivan and Milt Schmidt, 1974-75; Milt Schmidt and Tom McVie, 1975-76; Tom McVie, 1976-77, 1977-78; Danny Belisle, 1978-79; Danny Belisle and Gary Green, 1979-80; Gary Green, 1980-81; Gary Green, Roger Crozier and Bryan Murray, 1981-82; Bryan Murray, 1982-83 to 1988-89; Bryan Murray and Terry Murray, 1989-90; Terry Murray, 1990-91 to 1992-93; Terry Murray and Jim Schoenfeld, 1993-94; Jim Schoenfeld, 1994-95 to 1996-97; Ron Wilson, 1997-98 to 2001-02; Bruce Cassidy, 2002-03; Bruce Cassidy and Glen Hanlon, 2003-04; Glen Hanlon, 2004-05 to date.

Club Records

Team

(Figures in brackets for season records are games played; records for fewest points, wins, ties, losses, goals, goals against are for 70 or more games)

Record		
Most Points	**107**	1985-86 (80)
Most Wins	**50**	1985-86 (80)
Most Ties	**18**	1980-81 (80)
Most Losses	**67**	1974-75 (80)
Most Goals	**330**	1991-92 (80)
Most Goals Against	***446**	1974-75 (80)
Fewest Points	***21**	1974-75 (80)
Fewest Wins	***8**	1974-75 (80)
Fewest Ties	**5**	1974-75 (80), 1983-84 (80)
Fewest Losses	**23**	1985-86 (80)
Fewest Goals	**181**	1974-75 (80)
Fewest Goals Against	**194**	1999-00 (82)
Longest Winning Streak		
Overall	**10**	Jan. 27-Feb. 18/84
Home	**10**	Jan. 4-Feb. 23/00
Away	**6**	Feb. 26-Apr. 1/84
Longest Undefeated Streak		
Overall	**14**	Nov. 24-Dec. 23/82 (9 wins, 5 ties), Jan. 17-Feb. 18/84 (13 wins, 1 tie)
Home	**13**	Nov. 25/92-Jan. 31/93 (9 wins, 4 ties), Dec. 27/99-Feb. 23/00 (11 wins, 2 ties)
Away	**10**	Nov. 24/82-Jan. 8/83 (6 wins, 4 ties)
Longest Losing Streak		
Overall	***17**	Feb. 18-Mar. 26/75
Home	***11**	Feb. 18-Mar. 30/75
Away	**37**	Oct. 9/74-Mar. 26/75
Longest Winless Streak		
Overall	**25**	Nov. 29/75-Jan. 21/76 (22 losses, 3 ties)
Home	**14**	Dec. 3/75-Jan. 21/76 (11 losses, 3 ties)
Away	**37**	Oct. 9/74-Mar. 26/75 (37 losses)
Most Shutouts, Season	**9**	1995-96 (82)
Most PIM, Season	**2,204**	1989-90 (80)
Most Goals, Game	**12**	Feb. 6/90 (Que. 2 at Wsh. 12), Jan. 11/03 (Fla. 2 at Wsh. 12)

Individual

Record		
Most Seasons	**15**	Calle Johansson
Most Games	**983**	Calle Johansson
Most Goals, Career	**472**	Peter Bondra
Most Assists, Career	**418**	Michal Pivonka
Most Points, Career	**825**	Peter Bondra (472G, 353A)
Most PIM, Career	**2,003**	Dale Hunter
Most Shutouts, Career	**34**	Olaf Kolzig
Longest Consecutive Games Streak	**422**	Bob Carpenter (Oct. 7/81-Nov. 22/86)
Most Goals, Season	**60**	Dennis Maruk (1981-82)
Most Assists, Season	**76**	Dennis Maruk (1981-82)
Most Points, Season	**136**	Dennis Maruk (1981-82; 60G, 76A)
Most PIM, Season	**339**	Alan May (1989-90)
Most Points, Defenseman, Season	**81**	Larry Murphy (1986-87; 23G, 58A)
Most Points, Center, Season	**136**	Dennis Maruk (1981-82; 60G, 76A)
Most Points, Right Wing, Season	**102**	Mike Gartner (1984-85; 50G, 52A)
Most Points, Left Wing, Season	**106**	Alex Ovechkin (2005-06; 52G, 54A)
Most Points, Rookie, Season	**106**	Alex Ovechkin (2005-06; 52G, 54A)
Most Shutouts, Season	**9**	Jim Carey (1995-96)
Most Goals, Game	**5**	Bengt Gustafsson (Jan. 8/84), Peter Bondra (Feb. 5/94)
Most Assists, Game	**6**	Mike Ridley (Jan. 7/89)
Most Points, Game	**7**	Dino Ciccarelli (Mar. 18/89; 4G, 3A)

* NHL Record.

Retired Numbers

5	Rod Langway	1982-1993
7	Yvon Labre	1974-1981
32	Dale Hunter	1987-1999

Captains' History

Doug Mohns, 1974-75; Bill Clement and Yvon Labre, 1975-76; Yvon Labre, 1976-77, 1977-78; Guy Charron, 1978-79; Ryan Walter, 1979-80 to 1981-82; Rod Langway, 1982-83 to 1991-92; Rod Langway and Kevin Hatcher, 1992-93; Kevin Hatcher, 1993-94; Dale Hunter, 1994-95 to 1998-99; Adam Oates, 1999-2000, 2000-01; Brendan Witt and Steve Konowalchuk, 2001-02; Steve Konowalchuk, 2002-03, 2003-04; Jeff Halpern, 2005-06; Chris Clark, 2006-07 to date.

All-time Record vs. Other Clubs

Regular Season

	At Home								On Road								Total							
	GP	W	L	T	OL	GF	GA	PTS	GP	W	L	T	OL	GF	GA	PTS	GP	W	L	T	OL	GF	GA	PTS
Anaheim	10	4	6	0	0	17	28	8	10	3	6	1	0	25	31	7	20	7	12	1	0	42	59	15
Atlanta	21	12	5	3	1	75	61	28	21	8	9	2	2	61	61	20	42	20	14	5	3	136	122	48
Boston	59	17	27	12	3	164	204	49	60	16	32	9	3	160	220	44	119	33	59	21	6	324	424	93
Buffalo	60	16	34	9	1	153	211	42	60	16	38	6	0	159	237	38	120	32	72	15	1	312	448	80
Calgary	41	21	14	6	0	153	139	48	39	8	24	7	0	97	159	23	80	29	38	13	0	250	298	71
Carolina	55	32	18	4	1	187	144	69	57	27	18	10	2	177	160	66	112	59	36	14	3	364	304	135
Chicago	42	21	15	5	1	148	131	48	40	12	22	6	0	120	151	30	82	33	37	11	1	268	282	78
Colorado	33	18	10	4	1	131	105	41	35	15	15	5	0	121	108	35	68	33	25	9	1	252	213	76
Columbus	3	2	0	1	0	11	7	5	4	3	1	0	0	15	11	6	7	5	1	1	0	26	18	11
Dallas	41	16	17	8	0	124	132	40	42	12	22	8	0	111	156	32	83	28	39	16	0	235	288	72
Detroit	47	21	21	5	0	171	151	47	47	15	20	11	1	135	161	42	94	36	41	16	1	306	312	89
Edmonton	29	18	9	2	0	118	93	38	30	10	16	4	0	91	124	24	59	28	25	6	0	209	217	62
Florida	36	17	10	5	4	106	89	43	36	15	16	4	1	91	97	35	72	32	26	9	5	197	186	78
Los Angeles	47	19	21	7	0	189	174	45	48	15	27	6	0	147	189	36	95	34	48	13	0	336	363	81
Minnesota	3	2	1	0	0	7	6	4	4	0	3	0	1	3	9	1	7	2	4	0	1	10	15	5
Montreal	63	28	26	9	0	175	188	65	64	18	37	8	1	138	242	45	127	46	63	17	1	313	430	110
Nashville	5	3	2	0	0	12	13	6	5	1	3	1	0	11	16	3	10	4	5	1	0	23	29	9
New Jersey	83	49	26	6	2	317	238	106	83	34	39	7	3	237	256	78	166	83	65	13	5	554	494	184
NY Islanders	85	42	32	11	0	279	265	95	85	37	46	2	0	261	317	76	170	79	78	13	0	540	582	171
NY Rangers	88	45	31	9	3	328	282	102	86	35	41	9	1	290	321	80	174	80	72	18	4	618	603	182
Ottawa	28	13	11	4	0	89	81	30	27	11	15	1	0	76	99	23	55	24	26	5	0	165	180	53
Philadelphia	84	36	35	13	0	276	268	85	87	26	55	6	0	234	331	58	171	62	90	19	0	510	599	143
Phoenix	32	18	8	5	1	121	88	42	31	9	15	7	0	111	113	25	63	27	23	12	1	232	201	67
Pittsburgh	90	46	33	9	2	374	330	103	87	29	51	7	0	268	340	65	177	75	84	16	2	642	670	168
St. Louis	40	21	15	4	0	141	121	46	41	13	20	8	0	127	165	34	81	34	35	12	0	268	286	80
San Jose	13	5	7	0	1	36	39	11	11	3	7	1	0	27	33	7	24	8	14	1	1	63	72	18
Tampa Bay	37	22	9	4	2	132	92	50	37	20	13	2	2	115	94	44	74	42	22	6	4	247	186	94
Toronto	54	31	18	4	1	197	157	67	52	18	27	6	1	175	225	43	106	49	45	10	2	372	382	110
Vancouver	40	22	14	4	0	132	120	48	40	16	18	5	1	125	139	38	80	38	32	9	1	257	259	86
Defunct Clubs	10	2	8	0	0	28	42	4	10	4	5	1	0	30	39	9	20	6	13	1	0	58	81	13
Totals	**1279**	**619**	**483**	**153**	**24**	**4391**	**3999**	**1415**	**1279**	**449**	**661**	**150**	**19**	**3738**	**4604**	**1067**	**2558**	**1068**	**1144**	**303**	**43**	**8129**	**8603**	**2482**

Playoffs

	Series	W	L	GP	W	L	T	GF	GA	Last Mtg.	Rnd.	Result
Boston	2	1	1	10	4	6	0	21	28	1998	CQF	W 4-2
Buffalo	1	1	0	6	4	2	0	13	11	1998	CF	W 4-2
Detroit	1	0	1	4	0	4	0	7	13	1998	F	L 0-4
New Jersey	2	1	1	13	7	6	0	44	43	1990	DSF	W 4-2
NY Islanders	6	1	5	30	12	18	0	88	99	1993	DSF	L 2-4
NY Rangers	4	2	2	22	11	11	0	75	71	1994	CSF	L 1-4
Ottawa	1	1	0	5	4	1	0	18	7	1998	CSF	W 4-1
Philadelphia	3	2	1	16	9	7	0	65	55	1989	DSF	L 2-4
Pittsburgh	7	1	6	42	16	26	0	121	137	2001	CQF	L 2-4
Tampa Bay	1	0	1	6	2	4	0	15	14	2003	CQF	L 2-4
Totals	**28**	**10**	**18**	**154**	**69**	**85**	**0**	**467**	**478**			

Playoff Results 2007-2002

Year	Round	Opponent	Result	GF	GA
2003	CQF	Tampa Bay	L 2-4	15	14

Abbreviations: Round: F – Final; **CF** – conference final; **CSF** – conference semi-final; **CQF** – conference quarter-final; **DSF** – division semi-final.

Calgary totals include Atlanta Flames, 1974-75 to 1979-80. Carolina totals include Hartford, 1979-80 to 1996-97.
Colorado totals include Quebec, 1979-80 to 1994-95. Dallas totals include Minnesota North Stars, 1974-75 to 1992-93.
New Jersey totals include Kansas City, 1974-75, 1975-76, and Colorado Rockies, 1976-77 to 1981-82.
Phoenix totals include Winnipeg, 1979-80 to 1995-96.

2006-07 Results

Month	Day	Opponent	Score
Oct.	5	at NY Rangers	2-5
	7	Carolina	5-2
	12	at Minnesota	2-3†
	14	Atlanta	3-4*
	18	Florida	5-2
	19	at Atlanta	3-4†
	21	Tampa Bay	4-6
	25	at Colorado	5-3
	27	at Vancouver	2-3†
	28	at Edmonton	0-4
	30	at Calgary	4-2
Nov.	3	Atlanta	3-4
	4	at Philadelphia	5-3
	6	Ottawa	4-3*
	9	at Carolina	0-5
	11	NY Rangers	3-1
	13	at Florida	4-1
	15	Boston	2-3†
	17	Carolina	1-4
	18	at Boston	2-3*
	22	Atlanta	2-4
	24	Toronto	1-7
	25	at NY Islanders	1-4
	28	at Tampa Bay	5-2
	30	Dallas	4-3
Dec.	2	Buffalo	7-4
	6	Ottawa	6-2
	8	Anaheim	1-6
	9	at Philadelphia	5-3
	11	Pittsburgh	4-5†
	15	at Atlanta	3-2*
	16	Philadelphia	4-1
	19	Tampa Bay	4-5
	22	New Jersey	1-4
	23	at Toronto	3-2
	26	at Buffalo	3-6
	27	Montreal	1-4
	29	at New Jersey	3-4
	30	at NY Rangers	1-4
Jan.	1	Phoenix	2-3
	4	Montreal	5-1
	6	Atlanta	3-2*
	9	Philadelphia	6-2
	11	at Tampa Bay	4-5
	13	at Florida	3-7
	16	at Ottawa	2-5
	18	at Carolina	5-2
	20	Florida	1-4
	26	at Carolina	2-6
	27	Carolina	7-3
	30	at Ottawa	2-3
Feb.	1	at Florida	3-6
	3	at Pittsburgh	0-2
	4	NY Islanders	2-1†
	6	Boston	2-3†
	8	Los Angeles	4-3*
	10	NY Rangers	2-5
	15	at Tampa Bay	2-3†
	18	at Pittsburgh	2-3
	20	at Montreal	3-5
	21	San Jose	2-3†
	24	at New Jersey	4-2
	25	New Jersey	2-3
	27	Florida	5-6†
Mar.	1	Tampa Bay	4-5†
	3	NY Islanders	2-6
	6	at Toronto	0-3
	9	Carolina	0-3
	10	at NY Islanders	2-5
	12	at Atlanta	2-4
	15	at Boston	3-4†
	16	Toronto	5-1
	18	Tampa Bay	7-1
	21	at Buffalo	2-5
	22	at Carolina	3-4
	24	at Montreal	1-4
	27	Pittsburgh	3-4
	30	at Florida	2-3*
	31	at Tampa Bay	2-5
Apr.	3	Florida	1-0
	4	at Atlanta	3-2
	7	Buffalo	0-2

* – Overtime † – Shootout

Entry Draft Selections 2007-1993

2007
Pick	
5	Karl Alzner
34	Josh Godfrey
46	Ted Ruth
84	Phil Desimone
108	Brett Bruneteau
125	Brett Leffler
154	Dan Dunn
180	Justin Taylor
185	Nick Larson
199	Andrew Glass

2006
Pick	
4	Nicklas Backstrom
23	Simeon Varlamov
34	Michal Neuvirth
35	Francois Bouchard
52	Keith Seabrook
97	Oskar Osala
122	Luke Lynes
127	Maxime Lacroix
157	Brent Gwidt
177	Mathieu Perreault

2005
Pick	
14	Sasha Pokulok
27	Joe Finley
109	Andrew Thomas
118	Patrick McNeill
143	Daren Machesney
181	Tim Kennedy
209	Ineligible Claim
209	Viktor Dovgan

2004
Pick	
1	Alex Ovechkin
27	Jeff Schultz
29	Mike Green
33	Chris Bourque
62	Mikhail Yunkov
66	Sami Lepisto
88	Clayton Barthel
132	Oscar Hedman
138	Pasi Salonen
166	Peter Guggisberg
197	Andrew Gordon
230	Justin Mrazek
263	Travis Morin

2003
Pick	
18	Eric Fehr
83	Steve Werner
109	Andreas Valdix
155	Josh Robertson
249	Andrew Joudrey
279	Mark Olafson

2002
Pick	
12	Steve Eminger
13	Alexander Semin
17	Boyd Gordon
59	Maxime Daigneault
77	Patrick Wellar
92	Derek Krestanovich
109	Jevon Desautels
118	Petr Dvorak
145	Rob Gherson
179	Marian Havel
209	Joni Lindlof
242	Igor Ignatushkin
272	Patric Blomdahl

2001
Pick	
58	Nathan Paetsch
90	Owen Fussey
125	Jeff Lucky
160	Artem Ternavsky
191	Zbynek Novak
221	Johnny Oduya
249	Matt Maglione
254	Peter Polcik
275	Robert Muller
284	Viktor Hubl

2000
Pick	
26	Brian Sutherby
43	Matt Pettinger
61	Jakub Cutta
121	Ryan Vanbuskirk
163	Ivan Nepryayev
289	Bjorn Nord

1999
Pick	
7	Kris Beech
29	Michal Sivek
31	Charlie Stephens
34	Ross Lupaschuk
37	Nolan Yonkman
132	Roman Tvrdon
175	Kyle Clark
192	David Bornhammar
219	Maxim Orlov
249	Igor Shadilov

1998
Pick	
49	Jomar Cruz
59	Todd Hornung
106	Krys Barch
107	Chris Corrinet
118	Mike Siklenka
125	Erik Wendell
179	Nate Forster
193	Rastislav Stana
220	Mike Farrell
251	Blake Evans

1997
Pick	
9	Nick Boynton
35	Jean-Francois Fortin
89	Curtis Cruickshank
116	Kevin Caulfield
143	Henrik Petre
200	Pierre-Luc Therrien
226	Matt Oikawa

1996
Pick	
4	Alexandre Volchkov
17	Jaroslav Svejkovsky
43	Jan Bulis
58	Sergei Zimakov
74	Dave Weninger
78	Shawn McNeil
85	Justin Davis
126	Matthew Lahey
153	Andrew Van Bruggen
180	Michael Anderson
206	Oleg Orekhovsky
232	Chad Cavanagh

1995
Pick	
17	Brad Church
23	Miika Elomo
43	Dwayne Hay
93	Sebastien Charpentier
95	Joel Theriault
105	Benoit Gratton
124	Joel Cort
147	Frederick Jobin
199	Vasili Turkovsky
225	Scott Swanson

1994
Pick	
10	Nolan Baumgartner
15	Alexander Kharlamov
41	Scott Cherrey
93	Matt Herr
119	Yanick Jean
145	Dmitri Mekeshkin
171	Daniel Reja
197	Chris Patrick
223	John Tuohy
249	Richard Zednik
275	Sergei Tertyshny

1993
Pick	
11	Brendan Witt
17	Jason Allison
69	Patrick Boileau
147	Frank Banham
173	Daniel Hendrickson
174	Andrew Brunette
199	Joel Poirier
225	Jason Gladney
251	Marc Seliger
277	Dany Bousquet

General Managers' History

Milt Schmidt, 1974-75; Milt Schmidt and Max McNab, 1975-76; Max McNab, 1976-77 to 1980-81; Max McNab and Roger Crozier, 1981-82; David Poile, 1982-83 to 1996-97; George McPhee, 1997-98 to date.

Vice President and General Manager

GEORGE McPHEE
Vice President/General Manager, Washington Capitals.
Born in Wallaceburg, Ont., July 2, 1958.

On June 9, 1997, George McPhee became the fifth general manager of the Washington Capitals. In his first year on the job, McPhee led the Caps to the Stanley Cup Finals for the first time in franchise history. He has begun rebuilding the Capitals with younger players and used the first overall choice at the 2004 NHL Entry Draft to select Alex Ovechkin.

Prior to joining the Capitals, McPhee spent five years in the front office of the Vancouver Canucks where he served as vice president of hockey operations and alternate governor. He has earned degrees in both law and business and, while attending law school at Rutgers University, interned at the United States Court of International Trade in 1991.

A back injury forced McPhee to retire as an active player at the conclusion of the 1988-89 season, after a seven year playing career with the New York Rangers and New Jersey Devils. McPhee originally signed as a free agent with the Rangers in July, 1982, after graduating from Bowling Green State University with a business degree. McPhee did not waste any time in college, tallying 40 goals and 48 assists in his freshman season and easily winning CCHA rookie of the year honors. His outstanding collegiate hockey career was capped off when he was named the recipient of the Hobey Baker Award as the top U.S. collegiate player in his senior season. McPhee also earned All-America honors as a senior and finished his career at Bowling Green as the CCHA's all-time leading scorer with 114-153-267. He was the first player in CCHA history to make the Conference's all-academic team three straight seasons.

Club Directory

Verizon Center

Washington Capitals
627 N. Glebe Road, Suite 850
Arlington, VA 22203
Phone **202/266-2200**
PR FAX 202/266-2360
www.washingtoncaps.com
Capacity: 18,277

Ownership (Lincoln Holdings LLC)	
Chairman & Majority Owner	Ted Leonsis
President & Owner	Dick Patrick
Owners	Jack Davies, Richard Fairbank, Raul Fernandez, Sheila Johnson, Richard Kay, Jeong Kim, Mark D. Lerner, George Stamas
Director of Office Admin./Exec. Assistant	Michelle Trostle
Hockey Operations	
Vice President & General Manager	George McPhee
Director of Legal Affairs/Hockey Admin.	Don Fishman
Head Coach	Glen Hanlon
Assistant Coaches	Jay Leach, Dean Evason
Goaltending Coach	Dave Prior
Physiologist	Jack Blatherwick
Video Coach	Blaine Forsythe
Hockey Operations Assistants	Eric Garvey, Evan Gold
Executive Assistant	Katy Headman
Security Representative	James Wiseman
Scouting Staff	
Director of Player Personnel	Brian MacLellan
Pro Scout	Larry Carriere
Player Development	Steve Richmond
Director of Amateur Scouting	Ross Mahoney
Amateur Scouts	Steve Bowman, Ed McColgan, Martin Pouliot, Todd Woodcroft, Gleb Chistyakov
European Scouts	Vojtech Kucera, Petri Skriko, Mats Weiderstal
Director of Scouting Operations	Kris Wagner
Medical Staff	
Head Athletic Trainer	Greg Smith
Massage Therapist	Curt Millar
Team Physician	Ben Shaffer, MD
Team Internist	Chris Walsh, MD
Team Ophthalmologist	Bill Rich, MD
Team Dentist	Thomas Lenz, DDS, PC
Training Staff	
Head Equipment Manager	Brock Myles
Assistant Equipment Manager	Craig Leydig
Equipment Assistant	Brian Metzger
Business Operations	
Senior Director of Operations	George Parr
Information Technology Manager	Brian McPartland
Office Assistant	Valerie Garrett
Receptionist	Chuquita Pettus
Marketing and Communications	
Sr. Vice President, Chief Marketing Officer	Tim McDermott
Vice President, Communications, CCO	Kurt Kehl
Director of Media Relations	Nate Ewell
Manager of Media Relations	Paul Rovnak
Communications Coordinator	Julie Petri
Senior Director of Game Operations	Mark Tamar
Game Operations Coordinator	James Dowd
Mascot Coordinator	Chris Monihan
Manager of Community Relations	Elizabeth Wodatch
Community Relations Coordinator	Jennifer Vassil
Director of New Media	Sean Parker
Senior Writer	Mike Vogel
Website & Publications Coordinator	Andrew Mattice
Director of Promotions	Chris Lewis
Manager, Fan Development & Promotions	Gail Rodriguez
Finance	
Vice President, Finance	Keith Burrows
Accounting Manager	Jill Ruehle
Accounts Payable Manager	Adam Porcelli
Staff Accountant	Marta Sokol
Sales	
Sr. Director, Corporate Sponsorships	John Greeley
Director of Group Sales	Darren Montgomery
Director, Season Ticket Sales	Anthony Aspaas
Sr. Regional Sales Manager, Groups	Tim Bronaugh
Sr. Regional Sales Managers	Dave Boettinger, Audrius Zubrus
Regional Sales Managers, Groups	Ian Anderson, Jeff Keeney
Regional Sales Manager	Nova Ackerman, Jaclyn Benjamin, Wes Delancey, Matt MacDonald, Joseph O'Neill, Aaron Pearl, Letitia Petrillo, Jason Rocco, Harry Schroeder, Matt Winkler
Sponsorship Activation Manager	Julie DiBella
Client Relations Coordinator	Taylor Kettler
Executive Assistant	Lauren Gilmore
Ticket Operations	
Director, Ticket Operations	Chris Sheap
Manager, Ticket Operations	Jordan Cookler
Coordinators, Ticket Operations	Stephen Kaufman, Bryan Weir
Guest Services	
Director, Guest Services	Greg Monares
Manager, Guest Services	Chris Roberts
Coordinator, Guest Services	Justine Itté
Broadcasting	
Television Rights Holder	Comcast SportsNet
Television Play-by-Play	Joe Beninati
Television Analyst	Craig Laughlin
Television Reporter	Al Koken
Radio Play-by-Play	Steve Kolbe
Radio Analyst	Ken Sabourin

2006-2007 Final Statistics

Standings

Abbreviations: GP – games played; **W** – wins; **L** – losses; **OT** – overtime and shootout losses; **GF** – goals for; **GA** – goals against; **PTS** – points.

EASTERN CONFERENCE

Northeast Division

	GP	W	L	OT	GF	GA	PTS
Buffalo	82	53	22	7	308	242	113
Ottawa	82	48	25	9	288	222	105
Toronto	82	40	31	11	258	269	91
Montreal	82	42	34	6	245	256	90
Boston	82	35	41	6	219	289	76

Atlantic Division

	GP	W	L	OT	GF	GA	PTS
New Jersey	82	49	24	9	216	201	107
Pittsburgh	82	47	24	11	277	246	105
NY Rangers	82	42	30	10	242	216	94
NY Islanders	82	40	30	12	248	240	92
Philadelphia	82	22	48	12	214	303	56

Southeast Division

	GP	W	L	OT	GF	GA	PTS
Atlanta	82	43	28	11	246	245	97
Tampa Bay	82	44	33	5	253	261	93
Carolina	82	40	34	8	241	253	88
Florida	82	35	31	16	247	257	86
Washington	82	28	40	14	235	286	70

WESTERN CONFERENCE

Central Division

	GP	W	L	OT	GF	GA	PTS
Detroit	82	50	19	13	254	199	113
Nashville	82	51	23	8	272	212	110
St. Louis	82	34	35	13	214	254	81
Columbus	82	33	42	7	201	249	73
Chicago	82	31	42	9	201	258	71

Pacific Division

	GP	W	L	OT	GF	GA	PTS
Anaheim	82	48	20	14	258	208	110
San Jose	82	51	26	5	258	199	107
Dallas	82	50	25	7	226	197	107
Los Angeles	82	27	41	14	227	283	68
Phoenix	82	31	46	5	216	284	67

Northwest Division

	GP	W	L	OT	GF	GA	PTS
Vancouver	82	49	26	7	222	201	105
Minnesota	82	48	26	8	235	191	104
Calgary	82	43	29	10	258	226	96
Colorado	82	44	31	7	272	251	95
Edmonton	82	32	43	7	195	248	71

Tampa Bay's Martin St. Louis and Vincent Lecavalier flank Sidney Crosby of the Pittsburgh Penguins. Crosby led the league in points and Lecavalier in goals. St. Louis ranked among the leaders in both categories.

INDIVIDUAL LEADERS

Goal Scoring

Player	Team	GP	G
Vincent Lecavalier	Tampa Bay	82	52
Dany Heatley	Ottawa	82	50
Teemu Selanne	Anaheim	82	48
Alex Ovechkin	Washington	82	46
Marian Hossa	Atlanta	82	43
Martin St. Louis	Tampa Bay	82	43
Thomas Vanek	Buffalo	82	43
Ilya Kovalchuk	Atlanta	82	42
Simon Gagne	Philadelphia	76	41
Jason Blake	NY Islanders	82	40

Assists

Player	Team	GP	A
Joe Thornton	San Jose	82	92
Sidney Crosby	Pittsburgh	79	84
Marc Savard	Boston	82	74
Henrik Sedin	Vancouver	82	71
Jaromir Jagr	NY Rangers	82	66
Joe Sakic	Colorado	82	64
Daniel Briere	Buffalo	81	63
Pavel Datsyuk	Detroit	79	60
Alex Tanguay	Calgary	81	59
Martin St. Louis	Tampa Bay	82	59

Power-play Goals

Player	Team	GP	PP
Teemu Selanne	Anaheim	82	25
Sheldon Souray	Montreal	81	19
Ilya Kovalchuk	Atlanta	82	18
Chris Drury	Buffalo	77	17
Alexander Semin	Washington	77	17
Marian Hossa	Atlanta	82	17
Michael Ryder	Montreal	82	17
Dany Heatley	Ottawa	82	17

Shorthand Goals

Player	Team	GP	SH
Jordan Staal	Pittsburgh	81	7
Kris Draper	Detroit	81	5
Martin St. Louis	Tampa Bay	82	5
Vincent Lecavalier	Tampa Bay	82	5
Mike Richards	Philadelphia	59	4
Chris Clark	Washington	74	4
Maxime Talbot	Pittsburgh	75	4
Matthew Lombardi	Calgary	81	4
Bryan Smolinski	Chi., Van.	82	4

Game-winning Goals

Player	Team	GP	GW
Henrik Zetterberg	Detroit	63	10
Teemu Selanne	Anaheim	82	10
Dany Heatley	Ottawa	82	10
Chris Drury	Buffalo	77	9
Patrick Marleau	San Jose	77	9
Milan Michalek	San Jose	78	9

Shots

Player	Team	GP	S
Alex Ovechkin	Washington	82	392
Olli Jokinen	Florida	82	351
Marian Hossa	Atlanta	82	340
Vincent Lecavalier	Tampa Bay	82	339
Ilya Kovalchuk	Atlanta	82	336

Shooting Percentage

(minimum 82 shots)

Player	Team	GP	G	S	%
Jordan Staal	Pittsburgh	81	29	131	22.1
Jason Spezza	Ottawa	67	34	162	21.0
Alex Tanguay	Calgary	81	22	107	20.6
Kristian Huselius	Calgary	81	34	173	19.7
Alexander Radulov	Nashville	64	18	96	18.8

Penalty Minutes

Player	Team	GP	PIM
Ben Eager	Philadelphia	63	233
Josh Gratton	Phoenix	52	188
Chris Neil	Ottawa	82	177
Shane O'Brien	Ana., T.B	80	176
Sean Avery	L.A., NYR	84	174

Plus/Minus

Player	Team	GP	+/–
Thomas Vanek	Buffalo	82	47
Daniel Alfredsson	Ottawa	77	42
Nicklas Lidstrom	Detroit	80	40
Tom Preissing	Ottawa	80	40
Derek Roy	Buffalo	75	37
Anton Volchenkov	Ottawa	78	37

Individual Leaders

Abbreviations: GP – games played; **G** – goals; **A** – assists; **Pts** – points; **+/–** – difference between Goals For (**GF**) scored when a player is on the ice with his team at even strength or short-handed and Goals Against (**GA**) scored when the same player is on the ice with his team at even strength or on a power play; **PIM** – penalties in minutes; **PP** – power play goals; **SH** – short-handed goals; **GW** – game-winning goals; **GT** – game-tying goals; **S** – shots on goal; **%** – percentage of shots on goal resulting in goals.

Individual Scoring Leaders for Art Ross Trophy

Player	Team	GP	G	A	Pts	+/–	PIM	PP	SH	GW	S	%
Sidney Crosby	Pittsburgh	79	36	84	120	10	60	13	0	4	250	14.4
Joe Thornton	San Jose	82	22	92	114	24	44	10	0	5	213	10.3
Vincent Lecavalier	Tampa Bay	82	52	56	108	2	44	16	5	7	339	15.3
Dany Heatley	Ottawa	82	50	55	105	31	74	17	3	10	310	16.1
Martin St. Louis	Tampa Bay	82	43	59	102	7	28	14	5	7	273	15.8
Marian Hossa	Atlanta	82	43	57	100	18	49	17	3	5	340	12.6
Joe Sakic	Colorado	82	36	64	100	2	46	16	0	4	258	14.0
Jaromir Jagr	NY Rangers	82	30	66	96	26	78	7	0	5	324	9.3
Marc Savard	Boston	82	22	74	96	–19	96	10	1	3	221	10.0
Daniel Briere	Buffalo	81	32	63	95	17	89	9	0	6	234	13.7
Teemu Selanne	Anaheim	82	48	46	94	26	82	25	0	10	257	18.7
Jarome Iginla	Calgary	70	39	55	94	12	40	13	1	7	264	14.8
Alex Ovechkin	Washington	82	46	46	92	–19	52	16	0	8	392	11.7
Olli Jokinen	Florida	82	39	52	91	18	78	9	1	8	351	11.1
Jason Spezza	Ottawa	67	34	53	87	19	45	13	1	5	162	21.0
Daniel Alfredsson	Ottawa	77	29	58	87	42	42	7	2	7	240	12.1
Pavel Datsyuk	Detroit	79	27	60	87	36	20	5	2	5	207	13.0
Evgeni Malkin	Pittsburgh	78	33	52	85	2	80	16	0	6	242	13.6
Thomas Vanek	Buffalo	82	43	41	84	47	40	15	0	5	237	18.1
Daniel Sedin	Vancouver	81	36	48	84	19	36	16	0	8	236	15.3
Ray Whitney	Carolina	81	32	51	83	–5	46	6	0	6	215	14.9
Andrew Brunette	Colorado	82	27	56	83	–8	36	9	0	2	173	15.6
Michael Nylander	NY Rangers	79	26	57	83	12	42	14	0	4	193	13.5
Rod Brind'Amour	Carolina	78	26	56	82	7	46	9	2	5	181	14.4
Alex Tanguay	Calgary	81	22	59	81	12	44	5	0	0	107	20.6
Henrik Sedin	Vancouver	82	10	71	81	19	66	1	0	2	134	7.5

Defencemen Scoring Leaders

Player	Team	GP	G	A	Pts	+/–	PIM	PP	SH	GW	S	%
Scott Niedermayer	Anaheim	79	15	54	69	6	86	9	0	3	172	8.7
Sergei Gonchar	Pittsburgh	82	13	54	67	–5	72	10	1	3	191	6.8
Sheldon Souray	Montreal	81	26	38	64	–28	135	19	1	6	224	11.6
Dan Boyle	Tampa Bay	82	20	43	63	–5	62	10	1	4	203	9.9
Nicklas Lidstrom	Detroit	80	13	49	62	40	46	10	0	1	224	5.8
Ryan Whitney	Pittsburgh	81	14	45	59	9	77	9	0	2	129	10.9
Chris Pronger	Anaheim	66	13	46	59	27	69	8	0	2	166	7.8
Lubomir Visnovsky	Los Angeles	69	18	40	58	1	26	8	0	0	159	11.3
Tomas Kaberle	Toronto	74	11	47	58	3	20	2	0	1	128	8.6
Bryan McCabe	Toronto	82	15	42	57	3	115	11	0	1	207	7.2
Kimmo Timonen	Nashville	80	13	42	55	20	42	8	0	2	121	10.7
Brian Rafalski	New Jersey	82	8	47	55	4	34	3	1	4	148	5.4
Sergei Zubov	Dallas	78	12	42	54	0	26	9	0	3	156	7.7
Mathieu Schneider	Detroit	68	11	41	52	12	66	2	1	2	184	6.0
Philippe Boucher	Dallas	76	19	32	51	2	104	12	0	4	222	8.6

Ducks teammates Scott Niedermayer and Teemu Selanne celebrate. Niedermayer led all NHL defensemen in scoring, while Selanne became the only player in NHL history to post consecutive 40-goal seasons after the age of 35.

CONSECUTIVE SCORING STREAKS

Goals

Games	Player	Team	G
6	Dany Heatley	Ottawa	8
6	Ilya Kovalchuk	Atlanta	8
6	Jarome Iginla	Calgary	7
6	Martin Havlat	Chicago	7
6	Evgeni Malkin	Pittsburgh	7
6	Daniel Alfredsson	Ottawa	6
6	Vincent Lecavalier	Tampa Bay	6
6	Jason Pominville	Buffalo	6
6	Sidney Crosby	Pittsburgh	6
5	Alexander Semin	Washington	8
5	Vincent Lecavalier	Tampa Bay	7
5	Simon Gagne	Philadelphia	7
5	Dany Heatley	Ottawa	7
5	Jordan Staal	Pittsburgh	7
5	Yanic Perreault	Phoenix	6
5	Olli Jokinen	Florida	6
5	Martin St. Louis	Tampa Bay	6
5	Vincent Lecavalier	Tampa Bay	6
5	Dany Heatley	Ottawa	6
5	Geoff Sanderson	Philadelphia	5
5	Pavol Demitra	Minnesota	5
5	Milan Hejduk	Colorado	5
5	Mike Fisher	Ottawa	5

Assists

Games	Player	Team	A
10	Joe Sakic	Colorado	14
10	Martin St. Louis	Tampa Bay	11
9	Mathieu Schneider	Detroit	12
9	Daniel Briere	Buffalo	12
8	Andrew Brunette	Colorado	12
8	Brad Richards	Tampa Bay	12
8	Daniel Alfredsson	Ottawa	11
8	Marc Savard	Boston	11
8	Scott Niedermayer	Anaheim	10
8	Brian Rafalski	New Jersey	9
7	Sidney Crosby	Pittsburgh	13
7	Alex Ovechkin	Washington	10
7	Sidney Crosby	Pittsburgh	10
7	Martin Straka	NY Rangers	9
7	Ryan Whitney	Pittsburgh	9
7	Patrick O'Sullivan	Los Angeles	8
6	Sidney Crosby	Pittsburgh	12
6	Joe Thornton	San Jose	11
6	Joe Thornton	San Jose	10
6	Jaromir Jagr	NY Rangers	9
6	Marc Savard	Boston	9
6	Michael Nylander	NY Rangers	8
6	Martin St. Louis	Tampa Bay	8
6	Dany Heatley	Ottawa	8
6	Michel Ouellet	Pittsburgh	8
6	Jussi Jokinen	Dallas	8
6	Chris Pronger	Anaheim	7
6	Pavol Demitra	Minnesota	7
6	Milan Hejduk	Colorado	7
6	Daymond Langkow	Calgary	7
6	Kristian Huselius	Calgary	7
6	Scott Gomez	New Jersey	7
6	Andy McDonald	Anaheim	7

Points

Games	Player	Team	G	A	PTS
20	Paul Stastny	Colorado	11	18	29
16	Dany Heatley	Ottawa	11	13	24
15	Kristian Huselius	Calgary	10	11	21
13	Alex Ovechkin	Washington	8	12	20
12	Joe Sakic	Colorado	6	14	20
12	Pavel Datsyuk	Detroit	5	13	18
12	Martin St. Louis	Tampa Bay	6	11	17
12	M. Schneider	Detroit	2	13	15
11	Martin St. Louis	Tampa Bay	10	10	20
11	Martin Straka	NY Rangers	7	12	19
11	Jason Spezza	Ottawa	7	12	19
11	Marian Hossa	Atlanta	7	11	18
11	Vincent Lecavalier	Tampa Bay	8	10	18
11	Andrew Brunette	Colorado	5	12	17
10	Sidney Crosby	Pittsburgh	7	16	23
10	Joe Thornton	San Jose	5	17	22
10	Patrice Bergeron	Boston	6	11	17
10	Vincent Lecavalier	Tampa Bay	9	7	16
10	Daniel Briere	Buffalo	3	12	15
10	Jason Spezza	Ottawa	8	7	15
10	Steve Sullivan	Nashville	6	8	14
9	Brad Richards	Tampa Bay	4	12	16
9	Pavol Demitra	Minnesota	7	8	15
9	J. Langenbrunner	New Jersey	3	11	14
9	Milan Hejduk	Colorado	7	7	14
9	Bryan Mccabe	Toronto	4	9	13
9	D. Langkow	Calgary	3	10	13
9	Ryan Whitney	Pittsburgh	2	10	12
9	Patrice Bergeron	Boston	2	10	12
8	Alex Ovechkin	Washington	7	11	18
8	Olli Jokinen	Florida	6	11	17
8	Sidney Crosby	Pittsburgh	4	13	17

Individual Rookie Scoring Leaders

Rookie	Team	GP	G	A	Pts	+/–	PIM	PP	SH	GW	S	%
Evgeni Malkin	Pittsburgh	78	33	52	85	2	80	16	0	6	242	13.6
Paul Stastny	Colorado	82	28	50	78	4	42	11	0	6	185	15.1
Anze Kopitar	Los Angeles	72	20	41	61	–12	24	7	2	1	193	10.4
Wojtek Wolski	Colorado	76	22	28	50	2	14	7	0	2	165	13.3
Dustin Penner	Anaheim	82	29	16	45	–2	58	9	0	5	204	14.2
Jordan Staal	Pittsburgh	81	29	13	42	16	24	4	7	4	131	22.1
Travis Zajac	New Jersey	80	17	25	42	1	16	6	0	2	134	12.7
Matthew Carle	San Jose	77	11	31	42	9	30	8	0	1	111	9.9
Alexander Radulov	Nashville	64	18	19	37	19	26	5	0	4	96	18.8
Ryane Clowe	San Jose	58	16	18	34	4	78	4	0	3	93	17.2
G. Latendresse	Montreal	80	16	13	29	–20	47	5	0	3	121	13.2
Phil Kessel	Boston	70	11	18	29	–12	12	1	0	0	170	6.5
Joe Pavelski	San Jose	46	14	14	28	4	18	5	0	3	111	12.6
Drew Stafford	Buffalo	41	13	14	27	5	33	3	0	3	67	19.4
Ian White	Toronto	76	3	23	26	8	40	1	0	1	138	2.2
Marc-Edouard Vlasic	San Jose	81	3	23	26	13	18	2	0	0	66	4.5

Goal Scoring

Name	Team	GP	G
Evgeni Malkin	Pittsburgh	78	33
Jordan Staal	Pittsburgh	81	29
Dustin Penner	Anaheim	82	29
Paul Stastny	Colorado	82	28
Wojtek Wolski	Colorado	76	22
Anze Kopitar	Los Angeles	72	20
Alexander Radulov	Nashville	64	18
Travis Zajac	New Jersey	80	17
Ryane Clowe	San Jose	58	16
G. Latendresse	Montreal	80	16

Assists

Name	Team	GP	A
Evgeni Malkin	Pittsburgh	78	52
Paul Stastny	Colorado	82	50
Anze Kopitar	Los Angeles	72	41
Matthew Carle	San Jose	77	31
Wojtek Wolski	Colorado	76	28
Travis Zajac	New Jersey	80	25
Ian White	Toronto	76	23
Marc-Edouard Vlasic	San Jose	81	23
Nathan Paetsch	Buffalo	63	22
Alexandre Picard	Philadelphia	62	19
Alexander Radulov	Nashville	64	19

Power-play Goals

Name	Team	GP	PP
Evgeni Malkin	Pittsburgh	78	16
Paul Stastny	Colorado	82	11
Dustin Penner	Anaheim	82	9
Matthew Carle	San Jose	77	8
Anze Kopitar	Los Angeles	72	7
Wojtek Wolski	Colorado	76	7
Travis Zajac	New Jersey	80	6
Joe Pavelski	San Jose	46	5
Alexander Radulov	Nashville	64	5
G. Latendresse	Montreal	80	5

Shorthand Goals

Name	Team	GP	SH
Jordan Staal	Pittsburgh	81	7
Anze Kopitar	Los Angeles	72	2
Maxim Lapierre	Montreal	46	1
Karl Stewart	Pit., Chi., T.B	47	1
Patrick Thoresen	Edmonton	68	1

Game-winning Goals

Name	Team	GP	GW
Evgeni Malkin	Pittsburgh	78	6
Paul Stastny	Colorado	82	6
Dustin Penner	Anaheim	82	5
Alexander Radulov	Nashville	64	4
Jiri Hudler	Detroit	76	4
Jordan Staal	Pittsburgh	81	4
Drew Stafford	Buffalo	41	3
Joe Pavelski	San Jose	46	3
Ryane Clowe	San Jose	58	3
G. Latendresse	Montreal	80	3

Shots

Name	Team	GP	S
Evgeni Malkin	Pittsburgh	78	242
Dustin Penner	Anaheim	82	204
Anze Kopitar	Los Angeles	72	193
Paul Stastny	Colorado	82	185
Phil Kessel	Boston	70	170
Wojtek Wolski	Colorado	76	165
Ian White	Toronto	76	138
Travis Zajac	New Jersey	80	134
Jordan Staal	Pittsburgh	81	131
G. Latendresse	Montreal	80	121

Shooting Percentage

(minimum 82 shots)

Name	Team	GP	G	S	%
Jordan Staal	Pittsburgh	81	29	131	22.1
Alexander Radulov	Nashville	64	18	96	18.8
Ryane Clowe	San Jose	58	16	93	17.2
Paul Stastny	Colorado	82	28	185	15.1
Dustin Penner	Anaheim	82	29	204	14.2
Jiri Hudler	Detroit	76	15	107	14.0
Evgeni Malkin	Pittsburgh	78	33	242	13.6
Wojtek Wolski	Colorado	76	22	165	13.3
G. Latendresse	Montreal	80	16	121	13.2
Travis Zajac	New Jersey	80	17	134	12.7

Penalty Minutes

Name	Team	GP	PIM
Ben Eager	Philadelphia	63	233
Josh Gratton	Phoenix	52	188
Shane O'Brien	Ana., T.B	80	176
Ole-Kristian Tolle	Columbus	70	123
Zachery Stortini	Edmonton	29	105
David Koci	Chicago	9	88
Brad Winchester	Edmonton	59	86
Nick Tarnasky	Tampa Bay	77	80
Evgeni Malkin	Pittsburgh	78	80
Ryane Clowe	San Jose	58	78

Plus/Minus

Name	Team	GP	+/-
Alexander Radulov	Nashville	64	19
Jiri Hudler	Detroit	76	16
Jordan Staal	Pittsburgh	81	16
Marc-Edouard Vlasic	San Jose	81	13
Nathan Paetsch	Buffalo	63	10
Matthew Carle	San Jose	77	9
Valtteri Filppula	Detroit	73	8
Ian White	Toronto	76	8
Mark Stuart	Boston	15	7
Daniel Girardi	NY Rangers	34	7
Mark Giordano	Calgary	48	7

Three-or-More-Goal Games

Player	Team	Date	Final Score	G
Jason Blake	NY Islanders	Dec. 19	NYI 4 NYR 3	3
Jason Blake	NY Islanders	Feb. 27	Phi. 5 NYI 6	3
Philippe Boucher	Dallas	Nov. 24	L.A. 3 Dal. 5	3
Dan Boyle	Tampa Bay	Dec. 23	NYR 3 T.B. 4	3
Daniel Briere	Buffalo	Dec. 5	Buf. 4 T.B. 1	3
Daniel Briere	Buffalo	Jan. 30	Bos. 1 Buf. 7	3
Andrew Brunette	Colorado	Dec. 19	Col. 7 Edm. 6	3
Jonathan Cheechoo	San Jose	Oct. 12	S.J. 4 Edm. 6	3
Jonathan Cheechoo	San Jose	Mar. 22	S.J. 5 Atl. 1	3
Jonathan Cheechoo	San Jose	Apr. 1	L.A. 2 S.J. 6	3
Chris Clark	Washington	Mar. 15	Wsh. 3 Bos. 4	3
Daniel Cleary	Detroit	Dec. 28	Det. 7 Cbj. 4	3
Ryane Clowe	San Jose	Jan. 6	Cbj. 2 S.J 5	3
Erik Cole	Carolina	Nov. 9	Wsh. 0 Car. 5	3
Sidney Crosby	Pittsburgh	Oct. 28	Pit. 8 Phi. 2	3
Chris Drury	Buffalo	Oct. 14	NYR. 4 Buf. 7	3
Nils Ekman	Pittsburgh	Nov. 8	T.B. 4 Pit. 3	3
Brian Gionta	New Jersey	Oct. 12	Tor. 6 N.J. 7	3
Bill Guerin	St. Louis	Feb. 13	S.J. 6 St.L. 5	3
Bill Guerin	San Jose	Mar. 13	Chi. 1 S.J. 7	3
Jeffrey Hamilton	Chicago	Dec. 2	Chi. 4 Nsh. 3	3
Jeffrey Hamilton	Chicago	Mar. 10	Chi. 7 Phx. 5	3
Dany Heatley	Ottawa	Oct. 26	Tor. 2 Ott. 7	3
Dany Heatley	Ottawa	Nov. 24	Ott. 6 Fla. 4	3
Dany Heatley	Ottawa	Jan. 3	Buf. 3 Ott. 6	3
Milan Hejduk	Colorado	Feb. 15	Col. 7 Cgy. 5	3
Milan Hejduk	Colorado	Apr. 5	Col. 3 Van. 1	3
Tomas Holmstrom	Detroit	Jan. 11	Det. 5 Phx. 1	3
Tomas Holmstrom	Detroit	Feb. 24	Det. 3 Nsh. 4	3
Marian Hossa	Atlanta	Nov. 30	To.r 0 Atl. 5	3
Marian Hossa	Atlanta	Jan. 16	L.A. 2 Atl. 6	3
Jarome Iginla	Calgary	Mar. 29	Cgy. 4 Min. 2	3
Olli Jokinen	Florida	Nov. 16	Mtl. 1 Fla. 5	3
Olli Jokinen	Florida	Jan. 10	Pit. 2 Fla. 5	3
Olli Jokinen	Florida	Feb. 27	Fla. 6 Wsh. 5	3
Tomas Kaberle	Toronto	Oct. 28	Tor. 5 Mtl. 4	3
Ilya Kovalchuk	Atlanta	Oct. 23	Atl. 6 Fla. 3	3
Ilya Kovalchuk	Atlanta	Nov. 6	Bos. 3 Atl. 5	3
Viktor Kozlov	NY Islanders	Dec. 3	NYI 7 NYR 4	4
Vyacheslav Kozlov	Atlanta	Nov. 8	Ott. 4 Atl. 5	3
Chris Kunitz	Anaheim	Nov. 19	Phx. 4 Ana. 6	3
Vincent Lecavalier	Tampa Bay	Dec. 7	Atl. 0 T.B. 8	3
David Legwand	Nashville	Jan. 20	Chi. 3 Nsh. 6	3
Ryan Malone	Pittsburgh	Dec. 15	NYI 4 Pit. 7	3
Ryan Malone	Pittsburgh	Feb. 19	Pit. 5 NYI 6	3
Patrick Marleau	San Jose	Nov. 9	S.J. 7 L.A. 3	3
Alex Ovechkin	Washington	Dec. 15	Wsh. 3 Atl. 2	3
Mark Parrish	Minnesota	Dec. 9	Chi. 4 Min. 5	3
Mark Recchi	Pittsburgh	Jan. 20	Tor. 2 Pit. 8	3
Jeremy Roenick	Phoenix	Dec. 30	S.J. 0 Phx. 8	3
Michael Ryder	Montreal	Apr. 7	Mtl. 5 Tor. 6	3
Mathieu Schneider	Detroit	Oct. 11	Phx. 2 Det. 9	3
Daniel Sedin	Vancouver	Feb. 6	Van 5 Edm. 2	3
Teemu Selanne	Anaheim	Jan. 11	Ana. 5 Dal. 1	3
Alexander Semin	Washington	Oct. 7	Car. 2 Wsh. 5	3
Alexander Semin	Washington	Mar. 18	T.B 1 Wsh. 7	3
Brendan Shanahan	Ny Rangers	Dec. 3	NYI 7 NYR 4	3
Ryan Smyth	Edmonton	Oct. 12	S.J 4 Edm. 6	3
Martin St. Louis	Tampa Bay	Oct. 26	Car. 1 T.B. 5	3
Eric Staal	Carolina	Nov. 18	Dal. 4 Car. 5	3
Jordan Staal	Pittsburgh	Feb. 10	Pit. 6 Tor. 5	3
Alex Steen	Toronto	Jan. 4	Tor. 10 Bos. 2	3
Martin Straka	NY Rangers	Jan. 4	Phi. 2 NYR 3	3
Marco Sturm	Boston	Dec. 19	Bos. 7 Ott. 2	3
Steve Sullivan	Nashville	Dec. 14	Ott. 0 Nsh. 6	3
Mats Sundin	Toronto	Oct. 14	Cgy. 4 Tor. 5	3
Stephen Weiss	Florida	Jan. 13	Wsh. 3 Fla. 7	3
Kyle Wellwood	Toronto	Dec. 16	NYR 2 Tor. 9	3
Ray Whitney	Carolina	Feb. 8	Car. 5 Bos. 2	3
Justin Williams	Carolina	Oct. 16	Car. 5 T.B. 1	3
Henrik Zetterberg	Detroit	Feb. 17	Det. 4 Phx. 1	3

2006-07 Penalty Shots

(For shootout statistics, see page 143.)

Scored

Mats Sundin (Toronto) scored against Martin Gerber (Ottawa) October 4. Final Score: Ottawa 4 at Toronto 1

Marian Hossa (Atlanta) scored against Alexander Auld (Florida) October 21. Final Score: Florida 2 at Atlanta 4

Jordan Staal (Pittsburgh) scored against Fredrik Norrena (Columbus) October 21. Final Score: Columbus 3 at Pittsburgh 5

Brian Rolston (Minnesota) scored against Roberto Luongo (Vancouver) November 2. Final Score: Vancouver 2 at Minnesota 5

Andy McDonald (Anaheim) scored against Curtis Joseph (Phoenix) November 3. Final Score: Phoenix 2 at Anaheim 6

Brian Rolston (Minnesota) scored against Ray Emery (Ottawa) November 20. Final Score: Minnesota 3 at Ottawa 5

Nils Ekman (Pittsburgh) scored against Henrik Lundqvist (NY Rangers) December 7. Final Score: Pittsburgh 2 at NY Rangers 3

Jarret Stoll (Edmonton) scored against Nikolai Khabibulin (Chicago) December 10. Final Score: Edmonton 1 at Chicago 4

Mats Sundin (Toronto) scored against Olaf Kolzig (Washington) December 23. Final Score: Washington 3 at Toronto 2

David Legwand (Nashville) scored against Dan Cloutier (Los Angeles) December 23. Final Score: Los Angeles 0 at Nashville 7

John Pohl (Toronto) scored against Manny Fernandez (Minnesota) December 26. Final Score: Minnesota 3 at Toronto 4

Ales Kotalik (Buffalo) scored against John Grahame (Carolina) December 28. Final Score: Carolina 1 at Buffalo 4

Marco Sturm (Boston) scored against Ray Emery (Ottawa) January 9. Final Score: Boston 2 at Ottawa 5

Jed Ortmeyer (NY Rangers) scored against Tim Thomas (Boston) January 13. Final Score: Boston 1 at NY Rangers 3

Jarkko Ruutu (Pittsburgh) scored against Andrew Raycroft (Toronto) January 20. Final Score: Toronto 2 at Pittsburgh 8

Jere Lehtinen (Dallas) scored against J.S. Giguere (Anaheim) January 28. Final Score: Dallas 1 at Anaheim 4

Brendan Shanahan (NY Rangers) scored against Hannu Toivonen (Boston) January 29. Final Score: NY Rangers 6 at Boston 1

Gaetan Latendresse (Montreal) scored against Ray Emery (Ottawa) Feburary 8. Final Score: Montreal 1 at Ottawa 4

Marc-Antoine Pouliot (Edmonton) scored against Andrew Raycroft (Toronto) Feburary 17. Final Score: Edmonton 3 at Toronto 4

Tomas Plekanec (Montreal) scored against Cam Ward (Carolina) Feburary 17. Final Score: Carolina 5 at Montreal 3

Pierre-Marc Bouchard (Minnesota) scored against Tomas Vokoun (Nashville) Feburary 17. Final Score: Minnesota 4 at Nashville 1

Jean-Pierre Dumont (Nashville) scored against Curtis Joseph (Phoenix) Feburary 19. Final Score: Phoenix 1 at Nashville 4

Ville Peltonen (Florida) scored against Marc Denis (Tampa Bay) March 3. Final Score: Tampa Bay 2 at Florida 6

Ryan Smyth (NY Islanders) scored against David Aebischer (Montreal) March 13. Final Score: NY Islanders 3 at Montreal 5

Bill Guerin (San Jose) scored against Patrick Lalime (Chicago) March 13. Final Score: Chicago 1 at San Jose 7

Stopped

Dwayne Roloson (Edmonton) stopped Jarome Iginla (Calgary) October 5. Final Score: Calgary 1 at Edmonton 3

Ryan Miller (Buffalo) stopped Mike Richards (Philadelphia) October 17. Final Score: Philadelphia 1 at Buffalo 9

Brian Boucher (Chicago) stopped Niklas Hagman (Dallas) October 20. Final Score: Chicago 4 at Dallas 5

Curtis Joseph (Phoenix) stopped Daymond Langkow (Calgary) October 24. Final Score: Phoenix 1 at Calgary 6

Dan Cloutier (Los Angeles) stopped Todd White (Minnesota) October 25. Final Score: Los Angeles 1 at Minnesota 3

Peter Budaj (Colorado) stopped Alexander Ovechkin (Washington) October 25. Final Score: Washington 5 at Colorado 3

Alexander Auld (Florida) stopped Thomas Vanek (Buffalo) November 10. Final Score: Florida 4 at Buffalo 5

Kari Lehtonen (Atlanta) stopped Martin St. Louis (Tampa Bay) November 11. Final Score: Atlanta 3 at Tampa Bay 5

Niklas Backstrom (Minnesota) stopped Paul Kariya (Nashville) November 16. Final Score: Minnesota 7 at Nashville 6

Brent Johnson (Washington) stopped Marco Sturm (Boston) November 18. Final Score: Washington 2 at Boston 3

Alexander Auld (Florida) stopped Vincent Lecavalier (Tampa Bay) November 22. Final Score: Tampa Bay 6 at Florida 4

Tomas Vokoun (Nashville) stopped Mike Modano (Dallas) November 22. Final Score: Nashville 0 at Dallas 1

Henrik Lundqvist (NY Rangers) stopped Jordan Staal (Pittsburgh) November 25. Final Score: NY Rangers 2 at Pittsburgh 1

Mike Smith (Dallas) stopped Alexander Ovechkin (Washington) November 30. Final Score: Dallas 3 at Washington 4

Kari Lehtonen (Atlanta) stopped Gregory Campbell (Florida) December 2. Final Score: Atlanta 3 at Florida 1

Jose Theodore (Colorado) stopped Mike Grier (San Jose) December 7. Final Score: Colorado 5 at San Jose 2

Roberto Luongo (Vancouver) stopped Eric Staal (Carolina) December 8. Final Score: Carolina 3 at Vancouver 4

Pascal Leclaire (Columbus) stopped Peter Schaefer (Ottawa) December 10. Final Score: Ottawa 2 at Columbus 6

Cam Ward (Carolina) stopped John Pohl (Toronto) December 15. Final Score: Toronto 4 at Carolina 3

Ryan Miller (Buffalo) stopped Jason Spezza (Ottawa) December 16. Final Score: Ottawa 3 at Buffalo 1

David Aebischer (Montreal) stopped R.J. Umberger (Philadelphia) December 21. Final Score: Philadelphia 2 at Montreal 4

Dan Cloutier (Los Angeles) stopped Paul Kariya (Nashville) December 23. Final Score: Los Angeles 0 at Nashville 7

Olaf Kolzig (Washington) stopped Karel Rachunek (NY Rangers) December 30. Final Score: Washington 1 at NY Rangers 4

Nikolai Khabibulin (Chicago) stopped Rick Nash (Columbus) December 31. Final Score: Chicago 1 at Columbus 3

Fredrik Norrena (Columbus) stopped Teemu Selanne (Anaheim) January 5. Final Score: Columbus 4 at Anaheim 3

Olaf Kolzig (Washington) stopped Jean-Pierre Vigier (Atlanta) January 6. Final Score: Atlanta 2 at Washington 3

Rick DiPietro (NY Islanders) stopped Erik Cole (Carolina) January 6. Final Score: NY Islanders 2 at Carolina 4

Henrik Lundqvist (NY Rangers) stopped Marian Hossa (Atlanta) January 20. Final Score: Atlanta 3 at NY Rangers 1

Fredrik Norrena (Columbus) stopped Daniel Paille (Buffalo) January 26. Final Score: Buffalo 2 at Columbus 3

Andrew Raycroft (Toronto) stopped Eric Belanger (Carolina) January 30. Final Score: Toronto 4 at Carolina 1

Mike Dunham (NY Islanders) stopped Marian Hossa (Atlanta) Feburary 1. Final Score: NY Islanders 5 at Atlanta 2

David Aebischer (Montreal) stopped Erik Rasmussen (New Jersey) Feburary 14. Final Score: Montreal 2 at New Jersey 5

Stephen Valiquette (NY Rangers) stopped Dimitry Afanasenkov (Philadelphia) Feburary 17. Final Score: Philadelphia 5 at NY Rangers 3

Jocelyn Thibault (Pittsburgh) stopped Alexander Semin (Washington) Feburary 18. Final Score: Washington 2 at Pittsburgh 3

Ray Emery (Ottawa) stopped Thomas Vanek (Buffalo) Feburary 24. Final Score: Buffalo 5 at Ottawa 6

Evgeni Nabokov (San Jose) stopped Martin Erat (Nashville) Feburary 28. Final Score: Nashville 4 at San Jose 3

Peter Budaj (Colorado) stopped Tomas Holmstrom (Detroit) March 4. Final Score: Colorado 4 at Detroit 3

Curtis Joseph (Phoenix) stopped Daniel Sedin (Vancouver) March 8. Final Score: Vancouver 4 at Phoenix 2

Ryan Miller (Buffalo) stopped Marian Gaborik (Minnesota) March 9. Final Score: Minnesota 5 at Buffalo 1

Marty Turco (Dallas) stopped Shane Doan (Phoenix) March 18. Final Score: Phoenix 4 at Dallas 5

Mathieu Garon (Los Angeles) stopped Teemu Selanne (Anaheim) March 18. Final Score: Los Angeles 5 at Anaheim 3

Rick DiPietro (NY Islanders) stopped Evgeni Malkin (Pittsburgh) March 22. Final Score: Pittsburgh 1 at NY Islanders 3

Martin Biron (Philadelphia) stopped Justin Williams (Carolina) March 28. Final Score: Carolina 1 at Philadelphia 5

Brian Boucher (Columbus) stopped Duncan Keith (Chicago) March 30. Final Score: Columbus 1 at Chicago 3

John Grahame (Carolina) stopped Bryan Allen (Florida) April 7. Final Score: Florida 4 at Carolina 5

Summary

70 penalty shots resulted in 25 goals.

Goaltending Leaders

Minimum 25 games

Goals Against Average

Goaltender	Team	GPI	MINS	GA	Avg
Niklas Backstrom	Minnesota	41	2227	73	1.97
Dominik Hasek	Detroit	56	3341	114	2.05
Martin Brodeur	New Jersey	78	4697	171	2.18
Marty Turco	Dallas	67	3764	140	2.23
J.S. Giguere	Anaheim	56	3245	122	2.26
Roberto Luongo	Vancouver	76	4490	171	2.29
Evgeni Nabokov	San Jose	50	2778	106	2.29

Save Percentage

Goaltender	Team	GPI	MINS	GA	SA	S%	W	L	OT
Niklas Backstrom	Minnesota	41	2227	73	1028	.929	23	8	6
Chris Mason	Nashville	40	2342	93	1244	.925	24	11	4
Martin Brodeur	New Jersey	78	4697	171	2182	.922	48	23	7
Roberto Luongo	Vancouver	76	4490	171	2169	.921	47	22	6
Tomas Vokoun	Nashville	44	2601	104	1299	.920	27	12	4
Rick DiPietro	NY Islanders	62	3627	156	1917	.919	32	19	9
Ray Emery	Ottawa	58	3351	138	1691	.918	33	16	6

Wins

Goaltender	Team	GPI	MINS	W	L	OT
Martin Brodeur	New Jersey	78	4697	48	23	7
Roberto Luongo	Vancouver	76	4490	47	22	6
Ryan Miller	Buffalo	63	3692	40	16	6
Marc-Andre Fleury	Pittsburgh	67	3905	40	16	9
Miikka Kiprusoff	Calgary	74	4419	40	24	9
Dominik Hasek	Detroit	56	3341	38	11	6
Marty Turco	Dallas	67	3764	38	20	5

Shutouts

Goaltender	Team	GPI	MINS	SO	W	L	OT
Martin Brodeur	New Jersey	78	4697	12	48	23	7
Dominik Hasek	Detroit	56	3341	8	38	11	6
Evgeni Nabokov	San Jose	50	2778	7	25	16	4
Miikka Kiprusoff	Calgary	74	4419	7	40	24	9
Marty Turco	Dallas	67	3764	6	38	20	5
Niklas Backstrom	Minnesota	41	2227	5	23	8	6
Chris Mason	Nashville	40	2342	5	24	11	4

Team-by-Team Point Totals

2001-02 to 2006-07

(Ranked by five-year point %)

Team	06-07	05-06	03-04	02-03	01-02	Pts%
Detroit	113	124	109	110	116	.698
Ottawa	105	113	102	113	94	.643
Dallas	107	112	97	111	90	.630
New Jersey	107	101	100	108	95	.623
Vancouver	105	92	101	104	94	.605
Colorado	95	95	100	105	99	.602
San Jose	107	99	104	73	99	.588
Toronto	91	90	103	98	100	.588
Buffalo	113	110	85	72	82	.563
Philadelphia	56	101	101	107	97	.563
Tampa Bay	93	92	106	93	69	.552
Nashville	110	106	91	74	69	.549
Anaheim	110	98	76	95	69	.546
Calgary	96	103	94	75	79	.545
Boston	76	74	104	87	101	.539
NY Islanders	92	78	91	83	96	.537
Montreal	90	93	93	77	87	.537
Minnesota	104	84	83	95	73	.535
Edmonton	71	95	89	92	92	.535
Carolina	88	112	76	61	91	.522
St. Louis	81	57	91	99	98	.520
NY Rangers	94	100	69	78	80	.513
Los Angeles	68	89	81	78	95	.501
Atlanta	97	90	78	74	54	.479
Phoenix	67	81	68	78	95	.474
Washington	70	70	60	92	85	.460
Florida	86	85	75	70	60	.459
Chicago	71	65	59	79	96	.451
Pittsburgh	105	58	58	65	69	.433
Columbus	73	74	62	69	57	.409

Team Record When Scoring First Goal of a Game

Team	FG	W	L	OT
Anaheim	48	34	5	9
Atlanta	44	27	11	6
Boston	43	25	12	6
Buffalo	48	35	11	2
Calgary	46	31	12	3
Carolina	33	24	7	2
Chicago	40	22	12	6
Colorado	39	26	10	3
Columbus	33	23	5	5
Dallas	41	32	7	2
Detroit	43	34	5	4
Edmonton	40	22	14	4
Florida	37	24	7	6
Los Angeles	37	17	12	8
Minnesota	41	30	7	4
Montreal	31	23	6	2
Nashville	52	38	10	4
New Jersey	46	34	7	5
NY Islanders	42	31	6	5
NY Rangers	45	30	10	5
Ottawa	48	36	8	4
Philadelphia	30	15	8	7
Phoenix	29	18	8	3
Pittsburgh	43	29	8	6
San Jose	42	35	4	3
St. Louis	44	25	10	9
Tampa Bay	41	28	11	2
Toronto	41	27	10	4
Vancouver	44	34	6	4
Washington	37	21	8	8

Team Plus/Minus Differential

Team	GF	PPGF	Net GF	GA	PPGA	Net GA	Goal Differential
Buffalo	308	71	237	242	72	170	+67
Ottawa	288	72	216	222	61	161	+55
Detroit	254	68	186	199	63	136	+50
Nashville	272	71	201	212	55	157	+44
Calgary	258	73	185	226	81	145	+40
NY Islanders	248	63	185	240	79	161	+24
Anaheim	258	89	169	208	61	147	+22
San Jose	258	92	166	199	55	144	+22
Minnesota	235	72	163	191	48	143	+20
NY Rangers	242	75	167	216	65	151	+16
Atlanta	246	67	179	245	79	166	+13
Colorado	272	79	193	251	70	181	+12
Pittsburgh	277	94	183	246	75	171	+12
Dallas	226	79	147	197	59	138	+9
Toronto	258	71	187	269	90	179	+8
Vancouver	222	70	152	201	57	144	8
Florida	247	61	186	257	78	179	7
St. Louis	214	46	168	254	83	171	–3
New Jersey	216	65	151	201	40	161	–10
Tampa Bay	253	69	184	261	66	195	–11
Carolina	241	67	174	253	61	192	–18
Chicago	201	43	158	258	77	181	–23
Montreal	245	86	159	256	69	187	–28
Columbus	201	65	136	249	85	164	–28
Washington	235	67	168	286	82	204	–36
Phoenix	216	66	150	284	92	192	–42
Los Angeles	227	81	146	283	91	192	–46
Edmonton	195	53	142	248	59	189	–47
Boston	219	71	148	289	81	208	–60
Philadelphia	214	53	161	303	65	238	–77

Team Record When Leading, Trailing, Tied

Team	Leading after 1 period			Leading after 2 periods			Trailing after 1 period			Trailing after 2 periods			Tied after 1 period			Tied after 2 periods		
	W	L	OT	W	L	OT	W	L	OT	W	L	OT	W	L	OT	W	L	OT
Anaheim	21	3	5	32	1	5	9	8	3	5	15	5	18	9	6	11	4	4
Atlanta	20	5	5	24	4	5	11	17	2	7	23	2	12	6	4	12	1	4
Boston	17	8	3	18	2	5	5	22	0	5	30	0	13	11	3	12	9	1
Buffalo	25	3	0	39	5	2	8	6	3	5	13	1	20	13	4	9	4	4
Calgary	25	5	1	28	1	1	6	10	6	4	19	4	12	14	3	11	9	5
Carolina	23	1	2	27	3	0	11	18	3	5	25	2	6	15	3	8	6	6
Chicago	16	9	3	17	4	2	5	23	0	8	33	2	10	10	6	6	5	5
Colorado	18	6	2	27	4	2	10	12	2	3	19	1	16	13	3	14	8	4
Columbus	16	1	3	21	1	4	3	28	1	6	36	1	14	13	3	6	5	2
Dallas	25	1	2	30	3	1	10	17	2	10	20	1	15	7	3	10	2	5
Detroit	20	3	4	33	1	3	11	7	4	9	15	4	19	9	5	8	3	6
Edmonton	15	3	4	22	0	2	7	25	1	4	38	2	10	15	2	6	5	3
Florida	16	3	6	26	3	5	4	17	6	3	25	3	15	11	4	6	3	8
Los Angeles	12	4	5	17	2	5	4	25	5	3	32	5	11	12	4	7	7	4
Minnesota	22	4	1	28	1	0	11	13	2	5	19	3	15	9	5	15	6	5
Montreal	14	3	2	26	2	2	11	23	3	10	24	4	17	8	1	6	8	0
Nashville	29	7	3	35	1	5	7	9	1	4	15	1	15	7	4	12	7	2
New Jersey	18	2	3	31	2	1	9	11	4	5	17	4	22	11	2	13	5	4
NY Islanders	23	1	4	29	1	5	7	21	6	5	26	1	10	8	2	6	3	6
NY Rangers	20	7	4	27	3	5	6	15	3	8	20	3	16	8	3	7	7	2
Ottawa	30	4	4	36	5	4	7	9	0	4	18	4	11	12	5	8	2	1
Philadelphia	10	1	5	12	0	1	4	31	2	2	38	5	8	16	5	8	10	6
Phoenix	15	4	2	19	1	4	7	32	2	5	38	1	9	10	1	7	7	0
Pittsburgh	25	6	6	28	0	5	9	9	3	6	20	4	13	9	2	13	4	2
San Jose	29	3	2	41	2	3	8	17	1	3	19	0	14	6	2	7	5	2
St. Louis	13	6	7	23	3	4	5	19	1	5	26	4	16	10	5	6	6	5
Tampa Bay	20	4	2	22	2	3	13	22	0	10	22	1	11	6	4	12	8	2
Toronto	20	3	3	28	3	4	4	17	2	4	25	3	16	11	6	8	3	4
Vancouver	21	4	2	30	1	5	6	15	4	5	16	1	22	6	2	14	8	2
Washington	19	7	6	21	1	5	4	23	4	2	36	3	5	10	4	5	3	6

In 2006-07, Marc-Andre Fleury joined Tom Barrasso as the only Pittsburgh goaltenders to record 40 wins in a single season.

Team Statistics

TEAMS' HOME AND ROAD RECORD

Eastern Conference

Team	Home GP	W	L	OT	GF	GA	PTS	Road GP	W	L	OT	GF	GA	PTS
BUF	41	28	10	3	166	124	59	41	25	12	4	142	118	54
N.J.	41	25	10	6	107	99	56	41	24	14	3	109	102	51
OTT	41	25	13	3	146	100	53	41	23	12	6	142	122	52
PIT	41	26	10	5	136	104	57	41	21	14	6	141	142	48
ATL	41	23	12	6	133	119	52	41	20	16	5	113	126	45
NYR	41	21	15	5	127	107	47	41	21	15	5	115	109	47
T.B.	41	22	18	1	119	117	45	41	22	15	4	134	144	48
NYI	41	22	13	6	119	103	50	41	18	17	6	129	137	42
TOR	41	21	15	5	127	128	47	41	19	16	6	131	141	44
MTL	41	26	12	3	134	115	55	41	16	22	3	111	141	35
CAR	41	21	16	4	128	131	46	41	19	18	4	113	122	42
FLA	41	23	12	6	145	125	52	41	12	19	10	102	132	34
BOS	41	18	19	4	110	142	40	41	17	22	2	109	147	36
WSH	41	17	17	7	130	135	41	41	11	23	7	105	151	29
PHI	41	10	24	7	115	152	27	41	12	24	5	99	151	29
Total	**615**	**328**	**216**	**71**	**1942**	**1801**	**727**	**615**	**280**	**259**	**76**	**1795**	**1985**	**636**

Western Conference

Team	Home GP	W	L	OT	GF	GA	PTS	Road GP	W	L	OT	GF	GA	PTS
DET	41	29	4	8	145	87	66	41	21	15	5	109	112	47
NAS	41	28	8	5	153	105	61	41	23	15	3	119	107	49
ANA	41	26	6	9	144	105	61	41	22	14	5	114	103	49
S.J.	41	25	12	4	135	94	54	41	26	14	1	123	105	53
DAL	41	28	11	2	119	99	58	41	22	14	5	107	98	49
VAN	41	26	11	4	113	103	56	41	23	15	3	109	98	49
MIN	41	29	7	5	123	81	63	41	19	19	3	112	110	41
CAL	41	30	9	2	144	92	62	41	13	20	8	114	134	34
COL	41	22	16	3	132	124	47	41	22	15	4	140	127	48
ST.L.	41	18	19	4	110	122	40	41	16	16	9	104	132	41
CBJ	41	18	19	4	111	126	40	41	15	23	3	90	123	33
EDM	41	19	19	3	114	127	41	41	13	24	4	81	121	30
CHI	41	17	20	4	88	107	38	41	14	22	5	113	151	33
L.A.	41	16	16	9	116	129	41	41	11	25	5	111	154	27
PHX	41	18	20	3	120	135	39	41	13	26	2	96	149	28
Total	**615**	**349**	**197**	**69**	**1867**	**1636**	**767**	**615**	**273**	**277**	**65**	**1642**	**1824**	**611**
	1230	**677**	**413**	**140**	**3809**	**3437**	**1494**	**1230**	**553**	**536**	**141**	**3437**	**3809**	**1247**

Pittsburgh's Jordan Staal scored 29 goals as a rookie, including a league-leading seven while the Penguins were shorthanded.

TEAMS' DIVISIONAL RECORD

Northeast Division

	Against Own Division GP	W	L	OT	GF	GA	PTS	Against Other Divisions GP	W	L	OT	GF	GA	PTS
BUF	32	18	11	3	119	105	39	50	35	11	4	189	137	74
OTT	32	19	10	3	119	92	41	50	29	15	6	169	130	64
TOR	32	13	14	5	102	107	31	50	27	17	6	156	162	60
MON	32	16	12	4	101	112	36	50	26	22	2	144	144	54
BOS	32	14	17	1	85	110	29	50	21	24	5	134	179	47
Total								**250**	**138**	**89**	**23**	**792**	**752**	**299**

Atlantic Division

	GP	W	L	OT	GF	GA	PTS	GP	W	L	OT	GF	GA	PTS
N.J.	32	23	6	3	90	69	49	50	26	18	6	126	132	58
PIT	32	20	9	3	111	89	43	50	27	15	8	166	157	62
NYR	32	15	12	5	82	88	35	50	27	18	5	160	128	59
NYI	32	17	11	4	93	85	38	50	23	19	8	155	155	54
PHI	32	5	20	7	82	127	17	50	17	28	5	132	176	39
Total								**250**	**120**	**98**	**32**	**739**	**748**	**272**

Southeast Division

	GP	W	L	OT	GF	GA	PTS	GP	W	L	OT	GF	GA	PTS
ATL	32	18	7	7	95	87	43	50	25	21	4	151	158	54
T.B.	32	19	11	2	113	106	40	50	25	22	3	140	155	53
CAR	32	19	11	2	108	100	40	50	21	23	6	133	153	48
FLA	32	13	14	5	100	108	31	50	22	17	11	147	149	55
WSH	32	11	15	6	101	116	28	50	17	25	8	134	170	42
Total								**250**	**110**	**108**	**32**	**705**	**785**	**252**

Central Division

	GP	W	L	OT	GF	GA	PTS	GP	W	L	OT	GF	GA	PTS
DET	32	22	4	6	112	70	50	50	28	15	7	142	129	63
NSH	32	21	8	3	106	82	45	50	30	15	5	166	130	65
ST.L.	32	12	16	4	73	103	28	50	22	19	9	141	151	53
CBJ	32	11	17	4	83	104	26	50	22	25	3	118	145	47
CHI	32	14	17	1	94	109	29	50	17	25	8	107	149	42
Total								**250**	**119**	**99**	**32**	**674**	**704**	**270**

Pacific Division

	GP	W	L	OT	GF	GA	PTS	GP	W	L	OT	GF	GA	PTS
ANA	32	19	8	5	99	79	43	50	29	12	9	159	129	67
S.J.	32	18	13	1	96	85	37	50	33	13	4	162	114	70
DAL	32	24	7	1	94	68	49	50	26	18	6	132	129	58
L.A.	32	10	18	4	90	117	24	50	17	23	10	137	166	44
PHX	32	9	18	5	77	107	23	50	22	28	0	139	177	44
Total								**250**	**127**	**94**	**29**	**729**	**715**	**283**

Northwest Division

	GP	W	L	OT	GF	GA	PTS	GP	W	L	OT	GF	GA	PTS
VAN	32	16	13	3	87	90	35	50	33	13	4	135	111	70
MIN	32	18	8	6	82	67	42	50	30	18	2	153	124	62
CGY	32	17	12	3	98	84	37	50	26	17	7	160	142	59
COL	32	18	11	3	106	96	39	50	26	20	4	166	155	56
EDM	32	11	20	1	64	100	23	50	21	23	6	131	148	48
Total								**250**	**136**	**91**	**23**	**745**	**680**	**295**

TEAM STREAKS

Consecutive Wins

Games	Team	From	To
10	Buffalo	Oct. 4	Oct. 26
9	Detroit	Oct. 25	Nov. 14
9	Minnesota	Mar. 8	Mar. 24
7	Vancouver	Dec. 26	Jan. 7
7	Phoenix	Dec. 28	Jan. 9
6	Minnesota	Oct. 5	Oct. 18
6	Calgary	Nov. 4	Nov. 17
6	Nashville	Jan. 5	Jan. 15
6	Pittsburgh	Jan. 20	Feb. 3
6	Pittsburgh	Feb. 6	Feb. 18
6	Vancouver	Feb. 10	Feb. 22
6	Calgary	Mar. 20	Mar. 31

Consecutive Home Wins

Games	Team	From	To
13	Detroit	Dec. 20	Feb. 21
10	Calgary	Nov. 7	Dec. 12
9	Montreal	Feb. 20	Apr. 3
9	Toronto	Mar. 6	Apr. 7
8	Minnesota	Oct. 5	Nov. 2
8	Minnesota	Dec. 5	Jan. 2
8	Vancouver	Dec. 8	Jan. 7
8	Calgary	Jan. 4	Feb. 3
8	Nashville	Jan. 6	Feb. 8
8	Pittsburgh	Jan. 16	Feb. 18

Consecutive Road Wins

Games	Team	From	To
10	Buffalo	Oct. 4	Nov. 13
7	Nashville	Oct. 16	Nov. 4
7	Anaheim	Nov. 28	Dec. 13
7	Tampa Bay	Jan. 7	Feb. 1
6	Vancouver	Dec. 26	Jan. 18
6	Phoenix	Dec. 28	Jan. 9
5	Ottawa	Dec. 16	Jan. 20
5	New Jersey	Dec. 30	Jan. 26
5	New Jersey	Feb. 1	Feb. 27
5	Vancouver	Feb. 6	Feb. 22
5	Minnesota	Mar. 8	Mar. 17

TEAM PENALTIES

Abbreviations: GP – games played; **PEN** – total penalty minutes including bench minutes; **BMI** – total bench minor minutes; **AVG** – average penalty minutes/game calculated by dividing total penalty minutes by games played

Team	GP	PEN	BMI	AVG	Team	GP	PEN	BMI	AVG
N.J.	82	830	8	10.1	BUF	82	1200	18	14.6
MIN	82	862	12	10.5	CGY	82	1204	22	14.7
COL	82	884	20	10.8	VAN	82	1206	16	14.7
T.B.	82	897	6	10.9	STL	82	1223	20	14.9
S.J.	82	955	16	11.6	WSH	82	1233	16	15.0
DET	82	982	24	12.0	L.A.	82	1239	24	15.1
CAR	82	1021	14	12.5	PIT	82	1249	38	15.2
NYI	82	1062	24	13.0	BOS	82	1256	24	15.3
ATL	82	1097	26	13.4	EDM	82	1285	22	15.7
NYR	82	1109	22	13.5	PHI	82	1301	16	15.9
DAL	82	1133	22	13.8	CHI	82	1332	16	16.2
MTL	82	1133	14	13.8	CBJ	82	1357	20	16.5
TOR	82	1139	12	13.9	PHX	82	1445	28	17.6
OTT	82	1173	12	14.3	ANA	82	1457	30	17.8
FLA	82	1181	18	14.4	**Total**	**1230**	**34624**	**584**	
NSH	82	1179	24	14.4	**Two-Team Avg. PIM/GP**				**28.1**

Sheldon Souray's 19 power-play goals with the Canadiens last season ranked second in the NHL to Teemu Selanne's 25 and set a new record for defensemen.

TEAMS' POWER-PLAY RECORD

Abbreviations: ADV – total advantages; **PPGF** – power-play goals for;
% – calculated by dividing number of power-play goals by total advantages.

	Home					Road					Overall				
	Team	GP	ADV	PPGF	%	Team	GP	ADV	PPGF	%	Team	GP	ADV	PPGF	%
1	MTL	41	182	46	25.3	ANA	41	180	38	21.1	MTL	82	378	86	22.8
2	MIN	41	206	49	23.8	S.J	41	187	39	20.9	S.J	82	410	92	22.4
3	S.J	41	223	53	23.8	L.A	41	212	44	20.8	ANA	82	398	89	22.4
4	COL	41	195	46	23.6	MTL	41	196	40	20.4	COL	82	374	79	21.1
5	ANA	41	218	51	23.4	NYI	41	177	36	20.3	PIT	82	463	94	20.3
6	FLA	41	172	37	21.5	PIT	41	210	41	19.5	MIN	82	380	72	18.9
7	BUF	41	203	43	21.2	OTT	41	192	36	18.8	DAL	82	427	79	18.5
8	PIT	41	253	53	20.9	VAN	41	202	38	18.8	NYR	82	406	75	18.5
9	CGY	41	215	44	20.5	T.B	41	188	35	18.6	T.B	82	374	69	18.4
10	NSH	41	219	44	20.1	COL	41	179	33	18.4	L.A	82	442	81	18.3
11	NYR	41	197	39	19.8	DAL	41	195	34	17.4	CGY	82	401	73	18.2
12	DAL	41	232	45	19.4	N.J	41	173	30	17.3	NYI	82	348	63	18.1
13	ATL	41	214	41	19.2	NYR	41	209	36	17.2	FLA	82	337	61	18.1
14	TOR	41	203	38	18.7	PHX	41	182	31	17.0	OTT	82	403	72	17.9
15	BOS	41	212	39	18.4	DET	41	189	32	16.9	TOR	82	401	71	17.7
16	CBJ	41	224	41	18.3	TOR	41	198	33	16.7	N.J	82	367	65	17.7
17	T.B	41	186	34	18.3	CAR	41	210	34	16.2	BUF	82	407	71	17.4
18	N.J	41	194	35	18.0	BOS	41	200	32	16.0	NSH	82	408	71	17.4
19	DET	41	209	36	17.2	CGY	41	186	29	15.6	VAN	82	407	70	17.2
20	WSH	41	221	38	17.2	WSH	41	187	29	15.5	BOS	82	412	71	17.2
21	OTT	41	211	36	17.1	CHI	41	184	27	14.7	DET	82	398	68	17.1
22	PHI	41	191	32	16.8	FLA	41	165	24	14.5	ATL	82	407	67	16.5
23	PHX	41	218	35	16.1	NSH	41	189	27	14.3	PHX	82	400	66	16.5
24	L.A	41	230	37	16.1	BUF	41	204	28	13.7	WSH	82	408	67	16.4
25	NYI	41	171	27	15.8	EDM	41	190	26	13.7	CAR	82	447	67	15.0
26	VAN	41	205	32	15.6	ATL	41	193	26	13.5	CBJ	82	438	65	14.8
27	EDM	41	183	27	14.8	MIN	41	174	23	13.2	EDM	82	373	53	14.2
28	STL	41	207	30	14.5	PHI	41	185	21	11.4	PHI	82	376	53	14.1
29	CAR	41	237	33	13.9	CBJ	41	214	24	11.2	STL	82	381	46	12.1
30	CHI	41	180	16	8.9	STL	41	174	16	9.2	CHI	82	364	43	11.8
TOTAL		**1230**	**6211**	**1157**	**18.6**		**1230**	**5724**	**942**	**16.5**		**1230**	**11935**	**2099**	**17.6**

TEAMS' PENALTY KILLING RECORD

Abbreviations: TSH – total times short-handed; **PPGA** – power-play goals against;
% – calculated by dividing times short minus power-play goals against by times short.

	Home					Road					Overall				
	Team	GP	TSH	PPGA	%	Team	GP	TSH	PPGA	%	Team	GP	TSH	PPGA	%
1	VAN	41	192	20	89.6	EDM	41	197	22	88.8	VAN	82	436	57	86.9
2	DET	41	188	22	88.3	ANA	41	210	28	86.7	MIN	82	342	48	86.0
3	PIT	41	213	26	87.8	MIN	41	172	24	86.0	NSH	82	387	55	85.8
4	CHI	41	200	25	87.5	NSH	41	191	27	85.9	N.J	82	271	40	85.2
5	OTT	41	201	26	87.1	DAL	41	194	28	85.6	ANA	82	410	61	85.1
6	S.J	41	167	23	86.2	VAN	41	244	37	84.8	CAR	82	395	61	84.6
7	PHI	41	203	28	86.2	N.J	41	127	20	84.3	DET	82	408	63	84.6
8	N.J	41	144	20	86.1	CAR	41	203	32	84.2	EDM	82	382	59	84.6
9	MIN	41	170	24	85.9	BUF	41	210	34	83.8	OTT	82	394	61	84.5
10	NSH	41	196	28	85.7	PHI	41	217	37	82.9	PHI	82	420	65	84.5
11	NYR	41	179	26	85.5	FLA	41	226	39	82.7	DAL	82	377	59	84.4
12	CAR	41	192	29	84.9	MTL	41	223	39	82.5	NYR	82	400	65	83.8
13	MTL	41	196	30	84.7	NYR	41	221	39	82.4	MTL	82	419	69	83.5
14	STL	41	196	31	84.2	OTT	41	193	35	81.9	S.J	82	330	55	83.3
15	ANA	41	200	33	83.5	NYI	41	232	42	81.9	CHI	82	443	77	82.6
16	DAL	41	183	31	83.1	DET	41	220	41	81.4	FLA	82	443	78	82.4
17	BOS	41	221	39	82.4	BOS	41	221	42	81.0	PIT	82	419	75	82.1
18	ATL	41	181	32	82.3	CBJ	41	246	48	80.5	NYI	82	433	79	81.8
19	CGY	41	198	35	82.3	S.J	41	163	32	80.4	BOS	82	442	81	81.7
20	CBJ	41	207	37	82.1	COL	41	175	35	80.0	BUF	82	386	72	81.3
21	FLA	41	217	39	82.0	WSH	41	209	42	79.9	CBJ	82	453	85	81.2
22	NYI	41	201	37	81.6	PHX	41	224	47	79.0	CGY	82	414	81	80.4
23	WSH	41	205	40	80.5	CGY	41	216	46	78.7	COL	82	353	70	80.2
24	TOR	41	193	38	80.3	CHI	41	243	52	78.6	WSH	82	414	82	80.2
25	COL	41	178	35	80.3	ATL	41	210	47	77.6	STL	82	414	83	80.0
26	T.B	41	137	27	80.3	TOR	41	225	52	76.9	ATL	82	391	79	79.8
27	EDM	41	185	37	80.0	T.B	41	168	39	76.8	TOR	82	418	90	78.5
28	L.A	41	204	41	79.9	PIT	41	206	49	76.2	T.B	82	305	66	78.4
29	BUF	41	176	38	78.4	STL	41	218	52	76.1	PHX	82	425	92	78.4
30	PHX	41	201	45	77.6	L.A	41	207	50	75.8	L.A	82	411	91	77.9
TOTAL		**1230**	**5724**	**942**	**83.5**		**1230**	**6211**	**1157**	**81.4**		**1230**	**11935**	**2099**	**82.4**

SHORTHAND GOALS FOR

	Home			Road			Overall		
	Team	GP	SHGF	Team	GP	SHGF	Team	GP	SHGF
1	OTT	41	9	PHI	41	9	OTT	82	17
2	PIT	41	8	CGY	41	9	MTL	82	17
3	DET	41	8	MTL	41	9	PHI	82	15
4	MTL	41	8	OTT	41	8	CGY	82	15
5	BUF	41	7	WSH	41	7	T.B.	82	14
6	T.B.	41	7	T.B.	41	7	PIT	82	14
7	CAR	41	6	BOS	41	7	CAR	82	12
8	NYR	41	6	CHI	41	6	WSH	82	12
9	PHI	41	6	CAR	41	6	DET	82	12
10	CHI	41	6	NSH	41	6	CHI	82	12
11	CGY	41	6	PIT	41	6	NYR	82	11
12	ATL	41	5	STL	41	5	ATL	82	9
13	WSH	41	5	NYR	41	5	MIN	82	9
14	MIN	41	4	MIN	41	5	BUF	82	8
15	PHX	41	4	COL	41	4	NSH	82	8
16	S.J.	41	4	NYI	41	4	BOS	82	8
17	VAN	41	4	DET	41	4	COL	82	7
18	COL	41	3	CBJ	41	4	NYI	82	7
19	FLA	41	3	EDM	41	4	S.J.	82	7
20	L.A.	41	3	ATL	41	4	STL	82	7
21	NYI	41	3	N.J.	41	3	EDM	82	6
22	NSH	41	2	L.A.	41	3	CBJ	82	6
23	EDM	41	2	S.J.	41	3	L.A.	82	6
24	CBJ	41	2	TOR	41	2	VAN	82	5
25	ANA	41	2	FLA	41	2	PHX	82	5
26	DAL	41	2	ANA	41	2	FLA	82	5
27	STL	41	2	BUF	41	1	N.J.	82	4
28	TOR	41	1	DAL	41	1	ANA	82	4
29	N.J.	41	1	VAN	41	1	TOR	82	3
30	BOS	41	1	PHX	41	1	DAL	82	3
TOTAL		**1230**	**130**		**1230**	**138**		**1230**	**268**

SHORTHAND GOALS AGAINST

	Home			Road			Overall		
	Team	GP	SHGA	Team	GP	SHGA	Team	GP	SHGA
1	EDM	41	1	NYR	41	0	NSH	82	2
2	NSH	41	2	NSH	41	0	EDM	82	4
3	FLA	41	2	ANA	41	0	S.J.	82	4
4	DAL	41	2	S.J.	41	1	ANA	82	4
5	CHI	41	2	VAN	41	2	CGY	82	5
6	CGY	41	2	MTL	41	2	DAL	82	6
7	DET	41	3	COL	41	3	NYR	82	6
8	S.J.	41	3	CGY	41	3	CHI	82	6
9	CBJ	41	3	STL	41	3	FLA	82	6
10	L.A.	41	3	L.A.	41	3	MTL	82	6
11	NYI	41	3	EDM	41	3	L.A.	82	6
12	CAR	41	4	MIN	41	3	CAR	82	8
13	PHX	41	4	BUF	41	4	VAN	82	8
14	ANA	41	4	DAL	41	4	MIN	82	8
15	T.B.	41	4	CHI	41	4	COL	82	9
16	MTL	41	4	CAR	41	4	NYI	82	9
17	MIN	41	5	FLA	41	4	ATL	82	10
18	N.J.	41	5	ATL	41	4	STL	82	10
19	TOR	41	6	OTT	41	5	CBJ	82	10
20	COL	41	6	TOR	41	5	TOR	82	11
21	NYR	41	6	NYI	41	6	T.B.	82	11
22	ATL	41	6	N.J.	41	6	DET	82	11
23	PIT	41	6	WSH	41	7	N.J.	82	11
24	VAN	41	6	T.B.	41	7	OTT	82	12
25	OTT	41	7	PHI	41	7	BUF	82	13
26	PHI	41	7	CBJ	41	7	PIT	82	13
27	WSH	41	7	PIT	41	7	PHX	82	13
28	STL	41	7	DET	41	8	WSH	82	14
29	BUF	41	9	BOS	41	9	PHI	82	14
30	BOS	41	9	PHX	41	9	BOS	82	18
TOTAL		**1230**	**138**		**1230**	**130**		**1230**	**268**

Regular-Season Overtime Results

2006-07 to 1986-87

	2006-07				2005-06				2003-04				2002-03				2001-02			
Team	**GP**	**W**	**L**	**SO**	**GP**	**W**	**L**	**SO**	**GP**	**W**	**L**	**T**	**GP**	**W**	**L**	**T**	**GP**	**W**	**L**	**T**
ANA	23	5	4	14	18	3	5	10	22	4	8	10	21	6	6	9	14	3	3	8
ATL	25	7	7	11	18	5	3	10	18	6	4	8	19	7	5	7	19	3	5	11
BOS	19	4	2	13	22	4	8	10	30	8	7	15	21	6	4	11	24	9	9	6
BUF	22	5	3	14	17	6	1	10	13	2	4	7	21	3	8	10	16	4	1	11
CGY	15	2	5	8	15	2	4	9	13	3	3	7	19	2	6	11	17	2	3	12
CAR/HFD	14	6	3	5	20	4	6	10	25	5	6	14	15	4	3	8	27	6	5	16
CHI	18	3	2	13	22	7	7	8	23	4	8	11	23	6	4	13	17	3	1	13
COL/QUE	15	3	3	9	15	3	3	9	28	8	7	13	23	4	6	13	13	4	1	8
CBJ	16	4	2	10	18	6	1	11	18	6	4	8	28	7	8	13	15	2	5	8
DAL/MIN	22	6	3	13	21	3	5	13	18	3	2	13	24	5	4	15	21	3	5	13
DET	18	3	5	10	15	3	5	7	20	7	2	11	21	7	4	10	24	10	4	10
EDM	11	1	4	6	26	6	4	16	23	6	5	12	27	7	9	11	19	3	4	12
FLA	21	3	8	10	23	8	6	9	24	5	4	15	26	4	9	13	16	0	6	10
L.A.	20	2	8	10	15	4	4	7	27	2	9	16	19	6	7	6	18	3	4	11
MIN	25	7	1	17	14	1	5	8	24	1	3	20	19	8	1	10	21	0	9	12
MTL	14	2	1	11	18	7	6	5	16	5	4	7	19	2	9	8	17	2	3	12
NSH	17	3	3	11	17	3	5	9	22	7	4	11	24	8	6	10	18	5	0	13
N.J.	22	3	1	18	22	4	5	13	21	7	2	12	25	5	7	13	19	6	4	9
NYI	22	2	7	13	18	3	3	12	17	2	4	11	18	5	2	11	18	6	4	8
NYR	22	3	5	14	23	4	8	11	18	3	8	7	20	6	4	10	13	5	4	4
OTT	13	2	3	8	13	2	3	8	19	3	6	10	16	7	1	8	19	3	7	9
PHI	16	3	6	7	22	7	5	10	23	2	6	15	23	6	4	13	16	3	3	10
PHX/WPG	12	2	3	7	15	6	2	7	29	5	6	18	20	4	5	11	19	4	6	9
PIT	27	6	5	16	19	4	8	7	19	7	4	8	14	3	5	6	20	7	5	8
ST.L.	23	4	7	12	22	3	7	12	24	11	2	11	19	2	8	9	18	6	4	8
S.J.	8	1	3	4	21	9	4	8	21	3	6	12	23	6	6	11	13	2	3	8
T.B.	20	5	3	12	18	6	2	10	18	4	6	8	23	2	5	16	19	4	4	11
TOR	19	4	4	11	18	7	1	10	17	4	3	10	17	7	3	7	17	3	4	10
VAN	24	12	3	9	16	4	4	8	26	11	5	10	19	5	1	13	14	4	3	7
WSH	19	4	3	12	21	2	6	13	14	1	3	10	20	6	6	8	19	6	2	11
Totals	**281**	**117**		**164**	**281**	**136**		**145**	**315**	**145**		**170**	**313**	**156**		**157**	**270**	**121**		**149**

	2000-01				1999-2000				1998-99				1997-98				1996-97			
Team	**GP**	**W**	**L**	**T**	**GP**	**W**	**L**	**T**	**GP**	**W**	**L**	**T**	**GP**	**W**	**L**	**T**	**GP**	**W**	**L**	**T**
ANA	20	4	5	11	18	3	3	12	17	1	3	13	20	3	4	13	16	3	0	13
ATL	16	2	2	12	11	0	4	7	...	...	...	...	...	...	...	...	...	...	...	...
BOS	20	4	8	8	26	1	6	19	17	2	2	13	17	3	1	13	15	3	3	9
BUF	10	4	1	5	20	5	4	11	23	3	3	17	21	3	1	17	21	5	4	12
CGY	22	3	4	15	26	11	5	10	16	3	1	12	22	4	3	15	16	3	4	9
CAR/HFD	18	6	3	9	14	4	0	10	24	1	5	18	12	2	2	8	18	3	4	11
CHI	15	2	5	8	17	5	2	10	15	1	2	12	18	1	4	13	19	1	5	13
COL/QUE	20	6	4	10	17	5	1	11	12	2	0	10	22	2	3	17	15	2	3	10
CBJ	18	3	6	9	...	...	...	...	...	...	...	...	...	...	...	...	...	...	...	...
DAL/MIN	16	6	2	8	19	3	6	10	16	3	1	12	17	5	1	11	15	4	3	8
DET	23	10	4	9	16	4	2	10	10	2	1	7	15	0	0	15	27	7	2	18
EDM	20	5	3	12	27	3	8	16	20	3	5	12	15	3	2	10	16	1	6	9
FLA	24	2	9	13	15	3	6	6	21	1	2	18	20	3	2	15	26	3	4	19
L.A.	19	3	3	13	21	5	4	12	12	5	2	5	16	3	2	11	14	0	3	11
MIN	22	4	5	13	...	...	...	...	...	...	...	...	...	...	...	...	...	...	...	...
MTL	16	2	6	8	17	4	4	9	15	0	4	11	20	3	4	13	21	2	4	15
NSH	17	5	3	9	18	4	7	7	10	1	2	7	...	...	...	...	...	...	...	...
N.J.	20	5	3	12	16	3	5	8	15	3	1	11	16	2	3	11	17	1	2	14
NYI	12	2	3	7	15	5	1	9	17	1	6	10	13	0	2	11	17	3	2	12
NYR	11	5	1	5	21	6	3	12	19	5	3	11	24	2	4	18	13	3	0	10
OTT	16	3	4	9	15	2	2	11	18	1	2	15	17	2	0	15	17	0	2	15
PHI	19	5	3	11	21	6	3	12	24	2	3	19	15	3	1	11	18	3	2	13
PHX/WPG	23	3	3	17	16	4	4	8	15	2	1	12	14	0	2	12	16	5	4	7
PIT	15	3	3	9	17	3	6	8	22	7	1	14	23	3	2	18	13	1	4	8
ST.L.	23	6	5	12	17	5	1	11	15	1	1	13	12	2	2	8	13	1	1	11
S.J.	22	7	3	12	21	4	7	10	21	1	2	18	12	0	2	10	12	3	1	8
T.B.	13	2	5	6	16	0	7	9	12	1	2	9	13	0	3	10	16	4	2	10
TOR	19	3	5	11	17	7	3	7	14	6	1	7	10	1	0	9	10	1	1	8
VAN	23	5	7	11	27	4	8	15	13	0	1	12	17	0	3	14	14	5	2	7
WSH	16	2	4	10	19	5	2	12	11	2	3	6	17	4	1	12	13	2	2	9
Totals	**274**	**122**		**152**	**260**	**114**		**146**	**222**	**60**		**162**	**219**	**54**		**165**	**214**	**70**		**144**

2006-07
Home Team Wins: **62**
Visiting Team Wins: **55**

	1995-96				1994-95				1993-94				1992-93				1991-92			
Team	**GP**	**W**	**L**	**T**	**GP**	**W**	**L**	**T**	**GP**	**W**	**L**	**T**	**GP**	**W**	**L**	**T**	**GP**	**W**	**L**	**T**
ANA	16	6	2	8	7	2	0	5	12	2	5	5	...	...	...	...	...	...	...	...
ATL	...	...	...	...	...	...	...	...	...	...	...	...	...	...	...	...	...	...	...	...
BOS	19	2	6	11	8	2	3	3	17	2	2	13	15	5	3	7	20	6	2	12
BUF	15	2	6	7	9	1	1	7	13	0	4	9	18	4	4	10	16	2	2	12
CGY	16	2	3	11	9	1	1	7	18	3	2	13	19	4	4	11	19	2	5	12
CAR/HFD	14	2	3	9	9	1	1	7	14	4	1	9	18	3	9	6	18	2	3	13
CHI	19	1	4	14	7	2	0	5	16	2	5	9	16	1	3	12	19	2	2	15
COL/QUE	6	1	0	5	8	0	0	8	15	3	3	9	15	4	1	10	17	0	5	12
CBJ	...	...	...	...	...	...	...	...	...	...	...	...	...	...	...	...	...	...	...	...
DAL/MIN	15	1	0	14	9	0	1	8	22	6	3	13	10	0	0	10	8	0	2	6
DET	11	3	1	7	4	0	0	4	15	5	2	8	11	2	0	9	16	3	1	12
EDM	14	4	2	8	7	1	2	4	21	1	6	14	17	5	4	8	12	0	2	10
FLA	13	0	3	10	9	0	3	6	24	2	5	17	...	...	...	...	...	...	...	...
L.A.	23	3	2	18	9	0	0	9	18	3	3	12	13	2	1	10	16	1	1	14
MIN	...	...	...	...	...	...	...	...	...	...	...	...	...	...	...	...	...	...	...	...
MTL	15	2	3	10	10	1	2	7	19	3	2	14	14	5	3	6	20	6	3	11
NSH	...	...	...	...	...	...	...	...	...	...	...	...	...	...	...	...	...	...	...	...
N.J.	19	7	0	12	11	1	2	8	14	1	1	12	11	4	0	7	17	2	4	11
NYI	17	2	5	10	7	1	1	5	19	5	2	12	13	3	3	7	16	3	2	11
NYR	17	2	1	14	3	0	0	3	12	3	1	8	17	2	4	11	11	5	1	5
OTT	8	0	3	5	7	1	1	5	17	4	4	9	10	0	6	4	...	...	...	...
PHI	20	4	3	13	8	3	1	4	18	3	5	10	17	4	2	11	17	2	4	11
PHX/WPG	8	2	0	6	9	0	2	7	15	1	5	9	11	2	2	7	20	1	4	15
PIT	9	3	2	4	5	1	1	3	19	4	2	13	10	3	0	7	12	2	1	9
ST.L.	18	1	1	16	7	1	1	5	17	4	2	11	17	2	4	11	15	2	2	11
S.J.	9	1	1	7	5	1	0	4	19	2	1	16	10	3	5	2	9	1	3	5
T.B.	18	3	3	12	7	2	2	3	18	3	4	11	14	3	4	7	...	...	...	...
TOR	18	4	2	12	8	0	0	8	17	4	1	12	13	1	1	11	11	4	0	7
VAN	20	1	4	15	13	0	1	12	12	5	4	3	10	1	0	9	17	4	1	12
WSH	16	4	1	11	9	0	1	8	14	2	2	10	11	2	2	7	12	2	2	8
Totals	**201**	**64**		**137**	**101**	**26**		**75**	**214**	**74**		**140**	**165**	**65**		**100**	**169**	**52**		**117**

	1990-91				1989-90				1988-89				1987-88				1986-87			
Team	**GP**	**W**	**L**	**T**	**GP**	**W**	**L**	**T**	**GP**	**W**	**L**	**T**	**GP**	**W**	**L**	**T**	**GP**	**W**	**L**	**T**
ANA	...	...	...	...	...	...	...	...	...	...	...	...	...	...	...	...	...	...	...	...
ATL	...	...	...	...	...	...	...	...	...	...	...	...	...	...	...	...	...	...	...	...
BOS	17	5	0	12	14	3	2	9	19	3	2	14	14	4	4	6	12	2	3	7
BUF	24	3	2	19	15	4	3	8	13	2	4	7	12	0	1	11	13	1	4	8
CGY	15	3	4	8	21	3	3	15	17	5	3	9	15	2	4	9	4	1	0	3
CAR/HFD	9	1	1	7	9	0	0	9	10	1	4	5	12	3	2	7	9	2	0	7
CHI	12	3	1	8	10	2	2	6	17	2	3	12	15	4	2	9	15	1	0	14
COL/QUE	18	1	3	14	8	0	1	7	10	2	1	7	9	2	2	5	14	0	4	10
CBJ	...	...	...	...	...	...	...	...	...	...	...	...	...	...	...	...	...	...	...	...
DAL/MIN	17	0	3	14	11	3	4	4	17	0	1	16	16	1	2	13	14	2	2	10
DET	14	2	4	8	17	2	1	14	16	3	1	12	16	2	3	11	17	2	5	10
EDM	15	4	5	6	20	5	1	14	15	4	3	8	16	3	2	11	14	5	3	6
FLA	...	...	...	...	...	...	...	...	...	...	...	...	...	...	...	...	...	...	...	...
L.A.	16	4	2	10	12	3	2	7	14	6	1	7	12	1	3	8	12	2	2	8
MIN	...	...	...	...	...	...	...	...	...	...	...	...	...	...	...	...	...	...	...	...
MTL	17	3	3	11	17	4	2	11	11	2	0	9	16	1	2	13	16	2	4	10
NSH	...	...	...	...	...	...	...	...	...	...	...	...	...	...	...	...	...	...	...	...
N.J.	17	1	1	15	16	3	4	9	17	1	4	12	12	4	2	6	13	3	4	6
NYI	15	2	3	10	16	3	2	11	11	3	3	5	13	3	0	10	19	4	3	12
NYR	16	1	2	13	17	2	2	13	10	1	1	8	11	0	1	10	19	5	6	8
OTT	...	...	...	...	...	...	...	...	...	...	...	...	...	...	...	...	...	...	...	...
PHI	11	1	0	10	18	2	5	11	14	1	5	8	13	1	3	9	10	1	1	8
PHX/WPG	14	1	2	11	19	4	4	11	20	6	2	12	21	8	2	11	11	2	1	8
PIT	12	4	2	6	14	3	3	8	10	2	1	7	16	5	2	9	21	5	4	12
ST.L.	18	3	4	11	15	2	4	9	16	3	1	12	14	2	4	8	21	4	2	15
S.J.	...	...	...	...	...	...	...	...	...	...	...	...	...	...	...	...	...	...	...	...
T.B.	...	...	...	...	...	...	...	...	...	...	...	...	...	...	...	...	...	...	...	...
TOR	17	4	2	11	11	3	4	4	11	1	4	6	13	1	2	10	13	3	4	6
VAN	15	3	3	9	21	2	5	14	14	2	4	8	11	0	2	9	10	2	0	8
WSH	14	4	3	7	9	2	1	6	16	2	4	10	15	2	4	9	17	5	2	10
Totals	**166**	**54**		**112**	**155**	**55**		**100**	**149**	**52**		**97**	**146**	**49**		**97**	**147**	**54**		**93**

Abbreviations: GP – games played; **W** – overtime win; **L** – overtime loss;
SO – game tied after overtime. Game decided in shootout. (2005-06 to date); See page 143.
T – game tied after overtime. (Up to and including 2003-04.)

2006-07 Shootout Summary

Team Shootout Statistics

Team	GP	W	L	G	S	S%	SA	GA	Sv%	W	L	G	S	S%	SA	GA	Sv%	W	L	G	S	S%	SA	GA	Sv%
	OVERALL									HOME								ROAD							
ANA	14	4	10	14	55	.255	19	52	.635	1	7	8	33	.242	14	31	.548	3	3	6	22	.273	5	21	.762
ATL	11	7	4	15	29	.517	10	30	.667	4	2	9	18	.500	6	17	.647	3	2	6	11	.545	4	13	.692
BOS	13	9	4	18	54	.333	13	57	.772	5	3	12	35	.343	10	36	.722	4	1	6	19	.316	3	21	.857
BUF	14	10	4	17	47	.362	9	46	.804	5	2	7	28	.250	3	26	.885	5	2	10	19	.526	6	20	.700
CGY	8	3	5	9	29	.310	11	27	.593	2	1	3	8	.375	2	7	.714	1	4	6	21	.286	9	20	.550
CAR	5	0	5	1	17	.059	8	17	.529	0	3	0	9	.000	4	8	.500	0	2	1	8	.125	4	9	.556
CHI	13	6	7	17	47	.362	19	45	.578	2	3	5	19	.263	7	18	.611	4	4	12	28	.429	12	27	.556
COL	9	5	4	12	33	.364	11	33	.667	1	2	2	9	.222	3	8	.625	4	2	10	24	.417	8	25	.680
CBJ	10	5	5	13	42	.310	14	42	.667	1	3	6	21	.286	8	20	.600	4	2	7	21	.333	6	22	.727
DAL	13	9	4	18	51	.353	11	49	.776	2	2	4	13	.308	3	10	.700	7	2	14	38	.368	8	39	.795
DET	10	2	8	10	39	.256	17	37	.541	1	6	5	25	.200	11	23	.522	1	2	5	14	.357	6	14	.571
EDM	6	3	3	6	22	.273	8	24	.667	2	1	4	14	.286	4	14	.714	1	2	2	8	.250	4	10	.600
FLA	10	2	8	9	38	.237	15	35	.571	1	2	3	9	.333	3	6	.500	1	6	6	29	.207	12	29	.586
L.A.	10	4	6	18	46	.391	19	45	.578	3	5	14	38	.368	14	36	.611	1	1	4	8	.500	5	9	.444
MIN	17	10	7	27	62	.435	25	67	.627	7	4	17	39	.436	14	42	.667	3	3	10	23	.435	11	25	.560
MTL	11	6	5	15	39	.385	16	40	.600	4	3	10	26	.385	10	26	.615	2	2	5	13	.385	6	14	.571
NSH	11	6	5	14	34	.412	13	37	.649	2	3	6	16	.375	8	18	.556	4	2	8	18	.444	5	19	.737
N.J.	18	10	8	25	62	.403	23	66	.652	6	6	17	46	.370	17	48	.646	4	2	8	16	.500	6	18	.667
NYI	13	8	5	16	58	.276	13	58	.776	4	1	6	20	.300	3	20	.850	4	4	10	38	.263	10	38	.737
NYR	14	9	5	17	57	.298	12	57	.789	4	2	8	19	.421	5	19	.737	5	3	9	38	.237	7	38	.816
OTT	8	2	6	9	31	.290	11	29	.621	1	2	4	11	.364	4	10	.600	1	4	5	20	.250	7	19	.632
PHI	7	1	6	2	28	.071	10	28	.643	1	4	2	23	.087	7	23	.696	0	2	0	5	.000	3	5	.400
PHX	7	5	2	8	26	.308	6	29	.793	3	1	5	16	.313	3	17	.824	2	1	3	10	.300	3	12	.750
PIT	16	10	6	17	47	.362	12	44	.727	5	3	9	24	.375	5	21	.762	5	3	8	23	.348	7	23	.696
STL	12	6	6	14	36	.389	14	37	.622	2	1	4	8	.500	3	8	.625	4	5	10	28	.357	11	29	.621
S.J.	4	2	2	7	12	.583	7	13	.462	0	2	3	7	.429	5	7	.286	2	0	4	5	.800	2	6	.667
T.B.	12	10	2	16	53	.302	6	53	.887	4	0	7	16	.438	2	15	.867	6	2	9	37	.243	4	38	.895
TOR	11	4	7	14	44	.318	16	43	.628	1	3	4	13	.308	5	12	.583	3	4	10	31	.323	11	31	.645
VAN	9	5	4	15	37	.405	12	35	.657	4	2	10	27	.370	7	25	.720	1	2	5	10	.500	5	10	.500
WSH	12	1	11	5	40	.125	18	40	.550	1	6	4	27	.148	10	27	.630	0	5	1	13	.077	8	13	.385

Team Shootout Leaders

Wins

	W	L	Win%
T.B.	10	2	.833
BUF	10	4	.714
PIT	10	6	.625
MIN	10	7	.588
N.J.	10	8	.556
BOS	9	4	.692
DAL	9	4	.692
NYR	9	5	.643
NYI	8	5	.615
ATL	7	4	.636

Goals Scored

	G	S	S%
MIN	27	62	.435
N.J.	25	62	.403
L.A.	18	46	.391
DAL	18	51	.353
BOS	18	54	.333
PIT	17	47	.362
BUF	17	47	.362
CHI	17	47	.362
NYR	17	57	.298
T.B.	16	53	.302
NYI	16	58	.276

Fewest Goals Against

	GA	SA	Sv%
PHX	6	29	.793
T.B.	6	53	.887
S.J.	7	13	.462
CAR	8	17	.529
EDM	8	24	.667
BUF	9	46	.804
PHI	10	28	.643
ATL	10	30	.667
CGY	11	27	.593
OTT	11	29	.621
COL	11	33	.667
DAL	11	49	.776

Winning Percentage

	W	L	Win%
T.B.	10	2	.833
PHX	5	2	.714
BUF	10	4	.714
DAL	9	4	.692
BOS	9	4	.692
NYR	9	5	.643
ATL	7	4	.636
PIT	10	6	.625
NYI	8	5	.615
MIN	10	7	.588

Shootout Abbreviations

G........Goals Scored
GA......Goals Against
GDG ...Game Deciding Goal
S.........Shots Taken
SA ......Shots Against
S% ....Goal Scoring %
Sv%....Save %

Individual Shootout Leaders – Goaltenders

Goaltender Shootout Wins

	Team	W	L
Miller, Ryan	BUF	10	4
Brodeur, Martin	N.J.	10	6
Fleury, Marc-Andre	PIT	9	5
Thomas, Tim	BOS	8	2
Turco, Marty	DAL	8	4
Lundqvist, Henrik	NYR	8	4
Fernandez, Manny	MIN	7	1
Lehtonen, Kari	ATL	7	4
Holmqvist, Johan	T.B.	6	1
Legace, Manny	STL	5	3
Luongo, Roberto	VAN	5	3
DiPietro, Rick	NYI	5	4
4 Goaltenders with …		4	

Goaltender Shootout Shots Against

	Team	SA	GA	Sv%
Brodeur, Martin	N.J.	60	20	.667
Lundqvist, Henrik	NYR	50	9	.820
Thomas, Tim	BOS	46	8	.826
Miller, Ryan	BUF	46	9	.804
Turco, Marty	DAL	46	11	.761
DiPietro, Rick	NYI	44	9	.795
Fleury, Marc-Andre	PIT	39	9	.769
Giguere, J-S	ANA	39	13	.667

Goaltender Shootout Save Percentage

(min. 10 shots faced)	Team	Sv%	SA	GA
Denis, Marc	T.B.	.900	20	2
Holmqvist, Johan	T.B.	.879	33	4
Joseph, Curtis	PHX	.846	13	2
Thomas, Tim	BOS	.826	46	8
Lundqvist, Henrik	NYR	.820	50	9
Miller, Ryan	BUF	.804	46	9
DiPietro, Rick	NYI	.795	44	9
Fleury, Marc-Andre	PIT	.769	39	9
Turco, Marty	DAL	.761	46	11
Tellqvist, Mikael	PHX	.750	16	4

Atlanta's Slava Kozlov beats the Devils' Martin Brodeur in a shootout. Kozlov led the NHL with five shootout game-deciding goals.

Individual Shootout Leaders – Skaters

Shootout Goals Scored

	Team	G	S	S%
Christensen, Erik	PIT	8	14	.571
Koivu, Mikko	MIN	8	15	.533
Kozlov, Vyacheslav	ATL	7	11	.636
Kariya, Paul	NSH	7	11	.636
Gionta, Brian	N.J.	7	13	.539
Parise, Zach	N.J.	7	14	.500
7 players with		6		

Shootout Shots Taken

	Team	S	G	S%
Koivu, Mikko	MIN	15	8	.533
Crosby, Sidney	PIT	15	5	.333
Christensen, Erik	PIT	14	8	.571
Parise, Zach	N.J.	14	7	.500
Demitra, Pavol	MIN	14	6	.429
Briere, Daniel	BUF	14	6	.429
4 Players with		13		

Shootout Scoring Percentage

(min. 5 shots taken)	Team	S%	S	G
Nummelin, Petteri	MIN	.857	7	6
Kotalik, Ales	BUF	.714	7	5
Morrison, Brendan	VAN	.667	9	6
Madden, John	N.J.	.667	6	4
Nagy, Ladislav	PHX-DAL	.667	6	4
Kozlov, Vyacheslav	ATL	.636	11	7
Kariya, Paul	NSH	.636	11	7
Langenbrunner, Jamie	N.J.	.600	5	3

Shootout Game-Deciding Goals

	Team	GDG	S	G
Kozlov, Vyacheslav	ATL	5	11	7
Koivu, Mikko	MIN	4	15	8
Kotalik, Ales	BUF	4	7	5
Crosby, Sidney	PIT	4	15	5
Nagy, Ladislav	PHX-DAL	4	6	4
Kessel, Phil	BOS	4	7	4
Christensen, Erik	PIT	3	14	8
Briere, Daniel	BUF	3	14	6
Madden, John	N.J.	3	6	4
Stempniak, Lee	STL	3	8	4
St. Louis, Martin	T.B.	3	10	4
Hossa, Marcel	NYR	3	4	3

Shootout Register, 2006-07

Skaters

Player	Team	S	G	S%	GDG
Adams, Kevyn	PHX	1	0	.000	0
Afanasenkov, Dimitri	T.B.	2	1	.500	1
Afinogenov, Maxim	BUF	6	2	.333	1
Alexeev, Nikita	CHI	1	1	1.000	1
Alfredsson, Daniel	OTT	2	0	.000	0
Amonte, Anthony	CGY	2	0	.000	0
Antropov, Nikolai	TOR	2	0	.000	0
Arkhipov, Denis	CHI	2	0	.000	0
Armstrong, Derek	L.A.	1	0	.000	0
Avery, Sean	L.A.	1	0	.000	0
Axelsson, P-J	BOS	2	0	.000	0
Barnes, Stu	DAL	2	1	.500	1
Bates, Shawn	NYI	1	0	.000	0
Beech, Kris	WSH	1	0	.000	0
Belanger, Eric	ATL	1	0	.000	0
Bergeron, Patrice	BOS	11	6	.546	1
Bertuzzi, Todd	FLA-DET	4	0	.000	0
Betts, Blair	NYR	1	0	.000	0
Bieksa, Kevin	VAN	1	0	.000	0
Blake, Jason	NYI	6	1	.167	1
Bochenski, Brandon	CHI-BOS	4	0	.000	0
Bouchard, Pierre-Marc	MIN	6	1	.167	1
Bourque, Rene	CHI	1	0	.000	0
Bouwmeester, Jay	FLA	1	0	.000	0
Boyd, Dustin	CGY	1	0	.000	0
Boyes, Brad	BOS-STL	6	0	.000	0
Boyle, Dan	T.B.	1	0	.000	0
Bradley, Matt	WSH	1	0	.000	0
Brashear, Donald	WSH	1	0	.000	0
Briere, Daniel	BUF	14	6	.429	3
Brind'Amour, Rod	CAR	2	1	.500	0
Brown, Dustin	L.A.	8	4	.500	1
Brule, Gilbert	CBJ	1	0	.000	0
Brunette, Andrew	COL	1	0	.000	0
Brylin, Sergei	N.J.	8	1	.125	0
Bulis, Jan	VAN	1	0	.000	0
Calder, Kyle	PHI	1	0	.000	0
Cammalleri, Mike	L.A.	6	2	.333	0
Carcillo, Daniel	PHX	1	0	.000	0
Carter, Anson	CBJ	1	1	1.000	0
Carter, Jeff	PHI	2	0	.000	0
Chara, Zdeno	BOS	2	1	.500	1
Cheechoo, Jonathan	S.J.	3	2	.667	1
Chimera, Jason	CBJ	4	1	.250	1
Christensen, Erik	PIT	14	8	.571	3
Clark, Chris	WSH	1	0	.000	0
Clarke, Noah	L.A.	1	0	.000	0
Cleary, Daniel	DET	4	2	.500	0
Clowe, Ryane	S.J.	4	2	.500	1
Clymer, Ben	WSH	1	0	.000	0
Cole, Erik	CAR	2	0	.000	0
Comrie, Mike	PHX-OTT	7	3	.429	1
Craig, Ryan	T.B.	1	0	.000	0
Crosby, Sidney	PIT	15	5	.333	4
Cullen, Matt	NYR	8	3	.375	2
Datsyuk, Pavel	DET	10	5	.500	0
Dawes, Nigel	NYR	1	0	.000	0
Demitra, Pavol	MIN	14	6	.429	2
Doan, Shane	PHX	3	2	.667	1
Drury, Chris	BUF	1	0	.000	0
Dumont, Jean-Pierre	NSH	3	1	.333	1
Dupuis, Pascal	MIN	1	0	.000	0
Ekman, Nisse	PIT	1	0	.000	0
Elias, Patrik	N.J.	11	2	.182	1
Erat, Martin	NSH	7	1	.143	1
Eriksson, Anders	CBJ	1	0	.000	0
Eriksson, Loui	DAL	2	0	.000	0
Fedorov, Sergei	CBJ	3	2	.667	1
Fedotenko, Ruslan	T.B.	2	0	.000	0
Fehr, Eric	WSH	1	0	.000	0
Filppula, Valtteri	DET	2	0	.000	0
Fischer, Patrick	PHX	1	0	.000	0
Fisher, Mike	OTT	4	1	.250	0
Fleischmann, Tomas	WSH	1	0	.000	0
Forsberg, Peter	PHI-NSH	6	1	.167	1
Franzen, Johan	DET	2	1	.500	1
Friesen, Jeff	CGY	1	0	.000	0
Frolov, Alexander	L.A.	9	4	.444	1
Gaborik, Marian	MIN	2	0	.000	0
Gagne, Simon	PHI	6	1	.167	0
Gelinas, Martin	FLA	1	0	.000	0
Getzlaf, Ryan	ANA	12	5	.417	2
Gionta, Brian	N.J.	13	7	.539	2
Gomez, Scott	N.J.	1	0	.000	0
Gonchar, Sergei	PIT	2	0	.000	0
Green, Josh	VAN	3	1	.333	1
Green, Mike	WSH	1	0	.000	0
Guerin, Bill	STL	2	1	.500	1
Hagman, Niklas	DAL	1	0	.000	0
Hainsey, Ron	CBJ	1	0	.000	0
Hall, Adam	NYR	2	0	.000	0
Hamilton, Jeff	CHI	10	5	.500	0
Havlat, Martin	CHI	6	2	.333	1
Heatley, Dany	OTT	4	1	.250	0
Hecht, Jochen	BUF	1	0	.000	0
Hejduk, Milan	COL	7	2	.286	2
Hemsky, Ales	EDM	6	1	.167	0
Higgins, Christopher	MTL	4	1	.250	0
Hilbert, Andy	NYI	3	1	.333	1
Hollweg, Ryan	NYR	1	0	.000	0
Holmqvist, Michael	CHI	3	0	.000	0
Holmstrom, Tomas	DET	2	0	.000	0
Horton, Nathan	FLA	7	2	.286	1
Hossa, Marcel	NYR	4	3	.750	3
Hossa, Marian	ATL	10	5	.500	1
Hudler, Jiri	DET	3	0	.000	0
Hunter, Trent	NYI	5	0	.000	0
Huselius, Kristian	CGY	5	1	.200	0
Iginla, Jarome	CGY	4	3	.750	1
Jagr, Jaromir	NYR	9	3	.333	1
Jokinen, Jussi	DAL	12	5	.417	2
Jokinen, Olli	FLA	6	1	.167	0
Kaberle, Tomas	TOR	3	1	.333	0
Kapanen, Niko	PHX	1	0	.000	0
Kapanen, Sami	PHI	1	0	.000	0
Kariya, Paul	NSH	11	7	.636	1
Kastsitsyn, Andrei	MTL	2	1	.500	1
Kesler, Ryan	VAN	3	2	.667	1
Kessel, Phil	BOS	7	4	.571	4
Knuble, Mike	PHI	1	0	.000	0
Kobasew, Chuck	CGY	1	0	.000	0
Koivu, Mikko	MIN	15	8	.533	4
Koivu, Saku	MTL	9	5	.556	2
Kolnik, Juraj	FLA	1	0	.000	0
Konopka, Zenon	CBJ	1	0	.000	0
Kopitar, Anze	L.A.	9	5	.556	2
Kostopoulos, Tom	L.A.	1	0	.000	0
Kotalik, Ales	BUF	7	5	.714	4
Kovalchuk, Ilya	ATL	4	1	.250	0
Kovalev, Alex	MTL	9	4	.444	1
Kozlov, Viktor	NYI	13	5	.385	2
Kozlov, Vyacheslav	ATL	11	7	.636	5
Kuba, Filip	T.B.	2	0	.000	0
Kunitz, Chris	ANA	6	2	.333	0
Kwiatkowski, Joel	FLA	1	0	.000	0
Laich, Brooks	WSH	2	0	.000	0
Lang, Robert	DET	2	0	.000	0
Langenbrunner, Jamie	N.J.	5	3	.600	1
Langkow, Daymond	CGY	1	0	.000	0
Latendresse, Guillaume	MTL	1	0	.000	0
Lecavalier, Vincent	T.B.	12	3	.250	2
Lehtinen, Jere	DAL	3	1	.333	1
Linden, Trevor	VAN	3	2	.667	1
Lindros, Eric	DAL	1	1	1.000	0
Lombardi, Matthew	CGY	2	0	.000	0
Lundmark, Jamie	L.A.	3	2	.667	0
Lupul, Joffrey	EDM	2	0	.000	0
MacArthur, Clarke	BUF	1	0	.000	0
Madden, John	N.J.	6	4	.667	3
Malhotra, Manny	CBJ	2	1	.500	1
Malkin, Evgeni	PIT	12	3	.250	2
Marleau, Patrick	S.J.	1	0	.000	0
McAmmond, Dean	OTT	5	2	.400	1
McDonald, Andy	ANA	10	1	.100	0
McLean, Brett	COL	3	2	.667	1
Metropolit, Glen	STL	1	0	.000	0
Meyer IV, Freddie	PHI	1	0	.000	0
Miettinen, Antti	DAL	3	0	.000	0
Modano, Mike	DAL	3	0	.000	0
Modin, Fredrik	CBJ	3	0	.000	0
Montador, Steve	FLA	2	1	.500	0
Morrison, Brendan	VAN	9	6	.667	0
Murray, Glen	BOS	4	0	.000	0
Nagy, Ladislav	PHX-DAL	6	4	.667	4
Nash, Rick	CBJ	5	1	.200	0
Naslund, Markus	VAN	7	2	.286	1
Nedved, Petr	PHI	2	0	.000	0
Niedermayer, Rob	ANA	2	0	.000	0
Nielsen, Frans	NYI	1	1	1.000	0
Nieuwendyk, Joe	FLA	2	0	.000	0
Nolan, Owen	PHX	1	0	.000	0
Novotny, Jiri	WSH	1	0	.000	0
Nummelin, Petteri	MIN	7	6	.857	1
Nylander, Michael	NYR	13	5	.385	1
O'Neill, Jeff	TOR	2	1	.500	1
O'Sullivan, Patrick	L.A.	2	0	.000	0
Olesz, Rostislav	FLA	3	0	.000	0
Ouellet, Michel	PIT	1	0	.000	0
Ovechkin, Alex	WSH	12	2	.167	0
Pahlsson, Samuel	ANA	1	0	.000	0
Parise, Zach	N.J.	14	7	.500	2
Parrish, Mark	MIN	2	0	.000	0
Pavelski, Joe	S.J.	3	3	1.000	0
Peltonen, Ville	FLA	7	3	.429	0
Perezhogin, Alexander	MTL	2	0	.000	0
Perreault, Yanic	PHX-TOR	6	2	.333	0
Perrin, Eric	T.B.	4	0	.000	0
Perry, Corey	ANA	6	1	.167	1
Pettinger, Matt	WSH	4	1	.250	0
Phaneuf, Dion	CGY	2	0	.000	0
Picard, Alexandre	CBJ	1	0	.000	0
Pisani, Fernando	EDM	3	1	.333	0
Pitkanen, Joni	PHI	1	0	.000	0
Platt, Geoff	CBJ	1	0	.000	0
Plekanec, Tomas	MTL	3	1	.333	0
Pohl, John	TOR	2	1	.500	1
Pominville, Jason	BUF	2	0	.000	0
Ponikarovsky, Alexei	TOR	7	0	.000	0
Pothier, Brian	WSH	1	0	.000	0
Poti, Tom	NYI	2	0	.000	0
Pronger, Chris	ANA	1	0	.000	0
Prospal, Vaclav	T.B.	5	2	.400	1
Prucha, Petr	NYR	6	0	.000	0
Pyatt, Taylor	VAN	2	0	.000	0
Radulov, Alexander	NSH	6	3	.500	2
Reasoner, Marty	EDM	1	1	1.000	1
Reinprecht, Steven	PHX	2	0	.000	0
Ribeiro, Mike	DAL	9	4	.444	2
Richards, Brad	T.B.	12	5	.417	2
Richards, Mike	PHI	3	0	.000	0
Ritchie, Byron	CGY	3	2	.667	0
Roberts, Gary	FLA	1	0	.000	0
Robitaille, Randy	PHI-NYI	4	2	.500	1
Roenick, Jeremy	PHX	1	0	.000	0
Rolston, Brian	MIN	12	5	.417	1
Roy, Derek	BUF	1	0	.000	0
Rozsival, Michal	NYR	1	0	.000	0
Rucinsky, Martin	STL	6	2	.333	1
Ruutu, Jarkko	PIT	2	1	.500	1
Ruutu, Tuomo	CHI	4	2	.500	1
Ruzicka, Stefan	PHI	1	0	.000	0
Ryder, Michael	MTL	4	1	.250	1
Sakic, Joe	COL	8	4	.500	2
Salmelainen, Tony	CHI	1	0	.000	0
Samsonov, Sergei	MTL	3	1	.333	0
Samuelsson, Mikael	DET	2	0	.000	0
Sanderson, Geoff	PHI	1	0	.000	0
Satan, Miroslav	NYI	13	5	.385	2
Savard, Marc	BOS	6	1	.167	0
Sedin, Daniel	VAN	6	1	.167	1
Sedin, Henrik	VAN	1	0	.000	0
Sejna, Peter	STL	1	0	.000	0
Selanne, Teemu	ANA	12	4	.333	1
Semin, Alexander	WSH	10	2	.200	1
Shanahan, Brendan	NYR	8	3	.375	2
Shannon, Ryan	ANA	5	1	.200	0
Sharp, Patrick	CHI	3	2	.667	1
Sillinger, Mike	NYI	2	0	.000	0
Sim, Jonathan	ATL	2	1	.500	1
Smolinski, Bryan	CHI-VAN	4	2	.500	0
Smyth, Ryan	EDM-NYI	4	1	.250	1
Souray, Sheldon	MTL	1	1	1.000	1
Spezza, Jason	OTT	3	0	.000	0
St. Louis, Martin	T.B.	10	4	.400	3
St. Pierre, Martin	CHI	1	0	.000	0
Staal, Eric	CAR	3	0	.000	0
Stafford, Drew	BUF	3	2	.667	1
Stajan, Matthew	TOR	3	1	.333	0
Stastny, Paul	COL	3	0	.000	0
Steen, Alexander	TOR	2	1	.500	0
Stefan, Patrik	DAL	1	0	.000	0
Stempniak, Lee	STL	8	4	.500	3
Stoll, Jarret	EDM	1	0	.000	0
Straka, Martin	NYR	2	0	.000	0
Streit, Mark	MTL	1	0	.000	0
Stumpel, Jozef	FLA	4	2	.500	1
Sturm, Marco	BOS	11	4	.364	2
Sullivan, Steve	NSH	4	2	.500	1
Sundin, Mats	TOR	11	6	.546	1
Svatos, Marek	COL	5	1	.200	0
Svitov, Alexander	CBJ	1	0	.000	0
Sykora, Petr	EDM	5	1	.200	0
Taffe, Jeff	PHX	1	0	.000	0
Tambellini, Jeff	NYI	1	0	.000	0
Tanguay, Alex	CGY	7	3	.429	2
Tarnasky, Nick	T.B.	1	1	1.000	1
Tenkrat, Petr	BOS	3	2	.667	1
Thoresen, Patrick	EDM	1	0	.000	0
Thornton, Joe	S.J.	1	0	.000	0
Tkachuk, Keith	STL-ATL	6	2	.333	0
Torres, Raffi	EDM	1	1	1.000	1
Tucker, Darcy	TOR	6	1	.167	0
Umberger, R.J.	PHI	1	0	.000	0
Upshall, Scottie	PHI	1	0	.000	0
Vanek, Thomas	BUF	11	2	.182	1
Vasicek, Josef	NSH	1	0	.000	0
Vermette, Antoine	OTT	8	3	.375	1
Visnovsky, Lubomir	L.A.	3	1	.333	1
Vrbata, Radim	CHI	7	2	.286	2
Vyborny, David	CBJ	9	5	.556	1
Walker, Scott	CAR	1	0	.000	0
Walz, Wes	MIN	1	0	.000	0
Ward, Jason	NYR-T.B.	2	0	.000	0
Weight, Doug	STL	11	6	.546	1
Weiss, Stephen	FLA	1	0	.000	0
Wellwood, Kyle	TOR	4	1	.250	1
White, Todd	MIN	2	1	.500	1
Whitney, Ray	CAR	5	0	.000	0
Wideman, Dennis	STL	1	0	.000	0
Williams, Jason	DET-CHI	9	3	.333	0
Williams, Justin	CAR	4	0	.000	0
Willsie, Brian	L.A.	2	0	.000	0
Wolski, Wojtek	COL	6	3	.500	0
Yashin, Alexei	NYI	3	0	.000	0
York, Mike	NYI	3	1	.333	1
Zajac, Travis	N.J.	4	1	.250	1
Zednik, Richard	WSH	1	0	.000	0
Zetterberg, Henrik	DET	4	1	.250	1
Zherdev, Nikolai	CBJ	8	2	.250	1
Zidlicky, Marek	NSH	1	0	.000	0
Zigomanis, Mike	PHX	4	1	.250	0
Zubov, Sergei	DAL	12	5	.417	2
Zubrus, Dainius	WSH	1	0	.000	0

Goaltenders

Goaltender	Team	W	L	SA	GA	Sv %
Aebischer, David	MTL	2	2	18	6	.667
Anderson, Craig	FLA	1	0	2	0	1.000
Aubin, J-S	TOR	1	1	11	3	.727
Auld, Alex	FLA	0	3	8	6	.250
Bacashihua, Jason	STL	1	1	6	2	.667
Backstrom, Niklas	MIN	3	5	32	15	.531
Belfour, Ed	FLA	1	5	25	9	.640
Biron, Martin	PHI	0	1	3	2	.333
Boucher, Brian	CHI	0	2	4	4	.000
Brodeur, Martin	N.J.	10	6	60	20	.667
Brust, Barry	L.A.	1	1	5	1	.800
Bryzgalov, Ilya	ANA	0	4	13	6	.538
Budaj, Peter	COL	3	4	27	11	.593
Burke, Sean	L.A.	2	2	22	11	.500
Cassivi, Frederic	WSH	0	1	3	2	.333
Clemmensen, Scott	N.J.	0	2	6	3	.500
Conklin, Ty	CBJ	1	1	5	2	.600
Denis, Marc	T.B.	4	1	20	2	.900
DiPietro, Rick	NYI	5	4	44	9	.795
Dubielewicz, Wade	NYI	2	0	6	1	.833
Dunham, Mike	NYI	1	1	8	3	.625
Emery, Ray	OTT	1	4	19	8	.579
Esche, Robert	PHI	0	1	2	2	.000
Fernandez, Manny	MIN	7	1	32	9	.719
Fleury, Marc-Andre	PIT	9	5	39	9	.769
Garon, Mathieu	L.A.	1	3	18	7	.611
Gerber, Martin	OTT	1	2	10	3	.700
Giguere, J-S	ANA	4	6	39	13	.667
Grahame, John	CAR	0	1	3	2	.333
Halak, Jaroslav	MTL	2	0	8	2	.750
Harding, Josh	MIN	0	1	3	1	.667
Hasek, Dominik	DET	1	5	16	8	.500
Holmqvist, Johan	T.B.	6	1	33	4	.879
Huet, Cristobal	MTL	2	3	14	8	.429
Johnson, Brent	WSH	0	5	20	7	.650
Joseph, Curtis	PHX	2	1	13	2	.846
Khabibulin, Nikolai	CHI	4	4	33	11	.667
Kiprusoff, Miikka	CGY	3	4	16	7	.563
Kolzig, Olaf	WSH	1	5	17	9	.471
Lalime, Patrick	CHI	2	1	8	4	.500
Leclaire, Pascal	CBJ	1	1	15	4	.733
Legace, Manny	STL	5	3	25	7	.720
Lehtonen, Kari	ATL	7	4	30	10	.667
Lundqvist, Henrik	NYR	8	4	50	9	.820
Luongo, Roberto	VAN	5	3	31	10	.677
MacDonald, Joey	DET-BOS	0	2	10	5	.500
Markkanen, Jussi	EDM	0	1	3	2	.333
Mason, Chris	NSH	4	2	20	6	.700
McLennan, Jamie	CGY	0	1	11	4	.636
Miller, Ryan	BUF	10	4	46	9	.804
Nabokov, Yevgeni	S.J.	2	1	10	4	.600
Niittymaki, Antero	PHI	1	4	23	6	.739
Norrena, Fredrik	CBJ	3	3	22	8	.636
Osgood, Chris	DET	2	2	14	6	.571
Raycroft, Andrew	TOR	3	6	32	13	.594
Roloson, Dwayne	EDM	3	2	21	6	.714
Sabourin, Dany	VAN	0	1	4	2	.500
Sanford, Curtis	STL	0	2	6	5	.167
Smith, Mike	DAL	1	0	3	0	1.000
Tellqvist, Mikael	PHX	3	1	16	4	.750
Theodore, Jose	COL	2	0	6	0	1.000
Thibault, Jocelyn	PIT	1	1	5	3	.400
Thomas, Tim	BOS	8	2	46	8	.826
Toivonen, Hannu	BOS	1	1	8	3	.625
Toskala, Vesa	S.J.	0	1	3	3	.000
Turco, Marty	DAL	8	4	46	11	.761
Valiquette, Stephen	NYR	1	0	4	2	.500
Vokoun, Tomas	NSH	2	3	17	7	.588
Ward, Cam	CAR	0	4	14	6	.571
Weekes, Kevin	NYR	0	1	3	1	.667

NHL Record Book

All-Time Standings of NHL Teams

(ranked by percentage)

Active Clubs

Team	Games	Wins	Losses	Ties	OT Losses	SO Losses	Goals For	Goals Against	Points	Pts %	First Season
Montreal	5710	2933	1899	837	33	8	18773	15289	6744	.591	1917-18
Philadelphia	3096	1535	1062	457	30	12	10512	9119	3569	.576	1967-68
Buffalo	2870	1362	1068	409	22	9	9665	8733	3164	.551	1970-71
Boston	5550	2628	2075	791	44	12	17902	16444	6103	.550	1924-25
Edmonton	2158	1013	834	262	37	12	7838	7290	2337	.541	1979-80
Calgary	2714	1231	1064	379	28	12	9267	8737	2881	.531	1972-73
Detroit	5484	2467	2165	815	26	11	17095	16382	5786	.528	1926-27
Colorado	2158	984	876	261	27	10	7455	7200	2266	.525	1979-80
Minnesota	492	209	194	55	24	10	1215	1215	507	.515	2000-01
St. Louis	3096	1343	1275	432	32	14	9763	9862	3164	.511	1967-68
Toronto	5710	2499	2391	783	23	14	17708	17590	5818	.509	1917-18
NY Islanders	2714	1188	1147	347	24	8	9067	8695	2755	.508	1972-73
Nashville	656	283	276	60	29	8	1701	1793	663	.505	1998-99
Dallas	3096	1308	1297	459	27	5	9666	9929	3107	.502	1967-68
Ottawa	1118	483	482	115	26	12	3257	3297	1119	.500	1992-93
NY Rangers	5484	2317	2317	808	33	9	16976	17147	5484	.500	1926-27
Anaheim	1034	429	447	107	34	17	2732	2875	1016	.491	1993-94
Chicago	5484	2233	2393	814	31	13	16255	16679	5324	.485	1926-27
Washington	2558	1068	1144	303	26	17	8129	8603	2482	.485	1974-75
Florida	1034	394	437	142	47	14	2711	2956	991	.479	1993-94
Pittsburgh	3096	1268	1397	383	36	12	10459	11121	2967	.479	1967-68
New Jersey	2558	1029	1163	328	26	12	7857	8575	2424	.474	1974-75
Los Angeles	3096	1230	1397	424	38	7	10214	10920	2929	.473	1967-68
San Jose	1198	477	557	121	34	9	3334	3709	1118	.467	1991-92
Phoenix	2158	854	1004	266	29	5	6959	7694	2008	.465	1979-80
Carolina	2158	853	1006	263	29	7	6638	7386	2005	.465	1979-80
Vancouver	2870	1115	1325	391	31	8	9136	9984	2660	.463	1970-71
Tampa Bay	1118	415	553	112	32	6	2926	3515	980	.438	1992-93
Atlanta	574	204	286	45	30	9	1535	1937	492	.429	1999-2000
Columbus	492	172	258	33	21	8	1168	1517	406	.413	2000-01

Defunct Clubs

Team	Games	Wins	Losses	Ties	Goals For	Goals Against	Points	Pts %	First Season	Last Season
Ottawa Senators	542	258	221	63	1458	1333	579	.534	1917-18	1933-34
Montreal Maroons	622	271	260	91	1474	1405	633	.509	1924-25	1937-38
NY/Brooklyn Americans	784	255	402	127	1643	2182	637	.406	1925-26	1941-42
Hamilton Tigers	126	47	78	1	414	475	95	.377	1920-21	1924-25
Cleveland Barons	160	47	87	26	470	617	120	.375	1976-77	1977-78
Pittsburgh Pirates	212	67	122	23	376	519	157	.370	1925-26	1929-30
Calif./Oakland Seals	698	182	401	115	1826	2580	479	.343	1967-68	1975-76
St. Louis Eagles	48	11	31	6	86	144	28	.292	1934-35	1934-35
Quebec Bulldogs	24	4	20	0	91	177	8	.167	1919-20	1919-20
Montreal Wanderers	6	1	5	0	17	35	2	.167	1917-18	1917-18
Philadelphia Quakers	44	4	36	4	76	184	12	.136	1930-31	1930-31

Calgary totals include Atlanta Flames, 1972-73 to 1979-80.
Carolina totals include Hartford, 1979-80 to 1996-97.
Colorado totals include Quebec, 1979-80 to 1994-95.
Dallas totals include Minnesota North Stars, 1967-68 to 1992-93.
Detroit totals include Cougars, 1926-27 to 1929-30, and Falcons, 1930-31 to 1931-32.
New Jersey totals include Kansas City, 1974-75 to 1975-76, and Colorado Rockies, 1976-77 to 1981-82.
Phoenix totals include Winnipeg, 1979-80 to 1995-96.
Toronto totals include Arenas, 1917-18 to 1918-19, and St. Patricks, 1919-20 to 1925-26.

Year-By-Year Final Standings & Leading Scorers

*Stanley Cup winner

1917-18

First Half

Team	GP	W	L	T	GF	GA	PTS
Montreal	14	10	4	0	81	47	20
Toronto	14	8	6	0	71	75	16
Ottawa	14	5	9	0	67	79	10
**Mtl. Wanderers	6	1	5	0	17	35	2

**Montreal Arena burned down and Wanderers forced to withdraw from League. Montreal Canadiens and Toronto each counted a win for defaulted games with Wanderers.

Second Half

Team	GP	W	L	T	GF	GA	PTS
*Toronto	8	5	3	0	37	34	10
Ottawa	8	4	4	0	35	35	8
Montreal	8	3	5	0	34	37	6

Leading Scorers

Player	Club	GP	G	A	PTS	PIM
Joe Malone	Montreal	20	44	4	48	30
Cy Denneny	Ottawa	20	36	10	46	80
Reg Noble	Toronto	20	30	10	40	35
Newsy Lalonde	Montreal	14	23	7	30	51
Corb Denneny	Toronto	21	20	9	29	14
Harry Cameron	Toronto	21	17	10	27	28
Didier Pitre	Montreal	20	17	6	23	29
Eddie Gerard	Ottawa	20	13	7	20	26
Jack Darragh	Ottawa	18	14	5	19	26
Frank Nighbor	Ottawa	10	11	8	19	6
Harry Meeking	Toronto	21	10	9	19	28

1918-19

First Half

Team	GP	W	L	T	GF	GA	PTS
• Montreal	10	7	3	0	57	50	14
Ottawa	10	5	5	0	39	39	10
Toronto	10	3	7	0	42	49	6

Second Half

Team	GP	W	L	T	GF	GA	PTS
Ottawa	8	7	1	0	32	14	14
Montreal	8	3	5	0	31	28	6
Toronto	8	2	6	0	22	43	4

• NHL Champion. Stanley Cup not awarded due to influenza epidemic.

Leading Scorers

Player	Club	GP	G	A	PTS	PIM
Newsy Lalonde	Montreal	17	22	10	32	40
Odie Cleghorn	Montreal	17	22	6	28	22
Frank Nighbor	Ottawa	18	19	9	28	27
Cy Denneny	Ottawa	18	18	4	22	58
Didier Pitre	Montreal	17	14	5	19	12
Alf Skinner	Toronto	17	12	4	16	26
Harry Cameron	Tor., Ott.	14	11	3	14	35
Jack Darragh	Ottawa	14	11	3	14	33
Ken Randall	Toronto	15	8	6	14	27
Sprague Cleghorn	Ottawa	18	7	6	13	27

1919-20

First Half

Team	GP	W	L	T	GF	GA	PTS
Ottawa	12	9	3	0	59	23	18
Montreal	12	8	4	0	62	51	16
Toronto	12	5	7	0	52	62	10
Quebec	12	2	10	0	44	81	4

Second Half

Team	GP	W	L	T	GF	GA	PTS
*Ottawa	12	10	2	0	62	41	20
Toronto	12	7	5	0	67	44	14
Montreal	12	5	7	0	67	62	10
Quebec	12	2	10	0	47	96	4

Leading Scorers

Player	Club	GP	G	A	PTS	PIM
Joe Malone	Quebec	24	39	10	49	12
Newsy Lalonde	Montreal	23	37	9	46	34
Frank Nighbor	Ottawa	23	26	15	41	18
Corb Denneny	Toronto	24	24	12	36	20
Jack Darragh	Ottawa	23	22	14	36	22
Reg Noble	Toronto	24	24	9	33	52
Amos Arbour	Montreal	22	21	5	26	13
Cully Wilson	Toronto	23	20	6	26	86
Didier Pitre	Montreal	22	14	12	26	6
Punch Broadbent	Ottawa	21	19	6	25	40

1920-21

First Half

Team	GP	W	L	T	GF	GA	PTS
*Ottawa	10	8	2	0	49	23	16
Toronto	10	5	5	0	39	47	10
Montreal	10	4	6	0	37	51	8
Hamilton	10	3	7	0	34	38	6

Second Half

Team	GP	W	L	T	GF	GA	PTS
Toronto	14	10	4	0	66	53	20
Montreal	14	9	5	0	75	48	18
Ottawa	14	6	8	0	48	52	12
Hamilton	14	3	11	0	58	94	6

Leading Scorers

Player	Club	GP	G	A	PTS	PIM
Newsy Lalonde	Montreal	24	33	10	43	36
Babe Dye	Ham., Tor.	24	35	5	40	32
Cy Denneny	Ottawa	24	34	5	39	10
Joe Malone	Hamilton	20	28	9	37	6
Frank Nighbor	Ottawa	24	19	10	29	10
Reg Noble	Toronto	24	19	8	27	54
Harry Cameron	Toronto	24	18	9	27	35
Goldie Prodgers	Hamilton	24	18	9	27	8
Corb Denneny	Toronto	20	19	7	26	29
Jack Darragh	Ottawa	24	11	15	26	20

1921-22

Team	GP	W	L	T	GF	GA	PTS
Ottawa	24	14	8	2	106	84	30
*Toronto	24	13	10	1	98	97	27
Montreal	24	12	11	1	88	94	25
Hamilton	24	7	17	0	88	105	14

Leading Scorers

Player	Club	GP	G	A	PTS	PIM
Punch Broadbent	Ottawa	24	32	14	46	28
Cy Denneny	Ottawa	22	27	12	39	20
Babe Dye	Toronto	24	31	7	38	39
Harry Cameron	Toronto	24	18	17	35	22
Joe Malone	Hamilton	24	24	7	31	4
Corb Denneny	Toronto	24	19	9	28	28
Reg Noble	Toronto	24	17	11	28	19
Sprague Cleghorn	Montreal	24	17	9	26	80
Georges Boucher	Ottawa	23	13	12	25	12
Odie Cleghorn	Montreal	23	21	3	24	26

1922-23

Team	GP	W	L	T	GF	GA	PTS
*Ottawa	24	14	9	1	77	54	29
Montreal	24	13	9	2	73	61	28
Toronto	24	13	10	1	82	88	27
Hamilton	24	6	18	0	81	110	12

Leading Scorers

Player	Club	GP	G	A	PTS	PIM
Babe Dye	Toronto	22	26	11	37	19
Cy Denneny	Ottawa	24	23	11	34	28
Billy Boucher	Montreal	24	24	7	31	55
Jack Adams	Toronto	23	19	9	28	42
Mickey Roach	Hamilton	24	17	10	27	8
Odie Cleghorn	Montreal	24	19	6	25	18
Georges Boucher	Ottawa	24	14	9	23	58
Reg Noble	Toronto	24	12	11	23	47
Cully Wilson	Hamilton	23	16	5	21	46
Aurel Joliat	Montreal	24	12	9	21	37

1923-24

Team	GP	W	L	T	GF	GA	PTS
Ottawa	24	16	8	0	74	54	32
*Montreal	24	13	11	0	59	48	26
Toronto	24	10	14	0	59	85	20
Hamilton	24	9	15	0	63	68	18

Leading Scorers

Player	Club	GP	G	A	PTS	PIM
Cy Denneny	Ottawa	22	22	2	24	10
Georges Boucher	Ottawa	21	13	10	23	38
Billy Boucher	Montreal	23	16	6	22	48
Billy Burch	Hamilton	24	16	6	22	6
Aurel Joliat	Montreal	24	15	5	20	27
Babe Dye	Toronto	19	16	3	19	23
Jack Adams	Toronto	22	14	4	18	51
Reg Noble	Toronto	23	12	5	17	79
Howie Morenz	Montreal	24	13	3	16	20
King Clancy	Ottawa	24	8	8	16	26

1924-25

Team	GP	W	L	T	GF	GA	PTS
Hamilton	30	19	10	1	90	60	39
Toronto	30	19	11	0	90	84	38
• Montreal	30	17	11	2	93	56	36
Ottawa	30	17	12	1	83	66	35
Mtl. Maroons	30	9	19	2	45	65	20
Boston	30	6	24	0	49	119	12

• NHL Champion (Stanley Cup won by Victoria Cougars, WCHL)

Leading Scorers

Player	Club	GP	G	A	PTS	PIM
Babe Dye	Toronto	29	38	8	46	41
Cy Denneny	Ottawa	29	27	15	42	16
Aurel Joliat	Montreal	25	30	11	41	85
Howie Morenz	Montreal	30	28	11	39	46
Red Green	Hamilton	30	19	15	34	81
Jack Adams	Toronto	27	21	10	31	67
Billy Boucher	Montreal	30	17	13	30	92
Billy Burch	Hamilton	27	20	7	27	10
Jimmy Herberts	Boston	30	17	7	24	55
Hooley Smith	Ottawa	30	10	13	23	81

1925-26

Team	GP	W	L	T	GF	GA	PTS
Ottawa	36	24	8	4	77	42	52
*Mtl. Maroons	36	20	11	5	91	73	45
Pittsburgh	36	19	16	1	82	70	39
Boston	36	17	15	4	92	85	38
NY Americans	36	12	20	4	68	89	28
Toronto	36	12	21	3	92	114	27
Montreal	36	11	24	1	79	108	23

Leading Scorers

Player	Club	GP	G	A	PTS	PIM
Nels Stewart	Mtl. Maroons	36	34	8	42	119
Cy Denneny	Ottawa	36	24	12	36	18
Carson Cooper	Boston	36	28	3	31	10
Jimmy Herberts	Boston	36	26	5	31	47
Howie Morenz	Montreal	31	23	3	26	39
Jack Adams	Toronto	36	21	5	26	52
Aurel Joliat	Montreal	35	17	9	26	52
Billy Burch	NY Americans	36	22	3	25	33
Hooley Smith	Ottawa	28	16	9	25	53
Frank Nighbor	Ottawa	35	12	13	25	40

1926-27

Canadian Division

Team	GP	W	L	T	GF	GA	PTS
*Ottawa	44	30	10	4	86	69	64
Montreal	44	28	14	2	99	67	58
Mtl. Maroons	44	20	20	4	71	68	44
NY Americans	44	17	25	2	82	91	36
Toronto	44	15	24	5	79	94	35

American Division

Team	GP	W	L	T	GF	GA	PTS
NY Rangers	44	25	13	6	95	72	56
Boston	44	21	20	3	97	89	45
Chicago	44	19	22	3	115	116	41
Pittsburgh	44	15	26	3	79	108	33
Detroit	44	12	28	4	76	105	28

Leading Scorers

Player	Club	GP	G	A	PTS	PIM
Bill Cook	NY Rangers	44	33	4	37	58
Dick Irvin	Chicago	43	18	18	36	34
Howie Morenz	Montreal	44	25	7	32	49
Frank Fredrickson	Det., Bos.	41	18	13	31	46
Babe Dye	Chicago	41	25	5	30	14
Ace Bailey	Toronto	42	15	13	28	82
Frank Boucher	NY Rangers	44	13	15	28	17
Billy Burch	NY Americans	43	19	8	27	40
Harry Oliver	Boston	42	18	6	24	17
Duke Keats	Bos., Det.	42	16	8	24	52

1927-28

Canadian Division

Team	GP	W	L	T	GF	GA	PTS
Montreal	44	26	11	7	116	48	59
Mtl. Maroons	44	24	14	6	96	77	54
Ottawa	44	20	14	10	78	57	50
Toronto	44	18	18	8	89	88	44
NY Americans	44	11	27	6	63	128	28

American Division

Team	GP	W	L	T	GF	GA	PTS
Boston	44	20	13	11	77	70	51
*NY Rangers	44	19	16	9	94	79	47
Pittsburgh	44	19	17	8	67	76	46
Detroit	44	19	19	6	88	79	44
Chicago	44	7	34	3	68	134	17

Leading Scorers

Player	Club	GP	G	A	PTS	PIM
Howie Morenz	Montreal	43	33	18	51	66
Aurel Joliat	Montreal	44	28	11	39	105
Frank Boucher	NY Rangers	44	23	12	35	15
George Hay	Detroit	42	22	13	35	20
Nels Stewart	Mtl. Maroons	41	27	7	34	104
Art Gagne	Montreal	44	20	10	30	75
Bun Cook	NY Rangers	44	14	14	28	45
Bill Carson	Toronto	32	20	6	26	36
Frank Finnigan	Ottawa	38	20	5	25	34
Bill Cook	NY Rangers	43	18	6	24	42
Duke Keats	Det., Chi.	38	14	10	24	60

1928-29

Canadian Division

Team	GP	W	L	T	GF	GA	PTS
Montreal	44	22	7	15	71	43	59
NY Americans	44	19	13	12	53	53	50
Toronto	44	21	18	5	85	69	47
Ottawa	44	14	17	13	54	67	41
Mtl. Maroons	44	15	20	9	67	65	39

American Division

Team	GP	W	L	T	GF	GA	PTS
*Boston	44	26	13	5	89	52	57
NY Rangers	44	21	13	10	72	65	52
Detroit	44	19	16	9	72	63	47
Pittsburgh	44	9	27	8	46	80	26
Chicago	44	7	29	8	33	85	22

Leading Scorers

Player	Club	GP	G	A	PTS	PIM
Ace Bailey	Toronto	44	22	10	32	78
Nels Stewart	Mtl. Maroons	44	21	8	29	74
Carson Cooper	Detroit	43	18	9	27	14
Howie Morenz	Montreal	42	17	10	27	47
Andy Blair	Toronto	44	12	15	27	41
Frank Boucher	NY Rangers	44	10	16	26	8
Harry Oliver	Boston	43	17	6	23	24
Bill Cook	NY Rangers	43	15	8	23	41
Jimmy Ward	Mtl. Maroons	43	14	8	22	46

Seven players tied with 19 points

1929-30

Canadian Division

Team	GP	W	L	T	GF	GA	PTS
Mtl. Maroons	44	23	16	5	141	114	51
*Montreal	44	21	14	9	142	114	51
Ottawa	44	21	15	8	138	118	50
Toronto	44	17	21	6	116	124	40
NY Americans	44	14	25	5	113	161	33

American Division

Team	GP	W	L	T	GF	GA	PTS
Boston	44	38	5	1	179	98	77
Chicago	44	21	18	5	117	111	47
NY Rangers	44	17	17	10	136	143	44
Detroit	44	14	24	6	117	133	34
Pittsburgh	44	5	36	3	102	185	13

Leading Scorers

Player	Club	GP	G	A	PTS	PIM
Cooney Weiland	Boston	44	43	30	73	27
Frank Boucher	NY Rangers	42	26	36	62	16
Dit Clapper	Boston	44	41	20	61	48
Bill Cook	NY Rangers	44	29	30	59	56
Hec Kilrea	Ottawa	44	36	22	58	72
Nels Stewart	Mtl. Maroons	44	39	16	55	81
Howie Morenz	Montreal	44	40	10	50	72
Normie Himes	NY Americans	44	28	22	50	15
Joe Lamb	Ottawa	44	29	20	49	119
Dutch Gainor	Boston	42	18	31	49	39

1930-31

Canadian Division

Team	GP	W	L	T	GF	GA	PTS
*Montreal	44	26	10	8	129	89	60
Toronto	44	22	13	9	118	99	53
Mtl. Maroons	44	20	18	6	105	106	46
NY Americans	44	18	16	10	76	74	46
Ottawa	44	10	30	4	91	142	24

American Division

Team	GP	W	L	T	GF	GA	PTS
Boston	44	28	10	6	143	90	62
Chicago	44	24	17	3	108	78	51
NY Rangers	44	19	16	9	106	87	47
Detroit	44	16	21	7	102	105	39
Philadelphia	44	4	36	4	76	184	12

Leading Scorers

Player	Club	GP	G	A	PTS	PIM
Howie Morenz	Montreal	39	28	23	51	49
Ebbie Goodfellow	Detroit	44	25	23	48	32
Charlie Conacher	Toronto	37	31	12	43	78
Bill Cook	NY Rangers	43	30	12	42	39
Ace Bailey	Toronto	40	23	19	42	46
Joe Primeau	Toronto	38	9	32	41	18
Nels Stewart	Mtl. Maroons	42	25	14	39	75
Frank Boucher	NY Rangers	44	12	27	39	20
Cooney Weiland	Boston	44	25	13	38	14
Bun Cook	NY Rangers	44	18	17	35	72
Aurel Joliat	Montreal	43	13	22	35	73

1931-32

Canadian Division

Team	GP	W	L	T	GF	GA	PTS
Montreal	48	25	16	7	128	111	57
*Toronto	48	23	18	7	155	127	53
Mtl. Maroons	48	19	22	7	142	139	45
NY Americans	48	16	24	8	95	142	40

American Division

Team	GP	W	L	T	GF	GA	PTS
NY Rangers	48	23	17	8	134	112	54
Chicago	48	18	19	11	86	101	47
Detroit	48	18	20	10	95	108	46
Boston	48	15	21	12	122	117	42

Leading Scorers

Player	Club	GP	G	A	PTS	PIM
Busher Jackson	Toronto	48	28	25	53	63
Joe Primeau	Toronto	46	13	37	50	25
Howie Morenz	Montreal	48	24	25	49	46
Charlie Conacher	Toronto	44	34	14	48	66
Bill Cook	NY Rangers	48	34	14	48	33
Dave Trottier	Mtl. Maroons	48	26	18	44	94
Hooley Smith	Mtl. Maroons	43	11	33	44	49
Babe Siebert	Mtl. Maroons	48	21	18	39	64
Dit Clapper	Boston	48	17	22	39	21
Aurel Joliat	Montreal	48	15	24	39	46

1932-33

Canadian Division

Team	GP	W	L	T	GF	GA	PTS
Toronto	48	24	18	6	119	111	54
Mtl. Maroons	48	22	20	6	135	119	50
Montreal	48	18	25	5	92	115	41
NY Americans	48	15	22	11	91	118	41
Ottawa	48	11	27	10	88	131	32

American Division

Team	GP	W	L	T	GF	GA	PTS
Boston	48	25	15	8	124	88	58
Detroit	48	25	15	8	111	93	58
*NY Rangers	48	23	17	8	135	107	54
Chicago	48	16	20	12	88	101	44

Leading Scorers

Player	Club	GP	G	A	PTS	PIM
Bill Cook	NY Rangers	48	28	22	50	51
Busher Jackson	Toronto	48	27	17	44	43
Baldy Northcott	Mtl. Maroons	48	22	21	43	30
Hooley Smith	Mtl. Maroons	48	20	21	41	66
Paul Haynes	Mtl. Maroons	48	16	25	41	18
Aurel Joliat	Montreal	48	18	21	39	53
Marty Barry	Boston	48	24	13	37	40
Bun Cook	NY Rangers	48	22	15	37	35
Nels Stewart	Boston	47	18	18	36	62
Howie Morenz	Montreal	46	14	21	35	32
Johnny Gagnon	Montreal	48	12	23	35	64
Eddie Shore	Boston	48	8	27	35	102
Frank Boucher	NY Rangers	46	7	28	35	4

1933-34

Canadian Division

Team	GP	W	L	T	GF	GA	PTS
Toronto	48	26	13	9	174	119	61
Montreal	48	22	20	6	99	101	50
Mtl. Maroons	48	19	18	11	117	122	49
NY Americans	48	15	23	10	104	132	40
Ottawa	48	13	29	6	115	143	32

American Division

Team	GP	W	L	T	GF	GA	PTS
Detroit	48	24	14	10	113	98	58
*Chicago	48	20	17	11	88	83	51
NY Rangers	48	21	19	8	120	113	50
Boston	48	18	25	5	111	130	41

Leading Scorers

Player	Club	GP	G	A	PTS	PIM
Charlie Conacher	Toronto	42	32	20	52	38
Joe Primeau	Toronto	45	14	32	46	8
Frank Boucher	NY Rangers	48	14	30	44	4
Marty Barry	Boston	48	27	12	39	12
Cecil Dillon	NY Rangers	48	13	26	39	10
Nels Stewart	Boston	48	21	17	38	68
Busher Jackson	Toronto	38	20	18	38	38
Aurel Joliat	Montreal	48	22	15	37	27
Reg Smith	Mtl. Maroons	47	18	19	37	58
Paul Thompson	Chicago	48	20	16	36	17

1934-35

Canadian Division

Team	GP	W	L	T	GF	GA	PTS
Toronto	48	30	14	4	157	111	64
*Mtl. Maroons	48	24	19	5	123	92	53
Montreal	48	19	23	6	110	145	44
NY Americans	48	12	27	9	100	142	33
St. Louis	48	11	31	6	86	144	28

American Division

Team	GP	W	L	T	GF	GA	PTS
Boston	48	26	16	6	129	112	58
Chicago	48	26	17	5	118	88	57
NY Rangers	48	22	20	6	137	139	50
Detroit	48	19	22	7	127	114	45

Leading Scorers

Player	Club	GP	G	A	PTS	PIM
Charlie Conacher	Toronto	47	36	21	57	24
Syd Howe	St.L., Det.	50	22	25	47	34
Larry Aurie	Detroit	48	17	29	46	24
Frank Boucher	NY Rangers	48	13	32	45	2
Busher Jackson	Toronto	42	22	22	44	27
Herbie Lewis	Detroit	47	16	27	43	26
Art Chapman	NY Americans	47	9	34	43	4
Marty Barry	Boston	48	20	20	40	33
Sweeney Schriner	NY Americans	48	18	22	40	6
Nels Stewart	Boston	47	21	18	39	45
Paul Thompson	Chicago	48	16	23	39	20

1935-36

Canadian Division

Team	GP	W	L	T	GF	GA	PTS
Mtl. Maroons	48	22	16	10	114	106	54
Toronto	48	23	19	6	126	106	52
NY Americans	48	16	25	7	109	122	39
Montreal	48	11	26	11	82	123	33

American Division

Team	GP	W	L	T	GF	GA	PTS
*Detroit	48	24	16	8	124	103	56
Boston	48	22	20	6	92	83	50
Chicago	48	21	19	8	93	92	50
NY Rangers	48	19	17	12	91	96	50

Leading Scorers

Player	Club	GP	G	A	PTS	PIM
Sweeney Schriner	NY Americans	48	19	26	45	8
Marty Barry	Detroit	48	21	19	40	16
Paul Thompson	Chicago	45	17	23	40	19
Bill Thoms	Toronto	48	23	15	38	29
Charlie Conacher	Toronto	44	23	15	38	74
Hooley Smith	Mtl. Maroons	47	19	19	38	75
Doc Romnes	Chicago	48	13	25	38	6
Art Chapman	NY Americans	47	10	28	38	14
Herbie Lewis	Detroit	45	14	23	37	25
Baldy Northcott	Mtl. Maroons	48	15	21	36	41

1936-37

Canadian Division

Team	GP	W	L	T	GF	GA	PTS
Montreal	48	24	18	6	115	111	54
Mtl. Maroons	48	22	17	9	126	110	53
Toronto	48	22	21	5	119	115	49
NY Americans	48	15	29	4	122	161	34

American Division

Team	GP	W	L	T	GF	GA	PTS
*Detroit	48	25	14	9	128	102	59
Boston	48	23	18	7	120	110	53
NY Rangers	48	19	20	9	117	106	47
Chicago	48	14	27	7	99	131	35

Leading Scorers

Player	Club	GP	G	A	PTS	PIM
Sweeney Schriner	NY Americans	48	21	25	46	17
Syl Apps	Toronto	48	16	29	45	10
Marty Barry	Detroit	48	17	27	44	6
Larry Aurie	Detroit	45	23	20	43	20
Busher Jackson	Toronto	46	21	19	40	12
Johnny Gagnon	Montreal	48	20	16	36	38
Bob Gracie	Mtl. Maroons	47	11	25	36	18
Nels Stewart	Bos., NYA	43	23	12	35	37
Paul Thompson	Chicago	47	17	18	35	28
Bill Cowley	Boston	46	13	22	35	4

1937-38

Canadian Division

Team	GP	W	L	T	GF	GA	PTS
Toronto	48	24	15	9	151	127	57
NY Americans	48	19	18	11	110	111	49
Montreal	48	18	17	13	123	128	49
Mtl. Maroons	48	12	30	6	101	149	30

American Division

Team	GP	W	L	T	GF	GA	PTS
Boston	48	30	11	7	142	89	67
NY Rangers	48	27	15	6	149	96	60
*Chicago	48	14	25	9	97	139	37
Detroit	48	12	25	11	99	133	35

Leading Scorers

Player	Club	GP	G	A	PTS	PIM
Gordie Drillon	Toronto	48	26	26	52	4
Syl Apps	Toronto	47	21	29	50	9
Paul Thompson	Chicago	48	22	22	44	14
Georges Mantha	Montreal	47	23	19	42	12
Cecil Dillon	NY Rangers	48	21	18	39	6
Bill Cowley	Boston	48	17	22	39	8
Sweeney Schriner	NY Americans	49	21	17	38	22
Bill Thoms	Toronto	48	14	24	38	14
Clint Smith	NY Rangers	48	14	23	37	0
Nels Stewart	NY Americans	48	19	17	36	29
Neil Colville	NY Rangers	45	17	19	36	11

1938-39

Team	GP	W	L	T	GF	GA	PTS
*Boston	48	36	10	2	156	76	74
NY Rangers	48	26	16	6	149	105	58
Toronto	48	19	20	9	114	107	47
NY Americans	48	17	21	10	119	157	44
Detroit	48	18	24	6	107	128	42
Montreal	48	15	24	9	115	146	39
Chicago	48	12	28	8	91	132	32

Leading Scorers

Player	Club	GP	G	A	PTS	PIM
Toe Blake	Montreal	48	24	23	47	10
Sweeney Schriner	NY Americans	48	13	31	44	20
Bill Cowley	Boston	34	8	34	42	2
Clint Smith	NY Rangers	48	21	20	41	2
Marty Barry	Detroit	48	13	28	41	4
Syl Apps	Toronto	44	15	25	40	4
Tom Anderson	NY Americans	48	13	27	40	14
Johnny Gottselig	Chicago	48	16	23	39	15
Paul Haynes	Montreal	47	5	33	38	27
Roy Conacher	Boston	47	26	11	37	12
Lorne Carr	NY Americans	46	19	18	37	16
Neil Colville	NY Rangers	48	18	19	37	12
Phil Watson	NY Rangers	48	15	22	37	42

1939-40

Team	GP	W	L	T	GF	GA	PTS
Boston	48	31	12	5	170	98	67
*NY Rangers	48	27	11	10	136	77	64
Toronto	48	25	17	6	134	110	56
Chicago	48	23	19	6	112	120	52
Detroit	48	16	26	6	91	126	38
NY Americans	48	15	29	4	106	140	34
Montreal	48	10	33	5	90	168	25

Leading Scorers

Player	Club	GP	G	A	PTS	PIM
Milt Schmidt	Boston	48	22	30	52	37
Woody Dumart	Boston	48	22	21	43	16
Bobby Bauer	Boston	48	17	26	43	2
Gordie Drillon	Toronto	43	21	19	40	13
Bill Cowley	Boston	48	13	27	40	24
Bryan Hextall	NY Rangers	48	24	15	39	52
Neil Colville	NY Rangers	48	19	19	38	22
Syd Howe	Detroit	46	14	23	37	17
Toe Blake	Montreal	48	17	19	36	48
Murray Armstrong	NY Americans	48	16	20	36	12

1940-41

Team	GP	W	L	T	GF	GA	PTS
*Boston	48	27	8	13	168	102	67
Toronto	48	28	14	6	145	99	62
Detroit	48	21	16	11	112	102	53
NY Rangers	48	21	19	8	143	125	50
Chicago	48	16	25	7	112	139	39
Montreal	48	16	26	6	121	147	38
NY Americans	48	8	29	11	99	186	27

Leading Scorers

Player	Club	GP	G	A	PTS	PIM
Bill Cowley	Boston	46	17	45	62	16
Bryan Hextall	NY Rangers	48	26	18	44	16
Gordie Drillon	Toronto	42	23	21	44	2
Syl Apps	Toronto	41	20	24	44	6
Lynn Patrick	NY Rangers	48	20	24	44	12
Syd Howe	Detroit	48	20	24	44	8
Neil Colville	NY Rangers	48	14	28	42	28
Eddie Wiseman	Boston	48	16	24	40	10
Bobby Bauer	Boston	48	17	22	39	2
Sweeney Schriner	Toronto	48	24	14	38	6
Roy Conacher	Boston	40	24	14	38	7
Milt Schmidt	Boston	44	13	25	38	23

1941-42

Team	GP	W	L	T	GF	GA	PTS
NY Rangers	48	29	17	2	177	143	60
*Toronto	48	27	18	3	158	136	57
Boston	48	25	17	6	160	118	56
Chicago	48	22	23	3	145	155	47
Detroit	48	19	25	4	140	147	42
Montreal	48	18	27	3	134	173	39
Brooklyn	48	16	29	3	133	175	35

Leading Scorers

Player	Club	GP	G	A	PTS	PIM
Bryan Hextall	NY Rangers	48	24	32	56	30
Lynn Patrick	NY Rangers	47	32	22	54	18
Don Grosso	Detroit	48	23	30	53	13
Phil Watson	NY Rangers	48	15	37	52	48
Sid Abel	Detroit	48	18	31	49	45
Toe Blake	Montreal	47	17	28	45	19
Bill Thoms	Chicago	47	15	30	45	8
Gordie Drillon	Toronto	48	23	18	41	6
Syl Apps	Toronto	38	18	23	41	0
Tom Anderson	Brooklyn	48	12	29	41	54

1942-43

Team	GP	W	L	T	GF	GA	PTS
*Detroit	50	25	14	11	169	124	61
Boston	50	24	17	9	195	176	57
Toronto	50	22	19	9	198	159	53
Montreal	50	19	19	12	181	191	50
Chicago	50	17	18	15	179	180	49
NY Rangers	50	11	31	8	161	253	30

Leading Scorers

Player	Club	GP	G	A	PTS	PIM
Doug Bentley	Chicago	50	33	40	73	18
Bill Cowley	Boston	48	27	45	72	10
Max Bentley	Chicago	47	26	44	70	2
Lynn Patrick	NY Rangers	50	22	39	61	28
Lorne Carr	Toronto	50	27	33	60	15
Billy Taylor	Toronto	50	18	42	60	2
Bryan Hextall	NY Rangers	50	27	32	59	28
Toe Blake	Montreal	48	23	36	59	28
Elmer Lach	Montreal	45	18	40	58	14
Buddy O'Connor	Montreal	50	15	43	58	2

1943-44

Team	GP	W	L	T	GF	GA	PTS
*Montreal	50	38	5	7	234	109	83
Detroit	50	26	18	6	214	177	58
Toronto	50	23	23	4	214	174	50
Chicago	50	22	23	5	178	187	49
Boston	50	19	26	5	223	268	43
NY Rangers	50	6	39	5	162	310	17

Leading Scorers

Player	Club	GP	G	A	PTS	PIM
Herb Cain	Boston	48	36	46	82	4
Doug Bentley	Chicago	50	38	39	77	22
Lorne Carr	Toronto	50	36	38	74	9
Carl Liscombe	Detroit	50	36	37	73	17
Elmer Lach	Montreal	48	24	48	72	23
Clint Smith	Chicago	50	23	49	72	4
Bill Cowley	Boston	36	30	41	71	12
Bill Mosienko	Chicago	50	32	38	70	10
Art Jackson	Boston	49	28	41	69	8
Gus Bodnar	Toronto	50	22	40	62	18

1944-45

Team	GP	W	L	T	GF	GA	PTS
Montreal	50	38	8	4	228	121	80
Detroit	50	31	14	5	218	161	67
*Toronto	50	24	22	4	183	161	52
Boston	50	16	30	4	179	219	36
Chicago	50	13	30	7	141	194	33
NY Rangers	50	11	29	10	154	247	32

Leading Scorers

Player	Club	GP	G	A	PTS	PIM
Elmer Lach	Montreal	50	26	54	80	37
Maurice Richard	Montreal	50	50	23	73	36
Toe Blake	Montreal	49	29	38	67	15
Bill Cowley	Boston	49	25	40	65	2
Ted Kennedy	Toronto	49	29	25	54	14
Bill Mosienko	Chicago	50	28	26	54	0
Joe Carveth	Detroit	50	26	28	54	6
Ab DeMarco	NY Rangers	50	24	30	54	10
Clint Smith	Chicago	50	23	31	54	0
Syd Howe	Detroit	46	17	36	53	6

1945-46

Team	GP	W	L	T	GF	GA	PTS
*Montreal	50	28	17	5	172	134	61
Boston	50	24	18	8	167	156	56
Chicago	50	23	20	7	200	178	53
Detroit	50	20	20	10	146	159	50
Toronto	50	19	24	7	174	185	45
NY Rangers	50	13	28	9	144	191	35

Leading Scorers

Player	Club	GP	G	A	PTS	PIM
Max Bentley	Chicago	47	31	30	61	6
Gaye Stewart	Toronto	50	37	15	52	8
Toe Blake	Montreal	50	29	21	50	2
Clint Smith	Chicago	50	26	24	50	2
Maurice Richard	Montreal	50	27	21	48	50
Bill Mosienko	Chicago	40	18	30	48	12
Ab DeMarco	NY Rangers	50	20	27	47	20
Elmer Lach	Montreal	50	13	34	47	34
Alex Kaleta	Chicago	49	19	27	46	17
Billy Taylor	Toronto	48	23	18	41	14
Pete Horeck	Chicago	50	20	21	41	34

1946-47

Team	GP	W	L	T	GF	GA	PTS
Montreal	60	34	16	10	189	138	78
*Toronto	60	31	19	10	209	172	72
Boston	60	26	23	11	190	175	63
Detroit	60	22	27	11	190	193	55
NY Rangers	60	22	32	6	167	186	50
Chicago	60	19	37	4	193	274	42

Leading Scorers

Player	Club	GP	G	A	PTS	PIM
Max Bentley	Chicago	60	29	43	72	12
Maurice Richard	Montreal	60	45	26	71	69
Billy Taylor	Detroit	60	17	46	63	35
Milt Schmidt	Boston	59	27	35	62	40
Ted Kennedy	Toronto	60	28	32	60	27
Doug Bentley	Chicago	52	21	34	55	18
Bobby Bauer	Boston	58	30	24	54	4
Roy Conacher	Detroit	60	30	24	54	6
Bill Mosienko	Chicago	59	25	27	52	2
Woody Dumart	Boston	60	24	28	52	12

1947-48

Team	GP	W	L	T	GF	GA	PTS
*Toronto	60	32	15	13	182	143	77
Detroit	60	30	18	12	187	148	72
Boston	60	23	24	13	167	168	59
NY Rangers	60	21	26	13	176	201	55
Montreal	60	20	29	11	147	169	51
Chicago	60	20	34	6	195	225	46

Leading Scorers

Player	Club	GP	G	A	PTS	PIM
Elmer Lach	Montreal	60	30	31	61	72
Buddy O'Connor	NY Rangers	60	24	36	60	8
Doug Bentley	Chicago	60	20	37	57	16
Gaye Stewart	Tor., Chi.	61	27	29	56	83
Max Bentley	Chi., Tor.	59	26	28	54	14
Bud Poile	Tor., Chi.	58	25	29	54	17
Maurice Richard	Montreal	53	28	25	53	89
Syl Apps	Toronto	55	26	27	53	12
Ted Lindsay	Detroit	60	33	19	52	95
Roy Conacher	Chicago	52	22	27	49	4

1948-49

Team	GP	W	L	T	GF	GA	PTS
Detroit	60	34	19	7	195	145	75
Boston	60	29	23	8	178	163	66
Montreal	60	28	23	9	152	126	65
*Toronto	60	22	25	13	147	161	57
Chicago	60	21	31	8	173	211	50
NY Rangers	60	18	31	11	133	172	47

Leading Scorers

Player	Club	GP	G	A	PTS	PIM
Roy Conacher	Chicago	60	26	42	68	8
Doug Bentley	Chicago	58	23	43	66	38
Sid Abel	Detroit	60	28	26	54	49
Ted Lindsay	Detroit	50	26	28	54	97
Jim Conacher	Det., Chi.	59	26	23	49	43
Paul Ronty	Boston	60	20	29	49	11
Harry Watson	Toronto	60	26	19	45	0
Billy Reay	Montreal	60	22	23	45	33
Gus Bodnar	Chicago	59	19	26	45	14
Johnny Peirson	Boston	59	22	21	43	45

1949-50

Team	GP	W	L	T	GF	GA	PTS
*Detroit	70	37	19	14	229	164	88
Montreal	70	29	22	19	172	150	77
Toronto	70	31	27	12	176	173	74
NY Rangers	70	28	31	11	170	189	67
Boston	70	22	32	16	198	228	60
Chicago	70	22	38	10	203	244	54

Leading Scorers

Player	Club	GP	G	A	PTS	PIM
Ted Lindsay	Detroit	69	23	55	78	141
Sid Abel	Detroit	69	34	35	69	46
Gordie Howe	Detroit	70	35	33	68	69
Maurice Richard	Montreal	70	43	22	65	114
Paul Ronty	Boston	70	23	36	59	8
Roy Conacher	Chicago	70	25	31	56	16
Doug Bentley	Chicago	64	20	33	53	28
Johnny Peirson	Boston	57	27	25	52	49
Metro Prystai	Chicago	65	29	22	51	31
Bep Guidolin	Chicago	70	17	34	51	42

1950-51

Team	GP	W	L	T	GF	GA	PTS
Detroit	70	44	13	13	236	139	101
*Toronto	70	41	16	13	212	138	95
Montreal	70	25	30	15	173	184	65
Boston	70	22	30	18	178	197	62
NY Rangers	70	20	29	21	169	201	61
Chicago	70	13	47	10	171	280	36

Leading Scorers

Player	Club	GP	G	A	PTS	PIM
Gordie Howe	Detroit	70	43	43	86	74
Maurice Richard	Montreal	65	42	24	66	97
Max Bentley	Toronto	67	21	41	62	34
Sid Abel	Detroit	69	23	38	61	30
Milt Schmidt	Boston	62	22	39	61	33
Ted Kennedy	Toronto	63	18	43	61	32
Ted Lindsay	Detroit	67	24	35	59	110
Tod Sloan	Toronto	70	31	25	56	105
Red Kelly	Detroit	70	17	37	54	24
Sid Smith	Toronto	70	30	21	51	10
Cal Gardner	Toronto	66	23	28	51	42

1951-52

Team	GP	W	L	T	GF	GA	PTS
*Detroit	70	44	14	12	215	133	100
Montreal	70	34	26	10	195	164	78
Toronto	70	29	25	16	168	157	74
Boston	70	25	29	16	162	176	66
NY Rangers	70	23	34	13	192	219	59
Chicago	70	17	44	9	158	241	43

Leading Scorers

Player	Club	GP	G	A	PTS	PIM
Gordie Howe	Detroit	70	47	39	86	78
Ted Lindsay	Detroit	70	30	39	69	123
Elmer Lach	Montreal	70	15	50	65	36
Don Raleigh	NY Rangers	70	19	42	61	14
Sid Smith	Toronto	70	27	30	57	6
Bernie Geoffrion	Montreal	67	30	24	54	66
Bill Mosienko	Chicago	70	31	22	53	10
Sid Abel	Detroit	62	17	36	53	32
Ted Kennedy	Toronto	70	19	33	52	33
Milt Schmidt	Boston	69	21	29	50	57
Johnny Peirson	Boston	68	20	30	50	30

1952-53

Team	GP	W	L	T	GF	GA	PTS
Detroit	70	36	16	18	222	133	90
*Montreal	70	28	23	19	155	148	75
Boston	70	28	29	13	152	172	69
Chicago	70	27	28	15	169	175	69
Toronto	70	27	30	13	156	167	67
NY Rangers	70	17	37	16	152	211	50

Leading Scorers

Player	Club	GP	G	A	PTS	PIM
Gordie Howe	Detroit	70	49	46	95	57
Ted Lindsay	Detroit	70	32	39	71	111
Maurice Richard	Montreal	70	28	33	61	112
Wally Hergesheimer	NY Rangers	70	30	29	59	10
Alex Delvecchio	Detroit	70	16	43	59	28
Paul Ronty	NY Rangers	70	16	38	54	20
Metro Prystai	Detroit	70	16	34	50	12
Red Kelly	Detroit	70	19	27	46	8
Bert Olmstead	Montreal	69	17	28	45	83
Fleming Mackell	Boston	65	27	17	44	63
Jim McFadden	Chicago	70	23	21	44	29

1953-54

Team	GP	W	L	T	GF	GA	PTS
*Detroit	70	37	19	14	191	132	88
Montreal	70	35	24	11	195	141	81
Toronto	70	32	24	14	152	131	78
Boston	70	32	28	10	177	181	74
NY Rangers	70	29	31	10	161	182	68
Chicago	70	12	51	7	133	242	31

Leading Scorers

Player	Club	GP	G	A	PTS	PIM
Gordie Howe	Detroit	70	33	48	81	109
Maurice Richard	Montreal	70	37	30	67	112
Ted Lindsay	Detroit	70	26	36	62	110
Bernie Geoffrion	Montreal	54	29	25	54	87
Bert Olmstead	Montreal	70	15	37	52	85
Red Kelly	Detroit	62	16	33	49	18
Dutch Reibel	Detroit	69	15	33	48	18
Ed Sandford	Boston	70	16	31	47	42
Fleming Mackell	Boston	67	15	32	47	60
Ken Mosdell	Montreal	67	22	24	46	64
Paul Ronty	NY Rangers	70	13	33	46	18

1954-55

Team	GP	W	L	T	GF	GA	PTS
*Detroit	70	42	17	11	204	134	95
Montreal	70	41	18	11	228	157	93
Toronto	70	24	24	22	147	135	70
Boston	70	23	26	21	169	188	67
NY Rangers	70	17	35	18	150	210	52
Chicago	70	13	40	17	161	235	43

Leading Scorers

Player	Club	GP	G	A	PTS	PIM
Bernie Geoffrion	Montreal	70	38	37	75	57
Maurice Richard	Montreal	67	38	36	74	125
Jean Béliveau	Montreal	70	37	36	73	58
Dutch Reibel	Detroit	70	25	41	66	15
Gordie Howe	Detroit	64	29	33	62	68
Red Sullivan	Chicago	69	19	42	61	51
Bert Olmstead	Montreal	70	10	48	58	103
Sid Smith	Toronto	70	33	21	54	14
Ken Mosdell	Montreal	70	22	32	54	82
Danny Lewicki	NY Rangers	70	29	24	53	8

1955-56

Team	GP	W	L	T	GF	GA	PTS
*Montreal	70	45	15	10	222	131	100
Detroit	70	30	24	16	183	148	76
NY Rangers	70	32	28	10	204	203	74
Toronto	70	24	33	13	153	181	61
Boston	70	23	34	13	147	185	59
Chicago	70	19	39	12	155	216	50

Leading Scorers

Player	Club	GP	G	A	PTS	PIM
Jean Béliveau	Montreal	70	47	41	88	143
Gordie Howe	Detroit	70	38	41	79	100
Maurice Richard	Montreal	70	38	33	71	89
Bert Olmstead	Montreal	70	14	56	70	94
Tod Sloan	Toronto	70	37	29	66	100
Andy Bathgate	NY Rangers	70	19	47	66	59
Bernie Geoffrion	Montreal	59	29	33	62	66
Dutch Reibel	Detroit	68	17	39	56	10
Alex Delvecchio	Detroit	70	25	26	51	24
Dave Creighton	NY Rangers	70	20	31	51	43
Bill Gadsby	NY Rangers	70	9	42	51	84

1956-57

Team	GP	W	L	T	GF	GA	PTS
Detroit	70	38	20	12	198	157	88
*Montreal	70	35	23	12	210	155	82
Boston	70	34	24	12	195	174	80
NY Rangers	70	26	30	14	184	227	66
Toronto	70	21	34	15	174	192	57
Chicago	70	16	39	15	169	225	47

Leading Scorers

Player	Club	GP	G	A	PTS	PIM
Gordie Howe	Detroit	70	44	45	89	72
Ted Lindsay	Detroit	70	30	55	85	103
Jean Béliveau	Montreal	69	33	51	84	105
Andy Bathgate	NY Rangers	70	27	50	77	60
Ed Litzenberger	Chicago	70	32	32	64	48
Maurice Richard	Montreal	63	33	29	62	74
Don McKenney	Boston	69	21	39	60	31
Dickie Moore	Montreal	70	29	29	58	56
Henri Richard	Montreal	63	18	36	54	71
Norm Ullman	Detroit	64	16	36	52	47

1957-58

Team	GP	W	L	T	GF	GA	PTS
*Montreal	70	43	17	10	250	158	96
NY Rangers	70	32	25	13	195	188	77
Detroit	70	29	29	12	176	207	70
Boston	70	27	28	15	199	194	69
Chicago	70	24	39	7	163	202	55
Toronto	70	21	38	11	192	226	53

Leading Scorers

Player	Club	GP	G	A	PTS	PIM
Dickie Moore	Montreal	70	36	48	84	65
Henri Richard	Montreal	67	28	52	80	56
Andy Bathgate	NY Rangers	65	30	48	78	42
Gordie Howe	Detroit	64	33	44	77	40
Bronco Horvath	Boston	67	30	36	66	71
Ed Litzenberger	Chicago	70	32	30	62	63
Fleming Mackell	Boston	70	20	40	60	72
Jean Béliveau	Montreal	55	27	32	59	93
Alex Delvecchio	Detroit	70	21	38	59	22
Don McKenney	Boston	70	28	30	58	22

1958-59

Team	GP	W	L	T	GF	GA	PTS
*Montreal	70	39	18	13	258	158	91
Boston	70	32	29	9	205	215	73
Chicago	70	28	29	13	197	208	69
Toronto	70	27	32	11	189	201	65
NY Rangers	70	26	32	12	201	217	64
Detroit	70	25	37	8	167	218	58

Leading Scorers

Player	Club	GP	G	A	PTS	PIM
Dickie Moore	Montreal	70	41	55	96	61
Jean Béliveau	Montreal	64	45	46	91	67
Andy Bathgate	NY Rangers	70	40	48	88	48
Gordie Howe	Detroit	70	32	46	78	57
Ed Litzenberger	Chicago	70	33	44	77	37
Bernie Geoffrion	Montreal	59	22	44	66	30
Red Sullivan	NY Rangers	70	21	42	63	56
Andy Hebenton	NY Rangers	70	33	29	62	8
Don McKenney	Boston	70	32	30	62	20
Tod Sloan	Chicago	59	27	35	62	79

1959-60

Team	GP	W	L	T	GF	GA	PTS
*Montreal	70	40	18	12	255	178	92
Toronto	70	35	26	9	199	195	79
Chicago	70	28	29	13	191	180	69
Detroit	70	26	29	15	186	197	67
Boston	70	28	34	8	220	241	64
NY Rangers	70	17	38	15	187	247	49

Leading Scorers

Player	Club	GP	G	A	PTS	PIM
Bobby Hull	Chicago	70	39	42	81	68
Bronco Horvath	Boston	68	39	41	80	60
Jean Béliveau	Montreal	60	34	40	74	57
Andy Bathgate	NY Rangers	70	26	48	74	28
Henri Richard	Montreal	70	30	43	73	66
Gordie Howe	Detroit	70	28	45	73	46
Bernie Geoffrion	Montreal	59	30	41	71	36
Don McKenney	Boston	70	20	49	69	28
Vic Stasiuk	Boston	69	29	39	68	121
Dean Prentice	NY Rangers	70	32	34	66	43

1960-61

Team	GP	W	L	T	GF	GA	PTS
Montreal	70	41	19	10	254	188	92
Toronto	70	39	19	12	234	176	90
*Chicago	70	29	24	17	198	180	75
Detroit	70	25	29	16	195	215	66
NY Rangers	70	22	38	10	204	248	54
Boston	70	15	42	13	176	254	43

Leading Scorers

Player	Club	GP	G	A	PTS	PIM
Bernie Geoffrion	Montreal	64	50	45	95	29
Jean Béliveau	Montreal	69	32	58	90	57
Frank Mahovlich	Toronto	70	48	36	84	131
Andy Bathgate	NY Rangers	70	29	48	77	22
Gordie Howe	Detroit	64	23	49	72	30
Norm Ullman	Detroit	70	28	42	70	34
Red Kelly	Toronto	64	20	50	70	12
Dickie Moore	Montreal	57	35	34	69	62
Henri Richard	Montreal	70	24	44	68	91
Alex Delvecchio	Detroit	70	27	35	62	26

1961-62

Team	GP	W	L	T	GF	GA	PTS
Montreal	70	42	14	14	259	166	98
*Toronto	70	37	22	11	232	180	85
Chicago	70	31	26	13	217	186	75
NY Rangers	70	26	32	12	195	207	64
Detroit	70	23	33	14	184	219	60
Boston	70	15	47	8	177	306	38

Leading Scorers

Player	Club	GP	G	A	PTS	PIM
Bobby Hull	Chicago	70	50	34	84	35
Andy Bathgate	NY Rangers	70	28	56	84	44
Gordie Howe	Detroit	70	33	44	77	54
Stan Mikita	Chicago	70	25	52	77	97
Frank Mahovlich	Toronto	70	33	38	71	87
Alex Delvecchio	Detroit	70	26	43	69	18
Ralph Backstrom	Montreal	66	27	38	65	29
Norm Ullman	Detroit	70	26	38	64	54
Bill Hay	Chicago	60	11	52	63	34
Claude Provost	Montreal	70	33	29	62	22

1962-63

Team	GP	W	L	T	GF	GA	PTS
*Toronto	70	35	23	12	221	180	82
Chicago	70	32	21	17	194	178	81
Montreal	70	28	19	23	225	183	79
Detroit	70	32	25	13	200	194	77
NY Rangers	70	22	36	12	211	233	56
Boston	70	14	39	17	198	281	45

Leading Scorers

Player	Club	GP	G	A	PTS	PIM
Gordie Howe	Detroit	70	38	48	86	100
Andy Bathgate	NY Rangers	70	35	46	81	54
Stan Mikita	Chicago	65	31	45	76	69
Frank Mahovlich	Toronto	67	36	37	73	56
Henri Richard	Montreal	67	23	50	73	57
Jean Béliveau	Montreal	69	18	49	67	68
John Bucyk	Boston	69	27	39	66	36
Alex Delvecchio	Detroit	70	20	44	64	8
Bobby Hull	Chicago	65	31	31	62	27
Murray Oliver	Boston	65	22	40	62	38

1963-64

Team	GP	W	L	T	GF	GA	PTS
Montreal	70	36	21	13	209	167	85
Chicago	70	36	22	12	218	169	84
*Toronto	70	33	25	12	192	172	78
Detroit	70	30	29	11	191	204	71
NY Rangers	70	22	38	10	186	242	54
Boston	70	18	40	12	170	212	48

Leading Scorers

Player	Club	GP	G	A	PTS	PIM
Stan Mikita	Chicago	70	39	50	89	146
Bobby Hull	Chicago	70	43	44	87	50
Jean Béliveau	Montreal	68	28	50	78	42
Andy Bathgate	NYR, Tor.	71	19	58	77	34
Gordie Howe	Detroit	69	26	47	73	70
Kenny Wharram	Chicago	70	39	32	71	18
Murray Oliver	Boston	70	24	44	68	41
Phil Goyette	NY Rangers	67	24	41	65	15
Rod Gilbert	NY Rangers	70	24	40	64	62
Dave Keon	Toronto	70	23	37	60	6

1964-65

Team	GP	W	L	T	GF	GA	PTS
Detroit	70	40	23	7	224	175	87
*Montreal	70	36	23	11	211	185	83
Chicago	70	34	28	8	224	176	76
Toronto	70	30	26	14	204	173	74
NY Rangers	70	20	38	12	179	246	52
Boston	70	21	43	6	166	253	48

Leading Scorers

Player	Club	GP	G	A	PTS	PIM
Stan Mikita	Chicago	70	28	59	87	154
Norm Ullman	Detroit	70	42	41	83	70
Gordie Howe	Detroit	70	29	47	76	104
Bobby Hull	Chicago	61	39	32	71	32
Alex Delvecchio	Detroit	68	25	42	67	16
Claude Provost	Montreal	70	27	37	64	28
Rod Gilbert	NY Rangers	70	25	36	61	52
Pierre Pilote	Chicago	68	14	45	59	162
John Bucyk	Boston	68	26	29	55	24
Ralph Backstrom	Montreal	70	25	30	55	41
Phil Esposito	Chicago	70	23	32	55	44

1965-66

Team	GP	W	L	T	GF	GA	PTS
*Montreal	70	41	21	8	239	173	90
Chicago	70	37	25	8	240	187	82
Toronto	70	34	25	11	208	187	79
Detroit	70	31	27	12	221	194	74
Boston	70	21	43	6	174	275	48
NY Rangers	70	18	41	11	195	261	47

Leading Scorers

Player	Club	GP	G	A	PTS	PIM
Bobby Hull	Chicago	65	54	43	97	70
Stan Mikita	Chicago	68	30	48	78	58
Bobby Rousseau	Montreal	70	30	48	78	20
Jean Béliveau	Montreal	67	29	48	77	50
Gordie Howe	Detroit	70	29	46	75	83
Norm Ullman	Detroit	70	31	41	72	35
Alex Delvecchio	Detroit	70	31	38	69	16
Bob Nevin	NY Rangers	69	29	33	62	10
Henri Richard	Montreal	62	22	39	61	47
Murray Oliver	Boston	70	18	42	60	30

1966-67

Team	GP	W	L	T	GF	GA	PTS
Chicago	70	41	17	12	264	170	94
Montreal	70	32	25	13	202	188	77
*Toronto	70	32	27	11	204	211	75
NY Rangers	70	30	28	12	188	189	72
Detroit	70	27	39	4	212	241	58
Boston	70	17	43	10	182	253	44

Leading Scorers

Player	Club	GP	G	A	PTS	PIM
Stan Mikita	Chicago	70	35	62	97	12
Bobby Hull	Chicago	66	52	28	80	52
Norm Ullman	Detroit	68	26	44	70	26
Kenny Wharram	Chicago	70	31	34	65	21
Gordie Howe	Detroit	69	25	40	65	53
Bobby Rousseau	Montreal	68	19	44	63	58
Phil Esposito	Chicago	69	21	40	61	40
Phil Goyette	NY Rangers	70	12	49	61	6
Doug Mohns	Chicago	61	25	35	60	58
Henri Richard	Montreal	65	21	34	55	28
Alex Delvecchio	Detroit	70	17	38	55	10

1967-68

East Division

Team	GP	W	L	T	GF	GA	PTS
*Montreal	74	42	22	10	236	167	94
NY Rangers	74	39	23	12	226	183	90
Boston	74	37	27	10	259	216	84
Chicago	74	32	26	16	212	222	80
Toronto	74	33	31	10	209	176	76
Detroit	74	27	35	12	245	257	66

West Division

Team	GP	W	L	T	GF	GA	PTS
Philadelphia	74	31	32	11	173	179	73
Los Angeles	74	31	33	10	200	224	72
St. Louis	74	27	31	16	177	191	70
Minnesota	74	27	32	15	191	226	69
Pittsburgh	74	27	34	13	195	216	67
Oakland	74	15	42	17	153	219	47

Leading Scorers

Player	Club	GP	G	A	PTS	PIM
Stan Mikita	Chicago	72	40	47	87	14
Phil Esposito	Boston	74	35	49	84	21
Gordie Howe	Detroit	74	39	43	82	53
Jean Ratelle	NY Rangers	74	32	46	78	18
Rod Gilbert	NY Rangers	73	29	48	77	12
Bobby Hull	Chicago	71	44	31	75	39
Norm Ullman	Det., Tor.	71	35	37	72	28
Alex Delvecchio	Detroit	74	22	48	70	14
John Bucyk	Boston	72	30	39	69	8
Kenny Wharram	Chicago	74	27	42	69	18

1968-69

East Division

Team	GP	W	L	T	GF	GA	PTS
*Montreal	76	46	19	11	271	202	103
Boston	76	42	18	16	303	221	100
NY Rangers	76	41	26	9	231	196	91
Toronto	76	35	26	15	234	217	85
Detroit	76	33	31	12	239	221	78
Chicago	76	34	33	9	280	246	77

West Division

Team	GP	W	L	T	GF	GA	PTS
St. Louis	76	37	25	14	204	157	88
Oakland	76	29	36	11	219	251	69
Philadelphia	76	20	35	21	174	225	61
Los Angeles	76	24	42	10	185	260	58
Pittsburgh	76	20	45	11	189	252	51
Minnesota	76	18	43	15	189	270	51

Leading Scorers

Player	Club	GP	G	A	PTS	PIM
Phil Esposito	Boston	74	49	77	126	79
Bobby Hull	Chicago	74	58	49	107	48
Gordie Howe	Detroit	76	44	59	103	58
Stan Mikita	Chicago	74	30	67	97	52
Ken Hodge	Boston	75	45	45	90	75
Yvan Cournoyer	Montreal	76	43	44	87	31
Alex Delvecchio	Detroit	72	25	58	83	8
Red Berenson	St. Louis	76	35	47	82	43
Jean Béliveau	Montreal	69	33	49	82	55
Frank Mahovlich	Detroit	76	49	29	78	38
Jean Ratelle	NY Rangers	75	32	46	78	26

1969-70

East Division

Team	GP	W	L	T	GF	GA	PTS
Chicago	76	45	22	9	250	170	99
*Boston	76	40	17	19	277	216	99
Detroit	76	40	21	15	246	199	95
NY Rangers	76	38	22	16	246	189	92
Montreal	76	38	22	16	244	201	92
Toronto	76	29	34	13	222	242	71

West Division

Team	GP	W	L	T	GF	GA	PTS
St. Louis	76	37	27	12	224	179	86
Pittsburgh	76	26	38	12	182	238	64
Minnesota	76	19	35	22	224	257	60
Oakland	76	22	40	14	169	243	58
Philadelphia	76	17	35	24	197	225	58
Los Angeles	76	14	52	10	168	290	38

Leading Scorers

Player	Club	GP	G	A	PTS	PIM
Bobby Orr	Boston	76	33	87	120	125
Phil Esposito	Boston	76	43	56	99	50
Stan Mikita	Chicago	76	39	47	86	50
Phil Goyette	St. Louis	72	29	49	78	16
Walt Tkaczuk	NY Rangers	76	27	50	77	38
Jean Ratelle	NY Rangers	75	32	42	74	28
Red Berenson	St. Louis	67	33	39	72	38
Jean-Paul Parise	Minnesota	74	24	48	72	72
Gordie Howe	Detroit	76	31	40	71	58
Frank Mahovlich	Detroit	74	38	32	70	59
Dave Balon	NY Rangers	76	33	37	70	100
John McKenzie	Boston	72	29	41	70	114

1970-71

East Division

Team	GP	W	L	T	GF	GA	PTS
Boston	78	57	14	7	399	207	121
NY Rangers	78	49	18	11	259	177	109
*Montreal	78	42	23	13	291	216	97
Toronto	78	37	33	8	248	211	82
Buffalo	78	24	39	15	217	291	63
Vancouver	78	24	46	8	229	296	56
Detroit	78	22	45	11	209	308	55

West Division

Team	GP	W	L	T	GF	GA	PTS
Chicago	78	49	20	9	277	184	107
St. Louis	78	34	25	19	223	208	87
Philadelphia	78	28	33	17	207	225	73
Minnesota	78	28	34	16	191	223	72
Los Angeles	78	25	40	13	239	303	63
Pittsburgh	78	21	37	20	221	240	62
California	78	20	53	5	199	320	45

Leading Scorers

Player	Club	GP	G	A	PTS	PIM
Phil Esposito	Boston	78	76	76	152	71
Bobby Orr	Boston	78	37	102	139	91
John Bucyk	Boston	78	51	65	116	8
Ken Hodge	Boston	78	43	62	105	113
Bobby Hull	Chicago	78	44	52	96	32
Norm Ullman	Toronto	73	34	51	85	24
Wayne Cashman	Boston	77	21	58	79	100
John McKenzie	Boston	65	31	46	77	120
Dave Keon	Toronto	76	38	38	76	4
Jean Béliveau	Montreal	70	25	51	76	40
Fred Stanfield	Boston	75	24	52	76	12

1971-72

East Division

Team	GP	W	L	T	GF	GA	PTS
*Boston	78	54	13	11	330	204	119
NY Rangers	78	48	17	13	317	192	109
Montreal	78	46	16	16	307	205	108
Toronto	78	33	31	14	209	208	80
Detroit	78	33	35	10	261	262	76
Buffalo	78	16	43	19	203	289	51
Vancouver	78	20	50	8	203	297	48

West Division

Team	GP	W	L	T	GF	GA	PTS
Chicago	78	46	17	15	256	166	107
Minnesota	78	37	29	12	212	191	86
St. Louis	78	28	39	11	208	247	67
Pittsburgh	78	26	38	14	220	258	66
Philadelphia	78	26	38	14	200	236	66
California	78	21	39	18	216	288	60
Los Angeles	78	20	49	9	206	305	49

Leading Scorers

Player	Club	GP	G	A	PTS	PIM
Phil Esposito	Boston	76	66	67	133	76
Bobby Orr	Boston	76	37	80	117	106
Jean Ratelle	NY Rangers	63	46	63	109	4
Vic Hadfield	NY Rangers	78	50	56	106	142
Rod Gilbert	NY Rangers	73	43	54	97	64
Frank Mahovlich	Montreal	76	43	53	96	36
Bobby Hull	Chicago	78	50	43	93	24
Yvan Cournoyer	Montreal	73	47	36	83	15
John Bucyk	Boston	78	32	51	83	4
Bobby Clarke	Philadelphia	78	35	46	81	87
Jacques Lemaire	Montreal	77	32	49	81	26

1972-73

East Division

Team	GP	W	L	T	GF	GA	PTS
*Montreal	78	52	10	16	329	184	120
Boston	78	51	22	5	330	235	107
NY Rangers	78	47	23	8	297	208	102
Buffalo	78	37	27	14	257	219	88
Detroit	78	37	29	12	265	243	86
Toronto	78	27	41	10	247	279	64
Vancouver	78	22	47	9	233	339	53
NY Islanders	78	12	60	6	170	347	30

West Division

Team	GP	W	L	T	GF	GA	PTS
Chicago	78	42	27	9	284	225	93
Philadelphia	78	37	30	11	296	256	85
Minnesota	78	37	30	11	254	230	85
St. Louis	78	32	34	12	233	251	76
Pittsburgh	78	32	37	9	257	265	73
Los Angeles	78	31	36	11	232	245	73
Atlanta	78	25	38	15	191	239	65
California	78	16	46	16	213	323	48

Leading Scorers

Player	Club	GP	G	A	PTS	PIM
Phil Esposito	Boston	78	55	75	130	87
Bobby Clarke	Philadelphia	78	37	67	104	80
Bobby Orr	Boston	63	29	72	101	99
Rick MacLeish	Philadelphia	78	50	50	100	69
Jacques Lemaire	Montreal	77	44	51	95	16
Jean Ratelle	NY Rangers	78	41	53	94	12
Mickey Redmond	Detroit	76	52	41	93	24
John Bucyk	Boston	78	40	53	93	12
Frank Mahovlich	Montreal	78	38	55	93	51
Jim Pappin	Chicago	76	41	51	92	82

Rod Gilbert overcame a broken back in junior hockey and more back surgery later in his career to become an NHL star. He had a career-high 97 points in 1971-72.

1973-74

East Division

Team	GP	W	L	T	GF	GA	PTS
Boston	78	52	17	9	349	221	113
Montreal	78	45	24	9	293	240	99
NY Rangers	78	40	24	14	300	251	94
Toronto	78	35	27	16	274	230	86
Buffalo	78	32	34	12	242	250	76
Detroit	78	29	39	10	255	319	68
Vancouver	78	24	43	11	224	296	59
NY Islanders	78	19	41	18	182	247	56

West Division

Team	GP	W	L	T	GF	GA	PTS
*Philadelphia	78	50	16	12	273	164	112
Chicago	78	41	14	23	272	164	105
Los Angeles	78	33	33	12	233	231	78
Atlanta	78	30	34	14	214	238	74
Pittsburgh	78	28	41	9	242	273	65
St. Louis	78	26	40	12	206	248	64
Minnesota	78	23	38	17	235	275	63
California	78	13	55	10	195	342	36

Leading Scorers

Player	Club	GP	G	A	PTS	PIM
Phil Esposito	Boston	78	68	77	145	58
Bobby Orr	Boston	74	32	90	122	82
Ken Hodge	Boston	76	50	55	105	43
Wayne Cashman	Boston	78	30	59	89	111
Bobby Clarke	Philadelphia	77	35	52	87	113
Rick Martin	Buffalo	78	52	34	86	38
Syl Apps Jr.	Pittsburgh	75	24	61	85	37
Darryl Sittler	Toronto	78	38	46	84	55
Lowell MacDonald	Pittsburgh	78	43	39	82	14
Brad Park	NY Rangers	78	25	57	82	148
Dennis Hextall	Minnesota	78	20	62	82	138

1974-75

PRINCE OF WALES CONFERENCE

Norris Division

Team	GP	W	L	T	GF	GA	PTS
Montreal	80	47	14	19	374	225	113
Los Angeles	80	42	17	21	269	185	105
Pittsburgh	80	37	28	15	326	289	89
Detroit	80	23	45	12	259	335	58
Washington	80	8	67	5	181	446	21

Adams Division

Team	GP	W	L	T	GF	GA	PTS
Buffalo	80	49	16	15	354	240	113
Boston	80	40	26	14	345	245	94
Toronto	80	31	33	16	280	309	78
California	80	19	48	13	212	316	51

CLARENCE CAMPBELL CONFERENCE

Patrick Division

Team	GP	W	L	T	GF	GA	PTS
*Philadelphia	80	51	18	11	293	181	113
NY Rangers	80	37	29	14	319	276	88
NY Islanders	80	33	25	22	264	221	88
Atlanta	80	34	31	15	243	233	83

Smythe Division

Team	GP	W	L	T	GF	GA	PTS
Vancouver	80	38	32	10	271	254	86
St. Louis	80	35	31	14	269	267	84
Chicago	80	37	35	8	268	241	82
Minnesota	80	23	50	7	221	341	53
Kansas City	80	15	54	11	184	328	41

Leading Scorers

Player	Club	GP	G	A	PTS	PIM
Bobby Orr	Boston	80	46	89	135	101
Phil Esposito	Boston	79	61	66	127	62
Marcel Dionne	Detroit	80	47	74	121	14
Guy Lafleur	Montreal	70	53	66	119	37
Pete Mahovlich	Montreal	80	35	82	117	64
Bobby Clarke	Philadelphia	80	27	89	116	125
Rene Robert	Buffalo	74	40	60	100	75
Rod Gilbert	NY Rangers	76	36	61	97	22
Gilbert Perreault	Buffalo	68	39	57	96	36
Rick Martin	Buffalo	68	52	43	95	72

1975-76

PRINCE OF WALES CONFERENCE

Norris Division

Team	GP	W	L	T	GF	GA	PTS
*Montreal	80	58	11	11	337	174	127
Los Angeles	80	38	33	9	263	265	85
Pittsburgh	80	35	33	12	339	303	82
Detroit	80	26	44	10	226	300	62
Washington	80	11	59	10	224	394	32

Adams Division

Team	GP	W	L	T	GF	GA	PTS
Boston	80	48	15	17	313	237	113
Buffalo	80	46	21	13	339	240	105
Toronto	80	34	31	15	294	276	83
California	80	27	42	11	250	278	65

CLARENCE CAMPBELL CONFERENCE

Patrick Division

Team	GP	W	L	T	GF	GA	PTS
Philadelphia	80	51	13	16	348	209	118
NY Islanders	80	42	21	17	297	190	101
Atlanta	80	35	33	12	262	237	82
NY Rangers	80	29	42	9	262	333	67

Smythe Division

Team	GP	W	L	T	GF	GA	PTS
Chicago	80	32	30	18	254	261	82
Vancouver	80	33	32	15	271	272	81
St. Louis	80	29	37	14	249	290	72
Minnesota	80	20	53	7	195	303	47
Kansas City	80	12	56	12	190	351	36

Leading Scorers

Player	Club	GP	G	A	PTS	PIM
Guy Lafleur	Montreal	80	56	69	125	36
Bobby Clarke	Philadelphia	76	30	89	119	136
Gilbert Perreault	Buffalo	80	44	69	113	36
Bill Barber	Philadelphia	80	50	62	112	104
Pierre Larouche	Pittsburgh	76	53	58	111	33
Jean Ratelle	Bos., NYR	80	36	69	105	18
Pete Mahovlich	Montreal	80	34	71	105	76
Jean Pronovost	Pittsburgh	80	52	52	104	24
Darryl Sittler	Toronto	79	41	59	100	90
Syl Apps Jr.	Pittsburgh	80	32	67	99	24

1976-77

PRINCE OF WALES CONFERENCE

Norris Division

Team	GP	W	L	T	GF	GA	PTS
*Montreal	80	60	8	12	387	171	132
Los Angeles	80	34	31	15	271	241	83
Pittsburgh	80	34	33	13	240	252	81
Washington	80	24	42	14	221	307	62
Detroit	80	16	55	9	183	309	41

Adams Division

Team	GP	W	L	T	GF	GA	PTS
Boston	80	49	23	8	312	240	106
Buffalo	80	48	24	8	301	220	104
Toronto	80	33	32	15	301	285	81
Cleveland	80	25	42	13	240	292	63

CLARENCE CAMPBELL CONFERENCE

Patrick Division

Team	GP	W	L	T	GF	GA	PTS
Philadelphia	80	48	16	16	323	213	112
NY Islanders	80	47	21	12	288	193	106
Atlanta	80	34	34	12	264	265	80
NY Rangers	80	29	37	14	272	310	72

Smythe Division

Team	GP	W	L	T	GF	GA	PTS
St. Louis	80	32	39	9	239	276	73
Minnesota	80	23	39	18	240	310	64
Chicago	80	26	43	11	240	298	63
Vancouver	80	25	42	13	235	294	63
Colorado	80	20	46	14	226	307	54

Leading Scorers

Player	Club	GP	G	A	PTS	PIM
Guy Lafleur	Montreal	80	56	80	136	20
Marcel Dionne	Los Angeles	80	53	69	122	12
Steve Shutt	Montreal	80	60	45	105	28
Rick MacLeish	Philadelphia	79	49	48	97	42
Gilbert Perreault	Buffalo	80	39	56	95	30
Tim Young	Minnesota	80	29	66	95	58
Jean Ratelle	Boston	78	33	61	94	22
Lanny McDonald	Toronto	80	46	44	90	77
Darryl Sittler	Toronto	73	38	52	90	89
Bobby Clarke	Philadelphia	80	27	63	90	71

1977-78

PRINCE OF WALES CONFERENCE

Norris Division

Team	GP	W	L	T	GF	GA	PTS
*Montreal	80	59	10	11	359	183	129
Detroit	80	32	34	14	252	266	78
Los Angeles	80	31	34	15	243	245	77
Pittsburgh	80	25	37	18	254	321	68
Washington	80	17	49	14	195	321	48

Adams Division

Team	GP	W	L	T	GF	GA	PTS
Boston	80	51	18	11	333	218	113
Buffalo	80	44	19	17	288	215	105
Toronto	80	41	29	10	271	237	92
Cleveland	80	22	45	13	230	325	57

CLARENCE CAMPBELL CONFERENCE

Patrick Division

Team	GP	W	L	T	GF	GA	PTS
NY Islanders	80	48	17	15	334	210	111
Philadelphia	80	45	20	15	296	200	105
Atlanta	80	34	27	19	274	252	87
NY Rangers	80	30	37	13	279	280	73

Smythe Division

Team	GP	W	L	T	GF	GA	PTS
Chicago	80	32	29	19	230	220	83
Colorado	80	19	40	21	257	305	59
Vancouver	80	20	43	17	239	320	57
St. Louis	80	20	47	13	195	304	53
Minnesota	80	18	53	9	218	325	45

Leading Scorers

Player	Club	GP	G	A	PTS	PIM
Guy Lafleur	Montreal	78	60	72	132	26
Bryan Trottier	NY Islanders	77	46	77	123	46
Darryl Sittler	Toronto	80	45	72	117	100
Jacques Lemaire	Montreal	76	36	61	97	14
Denis Potvin	NY Islanders	80	30	64	94	81
Mike Bossy	NY Islanders	73	53	38	91	6
Terry O'Reilly	Boston	77	29	61	90	211
Gilbert Perreault	Buffalo	79	41	48	89	20
Bobby Clarke	Philadelphia	71	21	68	89	83
Lanny McDonald	Toronto	74	47	40	87	54
Wilf Paiement	Colorado	80	31	56	87	114

1978-79

PRINCE OF WALES CONFERENCE

Norris Division

Team	GP	W	L	T	GF	GA	PTS
*Montreal	80	52	17	11	337	204	115
Pittsburgh	80	36	31	13	281	279	85
Los Angeles	80	34	34	12	292	286	80
Washington	80	24	41	15	273	338	63
Detroit	80	23	41	16	252	295	62

Adams Division

Team	GP	W	L	T	GF	GA	PTS
Boston	80	43	23	14	316	270	100
Buffalo	80	36	28	16	280	263	88
Toronto	80	34	33	13	267	252	81
Minnesota	80	28	40	12	257	289	68

CLARENCE CAMPBELL CONFERENCE

Patrick Division

Team	GP	W	L	T	GF	GA	PTS
NY Islanders	80	51	15	14	358	214	116
Philadelphia	80	40	25	15	281	248	95
NY Rangers	80	40	29	11	316	292	91
Atlanta	80	41	31	8	327	280	90

Smythe Division

Team	GP	W	L	T	GF	GA	PTS
Chicago	80	29	36	15	244	277	73
Vancouver	80	25	42	13	217	291	63
St. Louis	80	18	50	12	249	348	48
Colorado	80	15	53	12	210	331	42

Leading Scorers

Player	Club	GP	G	A	PTS	PIM
Bryan Trottier	NY Islanders	76	47	87	134	50
Marcel Dionne	Los Angeles	80	59	71	130	30
Guy Lafleur	Montreal	80	52	77	129	28
Mike Bossy	NY Islanders	80	69	57	126	25
Bob MacMillan	Atlanta	79	37	71	108	14
Guy Chouinard	Atlanta	80	50	57	107	14
Denis Potvin	NY Islanders	73	31	70	101	58
Bernie Federko	St. Louis	74	31	64	95	14
Dave Taylor	Los Angeles	78	43	48	91	124
Clark Gillies	NY Islanders	75	35	56	91	68

1979-80

PRINCE OF WALES CONFERENCE

Norris Division

Team	GP	W	L	T	GF	GA	PTS
Montreal	80	47	20	13	328	240	107
Los Angeles	80	30	36	14	290	313	74
Pittsburgh	80	30	37	13	251	303	73
Hartford	80	27	34	19	303	312	73
Detroit	80	26	43	11	268	306	63

Adams Division

Team	GP	W	L	T	GF	GA	PTS
Buffalo	80	47	17	16	318	201	110
Boston	80	46	21	13	310	234	105
Minnesota	80	36	28	16	311	253	88
Toronto	80	35	40	5	304	327	75
Quebec	80	25	44	11	248	313	61

CLARENCE CAMPBELL CONFERENCE

Patrick Division

Team	GP	W	L	T	GF	GA	PTS
Philadelphia	80	48	12	20	327	254	116
*NY Islanders	80	39	28	13	281	247	91
NY Rangers	80	38	32	10	308	284	86
Atlanta	80	35	32	13	282	269	83
Washington	80	27	40	13	261	293	67

Smythe Division

Team	GP	W	L	T	GF	GA	PTS
Chicago	80	34	27	19	241	250	87
St. Louis	80	34	34	12	266	278	80
Vancouver	80	27	37	16	256	281	70
Edmonton	80	28	39	13	301	322	69
Winnipeg	80	20	49	11	214	314	51
Colorado	80	19	48	13	234	308	51

Leading Scorers

Player	Club	GP	G	A	PTS	PIM
Marcel Dionne	Los Angeles	80	53	84	137	32
Wayne Gretzky	Edmonton	79	51	86	137	21
Guy Lafleur	Montreal	74	50	75	125	12
Gilbert Perreault	Buffalo	80	40	66	106	57
Mike Rogers	Hartford	80	44	61	105	10
Bryan Trottier	NY Islanders	78	42	62	104	68
Charlie Simmer	Los Angeles	64	56	45	101	65
Blaine Stoughton	Hartford	80	56	44	100	16
Darryl Sittler	Toronto	73	40	57	97	62
Blair MacDonald	Edmonton	80	46	48	94	6
Bernie Federko	St. Louis	79	38	56	94	24

1980-81

PRINCE OF WALES CONFERENCE

Norris Division

Team	GP	W	L	T	GF	GA	PTS
Montreal	80	45	22	13	332	232	103
Los Angeles	80	43	24	13	337	290	99
Pittsburgh	80	30	37	13	302	345	73
Hartford	80	21	41	18	292	372	60
Detroit	80	19	43	18	252	339	56

Adams Division

Team	GP	W	L	T	GF	GA	PTS
Buffalo	80	39	20	21	327	250	99
Boston	80	37	30	13	316	272	87
Minnesota	80	35	28	17	291	263	87
Quebec	80	30	32	18	314	318	78
Toronto	80	28	37	15	322	367	71

CLARENCE CAMPBELL CONFERENCE

Patrick Division

Team	GP	W	L	T	GF	GA	PTS
*NY Islanders	80	48	18	14	355	260	110
Philadelphia	80	41	24	15	313	249	97
Calgary	80	39	27	14	329	298	92
NY Rangers	80	30	36	14	312	317	74
Washington	80	26	36	18	286	317	70

Smythe Division

Team	GP	W	L	T	GF	GA	PTS
St. Louis	80	45	18	17	352	281	107
Chicago	80	31	33	16	304	315	78
Vancouver	80	28	32	20	289	301	76
Edmonton	80	29	35	16	328	327	74
Colorado	80	22	45	13	258	344	57
Winnipeg	80	9	57	14	246	400	32

Leading Scorers

Player	Club	GP	G	A	PTS	PIM
Wayne Gretzky	Edmonton	80	55	109	164	28
Marcel Dionne	Los Angeles	80	58	77	135	70
Kent Nilsson	Calgary	80	49	82	131	26
Mike Bossy	NY Islanders	79	68	51	119	32
Dave Taylor	Los Angeles	72	47	65	112	130
Peter Stastny	Quebec	77	39	70	109	37
Charlie Simmer	Los Angeles	65	56	49	105	62
Mike Rogers	Hartford	80	40	65	105	32
Bernie Federko	St. Louis	78	31	73	104	47
Jacques Richard	Quebec	78	52	51	103	39
Rick Middleton	Boston	80	44	59	103	16
Bryan Trottier	NY Islanders	73	31	72	103	74

1981-82

CLARENCE CAMPBELL CONFERENCE

Norris Division

Team	GP	W	L	T	GF	GA	PTS
Minnesota	80	37	23	20	346	288	94
Winnipeg	80	33	33	14	319	332	80
St. Louis	80	32	40	8	315	349	72
Chicago	80	30	38	12	332	363	72
Toronto	80	20	44	16	298	380	56
Detroit	80	21	47	12	270	351	54

Smythe Division

Team	GP	W	L	T	GF	GA	PTS
Edmonton	80	48	17	15	417	295	111
Vancouver	80	30	33	17	290	286	77
Calgary	80	29	34	17	334	345	75
Los Angeles	80	24	41	15	314	369	63
Colorado	80	18	49	13	241	362	49

PRINCE OF WALES CONFERENCE

Adams Division

Team	GP	W	L	T	GF	GA	PTS
Montreal	80	46	17	17	360	223	109
Boston	80	43	27	10	323	285	96
Buffalo	80	39	26	15	307	273	93
Quebec	80	33	31	16	356	345	82
Hartford	80	21	41	18	264	351	60

Patrick Division

Team	GP	W	L	T	GF	GA	PTS
*NY Islanders	80	54	16	10	385	250	118
NY Rangers	80	39	27	14	316	306	92
Philadelphia	80	38	31	11	325	313	87
Pittsburgh	80	31	36	13	310	337	75
Washington	80	26	41	13	319	338	65

Leading Scorers

Player	Club	GP	G	A	PTS	PIM
Wayne Gretzky	Edmonton	80	92	120	212	26
Mike Bossy	NY Islanders	80	64	83	147	22
Peter Stastny	Quebec	80	46	93	139	91
Dennis Maruk	Washington	80	60	76	136	128
Bryan Trottier	NY Islanders	80	50	79	129	88
Denis Savard	Chicago	80	32	87	119	82
Marcel Dionne	Los Angeles	78	50	67	117	50
Bobby Smith	Minnesota	80	43	71	114	82
Dino Ciccarelli	Minnesota	76	55	51	106	138
Dave Taylor	Los Angeles	78	39	67	106	130

1982-83

CLARENCE CAMPBELL CONFERENCE

Norris Division

Team	GP	W	L	T	GF	GA	PTS
Chicago	80	47	23	10	338	268	104
Minnesota	80	40	24	16	321	290	96
Toronto	80	28	40	12	293	330	68
St. Louis	80	25	40	15	285	316	65
Detroit	80	21	44	15	263	344	57

Smythe Division

Team	GP	W	L	T	GF	GA	PTS
Edmonton	80	47	21	12	424	315	106
Calgary	80	32	34	14	321	317	78
Vancouver	80	30	35	15	303	309	75
Winnipeg	80	33	39	8	311	333	74
Los Angeles	80	27	41	12	308	365	66

PRINCE OF WALES CONFERENCE

Adams Division

Team	GP	W	L	T	GF	GA	PTS
Boston	80	50	20	10	327	228	110
Montreal	80	42	24	14	350	286	98
Buffalo	80	38	29	13	318	285	89
Quebec	80	34	34	12	343	336	80
Hartford	80	19	54	7	261	403	45

Patrick Division

Team	GP	W	L	T	GF	GA	PTS
Philadelphia	80	49	23	8	326	240	106
*NY Islanders	80	42	26	12	302	226	96
Washington	80	39	25	16	306	283	94
NY Rangers	80	35	35	10	306	287	80
New Jersey	80	17	49	14	230	338	48
Pittsburgh	80	18	53	9	257	394	45

Leading Scorers

Player	Club	GP	G	A	PTS	PIM
Wayne Gretzky	Edmonton	80	71	125	196	59
Peter Stastny	Quebec	75	47	77	124	78
Denis Savard	Chicago	78	35	86	121	99
Mike Bossy	NY Islanders	79	60	58	118	20
Marcel Dionne	Los Angeles	80	56	51	107	22
Barry Pederson	Boston	77	46	61	107	47
Mark Messier	Edmonton	77	48	58	106	72
Michel Goulet	Quebec	80	57	48	105	51
Glenn Anderson	Edmonton	72	48	56	104	70
Kent Nilsson	Calgary	80	46	58	104	10
Jari Kurri	Edmonton	80	45	59	104	22

1983-84

CLARENCE CAMPBELL CONFERENCE

Norris Division

Team	GP	W	L	T	GF	GA	PTS
Minnesota	80	39	31	10	345	344	88
St. Louis	80	32	41	7	293	316	71
Detroit	80	31	42	7	298	323	69
Chicago	80	30	42	8	277	311	68
Toronto	80	26	45	9	303	387	61

Smythe Division

Team	GP	W	L	T	GF	GA	PTS
*Edmonton	80	57	18	5	446	314	119
Calgary	80	34	32	14	311	314	82
Vancouver	80	32	39	9	306	328	73
Winnipeg	80	31	38	11	340	374	73
Los Angeles	80	23	44	13	309	376	59

PRINCE OF WALES CONFERENCE

Adams Division

Team	GP	W	L	T	GF	GA	PTS
Boston	80	49	25	6	336	261	104
Buffalo	80	48	25	7	315	257	103
Quebec	80	42	28	10	360	278	94
Montreal	80	35	40	5	286	295	75
Hartford	80	28	42	10	288	320	66

Patrick Division

Team	GP	W	L	T	GF	GA	PTS
NY Islanders	80	50	26	4	357	269	104
Washington	80	48	27	5	308	226	101
Philadelphia	80	44	26	10	350	290	98
NY Rangers	80	42	29	9	314	304	93
New Jersey	80	17	56	7	231	350	41
Pittsburgh	80	16	58	6	254	390	38

Leading Scorers

Player	Club	GP	G	A	PTS	PIM
Wayne Gretzky	Edmonton	74	87	118	205	39
Paul Coffey	Edmonton	80	40	86	126	104
Michel Goulet	Quebec	75	56	65	121	76
Peter Stastny	Quebec	80	46	73	119	73
Mike Bossy	NY Islanders	67	51	67	118	8
Barry Pederson	Boston	80	39	77	116	64
Jari Kurri	Edmonton	64	52	61	113	14
Bryan Trottier	NY Islanders	68	40	71	111	59
Bernie Federko	St. Louis	79	41	66	107	43
Rick Middleton	Boston	80	47	58	105	14

1984-85

CLARENCE CAMPBELL CONFERENCE

Norris Division

Team	GP	W	L	T	GF	GA	PTS
St. Louis	80	37	31	12	299	288	86
Chicago	80	38	35	7	309	299	83
Detroit	80	27	41	12	313	357	66
Minnesota	80	25	43	12	268	321	62
Toronto	80	20	52	8	253	358	48

Smythe Division

Team	GP	W	L	T	GF	GA	PTS
*Edmonton	80	49	20	11	401	298	109
Winnipeg	80	43	27	10	358	332	96
Calgary	80	41	27	12	363	302	94
Los Angeles	80	34	32	14	339	326	82
Vancouver	80	25	46	9	284	401	59

PRINCE OF WALES CONFERENCE

Adams Division

Team	GP	W	L	T	GF	GA	PTS
Montreal	80	41	27	12	309	262	94
Quebec	80	41	30	9	323	275	91
Buffalo	80	38	28	14	290	237	90
Boston	80	36	34	10	303	287	82
Hartford	80	30	41	9	268	318	69

Patrick Division

Team	GP	W	L	T	GF	GA	PTS
Philadelphia	80	53	20	7	348	241	113
Washington	80	46	25	9	322	240	101
NY Islanders	80	40	34	6	345	312	86
NY Rangers	80	26	44	10	295	345	62
New Jersey	80	22	48	10	264	346	54
Pittsburgh	80	24	51	5	276	385	53

Leading Scorers

Player	Club	GP	G	A	PTS	PIM
Wayne Gretzky	Edmonton	80	73	135	208	52
Jari Kurri	Edmonton	73	71	64	135	30
Dale Hawerchuk	Winnipeg	80	53	77	130	74
Marcel Dionne	Los Angeles	80	46	80	126	46
Paul Coffey	Edmonton	80	37	84	121	97
Mike Bossy	NY Islanders	76	58	59	117	38
John Ogrodnick	Detroit	79	55	50	105	30
Denis Savard	Chicago	79	38	67	105	56
Bernie Federko	St. Louis	76	30	73	103	27
Mike Gartner	Washington	80	50	52	102	71

1985-86

CLARENCE CAMPBELL CONFERENCE

Norris Division

Team	GP	W	L	T	GF	GA	PTS
Chicago	80	39	33	8	351	349	86
Minnesota	80	38	33	9	327	305	85
St. Louis	80	37	34	9	302	291	83
Toronto	80	25	48	7	311	386	57
Detroit	80	17	57	6	266	415	40

Smythe Division

Team	GP	W	L	T	GF	GA	PTS
Edmonton	80	56	17	7	426	310	119
Calgary	80	40	31	9	354	315	89
Winnipeg	80	26	47	7	295	372	59
Vancouver	80	23	44	13	282	333	59
Los Angeles	80	23	49	8	284	389	54

PRINCE OF WALES CONFERENCE

Adams Division

Team	GP	W	L	T	GF	GA	PTS
Quebec	80	43	31	6	330	289	92
*Montreal	80	40	33	7	330	280	87
Boston	80	37	31	12	311	288	86
Hartford	80	40	36	4	332	302	84
Buffalo	80	37	37	6	296	291	80

Patrick Division

Team	GP	W	L	T	GF	GA	PTS
Philadelphia	80	53	23	4	335	241	110
Washington	80	50	23	7	315	272	107
NY Islanders	80	39	29	12	327	284	90
NY Rangers	80	36	38	6	280	276	78
Pittsburgh	80	34	38	8	313	305	76
New Jersey	80	28	49	3	300	374	59

Leading Scorers

Player	Club	GP	G	A	PTS	PIM
Wayne Gretzky	Edmonton	80	52	163	215	52
Mario Lemieux	Pittsburgh	79	48	93	141	43
Paul Coffey	Edmonton	79	48	90	138	120
Jari Kurri	Edmonton	78	68	63	131	22
Mike Bossy	NY Islanders	80	61	62	123	14
Peter Stastny	Quebec	76	41	81	122	60
Denis Savard	Chicago	80	47	69	116	111
Mats Naslund	Montreal	80	43	67	110	16
Dale Hawerchuk	Winnipeg	80	46	59	105	44
Neal Broten	Minnesota	80	29	76	105	47

1986-87

CLARENCE CAMPBELL CONFERENCE

Norris Division

Team	GP	W	L	T	GF	GA	PTS
St. Louis	80	32	33	15	281	293	79
Detroit	80	34	36	10	260	274	78
Chicago	80	29	37	14	290	310	72
Toronto	80	32	42	6	286	319	70
Minnesota	80	30	40	10	296	314	70

Smythe Division

Team	GP	W	L	T	GF	GA	PTS
*Edmonton	80	50	24	6	372	284	106
Calgary	80	46	31	3	318	289	95
Winnipeg	80	40	32	8	279	271	88
Los Angeles	80	31	41	8	318	341	70
Vancouver	80	29	43	8	282	314	66

PRINCE OF WALES CONFERENCE

Adams Division

Team	GP	W	L	T	GF	GA	PTS
Hartford	80	43	30	7	287	270	93
Montreal	80	41	29	10	277	241	92
Boston	80	39	34	7	301	276	85
Quebec	80	31	39	10	267	276	72
Buffalo	80	28	44	8	280	308	64

Patrick Division

Team	GP	W	L	T	GF	GA	PTS
Philadelphia	80	46	26	8	310	245	100
Washington	80	38	32	10	285	278	86
NY Islanders	80	35	33	12	279	281	82
NY Rangers	80	34	38	8	307	323	76
Pittsburgh	80	30	38	12	297	290	72
New Jersey	80	29	45	6	293	368	64

Leading Scorers

Player	Club	GP	G	A	PTS	PIM
Wayne Gretzky	Edmonton	79	62	121	183	28
Jari Kurri	Edmonton	79	54	54	108	41
Mario Lemieux	Pittsburgh	63	54	53	107	57
Mark Messier	Edmonton	77	37	70	107	73
Doug Gilmour	St. Louis	80	42	63	105	58
Dino Ciccarelli	Minnesota	80	52	51	103	92
Dale Hawerchuk	Winnipeg	80	47	53	100	54
Michel Goulet	Quebec	75	49	47	96	61
Tim Kerr	Philadelphia	75	58	37	95	57
Raymond Bourque	Boston	78	23	72	95	36

1987-88

CLARENCE CAMPBELL CONFERENCE

Norris Division

Team	GP	W	L	T	GF	GA	PTS
Detroit	80	41	28	11	322	269	93
St. Louis	80	34	38	8	278	294	76
Chicago	80	30	41	9	284	328	69
Toronto	80	21	49	10	273	345	52
Minnesota	80	19	48	13	242	349	51

Smythe Division

Team	GP	W	L	T	GF	GA	PTS
Calgary	80	48	23	9	397	305	105
*Edmonton	80	44	25	11	363	288	99
Winnipeg	80	33	36	11	292	310	77
Los Angeles	80	30	42	8	318	359	68
Vancouver	80	25	46	9	272	320	59

PRINCE OF WALES CONFERENCE

Adams Division

Team	GP	W	L	T	GF	GA	PTS
Montreal	80	45	22	13	298	238	103
Boston	80	44	30	6	300	251	94
Buffalo	80	37	32	11	283	305	85
Hartford	80	35	38	7	249	267	77
Quebec	80	32	43	5	271	306	69

Patrick Division

Team	GP	W	L	T	GF	GA	PTS
NY Islanders	80	39	31	10	308	267	88
Washington	80	38	33	9	281	249	85
Philadelphia	80	38	33	9	292	292	85
New Jersey	80	38	36	6	295	296	82
NY Rangers	80	36	34	10	300	283	82
Pittsburgh	80	36	35	9	319	316	81

Leading Scorers

Player	Club	GP	G	A	PTS	PIM
Mario Lemieux	Pittsburgh	77	70	98	168	92
Wayne Gretzky	Edmonton	64	40	109	149	24
Denis Savard	Chicago	80	44	87	131	95
Dale Hawerchuk	Winnipeg	80	44	77	121	59
Luc Robitaille	Los Angeles	80	53	58	111	82
Peter Stastny	Quebec	76	46	65	111	69
Mark Messier	Edmonton	77	37	74	111	103
Jimmy Carson	Los Angeles	80	55	52	107	45
Hakan Loob	Calgary	80	50	56	106	47
Michel Goulet	Quebec	80	48	58	106	56

1988-89

CLARENCE CAMPBELL CONFERENCE

Norris Division

Team	GP	W	L	T	GF	GA	PTS
Detroit	80	34	34	12	313	316	80
St. Louis	80	33	35	12	275	285	78
Minnesota	80	27	37	16	258	278	70
Chicago	80	27	41	12	297	335	66
Toronto	80	28	46	6	259	342	62

Smythe Division

Team	GP	W	L	T	GF	GA	PTS
*Calgary	80	54	17	9	354	226	117
Los Angeles	80	42	31	7	376	335	91
Edmonton	80	38	34	8	325	306	84
Vancouver	80	33	39	8	251	253	74
Winnipeg	80	26	42	12	300	355	64

PRINCE OF WALES CONFERENCE

Adams Division

Team	GP	W	L	T	GF	GA	PTS
Montreal	80	53	18	9	315	218	115
Boston	80	37	29	14	289	256	88
Buffalo	80	38	35	7	291	299	83
Hartford	80	37	38	5	299	290	79
Quebec	80	27	46	7	269	342	61

Patrick Division

Team	GP	W	L	T	GF	GA	PTS
Washington	80	41	29	10	305	259	92
Pittsburgh	80	40	33	7	347	349	87
NY Rangers	80	37	35	8	310	307	82
Philadelphia	80	36	36	8	307	285	80
New Jersey	80	27	41	12	281	325	66
NY Islanders	80	28	47	5	265	325	61

Leading Scorers

Player	Club	GP	G	A	PTS	PIM
Mario Lemieux	Pittsburgh	76	85	114	199	100
Wayne Gretzky	Los Angeles	78	54	114	168	26
Steve Yzerman	Detroit	80	65	90	155	61
Bernie Nicholls	Los Angeles	79	70	80	150	96
Rob Brown	Pittsburgh	68	49	66	115	118
Paul Coffey	Pittsburgh	75	30	83	113	193
Joe Mullen	Calgary	79	51	59	110	16
Jari Kurri	Edmonton	76	44	58	102	69
Jimmy Carson	Edmonton	80	49	51	100	36
Luc Robitaille	Los Angeles	78	46	52	98	65

1989-90

CLARENCE CAMPBELL CONFERENCE

Norris Division

Team	GP	W	L	T	GF	GA	PTS
Chicago	80	41	33	6	316	294	88
St. Louis	80	37	34	9	295	279	83
Toronto	80	38	38	4	337	358	80
Minnesota	80	36	40	4	284	291	76
Detroit	80	28	38	14	288	323	70

Smythe Division

Team	GP	W	L	T	GF	GA	PTS
Calgary	80	42	23	15	348	265	99
*Edmonton	80	38	28	14	315	283	90
Winnipeg	80	37	32	11	298	290	85
Los Angeles	80	34	39	7	338	337	75
Vancouver	80	25	41	14	245	306	64

PRINCE OF WALES CONFERENCE

Adams Division

Team	GP	W	L	T	GF	GA	PTS
Boston	80	46	25	9	289	232	101
Buffalo	80	45	27	8	286	248	98
Montreal	80	41	28	11	288	234	93
Hartford	80	38	33	9	275	268	85
Quebec	80	12	61	7	240	407	31

Patrick Division

Team	GP	W	L	T	GF	GA	PTS
NY Rangers	80	36	31	13	279	267	85
New Jersey	80	37	34	9	295	288	83
Washington	80	36	38	6	284	275	78
NY Islanders	80	31	38	11	281	288	73
Pittsburgh	80	32	40	8	318	359	72
Philadelphia	80	30	39	11	290	297	71

Leading Scorers

Player	Club	GP	G	A	PTS	PIM
Wayne Gretzky	Los Angeles	73	40	102	142	42
Mark Messier	Edmonton	79	45	84	129	79
Steve Yzerman	Detroit	79	62	65	127	79
Mario Lemieux	Pittsburgh	59	45	78	123	78
Brett Hull	St. Louis	80	72	41	113	24
Bernie Nicholls	L.A., NYR	79	39	73	112	86
Pierre Turgeon	Buffalo	80	40	66	106	29
Pat LaFontaine	NY Islanders	74	54	51	105	38
Paul Coffey	Pittsburgh	80	29	74	103	95
Joe Sakic	Quebec	80	39	63	102	27
Adam Oates	St. Louis	80	23	79	102	30

1990-91

CLARENCE CAMPBELL CONFERENCE

Norris Division

Team	GP	W	L	T	GF	GA	PTS
Chicago	80	49	23	8	284	211	106
St. Louis	80	47	22	11	310	250	105
Detroit	80	34	38	8	273	298	76
Minnesota	80	27	39	14	256	266	68
Toronto	80	23	46	11	241	318	57

Smythe Division

Team	GP	W	L	T	GF	GA	PTS
Los Angeles	80	46	24	10	340	254	102
Calgary	80	46	26	8	344	263	100
Edmonton	80	37	37	6	272	272	80
Vancouver	80	28	43	9	243	315	65
Winnipeg	80	26	43	11	260	288	63

PRINCE OF WALES CONFERENCE

Adams Division

Team	GP	W	L	T	GF	GA	PTS
Boston	80	44	24	12	299	264	100
Montreal	80	39	30	11	273	249	89
Buffalo	80	31	30	19	292	278	81
Hartford	80	31	38	11	238	276	73
Quebec	80	16	50	14	236	354	46

Patrick Division

Team	GP	W	L	T	GF	GA	PTS
*Pittsburgh	80	41	33	6	342	305	88
NY Rangers	80	36	31	13	297	265	85
Washington	80	37	36	7	258	258	81
New Jersey	80	32	33	15	272	264	79
Philadelphia	80	33	37	10	252	267	76
NY Islanders	80	25	45	10	223	290	60

Leading Scorers

Player	Club	GP	G	A	PTS	PIM
Wayne Gretzky	Los Angeles	78	41	122	163	16
Brett Hull	St. Louis	78	86	45	131	22
Adam Oates	St. Louis	61	25	90	115	29
Mark Recchi	Pittsburgh	78	40	73	113	48
John Cullen	Pit., Hfd.	78	39	71	110	101
Joe Sakic	Quebec	80	48	61	109	24
Steve Yzerman	Detroit	80	51	57	108	34
Theoren Fleury	Calgary	79	51	53	104	136
Al MacInnis	Calgary	78	28	75	103	90
Steve Larmer	Chicago	80	44	57	101	79

1991-92

CLARENCE CAMPBELL CONFERENCE

Norris Division

Team	GP	W	L	T	GF	GA	PTS
Detroit	80	43	25	12	320	256	98
Chicago	80	36	29	15	257	236	87
St. Louis	80	36	33	11	279	266	83
Minnesota	80	32	42	6	246	278	70
Toronto	80	30	43	7	234	294	67

Smythe Division

Team	GP	W	L	T	GF	GA	PTS
Vancouver	80	42	26	12	285	250	96
Los Angeles	80	35	31	14	287	296	84
Edmonton	80	36	34	10	295	297	82
Winnipeg	80	33	32	15	251	244	81
Calgary	80	31	37	12	296	305	74
San Jose	80	17	58	5	219	359	39

PRINCE OF WALES CONFERENCE

Adams Division

Team	GP	W	L	T	GF	GA	PTS
Montreal	80	41	28	11	267	207	93
Boston	80	36	32	12	270	275	84
Buffalo	80	31	37	12	289	299	74
Hartford	80	26	41	13	247	283	65
Quebec	80	20	48	12	255	318	52

Patrick Division

Team	GP	W	L	T	GF	GA	PTS
NY Rangers	80	50	25	5	321	246	105
Washington	80	45	27	8	330	275	98
*Pittsburgh	80	39	32	9	343	308	87
New Jersey	80	38	31	11	289	259	87
NY Islanders	80	34	35	11	291	299	79
Philadelphia	80	32	37	11	252	273	75

Leading Scorers

Player	Club	GP	G	A	PTS	PIM
Mario Lemieux	Pittsburgh	64	44	87	131	94
Kevin Stevens	Pittsburgh	80	54	69	123	254
Wayne Gretzky	Los Angeles	74	31	90	121	34
Brett Hull	St. Louis	73	70	39	109	48
Luc Robitaille	Los Angeles	80	44	63	107	95
Mark Messier	NY Rangers	79	35	72	107	76
Jeremy Roenick	Chicago	80	53	50	103	23
Steve Yzerman	Detroit	79	45	58	103	64
Brian Leetch	NY Rangers	80	22	80	102	26
Adam Oates	St.L., Bos.	80	20	79	99	22

1992-93

CLARENCE CAMPBELL CONFERENCE

Norris Division

Team	GP	W	L	T	GF	GA	PTS
Chicago	84	47	25	12	279	230	106
Detroit	84	47	28	9	369	280	103
Toronto	84	44	29	11	288	241	99
St. Louis	84	37	36	11	282	278	85
Minnesota	84	36	38	10	272	293	82
Tampa Bay	84	23	54	7	245	332	53

Smythe Division

Team	GP	W	L	T	GF	GA	PTS
Vancouver	84	46	29	9	346	278	101
Calgary	84	43	30	11	322	282	97
Los Angeles	84	39	35	10	338	340	88
Winnipeg	84	40	37	7	322	320	87
Edmonton	84	26	50	8	242	337	60
San Jose	84	11	71	2	218	414	24

PRINCE OF WALES CONFERENCE

Adams Division

Team	GP	W	L	T	GF	GA	PTS
Boston	84	51	26	7	332	268	109
Quebec	84	47	27	10	351	300	104
*Montreal	84	48	30	6	326	280	102
Buffalo	84	38	36	10	335	297	86
Hartford	84	26	52	6	284	369	58
Ottawa	84	10	70	4	202	395	24

Patrick Division

Team	GP	W	L	T	GF	GA	PTS
Pittsburgh	84	56	21	7	367	268	119
Washington	84	43	34	7	325	286	93
NY Islanders	84	40	37	7	335	297	87
New Jersey	84	40	37	7	308	299	87
Philadelphia	84	36	37	11	319	319	83
NY Rangers	84	34	39	11	304	308	79

Leading Scorers

Player	Club	GP	G	A	PTS	PIM
Mario Lemieux	Pittsburgh	60	69	91	160	38
Pat LaFontaine	Buffalo	84	53	95	148	63
Adam Oates	Boston	84	45	97	142	32
Steve Yzerman	Detroit	84	58	79	137	44
Teemu Selanne	Winnipeg	84	76	56	132	45
Pierre Turgeon	NY Islanders	83	58	74	132	26
Alexander Mogilny	Buffalo	77	76	51	127	40
Doug Gilmour	Toronto	83	32	95	127	100
Luc Robitaille	Los Angeles	84	63	62	125	100
Mark Recchi	Philadelphia	84	53	70	123	95

1993-94

EASTERN CONFERENCE

Northeast Division

Team	GP	W	L	T	GF	GA	PTS
Pittsburgh	84	44	27	13	299	285	101
Boston	84	42	29	13	289	252	97
Montreal	84	41	29	14	283	248	96
Buffalo	84	43	32	9	282	218	95
Quebec	84	34	42	8	277	292	76
Hartford	84	27	48	9	227	288	63
Ottawa	84	14	61	9	201	397	37

Atlantic Division

Team	GP	W	L	T	GF	GA	PTS
*NY Rangers	84	52	24	8	299	231	112
New Jersey	84	47	25	12	306	220	106
Washington	84	39	35	10	277	263	88
NY Islanders	84	36	36	12	282	264	84
Florida	84	33	34	17	233	233	83
Philadelphia	84	35	39	10	294	314	80
Tampa Bay	84	30	43	11	224	251	71

WESTERN CONFERENCE

Central Division

Team	GP	W	L	T	GF	GA	PTS
Detroit	84	46	30	8	356	275	100
Toronto	84	43	29	12	280	243	98
Dallas	84	42	29	13	286	265	97
St. Louis	84	40	33	11	270	283	91
Chicago	84	39	36	9	254	240	87
Winnipeg	84	24	51	9	245	344	57

Pacific Division

Team	GP	W	L	T	GF	GA	PTS
Calgary	84	42	29	13	302	256	97
Vancouver	84	41	40	3	279	276	85
San Jose	84	33	35	16	252	265	82
Anaheim	84	33	46	5	229	251	71
Los Angeles	84	27	45	12	294	322	66
Edmonton	84	25	45	14	261	305	64

Leading Scorers

Player	Club	GP	G	A	PTS	PIM
Wayne Gretzky	Los Angeles	81	38	92	130	20
Sergei Fedorov	Detroit	82	56	64	120	34
Adam Oates	Boston	77	32	80	112	45
Doug Gilmour	Toronto	83	27	84	111	105
Pavel Bure	Vancouver	76	60	47	107	86
Jeremy Roenick	Chicago	84	46	61	107	125
Mark Recchi	Philadelphia	84	40	67	107	46
Brendan Shanahan	St. Louis	81	52	50	102	211
Dave Andreychuk	Toronto	83	53	46	99	98
Jaromir Jagr	Pittsburgh	80	32	67	99	61

1994-95

EASTERN CONFERENCE

Northeast Division

Team	GP	W	L	T	GF	GA	PTS
Quebec	48	30	13	5	185	134	65
Pittsburgh	48	29	16	3	181	158	61
Boston	48	27	18	3	150	127	57
Buffalo	48	22	19	7	130	119	51
Hartford	48	19	24	5	127	141	43
Montreal	48	18	23	7	125	148	43
Ottawa	48	9	34	5	117	174	23

Atlantic Division

Team	GP	W	L	T	GF	GA	PTS
Philadelphia	48	28	16	4	150	132	60
*New Jersey	48	22	18	8	136	121	52
Washington	48	22	18	8	136	120	52
NY Rangers	48	22	23	3	139	134	47
Florida	48	20	22	6	115	127	46
Tampa Bay	48	17	28	3	120	144	37
NY Islanders	48	15	28	5	126	158	35

WESTERN CONFERENCE

Central Division

Team	GP	W	L	T	GF	GA	PTS
Detroit	48	33	11	4	180	117	70
St. Louis	48	28	15	5	178	135	61
Chicago	48	24	19	5	156	115	53
Toronto	48	21	19	8	135	146	50
Dallas	48	17	23	8	136	135	42
Winnipeg	48	16	25	7	157	177	39

Pacific Division

Team	GP	W	L	T	GF	GA	PTS
Calgary	48	24	17	7	163	135	55
Vancouver	48	18	18	12	153	148	48
San Jose	48	19	25	4	129	161	42
Los Angeles	48	16	23	9	142	174	41
Edmonton	48	17	27	4	136	183	38
Anaheim	48	16	27	5	125	164	37

Leading Scorers

Player	Club	GP	G	A	PTS	PIM
Jaromir Jagr	Pittsburgh	48	32	38	70	37
Eric Lindros	Philadelphia	46	29	41	70	60
Alex Zhamnov	Winnipeg	48	30	35	65	20
Joe Sakic	Quebec	47	19	43	62	30
Ron Francis	Pittsburgh	44	11	48	59	18
Theoren Fleury	Calgary	47	29	29	58	112
Paul Coffey	Detroit	45	14	44	58	72
Mikael Renberg	Philadelphia	47	26	31	57	20
John LeClair	Mtl., Phi.	46	26	28	54	30
Mark Messier	NY Rangers	46	14	39	53	40
Adam Oates	Boston	48	12	41	53	8

1995-96

EASTERN CONFERENCE

Northeast Division

Team	GP	W	L	T	GF	GA	PTS
Pittsburgh	82	49	29	4	362	284	102
Boston	82	40	31	11	282	269	91
Montreal	82	40	32	10	265	248	90
Hartford	82	34	39	9	237	259	77
Buffalo	82	33	42	7	247	262	73
Ottawa	82	18	59	5	191	291	41

Atlantic Division

Team	GP	W	L	T	GF	GA	PTS
Philadelphia	82	45	24	13	282	208	103
NY Rangers	82	41	27	14	272	237	96
Florida	82	41	31	10	254	234	92
Washington	82	39	32	11	234	204	89
Tampa Bay	82	38	32	12	238	248	88
New Jersey	82	37	33	12	215	202	86
NY Islanders	82	22	50	10	229	315	54

WESTERN CONFERENCE

Central Division

Team	GP	W	L	T	GF	GA	PTS
Detroit	82	62	13	7	325	181	131
Chicago	82	40	28	14	273	220	94
Toronto	82	34	36	12	247	252	80
St. Louis	82	32	34	16	219	248	80
Winnipeg	82	36	40	6	275	291	78
Dallas	82	26	42	14	227	280	66

Pacific Division

Team	GP	W	L	T	GF	GA	PTS
*Colorado	82	47	25	10	326	240	104
Calgary	82	34	37	11	241	240	79
Vancouver	82	32	35	15	278	278	79
Anaheim	82	35	39	8	234	247	78
Edmonton	82	30	44	8	240	304	68
Los Angeles	82	24	40	18	256	302	66
San Jose	82	20	55	7	252	357	47

Leading Scorers

Player	Club	GP	G	A	PTS	PIM
Mario Lemieux	Pittsburgh	70	69	92	161	54
Jaromir Jagr	Pittsburgh	82	62	87	149	96
Joe Sakic	Colorado	82	51	69	120	44
Ron Francis	Pittsburgh	77	27	92	119	56
Peter Forsberg	Colorado	82	30	86	116	47
Eric Lindros	Philadelphia	73	47	68	115	163
Paul Kariya	Anaheim	82	50	58	108	20
Teemu Selanne	Wpg., Ana.	79	40	68	108	22
Alexander Mogilny	Vancouver	79	55	52	107	16
Sergei Fedorov	Detroit	78	39	68	107	48

1996-97

EASTERN CONFERENCE

Northeast Division

Team	GP	W	L	T	GF	GA	PTS
Buffalo	82	40	30	12	237	208	92
Pittsburgh	82	38	36	8	285	280	84
Ottawa	82	31	36	15	226	234	77
Montreal	82	31	36	15	249	276	77
Hartford	82	32	39	11	226	256	75
Boston	82	26	47	9	234	300	61

Atlantic Division

Team	GP	W	L	T	GF	GA	PTS
New Jersey	82	45	23	14	231	182	104
Philadelphia	82	45	24	13	274	217	103
Florida	82	35	28	19	221	201	89
NY Rangers	82	38	34	10	258	231	86
Washington	82	33	40	9	214	231	75
Tampa Bay	82	32	40	10	217	247	74
NY Islanders	82	29	41	12	240	250	70

WESTERN CONFERENCE

Central Division

Team	GP	W	L	T	GF	GA	PTS
Dallas	82	48	26	8	252	198	104
*Detroit	82	38	26	18	253	197	94
Phoenix	82	38	37	7	240	243	83
St. Louis	82	36	35	11	236	239	83
Chicago	82	34	35	13	223	210	81
Toronto	82	30	44	8	230	273	68

Pacific Division

Team	GP	W	L	T	GF	GA	PTS
Colorado	82	49	24	9	277	205	107
Anaheim	82	36	33	13	245	233	85
Edmonton	82	36	37	9	252	247	81
Vancouver	82	35	40	7	257	273	77
Calgary	82	32	41	9	214	239	73
Los Angeles	82	28	43	11	214	268	67
San Jose	82	27	47	8	211	278	62

Leading Scorers

Player	Club	GP	G	A	PTS	PIM
Mario Lemieux	Pittsburgh	76	50	72	122	65
Teemu Selanne	Anaheim	78	51	58	109	34
Paul Kariya	Anaheim	69	44	55	99	6
John LeClair	Philadelphia	82	50	47	97	58
Wayne Gretzky	NY Rangers	82	25	72	97	28
Jaromir Jagr	Pittsburgh	63	47	48	95	40
Mats Sundin	Toronto	82	41	53	94	59
Ziggy Palffy	NY Islanders	80	48	42	90	43
Ron Francis	Pittsburgh	81	27	63	90	20
Brendan Shanahan	Hfd., Det.	81	47	41	88	131

1997-98

EASTERN CONFERENCE

Northeast Division

Team	GP	W	L	T	GF	GA	PTS
Pittsburgh	82	40	24	18	228	188	98
Boston	82	39	30	13	221	194	91
Buffalo	82	36	29	17	211	187	89
Montreal	82	37	32	13	235	208	87
Ottawa	82	34	33	15	193	200	83
Carolina	82	33	41	8	200	219	74

Atlantic Division

Team	GP	W	L	T	GF	GA	PTS
New Jersey	82	48	23	11	225	166	107
Philadelphia	82	42	29	11	242	193	95
Washington	82	40	30	12	219	202	92
NY Islanders	82	30	41	11	212	225	71
NY Rangers	82	25	39	18	197	231	68
Florida	82	24	43	15	203	256	63
Tampa Bay	82	17	55	10	151	269	44

WESTERN CONFERENCE

Central Division

Team	GP	W	L	T	GF	GA	PTS
Dallas	82	49	22	11	242	167	109
*Detroit	82	44	23	15	250	196	103
St. Louis	82	45	29	8	256	204	98
Phoenix	82	35	35	12	224	227	82
Chicago	82	30	39	13	192	199	73
Toronto	82	30	43	9	194	237	69

Pacific Division

Team	GP	W	L	T	GF	GA	PTS
Colorado	82	39	26	17	231	205	95
Los Angeles	82	38	33	11	227	225	87
Edmonton	82	35	37	10	215	224	80
San Jose	82	34	38	10	210	216	78
Calgary	82	26	41	15	217	252	67
Anaheim	82	26	43	13	205	261	65
Vancouver	82	25	43	14	224	273	64

Leading Scorers

Player	Club	GP	G	A	PTS	PIM
Jaromir Jagr	Pittsburgh	77	35	67	102	64
Peter Forsberg	Colorado	72	25	66	91	94
Pavel Bure	Vancouver	82	51	39	90	48
Wayne Gretzky	NY Rangers	82	23	67	90	28
John LeClair	Philadelphia	82	51	36	87	32
Ziggy Palffy	NY Islanders	82	45	42	87	34
Ron Francis	Pittsburgh	81	25	62	87	20
Teemu Selanne	Anaheim	73	52	34	86	30
Jason Allison	Boston	81	33	50	83	60
Jozef Stumpel	Los Angeles	77	21	58	79	53

1998-99

EASTERN CONFERENCE

Northeast Division

Team	GP	W	L	T	GF	GA	PTS
Ottawa	82	44	23	15	239	179	103
Toronto	82	45	30	7	268	231	97
Boston	82	39	30	13	214	181	91
Buffalo	82	37	28	17	207	175	91
Montreal	82	32	39	11	184	209	75

Atlantic Division

Team	GP	W	L	T	GF	GA	PTS
New Jersey	82	47	24	11	248	196	105
Philadelphia	82	37	26	19	231	196	93
Pittsburgh	82	38	30	14	242	225	90
NY Rangers	82	33	38	11	217	227	77
NY Islanders	82	24	48	10	194	244	58

Southeast Division

Team	GP	W	L	T	GF	GA	PTS
Carolina	82	34	30	18	210	202	86
Florida	82	30	34	18	210	228	78
Washington	82	31	45	6	200	218	68
Tampa Bay	82	19	54	9	179	292	47

WESTERN CONFERENCE

Central Division

Team	GP	W	L	T	GF	GA	PTS
Detroit	82	43	32	7	245	202	93
St Louis	82	37	32	13	237	209	87
Chicago	82	29	41	12	202	248	70
Nashville	82	28	47	7	190	261	63

Pacific Division

Team	GP	W	L	T	GF	GA	PTS
*Dallas	82	51	19	12	236	168	114
Phoenix	82	39	31	12	205	197	90
Anaheim	82	35	34	13	215	206	83
San Jose	82	31	33	18	196	191	80
Los Angeles	82	32	45	5	189	222	69

Northwest Division

Team	GP	W	L	T	GF	GA	PTS
Colorado	82	44	28	10	239	205	98
Edmonton	82	33	37	12	230	226	78
Calgary	82	30	40	12	211	234	72
Vancouver	82	23	47	12	192	258	58

Leading Scorers

Player	Club	GP	G	A	PTS	PIM
Jaromir Jagr	Pittsburgh	81	44	83	127	66
Teemu Selanne	Anaheim	75	47	60	107	30
Paul Kariya	Anaheim	82	39	62	101	40
Peter Forsberg	Colorado	78	30	67	97	108
Joe Sakic	Colorado	73	41	55	96	29
Alexei Yashin	Ottawa	82	44	50	94	54
Eric Lindros	Philadelphia	71	40	53	93	120
Theoren Fleury	Cgy., Col.	75	40	53	93	86
John LeClair	Philadelphia	76	43	47	90	30
Pavol Demitra	St Louis	82	37	52	89	16

1999-2000

EASTERN CONFERENCE

Northeast Division

Team	GP	W	L	T	OTL	GF	GA	PTS
Toronto	82	45	27	7	3	246	222	100
Ottawa	82	41	28	11	2	244	210	95
Buffalo	82	35	32	11	4	213	204	85
Montreal	82	35	34	9	4	196	194	83
Boston	82	24	33	19	6	210	248	73

Atlantic Division

Team	GP	W	L	T	OTL	GF	GA	PTS
Philadelphia	82	45	22	12	3	237	179	105
*New Jersey	82	45	24	8	5	251	203	103
Pittsburgh	82	37	31	8	6	241	236	88
NY Rangers	82	29	38	12	3	218	246	73
NY Islanders	82	24	48	9	1	194	275	58

Southeast Division

Team	GP	W	L	T	OTL	GF	GA	PTS
Washington	82	44	24	12	2	227	194	102
Florida	82	43	27	6	6	244	209	98
Carolina	82	37	35	10	0	217	216	84
Tampa Bay	82	19	47	9	7	204	310	54
Atlanta	82	14	57	7	4	170	313	39

WESTERN CONFERENCE

Central Division

Team	GP	W	L	T	OTL	GF	GA	PTS
St. Louis	82	51	19	11	1	248	165	114
Detroit	82	48	22	10	2	278	210	108
Chicago	82	33	37	10	2	242	245	78
Nashville	82	28	40	7	7	199	240	70

Pacific Division

Team	GP	W	L	T	OTL	GF	GA	PTS
Dallas	82	43	23	10	6	211	184	102
Los Angeles	82	39	27	12	4	245	228	94
Phoenix	82	39	31	8	4	232	228	90
San Jose	82	35	30	10	7	225	214	87
Anaheim	82	34	33	12	3	217	227	83

Northwest Division

Team	GP	W	L	T	OTL	GF	GA	PTS
Colorado	82	42	28	11	1	233	201	96
Edmonton	82	32	26	16	8	226	212	88
Vancouver	82	30	29	15	8	227	237	83
Calgary	82	31	36	10	5	211	256	77

Leading Scorers

Player	Club	GP	G	A	PTS	PIM
Jaromir Jagr	Pittsburgh	63	42	54	96	50
Pavel Bure	Florida	74	58	36	94	16
Mark Recchi	Philadelphia	82	28	63	91	50
Paul Kariya	Anaheim	74	42	44	86	24
Teemu Selanne	Anaheim	79	33	52	85	12
Owen Nolan	San Jose	78	44	40	84	110
Tony Amonte	Chicago	82	43	41	84	48
Mike Modano	Dallas	77	38	43	81	48
Joe Sakic	Colorado	60	28	53	81	28
Steve Yzerman	Detroit	78	35	44	79	34

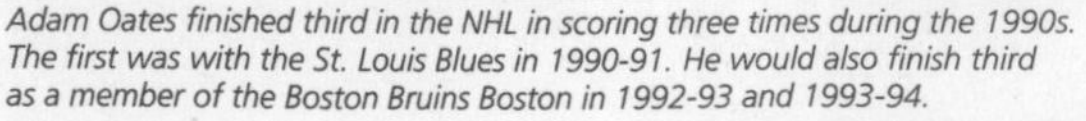

Adam Oates finished third in the NHL in scoring three times during the 1990s. The first was with the St. Louis Blues in 1990-91. He would also finish third as a member of the Boston Bruins Boston in 1992-93 and 1993-94.

Though neither finished among the NHL's top 10 scorers with Phoenix, Keith Tkachuk (left) led the NHL in goals with 52 for the Coyotes in 1996-97. Jeremy Roenick reached the top 10 with the Blackhawks in 1991-92 and 1993-94.

2000-01

EASTERN CONFERENCE

Northeast Division

Team	GP	W	L	T	OTL	GF	GA	PTS
Ottawa	82	48	21	9	4	274	205	109
Buffalo	82	46	30	5	1	218	184	98
Toronto	82	37	29	11	5	232	207	90
Boston	82	36	30	8	8	227	249	88
Montreal	82	28	40	8	6	206	232	70

Atlantic Division

Team	GP	W	L	T	OTL	GF	GA	PTS
New Jersey	82	48	19	12	3	295	195	111
Philadelphia	82	43	25	11	3	240	207	100
Pittsburgh	82	42	28	9	3	281	256	96
NY Rangers	82	33	43	5	1	250	290	72
NY Islanders	82	21	51	7	3	185	268	52

Southeast Division

Team	GP	W	L	T	OTL	GF	GA	PTS
Washington	82	41	27	10	4	233	211	96
Carolina	82	38	32	9	3	212	225	88
Florida	82	22	38	13	9	200	246	66
Atlanta	82	23	45	12	2	211	289	60
Tampa Bay	82	24	47	6	5	201	280	59

WESTERN CONFERENCE

Central Division

Team	GP	W	L	T	OTL	GF	GA	PTS
Detroit	82	49	20	9	4	253	202	111
St. Louis	82	43	22	12	5	249	195	103
Nashville	82	34	36	9	3	186	200	80
Chicago	82	29	40	8	5	210	246	71
Columbus	82	28	39	9	6	190	233	71

Pacific Division

Team	GP	W	L	T	OTL	GF	GA	PTS
Dallas	82	48	24	8	2	241	187	106
San Jose	82	40	27	12	3	217	192	95
Los Angeles	82	38	28	13	3	252	228	92
Phoenix	82	35	27	17	3	214	212	90
Anaheim	82	25	41	11	5	188	245	66

Northwest Division

Team	GP	W	L	T	OTL	GF	GA	PTS
*Colorado	82	52	16	10	4	270	192	118
Edmonton	82	39	28	12	3	243	222	93
Vancouver	82	36	28	11	7	239	238	90
Calgary	82	27	36	15	4	197	236	73
Minnesota	82	25	39	13	5	168	210	68

Leading Scorers

Player	Club	GP	G	A	PTS	PIM
Jaromir Jagr	Pittsburgh	81	52	69	121	42
Joe Sakic	Colorado	82	54	64	118	30
Patrik Elias	New Jersey	82	40	56	96	51
Alex Kovalev	Pittsburgh	79	44	51	95	96
Jason Allison	Boston	82	36	59	95	85
Martin Straka	Pittsburgh	82	27	68	95	38
Pavel Bure	Florida	82	59	33	92	58
Doug Weight	Edmonton	82	25	65	90	91
Ziggy Palffy	Los Angeles	73	38	51	89	20
Peter Forsberg	Colorado	73	27	62	89	54

2001-02

EASTERN CONFERENCE

Northeast Division

Team	GP	W	L	T	OTL	GF	GA	PTS
Boston	82	43	24	6	9	236	201	101
Toronto	82	43	25	10	4	249	207	100
Ottawa	82	39	27	9	7	243	208	94
Montreal	82	36	31	12	3	207	209	87
Buffalo	82	35	35	11	1	213	200	82

Atlantic Division

Team	GP	W	L	T	OTL	GF	GA	PTS
Philadelphia	82	42	27	10	3	234	192	97
NY Islanders	82	42	28	8	4	239	220	96
New Jersey	82	41	28	9	4	205	187	95
NY Rangers	82	36	38	4	4	227	258	80
Pittsburgh	82	28	41	8	5	198	249	69

Southeast Division

Team	GP	W	L	T	OTL	GF	GA	PTS
Carolina	82	35	26	16	5	217	217	91
Washington	82	36	33	11	2	228	240	85
Tampa Bay	82	27	40	11	4	178	219	69
Florida	82	22	44	10	6	180	250	60
Atlanta	82	19	47	11	5	187	288	54

WESTERN CONFERENCE

Central Division

Team	GP	W	L	T	OTL	GF	GA	PTS
*Detroit	82	51	17	10	4	251	187	116
St. Louis	82	43	27	8	4	227	188	98
Chicago	82	41	27	13	1	216	207	96
Nashville	82	28	41	13	0	196	230	69
Columbus	82	22	47	8	5	164	255	57

Pacific Division

Team	GP	W	L	T	OTL	GF	GA	PTS
San Jose	82	44	27	8	3	248	199	99
Phoenix	82	40	27	9	6	228	210	95
Los Angeles	82	40	27	11	4	214	190	95
Dallas	82	36	28	13	5	215	213	90
Anaheim	82	29	42	8	3	175	198	69

Northwest Division

Team	GP	W	L	T	OTL	GF	GA	PTS
Colorado	82	45	28	8	1	212	169	99
Vancouver	82	42	30	7	3	254	211	94
Edmonton	82	38	28	12	4	205	182	92
Calgary	82	32	35	12	3	201	220	79
Minnesota	82	26	35	12	9	195	238	73

Leading Scorers

Player	Club	GP	G	A	PTS	PIM
Jarome Iginla	Calgary	82	52	44	96	77
Markus Naslund	Vancouver	81	40	50	90	50
Todd Bertuzzi	Vancouver	72	36	49	85	110
Mats Sundin	Toronto	82	41	39	80	94
Jaromir Jagr	Washington	69	31	48	79	30
Joe Sakic	Colorado	82	26	53	79	18
Pavol Demitra	St. Louis	82	35	43	78	46
Adam Oates	Wsh., Phi.	80	14	64	78	28
Mike Modano	Dallas	78	34	43	77	38
Ron Francis	Carolina	80	27	50	77	18

2002-03

EASTERN CONFERENCE

Northeast Division

Team	GP	W	L	T	OTL	GF	GA	PTS
Ottawa	82	52	21	8	1	263	182	113
Toronto	82	44	28	7	3	236	208	98
Boston	82	36	31	11	4	245	237	87
Montreal	82	30	35	8	9	206	234	77
Buffalo	82	27	37	10	8	190	219	72

Atlantic Division

Team	GP	W	L	T	OTL	GF	GA	PTS
*New Jersey	82	46	20	10	6	216	166	108
Philadelphia	82	45	20	13	4	211	166	107
NY Islanders	82	35	34	11	2	224	231	83
NY Rangers	82	32	36	10	4	210	231	78
Pittsburgh	82	27	44	6	5	189	255	65

Southeast Division

Team	GP	W	L	T	OTL	GF	GA	PTS
Tampa Bay	82	36	25	16	5	219	210	93
Washington	82	39	29	8	6	224	220	92
Atlanta	82	31	39	7	5	226	284	74
Florida	82	24	36	13	9	176	237	70
Carolina	82	22	43	11	6	171	240	61

WESTERN CONFERENCE

Central Division

Team	GP	W	L	T	OTL	GF	GA	PTS
Detroit	82	48	20	10	4	269	203	110
St. Louis	82	41	24	11	6	253	222	99
Chicago	82	30	33	13	6	207	226	79
Nashville	82	27	35	13	7	183	206	74
Columbus	82	29	42	8	3	213	263	69

Pacific Division

Team	GP	W	L	T	OTL	GF	GA	PTS
Dallas	82	46	17	15	4	245	169	111
Anaheim	82	40	27	9	6	203	193	95
Los Angeles	82	33	37	6	6	203	221	78
Phoenix	82	31	35	11	5	204	230	78
San Jose	82	28	37	9	8	214	239	73

Northwest Division

Team	GP	W	L	T	OTL	GF	GA	PTS
Colorado	82	42	19	13	8	251	194	105
Vancouver	82	45	23	13	1	264	208	104
Minnesota	82	42	29	10	1	198	178	95
Edmonton	82	36	26	11	9	231	230	92
Calgary	82	29	36	13	4	186	228	75

Leading Scorers

Player	Club	GP	G	A	PTS	PIM
Peter Forsberg	Colorado	75	29	77	106	70
Markus Naslund	Vancouver	82	48	56	104	52
Joe Thornton	Boston	77	36	65	101	109
Milan Hejduk	Colorado	82	50	48	98	52
Todd Bertuzzi	Vancouver	82	46	51	97	144
Pavol Demitra	St. Louis	78	36	57	93	32
Glen Murray	Boston	82	44	48	92	64
Mario Lemieux	Pittsburgh	67	28	63	91	43
Danny Heatley	Atlanta	77	41	48	89	58
Ziggy Palffy	Los Angeles	76	37	48	85	47
Mike Modano	Dallas	79	28	57	85	30

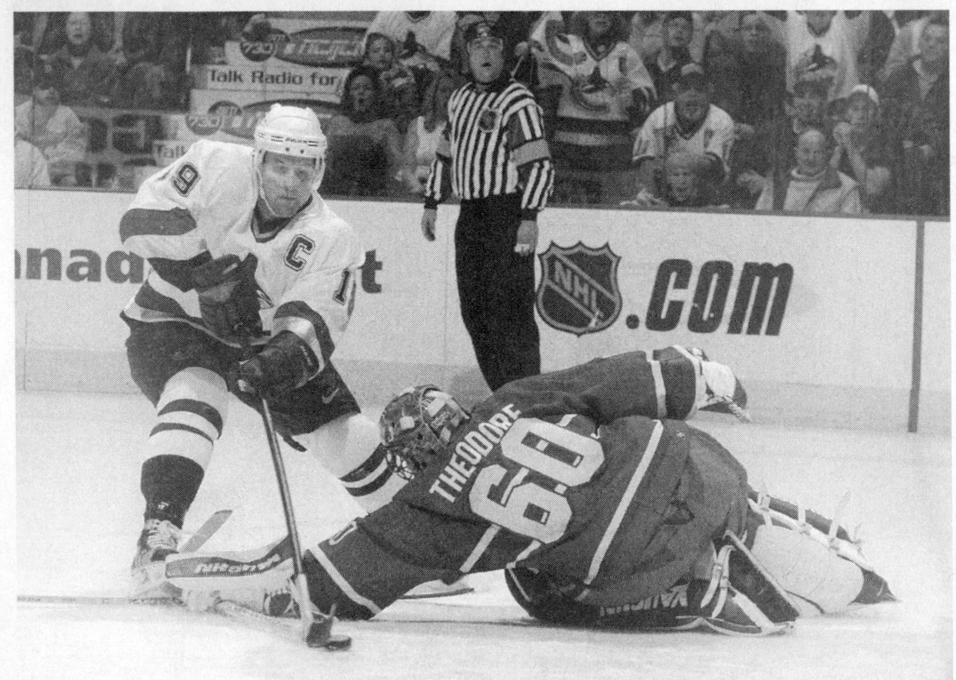

Canucks captain Markus Naslund was second in scoring two years in a row. He finished as the runner-up to Jarome Iginla with 90 points in 2001-02 and was edged out by fellow Swede Peter Forsberg, who had 106 points to Naslund's 104, in 2002-03.

2003-04

EASTERN CONFERENCE

Northeast Division

Team	GP	W	L	T	OTL	GF	GA	PTS
Boston	82	41	19	15	7	209	188	104
Toronto	82	45	24	10	3	242	204	103
Ottawa	82	43	23	10	6	262	189	102
Montreal	82	41	30	7	4	208	192	93
Buffalo	82	37	34	7	4	220	221	85

Atlantic Division

Team	GP	W	L	T	OTL	GF	GA	PTS
Philadelphia	82	40	21	15	6	229	186	101
New Jersey	82	43	25	12	2	213	164	100
NY Islanders	82	38	29	11	4	237	210	91
NY Rangers	82	27	40	7	8	206	250	69
Pittsburgh	82	23	47	8	4	190	303	58

Southeast Division

Team	GP	W	L	T	OTL	GF	GA	PTS
*Tampa Bay	82	46	22	8	6	245	192	106
Atlanta	82	33	37	8	4	214	243	78
Carolina	82	28	34	14	6	172	209	76
Florida	82	28	35	15	4	188	221	75
Washington	82	23	46	10	3	186	253	59

WESTERN CONFERENCE

Central Division

Team	GP	W	L	T	OTL	GF	GA	PTS
Detroit	82	48	21	11	2	255	189	109
St. Louis	82	39	30	11	2	191	198	91
Nashville	82	38	29	11	4	216	217	91
Columbus	82	25	45	8	4	177	238	62
Chicago	82	20	43	11	8	188	259	59

Pacific Division

Team	GP	W	L	T	OTL	GF	GA	PTS
San Jose	82	43	21	12	6	219	183	104
Dallas	82	41	26	13	2	194	175	97
Los Angeles	82	28	29	16	9	205	217	81
Anaheim	82	29	35	10	8	184	213	76
Phoenix	82	22	36	18	6	188	245	68

Northwest Division

Team	GP	W	L	T	OTL	GF	GA	PTS
Vancouver	82	43	24	10	5	235	194	101
Colorado	82	40	22	13	7	236	198	100
Calgary	82	42	30	7	3	200	176	94
Edmonton	82	36	29	12	5	221	208	89
Minnesota	82	30	29	20	3	188	183	83

Leading Scorers

Player	Club	GP	G	A	PTS	PIM
Martin St. Louis	Tampa Bay	82	38	56	94	24
Ilya Kovalchuk	Atlanta	81	41	46	87	63
Joe Sakic	Colorado	81	33	54	87	42
Markus Naslund	Vancouver	78	35	49	84	58
Marian Hossa	Ottawa	81	36	46	82	46
Patrik Elias	New Jersey	82	38	43	81	44
Daniel Alfredsson	Ottawa	77	32	48	80	24
Cory Stillman	Tampa Bay	81	25	55	80	36
Robert Lang	Wsh., Det.	69	30	49	79	24
Brad Richards	Tampa Bay	82	26	53	79	12
Alex Tanguay	Colorado	69	25	54	79	42

2004-05

SEASON CANCELLED

2005-06

EASTERN CONFERENCE

Northeast Division

Team	GP	W	L	OL	GF	GA	PTS
Ottawa	82	52	21	9	314	211	113
Buffalo	82	52	24	6	281	239	110
Montreal	82	42	31	9	243	247	93
Toronto	82	41	33	8	257	270	90
Boston	82	29	37	16	230	266	74

Atlantic Division

Team	GP	W	L	OL	GF	GA	PTS
New Jersey	82	46	27	9	242	229	101
Philadelphia	82	45	26	11	267	259	101
NY Rangers	82	44	26	12	257	215	100
NY Islanders	82	36	40	6	230	278	78
Pittsburgh	82	22	46	14	244	316	58

Southeast Division

Team	GP	W	L	OL	GF	GA	PTS
*Carolina	82	52	22	8	294	260	112
Tampa Bay	82	43	33	6	252	260	92
Atlanta	82	41	33	8	281	275	90
Florida	82	37	34	11	240	257	85
Washington	82	29	41	12	237	306	70

WESTERN CONFERENCE

Central Division

Team	GP	W	L	OL	GF	GA	PTS
Detroit	82	58	16	8	305	209	124
Nashville	82	49	25	8	259	227	106
Columbus	82	35	43	4	223	279	74
Chicago	82	26	43	13	211	285	65
St. Louis	82	21	46	15	197	292	57

Pacific Division

Team	GP	W	L	OL	GF	GA	PTS
Dallas	82	53	23	6	265	218	112
San Jose	82	44	27	11	266	242	99
Anaheim	82	43	27	12	254	229	98
Los Angeles	82	42	35	5	249	270	89
Phoenix	82	38	39	5	246	271	81

Northwest Division

Team	GP	W	L	OL	GF	GA	PTS
Calgary	82	46	25	11	218	200	103
Colorado	82	43	30	9	283	257	95
Edmonton	82	41	28	13	256	251	95
Vancouver	82	42	32	8	256	255	92
Minnesota	82	38	36	8	231	215	84

Leading Scorers

Player	Club	GP	G	A	PTS	PIM
Joe Thornton	Bos., S.J.	81	29	96	125	61
Jaromir Jagr	NY Rangers	82	54	69	123	72
Alex Ovechkin	Washington	81	52	54	106	52
Dany Heatley	Ottawa	82	50	53	103	86
Daniel Alfredsson	Ottawa	77	43	60	103	50
Sidney Crosby	Pittsburgh	81	39	63	102	110
Eric Staal	Carolina	82	45	55	100	81
Ilya Kovalchuk	Atlanta	78	52	46	98	68
Marc Savard	Atlanta	82	28	69	97	100
Jonathan Cheechoo	San Jose	82	56	37	93	58

2006-07

EASTERN CONFERENCE

Northeast Division

Team	GP	W	L	OL	GF	GA	PTS
Buffalo	82	53	22	7	308	242	113
Ottawa	82	48	25	9	288	222	105
Toronto	82	40	31	11	258	269	91
Montreal	82	42	34	6	245	256	90
Boston	82	35	41	6	219	289	76

Atlantic Division

Team	GP	W	L	OL	GF	GA	PTS
New Jersey	82	49	24	9	216	201	107
Pittsburgh	82	47	24	11	277	246	105
NY Rangers	82	42	30	10	242	216	94
NY Islanders	82	40	30	12	248	240	92
Philadelphia	82	22	48	12	214	303	56

Southeast Division

Team	GP	W	L	OL	GF	GA	PTS
Atlanta	82	43	28	11	246	245	97
Tampa Bay	82	44	33	5	253	261	93
Carolina	82	40	34	8	241	253	88
Florida	82	35	31	16	247	257	86
Washington	82	28	40	14	235	286	70

WESTERN CONFERENCE

Central Division

Team	GP	W	L	OL	GF	GA	PTS
Detroit	82	50	19	13	254	199	113
Nashville	82	51	23	8	272	212	110
St. Louis	82	34	35	13	214	254	81
Columbus	82	33	42	7	201	249	73
Chicago	82	31	42	9	201	258	71

Pacific Division

Team	GP	W	L	OL	GF	GA	PTS
*Anaheim	82	48	20	14	258	208	110
San Jose	82	51	26	5	258	199	107
Dallas	82	50	25	7	226	197	107
Los Angeles	82	27	41	14	227	283	68
Phoenix	82	31	46	5	216	284	67

Northwest Division

Team	GP	W	L	OL	GF	GA	PTS
Vancouver	82	49	26	7	222	201	105
Minnesota	82	48	26	8	235	191	104
Calgary	82	43	29	10	258	226	96
Colorado	82	44	31	7	272	251	95
Edmonton	82	32	43	7	195	248	71

Leading Scorers

Player	Club	GP	G	A	PTS	PIM
Sidney Crosby	Pittsburgh	79	36	84	120	60
Joe Thornton	San Jose	82	22	92	114	44
Vincent Lecavalier	Tampa Bay	82	52	56	108	44
Dany Heatley	Ottawa	82	50	55	105	74
Martin St. Louis	Tampa Bay	82	43	59	102	28
Marian Hossa	Atlanta	82	43	57	100	49
Joe Sakic	Colorado	82	36	64	100	46
Jaromir Jagr	NY Rangers	82	30	66	96	78
Marc Savard	Boston	82	22	74	96	96
Daniel Briere	Buffalo	81	32	63	95	89

Note: Detailed statistics for 2006-07 are listed in the Final Statistics, 2006-07 section of the *NHL Guide & Record Book*. **See page 135.**

Marc Savard (far left) made his second straight appearance in the NHL top ten in 2006-07, this time as a member of the Boston Bruins. Daniel Briere (left) made his first appearance in his last season with the Buffalo Sabres.

Team Records

Regular Season

FINAL STANDINGS

MOST POINTS, ONE SEASON:
132 – Montreal Canadiens, 1976-77. 60W-8L-12T. 80GP
131 – Detroit Red Wings, 1995-96. 62W-13L-7T. 82GP
129 – Montreal Canadiens, 1977-78. 59W-10L-11T. 80GP

BEST POINTS PERCENTAGE, ONE SEASON:
.875 – Boston Bruins, 1929-30. 38W-5L-1T. 77PTS in 44GP
.830 – Montreal Canadiens, 1943-44. 38W-5L-7T. 83PTS in 50GP
.825 – Montreal Canadiens, 1976-77. 60W-8L-12T. 132PTS in 80GP
.806 – Montreal Canadiens, 1977-78. 59W-10L-11T. 129PTS in 80GP
.800 – Montreal Canadiens, 1944-45. 38W-8L-4T. 80PTS in 50GP

FEWEST POINTS, ONE SEASON:
8 – Quebec Bulldogs, 1919-20. 4W-20L-0T. 24GP
10 – Toronto Arenas, 1918-19. 5W-13L-0T. 18GP
12 – Hamilton Tigers, 1920-21. 6W-18L-0T. 24GP
– Hamilton Tigers, 1922-23. 6W-18L-0T. 24GP
– Boston Bruins, 1924-25. 6W-24L-0T. 30GP
– Philadelphia Quakers, 1930-31. 4W-36L-4T. 44GP

FEWEST POINTS, ONE SEASON (MINIMUM 70-GAME SCHEDULE):
21 – Washington Capitals, 1974-75. 8W-67L-5T. 80GP
24 – Ottawa Senators, 1992-93. 10W-70L-4T. 84GP
– San Jose Sharks, 1992-93. 11W-71L-2T. 84GP
30 – New York Islanders, 1972-73. 12W-60L-6T. 78GP

WORST POINTS PERCENTAGE, ONE SEASON:
.131 – Washington Capitals, 1974-75. 8W-67L-5T. 21PTS in 80GP
.136 – Philadelphia Quakers, 1930-31. 4W-36L-4T. 12PTS in 44GP
.143 – Ottawa Senators, 1992-93. 10W-70L-4T. 24PTS in 84GP
– San Jose Sharks, 1992-93. 11W-71L-2T. 24PTS in 84GP
.148 – Pittsburgh Pirates, 1929-30. 5W-36L-3T. 13PTS in 44GP

TEAM WINS

Most Wins

MOST WINS, ONE SEASON:
62 – Detroit Red Wings, 1995-96. 82GP
60 – Montreal Canadiens, 1976-77. 80GP
59 – Montreal Canadiens, 1977-78. 80GP

MOST HOME WINS, ONE SEASON:
36 – Philadelphia Flyers, 1975-76. 40GP
– Detroit Red Wings, 1995-96. 41GP
33 – Boston Bruins, 1970-71. 39GP
– Boston Bruins, 1973-74. 39GP
– Montreal Canadiens, 1976-77. 40GP
– Philadelphia Flyers, 1976-77. 40GP
– New York Islanders, 1981-82. 40GP
– Philadelphia Flyers, 1985-86. 40GP

MOST ROAD WINS, ONE SEASON:
31 – Detroit Red Wings, 2005-06. 41GP
28 – New Jersey Devils, 1998-99. 41GP
27 – Montreal Canadiens, 1976-77. 40GP
– Montreal Canadiens, 1977-78. 40GP
– St. Louis Blues, 1999-2000. 41GP
26 – Boston Bruins, 1971-72. 39GP
– Montreal Canadiens, 1975-76. 40GP
– Edmonton Oilers, 1983-84. 40GP
– Detroit Red Wings, 1995-96. 41GP
– San Jose Sharks, 2006-07. 41GP

Fewest Wins

FEWEST WINS, ONE SEASON:
4 – Quebec Bulldogs, 1919-20. 24GP
– Philadelphia Quakers, 1930-31. 44GP
5 – Toronto Arenas, 1918-19. 18GP
Pittsburgh Pirates, 1929-30. 44GP

FEWEST WINS, ONE SEASON (MINIMUM 70-GAME SCHEDULE):
8 – Washington Capitals, 1974-75. 80GP
9 – Winnipeg Jets, 1980-81. 80GP
10 – Ottawa Senators, 1992-93. 84GP

FEWEST HOME WINS, ONE SEASON:
2 – Chicago Blackhawks, 1927-28. 22GP
3 – Boston Bruins, 1924-25. 15GP
– Chicago Blackhawks, 1928-29. 22GP
– Philadelphia Quakers, 1930-31. 22GP

FEWEST HOME WINS, ONE SEASON (MINIMUM 70-GAME SCHEDULE):
6 – Chicago Blackhawks, 1954-55. 35GP
– Washington Capitals, 1975-76. 40GP
7 – Boston Bruins, 1962-63. 35GP
– Washington Capitals, 1974-75. 40GP
– Winnipeg Jets, 1980-81. 40GP
– Pittsburgh Penguins, 1983-84. 40GP

FEWEST ROAD WINS, ONE SEASON:
0 – Toronto Arenas, 1918-19. 9GP
– Quebec Bulldogs, 1919-20. 12GP
– Pittsburgh Pirates, 1929-30. 22GP
1 – Hamilton Tigers, 1921-22. 12GP
– Toronto St. Patricks, 1925-26. 18GP
– Philadelphia Quakers, 1930-31. 22GP
– New York Americans, 1940-41. 24GP
– Washington Capitals, 1974-75. 40GP
* – Ottawa Senators, 1992-93. 41GP

FEWEST ROAD WINS, ONE SEASON (MINIMUM 70-GAME SCHEDULE):
1 – Washington Capitals, 1974-75. 40GP
*** – Ottawa Senators**, 1992-93. 41GP
2 – Boston Bruins, 1960-61. 35GP
– Los Angeles Kings, 1969-70. 38GP
– New York Islanders, 1972-73. 39GP
– California Golden Seals, 1973-74. 39GP
– Colorado Rockies, 1977-78. 40GP
– Winnipeg Jets, 1980-81. 40GP
– Quebec Nordiques, 1991-92. 40GP

TEAM LOSSES

Fewest Losses

FEWEST LOSSES, ONE SEASON:
5 – Ottawa Senators, 1919-20. 24GP
– Boston Bruins, 1929-30. 44GP
– Montreal Canadiens, 1943-44. 50GP

FEWEST HOME LOSSES, ONE SEASON:
0 – Ottawa Senators, 1922-23. 12GP
– Montreal Canadiens, 1943-44. 25GP
1 – Toronto Arenas, 1917-18. 11GP
– Ottawa Senators, 1918-19. 9GP
– Ottawa Senators, 1919-20. 12GP
– Toronto St. Patricks, 1922-23. 12GP
– Boston Bruins, 1929-30. 22GP
– Boston Bruins, 1930-31. 22GP
– Montreal Canadiens, 1976-77. 40GP
– Quebec Nordiques, 1994-95. 24GP

FEWEST ROAD LOSSES, ONE SEASON:
3 – Montreal Canadiens, 1928-29. 22GP
4 – Ottawa Senators, 1919-20. 12GP
– Montreal Canadiens, 1927-28. 22GP
– Boston Bruins, 1929-30. 20GP
– Boston Bruins, 1940-41. 24GP

FEWEST LOSSES, ONE SEASON (MINIMUM 70-GAME SCHEDULE):
8 – Montreal Canadiens, 1976-77. 80GP
10 – Montreal Canadiens, 1972-73. 78GP
– Montreal Canadiens, 1977-78. 80GP
11 – Montreal Canadiens, 1975-76. 80GP

FEWEST HOME LOSSES, ONE SEASON (MINIMUM 70-GAME SCHEDULE):
1 – Montreal Canadiens, 1976-77. 40GP
2 – Montreal Canadiens, 1961-62. 35GP
– New York Rangers, 1970-71. 39GP
– Philadelphia Flyers, 1975-76. 40GP

FEWEST ROAD LOSSES, ONE SEASON (MINIMUM 70-GAME SCHEDULE):
6 – Montreal Canadiens, 1972-73. 39GP
– Montreal Canadiens, 1974-75. 40GP
– Montreal Canadiens, 1977-78. 40GP
7 – Detroit Red Wings, 1951-52. 35GP
– Montreal Canadiens, 1976-77. 40GP
– Philadelphia Flyers, 1979-80. 40GP
– Boston Bruins, 2003-04. 41GP
– Detroit Red Wings, 2005-06. 41GP

Most Losses

MOST LOSSES, ONE SEASON:
71 – San Jose Sharks, 1992-93. 84GP
70 – Ottawa Senators, 1992-93. 84GP
67 – Washington Capitals, 1974-75. 80GP
61 – Quebec Nordiques, 1989-90. 80GP
– Ottawa Senators, 1993-94. 84GP

MOST HOME LOSSES, ONE SEASON:
***32 – San Jose Sharks**, 1992-93. 41GP
29 – Pittsburgh Penguins, 1983-84. 40GP
* – Ottawa Senators, 1993-94. 41GP

MOST ROAD LOSSES, ONE SEASON:
***40 – Ottawa Senators**, 1992-93. 41GP
39 – Washington Capitals, 1974-75. 40GP
37 – California Golden Seals, 1973-74. 39GP
* – San Jose Sharks, 1992-93. 41GP

* – Does not include neutral site games

TEAM TIES

Most Ties

MOST TIES, ONE SEASON:
24 – Philadelphia Flyers, 1969-70. 76GP
23 – Montreal Canadiens, 1962-63. 70GP
– Chicago Blackhawks, 1973-74. 78GP

MOST HOME TIES, ONE SEASON:
13 – New York Rangers, 1954-55. 35GP
– Philadelphia Flyers, 1969-70. 38GP
– California Golden Seals, 1971-72. 39GP
– California Golden Seals, 1972-73. 39GP
– Chicago Blackhawks, 1973-74. 39GP

MOST ROAD TIES, ONE SEASON:
15 – Philadelphia Flyers, 1976-77. 40GP
14 – Montreal Canadiens, 1952-53. 35GP
– Montreal Canadiens, 1974-75. 40GP
– Philadelphia Flyers, 1975-76. 40GP

Fewest Ties

FEWEST TIES, ONE SEASON (Since 1926-27):
1 – Boston Bruins, 1929-30. 44GP
2 – Montreal Canadiens, 1926-27. 44GP
– New York Americans, 1926-27. 44GP
– Boston Bruins, 1938-39. 48GP
– New York Rangers, 1941-42. 48GP
– San Jose Sharks, 1992-93. 84GP

FEWEST TIES, ONE SEASON (MINIMUM 70-GAME SCHEDULE):
2 – San Jose Sharks, 1992-93. 84GP
3 – New Jersey Devils, 1985-86. 80GP
– Calgary Flames, 1986-87. 80GP
– Vancouver Canucks, 1993-94. 84GP

WINNING STREAKS

LONGEST WINNING STREAK, ONE SEASON:
17 Games – Pittsburgh Penguins, Mar. 9 – Apr. 10, 1993.
15 Games – New York Islanders, Jan. 21 – Feb. 20, 1982.
14 Games – Boston Bruins, Dec. 3, 1929 – Jan. 9, 1930.

LONGEST HOME WINNING STREAK, ONE SEASON:
20 Games – Boston Bruins, Dec. 3, 1929 – Mar. 18, 1930.
– Philadelphia Flyers, Jan. 4 – Apr. 3, 1976.

LONGEST ROAD WINNING STREAK, ONE SEASON:
12 Games – Detroit Red Wings, Mar. 1 – Apr. 15, 2006.
10 Games – Buffalo Sabres, Dec. 10, 1983 – Jan. 23, 1984.
– St. Louis Blues, Jan. 21 – Mar. 2, 2000.
– New Jersey Devils, Feb. 27 – Apr. 7, 2001.
– Buffalo Sabres, Oct. 4 – Nov. 13, 2006.

LONGEST WINNING STREAK FROM START OF SEASON:
10 Games – Toronto Maple Leafs, 1993-94.
– Buffalo Sabres, 2006-07.
8 Games – Toronto Maple Leafs, 1934-35.
– Buffalo Sabres, 1975-76.
– Nashville Predators, 2005-06.
7 Games – Edmonton Oilers, 1983-84.
– Quebec Nordiques, 1985-86.
– Pittsburgh Penguins, 1986-87.
– Pittsburgh Penguins, 1994-95.

LONGEST HOME WINNING STREAK FROM START OF SEASON:
11 Games – Chicago Blackhawks, 1963-64.
10 Games – Ottawa Senators, 1925-26.
9 Games – Montreal Canadiens, 1953-54.
– Chicago Blackhawks, 1971-72.

LONGEST ROAD WINNING STREAK FROM START OF SEASON:
7 Games – Toronto Maple Leafs, Nov. 14 – Dec. 15, 1940.
– Philadelphia Flyers, Oct. 12 – Nov. 16, 1985.
– Detroit Red Wings, Oct. 6 – Nov. 6, 2005.

LONGEST WINNING STREAK, INCLUDING PLAYOFFS:
15 Games – Detroit Red Wings, Feb. 27 – Apr. 5, 1955.
(9 regular-season games, 6 playoff games)
– New Jersey Devils, Mar. 28 – Apr. 29, 2006.
(11 regular-season games, 4 playoff games)

LONGEST HOME WINNING STREAK, INCLUDING PLAYOFFS:
24 Games – Philadelphia Flyers, Jan. 4 – Apr. 25, 1976.
(20 regular-season games, 4 playoff games)

LONGEST ROAD WINNING STREAK, INCLUDING PLAYOFFS:
11 Games – New Jersey Devils, Feb. 27 – Apr. 17, 2001.
(10 regular-season games, 1 playoff game)

UNDEFEATED STREAKS

LONGEST UNDEFEATED STREAK, ONE SEASON:
35 Games – Philadelphia Flyers, Oct. 14, 1979 – Jan. 6, 1980. 25W-10T
28 Games – Montreal Canadiens, Dec. 18, 1977 – Feb. 23, 1978. 23W-5T

LONGEST HOME UNDEFEATED STREAK, ONE SEASON:
34 Games – Montreal Canadiens, Nov. 1, 1976 – Apr. 2, 1977. 28W-6T
27 Games – Boston Bruins, Nov. 22, 1970 – Mar. 20, 1971. 26W-1T

LONGEST ROAD UNDEFEATED STREAK, ONE SEASON:
23 Games – Montreal Canadiens, Nov. 27, 1974 – Mar. 12, 1975. 14W-9T
17 Games – Montreal Canadiens, Dec. 18, 1977 – Mar. 1, 1978. 14W-3T

LONGEST UNDEFEATED STREAK FROM START OF SEASON:
15 Games – Edmonton Oilers, 1984-85. 12W-3T
14 Games – Montreal Canadiens, 1943-44. 11W-3T

LONGEST HOME UNDEFEATED STREAK FROM START OF SEASON:
26 Games – Philadelphia Flyers, Oct. 11, 1979 – Feb. 3, 1980. 19W-7T

LONGEST ROAD UNDEFEATED STREAK FROM START OF SEASON:
15 Games – Detroit Red Wings, Oct. 18 – Dec. 20, 1951. 10W-5T

LONGEST UNDEFEATED STREAK, INCLUDING PLAYOFFS:
24 Games – Montreal Canadiens, Feb. 21 – Apr. 11, 1980.
15W-6T in regular season and 3W in playoffs.
21 Games – Pittsburgh Penguins, Mar. 9 – Apr. 22, 1993.
17W-1T in regular season and 3W in playoffs.

LONGEST HOME UNDEFEATED STREAK, INCLUDING PLAYOFFS:
38 Games – Montreal Canadiens, Nov. 1, 1976 – Apr. 26, 1977.
28W-6T in regular season and 4W in playoffs.

LONGEST ROAD UNDEFEATED STREAK, INCLUDING PLAYOFFS:
13 Games – Philadelphia Flyers, Feb. 26 – Apr. 21, 1977. 6W-4T in regular season and 3W in playoffs.
– Montreal Canadiens, Feb. 26 – Apr. 20, 1980. 6W-4T in regular season and 3W in playoffs.
– New York Islanders, Mar. 16 – May 1, 1980. 3W-3T in regular season and 7W in playoffs.

LOSING STREAKS

LONGEST LOSING STREAK, ONE SEASON:
17 Games – Washington Capitals, Feb. 18 – Mar. 26, 1975.
– San Jose Sharks, Jan. 4 – Feb. 12, 1993.
15 Games – Philadelphia Quakers, Nov. 29, 1930 – Jan. 8, 1931.

LONGEST HOME LOSING STREAK, ONE SEASON:
14 Games – Pittsburgh Penguins, Dec. 31, 2003 – Feb. 22, 2004.
11 Games – Boston Bruins, Dec. 8, 1924 – Feb. 17, 1925.
– Washington Capitals, Feb. 18 – Mar. 30, 1975.
– Ottawa Senators, Oct. 27 – Dec. 8, 1993.
– Atlanta Thrashers, Jan. 24 – Mar. 16, 2000.

LONGEST ROAD LOSING STREAK, ONE SEASON:
***38 Games – Ottawa Senators**, Oct. 10, 1992 – Apr. 3, 1993.
37 Games – Washington Capitals, Oct. 9, 1974 – Mar. 26, 1975.

LONGEST LOSING STREAK FROM START OF SEASON:
11 Games – New York Rangers, 1943-44.
7 Games – Montreal Canadiens, 1938-39.
– Chicago Blackhawks, 1947-48.
– Washington Capitals, 1983-84.
– Chicago Blackhawks, 1997-98.

LONGEST HOME LOSING STREAK FROM START OF SEASON:
8 Games – Los Angeles Kings, Oct. 13 – Nov. 6, 1971.

LONGEST ROAD LOSING STREAK FROM START OF SEASON:
***38 Games – Ottawa Senators**, Oct. 10, 1992 – Apr. 3, 1993.

WINLESS STREAKS

LONGEST WINLESS STREAK, ONE SEASON:
30 Games – Winnipeg Jets, Oct. 19 – Dec. 20, 1980. 23L-7T
27 Games – Kansas City Scouts, Feb. 12 – Apr. 4, 1976. 21L-6T
25 Games – Washington Capitals, Nov. 29, 1975 – Jan. 21, 1976. 22L-3T

LONGEST HOME WINLESS STREAK, ONE SEASON:
17 Games – Ottawa Senators, Oct. 28, 1995 – Jan. 27, 1996. 15L-2T
– Atlanta Thrashers, Jan. 19 – Mar. 29, 2000. 15L-2T
16 Games – Pittsburgh Penguins, Dec. 31, 2003 – Mar. 4, 2004. 15L-1T

LONGEST ROAD WINLESS STREAK, ONE SEASON:
***38 Games – Ottawa Senators**, Oct. 10, 1992 – Apr. 3, 1993. 38L
37 Games – Washington Capitals, Oct. 9, 1974 – Mar. 26, 1975. 37L

LONGEST WINLESS STREAK FROM START OF SEASON:
15 Games – New York Rangers, 1943-44. 14L-1T
11 Games – Pittsburgh Pirates, 1927-28. 8L-3T
– Minnesota North Stars, 1973-74. 5L-6T
– San Jose Sharks, 1995-96. 7L-4T

LONGEST HOME WINLESS STREAK FROM START OF SEASON:
11 Games – Pittsburgh Penguins, Oct. 8 – Nov. 19, 1983. 9L-2T

LONGEST ROAD WINLESS STREAK FROM START OF SEASON:
***38 Games – Ottawa Senators**, Oct. 10, 1992 – Apr. 3, 1993. 38L

NON-SHUTOUT STREAKS

LONGEST NON-SHUTOUT STREAK:
264 Games – Calgary Flames, Nov. 12, 1981 – Jan. 9, 1985.
261 Games – Los Angeles Kings, Mar. 15, 1986 – Oct. 22, 1989.
244 Games – Washington Capitals, Oct. 31, 1989 – Nov. 11, 1993.
236 Games – New York Rangers, Dec. 20, 1989 – Dec. 13, 1992.
230 Games – Quebec Nordiques, Feb. 10, 1980 – Jan. 12, 1983.

LONGEST NON-SHUTOUT STREAK, INCLUDING PLAYOFFS:
264 Games – Los Angeles Kings, Mar. 15, 1986 – Apr. 6, 1989.
(5 playoff games in 1987; 5 in 1988; 2 in 1989).
262 Games – Chicago Blackhawks, Mar. 14, 1970 – Feb. 21, 1973.
(8 playoff games in 1970; 18 in 1971; 8 in 1972).
251 Games – Quebec Nordiques, Feb. 10, 1980 – Jan. 12, 1983.
(5 playoff games in 1981; 16 in 1982).
246 Games – Pittsburgh Penguins, Jan. 7, 1989 – Oct. 26, 1991.
(11 playoff games in 1989; 24 in 1991).

* – Does not include neutral site games

TEAM GOALS

Most Goals

MOST GOALS, ONE SEASON:
446 – Edmonton Oilers, 1983-84. 80GP
426 – Edmonton Oilers, 1985-86. 80GP
424 – Edmonton Oilers, 1982-83. 80GP
417 – Edmonton Oilers, 1981-82. 80GP
401 – Edmonton Oilers, 1984-85. 80GP

MOST GOALS, ONE TEAM, ONE GAME:
16 – Montreal Canadiens, Mar. 3, 1920, at Quebec. Montreal won 16-3.

MOST GOALS, BOTH TEAMS, ONE GAME:
21 – Montreal Canadiens (14), Toronto St. Patricks (7), Jan. 10, 1920, at Montreal.
– Edmonton Oilers (12), Chicago Blackhawks (9), Dec. 11, 1985, at Chicago.
20 – Edmonton Oilers (12), Minnesota North Stars (8), Jan. 4, 1984, at Edmonton.
– Toronto Maple Leafs (11), Edmonton Oilers (9), Jan. 8, 1986, at Toronto.
19 – Montreal Wanderers (10), Toronto Arenas (9), Dec. 19, 1917, at Montreal.
– Montreal Canadiens (16), Quebec Bulldogs (3), Mar. 3, 1920, at Quebec.
– Montreal Canadiens (13), Hamilton Tigers (6), Feb. 26, 1921, at Montreal.
– Boston Bruins (10), New York Rangers (9), Mar. 4, 1944, at Boston.
– Detroit Red Wings (10), Boston Bruins (9), Mar. 16, 1944, at Detroit.
– Vancouver Canucks (10), Minnesota North Stars (9), Oct. 7, 1983, at Vancouver.

MOST GOALS, ONE TEAM, ONE PERIOD:
9 – Buffalo Sabres, Mar. 19, 1981, at Buffalo, second period during 14-4 win over Toronto.
8 – Detroit Red Wings, Jan. 23, 1944, at Detroit, third period during 15-0 win over NY Rangers.
– Boston Bruins, Mar. 16, 1969, at Boston, second period during 11-3 win over Toronto.
– New York Rangers, Nov. 21, 1971, at NY Rangers, third period during 12-1 win over California.
– Philadelphia Flyers, Mar. 31, 1973, at Philadelphia, second period during 10-2 win over NY Islanders.
– Buffalo Sabres, Dec. 21, 1975, at Buffalo, third period during 14-2 win over Washington.
– Minnesota North Stars, Nov. 11, 1981, at Minnesota, second period during 15-2 win over Winnipeg.
– Pittsburgh Penguins, Dec. 17, 1991, at Pittsburgh, second period during 10-2 win over San Jose.
– Washington Capitals, Feb. 3, 1999, at Washington, second period during 10-1 win over Tampa Bay.

MOST GOALS, BOTH TEAMS, ONE PERIOD:
12 – Buffalo Sabres (9), Toronto Maple Leafs (3), Mar. 19, 1981, at Buffalo, second period. Buffalo won 14-4.
– Edmonton Oilers (6), Chicago Blackhawks (6), Dec. 11, 1985, at Chicago, second period. Edmonton won 12-9.
10 – New York Rangers (7), New York Americans (3), Mar. 16, 1939, at NY Americans, third period. NY Rangers won 11-5.
– Toronto Maple Leafs (6), Detroit Red Wings (4), Mar. 17, 1946, at Detroit, third period. Toronto won 11-7.
– Buffalo Sabres (6), Vancouver Canucks (4), Jan. 8, 1976, at Buffalo, third period. Buffalo won 8-5.
– Buffalo Sabres (5), Montreal Canadiens (5), Oct. 26, 1982, at Montreal, first period. Teams tied 7-7.
– Quebec Nordiques (6), Boston Bruins (4), Dec. 7, 1982, at Quebec, second period. Quebec won 10-5.
– Vancouver Canucks (6), Calgary Flames (4), Jan. 16, 1987, at Vancouver, first period. Vancouver won 9-5.
– Detroit Red Wings (7), Winnipeg Jets (3), Nov. 25, 1987, at Detroit, third period. Detroit won 10-8.
– Chicago Blackhawks (5), St. Louis Blues (5), Mar. 15, 1988, at St. Louis, third period. Teams tied 7-7.

MOST CONSECUTIVE GOALS, ONE TEAM, ONE GAME:
15 – Detroit Red Wings, Jan. 23, 1944, at Detroit during 15-0 win over NY Rangers.

Fewest Goals

FEWEST GOALS, ONE SEASON:
33 – Chicago Blackhawks, 1928-29. 44GP
45 – Montreal Maroons, 1924-25. 30GP
46 – Pittsburgh Pirates, 1928-29. 44GP

FEWEST GOALS, ONE SEASON (MINIMUM 70-GAME SCHEDULE):
133 – Chicago Blackhawks, 1953-54. 70GP
147 – Toronto Maple Leafs, 1954-55. 70GP
– Boston Bruins, 1955-56. 70GP
150 – New York Rangers, 1954-55. 70GP

TEAM POWER-PLAY GOALS

MOST POWER-PLAY GOALS, ONE SEASON:
119 – Pittsburgh Penguins, 1988-89. 80GP
113 – Detroit Red Wings, 1992-93. 84GP
111 – New York Rangers, 1987-88. 80GP
110 – Pittsburgh Penguins, 1987-88. 80GP
– Winnipeg Jets, 1987-88. 80GP

TEAM SHORTHAND GOALS

MOST SHORTHAND GOALS, ONE SEASON:
36 – Edmonton Oilers, 1983-84. 80GP
28 – Edmonton Oilers, 1986-87. 80GP
27 – Edmonton Oilers, 1985-86. 80GP
– Edmonton Oilers, 1988-89. 80GP

TEAM GOALS-PER-GAME

HIGHEST GOALS-PER-GAME AVERAGE, ONE SEASON:
5.58 – Edmonton Oilers, 1983-84. 446G in 80GP.
5.38 – Montreal Canadiens, 1919-20. 129G in 24GP.
5.33 – Edmonton Oilers, 1985-86. 426G in 80GP.
5.30 – Edmonton Oilers, 1982-83. 424G in 80GP.
5.23 – Montreal Canadiens, 1917-18. 115G in 22GP.

LOWEST GOALS-PER-GAME AVERAGE, ONE SEASON:
0.75 – Chicago Blackhawks, 1928-29. 33G in 44GP.
1.05 – Pittsburgh Pirates, 1928-29. 46G in 44GP.
1.20 – New York Americans, 1928-29. 53G in 44GP.

TEAM ASSISTS

MOST ASSISTS, ONE SEASON:
737 – Edmonton Oilers, 1985-86. 80GP
736 – Edmonton Oilers, 1983-84. 80GP
706 – Edmonton Oilers, 1981-82. 80GP

FEWEST ASSISTS, ONE SEASON (Since 1926-27):
45 – New York Rangers, 1926-27. 44GP

FEWEST ASSISTS, ONE SEASON (MINIMUM 70-GAME SCHEDULE):
206 – Chicago Blackhawks, 1953-54. 70GP

TEAM TOTAL POINTS

MOST SCORING POINTS, ONE SEASON:
1,182 – Edmonton Oilers, 1983-84. (446G-736A) 80GP
1,163 – Edmonton Oilers, 1985-86. (426G-737A) 80GP
1,123 – Edmonton Oilers, 1981-82. (417G-706A) 80GP

MOST SCORING POINTS, ONE TEAM, ONE GAME:
40 – Buffalo Sabres, Dec. 21, 1975, at Buffalo. Buffalo defeated Washington 14-2, and had 26A.
39 – Minnesota North Stars, Nov. 11, 1981, at Minnesota. Minnesota defeated Winnipeg 15-2, and had 24A.
37 – Detroit Red Wings, Jan. 23, 1944, at Detroit. Detroit defeated NY Rangers 15-0, and had 22A.
– Toronto Maple Leafs, Mar. 16, 1957, at Toronto. Toronto defeated NY Rangers 14-1, and had 23A.
– Buffalo Sabres, Feb. 25, 1978, at Cleveland. Buffalo defeated Cleveland 13-3, and had 24A.
– Calgary Flames, Feb. 10, 1993, at Calgary. Calgary defeated San Jose 13-1, and had 24A.

MOST SCORING POINTS, BOTH TEAMS, ONE GAME:
62 – Edmonton Oilers, Chicago Blackhawks, Dec. 11, 1985, at Chicago. Edmonton won 12-9. Edmonton had 24A, Chicago, 17A.
53 – Quebec Nordiques, Washington Capitals, Feb. 22, 1981, at Washington. Quebec won 11-7. Quebec had 22A, Washington, 13A.
– Edmonton Oilers, Minnesota North Stars, Jan. 4, 1984, at Edmonton. Edmonton won 12-8. Edmonton had 20A, Minnesota, 13A.
– Minnesota North Stars, St. Louis Blues, Jan. 27, 1984, at St. Louis. Minnesota won 10-8. Minnesota had 19A, St. Louis, 16A.
– Toronto Maple Leafs, Edmonton Oilers, Jan. 8, 1986, at Toronto. Toronto won 11-9. Toronto had 17A, Edmonton, 16A.
52 – Montreal Maroons, New York Americans, Feb. 18, 1936, at NY Americans. Teams tied 8-8. NY Americans had 20A, Montreal, 16A. (3A allowed for each goal.)
– Vancouver Canucks, Minnesota North Stars, Oct. 7, 1983, at Vancouver. Vancouver won 10-9. Vancouver had 16A, Minnesota, 17A.

MOST SCORING POINTS, ONE TEAM, ONE PERIOD:
23 – New York Rangers, Nov. 21, 1971, at NY Rangers, third period during 12-1 win over California. NY Rangers had 8G, 15A.
– Buffalo Sabres, Dec. 21, 1975, at Buffalo, third period during 14-2 win over Washington. Buffalo had 8G, 15A.
– Buffalo Sabres, Mar. 19, 1981, at Buffalo, second period during 14-4 win over Toronto. Buffalo had 9G, 14A.
22 – Detroit Red Wings, Jan. 23, 1944, at Detroit, third period during 15-0 win over NY Rangers. Detroit had 8G, 14A.
– Boston Bruins, Mar. 16, 1969, at Boston, second period during 11-3 win over Toronto. Boston had 8G, 14A.
– Minnesota North Stars, Nov. 11, 1981, at Minnesota, second period during 15-2 win over Winnipeg. Minnesota had 8G, 14A.
– Pittsburgh Penguins, Dec. 17, 1991, at Pittsburgh, second period during 10-2 win over San Jose. Pittsburgh had 8G, 14A.
– Washington Capitals, Feb. 3, 1999, at Washington, second period during 10-1 win over Tampa Bay. Washington had 8G, 14A.

MOST SCORING POINTS, BOTH TEAMS, ONE PERIOD:
35 – Edmonton, Oilers, Chicago Blackhawks, Dec. 11, 1985, at Chicago, second period. Edmonton won 12-9. Edmonton had 6G, 12A; Chicago, 6G, 11A.
31 – Buffalo Sabres, Toronto Maple Leafs, Mar. 19, 1981, at Buffalo, second period. Buffalo won 14-4. Buffalo had 9G, 14A; Toronto, 3G, 5A.
29 – Winnipeg Jets, Detroit Red Wings, Nov. 25, 1987, at Detroit, third period. Detroit won 10-8. Detroit had 7G, 13A; Winnipeg, 3G, 6A.
– Chicago Blackhawks, St. Louis Blues, Mar. 15, 1988, at St. Louis, third period. Teams tied 7-7. St. Louis had 5G, 10A; Chicago, 5G, 9A.

FASTEST GOALS

FASTEST SIX GOALS, BOTH TEAMS:

3:00 – Quebec Nordiques, Washington Capitals, Feb. 22, 1981, at Washington. Scorers: Peter Stastny, Quebec, 18:51; Pierre Lacroix, Quebec, 19:57 (first period); Anton Stastny, Quebec, 0:34; Jacques Richard, Quebec, 1:07 and 1:37; Rick Green, Washington, 1:51 (second period). Quebec won 11-7.

3:15 – Montreal Canadiens, Toronto Maple Leafs, Jan. 4, 1944, at Montreal, first period. Scorers: Maurice Richard, Montreal, 14:10; Don Webster, Toronto, 15:13; Fern Majeau, Montreal, 15:41; Phil Watson, Montreal, 15:52; Lorne Carr, Toronto, 16:55; Butch Bouchard, Montreal, 17:25. Montreal won 6-3.

FASTEST FIVE GOALS, BOTH TEAMS:

1:24 – Chicago Blackhawks, Toronto Maple Leafs, Oct. 15, 1983, at Toronto, second period. Scorers: Gaston Gingras, Toronto, 16:49; Denis Savard, Chicago, 17:12; Steve Larmer, Chicago, 17:27; Denis Savard, Chicago, 17:42; John Anderson, Toronto, 18:13. Toronto won 10-8.

1:39 – Detroit Red Wings, Toronto Maple Leafs, Nov. 15, 1944, at Toronto, third period. Scorers: Ted Kennedy, Toronto, 10:36 and 10:55; Harold Jackson, Detroit, 11:48; Steve Wojciechowski, Detroit, 12:02; Don Grosso, Detroit, 12:15. Detroit won 8-4.

FASTEST FIVE GOALS, ONE TEAM:

2:07 – Pittsburgh Penguins, Nov. 22, 1972, at Pittsburgh, third period. Scorers: Bryan Hextall, Jr., 12:00; Jean Pronovost, 12:18; Al McDonough, 13:40; Ken Schinkel, 13:49; Ron Schock, 14:07. Pittsburgh defeated St. Louis 10-4.

2:37 – New York Islanders, Jan. 26, 1982, at NY Islanders, first period. Scorers: Duane Sutter, 1:31; John Tonelli, 2:30; Bryan Trottier, 2:46 and 3:31; Duane Sutter, 4:08. NY Islanders defeated Pittsburgh 9-2.

2:55 – Boston Bruins, Dec. 19, 1974, at Boston. Scorers: Bobby Schmautz, 19:13 (first period); Ken Hodge, 0:18; Phil Esposito, 0:43; Don Marcotte, 0:58; John Bucyk, 2:08 (second period). Boston defeated NY Rangers 11-3.

FASTEST FOUR GOALS, BOTH TEAMS:

0:53 – Chicago Blackhawks, Toronto Maple Leafs, Oct. 15, 1983, at Toronto, second period. Scorers: Gaston Gingras, Toronto, 16:49; Denis Savard, Chicago, 17:12; Steve Larmer, Chicago, 17:27; Denis Savard, Chicago, 17:42. Toronto won 10-8.

0:57 – Quebec Nordiques, Detroit Red Wings, Jan. 27, 1990, at Quebec, first period. Scorers: Paul Gillis, Quebec, 18:01; Claude Loiselle, Quebec, 18:12; Joe Sakic, Quebec, 18:27; Jimmy Carson, Detroit, 18:58. Detroit won 8-6.

1:01 – Colorado Rockies, New York Rangers, Jan. 15, 1980, at NY Rangers, first period. Scorers: Doug Sulliman, NY Rangers, 7:52; Eddie Johnstone, NY Rangers, 7:57; Warren Miller, NY Rangers, 8:20; Rob Ramage, Colorado, 8:53. Teams tied 6-6.

– Chicago Blackhawks, Toronto Maple Leafs, Oct. 15, 1983, at Toronto, second period. Scorers: Denis Savard, Chicago, 17:12; Steve Larmer, Chicago, 17:27; Denis Savard, Chicago, 17:42; John Anderson, Toronto, 18:13. Toronto won 10-8.

FASTEST FOUR GOALS, ONE TEAM:

1:20 – Boston Bruins, Jan. 21, 1945, at Boston, second period. Scorers: Bill Thoms, 6:34; Frank Mario, 7:08 and 7:27; Ken Smith, 7:54. Boston defeated NY Rangers 14-3.

FASTEST THREE GOALS, BOTH TEAMS:

0:15 – Minnesota North Stars, New York Rangers, Feb. 10, 1983, at Minnesota, second period. Scorers: Mark Pavelich, NY Rangers, 19:18; Ron Greschner, NY Rangers, 19:27; Willi Plett, Minnesota, 19:33. Minnesota won 7-5.

0:18 – Montreal Canadiens, New York Rangers, Dec. 12, 1963, at Montreal, first period. Scorers: Dave Balon, Montreal, 0:58; Gilles Tremblay, Montreal, 1:04; Camille Henry, NY Rangers, 1:16. Montreal won 6-4.

– California Golden Seals, Buffalo Sabres, Feb. 1, 1976, at California, third period. Scorers: Jim Moxey, California, 19:38; Wayne Merrick, California, 19:45; Danny Gare, Buffalo, 19:56. Buffalo won 9-5.

FASTEST THREE GOALS, ONE TEAM:

0:20 – Boston Bruins, Feb. 25, 1971, at Boston, third period. Scorers: John Bucyk, 4:50; Ed Westfall, 5:02; Ted Green, 5:10. Boston defeated Vancouver 8-3.

0:21 – Chicago Blackhawks, Mar. 23, 1952, at NY Rangers, third period. Bill Mosienko scored all three goals, at 6:09, 6:20 and 6:30. Chicago defeated NY Rangers 7-6.

– Washington Capitals, Nov. 23, 1990, at Washington, first period. Scorers: Michal Pivonka, 16:18; Stephen Leach, 16:29 and 16:39. Washington defeated Pittsburgh 7-3.

FASTEST THREE GOALS FROM START OF PERIOD, BOTH TEAMS:

1:05 – Hartford Whalers, Montreal Canadiens, Mar. 11, 1989, at Montreal, second period. Scorers: Kevin Dineen, Hartford, 0:11; Guy Carbonneau, Montreal, 0:36; Petr Svoboda, Montreal, 1:05. Montreal won 5-3.

FASTEST THREE GOALS FROM START OF PERIOD, ONE TEAM:

0:53 – Calgary Flames, Feb. 10, 1993, at Calgary, third period. Scorers: Gary Suter, 0:17; Chris Lindberg, 0:40; Ron Stern, 0:53. Calgary defeated San Jose 13-1.

FASTEST TWO GOALS, BOTH TEAMS:

0:02 – St. Louis Blues, Boston Bruins, Dec. 19, 1987, at Boston, third period. Scorers: Ken Linseman, Boston, 19:50; Doug Gilmour, St. Louis, 19:52. St. Louis won 7-5.

0:03 – Chicago Blackhawks, Minnesota North Stars, Nov. 5, 1988, at Minnesota, third period. Scorers: Steve Thomas, Chicago, 6:03; Dave Gagner, Minnesota, 6:06. Teams tied 5-5.

FASTEST TWO GOALS, ONE TEAM:

0:03 – Minnesota Wild, Jan. 21, 2004, at Minnesota, third period. Scorers: Jim Dowd, 19:44; Richard Park, 19:47. Minnesota defeated Chicago 4-2.

0:04 – Montreal Maroons, Jan. 3, 1931, at Montreal, third period. Nels Stewart scored both goals, at 8:24 and 8:28. Mtl. Maroons defeated Boston 5-3.

– Buffalo Sabres, Oct. 17, 1974, at Buffalo, third period. Scorers: Lee Fogolin, Jr., 14:55; Don Luce, 14:59. Buffalo defeated California 6-1.

– Toronto Maple Leafs, Dec. 29, 1988, at Quebec, third period. Scorers: Ed Olczyk, 5:24; Gary Leeman, 5:28. Toronto defeated Quebec 6-5.

– Calgary Flames, Oct. 17, 1989, at Quebec, third period. Scorers: Doug Gilmour, 19:45; Paul Ranheim, 19:49. Teams tied 8-8.

– Winnipeg Jets, Dec. 15, 1995, at Winnipeg, second period. Deron Quint scored both goals, at 7:51 and 7:55. Winnipeg defeated Edmonton 9-4.

FASTEST TWO GOALS FROM START OF GAME, ONE TEAM:

0:24 – Edmonton Oilers, Mar. 28, 1982, at Los Angeles. Scorers: Mark Messier, 0:14; Dave Lumley, 0:24. Edmonton defeated Los Angeles 6-2.

0:27 – Boston Bruins, Feb. 14, 2003, at Florida. Mike Knuble scored both goals, at 0:10 and 0:27. Calgary defeated Hartford 6-1.

0:29 – Pittsburgh Penguins, Dec. 6, 1980, at Pittsburgh. Scorers: George Ferguson, 0:17; Greg Malone, 0:29. Pittsburgh defeated Chicago 6-4.

FASTEST TWO GOALS FROM START OF PERIOD, BOTH TEAMS:

0:14 – New York Rangers, Quebec Nordiques, Nov. 5, 1983, at Quebec, third period. Scorers: Andre Savard, Quebec, 0:08; Pierre Larouche, NY Rangers, 0:14. Teams tied 4-4.

0:25 – St. Louis Blues, Chicago Blackhawks, Feb. 2, 2006, at St. Louis, second period. Scorers: Peter Cajanek, St. Louis, 0:10; Tyler Arnason, Chicago, 0:25. St. Louis won 6-5.

0:28 – Boston Bruins, Montreal Canadiens, Oct. 11, 1989, at Montreal, third period. Scorers: Jim Wiemer, Boston 0:10; Tom Chorske, Montreal 0:28. Montreal won 4-2.

FASTEST TWO GOALS FROM START OF PERIOD, ONE TEAM:

0:21 – Chicago Blackhawks, Nov. 5, 1983, at Minnesota, second period. Scorers: Ken Yaremchuk, 0:12; Darryl Sutter, 0:21. Minnesota defeated Chicago 10-5.

0:24 – Edmonton Oilers, Mar. 28, 1982, at Los Angeles, first period. Scorers: Mark Messier, 0:14; Dave Lumley, 0:24. Edmonton defeated Los Angeles 6-2.

0:29 – Pittsburgh Penguins, Dec. 6, 1980, at Pittsburgh, first period. Scorers: George Ferguson, 0:17; Greg Malone, 0:29. Pittsburgh defeated Chicago 6-4.

50, 40, 30, 20-GOAL SCORERS

MOST 50-OR-MORE GOAL SCORERS, ONE SEASON:

3 – Edmonton Oilers, 1983-84. 80GP. Wayne Gretzky, 87; Glenn Anderson, 54; Jari Kurri, 52.
– Edmonton Oilers, 1985-86. 80GP. Jari Kurri, 68; Glenn Anderson, 54; Wayne Gretzky, 52.
2 – Boston Bruins, 1970-71. 78GP. Phil Esposito, 76; John Bucyk, 51.
– Boston Bruins, 1973-74. 78GP. Phil Esposito, 68; Ken Hodge, 50.
– Philadelphia Flyers, 1975-76. 80GP. Reggie Leach, 61; Bill Barber, 50.
– Pittsburgh Penguins, 1975-76. 80GP. Pierre Larouche, 53; Jean Pronovost, 52.
– Montreal Canadiens, 1976-77. 80GP. Steve Shutt, 60; Guy Lafleur, 56.
– Los Angeles Kings, 1979-80. 80GP. Charlie Simmer, 56; Marcel Dionne, 53.
– Montreal Canadiens, 1979-80. 80GP. Pierre Larouche, 50; Guy Lafleur, 50.
– Los Angeles Kings, 1980-81. 80GP. Marcel Dionne, 58; Charlie Simmer, 56.
– Edmonton Oilers, 1981-82. 80GP. Wayne Gretzky, 92; Mark Messier, 50.
– New York Islanders, 1981-82. 80GP. Mike Bossy, 64; Bryan Trottier, 50.
– Edmonton Oilers, 1984-85. 80GP. Wayne Gretzky, 73; Jari Kurri, 71.
– Washington Capitals, 1984-85. 80GP. Bob Carpenter, 53; Mike Gartner, 50.
– Edmonton Oilers, 1986-87. 80GP. Wayne Gretzky, 62; Jari Kurri, 54.
– Calgary Flames, 1987-88. 80GP. Joe Nieuwendyk, 51; Hakan Loob, 50.
– Los Angeles Kings, 1987-88. 80GP. Jimmy Carson, 55; Luc Robitaille, 53.
– Calgary Flames, 1988-89. 80GP. Joe Nieuwendyk, 51; Joe Mullen, 51.
– Los Angeles Kings, 1988-89. 80GP. Bernie Nicholls, 70; Wayne Gretzky, 54.
– Buffalo Sabres, 1992-93. 84GP. Alexander Mogilny, 76; Pat LaFontaine, 53.
– Pittsburgh Penguins, 1992-93. 84GP. Mario Lemieux, 69; Kevin Stevens, 55.
– St. Louis Blues, 1992-93. 84GP. Brett Hull, 54; Brendan Shanahan, 51.
– Detroit Red Wings, 1993-94. 84GP. Sergei Fedorov, 56; Ray Sheppard, 52.
– St. Louis Blues, 1993-94. 84GP. Brett Hull, 57; Brendan Shanahan, 52.
– Pittsburgh Penguins, 1995-96. 82GP. Mario Lemieux, 69; Jaromir Jagr, 62.

MOST 40-OR-MORE GOAL SCORERS, ONE SEASON:

4 – Edmonton Oilers, 1982-83. 80GP. Wayne Gretzky, 71; Glenn Anderson, 48; Mark Messier, 48; Jari Kurri, 45.
– Edmonton Oilers, 1983-84. 80GP. Wayne Gretzky, 87; Glenn Anderson, 54; Jari Kurri, 52; Paul Coffey, 40.
– Edmonton Oilers, 1984-85. 80GP. Wayne Gretzky, 73; Jari Kurri, 71; Mike Krushelnyski, 43; Glenn Anderson, 42.
– Edmonton Oilers, 1985-86. 80GP. Jari Kurri, 68; Glenn Anderson, 54; Wayne Gretzky, 52; Paul Coffey, 48.
– Calgary Flames, 1987-88. 80GP. Joe Nieuwendyk, 51; Hakan Loob, 50; Mike Bullard, 48; Joe Mullen, 40.
3 – Boston Bruins, 1970-71. 78GP. Phil Esposito, 76; John Bucyk, 51; Ken Hodge, 43.
– New York Rangers, 1971-72. 78GP. Vic Hadfield, 50; Jean Ratelle, 46; Rod Gilbert, 43.
– Buffalo Sabres, 1975-76. 80GP. Danny Gare, 50; Rick Martin, 49; Gilbert Perreault, 44.
– Montreal Canadiens, 1979-80. 80GP. Guy Lafleur, 50; Pierre Larouche, 50; Steve Shutt, 47.
– Buffalo Sabres, 1979-80. 80GP. Danny Gare, 56; Rick Martin, 45; Gilbert Perreault, 40.
– Los Angeles Kings, 1980-81. 80GP. Marcel Dionne, 58; Charlie Simmer, 56; Dave Taylor, 47.
– Los Angeles Kings, 1984-85. 80GP. Marcel Dionne, 46; Bernie Nicholls, 46; Dave Taylor, 41.
– New York Islanders, 1984-85. 80GP. Mike Bossy, 58; Brent Sutter, 42; John Tonelli, 42.
– Chicago Blackhawks, 1985-86. 80GP. Denis Savard, 47; Troy Murray, 45; Al Secord, 40.

– Chicago Blackhawks, 1987-88. 80GP. Denis Savard, 44; Rick Vaive, 43; Steve Larmer, 41.
– Edmonton Oilers, 1987-88. 80GP. Craig Simpson, 43; Jari Kurri, 43; Wayne Gretzky, 40.
– Los Angeles Kings, 1988-89. 80GP. Bernie Nicholls, 70; Wayne Gretzky, 54; Luc Robitaille, 46.
– Los Angeles Kings, 1990-91. 80GP. Luc Robitaille, 45; Tomas Sandstrom, 45; Wayne Gretzky, 41.
– Pittsburgh Penguins, 1991-92. 80GP. Kevin Stevens, 54; Mario Lemieux, 44; Joe Mullen, 42.
– Pittsburgh Penguins, 1992-93. 84GP. Mario Lemieux, 69; Kevin Stevens, 55; Rick Tocchet, 48.
– Calgary Flames, 1993-94. 84GP. Gary Roberts, 41; Robert Reichel, 40; Theoren Fleury, 40.
– Pittsburgh Penguins, 1995-96. 82GP. Mario Lemieux, 69; Jaromir Jagr, 62; Petr Nedved, 45.

MOST 30-OR-MORE GOAL SCORERS, ONE SEASON:
6 – Buffalo Sabres, 1974-75. 80GP. Rick Martin, 52; Rene Robert, 40; Gilbert Perreault, 39; Don Luce, 33; Rick Dudley, 31; Danny Gare, 31.
– New York Islanders, 1977-78. 80GP. Mike Bossy, 53; Bryan Trottier, 46; Clark Gillies, 35; Denis Potvin, 30; Bob Nystrom, 30; Bob Bourne, 30.
– Winnipeg Jets, 1984-85. 80GP. Dale Hawerchuk, 53; Paul MacLean, 41; Laurie Boschman, 32; Brian Mullen, 32; Doug Smail, 31; Thomas Steen, 30.
5 – Chicago Blackhawks, 1968-69. 76GP
– Boston Bruins, 1970-71. 78GP
– Montreal Canadiens, 1971-72. 78GP
– Philadelphia Flyers, 1972-73. 78GP
– Boston Bruins, 1973-74. 78GP
– Montreal Canadiens, 1974-75. 80GP
– Montreal Canadiens, 1975-76. 80GP
– Pittsburgh Penguins, 1975-76. 80GP
– New York Islanders, 1978-79. 80GP
– Detroit Red Wings, 1979-80. 80GP
– Philadelphia Flyers, 1979-80. 80GP
– New York Islanders, 1980-81. 80GP
– St. Louis Blues, 1980-81. 80GP
– Chicago Blackhawks, 1981-82. 80GP
– Edmonton Oilers, 1981-82. 80GP
– Montreal Canadiens, 1981-82. 80GP
– Quebec Nordiques, 1981-82. 80GP
– Washington Capitals, 1981-82. 80GP
– Edmonton Oilers, 1982-83. 80GP
– Edmonton Oilers, 1983-84. 80GP
– Edmonton Oilers, 1984-85. 80GP
– Los Angeles Kings, 1984-85. 80GP
– Edmonton Oilers, 1985-86. 80GP
– Edmonton Oilers, 1986-87. 80GP
– Edmonton Oilers, 1987-88. 80GP
– Edmonton Oilers, 1988-89. 80GP
– Detroit Red Wings, 1991-92. 80GP
– New York Rangers, 1991-92. 80GP
– Pittsburgh Penguins, 1991-92. 80GP
– Detroit Red Wings, 1992-93. 84GP
– Pittsburgh Penguins, 1992-93. 84GP

MOST 20-OR-MORE GOAL SCORERS, ONE SEASON:
11 – Boston Bruins, 1977-78. 80GP. Peter McNab, 41; Terry O'Reilly, 29; Bobby Schmautz, 27; Stan Jonathan, 27; Jean Ratelle, 25; Rick Middleton, 25; Wayne Cashman, 24; Gregg Sheppard, 23; Brad Park, 22; Don Marcotte, 20; Bob Miller, 20.
10 – Boston Bruins, 1970-71. 78GP
– Montreal Canadiens, 1974-75. 80GP
– St. Louis Blues, 1980-81. 80GP

100-POINT SCORERS

MOST 100 OR-MORE-POINT SCORERS, ONE SEASON:
4 – Boston Bruins, 1970-71. 78GP. Phil Esposito, 76G-76A-152PTS; Bobby Orr, 37G-102A-139PTS; John Bucyk, 51G-65A-116PTS; Ken Hodge, 43G-62A-105PTS.
– Edmonton Oilers, 1982-83. 80GP. Wayne Gretzky, 71G-125A-196PTS; Mark Messier, 48G-58A-106PTS; Glenn Anderson, 48G-56A-104PTS; Jari Kurri, 45G-59A-104PTS.
– Edmonton Oilers, 1983-84. 80GP. Wayne Gretzky, 87G-118A-205PTS; Paul Coffey, 40G-86A-126PTS; Jari Kurri, 52G-61A-113PTS; Mark Messier, 37G-64A-101PTS.
– Edmonton Oilers,1985-86. 80GP. Wayne Gretzky, 52G-163A-215PTS; Paul Coffey, 48G-90A-138PTS; Jari Kurri, 68G-63A-131PTS; Glenn Anderson, 54G-48A-102PTS.
– Pittsburgh Penguins,1992-93. 84GP. Mario Lemieux, 69G-91A-160PTS; Kevin Stevens, 55G-56A-111PTS; Rick Tocchet, 48G-61A-109PTS; Ron Francis, 24G-76A-100PTS.
3 – Boston Bruins, 1973-74. 78GP. Phil Esposito, 68G-77A-145PTS; Bobby Orr, 32G-90A-122PTS; Ken Hodge, 50G-55A-105PTS.
– New York Islanders, 1978-79. 80GP. Bryan Trottier, 47G-87A-134PTS; Mike Bossy, 69G-57A-126PTS; Denis Potvin, 31G-70A-101PTS.
– Los Angeles Kings, 1980-81. 80GP. Marcel Dionne, 58G-77A-135PTS; Dave Taylor, 47G-65A-112PTS; Charlie Simmer, 56G-49A-105PTS.
– Edmonton Oilers, 1984-85. 80GP. Wayne Gretzky, 73G-135A-208PTS; Jari Kurri, 71G-64A-135PTS; Paul Coffey, 37G-84A-121PTS.
– New York Islanders, 1984-85. 80GP. Mike Bossy, 58G-59A-117PTS; Brent Sutter, 42G-60A-102PTS; John Tonelli, 42G-58A-100PTS.
– Edmonton Oilers, 1986-87. 80GP. Wayne Gretzky, 62G-121A-183PTS; Jari Kurri, 54G-54A-108PTS; Mark Messier, 37G-70A-107PTS.
– Pittsburgh Penguins, 1988-89. 80GP. Mario Lemieux, 85G-114A-199PTS; Rob Brown, 49G-66A-115PTS; Paul Coffey, 30G-83A-113PTS.
– Pittsburgh Penguins, 1995-96. 82GP. Mario Lemieux, 69G-92A-161PTS; Jaromir Jagr, 62G-87A-149PTS; Ron Francis, 27G-92A-119PTS.

SHOTS ON GOAL

MOST SHOTS, BOTH TEAMS, ONE GAME:
141 – New York Americans, Pittsburgh Pirates, Dec. 26, 1925, at NY Americans. NY Americans won 3-1 with 73 shots; Pittsburgh had 68 shots.

MOST SHOTS, ONE TEAM, ONE GAME:
83 – Boston Bruins, Mar. 4, 1941, at Boston. Boston defeated Chicago 3-2.
73 – New York Americans, Dec. 26, 1925, at NY Americans. NY Americans defeated Pittsburgh 3-1.
– Boston Bruins, Mar. 21, 1991, at Boston. Boston tied Quebec 3-3.
72 – Boston Bruins, Dec. 10, 1970, at Boston. Boston defeated Buffalo 8-2.

MOST SHOTS, ONE TEAM, ONE PERIOD:
33 – Boston Bruins, Mar. 4, 1941, at Boston, second period. Boston defeated Chicago 3-2.

TEAM GOALS AGAINST

Fewest Goals Against

FEWEST GOALS AGAINST, ONE SEASON:
42 – Ottawa Senators, 1925-26. 36GP
43 – Montreal Canadiens, 1928-29. 44GP
48 – Montreal Canadiens, 1923-24. 24GP
– Montreal Canadiens, 1927-28. 44GP

FEWEST GOALS AGAINST, ONE SEASON (MINIMUM 70-GAME SCHEDULE):
131 – Toronto Maple Leafs, 1953-54. 70GP
– Montreal Canadiens, 1955-56. 70GP
132 – Detroit Red Wings, 1953-54. 70GP
133 – Detroit Red Wings, 1951-52. 70GP
– Detroit Red Wings, 1952-53. 70GP

LOWEST GOALS-AGAINST-PER-GAME AVERAGE, ONE SEASON:
0.98 – Montreal Canadiens, 1928-29. 43GA in 44GP.
1.09 – Montreal Canadiens, 1927-28. 48GA in 44GP.
1.17 – Ottawa Senators, 1925-26. 42GA in 36GP.

Most Goals Against

MOST GOALS AGAINST, ONE SEASON:
446 – Washington Capitals, 1974-75. 80GP
415 – Detroit Red Wings, 1985-86. 80GP
414 – San Jose Sharks, 1992-93. 84GP
407 – Quebec Nordiques, 1989-90. 80GP
403 – Hartford Whalers, 1982-83. 80GP

HIGHEST GOALS-AGAINST-PER-GAME AVERAGE, ONE SEASON:
7.38 – Quebec Bulldogs, 1919-20. 177GA in 24GP.
6.20 – New York Rangers, 1943-44. 310GA in 50GP.
5.58 – Washington Capitals, 1974-75. 446GA in 80GP.

MOST POWER-PLAY GOALS AGAINST, ONE SEASON:
122 – Chicago Blackhawks, 1988-89. 80GP
120 – Pittsburgh Penguins, 1987-88. 80GP
116 – Washington Capitals, 2005-06. 82GP
115 – New Jersey Devils, 1988-89. 80GP
– Ottawa Senators, 1992-93. 84GP
114 – Los Angeles Kings, 1992-93. 84GP

MOST SHORTHAND GOALS AGAINST, ONE SEASON:
22 – Pittsburgh Penguins, 1984-85. 80GP
– Minnesota North Stars, 1991-92. 80GP
– Colorado Avalanche, 1995-96. 82GP
21 – Calgary Flames, 1984-85. 80GP
– Pittsburgh Penguins, 1989-90. 80GP

SHUTOUTS

MOST SHUTOUTS, ONE SEASON:
22 – Montreal Canadiens, 1928-29. All by George Hainsworth. 44GP
16 – New York Americans, 1928-29. Roy Worters 13, Flat Walsh 3. 44GP
15 – Ottawa Senators, 1925-26. All by Alex Connell. 36GP
– Ottawa Senators, 1927-28. All by Alex Connell. 44GP
– Boston Bruins, 1927-28. All by Hal Winkler. 44GP
– Chicago Blackhawks, 1969-70. All by Tony Esposito. 76GP

MOST CONSECUTIVE SHUTOUTS, ONE SEASON:
6 – Ottawa Senators, Jan. 31 – Feb. 18, 1928. All by Alex Connell.

MOST CONSECUTIVE SHUTOUTS TO START SEASON:
5 – Toronto Maple Leafs, Nov. 13 – 22, 1930. Lorne Chabot 3, Benny Grant 2.

MOST GAMES SHUTOUT, ONE SEASON:
20 – Chicago Blackhawks, 1928-29. 44GP

MOST CONSECUTIVE GAMES SHUTOUT:
8 – Chicago Blackhawks, Feb. 7 – 28, 1929.

MOST CONSECUTIVE GAMES SHUTOUT TO START SEASON:
3 – Montreal Maroons, Nov. 11 – 18, 1930.

TEAM SHOOTOUT RECORDS

MOST SHOOTOUT GAMES, ONE SEASON:
18 – New Jersey, 2006-07
17 – Minnesota, 2006-07
16 – Edmonton, 2005-06
– Pittsburgh, 2006-07

MOST SHOOTOUT GAMES, ALL-TIME:
31 – New Jersey
26 – Dallas
25 – Minnesota, NY Islanders, NY Rangers, Washington

MOST SHOOTOUT WINS, ONE SEASON:
12 – Dallas, 2005-06, 13GP
10 – Tampa Bay, 2006-07, 12GP
– Buffalo, 2006-07, 14GP
– Pittsburgh, 2006-07, 16GP
– Minnesota, 2006-07, 17GP
– New Jersey, 2006-07, 18GP

MOST SHOOTOUT WINS, ALL-TIME:
21 – Dallas, 26GP
19 – New Jersey, 31GP
17 – NY Islanders, 25GP

MOST SHOOTOUT HOME WINS, ONE SEASON:
7 – Minnesota, 2006-07, 11GP
6 – NY Islanders, 2005-06, 7GP
– New Jersey, 2006-07, 12GP

MOST SHOOTOUT HOME WINS, ALL-TIME:
10 – NY Islanders, 12GP
– New Jersey, 17GP
9 – Minnesota, 14GP

MOST SHOOTOUT ROAD WINS, ONE SEASON:
7 – Dallas, 2005-06, 8GP
– Dallas, 2006-07, 9GP
6 – Tampa Bay, 2006-07, 8GP

MOST SHOOTOUT ROAD WINS, ALL-TIME:
14 – Dallas, 17GP
9 – Buffalo, 14GP
– Columbus, 14GP
– New Jersey, 14GP

MOST SHOOTOUT SHOTS TAKEN, ONE SEASON:
62 – Minnesota, 2006-07, 17GP
– New Jersey, 2006-07, 18GP
58 – NY Islanders, 2006-07, 13GP

MOST SHOOTOUT SHOTS TAKEN, ALL-TIME:
107 – New Jersey, 31GP
106 – NY Rangers, 25GP
99 – NY Islanders, 25GP

MOST SHOOTOUT GOALS SCORED, ONE SEASON:
27 – Minnesota, 2006-07, 17GP
25 – New Jersey, 2006-07, 18GP
24 – Dallas, 2005-06, 13GP

MOST SHOOTOUT GOALS SCORED, ALL-TIME:
43 – New Jersey, 31GP
42 – Dallas, 26GP
36 – Minnesota, 25GP

BEST SHOOTOUT SCORING PERCENTAGE, ONE SEASON:
.583 – San Jose, 2006-07, 4GP (7G, 12S)
.571 – Dallas, 2005-06, 13GP (24G, 42S)
.517 – Atlanta, 2006-07, 11GP (15G, 29S)

BEST SHOOTOUT SCORING PERCENTAGE, ALL-TIME:
.452 – Dallas, 26GP (42G, 93S)
.441 – Nashville, 20GP (26G, 59S)
.424 – Los Angeles, 17GP (28G, 66S)

FEWEST SHOOTOUT GOALS AGAINST, ONE SEASON:
3 – Los Angeles, 2005-06, 7GP (21SA)
4 – Montreal, 2005-06, 5GP (15SA)
6 – Phoenix, 2006-07, 7GP (29SA)
– Tampa Bay, 2006-07, 12GP (53SA)

FEWEST SHOOTOUT GOALS AGAINST, ALL-TIME:
13 – Phoenix, 14 GP (54SA)
15 – Tampa Bay, 22GP (80SA)
18 – Carolina, 15GP (53SA)

BEST SHOOTOUT WINNING PERCENTAGE, ONE SEASON:
.923 – Dallas, 2005-06, 13GP (12W)
.857 – Los Angeles, 2005-06, 7GP (6W)
.833 – Tampa Bay, 2006-07, 12GP (10W)

BEST SHOOTOUT WINNING PERCENTAGE, ALL-TIME:
.808 – Dallas, 26GP (21W)
.727 – Tampa Bay, 22GP (16W)
.680 – NY Islanders, 25GP (17W)

TEAM PENALTIES

MOST PENALTY MINUTES, ONE SEASON:
2,713 – Buffalo Sabres, 1991-92. 80GP
2,670 – Pittsburgh Penguins, 1988-89. 80GP
2,663 – Chicago Blackhawks, 1991-92. 80GP
2,643 – Calgary Flames, 1991-92. 80GP
2,621 – Philadelphia Flyers, 1980-81. 80GP

MOST PENALTIES, BOTH TEAMS, ONE GAME:
85 – Edmonton Oilers (44), Los Angeles Kings (41), Feb. 28, 1990, at Los Angeles. Edmonton received 26 minors, 7 majors, 6 10-minute misconducts, 4 game misconducts and 1 match penalty; Los Angeles received 26 minors, 9 majors, 3 10-minute misconducts and 3 game misconducts.

MOST PENALTY MINUTES, BOTH TEAMS, ONE GAME:
419 – Ottawa Senators (206), Philadelphia Flyers (213), Mar. 5, 2004, at Philadelphia. Ottawa received 8 minors, 10 majors, 4 10-minute misconducts and 10 game misconducts. Philadelphia received 9 minors, 11 majors, 4 10-minute misconducts and 10 game misconducts.

MOST PENALTIES, ONE TEAM, ONE GAME:
44 – Edmonton Oilers, Feb. 28, 1990, at Los Angeles. Edmonton received 26 minors, 7 majors, 6 10-minute misconducts, 4 game misconducts and 1 match penalty.
42 – Minnesota North Stars, Feb. 26, 1981, at Boston. Minnesota received 18 minors, 13 majors, 4 10-minute misconducts and 7 game misconducts.
– Boston Bruins, Feb. 26, 1981, at Boston vs. Minnesota. Boston received 20 minors, 13 majors, 3 10-minute misconducts and 6 game misconducts.

MOST PENALTY MINUTES, ONE TEAM, ONE GAME:
213 – Philadelphia Flyers, Mar. 5, 2004, at Philadelphia. Philadelphia received 9 minors, 11 majors, 4 10-minute misconducts and 10 game misconducts.

MOST PENALTIES, BOTH TEAMS, ONE PERIOD:
67 – Minnesota North Stars (34), Boston Bruins (33), Feb. 26, 1981, at Boston, first period. Minnesota received 15 minors, 8 majors, 4 10-minute misconducts and 7 game misconducts. Boston had 16 minors, 8 majors, 3 10-minute misconducts and 6 game misconducts.

MOST PENALTY MINUTES, BOTH TEAMS, ONE PERIOD:
409 – Ottawa Senators (200), Philadelphia Flyers (209), Mar. 5, 2004, at Philadelphia, third period. Ottawa received 5 minors, 10 majors, 4 10-minute misconducts and 10 game misconducts. Philadelphia received 7 minors, 11 majors, 4 10-minute misconducts and 10 game misconducts.

MOST PENALTIES, ONE TEAM, ONE PERIOD:
34 – Minnesota North Stars, Feb. 26, 1981, at Boston, first period. Minnesota received 15 minors, 8 majors, 4 10-minute misconducts and 7 game misconducts.

MOST PENALTY MINUTES, ONE TEAM, ONE PERIOD:
209 – Philadelphia Flyers, Mar. 5, 2004, at Philadelphia vs. Ottawa, third period. Philadelphia received 7 minors, 11 majors, 4 10-minute misconducts and 10 game misconducts.
200 – Ottawa Senators, Mar. 5, 2004, at Philadelphia, third period. Ottawa received 5 minors, 10 majors, 4 10-minute misconducts and 10 game misconducts.

Individual Records

Regular Season

SEASONS

MOST SEASONS:
26 – Gordie Howe, Detroit, 1946-47 – 1970-71; Hartford, 1979-80.
25 – Mark Messier, Edmonton, NY Rangers, Vancouver, 1979-80 – 2003-04.
24 – Alex Delvecchio, Detroit, 1950-51 – 1973-74.
– Tim Horton, Toronto, NY Rangers, Pittsburgh, Buffalo, 1949-50, 1951-52 – 1973-74.
23 – John Bucyk, Detroit, Boston, 1955-56 – 1977-78.
– Ron Francis, Hartford, Pittsburgh, Carolina, Toronto, 1981-82 – 2003-04.
– Al MacInnis, Calgary, St. Louis, 1981-82 – 2003-04.
– Dave Andreychuk, Buffalo, Toronto, New Jersey, Boston, Colorado, Tampa Bay, 1982-83 – 2003-04, 2005-06.
– Chris Chelios, Montreal, Chicago, Detroit, 1983-84 – 2003-04, 2005-06, 2006-07.

GAMES

MOST GAMES:
1,767 – Gordie Howe, Detroit, 1946-47 – 1970-71; Hartford, 1979-80.
1,756 – Mark Messier, Edmonton, NY Rangers, Vancouver, 1979-80 – 2003-04.
1,731 – Ron Francis, Hartford, Pittsburgh, Carolina, Toronto, 1981-82 – 2003-04.
1,639 – Dave Andreychuk, Buffalo, Toronto, New Jersey, Boston, Colorado, Tampa Bay, 1982-83 – 2003-04, 2005-06.
1,635 – Scott Stevens, Washington, St. Louis, New Jersey, 1982-83 – 2003-04.
1,615 – Larry Murphy, Los Angeles, Washington, Minnesota, Pittsburgh, Toronto, Detroit, 1980-81 – 2000-01.

MOST GAMES, INCLUDING PLAYOFFS:
1,992 – Mark Messier, Edmonton, NY Rangers, Vancouver, 1,756 regular-season games, 236 playoff games.
1,924 – Gordie Howe, Detroit, Hartford, 1,767 regular-season games, 157 playoff games.
1,902 – Ron Francis, Hartford, Pittsburgh, Carolina, Toronto, 1,731 regular-season games, 171 playoff games.
1,868 – Scott Stevens, Washington, St. Louis, New Jersey, 1,635 regular-season games, 233 playoff games.
1,830 – Larry Murphy, Los Angeles, Washington, Minnesota, Pittsburgh, Toronto, Detroit, 1,615 regular-season games, 215 playoff games.

MOST CONSECUTIVE GAMES:
964 – Doug Jarvis, Montreal, Washington, Hartford, Oct. 8, 1975 – Oct. 10, 1987.
914 – Garry Unger, Toronto, Detroit, St. Louis, Atlanta, Feb. 24, 1968 – Dec. 21, 1979.
884 – Steve Larmer, Chicago, Oct. 6, 1982 – Apr. 15, 1993.
776 – Craig Ramsay, Buffalo, Mar. 27, 1973 – Feb. 10, 1983.
630 – Andy Hebenton, NY Rangers, Boston, Oct. 7, 1955 – Mar. 22, 1964.

GOALS

MOST GOALS:
894 – Wayne Gretzky, Edmonton, Los Angeles, St. Louis, NY Rangers, in 20 seasons. 1,487GP
801 – Gordie Howe, Detroit, Hartford, in 26 seasons. 1,767GP
741 – Brett Hull, Calgary, St. Louis, Dallas, Detroit, Phoenix, in 19 seasons. 1,269GP
731 – Marcel Dionne, Detroit, Los Angeles, NY Rangers, in 18 seasons. 1,348GP
717 – Phil Esposito, Chicago, Boston, NY Rangers, in 18 seasons. 1,282GP

MOST GOALS, INCLUDING PLAYOFFS:
1,016 – Wayne Gretzky, Edmonton, Los Angeles, St. Louis, NY Rangers, 894G in 1,487 regular-season games, 122G in 208 playoff games.
869 – Gordie Howe, Detroit, Hartford, 801G in 1,767 regular-season games, 68G in 157 playoff games.
844 – Brett Hull, Calgary, St. Louis, Dallas, Detroit, Phoenix, 741G in 1,269 regular-season games, 103G in 202 playoff games.
803 – Mark Messier, Edmonton, NY Rangers, Vancouver, 694G in 1,756 regular-season games, 109G in 236 playoff games.
778 – Phil Esposito, Chicago, Boston, NY Rangers, 717G in 1,282 regular-season games, 61G in 130 playoff games.

MOST GOALS, ONE SEASON:
92 – Wayne Gretzky, Edmonton, 1981-82. 80GP – 80 game schedule.
87 – Wayne Gretzky, Edmonton, 1983-84. 74GP – 80 game schedule.
86 – Brett Hull, St. Louis, 1990-91. 78GP – 80 game schedule.
85 – Mario Lemieux, Pittsburgh, 1988-89. 76GP – 80 game schedule.
76 – Phil Esposito, Boston, 1970-71. 78GP – 78 game schedule.
– Alexander Mogilny, Buffalo, 1992-93. 77GP – 84 game schedule.
– Teemu Selanne, Winnipeg, 1992-93. 84GP – 84 game schedule.
73 – Wayne Gretzky, Edmonton, 1984-85. 80GP – 80 game schedule.
72 – Brett Hull, St. Louis, 1989-90. 80GP – 80 game schedule.
71 – Wayne Gretzky, Edmonton, 1982-83. 80GP – 80 game schedule.
– Jari Kurri, Edmonton, 1984-85. 73GP – 80 game schedule.
70 – Mario Lemieux, Pittsburgh, 1987-88. 77GP – 80 game schedule.
– Bernie Nicholls, Los Angeles, 1988-89. 79GP – 80 game schedule.
– Brett Hull, St. Louis, 1991-92. 73GP – 80 game schedule.

MOST GOALS, ONE SEASON, INCLUDING PLAYOFFS:
100 – Wayne Gretzky, Edmonton, 1983-84, 87G in 74 regular-season games, 13G in 19 playoff games.
97 – Wayne Gretzky, Edmonton, 1981-82, 92G in 80 regular-season games, 5G in 5 playoff games.
– Mario Lemieux, Pittsburgh, 1988-89, 85G in 76 regular-season games, 12G in 11 playoff games.
– Brett Hull, St. Louis, 1990-91, 86G in 78 regular-season games, 11G in 13 playoff games.
90 – Wayne Gretzky, Edmonton, 1984-85, 73G in 80 regular-season games, 17G in 18 playoff games.
– Jari Kurri, Edmonton, 1984-85, 71G in 80 regular-season games, 19G in 18 playoff games.
85 – Mike Bossy, NY Islanders, 1980-81, 68G in 79 regular-season games, 17G in 18 playoff games.
– Brett Hull, St. Louis, 1989-90, 72G in 80 regular-season games, 13G in 12 playoff games.
83 – Wayne Gretzky, Edmonton, 1982-83, 71G in 73 regular-season games, 12G in 16 playoff games.
– Alexander Mogilny, Buffalo, 1992-93, 76G in 77 regular-season games, 7G in 7 playoff games.

MOST GOALS, 50 GAMES FROM START OF SEASON:
61 – Wayne Gretzky, Edmonton, 1981-82. Oct. 7, 1981 – Jan. 22, 1982. (80-game schedule)
– Wayne Gretzky, Edmonton, 1983-84. Oct. 5, 1983 – Jan. 25, 1984. (80-game schedule)
54 – Mario Lemieux, Pittsburgh, 1988-89. Oct. 7, 1988 – Jan. 31, 1989. (80-game schedule)
53 – Wayne Gretzky, Edmonton, 1984-85. Oct. 11, 1984 – Jan. 28, 1985. (80-game schedule)
52 – Brett Hull, St. Louis, 1990-91. Oct. 4, 1990 – Jan. 26, 1991. (80-game schedule)
50 – Maurice Richard, Montreal, 1944-45. Oct. 28, 1944 – Mar. 18, 1945. (50-game schedule)
– Mike Bossy, NY Islanders, 1980-81. Oct. 11, 1980 – Jan. 24, 1981. (80-game schedule)
– Brett Hull, St. Louis, 1991-92. Oct. 5, 1991 – Jan. 28, 1992. (80-game schedule)

MOST GOALS, ONE GAME:
7 – Joe Malone, Quebec, Jan. 31, 1920, at Quebec. Quebec 10, Toronto 6.
6 – Newsy Lalonde, Montreal, Jan. 10, 1920, at Montreal. Montreal 14, Toronto 7.
– Joe Malone, Quebec, Mar. 10, 1920, at Quebec. Quebec 10, Ottawa 4.
– Corb Denneny, Toronto, Jan. 26, 1921, at Toronto. Toronto 10, Hamilton 3.
– Cy Denneny, Ottawa, Mar. 7, 1921, at Ottawa. Ottawa 12, Hamilton 5.
– Syd Howe, Detroit, Feb. 3, 1944, at Detroit. Detroit 12, NY Rangers 2.
– Red Berenson, St. Louis, Nov. 7, 1968, at Philadelphia. St. Louis 8, Philadelphia 0.
– Darryl Sittler, Toronto, Feb. 7, 1976, at Toronto. Toronto 11, Boston 4.

No player since Toronto's Darryl Sittler has scored six goals in an NHL game. Sittler's performance on February 7, 1976 came as part of his record-setting 10-point night.

The Islanders' Bryan Trottier tied a record with four goals in a single period versus the Philadelphia Flyers on February 13, 1982. He set another record with six points in a single period against the Rangers on December 23, 1978.

MOST GOALS, ONE ROAD GAME:

6 – Red Berenson, St. Louis, Nov. 7, 1968, at Philadelphia. St. Louis 8, Philadelphia 0.
5 – Joe Malone, Montreal, Dec. 19, 1917, at Ottawa. Montreal 7, Ottawa 4.
– Red Green, Hamilton, Dec. 5, 1924, at Toronto. Hamilton 10, Toronto 3.
– Babe Dye, Toronto, Dec. 22, 1924, at Boston. Toronto 10, Boston 1.
– Punch Broadbent, Mtl. Maroons, Jan. 7, 1925, at Hamilton. Mtl. Maroons 6, Hamilton 2.
– Don Murdoch, NY Rangers, Oct. 12, 1976, at Minnesota. NY Rangers 10, Minnesota 4.
– Tim Young, Minnesota, Jan. 15, 1979, at NY Rangers. Minnesota 8, NY Rangers 1.
– Willy Lindstrom, Winnipeg, Mar. 2, 1982, at Philadelphia. Winnipeg 7, Philadelphia 6.
– Bengt Gustafsson, Washington, Jan. 8, 1984, at Philadelphia. Washington 7, Philadelphia 1.
– Wayne Gretzky, Edmonton, Dec. 15, 1984, at St. Louis. Edmonton 8, St. Louis 2.
– Dave Andreychuk, Buffalo, Feb. 6, 1986, at Boston. Buffalo 8, Boston 6.
– Mats Sundin, Quebec, Mar. 5, 1992, at Hartford. Quebec 10, Hartford 4.
– Mario Lemieux, Pittsburgh, Apr. 9, 1993, at NY Rangers. Pittsburgh 10, NY Rangers 4.
– Mike Ricci, Quebec, Feb. 17, 1994, at San Jose. Quebec 8, San Jose 2.
– Alex Zhamnov, Winnipeg, Apr. 1, 1995, at Los Angeles. Winnipeg 7, Los Angeles 7.

MOST GOALS, ONE PERIOD:

4 – Busher Jackson, Toronto, Nov. 20, 1934, at St. Louis, third period. Toronto 5, St. Louis 2.
– Max Bentley, Chicago, Jan. 28, 1943, at Chicago, third period. Chicago 10, NY Rangers 1.
– Clint Smith, Chicago, Mar. 4, 1945, at Chicago, third period. Chicago 6, Montreal 4.
– Red Berenson, St. Louis, Nov. 7, 1968, at Philadelphia, second period. St. Louis 8, Philadelphia 0.
– Wayne Gretzky, Edmonton, Feb. 18, 1981, at Edmonton, third period. Edmonton 9, St. Louis 2.
– Grant Mulvey, Chicago, Feb. 3, 1982, at Chicago, first period. Chicago 9, St. Louis 5.
– Bryan Trottier, NY Islanders, Feb. 13, 1982, at NY Islanders, second period. NY Islanders 8, Philadelphia 2.
– Al Secord, Chicago, Jan. 7, 1987, at Chicago, second period. Chicago 6, Toronto 4.
– Joe Nieuwendyk, Calgary, Jan. 11, 1989, at Calgary, second period. Calgary 8, Winnipeg 3.
– Peter Bondra, Washington, Feb. 5, 1994, at Washington, first period. Washington 6, Tampa Bay 3.
– Mario Lemieux, Pittsburgh, Jan. 26, 1997, at Montreal, third period. Pittsburgh 5, Montreal 2.

ASSISTS

MOST ASSISTS:

1,963 – Wayne Gretzky, Edmonton, Los Angeles, St. Louis, NY Rangers, in 20 seasons. 1,487GP
1,249 – Ron Francis, Hartford, Pittsburgh, Carolina, Toronto, in 23 seasons. 1,731GP
1,193 – Mark Messier, Edmonton, NY Rangers, Vancouver, in 25 seasons. 1,756GP
1,169 – Raymond Bourque, Boston, Colorado, in 22 seasons. 1,612GP
1,135 – Paul Coffey, Edmonton, Pittsburgh, Los Angeles, Detroit, Hartford, Philadelphia, Chicago, Carolina, Boston, in 21 seasons. 1,409GP

MOST ASSISTS, INCLUDING PLAYOFFS:

2,223 – Wayne Gretzky, Edmonton, Los Angeles, St. Louis, NY Rangers, 1,963A in 1,487 regular-season games, 260A in 208 playoff games.
1,379 – Mark Messier, Edmonton, NY Rangers, Vancouver, 1,193A in 1,756 regular-season games, 186A in 236 playoff games.
1,346 – Ron Francis, Hartford, Pittsburgh, Carolina, Toronto, 1,249A in 1,731 regular-season games, 97A in 171 playoff games.
1,308 – Raymond Bourque, Boston, Colorado, 1,169A in 1,612 regular-season games, 139A in 214 playoff games.
1,272 – Paul Coffey, Edmonton, Pittsburgh, Los Angeles, Detroit, Hartford, Philadelphia, Chicago, Carolina, Boston, 1,135A in 1,409 regular-season games, 137A in 194 playoff games.

MOST ASSISTS, ONE SEASON:

163 – Wayne Gretzky, Edmonton, 1985-86. 80GP – 80 game schedule.
135 – Wayne Gretzky, Edmonton, 1984-85. 80GP – 80 game schedule.
125 – Wayne Gretzky, Edmonton, 1982-83. 80GP – 80 game schedule.
122 – Wayne Gretzky, Los Angeles, 1990-91. 78GP – 80 game schedule.
121 – Wayne Gretzky, Edmonton, 1986-87. 79GP – 80 game schedule.
120 – Wayne Gretzky, Edmonton, 1981-82. 80GP – 80 game schedule.
118 – Wayne Gretzky, Edmonton, 1983-84. 74GP – 80 game schedule.
114 – Mario Lemieux, Pittsburgh, 1988-89. 76GP – 80 game schedule.
– Wayne Gretzky, Los Angeles, 1988-89. 78GP – 80 game schedule.
109 – Wayne Gretzky, Edmonton, 1980-81. 80GP – 80 game schedule.
– Wayne Gretzky, Edmonton, 1987-88. 64GP – 80 game schedule.
102 – Bobby Orr, Boston, 1970-71. 78GP – 78 game schedule.
– Wayne Gretzky, Los Angeles, 1989-90. 73GP – 80 game schedule.

MOST ASSISTS, ONE SEASON, INCLUDING PLAYOFFS:

174 – Wayne Gretzky, Edmonton, 1985-86, 163A in 80 regular-season games, 11A in 10 playoff games.
165 – Wayne Gretzky, Edmonton, 1984-85, 135A in 80 regular-season games, 30A in 18 playoff games.
151 – Wayne Gretzky, Edmonton, 1982-83, 125A in 80 regular-season games, 26A in 16 playoff games.
150 – Wayne Gretzky, Edmonton, 1986-87, 121A in 79 regular-season games, 29A in 21 playoff games.
140 – Wayne Gretzky, Edmonton, 1983-84, 118A in 74 regular-season games, 22A in 19 playoff games.
– Wayne Gretzky, Edmonton, 1987-88, 109A in 64 regular-season games, 31A in 19 playoff games.
133 – Wayne Gretzky, Los Angeles, 1990-91, 122A in 78 regular-season games, 11A in 12 playoff games.
131 – Wayne Gretzky, Los Angeles, 1988-89, 114A in 78 regular-season games, 17A in 11 playoff games.
127 – Wayne Gretzky, Edmonton, 1981-82, 120A in 80 regular-season games, 7A in 5 playoff games.
123 – Wayne Gretzky, Edmonton, 1980-81, 109A in 80 regular-season games, 14A in 9 playoff games.
121 – Mario Lemieux, Pittsburgh, 1988-89, 114A in 76 regular-season games, 7A in 11 playoff games.

MOST ASSISTS, ONE GAME:

7 – Billy Taylor, Detroit, Mar. 16, 1947, at Chicago. Detroit 10, Chicago 6.
– Wayne Gretzky, Edmonton, Feb. 15, 1980, at Edmonton. Edmonton 8, Washington 2.
– Wayne Gretzky, Edmonton, Dec. 11, 1985, at Chicago. Edmonton 12, Chicago 9.
– Wayne Gretzky, Edmonton, Feb. 14, 1986, at Edmonton. Edmonton 8, Quebec 2.
6 – Six assists have been recorded in one game on 24 occasions since Elmer Lach of Montreal first accomplished the feat vs. Boston on Feb. 6, 1943. The most recent player is Eric Lindros of Philadelphia on Feb. 26, 1997 at Ottawa.

MOST ASSISTS, ONE ROAD GAME:

7 – Billy Taylor, Detroit, Mar. 16, 1947, at Chicago. Detroit 10, Chicago 6.
– Wayne Gretzky, Edmonton, Dec. 11, 1985, at Chicago. Edmonton 12, Chicago 9.
6 – Bobby Orr, Boston, Jan. 1, 1973, at Vancouver. Boston 8, Vancouver 2.
– Patrik Sundstrom, Vancouver, Feb. 29, 1984, at Pittsburgh. Vancouver 9, Pittsburgh 5.
– Mario Lemieux, Pittsburgh, Dec. 5, 1992, at San Jose. Pittsburgh 9, San Jose 4.
– Eric Lindros, Philadelphia, Feb. 26, 1997, at Ottawa. Philadelphia 8, Ottawa 5.

MOST ASSISTS, ONE PERIOD:

5 – Dale Hawerchuk, Winnipeg, Mar. 6, 1984, at Los Angeles, second period. Winnipeg 7, Los Angeles 3.
4 – Four assists have been recorded in one period on 67 occasions since Mickey Roach of Hamilton first accomplished the feat vs. Toronto on Feb. 23, 1921. The most recent player is Joe Thornton of San Jose on Apr. 1, 2007 vs. Los Angeles.

POINTS

MOST POINTS:

2,857 – Wayne Gretzky, Edmonton, Los Angeles, St. Louis, NY Rangers, in 20 seasons. 1,487GP (894G-1,963A)
1,887 – Mark Messier, Edmonton, NY Rangers, Vancouver, in 25 seasons. 1,756GP (694G-1,193A)
1,850 – Gordie Howe, Detroit, Hartford, in 26 seasons. 1,767GP (801G-1,049A)
1,798 – Ron Francis, Hartford, Pittsburgh, Carolina, Toronto, in 23 seasons. 1,731GP (549G-1,249A)
1,771 – Marcel Dionne, Detroit, Los Angeles, NY Rangers, in 18 seasons. 1,348GP (731G-1,040A)

MOST POINTS, INCLUDING PLAYOFFS:

3,239 – Wayne Gretzky, Edmonton, Los Angeles, St. Louis, NY Rangers, 2,857PTS in 1,487 regular-season games, 382PTS in 208 playoff games.
2,182 – Mark Messier, Edmonton, NY Rangers, Vancouver, 1,887PTS in 1,756 regular-season games, 295PTS in 236 playoff games.
2,010 – Gordie Howe, Detroit, Hartford, 1,850PTS in 1,767 regular-season games, 160PTS in 157 playoff games.
1,941 – Ron Francis, Hartford, Pittsburgh, Carolina, Toronto, 1,798PTS in 1,731 regular-season games, 143PTS in 171 playoff games
1,940 – Steve Yzerman, Detroit, 1,755PTS in 1,514 regular-season games, 185PTS in 196 playoff games.

MOST POINTS, ONE SEASON:

215 – Wayne Gretzky, Edmonton, 1985-86. 80GP – 80 game schedule.
212 – Wayne Gretzky, Edmonton, 1981-82. 80GP – 80 game schedule.
208 – Wayne Gretzky, Edmonton, 1984-85. 80GP – 80 game schedule.
205 – Wayne Gretzky, Edmonton, 1983-84. 74GP – 80 game schedule.
199 – Mario Lemieux, Pittsburgh, 1988-89. 76GP – 80 game schedule.
196 – Wayne Gretzky, Edmonton, 1982-83. 80GP – 80 game schedule.
183 – Wayne Gretzky, Edmonton, 1986-87. 79GP – 80 game schedule.
168 – Mario Lemieux, Pittsburgh, 1987-88, 77GP – 80 game schedule.
– Wayne Gretzky, Los Angeles, 1988-89. 78GP – 80 game schedule.
164 – Wayne Gretzky, Edmonton, 1980-81. 80GP – 80 game schedule.
163 – Wayne Gretzky, Los Angeles, 1990-91. 78GP – 80 game schedule.
161 – Mario Lemieux, Pittsburgh, 1995-96. 70GP – 82 game schedule.
160 – Mario Lemieux, Pittsburgh, 1992-93. 60GP – 84 game schedule.

MOST POINTS, ONE SEASON, INCLUDING PLAYOFFS:

255 – Wayne Gretzky, Edmonton, 1984-85, 208PTS in 80 regular-season games, 47PTS in 18 playoff games.
240 – Wayne Gretzky, Edmonton, 1983-84, 205PTS in 74 regular-season games, 35PTS in 19 playoff games.
234 – Wayne Gretzky, Edmonton, 1982-83, 196PTS in 80 regular-season games, 38PTS in 16 playoff games.
– Wayne Gretzky, Edmonton, 1985-86, 215PTS in 80 regular-season games, 19PTS in 10 playoff games.
224 – Wayne Gretzky, Edmonton, 1981-82, 212PTS in 80 regular-season games, 12PTS in 5 playoff games.
218 – Mario Lemieux, Pittsburgh, 1988-89, 199PTS in 76 regular-season games, 19PTS in 11 playoff games.
217 – Wayne Gretzky, Edmonton, 1986-87, 183PTS in 79 regular-season games, 34PTS in 21 playoff games.
192 – Wayne Gretzky, Edmonton, 1987-88, 149PTS in 64 regular-season games, 43PTS in 19 playoff games.
190 – Wayne Gretzky, Los Angeles, 1988-89, 168PTS in 78 regular-season games, 22PTS in 11 playoff games.
188 – Mario Lemieux, Pittsburgh, 1995-96, 161PTS in 70 regular-season games, 27PTS in 18 playoff games.
185 – Wayne Gretzky, Edmonton, 1980-81, 164PTS in 80 regular-season games, 21PTS in 9 playoff games.

MOST POINTS, ONE GAME:

10 – Darryl Sittler, Toronto, Feb. 7, 1976, at Toronto, 6G-4A. Toronto 11, Boston 4.
8 – Maurice Richard, Montreal, Dec. 28, 1944, at Montreal, 5G-3A. Montreal 9, Detroit 1.
– Bert Olmstead, Montreal, Jan. 9, 1954, at Montreal, 4G-4A. Montreal 12, Chicago 1.
– Tom Bladon, Philadelphia, Dec. 11, 1977, at Philadelphia, 4G-4A. Philadelphia 11, Cleveland 1.
– Bryan Trottier, NY Islanders, Dec. 23, 1978, at NY Islanders, 5G-3A. NY Islanders 9, NY Rangers 4.
– Peter Stastny, Quebec, Feb. 22, 1981, at Washington, 4G-4A. Quebec 11, Washington 7.
– Anton Stastny, Quebec, Feb. 22, 1981, at Washington, 3G-5A. Quebec 11, Washington 7.
– Wayne Gretzky, Edmonton, Nov. 19, 1983, at Edmonton, 3G-5A. Edmonton 13, New Jersey 4.
– Wayne Gretzky, Edmonton, Jan. 4, 1984, at Edmonton, 4G-4A. Edmonton 12, Minnesota 8.
– Paul Coffey, Edmonton, Mar. 14, 1986, at Edmonton, 2G-6A. Edmonton 12, Detroit 3.
– Mario Lemieux, Pittsburgh, Oct. 15, 1988, at Pittsburgh, 2G-6A. Pittsburgh 9, St. Louis 2.
– Bernie Nicholls, Los Angeles, Dec. 1, 1988, at Los Angeles, 2G-6A. Los Angeles 9, Toronto 3.
– Mario Lemieux, Pittsburgh, Dec. 31, 1988, at Pittsburgh, 5G-3A. Pittsburgh 8, New Jersey 6.

MOST POINTS, ONE ROAD GAME:

8 – Peter Stastny, Quebec, Feb. 22, 1981, at Washington. 4G-4A. Quebec 11, Washington 7.
– Anton Stastny, Quebec, Feb. 22, 1981, at Washington. 3G-5A. Quebec 11, Washington 7.
7 – Red Green, Hamilton, Dec. 5, 1924, at Toronto. 5G-2A. Hamilton 10, Toronto 3.
– Billy Taylor, Detroit, Mar. 16, 1947, at Chicago. 7A. Detroit 10, Chicago 6.
– Red Berenson, St. Louis, Nov. 7, 1968, at Philadelphia. 6G-1A. St. Louis 8, Philadelphia 0.
– Gilbert Perreault, Buffalo, Feb. 1, 1976, at California. 2G-5A. Buffalo 9, California 5.
– Peter Stastny, Quebec, Apr. 1, 1982, at Boston. 3G-4A. Quebec 8, Boston 5.
– Wayne Gretzky, Edmonton, Nov. 6, 1983, at Winnipeg. 4G-3A. Edmonton 8, Winnipeg 5.
– Patrik Sundstrom, Vancouver, Feb. 29, 1984, at Pittsburgh. 1G-6A. Vancouver 9, Pittsburgh 5.
– Wayne Gretzky, Edmonton, Dec. 11, 1985, at Chicago. 7A. Edmonton 12, Chicago 9.
– Cam Neely, Boston, Oct. 16, 1988, at Chicago. 3G-4A. Boston 10, Chicago 3.
– Mario Lemieux, Pittsburgh, Jan. 21, 1989, at Edmonton. 2G-5A. Pittsburgh 7, Edmonton 4.
– Dino Ciccarelli, Washington, Mar. 18, 1989, at Hartford. 4G-3A. Washington 8, Hartford 2.
– Mats Sundin, Quebec, Mar. 5, 1992, at Hartford. 5G-2A. Quebec 10, Hartford 4.
– Mario Lemieux, Pittsburgh, Dec. 5, 1992, at San Jose. 1G-6A. Pittsburgh 9, San Jose 4.
– Eric Lindros, Philadelphia, Feb. 26, 1997, at Ottawa. 1G-6A. Philadelphia 8, Ottawa 5.

Eight of Daniel Sedin's 36 goals for Vancouver last season were game winners, including a record-tying four in overtime. The single-season record for overtime goals dates back to the league's early days. Through its 90-year history, the NHL has employed a variety of formats governing regular-season overtime play.

MOST POINTS, ONE PERIOD:

6 – Bryan Trottier, NY Islanders, Dec. 23, 1978, at NY Islanders, second period. 3G-3A. NY Islanders 9, NY Rangers 4.
5 – Bill Cook, NY Rangers, Mar. 12, 1933, at NY Americans, third period. 3G-2A. NY Rangers 8, NY Americans 2.
– Les Cunningham, Chicago, Jan. 28, 1940, at Chicago, third period. 2G-3A. Chicago 8, Montreal 1.
– Max Bentley, Chicago, Jan. 28, 1943, at Chicago, third period. 4G-1A. Chicago 10, NY Rangers 1.
– Leo Labine, Boston, Nov. 28, 1954, at Boston, second period. 3G-2A. Boston 6, Detroit 2.
– Darryl Sittler, Toronto, Feb. 7, 1976, at Toronto, second period. 3G-2A. Toronto 11, Boston 4.
– Grant Mulvey, Chicago, Feb. 3, 1982, at Chicago, first period. 4G-1A. Chicago 9, St. Louis 5.
– Dale Hawerchuk, Winnipeg, Mar. 6, 1984, at Los Angeles, second period. 5A. Winnipeg 7, Los Angeles 3.
– Jari Kurri, Edmonton, Oct. 26, 1984, at Edmonton, second period. 2G-3A. Edmonton 8, Los Angeles 2.
– Pat Elynuik, Winnipeg, Jan. 20, 1989, at Winnipeg, second period. 2G-3A. Winnipeg 7, Pittsburgh 3.
– Ray Ferraro, Hartford, Dec. 9, 1989, at Hartford, first period. 3G-2A. Hartford 7, New Jersey 3.
– Stephane Richer, Montreal, Feb. 14, 1990, at Montreal, first period. 2G-3A. Montreal 10, Vancouver 1.
– Cliff Ronning, Vancouver, Apr. 15, 1993, at Los Angeles, third period. 3G-2A. Vancouver 8, Los Angeles 6.
– Peter Forsberg, Colorado, Mar. 3, 1999, at Florida, third period. 2G-3A. Colorado 7, Florida 5.

POWER-PLAY AND SHORTHAND GOALS

MOST POWER-PLAY GOALS, CAREER:

274 – Dave Andreychuk, Buffalo, Toronto, New Jersey, Boston, Colorado, Tampa Bay, in 23 seasons. 1,639GP
265 – Brett Hull, Calgary, St. Louis, Dallas, Detroit, Phoenix, in 19 seasons. 1,269GP
249 – Phil Esposito, Chicago, Boston, NY Rangers, in 18 seasons. 1,282GP

MOST POWER-PLAY GOALS, ONE SEASON:

34 – Tim Kerr, Philadelphia, 1985-86. 76GP – 80 game schedule.
32 – Dave Andreychuk, Buffalo, Toronto, 1992-93. 83GP – 84 game schedule.
31 – Joe Nieuwendyk, Calgary, 1987-88. 75GP – 80 game schedule.
– Mario Lemieux, Pittsburgh, 1988-89. 76GP – 80 game schedule.
– Mario Lemieux, Pittsburgh, 1995-96. 70GP – 82 game schedule.
29 – Michel Goulet, Quebec, 1987-88. 80GP – 80 game schedule.
– Brett Hull, St. Louis, 1990-91. 78GP – 80 game schedule.
– Brett Hull, St. Louis, 1992-93. 80GP – 84 game schedule.

MOST SHORTHAND GOALS, ONE SEASON:

13 – Mario Lemieux, Pittsburgh, 1988-89. 76GP – 80 game schedule.
12 – Wayne Gretzky, Edmonton, 1983-84. 74GP – 80 game schedule.
11 – Wayne Gretzky, Edmonton, 1984-85. 80GP – 80 game schedule.
10 – Marcel Dionne, Detroit, 1974-75. 80GP – 80 game schedule.
– Mario Lemieux, Pittsburgh, 1987-88. 77GP – 80 game schedule.
– Dirk Graham, Chicago, 1988-89. 80GP – 80 game schedule.

MOST SHORTHAND GOALS, ONE GAME:

3 – Theoren Fleury, Calgary, Mar. 9, 1991, at St. Louis. Calgary 8, St. Louis 4.

OVERTIME SCORING

MOST OVERTIME GOALS, CAREER:

15 – Mats Sundin, Quebec, Toronto.
– Jaromir Jagr, Pittsburgh, Washington, NY Rangers.
14 – Sergei Fedorov, Detroit, Anaheim, Columbus.
13 – Steve Thomas, Toronto, Chicago, NY Islanders, New Jersey, Anaheim.
12 – Nels Stewart, Mtl. Maroons, Boston, NY Americans.
– Brett Hull, Calgary, St. Louis, Dallas, Detroit, Phoenix.

MOST OVERTIME ASSISTS, CAREER:

18 – Mark Messier, Edmonton, NY Rangers, Vancouver.
– Nicklas Lidstrom, Detroit.
17 – Adam Oates, Detroit, St. Louis, Boston, Washington, Philadelphia, Anaheim.
15 – Wayne Gretzky, Edmonton, Los Angeles, St. Louis, NY Rangers.
– Doug Gilmour, St. Louis, Calgary, Toronto, New Jersey, Chicago, Buffalo, Montreal.
– Sergei Fedorov, Detroit, Anaheim, Columbus.

MOST OVERTIME POINTS, CAREER:

29 – Sergei Fedorov, Detroit, Anaheim, Columbus. 14G-15A
26 – Mark Messier, Edmonton, NY Rangers, Vancouver. 8G-18A
– Jaromir Jagr, Pittsburgh, Washington, NY Rangers. 15G-11A
– Mats Sundin, Quebec, Toronto. 15G-11A
23 – Steve Thomas, Toronto, Chicago, NY Islanders, New Jersey, Anaheim. 13G-10A

MOST OVERTIME GOALS, ONE SEASON:

4 – Howie Morenz, Montreal, 1929-30.
– Frank Finnigan, Ottawa, 1929-30.
– Johnny Gagnon, Montreal 1936-37.
– Mats Sundin, Toronto, 1999-2000.
– Scott Niedermayer, New Jersey, 2001-02.
– Patrik Elias, New Jersey, 2003-04.
– Markus Naslund, Vancouver, 2003-04.
– Olli Jokinen, Florida, 2005-06.
– Daniel Sedin, Vancouver 2006-07.

SHOOTOUT GOALS

MOST SHOOTOUT GOALS, ONE SEASON:

10 – Jussi Jokinen, Dallas, 2005-06, (13S)
8 – Viktor Kozlov, New Jersey, 2005-06, (12S)
– Erik Christensen, Pittsburgh, 2006-07, (14S)
– Mikko Koivu, Minnesota, 2006-07, (15S)

MOST SHOOTOUT GOALS, ALL-TIME:

15 – Jussi Jokinen, Dallas, (25S)
13 – Viktor Kozlov, New Jersey, (25S)
12 – Paul Kariya, Nashville, (18S)
– Vyacheslav Kozlov, Atlanta, (18S)
– Mikko Koivu, Minnesota, (21S)
– Miroslav Satan, NY Islanders, (23S)
– Sergei Zubov, Dallas, (24S)

MOST SHOOTOUT SHOTS TAKEN, ONE SEASON:

15 – Mikko Koivu, Minnesota, 2006-07, (8G)
– Sidney Crosby, Pittsburgh, 2006-07, (5G)
14 – Ales Hemsky, Edmonton, 2005-06, (5G)
– Erik Christensen, Pittsburgh, 2006-07, (8G)
– Zach Parise, New Jersey, 2006-07, (7G)
– Daniel Briere, Buffalo, 2006-07, (6G)
– Pavol Demitra, Minnesota, 2006-07, (6G)

MOST SHOOTOUT SHOTS TAKEN, ALL-TIME:

25 – Jussi Jokinen, Dallas, (15G).
– Viktor Kozlov, New Jersey, NY Islanders, (13G)
– Alex Ovechkin, Washington, (8G)
24 – Sergei Zubov, Dallas, (12G)
– Michael Nylander, NY Rangers, (10G)

BEST SHOOTOUT SCORING PERCENTAGE, ONE SEASON: *(minimum 5 shots)*

.857 – Petteri Nummelin, Minnesota, 2006-07, (6G, 7S)
.800 – Ray Whitney, Carolina, 2005-06, (4G, 5S)
.769 – Jussi Jokinen, Dallas, 2005-06, (10G, 13S)

BEST SHOOTOUT SCORING PERCENTAGE, ALL-TIME: *(minimum 10 shots)*

.667 – Paul Kariya, Nashville, (12G, 18S)
.667 – Vyacheslav Kozlov, Atlanta, (12G, 18S)
.600 – Jussi Jokinen, Dallas, (15G, 25S)

GAME DECIDING SHOOTOUT GOALS, ONE SEASON:

5 – Miroslav Satan, NY Islanders, 2005-06, (10S)
– Viktor Kozlov, New Jersey, 2005-06, (12S)
– Vyacheslav Kozlov, Atlanta, 2006-07, (11S)

GAME DECIDING SHOOTOUT GOALS, ALL-TIME:

7 – Vyacheslav Kozlov, Atlanta, (18S)
– Miroslav Satan, NY Islanders, (23S)
– Viktor Kozlov, New Jersey, NY Islanders, (25S)

SCORING BY A CENTER

MOST GOALS BY A CENTER, CAREER:
894 – Wayne Gretzky, Edmonton, Los Angeles, St. Louis, NY Rangers, in 20 seasons. 1,487GP
731 – Marcel Dionne, Detroit, Los Angeles, NY Rangers, in 18 seasons. 1,348GP
717 – Phil Esposito, Chicago, Boston, NY Rangers, in 18 seasons. 1,282GP
694 – Mark Messier, Edmonton, NY Rangers, Vancouver, in 25 seasons. 1,756GP
692 – Steve Yzerman, Detroit, in 22 seasons. 1,514GP

MOST GOALS BY A CENTER, ONE SEASON:
92 – Wayne Gretzky, Edmonton, 1981-82. 80GP – 80 game schedule.
87 – Wayne Gretzky, Edmonton, 1983-84. 74GP – 80 game schedule.
85 – Mario Lemieux, Pittsburgh, 1988-89. 76GP – 80 game schedule.
76 – Phil Esposito, Boston, 1970-71. 78GP – 78 game schedule.
73 – Wayne Gretzky, Edmonton, 1984-85. 80GP – 80 game schedule.

MOST ASSISTS BY A CENTER, CAREER:
1,963 – Wayne Gretzky, Edmonton, Los Angeles, St. Louis, NY Rangers, in 20 seasons. 1,487GP
1,249 – Ron Francis, Hartford, Pittsburgh, Carolina, Toronto, in 23 seasons. 1,731GP
1,193 – Mark Messier, Edmonton, NY Rangers, Vancouver, in 25 seasons. 1,756GP
1,079 – Adam Oates, Detroit, St. Louis, Boston, Washington, Philadelphia, Anaheim, Edmonton, in 19 seasons. 1,337GP
1,063 – Steve Yzerman, Detroit, in 22 seasons. 1,514GP

MOST ASSISTS BY A CENTER, ONE SEASON:
163 – Wayne Gretzky, Edmonton, 1985-86. 80GP – 80 game schedule.
135 – Wayne Gretzky, Edmonton, 1984-85. 80GP – 80 game schedule.
125 – Wayne Gretzky, Edmonton, 1982-83. 80GP – 80 game schedule.
122 – Wayne Gretzky, Los Angeles, 1990-91. 78GP – 80 game schedule.
121 – Wayne Gretzky, Edmonton, 1986-87. 79GP – 80 game schedule.

MOST POINTS BY A CENTER, CAREER:
2,857 – Wayne Gretzky, Edmonton, Los Angeles, St. Louis, NY Rangers, in 20 seasons. 1,487GP (894G-1,963A)
1,887 – Mark Messier, Edmonton, NY Rangers, Vancouver, in 25 seasons. 1,756GP (694G-1,193A)
1,798 – Ron Francis, Hartford, Pittsburgh, Carolina, Toronto, in 23 seasons. 1,731GP (549G-1,249A)
1,771 – Marcel Dionne, Detroit, Los Angeles, NY Rangers, in 18 seasons. 1,348GP (731G-1,040A)
1,755 – Steve Yzerman, Detroit, in 22 seasons. 1,514GP (682G-1,063A)

MOST POINTS BY A CENTER, ONE SEASON:
215 – Wayne Gretzky, Edmonton, 1985-86. 80GP – 80 game schedule.
212 – Wayne Gretzky, Edmonton, 1981-82. 80GP – 80 game schedule.
208 – Wayne Gretzky, Edmonton, 1984-85. 80GP – 80 game schedule.
205 – Wayne Gretzky, Edmonton, 1983-84. 74GP – 80 game schedule.
199 – Mario Lemieux, Pittsburgh, 1988-89. 76GP – 80 game schedule.

SCORING BY A LEFT WING

MOST GOALS BY A LEFT WING, CAREER:
668 – Luc Robitaille, Los Angeles, Pittsburgh, NY Rangers, Detroit, in 19 seasons. 1,431GP
640 – Dave Andreychuk, Buffalo, Toronto, New Jersey, Boston, Colorado, Tampa Bay, in 23 seasons. 1,639GP
627 – Brendan Shanahan, New Jersey, St. Louis, Hartford, Detroit, NY Rangers, in 19 seasons. 1,417GP
610 – Bobby Hull, Chicago, Winnipeg, Hartford, in 16 seasons. 1,063GP
556 – John Bucyk, Detroit, Boston, in 23 seasons. 1,540GP

Though Sidney Crosby has started reaching some significant milestones at younger ages than Wayne Gretzky did, a great many of "The Great One's" records should still be safe for years to come. Gretzky topped 200 points in a season four times in his career.

MOST GOALS BY A LEFT WING, ONE SEASON:
63 – Luc Robitaille, Los Angeles, 1992-93. 84GP – 84 game schedule.
60 – Steve Shutt, Montreal, 1976-77. 80GP – 80 game schedule.
58 – Bobby Hull, Chicago, 1968-69. 74GP – 76 game schedule.
57 – Michel Goulet, Quebec, 1982-83. 80GP – 80 game schedule.
56 – Charlie Simmer, Los Angeles, 1979-80. 64GP – 80 game schedule.
– Charlie Simmer, Los Angeles, 1980-81. 65GP – 80 game schedule.
– Michel Goulet, Quebec, 1983-84. 75GP – 80 game schedule.

MOST ASSISTS BY A LEFT WING, CAREER:
813 – John Bucyk, Detroit, Boston, in 23 seasons. 1,540GP
726 – Luc Robitaille, Los Angeles, Pittsburgh, NY Rangers, Detroit, in 19 seasons. 1,431GP
698 – Dave Andreychuk, Buffalo, Toronto, New Jersey, Boston, Colorado, Tampa Bay, in 23 seasons. 1,639GP
667 – Brendan Shanahan, New Jersey, St. Louis, Hartford, Detroit, NY Rangers, in 19 seasons. 1,417GP
604 – Michel Goulet, Quebec, Chicago, in 15 seasons. 1,089GP

MOST ASSISTS BY A LEFT WING, ONE SEASON:
70 – Joe Juneau, Boston, 1992-93. 84GP – 84 game schedule.
69 – Kevin Stevens, Pittsburgh, 1991-92. 80GP – 80 game schedule.
67 – Mats Naslund, Montreal, 1985-86. 80GP – 80 game schedule.
65 – John Bucyk, Boston, 1970-71. 78GP – 78 game schedule.
– Michel Goulet, Quebec, 1983-84. 75GP – 80 game schedule.
64 – Mark Messier, Edmonton, 1983-84. 73GP – 80 game schedule.

MOST POINTS BY A LEFT WING, CAREER:
1,394 – Luc Robitaille, Los Angeles, Pittsburgh, NY Rangers, Detroit, in 19 seasons. 1,431GP (668G-726A)
1,369 – John Bucyk, Detroit, Boston, in 23 seasons. 1,540GP (556G-813A)
1,338 – Dave Andreychuk, Buffalo, Toronto, New Jersey, Boston, Colorado, Tampa Bay, in 23 seasons. 1,639GP (640G-698A)
1,294 – Brendan Shanahan, New Jersey, St. Louis, Hartford, Detroit, NY Rangers, in 19 seasons. 1,417GP (627G-667A)
1,170 – Bobby Hull, Chicago, Winnipeg, Hartford, in 16 seasons. 1,063GP (610G-560A)

MOST POINTS BY A LEFT WING, ONE SEASON:
125 – Luc Robitaille, Los Angeles, 1992-93. 84GP – 84 game schedule.
123 – Kevin Stevens, Pittsburgh, 1991-92. 80GP – 80 game schedule.
121 – Michel Goulet, Quebec, 1983-84. 75GP – 80 game schedule.
116 – John Bucyk, Boston, 1970-71. 78GP – 78 game schedule.
112 – Bill Barber, Philadelphia, 1975-76. 80GP – 80 game schedule.

SCORING BY A RIGHT WING

MOST GOALS BY A RIGHT WING, CAREER:
801 – Gordie Howe, Detroit, Hartford, in 26 seasons. 1,767GP
741 – Brett Hull, Calgary, St. Louis, Dallas, Detroit, Phoenix, in 19 seasons. 1,269GP
708 – Mike Gartner, Washington, Minnesota, NY Rangers, Toronto, Phoenix, in 19 seasons. 1,432GP
621 – Jaromir Jagr, Pittsburgh, Washington, NY Rangers, in 16 seasons. 1,191GP
608 – Dino Ciccarelli, Minnesota, Washington, Detroit, Tampa Bay, Florida, in 19 seasons. 1,232GP

MOST GOALS BY A RIGHT WING, ONE SEASON:
86 – Brett Hull, St. Louis, 1990-91. 78GP – 80 game schedule.
76 – Alexander Mogilny, Buffalo, 1992-93. 77GP – 84 game schedule.
– Teemu Selanne, Winnipeg, 1992-93. 84GP – 84 game schedule.
72 – Brett Hull, St. Louis, 1989-90. 80GP – 80 game schedule.
71 – Jari Kurri, Edmonton, 1984-85. 73GP – 80 game schedule.
70 – Brett Hull, St. Louis, 1991-92. 73GP – 80 game schedule.

MOST ASSISTS BY A RIGHT WING, CAREER:
1,049 – Gordie Howe, Detroit, Hartford, in 26 seasons. 1,767GP
907 – Jaromir Jagr, Pittsburgh, Washington, NY Rangers, in 16 seasons. 1,191GP
825 – Mark Recchi, Pittsburgh, Philadelphia, Montreal, Carolina, in 18 seasons. 1,338GP
797 – Jari Kurri, Edmonton, Los Angeles, NY Rangers, Anaheim, Colorado, in 17 seasons. 1,251GP
793 – Guy Lafleur, Montreal, NY Rangers, Quebec, in 17 seasons. 1,126GP

MOST ASSISTS BY A RIGHT WING, ONE SEASON:
87 – Jaromir Jagr, Pittsburgh, 1995-96. 82GP – 82 game schedule.
83 – Mike Bossy, NY Islanders, 1981-82. 80GP – 80 game schedule.
– Jaromir Jagr, Pittsburgh, 1998-99. 81GP – 82 game schedule.
80 – Guy Lafleur, Montreal, 1976-77. 80GP – 80 game schedule.
77 – Guy Lafleur, Montreal, 1978-79. 80GP – 80 game schedule.

MOST POINTS BY A RIGHT WING, CAREER:

1,850 – Gordie Howe, Detroit, Hartford, in 26 seasons. 1,767GP (801G-1,049A)
1,528 – Jaromir Jagr, Pittsburgh, Washington, NY Rangers, in 16 seasons. 1,191GP (621G-907A)
1,398 – Jari Kurri, Edmonton, Los Angeles, NY Rangers, Anaheim, Colorado, in 17 seasons. 1,251GP (601G-797A)
1,390 – Brett Hull, Calgary, St. Louis, Dallas, Detroit, Phoenix, in 19 seasons. 1,269GP (741G-649A)
1,353 – Guy Lafleur, Montreal, NY Rangers, Quebec, in 17 seasons. 1,126GP (560G-793A)

MOST POINTS BY A RIGHT WING, ONE SEASON:

149 – Jaromir Jagr, Pittsburgh, 1995-96. 82GP – 82 game schedule.
147 – Mike Bossy, NY Islanders, 1981-82. 80GP – 80 game schedule.
136 – Guy Lafleur, Montreal, 1976-77. 80GP – 80 game schedule.
135 – Jari Kurri, Edmonton, 1984-85. 73GP – 80 game schedule.
132 – Guy Lafleur, Montreal, 1977-78. 78GP – 80 game schedule.
– Teemu Selanne, Winnipeg, 1992-93. 84GP – 84 game schedule.

SCORING BY A DEFENSEMAN

MOST GOALS BY A DEFENSEMAN, CAREER:

410 – Raymond Bourque, Boston, Colorado, in 22 seasons. 1,612GP
396 – Paul Coffey, Edmonton, Pittsburgh, Los Angeles, Detroit, Hartford, Philadelphia, Chicago, Carolina, Boston, in 21 seasons. 1,409GP
340 – Al MacInnis, Calgary, St. Louis, in 23 seasons. 1,416GP
338 – Phil Housley, Buffalo, Winnipeg, St. Louis, Calgary, New Jersey, Washington, Chicago, Toronto, in 21 seasons. 1,495GP
310 – Denis Potvin, NY Islanders, in 15 seasons. 1,060GP

MOST GOALS BY A DEFENSEMAN, ONE SEASON:

48 – Paul Coffey, Edmonton, 1985-86. 79GP – 80 game schedule.
46 – Bobby Orr, Boston, 1974-75. 80GP – 80 game schedule.
40 – Paul Coffey, Edmonton, 1983-84. 80GP – 80 game schedule.
39 – Doug Wilson, Chicago, 1981-82. 76GP – 80 game schedule.
37 – Bobby Orr, Boston, 1970-71. 78GP – 78 game schedule.
– Bobby Orr, Boston, 1971-72. 76GP – 78 game schedule.
– Paul Coffey, Edmonton, 1984-85. 80GP – 80 game schedule.

MOST GOALS BY A DEFENSEMAN, ONE GAME:

5 – Ian Turnbull, Toronto, Feb. 2, 1977, at Toronto. Toronto 9, Detroit 1.
4 – Harry Cameron, Toronto, Dec. 26, 1917, at Toronto. Toronto 7, Montreal 5.
– Harry Cameron, Montreal, Mar. 3, 1920, at Quebec. Montreal 16, Quebec 3.
– Sprague Cleghorn, Montreal, Jan. 14, 1922, at Montreal. Montreal 10, Hamilton 6.
– John McKinnon, Pittsburgh, Nov. 19, 1929, at Pittsburgh. Pittsburgh 10, Toronto 5.
– Hap Day, Toronto, Nov. 19, 1929, at Pittsburgh. Pittsburgh 10, Toronto 5.
– Tom Bladon, Philadelphia, Dec. 11, 1977, at Philadelphia. Philadelphia 11, Cleveland 1.
– Ian Turnbull, Los Angeles, Dec. 12, 1981, at Los Angeles. Los Angeles 7, Vancouver 5.
– Paul Coffey, Edmonton, Oct. 26, 1984, at Calgary. Edmonton 6, Calgary 5.

MOST ASSISTS BY A DEFENSEMAN, CAREER:

1,169 – Raymond Bourque, Boston, Colorado, in 22 seasons. 1,612GP
1,135 – Paul Coffey, Edmonton, Pittsburgh, Los Angeles, Detroit, Hartford, Philadelphia, Chicago, Carolina, Boston, in 21 seasons. 1,409GP
934 – Al MacInnis, Calgary, St. Louis, in 23 seasons. 1,416GP
929 – Larry Murphy, Los Angeles, Washington, Minnesota, Pittsburgh, Toronto, Detroit, in 21 seasons. 1,615GP
894 – Phil Housley, Buffalo, Winnipeg, St. Louis, Calgary, New Jersey, Washington, Chicago, Toronto, in 21 seasons. 1,495GP

MOST ASSISTS BY A DEFENSEMAN, ONE SEASON:

102 – Bobby Orr, Boston, 1970-71. 78GP – 78 game schedule.
90 – Bobby Orr, Boston, 1973-74. 74GP – 78 game schedule.
– Paul Coffey, Edmonton, 1985-86. 79GP – 80 game schedule.
89 – Bobby Orr, Boston, 1974-75. 80GP – 80 game schedule.
87 – Bobby Orr, Boston, 1969-70. 76GP – 78 game schedule.

MOST ASSISTS BY A DEFENSEMAN, ONE GAME:

6 – Babe Pratt, Toronto, Jan. 8, 1944, at Toronto. Toronto 12, Boston 3.
– Pat Stapleton, Chicago, Mar. 30, 1969, at Chicago. Chicago 9, Detroit 5.
– Bobby Orr, Boston, Jan. 1, 1973, at Vancouver. Boston 8, Vancouver 2.
– Ron Stackhouse, Pittsburgh, Mar. 8, 1975, at Pittsburgh. Pittsburgh 8, Philadelphia 2.
– Paul Coffey, Edmonton, Mar. 14, 1986, at Edmonton. Edmonton 12, Detroit 3.
– Gary Suter, Calgary, Apr. 4, 1986, at Calgary. Calgary 9, Edmonton 3.

MOST POINTS BY A DEFENSEMAN, CAREER:

1,579 – Raymond Bourque, Boston, Colorado, in 22 seasons. 1,612GP (410G-1,169A)
1,531 – Paul Coffey, Edmonton, Pittsburgh, Los Angeles, Detroit, Hartford, Philadelphia, Chicago, Carolina, Boston, in 21 seasons. 1,409GP (396G-1,135A)
1,274 – Al MacInnis, Calgary, St. Louis, in 23 seasons. 1,416GP (340G-934A)
1,232 – Phil Housley, Buffalo, Winnipeg, St. Louis, Calgary, New Jersey, Washington, Chicago, Toronto, in 21 seasons. 1,495GP (338G-894A)
1,216 – Larry Murphy, Los Angeles, Washington, Minnesota, Pittsburgh, Toronto, Detroit, in 21 seasons. 1,615GP (287G-929A)

MOST POINTS BY A DEFENSEMAN, ONE SEASON:

139 – Bobby Orr, Boston, 1970-71. 78GP – 78 game schedule.
138 – Paul Coffey, Edmonton, 1985-86. 79GP – 80 game schedule.
135 – Bobby Orr, Boston, 1974-75. 80GP – 80 game schedule.
126 – Paul Coffey, Edmonton, 1983-84. 80GP – 80 game schedule.
122 – Bobby Orr, Boston, 1973-74. 74GP – 78 game schedule.

MOST POINTS BY A DEFENSEMAN, ONE GAME:

8 – Tom Bladon, Philadelphia, Dec. 11, 1977, at Philadelphia. 4G-4A. Philadelphia 11, Cleveland 1.
– Paul Coffey, Edmonton, Mar. 14, 1986, at Edmonton. 2G-6A. Edmonton 12, Detroit 3.
7 – Bobby Orr, Boston, Nov. 15, 1973, at Boston. 3G-4A. Boston 10, NY Rangers 2.

SCORING BY A GOALTENDER

MOST POINTS BY A GOALTENDER, CAREER:

48 – Tom Barrasso, Buffalo, Pittsburgh, Ottawa, Carolina, Toronto, St. Louis, in 19 seasons. 777GP
46 – Grant Fuhr, Edmonton, Toronto, Buffalo, Los Angeles, St. Louis, Calgary, in 19 seasons. 868GP

MOST POINTS BY A GOALTENDER, ONE SEASON:

14 – Grant Fuhr, Edmonton, 1983-84. 45GP – 80 game schedule.
9 – Curtis Joseph, St. Louis, 1991-92. 60GP – 80 game schedule.
8 – Mike Palmateer, Washington, 1980-81. 49GP – 80 game schedule.
– Grant Fuhr, Edmonton, 1987-88. 75GP – 80 game schedule.
– Ron Hextall, Philadelphia, 1988-89. 64GP – 80 game schedule.
– Tom Barrasso, Pittsburgh, 1992-93. 63GP – 84 game schedule.

MOST POINTS BY A GOALTENDER, ONE GAME:

3 – Jeff Reese, Calgary, Feb. 10, 1993, at Calgary. Calgary 13, San Jose 1.

No defenseman in history has ever been more successful in the offensive end of the rink over an entire career than Raymond Bourque. Bourque is the all-time career leader in goals, assists and points among NHL blueliners.

SCORING BY A ROOKIE

MOST GOALS BY A ROOKIE, ONE SEASON:
76 – Teemu Selanne, Winnipeg, 1992-93. 84GP – 84 game schedule.
53 – Mike Bossy, NY Islanders, 1977-78. 73GP – 80 game schedule.
52 – Alex Ovechkin, Washington, 2005-06. 81GP – 82 game schedule.
51 – Joe Nieuwendyk, Calgary, 1987-88. 75GP – 80 game schedule.
45 – Dale Hawerchuk, Winnipeg, 1981-82. 80GP – 80 game schedule.
– Luc Robitaille, Los Angeles, 1986-87. 79GP – 80 game schedule.

MOST GOALS BY A PLAYER IN HIS FIRST NHL SEASON, ONE GAME:
5 – Howie Meeker, Toronto, Jan. 8, 1947, at Toronto. Toronto 10, Chicago 4.
– Don Murdoch, NY Rangers, Oct. 12, 1976, at Minnesota. NY Rangers 10, Minnesota 4.

MOST GOALS BY A PLAYER IN HIS FIRST NHL GAME:
3 – Alex Smart, Montreal, Jan. 14, 1943, at Montreal. Montreal 5, Chicago 1.
– Real Cloutier, Quebec, Oct. 10, 1979, at Quebec. Atlanta 5, Quebec 3.

MOST ASSISTS BY A ROOKIE, ONE SEASON:
70 – Peter Stastny, Quebec, 1980-81. 77GP – 80 game schedule.
– Joe Juneau, Boston, 1992-93. 84GP – 84 game schedule.
63 – Bryan Trottier, NY Islanders, 1975-76. 80GP – 80 game schedule.
– Sidney Crosby, Pittsburgh, 2005–06. 81GP – 82 game schedule.
62 – Sergei Makarov, Calgary, 1989-90. 80GP – 80 game schedule.
60 – Larry Murphy, Los Angeles, 1980-81. 80GP – 80 game schedule.

MOST ASSISTS BY A PLAYER IN HIS FIRST NHL SEASON, ONE GAME:
7 – Wayne Gretzky, Edmonton, Feb. 15, 1980, at Edmonton. Edmonton 8, Washington 2.
6 – Gary Suter, Calgary, Apr. 4, 1986, at Calgary. Calgary 9, Edmonton 3.

MOST ASSISTS BY A PLAYER IN HIS FIRST NHL GAME:
4 – Dutch Reibel, Detroit, Oct. 8, 1953, at Detroit. Detroit 4, NY Rangers 1.
– Roland Eriksson, Minnesota, Oct. 6, 1976, at NY Rangers. NY Rangers 6, Minnesota 5.
3 – Al Hill, Philadelphia, Feb. 14, 1977, at Philadelphia. Philadelphia 6, St. Louis 4.
– Jarno Kultanen, Boston, Oct. 5, 2000, at Boston. Boston 4, Ottawa 4.
– Stanislav Chistov, Anaheim, Oct. 10, 2002, at St. Louis. Anaheim 4, St. Louis 3.
– Dominic Moore, NY Rangers, Nov. 1, 2003, at Montreal. NY Rangers 5, Montreal 1.

MOST POINTS BY A ROOKIE, ONE SEASON:
132 – Teemu Selanne, Winnipeg, 1992-93. 84GP – 84 game schedule.
109 – Peter Stastny, Quebec, 1980-81. 77GP – 80 game schedule.
106 – Alex Ovechkin, Washington, 2005-06. 81GP – 82 game schedule.
103 – Dale Hawerchuk, Winnipeg, 1981-82. 80GP – 80 game schedule.
102 – Joe Juneau, Boston, 1992-93. 84GP – 84 game schedule.
– Sidney Crosby, Pittsburgh, 2005–06. 81GP – 82 game schedule.
100 – Mario Lemieux, Pittsburgh, 1984-85. 73GP – 80 game schedule.

MOST POINTS BY A PLAYER IN HIS FIRST NHL SEASON, ONE GAME:
8 – Peter Stastny, Quebec, Feb. 22, 1981, at Washington. 4G-4A. Quebec 11, Washington 7.
– Anton Stastny, Quebec, Feb. 22, 1981, at Washington. 3G-5A. Quebec 11, Washington 7.
7 – Wayne Gretzky, Edmonton, Feb. 15, 1980, at Edmonton. 7A. Edmonton 8, Washington 2.
– Sergei Makarov, Calgary, Feb. 25, 1990, at Calgary. 2G-5A. Calgary 10, Edmonton 4.
6 – Wayne Gretzky, Edmonton, Mar. 29, 1980, at Toronto. 2G-4A. Edmonton 8, Toronto 5.
– Gary Suter, Calgary, Apr. 4, 1986, at Calgary. 6A. Calgary 9, Edmonton 3.

MOST POINTS BY A PLAYER IN HIS FIRST NHL GAME:
5 – Al Hill, Philadelphia, Feb. 14, 1977, at Philadelphia. 2G-3A. Philadelphia 6, St. Louis 4.
4 – Alex Smart, Montreal, Jan. 14, 1943, at Montreal. 3G-1A. Montreal 5, Chicago 1.
– Dutch Reibel, Detroit, Oct. 8, 1953, at Detroit. 4A. Detroit 4, NY Rangers 1.
– Roland Eriksson, Minnesota, Oct. 6, 1976, at NY Rangers. 4A. NY Rangers 6, Minnesota 5.
– Stanislav Chistov, Anaheim, Oct. 10, 2002, at St. Louis. 1G-3A. Anaheim 4, St. Louis 3.

SCORING BY A ROOKIE DEFENSEMAN

MOST GOALS BY A ROOKIE DEFENSEMAN, ONE SEASON:
23 – Brian Leetch, NY Rangers, 1988-89. 68GP – 80 game schedule.
22 – Barry Beck, Colorado, 1977-78. 75GP – 80 game schedule.
20 – Dion Phaneuf, 2005-06. 82GP – 82 game schedule.

MOST ASSISTS BY A ROOKIE DEFENSEMAN, ONE SEASON:
60 – Larry Murphy, Los Angeles, 1980-81. 80GP – 80 game schedule.
55 – Chris Chelios, Montreal, 1984-85. 74GP – 80 game schedule.
50 – Stefan Persson, NY Islanders, 1977-78. 66GP – 80 game schedule.
– Gary Suter, Calgary, 1985-86. 80GP – 80 game schedule.
49 – Nicklas Lidstrom, Detroit, 1991-92. 80GP – 80 game schedule.

MOST POINTS BY A ROOKIE DEFENSEMAN, ONE SEASON:
76 – Larry Murphy, Los Angeles, 1980-81. 80GP – 80 game schedule.
71 – Brian Leetch, NY Rangers, 1988-89. 68GP – 80 game schedule.
68 – Gary Suter, Calgary, 1985-86. 80GP – 80 game schedule.
66 – Phil Housley, Buffalo, 1982-83. 77GP – 80 game schedule.
65 – Raymond Bourque, Boston, 1979-80. 80GP – 80 game schedule.

Teemu Selanne shattered the single season scoring records for rookies when he broke into the NHL with the Winnipeg Jets in 1992-93. He had an astounding 76 goals and added 56 assists for 132 points.

PER-GAME SCORING AVERAGES

HIGHEST GOALS-PER-GAME AVERAGE, CAREER (AMONG PLAYERS WITH 200-OR-MORE GOALS):

.762 – Mike Bossy, NY Islanders, 1977-78 – 1986-87, with 573G in 752GP.
.756 – Cy Denneny, Ottawa, Boston, 1917-18 – 1928-29, with 248G in 328GP.
.754 – Mario Lemieux, Pittsburgh, 1984-85 – 1996-97, 2000-01 – 2003-04, 2005-06, with 690G in 915GP.
.742 – Babe Dye, Toronto, Hamilton, Chicago, NY Americans, 1919-20 – 1930-31, with 201G in 271GP.
.623 – Pavel Bure, Vancouver, Florida, NY Rangers, 1991-92 – 2002-03, with 437G in 702GP.

HIGHEST GOALS-PER-GAME AVERAGE, ONE SEASON (AMONG PLAYERS WITH 20-OR-MORE GOALS):

2.20 – Joe Malone, Montreal, 1917-18, with 44G in 20GP.
1.80 – Cy Denneny, Ottawa, 1917-18, with 36G in 20GP.
1.64 – Newsy Lalonde, Montreal, 1917-18, with 23G in 14GP.
1.63 – Joe Malone, Quebec, 1919-20, with 39G in 24GP.
1.61 – Newsy Lalonde, Montreal, 1919-20, with 37G in 23GP.

HIGHEST GOALS-PER-GAME AVERAGE, ONE SEASON (AMONG PLAYERS WITH 50-OR-MORE GOALS):

1.18 – Wayne Gretzky, Edmonton, 1983-84, with 87G in 74GP.
1.15 – Wayne Gretzky, Edmonton, 1981-82, with 92G in 80GP.
– Mario Lemieux, Pittsburgh, 1992-93, with 69G in 60GP.
1.12 – Mario Lemieux, Pittsburgh, 1988-89, with 85G in 76GP.
1.10 – Brett Hull, St. Louis, 1990-91, with 86G in 78GP.
1.02 – Cam Neely, Boston, 1993-94, with 50G in 49GP.
1.00 – Maurice Richard, Montreal, 1944-45, with 50G in 50GP.

HIGHEST ASSISTS-PER-GAME AVERAGE, CAREER (AMONG PLAYERS WITH 300-OR-MORE ASSISTS):

1.320 – Wayne Gretzky, Edmonton, Los Angeles, St. Louis, NY Rangers, 1979-80 – 1998-99, with 1,963A in 1,487GP.
1.129 – Mario Lemieux, Pittsburgh, 1984-85 – 1996-97, 2000-01 – 2003-04, 2005-06, with 1,033A in 915GP.
.982 – Bobby Orr, Boston, Chicago, 1966-67 – 1978-79, with 645A in 657GP.
.894 – Peter Forsberg, Quebec, Colorado, Philadelphia, Nashville, 1994-95 – 2000-01, 2002-03 – 2003-04, 2005-06, 2006-07 with 623A in 697GP.
.808 – Peter Stastny, Quebec, New Jersey, St. Louis, 1980-81 – 1994-95, with 789A in 977GP.

HIGHEST ASSISTS-PER-GAME AVERAGE, ONE SEASON (AMONG PLAYERS WITH 35-OR-MORE ASSISTS):

2.04 – Wayne Gretzky, Edmonton, 1985-86, with 163A in 80GP.
1.70 – Wayne Gretzky, Edmonton, 1987-88, with 109A in 64GP.
1.69 – Wayne Gretzky, Edmonton, 1984-85, with 135A in 80GP.
1.59 – Wayne Gretzky, Edmonton, 1983-84, with 118A in 74GP.
1.56 – Wayne Gretzky, Edmonton, 1982-83, with 125A in 80GP.
– Wayne Gretzky, Los Angeles, 1990-91, with 122A in 78GP.
1.53 – Wayne Gretzky, Edmonton, 1986-87, with 121A in 79GP.
1.52 – Mario Lemieux, Pittsburgh, 1992-93, with 91A in 60GP.
1.50 – Wayne Gretzky, Edmonton, 1981-82, with 120A in 80GP.
– Mario Lemieux, Pittsburgh, 1988-89, with 114A in 76GP.

HIGHEST POINTS-PER-GAME AVERAGE, CAREER (AMONG PLAYERS WITH 500-OR-MORE POINTS):

1.921 – Wayne Gretzky, Edmonton, Los Angeles, St. Louis, NY Rangers, 1979-80 – 1998-99, with 2,857PTS (894G-1,963A) in 1,487GP.
1.883 – Mario Lemieux, Pittsburgh, 1984-85 – 1996-97, 2000-01 – 2003-04, 2005-06, with 1,723PTS (690G-1,033A) in 915GP.
1.497 – Mike Bossy, NY Islanders, 1977-78 – 1986-87, with 1,126PTS (573G-553A) in 752GP.
1.393 – Bobby Orr, Boston, Chicago, 1966-67 – 1978-79, with 915PTS (270G-645A) in 657GP.
1.314 – Marcel Dionne, Detroit, Los Angeles, NY Rangers, 1971-72 – 1988-89, with 1,771PTS (731G-1,040A) in 1,348GP.

HIGHEST POINTS-PER-GAME AVERAGE, ONE SEASON (AMONG PLAYERS WITH 50-OR-MORE POINTS):

2.77 – Wayne Gretzky, Edmonton, 1983-84, with 205PTS in 74GP.
2.69 – Wayne Gretzky, Edmonton, 1985-86, with 215PTS in 80GP.
2.67 – Mario Lemieux, Pittsburgh, 1992-93, with 160PTS in 60GP.
2.65 – Wayne Gretzky, Edmonton, 1981-82, with 212PTS in 80GP.
2.62 – Mario Lemieux, Pittsburgh, 1988-89, with 199PTS in 76GP.
2.60 – Wayne Gretzky, Edmonton, 1984-85, with 208PTS in 80GP.
2.45 – Wayne Gretzky, Edmonton, 1982-83, with 196PTS in 80GP.
2.33 – Wayne Gretzky, Edmonton, 1987-88, with 149PTS in 64GP.
2.32 – Wayne Gretzky, Edmonton, 1986-87, with 183PTS in 79GP.
2.30 – Mario Lemieux, Pittsburgh, 1995-96, with 161PTS in 70GP.
2.18 – Mario Lemieux, Pittsburgh, 1987-88, with 168PTS in 77GP.
2.15 – Wayne Gretzky, Los Angeles, 1988-89, with 168PTS in 78GP.
2.09 – Wayne Gretzky, Los Angeles, 1990-91, with 163PTS in 78GP.
2.08 – Mario Lemieux, Pittsburgh, 1989-90, with 123PTS in 59GP.

SCORING PLATEAUS

MOST 20-OR-MORE GOAL SEASONS:

22 – Gordie Howe, Detroit, Hartford, in 26 seasons.
20 – Ron Francis, Hartford, Pittsburgh, Carolina, Toronto, in 23 seasons.
19 – Dave Andreychuk, Buffalo, Toronto, New Jersey, Boston, Colorado, Tampa Bay, in 23 seasons.
18 – Brendan Shanahan, New Jersey, St. Louis, Hartford, Detroit, NY Rangers, in 19 seasons.
17 – Marcel Dionne, Detroit, Los Angeles, NY Rangers, in 18 seasons.
– Mike Gartner, Washington, Minnesota, NY Rangers, Toronto, Phoenix, in 18 seasons.
– Wayne Gretzky, Edmonton, Los Angeles, St. Louis, NY Rangers, in 20 seasons.
– Mark Messier, Edmonton, NY Rangers, Vancouver, in 25 seasons.
– Brett Hull, Calgary, St. Louis, Dallas, Detroit, Phoenix, in 19 seasons.
– Joe Sakic, Quebec, Colorado, in 18 seasons.

MOST CONSECUTIVE 20-OR-MORE GOAL SEASONS:

22 – Gordie Howe, Detroit, 1949-50 – 1970-71.
18 – Brendan Shanahan, New Jersey, St. Louis, Hartford, Detroit, NY Rangers, 1988-89 – 2006-07.
17 – Marcel Dionne, Detroit, Los Angeles, NY Rangers, 1971-72 – 1987-88.
– Brett Hull, Calgary, St. Louis, Dallas, Detroit, 1987-88 – 2003-04.
16 – Phil Esposito, Chicago, Boston, NY Rangers, 1964-65 – 1979-80.
– Jaromir Jagr, Pittsburgh, Washington, NY Rangers, 1990-91 – 2006-07.
– Mats Sundin, Quebec, Toronto, 1990-91 – 2006-07.

New York Islanders great Mike Bossy was the first rookie in NHL history to score 50 goals and topped this scoring benchmark nine times in ten seasons. With 573 career goals in 752 games, he has a goals-per-game rate of .762.

MOST 30-OR-MORE GOAL SEASONS:
17 – Mike Gartner, Washington, Minnesota, NY Rangers, Toronto, Phoenix, in 19 seasons.
15 – Jaromir Jagr, Pittsburgh, Washington, NY Rangers, in 16 seasons.
14 – Gordie Howe, Detroit, Hartford, in 26 seasons.
– Marcel Dionne, Detroit, Los Angeles, NY Rangers, in 18 seasons.
– Wayne Gretzky, Edmonton, Los Angeles, St. Louis, NY Rangers, in 20 seasons.
13 – Bobby Hull, Chicago, Winnipeg, Hartford, in 16 seasons.
– Phil Esposito, Chicago, Boston, NY Rangers, in 18 seasons.
– Brett Hull, Calgary, St. Louis, Dallas, Detroit, Phoenix, in 19 seasons.

MOST CONSECUTIVE 30-OR-MORE GOAL SEASONS:
15 – Mike Gartner, Washington, Minnesota, NY Rangers, Toronto, 1979-80 – 1993-94.
– Jaromir Jagr, Pittsburgh, Washington, NY Rangers, 1991-92 – 2006-07.
13 – Bobby Hull, Chicago, 1959-60 – 1971-72.
– Phil Esposito, Boston, NY Rangers, 1967-68 – 1979-80.
– Wayne Gretzky, Edmonton, Los Angeles, 1979-80 – 1991-92.

MOST 40-OR-MORE GOAL SEASONS:
12 – Wayne Gretzky, Edmonton, Los Angeles, St. Louis, NY Rangers, in 20 seasons.
10 – Marcel Dionne, Detroit, Los Angeles, NY Rangers, in 18 seasons.
– Mario Lemieux, Pittsburgh, in 17 seasons.
9 – Mike Bossy, NY Islanders, in 10 seasons.
– Mike Gartner, Washington, Minnesota, NY Rangers, Toronto, Phoenix, in 19 seasons.

MOST CONSECUTIVE 40-OR-MORE GOAL SEASONS:
12 – Wayne Gretzky, Edmonton, Los Angeles, 1979-80 – 1990-91.
9 – Mike Bossy, NY Islanders, 1977-78 – 1985-86.
8 – Luc Robitaille, Los Angeles, 1986-87 – 1993-94.
7 – Phil Esposito, Boston, 1968-69 – 1974-75.
– Michel Goulet, Quebec, 1981-82 – 1987-88.
– Jari Kurri, Edmonton, 1982-83 – 1988-89.

MOST 50-OR-MORE GOAL SEASONS:
9 – Mike Bossy, NY Islanders, in 10 seasons.
– Wayne Gretzky, Edmonton, Los Angeles, St. Louis, NY Rangers, in 20 seasons.
6 – Guy Lafleur, Montreal, NY Rangers, Quebec, in 17 seasons.
– Marcel Dionne, Detroit, Los Angeles, NY Rangers, in 18 seasons.
– Mario Lemieux, Pittsburgh, in 17 seasons.
5 – Bobby Hull, Chicago, Winnipeg, Hartford, in 16 seasons.
– Phil Esposito, Chicago, Boston, NY Rangers, in 18 seasons.
– Brett Hull, Calgary, St. Louis, Dallas, Detroit, Phoenix, in 19 seasons.
– Steve Yzerman, Detroit, in 22 seasons.
– Pavel Bure, Vancouver, Florida, NY Rangers, in 12 seasons.

MOST CONSECUTIVE 50-OR-MORE GOAL SEASONS:
9 – Mike Bossy, NY Islanders, 1977-78 – 1985-86.
8 – Wayne Gretzky, Edmonton, 1979-80 – 1986-87.
6 – Guy Lafleur, Montreal, 1974-75 – 1979-80.
5 – Phil Esposito, Boston, 1970-71 – 1974-75.
– Marcel Dionne, Los Angeles, 1978-79 – 1982-83.
– Brett Hull, St. Louis, 1989-90 – 1993-94.

MOST 60-OR-MORE GOAL SEASONS:
5 – Mike Bossy, NY Islanders, in 10 seasons.
– Wayne Gretzky, Edmonton, Los Angeles, St. Louis, NY Rangers, in 20 seasons.
4 – Phil Esposito, Chicago, Boston, NY Rangers, in 18 seasons.
– Mario Lemieux, Pittsburgh, in 17 seasons.

MOST CONSECUTIVE 60-OR-MORE GOAL SEASONS:
4 – Wayne Gretzky, Edmonton, 1981-82 – 1984-85.
3 – Mike Bossy, NY Islanders, 1980-81 – 1982-83.
– Brett Hull, St. Louis, 1989-90 – 1991-92.
2 – Phil Esposito, Boston, 1970-71 – 1971-72, 1973-74 – 1974-75.
– Jari Kurri, Edmonton, 1984-85 – 1985-86.
– Mario Lemieux, Pittsburgh, 1987-88 – 1988-89.
– Steve Yzerman, Detroit, 1988-89 – 1989-90.
– Pavel Bure, Vancouver, 1992-93 – 1993-94.

MOST 100-OR-MORE POINT SEASONS:
15 – Wayne Gretzky, Edmonton, Los Angeles, St. Louis, NY Rangers, in 20 seasons.
10 – Mario Lemieux, Pittsburgh, in 17 seasons.
8 – Marcel Dionne, Detroit, Los Angeles, NY Rangers, in 18 seasons.
7 – Mike Bossy, NY Islanders, in 10 seasons.
– Peter Stastny, Quebec, New Jersey, St. Louis, in 15 seasons.

MOST CONSECUTIVE 100-OR-MORE POINT SEASONS:
13 – Wayne Gretzky, Edmonton, Los Angeles, 1979-80 – 1991-92.
6 – Bobby Orr, Boston, 1969-70 – 1974-75.
– Guy Lafleur, Montreal, 1974-75 – 1979-80.
– Mike Bossy, NY Islanders,1980-81 – 1985-86.
– Peter Stastny, Quebec, 1980-81 – 1985-86.
– Mario Lemieux, Pittsburgh, 1984-85 – 1989-90.
– Steve Yzerman, Detroit, 1987-88 – 1992-93.

THREE-OR-MORE-GOAL GAMES

MOST THREE-OR-MORE GOAL GAMES, CAREER:
50 – Wayne Gretzky, Edmonton, Los Angeles, St. Louis, NY Rangers, in 20 seasons, 37 three-goal games, 9 four-goal games, 4 five-goal games.
40 – Mario Lemieux, Pittsburgh, in 17 seasons, 27 three-goal games, 10 four-goal games, 3 five-goal games.
39 – Mike Bossy, NY Islanders, in 10 seasons, 30 three-goal games, 9 four-goal games.
33 – Brett Hull, Calgary, St. Louis, Dallas, Detroit, Phoenix, in 19 seasons, 30 three-goal games, 3 four-goal games.
32 – Phil Esposito, Chicago, Boston, NY Rangers, in 18 seasons, 27 three-goal games, 5 four-goal games.

MOST THREE-OR-MORE GOAL GAMES, ONE SEASON:
10 – Wayne Gretzky, Edmonton, 1981-82. 6 three-goal games, 3 four-goal games, 1 five-goal game.
– Wayne Gretzky, Edmonton, 1983-84. 6 three-goal games, 4 four-goal games.
9 – Mike Bossy, NY Islanders, 1980-81. 6 three-goal games, 3 four-goal games.
– Mario Lemieux, Pittsburgh, 1988-89. 7 three-goal games, 1 four-goal game, 1 five-goal game.
8 – Brett Hull, St. Louis, 1991-92. 8 three-goal games.
7 – Joe Malone, Montreal, 1917-18. 2 three-goal games, 2 four-goal games, 3 five-goal games.
– Phil Esposito, Boston, 1970-71. 7 three-goal games.
– Rick Martin, Buffalo, 1975-76. 6 three-goal games, 1 four-goal game.
– Alexander Mogilny, Buffalo, 1992-93. 5 three-goal games, 2 four-goal games.

Mike Gartner's record of 15 consecutive 30-goal seasons was equaled by Jaromir Jagr in 2006-07. Gartner still holds the career record of 17 seasons with 30-or-more goals.

SCORING STREAKS

LONGEST CONSECUTIVE GOAL-SCORING STREAK:

16 Games – Punch Broadbent, Ottawa, 1921-22. 27G
14 Games – Joe Malone, Montreal, 1917-18. 35G
13 Games – Newsy Lalonde, Montreal, 1920-21. 24G
– Charlie Simmer, Los Angeles, 1979-80. 17G
12 Games – Cy Denneny, Ottawa, 1917-18. 23G
– Dave Lumley, Edmonton, 1981-82. 15G
– Mario Lemieux, Pittsburgh, 1992-93. 18G

LONGEST CONSECUTIVE ASSIST-SCORING STREAK:

23 Games – Wayne Gretzky, Los Angeles, 1990-91. 48A
18 Games – Adam Oates, Boston, 1992-93. 28A
17 Games – Wayne Gretzky, Edmonton, 1983-84. 38A
– Paul Coffey, Edmonton, 1985-86. 27A
– Wayne Gretzky, Los Angeles, 1989-90. 35A
16 Games – Jaromir Jagr, Pittsburgh, 2000-01. 24A

LONGEST CONSECUTIVE POINT-SCORING STREAK:

51 Games – Wayne Gretzky, Edmonton, 1983-84. 61G-92A-153PTS
46 Games – Mario Lemieux, Pittsburgh, 1989-90. 39G-64A-103PTS
39 Games – Wayne Gretzky, Edmonton, 1985-86. 33G-75A-108PTS
30 Games – Wayne Gretzky, Edmonton, 1982-83. 24G-52A-76PTS
– Mats Sundin, Quebec, 1992-93. 21G-25A-46PTS

LONGEST CONSECUTIVE POINT-SCORING STREAK FROM START OF SEASON:

51 Games – Wayne Gretzky, Edmonton, 1983-84. 61G-92A-153PTS. Streak ended by Los Angeles and goaltender Markus Mattsson on Jan. 28, 1984.

LONGEST CONSECUTIVE POINT-SCORING STREAK BY A DEFENSEMAN:

28 Games – Paul Coffey, Edmonton, 1985-86. 16G-39A-55PTS
19 Games – Raymond Bourque, Boston, 1987-88. 6G-21A-27PTS
17 Games – Raymond Bourque, Boston, 1984-85. 4G-24A-28PTS
– Brian Leetch, NY Rangers, 1991-92. 5G-24A-29PTS
16 Games – Gary Suter, Calgary, 1987-88. 8G-17A-25PTS
15 Games – Bobby Orr, Boston, 1970-71. 10G-23A-33PTS
– Bobby Orr, Boston, 1973-74. 8G-15A-23PTS
– Steve Duchesne, Quebec, 1992-93. 4G-17A-21PTS
– Chris Chelios, Chicago, 1995-96. 4G-16A-20PTS

LONGEST CONSECUTIVE POINT-SCORING STREAK BY A ROOKIE:

20 Games – Paul Stastny, Colorado, 1983-84. 11G-18A-29PTS
17 Games – Teemu Selanne, Winnipeg, 1992-93. 20G-14A-34PTS
16 Games – Peter Stastny, Quebec, 1980-81
15 Games – Jude Drouin, Minnesota North Stars, 1970-71

FASTEST GOALS AND ASSISTS

FASTEST GOAL FROM START OF A GAME:

0:05 – Doug Smail, Winnipeg, Dec. 20, 1981, at Winnipeg. Winnipeg 5, St. Louis 4.
– Bryan Trottier, NY Islanders, Mar. 22, 1984, at Boston. NY Islanders 3, Boston 3.
– Alexander Mogilny, Buffalo, Dec. 21, 1991, at Toronto. Buffalo 4, Toronto 1.
0:06 – Henry Boucha, Detroit, Jan. 28, 1973, at Montreal. Detroit 4, Montreal 2.
– Jean Pronovost, Pittsburgh, Mar. 25, 1976, at St. Louis. St. Louis 5, Pittsburgh 2.
0:07 – Charlie Conacher, Toronto, Feb. 6, 1932, at Toronto. Toronto 6, Boston 0.
– Danny Gare, Buffalo, Dec. 17, 1978, at Buffalo. Buffalo 6, Vancouver 3.
– Tiger Williams, Los Angeles, Feb. 14, 1987, at Los Angeles. Los Angeles 5, Harford 2.
0:08 – Ron Martin, NY Americans, Dec. 4, 1932, at NY Americans. NY Americans 4, Montreal 2.
– Chuck Arnason, Colorado, Jan. 28, 1977, at Atlanta. Colorado 3, Atlanta 3.
– Wayne Gretzky, Edmonton, Dec. 14, 1983, at NY Rangers. Edmonton 9, NY Rangers 4.
– Gaetan Duchesne, Washington, Mar. 14, 1987, at St. Louis. Washington 3, St. Louis 3.
– Tim Kerr, Philadelphia, Mar. 7, 1989, at Philadelphia. Philadelphia 4, Edmonton 4.
– Grant Ledyard, Buffalo, Dec. 4, 1991, at Winnipeg. Buffalo 4, Winnipeg 4.
– Brent Sutter, Chicago, Feb. 5, 1995, at Vancouver. Chicago 9, Vancouver 4.
– Paul Kariya, Anaheim, Mar. 9, 1997, at Colorado. Anaheim 2, Colorado 2.
– Tony Hrkac, Dallas, Nov. 7, 1998, at Los Angeles. Dallas 4, Los Angeles 3.
– Sergei Fedorov, Detroit, Nov. 21, 1998, at Vancouver. Detroit 4, Vancouver 2.
– Ronald Petrovicky, Atlanta, Dec. 20, 2003, at Pittsburgh. Atlanta 7, Pittsburgh 4.
– Mike Modano, Dallas, Dec. 27, 2003, at Columbus. Dallas 4, Columbus 3.
– Antti Laaksonen, Colorado, Feb. 10, 2006, at Columbus. Colorado 4, Columbus 1.

FASTEST GOAL FROM START OF A PERIOD:

0:04 – Claude Provost, Montreal, Nov. 9, 1957, at Montreal, second period. Montreal 4, Boston 2.
– Denis Savard, Chicago, Jan. 12, 1986, at Chicago, third period. Chicago 4, Hartford 2.

FASTEST GOAL BY A PLAYER IN HIS FIRST NHL GAME:

0:15 – Gus Bodnar, Toronto, Oct. 30, 1943, at Toronto. Toronto 5, NY Rangers 2.
0:18 – Danny Gare, Buffalo, Oct. 10, 1974, at Buffalo. Buffalo 9, Boston 5.
0:20 – Alexander Mogilny, Buffalo, Oct. 5, 1989, at Buffalo. Buffalo 4, Quebec 3.

FASTEST TWO GOALS FROM START OF A GAME:

0:27 – Mike Knuble, Boston, Feb. 14, 2003, at Florida. 0:10 and 0:27. Boston 6, Florida 5.

FASTEST TWO GOALS:

0:04 – Nels Stewart, Mtl. Maroons, Jan. 3, 1931, at Mtl. Maroons. 8:24 and 8:28, third period. Mtl. Maroons 5, Boston 3.
– Deron Quint, Winnipeg, Dec. 15, 1995, at Winnipeg. 7:51 and 7:55, second period. Winnipeg 9, Edmonton 4.
0:05 – Pete Mahovlich, Montreal, Feb. 20, 1971, at Montreal. 12:16 and 12:21, third period. Montreal 7, Chicago 1.
0:06 – Jim Pappin, Chicago, Feb. 16, 1972, at Chicago. 2:57 and 3:03, third period. Chicago 3, Philadelphia 3.
– Ralph Backstrom, Los Angeles, Nov. 2, 1972, at Los Angeles. 8:30 and 8:36, third period. Los Angeles 5, Boston 2.
– Lanny McDonald, Calgary, Mar. 22, 1984, at Calgary. 16:23 and 16:29, first period. Detroit 6, Calgary 4.
– Sylvain Turgeon, Hartford, Mar. 28, 1987, at Hartford. 13:59 and 14:05, second period. Hartford 5, Pittsburgh 4.

FASTEST THREE GOALS:

0:21 – Bill Mosienko, Chicago, Mar. 23, 1952, at NY Rangers, against goaltender Lorne Anderson. Mosienko scored at 6:09, 6:20 and 6:30 of third period, all with both teams at full strength. Chicago 7, NY Rangers 6.
0:44 – Jean Béliveau, Montreal, Nov. 5, 1955, at Montreal, against goaltender Terry Sawchuk. Béliveau scored at 0:42, 1:08 and 1:26 of second period, all with Montreal holding a 6-4 man advantage. Montreal 4, Boston 2.

FASTEST THREE ASSISTS:

0:21 – Gus Bodnar, Chicago, Mar. 23, 1952, at NY Rangers, Bodnar assisted on Bill Mosienko's three goals at 6:09, 6:20 and 6:30 of third period. Chicago 7, NY Rangers 6.
0:44 – Bert Olmstead, Montreal, Nov. 5, 1955, at Montreal, Olmstead assisted on Jean Béliveau's three goals at 0:42, 1:08 and 1:26 of second period. Montreal 4, Boston 2.

SHOTS ON GOAL

MOST SHOTS ON GOAL, ONE SEASON:

550 – Phil Esposito, Boston, 1970-71. 78GP – 78 game schedule.
429 – Paul Kariya, Anaheim, 1998-99. 82GP – 82 game schedule.
426 – Phil Esposito, Boston, 1971-72. 76GP – 78 game schedule.
425 – Alex Ovechkin, Washington, 2005-06. 81GP – 82 game schedule.
414 – Bobby Hull, Chicago, 1968-69. 74GP – 76 game schedule.

PENALTIES

MOST PENALTY MINUTES, CAREER:

3,966 – Tiger Williams, Toronto, Vancouver, Detroit, Los Angeles, Hartford, in 14 seasons. 962GP
3,565 – Dale Hunter, Quebec, Washington, Colorado, in 19 seasons. 1,407GP
3,515 – Tie Domi, Toronto, NY Rangers, Winnipeg, in 16 seasons. 1,020GP
3,381 – Marty McSorley, Pittsburgh, Edmonton, Los Angeles, NY Rangers, San Jose, Boston, in 17 seasons. 961GP
3,300 – Bob Probert, Detroit, Chicago, in 17 seasons. 935GP

MOST PENALTY MINUTES, CAREER, INCLUDING PLAYOFFS:

4,421 – Tiger Williams, Toronto, Vancouver, Detroit, Los Angeles, Hartford, 3,966 in 962 regular-season games; 455 in 83 playoff games.
4,294 – Dale Hunter, Quebec, Washington, Colorado, 3,565 in 1,407 regular-season games; 729 in 186 playoff games.
3,755 – Marty McSorley, Pittsburgh, Edmonton, Los Angeles, NY Rangers, San Jose, Boston, 3,381 in 961 regular-season games; 374 in 115 playoff games.
3,753 – Tie Domi, Toronto, NY Rangers, Winnipeg, 3,515 in 1,020 regular-season games; 238 in 98 playoff games.
3,584 – Chris Nilan, Montreal, NY Rangers, Boston, 3,043 in 688 regular-season games; 541 in 111 playoff games.

MOST PENALTY MINUTES, ONE SEASON:

472 – Dave Schultz, Philadelphia, 1974-75.
409 – Paul Baxter, Pittsburgh, 1981-82.
408 – Mike Peluso, Chicago, 1991-92.
405 – Dave Schultz, Los Angeles, Pittsburgh, 1977-78.

MOST PENALTIES, ONE GAME:

10 – Chris Nilan, Boston, Mar. 31, 1991, at Boston vs. Hartford. 6 minors, 2 majors, 1 10-minute misconduct, 1 game misconduct.
9 – Jim Dorey, Toronto, Oct. 16, 1968, at Toronto vs. Pittsburgh. 4 minors, 2 majors, 2 10-minute misconducts, 1 game misconduct.
– Dave Schultz, Pittsburgh, Apr. 6, 1978, at Detroit. 5 minors, 2 majors, 2 10-minute misconducts.
– Randy Holt, Los Angeles, Mar. 11, 1979, at Philadelphia. 1 minor, 3 majors, 2 10-minute misconducts, 3 game misconducts.
– Russ Anderson, Pittsburgh, Jan. 19, 1980, at Pittsburgh vs. Edmonton. 3 minors, 3 majors, 3 game misconducts.
– Kim Clackson, Quebec, Mar. 8, 1981, at Quebec vs. Chicago. 4 minors, 3 majors, 2 game misconducts.
– Terry O'Reilly, Boston, Dec. 19, 1984, at Hartford. 5 minors, 3 majors, 1 game misconduct.
– Larry Playfair, Los Angeles, Dec. 9, 1986, at NY Islanders. 6 minors, 2 majors, 1 10-minute misconduct.
– Marty McSorley, Los Angeles, Apr. 14, 1992, at Vancouver. 5 minors, 2 majors, 1 10-minute misconduct, 1 game misconduct.
– Reed Low, St. Louis, Dec. 31, 2002, at Detroit. 4 minors, 1 major, 1 10-minute misconduct, 3 game misconducts.

MOST PENALTY MINUTES, ONE GAME:

67 – Randy Holt, Los Angeles, Mar. 11, 1979, at Philadelphia. 1 minor, 3 majors, 2 10-minute misconducts, 3 game misconducts.
57 – Brad Smith, Toronto, Nov. 15, 1986, at Toronto vs. Detroit. 1 minor, 3 majors, 2 10-minute misconducts, 2 game misconducts.
– Reed Low, St. Louis, Feb. 28, 2002, at St. Louis vs. Calgary. 1 minor, 3 majors, 1 10-minute misconduct, 3 game misconducts.

MOST PENALTIES, ONE PERIOD:
9 – Randy Holt, Los Angeles, Mar. 11, 1979, at Philadelphia, first period. 1 minor, 3 majors, 2 10-minute misconducts, 3 game misconducts.

MOST PENALTY MINUTES, ONE PERIOD:
67 – Randy Holt, Los Angeles, Mar. 11, 1979, at Philadelphia, first period. 1 minor, 3 majors, 2 10-minute misconducts, 3 game misconducts.

GOALTENDING

MOST GAMES APPEARED IN BY A GOALTENDER, CAREER:
1,029 – Patrick Roy, Montreal, Colorado,1984-85 – 2002-03.
971 – Terry Sawchuk, Detroit, Boston, Toronto, Los Angeles, NY Rangers, 1949-50 – 1969-70.
963 – Ed Belfour, Chicago, San Jose, Dallas, Toronto, Florida, 1988-89 – 2003-04, 2005-06, 2006-07.
913 – Curtis Joseph, St. Louis, Edmonton, Toronto, Detroit, Phoenix, 1989-90 – 2003-04, 2005-06, 2006-07.
906 – Glenn Hall, Detroit, Chicago, St. Louis, 1952-53, 1954-55 – 1970-71.

MOST CONSECUTIVE COMPLETE GAMES BY A GOALTENDER:
502 – Glenn Hall, Detroit, Chicago. Played 502 games from beginning of 1955-56 season through first 12 games of 1962-63 season. In his 503rd straight game, Nov. 7, 1962, at Chicago, Hall was removed from the game against Boston with a back injury in the first period.

MOST GAMES APPEARED IN BY A GOALTENDER, ONE SEASON:
79 – Grant Fuhr, St. Louis, 1995-96.
78 – Martin Brodeur, New Jersey, 2006-07.
77 – Martin Brodeur, New Jersey, 1995-96.
– Bill Ranford, Edmonton, Boston, 1995-96.
– Arturs Irbe, Carolina, 2000-01.
– Marc Denis, Columbus, 2002-03.

MOST MINUTES PLAYED BY A GOALTENDER, CAREER:
60,235 – Patrick Roy, Montreal, Colorado, 1984-85 – 2002-03.
57,194 – Terry Sawchuk, Detroit, Boston, Toronto, Los Angeles, NY Rangers, 1949-50 – 1969-70.

MOST MINUTES PLAYED BY A GOALTENDER, ONE SEASON:
4,697 – Martin Brodeur, New Jersey, 2006-07.
4,555 – Martin Brodeur, New Jersey, 2003-04.
4,511 – Marc Denis, Columbus, 2002-03.

MOST SHUTOUTS, CAREER:
103 – Terry Sawchuk, Detroit, Boston, Toronto, Los Angeles, NY Rangers, in 21 seasons. (1949-50 – 1969-70)
94 – George Hainsworth, Montreal, Toronto, in 11 seasons. (1926-27 – 1936-37)
92 – Martin Brodeur, New Jersey, in 14 seasons. (1991-92, 1993-94 – 2003-04, 2005-06, 2006-07)

MOST SHUTOUTS, ONE SEASON:
22 – George Hainsworth, Montreal, 1928-29. 44GP
15 – Alec Connell, Ottawa, 1925-26. 36GP
– Alec Connell, Ottawa, 1927-28. 44GP
– Hal Winkler, Boston, 1927-28. 44GP
– Tony Esposito, Chicago, 1969-70. 63GP
14 – George Hainsworth, Montreal, 1926-27. 44GP

LONGEST SHUTOUT SEQUENCE BY A GOALTENDER:
461:29 – Alec Connell, Ottawa, 1927-28, six consecutive shutouts. (Forward passing not permitted in attacking zones in 1927-28.)
343:05 – George Hainsworth, Montreal, 1928-29, four consecutive shutouts. (Forward passing not permitted in attacking zones in 1928-29.)
332:01 – Brian Boucher, Phoenix, 2003-04, five consecutive shutouts.
324:40 – Roy Worters, NY Americans, 1930-31, four consecutive shutouts.
309:21 – Bill Durnan, Montreal, 1948-49, four consecutive shutouts.

MOST WINS BY A GOALTENDER, CAREER:
551 – Patrick Roy, Montreal, Colorado, in 19 seasons. 1,029GP
494 – Martin Brodeur, New Jersey, in 14 seasons. 891GP
484 – Ed Belfour, Chicago, San Jose, Dallas, Toronto, Florida, in 17 seasons. 963GP
447 – Terry Sawchuk, Detroit, Boston, Toronto, Los Angeles, NY Rangers, in 21 seasons. 971GP
446 – Curtis Joseph, St. Louis, Edmonton, Toronto, Detroit, Phoenix, in 17 seasons. 913GP

MOST WINS BY A GOALTENDER, ONE SEASON:
48 – Martin Brodeur, New Jersey, 2006-07. 78GP
47 – Bernie Parent, Philadelphia, 1973-74. 73GP
– Roberto Luongo, Vancouver, 2006-07. 76GP
44 – Terry Sawchuk, Detroit, 1950-51. 70GP
– Terry Sawchuk, Detroit, 1951-52. 70GP
– Bernie Parent, Philadelphia, 1974-75. 68GP

LONGEST WINNING STREAK BY A GOALTENDER, ONE SEASON:
17 – Gilles Gilbert, Boston, 1975-76.
14 – Tiny Thompson, Boston, 1929-30.
– Ross Brooks, Boston, 1973-74.
– Don Beaupre, Minnesota, 1985-86.
– Tom Barrasso, Pittsburgh, 1992-93.

LONGEST UNDEFEATED STREAK BY A GOALTENDER, ONE SEASON:
32 Games – Gerry Cheevers, Boston, 1971-72. 24W-8T
31 Games – Pete Peeters, Boston, 1982-83. 26W-5T
27 Games – Pete Peeters, Philadelphia, 1979-80. 22W-5T

LONGEST UNDEFEATED STREAK BY A GOALTENDER IN HIS FIRST NHL SEASON:
23 Games – Grant Fuhr, Edmonton, 1981-82. 15W-8T

LONGEST UNDEFEATED STREAK BY A GOALTENDER FROM START OF CAREER:
16 Games – Patrick Lalime, Pittsburgh, 1996-97. 14W-2T

MOST 30-OR-MORE WIN SEASONS BY A GOALTENDER:
13 – Patrick Roy, Montreal, Colorado, in 19 seasons.
11 – Martin Brodeur, New Jersey, in 14 seasons.
9 – Ed Belfour, Chicago, San Jose, Dallas, Toronto, Florida, in 17 seasons.
8 – Tony Esposito, Montreal, Chicago, in 16 seasons.
7 – Jacques Plante, Montreal, NY Rangers, St. Louis, Toronto, Boston, in 18 seasons.
– Ken Dryden, Montreal, in 8 seasons.
– Curtis Joseph, St. Louis, Edmonton, Toronto, Detroit, Phoenix, in 17 seasons.
– Dominik Hasek, Chicago, Buffalo, Detroit, Ottawa, in 15 seasons.

MOST CONSECUTIVE 30-OR-MORE WIN SEASONS BY A GOALTENDER:
11 – Martin Brodeur, New Jersey, 1995-96 – 2006-07.
8 – Patrick Roy, Montreal, Colorado, 1995-96 – 2002-03.
7 – Tony Esposito, Chicago, 1969-70 – 1975-76.
6 – Jacques Plante, Montreal, 1954-55 – 1959-60.
5 – Terry Sawchuk, Detroit, 1950-51 – 1954-55.
– Ken Dryden, Montreal, 1974-75 – 1978-79.

MOST 40-OR-MORE WIN SEASONS BY A GOALTENDER:
6 – Martin Brodeur, New Jersey, in 14 seasons.
3 – Terry Sawchuk, Detroit, Boston, Toronto, Los Angeles, NY Rangers, in 21 seasons.
– Jacques Plante, Montreal, NY Rangers, St. Louis, Toronto, Boston, in 18 seasons.
2 – Bernie Parent, Boston, Philadelphia, Toronto, in 13 seasons.
– Ken Dryden, Montreal, in 8 seasons.
– Ed Belfour, Chicago, San Jose, Dallas, Toronto, Florida, in 17 seasons.
– Miikka Kiprusoff, San Jose, Calgary, in 6 seasons.

MOST CONSECUTIVE 40-OR-MORE WIN SEASONS BY A GOALTENDER:
2 – Terry Sawchuk, Detroit, 1950-51 – 1951-52.
– Bernie Parent, Philadelphia, 1973-74 – 1974-75.
– Ken Dryden, Montreal, 1975-76 – 1976-77.
– Martin Brodeur, New Jersey, 1999-2000 – 2000-01.
– Martin Brodeur, New Jersey, 2005-06 – 2006-07.
– Miikka Kiprusoff, Calgary, 2005-06 – 2006-07.

MOST LOSSES BY A GOALTENDER, CAREER:
352 – Gump Worsley, NY Rangers, Montreal, Minnesota, in 21 seasons. 861GP
351 – Gilles Meloche, Chicago, California, Cleveland, Minnesota, Pittsburgh, in 18 seasons. 788GP
346 – John Vanbiesbrouck, NY Rangers, Florida, Philadelphia, NY Islanders, New Jersey, in 20 seasons. 882GP
341 – Sean Burke, New Jersey, Hartford, Carolina, Vancouver, Philadelphia, Florida, Phoenix, Tampa Bay, Los Angeles, in 18 seasons. 820GP
– Curtis Joseph, St. Louis, Edmonton, Toronto, Detroit, Phoenix, in 17 seasons. 913GP

MOST LOSSES BY A GOALTENDER, ONE SEASON:
48 – Gary Smith, California, 1970-71. 71GP
47 – Al Rollins, Chicago, 1953-54. 66GP
46 – Peter Sidorkiewicz, Ottawa, 1992-93. 64GP

GOALTENDER SHOOTOUT RECORDS

MOST SHOOTOUT WINS, ONE SEASON:
10 – Ryan Miller, Buffalo, 2006-07, (14GP)
– Martin Brodeur, New Jersey, 2006-07, (16GP)
9 – Marc-Andre Fleury, Pittsburgh, 2006-07, (14GP)

MOST SHOOTOUT WINS, ALL-TIME:
18 – Martin Brodeur, New Jersey, (27GP)
16 – Marty Turco, Dallas, (21GP)
13 – Ryan Miller, Buffalo, (19GP)
– Rick DiPietro, NY Islanders, (20GP)

MOST SHOOTOUT SHOTS AGAINST, ONE SEASON:
60 – Martin Brodeur, New Jersey, 2006-07, (20GA)
50 – Henrik Lundqvist, NY Rangers, 2006-07, (9GA)
46 – Tim Thomas, Boston, 2006-07, (8GA)
– Ryan Miller, Buffalo, 2006-07, (9GA)
– Marty Turco, Dallas, 2006-07, (11GA)

MOST SHOOTOUT SHOTS AGAINST, ALL-TIME:
98 – Martin Brodeur, New Jersey, (29GA)
87 – Henrik Lundqvist, NY Rangers, (18GA)
85 – Rick DiPietro, NY Islanders, (21GA)

BEST SHOOTOUT SAVE PERCENTAGE, ONE SEASON: *(minimum 20 shots)*
.900 – Marc Denis, Tampa Bay, 2006-07, (20S, 2GA)
.879 – Johan Holmqvist, Tampa Bay, 2006-07, (33S, 4GA)
.850 – Kari Lehtonen, Atlanta, 2005-06, (20S, 3GA)

BEST SHOOTOUT SAVE PERCENTAGE, ALL-TIME: *(minimum 40 shots)*
.793 – Henrik Lundqvist, NY Rangers, (87S, 18GA)
.779 – Tim Thomas, Boston, (77S, 17GA)
.777 – Ryan Miller, Buffalo, (63S, 14GA)

Active NHL Players' Three-or-More-Goal Games

Among Henrik Zetterberg's 33 goals for the Red Wings in 2006-07 was his first career hat trick on February 17, 2007. Zetterberg led Detroit to a 4-1 win over Phoenix.

Regular Season

Teams named are the ones the players were with at the time of their multiple-scoring games. Players listed alphabetically.

Player	Team	3-Goals	4-Goals	5-Goals
Adams, Kevyn	Carolina	2	—	—
Alfredsson, Daniel	Ottawa	4	1	—
Amonte, Tony	NYR, Chi.	7	—	—
Antropov, Nik	Toronto	1	—	—
Armstrong, Derek	Los Angeles	1	—	—
Arnason, Tyler	Chicago	1	—	—
Arnott, Jason	Edm., N.J., Dal.	5	—	—
Barnes, Stu	Wpg., Pit., Dal.	4	—	—
Battaglia, Bates	Carolina	1	—	—
Belanger, Eric	Los Angeles	1	—	—
Berard, Bryan	Columbus	1	—	—
Bergeron, Marc-Andre	Edmonton	1	—	—
Bertuzzi, Todd	Vancouver	5	—	—
Blake, Jason	NY Islanders	4	—	—
Blake, Rob	Los Angeles	1	—	—
Bochenski, Brandon	Ottawa	1	—	—
Bondra, Peter	Washington	12	5	1
Bonk, Radek	Ottawa	1	—	—
Boucher, Philippe	Dallas	1	—	—
Boyes, Brad	Boston	1	—	—
Boyle, Dan	Tampa Bay	1	—	—
Brind'Amour, Rod	Phi., Car.	2	—	—
Briere, Daniel	Buffalo	2	—	—
Brown, Curtis	Buffalo	1	—	—
Brunette, Andrew	Colorado	1	—	—
Bulis, Jan	Montreal	—	1	—
Burrows, Alexandre	Vancouver	1	—	—
Carter, Anson	Boston	1	—	—
Cheechoo, Jonathan	San Jose	8	—	—
Chouinard, Marc	Minnesota	1	—	—
Clark, Chris	Washington	2	—	—
Cleary, Daniel	Detroit	1	—	—
Clowe, Ryane	San Jose	1	—	—
Cole, Erik	Carolina	4	—	—
Conroy, Craig	St.L., L.A.	2	—	—
Crosby, Sidney	Pittsburgh	1	—	—
Demitra, Pavol	St.L., L.A.	4	—	—
Devereaux, Boyd	Edmonton	1	—	—
Donovan, Shean	Atlanta	1	—	—
Drury, Chris	Buffalo	1	—	—
Dumont, Jean-Pierre	Chi., Buf.	3	—	—
Dvorak, Radek	NY Rangers	1	1	—
Ekman, Nils	Pittsburgh	1	—	—
Elias, Patrik	New Jersey	6	1	—
Fedorov, Sergei	Detroit	4	1	1
Forsberg, Peter	Colorado	6	—	—
Friesen, Jeff	San Jose	2	—	—
Frolov, Alexander	Los Angeles	2	—	—
Gaborik, Marian	Minnesota	6	—	—
Gagne, Simon	Philadelphia	2	—	—
Gelinas, Martin	Edm., Van.	2	1	—
Gionta, Brian	New Jersey	1	—	—
Gomez, Scott	New Jersey	2	—	—
Gonchar, Sergei	Washington	1	—	—
Gratton, Chris	Tampa Bay	1	—	—
Grier, Mike	Edmonton	1	—	—
Guerin, Bill	N.J., Bos., Dal., St.L., S.J.	8	—	—
Hamilton, Jeff	Chicago	2	—	—
Handzus, Michal	St. Louis	1	—	—
Hartnell, Scott	Nashville	1	—	—
Havlat, Martin	Ottawa	3	1	—
Heatley, Dany	Atl., Ott.	5	1	—
Hecht, Jochen	Buffalo	1	—	—
Hedstrom, Jonathan	Anaheim	1	—	—
Hejduk, Milan	Colorado	3	—	—
Holik, Bobby	New Jersey	3	—	—
Holmstrom, Tomas	Detroit	3	—	—
Horcoff, Shawn	Edmonton	1	—	—
Horton, Nathan	Florida	1	—	—
Hossa, Marian	Ott., Atl.	5	1	—
Iginla, Jarome	Calgary	4	1	—
Jagr, Jaromir	Pit., NYR	13	1	—
Jokinen, Olli	Florida	4	—	—
Kaberle, Thomas	Toronto	1	—	—
Kapanen, Niko	Dallas	1	—	—
Kapanen, Sami	Carolina	3	—	—
Kariya, Paul	Ana., Nsh.	9	—	—
Kobasew, Chuck	Calgary	1	—	—
Koivu, Saku	Montreal	1	—	—
Kovalchuk, Ilya	Atlanta	6	1	—
Kovalev, Alex	NYR, Pit.	10	—	—
Kozlov, Viktor	Fla., NYI	1	1	—
Kozlov, Vyacheslav	Det., Atl.	4	1	—
Kunitz, Chris	Anaheim	1	—	—
Laaksonen, Antti	Minnesota	1	—	—
Lang, Robert	Washington	1	—	—
Langkow, Daymond	Phoenix	2	—	—
Laperriere, Ian	Los Angeles	1	—	—
Lapointe, Martin	Det., Bos.	2	—	—
Laraque, Georges	Edmonton	1	—	—
Lecavalier, Vincent	Tampa Bay	4	—	—
Legwand, David	Nashville	1	—	—
Lehtinen, Jere	Dallas	2	—	—
Linden, Trevor	Van., Mtl.	5	—	—
Lindros, Eric	Phi., NYR	12	1	—
Lombardi, Matthew	Calgary	1	—	—
Madden, John	New Jersey	1	1	—
Malone, Ryan	Pittsburgh	2	—	—
Maltby, Kirk	Detroit	1	—	—
Marleau, Patrick	San Jose	2	—	—
McCauley, Alyn	San Jose	1	—	—
Modano, Mike	Min., Dal.	6	1	—
Modin, Fredrik	Tampa Bay	3	—	—
Morrison, Brendan	Vancouver	1	—	—
Morrow, Brendan	Dallas	1	—	—
Murray, Glen	L.A., Bos.	5	—	—
Nagy, Ladislav	Phoenix	2	—	—
Nash, Rick	Columbus	1	—	—
Naslund, Markus	Pit., Van.	8	2	—
Nedved, Petr	Pit., NYR	6	1	—
Nolan, Owen	Que., S.J.	9	1	—
Nylander, Michael	Hfd., Chi.	1	1	—
O'Neill, Jeff	Hfd., Car., Tor.	3	—	—
Orszagh, Vladimir	Nashville	1	—	—
Ovechkin, Alex	Washington	2	—	—
Parrish, Mark	Fla., NYI, Min.	4	1	—
Peca, Michael	Buffalo	1	—	—
Perreault, Yanic	L.A., Tor., Mtl.	3	1	—
Petersen, Toby	Pittsburgh	1	—	—
Petrovicky, Ronald	Atlanta	1	—	—
Piros, Kamil	Atlanta	1	—	—
Pisani, Fernando	Edmonton	1	—	—
Pominville, Jason	Buffalo	1	—	—
Prospal, Vaclav	Ana., T.B.	2	—	—
Pyatt, Taylor	Buffalo	2	—	—
Quint, Deron	Columbus	1	—	—
Recchi, Mark	Pit., Mtl., Phi.	7	—	—
Reinprecht, Steve	Col., Phx.	2	—	—
Rheaume, Pascal	Atlanta	—	1	—
Ricci, Mike	Que., S.J.	1	—	1
Richards, Mike	Philadelphia	1	—	—
Roberts, Gary	Cgy., Car., Tor.	12	1	—
Roenick, Jeremy	Chi., Phx.	7	2	—
Rolston, Brian	N.J., Min.	2	—	—
Roy, Derek	Buffalo	2	—	—
Rucinsky, Martin	Montreal	2	—	—
Ryder, Michael	Montreal	2	—	—
Sakic, Joe	Que., Col.	13	1	—
Salo, Sami	Ottawa	1	—	—
Samsonov, Sergei	Boston	1	—	—
Sanderson, Geoff	Har., Buf., CBJ	7	1	—
Satan, Miroslav	Buf., NYI	6	1	—
Savard, Marc	Calgary	1	1	—
Scatchard, Dave	NY Islanders	2	—	—
Schneider, Mathieu	Detroit	2	—	—
Sedin, Daniel	Vancouver	1	1	—
Selanne, Teemu	Wpg., Ana., S.J.	17	2	—
Semin, Alexander	Washington	2	—	—
Shanahan, Brendan	N.J., St.L., Hfd., Det., NYR	17	1	—
Sim, Jon	Florida	1	—	—
Smolinski, Bryan	Bos., L.A.	3	—	—
Smyth, Ryan	Edmonton	5	—	—
Souray, Sheldon	Montreal	1	—	—
St. Louis, Martin	Tampa Bay	4	—	—
Staal, Eric	Carolina	3	—	—
Staal, Jordan	Pittsburgh	1	—	—
Steen, Alex	Toronto	1	—	—
Stillman, Cory	Cgy., St.L.	3	—	—
Straka, Martin	Pit., NYR	6	—	—
Stumpel, Jozef	Bos., L.A.	2	—	—
Sturm, Marco	S.J., Bos.	2	—	—
Sullivan, Steve	Tor., Chi., Nsh.	5	1	—
Sundin, Mats	Que., Tor.	6	1	1
Svatos, Marek	Colorado	2	—	—
Sydor, Darryl	Dallas	1	—	—
Tanguay, Alex	Colorado	2	—	—
Tenkrat, Petr	Nashville	1	—	—
Thornton, Joe	Boston	2	—	—
Thornton, Scott	San Jose	1	—	—
Tkachuk, Keith	Phoenix	7	2	—
Turgeon, Pierre	Buf., NYI, Mtl., St.L.	15	—	—
Vasicek, Josef	Carolina	1	—	—
Visnovsky, Lubomir	Los Angeles	1	—	—
Vrbata, Radim	Col., Car.	2	—	—
Vyborny, David	Columbus	1	—	—
Walker, Scott	Nashville	2	—	—
Weight, Doug	Edm., St.L.	2	—	—
Weiss, Stephen	Florida	1	—	—
Wellwood, Kyle	Toronto	1	—	—
Wesley, Glen	Boston	1	—	—
Whitney, Ray	CBJ, Car.	2	—	—
Williams, Jason	Detroit	1	—	—
Williams, Justin	Carolina	1	—	—
Willis, Shane	Carolina	1	—	—
Yashin, Alexei	Ott., NYI	8	—	—
Zednik, Richard	Washington	1	—	—
Zetterberg, Henrik	Detroit	1	—	—
Zubrus, Dainus	Montreal	1	—	—

Top 100 All-Time Goal-Scoring Leaders

* active player

	Player	Seasons	Games	Goals	Goals per game
1.	**Wayne Gretzky**, Edm., L.A., St.L., NYR	20	1487	**894**	.601
2.	**Gordie Howe**, Det., Hfd.	26	1767	**801**	.453
3.	**Brett Hull**, Cgy., St.L., Dal., Det., Phx.	20	1269	**741**	.584
4.	**Marcel Dionne**, Det., L.A., NYR	18	1348	**731**	.542
5.	**Phil Esposito**, Chi., Bos., NYR	18	1282	**717**	.559
6.	**Mike Gartner**, Wsh., Min., NYR, Tor., Phx.	19	1432	**708**	.494
7.	**Mark Messier**, Edm., NYR, Van.	25	1756	**694**	.395
8.	**Steve Yzerman**, Det.	22	1514	**692**	.457
9.	**Mario Lemieux**, Pit.	18	915	**690**	.754
10.	**Luc Robitaille**, L.A., Pit., NYR, Det.	19	1431	**668**	.467
11.	**Dave Andreychuk**, Buf., Tor., N.J., Bos., Col., T.B.	23	1639	**640**	.390
* 12.	**Brendan Shanahan**, N.J., St.L., Hfd., Det., NYR	19	1417	**627**	.442
* 13.	**Jaromir Jagr**, Pit., Wsh., NYR	16	1191	**621**	.521
* 14.	**Joe Sakic**, Que., Col.	18	1319	**610**	.462
15.	**Bobby Hull**, Chi., Wpg., Hfd.	16	1063	**610**	.574
16.	**Dino Ciccarelli**, Min., Wsh., Det., T.B., Fla.	19	1232	**608**	.494
17.	**Jari Kurri**, Edm., L.A., NYR, Ana., Col.	17	1251	**601**	.480
18.	**Mike Bossy**, NYI	10	752	**573**	.762
19.	**Joe Nieuwendyk**, Cgy., Dal., N.J., Tor., Fla.	20	1257	**564**	.449
20.	**Guy Lafleur**, Mtl., NYR, Que.	17	1126	**560**	.497
21.	**John Bucyk**, Det., Bos.	23	1540	**556**	.361
22.	**Ron Francis**, Hfd., Pit., Car., Tor.	23	1731	**549**	.317
23.	**Michel Goulet**, Que., Chi.	15	1089	**548**	.503
24.	**Maurice Richard**, Mtl.	18	978	**544**	.556
25.	**Stan Mikita**, Chi.	22	1394	**541**	.388
* 26.	**Teemu Selanne**, Wpg., Ana., S.J., Col.	14	1041	**540**	.519
27.	**Frank Mahovlich**, Tor., Det., Mtl.	18	1181	**533**	.451
28.	**Bryan Trottier**, NYI, Pit.	18	1279	**524**	.410
* 29.	**Mats Sundin**, Que., Tor.	16	1231	**523**	.425
30.	**Pat Verbeek**, N.J., Hfd., NYR, Dal., Det.	20	1424	**522**	.367
31.	**Dale Hawerchuk**, Wpg., Buf., St.L., Phi.	16	1188	**518**	.436
* 32.	**Pierre Turgeon**, Buf., NYI, Mtl., St.L., Dal., Col.	19	1294	**515**	.398
33.	**Gilbert Perreault**, Buf.	17	1191	**512**	.430
* 34.	**Mark Recchi**, Pit., Phi., Mtl., Car.	18	1338	**508**	.380
* 35.	**Mike Modano**, Min., Dal.	18	1238	**507**	.410
36.	**Jean Beliveau**, Mtl.	20	1125	**507**	.451
* 37.	**Peter Bondra**, Wsh., Ott., Atl., Chi.	16	1081	**503**	.465
38.	**Joe Mullen**, St.L., Cgy., Pit., Bos.	17	1062	**502**	.473
39.	**Lanny McDonald**, Tor., Col., Cgy.	16	1111	**500**	.450
40.	**Glenn Anderson**, Edm., Tor., NYR, St.L.	16	1129	**498**	.441
* 41.	**Jeremy Roenick**, Chi., Phx., Phi., L.A.	18	1252	**495**	.395
42.	**Jean Ratelle**, NYR, Bos.	21	1281	**491**	.383
43.	**Norm Ullman**, Det., Tor.	20	1410	**490**	.348
44.	**Brian Bellows**, Min., Mtl., T.B., Ana., Wsh.	17	1188	**485**	.408
45.	**Darryl Sittler**, Tor., Phi., Det.	15	1096	**484**	.442
46.	**Bernie Nicholls**, L.A., NYR, Edm., N.J., Chi., S.J.	18	1127	**475**	.421
* 47.	**Keith Tkachuk**, Wpg., Phx., St.L., Atl.	15	976	**473**	.485
48.	**Denis Savard**, Chi., Mtl., T.B.	17	1196	**473**	.395
49.	**Alexander Mogilny**, Buf., Van., N.J., Tor.	16	990	**473**	.478
50.	**Pat LaFontaine**, NYI, Buf., NYR	15	865	**468**	.541
* 51.	**Sergei Fedorov**, Det., Ana., CBJ	16	1128	**461**	.409
52.	**Alex Delvecchio**, Det.	24	1549	**456**	.294
53.	**Theoren Fleury**, Cgy., Col., NYR, Chi.	15	1084	**455**	.420
54.	**Peter Stastny**, Que., N.J., St.L.	15	977	**450**	.461
55.	**Doug Gilmour**, St.L., Cgy., Tor., N.J., Chi., Buf., Mtl.	20	1474	**450**	.305
56.	**Rick Middleton**, NYR, Bos.	14	1005	**448**	.446
57.	**Rick Vaive**, Van., Tor., Chi., Buf.	13	876	**441**	.503
58.	**Steve Larmer**, Chi., NYR	15	1006	**441**	.438
59.	**Rick Tocchet**, Phi., Pit., L.A., Bos., Wsh., Phx.	18	1144	**440**	.385
60.	**Pavel Bure**, Van., Fla., NYR	12	702	**437**	.623
61.	**Vincent Damphousse**, Tor., Edm., Mtl., S.J.	18	1378	**432**	.313
* 62.	**Gary Roberts**, Cgy., Car., Tor., Fla., Pit.	20	1156	**431**	.373
63.	**Dave Taylor**, L.A.	17	1111	**431**	.388
64.	**Yvan Cournoyer**, Mtl.	16	968	**428**	.442
65.	**Brian Propp**, Phi., Bos., Min., Hfd.	15	1016	**425**	.418
66.	**Steve Shutt**, Mtl., L.A.	13	930	**424**	.456
67.	**Steve Thomas**, Tor., Chi., NYI, N.J., Ana., Det.	20	1235	**421**	.341
68.	**Stephane Richer**, Mtl., N.J., T.B., St.L., Pit.	17	1054	**421**	.399
69.	**Bill Barber**, Phi.	14	903	**420**	.465
* 70.	**Tony Amonte**, NYR, Chi., Phx., Phi., Cgy.	16	1174	**416**	.354
71.	**Garry Unger**, Tor., Det., St.L., Atl., L.A., Edm.	16	1105	**413**	.374

Twice a 50-goal scorer with the Washington Capitals in the 1990s, including a league-leading 52 in 1997-98, Peter Bondra scored his 500th career goal as a member of the Chicago Blackhawks on December 22, 2006.

	Player	Seasons	Games	Goals	Goals per game
72.	**John MacLean**, N.J., S.J., NYR, Dal.	18	1194	**413**	.346
73.	**Raymond Bourque**, Bos., Col.	22	1612	**410**	.254
74.	**Ray Ferraro**, Hfd., NYI, NYR, L.A., Atl., St.L.	18	1258	**408**	.324
* 75.	**Rod Brind'Amour**, St.L., Phi., Car.	18	1265	**408**	.323
76.	**Rod Gilbert**, NYR	18	1065	**406**	.381
77.	**John LeClair**, Mtl., Phi., Pit.	16	967	**406**	.420
78.	**John Ogrodnick**, Det., Que., NYR	14	928	**402**	.433
79.	**Dave Keon**, Tor., Hfd.	18	1296	**396**	.306
80.	**Paul Coffey**, Edm., Pit., L.A., Det., Hfd., Phi., Chi., Car., Bos.	21	1409	**396**	.281
81.	**Pierre Larouche**, Pit., Mtl., Hfd., NYR	14	812	**395**	.486
82.	**Cam Neely**, Van., Bos.	13	726	**395**	.544
83.	**Tomas Sandstrom**, NYR, L.A., Pit., Det., Ana.	15	983	**394**	.401
84.	**Bernie Geoffrion**, Mtl., NYR	16	883	**393**	.445
85.	**Jean Pronovost**, Pit., Atl., Wsh.	14	998	**391**	.392
86.	**Dean Prentice**, NYR, Bos., Det., Pit., Min.	22	1378	**391**	.284
87.	**Rick Martin**, Buf., L.A.	11	685	**384**	.561
88.	**Reggie Leach**, Bos., Cal., Phi., Det.	13	934	**381**	.408
89.	**Ted Lindsay**, Det., Chi.	17	1068	**379**	.355
90.	**Claude Lemieux**, Mtl., N.J., Col., Phx., Dal.	20	1197	**379**	.317
91.	**Butch Goring**, L.A., NYI, Bos.	16	1107	**375**	.339
* 92.	**Eric Lindros**, Phi., NYR, Tor., Dal.	14	760	**372**	.489
93.	**Rick Kehoe**, Tor., Pit.	14	906	**371**	.409
94.	**Tim Kerr**, Phi., NYR, Hfd.	13	655	**370**	.565
95.	**Bernie Federko**, St.L., Det.	14	1000	**369**	.369
* 96.	**Trevor Linden**, Van., NYI, Mtl., Wsh.	18	1323	**368**	.278
97.	**Geoff Courtnall**, Bos., Edm., Wsh., St.L., Van.	17	1048	**367**	.350
* 98.	**Paul Kariya**, Ana., Col., Nsh.	12	821	**366**	.446
99.	**Jacques Lemaire**, Mtl.	12	853	**366**	.429
*100.	**Owen Nolan**, Que., Col., S.J., Tor., Phx.	15	991	**365**	.368

Top 100 Active Goal-Scoring Leaders

Pittsburgh's Mark Recchi acknowledges the cheers from the crowd after scoring his 500th career goal on the road at Dallas on January 26, 2007. It was the 16th of Recchi's 24 goals in 2006-07.

	Player	Seasons	Games	Goals	Goals per game
1.	**Brendan Shanahan**, N.J., St.L., Hfd., Det., NYR	19	1417	**627**	.442
2.	**Jaromir Jagr**, Pit., Wsh., NYR	16	1191	**621**	.521
3.	**Joe Sakic**, Que., Col.	18	1319	**610**	.462
4.	**Teemu Selanne**, Wpg., Ana., S.J., Col.	14	1041	**540**	.519
5.	**Mats Sundin**, Que., Tor.	16	1231	**523**	.425
6.	**Pierre Turgeon**, Buf., NYI, Mtl., St.L., Dal., Col.	19	1294	**515**	.398
7.	**Mark Recchi**, Pit., Phi., Mtl., Car.	18	1338	**508**	.380
8.	**Mike Modano**, Min., Dal.	18	1238	**507**	.410
9.	**Peter Bondra**, Wsh., Ott., Atl., Chi.	16	1081	**503**	.465
10.	**Jeremy Roenick**, Chi., Phx., Phi., L.A.	18	1252	**495**	.395
11.	**Keith Tkachuk**, Wpg., Phx., St.L., Atl.	15	976	**473**	.485
12.	**Sergei Fedorov**, Det., Ana., CBJ	16	1128	**461**	.409
13.	**Gary Roberts**, Cgy., Car., Tor., Fla., Pit.	20	1156	**431**	.373
14.	**Tony Amonte**, NYR, Chi., Phx., Phi., Cgy.	16	1174	**416**	.354
15.	**Rod Brind'Amour**, St.L., Phi., Car.	18	1265	**408**	.323
16.	**Eric Lindros**, Phi., NYR, Tor., Dal.	14	760	**372**	.489
17.	**Trevor Linden**, Van., NYI, Mtl., Wsh.	18	1323	**368**	.278
18.	**Paul Kariya**, Ana., Col., Nsh.	12	821	**366**	.446
19.	**Owen Nolan**, Que., Col., S.J., Tor., Phx.	15	991	**365**	.368
20.	**Bill Guerin**, N.J., Edm., Bos., Dal., St.L., S.J.	15	1026	**364**	.355
21.	**Geoff Sanderson**, Hfd., Car., Van., Buf., CBJ, Phx., Phi.	16	1063	**352**	.331
22.	**Markus Naslund**, Pit., Van.	13	953	**346**	.363
23.	**Alexei Yashin**, Ott., NYI	12	850	**337**	.396
24.	**Alex Kovalev**, NYR, Pit., Mtl.	14	991	**333**	.336
25.	**Jarome Iginla**, Cgy.	11	778	**324**	.416
26.	**Miroslav Satan**, Edm., Buf., NYI	11	867	**321**	.370
27.	**Glen Murray**, Bos., Pit., L.A.	15	946	**320**	.338
28.	**Petr Nedved**, Van., St.L., NYR, Pit., Edm., Phx., Phi.	15	982	**310**	.316
29.	**Bobby Holik**, Hfd., N.J., NYR, Atl.	16	1170	**307**	.262
30.	**Vyacheslav Kozlov**, Det., Buf., Atl.	15	963	**305**	.317
31.	**Jason Arnott**, Edm., N.J., Dal., Nsh.	13	892	**303**	.340
32.	**Martin Gelinas**, Edm., Que., Van., Car., Cgy., Fla.	18	1216	**300**	.247
33.	**Daniel Alfredsson**, Ott.	11	783	**291**	.372
34.	**Ryan Smyth**, Edm., NYI	12	788	**270**	.343
35.	**Marian Hossa**, Ott., Atl.	9	629	**270**	.429
36.	**Bryan Smolinski**, Bos., Pit., NYI, L.A., Ott., Chi., Van.	14	992	**266**	.268
37.	**Pavol Demitra**, Ott., St.L., L.A., Min.	13	682	**266**	.390
38.	**Milan Hejduk**, Col.	8	624	**256**	.410
39.	**Brian Rolston**, N.J., Col., Bos., Min.	12	896	**255**	.285
40.	**Doug Weight**, NYR, Edm., St.L., Car.	16	1064	**255**	.240
41.	**Ray Whitney**, S.J., Edm., Fla., CBJ, Det., Car.	15	844	**254**	.301
42.	**Stu Barnes**, Wpg., Fla., Pit., Buf., Dal.	15	1057	**249**	.236
43.	**Peter Forsberg**, Que., Col., Phi., Nsh.	12	697	**248**	.356
44.	**Petr Sykora**, N.J., Ana., NYR, Edm.	9	764	**247**	.323
45.	**Patrik Elias**, N.J.	11	671	**244**	.364
46.	**Martin Straka**, Pit., Ott., NYI, Fla., L.A., NYR	14	889	**243**	.273
47.	**Mike Ricci**, Phi., Que., Col., S.J., Phx.	16	1099	**243**	.221
48.	**Yanic Perreault**, Tor., L.A., Mtl., Nsh., Phx.	13	806	**238**	.295
49.	**Jeff O'Neill**, Hfd., Car., Tor.	11	821	**237**	.289
50.	**Martin Rucinsky**, Edm., Que., Col., Mtl., Dal., NYR, St.L., Van.	15	921	**236**	.256
51.	**Vincent Lecavalier**, T.B.	8	629	**233**	.370
52.	**Steve Sullivan**, N.J., Tor., Chi., Nsh.	11	723	**228**	.315
53.	**Todd Bertuzzi**, NYI, Van., Fla., Det.	11	725	**226**	.312
54.	**Mike Sillinger**, Det., Ana., Van., Phi., T.B., Fla., Ott., CBJ, Phx., St.L.	16	990	**224**	.226
55.	**Patrick Marleau**, S.J.	9	717	**219**	.305
56.	**Jeff Friesen**, S.J., Ana., N.J., Wsh., Cgy.	12	893	**218**	.244
57.	**Jere Lehtinen**, Dal.	11	721	**216**	.300
58.	**Rob Blake**, L.A., Col.	17	1056	**214**	.203
59.	**Robert Lang**, L.A., Bos., Pit., Wsh., Det.	13	799	**213**	.267
60.	**Joe Thornton**, Bos., S.J.	9	672	**211**	.314
61.	**Cory Stillman**, Cgy., St.L., T.B., Car.	8	760	**210**	.276
62.	**Fredrik Modin**, Tor., T.B., CBJ	10	741	**205**	.277
63.	**Chris Gratton**, T.B., Phi., Buf., Phx., Col., Fla.	13	1008	**204**	.202
64.	**Anson Carter**, Wsh., Bos., Edm., NYR, L.A., Van., CBJ, Car.	10	674	**202**	.300
65.	**Ilya Kovalchuk**, Atl.	5	387	**202**	.522
66.	**Nicklas Lidstrom**, Det.	15	1176	**202**	.172
67.	**Simon Gagne**, Phi.	6	502	**201**	.400
68.	**Mathieu Schneider**, Mtl., NYI, Tor., NYR, L.A., Det.	18	1132	**200**	.177
69.	**Shane Doan**, Wpg., Phx.	11	803	**199**	.248
70.	**Daymond Langkow**, T.B., Phi., Phx., Cgy.	11	788	**194**	.246
71.	**Chris Drury**, Col., Cgy., Buf.	8	628	**193**	.307
72.	**Mark Parrish**, Fla., NYI, L.A., Min.	8	594	**192**	.323
73.	**Jozef Stumpel**, Bos., L.A., Fla.	15	905	**189**	.209
74.	**Michael Nylander**, Hfd., Cgy., T.B., Chi., Wsh., Bos., NYR	13	808	**189**	.234
75.	**Sami Kapanen**, Hfd., Car., Phi.	11	757	**184**	.243
76.	**Martin St. Louis**, Cgy., T.B.	8	526	**183**	.348
77.	**Chris Chelios**, Mtl., Chi., Det.	23	1547	**182**	.118
78.	**Dany Heatley**, Atl., Ott.	5	354	**180**	.508
79.	**Darcy Tucker**, Mtl., T.B., Tor.	11	739	**179**	.242
80.	**Marco Sturm**, S.J., Bos.	9	680	**178**	.262
81.	**Sergei Samsonov**, Bos., Edm., Mtl.	9	596	**178**	.299
82.	**Martin Lapointe**, Det., Bos., Chi.	15	921	**175**	.190
83.	**Dallas Drake**, Det., Wpg., Phx., St.L.	14	944	**174**	.184
84.	**Olli Jokinen**, L.A., NYI, Fla.	9	641	**174**	.271
85.	**Sergei Gonchar**, Wsh., Bos., Pit.	12	826	**173**	.209
86.	**Andrew Brunette**, Wsh., Nsh., Atl., Min., Col.	11	706	**172**	.244
87.	**Radek Dvorak**, Fla., NYR, Edm., St.L.	11	828	**171**	.207
88.	**Steve Rucchin**, Ana., NYR, Atl.	12	735	**171**	.233
89.	**Radek Bonk**, Ott., Mtl.	12	824	**171**	.208
90.	**Viktor Kozlov**, S.J., Fla., N.J., NYI	12	749	**169**	.226
91.	**Richard Zednik**, Wsh., Mtl., NYI	11	621	**168**	.271
92.	**Jamie Langenbrunner**, Dal., N.J.	12	739	**167**	.226
93.	**Michael Peca**, Van., Buf., NYI, Edm., Tor.	12	728	**164**	.225
94.	**Dean McAmmond**, Chi., Edm., Phi., Cgy., Col., St.L., Ott.	14	804	**164**	.204
95.	**Marian Gaborik**, Min.	6	408	**164**	.402
96.	**Todd Marchant**, NYR, Edm., CBJ, Ana.	13	891	**162**	.182
97.	**Daniel Briere**, Phx., Buf.	9	483	**162**	.335
98.	**Saku Koivu**, Mtl.	11	650	**159**	.245
99.	**Mike Knuble**, Det., NYR, Bos., Phi.	10	656	**159**	.242
100.	**Alex Tanguay**, Col., Cgy.	7	531	**159**	.299

Top 100 All-Time Assist Leaders

* active player

	Player	Seasons	Games	Assists	Assists per game
1.	**Wayne Gretzky**, Edm., L.A., St.L., NYR	20	1487	**1963**	1.320
2.	**Ron Francis**, Hfd., Pit., Car., Tor.	23	1731	**1249**	.722
3.	**Mark Messier**, Edm., NYR, Van.	25	1756	**1193**	.679
4.	**Raymond Bourque**, Bos., Col.	22	1612	**1169**	.725
5.	**Paul Coffey**, Edm., Pit., L.A., Det., Hfd., Phi., Chi., Car., Bos.	21	1409	**1135**	.806
6.	**Adam Oates**, Det., St.L., Bos., Wsh., Phi., Ana., Edm.	19	1337	**1079**	.807
7.	**Steve Yzerman**, Det.	22	1514	**1063**	.702
8.	**Gordie Howe**, Det., Hfd.	26	1767	**1049**	.594
9.	**Marcel Dionne**, Det., L.A., NYR	18	1348	**1040**	.772
10.	**Mario Lemieux**, Pit.	18	915	**1033**	1.129
* 11.	**Joe Sakic**, Que., Col.	18	1319	**979**	.742
12.	**Doug Gilmour**, St.L., Cgy., Tor., N.J., Chi., Buf., Mtl.	20	1474	**964**	.654
13.	**Al MacInnis**, Cgy., St.L.	23	1416	**934**	.660
14.	**Larry Murphy**, L.A., Wsh., Min., Pit., Tor., Det.	21	1615	**929**	.575
15.	**Stan Mikita**, Chi.	22	1394	**926**	.664
* 16.	**Jaromir Jagr**, Pit., Wsh., NYR	16	1191	**907**	.762
17.	**Bryan Trottier**, NYI, Pit.	18	1279	**901**	.704
18.	**Phil Housley**, Buf., Wpg., St.L., Cgy., N.J., Wsh., Chi., Tor.	21	1495	**894**	.598
19.	**Dale Hawerchuk**, Wpg., Buf., St.L., Phi.	16	1188	**891**	.750
20.	**Phil Esposito**, Chi., Bos., NYR	18	1282	**873**	.681
21.	**Denis Savard**, Chi., Mtl., T.B.	17	1196	**865**	.723
22.	**Bobby Clarke**, Phi.	15	1144	**852**	.745
23.	**Alex Delvecchio**, Det.	24	1549	**825**	.533
* 24.	**Mark Recchi**, Pit., Phi., Mtl., Car.	18	1338	**825**	.617
25.	**Gilbert Perreault**, Buf.	17	1191	**814**	.683
26.	**John Bucyk**, Det., Bos.	23	1540	**813**	.528
* 27.	**Pierre Turgeon**, Buf., NYI, Mtl., St.L., Dal., Col.	19	1294	**812**	.628
28.	**Jari Kurri**, Edm., L.A., NYR, Ana., Col.	17	1251	**797**	.637
29.	**Guy Lafleur**, Mtl., NYR, Que.	17	1126	**793**	.704
30.	**Peter Stastny**, Que., N.J., St.L.	15	977	**789**	.808
31.	**Brian Leetch**, NYR, Tor., Bos.	18	1205	**781**	.648
32.	**Jean Ratelle**, NYR, Bos.	21	1281	**776**	.606
33.	**Vincent Damphousse**, Tor., Edm., Mtl., S.J.	18	1378	**773**	.561
34.	**Bernie Federko**, St.L., Det.	14	1000	**761**	.761
* 35.	**Chris Chelios**, Mtl., Chi., Det.	23	1547	**754**	.487
36.	**Larry Robinson**, Mtl., L.A.	20	1384	**750**	.542
37.	**Denis Potvin**, NYI	15	1060	**742**	.700
38.	**Norm Ullman**, Det., Tor.	20	1410	**739**	.524
39.	**Bernie Nicholls**, L.A., NYR, Edm., N.J., Chi., S.J.	18	1127	**734**	.651
40.	**Luc Robitaille**, L.A., Pit., NYR, Det.	19	1431	**726**	.507
* 41.	**Mats Sundin**, Que., Tor.	16	1231	**720**	.585
* 42.	**Mike Modano**, Min., Dal.	18	1238	**719**	.581
43.	**Jean Beliveau**, Mtl.	20	1125	**712**	.633
44.	**Scott Stevens**, Wsh., St.L., N.J.	22	1635	**712**	.435
45.	**Dave Andreychuk**, Buf., Tor., N.J., Bos., Col., T.B.	23	1639	**698**	.426
46.	**Dale Hunter**, Que., Wsh., Col.	19	1407	**697**	.495
* 47.	**Doug Weight**, NYR, Edm., St.L., Car.	16	1064	**689**	.648
48.	**Henri Richard**, Mtl.	20	1256	**688**	.548
49.	**Brad Park**, NYR, Bos., Det.	17	1113	**683**	.614
50.	**Bobby Smith**, Min., Mtl.	15	1077	**679**	.630
* 51.	**Jeremy Roenick**, Chi., Phx., Phi., L.A.	18	1252	**675**	.539
* 52.	**Brendan Shanahan**, N.J., St.L., Hfd., Det., NYR	19	1417	**667**	.471
* 53.	**Nicklas Lidstrom**, Det.	15	1176	**666**	.566
* 54.	**Rod Brind'Amour**, St.L., Phi., Car.	18	1265	**655**	.518
55.	**Brett Hull**, Cgy., St.L., Dal., Det., Phx.	20	1269	**650**	.512
56.	**Bobby Orr**, Bos., Chi.	12	657	**645**	.982
* 57.	**Sergei Fedorov**, Det., Ana., CBJ	16	1128	**644**	.571
58.	**Gary Suter**, Cgy., Chi., S.J.	17	1145	**641**	.560
59.	**Dave Taylor**, L.A.	17	1111	**638**	.574
60.	**Borje Salming**, Tor., Det.	17	1148	**637**	.555
61.	**Darryl Sittler**, Tor., Phi., Det.	15	1096	**637**	.581
62.	**Neal Broten**, Min., Dal., N.J., L.A.	17	1099	**634**	.577
63.	**Theoren Fleury**, Cgy., Col., NYR, Chi.	15	1084	**633**	.584
64.	**Mike Gartner**, Wsh., Min., NYR, Tor., Phx.	19	1432	**627**	.438
65.	**Andy Bathgate**, NYR, Tor., Det., Pit.	17	1069	**624**	.584
* 66.	**Peter Forsberg**, Que., Col., Phi., Nsh.	12	697	**623**	.894
67.	**Rod Gilbert**, NYR	18	1065	**615**	.577
68.	**Michel Goulet**, Que., Chi.	15	1089	**604**	.555
69.	**Kirk Muller**, N.J., Mtl., NYI, Tor., Fla., Dal.	19	1349	**602**	.446
70.	**Glenn Anderson**, Edm., Tor., NYR, St.L.	16	1129	**601**	.532
* 71.	**Teemu Selanne**, Wpg., Ana., S.J., Col.	14	1041	**595**	.572
72.	**Dino Ciccarelli**, Min., Wsh., Det., T.B., Fla.	19	1232	**592**	.481
73.	**Doug Wilson**, Chi., S.J.	16	1024	**590**	.576
74.	**Dave Keon**, Tor., Hfd.	18	1296	**590**	.455

Both Jaromir Jagr and Joe Sakic reached several impressive milestones in 2006-07. Jagr scored his 600th goal on November 19, 2006, notched his 1,500th point on February 10, 2007 and collected his 900th assist on March 17.

	Player	Seasons	Games	Assists	Assist per game
* 75.	**Sergei Zubov**, NYR, Pit., Dal.	14	1012	**584**	.577
76.	**Dave Babych**, Wpg., Hfd., Van., Phi., L.A.	19	1195	**581**	.486
77.	**Brian Propp**, Phi., Bos., Min., Hfd.	15	1016	**579**	.570
78.	**Steve Larmer**, Chi., NYR	15	1006	**571**	.568
79.	**Frank Mahovlich**, Tor., Det., Mtl.	18	1181	**570**	.483
80.	**Craig Janney**, Bos., St.L., S.J., Wpg., Phx., T.B., NYI	12	760	**563**	.741
81.	**Cliff Ronning**, St.L., Van., Phx., Nsh., L.A., Min., NYI	18	1137	**563**	.495
82.	**Joe Nieuwendyk**, Cgy., Dal., N.J., Tor., Fla.	20	1257	**562**	.447
83.	**Joe Mullen**, St.L., Cgy., Pit., Bos.	17	1062	**561**	.528
84.	**Bobby Hull**, Chi., Wpg., Hfd.	16	1063	**560**	.527
85.	**Alexander Mogilny**, Buf., Van., N.J., Tor.	16	990	**559**	.565
86.	**Thomas Steen**, Wpg.	14	950	**553**	.582
87.	**Mike Bossy**, NYI	10	752	**553**	.735
88.	**Ken Linseman**, Phi., Edm., Bos., Tor.	14	860	**551**	.641
89.	**Tom Lysiak**, Atl., Chi.	13	919	**551**	.600
90.	**Mark Howe**, Hfd., Phi., Det.	16	929	**545**	.587
91.	**Pat LaFontaine**, NYI, Buf., NYR	15	865	**545**	.630
92.	**Red Kelly**, Det., Tor.	20	1316	**542**	.412
93.	**Pat Verbeek**, N.J., Hfd., NYR, Dal., Det.	20	1424	**541**	.380
94.	**Rick Middleton**, NYR, Bos.	14	1005	**540**	.537
95.	**Brian Bellows**, Min., Mtl., T.B., Ana., Wsh.	17	1188	**537**	.452
96.	**Andrew Cassels**, Mtl., Hfd., Cgy., Van., CBJ, Wsh.	16	1015	**528**	.520
97.	**Steve Duchesne**, L.A., Phi., Que., St.L., Ott., Det.	16	1113	**525**	.472
98.	**Dennis Maruk**, Cal., Cle., Min., Wsh.	14	888	**522**	.588
99.	**Wayne Cashman**, Bos.	17	1027	**516**	.502
100.	**Butch Goring**, L.A., NYI, Bos.	16	1107	**513**	.463

Top 100 Active Assist Leaders

	Player	Seasons	Games	Assists	Assists per game
1.	**Joe Sakic**, Que., Col.	18	1319	**979**	.742
2.	**Jaromir Jagr**, Pit., Wsh., NYR	16	1191	**907**	.762
3.	**Mark Recchi**, Pit., Phi., Mtl., Car.	18	1338	**825**	.617
4.	**Pierre Turgeon**, Buf., NYI, Mtl., St.L., Dal., Col.	19	1294	**812**	.628
5.	**Chris Chelios**, Mtl., Chi., Det.	23	1547	**754**	.487
6.	**Mats Sundin**, Que., Tor.	16	1231	**720**	.585
7.	**Mike Modano**, Min., Dal.	18	1238	**719**	.581
8.	**Doug Weight**, NYR, Edm., St.L., Car.	16	1064	**689**	.648
9.	**Jeremy Roenick**, Chi., Phx., Phi., L.A.	18	1252	**675**	.539
10.	**Brendan Shanahan**, N.J., St.L., Hfd., Det., NYR	19	1417	**667**	.471
11.	**Nicklas Lidstrom**, Det.	15	1176	**666**	.566
12.	**Rod Brind'Amour**, St.L., Phi., Car.	18	1265	**655**	.518
13.	**Sergei Fedorov**, Det., Ana., CBJ	16	1128	**644**	.571
14.	**Peter Forsberg**, Que., Col., Phi., Nsh.	12	697	**623**	.894
15.	**Teemu Selanne**, Wpg., Ana., S.J., Col.	14	1041	**595**	.572
16.	**Sergei Zubov**, NYR, Pit., Dal.	14	1012	**584**	.577
17.	**Teppo Numminen**, Wpg., Phx., Dal., Buf.	18	1314	**505**	.384
18.	**Paul Kariya**, Ana., Col., Nsh.	12	821	**500**	.609
19.	**Eric Lindros**, Phi., NYR, Tor., Dal.	14	760	**493**	.649
20.	**Trevor Linden**, Van., NYI, Mtl., Wsh.	18	1323	**487**	.368
21.	**Tony Amonte**, NYR, Chi., Phx., Phi., Cgy.	16	1174	**484**	.412
22.	**Scott Niedermayer**, N.J., Ana.	15	1053	**468**	.444
23.	**Jozef Stumpel**, Bos., L.A., Fla.	15	905	**468**	.517
24.	**Daniel Alfredsson**, Ott.	11	783	**467**	.596
25.	**Mathieu Schneider**, Mtl., NYI, Tor., NYR, L.A., Det.	18	1132	**463**	.409
26.	**Alex Kovalev**, NYR, Pit., Mtl.	14	991	**459**	.463
27.	**Rob Blake**, L.A., Col.	17	1056	**457**	.433
28.	**Gary Roberts**, Cgy., Car., Tor., Fla., Pit.	20	1156	**457**	.395
29.	**Keith Tkachuk**, Wpg., Phx., St.L., Atl.	15	976	**453**	.464
30.	**Joe Thornton**, Bos., S.J.	9	672	**449**	.668
31.	**Alexei Yashin**, Ott., NYI	12	850	**444**	.522
32.	**Martin Straka**, Pit., Ott., NYI, Fla., L.A., NYR	14	889	**433**	.487
33.	**Markus Naslund**, Pit., Van.	13	953	**422**	.443
34.	**Michael Nylander**, Hfd., Cgy., T.B., Chi., Wsh., Bos., NYR	13	808	**420**	.520
35.	**Ray Whitney**, S.J., Edm., Fla., CBJ, Det., Car.	15	844	**419**	.496
36.	**Owen Nolan**, Que., Col., S.J., Tor., Phx.	15	991	**410**	.414
37.	**Petr Nedved**, Van., St.L., NYR, Pit., Edm., Phx., Phi.	15	982	**407**	.414
38.	**Vyacheslav Kozlov**, Det., Buf., Atl.	15	963	**405**	.421
39.	**Glen Wesley**, Bos., Hfd., Car., Tor.	19	1379	**402**	.292
40.	**Bobby Holik**, Hfd., N.J., NYR, Atl.	16	1170	**397**	.339
41.	**Chris Pronger**, Hfd., St.L., Edm., Ana.	13	868	**396**	.456
42.	**Jason Arnott**, Edm., N.J., Dal., Nsh.	13	892	**395**	.443
43.	**Peter Bondra**, Wsh., Ott., Atl., Chi.	16	1081	**389**	.360
44.	**Pavol Demitra**, Ott., St.L., L.A., Min.	13	682	**379**	.556
45.	**Sergei Gonchar**, Wsh., Bos., Pit.	12	826	**377**	.456
46.	**Darryl Sydor**, L.A., Dal., CBJ, T.B.	15	1097	**377**	.344
47.	**Saku Koivu**, Mtl.	11	650	**376**	.578
48.	**Roman Hamrlik**, T.B., Edm., NYI, Cgy.	14	999	**374**	.374
49.	**Alexei Zhitnik**, L.A., Buf., NYI, Phi., Atl.	14	1020	**370**	.363
50.	**Robert Lang**, L.A., Bos., Pit., Wsh., Det.	13	799	**368**	.461
51.	**Mike Ricci**, Phi., Que., Col., S.J., Phx.	16	1099	**362**	.329
52.	**Bryan Smolinski**, Bos., Pit., NYI, L.A., Ott., Chi., Van.	14	992	**360**	.363
53.	**Martin Rucinsky**, Edm., Que., Col., Mtl., Dal., NYR, St.L., Van.	15	921	**360**	.391
54.	**Bill Guerin**, N.J., Edm., Bos., Dal., St.L., S.J.	15	1026	**355**	.346
55.	**Steve Sullivan**, N.J., Tor., Chi., Nsh.	11	723	**349**	.483
56.	**Marc Savard**, NYR, Cgy., Atl., Bos.	9	585	**342**	.585
57.	**Jarome Iginla**, Cgy.	11	778	**340**	.437
58.	**Chris Gratton**, T.B., Phi., Buf., Phx., Col., Fla.	13	1008	**340**	.337
59.	**Martin Gelinas**, Edm., Que., Van., Car., Cgy., Fla.	18	1216	**340**	.280
60.	**Vaclav Prospal**, Phi., Ott., Fla., T.B., Ana.	10	712	**337**	.473
61.	**Geoff Sanderson**, Hfd., Car., Van., Buf., CBJ, Phx., Phi.	16	1063	**335**	.315
62.	**Scott Gomez**, N.J.	7	548	**334**	.609
63.	**Patrik Elias**, N.J.	11	671	**329**	.490
64.	**Cory Stillman**, Cgy., St.L., T.B., Car.	8	760	**327**	.430
65.	**Stu Barnes**, Wpg., Fla., Pit., Buf., Dal.	15	1057	**325**	.307
66.	**Miroslav Satan**, Edm., Buf., NYI	11	867	**323**	.373
67.	**Alex Tanguay**, Col., Cgy.	7	531	**322**	.606
68.	**Brian Rolston**, N.J., Col., Bos., Min.	12	896	**320**	.357
69.	**Andrew Brunette**, Wsh., Nsh., Atl., Min., Col.	11	706	**318**	.450
70.	**Steve Rucchin**, Ana., NYR, Atl.	12	735	**318**	.433
71.	**Petr Sykora**, N.J., Ana., NYR, Edm.	9	764	**318**	.416
72.	**Todd Bertuzzi**, NYI, Van., Fla., Det.	11	725	**314**	.433
73.	**Marian Hossa**, Ott., Atl.	9	629	**312**	.496
74.	**Brad Richards**, T.B.	6	490	**306**	.624
75.	**Glen Murray**, Bos., Pit., L.A.	15	946	**301**	.318
76.	**Patrice Brisebois**, Mtl., Col.	16	904	**301**	.333
77.	**Brendan Morrison**, N.J., Van.	9	635	**299**	.471
78.	**Jeff Friesen**, S.J., Ana., N.J., Wsh., Cgy.	12	893	**298**	.334
79.	**Dallas Drake**, Det., Wpg., Phx., St.L.	14	944	**297**	.315
80.	**Mike Sillinger**, Det., Ana., Van., Phi., T.B., Fla., Ott., CBJ, Phx., St.L.	16	990	**296**	.299
81.	**Daymond Langkow**, T.B., Phi., Phx., Cgy.	11	788	**296**	.376
82.	**Ryan Smyth**, Edm., NYI	12	788	**294**	.373
83.	**Craig Conroy**, Mtl., St.L., Cgy., L.A.	12	767	**290**	.378
84.	**Milan Hejduk**, Col.	8	624	**288**	.462
85.	**Tomas Kaberle**, Tor.	8	599	**288**	.481
86.	**Bryan McCabe**, NYI, Van., Chi., Tor.	11	863	**285**	.330
87.	**Radek Dvorak**, Fla., NYR, Edm., St.L.	11	828	**278**	.336
88.	**Vincent Lecavalier**, T.B.	8	629	**277**	.440
89.	**Wade Redden**, Ott.	10	758	**277**	.365
90.	**Shane Doan**, Wpg., Phx.	11	803	**273**	.340
91.	**Viktor Kozlov**, S.J., Fla., N.J., NYI	12	749	**273**	.364
92.	**Patrick Marleau**, S.J.	9	717	**272**	.379
93.	**Todd Marchant**, NYR, Edm., CBJ, Ana.	13	891	**272**	.305
94.	**Radek Bonk**, Ott., Mtl.	12	824	**272**	.330
95.	**Chris Drury**, Col., Cgy., Buf.	8	628	**271**	.432
96.	**Jamie Langenbrunner**, Dal., N.J.	12	739	**268**	.363
97.	**Brian Rafalski**, N.J.	7	541	**267**	.494
98.	**Sami Kapanen**, Hfd., Car., Phi.	11	757	**266**	.351
99.	**Janne Niinimaa**, Phi., Edm., NYI, Dal., Mtl.	10	741	**265**	.358
100.	**Yanic Perreault**, Tor., L.A., Mtl., Nsh., Phx.	13	806	**264**	.328

Doug Weight of the St. Louis Blues skated in his 1,000th NHL game on November 16, 2006 and collected his 900th career point on December 1. He enters the 2007-08 season within reach of 700 career assists and 1,000 points.

Top 100 All-Time Point Leaders

* active player

The Rangers' Brendan Shanahan was the first of three players (followed by teammate Jaromir Jagr and Colorado's Joe Sakic) to reach the 600-goal plateau in 2006-07.

	Player	Seasons	Games	Goals	Assists	Points	Points per game
1.	**Wayne Gretzky**, Edm., L.A., St.L., NYR	20	1487	894	1963	**2857**	1.921
2.	**Mark Messier**, Edm., NYR, Van.	25	1756	694	1193	**1887**	1.075
3.	**Gordie Howe**, Det., Hfd.	26	1767	801	1049	**1850**	1.047
4.	**Ron Francis**, Hfd., Pit., Car., Tor.	23	1731	549	1249	**1798**	1.039
5.	**Marcel Dionne**, Det., L.A., NYR	18	1348	731	1040	**1771**	1.314
6.	**Steve Yzerman**, Det.	22	1514	692	1063	**1755**	1.159
7.	**Mario Lemieux**, Pit.	18	915	690	1033	**1723**	1.883
8.	**Phil Esposito**, Chi., Bos., NYR	18	1282	717	873	**1590**	1.240
* 9.	**Joe Sakic**, Que., Col.	18	1319	610	979	**1589**	1.205
10.	**Raymond Bourque**, Bos., Col.	22	1612	410	1169	**1579**	.980
11.	**Paul Coffey**, Edm., Pit., L.A., Det., Hfd., Phi., Chi., Car., Bos.	21	1409	396	1135	**1531**	1.087
* 12.	**Jaromir Jagr**, Pit., Wsh., NYR	16	1191	621	907	**1528**	1.283
13.	**Stan Mikita**, Chi.	22	1394	541	926	**1467**	1.052
14.	**Bryan Trottier**, NYI, Pit.	18	1279	524	901	**1425**	1.114
15.	**Adam Oates**, Det., St.L., Bos., Wsh., Phi., Ana., Edm.	19	1337	341	1079	**1420**	1.062
16.	**Doug Gilmour**, St.L., Cgy., Tor., N.J., Chi., Buf., Mtl.	20	1474	450	964	**1414**	.959
17.	**Dale Hawerchuk**, Wpg., Buf., St.L., Phi.	16	1188	518	891	**1409**	1.186
18.	**Jari Kurri**, Edm., L.A., NYR, Ana., Col.	17	1251	601	797	**1398**	1.118
19.	**Luc Robitaille**, L.A., Pit., NYR, Det.	19	1431	668	726	**1394**	.974
20.	**Brett Hull**, Cgy., St.L., Dal., Det., Phx.	20	1269	741	650	**1391**	1.096
21.	**John Bucyk**, Det., Bos.	23	1540	556	813	**1369**	.889
22.	**Guy Lafleur**, Mtl., NYR, Que.	17	1126	560	793	**1353**	1.202
23.	**Denis Savard**, Chi., Mtl., T.B.	17	1196	473	865	**1338**	1.119
24.	**Dave Andreychuk**, Buf., Tor., N.J., Bos., Col., T.B.	23	1639	640	698	**1338**	.816
25.	**Mike Gartner**, Wsh., Min., NYR, Tor., Phx.	19	1432	708	627	**1335**	.932
* 26.	**Mark Recchi**, Pit., Phi., Mtl., Car.	18	1338	508	825	**1333**	.996
* 27.	**Pierre Turgeon**, Buf., NYI, Mtl., St.L., Dal., Col.	19	1294	515	812	**1327**	1.026
28.	**Gilbert Perreault**, Buf.	17	1191	512	814	**1326**	1.113
* 29.	**Brendan Shanahan**, N.J., St.L., Hfd., Det., NYR	19	1417	627	667	**1294**	.913
30.	**Alex Delvecchio**, Det.	24	1549	456	825	**1281**	.827
31.	**Al MacInnis**, Cgy., St.L.	23	1416	340	934	**1274**	.900
32.	**Jean Ratelle**, NYR, Bos.	21	1281	491	776	**1267**	.989
* 33.	**Mats Sundin**, Que., Tor.	16	1231	523	720	**1243**	1.010
34.	**Peter Stastny**, Que., N.J., St.L.	15	977	450	789	**1239**	1.268
35.	**Phil Housley**, Buf., Wpg., St.L., Cgy., N.J., Wsh., Chi., Tor.	21	1495	338	894	**1232**	.824
36.	**Norm Ullman**, Det., Tor.	20	1410	490	739	**1229**	.872
* 37.	**Mike Modano**, Min., Dal.	18	1238	507	719	**1226**	.990
38.	**Jean Beliveau**, Mtl.	20	1125	507	712	**1219**	1.084
39.	**Larry Murphy**, L.A., Wsh., Min., Pit., Tor., Det.	21	1615	287	929	**1216**	.753
40.	**Bobby Clarke**, Phi.	15	1144	358	852	**1210**	1.058
41.	**Bernie Nicholls**, L.A., NYR, Edm., N.J., Chi., S.J.	18	1127	475	734	**1209**	1.073
42.	**Vincent Damphousse**, Tor., Edm., Mtl., S.J.	18	1378	432	773	**1205**	.874
43.	**Dino Ciccarelli**, Min., Wsh., Det., T.B., Fla.	19	1232	608	592	**1200**	.974
* 44.	**Jeremy Roenick**, Chi., Phx., Phi., L.A.	18	1252	495	675	**1170**	.935
45.	**Bobby Hull**, Chi., Wpg., Hfd.	16	1063	610	560	**1170**	1.101
46.	**Michel Goulet**, Que., Chi.	15	1089	548	604	**1152**	1.058
* 47.	**Teemu Selanne**, Wpg., Ana., S.J., Col.	14	1041	540	595	**1135**	1.090
48.	**Bernie Federko**, St.L., Det.	14	1000	369	761	**1130**	1.130
49.	**Mike Bossy**, NYI	10	752	573	553	**1126**	1.497
50.	**Joe Nieuwendyk**, Cgy., Dal., N.J., Tor., Fla.	20	1257	564	562	**1126**	.896
51.	**Darryl Sittler**, Tor., Phi., Det.	15	1096	484	637	**1121**	1.023
* 52.	**Sergei Fedorov**, Det., Ana., CBJ	16	1128	461	644	**1105**	.980
53.	**Frank Mahovlich**, Tor., Det., Mtl.	18	1181	533	570	**1103**	.934
54.	**Glenn Anderson**, Edm., Tor., NYR, St.L.	16	1129	498	601	**1099**	.973
55.	**Theoren Fleury**, Cgy., Col., NYR, Chi.	15	1084	455	633	**1088**	1.004
56.	**Dave Taylor**, L.A.	17	1111	431	638	**1069**	.962
57.	**Joe Mullen**, St.L., Cgy., Pit., Bos.	17	1062	502	561	**1063**	1.001
58.	**Pat Verbeek**, N.J., Hfd., NYR, Dal., Det.	20	1424	522	541	**1063**	.746
* 59.	**Rod Brind'Amour**, St.L., Phi., Car.	18	1265	408	655	**1063**	.840
60.	**Denis Potvin**, NYI	15	1060	310	742	**1052**	.992
61.	**Henri Richard**, Mtl.	20	1256	358	688	**1046**	.833
62.	**Bobby Smith**, Min., Mtl.	15	1077	357	679	**1036**	.962
63.	**Alexander Mogilny**, Buf., Van., N.J., Tor.	16	990	473	559	**1032**	1.042
64.	**Brian Leetch**, NYR, Tor., Bos.	18	1205	247	781	**1028**	.853
65.	**Brian Bellows**, Min., Mtl., T.B., Ana., Wsh.	17	1188	485	537	**1022**	.860
66.	**Rod Gilbert**, NYR	18	1065	406	615	**1021**	.959
67.	**Dale Hunter**, Que., Wsh., Col.	19	1407	323	697	**1020**	.725
68.	**Pat LaFontaine**, NYI, Buf., NYR	15	865	468	545	**1013**	1.171
69.	**Steve Larmer**, Chi., NYR	15	1006	441	571	**1012**	1.006
70.	**Lanny McDonald**, Tor., Col., Cgy.	16	1111	500	506	**1006**	.905
71.	**Brian Propp**, Phi., Bos., Min., Hfd.	15	1016	425	579	**1004**	.988
72.	**Rick Middleton**, NYR, Bos.	14	1005	448	540	**988**	.983
73.	**Dave Keon**, Tor., Hfd.	18	1296	396	590	**986**	.761
74.	**Andy Bathgate**, NYR, Tor., Det., Pit.	17	1069	349	624	**973**	.910
75.	**Maurice Richard**, Mtl.	18	978	544	421	**965**	.987
76.	**Kirk Muller**, N.J., Mtl., NYI, Tor., Fla., Dal.	19	1349	357	602	**959**	.711
77.	**Larry Robinson**, Mtl., L.A.	20	1384	208	750	**958**	.692
78.	**Rick Tocchet**, Phi., Pit., L.A., Bos., Wsh., Phx.	18	1144	440	512	**952**	.832
* 79.	**Doug Weight**, NYR, Edm., St.L., Car.	16	1064	255	689	**944**	.887
* 80.	**Chris Chelios**, Mtl., Chi., Det.	23	1547	182	754	**936**	.605
81.	**Steve Thomas**, Tor., Chi., NYI, N.J., Ana., Det.	20	1235	421	512	**933**	.755
* 82.	**Keith Tkachuk**, Wpg., Phx., St.L., Atl.	15	976	473	453	**926**	.949
83.	**Neal Broten**, Min., Dal., N.J., L.A.	17	1099	289	634	**923**	.840
84.	**Bobby Orr**, Bos., Chi.	12	657	270	645	**915**	1.393
85.	**Scott Stevens**, Wsh., St.L., N.J.	22	1635	196	712	**908**	.555
* 86.	**Tony Amonte**, NYR, Chi., Phx., Phi., Cgy.	16	1174	416	484	**900**	.767
87.	**Ray Ferraro**, Hfd., NYI, NYR, L.A., Atl., St.L.	18	1258	408	490	**898**	.714
88.	**Brad Park**, NYR, Bos., Det.	17	1113	213	683	**896**	.805
* 89.	**Peter Bondra**, Wsh., Ott., Atl., Chi.	16	1081	503	389	**892**	.825
90.	**Butch Goring**, L.A., NYI, Bos.	16	1107	375	513	**888**	.802
* 91.	**Gary Roberts**, Cgy., Car., Tor., Fla., Pit.	20	1156	431	457	**888**	.768
92.	**Bill Barber**, Phi.	14	903	420	463	**883**	.978
93.	**Dennis Maruk**, Cal., Cle., Min., Wsh.	14	888	356	522	**878**	.989
* 94.	**Peter Forsberg**, Que., Col., Phi., Nsh.	12	697	248	623	**871**	1.250
95.	**Cliff Ronning**, St.L., Van., Phx., Nsh., L.A., Min., NYI	18	1137	306	563	**869**	.764
* 96.	**Nicklas Lidstrom**, Det.	15	1176	202	666	**868**	.738
* 97.	**Paul Kariya**, Ana., Col., Nsh.	12	821	366	500	**866**	1.055
98.	**Ivan Boldirev**, Bos., Cal., Chi., Atl., Van., Det.	15	1052	361	505	**866**	.823
* 99.	**Eric Lindros**, Phi., NYR, Tor., Dal.	14	760	372	493	**865**	1.138
100.	**Yvan Cournoyer**, Mtl.	16	968	428	435	**863**	.892

Top 100 Active Points Leaders

Player	Seasons	Games	Goals	Assists	Points	Points per game
1. **Joe Sakic**, Que., Col.	18	1319	610	979	**1589**	1.205
2. **Jaromir Jagr**, Pit., Wsh., NYR.	16	1191	621	907	**1528**	1.283
3. **Mark Recchi**, Pit., Phi., Mtl., Car.	18	1338	508	825	**1333**	.996
4. **Pierre Turgeon**, Buf., NYI, Mtl., St.L., Dal., Col.	19	1294	515	812	**1327**	1.026
5. **Brendan Shanahan**, N.J., St.L., Hfd., Det., NYR	19	1417	627	667	**1294**	.913
6. **Mats Sundin**, Que., Tor.	16	1231	523	720	**1243**	1.010
7. **Mike Modano**, Min., Dal.	18	1238	507	719	**1226**	.990
8. **Jeremy Roenick**, Chi., Phx., Phi., L.A.	18	1252	495	675	**1170**	.935
9. **Teemu Selanne**, Wpg., Ana., S.J., Col.	14	1041	540	595	**1135**	1.090
10. **Sergei Fedorov**, Det., Ana., CBJ.	16	1128	461	644	**1105**	.980
11. **Rod Brind'Amour**, St.L., Phi., Car.	18	1265	408	655	**1063**	.840
12. **Doug Weight**, NYR, Edm., St.L., Car.	16	1064	255	689	**944**	.887
13. **Chris Chelios**, Mtl., Chi., Det.	23	1547	182	754	**936**	.605
14. **Keith Tkachuk**, Wpg., Phx., St.L., Atl.	15	976	473	453	**926**	.949
15. **Tony Amonte**, NYR, Chi., Phx., Phi., Cgy.	16	1174	416	484	**900**	.767
16. **Peter Bondra**, Wsh., Ott., Atl., Chi.	16	1081	503	389	**892**	.825
17. **Gary Roberts**, Cgy., Car., Tor., Fla., Pit.	20	1156	431	457	**888**	.768
18. **Peter Forsberg**, Que., Col., Phi., Nsh.	12	697	248	623	**871**	1.250
19. **Nicklas Lidstrom**, Det.	15	1176	202	666	**868**	.738
20. **Paul Kariya**, Ana., Col., Nsh.	12	821	366	500	**866**	1.055
21. **Eric Lindros**, Phi., NYR, Tor., Dal.	14	760	372	493	**865**	1.138
22. **Trevor Linden**, Van., NYI, Mtl., Wsh.	18	1323	368	487	**855**	.646
23. **Alex Kovalev**, NYR, Pit., Mtl.	14	991	333	459	**792**	.799
24. **Alexei Yashin**, Ott., NYI	12	850	337	444	**781**	.919
25. **Owen Nolan**, Que., Col., S.J., Tor., Phx.	15	991	365	410	**775**	.782
26. **Markus Naslund**, Pit., Van.	13	953	346	422	**768**	.806
27. **Daniel Alfredsson**, Ott.	11	783	291	467	**758**	.968
28. **Sergei Zubov**, NYR, Pit., Dal.	14	1012	148	584	**732**	.723
29. **Bill Guerin**, N.J., Edm., Bos., Dal., St.L., S.J.	15	1026	364	355	**719**	.701
30. **Petr Nedved**, Van., St.L., NYR, Pit., Edm., Phx., Phi.	15	982	310	407	**717**	.730
31. **Vyacheslav Kozlov**, Det., Buf., Atl.	15	963	305	405	**710**	.737
32. **Bobby Holik**, Hfd., N.J., NYR, Atl.	16	1170	307	397	**704**	.602
33. **Jason Arnott**, Edm., N.J., Dal., Nsh.	13	892	303	395	**698**	.783
34. **Geoff Sanderson**, Hfd., Car., Van., Buf., CBJ, Phx., Phi.	16	1063	352	335	**687**	.646
35. **Martin Straka**, Pit., Ott., NYI, Fla., L.A., NYR.	14	889	243	433	**676**	.760
36. **Ray Whitney**, S.J., Edm., Fla., CBJ, Det., Car.	15	844	254	419	**673**	.797
37. **Rob Blake**, L.A., Col.	17	1056	214	457	**671**	.635
38. **Jarome Iginla**, Cgy.	11	778	324	340	**664**	.853
39. **Mathieu Schneider**, Mtl., NYI, Tor., NYR, L.A., Det.	18	1132	200	463	**663**	.586
40. **Joe Thornton**, Bos., S.J.	9	672	211	449	**660**	.982
41. **Jozef Stumpel**, Bos., L.A., Fla.	15	905	189	468	**657**	.726
42. **Pavol Demitra**, Ott., St.L., L.A., Min.	13	682	266	379	**645**	.946
43. **Miroslav Satan**, Edm., Buf., NYI	11	867	321	323	**644**	.743
44. **Martin Gelinas**, Edm., Que., Van., Car., Cgy., Fla.	18	1216	300	340	**640**	.526
45. **Bryan Smolinski**, Bos., Pit., NYI, L.A., Ott., Chi., Van.	14	992	266	360	**626**	.631
46. **Glen Murray**, Bos., Pit., L.A.	15	946	320	301	**621**	.656
47. **Teppo Numminen**, Wpg., Phx., Dal., Buf.	18	1314	115	505	**620**	.472
48. **Michael Nylander**, Hfd., Cgy., T.B., Chi., Wsh., Bos., NYR	13	808	189	420	**609**	.754
49. **Scott Niedermayer**, N.J., Ana.	15	1053	140	468	**608**	.577
50. **Mike Ricci**, Phi., Que., Col., S.J., Phx.	16	1099	243	362	**605**	.551
51. **Martin Rucinsky**, Edm., Que., Col., Mtl., Dal., NYR, St.L., Van.	15	921	236	360	**596**	.647
52. **Marian Hossa**, Ott., Atl.	9	629	270	312	**582**	.925
53. **Robert Lang**, L.A., Bos., Pit., Wsh., Det.	13	799	213	368	**581**	.727

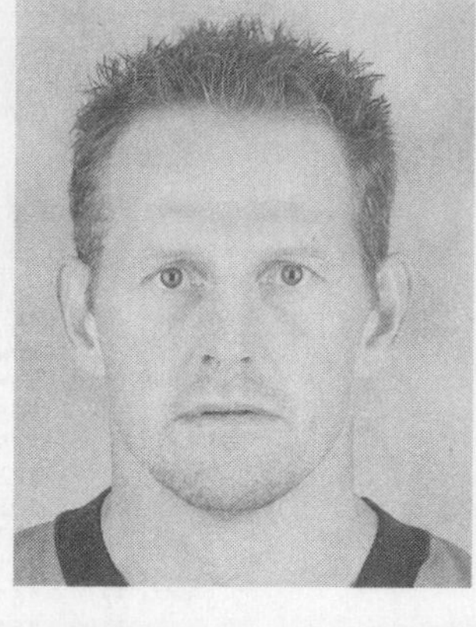

Acquired by Pittsburgh at the 2007 NHL trade deadline, Gary Roberts enters the 2007-08 season with 888 points split nearly evenly between goals (431) and assists (457).

Player	Seasons	Games	Goals	Assists	Points	Points per game
54. **Steve Sullivan**, N.J., Tor., Chi., Nsh.	11	723	228	349	**577**	.798
55. **Brian Rolston**, N.J., Col., Bos., Min.	12	896	255	320	**575**	.642
56. **Stu Barnes**, Wpg., Fla., Pit., Buf., Dal.	15	1057	249	325	**574**	.543
57. **Patrik Elias**, N.J.	11	671	244	329	**573**	.854
58. **Petr Sykora**, N.J., Ana., NYR, Edm.	9	764	247	318	**565**	.740
59. **Ryan Smyth**, Edm., NYI	12	788	270	294	**564**	.716
60. **Sergei Gonchar**, Wsh., Bos., Pit.	12	826	173	377	**550**	.666
61. **Chris Gratton**, T.B., Phi., Buf., Phx., Col., Fla.	13	1008	204	340	**544**	.540
62. **Milan Hejduk**, Col.	8	624	256	288	**544**	.872
63. **Todd Bertuzzi**, NYI, Van., Fla., Det.	11	725	226	314	**540**	.745
64. **Cory Stillman**, Cgy., St.L., T.B., Car.	8	760	210	327	**537**	.707
65. **Saku Koivu**, Mtl.	11	650	159	376	**535**	.823
66. **Glen Wesley**, Bos., Hfd., Car., Tor.	19	1379	127	402	**529**	.384
67. **Mike Sillinger**, Det., Ana., Van., Phi., T.B., Fla., Ott., CBJ, Phx., St.L.	16	990	224	296	**520**	.525
68. **Jeff Friesen**, S.J., Ana., N.J., Wsh., Cgy.	12	893	218	298	**516**	.578
69. **Chris Pronger**, Hfd., St.L., Edm., Ana.	13	868	119	396	**515**	.593
70. **Vincent Lecavalier**, T.B.	8	629	233	277	**510**	.811
71. **Roman Hamrlik**, T.B., Edm., NYI, Cgy.	14	999	131	374	**505**	.506
72. **Yanic Perreault**, Tor., L.A., Mtl., Nsh., Phx.	13	806	238	264	**502**	.623
73. **Marc Savard**, NYR, Cgy., Atl., Bos.	9	585	155	342	**497**	.850
74. **Jeff O'Neill**, Hfd., Car., Tor.	11	821	237	259	**496**	.604
75. **Patrick Marleau**, S.J.	9	717	219	272	**491**	.685
76. **Andrew Brunette**, Wsh., Nsh., Atl., Min., Col.	11	706	172	318	**490**	.694
77. **Daymond Langkow**, T.B., Phi., Phx., Cgy.	11	788	194	296	**490**	.622
78. **Steve Rucchin**, Ana., NYR, Atl.	12	735	171	318	**489**	.665
79. **Vaclav Prospal**, Phi., Ott., Fla., T.B., Ana.	10	712	146	337	**483**	.678
80. **Alex Tanguay**, Col., Cgy.	7	531	159	322	**481**	.906
81. **Shane Doan**, Wpg., Phx.	11	803	199	273	**472**	.588
82. **Dallas Drake**, Det., Wpg., Phx., St.L.	14	944	174	297	**471**	.499
83. **Darryl Sydor**, L.A., Dal., CBJ, T.B.	15	1097	94	377	**471**	.429
84. **Chris Drury**, Col., Cgy., Buf.	8	628	193	271	**464**	.739
85. **Alexei Zhitnik**, L.A., Buf., NYI, Phi., Atl.	14	1020	93	370	**463**	.454
86. **Scott Gomez**, N.J.	7	548	116	334	**450**	.821
87. **Sami Kapanen**, Hfd., Car., Phi.	11	757	184	266	**450**	.594
88. **Radek Dvorak**, Fla., NYR, Edm., St.L.	11	828	171	278	**449**	.542
89. **Brendan Morrison**, N.J., Van.	9	635	150	299	**449**	.707
90. **Radek Bonk**, Ott., Mtl.	12	824	171	272	**443**	.538
91. **Craig Conroy**, Mtl., St.L., Cgy., L.A.	12	767	153	290	**443**	.578
92. **Viktor Kozlov**, S.J., Fla., N.J., NYI	12	749	169	273	**442**	.590
93. **Brad Richards**, T.B.	6	490	132	306	**438**	.894
94. **Jere Lehtinen**, Dal.	11	721	216	220	**436**	.605
95. **Jamie Langenbrunner**, Dal., N.J.	12	739	167	268	**435**	.589
96. **Todd Marchant**, NYR, Edm., CBJ, Ana.	13	891	162	272	**434**	.487
97. **Martin St. Louis**, Cgy., T.B.	8	526	183	239	**422**	.802
98. **Anson Carter**, Wsh., Bos., Edm., NYR, L.A., Van., CBJ, Car.	10	674	202	219	**421**	.625
99. **Sergei Samsonov**, Bos., Edm., Mtl.	9	596	178	240	**418**	.701
100. **Michael Peca**, Van., Buf., NYI, Edm., Tor.	12	728	164	245	**409**	.562

Top 100 All-Time Games Played Leaders

* active player

	Player	Seasons	Games Played
1.	**Gordie Howe**, Det., Hfd.	26	**1767**
2.	**Mark Messier**, Edm., NYR, Van.	25	**1756**
3.	**Ron Francis**, Hfd., Pit., Car., Tor.	23	**1731**
4.	**Dave Andreychuk**, Buf., Tor., N.J., Bos., Col., T.B.	23	**1639**
5.	**Scott Stevens**, Wsh., St.L., N.J.	22	**1635**
6.	**Larry Murphy**, L.A., Wsh., Min., Pit., Tor., Det.	21	**1615**
7.	**Raymond Bourque**, Bos., Col.	22	**1612**
8.	**Alex Delvecchio**, Det.	24	**1549**
* 9.	**Chris Chelios**, Mtl., Chi., Det.	23	**1547**
10.	**John Bucyk**, Det., Bos.	23	**1540**
11.	**Steve Yzerman**, Det.	22	**1514**
12.	**Phil Housley**, Buf., Wpg., St.L., Cgy., N.J., Wsh., Chi., Tor.	21	**1495**
13.	**Wayne Gretzky**, Edm., L.A., St.L., NYR	20	**1487**
14.	**Doug Gilmour**, St.L., Cgy., Tor., N.J., Chi., Buf., Mtl.	20	**1474**
15.	**Tim Horton**, Tor., NYR, Pit., Buf.	24	**1446**
16.	**Mike Gartner**, Wsh., Min., NYR, Tor., Phx.	19	**1432**
17.	**Luc Robitaille**, L.A., Pit., NYR, Det.	19	**1431**
18.	**Scott Mellanby**, Phi., Edm., Fla., St.L., Atl.	21	**1431**
19.	**Pat Verbeek**, N.J., Hfd., NYR, Dal., Det.	20	**1424**
* 20.	**Brendan Shanahan**, N.J., St.L., Hfd., Det., NYR	19	**1417**
21.	**Al MacInnis**, Cgy., St.L.	23	**1416**
22.	**Harry Howell**, NYR, Oak., Cal., L.A.	21	**1411**
23.	**Norm Ullman**, Det., Tor.	20	**1410**
24.	**Paul Coffey**, Edm., Pit., L.A., Det., Hfd., Phi., Chi., Car., Bos.	21	**1409**
25.	**Dale Hunter**, Que., Wsh., Col.	19	**1407**
26.	**Stan Mikita**, Chi.	22	**1394**
27.	**Doug Mohns**, Bos., Chi., Min., Atl., Wsh.	22	**1390**
28.	**Larry Robinson**, Mtl., L.A.	20	**1384**
* 29.	**Glen Wesley**, Bos., Hfd., Car., Tor.	19	**1379**
30.	**Vincent Damphousse**, Tor., Edm., Mtl., S.J.	18	**1378**
31.	**Dean Prentice**, NYR, Bos., Det., Pit., Min.	22	**1378**
32.	**Ron Stewart**, Tor., Bos., St.L., NYR, Van., NYI	21	**1353**
33.	**Kirk Muller**, N.J., Mtl., NYI, Tor., Fla., Dal.	19	**1349**
34.	**Marcel Dionne**, Det., L.A., NYR	18	**1348**
* 35.	**Luke Richardson**, Tor., Edm., Phi., CBJ, T.B.	19	**1339**
* 36.	**Mark Recchi**, Pit., Phi., Mtl., Car.	18	**1338**
37.	**Adam Oates**, Det., St.L., Bos., Wsh., Phi., Ana., Edm.	19	**1337**
* 38.	**Trevor Linden**, Van., NYI, Mtl., Wsh.	18	**1323**
* 39.	**Joe Sakic**, Que., Col.	18	**1319**
40.	**Guy Carbonneau**, Mtl., St.L., Dal.	19	**1318**
41.	**Red Kelly**, Det., Tor.	20	**1316**
* 42.	**Teppo Numminen**, Wpg., Phx., Dal., Buf.	18	**1314**
43.	**Dave Keon**, Tor., Hfd.	18	**1296**
* 44.	**Pierre Turgeon**, Buf., NYI, Mtl., St.L., Dal., Col.	19	**1294**
45.	**Ken Daneyko**, N.J.	20	**1283**
46.	**Phil Esposito**, Chi., Bos., NYR	18	**1282**
47.	**Jean Ratelle**, NYR, Bos.	21	**1281**
48.	**James Patrick**, NYR, Hfd., Cgy., Buf.	21	**1280**
49.	**Bryan Trottier**, NYI, Pit.	18	**1279**
50.	**Brett Hull**, Cgy., St.L., Dal., Det., Phx.	20	**1269**
* 51.	**Rod Brind'Amour**, St.L., Phi., Car.	18	**1265**
52.	**Ray Ferraro**, Hfd., NYI, NYR, L.A., Atl., St.L.	18	**1258**
53.	**Joe Nieuwendyk**, Cgy., Dal., N.J., Tor., Fla.	20	**1257**
54.	**Craig Ludwig**, Mtl., NYI, Min., Dal.	17	**1256**
55.	**Henri Richard**, Mtl.	20	**1256**
56.	**Kevin Lowe**, Edm., NYR.	19	**1254**
* 57.	**Jeremy Roenick**, Chi., Phx., Phi., L.A.	18	**1252**
58.	**Jari Kurri**, Edm., L.A., NYR, Ana., Col.	17	**1251**
59.	**Bill Gadsby**, Chi., NYR, Det.	20	**1248**
60.	**Allan Stanley**, NYR, Chi., Bos., Tor., Phi.	21	**1244**
* 61.	**Mike Modano**, Min., Dal.	18	**1238**
62.	**Steve Thomas**, Tor., Chi., NYI, N.J., Ana., Det.	20	**1235**
63.	**Dino Ciccarelli**, Min., Wsh., Det., T.B., Fla.	19	**1232**
* 64.	**Mats Sundin**, Que., Tor.	16	**1231**
65.	**Ed Westfall**, Bos., NYI	18	**1226**
66.	**Brad McCrimmon**, Bos., Phi., Cgy., Det., Hfd., Phx.	18	**1222**
67.	**Eric Nesterenko**, Tor., Chi.	21	**1219**
* 68.	**Martin Gelinas**, Edm., Que., Van., Car., Cgy., Fla.	18	**1216**
69.	**Marcel Pronovost**, Det., Tor.	21	**1206**
70.	**Brian Leetch**, NYR, Tor., Bos.	18	**1205**
71.	**Claude Lemieux**, Mtl., N.J., Col., Phx., Dal.	20	**1197**
72.	**Denis Savard**, Chi., Mtl., T.B.	17	**1196**
73.	**Dave Babych**, Wpg., Hfd., Van., Phi., L.A.	19	**1195**
74.	**John MacLean**, N.J., S.J., NYR, Dal.	18	**1194**
* 75.	**Jaromir Jagr**, Pit., Wsh., NYR	16	**1191**
76.	**Gilbert Perreault**, Buf.	17	**1191**
77.	**Marc Bergevin**, Chi., NYI, Hfd., T.B., Det., St.L., Pit., Van.	20	**1191**
78.	**Dale Hawerchuk**, Wpg., Buf., St.L., Phi.	16	**1188**
79.	**Brian Bellows**, Min., Mtl., T.B., Ana., Wsh.	17	**1188**
80.	**Kevin Dineen**, Hfd., Phi., Car., Ott., CBJ	19	**1188**
81.	**George Armstrong**, Tor.	21	**1187**
82.	**Kelly Buchberger**, Edm., Atl., L.A., Phx., Pit.	18	**1182**
83.	**Scott Young**, Hfd., Pit., Que., Col., Ana., St.L., Dal.	17	**1181**
84.	**Frank Mahovlich**, Tor., Det., Mtl.	18	**1181**
85.	**Bob Carpenter**, Wsh., NYR, L.A., Bos., N.J.	19	**1178**
* 86.	**Nicklas Lidstrom**, Det.	15	**1176**
87.	**Don Marshall**, Mtl., NYR, Buf., Tor.	19	**1176**
* 88.	**Tony Amonte**, NYR, Chi., Phx., Phi., Cgy.	16	**1174**
89.	**Sylvain Cote**, Hfd., Wsh., Tor., Chi., Dal.	19	**1171**
* 90.	**Bobby Holik**, Hfd., N.J., NYR, Atl.	16	**1170**
91.	**Mike Keane**, Mtl., Col., NYR, Dal., St.L., Van.	16	**1161**
92.	**Bob Gainey**, Mtl.	16	**1160**
93.	**Kevin Hatcher**, Wsh., Dal., Pit., NYR, Car.	17	**1157**
94.	**Eric Weinrich**, N.J., Hfd., Chi., Mtl., Bos., Phi., St.L., Van.	17	**1157**
95.	**Shayne Corson**, Mtl., Edm., St.L., Tor., Dal.	19	**1156**
* 96.	**Gary Roberts**, Cgy., Car., Tor., Fla., Pit.	20	**1156**
97.	**Adam Graves**, Det., Edm., NYR, S.J.	16	**1152**
98.	**Leo Boivin**, Tor., Bos., Det., Pit., Min.	19	**1150**
99.	**Garry Galley**, L.A., Wsh., Bos., Phi., Buf., NYI	17	**1149**
100.	**Borje Salming**, Tor., Det.	17	**1148**

After helping the Atlanta Thrashers reach the playoffs for the first time in franchise history, Scott Mellanby announced his retirement on April 24, 2007. Mellanby played 1,431 games and finished with 364 goals and 476 assists.

Top 100 Active Games Played Leaders

Player	Seasons	Games Played
1. **Chris Chelios**, Mtl., Chi., Det.	23	**1547**
2. **Brendan Shanahan**, N.J., St.L., Hfd., Det., NYR	19	**1417**
3. **Glen Wesley**, Bos., Hfd., Car., Tor.	19	**1379**
4. **Luke Richardson**, Tor., Edm., Phi., CBJ, T.B.	19	**1339**
5. **Mark Recchi**, Pit., Phi., Mtl., Car.	18	**1338**
6. **Trevor Linden**, Van., NYI, Mtl., Wsh.	18	**1323**
7. **Joe Sakic**, Que., Col.	18	**1319**
8. **Teppo Numminen**, Wpg., Phx., Dal., Buf.	18	**1314**
9. **Pierre Turgeon**, Buf., NYI, Mtl., St.L., Dal., Col.	19	**1294**
10. **Rod Brind'Amour**, St.L., Phi., Car.	18	**1265**
11. **Jeremy Roenick**, Chi., Phx., Phi., L.A.	18	**1252**
12. **Mike Modano**, Min., Dal.	18	**1238**
13. **Mats Sundin**, Que., Tor.	16	**1231**
14. **Martin Gelinas**, Edm., Que., Van., Car., Cgy., Fla.	18	**1216**
15. **Jaromir Jagr**, Pit., Wsh., NYR	16	**1191**
16. **Nicklas Lidstrom**, Det.	15	**1176**
17. **Tony Amonte**, NYR, Chi., Phx., Phi., Cgy.	16	**1174**
18. **Bobby Holik**, Hfd., N.J., NYR, Atl.	16	**1170**
19. **Gary Roberts**, Cgy., Car., Tor., Fla., Pit.	20	**1156**
20. **Mathieu Schneider**, Mtl., NYI, Tor., NYR, L.A., Det.	18	**1132**
21. **Sergei Fedorov**, Det., Ana., CBJ	16	**1128**
22. **Mike Ricci**, Phi., Que., Col., S.J., Phx.	16	**1099**
23. **Darryl Sydor**, L.A., Dal., CBJ, T.B.	15	**1097**
24. **Peter Bondra**, Wsh., Ott., Atl., Chi.	16	**1081**
25. **Doug Weight**, NYR, Edm., St.L., Car.	16	**1064**
26. **Geoff Sanderson**, Hfd., Car., Van., Buf., CBJ, Phx., Phi.	16	**1063**
27. **Stu Barnes**, Wpg., Fla., Pit., Buf., Dal.	15	**1057**
28. **Rob Blake**, L.A., Col.	17	**1056**
29. **Scott Niedermayer**, N.J., Ana.	15	**1053**
30. **Teemu Selanne**, Wpg., Ana., S.J., Col.	14	**1041**
31. **Bill Guerin**, N.J., Edm., Bos., Dal., St.L., S.J.	15	**1026**
32. **Alexei Zhitnik**, L.A., Buf., NYI, Phi., Atl.	14	**1020**
33. **Sergei Zubov**, NYR, Pit., Dal.	14	**1012**
34. **Chris Gratton**, T.B., Phi., Buf., Phx., Col., Fla.	13	**1008**
35. **Derian Hatcher**, Min., Dal., Det., Phi.	15	**1001**
36. **Roman Hamrlik**, T.B., Edm., NYI, Cgy.	14	**999**
37. **Bryan Smolinski**, Bos., Pit., NYI, L.A., Ott., Chi., Van.	14	**992**
38. **Alex Kovalev**, NYR, Pit., Mtl.	14	**991**
39. **Owen Nolan**, Que., Col., S.J., Tor., Phx.	15	**991**
40. **Mike Sillinger**, Det., Ana., Van., Phi., T.B., Fla., Ott., CBJ, Phx., St.L.	16	**990**
41. **Petr Nedved**, Van., St.L., NYR, Pit., Edm., Phx., Phi.	15	**982**
42. **Keith Tkachuk**, Wpg., Phx., St.L., Atl.	15	**976**
43. **Vyacheslav Kozlov**, Det., Buf., Atl.	15	**963**
44. **Keith Carney**, Buf., Chi., Phx., Ana., Van., Min.	13	**957**
45. **Markus Naslund**, Pit., Van.	13	**953**
46. **Glen Murray**, Bos., Pit., L.A.	15	**946**
47. **Dallas Drake**, Det., Wpg., Phx., St.L.	14	**944**
48. **Adam Foote**, Que., Col., CBJ	15	**923**
49. **Bret Hedican**, St.L., Van., Fla., Car.	15	**922**
50. **Martin Lapointe**, Det., Bos., Chi.	15	**921**
51. **Martin Rucinsky**, Edm., Que., Col., Mtl., Dal., NYR, St.L., Van.	15	**921**
52. **Jozef Stumpel**, Bos., L.A., Fla.	15	**905**
53. **Patrice Brisebois**, Mtl., Col.	16	**904**
54. **Brian Rolston**, N.J., Col., Bos., Min.	12	**896**
55. **Scott Thornton**, Tor., Edm., Mtl., Dal., S.J., L.A.	16	**894**
56. **Jeff Friesen**, S.J., Ana., N.J., Wsh., Cgy.	12	**893**
57. **Jason Arnott**, Edm., N.J., Dal., Nsh.	13	**892**
58. **Todd Marchant**, NYR, Edm., CBJ, Ana.	13	**891**
59. **Martin Straka**, Pit., Ott., NYI, Fla., L.A., NYR	14	**889**
60. **Kris Draper**, Wpg., Det.	16	**885**
61. **Brad May**, Buf., Van., Phx., Col., Ana.	15	**882**
62. **Kirk Maltby**, Edm., Det.	13	**881**
63. **Jason Smith**, N.J., Tor., Edm.	12	**868**
64. **Chris Pronger**, Hfd., St.L., Edm., Ana.	13	**868**
65. **Miroslav Satan**, Edm., Buf., NYI	11	**867**
66. **Bryan McCabe**, NYI, Van., Chi., Tor.	11	**863**
67. **Darius Kasparaitis**, NYI, Pit., Col., NYR	14	**863**
68. **Ian Laperriere**, St.L., NYR, L.A., Col.	13	**857**
69. **Rob Niedermayer**, Fla., Cgy., Ana.	13	**854**
70. **Sean O'Donnell**, L.A., Min., N.J., Bos., Phx., Ana.	12	**850**
71. **Alexei Yashin**, Ott., NYI	12	**850**
72. **Donald Brashear**, Mtl., Van., Phi., Wsh.	13	**846**
73. **Ray Whitney**, S.J., Edm., Fla., CBJ, Det., Car.	15	**844**
74. **Sean Hill**, Mtl., Ana., Ott., Car., St.L., Fla., NYI	16	**841**
75. **Mattias Norstrom**, NYR, L.A., Dal.	13	**837**
76. **Matthew Barnaby**, Buf., Pit., T.B., NYR, Col., Chi., Dal.	14	**834**
77. **Sergei Gonchar**, Wsh., Bos., Pit.	12	**826**
78. **Radek Bonk**, Ott., Mtl.	12	**824**
79. **Jeff O'Neill**, Hfd., Car., Tor.	11	**821**
80. **Paul Kariya**, Ana., Col., Nsh.	12	**821**

Rob Blake of the Los Angeles Kings was the first of 10 NHL players to reach the 1,000 games-played plateau during the 2006-07 season. Blake's milestone game occurred on the road in Phoenix on November 4, 2006.

Player	Seasons	Games Played
81. **Michael Nylander**, Hfd., Cgy., T.B., Chi., Wsh., Bos., NYR	13	**808**
82. **Yanic Perreault**, Tor., L.A., Mtl., Nsh., Phx.	13	**806**
83. **Dean McAmmond**, Chi., Edm., Phi., Cgy., Col., St.L., Ott.	14	**804**
84. **Shane Doan**, Wpg., Phx.	11	**803**
85. **Robert Lang**, L.A., Bos., Pit., Wsh., Det.	13	**799**
86. **Richard Matvichuk**, Min., Dal., N.J.	14	**796**
87. **Ken Klee**, Wsh., Tor., N.J., Col.	12	**791**
88. **Daymond Langkow**, T.B., Phi., Phx., Cgy.	11	**788**
89. **Ryan Smyth**, Edm., NYI	12	**788**
90. **Daniel Alfredsson**, Ott.	11	**783**
91. **Jarome Iginla**, Cgy.	11	**778**
92. **Mike Grier**, Edm., Wsh., Buf., S.J.	10	**774**
93. **Shean Donovan**, S.J., Col., Atl., Pit., Cgy., Bos.	12	**774**
94. **Stephane Yelle**, Col., Cgy.	11	**770**
95. **Mike Rathje**, S.J., Phi.	13	**768**
96. **Craig Conroy**, Mtl., St.L., Cgy., L.A.	12	**767**
97. **Mathieu Dandenault**, Det., Mtl.	11	**766**
98. **Petr Sykora**, N.J., Ana., NYR, Edm.	9	**764**
99. **Cory Stillman**, Cgy., St.L., T.B., Car.	8	**760**
100. **Eric Lindros**, Phi., NYR, Tor., Dal.	14	**760**

Goaltending Records

All-Time Shutout Leaders (Minimum 46 Shutouts)

	Goaltender	Team	Seasons	Games	Shutouts
1.	**Terry Sawchuk** (1949-1970)	Detroit	14	734	85
		Boston	2	102	11
		Toronto	3	91	4
		Los Angeles	1	36	2
		NY Rangers	1	8	1
		Total	21	971	**103**
2.	**George Hainsworth** (1926-1937)	Montreal	7½	318	75
		Toronto	3½	147	19
		Total	11	465	**94**
3.	***Martin Brodeur** (1991-2007)	New Jersey	14	891	**92**
4.	**Glenn Hall** (1952-1971)	Detroit	4	148	17
		Chicago	10	618	51
		St. Louis	4	140	16
		Total	18	906	**84**
5.	**Jacques Plante** (1952-1973)	Montreal	11	556	58
		NY Rangers	2	98	5
		St. Louis	2	69	10
		Toronto	2¾	106	7
		Boston	¼	8	2
		Total	18	837	**82**
6.	**Tiny Thompson** (1928-1940)	Boston	10¼	468	74
		Detroit	1¾	85	7
		Total	12	553	**81**
7.	**Alex Connell** (1924-1937)	Ottawa	8	293	64
		Detroit	1	48	6
		NY Americans	1	1	0
		Mtl. Maroons	2	75	11
		Total	12	417	**81**
8.	***Dominik Hasek** (1990-2007)	Chicago	2	25	1
		Buffalo	9	491	55
		Detroit	3	135	15
		Ottawa	1	43	5
		Total	15	694	**76**
9.	**Tony Esposito** (1968-1984)	Montreal	1	13	2
		Chicago	15	873	74
		Total	16	886	**76**
10.	***Ed Belfour** (1988-2007)	Chicago	7⅔	415	30
		San Jose	⅓	13	1
		Dallas	5	307	27
		Toronto	3	170	17
		Florida	1	58	1
		Total	17	963	**76**
11.	**Lorne Chabot** (1926-1937)	NY Rangers	2	80	21
		Toronto	5	214	32
		Montreal	1	47	8
		Chicago	1	48	8
		Mtl. Maroons	1	16	2
		NY Americans	1	6	1
		Total	11	411	**72**
12.	**Harry Lumley** (1943-1960)	Detroit	6½	324	26
		NY Rangers	½	1	0
		Chicago	2	134	5
		Toronto	4	267	34
		Boston	3	78	6
		Total	16	804	**71**
13.	**Roy Worters** (1925-1937)	Pittsburgh Pirates	3	123	22
		NY Americans	9	360	45
		† Montreal		1	0
		Total	12	484	**67**
14.	**Patrick Roy** (1984-2003)	Montreal	11½	551	29
		Colorado	6½	478	37
		Total	19	1,029	**66**
15.	**Turk Broda** (1936-1952)	Toronto	14	629	**62**
16.	**Clint Benedict** (1917-1930)	Ottawa	7	158	19
		Mtl. Maroons	6	204	39
		Total	13	362	**58**
17.	**John Ross Roach** (1921-1935)	Toronto	7	222	13
		NY Rangers	4	89	30
		Detroit	3	180	15
		Total	14	491	**58**
18.	**Bernie Parent** (1965-1979)	Boston	2	57	1
		Philadelphia	9½	486	50
		Toronto	1½	65	3
		Total	13	608	**54**
19.	**Ed Giacomin** (1965-1978)	NY Rangers	10¼	539	49
		Detroit	2¾	71	5
		Total	13	610	**54**
20.	**Dave Kerr** (1930-1941)	Mtl. Maroons	3	101	11
		NY Americans	1	1	0
		NY Rangers	7	324	40
		Total	11	426	**51**
21.	**Rogie Vachon** (1966-1982)	Montreal	5¼	206	13
		Los Angeles	6¾	389	32
		Detroit	2	109	4
		Boston	2	91	2
		Total	16	795	**51**
22.	***Curtis Joseph** (1989-2007)	St. Louis	6	280	5
		Edmonton	3	177	14
		Toronto	4	249	17
		Detroit	2	92	7
		Phoenix	2	115	8
		Total	17	913	**51**
23.	**Ken Dryden** (1970-1979)	Montreal	8	397	**46**

* Active goalie
† Played 1 game for Montreal in 1929-30.

Ten or More Shutouts, One Season

Number of Shutouts	Goaltender	Team	Season	Length of Schedule
22	George Hainsworth	Montreal	1928-29	44
15	Alex Connell	Ottawa	1925-26	36
	Alex Connell	Ottawa	1927-28	44
	Hal Winkler	Boston	1927-28	44
	Tony Esposito	Chicago	1969-70	76
14	George Hainsworth	Montreal	1926-27	44
13	Clint Benedict	Mtl. Maroons	1926-27	44
	Alex Connell	Ottawa	1926-27	44
	George Hainsworth	Montreal	1927-28	44
	John Ross Roach	NY Rangers	1928-29	44
	Roy Worters	NY Americans	1928-29	44
	Harry Lumley	Toronto	1953-54	70
	Dominik Hasek	Buffalo	1997-98	82
12	Tiny Thompson	Boston	1928-29	44
	Charlie Gardiner	Chicago	1930-31	44
	Terry Sawchuk	Detroit	1951-52	70
	Terry Sawchuk	Detroit	1953-54	70
	Terry Sawchuk	Detroit	1954-55	70
	Glenn Hall	Detroit	1955-56	70
	Bernie Parent	Philadelphia	1973-74	78
	Bernie Parent	Philadelphia	1974-75	80
	Martin Brodeur	New Jersey	**2006-07**	82
11	Lorne Chabot	NY Rangers	1927-28	44
	Hap Holmes	Detroit	1927-28	44
	Roy Worters	Pittsburgh Pirates	1927-28	44
	Clint Benedict	Mtl. Maroons	1928-29	44
	Joe Miller	Pittsburgh Pirates	1928-29	44
	Lorne Chabot	Toronto	1928-29	44
	Tiny Thompson	Boston	1932-33	48
	Terry Sawchuk	Detroit	1950-51	70
	Dominik Hasek	Buffalo	2000-01	82
	Martin Brodeur	New Jersey	2003-04	82
10	Lorne Chabot	NY Rangers	1926-27	44
	Dolly Dolson	Detroit	1928-29	44
	John Ross Roach	Detroit	1932-33	48
	Charlie Gardiner	Chicago	1933-34	48
	Tiny Thompson	Boston	1935-36	48
	Frank Brimsek	Boston	1938-39	48
	Bill Durnan	Montreal	1948-49	60
	Harry Lumley	Toronto	1952-53	70
	Gerry McNeil	Montreal	1952-53	70
	Tony Esposito	Chicago	1973-74	78
	Ken Dryden	Montreal	1976-77	80
	Martin Brodeur	New Jersey	1996-97	82
	Martin Brodeur	New Jersey	1997-98	82
	Byron Dafoe	Boston	1998-99	82
	Roman Cechmanek	Philadelphia	2000-01	82
	Ed Belfour	Toronto	2003-04	82
	Miikka Kiprusoff	Calgary	2005-06	82

All-Time Win Leaders

(Minimum 240 Wins)

	Goaltender	Wins	GP	Dec.	Losses	OT/Ties
1.	Patrick Roy	**551**	1029	997	315	131
2.	* Martin Brodeur	**494**	891	876	263	119
3.	* Ed Belfour	**484**	963	929	320	125
4.	Terry Sawchuk	**447**	971	949	330	172
5.	* Curtis Joseph	**446**	913	882	341	95
6.	Jacques Plante	**437**	837	827	247	145
7.	Tony Esposito	**423**	886	880	306	151
8.	Glenn Hall	**407**	906	896	326	163
9.	Grant Fuhr	**403**	868	812	295	114
10.	Mike Vernon	**385**	781	750	273	92
11.	John Vanbiesbrouck	**374**	882	839	346	119
12.	Andy Moog	**372**	713	669	209	88
13.	Tom Barrasso	**369**	777	732	277	86
14.	* Dominik Hasek	**362**	694	667	213	92
15.	Rogie Vachon	**355**	795	773	291	127
16.	* Chris Osgood	**336**	621	599	186	77
17.	Gump Worsley	**335**	861	837	352	150
18.	Harry Lumley	**330**	803	801	329	142
19.	* Sean Burke	**324**	820	775	341	110
20.	Billy Smith	**305**	680	643	233	105
21.	Turk Broda	**302**	629	627	224	101
22.	Mike Richter	**301**	666	632	258	73
23.	Ron Hextall	**296**	608	579	214	69
24.	Mike Liut	**294**	663	639	271	74
25.	Ed Giacomin	**289**	610	594	208	97
26.	Dan Bouchard	**286**	655	631	232	113
27.	Tiny Thompson	**284**	553	553	194	75
28.	* Olaf Kolzig	**276**	657	628	272	80
29.	Bernie Parent	**271**	608	590	198	121
30.	Kelly Hrudey	**271**	677	624	265	88
31.	Gilles Meloche	**270**	788	752	351	131
32.	Don Beaupre	**268**	667	620	277	75
33.	Felix Potvin	**266**	635	611	260	85
34.	Ken Dryden	**258**	397	389	57	74
35.	Frank Brimsek	**252**	514	514	182	80
36.	Nikolai Khabibulin	**251**	586	559	239	69
37.	Johnny Bower	**250**	552	535	195	90
38.	George Hainsworth	**246**	465	465	145	74
39.	Pete Peeters	**246**	489	452	155	51
40.	Kirk McLean	**245**	612	579	262	72
41.	Bill Ranford	**240**	647	595	279	76

Active Shutout Leaders

(Minimum 25 Shutouts)

	Goaltender	Teams	Seasons	Games	Shutouts
1.	Martin Brodeur	N.J.	14	891	**92**
2.	Dominik Hasek	Chi., Buf., Det., Ott.	15	694	**76**
3.	Ed Belfour	Chi., S.J., Dal., Tor., Fla.	17	963	**76**
4.	Curtis Joseph	St.L., Edm., Tor., Det., Phx.	17	913	**51**
5.	Chris Osgood	Det., NYI, St.L.	13	621	**43**
6.	Sean Burke	N.J., Hfd., Car., Van., Phi., Fla., Phx., T.B., L.A.	18	820	**38**
7.	Jocelyn Thibault	Que., Col., Mtl., Chi., Pit.	13	574	**37**
8.	Nikolai Khabibulin	Wpg., Phx., T.B., Chi.	11	586	**36**
9.	Evgeni Nabokov	S.J.	7	353	**34**
10.	Patrick Lalime	Pit., Ott., St. L., Chi.	8	365	**34**
11.	Olaf Kolzig	Wsh.	15	657	**34**
12.	Roberto Luongo	NYI, Fla., Van.	7	417	**32**
13.	Marty Turco	Dal.	6	320	**30**
14.	Jean-Sebastien Giguere	Hfd., Cal., Ana.	9	353	**25**

All-Time Penalty-Minute Leaders

* active player

(Regular season. Minimum 2,000 minutes)

	Player	Seasons	Games	Penalty Minutes	Mins. per game
1.	**Tiger Williams**, Tor., Van., Det., L.A., Hfd.	14	962	**3966**	4.12
2.	**Dale Hunter**, Que., Wsh., Col.	19	1407	**3565**	2.53
3.	**Tie Domi**, Tor., NYR, Wpg.	16	1020	**3515**	3.45
4.	**Marty McSorley**, Pit., Edm., L.A., NYR, S.J., Bos.	17	961	**3381**	3.52
5.	**Bob Probert**, Det., Chi.	16	935	**3300**	3.53
6.	**Rob Ray**, Buf., Ott.	15	900	**3207**	3.56
7.	**Craig Berube**, Phi., Tor., Cgy., Wsh., NYI	17	1054	**3149**	2.99
8.	**Tim Hunter**, Cgy., Que., Van., S.J.	16	815	**3146**	3.86
9.	**Chris Nilan**, Mtl., NYR, Bos.	13	688	**3043**	4.42
10.	**Rick Tocchet**, Phi., Pit., L.A., Bos., Wsh., Phx.	18	1144	**2972**	2.60

Goals-Against Average Leaders (Minimum 25 games played)

(Exceptions: Minimum 13 games played, 1994-95; minimum 26 games played, 1992-93 to 1993-94; minimum 15 games played, 1917-18 to 1925-26)

Season	Goaltender and Club	GP	Mins.	GA	SO	AVG.
2006-07	Niklas Backstrom, Minnesota	41	2,227	73	5	1.97
2005-06	Miikka Kiprusoff, Calgary	74	4,380	151	10	2.07
2003-04	Miikka Kiprusoff, Calgary	38	2,301	65	4	1.69
2002-03	Marty Turco, Dallas	55	3,203	92	7	1.72
2001-02	Patrick Roy, Colorado	63	3,773	122	9	1.94
2000-01	Marty Turco, Dallas	26	1,266	40	3	1.90
99-2000	Brian Boucher, Philadelphia	35	2,038	65	4	1.91
1998-99	Ron Tugnutt, Ottawa	43	2,508	75	3	1.79
1997-98	Ed Belfour, Dallas	61	3,581	112	9	1.88
1996-97	Martin Brodeur, New Jersey	67	3,838	120	10	1.88
1995-96	Ron Hextall, Philadelphia	53	3,102	112	4	2.17
1994-95	Dominik Hasek, Buffalo	41	2,416	85	5	2.11
1993-94	Dominik Hasek, Buffalo	58	3,358	109	7	1.95
1992-93	Felix Potvin, Toronto	48	2,781	116	2	2.50
1991-92	Patrick Roy, Montreal	67	3,935	155	5	2.36
1990-91	Ed Belfour, Chicago	74	4,127	170	4	2.47
1989-90	Mike Liut, Hartford, Washington	37	2,161	91	4	2.53
1988-89	Patrick Roy, Montreal	48	2,744	113	4	2.47
1987-88	Pete Peeters, Washington	35	1,896	88	2	2.78
1986-87	Brian Hayward, Montreal	37	2,178	102	1	2.81
1985-86	Bob Froese, Philadelphia	51	2,728	116	5	2.55
1984-85	Tom Barrasso, Buffalo	54	3,248	144	5	2.66
1983-84	Pat Riggin, Washington	41	2,299	102	4	2.66
1982-83	Pete Peeters, Boston	62	3,611	142	8	2.36
1981-82	Denis Herron, Montreal	27	1,547	68	3	2.64
1980-81	Richard Sevigny, Montreal	33	1,777	71	2	2.40
1979-80	Bob Sauve, Buffalo	32	1,880	74	4	2.36
1978-79	Ken Dryden, Montreal	47	2,814	108	5	2.30
1977-78	Ken Dryden, Montreal	52	3,071	105	5	2.05
1976-77	Michel Larocque, Montreal	26	1,525	53	4	2.09
1975-76	Ken Dryden, Montreal	62	3,580	121	8	2.03
1974-75	Bernie Parent, Philadelphia	68	4,041	137	12	2.03
1973-74	Bernie Parent, Philadelphia	73	4,314	136	12	1.89
1972-73	Ken Dryden, Montreal	54	3,165	119	6	2.26
1971-72	Tony Esposito, Chicago	48	2,780	82	9	1.77
1970-71	Jacques Plante, Toronto	40	2,329	73	4	1.88
1969-70	Ernie Wakely, St. Louis	30	1,651	58	4	2.11
1968-69	Jacques Plante, St. Louis	37	2,139	70	5	1.96
1967-68	Gump Worsley, Montreal	40	2,213	73	6	1.98
1966-67	Glenn Hall, Chicago	32	1,664	66	2	2.38
1965-66	Johnny Bower, Toronto	35	1,998	75	3	2.25
1964-65	Johnny Bower, Toronto	34	2,040	81	3	2.38
1963-64	Johnny Bower, Toronto	51	3,009	106	5	2.11
1962-63	Don Simmons, Toronto	28	1,680	69	1	2.46
1961-62	Jacques Plante, Montreal	70	4,200	166	4	2.37
1960-61	Charlie Hodge, Montreal	30	1,800	74	4	2.47
1959-60	Jacques Plante, Montreal	69	4,140	175	3	2.54
1958-59	Jacques Plante, Montreal	67	4,000	144	9	2.16
1957-58	Jacques Plante, Montreal	57	3,386	119	9	2.11
1956-57	Jacques Plante, Montreal	61	3,660	122	9	2.00
1955-56	Jacques Plante, Montreal	64	3,840	119	7	1.86
1954-55	Harry Lumley, Toronto	69	4,140	134	8	1.94
1953-54	Harry Lumley, Toronto	69	4,140	128	13	1.86
1952-53	Terry Sawchuk, Detroit	63	3,780	120	9	1.90
1951-52	Terry Sawchuk, Detroit	70	4,200	133	12	1.90
1950-51	Al Rollins, Toronto	40	2,367	70	5	1.77
1949-50	Bill Durnan, Montreal	64	3,840	141	8	2.20
1948-49	Bill Durnan, Montreal	60	3,600	126	10	2.10
1947-48	Turk Broda, Toronto	60	3,600	143	5	2.38
1946-47	Bill Durnan, Montreal	60	3,600	138	4	2.30
1945-46	Bill Durnan, Montreal	40	2,400	104	4	2.60
1944-45	Bill Durnan, Montreal	50	3,000	121	1	2.42
1943-44	Bill Durnan, Montreal	50	3,000	109	2	2.18
1942-43	Johnny Mowers, Detroit	50	3,010	124	6	2.47
1941-42	Frank Brimsek, Boston	47	2,930	115	3	2.35
1940-41	Turk Broda, Toronto	48	2,970	99	5	2.00
1939-40	Dave Kerr, NY Rangers	48	3,000	77	8	1.54
1938-39	Frank Brimsek, Boston	43	2,610	68	10	1.56
1937-38	Tiny Thompson, Boston	48	2,970	89	7	1.80
1936-37	Normie Smith, Detroit	48	2,980	102	6	2.05
1935-36	Tiny Thompson, Boston	48	2,930	82	10	1.68
1934-35	Lorne Chabot, Chicago	48	2,940	88	8	1.80
1933-34	Wilf Cude, Detroit, Montreal	30	1,920	47	5	1.47
1932-33	Tiny Thompson, Boston	48	3,000	88	11	1.76
1931-32	Charlie Gardiner, Chicago	48	2,989	92	4	1.85
1930-31	Roy Worters, NY Americans	44	2,760	74	8	1.61
1929-30	Tiny Thompson, Boston	44	2,680	98	3	2.19
1928-29	George Hainsworth, Montreal	44	2,800	43	22	0.92
1927-28	George Hainsworth, Montreal	44	2,730	48	13	1.05
1926-27	Clint Benedict, Mtl. Maroons	43	2,748	65	13	1.42
1925-26	Alex Connell, Ottawa	36	2,251	42	15	1.12
1924-25	Georges Vèzina, Montreal	30	1,860	56	5	1.81
1923-24	Georges Vezina, Montreal	24	1,459	48	3	1.97
1922-23	Clint Benedict, Ottawa	24	1,478	54	4	2.18
1921-22	Clint Benedict, Ottawa	24	1,508	84	2	3.34
1920-21	Clint Benedict, Ottawa	24	1,457	75	2	3.09
1919-20	Clint Benedict, Ottawa	24	1,444	64	5	2.66
1918-19	Clint Benedict, Ottawa	18	1,113	53	2	2.86
1917-18	Georges Vezina, Montreal	21	1,282	84	1	3.93

All-Time Regular-Season NHL Coaching Register

Regular Season, 1917-2007

Coach	Team	Games Coached	Wins	Losses	O/T	Years	Cup Wins	Career
Abel, Sid	Chicago	140	39	79	22	2		
	Detroit	811	340	339	132	12		
	St. Louis	10	3	6	1	1		
	Kansas City	3	0	3	0	1		
	Total	964	382	427	155	16		1952-76
Adams, Jack	Detroit	964	413	390	161	20	3	1927-47
Agnew, Gary	Columbus	5	0	4	1	1		2006-07
Allen, Keith	Philadelphia	150	51	67	32	2		1967-69
Allison, Dave	Ottawa	25	2	22	1	1		1995-96
Anderson, Jim	Washington	54	4	45	5	1		1974-75
Angotti, Lou	St. Louis	32	6	20	6	2		
	Pittsburgh	80	16	58	6	1		
	Total	112	22	78	12	3		1973-84
Arbour, Al	St. Louis	107	42	40	25	3		
	NY Islanders	1499	739	537	223	19	4	
	Total	1606	781	577	248	22	4	1970-94
Armstrong, George	Toronto	47	17	26	4	1		1988-89
Babcock, Mike	Anaheim	164	69	76	19	3		
	Detroit	164	108	35	21	2		
	Total	328	177	111	40	5		2002-07
Barber, Bill	Philadelphia	136	73	46	17	2		2000-02
Barkley, Doug	Detroit	77	20	46	11	3		1970-76
Beaulieu, Andre	Minnesota	32	6	23	3	1		1977-78
Belisle, Danny	Washington	96	28	51	17	2		1978-80
Berenson, Red	St. Louis	204	100	72	32	3		1979-82
Bergeron, Michel	Quebec	634	265	283	86	8		
	NY Rangers	158	73	67	18	2		
	Total	792	338	350	104	10		1980-90
Berry, Bob	Los Angeles	240	107	94	39	3		
	Montreal	223	116	71	36	3		
	Pittsburgh	240	88	127	25	3		
	St. Louis	157	73	63	21	2		
	Total	860	384	355	121	11		1978-94
Beverley, Nick	Toronto	17	9	6	2	1		1995-96
Blackburn, Don	Hartford	140	42	63	35	2		1979-81
Blair, Wren	Minnesota	147	48	65	34	3		1967-70
Blake, Toe	Montreal	914	500	255	159	13	8	1955-68
Boileau, Marc	Pittsburgh	151	66	61	24	3		1973-76
Boivin, Leo	St. Louis	97	28	53	16	2		1975-78
Boucher, Frank	NY Rangers	527	181	263	83	11	1	1939-54
Boucher, Georges	Mtl. Maroons	12	6	5	1	1		
	Ottawa	48	13	29	6	1		
	St. Louis	35	9	20	6	1		
	Boston	70	22	32	16	1		
	Total	165	50	86	29	4		1930-50
Bowman, Scotty	St. Louis	238	110	83	45	4		
	Montreal	634	419	110	105	8	5	
	Buffalo	404	210	134	60	7		
	Pittsburgh	164	95	53	16	2	1	
	Detroit	701	410	204	87	9	3	
	Total	2141	1244	584	313	30	9	1967-02
Bowness, Rick	Winnipeg	28	8	17	3	1		
	Boston	80	36	32	12	1		
	Ottawa	235	39	178	18	4		
	NY Islanders	100	38	50	12	2		
	Phoenix	20	2	15	3	2		
	Total	463	123	292	48	10		1988-05
Brooks, Herb	NY Rangers	285	131	113	41	4		
	Minnesota	80	19	48	13	1		
	New Jersey	84	40	37	7	1		
	Pittsburgh	58	29	24	5	1		
	Total	507	219	222	66	7		1981-00
Brophy, John	Toronto	193	64	111	18	3		1986-89
Burnett, George	Edmonton	35	12	20	3	1		1994-95
Burns, Charlie	Minnesota	86	22	50	14	2		1969-75
Burns, Pat	Montreal	320	174	104	42	4		
	Toronto	281	133	107	41	4		
	Boston	254	105	103	46	4		
	New Jersey	164	89	53	22	3	1	
	Total	1019	501	367	151	15	1	1988-05
Bush, Eddie	Kansas City	32	1	23	8	1		1975-76
Campbell, Colin	NY Rangers	269	118	108	43	4		1994-98
Carbonneau, Guy	Montreal	82	42	34	6	1		2006-07
Carlyle, Randy	Anaheim	164	91	47	26	2	1	2005-07
Carpenter, Doug	New Jersey	290	100	166	24	4		
	Toronto	91	39	47	5	2		
	Total	381	139	213	29	6		1984-91
Carroll, Dick	Toronto	40	18	22	0	2	1	1917-19
Carroll, Frank	Toronto	24	15	9	0	1		1920-21
Cashman, Wayne	Philadelphia	61	32	20	9	1		1997-98
Cassidy, Bruce	Washington	110	47	54	9	3		2002-05
Chambers, Dave	Quebec	98	19	64	15	2		1990-92
Charron, Guy	Calgary	16	6	7	3	1		
	Anaheim	49	14	28	7	1		
	Total	65	20	35	10	2		1991-01
Cheevers, Gerry	Boston	376	204	126	46	5		1980-85
Cherry, Don	Boston	400	231	105	64	5		
	Colorado	80	19	48	13	1		
	Total	480	250	153	77	6		1974-80
Clancy, King	Mtl. Maroons	18	6	11	1	1		
	Toronto	210	80	81	49	3		
	Total	228	86	92	50	4		1937-56
Clapper, Dit	Boston	230	102	88	40	4		1945-49
Cleghorn, Odie	Pittsburgh	168	62	86	20	4		1925-29
Cleghorn, Sprague	Mtl. Maroons	48	19	22	7	1		1931-32
Colville, Neil	NY Rangers	93	26	41	26	2		1950-52
Conacher, Charlie	Chicago	162	56	84	22	3		1947-50
Conacher, Lionel	NY Americans	44	14	25	5	1		1929-30
Constantine, Kevin	San Jose	157	55	78	24	3		
	Pittsburgh	188	86	67	35	3		
	New Jersey	31	20	9	2	1		
	Total	376	161	154	61	7		1993-02
Cook, Bill	NY Rangers	117	34	59	24	2		1951-53
Crawford, Marc	Quebec	48	30	13	5	1		
	Colorado	246	135	75	36	3	1	
	Vancouver	529	246	213	70	8		
	Los Angeles	82	27	41	14	1		
	Total	905	438	342	125	13	1	1994-07
Creamer, Pierre	Pittsburgh	80	36	35	9	1		1987-88
Creighton, Fred	Atlanta	348	156	136	56	5		
	Boston	73	40	20	13	1		
	Total	421	196	156	69	6		1974-80
Crisp, Terry	Calgary	240	144	63	33	3	1	
	Tampa Bay	391	142	204	45	6		
	Total	631	286	267	78	9	1	1987-98
Crozier, Joe	Buffalo	192	77	80	35	3		
	Toronto	40	13	22	5	1		
	Total	232	90	102	40	4		1971-81
Crozier, Roger	Washington	1	0	1	0	1		1981-82
Cunniff, John	Hartford	13	3	9	1	1		
	New Jersey	133	59	56	18	2		
	Total	146	62	65	19	3		1982-91
Curry, Alex	Ottawa	36	24	8	4	1		1925-26
Dandurand, Leo	Montreal	163	78	76	9	6	1	1921-35
Day, Hap	Toronto	546	259	206	81	10	5	1940-50
Dea, Billy	Detroit	11	3	8	0	1		1981-82
Delvecchio, Alex	Detroit	245	82	131	32	4		1973-77
Demers, Jacques	Quebec	80	25	44	11	1		
	St. Louis	240	106	106	28	3		
	Detroit	320	137	136	47	4		
	Montreal	220	107	86	27	4	1	
	Tampa Bay	147	34	96	17	2		
	Total	1007	409	468	130	14	1	1979-99
Denneny, Cy	Boston	44	26	13	5	1	1	
	Ottawa	48	11	27	10	1		
	Total	92	37	40	15	2	1	1928-33
Dineen, Bill	Philadelphia	140	60	60	20	2		1991-93
Dudley, Rick	Buffalo	188	85	72	31	3		
	Florida	40	13	18	9	2		
	Total	228	98	90	40	5		1989-05
Duff, Dick	Toronto	2	0	2	0	1		1979-80
Dugal, Jules	Montreal	18	9	6	3	1		1938-39
Duncan, Art	Detroit	33	10	21	2	1		
	Toronto	47	21	16	10	2	1	
	Total	80	31	37	12	3	1	1926-32
Dutton, Red	NY Americans	288	90	151	47	6		
	Brooklyn	48	16	29	3	1		
	Total	336	106	180	50	7		1935-42
Eddolls, Frank	Chicago	70	13	40	17	1		1954-55
Esposito, Phil	NY Rangers	45	24	21	0	2		1986-89
Evans, Jack	California	80	27	42	11	1		
	Cleveland	160	47	87	26	2		
	Hartford	374	163	174	37	5		
	Total	614	237	303	74	8		1975-88
Fashoway, Gordie	Oakland	10	4	5	1	1		1967-68
Ferguson, John	NY Rangers	121	43	59	19	2		
	Winnipeg	14	7	6	1	1		
	Total	135	50	65	20	3		1975-86
Filion, Maurice	Quebec	6	1	3	2	1		1980-81
Francis, Bob	Phoenix	390	165	165	60	5		1999-04
Francis, Emile	NY Rangers	654	342	209	103	10		
	St. Louis	124	46	64	14	3		
	Total	778	388	273	117	13		1965-83
Fraser, Curt	Atlanta	279	64	184	31	4		1999-03
Fredrickson, Frank	Pittsburgh	44	5	36	3	1		1929-30
Ftorek, Robbie	Los Angeles	132	65	56	11	2		
	New Jersey	156	88	49	19	2		
	Boston	155	76	65	14	2		
	Total	443	229	170	44	6		1987-03
Gadsby, Bill	Detroit	78	35	31	12	2		1968-70
Gainey, Bob	Minnesota	244	95	119	30	3		
	Dallas	171	70	71	30	3		
	Montreal	41	23	15	3	1		
	Total	456	188	205	63	7		1990-06
Gallant, Gerard	Columbus	142	56	77	9	4		2003-07
Gardiner, Herb	Chicago	32	5	23	4	1		1929-30
Gardner, Jimmy	Hamilton	30	19	10	1	1		1924-25
Garvin, Ted	Detroit	11	2	8	1	1		1973-74
Geoffrion, Bernie	NY Rangers	43	22	18	3	1		

Coach	Team	Games Coached	Wins	Losses	O/T	Years	Cup Wins	Career
	Atlanta	208	77	92	39	3		
	Montreal	30	15	9	6	1		
	Total	281	114	119	48	5		1968-80
Gerard, Eddie	Ottawa	22	9	13	0	1		
	Mtl. Maroons	294	129	122	43	7	1	
	NY Americans	92	34	40	18	2		
	St. Louis	13	2	11	0	1		
	Total	421	174	186	61	11	1	1917-35
Gilbert, Greg	Calgary	121	42	62	17	3		2000-03
Gill, David	Ottawa	132	64	41	27	3	1	1926-29
Glover, Fred	Oakland	152	51	76	25	2		
	California	204	45	131	28	4		
	Los Angeles	68	18	42	8	1		
	Total	424	114	249	61	7		1968-74
Goodfellow, Ebbie	Chicago	140	30	91	19	2		1950-52
Gordon, Jackie	Minnesota	289	116	123	50	5		1970-75
Goring, Butch	Boston	93	42	38	13	2		
	NY Islanders	147	41	92	14	2		
	Total	240	83	130	27	4		1985-01
Gorman, Tommy	NY Americans	80	31	33	16	2		
	Chicago	73	28	28	17	2	1	
	Mtl. Maroons	174	74	71	29	4	1	
	Total	327	133	132	62	8	2	1925-38
Gottselig, Johnny	Chicago	187	62	105	20	4		1944-48
Goyette, Phil	NY Islanders	48	6	38	4	1		1972-73
Graham, Dirk	Chicago	59	16	35	8	1		1998-99
Granato, Tony	Colorado	133	72	44	17	2		2002-04
Green, Gary	Washington	157	50	78	29	3		1979-82
Green, Pete	Ottawa	150	94	52	4	6	3	1919-25
Green, Shorty	NY Americans	44	11	27	6	1		1927-28
Green, Ted	Edmonton	188	65	102	21	3		1991-94
Gretzky, Wayne	Phoenix	164	69	85	10	2		2005-07
Guidolin, Aldo	Colorado	59	12	39	8	1		1978-79
Guidolin, Bep	Boston	104	72	23	9	2		
	Kansas City	125	26	84	15	2		
	Total	229	98	107	24	4		1972-76
Hanlon, Glen	Washington	218	81	109	28	4		2003-07
Harkness, Ned	Detroit	38	12	22	4	1		1970-71
Harris, Ted	Minnesota	179	48	104	27	3		1975-78
Hart, Cecil	Montreal	394	196	125	73	9	2	1926-39
Hartley, Bob	Colorado	359	193	118	48	5	1	
	Atlanta	285	136	117	32	5		
	Total	644	329	235	80	9	1	1998-07
Hartsburg, Craig	Chicago	246	104	102	40	3		
	Anaheim	197	80	88	29	3		
	Total	443	184	190	69	6		1995-01
Harvey, Doug	NY Rangers	70	26	32	12	1		1961-62
Hay, Don	Phoenix	82	38	37	7	1		
	Calgary	68	23	32	13	1		
	Total	150	61	69	20	2		1996-01
Heffernan, Frank	Toronto	12	5	7	0	1		1919-20
Henning, Lorne	Minnesota	158	68	72	18	2		
	NY Islanders	65	19	39	7	2		
	Total	223	87	111	25	4		1985-01
Hitchcock, Ken	Dallas	503	277	166	60	7	1	
	Philadelphia	254	131	83	40	5		
	Columbus	62	28	29	5	1		
	Total	749	407	243	99	12	1	1995-07
Hlinka, Ivan	Pittsburgh	86	42	35	9	2		2000-02
Holmgren, Paul	Philadelphia	264	107	126	31	4		
	Hartford	161	54	93	14	4		
	Total	425	161	219	45	8		1988-96
Howell, Harry	Minnesota	11	3	6	2	1		1978-79
Imlach, Punch	Toronto	770	370	275	125	12	4	
	Buffalo	119	32	62	25	2		
	Total	889	402	337	150	14	4	1958-80
Ingarfield, Earl	NY Islanders	30	6	22	2	1		1972-73
Inglis, Bill	Buffalo	56	28	18	10	1		1978-79
Irvin, Dick	Chicago	126	45	62	19	3		
	Toronto	427	216	152	59	9	1	
	Montreal	896	431	313	152	15	3	
	Total	1449	692	527	230	27	4	1928-56
Ivan, Tommy	Detroit	470	262	118	90	7	3	
	Chicago	103	26	56	21	2		
	Total	573	288	174	111	9	3	1947-58
Iverson, Emil	Chicago	21	8	7	6	1		1932-33
Johnson, Bob	Calgary	400	193	155	52	5		
	Pittsburgh	80	41	33	6	1	1	
	Total	480	234	188	58	6	1	1982-91
Johnson, Tom	Boston	208	142	43	23	3	1	1970-73
Johnston, Eddie	Chicago	80	34	27	19	1		
	Pittsburgh	516	232	224	60	7		
	Total	596	266	251	79	8		1979-97
Johnston, Marshall	California	69	13	45	11	2		
	Colorado	56	15	32	9	1		
	Total	125	28	77	20	3		1973-82
Julien, Claude	Montreal	159	72	71	16	4		
	New Jersey	79	47	24	8			
	Total	238	119	95	24	5		2002-07
Kasper, Steve	Boston	164	66	78	20	2		1995-97
Keats, Duke	Detroit	11	2	7	2	1		1926-27
Keenan, Mike	Philadelphia	320	190	102	28	4		

Coach	Team	Games Coached	Wins	Losses	O/T	Years	Cup Wins	Career
	Chicago	320	153	126	41	4		
	NY Rangers	84	52	24	8	1	1	
	St. Louis	163	75	66	22	3		
	Vancouver	108	36	54	18	2		
	Boston	74	33	34	7	1		
	Florida	153	45	85	23	3		
	Total	1222	584	491	147	18	1	1984-04
Kehoe, Rick	Pittsburgh	160	55	91	14	2		2001-03
Kelly, Pat	Colorado	101	22	54	25	2		1977-79
Kelly, Red	Los Angeles	150	55	75	20	2		
	Pittsburgh	274	90	132	52	4		
	Toronto	318	133	123	62	4		
	Total	742	278	330	134	10		1967-77
King, Dave	Calgary	216	109	76	31	3		
	Columbus	204	64	119	21	3		
	Total	420	173	195	52	6		1992-03
Kingston, George	San Jose	164	28	129	7	2		1991-93
Kish, Larry	Hartford	49	12	32	5	1		1982-83
Kitchen, Mike	St. Louis	129	38	70	21	4		2003-07
Kromm, Bobby	Detroit	231	79	111	41	3		1977-80
Kurtenbach, Orland	Vancouver	125	36	62	27	2		1976-78
LaForge, Bill	Vancouver	20	4	14	2	1		1984-85
Lalonde, Newsy	Montreal	207	96	97	14	8		
	NY Americans	44	17	25	2	1		
	Ottawa	88	31	45	12	2		
	Total	339	144	167	28	11		1917-35
Lamorello, Lou	New Jersey	53	34	14	5	2		2005-07
Laperriere, Jacques	Montreal	1	0	1	0	1		1995-96
Lapointe, Ron	Quebec	89	33	50	6	2		1987-89
Laviolette, Peter	NY Islanders	164	77	68	19	2		
	Carolina	216	112	82	22	3	1	
	Total	380	189	150	41	6	1	2001-07
Laycoe, Hal	Los Angeles	24	5	18	1	1		
	Vancouver	156	44	96	16	2		
	Total	180	49	114	17	3		1969-72
Lehman, Hugh	Chicago	21	3	17	1	1		1927-28
Lemaire, Jacques	Montreal	97	48	37	12	2		
	New Jersey	378	199	122	57	5	1	
	Minnesota	492	213	211	68	7		
	Total	967	460	370	137	14	1	1983-07
Lepine, Pit	Montreal	48	10	33	5	1		1939-40
LeSueur, Percy	Hamilton	10	3	7	0	1		1923-24
Lewis, Dave*	Detroit	169	100	48	21	4		
	Boston	82	35	41	6	1		
	Total	251	135	89	27	5		1998-07

*Shared a record of 4-1-0 with co-coach Barry Smith in 1998-99

Coach	Team	Games Coached	Wins	Losses	O/T	Years	Cup Wins	Career
Ley, Rick	Hartford	160	69	71	20	2		
	Vancouver	124	47	50	27	2		
	Total	284	116	121	47	4		1989-96
Lindsay, Ted	Detroit	29	5	21	3	2		1979-81
Long, Barry	Winnipeg	205	87	93	25	3		1983-86
Loughlin, Clem	Chicago	144	61	63	20	3		1934-37
Lowe, Ron	Edmonton	341	139	162	40	5		
	NY Rangers	164	69	86	9	2		
	Total	505	208	248	49	7		1994-02
Lowe, Kevin	Edmonton	82	32	34	16	1		1999-00
Ludzik, Steve	Tampa Bay	121	31	76	14	2		1999-01
MacDonald, Parker	Minnesota	61	20	30	11	1		
	Los Angeles	42	13	24	5	1		
	Total	103	33	54	16	2		1973-82
MacLean, Doug	Florida	187	83	71	33	3		
	Columbus	79	24	47	8	2		
	Total	266	107	118	41	5		1995-04
MacMillan, Bill	Colorado	80	22	45	13	1		
	New Jersey	100	19	67	14	2		
	Total	180	41	112	27	3		1980-84
MacNeil, Al	Montreal	55	31	15	9	1	1	
	Atlanta	80	35	32	13	1		
	Calgary	171	72	66	33	3		
	Total	306	138	113	55	5		1970-03
MacTavish, Craig	Edmonton	492	222	203	67	7		2000-07
Magnuson, Keith	Chicago	132	49	57	26	2		1980-82
Mahoney, Bill	Minnesota	93	42	39	12	2		1983-85
Maloney, Dan	Toronto	160	45	100	15	2		
	Winnipeg	212	91	93	28	3		
	Total	372	136	193	43	5		1984-89
Maloney, Phil	Vancouver	232	95	105	32	4		1973-77
Mantha, Sylvio	Montreal	48	11	26	11	1		1935-36
Marshall, Bert	Colorado	24	3	17	4	1		1981-82
Martin, Jacques	St. Louis	160	66	71	23	2		
	Ottawa	692	341	255	96	9		
	Florida	164	72	65	27	3		
	Total	1016	479	391	146	14		1986-07
Matheson, Godfrey	Chicago	2	0	2	0	1		1932-33
Maurice, Paul	Hartford	152	61	72	19	2		
	Carolina	522	207	235	80	7		
	Toronto	82	40	31	11	1		
	Total	756	308	338	110	10		1995-07
Maxner, Wayne	Detroit	129	34	68	27	2		1980-82
McCammon, Bob	Philadelphia	218	119	68	31	4		
	Vancouver	294	102	156	36	4		
	Total	512	221	224	67	8		1978-91
McCreary, Bill	St. Louis	24	6	14	4	1		

Coach	Team	Games Coached	Wins	Losses	O/T	Years	Cup Wins	Career
	Vancouver	41	9	25	7	1		
	California	32	8	20	4	1		
	Total	**97**	**23**	**59**	**15**	**3**		**1971-75**
McGuire, Pierre	**Hartford**	**67**	**23**	**37**	**7**	**1**		**1993-94**
McLellan, John	**Toronto**	**310**	**126**	**139**	**45**	**4**		**1969-73**
McVie, Tom	Washington	204	49	122	33	3		
	Winnipeg	105	20	67	18	2		
	New Jersey	153	57	74	22	3		
	Total	**462**	**126**	**263**	**73**	**8**		**1975-92**
Meeker, Howie	**Toronto**	**70**	**21**	**34**	**15**	**1**		**1956-57**
Melrose, Barry	**Los Angeles**	**209**	**79**	**101**	**29**	**3**		**1992-95**
Milbury, Mike	Boston	160	90	49	21	2		
	NY Islanders	191	56	111	24	4		
	Total	**351**	**146**	**160**	**45**	**6**		**1989-99**
Molleken, Lorne	**Chicago**	**47**	**18**	**21**	**8**	**2**		**1998-00**
Muckler, John	Minnesota	35	6	23	6	1		
	Edmonton	160	75	65	20	2	1	
	Buffalo	268	125	109	34	4		
	NY Rangers	185	70	91	24	3		
	Total	**648**	**276**	**288**	**84**	**10**	**1**	**1968-00**
Muldoon, Pete	**Chicago**	**44**	**19**	**22**	**3**	**1**		**1926-27**
Munro, Dunc	**Mtl. Maroons**	**76**	**37**	**29**	**10**	**2**		**1929-31**
Murdoch, Bob	Chicago	80	30	41	9	1		
	Winnipeg	160	63	75	22	2		
	Total	**240**	**93**	**116**	**31**	**3**		**1987-91**
Murphy, Mike	Los Angeles	65	20	37	8	2		
	Toronto	164	60	87	17	2		
	Total	**229**	**80**	**124**	**25**	**4**		**1986-98**
Murray, Andy	Los Angeles	480	215	202	63	7		
	St. Louis	56	27	18	11	1		
	Total	**536**	**242**	**220**	**74**	**8**		**1999-07**
Murray, Bryan	Washington	672	343	246	83	9		
	Detroit	244	124	91	29	3		
	Florida	59	17	31	11	1		
	Anaheim	82	29	45	8	1		
	Ottawa	164	100	46	18	3		
	Total	**1221**	**613**	**459**	**149**	**17**		**1981-07**
Murray, Terry	Washington	325	163	134	28	5		
	Philadelphia	212	118	64	30	3		
	Florida	200	79	90	31	3		
	Total	**737**	**360**	**288**	**89**	**11**		**1989-01**
Nanne, Lou	**Minnesota**	**29**	**7**	**18**	**4**	**1**		**1977-78**
Neale, Harry	Vancouver	407	142	189	76	6		
	Detroit	35	8	23	4	1		
	Total	**442**	**150**	**212**	**80**	**7**		**1978-86**
Neilson, Roger	Toronto	160	75	62	23	2		
	Buffalo	80	39	20	21	1		
	Vancouver	133	51	61	21	3		
	Los Angeles	28	8	17	3	1		
	NY Rangers	280	141	104	35	4		
	Florida	132	53	56	23	2		
	Philadelphia	185	92	60	33	3		
	Ottawa	2	1	1	0	1		
	Total	**1000**	**460**	**381**	**159**	**17**		**1977-02**
Nolan, Ted	Buffalo	164	73	72	19	2		
	NY Islanders	82	40	30	12			
	Total	**246**	**113**	**102**	**31**	**3**		**1995-07**
Nykoluk, Mike	**Toronto**	**280**	**89**	**144**	**47**	**4**		**1980-84**
O'Connell, Mike	**Boston**	**9**	**3**	**3**	**3**	**1**		**2002-03**
O'Donoghue, George	**Toronto**	**29**	**15**	**13**	**1**	**2**	**1**	**1921-23**
O'Reilly, Terry	**Boston**	**227**	**115**	**86**	**26**	**3**		**1986-89**
Olczyk, Ed	**Pittsburgh**	**113**	**31**	**68**	**14**	**3**		**2003-06**
Oliver, Murray	**Minnesota**	**41**	**21**	**12**	**8**	**2**		**1981-83**
Olmstead, Bert	**Oakland**	**64**	**11**	**37**	**16**	**1**		**1967-68**
Paddock, John	**Winnipeg**	**281**	**106**	**138**	**37**	**4**		**1991-95**
Page, Pierre	Minnesota	160	63	77	20	2		
	Quebec	230	98	103	29	3		
	Calgary	164	66	78	20	2		
	Anaheim	82	26	43	13	1		
	Total	**636**	**253**	**301**	**82**	**8**		**1988-98**
Park, Brad	**Detroit**	**45**	**9**	**34**	**2**	**1**		**1985-86**
Paterson, Rick	**Tampa Bay**	**6**	**0**	**6**	**0**	**1**		**1997-98**
Patrick, Craig	NY Rangers	95	37	45	13	2		
	Pittsburgh	74	29	36	9	2		
	Total	**169**	**66**	**81**	**22**	**4**		**1980-97**
Patrick, Frank	**Boston**	**96**	**48**	**36**	**12**	**2**		**1934-36**
Patrick, Lester	**NY Rangers**	**604**	**281**	**216**	**107**	**13**	**2**	**1926-39**
Patrick, Lynn	NY Rangers	107	40	51	16	2		
	Boston	310	117	130	63	5		
	St. Louis	26	8	15	3	3		
	Total	**443**	**165**	**196**	**82**	**10**		**1948-76**
Patrick, Muzz	**NY Rangers**	**136**	**43**	**66**	**27**	**4**		**1953-63**
Perron, Jean	Montreal	240	126	84	30	3	1	
	Quebec	47	16	26	5	1		
	Total	**287**	**142**	**110**	**35**	**4**	**1**	**1985-89**
Perry, Don	**Los Angeles**	**168**	**52**	**85**	**31**	**3**		**1981-84**
Pike, Alf	**NY Rangers**	**123**	**36**	**66**	**21**	**2**		**1959-61**
Pilous, Rudy	**Chicago**	**387**	**162**	**151**	**74**	**6**	**1**	**1957-63**
Plager, Barclay	**St. Louis**	**178**	**49**	**96**	**33**	**4**		**1977-83**
Plager, Bob	**St. Louis**	**11**	**4**	**6**	**1**	**1**		**1992-93**
Playfair, Jim	**Calgary**	**82**	**43**	**29**	**10**	**1**		**2006-07**
Pleau, Larry	**Hartford**	**224**	**81**	**117**	**26**	**5**		**1980-89**
Polano, Nick	**Detroit**	**240**	**79**	**127**	**34**	**3**		**1982-85**
Popein, Larry	**NY Rangers**	**41**	**18**	**14**	**9**	**1**		**1973-74**
Powers, Eddie	**Toronto**	**66**	**31**	**32**	**3**	**2**		**1924-26**

Coach	Team	Games Coached	Wins	Losses	O/T	Years	Cup Wins	Career
Primeau, Joe	**Toronto**	**210**	**97**	**71**	**42**	**3**	**1**	**1950-53**
Pronovost, Marcel	**Buffalo**	**104**	**52**	**29**	**23**	**2**		**1977-79**
Pulford, Bob	Los Angeles	396	178	150	68	5		
	Chicago	433	185	180	68	7		
	Total	**829**	**363**	**330**	**136**	**12**		**1972-00**
Quenneville, Joel	St. Louis	593	307	209	77	8		
	Colorado	164	87	61	16	3		
	Total	**757**	**394**	**270**	**93**	**11**		**1996-07**
Querrie, Charles	**Toronto**	**72**	**29**	**38**	**5**	**3**		**1922-27**
Quinn, Mike	**Quebec**	**24**	**4**	**20**	**0**	**1**		**1919-20**
Quinn, Pat	Philadelphia	262	141	73	48	4		
	Los Angeles	202	75	101	26	3		
	Vancouver	280	141	111	28	5		
	Toronto	574	300	214	60	8		
	Total	**1318**	**657**	**499**	**162**	**19**		**1978-06**
Raeder, Cap	**San Jose**	**1**	**1**	**0**	**0**	**1**		**2002-03**
Ramsay, Craig	Buffalo	21	4	15	2	1		
	Philadelphia	28	12	12	4	1		
	Total	**49**	**16**	**27**	**6**	**2**		**1986-01**
Randall, Ken	**Hamilton**	**14**	**6**	**8**	**0**	**1**		**1923-24**
Reay, Billy	Toronto	90	26	50	14	2		
	Chicago	1012	516	335	161	14		
	Total	**1102**	**542**	**385**	**175**	**16**		**1957-77**
Regan, Larry	**Los Angeles**	**88**	**27**	**47**	**14**	**2**		**1970-72**
Renney, Tom	Vancouver	101	39	53	9	2		
	NY Rangers	184	91	71	22	4		
	Total	**285**	**130**	**124**	**31**	**6**		**1996-07**
Risebrough, Doug	**Calgary**	**144**	**71**	**56**	**17**	**2**		**1990-92**
Roberts, Jim	Buffalo	45	21	16	8	1		
	Hartford	80	26	41	13	1		
	St. Louis	9	3	3	3	1		
	Total	**134**	**50**	**60**	**24**	**3**		**1981-97**
Robinson, Larry	Los Angeles	328	122	161	45	4		
	New Jersey	173	87	62	24	4	1	
	Total	**501**	**209**	**223**	**69**	**8**	**1**	**1995-06**
Rodden, Mike	**Toronto**	**2**	**0**	**2**	**0**	**1**		**1926-27**
Romeril, Alex	**Toronto**	**13**	**7**	**5**	**1**	**1**		**1926-27**
Ross, Art	Mtl. Wanderers	6	1	5	0	1		
	Hamilton	24	6	18	0	1		
	Boston	728	361	277	90	16	1	
	Total	**758**	**368**	**300**	**90**	**18**	**1**	**1917-45**
Ruel, Claude	**Montreal**	**305**	**172**	**82**	**51**	**5**	**1**	**1968-81**
Ruff, Lindy	**Buffalo**	**738**	**358**	**289**	**91**	**10**		**1997-07**
Sather, Glen	Edmonton	842	464	268	110	11	4	
	NY Rangers	90	33	46	11	2		
	Total	**932**	**497**	**314**	**121**	**13**		**1979-04**
Sator, Ted	NY Rangers	99	41	48	10	2		
	Buffalo	207	96	89	22	3		
	Total	**306**	**137**	**137**	**32**	**5**		**1985-89**
Savard, Andre	**Quebec**	**24**	**10**	**13**	**1**	**1**		**1987-88**
Savard, Denis	**Chicago**	**61**	**24**	**30**	**7**	**1**		**2006-07**
Schinkel, Ken	**Pittsburgh**	**203**	**83**	**92**	**28**	**4**		**1972-77**
Schmidt, Milt	Boston	726	245	360	121	11		
	Washington	44	5	34	5	2		
	Total	**770**	**250**	**394**	**126**	**13**		**1954-76**
Schoenfeld, Jim	Buffalo	43	19	19	5	1		
	New Jersey	124	50	59	15	3		
	Washington	249	113	102	34	4		
	Phoenix	164	74	66	24	2		
	Total	**580**	**256**	**248**	**78**	**10**		**1985-99**
Shaughnessy, Tom	**Chicago**	**21**	**10**	**8**	**3**	**1**		**1929-30**
Shaw, Brad	**NY Islanders**	**40**	**18**	**18**	**4**	**1**		**2005-06**
Shero, Fred	Philadelphia	554	308	151	95	7	2	
	NY Rangers	180	82	74	24	3		
	Total	**734**	**390**	**225**	**119**	**10**	**2**	**1971-81**
Simpson, Joe	**NY Americans**	**144**	**42**	**72**	**30**	**3**		**1932-35**
Simpson, Terry	NY Islanders	187	81	82	24	3		
	Philadelphia	84	35	39	10	1		
	Winnipeg	97	43	47	7	2		
	Total	**368**	**159**	**168**	**41**	**6**		**1986-96**
Sims, Al	**San Jose**	**82**	**27**	**47**	**8**	**1**		**1996-97**
Sinden, Harry	**Boston**	**327**	**153**	**116**	**58**	**6**	**1**	**1966-85**
Skinner, Jimmy	**Detroit**	**247**	**123**	**78**	**46**	**4**	**1**	**1954-58**
Smeaton, Cooper	**Philadelphia**	**44**	**4**	**36**	**4**	**1**		**1930-31**
Smith, Alf	**Ottawa**	**18**	**12**	**6**	**0**	**1**		**1918-19**
Smith, Barry*	**Detroit**	**5**	**4**	**1**	**0**	**1**		**1998-99**

*Results shared with co-coach Dave Lewis.

Coach	Team	Games Coached	Wins	Losses	O/T	Years	Cup Wins	Career
Smith, Floyd	Buffalo	241	143	62	36	4		
	Toronto	68	30	33	5	1		
	Total	**309**	**173**	**95**	**41**	**5**		**1971-80**
Smith, Mike	**Winnipeg**	**23**	**2**	**17**	**4**	**1**		**1980-81**
Smith, Ron	**NY Rangers**	**44**	**15**	**22**	**7**	**1**		**1992-93**
Smythe, Conn	**Toronto**	**134**	**57**	**57**	**20**	**4**		**1927-31**
Sonmor, Glen	**Minnesota**	**417**	**174**	**161**	**82**	**7**		**1978-87**
Sproule, Harry	**Toronto**	**12**	**7**	**5**	**0**	**1**		**1919-20**
Stanley, Barney	**Chicago**	**23**	**4**	**17**	**2**	**1**		**1927-28**
Stasiuk, Vic	Philadelphia	154	45	68	41	2		
	California	75	21	38	16	1		
	Vancouver	78	22	47	9	1		
	Total	**307**	**88**	**153**	**66**	**4**		**1969-73**
Stevens, John	**Philadelphia**	**74**	**21**	**42**	**11**	**1**		**2006-07**
Stewart, Bill	**Chicago**	**69**	**22**	**35**	**12**	**2**	**1**	**1937-39**
Stewart, Bill	**NY Islanders**	**37**	**11**	**19**	**7**	**1**		**1998-99**
Stewart, Ron	NY Rangers	39	15	20	4	1		

Coach	Team	Games Coached	Wins	Losses	O/T	Years	Cup Wins	Career
	Los Angeles	80	31	34	15	1		
	Total	**119**	**46**	**54**	**19**	**2**		**1975-78**
Stirling, Steve	**NY Islanders**	**124**	**56**	**55**	**13**	**3**		**2003-06**
Suhonen, Alpo	**Chicago**	**82**	**29**	**45**	**8**	**1**		**2000-01**
Sullivan, Red	NY Rangers	196	58	103	35	4		
	Pittsburgh	150	47	79	24	2		
	Washington	18	2	16	0	1		
	Total	**364**	**107**	**198**	**59**	**7**		**1962-75**
Sullivan, Mike	**Boston**	**164**	**70**	**63**	**31**	**3**		**2003-06**
Sutherland, Bill	**Winnipeg**	**32**	**7**	**22**	**3**	**2**		**1979-81**
Sutter, Brian	St. Louis	320	153	124	43	4		
	Boston	216	120	73	23	3		
	Calgary	246	87	122	37	3		
	Chicago	246	91	118	37	4		
	Total	**1028**	**451**	**437**	**140**	**14**		**1988-05**
Sutter, Darryl	Chicago	216	110	80	26	3		
	San Jose	434	192	182	60	6		
	Calgary	210	107	77	26	4		
	Total	**860**	**409**	**339**	**112**	**12**		**1992-06**
Sutter, Duane	**Florida**	**72**	**22**	**42**	**8**	**2**		**2000-02**
Talbot, Jean-Guy	St. Louis	120	52	53	15	2		
	NY Rangers	80	30	37	13	1		
	Total	**200**	**82**	**90**	**28**	**3**		**1972-78**
Tessier, Orval	**Chicago**	**213**	**99**	**93**	**21**	**3**		**1982-85**
Therrien, Michel	Montreal	190	77	90	23	3		
	Pittsburgh	133	61	53	19	2		
	Total	**323**	**138**	**143**	**42**	**5**		**2000-07**
Thompson, Paul	**Chicago**	**272**	**104**	**127**	**41**	**7**		**1938-45**
Thompson, Percy	**Hamilton**	**48**	**13**	**35**	**0**	**2**		**1920-22**
Tippett, Dave	**Dallas**	**328**	**190**	**97**	**41**	**5**		**2002-07**
Tobin, Bill	**Chicago**	**71**	**29**	**29**	**13**	**2**		**1929-32**
Torchetti, John	Florida	27	10	13	4	1		
	Los Angeles	12	5	7	0	1		
	Total	**39**	**15**	**20**	**4**	**2**		**2003-06**
Tortorella, John	NY Rangers	4	0	3	1	1		
	Tampa Bay	453	208	198	47	6	1	
	Total	**457**	**208**	**201**	**48**	**7**	**1**	**1999-07**
Tremblay, Mario	**Montreal**	**159**	**71**	**63**	**25**	**2**		**1995-97**
Trottier, Bryan	**NY Rangers**	**54**	**21**	**27**	**6**	**1**		**2002-03**
Trotz, Barry	**Nashville**	**656**	**283**	**297**	**76**	**9**		**1998-07**
Ubriaco, Gene	**Pittsburgh**	**106**	**50**	**47**	**9**	**2**		**1988-90**
Vachon, Rogie	**Los Angeles**	**10**	**4**	**3**	**3**	**3**		**1983-95**
Vigneault, Alain	Montreal	266	109	122	35	4		
	Vancouver	82	49	26	7	1		
	Total	**348**	**158**	**148**	**42**	**5**		**1997-07**
Waddell, Don	**Atlanta**	**10**	**4**	**5**	**1**	**1**		**2002-03**
Watson, Bryan	**Edmonton**	**18**	**4**	**9**	**5**	**1**		**1980-81**
Watson, Phil	NY Rangers	295	119	124	52	5		
	Boston	84	16	55	13	2		
	Total	**379**	**135**	**179**	**65**	**7**		**1955-63**
Watt, Tom	Winnipeg	181	72	85	24	3		
	Vancouver	160	52	87	21	2		
	Toronto	149	52	80	17	2		
	Total	**490**	**176**	**252**	**62**	**7**		**1981-92**
Webster, Tom	NY Rangers	18	5	9	4	1		
	Los Angeles	240	115	94	31	3		
	Total	**258**	**120**	**103**	**35**	**4**		**1986-92**
Weiland, Cooney	**Boston**	**96**	**58**	**20**	**18**	**2**	**1**	**1939-41**
White, Bill	**Chicago**	**46**	**16**	**24**	**6**	**1**		**1976-77**
Wiley, Jim	**San Jose**	**57**	**17**	**37**	**3**	**1**		**1995-96**
Wilson, Johnny	Los Angeles	52	9	34	9	1		
	Detroit	145	67	56	22	2		
	Colorado	80	20	46	14	1		
	Pittsburgh	240	91	105	44	3		
	Total	**517**	**187**	**241**	**89**	**7**		**1969-80**
Wilson, Larry	**Detroit**	**36**	**3**	**29**	**4**	**1**		**1976-77**
Wilson, Rick	**Dallas**	**32**	**13**	**12**	**7**	**1**		**2001-02**
Wilson, Ron	Anaheim	296	120	145	31	4		
	Washington	410	192	167	51	5		
	San Jose	303	157	111	35	5		
	Total	**1009**	**469**	**423**	**117**	**14**		**1993-07**
Yawney, Trent	**Chicago**	**103**	**33**	**55**	**15**	**2**		**2005-07**
Young, Garry	California	12	2	7	3	1		
	St. Louis	98	41	41	16	2		
	Total	**110**	**43**	**48**	**19**	**3**		**1972-76**

Randy Carlyle (top) played 17 years in the NHL without winning the Stanley Cup, but got his name on the trophy in just his second year as an NHL coach with the Anaheim Ducks in 2007. Peter Laviolette of Carolina (middle) and John Tortorella with Tampa Bay were also first-time winners in recent years. In fact, since 1989, Scotty Bowman is the only head coach to have won the Stanley Cup more than once.

Year-by-Year Individual Regular-Season Leaders

Season	Goals	G	Assists	A	Points	Pts.	Penalty Minutes	PIM
1917-18	Joe Malone	44	Cy Denneny, Reg Noble, Harry Cameron	10	Joe Malone	48	Joe Hall	100
1918-19	Newsy Lalonde	22	Newsy Lalonde, Eddie Gerard	10	Newsy Lalonde	32	Joe Hall	135
1919-20	Joe Malone	39	Frank Nighbor	15	Joe Malone	49	Cully Wilson	86
1920-21	Babe Dye	35	Jack Darragh	15	Newsy Lalonde	43	Bert Corbeau	86
1921-22	Punch Broadbent	32	Harry Cameron	17	Punch Broadbent	46	Sprague Cleghorn	63
1922-23	Babe Dye	26	Edmond Bouchard	12	Babe Dye	37	Georges Boucher	58
1923-24	Cy Denneny	22	Georges Boucher	10	Cy Denneny	24	Bert Corbeau	55
1924-25	Babe Dye	38	Cy Denneny, Red Green	15	Babe Dye	46	Georges Boucher	95
1925-26	Nels Stewart	34	Frank Nighbor	13	Nels Stewart	42	Bert Corbeau	121
1926-27	Bill Cook	33	Dick Irvin	18	Bill Cook	37	Nels Stewart	133
1927-28	Howie Morenz	33	Howie Morenz	18	Howie Morenz	51	Eddie Shore	165
1928-29	Ace Bailey	22	Frank Boucher	16	Ace Bailey	32	Red Dutton	139
1929-30	Cooney Weiland	43	Frank Boucher	36	Cooney Weiland	73	Joe Lamb	119
1930-31	Charlie Conacher	31	Joe Primeau	32	Howie Morenz	51	Harvey Rockburn	118
1931-32	Charlie Conacher, Bill Cook	34	Joe Primeau	37	Busher Jackson	53	Red Dutton	107
1932-33	Bill Cook	28	Frank Boucher	28	Bill Cook	50	Red Horner	144
1933-34	Charlie Conacher	32	Joe Primeau	32	Charlie Conacher	52	Red Horner	126 *
1934-35	Charlie Conacher	36	Art Chapman	34	Charlie Conacher	57	Red Horner	125
1935-36	Charlie Conacher, Bill Thoms	23	Art Chapman	28	Sweeney Schriner	45	Red Horner	167
1936-37	Larry Aurie, Nels Stewart	23	Syl Apps	29	Sweeney Schriner	46	Red Horner	124
1937-38	Gordie Drillon	26	Syl Apps	29	Gordie Drillon	52	Red Horner	82 *
1938-39	Roy Conacher	26	Bill Cowley	34	Toe Blake	47	Red Horner	85
1939-40	Bryan Hextall	24	Milt Schmidt	30	Milt Schmidt	52	Red Horner	87
1940-41	Bryan Hextall	26	Bill Cowley	45	Bill Cowley	62	Jimmy Orlando	99
1941-42	Lynn Patrick	32	Phil Watson	37	Bryan Hextall	56	Pat Egan	124
1942-43	Doug Bentley	33	Bill Cowley	45	Doug Bentley	73	Jimmy Orlando	89 *
1943-44	Doug Bentley	38	Clint Smith	49	Herb Cain	82	Mike McMahon	98
1944-45	Maurice Richard	50	Elmer Lach	54	Elmer Lach	80	Pat Egan	86
1945-46	Gaye Stewart	37	Elmer Lach	34	Max Bentley	61	Jack Stewart	73
1946-47	Maurice Richard	45	Billy Taylor	46	Max Bentley	72	Gus Mortson	133
1947-48	Ted Lindsay	33	Doug Bentley	37	Elmer Lach	61	Bill Barilko	147
1948-49	Sid Abel	28	Doug Bentley	43	Roy Conacher	68	Bill Ezinicki	145
1949-50	Maurice Richard	43	Ted Lindsay	55	Ted Lindsay	78	Bill Ezinicki	144
1950-51	Gordie Howe	43	Gordie Howe, Ted Kennedy	43	Gordie Howe	86	Gus Mortson	142
1951-52	Gordie Howe	47	Elmer Lach	50	Gordie Howe	86	Gus Kyle	127
1952-53	Gordie Howe	49	Gordie Howe	46	Gordie Howe	95	Maurice Richard	112
1953-54	Maurice Richard	37	Gordie Howe	48	Gordie Howe	81	Gus Mortson	132
1954-55	Maurice Richard, Bernie Geoffrion	38	Bert Olmstead	48	Bernie Geoffrion	75	Fern Flaman	150
1955-56	Jean Beliveau	47	Bert Olmstead	56	Jean Beliveau	88	Lou Fontinato	202
1956-57	Gordie Howe	44	Ted Lindsay	55	Gordie Howe	89	Gus Mortson	147
1957-58	Dickie Moore	36	Henri Richard	52	Dickie Moore	84	Lou Fontinato	152
1958-59	Jean Beliveau	45	Dickie Moore	55	Dickie Moore	96	Ted Lindsay	184
1959-60	Bobby Hull, Bronco Horvath	39	Don McKenney	49	Bobby Hull	81	Carl Brewer	150
1960-61	Bernie Geoffrion	50	Jean Beliveau	58	Bernie Geoffrion	95	Pierre Pilote	165
1961-62	Bobby Hull	50	Andy Bathgate	56	Bobby Hull, Andy Bathgate	84	Lou Fontinato	167
1962-63	Gordie Howe	38	Henri Richard	50	Gordie Howe	86	Howie Young	273
1963-64	Bobby Hull	43	Andy Bathgate	58	Stan Mikita	89	Vic Hadfield	151
1964-65	Norm Ullman	42	Stan Mikita	59	Stan Mikita	87	Carl Brewer	177
1965-66	Bobby Hull	54	Stan Mikita, Bobby Rousseau, Jean Beliveau	48	Bobby Hull	97	Reggie Fleming	166
1966-67	Bobby Hull	52	Stan Mikita	62	Stan Mikita	97	John Ferguson	177
1967-68	Bobby Hull	44	Phil Esposito	49	Stan Mikita	87	Barclay Plager	153
1968-69	Bobby Hull	58	Phil Esposito	77	Phil Esposito	126	Forbes Kennedy	219
1969-70	Phil Esposito	43	Bobby Orr	87	Bobby Orr	120	Keith Magnuson	213
1970-71	Phil Esposito	76	Bobby Orr	102	Phil Esposito	152	Keith Magnuson	291
1971-72	Phil Esposito	66	Bobby Orr	80	Phil Esposito	133	Bryan Watson	212
1972-73	Phil Esposito	55	Phil Esposito	75	Phil Esposito	130	Dave Schultz	259
1973-74	Phil Esposito	68	Bobby Orr	90	Phil Esposito	145	Dave Schultz	348
1974-75	Phil Esposito	61	Bobby Orr, Bobby Clarke	89	Bobby Orr	135	Dave Schultz	472
1975-76	Reggie Leach	61	Bobby Clarke	89	Guy Lafleur	125	Steve Durbano	370
1976-77	Steve Shutt	60	Guy Lafleur	80	Guy Lafleur	136	Tiger Williams	338
1977-78	Guy Lafleur	60	Bryan Trottier	77	Guy Lafleur	132	Dave Schultz	405
1978-79	Mike Bossy	69	Bryan Trottier	87	Bryan Trottier	134	Tiger Williams	298
1979-80	Charlie Simmer, Danny Gare, Blaine Stoughton	56	Wayne Gretzky	86	Marcel Dionne, Wayne Gretzky	137	Jimmy Mann	287
1980-81	Mike Bossy	68	Wayne Gretzky	109	Wayne Gretzky	164	Tiger Williams	343
1981-82	Wayne Gretzky	92	Wayne Gretzky	120	Wayne Gretzky	212	Paul Baxter	409
1982-83	Wayne Gretzky	71	Wayne Gretzky	125	Wayne Gretzky	196	Randy Holt	275
1983-84	Wayne Gretzky	87	Wayne Gretzky	118	Wayne Gretzky	205	Chris Nilan	338
1984-85	Wayne Gretzky	73	Wayne Gretzky	135	Wayne Gretzky	208	Chris Nilan	358
1985-86	Jari Kurri	68	Wayne Gretzky	163	Wayne Gretzky	215	Joe Kocur	377
1986-87	Wayne Gretzky	62	Wayne Gretzky	121	Wayne Gretzky	183	Tim Hunter	361
1987-88	Mario Lemieux	70	Wayne Gretzky	109	Mario Lemieux	168	Bob Probert	398
1988-89	Mario Lemieux	85	Mario Lemieux, Wayne Gretzky	114	Mario Lemieux	199	Tim Hunter	375
1989-90	Brett Hull	72	Wayne Gretzky	102	Wayne Gretzky	142	Basil McRae	351
1990-91	Brett Hull	86	Wayne Gretzky	122	Wayne Gretzky	163	Rob Ray	350
1991-92	Brett Hull	70	Wayne Gretzky	90	Mario Lemieux	131	Mike Peluso	408
1992-93	Teemu Selanne, Alexander Mogilny	76	Adam Oates	97	Mario Lemieux	160	Marty McSorley	399
1993-94	Pavel Bure	60	Wayne Gretzky	92	Wayne Gretzky	130	Tie Domi	347
1994-95	Peter Bondra	34	Ron Francis	48	Jaromir Jagr, Eric Lindros	70	Enrico Ciccone	225
1995-96	Mario Lemieux	69	Mario Lemieux, Ron Francis	92	Mario Lemieux	161	Matthew Barnaby	335
1996-97	Keith Tkachuk	52	Mario Lemieux, Wayne Gretzky	72	Mario Lemieux	122	Gino Odjick	371
1997-98	Teemu Selanne, Peter Bondra	52	Jaromir Jagr, Wayne Gretzky	67	Jaromir Jagr	102	Donald Brashear	372
1998-99	Teemu Selanne	47	Jaromir Jagr	83	Jaromir Jagr	127	Rob Ray	261
99-2000	Pavel Bure	58	Mark Recchi	63	Jaromir Jagr	96	Denny Lambert	219
2000-01	Pavel Bure	59	Jaromir Jagr, Adam Oates	69	Jaromir Jagr	121	Matthew Barnaby	265
2001-02	Jarome Iginla	52	Adam Oates	64	Jarome Iginla	96	Peter Worell	354
2002-03	Milan Hejduk	50	Peter Forsberg	77	Peter Forsberg	106	Jody Shelley	249
2003-04	Rick Nash, Jarome Iginla, Ilya Kovalchuk	41	Scott Gomez, Martin St. Louis	56	Martin St. Louis	94	Sean Avery	261
2004-05	....	....	....	....	....	....	....	....
2005-06	Jonathan Cheechoo	56	Joe Thornton	96	Joe Thornton	125	Sean Avery	257
2006-07	Vincent Lecavalier	52	Joe Thornton	92	Sidney Crosby	120	Ben Eager	233

* Match Misconduct penalty not included in total penalty minutes.
1946-47 was the first season that a Match penalty was automaticaly written into the player's total penalty minutes as 20 minutes.
Beginning in 1947-48 all penalties, Match, Game Misconduct, and Misconduct, are written as 10 minutes.

One Season Scoring Records

Goals-Per-Game Leaders, One Season

(Among players with 20 goals or more in one season)

Player	Team	Season	Games	Goals	Average
Joe Malone	Montreal	1917-18	20	44	2.20
Cy Denneny	Ottawa	1917-18	20	36	1.80
Newsy Lalonde	Montreal	1917-18	14	23	1.64
Joe Malone	Quebec	1919-20	24	39	1.63
Newsy Lalonde	Montreal	1919-20	23	37	1.61
Reg Noble	Toronto	1917-18	20	30	1.50
Babe Dye	Ham., Tor.	1920-21	24	35	1.46
Cy Denneny	Ottawa	1920-21	24	34	1.42
Joe Malone	Hamilton	1920-21	20	28	1.40
Newsy Lalonde	Montreal	1920-21	24	33	1.38
Punch Broadbent	Ottawa	1921-22	24	32	1.33
Babe Dye	Toronto	1924-25	29	38	1.31
Babe Dye	Toronto	1921-22	24	31	1.29
Newsy Lalonde	Montreal	1918-19	17	22	1.29
Odie Cleghorn	Montreal	1918-19	17	22	1.29
Cy Denneny	Ottawa	1921-22	22	27	1.23
Aurel Joliat	Montreal	1924-25	25	30	1.20
Wayne Gretzky	Edmonton	1983-84	74	87	1.18
Babe Dye	Toronto	1922-23	22	26	1.18
Wayne Gretzky	Edmonton	1981-82	80	92	1.15
Mario Lemieux	Pittsburgh	1992-93	60	69	1.15
Frank Nighbor	Ottawa	1919-20	23	26	1.13
Mario Lemieux	Pittsburgh	1988-89	76	85	1.12
Brett Hull	St. Louis	1990-91	78	86	1.10
Cam Neely	Boston	1993-94	49	50	1.02
Maurice Richard	Montreal	1944-45	50	50	1.00
Reg Noble	Toronto	1919-20	24	24	1.00
Corb Denneny	Toronto	1919-20	24	24	1.00
Joe Malone	Hamilton	1921-22	24	24	1.00
Billy Boucher	Montreal	1922-23	24	24	1.00
Cy Denneny	Ottawa	1923-24	22	22	1.00
Alexander Mogilny	Buffalo	1992-93	77	76	0.99
Mario Lemieux	Pittsburgh	1995-96	70	69	0.99
Cooney Weiland	Boston	1929-30	44	43	0.98
Phil Esposito	Boston	1970-71	78	76	0.97
Jari Kurri	Edmonton	1984-85	73	71	0.97

Acquired in the trade that brought Sean Burke and Branko Radivojevic to Philadelphia, Ben Eager earned the club's Pelle Lindbergh trophy as the Flyers' most improved player. He was the only player in the NHL with more than 200 penalty minutes in 2006-07.

Assists-Per-Game Leaders, One Season

(Among players with 35 assists or more in one season)

Player	Team	Season	Games	Assists	Average
Wayne Gretzky	Edmonton	1985-86	80	163	2.04
Wayne Gretzky	Edmonton	1987-88	64	109	1.70
Wayne Gretzky	Edmonton	1984-85	80	135	1.69
Wayne Gretzky	Edmonton	1983-84	74	118	1.59
Wayne Gretzky	Edmonton	1982-83	80	125	1.56
Wayne Gretzky	Los Angeles	1990-91	78	122	1.56
Wayne Gretzky	Edmonton	1986-87	79	121	1.53
Mario Lemieux	Pittsburgh	1992-93	60	91	1.52
Wayne Gretzky	Edmonton	1981-82	80	120	1.50
Mario Lemieux	Pittsburgh	1988-89	76	114	1.50
Adam Oates	St. Louis	1990-91	61	90	1.48
Wayne Gretzky	Los Angeles	1988-89	78	114	1.46
Wayne Gretzky	Los Angeles	1989-90	73	102	1.40
Wayne Gretzky	Edmonton	1980-81	80	109	1.36
Mario Lemieux	Pittsburgh	1991-92	64	87	1.36
Mario Lemieux	Pittsburgh	1989-90	59	78	1.32
Bobby Orr	Boston	1970-71	78	102	1.31
Mario Lemieux	Pittsburgh	1995-96	70	92	1.31
Mario Lemieux	Pittsburgh	1987-88	77	98	1.27
Bobby Orr	Boston	1973-74	74	90	1.22
Wayne Gretzky	Los Angeles	1991-92	74	90	1.22
Joe Thornton	Bos., S.J.	2005-06	81	96	1.19
Ron Francis	Pittsburgh	1995-96	77	92	1.19
Mario Lemieux	Pittsburgh	1985-86	79	93	1.18
Bobby Clarke	Philadelphia	1975-76	76	89	1.17
Peter Stastny	Quebec	1981-82	80	93	1.16
Adam Oates	Boston	1992-93	84	97	1.15
Doug Gilmour	Toronto	1992-93	83	95	1.14
Wayne Gretzky	Los Angeles	1993-94	81	92	1.14
Paul Coffey	Edmonton	1985-86	79	90	1.14
Bobby Orr	Boston	1969-70	76	87	1.14
Bryan Trottier	NY Islanders	1978-79	76	87	1.14
Bobby Orr	Boston	1972-73	63	72	1.14
Bill Cowley	Boston	1943-44	36	41	1.14
Pat LaFontaine	Buffalo	1992-93	84	95	1.13
Steve Yzerman	Detroit	1988-89	80	90	1.13
Paul Coffey	Pittsburgh	1987-88	46	52	1.13
Joe Thornton	San Jose	**2006-07**	82	92	1.12
Bobby Orr	Boston	1974-75	80	89	1.11
Bobby Clarke	Philadelphia	1974-75	80	89	1.11
Paul Coffey	Pittsburgh	1988-89	75	83	1.11
Wayne Gretzky	Los Angeles	1992-93	45	49	1.11
Denis Savard	Chicago	1982-83	78	86	1.10
Denis Savard	Chicago	1981-82	80	87	1.09
Denis Savard	Chicago	1987-88	80	87	1.09
Wayne Gretzky	Edmonton	1979-80	79	86	1.09
Ron Francis	Pittsburgh	1994-95	44	48	1.09
Paul Coffey	Edmonton	1983-84	80	86	1.08
Elmer Lach	Montreal	1944-45	50	54	1.08
Peter Stastny	Quebec	1985-86	76	81	1.07
Jaromir Jagr	Pittsburgh	1995-96	82	87	1.06
Mark Messier	Edmonton	1989-90	79	84	1.06
Sidney Crosby	Pittsburgh	**2006-07**	79	84	1.06
Peter Forsberg	Colorado	1995-96	82	86	1.05
Paul Coffey	Edmonton	1984-85	80	84	1.05
Marcel Dionne	Los Angeles	1979-80	80	84	1.05
Bobby Orr	Boston	1971-72	76	80	1.05
Mike Bossy	NY Islanders	1981-82	80	83	1.04
Adam Oates	Boston	1993-94	77	80	1.04
Phil Esposito	Boston	1968-69	74	77	1.04
Bryan Trottier	NY Islanders	1983-84	68	71	1.04
Jason Spezza	Ottawa	2005-06	68	71	1.04
Pete Mahovlich	Montreal	1974-75	80	82	1.03
Kent Nilsson	Calgary	1980-81	80	82	1.03
Peter Stastny	Quebec	1982-83	75	77	1.03
Peter Forsberg	Colorado	2002-03	75	77	1.03
Denis Savard	Chicago	1988-89	58	59	1.02
Jaromir Jagr	Pittsburgh	1998-99	81	83	1.02
Doug Gilmour	Toronto	1993-94	83	84	1.01
Bernie Nicholls	Los Angeles	1988-89	79	80	1.01
Guy Lafleur	Montreal	1979-80	74	75	1.01
Guy Lafleur	Montreal	1976-77	80	80	1.00
Marcel Dionne	Los Angeles	1984-85	80	80	1.00
Brian Leetch	NY Rangers	1991-92	80	80	1.00
Bryan Trottier	NY Islanders	1977-78	77	77	1.00
Mike Bossy	NY Islanders	1983-84	67	67	1.00
Jean Ratelle	NY Rangers	1971-72	63	63	1.00
Steve Yzerman	Detroit	1993-94	58	58	1.00
Ron Francis	Hartford	1985-86	53	53	1.00
Guy Chouinard	Calgary	1980-81	52	52	1.00
Elmer Lach	Montreal	1943-44	48	48	1.00

Points-Per-Game Leaders, One Season

(Among players with 50 points or more in one season)

Player	Team	Season	Games	Points	Average
Wayne Gretzky	Edmonton	1983-84	74	205	2.77
Wayne Gretzky	Edmonton	1985-86	80	215	2.69
Mario Lemieux	Pittsburgh	1992-93	60	160	2.67
Wayne Gretzky	Edmonton	1981-82	80	212	2.65
Mario Lemieux	Pittsburgh	1988-89	76	199	2.62
Wayne Gretzky	Edmonton	1984-85	80	208	2.60
Wayne Gretzky	Edmonton	1982-83	80	196	2.45
Wayne Gretzky	Edmonton	1987-88	64	149	2.33
Wayne Gretzky	Edmonton	1986-87	79	183	2.32
Mario Lemieux	Pittsburgh	1995-96	70	161	2.30
Mario Lemieux	Pittsburgh	1987-88	77	168	2.18
Wayne Gretzky	Los Angeles	1988-89	78	168	2.15
Wayne Gretzky	Los Angeles	1990-91	78	163	2.09
Mario Lemieux	Pittsburgh	1989-90	59	123	2.08
Wayne Gretzky	Edmonton	1980-81	80	164	2.05
Mario Lemieux	Pittsburgh	1991-92	64	131	2.05
Bill Cowley	Boston	1943-44	36	71	1.97
Phil Esposito	Boston	1970-71	78	152	1.95
Wayne Gretzky	Los Angeles	1989-90	73	142	1.95
Steve Yzerman	Detroit	1988-89	80	155	1.94
Bernie Nicholls	Los Angeles	1988-89	79	150	1.90
Adam Oates	St. Louis	1990-91	61	115	1.89
Phil Esposito	Boston	1973-74	78	145	1.86
Jari Kurri	Edmonton	1984-85	73	135	1.85
Mike Bossy	NY Islanders	1981-82	80	147	1.84
Jaromir Jagr	Pittsburgh	1995-96	82	149	1.82
Mario Lemieux	Pittsburgh	1985-86	79	141	1.78
Bobby Orr	Boston	1970-71	78	139	1.78
Jari Kurri	Edmonton	1983-84	64	113	1.77
Mario Lemieux	Pittsburgh	2000-01	43	76	1.77
Pat LaFontaine	Buffalo	1992-93	84	148	1.76
Bryan Trottier	NY Islanders	1978-79	76	134	1.76
Mike Bossy	NY Islanders	1983-84	67	118	1.76
Paul Coffey	Edmonton	1985-86	79	138	1.75
Phil Esposito	Boston	1971-72	76	133	1.75
Peter Stastny	Quebec	1981-82	80	139	1.74
Wayne Gretzky	Edmonton	1979-80	79	137	1.73
Jean Ratelle	NY Rangers	1971-72	63	109	1.73
Marcel Dionne	Los Angeles	1979-80	80	137	1.71
Herb Cain	Boston	1943-44	48	82	1.71
Guy Lafleur	Montreal	1976-77	80	136	1.70
Dennis Maruk	Washington	1981-82	80	136	1.70
Phil Esposito	Boston	1968-69	74	126	1.70
Guy Lafleur	Montreal	1974-75	70	119	1.70
Mario Lemieux	Pittsburgh	1986-87	63	107	1.70
Adam Oates	Boston	1992-93	84	142	1.69
Bobby Orr	Boston	1974-75	80	135	1.69
Marcel Dionne	Los Angeles	1980-81	80	135	1.69
Guy Lafleur	Montreal	1977-78	78	132	1.69
Guy Lafleur	Montreal	1979-80	74	125	1.69
Rob Brown	Pittsburgh	1988-89	68	115	1.69
Jari Kurri	Edmonton	1985-86	78	131	1.68
Brett Hull	St. Louis	1990-91	78	131	1.68
Phil Esposito	Boston	1972-73	78	130	1.67
Cooney Weiland	Boston	1929-30	44	73	1.66
Alexander Mogilny	Buffalo	1992-93	77	127	1.65
Peter Stastny	Quebec	1982-83	75	124	1.65
Bobby Orr	Boston	1973-74	74	122	1.65

Player	Team	Season	Games	Points	Average
Kent Nilsson	Calgary	1980-81	80	131	1.64
Denis Savard	Chicago	1987-88	80	131	1.64
Wayne Gretzky	Los Angeles	1991-92	74	121	1.64
Steve Yzerman	Detroit	1992-93	84	137	1.63
Marcel Dionne	Los Angeles	1978-79	80	130	1.63
Dale Hawerchuk	Winnipeg	1984-85	80	130	1.63
Mark Messier	Edmonton	1989-90	79	129	1.63
Bryan Trottier	NY Islanders	1983-84	68	111	1.63
Pat LaFontaine	Buffalo	1991-92	57	93	1.63
Charlie Simmer	Los Angeles	1980-81	65	105	1.62
Guy Lafleur	Montreal	1978-79	80	129	1.61
Bryan Trottier	NY Islanders	1981-82	80	129	1.61
Phil Esposito	Boston	1974-75	79	127	1.61
Steve Yzerman	Detroit	1989-90	79	127	1.61
Peter Stastny	Quebec	1985-86	76	122	1.61
Mario Lemieux	Pittsburgh	1996-97	76	122	1.61
Michel Goulet	Quebec	1983-84	75	121	1.61
Wayne Gretzky	Los Angeles	1993-94	81	130	1.60
Bryan Trottier	NY Islanders	1977-78	77	123	1.60
Bobby Orr	Boston	1972-73	63	101	1.60
Guy Chouinard	Calgary	1980-81	52	83	1.60
Elmer Lach	Montreal	1944-45	50	80	1.60
Pierre Turgeon	NY Islanders	1992-93	83	132	1.59
Steve Yzerman	Detroit	1987-88	64	102	1.59
Mike Bossy	NY Islanders	1978-79	80	126	1.58
Paul Coffey	Edmonton	1983-84	80	126	1.58
Marcel Dionne	Los Angeles	1984-85	80	126	1.58
Bobby Orr	Boston	1969-70	76	120	1.58
Eric Lindros	Philadelphia	1995-96	73	115	1.58
Charlie Simmer	Los Angeles	1979-80	64	101	1.58
Teemu Selanne	Winnipeg	1992-93	84	132	1.57
Jaromir Jagr	Pittsburgh	1998-99	81	127	1.57
Bobby Clarke	Philadelphia	1975-76	76	119	1.57
Guy Lafleur	Montreal	1975-76	80	125	1.56
Dave Taylor	Los Angeles	1980-81	72	112	1.56
Denis Savard	Chicago	1982-83	78	121	1.55
Ron Francis	Pittsburgh	1995-96	77	119	1.55
Joe Thornton	Bos., S.J.	2005-06	81	125	1.54
Mike Bossy	NY Islanders	1985-86	80	123	1.54
Kevin Stevens	Pittsburgh	1991-92	80	123	1.54
Bobby Orr	Boston	1971-72	76	117	1.54
Mike Bossy	NY Islanders	1984-85	76	117	1.54
Kevin Stevens	Pittsburgh	1992-93	72	111	1.54
Doug Bentley	Chicago	1943-44	50	77	1.54
Doug Gilmour	Toronto	1992-93	83	127	1.53
Marcel Dionne	Los Angeles	1976-77	80	122	1.53
Sidney Crosby	Pittsburgh	**2006-07**	79	120	1.52
Jaromir Jagr	Pittsburgh	99-2000	63	96	1.52
Eric Lindros	Philadelphia	1996-97	52	79	1.52
Eric Lindros	Philadelphia	1994-95	46	70	1.52
Marcel Dionne	Detroit	1974-75	80	121	1.51
Mike Bossy	NY Islanders	1980-81	79	119	1.51
Paul Coffey	Edmonton	1984-85	80	121	1.51
Dale Hawerchuk	Winnipeg	1987-88	80	121	1.51
Paul Coffey	Pittsburgh	1988-89	75	113	1.51
Jaromir Jagr	Pittsburgh	1996-97	63	95	1.51
Cam Neely	Boston	1993-94	49	74	1.51

With 120 points in 79 games played last season, Sidney Crosby (being chased by the Rangers' Karel Rachunek) averaged 1.52 points per game. Crosby reached the 200-point plateau in his career at the age of 19 years and 207 days, 40 days younger than Wayne Gretzky.

Pittsburgh's Evgeni Malkin (right) led all rookies with 33 goals and 85 points in 2006-07. He began his NHL career with goals in six straight games, tying a record that had stood since the NHL's first season of 1917-18. Colorado's Paul Stastny had 85 points and set a rookie scoring record with points in 20 straight games from February 3 to March 17.

Rookie Scoring Records

All-Time Top 50 Goal-Scoring Rookies

	Rookie	Team	Position	Season	GP	G	A	PTS
1.	* Teemu Selanne	Winnipeg	Right wing	1992-93	84	76	56	132
2.	* Mike Bossy	NY Islanders	Right wing	1977-78	73	53	38	91
3.	* Alex Ovechkin	Washington	Left wing	2005-06	81	52	54	106
4.	* Joe Nieuwendyk	Calgary	Center	1987-88	75	51	41	92
5.	* Dale Hawerchuk	Winnipeg	Center	1981-82	80	45	58	103
	* Luc Robitaille	Los Angeles	Left wing	1986-87	79	45	39	84
7.	Rick Martin	Buffalo	Left wing	1971-72	73	44	30	74
	Barry Pederson	Boston	Center	1981-82	80	44	48	92
9.	* Steve Larmer	Chicago	Right wing	1982-83	80	43	47	90
	* Mario Lemieux	Pittsburgh	Center	1984-85	73	43	57	100
11.	Eric Lindros	Philadelphia	Center	1992-93	61	41	34	75
12.	Darryl Sutter	Chicago	Left wing	1980-81	76	40	22	62
	Sylvain Turgeon	Hartford	Left wing	1983-84	76	40	32	72
	Warren Young	Pittsburgh	Left wing	1984-85	80	40	32	72
15.	* Eric Vail	Atlanta	Left wing	1974-75	72	39	21	60
	* Peter Stastny	Quebec	Center	1980-81	77	39	70	109
	Anton Stastny	Quebec	Left wing	1980-81	80	39	46	85
	Steve Yzerman	Detroit	Center	1983-84	80	39	48	87
	Sidney Crosby	Pittsburgh	Center	2005-06	81	39	63	102
20.	* Gilbert Perreault	Buffalo	Center	1970-71	78	38	34	72
	Neal Broten	Minnesota	Center	1981-82	73	38	60	98
	Ray Sheppard	Buffalo	Right wing	1987-88	74	38	27	65
	Mikael Renberg	Philadelphia	Left wing	1993-94	83	38	44	82
24.	Jorgen Pettersson	St. Louis	Left wing	1980-81	62	37	36	73
	Jimmy Carson	Los Angeles	Center	1986-87	80	37	42	79
26.	Mike Foligno	Detroit	Right wing	1979-80	80	36	35	71
	Paul MacLean	Winnipeg	Right wing	1981-82	74	36	25	61
	Mike Bullard	Pittsburgh	Center	1981-82	75	36	27	63
	Tony Granato	NY Rangers	Right wing	1988-89	78	36	27	63
30.	Marian Stastny	Quebec	Right wing	1981-82	74	35	54	89
	Brian Bellows	Minnesota	Right wing	1982-83	78	35	30	65
	Tony Amonte	NY Rangers	Right wing	1991-92	79	35	34	69
33.	Nels Stewart	Mtl. Maroons	Center	1925-26	36	34	8	42
	* Danny Grant	Minnesota	Left wing	1968-69	75	34	31	65
	Norm Ferguson	Oakland	Right wing	1968-69	76	34	20	54
	Brian Propp	Philadelphia	Left wing	1979-80	80	34	41	75
	Wendel Clark	Toronto	Left wing	1985-86	66	34	11	45
	* Pavel Bure	Vancouver	Right wing	1991-92	65	34	26	60
39.	* Willi Plett	Atlanta	Right wing	1976-77	64	33	23	56
	Dale McCourt	Detroit	Center	1977-78	76	33	39	72
	Steve Bozek	Los Angeles	Center	1981-82	71	33	23	56
	Ron Flockhart	Philadelphia	Center	1981-82	72	33	39	72
	Mark Pavelich	NY Rangers	Center	1981-82	79	33	43	76
	Jason Arnott	Edmonton	Center	1993-94	78	33	35	68
	* Evgeni Malkin	Pittsburgh	Center	**2006-07**	78	33	52	85
46.	Bill Mosienko	Chicago	Right wing	1943-44	50	32	38	70
	Michel Bergeron	Detroit	Right wing	1975-76	72	32	27	59
	* Bryan Trottier	NY Islanders	Center	1975-76	80	32	63	95
	Don Murdoch	NY Rangers	Right wing	1976-77	59	32	24	56
	Jari Kurri	Edmonton	Left wing	1980-81	75	32	43	75
	Bobby Carpenter	Washington	Center	1981-82	80	32	35	67
	Petr Klima	Detroit	Left wing	1985-86	74	32	24	56
	Kjell Dahlin	Montreal	Right wing	1985-86	77	32	39	71
	Darren Turcotte	NY Rangers	Right wing	1989-90	76	32	34	66
	Joe Juneau	Boston	Center	1992-93	84	32	70	102
	Marek Svatos	Colorado	Right wing	2005-06	61	32	18	50

* Calder Trophy Winner

All-Time Top 50 Point-Scoring Rookies

	Rookie	Team	Position	Season	GP	G	A	PTS
1.	* Teemu Selanne	Winnipeg	Right wing	1992-93	84	76	56	132
2.	* Peter Stastny	Quebec	Center	1980-81	77	39	70	109
3.	* Alex Ovechkin	Washington	Left wing	2005-06	81	52	54	106
4.	* Dale Hawerchuk	Winnipeg	Center	1981-82	80	45	58	103
5.	Joe Juneau	Boston	Center	1992-93	84	32	70	102
	Sidney Crosby	Pittsburgh	Center	2005-06	81	39	63	102
7.	* Mario Lemieux	Pittsburgh	Center	1984-85	73	43	57	100
8.	Neal Broten	Minnesota	Center	1981-82	73	38	60	98
9.	* Bryan Trottier	NY Islanders	Center	1975-76	80	32	63	95
10.	Barry Pederson	Boston	Center	1981-82	80	44	48	92
	* Joe Nieuwendyk	Calgary	Center	1987-88	75	51	41	92
12.	* Mike Bossy	NY Islanders	Right wing	1977-78	73	53	38	91
13.	* Steve Larmer	Chicago	Right wing	1982-83	80	43	47	90
14.	Marian Stastny	Quebec	Right wing	1981-82	74	35	54	89
15.	Steve Yzerman	Detroit	Center	1983-84	80	39	48	87
16.	* Sergei Makarov	Calgary	Right wing	1989-90	80	24	62	86
17.	Anton Stastny	Quebec	Left wing	1980-81	80	39	46	85
18.	* Evgeni Malkin	Pittsburgh	Center	**2006-07**	78	33	52	85
19.	* Luc Robitaille	Los Angeles	Left wing	1986-87	79	45	39	84
20.	Mikael Renberg	Philadelphia	Left wing	1993-94	83	38	44	82
21.	Jimmy Carson	Los Angeles	Center	1986-87	80	37	42	79
	Sergei Fedorov	Detroit	Center	1990-91	77	31	48	79
	Alexei Yashin	Ottawa	Center	1993-94	83	30	49	79
24.	Paul Stastny	Colorado	Center	**2006-07**	82	28	50	78
25.	Marcel Dionne	Detroit	Center	1971-72	78	28	49	77
26.	Larry Murphy	Los Angeles	Defense	1980-81	80	16	60	76
	Mark Pavelich	NY Rangers	Center	1981-82	79	33	43	76
	Dave Poulin	Philadelphia	Center	1983-84	73	31	45	76
29.	Brian Propp	Philadelphia	Left wing	1979-80	80	34	41	75
	Jari Kurri	Edmonton	Left wing	1980-81	75	32	43	75
	Denis Savard	Chicago	Center	1980-81	76	28	47	75
	Mike Modano	Minnesota	Center	1989-90	80	29	46	75
	Eric Lindros	Philadelphia	Center	1992-93	61	41	34	75
34.	Rick Martin	Buffalo	Left wing	1971-72	73	44	30	74
	* Bobby Smith	Minnesota	Center	1978-79	80	30	44	74
36.	Jorgen Pettersson	St. Louis	Left wing	1980-81	62	37	36	73
37.	* Gilbert Perreault	Buffalo	Center	1970-71	78	38	34	72
	Dale McCourt	Detroit	Center	1977-78	76	33	39	72
	Ron Flockhart	Philadelphia	Center	1981-82	72	33	39	72
	Sylvain Turgeon	Hartford	Left wing	1983-84	76	40	32	72
	Carey Wilson	Calgary	Center	1984-85	74	24	48	72
	Warren Young	Pittsburgh	Left wing	1984-85	80	40	32	72
	Alex Zhamnov	Winnipeg	Center	1992-93	68	25	47	72
44.	Mike Foligno	Detroit	Right wing	1979-80	80	36	35	71
	Dave Christian	Winnipeg	Center	1980-81	80	28	43	71
	Mats Naslund	Montreal	Left wing	1982-83	74	26	45	71
	Kjell Dahlin	Montreal	Right wing	1985-86	77	32	39	71
	* Brian Leetch	NY Rangers	Defense	1988-89	68	23	48	71
49.	Bill Mosienko	Chicago	Right wing	1943-44	50	32	38	70
	* Scott Gomez	New Jersey	Center	99-2000	82	19	51	70

* Calder Trophy Winner

Rick Martin

Jean Pronovost

Wayne Gretzky

50-Goal Seasons

Player	Team	Date of 50th Goal	Score	Goaltender	Player's Game No.	Team Game No.	Total Goals	Total Games	Age When First 50th Scored (Yrs. & Mos.)
Maurice Richard	Mtl.	Mar. 18/45	Mtl. 4 at Bos. 2	Harvey Bennett	50	50	50	50	23.7
Bernie Geoffrion	Mtl.	Mar. 16/61	Tor. 2 at Mtl. 5	Cesare Maniago	62	68	50	64	30.1
Bobby Hull	Chi.	Mar. 25/62	Chi. 1 at NYR 4	Gump Worsley	70	70	50	70	23.2
Bobby Hull	Chi.	Mar. 2/66	Det. 4 at Chi. 5	Hank Bassen	52	57	54	65	
Bobby Hull	Chi.	Mar. 18/67	Chi. 5 at Tor. 9	Bruce Gamble	63	66	52	66	
Bobby Hull	Chi.	Mar. 5/69	NYR 4 at Chi. 4	Ed Giacomin	64	66	58	74	
Phil Esposito	Bos.	Feb. 20/71	Bos. 4 at L.A. 5	Denis DeJordy	58	58	76	78	29.0
John Bucyk	Bos.	Mar. 16/71	Bos. 11 at Det. 4	Roy Edwards	69	69	51	78	35.10
Phil Esposito	Bos.	Feb. 20/72	Bos. 3 at Chi. 1	Tony Esposito	60	60	66	76	
Bobby Hull	Chi.	Feb. 4/72	Det. 1 at Chi. 6	Andy Brown	78	78	50	78	
Vic Hadfield	NYR	Feb. 4/72	Mtl. 6 at NYR 5	Denis DeJordy	78	78	50	78	31.6
Phil Esposito	Bos.	Mar. 25/73	Buf. 1 at Bos. 6	Roger Crozier	75	75	55	78	
Mickey Redmond	Det.	Mar. 27/73	Det. 8 at Tor. 1	Ron Low	73	75	52	76	25.3
Rick MacLeish	Phi.	Apr. 1/73	Phi. 4 at Pit. 5	Cam Newton	78	78	50	78	23.2
Phil Esposito	Bos.	Feb. 20/74	Bos. 5 at Min. 5	Cesare Maniago	56	56	68	78	
Mickey Redmond	Det.	Mar. 23/74	NYR 3 at Det. 5	Ed Giacomin	69	71	51	76	
Ken Hodge	Bos.	Apr. 6/74	Bos. 2 at Mtl. 6	Michel Larocque	75	77	50	76	29.10
Rick Martin	Buf.	Apr. 7/74	St.L. 2 at Buf. 5	Wayne Stephenson	78	78	52	78	22.9
Phil Esposito	Bos.	Feb. 8/75	Bos. 8 at Det. 5	Jim Rutherford	54	54	61	79	
Guy Lafleur	Mtl.	Mar. 29/75	K.C. 1 at Mtl. 4	Denis Herron	66	76	53	70	23.6
Danny Grant	Det.	Apr. 2/75	Wsh. 3 at Det. 8	John Adams	78	78	50	80	29.2
Rick Martin	Buf.	Apr. 3/75	Bos. 2 at Buf. 4	Ken Broderick	67	79	52	68	
Reggie Leach	Phi.	Mar. 14/76	Atl. 1 at Phi. 6	Dan Bouchard	69	69	61	80	25.11
Jean Pronovost	Pit.	Mar. 24/76	Bos. 5 at Pit. 5	Gilles Gilbert	74	74	52	80	30.3
Guy Lafleur	Mtl.	Mar. 27/76	K.C. 2 at Mtl. 8	Denis Herron	76	76	56	80	
Bill Barber	Phi.	Apr. 3/76	Buf. 2 at Phi. 5	Al Smith	79	79	50	80	23.9
Pierre Larouche	Pit.	Apr. 3/76	Wsh. 5 at Pit. 4	Ron Low	75	79	53	76	20.5
Danny Gare	Buf.	Apr. 4/76	Tor. 2 at Buf. 5	Gord McRae	79	80	50	79	21.11
Steve Shutt	Mtl.	Mar. 1/77	Mtl. 5 at NYI 4	Glenn Resch	65	65	60	80	24.8
Guy Lafleur	Mtl.	Mar. 6/77	Mtl. 1 at Buf. 4	Don Edwards	68	68	56	80	
Marcel Dionne	L.A.	Apr. 2/77	Min. 2 at L.A. 7	Pete LoPresti	79	79	53	80	25.8
Guy Lafleur	Mtl.	Mar. 8/78	Wsh. 3 at Mtl. 4	Jim Bedard	63	65	60	78	
Mike Bossy	NYI	Apr. 1/78	Wsh. 2 at NYI 3	Bernie Wolfe	69	76	53	73	21.2
Mike Bossy	NYI	Feb. 24/79	Det. 1 at NYI 3	Rogie Vachon	58	58	69	80	
Marcel Dionne	L.A.	Mar. 11/79	L.A. 3 at Phi. 6	Wayne Stephenson	68	68	59	80	
Guy Lafleur	Mtl.	Mar. 31/79	Pit. 3 at Mtl. 5	Denis Herron	76	76	52	80	
Guy Chouinard	Atl.	Apr. 6/79	NYR 2 at Atl. 9	John Davidson	79	79	50	80	22.5
Marcel Dionne	L.A.	Mar. 12/80	L.A. 2 at Pit. 4	Nick Ricci	70	70	53	80	
Mike Bossy	NYI	Mar. 16/80	NYI 6 at Chi. 1	Tony Esposito	68	71	51	75	
Charlie Simmer	L.A.	Mar. 19/80	Det. 3 at L.A. 4	Jim Rutherford	57	73	56	64	26.0
Pierre Larouche	Mtl.	Mar. 25/80	Chi. 4 at Mtl. 8	Tony Esposito	72	75	50	73	
Danny Gare	Buf.	Mar. 27/80	Det. 1 at Buf. 10	Jim Rutherford	71	75	56	76	
Blaine Stoughton	Hfd.	Mar. 28/80	Hfd. 4 at Van. 4	Glen Hanlon	75	75	56	80	27.0
Guy Lafleur	Mtl.	Apr. 2/80	Mtl. 7 at Det. 2	Rogie Vachon	72	78	50	74	
Wayne Gretzky	Edm.	Apr. 2/80	Min. 1 at Edm. 1	Gary Edwards	78	79	51	79	19.2
Reggie Leach	Phi.	Apr. 3/80	Wsh. 2 at Phi. 4	empty net	75	79	50	76	
Mike Bossy	NYI	Jan. 24/81	Que. 3 at NYI 7	Ron Grahame	50	50	68	79	
Charlie Simmer	L.A.	Jan. 26/81	L.A. 7 at Que. 5	Michel Dion	51	51	56	65	
Marcel Dionne	L.A.	Mar. 8/81	L.A. 4 at Wpg. 1	Markus Mattsson	68	68	58	80	
Wayne Babych	St.L.	Mar. 12/81	St.L. 3 at Mtl. 4	Richard Sevigny	70	68	54	78	22.9
Wayne Gretzky	Edm.	Mar. 15/81	Edm. 3 at Cgy. 3	Pat Riggin	69	69	55	80	
Rick Kehoe	Pit.	Mar. 16/81	Pit. 7 at Edm. 6	Eddie Mio	70	70	55	80	29.7
Jacques Richard	Que.	Mar. 29/81	Mtl. 0 at Que. 4	Richard Sevigny	76	75	52	78	28.6
Dennis Maruk	Wsh.	Apr. 5/81	Det. 2 at Wsh. 7	Larry Lozinski	80	80	50	80	25.3
Wayne Gretzky	Edm.	Dec. 30/81	Phi. 5 at Edm. 7	empty net	39	39	92	80	
Dennis Maruk	Wsh.	Feb. 21/82	Wpg. 3 at Wsh. 6	Doug Soetaert	61	61	60	80	
Mike Bossy	NYI	Mar. 4/82	Tor. 1 at NYI 10	Michel Larocque	66	66	64	80	
Dino Ciccarelli	Min.	Mar. 8/82	St.L. 1 at Min. 8	Mike Liut	67	68	55	76	22.1
Rick Vaive	Tor.	Mar. 24/82	St.L. 3 at Tor. 4	Mike Liut	72	75	54	77	22.10
Blaine Stoughton	Hfd.	Mar. 28/82	Min. 5 at Hfd. 2	Gilles Meloche	76	76	52	80	
Rick Middleton	Bos.	Mar. 28/82	Bos. 5 at Buf. 9	Paul Harrison	72	77	51	75	28.11
Marcel Dionne	L.A.	Mar. 30/82	Cgy. 7 at L.A. 5	Pat Riggin	75	77	50	78	
Mark Messier	Edm.	Mar. 31/82	L.A. 3 at Edm. 7	Mario Lessard	78	79	50	78	21.3
Bryan Trottier	NYI	Apr. 3/82	Phi. 3 at NYI 6	Pete Peeters	79	79	50	80	25.9
Lanny McDonald	Cgy.	Feb. 18/83	Cgy. 1 at Buf. 5	Bob Sauve	60	60	66	80	30.0
Wayne Gretzky	Edm.	Feb. 19/83	Edm. 10 at Pit. 7	Nick Ricci	60	60	71	80	
Michel Goulet	Que.	Mar. 5/83	Hfd. 3 at Que. 10	Mike Veisor	67	67	57	80	22.11
Mike Bossy	NYI	Mar. 12/83	Wsh. 2 at NYI 6	Al Jensen	70	71	60	79	
Marcel Dionne	L.A.	Mar. 17/83	Que. 3 at L.A. 4	Dan Bouchard	71	71	56	80	
Al Secord	Chi.	Mar. 20/83	Tor. 3 at Chi. 7	Mike Palmateer	73	73	54	80	25.0
Rick Vaive	Tor.	Mar. 30/83	Tor. 4 at Det. 2	Gilles Gilbert	76	78	51	78	
Wayne Gretzky	Edm.	Jan. 7/84	Hfd. 3 at Edm. 5	Greg Millen	42	42	87	74	
Michel Goulet	Que.	Mar. 8/84	Que. 8 at Pit. 6	Denis Herron	63	69	56	75	
Rick Vaive	Tor.	Mar. 14/84	Min. 3 at Tor. 3	Gilles Meloche	69	72	52	76	
Mike Bullard	Pit.	Mar. 14/84	Pit. 6 at L.A. 7	Markus Mattsson	71	72	51	76	23.0
Jari Kurri	Edm.	Mar. 15/84	Edm. 2 at Mtl. 3	Rick Wamsley	57	73	52	64	23.10
Glenn Anderson	Edm.	Mar. 21/84	Hfd. 3 at Edm. 5	Greg Millen	76	76	54	80	23.6
Tim Kerr	Phi.	Mar. 22/84	Pit. 4 at Phi. 13	Denis Herron	74	75	54	79	24.3

Player	Team	Date of 50th Goal	Score		Goaltender	Player's Game No.	Team Game No.	Total Goals	Total Games	Age When First 50th Scored (Yrs. & Mos.)
Mike Bossy	NYI	Mar. 31/84	NYI 3	at Wsh. 1	Pat Riggin	67	79	51	67	
Wayne Gretzky	Edm.	Jan. 26/85	Pit. 3	at Edm. 6	Denis Herron	49	49	73	80	
Jari Kurri	Edm.	Feb. 3/85	Hfd. 3	at Edm. 6	Greg Millen	50	53	71	73	
Mike Bossy	NYI	Mar. 5/85	Phi. 5	at NYI 4	Bob Froese	61	65	58	76	
Michel Goulet	Que.	Mar. 6/85	Buf. 3	at Que. 4	Tom Barrasso	62	73	55	69	
Tim Kerr	Phi.	Mar. 7/85	Wsh. 6	at Phi. 9	Pat Riggin	63	65	54	74	
John Ogrodnick	Det.	Mar. 13/85	Det. 6	at Edm. 7	Grant Fuhr	69	69	55	79	25.9
Bob Carpenter	Wsh.	Mar. 21/85	Wsh. 2	at Mtl. 3	Steve Penney	72	72	53	80	21.9
Dale Hawerchuk	Wpg.	Mar. 29/85	Chi. 5	at Wpg. 5	W. Skorodenski	77	77	53	80	21.11
Mike Gartner	Wsh.	Apr. 7/85	Pit. 3	at Wsh. 7	Brian Ford	80	80	50	80	25.5
Jari Kurri	Edm.	Mar. 4/86	Edm. 6	at Van. 2	Richard Brodeur	63	65	68	78	
Mike Bossy	NYI	Mar. 11/86	Cgy. 4	at NYI 8	Reggie Lemelin	67	67	61	80	
Glenn Anderson	Edm.	Mar. 14/86	Det. 3	at Edm. 12	Greg Stefan	63	71	54	72	
Michel Goulet	Que.	Mar. 17/86	Que. 8	at Mtl. 6	Patrick Roy	67	72	53	75	
Wayne Gretzky	Edm.	Mar. 18/86	Wpg. 2	at Edm. 6	Brian Hayward	72	72	52	80	
Tim Kerr	Phi.	Mar. 20/86	Pit. 1	at Phi. 5	Roberto Romano	68	72	58	76	
Wayne Gretzky	Edm.	Feb. 4/87	Edm. 6	at Min. 5	Don Beaupre	55	55	62	79	
Dino Ciccarelli	Min.	Mar. 7/87	Pit. 7	at Min. 3	Gilles Meloche	66	66	52	80	
Mario Lemieux	Pit.	Mar. 12/87	Que. 3	at Pit. 6	Mario Gosselin	53	70	54	63	21.5
Tim Kerr	Phi.	Mar. 17/87	NYR 1	at Phi. 4	J. Vanbiesbrouck	67	71	58	75	
Jari Kurri	Edm.	Mar. 17/87	N.J. 4	at Edm. 7	Craig Billington	69	70	54	79	
Mario Lemieux	Pit.	Feb. 2/88	Wsh. 2	at Pit. 3	Pete Peeters	51	54	70	77	
Steve Yzerman	Det.	Mar. 1/88	Buf. 0	at Det. 4	Tom Barrasso	64	64	50	64	22.10
Joe Nieuwendyk	Cgy.	Mar. 12/88	Buf. 4	at Cgy. 10	Tom Barrasso	66	70	51	75	21.5
Craig Simpson	Edm.	Mar. 15/88	Buf. 4	at Edm. 6	Jacques Cloutier	71	71	56	80	21.1
Jimmy Carson	L.A.	Mar. 26/88	Chi. 5	at L.A. 9	Darren Pang	77	77	55	88	19.8
Luc Robitaille	L.A.	Apr. 1/88	L.A. 6	at Cgy. 3	Mike Vernon	79	79	53	80	21.10
Hakan Loob	Cgy.	Apr. 3/88	Min. 1	at Cgy. 4	Don Beaupre	80	80	50	80	27.9
Stephane Richer	Mtl.	Apr. 3/88	Mtl. 4	at Buf. 4	Tom Barrasso	72	80	50	72	21.10
Mario Lemieux	Pit.	Jan. 20/89	Pit. 3	at Wpg. 7	Pokey Reddick	44	46	85	76	
Bernie Nicholls	L.A.	Jan. 28/89	Edm. 7	at L.A. 6	Grant Fuhr	51	51	70	79	27.7
Steve Yzerman	Det.	Feb. 5/89	Det. 6	at Wpg. 2	Pokey Reddick	55	55	65	80	
Wayne Gretzky	L.A.	Mar. 4/89	Phi. 2	at L.A. 6	Ron Hextall	66	67	54	78	
Joe Nieuwendyk	Cgy.	Mar. 21/89	NYI 1	at Cgy. 4	Mark Fitzpatrick	72	74	51	77	
Joe Mullen	Cgy.	Mar. 31/89	Wpg. 1	at Cgy. 4	Bob Essensa	78	79	51	79	32.1
Brett Hull	St.L.	Feb. 6/90	Tor. 4	at St.L. 6	Jeff Reese	54	54	72	80	25.6
Steve Yzerman	Det.	Feb. 24/90	Det. 3	at NYI 3	Glenn Healy	63	63	62	79	
Cam Neely	Bos.	Mar. 10/90	Bos. 3	at NYI 3	Mark Fitzpatrick	69	71	55	76	24.9
Brian Bellows	Min.	Mar. 22/90	Min. 5	at Det. 1	Tim Cheveldae	75	75	55	80	25.6
Pat LaFontaine	NYI	Mar. 24/90	NYI 5	at Edm. 5	Bill Ranford	71	77	54	74	25.1
Stephane Richer	Mtl.	Mar. 24/90	Mtl. 4	at Hfd. 7	Peter Sidorkiewicz	75	77	51	75	
Gary Leeman	Tor.	Mar. 28/90	NYI 6	at Tor. 3	Mark Fitzpatrick	78	78	51	80	26.1
Luc Robitaille	L.A.	Mar. 31/90	L.A. 3	at Van. 6	Kirk McLean	79	79	52	80	
Brett Hull	St.L.	Jan. 25/91	St.L. 9	at Det. 4	David Gagnon	49	49	86	78	
Cam Neely	Bos.	Mar. 26/91	Bos. 7	at Que. 4	empty net	67	78	51	69	
Theoren Fleury	Cgy.	Mar. 26/91	Van. 2	at Cgy. 7	Bob Mason	77	77	51	79	22.9
Steve Yzerman	Det.	Mar. 30/91	NYR 5	at Det. 6	Mike Richter	79	79	51	80	
Brett Hull	St.L.	Jan. 28/92	St.L. 3	at L.A. 3	Kelly Hrudey	50	50	70	73	
Jeremy Roenick	Chi.	Mar. 7/92	Chi. 2	at Bos. 1	Daniel Berthiaume	67	67	53	80	22.2
Kevin Stevens	Pit.	Mar. 24/92	Pit. 3	at Det. 4	Tim Cheveldae	74	74	54	80	26.11
Gary Roberts	Cgy.	Mar. 31/92	Edm. 2	at Cgy. 5	Bill Ranford	73	77	53	76	25.10
Alexander Mogilny	Buf.	Feb. 3/93	Hfd. 2	at Buf. 3	Sean Burke	46	53	76	77	23.11
Teemu Selanne	Wpg.	Feb. 28/93	Min. 6	at Wpg. 7	Darcy Wakaluk	63	63	76	84	22.6
Pavel Bure	Van.	Mar. 1/93	Van. 5	at Buf. 2*	Grant Fuhr	63	63	60	83	21.11
Steve Yzerman	Det.	Mar. 10/93	Det. 6	at Edm. 3	Bill Ranford	70	70	58	84	
Luc Robitaille	L.A.	Mar. 15/93	L.A. 4	at Buf. 2	Grant Fuhr	69	69	63	84	
Brett Hull	St.L.	Mar. 20/93	St.L. 2	at L.A. 3	Robb Stauber	73	73	54	80	
Mario Lemieux	Pit.	Mar. 21/93	Pit. 6	at Edm. 4**	Ron Tugnutt	48	72	69	60	
Kevin Stevens	Pit.	Mar. 21/93	Pit. 6	at Edm. 4**	Ron Tugnutt	62	72	55	72	
Dave Andreychuk	Tor.	Mar. 23/93	Tor. 5	at Wpg. 4	Bob Essensa	72	73	54	83	29.6
Pat LaFontaine	Buf.	Mar. 28/93	Ott. 1	at Buf. 3	Peter Sidorkiewicz	75	75	53	84	
Pierre Turgeon	NYI	Apr. 2/93	NYI 3	at NYR 2	Mike Richter	75	76	58	83	23.8
Mark Recchi	Phi.	Apr. 3/93	T.B. 2	at Phi. 6	J-C Bergeron	77	77	53	84	25.2
Brendan Shanahan	St.L.	Apr. 15/93	T.B. 5	at St.L. 6	Pat Jablonski	71	84	51	71	24.3
Jeremy Roenick	Chi.	Apr. 15/93	Tor. 2	at Chi. 3	Felix Potvin	84	84	50	84	
Cam Neely	Bos.	Mar. 7/94	Wsh. 3	at Bos. 6	Don Beaupre	44	66	50	49	
Sergei Fedorov	Det.	Mar. 15/94	Van. 2	at Det. 5	Kirk McLean	67	69	56	82	24.3
Pavel Bure	Van.	Mar. 23/94	Van. 6	at L.A. 3	empty net	65	73	60	76	
Adam Graves	NYR	Mar. 23/94	NYR 5	at Edm. 3	Bill Ranford	74	74	51	84	25.11
Dave Andreychuk	Tor.	Mar. 24/94	S.J. 2	at Tor. 1	Arturs Irbe	73	74	53	83	
Brett Hull	St.L.	Mar. 25/94	Dal. 3	at St.L. 5	Andy Moog	71	74	52	81	
Ray Sheppard	Det.	Mar. 29/94	Hfd. 2	at Det. 6	Sean Burke	74	76	52	82	27.10
Brendan Shanahan	St.L.	Apr. 12/94	St.L. 5	at Dal. 9	Andy Moog	80	83	52	81	
Mike Modano	Dal.	Apr. 12/94	St.L. 5	at Dal. 9	Curtis Joseph	75	83	50	76	23.11
Mario Lemieux	Pit.	Feb. 23/96	Hfd. 4	at Pit. 5	Sean Burke	50	59	69	70	
Jaromir Jagr	Pit.	Feb. 23/96	Hfd. 4	at Pit. 5	Sean Burke	59	59	62	82	24.0
Alexander Mogilny	Van.	Feb. 29/96	St.L. 2	at Van. 2	Grant Fuhr	60	63	55	79	
Peter Bondra	Wsh.	Apr. 3/96	Wsh. 5	at Buf. 1	Andrei Trefilov	62	77	52	67	28.1
Joe Sakic	Col.	Apr. 7/96	Col. 4	at Dal. 1	empty net	79	79	51	82	26.7
John LeClair	Phi.	Apr. 10/96	Phi. 5	at N.J. 1	Corey Schwab	80	80	51	82	26.7
Keith Tkachuk	Wpg.	Apr. 12/96	L.A. 3	at Wpg. 5	empty net	75	81	50	76	24.0
Paul Kariya	Ana.	Apr. 14/96	Wpg. 2	at Ana. 5	N. Khabibulin	82	82	50	82	21.5
Keith Tkachuk	Phx.	Apr. 6/97	Phx. 1	at Col. 2	Patrick Roy	78	79	52	81	
Teemu Selanne	Ana.	Apr. 9/97	L.A. 1	at Ana. 4	empty net	77	81	51	78	
Mario Lemieux	Pit.	Apr. 11/97	Pit. 2	at Fla. 4	J. Vanbiesbrouck	75	81	50	76	

Bobby Carpenter

Brett Hull

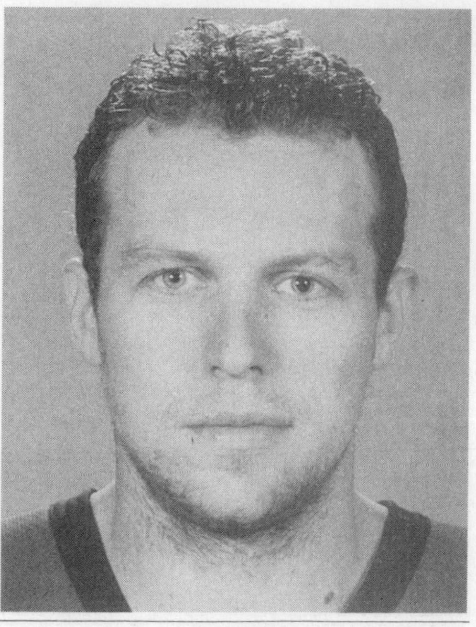

Dany Heatley

Vincent Lecavalier

Player	Team	Date of 50th Goal	Score		Goaltender	Player's Game No.	Team Game No.	Total Goals	Total Games	Age When First 50th Scored (Yrs. & Mos.)
John LeClair	Phi.	Apr. 13/97	N.J. 4	at Phi. 5	Mike Dunham	82	82	50	82	
Teemu Selanne	Ana.	Mar. 25/98	Ana. 3	at Chi. 2	Jeff Hackett	66	71	52	73	
John LeClair	Phi.	Apr. 13/98	Phi. 1	at Buf. 2	Dominik Hasek	79	79	51	82	
Pavel Bure	Van.	Apr. 17/98	Cgy. 4	at Van. 2	Dwayne Roloson	81	81	51	82	
Peter Bondra	Wsh.	Apr. 18/98	Wsh. 4	at Car. 3	Mike Fountain	75	80	52	76	
Pavel Bure	Fla.	Mar. 18/00	Fla. 4	at NYI 2	empty net	63	71	58	74	
Pavel Bure	Fla.	Mar. 16/01	Pit. 6	at Fla. 3	Johan Hedberg	72	72	59	82	
Joe Sakic	Col.	Apr. 4/01	Ana. 1	at Col. 1	J-S Giguere	80	80	54	82	
Jaromir Jagr	Pit.	Apr. 4/01	T.B. 2	at Pit. 4	Kevin Weekes	80	80	52	81	
Jarome Iginla	Cgy.	Apr. 7/02	Cgy. 2	at Chi. 3	Jocelyn Thibault	79	79	52	82	24.9
Milan Hejduk	Col.	Apr. 6/03	St. L. 2	at Col. 5	Brent Johnson	82	82	50	82	27.1
Jaromir Jagr	NYR	Mar. 24/06	NYR 2	at Fla. 3	Roberto Luongo	70	70	54	82	
Ilya Kovalchuk	Atl.	Apr. 6/06	Atl. 2	at T.B. 3	Sean Burke	72	76	52	78	22.11
Jonathan Cheechoo	S.J.	Apr. 10/06	S.J. 3	at Phx. 2	David LeNeveu	78	78	56	82	25.8
Alex Ovechkin	Wsh.	Apr. 13/06	Wsh. 3	at Atl. 5	Mike Dunham	78	79	52	81	20.6
Dany Heatley	Ott.	Apr. 18/06	Ott. 5	at NYR 1	Henrik Lundqvist	82	82	50	82	25.2
Vincent Lecavalier	T.B.	Mar. 30/07	T.B. 4	at Car. 2	Cam Ward	78	78	52	82	26.11
Dany Heatley	Ott.	Apr. 7/07	Ott. 6	at Bos. 3	Tim Thomas	82	82	50	82	

* neutral site game played at Hamilton; ** neutral site game played at Cleveland

100-Point Seasons

Jean Ratelle

Player	Team	Date of 100th Point	G or A	Score		Player's Game No.	Team Game No.	G - A PTS	Total Games	Age when first 100th point scored (Yrs. & Mos.)
Phil Esposito	Bos.	Mar. 2/69	(G)	Pit. 0	at Bos. 4	60	62	49-77 — 126	74	27.1
Bobby Hull	Chi.	Mar. 20/69	(G)	Chi. 5	at Bos. 5	71	71	58-49 — 107	76	30.2
Gordie Howe	Det.	Mar. 30/69	(G)	Det. 5	at Chi. 9	76	76	44-59 — 103	76	41.0
Bobby Orr	Bos.	Mar. 15/70	(G)	Det. 5	at Bos. 5	67	67	33-87 — 120	76	22.11
Phil Esposito	Bos.	Feb. 6/71	(A)	Buf. 3	at Bos. 4	51	51	76-76 — 152	78	
Bobby Orr	Bos.	Feb. 20/71	(A)	Bos. 4	at L.A. 5	58	58	37-102 — 139	78	
John Bucyk	Bos.	Mar. 13/71	(G)	Bos. 6	at Van. 3	68	68	51-65 — 116	78	35.10
Ken Hodge	Bos.	Mar. 21/71	(A)	Buf. 7	at Bos. 5	72	72	43-62 — 105	78	26.9
Jean Ratelle	NYR	Feb. 18/72	(A)	NYR 2	at Cal. 2	58	58	46-63 — 109	63	31.4
Phil Esposito	Bos.	Feb. 19/72	(A)	Bos. 6	at Min. 4	59	59	66-67 — 133	76	
Bobby Orr	Bos.	Mar. 2/72	(A)	Van. 3	at Bos. 7	64	64	37-80 — 117	76	
Vic Hadfield	NYR	Mar. 25/72	(A)	NYR 3	at Mtl. 3	74	74	50-56 — 106	78	31.5
Phil Esposito	Bos.	Mar. 3/73	(A)	Bos. 1	at Mtl. 5	64	64	55-75 — 130	78	
Bobby Clarke	Phi.	Mar. 29/73	(G)	Atl. 2	at Phi. 4	76	76	37-67 — 104	78	23.7
Bobby Orr	Bos.	Mar. 31/73	(G)	Bos. 3	at Tor. 7	62	77	29-72 — 101	63	
Rick MacLeish	Phi.	Apr. 1/73	(G)	Phi. 4	at Pit. 5	78	78	50-50 — 100	78	23.3
Phil Esposito	Bos.	Feb. 13/74	(A)	Bos. 9	at Cal. 6	53	53	68-77 — 145	78	
Bobby Orr	Bos.	Mar. 12/74	(A)	Buf. 0	at Bos. 4	62	66	32-90 — 122	74	
Ken Hodge	Bos.	Mar. 24/74	(A)	Mtl. 3	at Bos. 6	72	72	50-55 — 105	76	
Phil Esposito	Bos.	Feb. 8/75	(A)	Bos. 8	at Det. 5	54	54	61-66 — 127	79	
Bobby Orr	Bos.	Feb. 13/75	(A)	Bos. 1	at Buf. 3	57	57	46-89 — 135	80	
Guy Lafleur	Mtl.	Mar. 7/75	(G)	Wsh. 4	at Mtl. 8	56	66	53-66 — 119	70	24.6
Marcel Dionne	Det.	Mar. 9/75	(A)	Det. 5	at Phi. 8	67	67	47-74 — 121	80	23.7
Pete Mahovlich	Mtl.	Mar. 9/75	(G)	Mtl. 5	at NYR 3	67	67	35-82 — 117	80	29.5
Bobby Clarke	Phi.	Mar. 22/75	(A)	Min. 0	at Phi. 4	72	72	27-89 — 116	80	
Rene Robert	Buf.	Apr. 5/75	(A)	Buf. 4	at Tor. 2	74	80	40-60 — 100	74	26.4
Guy Lafleur	Mtl.	Mar. 10/76	(G)	Mtl. 5	at Chi. 1	69	69	56-69 — 125	80	
Bobby Clarke	Phi.	Mar. 11/76	(A)	Buf. 1	at Phi. 6	64	68	30-89 — 119	76	
Bill Barber	Phi.	Mar. 18/76	(A)	Van. 2	at Phi. 3	71	71	50-62 — 112	80	23.8
Gilbert Perreault	Buf.	Mar. 21/76	(A)	K.C. 1	at Buf. 3	73	73	44-69 — 113	80	25.4
Pierre Larouche	Pit.	Mar. 24/76	(G)	Bos. 5	at Pit. 5	70	74	53-58 — 111	76	20.4
Pete Mahovlich	Mtl.	Mar. 28/76	(A)	Mtl. 2	at Bos. 2	77	77	34-71 — 105	80	
Jean Ratelle	Bos.	Mar. 30/76	(G)	Buf. 4	at Bos. 4	77	77	36-69 — 105	80	
Jean Pronovost	Pit.	Apr. 3/76	(A)	Wsh. 5	at Pit. 4	79	79	52-52 — 104	80	30.4
Darryl Sittler	Tor.	Apr. 3/76	(A)	Bos. 4	at Tor. 2	78	79	41-59 — 100	79	25.7
Guy Lafleur	Mtl.	Feb. 26/77	(A)	Cle. 3	at Mtl. 5	63	63	56-80 — 136	80	
Marcel Dionne	L.A.	Mar. 5/77	(G)	Pit. 3	at L.A. 3	67	67	53-69 — 122	80	
Steve Shutt	Mtl.	Mar. 27/77	(A)	Mtl. 6	at Det. 0	77	77	60-45 — 105	80	24.9
Bryan Trottier	NYI	Feb. 25/78	(A)	Chi. 1	at NYI 7	59	60	46-77 — 123	77	21.7
Guy Lafleur	Mtl.	Feb. 28/78	(G)	Det. 3	at Mtl. 9	69	61	60-72 — 132	78	
Darryl Sittler	Tor.	Mar. 12/78	(A)	Tor. 7	at Pit. 1	67	67	45-72 — 117	80	
Guy Lafleur	Mtl.	Feb. 27/79	(A)	Mtl. 3	at NYI 7	61	61	52-77 — 129	80	
Bryan Trottier	NYI	Mar. 6/79	(A)	Buf. 3	at NYI 2	59	63	47-87 — 134	76	
Marcel Dionne	L.A.	Mar. 8/79	(G)	L.A. 4	at Buf. 6	66	66	59-71 — 130	80	
Mike Bossy	NYI	Mar. 11/79	(G)	NYI 4	at Bos. 4	66	66	69-57 — 126	80	22.2
Bob MacMillan	Atl.	Mar. 15/79	(A)	Atl. 4	at Phi. 5	68	69	37-71 — 108	79	26.6
Guy Chouinard	Atl.	Mar. 30/79	(G)	L.A. 3	at Atl. 5	75	75	50-57 — 107	80	22.5
Denis Potvin	NYI	Apr. 8/79	(A)	NYI 5	at NYR 2	73	80	31-70 — 101	73	25.5

Steve Shutt

Player	Team	Date of 100th Point	G or A	Score		Player's Game No.	Team Game No.	G - A PTS	Total Games	Age when first 100th point scored (Yrs. & Mos.)
Marcel Dionne	L.A.	Feb. 6/80	(A)	L.A. 3	at Hfd. 7	53	53	53-84 — 137	80	
Guy Lafleur	Mtl.	Feb. 10/80	(A)	Mtl. 3	at Bos. 2	55	55	50-75 — 125	74	
Wayne Gretzky	Edm.	Feb. 24/80	(A)	Bos. 4	at Edm. 2	61	62	51-86 — 137	79	19.2
Bryan Trottier	NYI	Mar. 30/80	(A)	NYI 9	at Que. 6	75	77	42-62 — 104	78	
Gilbert Perreault	Buf.	Apr. 1/80	(A)	Buf. 5	at Atl. 2	77	77	40-66 — 106	80	
Mike Rogers	Hfd.	Apr. 4/80	(A)	Que. 2	at Hfd. 9	79	79	44-61 — 105	80	25.5
Charlie Simmer	L.A.	Apr. 5/80	(G)	Van. 5	at L.A. 3	64	80	56-45 — 101	64	26.0
Blaine Stoughton	Hfd.	Apr. 6/80	(A)	Det. 3	at Hfd. 5	80	80	56-44 — 100	80	27.0
Wayne Gretzky	Edm.	Feb. 6/81	(G)	Wpg. 4	at Edm. 10	53	53	55-109 — 164	80	
Marcel Dionne	L.A.	Feb. 12/81	(A)	L.A. 5	at Chi. 5	58	58	58-77 — 135	80	
Charlie Simmer	L.A.	Feb. 14/81	(A)	Bos. 5	at L.A. 4	59	59	56-49 — 105	65	
Kent Nilsson	Cgy.	Feb. 27/81	(G)	Hfd. 1	at Cgy. 5	64	64	49-82 — 131	80	24.6
Mike Bossy	NYI	Mar. 3/81	(G)	Edm. 8	at NYI 8	65	66	68-51 — 119	79	
Dave Taylor	L.A.	Mar. 14/81	(G)	Min. 4	at L.A. 10	63	70	47-65 — 112	72	25.3
Mike Rogers	Hfd.	Mar. 22/81	(G)	Tor. 3	at Hfd. 3	74	74	40-65 — 105	80	
Bernie Federko	St.L.	Mar. 28/81	(A)	Buf. 4	at St.L. 7	74	76	31-73 — 104	78	24.10
Rick Middleton	Bos.	Mar. 28/81	(A)	Chi. 2	at Bos. 5	76	76	44-59 — 103	80	27.4
Bryan Trottier	NYI	Mar. 29/81	(G)	NYI 5	at Wsh. 4	69	76	31-72 — 103	73	
Jacques Richard	Que.	Mar. 29/81	(G)	Mtl. 0	at Que. 4	75	76	52-51 — 103	78	28.6
Peter Stastny	Que.	Mar. 29/81	(A)	Mtl. 0	at Que. 4	73	76	39-70 — 109	77	24.6
Wayne Gretzky	Edm.	Dec. 27/81	(G)	L.A. 3	at Edm. 10	38	38	92-120 — 212	80	
Mike Bossy	NYI	Feb. 13/82	(A)	Phi. 2	at NYI 8	55	55	64-83 — 147	80	
Peter Stastny	Que.	Feb. 16/82	(A)	Wpg. 3	at Que. 7	60	60	46-93 — 139	80	
Dennis Maruk	Wsh.	Feb. 20/82	(G)	Wsh. 3	at Min. 7	60	60	60-76 — 136	80	26.3
Bryan Trottier	NYI	Feb. 23/82	(G)	Chi. 1	at NYI 5	61	61	50-79 — 129	80	
Denis Savard	Chi.	Feb. 27/82	(A)	Chi. 5	at L.A. 3	64	64	32-87 — 119	80	21.1
Bobby Smith	Min.	Mar. 3/82	(A)	Det. 4	at Min. 6	66	66	43-71 — 114	80	24.1
Marcel Dionne	L.A.	Mar. 6/82	(G)	L.A. 6	at Hfd. 7	64	66	50-67 — 117	78	
Dave Taylor	L.A.	Mar. 20/82	(A)	Pit. 5	at L.A. 7	71	72	39-67 — 106	78	
Dale Hawerchuk	Wpg.	Mar. 24/82	(G)	L.A. 3	at Wpg. 5	74	74	45-58 — 103	80	18.11
Dino Ciccarelli	Min.	Mar. 27/82	(A)	Min. 6	at Bos. 5	72	76	55-52 — 107	76	21.8
Glenn Anderson	Edm.	Mar. 28/82	(G)	Edm. 6	at L.A. 2	78	78	38-67 — 105	80	21.7
Mike Rogers	NYR	Apr. 2/82	(G)	Pit. 7	at NYR 5	79	79	38-65 — 103	80	
Wayne Gretzky	Edm.	Jan. 5/83	(A)	Edm. 8	at Wpg. 3	42	42	71-125 — 196	80	
Mike Bossy	NYI	Mar. 3/83	(A)	Tor. 1	at NYI 5	66	67	60-58 — 118	79	
Peter Stastny	Que.	Mar. 5/83	(A)	Hfd. 3	at Que. 10	62	67	47-77 — 124	75	
Denis Savard	Chi.	Mar. 6/83	(G)	Mtl. 4	at Chi. 5	65	67	35-86 — 121	78	
Mark Messier	Edm.	Mar. 23/83	(G)	Edm. 4	at Wpg. 7	73	76	48-58 — 106	77	22.2
Barry Pederson	Bos.	Mar. 26/83	(A)	Hfd. 4	at Bos. 7	73	76	46-61 — 107	77	22.0
Marcel Dionne	L.A.	Mar. 26/83	(A)	Edm. 9	at L.A. 3	75	75	56-51 — 107	80	
Michel Goulet	Que.	Mar. 27/83	(A)	Que. 6	at Buf. 6	77	77	57-48 — 105	80	22.11
Glenn Anderson	Edm.	Mar. 29/83	(A)	Edm. 7	at Van. 4	70	78	48-56 — 104	72	
Jari Kurri	Edm.	Mar. 29/83	(A)	Edm. 7	at Van. 4	78	78	45-59 — 104	80	22.10
Kent Nilsson	Cgy.	Mar. 29/83	(G)	L.A. 3	at Cgy. 5	78	78	46-58 — 104	80	
Wayne Gretzky	Edm.	Dec. 18/83	(G)	Edm. 7	at Wpg. 5	34	34	87-118 — 205	74	
Paul Coffey	Edm.	Mar. 4/84	(A)	Mtl. 1	at Edm. 6	68	68	40-86 — 126	80	22.9
Michel Goulet	Que.	Mar. 4/84	(A)	Que. 1	at Buf. 1	62	67	56-65 — 121	75	
Jari Kurri	Edm.	Mar. 7/84	(G)	Chi. 4	at Edm. 7	53	69	52-61 — 113	64	
Peter Stastny	Que.	Mar. 8/84	(A)	Que. 8	at Pit. 6	69	69	46-73 — 119	80	
Mike Bossy	NYI	Mar. 8/84	(G)	Tor. 5	at NYI 9	56	68	51-67 — 118	67	
Barry Pederson	Bos.	Mar. 14/84	(A)	Bos. 4	at Det. 2	71	71	39-77 — 116	80	
Bryan Trottier	NYI	Mar. 18/84	(G)	NYI 4	at Hfd. 5	62	73	40-71 — 111	68	
Bernie Federko	St.L.	Mar. 20/84	(A)	Wpg. 3	at St.L. 9	75	76	41-66 — 107	79	
Rick Middleton	Bos.	Mar. 27/84	(G)	Bos. 6	at Que. 4	77	77	47-58 — 105	80	
Dale Hawerchuk	Wpg.	Mar. 27/84	(G)	Wpg. 3	at L.A. 3	77	77	37-65 — 102	80	
Mark Messier	Edm.	Mar. 27/84	(G)	Edm. 9	at Cgy. 2	72	79	37-64 — 101	73	
Wayne Gretzky	Edm.	Dec. 29/84	(A)	Det. 3	at Edm. 6	35	35	73-135 — 208	80	
Jari Kurri	Edm.	Jan. 29/85	(G)	Edm. 4	at Cgy. 2	48	51	71-64 — 135	73	
Mike Bossy	NYI	Feb. 23/85	(G)	Bos. 1	at NYI 7	56	60	58-59 — 117	76	
Dale Hawerchuk	Wpg.	Feb. 25/85	(A)	Wpg. 12	at NYR 5	64	64	53-77 — 130	80	
Marcel Dionne	L.A.	Mar. 5/85	(A)	Pit. 0	at L.A. 6	66	66	46-80 — 126	80	
Brent Sutter	NYI	Mar. 12/85	(A)	NYI 6	at St.L. 5	68	68	42-60 — 102	72	22.10
John Ogrodnick	Det.	Mar. 22/85	(A)	NYR 3	at Det. 5	73	73	55-50 — 105	79	25.9
Paul Coffey	Edm.	Mar. 26/85	(G)	Edm. 7	at NYI 5	74	74	37-84 — 121	80	
Denis Savard	Chi.	Mar. 29/85	(A)	Chi. 5	at Wpg. 5	75	76	38-67 — 105	79	
Peter Stastny	Que.	Apr. 2/85	(A)	Bos. 4	at Que. 6	74	77	32-68 — 100	75	
Bernie Federko	St.L.	Apr. 4/85	(A)	NYR 5	at St.L. 4	74	78	30-73 — 103	76	
Paul MacLean	Wpg.	Apr. 6/85	(A)	Wpg. 6	at Edm. 5	78	79	41-60 — 101	79	27.1
Bernie Nicholls	L.A.	Apr. 6/85	(A)	Van. 4	at L.A. 4	80	80	46-54 — 100	80	22.9
John Tonelli	NYI	Apr. 6/85	(G)	N.J. 5	at NYI 5	80	80	42-58 — 100	80	28.1
Mike Gartner	Wsh.	Apr. 7/85	(G)	Pit. 3	at Wsh. 7	80	80	50-52 — 102	80	25.6
Mario Lemieux	Pit.	Apr. 7/85	(G)	Pit. 3	at Wsh. 7	73	80	43-57 — 100	73	19.6
Wayne Gretzky	Edm.	Jan. 4/86	(A)	Hfd. 3	at Edm. 4	39	39	52-163 — 215	80	
Mario Lemieux	Pit.	Feb. 15/86	(G)	Van. 4	at Pit. 9	55	56	48-93 — 141	79	
Paul Coffey	Edm.	Feb. 19/86	(A)	Tor. 5	at Edm. 9	59	60	48-90 — 138	79	
Peter Stastny	Que.	Mar. 1/86	(A)	Buf. 8	at Que. 4	66	68	41-81 — 122	76	
Jari Kurri	Edm.	Mar. 2/86	(G)	Phi. 1	at Edm. 2	62	64	68-63 — 131	78	
Mike Bossy	NYI	Mar. 8/86	(G)	Wsh. 6	at NYI 2	65	65	61-62 — 123	80	
Denis Savard	Chi.	Mar. 12/86	(A)	Buf. 7	at Chi. 6	69	69	47-69 — 116	80	
Mats Naslund	Mtl.	Mar. 13/86	(A)	Mtl. 2	at Bos. 3	70	70	43-67 — 110	80	26.4
Michel Goulet	Que.	Mar. 24/86	(A)	Que. 1	at Min. 0	70	75	53-50 — 103	75	
Glenn Anderson	Edm.	Mar. 25/86	(G)	Edm. 7	at Det. 2	66	74	54-48 — 102	72	
Neal Broten	Min.	Mar. 26/86	(A)	Min. 6	at Tor. 1	76	76	29-76 — 105	80	26.4
Dale Hawerchuk	Wpg.	Mar. 31/86	(A)	Wpg. 5	at L.A. 2	78	78	46-59 — 105	80	
Bernie Federko	St.L.	Apr. 5/86	(G)	Chi. 5	at St.L. 7	79	79	34-68 — 102	80	

Dale Hawerchuk

Glenn Anderson

Bernie Nicholls

Denis Savard

Jimmy Carson

Luc Robitaille

Player	Team	Date of 100th Point	G or A	Score		Player's Game No.	Team Game No.	G - A PTS	Total Games	Age when first 100th point scored (Yrs. & Mos.)
Wayne Gretzky	Edm.	Jan. 11/87	(A)	Cgy. 3	at Edm. 5	42	42	62-121 — 183	79	
Jari Kurri	Edm.	Mar. 14/87	(A)	Buf. 3	at Edm. 5	67	68	54-54 — 108	79	
Mario Lemieux	Pit.	Mar. 18/87	(A)	St.L. 4	at Pit. 5	55	72	54-53 — 107	63	
Mark Messier	Edm.	Mar. 19/87	(A)	Edm. 4	at Cgy. 5	71	71	37-70 — 107	77	
Dino Ciccarelli	Min.	Mar. 30/87	(A)	NYR 6	at Min. 5	78	78	52-51 — 103	80	
Doug Gilmour	St.L.	Apr. 2/87	(A)	Buf. 3	at St.L. 5	78	78	42-63 — 105	80	23.10
Dale Hawerchuk	Wpg.	Apr. 5/87	(A)	Wpg. 3	at Cgy. 1	80	80	47-53 — 100	80	
Mario Lemieux	Pit.	Jan. 20/88	(G)	Pit. 8	at Chi. 3	45	48	70-98 — 168	77	
Wayne Gretzky	Edm.	Feb. 11/88	(A)	Edm. 7	at Van. 2	43	56	40-109 — 149	64	
Denis Savard	Chi.	Feb. 12/88	(A)	St.L. 3	at Chi. 4	57	57	44-87 — 131	80	
Dale Hawerchuk	Wpg.	Feb. 23/88	(G)	Wpg. 4	at Pit. 3	61	61	44-77 — 121	80	
Steve Yzerman	Det.	Feb. 27/88	(A)	Det. 4	at Que. 5	63	63	50-52 — 102	64	22.10
Peter Stastny	Que.	Mar. 8/88	(A)	Hfd. 4	at Que. 6	63	67	46-65 — 111	76	
Mark Messier	Edm.	Mar. 15/88	(A)	Buf. 4	at Edm. 6	68	71	37-74 — 111	77	
Jimmy Carson	L.A.	Mar. 26/88	(A)	Chi. 5	at L.A. 9	77	77	55-52 — 107	80	19.8
Hakan Loob	Cgy.	Mar. 26/88	(A)	Van. 1	at Cgy. 6	76	76	50-56 — 106	80	27.9
Mike Bullard	Cgy.	Mar. 26/88	(A)	Van. 1	at Cgy. 6	76	76	48-55 — 103	79	27.1
Michel Goulet	Que.	Mar. 27/88	(A)	Pit. 6	at Que. 3	76	76	48-58 — 106	80	
Luc Robitaille	L.A.	Mar. 30/88	(G)	Cgy. 7	at L.A. 9	78	78	53-58 — 111	80	22.1
Mario Lemieux	Pit.	Dec. 31/88	(A)	N.J. 6	at Pit. 8	36	38	85-114 — 199	76	
Wayne Gretzky	L.A.	Jan. 21/89	(A)	L.A. 4	at Hfd. 5	47	48	54-114 — 168	78	
Bernie Nicholls	L.A.	Jan. 21/89	(A)	L.A. 4	at Hfd. 5	48	48	70-80 — 150	79	
Steve Yzerman	Det.	Jan. 27/89	(G)	Tor. 1	at Det. 8	50	50	65-90 — 155	80	
Rob Brown	Pit.	Mar. 16/89	(A)	Pit. 2	at N.J. 1	60	72	49-66 — 115	68	20.11
Paul Coffey	Pit.	Mar. 20/89	(A)	Pit. 2	at Min. 7	69	74	30-83 — 113	75	
Joe Mullen	Cgy.	Mar. 23/89	(A)	L.A. 2	at Cgy. 4	74	75	51-59 — 110	79	32.1
Jari Kurri	Edm.	Mar. 29/89	(A)	Edm. 5	at Van. 2	75	79	44-58 — 102	76	
Jimmy Carson	Edm.	Apr. 2/89	(A)	Edm. 2	at Cgy. 4	80	80	49-51 — 100	80	
Mario Lemieux	Pit.	Jan. 28/90	(G)	Pit. 2	at Buf. 7	50	50	45-78 — 123	59	
Wayne Gretzky	L.A.	Jan. 30/90	(A)	N.J. 2	at L.A. 5	51	51	40-102 — 142	73	
Steve Yzerman	Det.	Feb. 19/90	(A)	Mtl. 5	at Det. 5	61	61	62-65 — 127	79	
Mark Messier	Edm.	Feb. 20/90	(A)	Edm. 4	at Van. 2	62	62	45-84 — 129	79	
Brett Hull	St.L.	Mar. 3/90	(A)	NYI 4	at St.L. 5	67	67	72-41 — 113	80	25.7
Bernie Nicholls	NYR	Mar. 12/90	(A)	L.A. 6	at NYR 2	70	71	39-73 — 112	79	
Pierre Turgeon	Buf.	Mar. 25/90	(G)	N.J. 4	at Buf. 3	76	76	40-66 — 106	80	20.7
Paul Coffey	Pit.	Mar. 25/90	(A)	Pit. 2	at Hfd. 4	77	77	29-74 — 103	80	
Pat LaFontaine	NYI	Mar. 27/90	(G)	Cgy. 4	at NYI 2	72	78	54-51 — 105	74	25.1
Adam Oates	St.L.	Mar. 29/90	(G)	Pit. 4	at St.L. 5	79	79	23-79 — 102	80	27.7
Joe Sakic	Que.	Mar. 31/90	(G)	Hfd. 3	at Que. 2	79	79	39-63 — 102	80	20.8
Ron Francis	Hfd.	Mar. 31/90	(G)	Hfd. 3	at Que. 2	79	79	32-69 — 101	80	27.0
Luc Robitaille	L.A.	Apr. 1/90	(A)	L.A. 4	at Cgy. 8	80	80	52-49 — 101	80	
Wayne Gretzky	L.A.	Jan. 30/91	(A)	N.J. 4	at L.A. 2	50	51	41-122 — 163	78	
Brett Hull	St.L.	Feb. 23/91	(G)	Bos. 2	at St.L. 9	60	62	86-45 — 131	78	
Mark Recchi	Pit.	Mar. 5/91	(G)	Van. 1	at Pit. 4	66	67	40-73 — 113	78	23.1
Steve Yzerman	Det.	Mar. 10/91	(G)	Det. 4	at St.L. 1	72	72	51-57 — 108	80	
John Cullen	Hfd.	Mar. 16/91	(G)	N.J. 2	at Hfd. 6	71	71	39-71 — 110	78	26.7
Adam Oates	St.L.	Mar. 17/91	(A)	St.L. 4	at Chi. 6	54	73	25-90 — 115	61	
Joe Sakic	Que.	Mar. 19/91	(G)	Edm. 7	at Que. 6	74	74	48-61 — 109	80	
Steve Larmer	Chi.	Mar. 24/91	(A)	Min. 4	at Chi. 5	76	76	44-57 — 101	80	29.9
Theoren Fleury	Cgy.	Mar. 26/91	(G)	Van. 2	at Cgy. 7	77	77	51-53 — 104	79	22.9
Al MacInnis	Cgy.	Mar. 28/91	(A)	Edm. 4	at Cgy. 4	78	78	28-75 — 103	78	27.8
Brett Hull	St.L.	Mar. 2/92	(G)	St.L. 5	at Van. 3	66	66	70-39 — 109	73	
Wayne Gretzky	L.A.	Mar. 3/92	(A)	Phi. 1	at L.A. 4	60	66	31-90 — 121	74	
Kevin Stevens	Pit.	Mar. 7/92	(A)	Pit. 3	at L.A. 5	66	66	54-69 — 123	80	26.11
Mario Lemieux	Pit.	Mar. 10/92	(A)	Cgy. 2	at Pit. 5	53	67	44-87 — 131	64	
Luc Robitaille	L.A.	Mar. 17/92	(A)	Wpg. 4	at L.A. 5	73	73	44-63 — 107	80	
Mark Messier	NYR	Mar. 22/92	(G)	N.J. 3	at NYR 6	74	75	35-72 — 107	79	
Jeremy Roenick	Chi.	Mar. 29/92	(A)	Tor. 1	at Chi. 5	77	77	53-50 — 103	80	22.2
Steve Yzerman	Det.	Apr. 14/92	(G)	Det. 7	at Min. 4	79	80	45-58 — 103	79	
Brian Leetch	NYR	Apr. 16/92	(G)	Pit. 1	at NYR 7	80	80	22-80 — 102	80	24.1
Mario Lemieux	Pit.	Dec. 31/92	(G)	Tor. 3	at Pit. 3	38	39	69-91 — 160	60	
Pat LaFontaine	Buf.	Feb. 10/93	(A)	Buf. 6	at Wpg. 2	55	55	53-95 — 148	84	
Adam Oates	Bos.	Feb. 14/93	(A)	Bos. 3	at T.B. 3	58	58	45-97 — 142	84	
Steve Yzerman	Det.	Feb. 24/93	(A)	Det. 7	at Buf. 10	64	64	58-79 — 137	84	
Pierre Turgeon	NYI	Feb. 28/93	(G)	NYI 7	at Hfd. 6	62	63	58-74 — 132	83	
Doug Gilmour	Tor.	Mar. 3/93	(A)	Min. 1	at Tor. 3	64	64	32-95 — 127	83	
Alexander Mogilny	Buf.	Mar. 5/93	(A)	Hfd. 4	at Buf. 2	58	65	76-51 — 127	77	24.1
Mark Recchi	Phi.	Mar. 7/93	(G)	Phi. 3	at N.J. 7	66	66	53-70 — 123	84	
Teemu Selanne	Wpg.	Mar. 9/93	(G)	Wpg. 4	at T.B. 2	68	68	76-56 — 132	84	22.7
Luc Robitaille	L.A.	Mar. 15/93	(A)	L.A. 4	at Buf. 2	69	69	63-62 — 125	84	
Kevin Stevens	Pit.	Mar. 23/93	(A)	S.J. 2	at Pit. 7	63	73	55-56 — 111	72	
Mats Sundin	Que.	Mar. 27/93	(G)	Phi. 3	at Que. 8	71	75	47-67 — 114	80	22.1
Pavel Bure	Van.	Apr. 1/93	(G)	Van. 5	at T.B. 3	77	77	60-50 — 110	83	22.0
Jeremy Roenick	Chi.	Apr. 4/93	(G)	St.L. 4	at Chi. 5	79	79	50-57 — 107	84	
Craig Janney	St.L.	Apr. 4/93	(G)	St.L. 4	at Chi. 5	79	79	24-82 — 106	84	25.7
Rick Tocchet	Pit.	Apr. 7/93	(G)	Mtl. 3	at Pit. 4	77	81	48-61 — 109	80	28.11
Joe Sakic	Que.	Apr. 8/93	(A)	Que. 2	at Bos. 6	75	81	48-57 — 105	78	
Ron Francis	Pit.	Apr. 9/93	(A)	Pit. 10	at NYR 4	82	82	24-76 — 100	84	
Brett Hull	St.L.	Apr. 11/93	(G)	Min. 1	at St.L. 5	78	82	54-47 — 101	80	
Theoren Fleury	Cgy.	Apr. 11/93	(G)	Cgy. 3	at Van. 6	82	82	34-66 — 100	83	
Joe Juneau	Bos.	Apr. 14/93	(A)	Bos. 4	at Ott. 2	84	84	32-70 — 102	84	25.3
Wayne Gretzky	L.A.	Feb. 14/94	(A)	Bos. 3	at L.A. 2	56	56	38-92 — 130	81	

Player	Team	Date of 100th Point	G or A	Score		Player's Game No.	Team Game No.	G - A	PTS	Total Games	Age when first 100th point scored (Yrs. & Mos.)
Sergei Fedorov	Det.	Mar. 1/94	(A)	Cgy. 2	at Det. 5	63	63	56-64	— 120	82	24.2
Doug Gilmour	Tor.	Mar. 23/94	(G)	Tor. 1	at Fla. 1	74	74	27-84	— 111	83	
Adam Oates	Bos.	Mar. 26/94	(A)	Mtl. 3	at Bos. 6	68	75	32-80	— 112	77	
Mark Recchi	Phi.	Mar. 27/94	(A)	Ana. 3	at Phi. 2	76	76	40-67	— 107	84	
Pavel Bure	Van.	Mar. 28/94	(A)	Tor. 2	at Van. 3	68	76	60-47	— 107	76	
Jeremy Roenick	Chi.	Mar. 31/94	(G)	Chi. 3	at Wsh. 6	78	78	46-61	— 107	84	
Brendan Shanahan	St.L.	Apr. 12/94	(G)	St.L. 5	at Dal. 9	80	83	52-50	— 102	81	25.2
Mario Lemieux	Pit.	Jan. 16/96	(G)	Col. 5	at Pit. 2	38	44	69-92	— 161	70	
Jaromir Jagr	Pit.	Feb. 6/96	(G)	Bos. 5	at Pit. 6	52	52	62-87	— 149	82	23.11
Ron Francis	Pit.	Mar. 9/96	(A)	N.J. 4	at Pit. 3	61	66	27-92	— 119	77	
Peter Forsberg	Col.	Mar. 9/96	(A)	Col. 7	at Van. 5	68	68	30-86	— 116	82	22.7
Joe Sakic	Col.	Mar. 17/96	(A)	Edm. 1	at Col. 8	70	70	51-69	— 120	82	
Eric Lindros	Phi.	Mar. 25/96	(A)	Hfd. 0	at Phi. 3	65	73	47-68	— 115	73	23
Teemu Selanne	Ana.	Mar. 25/96	(A)	Ana. 1	at Det. 5	70	73	40-68	— 108	79	
Alexander Mogilny	Van.	Mar. 25/96	(A)	L.A. 1	at Van. 4	72	75	55-52	— 107	79	
Wayne Gretzky	St.L.	Mar. 28/96	(A)	N.J. 4	at St.L. 4	76	75	23-79	— 102	80	
Doug Weight	Edm.	Mar. 30/96	(G)	Tor. 4	at Edm. 3	76	76	25-79	— 104	82	25.3
Sergei Fedorov	Det.	Apr. 2/96	(A)	Det. 3	at S.J. 6	72	76	39-68	— 107	78	
Paul Kariya	Ana.	Apr. 7/96	(G)	Ana. 5	at S.J. 3	78	78	50-58	— 108	82	21.5
Mario Lemieux	Pit.	Mar. 8/97	(A)	Phi. 2	at Pit. 3	61	65	50-72	— 122	76	
Teemu Selanne	Ana.	Apr. 1/97	(A)	Chi. 3	at Ana. 3	74	78	51-58	— 109	78	
Jaromir Jagr	Pit.	Apr. 15/98	(G)	T.B. 1	at Pit. 5	76	80	35-67	— 102	77	
Jaromir Jagr	Pit.	Mar. 13/99	(G)	Phi. 0	at Pit. 4	65	65	44-83	— 127	81	
Teemu Selanne	Ana.	Apr. 5/99	(A)	Ana. 2	at Det. 3	69	76	47-60	— 107	75	
Paul Kariya	Ana.	Apr. 17/99	(G)	Ana. 3	at S.J. 3	82	82	39-62	— 101	82	
Jaromir Jagr	Pit.	Mar. 10/01	(G)	Cgy. 3	at Pit. 6	68	68	52-69	— 121	81	
Joe Sakic	Col.	Mar. 18/01	(G)	Min. 3	at Col. 4	72	72	54-64	— 118	82	
Markus Naslund	Van.	Mar. 27/03	(A)	Phx. 1	at Van. 5	78	78	48-56	— 104	82	
Peter Forsberg	Col.	Mar. 31/03	(A)	S.J. 1	at Col. 3	72	79	29-77	— 106	79	
Joe Thornton	Bos.	Apr. 4/03	(A)	Buf. 5	at Bos. 8	77	82	36-65	— 101	77	23.9
Jaromir Jagr	NYR	Mar. 18/06	A	Tor. 2	at NYR 5	67	67	54-69	— 123	82	
Joe Thornton	S.J.	Mar. 21/06	A	S.J. 6	at St.L. 0	66	67	29-96	— 125	81	
Alex Ovechkin	Wsh.	Apr. 10/06	G	Wsh. 2	at Bos. 1	77	78	52-54	— 106	81	20.6
Dany Heatley	Ott.	Apr. 13/06	A	Fla. 5	at Ott. 4	80	80	50-53	— 103	82	25.2
Daniel Alfredsson	Ott.	Apr. 15/06	A	Fla. 5	at Ott. 4	76	81	43-60	— 103	77	33.4
Eric Staal	Car.	Apr. 15/06	A	Car. 2	at T.B. 3	81	81	45-55	— 100	82	21.5
Sidney Crosby	Pit.	Apr. 17/06	A	NYI 1	at Pit. 6	80	81	39-63	— 102	81	18.8
Sidney Crosby	Pit.	Mar. 10/07	G	NYR 2	at Pit. 3	65	68	36-84	— 120	79	
Joe Thornton	S.J.	Mar. 22/07	A	S.J. 5	at Atl. 1	75	75	22-92	— 114	82	
Vincent Lecavalier	T.B.	Mar. 24/07	A	Ott. 7	at T.B. 2	76	76	52-56	— 108	82	26.11
Dany Heatley	Ott.	Mar. 31/07	G	Ott. 5	at NYI 2	79	79	50-55	— 105	82	
Martin St. Louis	T.B.	Mar. 31/07	A	Wsh. 2	at T.B. 5	79	79	43-59	— 102	82	31.10
Marian Hossa	Atl.	Apr. 7/07	A	T.B. 2	at Atl. 3	82	82	43-57	— 100	82	28.3
Joe Sakic	Col.	Apr. 8/07	G	Cgy. 3	at Col. 6	82	82	36-64	— 100	82	

Sidney Crosby

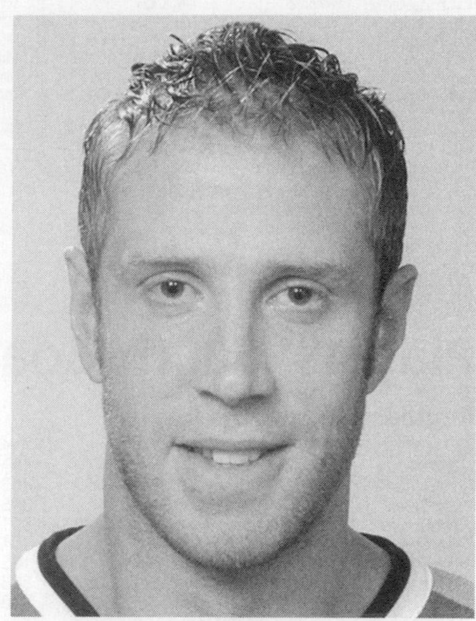

Joe Thornton

Joe Sakic

Marian Hossa

Martin St. Louis

Five-or-more-Goal Games

Player	Team	Date	Score			Opposing Goaltender
SEVEN GOALS						
Joe Malone	Quebec Bulldogs	Jan. 31/20	Tor. 6	at	Que. 10	Ivan Mitchell
SIX GOALS						
Newsy Lalonde	Montreal	Jan. 10/20	Tor. 7	at	Mtl. 14	Ivan Mitchell
Joe Malone	Quebec Bulldogs	Mar. 10/20	Ott. 4	at	Que. 10	Clint Benedict
Corb Denneny	Toronto St. Pats	Jan. 26/21	Ham. 3	at	Tor. 10	Howard Lockhart
Cy Denneny	Ottawa Senators	Mar. 7/21	Ham. 5	at	Ott. 12	Howard Lockhart
Syd Howe	Detroit	Feb. 3/44	NYR 2	at	Det. 12	Ken McAuley
Red Berenson	St. Louis	Nov. 7/68	St.L. 8	at	Phi. 0	Doug Favell
Darryl Sittler	Toronto	Feb. 7/76	Bos. 4	at	Tor. 11	Dave Reece
FIVE GOALS						
Joe Malone	Montreal	Dec. 19/17	Mtl. 7	at	Ott. 4	Clint Benedict
Harry Hyland	Mtl. Wanderers	Dec. 19/17	Tor. 9	at	Mtl. W. 10	Art Brooks, Sammy Hebert
Joe Malone	Montreal	Jan. 12/18	Ott. 4	at	Mtl. 9	Clint Benedict
Joe Malone	Montreal	Feb. 2/18	Tor. 2	at	Mtl. 11	Hap Holmes
Mickey Roach	Toronto St. Pats	Mar. 6/20	Que. 2	at	Tor. 11	Howard Lockhart
Newsy Lalonde	Montreal	Feb. 16/21	Ham. 5	at	Mtl. 10	Howard Lockhart
Babe Dye	Toronto St. Pats	Dec. 16/22	Mtl. 2	at	Tor. 7	Georges Vezina
Red Green	Hamilton Tigers	Dec. 5/24	Ham. 10	at	Tor. 3	John Ross Roach
Babe Dye	Toronto St. Pats	Dec. 22/24	Tor. 10	at	Bos. 1	Hec Fowler
Punch Broadbent	Mtl. Maroons	Jan. 7/25	Mtl. 6	at	Ham. 2	Jake Forbes
Pit Lepine	Montreal	Dec. 14/29	Ott. 4	at	Mtl. 6	Alex Connell
Howie Morenz	Montreal	Mar. 18/30	NYA 3	at	Mtl. 8	Roy Worters
Charlie Conacher	Toronto	Jan. 19/32	NYA 3	at	Tor. 11	Roy Worters (3) Al Shields (2)
Ray Getliffe	Montreal	Feb. 6/43	Bos. 3	at	Mtl. 8	Frank Brimsek
Maurice Richard	Montreal	Dec. 28/44	Det. 1	at	Mtl. 9	Harry Lumley
Howie Meeker	Toronto	Jan. 8/47	Chi. 4	at	Tor. 10	Paul Bibeault
Bernie Geoffrion	Montreal	Feb. 19/55	NYR 2	at	Mtl. 10	Gump Worsley
Bobby Rousseau	Montreal	Feb. 1/64	Det. 3	at	Mtl. 9	Roger Crozier
Yvan Cournoyer	Montreal	Feb. 15/75	Chi. 3	at	Mtl. 12	Mike Veisor
Don Murdoch	NY Rangers	Oct. 12/76	NYR 10	at	Min. 4	Gary Smith
Ian Turnbull	Toronto	Feb. 2/77	Det. 1	at	Tor. 9	Ed Giacomin (2) Jim Rutherford (3)
Bryan Trottier	NY Islanders	Dec. 23/78	NYR 4	at	NYI 9	Wayne Thomas (4) John Davidson (1)
Tim Young	Minnesota	Jan. 15/79	Min. 8	at	NYR 1	Doug Soetaert (3) Wayne Thomas (2)
John Tonelli	NY Islanders	Jan. 6/81	Tor. 3	at	NYI 6	Jiri Crha (4) empty net (1)
Wayne Gretzky	Edmonton	Feb. 18/81	St.L. 2	at	Edm. 9	Mike Liut (3) Ed Staniowski (2)
Wayne Gretzky	Edmonton	Dec. 30/81	Phi. 5	at	Edm. 7	Pete Peeters (4) empty net (1)
Grant Mulvey	Chicago	Feb. 3/82	St.L. 5	at	Chi. 9	Mike Liut (4) Gary Edwards (1)
Bryan Trottier	NY Islanders	Feb. 13/82	Phi. 2	at	NYI 8	Pete Peeters
Willy Lindstrom	Winnipeg	Mar. 2/82	Wpg. 7	at	Phi. 6	Pete Peeters
Mark Pavelich	NY Rangers	Feb. 23/83	Hfd. 3	at	NYR 11	Greg Millen
Jari Kurri	Edmonton	Nov. 19/83	N.J. 4	at	Edm. 13	Glenn Resch (3) Ron Low (2)
Bengt Gustafsson	Washington	Jan. 8/84	Wsh. 7	at	Phi. 1	Pelle Lindbergh
Pat Hughes	Edmonton	Feb. 3/84	Cgy. 5	at	Edm. 10	Don Edwards (3) Reggie Lemelin (2)
Wayne Gretzky	Edmonton	Dec. 15/84	Edm. 8	at	St.L. 2	Rick Wamsley (4) Mike Liut(1)
Dave Andreychuk	Buffalo	Feb. 6/86	Buf. 8	at	Bos. 6	Pat Riggin (1) Doug Keans (4)
Wayne Gretzky	Edmonton	Dec. 6/87	Min. 4	at	Edm. 10	Don Beaupre (4) Kari Takko (1)
Mario Lemieux	Pittsburgh	Dec. 31/88	N.J. 6	at	Pit. 8	Bob Sauve (3) Chris Terreri (2)
Joe Nieuwendyk	Calgary	Jan. 11/89	Wpg. 3	at	Cgy. 8	Daniel Berthiaume
Mats Sundin	Quebec	Mar. 5/92	Que. 10	at	Hfd. 4	Peter Sidorkiewicz (3) Kay Whitmore (2)
Mario Lemieux	Pittsburgh	Apr. 9/93	Pit. 10	at	NYR 4	Corey Hirsch (3) Mike Richter (2)
Peter Bondra	Washington	Feb. 5/94	T.B. 3	at	Wsh. 6	Daren Puppa (4) Pat Jablonski (1)
Mike Ricci	Quebec	Feb. 17/94	Que. 8	at	S.J. 2	Arturs Irbe (3) Jimmy Waite (2)
Alex Zhamnov	Winnipeg	Apr. 1/95	Wpg. 7	at	L.A. 7	Kelly Hrudey (3) Grant Fuhr (2)
Mario Lemieux	Pittsburgh	Mar. 26/96	St.L. 4	at	Pit. 8	Grant Fuhr (1) Jon Casey (4)
Sergei Fedorov	Detroit	Dec. 26/96	Wsh. 4	at	Det. 5	Jim Carey

Players' 500th Goals

Regular Season

Player	Team	Date	Game No.	Score			Opposing Goaltender	Total Goals	Total Games
Maurice Richard	Montreal	Oct. 19/57	863	Chi. 1	at	Mtl. 3	Glenn Hall	544	978
Gordie Howe	Detroit	Mar. 14/62	1,045	Det. 2	at	NYR 3	Gump Worsley	801	1,767
Bobby Hull	Chicago	Feb. 21/70	861	NYR. 2	at	Chi. 4	Ed Giacomin	610	1,063
Jean Béliveau	Montreal	Feb. 11/71	1,101	Min. 2	at	Mtl. 6	Gilles Gilbert	507	1,125
Frank Mahovlich	Montreal	Mar. 21/73	1,105	Van. 2	at	Mtl. 3	Dunc Wilson	533	1,181
Phil Esposito	Boston	Dec. 22/74	803	Det. 4	at	Bos. 5	Jim Rutherford	717	1,282
John Bucyk	Boston	Oct. 30/75	1,370	St.L. 2	at	Bos. 3	Yves Bélanger	556	1,540
Stan Mikita	Chicago	Feb. 27/77	1,221	Van. 4	at	Chi. 3	Cesare Maniago	541	1,394
Marcel Dionne	Los Angeles	Dec. 14/82	887	L.A. 2	at	Wsh. 7	Al Jensen	731	1,348
Guy Lafleur	Montreal	Dec. 20/83	918	Mtl. 6	at	N.J. 0	Glenn Resch	560	1,126
Mike Bossy	NY Islanders	Jan. 2/86	647	Bos. 5	at	NYI 7	empty net	573	752
Gilbert Perreault	Buffalo	Mar. 9/86	1,159	N.J. 3	at	Buf. 4	Alain Chevrier	512	1,191
Wayne Gretzky	Edmonton	Nov. 22/86	575	Van. 2	at	Edm. 5	empty net	894	1,487
Lanny McDonald	Calgary	Mar. 21/89	1,107	NYI 1	at	Cgy. 4	Mark Fitzpatrick	500	1,111
Bryan Trottier	NY Islanders	Feb. 13/90	1,104	Cgy. 4	at	NYI 2	Rick Wamsley	524	1,279
Mike Gartner	NY Rangers	Oct. 14/91	936	Wsh. 5	at	NYR 3	Mike Liut	708	1,432
Michel Goulet	Chicago	Feb. 16/92	951	Cgy. 5	at	Chi. 5	Jeff Reese	548	1,089
Jari Kurri	Los Angeles	Oct. 17/92	833	Bos. 6	at	L.A. 8	empty net	601	1,251
Dino Ciccarelli	Detroit	Jan. 8/94	946	Det. 6	at	L.A. 3	Kelly Hrudey	608	1,232
Mario Lemieux	Pittsburgh	Oct. 26/95	605	Pit. 7	at	NYI 5	Tommy Soderstrom	690	915
Mark Messier	NY Rangers	Nov. 6/95	1,141	Cgy. 2	at	NYR 4	Rick Tabaracci	694	1,756
Steve Yzerman	Detroit	Jan. 17/96	906	Col. 2	at	Det. 3	Patrick Roy	692	1,514
Dale Hawerchuk	St. Louis	Jan. 31/96	1,103	St.L. 4	at	Tor. 0	Felix Potvin	518	1,188
Brett Hull	St. Louis	Dec. 22/96	693	L.A. 4	at	St.L. 7	Stephane Fiset	741	1,269
Joe Mullen	Pittsburgh	Mar. 14/97	1,052	Pit. 3	at	Col. 6	Patrick Roy	502	1,062
Dave Andreychuk	New Jersey	Mar. 15/97	1,070	Wsh. 2	at	N.J. 3	Bill Ranford	640	1,639
Luc Robitaille	Los Angeles	Jan. 7/99	928	Buf. 2	at	L.A. 4	Dwayne Roloson	668	1,431
Pat Verbeek	Detroit	Mar. 22/00	1,285	Cgy. 2	at	Det. 2	Fred Brathwaite	522	1,424
Ron Francis	Carolina	Jan. 2/02	1,533	Bos. 6	at	Car. 3	Byron Dafoe	549	1,731
*Brendan Shanahan	Detroit	Mar. 23/02	1,100	Det. 2	at	Col. 0	Patrick Roy	627	1,417
*Joe Sakic	Colorado	Dec. 11/02	1,044	Col. 1	at	Van. 3	Dan Cloutier	610	1,319
Joe Nieuwendyk	New Jersey	Jan. 17/03	1,094	N.J. 2	at	Car. 1	Kevin Weekes	564	1,257
*Jaromir Jagr	Washington	Feb. 4/03	928	Wsh. 5	at	T.B. 1	John Grahame	621	1,191
*Pierre Turgeon	Colorado	Nov. 8/05	1,229	S.J. 2	at	Col. 5	Vesa Toskala	515	1,294
*Mats Sundin	Toronto	Oct. 14/06	1,162	Cgy. 4	at	Tor. 5	Miikka Kiprusoff	523	1,231
*Teemu Selanne	Anaheim	Nov. 22/06	982	Ana. 2	at	Col. 3	Jose Theodore	540	1,041
*Peter Bondra	Chicago	Dec. 22/06	1,050	Tor. 1	at	Chi. 3	J.S. Aubin	503	1,081
*Mark Recchi	Pittsburgh	Jan. 26/07	1,303	Pit. 4	at	Dal. 3	Marty Turco	508	1,338
*Mike Modano	Dallas	Mar. 13/07	1,225	Phi. 2	at	Dal. 3	Antero Niittymaki	507	1,238

*Active

Mats Sundin acknowledges the fans upon being named first star in a game on October 14, 2006 after his goal in overtime gave Toronto a 5-4 win over Calgary and capped a hat trick on a night that saw him score his the 500th regular-season NHL goal.

Players' 1,000th Points

Regular Season

Player	Team	Date	Game No.	G or A	Score	Total Points G-A-PTS	Total Games
Gordie Howe	Detroit	Nov. 27/60	938	(A)	Tor. 0 at Det. 2	801-1,049–1,850	1,767
Jean Béliveau	Montreal	Mar. 3/68	911	(G)	Mtl. 2 at Det. 5	507-712–1,219	1,125
Alex Delvecchio	Detroit	Feb. 16/69	1,143	(A)	L.A. 3 at Det. 6	456-825–1,281	1,549
Bobby Hull	Chicago	Dec. 13/70	909	(A)	Min. 2 at Chi. 5	610-560–1,170	1,063
Norm Ullman	Toronto	Oct. 16/71	1,113	(A)	NYR 5 at Tor. 3	490-739–1,229	1,410
Stan Mikita	Chicago	Oct. 15/72	924	(A)	St.L. 3 at Chi. 1	541-926–1,467	1,394
John Bucyk	Boston	Nov. 9/72	1,144	(G)	Det. 3 at Bos. 8	556-813–1,369	1,540
Frank Mahovlich	Montreal	Feb. 17/73	1,090	(A)	Phi. 7 at Mtl. 6	533-570–1,103	1,181
Henri Richard	Montreal	Dec. 20/73	1,194	(A)	Mtl. 2 at Buf. 2	358-688–1,046	1,256
Phil Esposito	Boston	Feb. 15/74	745	(A)	Bos. 4 at Van. 2	717-873–1,590	1,282
Rod Gilbert	NY Rangers	Feb. 19/77	1,027	(G)	NYR 2 at NYI 5	406-615–1,021	1,065
Jean Ratelle	Boston	Apr. 3/77	1,007	(A)	Tor. 4 at Bos. 7	491-776–1,267	1,281
Marcel Dionne	Los Angeles	Jan. 7/81	740	(G)	L.A. 5 at Hfd. 3	731-1,040–1,771	1,348
Guy Lafleur	Montreal	Mar. 4/81	720	(G)	Mtl. 9 at Wpg. 3	560-793–1,353	1,126
Bobby Clarke	Philadelphia	Mar. 19/81	922	(G)	Bos. 3 at Phi. 5	358-852–1,210	1,144
Gilbert Perreault	Buffalo	Apr. 3/82	871	(A)	Buf. 5 at Mtl. 4	512-814–1,326	1,191
Darryl Sittler	Philadelphia	Jan. 20/83	927	(G)	Cgy. 2 at Phi. 5	484-637–1,121	1,096
Wayne Gretzky	Edmonton	Dec. 19/84	424	(A)	L.A. 3 at Edm. 7	894-1,963–2,875	1,487
Bryan Trottier	NY Islanders	Jan. 29/85	726	(G)	Min. 4 at NYI 4	524-901–1,425	1,279
Mike Bossy	NY Islanders	Jan. 24/86	656	(A)	NYI 7 at Wsh. 5	573-553–1,126	752
Denis Potvin	NY Islanders	Apr. 4/87	987	(G)	Buf. 6 at NYI 6	310-742–1,052	1,060
Bernie Federko	St. Louis	Mar. 19/88	855	(A)	Hfd. 5 at St.L. 3	369-761–1,130	1,000
Lanny McDonald	Calgary	Mar. 7/89	1,101	(G)	Wpg. 5 at Cgy. 9	500-506–1,006	1,111
Peter Stastny	Quebec	Oct. 19/89	682	(G)	Que. 5 at Chi. 3	450-789–1,239	977
Jari Kurri	Edmonton	Jan. 2/90	716	(A)	Edm. 6 at St.L. 4	601-797–1,398	1,251
Denis Savard	Chicago	Mar. 11/90	727	(A)	St.L. 6 at Chi. 4	473-865–1,338	1,196
Paul Coffey	Pittsburgh	Dec. 22/90	770	(A)	Pit. 4 at NYI 3	396-1,135–1,531	1,409
Mark Messier	Edmonton	Jan. 13/91	822	(A)	Edm. 5 at Phi. 3	694-1,193–1,887	1,756
Dave Taylor	Los Angeles	Feb. 5/91	930	(A)	L.A. 3 at Phi. 2	431-638–1,069	1,111
Michel Goulet	Chicago	Feb. 23/91	878	(G)	Chi. 3 at Min. 3	548-604–1,152	1,089
Dale Hawerchuk	Buffalo	Mar. 8/91	781	(G)	Chi. 5 at Buf. 3	518-891–1,409	1,188
Bobby Smith	Minnesota	Nov. 30/91	986	(A)	Min. 4 at Tor. 3	357-679–1,036	1,077
Mike Gartner	NY Rangers	Jan. 4/92	971	(G)	NYR 4 at N.J. 6	708-627–1,335	1,432
Raymond Bourque	Boston	Feb. 29/92	933	(A)	Wsh. 5 at Bos. 5	410-1,169–1,579	1,612
Mario Lemieux	Pittsburgh	Mar. 24/92	513	(A)	Pit. 3 at Det. 4	690-1,033–1,723	915
Glenn Anderson	Toronto	Feb. 22/93	954	(G)	Tor. 8 at Van. 1	498-601–1,099	1,129
Steve Yzerman	Detroit	Feb. 24/93	737	(A)	Det. 7 at Buf. 10	692-1,063–1,755	1,514
Ron Francis	Pittsburgh	Oct. 28/93	893	(G)	Que. 7 at Pit. 3	549-1,249–1,798	1,731
Bernie Nicholls	New Jersey	Feb. 13/94	858	(G)	N.J. 3 at T.B. 3	475-734–1,209	1,127
Dino Ciccarelli	Detroit	Mar. 9/94	957	(G)	Det. 5 at Cgy. 1	608-592–1,200	1,232
Brian Propp	Hartford	Mar. 19/94	1,008	(G)	Hfd. 5 at Phi. 3	425-579–1,004	1,016
Joe Mullen	Pittsburgh	Feb. 7/95	935	(A)	Fla. 3 at Pit. 7	502-561–1,063	1,062
Steve Larmer	NY Rangers	Mar. 8/95	983	(A)	N.J. 4 at NYR 6	441-571–1,012	1,006
Doug Gilmour	Toronto	Dec. 23/95	935	(A)	Edm. 1 at Tor. 6	450-964–1,414	1,474
Larry Murphy	Toronto	Mar. 27/96	1,228	(G)	Tor. 6 at Van. 2	287-929–1,216	1,615
Dave Andreychuk	New Jersey	Apr. 7/96	998	(G)	NYR 2 at N.J. 4	640-698–1,338	1,639
Adam Oates	Washington	Oct. 8/97	830	(G)	Wsh. 6 at NYI 3	341-1,079–1,420	1,337
Phil Housley	Washington	Nov. 8/97	1,081	(A)	Edm. 1 at Wsh. 2	338-894–1,232	1,495
Dale Hunter	Washington	Jan. 9/98	1,308	(A)	Phi. 1 at Wsh. 4	323-697–1,020	1,407
Pat LaFontaine	NY Rangers	Jan. 22/98	847	(G)	Phi. 4 at NYR 3	468-545–1,013	865
Luc Robitaille	Los Angeles	Jan. 29/98	882	(A)	Cgy. 3 at L.A. 5	668-726–1,394	1,431
Al MacInnis	St. Louis	Apr. 7/98	1,056	(A)	St.L. 3 at Det. 5	340-934–1,274	1,416
Brett Hull	Dallas	Nov. 14/98	815	(A)	Dal. 3 at Bos. 1	741-650–1,391	1,269
Brian Bellows	Washington	Jan. 2/99	1,147	(A)	Tor. 2 at Wsh. 5	485-537–1,022	1,188
*Pierre Turgeon	St. Louis	Oct. 9/99	881	(G)	St.L. 4 at Edm. 3	515-812–1,327	1,294
*Joe Sakic	Colorado	Dec. 27/99	810	(A)	St.L. 1 at Col. 5	610-979–1,589	1,319
Pat Verbeek	Detroit	Feb. 27/00	1,275	(A)	T.B. 1 at Det. 3	522-541–1,063	1,424
V. Damphousse	San Jose	Oct. 14/00	1,090	(A)	Bos. 2 at S.J. 5	432-773–1,205	1,378
*Jaromir Jagr	Pittsburgh	Dec. 30/00	763	(G)	Ott. 3 at Pit. 5	621-907–1,528	1,191
*Mark Recchi	Philadelphia	Mar. 13/01	920	(A)	St.L. 2 at Phi. 5	508-825–1,333	1,338
Theoren Fleury	NY Rangers	Oct. 29/01	960	(A)	Dal. 2 at NYR 4	455-633–1,088	1,084
*B. Shanahan	Detroit	Jan. 12/02	1,073	(G)	Dal. 2 at Det. 5	627-667–1,294	1,417
*Jeremy Roenick	Philadelphia	Jan. 30/02	961	(G)	Phi. 1 at Ott. 3	495-675–1,170	1,252
*Mike Modano	Dallas	Nov. 15/02	965	(A)	Col. 2 at Dal. 4	507-719–1,226	1,238
Joe Nieuwendyk	New Jersey	Feb. 23/03	1,094	(G)	N.J. 4 at Pit. 3	564-562–1,126	1,257
*Mats Sundin	Toronto	Mar. 10/03	994	(G)	Tor. 3 at Edm. 2	523-720–1,243	1,231
*Sergei Fedorov	Anaheim	Feb. 14/04	965	(A)	Ana. 2 at Van. 1	461-644–1,105	1,128
Alexander Mogilny	Toronto	Mar. 15/04	946	(A)	Tor. 6 at Buf. 5	473-559–1,032	990
Brian Leetch	Boston	Oct. 18/05	1,151	(A)	Bos. 3 at Mtl. 4	247-781–1,028	1,205
*Teemu Selanne	Anaheim	Jan. 30/06	928	(G)	L.A. 3 at Ana. 4	540-595–1,135	1,041
*Rod Brind'Amour	Carolina	Nov. 4/06	1,202	(A)	Car. 3 at Ott. 2	408-655–1,063	1,265

*Active

Gordie Howe (top) became the NHL's first 1,000-point scorer on November 27, 1960. The Carolina Hurricanes' Rod Brind'Amour became the most recent player to reach this mark when he scored his 1,000th on November 4, 2006.

Individual Awards

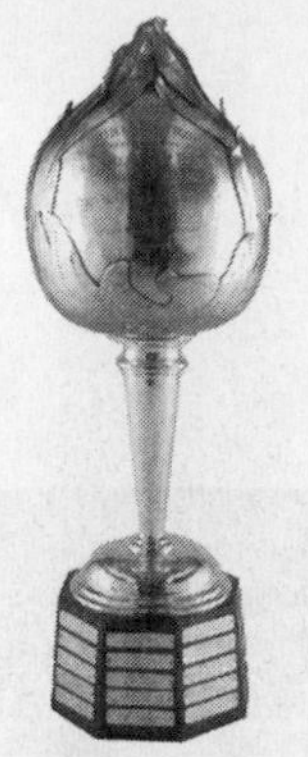

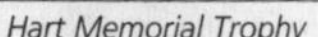

Hart Memorial Trophy

Art Ross Trophy

Calder Memorial Trophy

James Norris Memorial Trophy

HART MEMORIAL TROPHY

An annual award "to the player adjudged to be the most valuable to his team." Winner selected in a poll by the Professional Hockey Writers' Association in the 30 NHL cities at the end of the regular schedule.

History: The Hart Memorial Trophy was presented by the National Hockey League in 1960 after the original Hart Trophy was retired to the Hockey Hall of Fame. The original Hart Trophy was donated to the NHL in 1923 by Dr. David A. Hart, father of Cecil Hart, former manager-coach of the Montreal Canadiens.

2006-07 Winner: **Sidney Crosby, Pittsburgh Penguins**
Runners-up: **Roberto Luongo, Vancouver Canucks**
Martin Brodeur, New Jersey Devils

Center Sidney Crosby of the Pittsburgh Penguins captured the Hart Memorial Trophy, beating out goaltenders Roberto Luongo and Martin Brodeur by a comfortable margin. Crosby received 91 of 143 first-place votes for 1,225 points, besting Luongo of the Vancouver Canucks, who tallied 25 first-place votes and 801 points. Brodeur of the New Jersey Devils had 21 first-place votes and 763 points. Both Vincent Lecavalier of the Tampa Bay Lightning and Nicklas Lidstrom of the Detroit Red Wings also received first-place votes. Lecavalier had five first place votes and 362 points to finish fourth in the balloting, while Lidstrom had one first-place vote and 53 points to finish sixth. Joe Thornton of the San Jose Sharks finished fifth overall with 230 points, but had no first-place votes. Four months before his 20th birthday, Crosby finished the 2006-07 regular season as the first teenager in major pro team sports history to win a scoring title with 120 points (36 goals, 84 assists). NHL immortal Wayne Gretzky captured his first points title in 1980-81 at 20 years, three months. Crosby took the lead in the scoring race with a career-high six-point night December 13 against Philadelphia and stayed on top thereafter, never going more than three consecutive games without a point.

CALDER MEMORIAL TROPHY

An annual award "to the player selected as the most proficient in his first year of competition in the National Hockey League." Winner selected in a poll by the Professional Hockey Writers' Association at the end of the regular schedule.

History: From 1936-37 until his death in 1943, Frank Calder, NHL President, bought a trophy each year to be given permanently to the outstanding rookie. After Calder's death, the NHL presented the Calder Memorial Trophy in his memory and the trophy is to be kept in perpetuity. To be eligible for the award, a player cannot have played more than 25 games in any single preceding season nor in six or more games in each of any two preceding seasons in any major professional league. Beginning in 1990-91, to be eligible for this award a player must not have attained his twenty-sixth birthday by September 15th of the season in which he is eligible.

2006-07 Winner: **Evgeni Malkin, Pittsburgh Penguins**
Runners-up: **Paul Stastny, Colorado Avalanche**
Jordan Staal, Pittsburgh Penguins

Center Evgeni Malkin of the Pittsburgh Penguins captured the Calder Memorial Trophy. Malkin received 120 of 143 first-place votes and 1,357 points, outdistancing Colorado Avalanche center Paul Stastny, who polled 16 first-place votes and 965 points. Malkins teammate Jordan Staal received six first-place votes and 565 points. The final first-place vote went to Marc-Edouard Vlasic of the San Jose Sharks, but he finished sixth overall with 96 points behind Anze Kopitar of Los Angeles (417 points) and Dustin Penner of Anaheim (107).

Malkin launched his NHL career in memorable fashion, becoming the first player in 89 years to tally goals in each of his first six games. Before Malkin, only three players in NHL history had scored at least one goal in each of their first six (or more) games and all did so in 1917-18, the NHL's inaugural season. The 20-year-old went on to lead all rookies in goals (33), power-play goals (16), assists (52) and points (85). Malkin showed veteran savvy as a clutch goal-scorer; 25 of his 33 tallies came with the Penguins trailing or tied.

ART ROSS TROPHY

An annual award "to the player who leads the league in scoring points at the end of the regular season."

History: Arthur Howey Ross, former manager-coach of the Boston Bruins, presented the trophy to the National Hockey League in 1947. If two players finish the schedule with the same number of points, the trophy is awarded in the following manner: 1. Player with most goals. 2. Player with fewer games played. 3. Player scoring first goal of the season.

2006-07 Winner: **Sidney Crosby, Pittsburgh Penguins**
Runners-up: **Joe Thornton, San Jose Sharks**
Vincent Lecavalier, Tampa Bay Lightning

Center Sidney Crosby of the Pittsburgh Penguins won the Art Ross Trophy for the first time. His win marked the fifth season in a row that the award was won by a first-time winner following four straight wins by Jaromir Jagr from 1998 through 2001. Four months before his 20th birthday, Sidney Crosby finished the 2006-07 regular season as the first teenager in major pro team sports history to win a scoring title. NHL great Wayne Gretzky captured his first points title in 1980-81 at 20 years, three months. Crosby tallied 36 goals and 84 assists for 120 points — six ahead of San Jose Shark's center Joe Thornton, the 2005-06 Art Ross Trophy winner. Vincent Lecavalier finished third with an NHL-best 52 goals and 108 points. Crosby took the permanent scoring lead with a career-high six-point night against Philadelphia December 13 and never went more than three consecutive games without a point afterward.

JAMES NORRIS MEMORIAL TROPHY

An annual award "to the defense player who demonstrates throughout the season the greatest all-round ability in the position." Winner selected in a poll by the Professional Hockey Writers' Association at the end of the regular schedule.

History: The James Norris Memorial Trophy was presented in 1953 by the four children of the late James Norris in memory of the former owner-president of the Detroit Red Wings.

2006-07 Winner: **Nicklas Lidstrom, Detroit Red Wings**
Runners-up: **Scott Niedermayer, Anaheim Ducks**
Chris Pronger, Anaheim Ducks

For the fifth time in the past six seasons, Nicklas Lidstrom of the Detroit Red Wings has won the James Norris Memorial Trophy. Lidstrom received 87 first-place votes and 1,217 points. Anaheim Duck's defenseman Scott Niedermayer finished second in the balloting for the second consecutive season, receiving 46 first-place votes and 1,024 points. Duck's teammate Chris Pronger was third with six first-place votes and 608 points. Dan Boyle of Tampa Bay, Sergei Gonchar of Pittsburgh, Sheldon Souray of Montreal and Philippe Boucher of Dallas all received one first-place vote apiece.

Lidstrom tied for the NHL lead among defensemen in plus-minus with a +40 rating, ranked third among all players in ice time per game (27:29) and was fifth among defensemen in scoring with 62 points (13 goals, 49 assists). Lidstrom was one of just two defensemen, with Boston's Zdeno Chara, to average more than 5:00 of power-play and 4:00 of shorthanded time per game.

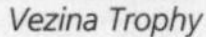

Vezina Trophy

Lady Byng Memorial Trophy

Frank J. Selke Trophy

Conn Smythe Trophy

VEZINA TROPHY

An annual award "to the goalkeeper adjudged to be the best at his position" as voted by the general managers of each of the 30 clubs.

History: Leo Dandurand, Louis Letourneau and Joe Cattarinich, former owners of the Montreal Canadiens, presented the trophy to the National Hockey League in 1926-27 in memory of Georges Vezina, outstanding goalkeeper of the Canadiens who collapsed during an NHL game on November 28, 1925, and died of tuberculosis a few months later. Until the 1981-82 season, the goalkeeper(s) of the team allowing the fewest number of goals during the regular season were awarded the Vezina Trophy.

2006-07 Winner: **Martin Brodeur, New Jersey Devils**
Runners-up: **Roberto Luongo, Vancouver Canucks**
Miikka Kiprusoff, Calgary Flames
Henrik Lundqvist, New York Rangers

Martin Brodeur of the New Jersey Devils captured the Vezina Trophy, winning the award for the third time in the past four seasons. Brodeur received first- or second-place votes from all 30 voters, including 16 first-place selections, and collected 122 points. Vancouver Canuck's goaltender Roberto Luongo finished a close second, garnering 14 first-place votes and 116 points. Both Miikka Kiprusoff of Calgary (last year's winner) and Henrik Lundqvist of the New York Rangers received seven third place votes to tie for third in the voting.

Brodeur won an NHL-record 48 games, surpassing Bernie Parent's 47 in 1973-74, led the NHL in shutouts (12), ranked third in goals-against average (2.18) and third in save percentage (.922). He finished the season in second place on the NHL's all-time victories list with 494, behind only Patrick Roy (551), and third on the all-time shutouts list with 92.

LADY BYNG MEMORIAL TROPHY

An annual award "to the player adjudged to have exhibited the best type of sportsmanship and gentlemanly conduct combined with a high standard of playing ability." Winner selected in a poll by the Professional Hockey Writers' Association at the end of the regular schedule.

History: Lady Byng, wife of Canada's Governor-General at the time, presented the Lady Byng Trophy in the 1924-25 season. After Frank Boucher of the New York Rangers won the award seven times in eight seasons, he was given the trophy to keep and Lady Byng donated another trophy in 1936. After Lady Byng's death in 1949, the National Hockey League presented a new trophy, changing the name to Lady Byng Memorial Trophy.

2006-07 Winner: **Pavel Datsyuk, Detroit Red Wings**
Runners-up: **Martin St. Louis, Tampa Bay Lightning**
Joe Sakic, Colorado Avalanche

Detroit Red Wings center Pavel Datsyuk won the Lady Byng Memorial Trophy for the second consecutive season. He is the first repeat winner of the Lady Byng since Paul Kariya won it in 1996 and 1997. Datsyuk received 38 first-place votes and 705 points, ahead of second-place Martin St. Louis of the Tampa Bay Lightning (26 first place votes, 513 points) and Joe Sakic (17 and 354).

Datsyuk led the Red Wings in scoring for the second consecutive season, matching a career high with 87 points (27 goals, 60 assists), and ranked second on the club and seventh in the NHL overall in plus-minus (+36). Datsyuk received just 20 penalty minutes in 79 games.

FRANK J. SELKE TROPHY

An annual award "to the forward who best excels in the defensive aspects of the game." Winner selected in a poll by the Professional Hockey Writers' Association at the end of the regular schedule.

History: Presented to the National Hockey League in 1977 by the Board of Governors of the NHL in honor of Frank J. Selke, one of the great architects of Montreal and Toronto championship teams.

2006-07 Winner: **Rod Brind'Amour, Carolina Hurricanes**
Runners-up: **Samuel Pahlsson, Anaheim Ducks**
Jay Pandolfo, New Jersey Devils

Carolina Hurricanes center Rod Brind'Amour captured his second consecutive Frank Selke Trophy. Brind'Amour was named on 76 of 141 ballots, including 16 first-place votes, and posted a narrow 15-point victory over Anaheim Duck's center Samuel Pahlsson, 420-405. Pahlsson actually received more first-place votes with 24. Jay Pandolfo of New Jersey was third in the voting with 16 first-place votes and 311 points. Chris Drury of the Buffalo Sabres received 18 first-place votes but only 300 points overall to finish fourth.

Brind'Amour ranked second among all NHL centers with a 59.2 faceoff win percentage and ranked third among NHL forwards in average ice time per game (23:19). He also led the Hurricanes in shorthanded ice time per game (3:37). Carolina's penalty killing finished the season ranked tied for sixth in the NHL at 84.6 percent and Brind'Amour was tied for first among Carolina players with five shorthanded points.

WILLIAM M. JENNINGS TROPHY

An annual award "to the goalkeeper(s) having played a minimum of 25 games for the team with the fewest goals scored against it." Winners selected on regular-season play.

History: The Jennings Trophy was presented in 1981-82 by the National Hockey League's Board of Governors to honor the late William M. Jennings, longtime governor and president of the New York Rangers and one of the great builders of hockey in the United States.

2006-07 Winner: **Niklas Backstrom/Manny Fernandez, Minnesota Wild**
Runners-up: **Marty Turco, Dallas Stars**
Dominik Hasek, Detroit Red Wings
Evgeni Nabokov/Vesa Toskala, San Jose Sharks

The netminding duo of Niklas Backstrom and Manny Fernandez captured the William M. Jennings Trophy after leading the Minnesota Wild to the best defensive record in the NHL for the first time. Backstrom and Fernandez split time in the Minnesota crease with 41 and 44 appearances, respectively, backstopping the Wild a league-low 191 team goals against. Backstrom also led all goaltenders in save percentage (.929), stopping 955 of 1,028 shots. Marty Turco saw most of the action in Detroit for a Stars team that allowed just 197 goals. Both the Detroit Red Wings, led by Dominik Hasek, and the San Jose Sharks, where Evgeni Nabokov and Vesa Toskala shared netminding duties, surrendered 199 goals.

CONN SMYTHE TROPHY

An annual award "to the most valuable player for his team in the playoffs." Winner selected by the Professional Hockey Writers' Association at the conclusion of the final game in the Stanley Cup Finals.

History: Presented by Maple Leaf Gardens Limited in 1964 to honor Conn Smythe, the former coach, manager, president and owner-governor of the Toronto Maple Leafs.

2006-07 Winner: **Scott Niedermayer, Anaheim Ducks**

Anaheim Ducks defenseman Scott Niedermayer, a four-time Stanley Cup champion, won the Conn Smythe Trophy for the first time. Niedermayer was one of only three Ducks defenseman to play in all 21 playoff games, and averaged 29:50 of ice time throughout the playoffs. He had three goals and 11 assists to rank third among defenseman in playoff scoring, but two of his three goals were overtime winners. With by far the most playoff experience on his team, the Ducks captain was a steadying influence at both ends of the ice.

William M. Jennings Trophy

Jack Adams Award

Bill Masterton Trophy

Lester Patrick Trophy

JACK ADAMS AWARD

An annual award presented by the National Hockey League Broadcasters' Association to "the NHL coach adjudged to have contributed the most to his team's success." Winner selected by a poll among members of the NHL Broadcasters' Association at the end of the regular season.

History: The award was presented by the NHL Broadcasters' Association in 1974 to commemorate the late Jack Adams, coach and general manager of the Detroit Red Wings, whose lifetime dedication to hockey serves as an inspiration to all who aspire to further the game.

2006-07 Winner: **Alain Vigneault, Vancouver Canucks**
Runners-up: **Lindy Ruff, Buffalo Sabres**
Michel Therrien, Pittsburgh Penguins

Vancouver Canucks head coach Alain Vigneault captured the Jack Adams Award for the first time.Vigneault received 18 first-place votes and 134 points, edging 2006 Adams winner Lindy Ruff of the Buffalo Sabres, who polled 11 first-place votes and 126 points. Michel Therrien of Pittsburgh and Barry Trotz of Nashville also received 11 first-place votes with Therrien finishing third overall with 91 points to Trotz's 89.

In his first year behind the Vancouver bench, Vigneault guided the Canucks to a franchise record-breaking season. They improved their wins record to 49 from a previous high of 46 and recorded the highest points total in club history with 105. The club also captured the fifth division title in franchise history. The Canucks were 29-11-7 in one-goal games and posted a league-best 32-8-6 mark after the Christmas break.

BILL MASTERTON MEMORIAL TROPHY

An annual award under the trusteeship of the Professional Hockey Writers' Association to "the National Hockey League player who best exemplifies the qualities of perseverance, sportsmanship and dedication to hockey." Winner selected by a poll among the 30 chapters of the PHWA at the end of the regular season. A $2,500 grant from the PHWA is awarded annually to the Bill Masterton Scholarship Fund, based in Bloomington, MN, in the name of the Masterton Trophy winner.

History: The trophy was presented by the NHL Writers' Association in 1968 to commemorate the late Bill Masterton, a player with the Minnesota North Stars, who exhibited to a high degree the qualities of perseverance, sportsmanship and dedication to hockey, and who died January 15, 1968.

2006-07 Winner: **Phil Kessel, Boston Bruins**

Boston Bruins center Phil Kessel is the 2006-2007 recipient of the Bill Masterton Memorial Trophy. In addition to the pressures of breaking into the NHL as a 19-year-old first-round draft pick, Kessel was diagnosed in early December with testicular cancer. He was actually able to maintain his focus well enough to play a December 9 game against New Jersey, knowing he'd be admitted to the hospital for what proved to be successful surgery on December 12, and then missed only 12 games before returning to Boston's lineup. He ranked among the NHL's rookie leaders with 11 goals and 29 points in 70 games in 2006-07, and was number-one among first-year players with four decisive shootout goals.

LESTER PATRICK TROPHY

An annual award "for outstanding service to hockey in the United States." Eligible recipients are players, officials, coaches, executives and referees. Winners are selected by an award committee consisting of the commissioner of the NHL, an NHL governor, a representative of the New York Rangers, a member of the Hockey Hall of Fame builder's section, a member of the Hockey Hall of Fame player's section, a member of the U.S. Hockey Hall of Fame, a member of the NHL Broadcasters' Association and a member of the Professional Hockey Writers' Association. Each except the League Commissioner is rotated annually. The winner receives a miniature of the trophy.

History: Presented by the New York Rangers in 1966 to honor the late Lester Patrick, longtime general manager and coach of the New York Rangers, whose teams finished out of the playoffs only once in his first 16 years with the club.

2006 Winners: **Steve Yzerman**
Red Berenson
Reed Larson
Glen Sonmor
Marcel Dionne

Steve Yzerman's 22-year playing career with the Detroit Red Wings can best be described in one word "excellence". He captained the Red Wings to three Stanley Cups, including back-to-back championships in 1997 and 1998. A 10-time NHL All-Star, Yzerman was a member of the NHL's All-Rookie team in 1984, won the Lester B. Pearson Award honoring the league's outstanding player in 1989, the Conn Smythe as the playoff MVP in 1998, the Frank J. Selke trophy as the league's top defensive forward in 2000 and Bill Masterton Memorial Trophy for his "perseverance, sportsmanship and dedication to hockey" in 2003.

Reed Larson is one of the all-time great players from Minnesota. He starred at Roosevelt High School and went on to capture the WCHA title in 1975 and NCAA title in 1976 with the University of Minnesota under the late Herb Brooks. A steady defenseman, Larson broke into the NHL with the Detroit Red Wings where he was runner up for the Calder Trophy as the league's top rookie. He was the first American-born player to score 200 career goals, recording five 20-goal seasons and eight 60-point campaigns in his 10 seasons with the Red Wings. He was elected to the U.S. Hockey Hall of Fame 1996.

Gordon "Red" Berenson became the first Canadian to enter the NHL straight from U.S. college hockey when he joined the NHL's Montreal Canadiens late in the 1961-62 season. After NHL expansion, Berenson went on to stardom with the St. Louis Blues. The opportunity of a lifetime came for Berenson in 1984 when he took the head coaching position at his alma mater, the University of Michigan. He has led the Wolverines to two NCAA championships, 15 consecutive NCAA tournament appearances, seven CCHA playoff championships and nine CCHA regular-season titles.

Glen Sonmor made his NHL debut with the New York Rangers in 1953. He became head coach of the Minnesota Golden Gophers in 1966 and was named the WCHA coach of the year for the 1969-70 season, and led the Golden Gophers to the WCHA title and NCAA runner-up in 1971. Sonmor left the Gophers in 1971 and took the head coaching position with the St. Paul Fighting Saints of the WHA. He returned to the NHL in 1978 and coached the North Stars, on three different occasions from 1978 to 1987, leading the club to its first Stanley Cup appearance against the New York Islanders in 1981.

Marcel Dionne entered the NHL with the Detroit Red Wings in 1971 as the second pick behind Guy Lafleur in the Amateur draft. By his fourth season, Dionne had emerged as an offensive superstar by scoring 121 points and winning the Lady Byng Trophy. He joined the Los Angeles Kings in 1975 and became the first player in club history to score 50-plus goals (53) and 100-plus points (122) in 1976-77. He posted the highest single-season point total of his career (137) to win the Art Ross Trophy as the leagues scoring champion in 1979-80. He was inducted into the Hockey Hall of Fame in 1992.

King Clancy Memorial Trophy

Presidents' Trophy

Maurice "Rocket" Richard Trophy

Lester B. Pearson Award

KING CLANCY MEMORIAL TROPHY

An annual award "to the player who best exemplifies leadership qualities on and off the ice and has made a noteworthy humanitarian contribution in his community."

History: The King Clancy Memorial Trophy was presented to the National Hockey League by the Board of Governors in 1988 to honor the late Frank "King" Clancy.

2006-07 Winner: Saku Koivu, Montreal Canadiens

Montreal Canadiens captain Saku Koivu's exemplary support of cancer treatment and research, and more particularly his personal demonstration of courage as a cancer survivor, is a source of inspiration and pride to his teammates, all who know him and particularly the many thousands of patients and their families who benefit from his selfless devotion.

After battling and beating non-Hodgkins lymphoma, Koivu went on to create the Saku Koivu Foundation in 2002. Through his personal financial generosity and leadership, the Foundation has raised $2.5 million, leading to the acquisition of the first PET/CT scans in Montreal. This advanced technology has proved invaluable in the treatment of thousands of cancer patients. In the spring of 2007, he announced that the Foundation is committed to raising $750,000 in support of cancer treatment initiatives at Montreal General Hospital.

Apart from monetary donations, Koivu meets patients after practices and games and signs personalized get well cards, inspiring and making wishes come true for children in need.

Having completed his seventh season as team captain, Koivu is the fourth-longest serving captain in franchise history, trailing only the legendary Jean Beliveau, Émile Bouchard and Bob Gainey. He also is longest tenured player on the Canadiens and led the club in assists (53) and points (75) this season.

MAURICE "ROCKET" RICHARD TROPHY

An annual award "presented to the player finishing the regular season as the League's goal-scoring leader."

History: A gift to the NHL from the Montreal Canadiens in 1999, the Maurice "Rocket" Richard Trophy honors one of the game's greatest stars. During his 18-year career with the Canadiens from 1942-43 through 1959-60, Richard was the first player in NHL history to score 50 goals in a season and 500 in his career. He played on eight Stanley Cup champions and led the League in goal scoring five times.

2006-07 Winner: Vincent Lecavalier, Tampa Bay Lightning
Runners-up: Dany Heatley, Ottawa Senators
Teemu Selanne, Anaheim Ducks

Center Vincent Lecavalier of the Tampa Bay Lightning tallied a club-record 52 goals to capture his first career Richard Trophy. Lecavalier, whose previous career high was 35 goals in 2005-06, also tied the franchise mark for power-play goals (16) and game-winners (seven). Scoring goals in bunches, the first overall pick in the 1998 Entry Draft registered a six-game goal-scoring streak from October 21 to November 2, tied for the longest in the NHL this season, and recorded two other five-game streaks.

Dany Heatley of the Ottawa Senators finished second in the NHL with 50 goals and became the first player with back-to-back 50-goal seasons since Pavel Bure in 1999-2000 and 2000-01. Teemu Selanne finished third with 48 goals and became the oldest player in NHL history with back-to-back 40-goal seasons.

PRESIDENTS' TROPHY

An annual award to the club finishing the regular-season with the best overall record.

History: Presented to the National Hockey League in 1985-86 by the NHL Board of Governors to recognize the team compiling the top regular-season record.

2006-07 Winner: Buffalo Sabres
Runners-up: Detroit Red Wings
Anaheim Ducks

The Buffalo Sabres captured the President's Trophy for the first time in franchise history, setting a franchise record with 53 wins in a season (53-22-7) and tying the franchise record for points in a season by matching the 113 in 1974-75. The Sabres were also the NHL's highest-scoring team with 308 goals. They also topped the Eastern Conference for the first time in franchise history and won their first Northeast Division title since 1996-97. Detroit won the Central Division for the fifth season in a row and tied the Sabres with 113 points, but had only 50 victories (50-19-13). The Anaheim Ducks won their first Pacific Division title with a record of 48-20-14 and 110 points.

LESTER B. PEARSON AWARD

The Lester B. Pearson Award is presented annually to the "most outstanding player" in the NHL as voted by fellow members of the National Hockey League Players' Association. The winner receives $20,000, and the two finalists receive $10,000 each to donate to the grassroots hockey program of their choice, through the NHLPA's Goals & Dreams Fund.

History: The award was first presented in 1970-71 by the NHLPA in honor of the late Lester B. Pearson, former Prime Minister of Canada.

2006-07 Winner: Sidney Crosby, Pittsburgh Penguins
Runners-up: Vincent Lecavalier, Tampa Bay Lightning
Roberto Luongo, Vancouver Canucks

Sidney Crosby of the Pittsburgh Penguins was selected as the recipient of the 2006-07 Lester B. Pearson Award. Crosby appeared in 79 games for the Pittsburgh Penguins, securing the NHL's top spot for points (120), power-play assists (48) and power-play points (61). In only his second season, the 19-year-old become the youngest player to ever post back-to-back 100 point seasons, and secured the Penguins their first playoff appearance since 2001. Crosby, who became the first teenager to win a major professional scoring title, becomes the youngest player to win the Lester B. Pearson Award, surpassing a 21-year-old Wayne Gretzky in 1981-82. Crosby also represents the Penguins' third Pearson recipient (Mario Lemieux, Jaromir Jagr), which ties them with the New York Rangers (Jean Ratelle, Mark Messier, Jagr) as the only two clubs to have three players win the Pearson in their respective jerseys.

2006-07 NHL Player of the Week/Month Award Winners

Player of the Week/Month

Period Ending	First Star	Second Star	Third Star
Oct. 15	**Marty Turco**, DAL	**Martin Havlat**, CHI	**Mats Sundin**, TOR
Oct. 22	**Maxim Afinogenov**, BUF	**J.S. Giguere**, ANA	**Sheldon Souray**, MTL
Oct. 29	**Ilya Kovalchuk**, ATL	**Martin Brodeur**, N.J.	**Evgeni Malkin**, PIT
October	**Ryan Miller**, BUF	**Ilya Kovalchuk**, ATL	**Scott Niedermayer**, ANA
Nov. 5	**Marc Savard**, BOS	**Andrew Raycroft**, TOR	**Brendan Shanahan**, NYR
Nov. 12	**Slava Kozlov**, ATL	**Miikka Kiprusoff**, CGY	**Dominik Hasek**, DET
Nov. 19	**Alexander Frolov**, L.A.	**Rod Brind'Amour**, CAR	**Tim Thomas**, BOS
Nov. 26	**Martin St. Louis**, T.B.	**Teemu Selanne**, ANA	**Mike Smith**, DAL
November	**Teemu Selanne**, ANA	**Marian Hossa**, ATL	**Cristobal Huet**, MTL
Dec. 3	**Viktor Kozlov**, NYI	**Nikolai Khabibulin**, CHI	**Marian Hossa**, ATL
Dec. 10	**Martin Brodeur**, N.J.	**Vincent Lecavalier**, T.B.	**Alex Ovechkin**, WSH
Dec. 17	**Sidney Crosby**, PIT	**Chris Mason**, NSH	**Jarome Iginla**, CGY
Dec. 24	**Tim Thomas**, BOS	**Manny Legace**, STL	**Vincent Lecavalier**, T.B.
Dec. 31	**Ray Emery**, OTT	**Alexander Frolov**, L.A.	**Daniel Sedin**, VAN
December	**Jarome Iginla**, CGY	**Dominik Hasek**, DET	**Sidney Crosby**, PIT
Jan. 7	**Roberto Luongo**, VAN	**Dany Heatley**, OTT	**Joe Thornton**, S.J.
Jan. 14	**Daniel Alfredsson**, OTT	**Miikka Kiprusoff**, CGY	Olli Jokinen, FLA
Jan. 21	**David Legwand**, NSH	**Marty Turco**, DAL	**Evgeni Malkin**, PIT
Jan. 28	**Mark Recchi**, PIT	**Fredrik Norrena**, CBJ	**Ryan Smyth**, EDM
January	**Dany Heatley**, OTT	**Sidney Crosby**, PIT	**Roberto Luongo**, VAN
Feb. 4	**Andrew Raycroft**, TOR	**Jamie Langenbrunner**, N.J.	**Nicklas Lidstrom**, DET
Feb. 11	**Henrik Zetterberg**, DET	**Martin Havlat**, CHI	**Mike Smith**, DAL
Feb. 18	**Henrik Zetterberg**, DET	**Teemu Selanne**, ANA	**Joe Sakic**, COL
Feb. 25	**Niklas Backstrom**, MIN	**Marc Savard**, BOS	**Brad Richards**, T.B.
February	**Henrik Zetterberg**, DET	**Rick DiPietro**, NYI	**Martin Brodeur**, N.J.
Mar. 4	**Kari Lehtonen**, ATL	Olli Jokinen, FLA	Peter Budaj, COL
Mar. 11	**Henrik Lundqvist**, NYR	**Jeff Hamilton**, CHI	**Evgeni Nabokov**, S.J.
Mar. 18	**Joe Thornton**, S.J.	**Joe Sakic**, COL	**Mike Modano**, DAL
Mar. 25	**Henrik Lundqvist**, NYR	**Jonathan Cheechoo**, S.J.	**Jaroslav Halak**, MTL
March	**Peter Budaj**, COL	**Joe Thornton**, S.J.	**Vincent Lecavalier**, T.B.
Apr. 1	**Miikka Kiprusoff**, CGY	**Olli Jokinen**, FLA	**Dominik Hasek**, DET
Apr. 8	**Wade Dubielewicz**, NYI	**Joe Sakic**, COL	**Niklas Backstrom**, MIN

Rookie of the Month

Month	Player
October	**Evgeni Malkin**, Pittsburgh
November	**Evgeni Malkin**, Pittsburgh
December	**Wojtek Wolski**, Colorado
January	**Ryane Clowe**, San Jose
February	**Paul Stastny**, Colorado
March	**Drew Stafford**, Buffalo

The NHL revamped its Player of the Week and Player of the Month awards in 2006-07, replacing separate offensive and defensive winners with three stars instead. Ottawa's Ray Emery (left) was honored as the First Star for the week ending December 31. Emery had three wins and a 0.66 goals-against average with two shutouts that week. Chicago's Martin Havlat (middle) was a Second Star for the week ending February 11. He had five goals and three assists to lead the Blackhawks to three wins in four road games. Atlanta's Marian Hossa (right) was Third Star for the week ending December 3 after enjoying back-to-back four-point games.

NATIONAL HOCKEY LEAGUE INDIVIDUAL AWARD WINNERS

ART ROSS TROPHY

	Winner	Runner-up
2007	Sidney Crosby, Pit.	Joe Thornton, S.J.
2006	Joe Thornton, Bos., S.J.	Jaromir Jagr, NYR
2005	....	....
2004	Martin St. Louis, T.B.	Ilya Kovalchuk, Atl.
2003	Peter Forsberg, Col.	Markus Naslund, Van.
2002	Jarome Iginla, Cgy.	Markus Naslund, Van.
2001	Jaromir Jagr, Pit.	Joe Sakic, Col.
2000	Jaromir Jagr, Pit.	Pavel Bure, Fla.
1999	Jaromir Jagr, Pit.	Teemu Selanne, Ana.
1998	Jaromir Jagr, Pit.	Peter Forsberg, Col.
1997	Mario Lemieux, Pit.	Teemu Selanne, Ana.
1996	Mario Lemieux, Pit.	Jaromir Jagr, Pit.
1995	Jaromir Jagr, Pit.	Eric Lindros, Phi.
1994	Wayne Gretzky, L.A.	Sergei Fedorov, Det.
1993	Mario Lemieux, Pit.	Pat LaFontaine, Buf.
1992	Mario Lemieux, Pit.	Kevin Stevens, Pit.
1991	Wayne Gretzky, L.A.	Brett Hull, St.L.
1990	Wayne Gretzky, L.A.	Mark Messier, Edm.
1989	Mario Lemieux, Pit.	Wayne Gretzky, L.A.
1988	Mario Lemieux, Pit.	Wayne Gretzky, Edm.
1987	Wayne Gretzky, Edm.	Jari Kurri, Edm.
1986	Wayne Gretzky, Edm.	Mario Lemieux, Pit.
1985	Wayne Gretzky, Edm.	Jari Kurri, Edm.
1984	Wayne Gretzky, Edm.	Paul Coffey, Edm.
1983	Wayne Gretzky, Edm.	Peter Stastny, Que.
1982	Wayne Gretzky, Edm.	Mike Bossy, NYI
1981	Wayne Gretzky, Edm.	Marcel Dionne, L.A.
1980	Marcel Dionne, L.A.	Wayne Gretzky, Edm.
1979	Bryan Trottier, NYI	Marcel Dionne, L.A.
1978	Guy Lafleur, Mtl.	Bryan Trottier, NYI
1977	Guy Lafleur, Mtl.	Marcel Dionne, L.A.
1976	Guy Lafleur, Mtl.	Bobby Clarke, Phi.
1975	Bobby Orr, Bos.	Phil Esposito, Bos.
1974	Phil Esposito, Bos.	Bobby Orr, Bos.
1973	Phil Esposito, Bos.	Bobby Clarke, Phi.
1972	Phil Esposito, Bos.	Bobby Orr, Bos.
1971	Phil Esposito, Bos.	Bobby Orr, Bos.
1970	Bobby Orr, Bos.	Phil Esposito, Bos.
1969	Phil Esposito, Bos.	Bobby Hull, Chi.
1968	Stan Mikita, Chi.	Phil Esposito, Bos.
1967	Stan Mikita, Chi.	Bobby Hull, Chi.
1966	Bobby Hull, Chi.	Stan Mikita, Chi.
1965	Stan Mikita, Chi.	Norm Ullman, Det.
1964	Stan Mikita, Chi.	Bobby Hull, Chi.
1963	Gordie Howe, Det.	Andy Bathgate, NYR
1962	Bobby Hull, Chi.	Andy Bathgate, NYR
1961	Bernie Geoffrion, Mtl.	Jean Beliveau, Mtl.
1960	Bobby Hull, Chi.	Bronco Horvath, Bos.
1959	Dickie Moore, Mtl.	Jean Beliveau, Mtl.
1958	Dickie Moore, Mtl.	Henri Richard, Mtl.
1957	Gordie Howe, Det.	Ted Lindsay, Det.
1956	Jean Beliveau, Mtl.	Gordie Howe, Det.
1955	Bernie Geoffrion, Mtl.	Maurice Richard, Mtl.
1954	Gordie Howe, Det.	Maurice Richard, Mtl.
1953	Gordie Howe, Det.	Ted Lindsay, Det.
1952	Gordie Howe, Det.	Ted Lindsay, Det.
1951	Gordie Howe, Det.	Maurice Richard, Mtl.
1950	Ted Lindsay, Det.	Sid Abel, Det.
1949	Roy Conacher, Chi.	Doug Bentley, Chi.
1948*	Elmer Lach, Mtl.	Buddy O'Connor, NYR
1947	Max Bentley, Chi.	Maurice Richard, Mtl.
1946	Max Bentley, Chi.	Gaye Stewart, Tor.
1945	Elmer Lach, Mtl.	Maurice Richard, Mtl.
1944	Herb Cain, Bos.	Doug Bentley, Chi.
1943	Doug Bentley, Chi.	Bill Cowley, Bos.
1942	Bryan Hextall, NYR	Lynn Patrick, NYR
1941	Bill Cowley, Bos.	Bryan Hextall, NYR
1940	Milt Schmidt, Bos.	Woody Dumart, Bos.
1939	Toe Blake, Mtl.	Sweeney Schriner, NYA
1938	Gordie Drillon, Tor.	Syl Apps, Tor.
1937	Sweeney Schriner, NYA	Syl Apps, Tor.
1936	Sweeney Schriner, NYA	Marty Barry, Det.
1935	Charlie Conacher, Tor.	Syd Howe, St.L., Det.
1934	Charlie Conacher, Tor.	Joe Primeau, Tor
1933	Bill Cook, NYR	Busher Jackson, Tor.
1932	Busher Jackson, Tor.	Joe Primeau, Tor.
1931	Howie Morenz, Mtl.	Ebbie Goodfellow, Det.
1930	Cooney Weiland, Bos.	Frank Boucher, NYR
1929	Ace Bailey, Tor.	Nels Stewart, Mtl.M
1928	Howie Morenz, Mtl.	Aurel Joliat, Mtl.
1927	Bill Cook, NYR	Dick Irvin, Chi.
1926	Nels Stewart, Mtl.M.	Cy Denneny, Ott.
1925	Babe Dye, Tor.	Cy Denneny, Ott.
1924	Cy Denneny, Ott.	Billy Boucher, Mtl.
1923	Babe Dye, Tor.	Cy Denneny, Ott.
1922	Punch Broadbent, Ott.	Cy Denneny, Ott.
1921	Newsy Lalonde, Mtl.	Babe Dye, Ham., Tor.
1920	Joe Malone, Que.	Newsy Lalonde, Mtl.
1919	Newsy Lalonde, Mtl.	Odie Cleghorn, Mtl.
1918	Joe Malone, Mtl.	Cy Denneny, Ott.

* Trophy first awarded in 1948.
Scoring leaders listed from 1918 to 1947.

HART MEMORIAL TROPHY

	Winner	Runner-up
2007	Sidney Crosby, Pit.	Roberto Luongo, Van.
2006	Joe Thornton, Bos., S.J.	Jaromir Jagr, NYR
2005	....	....
2004	Martin St. Louis, T.B.	Jarome Iginla, Cgy.
2003	Peter Forsberg, Col.	Markus Naslund, Van.
2002	Jose Theodore, Mtl.	Jarome Iginla, Cgy.
2001	Joe Sakic, Col.	Mario Lemieux, Pit.
2000	Chris Pronger, St.L.	Jaromir Jagr, Pit.
1999	Jaromir Jagr, Pit.	Alexei Yashin, Ott.
1998	Dominik Hasek, Buf.	Jaromir Jagr, Pit.
1997	Dominik Hasek, Buf.	Paul Kariya, Ana.
1996	Mario Lemieux, Pit.	Mark Messier, NYR
1995	Eric Lindros, Phi.	Jaromir Jagr, Pit.
1994	Sergei Fedorov, Det.	Dominik Hasek, Buf.
1993	Mario Lemieux, Pit.	Doug Gilmour, Tor.
1992	Mark Messier, NYR	Patrick Roy, Mtl.
1991	Brett Hull, St.L.	Wayne Gretzky, L.A.
1990	Mark Messier, Edm.	Raymond Bourque, Bos.
1989	Wayne Gretzky, L.A.	Mario Lemieux, Pit.
1988	Mario Lemieux, Pit.	Grant Fuhr, Edm.
1987	Wayne Gretzky, Edm.	Raymond Bourque, Bos.
1986	Wayne Gretzky, Edm.	Mario Lemieux, Pit.
1985	Wayne Gretzky, Edm.	Dale Hawerchuk, Wpg.
1984	Wayne Gretzky, Edm.	Rod Langway, Wsh.
1983	Wayne Gretzky, Edm.	Pete Peeters, Bos.
1982	Wayne Gretzky, Edm.	Bryan Trottier, NYI
1981	Wayne Gretzky, Edm.	Mike Liut, St.L.
1980	Wayne Gretzky, Edm.	Marcel Dionne, L.A.
1979	Bryan Trottier, NYI	Guy Lafleur, Mtl
1978	Guy Lafleur, Mtl.	Bryan Trottier, NYI
1977	Guy Lafleur, Mtl.	Bobby Clarke, Phi.
1976	Bobby Clarke, Phi.	Denis Potvin, NYI
1975	Bobby Clarke, Phi.	Rogie Vachon, L.A.
1974	Phil Esposito, Bos.	Bernie Parent, Phi.
1973	Bobby Clarke, Phi.	Phil Esposito, Bos.
1972	Bobby Orr, Bos.	Ken Dryden, Mtl.
1971	Bobby Orr, Bos.	Phil Esposito, Bos.
1970	Bobby Orr, Bos.	Tony Esposito, Chi.
1969	Phil Esposito, Bos.	Jean Beliveau, Mtl.
1968	Stan Mikita, Chi.	Jean Beliveau, Mtl.
1967	Stan Mikita, Chi.	Ed Giacomin, NYR
1966	Bobby Hull, Chi.	Jean Beliveau, Mtl.
1965	Bobby Hull, Chi.	Norm Ullman, Det.
1964	Jean Beliveau, Mtl.	Bobby Hull, Chi.
1963	Gordie Howe, Det.	Stan Mikita, Chi.
1962	Jacques Plante, Mtl.	Doug Harvey, NYR
1961	Bernie Geoffrion, Mtl.	Johnny Bower, Tor.
1960	Gordie Howe, Det.	Bobby Hull, Chi.
1959	Andy Bathgate, NYR	Gordie Howe, Det.
1958	Gordie Howe, Det.	Andy Bathgate, NYR
1957	Gordie Howe, Det.	Jean Beliveau, Mtl.
1956	Jean Beliveau, Mtl.	Tod Sloan, Tor.
1955	Ted Kennedy, Tor.	Harry Lumley, Tor.
1954	Al Rollins, Chi.	Red Kelly, Det.
1953	Gordie Howe, Det.	Al Rollins, Chi.
1952	Gordie Howe, Det.	Elmer Lach, Mtl.
1951	Milt Schmidt, Bos.	Maurice Richard, Mtl.
1950	Chuck Rayner, NYR	Ted Kennedy, Tor.
1949	Sid Abel, Det.	Bill Durnan, Mtl.
1948	Buddy O'Connor, NYR	Frank Brimsek, Bos.
1947	Maurice Richard, Mtl.	Milt Schmidt, Bos.
1946	Max Bentley, Chi.	Gaye Stewart, Tor.
1945	Elmer Lach, Mtl.	Maurice Richard, Mtl.
1944	Babe Pratt, Tor.	Bill Cowley, Bos.
1943	Bill Cowley, Bos.	Doug Bentley, Chi.
1942	Tom Anderson, Bro.	Syl Apps, Tor.
1941	Bill Cowley, Bos.	Dit Clapper, Bos.
1940	Ebbie Goodfellow, Det.	Syl Apps, Tor.
1939	Toe Blake, Mtl.	Syl Apps, Tor.
1938	Eddie Shore, Bos.	Paul Thompson, Chi.
1937	Babe Siebert, Mtl.	Lionel Conacher, Mtl.M
1936	Eddie Shore, Bos.	Hooley Smith, Mtl.M
1935	Eddie Shore, Bos.	Charlie Conacher, Tor.
1934	Aurel Joliat, Mtl.	Lionel Conacher, Chi.
1933	Eddie Shore, Bos.	Bill Cook, NYR
1932	Howie Morenz, Mtl.	Ching Johnson, NYR
1931	Howie Morenz, Mtl.	Eddie Shore, Bos.
1930	Nels Stewart, Mtl.M.	Lionel Hitchman, Bos.
1929	Roy Worters, NYA	Ace Bailey, Tor.
1928	Howie Morenz, Mtl.	Roy Worters, Pit.
1927	Herb Gardiner, Mtl.	Bill Cook, NYR
1926	Nels Stewart, Mtl.M.	Sprague Cleghorn, Bos.
1925	Billy Burch, Ham.	Howie Morenz, Mtl.
1924	Frank Nighbor, Ott.	Sprague Cleghorn, Mtl.

MAURICE "ROCKET" RICHARD TROPHY

2007	Vincent Lecavalier	Tampa Bay
2006	Jonathan Cheechoo	San Jose
2005	....	....
2004	Rick Nash	Columbus
	Jarome Iginla	Calgary
	Ilya Kovalchuk	Atlanta
2003	Milan Hejduk	Colorado
2002	Jarome Iginla	Calgary
2001	Pavel Bure	Florida
2000	Pavel Bure	Florida
1999	Teemu Selanne	Anaheim

WILLIAM M. JENNINGS TROPHY

	Winner	Runner-up
2007	Niklas Backstrom, Min.	Marty Turco, Dal.
	Manny Fernandez, Min.	
2006	Miikka Kiprusoff, Cgy.	Manny Legace, Det.
		Chris Osgood, Det.
2005	....	....
2004	Martin Brodeur, N.J.	Marty Turco, Dal.
2003	Martin Brodeur, N.J.	Marty Turco, Dal.
	Roman Cechmanek, Phi.	Ron Tugnutt, Dal.
	Robert Esche, Phi.	
2002	Patrick Roy, Col.	Tommy Salo, Edm.
2001	Dominik Hasek, Buf.	Ed Belfour, Dal.
		Marty Turco, Dal.
2000	Roman Turek, St.L.	John Vanbiesbrouck, Phi.
		Brian Boucher, Phi.
1999	Ed Belfour, Dal.	Dominik Hasek, Buf.
	Roman Turek, Dal.	
1998	Martin Brodeur, N.J.	Ed Belfour, Dal.
1997	Martin Brodeur, N.J.	Chris Osgood, Det.
	Mike Dunham, N.J.	Mike Vernon, Det.
1996	Chris Osgood, Det.	Martin Brodeur, N.J.
	Mike Vernon, Det.	
1995	Ed Belfour, Chi.	Mike Vernon, Det.
		Chris Osgood, Det.
1994	Dominik Hasek, Buf.	Martin Brodeur, N.J.
	Grant Fuhr, Buf.	Chris Terreri, N.J.
1993	Ed Belfour, Chi.	Felix Potvin, Tor.
		Grant Fuhr, Tor.
1992	Patrick Roy, Mtl.	Ed Belfour, Chi.
1991	Ed Belfour, Chi.	Patrick Roy, Mtl.
1990	Andy Moog, Bos.	Patrick Roy, Mtl.
	Reggie Lemelin, Bos.	Brian Hayward, Mtl.
1989	Patrick Roy, Mtl.	Mike Vernon, Cgy.
	Brian Hayward, Mtl.	Rick Wamsley, Cgy.
1988	Patrick Roy, Mtl.	Clint Malarchuk, Wsh.
	Brian Hayward, Mtl.	Pete Peeters, Wsh.
1987	Patrick Roy, Mtl.	Ron Hextall, Phi.
	Brian Hayward, Mtl.	
1986	Bob Froese, Phi.	Al Jensen, Wsh.
	Darren Jensen, Phi.	Pete Peeters, Wsh.
1985	Tom Barrasso, Buf.	Pat Riggin, Wsh.
	Bob Sauve, Buf.	
1984	Al Jensen, Wsh.	Tom Barrasso, Buf.
	Pat Riggin, Wsh.	Bob Sauve, Buf.
1983	Roland Melanson, NYI	Pete Peeters, Bos.
	Billy Smith, NYI	
1982	Rick Wamsley, Mtl.	Billy Smith, NYI
	Denis Herron, Mtl.	Roland Melanson, NYI

BILL MASTERTON MEMORIAL TROPHY

2007	Phil Kessel	Boston
2006	Teemu Selanne	Anaheim
2005	....	....
2004	Bryan Berard	Chicago
2003	Steve Yzerman	Detroit
2002	Saku Koivu	Montreal
2001	Adam Graves	NY Rangers
2000	Ken Daneyko	New Jersey
1999	John Cullen	Tampa Bay
1998	Jamie McLennan	St. Louis
1997	Tony Granato	San Jose
1996	Gary Roberts	Calgary
1995	Pat LaFontaine	Buffalo
1994	Cam Neely	Boston
1993	Mario Lemieux	Pittsburgh
1992	Mark Fitzpatrick	NY Islanders
1991	Dave Taylor	Los Angeles
1990	Gord Kluzak	Boston
1989	Tim Kerr	Philadelphia
1988	Bob Bourne	Los Angeles
1987	Doug Jarvis	Hartford
1986	Charlie Simmer	Boston
1985	Anders Hedberg	NY Rangers
1984	Brad Park	Detroit
1983	Lanny McDonald	Calgary
1982	Glenn Resch	Colorado
1981	Blake Dunlop	St. Louis
1980	Al MacAdam	Minnesota
1979	Serge Savard	Montreal
1978	Butch Goring	Los Angeles
1977	Ed Westfall	NY Islanders
1976	Rod Gilbert	NY Rangers
1975	Don Luce	Buffalo
1974	Henri Richard	Montreal
1973	Lowell MacDonald	Pittsburgh
1972	Bobby Clarke	Philadelphia
1971	Jean Ratelle	NY Rangers
1970	Pit Martin	Chicago
1969	Ted Hampson	Oakland
1968	Claude Provost	Montreal

LADY BYNG MEMORIAL TROPHY

	Winner	Runner-up
2007	Pavel Datsyuk, Det.	Martin St. Louis, T.B.
2006	Pavel Datsyuk, Det.	Brad Richards, T.B.
2005	....	....
2004	Brad Richards, T.B.	Daniel Alfredsson, Ott.
2003	Alexander Mogilny, Tor.	Nicklas Lidstrom, Det.
2002	Ron Francis, Car.	Joe Sakic, Col.
2001	Joe Sakic, Col.	Nicklas Lidstrom, Det.
2000	Pavol Demitra, St.L.	Nicklas Lidstrom, Det.
1999	Wayne Gretzky, NYR.	Nicklas Lidstrom, Det.
1998	Ron Francis, Pit.	Teemu Selanne, Ana.
1997	Paul Kariya, Ana.	Teemu Selanne, Ana.
1996	Paul Kariya, Ana.	Adam Oates, Bos.
1995	Ron Francis, Pit.	Adam Oates, Bos.
1994	Wayne Gretzky, L.A.	Adam Oates, Bos.
1993	Pierre Turgeon, NYI	Adam Oates, Bos.
1992	Wayne Gretzky, L.A.	Joe Sakic, Que.
1991	Wayne Gretzky, L.A.	Brett Hull, St.L.
1990	Brett Hull, St.L.	Wayne Gretzky, L.A.
1989	Joe Mullen, Cgy.	Wayne Gretzky, L.A.
1988	Mats Naslund, Mtl.	Wayne Gretzky, Edm.
1987	Joe Mullen, Cgy.	Wayne Gretzky, Edm.
1986	Mike Bossy, NYI	Jari Kurri, Edm.
1985	Jari Kurri, Edm.	Joe Mullen, St.L.
1984	Mike Bossy, NYI	Rick Middleton, Bos.
1983	Mike Bossy, NYI	Rick Middleton, Bos.
1982	Rick Middleton, Bos.	Mike Bossy, NYI
1981	Rick Kehoe, Pit.	Wayne Gretzky, Edm.
1980	Wayne Gretzky, Edm.	Marcel Dionne, L.A.
1979	Bob MacMillan, Atl.	Marcel Dionne, L.A.
1978	Butch Goring, L.A.	Peter McNab, Bos.
1977	Marcel Dionne, L.A.	Jean Ratelle, Bos.
1976	Jean Ratelle, NYR-Bos.	Jean Pronovost, Pit.
1975	Marcel Dionne, Det.	John Bucyk, Bos.
1974	John Bucyk, Bos.	Lowell MacDonald, Pit.
1973	Gilbert Perreault, Buf.	Jean Ratelle, NYR
1972	Jean Ratelle, NYR	John Bucyk, Bos.
1971	John Bucyk, Bos.	Dave Keon, Tor.
1970	Phil Goyette, St.L.	John Bucyk, Bos.
1969	Alex Delvecchio, Det.	Ted Hampson, Oak.
1968	Stan Mikita, Chi.	John Bucyk, Bos.
1967	Stan Mikita, Chi.	Dave Keon, Tor.
1966	Alex Delvecchio, Det.	Bobby Rousseau, Mtl.
1965	Bobby Hull, Chi.	Alex Delvecchio, Det.
1964	Kenny Wharram, Chi.	Dave Keon, Tor.
1963	Dave Keon, Tor.	Camille Henry, NYR
1962	Dave Keon, Tor.	Claude Provost, Mtl.
1961	Red Kelly, Tor.	Norm Ullman, Det.
1960	Don McKenney, Bos.	Andy Hebenton, NYR
1959	Alex Delvecchio, Det.	Andy Hebenton, NYR
1958	Camille Henry, NYR	Don Marshall, Mtl.
1957	Andy Hebenton, NYR	Dutch Reibel, Det.
1956	Dutch Reibel, Det.	Floyd Curry, Mtl.
1955	Sid Smith, Tor.	Danny Lewicki, NYR
1954	Red Kelly, Det.	Don Raleigh, NYR
1953	Red Kelly, Det.	Wally Hergesheimer, NYR
1952	Sid Smith, Tor.	Red Kelly, Det.
1951	Red Kelly, Det.	Woody Dumart, Bos.
1950	Edgar Laprade, NYR	Red Kelly, Det.
1949	Bill Quackenbush, Det.	Harry Watson, Tor.
1948	Buddy O'Connor, NYR	Syl Apps, Tor.
1947	Bobby Bauer, Bos.	Syl Apps, Tor.
1946	Toe Blake, Mtl.	Clint Smith, Chi.
1945	Bill Mosienko, Chi.	Syd Howe, Det.
1944	Clint Smith, Chi.	Herb Cain, Bos.
1943	Max Bentley, Chi.	Buddy O'Connor, Mtl.
1942	Syl Apps, Tor.	Gordie Drillon, Tor.
1941	Bobby Bauer, Bos.	Gordie Drillon, Tor.
1940	Bobby Bauer, Bos.	Clint Smith, NYR
1939	Clint Smith, NYR	Marty Barry, Det.
1938	Gordie Drillon, Tor.	Clint Smith, NYR
1937	Marty Barry, Det.	Gordie Drillon, Tor.
1936	Doc Romnes, Chi.	Sweeney Schriner, NYA
1935	Frank Boucher, NYR	Russ Blinco, Mtl.M
1934	Frank Boucher, NYR	Joe Primeau, Tor.
1933	Frank Boucher, NYR	Joe Primeau, Tor.
1932	Joe Primeau, Tor.	Frank Boucher, NYR
1931	Frank Boucher, NYR	Normie Himes, NYA
1930	Frank Boucher, NYR	Normie Himes, NYA
1929	Frank Boucher, NYR	Harold Darragh, Pit.
1928	Frank Boucher, NYR	George Hay, Det.
1927	Billy Burch, NYA	Dick Irvin, Chi.
1926	Frank Nighbor, Ott.	Billy Burch, NYA
1925	Frank Nighbor, Ott.	none

KING CLANCY MEMORIAL TROPHY

2007	Saku Koivu	Montreal
2006	Olaf Kolzig	Washington
2005	....	....
2004	Jarome Iginla	Calgary
2003	Brendan Shanahan	Detroit
2002	Ron Francis	Carolina
2001	Shjon Podein	Colorado
2000	Curtis Joseph	Toronto
1999	Rob Ray	Buffalo
1998	Kelly Chase	St. Louis
1997	Trevor Linden	Vancouver
1996	Kris King	Winnipeg
1995	Joe Nieuwendyk	Calgary
1994	Adam Graves	NY Rangers
1993	Dave Poulin	Boston
1992	Raymond Bourque	Boston
1991	Dave Taylor	Los Angeles
1990	Kevin Lowe	Edmonton
1989	Bryan Trottier	NY Islanders
1988	Lanny McDonald	Calgary

VEZINA TROPHY

	Winner	Runner-up
2007	Martin Brodeur, N.J.	Roberto Luongo, Van.
2006	Miikka Kiprusoff, Cgy.	Martin Brodeur, N.J.
2005	....	....
2004	Martin Brodeur, N.J.	Miikka Kiprusoff, Cgy.
2003	Martin Brodeur, N.J.	Marty Turco, Dal.
2002	Jose Theodore, Mtl.	Patrick Roy, Col.
2001	Dominik Hasek, Buf.	Roman Cechmanek, Phi.
2000	Olaf Kolzig, Wsh.	Roman Turek, St.L.
1999	Dominik Hasek, Buf.	Curtis Joseph, Tor.
1998	Dominik Hasek, Buf.	Martin Brodeur, N.J.
1997	Dominik Hasek, Buf.	Martin Brodeur, N.J.
1996	Jim Carey, Wsh.	Chris Osgood, Det.
1995	Dominik Hasek, Buf.	Ed Belfour, Chi.
1994	Dominik Hasek, Buf.	John Vanbiesbrouck, Fla.
1993	Ed Belfour, Chi.	Tom Barrasso, Pit.
1992	Patrick Roy, Mtl.	Kirk McLean, Van.
1991	Ed Belfour, Chi.	Patrick Roy, Mtl.
1990	Patrick Roy, Mtl.	Daren Puppa, Buf.
1989	Patrick Roy, Mtl.	Mike Vernon, Cgy.
1988	Grant Fuhr, Edm.	Tom Barrasso, Buf.
1987	Ron Hextall, Phi.	Mike Liut, Hfd.
1986	John Vanbiesbrouck, NYR	Bob Froese, Phi.
1985	Pelle Lindbergh, Phi.	Tom Barrasso, Buf.
1984	Tom Barrasso, Buf.	Reggie Lemelin, Cgy.
1983	Pete Peeters, Bos.	Roland Melanson, NYI
1982	Billy Smith, NYI	Grant Fuhr, Edm.
1981	Richard Sevigny, Mtl.	Pete Peeters, Phi.
	Denis Herron, Mtl.	Rick St. Croix, Phi.
	Michel Larocque, Mtl.	
1980	Bob Sauve, Buf.	Gerry Cheevers, Bos.
	Don Edwards, Buf.	Gilles Gilbert, Bos.
1979	Ken Dryden, Mtl.	Glenn Resch, NYI
	Michel Larocque, Mtl.	Billy Smith, NYI
1978	Ken Dryden, Mtl.	Bernie Parent, Phi.
	Michel Larocque, Mtl.	Wayne Stephenson, Phi.
1977	Ken Dryden, Mtl.	Glenn Resch, NYI
	Michel Larocque, Mtl.	Billy Smith, NYI
1976	Ken Dryden, Mtl.	Glenn Resch, NYI
		Billy Smith, NYI
1975	Bernie Parent, Phi.	Rogie Vachon, L.A.
		Gary Edwards, L.A.
1974	Bernie Parent, Phi. (tie)	Gilles Gilbert, Bos.
	Tony Esposito, Chi. (tie)	
1973	Ken Dryden, Mtl.	Ed Giacomin, NYR
		Gilles Villemure, NYR
1972	Tony Esposito, Chi.	Cesare Maniago, Min.
	Gary Smith, Chi.	Gump Worsley, Min.
1971	Ed Giacomin, NYR	Tony Esposito, Chi.
	Gilles Villemure, NYR	
1970	Tony Esposito, Chi.	Jacques Plante, St.L.
		Ernie Wakely, St.L.
1969	Jacques Plante, St.L.	Ed Giacomin, NYR
	Glenn Hall, St.L.	
1968	Gump Worsley, Mtl.	Johnny Bower, Tor.
	Rogie Vachon, Mtl.	Bruce Gamble, Tor.
1967	Glenn Hall, Chi.	Charlie Hodge, Mtl.
	Denis DeJordy, Chi.	
1966	Gump Worsley, Mtl.	Glenn Hall, Chi.
	Charlie Hodge, Mtl.	
1965	Terry Sawchuk, Tor.	Roger Crozier, Det.
	Johnny Bower, Tor.	
1964	Charlie Hodge, Mtl.	Glenn Hall, Chi.
1963	Glenn Hall, Chi.	Johnny Bower, Tor.
		Don Simmons, Tor.
1962	Jacques Plante, Mtl.	Johnny Bower, Tor.
1961	Johnny Bower, Tor.	Glenn Hall, Chi.
1960	Jacques Plante, Mtl.	Glenn Hall, Chi.
1959	Jacques Plante, Mtl.	Johnny Bower, Tor.
		Ed Chadwick, Tor.
1958	Jacques Plante, Mtl.	Gump Worsley, NYR
		Marcel Paille, NYR
1957	Jacques Plante, Mtl.	Glenn Hall, Det.
1956	Jacques Plante, Mtl.	Glenn Hall, Det.
1955	Terry Sawchuk, Det.	Harry Lumley, Tor.
1954	Harry Lumley, Tor.	Terry Sawchuk, Det.
1953	Terry Sawchuk, Det.	Gerry McNeil, Mtl.
1952	Terry Sawchuk, Det.	Al Rollins, Tor.
1951	Al Rollins, Tor.	Terry Sawchuk, Det.
1950	Bill Durnan, Mtl.	Harry Lumley, Det.
1949	Bill Durnan, Mtl.	Harry Lumley, Det.
1948	Turk Broda, Tor.	Harry Lumley, Det.
1947	Bill Durnan, Mtl.	Turk Broda, Tor.
1946	Bill Durnan, Mtl.	Frank Brimsek, Bos.
1945	Bill Durnan, Mtl.	Frank McCool, Tor. (tie)
		Harry Lumley, Det. (tie)
1944	Bill Durnan, Mtl.	Paul Bibeault, Tor.
1943	Johnny Mowers, Det.	Turk Broda, Tor.
1942	Frank Brimsek, Bos.	Turk Broda, Tor.
1941	Turk Broda, Tor.	Frank Brimsek, Bos. (tie)
		Johnny Mowers, Det. (tie)
1940	Dave Kerr, NYR	Frank Brimsek, Bos.
1939	Frank Brimsek, Bos.	Dave Kerr, NYR
1938	Tiny Thompson, Bos.	Dave Kerr, NYR
1937	Normie Smith, Det.	Dave Kerr, NYR
1936	Tiny Thompson, Bos.	Mike Karakas, Chi.
1935	Lorne Chabot, Chi.	Alex Connell, Mtl.M
1934	Charlie Gardiner, Chi.	Wilf Cude, Det.
1933	Tiny Thompson, Bos.	John Ross Roach, Det.
1932	Charlie Gardiner, Chi.	Alex Connell, Det.
1931	Roy Worters, NYA	Charlie Gardiner, Chi.
1930	Tiny Thompson, Bos.	Charlie Gardiner, Chi.
1929	George Hainsworth, Mtl.	Tiny Thompson, Bos.
1928	George Hainsworth, Mtl.	Alex Connell, Ott.
1927	George Hainsworth, Mtl.	Clint Benedict, Mtl.M

CALDER MEMORIAL TROPHY

	Winner	Runner-up
2007	Evgeni Malkin, Pit.	Paul Stastny, Col.
2006	Alex Ovechkin, Wsh.	Sidney Crosby, Pit.
2005	....	....
2004	Andrew Raycroft, Bos.	Michael Ryder, Mtl.
2003	Barret Jackman, St.L.	Henrik Zetterberg, Det.
2002	Dany Heatley, Atl.	Ilya Kovalchuk, Atl.
2001	Evgeni Nabokov, S.J.	Brad Richards, T.B.
2000	Scott Gomez, N.J.	Brad Stuart, S.J.
1999	Chris Drury, Col.	Marian Hossa, Ott.
1998	Sergei Samsonov, Bos.	Mattias Ohlund, Van.
1997	Bryan Berard, NYI	Jarome Iginla, Cgy.
1996	Daniel Alfredsson, Ott.	Eric Daze, Chi.
1995	Peter Forsberg, Que.	Jim Carey, Wsh.
1994	Martin Brodeur, N.J.	Jason Arnott, Edm.
1993	Teemu Selanne, Wpg.	Joe Juneau, Bos.
1992	Pavel Bure, Van.	Nicklas Lidstrom, Det
1991	Ed Belfour, Chi.	Sergei Fedorov, Det.
1990	Sergei Makarov, Cgy.	Mike Modano, Min.
1989	Brian Leetch, NYR	Trevor Linden, Van.
1988	Joe Nieuwendyk, Cgy.	Ray Sheppard, Buf.
1987	Luc Robitaille, L.A.	Ron Hextall, Phi.
1986	Gary Suter, Cgy.	Wendel Clark, Tor.
1985	Mario Lemieux, Pit.	Chris Chelios, Mtl.
1984	Tom Barrasso, Buf.	Steve Yzerman, Det.
1983	Steve Larmer, Chi.	Phil Housley, Buf.
1982	Dale Hawerchuk, Wpg.	Barry Pederson, Bos.
1981	Peter Stastny, Que.	Larry Murphy, L.A.
1980	Raymond Bourque, Bos.	Mike Foligno, Det.
1979	Bobby Smith, Min	Ryan Walter, Wsh.
1978	Mike Bossy, NYI	Barry Beck, Col.
1977	Willi Plett, Atl.	Don Murdoch, NYR
1976	Bryan Trottier, NYI	Glenn Resch, NYI
1975	Eric Vail, Atl.	Pierre Larouche, Pit.
1974	Denis Potvin, NYI	Tom Lysiak, Atl.
1973	Steve Vickers, NYR	Bill Barber, Phi.
1972	Ken Dryden, Mtl.	Rick Martin, Buf.
1971	Gilbert Perreault, Buf.	Jude Drouin, Min.
1970	Tony Esposito, Chi.	Bill Fairbairn, NYR
1969	Danny Grant, Min.	Norm Ferguson, Oak.
1968	Derek Sanderson, Bos.	Jacques Lemaire, Mtl.
1967	Bobby Orr, Bos.	Ed Van Impe, Chi.
1966	Brit Selby, Tor.	Bert Marshall, Det.
1965	Roger Crozier, Det.	Ron Ellis, Tor.
1964	Jacques Laperriere, Mtl.	John Ferguson, Mtl.
1963	Kent Douglas, Tor.	Doug Barkley, Det.
1962	Bobby Rousseau, Mtl.	Cliff Pennington, Bos.
1961	Dave Keon, Tor.	Bob Nevin, Tor.
1960	Bill Hay, Chi.	Murray Oliver, Det.
1959	Ralph Backstrom, Mtl.	Carl Brewer, Tor.
1958	Frank Mahovlich, Tor.	Bobby Hull, Chi.
1957	Larry Regan, Bos.	Ed Chadwick, Tor.
1956	Glenn Hall, Det.	Andy Hebenton, NYR
1955	Ed Litzenberger, Chi.	Don McKenney, Bos.
1954	Camille Henry, NYR	Dutch Reibel, Det.
1953	Gump Worsley, NYR	Gord Hannigan, Tor.
1952	Bernie Geoffrion, Mtl.	Hy Buller, NYR
1951	Terry Sawchuk, Det.	Al Rollins, Tor.
1950	Jack Gelineau, Bos.	Phil Maloney, Bos.
1949	Pentti Lund, NYR	Allan Stanley, NYR
1948	Jim McFadden, Det.	Pete Babando, Bos.
1947	Howie Meeker, Tor.	Jim Conacher, Det.
1946	Edgar Laprade, NYR	George Gee, Chi.
1945	Frank McCool, Tor.	Ken Smith, Bos.
1944	Gus Bodnar, Tor.	Bill Durnan, Mtl.
1943	Gaye Stewart, Tor.	Glen Harmon, Mtl.
1942	Grant Warwick, NYR	Buddy O'Connor, Mtl.
1941	John Quilty, Mtl.	Johnny Mowers, Det.
1940	Kilby MacDonald, NYR	Wally Stanowski, Tor.
1939	Frank Brimsek, Bos.	Roy Conacher, Bos.
1938	Cully Dahlstrom, Chi.	Murph Chamberlain, Tor.
1937	Syl Apps, Tor.	Gordie Drillon, Tor.
1936	Mike Karakas, Chi.	Bucko McDonald, Det.
1935	Sweeney Schriner, NYA	Bert Connelly, NYR
1934	Russ Blinco, Mtl.M.	none
1933	Carl Voss, Det.	none

FRANK J. SELKE TROPHY

	Winner	Runner-up
2007	Rod Brind'Amour, Car.	Samuel Pahlsson, Ana.
2006	Rod Brind'Amour, Car.	Jere Lehtinen, Dal.
2005	....	....
2004	Kris Draper, Det.	John Madden, N.J.
2003	Jere Lehtinen, Dal.	John Madden, N.J.
2002	Michael Peca, NYI	Craig Conroy, Cgy.
2001	John Madden, N.J.	Joe Sakic, Col.
2000	Steve Yzerman, Det.	Michal Handzus, St.L.
1999	Jere Lehtinen, Dal.	Magnus Arvedson, Ott.
1998	Jere Lehtinen, Dal.	Michael Peca, Buf.
1997	Michael Peca, Buf.	Peter Forsberg, Col.
1996	Sergei Fedorov, Det.	Ron Francis, Pit.
1995	Ron Francis, Pit.	Esa Tikkanen, St.L.
1994	Sergei Fedorov, Det.	Doug Gilmour, Tor.
1993	Doug Gilmour, Tor.	Dave Poulin, Bos.
1992	Guy Carbonneau, Mtl.	Sergei Fedorov, Det.
1991	Dirk Graham, Chi.	Esa Tikkanen, Edm.
1990	Rick Meagher, St.L.	Guy Carbonneau, Mtl.
1989	Guy Carbonneau, Mtl.	Esa Tikkanen, Edm.
1988	Guy Carbonneau, Mtl.	Steve Kasper, Bos.
1987	Dave Poulin, Phi.	Guy Carbonneau, Mtl.
1986	Troy Murray, Chi.	Ron Sutter, Phi.
1985	Craig Ramsay, Buf.	Doug Jarvis, Wsh.
1984	Doug Jarvis, Wsh.	Bryan Trottier, NYI
1983	Bobby Clarke, Phi.	Jari Kurri, Edm.
1982	Steve Kasper, Bos.	Bob Gainey, Mtl.
1981	Bob Gainey, Mtl.	Craig Ramsay, Buf.
1980	Bob Gainey, Mtl.	Craig Ramsay, Buf.
1979	Bob Gainey, Mtl.	Don Marcotte, Bos.
1978	Bob Gainey, Mtl.	Craig Ramsay, Buf.

CONN SMYTHE TROPHY

2007	Scott Niedermayer	Anaheim
2006	Cam Ward	Carolina
2005	....	....
2004	Brad Richards	Tampa Bay
2003	Jean-Sebastien Giguere	Anaheim
2002	Nicklas Lidstrom	Detroit
2001	Patrick Roy	Colorado
2000	Scott Stevens	New Jersey
1999	Joe Nieuwendyk	Dallas
1998	Steve Yzerman	Detroit
1997	Mike Vernon	Detroit
1996	Joe Sakic	Colorado
1995	Claude Lemieux	New Jersey
1994	Brian Leetch	NY Rangers
1993	Patrick Roy	Montreal
1992	Mario Lemieux	Pittsburgh
1991	Mario Lemieux	Pittsburgh
1990	Bill Ranford	Edmonton
1989	Al MacInnis	Calgary
1988	Wayne Gretzky	Edmonton
1987	Ron Hextall	Philadelphia
1986	Patrick Roy	Montreal
1985	Wayne Gretzky	Edmonton
1984	Mark Messier	Edmonton
1983	Billy Smith	NY Islanders
1982	Mike Bossy	NY Islanders
1981	Butch Goring	NY Islanders
1980	Bryan Trottier	NY Islanders
1979	Bob Gainey	Montreal
1978	Larry Robinson	Montreal
1977	Guy Lafleur	Montreal
1976	Reggie Leach	Philadelphia
1975	Bernie Parent	Philadelphia
1974	Bernie Parent	Philadelphia
1973	Yvan Cournoyer	Montreal
1972	Bobby Orr	Boston
1971	Ken Dryden	Montreal
1970	Bobby Orr	Boston
1969	Serge Savard	Montreal
1968	Glenn Hall	St. Louis
1967	Dave Keon	Toronto
1966	Roger Crozier	Detroit
1965	Jean Beliveau	Montreal

JAMES NORRIS MEMORIAL TROPHY

	Winner	Runner-up
2007	Nicklas Lidstrom, Det.	Scott Niedermayer, Ana.
2006	Nicklas Lidstrom, Det.	Scott Niedermayer, Ana.
2005	....	....
2004	Scott Niedermayer, N.J.	Zdeno Chara, Ott.
2003	Nicklas Lidstrom, Det.	Al MacInnis, St.L.
2002	Nicklas Lidstrom, Det.	Chris Chelios, Det.
2001	Nicklas Lidstrom, Det.	Raymond Bourque, Col.
2000	Chris Pronger, St.L.	Nicklas Lidstrom, Det.
1999	Al MacInnis, St.L.	Nicklas Lidstrom, Det.
1998	Rob Blake, L.A.	Nicklas Lidstrom, Det.
1997	Brian Leetch, NYR	V. Konstantinov, Det.
1996	Chris Chelios, Chi.	Raymond Bourque, Bos.
1995	Paul Coffey, Det.	Chris Chelios, Chi.
1994	Raymond Bourque, Bos.	Scott Stevens, N.J.
1993	Chris Chelios, Chi.	Raymond Bourque, Bos.
1992	Brian Leetch, NYR	Raymond Bourque, Bos.
1991	Raymond Bourque, Bos.	Al MacInnis, Cgy.
1990	Raymond Bourque, Bos.	Al MacInnis, Cgy.
1989	Chris Chelios, Mtl	Paul Coffey, Pit.
1988	Raymond Bourque, Bos.	Scott Stevens, Wsh.
1987	Raymond Bourque, Bos.	Mark Howe, Phi.
1986	Paul Coffey, Edm.	Mark Howe, Phi.
1985	Paul Coffey, Edm.	Raymond Bourque, Bos.
1984	Rod Langway, Wsh.	Paul Coffey, Edm.
1983	Rod Langway, Wsh.	Mark Howe, Phi.
1982	Doug Wilson, Chi.	Raymond Bourque, Bos.
1981	Randy Carlyle, Pit.	Denis Potvin, NYI
1980	Larry Robinson, Mtl.	Borje Salming, Tor.
1979	Denis Potvin, NYI	Larry Robinson, Mtl.
1978	Denis Potvin, NYI	Brad Park, Bos.
1977	Larry Robinson, Mtl.	Borje Salming, Tor.
1976	Denis Potvin, NYI	Brad Park, NYR-Bos.
1975	Bobby Orr, Bos.	Denis Potvin, NYI
1974	Bobby Orr, Bos.	Brad Park, NYR
1973	Bobby Orr, Bos.	Guy Lapointe, Mtl.
1972	Bobby Orr, Bos.	Brad Park, NYR
1971	Bobby Orr, Bos.	Brad Park, NYR
1970	Bobby Orr, Bos.	Brad Park, NYR
1969	Bobby Orr, Bos.	Tim Horton, Tor.
1968	Bobby Orr, Bos.	J.C. Tremblay, Mtl
1967	Harry Howell, NYR	Pierre Pilote, Chi.
1966	Jacques Laperriere, Mtl.	Pierre Pilote, Chi.
1965	Pierre Pilote, Chi.	Jacques Laperriere, Mtl.
1964	Pierre Pilote, Chi.	Tim Horton, Tor.
1963	Pierre Pilote, Chi.	Carl Brewer, Tor.
1962	Doug Harvey, NYR	Pierre Pilote, Chi.
1961	Doug Harvey, Mtl.	Marcel Pronovost, Det.
1960	Doug Harvey, Mtl.	Allan Stanley, Tor.
1959	Tom Johnson, Mtl.	Bill Gadsby, NYR
1958	Doug Harvey, Mtl.	Bill Gadsby, NYR
1957	Doug Harvey, Mtl.	Red Kelly, Det.
1956	Doug Harvey, Mtl.	Bill Gadsby, NYR
1955	Doug Harvey, Mtl.	Red Kelly, Det.
1954	Red Kelly, Det.	Doug Harvey, Mtl.

LESTER PATRICK TROPHY

2007	To be announced	
2006	Red Berenson Reed Larson Steve Yzerman	Marcel Dionne Glen Sonmor
2005	....	
2004	John Davidson Ray Miron	Mike Emrick
2003	Raymond Bourque Willie O'Ree	Ron DeGregorio
2002	Herb Brooks 1960 U.S. Olympic Team	Larry Pleau
2001	Gary Bettman David Poile	Scotty Bowman
2000	Mario Lemieux Lou Vairo	Craig Patrick
1999	Harry Sinden	
1998	U.S. Olympic Women's Team	
1998	Neal Broten John Mayasich	Peter Karmanos Max McNab
1997	Bill Cleary Pat LaFontaine	* Seymour H. Knox III
1996	George Gund Milt Schmidt	Ken Morrow
1995	Bob Fleming Joe Mullen	Brian Mullen
1994	Wayne Gretzky	Robert Ridder
1993	* Frank Boucher Bruce McNall	* Mervyn "Red" Dutton Gil Stein
1992	Al Arbour Lou Lamoriello	Art Berglund
1991	Rod Gilbert	Mike Ilitch
1990	Len Ceglarski	
1989	Dan Kelly * Lynn Patrick	Lou Nanne Bud Poile
1988	Keith Allen Bob Johnson	Fred Cusick
1987	* Hobey Baker	Frank Mathers
1986	John MacInnes	Jack Riley
1985	Jack Butterfield	Arthur M. Wirtz
1984	* Arthur Howey Ross	John A. Ziegler, Jr.
1983	Bill Torrey	
1982	Emile P. Francis	
1981	Charles M. Schulz	
1980	Bobby Clarke Edward M. Snider	Frederick A. Shero 1980 U.S. Olympic Team
1979	Bobby Orr	
1978	Phil Esposito William T. Tutt	Tom Fitzgerald William W. Wirtz
1977	Murray A. Armstrong John Mariucci	John P. Bucyk
1976	George A. Leader Bruce A. Norris	Stanley Mikita
1975	William L. Chadwick Thomas N. Ivan	Donald M. Clark
1974	* Weston W. Adams, Sr. Alex Delvecchio	* Charles L. Crovat Murray Murdoch
1973	Walter L. Bush, Jr.	
1972	Clarence S. Campbell * James D. Norris	John A. "Snooks" Kelly Ralph "Cooney" Weiland
1971	William M. Jennings * John B. Sollenberger	* Terrance G. Sawchuk
1970	* James C. V. Hendy	Edward W. Shore
1969	Robert M. Hull	* Edward J. Jeremiah
1968	* Walter A. Brown Thomas F. Lockhart	* Gen. John R. Kilpatrick
1967	* Charles F. Adams * James Norris, Sr.	Gordon Howe
1966	J.J. "Jack" Adams	

* awarded posthumously

PRESIDENTS' TROPHY

	Winner	Runner-up
2007	Buffalo Sabres	Detroit Red Wings
2006	Detroit Red Wings	Ottawa Senators
2005	....	....
2004	Detroit Red Wings	Tampa Bay Lightning
2003	Ottawa Senators	Dallas Stars
2002	Detroit Red Wings	Boston Bruins
2001	Colorado Avalanche	Detroit Red Wings
2000	St. Louis Blues	Detroit Red Wings
1999	Dallas Stars	New Jersey Devils
1998	Dallas Stars	New Jersey Devils
1997	Colorado Avalanche	Dallas Stars
1996	Detroit Red Wings	Colorado Avalanche
1995	Detroit Red Wings	Quebec Nordiques
1994	New York Rangers	New Jersey Devils
1993	Pittsburgh Penguins	Boston Bruins
1992	New York Rangers	Washington Capitals
1991	Chicago Blackhawks	St. Louis Blues
1990	Boston Bruins	Calgary Flames
1989	Calgary Flames	Montreal Canadiens
1988	Calgary Flames	Montreal Canadiens
1987	Edmonton Oilers	Philadelphia Flyers
1986	Edmonton Oilers	Philadelphia Flyers

LESTER B. PEARSON AWARD

2007	Sidney Crosby	Pittsburgh
2006	Jaromir Jagr	NY Rangers
2005	....	....
2004	Martin St. Louis	Tampa Bay
2003	Markus Naslund	Vancouver
2002	Jarome Iginla	Calgary
2001	Joe Sakic	Colorado
2000	Jaromir Jagr	Pittsburgh
1999	Jaromir Jagr	Pittsburgh
1998	Dominik Hasek	Buffalo
1997	Dominik Hasek	Buffalo
1996	Mario Lemieux	Pittsburgh
1995	Eric Lindros	Philadelphia
1994	Sergei Fedorov	Detroit
1993	Mario Lemieux	Pittsburgh
1992	Mark Messier	NY Rangers
1991	Brett Hull	St. Louis
1990	Mark Messier	Edmonton
1989	Steve Yzerman	Detroit
1988	Mario Lemieux	Pittsburgh
1987	Wayne Gretzky	Edmonton
1986	Mario Lemieux	Pittsburgh
1985	Wayne Gretzky	Edmonton
1984	Wayne Gretzky	Edmonton
1983	Wayne Gretzky	Edmonton
1982	Wayne Gretzky	Edmonton
1981	Mike Liut	St. Louis
1980	Marcel Dionne	Los Angeles
1979	Marcel Dionne	Los Angeles
1978	Guy Lafleur	Montreal
1977	Guy Lafleur	Montreal
1976	Guy Lafleur	Montreal
1975	Bobby Orr	Boston
1974	Phil Esposito	Boston
1973	Bobby Clarke	Philadelphia
1972	Jean Ratelle	NY Rangers
1971	Phil Esposito	Boston

JACK ADAMS AWARD

	Winner	Runner-up
2007	Alain Vigneault, Van.	Lindy Ruff, Buf.
2006	Lindy Ruff, Buf.	Peter Laviolette, NYR
2005	....	....
2004	John Tortorella, T.B.	Ron Wilson, S.J.
2003	Jacques Lemaire, Min.	John Tortorella, T.B.
2002	Bob Francis, Phx.	Brian Sutter, Chi.
2001	Bill Barber, Phi.	Scotty Bowman, Det.
2000	Joel Quenneville, St.L.	Alain Vigneault, Mtl.
1999	Jacques Martin, Ott.	Pat Quinn, Tor.
1998	Pat Burns, Bos.	Larry Robinson, L.A.
1997	Ted Nolan, Buf.	Ken Hitchcock, Dal.
1996	Scotty Bowman, Det.	Doug MacLean, Fla.
1995	Marc Crawford, Que.	Scotty Bowman, Det.
1994	Jacques Lemaire, N.J.	Kevin Constantine, S.J.
1993	Pat Burns, Tor.	Brian Sutter, Bos.
1992	Pat Quinn, Van.	Roger Neilson, NYR
1991	Brian Sutter, St.L.	Tom Webster, L.A.
1990	Bob Murdoch, Wpg.	Mike Milbury, Bos.
1989	Pat Burns, Mtl.	Bob McCammon, Van.
1988	Jacques Demers, Det.	Terry Crisp, Cgy.
1987	Jacques Demers, Det.	Jack Evans, Hfd.
1986	Glen Sather, Edm.	Jacques Demers, St.L.
1985	Mike Keenan, Phi.	Barry Long, Wpg.
1984	Bryan Murray, Wsh.	Scotty Bowman, Buf.
1983	Orval Tessier, Chi.	
1982	Tom Watt, Wpg.	
1981	Red Berenson, St.L.	Bob Berry, L.A.
1980	Pat Quinn, Phi.	
1979	Al Arbour, NYI	Fred Shero, NYR
1978	Bobby Kromm, Det.	Don Cherry, Bos.
1977	Scotty Bowman, Mtl.	Tom McVie, Wsh.
1976	Don Cherry, Bos.	
1975	Bob Pulford, L.A.	
1974	Fred Shero, Phi.	

NHL Entry Draft

History

Year	Location	Date	Players Drafted
1963	Queen Elizabeth Hotel, Montreal	June 5	21
1964	Queen Elizabeth Hotel, Montreal	June 11	24
1965	Queen Elizabeth Hotel, Montreal	April 27	11
1966	Mount Royal Hotel, Montreal	April 25	24
1967	Queen Elizabeth Hotel, Montreal	June 7	18
1968	Queen Elizabeth Hotel, Montreal	June 13	24
1969	Queen Elizabeth Hotel, Montreal	June 12	84
1970	Queen Elizabeth Hotel, Montreal	June 11	115
1971	Queen Elizabeth Hotel, Montreal	June 10	117
1972	Queen Elizabeth Hotel, Montreal	June 8	152
1973	Mount Royal Hotel, Montreal	May 15	168
1974	NHL Montreal Office	May 28	247
1975	NHL Montreal Office	June 3	217
1976	NHL Montreal Office	June 1	135
1977	NHL Montreal Office	June 14	185
1978	Queen Elizabeth Hotel, Montreal	June 15	234
1979	Queen Elizabeth Hotel, Montreal	August 9	126
1980	Montreal Forum	June 11	210
1981	Montreal Forum	June 10	211
1982	Montreal Forum	June 9	252
1983	Montreal Forum	June 8	242
1984	Montreal Forum	June 9	250
1985	Toronto Convention Centre	June 15	252
1986	Montreal Forum	June 21	252
1987	Joe Louis Arena, Detroit	June 13	252
1988	Montreal Forum	June 11	252
1989	Met Sports Center, Minnesota	June 17	252
1990	B.C. Place, Vancouver	June 16	250
1991	Memorial Auditorium, Buffalo	June 22	264
1992	Montreal Forum	June 20	264
1993	Le Colisée, Quebec	June 26	286
1994	Hartford Civic Center	June 28-29	286
1995	Edmonton Coliseum	July 8	234
1996	Kiel Center, St. Louis	June 22	241
1997	Civic Arena, Pittsburgh	June 21	246
1998	Marine Midland Arena, Buffalo	June 27	258
1999	FleetCenter, Boston	June 26	272
2000	Saddledome, Calgary	June 24-25	293
2001	National Car Rental Center, Florida	June 23-24	289
2002	Air Canada Centre, Toronto	June 22-23	290
2003	Gaylord Entertainment Center, Nashville	June 21-22	292
2004	RBC Center, Carolina	June 26-27	291
2005	Sheraton Hotel and Towers, Ottawa	July 30	230
2006	General Motors Place, Vancouver	June 24	213
2007	Nationwide Arena, Columbus	June 22-23	211

First Selections

Year	Player	Pos	Team	Drafted From	Age
1963	Garry Monahan	LW	Montreal	St. Michael's Juveniles	16.7
1964	Claude Gauthier		Detroit	Comite des jeunes (Rosemont)	
1965	Andre Veilleux	RW	NY Rangers	Montreal Ranger Jr. B	
1966	Barry Gibbs	D	Boston	Estevan Bruins	17.7
1967	Rick Pagnutti	D	Los Angeles	Garson Native Sons	20.6
1968	Michel Plasse	G	Montreal	Drummondville Rangers	20.0
1969	Rejean Houle	LW	Montreal	Montreal Jr. Canadiens	19.8
1970	Gilbert Perreault	C	Buffalo	Montreal Jr. Canadiens	19.7
1971	Guy Lafleur	RW	Montreal	Quebec Remparts	19.9
1972	Billy Harris	RW	NY Islanders	Toronto Marlboros	20.4
1973	Denis Potvin	D	NY Islanders	Ottawa 67's	19.7
1974	Greg Joly	D	Washington	Regina Pats	20.0
1975	Mel Bridgman	C	Philadelphia	Victoria Cougars	20.1
1976	Rick Green	D	Washington	London Knights	20.3
1977	Dale McCourt	C	Detroit	St. Catharines Fincups	20.4
1978	Bobby Smith	C	Minnesota	Ottawa 67's	20.4
1979	Rob Ramage	D	Colorado	London Knights	20.5
1980	Doug Wickenheiser	C	Montreal	Regina Pats	19.2
1981	Dale Hawerchuk	C	Winnipeg	Cornwall Royals	18.2
1982	Gord Kluzak	D	Boston	Nanaimo Islanders	18.3
1983	Brian Lawton	C	Minnesota	Mount St. Charles HS	18.11
1984	Mario Lemieux	C	Pittsburgh	Laval Voisins	18.8
1985	Wendel Clark	LW/D	Toronto	Saskatoon Blades	18.7
1986	Joe Murphy	C	Detroit	Michigan State Spartans	18.8
1987	Pierre Turgeon	C	Buffalo	Granby Bisons	17.10
1988	Mike Modano	C	Minnesota	Prince Albert Raiders	18.0
1989	Mats Sundin	RW	Quebec	Nacka (Sweden)	18.4
1990	Owen Nolan	RW	Quebec	Cornwall Royals	18.4
1991	Eric Lindros	C	Quebec	Oshawa Generals	18.3
1992	Roman Hamrlik	D	Tampa Bay	ZPS Zlin (Czech.)	18.2
1993	Alexandre Daigle	C	Ottawa	Victoriaville Tigres	18.5
1994	Ed Jovanovski	D	Florida	Windsor Spitfires	18.0
1995	Bryan Berard	D	Ottawa	Detroit Jr. Red Wings	18.4
1996	Chris Phillips	D	Ottawa	Prince Albert Raiders	18.3
1997	Joe Thornton	C	Boston	Sault Ste. Marie Greyhounds	17.11
1998	Vincent Lecavalier	C	Tampa Bay	Rimouski Oceanic	18.2
1999	Patrik Stefan	C	Atlanta	Long Beach Ice Dogs (IHL)	18.9
2000	Rick DiPietro	G	NY Islanders	Boston University Terriers	18.9
2001	Ilya Kovalchuk	LW	Atlanta	Spartak (Russia)	18.2
2002	Rick Nash	LW	Columbus	London Knights	18.0
2003	Marc-Andre Fleury	G	Pittsburgh	Cape Breton Screaming Eagles	18.0
2004	Alex Ovechkin	LW	Washington	Dynamo Moscow (Russia)	18.9
2005	Sidney Crosby	C	Pittsburgh	Rimouski Oceanic	17.11
2006	Erik Johnson	D	St. Louis	U.S. National U-18	18.3
2007	Patrick Kane	RW	Chicago	London Knights	18.7

Draft Summary

Following is a summary of the players drafted from the Ontario Hockey League (OHL), Quebec Major Junior Hockey League (QMJHL), Western Hockey League (WHL), United States colleges, United States high schools, European leagues and other North American leagues since 1969. "Other" may include Canadian and U.S. Jr. A and Jr. B, minor professional leagues (AHL, IHL), midget and other teams playing in leagues not listed above.

Year	Total	OHL		QMJHL		WHL		College		Hi School		Int'l		Other	
	Picks	Picks	%	Picks	%	Picks	%	Picks	%	Picks	%	Picks	%	Picks	%
1969	84	36	42.9	11	13.1	20	23.8	7	8.3	-	-	1	1.2	9	10.7
1970	115	51	44.3	13	11.3	22	19.1	16	13.9	-	-	-	-	13	11.3
1971	117	41	35.0	13	11.1	28	23.9	22	18.8	-	-	-	-	13	11.1
1972	152	46	30.3	30	19.7	44	28.9	21	13.8	-	-	-	-	11	7.2
1973	168	56	33.3	24	14.3	49	29.2	25	14.9	-	-	-	-	14	8.3
1974	247	69	27.9	40	16.2	66	26.7	41	16.6	-	-	6	2.4	25	10.1
1975	217	55	25.3	28	12.9	57	26.3	59	27.2	-	-	6	2.8	12	5.5
1976	135	47	34.8	18	13.3	33	24.4	26	19.3	-	-	8	5.9	3	2.2
1977	185	42	22.7	40	21.6	44	23.8	49	26.5	-	-	5	2.7	5	2.7
1978	234	59	25.2	22	9.4	48	20.5	73	31.2	-	-	16	6.8	16	6.8
1979	126	48	38.1	19	15.1	37	29.4	15	11.9	-	-	6	4.8	1	0.8
1980	210	73	34.8	24	11.4	41	19.5	42	20.0	7	3.3	13	6.2	10	4.8
1981	211	59	28.0	28	13.3	37	17.5	21	10.0	17	8.1	32	15.2	17	8.1
1982	252	60	23.8	17	6.7	55	21.8	20	7.9	47	18.7	35	13.9	18	7.1
1983	242	57	23.6	24	9.9	41	16.9	14	5.8	35	14.5	34	14.0	37	15.3
1984	250	55	22.0	16	6.4	37	14.8	22	8.8	44	17.6	40	16.0	36	14.4
1985	252	59	23.4	15	6.0	48	19.0	20	7.9	48	19.0	31	12.3	31	12.3
1986	252	66	26.2	22	8.7	32	12.7	22	8.7	40	15.9	28	11.1	42	16.7
1987	252	32	12.7	17	6.7	36	14.3	40	15.9	69	27.4	38	15.1	20	7.9
1988	252	32	12.7	22	8.7	30	11.9	48	19.0	56	22.2	39	15.5	25	9.9
1989	252	39	15.5	16	6.3	44	17.5	48	19.0	47	18.7	38	15.1	20	7.9
1990	250	39	15.6	14	5.6	33	13.2	38	15.2	57	22.8	53	21.2	16	6.4
1991	264	43	16.3	25	9.5	40	15.2	43	16.3	37	14.0	55	20.8	21	8.0
1992	264	57	21.6	22	8.3	45	17.0	9	3.4	25	9.5	84	31.8	22	8.3
1993	286	60	21.0	23	8.0	44	15.4	17	5.9	33	11.5	78	27.3	31	10.8
1994	286	45	15.7	28	9.8	66	23.1	6	2.1	28	9.8	80	28.0	33	11.5
1995	234	54	23.1	35	15.0	55	23.5	5	2.1	2	0.9	69	29.5	14	6.0
1996	241	51	21.2	31	12.9	54	22.4	25	10.4	6	2.5	58	24.1	16	6.6
1997	246	52	21.1	19	7.7	63	25.6	26	10.6	4	1.6	63	25.6	19	7.7
1998	258	50	19.4	41	15.9	44	17.1	27	10.5	7	2.7	75	29.1	14	5.4
1999	272	52	19.1	20	7.4	40	14.7	36	13.2	9	3.3	94	34.6	21	7.7
2000	293	39	13.3	21	7.2	41	14.0	35	11.9	7	2.4	123	42.0	27	9.2
2001	289	41	14.2	26	9.0	45	15.6	24	8.3	8	2.8	119	41.2	26	9.0
2002	290	35	12.1	23	7.9	43	14.8	41	14.1	6	2.1	110	37.9	32	11.0
2003	292	44	15.1	38	13.0	41	14.0	23	7.9	10	3.4	93	31.8	43	14.7
2004	291	42	14.4	27	9.3	44	15.1	28	9.6	18	6.2	88	30.2	44	15.1
2005	230	43	18.7	23	10.0	43	18.7	13	5.6	18	7.8	50	21.7	40	17.4
2006	213	29	13.6	25	11.7	24	11.2	18	8.4	19	8.9	63	29.5	35	16.4
2007	211	35	16.6	25	11.8	37	17.5	8	3.8	14	6.6	36	17.0	56	56.5
Total		**1893**	**21.2**	**925**	**10.4**	**1651**	**18.5**	**1073**	**12.0**	**718**	**8.0**	**1767**	**19.8**	**888**	**10.0**

Total Players Drafted (1969-2007): 8,915

The Chicago Blackhawks selected Patrick Kane first overall at the 2007 Entry Draft. The Buffalo-born right winger came with an impeccable pedigree after 160 points in midget hockey, two productive seasons with the U.S. National Team Development Program and an OHL scoring title as a major junior rookie with the London Knights.

Ontario Hockey League Draft Selections by Club

Total	Club	'07	'06	'05	'04	'03	'02	'01	'00	'99	'98	'97	'96	'95	'94	'93	'92	'91	'90	'89	'88	'87	'86	'85	'84	'83	'82	'81	'80	'79	'78	'77	'69 to '76
162	Peterborough	1	1	2	5	5	1	2	1	4	1	5	4	5	2	4	4	3	4	2	2	5	2	9	3	7	5	3	10	9	6	4	41
148	Oshawa	2	2	–	3	3	3	1	2	3	4	3	1	10	1	4	4	4	2	4	2	3	6	6	6	5	5	9	2	3	3	1	41
141	London	3	1	3	6	4	2	2	1	4	8	1	4	1	1	4	3	1	3	3	6	2	3	1	7	3	5	5	2	6	3	4	39
140	Kitchener	4	–	4	2	1	4	1	1	–	5	3	2	4	2	4	1	3	5	7	1	2	3	6	4	8	5	5	4	4	4	3	38
133	Ottawa	1	1	2	3	2	–	3	2	6	2	5	2	1	1	4	6	5	5	–	1	2	3	3	2	2	9	4	8	3	5	5	35
108	Sudbury	1	2	4	–	1	1	2	–	5	5	3	1	2	2	10	2	8	2	1	–	1	3	5	2	–	4	2	7	3	4	4	21
107	Sault Ste. Marie	3	–	1	3	1	2	1	1	1	4	1	4	3	4	3	7	2	1	3	2	1	7	5	4	6	1	8	3	3	5	1	16
97	Kingston	–	4	2	–	1	1	2	–	4	1	4	4	3	2	5	3	2	2	–	1	1	4	3	3	1	2	5	8	2	9	4	14
78	Windsor	2	2	3	2	2	2	2	2	2	1	5	1	4	3	–	3	–	1	2	5	–	7	3	2	2	3	5	3	2	4	1	2
68	Guelph	1	1	2	2	1	2	4	1	3	5	1	6	5	7	2	2	–	–	4	–	2	8	3	5	1	–	–	–	–	–	–	–
64	Saginaw/N. Bay	–	2	3	1	2	2	3	2	2	2	1	1	2	7	2	5	2	4	1	3	3	3	3	4	4	–	–	–	–	–	–	–
61	Belleville	4	2	2	–	–	2	3	1	5	2	5	–	3	3	–	4	1	2	4	–	2	5	4	4	3	–	–	–	–	–	–	–
56	Plymouth	3	2	3	3	3	3	3	6	2	2	4	3	6	2	7	2	2	–	–	–	–	–	–	–	–	–	–	–	–	–	–	–
30	Sarnia	1	1	3	–	5	2	1	3	1	3	2	7	1	–	–	–	–	–	–	–	–	–	–	–	–	–	–	–	–	–	–	–
28	Brampton	–	4	4	2	4	3	3	6	2	–	–	–	–	–	–	–	–	–	–	–	–	–	–	–	–	–	–	–	–	–	–	–
28	Owen Sound	1	2	2	1	1	1	–	1	–	1	2	3	2	3	4	2	1	1	–	–	–	–	–	–	–	–	–	–	–	–	–	–
22	Barrie	–	1	–	–	1	1	1	3	6	3	4	2	–	–	–	–	–	–	–	–	–	–	–	–	–	–	–	–	–	–	–	–
22	Erie	5	–	2	2	–	2	2	3	2	1	3	–	–	–	–	–	–	–	–	–	–	–	–	–	–	–	–	–	–	–	–	–
16	St. Michael's	–	–	–	4	5	1	5	1	–	–	–	–	–	–	–	–	–	–	–	–	–	–	–	–	–	–	–	–	–	–	–	–
12	Mississauga	3	1	1	3	2	–	–	2	–	–	–	–	–	–	–	–	–	–	–	–	–	–	–	–	–	–	–	–	–	–	–	–

Teams no longer operating

Total	Club	'07	'06	'05	'04	'03	'02	'01	'00	'99	'98	'97	'96	'95	'94	'93	'92	'91	'90	'89	'88	'87	'86	'85	'84	'83	'82	'81	'80	'79	'78	'77	'69 to '76
97	Toronto	–	–	–	–	–	–	–	–	–	–	–	–	–	–	–	–	–	–	2	2	1	4	3	4	4	6	2	10	4	5	7	43
72	Niagara Falls	–	–	–	–	–	–	–	–	–	–	–	6	2	3	4	4	4	4	4	–	–	–	–	–	–	6	6	8	5	3	2	11
62	Hamilton	–	–	–	–	–	–	–	–	–	–	–	–	–	–	–	–	2	–	–	4	4	6	3	–	–	–	–	–	1	8	–	34
52	St. Catharines	–	–	–	–	–	–	–	–	–	–	–	–	–	–	–	–	–	–	–	–	–	–	–	–	–	–	–	–	–	–	6	46
37	Cornwall	–	–	–	–	–	–	–	–	–	–	–	–	–	–	–	5	3	3	2	3	3	2	2	3	4	7	–	–	–	–	–	–
27	Brantford	–	–	–	–	–	–	–	–	–	–	–	–	–	–	–	–	–	–	–	–	–	–	–	2	7	2	5	8	3	–	–	–
20	Montreal	–	–	–	–	–	–	–	–	–	–	–	–	–	–	–	–	–	–	–	–	–	–	–	–	–	–	–	–	–	–	–	20
5	Newmarket	–	–	–	–	–	–	–	–	–	–	–	–	–	2	3	–	–	–	–	–	–	–	–	–	–	–	–	–	–	–	–	–

Quebec Major Junior Hockey League Draft Selections by Club

Total	Club	'07	'06	'05	'04	'03	'02	'01	'00	'99	'98	'97	'96	'95	'94	'93	'92	'91	'90	'89	'88	'87	'86	'85	'84	'83	'82	'81	'80	'79	'78	'77	'69 to '76
75	Lewiston/Sher.	3	2	5	2	1	–	3	–	–	5	1	–	4	2	3	–	–	–	–	–	–	–	–	–	–	2	5	1	4	3	6	23
75	Shawinigan	1	1	1	3	2	2	1	1	1	3	1	4	2	1	1	3	2	–	2	–	1	2	–	2	5	5	2	2	–	–	3	21
73	Gatineau/Hull	1	2	–	4	4	5	2	–	4	3	–	3	3	1	3	3	3	3	2	2	3	4	–	1	3	–	1	3	–	3	2	5
54	Drummondville	–	2	2	1	1	–	1	1	–	2	2	3	4	1	2	2	4	–	1	4	2	2	2	1	–	–	–	–	–	–	–	14
51	Chicoutimi	–	–	4	–	1	3	1	1	–	1	2	–	2	3	1	1	–	1	1	2	2	1	3	–	3	1	6	3	1	1	5	1
31	Victoriaville	1	–	–	–	–	3	1	3	2	1	2	3	1	1	6	2	–	1	–	4	–	–	–	–	–	–	–	–	–	–	–	–
30	Halifax	2	3	1	3	6	–	3	2	–	3	3	1	3	–	–	–	–	–	–	–	–	–	–	–	–	–	–	–	–	–	–	–
26	Rimouski	4	–	2	3	4	–	4	2	2	5	–	–	–	–	–	–	–	–	–	–	–	–	–	–	–	–	–	–	–	–	–	–
21	Quebec	2	2	2	1	3	1	3	–	3	4	–	–	–	–	–	–	–	–	–	–	–	–	–	–	–	–	–	–	–	–	–	–
21	Val-d'Or	–	–	2	1	1	1	2	2	3	–	2	4	2	1	–	–	–	–	–	–	–	–	–	–	–	–	–	–	–	–	–	–
20	PEI/Mtl. Rocket	2	–	2	8	1	3	1	1	2	–	–	–	–	–	–	–	–	–	–	–	–	–	–	–	–	–	–	–	–	–	–	–
18	Baie-Comeau	1	3	–	3	2	1	3	2	–	3	–	–	–	–	–	–	–	–	–	–	–	–	–	–	–	–	–	–	–	–	–	–
18	Moncton	1	3	1	2	3	2	–	–	2	2	1	1	–	–	–	–	–	–	–	–	–	–	–	–	–	–	–	–	–	–	–	–
15	Rouyn-Noranda	1	3	1	–	2	–	–	4	1	3	–	–	–	–	–	–	–	–	–	–	–	–	–	–	–	–	–	–	–	–	–	–
13	Cape Breton	–	1	–	3	2	2	1	1	–	3	–	–	–	–	–	–	–	–	–	–	–	–	–	–	–	–	–	–	–	–	–	–
9	Acadie-Bathurst	–	2	–	–	3	2	–	–	2	–	–	–	–	–	–	–	–	–	–	–	–	–	–	–	–	–	–	–	–	–	–	–
4	St. John's	4	–	–	–	–	–	–	–	–	–	–	–	–	–	–	–	–	–	–	–	–	–	–	–	–	–	–	–	–	–	–	–
3	Saint John	2	1	–	–	–	–	–	–	–	–	–	–	–	–	–	–	–	–	–	–	–	–	–	–	–	–	–	–	–	–	–	–

Teams no longer operating

Total	Club	'07	'06	'05	'04	'03	'02	'01	'00	'99	'98	'97	'96	'95	'94	'93	'92	'91	'90	'89	'88	'87	'86	'85	'84	'83	'82	'81	'80	'79	'78	'77	'69 to '76
54	Laval	–	–	–	–	–	–	–	–	–	3	1	2	4	5	2	1	4	3	3	1	3	5	–	2	1	2	–	–	1	2	4	5
47	Quebec	–	–	–	–	–	–	–	–	–	–	–	–	–	–	–	–	–	–	–	–	–	–	3	2	2	1	2	2	3	1	7	24
47	Trois Rivieres	–	–	–	–	–	–	–	–	–	–	–	–	–	–	–	1	2	1	3	3	1	–	3	–	3	1	2	2	2	3	6	14
45	Cornwall	–	–	–	–	–	–	–	–	–	–	–	–	–	–	–	–	–	–	–	–	–	–	–	–	–	–	5	5	1	6	1	27
32	Montreal	–	–	–	–	–	–	–	–	–	–	–	–	–	–	–	–	–	–	–	–	–	–	–	–	–	3	–	3	4	2	3	17
30	Granby	–	–	–	–	–	–	–	–	–	–	1	3	2	5	1	–	2	–	2	–	4	2	2	3	1	2	–	–	–	–	–	–
28	Sorel	–	–	–	–	–	–	–	–	–	–	–	–	–	–	–	–	–	–	–	–	–	–	–	–	–	–	5	–	–	–	3	20
27	Verdun	–	–	–	–	–	–	–	–	–	–	–	–	–	–	–	3	–	–	1	3	0	3	–	3	3	–	–	3	3	1	–	4
21	Beauport	–	–	–	–	–	–	–	–	–	–	3	3	7	3	1	3	1	–	–	–	–	–	–	–	–	–	–	–	–	–	–	–
16	St. Jean	–	–	–	–	–	–	–	–	–	–	–	–	1	1	2	1	3	–	1	3	0	1	1	–	2	–	–	–	–	–	–	–
15	St. Hyacinthe	–	–	–	–	–	–	–	–	–	–	–	4	–	4	1	2	1	3	–	–	–	–	–	–	–	–	–	–	–	–	–	–
12	Longueuil	–	–	–	–	–	–	–	–	–	–	–	–	–	–	–	–	3	2	–	–	1	2	1	2	1	–	–	–	–	–	–	–
2	St. Jerome	–	–	–	–	–	–	–	–	–	–	–	–	–	–	–	–	–	–	–	–	–	–	–	–	–	–	–	–	–	–	–	2

Boston's Patrice Bergeron (top) was drafted 45th overall by the Bruins from Acadie-Bathurst of the QMJHL in 2003. Montreal selected Guillaume Latendresse from Drummondville in the "Q" with the 45th pick in 2005.

2007 NHL Entry Draft Order of Selection

The first 14 picks of the 2007 Entry Draft are determined by the NHL's annual Draft Drawing, a weighted lottery system that is used to determine the order of selection.

The 14 teams that did not qualify for the 2007 Stanley Cup Playoffs, or clubs that acquired those clubs' 2007 first-round draft picks, participated in the drawing.

The Club selected in the drawing may not move up more than four positions in the draft order, thus only the five Clubs with the fewest regular-season points have the opportunity to select first overall. No Club can move down more than one position as a result of the Draft Drawing. For 2007, Chicago won the right to the first overall pick.

In the first round of the 2007 Entry Draft, the order of selection was as follows:

a) The winner of the Draft Drawing (Chicago) followed by the remaining non-playoff teams, in inverse order of points;

1. Chicago
2. Philadelphia
3. Phoenix
4. Los Angeles
5. Washington
6. Edmonton
7. Columbus
8. Boston
9. St. Louis
10. Florida
11. Carolina
12. Montreal
13. Toronto
14. Colorado

b) Clubs eliminated in the first two rounds of the 2007 Stanley Cup Playoffs, regular-season division winners excluded, in inverse order of points;

15. NY Islanders
16. Tampa Bay
17. NY Rangers
18. Calgary
19. Minnesota
20. Pittsburgh
21. Dallas
22. San Jose
23. Nashville

c) Regular-season division winning clubs eliminated in the first two rounds of the 2007 Stanley Cup Playoffs, in inverse order of points;

24. Atlanta
25. Vancouver
26. New Jersey

d) Clubs eliminated in the 2007 Conference Finals, in inverse order of points;

27. Buffalo
28. Detroit

e) Loser of Stanley Cup Final

29. Ottawa

f) Stanley Cup champion

30. Anaheim

In the second and subsequent rounds the order of selection is identical to that of the first round, except that all non-playoff clubs select in inverse order of points:

1. Philadelphia
2. Phoenix
3. Los Angeles
4. Washington
5. Chicago
6. Edmonton
7. Columbus
8. Boston
9. St. Louis
10. Florida
11. Carolina
12. Montreal
13. Toronto
14. Colorado

b) All other clubs select in the same order used in the first round.

Western Hockey League Draft Selections by Club

Total	Club	'07	'06	'05	'04	'03	'02	'01	'00	'99	'98	'97	'96	'95	'94	'93	'92	'91	'90	'89	'88	'87	'86	'85	'84	'83	'82	'81	'80	'79	'78	'77	'69 to '76
108	Regina	3	1	1	–	2	1	2	2	4	2	3	4	2	3	–	4	–	1	5	–	2	3	4	4	8	6	5	3	1	4	1	27
106	Kamloops	1	1	2	5	2	5	2	4	4	1	3	4	5	9	2	3	6	4	5	1	3	4	4	4	4	2	–	–	–	–	4	12
106	Portland	2	1	3	2	1	2	–	6	1	3	3	1	2	3	4	4	1	1	4	1	3	4	2	5	7	7	6	8	7	8	4	–
105	Saskatoon	3	–	4	1	–	–	4	1	4	2	2	2	2	4	2	3	2	2	3	4	4	5	1	3	5	5	3	2	2	1	4	25
104	Medicine Hat	–	2	4	2	3	3	2	–	1	3	2	7	2	6	1	3	3	1	4	1	5	2	6	1	2	1	2	4	–	4	5	22
98	Brandon	1	1	2	–	3	4	2	–	–	4	5	2	6	5	2	1	1	1	–	3	3	1	2	3	1	2	2	5	10	1	3	22
92	Seattle	1	1	3	2	5	1	5	4	6	2	8	1	5	5	4	2	3	6	2	4	2	1	3	1	–	6	–	3	2	4	–	–
88	Lethbridge	2	1	–	2	2	2	1	3	–	1	5	1	3	3	4	3	7	4	3	3	–	1	5	1	2	7	4	1	4	5	3	5
80	Prince Albert	–	–	2	4	2	1	4	2	3	3	5	3	4	3	5	2	6	4	3	3	1	6	6	2	2	4	–	–	–	–	–	–
60	Spokane	3	1	4	1	–	3	3	2	1	1	4	5	4	4	4	7	5	1	2	3	1	–	–	–	–	–	1	–	–	–	–	–
60	Swift Current	2	2	1	2	2	4	1	3	1	2	2	1	4	4	5	1	1	2	2	2	5	–	–	–	–	–	–	–	–	–	–	11
59	Moose Jaw	1	1	3	3	3	3	3	5	1	2	4	4	4	3	2	3	2	1	3	–	3	1	4	–	–	–	–	–	–	–	–	–
51	Tri-City	–	–	2	4	1	3	2	2	1	4	1	6	6	2	2	5	3	3	4	–	–	–	–	–	–	–	–	–	–	–	–	–
42	Red Deer	1	1	1	1	4	4	6	1	1	5	3	4	2	5	3	–	–	–	–	–	–	–	–	–	–	–	–	–	–	–	–	–
34	Calgary	4	1	2	5	3	2	1	4	6	3	–	3	–	–	–	–	–	–	–	–	–	–	–	–	–	–	–	–	–	–	–	–
30	Kelowna	2	–	2	4	4	1	1	1	2	2	7	4	–	–	–	–	–	–	–	–	–	–	–	–	–	–	–	–	–	–	–	–
26	Prince George	1	4	1	2	2	–	4	–	2	4	2	2	2	–	–	–	–	–	–	–	–	–	–	–	–	–	–	–	–	–	–	–
16	Kootenay	1	1	3	2	1	3	2	1	2	–	–	–	–	–	–	–	–	–	–	–	–	–	–	–	–	–	–	–	–	–	–	–
12	Vancouver	4	1	3	2	1	1	–	–	–	–	–	–	–	–	–	–	–	–	–	–	–	–	–	–	–	–	–	–	–	–	–	–
7	Everett	3	4	–	–	–	–	–	–	–	–	–	–	–	–	–	–	–	–	–	–	–	–	–	–	–	–	–	–	–	–	–	–
2	Chilliwack	2	–	–	–	–	–	–	–	–	–	–	–	–	–	–	–	–	–	–	–	–	–	–	–	–	–	–	–	–	–	–	–
Teams no longer operating																																	
70	Victoria	–	–	–	–	–	–	–	–	–	–	–	–	–	2	2	1	–	2	4	4	2	1	2	4	3	2	6	8	1	3	3	29
66	Calgary	–	–	–	–	–	–	–	–	–	–	–	–	–	–	–	–	–	–	–	–	–	2	3	3	3	4	5	2	–	3	4	37
62	New Westm'r	–	–	–	–	–	–	–	–	–	–	–	–	–	–	–	–	–	–	–	1	2	1	1	2	–	–	–	1	5	6	8	35
39	Flin Flon	–	–	–	–	–	–	–	–	–	–	–	–	–	–	–	–	–	–	–	–	–	–	–	–	–	–	–	–	–	5	1	33
38	Edmonton	–	–	–	–	–	–	–	–	–	–	4	–	–	–	–	–	–	–	–	–	–	–	–	–	–	–	–	–	2	–	–	32
34	Winnipeg	–	–	–	–	–	–	–	–	–	–	–	–	–	–	–	–	–	–	–	–	–	–	–	–	1	4	1	–	–	–	4	24
13	Billings	–	–	–	–	–	–	–	–	–	–	–	–	–	–	–	–	–	–	–	–	–	–	–	–	–	–	2	4	3	4	–	–
12	Estevan	–	–	–	–	–	–	–	–	–	–	–	–	–	–	–	–	–	–	–	–	–	–	–	–	–	–	–	–	–	–	–	12
12	Tacoma	–	–	–	–	–	–	–	–	–	–	–	–	2	5	2	3	–	–	–	–	–	–	–	–	–	–	–	–	–	–	–	–
11	Kelowna	–	–	–	–	–	–	–	–	–	–	–	–	–	–	–	–	–	–	–	–	–	–	5	4	2	–	–	–	–	–	–	–
6	Nanaimo	–	–	–	–	–	–	–	–	–	–	–	–	–	–	–	–	–	–	–	–	–	–	–	–	1	5	–	–	–	–	–	–
2	Vancouver	–	–	–	–	–	–	–	–	–	–	–	–	–	–	–	–	–	–	–	–	–	–	–	–	–	–	–	–	–	–	–	2

U.S. College Hockey Draft Selections by School

Total	Club	'07	'06	'05	'04	'03	'02	'01	'00	'99	'98	'97	'96	'95	'94	'93	'92	'91	'90	'89	'88	'87	'86	'85	'84	'83	'82	'81	'80	'79	'78	'77	'69 to '76
68	Minnesota	1	1	1	–	2	3	–	3	3	1	2	3	2	–	–	–	–	–	1	1	1	2	–	–	1	1	1	3	2	5	5	23
67	Michigan	1	2	1	3	2	3	2	1	2	3	1	3	–	1	1	2	4	5	3	2	1	–	1	1	–	–	–	4	–	6	1	11
51	Boston U.	–	1	–	1	–	3	2	1	3	2	1	1	1	–	1	1	2	2	1	3	2	2	1	1	–	–	1	–	1	5	4	8
48	Michigan State	–	1	–	2	1	4	–	2	2	1	1	1	–	1	1	1	4	5	4	4	1	1	–	2	–	2	–	2	–	–	–	5
46	Michigan Tech	–	–	–	–	–	–	1	–	–	–	–	1	–	2	1	–	2	1	2	1	1	2	2	2	–	1	–	4	1	2	1	19
43	Denver	–	–	2	1	–	1	–	–	1	–	3	–	–	–	–	–	–	–	1	1	4	2	1	–	–	1	–	1	2	2	2	18
41	Wisconsin	–	–	–	–	–	–	–	3	2	–	–	–	–	–	–	–	1	–	1	–	1	–	1	1	–	2	3	–	1	–	3	22
39	North Dakota	–	1	–	1	1	1	–	1	1	–	2	–	–	–	–	–	1	1	2	–	–	–	–	1	–	–	1	3	3	2	1	16
37	Boston College	–	1	1	1	1	3	2	3	–	3	3	2	–	–	–	–	–	–	2	–	2	1	–	–	–	1	1	2	–	5	–	3
36	Providence	–	2	–	–	1	1	–	2	–	2	1	–	–	–	–	–	–	1	–	–	–	1	1	–	2	1	4	5	–	4	3	5
34	Cornell	–	–	1	2	2	1	–	2	2	–	1	–	–	–	–	–	–	2	5	2	1	–	2	1	–	1	1	1	–	1	1	5
34	Harvard	–	–	1	–	–	3	2	2	1	2	1	3	–	1	2	–	–	–	2	1	1	–	2	–	1	1	–	–	–	2	2	4
33	Clarkson	–	1	–	–	–	–	–	1	1	3	–	–	–	–	1	1	2	3	1	1	1	–	–	1	1	1	1	1	1	2	2	7
33	Colorado	1	–	1	–	2	1	1	2	1	3	–	–	1	–	–	–	–	2	–	1	–	1	–	3	–	–	–	1	–	2	2	8
32	Notre Dame	1	1	–	2	–	2	1	1	2	–	2	1	–	–	–	–	–	–	–	–	–	–	–	–	–	–	–	1	1	3	–	14
31	New Hampshire	–	–	–	1	–	1	–	2	1	–	1	–	–	–	–	–	–	–	1	–	–	–	–	2	1	1	1	2	1	1	4	11
28	Bowling Green	–	1	1	–	–	1	1	–	1	1	1	–	–	–	–	1	3	1	2	3	–	–	–	–	1	–	–	1	1	1	1	6
25	RPI	–	–	–	–	–	–	1	2	2	–	1	–	–	–	–	1	3	–	–	2	2	–	1	–	1	1	2	1	–	3	1	1
24	Lake Superior	–	–	–	–	–	1	–	–	1	–	1	1	–	–	1	–	1	3	2	3	–	3	–	1	–	–	–	–	–	3	–	3
24	W. Michigan	–	1	–	–	–	1	–	–	–	1	1	–	–	–	2	–	4	1	1	1	1	2	–	2	2	–	–	2	–	–	2	–
23	St. Lawrence	–	–	–	–	–	1	–	–	1	–	1	1	–	–	1	–	2	1	1	1	1	1	1	1	–	3	–	–	–	4	1	1
22	Maine	–	1	–	1	2	–	–	1	4	1	1	1	–	–	1	–	–	1	2	3	–	1	–	–	1	1	–	–	–	–	–	–
22	Northern Mich.	–	–	–	2	2	–	–	1	–	–	–	1	–	–	–	–	1	–	2	1	4	–	–	–	–	1	2	1	–	4	–	–
21	Miami U.	1	1	1	2	–	1	1	–	–	1	–	–	–	–	1	1	2	–	2	4	2	–	1	–	–	–	–	–	–	–	–	–
21	Ohio State	–	–	1	–	1	2	2	–	1	–	1	1	–	–	1	1	1	1	–	2	2	–	–	1	–	–	–	–	–	1	2	–
20	Vermont	–	–	1	–	–	–	2	–	–	–	–	1	–	1	–	–	1	–	–	1	–	–	2	1	1	–	1	1	–	1	1	5
16	Yale	–	1	–	2	–	3	–	–	–	–	–	–	–	–	1	–	–	–	1	–	2	1	–	–	–	–	–	1	–	2	–	2
13	Brown	–	–	–	1	–	–	–	1	–	–	–	–	–	–	–	–	1	–	–	–	–	–	–	–	–	1	–	–	–	2	3	4
13	Colgate	–	1	–	1	–	1	–	–	–	–	–	–	–	–	–	–	2	2	1	1	–	–	–	–	–	–	–	–	1	2	–	1
13	Minn.-Duluth	–	–	–	–	–	–	–	–	–	1	–	–	–	–	–	–	1	2	1	2	–	–	–	–	–	–	1	–	–	1	1	3
10	Dartmouth	1	–	–	1	2	–	–	1	–	–	–	–	–	–	–	–	1	–	–	–	1	–	–	–	–	–	–	1	–	1	–	1
10	Northeastern	–	–	–	–	–	–	–	–	1	1	–	–	–	–	–	–	–	1	1	–	–	1	1	–	1	–	–	1	–	1	–	1
10	Princeton	–	–	–	–	–	–	1	–	–	1	–	–	–	–	1	–	–	–	1	–	1	–	–	–	1	–	1	1	–	1	–	1

Colleges with fewer than 10 players selected: 8 - Ferris State, Merrimack; 7 - Mass.-Lowell, St.Cloud State; 6 - Illinois-Chicago, St. Louis; 5 - Pennsylvania, Union College, Mass.-Amherst; 4 - Alaska-Anchorage, Nebraska-Omaha; 3 - Babson College, Alaska (Fairbanks), Minnesota State (Mankato); 1 - Air Force, American International College, Army, Bemidji State, Greenway, Hamilton, St. Anselm College, St. Thomas, Salem State, San Diego U., Wisconsin-River Falls.

U.S. High and Prep Schools Draft Selections by School (10 or more players drafted)

Total	School	'07	'06	'05	'04	'03	'02	'01	'00	'99	'98	'97	'96	'95	'94	'93	'92	'91	'90	'89	'88	'87	'86	'85	'84	'83	'82	'81	'80
21	Cushing Acad. (MA)	–	1	1	2	–	–	1	–	–	–	1	1	–	2	2	–	1	3	2	3	–	–	–	1	–	–	–	–
20	Northwood Prep (NY)	–	–	–	1	–	–	–	1	–	–	–	–	–	1	1	–	–	3	1	1	4	2	2	–	1	2	–	–
17	Belmont Hill (MA)	–	1	–	–	–	–	–	–	–	–	–	–	–	1	–	2	1	2	3	1	2	1	2	–	1	–	–	–
15	Edina (MN)	–	–	–	–	–	–	–	–	–	–	–	–	–	–	–	1	–	1	2	2	1	–	–	2	2	4	–	–
15	Hill-Murray (MN)	–	–	–	–	–	–	–	–	–	–	–	–	–	1	–	–	–	3	2	–	3	3	–	3	–	–	–	–
14	Catholic Memorial (MA)	–	–	–	2	–	–	–	–	–	1	–	–	–	2	1	2	–	–	2	1	1	–	2	–	–	–	–	–
14	Deerfield (IL)	1	–	–	1	1	1	–	2	1	–	–	–	–	–	–	–	1	–	2	1	1	–	1	1	–	–	–	–
13	Mount St. Charles (RI)	–	–	–	–	–	–	–	–	–	–	–	–	–	–	–	–	–	1	1	3	1	2	–	1	3	–	1	–
13	St. Sebastian's (MA)	–	1	–	–	4	1	1	–	–	1	–	–	–	1	2	2	–	–	–	–	–	–	–	–	–	–	–	–
12	Culver Mil. Acad. (IN)	–	–	–	–	–	–	–	–	–	–	–	–	–	–	2	2	1	2	2	1	2	–	–	–	–	–	–	–
11	Avon Old Farms (CT)	1	–	–	–	–	–	–	–	–	1	1	–	–	–	–	–	–	3	3	–	–	1	1	–	–	–	–	–
11	Canterbury (CT)	–	–	–	–	1	–	–	–	–	–	–	–	–	–	1	2	–	2	–	3	–	2	–	–	–	–	–	–
11	Hotchkiss (CT)	–	–	–	1	–	–	1	–	–	–	–	2	1	3	–	–	–	1	–	1	–	–	1	–	–	–	–	–
10	Choate-Rosemary (CT)	–	–	–	–	–	–	–	1	–	–	–	–	–	–	–	1	1	1	–	3	2	–	1	–	–	–	–	–
10	Lawrence Acad. (MA)	–	–	–	–	–	–	–	–	–	–	–	1	–	1	1	–	1	1	–	2	–	–	2	–	1	–	–	–
10	Matignon (MA)	–	–	–	–	–	–	–	–	–	–	–	–	–	–	–	–	1	–	–	–	3	–	–	3	–	1	1	1
10	Roseau (MN)	–	–	–	–	–	–	–	–	–	–	–	–	–	–	–	–	1	3	1	–	–	1	–	1	1	1	–	1
10	Thayer Acad. (MA)	–	–	2	1	–	–	–	–	2		–	–	–	–	–	2	–	–	–	2	–	1	–	–	–	–	–	–

U.S. College and High School Firsts

1967 – First U.S. College Player Drafted • Michigan Tech center Al Karlander was selected 17th overall by the Detroit Red Wings.

1979 – First U.S. College First- Round Selection • Minnesota-born defenseman Mike Ramsey (currently an assistant coach with the Minnesota Wild) was selected 11th overall by the Buffalo Sabres.

1980 – First U.S. High School Player Drafted • Center Jay North of Bloomington-Jefferson H.S. was taken 62nd overall by the Buffalo Sabres in 1980.

1981 – First U.S. High School First- Round Selection • Center Bob Carpenter of St. John's prep school was selected third overall by Washington in 1981.

1983 – First U.S. High School Player Drafted First Overall • Minnesota North Stars selected left winger Brian Lawton from Mount St. Charles H.S. first overall in 1983.

1986 – First U.S. College Player Drafted First Overall • Detroit selected right winger Joe Murphy from Michigan State first overall in 1986.

2005 – Most U.S. College Players Selected in the First Round • The 2005 draft saw eight U.S. college players selected in the first round, the most in Entry Draft history. Seven were selected in the first round in 2003 and 1986, six in 2000, five in 2002, four in 2001 and three in each of the 1986 and 1999 Entry Drafts.

Records Set for U.S.-Born Players in the 2007 Entry Draft

A record 29.9% of the players selected in the 2007 NHL Entry Draft (63 of 211) were U.S.-born and for the first time, U.S.-born players were selected with the top two picks as Patrick Kane (Chi.) and James vanRiemsdyk (Phi.) went first and second overall. This also marked the first time U.S.-born players were selected first overall in consecutive years – Kane this year and Erik Johnson (St.L.) in 2006. As well, a total of 10 Americans were selected in the first round of the 2007 Entry Draft, tying a record set in 2006. A record 21 Americans were selected in the first two rounds of 2007.

The United States Hockey League had 26 current or former players selected in the Draft, while two players from the North American Hockey League were chosen. Sixteen players who had skated with U.S. National Team Development Program were selected.

Players from 14 different states were selected in the 2007 Entry Draft, including California, Connecticut, Illinois, Massachusetts, Michigan, Minnesota, Missouri, North Dakota, New Jersey, New York, Ohio, Pennsylvania, Texas and Wisconsin.

International

Total	Country	'07	'06	'05	'04	'03	'02	'01	'00	'99	'98	'97	'96	'95	'94	'93	'92	'91	'90	'89	'88	'87	'86	'85	'84	'83	'82	'81	'80	'79	'78	'77	'69 to '76
510	USSR/CIS/Russia	7	16	11	24	32	33	36	44	29	22	16	17	27	35	31	45	25	14	18	11	2	1	2	1	5	3	–	–	–	2	–	1
444	Sweden	16	18	15	18	19	24	14	24	24	19	14	16	8	17	18	11	11	7	9	14	15	9	16	14	10	14	14	9	5	8	2	12
403	CzRep/Slovakia	4	11	15	24	20	21	28	28	20	20	17	14	21	18	15	17	9	21	8	5	11	6	8	13	9	13	4	–	1	2	–	–
306	Finland	4	13	8	14	12	26	29	19	17	12	11	7	12	8	9	8	6	9	3	7	6	10	4	10	9	5	12	4	–	2	3	7
44	Germany	4	2	1	1	4	1	7	1	–	–	1	3	1	1	3	2	1	–	–	2	1	–	1	2	1	–	2	–	–	2	–	–
43	Switzerland	1	3	–	4	5	4	5	7	3	2	3	1	–	1	2	–	1	–	–	–	–	–	–	–	–	–	–	–	–	–	–	1
7	Norway	–	–	–	–	–	1	–	–	–	–	1	–	–	–	–	–	1	2	–	–	2	–	–	–	–	–	–	–	–	–	–	–
4	Denmark	–	–	–	2	–	–	–	–	–	–	–	–	–	–	–	–	–	–	–	–	1	1	–	–	–	–	–	–	–	–	–	–
2	Japan	–	–	–	1	–	–	–	–	–	–	–	–	–	–	–	1	–	–	–	–	–	–	–	–	–	–	–	–	–	–	–	–
2	Poland	–	–	–	–	1	–	–	–	–	–	–	–	–	–	–	–	1	–	–	–	–	–	–	–	–	–	–	–	–	–	–	–
1	Scotland	–	–	–	–	–	–	–	–	–	–	–	–	–	–	–	–	–	–	–	–	–	1	–	–	–	–	–	–	–	–	–	–
1	Hungary	–	–	–	–	–	–	–	–	1	–	–	–	–	–	–	–	–	–	–	–	–	–	–	–	–	–	–	–	–	–	–	–

Czech Republic and Slovakia

Total	Club	'07	'06	'05	'04	'03	'02	'01	'00	'99	'98	'97	'96	'95	'94	'93	'92	'91	'90	'89	'88	'87	'86	'85	'84	'83	'82	'81	'80	'79	'78	'77	'69 to '76
34	Chemo. Litv.[1]	–	–	–	3	2	–	1	–	1	1	2	2	2	4	2	3	1	2	2	–	–	–	–	2	1	3	–	–	–	–	–	–
31	HC Ceske Bud.[2]	–	2	2	1	2	–	2	3	1	1	2	1	3	2	1	–	–	2	1	–	1	–	–	1	1	2	–	–	–	–	–	–
30	Dukla Trencin	1	1	1	4	3	–	2	3	2	–	1	2	1	–	2	2	–	2	1	1	–	–	–	1	–	–	–	–	–	–	–	–
28	Dukla Jihlava	–	–	–	–	–	–	–	1	–	–	–	2	2	1	1	1	2	3	1	1	3	–	1	3	4	2	–	–	–	–	–	–
28	Sparta Praha	–	1	2	4	1	1	2	1	–	1	1	–	1	–	1	1	–	2	1	2	1	1	1	2	–	1	–	–	–	–	–	–
28	Slavia Praha	1	–	1	1	2	2	5	3	2	5	4	–	–	–	1	–	–	–	–	–	–	–	–	1	–	–	–	–	–	–	–	–
23	HC Kladno[3]	–	3	1	1	1	–	1	1	2	–	–	2	–	2	1	–	2	1	–	–	–	1	–	1	–	1	2	–	–	–	–	–
22	Slovan Bratis.	–	–	–	–	3	1	–	2	2	1	1	1	–	3	–	–	–	1	–	–	1	1	1	–	–	2	–	–	1	1	–	–
21	ZPS Zlin[4]	–	–	1	2	–	–	2	–	2	2	1	–	2	–	1	2	2	–	–	–	1	1	1	–	1	–	–	–	–	–	–	–
19	HC Vitkovice[5]	–	1	1	2	–	2	–	1	1	1	–	1	1	1	3	1	–	1	–	–	–	–	–	–	–	–	1	–	–	1	–	–
15	HC Kosice[6]	–	1	1	–	–	–	1	–	1	1	1	1	–	–	–	–	–	2	–	–	–	1	–	2	–	2	1	–	–	–	–	–
14	HC Vsetin	1	1	–	1	1	3	2	2	–	1	2	–	–	–	–	–	–	–	–	–	–	–	–	–	–	–	–	–	–	–	–	–
13	HC Pardubice[7]	–	–	–	–	–	3	1	–	–	–	1	–	1	2	–	–	–	–	–	–	1	–	2	–	2	–	–	–	–	–	–	–
13	Interconex Plzen[8]	–	–	–	–	–	2	1	1	–	1	–	–	1	1	–	3	–	1	1	–	–	1	–	–	–	–	–	–	–	–	–	–
8	Zelezarny Trinec	–	1	1	–	1	1	1	1	2	–	–	–	–	–	–	–	–	–	–	–	–	–	–	–	–	–	–	–	–	–	–	–
8	Zetor Brno	–	–	–	–	–	–	–	–	–	1	–	–	–	–	–	1	–	2	–	–	3	–	1	–	–	–	–	–	–	–	–	–
7	AC Nitra	–	–	–	–	1	–	1	–	–	1	–	1	–	–	1	–	2	–	–	–	–	–	–	–	–	–	–	–	–	–	–	–
7	HC Olomouc[9]	–	–	–	–	–	–	–	–	–	1	–	–	2	1	–	2	–	–	1	–	–	–	–	–	–	–	–	–	–	–	–	–
7	ZTK Zvolen	–	–	–	–	–	–	–	2	2	–	–	1	1	–	–	1	–	–	–	–	–	–	–	–	–	–	–	–	–	–	–	–
6	ZTS Martin	–	–	–	1	–	–	1	1	–	–	–	–	2	–	–	–	–	–	–	1	–	–	–	–	–	–	–	–	–	–	–	–
4	HC Karlovy Vary	–	–	–	–	1	1	1	1	–	–	–	–	–	–	–	–	–	–	–	–	–	–	–	–	–	–	–	–	–	–	–	–
4	HC Liberec	–	–	1	1	–	–	2	–	–	–	–	–	–	–	–	–	–	–	–	–	–	–	–	–	–	–	–	–	–	–	–	–
3	Havirov	–	–	–	–	–	2	–	1	–	–	–	–	–	–	–	–	–	–	–	–	–	–	–	–	–	–	–	–	–	–	–	–
3	ZPA Presov	–	–	1	–	–	–	–	–	–	–	1	–	–	–	1	–	–	–	–	–	–	–	–	–	–	–	–	–	–	–	–	–

Former club names: [1]–CHZ Litvinov, [2]–Motor Ceske Budejovice, [3]–Poldi Kladno, [4]–TJ Gottwaldov, TJ Zlin, [5]–TJ Vitkovice, [6]–VSZ Kosice, [7]–Tesla Pardubice, [8]–Skoda Plzen, [9]–DS Olomouc. **Teams with two players selected:** Ingstav Brno, IS Banska Bystrica, Dubnica, Michalovce, Partizan Liptovsky Mikulas, VTJ Pisek, Skalica, Spisska Nova Ves, Topolcany. **Teams with one player selected:** Banik Sokolov, KLH Chomutov, Havlickuv Brod, Ostrava, KC SKP Poprad, Povazska Bystrica, HK Trnava, KHM Zvolen.

Finland

Total	Club	'07	'06	'05	'04	'03	'02	'01	'00	'99	'98	'97	'96	'95	'94	'93	'92	'91	'90	'89	'88	'87	'86	'85	'84	'83	'82	'81	'80	'79	'78	'77	'69 to '76
39	HIFK Helsinki	–	4	1	2	–	5	2	2	4	2	1	–	1	–	2	–	–	–	1	2	–	–	1	2	2	1	1	–	–	–	1	2
36	Jokerit	–	2	–	1	2	6	4	3	3	1	1	1	–	1	–	3	–	2	–	1	1	–	–	1	–	–	1	2	–	–	–	–
34	TPS Turku	–	–	–	1	1	1	3	3	1	3	3	1	3	2	3	–	–	–	–	–	–	1	1	–	–	–	6	1	–	–	–	–
33	Ilves	–	3	3	–	–	2	4	3	1	2	–	–	2	–	–	–	1	1	–	1	–	1	–	2	2	–	2	–	–	2	1	–
24	Karpat	–	–	2	2	3	3	3	–	–	1	1	–	–	–	1	–	1	–	–	–	2	2	–	1	–	1	–	1	–	–	–	–
22	Tappara	2	–	–	1	1	2	2	1	–	–	2	1	1	–	–	–	–	1	–	1	–	4	–	–	–	2	–	–	–	–	–	1
19	Lukko	1	–	–	1	1	1	3	1	2	–	–	–	–	–	–	1	–	1	–	–	1	–	1	–	2	–	–	–	–	–	1	2
16	Assat	–	2	–	–	–	1	–	–	–	1	–	–	1	1	1	–	–	1	–	1	–	–	–	2	2	–	1	–	–	–	–	2
16	Blues Espoo	–	–	1	1	–	1	2	–	2	–	1	–	1	2	–	2	1	1	–	1	–	–	–	–	–	–	–	–	–	–	–	–
12	HPK	–	1	–	–	–	1	1	3	1	1	1	–	–	–	–	2	–	–	1	–	–	–	–	–	–	–	–	–	–	–	–	–
11	JyP Jyvaskyla	–	–	–	1	–	2	1	–	3	–	1	2	–	–	–	–	–	–	–	–	1	–	–	–	–	–	–	–	–	–	–	–
10	KalPa Kuopio	–	1	–	–	1	–	2	1	–	1	–	–	–	2	1	–	–	–	–	–	1	–	–	–	–	–	–	–	–	–	–	–
9	Pelicans	1	–	–	1	–	–	–	–	–	–	–	1	–	–	1	–	2	–	–	–	–	–	–	1	1	1	–	–	–	–	–	–
7	SaiPa Lappeen.	–	–	1	1	1	–	1	1	–	–	–	–	–	–	–	–	–	1	–	–	–	–	–	–	–	–	1	–	–	–	–	–
3	Kiekoo-67	–	–	–	–	–	–	–	–	–	–	–	–	3	–	–	–	–	–	–	–	–	–	–	–	–	–	–	–	–	–	–	–

Teams with two players selected: KooKoo Kouvola, Sapko Savonlinna, Sport Vaasa, TuTo.
Teams with one player selected: Ahmat Hyvinkaa, Hermes Kokkola, Junkkarit Kalajoki, GrIFK Kauniainen, LeKi, S-Kiekko Seinajoki.

Buffalo selected Austrian Thomas Vanek (top) from the University of Minnesota with the fifth pick in the 2003 Entry Draft. Toronto's Tomas Kaberle was selected from Kladno in the Czech Repbulic with the 204th pick in 1996.

Note: International draft selections played outside North America in their draft year.

European-born players drafted from the OHL, QMJHL, WHL, U.S. colleges or other North American leagues are not counted as International players.

For analysis by birthplace, see the following page.

USSR/CIS/Russia

Total	Club	'07	'06	'05	'04	'03	'02	'01	'00	'99	'98	'97	'96	'95	'94	'93	'92	'91	'90	'89	'88	'87	'86	'85	'84	'83	'82	'81	'80	'79	'78	'77	'69 to '76
63	CSKA Moscow	2	1	1	3	3	–	–	–	3	1	–	3	2	5	3	7	4	3	8	5	1	1	1	–	4	1	–	–	–	1	–	–
46	Dynamo Moscow	1	–	–	1	1	–	–	2	2	1	1	1	7	1	2	10	7	4	3	2	–	–	–	–	–	–	–	–	–	–	–	–
33	Krylja Sovetov	–	1	1	2	–	1	1	1	2	1	1	2	3	5	1	3	4	2	1	1	–	–	–	–	–	–	–	–	–	–	–	–
29	Lokomotiv Yaro.2	1	3	2	–	3	1	1	9	–	4	2	2	1	–	–	–	–	–	–	–	–	–	–	–	–	–	–	–	–	–	–	–
22	Lokomotiv Yaro.[1]	–	–	–	–	4	2	–	1	1	3	1	1	5	1	–	–	2	1	–	–	–	–	–	–	–	–	–	–	–	–	–	–
22	Spartak Moscow	–	–	–	–	–	–	6	–	1	–	–	–	1	6	–	4	1	–	–	–	1	–	1	–	–	1	–	–	–	–	–	–
20	Traktor Chelyabinsk	1	1	2	–	–	1	–	–	–	1	1	–	1	1	7	2	–	–	2	–	–	–	–	–	–	–	–	–	–	–	–	–
18	Lada Togliatti	–	2	–	2	–	2	–	2	2	1	3	1	–	–	2	1	–	–	–	–	–	–	–	–	–	–	–	–	–	–	–	–
16	Dynamo 2	–	–	–	–	1	–	–	4	–	3	3	–	–	2	1	2	–	–	–	–	–	–	–	–	–	–	–	–	–	–	–	–
16	Elektrostal	–	–	–	–	2	9	1	–	–	–	1	–	–	–	–	3	–	–	–	–	–	–	–	–	–	–	–	–	–	–	–	–
14	Voskresensk	–	–	–	–	1	–	1	1	–	2	–	–	–	1	–	2	1	3	1	–	–	–	–	–	1	–	–	–	–	–	–	–
13	Severstal Cher.[2]	–	1	–	–	2	–	–	1	5	–	–	1	1	–	1	1	–	–	–	–	–	–	–	–	–	–	–	–	–	–	–	–
11	CSKA Moscow 2	–	2	1	1	2	–	–	–	–	–	2	2	–	1	–	–	–	–	–	–	–	–	–	–	–	–	–	–	–	–	–	–
11	HC CSKA	–	–	–	–	–	4	–	5	2	–	–	–	–	–	–	–	–	–	–	–	–	–	–	–	–	–	–	–	–	–	–	–
11	SKA St. Pete.[3]	–	–	–	–	–	–	2	1	2	–	–	–	–	1	–	1	2	–	–	–	–	–	–	–	–	1	–	–	–	1	–	–
11	Sokol Kiev	–	–	–	–	–	–	–	–	–	–	–	–	2	–	1	3	2	1	–	1	–	–	–	1	–	–	–	–	–	–	–	–
10	Pardaugava Riga[4]	–	–	–	–	–	–	–	–	–	–	–	–	–	–	1	4	1	–	2	1	–	–	–	–	–	–	–	–	–	–	–	1
9	Avangard Omsk	–	–	–	–	–	1	3	1	–	–	–	1	–	3	–	–	–	–	–	–	–	–	–	–	–	–	–	–	–	–	–	–
9	THC Tver	–	–	–	3	3	–	1	2	–	–	–	–	–	–	–	–	–	–	–	–	–	–	–	–	–	–	–	–	–	–	–	–
9	Ufa	–	–	–	–	1	–	–	1	–	–	1	1	1	2	2	–	–	–	–	–	–	–	–	–	–	–	–	–	–	–	–	–
9	Ust-Kamenogorsk	–	–	–	–	1	–	–	–	1	2	–	–	1	2	1	1	–	–	–	–	–	–	–	–	–	–	–	–	–	–	–	–
7	Magnitogorsk	–	1	–	1	1	1	3	–	–	–	–	–	–	–	–	–	–	–	–	–	–	–	–	–	–	–	–	–	–	–	–	–
7	Novokuznetsk	–	–	–	1	1	–	1	2	2	–	–	–	–	–	–	–	–	–	–	–	–	–	–	–	–	–	–	–	–	–	–	–
6	Lada Togliatti 2	–	–	1	–	–	–	2	2	1	–	–	–	–	–	–	–	–	–	–	–	–	–	–	–	–	–	–	–	–	–	–	–
6	Nizhnekamsk	–	–	–	1	–	–	2	2	–	–	1	–	–	–	–	–	–	–	–	–	–	–	–	–	–	–	–	–	–	–	–	–
5	AK Bars Kazan	–	–	–	–	1	–	1	1	–	1	–	–	–	1	–	–	–	–	–	–	–	–	–	–	–	–	–	–	–	–	–	–
5	Avangard Omsk 2	–	–	–	1	1	–	3	–	–	–	–	–	–	–	–	–	–	–	–	–	–	–	–	–	–	–	–	–	–	–	–	–
5	CSK VVS Samara	–	–	–	1	1	–	1	–	1	–	–	–	1	–	–	–	–	–	–	–	–	–	–	–	–	–	–	–	–	–	–	–
5	Perm	–	–	–	–	–	1	1	1	–	–	–	–	1	1	–	–	–	–	–	–	–	–	–	–	–	–	–	–	–	–	–	–
5	Tivali Minsk[5]	–	–	–	1	–	–	–	–	–	–	–	–	–	1	2	–	–	–	–	1	–	–	–	–	–	–	–	–	–	–	–	–
4	Dyn-Energ. Yekat.[6]	–	–	–	–	1	–	–	–	1	1	–	1	–	–	–	–	–	–	–	–	–	–	–	–	–	–	–	–	–	–	–	–
4	Krylja Sovetov 2	–	–	–	–	–	3	–	–	–	–	–	–	–	–	1	–	–	–	–	–	–	–	–	–	–	–	–	–	–	–	–	–
4	Nizhny Novgorod[7]	–	–	–	–	–	–	–	1	–	–	–	–	–	–	–	2	–	1	–	–	–	–	–	–	–	–	–	–	–	–	–	–
3	Ak-Bars Kazan 2	–	–	–	–	1	–	1	–	1	–	–	–	–	–	–	–	–	–	–	–	–	–	–	–	–	–	–	–	–	–	–	–
3	Kristall Saratov	–	–	–	1	–	–	1	–	–	–	–	–	–	–	1	–	–	–	–	–	–	–	–	–	–	–	–	–	–	–	–	–
3	Severstal Cher. 2	–	–	–	–	–	1	–	1	1	–	–	–	–	–	–	–	–	–	–	–	–	–	–	–	–	–	–	–	–	–	–	–

Former club names: 1–Torpedo Yaroslavl, 2–Metallurg Cherepovets, 3–SKA Leningrad, 4–Dynamo Riga, HC Riga, 5–Dynamo Minsk, 6–Avtomobilist Yekaterinburg, 7–Torpedo Gorky.
Teams with two players selected: Dizelist Penza, Metallurg Novokuznetsk 2, Salavat Yulayev Ufa 2, Spartak Moscow 2, Torpedo Nizhny Novgorod 2, Yunost Minsk.
Teams with one player selected: Amur Khabarovsk, Argus Moscow, Avangard Omsk, HC CSKA Moscow 2, Dynamo Khazov, Dynamo-81 Riga, Gazovik Tyumen, HK Gomel, Izohets St. Petersburg, Kapitan Stupino, Khimik Novopolotsk, Khimik Voskresensk 2, Mechel Chelyabinsk, Metallurg Magnitogorsk 2, Metalurgs Liepaja, Mostovik Kurgan, Neftekhimik Nizhnekamsk 2, Neftyanik Almetjevsk, SKA St. Petersburg 2, Spartak St. Petersburg, Sibir Novosibirsk 2, Stalkers-Juniors, Torpedo Nizhny Novgorod 2, THC Tver, Vityaz Podolsk, Vityaz Podolsk 2.

Sweden

Total	Club	'07	'06	'05	'04	'03	'02	'01	'00	'99	'98	'97	'96	'95	'94	'93	'92	'91	'90	'89	'88	'87	'86	'85	'84	'83	'82	'81	'80	'79	'78	'77	'69 to '76
42	Frolunda	5	3	3	4	2	3	3	4	2	1	–	1	1	3	–	1	–	–	1	1	1	–	1	2	–	–	–	–	–	–	–	–
38	Djurgarden	–	1	1	2	–	2	1	4	1	–	2	2	3	–	1	1	2	1	1	–	2	1	–	1	2	1	–	2	1	–	–	3
36	MoDo	–	–	1	1	–	3	–	3	7	–	3	3	–	–	5	2	2	–	–	–	1	–	–	2	–	1	–	–	1	–	–	1
33	Farjestad	–	1	–	–	–	2	1	–	1	6	3	–	2	–	1	2	1	–	1	–	–	–	2	1	1	1	2	1	–	2	2	–
30	Leksand	–	1	1	–	2	–	–	5	–	2	–	1	–	2	2	–	2	–	1	2	1	1	2	2	–	1	–	–	1	–	–	1
25	Brynas Gavle	1	1	–	–	2	–	2	1	1	2	1	1	–	–	1	–	–	–	–	–	4	–	–	2	1	–	1	1	1	1	–	1
25	Sodertalje	1	2	3	1	2	–	1	1	–	1	–	–	–	–	1	–	–	–	2	–	–	2	2	2	1	1	1	–	–	1	–	–
24	AIK Solna	–	–	–	–	–	1	1	–	3	1	1	–	–	1	–	1	1	1	–	–	–	–	4	–	1	3	2	–	1	1	–	1
23	HV 71	1	–	1	2	1	1	–	1	3	4	1	2	–	2	–	–	–	1	–	1	1	–	–	–	–	–	1	–	–	–	–	–
17	Malmo	1	1	1	1	1	4	–	1	1	–	–	2	–	1	1	1	–	–	–	1	–	–	–	–	–	–	–	–	–	–	–	–
15	Vasteras	1	3	–	1	–	1	–	1	–	–	–	–	–	1	1	–	1	1	2	2	–	–	–	–	–	–	–	–	–	–	–	–
14	Lulea	3	–	–	1	–	–	–	2	–	1	1	–	–	–	–	1	–	–	–	1	1	1	–	–	–	–	1	1	–	–	–	–
10	Hammarby	–	1	–	–	–	3	–	1	–	–	1	–	–	–	1	1	–	–	–	–	–	–	–	–	–	–	–	1	1	–	–	–
10	Rogle	1	–	–	–	–	–	–	–	1	–	–	–	1	2	2	–	–	–	–	2	1	–	–	–	–	–	–	–	–	–	–	–
10	Skelleftea	–	–	–	–	–	–	–	–	–	–	1	–	–	–	1	–	–	–	–	1	–	–	–	1	2	1	1	–	–	–	–	2
8	Bjorkloven	–	2	1	–	–	–	–	–	–	–	–	–	–	–	–	–	–	–	–	1	–	–	1	–	–	–	1	2	–	–	–	–
8	Timra	–	–	–	–	–	1	–	–	1	–	–	–	–	1	–	–	–	–	–	–	–	1	1	–	–	–	2	1	–	–	–	–
7	Huddinge	–	1	–	–	–	1	1	–	1	–	–	2	–	–	–	–	1	–	–	–	–	–	–	–	–	–	–	–	–	–	–	–
6	Mora	–	–	–	–	1	–	1	–	–	–	1	1	–	–	–	–	–	–	–	–	–	1	–	–	1	–	–	–	–	–	–	–
6	Orebro	–	–	–	1	–	–	–	–	–	–	–	–	–	–	–	–	–	–	–	–	1	–	1	–	1	–	–	–	–	1	–	1
4	Linkoping	1	1	1	1	–	–	–	–	–	–	–	–	–	–	–	–	–	–	–	–	–	–	–	–	–	–	–	–	–	–	–	–
4	Nacka	–	–	–	–	–	–	–	–	–	–	–	–	–	–	–	2	–	–	1	–	–	1	–	–	–	–	–	–	–	–	–	–
4	Troja/Ljungby	–	–	–	–	1	–	–	–	1	–	–	–	–	–	–	–	–	–	–	1	–	–	1	–	–	–	–	–	–	–	–	–
3	Boden	–	–	–	–	–	–	–	–	–	–	–	–	–	1	–	–	–	–	–	–	–	1	–	–	–	–	–	–	–	–	–	1
3	Falun	–	–	–	–	–	–	–	–	–	–	–	–	–	–	–	–	1	–	–	1	–	–	–	–	–	–	1	–	–	–	–	–
3	Grums	–	–	–	–	–	–	–	1	1	–	–	–	–	1	–	–	–	–	–	–	–	–	–	–	–	–	–	–	–	–	–	–
3	Morrum	–	–	–	–	–	2	1	–	–	–	–	–	–	–	–	–	–	–	–	–	–	–	–	–	–	–	–	–	–	–	–	–
3	Pitea	–	–	–	–	–	–	–	–	–	–	–	–	–	1	–	–	–	1	–	–	–	–	–	–	–	1	–	–	–	–	–	–
3	Stocksund	–	–	–	2	–	–	–	–	–	–	–	–	–	–	–	–	–	–	–	–	–	–	–	–	–	1	–	–	–	–	–	–
3	Team Kiruna	–	–	–	–	–	–	–	–	–	–	–	–	–	–	1	–	–	–	–	–	–	–	–	–	–	1	–	–	–	1	–	–

Teams with two players selected: Hasten, Ostersund, Tingsryd. **Teams with one player selected:** Almtuna, Arboga, Arvika, Bofors, Danderyd Hockey, Fagersta, Jamtland, Karskoga, Kumla, Stocksund, S/G Hockey 83 Gavle, Skovde, Sunne, Talje, Tunabro, Uppsala, Vallentuna, Vasby. Karskoga, Kumla, Stocksund, S/G Hockey 83 Gavle, Skovde, Sunne, Talje, Tunabro, Uppsala, Vallentuna, Vasby.

European Draft Firsts

1969 – First European (and Finn) • LW Tommi Salmelainen, 66th overall by St. Louis.

1974 – First Swede • C Per Alexandersson, 49th overall by Toronto. Four other Swedish-born players were selected that year, including defenseman Stefan Persson, 214th overall by the NY Islanders, who became the first European-trained player to be part of a Stanley Cup winner. (four times, 1980-83).

1975 – First Russian • C Viktor Khatulev, 160th overall by Philadelphia.

1976 – First European Taken in the First Round • Swedish D Bjorn Johansson, 5th overall by the California Seals.

1976 – First Swiss • C Jacques Soguel, 121st overall by St. Louis.

1978 – First Czechoslovak • LW Ladislav Svozil, 194th overall by Detroit.

1978 – First Germans • G Bernard Englbrecht, 196th overall by Atlanta and F Gerd Truntschka, 200th overall by St. Louis.

1989 – First European Taken First Overall • Swedish C Mats Sundin, first overall by Quebec in 1989.

2007 Entry Draft Analysis

BY BIRTHPLACE

Country of Origin

Country	Players Drafted
Canada	102
USA	63
Sweden	17
Russia	8
Czech Republic	5
Finland	4
Germany	3
Slovakia	3
Switzerland	2
Denmark	1
Kazakhstan	1
Nigeria	1
Ukraine	1
Total	**211**

U.S.-Born Players

State	Players Drafted
Michigan	14
Minnesota	14
Connecticut	5
New York	5
Illinois	4
Massachusetts	4
California	3
Ohio	3
Pennsylvania	3
Wisconsin	3
New Jersey	2
Missouri	1
North Dakota	1
Texas	1
Total	**63**

Canadian-Born Players

Province	Players Drafted
Ontario	40
Alberta	19
British Columbia	14
Quebec	10
Manitoba	6
Saskatchewan	5
Nova Scotia	4
New Brunswick	2
Prince Edward Island	2
Total	**102**

BY BIRTH YEAR

Year	Players Drafted
1989	127
1988	66
1987	15
1986	3

BY POSITION

Position	Players Drafted
Defense	60
Center	71
Right Wing	29
Left Wing	31
Goaltender	20

Notes on 2007 First-Round Selections

1. CHICAGO • **PATRICK KANE** • RW • A skilled playmaker with great hockey sense, Patrick Kane is very good at anticipating the play and has a good wrist shot. Though he stands only 5'9" and weighs 160 pounds, he is not afraid to take the puck into traffic and is able to fight through checks. A product of the U.S. National Team Development program, he led the Ontario Hockey League in scoring as a rookie in 2006-07 and helped the United States win a bronze medal at the World Junior Championship.

2. PHILADELPHIA • **JAMES vanRIEMSDYK** • LW • A power forward with great physical presence and ability to protect the puck, James vanRiemsdyk does not give up on the play and has an impressive work ethic. He is a good skater with great acceleration, good stickhandling skill and a hard shot. He stands 6'3"and weighs 200 pounds. A product of the U.S. National Team Development program, vanRiemsdyk won a gold medal at the 2006 Under-18 Tournament.

3. PHOENIX • **KYLE TURRIS** • C • A skilled forward with great playmaking ability, Kyle Turris has good on-ice awareness and a good work ethic. He is a fluid skater with a nose for the net and the ability to control the flow of the game. Turris has an accurate shot with a quick release. He is not afraid of taking a hit and can perform under pressure. He was named MVP of the British Columbia Hockey League in 2007 and was MVP of the 2006 Royal Bank Cup.

4. LOS ANGELES • **THOMAS HICKEY** • D • A defenseman with good offensive instincts, Thomas Hickey positions himself well and has good anticipation of the play. He is able to skate the puck out of the defensive zone and make good outlet passes. Hickey controls the power-play with patience and is smart with the puck. He was named rookie of the year with the Seattle Thunderbirds in 2005-06 and played for Team Pacific at the World Under-17 Challenge.

5. WASHINGTON • **KARL ALZNER** • D • A stay-at-home defenseman who is calm under pressure and composed with the puck, Karl Alzner has good positioning and reads the play well. Alzner stands 6'2" and weighs 206 pounds and wins the battles along the boards in his own zone. He has good skating ability and a strong shot from the point. Alzner won a gold medal with Team Canada at the 2007 World Junior Championship and at the 2005 Under-18 World Cup.

6. EDMONTON • **SAM GAGNER** • C/W • The son of former NHL Dave Gagner, Sam Gagner is a skilled forward with the ability to make the big play. He has very good hands and is creative with the puck. Gagner has a good wrist shot with a quick release and has high-end passing skills both forehand and backhand. He was the youngest player on Canada's gold medal-winning team at the 2007 World Junior Championship.

7. COLUMBUS • **JAKUB VORACEK** • RW • A European player who has adjusted well to the North American game, Jakub Voracek is a skilled forward who can execute plays at high speed. He has good passing ability and can play in traffic. He was named the top offensive rookie in the Quebec Major Junior Hockey League in 2006-07 and represented the Czech Republic at the World Junior and Under-18 Championships.

8. BOSTON • **ZACH HAMILL** • C • A playmaking forward with good stickhandling ability, Zach Hamill is very good on specialty teams and especially effective on the power-play. Hamill sees the ice well and sets up his teammates with good passing ability. He led the Western Hockey League in scoring in 2006-07 and was a key member of Canada's gold medal team at the 2005 Under-18 Junior World Cup.

9. SAN JOSE • **LOGAN COUTURE** • C • A player with good offensive instincts who sees the ice well, Logan Couture plays with energy and protects the puck well with his long reach. He has good playmaking skills, but needs to improve his balance. He won the shooting accuracy competition at the 2007 Ontario Hockey League All-Star Game and played for Team Canada at the World Under-18 Championship.

10. FLORIDA • **KEATON ELLERBY** • D • A cousin of Phoenix Coyotes captain Shane Doan, Keaton Ellerby is a playmaking offensive defenseman that also finishes his checks well. He stands 6'4" and weighs 186 pounds and is a good skater with great mobility. He handles the puck well and uses his long reach effectively. Ellerby won the hardest shot competition (95.6 mph) at the 2007 CHL Top Prospects Game.

11. CAROLINA • **BRANDON SUTTER** • C/RW • The son of former NHLer Brent Sutter (who coached him at Red Deer), Brandon Sutter has a good work ethic and excellent puck-pursuit. He is a skilled forward who is opportunistic in the offensive end and very smart with the puck. Sutter can be used in all situations. He was one of three underage players on Canada's gold medal team at the 2006 Under-18 World Cup and played at the 2007 World Under-18 Championship.

12. MONTREAL • **RYAN McDONAGH** • D • Named "Mr. Hockey" as the top high school prospect in Minnesota, Ryan McDonagh is an offensive defenseman with the skill to rush the puck. He has good first-step quickness and makes quick, accurate passes out of his own end. McDonagh has a good shot from the point and is strong along the boards and in the corners. He was a member of the USA's silver medal-winning team at the 2007 World Under-18 Championship.

13. ST. LOUIS • **LARS ELLER** • C/W • A Danish-born forward playing junior hockey in Sweden, Lars Eller is a skilled playmaker with good mobility and breakaway speed. He competes for the puck and controls it well, using his size and strength to his advantage. Eller possesses an excellent shot with a quick release and he sees the ice well. He competed for Denmark at both the World Junior Division I Championship and the World Under-18 Division I Championship in 2007.

14. COLORADO • **KEVIN SHATTENKIRK** • D • An offensive defenseman with good puck skills, Kevin Shattenkirk reads the play well and is clever in transition. He has good mobility and quick feet. A product of the U.S. National Team Development Program, Shattenkirk captained the Under-18 team in 2006–07 and won a silver medal at the 2007 World Under-18 Championship. He also won silver at the 2006 World Under-17 Challenge.

15. EDMONTON • **ALEX PLANTE** • D • Though his father Cam set a Western Hockey League record for points by a defenseman, Alex Plante is a stay-at-home blueliner who can skate the puck out of his zone with his long stride. Standing 6'3" and weighing 225 pounds, Plante plays a sound positional game. He can handle and shoot the puck well, but will need to improve his speed and agility. He is steady and efficient, and though not flashy, he is a solid player.

16. MINNESOTA • **COLTON GILLIES** • C • The nephew of former New York Islanders great Clark Gillies, Colton Gillies is a 6'4" power forward. He has great speed and uses his reach to his advantage on the penalty kill. Gillies out-muscles his opponents and has the ability to land punishing checks, but needs to get better around the net. He was a member of Team Canada at the 2007 Under-18 Championship, and won a gold medal at the 2006 Under-18 Junior World Cup.

17. NY RANGERS • **ALEXEI CHEREPANOV** • RW • With good puckhandling and good decision making, Alexei Cherepanov is an offensive forward with great acceleration and a nose for the net. He has a quick release and can shoot the puck at top speed. Cherepanov broke Pavel Bure's rookie record with 18 goals in the Russian league in 2006-07 and was named top forward at the World Junior Championship.

18. ST. LOUIS • **IAN COLE** • D • A stay-at-home defenseman with good hockey sense, Ian Cole has quick feet and a good shot from the point. He has good passing ability and likes to make the long stretch pass. A product of the U.S. National Team Development Program, Cole won a silver medal at the 2007 World Under-18 Championship and at the 2006 World Under-17 Hockey Challenge.

19. ANAHEIM • **LOGAN MacMILLAN** • D • The son of former NHLer Bob MacMillan, Logan MacMillan is a power forward who plays with an edge. He has good acceleration and mobility and goes hard to the net. He protects the puck and is defensively responsible. MacMillan won gold with Team Canada at the 2006 Under-18 Junior World Cup and was captain of Team Atlantic at the World Under-17 challenge.

20. PITTSBURGH • **ANGELO ESPOSITO** • C • An excellent skater with top-end speed and mobility, Angelo Esposito sees the ice well and has the ability to make pinpoint passes. A Memorial Cup champion and top offensive rookie with the Quebec Remparts in 2006, Esposito captained Team Canada at the 2006 Under-18 Junior World Cup and played at the 2007 World Under-18 Championship.

21. EDMONTON • **RILEY NASH** • C • A shifty center with good skating ability, Riley Nash was named 2007 rookie of the year in the British Columbia Hockey League after leading his team in scoring. Nash handles the puck with ease and is smart positionally, though he needs to be more consistent through 60 minutes. He was a member of Team Pacific at the 2006 World Under-17 Challenge.

22. MONTREAL • **MAX PACIORETTY** • LW • A competitive power forward with a good physical presence, Max Pacioretty does what it takes to help his team win. Pacioretty is a good skater with excellent first-step quickness. He has a very good wrist shot with a quick release and is strong in the face-off circle. At 6'1" and 203 pounds, he has good size and hits hard. He played in the 2007 USHL All-Star Game as a rookie.

23. NASHVILLE • **JONATHON BLUM** • D • A mobile, heads-up defenseman, Jonathon Blum makes good decisions with the puck and has high-end passing ability. Blum has good positioning and rarely gets beat, though he needs to get tougher along the boards and improve his physical presence. He is good on special teams and very patient with the puck. Blum has won back-to-back Western Hockey League titles and the 2007 Memorial Cup with the Vancouver Giants.

24. CALGARY • **MIKAEL BACKLUND** • C • A smart center with excellent speed, Mikael Backlund has soft hands and high-end passing ability. He sees the ice well and has good hockey sense. Backlund has a strong shot and a nose for the net. He did not play a lot due to an injury in 2006-07, but he helped Sweden win a bronze medal at the 2007 World Under-18 Championship and was the tournament's top goal scorer. He was MVP of the 2006 Mac's Midget Tournament.

25. VANCOUVER • **PATRICK WHITE**• C • A strong player with a physical presence, Patrick White plays tough in the corners and in traffic. He is also a skilled forward who can play right wing and get off his wrist shot with ease. White was the Associated Press player of the year for Minnesota boys hockey and led his high school to the Class AA state championship title game two years in a row. He won a silver medal with the U.S. team at the 2007 World Under-18 Championship.

26. ST. LOUIS • **DAVID PERRON** • LW • A hard-working, skilled forward, David Perron is very smart defensively and forces the play with his tenacious forechecking. His quick stick and quick hands often take defenders by surprise. Perron is heads up with the puck and makes impressive passes through traffic. Perron led all rookies in goals (39) and plus-minus (+37) in the Quebec Major Junior Hockey League in 2006-07 and helped Lewiston win the league championship.

27. DETROIT • **BRENDAN SMITH** • D • A skilled defenseman who's good with the puck, Brendan Smith has good mobility and a good skating stride. He is able to join the rush well and also gets involved physically, but needs to make better decisions with the puck. He led all defenseman in scoring with the St. Michael's Buzzers in 2006-07. He was an All-Star in 2006 and played for Canada East at the World Junior A Championship, winning a silver medal.

28. SAN JOSE • **NICHOLAS PETRECKI** • D • A stay-at-home defenseman with excellent speed and lateral quickness, Nicholas Petrecki has a strong physical presence on the ice with the ability to make big hits. He is quick to the puck and makes hard, accurate passes. Petrecki was fourth among USHL defensemen with 11 goals in 2006-07 and was sixth in plus-minus (+17). As a boy, he played at the Quebec Pee Wee tournament and considers it his most memorable experience..

29. OTTAWA • **JAMES O'BRIEN** • C • A skilled forward with good on-ice awareness, James O'Brien has a good work ethic. He handles the puck well and has a good wrist shot. O'Brien was the youngest player in Division I college at the University of Minnesota in 2006-07. A product of the U.S. National Team Development Program, he won a silver medal at the 2007 World Under-18 Championship.

30. PHOENIX • **NICK ROSS** • D • A playmaking defenseman who's very good at reading the ice, Nick Ross has good speed and is able to jump into the rush. He also has a strong physical presence and can deliver the big hit, though at times his play appears to be too casual. He finished third in the Western Hockey League among all 16-year old defensemen in 2005-06 and played in the 2007 CHL Top Prospects game.

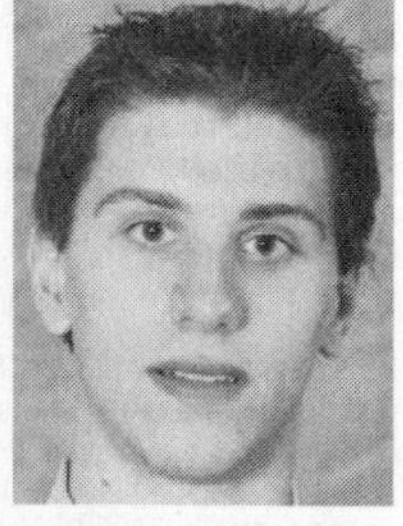

Players selected first through tenth in the 2007 NHL Entry Draft. (All rows left to right):
Top row: 1. Patrick Kane, RW, Chicago;
2. James vanRiemsdyk, LW, Philadelphia.
Second row: 3. Kyle Turris, C, Phoenix;
4. Thomas Hickey, D, Los Angeles.
Third row: 5. Karl Alzner, D, Washington;
6. Sam Gagner, C/W, Edmonton.
Fourth row: 7. Jakub Voracek, RW, Columbus;
8. Zach Hamill, C, Boston.
Bottom row: 9. Logan Couture, C, San Jose;
10. Keaton Ellerby, D, Florida.

2007 NHL ENTRY DRAFT

FIRST ROUND

Pick	Claimed by		Amateur Club	Position
1	CHI	Patrick Kane	London	RW
2	PHI	James vanRiemsdyk	USA U-18	LW
3	PHX	Kyle Turris	Burnaby	C
4	LA	Thomas Hickey	Seattle	D
5	WSH	Karl Alzner	Calgary	D
6	EDM	Sam Gagner	London	C/W
7	CBJ	Jakub Voracek	Halifax	RW
8	BOS	Zach Hamill	Everett	C
9	SJ	Logan Couture	Ottawa	C
10	FLA	Keaton Ellerby	Kamloops	D
11	CAR	Brandon Sutter	Red Deer	C/RW
12	MTL	Ryan McDonagh	Cretin-Derham	D
13	STL	Lars Eller	Frolunda Jr.	C
14	COL	Kevin Shattenkirk	USA U-18	D
15	EDM	Alex Plante	Calgary	D
16	MIN	Colton Gillies	Saskatoon	C
17	NYR	Alexei Cherepanov	Omsk	RW
18	STL	Ian Cole	USA U-18	D
19	ANA	Logan MacMillan	Halifax	C
20	PIT	Angelo Esposito	Quebec	C
21	EDM	Riley Nash	Salmon Arm	C
22	MTL	Max Pacioretty	Sioux City	LW
23	NSH	Jonathon Blum	Vancouver	D
24	CGY	Mikael Backlund	Vasteras	C
25	VAN	Patrick White	Tri-City	C
26	STL	David Perron	Lewiston	LW
27	DET	Brendan Smith	St. Michael's	D
28	SJ	Nicholas Petrecki	Omaha	D
29	OTT	James O'Brien	U of Minnesota	C
30	PHX	Nick Ross	Regina	D

SECOND ROUND

Pick	Claimed by		Amateur Club	Position
31	BUF	T.J. Brennan	St. John's	D
32	PHX	Brett MacLean	Oshawa	LW
33	VAN	Taylor Ellington	Everett	D
34	WSH	Josh Godfrey	Sault Ste. Marie	D
35	BOS	Tommy Cross	Westminster	D
36	PHX	Joel Gistedt	Frolunda	G
37	CBJ	Stefan Legein	Mississauga	RW
38	CHI	William Sweatt	Colorado College	LW
39	STL	Simon Hjalmarsson	Frolunda Jr.	RW
40	FLA	Michal Repik	Vancouver	RW
41	PHI	Kevin Marshall	Lewiston	D
42	ANA	Eric Tangradi	Belleville	C
43	MTL	P.K. Subban	Belleville	D
44	STL	Aaron Palushaj	Des Moines	RW
45	COL	Colby Cohen	Lincoln	D
46	WSH	Theo Ruth	USA U-18	D
47	TB	Dana Tyrell	Prince George	C/RW
48	NYR	Antoine Lafleur	PEI	G
49	COL	Trevor Cann	Peterborough	G
50	LA	Nico Sacchetti	Virginia High	C
51	PIT	Keven Veilleux	Victoriaville	C
52	L.A	Oscar Moller	Chilliwack	RW
53	CBJ	Will Weber	Gaylord High	D
54	NSH	Jeremy Smith	Plymouth	G
55	COL	T.J. Galiardi	Dartmouth	W
56	CHI	Akim Aliu	Sudbury	C/RW
57	NJ	Mike Hoeffel	USA U-18	W
58	NSH	Nick Spaling	Kitchener	C
59	BUF	Drew Schiestel	Mississauga	D
60	OTT	Ruslan Bashkirov	Quebec	LW
61	LA	Wayne Simmonds	Owen Sound	RW

THIRD ROUND

Pick	Claimed by		Amateur Club	Position
62	NYI	Mark Katic	Sarnia	D
63	ANA	Maxime Macenauer	Rouyn-Noranda	C
64	DAL	Sergei Korostin	Dynamo Moscow	RW
65	MTL	Olivier Fortier	Rimouski	C
66	PHI	Garrett Klotz	Saskatoon	LW
67	ATL	Spencer Machacek	Vancouver	RW
68	CBJ	Jake Hansen	Sioux Falls	W
69	CHI	Maxime Tanguay	Rimouski	C
70	CGY	John Negrin	Kootenay	D
71	FLA	Yevgeny Dadonov	Chelyabinsk	RW
72	CAR	Drayson Bowman	Spokane	C/LW
73	MTL	Yannick Weber	Kitchener	D
74	TOR	Dale Mitchell	Oshawa	RW
75	T.B	Luca Cunti	GCK Zurich Jr.	C
76	NYI	Jason Gregoire	Lincoln	LW
77	TB	Alexander Killorn	Deerfield	C
78	PIT	Robert Bortuzzo	Kitchener	D
79	NJ	Nick Palmieri	Erie	RW
80	PIT	Casey Pierro-Zabotel	Merritt	C
81	NSH	Ryan Thang	U of Notre Dame	LW
82	LA	Bryan Cameron	Belleville	C/RW
83	S.J	Timo Pielmeier	Koln Jr.	G
84	WSH	Phil Desimone	Sioux City	C
85	STL	Brett Sonne	Calgary	C/LW
86	CHI	Josh Unice	USA U-18	G
87	NJ	Corbin McPherson	Cowichan Valley	D
88	DET	Joakim Andersson	Frolunda Jr.	C
89	BUF	Corey Tropp	Sioux Falls	RW
90	OTT	Louie Caporusso	St. Michaels	C/LW
91	SJ	Tyson Sexsmith	Vancouver	G

FOURTH ROUND

Pick	Claimed by		Amateur Club	Position
92	ANA	Justin Vaive	USA U-18	LW
93	ANA	Steven Kampfer	U of Michigan	D
94	CBJ	Maxim Mayorov	Almetjevsk	LW
95	LA	Alec Martinez	Miami U.	D
96	STL	Cade Fairchild	USA U-18	D
97	EDM	Linus Omark	Lulea	LW
98	ANA	Sebastian Stefaniszin	Eisb. Jrs. Berlin	G
99	TOR	Matt Frattin	Fort Saskatchewan	RW
100	STL	Travis Erstad	Lincoln	C/RW
101	FLA	Matt Rust	USA U-18	C
102	CAR	Justin McCrae	Saskatoon	C
103	PHX	Vladimir Ruzicka	Slavia Jr.	C
104	TOR	Ben Winnett	Salmon Arm	LW
105	COL	Brad Malone	Sioux Falls	C/LW
106	NYI	Maxim Gratchev	Rimouski	LW
107	TB	Mitch Fadden	Lethbridge	C
108	WSH	Brett Bruneteau	Omaha	C
109	LA	Dwight King	Lethbridge	C/LW
110	MIN	Justin Falk	Spokane	D
111	PIT	Luca Caputi	Mississauga	LW
112	DAL	Colton Sceviour	Portland	C/RW
113	SJ	Kent Patterson	Cedar Rapids	G
114	NSH	Ben Ryan	Des Moines	C
115	ATL	Niclas Lucenius	Tappara Jr.	C
116	CGY	Keith Aulie	Brandon	D
117	NJ	Matt Halischuk	Kitchener	RW
118	PIT	Alex Grant	Saint John	D
119	NSH	Mark Santorelli	Chilliwack	C
120	OTT	Ben Blood	Shat.St.Mary's	D
121	ANA	Mattias Modig	Lulea	G

FIFTH ROUND

Pick	Claimed by		Amateur Club	Position
122	PHI	Mario Kempe	St. John's	RW
123	PHX	Maxim Goncharov	CSKA	D
124	LA	Linden Rowat	Regina	G
125	WSH	Brett Leffler	Regina	RW
126	CHI	Joseph Lavin	USA U-18	D
127	EDM	Milan Kytnar	Topolcany	C
128	DAL	Austin Smith	The Gunnery	RW
129	DAL	Jamie Benn	Victoria	LW
130	BOS	Denis Reul	Heil./Mann. Jr.	D
131	FLA	John Lee	Waterloo	D
132	CAR	Chris Terry	Plymouth	LW
133	MTL	Joe Stejskal	Grand Rapids	D
134	TOR	Juraj Mikus	Trencin	D
135	COL	Paul Carey	Salisbury	C
136	DAL	Ondrej Roman	Spokane	C
137	LA	Joshua Turnbull	Waterloo	C
138	NYR	Max Campbell	Strathroy	C
139	BUF	Bradley Eidsness	Okotoks	G
140	MIN	Cody Almond	Kelowna	C
141	PIT	Jake Muzzin	Sault Ste. Marie	D
142	MTL	Andrew Conboy	Omaha	LW
143	CGY	Mickey Renaud	Windsor	C
144	NSH	Andreas Thuresson	Malmo	C
145	VAN	Charles-Antoine Messier	Baie-Comeau	C
146	VAN	Ilja Kablukov	CSKA	C
147	BUF	Jean-Simon Allard	St. John's	C
148	DET	Randy Cameron	Moncton	C
149	DAL	Michael Neal	Belleville	LW
150	TB	Matt Marshall	Nobles	C/RW
151	ANA	Brett Morrison	PEI	C

SIXTH ROUND

Pick	Claimed by		Amateur Club	Position
152	PHI	Jonathon Kalinski	Minnesota State	LW
153	PHX	Scott Darling	Capital District	G
154	WSH	Dan Dunn	Wellington	G
155	COL	Jens Hellgren	Frolunda Jr.	D
156	CHI	Richard Greenop	Windsor	C
157	EDM	William Quist	Tingsryd	LW
158	CBJ	Allen York	Camrose	G
159	BOS	Alain Goulet	Aurora	D
160	STL	Anthony Peluso	Erie	D
161	PHI	Patrick Maroon	St. Louis	LW
162	CAR	Brett Bellemore	Plymouth	D
163	MTL	Nichlas Torp	HV 71 Jr.	D
164	TOR	Christopher DiDomenico	Saint John	C
165	S.J	Patrik Zackrisson	Rogle	RW
166	NYI	Blake Kessel	Waterloo	D
167	T.B	Johan Harju	Lulea	LW
168	NYR	Carl Hagelin	Sodertalje Jr.	LW
169	BOS	Radim Ostrcil	Vsetin	D
170	MIN	Harri Ilvonen	Tappara Jr.	D
171	PIT	Dustin Jeffrey	Sault Ste. Marie	C
172	DAL	Luke Gazdic	Erie	LW
173	SJ	Nick Bonino	Avon Old Farms	C
174	NSH	Robert Dietrich	Dusseldorf	D
175	ATL	John Albert	USA U-18	C
176	VAN	Taylor Matson	Des Moines	C
177	N.J	Vili Sopanen	Pelicans Jr.	RW
178	DET	Zack Torquato	Erie	C
179	BUF	Paul Byron	Gatineau	C
180	WSH	Justin Taylor	London	C
181	FLA	Corey Syvret	Guelph	D

SEVENTH ROUND

Pick	Claimed by	Amateur Club	Position
182 PHI	Brad Phillips	USA U-18	G
183 TB	Torrie Jung	Kelowna	G
184 LA	Josh Kidd	Erie	D
185 WSH	Nick Larson	Omaha	C
186 CGY	C.J. Severyn	USA U-18	LW
187 BUF	Nick Eno	Green Mountain	G
188 LA	Matt Fillier	St. John's	C/LW
189 BOS	Jordan Knackstedt	Moose Jaw	RW
190 STL	Trevor Nill	Compuware Midget	C
191 FLA	Ryan Watson	Cambridge	LW
192 MTL	Scott Kishel	Virginia High	D
193 NYR	David Skokan	Rimouski	C
194 TOR	Carl Gunnarsson	Linkoping	D
195 COL	Johan Alcen	Brynas	RW
196 NYI	Simon Lacroix	Shawinigan	D
197 TB	Michael Ward	Lewiston	D
198 NYR	Danny Hobbs	Ohio	C/RW
199 WSH	Andrew Glass	Nobles	LW
200 MIN	Carson McMillan	Calgary	RW
201 SJ	Justin Braun	Mass-Amherst	D
202 FLA	Sergei Gaiduchenko	Yaroslavl 2	G
203 SJ	Frazer McLaren	Portland	LW
204 NSH	Atte Engren	Lukko Jr.	G
205 ATL	Paul Postma	Swift Current	D
206 VAN	Dan Gendur	Everett	RW
207 NJ	Ryan Molle	Swift Current	D
208 DET	Bryan Rufenach	Lindsay	D
209 BUF	Drew Mackenzie	Taft School	D
210 TB	Justin Courtnall	Burnaby	LW
211 CBJ	Trent Vogelhuber	St. Louis - NAHL	RW

First Two Rounds
2006–2004

2006

FIRST ROUND

Pick	Claimed by	Amateur Club	Position
1 St.L.	Erik Johnson	USA U-18	D
2 Pit.	Jordan Staal	Peterborough	C
3 Chi.	Jonathan Toews	U. of North Dakota	C
4 Wsh.	Nicklas Backstrom	Brynas	C
5 Bos.	Phil Kessel	U. of Minnesota	C
6 CBJ	Derick Brassard	Drummondville	C
7 NYI	Kyle Okposo	Des Moines	RW
8 Phx.	Peter Mueller	Everett	C
9 Min.	James Sheppard	Cape Breton	C
10 Fla.	Michael Frolik	Kladno	C
11 L.A.	Jonathan Bernier	Lewiston	G
12 Atl.	Bryan Little	Barrie	C
13 Tor.	Jiri Tlusty	Kladno	C
14 Van.	Michael Grabner	Spokane	RW
15 T.B.	Riku Helenius	Ilves	G
16 S.J.	Ty Wishart	Prince George	D
17 L.A.	Trevor Lewis	Des Moines	C
18 Col.	Chris Stewart	Kingston	RW
19 Ana.	Mark Mitera	U. of Michigan	D
20 Mtl.	David Fischer	Apple Valley	D
21 NYR	Bobby Sanguinetti	Owen Sound	D
22 Phi.	Claude Giroux	Gatineau	RW
23 Wsh.	Simeon Varlamov	Yaroslavl 2	G
24 Buf.	Dennis Persson	Vasteras	D
25 St.L.	Patrik Berglund	Vasteras	C
26 Cgy.	Leland Irving	Everett	G
27 Dal.	Ivan Vishnevskiy	Rouyn Noranda	D
28 Ott.	Nick Foligno	Sudbury	LW
29 Phx.	Chris Summers	USA U-18	D
30 N.J.	Matthew Corrente	Saginaw	D

SECOND ROUND

Pick	Claimed by	Amateur Club	Position
31 St.L.	Tomas Kana	Vitkovice	C
32 Pit.	Carl Sneep	Brainerd	D
33 Chi.	Igor Makarov	Krylja	RW
34 Wsh.	Michal Neuvirth	Sparta Jr.	G
35 Wsh.	Francois Bouchard	Baie Comeau	RW
36 S.J.	Jamie Mcginn	Ottawa	LW
37 Bos.	Yuri Alexandrov	Cherepovets	D
38 Ana.	Bryce Swan	Halifax	RW
39 Phi.	Andreas Nodl	Sioux Falls	RW
40 Min.	Ondrej Fiala	Everett	C
41 Det.	Cory Emmerton	Kingston	C
42 Phi.	Michael Ratchuk	USA U-18	D
43 Atl.	Riley Holzapfel	Moose Jaw	C
44 Tor.	Nikolai Kulemin	Magnitogorsk	W
45 Edm.	Jeff Petry	Des Moines	D
46 Buf.	Jhonas Enroth	Sodertalje	G
47 Det.	Shawn Matthias	Belleville	C
48 L.A.	Joe Ryan	Quebec	D
49 Mtl.	Ben Maxwell	Kootenay	C
50 Bos.	Milan Lucic	Vancouver	LW
51 Col.	Nigel Williams	USA U-18	D
52 Wsh.	Keith Seabrook	Burnaby	D
53 Mtl.	Mathieu Carle	Acadie-Bathurst	D
54 NYR	Artem Anisimov	Yaroslavl	C
55 Phi.	Denis Bodrov	Togliatti	D
56 Nsh.	Blake Geoffrion	USA U-18	LW
57 Buf.	Mike Weber	Windsor	D
58 N.J.	Alexander Vasyunov	Yaroslavl 2	LW
59 Col.	Codey Burki	Brandon	C
60 NYI	Jesse Joensuu	Assat	W
61 Chi.	Simon Danis-Pepin	U. of Maine	D
62 Det.	Dick Axelsson	Huddinge	W
63 Car.	Jamie Mcbain	USA U-18	D

2005

FIRST ROUND

Pick	Claimed by	Amateur Club	Position
1 Pit.	Sidney Crosby	Rimouski	C
2 Ana.	Bobby Ryan	Owen Sound	RW
3 Car.	Jack Johnson	USA U-18	D
4 Min.	Benoit Pouliot	Sudbury	LW
5 Mtl.	Carey Price	Tri-City	G
6 CBJ	Gilbert Brule	Vancouver	C
7 Chi.	Jack Skille	USA U-18	RW
8 S.J.	Devin Setoguchi	Saskatoon	RW
9 Ott.	Brian Lee	Moorhead	D
10 Van.	Luc Bourdon	Val D'or	D
11 L.A.	Anze Kopitar	Sodertalje Jr.	C
12 NYR	Marc Staal	Sudbury	D
13 Buf.	Marek Zagrapan	Chicoutimi	C
14 Wsh.	Sasha Pokulok	Cornell	D
15 NYI	Ryan O'Marra	Erie	C
16 Atl.	Alex Bourret	Lewiston	RW
17 Phx.	Martin Hanzal	C. Budejovice	C
18 Nsh.	Ryan Parent	Guelph	D
19 Det.	Jakub Kindl	Kitchener	D
20 Fla.	Kenndal McArdle	Moose Jaw	LW
21 Tor.	Tuukka Rask	Ilves Jr.	G
22 Bos.	Matt Lashoff	Kitchener	D
23 N.J.	Nicklas Bergfors	Sodertalje	RW
24 St.L.	T.J. Oshie	Warroad	C
25 Edm.	Andrew Cogliano	St. Mike's B's	C
26 Cgy.	Matt Pelech	Sarnia	D
27 Wsh.	Joe Finley	Sioux Falls	D
28 Dal.	Matt Niskanen	Virginia	D
29 Phi.	Steve Downie	Windsor	RW
30 T.B.	Vladimir Mihalik	Presov	D

SECOND ROUND

Pick	Claimed by	Amateur Club	Position
31 Ana.	Brendan Mikkelson	Portland	D
32 Fla.	Tyler Plante	Brandon	G
33 Dal.	James Neal	Plymouth	LW
34 Col.	Ryan Stoa	USA U-18	C
35 S.J.	Marc-Edouard Vlasic	Quebec	D
36 Edm.	Taylor Chorney	Shat.-St. Mary's	D
37 St.L.	Scott Jackson	Seattle	D
38 N.J.	Jeff Frazee	USA U-18	G
39 Bos.	Petr Kalus	Vitkovice Jr.	LW
40 NYR	Michael Sauer	Portland	D
41 Atl.	Ondrej Pavelec	Kladno Jr.	G
42 Det.	Justin Abdelkader	Cedar Rapids	LW
43 Chi.	Michael Blunden	Erie	RW
44 Col.	Paul Stastny	U. of Denver	C
45 Mtl.	Guillaume Latendresse	Drummondville	RW
46 NYI	Dustin Kohn	Calgary	D
47 Col.	Tom Fritsche	Ohio State	LW
48 Buf.	Philip Gogulla	Koln	RW
49 Atl.	Chad Denny	Lewiston	D
50 L.A.	Dany Roussin	Rimouski	LW
51 Van.	Mason Raymond	Camrose	LW
52 Col.	Chris Durand	Seattle	C
53 Atl.	Andrew Kozek	South Surrey	W
54 Chi.	Dan Bertram	Boston College	RW
55 CBJ	Adam McQuaid	Sudbury	D
56 NYR	Marc-Andre Cliche	Lewiston	RW
57 Min.	Matt Kassian	Kamloops	LW
58 Car.	Nathan Hagemo	U. of Minnesota	D
59 Phx.	Pier-Olivier Pelletier	Drummondville	G
60 L.A.	T.J. Fast	Camrose	D
61 Pit.	Michael Gergen	Shat.-St. Mary's	W

2004

FIRST ROUND

Pick	Claimed by	Amateur Club	Position
1 Wsh.	Alex Ovechkin	Dynamo	LW
2 Pit.	Evgeni Malkin	Magnitogorsk	C
3 Chi.	Cam Barker	Medicine Hat	D
4 Car.	Andrew Ladd	Calgary	LW
5 Phx.	Blake Wheeler	Breck	RW
6 NYR	Al Montoya	U. of Michigan	G
7 Fla.	Rostislav Olesz	Vitkovice	C
8 CBJ	Alexandre Picard	Lewiston	LW
9 Ana.	Ladislav Smid	Liberec	D
10 Atl.	Boris Valabik	Kitchener	D
11 L.A.	Lauri Tukonen	Blues Espoo	RW
12 Min.	A.J. Thelen	Michigan State	D
13 Buf.	Drew Stafford	U. of North Dakota	RW
14 Edm.	Devan Dubnyk	Kamloops	G
15 Nsh.	Alexander Radulov	Tver	LW
16 NYI	Petteri Nokelainen	SaiPa	C
17 St.L.	Marek Schwarz	Sparta Praha	G
18 Mtl.	Kyle Chipchura	Prince Albert	C
19 NYR	Lauri Korpikoski	TPS Turku Jr.	LW
20 N.J.	Travis Zajac	Salmon Arm	C
21 Col.	Wojtek Wolski	Brampton	LW
22 S.J.	Lukas Kaspar	Litvinov	RW
23 Ott.	Andrej Meszaros	Trencin	D
24 Cgy.	Kris Chucko	Salmon Arm	LW
25 Edm.	Rob Schremp	London	C
26 Van.	Cory Schneider	Phillips-Andover	G
27 Wsh.	Jeff Schultz	Calgary	D
28 Dal.	Mark Fistric	Vancouver	D
29 Wsh.	Mike Green	Saskatoon	D
30 T.B.	Andy Rogers	Calgary	D

Since Marc-Andre Fleury was selected first overall by the Pittsburgh Penguins in 2003, just two goaltenders have been taken in the top ten at the NHL Entry Draft: the New York Rangers used the sixth pick in 2004 to select Al Montoya (top), and the Montreal Canadiens used the fifth pick in 2005 to select Carey Price.

SECOND ROUND

Pick	Claimed by	Amateur Club	Position
31 Pit.	Johannes Salmonsson	Djurgarden	LW
32 Chi.	Dave Bolland	London	C/RW
33 Wsh.	Christopher Bourque	Cushing Academy	C
34 Dal.	Johan Fransson	Lulea	D
35 Phx.	Logan Stephenson	Tri-City	D
36 NYR	Darin Olver	Northern Michigan	C
37 Fla.	David Shantz	Mississauga	G
38 Car.	Justin Peters	St. Michael's	G
39 Ana.	Jordan Smith	Sault Ste. Marie	D
40 Atl.	Grant Lewis	Dartmouth	D
41 Chi.	Bryan Bickell	Ottawa	LW
42 Min.	Roman Voloshenko	Krylja Sovetov	LW
43 Buf.	Michael Funk	Portland	D
44 Edm.	Roman Teslyuk	Kamloops	D
45 Chi.	Ryan Garlock	Windsor	C
46 CBJ	Adam Pineault	Boston College	RW
47 NYI	Blake Comeau	Kelowna	RW
48 NYR	Dane Byers	Prince Albert	LW
49 St.L.	Carl Soderberg	Malmo	C
50 Phx.	Enver Lisin	Saratov	RW
51 NYR	Bruce Graham	Moncton	C
52 Dal.	Raymond Sawada	Nanaimo	RW
53 Fla.	David Booth	Michigan State	LW
54 Chi.	Jakub Sindel	Sparta Praha	C
55 Col.	Victor Oreskovich	Green Bay	RW
56 Dal.	Niklas Grossman	Sodertalje Jr.	D
57 Edm.	Geoff Paukovich	U.S. Nat'l U-18	LW
58 Ott.	Kirill Lyamin	CSKA Moscow	D
59 CBJ	Kyle Wharton	Ottawa	D
60 NYR	Brandon Dubinsky	Portland	C
61 Pit.	Alex Goligoski	Sioux Falls	D
62 Wsh.	Michail Yunkov	Krylja	C
63 Bos.	David Krejci	Kladno Jr.	C
64 Bos.	Martins Karsums	Moncton	RW
65 T.B.	Mark Tobin	Rimouski	LW

First Round and Other Notable Selections 2003–1969

2003

FIRST ROUND

Pick	Claimed by		Amateur Club	Position
1	Pit.	Marc-Andre Fleury	Cape Breton	G
2	Car.	Eric Staal	Peterborough	C
3	Fla.	Nathan Horton	Oshawa	C
4	CBJ	Nikolai Zherdev	CSKA Moscow	W
5	Buf.	Thomas Vanek	U. of Minnesota	LW
6	S.J.	Milan Michalek	Budejovice	RW
7	Nsh.	Ryan Suter	U.S. National U-18	D
8	Atl.	Braydon Coburn	Portland	D
9	Cgy.	Dion Phaneuf	Red Deer	D
10	Mtl.	Andrei Kostitsyn	CSKA Moscow 2	RW
11	Phi.	Jeff Carter	Sault Ste. Marie	C
12	NYR	Hugh Jessiman	Dartmouth	RW
13	L.A.	Dustin Brown	Guelph	RW
14	Chi.	Brent Seabrook	Lethbridge	D
15	NYI	Robert Nilsson	Leksand	RW
16	S.J.	Steve Bernier	Moncton	RW
17	N.J.	Zach Parise	North Dakota	C
18	Wsh.	Eric Fehr	Brandon	RW
19	Ana.	Ryan Getzlaf	Calgary	C
20	Min.	Brent Burns	Brampton	RW
21	Bos.	Mark Stuart	Colorado College	D
22	Edm.	Marc-Antoine Pouliot	Rimouski	C
23	Van.	Ryan Kesler	Ohio State	C
24	Phi.	Mike Richards	Kitchener	C
25	Fla.	Anthony Stewart	Kingston	C
26	L.A.	Brian Boyle	St. Sebastian's H.S.	C
27	L.A.	Jeff Tambellini	U. of Michigan	LW
28	Ana.	Corey Perry	London	RW
29	Ott.	Patrick Eaves	Boston College	RW
30	St.L.	Shawn Belle	Tri-City	D

OTHER NOTABLE SELECTIONS

Pick	Claimed by		Amateur Club	Position
45	Bos.	Patrice Bergeron	Acadie-Bathurst	C
47	S.J.	Matt Carle	River City	D
49	Nsh.	Shea Weber	Kelowna	D
61	Mtl.	Maxim Lapierre	Montreal	C
148	St.L.	Lee Stempniak	Dartmouth	RW
271	Mtl.	Jaroslav Halak	Bratislava Jr.	G

2002

FIRST ROUND

Pick	Claimed by		Amateur Club	Position
1	CBJ	Rick Nash	London	LW
2	Atl.	Kari Lehtonen	Jokerit	G
3	Fla.	Jay Bouwmeester	Medicine Hat	D
4	Phi.	Joni Pitkanen	Karpat	D
5	Pit.	Ryan Whitney	Boston U.	D
6	Nsh.	Scottie Upshall	Kamloops	RW
7	Ana.	Joffrey Lupul	Medicine Hat	C
8	Min.	Pierre-Marc Bouchard	Chicoutimi	C
9	Fla.	Petr Taticek	Sault Ste. Marie	C
10	Cgy.	Eric Nystrom	U. of Michigan	LW
11	Buf.	Keith Ballard	U. of Minnesota	D
12	Wsh.	Steve Eminger	Kitchener	D
13	Wsh.	Alexander Semin	Chelyabinsk	LW
14	Mtl.	Christopher Higgins	Yale	C
15	Edm.	Jesse Niinimaki	Ilves Tampere	C
16	Ott.	Jakub Klepis	Portland	C
17	Wsh.	Boyd Gordon	Red Deer	RW
18	L.A.	Denis Grebeshkov	Yaroslavl	D
19	Phx.	Jakub Koreis	Plzen	C
20	Buf.	Dan Paille	Guelph	LW
21	Chi.	Anton Babchuk	Elektrostal	D
22	NYI	Sean Bergenheim	Jokerit	C
23	Phx.	Ben Eager	Oshawa	LW
24	Tor.	Alexander Steen	Vastra Frolunda	C
25	Car.	Cam Ward	Red Deer	G
26	Dal.	Martin Vagner	Hull	D
27	S.J.	Mike Morris	St. Sebastian's H.S.	RW
28	Col.	Jonas Johansson	HV 71 Jonkoping Jr.	RW
29	Bos.	Hannu Toivonen	HPK Jr.	G
30	Atl.	Jim Slater	Michigan State	C

OTHER NOTABLE SELECTIONS

Pick	Claimed by		Amateur Club	Position
36	Edm.	Jarret Stoll	Kootenay	C
43	Dal.	Trevor Daley	Sault Ste. Marie	D
44	Edm.	Matt Greene	Green Bay	D
46	Phx.	David Leneveu	Cornell	G
57	Tor.	Matt Stajan	Belleville	C
58	Det.	Jiri Hudler	Vsetin	C
90	Cgy.	Matthew Lomardi	Victoriaville	C
117	N.J.	Cam Janssen	Windsor	RW
133	CBJ	Lasse Pirjeta	Karpat	D
191	Tor.	Ian White	Swift Current	D
240	NYR	Petr Prucha	Pardubice	RW
254	Tor.	Jarkko Immonen	Assat	C
259	Bos.	Jan Stastny	U. of Notre Dame	C

2001

FIRST ROUND

Pick	Claimed by		Amateur Club	Position
1	Atl.	Ilya Kovalchuk	Spartak	LW
2	Ott.	Jason Spezza	Windsor	C
3	T.B.	Alexander Svitov	Avangard Omsk	C
4	Fla.	Stephen Weiss	Plymouth	C
5	Ana.	Stanislav Chistov	Avangard Omsk	LW
6	Min.	Mikko Koivu	TPS Turku	C
7	Mtl.	Mike Komisarek	U. of Michigan	D
8	CBJ	Pascal Leclaire	Halifax	G
9	Chi.	Tuomo Ruutu	Jokerit	C/LW
10	NYR	Dan Blackburn	Kootenay	G
11	Phx.	Fredrik Sjostrom	Vastra Frolunda	RW
12	Nsh.	Dan Hamhuis	Prince George	D
13	Edm.	Ales Hemsky	Hull	RW
14	Cgy.	Chuck Kobasew	Boston College	C
15	Car.	Igor Knyazev	Spartak	D
16	Van.	R.J. Umberger	Ohio State	C
17	Tor.	Carlo Colaiacovo	Erie	D
18	L.A.	Jens Karlsson	Vastra Frolunda	RW
19	Bos.	Shaone Morrisonn	Kamloops	D
20	S.J.	Marcel Goc	Schwenningen	C
21	Pit.	Colby Armstrong	Red Deer	RW
22	Buf.	Jiri Novotny	Budejovice	C
23	Ott.	Tim Gleason	Windsor	D
24	Fla.	Lukas Krajicek	Peterborough	D
25	Mtl.	Alexander Perezhogin	Avangard Omsk	C
26	Dal.	Jason Bacashihua	Chicago (NAHL)	G
27	Phi.	Jeff Woywitka	Red Deer	D
28	N.J.	Adrian Foster	Saskatoon	C
29	Chi.	Adam Munro	Erie	G
30	L.A.	Dave Steckel	Ohio State	C

OTHER NOTABLE SELECTIONS

Pick	Claimed by		Amateur Club	Position
32	Buf.	Derek Roy	Kitchener	C
49	L.A.	Mike Cammalleri	U. of Michigan	C
99	Ott.	Ray Emery	S.S. Marie	G
98	Nsh.	Jordin Tootoo	Brandon	RW
106	S.J.	Christoph Ehrhoff	Krefeld	D
132	NYI	Dusan Salficky	Plzen	G
134	Tor.	Kyle Wellwood	Belleville	C
172	Phi.	Dennis Seidenberg	Mannheim	D
176	Nsh.	Marek Zidlicky	HIFK	D
189	Atl.	Pasi Nurminen	Jokerit	G
214	L.A.	Cristobal Huet	Lugano	G
232	Ana.	Martin Gerber	Langnau	G
253	St.L.	Petr Cajanek	Zlin	RW

2000

FIRST ROUND

Pick	Claimed by		Amateur Club	Position
1	NYI	Rick DiPietro	Boston U.	G
2	Atl.	Dany Heatley	U. of Wisconsin	RW
3	Min.	Marian Gaborik	Dukla Trencin	RW
4	CBJ	Rostislav Klesla	Brampton	D
5	NYI	Raffi Torres	Brampton	LW
6	Nsh.	Scott Hartnell	Prince Albert	LW
7	Bos.	Lars Jonsson	Leksand	D
8	T.B.	Nikita Alexeev	Erie	RW
9	Cgy.	Brent Krahn	Calgary	G
10	Chi.	Mikhail Yakubov	Lada Togliatti	C
11	Chi.	Pavel Vorobiev	Yaroslavl	RW
12	Ana.	Alexei Smirnov	Tver	LW
13	Mtl.	Ron Hainsey	U. of Mass-Lowell	D
14	Col.	Vaclav Nedorost	Budejovice	C
15	Buf.	Artem Kryukov	Yaroslavl	C
16	Mtl.	Marcel Hossa	Portland	LW
17	Edm.	Alexei Mikhnov	Yaroslavl	LW
18	Pit.	Brooks Orpik	Boston College	D
19	Phx.	Krys Kolanos	Boston College	C
20	L.A.	Alexander Frolov	Yaroslavl 2	LW
21	Ott.	Anton Volchenkov	HC Moscow	D
22	N.J.	David Hale	Sioux City	D
23	Van.	Nathan Smith	Swift Current	C
24	Tor.	Brad Boyes	Erie	C
25	Dal.	Steve Ott	Windsor	C
26	Wsh.	Brian Sutherby	Moose Jaw	C
27	Bos.	Martin Samuelsson	MoDo Ornskoldsvik	RW
28	Phi.	Justin Williams	Plymouth	RW
29	Det.	Niklas Kronwall	Djurgarden	D
30	St.L.	Jeff Taffe	U. of Minnesota	C

OTHER NOTABLE SELECTIONS

Pick	Claimed by		Amateur Club	Position
33	Min.	Nick Schultz	Prince Albert	D
43	Wsh.	Matt Pettinger	Calgary	LW
44	Ana.	Ilya Bryzgalov	Lada Togliatti	G
46	Cgy.	Jarret Stoll	Kootenay	C
54	L.A.	Andreas Lilja	Malmo	D
76	N.J.	Michael Rupp	Erie	LW
97	Car.	Niclas Wallin	Brynas	D
118	L.A.	Lubomir Visnovsky	Bratislava	D
155	Cgy.	Travis Moen	Kelowna	LW
159	Col.	John-Michael Liles	Michigan State	D
171	Phi.	Roman Cechmanek	Vsetin	G
220	Buf.	Paul Gaustad	Portland	C

1999

FIRST ROUND

Pick	Claimed by		Amateur Club	Position
1	Atl.	Patrik Stefan	Long Beach	C
2	Van.	Daniel Sedin	MoDo Ornskoldsvik	LW
3	Van.	Henrik Sedin	MoDo Ornskoldsvik	C
4	NYR	Pavel Brendl	Calgary	RW
5	NYI	Tim Connolly	Erie	C
6	Nsh.	Brian Finley	Barrie	G
7	Wsh.	Kris Beech	Calgary	C
8	NYI	Taylor Pyatt	Sudbury	LW
9	NYR	Jamie Lundmark	Moose Jaw	C
10	NYI	Branislav Mezei	Belleville	D
11	Cgy.	Oleg Saprykin	Seattle	LW
12	Fla.	Denis Shvidki	Barrie	RW
13	Edm.	Jani Rita	Jokerit	LW
14	S.J.	Jeff Jillson	U. of Michigan	D
15	Phx.	Scott Kelman	Seattle	C
16	Car.	David Tanabe	U. of Wisconsin	D
17	St.L.	Barret Jackman	Regina	D
18	Pit.	Konstantin Koltsov	Cherepovets	RW
19	Phx.	Kirill Safronov	St. Petersburg	D
20	Buf.	Barrett Heisten	U. of Maine	LW
21	Bos.	Nick Boynton	Ottawa	D
22	Phi.	Maxime Ouellet	Quebec	G
23	Chi.	Steve McCarthy	Kootenay	D
24	Tor.	Luca Cereda	Ambri	C
25	Col.	Mikhail Kuleshov	Cherepovets	LW
26	Ott.	Martin Havlat	Trinec	LW
27	N.J.	Ari Ahonen	JyP HT Jr.	G
28	NYI	Kristian Kudroc	Michalovce	D

OTHER NOTABLE SELECTIONS

Pick	Claimed by		Amateur Club	Position
42	N.J.	Mike Commodore	North Dakota	D
70	Fla.	Niklas Hagman	HIFK Helsinki	LW
76	L.A.	Frantisek Kaberle	MoDo Ornskoldsvik	D
83	Ana.	Niclas Havelid	Malmo	D
91	Edm.	Mike Comrie	U. of Michigan	C
115	Pit.	Ryan Malone	Omaha	LW
191	Nsh.	Martin Erat	ZPS Zlin Jr.	LW
210	Det.	Henrik Zetterberg	Timra	LW
212	Col.	Radim Vrbata	Hull	RW
232	St.L.	Alexander Khavanov	Dynamo	D
247	Bos.	Mikko Eloranta	TPS Turku	LW

1998

FIRST ROUND

Pick	Claimed by		Amateur Club	Position
1	T.B.	Vincent Lecavalier	Rimouski	C
2	Nsh.	David Legwand	Plymouth	C
3	S.J.	Brad Stuart	Regina	D
4	Van.	Bryan Allen	Oshawa	D
5	Ana.	Vitaly Vishnevski	Yaroslavl 2	D
6	Cgy.	Rico Fata	London	RW
7	NYR	Manny Malhotra	Guelph	C
8	Chi.	Mark Bell	Ottawa	C
9	NYI	Mike Rupp	Erie	RW
10	Tor.	Nik Antropov	Ust-Kamenogorsk	C
11	Car.	Jeff Heerema	Sarnia	RW
12	Col.	Alex Tanguay	Halifax	LW
13	Edm.	Michael Henrich	Barrie	RW
14	Phx.	Patrick DesRochers	Sarnia	G
15	Ott.	Mathieu Chouinard	Shawinigan	G
16	Mtl.	Eric Chouinard	Quebec	LW
17	Col.	Martin Skoula	Barrie	D
18	Buf.	Dmitri Kalinin	Chelyabinsk	D
19	Col.	Robyn Regehr	Kamloops	D
20	Col.	Scott Parker	Kelowna	RW
21	L.A.	Mathieu Biron	Shawinigan	D
22	Phi.	Simon Gagne	Quebec	LW
23	Pit.	Milan Kraft	Keramika Plzen Jr.	C
24	St.L.	Christian Backman	Vastra Frolunda Jr.	D
25	Det.	Jiri Fischer	Hull	D
26	N.J.	Mike Van Ryn	U. of Michigan	D
27	N.J.	Scott Gomez	Tri-City	C

OTHER NOTABLE SELECTIONS

Pick	Claimed by		Amateur Club	Position
29	S.J.	Jonathan Cheechoo	Belleville	RW
43	Phx.	Ossi Vaananen	Jokerit Jr.	D
44	Ott.	Mike Fisher	Sudbury	C
64	T.B.	Brad Richards	Rimouski	C
71	Car.	Erik Cole	Clarkson	LW
87	Tor.	Alexei Ponikarovsky	Dyn-2 Moscow	LW
91	Car.	Josef Vasicek	Slavia Praha Jr.	C
99	Edm.	Shawn Horcoff	Michigan State	C
117	Fla.	Jaroslav Spacek	Farjestad Karlstad	D
135	Bos.	Andrew Raycroft	Sudbury	G
150	Ana.	Trent Hunter	Prince George	RW
162	Mtl.	Andrei Markov	Khimik	D
171	Det.	Pavel Datsyuk	Yekateringburg	C
216	Mtl.	Michael Ryder	Hull	RW
230	Nsh.	Karlis Skrastins	TPS Turku	D

1997

FIRST ROUND

Pick	Claimed by		Amateur Club	Position
1	Bos.	Joe Thornton	Sault Ste. Marie	C
2	S.J.	Patrick Marleau	Seattle	C
3	L.A.	Olli Jokinen	HIFK Helsinki	C
4	NYI	Roberto Luongo	Val-d'Or	G
5	NYI	Eric Brewer	Prince George	D
6	Cgy.	Daniel Tkaczuk	Barrie	C
7	T.B.	Paul Mara	Sudbury	D
8	Bos.	Sergei Samsonov	Detroit	LW
9	Wsh.	Nick Boynton	Ottawa	D
10	Van.	Brad Ference	Spokane	D
11	Mtl.	Jason Ward	Erie	RW
12	Ott.	Marian Hossa	Dukla Trencin	RW
13	Chi.	Daniel Cleary	Belleville	RW
14	Edm.	Michel Riesen	Biel-Bienne	RW
15	L.A.	Matt Zultek	Ottawa	LW
16	Chi.	Ty Jones	Spokane	RW
17	Pit.	Robert Dome	Las Vegas (IHL)	RW
18	Ana.	Mikael Holmqvist	Djurgarden	C
19	NYR	Stefan Cherneski	Brandon	RW
20	Fla.	Mike Brown	Red Deer	LW
21	Buf.	Mika Noronen	Tappara Tampere	G
22	Car.	Nikos Tselios	Belleville	D
23	S.J.	Scott Hannan	Kelowna	D
24	N.J.	J-F Damphousse	Moncton	G
25	Dal.	Brenden Morrow	Portland	LW
26	Col.	Kevin Grimes	Kingston	D

OTHER NOTABLE SELECTIONS

Pick	Claimed by		Amateur Club	Position
27	Bos.	Ben Clymer	Minnesota-Duluth	LW
48	Buf.	Henrik Tallinder	AIK Solna	D
69	Buf.	Maxim Afinogenov	Dynamo Moscow	RW
119	Ott.	Magnus Arvedson	Farjestad Karlstad	LW
130	Chi.	Kyle Calder	Regina	LW
136	NYR	Mike York	Michigan State	LW
144	Van.	Matt Cooke	Windsor	C
156	Buf.	Brian Campbell	Ottawa	D
161	Col.	David Aebischer	Fribourg-Gotteron	G
177	St.L.	Ladislav Nagy	Dragon Presov	LW
191	Bos.	Antti Laaksonen	U. of Denver	LW
208	Pit.	Andrew Ference	Portland	D
242	Chi.	Brett McLean	Kelowna	C

1996

FIRST ROUND

Pick	Claimed by		Amateur Club	Position
1	Ott.	Chris Phillips	Prince Albert	D
2	S.J.	Andrei Zyuzin	Salavat Yulayev Ufa	D
3	NYI	J.P. Dumont	Val-d'Or	RW
4	Wsh.	Alexandre Volchkov	Barrie	C
5	Dal.	Ric Jackman	Sault Ste. Marie	D
6	Edm.	Boyd Devereaux	Kitchener	C
7	Buf.	Erik Rasmussen	U. of Minnesota	LW/C
8	Bos.	Johnathan Aitken	Medicine Hat	D
9	Ana.	Ruslan Salei	Las Vegas (IHL)	D
10	N.J.	Lance Ward	Red Deer	D
11	Phx.	Dan Focht	Tri-City	D
12	Van.	Josh Holden	Regina	C
13	Cgy.	Derek Morris	Regina	D
14	St.L.	Marty Reasoner	Boston College	C
15	Phi.	Dainius Zubrus	Pembroke Jr. A	RW
16	T.B.	Mario Larocque	Hull	D
17	Wsh.	Jaroslav Svejkovsky	Tri-City	RW
18	Mtl.	Matt Higgins	Moose Jaw	C
19	Edm.	Matthieu Descoteaux	Shawinigan	D
20	Fla.	Marcus Nilson	Djurgarden	LW
21	S.J.	Marco Sturm	Landshut	LW
22	NYR	Jeff Brown	Sarnia	D
23	Pit.	Craig Hillier	Ottawa	G
24	Phx.	Daniel Briere	Drummondville	C
25	Col.	Peter Ratchuk	Shattuck St. Mary's H.S.	D
26	Det.	Jesse Wallin	Red Deer	D

OTHER NOTABLE SELECTIONS

Pick	Claimed by		Amateur Club	Position
35	Ana.	Matt Cullen	St. Cloud State	C
49	N.J.	Colin White	Hull	D
56	NYI	Zdeno Chara	Dukla Trencin	D
59	Edm.	Tom Poti	Cushing Academy	D
65	Fla.	Oleg Kvasha	CSKA Moscow	LW/C
79	Col.	Mark Parrish	St. Cloud State	RW
105	Pit.	Michal Rozsival	Dukla Jihlava	D
136	Ott.	Andreas Dackell	Brynas Gavle	RW
139	Phx.	Robert Esche	Detroit	G
174	Phx.	Trevor Letowski	Sarnia	RW
176	Col.	Samuel Pahlsson	MoDo	C
179	T.B.	Pavel Kubina	Vitkovice	D
204	Tor.	Tomas Kaberle	Kladno	D

1995

FIRST ROUND

Pick	Claimed by		Amateur Club	Position
1	Ott.	Bryan Berard	Detroit	D
2	NYI	Wade Redden	Brandon	D
3	L.A.	Aki Berg	Kiekko-67 Turku	D
4	Ana.	Chad Kilger	Kingston	C
5	T.B.	Daymond Langkow	Tri-City	C
6	Edm.	Steve Kelly	Prince Albert	C
7	Wpg.	Shane Doan	Kamloops	RW
8	Mtl.	Terry Ryan	Tri-City	LW
9	Bos.	Kyle McLaren	Tacoma	D
10	Fla.	Radek Dvorak	HC Ceske Budejovice	RW
11	Dal.	Jarome Iginla	Kamloops	RW
12	S.J.	Teemu Riihijarvi	Kiekko-Espoo	LW
13	Hfd.	Jean-Sebastien Giguere	Halifax	G
14	Buf.	Jay McKee	Niagara Falls	D
15	Tor.	Jeff Ware	Oshawa	D
16	Buf.	Martin Biron	Beauport	G
17	Wsh.	Brad Church	Prince Albert	LW
18	N.J.	Petr Sykora	Detroit	RW
19	Chi.	Dmitri Nabokov	Krylja Sovetov	C/LW
20	Cgy.	Denis Gauthier	Drummondville	D
21	Bos.	Sean Brown	Belleville	D
22	Phi.	Brian Boucher	Tri-City	G
23	Wsh.	Miika Elomo	Kiekko-67 Turku	LW
24	Pit.	Aleksey Morozov	Krylja Sovetov	RW
25	Col.	Marc Denis	Chicoutimi	G
26	Det.	Maxim Kuznetsov	Dynamo	D

OTHER NOTABLE SELECTIONS

Pick	Claimed by		Amateur Club	Position
31	Edm.	Georges Laraque	St-Jean	RW
45	Chi.	Christian Laflamme	Beauport	D
49	St.L.	Jochen Hecht	Mannheim	C
66	Van.	Peter Schaefer	Brandon	LW
67	Wpg.	Brad Isbister	Portland	LW
79	N.J.	Alyn McCauley	Ottawa	C
87	Hfd.	Sami Kapanen	HIFK Helsinki	RW
91	NYR	Marc Savard	Oshawa	C
101	St.L.	Michal Handzus	IS Banska Bystrica	C
116	S.J.	Miikka Kiprusoff	TPS Turku Jr.	G
128	Pit.	Jan Hrdina	Seattle	C
144	Van.	Brent Sopel	Swift Current	D
166	Fla.	Peter Worrell	Hull	LW
177	Bos.	P.J. Axelsson	Vastra Frolunda	LW
223	Tor.	Danny Markov	Spartak	D

1994

FIRST ROUND

Pick	Claimed by		Amateur Club	Position
1	Fla.	Ed Jovanovski	Windsor	D
2	Ana.	Oleg Tverdovsky	Krylja Sovetov	D
3	Ott.	Radek Bonk	Las Vegas (IHL)	C
4	Edm.	Jason Bonsignore	Niagara Falls	C
5	Hfd.	Jeff O'Neill	Guelph	RW
6	Edm.	Ryan Smyth	Moose Jaw	LW
7	L.A.	Jamie Storr	Owen Sound	G
8	T.B.	Jason Wiemer	Portland	C
9	NYI	Brett Lindros	Kingston	RW
10	Wsh.	Nolan Baumgartner	Kamloops	D
11	S.J.	Jeff Friesen	Regina	LW
12	Que.	Wade Belak	Saskatoon	D/RW
13	Van.	Mattias Ohlund	Pitea	D
14	Chi.	Ethan Moreau	Niagara Falls	LW
15	Wsh.	Alexander Kharlamov	CSKA Moscow	C
16	Tor.	Eric Fichaud	Chicoutimi	G
17	Buf.	Wayne Primeau	Owen Sound	C
18	Mtl.	Brad Brown	North Bay	D
19	Cgy.	Chris Dingman	Brandon	LW
20	Dal.	Jason Botterill	U. of Michigan	LW
21	Bos.	Evgeni Ryabchikov	Molot Perm	G
22	Que.	Jeffrey Kealty	Catholic Memorial H.S.	D
23	Det.	Yan Golubovsky	Dynamo 2	D
24	Pit.	Chris Wells	Seattle	C
25	N.J.	Vadim Sharifijanov	Salavat Yulayev Ufa	LW
26	NYR	Dan Cloutier	Sault Ste. Marie	G

OTHER NOTABLE SELECTIONS

Pick	Claimed by		Amateur Club	Position
27	Fla.	Rhett Warrener	Saskatoon	D
43	Buf.	Curtis Brown	Moose Jaw	C/LW
49	Det.	Mathieu Dandenault	Sherbrooke	RW/D
51	N.J.	Patrik Elias	Kladno	C
64	Tor.	Fredrik Modin	Timra	LW
72	Que.	Chris Drury	Fairfield Prep	C
87	Que.	Milan Hejduk	Pardubice	RW
124	Dal.	Marty Turco	Cambridge Jr. A	G
132	Ana.	Bates Battaglia	Caledon Jr. A	LW
133	Ott.	Daniel Alfredsson	Vastra Frolunda	RW
210	N.J.	Steve Sullivan	Sault Ste. Marie	RW
219	S.J.	Evgeni Nabokov	Ust-Kamengorsk	G
272	NYI	Dick Tarnstrom	AIK Solna	D

1993

FIRST ROUND

Pick	Claimed by		Amateur Club	Position
1	Ott.	Alexandre Daigle	Victoriaville	C
2	Hfd.	Chris Pronger	Peterborough	D
3	T.B.	Chris Gratton	Kingston	C
4	Ana.	Paul Kariya	U. of Maine	LW
5	Fla.	Rob Niedermayer	Medicine Hat	C
6	S.J.	Viktor Kozlov	Dynamo	C
7	Edm.	Jason Arnott	Oshawa	C
8	NYR	Niklas Sundstrom	MoDo Ornskoldsvik	RW
9	Dal.	Todd Harvey	Detroit	RW/C
10	Que.	Jocelyn Thibault	Sherbrooke	G
11	Wsh.	Brendan Witt	Seattle	D
12	Tor.	Kenny Jonsson	Rogle Angelholm	D
13	N.J.	Denis Pederson	Prince Albert	C/RW
14	Que.	Adam Deadmarsh	Portland	RW
15	Wpg.	Mats Lindgren	Skelleftea	C/LW
16	Edm.	Nick Stajduhar	London	D
17	Wsh.	Jason Allison	London	C
18	Cgy.	Jesper Mattsson	Malmo	C
19	Tor.	Landon Wilson	Dubuque Jr. A	RW
20	Van.	Mike Wilson	Sudbury	D
21	Mtl.	Saku Koivu	TPS Turku	C
22	Det.	Anders Eriksson	MoDo Ornskoldsvik	D
23	NYI	Todd Bertuzzi	Guelph	RW
24	Chi.	Eric Lecompte	Hull	LW
25	Bos.	Kevyn Adams	Miami of Ohio	C
26	Pit.	Stefan Bergkvist	Leksand	D

OTHER NOTABLE SELECTIONS

Pick	Claimed by		Amateur Club	Position
28	S.J.	Shean Donovan	Ottawa	RW
71	Phi.	Vaclav Prospal	Motor Ceske Budejovice	C
72	Hfd.	Marek Malik	Vitkovice	D
90	Chi.	Eric Daze	Beauport	RW
111	Edm.	Miroslav Satan	Dukla Trencin	LW
118	NYI	Tommy Salo	Vasteras	G
124	Van.	Scott Walker	Owen Sound	RW
151	Mtl.	Darcy Tucker	Kamloops	RW
164	NYR	Todd Marchant	Clarkson	C
207	Bos.	Hal Gill	Nashoba H.S.	D
219	St.L.	Mike Grier	St. Sebastian's H.S.	RW
227	Ott.	Pavol Demitra	Dukla Trencin	LW
252	Cgy.	German Titov	TPS Turku	LW

1992

FIRST ROUND

Pick	Claimed by		Amateur Club	Position
1	T.B. •	Roman Hamrlik	ZPS Zlin	D
2	Ott.	Alexei Yashin	Dynamo	C
3	S.J.	Mike Rathje	Medicine Hat	D
4	Que.	Todd Warriner	Windsor	LW
5	NYI	Darius Kasparaitis	Dynamo	D
6	Cgy.	Cory Stillman	Windsor	LW
7	Phi.	Ryan Sittler	Nichols H.S.	LW
8	Tor.	Brandon Convery	Sudbury	C
9	Hfd.	Robert Petrovicky	Dukla Trencin	C
10	S.J.	Andrei Nazarov	Dynamo	LW
11	Buf.	David Cooper	Medicine Hat	D
12	Chi.	Sergei Krivokrasov	CSKA Moscow	RW
13	Edm.	Joe Hulbig	St. Sebastian's H.S.	LW
14	Wsh.	Sergei Gonchar	Chelyabinsk	D
15	Phi.	Jason Bowen	Tri-City	D
16	Bos.	Dmitri Kvartalnov	San Diego (IHL)	LW
17	Wpg.	Sergei Bautin	Dynamo	D
18	N.J.	Jason Smith	Regina	D
19	Pit.	Martin Straka	HC Skoda Plzen	C
20	Mtl.	David Wilkie	Kamloops	D
21	Van.	Libor Polasek	Vitkovice	C
22	Det.	Curtis Bowen	Ottawa	LW
23	Tor.	Grant Marshall	Ottawa	RW
24	NYR	Peter Ferraro	Waterloo Jr. A	LW

OTHER NOTABLE SELECTIONS

Pick	Claimed by		Amateur Club	Position
27	Wpg.	Boris Mironov	CSKA Moscow	D
33	Mtl.	Valeri Bure	Spokane	RW
36	Chi.	Jeff Shantz	Regina	C
38	St.L.	Igor Korolev	Dynamo	C
40	Van.	Michael Peca	Ottawa	C
42	N.J.	Sergei Brylin	CSKA Moscow	C
46	Det.	Darren McCarty	Bellevile	RW
48	NYR	Mattias Norstrom	AIK Solna	D
65	Edm.	Kirk Maltby	Owen Sound	RW
78	Cgy.	Robert Svehla	Dukla Trencin	D
83	Buf.	Matthew Barnaby	Beauport	RW
158	St.L.	Ian Laperriere	Drummondville	C/RW
186	N.J.	Stephane Yelle	Oshawa	C
204	Wpg.	Nikolai Khabibulin	CSKA Moscow	G

1991

FIRST ROUND

Pick	Claimed by		Amateur Club	Position
1	Que.	Eric Lindros	Oshawa	C
2	S.J.	Pat Falloon	Spokane	RW
3	N.J.	Scott Niedermayer	Kamloops	D
4	NYI	Scott Lachance	Boston U.	D
5	Wpg.	Aaron Ward	U. of Michigan	D
6	Phi.	Peter Forsberg	MoDo Ornskoldsvik	C
7	Van.	Alek Stojanov	Hamilton	RW
8	Min.	Richard Matvichuk	Saskatoon	D
9	Hfd.	Patrick Poulin	St-Hyacinthe	C
10	Det.	Martin Lapointe	Laval	RW
11	N.J.	Brian Rolston	Detroit Compuware Jr. A	C/RW
12	Edm.	Tyler Wright	Swift Current	C
13	Buf.	Philippe Boucher	Granby	D
14	Wsh.	Pat Peake	Detroit	C
15	NYR	Alex Kovalev	Dynamo	RW
16	Pit.	Markus Naslund	MoDo Ornskoldsvik	LW
17	Mtl.	Brent Bilodeau	Seattle	D
18	Bos.	Glen Murray	Sudbury	RW
19	Cgy.	Niklas Sundblad	AIK Solna	RW
20	Edm.	Martin Rucinsky	CHZ Litvinov	LW
21	Wsh.	Trevor Halverson	North Bay	LW
22	Chi.	Dean McAmmond	Prince Albert	LW

OTHER NOTABLE SELECTIONS

Pick	Claimed by		Amateur Club	Position
23	S.J.	Ray Whitney	Spokane	LW
26	NYI	Ziggy Palffy	AC Nitra	RW
30	S.J.	Sandis Ozolinsh	Dynamo Riga	D
40	Bos.	Jozef Stumpel	AC Nitra	C
52	Cgy.	Sandy McCarthy	Laval	RW
58	Wsh.	Steve Konowalchuk	Portland	LW
59	Hfd.	Michael Nylander	Huddinge	C
71	Chi.	Igor Kravchuk	CSKA Moscow	D
81	L.A.	Alexei Zhitnik	Sokol Kiev	D
103	Que.	Bill Lindsay	Tri-City	RW
106	Bos.	Mariusz Czerkawski	GKS Tychy	RW
122	Phi.	Dmitry Yushkevich	Yaroslavl	D
203	Wpg.	Igor Ulanov	Khimik Voskresensk	D

1990

FIRST ROUND

Pick	Claimed by		Amateur Club	Position
1	Que.	Owen Nolan	Cornwall	RW
2	Van.	Petr Nedved	Seattle	C
3	Det.	Keith Primeau	Niagara Falls	C
4	Phi.	Mike Ricci	Peterborough	C
5	Pit.	Jaromir Jagr	Kladno	RW
6	NYI	Scott Scissons	Saskatoon	C
7	L.A.	Darryl Sydor	Kamloops	D
8	Min.	Derian Hatcher	North Bay	D
9	Wsh.	John Slaney	Cornwall	D
10	Tor.	Drake Berehowsky	Kingston	D
11	Cgy.	Trevor Kidd	Brandon	G
12	Mtl.	Turner Stevenson	Seattle	RW
13	NYR	Michael Stewart	Michigan State	D
14	Buf.	Brad May	Niagara Falls	LW
15	Hfd.	Mark Greig	Lethbridge	RW
16	Chi.	Karl Dykhuis	Hull	D
17	Edm.	Scott Allison	Prince Albert	C
18	Van.	Shawn Antoski	North Bay	LW
19	Wpg.	Keith Tkachuk	Malden Catholic H.S.	LW
20	N.J.	Martin Brodeur	St-Hyacinthe	G
21	Bos.	Bryan Smolinski	Michigan State	C

OTHER NOTABLE SELECTIONS

Pick	Claimed by		Amateur Club	Position
23	Van.	Jiri Slegr	CHZ Litvinov	D
31	Tor.	Felix Potvin	Chicoutimi	G
34	NYR	Doug Weight	Lake Superior State	C
36	Hfd.	Geoff Sanderson	Swift Current	LW
45	Det.	Vyacheslav Kozlov	Khimik Voskresensk	RW
85	NYR	Sergei Zubov	CSKA Moscow	D
86	Van.	Gino Odjick	Laval	RW
97	Buf.	Richard Smehlik	Vitkovice	D
133	L.A.	Robert Lang	CHZ Litvinov	C
156	Wsh.	Peter Bondra	Kosice	RW
177	Wsh.	Ken Klee	Bowling Green	D
244	NYR	Sergei Nemchinov	Krylja Sovetov	LW

1989

FIRST ROUND

Pick	Claimed by		Amateur Club	Position
1	Que.	Mats Sundin	Nacka	C
2	NYI	Dave Chyzowski	Kamloops	LW
3	Tor.	Scott Thornton	Belleville	LW
4	Wpg.	Stu Barnes	Tri-City	C
5	N.J.	Bill Guerin	Springfield Jr. B.	RW
6	Chi.	Adam Bennett	Sudbury	D
7	Min.	Doug Zmolek	John Marshall H.S.	D
8	Van.	Jason Herter	North Dakota	D
9	St.L.	Jason Marshall	Vernon Jr. A	D
10	Hfd.	Bobby Holik	Dukla Jihlava	C
11	Det.	Mike Sillinger	Regina	C
12	Tor.	Rob Pearson	Belleville	RW
13	Mtl.	Lindsay Vallis	Seattle	D
14	Buf.	Kevin Haller	Regina	D
15	Edm.	Jason Soules	Niagara Falls	D
16	Pit.	Jamie Heward	Regina	D
17	Bos.	Shayne Stevenson	Kitchener	RW
18	N.J.	Jason Miller	Medicine Hat	LW
19	Wsh.	Olaf Kolzig	Tri-City	G
20	NYR	Steven Rice	Kitchener	RW
21	Tor.	Steve Bancroft	Belleville	D

OTHER NOTABLE SELECTIONS

Pick	Claimed by		Amateur Club	Position
22	Que.	Adam Foote	Sault Ste. Marie	D
23	NYI	Travis Green	Spokane	C
53	Det.	Nicklas Lidstrom	Vasteras	D
62	Wpg.	Kris Draper	Canadian National	C
73	Hfd.	Jim McKenzie	Victoria	LW
74	Det.	Sergei Fedorov	CSKA Moscow	C
82	Wsh.	Trent Klatt	Osseo H.S.	RW
113	Van.	Pavel Bure	CSKA Moscow	RW
116	Det.	Dallas Drake	Northern Michigan	RW
183	Buf.	Donald Audette	Laval	RW
196	Min.	Arturs Irbe	Dynamo Riga	G
221	Det.	Vladimir Konstantinov	CSKA Moscow	D

1988

FIRST ROUND

Pick	Claimed by		Amateur Club	Position
1	Min.	Mike Modano	Prince Albert	C
2	Van.	Trevor Linden	Medicine Hat	RW
3	Que.	Curtis Leschyshyn	Saskatoon	D
4	Pit.	Darrin Shannon	Windsor	LW
5	Que.	Daniel Dore	Drummondville	RW
6	Tor.	Scott Pearson	Kingston	LW
7	L.A.	Martin Gelinas	Hull	LW
8	Chi.	Jeremy Roenick	Thayer Academy	C
9	St.L.	Rod Brind'Amour	Notre Dame Jr. A	C
10	Wpg.	Teemu Selanne	Jokerit	RW
11	Hfd.	Chris Govedaris	Toronto	LW
12	N.J.	Corey Foster	Peterborough	D
13	Buf.	Joel Savage	Victoria	RW
14	Phi.	Claude Boivin	Drummondville	LW
15	Wsh.	Reggie Savage	Victoriaville	C
16	NYI	Kevin Cheveldayoff	Brandon	D
17	Det.	Kory Kocur	Saskatoon	RW
18	Bos.	Rob Cimetta	Toronto	W
19	Edm.	Francois Leroux	St-Jean	D
20	Mtl.	Eric Charron	Trois-Rivieres	D
21	Cgy.	Jason Muzzatti	Michigan State	G

OTHER NOTABLE SELECTIONS

Pick	Claimed by		Amateur Club	Position
27	Tor.	Tie Domi	Peterborough	RW
60	Bos.	Steve Heinze	Lawrence Academy	RW
67	Pit.	Mark Recchi	Kamloops	RW
68	NYR	Tony Amonte	Thayer Academy	RW
89	Buf.	Alexander Mogilny	CSKA Moscow	RW
97	Buf.	Rob Ray	Cornwall	RW
120	Wsh.	Dmitri Khristich	Sokol Kiev	LW/C
163	NYI	Marty McInnis	Milton Academy	RW
198	St.L.	Bret Hedican	North St. Paul H.S.	D
234	Que.	Claude Lapointe	Laval	LW/C

1987

FIRST ROUND

Pick	Claimed by		Amateur Club	Position
1	Buf.	Pierre Turgeon	Granby	C
2	N.J.	Brendan Shanahan	London	LW
3	Bos.	Glen Wesley	Portland	D
4	L.A.	Wayne McBean	Medicine Hat	D
5	Pit.	Chris Joseph	Seattle	D
6	Min.	Dave Archibald	Portland	C/LW
7	Tor.	Luke Richardson	Peterborough	D
8	Chi.	Jimmy Waite	Chicoutimi	G
9	Que.	Bryan Fogarty	Kingston	D
10	NYR	Jay More	New Westminster	D
11	Det.	Yves Racine	Longueuil	D
12	St.L.	Keith Osborne	North Bay	RW
13	NYI	Dean Chynoweth	Medicine Hat	D
14	Bos.	Stephane Quintal	Granby	D
15	Que.	Joe Sakic	Swift Current	C
16	Wpg.	Bryan Marchment	Belleville	D
17	Mtl.	Andrew Cassels	Ottawa	C
18	Hfd.	Jody Hull	Peterborough	RW
19	Cgy.	Bryan Deasley	U. of Michigan	LW
20	Phi.	Darren Rumble	Kitchener	D
21	Edm.	Peter Soberlak	Swift Current	LW

OTHER NOTABLE SELECTIONS

Pick	Claimed by		Amateur Club	Position
25	Cgy.	Stephane Matteau	Hull	LW
33	Mtl.	John LeClair	Bellows Academy	LW
38	Mtl.	Eric Desjardins	Granby	D
44	Mtl.	Mathieu Schneider	Cornwall	D
71	Tor.	Joe Sacco	Medford H.S.	RW
108	Van.	Garry Valk	Sherwood Park Jr. A	RW
110	Pit.	Shawn McEachern	Matignon H.S.	RW
159	St.L.	Guy Hebert	Hamilton College	G
166	Cgy.	Theoren Fleury	Moose Jaw	RW

1986

FIRST ROUND

Pick	Claimed by		Amateur Club	Position
1	Det.	Joe Murphy	Michigan State	RW
2	L.A.	Jimmy Carson	Verdun	C
3	N.J.	Neil Brady	Medicine Hat	C
4	Pit.	Zarley Zalapski	Canadian National	D
5	Buf.	Shawn Anderson	Canadian National	D
6	Tor.	Vincent Damphousse	Laval	C
7	Van.	Dan Woodley	Portland	RW
8	Wpg.	Pat Elynuik	Prince Albert	RW
9	NYR	Brian Leetch	Avon Old Farms H.S.	D
10	St.L.	Jocelyn Lemieux	Laval	RW
11	Hfd.	Scott Young	Boston U.	RW
12	Min.	Warren Babe	Lethbridge	LW
13	Bos.	Craig Janney	Boston College	C
14	Chi.	Everett Sanipass	Verdun	LW
15	Mtl.	Mark Pederson	Medicine Hat	LW
16	Cgy.	George Pelawa	Bemidji H.S.	RW
17	NYI	Tom Fitzgerald	Austin Prep	RW
18	Que.	Ken McRae	Sudbury	C
19	Wsh.	Jeff Greenlaw	Canadian National	LW
20	Phi.	Kerry Huffman	Guelph	D
21	Edm.	Kim Issel	Prince Albert	RW

OTHER NOTABLE SELECTIONS

Pick	Claimed by		Amateur Club	Position
22	Det.	Adam Graves	Windsor	LW
27	Mtl.	Benoit Brunet	Hull	LW
29	Wpg.	Teppo Numminen	Tappara Tampere	D
47	Buf.	Bob Corkum	U. of Maine	C
57	Mtl.	Jyrki Lumme	Ilves Tampere	D
67	Pit.	Rob Brown	Kamloops	RW
72	NYR	Mark Janssens	Regina	C
85	Det.	Johan Garpenlov	Nacka	LW
114	NYR	Darren Turcotte	North Bay	C
141	Mtl.	Lyle Odelein	Moose Jaw	D
143	NYI	Rich Pilon	Prince Albert AAA	D
167	Phi.	Murray Baron	Vernon Jr. A	D

1985

FIRST ROUND

Pick	Claimed by		Amateur Club	Position
1	Tor.	Wendel Clark	Saskatoon	LW/D
2	Pit.	Craig Simpson	Michigan State	LW
3	N.J.	Craig Wolanin	Kitchener	D
4	Van.	Jim Sandlak	London	RW
5	Hfd.	Dana Murzyn	Calgary	D
6	NYI	Brad Dalgarno	Hamilton	RW
7	NYR	Ulf Dahlen	Ostersund	LW
8	Det.	Brent Fedyk	Regina	LW
9	L.A.	Craig Duncanson	Sudbury	LW
10	L.A.	Dan Gratton	Oshawa	C
11	Chi.	Dave Manson	Prince Albert	D
12	Mtl.	Jose Charbonneau	Drummondville	RW
13	NYI	Derek King	Sault Ste. Marie	LW
14	Buf.	Calle Johansson	Vastra Frolunda	D
15	Que.	David Latta	Kitchener	LW
16	Mtl.	Tom Chorske	Minneapolis SW H.S.	LW
17	Cgy.	Chris Biotti	Belmont Hill H.S.	D
18	Wpg.	Ryan Stewart	Kamloops	C
19	Wsh.	Yvon Corriveau	Toronto	LW
20	Edm.	Scott Metcalfe	Kingston	LW
21	Phi.	Glen Seabrooke	Peterborough	C

OTHER NOTABLE SELECTIONS

Pick	Claimed by		Amateur Club	Position
24	N.J.	Sean Burke	Toronto	G
27	Cgy.	Joe Nieuwendyk	Cornell	C
28	NYR	Mike Richter	Northwood Prep	G
32	N.J.	Eric Weinrich	North Yarmouth Academy	D
35	Buf.	Benoit Hogue	St-Jean	C
44	St.L.	Nelson Emerson	Stratford Jr.A	RW
52	Bos.	Bill Ranford	New Westminster	G
81	Wpg.	Fredrik Olausson	Farjestad Karlstad	D
113	Det.	Randy McKay	Michigan Tech	RW
119	Buf.	Joe Reekie	Cornwall	D
188	Edm.	Kelly Buchberger	Moose Jaw	RW
214	Van.	Igor Larionov	CSKA Moscow	C

1984

FIRST ROUND

Pick	Claimed by		Amateur Club	Position
1	Pit.	Mario Lemieux	Laval	C
2	N.J.	Kirk Muller	Guelph	LW
3	Chi.	Eddie Olczyk	Team USA	C
4	Tor.	Al Iafrate	Belleville	D
5	Mtl.	Petr Svoboda	CHZ Litvinov	D
6	L.A.	Craig Redmond	U. of Denver	D
7	Det.	Shawn Burr	Kitchener	LW/C
8	Mtl.	Shayne Corson	Brantford	LW
9	Pit.	Doug Bodger	Kamloops	D
10	Van.	J.J. Daigneault	Longueuil	D
11	Hfd.	Sylvain Cote	Quebec	D
12	Cgy.	Gary Roberts	Ottawa	LW
13	Min.	David Quinn	Kent H.S.	D

Pick	Claimed by		Amateur Club	Position
14	NYR	Terry Carkner	Peterborough	D
15	Que.	Trevor Stienburg	Guelph	RW
16	Pit.	Roger Belanger	Kingston	C
17	Wsh.	Kevin Hatcher	North Bay	D
18	Buf.	Mikael Andersson	Vastra Frolunda	LW
19	Bos.	Dave Pasin	Prince Albert	RW
20	NYI	Duncan MacPherson	Saskatoon	D
21	Edm.	Selmar Odelein	Regina	D

OTHER NOTABLE SELECTIONS

Pick	Claimed by		Amateur Club	Position
25	Tor.	Todd Gill	Windsor	D
27	Phi.	Scott Mellanby	Henry Carr Jr. B	RW
29	Mtl.	Stephane Richer	Granby	RW
38	Cgy.	Paul Ranheim	Edina H.S.	LW
51	Mtl.	Patrick Roy	Granby	G
59	Wsh.	Michal Pivonka	Kladno	C
60	Buf.	Ray Sheppard	Cornwall	RW
117	Cgy.	Brett Hull	Penticton Jr. A.	RW
119	NYR	Kjell Samuelsson	Leksand	D
134	St.L.	Cliff Ronning	New Westminster	C
166	Bos.	Don Sweeney	St. Paul's H.S.	D
171	L.A.	Luc Robitaille	Hull	LW
180	Cgy.	Gary Suter	U. of Wisconsin	D

1983

FIRST ROUND

Pick	Claimed by		Amateur Club	Position
1	Min.	Brian Lawton	Mount St. Charles H.S.	LW
2	Hfd.	Sylvain Turgeon	Hull	LW
3	NYI	Pat LaFontaine	Verdun	C
4	Det.	Steve Yzerman	Peterborough	C
5	Buf.	Tom Barrasso	Acton-Boxborough	G
6	N.J.	John MacLean	Oshawa	RW
7	Tor.	Russ Courtnall	Victoria	RW
8	Wpg.	Andrew McBain	North Bay	RW
9	Van.	Cam Neely	Portland	RW
10	Buf.	Normand Lacombe	New Hampshire	RW
11	Buf.	Adam Creighton	Ottawa	C
12	NYR	Dave Gagner	Brantford	C
13	Cgy.	Dan Quinn	Belleville	C
14	Wpg.	Bobby Dollas	Laval	D
15	Pit.	Bob Errey	Peterborough	LW
16	NYI	Gerald Diduck	Lethbridge	D
17	Mtl.	Alfie Turcotte	Portland	C
18	Chi.	Bruce Cassidy	Ottawa	D
19	Edm.	Jeff Beukeboom	Sault Ste. Marie	D
20	Hfd.	David Jensen	Lawrence Academy	C
21	Bos.	Nevin Markwart	Regina	LW

OTHER NOTABLE SELECTIONS

Pick	Claimed by		Amateur Club	Position
26	Mtl.	Claude Lemieux	Trois-Rivieres	RW
46	Det.	Bob Probert	Brantford	LW
60	Chi.	Marc Bergevin	Chicoutimi	D
82	Edm.	Esa Tikkanen	HIFK Helsinki	LW
88	Det.	Petr Klima	Dukla Jihlava	W
91	Det.	Joe Kocur	Saskatoon	RW
103	L.A.	Garry Galley	Bowling Green	D
114	Van.	Dave Lowry	London	LW
125	Phi.	Rick Tocchet	Sault Ste. Marie	RW
150	N.J.	Viacheslav Fetisov	CSKA Moscow	D
207	Chi.	Dominik Hasek	Pardubice	G
223	Buf.	Uwe Krupp	Koln	D
241	Cgy.	Sergei Makarov	CSKA Moscow	RW

1982

FIRST ROUND

Pick	Claimed by		Amateur Club	Position
1	Bos.	Gord Kluzak	Billings	D
2	Min.	Brian Bellows	Kitchener	LW
3	Tor.	Gary Nylund	Portland	D
4	Phi.	Ron Sutter	Lethbridge	C
5	Wsh.	Scott Stevens	Kitchener	D
6	Buf.	Phil Housley	South St. Paul H.S.	D
7	Chi.	Ken Yaremchuk	Portland	C
8	N.J.	Rocky Trottier	Nanaimo	RW
9	Buf.	Paul Cyr	Victoria	LW
10	Pit.	Rich Sutter	Lethbridge	RW
11	Van.	Michel Petit	Sherbrooke	D
12	Wpg.	Jim Kyte	Cornwall	D
13	Que.	David Shaw	Kitchener	D
14	Hfd.	Paul Lawless	Windsor	LW
15	NYR	Chris Kontos	Toronto	LW/C
16	Buf.	Dave Andreychuk	Oshawa	LW
17	Det.	Murray Craven	Medicine Hat	LW
18	N.J.	Ken Daneyko	Seattle	D
19	Mtl.	Alain Heroux	Chicoutimi	LW
20	Edm.	Jim Playfair	Portland	D
21	NYI	Pat Flatley	U. of Wisconsin	RW

OTHER NOTABLE SELECTIONS

Pick	Claimed by		Amateur Club	Position
36	NYR	Tomas Sandstrom	Farjestad Karlstad	RW
43	N.J.	Pat Verbeek	Sudbury	RW
45	Tor.	Ken Wregget	Lethbridge	G
56	Hfd.	Kevin Dineen	U. of Denver	RW
60	Bos.	Dave Reid	Peterborough	LW
67	Hfd.	Ulf Samuelsson	Leksand	D
75	Wpg.	Dave Ellett	Ottawa Jr. A.	D
80	Min.	Bob Rouse	Nanaimo	D
88	Hfd.	Ray Ferraro	Penticton Jr. A	C
119	Phi.	Ron Hextall	Brandon	G
120	NYR	Tony Granato	Northwood Prep	RW
134	St.L.	Doug Gilmour	Cornwall	C
140	Phi.	Dave Brown	Saskatoon	RW
181	Que.	Mike Hough	Kitchener	LW
183	NYR	Kelly Miller	Michigan State	LW

1981

FIRST ROUND

Pick	Claimed by		Amateur Club	Position
1	Wpg.	Dale Hawerchuk	Cornwall	C
2	L.A.	Doug Smith	Ottawa	C
3	Wsh.	Bob Carpenter	St. John's Prep.	C
4	Hfd.	Ron Francis	Sault Ste. Marie	C
5	Col.	Joe Cirella	Oshawa	D
6	Tor.	Jim Benning	Portland	D
7	Mtl.	Mark Hunter	Brantford	RW
8	Edm.	Grant Fuhr	Victoria	G
9	NYR	James Patrick	Prince Albert	D
10	Van.	Garth Butcher	Regina	D
11	Que.	Randy Moller	Lethbridge	D
12	Chi.	Tony Tanti	Oshawa	RW
13	Min.	Ron Meighan	Niagara Falls	D
14	Bos.	Normand Leveille	Chicoutimi	LW
15	Cgy.	Al MacInnis	Kitchener	D
16	Phi.	Steve Smith	Sault Ste. Marie	D
17	Buf.	Jiri Dudacek	Kladno	RW
18	Mtl.	Gilbert Delorme	Chicoutimi	D
19	Mtl.	Jan Ingman	Farjestad Karlstad	LW
20	St.L.	Marty Ruff	Lethbridge	D
21	NYI	Paul Boutilier	Sherbrooke	D

OTHER NOTABLE SELECTIONS

Pick	Claimed by		Amateur Club	Position
40	Mtl.	Chris Chelios	Moose Jaw	D
56	Cgy.	Mike Vernon	Calgary	G
72	NYR	John Vanbiesbrouck	Sault Ste. Marie	G
108	Col.	Bruce Driver	U. of Wisconsin	D
111	Edm.	Steve Smith	London	D
116	Que.	Mike Eagles	Kitchener	C/LW
145	Mtl.	Tom Kurvers	Minnesota-Duluth	D
152	Wsh.	Gaetan Duchesne	Quebec	LW

1980

FIRST ROUND

Pick	Claimed by		Amateur Club	Position
1	Mtl.	Doug Wickenheiser	Regina	C
2	Wpg.	Dave Babych	Portland	D
3	Chi.	Denis Savard	Montreal	C
4	L.A.	Larry Murphy	Peterborough	D
5	Wsh.	Darren Veitch	Regina	D
6	Edm.	Paul Coffey	Kitchener	D
7	Van.	Rick Lanz	Oshawa	D
8	Hfd.	Fred Arthur	Cornwall	D
9	Pit.	Mike Bullard	Brantford	C
10	L.A.	Jim Fox	Ottawa	RW
11	Det.	Mike Blaisdell	Regina	RW
12	St.L.	Rik Wilson	Kingston	D
13	Cgy.	Denis Cyr	Montreal	RW
14	NYR	Jim Malone	Toronto	C
15	Chi.	Jerome Dupont	Toronto	D
16	Min.	Brad Palmer	Victoria	LW
17	NYI	Brent Sutter	Red Deer Jr. A	C
18	Bos.	Barry Pederson	Victoria	C
19	Col.	Paul Gagne	Windsor	LW
20	Buf.	Steve Patrick	Brandon	RW
21	Phi.	Mike Stothers	Kingston	D

OTHER NOTABLE SELECTIONS

Pick	Claimed by		Amateur Club	Position
37	Min.	Don Beaupre	Sudbury	G
38	NYI	Kelly Hrudey	Medicine Hat	G
39	Cgy.	Steve Konroyd	Oshawa	D
46	Det.	Mark Osborne	Niagara Falls	LW
61	Mtl.	Craig Ludwig	North Dakota	D
69	Edm.	Jari Kurri	Jokerit	RW
73	L.A.	Bernie Nicholls	Kingston	C
80	NYI	Greg Gilbert	Toronto	LW
81	Bos.	Steve Kasper	Verdun	C
106	Col.	Aaron Broten	Minnesota-Duluth	LW/C
120	Chi.	Steve Larmer	Niagara Falls	RW
124	Mtl.	Mike McPhee	RPI	LW
128	Wpg.	Brian Mullen	U.S. Jr. National	RW
132	Edm.	Andy Moog	Billings	G
133	Van.	Doug Lidster	Colorado College	D
167	Buf.	Randy Cunneyworth	Ottawa	LW

1979

FIRST ROUND

Pick	Claimed by		Amateur Club	Position
1	Col.	Rob Ramage	London	D
2	St.L.	Perry Turnbull	Portland	C
3	Det.	Mike Foligno	Sudbury	RW
4	Wsh.	Mike Gartner	Niagara Falls	RW
5	Van.	Rick Vaive	Sherbrooke	RW
6	Min.	Craig Hartsburg	Sault Ste. Marie	D
7	Chi.	Keith Brown	Portland	D
8	Bos.	Raymond Bourque	Verdun	D
9	Tor.	Laurie Boschman	Brandon	C
10	Min.	Tom McCarthy	Oshawa	LW
11	Buf.	Mike Ramsey	U. of Minnesota	D
12	Atl.	Paul Reinhart	Kitchener	D
13	NYR	Doug Sulliman	Kitchener	RW
14	Phi.	Brian Propp	Brandon	LW
15	Bos.	Brad McCrimmon	Brandon	D
16	L.A.	Jay Wells	Kingston	D
17	NYI	Duane Sutter	Lethbridge	RW
18	Hfd.	Ray Allison	Brandon	RW
19	Wpg.	Jimmy Mann	Sherbrooke	RW
20	Que.	Michel Goulet	Quebec	LW
21	Edm.	Kevin Lowe	Quebec	D

OTHER NOTABLE SELECTIONS

Pick	Claimed by		Amateur Club	Position
26	Van.	Brent Ashton	Saskatoon	LW
30	L.A.	Mark Hardy	Montreal	D
32	Buf.	Lindy Ruff	Lethbridge	D/LW
37	Mtl.	Mats Naslund	Brynas Gavle	LW
40	Wpg.	Dave Christian	North Dakota	RW
41	Que.	Dale Hunter	Sudbury	C
42	Min.	Neal Broten	Minnesota-Duluth	C
44	Mtl.	Guy Carbonneau	Chicoutimi	C
48	Edm.	Mark Messier	St. Albert Jr. A	C
54	Atl.	Tim Hunter	Seattle	RW
66	Det.	John Ogrodnick	New Westminster	LW
69	Edm.	Glenn Anderson	U. of Denver	RW
75	Atl.	Jim Peplinski	Toronto	RW
83	Que.	Anton Stastny	Slovan Bratislava	LW
89	Van.	Dirk Graham	Regina	RW/LW
103	Wpg.	Thomas Steen	Leksand	C
120	Bos.	Mike Krushelnyski	Montreal	LW/C

1978

FIRST ROUND

Pick	Claimed by		Amateur Club	Position
1	Min.	Bobby Smith	Ottawa	C
2	Wsh.	Ryan Walter	Seattle	C/LW
3	St.L.	Wayne Babych	Portland	RW
4	Van.	Bill Derlago	Brandon	C
5	Col.	Mike Gillis	Kingston	LW
6	Phi.	Behn Wilson	Kingston	D
7	Phi.	Ken Linseman	Kingston	C
8	Mtl.	Danny Geoffrion	Cornwall	RW
9	Det.	Willie Huber	Hamilton	D
10	Chi.	Tim Higgins	Ottawa	RW
11	Atl.	Brad Marsh	London	D
12	Det.	Brent Peterson	Portland	C
13	Buf.	Larry Playfair	Portland	D
14	Phi.	Danny Lucas	Sault Ste. Marie	RW
15	NYI	Steve Tambellini	Lethbridge	C
16	Bos.	Al Secord	Hamilton	LW
17	Mtl.	Dave Hunter	Sudbury	LW
18	Wsh.	Tim Coulis	Hamilton	LW

OTHER NOTABLE SELECTIONS

Pick	Claimed by		Amateur Club	Position
19	Min.	Steve Payne	Ottawa	LW
21	Tor.	Joel Quenneville	Windsor	D
26	NYR	Don Maloney	Kitchener	LW
32	Buf.	Tony McKegney	Kingston	LW
40	Van.	Stan Smyl	New Westminster	RW
54	Min.	Curt Giles	Minnesota-Duluth	D
55	Wsh.	Bengt-Ake Gustafsson	Farjestad Karlstad	RW
93	NYR	Tom Laidlaw	Northern Michigan	D
103	Mtl.	Keith Acton	Peterborough	C
109	St.L.	Paul MacLean	Hull	RW
153	Bos.	Craig MacTavish	University of Lowell	C
173	St.L.	Risto Siltanen	Ilves Tampere	D
179	Chi.	Darryl Sutter	Lethbridge	LW
231	Mtl.	Chris Nilan	Northeastern	RW

1977

FIRST ROUND

Pick	Claimed by		Amateur Club	Position
1	Det.	Dale McCourt	St. Catharines	C
2	Col.	Barry Beck	New Westminster	D
3	Wsh.	Robert Picard	Montreal	D
4	Van.	Jere Gillis	Sherbrooke	LW
5	Cle.	Mike Crombeen	Kingston	RW
6	Chi.	Doug Wilson	Ottawa	D
7	Min.	Brad Maxwell	New Westminster	D
8	NYR	Lucien DeBlois	Sorel	C
9	St.L.	Scott Campbell	London	D
10	Mtl.	Mark Napier	Toronto	RW

Pick	Claimed by		Amateur Club	Position
11	Tor.	John Anderson	Toronto	RW
12	Tor.	Trevor Johansen	Toronto	D
13	NYR	Ron Duguay	Sudbury	C/RW
14	Buf.	Ric Seiling	St. Catharines	RW/C
15	NYI	Mike Bossy	Laval	RW
16	Bos.	Dwight Foster	Kitchener	RW
17	Phi.	Kevin McCarthy	Winnipeg	D
18	Mtl.	Norm Dupont	Montreal	LW

OTHER NOTABLE SELECTIONS

Pick	Claimed by		Amateur Club	Position
25	Min.	Dave Semenko	Brandon	LW
33	NYI	John Tonelli	Toronto	LW
36	Mtl.	Rod Langway	New Hampshire	D
43	Mtl.	Alain Cote	Chicoutimi	LW
54	Mtl.	Gordie Roberts	Victoria	D
62	NYR	Mario Marois	Quebec	D
66	Pit.	Mark Johnson	U. of Wisconsin	C
102	Pit.	Greg Millen	Peterborough	G
118	Atl.	Bobby Gould	New Hampshire	RW
135	Phi.	Pete Peeters	Medicine Hat	G
162	Mtl.	Craig Laughlin	Clarkson	RW

1976

FIRST ROUND

Pick	Claimed by		Amateur Club	Position
1	Wsh.	Rick Green	London	D
2	Pit.	Blair Chapman	Saskatoon	RW
3	Min.	Glen Sharpley	Hull	C
4	Det.	Fred Williams	Saskatoon	C
5	Cal.	Bjorn Johansson	Orebro	D
6	NYR	Don Murdoch	Medicine Hat	RW
7	St.L.	Bernie Federko	Saskatoon	C
8	Atl.	Dave Shand	Peterborough	D
9	Chi.	Real Cloutier	Quebec	RW
10	Atl.	Harold Phillipoff	New Westminster	LW
11	K.C.	Paul Gardner	Oshawa	C
12	Mtl.	Peter Lee	Ottawa	RW
13	Mtl.	Rod Schutt	Sudbury	LW
14	NYI	Alex McKendry	Sudbury	W
15	Wsh.	Greg Carroll	Medicine Hat	C
16	Bos.	Clayton Pachal	New Westminster	C/LW
17	Phi.	Mark Suzor	Kingston	D
18	Mtl.	Bruce Baker	Ottawa	RW

OTHER NOTABLE SELECTIONS

Pick	Claimed by		Amateur Club	Position
20	St.L.	Brian Sutter	Lethbridge	LW
22	Det.	Reed Larson	Minnesota-Duluth	D
30	Tor.	Randy Carlyle	Sudbury	D
42	NYR	Mike McEwen	Toronto	D
45	Chi.	Thomas Gradin	MoDo Ornskoldsvik	C
47	Pit.	Morris Lukowich	Medicine Hat	LW
56	St.L.	Mike Liut	Bowling Green	G
64	Atl.	Kent Nilsson	Djurgarden	C
68	NYI	Ken Morrow	Bowling Green	D
133	Mtl.	Ron Wilson	St. Catharines	C

1975

FIRST ROUND

Pick	Claimed by		Amateur Club	Position
1	Phi.	Mel Bridgman	Victoria	C
2	K.C.	Barry Dean	Medicine Hat	LW
3	Cal.	Ralph Klassen	Saskatoon	C
4	Min.	Bryan Maxwell	Medicine Hat	D
5	Det.	Rick Lapointe	Victoria	D
6	Tor.	Don Ashby	Calgary	C
7	Chi.	Greg Vaydik	Medicine Hat	C
8	Atl.	Richard Mulhern	Sherbrooke	D
9	Mtl.	Robin Sadler	Edmonton	D
10	Van.	Rick Blight	Brandon	RW
11	NYI	Pat Price	Saskatoon	D
12	NYR	Wayne Dillon	Toronto	C
13	Pit.	Gord Laxton	New Westminster	G
14	Bos.	Doug Halward	Peterborough	D
15	Mtl.	Pierre Mondou	Montreal	C
16	L.A.	Tim Young	Ottawa	C

OTHER NOTABLE SELECTIONS

Pick	Claimed by		Amateur Club	Position
17	Buf.	Bob Sauve	Laval	G
21	Cal.	Dennis Maruk	London	C
24	Tor.	Doug Jarvis	Peterborough	C
43	Chi.	Mike O'Connell	Kingston	D
57	Cal.	Greg Smith	Colorado College	D
80	Atl.	Willi Plett	St. Catharines	RW
108	Phi.	Paul Holmgren	U. of Minnesota	RW
210	L.A.	Dave Taylor	Clarkson	RW

1974

FIRST ROUND

Pick	Claimed by		Amateur Club	Position
1	Wsh.	Greg Joly	Regina	D
2	K.C.	Wilf Paiement	St. Catharines	RW
3	Cal.	Rick Hampton	St. Catharines	LW/D
4	NYI	Clark Gillies	Regina	LW
5	Mtl.	Cam Connor	Flin Flon	RW
6	Min.	Doug Hicks	Flin Flon	D
7	Mtl.	Doug Risebrough	Kitchener	C
8	Pit.	Pierre Larouche	Sorel	C
9	Det.	Bill Lochead	Oshawa	LW
10	Mtl.	Rick Chartraw	Kitchener	D/RW
11	Buf.	Lee Fogolin Jr.	Oshawa	D
12	Mtl.	Mario Tremblay	Montreal	RW
13	Tor.	Jack Valiquette	Sault Ste. Marie	C
14	NYR	Dave Maloney	Kitchener	D
15	Mtl.	Gord McTavish	Sudbury	C
16	Chi.	Grant Mulvey	Calgary	RW
17	Cal.	Ron Chipperfield	Brandon	C
18	Bos.	Don Larway	Swift Current	RW

OTHER NOTABLE SELECTIONS

Pick	Claimed by		Amateur Club	Position
22	NYI	Bryan Trottier	Swift Current	C
25	Bos.	Mark Howe	Toronto	D
29	Buf.	Danny Gare	Calgary	RW
31	Tor.	Tiger Williams	Swift Current	LW
32	NYR	Ron Greschner	New Westminster	D
38	K.C.	Bob Bourne	Saskatoon	C
39	Cal.	Charlie Simmer	Sault Ste. Marie	LW
52	Chi.	Bob Murray	Cornwall	D
59	Van.	Harold Snepsts	Edmonton	D
70	Chi.	Terry Ruskowski	Swift Current	C
125	Phi.	Reggie Lemelin	Sherbrooke	G
199	Mtl.	Dave Lumley	New Hampshire	RW
214	NYI	Stefan Persson	Brynas Gavle	D

1973

FIRST ROUND

Pick	Claimed by		Amateur Club	Position
1	NYI	Denis Potvin	Ottawa	D
2	Atl.	Tom Lysiak	Medicine Hat	C
3	Van.	Dennis Ververgaert	London	RW
4	Tor.	Lanny McDonald	Medicine Hat	RW
5	St.L.	John Davidson	Calgary	G
6	Bos.	Andre Savard	Quebec	C
7	Pit.	Blaine Stoughton	Flin Flon	RW
8	Mtl.	Bob Gainey	Peterborough	LW
9	Van.	Bob Dailey	Toronto	D
10	Tor.	Bob Neely	Peterborough	LW
11	Det.	Terry Richardson	New Westminster	G
12	Buf.	Morris Titanic	Sudbury	LW
13	Chi.	Darcy Rota	Edmonton	LW
14	NYR	Rick Middleton	Oshawa	RW
15	Tor.	Ian Turnbull	Ottawa	D
16	Atl.	Vic Mercredi	New Westminster	C

OTHER NOTABLE SELECTIONS

Pick	Claimed by		Amateur Club	Position
21	Atl.	Eric Vail	Sudbury	LW
27	Pit.	Colin Campbell	Peterborough	D
30	NYR	Pat Hickey	Hamilton	LW
33	NYI	Dave Lewis	Saskatoon	D
49	NYI	Andre St. Laurent	Montreal	C
85	Atl.	Ken Houston	Chatham Jr. B	RW
130	Cal.	Larry Patey	Braintree H.S.	C
134	Pit.	Gord Lane	New Westminster	D
162	Atl.	Greg Fox	U. of Michigan	D

1972

FIRST ROUND

Pick	Claimed by		Amateur Club	Position
1	NYI	Billy Harris	Toronto	RW
2	Atl.	Jacques Richard	Quebec	LW
3	Van.	Don Lever	Niagara Falls	LW
4	Mtl.	Steve Shutt	Toronto	LW
5	Buf.	Jim Schoenfeld	Niagara Falls	D
6	Mtl.	Michel Larocque	Ottawa	G
7	Phi.	Bill Barber	Kitchener	LW
8	Mtl.	Dave Gardner	Toronto	C
9	St.L.	Wayne Merrick	Ottawa	C
10	NYR	Al Blanchard	Kitchener	LW
11	Tor.	George Ferguson	Toronto	C
12	Min.	Jerry Byers	Kitchener	LW
13	Chi.	Phil Russell	Edmonton	D
14	Mtl.	John Van Boxmeer	Guelph	D
15	NYR	Bob MacMillan	St. Catharines	RW
16	Bos.	Mike Bloom	St. Catharines	LW

OTHER NOTABLE SELECTIONS

Pick	Claimed by		Amateur Club	Position
17	NYI	Lorne Henning	New Westminster	C
23	Phi.	Tom Bladon	Edmonton	D
33	NYI	Bob Nystrom	Calgary	RW
39	Phi.	Jimmy Watson	Calgary	D
55	Phi.	Al MacAdam	University of PEI	RW
85	Buf.	Peter McNab	U. of Denver	C
97	NYI	Richard Brodeur	Cornwall	G
139	Tor.	Pat Boutette	Minnesota-Duluth	C/RW
144	NYI	Garry Howatt	Flin Flon	LW

1971

FIRST ROUND

Pick	Claimed by		Amateur Club	Position
1	Mtl.	Guy Lafleur	Quebec	RW
2	Det.	Marcel Dionne	St. Catharines	C
3	Van.	Jocelyn Guevremont	Montreal	D
4	St.L.	Gene Carr	Flin Flon	C
5	Buf.	Rick Martin	Montreal	LW
6	Bos.	Ron Jones	Edmonton	D
7	Mtl.	Chuck Arnason	Flin Flon	RW
8	Phi.	Larry Wright	Regina	C
9	Phi.	Pierre Plante	Drummondville	RW
10	NYR	Steve Vickers	Toronto	LW
11	Mtl.	Murray Wilson	Ottawa	LW
12	Chi.	Dan Spring	Edmonton	C
13	NYR	Steve Durbano	Toronto	D
14	Bos.	Terry O'Reilly	Oshawa	RW

OTHER NOTABLE SELECTIONS

Pick	Claimed by		Amateur Club	Position
17	Van.	Bobby Lalonde	Montreal	C
19	Buf.	Craig Ramsay	Peterborough	LW
20	Mtl.	Larry Robinson	Kitchener	D
22	Tor.	Rick Kehoe	Hamilton	RW
33	Buf.	Bill Hajt	Saskatoon	D
48	L.A.	Neil Komadoski	Winnipeg	D
55	NYR	Jerry Butler	Hamilton	RW

1970

FIRST ROUND

Pick	Claimed by		Amateur Club	Position
1	Buf.	Gilbert Perreault	Montreal	C
2	Van.	Dale Tallon	Toronto	D
3	Bos.	Reggie Leach	Flin Flon	RW
4	Bos.	Rick MacLeish	Peterborough	C
5	Mtl.	Ray Martyniuk	Flin Flon	G
6	Mtl.	Chuck Lefley	Canadian National	LW
7	Pit.	Greg Polis	Estevan	LW
8	Tor.	Darryl Sittler	London	C
9	Bos.	Ron Plumb	Peterborough	D
10	Cal.	Chris Oddleifson	Winnipeg	C
11	NYR	Norm Gratton	Montreal	LW
12	Det.	Serge Lajeunesse	Montreal	D/RW
13	Bos.	Bob Stewart	Oshawa	D
14	Chi.	Dan Maloney	London	LW

OTHER NOTABLE SELECTIONS

Pick	Claimed by		Amateur Club	Position
18	Phi.	Bill Clement	Ottawa	C
22	Tor.	Errol Thompson	Charlottetown Sr.	LW
25	NYR	Mike Murphy	Toronto	RW
27	Bos.	Dan Bouchard	London	G
32	Phi.	Bob Kelly	Oshawa	LW
40	Det.	Yvon Lambert	Drummondville	LW
59	L.A.	Billy Smith	Cornwall	G
70	Chi.	Gilles Meloche	Verdun	G
88	Oak.	Terry Murray	Ottawa	D
103	Tor.	Ron Low	Dauphin Jr. A	G

1969

FIRST ROUND

Pick	Claimed by		Amateur Club	Position
1	Mtl.	Rejean Houle	Montreal	W
2	Mtl.	Marc Tardif	Montreal	LW
3	Bos.	Don Tannahill	Niagara Falls	LW
4	Bos.	Frank Spring	Edmonton	RW
5	Min.	Dick Redmond	St. Catharines	D
6	Phi.	Bob Currier	Cornwall	C
7	Oak.	Tony Featherstone	Peterborough	RW
8	NYR	Andre Dupont	Montreal	D
9	Tor.	Ernie Moser	Estevan	RW
10	Det.	Jim Rutherford	Hamilton	G
11	Bos.	Ivan Boldirev	Oshawa	C
12	NYR	Pierre Jarry	Ottawa	LW

OTHER NOTABLE SELECTIONS

Pick	Claimed by		Amateur Club	Position
17	Phi.	Bobby Clarke	Flin Flon	C
18	Oak.	Ron Stackhouse	Peterborough	D
25	Min.	Gilles Gilbert	London	G
26	Pit.	Michel Briere	Shawinigan	C
51	L.A.	Butch Goring	Dauphin Jr. A	C
52	Phi.	Dave Schultz	Sorel	LW
55	Tor.	Brian Spencer	Swift Current	LW
64	Phi.	Don Saleski	Regina	RW

NHL All-Stars

Active Players' All-Star Selection Records

Player	First Team Selections		Second Team Selections		Total
GOALTENDER					
Dominik Hasek	(6)	1993-94; 1994-95; 1996-97; 1997-98; 1998-99; 2000-01.	(0)		6
Martin Brodeur	(3)	2002-03; 2003-04; 2006-07	(3)	1996-97; 1997-98; 2005-06.	6
Ed Belfour	(2)	1990-91; 1992-93.	(1)	1994-95	3
Roberto Luongo	(0)		(2)	2003-04; 2006-07	2
Olie Kolzig	(1)	99-2000.	(0)		1
Miikka Kiprusoff	(1)	2005-06.	(0)		1
Chris Osgood	(0)		(1)	1995-96.	1
Jose Theodore	(0)		(1)	2001-02.	1
Marty Turco	(0)		(1)	2002-03.	1
DEFENSE					
Nicklas Lidstrom	(8)	1997-98; 1998-99; 99-2000; 2000-01; 2001-02; 2002-03; 2005-06; 2006-07	(0)		8
Chris Chelios	(5)	1988-89; 1992-93; 1994-95; 1995-96; 2001-02.	(2)	1990-91; 1996-97.	7
Scott Niedermayer	(3)	2003-04; 2005-06; 2006-07	(1)	2002-03.	4
Rob Blake	(1)	1997-98.	(3)	99-2000; 2000-01; 2001-02.	4
Chris Pronger	(1)	99-2000.	(3)	1997-98; 2003-04; 2006-07	4
Zdeno Chara	(1)	2003-04.	(1)	2005-06.	2
Sergei Gonchar	(0)		(2)	2001-02; 2002-03.	2
Derian Hatcher	(0)		(1)	2002-03.	1
Bryan McCabe	(0)		(1)	2003-04.	1
Sergei Zubov	(0)		(1)	2005-06.	1
Dan Boyle	(0)		(1)	2006-07.	1
CENTER					
Peter Forsberg	(3)	1997-98; 1998-99; 2002-03.	(0)		3
Joe Sakic	(3)	2000-01; 2001-02; 2003-04.	(0)		3
Eric Lindros	(1)	1994-95.	(1)	1995-96.	2
Joe Thornton	(1)	2005-06.	(1)	2002-03.	2
Mats Sundin	(0)		(2)	2001-02; 2003-04.	2
Sergei Fedorov	(1)	1993-94.	(0)		1
Sidney Crosby	(1)	2006-07.	(0)		1
Alexei Yashin	(0)		(1)	1998-99.	1
Mike Modano	(0)		(1)	99-2000.	1
Eric Staal	(0)		(1)	2005-06.	1
Vincent Lecavalier	(0)		(1)	2006-07.	1
RIGHT WING					
Jaromir Jagr	(7)	1994-95; 1995-96; 1997-98; 1998-99; 99-2000; 2000-01; 2005-06.	(1)	1996-97.	8
Teemu Selanne	(2)	1992-93; 1996-97.	(2)	1997-98; 1998-99.	4
Jarome Iginla	(1)	2001-02.	(1)	2003-04.	2
Martin St. Louis	(1)	2003-04.	(1)	2006-07.	2
Todd Bertuzzi	(1)	2002-03.	(0)		1
Dany Heatley	(1)	2006-07.	(0)		1
Mark Recchi	(0)		(1)	1991-92.	1
Bill Guerin	(0)		(1)	2001-02.	1
Milan Hejduk	(0)		(1)	2002-03.	1
Daniel Alfredsson	(0)		(1)	2005-06.	1
LEFT WING					
Paul Kariya	(3)	1995-96; 1996-97; 1998-99.	(2)	99-2000; 2002-03.	5
Markus Naslund	(3)	2001-02; 2002-03; 2003-04.	(0)		3
Brendan Shanahan	(2)	1993-94; 99-2000.	(1)	2001-02.	3
Alex Ovechkin	(2)	2005-06; 2006-07	(0)		2
Keith Tkachuk	(0)		(2)	1994-95; 1997-98.	2
Patrik Elias	(1)	2000-01.	(0)		1
Ilya Kovalchuk	(0)		(1)	2003-04.	1
Dany Heatley	(0)		(1)	2005-06.	1
Thomas Vanek	(0)		(1)	2006-07.	1

Leading NHL All-Stars 1930-31 to 2006-07

Player	Pos	Team	NHL Seasons	First Team Selections	Second Team Selections	Total Selections
Howe, Gordie	RW	Detroit	26	12	9	21
Bourque, Raymond	D	Bos., Col.	22	13	6	19
Gretzky, Wayne	C	Edm., L.A., NYR	20	8	7	15
Richard, Maurice	RW	Montreal	18	8	6	14
Hull, Bobby	LW	Chicago	16	10	2	12
Harvey, Doug	D	Mtl., NYR	19	10	1	11
Hall, Glenn	G	Det., Chi., St.L.	18	7	4	11
Beliveau, Jean	C	Montreal	20	6	4	10
Seibert, Earl	D	NYR, Chi.	15	4	6	10
Orr, Bobby	D	Boston	12	8	1	9
Lindsay, Ted	LW	Detroit	17	8	1	9
Lemieux, Mario	C	Pittsburgh	17	5	4	9
Mahovlich, Frank	LW	Tor., Det., Mtl.	18	3	6	9
* Lidstrom, Niklas	D	Detroit	15	8	0	8
Shore, Eddie	D	Boston	14	7	1	8
Esposito, Phil	C	Boston	18	6	2	8
Kelly, Red	D	Detroit	20	6	2	8
Mikita, Stan	C	Chicago	22	6	2	8
Bossy, Mike	RW	NY Islanders	10	5	3	8
Pilote, Pierre	D	Chicago	14	5	3	8
Robitaille, Luc	LW	Los Angeles	19	5	3	8
Coffey, Paul	D	Edm., Pit., Det.	21	4	4	8
Brimsek, Frank	G	Boston	10	2	6	8
* Jagr, Jaromir	RW	Pit., NYR	16	7	1	8
Potvin, Denis	D	NY Islanders	15	5	2	7
Park, Brad	D	NYR, Bos.	17	5	2	7
* Chelios, Chris	D	Mtl., Chi.	23	5	2	7
MacInnis, Al	D	Cgy., St.L.	23	4	3	7
Plante, Jacques	G	Mtl., Tor.	18	3	4	7
Gadsby, Bill	D	Chi., NYR, Det.	20	3	4	7
Sawchuk, Terry	G	Detroit	21	3	4	7
Durnan, Bill	G	Montreal	7	6	0	6
* Hasek, Dominik	G	Buffalo	14	6	0	6
Lafleur, Guy	RW	Montreal	17	6	0	6
Dryden, Ken	G	Montreal	8	5	1	6
Roy, Patrick	G	Montreal	19	4	2	6
* Brodeur, Martin	G	New Jersey	14	3	3	6
Clapper, Dit	RW/D	Boston	20	3	3	6
Robinson, Larry	D	Montreal	20	3	3	6
Horton, Tim	D	Toronto	24	3	3	6
Salming, Borje	D	Toronto	17	1	5	6
Cowley, Bill	C	Boston	13	4	1	5
Jackson, Busher	LW	Toronto	15	4	1	5
Messier, Mark	LW/C	Edm., NYR	25	4	1	5
* Kariya, Paul	LW	Anaheim	12	3	2	5
Conacher, Charlie	RW	Toronto	12	3	2	5
Stewart, Jack	D	Detroit	12	3	2	5
Blake, Toe	LW	Montreal	14	3	2	5
Lach, Elmer	C	Montreal	14	3	2	5
Quackenbush, Bill	D	Det., Bos.	14	3	2	5
Goulet, Michel	LW	Quebec	15	3	2	5
Esposito, Tony	G	Chicago	16	3	2	5
Reardon, Ken	D	Montreal	7	2	3	5
Apps, Syl	C	Toronto	10	2	3	5
LeClair, John	LW	Mtl., Phi.	16	2	3	5
Giacomin, Ed	G	NY Rangers	13	2	3	5
Leetch, Brian	D	NY Rangers	17	2	3	5
Kurri, Jari	RW	Edmonton	17	2	3	5
Stevens, Scott	D	Wsh., N.J.	21	2	3	5

* Active

Position Leaders in All-Star Selections

Position	Player	First Team	Second Team	Total
GOALTENDER	Glenn Hall	7	4	11
	Frank Brimsek	2	6	8
	Jacques Plante	3	4	7
	Terry Sawchuk	3	4	7
	Bill Durnan	6	0	6
	* Dominik Hasek	6	0	6
	Ken Dryden	5	1	6
	Patrick Roy	4	2	6
	* Martin Brodeur	3	3	6
DEFENSE	Raymond Bourque	13	6	19
	Doug Harvey	10	1	11
	Earl Seibert	4	6	10
	Bobby Orr	8	1	9
	* Nicklas Lidstrom	8	0	8
	Eddie Shore	7	1	8
	Red Kelly	6	2	8
	Pierre Pilote	5	3	8
	Paul Coffey	4	4	8
CENTER	Wayne Gretzky	8	7	15
	Jean Beliveau	6	4	10
	Mario Lemieux	5	4	9
	Phil Esposito	6	2	8
	Stan Mikita	6	2	8
RIGHT WING	Gordie Howe	12	9	21
	Maurice Richard	8	6	14
	* Jaromir Jagr	7	1	8
	Mike Bossy	5	3	8
	Guy Lafleur	6	0	6
LEFT WING	Bobby Hull	10	2	12
	Ted Lindsay	8	1	9
	Frank Mahovlich	3	6	9
	Luc Robitaille	5	3	8

* active player

All-Star Teams

1930-2007

Voting for the NHL All-Star Team is conducted among the representatives of the Professional Hockey Writers' Association at the end of the season.

Following is a list of the First and Second All-Star Teams since their inception in 1930-31.

2006-07

First Team		Second Team
Martin Brodeur, N.J.	G	Roberto Luongo, Fla.
Nicklas Lidstrom, Det.	D	Chris Pronger, Ana.
Scott Niedermayer, Ana.	D	Dan Boyle, T.B.
Sidney Crosby, Pit.	C	Vincent Lecavalier, T.B.
Dany Heatley, Ott.	RW	Martin St. Louis, T.B.
Alex Ovechkin, Wsh.	LW	Thomas Vanek, Buf.

2005-06

First Team		Second Team
Miikka Kiprusoff, Cgy.	G	Martin Brodeur, N.J.
Nicklas Lidstrom, Det.	D	Zdeno Chara, Ott.
Scott Niedermayer, Ana.	D	Sergei Zubov, Dal.
Joe Thornton, Bos., S.J.	C	Eric Staal, Car.
Jaromir Jagr, NYR	RW	Daniel Alfredsson, Ott.
Alex Ovechkin, Wsh.	LW	Dany Heatley, Ott.

2004-05

Season Cancelled

2003-04

First Team		Second Team
Martin Brodeur, N.J.	G	Roberto Luongo, Fla.
Scott Niedermayer, N.J.	D	Chris Pronger, St.L.
Zdeno Chara, Ott.	D	Bryan McCabe, Tor.
Joe Sakic, Col.	C	Mats Sundin, Tor.
Martin St. Louis, T.B.	RW	Jarome Iginla, Cgy.
Markus Naslund, Van.	LW	Ilya Kovalchuk, Atl.

2002-03

First Team		Second Team
Martin Brodeur, N.J.	G	Marty Turco, Dal.
Al MacInnis, St.L.	D	Sergei Gonchar, Wsh.
Nicklas Lidstrom, Det.	D	Derian Hatcher, Dal.
Peter Forsberg, Col.	C	Joe Thornton, Bos.
Todd Bertuzzi, Van.	RW	Milan Hejduk, Col.
Markus Naslund, Van.	LW	Paul Kariya, Ana.

2001-02

First Team		Second Team
Patrick Roy, Col.	G	Jose Theodore, Mtl.
Nicklas Lidstrom, Det.	D	Rob Blake, Col.
Chris Chelios, Det.	D	Sergei Gonchar, Wsh.
Joe Sakic, Col.	C	Mats Sundin, Tor.
Jarome Iginla, Cgy.	RW	Bill Guerin, Bos.
Markus Naslund, Van.	LW	Brendan Shanahan, Det.

2000-01

First Team		Second Team
Dominik Hasek, Buf.	G	Roman Cechmanek, Phi.
Nicklas Lidstrom, Det.	D	Rob Blake, L.A., Col.
Raymond Bourque, Col.	D	Scott Stevens, N.J.
Joe Sakic, Col.	C	Mario Lemieux, Pit.
Jaromir Jagr, Pit.	RW	Pavel Bure, Fla.
Patrik Elias, N.J.	LW	Luc Robitaille, L.A.

1999-2000

First Team		Second Team
Olaf Kolzig, Wsh.	G	Roman Turek, St.L.
Chris Pronger, St.L.	D	Rob Blake, L.A.
Nicklas Lidstrom, Det.	D	Eric Desjardins, Phi.
Steve Yzerman, Det.	C	Mike Modano, Dal.
Jaromir Jagr, Pit.	RW	Pavel Bure, Fla.
Brendan Shanahan, Det.	LW	Paul Kariya, Ana.

1998-99

First Team		Second Team
Dominik Hasek, Buf.	G	Byron Dafoe, Bos.
Al MacInnis, St.L.	D	Raymond Bourque, Bos.
Nicklas Lidstrom, Det.	D	Eric Desjardins, Phi.
Peter Forsberg, Col.	C	Alexei Yashin, Ott.
Jaromir Jagr, Pit.	RW	Teemu Selanne, Ana.
Paul Kariya, Ana.	LW	John LeClair, Phi.

1997-98

First Team		Second Team
Dominik Hasek, Buf.	G	Martin Brodeur, N.J.
Nicklas Lidstrom, Det.	D	Chris Pronger, St.L.
Rob Blake, L.A.	D	Scott Niedermayer, N.J.
Peter Forsberg, Col.	C	Wayne Gretzky, NYR
Jaromir Jagr, Pit.	RW	Teemu Selanne, Ana.
John LeClair, Phi.	LW	Keith Tkachuk, Phx.

1996-97

First Team		Second Team
Dominik Hasek, Buf.	G	Martin Brodeur, N.J.
Brian Leetch, NYR	D	Chris Chelios, Chi.
Sandis Ozolinsh, Col.	D	Scott Stevens, N.J.
Mario Lemieux, Pit.	C	Wayne Gretzky, NYR
Teemu Selanne, Ana.	RW	Jaromir Jagr, Pit.
Paul Kariya, Ana.	LW	John LeClair, Phi.

1995-96

First Team		Second Team
Jim Carey, Wsh.	G	Chris Osgood, Det.
Chris Chelios, Chi.	D	V. Konstantinov, Det.
Raymond Bourque, Bos.	D	Brian Leetch, NYR
Mario Lemieux, Pit.	C	Eric Lindros, Phi.
Jaromir Jagr, Pit.	RW	Alexander Mogilny, Van.
Paul Kariya, Ana.	LW	John LeClair, Phi.

1994-95

First Team		Second Team
Dominik Hasek, Buf.	G	Ed Belfour, Chi.
Paul Coffey, Det.	D	Raymond Bourque, Bos.
Chris Chelios, Chi.	D	Larry Murphy, Pit.
Eric Lindros, Phi.	C	Alexei Zhamnov, Wpg.
Jaromir Jagr, Pit.	RW	Theoren Fleury, Cgy.
John LeClair, Mtl., Phi.	LW	Keith Tkachuk, Wpg.

1993-94

First Team		Second Team
Dominik Hasek, Buf.	G	John Vanbiesbrouck, Fla.
Raymond Bourque, Bos.	D	Al MacInnis, Cgy.
Scott Stevens, N.J.	D	Brian Leetch, NYR
Sergei Fedorov, Det.	C	Wayne Gretzky, L.A.
Pavel Bure, Van.	RW	Cam Neely, Bos.
Brendan Shanahan, St.L.	LW	Adam Graves, NYR

1992-93

First Team		Second Team
Ed Belfour, Chi.	G	Tom Barrasso, Pit.
Chris Chelios, Chi.	D	Larry Murphy, Pit.
Raymond Bourque, Bos.	D	Al Iafrate, Wsh.
Mario Lemieux, Pit.	C	Pat LaFontaine, Buf.
Teemu Selanne, Wpg.	RW	Alexander Mogilny, Buf.
Luc Robitaille, L.A.	LW	Kevin Stevens, Pit.

1991-92

First Team		Second Team
Patrick Roy, Mtl.	G	Kirk McLean, Van.
Brian Leetch, NYR	D	Phil Housley, Wpg.
Raymond Bourque, Bos.	D	Scott Stevens, N.J.
Mark Messier, NYR	C	Mario Lemieux, Pit.
Brett Hull, St.L.	RW	Mark Recchi, Pit., Phi.
Kevin Stevens, Pit.	LW	Luc Robitaille, L.A.

1990-91

First Team		Second Team
Ed Belfour, Chi.	G	Patrick Roy, Mtl.
Raymond Bourque, Bos.	D	Chris Chelios, Chi.
Al MacInnis, Cgy.	D	Brian Leetch, NYR
Wayne Gretzky, L.A.	C	Adam Oates, St.L.
Brett Hull, St.L.	RW	Cam Neely, Bos.
Luc Robitaille, L.A.	LW	Kevin Stevens, Pit.

1989-90

First Team		Second Team
Patrick Roy, Mtl.	G	Daren Puppa, Buf.
Raymond Bourque, Bos.	D	Paul Coffey, Pit.
Al MacInnis, Cgy.	D	Doug Wilson, Chi.
Mark Messier, Edm.	C	Wayne Gretzky, L.A.
Brett Hull, St.L.	RW	Cam Neely, Bos.
Luc Robitaille, L.A.	LW	Brian Bellows, Min.

1988-89

First Team		Second Team
Patrick Roy, Mtl.	G	Mike Vernon, Cgy.
Chris Chelios, Mtl.	D	Al MacInnis, Cgy.
Paul Coffey, Pit.	D	Raymond Bourque, Bos.
Mario Lemieux, Pit.	C	Wayne Gretzky, L.A.
Joe Mullen, Cgy.	RW	Jari Kurri, Edm.
Luc Robitaille, L.A.	LW	Gerard Gallant, Det.

1987-88

First Team		Second Team
Grant Fuhr, Edm.	G	Patrick Roy, Mtl.
Raymond Bourque, Bos.	D	Gary Suter, Cgy.
Scott Stevens, Wsh.	D	Brad McCrimmon, Cgy.
Mario Lemieux, Pit.	C	Wayne Gretzky, Edm.
Hakan Loob, Cgy.	RW	Cam Neely, Bos.
Luc Robitaille, L.A.	LW	Michel Goulet, Que.

1986-87

First Team		Second Team
Ron Hextall, Phi.	G	Mike Liut, Hfd.
Raymond Bourque, Bos.	D	Larry Murphy, Wsh.
Mark Howe, Phi.	D	Al MacInnis, Cgy.
Wayne Gretzky, Edm.	C	Mario Lemieux, Pit.
Jari Kurri, Edm.	RW	Tim Kerr, Phi.
Michel Goulet, Que.	LW	Luc Robitaille, L.A.

1985-86

First Team		Second Team
John Vanbiesbrouck, NYR	G	Bob Froese, Phi.
Paul Coffey, Edm.	D	Larry Robinson, Mtl.
Mark Howe, Phi.	D	Raymond Bourque, Bos.
Wayne Gretzky, Edm.	C	Mario Lemieux, Pit.
Mike Bossy, NYI	RW	Jari Kurri, Edm.
Michel Goulet, Que.	LW	Mats Naslund, Mtl.

1984-85

First Team		Second Team
Pelle Lindbergh, Phi.	G	Tom Barrasso, Buf.
Paul Coffey, Edm.	D	Rod Langway, Wsh.
Raymond Bourque, Bos.	D	Doug Wilson, Chi.
Wayne Gretzky, Edm.	C	Dale Hawerchuk, Wpg.
Jari Kurri, Edm.	RW	Mike Bossy, NYI
John Ogrodnick, Det.	LW	John Tonelli, NYI

1983-84

First Team		Second Team
Tom Barrasso, Buf.	G	Pat Riggin, Wsh.
Rod Langway, Wsh.	D	Paul Coffey, Edm.
Raymond Bourque, Bos.	D	Denis Potvin, NYI
Wayne Gretzky, Edm.	C	Bryan Trottier, NYI
Mike Bossy, NYI	RW	Jari Kurri, Edm.
Michel Goulet, Que.	LW	Mark Messier, Edm.

1982-83

First Team		Second Team
Pete Peeters, Bos.	G	Roland Melanson, NYI
Mark Howe, Phi.	D	Raymond Bourque, Bos.
Rod Langway, Wsh.	D	Paul Coffey, Edm.
Wayne Gretzky, Edm.	C	Denis Savard, Chi.
Mike Bossy, NYI	RW	Lanny McDonald, Cgy.
Mark Messier, Edm.	LW	Michel Goulet, Que.

1981-82

First Team		Second Team
Billy Smith, NYI	G	Grant Fuhr, Edm.
Doug Wilson, Chi.	D	Paul Coffey, Edm.
Raymond Bourque, Bos.	D	Brian Engblom, Mtl.
Wayne Gretzky, Edm.	C	Bryan Trottier, NYI
Mike Bossy, NYI	RW	Rick Middleton, Bos.
Mark Messier, Edm.	LW	John Tonelli, NYI

1980-81

First Team		Second Team
Mike Liut, St.L.	G	Mario Lessard, L.A.
Denis Potvin, NYI	D	Larry Robinson, Mtl.
Randy Carlyle, Pit.	D	Raymond Bourque, Bos.
Wayne Gretzky, Edm.	C	Marcel Dionne, L.A.
Mike Bossy, NYI	RW	Dave Taylor, L.A.
Charlie Simmer, L.A.	LW	Bill Barber, Phi.

1979-80

First Team		Second Team
Tony Esposito, Chi.	G	Don Edwards, Buf.
Larry Robinson, Mtl.	D	Borje Salming, Tor.
Raymond Bourque, Bos.	D	Jim Schoenfeld, Buf.
Marcel Dionne, L.A.	C	Wayne Gretzky, Edm.
Guy Lafleur, Mtl.	RW	Danny Gare, Buf.
Charlie Simmer, L.A.	LW	Steve Shutt, Mtl.

1978-79

First Team		Second Team
Ken Dryden, Mtl.	G	Glenn Resch, NYI
Denis Potvin, NYI	D	Borje Salming, Tor.
Larry Robinson, Mtl.	D	Serge Savard, Mtl.
Bryan Trottier, NYI	C	Marcel Dionne, L.A.
Guy Lafleur, Mtl.	RW	Mike Bossy, NYI
Clark Gillies, NYI	LW	Bill Barber, Phi.

1977-78

First Team		Second Team
Ken Dryden, Mtl.	G	Don Edwards, Buf.
Denis Potvin, NYI	D	Larry Robinson, Mtl.
Brad Park, Bos.	D	Borje Salming, Tor.
Bryan Trottier, NYI	C	Darryl Sittler, Tor.
Guy Lafleur, Mtl.	RW	Mike Bossy, NYI
Clark Gillies, NYI	LW	Steve Shutt, Mtl.

1976-77

First Team		Second Team
Ken Dryden, Mtl.	G	Rogie Vachon, L.A.
Larry Robinson, Mtl.	D	Denis Potvin, NYI
Borje Salming, Tor.	D	Guy Lapointe, Mtl.
Marcel Dionne, L.A.	C	Gilbert Perreault, Buf.
Guy Lafleur, Mtl.	RW	Lanny McDonald, Tor.
Steve Shutt, Mtl.	LW	Rick Martin, Buf.

1975-76

First Team		Second Team
Ken Dryden, Mtl.	G	Glenn Resch, NYI
Denis Potvin, NYI	D	Borje Salming, Tor.
Brad Park, Bos.	D	Guy Lapointe, Mtl.
Bobby Clarke, Phi.	C	Gilbert Perreault, Buf.
Guy Lafleur, Mtl.	RW	Reggie Leach, Phi.
Bill Barber, Phi.	LW	Rick Martin, Buf.

1974-75

First Team		Second Team
Bernie Parent, Phi.	G	Rogie Vachon, L.A.
Bobby Orr, Bos.	D	Guy Lapointe, Mtl.
Denis Potvin, NYI	D	Borje Salming, Tor.
Bobby Clarke, Phi.	C	Phil Esposito, Bos.
Guy Lafleur, Mtl.	RW	René Robert, Buf.
Rick Martin, Buf.	LW	Steve Vickers, NYR

1973-74

First Team		Second Team
Bernie Parent, Phi.	G	Tony Esposito, Chi.
Bobby Orr, Bos.	D	Bill White, Chi.
Brad Park, NYR	D	Barry Ashbee, Phi.
Phil Esposito, Bos.	C	Bobby Clarke, Phi.
Ken Hodge, Bos.	RW	Mickey Redmond, Det.
Rick Martin, Buf.	LW	Wayne Cashman, Bos.

1972-73

First Team		Second Team
Ken Dryden, Mtl.	G	Tony Esposito, Chi.
Bobby Orr, Bos.	D	Brad Park, NYR
Guy Lapointe, Mtl.	D	Bill White, Chi.
Phil Esposito, Bos.	C	Bobby Clarke, Phi.
Mickey Redmond, Det.	RW	Yvan Cournoyer, Mtl.
Frank Mahovlich, Mtl.	LW	Dennis Hull, Chi.

1971-72

First Team		Second Team
Tony Esposito, Chi.	G	Ken Dryden, Mtl.
Bobby Orr, Bos.	D	Bill White, Chi.
Brad Park, NYR	D	Pat Stapleton, Chi.
Phil Esposito, Bos.	C	Jean Ratelle, NYR
Rod Gilbert, NYR	RW	Yvan Cournoyer, Mtl.
Bobby Hull, Chi.	LW	Vic Hadfield, NYR

1970-71

First Team		Second Team
Ed Giacomin, NYR	G	Jacques Plante, Tor.
Bobby Orr, Bos.	D	Brad Park, NYR
J.C. Tremblay, Mtl.	D	Pat Stapleton, Chi.
Phil Esposito, Bos.	C	Dave Keon, Tor.
Ken Hodge, Bos.	RW	Yvan Cournoyer, Mtl.
John Bucyk, Bos.	LW	Bobby Hull, Chi.

1969-70

First Team		Second Team
Tony Esposito, Chi.	G	Ed Giacomin, NYR
Bobby Orr, Bos.	D	Carl Brewer, Det.
Brad Park, NYR	D	Jacques Laperriere, Mtl.
Phil Esposito, Bos.	C	Stan Mikita, Chi.
Gordie Howe, Det.	RW	John McKenzie, Bos.
Bobby Hull, Chi.	LW	Frank Mahovlich, Det.

1968-69

First Team		Second Team
Glenn Hall, St.L.	G	Ed Giacomin, NYR
Bobby Orr, Bos.	D	Ted Green, Bos.
Tim Horton, Tor.	D	Ted Harris, Mtl.
Phil Esposito, Bos.	C	Jean Béliveau, Mtl.
Gordie Howe, Det.	RW	Yvan Cournoyer, Mtl.
Bobby Hull, Chi.	LW	Frank Mahovlich, Det.

1967-68

First Team		Second Team
Gump Worsley, Mtl.	G	Ed Giacomin, NYR
Bobby Orr, Bos.	D	J.C. Tremblay, Mtl.
Tim Horton, Tor.	D	Jim Neilson, NYR
Stan Mikita, Chi.	C	Phil Esposito, Bos.
Gordie Howe, Det.	RW	Rod Gilbert, NYR
Bobby Hull, Chi.	LW	John Bucyk, Bos.

1966-67

First Team		Second Team
Ed Giacomin, NYR	G	Glenn Hall, Chi.
Pierre Pilote, Chi.	D	Tim Horton, Tor.
Harry Howell, NYR	D	Bobby Orr, Bos.
Stan Mikita, Chi.	C	Norm Ullman, Det.
Kenny Wharram, Chi.	RW	Gordie Howe, Det.
Bobby Hull, Chi.	LW	Don Marshall, NYR

1965-66

First Team		Second Team
Glenn Hall, Chi.	G	Gump Worsley, Mtl.
Jacques Laperriere, Mtl.	D	Allan Stanley, Tor.
Pierre Pilote, Chi.	D	Pat Stapleton, Chi.
Stan Mikita, Chi.	C	Jean Béliveau, Mtl.
Gordie Howe, Det.	RW	Bobby Rousseau, Mtl.
Bobby Hull, Chi.	LW	Frank Mahovlich, Tor.

1964-65

First Team		Second Team
Roger Crozier, Det.	G	Charlie Hodge, Mtl.
Pierre Pilote, Chi.	D	Bill Gadsby, Det.
Jacques Laperriere, Mtl.	D	Carl Brewer, Tor.
Norm Ullman, Det.	C	Stan Mikita, Chi.
Claude Provost, Mtl.	RW	Gordie Howe, Det.
Bobby Hull, Chi.	LW	Frank Mahovlich, Tor.

1963-64

First Team		Second Team
Glenn Hall, Chi.	G	Charlie Hodge, Mtl.
Pierre Pilote, Chi.	D	Moose Vasko, Chi.
Tim Horton, Tor.	D	Jacques Laperriere, Mtl.
Stan Mikita, Chi.	C	Jean Béliveau, Mtl.
Kenny Wharram, Chi.	RW	Gordie Howe, Det.
Bobby Hull, Chi.	LW	Frank Mahovlich, Tor.

1962-63

First Team		Second Team
Glenn Hall, Chi.	G	Terry Sawchuk, Det.
Pierre Pilote, Chi.	D	Tim Horton, Tor.
Carl Brewer, Tor.	D	Moose Vasko, Chi.
Stan Mikita, Chi.	C	Henri Richard, Mtl.
Gordie Howe, Det.	RW	Andy Bathgate, NYR
Frank Mahovlich, Tor.	LW	Bobby Hull, Chi.

1961-62

First Team		Second Team
Jacques Plante, Mtl.	G	Glenn Hall, Chi.
Doug Harvey, NYR	D	Carl Brewer, Tor.
Jean-Guy Talbot, Mtl.	D	Pierre Pilote, Chi.
Stan Mikita, Chi.	C	Dave Keon, Tor.
Andy Bathgate, NYR	RW	Gordie Howe, Det.
Bobby Hull, Chi.	LW	Frank Mahovlich, Tor.

1960-61

First Team		Second Team
Johnny Bower, Tor.	G	Glenn Hall, Chi.
Doug Harvey, Mtl.	D	Allan Stanley, Tor.
Marcel Pronovost, Det.	D	Pierre Pilote, Chi.
Jean Béliveau, Mtl.	C	Henri Richard, Mtl.
Bernie Geoffrion, Mtl.	RW	Gordie Howe, Det.
Frank Mahovlich, Tor.	LW	Dickie Moore, Mtl.

1959-60

First Team		Second Team
Glenn Hall, Chi.	G	Jacques Plante, Mtl.
Doug Harvey, Mtl.	D	Allan Stanley, Tor.
Marcel Pronovost, Det.	D	Pierre Pilote, Chi.
Jean Béliveau, Mtl.	C	Bronco Horvath, Bos.
Gordie Howe, Det.	RW	Bernie Geoffrion, Mtl.
Bobby Hull, Chi.	LW	Dean Prentice, NYR

1958-59

First Team		Second Team
Jacques Plante, Mtl.	G	Terry Sawchuk, Det.
Tom Johnson, Mtl.	D	Marcel Pronovost, Det.
Bill Gadsby, NYR	D	Doug Harvey, Mtl.
Jean Béliveau, Mtl.	C	Henri Richard, Mtl.
Andy Bathgate, NYR	RW	Gordie Howe, Det.
Dickie Moore, Mtl.	LW	Alex Delvecchio, Det.

1957-58

First Team		Second Team
Glenn Hall, Chi.	G	Jacques Plante, Mtl.
Doug Harvey, Mtl.	D	Fern Flaman, Bos.
Bill Gadsby, NYR	D	Marcel Pronovost, Det.
Henri Richard, Mtl.	C	Jean Béliveau, Mtl.
Gordie Howe, Det.	RW	Andy Bathgate, NYR
Dickie Moore, Mtl.	LW	Camille Henry, NYR

1956-57

First Team		Second Team
Glenn Hall, Det.	G	Jacques Plante, Mtl.
Doug Harvey, Mtl.	D	Fern Flaman, Bos.
Red Kelly, Det.	D	Bill Gadsby, NYR
Jean Béliveau, Mtl.	C	Ed Litzenberger, Chi.
Gordie Howe, Det.	RW	Maurice Richard, Mtl.
Ted Lindsay, Det.	LW	Real Chevrefils, Bos.

1955-56

First Team		Second Team
Jacques Plante, Mtl.	G	Glenn Hall, Det.
Doug Harvey, Mtl.	D	Red Kelly, Det.
Bill Gadsby, NYR	D	Tom Johnson, Mtl.
Jean Béliveau, Mtl.	C	Tod Sloan, Tor.
Maurice Richard, Mtl.	RW	Gordie Howe, Det.
Ted Lindsay, Det.	LW	Bert Olmstead, Mtl.

1954-55

First Team		Second Team
Harry Lumley, Tor.	G	Terry Sawchuk, Det.
Doug Harvey, Mtl.	D	Bob Goldham, Det.
Red Kelly, Det.	D	Fern Flaman, Bos.
Jean Béliveau, Mtl.	C	Ken Mosdell, Mtl.
Maurice Richard, Mtl.	RW	Bernie Geoffrion, Mtl.
Sid Smith, Tor.	LW	Danny Lewicki, NYR

1953-54

First Team		Second Team
Harry Lumley, Tor.	G	Terry Sawchuk, Det.
Red Kelly, Det.	D	Bill Gadsby, Chi.
Doug Harvey, Mtl.	D	Tim Horton, Tor.
Ken Mosdell, Mtl.	C	Ted Kennedy, Tor.
Gordie Howe, Det.	RW	Maurice Richard, Mtl.
Ted Lindsay, Det.	LW	Ed Sandford, Bos.

1952-53

First Team		Second Team
Terry Sawchuk, Det.	G	Gerry McNeil, Mtl.
Red Kelly, Det.	D	Bill Quackenbush, Bos.
Doug Harvey, Mtl.	D	Bill Gadsby, Chi.
Fleming MacKell, Bos.	C	Alex Delvecchio, Det.
Gordie Howe, Det.	RW	Maurice Richard, Mtl.
Ted Lindsay, Det.	LW	Bert Olmstead, Mtl.

1951-52

First Team		Second Team
Terry Sawchuk, Det.	G	Jim Henry, Bos.
Red Kelly, Det.	D	Hy Buller, NYR
Doug Harvey, Mtl.	D	Jimmy Thomson, Tor.
Elmer Lach, Mtl.	C	Milt Schmidt, Bos.
Gordie Howe, Det.	RW	Maurice Richard, Mtl.
Ted Lindsay, Det.	LW	Sid Smith, Tor.

1950-51

First Team		Second Team
Terry Sawchuk, Det.	G	Chuck Rayner, NYR
Red Kelly, Det.	D	Jimmy Thomson, Tor.
Bill Quackenbush, Bos.	D	Leo Reise Jr., Det.
Milt Schmidt, Bos.	C	Sid Abel, Det.
		Ted Kennedy, Tor. (tied)
Gordie Howe, Det.	RW	Maurice Richard, Mtl.
Ted Lindsay, Det.	LW	Sid Smith, Tor.

1949-50

First Team		Second Team
Bill Durnan, Mtl.	G	Chuck Rayner, NYR
Gus Mortson, Tor.	D	Leo Reise Jr., Det.
Ken Reardon, Mtl.	D	Red Kelly, Det.
Sid Abel, Det.	C	Ted Kennedy, Tor.
Maurice Richard, Mtl.	RW	Gordie Howe, Det.
Ted Lindsay, Det.	LW	Tony Leswick, NYR

1948-49

First Team		Second Team
Bill Durnan, Mtl.	G	Chuck Rayner, NYR
Bill Quackenbush, Det.	D	Glen Harmon, Mtl.
Jack Stewart, Det.	D	Ken Reardon, Mtl.
Sid Abel, Det.	C	Doug Bentley, Chi.
Maurice Richard, Mtl.	RW	Gordie Howe, Det.
Roy Conacher, Chi.	LW	Ted Lindsay, Det.

1947-48

First Team		Second Team
Turk Broda, Tor.	G	Frank Brimsek, Bos.
Bill Quackenbush, Det.	D	Ken Reardon, Mtl.
Jack Stewart, Det.	D	Neil Colville, NYR
Elmer Lach, Mtl.	C	Buddy O'Connor, NYR
Maurice Richard, Mtl.	RW	Bud Poile, Chi.
Ted Lindsay, Det.	LW	Gaye Stewart, Chi.

1946-47

First Team		Second Team
Bill Durnan, Mtl.	G	Frank Brimsek, Bos.
Ken Reardon, Mtl.	D	Jack Stewart, Det.
Butch Bouchard, Mtl.	D	Bill Quackenbush, Det.
Milt Schmidt, Bos.	C	Max Bentley, Chi.
Maurice Richard, Mtl.	RW	Bobby Bauer, Bos.
Doug Bentley, Chi.	LW	Woody Dumart, Bos.

1945-46

First Team		Second Team
Bill Durnan, Mtl.	G	Frank Brimsek, Bos.
Jack Crawford, Bos.	D	Ken Reardon, Mtl.
Butch Bouchard, Mtl.	D	Jack Stewart, Det.
Max Bentley, Chi.	C	Elmer Lach, Mtl.
Maurice Richard, Mtl.	RW	Bill Mosienko, Chi.
Gaye Stewart, Tor.	LW	Toe Blake, Mtl.
Dick Irvin, Mtl.	Coach	Johnny Gottselig, Chi.

1944-45

First Team		Second Team
Bill Durnan, Mtl.	G	Mike Karakas, Chi.
Butch Bouchard, Mtl.	D	Glen Harmon, Mtl.
Flash Hollett, Det.	D	Babe Pratt, Tor.
Elmer Lach, Mtl.	C	Bill Cowley, Bos.
Maurice Richard, Mtl.	RW	Bill Mosienko, Chi.
Toe Blake, Mtl.	LW	Syd Howe, Det.
Dick Irvin, Mtl.	Coach	Jack Adams, Det.

1943-44

First Team		Second Team
Bill Durnan, Mtl.	G	Paul Bibeault, Tor.
Earl Seibert, Chi.	D	Butch Bouchard, Mtl.
Babe Pratt, Tor.	D	Dit Clapper, Bos.
Bill Cowley, Bos.	C	Elmer Lach, Mtl.
Lorne Carr, Tor.	RW	Maurice Richard, Mtl.
Doug Bentley, Chi.	LW	Herb Cain, Bos.
Dick Irvin, Mtl.	Coach	Hap Day, Tor.

1942-43

First Team		Second Team
Johnny Mowers, Det.	G	Frank Brimsek, Bos.
Earl Seibert, Chi.	D	Jack Crawford, Bos.
Jack Stewart, Det.	D	Flash Hollett, Bos.
Bill Cowley, Bos.	C	Syl Apps, Tor.
Lorne Carr, Tor.	RW	Bryan Hextall, NYR
Doug Bentley, Chi.	LW	Lynn Patrick, NYR
Jack Adams, Det.	Coach	Art Ross, Bos.

1941-42

First Team		Second Team
Frank Brimsek, Bos.	G	Turk Broda, Tor.
Earl Seibert, Chi.	D	Pat Egan, Bro.
Tom Anderson, Bro.	D	Bucko McDonald, Tor.
Syl Apps, Tor.	C	Phil Watson, NYR
Bryan Hextall, NYR	RW	Gordie Drillon, Tor.
Lynn Patrick, NYR	LW	Sid Abel, Det.
Frank Boucher, NYR	Coach	Paul Thompson, Chi.

1940-41

First Team		Second Team
Turk Broda, Tor.	G	Frank Brimsek, Bos.
Dit Clapper, Bos.	D	Earl Seibert, Chi.
Wally Stanowski, Tor.	D	Ott Heller, NYR
Bill Cowley, Bos.	C	Syl Apps, Tor.
Bryan Hextall, NYR	RW	Bobby Bauer, Bos.
Sweeney Schriner, Tor.	LW	Woody Dumart, Bos.
Cooney Weiland, Bos.	Coach	Dick Irvin, Mtl.

1939-40

First Team		Second Team
Dave Kerr, NYR	G	Frank Brimsek, Bos.
Dit Clapper, Bos.	D	Art Coulter, NYR
Ebbie Goodfellow, Det.	D	Earl Seibert, Chi.
Milt Schmidt, Bos.	C	Neil Colville, NYR
Bryan Hextall, NYR	RW	Bobby Bauer, Bos.
Toe Blake, Mtl.	LW	Woody Dumart, Bos.
Paul Thompson, Chi.	Coach	Frank Boucher, NYR

1938-39

First Team		Second Team
Frank Brimsek, Bos.	G	Earl Robertson, NYA
Eddie Shore, Bos.	D	Earl Seibert, Chi.
Dit Clapper, Bos.	D	Art Coulter, NYR
Syl Apps, Tor.	C	Neil Colville, NYR
Gordie Drillon, Tor.	RW	Bobby Bauer, Bos.
Toe Blake, Mtl.	LW	Johnny Gottselig, Chi.
Art Ross, Bos.	Coach	Red Dutton, NYA

1937-38

First Team		Second Team
Tiny Thompson, Bos.	G	Dave Kerr, NYR
Eddie Shore, Bos.	D	Art Coulter, NYR
Babe Siebert, Mtl.	D	Earl Seibert, Chi.
Bill Cowley, Bos.	C	Syl Apps, Tor.
Cecil Dillon, NYR	RW	
Gordie Drillon, Tor. *(tied)*		
Paul Thompson, Chi.	LW	Toe Blake, Mtl.
Lester Patrick, NYR	Coach	Art Ross, Bos.

1936-37

First Team		Second Team
Normie Smith, Det.	G	Wilf Cude, Mtl.
Babe Siebert, Mtl.	D	Earl Seibert, Chi.
Ebbie Goodfellow, Det.	D	Lionel Conacher, Mtl. M.
Marty Barry, Det.	C	Art Chapman, NYA
Larry Aurie, Det.	RW	Cecil Dillon, NYR
Busher Jackson, Tor.	LW	Sweeney Schriner, NYA
Jack Adams, Det.	Coach	Cecil Hart, Mtl.

1935-36

First Team		Second Team
Tiny Thompson, Bos.	G	Wilf Cude, Mtl.
Eddie Shore, Bos.	D	Earl Seibert, Chi.
Babe Siebert, Bos.	D	Ebbie Goodfellow, Det.
Hooley Smith, Mtl. M.	C	Bill Thoms, Tor.
Charlie Conacher, Tor.	RW	Cecil Dillon, NYR
Sweeney Schriner, NYA	LW	Paul Thompson, Chi.
Lester Patrick, NYR	Coach	Tommy Gorman, Mtl. M.

1934-35

First Team		Second Team
Lorne Chabot, Chi.	G	Tiny Thompson, Bos.
Eddie Shore, Bos.	D	Cy Wentworth, Mtl. M.
Earl Seibert, NYR	D	Art Coulter, Chi.
Frank Boucher, NYR	C	Cooney Weiland, Det.
Charlie Conacher, Tor.	RW	Dit Clapper, Bos.
Busher Jackson, Tor.	LW	Aurel Joliat, Mtl.
Lester Patrick, NYR	Coach	Dick Irvin, Tor.

1933-34

First Team		Second Team
Charlie Gardiner, Chi.	G	Roy Worters, NYA
King Clancy, Tor.	D	Eddie Shore, Bos.
Lionel Conacher, Chi.	D	Ching Johnson, NYR
Frank Boucher, NYR	C	Joe Primeau, Tor.
Charlie Conacher, Tor.	RW	Bill Cook, NYR
Busher Jackson, Tor.	LW	Aurel Joliat, Mtl.
Lester Patrick, NYR	Coach	Dick Irvin, Tor.

1932-33

First Team		Second Team
John Ross Roach, Det.	G	Charlie Gardiner, Chi.
Eddie Shore, Bos.	D	King Clancy, Tor.
Ching Johnson, NYR	D	Lionel Conacher, Mtl. M.
Frank Boucher, NYR	C	Howie Morenz, Mtl.
Bill Cook, NYR	RW	Charlie Conacher, Tor.
Baldy Northcott, Mtl. M.	LW	Busher Jackson, Tor.
Lester Patrick, NYR	Coach	Dick Irvin, Tor.

1931-32

First Team		Second Team
Charlie Gardiner, Chi.	G	Roy Worters, NYA
Eddie Shore, Bos.	D	Sylvio Mantha, Mtl.
Ching Johnson, NYR	D	King Clancy, Tor.
Howie Morenz, Mtl.	C	Hooley Smith, Mtl. M.
Bill Cook, NYR	RW	Charlie Conacher, Tor.
Busher Jackson, Tor.	LW	Aurel Joliat, Mtl.
Lester Patrick, NYR	Coach	Dick Irvin, Tor.

1930-31

First Team		Second Team
Charlie Gardiner, Chi.	G	Tiny Thompson, Bos.
Eddie Shore, Bos.	D	Sylvio Mantha, Mtl.
King Clancy, Tor.	D	Ching Johnson, NYR
Howie Morenz, Mtl.	C	Frank Boucher, NYR
Bill Cook, NYR	RW	Dit Clapper, Bos.
Aurel Joliat, Mtl.	LW	Bun Cook, NYR
Lester Patrick, NYR	Coach	Dick Irvin, Chi.

NHL ALL-ROOKIE TEAM

Voting for the NHL All-Rookie Team is conducted among the representatives of the Professional Hockey Writers' Association at the end of the season. The rookie all-star team was first selected for the 1982-83 season.

	2006-07
Goal	Mike Smith, Dallas
Defense	Matt Carle, San Jose
Defense	Marc-Edouard Vlasic, San Jose
Forward	Evgeni Malkin, Pittsburgh
Forward	Jordan Staal, Pittsburgh
Forward	Paul Stastny, Colorado

	2005-06
Goal	Henrik Lundqvist, NY Rangers
Defense	Andrej Meszaros, Ottawa
Defense	Dion Phaneuf, Calgary
Forward	Brad Boyes, Boston
Forward	Sidney Crosby, Pittsburgh
Forward	Alex Ovechkin, Washington

	2004-05
Goal	
Defense	
Defense	*Season Cancelled*
Forward	
Forward	
Forward	

	2003-04
Goal	Andrew Raycroft, Boston
Defense	John-Michael Liles, Colorado
Defense	Joni Pitkanen, Philadelphia
Forward	Trent Hunter, NY Islanders
Forward	Ryan Malone, Pittsburgh
Forward	Michael Ryder, Montreal

	2002-03
Goal	Sebastien Caron, Pittsburgh
Defense	Jay Bouwmeester, Florida
Defense	Barret Jackman, St. Louis
Forward	Tyler Arnason, Chicago
Forward	Rick Nash, Columbus
Forward	Henrik Zetterberg, Detroit

2001-02
Dan Blackburn, NY Rangers
Nick Boynton, Boston
Rostislav Klesla, Columbus
Dany Heatley, Atlanta
Ilya Kovalchuk, Atlanta
Kristian Huselius, Florida

2000-01
Evgeni Nabokov, San Jose
Lubomir Visnovsky, Los Angeles
Colin White, New Jersey
Martin Havlat, Ottawa
Brad Richards, Tampa Bay
Shane Willis, Carolina

1999-2000
Brian Boucher, Philadelphia
Brian Rafalski, New Jersey
Brad Stuart, San Jose
Simon Gagne, Philadelphia
Scott Gomez, New Jersey
Michael York, NY Rangers

1998-99
Jamie Storr, Los Angeles
Tom Poti, Edmonton
Sami Salo, Ottawa
Chris Drury, Colorado
Milan Hejduk, Colorado
Marian Hossa, Ottawa

1997-98
Jamie Storr, Los Angeles
Mattias Ohlund, Vancouver
Derek Morris, Calgary
Sergei Samsonov, Boston
Patrick Elias, New Jersey
Mike Johnson, Toronto

1996-97
Patrick Lalime, Pittsburgh
Bryan Berard, NY Islanders
Janne Niinimaa, Philadelphia
Jarome Iginla, Calgary
Jim Campbell, St. Louis
Sergei Berezin, Toronto

1995-96
Corey Hirsch, Vancouver
Ed Jovanovski, Florida
Kyle McLaren, Boston
Daniel Alfredsson, Ottawa
Eric Daze, Chicago
Petr Sykora, New Jersey

1994-95
Jim Carey, Washington
Chris Therien, Philadelphia
Kenny Jonsson, Toronto
Peter Forsberg, Quebec
Jeff Friesen, San Jose
Paul Kariya, Anaheim

1993-94
Martin Brodeur, New Jersey
Chris Pronger, Hartford
Boris Mironov, Wpg./Edm.
Jason Arnott, Edmonton
Mikael Renberg, Philadelphia
Oleg Petrov, Montreal

1992-93
Felix Potvin, Toronto
Vladimir Malakhov, NY Islanders
Scott Niedermayer, New Jersey
Eric Lindros, Philadelphia
Teemu Selanne, Winnipeg
Joe Juneau, Boston

1991-92
Dominik Hasek, Chicago
Nicklas Lidstrom, Detroit
Vladimir Konstantinov, Detroit
Kevin Todd, New Jersey
Tony Amonte, NY Rangers
Gilbert Dionne, Montreal

1990-91
Ed Belfour, Chicago
Eric Weinrich, New Jersey
Rob Blake, Los Angeles
Sergei Fedorov, Detroit
Ken Hodge, Boston
Jaromir Jagr, Pittsburgh

1989-90
Bob Essensa, Winnipeg
Brad Shaw, Hartford
Geoff Smith, Edmonton
Mike Modano, Minnesota
Sergei Makarov, Calgary
Rod Brind'Amour, St. Louis

1988-89
Peter Sidorkiewicz, Hartford
Brian Leetch, NY Rangers
Zarley Zalapski, Pittsburgh
Trevor Linden, Vancouver
Tony Granato, NY Rangers
David Volek, NY Islanders

1987-88
Darren Pang, Chicago
Glen Wesley, Boston
Calle Johansson, Buffalo
Joe Nieuwendyk, Calgary
Ray Sheppard, Buffalo
Iain Duncan, Winnipeg

1986-87
Ron Hextall, Philadelphia
Steve Duchesne, Los Angeles
Brian Benning, St. Louis
Jimmy Carson, Los Angeles
Jim Sandlak, Vancouver
Luc Robitaille, Los Angeles

1985-86
Patrick Roy, Montreal
Gary Suter, Calgary
Dana Murzyn, Hartford
Mike Ridley, NY Rangers
Kjell Dahlin, Montreal
Wendel Clark, Toronto

1984-85
Steve Penney, Montreal
Chris Chelios, Montreal
Bruce Bell, Quebec
Mario Lemieux, Pittsburgh
Tomas Sandstrom, NY Rangers
Warren Young, Pittsburgh

1983-84
Tom Barrasso, Buffalo
Thomas Eriksson, Philadelphia
Jamie Macoun, Calgary
Steve Yzerman, Detroit
Hakan Loob, Calgary
Sylvain Turgeon, Hartford

1982-83
Pelle Lindbergh, Philadelphia
Scott Stevens, Washington
Phil Housley, Buffalo
Dan Daoust, Mtl./Tor.
Steve Larmer, Chicago
Mats Naslund, Montreal

2007 All-Star Game Summary

JANUARY 24, 2007 at Dallas, TX West 12, East 9

PLAYERS ON ICE: **East** — R. Miller, Brodeur, Huet, B. Campbell, Souray, Bouwmeester, Chara, T. Kaberle, Rafalski, Crosby, Ovechkin, Briere, J. Blake, Gagne, Heatley, Marian Hossa, Lecavalier, St. Louis, Shanahan, E. Staal, Justin Williams

West — Luongo, Kiprusoff, Turco,S. Niedermayer, Lidstrom, P. Boucher, Jovanovski, Phaneuf, Timonen, Visnovsky, J. Thornton, Sakic, Cheechoo, Guerin, Havlat, Marleau, McDonald, R. Nash, Y. Perreault, Rolston, Selanne, Smyth

SUMMARY

First Period

1.	East	Briere	(Heatley, Hossa)	3:38
2.	West	Perreault	(Rolston, Guerin)	5:08
3.	West	Selanne	(unassisted)	6:17
4.	East	St. Louis	(Lecavalier, Rafalski)	13:07
5.	East	Stall	(Wiliams, Blake)	13:43
6.	West	Visnovsky	(Sakic, Nash)	18:55

PENALTIES: None

Second Period

7.	West	Marleau	(Cheechoo, Lidstrom)	2:41
8.	East	Williams	(Blake)	5:19
9.	East	Chara	(Briere, Rafalski)	6:29
10.	West	Rolston	(unassisted)	8:30
11.	West	Nash	(Sakic, Phaneuf)	10:40
12.	West	Havlat	(Sakic, Nash)	11:34
13.	West	Perreault	(Guerin, Rolston)	12:47
14.	East	Ovechkin	(Briere, Souray)	13:32
15.	West	Rolston	(Jovanovski)	18:58

PENALTIES: None

Third Period

16.	East	Heatley	(Briere, Hossa)	2:01
17.	West	Nash	(Sakic, Havlat)	7:12
18.	East	Chara	(Hossa, Briere)	10:37
19.	West	Havlat	(Smyth, Jovanovski)	19:00
20.	East	Souray	(Hossa, Heatley)	19:25
21.	West	Phaneuf	(Visnovsky)	19:48

PENALTIES: None

SHOTS ON GOAL BY:

East	12	11	15	**38**
West	12	16	11	**39**

	Goaltenders:	Time	SA	GA	ENG	Dec
East	Miller	20:00	12	3	0	
East	Brodeur	20:00	16	6	0	
East	Huet	19:27	10	2	1	L
West	Luongo	20:00	12	3	0	
West	Kiprusoff	20:00	11	3	0	
West	Turco	20:00	15	3	0	W

PP Conversions: East 0/0; West 0/0.

Referees: Mike Leggo, Greg Kimmerly

Linesmen: Lonnie Cameron, Jay Sharrers
Attendance: 18,532

Dallas Stars backup goaltender Mike Smith was named to the NHL All-Rookie Team for 2006-07. Smith was 12-5-2 with a 2.23 goals-against average and .912 save percentage in 23 games played.

All-Star Game Results

Year	Venue	Score	Coaches	Attendance
2007	Dallas	West 12, East 9	Lindy Ruff, Randy Carlyle	18,532
2004	Minnesota	East 6, West 4	Pat Quinn, Dave Lewis	19,434
2003	Florida	West 6, East 5	Marc Crawford, Jacques Martin	19,250
2002	Los Angeles	World 8, North America 5	Scotty Bowman, Pat Quinn	18,118
2001	Colorado	North America 14, World 12	Joel Quenneville, Jacques Martin	18,646
2000	Toronto	World 9, North America 4	Scotty Bowman, Pat Quinn	19,300
1999	Tampa Bay	North America 8, World 6	Lindy Ruff, Ken Hitchcock	19,758
1998	Vancouver	North America 8, World 7	Jacques Lemaire, Ken Hitchcock	18,422
1997	San Jose	East 11, West 7	Doug MacLean, Ken Hitchcock	17,422
1996	Boston	East 5, West 4	Doug MacLean, Scotty Bowman	17,565
1994	NY Rangers	East 9, West 8	Jacques Demers, Barry Melrose	18,200
1993	Montreal	Wales 16, Campbell 6	Scotty Bowman, Mike Keenan	17,137
1992	Philadelphia	Campbell 10, Wales 6	Bob Gainey, Scotty Bowman	17,380
1991	Chicago	Campbell 11, Wales 5	John Muckler, Mike Milbury	18,472
1990	Pittsburgh	Wales 12, Campbell 7	Pat Burns, Terry Crisp	16,236
1989	Edmonton	Campbell 9, Wales 5	Glen Sather, Terry O'Reilly	17,503
1988	St. Louis	Wales 6, Campbell 5 OT	Mike Keenan, Glen Sather	17,878
1986	Hartford	Wales 4, Campbell 3 OT	Mike Keenan, Glen Sather	15,100
1985	Calgary	Wales 6, Campbell 4	Al Arbour, Glen Sather	16,825
1984	New Jersey	Wales 7, Campbell 6	Al Arbour, Glen Sather	18,939
1983	NY Islanders	Campbell 9, Wales 3	Roger Neilson, Al Arbour	15,230
1982	Washington	Wales 4, Campbell 2	Al Arbour, Glen Sonmor	18,130
1981	Los Angeles	Campbell 4, Wales 1	Pat Quinn, Scotty Bowman	15,761
1980	Detroit	Wales 6, Campbell 3	Scotty Bowman, Al Arbour	21,002
1978	Buffalo	Wales 3, Campbell 2 OT	Scotty Bowman, Fred Shero	16,433
1977	Vancouver	Wales 4, Campbell 3	Scotty Bowman, Fred Shero	15,607
1976	Philadelphia	Wales 7, Campbell 5	Floyd Smith, Fred Shero	16,436
1975	Montreal	Wales 7, Campbell 1	Bep Guidolin, Fred Shero	16,080
1974	Chicago	West 6, East 4	Billy Reay, Scotty Bowman	16,426
1973	NY Rangers	East 5, West 4	Tom Johnson, Billy Reay	16,986
1972	Minnesota	East 3, West 2	Al MacNeil, Billy Reay	15,423
1971	Boston	West 2, East 1	Scotty Bowman, Harry Sinden	14,790
1970	St. Louis	East 4, West 1	Claude Ruel, Scotty Bowman	16,587
1969	Montreal	East 3, West 3	Toe Blake, Scotty Bowman	16,260
1968	Toronto	Toronto 4, All-Stars 3	Punch Imlach, Toe Blake	15,753
1967	Montreal	Montreal 3, All-Stars 0	Toe Blake, Sid Abel	14,284
1965	Montreal	All-Stars 5, Montreal 2	Billy Reay, Toe Blake	13,529
1964	Toronto	All-Stars 3, Toronto 2	Sid Abel, Punch Imlach	14,232
1963	Toronto	All-Stars 3, Toronto 3	Sid Abel, Punch Imlach	14,034
1962	Toronto	Toronto 4, All-Stars 1	Punch Imlach, Rudy Pilous	14,236
1961	Chicago	All-Stars 3, Chicago 1	Sid Abel, Rudy Pilous	14,534
1960	Montreal	All-Stars 2, Montreal 1	Punch Imlach, Toe Blake	13,949
1959	Montreal	Montreal 6, All-Stars 1	Toe Blake, Punch Imlach	13,818
1958	Montreal	Montreal 6, All-Stars 3	Toe Blake, Milt Schmidt	13,989
1957	Montreal	All-Stars 5, Montreal 3	Milt Schmidt, Toe Blake	13,003
1956	Montreal	All-Stars 1, Montreal 1	Jim Skinner, Toe Blake	13,095
1955	Detroit	Detroit 3, All-Stars 1	Jim Skinner, Dick Irvin	10,111
1954	Detroit	All-Stars 2, Detroit 2	King Clancy, Jim Skinner	10,689
1953	Montreal	All-Stars 3, Montreal 1	Lynn Patrick, Dick Irvin	14,153
1952	Detroit	1st Team 1, 2nd Team 1	Tommy Ivan, Dick Irvin	10,680
1951	Toronto	1st Team 2, 2nd Team 2	Joe Primeau, Dick Irvin	11,469
1950	Detroit	Detroit 7, All-Stars 1	Tommy Ivan, Lynn Patrick	9,166
1949	Toronto	All-Stars 3, Toronto 1	Tommy Ivan, Hap Day	13,541
1948	Chicago	All-Stars 3, Toronto 1	Tommy Ivan, Hap Day	12,794
1947	Toronto	All-Stars 4, Toronto 3	Dick Irvin, Hap Day	14,169

There was no All-Star contest during the calendar year of 1966 because the game was moved from the start of season to mid-season. In 1979, the Challenge Cup series between the Soviet Union and Team NHL replaced the All-Star Game. In 1987, Rendez-Vous '87, two games between the Soviet Union and Team NHL replaced the All-Star Game. Rendez-Vous '87 scores: game one, NHL All-Stars 4, Soviet Union 3; game two, Soviet Union 5, NHL All-Stars 3. No All-Star Games were played in 1995, 2005 and 2006.

NHL ALL-STAR GAME MVP

Year	MVP	Year	MVP	Year	MVP
1962	Eddie Shack, Tor.	1977	Rick Martin, Buf.	1993	Mike Gartner, NYR
1963	Frank Mahovlich, Tor.	1978	Billy Smith, NYI	1994	Mike Richter, NYR
1964	Jean Beliveau, Mtl.	1980	Reggie Leach, Phi.	1996	Raymond Bourque, Bos.
1965	Gordie Howe, Det.	1981	Mike Liut, St.L.	1997	Mark Recchi, Mtl.
1967	Henri Richard, Mtl.	1982	Mike Bossy, NYI	1998	Teemu Selanne, Ana.
1968	Bruce Gamble, Tor.	1983	Wayne Gretzky, Edm.	1999	Wayne Gretzky, NYR
1969	Frank Mahovlich, Det.	1984	Don Maloney, NYR	2000	Pavel Bure, Fla.
1970	Bobby Hull, Chi.	1985	Mario Lemieux, Pit.	2001	Bill Guerin, Bos.
1971	Bobby Hull, Chi.	1986	Grant Fuhr, Edm.	2002	Eric Daze, Chi.
1972	Bobby Orr, Bos.	1988	Mario Lemieux, Pit.	2003	Dany Heatley, Atl.
1973	Greg Polis, Pit.	1989	Wayne Gretzky, L.A.	2004	Joe Sakic, Col..
1974	Garry Unger, St.L.	1990	Mario Lemieux, Pit.	2007	Daniel Briere, Buf.
1975	Syl Apps Jr., Pit.	1991	Vincent Damphousse, Tor.		
1976	Pete Mahovlich, Mtl.	1992	Brett Hull, St.L.		

All-Star Game Records 1947 through 2007

TEAM RECORDS

MOST GOALS, BOTH TEAMS, ONE GAME:
26 — North America 14, World 12, 2001 at Colorado
22 — Wales 16, Campbell 6, 1993 at Montreal
21 — West 12, East 9, 2007 at Dallas
19 — Wales 12, Campbell 7, 1990 at Pittsburgh
18 — East 11, West 7, 1997 at San Jose
17 — East 9, West 8, 1994 at NY Rangers
16 — Campbell 11, Wales 5, 1991 at Chicago
— Campbell 10, Wales 6, 1992 at Philadelphia

FEWEST GOALS, BOTH TEAMS, ONE GAME:
2 — First Team All-Stars 1, Second Team All-Stars 1, 1952 at Detroit
— NHL All-Stars 1, Montreal Canadiens 1, 1956 at Montreal
3 — NHL All-Stars 2, Montreal Canadiens 1, 1960 at Montreal
— Montreal Canadiens 3, NHL All-Stars 0, 1967 at Montreal
— West 2, East 1, 1971 at Boston

MOST GOALS, ONE TEAM, ONE GAME:
16 — Wales 16, Campbell 6, 1993 at Montreal
14 — North America 14, World 12, 2001 at Colorado
12 — Wales 12, Campbell 7, 1990 at Pittsburgh
— World 12, North America 14, 2001 at Colorado
— West 12, East 9, 2007 at Dallas

FEWEST GOALS, ONE TEAM, ONE GAME:
0 — NHL All-Stars 0, Montreal Canadiens 3, 1967 at Montreal
1 — 17 times (1981, 1975, 1971, 1970, 1962, 1961, 1960, 1959, both teams 1956, 1955, 1953, both teams 1952, 1950, 1949, 1948)

MOST SHOTS, BOTH TEAMS, ONE GAME (SINCE 1955):
102 — 1994 at NY Rangers — East 9 (56 shots), West 8 (46 shots)
98 — 2001 at Colorado — North America 14 (53 shots), World 12 (45 shots)
90 — 1993 at Montreal — Wales 16 (49 shots), Campbell 6 (41 shots)
89 — 2002 at Los Angeles — World 8 (39 shots), North America 5 (50 shots)

FEWEST SHOTS, BOTH TEAMS, ONE GAME (SINCE 1955):
52 — 1978 at Buffalo — Campbell 2 (12 shots) Wales 3 (40 shots)
53 — 1960 at Montreal — NHL All-Stars 2 (27 shots) Montreal Canadiens 1 (26 shots)
55 — 1956 at Montreal — NHL All-Stars 1 (28 shots) Montreal Canadiens 1 (27 shots)
— 1971 at Boston — West 2 (28 shots) East 1 (27 shots)

MOST SHOTS, ONE TEAM, ONE GAME (SINCE 1955):
56 — 1994 at NY Rangers — East (9-8 vs. West)
53 — 2001 at Colorado — North America (14-12 vs. World)
50 — 2002 at Los Angeles — North America (5-8 vs. World)
49 — 1993 at Montreal — Wales (16-6 vs. Campbell)
— 1999 at Tampa Bay — North America (8-6 vs. World)

FEWEST SHOTS, ONE TEAM, ONE GAME (SINCE 1955):
12 — 1978 at Buffalo — Campbell (2-3 vs. Wales)
17 — 1970 at St. Louis — West (1-4 vs. East)
23 — 1961 at Chicago — Chicago Black Hawks (1-3 vs. NHL All-Stars)
24 — 1976 at Philadelphia — Campbell (5-7 vs. Wales)

MOST POWER-PLAY GOALS, BOTH TEAMS, ONE GAME (SINCE 1950):
3 — 1953 at Montreal — NHL All-Stars 3 (2 power-play goals), Montreal Canadiens 1 (1 power-play goal)
— 1954 at Detroit — NHL All-Stars 2 (1 power-play goal) Detroit Red Wings 2 (2 power-play goals)
— 1958 at Montreal — NHL All-Stars 3 (1 power-play goal) Montreal Canadiens 6 (2 power-play goals)

FEWEST POWER-PLAY GOALS, BOTH TEAMS, ONE GAME (SINCE 1950):
0 — 23 times (1952, 1959, 1960, 1967, 1968, 1969, 1972, 1973, 1976, 1980, 1981, 1984, 1985, 1992, 1994, 1996, 1999, 2000, 2001, 2002, 2003, 2004, 2007)

FASTEST TWO GOALS, BOTH TEAMS, FROM START OF GAME:
0:37 — 1970 at St. Louis — Jacques Laperriere of East scored at 0:20 and Dean Prentice of West scored at 0:37. Final score: East 4, West 1.

2:15 — 1998 at Vancouver — Teemu Selanne scored at 0:53 and Jaromir Jagr scored at 2:15 for World. Final score: North America 8, World 7.

3:37 — 1993 at Montreal — Mike Gartner scored at 3:15 and at 3:37 for Wales. Final score: Wales 16, Campbell 6.

FASTEST TWO GOALS, BOTH TEAMS:
0:08 — 1997 at San Jose — Owen Nolan scored at 18:54 and 19:02 of second period for West. Final Score: East 11, West 7.

0:10 — 1976 at Philadelphia — Dennis Ververgaert scored at 4:33 and at 4:43 of third period for Campbell. Final score: Wales 7, Campbell 5.

0:13 — 1998 at Vancouver — Teemu Selanne scored at 4:00 of first period for World and John LeClair scored at 4:13 for North America. Final score: North America 8, World 7.

FASTEST THREE GOALS, BOTH TEAMS:
0:48 — 2007 at Dallas — Martin Havlat scored at 19:00 of third period for West; Sheldon Souray scored at 19:25 for East; Dion Phaneuf scored at 19:48 for West. Final score: West 12, East 9.

1:08 — 1993 at Montreal — all by Wales — Mike Gartner scored at 3:15 and at 3:37 of first period; Peter Bondra scored at 4:23. Final score: Wales 16, Campbell 6.

1:14 — 1994 at NY Rangers — Bob Kudelski scored at 9:46 of first period for East; Sergei Fedorov scored at 10:20 for West; Eric Lindros scored at 11:00 for East. Final score: East 9, West 8.

FASTEST FOUR GOALS, BOTH TEAMS:
2:24 — 1997 at San Jose — Brendan Shanahan scored at 16:38 of second period for West; Dale Hawerchuk scored at 17:28 for East; Owen Nolan scored at 18:54 and 19:02 for West. Final score: East 11, West 7.

2:52 — 2007 at Dallas — Rick Nash scored at 10:40 of second period for West; Martin Havlat scored at 11:34 for West; Yanic Perreault scored at 12:47 for West; Alex Ovechkin scored at 13:32 for East. Final score: West 12, East 9.

2:57 — 2002 at Los Angeles — Sergei Fedorov scored at 16:59 of third period for World; Markus Naslund scored at 18:17 for World; Alex Zhamnov scored at 19:12 for World; Sami Kapanen scored at 19:56 for World. Final score: World 8, North America 5.

FASTEST TWO GOALS, ONE TEAM, FROM START OF GAME:
2:15 — 1998 at Vancouver — World — Teemu Selanne scored at 0:53 and Jaromir Jagr scored at 2:15. Final score: North America 8, World 7.

3:37 — 1993 at Montreal — Wales — Mike Gartner scored at 3:15 and at 3:37. Final score: Wales 16, Campbell 6.

4:19 — 1980 at Detroit — Wales — Larry Robinson scored at 3:58 and Steve Payne scored at 4:19. Final score: Wales 6, Campbell 3.

FASTEST TWO GOALS, ONE TEAM:
0:08 — 1997 at San Jose — West — Owen Nolan scored at 18:54 and at 19:02 of second period. Final score: East 11, West 7.

0:10 — 1976 at Philadelphia — Campbell — Dennis Ververgaert scored at 4:33 and at 4:43 of third period. Final score: Wales 7, Campbell 5.

0:14 — 1989 at Edmonton — Campbell — Steve Yzerman and Gary Leeman scored at 17:21 and 17:35 of second period. Final score: Campbell 9, Wales 5.

FASTEST THREE GOALS, ONE TEAM:
1:08 — 1993 at Montreal — Wales — Mike Gartner scored at 3:15 and 3:37 of first period; Peter Bondra scored at 4:23. Final score: Wales 16, Campbell 6.

1:32 — 1980 at Detroit — Wales — Ron Stackhouse scored at 11:40 of third period; Craig Hartsburg scored at 12:40; Reed Larson scored at 13:12. Final score: Wales 6, Campbell 3.

1:39 — 2002 at Los Angeles — Markus Naslund scored at 18:17 of third period; Alex Zhamnov scored at 19:12; Sami Kapanen scored at 19:56. Final score: World 8, North America 5.

FASTEST FOUR GOALS, ONE TEAM:
2:57 — 2002 at Los Angeles — World — Sergei Fedorov scored at 16:59 of third period; Markus Naslund scored at 18:17; Alex Zhamnov scored at 19:12; Sami Kapanen scored at 19:56. Final score: World 8, North America 5.

4:17 — 2007 at Dallas — Brian Rolston scored at 8:30 of second period; Rick Nash scored at 10:40; Martin Havlat scored at 11:34; Yanic Perreault scored at 12:47. Final score: West 12, East 9.

4:19 — 1992 at Philadelphia — Campbell — Brian Bellows scored at 7:40 of second period; Jeremy Roenick scored at 8:13; Theoren Fleury scored at 11:06, Brett Hull scored at 11:59. Final score: Campbell 10, Wales 6.

MOST GOALS, BOTH TEAMS, ONE PERIOD:
10 — 1997 at San Jose — Second period — East (6), West (4). Final score: East 11, West 7.

— 2001 at Colorado — Second period — North America (6), World (4). Final score: North America 14, World 12.

— 2001 at Colorado — Third period — North America (5), World (5). Final score: North America 14, World 12.

9 — 1990 at Pittsburgh — First period — Wales (7), Campbell (2). Final score: Wales 12, Campbell 7.

— 2007 at Dallas — Second period — West (6), East (3). Final score: West 12, East 9.

MOST GOALS, ONE TEAM, ONE PERIOD:
7 — 1990 at Pittsburgh — First period — Wales. Final score: Wales 12, Campbell 7.

6 — 1983 at NY Islanders — Third period — Campbell. Final score: Campbell 9, Wales 3.

— 1992 at Philadelphia — Second period — Campbell. Final score: Campbell 10, Wales 6.

— 1993 at Montreal — First period — Wales. Final score: Wales 16, Campbell 6.

— 1993 at Montreal — Second period — Wales. Final score: Wales 16, Campbell 6.

— 1997 at San Jose — Second period — East. Final score: East 11, West 7.

— 2001 at Colorado — Second period — North America. Final score: North America 14, World 12.

— 2007 at Dallas — Second period — West. Final score: West 12, East 9.

MOST SHOTS, BOTH TEAMS, ONE PERIOD:
39 — 1994 at NY Rangers — Second period — West (21), East (18). Final score: East 9, West 8.

— 2001 at Colorado — Third period — World (23), North America (16). Final score: North America 14, World 12.

36 — 1990 at Pittsburgh — Third period — Campbell (22), Wales (14). Final score: Wales 12, Campbell 7.

— 1994 at NY Rangers — First period — East (19), West (17). Final score: East 9, West 8.

— 2002 at Los Angeles — Third period — North America (20), World (16). Final score: World 8, North America 5.

MOST SHOTS, ONE TEAM, ONE PERIOD:
23 — 2001 at Colorado — Third period — World. Final score: North America 14, World 12.

22 — 1990 at Pittsburgh — Third period — Campbell. Final score: Wales 12, Campbell 7.

— 1991 at Chicago — Third period — Wales. Final score: Campbell 11, Wales 5.

— 1993 at Montreal — First period — Wales. Final score: Wales 16, Campbell 6.

FEWEST SHOTS, BOTH TEAMS, ONE PERIOD:
9 — 1971 at Boston — Third period — East (2), West (7). Final score: West 2, East 1.

— 1980 at Detroit — Second period — Campbell (4), Wales (5). Final score: Wales 6, Campbell 3.

13 — 1982 at Washington — Third period — Campbell (6), Wales (7). Final score: Wales 4, Campbell 2.

14 — 1978 at Buffalo — First period — Campbell (7), Wales (7). Final score: Wales 3, Campbell 2.

— 1986 at Hartford — First period — Campbell (6), Wales (8). Final score: Wales 4, Campbell 3.

FEWEST SHOTS, ONE TEAM, ONE PERIOD:
2 — 1971 at Boston — Third period — East. Final score: West 2, East 1.

— 1978 at Buffalo — Second period — Campbell. Final score: Wales 3, Campbell 2.

3 — 1978 at Buffalo — Third period — Campbell. Final score: Wales 3, Campbell 2.

4 — 1955 at Detroit — First period — NHL All-Stars. Final score: Detroit Red Wings 3, NHL All-Stars 1.

— 1980 at Detroit — Second period — Campbell. Final score: Wales 6, Campbell 3.

Playing in his 12th All-Star Game in 2007, Joe Sakic picked up four assists to become the all-time All-Star leader in that category with 16. His six All-Star Game goals give him 22 points, ranking him third in all-time All-Star scoring.

INDIVIDUAL RECORDS

Games

MOST GAMES PLAYED:
23 — Gordie Howe from 1948 through 1980
19 — Raymond Bourque from 1981 through 2001
18 — Wayne Gretzky from 1980 through 1999
15 — Frank Mahovlich from 1959 through 1974
— Mark Messier from 1982 through 2004

Goals

MOST GOALS (CAREER):
13 — Wayne Gretzky in 18GP
— Mario Lemieux in 10GP
10 — Gordie Howe in 23GP
9 — Teemu Selanne in 10GP
8 — Frank Mahovlich in 15GP
— Luc Robitaille in 8GP

MOST GOALS, ONE GAME:
4 — Wayne Gretzky, Campbell, 1983
— Mario Lemieux, Wales, 1990
— Vince Damphousse, Campbell, 1991
— Mike Gartner, Wales, 1993
— Dany Heatley, East, 2003
3 — Ted Lindsay, Detroit, 1950
— Mario Lemieux, Wales, 1988
— Pierre Turgeon, Wales, 1993
— Mark Recchi, East, 1997
— Owen Nolan, West, 1997
— Teemu Selanne, World, 1998
— Pavel Bure, World, 2000
— Bill Guerin, North America, 2001
— Joe Sakic, West, 2004

MOST GOALS, ONE PERIOD:
4 — Wayne Gretzky, Campbell, Third period, 1983
3 — Mario Lemieux, Wales, First period, 1990
— Vincent Damphousse, Campbell, Third period, 1991
— Mike Gartner, Wales, First period, 1993

Assists

MOST ASSISTS (CAREER):
16 — Joe Sakic in 12GP
14 — Mark Messier in 15GP
13 — Raymond Bourque in 19GP
12 — Adam Oates in 5GP
— Mats Sundin in 8GP
— Wayne Gretzky in 18GP

MOST ASSISTS, ONE GAME:
5 — Mats Naslund, Wales, 1988
4 — Raymond Bourque, Wales, 1985
— Adam Oates, Campbell, 1991
— Adam Oates, Wales, 1993
— Mark Recchi, Wales, 1993
— Pierre Turgeon, East, 1994
— Fredrik Modin, World, 2001
— Joe Sakic, West, 2007
— Daniel Briere, East, 2007
— Marian Hossa, East, 2007

MOST ASSISTS, ONE PERIOD:
4 — Adam Oates, Wales, First period, 1993
3 — Mark Messier, Campbell, Third period, 1983
3 — Marian Hossa, East, Third period, 2007

Points

MOST POINTS, CAREER:
25 — Wayne Gretzky (13G-12A in 18GP)
23 — Mario Lemieux (13G-10A in 10GP)
22 — Joe Sakic (6G-16A in 12GP)
20 — Mark Messier (6G-14A in 15GP)
19 — Gordie Howe (10G-9A in 23GP)

MOST POINTS, ONE GAME:
6 — Mario Lemieux, Wales, 1988 (3G-3A)
5 — Mats Naslund, Wales, 1988 (5A)
— Adam Oates, Campbell, 1991 (1G-4A)
— Mike Gartner, Wales, 1993 (4G-1A)
— Mark Recchi, Wales, 1993 (1G-4A)
— Pierre Turgeon, Wales, 1993 (3G-2A)
— Bill Guerin, North America, 2001 (3G-2A)
— Dany Heatley, East, 2003 (4G-1A)
— Daniel Briere, East, 2007 (1G-4A)

MOST POINTS, ONE PERIOD:
4 — Wayne Gretzky, Campbell, Third period, 1983 (4G)
— Mike Gartner, Wales, First period, 1993 (3G-1A)
— Adam Oates, Wales, First period, 1993 (4A)
3 — Gordie Howe, NHL All-Stars, Second period, 1965 (1G-2A)
— Pete Mahovlich, Wales, First period, 1976 (1G-2A)
— Mark Messier, Campbell, Third period, 1983 (3A)
— Mario Lemieux, Wales, Second period, 1988 (1G-2A)
— Mario Lemieux, Wales, First period, 1990 (3G)
— Vince Damphousse, Campbell, Third period, 1991 (3G)
— Mark Recchi, Wales, Second period, 1993 (1G-2A)
— Tony Amonte, North America, Second period, 2001 (2G-1A)
— Daniel Alfredsson, East, Second period, 2004 (2G-1A)
— Marian Hossa, East, Third period, 2007 (3A)

Power-Play Goals

MOST POWER-PLAY GOALS, CAREER:
6 — Gordie Howe in 23GP
3 — Bobby Hull in 12GP
— Maurice Richard in 13GP

Fastest Goals

FASTEST GOAL FROM START OF GAME:
0:19 — Ted Lindsay, Detroit, 1950
0:20 — Jacques Laperriere, East, 1970
0:21 — Mario Lemieux, Wales, 1990
0:35 — Vincent Damphousse, North America, 2002
0:36 — Chico Maki, West, 1971

FASTEST GOAL FROM START OF A PERIOD:
0:17 — Raymond Bourque, North America, 1999 (second period)
0:19 — Ted Lindsay, Detroit, 1950 (first period)
— Rick Tocchet, Wales, 1993 (second period)
0:20 — Jacques Laperriere, East, 1970 (first period)
0:21 — Mario Lemieux, Wales, 1990 (first period)
0:26 — Wayne Gretzky, Campbell, 1982 (second period)

FASTEST TWO GOALS (ONE PLAYER) FROM START OF GAME:
3:37 — Mike Gartner, Wales, 1993, at 3:15 and 3:37.
4:00 — Teemu Selanne, World, 1998, at 0:53 and 4:00
5:25 — Wally Hergesheimer, NHL All-Stars, 1953, at 4:06 and 5:25.

FASTEST TWO GOALS (ONE PLAYER) FROM START OF A PERIOD:
3:37 — Mike Gartner, Wales, 1993, at 3:15 and 3:37 of first period.
4:00 — Teemu Selanne, World, 1998, at 0:53 and 4:00 of first period.
4:43 — Dennis Ververgaert, Campbell, 1976, at 4:33 and 4:43 of third period.

FASTEST TWO GOALS (ONE PLAYER):
0:08 — Owen Nolan, West, 1997. Scored at 18:54 and 19:02 of second period.
0:10 — Dennis Ververgaert, Campbell, 1976. Scored at 4:33 and 4:43 of third period.
0:22 — Mike Gartner, Wales, 1993. Scored at 3:15 and 3:37 of first period.

Penalties

MOST PENALTY MINUTES:
25 — Gordie Howe in 23GP
21 — Gus Mortson in 9GP
16 — Harry Howell in 7GP

Goaltenders

MOST GAMES PLAYED:
13 — Glenn Hall from 1955 through 1969
11 — Terry Sawchuk from 1950 through 1968
— Patrick Roy from 1988 through 2003
9 — Martin Brodeur from 1996 through 2007
8 — Jacques Plante from 1956 through 1970

MOST MINUTES PLAYED:
540 — Glenn Hall in 13GP
467 — Terry Sawchuk in 11GP
370 — Jacques Plante in 8GP
250 — Patrick Roy in 11GP
209 — Turk Broda in 4GP

MOST GOALS AGAINST:
31 — Patrick Roy in 11GP
22 — Glenn Hall in 13GP
21 — Mike Vernon in 5GP
19 — Terry Sawchuk in 11GP
18 — Jacques Plante in 8GP
— Andy Moog in 4GP

BEST GOALS-AGAINST-AVERAGE AMONG THOSE WITH AT LEAST TWO GAMES PLAYED:
0.68 — Gilles Villemure in 3GP
1.49 — Gerry McNeil in 3GP
1.50 — Johnny Bower in 4GP
1.51 — Frank Brimsek in 3GP
1.64 — Gump Worsley in 4GP

No defenseman in NHL history has ever played more games than Scott Stevens, who played 1,635 in the regular season and 233 in the playoffs. Stevens captained the New Jersey Devils to three Stanley Cup titles between 1995 and 2003.

Hockey Hall of Fame

(Year of induction is listed after each Honoured Members name)

Location: Brookfield Place, at the corner of Front and Yonge Streets in the heart of downtown Toronto. Easy access from all major highways running into Toronto. Close to TTC subway and Union Station.

Telephone: administration (416) 360-7735; information (416) 360-7765.

Public Hours of Operation: Open every day except Christmas Day, New Year's Day and Induction Day (November 12, 2007). Please call our information number (above) or visit our website (below) for times.

The Hockey Hall of Fame can be booked for private functions after hours.

Website address: www.hhof.com

History: The Hockey Hall of Fame was established in 1943. Members were first honoured in 1945. On August 26, 1961, the Hockey Hall of Fame opened its doors to the public in a building located on the grounds of the Canadian National Exhibition in Toronto. The Hockey Hall of Fame relocated to its new site at BCE Place and welcomed the hockey world on June 18, 1993.

Honour Roll: There are 348 Honoured Members in the Hockey Hall of Fame. 238 have been inducted as players, 96 as builders and 14 as Referees/Linesmen. In addition, there are 78 media honourees.

Founding/Premiere Sponsors: Imperial Oil, International Ice Hockey Federation, MCI Canada, Molson Canada, National Hockey League, National Hockey League Players' Association, Panasonic Canada, Pepsi-Cola Canada, The Toronto Sun, The Sports Network (TSN/RDS).

PLAYERS

* Abel, Sidney Gerald 1969
* Adams, John James "Jack" 1959
* Apps, Charles Joseph Sylvanus "Syl" 1961
Armstrong, George Edward 1975
* Bailey, Irvine Wallace "Ace" 1975
* Bain, Donald H. "Dan" 1949
* Baker, Hobart "Hobey" 1945
Barber, William Charles "Bill" 1990
* Barry, Martin J. "Marty" 1965
Bathgate, Andrew James "Andy" 1978
* Bauer, Robert Theodore "Bobby" 1996
Béliveau, Jean Arthur 1972
* Benedict, Clinton S. 1965
* Bentley, Douglas Wagner 1964
* Bentley, Maxwell H. L. 1966
* Blake, Hector "Toe" 1966
Boivin, Leo Joseph 1986
* Boon, Richard R. "Dickie" 1952
Bossy, Michael 1991
Bouchard, Emile Joseph "Butch" 1966
* Boucher, Frank 1958
* Boucher, Georges "Buck" 1960
Bourque, Raymond 2004
Bower, John William 1976
* Bowie, Russell 1947
* Brimsek, Francis Charles 1966
* Broadbent, Harry L. "Punch" 1962
* Broda, Walter Edward "Turk" 1967
Bucyk, John Paul 1981
* Burch, Billy 1974
* Cameron, Harold Hugh "Harry" 1962
Cheevers, Gerald Michael "Gerry" 1985
* Clancy, Francis Michael "King" 1958
* Clapper, Aubrey "Dit" 1947
Clarke, Robert "Bobby" 1987
* Cleghorn, Sprague 1958
Coffey, Paul 2004
* Colville, Neil MacNeil 1967
* Conacher, Charles W. 1961
* Conacher, Lionel Pretoria 1994
* Conacher, Roy Gordon 1998
* Connell, Alex 1958
* Cook, Fred "Bun" 1995
* Cook, William Osser 1952
* Coulter, Arthur Edmund 1974
Cournoyer, Yvan Serge 1982
* Cowley, William Mailes 1968
* Crawford, Samuel Russell "Rusty" 1962
* Darragh, John Proctor "Jack" 1962
* Davidson, Allan M. "Scotty" 1950
* Day, Clarence Henry "Hap" 1961
Delvecchio, Alex 1977
* Denneny, Cyril "Cy" 1959
Dionne, Marcel 1992
* Drillon, Gordon Arthur 1975
* Drinkwater, Charles Graham 1950
Dryden, Kenneth Wayne 1983
Duff, Dick 2006
* Dumart, Woodrow "Woody" 1992
* Dunderdale, Thomas 1974
* Durnan, William Ronald 1964
* Dutton, Mervyn A. "Red" 1958
* Dye, Cecil Henry "Babe" 1970
Esposito, Anthony James "Tony" 1988
Esposito, Philip Anthony 1984
* Farrell, Arthur F. 1965
Federko, Bernie 2002
Fetisov, Viacheslav 2001
Flaman, Ferdinand Charles "Fern" 1990
* Foyston, Frank 1958
Francis, Ron 2007
* Fredrickson, Frank 1958
Fuhr, Grant 2003
Gadsby, William Alexander 1970
Gainey, Bob 1992
* Gardiner, Charles Robert "Chuck" 1945
* Gardiner, Herbert Martin "Herb" 1958
* Gardner, James Henry "Jimmy" 1962
Gartner, Michael Alfred 2001
* Geoffrion, Jos. A. Bernard "Boom Boom" 1972
* Gerard, Eddie 1945
Giacomin, Edward "Eddie" 1987
Gilbert, Rodrigue Gabriel "Rod" 1982
Gillies, Clark 2002
* Gilmour, Hamilton Livingstone "Billy" 1962
* Goheen, Frank Xavier "Moose" 1952
* Goodfellow, Ebenezer R. "Ebbie" 1963
Goulet, Michel 1998
* Grant, Michael "Mike" 1950
* Green, Wilfred "Shorty" 1962
Gretzky, Wayne Douglas 1999
* Griffis, Silas Seth "Si" 1950
* Hainsworth, George 1961
Hall, Glenn Henry 1975
* Hall, Joseph Henry 1961
* Harvey, Douglas Norman 1973
Hawerchuk, Dale Martin 2001
* Hay, George 1958
* Hern, William Milton "Riley" 1962
* Hextall, Bryan Aldwyn 1969
* Holmes, Harry "Hap" 1972
* Hooper, Charles Thomas "Tom" 1962
* Horner, George Reginald "Red" 1965
* Horton, Miles Gilbert "Tim" 1977
Howe, Gordon 1972
* Howe, Sydney Harris 1965
Howell, Henry Vernon "Harry" 1979
Hull, Robert Marvin 1983
* Hutton, John Bower "Bouse" 1962
* Hyland, Harry M. 1962
* Irvin, James Dickenson "Dick" 1958
* Jackson, Harvey "Busher" 1971
* Johnson, Ernest "Moose" 1952
* Johnson, Ivan "Ching" 1958
Johnson, Thomas Christian 1970
* Joliat, Aurel 1947
* Keats, Gordon "Duke" 1958
Kelly, Leonard Patrick "Red" 1969
Kennedy, Theodore Samuel "Teeder" 1966
Keon, David Michael 1986
* Kharlamov, Valeri 2005
Kurri, Jari 2001
Lach, Elmer James 1966
Lafleur, Guy Damien 1988
LaFontaine, Pat 2003
* Lalonde, Edouard Charles "Newsy" 1950
Langway, Rod Corry 2002
Laperriere, Jacques 1987
Lapointe, Guy 1993
Laprade, Edgar 1993
* Laviolette, Jean Baptiste "Jack" 1962
* Lehman, Hugh 1958
Lemaire, Jacques Gerard 1984
Lemieux, Mario 1997
* LeSueur, Percy 1961
* Lewis, Herbert A. 1989
Lindsay, Robert Blake Theodore "Ted" 1966
* Lumley, Harry 1980
MacInnis, Al 2007
* MacKay, Duncan "Mickey" 1952
Mahovlich, Frank William 1981
* Malone, Joseph "Joe" 1950
* Mantha, Sylvio 1960
* Marshall, John "Jack" 1965
* Maxwell, Fred G. "Steamer" 1962
McDonald, Lanny 1992
* McGee, Frank 1945
* McGimsie, William George "Billy" 1962
* McNamara, George 1958
Messier, Mark 2007
Mikita, Stanley 1983
Moore, Richard Winston "Dickie" 1974
* Moran, Patrick Joseph "Paddy" 1958
* Morenz, Howie 1945
* Mosienko, William "Billy" 1965
Mullen, Joseph P. 2000
Murphy, Larry 2004
Neely, Cam 2005
* Nighbor, Frank 1947
* Noble, Edward Reginald "Reg" 1962
* O'Connor, Herbert William "Buddy" 1988
* Oliver, Harry 1967
Olmstead, Murray Bert "Bert" 1985
Orr, Robert Gordon 1979
Parent, Bernard Marcel 1984

Park, Douglas Bradford "Brad" 1988
* Patrick, Joseph Lynn 1980
* Patrick, Lester 1947
Perreault, Gilbert 1990
* Phillips, Tommy 1945
Pilote, Joseph Albert Pierre Paul 1975
* Pitre, Didier "Pit" 1962
* Plante, Joseph Jacques Omer 1978
Potvin, Denis 1991
* Pratt, Walter "Babe" 1966
* Primeau, A. Joseph 1963
Pronovost, Joseph René Marcel 1978
Pulford, Bob 1991
* Pulford, Harvey 1945
* Quackenbush, Hubert George "Bill" 1976
* Rankin, Frank 1961
Ratelle, Joseph Gilbert Yvan Jean "Jean" 1985
* Rayner, Claude Earl "Chuck" 1973
Reardon, Kenneth Joseph 1966
Richard, Joseph Henri 1979
* Richard, Joseph Henri Maurice "Rocket" 1961
* Richardson, George Taylor 1950
* Roberts, Gordon 1971
Robinson, Larry 1995
* Ross, Arthur Howey 1949
Roy, Patrick 2006
* Russel, Blair 1965
* Russell, Ernest 1965
* Ruttan, J.D. "Jack" 1962
Salming, Borje Anders 1996
Savard, Denis Joseph 2000
Savard, Serge 1986
* Sawchuk, Terrance Gordon "Terry" 1971
* Scanlan, Fred 1965
Schmidt, Milton Conrad "Milt" 1961
* Schriner, David "Sweeney" 1962
* Seibert, Earl Walter 1963
* Seibert, Oliver Levi 1961
* Shore, Edward W. "Eddie" 1947
Shutt, Stephen 1993
* Siebert, Albert C. "Babe" 1964
* Simpson, Harold Edward "Bullet Joe" 1962
Sittler, Darryl Glen 1989
* Smith, Alfred E. 1962
Smith, Clint 1991
* Smith, Reginald "Hooley" 1972
* Smith, Thomas James 1973
Smith, William John "Billy" 1993
Stanley, Allan Herbert 1981
* Stanley, Russell "Barney" 1962
Stastny, Peter 1998
Stevens, Scott 2007
* Stewart, John Sherratt "Black Jack" 1964
* Stewart, Nelson "Nels" 1952
* Stuart, Bruce 1961
* Stuart, Hod 1945
* Taylor, Frederick "Cyclone" (O.B.E.) 1947
* Thompson, Cecil R. "Tiny" 1959
Tretiak, Vladislav 1989
* Trihey, Col. Harry J. 1950
Trottier, Bryan 1997
Ullman, Norman V. Alexander "Norm" 1982
* Vezina, Georges 1945
* Walker, John Phillip "Jack" 1960
* Walsh, Martin "Marty" 1962
* Watson, Harry E. 1962
* Watson, Harry 1994
* Weiland, Ralph "Cooney" 1971
* Westwick, Harry 1962
* Whitcroft, Fred 1962
* Wilson, Gordon Allan "Phat" 1962
* Worsley, Lorne John "Gump" 1980
* Worters, Roy 1969

BUILDERS

* Adams, Charles 1960
* Adams, Weston W. 1972
* Ahearn, Thomas Franklin "Frank" 1962
* Ahearne, John Francis "Bunny" 1977
* Allan, Sir Montagu (C.V.O.) 1945
Allen, Keith 1992
Arbour, Alger Joseph "Al" 1996
* Ballard, Harold Edwin 1977
* Bauer, Father David 1989
* Bickell, John Paris 1978
Bowman, Scotty 1991
* Brooks, Herb 2006
* Brown, George V. 1961
* Brown, Walter A. 1962
* Buckland, Frank 1975
Bush, Walter 2000
Butterfield, Jack Arlington 1980
* Calder, Frank 1947
* Campbell, Angus D. 1964
* Campbell, Clarence Sutherland 1966
* Cattarinich, Joseph 1977
Costello, Murray 2005
* Dandurand, Joseph Viateur "Leo" 1963
* Dilio, Francis Paul 1964
* Dudley, George S. 1958
* Dunn, James A. 1968
Fletcher, Cliff 2004
Francis, Emile 1982
* Gibson, Dr. John L. "Jack" 1976
* Gorman, Thomas Patrick "Tommy" 1963
Gregory, Jim 2007
* Griffiths, Frank A. 1993
* Hanley, William 1986
* Hay, Charles 1974
* Hendy, James C. 1968
* Hewitt, Foster 1965
* Hewitt, William Abraham 1947
Hotchkiss, Harley 2006
* Hume, Fred J. 1962
Illitch, Mike 2003
* Imlach, George "Punch" 1984
* Ivan, Thomas N. 1974
* Jennings, William M. 1975
* Johnson, Bob 1992
* Juckes, Gordon W. 1979
* Kilpatrick, Gen. John Reed 1960
Kilrea, Brian Blair 2003
* Knox, Seymour H. III 1993
* Leader, George Alfred 1969
* LeBel, Robert 1970
* Lockhart, Thomas F. 1965
* Loicq, Paul 1961
* Mariucci, John 1985
* Mathers, Frank 1992
* McLaughlin, Major Frederic 1963
* Milford, John "Jake" 1984
* Molson, Hon. Hartland de Montarville 1973
Morrison, Ian "Scotty" 1999
* Murray, Monsignor Athol 1998
* Neilson, Roger 2002
* Nelson, Francis 1947
* Norris, Bruce A. 1969
* Norris, Sr., James 1958
* Norris, James Dougan 1962
* Northey, William M. 1947
* O'Brien, John Ambrose 1962
O'Neill, Brian 1994
* Page, Fred 1993
Patrick, Craig 2001
* Patrick, Frank 1950
* Pickard, Allan W. 1958
* Pilous, Rudy 1985
* Poile, Norman "Bud" 1990
Pollock, Samuel Patterson Smyth 1978
* Raymond, Sen. Donat 1958
* Robertson, John Ross 1947
* Robinson, Claude C. 1947
* Ross, Philip D. 1976
* Sabetzki, Dr. Gunther 1995
Sather, Glen 1997
* Selke, Frank J. 1960
Sinden, Harry James 1983
* Smith, Frank D. 1962
* Smythe, Conn 1958
Snider, Edward M. 1988
* Stanley of Preston, Lord (G.C.B.) 1945
* Sutherland, Cap. James T. 1947
* Tarasov, Anatoli V. 1974
Torrey, Bill 1995
* Turner, Lloyd 1958
* Tutt, William Thayer 1978
* Voss, Carl Potter 1974
* Waghorne, Fred 1961
* Wirtz, Arthur Michael 1971
Wirtz, William W. "Bill" 1976
Ziegler, John A. Jr. 1987

REFEREES/LINESMEN

Armstrong, Neil 1991
Ashley, John George 1981
Chadwick, William L. 1964
* D'Amico, John 1993
* Elliott, Chaucer 1961
* Hayes, George William 1988
* Hewitson, Robert W. 1963
* Ion, Fred J. "Mickey" 1961
Pavelich, Matt 1987
* Rodden, Michael J. "Mike" 1962
* Smeaton, J. Cooper 1961
* Storey, Roy Alvin "Red" 1967
Udvari, Frank Joseph 1973
Van Hellemond, Andy 1999

8th Annual Hockey Hall of Fame Game
Saturday, November 10, 2007
New York Rangers vs. Toronto Maple Leafs
at Air Canada Centre in Toronto.

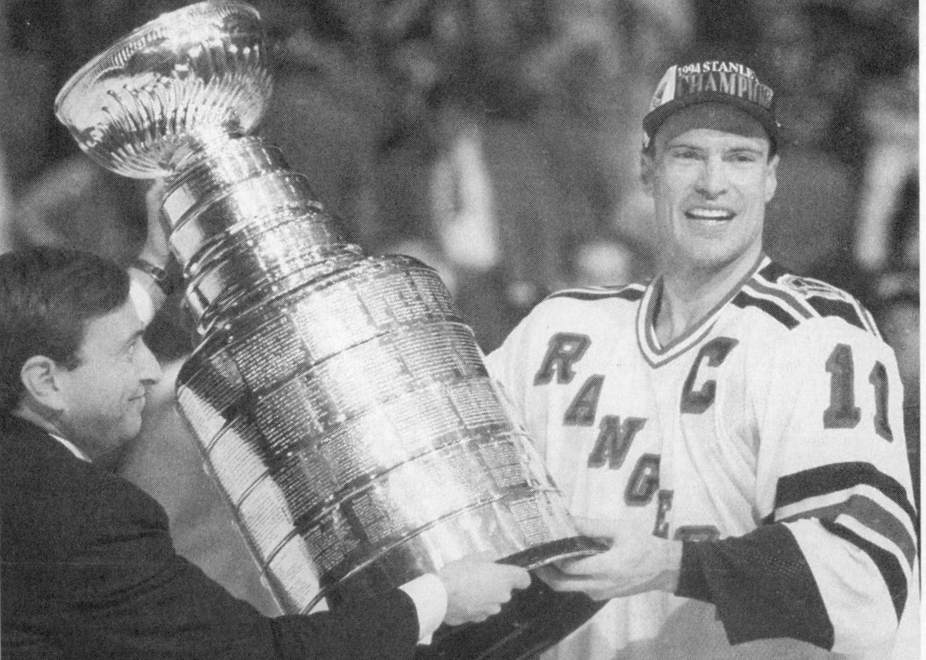

After winning the Stanley Cup five times in Edmonton, Mark Messier led the Rangers to the promised land in 1994, ending a 54-year Stanley Cup drought. With 694 goals and 1,193 assists, Messier's 1,887 rank as the second-highest total in the history of the NHL.

Elmer Ferguson Memorial Award Winners

In recognition of distinguished members of the newspaper profession whose words have brought honor to journalism and to hockey. Selected by the Professional Hockey Writers' Association.

* Barton, Charlie, Buffalo-Courier Express 1985
* Beauchamp, Jacques, Montreal Matin/Journal de Montréal 1984
* Brennan, Bill, Detroit News 1987
* Burchard, Jim, New York World Telegram 1984
* Burnett, Red, Toronto Star 1984
* Carroll, Dink, Montreal Gazette 1984
* Coleman, Jim, Southam Newspapers 1984

Conway, Russ, Eagle-Tribune 1999
* Damata, Ted, Chicago Tribune 1984

Delano, Hugh, New York Post 1991
Desjardins, Marcel, Montréal La Presse 1984
Duhatschek, Eric, Calgary Herald/Globe and Mail 2001
* Dulmage, Jack, Windsor Star 1984

Dunnell, Milt, Toronto Star 1984
Dupont, Kevin Paul, Boston Globe 2002
Elliott, Helene, Los Angeles Times 2005
Farber, Michael, Montreal Gazette/Sports Illustrated 2003
Fay, Dave, Washington Times 2007
* Ferguson, Elmer, Montreal Herald/Star 1984
* Fitzgerald, Tom, Boston Globe 1984

Frayne, Trent, Toronto Telegram/Globe and Mail/Sun 1984
Gatecliff, Jack, St. Catharines Standard 1995
Gross, George, Toronto Telegram/Sun 1985
Johnston, Dick, Buffalo News 1986
Kelley, Jim, Buffalo News 2004
* Laney, Al, New York Herald-Tribune 1984
* Larochelle, Claude, Le Soleil 1989

L'Esperance, Zotique, Journal de Montréal/ le Petit Journal 1985
* MacLeod, Rex, Toronto Globe and Mail/Star 1987

Matheson, Jim, Edmonton Journal 2000
* Mayer, Charles, Journal de Montréal/la Patrie 1985
* McKenzie, Ken, The Hockey News 1997

Monahan, Leo, Boston Daily Record/Record-American/Herald American 1986
Moriarty, Tim, UPI/Newsday 1986
Morrison, Scott, Toronto Sun/Rogers Sportsnet 2006
* Nichols, Joe, New York Times 1984
* O'Brien, Andy, Weekend Magazine 1985

Orr, Frank, Toronto Star 1989
Olan, Ben, New York Associated Press 1987
* O'Meara, Basil, Montreal Star 1984

Pedneault, Yvon, La Presse/Journal de Montréal 1998
* Proudfoot, Jim, Toronto Star 1988

Raymond, Bertrand, Journal de Montréal 1990
Rosa, Fran, Boston Globe 1987
Strachan, Al, Globe and Mail/Toronto Sun 1993
* Vipond, Jim, Toronto Globe and Mail 1984

Walter, Lewis, Detroit Times 1984
* Young, Scott, Toronto Globe and Mail/Telegram 1988

Foster Hewitt Memorial Award Winners

In recognition of members of the radio and television industry who made outstanding contributions to their profession and the game during their career in hockey broadcasting. Selected by the NHL Broadcasters' Association.

Cole, Bob, Hockey Night in Canada 1996
Cusick, Fred, Boston 1984
* Darling, Ted, Buffalo 1994
* Gallivan, Danny, Montreal 1984

Garneau, Richard, Montreal 1999
* Hart, Gene, Philadelphia 1997

Hewitt, Bill, Hockey Night in Canada 2007
* Hewitt, Foster, Toronto 1984

Irvin, Dick, Montreal 1988
Kaiton, Chuck, Hartford/Carolina 2004
* Kelly, Dan, St. Louis 1989

Lange, Mike, Pittsburgh 2001
* Lecavelier, René, Montreal 1984

Lynch, Budd, Detroit 1985
Maher, Peter, Calgary 2006
Martyn, Bruce, Detroit 1991
McDonald, Jiggs, Los Angeles, Atlanta, NY Islanders 1990
McFarlane, Brian, Hockey Night in Canada 1995
* McKnight, Wes, Toronto 1986

Meeker, Howie, Hockey Night in Canada 1998
Messina, Sal, New York 2005
Miller, Bob, Los Angeles 2000
Pettit, Lloyd, Chicago 1986
Phillips, Rod, Edmonton 2003

United States Hockey Hall of Fame

On May 11, 2007, the U.S. Hockey Hall of Fame and USA Hockey came to an historic agreement that transferred rights to the selection process and induction event associated with the Hall, including the Wayne Gretzky International Award, to USA Hockey. As part of the agreement, the U.S. Hockey Hall of Fame Museum, located in Eveleth, Minn., formed a separate Board of Directors to govern the national shrine for American Hockey.

The United States Hockey Hall of Fame Museum was opened on June 21, 1973. It is dedicated to honoring the sport of ice hockey in the United States by preserving those precious memories and legends of the game. It is located in Eveleth, Minnesota, 60 miles north of Duluth on Highway 53. The facility is open Monday to Saturday, 9 a.m. to 5 p.m. and Sundays from 10 a.m. to 3 p.m. Admission is $8.00 for adults, $7.00 for seniors and youths (13-17) and $6.00 for children (6-12). Children under 6 are free. Call for further information: 800-443-7825 or 218-744-5157. Web site address: www.ushockeyhall.com.

There are 134 enshrined members consisting of 83 players, 26 coaches, 20 administrators, two player/administrators, one referee and two teams. New members are inducted annually and must have made a significant contribution to hockey in the United States during the course of their career. A special Wayne Gretzky International Award pays tribute to international individuals who have made major contributions to hockey in the USA.

PLAYERS

* Abel, Clarence "Taffy" 1973
* Baker, Hobart "Hobey" 1973
* Bartholome, Earl 1977
* Bessone, Peter 1978

Blake, Robert 1985
Boucha, Henry 1995
* Brimsek, Frank 1973

Brink, Milton "Curly" 2006
Broten, Aaron 2007
Broten, Neal 2000
Carpenter, Bobby 2007
Cavanagh, Joe 1994
* Chaisson, Ray 1974
* Chase, John P. 1973

Christian, Dave 2001
Christian, Roger 1989
Christian, William "Bill" 1984
Christiansen, Keith 2005
Cleary, Robert 1981
Cleary, William 1976
* Conroy, Anthony 1975

Coppo, Paul, 2004
Curran, Mike 1998
* Dahlstrom, Carl "Cully" 1973
* Desjardins, Victor 1974
* Desmond, Richard 1988
* Dill, Robert 1979

Dougherty, Richard "Dick" 2003
* Everett, Doug 1974

Fusco, Mark 2002
Fusco, Scott 2002
Ftorek, Robbie 1991
Gambucci, Gary 2006
* Garrison, John B. 1973

Garrity, Jack 1986
* Goheen, Frank "Moose" 1973

Grant, Wally 1994
* Harding, Francis "Austie" 1975

Housley, Phil 2004
Howe, Mark 2003
* Iglehart, Stewart 1975

Johnson, Mark 2004
Johnson, Paul 2001
* Johnson, Virgil 1974
* Karakas, Mike 1973

Kirrane, Jack 1987
LaFontaine, Pat 2003
* Lane, Myles J. 1973

Langevin, David R. 1993
Langway, Rod 1999
Larson, Reed 1996
* Linder, Joseph 1975
* LoPresti, Sam L. 1973

MacDonald, Lane 2005
* Mariucci, John 1973

Matchefts, John 1991
* Mather, Bruce 1998

Mayasich, John 1976
McCartan, Jack 1983
* Moe, William 1974

Morrow, Ken 1995
* Moseley, Fred 1975

Mullen, Joe 1998
* Murray, Sr., Hugh "Muzz" 1987
* Nelson, Hubert "Hub" 1978
* Nyrop, William D. 1997
* Olson , Eddie 1977
* Owen, Jr., George 1973
* Palmer, Winthrop 1973

Paradise, Robert 1989
* Purpur, Clifford "Fido" 1974

Ramsey, Mike 2001
* Riley, Joe 2002
* Riley, William 1977

Roberts, Gordie 1999
* Roberts, Moe 2005
* Romnes, Elwin "Doc" 1973
* Rondeau, Richard 1985

Sheehy, Timothy K. 1997
Vanbiesbrouck, John 2007
* Williams, Thomas 1981
* Winters, Frank "Coddy" 1973
* Yackel, Ken 1986

COACHES

* Almquist, Oscar 1983

Bessone, Amo 1992
* Brooks, Herb 1990

Ceglarski, Len 1992
* Cunniff, John 2003
* Fullerton, James 1992

Gambucci, Sergio 1996
* Gordon, Malcolm K. 1973

Harkness, Nevin D. "Ned" 1994
* Heyliger, Victor 1974
* Holt, Jr. Charles E. 1997

Ikola, Willard 1990
* Jeremiah, Edward J. 1973
* Johnson, Bob 1991
* Kelley, John "Snooks" 1974

Kelley, John H. "Jack" 1993
Patrick, Craig 1996
* Pleban, Jon "Connie" 1990

Riley, Jack 1979
* Ross, Larry 1988
* Thompson, Clifford, R. 1973
* Stewart, William 1982

Williamson, Murray 2005
* Winsor, Alfred "Ralph" 1973

Woog, Doug 2002

ADMINISTRATORS

* Brown, George V. 1973
* Brown, Walter A. 1973

Bush, Walter 1980
* Clark, Donald 1978

Claypool, James 1995
* Gibson, J.C. "Doc" 1973

Ilitch, Mike 2004
* Jennings, William M. 1981
* Kahler, Nick 1980
* Lockhart, Thomas F. 1973

MacInnes, John 2007
* Marvin, Cal 1982

Palazzari, Doug 2000
Pleau, Larry 2000
* Ridder, Robert 1976
* Schulz, Charles M. 1993

Trumble, Harold 1985
* Tutt, William Thayer 1973
* Watson, Sid 1999

Wirtz, William W. "Bill" 1984
* Wright, Lyle Z.1973

PLAYER/ADMINISTRATOR

Milbury, Mike 2006
Nanne, Lou 1998

REFEREE

Chadwick, William 1974

TEAMS

1960 Olympic Team, 2000
1980 Olympic Team, 2003

WAYNE GRETZKY INTERNATIONAL AWARD

Wayne Gretzky 1999
The Howe family 2000
Scotty Morrison 2001
Scotty Bowman 2002
Bobby Hull 2003
* Herb Brooks 2004

*Deceased

International Ice Hockey Federation Hall of Fame

The IIHF Hall of Fame was founded in 1997.

Candidates for election as Honoured Members in the player category shall be chosen on the basis of their playing ability, sportsmanship, character and their contribution to their team or teams and to the game of ice hockey in general.

Candidates for election as Honoured Members in the builder category shall be chosen on the basis of their coaching, managerial or executive ability, where applicable, their sportsmanship and character, and their contribution to their organization or organizations and to the game of ice hockey in general.

Candidates for election as Honoured Members in the referee or linesman category shall be chosen on the basis of their officiating ability, sportsmanship, character and their contribution to the game of ice hockey in general. The Paul Loicq Award, named for the longtime former IIHF president, is presented to honor a person for his service to the international hockey community.

Inductees' names are followed by their country and year of induction.

PLAYERS

Alexandrov, Veniamin, RUS, 2007
Balderis, Helmut, LAT, 1998
Ball, Rudi, GER, 2004
Bergqvist, Sven, SWE, 1999
Bjorn, Lars, SWE, 1998
Bobrov, Vsevolod, RUS, 1997
Bourbonnais, Roger, CAN, 1999
Bouzek, Vladimir, CzRep, 2007
Bubnik, Vlastimil, CzRep, 1997
Cattini, Ferdinand, SUI, 1998
Cattini, Hans, SUI, 1998
Cerny, Josef, CzRep, 2007
Christian, Bill, USA, 1998
Cleary, Bill, USA, 1997
Cosby, Gerry, USA, 1997
Craig, Jim, USA, 1999
Curran, Mike, USA, 1999
Davydov, Vitaly, RUS, 2004
Drobny, Jaroslav, CzRep, 1997
Dzurilla, Vladimir, SVK, 1998
Erhardt, Carl, G.B., 1998
Fetisov, Vyacheslav, RUS, 2005
Firsov, Anatoli, RUS, 1998
Golonka, Josef, SVK, 1998
Gretzky, Wayne, CAN, 2000
Gruth, Henryk, POL, 2006
Gustafsson, Bengt-Ake, SWE, 2003
Gut, Karel, CzRep, 1998
Hedberg, Anders, SWE, 1997
Hlinka, Ivan, CzRep, 2002
Holecek, Jiri, CzRep, 1998
Holik, Jiri, CzRep, 1999
Holmqvist, Leif, SWE, 1999
Huck, Fran, CAN, 1999
Jaenecke, Gustav, GER, 1998
Johnson, Mark, USA, 1999
Johnston, Marshall, CAN, 1998
Jonsson, Tomas, SWE, 2000
Jutila, Timo, FIN, 2003
Keinonen, Matti, FIN, 2002
Kharlamov, Valeri, RUS, 1998
Kiessling, Udo, GER, 2000
Kolliker, Jakob, SUI, 2007
Konovalenko, Viktor, RUS, 2007
Kuhnhackl, Erich, GER, 1997
Kurri, Jari, FIN, 2000
Kuzkin, Viktor, RUS, 2005
Lacarriere, Jacques, FRA, 1998
Loktev, Konstantin, RUS, 2007
Loob, Hakan, SWE, 1998
Lundquist, Vic, CAN, 1997
Machac, Oldrich, CzRep, 1999
MacKenzie, Barry, CAN, 1999
Makarov, Sergei, RUS, 2001
Malecek, Josef, CzRep, 2003
Maltsev, Alexander, RUS, 1999
Marjamaki, Pekka, FIN, 1998
Martin, Seth, CAN, 1997
Martinec, Vladimir, CzRep, 2001
Mayasich, John, USA, 1997
Mayorov, Boris, RUS, 1999
McCartan, Jack, USA, 1998
McLeod, Jackie, CAN, 1999
Mikhailov, Boris, RUS, 2000
Nanne, Lou, USA, 2004
Naslund, Mats, SWE, 2005
Nedomansky, Vaclav, CzRep, 1997
Nilsson, Kent, SWE, 2006
Nilsson, Nisse, SWE, 2002
O'Malley, Terry, CAN, 1998
Oksanen, Lasse, FIN, 1999
Pana, Eduard, ROM, 1998
Patton, Peter, G.B., 2002
Peltonen, Esa, FIN, 2007
Petrov, Vladimir, RUS, 2006
Pettersson, Ronald, SWE, 2004
Pospisil, Frantisek, CzRep, 1999
Puschnig, Josef, AUT, 1999
Ragulin, Alexander, RUS, 1997
Rampf, Hans, GER, 2001
Rundqvist, Thomas, SWE, 2007
Salming, Borje, SWE, 1998
Schloder, Alois, GER, 2005
Sinden, Harry, CAN, 1997
Sologubov, Nikolai, RUS, 2004
Starshinov, Vyacheslav, RUS, 2007
Stastny, Peter, SVK, 2000
Sterner, Ulf, SWE, 2001
Stoltz, Roland, SWE, 1999
Tikal, Frantisek, CzRep, 2004
Torriani, Bibi, SUI, 1997
Tretiak, Vladislav, RUS, 1997
Tumba, Sven, SWE, 1997
Valtonen, Jorma, FIN, 1999
Vasiliev, Valeri, RUS, 1998
Wahlsten, Vladimir, FIN, 2006
Watson, Harry, CAN, 1998
Yakushev, Alexander, RUS, 2003
Ylonen, Urpo, FIN, 1997
Zabrodsky, Vladimir, CzRep, 1997
Ziesche, Joachim, GER, 1999

BUILDERS

Ahearne, Bunny, G.B., 1997
Aljancic Sr., Ernest, SLO, 2002
Bauer, Father David, CAN, 1997
Berglund, Curt, SWE, 2003
Bokac, Ludek, CzRep, 2007
Brooks, Herb, USA, 1999
Brown, Walter, USA, 1997
Buckna, Mike, CAN, 2004
Calcaterra, Enrico, ITA, 1999
Chernyshev, Arkady, RUS, 1999
Dimitriev, Igor, RUS, 2007
Dobida, Hans, AUT, 2007
Eklow, Rudolf, SWE, 1999
Grunander, Arne, SWE, 1997
Henschel, Heinz, GER, 2003
Hewitt, William, CAN, 1998
Holmes, Derek, CAN, 1999
Horsky, Ladislav, SVK, 2004
Hviid, Jorgen, DEN, 2005
Johannessen, Tore, NOR, 1999
Juckes, Gordon, CAN, 1997
Kawabuchi, Tsutomu, JPN, 2004
Khorozov, Anatoli, UKR, 2006
King, Dave, CAN, 2001
Kostka, Vladimir, CzRep, 1997
LeBel, Bob, CAN, 1997
Lindblad, Harry, FIN, 1999
Loicq, Paul, BEL, 1997
Luhti, Cesar W., SUI, 1998
Magnus, Louis, FRA, 1997
Pasztor, Gyorgy, HUN, 2001
Renwick, Gordon, CAN, 2002
Ridder, Bob, USA, 1998
Riley, Jack, USA, 1998
Sabetzki, Dr. Gunther, GER, 1997
Starovoitov, Andrei, RUS, 1997
Starsi, Jan, SVK, 1999
Stromberg, Arne, SWE, 1998
Stubb, Goran, FIN, 2000
Subrt, Miroslav, CzRep, 2004
Tarasov, Anatoli, RUS, 1997
Tikhonov, Viktor, RUS, 1998
Tomita, Shoichi, JPN, 2006
Trumble, Hal, USA, 1999
Tsutsumi, Yoshiaki, JPN, 1999
Tutt, Thayer, USA, 2002
Unsinn, Xaver, GER, 1998
Wasservogel, Walter, AUT, 1997
Yurzinov, Vladimir, RUS, 2002

REFEREES

Adamec, Quido, CzRep, 2005
Dahlberg, Ove, SWE, 2004
Karandin, Yuri, RUS, 2004
Kompalla, Josef, GER, 2003
Wiitala, Unto, FIN, 2003

PAUL LOICQ AWARD

Montag, Wolf-Dieter, GER, 1998
Neumayer, Roman, GER, 1999
Kukushkin, Vsevolod, RUS, 2000
Kataoka, Isao, JPN, 2001
Marsh, Pat, G.B., 2002
Nagobads, George, USA, 2003
Kukulowicz, Aggie, CAN, 2004
Hrabcek, Rita, AUS, 2005
Tovland, Bo, SWE, 2006
Nadin, Paul, CAN, 2007

Valeri Vasiliev (checking Ron Ellis during the 1972 Canada-Russia Summit Series) was a member of the Soviet national team from 1970 to 1982, winning nine World Championship titles and two Olympic gold medals. He was the most physical Soviet defensemen of his era.

2007 Stanley Cup Playoffs

Results

CONFERENCE QUARTER-FINALS
(Best-of-seven series)

Eastern Conference

Series 'A'

Thu. Apr. 12	NY Islanders 1	at	Buffalo 4
Sat. Apr. 14	NY Islanders 3	at	Buffalo 2
Mon. Apr. 16	Buffalo 3	at	NY Islanders 2
Wed. Apr. 18	Buffalo 4	at	NY Islanders 2
Fri. Apr. 20	NY Islanders 3	at	Buffalo 4

(Buffalo won series 4-1)

Series 'B'

Thu. Apr. 12	Tampa Bay 3	at	New Jersey 5
Sat. Apr. 14	Tampa Bay 3	at	New Jersey 2
Mon. Apr. 16	New Jersey 2	at	Tampa Bay 3
Wed. Apr. 18	New Jersey 4	at	Tampa Bay 3*
Fri. Apr. 20	Tampa Bay 0	at	New Jersey 3
Sun. Apr. 22	New Jersey 3	at	Tampa Bay 2

*Scott Gomez scored at 12:54 of overtime
(New Jersey won series 4-2)

Series 'C'

Thu. Apr. 12	NY Rangers 4	at	Atlanta 3
Sat. Apr. 14	NY Rangers 2	at	Atlanta 1
Tue. Apr. 17	Atlanta 0	at	NY Rangers 7
Wed. Apr. 18	Atlanta 2	at	NY Rangers 4

(NY Rangers won series 4-0)

Series 'D'

Wed. Apr. 11	Pittsburgh 3	at	Ottawa 6
Sat. Apr. 14	Pittsburgh 4	at	Ottawa 3
Sun. Apr. 15	Ottawa 4	at	Pittsburgh 2
Tue. Apr. 17	Ottawa 2	at	Pittsburgh 1
Thu. Apr. 19	Pittsburgh 0	at	Ottawa 3

(Ottawa won series 4-1)

Western Conference

Series 'E'

Thu. Apr. 12	Calgary 1	at	Detroit 4
Sun. Apr. 15	Calgary 1	at	Detroit 3
Tue. Apr. 17	Detroit 2	at	Calgary 3
Thu. Apr. 19	Detroit 2	at	Calgary 3
Sat. Apr. 21	Calgary 1	at	Detroit 5
Sun. Apr. 22	Detroit 2	at	Calgary 1*

*Johan Franzen scored at 24:23 of overtime
(Detroit won series 4-2)

Series 'F'

Wed. Apr. 11	Minnesota 1	at	Anaheim 2
Fri. Apr. 13	Minnesota 2	at	Anaheim 3
Sun. Apr. 15	Anaheim 2	at	Minnesota 1
Tue. Apr. 17	Anaheim 1	at	Minnesota 4
Thu. Apr. 19	Minnesota 1	at	Anaheim 4

(Anaheim won series 4-1)

Series 'G'

Wed. Apr. 11	Dallas 4	at	Vancouver 5*
Fri. Apr. 13	Dallas 2	at	Vancouver 0
Sun. Apr. 15	Vancouver 2	at	Dallas 1**
Tue. Apr. 17	Vancouver 2	at	Dallas 1
Thu. Apr. 19	Dallas 1	at	Vancouver 0***
Sat. Apr. 21	Vancouver 0	at	Dallas 2
Mon. Apr. 23	Dallas 1	at	Vancouver 4

*Henrik Sedin scored at 78:06 of overtime
**Taylor Pyatt scored at 7:47 of overtime
***Brenden Morrow scored at 6:22 of overtime
(Vancouver won series 4-3)

Series 'H'

Wed. Apr. 11	San Jose 5	at	Nashville 4*
Fri. Apr. 13	San Jose 2	at	Nashville 5
Mon. Apr. 16	Nashville 1	at	San Jose 3
Wed. Apr. 18	Nashville 2	at	San Jose 3
Fri. Apr. 20	San Jose 3	at	Nashville 2

*Patrick Rissmiller scored at 28:14 of overtime
(San Jose won series 4-1)

CONFERENCE SEMI-FINALS
(Best-of-seven series)

Eastern Conference

Series 'I'

Wed. Apr. 25	NY Rangers 2	at	Buffalo 5
Fri. Apr. 27	NY Rangers 2	at	Buffalo 3
Sun. Apr. 29	Buffalo 1	at	NY Rangers 2*
Tue. May 1	Buffalo 1	at	NY Rangers 2
Fri. May 4	NY Rangers 1	at	Buffalo 2**
Sun. May 6	Buffalo 5	at	NY Rangers 4

*Michal Rozsival scored at 36:43 of overtime
**Maxim Afinogenov scored at 4:39 of overtime
(Buffalo won series 4-2)

Series 'J'

Thu. Apr. 26	Ottawa 5	at	New Jersey 4
Sat. Apr. 28	Ottawa 2	at	New Jersey 3*
Mon. Apr. 30	New Jersey 0	at	Ottawa 2
Wed. May 2	New Jersey 2	at	Ottawa 3
Sat. May 5	Ottawa 3	at	New Jersey 2

*Jamie Langenbrunner scored at 21:55 of overtime
(Ottawa won series 4-1)

Western Conference

Series 'K'

Thu. Apr. 26	San Jose 2	at	Detroit 0
Sat. Apr. 28	San Jose 2	at	Detroit 3
Mon. Apr. 30	Detroit 1	at	San Jose 2
Wed. May 2	Detroit 3	at	San Jose 2*
Sat. May 5	San Jose 1	at	Detroit 4
Mon. May 7	Detroit 2	at	San Jose 0

*Mathieu Schneider scored at 16:04 of overtime
(Detroit won series 4-2)

Series 'L'

Wed. Apr. 25	Vancouver 1	at	Anaheim 5
Fri. Apr. 27	Vancouver 2	at	Anaheim 1*
Sun. Apr. 29	Anaheim 3	at	Vancouver 2
Tue. May 1	Anaheim 3	at	Vancouver 2**
Thu. May 3	Vancouver 1	at	Anaheim 2***

*Jeff Cowan scored at 27:49 of overtime
**Travis Moen scored at 2:07 of overtime
***Scott Niedermayer scored at 24:30 of overtime
(Anaheim won series 4-1)

CONFERENCE FINALS
(Best-of-seven series)

Eastern Conference

Series 'M'

Thu. May 10	Ottawa 5	at	Buffalo 2
Sat. May 12	Ottawa 4	at	Buffalo 3*
Mon. May 14	Buffalo 0	at	Ottawa 1
Wed. May 16	Buffalo 3	at	Ottawa 2
Sat. May 19	Ottawa 3	at	Buffalo 2**

*Joe Corvo scored at 24:58 of overtime
**Daniel Alfredsson scored at 9:32 of overtime
(Ottawa won series 4-1)

Western Conference

Series 'N'

Fri. May 11	Anaheim 1	at	Detroit 2
Sun. May 13	Anaheim 4	at	Detroit 3*
Tue. May 15	Detroit 5	at	Anaheim 0
Thu. May 17	Detroit 3	at	Anaheim 5
Sun. May 20	Anaheim 2	at	Detroit 1**
Tue. May 22	Detroit 3	at	Anaheim 4

*Scott Niedermayer scored at 14:17 of overtime
**Teemu Selanne scored at 11:57 of overtime
(Anaheim won series 4-2)

STANLEY CUP FINAL
(Best-of-seven series)

Series 'O'

Mon. May 28	Ottawa 2	at	Anaheim 3
Wed. May 30	Ottawa 0	at	Anaheim 1
Sat. June 2	Anaheim 3	at	Ottawa 5
Mon. June 4	Anaheim 3	at	Ottawa 2
Wed. June 6	Ottawa 2	at	Anaheim 6

(Anaheim won series 4-1)

Team Playoff Records

	GP	W	L	GF	GA	%
Anaheim	21	16	5	58	45	.762
Ottawa	20	13	7	59	47	.650
Detroit	18	10	8	48	35	.556
Buffalo	16	9	7	44	39	.563
NY Rangers	10	6	4	30	23	.600
San Jose	11	6	5	25	27	.545
New Jersey	11	5	6	30	29	.455
Vancouver	12	5	7	21	26	.417
Dallas	7	3	4	12	13	.429
Tampa Bay	6	2	4	14	19	.333
Calgary	6	2	4	10	18	.333
Nashville	5	1	4	14	16	.200
Minnesota	5	1	4	9	12	.200
NY Islanders	5	1	4	11	17	.200
Pittsburgh	5	1	4	10	18	.200
Atlanta	4	0	4	6	17	.000

Individual Leaders

Abbreviations: GP – games played; **G** – goals; **A** – assists; **PTS** – points; **+/–** – difference between Goals For (**GF**) scored when a player is on the ice with his team at even strength or short-handed and Goals Against (**GA**) scored when the same player is on the ice with his team at even strength or on a power play; **PIM** – penalties in minutes; **PP** – power play goals; **SH** – short-handed goals; **GW** – game-winning goals; **OT** – overtime goals; **S** – shots on goal; **%** – percentage of shots resulting in goals.

Playoff Scoring Leaders

Player	Team	GP	G	A	PTS	+/–	PIM	PP	SH	GW	OT	S	%
Daniel Alfredsson	Ottawa	20	14	8	22	4	10	6	1	4	1	66	21.2
Dany Heatley	Ottawa	20	7	15	22	4	14	2	0	2	0	59	11.9
Jason Spezza	Ottawa	20	7	15	22	5	10	3	0	0	0	49	14.3
Nicklas Lidstrom	Detroit	18	4	14	18	0	6	4	0	2	0	39	10.3
Ryan Getzlaf	Anaheim	21	7	10	17	1	32	3	1	3	0	57	12.3
Pavel Datsyuk	Detroit	18	8	8	16	2	8	4	0	2	0	66	12.1
Corey Perry	Anaheim	21	6	9	15	5	37	1	0	1	0	58	10.3
Teemu Selanne	Anaheim	21	5	10	15	1	10	0	0	2	1	60	8.3
Daniel Briere	Buffalo	16	3	12	15	3	16	2	0	1	0	49	6.1
Chris Pronger	Anaheim	19	3	12	15	10	26	1	0	0	0	58	5.2
Andy McDonald	Anaheim	21	10	4	14	6	10	5	0	0	0	64	15.6
Henrik Zetterberg	Detroit	18	6	8	14	1	12	3	0	1	0	78	7.7
Scott Gomez	New Jersey	11	4	10	14	6	14	0	0	1	1	37	10.8
Chris Drury	Buffalo	16	8	5	13	3	2	3	0	3	0	43	18.6
Michael Nylander	NY Rangers	10	6	7	13	9	0	2	0	2	0	23	26.1
Travis Moen	Anaheim	21	7	5	12	5	22	0	0	3	1	34	20.6
Daniel Cleary	Detroit	18	4	8	12	2	30	1	2	0	0	53	7.5
Samuel Pahlsson	Anaheim	21	3	9	12	10	20	0	0	2	0	30	10.0
Jaromir Jagr	NY Rangers	10	5	6	11	6	12	2	0	0	0	48	10.4
Mikael Samuelsson	Detroit	18	3	8	11	2	14	1	0	1	0	45	6.7
Scott Niedermayer	Anaheim	21	3	8	11	2	26	1	0	2	2	42	7.1
Joe Thornton	San Jose	11	1	10	11	2	10	0	0	0	0	23	4.3

Playoff Defencemen Scoring Leaders

Player	Team	GP	G	A	PTS	+/–	PIM	PP	SH	GW	OT	S	%
Nicklas Lidstrom	Detroit	18	4	14	18	0	6	4	0	2	0	39	10.3
Chris Pronger	Anaheim	19	3	12	15	10	26	1	0	0	0	58	5.2
Scott Niedermayer	Anaheim	21	3	8	11	2	26	1	0	2	2	42	7.1
Wade Redden	Ottawa	20	3	7	10	6	10	3	0	1	0	23	13.0
Joseph Corvo	Ottawa	20	2	7	9	4	6	1	0	1	1	49	4.1
Francois Beauchemin	Anaheim	20	4	4	8	2	16	4	0	0	0	58	6.9
Brian Rafalski	New Jersey	11	2	6	8	-1	8	2	0	0	0	11	18.2
Michal Rozsival	NY Rangers	10	3	4	7	6	10	2	0	1	1	18	16.7
Brian Campbell	Buffalo	16	3	4	7	0	14	2	0	0	0	29	10.3
Mattias Ohlund	Vancouver	12	2	5	7	3	12	1	0	0	0	29	6.9
Tom Preissing	Ottawa	20	2	5	7	3	10	1	0	1	0	21	9.5
Chris Chelios	Detroit	18	1	6	7	7	12	0	1	0	0	27	3.7
Andrej Meszaros	Ottawa	20	1	6	7	5	12	0	0	0	0	26	3.8

GOALTENDING LEADERS

Goals Against Average

Goaltender	Team	GP	Mins	GA	Avg.
Marty Turco	Dallas	7	509	11	1.30
Roberto Luongo	Vancouver	12	847	25	1.77
Dominik Hasek	Detroit	18	1140	34	1.79
Jean-Sebastien Giguere	Anaheim	18	1067	35	1.97
Henrik Lundqvist	NY Rangers	10	637	22	2.07

Wins

Goaltender	Team	GP	Mins	W	L
Jean-Sebastien Giguere	Anaheim	18	1067	13	4
Ray Emery	Ottawa	20	1249	13	7
Dominik Hasek	Detroit	18	1140	10	8
Ryan Miller	Buffalo	16	1029	9	7
Henrik Lundqvist	NY Rangers	10	637	6	4
Evgeni Nabokov	San Jose	11	701	6	5

Save Percentage

Goaltender	Team	GP	Mins	GA	SA	S%	W	L
Marty Turco	Dallas	7	509	11	229	.952	3	4
Roberto Luongo	Vancouver	12	847	25	427	.941	5	7
Henrik Lundqvist	NY Rangers	10	637	22	291	.924	6	4
Dominik Hasek	Detroit	18	1140	34	444	.923	10	8
Jean-Sebastien Giguere	Anaheim	18	1067	35	451	.922	13	4
Ryan Miller	Buffalo	16	1029	38	489	.922	9	7

Shutouts

Goaltender	Team	GP	Mins	SO
Marty Turco	Dallas	7	509	3
Ray Emery	Ottawa	20	1249	3
Dominik Hasek	Detroit	18	1140	2
Henrik Lundqvist	NY Rangers	10	637	1
Martin Brodeur	New Jersey	11	688	1
Evgeni Nabokov	San Jose	11	701	1
Jean-Sebastien Giguere	Anaheim	18	1067	1

Goals

Name	Team	GP	G
Daniel Alfredsson	Ottawa	20	14
Andy McDonald	Anaheim	21	10
Brian Gionta	New Jersey	11	8
Chris Drury	Buffalo	16	8
Pavel Datsyuk	Detroit	18	8
Zach Parise	New Jersey	11	7
Dany Heatley	Ottawa	20	7
Jason Spezza	Ottawa	20	7
Travis Moen	Anaheim	21	7
Ryan Getzlaf	Anaheim	21	7
Michael Nylander	NY Rangers	10	6
Thomas Vanek	Buffalo	16	6
Henrik Zetterberg	Detroit	18	6
Corey Perry	Anaheim	21	6

Assists

Name	Team	GP	A
Dany Heatley	Ottawa	20	15
Jason Spezza	Ottawa	20	15
Nicklas Lidstrom	Detroit	18	14
Daniel Briere	Buffalo	16	12
Chris Pronger	Anaheim	19	12
Joe Thornton	San Jose	11	10
Scott Gomez	New Jersey	11	10
Teemu Selanne	Anaheim	21	10
Ryan Getzlaf	Anaheim	21	10
Patrik Elias	New Jersey	10	9
Tim Connolly	Buffalo	16	9
Samuel Pahlsson	Anaheim	21	9
Corey Perry	Anaheim	21	9

Power-play Goals

Name	Team	GP	PP
Daniel Alfredsson	Ottawa	20	6
Andy McDonald	Anaheim	21	5
Tomas Holmstrom	Detroit	15	4
Nicklas Lidstrom	Detroit	18	4
Pavel Datsyuk	Detroit	18	4
Francois Beauchemin	Anaheim	20	4

Game-winning Goals

Name	Team	GP	GW
Daniel Alfredsson	Ottawa	20	4
Chris Drury	Buffalo	16	3
Travis Moen	Anaheim	21	3
Ryan Getzlaf	Anaheim	21	3
13 others with 2			

Short-handed Goals

Name	Team	GP	SH
Daniel Cleary	Detroit	18	2
Jean-Pierre Dumont	Nashville	5	1
Andrei Zyuzin	Calgary	5	1
Marian Gaborik	Minnesota	5	1
Filip Kuba	Tampa Bay	6	1
Chris Chelios	Detroit	18	1
Dean Mcammond	Ottawa	18	1
Kirk Maltby	Detroit	18	1
Daniel Alfredsson	Ottawa	20	1
Mike Fisher	Ottawa	20	1
Rob Niedermayer	Anaheim	21	1
Ryan Getzlaf	Anaheim	21	1

Overtime Goals

Name	Team	GP	OT
Scott Niedermayer	Anaheim	21	2
15 others with 1			

Shots

Name	Team	GP	S
Henrik Zetterberg	Detroit	18	78
Pavel Datsyuk	Detroit	18	66
Daniel Alfredsson	Ottawa	20	66
Andy McDonald	Anaheim	21	64
Teemu Selanne	Anaheim	21	60

Plus/Minus

Name	Team	GP	+/–
Teppo Numminen	Buffalo	16	10
Chris Pronger	Anaheim	19	10
Samuel Pahlsson	Anaheim	21	10
Michael Nylander	NY Rangers	10	9
Dmitri Kalinin	Buffalo	16	9
Rob Niedermayer	Anaheim	21	9

TEAMS' PLAYOFF HOME/ROAD RECORD

	HOME					Win	ROAD					Win
	GP	W	L	GF	GA	%	GP	W	L	GF	GA	%
ANA	12	10	2	36	23	.833	9	6	3	22	22	.667
OTT	9	6	3	27	18	.667	11	7	4	32	29	.636
DET	9	6	3	25	15	.667	9	4	5	23	20	.444
BUF	9	5	4	27	24	.556	7	4	3	17	15	.571
NYR	5	4	1	19	9	.800	5	2	3	11	14	.400
S.J.	5	3	2	10	9	.600	6	3	3	15	18	.500
N.J.	6	3	3	19	16	.500	5	2	3	11	13	.400
VAN	6	2	4	13	14	.333	6	3	3	8	12	.500
DAL	3	1	2	4	4	.333	4	2	2	8	9	.500
T.B.	3	1	2	8	9	.333	3	1	2	6	10	.333
CGY	3	2	1	7	6	.667	3	0	3	3	12	.000
NSH	3	1	2	11	10	.333	2	0	2	3	6	.000
MIN	2	1	1	5	3	.500	3	0	3	4	9	.000
NYI	2	0	2	4	7	.000	3	1	2	7	10	.333
PIT	2	0	2	3	6	.000	3	1	2	7	12	.333
ATL	2	0	2	4	6	.000	2	0	2	2	11	.000
Total	**81**	**45**	**36**	**222**	**179**	**.556**	**81**	**36**	**45**	**179**	**222**	**.444**

TEAM PENALTIES

Abbreviations: GP – games played; **PEN** – total penalty minutes, including bench penalties; **BMI** – total bench minor minutes; **AVG** – average penalty minutes per game. 89 games played.

Team	GP	PEN	BMI	AVG
BUF	16	162	0	10.1
NYI	5	54	2	10.8
N.J.	11	126	4	11.5
OTT	20	246	6	12.3
DET	18	244	10	13.6
DAL	7	104	4	14.9
S.J.	11	165	4	15.0
NYR	10	151	0	15.1
PIT	5	78	0	15.6
MIN	5	79	0	15.8
VAN	12	190	4	15.8
ANA	21	371	6	17.7
T.B.	6	110	2	18.3
CGY	6	117	0	19.5
ATL	4	115	2	28.8
NSH	5	148	0	29.6
Total	**81**	**2460**	**44**	
Two-Team average PIM/GP				**30.4**

TEAMS' POWER-PLAY RECORD

Abbreviations: ADV-total advantages; **PPGF**-power play goals for; **%** arrived by dividing number of power-play goals by total advantages.

	HOME					ROAD					OVERALL				
Team		GP	ADV	PPGF	%	Team	GP	ADV	PPGF	%	Team	GP	ADV	PPGF	%
1	NYR	5	28	9	32.1	OTT	11	46	12	26.1	NYR	10	54	13	24.1
2	CGY	3	16	4	25.0	PIT	3	19	4	21.1	N.J.	11	50	10	20.0
3	N.J.	6	25	6	24.0	NSH	2	5	1	20.0	OTT	20	95	18	18.9
4	T.B.	3	14	3	21.4	N.J.	5	25	4	16.0	DET	18	103	19	18.4
5	DET	9	53	11	20.8	DET	9	50	8	16.0	CGY	6	34	6	17.6
6	MIN	2	12	2	16.7	NYR	5	26	4	15.4	T.B.	6	26	4	15.4
7	ANA	12	61	10	16.4	BUF	7	36	5	13.9	ANA	21	105	16	15.2
8	NYI	2	8	1	12.5	ANA	9	44	6	13.6	PIT	5	28	4	14.3
9	ATL	2	8	1	12.5	CGY	3	18	2	11.1	NSH	5	22	3	13.6
10	OTT	9	49	6	12.2	S.J.	6	32	3	9.4	BUF	16	88	11	12.5
11	DAL	3	17	2	11.8	NYI	3	11	1	9.1	NYI	5	19	2	10.5
12	NSH	3	17	2	11.8	DAL	4	23	2	8.7	DAL	7	40	4	10.0
13	BUF	9	52	6	11.5	T.B.	3	12	1	8.3	MIN	5	27	2	7.4
14	VAN	6	38	4	10.5	ATL	2	9	0	.0	S.J.	11	57	4	7.0
15	S.J.	5	25	1	4.0	MIN	3	15	0	.0	VAN	12	67	4	6.0
16	PIT	2	9	0	.0	VAN	6	29	0	.0	ATL	4	17	1	5.9
Total		**81**	**432**	**68**	**15.7**		**81**	**400**	**53**	**13.3**		**81**	**832**	**121**	**14.5**

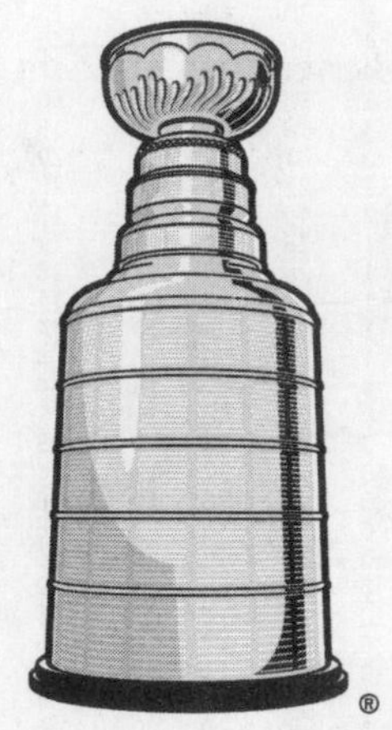

TEAMS' PENALTY KILLING RECORD

Abbreviations: TSH – Total times short-handed; **PPGA** – power-play goals against; **%** arrived by dividing times short-handed minus power-play goals against by times short.

	HOME					ROAD					OVERALL				
Team		GP	TSH	PPGA	%	Team	GP	TSH	PPGA	%	Team	GP	TSH	PPGA	%
1	CGY	3	15	0	100.0	NSH	2	11	0	100.0	NSH	5	30	2	93.3
2	DAL	3	11	0	100.0	OTT	11	54	5	90.7	DAL	7	38	3	92.1
3	NYR	5	26	2	92.3	VAN	6	40	4	90.0	VAN	12	76	8	89.5
4	DET	9	48	4	91.7	DAL	4	27	3	88.9	NYR	10	52	6	88.5
5	ANA	12	69	7	89.9	NYI	3	15	2	86.7	OTT	20	99	12	87.9
6	NSH	3	19	2	89.5	N.J.	5	22	3	86.4	CGY	6	38	5	86.8
7	ATL	2	9	1	88.9	S.J.	6	29	4	86.2	DET	18	91	12	86.8
8	VAN	6	36	4	88.9	NYR	5	26	4	84.6	ANA	21	121	16	86.8
9	OTT	9	45	7	84.4	ANA	9	52	9	82.7	NYI	5	24	4	83.3
10	BUF	9	42	8	81.0	BUF	7	33	6	81.8	S.J.	11	47	8	83.0
11	T.B.	3	15	3	80.0	DET	9	43	8	81.4	N.J.	11	46	8	82.6
12	N.J.	6	24	5	79.2	CGY	3	23	5	78.3	BUF	16	75	14	81.3
13	NYI	2	9	2	77.8	PIT	3	18	4	77.8	ATL	4	24	5	79.2
14	S.J.	5	18	4	77.8	ATL	2	15	4	73.3	PIT	5	24	6	75.0
15	MIN	2	8	2	75.0	MIN	3	11	3	72.7	T.B.	6	28	7	75.0
16	PIT	2	6	2	66.7	T.B.	3	13	4	69.2	MIN	5	19	5	73.7
Total		**81**	**400**	**53**	**86.8**		**81**	**432**	**68**	**84.3**		**81**	**832**	**121**	**85.5**

SHORT HAND GOALS

GOALS FOR			GOALS AGAINST		
Team	GP	GF	Team	GP	GA
DET	18	4	OTT	20	0
OTT	20	3	VAN	12	0
ANA	21	2	NYR	10	0
MIN	5	1	DAL	7	0
NSH	5	1	T.B.	6	0
T.B.	6	1	NYI	5	0
CGY	6	1	PIT	5	0
ATL	4	0	NSH	5	0
NYI	5	0	ATL	4	0
PIT	5	0	BUF	16	1
DAL	7	0	MIN	5	1
NYR	10	0	DET	18	2
N.J.	11	0	N.J.	11	2
S.J.	11	0	S.J.	11	2
VAN	12	0	CGY	6	2
BUF	16	0	ANA	21	3
Total	**81**	**13**		**81**	**13**

Ottawa's Daniel Alfredsson led all playoff scorers with 14 goals in 2007. His 22 points tied him for top spot with linemates Dany Heatley and Jason Spezza.

Stanley Cup Record Book

History: The Stanley Cup, the oldest trophy competed for by professional athletes in North America, was donated by Frederick Arthur, Lord Stanley of Preston and son of the Earl of Derby, in 1893. Lord Stanley purchased the trophy for 10 guineas ($50 at that time) for presentation to the amateur hockey champions of Canada. Since 1906, when Canadian teams began to pay their players openly, the Stanley Cup has been the symbol of professional hockey supremacy. It has been competed for only by NHL teams since 1926-27 and has been under the exclusive control of the NHL since 1947.

Stanley Cup Standings

1918-2007

(ranked by Cup wins)

Teams	Cup Wins	Yrs.	Series	Wins	Losses	Games	Wins	Losses	Ties	Goals For	Goals Against	Winning %
Montreal[1,2]	23	75	138	86	51	667	393	266	8	2050	1673	.595
Toronto[3]	13	64	109	58	51	524	251	269	4	1350	1427	.483
Detroit	10	55	103	58	45	518	269	248	1	1450	1332	.520
Boston	5	62	104	47	57	512	242	264	6	1488	1516	.479
Edmonton	5	20	49	34	15	251	152	99	0	938	763	.606
NY Rangers	4	50	89	43	46	400	189	203	8	1125	1154	.483
NY Islanders	4	21	47	30	17	240	134	106	0	792	714	.558
Chicago	3	53	90	40	50	411	188	218	5	1176	1311	.464
New Jersey[4]	3	18	37	22	15	213	117	96	0	593	513	.549
Philadelphia	2	31	65	36	29	346	180	166	0	1046	1016	.520
Pittsburgh	2	22	40	20	20	213	110	103	0	654	659	.516
Colorado[5]	2	19	41	24	17	233	126	107	0	689	651	.541
Dallas[6]	1	28	53	26	27	289	144	145	0	852	869	.498
Calgary[7]	1	24	38	15	23	195	89	106	0	605	661	.456
Carolina[8]	1	12	19	8	11	109	51	58	0	277	314	.469
Anaheim	1	5	14	10	4	73	44	29	0	180	168	.603
Tampa Bay	1	5	9	5	4	51	26	25	0	122	140	.510
St. Louis	0	34	57	23	34	303	138	165	0	857	943	.455
Buffalo	0	27	48	21	27	243	119	124	0	730	727	.490
Los Angeles	0	23	34	11	23	170	65	105	0	511	649	.382
Vancouver	0	21	32	11	21	167	71	96	0	473	552	.425
Washington	0	18	28	10	18	154	69	85	0	467	478	.448
Phoenix[9]	0	16	18	2	16	92	29	63	0	245	343	.315
San Jose	0	10	18	8	10	106	51	55	0	267	320	.481
Ottawa[10]	0	10	18	8	10	99	49	50	0	230	225	.495
Florida	0	3	6	3	3	31	13	18	0	77	82	.419
Nashville	0	3	3	0	3	16	4	12	0	33	45	.250
Minnesota	0	2	4	2	2	23	9	14	0	52	55	.391
Atlanta	0	1	1	0	1	4	0	4	0	6	17	.000
Columbus	0	0	0	0	0	0	0	0	0	0	0	.000

1 Montreal also won the Stanley Cup in 1916.
2 1919 final incomplete due to influenza epidemic.
3 Toronto Blueshirts also won the Stanley Cup in 1914.
4 Includes totals of Colorado Rockies 1976-82.
5 Includes totals of Quebec Nordiques 1979-95.
6 Includes totals of Minnesota North Stars 1967-93.
7 Includes totals of Atlanta Flames 1972-80.
8 Includes totals of Hartford Whalers 1979-97.
9 Includes totals of Winnipeg Jets 1979-96.
10 Modern Ottawa Senators franchise only, 1992 to date.

Stanley Cup Winners Prior to Formation of NHL in 1917

Season	Champions	Manager	Coach
1916-17	Seattle Metropolitans	Pete Muldoon	Pete Muldoon
1915-16	Montreal Canadiens	George Kennedy	George Kennedy
1914-15	Vancouver Millionaires	Frank Patrick	Frank Patrick
1913-14	Toronto Blueshirts	Jack Marshall	Scotty Davidson*
1912-13**	Quebec Bulldogs	M.J. Quinn	Joe Malone*
1911-12	Quebec Bulldogs	M.J. Quinn	C. Nolan
1910-11	Ottawa Senators		Percy LeSueur
1909-10	Montreal Wanderers (Mar. 1910)	Dickie Boon	Pud Glass*
1909-10	Ottawa Senators (Jan. 1910)		Bruce Stuart*
1908-09	Ottawa Senators		Bruce Stuart*
1907-08	Montreal Wanderers	Dickie Boon	Cecil Blachford
1906-07	Montreal Wanderers (Mar. 1907)	Dickie Boon	Cecil Blachford
1906-07	Kenora Thistles (Jan./Mar. 1907)	F.A. Hudson	Tom Phillips*
1905-06	Montreal Wanderers (Mar. 1906)	Cecil Blachford*	
1905-06	Ottawa Silver Seven (Feb. 1906)		Alf Smith
1904-05	Ottawa Silver Seven		Alf Smith
1903-04	Ottawa Silver Seven		Alf Smith
1902-03	Ottawa Silver Seven (Mar. 1903)		Alf Smith
1902-03	Montreal A.A.A. (Feb. 1903)		C. McKerrow
1901-02	Montreal A.A.A. (Mar. 1902)		C. McKerrow
1901-02	Winnipeg Victorias (Jan. 1902)		
1900-01	Winnipeg Victorias		Dan Bain*
1899-1900	Montreal Shamrocks		Harry Trihey*
1898-99	Montreal Shamrocks (Mar. 1899)		Harry Trihey*
1898-99	Montreal Victorias (Feb. 1899)		Mike Grant*
1897-98	Montreal Victorias		Frank Richardson
1896-97	Montreal Victorias		Mike Grant*
1895-96	Montreal Victorias (Dec. 1896)		Mike Grant*
1895-96	Winnipeg Victorias (Feb. 1896)		Jack Armitage
1894-95	Montreal Victorias		Mike Grant*
1893-94	Montreal A.A.A.		
1892-93	Montreal A.A.A.		

* In the early years the teams were frequently run by the Captain. *Indicates Captain
** Victoria defeated Quebec in challenge series. No official recognition.

Stanley Cup Winners

Year	W-L-T in Finals	Winner	Coach	Finalist	Coach
2007	4-1	Anaheim	Randy Carlyle	Ottawa	Bryan Murray
2006	4-3	Carolina	Peter Laviolette	Edmonton	Craig MacTavish
2005	....			....	....
2004	4-3	Tampa Bay	John Tortorella	Calgary	Darryl Sutter
2003	4-3	New Jersey	Pat Burns	Anaheim	Mike Babcock
2002	4-1	Detroit	Scotty Bowman	Carolina	Paul Maurice
2001	4-3	Colorado	Bob Hartley	New Jersey	Larry Robinson
2000	4-2	New Jersey	Larry Robinson	Dallas	Ken Hitchcock
1999	4-2	Dallas	Ken Hitchcock	Buffalo	Lindy Ruff
1998	4-0	Detroit	Scotty Bowman	Washington	Ron Wilson
1997	4-0	Detroit	Scotty Bowman	Philadelphia	Terry Murray
1996	4-0	Colorado	Marc Crawford	Florida	Doug MacLean
1995	4-0	New Jersey	Jacques Lemaire	Detroit	Scotty Bowman
1994	4-3	NY Rangers	Mike Keenan	Vancouver	Pat Quinn
1993	4-1	Montreal	Jacques Demers	Los Angeles	Barry Melrose
1992	4-0	Pittsburgh	Scotty Bowman	Chicago	Mike Keenan
1991	4-2	Pittsburgh	Bob Johnson	Minnesota	Bob Gainey
1990	4-1	Edmonton	John Muckler	Boston	Mike Milbury
1989	4-2	Calgary	Terry Crisp	Montreal	Pat Burns
1988	4-0	Edmonton	Glen Sather	Boston	Terry O'Reilly
1987	4-3	Edmonton	Glen Sather	Philadelphia	Mike Keenan
1986	4-1	Montreal	Jean Perron	Calgary	Bob Johnson
1985	4-1	Edmonton	Glen Sather	Philadelphia	Mike Keenan
1984	4-1	Edmonton	Glen Sather	NY Islanders	Al Arbour
1983	4-0	NY Islanders	Al Arbour	Edmonton	Glen Sather
1982	4-0	NY Islanders	Al Arbour	Vancouver	Roger Neilson
1981	4-1	NY Islanders	Al Arbour	Minnesota	Glen Sonmor
1980	4-2	NY Islanders	Al Arbour	Philadelphia	Pat Quinn
1979	4-1	Montreal	Scotty Bowman	NY Rangers	Fred Shero
1978	4-2	Montreal	Scotty Bowman	Boston	Don Cherry
1977	4-0	Montreal	Scotty Bowman	Boston	Don Cherry
1976	4-0	Montreal	Scotty Bowman	Philadelphia	Fred Shero
1975	4-2	Philadelphia	Fred Shero	Buffalo	Floyd Smith
1974	4-2	Philadelphia	Fred Shero	Boston	Bep Guidolin
1973	4-2	Montreal	Scotty Bowman	Chicago	Billy Reay
1972	4-2	Boston	Tom Johnson	NY Rangers	Emile Francis
1971	4-3	Montreal	Al MacNeil	Chicago	Billy Reay
1970	4-0	Boston	Harry Sinden	St. Louis	Scotty Bowman
1969	4-0	Montreal	Claude Ruel	St. Louis	Scotty Bowman
1968	4-0	Montreal	Toe Blake	St. Louis	Scotty Bowman
1967	4-2	Toronto	Punch Imlach	Montreal	Toe Blake
1966	4-2	Montreal	Toe Blake	Detroit	Sid Abel
1965	4-3	Montreal	Toe Blake	Chicago	Billy Reay
1964	4-3	Toronto	Punch Imlach	Detroit	Sid Abel
1963	4-1	Toronto	Punch Imlach	Detroit	Sid Abel
1962	4-2	Toronto	Punch Imlach	Chicago	Rudy Pilous
1961	4-2	Chicago	Rudy Pilous	Detroit	Sid Abel
1960	4-0	Montreal	Toe Blake	Toronto	Punch Imlach
1959	4-1	Montreal	Toe Blake	Toronto	Punch Imlach
1958	4-2	Montreal	Toe Blake	Boston	Milt Schmidt
1957	4-1	Montreal	Toe Blake	Boston	Milt Schmidt
1956	4-1	Montreal	Toe Blake	Detroit	Jimmy Skinner
1955	4-3	Detroit	Jimmy Skinner	Montreal	Dick Irvin
1954	4-3	Detroit	Tommy Ivan	Montreal	Dick Irvin
1953	4-1	Montreal	Dick Irvin	Boston	Lynn Patrick
1952	4-0	Detroit	Tommy Ivan	Montreal	Dick Irvin
1951	4-1	Toronto	Joe Primeau	Montreal	Dick Irvin
1950	4-3	Detroit	Tommy Ivan	NY Rangers	Lynn Patrick
1949	4-0	Toronto	Hap Day	Detroit	Tommy Ivan
1948	4-0	Toronto	Hap Day	Detroit	Tommy Ivan
1947	4-2	Toronto	Hap Day	Montreal	Dick Irvin
1946	4-1	Montreal	Dick Irvin	Boston	Dit Clapper
1945	4-3	Toronto	Hap Day	Detroit	Jack Adams
1944	4-0	Montreal	Dick Irvin	Chicago	Paul Thompson
1943	4-0	Detroit	Jack Adams	Boston	Art Ross
1942	4-3	Toronto	Hap Day	Detroit	Jack Adams
1941	4-0	Boston	Cooney Weiland	Detroit	Ebbie Goodfellow
1940	4-2	NY Rangers	Frank Boucher	Toronto	Dick Irvin
1939	4-1	Boston	Art Ross	Toronto	Dick Irvin
1938	3-1	Chicago	Bill Stewart	Toronto	Dick Irvin
1937	3-2	Detroit	Jack Adams	NY Rangers	Lester Patrick
1936	3-1	Detroit	Jack Adams	Toronto	Dick Irvin
1935	3-0	Mtl. Maroons	Tommy Gorman	Toronto	Dick Irvin
1934	3-1	Chicago	Tommy Gorman	Detroit	Herbie Lewis
1933	3-1	NY Rangers	Lester Patrick	Toronto	Dick Irvin
1932	3-0	Toronto	Dick Irvin	NY Rangers	Lester Patrick
1931	3-2	Montreal	Cecil Hart	Chicago	Dick Irvin
1930	2-0	Montreal	Cecil Hart	Boston	Art Ross
1929	2-0	Boston	Cy Denneny	NY Rangers	Lester Patrick
1928	3-2	NY Rangers	Lester Patrick	Mtl. Maroons	Eddie Gerard
1927	2-0-2	Ottawa	Dave Gill	Boston	Art Ross
		The National Hockey League assumed control of Stanley Cup competition after 1926			
1926	3-1	Mtl. Maroons	Eddie Gerard	Victoria	Lester Patrick
1925	3-1	Victoria	Lester Patrick	Montreal	Leo Dandurand
1924	2-0	Montreal	Leo Dandurand	Cgy. Tigers	Eddie Oatman
1923	2-0	Ottawa	Pete Green	Edm. Eskimos	Ken McKenzie
1922	3-2	Tor. St. Pats	George O'Donoghue	Van. Millionaires	Lloyd Cook/Frank Patrick
1921	3-2	Ottawa	Pete Green	Van. Millionaires	Lloyd Cook/Frank Patrick
1920	3-2	Ottawa	Pete Green	Seattle	Pete Muldoon
1919	2-2-1	No decision - series between Montreal and Seattle cancelled due to influenza epidemic			
1918	3-2	Tor. Arenas	Dick Carroll	Van. Millionaires	Frank Patrick

Championship Trophies

PRINCE OF WALES TROPHY

Beginning with the 1993-94 season, the club which advances to the Stanley Cup Finals as the winner of the Eastern Conference Championship is presented with the Prince of Wales Trophy.

History: His Royal Highness, the Prince of Wales, donated the trophy to the National Hockey League in 1925. It was originally awarded to the winner of the first game played in Madison Square Garden, December 15, 1925 (Montreal Canadiens 3 at NY Americans 1). It was then awarded to the NHL playoff champion in 1925-26 and 1926-27. From 1927-28 through 1937-38, the award was presented to the regular-season champion of the American Division of the NHL. (The team finishing first in the Canadian Division received the O'Brien Trophy during these years.) From 1938-39, when the NHL reverted to one section, to 1966-67, it was presented to the team winning the NHL regular-season championship. With expansion in 1967-68, it again became a divisional trophy, awarded to the regular-season champions of the East Division through to the end of the 1973-74 season. Beginning in 1974-75, it was awarded to the regular-season winner of the conference bearing the name of the trophy. From 1981-82 to 1992-93 the trophy was presented to the playoff champion in the Wales Conference. Since 1993-94, the trophy has been presented to the playoff champion in the Eastern Conference.

2006-07 Winner: Ottawa Senators

The Ottawa Senators won the Prince of Wales Trophy on May 19, 2007 after defeating the Buffalo Sabres 3-2 in overtime in game 5 of the Eastern Conference Finals. Before defeating the Sabres, the Senators had series wins over the Pittsburgh Penguins and the New Jersey Devils.

PRINCE OF WALES TROPHY WINNERS

2006-07	Ottawa	1977-78	Montreal	1949-50	Detroit
2005-06	Carolina	1976-77	Montreal	1948-49	Detroit
2003-04	Tampa Bay	1975-76	Montreal	1947-48	Toronto
2002-03	New Jersey	1974-75	Buffalo	1946-47	Montreal
2001-02	Carolina	1973-74	Boston	1945-46	Montreal
2000-01	New Jersey	1972-73	Montreal	1944-45	Montreal
99-2000	New Jersey	1971-72	Boston	1943-44	Montreal
1998-99	Buffalo	1970-71	Boston	1942-43	Detroit
1997-98	Washington	1969-70	Chicago	1941-42	NY Rangers
1996-97	Philadelphia	1968-69	Montreal	1940-41	Boston
1995-96	Florida	1967-68	Montreal	1939-40	Boston
1994-95	New Jersey	1966-67	Chicago	1938-39	Boston
1993-94	NY Rangers	1965-66	Montreal	1937-38	Boston
1992-93	Montreal	1964-65	Detroit	1936-37	Detroit
1991-92	Pittsburgh	1963-64	Montreal	1935-36	Detroit
1990-91	Pittsburgh	1962-63	Toronto	1934-35	Boston
1989-90	Boston	1961-62	Montreal	1933-34	Detroit
1988-89	Montreal	1960-61	Montreal	1932-33	Boston
1987-88	Boston	1959-60	Montreal	1931-32	NY Rangers
1986-87	Philadelphia	1958-59	Montreal	1930-31	Boston
1985-86	Montreal	1957-58	Montreal	1929-30	Boston
1984-85	Philadelphia	1956-57	Detroit	1928-29	Boston
1983-84	NY Islanders	1955-56	Montreal	1927-28	Boston
1982-83	NY Islanders	1954-55	Detroit	1926-27	Ottawa
1981-82	NY Islanders	1953-54	Detroit	1925-26	Mtl. Maroons
1980-81	Montreal	1952-53	Detroit	Dec. 15/25	Montreal
1979-80	Buffalo	1951-52	Detroit	1923-24	Montreal*
1978-79	Montreal	1950-51	Detroit		

* Engraved by Montreal Canadiens in 1925-26.

Prince of Wales Trophy

Clarence S. Campbell Bowl

Stanley Cup

CLARENCE S. CAMPBELL BOWL

Beginning with the 1993-94 season, the club which advances to the Stanley Cup Finals as the winner of the Western Conference Championship is presented with the Clarence S. Campbell Bowl.

History: Presented by the member clubs in 1968 for perpetual competition by the National Hockey League in recognition of the services of Clarence S. Campbell, President of the NHL from 1946 to 1977. From 1967-68 through 1973-74, the trophy was awarded to the regular-season champions of the West Division. Beginning in 1974-75, it was awarded to the regular-season winner of the conference bearing the name of the trophy. From 1981-82 to 1992-93 the trophy was presented to the playoff champion in the Campbell Conference. Since 1993-94, the trophy has been presented to the playoff champion in the Western Conference. The trophy itself is a hallmark piece made of sterling silver and was crafted by a British silversmith in 1878.

2006-07 Winner: Anaheim Ducks

The Anaheim Ducks won their second Clarence Campbell Bowl on May 22, 2007 after defeating the Detroit Red Wings 4-3 in game 6 of the Western Conference Finals. Before defeating the Red Wings, the Ducks had series wins over the Minnesota Wild and the Vancouver Canucks.

CLARENCE S. CAMPBELL BOWL WINNERS

2006-07	Anaheim	1992-93	Los Angeles	1979-80	Philadelphia
2005-06	Edmonton	1991-92	Chicago	1978-79	NY Islanders
2003-04	Calgary	1990-91	Minnesota	1977-78	NY Islanders
2002-03	Anaheim	1989-90	Edmonton	1976-77	Philadelphia
2001-02	Detroit	1988-89	Calgary	1975-76	Philadelphia
2000-01	Colorado	1987-88	Edmonton	1974-75	Philadelphia
99-2000	Dallas	1986-87	Edmonton	1973-74	Philadelphia
1998-99	Dallas	1985-86	Calgary	1972-73	Chicago
1997-98	Detroit	1984-85	Edmonton	1971-72	Chicago
1996-97	Detroit	1983-84	Edmonton	1970-71	Chicago
1995-96	Colorado	1982-83	Edmonton	1969-70	St. Louis
1994-95	Detroit	1981-82	Vancouver	1968-69	St. Louis
1993-94	Vancouver	1980-81	NY Islanders	1967-68	Philadelphia

Stanley Cup Winners

Rosters and Final Series Scores

2006-07 — Anaheim Ducks — Scott Niedermayer (Captain), Francois Beauchemin, Ilya Bryzgalov, Ryan Carter, Joe DiPenta, Ryan Getzlaf, Jean-Sebastien Giguere, Kent Huskins, Ric Jackman, Chris Kunitz, Todd Marchant, Brad May, Andy McDonald, Drew Miller, Travis Moen, Joe Motzko, Rob Niedermayer, Sean O'Donnell, Samuel Pahlsson, George Parros, Dustin Penner, Corey Perry, Chris Pronger, Teemu Selanne, Ryan Shannon, Shawn Thornton, Henry Samueli (Owner), Susan Samueli (Owner), Michael Schulman (CEO), Brian Burke (Executive Vice-President/General Manager), Tim Ryan (Executive Vice-President/COO), Bob Murray (Senior Vice-President/Hockey Operations), David McNab (Assistant General Manager), Randy Carlyle (Head Coach), Dave Farrish (Assistant Coach), Newell Brown (Assistant Coach), Francois Allaire (Goaltending Consultant), Joe Trotta (Video Coordinator), Tim Clark (Head Trainer), Mark O'Neill (Equipment Manager), John Allaway (Assistant Equipment Manager), Sean Skahan (Strength and Conditioning Coach), James Partida (Massage Therapist), Rick Paterson (Director of Professional Scouting), Alain Chainey (Director of Amateur Scouting), Al Coates (Senior Advisor to GM).

Scores: May 28, at Anaheim - Anaheim 3, Ottawa 2; May 30, at Anaheim - Anaheim 1, Ottawa 0; June 2, at Ottawa - Ottawa 5, Anaheim 3; June 4, at Ottawa - Anaheim 3, Ottawa 2; June 6, at Anaheim - Anaheim 6, Ottawa 2.

2005-06 — Carolina Hurricanes — Rod Brind'Amour (Captain), Craig Adams, Kevyn Adams, Anton Babchuk, Erik Cole, Mike Commodore, Matt Cullen, Martin Gerber, Bret Hedican, Andrew Hutchinson, Frantisek Kaberle, Chad LaRose, Andrew Ladd, Mark Recchi, Eric Staal, Cory Stillman, Oleg Tverdovsky, Josef Vasicek, Niclas Wallin, Aaron Ward, Cam Ward, Doug Weight, Glen Wesley, Ray Whitney, Justin Williams, Peter Karmanos Jr. (Owner), Thomas Thewes (Owner), Jim Rutherford (President and General Manager), Jason Karmanos (Vice President and Assistant General Manager), Mike Amendola (Chief Financial Officer), Peter Laviolette (Head Coach), Kevin McCarthy, Jeff Daniels (Assistant Coaches), Greg Stefan (Goaltending Coach), Chris Huffine (Video Coordinator), Skip Cunningham, Wally Tatomir, Bob Gorman (Equipment Managers), Peter Friesen (Head Athletic Therapist and Strength and Conditioning Coach), Chris Stewart (Associate Athletic Trainer), Brian Tatum (Team Services Manager), Kelly Kirwin (Event Coordinator for Hockey Operations), Marshall Johnston (Director of Professional Scouting), Claude Larose, Ron Smith (Professional Scouts), Sheldon Ferguson (Director of Amateur Scouting), Tony MacDonald, Albert Marshall, Martin Madden (Amateur Scouts), Tom Rowe (Head Coach, Lowell Lock Monsters), Mike Sundheim (Director of Media Relations), Kyle Hanlin (Manager of Media Relations).

Scores: June 5, at Carolina - Carolina 5, Edmonton 4; June 7, at Carolina - Carolina 5, Edmonton 0; June 10, at Edmonton - Edmonton 2, Carolina 1; June 12, at Edmonton - Carolina 2, Edmonton 1; June 14, at Carolina - Edmonton 4, Carolina 3; June 17, at Edmonton - Edmonton 4, Carolina 0; June 19, at Carolina - Carolina 3, Edmonton 1.

2003-04 — Tampa Bay Lightning — Dave Andreychuk (Captain), Dimitry Afanasenkov, Dan Boyle, Martin Cibak, Ben Clymer, Jassen Cullimore, Chris Dingman, Ruslan Fedotenko, John Grahame, Nikolai Khabibulin, Pavel Kubina, Vincent Lecavalier, Brad Lukowich, Fredrik Modin, Stan Neckar, Eric Perrin, Nolan Pratt, Brad Richards, Andre Roy, Martin St. Louis, Cory Sarich, Cory Stillman, Darryl Sydor, Tim Taylor, Bill Davidson (Owner), Tom Wilson (Governor), Ron Campbell (President), Jay Feaster (General Manager), Bill Barber (Director of Player Personnel), John Tortorella (Head Coach), Craig Ramsay (Assistant Coach), Jeff Reese (Assistant Coach), Eric Lawson (Strength and Conditioning Coach), Nigel Kinwan (Video Coach), Jack Goertzen (Head Scout), Rick Paterson (Chief Professional Scout), Mikael Andersson, Stephen Baker, Larry Bernard, Dirk Graham, Dave Heitz, Karri Kettunen, Yuri Yanchenkov, Darrell Young, Glen Zacharias (Scouts),Phil Thibodeau (Director of Team Services), Thomas Mulligan (Trainer), Adam Rambo (Assistant Trainer), Mike Griebel (Massage Therapist), Ray Thill (Equipment Manager), Dana Heinze, Jim Pickard (Assistant Equipment Managers).

Scores: May 25, at Tampa Bay - Calgary 4, Tampa Bay 1; May 27, at Tampa Bay - Tampa Bay 4, Calgary 1; May 29, at Calgary - Calgary 3, Tampa Bay 0; May 31, at Calgary - Tampa Bay 1, Calgary 0; June 3, at Tampa Bay - Calgary 3, Tampa Bay 2; June 5, at Calgary - Tampa Bay 3, Calgary 2; June 7, at Tampa Bay - Tampa Bay 2, Calgary 1.

2002-03 — New Jersey Devils — Scott Stevens (Captain), Tommy Albelin, Jiri Bicek, Martin Brodeur, Sergei Brylin, Ken Daneyko, Patrik Elias, Jeff Friesen, Brian Gionta, Scott Gomez, Jamie Langenbrunner, John Madden, Grant Marshall, Jim McKenzie, Scott Niedermayer, Joe Nieuwendyk, Jay Pandolfo, Brian Rafalski, Pascal Rheaume, Mike Rupp, Corey Schwab, Richard Smehlik, Turner Stevenson, Oleg Tverdovsky, Colin White, Lou Lamoriello (CEO/President/General Manager), Pat Burns (Head Coach), Bob Carpenter (Assistant Coach), John MacLean (Assistant Coach), Jacques Caron (Goaltending Coach), Larry Robinson (Special Assignment Coach), David Conte (Director, Scouting), Claude Carrier (Assistant Director, Scouting), Chris Lamoriello (Scout/Albany GM), Milt Fisher (Scout), Dan Labraaten (Scout), Marcel Pronovost (Scout), Bob Hoffmeyer (Pro Scout), Jan Ludvig (Pro Scout), Dr. Barry Fisher (Orthopedist), Vladimir Bure (Fitness Consultant), Taran Singleton (Hockey Operations), Bill Murray (Medical Trainer), Michael Vasalani (Strength/Conditioning Coordinator), Rich Matthews (Equipment Manager), Juergen Merz (Massage Therapist), Alex Abasto (Assistant Equipment Manager).

Scores: May 27, at New Jersey - New Jersey 3, Anaheim 0; May 29, at New Jersey - New Jersey 3, Anaheim 0; May 31, at Anaheim - Anaheim 3, New Jersey 2; June 2, at Anaheim - Anaheim 1, New Jersey 0; June 5, at New Jersey - New Jersey 6, Anaheim 3; June 7, at Anaheim - Anaheim 5, New Jersey 2; June 9, at New Jersey - New Jersey 3, Anaheim 0.

2001-02 — Detroit Red Wings — Steve Yzerman (Captain), Chris Chelios, Mathieu Dandenault, Pavel Datsyuk, Boyd Devereaux, Kris Draper, Steve Duchesne, Sergei Fedorov, Jiri Fischer, Dominik Hasek, Tomas Holmstrom, Brett Hull, Igor Larionov, Manny Legace, Nicklas Lidstrom, Kirk Maltby, Darren McCarty, Fredrik Olausson, Luc Robitaille, Brendan Shanahan, Jiri Slegr, Jason Williams, Michael Ilitch (Owner/Governor) Marian Ilitch (Owner/Secretary Treasurer), Ronald Ilitch, Michael Ilitch Jr., Lisa Ilitch Murray, Atanas Ilitch, Carole Ilitch Trepeck, Jim Devallano (Senior Vice President), Christopher Ilitch (Vice President), Denise Ilitch (Alternate Governor), Ken Holland (General Manager), Jim Nill (Assistant General Manager), Scotty Bowman (Head Coach), Dave Lewis (Associate Coach), Barry Smith (Associate Coach), Jim Berard (Goaltending Consultant), Joe Kocur (Video Coordinator), John Wharton (Athletic Trainer), Paul Boyer (Equipment Manager), Piet Van Zant (Assistant Athletic Trainer), Tim Abbott (Assistant Equipment Manager), Sergei Tchekmarev (Masseur), Dan Belisle (Pro Scout), Mark Howe (Pro Scout), Bob McCammon (Pro Scout), Hakan Andersson (Director of European Scouting), Mark Leach (Scout), Bruce Haralson (Scout), Joe McDonnell (Scout), Glenn Merkosky (Scout).

Scores: June 4, at Detroit - Carolina 3, Detroit 2; June 6, at Detroit - Detroit 3, Carolina 1; June 8, at Carolina - Detroit 3, Carolina 2; June 10, at Carolina - Detroit 3, Carolina 0; June 13, at Detroit - Detroit 3, Carolina 1.

2000-01 — Colorado Avalanche — Joe Sakic (Captain), David Aebischer, Rob Blake, Raymond Bourque, Greg de Vries, Chris Dingman, Chris Drury, Adam Foote, Peter Forsberg, Milan Hejduk, Dan Hinote, Jon Klemm, Eric Messier, Bryan Muir, Ville Nieminen, Scott Parker, Shjon Podein, Nolan Pratt, Dave Reid, Steve Reinprecht, Patrick Roy, Martin Skoula, Alex Tanguay, Stephane Yelle, E. Stanley Kroenke (Owner/Governor), Pierre Lacroix (President and General Manager), Bob Hartley (Head Coach), Jacques Cloutier (Assistant Coach), Bryan Trottier (Assistant Coach), Paul Fixter (Video Coach), Francois Giguere (Vice President of Hockey Operations), Brian MacDonald (Assistant General Manager), Michel Goulet (Vice President of Player Personnel), Jean Martineau (Vice President of Communications/Team Services), Pat Karns (Head Athletic Trainer), Matthew Sokolowski (Assistant Athletic Trainer), Wayne Flemming (Equipment Manager), Mark Miller (Equipment Manager), Dave Randolph (Assistant Equipment Manager), Paul Goldberg (Strength and Conditioning Coach), Gregorio Pradera (Massage Therapist), Brad Smith (Pro Scout), Jim Hammett (Chief Scout), Garth Joy, Steve Lyons, Joni Lehto, Orval Tessier (Scouts), Charlotte Grahame (Director of Hockey Operations).

Scores: May 26, at Colorado - Colorado 5, New Jersey 0; May 29, at Colorado - New Jersey 2, Colorado 1; May 31, at New Jersey - Colorado 3, New Jersey 1; June 2, at New Jersey - New Jersey 3, Colorado 2; June 4, at Colorado - New Jersey 4, Colorado 1; June 7, at New Jersey - Colorado 4, New Jersey 0; June 9, at Colorado - Colorado 3, New Jersey 1.

1999-2000 — New Jersey Devils — Scott Stevens (Captain), Jason Arnott, Brad Bombardir, Martin Brodeur, Steve Brule, Sergei Brylin, Ken Daneyko, Patrik Elias, Scott Gomez, Bobby Holik, Steve Kelly, Claude Lemieux, John Madden, Vladimir Malakhov, Randy McKay, Alexander Mogilny, Sergei Nemchinov, Scott Niedermayer, Krzysztof Oliwa, Jay Pandolfo, Brian Rafalski, Ken Sutton, Petr Sykora, Chris Terreri, Colin White, Dr. John J. McMullen (Owner/Chairman), Peter S. McMullen (Owner), Lou Lamoriello (President/General Manager), Larry Robinson (Head Coach), Viacheslav Fetisov (Assistant Coach), Bob Carpenter (Assistant Coach), Jacques Caron (Goaltending Coach), John Cunniff (AHL Coach), David Conte (Director of Scouting), Milt Fisher (Scout), Claude Carrier (Assistant Director of Scouting), Dan Labraaten (Scout), Marcel Pronovost (Scout), Bob Hoffmeyer (Pro Scout), Dr. Barry Fisher (Orthopedist), Dennis Gendron (AHL Assistant Coach), Robbie Ftorek (Coach), Vladimir Bure (Consultant), Taran Singleton (Hockey Operations), Marie Carnevale (Hockey Operations), Callie Smith (Hockey Operations), Bill Murray (Medical Trainer), Michael Vasalani (Strength/Conditioning Coordinator), Dana McGuane (Equipment Manager), Juergen Merz (Massage Therapist), Harry Bricker (Assistant Equipment Manager), Lou Centanni (Assistant Equipment Manager).

Scores: May 30, at New Jersey - New Jersey 7, Dallas 3; June 1, at New Jersey - Dallas 2, New Jersey 1; June 3, at Dallas - New Jersey 2, Dallas 1; June 5, at Dallas - New Jersey 3, Dallas 1; June 8, at New Jersey - Dallas 1 - New Jersey 0; at Dallas, New Jersey 2 - Dallas 1.

1998-99 — Dallas Stars — Derian Hatcher (Captain), Ed Belfour, Guy Carbonneau, Shawn Chambers, Benoit Hogue, Tony Hrkac, Brett Hull, Mike Keane, Jamie Langenbrunner, Jere Lehtinen, Craig Ludwig, Grant Marshall, Richard Matvichuk, Mike Modano, Joe Nieuwendyk, Derek Plante, Dave Reid, Jon Sim, Brian Skrudland, Blake Sloan, Darryl Sydor, Roman Turek, Pat Verbeek, Sergei Zubov, Thomas Hicks (Chairman of the Board and Owner), Jim Lites (President), Bob Gainey (Vice President, Hockey Operations and General Manager), Doug Armstrong (Assistant General Manager), Craig Button (Director of Player Personnel), Ken Hitchcock (Head Coach), Doug Jarvis (Assistant Coach), Rick Wilson (Assistant Coach), Rick McLaughlin (Vice President and Chief Financial Officer), Jeff Cogen (Vice President, Marketing and Promotion), Bill Strong (Vice President, Marketing and Broadcasting), Tim Bernhardt (Director of Amateur Scouting), Doug Overton (Director of Pro Scouting), Bob Gernander (Chief Scout), Stu MacGregor (Western Scout), Dave Suprenant (Medical Trainer), Dave Smith (Equipment Manager), Rich Matthews (Equipment Manager), J.J. McQueen (Strength and Conditioning Coach), Rick St. Croix (Goaltending Consultant), Dan Stuchal (Director of Team Services), Larry Kelly (Director of Public Relations).

Scores: June 8, at Dallas - Buffalo 3, Dallas 2; June 10, at Dallas - Dallas 4, Buffalo 2; June 12, at Buffalo - Dallas 2, Buffalo 1; June 15, at Buffalo - Buffalo 2, Dallas 1; June 17, at Dallas - Dallas 2, Buffalo 0; June 19, at Buffalo - Dallas 2, Buffalo 1.

1997-98 — Detroit Red Wings — Steve Yzerman (Captain), Doug Brown, Mathieu Dandenault, Kris Draper, Anders Eriksson, Sergei Fedorov, Viacheslav Fetisov, Brent Gilchrist, Kevin Hodson, Tomas Holmstrom, Mike Knuble, Joe Kocur, Vladimir Konstantinov, Vyacheslav Kozlov, Martin Lapointe, Igor Larionov, Nicklas Lidstrom, Jamie Macoun, Kirk Maltby, Darren McCarty, Dmitri Mironov, Larry Murphy, Chris Osgood, Bob Rouse, Brendan Shanahan, Aaron Ward, Mike Ilitch, (Owner/Chairman), Marian Ilitch (Owner), Atanas Ilitch (Vice President), Christopher Ilitch (Vice President), Denise Ilitch, Ronald Ilitch, Michael Ilitch Jr., Lisa Ilitch Murray, Carole Ilitch Trepeck, Jim Devellano (Senior Vice President), Scotty Bowman (Head Coach), Ken Holland (General Manager), Don Waddell (Assistant General Manager), Barry Smith (Associate Coach), Dave Lewis (Associate Coach), Jim Bedard (Goaltending Consultant), Jim Nill (Director of Player Development), Dan Belisle (Pro Scout), Mark Howe (Pro Scout), Hakan Andersson (Director of European Scouting), Mark Leach (USA Scout), Moe McDonnell (Eastern Scout), Bruce Haralson (Western Scout), John Wharton (Athletic Trainer), Paul Boyer (Equipment Manager) Tim Abbott (Assistant Equipment Manager), Bob Huddleston (Masseur), Sergei Mnatsakanov (Masseur), Wally Crossman (Dressing Room Assistant).

Scores: June 9, at Detroit — Detroit 2, Washington 1; June 11, at Detroit — Detroit 5, Washington 4; June 13, at Washington — Detroit 2, Washington 1; June 16, at Washington — Detroit 4, Washington 1.

1996-97 — Detroit Red Wings — Steve Yzerman (Captain), Doug Brown, Mathieu Dandenault, Kris Draper, Sergei Fedorov, Viacheslav Fetisov, Kevin Hodson, Tomas Holmstrom, Joe Kocur, Vladimir Konstantinov, Vyacheslav Kozlov, Martin Lapointe, Igor Larionov, Nicklas Lidstrom, Kirk Maltby, Darren McCarty, Larry Murphy, Chris Osgood, Jamie Pushor, Bob Rouse, Tomas Sandstrom, Brendan Shanahan, Tim Taylor, Mike Vernon, Aaron Ward, Mike Ilitch (Owner/Chairman), Marian Ilitch (Owner), Atanas Ilitch (Vice President), Christopher Ilitch (Vice President), Denise Ilitch Lites, Ronald Ilitch, Michael Ilitch, Jr., Lisa Ilitch Murray, Carole Ilitch Trepeck, Jim Devellano (Senior Vice President), Scotty Bowman (Head Coach/Director of Player Personnel), Ken Holland (Assistant General Manager), Barry Smith (Associate Coach), Dave Lewis (Associate Coach), Mike Krushelnyski (Assistant Coach). Jim Nill (Director of Player Development), Dan Belisle (Pro Scout), Mark Howe (Pro Scout), Hakan Andersson (Director of European Scouting), John Wharton (Athletic Trainer), Paul Boyer (Equipment Manager) Tim Abbott (Assistant Equipment Manager), Sergei Mnatsakanov (Masseur).

Scores: May 31, at Philadelphia — Detroit 4, Philadelphia 2; June 3, at Philadelphia — Detroit 4, Philadelphia 2; June 5, at Detroit — Detroit 6, Philadelphia 1; June 7, at Detroit — Detroit 2, Philadelphia 1.

1995-96 — Colorado Avalanche — Joe Sakic (Captain), Rene Corbet, Adam Deadmarsh, Stephane Fiset, Adam Foote, Peter Forsberg, Alexei Gusarov, Dave Hannan, Valeri Kamensky, Mike Keane, Jon Klemm, Uwe Krupp, Sylvain Lefebvre, Claude Lemieux, Curtis Leschyshyn, Troy Murray, Sandis Ozolinsh, Mike Ricci, Patrick Roy, Warren Rychel, Chris Simon, Craig Wolanin, Stephane Yelle, Scott Young, Charlie Lyons (Chairman, CEO), Pierre Lacroix (Exec. V.P., G.M.), Marc Crawford (Head Coach), Joel Quenneville (Assistant Coach), Jacques Cloutier (Assistant Coach), Francois Giguere (Assistant General Manager), Michel Goulet (Director of Player Personnel), Dave Draper (Chief Scout), Jean Martineau (Director of Public Relations), Pat Karns (Trainer), Matthew Sokolowski (Assistant Trainer), Rob McLean (Equipment Manager), Mike Kramer (Assistant Equipment Manager), Brock Gibbins (Assistant Equipment Manager), Skip Allen (Strength and Conditioning Coach), Paul Fixter (Video Coordinator), Leo Vyssokov (Massage Therapist).

Scores: June 4, at Colorado — Colorado 3, Florida 1; June 6, at Colorado — Colorado 8, Florida 1; June 8, at Florida — Colorado 3, Florida 2; June 10, at Florida — Colorado 1, Florida 0.

1994-95 — New Jersey Devils — Scott Stevens (Captain), Tommy Albelin, Martin Brodeur, Neal Broten, Sergei Brylin, Bob Carpenter, Shawn Chambers, Tom Chorske, Danton Cole, Ken Daneyko, Kevin Dean, Jim Dowd, Bruce Driver (Alternate Captain), Bill Guerin, Bobby Holik, Claude Lemieux, John MacLean (Alternate Captain), Chris McAlpine, Randy McKay, Scott Niedermayer, Mike Peluso, Stephane Richer, Brian Rolston, Chris Terreri, Valeri Zelepukin, Dr. John J. McMullen (Owner/Chairman), Peter S. McMullen (Owner), Lou Lamoriello (President/General Manager), Jacques Lemaire (Head Coach), Jacques Caron (Goaltender Coach), Dennis Gendron (Assistant Coach), Larry Robinson (Assistant Coach), Robbie Ftorek (AHL Coach), Alex Abasto (Assistant Equipment Manager), Bob Huddleston (Massage Therapist), David Nichols (Equipment Manager), Ted Schuch (Medical Trainer), Mike Vasalani (Strength Coach), David Conte (Director of Scouting) Claude Carrier (Scout), Milt Fisher (Scout), Dan Labraaten (Scout), Marcel Pronovost (Scout).

Scores: June 17, at Detroit — New Jersey 2, Detroit 1; June 20, at Detroit — New Jersey 4, Detroit 2; June 22, at New Jersey — New Jersey 5, Detroit 2; June 24, at New Jersey — New Jersey 5, Detroit 2.

1993-94 — New York Rangers — Mark Messier (Captain), Brian Leetch, Kevin Lowe, Adam Graves, Steve Larmer, Glenn Anderson, Jeff Beukeboom, Greg Gilbert, Mike Hartman, Glenn Healy, Mike Hudson, Alexander Karpovtsev, Joe Kocur, Alexei Kovalev, Nick Kypreos, Doug Lidster, Stephane Matteau, Craig MacTavish, Sergei Nemchinov, Brian Noonan, Ed Olczyk, Mike Richter, Esa Tikkanen, Jay Wells, Sergei Zubov, Neil Smith (President, General Manager and Governor), Robert Gutkowski, Stanley Jaffe, Kenneth Munoz (Governors), Larry Pleau (Assistant General Manager), Mike Keenan (Head Coach), Colin Campbell (Associate Coach), Dick Todd (Assistant Coach), Matthew Loughren (Manager, Team Operations), Barry Watkins (Director, Communications), Christer Rockstrom, Tony Feltrin, Martin Madden, Herb Hammond, Darwin Bennett (Scouts), Dave Smith, Joe Murphy, Mike Folga, Bruce Lifrieri (Trainers).
Scores: May 31, at New York — Vancouver 3, NY Rangers 2; June 2, at New York — NY Rangers 3, Vancouver 1; June 4, at Vancouver — NY Rangers 5, Vancouver 1; June 7, at Vancouver — NY Rangers 4, Vancouver 2; June 9, at New York — Vancouver 6, at NY Rangers 3; June 11, at Vancouver — Vancouver 4, NY Rangers 1; June 14, at New York — NY Rangers 3, Vancouver 2.

1992-93 — Montreal Canadiens — Guy Carbonneau (Captain), Patrick Roy, Mike Keane, Eric Desjardins, Stephan Lebeau, Mathieu Schneider, J-J Daigneault, Denis Savard, Lyle Odelein, Todd Ewen, Kirk Muller, John LeClair, Gilbert Dionne, Benoit Brunet, Patrice Brisebois, Paul DiPietro, Andre Racicot, Donald Dufresne, Mario Roberge, Sean Hill, Ed Ronan, Kevin Haller, Vincent Damphousse, Brian Bellows, Gary Leeman, Rob Ramage, Ronald Corey (President), Serge Savard (Managing Director & Vice-President Hockey), Jacques Demers (Head Coach), Jacques Laperriere (Assistant Coach), Charles Thiffault (Assistant Coach), Francois Allaire (Goaltending Instructor), Jean Béliveau (Senior Vice-President, Corporate Affairs), Fred Steer (Vice-President, Finance & Adminstration), Aldo Giampaolo (Vice-President, Operations), Bernard Brisset (Vice-President, Marketing & Communications), André Boudrias (Assistant to the Managing Director & Director of Scouting), Jacques Lemaire (Assistant to the Managing Director), Gaeten Lefebvre (Athletic Trainer), John Shipman (Assistant to the Athletic Trainer), Eddy Palchak (Equipment Manager), Pierre Gervais (Assistant to the Equipment Manager), Robert Boulanger (Assistant to the Equipment Manager), Pierre Ouellete (Assistant to the Equipment Manager).
Scores: June 1, at Montreal — Los Angeles 4, Montreal 1; June 2, at Montreal — Montreal 3, Los Angeles 2; June 5, at Los Angeles — Montreal 4, Los Angeles 3; June 7, at Los Angeles — Montreal 3, Los Angeles 2; June 9, at Montreal — Montreal 4, Los Angeles 1.

1991-92 — Pittsburgh Penguins — Mario Lemieux (Captain), Ron Francis, Bryan Trottier, Kevin Stevens, Bob Errey, Phil Bourque, Troy Loney, Rick Tocchet, Joe Mullen, Jaromir Jagr, Jiri Hrdina, Shawn McEachern, Ulf Samuelsson, Kjell Samuelsson, Larry Murphy, Gordie Roberts, Jim Paek, Paul Stanton, Tom Barrasso, Ken Wregget, Jay Caufield, Jamie Leach, Wendell Young, Grant Jennings, Peter Taglianetti, Jock Callander, Dave Michayluk, Mike Needham, Jeff Chychrun, Ken Priestlay, Jeff Daniels, Howard Baldwin (Owner and President), Morris Belzberg (Owner), Thomas Ruta (Owner), Donn Patton (Executive Vice President and Chief Financial Officer), Paul Martha (Executive Vice President and General Counsel), Craig Patrick (Executive Vice President and General Manager), Bob Johnson (Coach), Scotty Bowman (Director of Player Development and Coach), Barry Smith, Rick Kehoe, Pierre McGuire, Gilles Meloche, Rick Paterson (Assistant Coaches), Steve Latin (Equipment Manager), Skip Thayer (Trainer), John Welday (Strength and Conditioning Coach), Greg Malone, Les Binkley, Charlie Hodge, John Gill, Ralph Cox (Scouts).
Scores: May 26, at Pittsburgh — Pittsburgh 5, Chicago 4; May 28, at Pittsburgh — Pittsburgh 3, Chicago 1; May 30, at Chicago — Pittsburgh 1, Chicago 0; June 1, at Chicago — Pittsburgh 6, Chicago 5.

1990-91 — Pittsburgh Penguins — Mario Lemieux (Captain), Paul Coffey, Randy Hillier, Bob Errey, Tom Barrasso, Phil Bourque, Jay Caufield, Ron Francis, Randy Gilhen, Jiri Hrdina, Jaromir Jagr, Grant Jennings, Troy Loney, Joe Mullen, Larry Murphy, Jim Paek, Frank Pietrangelo, Barry Pederson, Mark Recchi, Gordie Roberts, Ulf Samuelsson, Paul Stanton, Kevin Stevens, Peter Taglianetti, Bryan Trottier, Scott Young, Wendell Young, Edward J. DeBartolo, Sr. (Owner), Marie D. DeBartolo York (President), Paul Martha (Vice-President & General Counsel), Craig Patrick (General Manager), Scotty Bowman (Director of Player Development & Recruitment), Bob Johnson (Coach), Rick Kehoe (Assistant Coach), Gilles Meloche (Goaltending Coach & Scout), Rick Paterson (Assistant Coach), Barry Smith (Assistant Coach), Steve Latin (Equipment Manager), Skip Thayer (Trainer), John Welday (Strength & Conditioning Coach), Greg Malone (Scout).
Scores: May 15, at Pittsburgh — Minnesota 5, Pittsburgh 4; May 17, at Pittsburgh — Pittsburgh 4, Minnesota 1; May 19, at Minnesota — Minnesota 3, Pittsburgh 1; May 21, at Minnesota — Pittsburgh 5, Minnesota 3; May 23, at Pittsburgh — Pittsburgh 6, Minnesota 4; May 25, at Minnesota — Pittsburgh 8, Minnesota 0.

1989-90 — Edmonton Oilers — Kevin Lowe, Steve Smith, Jeff Beukeboom, Mark Lamb, Joe Murphy, Glenn Anderson, Mark Messier (Captain), Adam Graves, Craig MacTavish, Kelly Buchberger, Jari Kurri, Craig Simpson, Martin Gelinas, Randy Gregg, Charlie Huddy, Geoff Smith, Reijo Ruotsalainen, Craig Muni, Bill Ranford, Dave Brown, Pokey Reddick, Petr Klima, Esa Tikkanen, Grant Fuhr, Peter Pocklington (Owner), Glen Sather (President/General Manager), John Muckler (Coach), Ted Green (Co-Coach), Ron Low (Ass't Coach), Bruce MacGregor (Ass't General Manager), Barry Fraser (Director of Player Personnel), John Blackwell (Director of Operations, AHL), Ace Bailey, Ed Chadwick, Lorne Davis, Harry Howell, Matti Vaisanen and Albert Reeves (Scouts), Bill Tuele (Director of Public Relations), Werner Baum (Controller), Dr. Gordon Cameron (Medical Chief of Staff), Dr. David Reid (Team Physician), Barrie Stafford (Athletic Trainer), Ken Lowe (Athletic Therapist), Stuart Poirier (Massage Therapist), Lyle Kulchisky (Ass't Trainer).
Scores: May 15, at Boston — Edmonton 3, Boston 2; May 18, at Boston — Edmonton 7, Boston 2; May 20, at Edmonton — Boston 2, Edmonton 1; May 22, at Edmonton — Edmonton 5, Boston 1; May 24, at Boston — Edmonton 4, Boston 1.

1988-89 — Calgary Flames — Mike Vernon, Rick Wamsley, Al MacInnis, Brad McCrimmon, Dana Murzyn, Ric Nattress, Joe Mullen, Lanny McDonald (Co-captain), Gary Roberts, Colin Patterson, Hakan Loob, Theoren Fleury, Jiri Hrdina, Tim Hunter (Ass't. captain), Gary Suter, Mark Hunter, Jim Peplinski (Co-captain), Joe Nieuwendyk, Brian MacLellan, Joel Otto, Jamie Macoun, Doug Gilmour, Rob Ramage. Norman Green, Harley Hotchkiss, Norman Kwong, Sonia Scurfield, B.J. Seaman, D.K. Seaman (Owners), Cliff Fletcher (President and General Manager), Al MacNeil (Ass't General Manager), Al Coates (Ass't to the President), Terry Crisp (Head Coach), Doug Risebrough, Tom Watt (Ass't Coaches), Glenn Hall (Goaltending Consultant), Jim Murray (Trainer), Bob Stewart (Equipment Manager), Al Murray (Ass't Trainer).
Scores: May 14, at Calgary — Calgary 3, Montreal 2; May 17, at Calgary— Montreal 4, Calgary 2; May 19, at Montreal — Montreal 4, Calgary 3; May 21, at Montreal — Calgary 4, Montreal 2; May 23, at Calgary — Calgary 3, Montreal 2; May 25, at Montreal — Calgary 4, Montreal 2.

1987-88 — Edmonton Oilers — Keith Acton, Glenn Anderson, Jeff Beukeboom, Geoff Courtnall, Grant Fuhr, Randy Gregg, Wayne Gretzky (Captain), Dave Hannan, Charlie Huddy, Mike Krushelnyski, Jari Kurri, Normand Lacombe, Kevin Lowe, Craig MacTavish, Kevin McClelland, Marty McSorley, Mark Messier, Craig Muni, Bill Ranford, Craig Simpson, Steve Smith, Esa Tikkanen, Peter Pocklington (Owner), Glen Sather (General Manager/Coach), John Muckler (Co-Coach), Ted Green (Ass't Coach), Bruce MacGregor (Ass't General Manager), Barry Fraser (Director of Player Personnel), Bill Tuele (Director of Public Relations), Dr. Gordon Cameron (Team Physician), Peter Millar (Athletic Therapist), Barrie Stafford (Trainer), Juergen Mers (Massage Therapist), Lyle Kulchisky (Ass't Trainer).
Scores: May 18, at Edmonton — Edmonton 2, Boston 1; May 20, at Edmonton — Edmonton 4, Boston 2; May 22, at Boston — Edmonton 6, Boston 3; May 24, at Boston — Boston 3, Edmonton 3 (suspended due to power failure); May 26, at Edmonton — Edmonton 6, Boston 3.

1986-87 — Edmonton Oilers — Glenn Anderson, Jeff Beukeboom, Kelly Buchberger, Paul Coffey, Grant Fuhr, Randy Gregg, Wayne Gretzky (Captain), Charlie Huddy, Dave Hunter, Mike Krushelnyski, Jari Kurri, Moe Lemay, Kevin Lowe, Craig MacTavish, Kevin McClelland, Marty McSorley, Mark Messier, Andy Moog, Craig Muni, Kent Nilsson, Jaroslav Pouzar, Reijo Ruotsalainen, Steve Smith, Esa Tikkanen, Peter Pocklington (Owner), Glen Sather (General Manager/Coach), John Muckler (Co-Coach), Ted Green (Ass't. Coach), Ron Low (Ass't. Coach), Bruce MacGregor (Ass't. General Manager), Barry Fraser (Director of Player Personnel), Peter Millar (Athletic Therapist), Barrie Stafford (Trainer), Lyle Kulchisky (Ass't Trainer).
Scores: May 17, at Edmonton — Edmonton 4, Philadelphia 2; May 20, at Edmonton — Edmonton 3, Philadelphia 2; May 22, at Philadelphia — Philadelphia 5, Edmonton 3; May 24, at Philadelphia — Edmonton 4, Philadelphia 1; May 26, at Edmonton — Philadelphia 4, Edmonton 3; May 28, at Philadelphia — Philadelphia 3, Edmonton 2; May 31, at Edmonton — Edmonton 3, Philadelphia 1.

1985-86 — Montreal Canadiens — Bob Gainey (Captain), Doug Soetaert, Patrick Roy, Rick Green, David Maley, Ryan Walter, Serge Boisvert, Mario Tremblay, Bobby Smith, Craig Ludwig, Tom Kurvers, Kjell Dahlin, Larry Robinson, Guy Carbonneau, Chris Chelios, Petr Svoboda, Mats Naslund, Lucien DeBlois, Steve Rooney, Gaston Gingras, Mike Lalor, Chris Nilan, John Kordic, Claude Lemieux, Mike McPhee, Brian Skrudland, Stephane Richer, Ronald Corey (President), Serge Savard (General Manager), Jean Perron (Coach), Jacques Laperrière (Ass't. Coach), Jean Béliveau (Vice President), Francois-Xavier Seigneur (Vice President), Fred Steer (Vice President), Jacques Lemaire (Ass't. General Manager), André Boudrias (Ass't. General Manager), Claude Ruel (Scouting), Yves Belanger (Athletic Therapist), Gaetan Lefebvre (Ass't. Athletic Therapist), Eddy Palchak (Trainer), Sylvain Toupin (Ass't. Trainer).
Scores: May 16, at Calgary — Calgary 5, Montreal 2; May 18, at Calgary — Montreal 3, Calgary 2; May 20, at Montreal — Montreal 5, Calgary 3; May 22, at Montreal — Montreal 1, Calgary 0; May 24, at Calgary — Montreal 4, Calgary 3.

1984-85 — Edmonton Oilers — Glenn Anderson, Billy Carroll, Paul Coffey, Lee Fogolin, Grant Fuhr, Randy Gregg, Wayne Gretzky (Captain), Charlie Huddy, Pat Hughes, Dave Hunter, Don Jackson, Mike Krushelnyski, Jari Kurri, Willy Lindstrom, Kevin Lowe, Dave Lumley, Kevin McClelland, Larry Melnyk, Mark Messier, Andy Moog, Mark Napier, Jaroslav Pouzar, Dave Semenko, Esa Tikkanen, Peter Pocklington (Owner), Glen Sather (General Manager/Coach), John Muckler (Ass't. Coach), Ted Green (Ass't. Coach), Bruce MacGregor (Ass't. General Manager), Barry Fraser (Director of Player Personnel/Chief Scout), Peter Millar (Athletic Therapist), Barrie Stafford, Lyle Kulchisky (Trainers)
Scores: May 21, at Philadelphia — Philadelphia 4, Edmonton 1; May 23, at Philadelphia — Edmonton 3, Philadelphia 1; May 25, at Edmonton — Edmonton 4, Philadelphia 3; May 28, at Edmonton — Edmonton 5, Philadelphia 3; May 30, at Edmonton — Edmonton 8, Philadelphia 3.

1983-84 — Edmonton Oilers — Glenn Anderson, Paul Coffey, Pat Conacher, Lee Fogolin, Grant Fuhr, Randy Gregg, Wayne Gretzky (Captain), Charlie Huddy, Pat Hughes, Dave Hunter, Don Jackson, Jari Kurri, Willy Lindstrom, Ken Linseman, Kevin Lowe, Dave Lumley, Kevin McClelland, Mark Messier, Andy Moog, Jaroslav Pouzar, Dave Semenko, Peter Pocklington (Owner), Glen Sather (General Manager/Coach), John Muckler (Ass't. Coach), Ted Green (Ass't. Coach), Bruce MacGregor (Ass't. General Manager), Barry Fraser (Director of Player Personnel/Chief Scout), Peter Millar (Athletic Therapist), Barrie Stafford (Trainer)
Scores: May 10, at New York — Edmonton 1, NY Islanders 0; May 12, at New York — NY Islanders 6, Edmonton 1; May 15, at Edmonton — Edmonton 7, NY Islanders 2; May 17, at Edmonton — Edmonton 7, NY Islanders 2; May 19, at Edmonton — Edmonton 5, NY Islanders 2.

1982-83 — New York Islanders — Mike Bossy, Bob Bourne, Paul Boutilier, Billy Carroll, Greg Gilbert, Clark Gillies, Butch Goring, Mats Hallin, Tomas Jonsson, Anders Kallur, Gord Lane, Dave Langevin, Mike McEwen, Roland Melanson, Wayne Merrick, Ken Morrow, Bob Nystrom, Stefan Persson, Denis Potvin (Captain), Billy Smith, Brent Sutter, Duane Sutter, John Tonelli, Bryan Trottier, Al Arbour (Coach), Lorne Henning (Ass't. Coach), Bill Torrey (General Manager), Ron Waske, Jim Pickard (Trainers)
Scores: May 10, at Edmonton — NY Islanders 2, Edmonton 0; May 12, at Edmonton — NY Islanders 6, Edmonton 3; May 14, at New York — NY Islanders 5, Edmonton 1; May 17, at New York — NY Islanders 4, Edmonton 2

1981-82 — New York Islanders — Mike Bossy, Bob Bourne, Billy Carroll, Butch Goring, Greg Gilbert, Clark Gillies, Tomas Jonsson, Anders Kallur, Gord Lane, Dave Langevin, Hector Marini, Mike McEwen, Roland Melanson, Wayne Merrick, Ken Morrow, Bob Nystrom, Stefan Persson, Denis Potvin (Captain), Billy Smith, Brent Sutter, Duane Sutter, John Tonelli, Bryan Trottier, Al Arbour (Coach), Lorne Henning (Ass't. Coach), Bill Torrey (General Manager), Jim Devellano (ass't. general manager/dir. of scouting), Ron Waske, Jim Pickard (Trainers)
Scores: May 8, at New York — NY Islanders 6, Vancouver 5; May 11, at New York — NY Islanders 6, Vancouver 4; May 13, at Vancouver — NY Islanders 3, Vancouver 0; May 16, at Vancouver — NY Islanders 3, Vancouver 1

1980-81 — New York Islanders — Denis Potvin (Captain), Mike McEwen, Ken Morrow, Gord Lane, Bob Lorimer, Stefan Persson, Dave Langevin, Mike Bossy, Bryan Trottier, Butch Goring, Wayne Merrick, Clark Gillies, John Tonelli, Bob Nystrom, Billy Carroll, Bob Bourne, Hector Marini, Anders Kallur, Duane Sutter, Garry Howatt, Lorne Henning, Billy Smith, Roland Melanson, Al Arbour (Coach), Bill Torrey (General Manager), Jim Devellano (Chief Scout), Ron Waske, Jim Pickard (Trainers).
Scores: May 12, at New York — NY Islanders 6, Minnesota 3; May 14, at New York — NY Islanders 6, Minnesota 3; May 17, at Minnesota — NY Islanders 7, Minnesota 5; May 19, at Minnesota— Minnesota 4, NY Islanders 2; May 21, at New York — NY Islanders 5, Minnesota 1.

1979-80 — New York Islanders — Gord Lane, Jean Potvin, Bob Lorimer, Denis Potvin (Captain), Stefan Persson, Ken Morrow, Dave Langevin, Duane Sutter, Garry Howatt, Clark Gillies, Lorne Henning, Wayne Merrick, Bob Bourne, Steve Tambellini, Bryan Trottier, Mike Bossy, Bob Nystrom, John Tonelli, Anders Kallur, Butch Goring, Alex McKendry, Glenn Resch, Billy Smith, Al Arbour (Coach), Bill Torrey (General Manager), Jim Devellano (Chief Scout), Ron Waske, Jim Pickard (Trainers).
Scores: May 13, at Philadelphia — NY Islanders 4, Philadelphia 3; May 15, at Philadelphia — Philadelphia 8, NY Islanders 3; May 17, at New York — NY Islanders 6, Philadelphia 2; May 19, at New York — NY Islanders 5, Philadelphia 2; May 22 at Philadelphia — Philadelphia 6, NY Islanders 3; May 24, at New York — NY Islanders 5, Philadelphia 4.

1978-79 — Montreal Canadiens — Ken Dryden, Larry Robinson, Serge Savard, Guy Lapointe, Brian Engblom, Gilles Lupien, Rick Chartraw, Guy Lafleur, Steve Shutt, Jacques Lemaire, Yvan Cournoyer (Captain), Réjean Houle, Pierre Mondou, Bob Gainey, Doug Jarvis, Yvon Lambert, Doug Risebrough, Pierre Larouche, Mario Tremblay, Cam Connor, Pat Hughes, Rod Langway, Mark Napier, Michel Larocque, Richard Sévigny, Scotty Bowman (Coach), Irving Grundman (Managing Director), Eddy Palchak, Pierre Meilleur (Trainers).
Scores: May 13, at Montreal — NY Rangers 4, Montreal 1; May 15, at Montreal — Montreal 6, NY Rangers 2; May 17, at New York — Montreal 4, NY Rangers 1; May 19, at New York — Montreal 4, NY Rangers 3; May 21, at Montreal — Montreal 4, NY Rangers 1.

1977-78 — Montreal Canadiens — Ken Dryden, Larry Robinson, Serge Savard, Guy Lapointe, Bill Nyrop, Pierre Bouchard, Brian Engblom, Gilles Lupien, Rick Chartraw, Guy Lafleur, Steve Shutt, Jacques Lemaire, Yvan Cournoyer (Captain), Réjean Houle, Pierre Mondou, Bob Gainey, Doug Jarvis, Yvon Lambert, Doug Risebrough, Pierre Larouche, Mario Tremblay, Michel Larocque, Murray Wilson, Scotty Bowman (Coach), Sam Pollock (General Manager), Eddy Palchak, Pierre Meilleur (Trainers).
Scores: May 13, at Montreal — Montreal 4, Boston 1; May 16, at Montreal — Montreal 3, Boston 2; May 18, at Boston — Boston 4, Montreal 0; May 21, at Boston — Boston 4, Montreal 3; May 23, at Montreal — Montreal 4, Boston 1; May 25, at Boston — Montreal 4, Boston 1.

1976-77 — Montreal Canadiens — Ken Dryden, Guy Lapointe, Larry Robinson, Serge Savard, Jimmy Roberts, Rick Chartraw, Bill Nyrop, Pierre Bouchard, Brian Engblom, Yvan Cournoyer (Captain), Guy Lafleur, Jacques Lemaire, Steve Shutt, Pete Mahovlich, Murray Wilson, Doug Jarvis, Yvon Lambert, Bob Gainey, Doug Risebrough, Mario Tremblay, Rejean Houle, Pierre Mondou, Mike Polich, Michel Larocque, Scotty Bowman (Coach), Sam Pollock (General Manager), Eddy Palchak, Pierre Meilleur (Trainers).
Scores: May 7, at Montreal — Montreal 7, Boston 3; May 10, at Montreal — Montreal 3, Boston 0; May 12, at Boston — Montreal 4, Boston 2; May 14, at Boston — Montreal 2, Boston 1.

1975-76 — Montreal Canadiens — Ken Dryden, Serge Savard, Guy Lapointe, Larry Robinson, Bill Nyrop, Pierre Bouchard, Jimmy Roberts, Guy Lafleur, Steve Shutt, Pete Mahovlich, Yvan Cournoyer (Captain), Jacques Lemaire, Yvon Lambert, Bob Gainey, Doug Jarvis, Doug Risebrough, Murray Wilson, Mario Tremblay, Rick Chartraw, Michel Larocque, Scotty Bowman (Coach), Sam Pollock (General Manager), Eddy Palchak, Pierre Meilleur (Trainers).
Scores: May 9, at Montreal — Montreal 4, Philadelphia 3; May 11, at Montreal — Montreal 2, Philadelphia 1; May 13, at Philadelphia — Montreal 3, Philadelphia 2; May 16, at Philadelphia — Montreal 5, Philadelphia 3.

1974-75 — Philadelphia Flyers — Bernie Parent, Wayne Stephenson, Ed Van Impe, Tom Bladon, André Dupont, Joe Watson, Jimmy Watson, Ted Harris, Larry Goodenough, Rick MacLeish, Bobby Clarke (Captain), Bill Barber, Reggie Leach, Gary Dornhoefer, Ross Lonsberry, Bob Kelly, Terry Crisp, Don Saleski, Dave Schultz, Orest Kindrachuk, Bill Clement, Fred Shero (Coach), Keith Allen (general manager), Frank Lewis, Jim McKenzie (Trainers).
Scores: May 15, at Philadelphia — Philadelphia 4, Buffalo 1; May 18, at Philadelphia — Philadelphia 2, Buffalo 1; May 20, at Buffalo — Buffalo 5, Philadelphia 4; May 22, at Buffalo — Buffalo 4, Philadelphia 2; May 25, at Philadelphia — Philadelphia 5, Buffalo 1; May 27, at Buffalo — Philadelphia 2, Buffalo 0.

1973-74 — Philadelphia Flyers — Bernie Parent, Ed Van Impe, Tom Bladon, André Dupont, Joe Watson, Jimmy Watson, Barry Ashbee, Bill Barber, Dave Schultz, Don Saleski, Gary Dornhoefer, Terry Crisp, Bobby Clarke (Captain), Simon Nolet, Ross Lonsberry, Rick MacLeish, Bill Flett, Orest Kindrachuk, Bill Clement, Bob Kelly, Bruce Cowick, Al MacAdam, Bobby Taylor, Fred Shero (Coach), Keith Allen (General Manager), Frank Lewis, Jim McKenzie (Trainers).
Scores: May 7, at Boston — Boston 3, Philadelphia 2; May 9, at Boston — Philadelphia 3, Boston 2; May 12, at Philadelphia — Philadelphia 4, Boston 1; May 14, at Philadelphia — Philadelphia 4, Boston 2; May 16, at Boston — Boston 5, Philadelphia 1; May 19, at Philadelphia — Philadelphia 1, Boston 0.

1972-73 — Montreal Canadiens — Ken Dryden, Guy Lapointe, Serge Savard, Larry Robinson, Jacques Laperrière, Bob Murdoch, Pierre Bouchard, Jimmy Roberts, Yvan Cournoyer, Frank Mahovlich, Jacques Lemaire, Pete Mahovlich, Marc Tardif, Henri Richard (Captain), Réjean Houle, Guy Lafleur, Chuck Lefley, Claude Larose, Murray Wilson, Steve Shutt, Michel Plasse, Scotty Bowman (Coach), Sam Pollock (General Manager), Eddy Palchak, Bob Williams (Trainers).
Scores: April 29, at Montreal — Montreal 8, Chicago 3; May 1, at Montreal — Montreal 4, Chicago 1; May 3, at Chicago — Chicago 7, Montreal 4; May 6, at Chicago — Montreal 4, Chicago 0; May 8, at Montreal — Chicago 8, Montreal 7; May 10, at Chicago — Montreal 6, Chicago 4.

1971-72 — Boston Bruins — Gerry Cheevers, Eddie Johnston, Bobby Orr, Ted Green, Carol Vadnais, Dallas Smith, Don Awrey, Phil Esposito, Ken Hodge, John Bucyk, Mike Walton, Wayne Cashman, Garnet Bailey, Derek Sanderson, Fred Stanfield, Ed Westfall, John McKenzie, Don Marcotte, Garry Peters, Chris Hayes, Tom Johnson (Coach), Milt Schmidt (General Manager), Dan Canney, John Forristall (Trainers).
Scores: April 30, at Boston — Boston 6, NY Rangers 5; May 2, at Boston — Boston 2, NY Rangers 1; May 4, at New York — NY Rangers 5, Boston 2; May 7, at New York — Boston 3, NY Rangers 2; May 9, at Boston — NY Rangers 3, Boston 2; May 11, at New York — Boston 3, NY Rangers 0.

1970-71 — Montreal Canadiens — Ken Dryden, Rogie Vachon, Jacques Laperrière, J.C. Tremblay, Guy Lapointe, Terry Harper, Pierre Bouchard, Jean Béliveau (Captain), Marc Tardif, Yvan Cournoyer, Réjean Houle, Claude Larose, Henri Richard, Phil Roberto, Pete Mahovlich, Leon Rochefort, John Ferguson, Bobby Sheehan, Jacques Lemaire, Frank Mahovlich, Bob Murdoch, Chuck Lefley, Al MacNeil (Coach), Sam Pollock (General Manager), Yvon Belanger, Eddy Palchak (Trainers).
Scores: May 4, at Chicago — Chicago 2, Montreal 1; May 6, at Chicago — Chicago 5, Montreal 3; May 9, at Montreal — Montreal 4, Chicago 2; May 11, at Montreal — Montreal 5, Chicago 2; May 13, at Chicago — Chicago 2, Montreal 0; May 16, at Montreal — Montreal 4, Chicago 3; May 18, at Chicago — Montreal 3, Chicago 2.

1969-70 — Boston Bruins — Gerry Cheevers, Eddie Johnston, Bobby Orr, Rick Smith, Dallas Smith, Bill Speer, Gary Doak, Don Awrey, Phil Esposito, Ken Hodge, John Bucyk, Wayne Carleton, Wayne Cashman, Derek Sanderson, Fred Stanfield, Ed Westfall, John McKenzie, Jim Lorentz, Don Marcotte, Bill Lesuk, Danny Schock, Harry Sinden (Coach), Milt Schmidt (General Manager), Dan Canney, John Forristall (Trainers).
Scores: May 3, at St. Louis — Boston 6, St. Louis 1; May 5, at St. Louis — Boston 6, St. Louis 2; May 7, at Boston — Boston 4, St. Louis 1; May 10, at Boston — Boston 4, St. Louis 3.

1968-69 — Montreal Canadiens — Gump Worsley, Rogie Vachon, Jacques Laperrière, J.C. Tremblay, Ted Harris, Serge Savard, Terry Harper, Larry Hillman, Jean Béliveau (Captain), Ralph Backstrom, Dick Duff, Yvan Cournoyer, Claude Provost, Bobby Rousseau, Henri Richard, John Ferguson, Christian Bordeleau, Mickey Redmond, Jacques Lemaire, Lucien Grenier, Tony Esposito, Claude Ruel (Coach), Sam Pollock (General Manager), Larry Aubut, Eddy Palchak (Trainers).
Scores: April 27, at Montreal — Montreal 3, St. Louis 1; April 29, at Montreal — Montreal 3, St. Louis 1; May 1 at St. Louis — Montreal 4, St. Louis 0; May 4, at St. Louis — Montreal 2, St. Louis 1.

1967-68 — Montreal Canadiens — Gump Worsley, Rogie Vachon, Jacques Laperrière, J.C. Tremblay, Ted Harris, Serge Savard, Terry Harper, Carol Vadnais, Jean Béliveau (Captain), Gilles Tremblay, Ralph Backstrom, Dick Duff, Claude Larose, Yvan Cournoyer, Claude Provost, Bobby Rousseau, Henri Richard, John Ferguson, Danny Grant, Jacques Lemaire, Mickey Redmond, Toe Blake (Coach), Sam Pollock (General Manager), Larry Aubut, Eddy Palchak (Trainers).
Scores: May 5, at St. Louis — Montreal 3, St. Louis 2; May 7, at St. Louis — Montreal 1, St. Louis 0; May 9, at Montreal — Montreal 4, St. Louis 3; May 11, at Montreal — Montreal 3, St. Louis 2.

1966-67 — Toronto Maple Leafs — Johnny Bower, Terry Sawchuk, Larry Hillman, Marcel Pronovost, Tim Horton, Bob Baun, Aut Erickson, Allan Stanley, Red Kelly, Ron Ellis, George Armstrong (Captain), Pete Stemkowski, Dave Keon, Mike Walton, Jim Pappin, Bob Pulford, Brian Conacher, Eddie Shack, Frank Mahovlich, Milan Marcetta, Larry Jeffrey, Bruce Gamble, Punch Imlach (Manager-Coach), Bob Haggart (Trainer).
Scores: April 20, at Montreal — Toronto 2, Montreal 6; April 22, at Montreal — Toronto 3, Montreal 0; April 25, at Toronto — Toronto 3, Montreal 2; April 27, at Toronto — Toronto 2, Montreal 6; April 29, at Montreal — Toronto 4, Montreal 1; May 2, at Toronto — Toronto 3, Montreal 1.

1965-66 — Montreal Canadiens — Gump Worsley, Charlie Hodge, J.C. Tremblay, Ted Harris, Jean-Guy Talbot, Terry Harper, Jacques Laperrière, Noel Price, Jean Béliveau (Captain), Ralph Backstrom, Dick Duff, Gilles Tremblay, Claude Larose, Yvan Cournoyer, Claude Provost, Bobby Rousseau, Henri Richard, Dave Balon, John Ferguson, Leon Rochefort, Jimmy Roberts, Toe Blake (Coach), Sam Pollock (general manager), Larry Aubut, Andy Galley (Trainers).
Scores: April 24, at Montreal — Detroit 3, Montreal 2; April 26, at Montreal — Detroit 5, Montreal 2; April 28, at Detroit — Montreal 4, Detroit 2; May 1, at Detroit — Montreal 2, Detroit 1; May 3, at Montreal — Montreal 5, Detroit 1; May 5, at Detroit — Montreal 3, Detroit 2.

1964-65 — Montreal Canadiens — Gump Worsley, Charlie Hodge, J.C. Tremblay, Ted Harris, Jean-Guy Talbot, Terry Harper, Jacques Laperrière, Jean Gauthier, Noel Picard, Jean Béliveau (Captain), Ralph Backstrom, Dick Duff, Claude Larose, Yvan Cournoyer, Claude Provost, Bobby Rousseau, Henri Richard, Dave Balon, John Ferguson, Red Berenson, Jimmy Roberts, Toe Blake (Coach), Sam Pollock (general manager), Larry Aubut, Andy Galley (Trainers).
Scores: April 17, at Montreal — Montreal 3, Chicago 2; April 20, at Montreal — Montreal 2, Chicago 0; April 22, at Chicago — Montreal 1, Chicago 3; April 25, at Chicago — Montreal 1, Chicago 5; April 7, at Montreal — Montreal 6, Chicago 0; April 29, at Chicago — Montreal 1, Chicago 2; May 1, at Montreal — Montreal 4, Chicago 0.

1963-64 — Toronto Maple Leafs — Johnny Bower, Don Simmons, Carl Brewer, Tim Horton, Bob Baun, Allan Stanley, Larry Hillman, Al Arbour, Red Kelly, Gerry Ehman, Andy Bathgate, George Armstrong (Captain), Ron Stewart, Dave Keon, Billy Harris, Don McKenney, Jim Pappin, Bob Pulford, Eddie Shack, Frank Mahovlich, Ed Litzenberger, Punch Imlach (Manager-Coach), Bob Haggert (Trainer).
Scores April 11, at Toronto — Toronto 3, Detroit 2; April 14, at Toronto — Toronto 3, Detroit 4; April 16, at Detroit — Toronto 3, Detroit 4; April 18, at Detroit — Toronto 4, Detroit 2; April 21, at Toronto — Toronto 1, Detroit 2; April 23, at Detroit — Toronto 4, Detroit 3; April 25, at Toronto — Toronto 4, Detroit 0.

1962-63 — Toronto Maple Leafs — Johnny Bower, Don Simmons, Carl Brewer, Tim Horton, Kent Douglas, Allan Stanley, Bob Baun, Larry Hillman, Red Kelly, Dick Duff, George Armstrong (Captain), Bob Nevin, Ron Stewart, Dave Keon, Billy Harris, Bob Pulford, Eddie Shack, Ed Litzenberger, Frank Mahovlich, John MacMillan, Punch Imlach (Manager-Coach), Bob Haggert (Trainer).
Scores: April 9, at Toronto — Toronto 4, Detroit 2; April 11, at Toronto — Toronto 4, Detroit 2; April 14, at Detroit — Toronto 2, Detroit 3; April 16, at Detroit — Toronto 4, Detroit 2; April 18, at Toronto — Toronto 3, Detroit 1.

1961-62 — Toronto Maple Leafs — Johnny Bower, Don Simmons, Carl Brewer, Tim Horton, Bob Baun, Allan Stanley, Al Arbour, Larry Hillman, Red Kelly, Dick Duff, George Armstrong (Captain), Frank Mahovlich, Bob Nevin, Ron Stewart, Billy Harris, Bert Olmstead, Bob Pulford, Eddie Shack, Dave Keon, Ed Litzenberger, John MacMillan, Punch Imlach (Manager-Coach), Bob Haggert (Trainer).
Scores: April 10, at Toronto — Toronto 4, Chicago 1; April 12, at Toronto — Toronto 3, Chicago 2; April 15, at Chicago — Toronto 0, Chicago 3; April 17, at Chicago — Toronto 1, Chicago 4; April 19, at Toronto —Toronto 8, Chicago 4; April 22, at Chicago — Toronto 2, Chicago 1.

1960-61 — Chicago Black Hawks — Glenn Hall, Al Arbour, Pierre Pilote, Moose Vasko, Jack Evans, Dollard St. Laurent, Reggie Fleming, Tod Sloan, Ron Murphy, Ed Litzenberger (Captain), Bill Hay, Wayne Hillman, Bobby Hull, Ab McDonald, Eric Nesterenko, Kenny Wharram, Earl Balfour, Stan Mikita, Murray Balfour, Chico Maki, Wayne Hicks, Tommy Ivan (Manager), Rudy Pilous (Coach), Nick Garen (Trainer).
Scores: April 6, at Chicago — Chicago 3, Detroit 2; April 8, at Detroit — Detroit 3, Chicago 1; April 10, at Chicago — Chicago 3, Detroit 1; April 12, at Detroit — Detroit 2, Chicago 1; April 14, at Chicago — Chicago 6, Detroit 3; April 16, at Detroit — Chicago 5, Detroit 1.

1959-60 — Montreal Canadiens — Jacques Plante, Charlie Hodge, Doug Harvey, Tom Johnson, Bob Turner, Jean-Guy Talbot, Albert Langlois, Ralph Backstrom, Jean Béliveau, Marcel Bonin, Bernie Geoffrion, Phil Goyette, Bill Hicke, Don Marshall, Ab McDonald, Dickie Moore, André Pronovost, Claude Provost, Henri Richard, Maurice Richard (Captain), Frank Selke (Manager), Toe Blake (Coach), Hector Dubois, Larry Aubut (Trainers).
Scores: April 7, at Montreal — Montreal 4, Toronto 2; April 9, at Montreal — Montreal 2, Toronto 1; April 12, at Toronto — Montreal 5, Toronto 2; April 14, at Toronto — Montreal 4, Toronto 0.

1958-59 — Montreal Canadiens — Jacques Plante, Charlie Hodge, Doug Harvey, Tom Johnson, Bob Turner, Jean-Guy Talbot, Albert Langlois, Bernie Geoffrion, Ralph Backstrom, Bill Hicke, Maurice Richard (Captain), Dickie Moore, Claude Provost, Ab McDonald, Henri Richard, Marcel Bonin, Phil Goyette, Don Marshall, André Pronovost, Jean Béliveau, Ian Cushenan, Frank Selke (Manager), Toe Blake (Coach), Hector Dubois, Larry Aubut (Trainers).
Scores: April 9, at Montreal — Montreal 5, Toronto 3; April 11, at Montreal — Montreal 3, Toronto 1; April 14, at Toronto — Toronto 3, Montreal 2; April 16, at Toronto — Montreal 3, Toronto 2; April 18, at Montreal — Montreal 5, Toronto 3.

1957-58 — Montreal Canadiens — Jacques Plante, Gerry McNeil, Doug Harvey, Tom Johnson, Bob Turner, Dollard St-Laurent, Jean-Guy Talbot, Albert Langlois, Jean Béliveau, Bernie Geoffrion, Maurice Richard (Captain), Dickie Moore, Claude Provost, Floyd Curry, Bert Olmstead, Henri Richard, Marcel Bonin, Phil Goyette, Don Marshall, André Pronovost, Connie Broden, Ab McDonald, Frank Selke (Manager), Toe Blake (Coach), Hector Dubois, Larry Aubut (Trainers).
Scores: April 8, at Montreal —Montreal 2, Boston 1; April 10, at Montreal — Boston 5, Montreal 2; April 13, at Boston — Montreal 3, Boston 0; April 15, at Boston — Boston 3, Montreal 1; April 17, at Montreal — Montreal 3, Boston 2; April 20, at Boston — Montreal 5, Boston 3.

1956-57 — Montreal Canadiens — Jacques Plante, Gerry McNeil, Doug Harvey, Tom Johnson, Bob Turner, Dollard St-Laurent, Jean-Guy Talbot, Jean Béliveau, Bernie Geoffrion, Floyd Curry, Dickie Moore, Maurice Richard (Captain), Claude Provost, Bert Olmstead, Henri Richard, Phil Goyette, Don Marshall, André Pronovost, Connie Broden, Jackie Leclair, Frank Selke (Manager), Toe Blake (Coach), Hector Dubois, Larry Aubut (Trainers).
Scores: April 6, at Montreal — Montreal 5, Boston 1; April 9, at Montreal — Montreal 1, Boston 0; April 11, at Boston — Montreal 4, Boston 2; April 14, at Boston — Boston 2, Montreal 0; April 16, at Montreal — Montreal 5, Boston 1.

1955-56 — Montreal Canadiens — Jacques Plante, Doug Harvey, Butch Bouchard (Captain), Bob Turner, Tom Johnson, Jean-Guy Talbot, Dollard St-Laurent, Jean Béliveau, Bernie Geoffrion, Bert Olmstead, Floyd Curry, Jackie Leclair, Maurice Richard, Dickie Moore, Henri Richard, Ken Mosdell, Don Marshall, Claude Provost, Frank Selke (Manager), Toe Blake (Coach), Hector Dubois (Trainer).
Scores: March 31, at Montreal — Montreal 6, Detroit 4; April 3, at Montreal — Montreal 5, Detroit 1; April 5, at Detroit — Detroit 3, Montreal 1; April 8, at Detroit — Montreal 3, Detroit 0; April 10, at Montreal — Montreal 3, Detroit 1.

1954-55 — Detroit Red Wings — Terry Sawchuk, Red Kelly, Bob Goldham, Marcel Pronovost, Benny Woit, Jim Hay, Larry Hillman, Ted Lindsay (Captain), Tony Leswick, Gordie Howe, Alex Delvecchio, Marty Pavelich, Glen Skov, Earl Reibel, Johnny Wilson, Bill Dineen, Vic Stasiuk, Marcel Bonin, Jack Adams (Manager), Jimmy Skinner (Coach), Carl Mattson (Trainer).
Scores: April 3, at Detroit — Detroit 4, Montreal 2; April 5, at Detroit — Detroit 7, Montreal 1, April 7, at Montreal — Montreal 4, Detroit 2; April 9, at Montreal — Montreal 5, Detroit 3; April 10, at Detroit — Detroit 5, Montreal 1; April 12, at Montreal — Montreal 6, Detroit 3; April 14, at Detroit — Detroit 3, Montreal 1.

1953-54 — Detroit Red Wings — Terry Sawchuk, Red Kelly, Bob Goldham, Benny Woit, Marcel Pronovost, Al Arbour, Keith Allen, Ted Lindsay (Captain), Tony Leswick, Gordie Howe, Marty Pavelich, Alex Delvecchio, Gilles Dube, Metro Prystai, Glen Skov, Johnny Wilson, Bill Dineen, Jimmy Peters, Earl Reibel, Vic Stasiuk, Jack Adams (Manager), Tommy Ivan (Coach), Carl Mattson (Trainer).
Scores: April 4, at Detroit — Detroit 3, Montreal 1; April 6, at Detroit — Montreal 3, Detroit 1; April 8, at Montreal — Detroit 5, Montreal 2; April 10, at Montreal — Detroit 2, Montreal 0; April 11, at Detroit — Montreal 1, Detroit 0; April 13, at Montreal — Montreal 4, Detroit 1; April 16, at Detroit — Detroit 2, Montreal 1.

1952-53 — Montreal Canadiens — Gerry McNeil, Jacques Plante, Doug Harvey, Butch Bouchard (Captain), Tom Johnson, Dollard St. Laurent, Bud MacPherson, Maurice Richard, Elmer Lach, Paul Meger, Bert Olmstead, Bernie Geoffrion, Floyd Curry, Paul Masnick, Billy Reay, Dickie Moore, Ken Mosdell, Dick Gamble, John McCormack, Lorne Davis, Calum MacKay, Eddie Mazur, Frank Selke (Manager), Dick Irvin (Coach), Hector Dubois (Trainer).
Scores: April 9, at Montreal — Montreal 4, Boston 2; April 11, at Montreal — Boston 4, Montreal 1; April 12, at Boston — Montreal 3, Boston 0; April 14, at Boston — Montreal 7, Boston 3; April 16, at Montreal — Montreal 1, Boston 0.

1951-52 — Detroit Red Wings — Terry Sawchuk, Bob Goldham, Benny Woit, Red Kelly, Leo Reise Jr., Marcel Pronovost, Ted Lindsay, Tony Leswick, Gordie Howe, Metro Prystai, Marty Pavelich, Sid Abel (Captain), Glen Skov, Alex Delvecchio, John Wilson, Vic Stasiuk, Larry Zeidel, Fred Glover, Jack Adams (Manager) Tommy Ivan (Coach), Carl Mattson (Trainer).
Scores: April 10, at Montreal — Detroit 3, Montreal 1; April 12, at Montreal — Detroit 2, Montreal 1; April 13, at Detroit — Detroit 3, Montreal 0; April 15, at Detroit — Detroit 3, Montreal 0.

1950-51 — Toronto Maple Leafs — Turk Broda, Al Rollins, Jimmy Thomson, Gus Mortson, Bill Barilko, Bill Juzda, Fern Flaman, Hugh Bolton, Ted Kennedy (Captain), Sid Smith, Tod Sloan, Cal Gardner, Howie Meeker, Harry Watson, Max Bentley, Joe Klukay, Danny Lewicki, Ray Timgren, Fleming Mackell, John McCormack, Bob Hassard, Conn Smythe (Manager), Joe Primeau (Coach), Tim Daly (Trainer).
Scores: April 11, at Toronto — Toronto 3, Montreal 2; April 14, at Toronto — Montreal 3, Toronto 2; April 17, at Montreal — Toronto 2, Montreal 1; April 19, at Montreal — Toronto 3, Montreal 2; April 21, at Toronto — Toronto 3, Montreal 2.

Bill Barilko's overtime goal to win the 1951 Stanley Cup Final became the stuff of legend when he disappeared in a plane crash that summer. The Maple Leafs did not win the Stanley Cup again until 1962; the year Barilko's remains were discovered in remote bush.

1949-50 — Detroit Red Wings — Harry Lumley, Jack Stewart, Leo Reise Jr., Clare Martin, Doug McKay, Al Dewsbury, Lee Fogolin, Marcel Pronovost, Red Kelly, Gord Haidy, Ted Lindsay, Sid Abel (Captain), Gordie Howe, George Gee, Jimmy Peters, Marty Pavelich, Jim McFadden, Pete Babando, Max McNab, Gerry Couture, Joe Carveth, Steve Black, Johnny Wilson, Larry Wilson, Jack Adams (Manager), Tommy Ivan (Coach), Carl Mattson (Trainer).
Scores: April 11, at Detroit — Detroit 4, NY Rangers 1; April 13, at Toronto* — NY Rangers 3, Detroit 1; April 15, at Toronto — Detroit 4, NY Rangers 0; April 18, at Detroit — NY Rangers 4, Detroit 3; April 20, at Detroit — NY Rangers 2, Detroit 1; April 22, at Detroit — Detroit 5, NY Rangers 4; April 23, at Detroit — Detroit 4, NY Rangers 3.

* Ice was unavailable in Madison Square Garden and Rangers elected to play second and third games on Toronto ice.

1948-49 — Toronto Maple Leafs — Turk Broda, Jimmy Thomson, Gus Mortson, Bill Barilko, Garth Boesch, Bill Juzda, Ted Kennedy (Captain), Howie Meeker, Vic Lynn, Harry Watson, Bill Ezinicki, Cal Gardner, Max Bentley, Joe Klukay, Sid Smith, Don Metz, Ray Timgren, Fleming Mackell, Harry Taylor, Bob Dawes, Tod Sloan, Conn Smythe (Manager), Hap Day (Coach), Tim Daly (Trainer).
Scores: April 8, at Detroit — Toronto 3, Detroit 2; April 10, at Detroit — Toronto 3, Detroit 1; April 13, at Toronto — Toronto 3, Detroit 1; April 16, at Toronto — Toronto 3, Detroit 1.

1947-48 — Toronto Maple Leafs — Turk Broda, Jimmy Thomson, Wally Stanowski, Garth Boesch, Bill Barilko, Gus Mortson, Phil Samis, Syl Apps (Captain), Bill Ezinicki, Harry Watson, Ted Kennedy, Howie Meeker, Vic Lynn, Nick Metz, Max Bentley, Joe Klukay, Les Costello, Don Metz, Sid Smith, Conn Smythe (Manager), Hap Day (Coach), Tim Daly (Trainer).
Scores: April 7, at Toronto — Toronto 5, Detroit 3; April 10, at Toronto — Toronto 4, Detroit 2; April 11, at Detroit — Toronto 2, Detroit 0; April 14, at Detroit — Toronto 7, Detroit 2.

1946-47 — Toronto Maple Leafs — Turk Broda, Garth Boesch, Gus Mortson, Jimmy Thomson, Wally Stanowski, Bill Barilko, Harry Watson, Bud Poile, Ted Kennedy, Syl Apps (Captain), Don Metz, Nick Metz, Bill Ezinicki, Vic Lynn, Howie Meeker, Gaye Stewart, Joe Klukay, Gus Bodnar, Bob Goldham, Conn Smythe (Manager), Hap Day (Coach), Tim Daly (Trainer).
Scores: April 8, at Montreal — Montreal 6, Toronto 0; April 10, at Montreal — Toronto 4, Montreal 0; April 12, at Toronto — Toronto 4, Montreal 2; April 15, at Toronto — Toronto 2, Montreal 1; April 17, at Montreal — Montreal 3, Toronto 1; April 19, at Toronto — Toronto 2, Montreal 1.

1945-46 — Montreal Canadiens — Elmer Lach, Toe Blake (Captain), Maurice Richard, Bob Fillion, Dutch Hiller, Murph Chamberlain, Ken Mosdell, Buddy O'Connor, Glen Harmon, Jimmy Peters, Butch Bouchard, Billy Reay, Ken Reardon, Leo Lamoureux, Frank Eddolls, Gerry Plamondon, Bill Durnan, Tommy Gorman (Manager), Dick Irvin (Coach), Ernie Cook (Trainer).
Scores: March 30, at Montreal — Montreal 4, Boston 3; April 2, at Montreal — Montreal 3, Boston 2; April 4, at Boston — Montreal 4, Boston 2; April 7, at Boston — Boston 3, Montreal 2; April 9, at Montreal — Montreal 6, Boston 3.

1944-45 — Toronto Maple Leafs — Don Metz, Frank McCool, Wally Stanowski, Reg Hamilton, Moe Morris, John McCreedy, Tom O'Neill, Ted Kennedy, Babe Pratt, Gus Bodnar, Art Jackson, Jack McLean, Mel Hill, Nick Metz, Bob Davidson (Captain), Sweeney Schriner, Lorne Carr, Pete Backor, Ross Johnstone, Conn Smythe (Manager), Frank Selke (Business Manager), Hap Day (Coach), Tim Daly (Trainer).
Scores: April 6, at Detroit — Toronto 1, Detroit 0; April 8, at Detroit — Toronto 2, Detroit 0; April 12, at Toronto — Toronto 1, Detroit 0; April 14, at Toronto — Detroit 5, Toronto 3; April 19, at Detroit — Detroit 2, Toronto 0; April 21, at Toronto — Detroit 1, Toronto 0; April 22, at Detroit — Toronto 2, Detroit 1.

1943-44 — Montreal Canadiens — Toe Blake (Captain), Maurice Richard, Elmer Lach, Ray Getliffe, Murph Chamberlain, Phil Watson, Butch Bouchard, Glen Harmon, Buddy O'Connor, Gerry Heffernan, Mike McMahon, Leo Lamoureux, Fern Majeau, Bob Fillion, Bill Durnan, Tommy Gorman (Manager), Dick Irvin (Coach), Ernie Cook (Trainer).
Scores: April 4, at Montreal — Montreal 5, Chicago 1; April 6, at Chicago — Montreal 3, Chicago 1; April 9, at Chicago — Montreal 3, Chicago 2; April 13, at Montreal — Montreal 5, Chicago 4.

1942-43 — Detroit Red Wings — Jack Stewart, Jimmy Orlando, Sid Abel (Captain), Alex Motter, Harry Watson, Joe Carveth, Mud Bruneteau, Eddie Wares, Johnny Mowers, Cully Simon, Don Grosso, Carl Liscombe, Connie Brown, Syd Howe, Les Douglas, Harold Jackson, Joe Fisher, Adam Brown, Jack Adams (Manager), Ebbie Goodfellow (Playing Coach), Honey Walker (Trainer).
Scores: April 1, at Detroit — Detroit 6, Boston 2; April 4, at Detroit — Detroit 4, Boston 3; April 7, at Boston — Detroit 4, Boston 0; April 8, at Boston — Detroit 2, Boston 0.

1941-42 — Toronto Maple Leafs — Wally Stanowski, Syl Apps (Captain), Bob Goldham, Gordie Drillon, Hank Goldup, Ernie Dickens, Sweeney Schriner, Bucko McDonald, Bob Davidson, Nick Metz, Bingo Kampman, Don Metz, Gaye Stewart, Turk Broda, John McCreedy, Lorne Carr, Pete Langelle, Billy Taylor, Conn Smythe (Manager), Hap Day (Coach), Frank Selke (Business Manager), Tim Daly (Trainer).
Scores: April 4, at Toronto — Detroit 3, Toronto 2; April 7, at Toronto — Detroit 4, Toronto 2; April 9, at Detroit — Detroit 5, Toronto 2; April 12, at Detroit — Toronto 4, Detroit 3; April 14, at Toronto — Toronto 9, Detroit 3; April 16, at Detroit — Toronto 3, Detroit 0; April 18, at Toronto — Toronto 3, Detroit 1.

1940-41 — Boston Bruins — Bill Cowley, Des Smith, Dit Clapper (Captain), Frank Brimsek, Flash Hollett, Jack Crawford, Bobby Bauer, Pat McReavy, Herb Cain, Mel Hill, Milt Schmidt, Woody Dumart, Roy Conacher, Terry Reardon, Art Jackson, Eddie Wiseman, Jack Shewchuk, Art Ross (Manager), Cooney Weiland (Coach), Win Green (Trainer).
Scores: April 6, at Boston — Detroit 2, Boston 3; April 8, at Boston — Detroit 1, Boston 2; April 10, at Detroit — Boston 4, Detroit 2; April 12, at Detroit — Boston 3, Detroit 1.

1939-40 — New York Rangers — Dave Kerr, Art Coulter (Captain), Ott Heller, Alex Shibicky, Mac Colville, Neil Colville, Phil Watson, Lynn Patrick, Clint Smith, Muzz Patrick, Babe Pratt, Bryan Hextall, Kilby MacDonald, Dutch Hiller, Alf Pike, Stan Smith, Lester Patrick (Manager), Frank Boucher (Coach), Harry Westerby (Trainer).
Scores: April 2, at New York — NY Rangers 2, Toronto 1; April 3, at New York — NY Rangers 6, Toronto 2; April 6, at Toronto — NY Rangers 1, Toronto 2; April 9, at Toronto — NY Rangers 0, Toronto 3; April 11, at Toronto — NY Rangers 2, Toronto 1; April 13, at Toronto — NY Rangers 3, Toronto 2.

1938-39 — Boston Bruins — Bobby Bauer, Mel Hill, Flash Hollett, Roy Conacher, Gord Pettinger, Charlie Sands, Milt Schmidt, Woody Dumart, Jack Crawford, Ray Getliffe, Frank Brimsek, Eddie Shore, Dit Clapper, Bill Cowley, Jack Portland, Red Hamill, Cooney Weiland (Captain), Art Ross (Manager-Coach), Win Green (Trainer).
Scores: April 6, at Boston — Toronto 1, Boston 2; April 9, at Boston — Toronto 3, Boston 2; April 11, at Toronto — Toronto 1, Boston 3; April 13, at Toronto — Toronto 0, Boston 2; April 16, at Boston — Toronto 1, Boston 3.

1937-38 — Chicago Black Hawks — Art Wiebe, Carl Voss, Harold Jackson, Mike Karakas, Mush March, Jack Shill, Earl Seibert, Cully Dahlstrom, Alex Levinsky, Johnny Gottselig (Captain), Lou Trudel, Pete Palangio, Bill MacKenzie, Doc Romnes, Paul Thompson, Roger Jenkins, Alfie Moore, Bert Connelly, Virgil Johnson, Paul Goodman, Bill Stewart (Manager-Coach), Eddie Froelich (Trainer).
Scores: April 5, at Toronto — Chicago 3, Toronto 1; April 7, at Toronto — Chicago 1, Toronto 5; April 10, at Chicago — Chicago 2, Toronto 1; April 12, at Chicago — Chicago 4, Toronto 1.

1936-37 — Detroit Red Wings — Normie Smith, Pete Kelly, Larry Aurie, Herbie Lewis, Hec Kilrea, Mud Bruneteau, Syd Howe, Wally Kilrea, Jimmy Franks, Bucko McDonald, Gord Pettinger, Ebbie Goodfellow, John Gallagher, Ralph Bowman, John Sorrell, Marty Barry, Earl Robertson, John Sherf, Howie Mackie, Rolly Roulston, Doug Young (Captain), Jack Adams (Manager-Coach), Honey Walker (Trainer).
Scores: April 6, at New York — Detroit 1, NY Rangers 5; April 8, at Detroit — Detroit 4, NY Rangers 2; April 11, at Detroit — Detroit 0, NY Rangers 1; April 13, at Detroit — Detroit 1, NY Rangers 0; April 15, at Detroit — Detroit 3, NY Rangers 0.

1935-36 — Detroit Red Wings — John Sorrell, Syd Howe, Marty Barry, Herbie Lewis, Mud Bruneteau, Wally Kilrea, Hec Kilrea, Gord Pettinger, Bucko McDonald, Ralph Bowman, Pete Kelly, Doug Young (Captain), Ebbie Goodfellow, Normie Smith, Larry Aurie, Jack Adams (Manager-Coach), Honey Walker (Trainer).
Scores: April 5, at Detroit — Detroit 3, Toronto 1; April 7, at Detroit — Detroit 9, Toronto 4; April 9, at Toronto — Detroit 3, Toronto 4; April 11, at Toronto — Detroit 3, Toronto 2.

1934-35 — Montreal Maroons — Lionel Conacher, Cy Wentworth, Alex Connell, Toe Blake, Stewart Evans, Earl Robinson, Bill Miller, Dave Trottier, Jimmy Ward, Baldy Northcott, Hooley Smith, Russ Blinco, Al Shields, Sammy McManus, Gus Marker, Bob Gracie, Herb Cain, Dutch Gainor, Tommy Gorman (Manager-Coach), Bill O'Brien (Trainer).
Scores: April 4, at Toronto — Mtl. Maroons 3, Toronto 2; April 6, at Toronto — Mtl. Maroons 3, Toronto 1; April 9, at Montreal — Mtl. Maroons 4, Toronto 1.

1933-34 — Chicago Black Hawks — Clarence Abel, Rosie Couture, Lou Trudel, Lionel Conacher, Paul Thompson, Leroy Goldsworthy, Art Coulter, Roger Jenkins, Don McFadyen, Tom Cook, Doc Romnes, Johnny Gottselig, Mush March, Johnny Sheppard, Charlie Gardiner (Captain), Bill Kendall, Jack Leswick, Tommy Gorman (Manager-Coach), Eddie Froelich (Trainer).
Scores: April 3, at Detroit — Chicago 2, Detroit 1; April 5, at Detroit — Chicago 4, Detroit 1; April 8, at Chicago — Detroit 5, Chicago 2; April 10, at Chicago — Chicago 1, Detroit 0.

1932-33 — New York Rangers — Ching Johnson, Butch Keeling, Frank Boucher, Art Somers, Babe Siebert, Bun Cook, Andy Aitkenhead, Ott Heller, Oscar Asmundson, Gord Pettinger, Doug Brennan, Cecil Dillon, Bill Cook (Captain), Murray Murdoch, Earl Seibert, Lester Patrick (Manager-Coach), Harry Westerby (Trainer).
Scores: April 4, at New York — NY Rangers 5, Toronto 1; April 8, at Toronto — NY Rangers 3, Toronto 1; April 11, at Toronto — Toronto 3, NY Rangers 2; April 13, at Toronto — NY Rangers 1, Toronto 0.

1931-32 — Toronto Maple Leafs — Charlie Conacher, Busher Jackson, King Clancy, Andy Blair, Red Horner, Lorne Chabot, Alex Levinsky, Joe Primeau, Harold Darragh, Baldy Cotton, Frank Finnigan, Hap Day (Captain), Ace Bailey, Bob Gracie, Fred Robertson, Earl Miller, Conn Smythe (Manager), Dick Irvin (Coach), Tim Daly (Trainer).
Scores: April 5, at New York — Toronto 6, NY Rangers 4; April 7, at Boston* — Toronto 6, NY Rangers 2; April 9, at Toronto — Toronto 6, NY Rangers 4.

* Ice was unavailable in Madison Square Garden and Rangers elected to play the second game on neutral ice.

1930-31 — Montreal Canadiens — George Hainsworth, Wildor Larochelle, Marty Burke, Sylvio Mantha (Captain), Howie Morenz, Johnny Gagnon, Aurel Joliat, Armand Mondou, Pit Lepine, Albert Leduc, Georges Mantha, Art Lesieur, Nick Wasnie, Bert McCaffrey, Gus Rivers, Jean Pusie, Léo Dandurand (Manager), Cecil Hart (Coach), Ed Dufour (Trainer).
Scores: April 3, at Chicago — Montreal 2, Chicago 1; April 5, at Chicago — Chicago 2, Montreal 1; April 9, at Montreal — Chicago 3, Montreal 2; April 11, at Montreal — Montreal 4, Chicago 2; April 14, at Montreal — Montreal 2, Chicago 0.

1929-30 — Montreal Canadiens — George Hainsworth, Marty Burke, Sylvio Mantha (Captain), Howie Morenz, Bert McCaffrey, Aurel Joliat, Albert Leduc, Pit Lepine, Wildor Larochelle, Nick Wasnie, Gerry Carson, Armand Mondou, Georges Mantha, Gus Rivers, Léo Dandurand (Manager), Cecil Hart (Coach), Ed Dufour (Trainer).
Scores: April 1, at Boston — Montreal 3, Boston 0; April 3, at Montreal — Montreal 4, Boston 3.

1928-29 — Boston Bruins — Tiny Thompson, Eddie Shore, Lionel Hitchman (Captain), Percy Galbraith, Eric Pettinger, Frank Fredrickson, Mickey Mackay, Red Green, Dutch Gainor, Harry Oliver, Eddie Rodden, Dit Clapper, Cooney Weiland, Lloyd Klein, Cy Denneny, Bill Carson, George Owen, Myles Lane, Art Ross (Manager-Coach), Win Green (Trainer).
Scores: March 28, at Boston — Boston 2, NY Rangers 0; March 29, at New York — Boston 2, NY Rangers 1.

1927-28 — New York Rangers — Lorne Chabot, Clarence Abel, Leo Bourgeault, Ching Johnson, Bill Cook (Captain), Bun Cook, Frank Boucher, Bill Boyd, Murray Murdoch, Paul Thompson, Alex Gray, Joe Miller, Patsy Callighen, Lester Patrick (Manager-Coach), Harry Westerby (Trainer).
Scores: April 5, at Montreal — Mtl. Maroons 2, NY Rangers 0; April 7, at Montreal — NY Rangers 2, Mtl. Maroons 1; April 10, at Montreal — Mtl. Maroons 2, NY Rangers 0; April 12, at Montreal — NY Rangers 1, Mtl. Maroons 0; April 14, at Montreal — NY Rangers 2, Mtl. Maroons 1.

1926-27 — Ottawa Senators — Alex Connell, King Clancy, Georges Boucher, Ed Gorman, Frank Finnigan, Alex Smith, Hec Kilrea, Hooley Smith, Cy Denneny, Frank Nighbor, Jack Adams, Milt Halliday, Dave Gill (Manager-Coach).
Scores: April 7, at Boston — Ottawa 0, Boston 0; April 9, at Boston — Ottawa 3, Boston 1; April 11, at Ottawa — Boston 1, Ottawa 1; April 13, at Ottawa — Ottawa 3, Boston 1.

In 1926, the Montreal Maroons won the Stanley Cup in just their second season in the NHL. The Maroons beat the Victoria Cougars of the Western Hockey League, who had been Stanley Cup champions in 1925. The next Cup win for a west coast team would be 82 years later when the Anaheim Ducks won in 2007.

1925-26 — Montreal Maroons — Clint Benedict, Reg Noble, Frank Carson, Dunc Munro, Nels Stewart, Punch Broadbent, Babe Siebert, Chuck Dinsmore, Merlyn Phillips, Hobie Kitchen, Sam Rothschild, Albert Holway, George Horne, Bernie Brophy, Eddie Gerard (Manager-Coach), Bill O'Brien (Trainer).
Scores: March 30, at Montreal — Mtl. Maroons 3, Victoria 0; April 1, at Montreal — Mtl. Maroons 3, Victoria 0; April 3, at Montreal — Victoria 3, Mtl. Maroons 2; April 6, at Montreal — Mtl. Maroons 2, Victoria 0.

The series in the spring of 1926 ended the annual playoffs between the champions of the East and the champions of the West. Since 1926-27 the annual playoffs in the National Hockey League have decided the Stanley Cup champions.

1924-25 — Victoria Cougars — Hap Holmes, Clem Loughlin, Gord Fraser, Frank Fredrickson, Jack Walker, Gizzy Hart, Harold Halderson, Frank Foyston, Wally Elmer, Harry Meeking, Jocko Anderson, Lester Patrick (Manager-Coach).
Scores: March 21, at Victoria — Victoria 5, Montreal 2; March 23, at Vancouver — Victoria 3, Montreal 1; March 27, at Victoria — Montreal 4, Victoria 2; March 30, at Victoria — Victoria 6, Montreal 1.

1923-24 — Montreal Canadiens — Georges Vezina, Sprague Cleghorn (Captain), Billy Coutu, Howie Morenz, Aurel Joliat, Billy Boucher, Odie Cleghorn, Sylvio Mantha, Bobby Boucher, Billy Bell, Billy Cameron, Joe Malone, Charles Fortier, Leo Dandurand (Manager-Coach).
Scores: March 22, at Montreal — Montreal 6, Cgy. Tigers 1; March 25, at Ottawa* — Montreal 3, Cgy. Tigers 0.

* Game transferred to Ottawa to benefit from artificial ice surface.

1922-23 — Ottawa Senators — Georges Boucher, Lionel Hitchman, Frank Nighbor, King Clancy, Harry Helman, Clint Benedict, Jack Darragh, Eddie Gerard, Cy Denneny, Punch Broadbent, Tommy Gorman (Manager), Pete Green (Coach), F. Dolan (Trainer).
Scores: March 29, at Vancouver — Ottawa 2, Edm. Eskimos 1; March 31, at Vancouver — Ottawa 1, Edm. Eskimos 0.

1921-22 — Toronto St. Patricks — Ted Stackhouse, Corb Denneny, Rod Smylie, Lloyd Andrews, John Ross Roach, Harry Cameron, Billy Stuart, Babe Dye, Ken Randall, Reg Noble, Eddie Gerard (borrowed for one game from Ottawa), Stan Jackson, Ivan Mitchell, Charlie Querrie (Manager), George O'Donoghue (Coach).
Scores: March 17, at Toronto — Van. Millionaires 4, Toronto 3; March 20, at Toronto — Toronto 2, Van. Millionaires 1; March 23, at Toronto — Van. Millionaires 3, Toronto 0; March 25, at Toronto — Toronto 6, Van. Millionaires 0; March 28, at Toronto — Toronto 5, Van. Millionaires 1.

1920-21 — Ottawa Senators — Jack MacKell, Jack Darragh, Morley Bruce, Georges Boucher, Eddie Gerard, Clint Benedict, Sprague Cleghorn, Frank Nighbor, Punch Broadbent, Cy Denneny, Leth Graham, Tommy Gorman (Manager),Pete Green (Coach), F. Dolan (Trainer).
Scores: March 21, at Vancouver — Van. Millionaires 2, Ottawa 1; March 24, at Vancouver — Ottawa 4, Van. Millionaires 3; March 28, at Vancouver — Ottawa 3, Van. Millionaires 2; March 31, at Vancouver — Van. Millionaires 3, Ottawa 2; April 4, at Vancouver — Ottawa 2, Van. Millionaires 1

1919-20 — Ottawa Senators — Jack MacKell, Jack Darragh, Morley Bruce, Horrace Merrill, Georges Boucher, Eddie Gerard, Clint Benedict, Sprague Cleghorn, Frank Nighbor, Punch Broadbent, Cy Denneny, Tommy Gorman (Manager), Pete Green (Coach).
Scores: March 22, at Ottawa — Ottawa 3, Seattle 2; March 24, at Ottawa — Ottawa 3, Seattle 0; March 27, at Ottawa — Seattle 3, Ottawa 1; March 30, at Toronto* — Seattle 5, Ottawa 2; April 1, at Toronto* — Ottawa 6, Seattle 1.

* Games transferred to Toronto to benefit from artificial ice surface.

1918-19 — No decision, Series halted by Spanish influenza epidemic, illness of several players and death of Joe Hall of Montreal Canadiens from flu. Five games had been played when the series was halted, each team having won two and tied one. The results are shown:
Scores: March 19, at Seattle — Seattle 7, Montreal 0; March 22, at Seattle — Montreal 4, Seattle 2; March 24, at Seattle — Seattle 7, Montreal 2; March 26, at Seattle — Montreal 0, Seattle 0; March 30, at Seattle — Montreal 4, Seattle 3.

1917-18 — Toronto Arenas — Rusty Crawford, Harry Meeking, Ken Randall, Corb Denneny, Harry Cameron, Jack Adams, Alf Skinner, Harry Mummery, Hap Holmes, Reg Noble, Sammy Hebert, Jack Marks, Jack Coughlin, Charlie Querrie (Manager), Dick Carroll (Coach), Frank Carroll (Trainer).
Scores: March 20, at Toronto — Toronto 5, Van. Millionaires 3; March 23, at Toronto — Van. Millionaires 6, Toronto 4; March 26, at Toronto — Toronto 6, Van. Millionaires 3; March 28, at Toronto — Van. Millionaires 8, Toronto 1; March 30, at Toronto — Toronto 2, Van. Millionaires 1.

1916-17 — Seattle Metropolitans — Hap Holmes, Ed Carpenter, Cully Wilson, Jack Walker, Bernie Morris, Frank Foyston, Roy Rickey, Jim Riley, Bobby Rowe (Captain), Peter Muldoon (Manager).
Scores: March 17, at Seattle — Montreal 8, Seattle 4; March 20, at Seattle — Seattle 6, Montreal 1; March 23, at Seattle — Seattle 4, Montreal 1; March 25, at Seattle — Seattle 9, Montreal 1.

1915-16 — Montreal Canadiens — Georges Vezina, Bert Corbeau, Jack Laviolette, Newsy Lalonde, Louis Berlinquette, Goldie Prodgers, Howard McNamara (Captain), Didier Pitre, Skene Ronan, Amos Arbour, Skinner Poulin, Jack Fournier, George Kennedy (Manager).
Scores: March 20, at Montreal — Portland 2, Montreal 0; March 22, at Montreal — Montreal 2, Portland 1; March 25, at Montreal — Montreal 6, Portland 3; March 28, at Montreal — Portland 6, Montreal 5; March 30, at Montreal — Montreal 2, Portland 1.

1914-15 — Vancouver Millionaires — Ken Mallen, Frank Nighbor, Cyclone Taylor, Hugh Lehman, Lloyd Cook, Mickey Mackay, Barney Stanley, Jim Seaborn, Si Griffis (Captain), Johnny Matz, Frank Patrick (Playing Manager).
Scores: March 22, at Vancouver — Van. Millionaires 6, Ottawa 2; March 24, at Vancouver — Van. Millionaires 8, Ottawa 3; March 26, at Vancouver — Van. Millionaires 12, Ottawa 3.

1913-14 — Toronto Blueshirts — Con Corbeau, Roy McGiffen, Jack Walker, George McNamara, Cully Wilson, Frank Foyston, Harry Cameron, Hap Holmes, Scotty Davidson (Captain), Harriston, Jack Marshall (Playing Manager), Frank and Dick Carroll (Trainers).
Scores: March 14, at Toronto — Toronto 5, Victoria 2; March 17, at Toronto — Toronto 6, Victoria 5; March 19, at Toronto — Toronto 2, Victoria 1.

1912-13 — Quebec Bulldogs — Joe Malone, Joe Hall, Paddy Moran, Harry Mummery, Tommy Smith, Jack Marks, Rusty Crawford, Billy Creighton, Jeff Malone, Rocket Power, M.J. Quinn (Manager), D. Beland (Trainer).
Scores: March 8, at Quebec — Que. Bulldogs 14, Sydney 3; March 10, at Quebec — Que. Bulldogs 6, Sydney 2.

Victoria challenged Quebec but the Bulldogs refused to put the Stanley Cup in competition so the two teams played an exhibition series with Victoria winning two games to one by scores of 7-5, 3-6, 6-1. It was the first meeting between the Eastern champions and the Western champions. The following year, and until the Western Hockey League disbanded after the 1926 playoffs, the Cup went to the winner of the series between East and West.

1911-12 — Quebec Bulldogs — Goldie Prodgers, Joe Hall, Walter Rooney, Paddy Moran, Jack Marks, Jack McDonald, Eddie Oatman, George Leonard, Joe Malone (Captain), C. Nolan (Coach), M.J. Quinn (Manager), D. Beland (Trainer).
Scores: March 11, at Quebec — Que. Bulldogs 9, Moncton 3; March 13, at Quebec — Que. Bulldogs 8, Moncton 0.

Prior to 1912, teams could challenge the Stanley Cup champions for the title, thus there was more than one Championship Series played in most of the seasons between 1894 and 1911.

1910-11 — Ottawa Senators — Hamby Shore, Percy LeSueur (Captain), Jack Darragh, Bruce Stuart, Marty Walsh, Bruce Ridpath, Fred Lake, Dubbie Kerr, Alex Currie, Horace Gaul.
Scores: March 13, at Ottawa — Ottawa 7, Galt 4; March 16, at Ottawa — Ottawa 13, Port Arthur 4.

1909-10 (March) **— Montreal Wanderers —** Cecil Blachford, Moose Johnson, Ernie Russell, Riley Hern, Harry Hyland, Jack Marshall, Pud Glass (Captain), Jimmy Gardner, Dickie Boon (Manager).
Scores: March 12, at Montreal — Mtl. Wanderers 7, Berlin (Kitchener) 3.

1909-10 (January) **— Ottawa Senators —** Dubbie Kerr, Fred Lake, Percy LeSueur, Ken Mallen, Bruce Ridpath, Gord Roberts, Hamby Shore, Bruce Stuart, Marty Walsh.
Scores: January 5, at Ottawa — Ottawa 12, Galt 3; January 7, at Ottawa — Ottawa 3, Galt 1; January 18, at Ottawa — Ottawa 8, Edmonton 4; January 20, at Ottawa — Ottawa 13, Edmonton 7.

1908-09 — Ottawa Senators — Fred Lake, Percy LeSueur, Cyclone Taylor, Billy Gilmour, Dubbie Kerr, Edgar Dey, Marty Walsh, Bruce Stuart (Captain).
Scores: Ottawa, as champions of the Eastern Canada Hockey Association took over the Stanley Cup in 1909 and, although a challenge was accepted by the Cup trustees from Winnipeg Shamrocks, games could not be arranged because of the lateness of the season. No other challenges were made in 1909. The following season — 1909-10 — however, the Senators accepted two challenges as defending Cup Champions. The first was against Galt in a two-game, total-goals series, and the second against Edmonton, also a two-game, total-goals series. Results: January 5, at Ottawa —Ottawa 12, Galt 3; January 7, at Ottawa — Ottawa 3, Galt 1. January 18, at Ottawa — Ottawa 8, Edm. Eskimos 4; January 20, at Ottawa — Ottawa 13, Edm. Eskimos 7.

1907-08 — Montreal Wanderers — Riley Hern, Art Ross, Walter Smaill, Pud Glass, Bruce Stuart, Ernie Russell, Moose Johnson, Cecil Blachford (Captain), Tom Hooper, Larry Gilmour, Ernie Liffiton, Dickie Boon (Manager).
Scores: Wanderers accepted four challenges for the Cup: January 9, at Montreal — Mtl. Wanderers 9, Ott. Victorias 3; January 13, at Montreal — Mtl. Wanderers 13, Ott. Victorias 1; March 10, at Montreal — Mtl. Wanderers 11, Wpg. Maple Leafs 5; March 12, at Montreal — Mtl. Wanderers 9, Wpg. Maple Leafs 3; March 14, at Montreal — Mtl. Wanderers 6, Toronto (OPHL) 4. At start of following season, 1908-09, Wanderers were challenged by Edmonton. Results: December 28, at Montreal — Mtl. Wanderers 7, Edm. Eskimos 3; December 30, at Montreal — Edm. Eskimos 7, Mtl. Wanderers 6. Total goals: Mtl. Wanderers 13, Edm. Eskimos 10.

1906-07 — (March 25) **— Montreal Wanderers —** Billy Strachan, Riley Hern, Lester Patrick, Hod Stuart, Pud Glass, Ernie Russell, Cecil Blachford (Captain), Moose Johnson, Rod Kennedy, Jack Marshall, Dickie Boon (Manager).

1906-07 — (March 18) **— Kenora Thistles —** Eddie Giroux, Si Griffis, Tom Hooper, Fred Whitcroft, Alf Smith, Harry Westwick, Roxy Beaudro, Tom Phillips (Captain), Russell Phillips.
Scores: March 16, at Winnipeg — Kenora 8, Brandon 6; March 18, at Winnipeg — Kenora 4, Brandon 1; March 23, at Winnipeg — Mtl. Wanderers 7, Kenora 2; March 25, at Winnipeg — Kenora 6, Mtl. Wanderers 5. Total goals: Mtl. Wanderers 12, Kenora 8.

1906-07 — (January) **— Kenora Thistles —** Eddie Giroux, Art Ross, Si Griffis, Tom Hooper, Billy McGimsie, Roxy Beaudro, Tommy Phillips (Captain), Joe Hall, Russell Phillips.
Scores: January 17, at Montreal — Kenora 4, Mtl. Wanderers 2; Jan. 21, at Montreal — Kenora 8, Mtl. Wanderers 6.

1905-06 — (March) **— Montreal Wanderers —** Henri Menard, Billy Strachan, Rod Kennedy, Lester Patrick, Pud Glass, Ernie Russell, Moose Johnson, Cecil Blachford (Captain), Josh Arnold, Dickie Boon (Manager).
Scores: March 14, at Montreal — Mtl. Wanderers 9, Ottawa 1; March 17, at Ottawa — Ottawa 9, Mtl. Wanderers 3. Total goals: Mtl. Wanderers 12, Ottawa 10. Wanderers accepted a challenge from New Glasgow, N.S., prior to the start of the 1906-07 season. Results: December 27, at Montreal — Mtl. Wanderers 10, New Glasgow 3; December 29, at Montreal — Mtl. Wanderers 7, New Glasgow 2.

1905-06 — (February) **— Ottawa Silver Seven —** Harvey Pulford (Captain), Arthur Moore, Harry Westwick, Frank McGee, Alf Smith (Playing Coach), Billy Gilmour, Billy Hague, Percy LeSueur, Harry Smith, Tommy Smith, Dion, Ebbs.
Scores: February 27, at Ottawa — Ottawa 16, Queen's University 7; February 28, at Ottawa — Ottawa 12, Queen's University 7; March 6, at Ottawa — Ottawa 6, Smiths Falls 5; March 8, at Ottawa — Ottawa 8, Smiths Falls 2.

1904-05 — Ottawa Silver Seven — Dave Finnie, Harvey Pulford (Captain), Arthur Moore, Harry Westwick, Frank McGee, Alf Smith (Playing Coach), Billy Gilmour, Frank White, Horace Gaul, Hamby Shore, Bones Allen.
Scores: January 13, at Ottawa — Ottawa 9, Dawson City 2; January 16, at Ottawa — Ottawa 23, Dawson City 2; March 7, at Ottawa — Rat Portage 9, Ottawa 3; March 9, at Ottawa — Ottawa 4, Rat Portage 2; March 11, at Ottawa — Ottawa 5, Rat Portage 4.

1903-04 — Ottawa Silver Seven — Suddy Gilmour, Arthur Moore, Frank McGee, Bouse Hutton, Billy Gilmour, Jim McGee, Harry Westwick, Harvey Pulford (Captain), Scott, Alf Smith (Playing Coach).
Scores: December 30, at Ottawa — Ottawa 9, Wpg. Rowing Club 1; January 1, at Ottawa — Wpg. Rowing Club 6, Ottawa 2; January 4, at Ottawa — Ottawa 2, Wpg. Rowing Club 0. February 23, at Ottawa — Ottawa 6, Tor. Marlboros 3; February 25, at Ottawa — Ottawa 11, Tor. Marlboros 2; March 2, at Montreal — Ottawa 5, Mtl. Wanderers 5. Following the tie game, a new two-game series was ordered to be played in Ottawa but the Wanderers refused unless the tie game was replayed in Montreal. When no settlement could be reached, the series was abandoned and Ottawa retained the Cup and accepted a two-game challenge from Brandon. Results: (both games at Ottawa), March 9, Ottawa 6, Brandon 3; March 11, Ottawa 9, Brandon 3.

1902-03 — (March) **— Ottawa Silver Seven —** Suddy Gilmour, Percy Sims, Bouse Hutton, Dave Gilmour, Billy Gilmour, Harry Westwick, Frank McGee, F.H. Wood, A.A. Fraser, Charles Spittal, Harvey Pulford (Captain), Arthur Moore, Alf Smith (coach.)
Scores: March 7, at Montreal — Ottawa 1, Mtl. Victorias 1; March 10, at Ottawa — Ottawa 8, Mtl. Victorias 0. Total goals: Ottawa 9, Mtl. Victorias 1; March 12, at Ottawa — Ottawa 6, Rat Portage 2; March 14, at Ottawa — Ottawa 4, Rat Portage 2.

1902-03 — (February) **— Montreal AAA —** Tom Hodge, Dickie Boon, Billy Nicholson, Tommy Phillips, Art Hooper, Billy Bellingham, Charles Liffiton, Jack Marshall, Jimmy Gardner, Cecil Blachford, George Smith.
Scores: January 29, at Montreal — Mtl. AAA 8, Wpg. Victorias 1; January 31, at Montreal — Wpg. Victorias 2, Mtl. AAA 2; February 2, at Montreal — Wpg. Victorias 4, Mtl. AAA 2; February 4, at Montreal — Mtl. AAA 5, Wpg. Victorias 1.

1901-02 — (March) **— Montreal AAA —** Tom Hodge, Dickie Boon, Billy Nicholson, Archie Hooper, Billy Bellingham, Charles Liffiton, Jack Marshall, Roland Elliott, Jimmy Gardner.
Scores: March 13, at Winnipeg — Wpg. Victorias 1, Mtl. AAA 0; March 15, at Winnipeg — Mtl. AAA 5, Wpg. Victorias 0; March 17, at Winnipeg — Mtl. AAA 2, Wpg. Victorias 1.

1901-02 — (January) **— Winnipeg Victorias —** Burke Wood, Tony Gingras, Charles Johnstone, Rod Flett, Magnus Flett, Dan Bain (Captain), Fred Scanlon, F. Cadham, G. Brown.
Scores: January 21, at Winnipeg — Wpg. Victorias 5, Tor Wellingtons 3; January 23, at Winnipeg — Wpg. Victorias 5, Tor. Wellingtons 3.

1900-01 — Winnipeg Victorias — Burke Wood, Jack Marshall, Tony Gingras, Charles Johnstone, Rod Flett, Magnus Flett, Dan Bain (Captain), Art Brown, George Carruthers.
Scores: January 29, at Montreal — Wpg. Victorias 4, Mtl. Shamrocks 3; January 31, at Montreal — Wpg. Victorias 2, Mtl. Shamrocks 1.

1899-1900 — Montreal Shamrocks — Joe McKenna, Frank Tansey, Frank Wall, Art Farrell, Fred Scanlon, Harry Trihey (Captain), Jack Brannen.
Scores: February 12, at Montreal — Mtl. Shamrocks 4, Wpg. Victorias 3; February 14, at Montreal — Wpg. Victorias 3, Mtl. Shamrocks 2; February 16, at Montreal — Mtl. Shamrocks 5, Wpg. Victorias 4; March 5, at Montreal — Mtl. Shamrocks 10, Halifax 2; March 7, at Montreal — Mtl. Shamrocks 11, Halifax 0.

1898-99 — (March) **— Montreal Shamrocks —** Joe McKenna, Frank Tansey, Frank Wall, Harry Trihey (Captain), Art Farrell, Fred Scanlon, Jack Brannen, John Dobby, Charles Hoerner.
Scores: March 14, at Montreal — Mtl. Shamrocks 6, Queen's University 2.

1898-99 — (February) **— Montreal Victorias —** Gordon Lewis, Mike Grant, Graham Drinkwater, Cam Davidson, Bob McDougall, Ernie McLea, Frank Richardson, Jack Ewing, Russell Bowie, Douglas Acer, Fred McRobie.
Scores: February 15, at Montreal — Mtl. Victorias 2, Wpg. Victorias 1; February 18, at Montreal — Mtl. Victorias 3, Wpg. Victorias 2.

1897-98 — Montreal Victorias — Gordon Lewis, Hartland McDougall, Mike Grant, Graham Drinkwater, Cam Davidson, Bob McDougall, Ernie McLea, Frank Richardson (Captain), Jack Ewing. The Victorias as champions of the Amateur Hockey Association, retained the Cup and were not called upon to defend it.

1896-97 — Montreal Victorias — Gordon Lewis, Harold Henderson, Mike Grant (Captain), Cam Davidson, Graham Drinkwater, Bob McDougall, Ernie McLea, Shirley Davidson, Hartland McDougall, Jack Ewing, Percy Molson, David Gillilan, McLellan.
Scores: December 27, at Montreal — Mtl. Victorias 15, Ott. Capitals 2.

1895-96 — (December) **— Montreal Victorias —** Harold Henderson, Mike Grant (Captain), Bob McDougall, Graham Drinkwater, Shirley Davidson, Ernie McLea, W. Wallace, Robert Jones, Cam Davidson, David Gillilan, Stanley Willett.
Scores: December 30, at Winnipeg — Mtl. Victorias 6, Wpg. Victorias 5.

1895-96 — (February) **— Winnipeg Victorias —** Whitey Merritt, Rod Flett, Fred Higginbotham, Jack Armitage (Captain), Tote Campbell, Dan Bain, Bobby Benson, Attie Howard.
Scores: February 14, at Montreal — Wpg. Victorias 2, Mtl. Victorias 0.

1894-95 — Montreal Victorias — Robert Jones, Harold Henderson, Mike Grant (Captain), Shirley Davidson, Bob McDougall, Norman Rankin, Graham Drinkwater, Roland Elliot, William Pullan, Hartland McDougall, Art Fenwick, A. McDougall. Montreal Victorias, as champions of the Amateur Hockey Association, were prepared to defend the Stanley Cup. However, the Stanley Cup trustees had already accepted a challenge match between the 1894 champion Montreal AAA and Queen's University. It was declared that if Montreal AAA defeated Queen's University, Montreal Victorias would be declared Stanley Cup champions. If Queen's University won, the Cup would go to the university club. In a game played March 9, 1895, Montreal AAA defeated Queen's University 5-1. As a result, Montreal Victorias were awarded the Stanley Cup.

1893-94 — Montreal AAA — Herb Collins, Allan Cameron, George James, Billy Barlow, Clare Mussen, Archie Hodgson, Haviland Routh, Alex Irving, James Stewart, E. O'Brien, A.C. (Toad) Wand, A.B. Kingan.
Scores: March 17, at Mtl. Victorias — Mtl. AAA 3, Mtl. Victorias 2; March 22, at Montreal — Mtl. AAA 3, Ott. Capitals 1.

1892-93 — Montreal AAA — Tom Paton, James Stewart, Allan Cameron, Haviland Routh, Archie Hodgson, Billy Barlow, A.B. Kingan, G.S. Lowe.
In accordance with the terms governing the presentation of the Stanley Cup, it was awarded for the first time to the Montreal AAA as champions of the Amateur Hockey Association in 1893. Once Montreal AAA had been declared holders of the Stanley Cup, any Canadian hockey team could challenge for the trophy.

All-Time NHL Playoff Formats

1917-18 — The regular-season was split into two halves. The winners of both halves faced each other in a two-game, total-goals series for the NHL championship and the right to meet the PCHA champion in the best-of-five Stanley Cup Finals.

1918-19 — Same as 1917-18, except that the Stanley Cup Finals was extended to a best-of-seven series.

1919-20 — Same as 1917-1918, except that Ottawa won both halves of the split regular-season schedule to earn an automatic berth into the best-of-five Stanley Cup Finals against the PCHA champions.

1921-22 — The top two teams at the conclusion of the regular-season faced each other in a two-game, total-goals series for the NHL championship. The NHL champion then moved on to play the winner of the PCHA-WCHL playoff series in the best-of-five Stanley Cup Finals.

1922-23 — The top two teams at the conclusion of the regular-season faced each other in a two-game, total-goals series for the NHL championship. The NHL champion then moved on to play the PCHA champion in the best-of-three Stanley Cup Semi-Finals, and the winner of the Semi-Finals played the WCHL champion, which had been given a bye, in the best-of-three Stanley Cup Finals.

1923-24 — The top two teams at the conclusion of the regular-season faced each other in a two-game, total-goals series for the NHL championship. The NHL champion then moved on to play the loser of the PCHA-WCHL playoff (the winner of the PCHA-WCHL playoff earned a bye into the Stanley Cup Finals) in the best-of-three Stanley Cup Semi-Finals. The winner of this series met the PCHA-WCHL playoff winner in the best-of-three Stanley Cup Finals.

1924-25 — The first place team (Hamilton) at the conclusion of the regular-season was supposed to play the winner of a two-game, total-goals series between the second (Toronto) and third (Montreal) place clubs. However, Hamilton refused to abide by this new format, demanding greater compensation than offered by the League. Thus, Toronto and Montreal played their two-game, total-goals series, and the winner (Montreal) earned the NHL title and then played the WCHL champion (Victoria) in the best-of-five Stanley Cup Finals.

1925-26 — The format which was intended for 1924-25 went into effect. The winner of the two-game, total-goals series between the second and third place teams squared off against the first place team in the two-game, total-goals NHL championship series. The NHL champion then moved on to play the WHL champion in the best-of-five Stanley Cup Finals.

After the 1925-26 season, the NHL was the only major professional hockey league still in existence and consequently took over sole control of the Stanley Cup competition.

1926-27 — The 10-team league was divided into two divisions — Canadian and American — of five teams apiece. In each division, the winner of the two-game, total-goals series between the second and third place teams faced the first place team in a two-game, total-goals series for the division title. The two division title winners then met in the best-of-five Stanley Cup Finals.

1928-29 — Both first place teams in the two divisions played each other in a best-of-five series. Both second place teams in the two divisions played each other in a two-game, total-goals series as did the two third place teams. The winners of these latter two series then played each other in a best-of-three series for the right to meet the winner of the series between the two first place clubs. This Stanley Cup Final was a best-of-three.

Series A: First in Canadian Division vs. first in American (best-of-five)
Series B: Second in Canadian Division vs. second in American (two-game, total-goals)
Series C: Third in Canadian Division vs. third in American (two-game, total-goals)
Series D: Winner of Series B vs. winner of Series C (best-of-three)
Series E: Winner of Series A vs. winner of Series D (best-of-three) for Stanley Cup

1931-32 — Same as 1928-29, except that Series D was changed to a two-game, total-goals format and Series E was changed to best-of-five.

1936-37 — Same as 1931-32, except that Series B, C, and D were each best-of-three.

1938-39 — With the NHL reduced to seven teams, the two-division system was replaced by one seven-team league. Based on final regular-season standings, the following playoff format was adopted:

Series A: First vs. Second (best-of-seven)
Series B: Third vs. Fourth (best-of-three)
Series C: Fifth vs. Sixth (best-of-three)
Series D: Winner of Series B vs. winner of Series C (best-of-three)
Series E: Winner of Series A vs. winner of Series D (best-of-seven)

1942-43 — With the NHL reduced to six teams (the "original six"), only the top four finishers qualified for playoff action. The best-of-seven Semi-Finals pitted Team #1 vs. Team #3 and Team #2 vs. Team #4. The winners of each Semi-Final series met in the best-of-seven Stanley Cup Finals.

1967-68 — When it doubled in size from 6 to 12 teams, the NHL once again was divided into two divisions — East and West — of six teams apiece. The top four clubs in each division qualified for the playoffs (all series were best-of-seven):

Series A: Team #1 (East) vs. Team #3 (East)
Series B: Team #2 (East) vs. Team #4 (East)
Series C: Team #1 (West) vs. Team #3 (West)
Series D: Team #2 (West) vs. Team #4 (West)
Series E: Winner of Series A vs. winner of Series B
Series F: Winner of Series C vs. winner of Series D
Series G: Winner of Series E vs. Winner of Series F

1970-71 — Same as 1967-68 except that Series E matched the winners of Series A and D, and Series F matched the winners of Series B and C.

1971-72 — Same as 1970-71, except that Series A and C matched Team #1 vs. Team #4, and Series B and D matched Team #2 vs. Team #3.

1974-75 — With the League now expanded to 18 teams in four divisions, a completely new playoff format was introduced. First, the #2 and #3 teams in each of the four divisions were pooled together in the Preliminary round. These eight (#2 and #3) clubs were ranked #1 to #8 based on regular-season record:

Series A: Team #1 vs. Team #8 (best-of-three)
Series B: Team #2 vs. Team #7 (best-of-three)
Series C: Team #3 vs. Team #6 (best-of-three)
Series D: Team #4 vs. Team #5 (best-of-three)
The winners of this Preliminary round then pooled together with the four division winners, which had received byes into this Quarter-Final round. These eight teams were again ranked #1 to #8 based on regular-season record:
Series E: Team #1 vs. Team #8 (best-of-seven)
Series F: Team #2 vs. Team #7 (best-of-seven)
Series G: Team #3 vs. Team #6 (best-of-seven)
Series H: Team #4 vs. Team #5 (best-of-seven)
The four Quarter-Finals winners, which moved on to the Semi-Finals, were then ranked #1 to #4 based on regular season record:
Series I: Team #1 vs. Team #4 (best-of-seven)
Series J: Team #2 vs. Team #3 (best-of-seven)
Series K: Winner of Series I vs. winner of Series J (best-of-seven)

1977-78 — Same as 1974-75, except that the Preliminary round consisted of the #2 teams in the four divisions and the next four teams based on regular-season record (not their standings within their divisions).

1979-80 — With the addition of four WHA franchises, the League expanded its playoff structure to include 16 of its 21 teams. The four first place teams in the four divisions automatically earned playoff berths. Among the 17 other clubs, the top 12, according to regular-season record, also earned berths. All 16 teams were then pooled together and ranked #1 to #16 based on regular-season record:

Series A: Team #1 vs. Team #16 (best-of-five)
Series B: Team #2 vs. Team #15 (best-of-five)
Series C: Team #3 vs. Team #14 (best-of-five)
Series D: Team #4 vs. Team #13 (best-of-five)
Series E: Team #5 vs. Team #12 (best-of-five)
Series F: Team #6 vs. Team #11 (best-of-five)
Series G: Team #7 vs. Team #10 (best-of-five)
Series H: Team #8 vs. Team # 9 (best-of-five)
The eight Preliminary round winners, ranked #1 to #8 based on regular-season record, moved on to the Quarter-Finals:
Series I: Team #1 vs. Team #8 (best-of-seven)
Series J: Team #2 vs. Team #7 (best-of-seven)
Series K: Team #3 vs. Team #6 (best-of-seven)
Series L: Team #4 vs. Team #5 (best-of-seven)
The four Quarter-Finals winners, ranked #1 to #4 based on regular-season record, moved on to the semi-finals:
Series M: Team #1 vs. Team #4 (best-of-seven)
Series N: Team #2 vs. Team #3 (best-of-seven)
Series O: Winner of Series M vs. winner of Series N (best-of-seven)

1981-82 — The first four teams in each division earned playoff berths. In each division, the first-place team opposed the fourth-place team and the second-place team opposed the third-place team in a best-of-five Division Semi-Final series (DSF). In each division, the two winners of the DSF met in a best-of-seven Division Final series (DF). The two DF winners in each conference met in a best-of-seven Conference Final series (CF). In the Prince of Wales Conference, the Adams Division winner opposed the Patrick Division winner; in the Clarence Campbell Conference, the Smythe Division winner opposed the Norris Division winner. The two CF winners met in a best-of-seven Stanley Cup Final (F) series.

1986-87 — Division Semi-Final series changed from best-of-five to best-of-seven.

1993-94 — The NHL's playoff draw is conference-based rather than division-based. At the conclusion of the regular season, the top eight teams in each of the Eastern and Western Conferences qualify for the playoffs. The teams that finish in first place in each of the League's divisions are seeded first and second in each conference's playoff draw and are assured of home ice advantage in the first two playoff rounds. The remaining teams are seeded based on their regular-season point totals. In each conference, the team seeded #1 plays #8; #2 vs. #7; #3 vs. #6; and #4 vs. #5. All series are best-of-seven with home ice rotating on a 2-2-1-1-1 basis, with the exception of matchups between Central and Pacific Division teams. These matchups will be played on a 2-3-2 basis to reduce travel. In a 2-3-2 series, the team with the most points will have its choice to start the series at home or on the road. The Eastern Conference champion will face the Western Conference champion in the Stanley Cup Final.

1994-95 — Same as 1993-94, except that in first, second or third-round playoff series involving Central and Pacific Division teams, the team with the better record has the choice of using either a 2-3-2 or a 2-2-1-1-1 format. When a 2-3-2 format is selected, the higher-ranked team also has the choice of playing games 1, 2, 6 and 7 at home or playing games 3, 4 and 5 at home. The format for the Stanley Cup Final remains 2-2-1-1-1.

1998-99 — The NHL's clubs are re-aligned into two conferences each consisting of three divisions. The number of teams qualifying for the Stanley Cup Playoffs remains unchanged at 16.

First-round playoff berths will be awarded to the first-place team in each division as well as to the next five best teams based on regular-season point totals in each conference. The three division winners in each conference will be seeded first through third, in order of points, for the playoffs and the next five best teams, in order of points, will be seeded fourth through eighth. In each conference, the team seeded #1 will play #8; #2 vs. #7; #3 vs. #6; and #4 vs. #5 in the quarterfinal round. Home-ice in the Conference Quarter-Finals is granted to those teams seeded first through fourth in each conference.

In the Conference Semi-Finals and Conference Finals, teams will be re-seeded according to the same criteria as the Conference Quarter-Finals. Higher seeded teams will have home-ice advantage.

Home-ice advantage for the Stanley Cup Finals will be determined by points.

All series remain best-of-seven.

The Anaheim Ducks went 10-2 at home during the 2007 playoffs en route to winning the Stanley Cup. Only two teams in history (New Jersey in 2003 with 12 and Edmonton in 1998 with 11) have won more than 10 games at home during one postseason.

Team Records

1918-2007

GAMES PLAYED

MOST GAMES PLAYED BY ALL TEAMS, ONE PLAYOFF YEAR:
92 — 1991. There were 51 DSF, 24 DF, 11 CF and 6 F games.
90 — 1994. There were 48 CQF, 23 CSF, 12 CF and 7 F games.
— 2002. There were 47 CQF, 25 CSF, 13 CF and 5 F games.

MOST GAMES PLAYED, ONE TEAM, ONE PLAYOFF YEAR:
26 — Philadelphia Flyers, 1987. Won DSF 4-2 vs. NY Rangers, DF 4-3 vs. NY Islanders, CF 4-2 vs. Montreal, and lost F 4-3 vs. Edmonton.
— Calgary Flames, 2004. Won DSF 4-3 vs. Vancouver, DF 4-2 vs. Detroit, CF 4-2 vs. San Jose, and lost F 4-3 vs. Tampa Bay.
25 — New Jersey Devils, 2001. Won CQF 4-2 vs. Carolina, CSF 4-3 vs. Toronto, CF 4-1 vs. Pittsburgh, and lost F 4-3 vs. Colorado.
— Carolina Hurricanes, 2006. Won CQF 4-2 vs. Montreal, CSF 4-1 vs. New Jersey, CF 4-3 vs. Buffalo, and F 4-3 vs. Edmonton

PLAYOFF APPEARANCES

MOST STANLEY CUP CHAMPIONSHIPS:
23 — Montreal Canadiens (1924-30-31-44-46-53-56-57-58-59-60-65-66-68-69-71-73-76-77-78-79-86-93)
13 — Toronto Maple Leafs (1918-22-32-42-45-47-48-49-51-62-63-64-67)
10 — Detroit Red Wings (1936-37-43-50-52-54-55-97-98-02)

MOST CONSECUTIVE STANLEY CUP CHAMPIONSHIPS:
5 — Montreal Canadiens (1956-57-58-59-60)
4 — Montreal Canadiens (1976-77-78-79)
— NY Islanders (1980-81-82-83)

MOST FINAL SERIES APPEARANCES:
32 — Montreal Canadiens in 89-year history.
22 — Detroit Red Wings in 80-year history.
21 — Toronto Maple Leafs in 89-year history.

MOST CONSECUTIVE FINAL SERIES APPEARANCES:
10 — Montreal Canadiens, (1951-60, inclusive)
5 — Montreal Canadiens, (1965-69, inclusive)
— NY Islanders, (1980-84, inclusive)

MOST YEARS IN PLAYOFFS:
75 — Montreal Canadiens in 89-year history.
64 — Toronto Maple Leafs in 89-year history.
62 — Boston Bruins in 82-year history.

MOST CONSECUTIVE PLAYOFF APPEARANCES:
29 — Boston Bruins (1968-96, inclusive)
28 — Chicago Blackhawks (1970-97, inclusive)
25 — St. Louis Blues (1980-2004, inclusive)
24 — Montreal Canadiens (1971-94, inclusive)
21 — Montreal Canadiens (1949-69, inclusive)

TEAM WINS

MOST HOME WINS, ONE TEAM, ONE PLAYOFF YEAR:
12 — New Jersey Devils, 2003 in 13 home games.
11 — Edmonton Oilers, 1988 in 11 home games.
10 — Edmonton Oilers, 1985 in 10 home games.
— Montreal Canadiens, 1986 in 11 home games.
— Montreal Canadiens, 1993 in 11 home games.
— Carolina Hurricanes, 2006 in 14 home games.
— Anaheim Ducks, 2007 in 12 home games.

MOST HOME WINS, ALL TEAMS, ONE PLAYOFF YEAR:
57 — 1991. Of 92 games played, home teams won 57 (29 DSF, 17 DF, 8 CF and 3 in F).

MOST ROAD WINS, ONE TEAM, ONE PLAYOFF YEAR:
10 — New Jersey Devils, 1995. Won three at Boston in CQF; two at Pittsburgh in CSF; three at Philadelphia in CF; and two at Detroit in F.
— New Jersey Devils, 2000. Won two at Florida in CQF; two at Toronto in CSF; three at Philadelphia in CF; and three at Dallas in F.
— Calgary Flames, 2004. Won three at Vancouver in DSF; two at Detroit in DF; three at San Jose in CF; and two at Tampa Bay in F.
8 — NY Islanders, 1980. Won two at Los Angeles in PR; three at Boston in QF; two at Buffalo in SF; and one at Philadelphia in F.
— Philadelphia Flyers, 1987. Won two at NY Rangers in DSF; two at NY Islanders in DF; three at Montreal in CF; and one at Edmonton in F.
— Edmonton Oilers, 1990. Won one at Winnipeg in DSF; two at Los Angeles in DF; two at Chicago in CF and three at Boston in F.
— Pittsburgh Penguins, 1992. Won two at Washington in DSF; two at NY Rangers in DF; two at Boston in CF; and two at Chicago in F.
— Vancouver Canucks, 1994. Won three at Calgary in CQF; two at Dallas in CSF; one at Toronto in CF; and two at NY Rangers in F.
— Colorado Avalanche, 1996. Won two at Vancouver in CQF; two at Chicago in CSF; two at Detroit in CF; and two at Florida in F.
— Detroit Red Wings, 1998. Won two at Phoenix in CQF; three at St. Louis in CSF; one at Dallas in CF; and two at Washington in F.
— Colorado Avalanche, 1999. Won three at San Jose in CQF; three at Detroit in CSF; and two at Dallas in CF.
— New Jersey Devils, 2001. Won two at Carolina in CQF; two at Toronto in CSF; two at Pittsburgh in CF; and two at Colorado in F.
— Detroit Red Wings, 2002. Won three at Vancouver in CQF; one at St. Louis in CSF; two at Colorado in CF; and two at Carolina in F.

MOST ROAD WINS, ALL TEAMS, ONE PLAYOFF YEAR:
46 — 1987. Of 87 games played, road teams won 46 (22 DSF, 14 DF, 8 CF and 2 in F).

MOST OVERTIME WINS, ONE TEAM, ONE PLAYOFF YEAR:
10 — Montreal Canadiens, 1993. Won two vs. Quebec in DSF; three vs. Buffalo in DF; two vs. NY Islanders in CF; and three vs. Los Angeles in F.
7 — Carolina Hurricanes, 2002. Won two vs. New Jersey in CQF; one vs. Montreal in CSF; three vs. Toronto in CF; and one vs. Detroit in F.
— Anaheim Mighty Ducks, 2003. Won two vs. Detroit in CQF; two vs. Dallas in CSF; one vs. Minnestoa in CF; and two vs. New Jersey in F.

MOST OVERTIME WINS AT HOME, ONE TEAM, ONE PLAYOFF YEAR:
4 — St. Louis Blues, 1968. Won one vs. Philadelphia in QF; three vs. Minnesota in SF.
— Montreal Canadiens, 1993. Won one vs. Quebec in DSF; one vs. Buffalo in DF, one vs. NY Islanders in CF; one vs. Los Angeles in F.

MOST OVERTIME WINS ON THE ROAD, ONE TEAM, ONE PLAYOFF YEAR:
6 — Montreal Canadiens, 1993. Won one vs. Quebec in DSF; two vs. Buffalo in DF; one vs. NY Islanders in CF; two vs. Los Angeles in F.

TEAM LOSSES

MOST LOSSES, ONE TEAM, ONE PLAYOFF YEAR:
11 — Philadelphia Flyers, 1987. Lost two vs. NY Rangers in DSF; three vs. NY Islanders in DF; two vs. Montreal in CF; four vs. Edmonton in F.
— Calgary Flames, 2004. Lost three vs. Vancouver in CQF; two vs. Detroit in CSF; two vs. San Jose in CF; four vs. Tampa Bay in F

MOST HOME LOSSES, ONE TEAM, ONE PLAYOFF YEAR:
7 — Calgary Flames, 2004. Lost two vs. Vancouver in DSF; one vs. Detroit in DF; two vs. San Jose in CF; two vs. Tampa Bay in F.
6 — Philadelphia Flyers, 1987. Lost one vs. NY Rangers in DSF; two vs. NY Islanders in DF; two vs. Montreal in CF; one vs. Edmonton in F.
— Washington Capitals, 1998. Lost two vs. Boston in CQF; two vs. Buffalo in CF; two vs. Detroit in F.
— Colorado Avalanche, 1999. Lost two vs. San Jose in CQF; two vs. Detroit in CSF; two vs. Dallas in CF.
— New Jersey Devils, 2001. Lost one vs. Carolina in CQF; two vs. Toronto in CSF; one vs. Pittsburgh in CF; two vs Colorado in F.
— Minnesota Wild, 2003. Lost two vs. Colorado in CQF; two vs. Vancouver in CSF; two vs. Anaheim in CF.

MOST ROAD LOSSES, ONE TEAM, ONE PLAYOFF YEAR:
7 — New Jersey Devils, 2003. Lost one at Boston in CQF; one at Tampa Bay in CSF; two at Ottawa in CF; three at Anaheim in F.

MOST OVERTIME LOSSES, ONE TEAM, ONE PLAYOFF YEAR:
4 — Montreal Canadiens, 1951. Lost four vs. Toronto in F.
— St. Louis Blues, 1968. Lost one vs. Philadelphia in QF; one vs. Minnesota in SF; two vs. Montreal in F.
— New York Rangers, 1979. Lost one vs. Philadelphia in QF; two vs. NY Islanders in SF; one vs. Montreal in F.
— Los Angeles Kings, 1991. Lost one vs. Vancouver in DSF; three vs. Edmonton in DF.
— Los Angeles Kings, 1993. Lost one vs. Toronto in CF; three vs. Montreal in F.
— New Jersey Devils, 1994. Lost one vs. Buffalo in CQF; one vs. Boston in CSF; two vs. NY Rangers in CF.
— Chicago Blackhawks, 1995. Lost one vs. Toronto in CQF; three vs. Detroit in CF.
— Philadelphia Flyers, 1996. Lost two vs. Tampa Bay in CQF; two vs. Florida in CSF.
— Dallas Stars, 1999. Lost two vs. St. Louis in CSF; one vs. Colorado in CF; one vs. Buffalo in F.
— Detroit Red Wings, 2002. Lost one vs. Vancouver in CQF; two vs. Colorado in CF; one vs. Carolina in F.
— New Jersey Devils, 2003. Lost two vs. Ottawa in CF; two vs. Anaheim in F.

MOST OVERTIME LOSSES AT HOME, ONE TEAM, ONE PLAYOFF YEAR:
4 — Detroit Red Wings, 2002. Lost one vs. Vancouver in CQF; two vs. Colorado in CF; one vs. Carolina in F.

MOST OVERTIME LOSSES ON THE ROAD, ONE TEAM, ONE PLAYOFF YEAR:
3 — Los Angeles Kings, 1991. Lost one at Vancouver in DSF; two at Edmonton in DF.
— Chicago Blackhawks, 1995. Lost one at Toronto in CQF; two at Detroit in CF.
— St. Louis Blues, 1996. Lost two at Toronto in CQF; one at Detroit in CSF.
— Dallas Stars, 1999. Lost two at St. Louis in CSF; one at Colorado in CF.
— New Jersey Devils, 2003. Lost one at Ottawa in CF; two at Anaheim in F.

PLAYOFF WINNING STREAKS

LONGEST PLAYOFF WINNING STREAK:
14 — Pittsburgh Penguins. Streak started May 9, 1992 as Pittsburgh won the first of three straight games in DF vs. NY Rangers. Continued with four wins vs. Boston in 1992 CF and four wins vs. Chicago in 1992 F. Pittsburgh then won the first three games of 1993 DSF vs. New Jersey. New Jersey ended the streak April 25, 1993, at New Jersey with a 4-1 win vs. Pittsburgh in the fourth game of 1993 DSF.
12 — Edmonton Oilers. Streak started May 15, 1984 as Edmonton won the first of three straight games in F vs. NY Islanders. Continued with three wins vs. Los Angeles in 1985 DSF and four wins vs. Winnipeg in 1985 DF. Edmonton then won the first two games of 1985 CF vs. Chicago. Chicago ended the streak May 9, 1985, at Chicago with a 5-2 win vs. Edmonton in the third game of 1985 CF.

MOST CONSECUTIVE WINS, ONE TEAM, ONE PLAYOFF YEAR:
11 — Chicago Blackhawks in 1992. Chicago won last three games of DSF vs. St. Louis to win series 4-2, defeated Detroit 4-0 in DF and Edmonton 4-0 in CF.
— Pittsburgh Penguins in 1992. Pittsburgh won last three games of DF vs. NY Rangers to win series 4-2, defeated Boston 4-0 in CF and Chicago 4-0 in F.
— Montreal Canadiens in 1993. Montreal won last four games of DSF vs. Quebec to win series 4-2, defeated Buffalo 4-0 in DF and won first three games of CF vs. NY Islanders.

PLAYOFF LOSING STREAKS

LONGEST PLAYOFF LOSING STREAK:
16 — Chicago Black Hawks. Streak started April 20, 1975 at Chicago with a 6-2 loss in fourth game of QF vs. Buffalo, won by Buffalo 4-1. Continued with four consecutive losses vs. Montreal, in 1976 QF and two straight losses vs. NY Islanders in 1977 best-of-three PRE. Chicago then lost four games vs. Boston in 1978 QF and four games vs. NY Islanders in 1979 QF. Chicago ended the streak April 8, 1980, at Chicago with a 3-2 win vs. St. Louis in the opening game of 1980 PRE.
— Los Angeles Kings. Streak started June 3, 1993 at Montreal with a 3-2 loss in second game of F vs. Montreal, won by Montreal 4-1. Los Angeles failed to qualify for the playoffs for the next four years. Then Los Angeles lost four games vs. St. Louis in 1998 CQF; missed the 1999 playoffs and lost four games vs. Detroit in 2002 CQF. Los Angeles then lost the first two games of 2001 CQF vs. Detroit. Los Angeles ended the streak April 15, 2001, at Los Angeles with a 2-1 win vs. Detroit in the third game of 2001 CQF.

Canadiens goaltender Gerry McNeil sprawls to make a save during the 1951 Stanley Cup Final against the Maple Leafs. Toronto won the series in five games, with every outcome determined in overtime. Montreal is the only team in NHL history to lose four overtime games in a single series.

MOST GOALS IN A SERIES, ONE TEAM

MOST GOALS, ONE TEAM, ONE PLAYOFF SERIES:
44 — Edmonton Oilers in 1985. Edmonton won best-of-seven CF 4-2, outscoring Chicago 44-25.
35 — Edmonton Oilers in 1983. Edmonton won best-of-seven DF 4-1, outscoring Calgary 35-13.
— Calgary Flames in 1995. Calgary lost best-of-seven CQF 4-3, outscoring San Jose 35-26.

MOST GOALS, ONE TEAM, TWO-GAME SERIES:
11 — Buffalo Sabres in 1977. Buffalo won best-of-three PRE 2-0, outscoring Minnesota 11-3.
— Toronto Maple Leafs in 1978. Toronto won best-of-three PRE 2-0, outscoring Los Angeles 11-3.

MOST GOALS, ONE TEAM, THREE-GAME SERIES:
23 — Chicago Blackhawks in 1985. Chicago won best-of-five DSF 3-0, outscoring Detroit 23-8.
20 — Minnesota North Stars in 1981. Minnesota won best-of-five PRE 3-0, outscoring Boston 20-13.
— NY Islanders in 1981. NY Islanders won best-of-five PRE 3-0, outscoring Toronto 20-4.

MOST GOALS, ONE TEAM, FOUR-GAME SERIES:
28 — Boston Bruins in 1972. Boston won best-of-seven SF 4-0, outscoring St. Louis 28-8.

MOST GOALS, ONE TEAM, FIVE-GAME SERIES:
35 — Edmonton Oilers in 1983. Edmonton won best-of-seven DF 4-1, outscoring Calgary 35-13.
32 — Edmonton Oilers in 1987. Edmonton won best-of-seven DSF 4-1, outscoring Los Angeles 32-20.
30 — Calgary Flames in 1988. Calgary won best-of-seven DSF 4-1, outscoring Los Angeles 30-18.

MOST GOALS, ONE TEAM, SIX-GAME SERIES:
44 — Edmonton Oilers in 1985. Edmonton won best-of-seven CF 4-2, outscoring Chicago 44-25.
33 — Montreal Canadiens in 1973. Montreal won best-of-seven F 4-2, outscoring Chicago 33-23.
— Chicago Blackhawks in 1985. Chicago won best-of-seven DF 4-2, outscoring Minnesota 33-29.
— Los Angeles Kings in 1993. Los Angeles won best-of-seven DSF 4-2, outscoring Calgary 33-28.

MOST GOALS, ONE TEAM, SEVEN-GAME SERIES:
35 — Calgary Flames in 1995. Calgary lost best-of-seven CQF 4-3, outscoring San Jose 35-26.
33 — Philadelphia Flyers in 1976. Philadelphia won best-of-seven QF 4-3, outscoring Toronto 33-23.
— Boston Bruins in 1983. Boston won best-of-seven DF 4-3, outscoring Buffalo 33-23.
— Edmonton Oilers in 1984. Edmonton won best-of-seven DF 4-3, outscoring Calgary 33-27.

FEWEST GOALS IN A SERIES, ONE TEAM

FEWEST GOALS, ONE TEAM, TWO-GAME SERIES:
0 — Toronto St. Patricks in 1921. Toronto lost two-game, total-goals NHL F 7-0 vs. Ottawa.
— New York Americans in 1929. NY Americans lost two-game, total-goals QF 1-0 vs. NY Rangers.
— New York Rangers in 1931. NY Rangers lost two-game, total-goals SF 3-0 vs. Chicago.
— Chicago Black Hawks in 1935. Chicago lost two-game, total-goals SF 1-0 vs. Mtl. Maroons.
— Montreal Maroons in 1937. Mtl. Maroons lost best-of-three SF 2-0, outscored by NY Rangers 5-0.
— New York Americans in 1939. NY Americans lost best-of-three QF 2-0, outscored by Toronto 5-0.

FEWEST GOALS, ONE TEAM, THREE-GAME SERIES:
1 — Montreal Maroons in 1936. Mtl. Maroons lost best-of-five SF 3-0, outscored by Detroit 6-1.

FEWEST GOALS, ONE TEAM, FOUR-GAME SERIES:
1 — Minnesota Wild in 2003. Minnesota lost best-of-seven CF 4-0, outscored by Anaheim 9-1.

FEWEST GOALS, ONE TEAM, FIVE-GAME SERIES:
2 — Philadelphia Flyers in 2002. Ottawa won best-of-seven CQF 4-1, while outscoring Philadelphia 11-2.

FEWEST GOALS, ONE TEAM, SIX-GAME SERIES:
5 — Boston Bruins in 1951. Toronto won best-of-seven SF 4-1 with 1 tie, outscoring Boston 17-5.

FEWEST GOALS, ONE TEAM, SEVEN-GAME SERIES:
9 — Toronto Maple Leafs, in 1945. Toronto won best-of- seven F 4-3; teams tied in scoring 9-9.
— Detroit Red Wings, in 1945. Toronto won best-of-seven F 4-3; teams tied in scoring 9-9.

Twice in NHL history there has only been one goal scored in an entire playoff series. Paul Thompson played in both. He lost to the Montreal Maroons as a member of the Chicago Blackhawks in 1935, but had set up the winning goal for the New York Rangers (scored by Butch Keeling) in 1929.

MOST GOALS IN A SERIES, BOTH TEAMS

MOST GOALS, BOTH TEAMS, ONE PLAYOFF SERIES:
69 — Edmonton Oilers (44), Chicago Black Hawks (25) in 1985. Edmonton won best-of-seven CF 4-2.
62 — Chicago Black Hawks (33), Minnesota North Stars (29) in 1985. Chicago won best-of-seven DF 4-2.
61 — Los Angeles Kings (33), Calgary Flames (28) in 1993. Los Angeles won best-of-seven DSF 4-2.
— Calgary Flames (35), San Jose Sharks (26) in 1995. San Jose won best-of-seven CQF 4-3.

MOST GOALS, BOTH TEAMS, TWO-GAME SERIES:
17 — Toronto St. Patricks (10), Montreal Canadiens (7) in 1918. Toronto won two-game total-goals NHL F.
15 — Boston Bruins (10), Chicago Black Hawks (5) in 1927. Boston won two-game total-goals QF.
— Pittsburgh Penguins (9), St. Louis Blues (6) in 1975. Pittsburgh won best-of-three PRE 2-0.

MOST GOALS, BOTH TEAMS, THREE-GAME SERIES:
33 — Minnesota North Stars (20), Boston Bruins (13) in 1981. Minnesota won best-of-five PRE 3-0.
31 — Chicago Black Hawks (23), Detroit Red Wings (8) in 1985. Chicago won best-of-five DSF 3-0.
28 — Toronto Maple Leafs (18), New York Rangers (10) in 1932. Toronto won best-of-five F 3-0.

MOST GOALS, BOTH TEAMS, FOUR-GAME SERIES:
36 — Boston Bruins (28), St. Louis Blues (8) in 1972. Boston won best-of-seven SF 4-0.
— Minnesota North Stars (18), Toronto Maple Leafs (18) in 1983. Minnesota won best-of-five DSF 3-1.
— Edmonton Oilers (25), Chicago Black Hawks (11) in 1983. Edmonton won best-of-seven CF 4-0.
35 — New York Rangers (23), Los Angeles Kings (12) in 1981. NY Rangers won best-of-five PRE 3-1.

MOST GOALS, BOTH TEAMS, FIVE-GAME SERIES:
52 — Edmonton Oilers (32), Los Angeles Kings (20) in 1987. Edmonton won best-of-seven DSF 4-1.
50 — Los Angeles Kings (27), Edmonton Oilers (23) in 1982. Los Angeles won best-of-five DSF 3-2.
48 — Edmonton Oilers (35), Calgary Flames (13) in 1983. Edmonton won best-of-seven DF 4-1.
— Calgary Flames (30), Los Angeles Kings (18) in 1988. Calgary won best-of-seven DSF 4-1.

MOST GOALS, BOTH TEAMS, SIX-GAME SERIES:
69 — Edmonton Oilers (44), Chicago Black Hawks (25) in 1985. Edmonton won best-of-seven CF 4-2.
62 — Chicago Black Hawks (33), Minnesota North Stars (29) in 1985. Chicago won best-of-seven DF 4-2.
61 — Los Angeles Kings (33), Calgary Flames (28) in 1993. Los Angeles won best-of-seven DSF 4-2.

MOST GOALS, BOTH TEAMS, SEVEN-GAME SERIES:
61 — Calgary Flames (35), San Jose Sharks (26) in 1995. San Jose won best-of-seven CQF 4-3.
60 — Edmonton Oilers (33), Calgary Flames (27) in 1984. Edmonton won best-of-seven DF 4-3.

FEWEST GOALS IN A SERIES, BOTH TEAMS

FEWEST GOALS, BOTH TEAMS, TWO-GAME SERIES:
1 — New York Rangers (1), New York Americans (0) in 1929. NY Rangers won two-game total-goals QF.
— Montreal Maroons (1), Chicago Black Hawks (0) in 1935. Mtl. Maroons won two-game total-goals SF.

FEWEST GOALS, BOTH TEAMS, THREE-GAME SERIES:
7 — Boston Bruins (5), Montreal Canadiens (2) in 1929. Boston won best-of-five SF 3-0.
— Detroit Red Wings (6), Montreal Maroons (1) in 1936. Detroit won best-of-five SF 3-0.

FEWEST GOALS, BOTH TEAMS, FOUR-GAME SERIES:
9 — Toronto Maple Leafs (7), Boston Bruins (2) in 1935. Toronto won best-of-five SF 3-1.

FEWEST GOALS, BOTH TEAMS, FIVE-GAME SERIES:
11 — Montreal Maroons (6), New York Rangers (5) in 1928. NY Rangers won best-of-five F 3-2.

FEWEST GOALS, BOTH TEAMS, SIX-GAME SERIES:
16 — Carolina Hurricanes (10), Toronto Maple Leafs (6) in 2002. Carolina won best-of-seven CF 4-2.

FEWEST GOALS, BOTH TEAMS, SEVEN-GAME SERIES:
18 — Toronto Maple Leafs (9), Detroit Red Wings (9) in 1945. Toronto won best-of-seven F 4-3.

MOST GOALS IN A GAME OR PERIOD

MOST GOALS, ONE TEAM, ONE GAME:
13 — Edmonton Oilers April 9, 1987, vs. Los Angeles at Edmonton. Edmonton won 13-3.
12 — Los Angeles Kings, April 10, 1990, vs. Calgary at Los Angeles. Los Angeles won 12-4.
11 — Montreal Canadiens, March 30, 1944, vs. Toronto at Montreal. Montreal won 11-0.
— Edmonton Oilers, May 4, 1985, vs. Chicago at Edmonton. Edmonton won 11-2.

MOST GOALS, ONE TEAM, ONE PERIOD:
7 — Montreal Canadiens, March 30, 1944, vs. Toronto at Montreal, third period. Montreal won 11-0.

MOST GOALS, BOTH TEAMS, ONE GAME:
18 — Los Angeles Kings (10), Edmonton Oilers (8), April 7, 1982, at Edmonton. Los Angeles won best-of-five DSF 3-2.
17 — Pittsburgh Penguins (10), Philadelphia Flyers (7), April 25, 1989, at Pittsburgh. Pittsburgh won best-of-seven DF 4-3.
16 — Edmonton Oilers (13), Los Angeles Kings (3), April 9, 1987, at Edmonton. Edmonton won best-of-seven DSF 4-1.
— Los Angeles Kings (12), Calgary Flames (4), April 10, 1990, at Los Angeles. Los Angeles won best-of-seven DF 4-2.

MOST GOALS, BOTH TEAMS, ONE PERIOD:
9 — New York Rangers (6), Philadelphia Flyers (3), April 24, 1979, third period, at Philadelphia. NY Rangers won 8-3.
— Los Angeles Kings (5), Calgary Flames (4), April 10, 1990, second period, at Los Angeles. Los Angeles won 12-4.
8 — Chicago Black Hawks (5), Montreal Canadiens (3), May 8, 1973, second period, at Montreal. Chicago won 8-7.
— Chicago Black Hawks (5), Edmonton Oilers (3), May 12, 1985, first period, at Chicago. Chicago won 8-6.
— Edmonton Oilers (6), Winnipeg Jets (2), April 6, 1988, third period, at Edmonton. Edmonton won 7-4.
— Hartford Whalers (5), Montreal Canadiens (3), April 10, 1988, third period, at Montreal. Hartford won 7-5.
— Vancouver Canucks (5), New York Rangers (3), June 9, 1994, third period, at NY Rangers. Vancouver won 6-3.

TEAM POWER-PLAY GOALS

MOST POWER-PLAY GOALS BY ALL TEAMS, ONE PLAYOFF YEAR:
199 — 1988 in 83 games.

MOST POWER-PLAY GOALS, ONE TEAM, ONE PLAYOFF YEAR:
35 — Minnesota North Stars, 1991 in 23 games.
32 — Edmonton Oilers, 1988 in 18 games.
31 — New York Islanders, 1981 in 18 games.

MOST POWER-PLAY GOALS, ONE TEAM, ONE SERIES:
15 — New York Islanders in 1980 F vs. Philadelphia. NY Islanders won series 4-2.
— Minnesota North Stars in 1991 DSF vs. Chicago. Minnesota won series 4-2.
13 — New York Islanders in 1981 QF vs. Edmonton. NY Islanders won series 4-2.
— Calgary Flames in 1986 CF vs. St. Louis. Calgary won series 4-3.
12 — Toronto Maple Leafs in 1976 QF vs. Philadelphia. Philadelphia won series 4-3.

MOST POWER-PLAY GOALS, BOTH TEAMS, ONE SERIES:
21 — New York Islanders (15), Philadelphia Flyers (6) in 1980 best-of-seven F won by NY Islanders 4-2.
— New York Islanders (13), Edmonton Oilers (8) in 1981 best-of-seven QF won by NY Islanders 4-2.
— Philadelphia Flyers (11), Pittsburgh Penguins (10) in 1989 best-of-seven DF won by Philadelphia 4-3.
— Minnesota North Stars (15), Chicago Black Hawks (6) in 1991 best-of-seven DSF won by Minnesota 4-2.
20 — Toronto Maple Leafs (12), Philadelphia Flyers (8) in 1976 best-of-seven QF won by Philadelphia 4-3.

MOST POWER-PLAY GOALS, ONE TEAM, ONE GAME:
6 — Boston Bruins, April 2, 1969, at Boston vs. Toronto. Boston won 10-0.

MOST POWER-PLAY GOALS, BOTH TEAMS, ONE GAME:
8 — Minnesota North Stars (4), St. Louis Blues (4), April 24, 1991, at Minnesota. Minnesota won 8-4.
7 — Minnesota North Stars (4), Edmonton Oilers (3), April 28, 1984, at Minnesota. Edmonton won 8-5.
— Philadelphia Flyers (4), NY Rangers (3), April 13, 1985, at NY Rangers. Philadelphia won 6-5.
— Chicago Black Hawks (5), Edmonton Oilers (2), May 14, 1985, at Edmonton. Edmonton won 10-5.
— Edmonton Oilers (5), Los Angeles Kings (2), April 9, 1987, at Edmonton. Edmonton won 13-3.
— Vancouver Canucks (4), Calgary Flames (3), April 9, 1989, at Vancouver. Vancouver won 5-3.

MOST POWER-PLAY GOALS, ONE TEAM, ONE PERIOD:
4 — Toronto Maple Leafs, March 26, 1936, second period vs. Boston at Toronto. Toronto won 8-3.
— Minnesota North Stars, April 28, 1984, second period vs. Edmonton at Minnesota. Edmonton won 8-5.
— Boston Bruins, April 11, 1991, third period vs. Hartford at Boston. Boston won 6-1.
— Minnesota North Stars, April 24, 1991, second period vs. St. Louis at Minnesota. Minnesota won 8-4.
— St. Louis Blues, April 27, 1998, third period at Los Angeles. St. Louis won 4-3.

MOST POWER-PLAY GOALS, BOTH TEAMS, ONE PERIOD:
5 — Minnesota North Stars (4), Edmonton Oilers (1), April 28, 1984, at Minnesota. Edmonton won 8-5.
— Vancouver Canucks (3), Calgary Flames (2), April 9, 1989, at Vancouver. Vancouver won 5-3.
— Minnesota North Stars (4), St. Louis Blues (1), April 24, 1991, at Minnesota. Minnesota won 8-4.

TEAM SHORTHAND GOALS

MOST SHORTHAND GOALS BY ALL TEAMS, ONE PLAYOFF YEAR:
33 — 1988, in 83 games.

MOST SHORTHAND GOALS, ONE TEAM, ONE PLAYOFF YEAR:
10 — Edmonton Oilers, 1983, in 16 games.
9 — New York Islanders, 1981, in 19 games.
8 — Philadelphia Flyers, 1989, in 19 games.

MOST SHORTHAND GOALS, ONE TEAM, ONE SERIES:
6 — Calgary Flames in 1995 vs. San Jose in best-of-seven CQF won by San Jose 4-3.
— Vancouver Canucks in 1995 vs. St. Louis in best-of-seven CQF won by Vancouver 4-3.
5 — NY Rangers in 1979 vs. Philadelphia in best-of-seven QF won by NY Rangers 4-1.
— Edmonton Oilers in 1983 vs. Calgary in best-of-seven DF won by Edmonton 4-1.

MOST SHORTHAND GOALS, BOTH TEAMS, ONE SERIES:
7 — Boston Bruins (4), NY Rangers (3), in 1958 SF won by Boston 4-2.
— Edmonton Oilers (5), Calgary Flames (2), in 1983 DF won by Edmonton 4-1.
— Vancouver Canucks (6), St. Louis Blues (1), in 1995 CQF won by Vancouver 4-3.

MOST SHORTHAND GOALS, ONE TEAM, ONE GAME:
3 — Boston Bruins, April 11, 1981, at Minnesota North Stars. Minnesota won 6-3.
— New York Islanders, April 17, 1983, at NY Rangers. NY Rangers won 7-6.
— Toronto Maple Leafs, May 8, 1994, at San Jose Sharks. Toronto won 8-3.

MOST SHORTHAND GOALS, BOTH TEAMS, ONE GAME:

4 — **Boston Bruins (3), Minnesota North Stars (1),** April 11, 1981, at Minnesota. Minnesota won 6-3.
— **New York Islanders (3), New York Rangers (1),** April 17, 1983, at NY Rangers. NY Rangers won 7-6.
— **Toronto Maple Leafs (3), San Jose Sharks (1),** May 8, 1994, at San Jose. Toronto won 8-3.
3 — Toronto Maple Leafs (2), Detroit Red Wings (1), April 5, 1947, at Toronto. Toronto won 6-1.
— New York Rangers (2), Boston Bruins (1), April 1, 1958, at Boston. NY Rangers won 5-2.
— Minnesota North Stars (2), Philadelphia Flyers (1), May 4, 1980, at Minnesota. Philadelphia won 5-3.
— Winnipeg Jets (2), Edmonton Oilers (1), April 9, 1988, at Winnipeg. Winnipeg won 6-4.
— New York Islanders (2), New Jersey Devils (1), April 14, 1988, at New Jersey. New Jersey won 6-5.
— Montreal Canadiens (2), New Jersey Devils (1), April 17, 1997, at New Jersey. New Jersey won 5-2.
— Dallas Stars (2), San Jose Sharks (1), May 5, 2000, at San Jose. Dallas won 5-4.
— Detroit Red Wings (2), Calgary Flames (1), April 21, 2007, at Detroit. Detroit won 5-1.

MOST SHORTHAND GOALS, ONE TEAM, ONE PERIOD:

2 — **Toronto Maple Leafs,** April 5, 1947, first period vs. Detroit at Toronto. Toronto won 6-1.
— **Toronto Maple Leafs,** April 13, 1965, first period vs. Montreal at Toronto. Montreal won 4-3.
— **Boston Bruins,** April 20, 1969, first period vs. Montreal at Boston. Boston won 3-2.
— **Boston Bruins,** April 8, 1970, second period vs. NY Rangers at Boston. Boston won 8-2.
— **Boston Bruins,** April 30, 1972, first period vs. NY Rangers at Boston. Boston won 6-5.
— **Chicago Black Hawks,** May 3, 1973, first period vs. Montreal at Chicago. Chicago won 7-4.
— **Montreal Canadiens,** April 23, 1978, first period at Detroit. Montreal won 8-0.
— **New York Islanders,** April 8, 1980, second period vs. Los Angeles at NY Islanders. NY Islanders won 8-1.
— **Los Angeles Kings,** April 9, 1980, first period at NY Islanders. Los Angeles won 6-3.
— **Boston Bruins,** April 13, 1980, second period at Pittsburgh. Boston won 8-3.
— **Minnesota North Stars,** May 4, 1980, second period vs. Philadelphia at Minnesota. Philadelphia won 5-3.
— **Boston Bruins,** April 11, 1981, third period at Minnesota North Stars. Minnesota won 6-3.
— **New York Islanders,** May 12, 1981, first period vs. Minnesota North Stars at NY Islanders. NY Islanders won 6-3.
— **Montreal Canadiens,** April 7, 1982, third period vs. Quebec at Montreal. Montreal won 5-1.
— **Edmonton Oilers,** April 24, 1983, third period vs. Chicago at Edmonton. Edmonton won 8-4.
— **Winnipeg Jets,** April 14, 1985, second period at Calgary. Winnipeg won 5-3.
— **Boston Bruins,** April 6, 1988, first period vs. Buffalo at Boston. Boston won 7-3.
— **New York Islanders,** April 14, 1988, third period at New Jersey. New Jersey won 6-5.
— **Detroit Red Wings,** April 29, 1993, second period at Toronto. Detroit won 7-3.
— **Toronto Maple Leafs,** May 8, 1994, third period at San Jose. Toronto won 8-3.
— **Calgary Flames,** May 11, 1995, first period at San Jose. Calgary won 9-2.
— **Vancouver Canucks,** May 15, 1995, second period at St. Louis. Vancouver won 6-5.
— **Montreal Canadiens,** April 17, 1997, second period at New Jersey. New Jersey won 5-2.
— **Philadelphia Flyers,** April 26, 1997, first period vs. Pittsburgh at Philadelphia. Philadelphia won 6-3.
— **Phoenix Coyotes,** April 24, 1998, second period at Detroit. Phoenix won 7-4.
— **Buffalo Sabres,** April 27, 1998, second period vs. Philadelphia at Buffalo. Buffalo won 6-1.
— **San Jose Sharks,** April 30, 1999, third period at Colorado. San Jose won 7-3.
— **Detroit Red Wings,** April 27, 2002, second period at Vancouver. Detroit won 6-4.
— **Detroit Red Wings,** April 21, 2007, second period at Detroit. Detroit won 5-1.

MOST SHORTHAND GOALS, BOTH TEAMS, ONE PERIOD:

3 — **Toronto Maple Leafs (2), Detroit Red Wings (1),** April 5, 1947, first period at Toronto. Toronto won 6-1.
— **Toronto Maple Leafs (2), San Jose Sharks (1),** May 8, 1994, third period at San Jose. Toronto won 8-3.

FASTEST GOALS

FASTEST FIVE GOALS, BOTH TEAMS:

3:06 — Minnesota North Stars, Chicago Black Hawks, April 21, 1985, at Chicago. Keith Brown scored for Chicago at 1:12 of the second period; Ken Yaremchuk, Chicago, 1:27; Dino Ciccarelli, Minnesota, 2:48; Tony McKegney, Minnesota, 4:07; and Curt Fraser, Chicago, 4:18. Chicago won 6-2 and won best-of-seven DF 4-2.

3:20 — Minnesota North Stars, Philadelphia Flyers, April 29, 1980, at Philadelphia. Paul Shmyr scored for Minnesota at 13:20 of the first period; Steve Christoff, Minnesota, 13:59; Ken Linseman, Philadelphia, 14:54; Tom Gorence, Philadelphia, 15:36; and Ken Linseman, Philadelphia, 16:40. Minnesota won 6-5. Philadelphia won best-of-seven SF 4-1.

4:00 — Los Angeles Kings, Detroit Red Wings, April 15, 2000, at Detroit. Brendan Shanahan scored for Detroit at 0:55 of the first period; Martin Lapointe, Detroit, 1:33; Luc Robitaille, Los Angeles, 2:04; Kris Draper, Detroit, 3:32; and Ziggy Palffy, Los Angeles, 4:55. Detroit won 8-5 and won best-of-seven CQF 4-0.

FASTEST FIVE GOALS, ONE TEAM:

3:36 — Montreal Canadiens, March 30, 1944, at Montreal vs. Toronto. Toe Blake scored at 7:58 and 8:37 of the third period; Maurice Richard, 9:17; Ray Getliffe, 10:33; and Buddy O'Connor, 11:34. Canadiens won 11-0 and won best-of-seven SF 4-1.

FASTEST FOUR GOALS, BOTH TEAMS:

1:33 — Toronto Maple Leafs, Philadelphia Flyers, April 20, 1976, at Philadelphia. Don Saleski scored for Philadelphia at 10:04 of the second period; Bob Neely, Toronto, 10:42; Gary Dornhoefer, Philadelphia, 11:24; and Don Saleski, Philadelphia, 11:37. Philadelphia won 7-1 and won best-of-seven SF 4-3.

1:34 — Calgary Flames, Montreal Canadiens, May 20, 1986, at Montreal. Joel Otto scored for Calgary at 17:59 of the first period; Bobby Smith, Montreal, 18:25; Mats Naslund, Montreal, 19:17; and Bob Gainey, Montreal, 19:33. Montreal won 5-3 and won best-of-seven F 4-1.

1:38 — Boston Bruins, Philadelphia Flyers, April 26, 1977, at Philadelphia. Gregg Sheppard scored for Boston at 14:01 of the second period; Mike Milbury, Boston, 15:01; Gary Dornhoefer, Philadelphia, 15:16; and Jean Ratelle, Boston, 15:39. Boston won 5-4 and won best-of-seven SF 4-0.

FASTEST FOUR GOALS, ONE TEAM:

2:35 — Montreal Canadiens, March 30, 1944, at Montreal. Toe Blake scored at 7:58 and 8:37 of the third period; Maurice Richard, 9:17; and Ray Getliffe, 10:33. Montreal won 11-0 and won best-of-seven SF 4-1.

FASTEST THREE GOALS, BOTH TEAMS:

0:21 — Chicago Black Hawks, Edmonton Oilers, May 7, 1985, at Edmonton. Behn Wilson scored for Chicago at 19:22 of the third period; Jari Kurri, Edmonton, 19:36; and Glenn Anderson, Edmonton, 19:43. Edmonton won 7-3 and won best-of-seven CF 4-2.

0:27 — Phoenix Coyotes, Detroit Red Wings, April 24, 1998, at Detroit. Jeremy Roenick scored for Phoenix at 13:24 of the second period; Mathieu Dandenault, Detroit, 13:32; and Keith Tkachuk, Phoenix, 13:51. Phoenix won 7-4. Detroit won best-of-seven CQF 4-2.

0:30 — Pittsburgh Penguins, Chicago Blackhawks, June 1, 1992, at Chicago. Dirk Graham scored for Chicago at 6:21 of the first period; Kevin Stevens, Pittsburgh, 6:33; and Dirk Graham, Chicago, 6:51. Pittsburgh won 6-5 and won best-of-seven F 4-0.

FASTEST THREE GOALS, ONE TEAM:

0:23 — Toronto Maple Leafs, April 12, 1979, at Toronto vs. Atlanta Flames. Darryl Sittler scored at 4:04 and 4:16 of the first period; and Ron Ellis, 4:27. Toronto won 7-4 and won best-of-three PRE 2-0.

0:38 — New York Rangers, April 12, 1986, at NY Rangers vs. Philadelphia. Jim Weimer scored at 12:29 of the third period; Bob Brooke, 12:43; and Ron Greschner, 13:07. NY Rangers won 5-2 and won best-of-five DSF 3-2.
— Colorado Avalanche, April 18, 2001, at Vancouver. Peter Forsberg scored at 9:11 of the third period; Joe Sakic, 9:28; and Eric Messier, 9:49. Colorado won 5-1 and won best-of-seven CQF 4-0.

FASTEST TWO GOALS, BOTH TEAMS:

0:05 — Pittsburgh Penguins, Buffalo Sabres, April 14, 1979, at Buffalo. Gilbert Perreault scored for Buffalo at 12:59 of the first period; and Jim Hamilton, Pittsburgh, 13:04. Pittsburgh won 4-3 and won best-of-three PRE 2-1.

0:08 — St. Louis Blues, Minnesota North Stars, April 9, 1989, at Minnesota. Bernie Federko scored for St. Louis at 2:28 of the third period; and Perry Berezan, Minnesota, 2:36. Minnesota won 5-4. St. Louis won best-of-seven DSF 4-1.
— Phoenix Coyotes, Detroit Red Wings, April 24, 1998, at Detroit. Jeremy Roenick scored for Phoenix at 13:24 of the second period; and Mathieu Dandenault, Detroit, 13:32. Phoenix won 7-4. Detroit won best-of-seven CQF 4-2.

FASTEST TWO GOALS, ONE TEAM:

0:05 — Detroit Red Wings, April 11, 1965, at Detroit vs. Chicago. Norm Ullman scored at 17:35 and 17:40 of the second period. Detroit won 4-2. Chicago won best-of-seven SF 4-3.

Jean-Sebastien Giguere set records en route to winning the Conn Smythe Trophy as playoff MVP in 2003, despite losing the Final to New Jersey. He didn't win the award in 2007, but the results were more rewarding as his Ducks won the Stanley Cup.

OVERTIME

SHORTEST OVERTIME:
0:09 — Montreal Canadiens, Calgary Flames, May 18, 1986, at Calgary. Montreal won 3-2 on Brian Skrudland's goal at 0:09 of the first overtime period. Montreal won best-of-seven F 4-1.
0:11 — New York Islanders, New York Rangers, April 11, 1975, at NY Rangers. NY Islanders won 4-3 on J.P. Parise's goal at 0:11 of the first overtime period. NY Islanders won best-of-three PRE 2-1.

LONGEST OVERTIME:
116:30 — Detroit Red Wings, Montreal Maroons, March 24, 1936, at Montreal. Mtl. Maroons won 1-0 on Mud Bruneteau's goal at 16:30 of the sixth overtime period. Detroit won best-of-five SF 3-0.

MOST OVERTIME GAMES, ONE PLAYOFF YEAR:
28 — 1993. Of 85 games played, 28 went into overtime.
26 — 2001. Of 86 games played, 26 went into overtime.
22 — 2003. Of 89 games played, 22 went into overtime.

FEWEST OVERTIME GAMES, ONE PLAYOFF YEAR:
0 — 1963. None of the 16 games went into overtime, the only year since 1926 that no overtime was required in any playoff series.

MOST OVERTIME GAMES, ONE SERIES:
5 — Toronto Maple Leafs, Montreal Canadiens in 1951. Toronto won best-of-seven F 4-1.
4 — Toronto Maple Leafs, Boston Bruins in 1933. Toronto won best-of-five SF 3-2.
— Boston Bruins, NY Rangers in 1939. Boston won best-of-seven SF 4-3.
— St. Louis Blues, Minnesota North Stars in 1968. St. Louis won best-of-seven SF 4-3.
— Dallas Stars, St. Louis Blues in 1999. Dallas won best-of-seven CSF 4-2.
— Dallas Stars, Edmonton Oilers in 2001. Dallas won best-of-seven CQF 4-2.

TEAM HAT-TRICKS

MOST HAT-TRICKS, BY ALL TEAMS, ONE PLAYOFF YEAR:
12 — 1983 in 66 games.
— 1988 in 83 games.
11 — 1985 in 70 games.
— 1992 in 86 games.

MOST HAT-TRICKS, ONE TEAM, ONE PLAYOFF YEAR:
6 — Edmonton Oilers in 16 games, 1983.
— Edmonton Oilers in 18 games, 1985.

SHUTOUTS

MOST SHUTOUTS, ONE PLAYOFF YEAR, ALL TEAMS:
25 — 2002. Of 90 games played, Detroit had 6; Ottawa had 4; Carolina, Colorado, St. Louis and Toronto had 3 each; while Los Angeles, New Jersey and Philadelphia had 1 each.
23 — 2004. Of 89 games played, Tampa Bay and Calgary had 5 each; Toronto and San Jose had 3 each; while Boston, Colorado, Detroit, Montreal, Nashville, NY Islanders and Philadelphia had 1 each.
19 — 2001. Of 86 games played, Colorado and New Jersey had 4 each, Toronto had 3, Pittsburgh and Los Angeles had 2 each, while Buffalo, Washington, Detroit and San Jose had 1 each.

FEWEST SHUTOUTS, ONE PLAYOFF YEAR, ALL TEAMS:
0 — 1959. 18 games played.

MOST SHUTOUTS, BOTH TEAMS, ONE SERIES:
5 — Toronto Maple Leafs (3), Detroit Red Wings (2), in 1945. Toronto won best-of-seven F 4-3.
— Toronto Maple Leafs (3), Detroit Red Wings (2), in 1950. Detroit won best-of-seven SF 4-3.

TEAM PENALTIES

FEWEST PENALTIES, BOTH TEAMS, BEST-OF-SEVEN SERIES:
19 — Detroit Red Wings, Toronto Maple Leafs in 1945. Detroit received 10 minors, Toronto received 9 minors. Detroit won best-of-seven F 4-3.

FEWEST PENALTIES, ONE TEAM, BEST-OF-SEVEN SERIES:
9 — Toronto Maple Leafs in 1945 vs. Detroit. Toronto received 9 minors. Detroit won best-of-seven F 4-3.

MOST PENALTIES, BOTH TEAMS, ONE SERIES:
218 — New Jersey Devils, Washington Capitals in 1988. New Jersey received 97 minors, 11 majors, 9 misconducts and 1 match penalty. Washington received 80 minors, 11 majors, 8 misconducts and 1 match penalty. New Jersey won best-of-seven DF 4-3.

MOST PENALTY MINUTES, BOTH TEAMS, ONE SERIES:
654 — New Jersey Devils (349), Washington Capitals (305) in 1988. New Jersey won best-of-seven DF 4-3.

MOST PENALTIES, ONE TEAM, ONE SERIES:
118 — New Jersey Devils in 1988 vs. Washington. New Jersey received 97 minors, 11 majors, 9 misconducts and 1 match penalty. New Jersey won best-of-seven DF 4-3.

MOST PENALTY MINUTES, ONE TEAM, ONE SERIES:
349 — New Jersey Devils in 1988 vs. Washington. New Jersey won best-of-seven DF 4-3.

MOST PENALTIES, BOTH TEAMS, ONE GAME:
66 — Detroit Red Wings (33), St. Louis Blues (33), April 12, 1991, at St. Louis. St. Louis won 6-1.
63 — Minnesota North Stars (34), Chicago Blackhawks (29), April 6, 1990, at Chicago. Chicago won 5-3.
62 — New Jersey Devils (32), Washington Capitals (30), April 22, 1988, at New Jersey. New Jersey won 10-4.

MOST PENALTY MINUTES, BOTH TEAMS, ONE GAME:
298 — Detroit Red Wings (152), St. Louis Blues (146), April 12, 1991, at St. Louis. Detroit received 33 penalties; St. Louis received 33 penalties. St. Louis won 6-1.
267 — New York Rangers (142), Los Angeles Kings (125), April 9, 1981, at Los Angeles. NY Rangers received 31 penalties; Los Angeles received 28 penalties. Los Angeles won 5-4.

MOST PENALTIES, ONE TEAM, ONE GAME:
34 — Minnesota North Stars, April 6, 1990, at Chicago. Chicago won 5-3.
33 — Detroit Red Wings, April 12, 1991, at St. Louis. St. Louis won 6-1.
— St. Louis Blues, April 12, 1991, at St. Louis vs. Detroit. St. Louis won 6-1.

MOST PENALTY MINUTES, ONE TEAM, ONE GAME:
152 — Detroit Red Wings, April 12, 1991, at St. Louis. St. Louis won 6-1.
146 — St. Louis Blues, April 12, 1991, at St. Louis vs. Detroit. St. Louis won 6-1.
142 — New York Rangers, April 9, 1981, at Los Angeles. Los Angeles won 5-4.

MOST PENALTIES, BOTH TEAMS, ONE PERIOD:
43 — New York Rangers (24), Los Angeles Kings (19), April 9, 1981, first period at Los Angeles. Los Angeles won 5-4.

MOST PENALTY MINUTES, BOTH TEAMS, ONE PERIOD:
248 — New York Islanders (124), Boston Bruins (124), April 17, 1980, first period at Boston. NY Islanders won 5-4.

MOST PENALTIES, ONE TEAM, ONE PERIOD:
24 — New York Rangers, April 9, 1981, first period at Los Angeles. Los Angeles won 5-4.

MOST PENALTY MINUTES, ONE TEAM, ONE PERIOD:
125 — New York Rangers, April 9, 1981, first period at Los Angeles. Los Angeles won 5-4.

Individual Records

GAMES PLAYED

MOST YEARS IN PLAYOFFS:
22 — Chris Chelios, Montreal, Chicago, Detroit (1984-97 inclusive; 1999-2004 inclusive, 2006, 2007)
21 — Raymond Bourque, Boston, Colorado (1980-96 inclusive; 98-2001 inclusive)
20 — Gordie Howe, Detroit, Hartford
— Larry Robinson, Montreal, Los Angeles
— Larry Murphy, Los Angeles, Washington, Minnesota, Pittsburgh, Toronto, Detroit
— Scott Stevens, Washington, St. Louis, New Jersey
— Steve Yzerman, Detroit

MOST CONSECUTIVE YEARS IN PLAYOFFS:
20 — Larry Robinson, Montreal, Los Angeles (1973-92, inclusive).
19 — Brett Hull, Calgary, St. Louis, Dallas, Detroit (1986-2004, inclusive).
18 — Larry Murphy, Los Angeles, Washington, Minnesota, Pittsburgh, Toronto, Detroit (1984-2001, inclusive).
17 — Brad Park, NY Rangers, Boston, Detroit (1969-85, inclusive).
— Raymond Bourque, Boston (1980-96, inclusive).

MOST PLAYOFF GAMES:
247 — Patrick Roy, Montreal, Colorado
246 — Chris Chelios, Montreal, Chicago, Detroit
236 — Mark Messier, Edmonton, NY Rangers
233 — Claude Lemieux, Montreal, New Jersey, Colorado, Phoenix
— Scott Stevens, Washington, St. Louis, New Jersey

GOALS

MOST GOALS IN PLAYOFFS (CAREER):
122 — Wayne Gretzky, Edmonton, Los Angeles, St. Louis, NY Rangers
109 — Mark Messier, Edmonton, NY Rangers
106 — Jari Kurri, Edmonton, Los Angeles, NY Rangers, Anaheim
103 — Brett Hull, Calgary, St. Louis, Dallas, Detroit
93 — Glenn Anderson, Edmonton, Toronto, NY Rangers, St. Louis

MOST GOALS, ONE PLAYOFF YEAR:
19 — Reggie Leach, Philadelphia, 1976. 16 games.
— Jari Kurri, Edmonton, 1985. 18 games.
18 — Joe Sakic, Colorado, 1996. 22 games.
17 — Newsy Lalonde, Montreal, 1919. 10 games.
— Mike Bossy, NY Islanders, 1981. 18 games.
— Steve Payne, Minnesota, 1981. 19 games.
— Mike Bossy, NY Islanders, 1982. 19 games.
— Mike Bossy, NY Islanders, 1983. 19 games
— Wayne Gretzky, Edmonton, 1985. 18 games.
— Kevin Stevens, Pittsburgh, 1991. 24 games.

MOST GOALS IN ONE SERIES (OTHER THAN FINAL):
12 — Jari Kurri, Edmonton, in 1985 CF, 6 games vs. Chicago.
11 — Newsy Lalonde, Montreal, in 1919 NHL F, 5 games vs. Ottawa.
10 — Tim Kerr, Philadelphia, in 1989 DF, 7 games vs. Pittsburgh.
9 — Reggie Leach, Philadelphia, in 1976 SF, 5 games vs. Boston.
— Bill Barber, Philadelphia, in 1980 SF, 5 games vs. Minnesota.
— Mike Bossy, NY Islanders, in 1983 CF, 6 games vs. Boston.
— Mario Lemieux, Pittsburgh, in 1989 DF, 7 games vs. Philadelphia.

MOST GOALS IN FINAL SERIES (NHL PLAYERS ONLY):
9 — Babe Dye, Toronto, in 1922, 5 games vs. Van. Millionaires.
8 — Alf Skinner, Toronto, in 1918, 5 games vs. Van. Millionaires.
7 — Jean Beliveau, Montreal, in 1956, 5 games vs. Detroit.
— Mike Bossy, NY Islanders, in 1982, 4 games vs. Vancouver.
— Wayne Gretzky, Edmonton, in 1985, 5 games vs. Philadelphia.

MOST GOALS, ONE GAME:
5 — Newsy Lalonde, Montreal, March 1, 1919, at Montreal. Final score: Montreal 6, Ottawa 3.
— Maurice Richard, Montreal, March 23, 1944, at Montreal. Final score: Montreal 5, Toronto 1.
— Darryl Sittler, Toronto, April 22, 1976, at Toronto. Final score: Toronto 8, Philadelphia 5.
— Reggie Leach, Philadelphia, May 6, 1976, at Philadelphia. Final score: Philadelphia 6, Boston 3.
— Mario Lemieux, Pittsburgh, April 25, 1989, at Pittsburgh. Final score: Pittsburgh 10, Philadelphia 7.

MOST GOALS, ONE PERIOD:
4 — Tim Kerr, Philadelphia, April 13, 1985, at NY Rangers, second period. Final score: Philadelphia 6, NY Rangers 5.
— Mario Lemieux, Pittsburgh, April 25, 1989, at Pittsburgh vs. Philadelphia, first period. Final score: Pittsburgh 10, Philadelphia 7.

ASSISTS

MOST ASSISTS IN PLAYOFFS (CAREER):
260 — Wayne Gretzky, Edmonton, Los Angeles, St. Louis, NY Rangers
186 — Mark Messier, Edmonton, NY Rangers
139 — Raymond Bourque, Boston, Colorado
137 — Paul Coffey, Edmonton, Pittsburgh, Los Angeles, Detroit, Philadelphia, Carolina
128 — Doug Gilmour, St. Louis, Calgary, Toronto, New Jersey, Buffalo, Montreal

MOST ASSISTS, ONE PLAYOFF YEAR:
31 — Wayne Gretzky, Edmonton, 1988. 19 games.
30 — Wayne Gretzky, Edmonton, 1985. 18 games.
29 — Wayne Gretzky, Edmonton, 1987. 21 games.
28 — Mario Lemieux, Pittsburgh, 1991. 23 games.
26 — Wayne Gretzky, Edmonton, 1983. 16 games.

MOST ASSISTS IN ONE SERIES (OTHER THAN FINAL):
14 — Rick Middleton, Boston, in 1983 DF, 7 games vs. Buffalo.
— Wayne Gretzky, Edmonton, in 1985 CF, 6 games vs. Chicago.
13 — Wayne Gretzky, Edmonton, in 1987 DSF, 5 games vs. Los Angeles.
— Doug Gilmour, Toronto, in 1994 CSF, 7 games vs. San Jose.
11 — Al MacInnis, Calgary, in 1984 DF, 7 games vs. Edmonton.
— Mark Messier, Edmonton, in 1989 DSF, 7 games vs. Los Angeles.
— Mike Ridley, Washington, in 1992 DSF, 7 games vs. Pittsburgh.
— Ron Francis, Pittsburgh, in 1995 CQF, 7 games vs. Washington.
10 — Fleming Mackell, Boston, in 1958 SF, 6 games vs. NY Rangers.
— Stan Mikita, Chicago, in 1962 SF, 6 games vs. Montreal.
— Bob Bourne, NY Islanders, in 1983 DF, 6 games vs. NY Rangers.
— Wayne Gretzky, Edmonton, in 1988 DSF, 5 games vs. Winnipeg.
— Mario Lemieux, Pittsburgh, in 1992 DSF, 6 games vs. Washington.

MOST ASSISTS IN FINAL SERIES:
10 — Wayne Gretzky, Edmonton, in 1988, 4 games plus suspended game vs. Boston.
9 — Jacques Lemaire, Montreal, in 1973, 6 games vs. Chicago.
— Wayne Gretzky, Edmonton, in 1987, 7 games vs. Philadelphia.
— Larry Murphy, Pittsburgh, in 1991, 6 games vs. Minnesota.

MOST ASSISTS, ONE GAME:
6 — Mikko Leinonen, NY Rangers, April 8, 1982, at NY Rangers. Final score: NY Rangers 7, Philadelphia 3.
— Wayne Gretzky, Edmonton, April 9, 1987, at Edmonton. Final score: Edmonton 13, Los Angeles 3.
5 — Toe Blake, Montreal, March 23, 1944, at Montreal. Final score: Montreal 5, Toronto 1.
— Maurice Richard, Montreal, March 27, 1956, at Montreal. Final score: Montreal 7, NY Rangers 0.
— Bert Olmstead, Montreal, March 30, 1957, at Montreal. Final score: Montreal 8, NY Rangers 3.
— Don McKenney, Boston, April 5, 1958, at Boston. Final score: Boston 8, NY Rangers 2.
— Stan Mikita, Chicago, April 4, 1973, at Chicago. Final score: Chicago 7, St. Louis 1.
— Wayne Gretzky, Edmonton, April 8, 1981, at Montreal. Final score: Edmonton 6, Montreal 3.
— Paul Coffey, Edmonton, May 14, 1985, at Edmonton. Final score: Edmonton 10, Chicago 5.
— Doug Gilmour, St. Louis, April 15, 1986, at Minnesota. Final score: St. Louis 6, Minnesota 3.
— Risto Siltanen, Quebec, April 14, 1987, at Hartford. Final score: Quebec 7, Hartford 5.
— Patrik Sundstrom, New Jersey, April 22, 1988, at New Jersey. Final score: New Jersey 10, Washington 4.
— Geoff Courtnall, St. Louis, April 23, 1998, at St. Louis. Final score: St. Louis 8, Los Angeles 3.

MOST ASSISTS, ONE PERIOD:
3 — Three assists by one player in one period of a playoff game has been recorded on 80 occasions. Mikael Samuelsson of the Detroit Red Wings is the most recent to equal this mark with 3 assists in the third period at Anaheim, May 22, 2007. Final score: Anaheim 4, Detroit 3.
— Wayne Gretzky has had 3 assists in one period 5 times; Raymond Bourque, 3 times; Toe Blake, Jean Beliveau, Doug Harvey and Bobby Orr, twice each. Joe Primeau of Toronto was the first player to be credited with 3 assists in one period of a playoff game; third period at Boston vs. NY Rangers, April 7, 1932. Final score: Toronto 6, NY Rangers 2.

POINTS

MOST POINTS IN PLAYOFFS (CAREER):
382 — Wayne Gretzky, Edmonton, Los Angeles, St. Louis, NY Rangers, 122G, 260A
295 — Mark Messier, Edmonton, NY Rangers, 109G, 186A
233 — Jari Kurri, Edmonton, Los Angeles, NY Rangers, Anaheim, 106G, 127A
214 — Glenn Anderson, Edmonton, Toronto, NY Rangers, St. Louis, 93G, 121A
196 — Paul Coffey, Edmonton, Pittsburgh, Los Angeles, Detroit, Philadelphia, Carolina, 59G, 137A

MOST POINTS, ONE PLAYOFF YEAR:
47 — Wayne Gretzky, Edmonton, in 1985. 17 goals, 30 assists in 18 games.
44 — Mario Lemieux, Pittsburgh, in 1991. 16 goals, 28 assists in 23 games.
43 — Wayne Gretzky, Edmonton, in 1988. 12 goals, 31 assists in 19 games.
40 — Wayne Gretzky, Los Angeles, in 1993. 15 goals, 25 assists in 24 games.
38 — Wayne Gretzky, Edmonton, in 1983. 12 goals, 26 assists in 16 games.

MOST POINTS IN ONE SERIES (OTHER THAN FINAL):
19 — Rick Middleton, Boston, in 1983 DF, 7 games vs. Buffalo. 5 goals, 14 assists.
18 — Wayne Gretzky, Edmonton, in 1985 CF, 6 games vs. Chicago. 4 goals, 14 assists.
17 — Mario Lemieux, Pittsburgh, in 1992 DSF, 6 games vs. Washington. 7 goals, 10 assists.
16 — Barry Pederson, Boston, in 1983 DF, 7 games vs. Buffalo. 7 goals, 9 assists.
— Doug Gilmour, Toronto, in 1994 CSF, 7 games vs. San Jose. 3 goals, 13 assists.
15 — Jari Kurri, Edmonton, in 1985 CF, 6 games vs. Chicago. 12 goals, 3 assists.
— Wayne Gretzky, Edmonton, in 1987 DSF, 5 games vs. Los Angeles. 2 goals, 13 assists.
— Tim Kerr, Philadelphia, in 1989 DF, 7 games vs. Pittsburgh. 10 goals, 5 assists.
— Mario Lemieux, Pittsburgh, in 1991 CF, 6 games vs. Boston. 6 goals, 9 assists.

MOST POINTS IN FINAL SERIES:
13 — Wayne Gretzky, Edmonton, in 1988, 4 games plus suspended game vs. Boston. 3 goals, 10 assists.
12 — Gordie Howe, Detroit, in 1955, 7 games vs. Montreal. 5 goals, 7 assists.
— Yvan Cournoyer, Montreal, in 1973, 6 games vs. Chicago. 6 goals, 6 assists.
— Jacques Lemaire, Montreal, in 1973, 6 games vs. Chicago. 3 goals, 9 assists.
— Mario Lemieux, Pittsburgh, in 1991, 5 games vs. Minnesota. 5 goals, 7 assists.

MOST POINTS, ONE GAME:
8 — Patrik Sundstrom, New Jersey, April 22, 1988, at New Jersey in 10-4 win over Washington. Sundstrom had 3 goals, 5 assists.
— Mario Lemieux, Pittsburgh, April 25, 1989, at Pittsburgh in 10-7 win over Philadelphia. Lemieux had 5 goals, 3 assists.
7 — Wayne Gretzky, Edmonton, April 17, 1983, at Calgary in 10-2 win. Gretzky had 4 goals, 3 assists.
— Wayne Gretzky, Edmonton, April 25,1985, at Winnipeg in 8-3 win. Gretzky had 3 goals, 4 assists.
— Wayne Gretzky, Edmonton, April 9, 1987, at Edmonton in 13-3 win over Los Angeles. Gretzky had 1 goal, 6 assists.
6 — Dickie Moore, Montreal, March 25, 1954, at Montreal in 8-1 win over Boston. Moore had 2 goals, 4 assists.
— Phil Esposito, Boston, April 2, 1969, at Boston in 10-0 win over Toronto. Esposito had 4 goals, 2 assists.
— Darryl Sittler, Toronto, April 22, 1976, at Toronto in 8-5 win over Philadelphia. Sittler had 5 goals, 1 assist.
— Guy Lafleur, Montreal, April 11, 1977, at Montreal in 7-2 win over St. Louis. Lafleur had 3 goals, 3 assists.
— Mikko Leinonen, NY Rangers, April 8, 1982, at NY Rangers in 7-3 win over Philadelphia. Leinonen had 6 assists.
— Paul Coffey, Edmonton, May 14, 1985, at Edmonton in 10-5 win over Chicago. Coffey had 1 goal, 5 assists.
— John Anderson, Hartford, April 12, 1986, at Hartford in 9-4 win over Quebec. Anderson had 2 goals, 4 assists.
— Mario Lemieux, Pittsburgh, April 23, 1992, at Pittsburgh in 6-4 win over Washington. Lemieux had 3 goals, 3 assists.
— Geoff Courtnall, St. Louis, April 23, 1998, at St. Louis in 8-3 win over Los Angeles. Courtnall had 1 goal, 5 assists.

MOST POINTS, ONE PERIOD:
4 — Maurice Richard, Montreal, March 29, 1945, at Montreal, third period, in 10-3 win vs. Toronto. 3 goals, 1 assist.
— Dickie Moore, Montreal, March 25, 1954, at Montreal, first period, in 8-1 win vs. Boston. 2 goals, 2 assists.
— Barry Pederson, Boston, April 8, 1982, at Boston, second period, in 7-3 win vs. Buffalo. 3 goals, 1 assist.
— Peter McNab, Boston, April 11, 1982, at Buffalo, second period, in 5-2 win vs. Buffalo. 1 goal, 3 assists.
— Tim Kerr, Philadelphia, April 13, 1985, at NY Rangers, second period, in 6-5 win vs. NY Rangers. 4 goals.
— Ken Linseman, Boston, April 14, 1985, at Boston, second period, in 7-6 win vs. Montreal. 2 goals, 2 assists.
— Wayne Gretzky, Edmonton, April 12, 1987, at Los Angeles, third period, in 6-3 win vs. Los Angeles. 1 goal, 3 assists.
— Glenn Anderson, Edmonton, April 6, 1988, at Edmonton, third period, in 7-4 win vs. Winnipeg. 3 goals, 1 assist.
— Mario Lemieux, Pittsburgh, April 25, 1989, at Pittsburgh, first period, in 10-7 win vs. Philadelphia. 4 goals.
— Dave Gagner, Minnesota North Stars, April 8, 1991, at Minnesota, first period, in 6-5 loss vs. Chicago. 2 goals, 2 assists.
— Mario Lemieux, Pittsburgh, April 23, 1992, at Pittsburgh, second period, in 6-4 win vs. Washington. 2 goals, 2 assists.
— Alexander Mogilny, New Jersey, April 28, 2001, at New Jersey, second period, in 6-5 win vs. Toronto. 1 goal, 3 assists.

POWER-PLAY GOALS

MOST POWER-PLAY GOALS IN PLAYOFFS (CAREER):
38 — Brett Hull, St. Louis, Dallas, Detroit
35 — Mike Bossy, NY Islanders
34 — Dino Ciccarelli, Minnesota, Washington, Detroit
— Wayne Gretzky, Edmonton, Los Angeles, St. Louis, NY Rangers
29 — Mario Lemieux, Pittsburgh

MOST POWER-PLAY GOALS, ONE PLAYOFF YEAR:
9 — Mike Bossy, NY Islanders, 1981. 18 games vs. Toronto, Edmonton, NY Rangers and Minnesota.
— Cam Neely, Boston, 1991. 19 games vs. Hartford, Montreal and Pittsburgh.
8 — Tim Kerr, Philadelphia, 1989. 19 games.
— John Druce, Washington, 1990. 15 games.
— Brian Propp, Minnesota, 1991. 23 games.
— Mario Lemieux, Pittsburgh, 1992. 15 games.

MOST POWER-PLAY GOALS, ONE PLAYOFF SERIES:
6 — Chris Kontos, Los Angeles, 1989 DSF vs. Edmonton, won by Los Angeles 4-3.
5 — Andy Bathgate, Detroit, 1966 SF vs. Chicago, won by Detroit 4-2.
— Denis Potvin, NY Islanders, 1981 QF vs. Edmonton, won by NY Islanders 4-2.
— Ken Houston, Calgary, 1981 QF vs. Philadelphia, won by Calgary 4-3.
— Rick Vaive, Chicago, 1988 DSF vs. St. Louis, won by St. Louis 4-1.
— Tim Kerr, Philadelphia, 1989 DF vs. Pittsburgh, won by Philadelphia 4-3.
— Mario Lemieux, Pittsburgh, 1989 DF vs. Philadelphia, won by Philadelphia 4-3.
— John Druce, Washington, 1990 DF vs. NY Rangers, won by Washington 4-1.
— Pat LaFontaine, Buffalo, 1992 DSF vs. Boston, won by Boston 4-3.
— Adam Graves, NY Rangers, 1996 CQF vs Montreal, won by NY Rangers 4-2.

MOST POWER-PLAY GOALS, ONE GAME:
3 — Syd Howe, Detroit, March 23, 1939, at Detroit vs. Montreal. Detroit won 7-3.
— Sid Smith, Toronto, April 10, 1949, at Detroit. Toronto won 3-1.
— Phil Esposito, Boston, April 2, 1969, at Boston vs. Toronto. Boston won 10-0.
— John Bucyk, Boston, April 21, 1974, at Boston vs. Chicago. Boston won 8-6.
— Denis Potvin, NY Islanders, April 17, 1981, at NY Islanders vs. Edmonton. NY Islanders won 6-3.
— Tim Kerr, Philadelphia, April 13, 1985, at NY Rangers. Philadelphia won 6-5.
— Jari Kurri, Edmonton, April 9, 1987, at Edmonton vs. Los Angeles. Edmonton won 13-3.
— Mark Johnson, New Jersey, April 22, 1988, at New Jersey vs. Washington. New Jersey won 10-4.
— Dino Ciccarelli, Detroit, April 29, 1993, at Toronto. Detroit won 7-3.
— Dino Ciccarelli, Detroit, May 11, 1995, at Dallas. Detroit won 5-1.
— Valeri Kamensky, Colorado, April 24, 1997, at Colorado vs. Chicago. Colorado won 7-0.

MOST POWER-PLAY GOALS, ONE PERIOD:
3 — Tim Kerr, Philadelphia, April 13, 1985, at NY Rangers, second period in 6-5 win.
2 — Two power-play goals have been scored by one player in one period on 55 occasions. Charlie Conacher of Toronto was the first to score two power-play goals in one period, setting the mark with two power-play goals in the second period at Toronto vs. Boston, March 26, 1936. Final score: Toronto 8, Boston 3. Brad Richards of the Tampa Bay Lightning is the most recent to equal this mark with two power-play goals in the second period at Calgary, June 5, 2004. Final score: Tampa Bay 3, Calgary 2.

SHORTHAND GOALS

MOST SHORTHAND GOALS IN PLAYOFFS (CAREER):
14 — Mark Messier, Edmonton, NY Rangers
11 — Wayne Gretzky, Edmonton, Los Angeles, St. Louis
10 — Jari Kurri, Edmonton, Los Angeles, NY Rangers
8 — Ed Westfall, Boston, NY Islanders
— Hakan Loob, Calgary

MOST SHORTHAND GOALS, ONE PLAYOFF YEAR:
3 — Derek Sanderson, Boston, 1969. 1 vs. Toronto in QF, won by Boston 4-0; 2 vs. Montreal in SF, won by Montreal, 4-2.
— Bill Barber, Philadelphia, 1980. All vs. Minnesota in SF, won by Philadelphia 4-1.
— Lorne Henning, NY Islanders, 1980. 1 vs. Boston in QF, won by NY Islanders 4-1; 1 vs. Buffalo in SF, won by NY Islanders 4-2, 1 vs. Philadelphia in F, won by NY Islanders 4-2.
— Wayne Gretzky, Edmonton, 1983. 2 vs. Winnipeg in DSF, won by Edmonton 3-0; 1 vs. Calgary in DF, won by Edmonton 4-1.
— Wayne Presley, Chicago, 1989. All vs. Detroit in DSF, won by Chicago 4-2.
— Todd Marchant, Edmonton, 1997. 1 vs. Dallas in CQF, won by Edmonton 4-3; 2 vs. Colorado in CSF, won by Colorado 4-1.

Detroit's Daniel Cleary scored two shorthand goals during the 2007 playoffs. They came a week apart, in two different playoff rounds. Cleary's first came in game five versus Calgary on April 21 and the second on April 28 in game two versus San Jose.

MOST SHORTHAND GOALS, ONE PLAYOFF SERIES:

3 — Bill Barber, Philadelphia, 1980 SF vs. Minnesota, won by Philadelphia 4-1.
— Wayne Presley, Chicago, 1989 DSF vs. Detroit, won by Chicago 4-2.
2 — Mac Colville, NY Rangers, 1940 SF vs. Boston, won by NY Rangers 4-2.
— Jerry Toppazzini, Boston, 1958 SF vs. NY Rangers, won by Boston 4-2.
— Dave Keon, Toronto, 1963 F vs. Detroit, won by Toronto 4-1.
— Bob Pulford, Toronto, 1964 F vs. Detroit, won by Toronto 4-3.
— Serge Savard, Montreal, 1968 F vs. St. Louis, won by Montreal 4-0.
— Derek Sanderson, Boston, 1969 SF vs. Montreal, won by Montreal 4-2.
— Bryan Trottier, NY Islanders, 1980 PR vs. Los Angeles, won by NY Islanders 3-1.
— Bobby Lalonde, Boston, 1981 PR vs. Minnesota, won by Minnesota 3-0.
— Butch Goring, NY Islanders, 1981 SF vs. NY Rangers, won by NY Islanders 4-0.
— Wayne Gretzky, Edmonton, 1983 DSF vs. Winnipeg, won by Edmonton 3-0.
— Mark Messier, Edmonton, 1983 DF vs. Calgary, won by Edmonton 4-1.
— Jari Kurri, Edmonton, 1983 CF vs. Chicago, won by Edmonton 4-0.
— Wayne Gretzky, Edmonton, 1985 DF vs. Winnipeg, won by Edmonton 4-0.
— Kevin Lowe, Edmonton, 1987 F vs. Philadelphia, won by Edmonton 4-3.
— Bob Gould, Washington, 1988 DSF vs. Philadelphia, won by Washington 4-3.
— Dave Poulin, Philadelphia, 1989 DF vs. Pittsburgh, won by Philadelphia 4-3.
— Russ Courtnall, Montreal, 1991 DF vs. Boston, won by Boston 4-3.
— Sergei Fedorov, Detroit, 1992 DSF vs. Minnesota, won by Detroit 4-3.
— Mark Messier, NY Rangers, 1992 DSF vs. New Jersey, won by NY Rangers 4-3.
— Tom Fitzgerald, NY Islanders, 1993 DF vs. Pittsburgh, won by NY Islanders 4-3.
— Mark Osborne, Toronto, 1994 CSF vs. San Jose, won by Toronto 4-3.
— Tony Amonte, Chicago, 1997 CQF vs. Colorado, won by Colorado 4-2.
— Brian Rolston, New Jersey, 1997 CQF vs. Montreal, won by New Jersey 4-1.
— Rod Brind'Amour, Philadelphia, 1997 CQF vs. Pittsburgh, won by Philadelphia 4-1.
— Todd Marchant, Edmonton, 1997 CSF vs. Colorado, won by Colorado 4-1.
— Jeremy Roenick, Phoenix, 1998 CQF vs. Detroit, won by Detroit 4-2.
— Vincent Damphousse, San Jose, 1999 CQF vs. Colorado, won by Colorado 4-2.
— Dixon Ward, Buffalo, 1999 CF vs. Toronto, won by Buffalo 4-1.
— Curtis Brown, Buffalo, 2001 CSF vs. Pittsburgh, won by Pittsburgh 4-3.
— John Madden, New Jersey, 2006 CQF vs. NY Rangers, won by New Jersey 4-0.

MOST SHORTHAND GOALS, ONE GAME:

2 — Dave Keon, Toronto, April 18, 1963, at Toronto, in 3-1 win vs. Detroit.
— Bryan Trottier, NY Islanders, April 8, 1980, at NY Islanders, in 8-1 win vs. Los Angeles.
— Bobby Lalonde, Boston, April 11, 1981, at Minnesota, in 6-3 loss vs. Minnesota.
— Wayne Gretzky, Edmonton, April 6, 1983, at Edmonton, in 6-3 win vs. Winnipeg.
— Jari Kurri, Edmonton, April 24, 1983, at Edmonton, in 8-3 win vs. Chicago.
— Wayne Gretzky, Edmonton, April 25, 1985, at Winnipeg, in 8-3 win by Edmonton.
— Mark Messier, NY Rangers, April 21, 1992, at NY Rangers, in 7-3 loss vs. New Jersey.
— Tom Fitzgerald, NY Islanders, May 8, 1993, at NY Islanders, in 6-5 win vs. Pittsburgh.
— Rod Brind'Amour, Philadelphia, April 26, 1997, at Philadelphia, in 6-3 win vs. Pittsburgh.
— Jeremy Roenick, Phoenix, April 24, 1998, at Detroit, in 7-4 win by Phoenix.
— Vincent Damphousse, San Jose, April 30, 1999, at Colorado, in 7-3 win by San Jose.
— John Madden, New Jersey, April 24, 2006, at New Jersey, in 4-1 win vs. NY Rangers.

MOST SHORTHAND GOALS, ONE PERIOD:

2 — Bryan Trottier, NY Islanders, April 8, 1980, second period, at NY Islanders, in 8-1 win vs. Los Angeles.
— Bobby Lalonde, Boston, April 11, 1981, third period, at Minnesota, in 6-3 loss vs. Minnesota.
— Jari Kurri, Edmonton, April 24, 1983, third period, at Edmonton, in 8-4 win vs. Chicago.
— Rod Brind'Amour, Philadelphia, April 26, 1997, first period, at Philadelphia, in 6-3 win vs. Pittsburgh.
— Jeremy Roenick, Phoenix, April 24, 1998, second period, at Detroit, in 7-4 win by Phoenix.
— Vincent Damphousse, San Jose, April 30, 1999, third period, at Colorado, in 7-3 win vs. Colorado.

GAME-WINNING GOALS

MOST GAME-WINNING GOALS IN PLAYOFFS, CAREER:

24 — Wayne Gretzky, Edmonton, Los Angeles, St. Louis, NY Rangers
— Brett Hull, St. Louis, Dallas, Detroit
19 — Claude Lemieux, Montreal, New Jersey, Colorado
18 — Maurice Richard, Montreal
— Joe Sakic, Colorado

MOST GAME-WINNING GOALS, ONE PLAYOFF YEAR:

7 — Brad Richards, Tampa Bay, 2004. 23 games.
6 — Joe Sakic, Colorado, 1996. 22 games.
— Joe Nieuwendyk, Dallas, 1999. 23 games.
5 — Mike Bossy, NY Islanders, 1983. 19 games.
— Jari Kurri, Edmonton, 1987. 21 games.
— Bobby Smith, Minnesota, 1991. 23 games.
— Mario Lemieux, Pittsburgh, 1992. 15 games.
— Fernando Pisani, Edmonton, 2006. 24 games.

MOST GAME-WINNING GOALS, ONE PLAYOFF SERIES:

4 — Mike Bossy, NY Islanders, 1983 CF vs. Boston, won by NY Islanders 4-2.

OVERTIME GOALS

MOST OVERTIME GOALS IN PLAYOFFS, CAREER:

7 — Joe Sakic, Colorado (2 in 1996; 1 in 1998; 1 in 2001; 2 in 2004; 1 in 2006)
6 — Maurice Richard, Montreal
5 — Glenn Anderson, Edmonton, Toronto, St. Louis
4 — Bob Nystrom, NY Islanders
— Dale Hunter, Quebec, Washington
— Wayne Gretzky, Edmonton, Los Angeles
— Stephane Richer, Montreal, New Jersey
— Joe Murphy, Edmonton, Chicago
— Esa Tikkanen, Edmonton, NY Rangers
— Jaromir Jagr, Pittsburgh
— Kirk Muller, Montreal, Dallas
— Jeremy Roenick, Chicago, Philadelphia
— Chris Drury, Colorado, Buffalo
— Jamie Langenbrunner, Dallas, New Jersey

MOST OVERTIME GOALS, ONE PLAYOFF YEAR:

3 — Mel Hill, Boston, 1939. All vs. NY Rangers in best-of-seven SF, won by Boston 4-3.
— Maurice Richard, Montreal, 1951. 2 vs. Detroit in best-of-seven SF, won by Montreal 4-2; 1 vs. Toronto best-of-seven F, won by Toronto 4-1.

MOST OVERTIME GOALS, ONE PLAYOFF SERIES:

3 — Mel Hill, Boston, 1939, SF vs. NY Rangers, won by Boston 4-3. Hill scored at 59:25 of overtime March 21 for a 2-1 win; at 8:24 of overtime, March 23 for a 3-2 win; and at 48:00 of overtime, April 2 for a 2-1 win.

Tampa Bay's Brad Richards, seen here scoring on Calgary's Miikka Kiprusoff during the 2004 Stanley Cup Final, scored a record seven game-winning goals during the 2004 postseason.

SCORING BY A DEFENSEMAN

MOST GOALS BY A DEFENSEMAN, ONE PLAYOFF YEAR:
12 — Paul Coffey, Edmonton, 1985. 18 games.
11 — Brian Leetch, NY Rangers, 1994. 23 games.
9 — Bobby Orr, Boston, 1970. 14 games.
— Brad Park, Boston, 1978. 15 games.
8 — Denis Potvin, NY Islanders, 1981. 18 games.
— Raymond Bourque, Boston, 1983. 17 games.
— Denis Potvin, NY Islanders, 1983. 20 games.
— Paul Coffey, Edmonton, 1984. 19 games.

MOST GOALS BY A DEFENSEMAN, ONE GAME:
3 — Bobby Orr, Boston, April 11, 1971, at Montreal. Final score: Boston 5, Montreal 2.
— Dick Redmond, Chicago, April 4, 1973, at Chicago. Final score: Chicago 7, St. Louis 1.
— Denis Potvin, NY Islanders, April 17, 1981, at NY Islanders. Final score: NY Islanders 6, Edmonton 3.
— Paul Reinhart, Calgary, April 14, 1983, at Edmonton. Final score: Edmonton 6, Calgary 3.
— Doug Halward, Vancouver, April 7, 1984, at Vancouver. Final score: Vancouver 7, Calgary 0.
— Paul Reinhart, Calgary, April 8, 1984, at Vancouver. Final score: Calgary 5, Vancouver 1.
— Al Iafrate, Washington, April 26, 1993, at Washington. Final score: Washington 6, NY Islanders 4.
— Eric Desjardins, Montreal, June 3, 1993, at Montreal. Final score: Montreal 3, Los Angeles 2.
— Gary Suter, Chicago, April 24, 1994, at Chicago. Final score: Chicago 4, Toronto 3.
— Brian Leetch, NY Rangers, May 22, 1995, at Philadelphia. Final score: Philadelphia 4, NY Rangers 3.
— Andy Delmore, Philadelphia, May 7, 2000, at Philadelphia. Final score: Philadelphia 6, Pittsburgh 3.

MOST ASSISTS BY A DEFENSEMAN, ONE PLAYOFF YEAR:
25 — Paul Coffey, Edmonton, 1985. 18 games.
24 — Al MacInnis, Calgary, 1989. 22 games.
23 — Brian Leetch, NY Rangers, 1994. 23 games.
19 — Bobby Orr, Boston, 1972. 15 games.
18 — Raymond Bourque, Boston, 1988. 23 games.
— Raymond Bourque, Boston, 1991. 19 games.
— Larry Murphy, Pittsburgh, 1991. 23 games.

MOST ASSISTS BY A DEFENSEMAN, ONE GAME:
5 — Paul Coffey, Edmonton, May 14, 1985 at Edmonton vs. Chicago. Edmonton won 10-5.
— Risto Siltanen, Quebec, April 14, 1987 at Hartford. Quebec won 7-5.

MOST POINTS BY A DEFENSEMAN, ONE PLAYOFF YEAR:
37 — Paul Coffey, Edmonton, 1985. 12 goals, 25 assists in 18 games.
34 — Brian Leetch, NY Rangers, 1994. 11 goals, 23 assists in 23 games.
31 — Al MacInnis, Calgary, 1989. 7 goals, 24 assists in 22 games.
25 — Denis Potvin, NY Islanders, 1981. 8 goals, 17 assists in 18 games.
— Raymond Bourque, Boston, 1991. 7 goals, 18 assists in 19 games.

MOST POINTS BY A DEFENSEMAN, ONE GAME:
6 — Paul Coffey, Edmonton, May 14, 1985 at Edmonton vs. Chicago. 1 goal, 5 assists. Edmonton won 10-5.
5 — Eddie Bush, Detroit, April 9, 1942, at Detroit vs. Toronto. 1 goal, 4 assists. Detroit won 5-2.
— Bob Dailey, Philadelphia, May 1, 1980, at Philadelphia vs. Minnesota. 1 goal, 4 assists. Philadelphia won 7-0.
— Denis Potvin, NY Islanders, April 17, 1981, at NY Islanders vs. Edmonton. 3 goals, 2 assists. NY Islanders won 6-3.
— Risto Siltanen, Quebec, April 14, 1987, at Hartford. 5 assists. Quebec won 7-5.

SCORING BY A ROOKIE

MOST GOALS BY A ROOKIE, ONE PLAYOFF YEAR:
14 — Dino Ciccarelli, Minnesota, 1981. 19 games.
11 — Jeremy Roenick, Chicago, 1990. 20 games.
10 — Claude Lemieux, Montreal, 1986. 20 games.
9 — Pat Flatley, NY Islanders, 1984. 21 games
8 — Steve Christoff, Minnesota, 1980. 14 games.
— Brad Palmer, Minnesota, 1981. 19 games.
— Mike Krushelnyski, Boston, 1983. 17 games.
— Bob Joyce, Boston, 1988. 23 games.

MOST POINTS BY A ROOKIE, ONE PLAYOFF YEAR:
21 — Dino Ciccarelli, Minnesota, 1981. 14 goals, 7 assists in 19 games.
20 — Don Maloney, NY Rangers, 1979. 7 goals, 13 assists in 18 games.

THREE-OR-MORE-GOAL GAMES

MOST THREE-OR-MORE-GOAL GAMES IN PLAYOFFS, CAREER:
10 — Wayne Gretzky, Edmonton, Los Angeles, NY Rangers. Eight three-goal games; two four-goal games.
7 — Maurice Richard, Montreal. Four three-goal games; two four-goal games; one five-goal game.
— Jari Kurri, Edmonton. Six three-goal games; one four-goal game.
6 — Dino Ciccarelli, Minnesota, Washington, Detroit. Five three-goal games; one four-goal game.
5 — Mike Bossy, NY Islanders. Four three-goal games; one four-goal game.

MOST THREE-OR-MORE-GOAL GAMES, ONE PLAYOFF YEAR:
4 — Jari Kurri, Edmonton, 1985. 1 four-goal game, 3 three-goal games.
3 — Mark Messier, Edmonton, 1983. 3 three-goal games.
— Mike Bossy, NY Islanders, 1983. 1 four-goal game, 2 three-goal games
2 — Newsy Lalonde, Montreal, 1919. 1 five-goal game, 1 four-goal game.
— Maurice Richard, Montreal, 1944. 1 five-goal game; 1 three-goal game.
— Doug Bentley, Chicago, 1944. 2 three-goal games.
— Norm Ullman, Detroit, 1964. 2 three-goal games.
— Phil Esposito, Boston, 1970. 2 three-goal games.
— Pit Martin, Chicago, 1973. 2 three-goal games.
— Rick MacLeish, Philadelphia, 1975. 2 three-goal games.
— Lanny McDonald, Toronto, 1977. 1 four-goal game; 1 three-goal game.
— Wayne Gretzky, Edmonton, 1981. 2 three-goal games.
— Wayne Gretzky, Edmonton, 1983. 2 four-goal games.
— Wayne Gretzky, Edmonton, 1985. 2 three-goal games.
— Petr Klima, Detroit, 1988. 2 three-goal games.
— Cam Neely, Boston, 1991. 2 three-goal games.
— Wayne Gretzky, NY Rangers, 1997. 2 three-goal games.
— Daniel Alfredsson, Ottawa, 1998. 2 three-goal games.
— Patrick Marleau, San Jose, 2004. 2 three-goal games.

MOST THREE-OR-MORE-GOAL GAMES, ONE PLAYOFF SERIES:
3 — Jari Kurri, Edmonton, 1985 CF vs. Chicago, won by Edmonton 4-2. Kurri scored 3 goals May 7 at Edmonton in 7-3 win, 3 goals May 14 at Edmonton in 10-5 win and 4 goals May 16 at Chicago in 8-2 win.
2 — Doug Bentley, Chicago, 1944 SF vs. Detroit, won by Chicago 4-1. Bentley scored 3 goals March 28 at Chicago in 7-1 win and 3 goals March 30 at Detroit in 5-2 win.
— Norm Ullman, Detroit, 1964 SF vs. Chicago, won by Detroit 4-3. Ullman scored 3 goals March 29 at Chicago in 5-4 win and 3 goals April 7 at Detroit in 7-2 win.
— Mark Messier, Edmonton, 1983 DF vs. Calgary, won by Edmonton 4-1. Messier scored 4 goals April 14 at Edmonton in 6-3 win and 3 goals April 17 at Calgary in 10-2 win.
— Mike Bossy, NY Islanders, 1983 CF vs. Boston, won by NY Islanders 4-2. Bossy scored 3 goals May 3 at NY Islanders in 8-3 win and 4 goals May 7 at New York in 8-4 win.

SCORING STREAKS

LONGEST CONSECUTIVE GOAL-SCORING STREAK, ONE PLAYOFF YEAR:
10 Games — Reggie Leach, Philadelphia, 1976. Streak started April 17 at Toronto and ended May 9 at Montreal. He scored one goal in each of eight games; two in one game; and five in another; a total of 15 goals.

LONGEST CONSECUTIVE POINT-SCORING STREAK, ONE PLAYOFF YEAR:
18 games — Bryan Trottier, NY Islanders, 1981. 11 goals, 18 assists, 29 points.
17 games — Wayne Gretzky, Edmonton, 1988. 12 goals, 29 assists, 41 points.
— Al MacInnis, Calgary, 1989. 7 goals, 19 assists, 26 points.

LONGEST CONSECUTIVE POINT-SCORING STREAK, MORE THAN ONE PLAYOFF YEAR:
27 games — Bryan Trottier, NY Islanders, 1980, 1981 and 1982. 7 games in 1980 (3 goals, 5 assists, 8 points), 18 games in 1981 (11 goals, 18 assists, 29 points), and two games in 1982 (2 goals, 3 assists, 5 points). Total points, 42.
19 games — Wayne Gretzky, Edmonton, Los Angeles, 1988 and 1989. 17 games in 1988 (12 goals, 29 assists, 41 points with Edmonton), 2 games in 1989 (1 goal, 2 assists, 3 points with Los Angeles). Total points, 44.
— Al MacInnis, Calgary, 1989 and 1990. 17 games in 1989 (7 goals, 19 assists, 26 points), and two games in 1990 (2 goals, 1 assist, 3 points). Total points, 29.

FASTEST GOALS

FASTEST GOAL FROM START OF GAME:
0:06 — Don Kozak, Los Angeles, April 17, 1977, at Los Angeles vs. Boston and goaltender Gerry Cheevers. Los Angeles won 7-4.
0:07 — Bob Gainey, Montreal, May 5, 1977, at NY Islanders vs. goaltender Chico Resch. Montreal won 2-1.
— Terry Murray, Philadelphia, April 12, 1981, at Quebec vs. goaltender Dan Bouchard. Quebec won 4-3 in overtime.

FASTEST GOAL FROM START OF PERIOD (OTHER THAN FIRST):
0:06 — Pelle Eklund, Philadelphia, April 25, 1989, at Pittsburgh vs. goaltender Tom Barrasso, second period. Pittsburgh won 10-7.
0:09 — Bill Collins, Minnesota, April 9, 1968, at Minnesota vs. Los Angeles and goaltender Wayne Rutledge, third period. Minnesota won 7-5.
— Dave Balon, Minnesota, April 25, 1968, at St. Louis vs. goaltender Glenn Hall, third period. Minnesota won 5-1.
— Murray Oliver, Minnesota, April 8, 1971, at St. Louis vs. goaltender Ernie Wakely, third period. St. Louis won 4-2.
— Clark Gillies, NY Islanders, April 15, 1977, at Buffalo vs. goaltender Don Edwards, third period. NY Islanders won 4-3.
— Eric Vail, Atlanta, April 11, 1978, at Atlanta vs. Detroit and goaltender Ron Low, third period. Detroit won 5-3.
— Stan Smyl, Vancouver, April 10, 1979, at Philadelphia vs. goaltender Wayne Stephenson, third period. Vancouver won 3-2.
— Wayne Gretzky, Edmonton, April 6, 1983, at Edmonton vs. Winnipeg and goaltender Brian Hayward, second period. Edmonton won 6-3.
— Mark Messier, Edmonton, April 16, 1984, at Calgary vs. goaltender Don Edwards, third period. Edmonton won 5-3.
— Brian Skrudland, Montreal, May 18, 1986, at Calgary vs. goaltender Mike Vernon, first overtime period. Montreal won 3-2.

FASTEST TWO GOALS:
0:05 — Norm Ullman, Detroit, April 11, 1965, at Detroit vs. Chicago and goaltender Glenn Hall. Ullman scored at 17:35 and 17:40 of second period. Detroit won 4-2.

FASTEST TWO GOALS FROM START OF A GAME:
1:08 — **Dick Duff, Toronto,** April 9, 1963, at Toronto vs. Detroit and goaltender Terry Sawchuk. Duff scored at 0:49 and 1:08. Toronto won 4-2.

FASTEST TWO GOALS FROM START OF A PERIOD:
0:35 — **Pat LaFontaine, NY Islanders,** May 19, 1984, at Edmonton vs. goaltender Andy Moog. LaFontaine scored at 0:13 and 0:35 of third period. Edmonton won 5-2.

PENALTIES

MOST PENALTY MINUTES IN PLAYOFFS, CAREER:
729 — Dale Hunter, Quebec, Washington, Colorado
541 — Chris Nilan, Montreal, NY Rangers, Boston
529 — Claude Lemieux, Montreal, New Jersey, Colorado, Phoenix
471 — Rick Tocchet, Philadelphia, Pittsburgh, Boston, Phoenix
466 — Willi Plett, Atlanta, Calgary, Minnesota, Boston

MOST PENALTIES, ONE GAME:
8 — **Forbes Kennedy, Toronto,** April 2, 1969, at Boston. Kennedy was assessed 4 minors, 2 majors, 1 10-minute misconduct, 1 game misconduct. Boston won 10-0.
— **Kim Clackson, Pittsburgh,** April 14, 1980, at Boston. Clackson was assessed 5 minors, 2 majors, 1 10-minute misconduct. Boston won 6-2.

MOST PENALTY MINUTES, ONE GAME:
42 — **Dave Schultz, Philadelphia,** April 22, 1976, at Toronto. Schultz was assessed 1 minor, 2 majors, 1 10-minute misconduct and 2 game-misconducts. Toronto won 8-5.

MOST PENALTIES, ONE PERIOD AND MOST PENALTY MINUTES, ONE PERIOD:
6 Penalties; 39 Minutes — Ed Hospodar, NY Rangers, April 9, 1981, at Los Angeles, first period. Hospodar was assessed 2 minors, 1 major, 1 10-minute misconduct, 2 game misconducts. Los Angeles won 5-4.

GOALTENDING

MOST PLAYOFF GAMES APPEARED IN BY A GOALTENDER, CAREER:
247 — Patrick Roy, Montreal, Colorado
164 — Martin Brodeur, New Jersey
161 — Ed Belfour, Chicago, Dallas, Toronto
150 — Grant Fuhr, Edmonton, Buffalo, St. Louis
138 — Mike Vernon, Calgary, Detroit, San Jose, Florida

MOST MINUTES PLAYED BY A GOALTENDER, CAREER:
15,209 — Patrick Roy, Montreal, Colorado
10,221 — Martin Brodeur, New Jersey
9,945 — Ed Belfour, Chicago, Dallas, Toronto
8,834 — Grant Fuhr, Edmonton, Buffalo, St. Louis
8,214 — Mike Vernon, Calgary, Detroit, San Jose, Florida

MOST MINUTES PLAYED BY A GOALTENDER, ONE PLAYOFF YEAR:
1,655 — Miikka Kiprusoff, Calgary, 2004. 26 games.
1,544 — Kirk McLean, Vancouver, 1994. 24 games.
— Ed Belfour, Dallas, 1999. 23 games.
1,540 — Ron Hextall, Philadelphia, 1987. 26 games.
1,505 — Martin Brodeur, New Jersey, 2001. 25 games.

MOST SHUTOUTS IN PLAYOFFS (CAREER):
23 — Patrick Roy, Montreal, Colorado
22 — Martin Brodeur, New Jersey
16 — Curtis Joseph, St. Louis, Edmonton, Toronto

MOST SHUTOUTS, ONE PLAYOFF YEAR:
7 — Martin Brodeur, New Jersey, 2003. 24 games.
6 — Dominik Hasek, Detroit, 2002. 23 games.
5 — Jean-Sebastien Giguere, Anaheim, 2003. 21 games.
— Nikolai Khabibulin, Tampa Bay, 2004. 23 games.
— Miikka Kiprusoff, Calgary, 2004. 26 games.

MOST SHUTOUTS, ONE PLAYOFF SERIES:
3 — **Clint Benedict, Mtl. Maroons,** 1926 F vs. Victoria. 4 games.
— **Dave Kerr, NY Rangers,** 1940 SF vs. Boston. 6 games.
— **Frank McCool, Toronto,** 1945 F vs. Detroit. 7 games.
— **Turk Broda, Toronto,** 1950 SF vs. Detroit. 7 games.
— **Felix Potvin, Toronto,** 1994 CQF vs. Chicago. 6 games.
— **Martin Brodeur, New Jersey,** 1995 CQF vs. Boston. 7 games.
— **Brent Johnson, St. Louis,** 2002 CQF vs. Chicago. 5 games.
— **Patrick Lalime, Ottawa,** 2002 CQF vs. Philadelphia. 5 games.
— **Jean-Sebastien Giguere, Anaheim,** 2003 CF vs. Minnesota. 4 games.
— **Martin Brodeur, New Jersey,** 2003 F vs. Anaheim. 7 games.
— **Ed Belfour, Toronto,** 2004 CQF vs. Ottawa. 7 games.
— **Nikolai Khabibulin, Tampa Bay,** 2004 CQF vs. NY Islanders. 5 games.

MOST WINS BY A GOALTENDER, (CAREER):
151 — Patrick Roy, Montreal, Colorado
94 — Martin Brodeur, New Jersey
92 — Grant Fuhr, Edmonton, Buffalo, St. Louis
88 — Billy Smith, NY Islanders
— Ed Belfour, Chicago, Dallas, Toronto

MOST WINS BY A GOALTENDER, ONE PLAYOFF YEAR:
16 — Sixteen wins by a goaltender in one playoff year has been recorded on 16 occasions. Nikolai Khabibulin of the Tampa Bay Lightning is the most recent to equal this mark, posting a record of 16 wins and 7 losses in 23 games in 2004. It was first accomplished by Grant Fuhr in 1988.

MOST CONSECUTIVE WINS BY A GOALTENDER, MORE THAN ONE PLAYOFF YEAR:
14 — **Tom Barrasso, Pittsburgh,** 1992, 1993; 3 wins vs. NY Rangers in 1992 DF, won by Pittsburgh 4-2; 4 wins vs. Boston in 1992 CF, won by Pittsburgh 4-0; 4 wins vs. Chicago in 1992 F, won by Pittsburgh 4-0; 3 wins vs. New Jersey in 1993 DSF, won by Pittsburgh 4-1.

MOST CONSECUTIVE WINS BY A GOALTENDER, ONE PLAYOFF YEAR:
11 — **Ed Belfour, Chicago,** 1992. 3 wins vs. St. Louis in DSF, won by Chicago 4-2; 4 wins vs. Detroit in DF, won by Chicago 4-0; and 4 wins vs. Edmonton in CF, won by Chicago 4-0.
— **Tom Barrasso, Pittsburgh,** 1992. 3 wins vs. NY Rangers in DF, won by Pittsburgh 4-2; 4 wins vs. Boston in CF, won by Pittsburgh 4-0; and 4 wins vs. Chicago in F, won by Pittsburgh 4-0.
— **Patrick Roy, Montreal,** 1993. 4 wins vs. Quebec in DSF, won by Montreal 4-2; 4 wins vs. Buffalo in DF, won by Montreal 4-0; and 3 wins vs. NY Islanders in CF, won by Montreal 4-1.

LONGEST SHUTOUT SEQUENCE:
270:08 — George Hainsworth, Montreal, 1930. Hainsworth's shutout streak began after Murray Murdoch scored a goal for the NY Rangers at 15:34 of the first period in the first game of a SF series on March 28, 1930. Hainsworth did not allow another goal in the final 113:18 of that game, won by Montreal 2-1 at 8:52 of the 4th overtime period. Hainsworth then shutout the NY Rangers in the next and final game of the series on March 30, 1930, won by Montreal 2-0. The streak continued with a 3-0 win over Boston in the opening game of the F series on April 1, 1930. His streak ended on April 3, 1930 when Boston's Eddie Shore scored at 16:50 of the second period in the second game of the F series.

MOST CONSECUTIVE SHUTOUTS:
3 — **Clint Benedict, Mtl. Maroons,** 1926. Benedict shut out Ottawa 1-0, Mar. 27; he then shut out Victoria twice, 3-0, Mar. 30; 3-0, Apr. 1. Mtl. Maroons won NHL F vs. Ottawa 2 goals to 1 and won the best-of-five F vs. Victoria 3-1.
— **John Ross Roach, NY Rangers,** 1929. Roach shut out NY Americans twice, 0-0, Mar. 19; 1-0, Mar. 21; he then shut out Toronto 1-0, Mar. 24. NY Rangers won QF vs. NY Americans 1 goal to 0 and won the best-of-three SF vs. Toronto 2-0.
— **Frank McCool, Toronto,** 1945. McCool shut out Detroit 1-0, April 6; 2-0, April 8; 1-0, April 12. Toronto won the best-of-seven F 4-3.
— **Brent Johnson, St. Louis,** 2002. Johnson shut out Chicago three times; 2-0, April 20; 4-0, April 21; 1-0, April 23. St. Louis won the best-of-seven CQF 4-1.
— **Patrick Lalime, Ottawa,** 2002. Lalime shut out Philadelphia three times; 3-0, April 20; 3-0, April 22; 3-0, April 24. Ottawa won the best-of-seven CQF 4-1.
— **Jean-Sebastien Giguere, Anaheim,** 2003. Giguere shut out Minnesota 1-0, May 10; 2-0, May 12; 4-0, May 14. Anaheim won the best-of-seven CF 4-0.

Early Playoff Records

1893-1918

Team Records

MOST GOALS, BOTH TEAMS, ONE GAME:
25 — **Ottawa Silver Seven, Dawson City** at Ottawa, Jan. 16, 1905. Ottawa 23, Dawson City 2. Ottawa won best-of-three series 2-0.

MOST GOALS, ONE TEAM, ONE GAME:
23 — **Ottawa Silver Seven** at Ottawa, Jan. 16, 1905. Ottawa defeated Dawson City 23-2.

MOST GOALS, BOTH TEAMS, BEST-OF-THREE SERIES:
42 — **Ottawa Silver Seven, Queen's University** at Ottawa, 1906. Ottawa defeated Queen's 16-7, Feb. 27, and 12-7, Feb. 28.

MOST GOALS, ONE TEAM, BEST-OF-THREE SERIES:
32 — **Ottawa Silver Seven** in 1905 at Ottawa. Defeated Dawson City 9-2, Jan. 13, and 23-2, Jan. 16.

MOST GOALS, BOTH TEAMS, BEST-OF-FIVE SERIES:
39 — **Toronto Arenas, Vancouver Millionaires** at Toronto, 1918. Toronto won 5-3, Mar. 20; 6-3, Mar. 26; 2-1, Mar. 30. Vancouver won 6-4, Mar. 23, and 8-1, Mar. 28. Toronto scored 18 goals; Vancouver 21.

MOST GOALS, ONE TEAM, BEST-OF-FIVE SERIES:
26 — **Vancouver Millionaires** in 1915 at Vancouver. Defeated Ottawa Senators 6-2, Mar. 22; 8-3, Mar. 24; and 12-3, Mar. 26.

Individual Records

MOST GOALS IN PLAYOFFS:
63 — **Frank McGee, Ottawa Silver Seven,** in 22 playoff games. Seven goals in four games, 1903; 21 goals in eight games, 1904; 18 goals in four games, 1905; 17 goals in six games, 1906.

MOST GOALS, ONE PLAYOFF SERIES:
15 — **Frank McGee, Ottawa Silver Seven,** in two games in 1905 at Ottawa. Scored one goal, Jan. 13, in 9-2 victory over Dawson City and 14 goals, Jan. 16, in 23-2 victory.

MOST GOALS, ONE PLAYOFF GAME:
14 — **Frank McGee, Ottawa Silver Seven,** at Ottawa, Jan. 16, 1905, in 23-2 victory over Dawson City.

FASTEST THREE GOALS:
40 Seconds — **Marty Walsh, Ottawa Senators,** at Ottawa, March 16, 1911, at 3:00, 3:10, and 3:40 of third period. Ottawa defeated Port Arthur 13-4.

All-Time Playoff Goal Leaders since 1918

(40 or more goals)

Player	Teams	Yrs.	GP	G
Wayne Gretzky	Edm., L.A., St.L., NYR	16	208	122
Mark Messier	Edm., NYR, Van.	17	236	109
Jari Kurri	Edm., L.A., NYR, Ana., Col.	15	200	106
Brett Hull	Cgy., St.L., Dal., Det., Phx.	19	202	103
Glenn Anderson	Edm., Tor., NYR, St.L.	15	225	93
Mike Bossy	NYI	10	129	85
Maurice Richard	Mtl.	15	133	82
* Joe Sakic	Que., Col.	12	162	82
Claude Lemieux	Mtl., N.J., Col., Phx., Dal.	17	233	80
Jean Beliveau	Mtl.	17	162	79
Mario Lemieux	Pit.	8	107	76
Dino Ciccarelli	Min., Wsh., Det., T.B., Fla.	14	141	73
* Jaromir Jagr	Pit., Wsh., NYR	14	159	72
Esa Tikkanen	Edm., NYR, St.L., N.J., Van., Fla., Wsh.	13	186	72
Bryan Trottier	NYI, Pit.	17	221	71
Steve Yzerman	Det.	20	196	70
Gordie Howe	Det., Hfd.	20	157	68
Joe Nieuwendyk	Cgy., Dal., N.J., Tor., Fla.	16	158	66
Denis Savard	Chi., Mtl., T.B.	16	169	66
Yvan Cournoyer	Mtl.	12	147	64
Brian Propp	Phi., Bos., Min., Hfd.	13	160	64
Bobby Smith	Min., Mtl.	13	184	64
* Peter Forsberg	Que., Col., Phi., Nsh.	12	144	63
Bobby Hull	Chi., Wpg., Hfd.	14	119	62
Phil Esposito	Chi., Bos., NYR	15	130	61
Jacques Lemaire	Mtl.	11	145	61
Joe Mullen	St.L., Cgy., Pit., Bos.	15	143	60
Doug Gilmour	St.L., Cgy., Tor., N.J., Chi., Buf., Mtl.	17	182	60
Stan Mikita	Chi.	18	155	59
Paul Coffey	Edm., Pit., L.A., Det., Hfd., Phi., Chi., Car., Bos.	16	194	59
Guy Lafleur	Mtl., NYR, Que.	14	128	58
Bernie Geoffrion	Mtl., NYR	16	132	58
Luc Robitaille	L.A., Pit., NYR, Det.	15	159	58
* Brendan Shanahan	N.J., St.L., Hfd., Det., NYR	17	167	58
Cam Neely	Van., Bos.	9	93	57
Steve Larmer	Chi., NYR	13	140	56
Denis Potvin	NYI	14	185	56
Rick MacLeish	Phi., Hfd., Pit., Det.	11	114	54
Steve Thomas	Tor., Chi., NYI, N.J., Ana., Det.	16	174	54
Bill Barber	Phi.	11	129	53
Stephane Richer	Mtl., N.J., T.B., St.L., Pit.	13	134	53
* Mike Modano	Min., Dal.	14	156	53
Rick Tocchet	Phi., Pit., L.A., Bos., Wsh., Phx.	13	145	52
* Jeremy Roenick	Chi., Phx., Phi., L.A.	15	136	51
Frank Mahovlich	Tor., Det., Mtl.	14	137	51
Brian Bellows	Min., Mtl., T.B., Ana., Wsh.	13	143	51
Steve Shutt	Mtl., L.A.	12	99	50
* Rod Brind'Amour	St.L., Phi., Car.	11	141	50
* Sergei Fedorov	Det., Ana., CBJ	13	162	50
Henri Richard	Mtl.	18	180	49
Reggie Leach	Bos., Cal., Phi., Det.	8	94	47
Ted Lindsay	Det., Chi.	16	133	47
* Mark Recchi	Pit., Phi., Mtl., Car.	12	140	47
Clark Gillies	NYI, Buf.	13	164	47
Kevin Stevens	Pit., Bos., L.A., NYR, Phi.	7	103	46
Dickie Moore	Mtl., Tor., St.L.	14	135	46
Ron Francis	Hfd., Pit., Car., Tor.	17	171	46
Rick Middleton	NYR, Bos.	12	114	45
Lanny McDonald	Tor., Col., Cgy.	13	117	44
Scott Young	Hfd., Pit., Que., Col., Ana., St.L., Dal.	14	141	44
* Daniel Alfredsson	Ott.	10	99	43
Ken Linseman	Phi., Edm., Bos., Tor.	11	113	43
* Chris Drury	Col., Cgy., Buf.	6	114	43
Mike Gartner	Wsh., Min., NYR, Tor., Phx.	15	122	43
Dave Andreychuk	Buf., Tor., N.J., Bos., Col., T.B.	18	162	43
* Vyacheslav Kozlov	Det., Buf., Atl.	10	118	42
Bernie Nicholls	L.A., NYR, Edm., N.J., Chi., S.J.	13	118	42
Bobby Clarke	Phi.	13	136	42
John LeClair	Mtl., Phi., Pit.	14	154	42
Adam Oates	Det., St.L., Bos., Wsh., Phi., Ana., Edm.	15	163	42
Dale Hunter	Que., Wsh., Col.	18	186	42
John Bucyk	Det., Bos.	14	124	41
Vincent Damphousse	Tor., Edm., Mtl., S.J.	14	140	41
Raymond Bourque	Bos., Col.	21	214	41
Tim Kerr	Phi., NYR, Hfd.	10	81	40
Peter McNab	Buf., Bos., Van., N.J.	10	107	40
Bob Bourne	NYI, L.A.	13	139	40
John Tonelli	NYI, Cgy., L.A., Chi., Que.	13	172	40

* Active

All-Time Playoff Assist Leaders since 1918

(60 or more assists)

Player	Teams	Yrs.	GP	A
Wayne Gretzky	Edm., L.A., St.L., NYR	16	208	260
Mark Messier	Edm., NYR, Van.	17	236	186
Raymond Bourque	Bos., Col.	21	214	139
Paul Coffey	Edm., Pit., L.A., Det., Hfd., Phi., Chi., Car., Bos.	16	194	137
Doug Gilmour	St.L., Cgy., Tor., N.J., Chi., Buf., Mtl.	17	182	128
Jari Kurri	Edm., L.A., NYR, Ana., Col.	15	200	127
Al MacInnis	Cgy., St.L.	19	177	121
Glenn Anderson	Edm., Tor., NYR, St.L.	15	225	121
Larry Robinson	Mtl., L.A.	20	227	116
Steve Yzerman	Det.	20	196	115
Larry Murphy	L.A., Wsh., Min., Pit., Tor., Det.	20	215	115
Adam Oates	Det., St.L., Bos., Wsh., Phi., Ana., Edm.	15	163	114
* Sergei Fedorov	Det., Ana., CBJ	13	162	113
Bryan Trottier	NYI, Pit.	17	221	113
* Chris Chelios	Mtl., Chi., Det.	22	246	113
Denis Savard	Chi., Mtl., T.B.	16	169	109
Denis Potvin	NYI	14	185	108
* Peter Forsberg	Que., Col., Phi., Nsh.	12	144	103
Jean Beliveau	Mtl.	17	162	97
Ron Francis	Hfd., Pit., Car., Tor.	17	171	97
* Nicklas Lidstrom	Det.	15	192	97
Mario Lemieux	Pit.	8	107	96
* Joe Sakic	Que., Col.	12	162	96
Bobby Smith	Min., Mtl.	13	184	96
* Jaromir Jagr	Pit., Wsh., NYR	14	159	94
Gordie Howe	Det., Hfd.	20	157	92
Scott Stevens	Wsh., St.L., N.J.	20	233	92
Stan Mikita	Chi.	18	155	91
Brad Park	NYR, Bos., Det.	17	161	90
* Sergei Zubov	NYR, Pit., Dal.	12	153	88
Brett Hull	Cgy., St.L., Dal., Det., Phx.	19	202	87
Craig Janney	Bos., St.L., S.J., Wpg., Phx., T.B., NYI	11	120	86
Brian Propp	Phi., Bos., Min., Hfd.	13	160	84
* Mike Modano	Min., Dal.	14	156	80
Henri Richard	Mtl.	18	180	80
Jacques Lemaire	Mtl.	11	145	78
Claude Lemieux	Mtl., N.J., Col., Phx., Dal.	17	233	78
Ken Linseman	Phi., Edm., Bos., Tor.	11	113	77
Bobby Clarke	Phi.	13	136	77
Guy Lafleur	Mtl., NYR, Que.	14	128	76
Phil Esposito	Chi., Bos., NYR	15	130	76
Dale Hunter	Que., Wsh., Col.	18	186	76
Mike Bossy	NYI	10	129	75
Steve Larmer	Chi., NYR	13	140	75
John Tonelli	NYI, Cgy., L.A., Chi., Que.	13	172	75
Peter Stastny	Que., N.J., St.L.	12	93	72
Bernie Nicholls	L.A., NYR, Edm., N.J., Chi., S.J.	13	118	72
Brian Bellows	Min., Mtl., T.B., Ana., Wsh.	13	143	71
Gilbert Perreault	Buf.	11	90	70
* Mark Recchi	Pit., Phi., Mtl., Car.	12	140	70
Geoff Courtnall	Bos., Edm., Wsh., St.L., Van.	15	156	70
Brian Leetch	NYR, Tor., Bos.	8	95	69
Dale Hawerchuk	Wpg., Buf., St.L., Phi.	15	97	69
Alex Delvecchio	Det.	14	121	69
* Patrik Elias	N.J.	10	121	69
* Chris Pronger	Hfd., St.L., Edm., Ana.	11	128	69
Luc Robitaille	L.A., Pit., NYR, Det.	15	159	69
* Brendan Shanahan	N.J., St.L., Hfd., Det., NYR	17	167	68
Bobby Hull	Chi., Wpg., Hfd.	14	119	67
Sandis Ozolinsh	S.J., Col., Car., Fla., Ana., NYR	10	137	67
Frank Mahovlich	Tor., Det., Mtl.	14	137	67
Igor Larionov	Van., S.J., Det., Fla., N.J.	13	150	67
Bobby Orr	Bos., Chi.	8	74	66
Bernie Federko	St.L., Det.	11	91	66
Jean Ratelle	NYR, Bos.	15	123	66
Charlie Huddy	Edm., L.A., Buf., St.L.	14	183	66
* Trevor Linden	Van., NYI, Mtl., Wsh.	12	124	65
* Jeremy Roenick	Chi., Phx., Phi., L.A.	15	136	65
Dickie Moore	Mtl., Tor., St.L.	14	135	64
Doug Harvey	Mtl., NYR, Det., St.L.	15	137	64
* Scott Niedermayer	N.J., Ana.	13	183	64
Neal Broten	Min., Dal., N.J., L.A.	13	135	63
Vincent Damphousse	Tor., Edm., Mtl., S.J.	14	140	63
Yvan Cournoyer	Mtl.	12	147	63
* Pierre Turgeon	Buf., NYI, Mtl., St.L., Dal., Col.	15	109	62
John Bucyk	Det., Bos.	14	124	62
Doug Wilson	Chi., S.J.	12	95	61
Steve Duchesne	L.A., Phi., Que., St.L., Ott., Det.	14	121	61
Kevin Stevens	Pit., Bos., L.A., NYR, Phi.	7	103	60
Bernie Geoffrion	Mtl., NYR	16	132	60
Rick Tocchet	Phi., Pit., L.A., Bos., Wsh., Phx.	13	145	60
Esa Tikkanen	Edm., NYR, St.L., N.J., Van., Fla., Wsh.	13	186	60

All-Time Playoff Point Leaders since 1918

(105 or more points)

Player	Teams	Yrs.	GP	G	A	Pts.
Wayne Gretzky	Edm., L.A., St.L., NYR	16	208	122	260	382
Mark Messier	Edm., NYR, Van.	17	236	109	186	295
Jari Kurri	Edm., L.A., NYR, Ana., Col.	15	200	106	127	233
Glenn Anderson	Edm., Tor., NYR, St.L.	15	225	93	121	214
Paul Coffey	Edm., Pit., L.A., Det., Hfd., Phi., Chi., Car., Bos.	16	194	59	137	196
Brett Hull	Cgy., St.L., Dal., Det., Phx.	19	202	103	87	190
Doug Gilmour	St.L., Cgy., Tor., N.J., Chi., Buf., Mtl.	17	182	60	128	188
Steve Yzerman	Det.	20	196	70	115	185
Bryan Trottier	NYI, Pit.	17	221	71	113	184
Raymond Bourque	Bos., Col.	21	214	41	139	180
* Joe Sakic	Que., Col.	12	162	82	96	178
Jean Beliveau	Mtl.	17	162	79	97	176
Denis Savard	Chi., Mtl., T.B.	16	169	66	109	175
Mario Lemieux	Pit.	8	107	76	96	172
* Peter Forsberg	Que., Col., Phi., Nsh.	12	144	63	103	166
* Jaromir Jagr	Pit., Wsh., NYR	14	159	72	94	166
Denis Potvin	NYI	14	185	56	108	164
* Sergei Fedorov	Det., Ana., CBJ	13	162	50	113	163
Mike Bossy	NYI	10	129	85	75	160
Gordie Howe	Det., Hfd.	20	157	68	92	160
Al MacInnis	Cgy., St.L.	19	177	39	121	160
Bobby Smith	Min., Mtl.	13	184	64	96	160
Claude Lemieux	Mtl., N.J., Col., Phx., Dal.	17	233	80	78	158
Adam Oates	Det., St.L., Bos., Wsh., Phi., Ana., Edm.	15	163	42	114	156
Larry Murphy	L.A., Wsh., Min., Pit., Tor., Det.	20	215	37	115	152
Stan Mikita	Chi.	18	155	59	91	150
Brian Propp	Phi., Bos., Min., Hfd.	13	160	64	84	148
Larry Robinson	Mtl., L.A.	20	227	28	116	144
* Chris Chelios	Mtl., Chi., Det.	22	246	31	113	144
Ron Francis	Hfd., Pit., Car., Tor.	17	171	46	97	143
Jacques Lemaire	Mtl.	11	145	61	78	139
Phil Esposito	Chi., Bos., NYR	15	130	61	76	137
* Nicklas Lidstrom	Det.	15	192	39	97	136
Guy Lafleur	Mtl., NYR, Que.	14	128	58	76	134
* Mike Modano	Min., Dal.	14	156	53	80	133
Esa Tikkanen	Edm., NYR, St.L., N.J., Van., Fla., Wsh.	13	186	72	60	132
Steve Larmer	Chi., NYR	13	140	56	75	131
Bobby Hull	Chi., Wpg., Hfd.	14	119	62	67	129
Henri Richard	Mtl.	18	180	49	80	129
Yvan Cournoyer	Mtl.	12	147	64	63	127
Luc Robitaille	L.A., Pit., NYR, Det.	15	159	58	69	127
Maurice Richard	Mtl.	15	133	82	44	126
* Brendan Shanahan	N.J., St.L., Hfd., Det., NYR	17	167	58	68	126
Brad Park	NYR, Bos., Det.	17	161	35	90	125
Brian Bellows	Min., Mtl., T.B., Ana., Wsh.	13	143	51	71	122
Ken Linseman	Phi., Edm., Bos., Tor.	11	113	43	77	120
Bobby Clarke	Phi.	13	136	42	77	119
Bernie Geoffrion	Mtl., NYR	16	132	58	60	118
Frank Mahovlich	Tor., Det., Mtl.	14	137	51	67	118
Dino Ciccarelli	Min., Wsh., Det., T.B., Fla.	14	141	73	45	118
Dale Hunter	Que., Wsh., Col.	18	186	42	76	118
Scott Stevens	Wsh., St.L., N.J.	20	233	26	92	118
* Mark Recchi	Pit., Phi., Mtl., Car.	12	140	47	70	117
* Jeremy Roenick	Chi., Phx., Phi., L.A.	15	136	51	65	116
Joe Nieuwendyk	Cgy., Dal., N.J., Tor., Fla.	16	158	66	50	116
John Tonelli	NYI, Cgy., L.A., Chi., Que.	13	172	40	75	115
Bernie Nicholls	L.A., NYR, Edm., N.J., Chi., S.J.	13	118	42	72	114
Rick Tocchet	Phi., Pit., L.A., Bos., Wsh., Phx.	13	145	52	60	112
* Sergei Zubov	NYR, Pit., Dal.	12	153	23	88	111
Craig Janney	Bos., St.L., S.J., Wpg., Phx., T.B., NYI	11	120	24	86	110
Dickie Moore	Mtl., Tor., St.L.	14	135	46	64	110
Geoff Courtnall	Bos., Edm., Wsh., St.L., Van.	15	156	39	70	109
Bill Barber	Phi.	11	129	53	55	108
Rick MacLeish	Phi., Hfd., Pit., Det.	11	114	54	53	107
* Rod Brind'Amour	St.L., Phi., Car.	11	141	50	57	107
Steve Thomas	Tor., Chi., NYI, N.J., Ana., Det.	16	174	54	53	107
Kevin Stevens	Pit., Bos., L.A., NYR, Phi.	7	103	46	60	106
Joe Mullen	St.L., Cgy., Pit., Bos.	15	143	60	46	106
Peter Stastny	Que., N.J., St.L.	12	93	33	72	105

Carolina's Eric Staal, cutting out from behind the New Jersey net during the Hurricanes' 2006 Eastern Semi-Final series with the Devils, capped a brilliant 2005-06 season by leading the playoffs in scoring with the highest point total since 1995-96.

Leading Playoff Scorers, 1918–2007

Season	Player and Club	Games Played	Goals	Assists	Points
2006-07	Daniel Alfredsson, Ottawa	20	14	8	22
	Dany Heatley, Ottawa	20	7	15	22
	Jason Spezza, Ottawa	20	7	15	22
2005-06	Eric Staal, Carolina	25	9	19	28
2004-05	*Season Cancelled*				
2003-04	Brad Richards, Tampa Bay	23	12	14	26
2002-03	Jamie Langenbrunner, New Jersey	24	11	7	18
	Scott Niedermayer, New Jersey	24	2	16	18
2001-02	Peter Forsberg, Colorado	20	9	18	27
2000-01	Joe Sakic, Colorado	21	13	13	26
99-2000	Brett Hull, Dallas	23	11	13	24
1998-99	Peter Forsberg, Colorado	19	8	16	24
1997-98	Steve Yzerman, Detroit	22	6	18	24
1996-97	Eric Lindros, Philadelphia	19	12	14	26
1995-96	Joe Sakic, Colorado	22	18	16	34
1994-95	Sergei Fedorov, Detroit	17	7	17	24
1993-94	Brian Leetch, NY Rangers	23	11	23	34
1992-93	Wayne Gretzky, Los Angeles	24	15	25	40
1991-92	Mario Lemieux, Pittsburgh	15	16	18	34
1990-91	Mario Lemieux, Pittsburgh	23	16	28	44
1989-90	Craig Simpson, Edmonton	22	16	15	31
	Mark Messier, Edmonton	22	9	22	31
1988-89	Al MacInnis, Calgary	22	7	24	31
1987-88	Wayne Gretzky, Edmonton	19	12	31	43
1986-87	Wayne Gretzky, Edmonton	21	5	29	34
1985-86	Doug Gilmour, St. Louis	19	9	12	21
	Bernie Federko, St. Louis	19	7	14	21
1984-85	Wayne Gretzky, Edmonton	18	17	30	47
1983-84	Wayne Gretzky, Edmonton	19	13	22	35
1982-83	Wayne Gretzky, Edmonton	16	12	26	38
1981-82	Bryan Trottier, NY Islanders	19	6	23	29
1980-81	Mike Bossy, NY Islanders	18	17	18	35
1979-80	Bryan Trottier, NY Islanders	21	12	17	29
1978-79	Jacques Lemaire, Montreal	16	11	12	23
	Guy Lafleur, Montreal	16	10	13	23
1977-78	Guy Lafleur, Montreal	15	10	11	21
	Larry Robinson, Montreal	15	4	17	21
1976-77	Guy Lafleur, Montreal	14	9	17	26
1975-76	Reggie Leach, Philadelphia	16	19	5	24
1974-75	Rick MacLeish, Philadelphia	17	11	9	20
1973-74	Rick MacLeish, Philadelphia	17	13	9	22
1972-73	Yvan Cournoyer, Montreal	17	15	10	25
1971-72	Phil Esposito, Boston	15	9	15	24
	Bobby Orr, Boston	15	5	19	24
1970-71	Frank Mahovlich, Montreal	20	14	13	27
1969-70	Phil Esposito, Boston	14	13	14	27
1968-69	Phil Esposito, Boston	10	8	10	18
1967-68	Bill Goldsworthy, Minnesota	14	8	7	15
1966-67	Jim Pappin, Toronto	12	7	8	15
1965-66	Norm Ullman, Detroit	12	6	9	15
1964-65	Bobby Hull, Chicago	14	10	7	17
1963-64	Gordie Howe, Detroit	14	9	10	19
1962-63	Gordie Howe, Detroit	11	7	9	16
	Norm Ullman, Detroit	11	4	12	16
1961-62	Stan Mikita, Chicago	12	6	15	21
1960-61	Gordie Howe, Detroit	11	4	11	15
	Pierre Pilote, Chicago	12	3	12	15
1959-60	Henri Richard, Montreal	8	3	9	12
	Bernie Geoffrion, Montreal	8	2	10	12
1958-59	Dickie Moore, Montreal	11	5	12	17
1957-58	Fleming MacKell, Boston	12	5	14	19
1956-57	Bernie Geoffrion, Montreal	11	11	7	18
1955-56	Jean Béliveau, Montreal	10	12	7	19
1954-55	Gordie Howe, Detroit	11	9	11	20
1953-54	Dickie Moore, Montreal	11	5	8	13
1952-53	Ed Sandford, Boston	11	8	3	11
1951-52	Ted Lindsay, Detroit	8	5	2	7
	Floyd Curry, Montreal	11	4	3	7
	Metro Prystai, Detroit	8	2	5	7
	Gordie Howe, Detroit	8	2	5	7
1950-51	Maurice Richard, Montreal	11	9	4	13
	Max Bentley, Toronto	11	2	11	13
1949-50	Pentti Lund, NY Rangers	12	6	5	11
1948-49	Gordie Howe, Detroit	11	8	3	11
1947-48	Ted Kennedy, Toronto	9	8	6	14
1946-47	Maurice Richard, Montreal	10	6	5	11
1945-46	Elmer Lach, Montreal	9	5	12	17
1944-45	Joe Carveth, Detroit	14	5	6	11
1943-44	Toe Blake, Montreal	9	7	11	18
1942-43	Carl Liscombe, Detroit	10	6	8	14
1941-42	Don Grosso, Detroit	12	8	6	14
	Syl Apps, Toronto	13	5	9	14
1940-41	Milt Schmidt, Boston	11	5	6	11
1939-40	Phil Watson, NY Rangers	12	3	6	9
	Neil Colville, NY Rangers	12	2	7	9
1938-39	Bill Cowley, Boston	12	3	11	14
1937-38	Johnny Gottselig, Chicago	10	5	3	8
	Gordie Drillon, Toronto	7	7	1	8
1936-37	Marty Barry, Detroit	10	4	7	11
1935-36	Frank Boll, Toronto	9	7	3	10
1934-35	Baldy Northcott, Mtl. Maroons	7	4	1	5
	Busher Jackson, Toronto	7	3	2	5
	Cy Wentworth, Mtl. Maroons	7	3	2	5
	Charlie Conacher, Toronto	7	1	4	5
1933-34	Larry Aurie, Detroit	9	3	7	10
1932-33	Cecil Dillon, NY Rangers	8	8	2	10
1931-32	Frank Boucher, NY Rangers	7	3	6	9
1930-31	Cooney Weiland, Boston	5	6	3	9
1929-30	Marty Barry, Boston	6	3	3	6
	Cooney Weiland, Boston	6	1	5	6
1928-29	Andy Blair, Toronto	4	3	0	3
	Butch Keeling, NY Rangers	6	3	0	3
	Ace Bailey, Toronto	4	1	2	3
1927-28	Frank Boucher, NY Rangers	9	7	3	10
1926-27	Harry Oliver, Boston	8	4	2	6
	Percy Galbraith, Boston	8	3	3	6
1925-26	Nels Stewart, Mtl. Maroons	8	6	3	9
1924-25	Howie Morenz, Montreal	6	7	1	8
1923-24	Howie Morenz, Montreal	6	7	3	10
1922-23	Punch Broadbent, Ottawa	8	6	1	7
1921-22	Babe Dye, Toronto	7	11	1	12
1920-21	Cy Denneny, Ottawa	7	4	2	6
1919-20	Frank Nighbor, Ottawa	5	6	1	7
	Jack Darragh, Ottawa	5	5	2	7
1918-19	Newsy Lalonde, Montreal	10	17	2	19
1917-18	Alf Skinner, Toronto	7	8	3	11

Three-or-more-Goal Games, Playoffs 1918 –2007

Player	Team	Date	City	Total Goals	Opposing Goaltender	Score	
Wayne Gretzky (10)	Edm.	Apr. 11/81	Edm.	3	Richard Sevigny	Edm. 6	Mtl. 2
		Apr. 19/81	Edm.	3	Billy Smith	Edm. 5	NYI 2
		Apr. 6/83	Edm.	4	Brian Hayward	Edm. 6	Wpg. 3
		Apr. 17/83	Cgy.	4	Reggie Lemelin	Edm. 10	Cgy. 2
		Apr. 25/85	Wpg.	3	Brian Hayward (2)		
					Marc Behrend (1)	Edm. 8	Wpg. 3
		May 25/85	Edm.	3	Pelle Lindbergh	Edm. 4	Phi. 3
		Apr. 24/86	Cgy.	3	Mike Vernon	Edm. 7	Cgy. 4
	L.A.	May 29/93	Tor.	3	Felix Potvin	L.A. 5	Tor. 4
	NYR	Apr. 23/97	NYR	3	John Vanbiesbrouck	NYR 3	Fla. 2
		May 18/97	Phi.	3	Garth Snow	NYR 5	Phi. 4
Maurice Richard (7)	Mtl.	Mar. 23/44	Mtl.	5	Paul Bibeault	Mtl. 5	Tor. 1
		Apr. 6/44	Chi.	3	Mike Karakas	Mtl. 3	Chi. 1
		Mar. 29/45	Mtl.	4	Frank McCool	Mtl. 10	Tor. 3
		Apr. 14/53	Bos.	3	Gord Henry	Mtl. 7	Bos. 3
		Mar. 20/56	Mtl.	3	Gump Worsley	Mtl. 7	NYR 1
		Apr. 6/57	Mtl.	4	Don Simmons	Mtl. 5	Bos. 1
		Apr. 1/58	Det.	3	Terry Sawchuk	Mtl. 4	Det. 3
Jari Kurri (7)	Edm.	Apr. 4/84	Edm.	3	Doug Soetaert (1)		
					Mike Veisor (2)	Edm. 9	Wpg. 2
		Apr. 25/85	Wpg.	3	Brian Hayward (2)		
					Marc Behrend (1)	Edm. 8	Wpg. 3
		May 7/85	Edm.	3	Murray Bannerman	Edm. 7	Chi. 3
		May 14/85	Edm.	3	Murray Bannerman	Edm. 10	Chi. 5
		May 16/85	Chi.	4	Murray Bannerman	Edm. 8	Chi. 2
		Apr. 9/87	Edm.	4	Rollie Melanson (2)		
					Darren Eliot (2)	Edm. 13	L.A. 3
		May 18/90	Bos.	3	Andy Moog (2)		
					Reggie Lemelin (1)	Edm. 7	Bos. 2
Dino Ciccarelli (6)	Min.	May 5/81	Min.	3	Pat Riggin	Min. 7	Cgy. 4
		Apr. 10/82	Min.	3	Murray Bannerman	Min. 7	Chi. 1
	Wsh.	Apr. 5/90	N.J.	3	Sean Burke	Wsh. 5	N.J. 4
		Apr. 25/92	Pit.	4	Tom Barrasso (1)		
					Ken Wregget (3)	Wsh. 7	Pit. 2
	Det.	Apr. 29/93	Tor.	3	Felix Potvin (2)		
					Daren Puppa (1)	Det. 7	Tor. 3
		May 11/95	Dal.	3	Andy Moog (2)		
					Darcy Wakaluk (1)	Det. 5	Dal. 1
Mike Bossy (5)	NYI	Apr. 16/79	NYI	3	Tony Esposito	NYI 6	Chi. 2
		May 8/82	NYI	3	Richard Brodeur	NYI 6	Van. 5
		Apr. 10/83	Wsh.	3	Al Jensen	NYI 6	Wsh. 3
		May 3/83	NYI	3	Pete Peeters	NYI 8	Bos. 3
		May 7/83	NYI	4	Pete Peeters	NYI 8	Bos. 4
Phil Esposito (4)	Bos.	Apr. 2/69	Bos.	4	Bruce Gamble	Bos. 10	Tor. 0
		Apr. 8/70	Bos.	3	Ed Giacomin	Bos. 8	NYR 2
		Apr. 19/70	Chi.	3	Tony Esposito	Bos. 6	Chi. 3
		Apr. 8/75	Bos.	3	Tony Esposito (2)		
					Michel Dumas (1)	Bos. 8	Chi. 2
Mark Messier (4)	Edm.	Apr. 14/83	Edm.	4	Reggie Lemelin	Edm. 6	Cgy. 3
		Apr. 17/83	Cgy.	3	Reggie Lemelin (1)	Edm. 10	Cgy. 2
					Don Edwards (2)		
		Apr. 26/83	Edm.	3	Murray Bannerman	Edm. 8	Chi. 2
	NYR	May 25/94	N.J.	3	Martin Brodeur (2)	NYR 4	N.J. 2
					ENG (1)		
Steve Yzerman (4)	Det.	Apr. 6/89	Det.	3	Alain Chevrier	Chi. 5	Det. 4
		Apr. 4/91	St.L.	3	Vincent Riendeau (2)	Det. 6	St.L. 3
					Pat Jablonski (1)		
		May 8/96	St.L.	3	Jon Casey	St.L. 5	Det. 4
		Apr. 21/99	Det.	3	Guy Hebert (2)	Det. 5	Ana. 3
					Pat Jablonski (1)		
Bernie Geoffrion (3)	Mtl.	Mar. 27/52	Mtl.	3	Jim Henry	Mtl. 4	Bos. 0
		Apr. 7/55	Mtl.	3	Terry Sawchuk	Mtl. 4	Det. 2
		Mar. 30/57	Mtl.	3	Gump Worsley	Mtl. 8	NYR 3
Norm Ullman (3)	Det.	Mar. 29/64	Chi.	3	Glenn Hall	Det. 5	Chi. 4
		Apr. 7/64	Det.	3	Glenn Hall (2)		
					Denis DeJordy (1)	Det. 7	Chi. 2
		Apr. 11/65	Det.	3	Glenn Hall	Det. 4	Chi. 2
John Bucyk (3)	Bos.	May 3/70	St.L.	3	Jacques Plante (1)		
					Ernie Wakely (2)	Bos. 6	St.L. 1
		Apr. 20/72	Bos.	3	Jacques Caron (1)		
					Ernie Wakely (2)	Bos. 10	St.L. 2
		Apr. 21/74	Bos.	3	Tony Esposito	Bos. 8	Chi. 6
Rick MacLeish (3)	Phi.	Apr. 11/74	Phi.	3	Phil Myre	Phi. 5	Atl. 1
		Apr. 13/75	Phi.	3	Gord McRae	Phi. 6	Tor. 3
		May 13/75	Phi.	3	Glenn Resch	Phi. 4	NYI 1
Denis Savard (3)	Chi.	Apr. 19/82	Chi.	3	Mike Liut	Chi. 7	StL. 4
		Apr. 10/86	Chi.	4	Ken Wregget	Tor. 6	Chi. 4
		Apr. 9/88	St.L.	3	Greg Millen	Chi. 6	St.L. 3
Tim Kerr (3)	Phi.	Apr. 13/85	NYR	4	Glen Hanlon	Phi. 6	NYR 5
		Apr. 20/87	Phi.	3	Kelly Hrudey	Phi. 4	NYI 2
		Apr. 19/89	Pit.	3	Tom Barrasso	Phi. 4	Pit. 2
Cam Neely (3)	Bos.	Apr. 9/87	Mtl.	3	Patrick Roy	Mtl. 4	Bos. 3
		Apr. 5/91	Bos.	3	Peter Sidorkiewicz	Bos. 4	Hfd. 3
		Apr. 25/91	Bos.	3	Patrick Roy	Bos. 4	Mtl. 1
Petr Klima (3)	Det.	Apr. 7/88	Tor.	3	Alan Bester (2)		
					Ken Wregett (1)	Det. 6	Tor. 2
		Apr. 21/88	St.L.	3	Greg Millen	Det. 6	St.L. 0
	Edm.	May 4/91	Edm.	3	Jon Casey	Edm. 7	Min. 2
Esa Tikkanen (3)	Edm.	May 22/88	Edm.	3	Reggie Lemelin	Edm. 6	Bos. 3
		Apr. 16/91	Cgy.	3	Mike Vernon	Edm. 5	Cgy. 4
		Apr. 26/92	L.A.	3	Kelly Hrudey (2)	Edm. 5	L.A. 2
					Tom Askey (1)		
Mike Gartner (3)	NYR	Apr. 13/90	NYR	3	Mark Fitzpatrick (2)		
					Glenn Healy (1)	NYR 6	NYI 5
		Apr. 27/92	NYR	3	Chris Terreri	NYR 8	N.J. 5
	Tor.	Apr. 25/96	Tor.	3	Jon Casey	Tor. 5	St.L. 4
Mario Lemieux (3)	Pit.	Apr. 25/89	Pit.	5	Ron Hextall	Pit. 10	Phi. 7
		Apr. 23/92	Pit.	3	Don Beaupre	Pit. 6	Wsh. 4
		May 11/96	Pit.	3	Mike Richter	Pit. 7	NYR 3
Patrick Marleau (3)	S.J.	Apr. 10/04	S.J.	3	Chris Osgood	S.J. 3	St.L. 1
		Apr. 22/04	S.J.	3	David Aebischer	S.J. 5	Col. 2
		Apr. 27/06	S.J.	3	Chris Mason	Nsh. 4	S.J. 5
Newsy Lalonde (2)	Mtl.	Mar. 1/19	Mtl.	5	Clint Benedict	Mtl. 6	Ott. 3
		Mar. 22/19	Sea.	4	Hap Holmes	Mtl. 4	Sea. 2
Howie Morenz (2)	Mtl.	Mar. 22/24	Mtl.	3	Charles Reid	Mtl. 6	Cgy.T. 1
		Mar. 27/25	Mtl.	3	Hap Holmes	Mtl. 4	Vic. 2
Doug Bentley (2)	Chi.	Mar. 28/44	Chi.	3	Connie Dion	Chi. 7	Det. 1
		Mar. 30/44	Det.	3	Connie Dion	Chi. 5	Det. 2
Toe Blake (2)	Mtl.	Mar. 22/38	Mtl.	3	Mike Karakas	Mtl. 6	Chi. 4
		Mar. 26/46	Chi.	3	Mike Karakas	Mtl. 7	Chi. 2
Ted Kennedy (2)	Tor.	Apr. 14/45	Tor.	3	Harry Lumley	Det. 5	Tor. 3
		Mar. 27/48	Tor.	4	Frank Brimsek	Tor. 5	Bos. 3
F. St. Marseille (2)	St.L.	Apr. 28/70	St.L.	3	Al Smith	St.L. 5	Pit. 0
		Apr. 6/72	Min.	3	Cesare Maniago	Min. 6	St.L. 5
Bobby Hull (2)	Chi.	Apr. 7/63	Det.	3	Terry Sawchuk	Det. 7	Chi. 4
		Apr. 9/72	Pit.	3	Jim Rutherford	Chi. 6	Pit. 5
Pit Martin (2)	Chi.	Apr. 4/73	Chi.	3	Wayne Stephenson	Chi. 7	St.L. 1
		May 10/73	Chi.	3	Ken Dryden	Mtl. 6	Chi. 4
Yvan Cournoyer (2)	Mtl.	Apr. 5/73	Mtl.	3	Dave Dryden	Mtl. 7	Buf. 3
		Apr. 11/74	Mtl.	3	Ed Giacomin	Mtl. 4	NYR 1
Guy Lafleur (2)	Mtl.	May 1/75	Mtl.	3	Roger Crozier (1)		
					Gerry Desjardins (2)	Mtl. 7	Buf. 0
		Apr. 11/77	Mtl.	3	Ed Staniowski	Mtl. 7	St.L. 2
Lanny McDonald (2)	Tor.	Apr. 9/77	Pit.	3	Denis Herron	Tor. 5	Pit. 2
		Apr. 17/77	Tor.	4	Wayne Stephenson	Phi. 6	Tor. 5
Bill Barber (2)	Phi.	May 4/80	Min.	4	Gilles Meloche	Phi. 5	Min. 3
		Apr. 9/81	Phi.	3	Dan Bouchard	Phi. 8	Que. 5
Bryan Trottier (2)	NYI	Apr. 8/80	NYI	3	Doug Keans	NYI 8	L.A. 1
		Apr. 9/81	NYI	3	Michel Larocque	NYI 5	Tor. 1
Butch Goring (2)	L.A.	Apr. 9/77	L.A.	3	Phil Myre	L.A. 4	Atl. 2
	NYI	May 17/81	Min.	3	Gilles Meloche	NYI 7	Min. 5
Paul Reinhart (2)	Cgy.	Apr. 14/83	Edm.	3	Andy Moog	Edm. 6	Cgy. 3
		Apr. 8/84	Van	3	Richard Brodeur	Cgy. 5	Van. 1
Brian Propp (2)	Phi.	Apr. 22/81	Phi.	3	Pat Riggin	Phi. 9	Cgy. 4
		Apr. 21/85	Phi.	3	Billy Smith	Phi. 5	NYI 2
Peter Stastny (2)	Que.	Apr. 5/83	Bos.	3	Pete Peeters	Bos. 4	Que. 3
		Apr. 11/87	Que.	3	Mike Liut (2)		
					Steve Weeks (1)	Que. 5	Hfd. 1
Michel Goulet (2)	Que.	Apr. 23/85	Que.	3	Steve Penney	Que. 7	Mtl. 6
		Apr. 12/87	Que.	3	Mike Liut	Que. 4	Hfd. 1
Glenn Anderson (2)	Edm.	Apr. 26/83	Edm.	4	Murray Bannerman	Edm. 8	Chi. 2
		Apr. 6/88	Wpg.	3	Daniel Berthiaume	Edm. 7	Wpg. 4
Peter Zezel (2)	Phi.	Apr. 13/86	NYR	3	John Vanbiesbrouck	Phi. 7	NYR 1
	St.L.	Apr. 11/89	St.L.	3	Jon Casey (2)		
					Kari Takko (1)	St.L. 6	Min. 1
Geoff Courtnall (2)	Van.	Apr. 4/91	L.A.	3	Kelly Hrudey	Van. 6	L.A. 5
		Apr. 30/92	Van.	3	Rick Tabaracci	Van. 5	Win. 0
Joe Sakic (2)	Que.	May 6/95	Que.	3	Mike Richter	Que. 5	NYR 4
	Col.	Apr. 25/96	Col.	3	Corey Hirsch	Col. 5	Van. 4
Daniel Alfredsson (2)	Ott.	Apr. 28/98	Ott.	3	Martin Brodeur	Ott. 4	N.J. 3
		May 11/98	Ott.	3	Olaf Kolzig	Ott. 4	Wsh. 3
Harry Meeking	Tor.	Mar. 11/18	Tor.	3	Georges Vezina	Tor. 7	Mtl. 3
Alf Skinner	Tor.	Mar. 23/18	Tor.	3	Hugh Lehman	Van.M. 6	Tor. 4
Joe Malone	Mtl.	Feb. 23/19	Mtl.	3	Clint Benedict	Mtl. 8	Ott. 4
Odie Cleghorn	Mtl.	Feb. 27/19	Ott.	3	Clint Benedict	Mtl. 5	Ott. 3
Jack Darragh	Ott.	Apr. 1/20	Tor.	3	Hap Holmes	Ott. 6	Sea. 1
George Boucher	Ott.	Mar. 10/21	Ott.	3	Jake Forbes	Ott. 5	Tor. 0
Babe Dye	Tor.	Mar. 28/22	Tor.	4	Hugh Lehman	Tor. 5	Van.M. 1
Percy Galbraith	Bos.	Mar. 31/27	Bos.	3	Hugh Lehman	Bos. 4	Chi. 4
Busher Jackson	Tor.	Apr. 5/32	NYR	3	John Ross Roach	Tor. 6	NYR 4
Frank Boucher	NYR	Apr. 9/32	Tor.	3	Lorne Chabot	Tor. 6	NYR 4
Charlie Conacher	Tor.	Mar. 26/36	Tor.	3	Tiny Thompson	Tor. 8	Bos. 3
Syd Howe	Det.	Mar. 23/39	Det.	3	Claude Bourque	Det. 7	Mtl. 3
Bryan Hextall	NYR	Apr. 3/40	NYR	3	Turk Broda	NYR 6	Tor. 2
Joe Benoit	Mtl.	Mar. 22/41	Mtl.	3	Sam LoPresti	Mtl. 4	Chi. 3
Syl Apps	Tor.	Mar. 25/41	Tor.	3	Frank Brimsek	Tor. 7	Bos. 2
Jack McGill	Bos.	Mar. 29/42	Bos.	3	Johnny Mowers	Det. 6	Bos. 4
Don Metz	Tor.	Apr. 14/42	Tor.	3	Johnny Mowers	Tor. 9	Det. 3
Mud Bruneteau	Det.	Apr. 1/43	Det.	3	Frank Brimsek	Det. 6	Bos. 2
Don Grosso	Det.	Apr. 7/43	Bos.	3	Frank Brimsek	Det. 4	Bos. 0
Carl Liscombe	Det.	Apr. 3/45	Bos.	4	Paul Bibeault	Det. 5	Bos. 3
Billy Reay	Mtl.	Apr. 1/47	Bos.	4	Frank Brimsek	Mtl. 5	Bos. 1
Gerry Plamondon	Mtl.	Mar. 24/49	Det.	3	Harry Lumley	Mtl. 4	Det. 3
Sid Smith	Tor.	Apr. 10/49	Det.	3	Harry Lumley	Tor. 3	Det. 1
Pentti Lund	NYR	Apr. 2/50	NYR	3	Bill Durnan	NYR 4	Mtl. 1
Ted Lindsay	Det.	Apr. 5/55	Det.	4	Charlie Hodge (1)		
					Jacques Plante (3)	Det. 7	Mtl. 1
Gordie Howe	Det.	Apr. 10/55	Det.	3	Jacques Plante	Det. 5	Mtl. 1

Three-or-more-Goal Games, Playoffs *— continued*

Player	Team	Date	City	Total Goals	Opposing Goaltender	Score	
Phil Goyette	Mtl.	Mar. 25/58	Mtl.	3	Terry Sawchuk	Mtl. 8	Det. 1
Jerry Toppazzini	Bos.	Apr. 5/58	Bos.	3	Gump Worsley	Bos. 8	NYR 2
Bob Pulford	Tor.	Apr. 19/62	Tor.	3	Glenn Hall	Tor. 8	Chi. 4
Dave Keon	Tor.	Apr. 9/64	Mtl.	3	Charlie Hodge (2)	Tor. 3	Mtl. 1
					ENG (1)		
Henri Richard	Mtl.	Apr. 20/67	Mtl.	3	Terry Sawchuk (2)		
					Johnny Bower (1)	Mtl. 6	Tor. 2
Rosaire Paiement	Phi.	Apr. 13/68	Phi.	3	Glenn Hall (1)		
					Seth Martin (2)	Phi. 6	St.L. 1
Jean Beliveau	Mtl.	Apr. 20/68	Mtl.	3	Denis DeJordy	Mtl. 4	Chi. 1
Red Berenson	St.L.	Apr. 15/69	St.L.	3	Gerry Desjardins	St.L. 4	L.A. 0
Ken Schinkel	Pit.	Apr. 11/70	Oak.	3	Gary Smith	Pit. 5	Oak. 2
Jim Pappin	Chi.	Apr. 11/71	Phi.	3	Bruce Gamble	Chi. 6	Phi. 2
Bobby Orr	Bos.	Apr. 11/71	Mtl.	3	Ken Dryden	Bos. 5	Mtl. 2
Jacques Lemaire	Mtl.	Apr. 20/71	Mtl.	3	Gump Worsley	Mtl. 7	Min. 2
Vic Hadfield	NYR	Apr. 22/71	NYR	3	Tony Esposito	NYR 4	Chi. 1
Fred Stanfield	Bos.	Apr. 18/72	Bos.	3	Jacques Caron	Bos. 6	St.L. 1
Ken Hodge	Bos.	Apr. 30/72	Bos.	3	Ed Giacomin	Bos. 6	NYR 5
Dick Redmond	Chi.	Apr. 4/73	Chi.	3	Wayne Stephenson	Chi. 7	St.L. 1
Steve Vickers	NYR	Apr. 10/73	Bos.	3	Ross Brooks (2)		
					Eddie Johnston (1)	NYR 6	Bos. 3
Tom Williams	L.A.	Apr. 14/74	L.A.	3	Mike Veisor	L.A. 5	Chi. 1
Marcel Dionne	L.A.	Apr. 15/76	L.A.	3	Gilles Gilbert	L.A. 6	Bos. 4
Don Saleski	Phi.	Apr. 20/76	Phi.	3	Wayne Thomas	Phi. 7	Tor. 1
Darryl Sittler	Tor.	Apr. 22/76	Tor.	5	Bernie Parent	Tor. 8	Phi. 5
Reggie Leach	Phi.	May 6/76	Phi.	5	Gilles Gilbert	Phi. 6	Bos. 3
Jim Lorentz	Buf.	Apr. 7/77	Min.	3	Pete LoPresti (2)		
					Gary Smith (1)	Buf. 7	Min. 1
Bobby Schmautz	Bos.	Apr. 11/77	Bos.	3	Rogie Vachon	Bos. 8	L.A. 3
Billy Harris	NYI	Apr. 23/77	Mtl.	3	Ken Dryden	Mtl. 4	NYI 3
George Ferguson	Tor.	Apr. 11/78	Tor.	3	Rogie Vachon	Tor. 7	L.A. 3
Jean Ratelle	Bos.	May 3/79	Bos.	3	Ken Dryden	Bos. 4	Mtl. 3
Stan Jonathan	Bos.	May 8/79	Bos.	3	Ken Dryden	Bos. 5	Mtl. 2
Ron Duguay	NYR	Apr. 20/80	NYR	3	Pete Peeters	NYR 4	Phi. 2
Steve Shutt	Mtl.	Apr. 22/80	Mtl.	3	Gilles Meloche	Mtl. 6	Min. 2
Gilbert Perreault	Buf.	May 6/80	NYI	3	Billy Smith (2)		
					ENG (1)	Buf. 7	NYI 4
Paul Holmgren	Phi.	May 15/80	Phi.	3	Billy Smith	Phi. 8	NYI 3
Steve Payne	Min.	Apr. 8/81	Bos.	3	Rogie Vachon	Min. 5	Bos. 4
Denis Potvin	NYI	Apr. 17/81	NYI	3	Andy Moog	NYI 6	Edm. 3
Barry Pederson	Bos.	Apr. 8/82	Bos.	3	Don Edwards	Bos. 7	Buf. 3
Duane Sutter	NYI	Apr. 15/83	NYI	3	Glen Hanlon	NYI 5	NYR 0
Doug Halward	Van.	Apr. 7/84	Van.	3	Reggie Lemelin (2)		
					Don Edwards (1)	Van. 7	Cgy. 0
Jorgen Pettersson	St.L.	Apr. 8/84	Det.	3	Eddie Mio	St.L. 3	Det. 2
Clark Gillies	NYI	May 12/84	NYI	3	Grant Fuhr	NYI 6	Edm. 1
Ken Linseman	Bos.	Apr. 14/85	Bos.	3	Steve Penney	Bos. 7	Mtl. 6
Dave Andreychuk	Buf.	Apr. 14/85	Buf.	3	Dan Bouchard	Buf. 7	Que. 4
Greg Paslawski	St.L.	Apr. 15/86	Min.	3	Don Beaupre	St.L. 6	Min. 3
Doug Risebrough	Cgy.	May 4/86	Cgy.	3	Rick Wamsley	Cgy. 8	St.L. 2
Mike McPhee	Mtl.	Apr. 11/87	Bos.	3	Doug Keans	Mtl. 5	Bos. 4
John Ogrodnick	Que.	Apr. 14/87	Hfd.	3	Mike Liut	Que. 7	Hfd. 5
Pelle Eklund	Phi.	May 10/87	Mtl.	3	Patrick Roy (1)		
					Brian Hayward (2)	Phi. 6	Mtl. 3
John Tucker	Buf.	Apr. 9/88	Bos.	4	Andy Moog	Buf. 6	Bos. 2
Tony Hrkac	St.L.	Apr. 10/88	St.L.	4	Darren Pang	St.L. 6	Chi. 5
Hakan Loob	Cgy.	Apr. 10/88	Cgy.	3	Glenn Healy	Cgy. 7	L.A. 3
Ed Olczyk	Tor.	Apr. 12/88	Tor.	3	Greg Stefan (2)		
					Glen Hanlon (1)	Tor. 6	Det. 5
Aaron Broten	N.J.	Apr. 20/88	N.J.	3	Pete Peeters	N.J. 5	Wsh. 2
Mark Johnson	N.J.	Apr. 22/88	Wsh.	4	Pete Peeters	N.J. 10	Wsh. 4
Patrik Sundstrom	N.J.	Apr. 22/88	Wsh.	3	Pete Peeters (2)		
					Clint Malarchuk (1)	N.J. 10	Wsh. 4
Bob Brooke	Min.	Apr. 5/89	St.L.	3	Greg Millen	St.L. 4	Min. 3
Chris Kontos	L.A.	Apr. 6/89	L.A.	3	Grant Fuhr	L.A. 5	Edm. 2
Wayne Presley	Chi.	Apr. 13/89	Chi.	3	Greg Stefan (1)		
					Glen Hanlon (2)	Chi. 7	Det. 1
Tony Granato	L.A.	Apr. 10/90	L.A.	3	Mike Vernon (1)		
					Rick Wamsley (2)	L.A. 12	Cgy. 4
Tomas Sandstrom	L.A.	Apr. 10/90	L.A.	3	Mike Vernon (1)		
					Rick Wamsley (2)	L.A. 12	Cgy. 4
Dave Taylor	L.A.	Apr. 10/90	L.A.	3	Mike Vernon (1)		
					Rick Wamsley (2)	L.A. 12	Cgy. 4
Bernie Nicholls	NYR	Apr. 19/90	NYR	3	Mike Liut	NYR 7	Wsh. 3
John Druce	Wsh.	Apr. 21/90	NYR	3	John Vanbiesbrouck	Wsh. 6	NYR 3
Adam Oates	St.L.	Apr. 12/91	St.L.	3	Tim Chevaldae	St.L. 6	Det. 1
Luc Robitaille	L.A.	Apr. 26/91	L.A.	3	Grant Fuhr	L.A. 5	Edm. 2
Ray Sheppard	Det.	Apr. 24/92	Min.	3	Jon Casey	Min. 5	Det. 2
Pavel Bure	Van.	Apr. 28/92	Wpg.	3	Rick Tabaracci	Van. 8	Wpg. 3
Joe Murphy	Edm.	May 6/92	Edm.	3	Kirk McLean	Edm. 5	Van. 2
Ron Francis	Pit.	May 9/92	Pit.	3	Mike Richter (2)		
					John V'brouck (1)	Pit. 5	NYR. 4
Kevin Stevens	Pit.	May 21/92	Bos.	4	Andy Moog	Pit. 5	Bos. 2
Dirk Graham	Chi.	Jun. 1/92	Chi.	3	Tom Barrasso	Pit. 6	Chi. 5
Brian Noonan	Chi.	Apr. 18/93	Chi.	3	Curtis Joseph	St.L. 4	Chi. 3
Dale Hunter	Wsh.	Apr. 20/93	Wsh.	3	Glenn Healy	NYI 5	Wsh. 4
Teemu Selanne	Wpg.	Apr. 23/93	Wpg.	3	Kirk McLean	Wpg. 5	Van. 4
Ray Ferraro	NYI	Apr. 26/93	Wsh.	4	Don Beaupre	Wsh. 6	NYI 4
Al Iafrate	Wsh.	Apr. 26/93	Wsh.	3	Glenn Healy (2)		
					Mark Fitzpatrick (1)	Wsh. 6	NYI 4
Paul DiPietro	Mtl.	Apr. 28/93	Mtl.	3	Ron Hextall	Mtl. 6	Que. 2
Wendel Clark	Tor.	May 27/93	L.A.	3	Kelly Hrudey	L.A. 5	Tor. 4
Eric Desjardins	Mtl.	Jun. 3/93	Mtl.	3	Kelly Hrudey	Mtl. 3	L.A. 2
Tony Amonte	Chi.	Apr. 23/94	Chi.	4	Felix Potvin	Chi. 5	Tor. 4
Gary Suter	Chi.	Apr. 24/94	Chi.	3	Felix Potvin	Chi. 4	Tor. 3
Ulf Dahlen	S.J.	May 6/94	S.J.	3	Felix Potvin	S.J. 5	Tor. 2
Mike Sullivan	Cgy.	May 11/95	S.J.	3	Arturs Irbe (2)		
					Wade Flaherty (1)	Cgy. 9	S.J. 2
Theoren Fleury	Cgy.	May 13/95	S.J.	4	Arturs Irbe (3)		
					ENG (1)	Cgy. 6	S.J. 4
Brendan Shanahan	St.L.	May 13/95	Van.	3	Kirk McLean	St.L. 5	Van. 2
John LeClair	Phi.	May 21/95	Phi.	3	Mike Richter	Phi. 5	NYR 4
Brian Leetch	NYR	May 22/95	Phi.	3	Ron Hextall	Phi. 4	NYR 3
Trevor Linden	Van.	Apr. 25/96	Col.	3	Patrick Roy	Col. 5	Van. 4
Jaromir Jagr	Pit.	May 11/96	Pit.	3	Mike Richter	Pit. 7	NYR 3
Peter Forsberg	Col.	Jun. 6/96	Col.	3	John Vanbiesbrouck	Col. 8	Fla. 1
Valeri Zelepukin	N.J.	Apr. 22/97	Mtl.	3	Jocelyn Thibault	N.J. 6	Mtl. 4
Valeri Kamensky	Col.	Apr. 24/97	Col.	3	Jeff Hackett (2)		
					Chris Terreri (1)	Col. 7	Chi. 0
Eric Lindros	Phi.	May 20/97	NYR	3	Mike Richter	Phi. 6	NYR 3
Matthew Barnaby	Buf.	May 10/98	Buf.	3	Andy Moog (2)	Buf. 6	Mtl. 3
					ENG (1)		
Martin Straka	Pit.	Apr. 25/99	Pit.	3	Martin Brodeur	Pit. 4	N.J. 2
Martin Lapointe	Det.	Apr. 15/00	Det.	3	Stephane Fiset (2)	Det. 8	L.A. 5
					Jamie Storr (1)		
Doug Weight	Edm.	Apr. 16/00	Edm.	3	Ed Belfour	Edm. 5	Dal. 2
Bill Guerin	Edm.	Apr. 18/00	Edm.	3	Ed Belfour	Dal. 4	Edm. 3
Scott Young	St.L.	Apr. 23/00	S.J.	3	Steve Shields	St.L. 6	S.J. 2
Andy Delmore	Phi.	May 7/00	Phi.	3	Ron Tugnutt (2)	Phi. 6	Pit. 3
					Peter Skudra (1)		
Brett Hull	Det.	Apr. 27/02	Van.	3	Peter Skudra	Det. 6	Van. 4
Keith Tkachuk	St.L.	May 7/02	St.L.	3	Dominik Hasek	St.L. 6	Det. 1
Darren McCarty	Det.	May 18/02	Det.	3	Patrick Roy	Det. 5	Col. 3
Alexander Mogilny	Tor.	Apr. 9/03	Phi.	3	Roman Cechmanek (2)	Tor. 5	Phi. 3
					ENG (1)		
Mike Sillinger	St.L.	Apr. 12/04	St.L.	3	Evgeni Nabokov (2)	St.L. 4	S.J. 1
					ENG (1)		
Keith Primeau	Phi.	May 2/04	Phi.	3	Ed Belfour (2)	Phi. 7	Tor. 2
					Trevor Kidd (1)		
Jean-Pierre Dumont	Buf.	Apr. 24/06	Buf.	3	Antero Niitymaki (1)	Phi. 2	Buf. 8
					Robert Esche (2)		
John Madden	N.J.	Apr. 24/06	N.J.	3	Kevin Weekes	NYR 1	N.J. 4
Jason Pominville	Buf.	Apr. 24/06	Buf.	3	Antero Niittymaki (2)	Phi. 2	Buf. 8
					Robert Esche (1)		
Joffrey Lupul	Ana.	May 9/06	Col.	4	Jose Theodore	Ana. 4	Col. 3
Michael Nylander	NYR	Apr. 17/07	NYR	3	Kari Lehtonen	NYR 7	Atl. 0
Andy McDonald	Ana.	Apr. 25/07	Ana.	3	Dany Sabourin (1)	Ana. 5	Van. 1
					Roberto Luongo (2)		

Andy McDonald led the Ducks with 10 postseason goals during their playoff march to the 2007 Stanley Cup. McDonald had a hat trick in a 5-1 win over Vancouver to open the second round of the playoffs.

Overtime Games since 1918

Abbreviations: Teams/Cities: — **Ana.** - Anaheim; **Atl.** - Atlanta; **Bos.** - Boston; **Buf.** - Buffalo; **Cgy.** - Calgary; **Cgy. T.** - Calgary Tigers (Western Canada Hockey League); **Chi.** - Chicago; **Col.** - Colorado; **Dal.** - Dallas; **Det.** - Detroit; **Edm.** - Edmonton; **Edm. E.** - Edmonton Eskimos (WCHL); **Fla.** - Florida; **Hfd.** - Hartford; **L.A.** - Los Angeles; **Min.** - Minnesota; **Mtl.** - Montreal; **Mtl. M.** - Montreal Maroons; **N.J.** - New Jersey; **NYA** - NY Americans; **NYI** - New York Islanders; **NYR** - New York Rangers; **Oak.** - Oakland; **Ott.** - Ottawa; **Phi.** - Philadelphia; **Phx.** - Phoenix; **Pit.** - Pittsburgh; **Que.** - Quebec; **St.L.** - St. Louis; **Sea.** - Seattle Metropolitans (Pacific Coast Hockey Association); **S.J.** - San Jose; **T.B.** - Tampa Bay; **Tor.** - Toronto; **Van.** - Vancouver; **Van. M.** - Vancouver Millionaires (PCHA); **Vic.** - Victoria Cougars (WCHL); **Wpg.** - Winnipeg; **Wsh.** - Washington.

SERIES — **CF** - conference final; **CQF** - conference quarter-final; **CSF** - conference semi-final; **DF** - division final; **DSF** - division semi-final; **F** - final; **PRE** - preliminary round; **QF** - quarter-final; **SF** - semi-final.

Date	City	Series	Score		Scorer	Overtime	Series Winner
Mar. 26/19	Sea.	F	Mtl. 0	Sea. 0	no scorer	20:00	....
Mar. 30/19	Sea.	F	Mtl. 4	Sea. 3	Odie Cleghorn	15:57	....
Mar. 20/22	Tor.	F	Tor. 2	Van. M. 1	Babe Dye	4:50	Tor.
Mar. 29/23	Van.	F	Ott. 2	Edm. E. 1	Cy Denneny	2:08	Ott.
Mar. 31/27	Mtl.	QF	Mtl. 1	Mtl. M. 0	Howie Morenz	12:05	Mtl.
Apr. 7/27	Bos.	F	Ott. 0	Bos. 0	no scorer	20:00	Ott.
Apr. 11/27	Ott.	F	Bos. 1	Ott. 1	no scorer	20:00	Ott.
Apr. 3/28	Mtl.	QF	Mtl. M. 1	Mtl. 0	Russell Oatman	8:20	Mtl. M.
Apr. 7/28	Mtl.	F	NYR 2	Mtl. M. 1	Frank Boucher	7:05	NYR
Mar. 21/29	NYR	QF	NYR 1	NYA 0	Butch Keeling	29:50	NYR
Mar. 26/29	Tor.	SF	NYR 2	Tor. 1	Frank Boucher	2:03	NYR
Mar. 20/30	Mtl.	SF	Bos. 2	Mtl. M. 1	Harry Oliver	45:35	Bos.
Mar. 25/30	Bos.	SF	Mtl. M. 1	Bos. 0	Archie Wilcox	26:27	Bos.
Mar. 26/30	Mtl.	QF	Chi. 2	Mtl. 2	Howie Morenz (Mtl.)	51:43	Mtl.
Mar. 28/30	Mtl.	SF	Mtl. 2	NYR 1	Gus Rivers	68:52	Mtl.
Mar. 24/31	Bos.	SF	Bos. 5	Mtl. 4	Cooney Weiland	18:56	Mtl.
Mar. 26/31	Chi.	QF	Chi. 2	Tor. 1	Stew Adams	19:20	Chi.
Mar. 28/31	Mtl.	SF	Mtl. 4	Bos. 3	Georges Mantha	5:10	Mtl.
Apr. 1/31	Mtl.	SF	Mtl. 3	Bos. 2	Wildor Larochelle	19:00	Mtl.
Apr. 5/31	Chi.	F	Chi. 2	Mtl. 1	Johnny Gottselig	24:50	Mtl.
Apr. 9/31	Mtl.	F	Chi. 3	Mtl. 2	Cy Wentworth	53:50	Mtl.
Mar. 26/32	Mtl.	SF	NYR 4	Mtl. 3	Fred Cook	59:32	NYR
Apr. 2/32	Tor.	SF	Tor. 3	Mtl. M. 2	Bob Gracie	17:59	Tor.
Mar. 25/33	Bos.	SF	Bos. 2	Tor. 1	Marty Barry	14:14	Tor.
Mar. 28/33	Bos.	SF	Tor. 1	Bos. 0	Busher Jackson	15:03	Tor.
Mar. 30/33	Tor.	SF	Bos. 2	Tor. 1	Eddie Shore	4:23	Tor.
Apr. 3/33	Tor.	SF	Tor. 1	Bos. 0	Ken Doraty	104:46	Tor.
Apr. 13/33	Tor.	F	NYR 1	Tor. 0	Bill Cook	7:33	NYR
Mar. 22/34	Tor.	SF	Det. 2	Tor. 1	Herbie Lewis	1:33	Det.
Mar. 25/34	Chi.	QF	Chi. 1	Mtl. 1	Mush March (Chi)	11:05	Chi.
Apr. 3/34	Det.	F	Chi. 2	Det. 1	Paul Thompson	21:10	Chi.
Apr. 10/34	Chi.	F	Chi. 1	Det. 0	Mush March	30:05	Chi.
Mar. 23/35	Bos.	SF	Bos. 1	Tor. 0	Dit Clapper	33:26	Tor.
Mar. 26/35	Chi.	QF	Mtl. M. 1	Chi. 0	Baldy Northcott	4:02	Mtl. M.
Mar. 30/35	Tor.	SF	Tor. 2	Bos. 1	Pep Kelly	1:36	Tor.
Apr. 4/35	Tor.	F	Mtl. M. 3	Tor. 2	Dave Trottier	5:28	Mtl. M.
Mar. 24/36	Mtl.	SF	Det. 1	Mtl. M. 0	Mud Bruneteau	116:30	Det.
Apr. 9/36	Tor.	F	Tor. 4	Det. 3	Buzz Boll	0:31	Det.
Mar. 25/37	NYR	QF	NYR 2	Tor. 1	Babe Pratt	13:05	NYR
Apr. 1/37	Mtl.	SF	Det. 2	Mtl. 1	Hec Kilrea	51:49	Det.
Mar. 22/38	NYR	QF	NYA 2	NYR 1	John Sorrell	21:25	NYA
Mar. 24/38	Tor.	SF	Tor. 1	Bos. 0	George Parsons	21:31	Tor.
Mar. 26/38	Mtl.	QF	Chi. 3	Mtl. 2	Paul Thompson	11:49	Chi.
Mar. 27/38	NYR	QF	NYA 3	NYR 2	Lorne Carr	60:40	NYA
Mar. 29/38	Bos.	SF	Tor. 3	Bos. 2	Gordie Drillon	10:04	Tor.
Mar. 31/38	Chi.	SF	Chi. 1	NYA 0	Cully Dahlstrom	33:01	Chi.
Mar. 21/39	NYR	SF	Bos. 2	NYR 1	Mel Hill	59:25	Bos.
Mar. 23/39	Bos.	SF	Bos. 3	NYR 2	Mel Hill	8:24	Bos.
Mar. 26/39	Det.	QF	Det. 1	Mtl. 0	Marty Barry	7:47	Det.
Mar. 30/39	Bos.	SF	NYR 2	Bos. 1	Clint Smith	17:19	Bos.
Apr. 1/39	Tor.	SF	Tor. 5	Det. 4	Gordie Drillon	5:42	Tor.
Apr. 2/39	Bos.	SF	Bos. 2	NYR 1	Mel Hill	48:00	Bos.
Apr. 9/39	Bos.	F	Tor. 3	Bos. 2	Doc Romnes	10:38	Bos.
Mar. 19/40	Det.	QF	Det. 2	NYA 1	Syd Howe	0:25	Det.
Mar. 19/40	Tor.	QF	Tor. 3	Chi. 2	Syl Apps	6:35	Tor.
Apr. 2/40	NYR	F	NYR 2	Tor. 1	Alf Pike	15:30	NYR
Apr. 11/40	Tor.	F	NYR 2	Tor. 1	Muzz Patrick	31:43	NYR
Apr. 13/40	Tor.	F	NYR 3	Tor. 2	Bryan Hextall	2:07	NYR
Mar. 20/41	Det.	QF	Det. 2	NYR 1	Gus Giesebrecht	12:01	Det.
Mar. 22/41	Mtl.	QF	Mtl. 4	Chi. 3	Charlie Sands	34:04	Chi.
Mar. 29/41	Bos.	SF	Tor. 2	Bos. 1	Pete Langelle	17:31	Bos.
Mar. 30/41	Chi.	SF	Det. 2	Chi. 1	Gus Giesebrecht	9:15	Det.
Mar. 22/42	Chi.	QF	Bos. 2	Chi. 1	Des Smith	6:51	Bos.
Mar. 21/43	Bos.	SF	Bos. 5	Mtl. 4	Don Gallinger	12:30	Bos.
Mar. 23/43	Det.	SF	Tor. 3	Det. 2	Jack McLean	70:18	Det.
Mar. 25/43	Mtl.	SF	Bos. 3	Mtl. 2	Busher Jackson	3:20	Bos.
Mar. 30/43	Tor.	SF	Det. 3	Tor. 2	Adam Brown	9:21	Det.
Mar. 30/43	Bos.	SF	Bos. 5	Mtl. 4	Ab DeMarco	3:41	Bos.
Apr. 13/44	Mtl.	F	Mtl. 5	Chi. 4	Toe Blake	9:12	Mtl.
Mar. 27/45	Tor.	SF	Tor. 4	Mtl. 3	Gus Bodnar	12:36	Tor.
Mar. 29/45	Det.	SF	Det. 3	Bos. 2	Mud Bruneteau	17:12	Det.
Apr. 21/45	Tor.	F	Det. 1	Tor. 0	Eddie Bruneteau	14:16	Tor.
Mar. 28/46	Bos.	SF	Bos. 4	Det. 3	Don Gallinger	9:51	Bos.
Mar. 30/46	Mtl.	F	Mtl. 4	Bos. 3	Maurice Richard	9:08	Mtl.
Apr. 2/46	Mtl.	F	Mtl. 3	Bos. 2	Jimmy Peters	16:55	Mtl.
Apr. 7/46	Bos.	F	Bos. 3	Mtl. 2	Terry Reardon	15:13	Mtl.
Mar. 26/47	Tor.	SF	Tor. 3	Det. 2	Howie Meeker	3:05	Tor.
Mar. 27/47	Mtl.	SF	Mtl. 2	Bos. 1	Ken Mosdell	5:38	Mtl.
Apr. 3/47	Mtl.	SF	Mtl. 4	Bos. 3	John Quilty	36:40	Mtl.
Apr. 15/47	Tor.	F	Tor. 2	Mtl. 1	Syl Apps	16:36	Tor.
Mar. 24/48	Tor.	SF	Tor. 5	Bos. 4	Nick Metz	17:03	Tor.
Mar. 22/49	Det.	SF	Det. 2	Mtl. 1	Max McNab	44:52	Det.
Mar. 24/49	Det.	SF	Mtl. 4	Det. 3	Gerry Plamondon	2:59	Det.
Mar. 26/49	Tor.	SF	Bos. 5	Tor. 4	Woody Dumart	16:14	Tor.
Apr. 8/49	Det.	F	Tor. 3	Det. 2	Joe Klukay	17:31	Tor.
Apr. 4/50	Tor.	SF	Det. 2	Tor. 1	Leo Reise Jr.	20:38	Det.
Apr. 4/50	Mtl.	SF	Mtl. 3	NYR 2	Elmer Lach	15:19	NYR
Apr. 9/50	Det.	SF	Det. 1	Tor. 0	Leo Reise Jr.	8:39	Det.
Apr. 18/50	Det.	F	NYR 4	Det. 3	Don Raleigh	8:34	Det.
Apr. 20/50	Det.	F	NYR 2	Det. 1	Don Raleigh	1:38	Det.
Apr. 23/50	Det.	F	Det. 4	NYR 3	Pete Babando	28:31	Det.
Mar. 27/51	Det.	SF	Mtl. 3	Det. 2	Maurice Richard	61:09	Mtl.
Mar. 29/51	Det.	SF	Mtl. 1	Det. 0	Maurice Richard	42:20	Mtl.
Mar. 31/51	Tor.	SF	Bos. 1	Tor. 1	no scorer	20:00	Tor.
Apr. 11/51	Tor.	F	Tor. 3	Mtl. 2	Sid Smith	5:51	Tor.
Apr. 14/51	Tor.	F	Mtl. 3	Tor. 2	Maurice Richard	2:55	Tor.
Apr. 17/51	Mtl.	F	Tor. 2	Mtl. 1	Ted Kennedy	4:47	Tor.
Apr. 19/51	Mtl.	F	Tor. 3	Mtl. 2	Harry Watson	5:15	Tor.
Apr. 21/51	Tor.	F	Tor. 3	Mtl. 2	Bill Barilko	2:53	Tor.
Apr. 6/52	Bos.	SF	Mtl. 3	Bos. 2	Paul Masnick	27:49	Mtl.
Mar. 29/53	Bos.	SF	Bos. 2	Det. 1	Jack McIntyre	12:29	Bos.
Mar. 29/53	Chi.	SF	Chi. 2	Mtl. 1	Al Dewsbury	5:18	Mtl.
Apr. 16/53	Mtl.	F	Mtl. 1	Bos. 0	Elmer Lach	1:22	Mtl.
Apr. 1/54	Det.	SF	Det. 4	Tor. 3	Ted Lindsay	21:01	Det.
Apr. 11/54	Det.	F	Mtl. 1	Det. 0	Ken Mosdell	5:45	Det.
Apr. 16/54	Det.	F	Det. 2	Mtl. 1	Tony Leswick	4:29	Det.
Mar. 29/55	Bos.	SF	Mtl. 4	Bos. 3	Don Marshall	3:05	Mtl.
Mar. 24/56	Tor.	SF	Det. 5	Tor. 4	Ted Lindsay	4:22	Det.
Mar. 28/57	NYR	SF	NYR 4	Mtl. 3	Andy Hebenton	13:38	Mtl.
Apr. 4/57	Mtl.	SF	Mtl. 4	NYR 3	Maurice Richard	1:11	Mtl.
Mar. 27/58	NYR	SF	Bos. 4	NYR 3	Jerry Toppazzini	4:46	Bos.
Mar. 30/58	Det.	SF	Mtl. 2	Det. 1	André Pronovost	11:52	Mtl.
Apr. 17/58	Mtl.	F	Mtl. 3	Bos. 2	Maurice Richard	5:45	Mtl.
Mar. 28/59	Tor.	SF	Tor. 3	Bos. 2	Gerry Ehman	5:02	Tor.
Mar. 31/59	Tor.	SF	Tor. 3	Bos. 2	Frank Mahovlich	11:21	Tor.
Apr. 14/59	Tor.	F	Tor. 3	Mtl. 2	Dick Duff	10:06	Mtl.
Mar. 26/60	Mtl.	SF	Mtl. 4	Chi. 3	Doug Harvey	8:38	Mtl.
Mar. 27/60	Det.	SF	Tor. 5	Det. 4	Frank Mahovlich	43:00	Tor.
Mar. 29/60	Det.	SF	Det. 2	Tor. 1	Gerry Melnyk	1:54	Tor.
Mar. 22/61	Tor.	SF	Tor. 3	Det. 2	George Armstrong	24:51	Det.
Mar. 26/61	Chi.	SF	Chi. 2	Mtl. 1	Murray Balfour	52:12	Chi.
Apr. 5/62	Tor.	SF	Tor. 3	NYR 2	Red Kelly	24:23	Tor.
Apr. 2/64	Det.	SF	Chi. 3	Det. 2	Murray Balfour	8:21	Det.
Apr. 14/64	Tor.	F	Det. 4	Tor. 3	Larry Jeffrey	7:52	Tor.
Apr. 23/64	Det.	F	Tor. 4	Det. 3	Bob Baun	1:43	Tor.
Apr. 6/65	Tor.	SF	Tor. 3	Mtl. 2	Dave Keon	4:17	Mtl.
Apr. 13/65	Tor.	SF	Mtl. 4	Tor. 3	Claude Provost	16:33	Mtl.
May 5/66	Det.	F	Mtl. 3	Det. 2	Henri Richard	2:20	Mtl.
Apr. 13/67	NYR	SF	Mtl. 2	NYR 1	John Ferguson	6:28	Mtl.
Apr. 25/67	Tor.	F	Tor. 3	Mtl. 2	Bob Pulford	28:26	Tor.
Apr. 10/68	St.L.	QF	St.L. 3	Phi. 2	Larry Keenan	24:10	St.L.
Apr. 16/68	St.L.	QF	Phi. 2	St.L. 1	Don Blackburn	31:18	St.L.
Apr. 16/68	Min.	QF	Min. 4	L.A. 3	Milan Marcetta	9:11	Min.
Apr. 22/68	Min.	SF	Min. 3	St.L. 2	Parker MacDonald	3:41	St.L.
Apr. 27/68	St.L.	SF	St.L. 4	Min. 3	Gary Sabourin	1:32	St.L.
Apr. 28/68	Mtl.	SF	Mtl. 4	Chi. 3	Jacques Lemaire	2:14	Mtl.
Apr. 29/68	St.L.	SF	St.L. 3	Min. 2	Bill McCreary	17:27	St.L.
May 3/68	St.L.	SF	St.L. 2	Min. 1	Ron Schock	22:50	St.L.
May 5/68	St.L.	F	Mtl. 3	St.L. 2	Jacques Lemaire	1:41	Mtl.
May 9/68	Mtl.	F	Mtl. 4	St.L. 3	Bobby Rousseau	1:13	Mtl.
Apr. 2/69	Oak.	QF	L.A. 5	Oak. 4	Ted Irvine	0:19	L.A.
Apr. 10/69	Mtl.	SF	Mtl. 3	Bos. 2	Ralph Backstrom	0:42	Mtl.
Apr. 13/69	Mtl.	SF	Mtl. 4	Bos. 3	Mickey Redmond	4:55	Mtl.
Apr. 24/69	Bos.	SF	Mtl. 2	Bos. 1	Jean Béliveau	31:28	Mtl.
Apr. 12/70	Oak.	QF	Pit. 3	Oak. 2	Michel Briere	8:28	Pit.
May 10/70	Bos.	F	Bos. 4	St.L. 3	Bobby Orr	0:40	Bos.
Apr. 15/71	Tor.	QF	NYR 2	Tor. 1	Bob Nevin	9:07	NYR
Apr. 18/71	Chi.	SF	NYR 2	Chi. 1	Pete Stemkowski	1:37	Chi.
Apr. 27/71	Chi.	SF	Chi. 3	NYR 2	Bobby Hull	6:35	Chi.
Apr. 29/71	NYR	SF	NYR 3	Chi. 2	Pete Stemkowski	41:29	Chi.
May 4/71	Chi.	F	Chi. 2	Mtl. 1	Jim Pappin	21:11	Mtl.
Apr. 6/72	Bos.	QF	Tor. 4	Bos. 3	Jim Harrison	2:58	Bos.
Apr. 6/72	Min.	QF	Min. 6	St.L. 5	Bill Goldsworthy	1:36	St.L.
Apr. 9/72	Pit.	QF	Chi. 6	Pit. 5	Pit Martin	0:12	Chi.
Apr. 16/72	Min.	QF	St.L. 2	Min. 1	Kevin O'Shea	10:07	St.L.
Apr. 1/73	Mtl.	QF	Buf. 3	Mtl. 2	René Robert	9:18	Mtl.
Apr. 10/73	Phi.	QF	Phi. 3	Min. 2	Gary Dornhoefer	8:35	Phi.
Apr. 14/73	Mtl.	SF	Phi. 5	Mtl. 4	Rick MacLeish	2:56	Mtl.
Apr. 17/73	Mtl.	SF	Mtl. 4	Phi. 3	Larry Robinson	6:45	Mtl.
Apr. 14/74	Tor.	QF	Bos. 4	Tor. 3	Ken Hodge	1:27	Bos.
Apr. 14/74	Atl.	QF	Phi. 4	Atl. 3	Dave Schultz	5:40	Phi.
Apr. 16/74	Mtl.	QF	NYR 3	Mtl. 2	Ron Harris	4:07	NYR
Apr. 23/74	Chi.	SF	Chi. 4	Bos. 3	Jim Pappin	3:48	Bos.
Apr. 28/74	NYR	SF	NYR 2	Phi. 1	Rod Gilbert	4:20	Phi.
May 9/74	Bos.	F	Phi. 3	Bos. 2	Bobby Clarke	12:01	Phi.
Apr. 8/75	L.A.	PRE	L.A. 3	Tor. 2	Mike Murphy	8:53	Tor.
Apr. 10/75	Tor.	PRE	Tor. 3	L.A. 2	Blaine Stoughton	10:19	Tor.
Apr. 10/75	Chi.	PRE	Chi. 4	Bos. 3	Ivan Boldirev	7:33	Chi.
Apr. 11/75	NYR	PRE	NYI 4	NYR 3	Jean-Paul Parise	0:11	NYI
Apr. 17/75	Chi.	QF	Chi. 5	Buf. 4	Stan Mikita	2:31	Buf.
Apr. 19/75	Tor.	QF	Phi. 4	Tor. 3	André Dupont	1:45	Phi.
Apr. 22/75	Mtl.	QF	Mtl. 5	Van. 4	Guy Lafleur	17:06	Mtl.
Apr. 27/75	Buf.	SF	Buf. 6	Mtl. 5	Danny Gare	4:42	Buf.
May 1/75	Phi.	SF	Phi. 5	NYI 4	Bobby Clarke	2:56	Phi.
May 6/75	Buf.	SF	Buf. 5	Mtl. 4	René Robert	5:56	Buf.
May 7/75	NYI	SF	NYI 4	Phi. 3	Jude Drouin	1:53	Phi.
May 20/75	Buf.	F	Buf. 5	Phi. 4	René Robert	18:29	Phi.
Apr. 8/76	Buf.	PRE	Buf. 3	St.L. 2	Danny Gare	11:43	Buf.

Overtime Games since 1918 — *continued*

Date	City	Series	Score		Scorer	Overtime	Series Winner
Apr. 9/76	Buf.	PRE	Buf. 2	St.L. 1	Don Luce	14:27	Buf.
Apr. 13/76	Bos.	QF	L.A. 3	Bos. 2	Butch Goring	0:27	Bos.
Apr. 13/76	Buf.	QF	Buf. 3	NYI 2	Danny Gare	14:04	NYI
Apr. 22/76	L.A.	QF	L.A. 4	Bos. 3	Butch Goring	18:28	Bos.
Apr. 29/76	Phi.	SF	Phi. 2	Bos. 1	Reggie Leach	13:38	Phi.
Apr. 15/77	Tor.	QF	Phi. 4	Tor. 3	Rick MacLeish	2:55	Phi.
Apr. 17/77	Tor.	QF	Phi. 6	Tor. 5	Reggie Leach	19:10	Phi.
Apr. 24/77	Phi.	SF	Bos. 4	Phi. 3	Rick Middleton	2:57	Bos.
Apr. 26/77	Phi.	SF	Bos. 5	Phi. 4	Terry O'Reilly	30:07	Bos.
May 3/77	Mtl.	SF	NYI 4	Mtl. 3	Billy Harris	3:58	Mtl.
May 14/77	Bos.	F	Mtl. 2	Bos. 1	Jacques Lemaire	4:32	Mtl.
Apr. 11/78	Phi.	PRE	Phi. 3	Col. 2	Mel Bridgman	0:23	Phi.
Apr. 13/78	NYR	PRE	NYR 4	Buf. 3	Don Murdoch	1:37	Buf.
Apr. 19/78	Bos.	QF	Bos. 4	Chi. 3	Terry O'Reilly	1:50	Bos.
Apr. 19/78	NYI	QF	NYI 3	Tor. 2	Mike Bossy	2:50	Tor.
Apr. 21/78	Chi.	QF	Bos. 4	Chi. 3	Peter McNab	10:17	Bos.
Apr. 25/78	NYI	QF	NYI 2	Tor. 1	Bob Nystrom	8:02	Tor.
Apr. 29/78	NYI	QF	Tor. 2	NYI 1	Lanny McDonald	4:13	Tor.
May 2/78	Bos.	SF	Bos. 3	Phi. 2	Rick Middleton	1:43	Bos.
May 16/78	Mtl.	F	Mtl. 3	Bos. 2	Guy Lafleur	13:09	Mtl.
May 21/78	Bos.	F	Bos. 4	Mtl. 3	Bobby Schmautz	6:22	Mtl.
Apr. 12/79	L.A.	PRE	NYR 2	L.A. 1	Phil Esposito	6:11	NYR
Apr. 14/79	Buf.	PRE	Pit. 4	Buf. 3	George Ferguson	0:47	Pit.
Apr. 16/79	Phi.	QF	Phi. 3	NYR 2	Ken Linseman	0:44	NYR
Apr. 18/79	NYI	QF	NYI 1	Chi. 0	Mike Bossy	2:31	NYI
Apr. 21/79	Tor.	QF	Mtl. 4	Tor. 3	Cam Connor	25:25	Mtl.
Apr. 22/79	Tor.	QF	Mtl. 5	Tor. 4	Larry Robinson	4:14	Mtl.
Apr. 28/79	NYI	SF	NYI 4	NYR 3	Denis Potvin	8:02	NYR
May 3/79	NYR	SF	NYI 3	NYR 2	Bob Nystrom	3:40	NYR
May 3/79	Bos.	SF	Bos. 4	Mtl. 3	Jean Ratelle	3:46	Mtl.
May 10/79	Mtl.	SF	Mtl. 5	Bos. 4	Yvon Lambert	9:33	Mtl.
May 19/79	NYR	F	Mtl. 4	NYR 3	Serge Savard	7:25	Mtl.
Apr. 8/80	NYR	PRE	NYR 2	Atl. 1	Steve Vickers	0:33	NYR
Apr. 8/80	Phi.	PRE	Phi. 4	Edm. 3	Bobby Clarke	8:06	Phi.
Apr. 8/80	Chi.	PRE	Chi. 3	St.L. 2	Doug Lecuyer	12:34	Chi.
Apr. 11/80	Hfd.	PRE	Mtl. 4	Hfd. 3	Yvon Lambert	0:29	Mtl.
Apr. 11/80	Tor.	PRE	Min. 4	Tor. 3	Al MacAdam	0:32	Min.
Apr. 11/80	L.A.	PRE	NYI 4	L.A. 3	Ken Morrow	6:55	NYI
Apr. 11/80	Edm.	PRE	Phi. 3	Edm. 2	Ken Linseman	23:56	Phi.
Apr. 16/80	Bos.	QF	NYI 2	Bos. 1	Clark Gillies	1:02	NYI
Apr. 17/80	Bos.	QF	NYI 5	Bos. 4	Bob Bourne	1:24	NYI
Apr. 21/80	NYI	QF	Bos. 4	NYI 3	Terry O'Reilly	17:13	NYI
May 1/80	Buf.	SF	NYI 2	Buf. 1	Bob Nystrom	21:20	NYI
May 13/80	Phi.	F	NYI 4	Phi. 3	Denis Potvin	4:07	NYI
May 24/80	NYI	F	NYI 5	Phi. 4	Bob Nystrom	7:11	NYI
Apr. 8/81	Buf.	PRE	Buf. 3	Van. 2	Alan Haworth	5:00	Buf.
Apr. 8/81	Bos.	PRE	Min. 5	Bos. 4	Steve Payne	3:34	Min.
Apr. 11/81	Chi.	PRE	Cgy. 5	Chi. 4	Willi Plett	35:17	Cgy.
Apr. 12/81	Que.	PRE	Que. 4	Phi. 3	Dale Hunter	0:37	Phi.
Apr. 14/81	St.L.	PRE	St.L. 4	Pit. 3	Mike Crombeen	25:16	St.L.
Apr. 16/81	Buf.	QF	Min. 4	Buf. 3	Steve Payne	0:22	Min.
Apr. 20/81	Min.	QF	Buf. 5	Min. 4	Craig Ramsay	16:32	Min.
Apr. 20/81	Edm.	QF	NYI 5	Edm. 4	Ken Morrow	5:41	NYI
Apr. 7/82	Min.	DSF	Chi. 3	Min. 2	Greg Fox	3:34	Chi.
Apr. 8/82	Edm.	DSF	Edm. 3	L.A. 2	Wayne Gretzky	6:20	L.A.
Apr. 8/82	Van.	DSF	Van. 2	Cgy. 1	Tiger Williams	14:20	Van.
Apr. 10/82	Pit.	DSF	Pit. 2	NYI 1	Rick Kehoe	4:14	NYI
Apr. 10/82	L.A.	DSF	L.A. 6	Edm. 5	Daryl Evans	2:35	L.A.
Apr. 13/82	Mtl.	DSF	Que. 3	Mtl. 2	Dale Hunter	0:22	Que.
Apr. 13/82	NYI	DSF	NYI 4	Pit. 3	John Tonelli	6:19	NYI
Apr. 16/82	Van.	DF	L.A. 3	Van. 2	Steve Bozek	4:33	Van.
Apr. 18/82	Que.	DF	Que. 3	Bos. 2	Wilf Paiement	11:44	Que.
Apr. 18/82	NYR	DF	NYI 4	NYR 3	Bryan Trottier	3:00	NYI
Apr. 18/82	L.A.	DF	Van. 4	L.A. 3	Colin Campbell	1:23	Van.
Apr. 21/82	St.L.	DF	St.L. 3	Chi. 2	Bernie Federko	3:28	Chi.
Apr. 23/82	Que.	DF	Bos. 6	Que. 5	Peter McNab	10:54	Que.
Apr. 27/82	Chi.	CF	Van. 2	Chi. 1	Jim Nill	28:58	Van.
May 1/82	Que.	CF	NYI 5	Que. 4	Wayne Merrick	16:52	NYI
May 8/82	NYI	F	NYI 6	Van. 5	Mike Bossy	19:58	NYI
Apr. 5/83	Bos.	DSF	Bos. 4	Que. 3	Barry Pederson	1:46	Bos.
Apr. 6/83	Cgy.	DSF	Cgy. 4	Van. 3	Eddy Beers	12:27	Cgy.
Apr. 7/83	Min.	DSF	Min. 5	Tor. 4	Bobby Smith	5:03	Min.
Apr. 10/83	Tor.	DSF	Min. 5	Tor. 4	Dino Ciccarelli	8:05	Min.
Apr. 10/83	Van.	DSF	Cgy. 4	Van. 3	Greg Meredith	1:06	Cgy.
Apr. 18/83	Min.	DF	Chi. 4	Min. 3	Rich Preston	10:34	Chi.
Apr. 24/83	Bos.	DF	Bos. 3	Buf. 2	Brad Park	1:52	Bos.
Apr. 5/84	Edm.	DSF	Edm. 5	Wpg. 4	Randy Gregg	0:21	Edm.
Apr. 7/84	Det.	DSF	St.L. 4	Det. 3	Mark Reeds	37:07	St.L.
Apr. 8/84	Det.	DSF	St.L. 3	Det. 2	Jorgen Pettersson	2:42	St.L.
Apr. 10/84	NYI	DSF	NYI 3	NYR 2	Ken Morrow	8:56	NYI
Apr. 13/84	Min.	DF	St.L. 4	Min. 3	Doug Gilmour	16:16	Min.
Apr. 13/84	Edm.	DF	Cgy. 6	Edm. 5	Carey Wilson	3:42	Edm.
Apr. 13/84	NYI	DF	NYI 5	Wsh. 4	Anders Kallur	7:35	NYI
Apr. 16/84	Mtl.	DF	Que. 4	Mtl. 3	Bo Berglund	3:00	Mtl.
Apr. 20/84	Cgy.	DF	Cgy. 5	Edm. 4	Lanny McDonald	1:04	Edm.
Apr. 22/84	Min.	DF	Min. 4	St.L. 3	Steve Payne	6:00	Min.
Apr. 10/85	Phi.	DSF	Phi. 5	NYR 4	Mark Howe	8:01	Phi.
Apr. 10/85	Wsh.	DSF	Wsh. 4	NYI 3	Alan Haworth	2:28	NYI
Apr. 10/85	Edm.	DSF	Edm. 3	L.A. 2	Lee Fogolin	3:01	Edm.
Apr. 10/85	Wpg.	DSF	Wpg. 5	Cgy. 4	Brian Mullen	7:56	Wpg.
Apr. 11/85	Wsh.	DSF	Wsh. 2	NYI 1	Mike Gartner	21:23	NYI
Apr. 13/85	L.A.	DSF	Edm. 4	L.A. 3	Glenn Anderson	0:46	Edm.
Apr. 18/85	Mtl.	DF	Que. 2	Mtl. 1	Mark Kumpel	12:23	Que.
Apr. 23/85	Que.	DF	Que. 7	Mtl. 6	Dale Hunter	18:36	Que.
Apr. 25/85	Min.	DF	Chi. 7	Min. 6	Darryl Sutter	21:57	Chi.
Apr. 28/85	Chi.	DF	Min. 5	Chi. 4	Dennis Maruk	1:14	Chi.
Apr. 30/85	Min.	DF	Chi. 6	Min. 5	Darryl Sutter	15:41	Chi.
May 2/85	Mtl.	DF	Que. 3	Mtl. 2	Peter Stastny	2:22	Que.
May 5/85	Que.	CF	Que. 2	Phi. 1	Peter Stastny	6:20	Phi.
Apr. 9/86	Que.	DSF	Hfd. 3	Que. 2	Sylvain Turgeon	2:36	Hfd.
Apr. 12/86	Wpg.	DSF	Cgy. 4	Wpg. 3	Lanny McDonald	8:25	Cgy.
Apr. 17/86	Wsh.	DF	NYR 4	Wsh. 3	Brian MacLellan	1:16	NYR
Apr. 20/86	Edm.	DF	Edm. 6	Cgy. 5	Glenn Anderson	1:04	Cgy.
Apr. 23/86	Hfd.	DF	Hfd. 2	Mtl. 1	Kevin Dineen	1:07	Mtl.
Apr. 23/86	NYR	DF	NYR 6	Wsh. 5	Bob Brooke	2:40	NYR
Apr. 26/86	St L.	DF	St L. 4	Tor. 3	Mark Reeds	7:11	St L.
Apr. 29/86	Mtl.	DF	Mtl. 2	Hfd. 1	Claude Lemieux	5:55	Mtl.
May 5/86	NYR	CF	Mtl. 4	NYR 3	Claude Lemieux	9:41	Mtl.
May 12/86	St L.	CF	St L. 6	Cgy. 5	Doug Wickenheiser	7:30	Cgy.
May 18/86	Cgy.	F	Mtl. 3	Cgy. 2	Brian Skrudland	0:09	Mtl.
Apr. 8/87	Hfd.	DSF	Hfd. 3	Que. 2	Paul MacDermid	2:20	Que.
Apr. 9/87	Mtl.	DSF	Mtl. 4	Bos. 3	Mats Naslund	2:38	Mtl.
Apr. 9/87	St.L.	DSF	Tor. 3	St.L. 2	Rick Lanz	10:17	Tor.
Apr. 11/87	Wpg.	DSF	Cgy. 3	Wpg. 2	Mike Bullard	3:53	Wpg.
Apr. 11/87	Chi.	DSF	Det. 4	Chi. 3	Shawn Burr	4:51	Det.
Apr. 16/87	Que.	DSF	Que. 5	Hfd. 4	Peter Stastny	6:05	Que.
Apr. 18/87	Wsh.	DSF	NYI 3	Wsh. 2	Pat LaFontaine	68:47	NYI
Apr. 21/87	Edm.	DF	Edm. 3	Wpg. 2	Glenn Anderson	0:36	Edm.
Apr. 26/87	Que.	DF	Mtl. 3	Que. 2	Mats Naslund	5:30	Mtl.
Apr. 27/87	Tor.	DF	Tor. 3	Det. 2	Mike Allison	9:31	Det.
May 4/87	Phi.	CF	Phi. 4	Mtl. 3	Ilkka Sinislao	9:11	Phi.
May 20/87	Edm.	F	Edm. 3	Phi. 2	Jari Kurri	6:50	Edm.
Apr. 6/88	NYI	DSF	NYI 4	N.J. 3	Pat LaFontaine	6:11	N.J.
Apr. 10/88	Phi.	DSF	Phi. 5	Wsh. 4	Murray Craven	1:18	Wsh.
Apr. 10/88	N.J.	DSF	NYI 5	N.J. 4	Brent Sutter	15:07	N.J.
Apr. 10/88	Buf.	DSF	Buf. 6	Bos. 5	John Tucker	5:32	Bos.
Apr. 12/88	Det.	DSF	Tor. 6	Det. 5	Ed Olczyk	0:34	Det.
Apr. 16/88	Wsh.	DSF	Wsh. 5	Phi. 4	Dale Hunter	5:57	Wsh.
Apr. 21/88	Cgy.	DF	Edm. 5	Cgy. 4	Wayne Gretzky	7:54	Edm.
May 4/88	Bos.	CF	N.J. 3	Bos. 2	Doug Brown	17:46	Bos.
May 9/88	Det.	CF	Edm. 4	Det. 3	Jari Kurri	11:02	Edm.
Apr. 5/89	St.L.	DSF	St.L. 4	Min. 3	Brett Hull	11:55	St.L.
Apr. 5/89	Cgy.	DSF	Van. 4	Cgy. 3	Paul Reinhart	2:47	Cgy.
Apr. 6/89	St.L.	DSF	St.L. 4	Min. 3	Rick Meagher	5:30	St.L.
Apr. 6/89	Det.	DSF	Chi. 5	Det. 4	Duane Sutter	14:36	Chi.
Apr. 8/89	Hfd.	DSF	Mtl. 5	Hfd. 4	Stephane Richer	5:01	Mtl.
Apr. 8/89	Phi.	DSF	Wsh. 4	Phi. 3	Kelly Miller	0:51	Phi.
Apr. 9/89	Hfd.	DSF	Mtl. 4	Hfd. 3	Russ Courtnall	15:12	Mtl.
Apr. 15/89	Cgy.	DSF	Cgy. 4	Van. 3	Joel Otto	19:21	Cgy.
Apr. 18/89	Cgy.	DF	Cgy. 4	L.A. 3	Doug Gilmour	7:47	Cgy.
Apr. 19/89	Mtl.	DF	Mtl. 3	Bos. 2	Bobby Smith	12:24	Mtl.
Apr. 20/89	St.L.	DF	St.L. 5	Chi. 4	Tony Hrkac	33:49	Chi.
Apr. 21/89	Phi.	DF	Pit. 4	Phi. 3	Phil Bourque	12:08	Phi.
May 8/89	Chi.	CF	Cgy. 2	Chi. 1	Al MacInnis	15:05	Cgy.
May 9/89	Mtl.	CF	Phi. 2	Mtl. 1	Dave Poulin	5:02	Mtl.
May 19/89	Mtl.	F	Mtl. 4	Cgy. 3	Ryan Walter	38:08	Cgy.
Apr. 5/90	N.J.	DSF	Wsh. 5	N.J. 4	Dino Ciccarelli	5:34	Wsh.
Apr. 6/90	Edm.	DSF	Edm. 3	Wpg. 2	Mark Lamb	4:21	Edm.
Apr. 8/90	Tor.	DSF	St.L. 6	Tor. 5	Sergio Momesso	6:04	St.L.
Apr. 8/90	L.A.	DSF	L.A. 2	Cgy. 1	Tony Granato	8:37	L.A.
Apr. 9/90	Mtl.	DSF	Mtl. 2	Buf. 1	Brian Skrudland	12:35	Mtl.
Apr. 9/90	NYI	DSF	NYI 4	NYR 3	Brent Sutter	20:59	NYR
Apr. 10/90	Wpg.	DSF	Wpg. 4	Edm. 3	Dave Ellett	21:08	Edm.
Apr. 14/90	L.A.	DSF	L.A. 4	Cgy. 3	Mike Krushelnyski	23:14	L.A.
Apr. 15/90	Hfd.	DSF	Hfd. 3	Bos. 2	Kevin Dineen	12:30	Bos.
Apr. 21/90	Bos.	DF	Bos. 5	Mtl. 4	Garry Galley	3:42	Bos.
Apr. 24/90	L.A.	DF	Edm. 6	L.A. 5	Joe Murphy	4:42	Edm.
Apr. 25/90	Wsh.	DF	Wsh. 4	NYR 3	Rod Langway	0:34	Wsh.
Apr. 27/90	NYR	DF	Wsh. 2	NYR 1	John Druce	6:48	Wsh.
May 15/90	Bos.	F	Edm. 3	Bos. 2	Petr Klima	55:13	Edm.
Apr. 4/91	Chi.	DSF	Min. 4	Chi. 3	Brian Propp	4:14	Min.
Apr. 5/91	Pit.	DSF	Pit. 5	N.J. 4	Jaromir Jagr	8:52	Pit.
Apr. 6/91	L.A.	DSF	L.A. 3	Van. 2	Wayne Gretzky	11:08	L.A.
Apr. 8/91	Van.	DSF	Van. 2	L.A. 1	Cliff Ronning	3:12	L.A.
Apr. 11/91	NYR	DSF	Wsh. 5	NYR 4	Dino Ciccarelli	6:44	Wsh.
Apr. 11/91	Mtl.	DSF	Mtl. 4	Buf. 3	Russ Courtnall	5:56	Mtl.
Apr. 14/91	Edm.	DSF	Cgy. 2	Edm. 1	Theoren Fleury	4:40	Edm.
Apr. 16/91	Cgy.	DSF	Edm. 5	Cgy. 4	Esa Tikkanen	6:58	Edm.
Apr. 18/91	L.A.	DF	L.A. 4	Edm. 3	Luc Robitaille	2:13	Edm.
Apr. 19/91	Bos.	DF	Mtl. 4	Bos. 3	Stephane Richer	0:27	Bos.
Apr. 19/91	Pit.	DF	Pit. 7	Wsh. 6	Kevin Stevens	8:10	Pit.
Apr. 20/91	L.A.	DF	Edm. 4	L.A. 3	Petr Klima	24:48	Edm.
Apr. 22/91	Edm.	DF	Edm. 4	L.A. 3	Esa Tikkanen	20:48	Edm.
Apr. 27/91	Mtl.	DF	Mtl. 3	Bos. 2	Shayne Corson	17:47	Bos.
Apr. 28/91	Edm.	DF	Edm. 4	L.A. 3	Craig MacTavish	16:57	Edm.
May 3/91	Bos.	CF	Bos. 5	Pit. 4	Vladimir Ruzicka	8:14	Pit.
Apr. 21/92	Bos.	DSF	Bos. 3	Buf. 2	Adam Oates	11:14	Bos.
Apr. 22/92	Min.	DSF	Det. 5	Min. 4	Yves Racine	1:15	Det.
Apr. 22/92	St.L.	DSF	St.L. 5	Chi. 4	Brett Hull	23:33	Chi.
Apr. 25/92	Buf.	DSF	Bos. 5	Buf. 4	Ted Donato	2:08	Bos.
Apr. 28/92	Min.	DSF	Det. 1	Min. 0	Sergei Fedorov	16:13	Det.
Apr. 29/92	Hfd.	DSF	Hfd. 2	Mtl. 1	Yvon Corriveau	0:24	Mtl.
May 1/92	Mtl.	DSF	Mtl. 3	Hfd. 2	Russ Courtnall	25:26	Mtl.
May 3/92	Van.	DF	Edm. 4	Van. 3	Joe Murphy	8:36	Edm.
May 5/92	Mtl.	DF	Bos. 3	Mtl. 2	Peter Douris	3:12	Bos.
May 7/92	Pit.	DF	NYR 6	Pit. 5	Kris King	1:29	Pit.
May 9/92	Pit.	DF	Pit. 5	NYR 4	Ron Francis	2:47	Pit.
May 17/92	Pit.	CF	Pit. 4	Bos. 3	Jaromir Jagr	9:44	Pit.

The Anaheim Ducks celebrate Scott Niedermayer's overtime goal to beat the Detroit Red Wings on May 13, 2007. Niedermayer also scored an overtime winner to eliminate Vancouver in round two. He was the only player with two playoff overtime goals in 2007.

Date	City	Series	Score		Scorer	Overtime	Series Winner
May 20/92	Edm.	CF	Chi. 4	Edm. 3	Jeremy Roenick	2:45	Chi.
Apr. 18/93	Bos.	DSF	Buf. 5	Bos. 4	Bob Sweeney	11:03	Buf.
Apr. 18/93	Que.	DSF	Que. 3	Mtl. 2	Scott Young	16:49	Mtl.
Apr. 20/93	Wsh.	DSF	NYI 5	Wsh. 4	Brian Mullen	34:50	NYI
Apr. 22/93	Mtl.	DSF	Mtl. 2	Que. 1	Vincent Damphousse	10:30	Mtl.
Apr. 22/93	Buf.	DSF	Buf. 4	Bos. 3	Yuri Khmylev	1:05	Buf.
Apr. 22/93	NYI	DSF	NYI 4	Wsh. 3	Ray Ferraro	4:46	NYI
Apr. 24/93	Buf.	DSF	Buf. 6	Bos. 5	Brad May	4:48	Buf.
Apr. 24/93	NYI	DSF	NYI 4	Wsh. 3	Ray Ferraro	25:40	NYI
Apr. 25/93	St.L.	DSF	St.L. 4	Chi. 3	Craig Janney	10:43	St.L.
Apr. 26/93	Que.	DSF	Mtl. 5	Que. 4	Kirk Muller	8:17	Mtl.
Apr. 27/93	Det.	DSF	Tor. 5	Det. 4	Mike Foligno	2:05	Tor.
Apr. 27/93	Van.	DSF	Wpg. 4	Van. 3	Teemu Selanne	6:18	Van.
Apr. 29/93	Wpg.	DSF	Van. 4	Wpg. 3	Greg Adams	4:30	Van.
May 1/93	Det.	DSF	Tor. 4	Det. 3	Nikolai Borschevsky	2:35	Tor.
May 3/93	Tor.	DF	Tor. 2	St.L. 1	Doug Gilmour	23:16	Tor.
May 4/93	Mtl.	DF	Mtl. 4	Buf. 3	Guy Carbonneau	2:50	Mtl.
May 5/93	Tor.	DF	St.L. 2	Tor. 1	Jeff Brown	23:03	Tor.
May 6/93	Buf.	DF	Mtl. 4	Buf. 3	Gilbert Dionne	8:28	Mtl.
May 8/93	Buf.	DF	Mtl. 4	Buf. 3	Kirk Muller	11:37	Mtl.
May 11/93	Van.	DF	L.A. 4	Van. 3	Gary Shuchuk	26:31	L.A.
May 14/93	Pit.	DF	NYI 4	Pit. 3	Dave Volek	5:16	NYI
May 18/93	Mtl.	CF	Mtl. 4	NYI 3	Stephan Lebeau	26:21	Mtl.
May 20/93	NYI	CF	Mtl. 2	NYI 1	Guy Carbonneau	12:34	Mtl.
May 25/93	Tor.	CF	Tor. 3	L.A. 2	Glenn Anderson	19:20	L.A.
May 27/93	L.A.	CF	L.A. 5	Tor. 4	Wayne Gretzky	1:41	L.A.
Jun. 3/93	Mtl.	F	Mtl. 3	L.A. 2	Eric Desjardins	0:51	Mtl.
Jun. 5/93	L.A.	F	Mtl. 4	L.A. 3	John LeClair	0:34	Mtl.
Jun. 7/93	L.A.	F	Mtl. 3	L.A. 2	John LeClair	14:37	Mtl.
Apr. 20/94	Tor.	CQF	Tor. 1	Chi. 0	Todd Gill	2:15	Tor.
Apr. 22/94	St.L.	CQF	Dal. 5	St.L. 4	Paul Cavallini	8:34	Dal.
Apr. 24/94	Chi.	CQF	Chi. 4	Tor. 3	Jeremy Roenick	1:23	Tor.
Apr. 25/94	Bos.	CQF	Mtl. 2	Bos. 1	Kirk Muller	17:18	Bos.
Apr. 26/94	Cgy.	CQF	Van. 2	Cgy. 1	Geoff Courtnall	7:15	Van.
Apr. 27/94	Buf.	CQF	Buf. 1	N.J. 0	Dave Hannan	65:43	N.J.
Apr. 28/94	Van.	CQF	Van. 3	Cgy. 2	Trevor Linden	16:43	Van.
Apr. 30/94	Cgy.	CQF	Van. 4	Cgy. 3	Pavel Bure	22:20	Van.
May 3/94	N.J.	CSF	Bos. 6	N.J. 5	Don Sweeney	9:08	N.J.
May 7/94	Bos.	CSF	N.J. 5	Bos. 4	Stephane Richer	14:19	N.J.
May 8/94	Van.	CSF	Van. 2	Dal. 1	Sergio Momesso	11:01	Van.
May 12/94	Tor.	CSF	Tor. 3	S.J. 2	Mike Gartner	8:53	Tor.
May 15/94	NYR	CF	N.J. 4	NYR 3	Stephane Richer	35:23	NYR
May 16/94	Tor.	CF	Tor. 3	Van. 2	Peter Zezel	16:55	Van.
May 19/94	N.J.	CF	NYR 3	N.J. 2	Stephane Matteau	26:13	NYR
May 24/94	Van.	CF	Van. 4	Tor. 3	Greg Adams	20:14	Van.
May 27/94	NYR	CF	NYR 2	N.J. 1	Stephane Matteau	24:24	NYR
May 31/94	NYR	F	Van. 3	NYR 2	Greg Adams	19:26	NYR
May 7/95	Phi.	CQF	Phi. 4	Buf. 3	Karl Dykhuis	10:06	Phi.
May 9/95	Cgy.	CQF	S.J. 5	Cgy. 4	Ulf Dahlen	12:21	S.J.
May 12/95	NYR	CQF	NYR 3	Que. 2	Steve Larmer	8:09	NYR
May 12/95	N.J.	CQF	N.J. 1	Bos. 0	Randy McKay	8:51	N.J.
May 14/95	Pit.	CQF	Pit. 6	Wsh. 5	Luc Robitaille	4:30	Pit.
May 15/95	St.L.	CQF	Van. 6	St.L. 5	Cliff Ronning	1:48	Van.
May 17/95	Tor.	CQF	Tor. 5	Chi. 4	Randy Wood	10:00	Chi.
May 19/95	Cgy.	CQF	S.J. 5	Cgy. 4	Ray Whitney	21:54	S.J.
May 21/95	Phi.	CSF	Phi. 5	NYR 4	Eric Desjardins	7:03	Phi.
May 21/95	Chi.	CSF	Chi. 2	Van. 1	Joe Murphy	9:04	Chi.
May 22/95	Phi.	CSF	Phi. 4	NYR 3	Kevin Haller	0:25	Phi.
May 25/95	Van.	CSF	Chi. 3	Van. 2	Chris Chelios	6:22	Chi.
May 26/95	N.J.	CSF	N.J. 2	Pit. 1	Neal Broten	18:36	N.J.
May 27/95	Van.	CSF	Chi. 4	Van. 3	Chris Chelios	5:35	Chi.

Date	City	Series	Score		Scorer	Overtime	Series Winner
Jun. 1/95	Det.	CF	Det. 2	Chi. 1	Nicklas Lidstrom	1:01	Det.
Jun. 6/95	Chi.	CF	Det. 4	Chi. 3	Vladimir Konstantinov	29:25	Det.
Jun. 7/95	N.J.	CF	Phi. 3	N.J. 2	Eric Lindros	4:19	N.J.
Jun. 11/95	Det.	CF	Det. 2	Chi. 1	Vyacheslav Kozlov	22:25	Det.
Apr. 16/96	NYR	CQF	Mtl. 3	NYR 2	Vincent Damphousse	5:04	NYR
Apr. 18/96	Tor.	CQF	Tor. 5	St.L. 4	Mats Sundin	4:02	St.L.
Apr. 18/96	Phi.	CQF	T.B. 2	Phi. 1	Brian Bellows	9:05	Phi.
Apr. 21/96	St.L.	CQF	St.L. 3	Tor. 2	Glenn Anderson	1:24	St.L.
Apr. 21/96	T.B.	CQF	T.B. 5	Phi. 4	Alexander Selivanov	2:04	Phi.
Apr. 23/96	Cgy.	CQF	Chi. 2	Cgy. 1	Joe Murphy	50:02	Chi.
Apr. 24/96	Wsh.	CQF	Pit. 3	Wsh. 2	Petr Nedved	79:15	Pit.
Apr. 25/96	Col.	CQF	Col. 5	Van. 4	Joe Sakic	0:51	Col.
Apr. 25/96	Tor.	CQF	Tor. 5	St.L. 4	Mike Gartner	7:31	St.L.
May 2/96	Col.	CSF	Chi. 3	Col. 2	Jeremy Roenick	6:29	Col.
May 6/96	Chi.	CSF	Chi. 4	Col. 3	Sergei Krivokrasov	0:46	Col.
May 8/96	St.L.	CSF	St.L. 5	Det. 4	Igor Kravchuk	3:23	Det.
May 8/96	Chi.	CSF	Col. 3	Chi. 2	Joe Sakic	44:33	Col.
May 9/96	Fla.	CSF	Fla. 4	Phi. 3	Dave Lowry	4:06	Fla.
May 12/96	Phi.	CSF	Fla. 2	Phi. 1	Mike Hough	28:05	Fla.
May 13/96	Chi.	CSF	Col. 4	Chi. 3	Sandis Ozolinsh	25:18	Col.
May 16/96	Det.	CSF	Det. 1	St.L. 0	Steve Yzerman	21:15	Det.
May 19/96	Det.	CF	Col. 3	Det. 2	Mike Keane	17:31	Col.
Jun. 10/96	Fla.	F	Col. 1	Fla. 0	Uwe Krupp	44:31	Col.
Apr. 20/97	Chi.	CQF	Chi. 4	Col. 3	Sergei Krivokrasov	31:03	Col.
Apr. 20/97	Edm.	CQF	Edm. 4	Dal. 3	Kelly Buchberger	9:15	Edm.
Apr. 22/97	NYR	CQF	NYR 4	Fla. 3	Esa Tikkanen	16:29	NYR
Apr. 23/97	Ott.	CQF	Ott. 1	Buf. 0	Daniel Alfredsson	2:34	Buf.
Apr. 24/97	Mtl.	CQF	Mtl. 4	N.J. 3	Patrice Brisebois	47:37	N.J.
Apr. 25/97	Fla.	CQF	NYR 3	Fla. 2	Esa Tikkanen	12:02	NYR
Apr. 25/97	Dal.	CQF	Edm. 1	Dal. 0	Ryan Smyth	20:22	Edm.
Apr. 27/97	Phx.	CQF	Ana. 3	Phx. 2	Paul Kariya	7:29	Ana.
Apr. 29/97	Buf.	CQF	Buf. 3	Ott. 2	Derek Plante	5:24	Buf.
Apr. 29/97	Dal.	CQF	Edm. 4	Dal. 3	Todd Marchant	12:26	Edm.
May 2/97	Det.	CSF	Det. 2	Ana. 1	Martin Lapointe	0:59	Det.
May 4/97	Det.	CSF	Det. 3	Ana. 2	Vyacheslav Kozlov	41:31	Det.
May 8/97	Ana.	CSF	Det. 3	Ana. 2	Brendan Shanahan	37:03	Det.
May 9/97	Phi.	CSF	Buf. 5	Phi. 4	Ed Ronan	6:24	Phi.
May 9/97	Edm.	CSF	Col. 3	Edm. 2	Claude Lemieux	8:35	Col.
May 11/97	N.J.	CSF	NYR 2	N.J. 1	Adam Graves	14:08	NYR
Apr. 22/98	N.J.	CQF	Ott. 2	N.J. 1	Bruce Gardiner	5:58	Ott.
Apr. 23/98	Pit.	CQF	Mtl. 3	Pit. 2	Benoit Brunet	18:43	Mtl.
Apr. 24/98	Wsh.	CQF	Bos. 4	Wsh. 3	Darren Van Impe	20:54	Wsh.
Apr. 26/98	Ott.	CQF	Ott. 2	N.J. 1	Alexei Yashin	2:47	Ott.
Apr. 26/98	Bos.	CQF	Wsh. 3	Bos. 2	Joe Juneau	26:31	Wsh.
Apr. 26/98	Edm.	CQF	Col. 5	Edm. 4	Joe Sakic	15:25	Edm.
Apr. 28/98	S.J.	CQF	S.J. 1	Dal. 0	Andrei Zyuzin	6:31	Dal.
May 1/98	Phi.	CQF	Buf. 3	Phi. 2	Michal Grosek	5:40	Buf.
May 2/98	S.J.	CQF	Dal. 3	S.J. 2	Mike Keane	3:43	Dal.
May 3/98	Bos.	CQF	Wsh. 3	Bos. 2	Brian Bellows	15:24	Wsh.
May 3/98	Buf.	CSF	Buf. 3	Mtl. 2	Geoff Sanderson	2:37	Buf.
May 11/98	Edm.	CSF	Dal. 1	Edm. 0	Benoit Hogue	13:07	Dal.
May 12/98	Mtl.	CSF	Buf. 5	Mtl. 4	Michael Peca	21:24	Buf.
May 12/98	St.L.	CSF	Det. 3	St.L. 2	Brendan Shanahan	31:12	Det.
May 25/98	Wsh.	CF	Wsh. 3	Buf. 2	Todd Krygier	3:01	Wsh.
May 28/98	Buf.	CF	Wsh. 4	Buf. 3	Peter Bondra	9:37	Wsh.
Jun. 3/98	Dal.	CF	Dal. 3	Det. 2	Jamie Langenbrunner	0:46	Det.
Jun. 4/98	Buf.	CF	Wsh. 3	Buf. 2	Joe Juneau	6:24	Wsh.
Jun. 11/98	Det.	F	Det. 5	Wsh. 4	Kris Draper	15:24	Det.
Apr. 23/99	Ott.	CQF	Buf. 3	Ott. 2	Miroslav Satan	30:35	Buf.
Apr. 24/99	Car.	CQF	Car. 3	Bos. 2	Ray Sheppard	17:05	Bos.
Apr. 24/99	Phx.	CQF	Phx. 4	St.L. 3	Shane Doan	8:58	St.L.

Overtime Games since 1918 — *continued*

Date	City	Series	Score		Scorer	Overtime	Series Winner
Apr. 26/99	S.J.	CQF	Col. 2	S.J. 1	Milan Hejduk	7:53	Col.
Apr. 27/99	Edm.	CQF	Dal. 3	Edm. 2	Joe Nieuwendyk	57:34	Dal.
Apr. 30/99	Tor.	CQF	Tor. 2	Phi. 1	Yanic Perreault	11:51	Tor.
Apr. 30/99	Car.	CQF	Bos. 4	Car. 3	Anson Carter	34:45	Bos.
Apr. 30/99	Phx.	CQF	St.L. 2	Phx. 1	Scott Young	5:43	St.L.
May 2/99	Pit.	CQF	Pit. 3	N.J. 2	Jaromir Jagr	8:59	Pit.
May 3/99	S.J.	CQF	Col. 3	S.J. 2	Milan Hejduk	13:12	Col.
May 4/99	Phx.	CQF	St.L. 1	Phx. 0	Pierre Turgeon	17:59	St.L.
May 7/99	Col.	CSF	Det. 3	Col. 2	Kirk Maltby	4:18	Col.
May 8/99	Dal.	CSF	Dal. 5	St.L. 4	Joe Nieuwendyk	8:22	Dal.
May 10/99	St.L.	CSF	St.L. 3	Dal. 2	Pavol Demitra	2:43	Dal.
May 12/99	St.L.	CSF	St.L. 3	Dal. 2	Pierre Turgeon	5:52	Dal.
May 13/99	Pit.	CSF	Tor. 3	Pit. 2	Sergei Berezin	2:18	Tor.
May 17/99	Pit.	CSF	Tor. 4	Pit. 3	Garry Valk	1:57	Tor.
May 17/99	St.L.	CSF	Dal. 2	St.L. 1	Mike Modano	2:21	Dal.
May 28/99	Col.	CF	Col. 3	Dal. 2	Chris Drury	19:29	Dal.
Jun. 8/99	Dal.	F	Buf. 3	Dal. 2	Jason Woolley	15:30	Dal.
Jun. 19/99	Buf.	F	Dal. 2	Buf. 1	Brett Hull	54:51	Dal.
Apr. 15/00	Pit.	CQF	Pit. 2	Wsh. 1	Jaromir Jagr	5:49	Pit.
Apr. 18/00	Buf.	CQF	Buf. 3	Phi. 2	Stu Barnes	4:42	Phi.
Apr. 22/00	Tor.	CQF	Tor. 2	Ott. 1	Steve Thomas	14:47	Tor.
May 2/00	Pit.	CSF	Phi. 4	Pit. 3	Andy Delmore	11:01	Phi.
May 3/00	Det.	CSF	Col. 3	Det. 2	Chris Drury	10:21	Col.
May 4/00	Pit.	CSF	Phi. 2	Pit. 1	Keith Primeau	92:01	Phi.
May 23/00	Dal.	CF	Dal. 3	Col. 2	Joe Nieuwendyk	12:10	Dal.
Jun. 8/00	N.J.	F	Dal. 1	N.J. 0	Mike Modano	46:21	N.J.
Jun. 10/00	Dal.	F	N.J. 2	Dal. 1	Jason Arnott	28:20	N.J.
Apr. 11/01	Dal.	CQF	Dal. 2	Edm. 1	Jamie Langenbrunner	2:08	Dal.
Apr. 13/01	Ott.	CQF	Tor. 1	Ott. 0	Mats Sundin	10:49	Tor.
Apr. 14/01	Phi.	CQF	Buf. 4	Phi. 3	Jay McKee	18:02	Buf.
Apr. 15/01	Edm.	CQF	Dal. 3	Edm. 2	Benoit Hogue	19:48	Dal.
Apr. 16/01	Tor.	CQF	Tor. 3	Ott. 2	Cory Cross	2:16	Tor.
Apr. 16/01	Van.	CQF	Col. 4	Van. 3	Peter Forsberg	2:50	Col.
Apr. 17/01	Buf.	CQF	Buf. 4	Phi. 3	Curtis Brown	6:13	Buf.
Apr. 17/01	Edm.	CQF	Edm. 2	Dal. 1	Mike Comrie	17:19	Dal.
Apr. 18/01	Car.	CQF	Car. 3	N.J. 2	Rod Brind'Amour	:46	N.J.
Apr. 18/01	Pit.	CQF	Wsh. 4	Pit. 3	Jeff Halpern	4:01	Pit.
Apr. 18/01	L.A.	CQF	L.A. 4	Det. 3	Eric Belanger	2:36	L.A.
Apr. 19/01	Dal.	CQF	Dal. 4	Edm. 3	Kirk Muller	8:01	Dal.
Apr. 19/01	St.L.	CQF	St.L. 3	S.J. 2	Bryce Salvador	9:54	St.L.
Apr. 23/01	Pit.	CQF	Pit. 4	Wsh. 3	Martin Straka	13:04	Pit.
Apr. 23/01	L.A.	CQF	L.A. 3	Det. 2	Adam Deadmarsh	4:48	L.A.
Apr. 26/01	Col.	CSF	L.A. 4	Col. 3	Jaroslav Modry	14:23	Col.
Apr. 28/01	N.J.	CSF	N.J. 6	Tor. 5	Randy McKay	5:31	N.J.
May 1/01	Tor.	CSF	N.J. 3	Tor. 2	Brian Rafalski	7:00	N.J.
May 1/01	St.L.	CSF	St.L. 3	Dal. 2	Cory Stillman	29:26	St.L.
May 5/01	Buf.	CSF	Buf. 3	Pit. 2	Stu Barnes	8:34	Pit.
May 6/01	L.A.	CSF	L.A. 1	Col. 0	Glen Murray	22:41	Col.
May 8/01	Pit.	CSF	Pit. 3	Buf. 2	Martin Straka	11:29	Pit.
May 10/01	Buf.	CSF	Pit. 3	Buf. 2	Darius Kasparaitis	13:01	Pit.
May 16/01	St.L.	CF	St.L. 4	Col. 3	Scott Young	30:27	Col.
May 18/01	St.L.	CF	Col. 4	St.L. 3	Stephane Yelle	4:23	Col.
May 21/01	Col.	CF	Col. 2	St.L. 1	Joe Sakic	:24	Col.
Apr. 17/02	Phi.	CQF	Phi. 1	Ott. 0	Ruslan Fedotenko	7:47	Ott.
Apr. 17/02	Det.	CQF	Van. 4	Det. 3	Henrik Sedin	13:59	Det.
Apr. 19/02	Car.	CQF	Car. 2	N.J. 1	Bates Battaglia	15:26	Car.
Apr. 24/02	Car.	CQF	Car. 3	N.J. 2	Josef Vasicek	8:16	Car.
Apr. 25/02	Col.	CQF	L.A. 1	Col. 0	Craig Johnson	2:19	Col.
Apr. 26/02	Phi.	CQF	Ott. 2	Phi. 1	Martin Havlat	7:33	Ott.
May 4/02	Tor.	CSF	Tor. 3	Ott. 2	Gary Roberts	44:30	Tor.
May 7/02	Mtl.	CSF	Mtl. 2	Car. 1	Donald Audette	2:26	Car.
May 9/02	Mtl.	CSF	Car. 4	Mtl. 3	Niclas Wallin	3:14	Car.
May 13/02	S.J.	CSF	Col. 2	S.J. 1	Peter Forsberg	2:47	Col.
May 19/02	Car.	CF	Car. 2	Tor. 1	Niclas Wallin	13:42	Car.
May 20/02	Det.	CF	Col. 4	Det. 3	Chris Drury	2:17	Det.
May 21/02	Tor.	CF	Car. 2	Tor. 1	Jeff O'Neill	6:01	Car.
May 22/02	Col.	CF	Det. 2	Col. 1	Fredrik Olausson	12:44	Det.
May 27/02	Det.	CF	Col. 2	Det. 1	Peter Forsberg	6:24	Det.
May 28/02	Tor.	CF	Car. 2	Tor. 1	Martin Gelinas	8:05	Car.
Jun. 4/02	Det.	F	Car. 3	Det. 2	Ron Francis	:58	Det.
Jun. 8/02	Car.	F	Det. 3	Car. 2	Igor Larionov	54:47	Det.
Apr. 10/03	Det.	CQF	Ana. 2	Det. 1	Paul Kariya	43:18	Ana.
Apr. 14/03	NYI	CQF	Ott. 3	NYI 2	Todd White	22:25	Ott.
Apr. 14/03	Tor.	CQF	Tor. 4	Phi. 3	Tomas Kaberle	27:20	Phi.
Apr. 15/03	Wsh.	CQF	T.B. 4	Wsh. 3	Vincent Lecavalier	2:29	T.B.
Apr. 16/03	Tor.	CQF	Phi. 3	Tor. 2	Mark Recchi	53:54	Phi.
Apr. 16/03	Ana.	CQF	Ana. 3	Det. 2	Steve Rucchin	6:53	Ana.
Apr. 20/03	Wsh.	CQF	T.B. 2	Wsh. 1	Martin St. Louis	44:03	T.B.
Apr. 21/03	Tor.	CQF	Tor. 2	Phi. 1	Travis Green	30:51	Phi.
Apr. 21/03	Min.	CQF	Min. 3	Col. 2	Richard Park	4:22	Min.
Apr. 22/03	Col.	CQF	Min. 3	Col. 2	Andrew Brunette	3:25	Min.
Apr. 24/03	Dal.	CSF	Ana. 4	Dal. 3	Petr Sykora	80:48	Ana.
Apr. 25/03	Van.	CSF	Van. 4	Min. 3	Trent Klatt	3:42	Min.
Apr. 26/03	N.J.	CSF	N.J. 3	T.B. 2	Jamie Langenbrunner	2:09	N.J.
Apr. 26/03	Dal.	CSF	Ana. 3	Dal. 2	Mike Leclerc	1:44	Ana.
Apr. 29/03	Phi.	CSF	Ott. 3	Phi. 2	Wade Redden	6:43	Ott.
May 2/03	Min.	CSF	Van. 3	Min. 2	Brent Sopel	15:52	Min.
May 2/03	N.J.	CSF	N.J. 2	T.B. 1	Grant Marshall	51:12	N.J.
May 10/03	Min.	CF	Ana. 1	Min. 0	Petr Sykora	28:06	Ana.
May 10/03	Ott.	CF	Ott. 3	N.J. 2	Shaun Van Allen	3:08	N.J.
May 21/03	N.J.	CF	Ott. 2	N.J. 1	Chris Phillips	15:51	N.J.
May 31/03	Ana.	F	Ana. 3	N.J. 2	Ruslan Salei	6:59	N.J.
Jun. 2/03	Ana.	F	Ana. 1	N.J. 0	Steve Thomas	0:39	N.J.
Apr. 8/04	S.J.	CQF	S.J. 1	St.L. 0	Niko Dimitrakos	9:16	S.J.
Apr. 9/04	Bos.	CQF	Bos. 2	Mtl. 1	Patrice Bergeron	1:26	Mtl.
Apr. 12/04	Dal.	CQF	Dal. 4	Col. 3	Steve Ott	2:11	Col.
Apr. 13/04	Mtl.	CQF	Bos. 4	Mtl. 3	Glen Murray	29:27	Mtl.
Apr. 14/04	Dal.	CQF	Col. 3	Dal. 2	Marek Svatos	25:21	Col.
Apr. 16/04	T.B.	CQF	T.B. 3	NYI 2	Martin St. Louis	4:07	T.B.
Apr. 17/04	Cgy.	CQF	Van. 5	Cgy. 4	Brendan Morrison	42:28	Cgy.
Apr. 18/04	Ott.	CQF	Ott. 2	Tor. 1	Mike Fisher	21:47	Tor.
Apr. 19/04	Van.	CQF	Cgy. 3	Van. 2	Martin Gelinas	1:25	Cgy.
Apr. 22/04	Det.	CSF	Cgy. 2	Det. 1	Marcus Nilson	2:39	Cgy.
Apr. 27/04	Mtl.	CSF	T.B. 4	Mtl 3	Brad Richards	1:05	T.B.
Apr. 28/04	Col	CSF	Col. 1	S.J. 0	Joe Sakic	5:15	S.J.
May 1/04	S.J.	CSF	Col. 2	S.J. 1	Joe Sakic	1:54	S.J.
May 3/04	Cgy	CSF	Cgy. 1	Det. 0	Martin Gelinas	19:13	Cgy.
May 4/04	Phi.	CSF	Phi. 3	Tor. 2	Jeremy Roenick	7:39	Phi.
May 9/04	S.J.	CF	Cgy. 4	S.J. 3	Steve Montador	18:43	Cgy.
May 20/04	Phi.	CF	Phi. 5	T.B. 4	Simon Gagne	18:18	T.B.
Jun. 3/04	T.B.	F	Cgy. 3	T.B. 2	Oleg Saprykin	14:40	T.B.
Jun. 5/04	Cgy.	F	T.B. 3	Cgy. 2	Martin St. Louis	20:33	T.B.
Apr. 21/06	Det.	CQF	Det. 3	Edm. 2	Kirk Maltby	22:39	Edm.
Apr. 21/06	Cgy.	CQF	Cgy. 2	Ana. 1	Darren McCarty	9:45	Ana.
Apr. 22/06	Buf.	CQF	Buf. 3	Phi. 2	Daniel Briere	27:31	Buf.
Apr. 24/06	Car.	CQF	Mtl. 6	Car. 5	Michael Ryder	22:32	Car.
Apr. 24/06	Dal.	CQF	Col. 5	Dal. 4	Joe Sakic	4:36	Col.
Apr. 25/06	Edm.	CQF	Edm. 4	Det. 3	Jarret Stoll	28:44	Edm.
Apr. 26/06	Mtl.	CQF	Car. 2	Mtl. 1	Eric Staal	3:38	Car.
Apr. 26/06	Col.	CQF	Col. 4	Dal. 3	Alex Tanguay	1:09	Col.
Apr. 27/06	Ana.	CQF	Ana. 3	Cgy. 2	Sean O'Donnell	1:36	Ana.
Apr. 30/06	Dal.	CQF	Col. 3	Dal. 2	Andrew Brunette	13:55	Col.
May 2/06	Mtl.	CQF	Car. 2	Mtl. 1	Cory Stillman	1:19	Car.
May 5/06	Ott.	CSF	Buf. 7	Ott. 6	Chris Drury	0:18	Buf.
May 8/06	Car.	CSF	Car. 3	N.J. 2	Niclas Wallin	3:09	Car.
May 9/06	Col.	CSF	Ana. 4	Col. 3	Joffrey Lupul	16:30	Ana.
May 10/06	Buf.	CSF	Buf. 3	Ott. 2	J.P. Dumont	5:05	Buf.
May 10/06	Edm.	CSF	Edm. 3	S.J. 2	Shawn Horcoff	42:24	Edm.
May 13/06	Ott.	CSF	Buf. 3	Ott. 2	Jason Pominville	2:26	Buf.
May 28/06	Car.	CF	Car. 4	Buf. 3	Cory Stillman	8:46	Car.
May 30/06	Buf.	CF	Buf. 2	Car. 1	Daniel Briere	4:22	Car.
June 14/06	Car.	F	Edm. 4	Car. 3	Fernando Pisani	3:31	Car.
Apr. 11/07	Nas.	CQF	S.J. 5	Nas. 4	Patrick Rissmiller	28:14	S.J.
Apr. 11/07	Van.	CQF	Van. 5	Dal. 4	Henrik Sedin	78:06	Van.
Apr. 15/07	Dal.	CQF	Van. 2	Dal. 1	Taylor Pyatt	7:47	Van.
Apr. 18/07	T.B.	CQF	N.J. 4	T.B. 3	Scott Gomez	12:54	N.J.
Apr. 19/07	Van.	CQF	Dal. 1	Van. 0	Brendan Morrow	6:22	Van.
Apr. 22/07	Cgy.	CQF	Det. 2	Cgy. 1	Johan Franzen	24:23	Det.
Apr. 27/07	Ana.	CSF	Van. 2	Ana. 1	Jeff Cowan	27:49	Ana.
Apr. 28/07	N.J.	CSF	N.J. 3	Ott. 2	Jamie Langenbrunner	21:55	Ott.
Apr. 29/07	NYR	CSF	NYR 2	Buf. 1	Michal Rozsival	36:43	Buf.
May 1/07	Van.	CSF	Ana. 3	Van. 2	Travis Moen	2:07	Ana.
May 2/07	S.J.	CSF	Det. 3	S.J. 2	Mathieu Schnieder	16:04	Det.
May 3/07	Ana.	CSF	Ana. 2	Van. 1	Scott Niedermayer	24:30	Ana.
May 4/07	Buf.	CSF	Buf. 2	NYR 1	Maxim Afinogenov	4:39	Buf.
May 12/07	Buf.	CF	Ott. 4	Buf. 3	Joe Corvo	24:58	Ott.
May 13/07	Det.	CF	Ana. 4	Det. 3	Scott Niedermayer	14:17	Ana.
May 19/07	Buf.	CF	Ott. 3	Buf. 2	Daniel Alfredsson	9:32	Ott.
May 20/07	Det.	CF	Ana. 2	Det. 1	Teemu Selanne	11:57	Ana.

Ten Longest Overtime Games

Date	City	Series	Score		Scorer	Overtime	Series Winner
Mar. 24/36	Mtl.	SF	Det. 1	Mtl. M. 0	Mud Bruneteau	116:30	Det.
Apr. 3/33	Tor.	SF	Tor. 1	Bos. 0	Ken Doraty	104:46	Tor.
May 4/00	Pit.	CSF	Phi. 2	Pit. 1	Keith Primeau	92:01	Phi.
Apr. 24/03	Dal.	CSF	Ana. 4	Dal. 3	Petr Sykora	80:48	Ana.
Apr. 24/96	Wsh.	CQF	Pit. 3	Wsh. 2	Petr Nedved	79:15	Pit.
Apr. 11/07	**Van.**	**CQF**	**Van. 5**	**Dal. 4**	**Henrik Sedin**	**78:06**	**Van.**
Mar. 23/43	Det.	SF	Tor. 3	Det. 2	Jack McLean	70:18	Det.
Mar. 28/30	Mtl.	SF	Mtl. 2	NYR 1	Gus Rivers	68:52	Mtl.
Apr. 18/87	Wsh.	DSF	NYI 3	Wsh. 2	Pat LaFontaine	68:47	NYI
Apr. 27/94	Buf.	CQF	Buf. 1	N.J. 0	Dave Hannan	65:43	N.J.

Overtime Record of Current Teams

(Listed by number of OT games played)

	Overall				Home					Road				
Team	GP	W	L	T	GP	W	L	T	Last OT Game	GP	W	L	T	Last OT Game
Montreal	128	71	55	2	61	37	23	1	May 2/06	67	34	32	1	Apr. 24/06
Toronto	106	54	51	1	68	36	31	1	May 4/04	38	18	20	0	Apr. 18/04
Boston	100	40	57	3	46	21	24	1	Apr. 9/04	54	19	33	2	Apr. 13/04
Detroit	82	36	46	0	48	17	31	0	May 20/07	34	19	15	0	May 2/07
NY Rangers	65	31	34	0	28	13	15	0	Apr. 29/07	37	18	19	0	May 4/07
Chicago	62	30	30	2	30	16	13	1	Apr. 20/97	32	14	17	1	May 2/96
Dallas[1]	60	25	35	0	30	11	19	0	Apr. 15/07	30	14	16	0	Apr. 19/07
Philadelphia	59	28	31	0	26	13	13	0	May 20/04	33	15	18	0	Apr. 22/06
Buffalo	56	31	25	0	32	20	12	0	May 19/07	24	11	13	0	Apr. 29/07
Colorado[2]	53	31	22	0	21	10	11	0	May 9/06	32	21	11	0	Apr. 30/06
St. Louis	50	27	23	0	26	20	6	0	May 18/01	24	7	17	0	Apr. 8/04
Edmonton	42	24	18	0	23	13	10	0	May 10/06	19	11	8	0	Jun. 14/06
Vancouver	41	20	21	0	18	7	11	0	May 1/07	23	13	10	0	May 3/07
NY Islanders	40	29	11	0	18	14	4	0	Apr. 14/03	22	15	7	0	Apr. 16/04
Calgary[3]	40	17	23	0	19	6	13	0	Apr. 22/07	21	11	10	0	Apr. 27/06
New Jersey[4]	36	12	24	0	15	6	9	0	Apr. 28/07	21	6	15	0	Apr. 18/07
Los Angeles	35	17	18	0	19	11	8	0	May 6/01	16	6	10	0	Apr. 25/02
Washington	31	14	17	0	12	5	7	0	Apr. 20/03	19	9	10	0	Apr. 23/01
Carolina[5]	30	18	12	0	18	11	7	0	Jun. 14/06	12	7	5	0	May 30/06
Pittsburgh	28	15	13	0	18	10	8	0	May 8/01	10	5	5	0	May 10/01
Ottawa	22	11	11	0	8	4	4	0	May 13/06	14	7	7	0	May 19/07
Anaheim	19	14	5	0	7	5	2	0	May 3/07	12	9	3	0	May 20/07
San Jose	16	5	11	0	9	2	7	0	May 2/07	7	3	4	0	Apr. 11/07
Tampa Bay	12	7	5	0	4	2	2	0	Apr. 18/07	8	5	3	0	Jun. 5/04
Phoenix[6]	12	5	7	0	8	3	5	0	May 4/99	4	2	2	0	Apr. 27/93
Florida	5	2	3	0	3	1	2	0	Apr. 25/97	2	1	1	0	Apr. 22/97
Minnesota	5	2	3	0	3	1	2	0	May 10/03	2	1	1	0	Apr. 25/03
Nashville	1	0	1	0	1	0	1	0	Apr. 11/07	0	0	0	0	

[1] Totals include those of Minnesota North Stars 1967-93.
[2] Totals include those of Quebec 1979-95.
[3] Totals include those of Atlanta Flames 1972-80.
[4] Totals include those of Kansas City and Colorado Rockies 1974-82.
[5] Totals include those of Hartford 1979-97.
[6] Totals include those of Winnipeg 1979-96.

The Canucks' Henrik Sedin ended the longest game of the 2007 playoffs on the first night of the postseason with a goal at 18:06 of the fourth overtime period. Vancouver's win over the Dallas Stars clocks in as the sixth-longest game in NHL history.

Penalty Shots in Stanley Cup Playoff Games

Date	Player	Goaltender	Scored	Final Score	Series
Mar. 25/37	Lionel Conacher, Mtl. Maroons	Tiny Thompson, Boston	No	Mtl. M. 0 at Bos. 4	QF
Apr. 15/37	Alex Shibicky, NY Rangers	Earl Robertson, Detroit	No	NYR 0 at Det. 3	F
Mar. 24/38	Mush March, Chicago	Wilf Cude, Montreal	No	Mtl. 0 at Chi. 4	QF
Mar. 29/38	Lorne Carr, NY Americans	Mike Karakas, Chicago	No	Chi. 1 at NYA 3	SF
Apr. 10/38	Art Wiebe, Chicago	Turk Broda, Toronto	No	Tor. 1 at Chi. 2	F
Mar. 24/42	Charlie Sands, Montreal	Johnny Mowers, Detroit	No	Det. 0 at Mtl. 5	QF
Apr. 13/44	Virgil Johnson, Chicago	Bill Durnan, Montreal	No	Chi. 4 at Mtl. 5*	F
Apr. 9/68	Wayne Connelly, Minnesota	Terry Sawchuk, Los Angeles	Yes	L.A. 5 at Min. 7	QF
Apr. 27/68	Jim Roberts, St. Louis	Cesare Maniago, Minnesota	No	St.L. 4 at Min. 3	SF
May 16/71	Frank Mahovlich, Montreal	Tony Esposito, Chicago	No	Chi. 3 at Mtl. 4	F
May 7/75	Bill Barber, Philadelphia	Glenn Resch, NY Islanders	No	Phi. 3 at NYI 4*	SF
Apr. 20/79	Mike Walton, Chicago	Glenn Resch, NY Islanders	No	NYI 4 at Chi. 0	QF
Apr. 9/81	Peter McNab, Boston	Don Beaupre, Minnesota	No	Min. 5 at Bos. 4*	PR
Apr. 17/81	Anders Hedberg, NY Rangers	Mike Liut, St. Louis	Yes	NYR 6 at St.L. 4	QF
Apr. 9/83	Denis Potvin, NY Islanders	Pat Riggin, Washington	No	NYI 6 at Wsh. 2	DSF
Apr. 28/84	Wayne Gretzky, Edmonton	Don Beaupre, Minnesota	Yes	Edm. 8 at Min. 5	CF
May 1/84	Mats Naslund, Montreal	Billy Smith, NY Islanders	No	Mtl. 1 at NYI 3	CF
Apr. 14/85	Bob Carpenter, Washington	Billy Smith, NY Islanders	No	Wsh. 4 at NYI. 6	DF
May 28/85	Ron Sutter, Philadelphia	Grant Fuhr, Edmonton	No	Phi. 3 at Edm. 5	F
May 30/85	Dave Poulin, Philadelphia	Grant Fuhr, Edmonton	No	Phi. 3 at Edm. 8	F
Apr. 9/88	John Tucker, Buffalo	Andy Moog, Boston	Yes	Bos. 2 at Buf. 6	DSF
Apr. 9/88	Petr Klima, Detroit	Allan Bester, Toronto	Yes	Det. 6 at Tor. 3	DSF
Apr. 8/89	Neal Broten, Minnesota	Greg Millen, St. Louis	Yes	St.L. 5 at Min. 3	DSF
Apr. 4/90	Al MacInnis, Calgary	Kelly Hrudey, Los Angeles	Yes	L.A. 5 at Cgy. 3	DSF
Apr. 5/90	Randy Wood, NY Islanders	Mike Richter, NY Rangers	No	NYI 1 at NYR 2	DSF
May 3/90	Kelly Miller, Washington	Andy Moog, Boston	No	Wsh. 3 at Bos. 5	CF
May 18/90	Petr Klima, Edmonton	Reggie Lemelin, Boston	No	Edm. 7 at Bos. 2	F
Apr. 6/91	Basil McRae, Minnesota	Ed Belfour, Chicago	Yes	Min. 2 at Chi. 5	DSF
Apr. 10/91	Steve Duchesne, Los Angeles	Kirk McLean, Vancouver	Yes	L.A. 6 at Van. 1	DSF
May 11/92	Jaromir Jagr, Pittsburgh	John Vanbiesbrouck, NYR	Yes	Pit. 3 at NYR 2	DF
May 13/92	Shawn McEachern, Pittsburgh	John Vanbiesbrouck, NYR	No	NYR 1 at Pit. 5	DF
June 7/94	Pavel Bure, Vancouver	Mike Richter, NYR	No	NYR 4 at Van. 2	F
May 9/95	Patrick Poulin, Chicago	Felix Potvin, Toronto	No	Tor. 3 at Chi. 0	CQF
May 10/95	Michal Pivonka, Washington	Tom Barrasso, Pittsburgh	No	Pit. 2 at Wsh. 6	CQF
Apr. 24/96	Joe Juneau, Washington	Ken Wregget, Pittsburgh	No	Pit. 3 at Wsh. 2**	CQF
May 11/97	Eric Lindros, Philadelphia	Steve Shields, Buffalo	Yes	Phi. 6 at Buf. 3	CSF
Apr. 23/98	Aleksey Morozov, Pittsburgh	Andy Moog, Montreal	No	Mtl. 3 at Pit. 2**	CQF
Apr. 22/99	Mats Sundin, Toronto	John Vanbiesbrouck, Phi.	No	Phi. 3 at Tor. 0	CQF
May 29/99	Mats Sundin, Toronto	Dominik Hasek, Buffalo	Yes	Tor. 2 at Buf. 5	CF
Apr. 16/00	Eric Desjardins, Philadelphia	Dominik Hasek, Buffalo	No	Phi. 2 at Buf. 0	CQF
Apr. 11/01	Mark Recchi, Philadelphia	Dominik Hasek, Buffalo	No	Buf. 2 at Phi. 1	CQF
May 2/01	Martin Straka, Pittsburgh	Dominik Hasek, Buffalo	No	Buf. 5 at Pit. 2	CSF
May 12/01	Joe Sakic, Colorado	Roman Turek, St. Louis	Yes	St.L. 1 at Col. 4	CF
Apr. 21/02	Todd Bertuzzi, Vancouver	Dominik Hasek, Detroit	No	Det. 3 at Van. 1	CQF
Apr. 24/02	Shawn Bates, NY Islanders	Curtis Joseph, Toronto	Yes	Tor. 3 at NYI 4	CQF
Apr. 26/02	Mike Johnson, Phoenix	Evgeni Nabokov, San Jose	Yes	Phx. 1 at S.J. 4	CQF
Apr. 15/03	Dainius Zubrus, Washington	Nikolai Khabibulin, Tampa Bay	No	T.B. 4 at Wsh. 3	CQF
Apr. 21/03	Robert Reichel, Toronto	Roman Cechmanek, Philadelphia	No	Phi. 1 at Tor. 2	CQF
Apr. 7/04	Steve Sullivan, Nashville	Manny Legace, Detroit	No	Nsh. 1 at Det. 3	CQF
Apr. 28/06	Derek Roy, Buffalo	Robert Esche, Philadelphia	No	Buf. 4 at Phi. 5	CQF
June 5/06	Chris Pronger, Edmonton***	Cam Ward, Carolina	Yes	Edm. 4 at Car. 5	F
Apr. 21/07	Daniel Cleary, Detroit	Miikka Kiprusoff, Calgary	Yes	Cgy. 1 at Det. 5	CQF
June 5/07	Antoine Vermette, Ottawa	J.S. Giguere, Anaheim	No	Ott. 2 at Ana. 6	F

* Game was decided in overtime, but shot taken during regulation time.
** Shot taken in overtime.
*** First penalty shot scored in Stanley Cup Final history

There were two penalty shots during the 2007 playoffs. Detroit's Daniel Cleary scored on Calgary's Miikka Kiprusoff in the opening round. Ottawa's Antoine Vermette (above) was stopped by Jean-Sebastien Giguere during the Stanley Cup Final.

NHL Playoff Coaching Records

Coach	Team	Games Coached	Wins	Losses	Ties	Playoff Years	Cup Wins	Career
Abel, Sid	Chicago	7	3	4	0	1		
	Detroit	69	29	40	0	8		
	Total	76	32	44	0	9		1952-76
Adams, Jack	Detroit	105	52	52	1	15	3	1927-47
Allen, Keith	Philadelphia	11	3	8	0	2		1967-69
Arbour, Al	St. Louis	11	4	7	0	1		
	NY Islanders	198	119	79	0	15	4	
	Total	209	123	86	0	16	4	1970-94
Babcock, Mike	Anaheim	21	15	6	0	1		
	Detroit	24	12	12	0	2		
	Total	45	27	18	0	3		2002-07
Barber, Bill	Philadelphia	11	3	8	0	2		2000-02
Berenson, Red	St. Louis	14	5	9	0	2		1979-82
Bergeron, Michel	Quebec	68	31	37	0	7		1980-90
Berry, Bob	Los Angeles	10	2	8	0	3		
	Montreal	8	2	6	0	2		
	St. Louis	15	7	8	0	2		
	Total	33	11	22	0	7		1978-94
Beverley, Nick	Toronto	6	2	4	0	1		1995-96
Blackburn, Don	Hartford	3	0	3	0	1		1979-81
Blair, Wren	Minnesota	14	7	7	0	1		1967-70
Blake, Toe	Montreal	119	82	37	0	13	8	1955-68
Boileau, Marc	Pittsburgh	9	5	4	0	1		1973-76
Boivin, Leo	St. Louis	3	1	2	0	1		1975-78
Boucher, Frank	NY Rangers	27	13	14	0	4	1	1939-54
Boucher, Georges	Mtl. Maroons	2	0	2	0	1		1930-50
Bowman, Scotty	St. Louis	52	26	26	0	4		
	Montreal	98	70	28	0	8	5	
	Buffalo	36	18	18	0	5		
	Pittsburgh	33	23	10	0	2	1	
	Detroit	134	86	48	0	9	3	
	Total	353	223	130	0	28	9	1967-02
Bowness, Rick	Boston	15	8	7	0	1		1988-05
Brooks, Herb	NY Rangers	24	12	12	0	3		
	New Jersey	5	1	4	0	1		
	Pittsburgh	11	6	5	0	1		
	Total	40	19	21	0	5		1981-00
Brophy, John	Toronto	19	9	10	0	2		1986-89
Burns, Charlie	Minnesota	6	2	4	0	1		1969-75
Burns, Pat	Montreal	56	30	26	0	4		
	Toronto	46	23	23	0	3		
	Boston	18	8	10	0	3		
	New Jersey	29	17	12	0	2	1	
	Total	149	78	71	0	11	1	1988-05
Campbell, Colin	NY Rangers	36	18	18	0	3		1994-98
Carlyle, Randy	Anaheim	37	25	12	0	2	1	2005-07
Carpenter, Doug	Toronto	5	1	4	0	1		1984-91
Carroll, Dick	Toronto	7	4	3	0	1	1	1917-19
Cassidy, Bruce	Washington	6	2	4	0	1		2002-04
Cheevers, Gerry	Boston	34	15	19	0	4		1980-85
Cherry, Don	Boston	55	31	24	0	5		1974-80
Clancy, King	Toronto	14	2	12	0	3		1937-56
Clapper, Dit	Boston	25	8	17	0	4		1945-49
Cleghorn, Odie	Pittsburgh	4	1	2	1	2		1925-29
Cleghorn, Sprague	Mtl. Maroons	4	1	1	2	1		1931-32
Constantine, Kevin	San Jose	25	11	14	0	2		
	Pittsburgh	19	8	11	0	2		
	New Jersey	6	2	4	0	1		
	Total	50	21	29	0	5		1993-02
Crawford, Marc	Quebec	6	2	4	0	1		
	Colorado	46	29	17	0	3	1	
	Vancouver	31	12	19	0	4		
	Total	83	43	40	0	8	1	1994-07
Creighton, Fred	Atlanta	9	2	7	0	4		1974-80
Crisp, Terry	Calgary	37	22	15	0	3	1	
	Tampa Bay	6	2	4	0	1		
	Total	43	24	19	0	4	1	1987-98
Crozier, Joe	Buffalo	6	2	4	0	1		1971-81
Cunniff, John	New Jersey	6	2	4	0	1		1982-91
Curry, Alex	Ottawa	2	0	1	1	1		1925-26
Dandurand, Leo	Montreal	16	10	6	0	4	1	1921-35
Day, Hap	Toronto	80	49	31	0	9	5	1940-50
Demers, Jacques	St. Louis	33	16	17	0	3		
	Detroit	38	20	18	0	3		
	Montreal	27	19	8	0	2	1	
	Total	98	55	43	0	8	1	1979-99
Denneny, Cy	Boston	5	5	0	0	1	1	1928-33
Dudley, Rick	Buffalo	12	4	8	0	2		1989-04
Dugal, Jules	Montreal	3	1	2	0	1		1938-39
Duncan, Art	Toronto	2	0	1	1	1		1926-32
Dutton, Red	NY Americans	16	6	10	0	4		1935-42
Esposito, Phil	NY Rangers	10	2	8	0	2		1986-89
Evans, Jack	Hartford	16	8	8	0	2		1975-88
Ferguson, John	Winnipeg	3	0	3	0	1		1975-86
Francis, Bob	Phoenix	10	2	8	0	2		1999-04
Francis, Emile	NY Rangers	75	34	41	0	9		
	St. Louis	14	5	9	0	2		
	Total	89	39	50	0	11		1965-83
Ftorek, Robbie	Los Angeles	16	5	11	0	2		
	New Jersey	7	3	4	0	1		
	Boston	6	2	4	0	1		
	Total	29	10	19	0	4		1987-02
Gainey, Bob	Minnesota	30	17	13	0	2		
	Dallas	14	6	8	0	2		
	Montreal	6	2	4	0	1		
	Total	50	25	25	0	5		1990-06
Geoffrion, Bernie	Atlanta	4	0	4	0	1		1968-80
Gerard, Eddie	Mtl. Maroons	25	11	9	5	5	1	1917-35
Gill, David	Ottawa	8	3	2	3	2	1	1926-29
Glover, Fred	Oakland	11	3	8	0	2		1968-74
Gordon, Jackie	Minnesota	25	11	14	0	3		1970-75
Goring, Butch	Boston	3	0	3	0	1		1985-01
Gorman, Tommy	NY Americans	2	0	1	1	1		
	Chicago	8	6	1	1	1	1	
	Mtl. Maroons	15	7	6	2	3	1	
	Total	25	13	8	4	5	2	1925-38
Gottselig, Johnny	Chicago	4	0	4	0	1		1944-48
Granato, Tony	Colorado	18	9	9	0	2		2002-04
Green, Pete	Ottawa	26	14	9	3	6	3	1919-25
Green, Ted	Edmonton	16	8	8	0	1		1991-94
Guidolin, Bep	Boston	21	11	10	0	2		1972-76
Harris, Ted	Minnesota	2	0	2	0	1		1975-78
Hart, Cecil	Montreal	37	16	17	4	8	2	1926-39
Hartley, Bob	Colorado	80	49	31	0	4	1	
	Atlanta	4	0	0	0	1		
	Total	84	49	35	0	5	1	1998-07
Hartsburg, Craig	Chicago	16	8	8	0	2		
	Anaheim	4	0	4	0	1		
	Total	20	8	12	0	3		1995-01
Harvey, Doug	NY Rangers	6	2	4	0	1		1961-62
Hay, Don	Phoenix	7	3	4	0	1		1996-01
Henning, Lorne	Minnesota	5	2	3	0	1		1985-01
Hitchcock, Ken	Dallas	80	47	33	0	5	1	
	Philadelphia	37	19	18	0	3		
	Total	117	66	51	0	8	1	1995-07
Hlinka, Ivan	Pittsburgh	18	9	9	0	1		2000-02
Holmgren, Paul	Philadelphia	19	10	9	0	1		1988-96
Imlach, Punch	Toronto	92	44	48	0	11	4	1958-80
Inglis, Bill	Buffalo	3	1	2	0	1		1978-79
Irvin, Dick	Chicago	9	5	3	1	1		
	Toronto	66	33	32	1	9	1	
	Montreal	115	62	53	0	14	3	
	Total	190	100	88	2	24	4	1928-56
Ivan, Tommy	Detroit	67	36	31	0	7	3	1947-58
Johnson, Bob	Calgary	52	25	27	0	5		
	Pittsburgh	24	16	8	0	1	1	
	Total	76	41	35	0	6	1	1982-91
Johnson, Tom	Boston	22	15	7	0	2	1	1970-73
Johnston, Eddie	Chicago	7	3	4	0	1		
	Pittsburgh	46	22	24	0	5		
	Total	53	25	28	0	6		1979-97
Julien, Claude	Montreal	11	4	7	0	1		2002-07
Kasper, Steve	Boston	5	1	4	0	1		1995-97
Keenan, Mike	Philadelphia	57	32	25	0	4		
	Chicago	60	33	27	0	4		
	NY Rangers	23	16	7	0	1	1	
	St. Louis	20	10	10	0	2		
	Total	160	91	69	0	11	1	1984-04
Kelly, Pat	Colorado	2	0	2	0	1		1977-79
Kelly, Red	Los Angeles	18	7	11	0	2		
	Pittsburgh	14	6	8	0	2		
	Toronto	30	11	19	0	4		
	Total	62	24	38	0	8		1967-77
King, Dave	Calgary	20	8	12	0	3		1992-02
Kitchen, Mike	St. Louis	5	1	4	0	1		2003-07
Kromm, Bobby	Detroit	7	3	4	0	1		1977-80
Lalonde, Newsy	Montreal	16	7	6	3	4		
	Ottawa	2	0	1	1	1		
	Total	18	7	7	4	5		1917-35
Lamorello, Lou	New Jersey	20	10	10	0	2		2005-07
Laviolette, Peter	NY Islanders	12	4	8	0	2		
	Carolina	25	16	9	0	1	1	
	Total	37	20	17	0	3	1	2001-07
Lemaire, Jacques	Montreal	27	15	12	0	2		
	New Jersey	56	34	22	0	4	1	
	Minnesota	23	9	14	0	2		
	Total	106	58	48	0	8	1	1983-07
Lewis, Dave	Detroit	16	6	10	0	2		1999-07
Ley, Rick	Hartford	13	5	8	0	2		
	Vancouver	11	4	7	0	1		
	Total	24	9	15	0	3		1989-96
Long, Barry	Winnipeg	11	3	8	0	2		1983-86
Loughlin, Clem	Chicago	4	1	2	1	2		1934-37
Low, Ron	Edmonton	28	10	18	0	3		1994-02
Lowe, Kevin	Edmonton	5	1	4	0	1		1999-00
MacLean, Doug	Florida	27	13	14	0	2		1995-04

Coach	Team	Games Coached	Wins	Losses	Ties	Playoff Years	Cup Wins	Career
MacNeil, Al	Montreal	20	12	8	0	1	1	
	Atlanta	4	1	3	0	1		
	Calgary	19	9	10	0	2		
	Total	**43**	**22**	**21**	**0**	**4**	**1**	**1970-82**
MacTavish, Craig	**Edmonton**	**36**	**19**	**17**	**0**	**3**		**2000-07**
Magnuson, Keith	**Chicago**	**3**	**0**	**3**	**0**	**1**		**1980-82**
Mahoney, Bill	**Minnesota**	**16**	**7**	**9**	**0**	**1**		**1983-85**
Maloney, Dan	Toronto	10	6	4	0	1		
	Winnipeg	15	5	10	0	2		
	Total	**25**	**11**	**14**	**0**	**3**		**1984-89**
Maloney, Phil	**Vancouver**	**7**	**1**	**6**	**0**	**2**		**1973-77**
Martin, Jacques	St. Louis	16	7	9	0	2		
	Ottawa	69	31	38	0	8		
	Total	**85**	**38**	**47**	**0**	**10**		**1986-07**
Maurice, Paul	**Carolina**	**35**	**17**	**18**	**0**	**3**		**1995-07**
McCammon, Bob	Philadelphia	10	1	9	0	3		
	Vancouver	7	3	4	0	1		
	Total	**17**	**4**	**13**	**0**	**4**		**1978-91**
McLellan, John	**Toronto**	**11**	**3**	**8**	**0**	**2**		**1969-73**
McVie, Tom	**New Jersey**	**14**	**6**	**8**	**0**	**2**		**1975-92**
Melrose, Barry	**Los Angeles**	**24**	**13**	**11**	**0**	**1**		**1992-95**
Milbury, Mike	**Boston**	**40**	**23**	**17**	**0**	**2**		**1989-98**
Muckler, John	Edmonton	40	25	15	0	2	1	
	Buffalo	27	11	16	0	4		
	Total	**67**	**36**	**31**	**0**	**6**	**1**	**1968-00**
Muldoon, Pete	**Chicago**	**2**	**0**	**1**	**1**	**1**		**1926-27**
Munro, Dunc	**Mtl. Maroons**	**4**	**1**	**3**	**0**	**1**		**1929-31**
Murdoch, Bob	Chicago	5	1	4	0	1		
	Winnipeg	7	3	4	0	1		
	Total	**12**	**4**	**8**	**0**	**2**		**1987-91**
Murphy, Mike	**Los Angeles**	**5**	**1**	**4**	**0**	**1**		**1986-98**
Murray, Andy	**Los Angeles**	**24**	**10**	**14**	**0**	**3**		**1999-07**
Murray, Bryan	Washington	53	24	29	0	7		
	Detroit	25	10	15	0	3		
	Ottawa	30	18	12	0	2		
	Total	**108**	**52**	**56**	**0**	**12**		**1981-07**
Murray, Terry	Washington	39	18	21	0	4		
	Philadelphia	46	28	18	0	3		
	Florida	4	0	4	0	1		
	Total	**89**	**46**	**43**	**0**	**8**		**1989-01**
Neale, Harry	**Vancouver**	**14**	**3**	**11**	**0**	**4**		**1978-86**
Neilson, Roger	Toronto	19	8	11	0	2		
	Buffalo	8	4	4	0	1		
	Vancouver	21	12	9	0	2		
	NY Rangers	29	13	16	0	3		
	Philadelphia	29	14	15	0	3		
	Total	**106**	**51**	**55**	**0**	**11**		**1977-02**
Nolan, Ted	Buffalo	12	5	7	0	1		
	NY Islanders	5	1	4	0	1		
	Total	**17**	**6**	**11**	**0**	**2**		**1995-07**
Nykoluk, Mike	**Toronto**	**7**	**1**	**6**	**0**	**2**		**1980-84**
O'Connell, Mike	**Boston**	**5**	**1**	**4**	**0**	**1**		**2002-03**
O'Donoghue, George	**Toronto**	**7**	**4**	**2**	**1**	**1**	**1**	**1921-23**
O'Reilly, Terry	**Boston**	**37**	**17**	**19**	**1**	**3**		**1986-89**
Oliver, Murray	**Minnesota**	**13**	**5**	**8**	**0**	**2**		**1981-83**
Paddock, John	**Winnipeg**	**13**	**5**	**8**	**0**	**2**		**1991-95**
Page, Pierre	Minnesota	12	4	8	0	2		
	Quebec	6	2	4	0	1		
	Calgary	4	0	4	0	1		
	Total	**22**	**6**	**16**	**0**	**4**		**1988-98**
Patrick, Craig	NY Rangers	17	7	10	0	2		
	Pittsburgh	5	1	4	0	1		
	Total	**22**	**8**	**14**	**0**	**3**		**1980-97**
Patrick, Frank	**Boston**	**6**	**2**	**4**	**0**	**2**		**1934-36**
Patrick, Lester	**NY Rangers**	**65**	**32**	**26**	**7**	**12**	**2**	**1926-39**
Patrick, Lynn	NY Rangers	12	7	5	0	1		
	Boston	28	9	18	1	4		
	Total	**40**	**16**	**23**	**1**	**5**		**1948-76**
Perron, Jean	**Montreal**	**48**	**30**	**18**	**0**	**3**	**1**	**1985-89**
Perry, Don	**Los Angeles**	**10**	**4**	**6**	**0**	**1**		**1981-84**
Pilous, Rudy	**Chicago**	**41**	**19**	**22**	**0**	**5**	**1**	**1957-63**
Plager, Barclay	**St. Louis**	**4**	**1**	**3**	**0**	**1**		**1977-83**
Playfair, Jim	**Calgary**	**6**	**2**	**4**	**0**	**1**		**2006-07**
Pleau, Larry	**Hartford**	**10**	**2**	**8**	**0**	**2**		**1980-89**
Polano, Nick	**Detroit**	**7**	**1**	**6**	**0**	**2**		**1982-85**
Powers, Eddie	**Toronto**	**2**	**0**	**2**	**0**	**1**		**1924-26**
Primeau, Joe	**Toronto**	**15**	**8**	**6**	**1**	**2**	**1**	**1950-53**
Pronovost, Marcel	**Buffalo**	**8**	**3**	**5**	**0**	**1**		**1977-79**
Pulford, Bob	Los Angeles	26	10	16	0	4		
	Chicago	45	17	28	0	6		
	Total	**71**	**27**	**44**	**0**	**10**		**1972-00**
Quenneville, Joel	St. Louis	68	34	34	0	7		
	Colorado	9	4	5	0	1		
	Total	**77**	**38**	**39**	**0**	**8**		**1996-07**
Quinn, Pat	Philadelphia	39	22	17	0	3		
	Los Angeles	3	0	3	0	1		
	Vancouver	61	31	30	0	5		
	Toronto	80	41	39	0	6		
	Total	**183**	**94**	**89**	**0**	**15**		**1978-06**
Reay, Billy	**Chicago**	**116**	**56**	**60**	**0**	**12**		**1957-77**
Renney, Tom	**NY Rangers**	**14**	**6**	**8**	**0**	**2**		**1996-07**
Risebrough, Doug	**Calgary**	**7**	**3**	**4**	**0**	**1**		**1990-92**
Roberts, Jim	**Hartford**	**7**	**3**	**4**	**0**	**1**		**1981-97**
Robinson, Larry	Los Angeles	4	0	4	0	1		
	New Jersey	48	31	17	0	2	1	
	Total	**52**	**31**	**21**	**0**	**3**	**1**	**1995-06**
Ross, Art	**Boston**	**65**	**27**	**33**	**5**	**11**	**1**	**1917-45**
Ruel, Claude	**Montreal**	**27**	**18**	**9**	**0**	**3**	**1**	**1968-81**
Ruff, Lindy	**Buffalo**	**88**	**52**	**36**	**0**	**6**		**1997-07**
Sather, Glen	**Edmonton**	**127**	**89**	**37**	**1**	**10**	**4**	**1979-04**
Sator, Ted	NY Rangers	16	8	8	0	1		
	Buffalo	11	3	8	0	2		
	Total	**27**	**11**	**16**	**0**	**3**		**1985-89**
Schinkel, Ken	**Pittsburgh**	**6**	**2**	**4**	**0**	**2**		**1972-77**
Schmidt, Milt	**Boston**	**34**	**15**	**19**	**0**	**4**		**1954-76**
Schoenfeld, Jim	New Jersey	20	11	9	0	1		
	Washington	24	10	14	0	3		
	Phoenix	13	5	8	0	2		
	Total	**57**	**26**	**31**	**0**	**6**		**1985-99**
Shero, Fred	Philadelphia	83	48	35	0	6	2	
	NY Rangers	27	15	12	0	2		
	Total	**110**	**63**	**47**	**0**	**8**	**2**	**1971-81**
Simpson, Terry	NY Islanders	20	9	11	0	2		
	Winnipeg	6	2	4	0	1		
	Total	**26**	**11**	**15**	**0**	**3**		**1986-96**
Sinden, Harry	**Boston**	**43**	**24**	**19**	**0**	**5**	**1**	**1966-85**
Skinner, Jimmy	**Detroit**	**26**	**14**	**12**	**0**	**3**	**1**	**1954-58**
Smith, Alf	**Ottawa**	**5**	**1**	**4**	**0**	**1**		**1918-19**
Smith, Floyd	**Buffalo**	**32**	**16**	**16**	**0**	**3**		**1971-80**
Smythe, Conn	**Toronto**	**4**	**2**	**2**	**0**	**1**		**1927-31**
Sonmor, Glen	**Minnesota**	**43**	**25**	**18**	**0**	**3**		**1978-87**
Stasiuk, Vic	**Philadelphia**	**4**	**0**	**4**	**0**	**1**		**1969-73**
Stewart, Bill	**Chicago**	**10**	**7**	**3**	**0**	**1**	**1**	**1937-39**
Stewart, Ron	**Los Angeles**	**2**	**0**	**2**	**0**	**1**		**1975-78**
Stirling, Steve	**NY Islanders**	**5**	**1**	**4**	**0**	**1**		**2003-06**
Sullivan, Mike	**Boston**	**7**	**3**	**4**	**0**	**1**		**2003-06**
Sutter, Brian	St. Louis	41	20	21	0	4		
	Boston	22	7	15	0	3		
	Chicago	5	1	4	0	1		
	Total	**68**	**28**	**40**	**0**	**8**		**1988-05**
Sutter, Darryl	Chicago	26	11	15	0	3		
	San Jose	42	18	24	0	5		
	Calgary	33	18	15	0	2		
	Total	**101**	**47**	**54**	**0**	**10**		**1992-06**
Talbot, Jean-Guy	St. Louis	5	1	4	0	1		
	NY Rangers	3	1	2	0	1		
	Total	**8**	**2**	**6**	**0**	**2**		**1972-78**
Tessier, Orval	**Chicago**	**18**	**9**	**9**	**0**	**2**		**1982-85**
Therrien, Michel	Montreal	12	6	6	0	1		
	Pittsburgh	5	1	4	0	1		
	Total	**17**	**7**	**10**	**0**	**2**		**2000-07**
Thompson, Paul	**Chicago**	**19**	**7**	**12**	**0**	**4**		**1938-45**
Tippett, Dave	**Dallas**	**29**	**11**	**18**	**0**	**4**		**2002-07**
Tobin, Bill	**Chicago**	**4**	**1**	**2**	**1**	**2**		**1929-32**
Tortorella, John	**Tampa Bay**	**45**	**24**	**21**	**0**	**4**	**1**	**1999-07**
Tremblay, Mario	**Montreal**	**11**	**3**	**8**	**0**	**2**		**1995-97**
Trotz, Barry	**Nashville**	**16**	**4**	**12**	**0**	**3**		**1998-07**
Ubriaco, Gene	**Pittsburgh**	**11**	**7**	**4**	**0**	**1**		**1988-90**
Vigneault, Alain	Montreal	10	4	6	0	1		
	Vancouver	12	5	7	0	1		
	Total	**22**	**9**	**13**	**0**	**2**		**1997-07**
Watson, Phil	**NY Rangers**	**16**	**4**	**12**	**0**	**3**		**1955-63**
Watt, Tom	Winnipeg	7	1	6	0	2		
	Vancouver	3	0	3	0	1		
	Total	**10**	**1**	**9**	**0**	**3**		**1981-92**
Webster, Tom	**Los Angeles**	**28**	**12**	**16**	**0**	**3**		**1986-92**
Weiland, Cooney	**Boston**	**17**	**10**	**7**	**0**	**2**	**1**	**1939-41**
White, Bill	**Chicago**	**2**	**0**	**2**	**0**	**1**		**1976-77**
Wilson, Johnny	**Pittsburgh**	**12**	**4**	**8**	**0**	**2**		**1969-80**
Wilson, Ron	Anaheim	11	4	7	0	1		
	Washington	32	15	17	0	3		
	San Jose	39	22	17	0	3		
	Total	**82**	**41**	**41**	**0**	**7**		**1993-07**
Young, Garry	**St. Louis**	**2**	**0**	**2**	**0**	**1**		**1972-76**

Key to Prospect, NHL Player and Goaltender Registers

Demographics: Position, shooting side (catching hand for goaltenders), height, weight, place and date of birth as well as draft information, if any, is located on this line.

Major and tier-II junior, NCAA, minor pro, European and NHL clubs form a permanent part of each player's data panel. If a player sees action with more than one club in any of the above categories, a separate line is included for each one.

Olympic Team statistics are also listed.

Player's NHL organization as of August 14, 2007. This includes players under contract, unsigned draft choices and other players on reserve lists. Free agents as of this date show a blank here.

The complete career data panels of players with NHL experience who announced their retirement before the start of the 2007-08 season are included in the Player Register and Golatender Register.

These newly-retired players also show a blank here.

Each NHL club's minor-pro affiliates are listed on page 14.

PRONGER, Chris (PRAHN-guhr, KRIHS) **ANA.**

Defense. Shoots left. 6'6", 220 lbs. Born, Dryden, Ont., October 10, 1974. Hartford's 1st choice, 2nd overall, in 1993 Entry Draft.

Season	Club	League	Regular Season GP	G	A	Pts	PIM	PP	SH	GW	S	%	+/-	TF	F%	Min	Playoffs GP	G	A	Pts	PIM	PP	SH	GW	Min
1990-91	Stratford Cullitons	OHA-B	48	15	37	52	132	....	....	....	....	....	....	....	....	....	....	....	....	....	....	....	....	....	....
1991-92	Peterborough	OHL	63	17	45	62	90	....	....	....	....	....	....	....	....	....	10	1	8	9	28	....	....	....	....
1992-93	Peterborough	OHL	61	15	62	77	108	....	....	....	....	....	....	....	....	....	21	15	25	40	51	....	....	....	....
1993-94	**Hartford**	**NHL**	**81**	**5**	**25**	**30**	**113**	**2**	**0**	**0**	**174**	**2.9**	**–3**	....	....	....	....	....	....	....	....	....	....	....	....
1994-95	**Hartford**	**NHL**	**43**	**5**	**9**	**14**	**54**	**3**	**0**	**1**	**94**	**5.3**	**–12**	....	....	....	....	....	....	....	....	....	....	....	....
1995-96	**St. Louis**	**NHL**	**78**	**7**	**18**	**25**	**110**	**3**	**1**	**1**	**138**	**5.1**	**–18**	....	....	....	**13**	**1**	**5**	**6**	[illegible]	**0**	**0**	**0**	....
1996-97	**St. Louis**	**NHL**	**79**	**11**	**24**	**35**	**143**	**4**	**0**	**0**	**147**	**7.5**	**15**	....	....	....	**6**	**1**	**1**	**2**	[illegible]	**0**	**0**	**0**	....
1997-98	**St. Louis**	**NHL**	**81**	**9**	**27**	**36**	**180**	**1**	**0**	**2**	**145**	**6.2**	**47**	....	....	....	**10**	**1**	**9**	**10**	[illegible]	**0**	**0**	**0**	....
	Canada	Olympics	6	0	0	0	4	....	....	....	....	....	....	....	....	....	....	....	....	....	....	....	....	....	....
1998-99	**St. Louis**	**NHL**	**67**	**13**	**33**	**46**	**113**	**8**	**0**	**0**	**172**	**7.6**	**3**	**0**	**0.0**	**30:36**	**13**	**1**	**4**	**5**	[illegible]	**1**	**0**	**0**	**35:53**
99-2000	**St. Louis**	**NHL**	**79**	**14**	**48**	**62**	**92**	**8**	**0**	**3**	**192**	**7.3**	***52**	**1**	**0.0**	**30:14**	**7**	**3**	**4**	**7**	**32**	**2**	**0**	**2**	**30:14**
2000-01	**St. Louis**	**NHL**	**51**	**8**	**39**	**47**	**75**	**4**	**0**	**0**	**121**	**6.6**	**21**	**0**	**0.0**	**27:45**	**15**	**1**	**7**	**8**	**32**	**0**	**0**	**0**	**33:50**
2001-02	**St. Louis**	**NHL**	**78**	**7**	**40**	**47**	**120**	**4**	**1**	**3**	**204**	**3.4**	[illegible]	**0**	**0.0**	**29:28**	**9**	**1**	**7**	**8**	**24**	**0**	**0**	**0**	**27:51**
	Canada	Olympics	6	0	1	1	2	....	....	....	....	....	....	....	....	....	....	....	....	....	....	....	....	....	....
2002-03	**St. Louis**	**NHL**	**5**	**1**	**3**	**4**	**10**	**0**	**0**	**0**	**11**	**9.1**	[illegible]	**1**	**0.0**	**21:39**	**7**	**1**	**3**	**4**	**14**	**0**	**0**	**0**	**24:36**
2003-04	**St. Louis**	**NHL**	**80**	**14**	**40**	**54**	**88**	**7**	**0**	**3**	**203**	**6.9**	[illegible]	**2**	**0.0**	**27:28**	**5**	**0**	**1**	**1**	**16**	**0**	**0**	**0**	**27:54**
2004-05			DID NOT PLAY																						
2005-06	**Edmonton**	**NHL**	**80**	**12**	**44**	**56**	**74**	**10**	**0**	**3**	**155**	**7.7**	**2**	**1**	**0.0**	**27:59**	**24**	**5**	**16**	**21**	**26**	[illegible]	**0**	**0**	**30:57**
	Canada	Olympics	6	1	[illegible]	3	16	....	....	....	....	....	....	....	....	....	....	....	....	....	....	....	....	....	....
2006-07 ♦	**Anaheim**	**NHL**	**66**	**13**	**46**	**59**	**69**	**8**	**0**	**2**	**166**	**7.8**	**27**	**4**	**25.0**	**27:06**	**19**	**3**	**12**	**15**	**26**	[illegible]	**0**	**0**	**30:11**
	NHL Totals		**868**	**119**	**396**	[illegible]	**1241**	**62**	**2**	**18**	**1922**	**6.2**		**9**	**11.1**	**28:38**	**128**	**18**	**69**	**87**	**262**	[illegible]	**0**	**2**	**30:57**

OHL All-Rookie Team (1992) • OHL First All-Star Team (1993) • Canadian Major Junior First All-Star Team (1993) • Canadian Major Junior Defenseman of the Year (1993) • NHL All-Rookie Team (1994) • NHL Second All-Star Team (1998, 2004, 2007) • Bud Ice Plus/Minus Award (1998) • NHL First All-Star Team (2000) • Bud Light Plus/Minus Award (2000) • James Norris Memorial Trophy (2000) • Hart Memorial Trophy (2000)

Played in NHL All-Star Game (1999, 2000, 2002, 2004)

Traded to **St. Louis** by **Hartford** for Brendan Shanahan, July 27, 1995. • Missed majority of 2002-03 season recovering from wrist and knee surgery, September 10, 2002. Traded to **Edmonton** by **St. Louis** for Eric Brewer, Doug Lynch and Jeff Woywitka, August 2, 2005. Traded to **Anaheim** by **Edmonton** for Joffrey Lupul, Ladislav Smid, Anaheim's 1st round choice (later traded to Phoenix - Phoenix selected Nick Ross) in 2007 Entry Draft and Anaheim's 1st round choice in 2008 Entry Draft, July 3, 2006.

Diamond (♦) indicates member of Stanley Cup-winning team.

"Did not play" Indicates that a player did not participate in a professional, junior or college league for an entire season.

Asterisk (*) indicates league leader in this statistical category.

All trades, free agent signings and other transactions involving NHL clubs are listed in chronological order. First draft selection for players who re-enter the NHL Entry Draft is noted here. Other special notes are also listed here. These are highlighted with a bullet (•).

Dates for trades or free agent signings often differ depending upon source. Signings can be reported based on when contracts are filed with NHL Central Registry or on the date a club announces that it has made a trade or come to terms with a free agent.

All-Star Team selections and awards are listed below player's year-by-year data.

NHL All-Star Game appearances are listed above trade notes.

THIS 76TH EDITION OF THE *NHL Official Guide & Record Book* is the ninth to include additional statistical categories for forwards and defensemen in the National Hockey League. These categories are, from left to right in the sample panel above, power-play goals (PP), shorthand goals (SH), game-winning goals (GW), shots on goal (S), percentage of shots that score (%), plus-minus rating (+/–), total faceoffs taken (TF), faceoff winning percentage (F%), and average time-on-ice per game played (Min).

To integrate this data, the Player Register has been is split into two sections. The Prospect Register presents data on players who have yet to play in the NHL. The NHL Player Register, containing more information and a photo of each player, lists all active players who have appeared in an NHL regular-season or playoff game at any time.

Goaltenders, whether prospects or active NHLers, are included in one register. With the addition of the shootout to NHL regular-season play, the column formerly used to record tie games for goaltenders has been renamed "O/T." For NHL goaltenders beginning in 2005-06, it lists overtime losses and shootout losses; previous to 2005-06, it lists tie games.

Registers (with their starting page) are presented in the following order: Prospects (271), NHL Players (343), Goaltenders (581), Retired Players (606) and Retired Goaltenders (643).

League abbreviations, page 654. Late additions to the Registers, page 605.

Some information is unavailable at press time. Readers are encouraged to contribute. See page 5 for contact names and addresses.

Pronunciation of Player Names

United Press International phonetic style.

AY	long A as in mate
A	short A as in cat
AI	nasal A as on air
AH	short A as in father
AW	broad A as in talk
EE	long E as in meat
EH	short E as in get
UH	hollow E as in the
AY	French long E with acute accent as in Pathe
IH	middle E as in pretty
EW	EW dipthong as in few
IGH	long I as in time
EE	French long I as in machine
IH	short I as in pity
OH	long O as in note
AH	short O as in hot
AW	broad O as in fought
OI	OI dipthong as in noise
OO	long double OO as in fool
U	short double O as in foot
OW	OW dipthong as in how
EW	long U as in mule
OO	long U as in rule
U	middle U as in put
UH	short U as in shut or hurt
K	hard C as in cat
S	soft C as in cease
SH	soft CH as in machine
CH	hard CH or TCH as in catch
Z	hard S as in bells
S	soft S as in sun
G	hard G as in gang
J	soft G as in general
ZH	soft J as in French version of Joliet
KH	gutteral CH as in Scottish version of Loch

2007-08 Prospect Register

Note: The 2007-08 Prospect Register lists forwards and defensemen only. Goaltenders are listed separately. The Prospect Register lists every player drafted in the 2007 Entry Draft, players on NHL Reserve Lists and other players who have not yet played in the NHL. Trades and roster changes are current as of August 14, 2007.

Abbreviations: A – assists; **G** – goals; **GP** – games played; **PIM** – penalties in minutes; **Pts** – points; ***** – league-leading total.

NHL Player Register begins on page 343.
Goaltender Register begins on page 581.
League Abbreviations are listed on page 654.

ABDELKADER, Justin (abdehl-KAY-duhr, JUHS-tihn) DET.

Left wing. Shoots left. 6'1", 195 lbs. Born, Muskegon, MI, February 25, 1987.
(Detroit's 2nd choice, 42nd overall, in 2005 Entry Draft).

			Regular Season					Playoffs				
Season	Club	League	GP	G	A	Pts	PIM	GP	G	A	Pts	PIM
2003-04	Muskegon M.S.	High-MI	28	37	43	80	....	....	....	....	....	....
2004-05	Cedar Rapids	USHL	60	27	25	52	86	11	0	4	4	8
2005-06	Michigan State	CCHA	44	10	12	22	83	....	....	....	....	....
2006-07	Michigan State	CCHA	38	15	18	33	91	....	....	....	....	....

NCAA Championship All-Tournament Team (2007) • NCAA Championship Tournament MVP (2007)

AHNELOV, Jonas (AH-neh-lawv, YOH-nuhs) PHX.

Defense. Shoots left. 6'3", 205 lbs. Born, Huddinge, Sweden, December 11, 1987.
(Phoenix's 3rd choice, 88th overall, in 2006 Entry Draft).

			Regular Season					Playoffs				
Season	Club	League	GP	G	A	Pts	PIM	GP	G	A	Pts	PIM
2003-04	Huddinge IK U18	Swe-U18	6	0	3	3	8	....	....	....	....	....
	Huddinge IK Jr.	Swe-Jr.	9	0	1	1	6	....	....	....	....	....
2004-05	Huddinge IK U18	Swe-U18	2	0	0	0	2	....	....	....	....	....
	Huddinge IK Jr.	Swe-Jr.	29	3	3	6	94	3	0	0	0	2
2005-06	Frolunda Jr.	Swe-Jr.	29	4	11	15	84	7	2	4	6	22
	Frolunda	Sweden	15	0	0	0	2	....	....	....	....	....
2006-07	Frolunda Jr.	Swe-Jr.	9	4	5	9	22	8	2	3	5	8
	Frolunda	Sweden	46	1	3	4	20	....	....	....	....	....

AIELLO, Anthony (igh-EHL-oh, AN-thu-nee) MIN.

Defense. Shoots left. 6'1", 187 lbs. Born, Braintree, MA, May 19, 1986.
(Minnesota's 6th choice, 129th overall, in 2005 Entry Draft).

			Regular Season					Playoffs				
Season	Club	League	GP	G	A	Pts	PIM	GP	G	A	Pts	PIM
2003-04	Thayer Academy	High-MA	33	11	26	37	....	....	....	....	....	....
2004-05	Thayer Academy	High-MA	30	7	27	34	42	....	....	....	....	....
2005-06	Boston College	H-East	40	1	8	9	50	....	....	....	....	....
2006-07	Boston College	H-East	22	1	8	9	24	....	....	....	....	....

ALBERS, Paul (AL-buhrs, PAWL) MIN.

Defense. Shoots left. 6'1", 189 lbs. Born, Melville, Sask., October 15, 1985.

			Regular Season					Playoffs				
Season	Club	League	GP	G	A	Pts	PIM	GP	G	A	Pts	PIM
2001-02	Calgary Hitmen	WHL	54	1	5	6	32	7	0	0	0	6
2002-03	Calgary Hitmen	WHL	72	4	20	24	51	5	0	0	0	0
2003-04	Calgary Hitmen	WHL	8	0	1	1	6	....	....	....	....	....
	Regina Pats	WHL	54	5	18	23	30	4	0	0	0	2
2004-05	Regina Pats	WHL	23	0	4	4	6	....	....	....	....	....
	Vancouver Giants	WHL	48	4	19	23	42	6	2	3	5	0
2005-06	Vancouver Giants	WHL	70	17	45	62	33	18	3	*16	19	8
2006-07	Houston Aeros	AHL	5	0	0	0	2	....	....	....	....	....
	Texas Wildcatters	ECHL	68	12	31	43	32	9	1	5	6	8

WHL West First All-Star Team (2006) • Memorial Cup Tournament All-Star Team (2006) • ECHL All-Rookie Team (2007)

Signed as a free agent by **Minnesota**, July 5, 2006.

ALBERT, John (AL-buhrt, JAWN) ATL.

Center. Shoots left. 5'10", 180 lbs. Born, Cleveland, OH, January 19, 1989.
(Atlanta's 3rd choice, 175th overall, in 2007 Entry Draft).

			Regular Season					Playoffs				
Season	Club	League	GP	G	A	Pts	PIM	GP	G	A	Pts	PIM
2004-05	Cleveland Barons	MWEHL	67	34	60	94	....	....	....	....	....	....
	Cleveland Barons	NAHL	3	0	0	0	0	....	....	....	....	....
2005-06	USNTDP	U-17	19	8	15	23	25	....	....	....	....	....
	USNTDP	NAHL	36	8	15	23	23	....	....	....	....	....
2006-07	USNTDP	U-18	41	8	16	24	10	....	....	....	....	....
	USNTDP	NAHL	15	4	9	13	4	....	....	....	....	....

ALCEN, Johan (AL-sehn, YOH-hahn) COL.

Right wing. Shoots left. 6'1", 189 lbs. Born, Sandviken, Sweden, March 11, 1988.
(Colorado's 9th choice, 195th overall, in 2007 Entry Draft).

			Regular Season					Playoffs				
Season	Club	League	GP	G	A	Pts	PIM	GP	G	A	Pts	PIM
2003-04	Sandvikens IK	Sweden-4	STATISTICS NOT AVAILABLE									
2004-05	Brynas IF Gavle Jr.	Swe-Jr.	30	9	12	21	16	....	....	....	....	....
2005-06	Brynas U18	Swe-U18	2	1	3	4	4	....	....	....	....	....
	Brynas IF Gavle Jr.	Swe-Jr.	39	16	19	35	48	2	0	2	2	0
	Brynas IF Gavle	Sweden	3	0	0	0	0	....	....	....	....	....
2006-07	Brynas IF Gavle Jr.	Swe-Jr.	26	17	29	46	46	4	1	1	2	0
	IFK Arboga IK	Sweden-2	2	0	0	0	2	....	....	....	....	....
	Brynas IF Gavle	Sweden	32	0	0	0	0	1	0	0	0	0

ALEN, Juha (AL-ehn, YOO-haw) VAN.

Defense. Shoots left. 6'3", 218 lbs. Born, Tampere, Finland, October 25, 1981.
(Anaheim's 4th choice, 90th overall, in 2003 Entry Draft).

			Regular Season					Playoffs				
Season	Club	League	GP	G	A	Pts	PIM	GP	G	A	Pts	PIM
1998-99	KooVee Jr.	Fin-Jr.	36	6	7	13	42	....	....	....	....	....
99-2000	KooVee Jr.	Fin-Jr.	22	2	4	6	28	....	....	....	....	....
2000-01	Ilves Tampere Jr.	Fin-Jr.	42	2	12	14	62	....	....	....	....	....
2001-02	Soo Indians	NAHL	54	10	10	20	46	2	0	1	1	0
2002-03	Northern Mich.	CCHA	40	4	19	23	64	....	....	....	....	....
2003-04	Cincinnati	AHL	59	2	3	5	64	9	0	0	0	14
2004-05	Ilves Tampere	Finland	7	0	0	0	16	2	0	0	0	0
2005-06	Ilves Tampere	Finland	52	5	5	10	104	4	0	0	0	6
2006-07	Ilves Tampere	Finland	27	4	4	8	42	....	....	....	....	....
	Blues Espoo	Finland	12	0	0	0	4	....	....	....	....	....

• Missed majority of 2004-05 season recovering from off-season foot injury. Traded to **Vancouver** by **Anaheim** with Keith Carney for Brett Skinner and NY Islanders' 2nd round choice (previously acquired - Anaheim selected Bryce Swan) in 2006 Entry Draft, March 9, 2006.

ALEXANDROV, Viktor (al-ehx-AN-drawv, VIHK-tohr) ST.L.

Left wing. Shoots left. 5'11", 183 lbs. Born, Ust-Kamenogorsk, USSR, December 28, 1985.
(St. Louis' 3rd choice, 83rd overall, in 2004 Entry Draft).

			Regular Season					Playoffs				
Season	Club	League	GP	G	A	Pts	PIM	GP	G	A	Pts	PIM
2001-02	Ust-Kamenogorsk	Russia-2	45	12	17	29	48	2	0	1	1	2
2002-03	Yaroslavl	Russia	2	0	0	0	2	....	....	....	....	....
	Energiya Kemerovo	Russia-2	15	2	4	6	12	....	....	....	....	....
	Novokuznetsk	Russia	11	0	0	0	4	....	....	....	....	....
2003-04	Novokuznetsk	Russia	57	5	4	9	26	4	1	1	2	4
2004-05	Novokuznetsk	Russia	50	8	10	18	16	4	1	1	2	0
2005-06	SKA St. Petersburg	Russia	41	4	6	10	55	....	....	....	....	....
	St. Petersburg 2	Russia-3	1	0	3	3	0	....	....	....	....	....
2006-07	SKA St. Petersburg	Russia	19	1	10	11	18	....	....	....	....	....
	St. Petersburg 2	Russia-3	5	2	7	9	12	....	....	....	....	....
	MVD	Russia	20	2	6	8	8	2	0	2	2	2

ALEXANDROV, Yuri (al-ehx-AN-drawv, YOO-ree) BOS.

Defense. Shoots left. 6', 185 lbs. Born, Cherepovets, USSR, June 24, 1988.
(Boston's 2nd choice, 37th overall, in 2006 Entry Draft).

			Regular Season					Playoffs				
Season	Club	League	GP	G	A	Pts	PIM	GP	G	A	Pts	PIM
2003-04	Cherepovets 2	Russia-3	32	0	2	2	10	4	0	0	0	0
2004-05	Cherepovets 2	Russia-3	STATISTICS NOT AVAILABLE									
2005-06	Cherepovets	Russia	37	1	0	1	18	2	0	0	0	2
2006-07	Cherepovets	Russia	45	1	1	2	38	5	0	0	0	8

ALIU, Akim (a-LEE-00, A-kihm) CHI.

Center. Shoots right. 6'2", 200 lbs. Born, Okene, Nigeria, April 24, 1989.
(Chicago's 3rd choice, 56th overall, in 2007 Entry Draft).

			Regular Season					Playoffs				
Season	Club	League	GP	G	A	Pts	PIM	GP	G	A	Pts	PIM
2004-05	Toronto Marlboros	GTHL	68	35	50	85	197	....	....	....	....	....
2005-06	Windsor Spitfires	OHL	18	3	4	7	25	....	....	....	....	....
	Sudbury Wolves	OHL	29	7	6	13	54	6	0	1	1	7
2006-07	Sudbury Wolves	OHL	53	20	22	42	104	21	1	5	6	50

ALLARD, Jean-Simon (a-LAHR, ZHAWN-SEE-mohn) BUF.

Center. Shoots right. 6'2", 195 lbs. Born, St. Bruno, Que., May 24, 1989.
(Buffalo's 5th choice, 147th overall, in 2007 Entry Draft).

			Regular Season					Playoffs				
Season	Club	League	GP	G	A	Pts	PIM	GP	G	A	Pts	PIM
2004-05	Jonquiere Elites	QAAA	40	19	18	37	30	10	4	13	17	0
2005-06	St. John's	QMJHL	65	4	13	17	34	5	0	0	0	2
2006-07	St. John's	QMJHL	69	12	38	50	47	4	0	1	1	4

ALMOND, Cody (al-MUHND, KOH-dee) MIN.

Center. Shoots left. 6'2", 199 lbs. Born, Calgary, Alta., July 24, 1989.
(Minnesota's 3rd choice, 140th overall, in 2007 Entry Draft).

			Regular Season					Playoffs				
Season	Club	League	GP	G	A	Pts	PIM	GP	G	A	Pts	PIM
2004-05	Cgy. Stampeders	SAMHL	30	28	15	43	108	....	....	....	....	....
2005-06	Kelowna Rockets	WHL	23	2	1	3	7	8	0	0	0	0
2006-07	Kelowna Rockets	WHL	68	15	28	43	72	....	....	....	....	....

ALMTORP, Jonas (AHLM-tohrp, YOH-nuhs) EDM.

Center. Shoots left. 6'1", 189 lbs. Born, Uppsala, Sweden, November 17, 1983.
(Edmonton's 7th choice, 111th overall, in 2002 Entry Draft).

			Regular Season					Playoffs				
Season	Club	League	GP	G	A	Pts	PIM	GP	G	A	Pts	PIM
99-2000	MoDo U18	Swe-U18	22	*19	12	31	*55	....	....	....	....	....
	Malmo Jr.	Swe-Jr.	7	1	0	1	0	....	....	....	....	....
2000-01	MoDo U18	Swe-U18	12	11	1	12	30	....	....	....	....	....
	Malmo Jr.	Swe-Jr.	27	19	7	26	38	7	6	1	7	10
2001-02	MODO	Sweden	3	0	0	0	0	....	....	....	....	....
	Malmo Jr.	Swe-Jr.	37	26	18	44	102	2	1	1	2	4
2002-03	MODO	Sweden	28	1	1	2	22	....	....	....	....	....
	Ornskoldsviks SK	Sweden-2	12	5	4	9	49	....	....	....	....	....
	Malmo Jr.	Swe-Jr.	5	2	2	4	12	....	....	....	....	....
2003-04	Sundsvall	Sweden-2	32	9	9	18	65	....	....	....	....	....
	MODO	Sweden	20	0	0	0	4	3	0	0	0	0
	Malmo Jr.	Swe-Jr.	3	0	0	0	14	....	....	....	....	....
2004-05	Brynas IF Gavle	Sweden	3	0	0	0	0	....	....	....	....	....
	Almtuna	Sweden-2	44	16	20	36	56	3	0	3	3	2
2005-06	Brynas IF Gavle	Sweden	50	6	6	12	42	4	0	1	1	4
2006-07	Brynas IF Gavle	Sweden	46	4	7	11	30	7	2	0	2	6

ALZNER, Karl (ALZ-nuhr, KARL) WSH.

Defense. Shoots left. 6'2", 206 lbs. Born, Burnaby, B.C., September 24, 1988.
(Washington's 1st choice, 5th overall, in 2007 Entry Draft).

			Regular Season					Playoffs				
Season	Club	League	GP	G	A	Pts	PIM	GP	G	A	Pts	PIM
2003-04	Richmond	PIJHL	74	3	15	18	8	....	....	....	....	....
2004-05	Calgary Hitmen	WHL	66	0	10	10	19	12	0	3	3	9
2005-06	Calgary Hitmen	WHL	70	4	20	24	28	13	1	3	4	4
2006-07	Calgary Hitmen	WHL	63	8	39	47	32	18	1	12	13	4

WHL East Second All-Star Team (2007)

ANDERSEN, Niclas (AN-duhr-suhn, NIHK-luhs) L.A.

Defense. Shoots left. 6'1", 207 lbs. Born, Grums, Sweden, April 28, 1988.
(Los Angeles' 6th choice, 114th overall, in 2006 Entry Draft).

			Regular Season					Playoffs				
Season	Club	League	GP	G	A	Pts	PIM	GP	G	A	Pts	PIM
2003-04	Grums IK	Sweden-3	30	4	5	9	45	....	....	....	....	....
2004-05	Leksands IF Jr.	Swe-Jr.	26	3	2	5	91	5	0	2	2	2
2005-06	Leksands IF U18	Swe-U18	3	0	3	3	8	2	0	0	0	10
	Leksands IF Jr.	Swe-Jr.	36	5	6	11	214	....	....	....	....	....
	Leksands IF	Sweden-Q	3	0	0	0	2	....	....	....	....	....
	Leksands IF	Sweden	8	0	0	0	8	....	....	....	....	....
2006-07	Leksands IF Jr.	Swe-Jr.	4	1	1	2	47	....	....	....	....	....
	Leksands IF	Sweden-2	35	0	5	5	38	....	....	....	....	....

ANDERSON, R.J. (AN-duhr-suhn, AHR-JAY) PHI.

Defense. Shoots right. 5'11", 190 lbs. Born, Maple Wood, MN, July 16, 1986.
(Philadelphia's 2nd choice, 101st overall, in 2004 Entry Draft).

			Regular Season					Playoffs				
Season	Club	League	GP	G	A	Pts	PIM	GP	G	A	Pts	PIM
2002-03	Centennial	High-MN	24	6	35	41	10	....	....	....	....	....
2003-04	Centennial	High-MN	30	29	56	85	34	....	....	....	....	....
	Team Northeast	UMEHL	24	9	16	25	....	....	....	....	....	....
2004-05	Centennial	High-MN	28	23	36	59	....	....	....	....	....	....
2005-06	U. of Minnesota	WCHA	37	0	4	4	32	....	....	....	....	....
2006-07	U. of Minnesota	WCHA	32	0	6	6	20	....	....	....	....	....

ANDERSSON, Joakim (AN-duhr-suhn, YOH-ah-kihm) DET.

Center. Shoots left. 6'2", 198 lbs. Born, Munkedal, Sweden, February 5, 1989.
(Detroit's 2nd choice, 88th overall, in 2007 Entry Draft).

			Regular Season					Playoffs				
Season	Club	League	GP	G	A	Pts	PIM	GP	G	A	Pts	PIM
2004-05	Munkedals BK	Sweden-5	STATISTICS NOT AVAILABLE									
2005-06	Frolunda U18	Swe-U18	1	0	0	0	0	2	0	1	1	0
	Frolunda Jr.	Swe-Jr.	35	9	11	20	10	7	2	5	7	4
2006-07	Frolunda U18	Swe-U18	2	1	2	3	2	6	3	2	5	28
	Frolunda Jr.	Swe-Jr.	41	20	26	46	60	8	0	7	7	4
	Frolunda	Sweden	1	0	0	0	0	....	....	....	....	....

ANGELIDIS, Mike (AN-gehl-EE-dihs, MIGHK) CAR.

Left wing. Shoots left. 6'1", 210 lbs. Born, Woodbridge, Ont., June 27, 1985.

			Regular Season					Playoffs				
Season	Club	League	GP	G	A	Pts	PIM	GP	G	A	Pts	PIM
2002-03	Owen Sound	OHL	65	7	10	17	81	4	1	1	2	0
2003-04	Owen Sound	OHL	66	9	9	18	118	7	4	1	5	4
2004-05	Owen Sound	OHL	41	9	10	19	126	8	3	2	5	10
2005-06	Owen Sound	OHL	68	53	25	78	167	11	5	9	14	38
2006-07	Albany River Rats	AHL	27	4	5	9	44	4	0	0	0	10
	Florida Everblades	ECHL	24	10	8	18	54	....	....	....	....	....

OHL First All-Star Team (2006) • Canadian Major Junior Humanitarian Player of the Year (2006)

Signed as a free agent by **Carolina**, July 27, 2006.

ANIKEYENKO, Vitali (ah-nih-KEH-ehn-koh, vih-TAL-ee) OTT.

Defense. Shoots right. 6'3", 200 lbs. Born, Kiev, USSR, January 2, 1987.
(Ottawa's 2nd choice, 70th overall, in 2005 Entry Draft).

			Regular Season					Playoffs				
Season	Club	League	GP	G	A	Pts	PIM	GP	G	A	Pts	PIM
2003-04	Yaroslavl 2	Russia-3	40	2	9	11	68	....	....	....	....	....
2004-05	Yaroslavl 2	Russia-3	58	3	11	14	62	....	....	....	....	....
2005-06	Yaroslavl 2	Russia-3	19	3	5	8	20	....	....	....	....	....
	Yaroslavl	Russia	26	0	1	1	28	1	0	0	0	0
2006-07	Yaroslavl 2	Russia-3	15	1	6	7	59	....	....	....	....	....
	Yaroslavl	Russia	25	1	3	4	16	3	0	0	0	12

ANISIMOV, Artem (a-NEE-see-mawv, AHR-tehm) NYR

Center. Shoots left. 6'3", 187 lbs. Born, Yaroslavl, USSR, May 24, 1988.
(NY Rangers' 2nd choice, 54th overall, in 2006 Entry Draft).

			Regular Season					Playoffs				
Season	Club	League	GP	G	A	Pts	PIM	GP	G	A	Pts	PIM
2004-05	Yaroslavl 2	Russia-3	24	3	5	8	10	....	....	....	....	....
2005-06	Yaroslavl 2	Russia-3	32	15	12	27	28	....	....	....	....	....
	Yaroslavl	Russia	10	0	1	1	4	....	....	....	....	....
2006-07	Yaroslavl 2	Russia-3	2	2	0	2	0	....	....	....	....	....
	Yaroslavl	Russia	39	2	8	10	26	7	3	2	5	4

ANSHAKOV, Sergei (an-sha-KAHV, SAIR-gay) PIT.

Left wing. Shoots left. 6'3", 179 lbs. Born, Moscow, USSR, January 13, 1984.
(Los Angeles' 2nd choice, 50th overall, in 2002 Entry Draft).

			Regular Season					Playoffs				
Season	Club	League	GP	G	A	Pts	PIM	GP	G	A	Pts	PIM
2000-01	Dyn'o Moscow 18	Exhib.	6	7	1	8	2	....	....	....	....	....
2001-02	HK CSKA 2	Russia-3	3	3	1	4	0	....	....	....	....	....
	HK CSKA Moscow	Russia-2	46	20	12	22	10	....	....	....	....	....
2002-03	CSKA Moscow	Russia	25	1	2	3	4	....	....	....	....	....
2003-04	CSKA Moscow	Russia	33	3	2	5	12	....	....	....	....	....
2004-05	CSKA Moscow	Russia	11	0	0	0	2	....	....	....	....	....
	Ufa	Russia	23	9	3	12	4	....	....	....	....	....
2005-06	Ufa	Russia	6	1	1	2	12	....	....	....	....	....
	Dynamo Moscow	Russia	1	0	0	0	0	....	....	....	....	....
	HK MVD-THK Tver	Russia-3	1	2	0	2	0	....	....	....	....	....
	MVD	Russia	12	1	3	4	2	2	0	1	1	0
2006-07	CSKA Moscow	Russia	29	2	3	5	12	....	....	....	....	....
	Sibir Novosibirsk 2	Russia-3	2	2	1	3	0	....	....	....	....	....
	Sibir Novosibirsk	Russia	17	2	4	6	4	3	1	0	1	2

Traded to **Pittsburgh** by **Los Angeles** with Martin Strbak for Martin Straka, November 30, 2003.

ANTTILA, Marko (AN-tih-la, MAHR-koh) CHI.

Right wing. Shoots right. 6'7", 226 lbs. Born, Lempaala, Finland, May 27, 1985.
(Chicago's 17th choice, 260th overall, in 2004 Entry Draft).

			Regular Season					Playoffs				
Season	Club	League	GP	G	A	Pts	PIM	GP	G	A	Pts	PIM
2002-03	LeKi Lempaala U18	Fin-U18	11	17	8	25	41	....	....	....	....	....
2003-04	LeKi Lempaala Jr.	Fin-Jr.	12	11	11	22	26	....	....	....	....	....
	LeKi Lempaala	Finland-4	21	18	18	36	20	....	....	....	....	....
2004-05	Ilves Tampere Jr.	Fin-Jr.	27	14	6	20	44	9	5	7	12	14
	Ilves Tampere	Finland	28	2	1	3	10	3	0	0	0	0
2005-06	Ilves Tampere Jr.	Fin-Jr.	10	4	2	6	6	2	1	1	2	4
	Ilves Tampere	Finland	50	4	3	7	46	4	0	0	0	0
2006-07	Ilves Tampere	Finland	53	2	2	4	34	7	1	0	1	8

AQUINO, Luciano (a-KEE-noh, loo-chee-A-noh) NYI

Center/Left wing. Shoots left. 5'9", 198 lbs. Born, Mississauga, Ont., January 26, 1985.
(NY Islanders' 7th choice, 210th overall, in 2005 Entry Draft).

			Regular Season					Playoffs				
Season	Club	League	GP	G	A	Pts	PIM	GP	G	A	Pts	PIM
2003-04	U. of Maine	H-East	20	4	5	9	8	....	....	....	....	....
2004-05	Brampton	OHL	65	25	46	71	80	....	....	....	....	....
2005-06	Brampton	OHL	32	28	44	72	32	11	8	13	21	23
	Bridgeport	AHL	9	0	2	2	6	....	....	....	....	....
	Trenton Titans	ECHL	3	0	1	1	0	....	....	....	....	....
2006-07	Bridgeport	AHL	13	2	1	3	6	....	....	....	....	....
	Pensacola	ECHL	2	0	1	1	8	....	....	....	....	....
	Utah Grizzlies	ECHL	31	8	20	28	38	....	....	....	....	....

ARCHER, Andrew (AHR-chuhr, AN-droo) MTL.

Defense. Shoots right. 6'4", 213 lbs. Born, Calgary, Alta., May 15, 1983.
(Montreal's 7th choice, 203rd overall, in 2001 Entry Draft).

			Regular Season					Playoffs				
Season	Club	League	GP	G	A	Pts	PIM	GP	G	A	Pts	PIM
99-2000	Oshawa Generals	OHL	47	0	1	1	24	3	0	1	1	2
2000-01	Oshawa Generals	OHL	2	0	0	0	4	....	....	....	....	....
	Guelph Storm	OHL	50	0	2	2	59	4	0	0	0	4
2001-02	Guelph Storm	OHL	58	3	10	13	76	9	0	2	2	16
2002-03	Guelph Storm	OHL	65	2	16	18	138	11	2	2	4	18
2003-04	Hamilton Bulldogs	AHL	30	0	1	1	23	3	0	0	0	0
	Columbus	ECHL	6	0	1	1	19	....	....	....	....	....
2004-05	Hamilton Bulldogs	AHL	68	1	10	11	112	3	0	0	0	2
2005-06	Hamilton Bulldogs	AHL	42	0	3	3	62	....	....	....	....	....
2006-07	Hamilton Bulldogs	AHL	16	0	1	1	24	19	0	3	3	21

• Missed majority of 2003-04 season recovering from hernia injury suffered in training camp, September 15, 2003. • Missed majority of 2006-07 season recovering from off-season knee surgery.

ARDELAN, Mark (AHR-deh-lan, MAHRK) PIT.

Defense. Shoots left. 5'11", 202 lbs. Born, Regina, Sask., March 16, 1983.

			Regular Season					Playoffs				
Season	Club	League	GP	G	A	Pts	PIM	GP	G	A	Pts	PIM
99-2000	Brandon	WHL	63	4	16	20	60	....	....	....	....	....
2000-01	Brandon	WHL	66	2	14	16	65	6	0	1	1	9
2001-02	Vancouver Giants	WHL	66	8	29	37	50	....	....	....	....	....
2002-03	Vancouver Giants	WHL	71	13	35	48	64	4	0	1	1	0
2003-04	Prince Albert	WHL	72	19	54	73	29	6	1	4	5	0
2004-05	Portland Pirates	AHL	1	0	1	1	2	....	....	....	....	....
	South Carolina	ECHL	72	15	32	47	24	4	0	0	0	2
2005-06	Manchester	AHL	62	9	21	30	36	7	2	0	2	0
2006-07	Iowa Stars	AHL	79	8	30	38	32	11	0	5	5	4

Signed as a free agent by **Pittsburgh**, July 16, 2007.

ARMSTRONG, John (AHRM-stawng, JAWN) **CGY.**

Center. Shoots right. 6'2", 191 lbs. Born, Unionville, Ont., February 26, 1988.
(Calgary's 2nd choice, 87th overall, in 2006 Entry Draft).

			Regular Season					Playoffs				
Season	Club	League	GP	G	A	Pts	PIM	GP	G	A	Pts	PIM
2004-05	Plymouth Whalers	OHL	52	6	13	19	39	4	0	0	0	4
2005-06	Plymouth Whalers	OHL	65	14	23	37	75	13	4	7	11	18
2006-07	Plymouth Whalers	OHL	34	8	13	21	26	....	....	....	....	....
	Peterborough	OHL	27	11	13	24	34	....	....	....	....	....

ARMSTRONG, Riley (AHRM-stawng, RIGH-lee) **S.J.**

Right wing. Shoots right. 5'11", 185 lbs. Born, Saskatoon, Sask., November 8, 1984.

			Regular Season					Playoffs				
Season	Club	League	GP	G	A	Pts	PIM	GP	G	A	Pts	PIM
2001-02	Yorkton Terriers	SMHL	42	43	34	77	....	....	....	....	....	....
2002-03	Kootenay Ice	WHL	65	6	10	16	69	10	0	1	1	14
2003-04	Everett Silvertips	WHL	69	18	26	44	119	21	5	4	9	46
2004-05	Cleveland Barons	AHL	70	8	11	19	117	....	....	....	....	....
2005-06	Cleveland Barons	AHL	64	4	5	9	67	....	....	....	....	....
2006-07	Worcester Sharks	AHL	73	19	17	36	108	6	0	1	1	12

Signed as a free agent by **San Jose**, September 15, 2004.

ARSENE, Dean (ahr-SEH-nee, DEEN) **WSH.**

Defense. Shoots left. 6'2", 200 lbs. Born, Abbotsford, B.C., July 12, 1980.

			Regular Season					Playoffs				
Season	Club	League	GP	G	A	Pts	PIM	GP	G	A	Pts	PIM
1996-97	Regina Pats	WHL	62	0	8	8	53	3	0	0	0	2
1997-98	Regina Pats	WHL	31	2	7	9	47	....	....	....	....	....
	Edmonton Ice	WHL	43	0	12	12	90	....	....	....	....	....
1998-99	Kootenay Ice	WHL	68	1	4	5	111	4	0	0	0	4
99-2000	Kootenay Ice	WHL	66	4	7	11	150	21	1	2	3	59
2000-01	Kootenay Ice	WHL	68	1	10	11	178	11	0	1	1	34
2001-02	Charlotte	ECHL	63	3	10	13	101	5	0	2	2	16
2002-03	Hartford Wolf Pack	AHL	50	1	3	4	94	....	....	....	....	....
2003-04	Hershey Bears	AHL	22	0	2	2	44	....	....	....	....	....
	Reading Royals	ECHL	46	0	6	6	118	15	1	5	6	34
2004-05	Hershey Bears	AHL	56	1	5	6	140	....	....	....	....	....
2005-06	Hershey Bears	AHL	68	2	5	7	181	21	0	1	1	29
2006-07	Hershey Bears	AHL	61	3	12	15	187	6	0	2	2	8

Signed as a free agent by **Washington**, July 26, 2006.

ASTON, Peter (AS-tuhn, PEE-tuhr) **FLA.**

Defense. Shoots right. 6'1", 205 lbs. Born, Toronto, Ont., February 24, 1986.
(Florida's 5th choice, 155th overall, in 2006 Entry Draft).

			Regular Season					Playoffs				
Season	Club	League	GP	G	A	Pts	PIM	GP	G	A	Pts	PIM
2002-03	Pickering Panthers	OPJHL	45	4	20	24	52	....	....	....	....	....
2003-04	Peterborough	OHL	36	2	3	5	17	....	....	....	....	....
2004-05	Peterborough	OHL	52	0	15	15	16	14	0	4	4	6
2005-06	Peterborough	OHL	16	4	15	19	10	....	....	....	....	....
	Windsor Spitfires	OHL	49	12	21	33	21	7	2	1	3	2
2006-07	Assat Pori	Finland	21	2	1	3	14	....	....	....	....	....
	Oshawa Generals	OHL	41	8	24	32	38	9	1	7	8	8

ATYUSHOV, Vitali (a-tew-SHAWF, vih-TAL-ee) **OTT.**

Defense. Shoots left. 6'1", 205 lbs. Born, Penza, USSR, July 4, 1979.
(Ottawa's 8th choice, 276th overall, in 2002 Entry Draft).

			Regular Season					Playoffs				
Season	Club	League	GP	G	A	Pts	PIM	GP	G	A	Pts	PIM
1997-98	Krylja Sovetov	Russia	4	0	0	0	2	....	....	....	....	....
1998-99	Dizelist Penza 2	Russia-4	2	1	1	2	2	....	....	....	....	....
	Dizelist Penza	Russia-2	22	0	0	0	22	....	....	....	....	....
	Krylja Sovetov	Russia	17	1	0	1	20	....	....	....	....	....
	Krylja Sovetov	Russia-Q	21	0	5	5	50	....	....	....	....	....
99-2000	Perm	Russia	38	4	0	4	50	3	0	0	0	12
2000-01	Perm	Russia	44	3	9	12	32	....	....	....	....	....
2001-02	Perm	Russia	51	4	8	12	66	....	....	....	....	....
2002-03	Ak Bars Kazan	Russia	33	0	9	9	12	2	0	0	0	0
2003-04	Magnitogorsk	Russia	56	5	9	14	26	14	2	3	5	6
2004-05	Magnitogorsk	Russia	58	6	18	24	42	5	2	0	2	0
2005-06	Magnitogorsk	Russia	51	7	12	19	64	11	2	0	2	4
2006-07	Magnitogorsk	Russia	54	7	20	27	46	15	3	9	12	10

AUBIN, Brent (OH-behn, BREHNT) **TOR.**

Right wing. Shoots left. 5'9", 181 lbs. Born, St-Sophie, Que., June 18, 1986.

			Regular Season					Playoffs				
Season	Club	League	GP	G	A	Pts	PIM	GP	G	A	Pts	PIM
2002-03	Rouyn-Noranda	QMJHL	65	14	20	34	98	4	1	0	1	6
2003-04	Rouyn-Noranda	QMJHL	70	29	36	65	116	11	4	3	7	22
2004-05	Rouyn-Noranda	QMJHL	70	41	43	84	78	10	5	4	9	14
2005-06	Rouyn-Noranda	QMJHL	40	31	33	64	58	....	....	....	....	....
	Quebec Remparts	QMJHL	32	26	27	53	34	23	12	15	27	24
2006-07	Quebec Remparts	QMJHL	68	51	54	105	124	5	3	5	8	8
	Toronto Marlies	AHL	8	0	2	2	4	....	....	....	....	....

Signed as a free agent by **Toronto**, September 15, 2006.

AUBIN, Mathieu (oh-BEHN, MAT-yew) **MTL.**

Center. Shoots right. 6'2", 202 lbs. Born, Sorel, Que., September 18, 1986.
(Montreal's 4th choice, 130th overall, in 2005 Entry Draft).

			Regular Season					Playoffs				
Season	Club	League	GP	G	A	Pts	PIM	GP	G	A	Pts	PIM
2001-02	Antoine-Girouard	QAAA	19	5	10	15	10	....	....	....	....	....
2002-03	Antoine-Girouard	QAAA	42	19	35	54	28	....	....	....	....	....
	Sherbrooke	QMJHL	1	0	0	0	0	....	....	....	....	....
2003-04	Lewiston	QMJHL	68	19	23	42	34	7	1	1	2	2
2004-05	Lewiston	QMJHL	49	19	26	45	24	8	3	6	9	6
2005-06	Lewiston	QMJHL	70	47	56	103	63	6	3	4	7	4
2006-07	Hamilton Bulldogs	AHL	17	2	3	5	4	....	....	....	....	....
	Cincinnati	ECHL	38	12	25	37	32	10	4	5	9	10

AUFFREY, Matt (AWF-ree, MAT) **ANA.**

Right wing. Shoots right. 6'2", 214 lbs. Born, Cincinnati, OH, January 3, 1986.
(Anaheim's 5th choice, 172nd overall, in 2004 Entry Draft).

			Regular Season					Playoffs				
Season	Club	League	GP	G	A	Pts	PIM	GP	G	A	Pts	PIM
2001-02	Syracuse	OPJHL	....	33	39	72	....	....	....	....	....	....
2002-03	USNTDP	U-17	23	3	9	12	18	....	....	....	....	....
	USNTDP	NAHL	40	8	9	17	50	....	....	....	....	....
2003-04	USNTDP	U-18	44	13	14	27	....	....	....	....	....	....
	USNTDP	NAHL	10	1	2	3	8	....	....	....	....	....
2004-05	U. of Wisconsin	WCHA	25	3	5	8	18	....	....	....	....	....
2005-06	U. of Wisconsin	WCHA	1	0	0	0	0	....	....	....	....	....
	Kitchener Rangers	OHL	59	24	26	50	82	5	1	2	3	12
	Portland Pirates	AHL	2	0	1	1	6	....	....	....	....	....
2006-07	Kitchener Rangers	OHL	7	3	1	4	16	....	....	....	....	....
	Brampton	OHL	27	11	13	24	63	....	....	....	....	....
	Kingston	OHL	31	13	16	29	41	5	4	3	7	4

AUGER, Chris (AW-zhay, KRIHS) **CHI.**

Center. Shoots left. 5'10", 161 lbs. Born, Belleville, Ont., December 16, 1987.
(Chicago's 8th choice, 169th overall, in 2006 Entry Draft).

			Regular Season					Playoffs				
Season	Club	League	GP	G	A	Pts	PIM	GP	G	A	Pts	PIM
2004-05	Wellington Dukes	OPJHL	44	25	30	55	16	14	9	11	20	37
2005-06	Wellington Dukes	OPJHL	47	41	51	92	46	12	8	14	22	2
2006-07	U. Mass-Lowell	H-East	34	2	10	12	6	....	....	....	....	....

OPJHL East MVP (2006)

AULIE, Keith (AW-lee, KEETH) **CGY.**

Defense. Shoots left. 6'6", 208 lbs. Born, Regina, Sask., June 11, 1989.
(Calgary's 3rd choice, 116th overall, in 2007 Entry Draft).

			Regular Season					Playoffs				
Season	Club	League	GP	G	A	Pts	PIM	GP	G	A	Pts	PIM
2004-05	Notre Dame	SJHL	38	2	7	9	53	....	....	....	....	....
2005-06	Brandon	WHL	38	0	2	2	32	4	0	0	0	4
2006-07	Brandon	WHL	66	1	8	9	82	11	0	2	2	14

AXELSSON, Anton (AHX-ehl-suhn, AN-tawn) **DET.**

Left wing. Shoots left. 6', 183 lbs. Born, Ytterby, Sweden, January 16, 1986.
(Detroit's 5th choice, 192nd overall, in 2004 Entry Draft).

			Regular Season					Playoffs				
Season	Club	League	GP	G	A	Pts	PIM	GP	G	A	Pts	PIM
2003-04	V.Frolunda Jr.	Swe-Jr.	28	7	10	17	14	10	2	3	5	2
2004-05	Frolunda Jr.	Swe-Jr.	33	12	30	42	14	6	2	5	7	0
2005-06	Frolunda Jr.	Swe-Jr.	12	6	11	17	2	1	0	1	1	0
	Frolunda	Sweden	39	3	3	6	8	11	0	0	0	6
2006-07	Frolunda Jr.	Swe-Jr.	2	4	2	6	4	....	....	....	....	....
	Kungalvs IK	Sweden-3	1	1	3	4	0	....	....	....	....	....
	Frolunda	Sweden	52	5	7	12	14	....	....	....	....	....

AXELSSON, Dick (AHX-ehl-suhn, DIHK) **DET.**

Wing. Shoots left. 6'2", 198 lbs. Born, Stockholm, Sweden, April 25, 1987.
(Detroit's 3rd choice, 62nd overall, in 2006 Entry Draft).

			Regular Season					Playoffs				
Season	Club	League	GP	G	A	Pts	PIM	GP	G	A	Pts	PIM
2003-04	Huddinge IK U18	Swe-U18	13	3	1	4	38	....	....	....	....	....
2004-05	Huddinge IK U18	Swe-U18	1	0	0	0	0	....	....	....	....	....
	Huddinge IK Jr.	Swe-Jr.	31	12	4	16	34	3	1	0	1	0
2005-06	Huddinge IK Jr.	Swe-Jr.	28	19	15	34	157	....	....	....	....	....
	Huddinge IK	Sweden-3	31	23	6	29	14	5	1	2	3	6
2006-07	Huddinge IK	Sweden-2	33	16	15	31	145	....	....	....	....	....

AXELSSON, Emil (AHX-ehl-suhn, eh-MIHL) **NYI**

Defense. Shoots left. 6'3", 198 lbs. Born, Orebro, Sweden, March 19, 1986.
(NY Islanders' 7th choice, 210th overall, in 2004 Entry Draft).

			Regular Season					Playoffs				
Season	Club	League	GP	G	A	Pts	PIM	GP	G	A	Pts	PIM
2002-03	HC Orebro 90 Jr.	Swe-Jr.	27	7	9	16	2	....	....	....	....	....
2003-04	HC Orebro 90	Sweden-2	49	4	0	4	116	....	....	....	....	....
2004-05	Linkopings HC Jr.	Swe-Jr.	21	0	1	1	32	....	....	....	....	....
2005-06	IFK Arboga IK	Sweden-2	39	1	2	3	30	....	....	....	....	....
2006-07	IFK Arboga IK	Sweden-2	38	1	5	6	85	....	....	....	....	....
	Linkopings HC	Sweden	2	0	0	0	0	....	....	....	....	....
	VIK Vasteras HK	Sweden-2	5	0	0	0	2	2	0	0	0	0

BABIN, Noah (BA-bihn, NOH-ah) **CAR.**

Defense. Shoots right. 6', 200 lbs. Born, Palm Beach Gardens, FL, March 11, 1984.

			Regular Season					Playoffs				
Season	Club	League	GP	G	A	Pts	PIM	GP	G	A	Pts	PIM
2002-03	Green Bay	USHL	57	3	11	14	54	....	....	....	....	....
2003-04	U. of Notre Dame	CCHA	31	0	1	1	20	....	....	....	....	....
2004-05	U. of Notre Dame	CCHA	38	5	6	11	34	....	....	....	....	....
2005-06	U. of Notre Dame	CCHA	35	3	12	15	20	....	....	....	....	....
2006-07	U. of Notre Dame	CCHA	42	2	20	22	32	....	....	....	....	....
	Albany River Rats	AHL	11	1	6	7	2	5	0	0	0	2

Signed as a free agent by **Carolina**, March 26, 2007.

BABY, Stephen (BAH-bee, STEE-vehn)

Right wing. Shoots right. 6'5", 235 lbs. Born, Chicago, IL, January 31, 1980.
(Atlanta's 8th choice, 188th overall, in 1999 Entry Draft).

			Regular Season					Playoffs				
Season	Club	League	GP	G	A	Pts	PIM	GP	G	A	Pts	PIM
1997-98	Green Bay	USHL	56	17	17	34	85	4	1	3	4	8
1998-99	Green Bay	USHL	55	23	24	47	83	6	1	1	2	4
99-2000	Cornell Big Red	ECAC	31	4	10	14	52	....	....	....	....	....
2000-01	Cornell Big Red	ECAC	32	8	20	28	47	....	....	....	....	....
2001-02	Cornell Big Red	ECAC	35	9	23	32	42	....	....	....	....	....
2002-03	Cornell Big Red	ECAC	36	8	*33	41	60	....	....	....	....	....
2003-04	Chicago Wolves	AHL	68	14	12	26	72	10	1	4	5	6
2004-05	Chicago Wolves	AHL	64	6	3	9	115	6	0	0	0	12
2005-06	Chicago Wolves	AHL	39	7	15	22	44	....	....	....	....	....
2006-07	Chicago Wolves	AHL	8	1	2	3	21	....	....	....	....	....
	Springfield Falcons	AHL	23	2	1	3	24	....	....	....	....	....

ECAC Second All-Star Team (2002, 2003) • NCAA East Second All-American Team (2003)

Traded to **Tampa Bay** by **Atlanta** with Kyle Wanvig for Andy Delmore and Andre Deveaux, February 1, 2007.

BACKLUND, Mikael (BAHK-luhnd, mih-KIGH-ehl) **CGY.**

Center. Shoots left. 6', 194 lbs. Born, Vasteras, Sweden, March 17, 1989.
(Calgary's 1st choice, 24th overall, in 2007 Entry Draft).

			Regular Season					Playoffs				
Season	Club	League	GP	G	A	Pts	PIM	GP	G	A	Pts	PIM
2004-05	Vasteras U18	Swe-U18	14	5	6	11	14	4	2	1	3	2
2005-06	Vasteras Jr.	Swe-Jr.	25	15	16	31	30	....	....	....	....	....
	VIK Vasteras HK	Sweden-2	12	2	2	4	14	....	....	....	....	....
2006-07	Vasteras U18	Swe-U18	2	2	1	3	2	1	0	0	0	10
	Vasteras Jr.	Swe-Jr.	7	5	4	9	8	5	1	0	1	4
	VIK Vasteras HK	Sweden-2	18	1	2	3	14	....	....	....	....	....

BACKSTROM, Nicklas (BAK-struhm, NIHK-luhs) **WSH.**

Center. Shoots left. 6', 183 lbs. Born, Gavle, Sweden, November 23, 1987.
(Washington's 1st choice, 4th overall, in 2006 Entry Draft).

			Regular Season					Playoffs				
Season	Club	League	GP	G	A	Pts	PIM	GP	G	A	Pts	PIM
2001-02	Brynas U18	Swe-U18	2	0	0	0	0	....	....	....	....	....
2002-03	Brynas U18	Swe-U18	STATISTICS NOT AVAILABLE									
2003-04	Brynas U18	Swe-U18	6	9	5	14	4	3	0	3	3	0
	Brynas IF Gavle Jr.	Swe-Jr.	21	2	6	8	2	5	0	0	0	4
2004-05	Brynas IF Gavle Jr.	Swe-Jr.	29	17	17	34	24	....	....	....	....	....
	Brynas IF Gavle	Sweden	19	0	0	0	2	....	....	....	....	....
	Brynas IF Gavle	Sweden	19	0	0	0	2	....	....	....	....	....
2005-06	Brynas IF Gavle	Sweden	46	10	16	26	30	4	1	0	1	2
	Brynas IF Gavle Jr.	Swe-Jr.	....	....	....	....	....	1	0	0	0	2
2006-07	Brynas IF Gavle	Sweden	45	12	28	40	46	7	3	3	6	6

BACKSTROM, Nils (BAK-struhm, NIHLZ) **DET.**

Defense. Shoots right. 6', 183 lbs. Born, Stockholm, Sweden, June 29, 1986.
(Detroit's 8th choice, 290th overall, in 2004 Entry Draft).

			Regular Season					Playoffs				
Season	Club	League	GP	G	A	Pts	PIM	GP	G	A	Pts	PIM
2003-04	Stocksund Jr.	Swe-Jr.	12	1	6	7	26	....	....	....	....	....
2004-05	Djurgarden Jr.	Swe-Jr.	31	0	5	5	75	....	....	....	....	....
2005-06	Djurgarden Jr.	Swe-Jr.	41	7	11	18	70	4	0	1	1	4
	Djurgarden	Sweden	1	0	0	0	0	....	....	....	....	....
2006-07	Alaska Anchorage	WCHA	33	1	9	10	44	....	....	....	....	....

BAGNALL, Drew (BAG-nuhl, DROO) **FLA.**

Defense. Shoots left. 6'3", 205 lbs. Born, Oakbank, Man., October 26, 1983.
(Dallas' 9th choice, 195th overall, in 2003 Entry Draft).

			Regular Season					Playoffs				
Season	Club	League	GP	G	A	Pts	PIM	GP	G	A	Pts	PIM
2000-01	Battlefords	SJHL	58	7	20	27	205	....	....	....	....	....
2001-02	Battlefords	SJHL	60	16	23	39	247	....	....	....	....	....
2002-03	Battlefords	SJHL	55	17	46	63	248	4	0	1	1	4
2003-04	St. Lawrence	ECAC	40	5	13	18	61	....	....	....	....	....
2004-05	St. Lawrence	ECACHL	37	7	12	19	68	....	....	....	....	....
2005-06	St. Lawrence	ECACHL	24	1	9	10	32	....	....	....	....	....
2006-07	St. Lawrence	ECACHL	39	6	19	25	74	....	....	....	....	....

Traded to **Florida** by **Dallas** with Dallas' 2nd round compensatory choice (later traded to Phoenix - Phoenix selected Enver Lisin) in 2004 Entry Draft for Valeri Bure, March 8, 2004.

BAHENSKY, Zdenek (ba-HEHN-skee, z'DEHN-ehk) **NYR**

Right wing. Shoots left. 6'2", 195 lbs. Born, Most, Czech., January 3, 1986.
(NY Rangers' 7th choice, 73rd overall, in 2004 Entry Draft).

			Regular Season					Playoffs				
Season	Club	League	GP	G	A	Pts	PIM	GP	G	A	Pts	PIM
2001-02	Litvinov U17	CzR-U17	46	16	17	33	102	2	0	0	0	0
2002-03	Litvinov U17	CzR-U17	3	2	3	5	4	....	....	....	....	....
	Litvinov Jr.	CzRep-Jr.	31	4	2	6	8	....	....	....	....	....
2003-04	Litvinov Jr.	CzRep-Jr.	52	14	15	29	204	2	1	1	2	14
2004-05	Saskatoon Blades	WHL	66	14	17	31	101	4	0	0	0	2
2005-06	Saskatoon Blades	WHL	65	19	36	55	76	10	2	5	7	16
2006-07	Hartford Wolf Pack	AHL	13	0	1	1	4	2	0	0	0	0
	Charlotte	ECHL	58	9	14	23	118	4	0	1	1	0

BAIER, Paul (BAI-uhr, PAWL) **L.A.**

Defense. Shoots right. 6'3", 212 lbs. Born, Summit, NJ, February 2, 1985.
(Los Angeles' 2nd choice, 95th overall, in 2004 Entry Draft).

			Regular Season					Playoffs				
Season	Club	League	GP	G	A	Pts	PIM	GP	G	A	Pts	PIM
2002-03	Deerfield Academy	High-MA	25	2	15	17	24	....	....	....	....	....
2003-04	Deerfield Academy	High-MA	23	6	4	10	22	....	....	....	....	....
2004-05	Brown U.	ECACHL	32	2	8	10	24	....	....	....	....	....
2005-06	Brown U.	ECACHL	30	0	6	6	18	....	....	....	....	....
2006-07	Brown U.	ECACHL	32	1	4	5	55	....	....	....	....	....

BAILEY, Jason (BAY-lee, JAY-sohn) **ANA.**

Right wing. Shoots right. 6', 205 lbs. Born, Ottawa, Ont., June 4, 1987.
(Anaheim's 3rd choice, 63rd overall, in 2005 Entry Draft).

			Regular Season					Playoffs				
Season	Club	League	GP	G	A	Pts	PIM	GP	G	A	Pts	PIM
2003-04	Nepean Raiders	CJHL	45	14	14	28	119	18	2	7	9	35
2004-05	USNTDP	U-18	26	3	2	5	91	....	....	....	....	....
	USNTDP	NAHL	13	2	4	6	50	....	....	....	....	....
2005-06	U. of Michigan	CCHA	27	5	2	7	57	....	....	....	....	....
2006-07	U. of Michigan	CCHA	19	0	0	0	28	....	....	....	....	....
	Ottawa 67's	OHL	35	7	9	16	88	4	0	0	0	6

BAINES, Ajay (BAYNZ, AY-JAY)

Center. Shoots left. 5'9", 183 lbs. Born, Kamloops, B.C., March 25, 1978.

			Regular Season					Playoffs				
Season	Club	League	GP	G	A	Pts	PIM	GP	G	A	Pts	PIM
1994-95	Kamloops	BCAHA	52	45	79	124	139	....	....	....	....	....
1995-96	Kamloops Blazers	WHL	68	14	29	43	43	....	....	....	....	....
1996-97	Kamloops Blazers	WHL	70	32	43	75	106	5	4	1	5	6
1997-98	Kamloops Blazers	WHL	72	34	25	59	88	....	....	....	....	....
1998-99	Kamloops Blazers	WHL	72	33	32	65	145	15	7	6	13	20
99-2000	Greenville Grrrowl	ECHL	67	24	31	55	102	15	2	5	7	13
2000-01	Norfolk Admirals	AHL	73	18	18	36	92	9	0	1	1	2
2001-02	Norfolk Admirals	AHL	80	16	28	44	70	4	0	1	1	0
2002-03	Norfolk Admirals	AHL	74	8	14	22	108	9	2	1	3	18
2003-04	Norfolk Admirals	AHL	80	15	27	42	81	8	1	3	4	13
2004-05	Norfolk Admirals	AHL	70	7	16	23	60	6	3	2	5	16
2005-06	Norfolk Admirals	AHL	32	4	4	8	45	....	....	....	....	....
	Omaha	AHL	24	8	4	12	26	....	....	....	....	....
2006-07	Hamilton Bulldogs	AHL	77	13	13	26	72	22	6	4	10	8

Signed as a free agent by **Chicago**, August 1, 2001. Signed as a free agent by **Hamilton** (AHL), August 4, 2006.

BALAN, Stanislav (BAY-luhn, STAN-ihs-lahv) **NSH.**

Center. Shoots left. 6'2", 161 lbs. Born, Hodonin, Czech., January 30, 1986.
(Nashville's 8th choice, 209th overall, in 2004 Entry Draft).

			Regular Season					Playoffs				
Season	Club	League	GP	G	A	Pts	PIM	GP	G	A	Pts	PIM
2001-02	HC Zlin Jr.	CzRep-Jr.	48	21	23	44	60	4	1	1	2	0
2002-03	HC Zlin Jr.	CzRep-Jr.	35	24	21	45	59	3	2	0	2	16
2003-04	HC Zlin Jr.	CzRep-Jr.	53	23	33	56	122	5	2	0	2	31
	HC Hame Zlin	CzRep	4	1	0	1	2	....	....	....	....	....
2004-05	SHK Hodonin	CzRep-3	5	3	2	5	20	....	....	....	....	....
	HC Zlin Jr.	CzRep-Jr.	37	10	13	23	131	2	0	0	0	2
2005-06	Portland	WHL	67	14	23	37	102	12	1	4	5	18
2006-07	HC Hame Zlin	CzRep	44	4	3	7	48	5	0	0	0	2
	Trebic	CzRep-2	7	3	2	5	12	....	....	....	....	....

BALDWIN, Gord (BAHLD-wihn, GOHRD) **CGY.**

Defense. Shoots left. 6'5", 211 lbs. Born, Winnipeg, Man., March 1, 1987.
(Calgary's 2nd choice, 69th overall, in 2005 Entry Draft).

			Regular Season					Playoffs				
Season	Club	League	GP	G	A	Pts	PIM	GP	G	A	Pts	PIM
2003-04	Wpg. Thrashers	MMHL	39	5	16	21	66	....	....	....	....	....
2004-05	Medicine Hat	WHL	66	3	8	11	73	....	....	....	....	....
2005-06	Medicine Hat	WHL	71	4	20	24	119	13	0	9	9	22
2006-07	Medicine Hat	WHL	53	7	19	26	70	23	2	6	8	32

BARANKA, Ivan (ba-RAN-kuh, IGH-vuhn) **NYR**

Defense. Shoots left. 6'3", 205 lbs. Born, Ilava, Czech., May 19, 1985.
(NY Rangers' 2nd choice, 50th overall, in 2003 Entry Draft).

			Regular Season					Playoffs				
Season	Club	League	GP	G	A	Pts	PIM	GP	G	A	Pts	PIM
2002-03	Dubnica Jr.	Slovak-Jr.	27	1	7	8	44	....	....	....	....	....
	Dubnica	Slovak-2	2	0	0	0	0	....	....	....	....	....
2003-04	Everett Silvertips	WHL	58	3	12	15	69	20	3	5	8	26
2004-05	Everett Silvertips	WHL	64	7	16	23	64	11	3	1	4	6
	Hartford Wolf Pack	AHL	....	....	....	....	....	1	0	0	0	0
2005-06	Hartford Wolf Pack	AHL	59	5	16	21	87	....	....	....	....	....
2006-07	Hartford Wolf Pack	AHL	54	3	20	23	50	....	....	....	....	....

BARANOV, Konstantin (buh-RA-nawf, KAWN-stan-tihn) **PHI.**

Right wing. Shoots left. 6'2", 185 lbs. Born, Omsk, USSR, January 11, 1982.
(Philadelphia's 3rd choice, 126th overall, in 2002 Entry Draft).

			Regular Season					Playoffs				
Season	Club	League	GP	G	A	Pts	PIM	GP	G	A	Pts	PIM
1998-99	Omsk 2	Russia-4	23	18	8	26	40	....	....	....	....	....
	Avangard Omsk	Russia	1	0	0	0	0	2	0	0	0	0
99-2000	Omsk 2	Russia-3	33	15	8	23	46	....	....	....	....	....
	Avangard Omsk	Russia	1	0	0	0	2	....	....	....	....	....
2000-01	Kristall Saratov	Russia-2	26	6	9	15	26	....	....	....	....	....
	Ufa	Russia	8	1	0	1	4	....	....	....	....	....
2001-02	Avangard Omsk	Russia	5	0	0	0	6	....	....	....	....	....
	Mechel	Russia	6	1	2	3	2	....	....	....	....	....
	Lada Togliatti	Russia	20	2	4	6	18	3	0	2	2	0
2002-03	Avangard Omsk	Russia	6	0	1	1	2	....	....	....	....	....
	Ufa	Russia	11	2	2	4	0	....	....	....	....	....
	CSKA Moscow	Russia	14	4	1	5	10	....	....	....	....	....
	Omsk 2	Russia-3	3	4	6	10	2	....	....	....	....	....
2003-04	Avangard Omsk	Russia	51	6	10	16	50	11	2	2	4	6
2004-05	Omsk 2	Russia-3	7	5	7	12	20	....	....	....	....	....
	Avangard Omsk	Russia	21	3	2	5	16	....	....	....	....	....
2005-06	Dynamo Moscow	Russia	19	0	5	5	10	....	....	....	....	....
	SKA St. Petersburg	Russia	12	1	2	3	18	3	0	0	0	2
2006-07	Amur Khabarovsk	Russia	7	0	1	1	16	....	....	....	....	....
	Novokuznetsk	Russia	21	2	2	4	28	3	3	1	4	0

BARNES, Joe (BAHRNZ, JOH) **NYR**

Center. Shoots left. 6'3", 212 lbs. Born, Winnipeg, Man., June 16, 1986.
(Carolina's 3rd choice, 64th overall, in 2005 Entry Draft).

			Regular Season					Playoffs				
Season	Club	League	GP	G	A	Pts	PIM	GP	G	A	Pts	PIM
2001-02	Winnipeg Sharks	MMHL	STATISTICS NOT AVAILABLE									
	Saskatoon Blades	WHL	1	0	0	0	0	....	....	....	....	....
2002-03	Saskatoon Blades	WHL	54	9	7	16	48	....	....	....	....	....
2003-04	Saskatoon Blades	WHL	58	5	17	22	90	....	....	....	....	....
2004-05	Saskatoon Blades	WHL	72	30	32	62	73	4	0	1	1	0
2005-06	Saskatoon Blades	WHL	55	25	27	52	55	7	2	4	6	8
2006-07	Albany River Rats	AHL	15	2	1	3	19	....	....	....	....	....

Traded to **NY Rangers** by **Carolina** with Andrew Hutchinson and Carolina's 3rd round choice in 2008 Entry Draft for Matt Cullen, July 17, 2007.

BARRIBALL, Jay (BEHR-ih-bahl, JAY) ST.L.

Left wing. Shoots left. 5'9", 155 lbs. Born, Prior Lake, MN, May 27, 1987.
(San Jose's 6th choice, 203rd overall, in 2006 Entry Draft).

			Regular Season					Playoffs				
Season	Club	League	GP	G	A	Pts	PIM	GP	G	A	Pts	PIM
2004-05	Holy Angels	High-MN	30	32	49	81	....	....	....	....	....	....
2005-06	Holy Angels	High-MN	20	28	38	66	....	....	....	....	....	....
	Sioux Falls	USHL	13	5	7	12	2	5	2	1	3	0
2006-07	U. of Minnesota	WCHA	44	20	23	43	16	....	....	....	....	....

Traded to **St. Louis** by **San Jose** with Ville Nieminen and New Jersey's 1st round choice (previously acquired, St. Louis selected David Perron) in 2007 Entry Draft for Bill Guerin, February 27, 2007.

BARTULIS, Oskars (bahr-TEW-lihs, AWZ-kahrz) PHI.

Defense. Shoots left. 6'2", 195 lbs. Born, Ogre, USSR, January 21, 1987.
(Philadelphia's 2nd choice, 91st overall, in 2005 Entry Draft).

			Regular Season					Playoffs				
Season	Club	League	GP	G	A	Pts	PIM	GP	G	A	Pts	PIM
2001-02	Prizma '83 Riga	EEHL-B	3	1	0	1	2	....	....	....	....	....
	Prizma '83 Riga	Latvia	6	0	1	1	2	....	....	....	....	....
2002-03	Prizma '83 Riga	EEHL-B	12	5	5	10	12	....	....	....	....	....
	Vilki Riga	Latvia	....	0	1	1	12	....	....	....	....	....
2003-04	CSKA Moscow 2	Russia-3	65	3	9	12	....	....	....	....	....	....
2004-05	Moncton Wildcats	QMJHL	62	5	19	24	55	12	1	1	2	16
2005-06	Moncton Wildcats	QMJHL	54	6	25	31	84	21	1	9	10	22
2006-07	Cape Breton	QMJHL	55	13	35	48	52	16	3	9	12	24

QMJHL All-Rookie Team (2005) • Canadian Major Junior All-Rookie Team (2005) • QMJHL Second All-Star Team (2007)

BASHKIROV, Ruslan (bash-KIHR-ahv, roos-LAHN) OTT.

Left wing. Shoots left. 5'11", 186 lbs. Born, Moscow, USSR, March 7, 1989.
(Ottawa's 2nd choice, 60th overall, in 2007 Entry Draft).

			Regular Season					Playoffs				
Season	Club	League	GP	G	A	Pts	PIM	GP	G	A	Pts	PIM
2005-06	Spartak Moscow 2	Russia-3	35	16	9	25	44	....	....	....	....	....
2006-07	Quebec Remparts	QMJHL	64	30	37	67	117	5	1	3	4	6

BASS, Cody (BAS, KOH-dee) OTT.

Center. Shoots right. 6', 206 lbs. Born, Owen Sound, Ont., January 7, 1987.
(Ottawa's 3rd choice, 95th overall, in 2005 Entry Draft).

			Regular Season					Playoffs				
Season	Club	League	GP	G	A	Pts	PIM	GP	G	A	Pts	PIM
2003-04	Mississauga	OHL	61	3	7	10	30	24	2	3	5	21
2004-05	Mississauga	OHL	66	11	17	28	103	5	1	1	2	8
2005-06	Mississauga	OHL	67	16	25	41	152	....	....	....	....	....
	Binghamton	AHL	9	1	0	1	2	....	....	....	....	....
2006-07	Mississauga	OHL	23	5	11	16	37	....	....	....	....	....
	Saginaw Spirit	OHL	30	5	24	29	49	6	1	2	3	10
	Binghamton	AHL	5	0	2	2	9	....	....	....	....	....

BEARSON, Zach (BEER-suhn, ZAK) FLA.

Right wing. Shoots right. 6'1", 180 lbs. Born, Houston, TX, June 13, 1987.
(Florida's 8th choice, 224th overall, in 2005 Entry Draft).

			Regular Season					Playoffs				
Season	Club	League	GP	G	A	Pts	PIM	GP	G	A	Pts	PIM
2002-03	Team Illinois	MWEHL	....	21	29	50	....	....	....	....	....	....
2003-04	Waterloo	USHL	53	7	11	18	65	9	4	1	5	12
2004-05	Waterloo	USHL	51	18	18	36	56	5	0	1	1	2
2005-06	Waterloo	USHL	56	13	21	34	73	....	....	....	....	....
2006-07	U. of Wisconsin	WCHA	5	0	0	0	2	....	....	....	....	....

BEAULIEU, Josh (BOI-loh, JAWSH) PHI.

Right wing. Shoots right. 6'1", 180 lbs. Born, Windsor, Ont., January 10, 1987.
(Philadelphia's 4th choice, 152nd overall, in 2005 Entry Draft).

			Regular Season					Playoffs				
Season	Club	League	GP	G	A	Pts	PIM	GP	G	A	Pts	PIM
2003-04	London Knights	OHL	41	3	6	9	32	9	0	0	0	5
2004-05	London Knights	OHL	65	9	13	22	159	13	2	3	5	13
2005-06	London Knights	OHL	60	15	13	28	140	18	4	5	9	12
2006-07	London Knights	OHL	44	10	6	16	93	10	3	6	9	31

BEAVERSON, Luke (BEE-vuhr-suhn, LEWK) FLA.

Defense. Shoots left. 6'4", 208 lbs. Born, St. Paul, MN, December 11, 1984.
(Florida's 7th choice, 283rd overall, in 2004 Entry Draft).

			Regular Season					Playoffs				
Season	Club	League	GP	G	A	Pts	PIM	GP	G	A	Pts	PIM
2003-04	Green Bay	USHL	57	1	6	7	141	....	....	....	....	....
2004-05	Alaska Anchorage	WCHA	37	0	2	2	48	....	....	....	....	....
2005-06	Alaska Anchorage	WCHA	34	1	3	4	53	....	....	....	....	....
2006-07	Alaska Anchorage	WCHA	37	5	4	9	44	....	....	....	....	....

BELESKEY, Matt (beh-LEH-skee, MAT) ANA.

Left wing. Shoots left. 6', 202 lbs. Born, Windsor, Ont., June 7, 1988.
(Anaheim's 4th choice, 112th overall, in 2006 Entry Draft).

			Regular Season					Playoffs				
Season	Club	League	GP	G	A	Pts	PIM	GP	G	A	Pts	PIM
2004-05	Belleville Bulls	OHL	68	10	13	23	118	5	0	0	0	18
2005-06	Belleville Bulls	OHL	61	20	20	40	119	6	1	2	3	10
2006-07	Belleville Bulls	OHL	66	27	41	68	124	15	4	10	14	18

BELLAMY, Rob (BEHL-ah-mee, RAWB) PHI.

Right wing. Shoots right. 6', 205 lbs. Born, Providence, RI, May 30, 1985.
(Philadelphia's 1st choice, 92nd overall, in 2004 Entry Draft).

			Regular Season					Playoffs				
Season	Club	League	GP	G	A	Pts	PIM	GP	G	A	Pts	PIM
2002-03	Berkshire Bears	High-MA	32	21	21	42	128	....	....	....	....	....
2003-04	N.E. Jr. Coyotes	EJHL	36	19	21	40	95	....	....	....	....	....
2004-05	U. of Maine	H-East	28	3	4	7	34	....	....	....	....	....
2005-06	U. of Maine	H-East	40	6	9	15	77	....	....	....	....	....
2006-07	U. of Maine	H-East	37	1	7	8	82	....	....	....	....	....

BELLEMORE, Brett (BEHL-mohr, BREHT) CAR.

Defense. Shoots right. 6'4", 194 lbs. Born, Windsor, Ont., June 25, 1988.
(Carolina's 5th choice, 162nd overall, in 2007 Entry Draft).

			Regular Season					Playoffs				
Season	Club	League	GP	G	A	Pts	PIM	GP	G	A	Pts	PIM
2005-06	Plymouth Whalers	OHL	46	0	0	0	16	10	0	0	0	0
2006-07	Plymouth Whalers	OHL	50	0	12	12	50	20	0	5	5	28

BELLER, Greg (BEHL-uhr, GREHG) NYR

Wing. Shoots left. 6'3", 213 lbs. Born, Vancouver, B.C., January 22, 1987.
(NY Rangers' 8th choice, 178th overall, in 2005 Entry Draft).

			Regular Season					Playoffs				
Season	Club	League	GP	G	A	Pts	PIM	GP	G	A	Pts	PIM
2004-05	Lake of the Woods	High-MN	21	23	25	48	38	....	....	....	....	....
	Borderland	SJHL	6	2	5	7	0	2	0	1	1	2
2005-06	Green Bay	USHL	3	1	0	1	2	....	....	....	....	....
2006-07	Yale	ECACHL	24	2	3	5	18	....	....	....	....	....

• Missed majority of 2005-06 season recovering from collarbone injury suffered during the pre-season and re-injured in a game on November 29, 2005.

BENDFELD, Jordan (BENHD-felhd, JOHR-dahn) PHX.

Defense. Shoots right. 6'2", 222 lbs. Born, Leduc, Alta., February 9, 1988.
(Phoenix's 6th choice, 152nd overall, in 2006 Entry Draft).

			Regular Season					Playoffs				
Season	Club	League	GP	G	A	Pts	PIM	GP	G	A	Pts	PIM
2003-04	Leduc Oil Kings	AMHL	36	0	9	9	22	....	....	....	....	....
2004-05	Leduc Oil Kings	AMHL	21	1	5	6	96	....	....	....	....	....
	Medicine Hat	WHL	16	0	0	0	4	2	0	0	0	2
2005-06	Medicine Hat	WHL	65	2	10	12	92	13	0	4	4	27
2006-07	Medicine Hat	WHL	72	9	21	30	136	23	0	5	5	*62

BENN, Jamie (BEHN, JAY-mee) DAL.

Left wing. Shoots left. 6'2", 185 lbs. Born, Victoria, B.C., July 18, 1989.
(Dallas' 5th choice, 129th overall, in 2007 Entry Draft).

			Regular Season					Playoffs				
Season	Club	League	GP	G	A	Pts	PIM	GP	G	A	Pts	PIM
2004-05	Peninsula Eagles	BCAHA	STATISTICS NOT AVAILABLE									
	Peninsula Panthers	VIJHL	4	1	2	3	2	2	0	0	0	0
2005-06	Peninsula Panthers	VIJHL	38	31	24	55	92	7	5	7	10	20
2006-07	Victoria Grizzlies	BCHL	53	42	23	65	78	11	5	4	9	12

• Signed Letter of Intent to attend **University of Alaska** (CCHA) in fall of 2008.

BENTIVOGLIO, Sean (behn-tih-VOHG-lee-oh, SHAWN) NYI

Left wing. Shoots left. 5'10", 190 lbs. Born, Thorold, Ont., October 16, 1985.

			Regular Season					Playoffs				
Season	Club	League	GP	G	A	Pts	PIM	GP	G	A	Pts	PIM
2003-04	Niagara University	CHA	39	2	19	21	14	....	....	....	....	....
2004-05	Niagara University	CHA	36	9	18	27	20	....	....	....	....	....
2005-06	Niagara University	CHA	33	16	22	38	55	....	....	....	....	....
2006-07	Niagara University	CHA	37	16	30	46	53	....	....	....	....	....
	Providence Bruins	AHL	15	3	11	14	8	13	3	6	9	14

Signed as a free agent by **NY Islanders**, May 19, 2007.

BERGFORS, Nicklas (BUHRG-fohrs, NIHK-luhs) N.J.

Right wing. Shoots right. 5'11", 190 lbs. Born, Sodertalje, Sweden, March 7, 1987.
(New Jersey's 1st choice, 23rd overall, in 2005 Entry Draft).

			Regular Season					Playoffs				
Season	Club	League	GP	G	A	Pts	PIM	GP	G	A	Pts	PIM
2002-03	Sodertalje SK U18	Swe-U18	4	4	4	8	0	....	....	....	....	....
	Sodertalje SK Jr.	Swe-Jr.	13	1	5	6	4	....	....	....	....	....
2003-04	Sodertalje SK U18	Swe-U18	5	14	4	18	4	2	0	1	1	6
	Sodertalje SK Jr.	Swe-Jr.	31	13	17	30	22	2	1	1	2	0
2004-05	Sodertalje SK Jr.	Swe-Jr.	21	18	16	34	25	3	0	3	3	4
	Sodertalje SK	Sweden	25	1	0	1	2	2	0	0	0	0
2005-06	Albany River Rats	AHL	65	17	23	40	10	....	....	....	....	....
2006-07	Lowell Devils	AHL	60	13	19	32	8	....	....	....	....	....

BERGLUND, Patrik (BUHRG-luhnd, PAT-rihk) ST.L.

Center. Shoots left. 6'4", 187 lbs. Born, Vasteras, Sweden, June 2, 1988.
(St. Louis' 2nd choice, 25th overall, in 2006 Entry Draft).

			Regular Season					Playoffs				
Season	Club	League	GP	G	A	Pts	PIM	GP	G	A	Pts	PIM
2002-03	Vasteras U18	Swe-U18	1	0	1	1	0	....	....	....	....	....
2003-04	Vasteras U18	Swe-U18	10	4	1	5	18	....	....	....	....	....
2004-05	Vasteras U18	Swe-U18	5	2	1	3	4	3	0	1	1	6
	Vasteras Jr.	Swe-Jr.	25	5	5	10	14	....	....	....	....	....
2005-06	Vasteras Jr.	Swe-Jr.	27	17	12	29	38	....	....	....	....	....
	VIK Vasteras HK	Sweden-2	21	3	1	4	4	....	....	....	....	....
2006-07	VIK Vasteras HK	Sweden-2	35	21	27	48	30	1	0	0	0	2
	Vasteras Jr.	Swe-Jr.	....	....	....	....	....	5	4	5	9	6

BERNIER, Marc-Andre (BAIRN-yay, MAHRK-AWN-dray) VAN.

Right wing. Shoots right. 6'4", 203 lbs. Born, Laval, Que., February 5, 1985.
(Vancouver's 2nd choice, 60th overall, in 2003 Entry Draft).

			Regular Season					Playoffs				
Season	Club	League	GP	G	A	Pts	PIM	GP	G	A	Pts	PIM
99-2000	Laval-Laurentides	QAAA	15	2	3	5	10	9	1	0	1	2
2000-01	Laval-Laurentides	QAAA	26	6	12	18	16	8	3	2	5	6
2001-02	Halifax	QMJHL	49	0	6	6	20	2	0	0	0	0
2002-03	Halifax	QMJHL	67	29	29	58	43	21	9	8	17	8
2003-04	Cape Breton	QMJHL	58	27	23	50	27	5	1	3	4	2
2004-05	Halifax	QMJHL	65	27	23	50	51	12	4	5	9	8
2005-06	Manitoba Moose	AHL	16	0	0	0	7	....	....	....	....	....
	Columbia Inferno	ECHL	44	6	17	23	34	....	....	....	....	....
2006-07	Manitoba Moose	AHL	23	1	1	2	16	....	....	....	....	....
	Victoria	ECHL	40	18	15	33	32	6	1	1	2	8

BERNIKOV, Ruslan (BAIR-nih-kahf, roos-LAHN) **DAL.**

Right wing. Shoots left. 6'3", 216 lbs. Born, Vidnoye, USSR, December 4, 1977.
(Dallas' 6th choice, 139th overall, in 2000 Entry Draft).

			Regular Season					Playoffs				
Season	Club	League	GP	G	A	Pts	PIM	GP	G	A	Pts	PIM
1996-97	Dyn'o Moscow 2	Russia-3	32	11	4	15	20	....	....	....	....	....
	Dynamo Moscow	Russia	2	0	0	0	0	....	....	....	....	....
1997-98	Yekaterinburg 2	Russia-3	2	1	1	2	0	....	....	....	....	....
	Yekaterinburg	Russia	43	7	7	14	55	....	....	....	....	....
1998-99	Dynamo Moscow	Russia	6	0	1	1	2	....	....	....	....	....
	Krylja Sovetov	Russia	20	3	1	4	24	....	....	....	....	....
	CSKA Moscow	Russia	1	0	0	0	0	....	....	....	....	....
	Cherepovets	Russia	5	0	0	0	0	1	0	0	0	0
99-2000	Dynamo Moscow	Russia	6	2	1	3	2	....	....	....	....	....
	Amur Khabarovsk	Russia	14	3	6	9	10	5	3	1	4	2
2000-01	Amur Khabarovsk	Russia	33	1	4	5	40	....	....	....	....	....
2001-02	Amur Khabarovsk	Russia	38	7	10	17	20	....	....	....	....	....
2002-03	Krylja Sovetov	Russia	50	15	10	25	40	....	....	....	....	....
2003-04	Lada Togliatti	Russia	49	8	10	18	51	6	0	0	0	4
2004-05	Lada Togliatti	Russia	16	3	1	4	14	....	....	....	....	....
	Cherepovets	Russia	33	9	6	15	8	....	....	....	....	....
2005-06	Mytischi	Russia	21	2	3	5	40	....	....	....	....	....
	Ak Bars Kazan	Russia	5	0	0	0	0	....	....	....	....	....
	Ufa	Russia	16	3	2	5	26	6	1	0	1	4
2006-07	Ufa	Russia	32	6	3	9	14	5	1	1	2	6
	Ufa 2	Russia-3	4	4	3	7	28	....	....	....	....	....

BERRY, Alex (BAIR-ee, AL-ehx) **TOR.**

Right wing. Shoots right. 6'2", 212 lbs. Born, Danvers, MA, March 6, 1986.
(Toronto's 3rd choice, 153rd overall, in 2005 Entry Draft).

			Regular Season					Playoffs				
Season	Club	League	GP	G	A	Pts	PIM	GP	G	A	Pts	PIM
2003-04	Cushing	High-MA	31	19	16	35	50	....	....	....	....	....
2004-05	Junior Bruins	EJHL	53	17	25	42	170	....	....	....	....	....
2005-06	Massachusetts	H-East	24	1	1	2	33	....	....	....	....	....
2006-07	Massachusetts	H-East	29	7	6	13	34	....	....	....	....	....

BERTI, Adam (BUHR-tee, A-duhm) **CHI.**

Left wing. Shoots left. 6'3", 198 lbs. Born, Scarborough, Ont., July 1, 1986.
(Chicago's 6th choice, 68th overall, in 2004 Entry Draft).

			Regular Season					Playoffs				
Season	Club	League	GP	G	A	Pts	PIM	GP	G	A	Pts	PIM
2002-03	Oshawa Generals	OHL	15	3	3	6	12	....	....	....	....	....
2003-04	Oshawa Generals	OHL	66	17	29	46	44	7	0	2	2	4
2004-05	Oshawa Generals	OHL	66	23	28	51	53	....	....	....	....	....
2005-06	Oshawa Generals	OHL	23	16	18	34	28	....	....	....	....	....
	Erie Otters	OHL	39	17	12	29	24	....	....	....	....	....
2006-07	Norfolk Admirals	AHL	48	6	6	12	50	....	....	....	....	....

BERTRAM, Dan (BUHR-truhm, DAN) **CHI.**

Right wing. Shoots right. 5'11", 182 lbs. Born, Calgary, Alta., January 14, 1987.
(Chicago's 3rd choice, 54th overall, in 2005 Entry Draft).

			Regular Season					Playoffs				
Season	Club	League	GP	G	A	Pts	PIM	GP	G	A	Pts	PIM
2003-04	Camrose Kodiaks	AJHL	44	22	33	55	....	....	....	....	....	....
2004-05	Boston College	H-East	39	9	8	17	58	....	....	....	....	....
2005-06	Boston College	H-East	39	10	16	26	38	....	....	....	....	....
2006-07	Boston College	H-East	40	8	17	25	48	....	....	....	....	....

AJHL Rookie of the Year (2004)

BEZRUKOV, Dmitri (behz-ROO-kahv, dih-MEE-tree) **T.B.**

Left wing. Shoots left. 6'3", 187 lbs. Born, Kazan, USSR, November 9, 1977.
(Tampa Bay's 11th choice, 259th overall, in 2001 Entry Draft).

			Regular Season					Playoffs				
Season	Club	League	GP	G	A	Pts	PIM	GP	G	A	Pts	PIM
1997-98	Nizhnekamsk 2	Russia-3	8	0	1	1	6	....	....	....	....	....
	Nizhnekamsk	Russia	14	5	3	8	4	....	....	....	....	....
1998-99	Nizhnekamsk 2	Russia-4	1	3	0	3	0	....	....	....	....	....
	Nizhnekamsk	Russia	39	4	6	10	18	3	1	0	1	2
99-2000	Nizhnekamsk 2	Russia-3	4	0	0	0	6	....	....	....	....	....
	Leninogorsk	Russia-2	8	2	1	3	8	....	....	....	....	....
	Nizhnekamsk	Russia	28	5	6	11	45	3	0	1	1	2
2000-01	Nizhnekamsk	Russia	35	7	10	17	54	4	0	2	2	2
2001-02	Nizhnekamsk	Russia	38	5	6	11	45	....	....	....	....	....
2002-03	Spartak Moscow	Russia	51	10	12	22	24	....	....	....	....	....
2003-04	Nizhnekamsk	Russia	17	1	3	4	10	....	....	....	....	....
	Cherepovets	Russia	8	0	0	0	0	....	....	....	....	....
	Cherepovets 2	Russia-3	12	7	10	17	20	....	....	....	....	....
2004-05	Perm	Russia	27	1	3	4	18	....	....	....	....	....
	Nizhny Novgorod	Russia-2	18	7	5	12	16	6	0	1	1	4
2005-06	Nizhny Novgorod	Russia-2	25	4	4	8	32	....	....	....	....	....
	Almetjevsk 2	Russia-3	3	2	0	2	0	....	....	....	....	....
	Almetjevsk	Russia-2	18	3	4	7	18	8	0	0	0	8
2006-07	Almetjevsk	Russia-2	36	5	8	13	65	3	0	0	0	0

BIEGA, Alex (bee-AY-guh, AL-ehx) **BUF.**

Defense. Shoots right. 5'10", 191 lbs. Born, Montreal, Que., April 4, 1988.
(Buffalo's 5th choice, 147th overall, in 2006 Entry Draft).

			Regular Season					Playoffs				
Season	Club	League	GP	G	A	Pts	PIM	GP	G	A	Pts	PIM
2004-05	Salisbury School	High-CT	27	9	22	31	45	....	....	....	....	....
2005-06	Salisbury School	High-CT	28	10	17	27	51	....	....	....	....	....
2006-07	Harvard Crimson	ECACHL	33	6	12	18	36	....	....	....	....	....

ECACHL All-Rookie Team (2007)

BIRNER, Michal (BUHR-nuhr, MEE-khahl) **ST.L.**

Left wing. Shoots left. 6', 183 lbs. Born, Litomerice, Czech., March 2, 1986.
(St. Louis' 4th choice, 116th overall, in 2004 Entry Draft).

			Regular Season					Playoffs				
Season	Club	League	GP	G	A	Pts	PIM	GP	G	A	Pts	PIM
2000-01	Slavia U17	CzR-U17	48	16	24	40	20	7	0	1	1	6
2001-02	Slavia U17	CzR-U17	46	24	34	58	28	21	1	0	1	0
2002-03	Slavia U17	CzR-U17	5	5	6	11	14	5	4	3	7	20
	HC Slavia Praha Jr.	CzRep-Jr.	31	4	8	12	10	3	1	0	1	2
2003-04	HC Slavia Praha Jr.	CzRep-Jr.	55	25	35	60	112	2	0	1	1	4
	HC Slavia Praha	CzRep	1	0	0	0	0	....	....	....	....	....
2004-05	Barrie Colts	OHL	28	4	10	14	12	....	....	....	....	....
	Saginaw Spirit	OHL	31	7	21	28	29	....	....	....	....	....
2005-06	Saginaw Spirit	OHL	60	31	54	85	91	4	1	3	4	8
2006-07	Peoria Rivermen	AHL	66	11	17	28	20	....	....	....	....	....

BISSONNETTE, Paul (bih-sawn-EHT, PAWL) **PIT.**

Defense. Shoots left. 6'2", 211 lbs. Born, Welland, Ont., March 11, 1985.
(Pittsburgh's 5th choice, 121st overall, in 2003 Entry Draft).

			Regular Season					Playoffs				
Season	Club	League	GP	G	A	Pts	PIM	GP	G	A	Pts	PIM
2001-02	North Bay	OHL	57	3	3	6	21	5	0	0	0	2
2002-03	Saginaw Spirit	OHL	67	7	16	23	57	....	....	....	....	....
2003-04	Saginaw Spirit	OHL	67	5	14	19	96	....	....	....	....	....
2004-05	Saginaw Spirit	OHL	28	1	6	7	46	....	....	....	....	....
	Owen Sound	OHL	35	2	11	13	46	8	1	3	4	2
2005-06	Wilkes-Barre	AHL	55	1	5	6	60	11	0	1	1	4
	Wheeling Nailers	ECHL	14	3	7	10	4	....	....	....	....	....
2006-07	Wilkes-Barre	AHL	3	0	0	0	6	....	....	....	....	....
	Wheeling Nailers	ECHL	65	10	32	42	115	....	....	....	....	....

BITZ, Byron (BIHTZ, BIGH-ruhn) **BOS.**

Right wing. Shoots right. 6'5", 215 lbs. Born, Saskatoon, Sask., July 21, 1984.
(Boston's 4th choice, 107th overall, in 2003 Entry Draft).

			Regular Season					Playoffs				
Season	Club	League	GP	G	A	Pts	PIM	GP	G	A	Pts	PIM
2000-01	Saskatoon	SMBHL	40	17	35	52	....	....	....	....	....	....
2001-02	Saskatoon	SMHL	41	25	48	73	69	11	12	10	22	9
2002-03	Nanaimo Clippers	BCHL	58	27	46	73	59	....	....	....	....	....
2003-04	Cornell Big Red	ECAC	31	5	16	21	36	....	....	....	....	....
2004-05	Cornell Big Red	ECACHL	29	5	10	15	20	....	....	....	....	....
2005-06	Cornell Big Red	ECACHL	35	10	18	28	52	....	....	....	....	....
2006-07	Cornell Big Red	ECACHL	29	8	16	24	49	....	....	....	....	....

BLANCHARD, Nicolas (BLAN-shard, NIHK-oh-las) **CAR.**

Center/Right wing. Shoots left. 6'3", 200 lbs. Born, Granby, Que., May 31, 1987.
(Carolina's 8th choice, 192nd overall, in 2005 Entry Draft).

			Regular Season					Playoffs				
Season	Club	League	GP	G	A	Pts	PIM	GP	G	A	Pts	PIM
2003-04	Antoine-Girouard	QAAA	42	24	28	52	28	13	9	6	15	4
2004-05	Chicoutimi	QMJHL	69	13	26	39	31	17	2	2	4	10
2005-06	Chicoutimi	QMJHL	60	15	29	44	51	9	1	2	3	4
2006-07	Chicoutimi	QMJHL	62	22	35	57	41	4	0	2	2	8
	Albany River Rats	AHL	7	1	2	3	2	5	0	0	0	2

BLIZNAK, Mario (BLIZH-nak, MAHR-ee-oh) **VAN.**

Center. Shoots left. 6', 200 lbs. Born, Trencin, Czech., March 6, 1987.
(Vancouver's 6th choice, 205th overall, in 2005 Entry Draft).

			Regular Season					Playoffs				
Season	Club	League	GP	G	A	Pts	PIM	GP	G	A	Pts	PIM
2003-04	Dubnica U18	Svk-U18	46	25	26	51	62	....	....	....	....	....
	Dubnica Jr.	Slovak-Jr.	2	1	0	1	2	....	....	....	....	....
2004-05	Dubnica U18	Svk-U18	14	5	8	13	45	....	....	....	....	....
	Dubnica Jr.	Slovak-Jr.	36	22	17	39	38	....	....	....	....	....
	Dubnica	Slovakia	19	0	0	0	14	....	....	....	....	....
2005-06	Vancouver Giants	WHL	69	9	12	21	29	18	4	1	5	14
2006-07	Vancouver Giants	WHL	47	8	14	22	20	22	6	6	12	14

BLOOD, Ben (BLUHD, BEHN) **OTT.**

Defense. Shoots left. 6'3", 212 lbs. Born, Plymouth, MN, March 15, 1989.
(Ottawa's 4th choice, 120th overall, in 2007 Entry Draft).

			Regular Season					Playoffs				
Season	Club	League	GP	G	A	Pts	PIM	GP	G	A	Pts	PIM
2005-06	Shat.-St. Mary's	High-MN	73	3	22	25	32	....	....	....	....	....
2006-07	Shat.-St. Mary's	High-MN	63	11	25	36	144	....	....	....	....	....

• Signed Letter of Intent to attend **University of North Dakota** (WCHA) in fall of 2007.

BLUM, Jonathon (BLUHM, JAWN-ah-thuhn) **NSH.**

Defense. Shoots right. 6', 168 lbs. Born, Long Beach, CA, January 30, 1989.
(Nashville's 1st choice, 23rd overall, in 2007 Entry Draft).

			Regular Season					Playoffs				
Season	Club	League	GP	G	A	Pts	PIM	GP	G	A	Pts	PIM
2004-05	California Wave	Cal-Am	55	15	50	65	65	....	....	....	....	....
2005-06	Vancouver Giants	WHL	61	7	17	24	25	18	1	7	8	16
2006-07	Vancouver Giants	WHL	72	8	43	51	48	22	3	6	9	8

BODIE, Troy (BOH-dee, TROI) **EDM.**

Right wing. Shoots right. 6'4", 196 lbs. Born, Portage La Prairie, Man., January 25, 1985.
(Edmonton's 12th choice, 278th overall, in 2003 Entry Draft).

			Regular Season					Playoffs				
Season	Club	League	GP	G	A	Pts	PIM	GP	G	A	Pts	PIM
2001-02	Central Plains	MMMHL	40	22	21	43	10	....	....	....	....	....
2002-03	Kelowna Rockets	WHL	35	4	4	8	36	11	1	1	2	2
2003-04	Kelowna Rockets	WHL	71	8	12	20	112	17	7	3	10	6
2004-05	Kelowna Rockets	WHL	72	24	24	48	96	24	4	13	17	26
2005-06	Kelowna Rockets	WHL	72	28	25	53	117	12	5	4	9	8
2006-07	Hamilton Bulldogs	AHL	20	0	1	1	29	....	....	....	....	....
	Stockton Thunder	ECHL	46	21	17	38	80	6	0	2	2	6

BODNARCHUK, Andrew (BAWD-nahr-chuhk, AN-droo) **BOS.**

Defense. Shoots left. 5'11", 190 lbs. Born, Drumheller, Alta., July 11, 1988.
(Boston's 5th choice, 128th overall, in 2006 Entry Draft).

			Regular Season					Playoffs				
Season	Club	League	GP	G	A	Pts	PIM	GP	G	A	Pts	PIM
2003-04	Dartmouth	NSMHL	58	16	23	39	81	....	....	....	....	....
2004-05	St. Paul's School	High-NH	36	3	15	18	....	....	....	....	....	....
2005-06	Halifax	QMJHL	68	6	17	23	136	11	0	2	2	22
2006-07	Halifax	QMJHL	63	16	41	57	96	12	1	10	11	25
	Providence Bruins	AHL	....	....	....	....	....	1	0	0	0	0

QMJHL All-Rookie Team (2006)

BODROV, Denis (bawd-RAWV, DEH-nihs) **PHI.**

Defense. Shoots left. 6', 185 lbs. Born, Togliatti, USSR, August 22, 1986.
(Philadelphia's 4th choice, 55th overall, in 2006 Entry Draft).

			Regular Season					Playoffs				
Season	Club	League	GP	G	A	Pts	PIM	GP	G	A	Pts	PIM
2002-03	Lada Togliatti 2	Russia-3	9	0	0	0	2	....	....	....	....	....
2003-04	Lada Togliatti 2	Russia-3	45	3	4	7	58	....	....	....	....	....
2004-05	CSK VVS Samara	Russia-2	33	1	6	7	57	....	....	....	....	....
2005-06	Lada Togliatti	Russia	35	2	2	4	42	8	0	0	0	8
2006-07	Lada Togliatti	Russia	49	1	5	6	70	3	0	1	1	6

BOLL, Jared (BAWL, JAIR-ehd) CBJ

Right wing. Shoots right. 6'2", 190 lbs. Born, Crystal Lake, IL, May 13, 1986.
(Columbus' 4th choice, 101st overall, in 2005 Entry Draft).

			Regular Season					Playoffs				
Season	Club	League	GP	G	A	Pts	PIM	GP	G	A	Pts	PIM
2003-04	Lincoln Stars	USHL	57	6	8	14	*176	....	....	....	....	....
2004-05	Lincoln Stars	USHL	59	23	24	47	*294	4	1	3	4	25
2005-06	Plymouth Whalers	OHL	65	19	22	41	205	13	2	4	6	21
2006-07	Plymouth Whalers	OHL	66	28	27	55	198	20	6	4	10	*66

BOLT, Bobby (BOHLT, BAW-bee) ANA.

Left wing. Shoots left. 6'4", 226 lbs. Born, Thunder Bay, Ont., April 29, 1987.
(Anaheim's 4th choice, 127th overall, in 2005 Entry Draft).

			Regular Season					Playoffs				
Season	Club	League	GP	G	A	Pts	PIM	GP	G	A	Pts	PIM
2003-04	Strathroy Rockets	OHA-B	39	5	14	19	41	....	....	....	....	....
	London Knights	OHL	8	1	0	1	2	....	....	....	....	....
2004-05	Kingston	OHL	67	11	14	25	92	....	....	....	....	....
2005-06	Kingston	OHL	68	5	10	15	89	6	0	0	0	4
2006-07	Kingston	OHL	62	22	28	50	70	5	0	6	6	4
	Portland Pirates	AHL	5	1	1	2	2	....	....	....	....	....

BONINO, Nick (boh-NEE-noh, NIHK) S.J.

Center. Shoots left. 6'1", 180 lbs. Born, Hartford, CT, April 20, 1988.
(San Jose's 6th choice, 173rd overall, in 2007 Entry Draft).

			Regular Season					Playoffs				
Season	Club	League	GP	G	A	Pts	PIM	GP	G	A	Pts	PIM
2003-04	Farmington	High-CT	24	44	23	67	10	....	....	....	....	....
2004-05	Farmington	High-CT	24	68	23	91	12	....	....	....	....	....
2005-06	Avon Old Farms	High-CT	25	26	30	56	10	....	....	....	....	....
2006-07	Avon Old Farms	High-CT	26	24	42	66	14	....	....	....	....	....

• Signed Letter of Intent to attend **Boston University** (Hockey East) in fall of 2007.

BONNEAU, Jimmy (BAW-noh, JIHM-mee) MTL.

Left wing. Shoots left. 6'3", 214 lbs. Born, Baie-Comeau, Que., March 22, 1985.
(Montreal's 10th choice, 241st overall, in 2003 Entry Draft).

			Regular Season					Playoffs				
Season	Club	League	GP	G	A	Pts	PIM	GP	G	A	Pts	PIM
2000-01	Jonquiere Elites	QAAA	1	0	0	0	0	....	....	....	....	....
2001-02	Jonquiere Elites	QAAA	40	5	10	15	55	3	1	1	2	2
2002-03	Montreal Rocket	QMJHL	65	1	5	6	261	7	0	0	0	12
2003-04	PEI Rocket	QMJHL	70	7	12	19	263	11	1	0	1	12
2004-05	PEI Rocket	QMJHL	70	11	11	22	234	....	....	....	....	....
2005-06	Long Beach	ECHL	65	1	5	6	137	....	....	....	....	....
2006-07	Hamilton Bulldogs	AHL	9	0	0	0	59	....	....	....	....	....
	Cincinnati	ECHL	46	2	5	7	89	10	0	0	0	23

BOOGAARD, Aaron (BOO-gard, AIR-ruhn) PIT.

Right wing. Shoots right. 6'3", 220 lbs. Born, Newmarket, Ont., August 11, 1986.
(Minnesota's 9th choice, 175th overall, in 2004 Entry Draft).

			Regular Season					Playoffs				
Season	Club	League	GP	G	A	Pts	PIM	GP	G	A	Pts	PIM
2002-03	Calgary Hitmen	WHL	39	3	0	3	52	5	0	0	0	0
2003-04	Calgary Hitmen	WHL	12	0	1	1	24	....	....	....	....	....
	Tri-City Americans	WHL	23	3	1	4	33	6	0	0	0	8
2004-05	Tri-City Americans	WHL	65	4	11	15	96	5	0	0	0	4
2005-06	Tri-City Americans	WHL	65	6	4	10	211	5	0	2	2	4
2006-07	Tri-City Americans	WHL	69	10	11	21	173	5	1	0	1	14

Signed as a free agent by **Pittsburgh**, April 23, 2007.

BORER, Casey (BOHR-uhr, KAY-see) CAR.

Defense. Shoots left. 6'2", 205 lbs. Born, Minneapolis, MN, July 28, 1985.
(Carolina's 3rd choice, 69th overall, in 2004 Entry Draft).

			Regular Season					Playoffs				
Season	Club	League	GP	G	A	Pts	PIM	GP	G	A	Pts	PIM
2002-03	USNTDP	U-18	46	2	2	4	36	....	....	....	....	....
	USNTDP	NAHL	10	1	2	3	10	....	....	....	....	....
2003-04	St. Cloud State	WCHA	31	0	8	8	18	....	....	....	....	....
2004-05	St. Cloud State	WCHA	35	0	11	11	40	....	....	....	....	....
2005-06	St. Cloud State	WCHA	42	3	8	11	24	....	....	....	....	....
2006-07	St. Cloud State	WCHA	40	2	9	11	30	....	....	....	....	....
	Albany River Rats	AHL	1	0	0	0	0	....	....	....	....	....

BORTUZZO, Robert (bohr-TOOZ-oh, RAW-buhrt) PIT.

Defense. Shoots right. 6'3", 196 lbs. Born, Thunder Bay, Ont., March 18, 1989.
(Pittsburgh's 3rd choice, 78th overall, in 2007 Entry Draft).

			Regular Season					Playoffs				
Season	Club	League	GP	G	A	Pts	PIM	GP	G	A	Pts	PIM
2005-06	F-Wm. North Stars	SIJHL	40	4	18	22	....	....	....	....	....	....
2006-07	Kitchener Rangers	OHL	63	2	12	14	67	9	1	2	3	8

BOUCHARD, Francois (BOO-shahrd, frahn-SWUH) WSH.

Right wing. Shoots left. 6', 180 lbs. Born, Sherbrooke, Que., April 26, 1988.
(Washington's 4th choice, 35th overall, in 2006 Entry Draft).

			Regular Season					Playoffs				
Season	Club	League	GP	G	A	Pts	PIM	GP	G	A	Pts	PIM
2004-05	Baie-Comeau	QMJHL	54	11	13	24	13	6	1	1	2	2
2005-06	Baie-Comeau	QMJHL	69	33	69	102	66	4	1	0	1	6
2006-07	Baie-Comeau	QMJHL	68	45	*80	*125	72	11	7	11	18	4

QMJHL Second All-Star Team (2007)

BOURQUE, Chris (BOHRK, KRIHS) WSH.

Center. Shoots left. 5'8", 181 lbs. Born, Boston, MA, January 29, 1986.
(Washington's 4th choice, 33rd overall, in 2004 Entry Draft).

			Regular Season					Playoffs				
Season	Club	League	GP	G	A	Pts	PIM	GP	G	A	Pts	PIM
2002-03	Cushing	High-MA	28	31	26	57	49	....	....	....	....	....
2003-04	Cushing	High-MA	31	37	53	90	96	....	....	....	....	....
2004-05	Boston University	H-East	35	10	13	23	50	....	....	....	....	....
	Portland Pirates	AHL	6	1	1	2	2	....	....	....	....	....
2005-06	Hershey Bears	AHL	52	8	28	36	40	1	0	0	0	0
2006-07	Hershey Bears	AHL	76	25	33	58	49	19	2	6	8	18

Hockey East All-Rookie Team (2005)

BOURRET, Alex (BUHR-ray, AL-ehx) NYR

Right wing. Shoots left. 5'11", 205 lbs. Born, Drummondville, Que., October 5, 1986.
(Atlanta's 1st choice, 16th overall, in 2005 Entry Draft).

			Regular Season					Playoffs				
Season	Club	League	GP	G	A	Pts	PIM	GP	G	A	Pts	PIM
2001-02	Magog	QAAA	40	26	34	60	105	....	....	....	....	....
2002-03	Sherbrooke	QMJHL	61	13	15	28	73	12	1	1	2	10
2003-04	Lewiston	QMJHL	65	22	41	63	94	7	4	5	9	20
2004-05	Lewiston	QMJHL	65	31	55	86	172	8	6	8	14	25
2005-06	Shawinigan	QMJHL	67	44	70	114	133	7	3	4	7	14
2006-07	Chicago Wolves	AHL	45	11	21	32	46	....	....	....	....	....
	Hartford Wolf Pack	AHL	23	5	13	18	12	7	3	8	11	2

QMJHL Second All-Star Team (2005, 2006)

Traded to **NY Rangers** by **Atlanta** for Pascal Dupuis and NY Rangers' 3rd round choice (later traded to Pittsburgh - Pittsburgh selected Robert Bortuzzo) in 2007 Entry Draft, February 27, 2007.

BOWMAN, Drayson (BOH-muhn, DRAY-suhn) CAR.

Center/Left wing. Shoots left. 6', 181 lbs. Born, Grand Rapids, MI, March 8, 1989.
(Carolina's 2nd choice, 72nd overall, in 2007 Entry Draft).

			Regular Season					Playoffs				
Season	Club	League	GP	G	A	Pts	PIM	GP	G	A	Pts	PIM
2004-05	Kimberly	KIJHL	47	29	30	59	108	....	....	....	....	....
	Spokane Chiefs	WHL	4	0	0	0	0	....	....	....	....	....
2005-06	Spokane Chiefs	WHL	72	17	17	34	51	....	....	....	....	....
2006-07	Spokane Chiefs	WHL	61	24	19	43	55	6	2	5	7	4

BOYCHUK, Johnny (BOI-chuhk, JAW-nee) COL.

Defense. Shoots right. 6'2", 225 lbs. Born, Edmonton, Alta., January 19, 1984.
(Colorado's 2nd choice, 61st overall, in 2002 Entry Draft).

			Regular Season					Playoffs				
Season	Club	League	GP	G	A	Pts	PIM	GP	G	A	Pts	PIM
1998-99	Edm. Cycle	AMBHL	36	8	20	28	59	....	....	....	....	....
99-2000	Edm. Cycle	AMHL	35	6	17	23	59	....	....	....	....	....
2000-01	Calgary Hitmen	WHL	66	4	8	12	61	12	1	1	2	17
2001-02	Calgary Hitmen	WHL	70	8	32	40	85	7	1	1	2	6
2002-03	Calgary Hitmen	WHL	40	8	18	26	58	....	....	....	....	....
	Moose Jaw	WHL	27	5	17	22	32	13	2	6	8	29
2003-04	Moose Jaw	WHL	62	13	20	33	71	10	1	9	10	9
2004-05	Hershey Bears	AHL	80	3	12	15	69	....	....	....	....	....
2005-06	Lowell	AHL	74	6	26	32	73	....	....	....	....	....
2006-07	Albany River Rats	AHL	80	10	18	28	125	5	1	1	2	4

BOYLE, Brian (BOIL, BRIGH-uhn) L.A.

Center. Shoots left. 6'6", 222 lbs. Born, Dorchester, MA, December 18, 1984.
(Los Angeles' 2nd choice, 26th overall, in 2003 Entry Draft).

			Regular Season					Playoffs				
Season	Club	League	GP	G	A	Pts	PIM	GP	G	A	Pts	PIM
2000-01	St. Sebastian's	High-MA	25	20	19	39	....	....	....	....	....	....
2001-02	St. Sebastian's	High-MA	28	21	26	47	22	....	....	....	....	....
2002-03	St. Sebastian's	High-MA	31	32	31	62	46	....	....	....	....	....
2003-04	Boston College	H-East	35	5	3	8	36	....	....	....	....	....
2004-05	Boston College	H-East	40	19	8	27	64	....	....	....	....	....
2005-06	Boston College	H-East	42	22	*30	52	90	....	....	....	....	....
2006-07	Boston College	H-East	42	19	*34	*53	*104	....	....	....	....	....
	Manchester	AHL	2	0	0	0	2	16	3	5	8	13

Hockey East First All-Star Team (2006, 2007) • NCAA East Second All-American Team (2006) • NCAA East First All-American Team (2007) • NCAA Championship All-Tournament Team (2007)

BRADFORD, Brock (BRAD-fohrd, BRAWK) BOS.

Center. Shoots right. 5'9", 168 lbs. Born, Burnaby, B.C., January 7, 1987.
(Boston's 8th choice, 217th overall, in 2005 Entry Draft).

			Regular Season					Playoffs				
Season	Club	League	GP	G	A	Pts	PIM	GP	G	A	Pts	PIM
2002-03	Richmond	PIJHL	18	12	12	24	....	....	....	....	....	....
	Coquitlam Express	BCHL	36	11	23	34	14	....	....	....	....	....
2003-04	Coquitlam Express	BCHL	57	36	49	85	....	....	....	....	....	....
2004-05	Omaha Lancers	USHL	60	24	33	57	16	5	0	1	1	0
2005-06	Boston College	H-East	42	6	12	18	8	....	....	....	....	....
2006-07	Boston College	H-East	42	19	26	45	28	....	....	....	....	....

BRASSARD, Derick (bra-SAHRD, DAIR-ihk) CBJ

Center. Shoots left. 6'1", 180 lbs. Born, Hull, Que., September 22, 1987.
(Columbus' 1st choice, 6th overall, in 2006 Entry Draft).

			Regular Season					Playoffs				
Season	Club	League	GP	G	A	Pts	PIM	GP	G	A	Pts	PIM
2004-05	Drummondville	QMJHL	69	25	51	76	25	6	1	5	6	6
2005-06	Drummondville	QMJHL	58	44	72	116	92	7	5	4	9	10
2006-07	Drummondville	QMJHL	14	6	19	25	24	12	9	15	24	12

QMJHL First All-Star Team (2006)

• Missed majority of 2006-07 season recovering from a shoulder injury.

BRAUN, Constantin (BRAWN, kawn-stuhn-TIHN) L.A.

Left wing. Shoots left. 6'3", 198 lbs. Born, Lampertheim, West Germany, March 11, 1988.
(Los Angeles' 9th choice, 164th overall, in 2006 Entry Draft).

			Regular Season					Playoffs				
Season	Club	League	GP	G	A	Pts	PIM	GP	G	A	Pts	PIM
2003-04	Mannheim Jr.	Ger-Jr.	30	12	5	17	42	....	....	....	....	....
2004-05	Eisb. Jrs. Berlin	German-3	1	0	0	0	0	....	....	....	....	....
	Eisb. Jrs. Berl. Jr.	Ger-Jr.	29	14	20	34	125	6	5	4	9	16
2005-06	Eisb. Jrs. Berl. Jr.	Ger-Jr.	7	8	4	12	14	1	1	0	1	6
	Eisbaren Berlin	Germany	6	0	0	0	0	....	....	....	....	....
	Eisb. Jrs. Berlin	German-3	24	13	10	23	34	....	....	....	....	....
2006-07	Eisb. Jrs. Berlin	German-3	10	4	3	7	37	2	2	1	3	0
	Eisbaren Berlin	Germany	34	1	3	4	14	....	....	....	....	....

BRAUN, Justin (BRAWN, JUHS-tihn) S.J.

Defense. Shoots right. 6'1", 180 lbs. Born, St. Paul, MN, February 10, 1987.
(San Jose's 7th choice, 201st overall, in 2007 Entry Draft).

			Regular Season					Playoffs				
Season	Club	League	GP	G	A	Pts	PIM	GP	G	A	Pts	PIM
2004-05	White Bear Lake	High-MN	STATISTICS NOT AVAILABLE									
	Green Bay	USHL	10	0	0	0	2	....	....	....	....	....
2005-06	Green Bay	USHL	59	2	11	13	69	3	0	0	0	2
2006-07	Massachusetts	H-East	39	4	10	14	20	....	....	....	....	....

Hockey East All-Rookie Team (2007)

BREAULT, Benjamin (BRAWLT, BEHN-jah-mihn) BUF.

Center. Shoots left. 5'10", 177 lbs. Born, Pembroke, Ont., February 21, 1988.
(Buffalo's 6th choice, 207th overall, in 2006 Entry Draft).

			Regular Season					Playoffs				
Season	Club	League	GP	G	A	Pts	PIM	GP	G	A	Pts	PIM
2004-05	Baie-Comeau	QMJHL	54	13	27	40	27	4	2	0	2	0
2005-06	Baie-Comeau	QMJHL	68	30	38	68	60	4	0	2	2	4
2006-07	Baie-Comeau	QMJHL	65	40	40	80	60	11	4	7	11	12

BRENNAN, T.J. (BREH-nan, TEE-JAY) BUF.

Defense. Shoots left. 6', 204 lbs. Born, Willingboro, NJ, April 3, 1989.
(Buffalo's 1st choice, 31st overall, in 2007 Entry Draft).

			Regular Season					Playoffs				
Season	Club	League	GP	G	A	Pts	PIM	GP	G	A	Pts	PIM
2005-06	Phi. Little Flyers	AtJHL	42	9	23	32	....	....	....	....	....	....
2006-07	Saint John	QMJHL	68	16	25	41	79	4	1	1	2	4

BRINE, David (BRIGHN, DAY-vihd) FLA.

Center. Shoots left. 6'1", 201 lbs. Born, Truro, N.S., January 6, 1985.

			Regular Season					Playoffs				
Season	Club	League	GP	G	A	Pts	PIM	GP	G	A	Pts	PIM
2002-03	Truro Bearcats	MJrHL	52	21	32	53	29	....	....	....	....	....
2003-04	Halifax	QMJHL	70	22	25	47	20	....	....	....	....	....
2004-05	Halifax	QMJHL	67	14	37	51	36	13	6	7	13	8
2005-06	Halifax	QMJHL	70	34	66	100	80	11	1	5	6	23
	Manitoba Moose	AHL	....	....	....	....	....	9	0	1	1	2
2006-07	Rochester	AHL	22	4	4	8	4	....	....	....	....	....
	Florida Everblades	ECHL	52	9	21	30	22	15	6	4	10	22

Signed as a free agent by **Florida**, September 14, 2006.

BROOKS, Brendan (BROOKS, BREHN-duhn)

Center. Shoots right. 5'10", 185 lbs. Born, St. Catherines, Ont., November 26, 1978.

			Regular Season					Playoffs				
Season	Club	League	GP	G	A	Pts	PIM	GP	G	A	Pts	PIM
1997-98	Owen Sound	OHL	25	3	10	13	6	....	....	....	....	....
	North Bay	OHL	32	7	5	12	26	....	....	....	....	....
	Mississippi	ECHL	1	0	1	1	0	....	....	....	....	....
1998-99	Quad City	UHL	61	18	17	35	67	15	3	1	4	8
99-2000	Quad City	UHL	73	26	26	52	102	14	6	3	9	35
2000-01	Lowell	AHL	5	0	1	1	17	....	....	....	....	....
	Cincinnati	IHL	1	0	0	0	0	....	....	....	....	....
	Dayton Bombers	ECHL	65	29	18	47	95	8	2	3	5	20
2001-02	Manchester	AHL	9	0	2	2	10	....	....	....	....	....
2004-05	Worcester IceCats	AHL	79	20	18	38	36	....	....	....	....	....
2005-06	Peoria Rivermen	AHL	79	14	13	27	61	4	1	0	1	4
2006-07	Grand Rapids	AHL	51	9	8	17	44	....	....	....	....	....
	Manitoba Moose	AHL	7	0	0	0	0	8	1	0	1	6

Signed as a free agent by **Detroit**, August 7, 2006.

BROPHEY, Evan (BROH-fee, EN-vuhn) CHI.

Center/Left wing. Shoots left. 6'1", 203 lbs. Born, Kitchener, Ont., December 3, 1986.
(Chicago's 4th choice, 68th overall, in 2005 Entry Draft).

			Regular Season					Playoffs				
Season	Club	League	GP	G	A	Pts	PIM	GP	G	A	Pts	PIM
2002-03	Barrie Colts	OHL	61	12	14	26	36	6	0	0	0	2
2003-04	Barrie Colts	OHL	67	14	11	25	63	12	4	3	7	4
2004-05	Barrie Colts	OHL	10	3	7	10	13	....	....	....	....	....
	Belleville Bulls	OHL	53	25	36	61	42	5	2	1	3	2
2005-06	Belleville Bulls	OHL	22	9	17	26	39	....	....	....	....	....
	Plymouth Whalers	OHL	40	10	25	35	42	13	4	7	11	18
2006-07	Plymouth Whalers	OHL	68	36	71	107	91	20	9	14	23	26

BROSNIHAN, Pat (BRAWS-nih-han, PAT) PHX.

Right wing. Shoots right. 6'4", 214 lbs. Born, Worcester, MA, August 20, 1986.
(Phoenix's 5th choice, 212th overall, in 2005 Entry Draft).

			Regular Season					Playoffs				
Season	Club	League	GP	G	A	Pts	PIM	GP	G	A	Pts	PIM
2003-04	Worcester	High-MA	25	28	26	54	30	....	....	....	....	....
2004-05	Worcester	High-MA	26	20	44	64	48	....	....	....	....	....
2005-06	Yale	ECACHL	19	0	1	1	31	....	....	....	....	....
2006-07	Yale	ECACHL	27	3	2	5	37	....	....	....	....	....

BROWN, Mike (BROWN, MIGHK) VAN.

Right wing. Shoots right. 6', 210 lbs. Born, Northbrook, IL, June 24, 1985.
(Vancouver's 4th choice, 159th overall, in 2004 Entry Draft).

			Regular Season					Playoffs				
Season	Club	League	GP	G	A	Pts	PIM	GP	G	A	Pts	PIM
2000-01	Chicago Chill	USAHA	66	27	23	50	....	....	....	....	....	....
2001-02	USNTDP	U-17	17	6	4	10	13	....	....	....	....	....
	USNTDP	NAHL	46	5	11	16	56	....	....	....	....	....
2002-03	USNTDP	U-18	34	5	3	8	16	....	....	....	....	....
	USNTDP	NAHL	9	0	3	3	29	....	....	....	....	....
2003-04	U. of Michigan	CCHA	42	8	5	13	51	....	....	....	....	....
2004-05	U. of Michigan	CCHA	35	3	5	8	95	....	....	....	....	....
2005-06	Manitoba Moose	AHL	73	7	8	15	139	13	1	2	3	17
2006-07	Manitoba Moose	AHL	62	3	0	3	194	13	0	2	2	16

BROWNLEE, Chad (BROWN-lee, CHAD) VAN.

Defense. Shoots right. 6'2", 200 lbs. Born, Kelowna, B.C., July 12, 1984.
(Vancouver's 6th choice, 190th overall, in 2003 Entry Draft).

			Regular Season					Playoffs				
Season	Club	League	GP	G	A	Pts	PIM	GP	G	A	Pts	PIM
2001-02	Vernon Vipers	BCHL	55	6	12	18	62	....	....	....	....	....
2002-03	Vernon Vipers	BCHL	58	8	16	24	63	18	2	7	9	14
2003-04	Minnesota State	WCHA	35	2	1	3	44	....	....	....	....	....
2004-05	Minnesota State	WCHA	36	1	1	2	60	....	....	....	....	....
2005-06	Minnesota State	WCHA	29	1	1	2	47	....	....	....	....	....
2006-07	Minnesota State	WCHA	34	0	4	4	50	....	....	....	....	....

BRUNETEAU, Brett (BROO-neh-toh, BREHT) WSH.

Center. Shoots left. 5'11", 183 lbs. Born, San Francisco, CA, January 5, 1989.
(Washington's 5th choice, 108th overall, in 2007 Entry Draft).

			Regular Season					Playoffs				
Season	Club	League	GP	G	A	Pts	PIM	GP	G	A	Pts	PIM
2005-06	Omaha Lancers	USHL	54	7	12	19	31	3	0	0	0	0
2006-07	Omaha Lancers	USHL	55	12	28	40	55	5	0	1	1	6

• Signed Letter of Intent to attend **University of North Dakota** (WCHA) in fall of 2008.

BUCKLEY, Brendan (BUHK-lee, BREHN-duhn) L.A.

Defense. Shoots right. 6'1", 205 lbs. Born, Boston, MA, February 26, 1977.
(Anaheim's 3rd choice, 117th overall, in 1996 Entry Draft).

			Regular Season					Playoffs				
Season	Club	League	GP	G	A	Pts	PIM	GP	G	A	Pts	PIM
1994-95	Boston Jr. Bruins	Exhib.	48	22	43	65	164	....	....	....	....	....
1995-96	Boston College	H-East	34	0	4	4	72	....	....	....	....	....
1996-97	Boston College	H-East	38	2	6	8	90	....	....	....	....	....
1997-98	Boston College	H-East	41	1	12	13	69	....	....	....	....	....
1998-99	Boston College	H-East	43	1	13	14	75	....	....	....	....	....
99-2000	Cincinnati	AHL	4	0	0	0	6	....	....	....	....	....
	Quad City	UHL	61	1	10	11	73	9	1	0	1	10
2000-01	Wilkes-Barre	AHL	63	2	8	10	62	21	0	2	2	33
2001-02	Wilkes-Barre	AHL	80	1	19	20	116	....	....	....	....	....
2002-03	Wilkes-Barre	AHL	80	2	6	8	99	6	0	0	0	2
2003-04	Wilkes-Barre	AHL	45	2	4	6	61	....	....	....	....	....
	Syracuse Crunch	AHL	30	0	4	4	40	7	0	0	0	14
2004-05	Worcester IceCats	AHL	63	3	13	16	128	....	....	....	....	....
2005-06	Peoria Rivermen	AHL	73	2	9	11	104	4	0	0	0	4
2006-07	Manchester	AHL	63	2	7	9	107	16	0	3	3	13

Signed as a free agent by **Pittsburgh**, September 28, 2000. Traded to **Columbus** by **Pittsburgh** for Pauli Levokari, February 10, 2004. Signed as a free agent by **Worcester** (AHL), October 25, 2004. Signed as a free agent by **Los Angeles**, July 10, 2006.

BUMAGIN, Alexander (buh-MAH-gihn, al-EHX-AN-duhr) EDM.

Wing. Shoots left. 6', 180 lbs. Born, Togliatti, USSR, March 1, 1987.
(Edmonton's 5th choice, 170th overall, in 2006 Entry Draft).

			Regular Season					Playoffs				
Season	Club	League	GP	G	A	Pts	PIM	GP	G	A	Pts	PIM
2002-03	Lada Togliatti 2	Russia-3	9	4	1	5	2	....	....	....	....	....
2003-04	Lada Togliatti 2	Russia-3	22	4	9	13	12	4	0	1	1	4
2004-05	Lada Togliatti 2	Russia-3	STATISTICS NOT AVAILABLE									
	Lada Togliatti	Russia	7	2	0	2	2	....	....	....	....	....
	Lada Togliatti	Russia	7	2	0	2	2	....	....	....	....	....
2005-06	Lada Togliatti	Russia	40	9	12	21	28	8	0	3	3	4
2006-07	Lada Togliatti	Russia	41	2	3	5	18	3	0	0	0	0

BURAVCHIKOV, Vyacheslav (burh-AV-chih-kawf, V'YTACH-ih-slav) BUF.

Defense. Shoots left. 6', 189 lbs. Born, Moscow, USSR, May 22, 1987.
(Buffalo's 7th choice, 191st overall, in 2005 Entry Draft).

			Regular Season					Playoffs				
Season	Club	League	GP	G	A	Pts	PIM	GP	G	A	Pts	PIM
2003-04	Krylja Sovetov 2	Russia-3	STATISTICS NOT AVAILABLE									
2004-05	Krylja Sovetov 2	Russia-3	15	5	6	11	22	....	....	....	....	....
	Krylja Sovetov	Russia-2	26	4	1	5	14	3	0	0	0	2
2005-06	Mytischi	Russia	43	1	2	3	24	9	1	0	1	4
2006-07	Ak Bars Kazan	Russia	35	0	3	3	20	....	....	....	....	....

BURKI, Codey (BUHR-kee, KOH-dee) COL.

Center. Shoots left. 6', 190 lbs. Born, Winnipeg, Man., November 17, 1987.
(Colorado's 3rd choice, 59th overall, in 2006 Entry Draft).

			Regular Season					Playoffs				
Season	Club	League	GP	G	A	Pts	PIM	GP	G	A	Pts	PIM
2004-05	Brandon	WHL	68	10	13	23	48	24	6	5	11	13
2005-06	Brandon	WHL	70	27	34	61	69	6	0	3	3	2
2006-07	Brandon	WHL	70	36	49	85	83	11	6	5	11	4

BUSTO, Michael (BUHS-toh, MIGH-kuhl) NYR

Defense. Shoots right. 6'2", 210 lbs. Born, Burnaby, B.C., June 20, 1986.

			Regular Season					Playoffs				
Season	Club	League	GP	G	A	Pts	PIM	GP	G	A	Pts	PIM
2001-02	Moose Jaw	WHL	3	0	0	0	2	....	....	....	....	....
2002-03	Moose Jaw	WHL	50	1	7	8	54	7	1	0	1	0
2003-04	Moose Jaw	WHL	42	4	13	17	51	....	....	....	....	....
	Swift Current	WHL	26	0	0	0	29	5	0	0	0	2
2004-05	Kootenay Ice	WHL	71	8	21	29	79	16	1	5	6	27
2005-06	Kootenay Ice	WHL	69	8	35	43	77	4	0	4	4	4
2006-07	Kootenay Ice	WHL	70	20	43	63	79	6	1	2	3	9

Signed as a free agent by **NY Rangers**, April 27, 2007.

BUT, Anton (BOOT, AN-tawn) T.B.

Left wing. Shoots left. 6'1", 189 lbs. Born, Kharkov, USSR, July 3, 1980.
(New Jersey's 7th choice, 119th overall, in 1998 Entry Draft).

			Regular Season					Playoffs				
Season	Club	League	GP	G	A	Pts	PIM	GP	G	A	Pts	PIM
1995-96	Yaroslavl 2	CIS-2	60	30	12	42	10	....	....	....	....	....
1996-97	Yaroslavl 2	Russia-3	70	30	20	50	20	....	....	....	....	....
1997-98	Yaroslavl 2	Russia-2	48	12	5	17	28	....	....	....	....	....
1998-99	Yaroslavl 2	Russia-3	22	12	8	20	59	....	....	....	....	....
	Torpedo Yaroslavl	Russia	5	0	0	0	0	....	....	....	....	....
99-2000	Yaroslavl 2	Russia-3	1	0	0	0	2	....	....	....	....	....
	Torpedo Yaroslavl	Russia	26	2	5	7	16	8	2	1	3	0
2000-01	Yaroslavl	Russia	42	14	6	20	14	11	1	3	4	8
2001-02	Yaroslavl	Russia	48	14	11	25	14	6	0	1	1	2
2002-03	Yaroslavl	Russia	44	16	13	29	16	9	1	2	3	6
2003-04	Yaroslavl	Russia	51	11	10	21	24	3	0	0	0	0
2004-05	Yaroslavl	Russia	60	12	22	34	58	8	3	3	6	0
2005-06	Yaroslavl	Russia	49	16	21	37	26	11	2	1	3	2
2006-07	SKA St. Petersburg	Russia	52	13	13	26	61	2	0	1	1	2

Rights traded to **Tampa Bay** by **New Jersey** with Josef Boumedienne and Sascha Goc for Andrei Zyuzin, November 9, 2001.

BUTCHER, Matt (BUH-chuhr, MAT) VAN.

Center. Shoots left. 6'1", 188 lbs. Born, Bellingham, WA, January 1, 1987.
(Vancouver's 4th choice, 138th overall, in 2005 Entry Draft).

			Regular Season					Playoffs				
Season	Club	League	GP	G	A	Pts	PIM	GP	G	A	Pts	PIM
2003-04	Chilliwack Chiefs	BCHL	48	7	18	25	73	11	3	1	4	14
2004-05	Chilliwack Chiefs	BCHL	59	27	28	55	94	....	....	....	....	....
2005-06	Chilliwack Chiefs	BCHL	57	38	63	101	109	10	12	11	23	12
2006-07	Northern Mich.	CCHA	40	0	4	4	28	....	....	....	....	....

BUTLER, Chris (BUHT-luhr, KRIHS) BUF.

Defense. Shoots left. 6'1", 178 lbs. Born, St. Louis, MO, October 27, 1986.
(Buffalo's 4th choice, 96th overall, in 2005 Entry Draft).

			Regular Season					Playoffs				
Season	Club	League	GP	G	A	Pts	PIM	GP	G	A	Pts	PIM
2003-04	Sioux City	USHL	55	3	6	9	37	7	0	1	1	6
2004-05	Sioux City	USHL	60	6	22	28	90	13	1	6	7	10
2005-06	U. of Denver	WCHA	35	7	15	22	28	....	....	....	....	....
2006-07	U. of Denver	WCHA	39	10	17	27	42	....	....	....	....	....

USHL First All-Star Team (2005) • WCHA All-Rookie Team (2006)

BYERS, Dane (BIGH-uhrs, DAYN) NYR

Left wing. Shoots left. 6'3", 190 lbs. Born, Nipawin, Sask., February 21, 1986.
(NY Rangers' 4th choice, 48th overall, in 2004 Entry Draft).

			Regular Season					Playoffs				
Season	Club	League	GP	G	A	Pts	PIM	GP	G	A	Pts	PIM
2002-03	Prince Albert	WHL	49	8	6	14	46	....	....	....	....	....
2003-04	Prince Albert	WHL	51	9	8	17	134	6	1	2	3	17
2004-05	Prince Albert	WHL	65	11	9	20	181	17	4	6	10	18
2005-06	Prince Albert	WHL	71	21	27	48	157	....	....	....	....	....
	Hartford Wolf Pack	AHL	5	0	2	2	6	....	....	....	....	....
2006-07	Hartford Wolf Pack	AHL	78	17	30	47	213	7	2	0	2	16

BYRNE, Trevor (BUHR-ne, TREH-vuhr) DAL.

Defense. Shoots left. 6'3", 205 lbs. Born, Weymouth, MA, May 7, 1980.
(St. Louis' 4th choice, 143rd overall, in 1999 Entry Draft).

			Regular Season					Playoffs				
Season	Club	League	GP	G	A	Pts	PIM	GP	G	A	Pts	PIM
1997-98	Deerfield Academy	High-MA	25	5	14	19	16	....	....	....	....	....
1998-99	Deerfield Academy	High-MA	25	9	19	28	22	....	....	....	....	....
99-2000	Dartmouth	ECAC	30	3	9	12	40	....	....	....	....	....
2000-01	Dartmouth	ECAC	34	5	21	26	52	....	....	....	....	....
2001-02	Dartmouth	ECAC	32	5	16	21	38	....	....	....	....	....
2002-03	Dartmouth	ECAC	34	8	16	24	28	....	....	....	....	....
2003-04	Worcester IceCats	AHL	63	7	13	20	22	9	2	2	4	2
	Peoria Rivermen	ECHL	6	0	0	0	0	....	....	....	....	....
2004-05	Worcester IceCats	AHL	40	1	6	7	18	....	....	....	....	....
	Peoria Rivermen	ECHL	33	6	12	18	28	....	....	....	....	....
2005-06	Peoria Rivermen	AHL	51	3	18	21	47	3	0	1	1	0
	Wheeling Nailers	ECHL	2	0	3	3	0	....	....	....	....	....
2006-07	Hershey Bears	AHL	35	1	13	14	46	....	....	....	....	....
	Chicago Wolves	AHL	9	0	0	0	6	15	2	4	6	18

ECAC Second All-Star Team (2001, 2002, 2003)

Signed as a free agent by **Washington**, July 25, 2006. Signed as a free agent by **Dallas**, July 6, 2007.

BYRON, Paul (BIGH-ruhn, PAWL) BUF.

Center. Shoots left. 5'8", 135 lbs. Born, Ottawa, Ont., April 27, 1989.
(Buffalo's 6th choice, 179th overall, in 2007 Entry Draft).

			Regular Season					Playoffs				
Season	Club	League	GP	G	A	Pts	PIM	GP	G	A	Pts	PIM
2005-06	Ottawa West	OJHL-B	33	20	23	43	33	7	3	8	11	4
2006-07	Gatineau	QMJHL	68	21	23	44	46	5	5	1	6	2

CABANA, Frederik (kah-BAH-nuh, FREHD-uhr-ihk) PHI.

Center. Shoots left. 6', 200 lbs. Born, Fleurimont, Que., May 16, 1986.
(Philadelphia's 7th choice, 171st overall, in 2004 Entry Draft).

			Regular Season					Playoffs				
Season	Club	League	GP	G	A	Pts	PIM	GP	G	A	Pts	PIM
2001-02	Magog	QAAA	37	20	16	36	124	7	1	4	5	12
2002-03	Halifax	QMJHL	62	4	10	14	65	24	7	1	8	50
2003-04	Halifax	QMJHL	70	17	21	38	78	....	....	....	....	....
2004-05	Halifax	QMJHL	59	10	24	34	47	11	6	6	12	11
2005-06	Halifax	QMJHL	68	17	24	41	85	11	1	3	4	17
2006-07	Philadelphia	AHL	61	4	15	19	78	....	....	....	....	....

CALLA, Brady (KAL-luh, BRAY-dee) FLA.

Right wing. Shoots right. 6', 190 lbs. Born, North Vancouver, B.C., March 14, 1988.
(Florida's 2nd choice, 73rd overall, in 2006 Entry Draft).

			Regular Season					Playoffs				
Season	Club	League	GP	G	A	Pts	PIM	GP	G	A	Pts	PIM
2004-05	Everett Silvertips	WHL	68	11	10	21	38	11	1	1	2	0
2005-06	Everett Silvertips	WHL	66	8	25	33	52	11	1	2	3	4
2006-07	Everett Silvertips	WHL	29	3	6	9	23	....	....	....	....	....
	Moose Jaw	WHL	39	12	20	32	19	....	....	....	....	....

CALLAHAN, Joe (kal-AH-han, JOH) ANA.

Defense. Shoots right. 6'3", 221 lbs. Born, Brockton, MA, December 20, 1982.
(Phoenix's 4th choice, 70th overall, in 2002 Entry Draft).

			Regular Season					Playoffs				
Season	Club	League	GP	G	A	Pts	PIM	GP	G	A	Pts	PIM
2001-02	Yale	ECAC	31	3	8	11	20	....	....	....	....	....
2002-03	Yale	ECAC	32	2	11	13	38	....	....	....	....	....
2003-04	Yale	ECAC	31	6	14	20	38	....	....	....	....	....
	Springfield Falcons	AHL	13	0	4	4	12	....	....	....	....	....
2004-05	Utah Grizzlies	AHL	75	4	7	11	66	....	....	....	....	....
2005-06	San Antonio	AHL	80	1	5	6	88	....	....	....	....	....
2006-07	San Antonio	AHL	78	1	13	14	65	....	....	....	....	....

Signed as a free agent by **Anaheim**, July 12, 2007.

CAMERON, Bryan (KAM-ih-RUHN, BRIGH-uhn) L.A.

Center/Right wing. Shoots right. 5'10", 175 lbs. Born, Brampton, Ont., February 25, 1989.
(Los Angeles' 4th choice, 82nd overall, in 2007 Entry Draft).

			Regular Season					Playoffs				
Season	Club	League	GP	G	A	Pts	PIM	GP	G	A	Pts	PIM
2004-05	Toronto Marlboros	GTHL	75	73	47	120	76	....	....	....	....	....
2005-06	Belleville Bulls	OHL	64	20	9	29	46	6	1	2	3	6
2006-07	Belleville Bulls	OHL	60	33	25	58	50	15	4	8	12	15

CAMERON, Randy (KAM-ih-RUHN, RAN-dee) DET.

Center. Shoots right. 5'11", 175 lbs. Born, Cornwall, PEI, January 28, 1989.
(Detroit's 3rd choice, 148th overall, in 2007 Entry Draft).

			Regular Season					Playoffs				
Season	Club	League	GP	G	A	Pts	PIM	GP	G	A	Pts	PIM
2005-06	Summerside	MJrHL	52	21	50	71	16	11	2	6	8	6
2006-07	Moncton Wildcats	QMJHL	70	17	22	39	44	7	1	1	2	0

CAMPBELL, Max (KAM-behl, MAX) NYR

Center. Shoots left. 6', 170 lbs. Born, Strathroy, Ont., December 21, 1988.
(NY Rangers' 3rd choice, 138th overall, in 2007 Entry Draft).

			Regular Season					Playoffs				
Season	Club	League	GP	G	A	Pts	PIM	GP	G	A	Pts	PIM
2005-06	Strathroy Rockets	OJHL-B	48	17	18	35	10	....	....	....	....	....
2006-07	Strathroy Rockets	OJHL-B	46	46	49	95	84	....	....	....	....	....

CAPORUSSO, Louie (kap-oh-ROO-soh, LOO-ee) OTT.

Center/Left wing. Shoots left. 5'9", 185 lbs. Born, Toronto, Ont., June 21, 1989.
(Ottawa's 3rd choice, 90th overall, in 2007 Entry Draft).

			Regular Season					Playoffs				
Season	Club	League	GP	G	A	Pts	PIM	GP	G	A	Pts	PIM
2004-05	Tor. Red Wings	GTHL	53	38	28	66	28	....	....	....	....	....
2005-06	St. Michael's	OPJHL	48	29	44	73	44	25	8	10	18	16
2006-07	St. Michael's	OPJHL	37	23	27	50	45	20	14	19	33	14

CAPUTI, Luca (ka-POO-tee, LOO-ka) PIT.

Left wing. Shoots left. 6'2", 184 lbs. Born, Toronto, Ont., October 1, 1988.
(Pittsburgh's 5th choice, 111th overall, in 2007 Entry Draft).

			Regular Season					Playoffs				
Season	Club	League	GP	G	A	Pts	PIM	GP	G	A	Pts	PIM
2003-04	Tor. Jr. Canadiens	GTHL	53	52	55	107	127	....	....	....	....	....
2004-05	Mississauga	OHL	48	5	1	6	25	....	....	....	....	....
2005-06	Mississauga	OHL	32	3	0	3	43	....	....	....	....	....
2006-07	Mississauga	OHL	68	27	38	65	66	5	2	1	3	0

CAREFOOT, Mitch (KAIR-fut, MIHTCH) PHX.

Center. Shoots left. 6'1", 210 lbs. Born, Dauphin, Man., January 2, 1985.
(Atlanta's 8th choice, 237th overall, in 2004 Entry Draft).

			Regular Season					Playoffs				
Season	Club	League	GP	G	A	Pts	PIM	GP	G	A	Pts	PIM
2002-03	Salmon Arm	BCHL	56	19	36	55	51	11	4	3	7	26
2003-04	Cornell Big Red	ECAC	31	6	1	7	14	....	....	....	....	....
2004-05	Cornell Big Red	ECACHL	31	4	7	11	8	....	....	....	....	....
2005-06	Cornell Big Red	ECACHL	33	6	4	10	28	....	....	....	....	....
2006-07	Cornell Big Red	ECACHL	27	9	8	17	16	....	....	....	....	....

Signed as a free agent by **Phoenix** (AHL), August 8, 2007.

CAREY, Paul (KAIR-ee, PAWL) COL.

Center. Shoots left. 6', 175 lbs. Born, Boston, MA, September 24, 1988.
(Colorado's 7th choice, 135th overall, in 2007 Entry Draft).

			Regular Season					Playoffs				
Season	Club	League	GP	G	A	Pts	PIM	GP	G	A	Pts	PIM
2005-06	Salisbury School	High-CT	27	14	11	25	18	....	....	....	....	....
2006-07	Salisbury School	High-CT	24	16	11	27	16	....	....	....	....	....

CARLE, Mathieu (KAHRL, MA-tyew) MTL.

Defense. Shoots right. 5'11", 215 lbs. Born, Gatineau, Que., September 30, 1987.
(Montreal's 3rd choice, 53rd overall, in 2006 Entry Draft).

			Regular Season					Playoffs				
Season	Club	League	GP	G	A	Pts	PIM	GP	G	A	Pts	PIM
2004-05	Acadie-Bathurst	QMJHL	69	4	29	33	53	....	....	....	....	....
2005-06	Acadie-Bathurst	QMJHL	67	18	51	69	122	17	1	14	15	29
2006-07	Acadie-Bathurst	QMJHL	38	12	39	51	52	....	....	....	....	....
	Rouyn-Noranda	QMJHL	25	4	15	19	27	16	6	10	16	16

QMJHL All-Rookie Team (2004)

CARMAN, Michael (KAR-mahn, MIGH-kuhl) COL.

Center. Shoots left. 6', 180 lbs. Born, Augusta, GA, April 14, 1988.
(Colorado's 4th choice, 81st overall, in 2006 Entry Draft).

			Regular Season					Playoffs				
Season	Club	League	GP	G	A	Pts	PIM	GP	G	A	Pts	PIM
2003-04	Holy Angels	High-MN	29	19	40	59	....	....	....	....	....	....
2004-05	USNTDP	U-17	14	2	9	11	40	....	....	....	....	....
	USNTDP	NAHL	39	12	15	27	38	10	2	4	6	10
2005-06	USNTDP	U-18	43	15	23	38	78	....	....	....	....	....
	USNTDP	NAHL	17	6	10	16	24	....	....	....	....	....
2006-07	U. of Minnesota	WCHA	41	9	11	20	55	....	....	....	....	....

CARPENTIER, Hugo (kar-PUHNT-yay, HEW-goh) CGY.

Center. Shoots left. 6'2", 205 lbs. Born, Hull, Que., March 17, 1988.
(Calgary's 4th choice, 118th overall, in 2006 Entry Draft).

			Regular Season					Playoffs				
Season	Club	League	GP	G	A	Pts	PIM	GP	G	A	Pts	PIM
2004-05	Rouyn-Noranda	QMJHL	49	6	9	15	32	5	0	1	1	6
2005-06	Rouyn-Noranda	QMJHL	70	31	39	70	64	5	1	2	3	4
2006-07	Rouyn-Noranda	QMJHL	69	17	37	54	86	16	0	6	6	24

CARSON, Brett (KAR-suhn, BREHT) CAR.

Defense. Shoots right. 6'5", 220 lbs. Born, Regina, Sask., November 29, 1985.
(Carolina's 4th choice, 109th overall, in 2004 Entry Draft).

			Regular Season					Playoffs				
Season	Club	League	GP	G	A	Pts	PIM	GP	G	A	Pts	PIM
99-2000	Pipestone Valley	SSMHL	8	0	0	0	0	....	....	....	....	....
2000-01	Pipestone Valley	SSMHL	31	5	17	22	20	....	....	....	....	....
2001-02	Yorkton Terriers	SMHL	41	16	37	53	32	....	....	....	....	....
	Moose Jaw	WHL	6	0	0	0	0	12	2	0	2	0
2002-03	Moose Jaw	WHL	28	1	4	5	28	....	....	....	....	....
	Calgary Hitmen	WHL	30	3	6	9	4	5	2	1	3	0
2003-04	Calgary Hitmen	WHL	71	5	27	32	49	7	0	0	0	6
2004-05	Calgary Hitmen	WHL	61	8	16	24	61	8	2	2	4	8
2005-06	Calgary Hitmen	WHL	72	11	29	40	62	13	1	6	7	20
2006-07	Albany River Rats	AHL	63	2	16	18	26	5	0	2	2	0
	Florida Everblades	ECHL	3	1	1	2	0	....	....	....	....	....

WHL East First All-Star Team (2006)

CARUSO, Michael (kah-ROO-soh, MIGH-kuhl) FLA.

Defense. Shoots left. 6'2", 191 lbs. Born, Mississauga, Ont., July 5, 1988.
(Florida's 3rd choice, 103rd overall, in 2006 Entry Draft).

			Regular Season					Playoffs				
Season	Club	League	GP	G	A	Pts	PIM	GP	G	A	Pts	PIM
2004-05	Guelph Storm	OHL	56	0	3	3	31	4	0	0	0	2
2005-06	Guelph Storm	OHL	66	1	15	16	85	15	1	2	3	24
2006-07	Guelph Storm	OHL	64	4	16	20	119	4	0	0	0	8

CASHMAN, Reid (KASH-man, REED) TOR.

Defense. Shoots left. 6'2", 210 lbs. Born, Red Wing, MN, March 14, 1983.

			Regular Season					Playoffs				
Season	Club	League	GP	G	A	Pts	PIM	GP	G	A	Pts	PIM
2002-03	Waterloo	USHL	56	5	42	47	42	7	0	2	2	2
2003-04	Quinnipiac	AH	35	2	19	21	52	....	....	....	....	....
2004-05	Quinnipiac	AH	37	13	*32	*45	74	....	....	....	....	....
2005-06	Quinnipiac	ECACHL	39	5	*36	41	66	....	....	....	....	....
2006-07	Quinnipiac	ECACHL	40	3	*38	41	54	....	....	....	....	....
	Toronto Marlies	AHL	7	0	1	1	2	....	....	....	....	....

ECACHL First All-Star Team (2006, 2007) • NCAA East Second All-American Team (2006) • NCAA East First All-American Team (2007)

Signed as a free agent by **Toronto**, March 20, 2007.

CAVANAGH, Tom (KAV-a-naw, TAWM) S.J.

Left wing. Shoots left. 6', 200 lbs. Born, Warwick, RI, March 24, 1982.
(San Jose's 6th choice, 182nd overall, in 2001 Entry Draft).

			Regular Season					Playoffs				
Season	Club	League	GP	G	A	Pts	PIM	GP	G	A	Pts	PIM
1997-98	Toll Gate Titans	High-RI	15	5	17	22	6	4	2	8	10	4
1998-99	Toll Gate Titans	High-RI	15	9	20	29	26	5	5	4	9	6
99-2000	Toll Gate Titans	High-RI	18	25	29	*54	28	5	0	12	12	9
2000-01	Exeter	High-NH	31	*42	40	82	34	....	....	....	....	....
2001-02	Harvard Crimson	ECAC	34	8	17	25	4	....	....	....	....	....
2002-03	Harvard Crimson	ECAC	34	14	13	27	31	....	....	....	....	....
2003-04	Harvard Crimson	ECAC	36	16	20	36	26	....	....	....	....	....
2004-05	Harvard Crimson	ECACHL	34	10	19	29	22	....	....	....	....	....
2005-06	Cleveland Barons	AHL	62	10	11	21	36	....	....	....	....	....
2006-07	Worcester Sharks	AHL	74	12	32	44	56	6	1	0	1	6

ECACHL Second All-Star Team 2005)

CAVANAUGH, Dan (KAV-a-naw, DAN)

Center. Shoots right. 6'1", 190 lbs. Born, Springfield, MA, March 3, 1980.
(Calgary's 2nd choice, 38th overall, in 1999 Entry Draft).

			Regular Season					Playoffs				
Season	Club	League	GP	G	A	Pts	PIM	GP	G	A	Pts	PIM
1995-96	N.E. Jr. Whalers	EJHL	43	8	7	15	....	....	....	....	....	....
1996-97	N.E. Jr. Coyotes	EJHL	56	23	46	69	....	....	....	....	....	....
1997-98	N.E. Jr. Coyotes	EJHL	38	31	*47	*78	58	13	8	12	30	....
1998-99	Boston University	H-East	36	6	8	14	60	....	....	....	....	....
99-2000	Boston University	H-East	40	9	25	34	62	....	....	....	....	....
2000-01	Boston University	H-East	35	7	21	28	43	....	....	....	....	....
2001-02	Houston Aeros	AHL	70	3	16	19	41	5	0	0	0	0
2002-03	Houston Aeros	AHL	77	13	13	26	126	23	2	2	4	20
2003-04	Houston Aeros	AHL	73	16	23	39	94	2	0	1	1	2
2004-05	Houston Aeros	AHL	66	8	14	22	128	5	0	0	0	13
2005-06	Philadelphia	AHL	26	2	6	8	36	....	....	....	....	....
	Springfield Falcons	AHL	39	4	15	19	61	....	....	....	....	....
2006-07	Springfield Falcons	AHL	68	1	13	14	59	....	....	....	....	....

Rights traded to **Minnesota** by **Calgary** with Calgary's 8th round choice (Jake Riddle) in 2001 Entry Draft for Mike Vernon, June 23, 2000.

CEPEK, Cameron (SEE-pehk, KAM-ih-RUHN) MTL.

Defense. Shoots right. 6'1", 186 lbs. Born, Huntington Beach, CA, January 12, 1988.
(Montreal's 6th choice, 199th overall, in 2006 Entry Draft).

			Regular Season					Playoffs				
Season	Club	League	GP	G	A	Pts	PIM	GP	G	A	Pts	PIM
2003-04	California Wave	Cal-Am	65	18	30	48	120	....	....	....	....	....
2004-05	Portland	WHL	66	2	2	4	104	7	0	0	0	4
2005-06	Portland	WHL	21	2	8	10	71	12	0	1	1	10
2006-07	Portland	WHL	49	1	8	9	87	....	....	....	....	....

CEREDA, Luca (suh-REH-duh, LOO-ka) TOR.

Center. Shoots left. 6'2", 202 lbs. Born, Lugano, Switz., September 7, 1981.
(Toronto's 1st choice, 24th overall, in 1999 Entry Draft).

			Regular Season					Playoffs				
Season	Club	League	GP	G	A	Pts	PIM	GP	G	A	Pts	PIM
1996-97	HC Ambri-Piotta	Swiss	35	13	8	21	....	....	....	....	....	....
1997-98	HC Ambri-Piotta	Swiss	28	17	27	44	24	....	....	....	....	....
1998-99	Ambri Jr.	Swiss-Jr.	3	4	3	7	20	....	....	....	....	....
	HC Ambri-Piotta	Swiss	38	6	10	16	8	15	0	6	6	4
99-2000	HC Ambri-Piotta	Swiss	44	1	5	6	14	9	0	1	1	2
2000-01	Ottawa 67's	OHL	DID NOT PLAY									
2001-02	St. John's	AHL	71	5	8	13	23	11	2	1	3	10
2002-03	St. John's	AHL	68	7	18	25	26	....	....	....	....	....
2003-04	St. John's	AHL	22	0	2	2	8	....	....	....	....	....
	SC Bern	Swiss	9	1	3	4	22	15	4	0	4	4
2004-05	SC Bern	Swiss	37	1	1	2	6	11	0	1	1	2
2005-06	HC Ambri-Piotta	Swiss	42	6	16	22	51	7	1	1	2	4
2006-07	HC Ambri-Piotta	Swiss	30	3	14	17	26	6	0	1	1	16

• Missed entire 2000-01 season recovering from heart surgery, October 19, 2000. • Loaned to **Bern** (Swiss) by **Toronto**, January 21, 2004.

CHAPUT, Stefan (sha-PEW, STEH-fan) CAR.

Center. Shoots left. 6', 190 lbs. Born, Montreal, Que., March 11, 1988.
(Carolina's 4th choice, 153rd overall, in 2006 Entry Draft).

			Regular Season					Playoffs				
Season	Club	League	GP	G	A	Pts	PIM	GP	G	A	Pts	PIM
2003-04	West Island Lions	QAAA	29	7	12	19	32	7	1	3	4	4
2004-05	West Island Lions	QAAA	39	29	25	54	86	5	2	2	4	16
	Lewiston	QMJHL	8	2	3	5	2	8	1	0	1	2
2005-06	Lewiston	QMJHL	69	19	29	48	44	6	0	1	1	4
2006-07	Lewiston	QMJHL	57	17	29	46	43	17	6	5	11	20

CHARLEBOIS, Joe (SHAHR-luh-bwah, JOH) CHI.

Defense. Shoots right. 6'1", 210 lbs. Born, Potsdam, NY, February 18, 1986.
(Chicago's 10th choice, 188th overall, in 2005 Entry Draft).

			Regular Season					Playoffs				
Season	Club	League	GP	G	A	Pts	PIM	GP	G	A	Pts	PIM
2002-03	Cornwall Colts	CJHL	59	2	18	20	....	....	....	....	....	....
2003-04	USNTDP	U-18	35	0	2	2	10	....	....	....	....	....
	USNTDP	NAHL	12	1	0	1	6	7	0	1	1	4
2004-05	Sioux City	USHL	59	1	24	25	146	7	1	1	2	6
2005-06	New Hampshire	H-East	32	2	3	5	35	....	....	....	....	....
2006-07	New Hampshire	H-East	39	0	4	4	50	....	....	....	....	....

CHEREPANOV, Alexei (chair-ih-PAN-ahv, al-EHX-ay) NYR

Right wing. Shoots left. 6', 183 lbs. Born, Ozerki, USSR, January 15, 1989.
(NY Rangers' 1st choice, 17th overall, in 2007 Entry Draft).

			Regular Season					Playoffs				
Season	Club	League	GP	G	A	Pts	PIM	GP	G	A	Pts	PIM
2005-06	Omsk 2	Russia-3	5	2	0	2	2	....	....	....	....	....
2006-07	Avangard Omsk 2	Russia-3	3	1	0	1	0	....	....	....	....	....
	Avangard Omsk	Russia	46	18	11	29	45	10	3	5	8	0

CHIPCHURA, Kyle (chip-CHUHR-a, KIGHL) MTL.

Center. Shoots left. 6'2", 205 lbs. Born, Westlock, Alta., February 19, 1986.
(Montreal's 1st choice, 18th overall, in 2004 Entry Draft).

			Regular Season					Playoffs				
Season	Club	League	GP	G	A	Pts	PIM	GP	G	A	Pts	PIM
2000-01	Spruce Grove	AMBHL	36	26	34	60	48	....	....	....	....	....
2001-02	Ft. Saskatchewan	AMHL	33	15	36	51	78	17	16	20	36	....
2002-03	Prince Albert	WHL	63	9	21	30	89	....	....	....	....	....
2003-04	Prince Albert	WHL	64	15	33	48	118	6	2	4	6	12
2004-05	Prince Albert	WHL	28	14	18	32	32	14	4	7	11	25
2005-06	Prince Albert	WHL	59	21	34	55	81	....	....	....	....	....
	Hamilton Bulldogs	AHL	8	1	2	3	6	....	....	....	....	....
2006-07	Hamilton Bulldogs	AHL	80	12	27	39	56	22	6	7	13	20

WHL East Second All-Star Team (2006)

CHORNEY, Taylor (CHOHR-nee, TAY-luhr) EDM.

Defense. Shoots left. 5'11", 182 lbs. Born, Thunder Bay, Ont., April 27, 1987.
(Edmonton's 2nd choice, 36th overall, in 2005 Entry Draft).

			Regular Season					Playoffs				
Season	Club	League	GP	G	A	Pts	PIM	GP	G	A	Pts	PIM
2003-04	Shat.-St. Mary's	High-MN	74	12	44	56	58	....	....	....	....	....
2004-05	Shat.-St. Mary's	High-MN	50	4	30	34	52	....	....	....	....	....
2005-06	North Dakota	WCHA	44	3	15	18	54	....	....	....	....	....
2006-07	North Dakota	WCHA	39	8	23	31	48	....	....	....	....	....

WCHA Second All-Star Team (2007) • NCAA West Second All-American Team (2007)

CHRISTIE, Matt (KRIHS-tee, MAT) ANA.

Center. Shoots left. 5'10", 195 lbs. Born, Toronto, Ont., February 22, 1985.
(Anaheim's 7th choice, 236th overall, in 2004 Entry Draft).

			Regular Season					Playoffs				
Season	Club	League	GP	G	A	Pts	PIM	GP	G	A	Pts	PIM
2002-03	Aurora Tigers	OPJHL	40	21	30	51	22	15	6	7	13	10
2003-04	Miami U.	CCHA	41	21	14	35	22	....	....	....	....	....
2004-05	Miami U.	CCHA	33	15	21	36	14	....	....	....	....	....
2005-06	Miami U.	CCHA	39	7	17	24	10	....	....	....	....	....
2006-07	Miami U.	CCHA	37	8	17	25	6	....	....	....	....	....
	Portland Pirates	AHL	5	2	0	2	6	....	....	....	....	....

CHUCKO, Kris (CHUH-koh, KRIHS) CGY.

Left wing. Shoots right. 6'2", 211 lbs. Born, Burnaby, B.C., March 13, 1986.
(Calgary's 1st choice, 24th overall, in 2004 Entry Draft).

			Regular Season					Playoffs				
Season	Club	League	GP	G	A	Pts	PIM	GP	G	A	Pts	PIM
2002-03	Salmon Arm	BCHL	59	14	19	33	80	11	5	3	8	12
2003-04	Salmon Arm	BCHL	53	32	55	87	161	14	10	9	19	36
2004-05	U. of Minnesota	WCHA	44	10	11	21	61	....	....	....	....	....
2005-06	U. of Minnesota	WCHA	33	4	9	13	40	....	....	....	....	....
2006-07	Omaha	AHL	80	14	14	28	72	6	0	0	0	2

CLACKSON, Matt (KLAK-suhn, MA-thyew) PHI.

Left wing. Shoots right. 6', 196 lbs. Born, Saskatoon, Sask., April 26, 1985.
(Philadelphia's 6th choice, 215th overall, in 2005 Entry Draft).

			Regular Season					Playoffs				
Season	Club	League	GP	G	A	Pts	PIM	GP	G	A	Pts	PIM
2002-03	Pittsburgh Hornets	MWEHL	64	22	22	44	169	....	....	....	....	....
2003-04	Chicago Steel	USHL	42	5	4	9	108	5	0	1	1	8
2004-05	Chicago Steel	USHL	56	10	15	25	270	....	....	....	....	....
2005-06	Western Mich.	CCHA	34	1	1	2	52	....	....	....	....	....
2006-07	Western Mich.	CCHA	36	0	8	8	80	....	....	....	....	....

CLICHE, Marc-Andre (KLEESH, MAHRK-AWN-dray) L.A.

Right wing. Shoots right. 6'1", 190 lbs. Born, Rouyn-Noranda, Que., March 23, 1987.
(NY Rangers' 3rd choice, 56th overall, in 2005 Entry Draft).

			Regular Season					Playoffs				
Season	Club	League	GP	G	A	Pts	PIM	GP	G	A	Pts	PIM
2003-04	Lewiston	QMJHL	52	8	10	18	17	7	1	2	3	0
2004-05	Lewiston	QMJHL	19	4	4	8	8	....	....	....	....	....
2005-06	Lewiston	QMJHL	66	37	45	82	60	6	2	2	4	0
2006-07	Lewiston	QMJHL	52	24	30	54	42	16	6	16	22	10

Traded to **Los Angeles** by **NY Rangers** with Jason Ward, Jan Marek and future considerations for Sean Avery, John Seymour and future considerations, February 5, 2007.

CLITSOME, Grant (KLIHT-suhm, GRANT) CBJ

Defense. Shoots left. 6', 208 lbs. Born, Gloucester, Ont., April 14, 1985.
(Columbus' 12th choice, 271st overall, in 2004 Entry Draft).

			Regular Season					Playoffs				
Season	Club	League	GP	G	A	Pts	PIM	GP	G	A	Pts	PIM
2003-04	Nepean Raiders	CJHL	55	13	26	39	67	17	1	10	11	6
2004-05	Clarkson Knights	ECACHL	39	2	11	13	36	....	....	....	....	....
2005-06	Clarkson Knights	ECACHL	34	2	17	19	20	....	....	....	....	....
2006-07	Clarkson Knights	ECACHL	38	7	12	19	38	....	....	....	....	....

CLUNE, Richard (KLOON, RIH-chuhrd) DAL.

Left wing. Shoots left. 5'11", 195 lbs. Born, Toronto, Ont., April 25, 1987.
(Dallas' 3rd choice, 71st overall, in 2005 Entry Draft).

			Regular Season					Playoffs				
Season	Club	League	GP	G	A	Pts	PIM	GP	G	A	Pts	PIM
2003-04	Sarnia Sting	OHL	58	3	13	16	72	5	0	1	1	0
2004-05	Sarnia Sting	OHL	68	21	13	34	103	....	....	....	....	....
2005-06	Sarnia Sting	OHL	61	20	32	52	126	....	....	....	....	....
2006-07	Barrie Colts	OHL	67	32	46	78	151	8	3	4	7	8
	Iowa Stars	AHL	1	0	0	0	2	....	....	....	....	....

CLUTTERBUCK, Cal (KLUH-tuhr-buhck, KAL) MIN.

Right wing. Shoots right. 5'11", 213 lbs. Born, Welland, Ont., November 18, 1987.
(Minnesota's 3rd choice, 72nd overall, in 2006 Entry Draft).

			Regular Season					Playoffs				
Season	Club	League	GP	G	A	Pts	PIM	GP	G	A	Pts	PIM
2004-05	St. Michael's	OHL	38	10	6	16	55	....	....	....	....	....
	Oshawa Generals	OHL	27	9	9	18	42	....	....	....	....	....
2005-06	Oshawa Generals	OHL	66	35	33	68	139	....	....	....	....	....
2006-07	Oshawa Generals	OHL	65	35	54	89	153	9	8	5	13	21

COGLIANO, Andrew (kawg-lee-A-noh, AN-droo) EDM.

Center. Shoots left. 5'10", 178 lbs. Born, Toronto, Ont., June 14, 1987.
(Edmonton's 1st choice, 25th overall, in 2005 Entry Draft).

			Regular Season					Playoffs				
Season	Club	League	GP	G	A	Pts	PIM	GP	G	A	Pts	PIM
2002-03	Vaughan	GTHL	58	39	54	93	122	....	....	....	....	....
2003-04	St. Mike's B's	OPJHL	36	26	47	73	14	24	11	20	31	12
2004-05	St. Mike's B's	OPJHL	49	36	*66	*102	33	25	*22	*24	*46	20
2005-06	U. of Michigan	CCHA	39	12	16	28	38	....	....	....	....	....
2006-07	U. of Michigan	CCHA	38	24	26	50	12	....	....	....	....	....

CCHA All-Rookie Team (2006)

COHEN, Colby (KOH-uhn, KOHL-bee) COL.

Defense. Shoots right. 6'2", 200 lbs. Born, Villanova, PA, April 25, 1989.
(Colorado's 2nd choice, 45th overall, in 2007 Entry Draft).

			Regular Season					Playoffs				
Season	Club	League	GP	G	A	Pts	PIM	GP	G	A	Pts	PIM
2004-05	Syracuse Stars	EmJHL	50	13	30	41	....	....	....	....	....	....
2005-06	USNTDP	U-17	18	2	3	5	22	....	....	....	....	....
	USNTDP	NAHL	37	5	9	14	33	10	1	1	2	0
2006-07	USNTDP	NAHL	4	1	3	4	0	....	....	....	....	....
	Lincoln Stars	USHL	53	13	47	60	110	4	0	0	0	2

COLBERT, Will (KOHL-buhrt, WIHL) S.J.

Defense. Shoots left. 6'3", 225 lbs. Born, Arnprior, Ont., February 6, 1985.
(San Jose's 7th choice, 183rd overall, in 2005 Entry Draft).

			Regular Season					Playoffs				
Season	Club	League	GP	G	A	Pts	PIM	GP	G	A	Pts	PIM
2001-02	Pembroke	CJHL	52	2	6	8	20	....	....	....	....	....
2002-03	Ottawa 67's	OHL	56	1	6	7	23	23	1	5	6	7
2003-04	Ottawa 67's	OHL	55	3	18	21	28	7	0	4	4	0
2004-05	Ottawa 67's	OHL	68	6	26	32	65	21	3	8	11	8
2005-06	St. FX University	AUAA	28	3	8	11	10	....	....	....	....	....
2006-07	St. FX University	AUAA	27	2	9	11	28	....	....	....	....	....

• Re-entered NHL Entry Draft. Originally Ottawa's 7th choice, 228th overall, in 2003 Entry Draft.

CIS All-Rookie Team (2006)

COLE, Brad (KOHL, BRAD) CGY.

Defense. Shoots left. 6'3", 185 lbs. Born, Miniota, Man., October 21, 1986.

			Regular Season					Playoffs				
Season	Club	League	GP	G	A	Pts	PIM	GP	G	A	Pts	PIM
2003-04	Seattle	WHL	6	0	0	0	12	....	....	....	....	....
	Kootenay Ice	WHL	52	0	1	1	39	4	1	0	1	2
2004-05	Kootenay Ice	WHL	39	1	2	3	35	8	0	1	1	2
2005-06	Kootenay Ice	WHL	16	1	2	3	20	....	....	....	....	....
	Saskatoon Blades	WHL	56	3	12	15	64	9	1	0	1	23
2006-07	Saskatoon Blades	WHL	63	16	25	41	83	....	....	....	....	....

Signed as a free agent by **Calgary**, May 22, 2007.

COLE, Ian (KOHL, EE-an) ST.L.

Defense. Shoots left. 6'1", 211 lbs. Born, Ann Arbour, MI, February 21, 1989.
(St. Louis' 2nd choice, 18th overall, in 2007 Entry Draft).

			Regular Season					Playoffs				
Season	Club	League	GP	G	A	Pts	PIM	GP	G	A	Pts	PIM
2004-05	Det. Victory Honda	MWEHL	60	15	25	40	....	....	....	....	....	....
2005-06	USNTDP	U-17	18	2	1	3	14	....	....	....	....	....
	USNTDP	NAHL	40	2	8	10	75	12	0	3	3	14
2006-07	USNTDP	U-18	42	6	11	17	36	....	....	....	....	....
	USNTDP	NAHL	16	2	7	9	28	....	....	....	....	....

COLLINS, Chris (KAW-lihns, KRIHS) BOS.

Left wing. Shoots right. 5'10", 181 lbs. Born, Fairport, NY, June 8, 1984.

			Regular Season					Playoffs				
Season	Club	League	GP	G	A	Pts	PIM	GP	G	A	Pts	PIM
2001-02	Des Moines	USHL	60	26	39	65	112	3	1	2	3	10
2002-03	Boston College	H-East	39	11	12	23	53	....	....	....	....	....
2003-04	Boston College	H-East	41	9	10	19	42	....	....	....	....	....
2004-05	Boston College	H-East	40	9	8	17	58	....	....	....	....	....
2005-06	Boston College	H-East	40	*31	29	*60	26	....	....	....	....	....
2006-07	Providence Bruins	AHL	17	2	0	2	12	1	0	0	0	0
	Long Beach	ECHL	51	18	19	37	79	....	....	....	....	....

Hockey East First All-Star Team (2006) • NCAA East First All-American Team (2006) • NCAA Championship All-Tournament Team (2006)

Signed as a free agent by **Boston**, July 11, 2006.

COLLINS, Dan (KAW-lihns, DAN) FLA.

Right wing. Shoots right. 6'1", 185 lbs. Born, Syracuse, NY, February 26, 1987.
(Florida's 3rd choice, 90th overall, in 2005 Entry Draft).

			Regular Season					Playoffs				
Season	Club	League	GP	G	A	Pts	PIM	GP	G	A	Pts	PIM
2002-03	Syracuse	OPJHL	35	14	12	26	58	....	....	....	....	....
2003-04	Plymouth Whalers	OHL	59	9	13	22	30	9	0	1	1	0
2004-05	Plymouth Whalers	OHL	68	25	21	46	60	4	0	0	0	6
2005-06	Plymouth Whalers	OHL	44	26	23	49	56	4	3	2	5	2
2006-07	Plymouth Whalers	OHL	66	26	42	68	87	20	9	11	20	30

COLLINS, Sean (KAW-lihns, SHAWN) WSH.

Defense. Shoots right. 6'1", 212 lbs. Born, Troy, MI, October 30, 1983.

			Regular Season					Playoffs				
Season	Club	League	GP	G	A	Pts	PIM	GP	G	A	Pts	PIM
2002-03	Sioux City	USHL	59	6	22	28	89	4	0	1	1	2
2003-04	Ohio State	CCHA	41	3	12	15	57	....	....	....	....	....
2004-05	Ohio State	CCHA	40	9	17	26	40	....	....	....	....	....
2005-06	Ohio State	CCHA	39	7	11	18	63	....	....	....	....	....
2006-07	Ohio State	CCHA	37	9	19	28	50	....	....	....	....	....
	Hershey Bears	AHL	3	0	0	0	2	....	....	....	....	....

Signed as a free agent by **Washington**, March 19, 2007.

CONBOY, Andrew (KAWN-boi, AN-droo) MTL.

Left wing. Shoots left. 6'4", 196 lbs. Born, Burnsville, MN, May 16, 1988.
(Montreal's 7th choice, 142nd overall, in 2007 Entry Draft).

			Regular Season					Playoffs				
Season	Club	League	GP	G	A	Pts	PIM	GP	G	A	Pts	PIM
2005-06	Wichita Falls	NAHL	51	7	8	15	158	5	0	2	2	2
2006-07	Omaha Lancers	USHL	56	25	25	50	105	....	....	....	....	....

CONBOY, Tim (KAWN-boi, TIHM) CAR.

Defense. Shoots right. 6'2", 210 lbs. Born, Farmington, MN, March 22, 1982.
(San Jose's 6th choice, 217th overall, in 2002 Entry Draft).

			Regular Season					Playoffs				
Season	Club	League	GP	G	A	Pts	PIM	GP	G	A	Pts	PIM
99-2000	Brainerd	High-MN	22	20	26	46	....	....	....	....	....	....
2000-01	Rochester	USHL	51	5	9	14	256	....	....	....	....	....
2001-02	Rochester	USHL	14	1	6	7	65	....	....	....	....	....
	Topeka	USHL	29	4	15	19	128	....	....	....	....	....
2002-03	St. Cloud State	WCHA	31	3	12	15	48	....	....	....	....	....
2003-04	St. Cloud State	WCHA	32	5	5	10	68	....	....	....	....	....
	Cleveland Barons	AHL	....	....	....	....	....	3	0	3	3	4
2004-05	Cleveland Barons	AHL	61	4	11	15	134	....	....	....	....	....
2005-06	Cleveland Barons	AHL	78	6	14	20	124	....	....	....	....	....
2006-07	Albany River Rats	AHL	75	3	7	10	163	5	0	1	1	6

Signed as a free agent by **Carolina**, July 21, 2006.

CONDRA, Erik (KAWN-druh, AIR-ihk) OTT.

Right wing. Shoots right. 5'11", 180 lbs. Born, Trenton, MI, August 6, 1986.
(Ottawa's 7th choice, 211th overall, in 2006 Entry Draft).

			Regular Season					Playoffs				
Season	Club	League	GP	G	A	Pts	PIM	GP	G	A	Pts	PIM
2004-05	Lincoln Stars	USHL	60	30	30	60	56	4	0	2	2	4
2005-06	U. of Notre Dame	CCHA	36	6	28	34	32	....	....	....	....	....
2006-07	U. of Notre Dame	CCHA	42	14	34	48	18	....	....	....	....	....

CCHA All-Rookie Team (2006)

COOK, Tim (KUK, TIHM) OTT.

Defense. Shoots right. 6'4", 190 lbs. Born, Montclair, NJ, March 13, 1984.
(Ottawa's 5th choice, 142nd overall, in 2003 Entry Draft).

			Regular Season					Playoffs				
Season	Club	League	GP	G	A	Pts	PIM	GP	G	A	Pts	PIM
2000-01	Hotchkiss	High-CT	22	2	10	12	22	....	....	....	....	....
2001-02	Omaha Lancers	USHL	42	2	4	6	39	5	0	1	1	2
2002-03	River City Lancers	USHL	59	3	12	15	62	10	0	2	2	18
2003-04	U. of Michigan	CCHA	24	0	2	2	28	....	....	....	....	....
2004-05	U. of Michigan	CCHA	36	0	0	0	54	....	....	....	....	....
2005-06	U. of Michigan	CCHA	40	1	2	3	37	....	....	....	....	....
2006-07	U. of Michigan	CCHA	36	0	4	4	14	....	....	....	....	....

CORBIN, J.D. (KOHR-bihn, JAY-DEE) COL.

Left wing. Shoots left. 5'10", 185 lbs. Born, Littleton, CO, March 23, 1985.
(Colorado's 8th choice, 249th overall, in 2004 Entry Draft).

			Regular Season					Playoffs				
Season	Club	League	GP	G	A	Pts	PIM	GP	G	A	Pts	PIM
2001-02	USNTDP	U-17	14	3	9	12	26	....	....	....	....	....
	USNTDP	NAHL	29	3	4	7	20	....	....	....	....	....
2002-03	USNTDP	U-18	41	7	12	19	....	....	....	....	....	....
	USNTDP	NAHL	10	1	1	2	4	....	....	....	....	....
2003-04	U. of Denver	WCHA	39	3	6	9	18	....	....	....	....	....
2004-05	U. of Denver	WCHA	41	1	18	19	22	....	....	....	....	....
2005-06	U. of Denver	WCHA	38	5	15	20	16	....	....	....	....	....
2006-07	U. of Denver	WCHA	10	2	4	6	4	....	....	....	....	....

CORMIER, Kevin (KOHR-mee-ay, KEH-vihn) PHX.

Left wing. Shoots left. 6'3", 249 lbs. Born, Moncton, N.B., January 27, 1986.
(Phoenix's 6th choice, 168th overall, in 2004 Entry Draft).

			Regular Season					Playoffs				
Season	Club	League	GP	G	A	Pts	PIM	GP	G	A	Pts	PIM
2003-04	Moncton	MJrHL	42	3	2	5	235	4	0	0	0	52
	Halifax	QMJHL	1	0	0	0	5	....	....	....	....	....
2004-05	Halifax	QMJHL	60	2	5	7	235	9	0	0	0	8
2005-06	Halifax	QMJHL	69	16	11	27	202	11	0	1	1	18
2006-07	Rimouski Oceanic	QMJHL	28	5	4	9	97	....	....	....	....	....
	Shawinigan	QMJHL	25	7	5	12	70	3	0	0	0	4

CORRENTE, Matthew (kohr-REHN-tay, MA-thew) N.J.

Defense. Shoots right. 6', 195 lbs. Born, Mississauga, Ont., March 17, 1988.
(New Jersey's 1st choice, 30th overall, in 2006 Entry Draft).

			Regular Season					Playoffs				
Season	Club	League	GP	G	A	Pts	PIM	GP	G	A	Pts	PIM
2004-05	Saginaw Spirit	OHL	62	6	9	15	89	....	....	....	....	....
2005-06	Saginaw Spirit	OHL	61	6	24	30	172	4	1	1	2	8
2006-07	Saginaw Spirit	OHL	29	2	13	15	67	....	....	....	....	....
	Mississauga	OHL	14	1	10	11	27	5	0	1	1	8

COURTNALL, Justin (KOHRT-nawl, JUHS-tihn) T.B.

Left wing. Shoots left. 6'3", 185 lbs. Born, Victoria, B.C., May 21, 1989.
(Tampa Bay's 9th choice, 210th overall, in 2007 Entry Draft).

			Regular Season					Playoffs				
Season	Club	League	GP	G	A	Pts	PIM	GP	G	A	Pts	PIM
2005-06	Victoria Cougars	VIJHL	33	17	17	34	51	....	....	....	....	....
2006-07	Victoria Grizzlies	BCHL	5	0	0	0	14	....	....	....	....	....
	Burnaby Express	BCHL	48	5	9	14	55	12	0	2	2	19

COUTURE, Derek (koh-TYOOR, DAIR-ihk) **CGY.**

Right wing. Shoots right. 6'2", 206 lbs. Born, Calgary, Alta., April 24, 1984.

			Regular Season					Playoffs				
Season	**Club**	**League**	**GP**	**G**	**A**	**Pts**	**PIM**	**GP**	**G**	**A**	**Pts**	**PIM**
2001-02	Saskatoon Blades	WHL	61	6	10	16	159	7	0	0	0	10
2002-03	Saskatoon Blades	WHL	70	17	20	37	160	6	1	2	3	13
2003-04	Saskatoon Blades	WHL	45	3	9	12	99	....	....	....	....	....
2004-05	Seattle	WHL	71	20	18	38	154	12	3	6	9	18
2005-06	Omaha	AHL	66	7	12	19	88	....	....	....	....	....
2006-07	Omaha	AHL	46	3	6	9	76	6	0	1	1	4

Signed as a free agent by **Calgary**, August 5, 2005.

COUTURE, Logan (koh-TYOOR, LOH-guhn) **S.J.**

Center. Shoots left. 6', 195 lbs. Born, Guelph, Ont., March 28, 1989.
(San Jose's 1st choice, 9th overall, in 2007 Entry Draft).

			Regular Season					Playoffs				
Season	**Club**	**League**	**GP**	**G**	**A**	**Pts**	**PIM**	**GP**	**G**	**A**	**Pts**	**PIM**
2004-05	St. Thomas Stars	OJHL-B	48	24	22	46	....	....	....	....	....	....
2005-06	Ottawa 67's	OHL	65	25	39	64	52	6	3	4	7	0
2006-07	Ottawa 67's	OHL	54	26	52	78	24	5	1	7	8	4

CRABB, Joey (KRAB, JOH-ee) **ATL.**

Right wing. Shoots right. 6'1", 190 lbs. Born, Anchorage, AK, April 3, 1983.
(NY Rangers' 7th choice, 226th overall, in 2002 Entry Draft).

			Regular Season					Playoffs				
Season	**Club**	**League**	**GP**	**G**	**A**	**Pts**	**PIM**	**GP**	**G**	**A**	**Pts**	**PIM**
99-2000	USNTDP	NAHL	55	13	10	23	69	3	1	0	1	4
2000-01	USNTDP	U-18	39	10	10	20	22	....	....	....	....	....
	USNTDP	USHL	21	2	3	5	18	....	....	....	....	....
2001-02	Green Bay	USHL	61	15	27	42	94	7	4	8	12	21
2002-03	Colorado College	WCHA	35	4	4	8	40	....	....	....	....	....
2003-04	Colorado College	WCHA	39	15	12	27	20	....	....	....	....	....
2004-05	Colorado College	WCHA	43	16	16	32	44	....	....	....	....	....
2005-06	Colorado College	WCHA	42	18	25	43	45	....	....	....	....	....
2006-07	Chicago Wolves	AHL	63	7	15	22	25	6	0	0	0	0

Signed as a free agent by **Atlanta**, August 31, 2006.

CRACKNELL, Adam (krak-NEHL, A-duhm) **CGY.**

Right wing. Shoots right. 6'3", 214 lbs. Born, Prince Albert, Sask., July 15, 1985.
(Calgary's 10th choice, 279th overall, in 2004 Entry Draft).

			Regular Season					Playoffs				
Season	**Club**	**League**	**GP**	**G**	**A**	**Pts**	**PIM**	**GP**	**G**	**A**	**Pts**	**PIM**
2002-03	Kootenay Ice	WHL	67	7	4	11	37	11	0	0	0	2
2003-04	Kootenay Ice	WHL	72	26	35	61	63	4	1	1	2	2
2004-05	Kootenay Ice	WHL	72	19	29	48	65	16	8	8	16	6
2005-06	Kootenay Ice	WHL	72	42	51	93	85	6	1	4	5	6
	Omaha	AHL	6	1	2	3	2	....	....	....	....	....
2006-07	Las Vegas	ECHL	31	8	14	22	35	8	3	3	6	6

WHL West Second All-Star Team (2006)

CROMBEEN, B.J. (KRAWM-been, BEE-JAY) **DAL.**

Right wing. Shoots right. 6'2", 200 lbs. Born, Denver, CO, July 10, 1985.
(Dallas' 3rd choice, 54th overall, in 2003 Entry Draft).

			Regular Season					Playoffs				
Season	**Club**	**League**	**GP**	**G**	**A**	**Pts**	**PIM**	**GP**	**G**	**A**	**Pts**	**PIM**
2000-01	Newmarket	OPJHL	35	14	14	28	63	....	....	....	....	....
2001-02	Barrie Colts	OHL	60	12	13	25	118	20	1	1	2	31
2002-03	Barrie Colts	OHL	63	22	24	46	133	6	1	0	1	8
2003-04	Barrie Colts	OHL	62	21	29	50	154	12	5	7	12	35
2004-05	Barrie Colts	OHL	63	31	18	49	111	6	2	4	6	35
2005-06	Iowa Stars	AHL	52	5	7	12	97	5	1	0	1	9
	Idaho Steelheads	ECHL	8	5	3	8	5	....	....	....	....	....
2006-07	Assat Pori	Finland	55	13	9	22	152	....	....	....	....	....
	Idaho Steelheads	ECHL	13	7	4	11	43	22	5	5	10	45

Signed as a free agent by **Assat** (Finland), August 2, 2006.

CROSS, Tommy (KRAWS, TAW-mee) **BOS.**

Defense. Shoots left. 6'3", 198 lbs. Born, Hartford, CT, September 12, 1989.
(Boston's 2nd choice, 35th overall, in 2007 Entry Draft).

			Regular Season					Playoffs				
Season	**Club**	**League**	**GP**	**G**	**A**	**Pts**	**PIM**	**GP**	**G**	**A**	**Pts**	**PIM**
2004-05	Simsbury	High-CT	23	5	40	45	18	....	....	....	....	....
2005-06	Simsbury	High-CT	22	15	35	50		....	....	....	....	....
2006-07	Westminster	High-CT	25	8	12	20	20	....	....	....	....	....
	USNTDP	NAHL	2	0	2	2	0	....	....	....	....	....

• Signed Letter of Intent to attend **Boston College** (Hockey East) in fall of 2008.

CROWDER, Tim (KROW-duhr, TIHM) **PIT.**

Right wing. Shoots right. 6'2", 180 lbs. Born, Victoria, B.C., October 16, 1986.
(Pittsburgh's 5th choice, 126th overall, in 2005 Entry Draft).

			Regular Season					Playoffs				
Season	**Club**	**League**	**GP**	**G**	**A**	**Pts**	**PIM**	**GP**	**G**	**A**	**Pts**	**PIM**
2002-03	Powell River Kings	BCHL	52	6	6	12	....	....	....	....	....	....
2003-04	Powell River Kings	BCHL	57	21	34	55	44	7	3	3	6	8
2004-05	South Surrey	BCHL	56	23	27	50	30	....	....	....	....	....
2005-06	Michigan State	CCHA	44	17	13	30	29	....	....	....	....	....
2006-07	Michigan State	CCHA	41	14	11	25	18	....	....	....	....	....

CROWLEY, Dane (KROH-lee, DAYN) **T.B.**

Defense. Shoots right. 6'2", 210 lbs. Born, Winnipeg, Man., January 22, 1987.
(Tampa Bay's 3rd choice, 168th overall, in 2006 Entry Draft).

			Regular Season					Playoffs				
Season	**Club**	**League**	**GP**	**G**	**A**	**Pts**	**PIM**	**GP**	**G**	**A**	**Pts**	**PIM**
2003-04	Saskatoon Blades	WHL	28	1	3	4	28	....	....	....	....	....
2004-05	Saskatoon Blades	WHL	52	1	3	4	101	4	0	0	0	8
2005-06	Saskatoon Blades	WHL	42	0	9	9	85	....	....	....	....	....
	Swift Current	WHL	29	1	11	12	64	4	0	2	2	23
2006-07	Swift Current	WHL	33	4	15	19	96	....	....	....	....	....
	Everett Silvertips	WHL	29	4	13	17	28	12	0	3	3	8

CUNNING, Cam (KUH-nihng, KAM) **CGY.**

Left wing. Shoots left. 6'1", 215 lbs. Born, Powell River, B.C., June 4, 1985.
(Calgary's 8th choice, 240th overall, in 2003 Entry Draft).

			Regular Season					Playoffs				
Season	**Club**	**League**	**GP**	**G**	**A**	**Pts**	**PIM**	**GP**	**G**	**A**	**Pts**	**PIM**
2002-03	Kamloops Blazers	WHL	71	7	12	19	54	6	1	0	1	2
2003-04	Kamloops Blazers	WHL	65	14	13	27	62	5	1	1	2	10
2004-05	Kamloops Blazers	WHL	39	14	8	22	63	....	....	....	....	....
	Vancouver Giants	WHL	30	3	7	10	19	6	1	3	4	14
2005-06	Red Deer Rebels	WHL	40	19	13	32	52	....	....	....	....	....
	Omaha	AHL	30	2	4	6	24	....	....	....	....	....
2006-07	Omaha	AHL	60	12	5	17	45	6	0	2	2	2

CUNTI, Luca (KOON-tee, LOO-ka) **T.B.**

Center. Shoots left. 6', 190 lbs. Born, Zurich, Switz., July 4, 1989.
(Tampa Bay's 2nd choice, 75th overall, in 2007 Entry Draft).

			Regular Season					Playoffs				
Season	**Club**	**League**	**GP**	**G**	**A**	**Pts**	**PIM**	**GP**	**G**	**A**	**Pts**	**PIM**
2004-05	GCK Zurich Jr.	Swiss-Jr.	32	12	10	22	18	....	....	....	....	....
2005-06	GCK Lions Zurich	Swiss-2	7	0	0	0	2	....	....	....	....	....
	GCK Zurich Jr.	Swiss-Jr.	48	20	24	44	34	....	....	....	....	....
2006-07	GCK Zurich Jr.	Swiss-Jr.	13	9	7	16	22	....	....	....	....	....
	Switzerland U20	Swiss-2	3	0	0	0	2	....	....	....	....	....
	HC Thurgau	Swiss-2	5	1	0	1	6	....	....	....	....	....
	GCK Lions Zurich	Swiss-2	5	1	1	2	0	....	....	....	....	....
	EHC Dubendorf	Swiss-3	STATISTICS NOT AVAILABLE									

CURRY, Mike (KUH-ree, MIGHK) **L.A.**

Right wing. Shoots right. 6'4", 190 lbs. Born, Fort Benning, GA, September 20, 1984.
(Los Angeles' 6th choice, 205th overall, in 2004 Entry Draft).

			Regular Season					Playoffs				
Season	**Club**	**League**	**GP**	**G**	**A**	**Pts**	**PIM**	**GP**	**G**	**A**	**Pts**	**PIM**
2002-03	Sioux City	USHL	52	6	13	19	58	4	1	2	3	2
2003-04	Sioux City	USHL	60	20	20	40	119	7	2	5	7	16
2004-05	U. Minn-Duluth	WCHA	22	3	6	9	35	....	....	....	....	....
2005-06	U. Minn-Duluth	WCHA	36	2	3	5	68	....	....	....	....	....
2006-07	U. Minn-Duluth	WCHA	36	3	11	14	60	....	....	....	....	....

CURRY, Sean (KUH-ree, SHAWN) **BOS.**

Defense. Shoots right. 6'4", 230 lbs. Born, Burnsville, MN, April 29, 1982.
(Carolina's 6th choice, 211th overall, in 2001 Entry Draft).

			Regular Season					Playoffs				
Season	**Club**	**League**	**GP**	**G**	**A**	**Pts**	**PIM**	**GP**	**G**	**A**	**Pts**	**PIM**
99-2000	Burnsville	High-MN	23	8	18	26	....	....	....	....	....	....
2000-01	Tri-City Americans	WHL	72	5	12	17	113	....	....	....	....	....
2001-02	Tri-City Americans	WHL	36	6	6	12	84	....	....	....	....	....
	Medicine Hat	WHL	24	4	13	17	43	....	....	....	....	....
2002-03	Lowell	AHL	35	0	2	2	62	....	....	....	....	....
	Florida Everblades	ECHL	32	1	6	7	77	1	0	0	0	0
2003-04	Lowell	AHL	74	1	8	9	66	....	....	....	....	....
2004-05	Lowell	AHL	61	2	7	9	103	7	0	1	1	4
2005-06	Providence Bruins	AHL	72	4	4	8	144	6	0	1	1	20
2006-07	Providence Bruins	AHL	64	5	8	13	122	13	2	9	11	28

Signed as a free agent by **Boston**, August 8, 2007.

DADONOV, Evgeni (do-DON-nauv, ehv-GEH-nee) **FLA.**

Right wing. Shoots left. 5'10", 178 lbs. Born, Chelyabinsk, USSR, March 12, 1989.
(Florida's 3rd choice, 71st overall, in 2007 Entry Draft).

			Regular Season					Playoffs				
Season	**Club**	**League**	**GP**	**G**	**A**	**Pts**	**PIM**	**GP**	**G**	**A**	**Pts**	**PIM**
2005-06	Chelyabinsk 2	Russia-3	12	1	4	5	2	....	....	....	....	....
	Chelyabinsk	Russia-2	....	....	....	....	....	1	0	0	0	0
2006-07	Chelyabinsk 2	Russia-3	4	2	0	2	14	....	....	....	....	....
	Chelyabinsk	Russia	24	1	1	2	8	....	....	....	....	....

D'AGOSTINI, Matt (DAG-uh-stee-noh, MAT) **MTL.**

Right wing. Shoots right. 6', 182 lbs. Born, Sault Ste. Marie, Ont., October 23, 1986.
(Montreal's 5th choice, 190th overall, in 2005 Entry Draft).

			Regular Season					Playoffs				
Season	**Club**	**League**	**GP**	**G**	**A**	**Pts**	**PIM**	**GP**	**G**	**A**	**Pts**	**PIM**
2003-04	Soo North Stars	GNML	36	36	23	59	41	....	....	....	....	....
2004-05	Guelph Storm	OHL	59	24	22	46	29	4	0	2	2	8
2005-06	Guelph Storm	OHL	66	25	54	79	81	15	8	20	28	16
2006-07	Hamilton Bulldogs	AHL	63	21	28	49	33	22	4	9	13	18

D'AMOUR, Dominic (dah-MOHR, DOHM-ihn-ihk)

Defense. Shoots left. 6'3", 202 lbs. Born, LaSalle, Que., January 28, 1984.
(Toronto's 4th choice, 88th overall, in 2002 Entry Draft).

			Regular Season					Playoffs				
Season	**Club**	**League**	**GP**	**G**	**A**	**Pts**	**PIM**	**GP**	**G**	**A**	**Pts**	**PIM**
99-2000	Charles-Lemoyne	QAAA	35	3	8	11	47	16	1	1	2	14
2000-01	Charles-Lemoyne	QAAA	11	1	4	5	36	....	....	....	....	....
	Rouyn-Noranda	QMJHL	18	0	0	0	10	....	....	....	....	....
2001-02	Hull Olympiques	QMJHL	68	5	5	10	225	12	0	3	3	32
2002-03	Hull Olympiques	QMJHL	65	5	25	30	211	17	2	3	5	51
2003-04	Gatineau	QMJHL	61	15	38	53	211	15	3	6	9	*41
2004-05	St. John's	AHL	26	1	1	2	60	1	0	0	0	0
	Pensacola	ECHL	22	4	8	12	33	4	0	0	0	2
2005-06	Toronto Marlies	AHL	30	1	3	4	25	....	....	....	....	....
2006-07	Toronto Marlies	AHL	42	2	9	11	59	....	....	....	....	....

DANIS-PEPIN, Simon (da-NEE-peh-PEH, see-MOHN) **CHI.**

Defense. Shoots right. 6'7", 217 lbs. Born, Gatineau, Que., April 11, 1988.
(Chicago's 3rd choice, 61st overall, in 2006 Entry Draft).

			Regular Season					Playoffs				
Season	**Club**	**League**	**GP**	**G**	**A**	**Pts**	**PIM**	**GP**	**G**	**A**	**Pts**	**PIM**
2003-04	Gatineau Intrepide	QAAA	33	2	14	16	20	2	0	0	0	0
2004-05	Gatineau Intrepide	QAAA	39	6	31	37	64	14	6	7	13	25
2005-06	N.H. Jr. Monarchs	EJHL	2	0	0	0	0	....	....	....	....	....
	U. of Maine	H-East	23	0	5	5	14	....	....	....	....	....
2006-07	U. of Maine	H-East	40	2	4	6	18	....	....	....	....	....

DASILVA, Dan (duh-SIHL-vah, DAN) **COL.**

Right wing. Shoots right. 6'1", 195 lbs. Born, Saskatoon, Sask., April 30, 1985.

			Regular Season					Playoffs				
Season	Club	League	GP	G	A	Pts	PIM	GP	G	A	Pts	PIM
2002-03	Portland	WHL	64	9	13	22	81	7	0	4	4	16
2003-04	Portland	WHL	65	36	20	56	120	5	0	1	1	6
2004-05	Portland	WHL	71	31	42	73	127	5	1	1	2	6
2005-06	Lowell	AHL	25	3	2	5	27	....	....	....	....	....
	San Diego Gulls	ECHL	4	5	3	8	2	....	....	....	....	....
2006-07	Albany River Rats	AHL	43	11	8	19	33	....	....	....	....	....
	Arizona Sundogs	CHL	14	9	13	22	10	....	....	....	....	....

Signed as a free agent by **Colorado**, October 11, 2005.

DAUGAVINS, Kaspars (DAH-gah-vihnsh, KAS-purz) **OTT.**

Left wing. Shoots left. 5'11", 181 lbs. Born, Riga, USSR, May 18, 1988.
(Ottawa's 3rd choice, 91st overall, in 2006 Entry Draft).

			Regular Season					Playoffs				
Season	Club	League	GP	G	A	Pts	PIM	GP	G	A	Pts	PIM
2003-04	HK Riga 2000	EEHL	2	0	1	1	0	....	....	....	....	....
	Prizma/Riga 86	Latvia	14	6	6	12	10	2	1	1	2	4
2004-05	CSKA Moscow 2	Russia-3	STATISTICS NOT AVAILABLE									
2005-06	HK Riga 2000	Latvia	....	4	6	10	16	....	....	....	....	....
	HK Riga 2000	BelOpen	45	4	11	15	16	....	....	....	....	....
2006-07	St. Michael's	OHL	61	18	42	60	64	....	....	....	....	....
	Binghamton	AHL	11	2	0	2	9	....	....	....	....	....

OHL All-Rookie Team (2007)

D'AVERSA, Jonathan (dah-VEHR-sah, JAWN-ah-thuhn) **PIT.**

Defense. Shoots right. 6'2", 200 lbs. Born, Richmond Hill, Ont., March 2, 1986.

			Regular Season					Playoffs				
Season	Club	League	GP	G	A	Pts	PIM	GP	G	A	Pts	PIM
2002-03	Stouffville Spirit	OPJHL	49	4	21	25	18	....	....	....	....	....
2003-04	Sudbury Wolves	OHL	63	1	14	15	22	7	0	1	1	2
2004-05	Sudbury Wolves	OHL	67	5	24	29	42	12	4	6	10	8
2005-06	Sudbury Wolves	OHL	62	7	39	46	83	10	2	0	2	17
2006-07	Sudbury Wolves	OHL	67	13	47	60	53	21	3	15	18	16

Signed as a free agent by **Pittsburgh**, May 24, 2007.

DAVIS, Nathan (DAY-vihs, NAY-thuhn) **CHI.**

Center/Left wing. Shoots left. 6'1", 193 lbs. Born, Cleveland, OH, May 23, 1986.
(Chicago's 6th choice, 113th overall, in 2005 Entry Draft).

			Regular Season					Playoffs				
Season	Club	League	GP	G	A	Pts	PIM	GP	G	A	Pts	PIM
2002-03	USNTDP	NAHL	20	2	3	5	23	....	....	....	....	....
2003-04	USNTDP	U-18	46	7	8	15	16	....	....	....	....	....
	USNTDP	NAHL	11	3	6	9	17	....	....	....	....	....
2004-05	Miami U.	CCHA	38	14	11	25	30	....	....	....	....	....
2005-06	Miami U.	CCHA	37	20	20	40	34	....	....	....	....	....
2006-07	Miami U.	CCHA	42	21	29	50	24	....	....	....	....	....

CCHA First All-Star Team (2006) • CCHA Second All-Star Team (2007) • NCAA West Second All-American Team (2007)

DAVIS, Patrick (DAY-vihs, PAT-rihk) **N.J.**

Center. Shoots right. 6'3", 205 lbs. Born, Sterling, MI, December 28, 1986.
(New Jersey's 4th choice, 99th overall, in 2005 Entry Draft).

			Regular Season					Playoffs				
Season	Club	League	GP	G	A	Pts	PIM	GP	G	A	Pts	PIM
2002-03	Detroit Belle Tire	MWEHL	STATISTICS NOT AVAILABLE									
	Sioux City	USHL	16	3	2	5	8	1	0	0	0	2
2003-04	Kitchener Rangers	OHL	27	8	10	18	21	....	....	....	....	....
2004-05	Kitchener Rangers	OHL	59	20	30	50	41	14	3	4	7	20
2005-06	Kitchener Rangers	OHL	22	13	4	17	30	....	....	....	....	....
	Windsor Spitfires	OHL	38	22	29	51	64	7	2	6	8	12
	Albany River Rats	AHL	3	0	0	0	2	....	....	....	....	....
2006-07	Lowell Devils	AHL	41	5	13	18	26	....	....	....	....	....

DAY, Brian (DAY, BRIGH-uhn) **NYI**

Right wing. Shoots right. 6', 186 lbs. Born, Boston, MA, August 4, 1988.
(NY Islanders' 11th choice, 171st overall, in 2006 Entry Draft).

			Regular Season					Playoffs				
Season	Club	League	GP	G	A	Pts	PIM	GP	G	A	Pts	PIM
2003-04	Gov. Dummer	High-MA	25	8	15	23	....	....	....	....	....	....
2004-05	Gov. Dummer	High-MA	25	11	13	24	30	....	....	....	....	....
2005-06	Gov. Dummer	High-MA	28	9	13	22	34	....	....	....	....	....
2006-07	Gov. Academy	High-MA	27	20	18	38	....	....	....	....	....	....

• Signed Letter of Intent to attend **Colgate University** (ECACHL) in fall of 2007.

DEE, Robby (DEE, RAW-bee) **EDM.**

Center/Wing. Shoots left. 6'2", 185 lbs. Born, Minneapolis, MN, April 9, 1987.
(Edmonton's 4th choice, 86th overall, in 2005 Entry Draft).

			Regular Season					Playoffs				
Season	Club	League	GP	G	A	Pts	PIM	GP	G	A	Pts	PIM
2004-05	Breck Mustangs	High-MN	28	49	38	87	14	....	....	....	....	....
2005-06	Omaha Lancers	USHL	32	6	6	12	20	3	1	0	1	2
2006-07	Omaha Lancers	USHL	34	11	14	25	60	....	....	....	....	....

DEGON, Marvin (DEE-gawn, MAR-vihn) **MTL.**

Defense. Shoots right. 5'11", 190 lbs. Born, Worcester, MA, July 20, 1983.

			Regular Season					Playoffs				
Season	Club	League	GP	G	A	Pts	PIM	GP	G	A	Pts	PIM
2002-03	Massachusetts	H-East	36	2	14	16	14	....	....	....	....	....
2003-04	Massachusetts	H-East	36	5	15	20	18	....	....	....	....	....
2004-05	Massachusetts	H-East	38	10	8	18	44	....	....	....	....	....
2005-06	Massachusetts	H-East	36	10	19	29	33	....	....	....	....	....
	Hartford Wolf Pack	AHL	14	2	4	6	4	13	0	5	5	6
2006-07	Hartford Wolf Pack	AHL	71	8	26	34	40	7	0	1	1	0

Signed as a free agent by **Montreal**, July 5, 2007.

DEGRAY, John (DIH-gray, JAWN) **ANA.**

Defense. Shoots left. 6'4", 210 lbs. Born, Richmond Hill, Ont., March 14, 1988.
(Anaheim's 3rd choice, 83rd overall, in 2006 Entry Draft).

			Regular Season					Playoffs				
Season	Club	League	GP	G	A	Pts	PIM	GP	G	A	Pts	PIM
2003-04	Richmond Hill	Minor-ON	76	5	35	40	107	....	....	....	....	....
2004-05	Brampton	OHL	52	2	8	10	51	6	0	0	0	2
2005-06	Brampton	OHL	68	0	10	10	103	11	0	0	0	8
2006-07	Brampton	OHL	65	4	13	17	75	4	1	0	1	10

DELORY, James (deh-LOR-ee, JAYMZ) **S.J.**

Defense. Shoots right. 6'4", 220 lbs. Born, Scarborough, Ont., March 3, 1988.
(San Jose's 3rd choice, 98th overall, in 2006 Entry Draft).

			Regular Season					Playoffs				
Season	Club	League	GP	G	A	Pts	PIM	GP	G	A	Pts	PIM
2004-05	Oshawa Generals	OHL	61	1	4	5	82	....	....	....	....	....
2005-06	Oshawa Generals	OHL	67	6	26	32	136	....	....	....	....	....
2006-07	Oshawa Generals	OHL	61	4	21	25	167	9	0	4	4	16

DEMEN-WILLAUME, Richard (deh-MEHN-WIHL-awm, RIH-kahrd) **COL.**

Defense. Shoots left. 6'3", 210 lbs. Born, Asa, Sweden, January 28, 1986.
(Colorado's 4th choice, 154th overall, in 2004 Entry Draft).

			Regular Season					Playoffs				
Season	Club	League	GP	G	A	Pts	PIM	GP	G	A	Pts	PIM
2001-02	V.Frolunda U18	Swe-U18	13	2	2	4	14	3	1	0	1	2
	V.Frolunda Jr.	Swe-Jr.	1	0	0	0	0	....	....	....	....	....
2002-03	V.Frolunda Jr.	Swe-Jr.	22	0	6	6	14	5	0	1	1	6
	V.Frolunda U18	Swe-U18	1	0	0	0	2	7	1	2	3	4
2003-04	V.Frolunda Jr.	Swe-Jr.	35	6	7	13	22	....	....	....	....	....
2004-05	Frolunda	Sweden	9	0	0	0	0	1	0	0	0	0
	Frolunda Jr.	Swe-Jr.	32	3	12	15	63	6	1	1	2	22
2005-06	Frolunda Jr.	Swe-Jr.	10	4	8	12	8	6	3	5	8	31
	Frolunda	Sweden	42	2	1	3	26	....	....	....	....	....
2006-07	Arizona Sundogs	CHL	9	0	2	2	16	....	....	....	....	....

DENISOV, Denis (den-NEES-ahf, deh-NEES) **BUF.**

Left wing. Shoots left. 6', 183 lbs. Born, Kalinin, USSR, December 31, 1981.
(Buffalo's 4th choice, 149th overall, in 2000 Entry Draft).

			Regular Season					Playoffs				
Season	Club	League	GP	G	A	Pts	PIM	GP	G	A	Pts	PIM
1997-98	HK CSKA Moscow	Russia	7	0	0	0	4	....	....	....	....	....
1998-99	HK CSKA Moscow	Russia-2	42	1	6	7	16	....	....	....	....	....
99-2000	HK Moscow	Russia-2	39	1	8	9	16	....	....	....	....	....
2000-01	HK Moscow	Russia-2	41	0	3	3	6	....	....	....	....	....
2001-02	Krylja Sovetov	Russia	47	3	4	7	37	....	....	....	....	....
	Krylja Sovetov 2	Russia-3	3	0	1	1	18	....	....	....	....	....
2002-03	Ufa	Russia	50	2	8	10	12	3	0	1	1	0
2003-04	Ak Bars Kazan	Russia	51	4	11	15	34	7	0	0	0	4
2004-05	Ak Bars Kazan	Russia	57	4	7	11	30	4	0	0	0	2
2005-06	Ak Bars Kazan	Russia	22	0	2	2	51	2	0	0	0	4
2006-07	Avangard Omsk	Russia	52	2	10	12	32	9	1	2	3	4

DENNY, Chad (DEHN-ee, CHAD) **ATL.**

Defense. Shoots left. 6'3", 220 lbs. Born, Sydney, N.S., March 27, 1987.
(Atlanta's 3rd choice, 49th overall, in 2005 Entry Draft).

			Regular Season					Playoffs				
Season	Club	League	GP	G	A	Pts	PIM	GP	G	A	Pts	PIM
2003-04	Lewiston	QMJHL	41	3	6	9	19	7	0	0	0	11
2004-05	Lewiston	QMJHL	53	8	18	26	98	8	2	2	4	14
2005-06	Lewiston	QMJHL	62	19	28	47	150	6	0	3	3	10
2006-07	Lewiston	QMJHL	59	17	48	65	89	17	10	9	19	32

DERLYUK, Roman (duhr-LYUHK, ROH-muhn) **FLA.**

Defense. Shoots left. 6'3", 198 lbs. Born, Leningrad, USSR, October 27, 1986.
(Florida's 7th choice, 164th overall, in 2005 Entry Draft).

			Regular Season					Playoffs				
Season	Club	League	GP	G	A	Pts	PIM	GP	G	A	Pts	PIM
2003-04	Lokom. St. Pete.	Russia-3	STATISTICS NOT AVAILABLE									
2004-05	Spartak St. Pet.	Russia-2	51	0	3	3	74	....	....	....	....	....
2005-06	SKA St. Petersburg	Russia	32	0	3	3	63	2	1	0	1	0
	St. Petersburg 2	Russia-3	2	0	1	1	0	....	....	....	....	....
2006-07	SKA St. Petersburg	Russia	6	0	1	1	4	....	....	....	....	....
	St. Petersburg 2	Russia-3	6	1	4	5	6	....	....	....	....	....
	THK Tver	Russia-3	2	0	2	2	0	....	....	....	....	....
	MVD	Russia	19	0	3	3	14	1	0	0	0	0

DESBIENS, Guillaume (deh-BYEHN, GEE-OHM) **ATL.**

Right wing. Shoots right. 6'2", 210 lbs. Born, Alma, Que., April 20, 1985.
(Atlanta's 3rd choice, 116th overall, in 2003 Entry Draft).

			Regular Season					Playoffs				
Season	Club	League	GP	G	A	Pts	PIM	GP	G	A	Pts	PIM
2001-02	Rouyn-Noranda	QMJHL	65	14	10	24	115	4	1	1	2	9
2002-03	Rouyn-Noranda	QMJHL	64	15	18	33	233	4	0	0	0	4
2003-04	Rouyn-Noranda	QMJHL	58	20	21	41	199	11	2	2	4	24
2004-05	Rouyn-Noranda	QMJHL	56	27	16	43	206	10	1	4	5	25
2005-06	Chicago Wolves	AHL	3	0	0	0	7	....	....	....	....	....
	Gwinnett	ECHL	65	33	27	60	187	17	10	6	16	38
2006-07	Chicago Wolves	AHL	54	3	6	9	118	6	0	1	1	2

DESIMONE, Phil (dih-SEE-mohn, FIHL) **WSH.**

Center. Shoots left. 6', 193 lbs. Born, East Amherst, NY, March 19, 1987.
(Washington's 4th choice, 84th overall, in 2007 Entry Draft).

			Regular Season					Playoffs				
Season	Club	League	GP	G	A	Pts	PIM	GP	G	A	Pts	PIM
2004-05	Sioux City	USHL	44	2	7	9	28	6	0	1	1	4
2006-07	Sioux City	USHL	60	26	47	73	60	7	6	6	12	2

• Signed Letter of Intent to attend **University of New Hampshire** (Hockey East) in fall of 2007.

DEVEAUX, Andre (de-VOH, AWN-dray)

Center. Shoots right. 6'3", 240 lbs. Born, Freeport, Bahamas, February 23, 1984.
(Montreal's 4th choice, 182nd overall, in 2002 Entry Draft).

			Regular Season					Playoffs				
Season	Club	League	GP	G	A	Pts	PIM	GP	G	A	Pts	PIM
2000-01	Belleville Bulls	OHL	58	3	6	9	65	10	3	6	9	6
2001-02	Belleville Bulls	OHL	64	8	13	21	89	11	1	2	3	30
2002-03	Belleville Bulls	OHL	34	6	12	18	93	....	....	....	....	....
	Owen Sound	OHL	29	9	10	19	33	4	2	2	4	6
2003-04	Owen Sound	OHL	64	16	30	46	151	7	3	3	6	21
2004-05	Springfield Falcons	AHL	73	4	8	12	210	....	....	....	....	....
2005-06	Springfield Falcons	AHL	59	6	5	11	135	....	....	....	....	....
	Johnstown Chiefs	ECHL	11	4	7	11	36	5	1	1	2	2
2006-07	Springfield Falcons	AHL	8	1	2	3	8	....	....	....	....	....
	Johnstown Chiefs	ECHL	21	6	8	14	51	....	....	....	....	....
	Chicago Wolves	AHL	28	4	4	8	105	14	3	2	5	48

Signed as a free agent by **Tampa Bay**, September 15, 2004. Traded to **Atlanta** by **Tampa Bay** with Andy Delmore for and Stephen Baby and Kyle Wanvig, February 1, 2007.

DiCASMIRRO, Nate (dee-KAZ-MIHR-oh, NAYT) BOS.

Left wing. Shoots left. 5'11", 205 lbs. Born, Atikokan, Ont., September 27, 1978.

			Regular Season					Playoffs				
Season	Club	League	GP	G	A	Pts	PIM	GP	G	A	Pts	PIM
1996-97	North Iowa	USHL	51	18	22	40	86	12	0	6	6	22
1997-98	North Iowa	USHL	52	29	45	74	118	11	5	5	10	34
1998-99	St. Cloud State	WCHA	34	6	8	14	46	....	....	....	....	....
99-2000	St. Cloud State	WCHA	40	19	24	43	26	....	....	....	....	....
2000-01	St. Cloud State	WCHA	32	9	20	29	26	....	....	....	....	....
2001-02	St. Cloud State	WCHA	41	17	33	50	58	....	....	....	....	....
	Hamilton Bulldogs	AHL	1	0	0	0	0	10	0	5	5	6
2002-03	Hamilton Bulldogs	AHL	49	5	12	17	22	16	2	1	3	8
2003-04	Toronto	AHL	71	17	18	35	37	2	0	1	1	0
2004-05	Edmonton	AHL	77	7	18	25	48	....	....	....	....	....
2005-06	Grand Rapids	AHL	72	16	36	52	97	16	3	3	6	20
2006-07	Providence Bruins	AHL	68	10	18	28	59	13	4	0	4	10

USHL First All-Star Team (1998) • USHL MVP (1998) • WCHA Second All-Star Team (2002)

Signed as a free agent by **Edmonton**, May 28, 2002. Signed as a free agent by **Boston**, July 17, 2006.

DIDIOMETE, Devin (dih-dee-OH-meht, DEH-vihn) CGY.

Left wing. Shoots left. 5'11", 189 lbs. Born, Stratford, Ont., May 9, 1988.
(Calgary's 7th choice, 187th overall, in 2006 Entry Draft).

			Regular Season					Playoffs				
Season	Club	League	GP	G	A	Pts	PIM	GP	G	A	Pts	PIM
2004-05	Sudbury Wolves	OHL	58	7	8	15	113	11	0	1	1	11
2005-06	Sudbury Wolves	OHL	60	15	21	36	202	10	0	4	4	26
2006-07	Sudbury Wolves	OHL	62	21	19	40	205	21	6	6	12	62

DIDOMENICO, Christopher (dee-DOH-mehn-ih-koh, KRIHS-tuh-fuh TOR.

Center. Shoots right. 5'11", 165 lbs. Born, Toronto, Ont., February 20, 1989.
(Toronto's 5th choice, 164th overall, in 2007 Entry Draft).

			Regular Season					Playoffs				
Season	Club	League	GP	G	A	Pts	PIM	GP	G	A	Pts	PIM
2005-06	North York	GTHL	36	28	35	63	....	....	....	....	....	....
	North York	OPJHL	2	2	0	2	0	....	....	....	....	....
2006-07	Saint John	QMJHL	70	25	50	75	60	....	....	....	....	....

QMJHL All-Rookie Team (2007)

DIETRICH, Robert (DEET-rihkh, RAW-buhrt) NSH.

Defense. Shoots left. 5'10", 172 lbs. Born, Ordzhonikidze, USSR, July 25, 1986.
(Nashville's 8th choice, 174th overall, in 2007 Entry Draft).

			Regular Season					Playoffs				
Season	Club	League	GP	G	A	Pts	PIM	GP	G	A	Pts	PIM
2001-02	Kaufbeuren Jr.	Ger-Jr.	9	1	2	3	2	....	....	....	....	....
2002-03	Mannheim Jr.	Ger-Jr.	33	4	13	17	39	3	0	1	1	4
2003-04	EC Peiting	German-3	42	5	9	24	83	....	....	....	....	....
2004-05	ETC Crimmitschau	German-2	45	3	14	17	34	10	0	0	0	6
2005-06	Straubing Tigers	German-2	46	5	3	8	55	15	0	1	1	8
	Dusseldorf	Germany	4	0	0	0	2	....	....	....	....	....
2006-07	Dusseldorf	Germany	52	3	19	22	28	9	2	4	6	22

DILLON, Spencer (DIH-luhn, SPEHN-suhr) FLA.

Defense. Shoots right. 6'4", 190 lbs. Born, Santa Cruz, CA, January 7, 1985.
(Florida's 6th choice, 267th overall, in 2004 Entry Draft).

			Regular Season					Playoffs				
Season	Club	League	GP	G	A	Pts	PIM	GP	G	A	Pts	PIM
2003-04	Salmon Arm	BCHL	42	0	7	7	160	14	0	2	2	22
2004-05	Green Bay	USHL	54	1	2	3	91	....	....	....	....	....
2005-06	Northern Mich.	CCHA	6	0	1	1	14	....	....	....	....	....
2006-07	Northern Mich.	CCHA	15	0	1	1	16	....	....	....	....	....

• Missed majority of 2005-06 season due to injury.

DINGLE, Ryan (DIHN-guhl, RIGH-uhn) ANA.

Left wing. Shoots left. 5'10", 190 lbs. Born, Steamboat Springs, CO, April 4, 1984.

			Regular Season					Playoffs				
Season	Club	League	GP	G	A	Pts	PIM	GP	G	A	Pts	PIM
2001-02	Des Moines	USHL	61	7	10	17	63	3	1	0	1	2
2002-03	Des Moines	USHL	26	8	6	14	16	....	....	....	....	....
	Tri-City Storm	USHL	32	17	17	34	31	3	0	0	0	6
2003-04	Tri-City Storm	USHL	38	13	23	36	14	9	3	7	10	4
2004-05	U. of Denver	WCHA	41	6	12	18	32	....	....	....	....	....
2005-06	U. of Denver	WCHA	38	27	16	43	37	....	....	....	....	....
2006-07	U. of Denver	WCHA	40	22	15	37	38	....	....	....	....	....
	Portland Pirates	AHL	4	0	1	1	4	....	....	....	....	....

Signed as a free agent by **Anaheim**, March 26, 2007.

DIXON, Stephen (DIHX-uhn, STEE-vehn) ANA.

Center. Shoots left. 5'11", 188 lbs. Born, Halifax, N.S., September 7, 1985.
(Pittsburgh's 9th choice, 229th overall, in 2003 Entry Draft).

			Regular Season					Playoffs				
Season	Club	League	GP	G	A	Pts	PIM	GP	G	A	Pts	PIM
2001-02	Cape Breton	QMJHL	64	16	15	31	12	16	3	5	8	12
2002-03	Cape Breton	QMJHL	72	28	42	70	54	4	0	0	0	6
2003-04	Cape Breton	QMJHL	55	22	50	72	33	5	1	0	1	0
2004-05	Cape Breton	QMJHL	45	17	34	51	40	....	....	....	....	....
2005-06	Wilkes-Barre	AHL	80	12	17	29	45	11	0	1	1	4
2006-07	Wilkes-Barre	AHL	80	17	24	41	43	11	2	3	5	6

Traded to **Anaheim** by **Pittsburgh** for Tim Brent, June 23, 2007.

DOBRYSHKIN, Yuri (doh-BRIHSH-kihn, YOO-ree) ATL.

Right wing. Shoots right. 6', 190 lbs. Born, Penza, USSR, July 19, 1979.
(Atlanta's 7th choice, 159th overall, in 1999 Entry Draft).

			Regular Season					Playoffs				
Season	Club	League	GP	G	A	Pts	PIM	GP	G	A	Pts	PIM
1996-97	Krylja Sovetov 2	Russia-3	35	13	5	18	42	....	....	....	....	....
	Krylja Sovetov	Russia	2	0	0	0	0	2	0	0	0	0
1997-98	Krylja Sovetov 2	Russia-3	26	12	5	17	68	....	....	....	....	....
	Krylja Sovetov	Russia	22	4	0	4	12	....	....	....	....	....
1998-99	Krylja Sovetov	Russia	50	11	5	16	86	....	....	....	....	....
99-2000	Ak Bars Kazan	Russia	27	6	9	15	24	17	2	0	2	10
2000-01	Ak Bars Kazan	Russia	40	10	5	15	32	4	2	0	2	2
2001-02	Ak Bars Kazan	Russia	38	9	8	17	22	11	0	2	2	6
2002-03	Cherepovets	Russia	49	19	7	26	82	12	5	2	7	12
2003-04	Cherepovets	Russia	53	11	7	18	75	....	....	....	....	....
2004-05	Magnitogorsk	Russia	54	14	6	20	42	2	0	0	0	0
2005-06	Magnitogorsk	Russia	15	3	1	4	22	8	0	0	0	0
	Magnitogorsk 2	Russia-3	2	3	1	4	2	....	....	....	....	....
2006-07	CSKA Moscow	Russia	50	5	10	15	65	12	3	0	3	12

DODGE, Nick (DAWGE, NIHK) CAR.

Right wing. Shoots right. 5'10", 175 lbs. Born, Oakville, Ont., May 1, 1986.
(Carolina's 5th choice, 183rd overall, in 2006 Entry Draft).

			Regular Season					Playoffs				
Season	Club	League	GP	G	A	Pts	PIM	GP	G	A	Pts	PIM
2004-05	Clarkson Knights	ECACHL	37	6	12	18	42	....	....	....	....	....
2005-06	Clarkson Knights	ECACHL	38	16	25	41	72	....	....	....	....	....
2006-07	Clarkson Knights	ECACHL	36	18	21	39	32	....	....	....	....	....

ECACHL First All-Star Team (2007) • NCAA East Second All-American Team (2007)

DOELL, Kevin (DOH-ehl, KEH-vihn)

Center. Shoots left. 5'11", 190 lbs. Born, Saskatoon, Sask., July 15, 1979.

			Regular Season					Playoffs				
Season	Club	League	GP	G	A	Pts	PIM	GP	G	A	Pts	PIM
99-2000	U. of Denver	WCHA	40	8	15	23	18	....	....	....	....	....
2000-01	U. of Denver	WCHA	36	9	10	19	26	....	....	....	....	....
2001-02	U. of Denver	WCHA	41	20	23	43	28	....	....	....	....	....
2002-03	U. of Denver	WCHA	41	25	26	51	34	....	....	....	....	....
2003-04	Chicago Wolves	AHL	8	1	1	2	6	1	0	0	0	0
	Gwinnett	ECHL	63	33	41	74	88	13	1	6	7	12
2004-05	Chicago Wolves	AHL	45	4	8	12	69	....	....	....	....	....
	Gwinnett	ECHL	11	6	9	15	14	8	2	1	3	14
2005-06	Chicago Wolves	AHL	78	17	34	51	72	....	....	....	....	....
2006-07	Chicago Wolves	AHL	80	14	19	33	107	15	2	4	6	14

ECHL All-Rookie Team (2004) • ECHL Rookie of the Year (2004)

Signed as a free agent by **Atlanta**, June 30, 2004. Signed as a free agent by **Espoo** (Finland), June 6, 2007.

DONALLY, Ryan (DAWN-ah-lee, RIGH-uhn) CGY.

Left wing. Shoots left. 6'5", 224 lbs. Born, Tecumseh, Ont., February 4, 1985.
(Calgary's 3rd choice, 97th overall, in 2003 Entry Draft).

			Regular Season					Playoffs				
Season	Club	League	GP	G	A	Pts	PIM	GP	G	A	Pts	PIM
2001-02	Windsor Spitfires	OHL	53	6	7	13	77	16	0	2	2	6
2002-03	Windsor Spitfires	OHL	65	11	15	26	108	7	0	1	1	8
2003-04	Windsor Spitfires	OHL	44	8	14	22	93	....	....	....	....	....
2004-05	Windsor Spitfires	OHL	29	2	3	5	87	....	....	....	....	....
	Kitchener Rangers	OHL	21	1	2	3	45	13	0	0	0	12
2005-06	Kitchener Rangers	OHL	8	0	0	0	29	....	....	....	....	....
	Sudbury Wolves	OHL	39	5	5	10	76	10	0	1	1	27
2006-07	Omaha	AHL	18	3	2	5	38	....	....	....	....	....
	Las Vegas	ECHL	33	3	5	8	79	3	0	0	0	4

DONIKA, Mikhail (DAW-nih-ka, mih-kigh-EHL) DAL.

Defense. Shoots left. 6', 185 lbs. Born, Yaroslavl, USSR, May 15, 1979.
(Dallas' 11th choice, 272nd overall, in 1999 Entry Draft).

			Regular Season					Playoffs				
Season	Club	League	GP	G	A	Pts	PIM	GP	G	A	Pts	PIM
1996-97	Yaroslavl 2	Russia-3	15	3	5	8	6	....	....	....	....	....
	Torpedo Yaroslavl	Russia	22	1	0	1	6	2	0	0	0	0
1997-98	Yaroslavl 2	Russia-2	19	1	2	3	32	....	....	....	....	....
	Torpedo Yaroslavl	Russia	30	0	2	2	14	....	....	....	....	....
1998-99	Yaroslavl 2	Russia-3	6	2	1	3	4	....	....	....	....	....
	Torpedo Yaroslavl	Russia	37	0	1	1	10	....	....	....	....	....
99-2000	Torpedo Yaroslavl	Russia	35	0	1	1	22	10	0	0	0	4
2000-01	Dynamo Moscow	Russia	43	1	3	4	12	....	....	....	....	....
2001-02	Amur Khabarovsk	Russia	51	1	3	4	66	....	....	....	....	....
2002-03	Spartak Moscow	Russia	51	4	7	11	16	....	....	....	....	....
2003-04	Spartak Moscow	Russia-2	55	4	14	18	14	12	2	1	3	2
2004-05	Spartak Moscow	Russia	49	0	2	2	34	....	....	....	....	....
2005-06	Perm	Russia	26	0	0	0	18	....	....	....	....	....
	Sibir Novosibirsk	Russia	14	1	3	4	8	3	0	1	1	0
2006-07	Nizhny Novgorod	Russia-2	47	8	16	24	38	14	3	0	3	14

DORSETT, Derek (DORH-seht, DAIR-ihk) CBJ

Right wing. Shoots right. 5'11", 176 lbs. Born, Kindersley, Sask., December 20, 1986.
(Columbus' 9th choice, 189th overall, in 2006 Entry Draft).

			Regular Season					Playoffs				
Season	Club	League	GP	G	A	Pts	PIM	GP	G	A	Pts	PIM
2004-05	Medicine Hat	WHL	51	5	11	16	108	13	5	1	6	35
2005-06	Medicine Hat	WHL	68	25	23	48	*279	13	8	4	12	53
2006-07	Medicine Hat	WHL	61	19	45	64	206	17	8	8	16	56

DOVGAN, Viktor (DAWV-guhn, VIHK-tohr) WSH.

Defense. Shoots left. 6'2", 205 lbs. Born, Moscow, USSR, February 27, 1987.
(Washington's 7th choice, 209th overall, in 2005 Entry Draft).

			Regular Season					Playoffs				
Season	Club	League	GP	G	A	Pts	PIM	GP	G	A	Pts	PIM
2003-04	CSKA Moscow 2	Russia-3	STATISTICS NOT AVAILABLE									
2004-05	CSKA Moscow 2	Russia-3	STATISTICS NOT AVAILABLE									
2005-06	CSKA Moscow 2	Russia-3	STATISTICS NOT AVAILABLE									
	CSK VVS Samara	Russia-2	8	1	2	3	20	3	0	1	1	4
2006-07	Hershey Bears	AHL	1	0	0	0	2	....	....	....	....	....
	South Carolina	ECHL	56	5	6	11	95	....	....	....	....	....

DOWELL, Jake (DOW-uhl, JAYK) CHI.

Center. Shoots left. 6', 202 lbs. Born, Eau Claire, WI, March 4, 1985.
(Chicago's 10th choice, 140th overall, in 2004 Entry Draft).

			Regular Season					Playoffs				
Season	Club	League	GP	G	A	Pts	PIM	GP	G	A	Pts	PIM
2000-01	Eau Claire Mem.	High-WI	24	25	30	55	....	....	....	....	....	....
2001-02	USNTDP	U-17	11	5	1	6	14	....	....	....	....	....
	USNTDP	NAHL	44	5	12	17	51	....	....	....	....	....
2002-03	USNTDP	U-18	54	8	17	25	54	....	....	....	....	....
	USNTDP	NAHL	9	2	2	4	13	....	....	....	....	....
2003-04	U. of Wisconsin	WCHA	37	6	13	19	48	....	....	....	....	....
2004-05	U. of Wisconsin	WCHA	38	12	14	26	74	....	....	....	....	....
2005-06	U. of Wisconsin	WCHA	43	5	15	20	42	....	....	....	....	....
2006-07	U. of Wisconsin	WCHA	41	19	6	25	54	....	....	....	....	....
	Norfolk Admirals	AHL	9	2	3	5	8	6	0	3	3	4

DOWNIE, Steve (DOW-nee, STEEV) PHI.

Right wing. Shoots right. 5'11", 200 lbs. Born, Newmarket, Ont., April 3, 1987.
(Philadelphia's 1st choice, 29th overall, in 2005 Entry Draft).

			Regular Season					Playoffs				
Season	Club	League	GP	G	A	Pts	PIM	GP	G	A	Pts	PIM
2002-03	Aurora Tigers	OPJHL	34	12	13	25	55	....	....	....	....	....
2003-04	Windsor Spitfires	OHL	49	7	9	16	90	4	0	1	1	27
2004-05	Windsor Spitfires	OHL	61	21	52	73	179	11	4	5	9	49
2005-06	Windsor Spitfires	OHL	1	3	0	3	4	....	....	....	....	....
	Peterborough	OHL	34	16	34	50	109	19	6	15	21	38
2006-07	Peterborough	OHL	28	23	36	59	92	....	....	....	....	....
	Kitchener Rangers	OHL	17	12	21	33	32	9	8	14	22	15
	Philadelphia	AHL	1	0	0	0	0	....	....	....	....	....

DRAVECKY, Vladimir (dra-VEH-kee, vla-DIH-meer) L.A.

Right wing. Shoots left. 5'10", 185 lbs. Born, Kosice, Czech., June 3, 1985.

			Regular Season					Playoffs				
Season	Club	League	GP	G	A	Pts	PIM	GP	G	A	Pts	PIM
2002-03	Trebisov	Slovak-2	2	0	1	1	0	....	....	....	....	....
2003-04	Presov Jr.	Slovak-Jr.	1	0	1	1	0	....	....	....	....	....
	Presov	Slovak-2	4	1	1	2	4	7	7	2	9	4
	HC Kosice	Slovakia	43	1	3	4	4	....	....	....	....	....
2004-05	HC Kosice Jr.	Slovak-Jr.	10	4	10	14	8	5	1	3	4	2
	HC Kosice	Slovakia	51	5	6	11	8	10	0	1	1	0
2005-06	HC Kosice	Slovakia	54	8	18	26	18	8	1	0	1	8
	HKm Humenne	Slovak-2	2	1	3	4	0	....	....	....	....	....
2006-07	HC Kosice	Slovakia	52	9	14	23	16	11	5	3	8	2
	HKm Humenne	Slovak-2	1	2	1	3	2	....	....	....	....	....

Signed as a free agent by **Los Angeles**, May 31, 2007.

DRAZENOVIC, Nicholas (DRAY-zehn-oh-vihk, NIHK-oh-las) ST.L.

Center. Shoots left. 6', 172 lbs. Born, Prince George, B.C., January 14, 1987.
(St. Louis' 6th choice, 171st overall, in 2005 Entry Draft).

			Regular Season					Playoffs				
Season	Club	League	GP	G	A	Pts	PIM	GP	G	A	Pts	PIM
2003-04	Prince George	WHL	65	7	30	37	38	....	....	....	....	....
2004-05	Prince George	WHL	72	18	38	56	24	....	....	....	....	....
2005-06	Prince George	WHL	71	30	33	63	51	5	0	0	0	4
2006-07	Prince George	WHL	58	18	32	50	63	15	9	10	19	6

DROZDETSKY, Alexander (drawz-DEHT-skee, al-EHX-AN-duhr) PHI.

Right wing. Shoots left. 6', 180 lbs. Born, Moscow, USSR, November 10, 1981.
(Philadelphia's 2nd choice, 94th overall, in 2000 Entry Draft).

			Regular Season					Playoffs				
Season	Club	League	GP	G	A	Pts	PIM	GP	G	A	Pts	PIM
1997-98	St. Petersburg 2	Russia-3	19	0	1	1	0	....	....	....	....	....
1998-99	St. Petersburg 2	Russia-4	24	5	3	8	12	....	....	....	....	....
99-2000	St. Petersburg 2	Russia-3	4	4	1	5	2	....	....	....	....	....
	SKA St. Petersburg	Russia	32	2	0	2	10	4	0	0	0	0
2000-01	SKA St. Petersburg	Russia	42	6	7	13	74	....	....	....	....	....
2001-02	CSKA Moscow	Russia	49	11	6	17	26	....	....	....	....	....
2002-03	CSKA Moscow	Russia	46	14	13	27	30	....	....	....	....	....
2003-04	Ak Bars Kazan	Russia	57	16	15	31	62	1	0	0	0	2
2004-05	Ak Bars Kazan	Russia	32	3	4	7	28	....	....	....	....	....
	Ak Bars Kazan 2	Russia-3	....	10	8	18	....	....	....	....	....	....
	Nizhnekamsk	Russia	7	5	1	6	4	....	....	....	....	....
2005-06	Avangard Omsk	Russia	30	6	6	12	26	....	....	....	....	....
	SKA St. Petersburg	Russia	16	4	10	14	6	3	0	0	0	0
2006-07	SKA St. Petersburg	Russia	45	11	15	26	66	3	0	2	2	0

DUDAS, Jesse (DOO-dah, JEH-see) CBJ

Defense. Shoots right. 6'1", 214 lbs. Born, St. Albert, Alta., March 31, 1988.
(Columbus' 8th choice, 159th overall, in 2006 Entry Draft).

			Regular Season					Playoffs				
Season	Club	League	GP	G	A	Pts	PIM	GP	G	A	Pts	PIM
2004-05	Lethbridge	WHL	44	1	3	4	28	2	0	1	1	0
2005-06	Lethbridge	WHL	18	0	7	7	12	....	....	....	....	....
	Prince George	WHL	6	0	4	4	15	....	....	....	....	....
2006-07	Prince George	WHL	32	2	27	29	51	....	....	....	....	....

DUFFY, Matt (DUHF-ee, MAT) FLA.

Defense. Shoots right. 6'2", 180 lbs. Born, Portland, ME, March 21, 1986.
(Florida's 5th choice, 104th overall, in 2005 Entry Draft).

			Regular Season					Playoffs				
Season	Club	League	GP	G	A	Pts	PIM	GP	G	A	Pts	PIM
2003-04	N.H. Jr. Monarchs	EJHL	33	9	13	22	....	....	....	....	....	....
2004-05	N.H. Jr. Monarchs	EJHL	54	19	26	45	147	....	....	....	....	....
2005-06	U. of Maine	H-East	28	3	5	8	43	....	....	....	....	....
2006-07	U. of Maine	H-East	39	5	5	10	41	....	....	....	....	....

DUPONT, Brodie (DOO-pawnt, BROH-dee) NYR

Center. Shoots left. 6'2", 210 lbs. Born, Russell, Man., February 17, 1987.
(NY Rangers' 4th choice, 66th overall, in 2005 Entry Draft).

			Regular Season					Playoffs				
Season	Club	League	GP	G	A	Pts	PIM	GP	G	A	Pts	PIM
2003-04	Swan Valley	MJHL	51	25	16	41	88	12	5	1	6	36
	Calgary Hitmen	WHL	2	0	1	1	0	....	....	....	....	....
2004-05	Calgary Hitmen	WHL	70	14	11	25	111	12	2	8	10	21
2005-06	Calgary Hitmen	WHL	72	30	23	53	123	13	4	5	9	24
2006-07	Calgary Hitmen	WHL	70	37	33	70	90	18	9	7	16	33

DUPUIS, Philippe (doo-PWEE, fihl-EEP) CBJ

Center. Shoots right. 6', 196 lbs. Born, Laval, Que., April 24, 1985.
(Columbus' 5th choice, 104th overall, in 2003 Entry Draft).

			Regular Season					Playoffs				
Season	Club	League	GP	G	A	Pts	PIM	GP	G	A	Pts	PIM
2000-01	Laval-Laurentides	QAAA	46	16	27	43	74	8	1	5	6	30
2001-02	Hull Olympiques	QMJHL	67	7	14	21	59	12	6	5	11	14
2002-03	Hull Olympiques	QMJHL	68	22	34	56	89	20	2	4	6	22
2003-04	Gatineau	QMJHL	60	18	37	55	77	15	6	10	16	14
2004-05	Rouyn-Noranda	QMJHL	62	34	50	84	60	10	5	3	8	8
2005-06	Moncton Wildcats	QMJHL	56	32	76	108	52	19	14	18	32	14
2006-07	Syracuse Crunch	AHL	51	11	11	22	18	....	....	....	....	....
	Dayton Bombers	ECHL	8	3	2	5	8	19	6	9	15	28

DURNO, Chris (DUHR-noh, KRIHS)

Center. Shoots left. 6'4", 205 lbs. Born, Scarborough, Ont., October 31, 1980.

			Regular Season					Playoffs				
Season	Club	League	GP	G	A	Pts	PIM	GP	G	A	Pts	PIM
99-2000	Michigan Tech	WCHA	24	1	1	2	30	....	....	....	....	....
2000-01	Michigan Tech	WCHA	35	9	6	15	46	....	....	....	....	....
2001-02	Michigan Tech	WCHA	36	7	8	15	48	....	....	....	....	....
2002-03	Michigan Tech	WCHA	35	5	11	16	60	....	....	....	....	....
2003-04	Gwinnett	ECHL	68	20	26	46	46	13	7	5	12	10
2004-05	Gwinnett	ECHL	66	20	36	56	101	8	5	2	7	8
2005-06	Gwinnett	ECHL	13	12	10	22	19	....	....	....	....	....
	Milwaukee	AHL	57	20	20	40	52	21	2	2	4	18
2006-07	Norfolk Admirals	AHL	22	4	1	5	61	....	....	....	....	....
	Portland Pirates	AHL	12	1	1	2	2	....	....	....	....	....
	Milwaukee	AHL	29	13	3	16	24	4	1	2	3	10

Signed as a free agent by **Chicago**, September 25, 2006. Traded to **Anaheim** by **Chicago** with Sebastiien Caron and Matt Keith for Pierre Parenteau and Bruno St. Jacques, December 28, 2006. Traded to **Nashville** by **Anaheim** for Shane Endicott, January 26, 2007.

DWYER, Patrick (DWIGH-uhr, PAT-rihk) CAR.

Right wing. Shoots right. 5'11", 175 lbs. Born, Great Falls, MT, June 22, 1983.
(Atlanta's 3rd choice, 116th overall, in 2002 Entry Draft).

			Regular Season					Playoffs				
Season	Club	League	GP	G	A	Pts	PIM	GP	G	A	Pts	PIM
2000-01	Great Falls	NWJHL	40	33	57	90	106	12	10	12	22	....
2001-02	Western Mich.	CCHA	38	17	17	34	26	....	....	....	....	....
2002-03	Western Mich.	CCHA	33	9	10	19	20	....	....	....	....	....
2003-04	Western Mich.	CCHA	35	13	13	26	22	....	....	....	....	....
2004-05	Western Mich.	CCHA	36	6	16	22	56	....	....	....	....	....
2005-06	Chicago Wolves	AHL	73	16	29	45	49	....	....	....	....	....
2006-07	Albany River Rats	AHL	79	16	25	41	39	5	0	1	1	5

CCHA All-Rookie Team (2002) • CCHA Rookie of the Year (2002)

Signed as a free agent by **Carolina**, July 7, 2006.

DYMENT, Chris (DIGH-mehnt, KRIHS)

Defense. Shoots right. 6'3", 207 lbs. Born, Reading, MA, October 24, 1979.
(Montreal's 3rd choice, 97th overall, in 1999 Entry Draft).

			Regular Season					Playoffs				
Season	Club	League	GP	G	A	Pts	PIM	GP	G	A	Pts	PIM
1997-98	Reading	High-MA	22	22	22	44	15	....	....	....	....	....
1998-99	Boston University	H-East	25	1	5	6	16	....	....	....	....	....
99-2000	Boston University	H-East	42	11	20	31	42	....	....	....	....	....
2000-01	Boston University	H-East	37	1	10	11	38	....	....	....	....	....
2001-02	Boston University	H-East	38	7	18	25	24	....	....	....	....	....
2002-03	Houston Aeros	AHL	40	2	3	5	64	17	0	1	1	8
2003-04	Houston Aeros	AHL	13	1	0	1	12	....	....	....	....	....
	Springfield Falcons	AHL	23	0	1	1	16	....	....	....	....	....
2004-05	Providence Bruins	AHL	48	3	4	7	112	5	0	0	0	0
2005-06	Providence Bruins	AHL	32	4	7	11	47	5	0	0	0	4
2006-07	Albany River Rats	AHL	7	0	0	0	4	....	....	....	....	....
	Florida Everblades	ECHL	56	7	10	17	62	2	1	1	2	2

Hockey East First All-Star Team (2000) • NCAA East Second All-American Team (2000) • Hockey East Second All-Star Team (2002)

Traded to **Minnesota** by **Montreal** for Minnesota's 5th round choice (later traded to Calgary – Calgary selected Jiri Cetkovsky) in 2002 Entry Draft, May 25, 2002. Traded to **Phoenix** by **Minnesota** for Michael Schutte, December 9, 2003. Signed as a free agent by **Boston**, September 8, 2004.

EARL, Robbie (UHRL, RAW-bee) TOR.

Left wing. Shoots left. 6', 195 lbs. Born, Chicago, IL, June 6, 1985.
(Toronto's 4th choice, 187th overall, in 2004 Entry Draft).

			Regular Season					Playoffs				
Season	Club	League	GP	G	A	Pts	PIM	GP	G	A	Pts	PIM
2000-01	L.A. Jr. Kings	Cal-Am	29	48	22	70	....	....	....	....	....	....
2001-02	USNTDP	U-17	15	8	9	17	....	....	....	....	....	....
	USNTDP	NAHL	43	14	7	21	43	....	....	....	....	....
2002-03	USNTDP	U-18	43	16	8	24	58	....	....	....	....	....
	USNTDP	NAHL	10	4	5	9	18	....	....	....	....	....
2003-04	U. of Wisconsin	WCHA	42	14	13	27	46	....	....	....	....	....
2004-05	U. of Wisconsin	WCHA	41	20	24	44	62	....	....	....	....	....
2005-06	U. of Wisconsin	WCHA	42	24	26	50	56	....	....	....	....	....
	Toronto Marlies	AHL	1	0	0	0	0	3	0	0	0	0
2006-07	Toronto Marlies	AHL	67	12	18	30	50	....	....	....	....	....

WCHA All-Rookie Team (2004) • WCHA Second All-Star Team (2005) • NCAA Championship All-Tournament Team (2006) • NCAA Championship Tournament MVP (2006)

EBBETT, Andrew (EH-beht, AN-droo) ANA.

Left wing. Shoots left. 5'10", 174 lbs. Born, Vernon, B.C., January 2, 1983.

			Regular Season					Playoffs				
Season	Club	League	GP	G	A	Pts	PIM	GP	G	A	Pts	PIM
2002-03	U. of Michigan	CCHA	43	9	18	27	22	....	....	....	....	....
2003-04	U. of Michigan	CCHA	43	9	28	37	56	....	....	....	....	....
2004-05	U. of Michigan	CCHA	40	6	31	37	28	....	....	....	....	....
2005-06	U. of Michigan	CCHA	41	14	28	42	25	....	....	....	....	....
2006-07	Binghamton	AHL	71	26	39	65	44	....	....	....	....	....

Signed as a free agent by **Anaheim**, May 16, 2007.

ECKFORD, Tyler (EHK-fuhrd, TIGH-luhr) N.J.

Defense. Shoots left. 6'1", 205 lbs. Born, Vancouver, B.C., September 8, 1985.
(New Jersey's 5th choice, 217th overall, in 2004 Entry Draft).

			Regular Season					Playoffs				
Season	Club	League	GP	G	A	Pts	PIM	GP	G	A	Pts	PIM
2003-04	South Surrey	BCHL	58	7	30	37	101	13	2	8	10	34
2004-05	South Surrey	BCHL	60	22	43	65	93	25	4	15	19	46
2005-06	Alaska	CCHA	38	3	15	18	43	....	....	....	....	....
2006-07	Alaska	CCHA	39	5	17	22	54	....	....	....	....	....

CCHA All-Rookie Team (2006)

EGENER, Mike (EHG-eh-nuhr, MIGHK) T.B.

Defense. Shoots left. 6'4", 216 lbs. Born, Lahr, West Germany, September 26, 1984.
(Tampa Bay's 1st choice, 34th overall, in 2003 Entry Draft).

			Regular Season					Playoffs				
Season	Club	League	GP	G	A	Pts	PIM	GP	G	A	Pts	PIM
99-2000	Calgary Bruins	CMHA	27	4	9	13	88	....	....	....	....	....
2000-01	Calgary Hitmen	WHL	52	1	0	1	91	6	0	0	0	5
2001-02	Calgary Hitmen	WHL	68	2	7	9	175	6	0	0	0	23
2002-03	Calgary Hitmen	WHL	40	2	8	10	210	3	1	0	1	8
2003-04	Calgary Hitmen	WHL	64	1	16	17	228	7	1	1	2	47
2004-05	Springfield Falcons	AHL	45	3	2	5	183	....	....	....	....	....
2005-06	Springfield Falcons	AHL	38	2	1	3	142	....	....	....	....	....
	Johnstown Chiefs	ECHL	18	2	2	4	66	....	....	....	....	....
2006-07	Springfield Falcons	AHL	75	0	3	3	152	....	....	....	....	....

ELLER, Lars (EHL-uhr, LARZ) ST.L.

Center. Shoots left. 6', 198 lbs. Born, Herlev, Denmark, May 8, 1989.
(St. Louis' 1st choice, 13th overall, in 2007 Entry Draft).

			Regular Season					Playoffs				
Season	Club	League	GP	G	A	Pts	PIM	GP	G	A	Pts	PIM
2004-05	Rodovre IK Jr.	Den-Jr.	28	21	26	47	20	....	....	....	....	....
	Rodovre	Denmark	1	3	1	4	0	....	....	....	....	....
2005-06	Frolunda U18	Swe-U18	8	2	4	6	10	2	0	0	0	0
	Frolunda Jr.	Swe-Jr.	36	7	7	14	6	2	0	0	0	0
2006-07	Frolunda U18	Swe-U18	3	1	4	5	6	6	3	2	5	8
	Frolunda Jr.	Swe-Jr.	39	18	37	55	58	8	4	1	5	24

ELLERBY, Keaton (EHL-uhr-bee, KEE-tuhn) FLA.

Defense. Shoots left. 6'4", 186 lbs. Born, Strathmore, Alta., November 5, 1988.
(Florida's 1st choice, 10th overall, in 2007 Entry Draft).

			Regular Season					Playoffs				
Season	Club	League	GP	G	A	Pts	PIM	GP	G	A	Pts	PIM
2003-04	Okotoks Oilers	AMHA	30	7	32	39	69	....	....	....	....	....
2004-05	Kamloops Blazers	WHL	60	0	1	1	77	6	0	0	0	16
2005-06	Kamloops Blazers	WHL	68	2	6	8	121	....	....	....	....	....
2006-07	Kamloops Blazers	WHL	69	2	23	25	120	4	1	2	3	12

ELLINGTON, Taylor (EHL-ihng-tuhn, TAY-luhr) VAN.

Defense. Shoots left. 6', 200 lbs. Born, Victoria, B.C., October 31, 1988.
(Vancouver's 2nd choice, 33rd overall, in 2007 Entry Draft).

			Regular Season					Playoffs				
Season	Club	League	GP	G	A	Pts	PIM	GP	G	A	Pts	PIM
2004-05	Everett Silvertips	WHL	47	0	0	0	48	8	0	1	1	4
2005-06	Everett Silvertips	WHL	63	0	7	7	62	15	1	2	3	16
2006-07	Everett Silvertips	WHL	60	5	8	13	65	6	1	0	1	2

ELLIOTT, Brandon (EHL-lee-awt, BRAN-duhn) T.B.

Left wing. Shoots left. 6'4", 225 lbs. Born, Orangeville, Ont., March 8, 1984.
(Tampa Bay's 4th choice, 158th overall, in 2004 Entry Draft).

			Regular Season					Playoffs				
Season	Club	League	GP	G	A	Pts	PIM	GP	G	A	Pts	PIM
2001-02	Orangeville	OHA-B	STATISTICS NOT AVAILABLE									
	Mississauga	OHL	7	0	0	0	14	....	....	....	....	....
2002-03	Collingwood Blues	OPJHL	STATISTICS NOT AVAILABLE									
2003-04	Collingwood Blues	OPJHL	25	6	15	21	138	....	....	....	....	....
	Mississauga	OHL	30	0	4	4	89	13	0	0	0	32
2004-05	Mississauga	OHL	22	1	4	5	74	....	....	....	....	....
	Springfield Falcons	AHL	2	0	0	0	7	....	....	....	....	....
	Victoria	ECHL	13	0	2	2	41	....	....	....	....	....
2005-06	Johnstown Chiefs	ECHL	68	10	7	17	207	5	0	0	0	0
2006-07	Springfield Falcons	AHL	10	0	1	1	27	....	....	....	....	....
	Johnstown Chiefs	ECHL	48	11	6	17	137	....	....	....	....	....

EMMERSON, Riley (EHM-uhr-sohn, RIGH-lee) MIN.

Right wing. Shoots left. 6'7", 238 lbs. Born, Burnaby, B.C., February 7, 1986.
(Minnesota's 7th choice, 199th overall, in 2005 Entry Draft).

			Regular Season					Playoffs				
Season	Club	League	GP	G	A	Pts	PIM	GP	G	A	Pts	PIM
2003-04	Chilliwack Chiefs	BCHL	52	0	6	6	137	6	0	0	0	0
2004-05	Tri-City Americans	WHL	35	0	0	0	61	....	....	....	....	....
2005-06	Tri-City Americans	WHL	66	1	1	2	109	2	0	0	0	0
2006-07	Texas Wildcatters	ECHL	42	2	1	3	99	....	....	....	....	....

EMMERTON, Cory (EHM-uhr-tuhn, KOH-ree) DET.

Center. Shoots left. 6', 177 lbs. Born, St. Thomas, Ont., June 1, 1988.
(Detroit's 1st choice, 41st overall, in 2006 Entry Draft).

			Regular Season					Playoffs				
Season	Club	League	GP	G	A	Pts	PIM	GP	G	A	Pts	PIM
2004-05	Kingston	OHL	58	17	21	38	8	....	....	....	....	....
2005-06	Kingston	OHL	66	26	64	90	32	6	2	0	2	6
2006-07	Kingston	OHL	40	29	37	66	22	5	5	2	7	2
	Grand Rapids	AHL	....	....	....	....	....	2	0	0	0	0

ENGASSER, Will (EHN-gahs-uhr, WIHL-yuhm) PHX.

Left wing. Shoots left. 6'2", 237 lbs. Born, Edina, MN, September 25, 1985.
(Phoenix's 9th choice, 261st overall, in 2004 Entry Draft).

			Regular Season					Playoffs				
Season	Club	League	GP	G	A	Pts	PIM	GP	G	A	Pts	PIM
2000-01	Blake Bears	High-MN	5	1	2	3	....	....	....	....	....	....
2001-02	Blake Bears	High-MN	26	7	24	31	....	....	....	....	....	....
2002-03	Blake Bears	High-MN	28	17	26	43	52	....	....	....	....	....
2003-04	Blake Bears	High-MN	28	22	30	52	20	....	....	....	....	....
	Team Southwest	UMEHL	24	9	5	14	....	....	....	....	....	....
2004-05	Yale	ECACHL	21	2	0	2	10	....	....	....	....	....
2005-06	Yale	ECACHL	18	2	2	4	6	....	....	....	....	....
2006-07	Yale	ECACHL	25	7	1	8	22	....	....	....	....	....

ENGELLAND, Deryk (ehn-GUHL-uhnd, DEH-rihk) PIT.

Defense. Shoots right. 6'2", 202 lbs. Born, Edmonton, Alta., April 5, 1982.
(New Jersey's 11th choice, 194th overall, in 2000 Entry Draft).

			Regular Season					Playoffs				
Season	Club	League	GP	G	A	Pts	PIM	GP	G	A	Pts	PIM
1998-99	Moose Jaw	WHL	2	0	0	0	0	....	....	....	....	....
99-2000	Moose Jaw	WHL	55	0	5	5	62	4	0	0	0	0
2000-01	Moose Jaw	WHL	65	4	11	15	157	4	0	0	0	10
2001-02	Moose Jaw	WHL	56	7	10	17	102	12	0	2	2	27
2002-03	Moose Jaw	WHL	65	3	8	11	199	13	1	1	2	20
2003-04	Lowell	AHL	26	0	0	0	34	....	....	....	....	....
	Las Vegas	ECHL	35	2	11	13	63	2	0	0	0	0
2004-05	Las Vegas	ECHL	72	5	16	21	138	....	....	....	....	....
2005-06	Hershey Bears	AHL	37	0	4	4	77	1	0	0	0	0
	South Carolina	ECHL	35	3	13	16	20	....	....	....	....	....
2006-07	Hershey Bears	AHL	44	4	6	10	95	14	0	0	0	14
	Reading Royals	ECHL	6	0	3	3	8	....	....	....	....	....

Signed as a free agent by **Calgary**, July, 2003. Signed as a free agent by **Pittsburgh**, July 16, 2007.

ENLUND, Jonas (EHN-luhnd, YOH-nuhs) ATL.

Center. Shoots left. 6', 185 lbs. Born, Helsinki, Finland, November 3, 1987.
(Atlanta's 5th choice, 165th overall, in 2006 Entry Draft).

			Regular Season					Playoffs				
Season	Club	League	GP	G	A	Pts	PIM	GP	G	A	Pts	PIM
2002-03	HIFK Helsinki U18	Fin-U18	24	11	3	14	0	2	1	0	1	0
2003-04	HIFK Helsinki U18	Fin-U18	30	15	16	31	30	7	3	5	8	2
	HIFK Helsinki Jr.	Fin-Jr.	3	0	0	0	0	....	....	....	....	....
2004-05	HIFK Helsinki U18	Fin-U18	....	....	....	....	....	7	4	3	7	8
	HIFK Helsinki Jr.	Fin-Jr.	38	15	15	30	18	2	1	1	2	0
2005-06	Suomi U20	Finland-2	4	1	1	2	0	....	....	....	....	....
	HIFK Helsinki Jr.	Fin-Jr.	37	24	18	42	14	....	....	....	....	....
2006-07	Tappara Jr.	Fin-Jr.	10	2	7	9	12	4	3	0	3	2
	Suomi U20	Finland-2	5	0	1	1	0	....	....	....	....	....
	Tappara Tampere	Finland	46	2	1	3	8	5	0	0	0	0

ENSTROM, Tobias (EHN-struhm, toh-BYE-uhs) ATL.

Defense. Shoots left. 5'10", 175 lbs. Born, Nordingra, Sweden, November 5, 1984.
(Atlanta's 8th choice, 239th overall, in 2003 Entry Draft).

			Regular Season					Playoffs				
Season	Club	League	GP	G	A	Pts	PIM	GP	G	A	Pts	PIM
99-2000	MoDo U18	Swe-U18	3	0	0	0	0	....	....	....	....	....
2000-01	MoDo U18	Swe-U18	16	7	6	13	18	....	....	....	....	....
	MoDo Jr.	Swe-Jr.	1	0	0	0	0	....	....	....	....	....
2001-02	MODO Jr.	Swe-Jr.	21	1	7	8	10	2	1	1	2	2
2002-03	MODO Jr.	Swe-Jr.	7	4	6	10	31	....	....	....	....	....
	MODO	Sweden	42	1	5	6	16	6	0	1	1	4
2003-04	MODO	Sweden	33	1	4	5	6	6	1	1	2	2
2004-05	MODO	Sweden	49	4	10	14	24	2	0	0	0	0
2005-06	MODO	Sweden	47	4	7	11	48	4	0	1	1	25
2006-07	MODO	Sweden	55	7	21	28	52	20	1	11	12	37

ERICSSON, Jonathan (AIR-ihk-suhn, JAWN-ah-thuhn) DET.

Defense. Shoots left. 6'4", 206 lbs. Born, Karlskrona, Sweden, March 2, 1984.
(Detroit's 10th choice, 291st overall, in 2002 Entry Draft).

			Regular Season					Playoffs				
Season	Club	League	GP	G	A	Pts	PIM	GP	G	A	Pts	PIM
2001-02	Hasten Jr.	Swe-Jr.	STATISTICS NOT AVAILABLE									
2002-03	Vita Hasten	Sweden-3	40	2	4	6	36	....	....	....	....	....
2003-04	Sodertalje SK	Sweden	42	1	0	1	12	....	....	....	....	....
2004-05	Sodertalje SK	Sweden	15	0	0	0	4	1	0	0	0	0
2005-06	Sodertalje SK Jr.	Swe-Jr.	1	0	0	0	2	....	....	....	....	....
	Almtuna	Sweden-2	19	2	3	5	44	....	....	....	....	....
	Sodertalje SK	Sweden	24	0	0	0	20	....	....	....	....	....
	Sodertalje SK	Sweden-Q	7	0	1	1	4	....	....	....	....	....
2006-07	Grand Rapids	AHL	67	5	24	29	102	7	0	0	0	8

ERSTAD, Travis (UHR-stad, TRA-vihs) ST.L.

Center/Right wing. Shoots right. 6'4", 182 lbs. Born, Madison, WI, November 9, 1988.
(St. Louis' 8th choice, 100th overall, in 2007 Entry Draft).

			Regular Season					Playoffs				
Season	Club	League	GP	G	A	Pts	PIM	GP	G	A	Pts	PIM
2005-06	Stevens Point High	High-WI	STATISTICS NOT AVAILABLE									
2006-07	Stevens Point High	High-WI	24	31	33	64	....	....	....	....	....	....
	Lincoln Stars	USHL	8	0	0	0	4	3	1	0	1	0

• Signed Letter of Intent to attend **University of Wisconsin** (WCHA) in fall of 2008.

ESPOSITO, Angelo (EHS-poh-ZEE-toh, AN-jul-loh) PIT.

Center. Shoots left. 6'1", 180 lbs. Born, Montreal, Que., February 20, 1989.
(Pittsburgh's 1st choice, 20th overall, in 2007 Entry Draft).

			Regular Season					Playoffs				
Season	Club	League	GP	G	A	Pts	PIM	GP	G	A	Pts	PIM
2004-05	Shat.-St. Mary's	High-MN	68	31	35	66	47	....	....	....	....	....
2005-06	Quebec Remparts	QMJHL	57	39	59	98	45	23	6	5	11	4
2006-07	Quebec Remparts	QMJHL	60	27	52	79	63	5	4	3	7	2

QMJHL All-Rookie Team (2006) • QMJHL Offensive Rookie of the Year (2006)

ESTRADA, Kevin (eh-STRA-duh, KEH-vihn)

Right wing. Shoots left. 5'11", 185 lbs. Born, Surrey, B.C., May 28, 1982.
(Carolina's 3rd choice, 91st overall, in 2001 Entry Draft).

			Regular Season					Playoffs				
Season	Club	League	GP	G	A	Pts	PIM	GP	G	A	Pts	PIM
1997-98	Chilliwack Chiefs	BCHL	35	1	5	6	17	....	....	....	....	....
1998-99	Chilliwack Chiefs	BCHL	58	13	29	42	58	....	....	....	....	....
99-2000	Chilliwack Chiefs	BCHL	45	9	20	29	29	30	6	27	33	14
2000-01	Chilliwack Chiefs	BCHL	59	34	*84	*118	65	....	....	....	....	....
2001-02	Michigan State	CCHA	40	4	7	11	24	....	....	....	....	....
2002-03	Michigan State	CCHA	35	7	4	11	16	....	....	....	....	....
2003-04	Michigan State	CCHA	34	6	10	16	43	....	....	....	....	....
2004-05	Michigan State	CCHA	26	3	1	4	16	....	....	....	....	....
2005-06	Lowell	AHL	59	5	10	15	36	....	....	....	....	....
	Florida Everblades	ECHL	7	1	5	6	6	8	1	4	5	4
2006-07	Albany River Rats	AHL	53	2	7	9	40	....	....	....	....	....
	Florida Everblades	ECHL	3	1	1	2	2	....	....	....	....	....

EVSEEV, Vladislav (yehv-SAY-ehv, VLA-dih-slav) **BOS.**

Left wing. Shoots left. 6'2", 196 lbs. Born, Moscow, USSR, September 10, 1984.
(Boston's 2nd choice, 56th overall, in 2002 Entry Draft).

			Regular Season					Playoffs				
Season	Club	League	GP	G	A	Pts	PIM	GP	G	A	Pts	PIM
99-2000	Dyn'o Moscow 2	Russia-3	5	2	3	5	6	....	....	....	....	....
2000-01	Dyn'o Moscow 2	Russia-3	6	5	2	7	2	....	....	....	....	....
2001-02	CSKA Moscow 2	Russia-3	8	2	1	3	2	....	....	....	....	....
	HK CSKA Moscow	Russia-2	15	2	5	7	10	....	....	....	....	....
2002-03	Dynamo Moscow	Russia	22	1	1	2	2	1	0	0	0	0
2003-04	Vityaz Podolsk	Russia-2	8	1	2	3	2	7	0	0	0	2
2004-05	Dynamo Moscow	Russia	12	1	1	2	2	....	....	....	....	....
	Ufa	Russia	5	0	0	0	2	....	....	....	....	....
2005-06	Cherepovets	Russia	30	3	0	3	18	....	....	....	....	....
2006-07	Dynamo Moscow	Russia	30	1	3	4	32	2	0	0	0	0

EZHOV, Denis (YEHZH-awf, DEH-nihs) **BUF.**

Defense. Shoots left. 5'11", 200 lbs. Born, Togliatti, USSR, February 28, 1985.
(Buffalo's 5th choice, 114th overall, in 2003 Entry Draft).

			Regular Season					Playoffs				
Season	Club	League	GP	G	A	Pts	PIM	GP	G	A	Pts	PIM
99-2000	Lada Togliatti 2	Russia-3	4	0	0	0	4	....	....	....	....	....
2000-01	Lada Togliatti 2	Russia-3	STATISTICS NOT AVAILABLE									
2001-02	Lada Togliatti 2	Russia-3	4	2	4	6	6	....	....	....	....	....
	Lada Togliatti	Russia	15	0	0	0	6	....	....	....	....	....
2002-03	Lada Togliatti 2	Russia-3	15	2	7	9	4	....	....	....	....	....
	CSK VVS Samara	Russia-2	9	0	1	1	8	....	....	....	....	....
2003-04	Novokuznetsk	Russia	19	0	1	1	2	3	0	0	0	0
	CSKA Moscow 2	Russia-3	4	1	2	3	2	....	....	....	....	....
2004-05	Novokuznetsk	Russia	28	0	0	0	16	4	0	0	0	2
2005-06	Mytischi	Russia	24	1	0	1	10	....	....	....	....	....
	Kristall Elektrostal	Russia-3	STATISTICS NOT AVAILABLE									
2006-07	Chelyabinsk	Russia	54	2	6	8	73	....	....	....	....	....

FADDEN, Mitch (FA-dehn, MIHTCH) **T.B.**

Center. Shoots left. 6', 174 lbs. Born, Victoria, B.C., April 3, 1988.
(Tampa Bay's 4th choice, 107th overall, in 2007 Entry Draft).

			Regular Season					Playoffs				
Season	Club	League	GP	G	A	Pts	PIM	GP	G	A	Pts	PIM
2003-04	Victoria Cougars	VIJHL	47	36	31	67	63	11	11	4	15	24
	Seattle	WHL	2	0	0	0	0	....	....	....	....	....
2004-05	Seattle	WHL	64	9	12	21	30	12	2	0	2	4
2005-06	Seattle	WHL	38	9	11	20	19	....	....	....	....	....
	Lethbridge	WHL	30	11	17	28	22	6	2	5	7	14
2006-07	Lethbridge	WHL	71	36	48	84	54	....	....	....	....	....

FAIRCHILD, Cade (FAIR-chighld, KAYD) **ST.L.**

Defense. Shoots left. 5'10", 186 lbs. Born, Duluth, MN, January 15, 1989.
(St. Louis' 7th choice, 96th overall, in 2007 Entry Draft).

			Regular Season					Playoffs				
Season	Club	League	GP	G	A	Pts	PIM	GP	G	A	Pts	PIM
2004-05	Duluth East	High-MN	29	10	32	42	....	....	....	....	....	....
2005-06	USNTDP	U-17	18	2	7	9	4	....	....	....	....	....
	USNTDP	NAHL	36	8	9	17	10	2	0	0	0	0
2006-07	USNTDP	U-18	36	3	16	19	34	....	....	....	....	....
	USNTDP	NAHL	13	1	6	7	16	....	....	....	....	....

FALK, Justin (FAWLK, JUHS-tihn) **MIN.**

Defense. Shoots left. 6'5", 215 lbs. Born, Snowflake, Man., October 11, 1988.
(Minnesota's 2nd choice, 110th overall, in 2007 Entry Draft).

			Regular Season					Playoffs				
Season	Club	League	GP	G	A	Pts	PIM	GP	G	A	Pts	PIM
2004-05	Swan Valley	MJHL	56	0	8	8	46	....	....	....	....	....
	Calgary Hitmen	WHL	4	0	0	0	2	5	0	0	0	0
2005-06	Calgary Hitmen	WHL	5	0	2	2	0	....	....	....	....	....
	Spokane Chiefs	WHL	48	0	8	8	35	....	....	....	....	....
2006-07	Spokane Chiefs	WHL	62	3	12	15	88	6	0	0	0	8

FAST, T.J. (FAST, TEE-JAY) **L.A.**

Defense. Shoots left. 6'1", 190 lbs. Born, Calgary, Alta., September 2, 1987.
(Los Angeles' 3rd choice, 60th overall, in 2005 Entry Draft).

			Regular Season					Playoffs				
Season	Club	League	GP	G	A	Pts	PIM	GP	G	A	Pts	PIM
2003-04	Cgy. North Stars	AMHL	31	7	7	14	42	....	....	....	....	....
2004-05	Camrose Kodiaks	AJHL	58	8	28	36	40	....	....	....	....	....
2005-06	U. of Denver	WCHA	39	1	6	7	26	....	....	....	....	....
2006-07	U. of Denver	WCHA	19	0	4	4	14	....	....	....	....	....
	Tri-City Americans	WHL	26	3	19	22	30	6	0	1	1	14

AJHL All-Rookie Team (2005)

FAYNE, Mark (FAYN, MAHRK) **N.J.**

Defense. Shoots right. 6'3", 195 lbs. Born, Nashua, NH, May 15, 1987.
(New Jersey's 5th choice, 155th overall, in 2005 Entry Draft).

			Regular Season					Playoffs				
Season	Club	League	GP	G	A	Pts	PIM	GP	G	A	Pts	PIM
2003-04	Nobles	High-MA	20	3	5	8	14	....	....	....	....	....
2004-05	Nobles	High-MA	24	1	17	18	16	....	....	....	....	....
2005-06	Nobles	High-MA	29	10	24	34	....	....	....	....	....	....
2006-07	Providence College	H-East	36	5	7	12	43	....	....	....	....	....

FEDOROV, Yevgeny (FEH-duh-rahf, yehv-GEH-nee) **L.A.**

Center. Shoots left. 5'10", 187 lbs. Born, Sverdlovsk, USSR, November 11, 1980.
(Los Angeles' 6th choice, 201st overall, in 2000 Entry Draft).

			Regular Season					Playoffs				
Season	Club	League	GP	G	A	Pts	PIM	GP	G	A	Pts	PIM
1997-98	Krylja Sovetov 2	Russia-3	20	1	6	7	48	....	....	....	....	....
	Krylja Sovetov	Russia	32	1	0	1	12	....	....	....	....	....
1998-99	Krylja Sovetov	Russia	52	5	3	8	61	....	....	....	....	....
99-2000	Perm	Russia	37	5	5	10	20	3	0	1	1	4
2000-01	Perm	Russia	43	9	9	18	18	....	....	....	....	....
2001-02	Ak Bars Kazan	Russia	45	10	12	22	12	11	0	0	0	2
2002-03	Ak Bars Kazan	Russia	46	4	11	15	26	5	1	0	1	2
2003-04	Ak Bars Kazan	Russia	47	7	4	11	14	4	0	0	0	0
2004-05	Ak Bars Kazan	Russia	47	4	10	14	10	....	....	....	....	....
2005-06	Dynamo Moscow	Russia	35	7	9	16	16	....	....	....	....	....
2006-07	Dynamo Moscow	Russia	48	15	9	24	42	3	0	0	0	0

FENTON, P.J. (FEHN-tuhn, PEE-JAY) **S.J.**

Left wing. Shoots left. 5'11", 180 lbs. Born, Springfield, MA, August 26, 1985.
(San Jose's 6th choice, 162nd overall, in 2005 Entry Draft).

			Regular Season					Playoffs				
Season	Club	League	GP	G	A	Pts	PIM	GP	G	A	Pts	PIM
2002-03	N.E. Jr. Coyotes	EJHL	35	8	17	25	....	....	....	....	....	....
2003-04	N.E. Jr. Coyotes	EJHL	37	16	17	33	61	....	....	....	....	....
2004-05	Massachusetts	H-East	36	12	12	24	24	....	....	....	....	....
2005-06	Massachusetts	H-East	35	5	12	17	61	....	....	....	....	....
2006-07	Massachusetts	H-East	39	10	15	25	16	....	....	....	....	....

Hockey East All-Rookie Team (2005)

FERNHOLM, Daniel (FUHRN-hohlm, DAN-yehl) **PIT.**

Defense. Shoots left. 6'4", 218 lbs. Born, Stockholm, Sweden, December 20, 1983.
(Pittsburgh's 4th choice, 101st overall, in 2002 Entry Draft).

			Regular Season					Playoffs				
Season	Club	League	GP	G	A	Pts	PIM	GP	G	A	Pts	PIM
99-2000	Mora IK Jr.	Swe-Jr.	33	3	3	6	8	1	0	0	0	0
2000-01	Mora IK Jr.	Swe-Jr.	3	0	1	1	2	....	....	....	....	....
	Mora IK	Sweden-2	2	0	0	0	0	....	....	....	....	....
2001-02	Djurgarden Jr.	Swe-Jr.	8	6	13	19	12	3	0	0	0	0
2002-03	Huddinge IK	Sweden-2	39	6	10	16	20	2	1	0	1	0
	Huddinge IK Jr.	Swe-Jr.	1	0	0	0	2	....	....	....	....	....
2003-04	Hammarby	Sweden-2	15	1	3	4	6	....	....	....	....	....
	Djurgarden	Sweden	37	4	7	11	28	4	0	0	0	4
2004-05	Djurgarden Jr.	Swe-Jr.	2	0	0	0	4	....	....	....	....	....
	HC Forst Bolzano	Italy	7	0	2	2	2	....	....	....	....	....
	Djurgarden	Sweden	31	3	2	5	22	11	0	0	0	14
2005-06	Wilkes-Barre	AHL	27	1	6	7	10	....	....	....	....	....
	Wheeling Nailers	ECHL	29	2	4	6	20	9	1	3	4	6
2006-07	Wheeling Nailers	ECHL	13	0	3	3	14	....	....	....	....	....
	Djurgarden	Sweden	32	4	12	16	16	....	....	....	....	....

FERRIERO, Benn (fuh-RAIR-oh, BEHN) **PHX.**

Center. Shoots right. 5'10", 191 lbs. Born, Boston, MA, April 29, 1987.
(Phoenix's 8th choice, 196th overall, in 2006 Entry Draft).

			Regular Season					Playoffs				
Season	Club	League	GP	G	A	Pts	PIM	GP	G	A	Pts	PIM
2001-02	Gov. Dummer	High-MA	STATISTICS NOT AVAILABLE									
2002-03	Gov. Dummer	High-MA	....	8	10	18	....	....	....	....	....	....
2003-04	Gov. Dummer	High-MA	28	19	24	43		....	....	....	....	....
2004-05	Gov. Dummer	High-MA	28	15	27	42		....	....	....	....	....
2005-06	Boston College	H-East	42	16	9	25	36	....	....	....	....	....
2006-07	Boston College	H-East	42	23	23	46	43	....	....	....	....	....

Hockey East All-Rookie Team (2006)

FESTERLING, Brett (FEHS-tuhr-lihng, BREHT) **ANA.**

Defense. Shoots left. 6'1", 208 lbs. Born, Quesnel, B.C., March 3, 1986.

			Regular Season					Playoffs				
Season	Club	League	GP	G	A	Pts	PIM	GP	G	A	Pts	PIM
2001-02	Quesnel Thunder	BCAHA	40	18	26	44	44	....	....	....	....	....
	Quesnel	BCHL	7	0	0	0	0	....	....	....	....	....
	Tri-City Americans	WHL	3	0	0	0	0	....	....	....	....	....
2002-03	Tri-City Americans	WHL	55	3	8	11	26	....	....	....	....	....
2003-04	Tri-City Americans	WHL	54	1	9	10	34	11	1	1	2	2
2004-05	Tri-City Americans	WHL	33	3	11	14	20	....	....	....	....	....
	Vancouver Giants	WHL	32	2	4	6	10	5	0	0	0	6
2005-06	Vancouver Giants	WHL	67	1	6	7	35	18	0	1	1	10
2006-07	Vancouver Giants	WHL	70	5	16	21	80	22	1	6	7	24

Signed as a free agent by **Anaheim**, September 14, 2005.

FIALA, Ondrej (fee-A-la, AWN-dray) **MIN.**

Center. Shoots left. 6'2", 198 lbs. Born, Sternberk, Czech., November 4, 1987.
(Minnesota's 2nd choice, 40th overall, in 2006 Entry Draft).

			Regular Season					Playoffs				
Season	Club	League	GP	G	A	Pts	PIM	GP	G	A	Pts	PIM
2000-01	HC Olomouc U17	CzR-U17	6	1	2	3	2	1	0	0	0	0
2001-02	HC Havirov U17	CzR-U17	16	6	9	15	8	....	....	....	....	....
	HC Trinec U17	CzR-U17	27	6	12	18	16	6	2	2	4	2
2002-03	HC Trinec U17	CzR-U17	40	26	30	56	54	2	1	1	2	2
	HC Trinec Jr.	CzRep-Jr.	2	0	0	0	0	6	1	0	1	2
2003-04	HC Trinec U17	CzR-U17	3	1	0	1	4	2	1	0	1	0
	HC Trinec Jr.	CzRep-Jr.	28	9	7	16	16	2	0	0	0	0
2004-05	HC Trinec Jr.	CzRep-Jr.	29	6	6	12	77	....	....	....	....	....
	HC Kladno Jr.	CzRep-Jr.	11	3	5	8	12	10	2	3	5	2
	HC Ocelari Trinec	CzRep	3	0	0	0	0	....	....	....	....	....
2005-06	Everett Silvertips	WHL	51	21	14	35	26	8	4	4	8	4
2006-07	Everett Silvertips	WHL	39	12	21	33	26	....	....	....	....	....

FIEDLER, Jonas (FIHD-luhr, YOH-nuhs) **CAR.**

Right wing. Shoots right. 6'2", 173 lbs. Born, Jihlava, Czech., May 29, 1984.
(Carolina's 7th choice, 235th overall, in 2004 Entry Draft).

			Regular Season					Playoffs				
Season	Club	League	GP	G	A	Pts	PIM	GP	G	A	Pts	PIM
99-2000	Jihlava Jr.	CzRep-Jr.	48	11	11	22	48	....	....	....	....	....
2000-01	Jihlava Jr.	CzRep-Jr.	44	29	33	62	167	....	....	....	....	....
2001-02	Plymouth Whalers	OHL	68	8	12	20	27	6	0	1	1	4
2002-03	Plymouth Whalers	OHL	63	7	21	28	59	18	5	9	14	10
2003-04	Plymouth Whalers	OHL	63	18	28	46	83	9	1	6	7	16
2004-05	Plymouth Whalers	OHL	61	19	18	37	71	4	1	0	1	2
	Florida Everblades	ECHL	2	0	0	0	0	....	....	....	....	....
2005-06	HC Dukla Jihlava	CzRep-2	46	8	9	17	122	6	0	2	2	22
2006-07	HC Dukla Jihlava	CzRep-2	51	6	25	31	149	4	0	0	0	30

• Re-entered NHL Entry Draft. Originally San Jose's 3rd choice, 86th overall, in 2002 Entry Draft.

FIGREN, Robin (FIH-grehn, RAW-bihn) **NYI**

Wing. Shoots right. 5'11", 176 lbs. Born, Stockholm, Sweden, March 7, 1988.
(NY Islanders' 3rd choice, 70th overall, in 2006 Entry Draft).

			Regular Season					Playoffs				
Season	Club	League	GP	G	A	Pts	PIM	GP	G	A	Pts	PIM
2003-04	Hammarby U18	Swe-U18	11	5	5	10	22	....	....	....	....	....
2004-05	Frolunda U18	Swe-U18	12	13	8	21	94	7	4	4	8	10
	Frolunda Jr.	Swe-Jr.	4	1	2	3	0	....	....	....	....	....
2005-06	Frolunda Jr.	Swe-Jr.	38	10	18	28	72	7	4	2	6	6
	Frolunda	Sweden	2	0	0	0	0	....	....	....	....	....
	Frolunda U18	Swe-U18	1	1	0	1	2	2	2	0	2	0
2006-07	Calgary Hitmen	WHL	62	10	17	27	54	18	4	4	8	18

FILEWICH, Jonathan (FIGHL-uh-which, JAWN-ah-thuhn) **PIT.**

Right wing. Shoots right. 6'2", 208 lbs. Born, Kelowna, B.C., October 2, 1984.
(Pittsburgh's 3rd choice, 70th overall, in 2003 Entry Draft).

			Regular Season					Playoffs				
Season	Club	League	GP	G	A	Pts	PIM	GP	G	A	Pts	PIM
1998-99	Sherwood Park	AMBHL	36	29	43	72	90	....	....	....	....	....
99-2000	Sherwood Park	AMHL	33	28	20	48	59	....	....	....	....	....
	Prince George	WHL	3	0	0	0	0	....	....	....	....	....
2000-01	Prince George	WHL	61	9	16	25	32	....	....	....	....	....
2001-02	Prince George	WHL	66	13	19	32	23	7	2	0	2	2
2002-03	Prince George	WHL	51	27	27	54	45	5	1	1	2	2
2003-04	Prince George	WHL	72	30	25	55	52	....	....	....	....	....
2004-05	Lethbridge	WHL	68	42	38	80	26	5	1	1	2	2
2005-06	Wilkes-Barre	AHL	73	22	14	36	40	11	6	4	10	6
2006-07	Wilkes-Barre	AHL	80	30	26	56	38	11	4	2	6	8

FILLIER, Matt (FIHL-ee-uhr, MAT) **L.A.**

Center/Left wing. Shoots left. 6'1", 180 lbs. Born, New Glasgow, N.S., October 5, 1988.
(Los Angeles' 10th choice, 188th overall, in 2007 Entry Draft).

			Regular Season					Playoffs				
Season	Club	League	GP	G	A	Pts	PIM	GP	G	A	Pts	PIM
2003-04	Pictou	NSMHL	27	3	8	11	10	....	....	....	....	....
2004-05	Pictou	NSMHL	31	19	37	56	36	8	2	8	10	6
2005-06	St. John's	QMJHL	59	7	12	19	75	5	0	0	0	4
2006-07	St. John's	QMJHL	63	18	18	36	118	4	0	1	1	2

FINLEY, Joe (FIHN-lee, JOH) **WSH.**

Defense. Shoots left. 6'7", 229 lbs. Born, Edina, MN, June 29, 1987.
(Washington's 2nd choice, 27th overall, in 2005 Entry Draft).

			Regular Season					Playoffs				
Season	Club	League	GP	G	A	Pts	PIM	GP	G	A	Pts	PIM
2004-05	Sioux Falls	USHL	55	3	10	13	181	....	....	....	....	....
2005-06	North Dakota	WCHA	43	0	3	3	96	....	....	....	....	....
2006-07	North Dakota	WCHA	41	1	6	7	72	....	....	....	....	....

FISCHER, David (FIH-shuhr, DAY-vihd) **MTL.**

Defense. Shoots right. 6'4", 192 lbs. Born, Minneapolis, MN, February 19, 1988.
(Montreal's 1st choice, 20th overall, in 2006 Entry Draft).

			Regular Season					Playoffs				
Season	Club	League	GP	G	A	Pts	PIM	GP	G	A	Pts	PIM
2003-04	Apple Valley	High-MN	27	2	9	11	10	....	....	....	....	....
2004-05	Apple Valley	High-MN	28	8	20	28	36	....	....	....	....	....
2005-06	Apple Valley	High-MN	28	8	31	39	22	....	....	....	....	....
2006-07	U. of Minnesota	WCHA	42	0	5	5	14	....	....	....	....	....

FISTRIC, Mark (FIHST-rihc, MAHRK) **DAL.**

Defense. Shoots left. 6'2", 232 lbs. Born, Edmonton, Alta., June 1, 1986.
(Dallas' 1st choice, 28th overall, in 2004 Entry Draft).

			Regular Season					Playoffs				
Season	Club	League	GP	G	A	Pts	PIM	GP	G	A	Pts	PIM
2000-01	Edmonton MLAC	AMBHL	34	13	13	26	144	....	....	....	....	....
2001-02	Edmonton MLAC	AMHL	30	8	10	18	85	....	....	....	....	....
	Vancouver Giants	WHL	4	0	2	2	0	....	....	....	....	....
2002-03	Vancouver Giants	WHL	63	2	7	9	81	4	0	0	0	8
2003-04	Vancouver Giants	WHL	72	1	11	12	192	11	0	2	2	10
2004-05	Vancouver Giants	WHL	15	1	5	6	32	6	1	1	2	16
2005-06	Vancouver Giants	WHL	60	7	22	29	148	18	1	9	10	30
2006-07	Iowa Stars	AHL	80	2	22	24	83	12	0	0	0	16

FITZGERALD, Zack (fihtz-JAIR-uhld, ZAK) **VAN.**

Defense. Shoots left. 6'2", 214 lbs. Born, Two Harbors, MN, June 16, 1985.
(St. Louis' 4th choice, 88th overall, in 2003 Entry Draft).

			Regular Season					Playoffs				
Season	Club	League	GP	G	A	Pts	PIM	GP	G	A	Pts	PIM
2000-01	Duluth East	High-MN	26	1	7	8	44	....	....	....	....	....
2001-02	Seattle	WHL	61	3	7	10	214	10	0	2	2	19
2002-03	Seattle	WHL	64	8	14	22	232	15	0	4	4	33
2003-04	Seattle	WHL	58	4	15	19	163	....	....	....	....	....
2004-05	Seattle	WHL	65	7	18	25	*244	9	0	3	3	24
2005-06	Peoria Rivermen	AHL	13	1	1	2	47	....	....	....	....	....
	Alaska Aces	ECHL	12	1	1	2	108	....	....	....	....	....
2006-07	Peoria Rivermen	AHL	29	0	2	2	86	....	....	....	....	....
	Alaska Aces	ECHL	10	0	1	1	48	14	2	3	5	*82

Traded to **Vancouver** by **St. Louis** for Francois-Pierre Guenette, August 1, 2007.

FLETCHER, Justin (FLEHTCH-uhr, JUHS-tihn) **T.B.**

Defense. Shoots left. 5'11", 180 lbs. Born, Maryville, IL, March 30, 1983.

			Regular Season					Playoffs				
Season	Club	League	GP	G	A	Pts	PIM	GP	G	A	Pts	PIM
2000-01	Sioux City	USHL	38	0	5	5	28	3	0	0	0	0
2001-02	Sioux City	USHL	56	3	10	13	48	12	2	1	3	6
2002-03	Sioux City	USHL	60	12	31	43	28	4	0	3	3	6
2003-04	St. Cloud State	WCHA	29	6	7	13	22	....	....	....	....	....
2004-05	St. Cloud State	WCHA	36	8	14	22	86	....	....	....	....	....
2005-06	St. Cloud State	WCHA	40	6	21	27	55	....	....	....	....	....
2006-07	St. Cloud State	WCHA	38	6	18	24	37	....	....	....	....	....
	Springfield Falcons	AHL	10	3	1	4	4	....	....	....	....	....

Signed as a free agent by **Tampa Bay**, April 30, 2007.

FLOOD, Mark (FLUD, MAHRK) **CAR.**

Defense. Shoots right. 6'1", 190 lbs. Born, Charlottetown, PEI, September 29, 1984.
(Montreal's 8th choice, 188th overall, in 2003 Entry Draft).

			Regular Season					Playoffs				
Season	Club	League	GP	G	A	Pts	PIM	GP	G	A	Pts	PIM
2000-01	Charlotwn AAA	PEIHA	STATISTICS NOT AVAILABLE									
	Charlotwn Abbies	MJrHL	11	0	2	2	2	....	....	....	....	....
2001-02	Peterborough	OHL	57	1	4	5	21	6	0	0	0	2
2002-03	Peterborough	OHL	68	5	24	29	18	7	1	2	3	0
2003-04	Peterborough	OHL	68	15	29	44	30	....	....	....	....	....
2004-05	Peterborough	OHL	60	4	38	42	14	14	2	7	9	0
2005-06	Syracuse Crunch	AHL	9	1	1	2	2	....	....	....	....	....
	Dayton Bombers	ECHL	50	11	14	25	20	....	....	....	....	....
2006-07	Syracuse Crunch	AHL	8	1	1	2	2	....	....	....	....	....
	Albany River Rats	AHL	36	3	7	10	20	....	....	....	....	....

Signed as a free agent by **Columbus**, August 22, 2005. Traded to **Carolina** by **Columbus** for Derrick Walser, November 29, 2006.

FLYNN, Ryan (FLIHN, RIGH-uhn) **NSH.**

Right wing. Shoots right. 6'2", 212 lbs. Born, St. Paul, MN, March 22, 1988.
(Nashville's 4th choice, 176th overall, in 2006 Entry Draft).

			Regular Season					Playoffs				
Season	Club	League	GP	G	A	Pts	PIM	GP	G	A	Pts	PIM
2003-04	Centennial	High-MN	30	29	39	68	....	....	....	....	....	....
2004-05	USNTDP	U-17	14	4	5	9	12	....	....	....	....	....
	USNTDP	NAHL	41	11	8	19	31	9	2	4	6	7
2005-06	USNTDP	U-18	42	10	12	22	57	....	....	....	....	....
	USNTDP	NAHL	17	6	5	11	20	....	....	....	....	....
2006-07	U. of Minnesota	WCHA	43	5	8	13	58	....	....	....	....	....

FOLIGNO, Nick (foh-LIHG-noh, NIHK) **OTT.**

Left wing. Shoots left. 6', 192 lbs. Born, Buffalo, NY, October 31, 1987.
(Ottawa's 1st choice, 28th overall, in 2006 Entry Draft).

			Regular Season					Playoffs				
Season	Club	League	GP	G	A	Pts	PIM	GP	G	A	Pts	PIM
2003-04	USNTDP	U-17	18	7	9	16	28	....	....	....	....	....
	USNTDP	NAHL	43	8	12	20	44	7	2	1	3	8
2004-05	USNTDP	U-18	4	2	1	3	0	....	....	....	....	....
	Sudbury Wolves	OHL	65	10	28	38	111	12	5	5	10	16
2005-06	Sudbury Wolves	OHL	65	24	46	70	146	10	1	3	4	28
2006-07	Sudbury Wolves	OHL	66	31	57	88	135	21	12	17	29	36

FOOTE, Jordan (FUT, JOHR-dahn) **NYR**

Left wing. Shoots left. 6'3", 213 lbs. Born, Edmonton, Alta., March 7, 1985.
(NY Rangers' 11th choice, 169th overall, in 2004 Entry Draft).

			Regular Season					Playoffs				
Season	Club	League	GP	G	A	Pts	PIM	GP	G	A	Pts	PIM
2003-04	Nanaimo Clippers	BCHL	58	23	26	49	73	....	....	....	....	....
2004-05	Michigan Tech	WCHA	13	1	1	2	6	....	....	....	....	....
2005-06	Michigan Tech	WCHA	31	2	0	2	33	....	....	....	....	....
2006-07	Michigan Tech	WCHA	39	2	7	9	34	....	....	....	....	....

FORD, Matthew (FOHRD, MA-thew) **CHI.**

Right wing. Shoots right. 6'1", 206 lbs. Born, West Hills, CA, October 9, 1984.
(Chicago's 16th choice, 256th overall, in 2004 Entry Draft).

			Regular Season					Playoffs				
Season	Club	League	GP	G	A	Pts	PIM	GP	G	A	Pts	PIM
2003-04	Sioux Falls	USHL	60	*37	31	68	60	....	....	....	....	....
2004-05	U. of Wisconsin	WCHA	21	5	5	10	18	....	....	....	....	....
2005-06	U. of Wisconsin	WCHA	31	5	2	7	14	....	....	....	....	....
2006-07	U. of Wisconsin	WCHA	39	7	6	13	38	....	....	....	....	....

FORNEY, Michael (FOHR-NEE, MIGH-kuhl) **ATL.**

Right wing. Shoots right. 6'2", 185 lbs. Born, Thief River Falls, MN, May 14, 1988.
(Atlanta's 3rd choice, 80th overall, in 2006 Entry Draft).

			Regular Season					Playoffs				
Season	Club	League	GP	G	A	Pts	PIM	GP	G	A	Pts	PIM
2002-03	Thief River Falls	High-MN	28	4	10	14	....	....	....	....	....	....
2003-04	Thief River Falls	High-MN	24	14	22	36	....	....	....	....	....	....
2004-05	Thief River Falls	High-MN	28	34	33	67	....	....	....	....	....	....
2005-06	Thief River Falls	High-MN	21	23	37	60	28	....	....	....	....	....
	Des Moines	USHL	3	0	0	0	0	....	....	....	....	....
2006-07	North Dakota	WCHA	16	0	2	2	10	....	....	....	....	....

FORREST, J.D. (FOH-rehst, JAY-DEE) **CAR.**

Defense. Shoots left. 5'9", 185 lbs. Born, Auburn, NY, April 15, 1981.
(Carolina's 5th choice, 181st overall, in 2000 Entry Draft).

			Regular Season					Playoffs				
Season	Club	League	GP	G	A	Pts	PIM	GP	G	A	Pts	PIM
1997-98	USNTDP	U-17	23	3	9	12	2	....	....	....	....	....
	USNTDP	USHL	5	2	0	2	17	....	....	....	....	....
	USNTDP	NAHL	41	2	16	18	20	5	0	1	1	2
1998-99	USNTDP	U-18	6	1	2	3	10	....	....	....	....	....
	USNTDP	USHL	48	5	21	26	34	....	....	....	....	....
	USNTDP	NAHL	2	1	0	1	4	....	....	....	....	....
99-2000	USNTDP	USHL	8	0	0	0	2	....	....	....	....	....
	USNTDP	NAHL	49	6	28	34	46	3	0	0	0	6
2000-01	Boston College	H-East	38	6	17	23	40	....	....	....	....	....
2001-02	Boston College	H-East	35	8	19	27	28	....	....	....	....	....
2002-03	Boston College	H-East	34	6	25	31	28	....	....	....	....	....
2003-04	Boston College	H-East	37	4	13	17	26	....	....	....	....	....
2004-05	SaiPa	Finland	53	7	12	19	44	....	....	....	....	....
2005-06	Assat Pori	Finland	43	6	5	11	69	14	0	4	4	14
2006-07	Albany River Rats	AHL	DID NOT PLAY – INJURED									

Hockey East Second All-Star Team (2003) • NCAA East Second All-American Team (2003)

Signed as a free agent by **SaiPa** (Finland), May 21, 2004. Signed as a free agent by **Carolina**, July 20, 2006. • Missed entire 2006-07 season recovering from knee injury suffered during the pre-season.

FORTIER, Olivier (FOHR-t'yay, OH-lihv-ee-ay) **MTL.**

Center. Shoots left. 5'11", 173 lbs. Born, Quebec City, Que., May 2, 1989.
(Montreal's 4th choice, 65th overall, in 2007 Entry Draft).

			Regular Season					Playoffs				
Season	Club	League	GP	G	A	Pts	PIM	GP	G	A	Pts	PIM
2004-05	St-Francois	QAAA	31	7	17	24	8	4	2	1	3	4
2005-06	Drummondville	QMJHL	13	2	2	4	14	....	....	....	....	....
	Rimouski Oceanic	QMJHL	27	4	8	12	16	....	....	....	....	....
2006-07	Rimouski Oceanic	QMJHL	69	28	36	64	28	....	....	....	....	....

FOSTER, Alex (FAW-stuhr, AL-ehx) **TOR.**

Center. Shoots left. 6'1", 200 lbs. Born, Canton, MI, August 26, 1984.

			Regular Season					Playoffs				
Season	Club	League	GP	G	A	Pts	PIM	GP	G	A	Pts	PIM
2002-03	Sioux Falls	USHL	57	6	15	21	72	3	0	1	1	8
2003-04	Sioux Falls	USHL	5	0	1	1	0	....	....	....	....	....
	Danville Wings	USHL	55	23	30	53	91	6	1	2	3	6
2004-05	Bowling Green	CCHA	34	8	23	31	31	....	....	....	....	....
2005-06	Bowling Green	CCHA	38	11	40	51	40	....	....	....	....	....
2006-07	Toronto Marlies	AHL	57	8	9	17	31	....	....	....	....	....
	Columbia Inferno	ECHL	9	1	10	11	6	....	....	....	....	....

CCHA Second All-Star Team (2006)

Signed as a free agent by **Toronto**, March 8, 2006.

FOX, T.J. (FAWX, TEE-JAY) **S.J.**

Left wing. Shoots left. 6'1", 200 lbs. Born, Oswego, NY, June 11, 1984.

			Regular Season					Playoffs				
Season	Club	League	GP	G	A	Pts	PIM	GP	G	A	Pts	PIM
2002-03	Green Bay	USHL	32	3	3	6	24	....	....	....	....	....
2003-04	Chicago Steel	USHL	56	11	16	27	62	5	1	0	1	4
2004-05	Chicago Steel	USHL	60	21	29	50	90	7	2	3	5	8
2005-06	Union College	ECACHL	30	8	12	20	34	....	....	....	....	....
2006-07	Union College	ECACHL	36	13	24	37	54	....	....	....	....	....

Signed as a free agent by **San Jose**, March 7, 2007.

FRANK, Chris (FRANK, KRIHS) **PHX.**

Defense. Shoots left. 6'1", 231 lbs. Born, Lynnwood, WA, January 8, 1986.
(Phoenix's 7th choice, 188th overall, in 2006 Entry Draft).

			Regular Season					Playoffs				
Season	Club	League	GP	G	A	Pts	PIM	GP	G	A	Pts	PIM
2003-04	Cowichan Valley	BCHL	55	3	16	19	277	6	1	0	1	26
2004-05	Cowichan Valley	BCHL	55	6	30	36	207	....	....	....	....	....
2005-06	Western Mich.	CCHA	38	2	2	4	127	....	....	....	....	....
2006-07	Western Mich.	CCHA	36	2	10	12	*109	....	....	....	....	....

FRANSON, Cody (FRAN-suhn, KOH-dee) **NSH.**

Defense. Shoots right. 6'4", 205 lbs. Born, Salmon Arm, B.C., August 8, 1987.
(Nashville's 3rd choice, 79th overall, in 2005 Entry Draft).

			Regular Season					Playoffs				
Season	Club	League	GP	G	A	Pts	PIM	GP	G	A	Pts	PIM
2002-03	Sicamous	BCAHA	65	44	82	126	42	....	....	....	....	....
	Vancouver Giants	WHL	3	0	0	0	0	....	....	....	....	....
2003-04	Beaver Valley	KIJHL	48	10	22	32	70	....	....	....	....	....
	Trail Smoke Eaters	BCHL	2	0	1	1	0	....	....	....	....	....
	Vancouver Giants	WHL	2	0	0	0	0	....	....	....	....	....
2004-05	Vancouver Giants	WHL	64	2	11	13	44	4	0	1	1	0
2005-06	Vancouver Giants	WHL	71	15	40	55	61	18	5	15	20	12
2006-07	Vancouver Giants	WHL	59	17	34	51	88	19	3	4	7	10

WHL West Second All-Star Team (2006) • WHL West First All-Star Team (2007) • Memorial Cup Tournament All-Star Team (2007)

FRANSSON, Johan (FRAN-suhn, YOH-han) **L.A.**

Defense. Shoots left. 6'1", 183 lbs. Born, Kalix, Sweden, February 18, 1985.
(Dallas' 2nd choice, 34th overall, in 2004 Entry Draft).

			Regular Season					Playoffs				
Season	Club	League	GP	G	A	Pts	PIM	GP	G	A	Pts	PIM
2000-01	Kalix HF	Sweden-3	19	0	6	6	8	....	....	....	....	....
2001-02	Lulea HF U18	Swe-U18	5	2	0	2	0	....	....	....	....	....
	Lulea HF Jr.	Swe-Jr.	29	4	4	8	28	5	0	1	1	8
2002-03	Lulea HF Jr.	Swe-Jr.	24	2	4	6	67	....	....	....	....	....
	Lulea HF U18	Swe-U18	2	0	0	0	2	....	....	....	....	....
	Lulea HF	Sweden	3	0	0	0	0	....	....	....	....	....
2003-04	Lulea HF Jr.	Swe-Jr.	5	0	2	2	10	....	....	....	....	....
	Lulea HF	Sweden	44	3	3	6	28	2	0	0	0	4
2004-05	Lulea HF Jr.	Swe-Jr.	1	1	1	2	0	7	1	2	3	4
	Lulea HF	Sweden	43	1	6	7	30	3	0	0	0	0
2005-06	Lulea HF	Sweden	50	3	5	8	74	6	1	1	2	6
2006-07	Frolunda	Sweden	35	0	6	6	18	....	....	....	....	....
	Assat Pori	Finland	6	0	1	1	2	....	....	....	....	....
	Linkopings HC	Sweden	8	0	0	0	4	15	0	0	0	2

Rights traded to **Los Angeles** by **Dallas** with Jaroslav Modry, Dallas' 2nd (Oscar Moller) and 3rd (Bryan Cameron) round choices in 2007 Entry Draft and Dallas' 1st round choice in 2008 Entry Draft for Mattias Norstrom, Konstantin Pushkarev and Los Angeles' 3rd (Sergei Korostin) and 4th (later traded to Columbus - Columbus selected Maxim Mayorov) round choices in 2007 Entry Draft, February 27, 2007.

FRASER, Jamie (FRAY-zuhr, JAY-mee) **NYI**

Defense. Shoots left. 6'1", 200 lbs. Born, Sarnia, Ont., November 17, 1985.

			Regular Season					Playoffs				
Season	Club	League	GP	G	A	Pts	PIM	GP	G	A	Pts	PIM
2002-03	Brampton	OHL	57	3	11	14	13	10	0	2	2	2
2003-04	Brampton	OHL	61	4	13	17	36	12	3	1	4	6
2004-05	Sarnia Sting	OHL	66	10	21	31	22	....	....	....	....	....
2005-06	Sarnia Sting	OHL	65	16	26	42	68	....	....	....	....	....
	South Carolina	ECHL	3	1	0	1	2	6	1	1	2	2
2006-07	Syracuse Crunch	AHL	2	0	0	0	0	....	....	....	....	....
	South Carolina	ECHL	27	5	23	28	6	....	....	....	....	....
	Bridgeport	AHL	43	3	11	14	16	....	....	....	....	....

Signed as a free agent by **NY Islanders**, February 22, 2007.

FRATTIN, Matt (FRA-tihn, MAT) **TOR.**

Right wing. Shoots right. 5'11", 187 lbs. Born, Edmonton, Alta., January 3, 1988.
(Toronto's 2nd choice, 99th overall, in 2007 Entry Draft).

			Regular Season					Playoffs				
Season	Club	League	GP	G	A	Pts	PIM	GP	G	A	Pts	PIM
2004-05	Gregg Distributors	AMHL	34	12	13	25	14	....	....	....	....	....
2005-06	Gregg Distributors	AMHL	34	20	17	37	48	6	5	1	6	4
	Ft. Saskatchewan	AJHL	3	2	0	2	0	....	....	....	....	....
2006-07	Ft. Saskatchewan	AJHL	58	49	34	83	75	15	5	6	11	10

• Signed Letter of Intent to attend **University of North Dakota** (WCHA) in fall of 2008.

FRECHETTE, Maxime (freh-SHEHT, max-EEM) **CBJ**

Defense. Shoots right. 6'5", 200 lbs. Born, Sorel, Que., May 9, 1988.
(Columbus' 7th choice, 142nd overall, in 2006 Entry Draft).

			Regular Season					Playoffs				
Season	Club	League	GP	G	A	Pts	PIM	GP	G	A	Pts	PIM
2004-05	Drummondville	QMJHL	50	2	3	5	50	1	0	0	0	0
2005-06	Drummondville	QMJHL	13	0	0	0	24	....	....	....	....	....
2006-07	Drummondville	QMJHL	53	0	2	2	154	7	2	1	3	16

• Missed majority of 2005-06 season recovering from shoulder injury.

FREDHEIM, Kris (FREHD-highm, KRIHS) **VAN.**

Defense. Shoots right. 6'2", 174 lbs. Born, Campbell River, B.C., February 23, 1987.
(Vancouver's 5th choice, 185th overall, in 2005 Entry Draft).

			Regular Season					Playoffs				
Season	Club	League	GP	G	A	Pts	PIM	GP	G	A	Pts	PIM
2003-04	Notre Dame	SMHL	41	9	21	30	38	....	....	....	....	....
2004-05	Notre Dame	SJHL	50	2	15	17	28	....	....	....	....	....
2005-06	Notre Dame	SJHL	52	12	23	35	75	11	2	9	11	15
2006-07	Colorado College	WCHA	23	1	3	4	16	....	....	....	....	....

FREDRIKSSON, David (FREHD-rihk-suhn, DAY-vihd) **ST.L.**

Right wing. Shoots left. 6'2", 214 lbs. Born, Jonkoping, Sweden, October 4, 1985.
(St. Louis' 7th choice, 211th overall, in 2004 Entry Draft).

			Regular Season					Playoffs				
Season	Club	League	GP	G	A	Pts	PIM	GP	G	A	Pts	PIM
2001-02	HV 71 Jr.	Swe-Jr.	14	6	2	8	20	....	....	....	....	....
2002-03	HV 71 Jr.	Swe-Jr.	27	9	10	19	24	8	10	0	10	10
	HV 71 Jonkoping	Sweden	1	0	0	0	0	....	....	....	....	....
2003-04	HV 71 Jr.	Swe-Jr.	18	9	3	12	42	2	1	0	1	2
	HV 71 Jonkoping	Sweden	9	0	0	0	2	6	0	0	0	0
2004-05	HV 71 Jr.	Swe-Jr.	19	8	5	13	48	....	....	....	....	....
	Morrums GoIS IK	Sweden-2	2	1	0	1	2	....	....	....	....	....
	HV 71 Jonkoping	Sweden	18	0	0	0	0	....	....	....	....	....
2005-06	HV 71 Jr.	Swe-Jr.	4	6	3	9	8	....	....	....	....	....
	HV 71 Jonkoping	Sweden	37	5	4	9	34	3	0	0	0	4
2006-07	HV 71 Jonkoping	Sweden	12	0	1	1	4	....	....	....	....	....
	VIK Vasteras HK	Sweden-2	3	0	1	1	2	....	....	....	....	....

FRITSCHE, Tom (FRIHCH, TAWM) **COL.**

Left wing. Shoots left. 5'11", 183 lbs. Born, Parma, OH, September 30, 1986.
(Colorado's 3rd choice, 47th overall, in 2005 Entry Draft).

			Regular Season					Playoffs				
Season	Club	League	GP	G	A	Pts	PIM	GP	G	A	Pts	PIM
2002-03	USNTDP	U-17	19	7	11	18	16	....	....	....	....	....
	USNTDP	NAHL	44	14	9	23	43	....	....	....	....	....
2003-04	USNTDP	U-18	46	19	23	42	46	....	....	....	....	....
	USNTDP	NAHL	11	5	4	9	0	....	....	....	....	....
2004-05	Ohio State	CCHA	42	11	*34	45	38	....	....	....	....	....
2005-06	Ohio State	CCHA	37	11	19	30	16	....	....	....	....	....
2006-07	Ohio State	CCHA	19	5	8	13	8	....	....	....	....	....

CCHA All-Rookie Team (2005) • CCHA Second All-Star Team (2005)

FRITZ, Mitch (FRIHTZ, MIHTCH) **NYR**

Left wing. Shoots left. 6'8", 258 lbs. Born, Osoyoos, B.C., November 24, 1980.

			Regular Season					Playoffs				
Season	Club	League	GP	G	A	Pts	PIM	GP	G	A	Pts	PIM
1998-99	Kelowna Rockets	WHL	52	9	0	9	156	2	0	0	0	0
99-2000	Kelowna Rockets	WHL	58	4	2	6	204	5	0	0	0	0
2000-01	Lowell	AHL	5	0	0	0	20	....	....	....	....	....
	Tallahassee	ECHL	42	5	3	8	79	....	....	....	....	....
2001-02	Hamilton Bulldogs	AHL	13	0	0	0	37	....	....	....	....	....
	Saint John Flames	AHL	11	0	0	0	34	....	....	....	....	....
	Columbus	ECHL	45	3	7	10	284	....	....	....	....	....
2002-03	Milwaukee	AHL	13	1	2	3	33	....	....	....	....	....
	Columbus	ECHL	33	2	4	6	144	....	....	....	....	....
2003-04	Worcester IceCats	AHL	4	0	0	0	10	4	0	0	0	4
	Columbus	ECHL	64	3	9	12	149	....	....	....	....	....
2004-05	Springfield Falcons	AHL	45	3	1	4	179	....	....	....	....	....
2005-06	Springfield Falcons	AHL	69	6	5	11	212	....	....	....	....	....
2006-07	Springfield Falcons	AHL	63	0	1	1	144	....	....	....	....	....

Yanick Dupre Memorial Award (Outstanding Humanitarian Contribution - AHL) (2006)

Signed as a free agent by **Tampa Bay**, August 5, 2005. Rights traded to **NY Rangers** by **Tampa Bay** for the rights to Bryce Lampman, July 4, 2007.

FROLIK, Michael (FROH-lihk, MIGH-kuhl) **FLA.**

Center. Shoots left. 6'1", 185 lbs. Born, Kladno, Czech., February 17, 1988.
(Florida's 1st choice, 10th overall, in 2006 Entry Draft).

			Regular Season					Playoffs				
Season	Club	League	GP	G	A	Pts	PIM	GP	G	A	Pts	PIM
2002-03	HC Kladno U17	CzR-U17	46	37	21	58	36	9	9	1	10	18
	HC Kladno Jr.	CzRep-Jr.	....	....	....	....	....	1	0	0	0	2
2003-04	HC Kladno U17	CzR-U17	1	0	1	1	2	....	....	....	....	....
	HC Kladno Jr.	CzRep-Jr.	53	21	23	44	22	7	3	1	4	6
2004-05	HC Kladno U17	CzR-U17	....	....	....	....	....	1	1	0	1	0
	HC Kladno Jr.	CzRep-Jr.	15	9	11	20	18	5	1	0	1	0
	HC Rabat Kladno	CzRep	27	3	1	4	6	1	0	0	0	0
2005-06	HC Kladno Jr.	CzRep-Jr.	3	1	2	3	0	6	3	9	12	6
	HC Rabat Kladno	CzRep	48	2	7	9	32	....	....	....	....	....
2006-07	Rimouski Oceanic	QMJHL	52	31	42	73	40	....	....	....	....	....

QMJHL All-Rookie Team (2007)

FULLER, Evan (FUL-lehr, EN-vuhn) **VAN.**

Right wing. Shoots right. 6'2", 196 lbs. Born, Salmon Arm, B.C., June 1, 1988.
(Vancouver's 5th choice, 197th overall, in 2006 Entry Draft).

			Regular Season					Playoffs				
Season	Club	League	GP	G	A	Pts	PIM	GP	G	A	Pts	PIM
2004-05	Prince George	WHL	55	5	3	8	66	....	....	....	....	....
2005-06	Prince George	WHL	56	2	5	7	87	5	0	0	0	7
2006-07	Prince George	WHL	72	8	12	20	70	15	3	6	9	12

FULTON, Jordan (FUL-tuhn, JOHR-dahn) **CGY.**

Center. Shoots left. 6', 191 lbs. Born, St. Louis Park, MN, September 12, 1987.
(Calgary's 6th choice, 179th overall, in 2006 Entry Draft).

			Regular Season					Playoffs				
Season	Club	League	GP	G	A	Pts	PIM	GP	G	A	Pts	PIM
2002-03	Breck Mustangs	High-MN	26	24	7	31	12	....	....	....	....	....
2003-04	Breck Mustangs	High-MN	31	30	36	66	24	....	....	....	....	....
2004-05	Breck Mustangs	High-MN	28	29	41	70	68	....	....	....	....	....
2005-06	Breck Mustangs	High-MN	28	45	36	81	76	....	....	....	....	....
2006-07	U. Minn-Duluth	WCHA	38	3	7	10	22	....	....	....	....	....

GAGNER, Sam (GAH-n'yay, SAM) **EDM.**

Center/Wing. Shoots right. 5'11", 191 lbs. Born, London, Ont., August 10, 1989.
(Edmonton's 1st choice, 6th overall, in 2007 Entry Draft).

			Regular Season					Playoffs				
Season	Club	League	GP	G	A	Pts	PIM	GP	G	A	Pts	PIM
2004-05	Toronto Marlboros	GTHL	70	62	118	180	56	....	....	....	....	....
2005-06	Sioux City	USHL	56	11	35	46	60	....	....	....	....	....
2006-07	London Knights	OHL	53	35	83	118	36	16	7	*22	29	22

USHL All-Rookie Team (2006) • OHL All-Rookie Team (2007)

GAGNON, Aaron (GAN-YAWN, AIR-ruhn) **DAL.**

Center. Shoots right. 5'10", 185 lbs. Born, Quesnel, B.C., April 24, 1986.
(Phoenix's 8th choice, 240th overall, in 2004 Entry Draft).

			Regular Season					Playoffs				
Season	Club	League	GP	G	A	Pts	PIM	GP	G	A	Pts	PIM
2001-02	North Okanoghan	BCAHA	41	59	59	118	60	....	....	....	....	....
	Seattle	WHL	2	0	0	0	0	....	....	....	....	....
2002-03	Seattle	WHL	60	5	13	18	14	15	3	2	5	4
2003-04	Seattle	WHL	63	21	15	36	29	....	....	....	....	....
2004-05	Seattle	WHL	72	31	34	65	29	12	4	5	9	16
2005-06	Seattle	WHL	62	24	21	45	40	7	5	3	8	6
2006-07	Seattle	WHL	59	42	38	80	58	11	6	2	8	10

WHL West First All-Star Team (2005, 2007)

Signed as a free agent by **Dallas**, February 2, 2007.

GALIARDI, T.J. (gal-ee-AR-dee, TEE-JAY) **COL.**

Wing. Shoots left. 6'2", 172 lbs. Born, Calgary, Alta., April 22, 1988.
(Colorado's 4th choice, 55th overall, in 2007 Entry Draft).

			Regular Season					Playoffs				
Season	Club	League	GP	G	A	Pts	PIM	GP	G	A	Pts	PIM
2004-05	Cgy. North Stars	AMHL	36	14	16	30	32	....	....	....	....	....
2005-06	Calgary Royals	AJHL	56	19	37	56	60	....	....	....	....	....
2006-07	Dartmouth	ECACHL	33	14	17	31	30	....	....	....	....	....

ECACHL All-Rookie Team (2007)

GAUTHIER, Mike (GOH-tyay, MIGHK)

Defense. Shoots right. 6'4", 185 lbs. Born, Vancouver, B.C., March 26, 1987.
(St. Louis' 5th choice, 169th overall, in 2005 Entry Draft).

			Regular Season					Playoffs				
Season	Club	League	GP	G	A	Pts	PIM	GP	G	A	Pts	PIM
2002-03	Delta Ice Hawks	PIJHL	36	6	15	21	288	....	....	....	....	....
	Prince Albert	WHL	3	0	0	0	2	....	....	....	....	....
2003-04	Prince Albert	WHL	52	1	0	1	130	5	0	0	0	2
2004-05	Prince Albert	WHL	40	2	1	3	93	13	0	0	0	18
2005-06	Prince Albert	WHL	69	4	8	12	169	....	....	....	....	....
2006-07	Prince Albert	WHL	69	5	19	24	*264	4	0	1	1	17

GAWRYLETZ, Travis (GAW-reh-lehtz, TRA-vihs) **PHI.**

Defense. Shoots right. 6'2", 190 lbs. Born, Trail, B.C., November 2, 1985.
(Philadelphia's 9th choice, 253rd overall, in 2004 Entry Draft).

			Regular Season					Playoffs				
Season	Club	League	GP	G	A	Pts	PIM	GP	G	A	Pts	PIM
2002-03	Trail Smoke Eaters	BCHL	56	4	28	32	42	14	6	6	12	10
2003-04	Trail Smoke Eaters	BCHL	51	9	21	30	51	10	1	3	4	6
2004-05	U. Minn-Duluth	WCHA	35	4	1	5	26	....	....	....	....	....
2005-06	U. Minn-Duluth	WCHA	32	0	7	7	12	....	....	....	....	....
2006-07	U. Minn-Duluth	WCHA	37	0	5	5	57	....	....	....	....	....

BCHL All-Rookie Team (2003) • BCHL Interior Division First All-Star Team (2004)

GAZDIC, Luke (GAZ-dihk, LEWK) **DAL.**

Left wing. Shoots left. 6'3", 210 lbs. Born, Toronto, Ont., July 25, 1989.
(Dallas' 8th choice, 172nd overall, in 2007 Entry Draft).

			Regular Season					Playoffs				
Season	Club	League	GP	G	A	Pts	PIM	GP	G	A	Pts	PIM
2005-06	Wexford Raiders	OPJHL	47	17	16	33	105	....	....	....	....	....
	North York	GTHL	38	13	16	29	24	....	....	....	....	....
2006-07	Erie Otters	OHL	58	5	8	13	136	....	....	....	....	....

GELECH, Randall (GEH-lehkh, RAN-duhl) **DET.**

Center. Shoots right. 6'3", 220 lbs. Born, Wynard, Sask., February 2, 1984.
(Phoenix's 5th choice, 208th overall, in 2003 Entry Draft).

			Regular Season					Playoffs				
Season	Club	League	GP	G	A	Pts	PIM	GP	G	A	Pts	PIM
2000-01	Kelowna Rockets	WHL	51	1	9	10	19	6	0	0	0	4
2001-02	Kelowna Rockets	WHL	48	6	2	8	33	15	2	1	3	15
2002-03	Kelowna Rockets	WHL	67	25	20	45	93	19	8	4	12	17
2003-04	Kelowna Rockets	WHL	71	30	19	49	117	17	10	4	14	22
2004-05	Utah Grizzlies	AHL	76	15	12	27	72	....	....	....	....	....
2005-06	San Antonio	AHL	75	9	12	21	39	....	....	....	....	....
2006-07	San Antonio	AHL	79	17	17	34	64	....	....	....	....	....

Memorial Cup Tournament All-Star Team (2004)

Signed as a free agent by **Detroit**, July 16, 2007.

GENDUR, Dan (JEHN-duhr, DAN) **VAN.**

Right wing. Shoots right. 5'11", 195 lbs. Born, Vancouver, B.C., May 21, 1987.
(Vancouver's 6th choice, 206th overall, in 2007 Entry Draft).

			Regular Season					Playoffs				
Season	Club	League	GP	G	A	Pts	PIM	GP	G	A	Pts	PIM
2003-04	Victoria Cougars	VIJHL	31	26	30	56	70	....	....	....	....	....
	Cowichan Valley	BCHL	17	3	8	11	22	1	0	0	0	0
2004-05	Prince George	WHL	60	2	6	8	75	....	....	....	....	....
2005-06	Prince George	WHL	19	2	1	3	24	....	....	....	....	....
2006-07	Prince George	WHL	13	2	5	7	18	....	....	....	....	....
	Everett Silvertips	WHL	48	20	22	42	44	12	4	4	8	8

GENEROUS, Matt (GEHN-uhr-uhs, MAT) **BUF.**

Defense. Shoots right. 6'3", 185 lbs. Born, Methuen, MA, May 4, 1985.
(Buffalo's 8th choice, 208th overall, in 2005 Entry Draft).

			Regular Season					Playoffs				
Season	Club	League	GP	G	A	Pts	PIM	GP	G	A	Pts	PIM
2003-04	N.E. Jr. Falcons	EJHL	43	6	9	15	134	....	....	....	....	....
2004-05	N.E. Jr. Falcons	EJHL	49	8	16	24	105	....	....	....	....	....
2005-06	St. Lawrence	ECACHL	34	4	11	15	34	....	....	....	....	....
2006-07	St. Lawrence	ECACHL	37	3	6	9	34	....	....	....	....	....

ECACHL All-Rookie Team (2006)

GENOWAY, Colby (JEHN-oh-way, KOHL-bee) **VAN.**

Right wing. Shoots right. 6'1", 201 lbs. Born, Morden, Man., December 12, 1983.

			Regular Season					Playoffs				
Season	Club	League	GP	G	A	Pts	PIM	GP	G	A	Pts	PIM
2002-03	North Dakota	WCHA	31	1	2	3	24	....	....	....	....	....
2003-04	North Dakota	WCHA	40	11	23	34	22	....	....	....	....	....
2004-05	North Dakota	WCHA	42	13	31	44	38	....	....	....	....	....
	Hartford Wolf Pack	AHL	4	0	0	0	0	....	....	....	....	....
2005-06	Hartford Wolf Pack	AHL	77	26	35	61	78	13	4	8	12	10
2006-07	Portland Pirates	AHL	41	8	21	29	36	....	....	....	....	....
	Manitoba Moose	AHL	32	1	11	12	12	13	1	1	2	6

Signed as a free agent by **Anaheim**, July 11, 2006. Traded to **Vancouver** by **Anaheim** for Joe Rullier, January 24, 2007.

GEOFFRION, Blake (JEHF-REE-ohn, BLAYK) **NSH.**

Left wing. Shoots left. 6'1", 196 lbs. Born, Plantation, FL, February 3, 1988.
(Nashville's 1st choice, 56th overall, in 2006 Entry Draft).

			Regular Season					Playoffs				
Season	Club	League	GP	G	A	Pts	PIM	GP	G	A	Pts	PIM
2003-04	Culver Academy	High-IN	45	....	....	65	....	....	....	....	....	....
2004-05	USNTDP	U-17	11	2	3	5	24	....	....	....	....	....
	USNTDP	NAHL	37	7	15	22	62	10	2	5	7	23
2005-06	USNTDP	U-18	41	12	14	26	38	....	....	....	....	....
	USNTDP	NAHL	13	6	9	15	30	....	....	....	....	....
2006-07	U. of Wisconsin	WCHA	36	2	4	6	62	....	....	....	....	....

GERBE, Nathan (GUHR-bee, NAY-thuhn) **BUF.**

Center. Shoots left. 5'5", 160 lbs. Born, Oxford, MI, July 24, 1987.
(Buffalo's 5th choice, 142nd overall, in 2005 Entry Draft).

			Regular Season					Playoffs				
Season	Club	League	GP	G	A	Pts	PIM	GP	G	A	Pts	PIM
2002-03	River City Lancers	USHL	25	3	3	6	49	7	1	1	2	2
2003-04	USNTDP	U-17	32	14	12	26	66	....	....	....	....	....
	USNTDP	NAHL	26	11	7	18	87	....	....	....	....	....
2004-05	USNTDP	U-18	26	6	11	17	48	....	....	....	....	....
	USNTDP	NAHL	12	7	5	12	25	....	....	....	....	....
2005-06	Boston College	H-East	39	11	7	18	75	....	....	....	....	....
2006-07	Boston College	H-East	41	*25	22	47	76	....	....	....	....	....

Hockey East Second Alll-Star Team (2007) • NCAA Championship All-Tournament Team (2007)

GERGEN, Michael (GUHR-gehn, MIGH-kuhl) **PIT.**

Left wing. Shoots left. 5'11", 185 lbs. Born, Hastings, MN, February 17, 1987.
(Pittsburgh's 2nd choice, 61st overall, in 2005 Entry Draft).

			Regular Season					Playoffs				
Season	Club	League	GP	G	A	Pts	PIM	GP	G	A	Pts	PIM
2003-04	Shat.-St. Mary's	High-MN	71	29	26	55	52	....	....	....	....	....
2004-05	Shat.-St. Mary's	High-MN	69	64	53	117	110	....	....	....	....	....
2005-06	U. Minn-Duluth	WCHA	39	14	8	22	63	....	....	....	....	....
2006-07	U. Minn-Duluth	WCHA	39	5	11	16	34	....	....	....	....	....

GIFFORD, Brian (GIH-fuhrd, BRIGH-uhn) **PIT.**

Center. Shoots left. 6'1", 173 lbs. Born, Fargo, ND, November 12, 1985.
(Pittsburgh's 5th choice, 85th overall, in 2004 Entry Draft).

			Regular Season					Playoffs				
Season	Club	League	GP	G	A	Pts	PIM	GP	G	A	Pts	PIM
2002-03	Moorhead Spuds	High-MN	30	18	20	38	32	....	....	....	....	....
2003-04	Moorhead Spuds	High-MN	26	19	37	56	26	....	....	....	....	....
2004-05	Indiana Ice	USHL	55	13	10	23	80	3	1	0	1	0
2005-06	Indiana Ice	USHL	56	12	14	26	55	5	0	2	2	0
2006-07	U. of Denver	WCHA	40	3	10	13	49	....	....	....	....	....

GILLIES, Colton (GIHL-eez, KOHL-tuhn) **MIN.**

Center. Shoots left. 6'4", 194 lbs. Born, White Rock, B.C., February 12, 1989.
(Minnesota's 1st choice, 16th overall, in 2007 Entry Draft).

			Regular Season					Playoffs				
Season	Club	League	GP	G	A	Pts	PIM	GP	G	A	Pts	PIM
2004-05	North Delta Flyers	PIJHL	44	9	17	26		....	....	....	....	....
	South Surrey	BCHL	3	1	0	1	0	....	....	....	....	....
	Saskatoon Blades	WHL	9	1	1	2	8	2	0	0	0	0
2005-06	Saskatoon Blades	WHL	63	6	6	12	57	8	0	0	0	4
2006-07	Saskatoon Blades	WHL	65	13	17	30	148	....	....	....	....	....

GIMAEV, Sergei (gih-MIGH-ehv, SAIR-gay) **OTT.**

Defense. Shoots left. 6'1", 183 lbs. Born, Moscow, USSR, February 16, 1984.
(Ottawa's 6th choice, 166th overall, in 2003 Entry Draft).

			Regular Season					Playoffs				
Season	Club	League	GP	G	A	Pts	PIM	GP	G	A	Pts	PIM
2001-02	CSKA Moscow 2	Russia-3	36	0	10	10	50	....	....	....	....	....
2002-03	Cherepovets	Russia	11	0	0	0	4	....	....	....	....	....
2003-04	Cherepovets	Russia	50	1	3	4	32	....	....	....	....	....
2004-05	Cherepovets	Russia	5	0	1	1	2	....	....	....	....	....
	Sibir Novosibirsk	Russia	31	1	6	7	34	....	....	....	....	....
2005-06	Dynamo Moscow	Russia	46	1	3	4	36	2	0	0	0	0
2006-07	Dynamo Moscow	Russia	23	0	2	2	28	2	0	0	0	6

GIONTA, Stephen (jee-OHN-tuh, STEE-vehn) **N.J.**

Right wing. Shoots right. 5'7", 185 lbs. Born, Rochester, NY, October 9, 1983.

			Regular Season					Playoffs				
Season	Club	League	GP	G	A	Pts	PIM	GP	G	A	Pts	PIM
2002-03	Boston College	H-East	33	5	10	15	36	....	....	....	....	....
2003-04	Boston College	H-East	41	9	15	24	36	....	....	....	....	....
2004-05	Boston College	H-East	38	8	11	19	44	....	....	....	....	....
2005-06	Boston College	H-East	37	11	21	32	66	....	....	....	....	....
	Albany River Rats	AHL	3	5	1	6	2	....	....	....	....	....
2006-07	Lowell Devils	AHL	67	7	8	15	15	....	....	....	....	....

Signed to an ATO (tryout) contract by **Albany** (AHL), April 12, 2006.

GIROUX, Claude (zhih-ROO, KLOHD) **PHI.**

Right wing. Shoots right. 5'11", 180 lbs. Born, Hearst, Ont., January 12, 1988.
(Philadelphia's 1st choice, 22nd overall, in 2006 Entry Draft).

			Regular Season					Playoffs				
Season	Club	League	GP	G	A	Pts	PIM	GP	G	A	Pts	PIM
2004-05	Cumberland	CJHL	48	13	27	40	30	....	....	....	....	....
2005-06	Gatineau	QMJHL	69	39	64	103	64	17	5	15	20	24
2006-07	Gatineau	QMJHL	63	48	64	112	49	5	2	5	7	2
	Philadelphia	AHL	5	1	1	2	6	....	....	....	....	....

QMJHL All-Rookie Team (2006)

GLADSKIKH, Evgeny (glad-SKEEKH, ehv-GEH-nee) **VAN.**

Right wing. Shoots left. 6', 198 lbs. Born, Magnitogorsk, USSR, April 24, 1982.
(Vancouver's 3rd choice, 114th overall, in 2001 Entry Draft).

			Regular Season					Playoffs				
Season	Club	League	GP	G	A	Pts	PIM	GP	G	A	Pts	PIM
1998-99	Magnitogorsk 2	Russia-4	16	3	3	6	6	....	....	....	....	....
99-2000	Magnitogorsk 2	Russia-3	39	17	2	19	24	....	....	....	....	....
	Magnitogorsk	Russia	1	0	0	0	0	....	....	....	....	....
2000-01	Magnitogorsk 2	Russia-3	11	10	7	17	6	....	....	....	....	....
	Magnitogorsk	Russia	31	3	5	8	10	12	0	2	2	2
2001-02	Magnitogorsk	Russia	32	5	6	11	6	4	0	0	0	4
2002-03	Magnitogorsk	Russia	42	4	7	11	18	3	0	0	0	2
2003-04	Magnitogorsk	Russia	47	13	13	26	22	14	3	1	4	10
2004-05	Magnitogorsk 2	Russia-3	2	0	2	2	0	....	....	....	....	....
	Magnitogorsk	Russia	42	11	12	23	24	4	1	0	1	4
2005-06	Magnitogorsk	Russia	43	12	8	20	20	7	1	1	2	2
2006-07	Magnitogorsk	Russia	47	5	9	14	16	15	2	4	6	6

GLASS, Andrew (GLAS, AN-droo) **WSH.**

Left wing. Shoots left. 5'11", 180 lbs. Born, Wrentham, MA, July 14, 1989.
(Washington's 10th choice, 199th overall, in 2007 Entry Draft).

			Regular Season					Playoffs				
Season	Club	League	GP	G	A	Pts	PIM	GP	G	A	Pts	PIM
2003-04	Junior Bruins	Minor-MA	61	15	23	38	2	....	....	....	....	....
2004-05	Little Bruins	Minor-MA	33	5	13	18	15	....	....	....	....	....
	Nobles	High-MA	29	7	15	22	6	....	....	....	....	....
2005-06	Little Bruins	Minor-MA	19	9	11	20	17	....	....	....	....	....
	Nobles	High-MA	29	15	24	39	8	....	....	....	....	....
2006-07	Little Bruins	Minor-MA	12	7	8	15	4	....	....	....	....	....
	Nobles	High-MA	18	7	10	17	6	....	....	....	....	....

• Signed Letter of Intent to attend **Boston University** (Hockey East) in fall of 2008.

GLASS, Tanner (GLAS, TA-nuhr) **FLA.**

Forward. Shoots left. 6', 196 lbs. Born, Regina, Sask., November 29, 1983.
(Florida's 13th choice, 265th overall, in 2003 Entry Draft).

			Regular Season					Playoffs				
Season	Club	League	GP	G	A	Pts	PIM	GP	G	A	Pts	PIM
2000-01	Yorkton Mallers	SMHL	39	31	29	60	120	4	3	1	4	10
2001-02	Penticton Panthers	BCHL	57	11	28	39	171	....	....	....	....	....
2002-03	Nanaimo Clippers	BCHL	18	8	14	22	46	....	....	....	....	....
	Penticton Panthers	BCHL	32	15	25	40	108	....	....	....	....	....
2003-04	Dartmouth	ECAC	26	4	7	11	18	....	....	....	....	....
2004-05	Dartmouth	ECACHL	33	7	8	15	32	....	....	....	....	....
2005-06	Dartmouth	ECACHL	33	12	16	28	56	....	....	....	....	....
2006-07	Dartmouth	ECACHL	32	8	20	28	92	....	....	....	....	....
	Rochester	AHL	4	0	1	1	5	....	....	....	....	....

GLASSER, Matthew (GLAS-uhr, MA-thew) **EDM.**

Left wing. Shoots left. 5'10", 175 lbs. Born, Saskatoon, Sask., January 11, 1987.
(Edmonton's 8th choice, 220th overall, in 2005 Entry Draft).

			Regular Season					Playoffs				
Season	Club	League	GP	G	A	Pts	PIM	GP	G	A	Pts	PIM
2003-04	Fort McMurray	AJHL	55	13	12	25	24	....	....	....	....	....
2004-05	Fort McMurray	AJHL	62	25	24	49	14	....	....	....	....	....
2005-06	Fort McMurray	AJHL	58	15	20	35	36	17	5	2	7	38
2006-07	U. of Denver	WCHA	12	0	0	0	2	....	....	....	....	....

GLAZACHEV, Konstantin (GLAH-zuh-chehv, KAWN-stan-tihn) **NSH.**

Left wing. Shoots right. 6', 186 lbs. Born, Arkhangelsk, USSR, February 18, 1985.
(Nashville's 2nd choice, 35th overall, in 2003 Entry Draft).

			Regular Season					Playoffs				
Season	Club	League	GP	G	A	Pts	PIM	GP	G	A	Pts	PIM
2001-02	Yaroslavl 2	Russia-3	7	5	6	11	6	....	....	....	....	....
2002-03	Yaroslavl 2	Russia-3	STATISTICS NOT AVAILABLE									
	Yaroslavl	Russia	13	3	4	7	4	4	0	0	0	0
2003-04	Yaroslavl	Russia	35	4	3	7	4	2	0	0	0	0
	Yaroslavl 2	Russia-3	9	6	5	11	8	....	....	....	....	....
2004-05	Sibir Novosibirsk	Russia	24	4	9	13	6	....	....	....	....	....
	Yaroslavl	Russia	9	0	3	3	2	....	....	....	....	....
	Yaroslavl 2	Russia-3	20	17	9	26	14	....	....	....	....	....
2005-06	Yaroslavl	Russia	29	7	4	11	8	9	0	2	2	0
2006-07	Yaroslavl	Russia	14	4	1	5	10	....	....	....	....	....
	Yaroslavl 2	Russia-3	4	2	5	7	0	....	....	....	....	....
	Amur Khabarovsk	Russia	22	4	7	11	14	....	....	....	....	....

GLUKHOV, Alexei (GLUH-khawv, al-EHX-ay) **T.B.**

Right wing. Shoots left. 6'3", 176 lbs. Born, Voskresensk, USSR, April 5, 1984.
(Tampa Bay's 12th choice, 286th overall, in 2002 Entry Draft).

			Regular Season					Playoffs				
Season	Club	League	GP	G	A	Pts	PIM	GP	G	A	Pts	PIM
99-2000	Voskresensk 2	Russia-3	10	2	2	4	2	....	....	....	....	....
2000-01	Voskresensk	Russia-2	9	0	1	1	6	....	....	....	....	....
2001-02	Voskresensk 2	Russia-3	34	8	22	30	54	....	....	....	....	....
	Voskresensk	Russia-2	4	0	0	0	0	....	....	....	....	....
2002-03	Voskresensk	Russia-2	38	4	4	8	30	....	....	....	....	....
2003-04	Voskresensk	Russia	28	0	0	0	12	....	....	....	....	....
2004-05	Springfield Falcons	AHL	3	0	1	1	6	....	....	....	....	....
	Voskresensk	Russia	9	0	0	0	6	....	....	....	....	....
2005-06	Mytischi	Russia	45	2	14	16	70	9	2	1	3	10
2006-07	Cherepovets	Russia	52	2	14	16	97	5	0	0	0	4

Signed to PTO (tryout) contract by **Springfield** (AHL), April 14, 2005.

GODFREY, Josh (GAWD-free, JAWSH) **WSH.**

Defense. Shoots right. 6'1", 195 lbs. Born, Collingwood, Ont., January 15, 1988.
(Washington's 2nd choice, 34th overall, in 2007 Entry Draft).

			Regular Season					Playoffs				
Season	Club	League	GP	G	A	Pts	PIM	GP	G	A	Pts	PIM
2004-05	Guelph Storm	OHL	18	0	4	4	9	1	0	0	0	0
2005-06	Guelph Storm	OHL	33	2	8	10	38	....	....	....	....	....
	Sault Ste. Marie	OHL	30	6	5	11	26	1	0	1	1	0
2006-07	Sault Ste. Marie	OHL	68	24	33	57	80	13	9	5	14	18

GOGULLA, Philip (GOH-goo-lah, FIHL-ihp) **BUF.**

Right wing. Shoots left. 6'2", 176 lbs. Born, Dusseldorf, West Germany, July 31, 1987.
(Buffalo's 2nd choice, 48th overall, in 2005 Entry Draft).

			Regular Season					Playoffs				
Season	Club	League	GP	G	A	Pts	PIM	GP	G	A	Pts	PIM
2002-03	Krefelder EV Jr.	Ger-Jr.	32	11	23	34	42	2	0	0	0	2
2003-04	Krefelder EV Jr.	Ger-Jr.	35	35	44	79	22	2	0	2	2	27
2004-05	Essen	German-2	3	0	0	0	0	....	....	....	....	....
	Koln Jr.	Ger-Jr.	7	4	5	9	18	....	....	....	....	....
	Kolner Haie	Germany	47	1	1	2	14	7	0	0	0	2
2005-06	Kolner Haie	Germany	48	7	15	22	49	9	3	2	5	40
2006-07	Kolner Haie	Germany	44	8	13	21	26	7	0	0	0	8

GOLIGOSKI, Alex (goh-lih-GAW-skee, AL-ehx) **PIT.**

Defense. Shoots right. 5'11", 180 lbs. Born, Grand Rapids, MN, July 30, 1985.
(Pittsburgh's 3rd choice, 61st overall, in 2004 Entry Draft).

			Regular Season					Playoffs				
Season	Club	League	GP	G	A	Pts	PIM	GP	G	A	Pts	PIM
2002-03	Grand Rapids	High-MN	28	14	20	34	22	....	....	....	....	....
2003-04	Grand Rapids	High-MN	26	25	31	56	16	....	....	....	....	....
	Sioux Falls	USHL	10	0	2	2	6	....	....	....	....	....
2004-05	U. of Minnesota	WCHA	33	5	15	20	44	....	....	....	....	....
2005-06	U. of Minnesota	WCHA	41	11	28	39	63	....	....	....	....	....
2006-07	U. of Minnesota	WCHA	44	9	30	39	51	....	....	....	....	....

WCHA All-Rookie Team (2005) • WCHA Second All-Star Team (2006) • WCHA First All-Star Team (2007) • NCAA West First All-American Team (2007)

GONCHAROV, Maxim (gohn-CHAR-ahv, mahx-EEM) **PHX.**

Defense. Shoots right. 6', 176 lbs. Born, Moscow, USSR, June 15, 1989.
(Phoenix's 6th choice, 123rd overall, in 2007 Entry Draft).

			Regular Season					Playoffs				
Season	Club	League	GP	G	A	Pts	PIM	GP	G	A	Pts	PIM
2005-06	CSKA Moscow 2	Russia-3	STATISTICS NOT AVAILABLE									
2006-07	CSKA Moscow 2	Russia-3	STATISTICS NOT AVAILABLE									
	CSKA Moscow	Russia	18	0	0	0	10	5	0	0	0	2

GORDON, Andrew (GOHR-duhn, AN-droo) **WSH.**

Right wing. Shoots right. 5'11", 180 lbs. Born, Halifax, N.S., December 13, 1985.
(Washington's 11th choice, 197th overall, in 2004 Entry Draft).

			Regular Season					Playoffs				
Season	**Club**	**League**	**GP**	**G**	**A**	**Pts**	**PIM**	**GP**	**G**	**A**	**Pts**	**PIM**
2002-03	Notre Dame	SJHL	58	20	27	47	12	....	....	....	....	....
2003-04	Notre Dame	SJHL	55	20	44	64	12	....	....	....	....	....
2004-05	St. Cloud State	WCHA	38	9	8	17	6	....	....	....	....	....
2005-06	St. Cloud State	WCHA	42	20	20	40	22	....	....	....	....	....
2006-07	St. Cloud State	WCHA	40	22	23	45	16	....	....	....	....	....

WCHA First All-Star Team (2007)

GOULET, Alain (goo-LAY, AL-eh) **BOS.**

Defense. Shoots right. 6'3", 178 lbs. Born, Kapuskasing, Ont., September 22, 1988.
(Boston's 4th choice, 159th overall, in 2007 Entry Draft).

			Regular Season					Playoffs				
Season	**Club**	**League**	**GP**	**G**	**A**	**Pts**	**PIM**	**GP**	**G**	**A**	**Pts**	**PIM**
2005-06	Ottawa Jr. Sens	CJHL	41	6	14	20	22	....	....	....	....	....
2006-07	Aurora Tigers	OPJHL	43	10	32	42	34	25	5	16	21	32

• Signed Letter of Intent to attend **University of Nebraska-Omaha** (CCHA) in fall of 2007.

GOULET, Stephane (goo-LAY, STEH-fan) **EDM.**

Right wing. Shoots left. 6'3", 185 lbs. Born, Levis, Que., January 7, 1986.
(Edmonton's 8th choice, 208th overall, in 2004 Entry Draft).

			Regular Season					Playoffs				
Season	**Club**	**League**	**GP**	**G**	**A**	**Pts**	**PIM**	**GP**	**G**	**A**	**Pts**	**PIM**
2002-03	Levis	QAAA	42	39	29	68	70	....	....	....	....	....
2003-04	Quebec Remparts	QMJHL	54	6	8	14	14	5	0	0	0	2
2004-05	Moncton Wildcats	QMJHL	69	22	25	47	37	12	3	7	10	12
2005-06	Moncton Wildcats	QMJHL	67	51	42	93	80	13	7	8	15	16
2006-07	Grand Rapids	AHL	2	0	0	0	2	....	....	....	....	....
	Stockton Thunder	ECHL	69	17	23	40	58	5	0	1	1	2

GRABNER, Michael (GRAB-nuhr, MIGH-kuhl) **VAN.**

Right wing. Shoots left. 6', 177 lbs. Born, Villach, Austria, October 5, 1987.
(Vancouver's 1st choice, 14th overall, in 2006 Entry Draft).

			Regular Season					Playoffs				
Season	**Club**	**League**	**GP**	**G**	**A**	**Pts**	**PIM**	**GP**	**G**	**A**	**Pts**	**PIM**
2002-03	EC Villacher SV Jr.	Austria-Jr.	13	6	4	10	4	....	....	....	....	....
2003-04	EC Villacher SV Jr.	Austria-Jr.	23	32	5	37	58	....	....	....	....	....
	EC Villacher SV	Austria	18	2	1	3	0	....	....	....	....	....
2004-05	Spokane Chiefs	WHL	58	13	11	24	18	....	....	....	....	....
2005-06	Spokane Chiefs	WHL	67	36	14	50	28	....	....	....	....	....
2006-07	Spokane Chiefs	WHL	55	39	16	55	34	6	0	1	1	2
	Manitoba Moose	AHL	2	1	1	2	0	6	0	0	0	0

GRACIK, Juraj (GRAH-chihk, YUHR-ay) **ATL.**

Right wing. Shoots right. 6'3", 190 lbs. Born, Topolcany, Czech., August 14, 1986.
(Atlanta's 5th choice, 142nd overall, in 2004 Entry Draft).

			Regular Season					Playoffs				
Season	**Club**	**League**	**GP**	**G**	**A**	**Pts**	**PIM**	**GP**	**G**	**A**	**Pts**	**PIM**
2002-03	Topolcany Jr.	Slovak-Jr.	24	10	7	17	28	....	....	....	....	....
2003-04	Topolcany Jr.	Slovak-Jr.	28	22	12	34	78	....	....	....	....	....
	Topolcany	Slovak-2	28	16	8	24	8	4	1	0	1	0
2004-05	Tri-City Americans	WHL	33	4	2	6	18	....	....	....	....	....
2005-06	Tri-City Americans	WHL	53	22	23	45	36	....	....	....	....	....
2006-07	Bratislava	Slovakia	37	5	1	6	6	3	0	0	0	0
	HC Topolcany	Slovak-2	7	8	1	9	18	....	....	....	....	....
	Ruzinov	Slovak-2	13	7	5	12	16	3	1	1	2	0

Signed as a free agent by **Bratislava** (Slovakia), October 14, 2006.

GRAGNANI, Marc-Andre (GRUH-na-nee, MAHRK-AWN-dray) **BUF.**

Defense. Shoots left. 6'1", 180 lbs. Born, Montreal, Que., March 11, 1987.
(Buffalo's 3rd choice, 87th overall, in 2005 Entry Draft).

			Regular Season					Playoffs				
Season	**Club**	**League**	**GP**	**G**	**A**	**Pts**	**PIM**	**GP**	**G**	**A**	**Pts**	**PIM**
2002-03	West Island Lions	QAAA	34	3	15	18	22	....	....	....	....	....
2003-04	PEI Rocket	QMJHL	61	2	13	15	42	11	0	0	0	4
2004-05	PEI Rocket	QMJHL	68	10	29	39	48	....	....	....	....	....
2005-06	PEI Rocket	QMJHL	62	16	55	71	75	6	1	4	5	14
2006-07	PEI Rocket	QMJHL	65	22	46	68	58	7	5	8	13	4

GRAHAM, Bruce (GRAY-uhm, BROOS) **NYR**

Center. Shoots left. 6'6", 230 lbs. Born, Moncton, N.B., December 2, 1985.
(NY Rangers' 5th choice, 51st overall, in 2004 Entry Draft).

			Regular Season					Playoffs				
Season	**Club**	**League**	**GP**	**G**	**A**	**Pts**	**PIM**	**GP**	**G**	**A**	**Pts**	**PIM**
2001-02	Moncton Flyers	NBMHL	STATISTICS NOT AVAILABLE									
	Moncton Wildcats	QMJHL	3	0	0	0	0	....	....	....	....	....
2002-03	Moncton Wildcats	QMJHL	66	15	13	28	80	6	0	2	2	0
2003-04	Moncton Wildcats	QMJHL	68	24	33	57	89	18	0	14	14	4
2004-05	Moncton Wildcats	QMJHL	47	23	19	42	56	12	4	5	9	19
2005-06	Hartford Wolf Pack	AHL	25	2	5	7	15	....	....	....	....	....
	Charlotte	ECHL	23	6	12	18	40	2	0	0	0	0
2006-07	Hartford Wolf Pack	AHL	7	0	1	1	0	2	0	0	0	0
	Charlotte	ECHL	65	33	23	56	83	5	1	2	3	8

GRANATH, Elias (GRA-nuth, EHL-ee-ahs)

Defense. Shoots left. 6'1", 174 lbs. Born, Borlange, Sweden, September 6, 1985.
(Dallas' 10th choice, 196th overall, in 2003 Entry Draft).

			Regular Season					Playoffs				
Season	**Club**	**League**	**GP**	**G**	**A**	**Pts**	**PIM**	**GP**	**G**	**A**	**Pts**	**PIM**
2001-02	Leksands IF U18	Swe-U18	11	0	1	1	8	4	0	0	0	2
	Leksands IF Jr.	Swe-Jr.	6	0	0	0	0	1	0	0	0	0
2002-03	Leksands IF Jr.	Swe-Jr.	29	0	4	4	49	....	....	....	....	....
	Leksands IF U18	Swe-U18	6	0	2	2	0	2	0	1	1	8
2003-04	Leksands IF Jr.	Swe-Jr.	25	4	4	8	34	....	....	....	....	....
	Leksands IF	Sweden-Q	10	0	0	0	4	....	....	....	....	....
2004-05	Leksands IF	Sweden-2	35	3	3	6	24	....	....	....	....	....
	Leksands IF Jr.	Swe-Jr.	5	0	2	2	8	5	1	0	1	2
2005-06	Leksands IF Jr.	Swe-Jr.	3	1	1	2	2	....	....	....	....	....
	Leksands IF	Sweden	46	0	0	0	55	....	....	....	....	....
2006-07	Leksands IF	Sweden-2	54	1	9	10	48	....	....	....	....	....

GRANT, Alex (GRANT, AL-ehx) **PIT.**

Defense. Shoots right. 6'2", 185 lbs. Born, Antigonish, N.S., January 20, 1989.
(Pittsburgh's 6th choice, 118th overall, in 2007 Entry Draft).

			Regular Season					Playoffs				
Season	**Club**	**League**	**GP**	**G**	**A**	**Pts**	**PIM**	**GP**	**G**	**A**	**Pts**	**PIM**
2004-05	Antigonish	MJrHL	50	7	9	16	36	3	1	1	2	2
2005-06	Saint John	QMJHL	47	4	9	13	58	....	....	....	....	....
2006-07	Saint John	QMJHL	68	12	20	32	108	....	....	....	....	....

GRATCHEV, Maxim (GRAT-chehv, mahx-EEM) **NYI**

Left wing. Shoots left. 5'11", 196 lbs. Born, Novosibirsk, USSR, September 26, 1988.
(NY Islanders' 3rd choice, 106th overall, in 2007 Entry Draft).

			Regular Season					Playoffs				
Season	**Club**	**League**	**GP**	**G**	**A**	**Pts**	**PIM**	**GP**	**G**	**A**	**Pts**	**PIM**
2003-04	Thayer Academy	High-MA	STATISTICS NOT AVAILABLE									
2004-05	Quebec Remparts	QMJHL	54	7	11	18	36	....	....	....	....	....
2005-06	Quebec Remparts	QMJHL	22	5	5	10	40	....	....	....	....	....
	Rimouski Oceanic	QMJHL	33	6	11	17	57	....	....	....	....	....
2006-07	Rimouski Oceanic	QMJHL	70	35	42	77	88	....	....	....	....	....

GREENING, Colin (GREEN-ihng, KAW-lihn) **OTT.**

Center/Left wing. Shoots left. 6'2", 191 lbs. Born, St. John's, Nfld., March 9, 1986.
(Ottawa's 8th choice, 204th overall, in 2005 Entry Draft).

			Regular Season					Playoffs				
Season	**Club**	**League**	**GP**	**G**	**A**	**Pts**	**PIM**	**GP**	**G**	**A**	**Pts**	**PIM**
2002-03	St. John's	NFAHA	60	24	34	58	48	....	....	....	....	....
2003-04	Upper Canada	High-ON	53	30	43	73	40	....	....	....	....	....
2004-05	Upper Canada	High-ON	35	24	22	46	24	....	....	....	....	....
2005-06	Nanaimo Clippers	BCHL	56	27	35	62	46	5	3	0	3	2
2006-07	Cornell Big Red	ECACHL	31	11	8	19	26	....	....	....	....	....

GREENOP, Richard (GREEN-awp, RIH-chuhrd) **CHI.**

Center. Shoots right. 6'3", 210 lbs. Born, Oshawa, Ont., February 24, 1989.
(Chicago's 7th choice, 156th overall, in 2007 Entry Draft).

			Regular Season					Playoffs				
Season	**Club**	**League**	**GP**	**G**	**A**	**Pts**	**PIM**	**GP**	**G**	**A**	**Pts**	**PIM**
2005-06	Oshawa	OPJHL	47	10	4	14	97	....	....	....	....	....
2006-07	Windsor Spitfires	OHL	48	3	9	12	149	....	....	....	....	....

GREENTREE, Kyle (GREEN-TREE, KIGHL) **PHI.**

Left wing. Shoots left. 6'3", 210 lbs. Born, Victoria, B.C., November 15, 1983.

			Regular Season					Playoffs				
Season	**Club**	**League**	**GP**	**G**	**A**	**Pts**	**PIM**	**GP**	**G**	**A**	**Pts**	**PIM**
2000-01	Victoria Salsa	BCHL	59	27	38	65	50	....	....	....	....	....
2003-04	Victoria Salsa	BCHL	59	62	53	115	170	5	4	5	9	29
2004-05	Alaska	CCHA	37	12	20	32	31	....	....	....	....	....
2005-06	Alaska	CCHA	39	8	19	27	58	....	....	....	....	....
2006-07	Philadelphia	AHL	8	2	0	2	2	....	....	....	....	....
	Alaska	CCHA	39	21	21	42	78	....	....	....	....	....

Signed as a free agent by **Philadelphia**, March 14, 2007.

GREER, Matt (GREER, MAT) **CBJ**

Left wing. Shoots right. 6'2", 190 lbs. Born, St. Paul, MN, November 21, 1985.
(Columbus' 11th choice, 233rd overall, in 2004 Entry Draft).

			Regular Season					Playoffs				
Season	**Club**	**League**	**GP**	**G**	**A**	**Pts**	**PIM**	**GP**	**G**	**A**	**Pts**	**PIM**
2003-04	White Bear Lake	High-MN	27	25	19	44	....	....	....	....	....	....
2004-05	Des Moines	USHL	60	14	18	32	16	....	....	....	....	....
2005-06	U. Minn-Duluth	WCHA	40	2	3	5	12	....	....	....	....	....
2006-07	U. Minn-Duluth	WCHA	32	4	4	8	24	....	....	....	....	....

GREGOIRE, Jason (GREHG-wahr, JAY-suhn) **NYI**

Left wing. Shoots left. 5'11", 175 lbs. Born, Winnipeg, Man., February 24, 1989.
(NY Islanders' 2nd choice, 76th overall, in 2007 Entry Draft).

			Regular Season					Playoffs				
Season	**Club**	**League**	**GP**	**G**	**A**	**Pts**	**PIM**	**GP**	**G**	**A**	**Pts**	**PIM**
2005-06	Winnipeg South	MJHL	57	22	28	50	46	14	12	11	23	....
2006-07	Lincoln Stars	USHL	32	16	20	36	10	4	4	0	4	2

• Signed Letter of Intent to attend **University of North Dakota** (WCHA) in fall of 2008.

GRIGORENKO, Igor (grih-goh-REHN-koh, EE-gohr) **DET.**

Right wing. Shoots right. 5'11", 183 lbs. Born, Togliatti, USSR, April 9, 1983.
(Detroit's 1st choice, 62nd overall, in 2001 Entry Draft).

			Regular Season					Playoffs				
Season	**Club**	**League**	**GP**	**G**	**A**	**Pts**	**PIM**	**GP**	**G**	**A**	**Pts**	**PIM**
1998-99	Lada Togliatti 2	Russia-4	19	3	3	6	2	....	....	....	....	....
99-2000	Lada Togliatti 2	Russia-3	38	17	18	35	36	....	....	....	....	....
2000-01	Lada Togliatti 2	Russia-3	6	5	4	9	....	....	....	....	....	....
	CSK VVS Samara	Russia-2	39	10	10	20	....	....	....	....	....	....
	Lada Togliatti	Russia	....	....	....	....	....	5	1	0	1	4
2001-02	Lada Togliatti	Russia	41	8	9	17	58	4	1	0	1	2
2002-03	Lada Togliatti	Russia	47	19	11	30	82	10	1	*6	7	10
2003-04	Lada Togliatti 2	Russia-3	6	2	2	4	0	2	0	1	1	0
	Lada Togliatti	Russia	....	....	....	....	....	3	0	0	0	0
2004-05	Lada Togliatti	Russia	11	0	1	1	6	....	....	....	....	....
	Ufa	Russia	30	11	7	18	22	....	....	....	....	....
2005-06	Cherepovets	Russia	50	13	20	33	26	4	1	1	2	8
2006-07	Lada Togliatti	Russia	49	14	13	27	71	2	2	1	3	2

• Missed majority of 2003-04 season recovering from injuries suffered in automobile accident, May 16, 2003.

GROT, Denis (GROHT, DEH-nihs) VAN.

Defense. Shoots left. 6', 185 lbs. Born, Minsk, USSR, January 6, 1984.
(Vancouver's 2nd choice, 55th overall, in 2002 Entry Draft).

			Regular Season					Playoffs				
Season	Club	League	GP	G	A	Pts	PIM	GP	G	A	Pts	PIM
2000-01	Yaroslavl 2	Russia-3	34	5	1	6	10	....	....	....	....	....
	Russia	Nat-Tm	5	0	2	2	8	....	....	....	....	....
2001-02	Yaroslavl 2	Russia-3	14	1	0	1	10	....	....	....	....	....
	Elektrostal 2	Russia-3	3	0	1	1	2	....	....	....	....	....
	Elektrostal	Russia-2	33	1	1	2	42	....	....	....	....	....
2002-03	HK Lipetsk	Russia-2	27	4	4	8	28	....	....	....	....	....
2003-04	Yaroslavl	Russia	31	0	2	2	4	3	0	0	0	2
2004-05	Yaroslavl 2	Russia-3	20	2	3	5	22	....	....	....	....	....
	Yaroslavl	Russia	1	0	0	0	2	....	....	....	....	....
	Sibir Novosibirsk	Russia	23	0	4	4	32	....	....	....	....	....
	Amur Khabarovsk	Russia-2	9	1	5	6	2	12	0	0	0	31
2005-06	Spartak Moscow	Russia	48	1	4	5	28	3	0	0	0	0
2006-07	Nizhnekamsk	Russia	38	2	7	9	59	1	0	0	0	2

GRYBA, Eric (GREE-buh, AIR-ihk) OTT.

Defense. Shoots right. 6'3", 215 lbs. Born, Saskatoon, Sask., April 14, 1988.
(Ottawa's 2nd choice, 68th overall, in 2006 Entry Draft).

			Regular Season					Playoffs				
Season	Club	League	GP	G	A	Pts	PIM	GP	G	A	Pts	PIM
2003-04	Sask. Contacts	SMHL	39	1	10	11	89	10	4	8	12	20
2004-05	Sask. Contacts	SMHL	32	11	29	40	83	11	5	7	12	22
2005-06	Green Bay	USHL	56	3	12	15	*205	3	1	1	2	27
2006-07	Boston University	H-East	38	1	3	4	76	....	....	....	....	....

GUENETTE, Francois-Pierre (gwih-NEHT, frahn-SWUH-PEE-air) ST.L.

Center. Shoots right. 6', 184 lbs. Born, Laval, Que., January 18, 1984.
(Vancouver's 7th choice, 222nd overall, in 2003 Entry Draft).

			Regular Season					Playoffs				
Season	Club	League	GP	G	A	Pts	PIM	GP	G	A	Pts	PIM
99-2000	Laval-Laurentides	QAAA	33	15	18	33	14	9	3	6	9	2
2000-01	Laval-Laurentides	QAAA	41	17	27	44	47	8	3	8	11	4
2001-02	Halifax	QMJHL	35	2	11	13	14	11	3	4	7	0
2002-03	Halifax	QMJHL	72	38	49	87	24	24	10	17	27	12
2003-04	Cape Breton	QMJHL	69	34	51	85	26	5	0	2	2	2
2004-05	Halifax	QMJHL	70	21	38	59	46	13	4	11	15	4
2005-06	Columbia Inferno	ECHL	68	12	30	42	34	....	....	....	....	....
2006-07	Victoria	ECHL	67	13	42	55	28	6	0	4	4	4

Traded to **St. Louis** by **Vancouver** for Zack Fitzgerald, August 1, 2007.

GUERIN, Marty (GAIR-ihn, MAHR-tee) L.A.

Right wing. Shoots right. 6'1", 190 lbs. Born, Manchester, NH, May 25, 1983.
(Los Angeles' 10th choice, 274th overall, in 2003 Entry Draft).

			Regular Season					Playoffs				
Season	Club	League	GP	G	A	Pts	PIM	GP	G	A	Pts	PIM
2000-01	Omaha Lancers	USHL	42	3	5	8	24	7	0	0	0	0
2001-02	Omaha Lancers	USHL	31	12	11	33	16	....	....	....	....	....
	Des Moines	USHL	7	2	1	3	2	....	....	....	....	....
2002-03	Des Moines	USHL	60	27	33	60	30	4	1	3	4	6
2003-04	Miami U.	CCHA	41	14	19	33	18	....	....	....	....	....
2004-05	Miami U.	CCHA	34	15	19	34	42	....	....	....	....	....
2005-06	Miami U.	CCHA	39	8	8	16	36	....	....	....	....	....
2006-07	Miami U.	CCHA	42	12	20	32	51	....	....	....	....	....

GUGGISBERG, Peter (GUH-gihs-buhrg, PEE-tuhr) WSH.

Right wing. Shoots right. 5'11", 183 lbs. Born, Davos, Switz., January 20, 1985.
(Washington's 10th choice, 166th overall, in 2004 Entry Draft).

			Regular Season					Playoffs				
Season	Club	League	GP	G	A	Pts	PIM	GP	G	A	Pts	PIM
2000-01	Langnau Jr.	Swiss-Jr.	12	3	3	6	0	2	1	0	1	2
2001-02	Langnau Jr.	Swiss-Jr.	15	12	4	16	2	4	2	3	5	4
	Langnau	Swiss	....	....	....	....	....	6	0	1	1	0
2002-03	Langnau Jr.	Swiss-Jr.	10	7	10	17	0	5	2	1	3	32
	Langnau	Swiss	34	6	7	13	0	....	....	....	....	....
2003-04	HC Davos	Swiss	39	11	9	20	2	6	0	0	0	4
2004-05	HC Davos	Swiss	36	12	7	19	8	15	3	5	8	4
2005-06	HC Davos	Swiss	43	7	9	16	10	15	3	2	5	2
2006-07	HC Davos	Swiss	43	6	6	12	6	19	6	5	11	4

GUNNARSSON, Carl (GUHN-nuhr-suhn, KARL) TOR.

Defense. Shoots left. 6'2", 189 lbs. Born, Orebro, Sweden, November 9, 1986.
(Toronto's 6th choice, 194th overall, in 2007 Entry Draft).

			Regular Season					Playoffs				
Season	Club	League	GP	G	A	Pts	PIM	GP	G	A	Pts	PIM
2003-04	HC Orebro 90	Sweden-2	43	0	4	4	16	....	....	....	....	....
2004-05	Linkopings HC U18	Swe-U18	1	0	1	1	2	....	....	....	....	....
	Linkopings HC Jr.	Swe-Jr.	22	2	5	7	24	....	....	....	....	....
2005-06	Linkopings HC Jr.	Swe-Jr.	30	7	6	13	26	4	1	0	1	4
	IFK Arboga IK	Sweden-2	12	1	5	6	8	....	....	....	....	....
	Linkopings HC	Sweden	14	0	0	0	0	....	....	....	....	....
2006-07	Linkopings HC Jr.	Swe-Jr.	6	0	5	5	6	....	....	....	....	....
	VIK Vasteras HK	Sweden-2	15	2	3	5	14	....	....	....	....	....
	Linkopings HC	Sweden	30	2	2	4	8	15	0	4	4	4

GUTHRIE, Shea (GUHTH-ree, SHAY) NYI

Wing. Shoots right. 6', 200 lbs. Born, Almonte, Ont., July 30, 1987.
(NY Islanders' 3rd choice, 76th overall, in 2005 Entry Draft).

			Regular Season					Playoffs				
Season	Club	League	GP	G	A	Pts	PIM	GP	G	A	Pts	PIM
2004-05	St. George's	High-RI	25	31	26	57	20	....	....	....	....	....
2005-06	Clarkson Knights	ECACHL	33	9	17	26	60	....	....	....	....	....
2006-07	Clarkson Knights	ECACHL	36	8	23	31	30	....	....	....	....	....

ECACHL All-Rookie Team (2006)

GWIDT, Brent (GWIGHT, BREHNT)

Center. Shoots left. 6'2", 198 lbs. Born, Minocqua, WI, February 20, 1988.
(Washington's 9th choice, 157th overall, in 2006 Entry Draft).

			Regular Season					Playoffs				
Season	Club	League	GP	G	A	Pts	PIM	GP	G	A	Pts	PIM
2004-05	Lakeland Union	High-WI	15	25	10	35	10	....	....	....	....	....
2005-06	Lakeland Union	High-WI	21	41	23	64	43	....	....	....	....	....
2006-07	Indiana Ice	USHL	55	8	5	13	26	7	0	2	2	4

HAGELIN, Carl (HAG-eh-lihn, KARL) NYR

Left wing. Shoots left. 5'11", 176 lbs. Born, Sodertalje, Sweden, August 23, 1988.
(NY Rangers' 4th choice, 168th overall, in 2007 Entry Draft).

			Regular Season					Playoffs				
Season	Club	League	GP	G	A	Pts	PIM	GP	G	A	Pts	PIM
2004-05	Sodertalje SK U18	Swe-U18	14	10	7	17	16	2	0	2	2	0
2005-06	Sodertalje SK U18	Swe-U18	7	4	8	12	2	....	....	....	....	....
	Sodertalje SK Jr.	Swe-Jr.	41	20	20	40	42	4	1	2	3	22
2006-07	Sodertalje SK Jr.	Swe-Jr.	40	24	31	55	42	3	1	5	6	20

HAGOS, Yared (HA-gohs, YAIR-ehd)

Center. Shoots left. 6'1", 202 lbs. Born, Stockholm, Sweden, March 27, 1983.
(Dallas' 2nd choice, 70th overall, in 2001 Entry Draft).

			Regular Season					Playoffs				
Season	Club	League	GP	G	A	Pts	PIM	GP	G	A	Pts	PIM
1998-99	AIK Solna Jr.	Swe-Jr.	32	8	12	20	22	....	....	....	....	....
99-2000	AIK Solna U18	Swe-U18	13	4	6	10	6	....	....	....	....	....
	AIK Solna Jr.	Swe-Jr.	17	6	4	10	10	....	....	....	....	....
2000-01	AIK Solna Jr.	Swe-Jr.	24	8	13	21	46	2	2	1	3	2
	AIK Solna	Sweden	....	....	....	....	....	5	0	0	0	0
2001-02	AIK Solna Jr.	Swe-Jr.	1	0	3	3	2	1	0	2	2	0
	AIK Solna	Sweden	45	4	6	10	36	....	....	....	....	....
	AIK Solna	Sweden-Q	9	0	0	0	12	....	....	....	....	....
2002-03	AIK Solna	Sweden-2	49	10	22	32	67	4	0	1	1	2
	AIK Solna Jr.	Swe-Jr.	1	0	1	1	0	....	....	....	....	....
2003-04	Timra IK	Sweden	48	9	11	20	75	10	3	1	4	6
2004-05	Timra IK	Sweden	49	6	15	21	38	7	1	0	1	2
2005-06	Iowa Stars	AHL	57	7	15	22	40	....	....	....	....	....
2006-07	Iowa Stars	AHL	75	8	14	22	48	12	1	1	2	16

HALISCHUK, Matt (huh-LIHS-chuhk, MAT) N.J.

Right wing. Shoots right. 5'11", 175 lbs. Born, Toronto, Ont., June 1, 1988.
(New Jersey's 4th choice, 117th overall, in 2007 Entry Draft).

			Regular Season					Playoffs				
Season	Club	League	GP	G	A	Pts	PIM	GP	G	A	Pts	PIM
2003-04	Tor. Jr. Canadiens	GTHL	53	37	48	85	27	....	....	....	....	....
2004-05	St. Michael's	OHL	30	3	3	6	4	....	....	....	....	....
2005-06	St. Michael's	OHL	61	13	18	31	16	4	1	1	2	0
2006-07	Kitchener Rangers	OHL	67	33	33	66	20	9	4	1	5	10

HAMILL, Zach (HA-mihl, ZAK) BOS.

Center. Shoots right. 6', 175 lbs. Born, Vancouver, B.C., September 23, 1988.
(Boston's 1st choice, 8th overall, in 2007 Entry Draft).

			Regular Season					Playoffs				
Season	Club	League	GP	G	A	Pts	PIM	GP	G	A	Pts	PIM
2003-04	Port Coquitlam	PIJHL	39	30	31	51	50	....	....	....	....	....
	Everett Silvertips	WHL	4	0	2	2	0	20	3	2	5	2
2004-05	Everett Silvertips	WHL	57	8	25	33	29	11	2	3	5	8
2005-06	Everett Silvertips	WHL	53	21	38	59	28	15	3	11	14	4
2006-07	Everett Silvertips	WHL	69	32	*61	*93	90	12	2	8	10	16

WHL West First All-Star Team (2007)

HAMILTON, Mike (HAM-ihl-tuhn, MIGHK) ATL.

Left wing. Shoots left. 6'1", 190 lbs. Born, Vancouver, B.C., May 2, 1983.
(Atlanta's 6th choice, 175th overall, in 2003 Entry Draft).

			Regular Season					Playoffs				
Season	Club	League	GP	G	A	Pts	PIM	GP	G	A	Pts	PIM
99-2000	Peninsula Panthers	VIJHL	44	33	42	75	94	....	....	....	....	....
2000-01	Peninsula Panthers	VIJHL	19	15	20	35	106	....	....	....	....	....
	Victoria Salsa	BCHL	31	2	5	7	18	....	....	....	....	....
2001-02	Victoria Salsa	BCHL	13	5	2	7	14	....	....	....	....	....
	Merritt	BCHL	45	23	36	59	64	....	....	....	....	....
2002-03	Merritt	BCHL	56	42	51	95	133	....	....	....	....	....
2003-04	U. of Maine	H-East	29	7	6	13	40	....	....	....	....	....
2004-05	U. of Maine	H-East	38	3	15	18	49	....	....	....	....	....
2005-06	U. of Maine	H-East	30	1	10	11	56	....	....	....	....	....
2006-07	U. of Maine	H-East	40	9	13	22	63	....	....	....	....	....

HAMILTON, Ryan (HAM-ihl-tuhn, RIGH-uhn) MIN.

Left wing. Shoots left. 6'2", 217 lbs. Born, Oshawa, Ont., April 15, 1985.

			Regular Season					Playoffs				
Season	Club	League	GP	G	A	Pts	PIM	GP	G	A	Pts	PIM
2002-03	Couchiching	OPJHL	11	5	8	13	2	....	....	....	....	....
	Peterborough Bees	OPJHL	27	3	10	13	43	....	....	....	....	....
	Trenton Sting	OPJHL	17	3	8	11	24	....	....	....	....	....
	Barrie Colts	OHL	24	3	2	5	10	6	1	0	1	0
2003-04	Kingston	OPJHL	14	1	5	6	23	....	....	....	....	....
	Barrie Colts	OHL	46	17	10	27	21	7	0	1	1	8
2004-05	Barrie Colts	OHL	37	13	11	24	6	6	2	0	2	2
2005-06	Barrie Colts	OHL	63	46	26	72	58	14	8	9	17	11
	Houston Aeros	AHL	....	....	....	....	....	1	0	0	0	0
2006-07	Houston Aeros	AHL	62	7	9	16	36	....	....	....	....	....

Signed as a free agent by **Minnesota**, July 5, 2006.

HANSEN, Jake (HAHN-suhn, JAYK) CBJ

Wing. Shoots right. 6'1", 170 lbs. Born, St.Paul, MN, August 21, 1989.
(Columbus' 4th choice, 68th overall, in 2007 Entry Draft).

			Regular Season					Playoffs				
Season	Club	League	GP	G	A	Pts	PIM	GP	G	A	Pts	PIM
2005-06	White Bear Lake	High-MN	STATISTICS NOT AVAILABLE									
2006-07	White Bear Lake	High-MN	25	28	43	71	....	....	....	....	....	....
	Sioux Falls	USHL	15	4	4	8	14	7	0	2	2	6

• Signed Letter of Intent to attend **University of Minnesota** (WCHA) in fall of 2008.

HANZAL, Martin (HAHN-zuhl, MAHR-tihn) **PHX.**

Center. Shoots left. 6'5", 208 lbs. Born, Pisek, Czech., February 20, 1987.
(Phoenix's 1st choice, 17th overall, in 2005 Entry Draft).

			Regular Season					Playoffs				
Season	**Club**	**League**	**GP**	**G**	**A**	**Pts**	**PIM**	**GP**	**G**	**A**	**Pts**	**PIM**
2002-03	C. Budejovice U17	CzR-U17	47	24	30	54	28	7	1	3	4	25
2003-04	C. Budejovice U17	CzR-U17	2	0	2	2	2	2	1	0	1	4
	C. Budejovice Jr.	CzRep-Jr.	53	15	7	22	32	....	....	....	....	....
2004-05	C. Budejovice Jr.	CzRep-Jr.	37	22	22	44	80	2	1	2	3	2
	C. Budejovice	CzRep-2	15	1	2	3	2	6	0	0	0	6
2005-06	C. Budejovice Jr.	CzRep-Jr.	7	3	5	8	20	....	....	....	....	....
	C. Budejovice	CzRep	19	0	1	1	10	....	....	....	....	....
	BK Mlada Boleslav	CzRep-2	5	2	0	2	0	....	....	....	....	....
	Omaha Lancers	USHL	19	4	15	19	30	5	1	0	1	4
2006-07	Red Deer Rebels	WHL	60	26	59	85	94	6	2	7	9	19

WHL East Second All-Star Team (2007)

HARANT, Tomas (HAH-rant, TAW-mahsh)

Defense. Shoots left. 6'3", 200 lbs. Born, Zilina, Czech., April 28, 1980.
(Nashville's 8th choice, 173rd overall, in 2000 Entry Draft).

			Regular Season					Playoffs				
Season	**Club**	**League**	**GP**	**G**	**A**	**Pts**	**PIM**	**GP**	**G**	**A**	**Pts**	**PIM**
1995-96	HKP Zilina Jr.	Slovak-Jr.	46	3	9	12	142	....	....	....	....	....
1996-97	HKP Zilina Jr.	Slovak-Jr.	44	1	4	5	18	....	....	....	....	....
1997-98	HK SKP Zilina Jr.	Slovak-Jr.	41	5	7	12	72	....	....	....	....	....
	HK SKP Zilina	Slovak-2	5	0	0	0	0	....	....	....	....	....
1998-99	HK SKP Zilina Jr.	Slovak-Jr.	33	1	6	7	108	....	....	....	....	....
99-2000	HK SKP PChZ Zilina	Slovak-2	26	0	3	3	34	....	....	....	....	....
2000-01	HC Trinec Jr.	CzRep-Jr.	5	1	2	3	8	1	0	0	0	4
	HC Ocelari Trinec	CzRep	15	1	2	3	14	....	....	....	....	....
2001-02	MsHK SKP Zilina	Slovakia	51	2	3	5	46	4	0	0	0	4
2002-03	MsHK SKP Zilina	Slovakia	28	2	3	5	86	4	1	0	1	24
	HC Havirov	CzRep	19	0	1	1	40	....	....	....	....	....
2003-04	Dynamo Moscow	Russia	31	1	0	1	18	3	0	0	0	0
2004-05	Dynamo Moscow	Russia	1	0	0	0	2	....	....	....	....	....
	Karlovy Vary	CzRep	37	1	5	6	57	....	....	....	....	....
2005-06	C. Budejovice	CzRep	45	2	7	9	90	10	4	2	6	40
2006-07	Lowell Devils	AHL	54	1	23	24	36	....	....	....	....	....

Signed as a free agent by **New Jersey**, July 24, 2006. Signed as a free agent by **Mora** (Sweden), July 9, 2007.

HARJU, Johan (HAHR-yoo, YOH-hahn) **T.B.**

Left wing. Shoots left. 6'3", 205 lbs. Born, Overtornea, Sweden, May 15, 1986.
(Tampa Bay's 6th choice, 167th overall, in 2007 Entry Draft).

			Regular Season					Playoffs				
Season	**Club**	**League**	**GP**	**G**	**A**	**Pts**	**PIM**	**GP**	**G**	**A**	**Pts**	**PIM**
2002-03	Lulea HF U18	Swe-U18	11	7	2	9	14	....	....	....	....	....
	Lulea HF Jr.	Swe-Jr.	7	2	0	2	0	....	....	....	....	....
2003-04	Lulea HF U18	Swe-U18	3	1	3	4	0	7	4	3	7	8
	Lulea HF Jr.	Swe-Jr.	35	14	12	26	8	....	....	....	....	....
2004-05	Lulea HF Jr.	Swe-Jr.	33	18	13	31	14	7	2	2	4	2
	Pitea HC	Sweden-2	1	0	0	0	0	....	....	....	....	....
	Lulea HF	Sweden	4	0	0	0	0	....	....	....	....	....
2005-06	Lulea HF Jr.	Swe-Jr.	17	14	9	23	4	4	3	1	4	8
	Lulea HF	Sweden	39	3	1	4	8	4	0	0	0	20
2006-07	Lulea HF	Sweden	55	12	10	22	30	4	2	0	2	4

HARRINGTON, Chris (HAYR-ihng-tuhn, KRIHS) **TOR.**

Defense. Shoots right. 6', 202 lbs. Born, St. Cloud, MN, May 7, 1982.

			Regular Season					Playoffs				
Season	**Club**	**League**	**GP**	**G**	**A**	**Pts**	**PIM**	**GP**	**G**	**A**	**Pts**	**PIM**
2000-01	Omaha Lancers	USHL	50	7	11	18	66	10	2	6	8	12
2001-02	Omaha Lancers	USHL	57	9	33	42	68	13	3	3	6	32
2002-03	U. of Minnesota	WCHA	45	4	14	18	60	....	....	....	....	....
2003-04	U. of Minnesota	WCHA	41	5	24	29	42	....	....	....	....	....
2004-05	U. of Minnesota	WCHA	43	2	24	26	98	....	....	....	....	....
2005-06	U. of Minnesota	WCHA	40	3	33	36	64	....	....	....	....	....
2006-07	Toronto Marlies	AHL	68	10	18	28	58	....	....	....	....	....

WCHA All-Rookie Team (2003)

Signed as a free agent by **Toronto**. April 19, 2006.

HEDLUND, Andy (HEHD-luhnd, AN-dee)

Defense. Shoots left. 6'3", 215 lbs. Born, Osseo, MN, May 16, 1978.

			Regular Season					Playoffs				
Season	**Club**	**League**	**GP**	**G**	**A**	**Pts**	**PIM**	**GP**	**G**	**A**	**Pts**	**PIM**
1997-98	Fargo-Moorhead	USHL	56	4	12	16	135	4	0	4	4	0
1998-99	Minnesota State	WCHA	34	1	2	3	34	....	....	....	....	....
99-2000	Minnesota State	WCHA	36	4	2	6	58	....	....	....	....	....
2000-01	Minnesota State	WCHA	38	6	6	12	64	....	....	....	....	....
2001-02	Minnesota State	WCHA	37	5	10	15	48	....	....	....	....	....
	Trenton Titans	ECHL	2	0	0	0	0	6	0	0	0	6
2002-03	Trenton Titans	ECHL	13	1	2	3	14	....	....	....	....	....
	Binghamton	AHL	59	1	7	8	48	10	0	0	0	0
2003-04	Binghamton	AHL	80	4	19	23	108	2	0	0	0	2
2004-05	Binghamton	AHL	75	2	13	15	103	6	0	2	2	25
2005-06	Krefeld Pinguine	Germany	52	12	22	34	100	5	0	2	2	6
2006-07	Binghamton	AHL	56	6	21	27	84	....	....	....	....	....
	Hershey Bears	AHL	21	0	8	8	30	19	0	3	3	28

Signed as a free agent by **Trenton** (ECHL), March 28, 2002. Signed as a free agent by **Binghamton** (AHL), November 3, 2002. Signed as a free agent by **Ottawa**, December 18, 2003. Traded to **Washington** by **Ottawa** with Ottawa's 6th round choice (Justin Taylor) in 2007 Entry Draft for Lawrence Nycholat, February 26, 2007.

HEDMAN, Anton (HEHD-man, AN-tawn) **BOS.**

Center. Shoots left. 6'2", 207 lbs. Born, Stockholm, Sweden, May 15, 1986.
(Boston's 7th choice, 255th overall, in 2004 Entry Draft).

			Regular Season					Playoffs				
Season	**Club**	**League**	**GP**	**G**	**A**	**Pts**	**PIM**	**GP**	**G**	**A**	**Pts**	**PIM**
2003-04	Stocksund Jr.	Swe-Jr.	14	5	5	10	14	....	....	....	....	....
2004-05	Djurgarden Jr.	Swe-Jr.	32	14	9	23	119	....	....	....	....	....
2005-06	Sudbury Wolves	OHL	60	18	16	34	126	8	1	3	4	19
2006-07	Owen Sound	OHL	39	12	12	24	73	....	....	....	....	....
	Guelph Storm	OHL	28	5	7	12	38	4	0	1	1	8

HEDMAN, Oscar (HEHD-man, AWZ-kuhr) **WSH.**

Defense. Shoots left. 6', 209 lbs. Born, Ornskoldsvik, Sweden, April 21, 1986.
(Washington's 8th choice, 132nd overall, in 2004 Entry Draft).

			Regular Season					Playoffs				
Season	**Club**	**League**	**GP**	**G**	**A**	**Pts**	**PIM**	**GP**	**G**	**A**	**Pts**	**PIM**
2002-03	MODO U18	Swe-U18	14	4	5	9	8	6	2	1	3	32
	Malmo Jr.	Swe-Jr.	5	0	1	1	2	....	....	....	....	....
2003-04	Malmo Jr.	Swe-Jr.	25	7	11	18	28	8	3	3	6	6
	MODO U18	Swe-U18	3	3	1	4	2	2	0	3	3	0
	MODO	Sweden	24	1	2	3	6	6	0	0	0	0
2004-05	MODO Jr.	Swe-Jr.	7	2	2	4	12	5	0	1	1	4
	MODO	Sweden	43	1	3	4	18	4	0	0	0	0
2005-06	MODO Jr.	Swe-Jr.	7	3	2	5	10	....	....	....	....	....
	MODO	Sweden	44	3	2	5	30	5	0	1	1	0
2006-07	MODO	Sweden	55	2	7	9	42	20	1	4	5	14

HELLGREN, Jens (HEHL-grehn, YEHNZ) **COL.**

Defense. Shoots left. 6'3", 192 lbs. Born, Bjorbo, Sweden, March 6, 1989.
(Colorado's 8th choice, 155th overall, in 2007 Entry Draft).

			Regular Season					Playoffs				
Season	**Club**	**League**	**GP**	**G**	**A**	**Pts**	**PIM**	**GP**	**G**	**A**	**Pts**	**PIM**
2004-05	Leksands IF U18	Swe-U18	STATISTICS NOT AVAILABLE									
2005-06	Frolunda U18	Swe-U18	12	1	0	1	2	2	0	0	0	2
	Frolunda Jr.	Swe-Jr.	22	0	0	0	4	6	0	0	0	0
2006-07	Frolunda U18	Swe-U18	3	0	2	2	0	4	2	2	4	6
	Frolunda Jr.	Swe-Jr.	40	4	6	10	26	7	0	0	0	2

HELLSTROM, Alexander (HEHL-struhm, al-EHX-AN-duhr) **ST.L.**

Defense. Shoots left. 6'2", 207 lbs. Born, Falun, Sweden, April 17, 1987.
(St. Louis' 9th choice, 184th overall, in 2006 Entry Draft).

			Regular Season					Playoffs				
Season	**Club**	**League**	**GP**	**G**	**A**	**Pts**	**PIM**	**GP**	**G**	**A**	**Pts**	**PIM**
2003-04	Bjorkloven U18	Swe-U18	7	0	2	2	8	....	....	....	....	....
2004-05	Bjorkloven U18	Swe-U18	STATISTICS NOT AVAILABLE									
	Bjorkloven Jr.	Swe-Jr.	3	0	2	2	2	....	....	....	....	....
	IF Bjorkloven Umea	Sweden-2	15	0	1	1	8	....	....	....	....	....
2005-06	Bjorkloven Jr.	Swe-Jr.	11	1	3	4	20	6	0	3	3	4
	IF Bjorkloven Umea	Sweden-2	31	1	0	1	45	....	....	....	....	....
2006-07	Bjorkloven Jr.	Swe-Jr.	8	2	2	4	26	....	....	....	....	....
	IF Bjorkloven Umea	Sweden-2	55	0	7	7	153	6	0	0	0	6

HELM, Darren (HEHLM, DAIR-ehn) **DET.**

Center/Left wing. Shoots left. 5'11", 172 lbs. Born, Winnipeg, Man., January 21, 1987.
(Detroit's 5th choice, 132nd overall, in 2005 Entry Draft).

			Regular Season					Playoffs				
Season	**Club**	**League**	**GP**	**G**	**A**	**Pts**	**PIM**	**GP**	**G**	**A**	**Pts**	**PIM**
2003-04	Selkirk Fishermen	MJBHL	34	39	32	71	34	....	....	....	....	....
2004-05	Medicine Hat	WHL	72	10	14	24	27	13	2	6	8	10
2005-06	Medicine Hat	WHL	70	41	38	79	37	13	5	4	9	2
2006-07	Medicine Hat	WHL	59	25	39	64	53	23	10	12	22	14

WHL East First All-Star Team (2006) • WHL East Second All-Star Team (2007) • Memorial Cup Tournament All-Star Team (2007)

HELMINEN, Dwight (HEHL-mih-nehn, DWIGHT)

Center. Shoots left. 5'10", 191 lbs. Born, Hancock, MI, June 22, 1983.
(Edmonton's 12th choice, 244th overall, in 2002 Entry Draft).

			Regular Season					Playoffs				
Season	**Club**	**League**	**GP**	**G**	**A**	**Pts**	**PIM**	**GP**	**G**	**A**	**Pts**	**PIM**
1998-99	Det. Compuware	MNHL	32	9	7	16	....	....	....	....	....	....
99-2000	USNTDP	USHL	30	5	7	12	10	....	....	....	....	....
	USNTDP	NAHL	30	7	10	17	8	....	....	....	....	....
2000-01	USNTDP	U-18	42	9	36	45	20	....	....	....	....	....
	USNTDP	USHL	24	12	7	19	8	....	....	....	....	....
	USNTDP	NAHL	1	0	1	1	2	....	....	....	....	....
2001-02	U. of Michigan	CCHA	39	10	8	18	10	....	....	....	....	....
2002-03	U. of Michigan	CCHA	39	17	16	33	34	....	....	....	....	....
2003-04	U. of Michigan	CCHA	41	17	11	28	4	....	....	....	....	....
2004-05	Charlotte	ECHL	28	5	16	21	10	15	7	3	10	2
	Hartford Wolf Pack	AHL	41	2	7	9	10	....	....	....	....	....
2005-06	Hartford Wolf Pack	AHL	77	32	24	56	40	13	3	5	8	10
2006-07	Hartford Wolf Pack	AHL	80	15	24	39	32	7	1	1	2	2

Traded to **NY Rangers** by **Edmonton** with Stephen Valiquette and Edmonton's 2nd round compensatory choice (Dane Byers) in 2004 Entry Draft for Petr Nedved and Jussi Markkanen, March 3, 2004. Signed as a free agent by **Jyvaskyla** (Finland), July 7, 2007.

HEMINGWAY, Brett (HEH-mihng-way, BREHT) **COL.**

Right wing. Shoots right. 6'1", 185 lbs. Born, Yorkton, Sask., September 28, 1983.
(Colorado's 6th choice, 225th overall, in 2003 Entry Draft).

			Regular Season					Playoffs				
Season	**Club**	**League**	**GP**	**G**	**A**	**Pts**	**PIM**	**GP**	**G**	**A**	**Pts**	**PIM**
2000-01	Port Coquitlam	PIJHL	36	22	19	41	24	....	....	....	....	....
2001-02	Coquitlam Express	BCHL	60	45	39	84	31	....	....	....	....	....
2002-03	Coquitlam Express	BCHL	60	42	50	92	50	7	7	5	12	4
2003-04	New Hampshire	H-East	34	7	12	19	8	....	....	....	....	....
2004-05	New Hampshire	H-East	42	22	21	43	14	....	....	....	....	....
2005-06	New Hampshire	H-East	38	19	22	41	22	....	....	....	....	....
2006-07	New Hampshire	H-East	36	13	19	32	45	....	....	....	....	....
	Albany River Rats	AHL	2	1	0	1	2	....	....	....	....	....

Hockey East All-Rookie Team (2004)

HENDRICKS, Matt (HEHN-drihks, MAT) **BOS.**

Center. Shoots left. 6', 215 lbs. Born, Blaine, MN, June 17, 1981.
(Nashville's 5th choice, 131st overall, in 2000 Entry Draft).

			Regular Season					Playoffs				
Season	**Club**	**League**	**GP**	**G**	**A**	**Pts**	**PIM**	**GP**	**G**	**A**	**Pts**	**PIM**
1998-99	Blaine Bengals	High-MN	22	23	34	57	42	....	....	....	....	....
99-2000	Blaine Bengals	High-MN	21	23	30	53	28	....	....	....	....	....
2000-01	St. Cloud State	WCHA	37	3	9	12	23	....	....	....	....	....
2001-02	St. Cloud State	WCHA	42	19	20	39	74	....	....	....	....	....
2002-03	St. Cloud State	WCHA	37	18	18	36	64	....	....	....	....	....
2003-04	St. Cloud State	WCHA	36	13	11	24	32	....	....	....	....	....
	Milwaukee	AHL	1	0	0	0	2	....	....	....	....	....
2004-05	Lowell	AHL	15	1	2	3	10	....	....	....	....	....
	Florida Everblades	ECHL	54	24	26	50	94	4	0	0	0	4
2005-06	Rochester	AHL	56	13	14	27	84	....	....	....	....	....
2006-07	Hershey Bears	AHL	65	18	26	44	105	19	8	4	12	18

Signed as a free agent by **Boston**, July 9, 2007.

HENDRIKX, Trevor (HEHN-drihx, TREH-vuhr) **CBJ**

Defense. Shoots right. 6'2", 205 lbs. Born, Russell, Ont., March 29, 1985.
(Columbus' 8th choice, 201st overall, in 2005 Entry Draft).

			Regular Season					Playoffs				
Season	Club	League	GP	G	A	Pts	PIM	GP	G	A	Pts	PIM
2000-01	Gloucester	OPJHL	26	2	3	5	25	....	....	....	....	....
2001-02	Peterborough	OHL	46	1	3	4	37	5	0	0	0	4
2002-03	Peterborough	OHL	56	1	8	9	128	7	0	0	0	4
2003-04	Peterborough	OHL	63	8	24	32	208	....	....	....	....	....
2004-05	Peterborough	OHL	68	15	33	48	100	14	5	7	12	14
2005-06	Peterborough	OHL	60	9	47	56	123	19	5	10	15	40
2006-07	Dayton Bombers	ECHL	41	5	6	11	88	15	2	2	4	6

• Re-entered NHL Entry Draft. Originally Columbus' 10th choice, 283rd overall, in 2003 Entry Draft.

HENDRY, Jordan (HEHN-dree, JOHR-dahn) **CHI.**

Defense. Shoots left. 6', 196 lbs. Born, Nokomis, Sask., February 23, 1984.

			Regular Season					Playoffs				
Season	Club	League	GP	G	A	Pts	PIM	GP	G	A	Pts	PIM
2002-03	Alaska	CCHA	35	3	5	8	10	....	....	....	....	....
2003-04	Alaska	CCHA	36	4	9	13	38	....	....	....	....	....
2004-05	Alaska	CCHA	3	0	1	1	21	....	....	....	....	....
2005-06	Alaska	CCHA	38	4	10	14	74	....	....	....	....	....
	Norfolk Admirals	AHL	13	1	4	5	13	3	0	0	0	2
2006-07	Norfolk Admirals	AHL	80	4	12	16	84	6	0	2	2	6

Signed as a free agent by **Chicago**, March 18, 2006.

HENRICH, Adam (HEHN-rihch, A-duhm)

Left wing. Shoots left. 6'4", 231 lbs. Born, Thornhill, Ont., January 19, 1984.
(Tampa Bay's 1st choice, 60th overall, in 2002 Entry Draft).

			Regular Season					Playoffs				
Season	Club	League	GP	G	A	Pts	PIM	GP	G	A	Pts	PIM
99-2000	Don Mills Flyers	GTHL	54	30	52	82	86	....	....	....	....	....
2000-01	Brampton	OHL	48	5	4	9	27	9	0	0	0	6
2001-02	Brampton	OHL	66	33	30	63	92	....	....	....	....	....
2002-03	Brampton	OHL	63	31	33	64	84	11	4	1	5	25
2003-04	Brampton	OHL	65	29	29	58	146	12	5	1	6	24
2004-05	Springfield Falcons	AHL	63	10	16	26	97	....	....	....	....	....
	Johnstown Chiefs	ECHL	6	2	1	3	15	....	....	....	....	....
2005-06	Springfield Falcons	AHL	12	0	3	3	14	....	....	....	....	....
	Johnstown Chiefs	ECHL	51	18	23	41	78	5	2	4	6	8
2006-07	Springfield Falcons	AHL	27	3	6	9	31	....	....	....	....	....
	Johnstown Chiefs	ECHL	32	15	19	34	119	2	0	0	0	2

HENSICK, T.J. (HEHN-sihk, TEE-JAY) **COL.**

Center. Shoots right. 5'10", 185 lbs. Born, Lansing, MI, December 10, 1985.
(Colorado's 5th choice, 88th overall, in 2005 Entry Draft).

			Regular Season					Playoffs				
Season	Club	League	GP	G	A	Pts	PIM	GP	G	A	Pts	PIM
2001-02	USNTDP	U-17	17	10	5	15	....	....	....	....	....	....
	USNTDP	NAHL	46	15	25	40	10	....	....	....	....	....
2002-03	USNTDP	U-18	48	24	24	48	11	....	....	....	....	....
	USNTDP	NAHL	10	6	7	13	0	....	....	....	....	....
2003-04	U. of Michigan	CCHA	43	12	*34	46	38	....	....	....	....	....
2004-05	U. of Michigan	CCHA	39	23	32	55	24	....	....	....	....	....
2005-06	U. of Michigan	CCHA	41	17	35	52	44	....	....	....	....	....
2006-07	U. of Michigan	CCHA	41	23	*46	*69	38	....	....	....	....	....

CCHA All-Rookie Team (2004) • CCHA First All-Star Team (2004, 2005, 2007) • CCHA Rookie of the Year (2004) • NCAA West First All-American Team (2005, 2007) • CCHA Second All-Star Team (2006)

HERSLEY, Patrik (HUHRS-lee, PAT-rihk) **L.A.**

Defense. Shoots right. 6'3", 205 lbs. Born, Malmo, Sweden, June 23, 1986.
(Los Angeles' 5th choice, 139th overall, in 2005 Entry Draft).

			Regular Season					Playoffs				
Season	Club	League	GP	G	A	Pts	PIM	GP	G	A	Pts	PIM
2002-03	Malmo U18	Swe-U18	9	3	4	7	53	4	1	2	3	4
	Malmo Jr.	Swe-Jr.	16	0	2	2	4	1	0	0	0	0
2003-04	Malmo U18	Swe-U18	2	2	0	2	4	....	....	....	....	....
	Malmo Jr.	Swe-Jr.	17	1	4	5	16	8	0	2	2	2
2004-05	Malmo Jr.	Swe-Jr.	31	8	14	22	104	3	2	1	3	6
	Malmo	Sweden	8	0	1	1	0	....	....	....	....	....
	Malmo	Sweden-Q	6	0	0	0	2	....	....	....	....	....
2005-06	Malmo Jr.	Swe-Jr.	13	10	9	19	38	....	....	....	....	....
	Malmo	Sweden-2	41	6	8	14	38	....	....	....	....	....
2006-07	Malmo Jr.	Swe-Jr.	2	1	3	4	14	....	....	....	....	....
	Malmo	Sweden	28	1	1	2	10	....	....	....	....	....
	IK Pantern Malmo	Sweden-3	2	1	1	2	8	....	....	....	....	....

HESHKA, Shaun (HEHSH-kah, SHAWN) **VAN.**

Defense. Shoots right. 6'1", 209 lbs. Born, Melville, Sask., July 30, 1985.

			Regular Season					Playoffs				
Season	Club	League	GP	G	A	Pts	PIM	GP	G	A	Pts	PIM
2002-03	Melville	SJHL	53	6	14	20	53	....	....	....	....	....
2003-04	Everett Silvertips	WHL	66	3	7	10	25	21	0	2	2	8
2004-05	Everett Silvertips	WHL	72	12	26	38	21	11	2	0	2	6
2005-06	Everett Silvertips	WHL	66	10	49	59	91	14	3	10	13	10
2006-07	Manitoba Moose	AHL	57	2	4	6	14	7	0	0	0	8
	Victoria	ECHL	3	0	1	1	4	....	....	....	....	....

WHL West First All-Star Team (2006)

Signed as a free agent by **Vancouver**, July 24, 2006.

HICKEY, Chris (HIH-kee, KRIHS) **MIN.**

Center. Shoots right. 6'1", 196 lbs. Born, St. Paul, MN, September 2, 1988.
(Minnesota's 7th choice, 192nd overall, in 2006 Entry Draft).

			Regular Season					Playoffs				
Season	Club	League	GP	G	A	Pts	PIM	GP	G	A	Pts	PIM
2003-04	Cretin-Derham	High-MN	27	19	13	32	32	....	....	....	....	....
2004-05	Cretin-Derham	High-MN	28	25	21	46	48	....	....	....	....	....
2005-06	Cretin-Derham	High-MN	31	37	28	65	36	....	....	....	....	....
2006-07	Cretin-Derham	High-MN	17	21	15	36	....	....	....	....	....	....
	Tri-City Storm	USHL	1	0	0	0	0	....	....	....	....	....

HICKEY, Thomas (HIH-kee, TAW-muhs) **L.A.**

Defense. Shoots left. 5'11", 182 lbs. Born, Calgary, Alta., February 8, 1989.
(Los Angeles' 1st choice, 4th overall, in 2007 Entry Draft).

			Regular Season					Playoffs				
Season	Club	League	GP	G	A	Pts	PIM	GP	G	A	Pts	PIM
2004-05	Calgary Royals	AJHL	33	9	13	22	36	....	....	....	....	....
	Seattle	WHL	5	2	1	3	6	....	....	....	....	....
2005-06	Seattle	WHL	69	1	27	28	53	7	1	3	4	10
2006-07	Seattle	WHL	68	9	41	50	70	11	3	4	7	4

WHL West Second All-Star Team (2007)

HILLIER, Ryan (HIHL-lee-uhr, RIGH-uhn) **NYR**

Left wing. Shoots left. 6'1", 190 lbs. Born, Halifax, N.S., January 25, 1988.
(NY Rangers' 3rd choice, 84th overall, in 2006 Entry Draft).

			Regular Season					Playoffs				
Season	Club	League	GP	G	A	Pts	PIM	GP	G	A	Pts	PIM
2003-04	Dartmouth	NSMHL	55	31	36	67	97	....	....	....	....	....
2004-05	Halifax	QMJHL	21	1	1	2	13	7	0	2	2	2
2005-06	Halifax	QMJHL	68	19	38	57	76	11	2	2	4	12
2006-07	Halifax	QMJHL	70	32	27	59	79	12	3	6	9	20

HIMELFARB, Eric (HIH-muhl-FAHRB, AIR-ihk)

Center. Shoots right. 5'9", 161 lbs. Born, Thornhill, Ont., January 1, 1983.
(Montreal's 6th choice, 171st overall, in 2001 Entry Draft).

			Regular Season					Playoffs				
Season	Club	League	GP	G	A	Pts	PIM	GP	G	A	Pts	PIM
1998-99	Don Mills Flyers	GTHL	40	40	31	71	42	....	....	....	....	....
99-2000	Sarnia Sting	OHL	62	14	33	47	26	7	1	4	5	4
2000-01	Sarnia Sting	OHL	49	31	44	75	48	4	1	7	8	4
2001-02	Sarnia Sting	OHL	67	35	48	83	67	5	1	4	5	11
2002-03	Barrie Colts	OHL	67	31	44	75	81	6	1	0	1	6
2003-04	Grand Rapids	AHL	7	2	3	5	2	4	0	3	3	0
	Kingston	OHL	67	37	70	107	80	5	4	4	8	8
2004-05	Grand Rapids	AHL	76	19	24	43	59	....	....	....	....	....
2005-06	Grand Rapids	AHL	62	10	18	28	60	16	0	0	0	12
2006-07	Grand Rapids	AHL	69	15	15	30	60	7	1	0	1	12

Signed as a free agent by **Detroit**, July 21, 2004. Signed as a free agent by **Lausanne** (Swiss), May 30, 2007.

HJALMARSSON, Niklas (H'YAHL-muhr-suhn, NIHK-luhs) **CHI.**

Defense. Shoots left. 6'3", 196 lbs. Born, Eksjo, Sweden , June 6, 1987.
(Chicago's 5th choice, 108th overall, in 2005 Entry Draft).

			Regular Season					Playoffs				
Season	Club	League	GP	G	A	Pts	PIM	GP	G	A	Pts	PIM
2003-04	HV 71 Jr.	Swe-Jr.	15	1	3	4	14	2	0	0	0	8
2004-05	HV 71 U18	Swe-U18	3	0	2	2	4	....	....	....	....	....
	HV 71 Jr.	Swe-Jr.	31	4	11	15	87	....	....	....	....	....
	HV 71 Jonkoping	Sweden	14	0	0	0	0	....	....	....	....	....
2005-06	HV 71 Jr.	Swe-Jr.	7	3	2	5	12	....	....	....	....	....
	HV 71 Jonkoping	Sweden	4	1	2	3	0	12	0	1	1	4
2006-07	HV 71 Jonkoping	Sweden	37	2	0	2	24	14	1	1	2	0
	IK Oskarshamn	Sweden-2	8	1	2	3	6	....	....	....	....	....
	HV 71 Jr.	Swe-Jr.	7	0	2	2	14	....	....	....	....	....

HJALMARSSON, Simon (H'YAHL-muhr-suhn, SEE-muhn) **ST.L.**

Right wing. Shoots left. 5'11", 161 lbs. Born, Varnamo, Sweden, February 1, 1989.
(St. Louis' 4th choice, 39th overall, in 2007 Entry Draft).

			Regular Season					Playoffs				
Season	Club	League	GP	G	A	Pts	PIM	GP	G	A	Pts	PIM
2004-05	Gislaveds SK Jr.	Swe-Jr.		STATISTICS NOT AVAILABLE								
2005-06	Frolunda U18	Swe-U18	6	2	3	5	4	2	0	0	0	2
	Frolunda Jr.	Swe-Jr.	31	8	10	18	8	7	2	3	5	2
2006-07	Frolunda U18	Swe-U18	3	4	3	7	33	6	3	8	11	2
	Gislaveds SK	Sweden-3	2	0	1	1	0	....	....	....	....	....
	Frolunda Jr.	Swe-Jr.	41	31	23	54	91	8	1	1	2	6

HLINKA, Jaroslav (huh-LIHN-kuh, YAHR-oh-slav) **COL.**

Center. Shoots left. 5'10", 185 lbs. Born, Prague, Czech., November 10, 1976.

			Regular Season					Playoffs				
Season	Club	League	GP	G	A	Pts	PIM	GP	G	A	Pts	PIM
1994-95	HC Sparta Praha	CzRep	4	0	2	2	0	5	1	1	2	0
1995-96	Usti n. L.	CzRep-2	3	1	1	2	2	....	....	....	....	....
	H+S Beroun	CzRep-2	6	2	1	3	0	....	....	....	....	....
	HC Sparta Praha	CzRep	18	3	1	4	6	12	1	4	5	0
1996-97	HC Sparta Praha	CzRep	48	8	18	26	12	6	0	0	0	0
	Karlovy Vary	CzRep-2	3	1	0	1	0	....	....	....	....	....
1997-98	HC Sparta Praha	CzRep	51	18	19	37	24	11	2	6	8	8
1998-99	HC Sparta Praha	CzRep	41	9	24	33	22	6	1	2	3	0
99-2000	HC Sparta Praha	CzRep	49	20	37	57	51	8	2	3	5	10
2000-01	HC Sparta Praha	CzRep	45	12	17	29	28	13	2	9	11	12
2001-02	HC Sparta Praha	CzRep	52	16	45	61	54	13	9	6	15	4
2002-03	Kloten Flyers	Swiss	41	18	30	48	16	....	....	....	....	....
2003-04	Kloten Flyers	Swiss	43	18	23	41	33	8	3	8	11	6
2004-05	Ak Bars Kazan	Russia	36	4	16	20	10	1	0	0	0	0
2005-06	Kloten Flyers	Swiss	37	12	23	35	18	....	....	....	....	....
	HC Sparta Praha	CzRep	9	3	8	11	14	17	10	6	16	10
2006-07	HC Sparta Praha	CzRep	46	19	38	57	46	16	4	12	16	38

Signed as a free agent by **Colorado**, June 1, 2007.

HOBBS, Danny (HAWBZ, DA-nee) **NYR**

Center/Right wing. Shoots left. 5'11", 178 lbs. Born, Shawville, Que., June 21, 1989.
(NY Rangers' 6th choice, 198th overall, in 2007 Entry Draft).

			Regular Season					Playoffs				
Season	Club	League	GP	G	A	Pts	PIM	GP	G	A	Pts	PIM
2005-06	Stanstead	QJHL	46	58	32	90	15	....	....	....	....	....
2006-07	Ohio	USHL	60	10	11	21	36	4	0	2	2	2

• Signed Letter of Intent to attend **University of Massachusetts** (Hockey East) in fall of 2008.

HOBSON, Adam (HAWB-sohn, A-duhm) CHI.

Center. Shoots left. 6', 210 lbs. Born, Lund, Sweden, January 9, 1987.
(Chicago's 12th choice, 203rd overall, in 2005 Entry Draft).

			Regular Season					Playoffs				
Season	Club	League	GP	G	A	Pts	PIM	GP	G	A	Pts	PIM
2002-03	Abbotsford Pilots	PIJHL	38	20	28	48	....	....	....	....	....	....
	Spokane Chiefs	WHL	1	0	0	0	2	....	....	....	....	....
2003-04	Spokane Chiefs	WHL	63	4	5	9	35	4	0	0	0	0
2004-05	Spokane Chiefs	WHL	72	10	27	37	47	....	....	....	....	....
2005-06	Spokane Chiefs	WHL	72	23	27	50	124	....	....	....	....	....
2006-07	Spokane Chiefs	WHL	43	14	18	32	59	6	3	0	3	6

HOEFFEL, Mike (HOH-fuhl, MIGHK) N.J.

Left wing. Shoots left. 6'2", 185 lbs. Born, North Oaks, MN, April 9, 1989.
(New Jersey's 1st choice, 57th overall, in 2007 Entry Draft).

			Regular Season					Playoffs				
Season	Club	League	GP	G	A	Pts	PIM	GP	G	A	Pts	PIM
2004-05	Hill-Murray	High-MN	26	24	19	43	10	....	....	....	....	....
2005-06	Hill-Murray	High-MN	30	27	46	73	20	....	....	....	....	....
2006-07	USNTDP	U-18	33	10	2	12	18	....	....	....	....	....
	USNTDP	NAHL	11	6	5	11	10	....	....	....	....	....

HOFFMAN, Mike (HAWF-muhn, MIGHK)

Right wing. Shoots right. 6'5", 248 lbs. Born, Weymouth, MA, September 20, 1980.

			Regular Season					Playoffs				
Season	Club	League	GP	G	A	Pts	PIM	GP	G	A	Pts	PIM
2002-03	Connecticut	MAAC	28	2	8	10	24	....	....	....	....	....
2003-04	Connecticut	MAAC	3	0	0	0	2	....	....	....	....	....
	Worcester IceCats	AHL	15	0	0	0	20	....	....	....	....	....
	Peoria Rivermen	ECHL	25	2	7	9	16	8	0	1	1	6
2004-05	Cleveland Barons	AHL	58	1	7	8	170	....	....	....	....	....
2005-06	Toronto Marlies	AHL	54	2	5	7	103	1	0	0	0	0
2006-07	Manchester	AHL	35	6	7	13	96	....	....	....	....	....
	Portland Pirates	AHL	21	4	5	9	43	....	....	....	....	....

Signed as a free agent by **Cleveland** (AHL), September 22, 2004. Signed as a free agent by **Toronto**, August 12, 2005.

HOGEBOOM, Greg (HOH-guh-BOOM, GREHG)

Right wing. Shoots right. 6', 190 lbs. Born, Toronto, Ont., September 26, 1982.
(Los Angeles' 6th choice, 152nd overall, in 2002 Entry Draft).

			Regular Season					Playoffs				
Season	Club	League	GP	G	A	Pts	PIM	GP	G	A	Pts	PIM
99-2000	Wexford Raiders	OPJHL	48	32	47	79	44	....	....	....	....	....
2000-01	Miami U.	CCHA	38	8	5	13	20	....	....	....	....	....
2001-02	Miami U.	CCHA	36	14	9	23	22	....	....	....	....	....
2002-03	Miami U.	CCHA	41	24	18	42	16	....	....	....	....	....
2003-04	Miami U.	CCHA	41	19	23	42	16	....	....	....	....	....
	Manchester	AHL	3	0	1	1	0	....	....	....	....	....
2004-05	Manchester	AHL	14	1	0	1	10	....	....	....	....	....
2005-06	Manchester	AHL	42	9	10	19	18	1	0	0	0	0
	Reading Royals	ECHL	19	9	18	27	4	....	....	....	....	....
2006-07	Manchester	AHL	15	0	1	1	6	....	....	....	....	....
	Reading Royals	ECHL	54	30	44	74	43	....	....	....	....	....

CCHA Second All-Star Team (2004)

HOLLOWAY, Bud (HAHL-OH-way, BUHD) L.A.

Center. Shoots right. 6', 190 lbs. Born, Wapella, Sask., March 1, 1988.
(Los Angeles' 5th choice, 86th overall, in 2006 Entry Draft).

			Regular Season					Playoffs				
Season	Club	League	GP	G	A	Pts	PIM	GP	G	A	Pts	PIM
2003-04	Yorkton Harvest	SMHL	43	15	21	36	22	....	....	....	....	....
	Seattle	WHL	2	0	0	0	0	....	....	....	....	....
2004-05	Seattle	WHL	67	4	11	15	27	12	0	1	1	0
2005-06	Seattle	WHL	72	21	13	34	18	7	3	2	5	4
2006-07	Seattle	WHL	71	27	38	65	50	11	3	3	6	8

HOLMQVIST, Andreas (HOHLM-kvihst, awn-DRAY-uhs) T.B.

Defense. Shoots right. 6'4", 195 lbs. Born, Stockholm, Sweden, July 23, 1981.
(Tampa Bay's 3rd choice, 61st overall, in 2001 Entry Draft).

			Regular Season					Playoffs				
Season	Club	League	GP	G	A	Pts	PIM	GP	G	A	Pts	PIM
99-2000	Hammarby Jr.	Swe-Jr.	33	8	12	20	16	6	1	2	3	4
2000-01	Hammarby Jr.	Swe-Jr.	47	6	15	21	40	....	....	....	....	....
2001-02	Hammarby	Sweden-2	42	11	13	24	97	....	....	....	....	....
2002-03	Linkopings HC	Sweden	43	4	9	13	28	....	....	....	....	....
	Linkopings HC	Sweden-Q	10	0	0	0	4	....	....	....	....	....
2003-04	Hamilton Bulldogs	AHL	4	0	0	0	0	....	....	....	....	....
	Pensacola	ECHL	63	4	33	37	16	5	0	4	4	0
2004-05	Springfield Falcons	AHL	42	3	9	12	22	....	....	....	....	....
2005-06	Linkopings HC	Sweden	46	6	16	22	64	13	1	3	4	24
2006-07	Linkopings HC	Sweden	49	7	21	28	54	12	4	5	9	35

HOLTET, Marius (HOHL-teht, MAIR-ee-uhs) DAL.

Center. Shoots right. 6'1", 188 lbs. Born, Hamar, Norway, August 31, 1984.
(Dallas' 4th choice, 42nd overall, in 2002 Entry Draft).

			Regular Season					Playoffs				
Season	Club	League	GP	G	A	Pts	PIM	GP	G	A	Pts	PIM
2000-01	Farjestad U18	Swe-U18	5	3	1	4	16	....	....	....	....	....
	Farjestad Jr.	Swe-Jr.	18	2	2	4	18	....	....	....	....	....
2001-02	Farjestad Jr.	Swe-Jr.	37	12	7	19	70	....	....	....	....	....
2002-03	Skare BK Karlstad	Sweden-3	STATISTICS NOT AVAILABLE									
	Bofors	Sweden-2	14	1	1	2	8	2	0	0	0	2
2003-04	Bofors	Sweden-2	43	11	3	14	90	5	2	0	2	4
2004-05	Louisiana	ECHL	4	0	0	0	0	....	....	....	....	....
	Houston Aeros	AHL	54	7	5	12	48	1	0	0	0	0
2005-06	Iowa Stars	AHL	68	9	13	22	61	7	2	0	2	2
2006-07	Iowa Stars	AHL	66	16	15	31	48	11	2	0	2	6

HOLZAPFEL, Riley (HOHL-za-fehl, RIGH-lee) ATL.

Center. Shoots left. 6', 185 lbs. Born, Regina, Sask., August 18, 1988.
(Atlanta's 2nd choice, 43rd overall, in 2006 Entry Draft).

			Regular Season					Playoffs				
Season	Club	League	GP	G	A	Pts	PIM	GP	G	A	Pts	PIM
2004-05	Moose Jaw	WHL	63	15	13	28	32	5	1	2	3	8
2005-06	Moose Jaw	WHL	64	19	38	57	46	22	7	9	16	20
2006-07	Moose Jaw	WHL	72	39	43	82	94	....	....	....	....	....

WHL East First All-Star Team (2007)

HOLZER, Korbinian (HOHL-zuhr, kohr-BEEHN-yuhn) TOR.

Defense. Shoots right. 6'3", 190 lbs. Born, Munich, West Germany, February 16, 1988.
(Toronto's 4th choice, 111th overall, in 2006 Entry Draft).

			Regular Season					Playoffs				
Season	Club	League	GP	G	A	Pts	PIM	GP	G	A	Pts	PIM
2004-05	EC Bad Tolz Jr.	Ger-Jr.	34	7	11	18	66	5	0	2	2	2
2005-06	EC Bad Tolz Jr.	Ger-Jr.	2	1	1	2	6	....	....	....	....	....
	Tolzer Lowen	German-2	46	3	3	6	94	....	....	....	....	....
2006-07	Regensburg	German-2	42	2	6	8	68	4	0	0	0	2

HORNQVIST, Patric (HOHRN-kwihst, PAT-rihk) NSH.

Right wing. Shoots left. 5'11", 194 lbs. Born, Sollentuna, Sweden, January 1, 1987.
(Nashville's 7th choice, 230th overall, in 2005 Entry Draft).

			Regular Season					Playoffs				
Season	Club	League	GP	G	A	Pts	PIM	GP	G	A	Pts	PIM
2003-04	Vasby Jr.	Swe-Jr.	10	7	10	17	30	....	....	....	....	....
	Vasby	Sweden-3	32	8	5	13	26	....	....	....	....	....
2004-05	Vasby	Sweden-3	28	12	12	24	36	....	....	....	....	....
	Djurgarden Jr.	Swe-Jr.	5	3	0	3	2	....	....	....	....	....
2005-06	Djurgarden Jr.	Swe-Jr.	4	2	1	3	2	4	1	2	3	2
	Djurgarden	Sweden	47	5	2	7	36	....	....	....	....	....
2006-07	Djurgarden	Sweden	49	23	11	34	38	....	....	....	....	....
	Djurgarden Jr.	Swe-Jr.	....	....	....	....	....	7	2	5	7	14

HRABAL, Josef (huh-RA-buhl, YOH-sehf) EDM.

Defense. Shoots left. 6'1", 176 lbs. Born, Prerov, Czech., August 17, 1985.
(Edmonton's 11th choice, 248th overall, in 2003 Entry Draft).

			Regular Season					Playoffs				
Season	Club	League	GP	G	A	Pts	PIM	GP	G	A	Pts	PIM
2001-02	HC Vsetin U17	CzR-U17	38	4	2	6	18	....	....	....	....	....
2002-03	HC Vsetin Jr.	CzRep-Jr.	30	6	7	13	12	9	2	4	6	10
	HC Vsetin	CzRep	6	0	0	0	4	....	....	....	....	....
2003-04	HC Vsetin	CzRep	13	0	0	0	2	....	....	....	....	....
	HC Vsetin Jr.	CzRep-Jr.	46	12	8	20	54	7	1	0	1	2
2004-05	HC Vsetin	CzRep	23	0	2	2	8	....	....	....	....	....
	HC Kometa Brno	CzRep-2	1	0	0	0	0	....	....	....	....	....
	HC Olomouc	CzRep-2	7	0	0	0	6	....	....	....	....	....
	HC Vsetin Jr.	CzRep-Jr.	19	6	8	14	42	8	3	4	7	16
2005-06	HC Vsetin	CzRep	34	3	9	12	34	....	....	....	....	....
	HC Vsetin Jr.	CzRep-Jr.	1	1	0	1	2	....	....	....	....	....
	HC Vsetin	CzRep-Q	....	....	....	....	....	6	0	2	2	2
2006-07	Cherepovets	Russia	20	3	4	7	24	5	0	1	1	2
	HC Vsetin	CzRep	21	3	7	10	30	....	....	....	....	....

HRDEL, Zbynek (HUHR-duhl, z'BIGH-nehk) T.B.

Center. Shoots right. 6'2", 194 lbs. Born, Pisek, Czech., August 19, 1985.
(Tampa Bay's 10th choice, 286th overall, in 2003 Entry Draft).

			Regular Season					Playoffs				
Season	Club	League	GP	G	A	Pts	PIM	GP	G	A	Pts	PIM
2000-01	Sparta U17	CzR-U17	46	11	11	22	22	....	....	....	....	....
2001-02	Sparta U17	CzR-U17	31	24	19	43	42	6	4	3	7	2
2002-03	Rimouski Oceanic	QMJHL	65	10	14	24	131	....	....	....	....	....
2003-04	Rimouski Oceanic	QMJHL	54	15	31	46	41	9	4	6	10	4
2004-05	Rimouski Oceanic	QMJHL	56	23	35	58	47	13	8	7	15	10
2005-06	Springfield Falcons	AHL	46	5	10	15	22	....	....	....	....	....
	Johnstown Chiefs	ECHL	15	6	5	11	10	4	1	2	3	8
2006-07	Springfield Falcons	AHL	4	0	0	0	4	....	....	....	....	....
	Johnstown Chiefs	ECHL	65	13	23	36	67	2	2	0	2	0

HROMAS, Karel (huh-ROM-mahs, KAH-rehl) CHI.

Left wing. Shoots left. 6'2", 208 lbs. Born, Beroun, Czech., January 27, 1986.
(Chicago's 8th choice, 123rd overall, in 2004 Entry Draft).

			Regular Season					Playoffs				
Season	Club	League	GP	G	A	Pts	PIM	GP	G	A	Pts	PIM
2000-01	Sparta U17	CzR-U17	34	4	18	22	6	....	....	....	....	....
2001-02	Sparta U17	CzR-U17	39	19	15	34	55	6	3	2	5	6
2002-03	Sparta U17	CzR-U17	1	3	1	4	0	....	....	....	....	....
	Sparta Jr.	CzRep-Jr.	32	6	7	13	14	3	0	1	1	4
2003-04	Sparta Jr.	CzRep-Jr.	21	10	10	20	16	....	....	....	....	....
	HC Sparta Praha	CzRep	13	0	0	0	2	2	0	0	0	0
2004-05	Everett Silvertips	WHL	65	18	11	29	22	11	2	2	4	4
2005-06	Everett Silvertips	WHL	52	11	11	22	14	14	2	0	2	10
2006-07	HC Sparta Praha	CzRep	48	1	0	1	20	11	1	0	1	0

HUGHES, Bobby (HEWZ, BAW-bee) CAR.

Center. Shoots left. 5'10", 180 lbs. Born, Richmond Hill, Ont., November 11, 1987.
(Carolina's 3rd choice, 123rd overall, in 2006 Entry Draft).

			Regular Season					Playoffs				
Season	Club	League	GP	G	A	Pts	PIM	GP	G	A	Pts	PIM
2003-04	Kingston	OHL	62	11	16	27	20	5	0	1	1	2
2004-05	Kingston	OHL	66	17	38	55	36	....	....	....	....	....
2005-06	Kingston	OHL	56	35	40	75	47	6	1	1	2	4
2006-07	Kingston	OHL	59	40	56	96	76	5	0	3	3	0
	Albany River Rats	AHL	....	....	....	....	....	1	0	0	0	0

HUNTER, Dylan (HUHN-tuhr, DIH-luhn) BUF.

Left wing. Shoots left. 5'11", 204 lbs. Born, Quebec City, Que., May 21, 1985.
(Buffalo's 8th choice, 273rd overall, in 2004 Entry Draft).

			Regular Season					Playoffs				
Season	Club	League	GP	G	A	Pts	PIM	GP	G	A	Pts	PIM
2001-02	London Knights	OHL	54	6	21	27	38	6	1	1	2	10
2002-03	London Knights	OHL	68	11	31	42	41	14	3	3	6	8
2003-04	London Knights	OHL	64	26	53	79	47	15	4	10	14	10
2004-05	London Knights	OHL	67	31	73	104	64	18	10	11	21	16
2005-06	London Knights	OHL	62	32	85	117	50	19	13	23	36	16
2006-07	Rochester	AHL	67	8	20	28	42	6	1	2	3	2

OHL First All-Star Team (2005) • OHL Second All-Star Team (2006)

HUNTER, Eric (HUHN-tuhr, AIR-ihk) NYR

Center. Shoots left. 6'2", 195 lbs. Born, Winnipeg, Man., August 11, 1986.
(NY Rangers' 6th choice, 174th overall, in 2006 Entry Draft).

			Regular Season					Playoffs				
Season	Club	League	GP	G	A	Pts	PIM	GP	G	A	Pts	PIM
2002-03	Prince George	WHL	66	16	18	34	70	5	1	0	1	6
2003-04	Prince George	WHL	70	19	23	42	122	....	....	....	....	....
2004-05	Prince George	WHL	47	12	18	30	57	....	....	....	....	....
2005-06	Prince George	WHL	71	40	32	72	125	5	3	1	4	10
2006-07	Prince George	WHL	69	24	31	55	109	6	2	2	4	6

• Re-entered NHL Entry Draft. Originally Chicago's 15th choice, 229th overall, in 2004 Entry Draft.

HUNTER, J.J. (HUHN-tuhr, JAY-JAY)

Right wing. Shoots left. 6'1", 185 lbs. Born, Shaunavon, Sask., July 6, 1980.

			Regular Season					Playoffs				
Season	Club	League	GP	G	A	Pts	PIM	GP	G	A	Pts	PIM
1998-99	Kelowna Rockets	WHL	66	18	32	50	61	6	1	2	3	2
99-2000	Kelowna Rockets	WHL	66	22	26	48	61	5	1	0	1	2
2000-01	Kelowna Rockets	WHL	12	1	5	6	4	....	....	....	....	....
	Prince Albert	WHL	58	28	17	45	40	....	....	....	....	....
2001-02	Hamilton Bulldogs	AHL	1	0	0	0	0	1	0	0	0	0
	Columbus	ECHL	60	23	22	45	59	....	....	....	....	....
2002-03	Hamilton Bulldogs	AHL	2	0	0	0	2	....	....	....	....	....
	Columbus	ECHL	70	17	36	53	82	....	....	....	....	....
2003-04	Toronto	AHL	56	12	16	28	53	3	1	1	2	2
	Columbus	ECHL	4	2	1	3	2	....	....	....	....	....
2004-05	Edmonton	AHL	64	13	11	24	51	....	....	....	....	....
2005-06	Hamilton Bulldogs	AHL	34	4	7	11	55	....	....	....	....	....
2006-07	Toronto Marlies	AHL	9	0	1	1	8	....	....	....	....	....
	Manitoba Moose	AHL	48	11	5	16	49	13	1	4	5	6

Signed as a free agent by **Edmonton**, August 19, 2002.

HUNWICK, Matt (HUHN-wihk, MAT) BOS.

Defense. Shoots left. 5'11", 190 lbs. Born, Warren, MI, May 21, 1985.
(Boston's 6th choice, 224th overall, in 2004 Entry Draft).

			Regular Season					Playoffs				
Season	Club	League	GP	G	A	Pts	PIM	GP	G	A	Pts	PIM
2001-02	USNTDP	U-17	14	3	4	7	6	....	....	....	....	....
	USNTDP	NAHL	29	2	1	3	30	....	....	....	....	....
2002-03	USNTDP	U-18	40	6	16	22	40	....	....	....	....	....
	USNTDP	NAHL	8	2	2	4	23	....	....	....	....	....
2003-04	U. of Michigan	CCHA	41	1	14	15	62	....	....	....	....	....
2004-05	U. of Michigan	CCHA	40	6	19	25	60	....	....	....	....	....
2005-06	U. of Michigan	CCHA	41	11	19	30	70	....	....	....	....	....
2006-07	U. of Michigan	CCHA	41	6	21	27	64	....	....	....	....	....

CCHA All-Rookie Team (2004) • CCHA Second All-Star Team (2005, 2006), CCHA First All-Star Team (2007) • NCAA West Second All-American Team (2007)

HYNES, Shane (HIGHNZ, SHAYN) ANA.

Right wing. Shoots right. 6'3", 210 lbs. Born, Montreal, Que., November 7, 1983.
(Anaheim's 3rd choice, 86th overall, in 2003 Entry Draft).

			Regular Season					Playoffs				
Season	Club	League	GP	G	A	Pts	PIM	GP	G	A	Pts	PIM
99-2000	Cgy. AAA Flames	AMHL	30	8	12	20	20	....	....	....	....	....
2000-01	Cgy. AAA Flames	AMHL	28	18	21	38	76	....	....	....	....	....
2001-02	Nanaimo Clippers	BCHL	50	38	36	74	183	....	....	....	....	....
2002-03	Cornell Big Red	ECAC	32	11	9	20	36	....	....	....	....	....
2003-04	Cornell Big Red	ECAC	30	9	9	18	54	....	....	....	....	....
2004-05	Cornell Big Red	ECACHL	33	7	21	28	40	....	....	....	....	....
2005-06	Portland Pirates	AHL	12	1	3	4	32	....	....	....	....	....
2006-07	Portland Pirates	AHL	5	0	0	0	0	....	....	....	....	....
	Augusta Lynx	ECHL	49	17	28	45	94	2	1	0	1	2

BCHL All-Rookie Team (2002)

• Missed majority of 2005-06 season recovering from a knee injury.

IGGULDEN, Mike (IHG-gul-den, MIGHK) S.J.

Right wing. Shoots right. 6'3", 215 lbs. Born, St. Catherines, Ont., November 9, 1982.

			Regular Season					Playoffs				
Season	Club	League	GP	G	A	Pts	PIM	GP	G	A	Pts	PIM
2001-02	Cornell Big Red	ECAC	30	1	3	4	6	....	....	....	....	....
2002-03	Cornell Big Red	ECAC	15	0	2	2	19	....	....	....	....	....
2003-04	Cornell Big Red	ECAC	30	2	8	10	10	....	....	....	....	....
2004-05	Cornell Big Red	ECACHL	35	10	8	18	8	....	....	....	....	....
	Rochester	AHL	6	1	0	1	7	....	....	....	....	....
2005-06	Cleveland Barons	AHL	77	22	26	48	57	....	....	....	....	....
2006-07	Worcester Sharks	AHL	73	30	27	57	55	6	3	3	6	0

Signed to an ATO (tryout) contract by **Rochester** (AHL), April 5, 2004. Signed to a PTO (tryout) contract by **Cleveland** (AHL), September 19, 2005. Signed as a free agent by **San Jose**, January 16, 2006.

IGNATUSHKIN, Igor (ihg-nah-TOOSH-kihn, EE-gohr) WSH.

Center. Shoots left. 5'11", 161 lbs. Born, Elektrostal, USSR, April 7, 1984.
(Washington's 12th choice, 242nd overall, in 2002 Entry Draft).

			Regular Season					Playoffs				
Season	Club	League	GP	G	A	Pts	PIM	GP	G	A	Pts	PIM
99-2000	Elektrostal 2	Russia-3	5	0	0	0	0	....	....	....	....	....
2000-01	Team Center 84	Exhib.	5	1	1	2	0	....	....	....	....	....
	Elektrostal 2	Russia-3	STATISTICS NOT AVAILABLE									
2001-02	Elektrostal 2	Russia-3	6	2	3	5	6	....	....	....	....	....
	Elektrostal	Russia-2	46	1	4	5	20	....	....	....	....	....
2002-03	Elektrostal	Russia-2	36	9	10	19	8	....	....	....	....	....
2003-04	Kristall Elektrostal	Russia-2	49	6	2	8	22	....	....	....	....	....
2004-05	Kristall Elektrostal	Russia-2	45	9	3	12	28	....	....	....	....	....
	Leninogorsk	Russia-2	6	1	1	2	6	4	1	0	1	4
2005-06	Mytischi	Russia	7	0	0	0	2	....	....	....	....	....
	Kristall Elektrostal	Russia-3	STATISTICS NOT AVAILABLE									
2006-07	Kristall Elektrostal	Russia-2	49	14	23	37	48	....	....	....	....	....

IHNACAK, Brian (ih-NAH-chehk, BRIGH-uhn) PIT.

Center. Shoots right. 6', 178 lbs. Born, Toronto, Ont., April 10, 1985.
(Pittsburgh's 12th choice, 259th overall, in 2004 Entry Draft).

			Regular Season					Playoffs				
Season	Club	League	GP	G	A	Pts	PIM	GP	G	A	Pts	PIM
2001-02	St. Mike's B's	OPJHL	48	6	13	19	22	....	....	....	....	....
2002-03	St. Mike's B's	OPJHL	46	40	46	86	66	10	8	7	15	8
2003-04	Brown U.	ECAC	31	10	20	30	20	....	....	....	....	....
2004-05	Brown U.	ECACHL	30	12	11	23	30	....	....	....	....	....
2005-06	Brown U.	ECACHL	15	3	6	9	31	....	....	....	....	....
2006-07	Brown U.	ECACHL	27	3	11	14	14	....	....	....	....	....

ECAC All-Rookie Team (2004) • ECAC Rookie of the Year (2004) (co-winner - David McKee)

ILVONEN, Harri (ihl-VOH-nehn, HAIR-ree) MIN.

Defense. Shoots left. 6'2", 187 lbs. Born, Helsinki, Finland, November 3, 1988.
(Minnesota's 4th choice, 170th overall, in 2007 Entry Draft).

			Regular Season					Playoffs				
Season	Club	League	GP	G	A	Pts	PIM	GP	G	A	Pts	PIM
2004-05	Tappara U18	Fin-U18	27	2	10	12	14	2	0	0	0	2
2005-06	Tappara U18	Fin-U18	10	3	5	8	10	3	0	2	2	4
	Tappara Jr.	Fin-Jr.	24	2	1	3	24	....	....	....	....	....
2006-07	Tappara Jr.	Fin-Jr.	39	9	21	30	38	10	0	2	2	22
	Suomi U20	Finland-2	10	0	2	2	12	....	....	....	....	....
	Tappara Tampere	Finland	7	0	0	0	2	....	....	....	....	....

IRMEN, Danny (UHR-mehn, DA-nee) MIN.

Center. Shoots right. 6', 190 lbs. Born, Fargo, ND, September 6, 1984.
(Minnesota's 3rd choice, 78th overall, in 2003 Entry Draft).

			Regular Season					Playoffs				
Season	Club	League	GP	G	A	Pts	PIM	GP	G	A	Pts	PIM
2001-02	Lincoln Stars	USHL	61	17	36	53	....	....	....	....	....	....
2002-03	Lincoln Stars	USHL	45	21	34	55	78	10	8	6	14	17
2003-04	U. of Minnesota	WCHA	44	14	8	22	40	....	....	....	....	....
2004-05	U. of Minnesota	WCHA	44	24	19	43	66	....	....	....	....	....
2005-06	U. of Minnesota	WCHA	30	16	22	38	40	....	....	....	....	....
	Houston Aeros	AHL	4	0	2	2	0	7	0	0	0	4
2006-07	Houston Aeros	AHL	80	17	20	37	45	....	....	....	....	....

USHL Second All-Star Team (2003) • USHL Playoff MVP (2003)

ISAKOV, Evgeni (ih-SA-kawf, ehv-GEH-nee) PIT.

Right wing. Shoots left. 6'1", 196 lbs. Born, Krasnoyarsk, USSR, October 13, 1984.
(Pittsburgh's 6th choice, 161st overall, in 2003 Entry Draft).

			Regular Season					Playoffs				
Season	Club	League	GP	G	A	Pts	PIM	GP	G	A	Pts	PIM
99-2000	Rubin Tyumen 2	Russia-3	7	0	2	2	16	....	....	....	....	....
2000-01	Rubin Tyumen 2	Russia-3						....	....	....	....	....
	Gazovik Tyumen	Russia-3	11	1	1	2	12	....	....	....	....	....
2001-02	Gazovik Tyumen	Russia-2	19	2	2	4	2	....	....	....	....	....
	Elektrostal	Russia-2	29	3	2	5	24	....	....	....	....	....
	Elektrostal 2	Russia-3	11	3	3	6	43	....	....	....	....	....
2002-03	Cherepovets	Russia	36	0	3	3	12	1	0	0	0	0
2003-04	Cherepovets	Russia	38	3	2	5	18	....	....	....	....	....
	Cherepovets 2	Russia-3	14	4	8	12	48	....	....	....	....	....
2004-05	Kristall Saratov	Russia-2	1	0	0	0	0	....	....	....	....	....
	Tyumen 2	Russia-3	2	1	3	4	14	....	....	....	....	....
	Gazovik Tyumen	Russia-2	4	0	2	2	2	3	0	0	0	2
2005-06	Gazovik Tyumen	Russia-2	46	9	12	21	90	3	0	0	0	6
2006-07	Gazovik Tyumen	Russia-2	51	6	11	17	48	....	....	....	....	....
	Tyumen 2	Russia-3	2	1	2	3	0	....	....	....	....	....

ISTOMIN, Denis (ihs-TOH-mihn, DEH-nihs) CHI.

Right wing. Shoots left. 6', 189 lbs. Born, Chelyabinsk, USSR, January 12, 1987.
(Chicago's 7th choice, 117th overall, in 2005 Entry Draft).

			Regular Season					Playoffs				
Season	Club	League	GP	G	A	Pts	PIM	GP	G	A	Pts	PIM
2003-04	Magnitogorsk 2	Russia-3	3	2	1	3	2	....	....	....	....	....
2004-05	Chelyabinsk 2	Russia-3	1	0	0	0	0	....	....	....	....	....
	Chelyabinsk	Russia-2	42	11	5	16	24	8	1	1	2	4
2005-06	Vityaz Chekhov	Russia	46	4	4	8	6	....	....	....	....	....
	Nizhny Novgorod	Russia-2	4	0	3	3	2	3	2	1	3	0
2006-07	Magnitogorsk	Russia	6	0	1	1	6	....	....	....	....	....
	Vityaz Chekhov	Russia	15	0	3	3	6	....	....	....	....	....

JAFFRAY, Jason (JAF-ray, JAY-suhn) VAN.

Left wing. Shoots left. 6'1", 205 lbs. Born, Rimbey, Alta., June 30, 1981.

			Regular Season					Playoffs				
Season	Club	League	GP	G	A	Pts	PIM	GP	G	A	Pts	PIM
1997-98	Edmonton Ice	WHL	6	0	1	1	0	....	....	....	....	....
1998-99	Kootenay Ice	WHL	57	14	12	26	50	7	1	2	3	6
99-2000	Kootenay Ice	WHL	71	24	28	52	104	21	10	9	19	17
2000-01	Kootenay Ice	WHL	70	31	42	73	108	11	5	7	12	10
2001-02	Kootenay Ice	WHL	32	15	19	34	38	....	....	....	....	....
	Swift Current	WHL	41	23	26	49	44	12	4	5	9	25
2002-03	Norfolk Admirals	AHL	2	0	0	0	0	....	....	....	....	....
	Roanoke Express	ECHL	64	34	51	85	89	4	0	3	3	4
2003-04	Wilkes-Barre	AHL	5	0	1	1	0	....	....	....	....	....
	Wheeling Nailers	ECHL	54	37	37	74	81	2	1	1	2	2
2004-05	Cleveland Barons	AHL	30	10	6	16	23	....	....	....	....	....
	Manitoba Moose	AHL	14	4	4	8	6	1	0	0	0	0
	Wheeling Nailers	ECHL	23	6	6	12	22	....	....	....	....	....
2005-06	Manitoba Moose	AHL	73	12	35	47	58	13	6	1	7	11
2006-07	Manitoba Moose	AHL	77	35	46	81	75	13	6	7	13	6

AHL Second All-Star Team (2007)

Signed as a free agent by **Vancouver**, July 3, 2007.

JEFFREY, Dustin (JEHF-ree, DUHS-tihn) PIT.

Center. Shoots left. 6'1", 205 lbs. Born, Sarnia, Ont., February 27, 1988.
(Pittsburgh's 8th choice, 171st overall, in 2007 Entry Draft).

			Regular Season					Playoffs				
Season	Club	League	GP	G	A	Pts	PIM	GP	G	A	Pts	PIM
2003-04	Lambton Sting	Minor-ON	40	44	23	67	22	....	....	....	....	....
2004-05	Mississauga	OHL	53	10	15	25	20	....	....	....	....	....
2005-06	Mississauga	OHL	30	6	9	15	26	....	....	....	....	....
	Sault Ste. Marie	OHL	39	12	11	23	10	4	1	2	3	2
2006-07	Sault Ste. Marie	OHL	68	34	58	92	40	13	6	12	18	11

JENSEN, Christian (JEHN-suhn, KRIHS-tyehn) S.J.

Defense. Shoots right. 6'3", 190 lbs. Born, Brooklyn, NY, January 6, 1986.
(San Jose's 10th choice, 289th overall, in 2004 Entry Draft).

			Regular Season					Playoffs				
Season	Club	League	GP	G	A	Pts	PIM	GP	G	A	Pts	PIM
2003-04	New Jersey Jrs.	AtJHL	48	6	23	29	62	....	....	....	....	....
2004-05	Jersey Hitmen	EJHL	48	1	9	10	22	....	....	....	....	....
2005-06	Chicago Steel	USHL	24	0	4	4	8	....	....	....	....	....
	Waterloo	USHL	18	1	4	5	14	....	....	....	....	....
2006-07	RPI Engineers	ECACHL	24	1	3	4	28	....	....	....	....	....

JENSEN, Joe (JEHN-suhn, JOH) PIT.

Center. Shoots left. 5'11", 180 lbs. Born, Maple Grove, MN, February 6, 1983.
(Pittsburgh's 10th choice, 232nd overall, in 2003 Entry Draft).

			Regular Season					Playoffs				
Season	Club	League	GP	G	A	Pts	PIM	GP	G	A	Pts	PIM
2000-01	Sioux City	USHL	56	14	20	34	59	8	2	4	6	12
2001-02	Sioux City	USHL	57	20	26	46	135	3	0	0	0	6
2002-03	St. Cloud State	WCHA	37	9	9	18	14	....	....	....	....	....
2003-04	St. Cloud State	WCHA	38	10	14	24	42	....	....	....	....	....
2004-05	St. Cloud State	WCHA	40	12	14	26	36	....	....	....	....	....
2005-06	St. Cloud State	WCHA	38	14	18	32	14	....	....	....	....	....
2006-07	Wilkes-Barre	AHL	26	6	5	11	16	7	2	1	3	6
	Wheeling Nailers	ECHL	28	11	18	29	45	....	....	....	....	....

JESSIMAN, Hugh (JEHS-ih-muhn, HEW) NYR

Right wing. Shoots right. 6'6", 231 lbs. Born, New York, NY, March 28, 1984.
(NY Rangers' 1st choice, 12th overall, in 2003 Entry Draft).

			Regular Season					Playoffs				
Season	Club	League	GP	G	A	Pts	PIM	GP	G	A	Pts	PIM
2001-02	Brunswick Bruins	High-CT	18	25	27	52	40	....	....	....	....	....
2002-03	Dartmouth	ECAC	34	23	24	47	48	....	....	....	....	....
2003-04	Dartmouth	ECAC	34	16	17	33	71	....	....	....	....	....
2004-05	Dartmouth	ECACHL	12	1	1	2	18	....	....	....	....	....
2005-06	Hartford Wolf Pack	AHL	46	7	11	18	66	2	0	0	0	0
	Charlotte	ECHL	25	13	10	23	56	....	....	....	....	....
2006-07	Hartford Wolf Pack	AHL	49	7	6	13	79	7	1	0	1	9
	Charlotte	ECHL	20	12	10	22	52	....	....	....	....	....

ECAC All-Rookie Team (2003) • ECAC Rookie of the Year (2003) • ECAC Second All-Star Team (2004)

JOENSUU, Jesse (YOH-ehn-soo, YEH-see) NYI

Wing. Shoots left. 6'4", 207 lbs. Born, Pori, Finland, October 5, 1987.
(NY Islanders' 2nd choice, 60th overall, in 2006 Entry Draft).

			Regular Season					Playoffs				
Season	Club	League	GP	G	A	Pts	PIM	GP	G	A	Pts	PIM
2002-03	Assat Pori U18	Fin-U18	26	8	10	18	53	3	1	2	3	0
	Assat Pori Jr.	Fin-Jr.	3	0	1	1	2	....	....	....	....	....
2003-04	Assat Pori U18	Fin-U18	6	7	2	9	8	....	....	....	....	....
	Assat Pori Jr.	Fin-Jr.	28	7	9	16	18	3	0	1	1	2
	Assat Pori	Finland	6	0	0	0	0	....	....	....	....	....
2004-05	Assat Pori Jr.	Fin-Jr.	17	7	13	20	20	2	1	1	2	2
	Assat Pori	Finland	39	1	1	2	4	....	....	....	....	....
	Assat Pori	Finland	39	1	1	2	4	....	....	....	....	....
2005-06	Suomi U20	Finland-2	2	1	0	1	12	....	....	....	....	....
	Assat Pori	Finland	51	4	8	12	57	14	0	2	2	12
2006-07	Assat Pori Jr.	Fin-Jr.	5	2	1	3	6	....	....	....	....	....
	Suomi U20	Finland-2	2	0	2	2	6	....	....	....	....	....
	Assat Pori	Finland	52	9	17	26	74	....	....	....	....	....

JOHANSSON, Fredrik (yoh-HAHN-suhn, FREHD-rihk) EDM.

Center. Shoots left. 5'11", 178 lbs. Born, Goteburg, Sweden, February 27, 1984.
(Edmonton's 14th choice, 274th overall, in 2002 Entry Draft).

			Regular Season					Playoffs				
Season	Club	League	GP	G	A	Pts	PIM	GP	G	A	Pts	PIM
2000-01	V.Frolunda Jr.	Swe-Jr.	22	3	4	7	8	3	0	1	1	4
	V.Frolunda U18	Swe-U18	6	5	1	6	4	....	....	....	....	....
2001-02	V.Frolunda Jr.	Swe-Jr.	42	13	23	36	39	....	....	....	....	....
	V.Frolunda U18	Swe-U18	1	0	1	1	0	....	....	....	....	....
2002-03	V.Frolunda Jr.	Swe-Jr.	30	13	34	47	24	3	0	2	2	2
	V.Frolunda	Sweden	9	0	0	0	2	5	0	0	0	0
2003-04	V.Frolunda Jr.	Swe-Jr.	7	1	2	3	4	4	2	4	6	0
	Halmstad	Sweden-2	1	0	0	0	0	....	....	....	....	....
	V.Frolunda	Sweden	48	1	3	4	6	10	0	0	0	0
2004-05	Vasteras	Sweden-2	46	15	15	30	32	5	0	3	3	8
2005-06	VIK Vasteras HK	Sweden-2	41	7	15	22	26	....	....	....	....	....
2006-07	Frolunda	Sweden	53	1	4	5	20	....	....	....	....	....
	Frolunda Jr.	Swe-Jr.	1	1	1	2	2	....	....	....	....	....

JOHANSSON, Kim (yoh-HAHN-suhn, KIHM) NYI

Wing. Shoots left. 6'1", 172 lbs. Born, Malmo, Sweden, January 21, 1988.
(NY Islanders' 9th choice, 141st overall, in 2006 Entry Draft).

			Regular Season					Playoffs				
Season	Club	League	GP	G	A	Pts	PIM	GP	G	A	Pts	PIM
2003-04	Malmo U18	Swe-U18	3	0	0	0	2	....	....	....	....	....
2004-05	Malmo U18	Swe-U18	14	4	1	5	14	2	1	1	2	4
	Malmo Jr.	Swe-Jr.	4	0	0	0	2	....	....	....	....	....
2005-06	Malmo U18	Swe-U18	6	1	2	3	27	6	1	0	1	16
	Malmo Jr.	Swe-Jr.	39	5	10	15	28	....	....	....	....	....
2006-07	Malmo Jr.	Swe-Jr.	38	10	20	30	79	4	0	2	2	10

JOHANSSON, Magnus CHI.

Defense. Shoots left. 5'11", 180 lbs. Born, Linkoping, Sweden, September 4, 1973.

			Regular Season					Playoffs				
Season	Club	League	GP	G	A	Pts	PIM	GP	G	A	Pts	PIM
1997-98	V.Frolunda	Sweden	46	5	8	13	24	....	....	....	....	....
1998-99	V.Frolunda	Sweden	48	10	9	19	4	4	0	1	1	4
99-2000	V.Frolunda	Sweden	49	12	22	34	20	....	....	....	....	....
2000-01	V.Frolunda	Sweden	50	6	28	34	26	5	2	1	3	14
2001-02	V.Frolunda	Sweden	48	14	21	35	36	10	1	5	6	8
2002-03	V.Frolunda	Sweden	50	11	15	26	14	16	2	3	5	20
2003-04	Langnau	Swiss	48	4	21	25	36	....	....	....	....	....
2004-05	Linkopings HC	Sweden	47	9	25	34	26	6	3	0	3	0
2005-06	Linkopings HC	Sweden	50	11	11	22	30	13	2	1	3	10
2006-07	Linkopings HC	Sweden	52	8	28	36	46	....	....	....	....	....

Signed as a free agent by **Chicago**, June 4, 2007.

JOHNER, Dustin (JAW-nuhr, DUHS-tihn)

Center. Shoots right. 5'11", 181 lbs. Born, Estevan, Sask., March 6, 1983.
(Florida's 8th choice, 169th overall, in 2001 Entry Draft).

			Regular Season					Playoffs				
Season	Club	League	GP	G	A	Pts	PIM	GP	G	A	Pts	PIM
1998-99	Red Deer Rebels	AMBHL	36	35	29	64	42	....	....	....	....	....
99-2000	Red Deer Chiefs	AMHL	36	24	31	55	80	....	....	....	....	....
	Seattle	WHL	6	0	1	1	0	....	....	....	....	....
2000-01	Seattle	WHL	72	25	31	56	45	9	1	5	6	6
2001-02	Seattle	WHL	71	33	48	81	71	8	4	3	7	8
2002-03	Seattle	WHL	71	36	41	77	97	15	7	6	13	14
2003-04	Seattle	WHL	71	26	31	57	54	....	....	....	....	....
	South Carolina	ECHL	4	2	4	6	0	7	4	3	7	4
2004-05	Lowell	AHL	23	4	8	12	12	11	1	0	1	4
	Las Vegas	ECHL	51	22	26	48	42	....	....	....	....	....
2005-06	Omaha	AHL	5	0	0	0	2	....	....	....	....	....
	Las Vegas	ECHL	9	2	2	4	8	....	....	....	....	....
	Rochester	AHL	16	1	1	2	8	....	....	....	....	....
	Florida Everblades	ECHL	36	15	21	36	24	8	5	4	9	4
2006-07	Rochester	AHL	2	0	0	0	0	....	....	....	....	....
	Florida Everblades	ECHL	67	29	35	64	66	16	7	6	13	12

Signed as a free agent by **Calgary**, July 6, 2004. Traded to **Florida** by **Calgary** with Steve Montador for Kristian Huselius, December 2, 2005.

JOHNSON, Erik (JAWN-suhn, AIR-ihk) ST.L.

Defense. Shoots right. 6'4", 222 lbs. Born, Bloomington, MN, March 21, 1988.
(St. Louis' 1st choice, 1st overall, in 2006 Entry Draft).

			Regular Season					Playoffs				
Season	Club	League	GP	G	A	Pts	PIM	GP	G	A	Pts	PIM
2003-04	Holy Angels	High-MN	31	13	21	34	....	....	....	....	....	....
2004-05	USNTDP	U-17	26	5	9	14	14	....	....	....	....	....
	USNTDP	NAHL	31	6	6	12	12	....	....	....	....	....
2005-06	USNTDP	U-18	36	12	22	34	78	....	....	....	....	....
	USNTDP	NAHL	11	4	11	15	10	....	....	....	....	....
2006-07	U. of Minnesota	WCHA	41	4	20	24	50	....	....	....	....	....

WCHA All-Rookie Team (2007)

JOHNSON, Nick (JAWN-suhn, NIHK) PIT.

Right wing. Shoots right. 6'1", 183 lbs. Born, Calgary, Alta., December 24, 1985.
(Pittsburgh's 4th choice, 67th overall, in 2004 Entry Draft).

			Regular Season					Playoffs				
Season	Club	League	GP	G	A	Pts	PIM	GP	G	A	Pts	PIM
2002-03	St. Albert Saints	AJHL	60	21	30	51	10	....	....	....	....	....
2003-04	St. Albert Saints	AJHL	51	35	36	71	33	4	0	2	2	0
2004-05	Dartmouth	ECACHL	35	18	17	35	16	....	....	....	....	....
2005-06	Dartmouth	ECACHL	33	15	10	25	24	....	....	....	....	....
2006-07	Dartmouth	ECACHL	33	14	16	30	46	....	....	....	....	....

ECACHL All-Rookie Team 2005)

JONES, David (JOHNZ, DAY-vihd) COL.

Right wing. Shoots right. 6'2", 220 lbs. Born, Guelph, Ont., August 10, 1984.
(Colorado's 8th choice, 288th overall, in 2003 Entry Draft).

			Regular Season					Playoffs				
Season	Club	League	GP	G	A	Pts	PIM	GP	G	A	Pts	PIM
2000-01	Port Coquitlam	PIJHL	40	18	11	29	33	....	....	....	....	....
2001-02	Coquitlam Express	BCHL	59	19	32	51	62	....	....	....	....	....
2002-03	Coquitlam Express	BCHL	35	9	19	28	55	7	2	6	8	8
2003-04	Coquitlam Express	BCHL	53	33	60	93	78	7	3	6	9	4
2004-05	Dartmouth	ECACHL	34	9	5	14	26	....	....	....	....	....
2005-06	Dartmouth	ECACHL	33	17	17	34	38	....	....	....	....	....
2006-07	Dartmouth	ECACHL	33	18	26	*44	22	....	....	....	....	....

ECACHL Second All-Star Team (2006) • ECACHL First All-Star Tearm (2007) • NCAA East First All-American Team (2007)

JONES, Ryan (JOHNZ, RIGH-uhn) MIN.

Right wing. Shoots right. 6'1", 207 lbs. Born, Chatham, Ont., June 14, 1984.
(Minnesota's 5th choice, 111th overall, in 2004 Entry Draft).

			Regular Season					Playoffs				
Season	Club	League	GP	G	A	Pts	PIM	GP	G	A	Pts	PIM
2002-03	Chatham Maroons	OHA-B	38	12	11	23	42	....	....	....	....	....
2003-04	Chatham Maroons	OHA-B	46	39	30	69	64	17	17	9	26	25
2004-05	Miami U.	CCHA	38	8	7	15	79	....	....	....	....	....
2005-06	Miami U.	CCHA	39	22	13	35	72	....	....	....	....	....
2006-07	Miami U.	CCHA	42	29	19	48	88	....	....	....	....	....

CCHA Second All-Star Team (2006, 2007)

JONSSON, Per (YAWN-suhn, PAIR) CGY.

Forward. Shoots left. 6', 172 lbs. Born, Karlstad, Sweden, April 20, 1988.
(Calgary's 8th choice, 209th overall, in 2006 Entry Draft).

			Regular Season					Playoffs				
Season	Club	League	GP	G	A	Pts	PIM	GP	G	A	Pts	PIM
2004-05	Farjestad U18	Swe-U18	12	2	2	4	10	2	0	0	0	2
2005-06	Farjestad U18	Swe-U18	14	3	1	4	38	8	1	1	2	22
2006-07	Farjestad	Sweden	11	0	1	1	0	....	....	....	....	....
	Skare BK Karlstad	Sweden-3	25	3	4	7	42	....	....	....	....	....

JOSLIN, Derek (JAWS-lihn, DAIR-ihk) S.J.

Defense. Shoots left. 6'1", 205 lbs. Born, Richmond Hill, Ont., March 17, 1987.
(San Jose's 5th choice, 149th overall, in 2005 Entry Draft).

			Regular Season					Playoffs				
Season	Club	League	GP	G	A	Pts	PIM	GP	G	A	Pts	PIM
2002-03	Vaughan	GTHL	60	9	18	27	72	....	....	....	....	....
2003-04	Aurora Tigers	OPJHL	36	4	12	16	....	....	....	....	....	....
	Ottawa 67's	OHL	7	0	0	0	4	....	....	....	....	....
2004-05	Ottawa 67's	OHL	68	6	24	30	44	21	0	3	3	24
2005-06	Ottawa 67's	OHL	68	11	37	48	40	6	1	5	6	10
	Cleveland Barons	AHL	2	0	0	0	0	....	....	....	....	....
2006-07	Ottawa 67's	OHL	68	11	38	49	66	5	1	4	5	4
	Worcester Sharks	AHL	3	0	0	0	0	4	0	0	0	2

JOUDREY, Andrew (JOO-dree, AN-droo) **WSH.**

Center. Shoots left. 5'11", 191 lbs. Born, Halifax, N.S., July 15, 1984.
(Washington's 5th choice, 249th overall, in 2003 Entry Draft).

			Regular Season					Playoffs				
Season	Club	League	GP	G	A	Pts	PIM	GP	G	A	Pts	PIM
2000-01	Dartmouth	NSMHL	82	51	70	121	....	....	....	....	....	....
2001-02	Notre Dame	SJHL	57	24	38	62	14	....	....	....	....	....
2002-03	Notre Dame	SJHL	53	27	51	78	16	....	....	....	....	....
2003-04	U. of Wisconsin	WCHA	42	7	15	22	2	....	....	....	....	....
2004-05	U. of Wisconsin	WCHA	41	7	17	24	18	....	....	....	....	....
2005-06	U. of Wisconsin	WCHA	37	8	10	18	14	....	....	....	....	....
2006-07	U. of Wisconsin	WCHA	40	9	20	29	18	....	....	....	....	....
	Hershey Bears	AHL	5	2	1	3	0	10	0	2	2	0

JOUKOV, Mishail (ZHOO-kawv, mee-shigh-EHL) **EDM.**

Left wing. Shoots left. 6'3", 200 lbs. Born, Leningrad, USSR, January 3, 1985.
(Edmonton's 4th choice, 72nd overall, in 2003 Entry Draft).

			Regular Season					Playoffs				
Season	Club	League	GP	G	A	Pts	PIM	GP	G	A	Pts	PIM
2000-01	Mora IK Jr.	Swe-Jr.	28	9	14	23	6	9	2	4	6	0
2001-02	IFK Arboga IK	Sweden-2	37	4	9	13	12	3	1	0	1	2
2002-03	IFK Arboga IK	Sweden-2	41	9	14	23	30	3	3	1	4	0
2003-04	Vasteras	Sweden-2	44	5	12	17	16	....	....	....	....	....
	HV 71 Jonkoping	Sweden	3	0	0	0	0	....	....	....	....	....
2004-05	Ak Bars Kazan 2	Russia-3	....	8	11	19	....	....	....	....	....	....
	Spartak Moscow	Russia	13	1	2	3	2	....	....	....	....	....
	Ak Bars Kazan	Russia	2	0	0	0	0	....	....	....	....	....
2005-06	Ak Bars Kazan	Russia	38	1	7	8	8	4	0	1	1	0
2006-07	Ak Bars Kazan	Russia	37	2	7	9	26	11	0	4	4	4

JUNLAND, Jonas (YUHN-land, YOH-nuhs) **ST.L.**

Defense. Shoots left. 6'2", 198 lbs. Born, Linkoping, Sweden, November 15, 1987.
(St. Louis' 4th choice, 64th overall, in 2006 Entry Draft).

			Regular Season					Playoffs				
Season	Club	League	GP	G	A	Pts	PIM	GP	G	A	Pts	PIM
2002-03	Linkopings HC U18	Swe-U18	7	0	0	0	6	....	....	....	....	....
2003-04	Linkopings HC U18	Swe-U18	4	0	0	0	4	....	....	....	....	....
	Linkopings HC Jr.	Swe-Jr.	19	1	0	1	12	....	....	....	....	....
2004-05	Linkopings HC U18	Swe-U18	11	6	5	11	35	....	....	....	....	....
	Linkopings HC Jr.	Swe-Jr.	32	3	5	8	96	....	....	....	....	....
2005-06	Linkopings HC Jr.	Swe-Jr.	32	17	23	40	44	....	....	....	....	....
	Linkopings HC U18	Swe-U18	1	5	0	5	2	....	....	....	....	....
	Linkopings HC	Sweden	4	0	0	0	0	....	....	....	....	....
2006-07	Linkopings HC Jr.	Swe-Jr.	9	6	7	13	26	....	....	....	....	....
	IK Oskarshamn	Sweden-2	4	0	3	3	4	....	....	....	....	....
	Linkopings HC	Sweden	41	1	4	5	22	15	0	5	5	20

JUUTILAINEN, Jan-Mikael (yoo-tih-LIGH-nehn, YAHN-mih-KAYL) **CHI.**

Center. Shoots left. 5'11", 183 lbs. Born, Espoo, Finland, January 5, 1988.
(Chicago's 7th choice, 156th overall, in 2006 Entry Draft).

			Regular Season					Playoffs				
Season	Club	League	GP	G	A	Pts	PIM	GP	G	A	Pts	PIM
2004-05	Jokerit U18	Fin-U18	30	15	6	21	4	7	1	1	2	0
	Jokerit Helsinki Jr.	Fin-Jr.	1	0	0	0	0	....	....	....	....	....
2005-06	Jokerit U18	Fin-U18	16	8	13	21	28	6	6	7	13	2
	Jokerit Helsinki Jr.	Fin-Jr.	36	3	12	15	35	4	0	0	0	2
	Suomi U20	Finland-2	1	0	0	0	0	....	....	....	....	....
2006-07	Waterloo	USHL	46	9	10	19	18	5	0	0	0	0

KABLUKOV, Ilja (ka-BLOO-hahv, IHL-yah) **VAN.**

Center. Shoots left. 6'2", 183 lbs. Born, Moscow, USSR, January 18, 1988.
(Vancouver's 4th choice, 146th overall, in 2007 Entry Draft).

			Regular Season					Playoffs				
Season	Club	League	GP	G	A	Pts	PIM	GP	G	A	Pts	PIM
2005-06	CSKA Moscow 2	Russia-3	STATISTICS NOT AVAILABLE									
2006-07	CSKA Moscow 2	Russia-3	STATISTICS NOT AVAILABLE									
	CSKA Moscow	Russia	24	0	0	0	2	2	0	0	0	2

KAIP, Rylan (KAYP, RIH-luhn) **ATL.**

Center. Shoots left. 6'1", 185 lbs. Born, Wilcox, Sask., March 19, 1984.
(Atlanta's 9th choice, 269th overall, in 2003 Entry Draft).

			Regular Season					Playoffs				
Season	Club	League	GP	G	A	Pts	PIM	GP	G	A	Pts	PIM
2000-01	Notre Dame	SJHL	5	0	0	0	0	1	0	0	0	0
2001-02	Notre Dame	SJHL	61	14	18	32	77	....	....	....	....	....
2002-03	Notre Dame	SJHL	57	20	36	56	164	6	1	6	7	21
2003-04	Notre Dame	SJHL	54	30	36	66	133	4	1	1	2	6
2004-05	North Dakota	WCHA	22	0	4	4	20	....	....	....	....	....
2005-06	North Dakota	WCHA	42	3	5	8	76	....	....	....	....	....
2006-07	North Dakota	WCHA	38	5	7	12	55	....	....	....	....	....

KALINSKI, Jonathon (kuh-LIHN-skee, JAWN-ah-thuhn) **PHI.**

Left wing. Shoots left. 6'1", 180 lbs. Born, Bonnyville , Alta., May 25, 1987.
(Philadelphia's 5th choice, 152nd overall, in 2007 Entry Draft).

			Regular Season					Playoffs				
Season	Club	League	GP	G	A	Pts	PIM	GP	G	A	Pts	PIM
2003-04	Bonneyville	AJHL	52	13	13	26	68	5	0	0	0	8
2004-05	Bonnyville Pontiacs	AJHL	58	16	25	41	195	4	2	0	2	6
2005-06	Minnesota State	WCHA	30	4	7	11	73	....	....	....	....	....
2006-07	Minnesota State	WCHA	37	17	10	27	74	....	....	....	....	....

KAMPFER, Steven (KAMP-fuhr, STEE-vehn) **ANA.**

Defense. Shoots right. 5'11", 204 lbs. Born, Ann Arbour, MI, September 24, 1988.
(Anaheim's 5th choice, 93rd overall, in 2007 Entry Draft).

			Regular Season					Playoffs				
Season	Club	League	GP	G	A	Pts	PIM	GP	G	A	Pts	PIM
2004-05	Sioux City	USHL	47	6	13	19	91	13	2	5	7	12
2005-06	Sioux City	USHL	56	6	10	16	99	....	....	....	....	....
2006-07	U. of Michigan	CCHA	35	1	3	4	24	....	....	....	....	....

KANA, Tomas (KA-nah, TAW-mahsh) **ST.L.**

Center. Shoots right. 6', 202 lbs. Born, Opava, Czech., November 29, 1987.
(St. Louis' 3rd choice, 31st overall, in 2006 Entry Draft).

			Regular Season					Playoffs				
Season	Club	League	GP	G	A	Pts	PIM	GP	G	A	Pts	PIM
2002-03	HC Vitkovice U17	CzR-U17	44	20	14	34	72	2	2	0	2	4
	HC Vitkovice Jr.	CzRep-Jr.	3	2	0	2	4	....	....	....	....	....
2003-04	HC Vitkovice U17	CzR-U17	8	2	9	11	33	7	4	5	9	18
	HC Vitkovice Jr.	CzRep-Jr.	50	12	7	19	78	....	....	....	....	....
2004-05	HC Vitkovice Jr.	CzRep-Jr.	46	12	22	34	155	2	0	0	0	2
	HC Vitkovice Steel	CzRep	1	0	0	0	0	....	....	....	....	....
2005-06	HC Vitkovice Steel	CzRep	42	5	9	14	50	6	0	1	1	2
	HC Vitkovice Jr.	CzRep-Jr.	5	4	3	7	16	....	....	....	....	....
2006-07	HC Vitkovice Steel	CzRep	44	9	7	16	54	....	....	....	....	....
	BK Mlada Boleslav	CzRep-2	6	2	1	3	16	6	1	0	1	16

KANE, Patrick (KAYN, PAT-rihk) **CHI.**

Right wing. Shoots left. 5'10", 163 lbs. Born, Buffalo, NY, November 19, 1988.
(Chicago's 1st choice, 1st overall, in 2007 Entry Draft).

			Regular Season					Playoffs				
Season	Club	League	GP	G	A	Pts	PIM	GP	G	A	Pts	PIM
2003-04	Det. Honeybaked	MWEHL	70	83	77	160	....	....	....	....	....	....
2004-05	USNTDP	U-17	23	16	17	33	8	....	....	....	....	....
	USNTDP	NAHL	40	16	21	37	8	9	7	8	15	2
2005-06	USNTDP	U-18	43	35	33	68	10	....	....	....	....	....
	USNTDP	NAHL	15	17	17	34	12	....	....	....	....	....
2006-07	London Knights	OHL	58	62	83	*145	52	16	10	21	*31	16

OHL All-Rookie Team (2007) • OHL First All-Star Team (2007) • OHL Rookie of the Year (2007) • Canadian Major Junior Rookie of the Year (2007)

KARIYA, Martin (kah-REE-ah, MAR-tihn) **ST.L.**

Right wing. Shoots right. 5'9", 175 lbs. Born, Vancouver, B.C., October 5, 1981.

			Regular Season					Playoffs				
Season	Club	League	GP	G	A	Pts	PIM	GP	G	A	Pts	PIM
1998-99	Victoria Salsa	BCJHL	59	25	80	105	14	....	....	....	....	....
99-2000	U. of Maine	H-East	35	8	17	25	6	....	....	....	....	....
2000-01	U. of Maine	H-East	39	12	14	36	10	....	....	....	....	....
2001-02	U. of Maine	H-East	43	16	28	44	14	....	....	....	....	....
2002-03	U. of Maine	H-East	39	14	36	50	6	....	....	....	....	....
	Portland Pirates	AHL	....	....	....	....	....	3	0	0	0	0
2003-04	Bridgeport	AHL	70	8	17	25	16	7	0	1	1	2
2004-05	HC Nikko Icebucks	AsianHL	15	6	12	18	20	....	....	....	....	....
2005-06	Stjernen Hockey	Norway	39	15	37	52	49	11	3	10	13	8
2006-07	Blues Espoo	Finland	51	18	43	61	58	....	....	....	....	....

Hockey East First All-Star Team (2003)

Signed to a PTO (tryout) contract by **Portland** (AHL), April 9, 2003. Signed as a free agent by **Bridgeport** (AHL), July 7, 2003. Signed as a free agent by **St. Louis**, June 1, 2007.

KARLSSON, Mattias (KARL-suhn, mat-TEE-uhs) **OTT.**

Defense. Shoots left. 6'2", 192 lbs. Born, Stora, Sweden, April 15, 1985.
(Ottawa's 4th choice, 135th overall, in 2003 Entry Draft).

			Regular Season					Playoffs				
Season	Club	League	GP	G	A	Pts	PIM	GP	G	A	Pts	PIM
2001-02	Brynas U18	Swe-U18	5	2	1	3	6	....	....	....	....	....
	Brynas IF Gavle Jr.	Swe-Jr.	13	0	1	1	12	....	....	....	....	....
2002-03	Brynas IF Gavle Jr.	Swe-Jr.	27	11	6	17	93	2	0	0	0	4
	Brynas IF Gavle	Sweden	3	0	0	0	0	....	....	....	....	....
	Brynas IF Gavle	Sweden-Q	3	0	0	0	0	....	....	....	....	....
2003-04	Brynas IF Gavle Jr.	Swe-Jr.	20	5	8	13	67	5	0	4	4	10
	Brynas IF Gavle	Sweden	39	0	0	0	6	....	....	....	....	....
2004-05	Brynas IF Gavle Jr.	Swe-Jr.	13	3	5	8	40	....	....	....	....	....
	Almtuna	Sweden-2	22	0	2	2	18	....	....	....	....	....
	Brynas IF Gavle	Sweden	9	0	0	0	2	....	....	....	....	....
	Brynas IF Gavle	Sweden-Q	1	0	0	0	0	....	....	....	....	....
2005-06	Almtuna Jr.	Swe-Jr.	2	0	1	1	4	....	....	....	....	....
	Almtuna	Sweden-2	32	3	4	7	40	....	....	....	....	....
2006-07	Bofors	Sweden-2	44	11	21	32	34	....	....	....	....	....

KARSUMS, Martins (KAHR-suhmz, MAHR-tihnsh) **BOS.**

Right wing. Shoots right. 5'10", 198 lbs. Born, Riga, USSR, February 26, 1986.
(Boston's 2nd choice, 64th overall, in 2004 Entry Draft).

			Regular Season					Playoffs				
Season	Club	League	GP	G	A	Pts	PIM	GP	G	A	Pts	PIM
2000-01	Prizma '83 Riga Jr.	Latvia-Jr.	2	0	0	0	0	....	....	....	....	....
	Lido Nafta Jr.	Latvia-Jr.	18	8	6	14	....	....	....	....	....	....
2001-02	Prizma '83 Riga	EEHL-B	16	7	8	15	4	....	....	....	....	....
	Prizma '83 Riga	Latvia	6	4	1	5	4	....	....	....	....	....
2002-03	HK Riga 2000	EEHL	2	0	0	0	0	....	....	....	....	....
	Vilki Riga	Latvia	STATISTICS NOT AVAILABLE									
2003-04	Moncton Wildcats	QMJHL	60	30	23	53	76	20	8	9	17	14
2004-05	Moncton Wildcats	QMJHL	30	14	12	26	31	2	0	0	0	0
2005-06	Moncton Wildcats	QMJHL	49	34	31	65	89	21	15	11	26	22
2006-07	Providence Bruins	AHL	54	13	22	35	41	12	3	1	4	2

QMJHL All-Rookie Team (2004)

KASPAR, Lukas (kas-PAHR, LOO-kahsh) **S.J.**

Right wing. Shoots left. 6'2", 210 lbs. Born, Most, Czech., September 23, 1985.
(San Jose's 1st choice, 22nd overall, in 2004 Entry Draft).

			Regular Season					Playoffs				
Season	Club	League	GP	G	A	Pts	PIM	GP	G	A	Pts	PIM
2000-01	Litvinov U17	CzR-U17	48	27	19	46	64	6	2	3	5	0
2001-02	Litvinov U17	CzR-U17	48	35	41	76	143	2	1	1	2	0
2002-03	Litvinov	CzRep	9	1	1	2	2	....	....	....	....	....
	Litvinov Jr.	CzRep-Jr.	26	14	14	28	40	....	....	....	....	....
2003-04	Litvinov Jr.	CzRep-Jr.	23	21	14	35	56	1	0	0	0	0
	Litvinov	CzRep	37	4	2	6	10	....	....	....	....	....
	Usti n. L.	CzRep-2	1	1	0	1	0	....	....	....	....	....
	SK HC Banik Most	CzRep-3	....	....	....	....	....	1	0	0	0	2
2004-05	Ottawa 67's	OHL	59	21	30	51	45	21	6	14	20	8
2005-06	Cleveland Barons	AHL	76	14	22	36	88	....	....	....	....	....
2006-07	Worcester Sharks	AHL	78	12	28	40	64	6	0	2	2	6

KASSIAN, Matt — (KAS-ee-uhn, MAT) — MIN.

Left wing. Shoots left. 6'4", 238 lbs. Born, Edmonton, Alta., October 28, 1986.
(Minnesota's 2nd choice, 57th overall, in 2005 Entry Draft).

			Regular Season					Playoffs				
Season	Club	League	GP	G	A	Pts	PIM	GP	G	A	Pts	PIM
2002-03	Sherwood Park	AJHL	33	5	7	12	38	....	....	....	....	....
2003-04	Vancouver Giants	WHL	37	1	0	1	42	3	0	0	0	4
2004-05	Vancouver Giants	WHL	41	0	3	3	89	....	....	....	....	....
	Kamloops Blazers	WHL	28	3	0	3	83	6	1	2	3	14
2005-06	Kamloops Blazers	WHL	67	5	6	11	147	....	....	....	....	....
2006-07	Kamloops Blazers	WHL	72	8	10	18	162	4	0	1	1	0

KATIC, Mark — (KA-tihk, MAHRK) — NYI

Defense. Shoots left. 5'10", 180 lbs. Born, Timmins, Ont., May 9, 1989.
(NY Islanders' 1st choice, 62nd overall, in 2007 Entry Draft).

			Regular Season					Playoffs				
Season	Club	League	GP	G	A	Pts	PIM	GP	G	A	Pts	PIM
2003-04	Timmins Majors	GNMHL	40	12	20	32	35	....	....	....	....	....
2004-05	Timmins Majors	GNMHL	35	11	21	32	74	....	....	....	....	....
2005-06	Sarnia Sting	OHL	51	5	29	34	33	....	....	....	....	....
2006-07	Sarnia Sting	OHL	68	5	35	40	31	4	1	3	4	8

KAZIONOV, Denis — (ka-zee-OH-nahv, DEH-nihs) — T.B.

Left wing. Shoots left. 6'3", 187 lbs. Born, Perm, USSR, December 8, 1987.
(Tampa Bay's 4th choice, 198th overall, in 2006 Entry Draft).

			Regular Season					Playoffs				
Season	Club	League	GP	G	A	Pts	PIM	GP	G	A	Pts	PIM
2003-04	CSKA Moscow 2	Russia-3	2	0	1	1	2	....	....	....	....	....
2004-05	Dyn'o Moscow 2	Russia-3	STATISTICS NOT AVAILABLE									
2005-06	HK MVD-THK Tver	Russia-3	31	6	13	19	34	....	....	....	....	....
	MVD	Russia	26	0	0	0	12	3	0	0	0	0
2006-07	THK Tver	Russia-3	13	23	15	38	42	....	....	....	....	....
	MVD	Russia	24	2	0	2	8	2	0	0	0	2

KAZIONOV, Dmitri — (ka-zee-OH-nahv, dih-MEE-tree) — T.B.

Center. Shoots left. 6'3", 185 lbs. Born, Moscow, USSR, May 13, 1984.
(Tampa Bay's 2nd choice, 100th overall, in 2002 Entry Draft).

			Regular Season					Playoffs				
Season	Club	League	GP	G	A	Pts	PIM	GP	G	A	Pts	PIM
99-2000	Dyn'o Moscow 2	Russia-3	2	1	0	1	0	....	....	....	....	....
2000-01	THK Tver	Russia-2	33	1	1	2	6	....	....	....	....	....
2001-02	HK CSKA Moscow	Russia-2	2	0	1	1	0	....	....	....	....	....
	HK CSKA 2	Russia-3	10	1	0	1	4	....	....	....	....	....
	Lada Togliatti	Russia	3	0	0	0	0	....	....	....	....	....
	Lada Togliatti 2	Russia-3	16	10	9	19	0	....	....	....	....	....
2002-03	Lada Togliatti	Russia	5	0	1	1	4	....	....	....	....	....
	Lada Togliatti 2	Russia-3	34	14	13	27	26	....	....	....	....	....
2003-04	Lada Togliatti 2	Russia-3	5	3	2	5	0	4	0	0	0	0
	Lada Togliatti	Russia	47	5	5	10	34	5	0	0	0	4
2004-05	Lada Togliatti	Russia	46	3	7	10	32	2	0	0	0	0
2005-06	Lada Togliatti	Russia	13	0	3	3	18	....	....	....	....	....
	Dynamo Moscow	Russia	27	2	2	4	24	4	1	0	1	6
2006-07	Ak Bars Kazan	Russia	48	10	11	21	34	13	2	3	5	4

KELLER, Justin — (KEHL-uhr, JUHS-tihn) — T.B.

Left wing. Shoots left. 5'11", 185 lbs. Born, Nelson, B.C., March 4, 1986.
(Tampa Bay's 8th choice, 245th overall, in 2004 Entry Draft).

			Regular Season					Playoffs				
Season	Club	League	GP	G	A	Pts	PIM	GP	G	A	Pts	PIM
2001-02	Spokane Chiefs	WHL	25	7	6	13	10	....	....	....	....	....
	Saskatoon Blades	WHL	36	7	6	13	6	2	0	0	0	2
2002-03	Saskatoon Blades	WHL	2	0	0	0	0	....	....	....	....	....
	Regina Pats	WHL	16	3	3	6	6	....	....	....	....	....
2003-04	Kelowna Rockets	WHL	72	25	21	46	44	17	4	5	9	18
2004-05	Kelowna Rockets	WHL	72	31	22	53	103	23	12	10	22	44
2005-06	Kelowna Rockets	WHL	72	*51	37	88	82	12	3	6	9	14
2006-07	Springfield Falcons	AHL	60	13	11	24	26	....	....	....	....	....

WHL West First All-Star Team (2006)

KEMP, T.J. — (KEHMP, TEE-JAY) — EDM.

Defense. Shoots left. 5'11", 197 lbs. Born, Pickering, Ont., July 3, 1981.

			Regular Season					Playoffs				
Season	Club	League	GP	G	A	Pts	PIM	GP	G	A	Pts	PIM
2001-02	Mercyhurst	MAAC	31	6	13	19	18	....	....	....	....	....
2002-03	Mercyhurst	MAAC	37	11	16	27	39	....	....	....	....	....
2003-04	Mercyhurst	AH	34	5	21	26	42	....	....	....	....	....
2004-05	Mercyhurst	AH	31	10	18	28	78	....	....	....	....	....
	Missouri	UHL	6	1	2	3	4	....	....	....	....	....
2005-06	Peoria Rivermen	AHL	3	0	0	0	2	....	....	....	....	....
	Iowa Stars	AHL	3	0	0	0	0	....	....	....	....	....
	Milwaukee	AHL	2	0	0	0	2	....	....	....	....	....
	Bridgeport	AHL	6	0	0	0	0	....	....	....	....	....
	Reading Royals	ECHL	60	13	27	40	54	4	1	1	2	2
2006-07	Manchester	AHL	65	5	33	38	56	14	2	5	7	12

Signed as a free agent by **Edmonton**, July 17, 2007.

KEMPE, Mario — (KEHM-peh, MAHR-ee-oh) — PHI.

Center. Shoots left. 6', 185 lbs. Born, Kramfors, Sweden, September 19, 1988.
(Philadelphia's 4th choice, 122nd overall, in 2007 Entry Draft).

			Regular Season					Playoffs				
Season	Club	League	GP	G	A	Pts	PIM	GP	G	A	Pts	PIM
2003-04	Hoga Kusten	Sweden-4	STATISTICS NOT AVAILABLE									
2004-05	MODO U18	Swe-U18	14	5	7	12	40	4	1	1	2	4
2005-06	MODO U18	Swe-U18	6	4	2	6	29	2	0	2	2	0
	MODO Jr.	Swe-Jr.	36	20	12	32	16	2	0	0	0	10
2006-07	St. John's	QMJHL	62	23	19	42	51	4	0	0	0	2

KENNEDY, Tim — (KEH-nuh-dee, TIHM) — BUF.

Left wing. Shoots left. 5'9", 176 lbs. Born, Buffalo, NY, April 30, 1986.
(Washington's 6th choice, 181st overall, in 2005 Entry Draft).

			Regular Season					Playoffs				
Season	Club	League	GP	G	A	Pts	PIM	GP	G	A	Pts	PIM
2003-04	Sioux City	USHL	56	9	10	19	42	7	2	2	4	6
2004-05	Sioux City	USHL	54	30	31	61	112	13	*6	*11	*17	18
2005-06	Michigan State	CCHA	29	4	15	19	31	....	....	....	....	....
2006-07	Michigan State	CCHA	42	18	25	43	49	....	....	....	....	....

USHL Second All-Star Team (2005) • NCAA Championship All-Tournament Team (2007)

Traded to **Buffalo** by **Washington** for Buffalo's 6th round choice (Mathieu Perreault) in 2006 Entry Draft, July 30, 2005.

KENNEDY, Tyler — (KEH-nuh-dee, TIGH-luhr) — PIT.

Center. Shoots right. 5'11", 183 lbs. Born, Sault Ste. Marie, Ont., July 15, 1986.
(Pittsburgh's 6th choice, 99th overall, in 2004 Entry Draft).

			Regular Season					Playoffs				
Season	Club	League	GP	G	A	Pts	PIM	GP	G	A	Pts	PIM
2002-03	Sault Ste. Marie	OHL	61	5	10	15	28	4	0	0	0	0
2003-04	Sault Ste. Marie	OHL	63	16	26	42	28	....	....	....	....	....
2004-05	Sault Ste. Marie	OHL	61	21	36	57	37	4	1	3	4	4
2005-06	Sault Ste. Marie	OHL	64	22	48	70	60	4	1	2	3	2
2006-07	Wilkes-Barre	AHL	40	12	25	37	20	....	....	....	....	....

KESSEL, Blake — (KEH-suhl, BLAYK) — NYI

Defense. Shoots right. 6'1", 210 lbs. Born, Madison, WI, April 13, 1989.
(NY Islanders' 4th choice, 166th overall, in 2007 Entry Draft).

			Regular Season					Playoffs				
Season	Club	League	GP	G	A	Pts	PIM	GP	G	A	Pts	PIM
2005-06	Madison Capitols	MAHL	62	33	47	80	....	....	....	....	....	....
2006-07	Waterloo	USHL	59	11	27	38	38	9	1	5	6	8

• Signed Letter of Intent to attend **University of New Hampshire** (Hockey East) in fall of 2008.

KHOMITSKI, Vadim — (khoh-MIHT-skee, va-DEEM) — DAL.

Defense. Shoots left. 6'1", 185 lbs. Born, Voskresensk, USSR, July 21, 1982.
(Dallas' 5th choice, 123rd overall, in 2000 Entry Draft).

			Regular Season					Playoffs				
Season	Club	League	GP	G	A	Pts	PIM	GP	G	A	Pts	PIM
1998-99	Voskresensk	Russia	9	0	0	0	10	....	....	....	....	....
99-2000	Voskresensk	Russia-2	17	0	0	0	31	....	....	....	....	....
	HK Moscow	Russia-2	11	0	1	1	10	....	....	....	....	....
2000-01	HK Moscow	Russia-2	44	2	7	9	89	....	....	....	....	....
2001-02	HK CSKA Moscow	Russia-2	68	2	18	20	63	....	....	....	....	....
2002-03	CSKA Moscow	Russia	51	3	2	5	58	....	....	....	....	....
2003-04	CSKA Moscow	Russia	54	3	3	6	46	....	....	....	....	....
2004-05	CSKA Moscow	Russia	60	1	5	6	105	....	....	....	....	....
2005-06	CSKA Moscow	Russia	51	5	6	11	110	7	0	0	0	6
2006-07	Iowa Stars	AHL	9	1	6	7	24	....	....	....	....	....
	Mytischi	Russia	29	6	5	11	50	9	1	1	2	22

KHOMUTOV, Ivan — (khoh-moo-TAWF, ee-VAHN) — N.J.

Center. Shoots left. 6'3", 210 lbs. Born, Saratov, USSR, March 11, 1985.
(New Jersey's 3rd choice, 93rd overall, in 2003 Entry Draft).

			Regular Season					Playoffs				
Season	Club	League	GP	G	A	Pts	PIM	GP	G	A	Pts	PIM
2001-02	HK CSKA 2	Russia-3	30	11	8	19	14	....	....	....	....	....
2002-03	Elektrostal	Russia-2	20	1	1	2	8	....	....	....	....	....
2003-04	London Knights	OHL	40	9	12	21	25	15	3	1	4	7
2004-05	Albany River Rats	AHL	66	6	11	17	30	....	....	....	....	....
2005-06	Albany River Rats	AHL	60	9	20	29	44	....	....	....	....	....
2006-07	Lowell Devils	AHL	3	1	1	2	2	....	....	....	....	....
	Trenton Titans	ECHL	5	0	1	1	2	....	....	....	....	....

KIDD, Josh — (KIHD, JAWSH) — L.A.

Defense. Shoots right. 6'5", 220 lbs. Born, Sundridge, Ont., November 16, 1988.
(Los Angeles' 9th choice, 184th overall, in 2007 Entry Draft).

			Regular Season					Playoffs				
Season	Club	League	GP	G	A	Pts	PIM	GP	G	A	Pts	PIM
2003-04	Richmond Hill	Minor-ON	75	7	14	21	126	....	....	....	....	....
2004-05	Erie Otters	OHL	57	0	0	0	11	4	0	0	0	0
2005-06	Erie Otters	OHL	68	4	6	10	53	....	....	....	....	....
2006-07	Erie Otters	OHL	64	9	18	27	96	....	....	....	....	....

KILLORN, Alexander — (KIHL-ohrn, al-ehx-AN-duhr) — T.B.

Center. Shoots left. 6', 161 lbs. Born, Halifax, N.S., September 14, 1989.
(Tampa Bay's 3rd choice, 77th overall, in 2007 Entry Draft).

			Regular Season					Playoffs				
Season	Club	League	GP	G	A	Pts	PIM	GP	G	A	Pts	PIM
2005-06	Lac St-Louis Lions	QAAA	43	18	34	52	94	10	9	6	15	8
2006-07	Deerfield Academy	High-MA	25	18	14	32	....	....	....	....	....	....

• Signed Letter of Intent to attend **Harvard University** (ECACHL) in fall of 2008.

KINCH, Matt — (KIHNCH, MATT) — OTT.

Defense. Shoots left. 5'11", 185 lbs. Born, Red Deer, Alta., February 17, 1980.
(Buffalo's 8th choice, 146th overall, in 1999 Entry Draft).

			Regular Season					Playoffs				
Season	Club	League	GP	G	A	Pts	PIM	GP	G	A	Pts	PIM
1995-96	Red Deer	AMHL	35	6	17	23	31	....	....	....	....	....
	Calgary Hitmen	WHL	1	0	1	1	2	....	....	....	....	....
1996-97	Calgary Hitmen	WHL	64	10	22	32	31	....	....	....	....	....
1997-98	Calgary Hitmen	WHL	55	7	24	31	13	18	3	2	5	4
1998-99	Calgary Hitmen	WHL	68	14	69	83	16	21	8	15	23	59
99-2000	Calgary Hitmen	WHL	62	14	61	75	24	13	2	12	14	8
2000-01	Calgary Hitmen	WHL	70	18	66	84	52	12	3	6	9	6
2001-02	Hartford Wolf Pack	AHL	40	1	7	8	4	....	....	....	....	....
	Charlotte	ECHL	26	3	12	15	13	5	3	2	5	0
2002-03	Hartford Wolf Pack	AHL	66	7	22	29	28	2	0	0	0	0
2003-04	Hartford Wolf Pack	AHL	67	1	19	20	38	1	0	0	0	0
2004-05	Salzburg	Austria	37	1	12	13	18	....	....	....	....	....
2005-06	Langnau	Swiss	25	1	4	5	14	....	....	....	....	....
	ERC Ingolstadt	Germany	16	1	2	3	16	7	0	0	0	4
2006-07	Straubing Tigers	Germany	51	4	20	24	36	....	....	....	....	....

WHL East First All-Star Team (1999, 2001) • Memorial Cup Tournament All-Star Team (1999) • Canadian Major Junior Sportsman of the Year (1999) • WHL East Second All-Star Team (2000) • Canadian Major Junior First All-Star Team (2001)

Signed as a free agent by **NY Rangers**, June 26, 2001. Signed as a free agent by **Salzburg** (Austria), August 11, 2004. Signed as a free agent by **Ottawa**, July 17, 2007.

KINDL, Jakub (KEEHN-duhl, YA-kuhb) DET.

Defense. Shoots left. 6'3", 199 lbs. Born, Sumperk, Czech., February 10, 1987.
(Detroit's 1st choice, 19th overall, in 2005 Entry Draft).

			Regular Season					Playoffs				
Season	Club	League	GP	G	A	Pts	PIM	GP	G	A	Pts	PIM
2002-03	HC Pardubice U17	CzR-U17	3	0	3	3	10	....	....	....	....	....
	HC Pardubice Jr.	CzRep-Jr.	27	0	3	3	46	....	....	....	....	....
	Pardubice	CzRep	1	0	0	0	0	....	....	....	....	....
2003-04	HC Pardubice U17	CzR-U17	2	0	1	1	6	....	....	....	....	....
	HC Pardubice Jr.	CzRep-Jr.	48	4	14	18	108	....	....	....	....	....
	Hr. Kralove	CzRep-2	1	0	0	0	0	1	0	0	0	0
2004-05	Kitchener Rangers	OHL	62	3	11	14	92	12	0	0	0	22
2005-06	Kitchener Rangers	OHL	60	12	46	58	112	5	1	0	1	10
	Grand Rapids	AHL	3	0	1	1	2	....	....	....	....	....
2006-07	Kitchener Rangers	OHL	54	11	44	55	142	9	2	9	11	8
	Grand Rapids	AHL	....	....	....	....	....	7	0	2	2	0

OHL Second All-Star Team (2007)

KING, Dwight (KIHNG, DWIGHT) L.A.

Center/Left wing. Shoots left. 6'2", 221 lbs. Born, Meadowlake, Sask., July 5, 1989.
(Los Angeles' 6th choice, 109th overall, in 2007 Entry Draft).

			Regular Season					Playoffs				
Season	Club	League	GP	G	A	Pts	PIM	GP	G	A	Pts	PIM
2004-05	Beardy's	SMHL	44	26	30	56	16	3	0	1	1	4
	Lethbridge	WHL	7	0	0	0	2	4	0	0	0	2
2005-06	Lethbridge	WHL	68	8	8	16	22	6	0	0	0	6
2006-07	Lethbridge	WHL	62	12	32	44	39	....	....	....	....	....

KISHEL, Scott (KIH-shuhl, SKAWT) MTL.

Defense. Shoots left. 5'11", 157 lbs. Born, Virginia, MN, April 21, 1989.
(Montreal's 9th choice, 192nd overall, in 2007 Entry Draft).

			Regular Season					Playoffs				
Season	Club	League	GP	G	A	Pts	PIM	GP	G	A	Pts	PIM
2004-05	Virginia Blue Devils	High-MN	....	4	9	13	....	....	....	....	....	....
2005-06	Virginia Blue Devils	High-MN	....	5	25	30	....	....	....	....	....	....
2006-07	Virginia Blue Devils	High-MN	24	14	34	48	....	....	....	....	....	....

• Signed Letter of Intent to attend **University of Minnesota-Duluth** (WCHA) in fall of 2008.

KLIMOV, Valeri (KLEE-mawf, VAL-uhr-ee) N.J.

Defense. Shoots left. 6'3", 200 lbs. Born, Moscow, USSR, July 17, 1986.
(New Jersey's 7th choice, 282nd overall, in 2004 Entry Draft).

			Regular Season					Playoffs				
Season	Club	League	GP	G	A	Pts	PIM	GP	G	A	Pts	PIM
2001-02	Spartak Moscow 2	Russia-3	24	1	1	2	6	....	....	....	....	....
2002-03	Spartak Moscow 2	Russia-3	5	2	1	3	8	....	....	....	....	....
2003-04	Spartak Moscow 2	Russia-3	4	1	0	1	0	....	....	....	....	....
2004-05	Spartak Moscow	Russia	6	0	0	0	2	....	....	....	....	....
2005-06	Spartak Moscow 2	Russia-3	17	1	4	5	20	....	....	....	....	....
	Spartak Moscow	Russia	23	1	0	1	4	2	0	0	0	2
2006-07	Khimik	Russia-2	3	0	1	1	2	....	....	....	....	....

KLOTZ, Garrett (KLAWTZ, GAIR-reht) PHI.

Left wing. Shoots left. 6'6", 225 lbs. Born, Regina, Sask., November 27, 1988.
(Philadelphia's 3rd choice, 66th overall, in 2007 Entry Draft).

			Regular Season					Playoffs				
Season	Club	League	GP	G	A	Pts	PIM	GP	G	A	Pts	PIM
2004-05	Reg. Midget Hawks	SMMHL	STATISTICS NOT AVAILABLE									
	Reg. Pat Canadians	SMHL	5	0	1	1	0	....	....	....	....	....
2005-06	Red Deer Rebels	WHL	35	2	0	2	26	....	....	....	....	....
2006-07	Saskatoon Blades	WHL	63	2	2	4	107	....	....	....	....	....

KLUBERTANZ, Kyle (KLOO-buhr-tanz, KIGHL) ANA.

Defense. Shoots right. 6', 186 lbs. Born, Madison, WI, September 23, 1985.
(Anaheim's 3rd choice, 74th overall, in 2004 Entry Draft).

			Regular Season					Playoffs				
Season	Club	League	GP	G	A	Pts	PIM	GP	G	A	Pts	PIM
2002-03	Green Bay	USHL	60	8	26	34	74	....	....	....	....	....
2003-04	Green Bay	USHL	57	6	21	27	124	....	....	....	....	....
2004-05	U. of Wisconsin	WCHA	41	3	15	18	64	....	....	....	....	....
2005-06	U. of Wisconsin	WCHA	43	4	17	21	44	....	....	....	....	....
2006-07	U. of Wisconsin	WCHA	34	1	12	13	46	....	....	....	....	....

WCHA All-Rookie Team (2005)

KNACKSTEDT, Jordan (NAK-stehd, JOHR-dahn) BOS.

Right wing. Shoots right. 6'3", 191 lbs. Born, Saskatoon, Sask., September 28, 1988.
(Boston's 6th choice, 189th overall, in 2007 Entry Draft).

			Regular Season					Playoffs				
Season	Club	League	GP	G	A	Pts	PIM	GP	G	A	Pts	PIM
2003-04	Beardy's	SMHL	44	22	19	41	20	4	2	1	3	0
2004-05	Red Deer Rebels	WHL	52	1	2	3	34	7	0	0	0	2
2005-06	Red Deer Rebels	WHL	72	12	28	40	36	....	....	....	....	....
2006-07	Red Deer Rebels	WHL	33	10	7	17	54	....	....	....	....	....
	Moose Jaw	WHL	39	13	26	39	44	....	....	....	....	....

KNYAZEV, Igor (kuh-NYA-zhev, EE-gohr) PHX.

Defense. Shoots left. 6', 208 lbs. Born, Elektrostal, USSR, January 27, 1983.
(Carolina's 1st choice, 15th overall, in 2001 Entry Draft).

			Regular Season					Playoffs				
Season	Club	League	GP	G	A	Pts	PIM	GP	G	A	Pts	PIM
99-2000	Spartak Moscow 2	Russia-3	13	2	4	6	74	....	....	....	....	....
	Spartak Moscow	Russia-2	26	1	1	2	6	....	....	....	....	....
2000-01	Spartak Moscow	Russia-2	53	6	5	11	101	....	....	....	....	....
2001-02	Spartak Moscow	Russia	3	0	0	0	8	....	....	....	....	....
	Spartak Moscow 2	Russia-3	2	0	1	1	0	....	....	....	....	....
	Ak Bars Kazan	Russia	14	0	1	1	4	3	0	0	0	0
2002-03	Lowell	AHL	68	2	5	7	68	....	....	....	....	....
2003-04	Springfield Falcons	AHL	72	1	6	7	61	....	....	....	....	....
2004-05	Voskresensk	Russia	29	0	2	2	57	....	....	....	....	....
2005-06	Mytischi	Russia	21	3	1	4	36	....	....	....	....	....
2006-07	Dynamo Moscow	Russia	14	0	2	2	22	....	....	....	....	....
	Vityaz Chekhov	Russia	12	0	0	0	82	3	0	0	0	2

Traded to **Phoenix** by **Carolina** with David Tanabe for Danny Markov and Edmonton's 3rd round choice (previously acquired, later traded to NY Rangers - NY Rangers selected Billy Ryan) in 2004 Entry Draft, June 21, 2003. Signed as a free agent by **Voskresensk** (Russia), September, 2004.

KOHN, Dustin (KOHN, DUHS-tihn) NYI

Defense. Shoots left. 6'2", 182 lbs. Born, Edmonton, Alta., February 2, 1987.
(NY Islanders' 2nd choice, 46th overall, in 2005 Entry Draft).

			Regular Season					Playoffs				
Season	Club	League	GP	G	A	Pts	PIM	GP	G	A	Pts	PIM
2003-04	Calgary Hitmen	WHL	52	3	6	9	13	7	0	1	1	2
2004-05	Calgary Hitmen	WHL	71	8	35	43	61	12	0	4	4	6
2005-06	Calgary Hitmen	WHL	38	2	12	14	20	....	....	....	....	....
	Brandon	WHL	31	2	13	15	30	6	0	4	4	10
	Bridgeport	AHL	2	0	0	0	0	....	....	....	....	....
2006-07	Brandon	WHL	61	5	45	50	77	11	1	8	9	18

KOISTINEN, Ville (KOIS-tih-nehn, VIHL-ee) NSH.

Defense. Shoots left. 5'11", 190 lbs. Born, Oulu, Finland, June 17, 1982.

			Regular Season					Playoffs				
Season	Club	League	GP	G	A	Pts	PIM	GP	G	A	Pts	PIM
1998-99	Ilves Tampere U18	Fin-U18	34	4	10	14	86	....	....	....	....	....
	Ilves Tampere Jr.	Fin-Jr.	1	0	0	0	2	....	....	....	....	....
99-2000	Ilves Tampere U18	Fin-U18	14	4	6	10	69	....	....	....	....	....
	Ilves Tampere Jr.	Fin-Jr.	34	4	2	6	40	....	....	....	....	....
2000-01	Ilves Tampere	Finland	6	0	0	0	0	5	0	1	1	0
	Ilves Tampere Jr.	Fin-Jr.	26	1	8	9	101	....	....	....	....	....
2001-02	Ilves Tampere	Finland	53	1	8	9	42	....	....	....	....	....
	Ilves Tampere Jr.	Fin-Jr.	6	2	2	4	16	....	....	....	....	....
2002-03	Ilves Tampere	Finland	18	4	1	5	8	....	....	....	....	....
	Ilves Tampere Jr.	Fin-Jr.	1	0	0	0	10	....	....	....	....	....
2003-04	Ilves Tampere	Finland	54	7	16	23	51	7	0	2	2	0
2004-05	Ilves Tampere	Finland	52	6	14	20	69	3	0	0	0	0
2005-06	Ilves Tampere	Finland	56	8	26	34	70	4	0	1	1	2
2006-07	Milwaukee	AHL	59	9	32	41	44	4	0	2	2	4

Signed as a free agent by **Nashville**, May 11, 2006.

KOLARIK, Chad (koh-LAHR-ihk, CHAD) PHX.

Center. Shoots right. 5'10", 175 lbs. Born, Abington, PA, January 26, 1986.
(Phoenix's 7th choice, 199th overall, in 2004 Entry Draft).

			Regular Season					Playoffs				
Season	Club	League	GP	G	A	Pts	PIM	GP	G	A	Pts	PIM
2002-03	USNTDP	U-17	21	14	10	24	4	....	....	....	....	....
	USNTDP	NAHL	44	16	22	38	43	....	....	....	....	....
2003-04	USNTDP	U-18	45	18	20	38	16	....	....	....	....	....
	USNTDP	NAHL	10	3	4	7	4	....	....	....	....	....
2004-05	U. of Michigan	CCHA	42	18	17	35	53	....	....	....	....	....
2005-06	U. of Michigan	CCHA	41	12	26	38	30	....	....	....	....	....
2006-07	U. of Michigan	CCHA	41	18	27	45	24	....	....	....	....	....

KOLEHMAINEN, Janne (koh-leh-MAYN-ehn, YAH-nee) OTT.

Left wing. Shoots left. 6'3", 209 lbs. Born, Lappeenranta, Finland, March 22, 1986.
(Ottawa's 5th choice, 115th overall, in 2005 Entry Draft).

			Regular Season					Playoffs				
Season	Club	League	GP	G	A	Pts	PIM	GP	G	A	Pts	PIM
2002-03	SaiPa U18	Fin-U18	23	11	8	19	77	....	....	....	....	....
	SaiPa Jr.	Fin-Jr.	1	0	0	0	0	....	....	....	....	....
2003-04	SaiPa U18	Fin-U18	6	3	1	4	18	....	....	....	....	....
	SaiPa Jr.	Fin-Jr.	30	4	7	11	26	4	3	0	3	4
	SaiPa	Finland	6	0	0	0	2	....	....	....	....	....
2004-05	SaiPa Jr.	Fin-Jr.	13	2	4	6	24	2	1	1	2	0
	SaiPa	Finland	29	1	1	2	8	....	....	....	....	....
2005-06	SaiPa Jr.	Fin-Jr.	12	3	2	5	12	3	2	0	2	14
	Suomi U20	Finland-2	3	0	0	0	2	....	....	....	....	....
	SaiPa	Finland	36	0	2	2	45	8	0	1	1	4
2006-07	SaiPa Jr.	Fin-Jr.	1	0	0	0	0	....	....	....	....	....
	SaiPa	Finland	50	4	5	9	40	....	....	....	....	....

KOLLAR, Tomas (koh-LAHR, TAW-mahsh)

Left wing. Shoots left. 6'2", 211 lbs. Born, Stockholm, Sweden, April 20, 1982.
(Detroit's 6th choice, 226th overall, in 2003 Entry Draft).

			Regular Season					Playoffs				
Season	Club	League	GP	G	A	Pts	PIM	GP	G	A	Pts	PIM
99-2000	Hammarby Jr.	Swe-Jr.	42	10	15	25	52	....	....	....	....	....
2000-01	Hammarby Jr.	Swe-Jr.	8	2	4	6	12	....	....	....	....	....
	Hammarby	Sweden-2	23	3	2	5	10	....	....	....	....	....
2001-02	Hammarby	Sweden-2	46	9	9	18	24	2	3	0	3	2
	Hammarby Jr.	Swe-Jr.	3	0	3	3	6	2	1	0	1	0
2002-03	Hammarby	Sweden-2	27	10	8	18	45	....	....	....	....	....
2003-04	Djurgarden	Sweden	50	6	8	14	22	4	0	0	0	0
2004-05	Skelleftea AIK HK	Sweden-2	17	9	5	14	16	....	....	....	....	....
	Djurgarden	Sweden	32	1	6	7	46	12	0	1	1	30
2005-06	Sodertalje SK	Sweden	50	7	8	15	111	....	....	....	....	....
	Sodertalje SK	Sweden-Q	9	2	3	5	45	....	....	....	....	....
2006-07	Sodertalje SK	Sweden-2	42	15	18	33	98	....	....	....	....	....

KOLOSOV, Sergei (KOH-leh-sawf, SAIR-gay) DET.

Defense. Shoots left. 6'4", 187 lbs. Born, Novopolotsk, USSR, May 22, 1986.
(Detroit's 3rd choice, 151st overall, in 2004 Entry Draft).

			Regular Season					Playoffs				
Season	Club	League	GP	G	A	Pts	PIM	GP	G	A	Pts	PIM
2003-04	Dynamo Minsk	Belarus	STATISTICS NOT AVAILABLE									
2004-05	Dynamo Minsk	BelOpen	37	2	6	8	24	....	....	....	....	....
	Yunost-Minsk	BelOpen	1	0	0	0	2	9	0	0	0	4
2005-06	Cedar Rapids	USHL	50	2	8	10	66	8	0	0	0	10
2006-07	Cedar Rapids	USHL	51	1	10	11	79	5	0	0	0	4

KOLTSOV, Ivan (kohlt-SAHV, ee-VAHN) EDM.

Defense. Shoots left. 6'2", 182 lbs. Born, Cherepovets, USSR, March 7, 1984.
(Edmonton's 6th choice, 106th overall, in 2002 Entry Draft).

			Regular Season					Playoffs				
Season	Club	League	GP	G	A	Pts	PIM	GP	G	A	Pts	PIM
2001-02	Cherepovets 2	Russia-3	27	2	2	4	24	....	....	....	....	....
2002-03	Leninogorsk	Russia-2	1	0	1	1	2	....	....	....	....	....
	Cherepovets 2	Russia-3	34	4	7	11	26	....	....	....	....	....
2003-04	Cherepovets 2	Russia-3	14	2	2	4	20	....	....	....	....	....
2004-05	HK Lipetsk	Russia-2	10	2	0	2	2	....	....	....	....	....
	HK Belgorod	Russia-2	30	1	2	3	32	....	....	....	....	....
2005-06	Dizel Penza	Russia-2	40	0	4	4	22	8	0	0	0	4
2006-07	Mechel	Russia-2	17	0	1	1	12	....	....	....	....	....

KOLTSOV, Kiril (kohlt-SAHV, kih-RIHL) VAN.

Defense. Shoots left. 5'11", 183 lbs. Born, Chelyabinsk, USSR, February 1, 1983.
(Vancouver's 1st choice, 49th overall, in 2002 Entry Draft).

			Regular Season					Playoffs				
Season	Club	League	GP	G	A	Pts	PIM	GP	G	A	Pts	PIM
1998-99	Streetsville Derbys	OPJHL	20	5	7	12	4	....	....	....	....	....
99-2000	Omsk 2	Russia-3	27	0	7	7	30	....	....	....	....	....
	Avangard Omsk	Russia	2	0	0	0	0	....	....	....	....	....
2000-01	Avangard Omsk	Russia	39	0	1	1	20	16	1	3	4	12
2001-02	Avangard Omsk	Russia	41	1	5	6	34	11	1	0	1	8
2002-03	Avangard Omsk	Russia	45	4	8	12	54	12	1	3	4	8
2003-04	Manitoba Moose	AHL	74	7	25	32	62	....	....	....	....	....
2004-05	Manitoba Moose	AHL	28	3	14	17	42	....	....	....	....	....
	Avangard Omsk	Russia	22	2	2	4	46	10	0	1	1	18
2005-06	Avangard Omsk	Russia	43	9	8	17	98	13	4	5	9	10
2006-07	Avangard Omsk	Russia	51	9	31	40	46	9	3	3	6	12

KOMADOSKI, Neil (koh-mah-DAW-skee, NEEL)

Defense. Shoots left. 6'1", 215 lbs. Born, Chesterfield, MO, February 10, 1982.
(Ottawa's 3rd choice, 81st overall, in 2001 Entry Draft).

			Regular Season					Playoffs				
Season	Club	League	GP	G	A	Pts	PIM	GP	G	A	Pts	PIM
1997-98	Aurora Tigers	OPJHL	1	0	0	0	0	....	....	....	....	....
1998-99	USNTDP	NAHL	49	3	11	14	222	....	....	....	....	....
99-2000	USNTDP	U-18	6	0	2	2	12	....	....	....	....	....
	USNTDP	USHL	50	7	8	15	202	....	....	....	....	....
	USNTDP	NAHL	1	1	0	1	0	....	....	....	....	....
2000-01	U. of Notre Dame	CCHA	30	2	5	7	106	....	....	....	....	....
2001-02	U. of Notre Dame	CCHA	37	2	9	11	100	....	....	....	....	....
2002-03	U. of Notre Dame	CCHA	40	1	23	24	46	....	....	....	....	....
2003-04	U. of Notre Dame	CCHA	39	5	15	20	48	....	....	....	....	....
	Binghamton	AHL	3	0	0	0	2	1	0	0	0	0
2004-05	Binghamton	AHL	36	2	1	3	68	....	....	....	....	....
2005-06	Binghamton	AHL	41	0	5	5	71	....	....	....	....	....
2006-07	Binghamton	AHL	68	3	4	7	81	....	....	....	....	....

KOMAROV, Leo (koh-mah-RAWV, L'YAY-oh) TOR.

Center. Shoots left. 5'10", 187 lbs. Born, Narva, USSR, January 23, 1987.
(Toronto's 7th choice, 180th overall, in 2006 Entry Draft).

			Regular Season					Playoffs				
Season	Club	League	GP	G	A	Pts	PIM	GP	G	A	Pts	PIM
2003-04	Sport Vaasa U18	Fin-U18	30	9	15	24	8	....	....	....	....	....
2004-05	Assat Pori U18	Fin-U18	9	4	5	9	62	....	....	....	....	....
	Assat Pori Jr.	Fin-Jr.	38	8	6	13	59	2	0	0	0	2
2005-06	Suomi U20	Finland-2	5	0	3	3	4	....	....	....	....	....
	Assat Pori Jr.	Fin-Jr.	10	5	6	11	59	2	2	1	3	10
	Assat Pori	Finland	44	3	3	6	106	14	1	3	4	22
2006-07	Suomi U20	Finland-2	1	1	0	1	0	....	....	....	....	....
	Pelicans Lahti	Finland	49	3	9	12	108	6	1	0	1	6

KONTIOLA, Petri (KAWN-tee-oh-la, PEH-tree) CHI.

Center. Shoots right. 6', 197 lbs. Born, Seinajoki, Finland, October 4, 1984.
(Chicago's 12th choice, 196th overall, in 2004 Entry Draft).

			Regular Season					Playoffs				
Season	Club	League	GP	G	A	Pts	PIM	GP	G	A	Pts	PIM
2001-02	Tappara U18	Fin-U18	22	5	3	8	8	2	1	0	1	2
2002-03	Tappara Jr.	Fin-Jr.	36	7	10	17	12	8	3	3	6	0
2003-04	Suomi U20	Finland-2	6	1	1	2	4	....	....	....	....	....
	Tappara Jr.	Fin-Jr.	12	3	12	15	8	10	4	4	8	10
	Tappara Tampere	Finland	39	4	9	13	29	3	1	1	2	0
2004-05	Tappara Jr.	Fin-Jr.	1	1	0	1	0	....	....	....	....	....
	Tappara Tampere	Finland	54	8	17	25	24	8	2	2	4	2
2005-06	Tappara Tampere	Finland	56	9	*35	44	55	6	1	3	4	0
2006-07	Tappara Tampere	Finland	51	12	35	47	50	5	1	3	4	8

KOOPMAN, Kevin (KOOP-man, KEH-vihn) OTT.

Defense. Shoots right. 6'3", 200 lbs. Born, Hope, B.C., June 30, 1988.
(Ottawa's 6th choice, 181st overall, in 2006 Entry Draft).

			Regular Season					Playoffs				
Season	Club	League	GP	G	A	Pts	PIM	GP	G	A	Pts	PIM
2004-05	Beaver Valley	KIJHL	41	4	14	18	45	....	....	....	....	....
2005-06	Beaver Valley	KIJHL	38	14	25	39	64	....	....	....	....	....
	Vernon Vipers	BCHL	8	1	0	1	9	....	....	....	....	....
2006-07	Vernon Vipers	BCHL	45	1	7	8	97	....	....	....	....	....

KIJHL MVP (2006)

KOREIS, Jakub (KOHR-ays, YA-kuhb)

Center. Shoots left. 6'3", 214 lbs. Born, Plzen, Czech., June 26, 1984.
(Phoenix's 1st choice, 19th overall, in 2002 Entry Draft).

			Regular Season					Playoffs				
Season	Club	League	GP	G	A	Pts	PIM	GP	G	A	Pts	PIM
99-2000	HC Plzen U17	CzR-U17	41	21	22	43	44	....	....	....	....	....
	HC Plzen Jr.	CzRep-Jr.	3	2	1	3	2	....	....	....	....	....
2000-01	HC Plzen U17	CzR-U17	9	7	10	17	28	....	....	....	....	....
	HC Plzen Jr.	CzRep-Jr.	43	14	15	29	83	....	....	....	....	....
2001-02	HC Plzen Jr.	CzRep-Jr.	23	14	14	28	38	....	....	....	....	....
	HC Keramika Plzen	CzRep	20	3	0	3	10	....	....	....	....	....
2002-03	HC Keramika Plzen	CzRep	23	1	6	7	8	....	....	....	....	....
	HC Plzen Jr.	CzRep-Jr.	10	3	5	8	28	....	....	....	....	....
2003-04	Guelph Storm	OHL	48	11	28	39	85	22	8	10	18	24
2004-05	Utah Grizzlies	AHL	79	5	6	11	96	....	....	....	....	....
2005-06	San Antonio	AHL	70	3	5	8	74	....	....	....	....	....
2006-07	San Antonio	AHL	77	6	19	25	70	....	....	....	....	....

KORNEEV, Konstantin (kor-NEE-ehv, KAWN-stan-tihn) MTL.

Defense. Shoots right. 5'11", 181 lbs. Born, Moscow, USSR, June 5, 1984.
(Montreal's 6th choice, 275th overall, in 2002 Entry Draft).

			Regular Season					Playoffs				
Season	Club	League	GP	G	A	Pts	PIM	GP	G	A	Pts	PIM
99-2000	Krylja Sovetov 2	Russia-3	1	0	0	0	0	....	....	....	....	....
2000-01	Russia Jr.	Exhib.	12	0	4	4	10	....	....	....	....	....
2001-02	Krylja Sovetov 2	Russia-3	26	9	19	28	44	....	....	....	....	....
	Krylja Sovetov	Russia	4	0	2	2	0	2	0	0	0	2
2002-03	Krylja Sovetov	Russia	49	2	8	10	28	....	....	....	....	....
2003-04	Ak Bars Kazan	Russia	55	1	4	5	8	8	0	1	1	2
2004-05	Ak Bars Kazan 2	Russia-3	....	6	16	22	....	....	....	....	....	....
	Ak Bars Kazan	Russia	35	0	4	4	10	1	0	0	0	0
2005-06	Ak Bars Kazan	Russia	30	1	3	4	14	4	0	0	0	0
2006-07	CSKA Moscow	Russia	54	8	14	22	40	12	2	4	6	6

KOROSTIN, Sergei (koh-ROH-stihn, SAIR-gay) DAL.

Right wing. Shoots left. 5'11", 180 lbs. Born, Prokopjevsk, USSR, July 5, 1989.
(Dallas' 2nd choice, 64th overall, in 2007 Entry Draft).

			Regular Season					Playoffs				
Season	Club	League	GP	G	A	Pts	PIM	GP	G	A	Pts	PIM
2005-06	Dyn'o Moscow 2	Russia-3	STATISTICS NOT AVAILABLE									
	Dynamo Moscow	Russia	1	0	0	0	0	....	....	....	....	....
2006-07	Dyn'o Moscow 2	Russia-3	STATISTICS NOT AVAILABLE									
	Dynamo Moscow	Russia	7	0	0	0	8	....	....	....	....	....

KORPIKOSKI, Lauri (kohr-pih-KAWS-kee, LOW-ree) NYR

Left wing. Shoots left. 6'1", 190 lbs. Born, Turku, Finland, July 28, 1986.
(NY Rangers' 2nd choice, 19th overall, in 2004 Entry Draft).

			Regular Season					Playoffs				
Season	Club	League	GP	G	A	Pts	PIM	GP	G	A	Pts	PIM
2002-03	TPS Turku U18	Fin-U18	21	7	4	11	10	....	....	....	....	....
2003-04	TPS Turku U18	Fin-U18	....	....	....	....	....	4	5	3	8	16
	TPS Turku Jr.	Fin-Jr.	36	12	8	20	20	4	0	2	2	4
2004-05	TPS Turku Jr.	Fin-Jr.	3	3	0	3	0	....	....	....	....	....
	TPS Turku	Finland	41	0	6	6	12	6	1	0	1	0
2005-06	TPS Turku Jr.	Fin-Jr.	1	1	0	1	2	....	....	....	....	....
	Suomi U20	Finland-2	3	1	3	4	0	....	....	....	....	....
	TPS Turku	Finland	51	3	4	7	16	2	0	1	1	0
	Hartford Wolf Pack	AHL	5	2	1	3	0	11	1	0	1	2
2006-07	Hartford Wolf Pack	AHL	78	11	27	38	23	7	0	0	0	0

KOSMACHEV, Dmitry (kaws-ma-CHEHV, dih-MEE-tree) CBJ

Defense. Shoots right. 6'3", 209 lbs. Born, Nizhny Novgorod, USSR, June 7, 1985.
(Columbus' 3rd choice, 71st overall, in 2003 Entry Draft).

			Regular Season					Playoffs				
Season	Club	League	GP	G	A	Pts	PIM	GP	G	A	Pts	PIM
2001-02	HK CSKA 2	Russia-3	6	1	0	1	2	....	....	....	....	....
	HK CSKA Moscow	Russia-2	49	0	1	1	12	....	....	....	....	....
2002-03	CSKA Moscow	Russia	27	0	0	0	2	....	....	....	....	....
2003-04	CSKA Moscow	Russia	34	0	2	2	12	....	....	....	....	....
2004-05	Nizhny Novgorod	Russia-2	34	3	4	7	22	15	0	1	1	0
2005-06	Mytischi	Russia	38	2	2	4	14	9	0	0	0	4
	Kristall Elektrostal	Russia-3	STATISTICS NOT AVAILABLE									
2006-07	Mytischi	Russia	32	0	0	0	18	9	0	0	0	2

KOSTITSYN, Sergei (kaws-TIHT-sihn, SAIR-gay) MTL.

Left wing. Shoots left. 5'11", 190 lbs. Born, Novopolotsk, USSR, March 20, 1987.
(Montreal's 6th choice, 200th overall, in 2005 Entry Draft).

			Regular Season					Playoffs				
Season	Club	League	GP	G	A	Pts	PIM	GP	G	A	Pts	PIM
2003-04	HK Gomel	EEHL	6	0	1	1	0	....	....	....	....	....
	HK Gomel 2	EEHL-B	6	7	2	9	14	....	....	....	....	....
	Yunior Minsk	EEHL-B	STATISTICS NOT AVAILABLE									
	Yunior Minsk	Belarus	3	0	0	0	0	....	....	....	....	....
	HK Gomel	Belarus	22	5	4	9	4	11	1	2	3	8
2004-05	HK Gomel	BelOpen	40	4	10	14	24	4	2	0	2	12
2005-06	London Knights	OHL	63	26	52	78	78	19	13	24	37	*44
2006-07	London Knights	OHL	59	40	*91	131	76	16	9	12	21	39

KOZAK, Rick (KOH-zak, RIHK) NYR

Right wing. Shoots right. 6'3", 225 lbs. Born, Norway House, Man., August 19, 1985.
(Philadelphia's 7th choice, 95th overall, in 2003 Entry Draft).

			Regular Season					Playoffs				
Season	Club	League	GP	G	A	Pts	PIM	GP	G	A	Pts	PIM
2000-01	Norman	MMMHL	31	17	27	44	166	....	....	....	....	....
2001-02	Swan Valley	MJHL	35	14	21	35	103	4	0	0	0	4
	Prince George	WHL	4	0	0	0	11	....	....	....	....	....
2002-03	Swan Valley	MJHL	25	17	20	37	99	....	....	....	....	....
	Brandon	WHL	38	9	6	15	87	16	6	5	11	51
2003-04	Brandon	WHL	25	5	3	8	83	....	....	....	....	....
	Kamloops Blazers	WHL	29	9	6	15	77	5	1	0	1	12
	Hartford Wolf Pack	AHL	2	0	1	1	0	....	....	....	....	....
2004-05	Kamloops Blazers	WHL	12	3	0	3	33	....	....	....	....	....
	Prince Albert	WHL	39	11	13	24	152	17	6	3	9	58
2005-06	Hartford Wolf Pack	AHL	3	0	0	0	4	....	....	....	....	....
	Charlotte	ECHL	28	7	9	16	68	3	0	0	0	6
2006-07	Charlotte	ECHL	16	3	3	6	79	....	....	....	....	....
	Memphis	CHL	18	14	6	20	61	....	....	....	....	....

Traded to **NY Rangers** by **Philadelphia** with Philadelphia's 2nd round choice (later traded to Atlanta - Atlanta selected Ondrej Pavelec) in 2005 Entry Draft for Vladimir Malakhov, March 8, 2004.

KOZEK, Andrew (KOH-zehk, AN-droo) ATL.

Left wing. Shoots left. 5'11", 190 lbs. Born, Revelstoke, B.C., May 26, 1986.
(Atlanta's 4th choice, 53rd overall, in 2005 Entry Draft).

			Regular Season					Playoffs				
Season	Club	League	GP	G	A	Pts	PIM	GP	G	A	Pts	PIM
2003-04	South Surrey	BCHL	58	19	22	41	67	....	....	....	....	....
2004-05	South Surrey	BCHL	60	48	49	97	81	....	....	....	....	....
2005-06	North Dakota	WCHA	46	7	6	13	22	....	....	....	....	....
2006-07	North Dakota	WCHA	41	5	6	11	12	....	....	....	....	....

KRIKUNOV, Ilia (krih-koo-NAWF, IHL-yah) VAN.

Left wing. Shoots left. 5'11", 169 lbs. Born, Elektrostal, USSR, February 27, 1984.
(Vancouver's 8th choice, 223rd overall, in 2002 Entry Draft).

			Regular Season					Playoffs				
Season	Club	League	GP	G	A	Pts	PIM	GP	G	A	Pts	PIM
2000-01	Elektrostal 2	Russia-3	4	0	0	0	2	....	....	....	....	....
2001-02	Elektrostal 2	Russia-3	5	3	6	9	4	....	....	....	....	....
	Elektrostal	Russia-2	48	12	10	22	28	....	....	....	....	....
2002-03	Elektrostal	Russia-2	48	19	9	28	34	....	....	....	....	....
2003-04	Voskresensk	Russia	50	10	9	19	14	....	....	....	....	....
2004-05	Voskresensk	Russia	58	9	14	23	20	....	....	....	....	....
2005-06	Mytischi	Russia	46	10	5	15	57	8	1	1	2	2
	Kristall Elektrostal	Russia-3	STATISTICS NOT AVAILABLE									
2006-07	Mytischi	Russia	48	9	6	15	56	9	2	1	3	12

KRUCHININ, Andrei (kroo-CHIHN-ihn, AWN-dray) **MTL.**

Defense. Shoots left. 5'11", 187 lbs. Born, Karaganda, USSR, May 18, 1978.
(Montreal's 7th choice, 189th overall, in 1998 Entry Draft).

			Regular Season					Playoffs				
Season	Club	League	GP	G	A	Pts	PIM	GP	G	A	Pts	PIM
1996-97	Lada Togliatti	Russia	19	0	1	1	8	11	0	0	0	0
1997-98	Lada Togliatti	Russia	43	0	4	4	73	....	....	....	....	....
1998-99	Lada Togliatti	Russia	41	1	4	5	56	6	0	1	1	2
99-2000	CSK VVS Samara	Russia	6	1	0	1	0	....	....	....	....	....
	Lada Togliatti	Russia	25	1	2	3	24	6	1	0	1	4
2000-01	Perm	Russia	14	1	3	4	10	....	....	....	....	....
	Lada Togliatti	Russia	14	0	2	2	12	3	0	0	0	0
2001-02	Avangard Omsk	Russia	21	0	0	0	6	....	....	....	....	....
	Nizhnekamsk	Russia	17	1	3	4	8	....	....	....	....	....
2002-03	Nizhnekamsk	Russia	30	1	6	7	16	....	....	....	....	....
2003-04	Nizhnekamsk	Russia	49	2	6	8	53	5	1	1	2	4
2004-05	Lada Togliatti	Russia	32	3	4	7	24	7	0	1	1	2
2005-06	Lada Togliatti	Russia	35	6	5	11	67	8	0	2	2	4
2006-07	Mytischi	Russia	43	4	2	6	24	9	0	0	0	6

KRUEGER, Justin (KROO-guhr, JUHS-tihn) **CAR.**

Defense. Shoots right. 6'2", 205 lbs. Born, Winnipeg, Man., October 6, 1986.
(Carolina's 6th choice, 213th overall, in 2006 Entry Draft).

			Regular Season					Playoffs				
Season	Club	League	GP	G	A	Pts	PIM	GP	G	A	Pts	PIM
2002-03	HC Davos Jr.	Swiss-Jr.	12	0	0	0	4	2	0	0	0	0
2003-04	HC Davos Jr.	Swiss-Jr.	33	2	0	2	14	....	....	....	....	....
2004-05	HC Davos Jr.	Swiss-Jr.	38	5	12	17	76	4	1	2	3	2
2005-06	Penticton Vees	BCHL	55	7	15	22	25	....	....	....	....	....
2006-07	Cornell Big Red	ECACHL	31	1	5	6	24	....	....	....	....	....

KRYSANOV, Anton (KREE-sa-nahf, AN-tawn) **PHX.**

Center. Shoots left. 6'3", 198 lbs. Born, Togliatti, USSR, March 25, 1987.
(Phoenix's 4th choice, 148th overall, in 2005 Entry Draft).

			Regular Season					Playoffs				
Season	Club	League	GP	G	A	Pts	PIM	GP	G	A	Pts	PIM
2002-03	Lada Togliatti 2	Russia-3	9	1	3	4	2	....	....	....	....	....
2003-04	Lada Togliatti 2	Russia-3	18	2	3	5	2	....	....	....	....	....
2004-05	Lada Togliatti 2	Russia-3	34	13	13	26	32	....	....	....	....	....
	Lada Togliatti	Russia	15	1	0	1	2	....	....	....	....	....
2005-06	Lada Togliatti	Russia	46	3	3	6	24	8	0	0	0	2
2006-07	Lada Togliatti	Russia	48	1	15	16	14	3	0	0	0	4

KRYUKOV, Artem (KREE-oo-kahf, AHR-tehm) **BUF.**

Center. Shoots left. 6'3", 180 lbs. Born, Novosibirsk, USSR, March 5, 1982.
(Buffalo's 1st choice, 15th overall, in 2000 Entry Draft).

			Regular Season					Playoffs				
Season	Club	League	GP	G	A	Pts	PIM	GP	G	A	Pts	PIM
1997-98	Torpedo Yaroslavl	Russia	7	0	0	0	2	....	....	....	....	....
1998-99	Yaroslavl 2	Russia-3	20	2	2	4	6	....	....	....	....	....
99-2000	Yaroslavl 2	Russia-3	14	1	1	2	12	....	....	....	....	....
	Torpedo Yaroslavl	Russia	3	0	0	0	4	....	....	....	....	....
2000-01	Yaroslavl 2	Russia-3	6	0	0	0	2	11	0	0	0	8
	SKA St. Petersburg	Russia	14	0	2	2	14	....	....	....	....	....
2001-02	Yaroslavl	Russia	15	1	3	4	10	6	1	0	1	8
2002-03	Sibir Novosibirsk	Russia	9	0	0	0	27	....	....	....	....	....
2003-04	Yaroslavl 2	Russia-3	30	5	4	9	26	....	....	....	....	....
	Yaroslavl	Russia	4	0	2	2	0	....	....	....	....	....
2004-05	Yaroslavl	Russia	60	8	9	17	44	7	1	0	1	4
2005-06	Yaroslavl	Russia	33	1	2	3	42	1	0	0	0	0
	Yaroslavl 2	Russia-3	6	3	3	6	18	....	....	....	....	....
2006-07	Vityaz Chekhov	Russia	12	0	0	0	20	....	....	....	....	....
	Yaroslavl 2	Russia-3	13	4	10	14	10	....	....	....	....	....
	Yaroslavl	Russia	19	1	3	4	20	....	....	....	....	....

KUDELKA, Tomas (koo-DEHL-kah, TAW-mahsh) **OTT.**

Defense. Shoots left. 6'2", 182 lbs. Born, Gottwaldov, Czech., March 10, 1987.
(Ottawa's 6th choice, 136th overall, in 2005 Entry Draft).

			Regular Season					Playoffs				
Season	Club	League	GP	G	A	Pts	PIM	GP	G	A	Pts	PIM
2002-03	HC Zlin U17	CzR-U17	45	1	16	17	28	3	1	0	1	12
2003-04	HC Zlin U17	CzR-U17	1	0	0	0	2	3	0	0	0	0
	HC Zlin Jr.	CzRep-Jr.	51	1	12	13	95	7	0	0	0	0
	HC Hame Zlin	CzRep	3	0	0	0	0	....	....	....	....	....
2004-05	HC Zlin Jr.	CzRep-Jr.	38	9	8	17	38	....	....	....	....	....
	HC Hame Zlin	CzRep	4	0	0	0	6	....	....	....	....	....
2005-06	Lethbridge	WHL	64	6	25	31	77	6	1	1	2	12
	Binghamton	AHL	5	0	0	0	4	....	....	....	....	....
2006-07	Lethbridge	WHL	59	14	27	41	74	....	....	....	....	....
	Binghamton	AHL	11	1	2	3	8	....	....	....	....	....

KUKUMBERG, Roman (KOO-kuhm-buhrg, ROH-muhn) **TOR.**

Center. Shoots right. 6'1", 198 lbs. Born, Bratislava, Czech., April 8, 1980.
(Toronto's 2nd choice, 113th overall, in 2004 Entry Draft).

			Regular Season					Playoffs				
Season	Club	League	GP	G	A	Pts	PIM	GP	G	A	Pts	PIM
2001-02	Dukla Trencin	Slovakia	46	12	9	21	20	4	0	0	0	2
2002-03	Dukla Trencin	Slovakia	53	18	18	36	60	12	6	5	11	12
2003-04	Dukla Trencin	Slovakia	51	16	20	36	93	11	4	8	12	14
2004-05	Nizhnekamsk	Russia	55	10	11	21	40	3	0	0	0	4
2005-06	Toronto Marlies	AHL	54	2	6	8	30	....	....	....	....	....
2006-07	Bratislava	Slovakia	45	12	17	29	62	14	6	9	15	10

KUKUSHKIN, Sergei (koo-KOOSH-kihn, SAIR-gay) **DAL.**

Center. Shoots left. 6'2", 187 lbs. Born, Minsk, USSR, July 24, 1985.
(Dallas' 8th choice, 218th overall, in 2004 Entry Draft).

			Regular Season					Playoffs				
Season	Club	League	GP	G	A	Pts	PIM	GP	G	A	Pts	PIM
2003-04	Yunost Minsk	Belarus		STATISTICS NOT AVAILABLE								
2004-05	N.E. Jr. Falcons	EJHL	21	9	13	22	30	....	....	....	....	....
	Indiana Ice	USHL	19	1	2	3	50	....	....	....	....	....
2005-06	Kapitan Stupino	Russia-2	45	21	11	32	67	8	4	3	7	10
2006-07	Dynamo Moscow	Russia	5	1	1	2	8	....	....	....	....	....
	Lada Togliatti	Russia	25	4	1	5	12	1	0	0	0	2

KULDA , Arturs (KOOL-da, AHR-tuhrs) **ATL.**

Defense. Shoots left. 6'2", 200 lbs. Born, Riga, USSR, July 25, 1988.
(Atlanta's 7th choice, 200th overall, in 2006 Entry Draft).

			Regular Season					Playoffs				
Season	Club	League	GP	G	A	Pts	PIM	GP	G	A	Pts	PIM
2003-04	Prizma/Riga 86	Latvia	11	0	0	0	8	2	0	0	0	0
2004-05	CSKA Moscow 2	Russia-3		STATISTICS NOT AVAILABLE								
2005-06	CSKA Moscow 2	Russia-3	44	5	12	17	....					
2006-07	Peterborough	OHL	58	2	9	11	83	....	....	....	....	....

KULEMIN, Nikolai (koo-LAY-mihn, NIH-koh-ligh) **TOR.**

Wing. Shoots left. 6'1", 183 lbs. Born, Magnitogorsk, USSR, July 14, 1986.
(Toronto's 2nd choice, 44th overall, in 2006 Entry Draft).

			Regular Season					Playoffs				
Season	Club	League	GP	G	A	Pts	PIM	GP	G	A	Pts	PIM
2003-04	Magnitogorsk 2	Russia-3	43	8	18	26	91	....	....	....	....	....
2004-05	Magnitogorsk 2	Russia-3	43	9	13	22	44	....	....	....	....	....
2005-06	Magnitogorsk	Russia	31	5	7	12	8	11	2	4	6	6
	Magnitogorsk 2	Russia-3	4	3	1	4	6	....	....	....	....	....
2006-07	Magnitogorsk	Russia	54	27	12	39	42	15	10	1	11	10

KULYASH, Denis (kuh-L'YASH, DEH-nihs) **NSH.**

Defense. Shoots left. 6'3", 199 lbs. Born, Omsk, USSR, May 31, 1983.
(Nashville's 9th choice, 243rd overall, in 2004 Entry Draft).

			Regular Season					Playoffs				
Season	Club	League	GP	G	A	Pts	PIM	GP	G	A	Pts	PIM
2003-04	CSK VVS Samara 2	Russia-3		STATISTICS NOT AVAILABLE								
	CSKA Moscow	Russia	10	1	0	1	8	....	....	....	....	....
2004-05	CSKA Moscow	Russia	59	8	10	18	58	....	....	....	....	....
2005-06	Dynamo Moscow	Russia	44	12	5	17	117	4	0	2	2	6
2006-07	Dynamo Moscow	Russia	48	3	9	12	58	2	0	0	0	2

KUNES, Tim (KOONZ, TIHM) **CAR.**

Defense. Shoots left. 6'1", 170 lbs. Born, Red Bank, NJ, February 12, 1987.
(Carolina's 6th choice, 145th overall, in 2005 Entry Draft).

			Regular Season					Playoffs				
Season	Club	League	GP	G	A	Pts	PIM	GP	G	A	Pts	PIM
2003-04	N.E. Jr. Falcons	EJHL	45	4	19	23	20	....	....	....	....	....
2004-05	N.E. Jr. Falcons	EJHL	50	12	28	40	51	....	....	....	....	....
2005-06	Boston College	H-East	28	1	3	4	31	....	....	....	....	....
2006-07	Boston College	H-East	27	1	4	5	6	....	....	....	....	....

KVAPIL, Marek (kuh-VAH-puhl, MAHR-ehk) **T.B.**

Right wing. Shoots right. 5'11", 172 lbs. Born, Ilava, Czech., January 5, 1985.
(Tampa Bay's 7th choice, 163rd overall, in 2005 Entry Draft).

			Regular Season					Playoffs				
Season	Club	League	GP	G	A	Pts	PIM	GP	G	A	Pts	PIM
2002-03	HC Slavia Praha Jr.	CzRep-Jr.	33	9	4	13	4	2	0	0	0	0
2003-04	HC Slavia Praha Jr.	CzRep-Jr.	42	19	17	36	43	2	1	0	1	0
	HC Slavia Praha	CzRep	11	0	0	0	0	....	....	....	....	....
	HC Kometa Brno	CzRep-2	4	0	2	2	4	....	....	....	....	....
2004-05	HC Slavia Praha Jr.	CzRep-Jr.	8	6	4	10	8	....	....	....	....	....
	Saginaw Spirit	OHL	53	25	37	62	14	....	....	....	....	....
2005-06	Springfield Falcons	AHL	79	18	27	45	24	....	....	....	....	....
2006-07	Springfield Falcons	AHL	72	12	15	27	33	....	....	....	....	....
	Johnstown Chiefs	ECHL	7	3	8	11	2	2	1	1	2	0

KVETON, David (KVEH-tuhn, DAY-vihd) **NYR**

Right wing. Shoots left. 6', 190 lbs. Born, Novy Jicin, Czech., January 3, 1988.
(NY Rangers' 4th choice, 104th overall, in 2006 Entry Draft).

			Regular Season					Playoffs				
Season	Club	League	GP	G	A	Pts	PIM	GP	G	A	Pts	PIM
2003-04	HC Vsetin U17	CzR-U17	14	9	11	20	35	....	....	....	....	....
	HC Vsetin Jr.	CzRep-Jr.	41	12	11	23	14	5	2	3	5	2
	TJ Novy Jicin	CzRep-3	1	0	1	1	0	....	....	....	....	....
	HC Vsetin	CzRep	1	0	0	0	0	....	....	....	....	....
2004-05	HC Vsetin U17	CzR-U17	1	1	0	1	0	....	....	....	....	....
	HC Vsetin Jr.	CzRep-Jr.	36	21	27	48	66	8	6	5	11	4
	TJ Novy Jicin	CzRep-3	7	0	1	1	6	....	....	....	....	....
	HC Vsetin	CzRep	6	1	0	1	0	....	....	....	....	....
2005-06	HC Vsetin Jr.	CzRep-Jr.	1	1	1	2	0	1	0	1	1	0
	HC Sareza Ostrava	CzRep-2	7	2	1	3	2	....	....	....	....	....
	HC Vsetin	CzRep	45	6	4	10	18	....	....	....	....	....
	TJ Novy Jicin	CzRep-3	....	....	....	....	....	5	5	0	5	18
	HC Vsetin	CzRep-Q	....	....	....	....	....	3	1	1	2	2
2006-07	Gatineau	QMJHL	31	5	27	32	17	5	0	0	0	4
	HC Vsetin	CzRep	19	2	0	2	8	....	....	....	....	....

KYTNAR, Milan (KIHT-nahr, MEE-lan) **EDM.**

Center. Shoots left. 6', 180 lbs. Born, Topolcany, Czech., May 19, 1989.
(Edmonton's 5th choice, 127th overall, in 2007 Entry Draft).

			Regular Season					Playoffs				
Season	Club	League	GP	G	A	Pts	PIM	GP	G	A	Pts	PIM
2003-04	Topolcany U18	Svk-U18	42	17	22	39	90	....	....	....	....	....
2004-05	Topolcany U18	Svk-U18	53	36	65	101	105	....	....	....	....	....
	Topolcany Jr.	Slovak-Jr.	10	2	2	4	8	....	....	....	....	....
2005-06	HK Trnava U18	Svk-U18	30	18	23	41	106	....	....	....	....	....
	HK Trnava Jr.	Slovak-Jr.	12	1	2	3	20	....	....	....	....	....
	Topolcany U18	Svk-U18	8	4	4	8	4	....	....	....	....	....
	Topolcany Jr.	Slovak-Jr.	6	6	4	10	8	....	....	....	....	....
2006-07	HC Topolcany U18	Svk-U18	53	37	54	91	84	....	....	....	....	....
	HC Topolcany	Slovak-2	22	4	7	11	53	5	1	1	2	4

LAAKSO, Teemu (LAK-soh, TEE-moo) **NSH.**

Defense. Shoots right. 6'1", 211 lbs. Born, Tuusula, Finland, August 27, 1987.
(Nashville's 2nd choice, 78th overall, in 2005 Entry Draft).

			Regular Season					Playoffs				
Season	Club	League	GP	G	A	Pts	PIM	GP	G	A	Pts	PIM
2002-03	KJT Jarvenpaa U18	Fin-U18	18	2	5	7	24	....	....	....	....	....
2003-04	HIFK Helsinki Jr.	Fin-Jr.	41	3	6	9	20	3	0	1	1	0
2004-05	HIFK Helsinki U18	Fin-U18	....	....	....	....	....	1	0	0	0	0
	HIFK Helsinki Jr.	Fin-Jr.	20	5	4	9	18	....	....	....	....	....
	HIFK Helsinki	Finland	15	0	2	2	2	....	....	....	....	....
2005-06	HIFK Helsinki Jr.	Fin-Jr.	6	1	2	3	32	....	....	....	....	....
	Suomi U20	Finland-2	6	2	0	2	10	....	....	....	....	....
	HIFK Helsinki	Finland	47	2	1	3	20	8	1	0	1	0
2006-07	Suomi U20	Finland-2	2	0	1	1	4	....	....	....	....	....
	HIFK Helsinki	Finland	50	3	6	9	70	5	0	1	1	0

LABRIE, Pierre-Cedric (la-BREE, pee-AIR-SHE-drihk) VAN.

Left wing. Shoots right. 6'2", 212 lbs. Born, Baie Comeau, Que., December 6, 1986.

			Regular Season					Playoffs				
Season	Club	League	GP	G	A	Pts	PIM	GP	G	A	Pts	PIM
2003-04	Coaticook	QJHL	46	13	12	25	96	....	....	....	....	....
	Quebec Remparts	QMJHL	1	0	0	0	0	....	....	....	....	....
2004-05	Coaticook	QJHL	15	3	4	7	59	....	....	....	....	....
2005-06	Restigouche Tigers	MJrHL	54	43	43	86	153	....	....	....	....	....
	Baie-Comeau	QMJHL	....	....	....	....	....	4	2	2	4	6
2006-07	Baie-Comeau	QMJHL	68	35	28	63	113	11	8	6	14	35

Signed as a free agent by **Vancouver**, July 3, 2007.

LACROIX, Maxime (luh-KWAH, max-EEM) WSH.

Left wing. Shoots left. 6', 180 lbs. Born, Quebec City, Que., June 5, 1987.
(Washington's 8th choice, 127th overall, in 2006 Entry Draft).

			Regular Season					Playoffs				
Season	Club	League	GP	G	A	Pts	PIM	GP	G	A	Pts	PIM
2003-04	St-Francois	QAAA	42	21	21	42	47	8	3	1	4	8
2004-05	Quebec Remparts	QMJHL	49	6	8	14	34	13	0	0	0	8
2005-06	Quebec Remparts	QMJHL	70	25	22	47	79	23	7	5	12	21
2006-07	Quebec Remparts	QMJHL	68	22	31	53	85	5	2	1	3	2

LACROIX, Simon (luh-KWAH, see-MOHN) NYI

Defense. Shoots right. 6'2", 172 lbs. Born, Ottawa, Ont., May 29, 1989.
(NY Islanders' 5th choice, 196th overall, in 2007 Entry Draft).

			Regular Season					Playoffs				
Season	Club	League	GP	G	A	Pts	PIM	GP	G	A	Pts	PIM
2005-06	Cumberland	CJHL	65	6	13	19	90	....	....	....	....	....
2006-07	Shawinigan	QMJHL	60	11	27	38	66	4	0	2	2	6

QMJHL All-Rookie Team (2007)

LAGERSTROM, Tony (LA-guhr-struhm, TOH-nee) CHI.

Center. Shoots left. 6'1", 189 lbs. Born, Stockholm, Sweden, July 19, 1988.
(Chicago's 4th choice, 76th overall, in 2006 Entry Draft).

			Regular Season					Playoffs				
Season	Club	League	GP	G	A	Pts	PIM	GP	G	A	Pts	PIM
2003-04	Huddinge IK U18	Swe-U18	12	5	1	6	6	....	....	....	....	....
2004-05	Sodertalje SK U18	Swe-U18	2	3	2	5	4	1	0	0	0	0
	Sodertalje SK Jr.	Swe-Jr.	28	13	11	24	16	3	2	1	3	2
2005-06	Sodertalje SK U18	Swe-U18	7	9	5	14	2	1	0	0	0	0
	Sodertalje SK Jr.	Swe-Jr.	37	14	19	33	69	4	1	2	3	14
	Sodertalje SK	Sweden	1	0	0	0	0	....	....	....	....	....
2006-07	Sodertalje SK Jr.	Swe-Jr.	23	7	11	18	16	3	0	3	3	6
	Sodertalje SK	Sweden-2	36	0	1	1	2	....	....	....	....	....

LAHTI, Janne (LAH-tee, yah-NAY) MTL.

Left wing. Shoots left. 6', 200 lbs. Born, Riihimaki, Finland, July 20, 1982.

			Regular Season					Playoffs				
Season	Club	League	GP	G	A	Pts	PIM	GP	G	A	Pts	PIM
1998-99	HPK U18	Fin-U18	36	10	6	16	18	....	....	....	....	....
99-2000	HPK U18	Fin-U18	12	5	7	12	2	....	....	....	....	....
	HPK Jr.	Fin-Jr.	18	6	5	11	8	....	....	....	....	....
2000-01	HPK Jr.	Fin-Jr.	35	9	11	20	16	....	....	....	....	....
2001-02	HPK Hameenlinna	Finland	36	1	0	1	2	4	0	0	0	0
	HPK Jr.	Fin-Jr.	22	22	11	33	18	4	1	3	4	2
2002-03	HPK Hameenlinna	Finland	17	1	0	1	2	1	0	0	0	0
	HPK Jr.	Fin-Jr.	22	23	19	42	35	....	....	....	....	....
2003-04	HPK Hameenlinna	Finland	43	14	6	20	26	8	1	0	1	0
2004-05	HPK Hameenlinna	Finland	52	6	9	15	22	8	2	2	4	4
	Haukat Jarvenpaa	Finland-2	4	2	2	4	2	....	....	....	....	....
2005-06	HPK Hameenlinna	Finland	51	9	13	22	30	13	5	4	9	6
2006-07	HPK Hameenlinna	Finland	56	20	14	34	87	9	8	1	9	4

Signed as a free agent by **Montreal**, May 31, 2007.

LAKOS, Andre (LA-kaws, AWN-dray) MIN.

Defense. Shoots right. 6'6", 230 lbs. Born, Vienna, Austria, July 29, 1979.
(New Jersey's 4th choice, 95th overall, in 1999 Entry Draft).

			Regular Season					Playoffs				
Season	Club	League	GP	G	A	Pts	PIM	GP	G	A	Pts	PIM
1995-96	Montreal-Bourassa	QAAA	40	2	13	15	68	....	....	....	....	....
1996-97	Shelburne Wolves	MTJHL	36	5	12	17	47	....	....	....	....	....
1997-98	St. Michael's	OHL	49	2	10	12	54	....	....	....	....	....
1998-99	Barrie Colts	OHL	62	4	23	27	40	12	3	3	6	8
99-2000	Albany River Rats	AHL	65	1	7	8	41	5	0	2	2	4
2000-01	Albany River Rats	AHL	51	1	20	21	29	....	....	....	....	....
2001-02	Albany River Rats	AHL	36	0	3	3	24	....	....	....	....	....
	Utah Grizzlies	AHL	26	0	1	1	28	1	0	0	0	0
	Austria	Olympics	4	0	0	0	6	....	....	....	....	....
2002-03	Augusta Lynx	ECHL	5	0	2	2	8	....	....	....	....	....
2003-04	Vienna Capitals	Austria	48	6	19	25	75	....	....	....	....	....
2004-05	Syracuse Crunch	AHL	51	1	12	13	51	....	....	....	....	....
2005-06	Salzburg	Austria	46	8	22	30	115	11	3	7	10	2
2006-07	Salzburg	Austria	52	16	28	44	125	8	3	4	7	6

Traded to **Dallas** by **New Jersey** with future considerations for Valeri Kamensky, January 16, 2002. Signed as a free agent by **Columbus**, July 7, 2004. Signed as a free agent by **Salzburg** (Austria), May 5, 2005. Signed as a free agent by **Minnesota**, June 16, 2007.

LALIBERTE, David (la-LIH-buhr-tee, DAY-vihd) PHI.

Right wing. Shoots right. 6'1", 194 lbs. Born, St-Jean-Sur-Richelieu, Que., March 17, 1986.
(Philadelphia's 3rd choice, 124th overall, in 2004 Entry Draft).

			Regular Season					Playoffs				
Season	Club	League	GP	G	A	Pts	PIM	GP	G	A	Pts	PIM
2001-02	Antoine-Girouard	QAAA	41	21	21	42	14	15	8	9	17	6
2002-03	Montreal Rocket	QMJHL	66	15	14	29	10	6	3	0	3	2
2003-04	PEI Rocket	QMJHL	70	21	22	43	51	11	1	3	4	6
2004-05	PEI Rocket	QMJHL	41	23	13	36	36	....	....	....	....	....
2005-06	PEI Rocket	QMJHL	34	12	11	23	41	6	3	1	4	6
2006-07	PEI Rocket	QMJHL	68	50	48	98	86	7	5	4	9	4

LAMBERT, Michael (lam-BAIR, MIGH-kuhl)

Left wing. Shoots left. 6'2", 205 lbs. Born, Trois-Rivieres, Que., March 10, 1984.
(Montreal's 3rd choice, 99th overall, in 2002 Entry Draft).

			Regular Season					Playoffs				
Season	Club	League	GP	G	A	Pts	PIM	GP	G	A	Pts	PIM
1998-99	Cap-d-Madeleine	QAAA	3	0	0	0	0	....	....	....	....	....
99-2000	Cap-d-Madeleine	QAAA	42	20	16	36	38	1	0	2	2	0
2000-01	Acadie-Bathurst	QMJHL	23	2	5	7	15	....	....	....	....	....
	Montreal Rocket	QMJHL	33	6	12	18	14	....	....	....	....	....
2001-02	Montreal Rocket	QMJHL	71	29	24	53	111	7	1	6	7	15
2002-03	Montreal Rocket	QMJHL	71	28	32	60	53	7	2	2	4	10
2003-04	PEI Rocket	QMJHL	67	42	42	84	53	11	6	7	13	6
2004-05	Hamilton Bulldogs	AHL	40	3	4	7	18	....	....	....	....	....
	Long Beach	ECHL	18	5	4	9	26	7	5	1	6	14
2005-06	Hamilton Bulldogs	AHL	39	10	7	17	25	....	....	....	....	....
	Long Beach	ECHL	20	11	7	18	16	5	2	1	3	12
2006-07	Hamilton Bulldogs	AHL	49	11	5	16	19	14	2	2	4	6

LAMMERS, John (LA-muhrs, JAWN) DAL.

Left wing. Shoots left. 5'11", 184 lbs. Born, Bowmanville, Ont., January 29, 1986.
(Dallas' 5th choice, 86th overall, in 2004 Entry Draft).

			Regular Season					Playoffs				
Season	Club	League	GP	G	A	Pts	PIM	GP	G	A	Pts	PIM
2001-02	Langley Bantams	BCAHA	64	51	69	120	30	....	....	....	....	....
	Lethbridge	WHL	5	0	0	0	0	....	....	....	....	....
2002-03	Lethbridge	WHL	53	17	15	32	11	....	....	....	....	....
2003-04	Lethbridge	WHL	62	21	24	45	31	....	....	....	....	....
2004-05	Lethbridge	WHL	66	17	30	47	43	5	0	0	0	2
2005-06	Everett Silvertips	WHL	70	38	37	75	25	15	5	6	11	12
2006-07	Iowa Stars	AHL	52	6	8	14	14	....	....	....	....	....
	Idaho Steelheads	ECHL	9	2	2	4	4	22	7	12	19	2

LANDRY, Jon (LAN-dree, JAWN) CBJ

Defense. Shoots right. 6'2", 180 lbs. Born, Lexington, MA, May 29, 1984.

			Regular Season					Playoffs				
Season	Club	League	GP	G	A	Pts	PIM	GP	G	A	Pts	PIM
2003-04	Holy Cross	AH	33	3	12	15	28	....	....	....	....	....
2004-05	Holy Cross	AH	35	3	12	15	52	....	....	....	....	....
2005-06	Holy Cross	AH	38	9	20	29	54	....	....	....	....	....
2006-07	Holy Cross	AH	27	9	18	27	54	....	....	....	....	....
	Augusta Lynx	ECHL	2	1	0	1	2	....	....	....	....	....

AH First All-Star Team (2006, 2007)

Signed as a free agent by **Columbus**, March 19, 2007.

LANNON, Ryan (LA-nuhn, RIGH-uhn) PIT.

Defense. Shoots left. 6'1", 198 lbs. Born, Worcester, MA, December 14, 1982.
(Pittsburgh's 10th choice, 239th overall, in 2002 Entry Draft).

			Regular Season					Playoffs				
Season	Club	League	GP	G	A	Pts	PIM	GP	G	A	Pts	PIM
1998-99	USNTDP	NAHL	56	3	4	7	36	....	....	....	....	....
99-2000	Cushing	High-MA	STATISTICS NOT AVAILABLE									
2000-01	Cushing	High-MA	STATISTICS NOT AVAILABLE									
2001-02	Harvard Crimson	ECAC	34	0	2	2	38	....	....	....	....	....
2002-03	Harvard Crimson	ECAC	34	3	11	14	39	....	....	....	....	....
2003-04	Harvard Crimson	ECAC	35	0	9	9	36	....	....	....	....	....
2004-05	Harvard Crimson	ECACHL	33	1	12	13	34	....	....	....	....	....
2005-06	Wilkes-Barre	AHL	74	2	8	10	65	11	0	0	0	8
2006-07	Wilkes-Barre	AHL	68	0	19	19	71	11	0	2	2	14

LAPOINT, Derrick (luh-POYNT, DAIR-ihk) FLA.

Defense. Shoots left. 6'3", 175 lbs. Born, Eau Claire, MA, May 13, 1988.
(Florida's 4th choice, 116th overall, in 2006 Entry Draft).

			Regular Season					Playoffs				
Season	Club	League	GP	G	A	Pts	PIM	GP	G	A	Pts	PIM
2004-05	Eau Claire North	High-WI	23	9	28	37	14	....	....	....	....	....
2005-06	Eau Claire North	High-WI	23	6	26	32	34	....	....	....	....	....
2006-07	Green Bay	USHL	59	13	36	49	48	4	0	2	2	2

LARSON, Nick (LAR-suhn, NIHK) WSH.

Center. Shoots right. 6'1", 175 lbs. Born, Edina, MN, January 16, 1989.
(Washington's 9th choice, 185th overall, in 2007 Entry Draft).

			Regular Season					Playoffs				
Season	Club	League	GP	G	A	Pts	PIM	GP	G	A	Pts	PIM
2004-05	Hill-Murray	High-MN	26	9	15	24	6	....	....	....	....	....
2005-06	Hill-Murray	High-MN	....	41	38	79		....	....	....	....	....
2006-07	Hill-Murray	High-MN	29	31	30	61	16	....	....	....	....	....
	Omaha Lancers	USHL	10	3	2	5	6	....	....	....	....	....

• Signed Letter of Intent to attend **University of Minnesota** (WCHA) in fall of 2007.

LASCEK, Stanislav (LASH-chehk, STAN-ihs-lahv) T.B.

Right wing. Shoots left. 6', 195 lbs. Born, Martin, Czech., January 17, 1986.
(Tampa Bay's 6th choice, 133rd overall, in 2005 Entry Draft).

			Regular Season					Playoffs				
Season	Club	League	GP	G	A	Pts	PIM	GP	G	A	Pts	PIM
2002-03	HKm Zvolen	Slovakia	1	0	0	0	2	....	....	....	....	....
	HKm Zvolen B	Slovak-2	19	2	4	6	29	....	....	....	....	....
2003-04	Chicoutimi	QMJHL	59	17	40	57	49	18	5	13	18	30
2004-05	Chicoutimi	QMJHL	53	18	72	90	42	17	4	18	22	26
2005-06	Chicoutimi	QMJHL	64	47	88	135	96	9	4	13	17	8
2006-07	Springfield Falcons	AHL	29	2	2	4	12	....	....	....	....	....
	Johnstown Chiefs	ECHL	25	12	15	27	26	....	....	....	....	....

QMJHL Second All-Star Team (2006)

LATAL, Martin (LAH-tuhl, MAHR-tihn) PHX.

Right wing. Shoots left. 5'11", 174 lbs. Born, Olomouc, Czech., March 17, 1988.
(Phoenix's 5th choice, 131st overall, in 2006 Entry Draft).

			Regular Season					Playoffs				
Season	Club	League	GP	G	A	Pts	PIM	GP	G	A	Pts	PIM
2002-03	Sparta U17	CzR-U17	24	2	6	8	12	2	0	0	0	0
2003-04	HC Kladno U17	CzR-U17	48	15	16	31	69	2	0	1	1	0
	HC Kladno Jr.	CzRep-Jr.	1	0	0	0	0	....	....	....	....	....
2004-05	HC Kladno U17	CzR-U17	3	3	3	6	22	4	3	1	4	10
	HC Kladno Jr.	CzRep-Jr.	41	7	8	15	86	6	1	1	2	12
2005-06	HC Plzen Jr.	CzRep-Jr.	6	2	1	3	2	....	....	....	....	....
	Plzen	CzRep	5	0	0	0	4	....	....	....	....	....
	HC Kladno Jr.	CzRep-Jr.	24	14	9	23	62	7	4	1	5	8
	HC Rabat Kladno	CzRep	20	0	0	0	0	....	....	....	....	....
2006-07	PEI Rocket	QMJHL	66	18	28	46	90	7	3	4	7	8

LATENDRESSE, Olivier (lah-TEHN-drehs, oh-LIHV-ee-ay) PHX.

Center. Shoots left. 5'10", 195 lbs. Born, LaSalle, Que., February 12, 1986.

			Regular Season					Playoffs				
Season	Club	League	GP	G	A	Pts	PIM	GP	G	A	Pts	PIM
2002-03	Val-d'Or Foreurs	QMJHL	55	11	14	25	22	8	0	2	2	0
2003-04	Val-d'Or Foreurs	QMJHL	53	19	46	65	44	7	1	5	6	14
2004-05	Val-d'Or Foreurs	QMJHL	68	27	47	74	34	....	....	....	....	....
2005-06	Val-d'Or Foreurs	QMJHL	70	41	84	125	83	4	5	2	7	2
2006-07	San Antonio	AHL	17	1	3	4	14	....	....	....	....	....
	Phoenix	ECHL	47	12	15	27	22	....	....	....	....	....

Signed as a free agent by **Phoenix**, September 15, 2004.

LaVALLEE, Jordan (LA-VA-lee, JOHR-dahn) ATL.

Left wing. Shoots left. 6'3", 220 lbs. Born, Corvallis, OR, May 11, 1986.
(Atlanta's 5th choice, 116th overall, in 2005 Entry Draft).

			Regular Season					Playoffs				
Season	Club	League	GP	G	A	Pts	PIM	GP	G	A	Pts	PIM
2002-03	Quebec Remparts	QMJHL	55	3	6	9	54	11	0	1	1	0
2003-04	Quebec Remparts	QMJHL	69	11	16	27	111	5	2	0	2	6
2004-05	Quebec Remparts	QMJHL	64	40	26	66	108	13	5	2	7	26
2005-06	Quebec Remparts	QMJHL	37	18	19	37	34	23	7	8	15	30
2006-07	Chicago Wolves	AHL	79	16	18	34	90	14	7	1	8	8

LAVIN, Joseph (LA-vihn, JOH-sehf) CHI.

Defense. Shoots left. 6'1", 195 lbs. Born, Worcester, MA, July 17, 1989.
(Chicago's 6th choice, 126th overall, in 2007 Entry Draft).

			Regular Season					Playoffs				
Season	Club	League	GP	G	A	Pts	PIM	GP	G	A	Pts	PIM
2004-05	Boston Jr. Bruins	EmJHL	64	11	44	55	....	....	....	....	....	....
2005-06	USNTDP	U-17	19	2	1	3	30	....	....	....	....	....
	USNTDP	NAHL	37	8	10	18	16	12	3	2	5	4
2006-07	USNTDP	U-18	23	1	0	1	18	....	....	....	....	....
	USNTDP	NAHL	18	1	8	9	22	6	0	2	2	4

LAVRENTIEV, Anton (lahv-REHN-tee-yehv, AN-tawn) NSH.

Defense. Shoots right. 6'4", 196 lbs. Born, Kazan, USSR, August 25, 1983.
(Nashville's 7th choice, 178th overall, in 2001 Entry Draft).

			Regular Season					Playoffs				
Season	Club	League	GP	G	A	Pts	PIM	GP	G	A	Pts	PIM
2000-01	Ak Bars Kazan 2	Russia-3	STATISTICS NOT AVAILABLE									
2001-02	Sudbury Wolves	OHL	10	0	0	0	17	....	....	....	....	....
	Ak Bars Kazan 2	Russia-3	STATISTICS NOT AVAILABLE									
2002-03	Yuzhny Ural Orsk	Russia-2	13	0	1	1	14	....	....	....	....	....
2003-04	HK Rybinsk	Russia-2	31	2	1	3	49	....	....	....	....	....
2004-05	Novopolotsk	BelOpen	23	2	3	5	26	1	0	0	0	2
2005-06	Naber. Chelny	Russia-3	70	8	6	14	214	....	....	....	....	....
2006-07	Naber. Chelny	Russia-3	67	10	21	31	270	....	....	....	....	....

LAWRENCE, Chris (LOH-rehnts, KRIHS) T.B.

Center. Shoots right. 6'4", 199 lbs. Born, Toronto, Ont., February 5, 1987.
(Tampa Bay's 3rd choice, 89th overall, in 2005 Entry Draft).

			Regular Season					Playoffs				
Season	Club	League	GP	G	A	Pts	PIM	GP	G	A	Pts	PIM
2003-04	Sault Ste. Marie	OHL	62	7	6	13	34	....	....	....	....	....
2004-05	Sault Ste. Marie	OHL	68	11	40	51	57	7	3	3	6	4
2005-06	Sault Ste. Marie	OHL	29	3	14	17	31	....	....	....	....	....
	Mississauga	OHL	38	20	16	36	60	....	....	....	....	....
2006-07	Mississauga	OHL	64	47	41	88	113	5	3	1	4	14

LAWSON, Kyle (LAW-suhn, KIGHL) CAR.

Defense. Shoots right. 5'11", 192 lbs. Born, Southfield, MI, January 11, 1987.
(Carolina's 9th choice, 198th overall, in 2005 Entry Draft).

			Regular Season					Playoffs				
Season	Club	League	GP	G	A	Pts	PIM	GP	G	A	Pts	PIM
2003-04	Det. Honeybaked	MWEHL	61	17	41	58	68	....	....	....	....	....
	Texarkana Bandits	NAHL	....	....	....	....	....	3	0	1	1	0
2004-05	USNTDP	U-18	23	2	12	14	6	....	....	....	....	....
	USNTDP	NAHL	8	1	3	4	0	....	....	....	....	....
2005-06	Tri-City Storm	USHL	49	9	13	22	40	1	0	0	0	0
2006-07	U. of Notre Dame	CCHA	38	4	15	19	14	....	....	....	....	....

CCHA All-Rookie Team (2007)

LEAVITT, Alex (LEH-viht, ALEHX) PHX.

Center. Shoots right. 5'10", 175 lbs. Born, Edmonton, Alta., January 31, 1984.

			Regular Season					Playoffs				
Season	Club	League	GP	G	A	Pts	PIM	GP	G	A	Pts	PIM
2001-02	U. of Wisconsin	WCHA	39	11	13	24	42	....	....	....	....	....
2002-03	U. of Wisconsin	WCHA	28	2	13	15	24	....	....	....	....	....
2003-04	Swift Current	WHL	71	27	41	68	67	5	2	2	4	8
2004-05	Swift Current	WHL	15	3	11	14	27	....	....	....	....	....
	Everett Silvertips	WHL	49	13	35	48	43	11	6	5	11	6
2005-06	Alaska Aces	ECHL	72	26	65	91	58	16	1	12	13	28
2006-07	Houston Aeros	AHL	23	2	9	11	14	....	....	....	....	....
	Texas Wildcatters	ECHL	30	10	14	24	30	....	....	....	....	....
	San Antonio	AHL	16	10	10	20	22	....	....	....	....	....

Signed as a free agent by **Phoenix**, March 15, 2007.

LEBLANC, Peter (luh-BLAHNK, PEE-tuhr) CHI.

Center. Shoots left. 5'10", 196 lbs. Born, Hamilton, Ont., February 3, 1988.
(Chicago's 9th choice, 186th overall, in 2006 Entry Draft).

			Regular Season					Playoffs				
Season	Club	League	GP	G	A	Pts	PIM	GP	G	A	Pts	PIM
2004-05	Hamilton	OPJHL	49	14	22	36	....	....	....	....	....	....
2005-06	Hamilton	OPJHL	22	10	12	22	25	....	....	....	....	....
2006-07	New Hampshire	H-East	39	1	4	5	4	....	....	....	....	....

OPJHL Rookie of the Year (2005)

• Missed majority of 2005-06 season due to mononucleosis.

LEE, Brian (LEE, BRIGH-uhn) OTT.

Defense. Shoots right. 6'2", 202 lbs. Born, Fargo, ND, March 26, 1987.
(Ottawa's 1st choice, 9th overall, in 2005 Entry Draft).

			Regular Season					Playoffs				
Season	Club	League	GP	G	A	Pts	PIM	GP	G	A	Pts	PIM
2003-04	Moorhead Spuds	High-MN	29	10	38	48	....	....	....	....	....	....
2004-05	Moorhead Spuds	High-MN	25	12	26	38	....	....	....	....	....	....
	Lincoln Stars	USHL	12	0	3	3	4	4	2	3	5	2
2005-06	North Dakota	WCHA	44	4	23	27	44	....	....	....	....	....
2006-07	North Dakota	WCHA	38	2	24	26	69	....	....	....	....	....

WCHA All-Rookie Team (2006)

LEE, Carter (LEE, KAHR-tuhr) S.J.

Right wing. Shoots right. 6'1", 190 lbs. Born, Toms River, NJ, July 2, 1984.
(San Jose's 11th choice, 276th overall, in 2003 Entry Draft).

			Regular Season					Playoffs				
Season	Club	League	GP	G	A	Pts	PIM	GP	G	A	Pts	PIM
2001-02	Christian Bros.	High-NJ	34	10	9	19	45	....	....	....	....	....
2002-03	Canterbury	High-CT	35	38	22	60	40	....	....	....	....	....
2003-04	Canterbury	High-CT	30	19	26	45	40	....	....	....	....	....
2004-05	Northeastern	H-East	11	2	1	3	4	....	....	....	....	....
2005-06	Northeastern	H-East	9	0	1	1	21	....	....	....	....	....
2006-07	Lake Superior	CCHA	DID NOT PLAY – TRANSFERRED COLLEGES									

LEE, John (LEE, JAWN) FLA.

Defense. Shoots right. 6'2", 173 lbs. Born, Fargo, ND, January 16, 1989.
(Florida's 5th choice, 131st overall, in 2007 Entry Draft).

			Regular Season					Playoffs				
Season	Club	League	GP	G	A	Pts	PIM	GP	G	A	Pts	PIM
2004-05	Moorhead Spuds	High-MN	3	0	1	1	0	....	....	....	....	....
2005-06	Moorhead Spuds	High-MN	26	6	21	27	50	....	....	....	....	....
2006-07	Moorhead Spuds	High-MN	26	6	33	39	62	....	....	....	....	....
	Waterloo	USHL	27	2	7	9	56	9	0	3	3	4

• Signed Letter of Intent to attend **University of Denver** (WCHA) in fall of 2008.

LEFFLER, Brett (LEHF-luhr, BREHT) WSH.

Right wing. Shoots right. 6'1", 198 lbs. Born, Wynyard, Sask., May 19, 1989.
(Washington's 6th choice, 125th overall, in 2007 Entry Draft).

			Regular Season					Playoffs				
Season	Club	League	GP	G	A	Pts	PIM	GP	G	A	Pts	PIM
2004-05	Tisdale Trojans	SMHL	43	20	27	80	....	5	1	0	1	8
	Regina Pats	WHL	7	0	1	1	2	....	....	....	....	....
2005-06	Regina Pats	WHL	42	2	7	9	54	....	....	....	....	....
2006-07	Regina Pats	WHL	69	13	13	26	114	10	2	0	2	14

LEGEIN, Stefan (LEE-gihn, STEH-fan) CBJ

Right wing. Shoots right. 5'9", 170 lbs. Born, Oakville, Ont., November 24, 1988.
(Columbus' 2nd choice, 37th overall, in 2007 Entry Draft).

			Regular Season					Playoffs				
Season	Club	League	GP	G	A	Pts	PIM	GP	G	A	Pts	PIM
2003-04	Tor. Red Wings	GTHL	33	19	14	33	63	....	....	....	....	....
2004-05	Mississauga	OHL	49	3	5	8	37	5	0	1	1	0
2005-06	Mississauga	OHL	59	7	9	16	101	....	....	....	....	....
2006-07	Mississauga	OHL	64	43	32	75	115	5	3	2	5	0

LEHMAN, Scott (LAY-man, SKAWT) ATL.

Defense. Shoots left. 6'2", 200 lbs. Born, Fort McMurray, Alta., January 6, 1986.
(Atlanta's 3rd choice, 76th overall, in 2004 Entry Draft).

			Regular Season					Playoffs				
Season	Club	League	GP	G	A	Pts	PIM	GP	G	A	Pts	PIM
2002-03	St. Michael's	OHL	53	3	10	13	50	19	1	3	4	34
2003-04	St. Michael's	OHL	66	5	27	32	189	18	2	2	4	38
2004-05	St. Michael's	OHL	57	2	19	21	189	10	2	2	4	31
2005-06	St. Michael's	OHL	68	5	50	55	175	4	0	2	2	15
2006-07	Chicago Wolves	AHL	3	0	0	0	14	....	....	....	....	....
	Gwinnett	ECHL	72	2	12	14	86	4	0	0	0	11

LEHTIVUORI, Joonas (leh-tee-VWOO-aw-ree, YOH-nuhs) PHI.

Defense. Shoots left. 5'11", 170 lbs. Born, Tempere, Finland, July 19, 1988.
(Philadelphia's 6th choice, 101st overall, in 2006 Entry Draft).

			Regular Season					Playoffs				
Season	Club	League	GP	G	A	Pts	PIM	GP	G	A	Pts	PIM
2004-05	Ilves Tampere U18	Fin-U18	25	5	11	16	12	5	1	1	2	8
2005-06	Ilves Tampere U18	Fin-U18	2	0	1	1	0	6	1	4	5	4
	Ilves Tampere Jr.	Fin-Jr.	39	9	16	25	22	3	0	0	0	4
	Ilves Tampere	Finland	1	0	0	0	0	....	....	....	....	....
2006-07	Ilves Tampere Jr.	Fin-Jr.	15	3	8	11	51	5	0	1	1	2
	Suomi U20	Finland-2	2	0	0	0	0	....	....	....	....	....
	Ilves Tampere	Finland	40	0	0	0	18	4	0	0	0	0

LEHTONEN, Mikko (LEH-tuh-nehn, MEE-koh) BOS.

Right wing. Shoots right. 6'5", 203 lbs. Born, Espoo, Finland, April 1, 1987.
(Boston's 3rd choice, 83rd overall, in 2005 Entry Draft).

			Regular Season					Playoffs				
Season	Club	League	GP	G	A	Pts	PIM	GP	G	A	Pts	PIM
2002-03	Blues Espoo U18	Fin-U18	11	1	3	4	2	1	0	0	0	0
2003-04	Blues Espoo U18	Fin-U18	20	8	7	15	22	....	....	....	....	....
	Blues Espoo Jr.	Fin-Jr.	19	3	0	3	0	5	0	0	0	0
2004-05	Blues Espoo U18	Fin-U18	2	0	2	2	0	....	....	....	....	....
	Blues Espoo Jr.	Fin-Jr.	37	6	9	15	38	6	3	1	4	0
	Blues Espoo	Finland	1	0	0	0	0	....	....	....	....	....
2005-06	Blues Espoo Jr.	Fin-Jr.	15	3	4	7	12	10	5	2	7	6
	Suomi U20	Finland-2	3	1	0	1	2	....	....	....	....	....
	Blues Espoo	Finland	25	4	0	4	0	....	....	....	....	....
2006-07	Suomi U20	Finland-2	3	0	3	3	0	....	....	....	....	....
	Blues Espoo	Finland	39	6	9	15	24	9	1	1	2	4

LEMIEUX, Francis (leh-M'YOO, FRAN-sihs) **MTL.**

Center. Shoots right. 5'11", 187 lbs. Born, Sherbrooke, Que., February 22, 1984.

			Regular Season					Playoffs				
Season	Club	League	GP	G	A	Pts	PIM	GP	G	A	Pts	PIM
2001-02	Chicoutimi	QMJHL	66	17	22	39	44	3	0	0	0	0
2002-03	Chicoutimi	QMJHL	66	28	35	63	36	4	0	0	0	2
2003-04	Chicoutimi	QMJHL	70	22	44	66	49	18	6	4	10	10
2004-05	Chicoutimi	QMJHL	70	32	50	82	52	13	4	5	9	6
2005-06	Hamilton Bulldogs	AHL	67	18	23	41	76	....	....	....	....	....
2006-07	Hamilton Bulldogs	AHL	44	6	11	17	34	11	0	2	2	6

Signed as a free agent by **Montreal**, December 8, 2005.

LEMTYUGOV, Nikolai (LEHM-tyuh-gawf, NIH-koh-ligh) **ST.L.**

Right wing. Shoots left. 6', 183 lbs. Born, Miass, USSR, January 15, 1986.
(St. Louis' 7th choice, 219th overall, in 2005 Entry Draft).

			Regular Season					Playoffs				
Season	Club	League	GP	G	A	Pts	PIM	GP	G	A	Pts	PIM
2003-04	CSKA Moscow 2	Russia-3	STATISTICS NOT AVAILABLE									
2004-05	CSKA Moscow 2	Russia-3	STATISTICS NOT AVAILABLE									
	CSKA Moscow	Russia	11	1	1	2	16	....	....	....	....	....
2005-06	CSKA Moscow	Russia	37	9	11	20	45	7	1	1	2	8
2006-07	Cherepovets	Russia	52	11	8	19	50	5	0	1	1	8

LEPISTO, Sami (LEH-pihs-toh, SA-mee) **WSH.**

Defense. Shoots left. 5'11", 176 lbs. Born, Espoo, Finland, October 17, 1984.
(Washington's 6th choice, 66th overall, in 2004 Entry Draft).

			Regular Season					Playoffs				
Season	Club	League	GP	G	A	Pts	PIM	GP	G	A	Pts	PIM
2001-02	Jokerit U18	Fin-U18	20	8	14	22	36	8	4	8	12	12
	Jokerit Helsinki Jr.	Fin-Jr.	14	0	5	5	2	....	....	....	....	....
2002-03	Jokerit Helsinki Jr.	Fin-Jr.	36	5	14	19	34	11	1	5	6	8
2003-04	Suomi U20	Finland-2	1	0	0	0	0	....	....	....	....	....
	Jokerit Helsinki	Finland	53	3	4	7	20	8	0	1	1	4
2004-05	Jokerit Helsinki	Finland	55	7	18	25	44	12	1	7	8	12
2005-06	Jokerit Helsinki	Finland	56	8	21	29	68	....	....	....	....	....
2006-07	Jokerit Helsinki	Finland	26	1	9	10	32	10	2	2	4	4

LESSARD, Pierre-Luc (leh-SAHR, PEE-air-LEWK) **OTT.**

Defense. Shoots left. 6', 180 lbs. Born, Thetford Mines, Que., January 16, 1988.
(Ottawa's 4th choice, 121st overall, in 2006 Entry Draft).

			Regular Season					Playoffs				
Season	Club	League	GP	G	A	Pts	PIM	GP	G	A	Pts	PIM
2004-05	Gatineau	QMJHL	48	3	6	9	9	10	0	2	2	0
2005-06	Gatineau	QMJHL	55	7	25	32	38	17	2	10	12	12
2006-07	PEI Rocket	QMJHL	70	12	22	34	77	7	0	2	2	0

LETESTU, Mark **PIT.**

Center. Shoots right. 5'11", 195 lbs. Born, Elk Point, Alta., February 4, 1985.

			Regular Season					Playoffs				
Season	Club	League	GP	G	A	Pts	PIM	GP	G	A	Pts	PIM
2003-04	Bonneyville	AJHL	58	22	27	49	24	....	....	....	....	....
2004-05	Bonnyville Pontiacs	AJHL	63	39	47	86	32	....	....	....	....	....
2006-07	Western Mich.	CCHA	37	24	22	46	14	....	....	....	....	....
	Wilkes-Barre	AHL	3	0	0	0	0	2	0	0	0	2

Signed as a free agent by **Pittsburgh**, March 20, 2007.

LETOURNEAU-LEBLOND, Pierre-Luc (leh-TOOR-noh-leh-BLAWN) **N.J.**

Right wing. Shoots left. 6'2", 215 lbs. Born, Levis, Que., June 4, 1985.
(New Jersey's 4th choice, 216th overall, in 2004 Entry Draft).

			Regular Season					Playoffs				
Season	Club	League	GP	G	A	Pts	PIM	GP	G	A	Pts	PIM
2003-04	Baie-Comeau	QMJHL	62	2	3	5	198	4	0	0	0	6
2004-05	Baie-Comeau	QMJHL	67	1	6	7	229	6	0	1	1	10
2005-06	Albany River Rats	AHL	27	1	1	2	130	....	....	....	....	....
	Adirondack	UHL	31	3	6	9	165	6	0	1	1	29
2006-07	Trenton Titans	ECHL	52	4	9	13	183	4	0	0	0	15

LEWIS, Grant (LOO-ihs, GRANT) **ATL.**

Defense. Shoots right. 6'3", 200 lbs. Born, Pittsburgh, PA, January 20, 1985.
(Atlanta's 2nd choice, 40th overall, in 2004 Entry Draft).

			Regular Season					Playoffs				
Season	Club	League	GP	G	A	Pts	PIM	GP	G	A	Pts	PIM
2002-03	Pittsburgh Forge	NAHL	50	2	7	9	59	....	....	....	....	....
2003-04	Dartmouth	ECAC	34	3	22	25	57	....	....	....	....	....
2004-05	Dartmouth	ECACHL	33	5	17	22	32	....	....	....	....	....
2005-06	Dartmouth	ECACHL	29	4	11	15	53	....	....	....	....	....
2006-07	Dartmouth	ECACHL	24	1	14	15	30	....	....	....	....	....

ECAC All-Rookie Team (2004) • ECAC First All-Star Team (2004) • ECACHL Second All-Star Team (2006)

LEWIS, Trevor (LOO-ihs, TREH-vuhr) **L.A.**

Center. Shoots right. 6'1", 192 lbs. Born, Salt Lake City, UT, January 8, 1987.
(Los Angeles' 2nd choice, 17th overall, in 2006 Entry Draft).

			Regular Season					Playoffs				
Season	Club	League	GP	G	A	Pts	PIM	GP	G	A	Pts	PIM
2004-05	Des Moines	USHL	52	10	12	22	70	....	....	....	....	....
2005-06	Des Moines	USHL	56	35	40	75	69	11	3	*13	*16	16
2006-07	Owen Sound	OHL	62	29	44	73	51	4	1	2	3	0
	Manchester	AHL	8	4	2	6	2	2	0	0	0	0

LINDGREN, Perttu (LIHND-gruhn, PUHR-too) **DAL.**

Center. Shoots left. 6', 185 lbs. Born, Tampere, Finland, August 26, 1987.
(Dallas' 4th choice, 75th overall, in 2005 Entry Draft).

			Regular Season					Playoffs				
Season	Club	League	GP	G	A	Pts	PIM	GP	G	A	Pts	PIM
2003-04	Ilves Tampere U18	Fin-U18	24	11	17	28	26	....	....	....	....	....
	Ilves Tampere Jr.	Fin-Jr.	2	0	0	0	0	....	....	....	....	....
2004-05	Ilves Tampere Jr.	Fin-Jr.	38	12	29	41	2	10	7	10	17	4
	Ilves Tampere	Finland	2	0	0	0	0	....	....	....	....	....
2005-06	Ilves Tampere Jr.	Fin-Jr.	2	1	0	1	0	....	....	....	....	....
	Suomi U20	Finland-2	3	0	3	3	0	....	....	....	....	....
	Ilves Tampere	Finland	51	13	24	37	16	4	0	0	0	0
2006-07	Suomi U20	Finland-2	2	1	1	2	2	....	....	....	....	....
	Ilves Tampere	Finland	43	4	22	26	38	7	4	2	6	2

LINDSTROM, Sanny (LIHND-struhm, SAN-nee) **COL.**

Defense. Shoots left. 6'2", 205 lbs. Born, Stockholm, Sweden, December 24, 1979.
(Colorado's 4th choice, 112th overall, in 1999 Entry Draft).

			Regular Season					Playoffs				
Season	Club	League	GP	G	A	Pts	PIM	GP	G	A	Pts	PIM
1997-98	Huddinge IK	Sweden-2	32	6	6	12	46	....	....	....	....	....
1998-99	Huddinge IK	Sweden-2	37	4	4	8	65	....	....	....	....	....
99-2000	Hershey Bears	AHL	42	1	2	3	57	....	....	....	....	....
	Baton Rouge	ECHL	11	1	2	3	16	....	....	....	....	....
2000-01	Hershey Bears	AHL	24	0	0	0	61	....	....	....	....	....
	Quad City	UHL	5	1	1	2	10	....	....	....	....	....
2001-02	Quad City	UHL	38	4	23	27	71	12	0	3	3	20
	Hershey Bears	AHL	2	0	0	0	0	....	....	....	....	....
2002-03	Timra IK	Sweden	39	1	1	2	81	9	0	1	1	0
2003-04	Timra IK	Sweden	48	1	3	4	91	10	2	0	2	24
2004-05	Timra IK	Sweden	50	5	6	11	109	7	0	1	1	10
2005-06	Timra IK	Sweden	50	2	4	6	83	....	....	....	....	....
2006-07	Timra IK	Sweden	42	4	7	11	88	7	1	0	1	8

• Missed majority of 2000-01 season recovering from knee injury suffered in practice, March 5, 2000.

LINGLET, Charles (LIHNG-leht, CHAHR-uhlz) **ST.L.**

Left wing. Shoots left. 6'2", 205 lbs. Born, Montreal, Que., June 22, 1982.

			Regular Season					Playoffs				
Season	Club	League	GP	G	A	Pts	PIM	GP	G	A	Pts	PIM
99-2000	Baie-Comeau	QMJHL	64	14	20	34	13	6	3	3	6	4
2000-01	Baie-Comeau	QMJHL	70	21	34	55	61	11	2	2	4	10
2001-02	Baie-Comeau	QMJHL	72	52	71	123	34	5	1	3	4	2
2002-03	Baie-Comeau	QMJHL	47	21	27	48	35	12	3	8	11	18
2003-04	Utah Grizzlies	AHL	7	0	0	0	2	....	....	....	....	....
	Alaska Aces	ECHL	62	20	35	55	61	7	2	5	7	4
2004-05	Alaska Aces	ECHL	72	28	34	62	44	15	6	10	16	14
2005-06	Peoria Rivermen	AHL	38	14	7	21	10	....	....	....	....	....
	Las Vegas	ECHL	16	5	9	14	15	12	5	4	9	20
2006-07	Peoria Rivermen	AHL	73	31	29	60	30	....	....	....	....	....

QMJHL First All-Star Team (2002)

Signed as a free agent by **St. Louis**, Jauary 1, 2007.

LITTLE, Bryan (LIH-tuhl, BRIGH-uhn) **ATL.**

Center. Shoots right. 5'11", 200 lbs. Born, Edmonton, Alta., November 12, 1987.
(Atlanta's 1st choice, 12th overall, in 2006 Entry Draft).

			Regular Season					Playoffs				
Season	Club	League	GP	G	A	Pts	PIM	GP	G	A	Pts	PIM
2003-04	Barrie Colts	OHL	64	34	24	58	18	12	5	5	10	7
2004-05	Barrie Colts	OHL	62	36	32	68	34	4	5	1	6	2
2005-06	Barrie Colts	OHL	64	42	67	109	99	14	8	15	23	19
2006-07	Barrie Colts	OHL	57	41	66	107	77	8	4	5	9	8
	Chicago Wolves	AHL	....	....	....	....	....	2	0	0	0	0

OHL Second All-Star Team (2007)

LOCKE, Corey (LAWK, KOH-ree) **MTL.**

Center. Shoots left. 5'9", 168 lbs. Born, Toronto, Ont., May 8, 1984.
(Montreal's 5th choice, 113th overall, in 2003 Entry Draft).

			Regular Season					Playoffs				
Season	Club	League	GP	G	A	Pts	PIM	GP	G	A	Pts	PIM
2000-01	Newmarket	OPJHL	49	34	51	85	16	16	10	12	22	14
2001-02	Ottawa 67's	OHL	55	18	25	43	18	13	6	7	13	10
2002-03	Ottawa 67's	OHL	66	*63	*88	*151	83	23	*19	19	*38	30
2003-04	Ottawa 67's	OHL	65	*51	67	*118	82	7	7	3	10	10
2004-05	Hamilton Bulldogs	AHL	78	16	27	43	20	4	0	0	0	2
2005-06	Hamilton Bulldogs	AHL	77	19	40	59	67	....	....	....	....	....
2006-07	Hamilton Bulldogs	AHL	80	20	35	55	54	22	*10	12	22	10

OHL First All-Star Team (2003, 2004) • OHL Player of the Year (2003, 2004) • Canadian Major Junior First All-Star Team (2003, 2004) • Canadian Major Junior Player of the Year (2003)

LOGINOV, Denis (LOG-gih-nawv, DEH-nihs) **ATL.**

Center. Shoots left. 6'1", 210 lbs. Born, Kazan, USSR, May 5, 1985.
(Atlanta's 7th choice, 203rd overall, in 2003 Entry Draft).

			Regular Season					Playoffs				
Season	Club	League	GP	G	A	Pts	PIM	GP	G	A	Pts	PIM
99-2000	Ak Bars Kazan 2	Russia-3	4	0	0	0	0	....	....	....	....	....
2000-01	Ak Bars Kazan 2	Russia-3	STATISTICS NOT AVAILABLE									
2001-02	Ak Bars Kazan 2	Russia-3	38	6	10	16	40	....	....	....	....	....
	Team Volga	Exhib.	3	0	3	3	27	....	....	....	....	....
2002-03	Ak Bars Kazan 2	Russia-3	52	17	24	41	98	....	....	....	....	....
	Perm	Russia	1	0	0	0	0	....	....	....	....	....
2003-04	Ak Bars Kazan	Russia	16	2	1	3	0	7	1	0	1	6
2004-05	Ak Bars Kazan	Russia	2	0	0	0	0	....	....	....	....	....
2005-06	Almetjevsk	Russia-2	7	1	0	1	8	....	....	....	....	....
	Ak Bars Kazan	Russia	16	1	1	2	10	....	....	....	....	....
2006-07	Ak Bars Kazan 2	Russia-3	STATISTICS NOT AVAILABLE									

LOUHIVAARA, Ossi (loo-hih-VAH-rah, AW-see) **OTT.**

Right wing. Shoots right. 6', 179 lbs. Born, Kotka, Finland, August 31, 1983.
(Ottawa's 8th choice, 260th overall, in 2003 Entry Draft).

			Regular Season					Playoffs				
Season	Club	League	GP	G	A	Pts	PIM	GP	G	A	Pts	PIM
99-2000	Titaanit Kotka	Finland-3	1	0	0	0	0	....	....	....	....	....
2000-01	Titaanit Kotka	Finland-3	32	10	12	22	10	3	1	2	3	2
2001-02	Titaanit Kotka	Finland-3	34	13	14	27	10	3	1	1	2	0
	HC Banik Most	CzRep-3	....	....	....	....	....	2	1	2	3	2
2002-03	KooKoo Kouvola	Finland-2	44	20	15	35	20	9	1	3	4	4
2003-04	KooKoo Kouvola	Finland-2	41	13	17	30	4	9	1	1	2	2
2004-05	JYP Jyvaskyla	Finland	56	4	9	13	12	3	0	0	0	0
2005-06	JYP Jyvaskyla	Finland	53	7	11	18	30	3	0	2	2	2
2006-07	JYP Jyvaskyla	Finland	34	8	4	12	10	....	....	....	....	....

LOVE, Mitch (LUHV, MIHTCH) **COL.**

Defense. Shoots left. 6', 200 lbs. Born, Quesnel, B.C., June 15, 1984.

			Regular Season					Playoffs				
Season	Club	League	GP	G	A	Pts	PIM	GP	G	A	Pts	PIM
2000-01	Moose Jaw	WHL	51	5	4	9	97	4	0	0	0	2
2001-02	Moose Jaw	WHL	16	0	1	1	40	....	....	....	....	....
	Swift Current	WHL	52	5	11	16	132	12	0	0	0	37
2002-03	Swift Current	WHL	70	2	15	17	*327	4	1	0	1	16
2003-04	Everett Silvertips	WHL	70	12	15	27	163	21	2	6	8	47
2004-05	Everett Silvertips	WHL	59	9	20	29	142	4	0	2	2	6
2005-06	Lowell	AHL	27	0	4	4	68	....	....	....	....	....
2006-07	Albany River Rats	AHL	69	1	5	6	184	....	....	....	....	....

Signed as a free agent by **Colorado**, October 25, 2005.

LUCENIUS, Niclas (loo-SEHN-ee-uhs, NIHK-luhs) **ATL.**

Center. Shoots left. 6', 190 lbs. Born, Turku, Finland, May 3, 1989.
(Atlanta's 2nd choice, 115th overall, in 2007 Entry Draft).

			Regular Season					Playoffs				
Season	Club	League	GP	G	A	Pts	PIM	GP	G	A	Pts	PIM
2005-06	Tappara U18	Fin-U18	11	6	5	11	10	3	2	0	2	25
	Tappara Jr.	Fin-Jr.	23	5	4	9	18	....	....	....	....	....
2006-07	Tappara U18	Fin-U18	7	5	3	8	32	....	....	....	....	....
	Tappara Jr.	Fin-Jr.	33	14	14	28	44	10	2	3	5	14
	Tappara Tampere	Finland	5	0	0	0	0	....	....	....	....	....

LUCHINKIN, Sergei (loo-CHIHN-kihn, SAIR-gay) **CBJ**

Center. Shoots left. 5'11", 172 lbs. Born, Dmitrov, USSR, October 16, 1976.
(Dallas' 9th choice, 202nd overall, in 1995 Entry Draft).

			Regular Season					Playoffs				
Season	Club	League	GP	G	A	Pts	PIM	GP	G	A	Pts	PIM
1994-95	Dynamo Moscow	CIS	6	1	0	1	4	....	....	....	....	....
1995-96	Dynamo Moscow	CIS	21	6	2	8	14	10	0	1	1	6
1996-97	Dynamo Moscow	Russia	18	1	5	6	4	....	....	....	....	....
	Dynamo Moscow	EuroHL	4	0	1	1	4	....	....	....	....	....
1997-98	Dynamo Moscow	EuroHL	1	0	0	0	0	....	....	....	....	....
	Dynamo Moscow	Russia	6	0	1	1	0	....	....	....	....	....
	Spartak Moscow	Russia	10	0	1	1	4	....	....	....	....	....
1998-99	Spartak Moscow	Russia	33	4	5	9	18	....	....	....	....	....
99-2000	Spartak Moscow 2	Russia-3	1	2	0	2	2	....	....	....	....	....
	Spartak Moscow	Russia-2	58	19	17	36	54	....	....	....	....	....
2001-02	HK CSKA Moscow	Russia-2	60	14	20	34	32	....	....	....	....	....
	Spartak Moscow	Russia	57	23	18	41	46	....	....	....	....	....
2002-03	CSKA Moscow	Russia	16	7	4	11	6	....	....	....	....	....
2003-04	CSKA Moscow	Russia	40	1	2	3	14	....	....	....	....	....
2005-06	MVD	Russia	27	3	1	4	22	....	....	....	....	....
	HK MVD-THK Tver	Russia-3	1	0	0	0	0	....	....	....	....	....
	Nizhnekamsk	Russia	17	4	5	9	10	5	0	2	2	10
2006-07	Nizhnekamsk	Russia	4	0	0	0	0	....	....	....	....	....
	Lada Togliatti	Russia	8	1	1	2	8	....	....	....	....	....

Claimed by **Columbus** from **Dallas** in Expansion Draft, June 23, 2000.

LUCIA, Tony (loo-CHEE-ah, TOH-nee) **S.J.**

Left wing. Shoots left. 6', 180 lbs. Born, Wayzata, MN, August 23, 1987.
(San Jose's 8th choice, 193rd overall, in 2005 Entry Draft).

			Regular Season					Playoffs				
Season	Club	League	GP	G	A	Pts	PIM	GP	G	A	Pts	PIM
2003-04	Wayzata	High-MN	31	13	22	35	....	....	....	....	....	....
2004-05	Wayzata	High-MN	24	27	36	63	32	....	....	....	....	....
	Omaha Lancers	USHL	11	1	0	1	0	....	....	....	....	....
2005-06	Omaha Lancers	USHL	56	12	23	35	25	5	0	0	0	2
2006-07	U. of Minnesota	WCHA	43	7	12	19	28	....	....	....	....	....

LUCIC, Milan (LOO-sihk, MEE-lan) **BOS.**

Left wing. Shoots left. 6'4", 220 lbs. Born, Vancouver, B.C., June 7, 1988.
(Boston's 3rd choice, 50th overall, in 2006 Entry Draft).

			Regular Season					Playoffs				
Season	Club	League	GP	G	A	Pts	PIM	GP	G	A	Pts	PIM
2004-05	Coquitlam Express	BCHL	50	9	14	23	100	....	....	....	....	....
	Vancouver Giants	WHL	1	0	0	0	2	2	0	0	0	0
2005-06	Vancouver Giants	WHL	62	9	10	19	149	18	3	4	7	23
2006-07	Vancouver Giants	WHL	70	30	38	68	147	22	7	12	19	26

Memorial Cup Tournament All-Star Team (2007) • Stafford Smythe Memorial Trophy (Memorial Cup Tournament MVP) (2007)

LUDWIG, Trevor (LUHD-wihg, TREH-vuhr) **DAL.**

Defense. Shoots left. 6'1", 200 lbs. Born, Rhinelander, WI, May 24, 1985.
(Dallas' 7th choice, 183rd overall, in 2004 Entry Draft).

			Regular Season					Playoffs				
Season	Club	League	GP	G	A	Pts	PIM	GP	G	A	Pts	PIM
2002-03	Texas Tornado	NAHL	55	4	5	9	39	....	....	....	....	....
2003-04	Texas Tornado	NAHL	54	5	25	30	50	....	....	....	....	....
2004-05	Providence College	H-East	33	1	6	7	36	....	....	....	....	....
2005-06	Providence College	H-East	27	0	2	2	6	....	....	....	....	....
2006-07	Providence College	H-East	26	0	2	2	37	....	....	....	....	....

NAHL All-Rookie Team (2003) • NAHL First All-Star Team (2004)

LUKACEVIC, Ned (loo-kuh-SAY-vihk, NEHD) **L.A.**

Left wing. Shoots left. 6', 185 lbs. Born, Podgorica, Serbia, February 11, 1986.
(Los Angeles' 3rd choice, 110th overall, in 2004 Entry Draft).

			Regular Season					Playoffs				
Season	Club	League	GP	G	A	Pts	PIM	GP	G	A	Pts	PIM
2000-01	Port Coquitlam	BCAHA	60	42	48	90	....	....	....	....	....	....
2001-02	Port Coquitlam	BCAHA	70	40	55	95	60	....	....	....	....	....
	Spokane Chiefs	WHL	1	1	0	1	0	....	....	....	....	....
2002-03	Spokane Chiefs	WHL	31	0	4	4	29	4	0	1	1	0
2003-04	Spokane Chiefs	WHL	72	19	14	33	65	4	1	1	2	2
2004-05	Spokane Chiefs	WHL	71	18	28	46	52	....	....	....	....	....
2005-06	Swift Current	WHL	63	25	28	53	71	4	1	0	1	5
	Manchester	AHL	....	....	....	....	....	7	1	0	1	4
2006-07	Manchester	AHL	12	1	0	1	9	....	....	....	....	....
	Reading Royals	ECHL	53	7	17	24	38	....	....	....	....	....

LUNDIN, Mike (LUHN-dihn, MIGHK) **T.B.**

Defense. Shoots left. 6'1", 195 lbs. Born, Burnsville, MN, September 24, 1984.
(Tampa Bay's 3rd choice, 102nd overall, in 2004 Entry Draft).

			Regular Season					Playoffs				
Season	Club	League	GP	G	A	Pts	PIM	GP	G	A	Pts	PIM
2002-03	Apple Valley	High-MN	27	8	20	27	....	....	....	....	....	....
2003-04	U. of Maine	H-East	44	3	16	19	34	....	....	....	....	....
2004-05	U. of Maine	H-East	40	1	13	14	2	....	....	....	....	....
2005-06	U. of Maine	H-East	36	3	13	16	4	....	....	....	....	....
2006-07	U. of Maine	H-East	40	6	14	20	2	....	....	....	....	....

Hockey East Second All-Star Team (2007)

LUTTINEN, Arttu (LOO-tuh-nehn, AHR-too) **OTT.**

Center. Shoots left. 5'11", 198 lbs. Born, Helsinki, Finland, September 3, 1983.
(Ottawa's 3rd choice, 75th overall, in 2002 Entry Draft).

			Regular Season					Playoffs				
Season	Club	League	GP	G	A	Pts	PIM	GP	G	A	Pts	PIM
99-2000	HIFK Helsinki U18	Fin-U18	17	5	9	14	10	2	0	0	0	2
2000-01	HIFK Helsinki U18	Fin-U18	20	14	20	34	141	3	0	3	3	2
	Ilves Tampere U18	Fin-U18	20	14	20	34	141	....	....	....	....	....
	HIFK Helsinki Jr.	Fin-Jr.	8	4	2	6	4	8	0	1	1	2
2001-02	HIFK Helsinki Jr.	Fin-Jr.	24	16	17	33	60	1	0	0	0	0
2002-03	HIFK Helsinki Jr.	Fin-Jr.	10	8	9	17	52	8	4	6	10	20
	FPS Forssa	Finland-2	2	0	1	1	4	....	....	....	....	....
	HIFK Helsinki	Finland	41	4	4	8	10	1	0	0	0	0
2003-04	HIFK Helsinki Jr.	Fin-Jr.	1	0	0	0	0	....	....	....	....	....
	Ahmat Hyvinkaa	Finland-2	4	3	2	5	2	....	....	....	....	....
	Haukat Jarvenpaa	Finland-2	1	0	0	0	0	....	....	....	....	....
	HIFK Helsinki	Finland	50	1	7	8	12	12	0	0	0	0
2004-05	HIFK Helsinki	Finland	56	12	13	25	67	5	1	0	1	0
2005-06	HIFK Helsinki	Finland	56	18	26	44	66	12	4	3	7	39
2006-07	Binghamton	AHL	74	12	17	29	53	....	....	....	....	....

LYAMIN, Kirill (L'YAH-mihn, kih-RIHL) **OTT.**

Defense. Shoots left. 6'2", 198 lbs. Born, Moscow, USSR, January 13, 1986.
(Ottawa's 2nd choice, 58th overall, in 2004 Entry Draft).

			Regular Season					Playoffs				
Season	Club	League	GP	G	A	Pts	PIM	GP	G	A	Pts	PIM
2001-02	Moscow 18	Exhib.	5	0	3	3	4	....	....	....	....	....
2002-03	CSKA Moscow 2	Russia-3	5	0	0	0	10	....	....	....	....	....
	Moscow 18	Exhib.	5	0	0	0	6	....	....	....	....	....
2003-04	CSKA Moscow 2	Russia-3	STATISTICS NOT AVAILABLE									
	CSKA Moscow	Russia	28	0	3	3	12	....	....	....	....	....
2004-05	CSKA Moscow 2	Russia-3	STATISTICS NOT AVAILABLE									
2005-06	CSKA Moscow	Russia	25	0	1	1	28	2	0	0	0	0
2006-07	CSKA Moscow	Russia	47	1	7	8	48	12	1	0	1	8

LYNES, Luke (LIGHNZ, LEWK) **WSH.**

Center. Shoots left. 6'1", 195 lbs. Born, Rochester Hills, MI, November 28, 1987.
(Washington's 7th choice, 122nd overall, in 2006 Entry Draft).

			Regular Season					Playoffs				
Season	Club	League	GP	G	A	Pts	PIM	GP	G	A	Pts	PIM
2003-04	Culver Academy	High-IN	46	32	29	61	....	....	....	....	....	....
2004-05	Brampton	OHL	68	11	13	24	60	6	0	0	0	4
2005-06	Brampton	OHL	65	34	28	62	61	11	2	6	8	10
2006-07	Brampton	OHL	68	34	31	65	63	4	2	0	2	7

LYUBUSHIN, Mikhail (l'yoo-BOOSH-ihn, mih-kigh-EHL) **L.A.**

Defense. Shoots left. 6'1", 183 lbs. Born, Moscow, USSR, July 24, 1983.
(Los Angeles' 9th choice, 215th overall, in 2002 Entry Draft).

			Regular Season					Playoffs				
Season	Club	League	GP	G	A	Pts	PIM	GP	G	A	Pts	PIM
99-2000	Vityaz Podolsk 2	Russia-3	24	2	2	4	69	....	....	....	....	....
2000-01	Krylja Sovetov	Russia-2	2	0	1	1	0	1	0	0	0	0
2001-02	Krylja Sovetov 2	Russia-3	20	3	6	9	24	....	....	....	....	....
	THK Tver	Russia-2	22	1	0	1	18	....	....	....	....	....
	Krylja Sovetov	Russia	13	0	1	1	14	3	0	0	0	0
2002-03	Krylja Sovetov	Russia	49	0	6	6	26	....	....	....	....	....
2003-04	Dynamo Moscow	Russia	38	1	2	3	18	2	0	0	0	2
2004-05	Voskresensk	Russia	21	1	2	3	16	....	....	....	....	....
	Vityaz Chekhov	Russia-2	8	0	2	2	6	14	1	0	1	8
2005-06	Cherepovets	Russia	23	1	4	5	10	....	....	....	....	....
	Avangard Omsk	Russia	26	0	1	1	20	8	0	0	0	4
2006-07	Avangard Omsk	Russia	21	0	1	1	16	3	0	0	0	2
	Avangard Omsk 2	Russia-3	2	0	1	1	4	....	....	....	....	....

MacDONALD, Andrew (MAK-DAWN-uhld, AN-droo) **NYI**

Defense. Shoots left. 6'1", 188 lbs. Born, Judique, N.S., September 7, 1986.
(NY Islanders' 10th choice, 160th overall, in 2006 Entry Draft).

			Regular Season					Playoffs				
Season	Club	League	GP	G	A	Pts	PIM	GP	G	A	Pts	PIM
2003-04	Truro Bearcats	MJrHL	50	8	20	28	43	10	0	0	0	....
2004-05	Truro Bearcats	MJrHL	56	11	22	33	60	17	6	7	13	....
2005-06	Moncton Wildcats	QMJHL	68	6	40	46	62	21	2	11	13	10
2006-07	Moncton Wildcats	QMJHL	65	14	44	58	81	7	1	5	6	4
	Bridgeport	AHL	3	0	0	0	0	....	....	....	....	....

QMJHL First All-Star Team (2007)

MacDONALD, David (MAK-DAWN-uhld, DAY-vihd) **S.J.**

Defense. Shoots right. 6'4", 230 lbs. Born, Halifax, N.S., April 30, 1985.
(San Jose's 7th choice, 225th overall, in 2004 Entry Draft).

			Regular Season					Playoffs				
Season	Club	League	GP	G	A	Pts	PIM	GP	G	A	Pts	PIM
2003-04	N.E. Jr. Coyotes	EJHL	37	1	5	6	81	....	....	....	....	....
2004-05	Harvard Crimson	ECACHL	33	0	2	2	22	....	....	....	....	....
2005-06	Harvard Crimson	ECACHL	22	0	3	3	24	....	....	....	....	....
2006-07	Harvard Crimson	ECACHL	26	0	2	2	35	....	....	....	....	....

MacDONALD, Franklin (MAK-DAWN-uhld, FRAN-klihn) FLA.

Defense. Shoots left. 6', 198 lbs. Born, Sydney, N.S., April 8, 1985.

			Regular Season					Playoffs				
Season	Club	League	GP	G	A	Pts	PIM	GP	G	A	Pts	PIM
2002-03	Truro Bearcats	MJrHL	48	2	10	12	65	....	....	....	....	....
2003-04	Halifax	QMJHL	63	4	8	12	52	....	....	....	....	....
2004-05	Halifax	QMJHL	65	5	11	16	93	13	0	5	5	24
2005-06	Halifax	QMJHL	58	12	33	45	129	11	4	2	6	22
2006-07	Rochester	AHL	11	0	2	2	12	....	....	....	....	....
	Florida Everblades	ECHL	56	4	20	24	58	16	1	5	6	20

Signed as a free agent by **Florida**, September 14, 2006.

MACENAUER, Maxime (MAK-ehn-owr, mahx-EEM) ANA.

Center. Shoots left. 5'11", 188 lbs. Born, Laval, Que., January 4, 1989.
(Anaheim's 3rd choice, 63rd overall, in 2007 Entry Draft).

			Regular Season					Playoffs				
Season	Club	League	GP	G	A	Pts	PIM	GP	G	A	Pts	PIM
2004-05	Ecole Montpetit	QAAA	37	17	22	39	56	3	0	0	0	0
2005-06	Rimouski Oceanic	QMJHL	41	8	14	22	30	....	....	....	....	....
2006-07	Rouyn-Noranda	QMJHL	14	1	3	4	10	....	....	....	....	....

MACHACEK, Spencer (muh-HA-chehk, SPEHN-suhr) ATL.

Right wing. Shoots right. 6'1", 195 lbs. Born, Lethbridge, Alta., October 14, 1988.
(Atlanta's 1st choice, 67th overall, in 2007 Entry Draft).

			Regular Season					Playoffs				
Season	Club	League	GP	G	A	Pts	PIM	GP	G	A	Pts	PIM
2004-05	Brooks Bandits	AJHL	59	16	20	36	41	10	2	2	4	8
2005-06	Vancouver Giants	WHL	70	23	22	45	53	18	6	8	14	8
2006-07	Vancouver Giants	WHL	63	21	24	45	32	22	9	11	20	14

MACIAS, Raymond (mah-CHEE-ahs, RAY-muhnd) COL.

Defense. Shoots right. 6'2", 195 lbs. Born, Long Beach, CA, September 18, 1986.
(Colorado's 6th choice, 124th overall, in 2005 Entry Draft).

			Regular Season					Playoffs				
Season	Club	League	GP	G	A	Pts	PIM	GP	G	A	Pts	PIM
2002-03	L.A. Jr. Kings	Cal-Am	49	37	26	63	100	....	....	....	....	....
	Kamloops Blazers	WHL	4	0	0	0	0	2	0	0	0	0
2003-04	Kamloops Blazers	WHL	69	12	17	29	14	5	2	0	2	0
2004-05	Kamloops Blazers	WHL	69	12	35	47	18	2	0	0	0	0
2005-06	Kamloops Blazers	WHL	68	12	26	38	34	....	....	....	....	....
2006-07	Kamloops Blazers	WHL	70	30	40	70	58	....	....	....	....	....

WHL West First All-Star Team (2007)

MacKENZIE, Aaron (muh-KEHN-zee, AIR-ruhn)

Defense. Shoots left. 6', 193 lbs. Born, Terrace Bay, Ont., March 7, 1981.

			Regular Season					Playoffs				
Season	Club	League	GP	G	A	Pts	PIM	GP	G	A	Pts	PIM
1998-99	Thunder Bay Flyers	USHL	49	8	12	20	123	3	0	1	1	0
99-2000	U. of Denver	WCHA	40	1	9	10	56	....	....	....	....	....
2000-01	U. of Denver	WCHA	37	2	6	8	45	....	....	....	....	....
2001-02	U. of Denver	WCHA	39	5	18	23	30	....	....	....	....	....
2002-03	U. of Denver	WCHA	41	11	21	32	33	....	....	....	....	....
2003-04	Worcester IceCats	AHL	66	5	9	14	108	10	0	2	2	10
2004-05	Worcester IceCats	AHL	75	2	13	15	106	....	....	....	....	....
2005-06	Peoria Rivermen	AHL	51	2	7	9	35	4	0	0	0	6
2006-07	Peoria Rivermen	AHL	67	1	6	7	46	....	....	....	....	....

WCHA First All-Star Team (2003)

Signed as a free agent by **Worcester** (AHL), October 6, 2003. Signed as a free agent by **St. Louis**, June 29, 2004.

MACKENZIE, Drew (muh-KEHN-zee , DROO) BUF.

Defense. Shoots left. 6'2", 200 lbs. Born, Stamford, CT, December 17, 1988.
(Buffalo's 8th choice, 209th overall, in 2007 Entry Draft).

			Regular Season					Playoffs				
Season	Club	League	GP	G	A	Pts	PIM	GP	G	A	Pts	PIM
2004-05	Taft Rhinos	High-CT	....	0	1	1	....	....	....	....	....	....
2005-06	Taft Rhinos	High-CT	....	0	11	11	....	....	....	....	....	....
2006-07	Taft Rhinos	High-CT	24	3	10	13	10	....	....	....	....	....

• Signed Letter of Intent to attend **University of Vermont** (Hockey East) in fall of 2008.

MACLEAN, Brett (muh-KLAIN, BREHT) PHX.

Left wing. Shoots right. 6'2", 197 lbs. Born, Port Elgin, Ont., December 24, 1988.
(Phoenix's 3rd choice, 32nd overall, in 2007 Entry Draft).

			Regular Season					Playoffs				
Season	Club	League	GP	G	A	Pts	PIM	GP	G	A	Pts	PIM
2003-04	Grey-Bruce	Minor-ON	66	71	47	118	117	....	....	....	....	....
	Listowel Cyclones	OJHL-B	9	4	6	10	10	2	3	2	5	12
2004-05	Erie Otters	OHL	68	7	16	23	31	6	1	1	2	6
2005-06	Erie Otters	OHL	13	3	5	8	6	....	....	....	....	....
	Oshawa Generals	OHL	35	13	25	38	29	....	....	....	....	....
2006-07	Oshawa Generals	OHL	68	47	53	100	43	7	6	9	15	9

OHL Second All-Star Team (2007)

MacMILLAN, Logan (muhk-MIHL-uhn , LOH-guhn) ANA.

Center. Shoots left. 6'1", 182 lbs. Born, Charlottetown, PEI, July 5, 1989.
(Anaheim's 1st choice, 19th overall, in 2007 Entry Draft).

			Regular Season					Playoffs				
Season	Club	League	GP	G	A	Pts	PIM	GP	G	A	Pts	PIM
2004-05	Notre Dame	SJHL	41	9	19	28	27	....	....	....	....	....
2005-06	Halifax	QMJHL	62	9	9	18	31	11	1	0	1	0
2006-07	Halifax	QMJHL	68	20	35	55	82	12	9	11	20	6

MacMURCHY, Ryan (muhk-MUHR-chee, RIGH-uhn)

Right wing. Shoots right. 5'11", 190 lbs. Born, Regina, Sask., April 27, 1983.
(St. Louis' 9th choice, 284th overall, in 2002 Entry Draft).

			Regular Season					Playoffs				
Season	Club	League	GP	G	A	Pts	PIM	GP	G	A	Pts	PIM
1998-99	Regina Capitals	SMHL	40	18	15	33	....	....	....	....	....	....
99-2000	Regina Capitals	SMHL	38	23	44	67	....	....	....	....	....	....
2000-01	Vernon Vipers	BCHL	30	4	6	10	....	....	....	....	....	....
2001-02	Notre Dame	AJHL	61	32	52	84	63	11	2	5	7	13
2002-03	U. of Wisconsin	WCHA	39	10	14	24	69	....	....	....	....	....
2003-04	U. of Wisconsin	WCHA	43	15	13	28	95	....	....	....	....	....
2004-05	U. of Wisconsin	WCHA	40	11	22	33	88	....	....	....	....	....
2005-06	U. of Wisconsin	WCHA	42	8	17	25	90	....	....	....	....	....
2006-07	Peoria Rivermen	AHL	24	4	1	5	20	....	....	....	....	....
	Alaska Aces	ECHL	18	4	6	10	52	15	4	1	5	63

MADILL, Mike (MA-dihl, MIGHK)

Defense. Shoots right. 6', 189 lbs. Born, Kirkland, Que., May 9, 1982.

			Regular Season					Playoffs				
Season	Club	League	GP	G	A	Pts	PIM	GP	G	A	Pts	PIM
2002-03	St. Lawrence	ECAC	35	1	8	9	26	....	....	....	....	....
2003-04	St. Lawrence	ECAC	41	2	4	6	47	....	....	....	....	....
2004-05	St. Lawrence	ECACHL	38	6	15	21	30	....	....	....	....	....
2005-06	St. Lawrence	ECACHL	40	5	22	27	54	....	....	....	....	....
2006-07	Houston Aeros	AHL	7	0	1	1	0	....	....	....	....	....
	Texas Wildcatters	ECHL	67	4	39	43	60	10	0	3	3	14

ECACHL First All-Star Team (2006)

Signed as a free agent by **Minnesota**, July 5, 2006.

MADSEN, Morten (MAD-sehn, MOHR-tuhn) MIN.

Right wing. Shoots left. 6'2", 205 lbs. Born, Rodovre, Denmark, January 16, 1987.
(Minnesota's 5th choice, 122nd overall, in 2005 Entry Draft).

			Regular Season					Playoffs				
Season	Club	League	GP	G	A	Pts	PIM	GP	G	A	Pts	PIM
2003-04	V.Frolunda U18	Swe-U18	11	13	8	21	0	7	3	1	4	4
	V.Frolunda Jr.	Swe-Jr.	16	3	2	5	0	1	0	0	0	0
2004-05	Frolunda U18	Swe-U18	2	1	2	3	0	6	7	7	14	6
	Frolunda Jr.	Swe-Jr.	32	7	14	21	14	6	3	2	5	0
2005-06	Frolunda Jr.	Swe-Jr.	36	10	32	42	60	7	5	3	8	4
	Frolunda	Sweden	5	0	0	0	2	....	....	....	....	....
2006-07	Victoriaville Tigres	QMJHL	62	32	68	100	86	6	3	6	9	4

MAENPAA, Mikko (MIGH-ehn-pah, MEE-koh) CBJ

Defense. Shoots left. 5'11", 180 lbs. Born, Tampere, Finland, April 19, 1983.

			Regular Season					Playoffs				
Season	Club	League	GP	G	A	Pts	PIM	GP	G	A	Pts	PIM
99-2000	Tappara Jr.	Fin-Jr.	31	10	5	15	60	....	....	....	....	....
2000-01	Tappara Jr.	Fin-Jr.	6	2	1	3	26	....	....	....	....	....
	Tappara Jr.	Fin-Jr.	35	10	8	18	30	5	1	0	1	4
2001-02	Tappara Jr.	Fin-Jr.	39	13	12	25	201	....	....	....	....	....
2002-03	JYP Jyvaskyla Jr.	Fin-Jr.	4	1	3	4	0	....	....	....	....	....
	JYP Jyvaskyla	Finland	9	0	0	0	4	....	....	....	....	....
2003-04	JYP Jyvaskyla	Finland	40	0	2	2	44	2	0	0	0	2
	JYP Jyvaskyla Jr.	Fin-Jr.	3	0	2	2	4	....	....	....	....	....
	Sport Vaasa	Finland-2	2	1	0	1	0	....	....	....	....	....
2004-05	JYP Jyvaskyla	Finland	14	0	1	1	6	....	....	....	....	....
	Pelicans Lahti	Finland	27	0	2	2	10	....	....	....	....	....
	Jukurit Mikkeli	Finland-2	4	0	2	2	4	....	....	....	....	....
2005-06	Jukurit Mikkeli	Finland-2	40	6	10	16	75	6	2	1	3	2
2006-07	HPK Hameenlinna	Finland	52	14	26	40	48	9	3	2	5	10

Signed as a free agent by **Columbus**, June 1, 2007.

MAGNAN-GRENIER, Olivier (MAHG-nah-GREH-n'yay) N.J.

Defense. Shoots left. 6'2", 200 lbs. Born, Sherbrooke, Que., May 1, 1986.
(New Jersey's 6th choice, 148th overall, in 2006 Entry Draft).

			Regular Season					Playoffs				
Season	Club	League	GP	G	A	Pts	PIM	GP	G	A	Pts	PIM
2004-05	Rouyn-Noranda	QMJHL	70	5	15	20	82	10	0	2	2	14
2005-06	Rouyn-Noranda	QMJHL	69	14	27	41	97	5	0	1	1	6
2006-07	Lowell Devils	AHL	24	1	1	2	13	....	....	....	....	....
	Trenton Titans	ECHL	45	1	9	10	63	1	0	0	0	0

MAKAROV, Igor (mak-AH-rawv, EE-gohr) CHI.

Right wing. Shoots right. 6'1", 183 lbs. Born, Moscow, USSR, September 19, 1987.
(Chicago's 2nd choice, 33rd overall, in 2006 Entry Draft).

			Regular Season					Playoffs				
Season	Club	League	GP	G	A	Pts	PIM	GP	G	A	Pts	PIM
2003-04	Krylja Sovetov 2	Russia-3	1	0	0	0	0	....	....	....	....	....
2004-05	Krylja Sovetov 2	Russia-3	38	13	15	28	44	....	....	....	....	....
	Krylja Sovetov	Russia-2	6	2	2	4	4	1	0	0	0	0
2005-06	Krylja Sovetov	Russia-2	35	9	7	16	20	17	3	4	7	20
2006-07	SKA St. Petersburg	Russia	49	7	2	9	47	3	1	0	1	2

MAKI, Ryan (MA-kee, RIGH-uhn) NSH.

Right wing. Shoots right. 6'1", 208 lbs. Born, Medford, NJ, April 23, 1985.
(Nashville's 5th choice, 176th overall, in 2005 Entry Draft).

			Regular Season					Playoffs				
Season	Club	League	GP	G	A	Pts	PIM	GP	G	A	Pts	PIM
2001-02	USNTDP	U-17	17	3	11	14	6	....	....	....	....	....
	USNTDP	NAHL	31	4	11	15	24	....	....	....	....	....
2002-03	USNTDP	U-18	42	5	6	11	18	....	....	....	....	....
	USNTDP	NAHL	10	1	0	1	8	....	....	....	....	....
2003-04	Harvard Crimson	ECAC	34	4	4	8	18	....	....	....	....	....
2004-05	Harvard Crimson	ECACHL	30	10	9	19	20	....	....	....	....	....
2005-06	Harvard Crimson	ECACHL	33	10	12	22	32	....	....	....	....	....
2006-07	Harvard Crimson	ECACHL	32	12	11	23	36	....	....	....	....	....
	Milwaukee	AHL	2	0	1	1	0	2	0	0	0	0

MALENKYKH, Vladimir (MAH-lihn-keh, vla-DIH-meer) PIT.

Defense. Shoots left. 6'1", 187 lbs. Born, Togliatti, USSR, October 1, 1980.
(Pittsburgh's 7th choice, 157th overall, in 1999 Entry Draft).

			Regular Season					Playoffs				
Season	Club	League	GP	G	A	Pts	PIM	GP	G	A	Pts	PIM
1997-98	Lada Togliatti 2	Russia-3	39	6	4	10	112	....	....	....	....	....
1998-99	Lada Togliatti 2	Russia-4	38	6	3	9	68	....	....	....	....	....
	Lada Togliatti	Russia	9	0	0	0	2	....	....	....	....	....
99-2000	Lada Togliatti 2	Russia-3	34	7	9	16	98	....	....	....	....	....
	CSK VVS Samara	Russia	7	0	1	1	14	....	....	....	....	....
	Lada Togliatti	Russia	1	0	0	0	0	....	....	....	....	....
	CSK VVS Samara 2	Russia-3	1	0	1	1	2	....	....	....	....	....
2000-01	Lada Togliatti	Russia	25	1	1	2	14	5	0	0	0	26
2001-02	Lada Togliatti	Russia	47	5	4	9	88	4	0	0	0	2
2002-03	Lada Togliatti	Russia	30	3	1	4	36	10	0	0	0	6
2003-04	Lada Togliatti	Russia	44	2	4	6	42	3	0	0	0	0
2004-05	Lada Togliatti	Russia	37	1	4	5	20	....	....	....	....	....
2005-06	Magnitogorsk	Russia	36	0	2	2	8	11	0	1	1	16
	Magnitogorsk 2	Russia-3	5	1	1	2	2	....	....	....	....	....
2006-07	Magnitogorsk	Russia	54	2	9	11	92	15	1	2	3	28

MALMIVAARA, Olli (mal-mih-VAH-ruh, OH-lee) N.J.

Defense. Shoots left. 6'7", 220 lbs. Born, Kajaani, Finland, March 13, 1982.
(Chicago's 6th choice, 117th overall, in 2000 Entry Draft).

			Regular Season					Playoffs				
Season	Club	League	GP	G	A	Pts	PIM	GP	G	A	Pts	PIM
1998-99	Jokerit U18	Fin-U18	35	1	8	9	10	7	0	0	0	2
99-2000	Jokerit U18	Fin-U18	14	6	6	12	14	1	0	0	0	2
	Jokerit U18	Fin-U18	27	3	3	6	12	12	0	2	2	2
2000-01	Jokerit Helsinki Jr.	Fin-Jr.	33	10	13	23	24	2	0	0	0	0
	Kiekko-Vantaa	Finland-2	4	1	0	1	2	....	....	....	....	....
	Jokerit Helsinki	Finland	5	0	0	0	2	....	....	....	....	....
2001-02	Jokerit Helsinki Jr.	Fin-Jr.	2	0	1	1	0	....	....	....	....	....
	Jokerit Helsinki	Finland	53	0	6	6	16	11	0	0	0	2
2002-03	Jokerit Helsinki Jr.	Fin-Jr.	1	0	0	0	0	....	....	....	....	....
	Kiekko-Vantaa	Finland-2	2	1	1	2	2	....	....	....	....	....
	Jokerit Helsinki	Finland	42	1	0	1	22	5	0	0	0	0
2003-04	Jokerit Helsinki	Finland	25	1	0	1	2	....	....	....	....	....
	SaiPa	Finland	11	1	0	1	6	....	....	....	....	....
2004-05	SaiPa	Finland	56	9	1	10	89	....	....	....	....	....
2005-06	SaiPa	Finland	54	11	9	20	134	8	1	0	1	12
2006-07	Lowell Devils	AHL	60	1	10	11	44	....	....	....	....	....

MALONE, Brad (MA-lohn, BRAD) COL.

Center/Left wing. Shoots left. 6'2", 207 lbs. Born, Miramichi, N.B., May 20, 1989.
(Colorado's 5th choice, 105th overall, in 2007 Entry Draft).

			Regular Season					Playoffs				
Season	Club	League	GP	G	A	Pts	PIM	GP	G	A	Pts	PIM
2005-06	Cushing	High-MA	STATISTICS NOT AVAILABLE									
2006-07	Sioux Falls	USHL	57	14	19	33	134	8	3	1	4	24

• Signed Letter of Intent to attend **University of North Dakota** (WCHA) in fall of 2007.

MALONEY, Brian (muh-LOH-nee, BRIGH-uhn)

Left wing. Shoots left. 6'1", 205 lbs. Born, Bassano, Alta., September 27, 1978.

			Regular Season					Playoffs				
Season	Club	League	GP	G	A	Pts	PIM	GP	G	A	Pts	PIM
1997-98	Olds Grizzlys	AJHL	31	21	13	34	....	....	....	....	....	....
	Chilliwack Chiefs	BCHL	27	4	12	16	36	....	....	....	....	....
1998-99	Chilliwack Chiefs	BCHL	60	40	75	115	121	....	....	....	....	....
99-2000	Michigan State	CCHA	42	12	19	31	87	....	....	....	....	....
2000-01	Michigan State	CCHA	41	15	22	37	86	....	....	....	....	....
2001-02	Michigan State	CCHA	37	17	16	33	71	....	....	....	....	....
2002-03	Michigan State	CCHA	39	19	16	35	48	....	....	....	....	....
	Chicago Wolves	AHL	4	0	1	1	11	....	....	....	....	....
2003-04	Chicago Wolves	AHL	69	9	11	20	56	10	1	1	2	17
2004-05	Chicago Wolves	AHL	77	7	10	17	164	18	2	1	3	38
2005-06	Chicago Wolves	AHL	68	16	18	34	143	....	....	....	....	....
2006-07	Binghamton	AHL	39	5	8	13	44	....	....	....	....	....

Signed as a free agent by **Atlanta**, April 2, 2003. Signed as a free agent by **Ottawa**, July 27, 2006. Signed as a free agent by **Krefeld** (Germany), June 27, 2007.

MARCHAND, Brad (mahr-SHAHND, BRAD) BOS.

Center. Shoots left. 5'9", 187 lbs. Born, Halifax, N.S., May 11, 1988.
(Boston's 4th choice, 71st overall, in 2006 Entry Draft).

			Regular Season					Playoffs				
Season	Club	League	GP	G	A	Pts	PIM	GP	G	A	Pts	PIM
2003-04	Dartmouth	NSMHL	60	47	47	94	104	....	....	....	....	....
2004-05	Moncton Wildcats	QMJHL	61	9	20	29	52	11	1	0	1	7
2005-06	Moncton Wildcats	QMJHL	68	29	37	66	83	20	5	14	19	34
2006-07	Val-d'Or Foreurs	QMJHL	57	33	47	80	108	20	*16	*24	*40	36

MARCINKO, Tomas (mahr-TSIHN-koh, TAW-mahsh) NYI

Center. Shoots right. 6'4", 187 lbs. Born, Poprad, Czech., April 11, 1988.
(NY Islanders' 6th choice, 115th overall, in 2006 Entry Draft).

			Regular Season					Playoffs				
Season	Club	League	GP	G	A	Pts	PIM	GP	G	A	Pts	PIM
2003-04	HC Kosice U18	Svk-U18	42	19	23	42	60	2	0	0	0	4
	HC Kosice Jr.	Slovak-Jr.	7	0	2	2	4	3	0	1	1	0
2004-05	HC Kosice	Slovakia	6	0	0	0	0	....	....	....	....	....
	HC Kosice Jr.	Slovak-Jr.	38	11	18	29	28	8	1	2	3	6
	HC Kosice	Slovakia	6	0	0	0	0	....	....	....	....	....
2005-06	HC Kosice Jr.	Slovak-Jr.	35	26	21	47	50	3	1	0	1	4
	HKm Humenne	Slovak-2	9	3	5	8	10	....	....	....	....	....
	HC Kosice	Slovakia	18	2	0	2	2	5	0	0	0	0
2006-07	Barrie Colts	OHL	56	19	21	40	56	8	0	1	1	8

MAREK, Jan (MAIR-ehk, YAHN) L.A.

Center. Shoots right. 5'10", 185 lbs. Born, Jindrichuv Hradec, Czech., December 31, 1979.
(NY Rangers' 10th choice, 243rd overall, in 2003 Entry Draft).

			Regular Season					Playoffs				
Season	Club	League	GP	G	A	Pts	PIM	GP	G	A	Pts	PIM
1998-99	Trinec	CzRep	32	2	2	4	2	6	0	0	0	0
99-2000	HC Trinec Jr.	CzRep-Jr.	6	5	5	10	10	1	0	0	0	0
	HC Slezan Opava	CzRep-2	3	0	1	1	4	....	....	....	....	....
	Jind. Hradec	CzRep-2	4	0	3	3	10	....	....	....	....	....
	HC Ocelari Trinec	CzRep	32	1	5	6	4	2	0	0	0	0
2000-01	HC Ocelari Trinec	CzRep	38	7	4	11	2	....	....	....	....	....
2001-02	HC Ocelari Trinec	CzRep	52	13	27	40	44	6	1	3	4	6
2002-03	HC Ocelari Trinec	CzRep	51	*32	30	62	42	12	6	4	10	22
2003-04	HC Sparta Praha	CzRep	50	21	30	51	62	11	4	9	13	26
2004-05	HC Sparta Praha	CzRep	38	7	21	28	26	5	2	2	4	2
2005-06	HC Sparta Praha	CzRep	48	22	32	*54	66	17	4	4	8	24
2006-07	Magnitogorsk	Russia	47	17	30	47	70	15	7	10	17	10

Traded to **Los Angeles** by **NY Rangers** with Jason Ward, Marc-Andre Cliche and future considerations for Sean Avery, John Seymour and future considerations, February 5, 2007.

MAROON, Patrick (ma-ROON, PAT-rihk) PHI.

Left wing. Shoots left. 6'4", 225 lbs. Born, St Louis, MO, April 23, 1988.
(Philadelphia's 6th choice, 161st overall, in 2007 Entry Draft).

			Regular Season					Playoffs				
Season	Club	League	GP	G	A	Pts	PIM	GP	G	A	Pts	PIM
2005-06	Texarkana Bandits	NAHL	57	23	37	60	61	8	3	1	4	22
2006-07	St. Louis Bandits	NAHL	57	40	55	*95	152	12	*10	*13	*23	12

• Signed Letter of Intent to attend **Ferris State University** (CCHA) in fall of 2007.

MARQUARDT, Matt (MAR-kwart, MAT) CBJ

Left wing. Shoots left. 6'2", 222 lbs. Born, North Bay, Ont., July 19, 1987.
(Columbus' 10th choice, 194th overall, in 2006 Entry Draft).

			Regular Season					Playoffs				
Season	Club	League	GP	G	A	Pts	PIM	GP	G	A	Pts	PIM
2003-04	Huntsville Wildcats	OPJHL	STATISTICS NOT AVAILABLE									
	Brockville Braves	CJHL	11	1	2	3	17	....	....	....	....	....
2004-05	Brockville Braves	CJHL	55	19	22	41	78	7	2	1	3	8
2005-06	Moncton Wildcats	QMJHL	68	16	9	25	69	20	5	3	8	12
2006-07	Moncton Wildcats	QMJHL	67	41	29	70	68	7	1	3	4	14

CJHL Rookie of the Year (2005)

MARR, Steve (MAHR, STEEV) CHI.

Defense. Shoots left. 6'2", 207 lbs. Born, Kamloops, B.C., June 6, 1984.

			Regular Season					Playoffs				
Season	Club	League	GP	G	A	Pts	PIM	GP	G	A	Pts	PIM
2001-02	Medicine Hat	WHL	63	0	0	0	50	....	....	....	....	....
2002-03	Medicine Hat	WHL	54	3	11	14	95	11	0	1	1	22
2003-04	Medicine Hat	WHL	71	2	9	11	80	20	1	2	3	*50
2004-05	Medicine Hat	WHL	54	11	8	19	105	13	2	3	5	22
2005-06	Omaha	AHL	32	0	0	0	31	....	....	....	....	....
	Las Vegas	ECHL	23	1	3	4	24	....	....	....	....	....
2006-07	Omaha	AHL	34	1	3	4	18	....	....	....	....	....

Signed as a free agent by **Calgary**, August 5, 2005. Traded to **Chicago** by **Calgary** with Andrei Zyuzin for Adrian Aucoin and Chicago's 7th round choice (C.J. Severyn) in 2007 Entry Draft, June 22, 2007.

MARSH, Tyson (MAHRSH, TIGH-suhn)

Defense. Shoots left. 6'1", 190 lbs. Born, Quesnel, B.C., June 20, 1984.

			Regular Season					Playoffs				
Season	Club	League	GP	G	A	Pts	PIM	GP	G	A	Pts	PIM
2000-01	Quesnel	BCHL	52	4	2	6	25	....	....	....	....	....
2001-02	Vancouver Giants	WHL	69	2	14	16	85	....	....	....	....	....
2002-03	Vancouver Giants	WHL	68	3	15	18	143	3	0	1	1	4
2003-04	Vancouver Giants	WHL	67	3	18	21	102	11	0	3	3	4
2004-05	St. John's	AHL	21	0	1	1	30	....	....	....	....	....
	Pensacola	ECHL	23	1	2	3	29	4	0	0	0	2
2005-06	Toronto Marlies	AHL	12	0	0	0	23	....	....	....	....	....
2006-07	Toronto Marlies	AHL	1	0	1	1	5	....	....	....	....	....
	Columbia Inferno	ECHL	48	2	19	21	97	....	....	....	....	....

Signed as a free agent by **Toronto**, September 18, 2002. • Missed majority of 2005-06 season recovering from an abdominal injury.

MARSHALL, Kevin (MAR-shuhl, KEH-vihn) PHI.

Defense. Shoots left. 6'1", 200 lbs. Born, Boucherville, Que., March 10, 1989.
(Philadelphia's 2nd choice, 41st overall, in 2007 Entry Draft).

			Regular Season					Playoffs				
Season	Club	League	GP	G	A	Pts	PIM	GP	G	A	Pts	PIM
2004-05	C.C. Lemoyne	QAAA	39	2	9	11	88	5	0	1	1	16
2005-06	Lewiston	QMJHL	60	1	10	11	112	6	0	1	1	14
2006-07	Lewiston	QMJHL	70	5	27	32	141	17	0	7	7	38

MARSHALL, Matt (MAR-shuhl, MAT) T.B.

Center/Right wing. Shoots right. 6'1", 175 lbs. Born, Boston, MA, August 30, 1988.
(Tampa Bay's 5th choice, 150th overall, in 2007 Entry Draft).

			Regular Season					Playoffs				
Season	Club	League	GP	G	A	Pts	PIM	GP	G	A	Pts	PIM
2005-06	Hingham	High-MA	STATISTICS NOT AVAILABLE									
2006-07	Nobles	High-MA	27	14	10	24	6	....	....	....	....	....

• Signed Letter of Intent to attend **Vermont** (Hockey East) in fall of 2008.

MARTIN, Jesse (MAHR-tihn, JEH-see) ATL.

Center. Shoots right. 5'11", 170 lbs. Born, Edmonton, Alta., September 7, 1988.
(Atlanta's 6th choice, 195th overall, in 2006 Entry Draft).

			Regular Season					Playoffs				
Season	Club	League	GP	G	A	Pts	PIM	GP	G	A	Pts	PIM
2003-04	K of C Pats	AMHL	34	10	11	21	6	....	....	....	....	....
2004-05	K of C Pats	AMHL	30	17	28	45	70	8	4	8	12	....
2005-06	Spruce Grove	AJHL	40	15	29	44	122	....	....	....	....	....
2006-07	Tri-City Storm	USHL	59	19	37	56	31	9	2	4	6	4

MARTINEZ, Alec (mar-TEE-nehz, AL-ehk) L.A.

Defense. Shoots left. 6', 188 lbs. Born, Rochester Hills, MI, July 26, 1987.
(Los Angeles' 5th choice, 95th overall, in 2007 Entry Draft).

			Regular Season					Playoffs				
Season	Club	League	GP	G	A	Pts	PIM	GP	G	A	Pts	PIM
2004-05	Cedar Rapids	USHL	58	10	11	21	30	11	1	2	3	8
2005-06	Miami U.	CCHA	39	3	8	11	31	....	....	....	....	....
2006-07	Miami U.	CCHA	42	9	15	24	40	....	....	....	....	....

MARVIN, Aaron (MAHR-vihn, AIR-ruhn) CGY.

Forward. Shoots left. 6'2", 191 lbs. Born, Warrod, MN, May 27, 1988.
(Calgary's 3rd choice, 89th overall, in 2006 Entry Draft).

			Regular Season					Playoffs				
Season	Club	League	GP	G	A	Pts	PIM	GP	G	A	Pts	PIM
2004-05	Warroad Warriors	High-MN	31	23	25	48	18	....	....	....	....	....
2005-06	Warroad Warriors	High-MN	23	9	21	30	40	....	....	....	....	....
2006-07	Tri-City Storm	USHL	13	1	3	4	8	9	1	0	1	8

MASON, Tyrell (MAY-sohn, TIGH-rehl) NYI

Defense. Shoots left. 6'1", 167 lbs. Born, Grand Prairie, Alta., March 12, 1986.
(NY Islanders' 5th choice, 180th overall, in 2005 Entry Draft).

			Regular Season					Playoffs				
Season	Club	League	GP	G	A	Pts	PIM	GP	G	A	Pts	PIM
2003-04	Salmon Arm	BCHL	59	7	29	36	36	....	....	....	....	....
2004-05	Salmon Arm	BCHL	51	6	36	42	78	....	....	....	....	....
2005-06	Clarkson Knights	ECACHL	38	1	5	6	38	....	....	....	....	....
2006-07	Clarkson Knights	ECACHL	39	1	11	12	62	....	....	....	....	....

MATSON, Taylor (MAT-suhn, TAY-luhr) VAN.

Center. Shoots right. 5'10", 165 lbs. Born, Mound, MN, September 16, 1988.
(Vancouver's 5th choice, 176th overall, in 2007 Entry Draft).

			Regular Season					Playoffs				
Season	Club	League	GP	G	A	Pts	PIM	GP	G	A	Pts	PIM
2005-06	Holy Angels	High-MN	27	30	40	70	28	....	....	....	....	....
2006-07	Holy Angels	High-MN	11	16	15	31	16	....	....	....	....	....
	Des Moines	USHL	10	1	2	3	6	6	0	1	1	10

MATSUMOTO, Jonathan (mat-suh-MOH-toh, JAWN-ah-thuhn) PHI.

Center. Shoots left. 6', 184 lbs. Born, Ottawa, Ont., October 13, 1986.
(Philadelphia's 5th choice, 79th overall, in 2006 Entry Draft).

			Regular Season					Playoffs				
Season	Club	League	GP	G	A	Pts	PIM	GP	G	A	Pts	PIM
2002-03	Cumberland	CJHL	8	2	3	5	2	10	4	7	11	2
2003-04	Cumberland	CJHL	51	31	32	63	26	7	5	5	10	6
2004-05	Bowling Green	CCHA	36	18	14	32	22	....	....	....	....	....
2005-06	Bowling Green	CCHA	36	20	28	48	43	....	....	....	....	....
2006-07	Bowling Green	CCHA	38	11	22	33	70	....	....	....	....	....
	Philadelphia	AHL	16	2	2	4	10	....	....	....	....	....

MATTHIAS, Shawn (muh-TIGH-uhs, SHAWN) FLA.

Center. Shoots left. 6'3", 211 lbs. Born, Mississauga, Ont., February 19, 1988.
(Detroit's 2nd choice, 47th overall, in 2006 Entry Draft).

			Regular Season					Playoffs				
Season	Club	League	GP	G	A	Pts	PIM	GP	G	A	Pts	PIM
2004-05	Belleville Bulls	OHL	37	1	1	2	15	3	0	0	0	0
2005-06	Belleville Bulls	OHL	67	13	21	34	42	6	3	0	3	2
2006-07	Belleville Bulls	OHL	64	38	35	73	61	15	13	5	18	10

Traded to **Florida** by **Detroit** with Detroit's 2nd round choice (later traded to Nashville - Nashville selected Nick Spaling) in 2007 Entry Draft for Todd Bertuzzi, February 27, 2007.

MAXWELL, Ben (MAX-wehl, BEHN) MTL.

Center. Shoots left. 6'1", 185 lbs. Born, North Vancouver, B.C., March 30, 1988.
(Montreal's 2nd choice, 49th overall, in 2006 Entry Draft).

			Regular Season					Playoffs				
Season	Club	League	GP	G	A	Pts	PIM	GP	G	A	Pts	PIM
2003-04	North Delta Ice	PIJHL	40	17	28	45	46	5	3	6	9	0
	South Surrey	BCHL	2	0	0	0	0	....	....	....	....	....
	Kootenay Ice	WHL	3	0	1	1	2	1	0	0	0	0
2004-05	Kootenay Ice	WHL	68	8	10	18	37	16	0	1	1	6
2005-06	Kootenay Ice	WHL	69	28	32	60	52	6	3	5	8	0
2006-07	Kootenay Ice	WHL	39	19	34	53	42	7	1	4	5	21

MAYOROV, Maxim (may-YOHR-ahv, mahx-EEM) CBJ

Left wing. Shoots left. 6'2", 187 lbs. Born, Magnitogorsk, USSR, March 26, 1989.
(Columbus' 5th choice, 94th overall, in 2007 Entry Draft).

			Regular Season					Playoffs				
Season	Club	League	GP	G	A	Pts	PIM	GP	G	A	Pts	PIM
2005-06	Ak Bars Kazan 2	Russia-3	STATISTICS NOT AVAILABLE									
2006-07	Leninogorsk	Russia-2	28	6	4	10	6	....	....	....	....	....
	Almetjevsk	Russia-2	6	1	1	2	0	4	0	0	0	2

McARDLE, Kenndal (muh-KAHR-duhl, KEHN-dahl) FLA.

Left wing. Shoots left. 5'11", 190 lbs. Born, Toronto, Ont., January 4, 1987.
(Florida's 1st choice, 20th overall, in 2005 Entry Draft).

			Regular Season					Playoffs				
Season	Club	League	GP	G	A	Pts	PIM	GP	G	A	Pts	PIM
2002-03	Burnaby	BCAHA	30	1	9	10	131	....	....	....	....	....
	Moose Jaw	WHL	2	0	0	0	0	....	....	....	....	....
2003-04	Moose Jaw	WHL	54	8	8	16	57	10	3	2	5	6
2004-05	Moose Jaw	WHL	70	37	37	74	122	5	1	0	1	16
2005-06	Moose Jaw	WHL	72	28	43	71	135	22	6	10	16	43
2006-07	Moose Jaw	WHL	26	10	10	20	75	....	....	....	....	....
	Vancouver Giants	WHL	37	9	13	22	54	22	*11	9	20	49

McBAIN, Jamie (muhk-BAYN, JAY-mee) CAR.

Defense. Shoots right. 6'1", 200 lbs. Born, Edina, MN, February 25, 1988.
(Carolina's 1st choice, 63rd overall, in 2006 Entry Draft).

			Regular Season					Playoffs				
Season	Club	League	GP	G	A	Pts	PIM	GP	G	A	Pts	PIM
2003-04	Shat.-St. Mary's	High-MN	73	6	27	33	....	....	....	....	....	....
2004-05	USNTDP	U-17	14	1	6	7	16	....	....	....	....	....
	USNTDP	NAHL	38	2	7	9	22	10	0	3	3	4
2005-06	USNTDP	U-18	41	9	16	25	35	....	....	....	....	....
	USNTDP	NAHL	14	0	5	5	6	....	....	....	....	....
2006-07	U. of Wisconsin	WCHA	36	3	15	18	36	....	....	....	....	....

WCHA All-Rookie Team (2007)

McCARTHY, John (muh-KAHR-thee, JAWN) S.J.

Left wing. Shoots left. 6'1", 205 lbs. Born, Boston, MA, August 9, 1986.
(San Jose's 5th choice, 202nd overall, in 2006 Entry Draft).

			Regular Season					Playoffs				
Season	Club	League	GP	G	A	Pts	PIM	GP	G	A	Pts	PIM
2004-05	Des Moines	USHL	60	8	10	18	32	....	....	....	....	....
2005-06	Boston University	H-East	33	2	2	4	12	....	....	....	....	....
2006-07	Boston University	H-East	39	2	3	5	18	....	....	....	....	....

McCLELLAN, Steve (muh-KLEHL-uhn, STEEV) COL.

Defense. Shoots left. 6'1", 180 lbs. Born, Boston, MA, April 22, 1985.
(Colorado's 9th choice, 281st overall, in 2004 Entry Draft).

			Regular Season					Playoffs				
Season	Club	League	GP	G	A	Pts	PIM	GP	G	A	Pts	PIM
2001-02	Catholic Memorial	High-MA	20	4	16	20	....	....	....	....	....	....
2002-03	Catholic Memorial	High-MA	28	3	9	12	....	....	....	....	....	....
2003-04	Catholic Memorial	High-MA	25	8	18	26	14	....	....	....	....	....
2004-05	Cushing	High-MA	34	6	20	26	....	....	....	....	....	....
2005-06	Northeastern	H-East	9	0	0	0	6	....	....	....	....	....
2006-07	Northeastern	H-East	DID NOT PLAY									

McCOLLEM, Matthew (muh-KAHL-uhm, MA-thew) ST.L.

Left wing. Shoots left. 6', 185 lbs. Born, Somerville, MA, May 6, 1988.
(St. Louis' 8th choice, 154th overall, in 2006 Entry Draft).

			Regular Season					Playoffs				
Season	Club	League	GP	G	A	Pts	PIM	GP	G	A	Pts	PIM
2004-05	Belmont Hill	High-MA	....	2	7	9	....	....	....	....	....	....
2005-06	Belmont Hill	High-MA	....	15	11	26	....	....	....	....	....	....
2006-07	Belmont Hill	High-MA	28	16	19	35	64	....	....	....	....	....

• Signed Letter of Intent to attend **Harvard University** (ECACHL) in fall of 2007.

McCRAE, Justin (muh-KRAY, JUHS-tihn) CAR.

Center. Shoots right. 6'1", 185 lbs. Born, Calgary, Alta., October 30, 1988.
(Carolina's 3rd choice, 102nd overall, in 2007 Entry Draft).

			Regular Season					Playoffs				
Season	Club	League	GP	G	A	Pts	PIM	GP	G	A	Pts	PIM
2003-04	Strathmore	AMHL	36	9	14	23	36	....	....	....	....	....
	Saskatoon Blades	WHL	6	0	0	0	2	....	....	....	....	....
2004-05	Saskatoon Blades	WHL	68	8	11	19	44	4	0	0	0	2
2005-06	Saskatoon Blades	WHL	71	17	24	41	58	9	1	2	3	10
2006-07	Saskatoon Blades	WHL	61	16	33	49	98	....	....	....	....	....

McCULLOCH, Scott (muh-KUHL-uh, SKAWT) CHI.

Left wing. Shoots left. 6', 212 lbs. Born, Edmonton, Alta., March 10, 1986.
(Chicago's 11th choice, 165th overall, in 2004 Entry Draft).

			Regular Season					Playoffs				
Season	Club	League	GP	G	A	Pts	PIM	GP	G	A	Pts	PIM
2003-04	Grand Prairie	AJHL	44	23	26	49	85	16	12	8	20	18
2004-05	Colorado College	WCHA	11	4	3	7	6	....	....	....	....	....
2005-06	Colorado College	WCHA	42	5	7	12	67	....	....	....	....	....
2006-07	Colorado College	WCHA	39	18	6	24	48	....	....	....	....	....

McCUTCHEON, Mark (muh-KUH-chuhn, MAHRK) COL.

Center. Shoots right. 6', 190 lbs. Born, Ithaca, NY, May 21, 1984.
(Colorado's 3rd choice, 146th overall, in 2003 Entry Draft).

			Regular Season					Playoffs				
Season	Club	League	GP	G	A	Pts	PIM	GP	G	A	Pts	PIM
2001-02	N.E. Jr. Coyotes	EJHL	36	24	26	50	84	....	....	....	....	....
2002-03	N.E. Jr. Coyotes	EJHL	35	27	22	49	76	10	8	5	13	24
2003-04	Cornell Big Red	ECAC	32	0	4	4	12	....	....	....	....	....
2004-05	Cornell Big Red	ECACHL	22	0	5	5	12	....	....	....	....	....
2005-06	Cornell Big Red	ECACHL	34	9	6	15	34	....	....	....	....	....
2006-07	Cornell Big Red	ECACHL	29	10	10	20	32	....	....	....	....	....

McDONAGH, Ryan (muhk-DUHN-uh, RIGH-uhn) MTL.

Defense. Shoots left. 6'1", 204 lbs. Born, St.Paul, MN, June 13, 1989.
(Montreal's 1st choice, 12th overall, in 2007 Entry Draft).

			Regular Season					Playoffs				
Season	Club	League	GP	G	A	Pts	PIM	GP	G	A	Pts	PIM
2004-05	Cretin-Derham	High-MN	28	12	18	30	....	....	....	....	....	....
2005-06	Cretin-Derham	High-MN	25	12	33	45	....	....	....	....	....	....
2006-07	Cretin-Derham	High-MN	26	14	26	40	....	....	....	....	....	....

• Signed Letter of Intent to attend **University of Wisconsin** (WCHA) in fall of 2007.

McDONALD, Colin (muhk-DAWN-uhld, KAW-lihn) EDM.

Right wing. Shoots right. 6'3", 205 lbs. Born, New Haven, CT, September 30, 1984.
(Edmonton's 2nd choice, 51st overall, in 2003 Entry Draft).

			Regular Season					Playoffs				
Season	Club	League	GP	G	A	Pts	PIM	GP	G	A	Pts	PIM
2001-02	N.E. Jr. Coyotes	EJHL	39	16	20	36	50	....	....	....	....	....
2002-03	N.E. Jr. Coyotes	EJHL	44	28	40	*68	59	....	....	....	....	....
2003-04	Providence College	H-East	37	10	6	16	47	....	....	....	....	....
2004-05	Providence College	H-East	26	11	5	16	14	....	....	....	....	....
2005-06	Providence College	H-East	36	9	19	28	29	....	....	....	....	....
2006-07	Providence College	H-East	36	13	4	17	30	....	....	....	....	....

Hockey East All-Rookie Team (2004)

McGINN, Jamie (muh-GIHN, JAY-mee) S.J.

Left wing. Shoots left. 6', 185 lbs. Born, Fergus, Ont., August 5, 1988.
(San Jose's 2nd choice, 36th overall, in 2006 Entry Draft).

			Regular Season					Playoffs				
Season	Club	League	GP	G	A	Pts	PIM	GP	G	A	Pts	PIM
2003-04	Tor. Jr. Canadiens	GTHL	31	....	....	48	....	18	14	18	32	....
2004-05	Ottawa 67's	OHL	59	10	12	22	35	18	4	7	11	0
2005-06	Ottawa 67's	OHL	65	26	31	57	113	6	2	2	4	4
2006-07	Ottawa 67's	OHL	68	46	43	89	49	5	5	1	6	2
	Worcester Sharks	AHL	4	1	1	2	4	6	0	0	0	8

McGRATH, Evan (muh-GRATH, EH-vuhn) DET.

Center. Shoots left. 6', 190 lbs. Born, Oakville, Ont., January 14, 1986.
(Detroit's 2nd choice, 128th overall, in 2004 Entry Draft).

			Regular Season					Playoffs				
Season	**Club**	**League**	**GP**	**G**	**A**	**Pts**	**PIM**	**GP**	**G**	**A**	**Pts**	**PIM**
2001-02	Oakville Blades	OPJHL	49	43	44	87	24	....	....	....	....	....
2002-03	Kitchener Rangers	OHL	64	16	31	47	40	21	6	2	8	6
2003-04	Kitchener Rangers	OHL	68	15	36	51	28	5	2	1	3	2
2004-05	Kitchener Rangers	OHL	67	28	59	87	51	15	7	6	13	6
2005-06	Kitchener Rangers	OHL	67	37	77	114	63	5	1	3	4	4
2006-07	Grand Rapids	AHL	59	6	8	14	41	7	0	0	0	0
	Toledo Storm	ECHL	9	6	9	15	12	....	....	....	....	....

OHL All-Rookie Team (2003)

McGUIRK, Brian (muh-GUHRK, BRIGH-uhn) CBJ

Left wing. Shoots left. 6', 191 lbs. Born, Danvers, MA, July 11, 1985.
(Columbus' 10th choice, 231st overall, in 2004 Entry Draft).

			Regular Season					Playoffs				
Season	**Club**	**League**	**GP**	**G**	**A**	**Pts**	**PIM**	**GP**	**G**	**A**	**Pts**	**PIM**
2003-04	Gov. Dummer	High-MA	25	16	16	32	....	....	....	....	....	....
2004-05	Boston University	H-East	33	0	1	1	18	....	....	....	....	....
2005-06	Boston University	H-East	39	5	4	9	18	....	....	....	....	....
2006-07	Boston University	H-East	36	1	4	5	24	....	....	....	....	....

McILVANE, Matthew (MAK-uhl-vay-nee, MA-thew) OTT.

Center. Shoots right. 6', 202 lbs. Born, Downers Grove, IL, November 2, 1985.
(Ottawa's 10th choice, 251st overall, in 2004 Entry Draft).

			Regular Season					Playoffs				
Season	**Club**	**League**	**GP**	**G**	**A**	**Pts**	**PIM**	**GP**	**G**	**A**	**Pts**	**PIM**
2003-04	Chicago Steel	USHL	59	22	24	46	53	3	1	2	3	0
2004-05	Ohio State	CCHA	42	1	5	6	30	....	....	....	....	....
2005-06	Ohio State	CCHA	37	3	10	13	45	....	....	....	....	....
2006-07	Ohio State	CCHA	36	6	11	17	18	....	....	....	....	....

McINTYRE, David (MAK-ihn-tigh-uhr, DAY-vihd) DAL.

Center. Shoots left. 5'11", 171 lbs. Born, Oakville, Ont., February 4, 1987.
(Dallas' 4th choice, 138th overall, in 2006 Entry Draft).

			Regular Season					Playoffs				
Season	**Club**	**League**	**GP**	**G**	**A**	**Pts**	**PIM**	**GP**	**G**	**A**	**Pts**	**PIM**
2004-05	Newmarket	OPJHL	46	17	14	31	33	16	8	7	15	20
2005-06	Newmarket	OPJHL	46	42	50	92	143	11	4	8	12	42
2006-07	Colgate	ECACHL	40	9	8	17	75	....	....	....	....	....

McKENZIE, Jim (muh-KEHN-zee, JIHM) OTT.

Right wing. Shoots right. 6'2", 209 lbs. Born, St. Paul, MN, June 10, 1984.
(Ottawa's 7th choice, 141st overall, in 2004 Entry Draft).

			Regular Season					Playoffs				
Season	**Club**	**League**	**GP**	**G**	**A**	**Pts**	**PIM**	**GP**	**G**	**A**	**Pts**	**PIM**
2000-01	Hill-Murray	High-MN	27	9	13	22	....	....	....	....	....	....
2001-02	USNTDP	U-18	13	7	8	15	10	....	....	....	....	....
	USNTDP	USHL	2	0	1	1	9	....	....	....	....	....
	USNTDP	NAHL	4	0	2	2	4	....	....	....	....	....
	Green Bay	USHL	17	1	2	3	34	....	....	....	....	....
2002-03	Sioux Falls	USHL	45	6	18	24	108	....	....	....	....	....
2003-04	Sioux Falls	USHL	59	26	38	64	168	....	....	....	....	....
2004-05	Michigan State	CCHA	34	11	7	18	44	....	....	....	....	....
2005-06	Michigan State	CCHA	43	11	17	28	85	....	....	....	....	....
2006-07	Michigan State	CCHA	35	12	18	30	56	....	....	....	....	....

McKNIGHT, Matt (muhk-NIGHT, MAT) DAL.

Forward. Shoots right. 6'2", 190 lbs. Born, Red Deer, Alta., June 14, 1984.
(Dallas' 10th choice, 280th overall, in 2004 Entry Draft).

			Regular Season					Playoffs				
Season	**Club**	**League**	**GP**	**G**	**A**	**Pts**	**PIM**	**GP**	**G**	**A**	**Pts**	**PIM**
2003-04	Camrose Kodiaks	AJHL	42	20	36	56	31	....	....	....	....	....
2004-05	U. Minn-Duluth	WCHA	30	6	13	19	16	....	....	....	....	....
2005-06	U. Minn-Duluth	WCHA	40	9	16	25	24	....	....	....	....	....
2006-07	U. Minn-Duluth	WCHA	29	4	5	9	16	....	....	....	....	....

McLAREN, Frazer (muh-KLAIR-uhn, FRAY-zuhr) S.J.

Left wing. Shoots left. 6'5", 230 lbs. Born, Winnipeg, Man., October 29, 1987.
(San Jose's 8th choice, 203rd overall, in 2007 Entry Draft).

			Regular Season					Playoffs				
Season	**Club**	**League**	**GP**	**G**	**A**	**Pts**	**PIM**	**GP**	**G**	**A**	**Pts**	**PIM**
2002-03	Kelvin	High-MB	56	27	24	51	136	....	....	....	....	....
2003-04	Portland	WHL	50	0	3	3	44	1	0	0	0	0
2004-05	Portland	WHL	71	6	5	11	124	7	0	0	0	10
2005-06	Portland	WHL	70	12	6	18	194	12	0	2	2	27
2006-07	Portland	WHL	61	19	12	31	186	....	....	....	....	....

McLEOD, Cody (muh-KLOWD, KOH-dee) COL.

Left wing. Shoots left. 6'2", 210 lbs. Born, Binscarth, Man., June 26, 1984.

			Regular Season					Playoffs				
Season	**Club**	**League**	**GP**	**G**	**A**	**Pts**	**PIM**	**GP**	**G**	**A**	**Pts**	**PIM**
2001-02	Portland	WHL	47	10	3	13	86	5	0	0	0	0
2002-03	Portland	WHL	71	15	18	33	153	7	1	1	2	13
2003-04	Portland	WHL	69	13	18	31	227	5	2	2	4	6
2004-05	Portland	WHL	70	31	29	60	195	7	0	3	3	8
	Adirondack	UHL	1	0	0	0	0	5	0	0	0	11
2005-06	Lowell	AHL	33	4	5	9	87	....	....	....	....	....
	San Diego Gulls	ECHL	16	4	5	9	48	2	2	1	3	14
2006-07	Albany River Rats	AHL	73	11	8	19	180	5	0	0	0	4

Signed as a free agent by **Colorado**, July 6, 2006.

McMILLAN, Carson (muhk-MIHL-lihn, KAHR-suhn) MIN.

Right wing. Shoots right. 6'1", 194 lbs. Born, Brandon, Man., September 10, 1988.
(Minnesota's 5th choice, 200th overall, in 2007 Entry Draft).

			Regular Season					Playoffs				
Season	**Club**	**League**	**GP**	**G**	**A**	**Pts**	**PIM**	**GP**	**G**	**A**	**Pts**	**PIM**
2003-04	Crocus Plains	High-MB	STATISTICS NOT AVAILABLE									
	Brandon	MMHL	4	0	0	0	0	....	....	....	....	....
2004-05	Brandon	MMHL	40	17	19	36	34	5	3	4	7	8
	Winkler Flyers	MJHL	4	1	1	2	2	....	....	....	....	....
2005-06	Calgary Hitmen	WHL	59	3	2	5	42	13	0	0	0	2
2006-07	Calgary Hitmen	WHL	72	7	15	22	76	18	2	0	2	17

McNEILL, Patrick (muhk-NEEL, PAT-rihk) WSH.

Defense. Shoots left. 6', 195 lbs. Born, Strathroy, Ont., March 17, 1987.
(Washington's 4th choice, 118th overall, in 2005 Entry Draft).

			Regular Season					Playoffs				
Season	**Club**	**League**	**GP**	**G**	**A**	**Pts**	**PIM**	**GP**	**G**	**A**	**Pts**	**PIM**
2002-03	Strathroy Rockets	OHA-B	45	6	13	19	53	....	....	....	....	....
2003-04	Saginaw Spirit	OHL	57	3	11	14	28	....	....	....	....	....
2004-05	Saginaw Spirit	OHL	66	7	26	33	31	....	....	....	....	....
2005-06	Saginaw Spirit	OHL	68	21	56	77	64	4	1	3	4	6
2006-07	Saginaw Spirit	OHL	58	22	36	58	49	6	3	2	5	6

OHL Second All-Star Team (2006)

McPHERSON, Corbin (muhk-FUHR-suhn, KOHR-bihn) N.J.

Defense. Shoots right. 6'4", 210 lbs. Born, Folsom, CA, September 7, 1988.
(New Jersey's 3rd choice, 87th overall, in 2007 Entry Draft).

			Regular Season					Playoffs				
Season	**Club**	**League**	**GP**	**G**	**A**	**Pts**	**PIM**	**GP**	**G**	**A**	**Pts**	**PIM**
2005-06	San Jose Jr. Sharks	Cal-Am	59	5	16	21	45	....	....	....	....	....
2006-07	Cowichan Valley	BCHL	44	4	10	14	63	18	1	3	4	14

McQUAID, Adam (muhk-WAYD, A-duhm) BOS.

Defense. Shoots right. 6'4", 209 lbs. Born, Charlottetown, PEI, October 12, 1986.
(Columbus' 2nd choice, 55th overall, in 2005 Entry Draft).

			Regular Season					Playoffs				
Season	**Club**	**League**	**GP**	**G**	**A**	**Pts**	**PIM**	**GP**	**G**	**A**	**Pts**	**PIM**
2003-04	Sudbury Wolves	OHL	47	3	6	9	25	7	0	1	1	2
2004-05	Sudbury Wolves	OHL	66	3	16	19	98	8	0	2	2	10
2005-06	Sudbury Wolves	OHL	68	3	14	17	107	10	0	1	1	16
2006-07	Sudbury Wolves	OHL	65	9	22	31	110	21	1	5	6	24

Traded to **Boston** by **Columbus** for Boston's 5th round choice (later traded to Dallas - Dallas selected Jamie Benn) in 2007 Entry Draft, May 16, 2007.

MECKLER, David (MEHK-luhr, DAY-vihd) L.A.

Center. Shoots right. 6', 184 lbs. Born, Highland Park, IL, July 9, 1987.
(Los Angeles' 7th choice, 134th overall, in 2006 Entry Draft).

			Regular Season					Playoffs				
Season	**Club**	**League**	**GP**	**G**	**A**	**Pts**	**PIM**	**GP**	**G**	**A**	**Pts**	**PIM**
2004-05	Waterloo	USHL	60	30	15	45	32	5	3	2	5	2
2005-06	Yale	ECACHL	31	7	3	10	28	....	....	....	....	....
2006-07	London Knights	OHL	67	38	35	73	53	16	*15	7	22	20

MEDVEC, Kyle (MEHD-vek, KIGHL) MIN.

Defense. Shoots left. 6'6", 205 lbs. Born, Westminster, CO, June 16, 1988.
(Minnesota's 4th choice, 102nd overall, in 2006 Entry Draft).

			Regular Season					Playoffs				
Season	**Club**	**League**	**GP**	**G**	**A**	**Pts**	**PIM**	**GP**	**G**	**A**	**Pts**	**PIM**
2003-04	Apple Valley	High-MN	27	1	12	13	30	....	....	....	....	....
2004-05	Apple Valley	High-MN	23	4	16	20	18	....	....	....	....	....
2005-06	Apple Valley	High-MN	28	13	22	35	44	....	....	....	....	....
	Sioux City	USHL	3	0	0	0	0	....	....	....	....	....
2006-07	Sioux City	USHL	57	4	14	18	83	7	0	0	0	4

MEGALINSKY, Dmitri (meh-gahl-IHN-skee, dih-MEE-tree) OTT.

Defense. Shoots left. 6'2", 212 lbs. Born, Perm, USSR, April 15, 1985.
(Ottawa's 7th choice, 186th overall, in 2005 Entry Draft).

			Regular Season					Playoffs				
Season	**Club**	**League**	**GP**	**G**	**A**	**Pts**	**PIM**	**GP**	**G**	**A**	**Pts**	**PIM**
2003-04	HK Voronezh	Russia-2	42	4	8	12	159	....	....	....	....	....
	Yaroslavl	Russia	1	0	0	0	0	....	....	....	....	....
	Yaroslavl 2	Russia-3	11	0	4	4	16	....	....	....	....	....
2004-05	Yaroslavl	Russia	1	0	0	0	2	....	....	....	....	....
	Yaroslavl 2	Russia-3	30	6	12	18	82	....	....	....	....	....
2005-06	Yaroslavl 2	Russia-3	12	4	10	14	6	....	....	....	....	....
	Yaroslavl	Russia	20	0	1	1	8	8	0	0	0	6
2006-07	Khimik	Russia-2	33	4	7	11	34	7	0	1	1	16

MELYAKOV, Igor (mehl-yuh-KAHF, EE-gohr) L.A.

Left wing. Shoots left. 5'10", 190 lbs. Born, Lipetsk, USSR, December 23, 1976.
(Los Angeles' 6th choice, 137th overall, in 1995 Entry Draft).

			Regular Season					Playoffs				
Season	**Club**	**League**	**GP**	**G**	**A**	**Pts**	**PIM**	**GP**	**G**	**A**	**Pts**	**PIM**
1993-94	Torpedo Yaroslavl	CIS	39	4	3	7	10	4	0	0	0	0
1994-95	Torpedo Yaroslavl	CIS	50	6	8	14	34	4	0	1	1	0
1995-96	Torpedo Yaroslavl	CIS	39	5	1	6	6	3	0	0	0	2
1996-97	Torpedo Yaroslavl	Russia	8	0	0	0	0	....	....	....	....	....
	Nizhny Novgorod	Russia	12	2	3	5	10	....	....	....	....	....
1997-98	Nizhny Novgorod	Russia	13	3	3	6	6	....	....	....	....	....
1998-99	Nizhny Novgorod	Russia-2	36	13	17	30	14	....	....	....	....	....
99-2000	Nizhny Novgorod	Russia	34	1	8	9	10	5	1	0	1	4
2000-01	Nizhny Novgorod	Russia	24	2	3	5	10	....	....	....	....	....
2001-02	HK Lipetsk	Russia-2	68	16	37	53	94	....	....	....	....	....
2002-03	Voskresensk	Russia-2	48	9	22	31	16	....	....	....	....	....
2003-04	Nizhny Novgorod	Russia	45	5	10	15	18	....	....	....	....	....
	Nizh. Novgorod 2	Russia-3	4	1	6	7	4	....	....	....	....	....
2004-05	Nizhny Novgorod	Russia-2	52	14	30	44	32	11	2	4	6	18
2005-06	Magnitogorsk	Russia	25	7	8	15	10	3	0	0	0	2
2006-07	Novokuznetsk	Russia	22	0	1	1	8	....	....	....	....	....
	Nizhny Novgorod	Russia-2	16	2	6	8	10	12	2	5	7	6

MERCIER, Justin (MUHR-see-uhr, JUHS-tihn) COL.

Forward. Shoots left. 5'11", 190 lbs. Born, Erie, PA, June 25, 1987.
(Colorado's 8th choice, 168th overall, in 2005 Entry Draft).

			Regular Season					Playoffs				
Season	**Club**	**League**	**GP**	**G**	**A**	**Pts**	**PIM**	**GP**	**G**	**A**	**Pts**	**PIM**
2003-04	St. Louis	USHL	60	12	9	21	....	....	....	....	....	....
2004-05	USNTDP	U-18	26	1	7	8	31	....	....	....	....	....
	USNTDP	NAHL	16	4	3	7	33	....	....	....	....	....
2005-06	Miami U.	CCHA	35	3	7	10	32	....	....	....	....	....
2006-07	Miami U.	CCHA	40	10	15	25	59	....	....	....	....	....

MESSIER, Charles-Antoine (MEH-see-ay, SHARL-AN-twuhn) VAN.

Center. Shoots left. 5'10", 176 lbs. Born, Boucherville, Que., November 4, 1988.
(Vancouver's 3rd choice, 145th overall, in 2007 Entry Draft).

			Regular Season					Playoffs				
Season	**Club**	**League**	**GP**	**G**	**A**	**Pts**	**PIM**	**GP**	**G**	**A**	**Pts**	**PIM**
2005-06	Baie-Comeau	QMJHL	57	4	11	15	33	4	2	0	2	2
2006-07	Baie-Comeau	QMJHL	69	27	21	48	67	11	0	3	3	14

MEYER, Stefan (MAY-uhr, STEH-fan) FLA.

Left wing. Shoots left. 6'2", 194 lbs. Born, Medicine Hat, Alta., July 20, 1985.
(Florida's 4th choice, 55th overall, in 2003 Entry Draft).

			Regular Season					Playoffs				
Season	Club	League	GP	G	A	Pts	PIM	GP	G	A	Pts	PIM
2000-01	Notre Dame	SBHL	50	36	52	88	71	....	....	....	....	....
2001-02	Medicine Hat	WHL	67	18	22	40	48	....	....	....	....	....
2002-03	Medicine Hat	WHL	70	36	16	52	90	11	3	3	6	14
2003-04	Medicine Hat	WHL	72	34	41	75	69	19	7	10	17	27
2004-05	Medicine Hat	WHL	69	34	43	77	104	13	2	4	6	8
2005-06	Rochester	AHL	68	12	16	28	139	....	....	....	....	....
2006-07	Rochester	AHL	63	13	9	22	90	6	0	2	2	8

MEYERS, Josh (MIGH-uhrs, JAWSH) L.A.

Defense. Shoots right. 6'2", 180 lbs. Born, Alexandria, MN, December 7, 1985.
(Los Angeles' 7th choice, 206th overall, in 2005 Entry Draft).

			Regular Season					Playoffs				
Season	Club	League	GP	G	A	Pts	PIM	GP	G	A	Pts	PIM
2003-04	Minnesota Blizzard	NAHL	27	2	12	14	....	....	....	....	....	....
2004-05	Sioux City	USHL	57	8	24	32	92	13	1	9	10	18
2005-06	U. Minn-Duluth	WCHA	27	3	7	10	20	....	....	....	....	....
2006-07	U. Minn-Duluth	WCHA	37	11	13	24	30	....	....	....	....	....

MIHALIK, Vladimir (mih-HAHL-ihk, vla-DIH-meer) T.B.

Defense. Shoots left. 6'7", 222 lbs. Born, Presov, Czech., January 29, 1987.
(Tampa Bay's 1st choice, 30th overall, in 2005 Entry Draft).

			Regular Season					Playoffs				
Season	Club	League	GP	G	A	Pts	PIM	GP	G	A	Pts	PIM
2003-04	Presov	Svk-U18	6	4	4	8	4	....	....	....	....	....
	Presov Jr.	Slovak-Jr.	23	6	10	16	44	....	....	....	....	....
2004-05	PHK Presov Jr.	Slovak-Jr.	23	6	10	16	44	....	....	....	....	....
	PHK Presov	Slovak-2	32	3	1	4	24	6	0	1	1	2
2005-06	Red Deer Rebels	WHL	62	3	9	12	86	....	....	....	....	....
2006-07	Prince George	WHL	53	7	19	26	91	15	1	2	3	17

MIKHAILISHIN, Alexander (mih-khigh-LIHSH-ihn, al-EHX-AN-duh N.J.

Defense. Shoots left. 6'4", 210 lbs. Born, Neustrelitz, East Germany, February 24, 1986.
(New Jersey's 2nd choice, 155th overall, in 2004 Entry Draft).

			Regular Season					Playoffs				
Season	Club	League	GP	G	A	Pts	PIM	GP	G	A	Pts	PIM
2001-02	Spartak Moscow 2	Russia-3	15	0	0	0	2	....	....	....	....	....
2002-03	Spartak Moscow 2	Russia-3	7	1	1	2	4	....	....	....	....	....
2003-04	Spartak Moscow 2	Russia-3	STATISTICS NOT AVAILABLE									
2004-05	Spartak Moscow	Russia	6	0	1	1	4	....	....	....	....	....
2005-06	Spartak Moscow 2	Russia-3	23	2	0	2	72	....	....	....	....	....
2006-07	Yuzhny Ural Orsk	Russia-2	22	0	0	0	128	....	....	....	....	....
	Krylja Sovetov 2	Russia-3	12	1	1	2	22	....	....	....	....	....

MIKKELSON, Brendan (MIGHK-ehl-sohn, BREHN-duhn) ANA.

Defense. Shoots left. 6'2", 202 lbs. Born, Regina, Sask., June 22, 1987.
(Anaheim's 2nd choice, 31st overall, in 2005 Entry Draft).

			Regular Season					Playoffs				
Season	Club	League	GP	G	A	Pts	PIM	GP	G	A	Pts	PIM
2003-04	Portland	WHL	65	3	12	15	43	5	1	0	1	0
2004-05	Portland	WHL	70	5	10	15	60	7	1	2	3	0
2005-06	Portland	WHL	3	1	1	2	4	....	....	....	....	....
	Vancouver Giants	WHL	19	1	8	9	37	....	....	....	....	....
2006-07	Vancouver Giants	WHL	69	6	23	29	60	21	3	7	10	10

Memorial Cup Tournament All-Star Team (2007)

• Missed majority of 2005-06 season recovering from shoulder and knee injuries.

MIKUS, Juraj (MEE-kuhsh, YUHR-ay) TOR.

Defense. Shoots left. 6'4", 185 lbs. Born, Trencin, Czech., November 30, 1988.
(Toronto's 4th choice, 134th overall, in 2007 Entry Draft).

			Regular Season					Playoffs				
Season	Club	League	GP	G	A	Pts	PIM	GP	G	A	Pts	PIM
2004-05	Piestany U18	Svk-U18	2	1	2	3	2	....	....	....	....	....
	Dukla Trencin U18	Svk-U18	39	2	7	9	20	5	0	0	0	0
2005-06	Piestany Jr.	Slovak-Jr.	6	0	4	4	2	....	....	....	....	....
	Dukla Trencin Jr.	Slovak-Jr.	17	1	4	5	2	....	....	....	....	....
	Dukla Trencin U18	Svk-U18	40	3	18	21	36	7	1	5	6	12
2006-07	Dukla Trencin Jr.	Slovak-Jr.	42	9	15	24	72	7	2	1	3	10
	P. Bystrica	Slovak-2	7	0	3	3	2	1	0	0	0	0
	Dukla Trencin	Slovakia	22	0	0	0	2	7	0	0	0	0

MILLER, Bryan (MIHL-luhr, BRIGH-uhn)

Defense. Shoots right. 5'10", 190 lbs. Born, Wayne, NJ, February 17, 1983.

			Regular Season					Playoffs				
Season	Club	League	GP	G	A	Pts	PIM	GP	G	A	Pts	PIM
2001-02	Boston University	H-East	34	4	15	19	12	....	....	....	....	....
2002-03	Boston University	H-East	42	5	18	23	48	....	....	....	....	....
2003-04	Boston University	H-East	38	5	15	20	24	....	....	....	....	....
2004-05	Boston University	H-East	39	6	20	26	42	....	....	....	....	....
	Albany River Rats	AHL	8	0	2	2	0	....	....	....	....	....
2005-06	Albany River Rats	AHL	40	3	15	18	36	....	....	....	....	....
2006-07	Lowell Devils	AHL	12	0	4	4	4	....	....	....	....	....
	Trenton Titans	ECHL	53	6	22	28	24	5	0	1	1	2

Signed as a free agent by **New Jersey**, August 6, 2005.

MILLER, T.J. (MIHL-luhr, TEE-JAY) N.J.

Defense. Shoots left. 6'4", 210 lbs. Born, Placetia, CA, September 15, 1986.
(New Jersey's 5th choice, 107th overall, in 2006 Entry Draft).

			Regular Season					Playoffs				
Season	Club	League	GP	G	A	Pts	PIM	GP	G	A	Pts	PIM
2004-05	South Surrey	BCHL	53	3	9	12	85	....	....	....	....	....
2005-06	Penticton Vees	BCHL	60	16	32	48	73	....	....	....	....	....
2006-07	Northern Mich.	CCHA	37	2	12	14	12	....	....	....	....	....

MINARD, Chris (mih-NAHRD, KRIHS) PIT.

Center. Shoots left. 6'1", 190 lbs. Born, Thompson, Man., November 18, 1981.

			Regular Season					Playoffs				
Season	Club	League	GP	G	A	Pts	PIM	GP	G	A	Pts	PIM
1997-98	Owen Sound	OHL	9	0	1	1	1	1	0	0	0	2
1998-99	Owen Sound	OHL	43	6	9	15	18	....	....	....	....	....
99-2000	Owen Sound	OHL	38	12	14	26	39	....	....	....	....	....
	St. Michael's	OHL	28	5	14	19	6	....	....	....	....	....
2000-01	St. Michael's	OHL	40	11	8	19	28	....	....	....	....	....
	Oshawa Generals	OHL	28	12	12	24	18	....	....	....	....	....
2001-02	Oshawa Generals	OHL	67	36	35	71	20	5	2	3	5	6
2002-03	Pensacola	ECHL	72	15	17	32	71	4	0	0	0	6
2003-04	San Angelo Saints	CHL	64	39	36	75	51	5	1	1	2	2
2004-05	Alaska Aces	ECHL	69	*49	29	78	54	15	4	4	8	12
	Milwaukee	AHL	1	0	0	0	0	....	....	....	....	....
2005-06	Albany River Rats	AHL	37	7	12	19	26	....	....	....	....	....
	Alaska Aces	ECHL	33	26	16	42	38	22	*14	5	19	*54
2006-07	Lowell Devils	AHL	65	32	17	49	30	....	....	....	....	....

Signed as a free agent by **Albany** (AHL), August 16, 2005. Signed as a free agent by **Pittsburgh**, July 12, 2007.

MIRNOV, Igor (mihr-NAWF, EE-gohr) OTT.

Left wing. Shoots left. 6', 187 lbs. Born, Chita, USSR, September 19, 1984.
(Ottawa's 2nd choice, 67th overall, in 2003 Entry Draft).

			Regular Season					Playoffs				
Season	Club	League	GP	G	A	Pts	PIM	GP	G	A	Pts	PIM
2001-02	Dyn'o Moscow 2	Russia-3	30	33	17	50	34	....	....	....	....	....
	Dynamo Moscow	Russia	6	0	0	0	0	....	....	....	....	....
2002-03	Dynamo Moscow	Russia	50	3	7	10	49	5	0	0	0	2
2003-04	Dynamo Moscow	Russia	53	11	10	21	26	3	0	0	0	2
2004-05	Dynamo Moscow	Russia	55	13	13	26	50	9	2	4	6	0
2005-06	Dynamo Moscow	Russia	32	8	10	18	36	4	0	2	2	4
2006-07	Dynamo Moscow	Russia	49	21	25	46	54	3	2	1	3	4

MISHARIN, Georgy (mih-SHAHR-ihn, g'YOHR-gee) MIN.

Defense. Shoots left. 6', 198 lbs. Born, Yekaterinburg, USSR, May 11, 1985.
(Minnesota's 6th choice, 207th overall, in 2003 Entry Draft).

			Regular Season					Playoffs				
Season	Club	League	GP	G	A	Pts	PIM	GP	G	A	Pts	PIM
2001-02	Yekaterinburg 2	Russia-3	STATISTICS NOT AVAILABLE									
	Magnitogorsk 2	Russia-3	STATISTICS NOT AVAILABLE									
2002-03	Yekaterinburg	Russia-2	28	1	3	4	16	....	....	....	....	....
2003-04	Saginaw Spirit	OHL	65	5	22	27	42	....	....	....	....	....
2004-05	Nizhnekamsk	Russia	47	1	3	4	38	3	0	0	0	4
2005-06	CSKA Moscow	Russia	50	4	9	13	46	7	0	0	0	31
2006-07	Dynamo Moscow	Russia	48	3	7	10	70	3	0	1	1	12

Signed as a free agent by **Dynamo Moscow** (Russia), August 31, 2006.

MITCHELL, Dale (MIH-chuhl, DAYL) TOR.

Right wing. Shoots right. 5'8", 207 lbs. Born, Etobicoke, Ont., April 9, 1989.
(Toronto's 1st choice, 74th overall, in 2007 Entry Draft).

			Regular Season					Playoffs				
Season	Club	League	GP	G	A	Pts	PIM	GP	G	A	Pts	PIM
2005-06	Oshawa Generals	OHL	65	20	23	43	63	....	....	....	....	....
2006-07	Oshawa Generals	OHL	67	43	37	80	81	9	1	4	5	12

MITCHELL, John (MIH-chuhl, JAWN) TOR.

Center. Shoots left. 6'1", 205 lbs. Born, Waterloo, Ont., January 22, 1985.
(Toronto's 4th choice, 158th overall, in 2003 Entry Draft).

			Regular Season					Playoffs				
Season	Club	League	GP	G	A	Pts	PIM	GP	G	A	Pts	PIM
2000-01	Waterloo Siskens	OPJHL	47	15	29	44	33	....	....	....	....	....
2001-02	Plymouth Whalers	OHL	62	9	9	18	23	6	1	0	1	4
2002-03	Plymouth Whalers	OHL	68	18	37	55	31	18	2	10	12	8
2003-04	Plymouth Whalers	OHL	65	28	54	82	45	9	6	6	12	6
2004-05	Plymouth Whalers	OHL	63	25	50	75	59	4	1	1	2	0
	St. John's	AHL	2	0	0	0	0	....	....	....	....	....
2005-06	Toronto Marlies	AHL	51	5	12	17	22	2	0	0	0	0
2006-07	Toronto Marlies	AHL	73	16	20	36	46	....	....	....	....	....

MITCHELL, Torrey (MIH-chuhl, TOH-ree) S.J.

Center. Shoots right. 5'11", 175 lbs. Born, Montreal, Que., January 30, 1985.
(San Jose's 3rd choice, 126th overall, in 2004 Entry Draft).

			Regular Season					Playoffs				
Season	Club	League	GP	G	A	Pts	PIM	GP	G	A	Pts	PIM
2002-03	Hotchkiss	High-CT	26	19	30	49	33	....	....	....	....	....
2003-04	Hotchkiss	High-CT	25	25	37	62	42	....	....	....	....	....
2004-05	U. of Vermont	ECACHL	38	11	19	30	74	....	....	....	....	....
2005-06	U. of Vermont	H-East	38	12	28	40	34	....	....	....	....	....
2006-07	U. of Vermont	H-East	39	12	23	35	46	....	....	....	....	....
	Worcester Sharks	AHL	11	2	5	7	27	6	1	1	2	15

ECACHL All-Rookie Team (2005)

MITERA, Mark (MIH-tair-a, MAHRK) ANA.

Defense. Shoots left. 6'3", 211 lbs. Born, Royal Oak, MI, October 22, 1987.
(Anaheim's 1st choice, 19th overall, in 2006 Entry Draft).

			Regular Season					Playoffs				
Season	Club	League	GP	G	A	Pts	PIM	GP	G	A	Pts	PIM
2003-04	USNTDP	U-17	16	2	6	8	22	....	....	....	....	....
	USNTDP	NAHL	43	2	13	15	69	7	0	2	2	10
2004-05	USNTDP	U-18	45	5	10	15	91	....	....	....	....	....
	USNTDP	NAHL	16	2	6	8	32	....	....	....	....	....
2005-06	U. of Michigan	CCHA	39	0	10	10	59	....	....	....	....	....
2006-07	U. of Michigan	CCHA	41	1	17	18	52	....	....	....	....	....

MOLLE, Ryan (MOHL, RIGH-uhn) N.J.

Defense. Shoots right. 6'3", 195 lbs. Born, Winnipeg, Man., January 29, 1989.
(New Jersey's 6th choice, 207th overall, in 2007 Entry Draft).

			Regular Season					Playoffs				
Season	Club	League	GP	G	A	Pts	PIM	GP	G	A	Pts	PIM
2004-05	Cgy. Stampeders	CBHL	STATISTICS NOT AVAILABLE									
	Vancouver Giants	WHL	1	0	0	0	0	....	....	....	....	....
2005-06	Calgary Flames	AMHL	35	3	16	19	60	....	....	....	....	....
	Vancouver Giants	WHL	2	0	0	0	0	....	....	....	....	....
2006-07	Swift Current	WHL	61	1	4	5	52	6	1	0	1	8

MOLLER, Oscar (MOH-luhr, OAWZ-kuhr) **L.A.**

Right wing. Shoots right. 5'11", 179 lbs. Born, Stockholm, Sweden, January 22, 1989.
(Los Angeles' 2nd choice, 52nd overall, in 2007 Entry Draft).

			Regular Season					Playoffs				
Season	Club	League	GP	G	A	Pts	PIM	GP	G	A	Pts	PIM
2003-04	Spanga U18	Swe-U18	32	28	12	40	68	....	....	....	....	....
2004-05	Spanga U18	Swe-U18	24	28	16	44	52	....	....	....	....	....
	Spanga Jr.	Swe-Jr.	4	6	1	7	6	....	....	....	....	....
	Spanga	Sweden-4	6	6	4	10	0	....	....	....	....	....
2005-06	Djurgarden U18	Swe-U18	8	8	5	13	6	2	1	0	1	0
	Djurgarden Jr.	Swe-Jr.	25	8	5	13	41	4	2	0	2	0
2006-07	Chilliwack Bruins	WHL	68	32	37	69	50	5	0	3	3	6

MONDOU, Benoit (mawn-DOO, BEHN-wah) **N.J.**

Center. Shoots right. 5'9", 175 lbs. Born, Sorel, Que., May 3, 1985.
(Boston's 9th choice, 247th overall, in 2003 Entry Draft).

			Regular Season					Playoffs				
Season	Club	League	GP	G	A	Pts	PIM	GP	G	A	Pts	PIM
2001-02	Baie-Comeau	QMJHL	64	25	45	70	36	5	1	5	6	4
2002-03	Baie-Comeau	QMJHL	25	5	16	21	12	....	....	....	....	....
	Shawinigan	QMJHL	35	6	35	41	21	9	3	8	11	8
2003-04	Shawinigan	QMJHL	68	34	61	95	32	10	4	9	13	2
2004-05	Shawinigan	QMJHL	57	16	43	59	44	4	2	3	5	9
2005-06	Shawinigan	QMJHL	59	46	52	98	57	8	5	4	9	6
2006-07	Trenton Titans	ECHL	62	25	31	56	36	5	2	1	3	6

QMJHL All-Rookie Team (2002) • Canadian Major Junior Sportsman of the Year (2004)

Signed as a free agent by **New Jersey**, June 24, 2006.

MONTGOMERY, Kevin (mawnt-GUHM-uhr-ee, KEH-vihn) **COL.**

Defense. Shoots left. 6'1", 185 lbs. Born, Rochester, NY, April 4, 1988.
(Colorado's 4th choice, 110th overall, in 2006 Entry Draft).

			Regular Season					Playoffs				
Season	Club	League	GP	G	A	Pts	PIM	GP	G	A	Pts	PIM
2003-04	Syracuse Jr. Stars	EmJHL	62	7	28	35	....	....	....	....	....	....
2004-05	USNTDP	U-17	8	1	4	5	4	....	....	....	....	....
	USNTDP	NAHL	38	4	12	16	46	9	1	3	4	6
2005-06	USNTDP	U-18	42	2	10	12	61	....	....	....	....	....
	USNTDP	NAHL	17	4	6	10	15	....	....	....	....	....
2006-07	Ohio State	CCHA	17	1	4	5	18	....	....	....	....	....
	London Knights	OHL	31	1	16	17	50	9	0	0	0	6

MONYCH, Lance (MOH-nihch, LANTS)

Right wing. Shoots right. 6'3", 203 lbs. Born, Red Deer, Alta., July 25, 1984.
(Phoenix's 6th choice, 97th overall, in 2002 Entry Draft).

			Regular Season					Playoffs				
Season	Club	League	GP	G	A	Pts	PIM	GP	G	A	Pts	PIM
99-2000	Brandon Hawks	MBHL	30	32	34	66	98	....	....	....	....	....
	Brandon	WHL	3	0	0	0	0	....	....	....	....	....
2000-01	Brandon	WHL	53	14	8	22	34	6	1	0	1	0
2001-02	Brandon	WHL	71	18	30	48	96	19	4	3	7	20
2002-03	Brandon	WHL	70	19	26	45	111	17	7	3	10	20
2003-04	Brandon	WHL	58	29	26	55	71	11	2	6	8	8
2004-05	Brandon	WHL	64	30	36	66	88	24	*19	7	26	44
2005-06	San Antonio	AHL	37	0	0	0	16	....	....	....	....	....
	Stockton Thunder	ECHL	26	11	10	21	14	....	....	....	....	....
	Laredo Bucks	CHL	3	4	0	4	0	....	....	....	....	....
2006-07	San Antonio	AHL	2	0	0	0	2	....	....	....	....	....
	Phoenix	ECHL	65	16	13	29	107	4	0	4	4	4

MOORE, Greg (MOOR, GREHG) **NYR**

Right wing. Shoots right. 6'1", 225 lbs. Born, Lisbon, ME, March 26, 1984.
(Calgary's 5th choice, 143rd overall, in 2003 Entry Draft).

			Regular Season					Playoffs				
Season	Club	League	GP	G	A	Pts	PIM	GP	G	A	Pts	PIM
99-2000	St. Dominic Saints	High-ME	31	32	40	72	....	....	....	....	....	....
2000-01	USNTDP	U-17	13	4	6	10	1	....	....	....	....	....
	USNTDP	NAHL	56	8	12	20	22	....	....	....	....	....
2001-02	USNTDP	U-18	35	8	20	28	14	....	....	....	....	....
	USNTDP	USHL	12	2	2	4	4	....	....	....	....	....
	USNTDP	NAHL	6	3	2	5	2	....	....	....	....	....
2002-03	U. of Maine	H-East	33	9	7	16	10	....	....	....	....	....
2003-04	U. of Maine	H-East	39	15	8	23	44	....	....	....	....	....
2004-05	U. of Maine	H-East	40	14	9	23	16	....	....	....	....	....
2005-06	U. of Maine	H-East	42	28	17	45	47	....	....	....	....	....
	Hartford Wolf Pack	AHL	2	1	1	2	2	13	2	5	7	6
2006-07	Hartford Wolf Pack	AHL	79	8	17	25	41	7	0	1	1	4

Hockey East First All-Star Team (2006) • NCAA East First All-American Team (2006)

Traded to **NY Rangers** by **Calgary** with Jamie McLennan and Blair Betts for Chris Simon and NY Rangers' 7th round choice (Matt Schneider) in 2004 Entry Draft, March 6, 2004.

MORIN, Travis (moh-REHN, TRA-vihs) **WSH.**

Center. Shoots left. 6'2", 175 lbs. Born, Minneapolis, MN, January 9, 1984.
(Washington's 13th choice, 263rd overall, in 2004 Entry Draft).

			Regular Season					Playoffs				
Season	Club	League	GP	G	A	Pts	PIM	GP	G	A	Pts	PIM
2001-02	Chicago Steel	USHL	20	5	8	13	....	4	0	0	0	2
2002-03	Chicago Steel	USHL	60	21	26	47	46	....	....	....	....	....
2003-04	Minnesota State	WCHA	38	9	12	21	14	....	....	....	....	....
2004-05	Minnesota State	WCHA	36	12	19	31	20	....	....	....	....	....
2005-06	Minnesota State	WCHA	39	20	22	42	16	....	....	....	....	....
2006-07	Minnesota State	WCHA	38	17	22	39	34	....	....	....	....	....
	South Carolina	ECHL	8	2	1	3	0	....	....	....	....	....

WCHA Second All-Star Team (2007)

MORMINA, Joey (mohr-MEE-nah, JOH-ee) **CAR.**

Defense. Shoots left. 6'6", 220 lbs. Born, Montreal, Que., June 29, 1982.
(Philadelphia's 6th choice, 193rd overall, in 2002 Entry Draft).

			Regular Season					Playoffs				
Season	Club	League	GP	G	A	Pts	PIM	GP	G	A	Pts	PIM
2000-01	Holderness School	High-NH	29	15	15	30	....	....	....	....	....	....
2001-02	Colgate	ECAC	34	2	13	15	28	....	....	....	....	....
2002-03	Colgate	ECAC	40	4	9	13	52	....	....	....	....	....
2003-04	Colgate	ECAC	28	2	10	12	26	....	....	....	....	....
2004-05	Colgate	ECACHL	39	8	8	16	50	....	....	....	....	....
2005-06	Manchester	AHL	61	0	13	13	70	7	0	0	0	4
2006-07	Manchester	AHL	62	2	9	11	108	1	0	0	0	2

Signed as a free agent by **Los Angeles**, August 24, 2005. Signed as a free agent by **Carolina**, July 2, 2007.

MORRIS, Mike (MOHR-his, MIGHK) **S.J.**

Right wing. Shoots right. 6'1", 185 lbs. Born, Dorchester, MA, July 14, 1983.
(San Jose's 1st choice, 27th overall, in 2002 Entry Draft).

			Regular Season					Playoffs				
Season	Club	League	GP	G	A	Pts	PIM	GP	G	A	Pts	PIM
2000-01	St. Sebastian's	High-MA	28	20	28	48	18	....	....	....	....	....
2001-02	St. Sebastian's	High-MA	31	29	29	58	26	....	....	....	....	....
2002-03	Northeastern	H-East	26	9	12	21	16	....	....	....	....	....
2003-04	Northeastern	H-East	34	10	20	30	14	....	....	....	....	....
2004-05	Northeastern	H-East	34	19	20	39	22	....	....	....	....	....
2005-06	Northeastern	H-East	DID NOT PLAY – INJURED									
2006-07	Northeastern	H-East	20	7	11	18	22	....	....	....	....	....

Hockey East Second All-Star Team (2005)

• Missed 2005-06 season due to head injury originally suffered in 2004.

MORRISON, Brett (MOHR-ih-suhn , BREHT) **ANA.**

Center. Shoots left. 5'11", 192 lbs. Born, Sydney, N.S., July 25, 1987.
(Anaheim's 8th choice, 151st overall, in 2007 Entry Draft).

			Regular Season					Playoffs				
Season	Club	League	GP	G	A	Pts	PIM	GP	G	A	Pts	PIM
2003-04	Cape Breton	NSMHL	36	43	41	84	22	....	....	....	....	....
2004-05	Gatineau	QMJHL	51	7	15	22	6	8	0	0	0	0
2005-06	Gatineau	QMJHL	64	33	39	72	53	16	2	5	7	4
2006-07	Gatineau	QMJHL	36	23	31	54	50	....	....	....	....	....
	PEI Rocket	QMJHL	28	12	24	36	26	7	8	8	16	10

MOULSON, Matt (MOWL-suhn, MAT) **L.A.**

Left wing. Shoots left. 6'1", 195 lbs. Born, North York, Ont., November 1, 1983.
(Pittsburgh's 11th choice, 263rd overall, in 2003 Entry Draft).

			Regular Season					Playoffs				
Season	Club	League	GP	G	A	Pts	PIM	GP	G	A	Pts	PIM
2001-02	Guelph	OHA-B	42	56	46	102	80	....	....	....	....	....
2002-03	Cornell Big Red	ECAC	33	13	10	23	22	....	....	....	....	....
2003-04	Cornell Big Red	ECAC	32	18	17	35	37	....	....	....	....	....
2004-05	Cornell Big Red	ECACHL	34	22	20	42	33	....	....	....	....	....
2005-06	Cornell Big Red	ECACHL	35	18	20	38	14	....	....	....	....	....
2006-07	Manchester	AHL	77	25	32	57	23	16	2	3	5	8

ECACHL First All-Star Team (2005) • NCAA East Second All-American Team (2005) • ECACHL Second All-Star Team (2006)

Signed as a free agent by **Los Angeles**, September 1, 2006.

MOZYAKIN, Sergei (mohz-YA-kihn, SAIR-gay) **CBJ**

Left wing. Shoots right. 5'10", 165 lbs. Born, Yaroslavl, USSR, March 30, 1981.
(Columbus' 13th choice, 263rd overall, in 2002 Entry Draft).

			Regular Season					Playoffs				
Season	Club	League	GP	G	A	Pts	PIM	GP	G	A	Pts	PIM
1998-99	Val-d'Or Foreurs	QMJHL	4	0	1	1	2	....	....	....	....	....
99-2000	HK Moscow 2	Russia-3	6	9	3	12	6	....	....	....	....	....
	HK Moscow	Russia-2	44	23	25	48	10	....	....	....	....	....
2000-01	HK Moscow	Russia-2	37	22	28	50	18	....	....	....	....	....
	CSKA Moscow	Russia	9	0	2	2	0	....	....	....	....	....
2001-02	HK CSKA Moscow	Russia-2	54	34	30	64	10	12	9	12	21	4
2002-03	CSKA Moscow	Russia	33	12	15	27	18	....	....	....	....	....
2003-04	CSKA Moscow	Russia	45	21	19	40	6	....	....	....	....	....
2004-05	CSKA Moscow	Russia	49	11	12	23	22	....	....	....	....	....
2005-06	CSKA Moscow	Russia	51	20	*31	*51	28	7	1	2	3	4
2006-07	Mytischi	Russia	54	27	33	60	10	9	5	3	8	4

MUELLER, Peter (MEW-luhr, PEE-tuhr) **PHX.**

Center. Shoots right. 6'2", 205 lbs. Born, Bloomington, MN, April 14, 1988.
(Phoenix's 1st choice, 8th overall, in 2006 Entry Draft).

			Regular Season					Playoffs				
Season	Club	League	GP	G	A	Pts	PIM	GP	G	A	Pts	PIM
2003-04	USNTDP	U-17	17	4	9	13	25	....	....	....	....	....
	USNTDP	NAHL	43	10	16	26	26	7	3	2	5	4
2004-05	USNTDP	U-18	43	27	27	64	75	....	....	....	....	....
	USNTDP	NAHL	14	11	13	24	16	....	....	....	....	....
2005-06	Everett Silvertips	WHL	52	26	32	58	44	15	7	6	13	10
2006-07	Everett Silvertips	WHL	51	21	57	78	45	12	7	9	16	12

WHL Rookie ot the Year (2006) • WHL West First All-Star Team (2007)

MUKHACHEV, Andrei (moo-khah-CHEHV, AWN-dray) **NSH.**

Defense. Shoots left. 6'3", 196 lbs. Born, Ekaterinburg, USSR, July 21, 1980.
(Nashville's 11th choice, 210th overall, in 2003 Entry Draft).

			Regular Season					Playoffs				
Season	Club	League	GP	G	A	Pts	PIM	GP	G	A	Pts	PIM
1998-99	HK CSKA Moscow	Russia-2	38	0	2	2	30	....	....	....	....	....
99-2000	HK Moscow	Russia-2	40	2	9	11	44	....	....	....	....	....
2000-01	CSKA Moscow 2	Russia-3	8	1	5	6	18	....	....	....	....	....
	HK Moscow	Russia-2	40	2	9	11	44	....	....	....	....	....
2001-02	HK CSKA Moscow	Russia-2	39	3	9	12	28	12	2	5	7	10
2002-03	CSKA Moscow	Russia	50	3	7	10	30	....	....	....	....	....
2003-04	CSKA Moscow	Russia	38	2	4	6	28	....	....	....	....	....
2004-05	CSKA Moscow	Russia	21	0	2	2	14	....	....	....	....	....
2005-06	CSKA Moscow	Russia	48	1	4	5	71	7	0	0	0	4
2006-07	Vityaz Chekhov	Russia	51	2	8	10	82	3	0	0	0	2

MURATOV, Yevgeny (muhr-A-tahf, yehv-GEH-nee) **EDM.**

Left wing. Shoots right. 5'10", 178 lbs. Born, Nizhny Tagil, USSR, January 28, 1981.
(Edmonton's 10th choice, 274th overall, in 2000 Entry Draft).

			Regular Season					Playoffs				
Season	Club	League	GP	G	A	Pts	PIM	GP	G	A	Pts	PIM
1997-98	Nizhnekamsk 2	Russia-3	39	7	7	14	2	....	....	....	....	....
1998-99	Nizhnekamsk 2	Russia-4	37	26	9	35	32	....	....	....	....	....
	Nizhnekamsk	Russia	4	0	0	0	0	3	1	0	1	2
99-2000	Nizhnekamsk	Russia	29	9	7	16	2	....	....	....	....	....
	Ak Bars Kazan	Russia	8	2	2	4	2	9	0	0	0	2
2000-01	Nizhnekamsk	Russia	42	9	8	17	14	4	0	0	0	0
2001-02	Nizhnekamsk	Russia	45	5	13	18	4	....	....	....	....	....
2002-03	Nizhnekamsk	Russia	51	10	11	21	41	....	....	....	....	....
2003-04	Nizhnekamsk	Russia	20	1	6	7	8	....	....	....	....	....
2004-05	Novokuznetsk	Russia	58	15	13	28	12	4	1	2	3	0
2005-06	SKA St. Petersburg	Russia	49	13	10	23	16	3	0	1	1	0
2006-07	SKA St. Petersburg	Russia	42	5	9	14	14	1	0	0	0	0
	St. Petersburg 2	Russia-3	5	5	5	10	2	....	....	....	....	....

Signed as a free agent by **Nizhnekamsk** (Russia), August 5, 2007.

MURPHY, Colin (MUHR-fee, KOHL-ihn)

Left wing. Shoots left. 6', 195 lbs. Born, Fort McMurray, Alta., April 11, 1980.

			Regular Season					Playoffs				
Season	Club	League	GP	G	A	Pts	PIM	GP	G	A	Pts	PIM
2001-02	Michigan Tech	WCHA	38	8	19	27	40	....	....	....	....	....
2002-03	Michigan Tech	WCHA	37	20	20	40	42	....	....	....	....	....
2003-04	Michigan Tech	WCHA	33	15	17	32	28	....	....	....	....	....
2004-05	Michigan Tech	WCHA	37	11	*42	53	40	....	....	....	....	....
	St. John's	AHL	12	1	7	8	34	5	1	3	4	17
2005-06	Toronto Marlies	AHL	53	16	17	33	44	4	0	0	0	0
2006-07	Toronto Marlies	AHL	73	20	36	56	126	....	....	....	....	....

WCHA First All-Star Team (2005) • NCAA West Second All-American Team (2005)

Signed as a free agent by **Toronto**, March 18, 2005.

MURPHY, Cory (MUHR-fee, KOH-ree) **FLA.**

Defense. Shoots left. 5'10", 185 lbs. Born, Kanata, Ont., February 13, 1978.

			Regular Season					Playoffs				
Season	Club	League	GP	G	A	Pts	PIM	GP	G	A	Pts	PIM
1997-98	Colgate	ECAC	35	8	19	27	38	....	....	....	....	....
1998-99	Colgate	ECAC	34	3	23	26	26	....	....	....	....	....
99-2000	Colgate	ECAC	35	10	19	29	26	....	....	....	....	....
2000-01	Colgate	ECAC	34	7	22	29	34	....	....	....	....	....
2001-02	Blues Espoo	Finland	46	9	15	24	38	3	0	1	1	0
2002-03	Blues Espoo	Finland	45	11	4	15	49	7	1	0	1	2
2003-04	Ilves Tampere	Finland	56	18	26	44	22	7	1	2	3	2
2004-05	Ilves Tampere	Finland	56	12	23	35	36	7	1	3	4	18
2005-06	Fribourg	Swiss	44	13	22	35	52	....	....	....	....	....
2006-07	HIFK Helsinki	Finland	45	13	37	50	46	....	....	....	....	....

Signed as a free agent by **Florida**, March 26, 2007.

MURPHY, Ryan (MUHR-fee, RIGH-uhn) **N.J.**

Left wing. Shoots left. 6'1", 205 lbs. Born, Van Nuys, CA, March 21, 1979.
(Carolina's 4th choice, 113th overall, in 1999 Entry Draft).

			Regular Season					Playoffs				
Season	Club	League	GP	G	A	Pts	PIM	GP	G	A	Pts	PIM
1995-96	Thornhill Islanders	MTJHL	32	13	16	29	49	1	0	0	0	0
1996-97	Thornhill Islanders	MTJHL	41	22	32	54	36	12	7	8	15	....
1997-98	Bowling Green	CCHA	36	3	9	12	27	....	....	....	....	....
1998-99	Bowling Green	CCHA	34	10	23	33	38	....	....	....	....	....
99-2000	Bowling Green	CCHA	36	9	10	19	63	....	....	....	....	....
2000-01	Bowling Green	CCHA	38	23	15	38	22	....	....	....	....	....
2001-02	Florida Everblades	ECHL	66	13	18	31	38	6	1	2	3	4
2002-03	Lowell	AHL	12	1	2	3	4	....	....	....	....	....
	Florida Everblades	ECHL	58	28	17	45	47	1	0	0	0	0
2003-04	Albany River Rats	AHL	71	10	9	19	28	....	....	....	....	....
2004-05	Albany River Rats	AHL	75	13	23	36	44	....	....	....	....	....
2005-06	Albany River Rats	AHL	17	4	2	6	12	....	....	....	....	....
2006-07	Lowell Devils	AHL	69	17	21	38	22	....	....	....	....	....

Signed as a free agent by **New Jersey**, July 20, 2003.

MURRAY, Andrew (MUHR-ree, AN-droo) **CBJ**

Center. Shoots left. 6'2", 210 lbs. Born, Selkirk, Man., November 6, 1981.
(Columbus' 11th choice, 242nd overall, in 2001 Entry Draft).

			Regular Season					Playoffs				
Season	Club	League	GP	G	A	Pts	PIM	GP	G	A	Pts	PIM
99-2000	Selkirk Steelers	MJHL	63	29	48	77	....	....	....	....	....	....
2000-01	Selkirk Steelers	MJHL	64	46	56	102	72	5	3	0	3	6
2001-02	Bemidji State	CHA	35	15	15	30	22	....	....	....	....	....
2002-03	Bemidji State	CHA	36	9	18	27	38	....	....	....	....	....
2003-04	Bemidji State	CHA	25	6	14	20	41	....	....	....	....	....
2004-05	Bemidji State	CHA	32	16	22	38	30	....	....	....	....	....
2005-06	Syracuse Crunch	AHL	77	13	16	29	73	6	0	1	1	17
2006-07	Syracuse Crunch	AHL	72	10	12	22	62	....	....	....	....	....

CHA All-Rookie Team (2002)

MURRAY, Brady (MUHR-ree, BRAY-dee) **L.A.**

Center. Shoots left. 5'9", 180 lbs. Born, Brandon, Man., August 17, 1984.
(Los Angeles' 6th choice, 152nd overall, in 2003 Entry Draft).

			Regular Season					Playoffs				
Season	Club	League	GP	G	A	Pts	PIM	GP	G	A	Pts	PIM
2001-02	Shat.-St. Mary's	High-MN	60	58	92	150	50	....	....	....	....	....
2002-03	Salmon Arm	BCHL	59	42	59	101	30	....	....	....	....	....
2003-04	North Dakota	WCHA	37	19	27	46	32	....	....	....	....	....
2004-05	North Dakota	WCHA	25	8	12	20	22	....	....	....	....	....
2005-06	Rapperswil	Swiss	36	3	9	12	28	10	3	2	5	10
2006-07	Rapperswil	Swiss	38	12	20	32	38	7	4	2	6	6

WCHA All-Rookie Team (2004) • WCHA Rookie of the Year (2004)

MURSAK , Jan (MUHR-sak, YAHN) **DET.**

Left wing. Shoots right. 5'11", 167 lbs. Born, Maribor, Yugoslavia, January 20, 1988.
(Detroit's 5th choice, 182nd overall, in 2006 Entry Draft).

			Regular Season					Playoffs				
Season	Club	League	GP	G	A	Pts	PIM	GP	G	A	Pts	PIM
2002-03	HK Maribor U18	Sloven-U18	13	27	18	45	14	....	....	....	....	....
2003-04	HK Maribor U18	Sloven-U18	22	27	17	44	14	....	....	....	....	....
	HK Maribor Jr.	Sloven-Jr.	19	8	8	16	37	....	....	....	....	....
	HK Maribor	Slovenia	14	3	3	6	16	....	....	....	....	....
2004-05	HK Maribor Jr.	Sloven-Jr.	19	17	16	33	39	....	....	....	....	....
	HK Maribor	Slovenia	24	16	29	45	10	....	....	....	....	....
2005-06	C. Budejovice Jr.	CzRep-Jr.	43	15	15	30	32	5	0	2	2	2
2006-07	Saginaw Spirit	OHL	62	27	53	80	50	6	1	2	3	10
	Grand Rapids	AHL	....	....	....	....	....	7	0	2	2	2

MUZZIN, Jake (MUH-zihn, JAYK) **PIT.**

Defense. Shoots left. 6'2", 206 lbs. Born, Woodstock, Ont., February 21, 1989.
(Pittsburgh's 7th choice, 141st overall, in 2007 Entry Draft).

			Regular Season					Playoffs				
Season	Club	League	GP	G	A	Pts	PIM	GP	G	A	Pts	PIM
2004-05	Brantford 99ers	Minor-ON	57	20	23	43	78	....	....	....	....	....
2005-06	Sault Ste. Marie	OHL	DID NOT PLAY – INJURED									
2006-07	Soo Thunderbirds	NOJHL	4	0	3	3	2	....	....	....	....	....
	Sault Ste. Marie	OHL	37	1	3	4	10	13	0	4	4	6

• Missed entire 2005-06 season recovering from off-season back surgery.

NASBY, Bret (NAZ-bee, BREHT) **FLA.**

Defense. Shoots right. 6'3", 188 lbs. Born, Grimsby, Ont., March 22, 1986.
(Florida's 5th choice, 152nd overall, in 2004 Entry Draft).

			Regular Season					Playoffs				
Season	Club	League	GP	G	A	Pts	PIM	GP	G	A	Pts	PIM
2002-03	Grimsby	OHA-C	53	6	14	20	63	....	....	....	....	....
2003-04	Oshawa Generals	OHL	56	0	7	7	41	7	0	3	3	6
2004-05	Oshawa Generals	OHL	66	4	13	17	71	....	....	....	....	....
2005-06	Oshawa Generals	OHL	20	5	9	14	42	....	....	....	....	....
	Erie Otters	OHL	32	4	13	17	30	....	....	....	....	....
2006-07	Florida Everblades	ECHL	31	1	3	4	19	....	....	....	....	....

NASH, Riley (NASH, RIGH-lee) **EDM.**

Center. Shoots right. 6'1", 175 lbs. Born, Consort, Alta., May 9, 1989.
(Edmonton's 3rd choice, 21st overall, in 2007 Entry Draft).

			Regular Season					Playoffs				
Season	Club	League	GP	G	A	Pts	PIM	GP	G	A	Pts	PIM
2005-06	Thompson Blazers	BCAHA	31	29	31	60	100	....	....	....	....	....
	Salmon Arm	BCHL	1	0	0	0	0	5	1	2	3	0
2006-07	Salmon Arm	BCHL	55	38	46	84	87	11	4	7	11	31

NASLUND, Fredrik (NAZ-luhnd, FREHD-rihk) **DAL.**

Left wing. Shoots right. 6'4", 211 lbs. Born, Stockholm, Sweden, February 11, 1986.
(Dallas' 6th choice, 104th overall, in 2004 Entry Draft).

			Regular Season					Playoffs				
Season	Club	League	GP	G	A	Pts	PIM	GP	G	A	Pts	PIM
2002-03	Vasteras Jr.	Swe-Jr.	34	12	9	21	8	....	....	....	....	....
2003-04	Vasteras Jr.	Swe-Jr.	17	13	15	28	6	3	0	1	1	4
	Vasteras	Sweden-2	32	2	4	6	0	....	....	....	....	....
2004-05	Vasteras	Sweden-2	3	0	0	0	0	....	....	....	....	....
	Vasteras Jr.	Swe-Jr.	21	7	7	14	2	....	....	....	....	....
2005-06	Peterborough	OHL	66	9	21	30	30	19	6	5	11	6
2006-07	Nykoping	Sweden-2	45	13	13	26	38	5	2	2	4	4

NAUROV, Alexander (naw-OO-rawf, al-EHX-AN-duhr) **DAL.**

Right wing. Shoots left. 5'11", 191 lbs. Born, Saratov, USSR, March 4, 1985.
(Dallas' 5th choice, 134th overall, in 2003 Entry Draft).

			Regular Season					Playoffs				
Season	Club	League	GP	G	A	Pts	PIM	GP	G	A	Pts	PIM
2001-02	Yaroslavl 2	Russia-3	12	0	0	0	16	....	....	....	....	....
2002-03	Yaroslavl 2	Russia-3	STATISTICS NOT AVAILABLE									
2003-04	Yaroslavl 2	Russia-3	24	9	5	14	73	....	....	....	....	....
2004-05	Yaroslavl 2	Russia-3	35	19	16	35	61	....	....	....	....	....
	Yaroslavl	Russia	11	2	2	4	2	....	....	....	....	....
2005-06	Kristall Saratov	Russia-2	52	11	13	24	42	....	....	....	....	....
2006-07	Idaho Steelheads	ECHL	16	1	6	7	8	8	0	0	0	2
	Assat Pori	Finland	11	0	2	2	8	....	....	....	....	....
	TuTo Turku	Finland-2	4	0	0	0	10	....	....	....	....	....

NEAL, James (NEEL, JAYMS) **DAL.**

Left wing. Shoots left. 6'2", 185 lbs. Born, Oshawa, Ont., September 3, 1987.
(Dallas' 2nd choice, 33rd overall, in 2005 Entry Draft).

			Regular Season					Playoffs				
Season	Club	League	GP	G	A	Pts	PIM	GP	G	A	Pts	PIM
2003-04	Bowmanville	OPJHL	43	28	27	55	....	....	....	....	....	....
	Plymouth Whalers	OHL	9	2	4	6	0	....	....	....	....	....
2004-05	Plymouth Whalers	OHL	67	18	26	44	32	4	1	1	2	6
2005-06	Plymouth Whalers	OHL	66	21	37	58	109	13	9	7	16	33
2006-07	Plymouth Whalers	OHL	45	27	38	65	94	20	13	12	25	54

OHL First All-Star Team (2007)

NEAL, Michael (NEEL, MIGH-kuhl) **DAL.**

Left wing. Shoots left. 6'2", 188 lbs. Born, Whitby, Ont., April 3, 1989.
(Dallas' 7th choice, 149th overall, in 2007 Entry Draft).

			Regular Season					Playoffs				
Season	Club	League	GP	G	A	Pts	PIM	GP	G	A	Pts	PIM
2004-05	Whitby Wildcats	Minor-ON	52	20	29	49	67	....	....	....	....	....
2005-06	Belleville Bulls	OHL	46	1	3	4	6	....	....	....	....	....
2006-07	Belleville Bulls	OHL	52	4	4	8	25	15	0	1	1	6

NEGRIN, John (NEH-grihn, JAWN) **CGY.**

Defense. Shoots left. 6'2", 195 lbs. Born, West Vancouver, B.C., March 25, 1989.
(Calgary's 2nd choice, 70th overall, in 2007 Entry Draft).

			Regular Season					Playoffs				
Season	Club	League	GP	G	A	Pts	PIM	GP	G	A	Pts	PIM
2004-05	North Delta Flyers	PIJHL	45	3	12	15	53	....	....	....	....	....
	Kootenay Ice	WHL	2	0	0	0	0	....	....	....	....	....
2005-06	Kootenay Ice	WHL	55	3	7	10	48	6	0	0	0	6
2006-07	Kootenay Ice	WHL	44	1	15	16	57	7	0	2	2	8

NELSON, Levi (NELH-sohn, LEE-vigh) **BOS.**

Center. Shoots left. 6', 184 lbs. Born, Calgary, Alta., April 28, 1988.
(Boston's 6th choice, 158th overall, in 2006 Entry Draft).

			Regular Season					Playoffs				
Season	Club	League	GP	G	A	Pts	PIM	GP	G	A	Pts	PIM
2004-05	Cgy. North Stars	AMHL	35	15	13	28	70	....	....	....	....	....
	Swift Current	WHL	2	1	0	1	0	....	....	....	....	....
2005-06	Swift Current	WHL	63	21	17	38	63	4	0	0	0	4
2006-07	Swift Current	WHL	66	18	34	52	125	6	4	3	7	4
	Providence Bruins	AHL	1	0	0	0	2	4	1	0	1	2

NEPRYAYEV, Ivan (neh-pree-YIGH-ehv, IGH-vuhn) **WSH.**

Center. Shoots left. 6'1", 180 lbs. Born, Yaroslavl, USSR, February 4, 1982.
(Washington's 5th choice, 163rd overall, in 2000 Entry Draft).

			Regular Season					Playoffs				
Season	Club	League	GP	G	A	Pts	PIM	GP	G	A	Pts	PIM
1997-98	Torpedo Yaroslavl	Russia	6	0	0	0	0	....	....	....	....	....
1998-99	Yaroslavl 2	Russia-3	15	1	0	1	0	....	....	....	....	....
99-2000	Yaroslavl 2	Russia-3	40	8	14	22	....	....	....	....	....	....
2000-01	Yaroslavl	Russia	10	0	0	0	2	....	....	....	....	....
2001-02	Yaroslavl 2	Russia-3	2	1	0	1	18	....	....	....	....	....
	Yaroslavl	Russia	36	3	8	11	28	....	....	....	....	....
2002-03	Yaroslavl	Russia	26	3	6	9	12	6	1	0	1	0
2003-04	Yaroslavl 2	Russia-3	13	5	10	15	12	....	....	....	....	....
2004-05	Yaroslavl	Russia	56	10	10	20	73	9	1	0	1	16
2005-06	Yaroslavl	Russia	43	7	16	23	70	11	0	0	0	8
	Russia	Olympics	2	0	0	0	2	....	....	....	....	....
2006-07	Yaroslavl	Russia	52	17	9	26	66	7	0	4	4	2

NESBITT, Derek

Right wing. Shoots left. 6', 185 lbs. Born, Egmondville, Ont., April 16, 1982.

			Regular Season					Playoffs				
Season	Club	League	GP	G	A	Pts	PIM	GP	G	A	Pts	PIM
2001-02	Ferris State	CCHA	36	9	11	20	16	....	....	....	....	....
2002-03	Ferris State	CCHA	42	20	33	53	26	....	....	....	....	....
2003-04	Ferris State	CCHA	38	11	17	28	36	....	....	....	....	....
2004-05	Ferris State	CCHA	38	19	21	40	44	....	....	....	....	....
	Bossier-Shreve.	CHL	7	0	5	5	0	....	....	....	....	....
2005-06	Gwinnett	ECHL	71	26	43	69	6	17	6	7	13	8
2006-07	Idaho Steelheads	ECHL	66	30	51	81	32	22	6	12	18	8

NICKERSON, Matt (NIH-kuhr-suhn, MAT) **DAL.**

Defense. Shoots right. 6'4", 230 lbs. Born, New London, CT, January 11, 1985.
(Dallas' 4th choice, 99th overall, in 2003 Entry Draft).

			Regular Season					Playoffs				
Season	Club	League	GP	G	A	Pts	PIM	GP	G	A	Pts	PIM
2000-01	Victoria Salsa	BCHL	....	....	....	....	196	....	....	....	....	....
2001-02	Texas Tornado	NAHL	47	1	12	13	97	6	0	0	0	6
2002-03	Texas Tornado	NAHL	47	6	23	29	277	6	0	1	1	*18
2003-04	Clarkson Knights	ECAC	38	5	9	14	*179	....	....	....	....	....
2004-05	Victoriaville Tigres	QMJHL	48	1	11	12	182	6	0	1	1	27
2005-06	Assat Pori	Finland	36	5	8	13	*236	14	1	0	1	50
2006-07	Iowa Stars	AHL	40	0	3	3	97	....	....	....	....	....
	Idaho Steelheads	ECHL	13	1	1	2	73	....	....	....	....	....

NIKITIN, Nikita (nih-KEE-tihn, nih-KEE-tuh) **ST.L.**

Defense. Shoots left. 6'3", 178 lbs. Born, Omsk, USSR, June 16, 1986.
(St. Louis' 5th choice, 136th overall, in 2004 Entry Draft).

			Regular Season					Playoffs				
Season	Club	League	GP	G	A	Pts	PIM	GP	G	A	Pts	PIM
2002-03	Omsk 2	Russia-3	34	3	7	10	4	....	....	....	....	....
2003-04	Omsk 2	Russia-3	34	3	8	11	22	....	....	....	....	....
2004-05	Avangard Omsk	Russia	12	0	0	0	2	3	0	0	0	0
	Omsk 2	Russia-3	31	3	8	11	20	....	....	....	....	....
2005-06	Avangard Omsk	Russia	43	1	2	3	22	13	1	2	3	6
	Omsk 2	Russia-3	1	0	0	0	0	....	....	....	....	....
2006-07	Avangard Omsk	Russia	54	1	15	16	99	9	0	4	4	35

NIKULIN, Alexander (nih-KOO-lihn, al-EHX-AN-duhr) **OTT.**

Center. Shoots left. 6'1", 195 lbs. Born, Moscow, USSR, August 25, 1985.
(Ottawa's 6th choice, 122nd overall, in 2004 Entry Draft).

			Regular Season					Playoffs				
Season	Club	League	GP	G	A	Pts	PIM	GP	G	A	Pts	PIM
2002-03	CSKA Moscow 2	Russia-3	46	22	14	36	....	....	....	....	....	....
2003-04	CSKA Moscow 2	Russia-3	47	21	20	41	46	....	....	....	....	....
2004-05	CSKA Moscow	Russia	16	3	3	6	0	....	....	....	....	....
2005-06	CSKA Moscow	Russia	51	10	12	22	22	7	1	0	1	2
2006-07	CSKA Moscow	Russia	33	5	11	16	8	12	4	2	6	4

NIKULIN, Ilja (nih-KOO-lihn, IHL-yah) **ATL.**

Defense. Shoots left. 6'3", 210 lbs. Born, Moscow, USSR, March 12, 1982.
(Atlanta's 2nd choice, 31st overall, in 2000 Entry Draft).

			Regular Season					Playoffs				
Season	Club	League	GP	G	A	Pts	PIM	GP	G	A	Pts	PIM
1998-99	Dyn'o Moscow 2	Russia-3	23	0	2	2	18	....	....	....	....	....
99-2000	Dyn'o Moscow 2	Russia-3	4	2	1	3	10	....	....	....	....	....
	THK Tver	Russia-2	39	3	6	9	84	....	....	....	....	....
2000-01	Dynamo Moscow	Russia	44	0	4	4	61	....	....	....	....	....
2001-02	Dyn'o Moscow 2	Russia-3	2	0	1	1	2	....	....	....	....	....
	Dynamo Moscow	Russia	47	2	1	3	44	3	0	0	0	0
2002-03	Dynamo Moscow	Russia	40	1	4	5	46	5	0	1	1	4
2003-04	Dynamo Moscow	Russia	54	1	5	6	56	3	0	0	0	2
2004-05	Dynamo Moscow	Russia	50	1	9	10	65	10	0	3	3	8
2005-06	Ak Bars Kazan	Russia	49	9	9	18	48	13	4	0	4	36
2006-07	Ak Bars Kazan	Russia	51	11	14	25	99	16	4	5	9	18

NILL, Trevor (NIHL, TREH-vuhr) **ST.L.**

Center. Shoots right. 6'1", 180 lbs. Born, Detroit, MI, April 11, 1989.
(St. Louis' 10th choice, 190th overall, in 2007 Entry Draft).

			Regular Season					Playoffs				
Season	Club	League	GP	G	A	Pts	PIM	GP	G	A	Pts	PIM
2004-05	Det. Compuware	MWEHL	25	10	8	18	8	4	2	1	3	0
2005-06	Det. Compuware	MWEHL	21	4	9	13	20	4	1	0	1	2
2006-07	Det. Compuware	MWEHL	24	6	10	16	23	6	2	4	6	2

• Signed Letter of Intent to attend **Michigan State University** (CCHA) in fall of 2008.

NISKALA, Janne (NIHS-kah-lah, YAH-nee) **NSH.**

Defense. Shoots left. 5'11", 199 lbs. Born, Vasteras, Sweden, September 22, 1981.
(Nashville's 5th choice, 147th overall, in 2004 Entry Draft).

			Regular Season					Playoffs				
Season	Club	League	GP	G	A	Pts	PIM	GP	G	A	Pts	PIM
1997-98	Lukko Rauma U18	Fin-U18	34	7	16	23	40	....	....	....	....	....
1998-99	Lukko Rauma U18	Fin-U18	14	7	4	11	42	....	....	....	....	....
	Lukko Rauma Jr.	Fin-Jr.	2	0	0	0	12	....	....	....	....	....
99-2000	Lukko Rauma Jr.	Fin-Jr.	40	14	15	29	50	8	0	2	2	8
2000-01	Lukko Rauma Jr.	Fin-Jr.	13	4	8	12	40	....	....	....	....	....
	Lukko Rauma	Finland	18	0	0	0	0	....	....	....	....	....
	Jaa-Kotkat	Finland-2	13	4	1	5	43	....	....	....	....	....
	Manchester Storm	Britain	16	0	1	1	14	....	....	....	....	....
2001-02	Lukko Rauma Jr.	Fin-Jr.	3	1	1	2	2	....	....	....	....	....
	Lukko Rauma	Finland	55	7	13	20	81	....	....	....	....	....
2002-03	Lukko Rauma	Finland	46	4	5	9	40	....	....	....	....	....
2003-04	Lukko Rauma	Finland	55	21	15	36	73	4	0	0	0	16
2004-05	Lukko Rauma	Finland	44	9	12	21	63	9	5	2	7	4
2005-06	EV Zug	Swiss	43	12	17	29	50	7	0	2	2	10
2006-07	Farjestad	Sweden	53	19	30	49	62	9	3	3	6	14

NISKANEN, Matt (NIHS-kah-nehn, MAT) **DAL.**

Defense. Shoots right. 6', 194 lbs. Born, Virginia, MN, December 6, 1986.
(Dallas' 1st choice, 28th overall, in 2005 Entry Draft).

			Regular Season					Playoffs				
Season	Club	League	GP	G	A	Pts	PIM	GP	G	A	Pts	PIM
2003-04	Virginia Blue Devils	High-MN	....	24	37	61	....	....	....	....	....	....
2004-05	Virginia Blue Devils	High-MN	29	27	38	65	34	....	....	....	....	....
2005-06	U. Minn-Duluth	WCHA	38	1	13	14	40	....	....	....	....	....
2006-07	U. Minn-Duluth	WCHA	39	9	22	31	42	....	....	....	....	....
	Iowa Stars	AHL	13	0	3	3	6	12	2	5	7	10

WCHA First All-Star Team (2007)

NODL, Andreas (NOHD'L, awn-DRAY-uhs) **PHI.**

Right wing. Shoots left. 6'1", 190 lbs. Born, Vienna, Austria, February 28, 1987.
(Philadelphia's 2nd choice, 39th overall, in 2006 Entry Draft).

			Regular Season					Playoffs				
Season	Club	League	GP	G	A	Pts	PIM	GP	G	A	Pts	PIM
2001-02	Wien Jr.	Austria-Jr.	1	0	0	0	0	....	....	....	....	....
2002-03	Wien Jr.	Austria-Jr.	STATISTICS NOT AVAILABLE									
2003-04	Vienna Capitals	Austria	25	15	22	37	26	....	....	....	....	....
	Wien Jr.	Austria-Jr.	15	11	10	21	47	....	....	....	....	....
2004-05	Sioux Falls	USHL	44	7	9	16	24	....	....	....	....	....
	Sioux Falls	USHL	44	7	9	16	24	....	....	....	....	....
2005-06	Sioux Falls	USHL	58	29	30	59	16	14	6	9	15	6
2006-07	St. Cloud State	WCHA	40	18	28	46	32	....	....	....	....	....

USHL First All-Star Team (2006) • WCHA All-Rookie Team (2007) • WCHA Rookie of the Year (2007)

NOLAN, Brandon (NOH-lan, BRAN-duhn) **CAR.**

Center/Left wing. Shoots left. 5'10", 185 lbs. Born, Sault Ste. Marie, Ont., July 18, 1983.
(Vancouver's 3rd choice, 111th overall, in 2003 Entry Draft).

			Regular Season					Playoffs				
Season	Club	League	GP	G	A	Pts	PIM	GP	G	A	Pts	PIM
99-2000	St. Catharines	OHA-B	47	18	13	31	10	....	....	....	....	....
2000-01	Oshawa Generals	OHL	52	15	23	38	21	....	....	....	....	....
2001-02	Oshawa Generals	OHL	57	30	28	58	78	5	2	4	6	4
2002-03	Oshawa Generals	OHL	68	36	52	88	57	13	10	7	17	4
2003-04	Manitoba Moose	AHL	48	7	10	17	18	....	....	....	....	....
	Columbia Inferno	ECHL	19	5	10	15	38	3	0	1	1	17
2004-05	Manitoba Moose	AHL	48	4	8	12	16	....	....	....	....	....
2005-06	Manitoba Moose	AHL	18	3	8	11	10	....	....	....	....	....
	Columbia Inferno	ECHL	43	20	31	51	94	....	....	....	....	....
2006-07	Bridgeport	AHL	40	9	13	22	59	....	....	....	....	....
	Vaxjo Lakers HC	Sweden-2	19	6	10	16	44	....	....	....	....	....

• Re-entered NHL Entry Draft. Originally New Jersey's 6th choice, 72nd overall, in 2001 Entry Draft.

OHL Second All-Star Team (2003)

Signed as a free agent by **Carolina**, July 2, 2007.

NOLET, Martin (noh-LAY, MAHR-tihn) **L.A.**

Defense. Shoots right. 6'3", 209 lbs. Born, Quebec, Que., October 2, 1986.
(Los Angeles' 8th choice, 144th overall, in 2006 Entry Draft).

			Regular Season					Playoffs				
Season	Club	League	GP	G	A	Pts	PIM	GP	G	A	Pts	PIM
2002-03	St-Francois	QAAA	31	3	3	6	62	....	....	....	....	....
2003-04	St-Francois	QAAA	31	5	11	16	91	8	2	2	4	24
2004-05	Champlain College	QJHL	43	4	23	27	97	14	2	3	5	14
2005-06	Champlain College	QJHL	19	5	7	12	26	10	1	1	2	24
2006-07	Massachusetts	H-East	32	1	3	4	35	....	....	....	....	....

• Missed majority of 2005-06 season recovering from off-season shoulder surgery.

NORTON, Pierce (NOHR-tuhn, PIHRS) **TOR.**

Right wing. Shoots right. 6'2", 200 lbs. Born, Boston, MA, June 7, 1985.
(Toronto's 6th choice, 285th overall, in 2004 Entry Draft).

			Regular Season					Playoffs				
Season	Club	League	GP	G	A	Pts	PIM	GP	G	A	Pts	PIM
2002-03	Thayer Academy	High-MA	29	16	18	34	....	....	....	....	....	....
2003-04	Thayer Academy	High-MA	34	21	34	55	84	....	....	....	....	....
2004-05	Thayer Academy	High-MA	29	*30	20	50	....	....	....	....	....	....
2005-06	Providence College	H-East	35	1	2	3	22	....	....	....	....	....
2006-07	Providence College	H-East	31	6	5	11	46	....	....	....	....	....

NYHOLM, Robert (NYOO-hohlm, RAW-buhrt) **CBJ**

Right wing. Shoots left. 6'1", 194 lbs. Born, Pietarsaari, Finland, March 7, 1988.
(Columbus' 5th choice, 129th overall, in 2006 Entry Draft).

			Regular Season					Playoffs				
Season	Club	League	GP	G	A	Pts	PIM	GP	G	A	Pts	PIM
2003-04	Lepplax U18	Fin-U18	26	76	32	108	36	....	....	....	....	....
2004-05	HIFK Helsinki U18	Fin-U18	1	1	0	1	2	3	0	2	2	6
	HIFK Helsinki Jr.	Fin-Jr.	33	6	5	11	35	....	....	....	....	....
2005-06	HIFK Helsinki U18	Fin-U18	2	2	3	5	4	7	4	3	7	4
	HIFK Helsinki Jr.	Fin-Jr.	39	11	9	20	24	....	....	....	....	....
2006-07	Kingston	OHL	66	13	21	34	29	5	0	3	3	2

O'BRIEN, James (oh-BRIGH-uhn, JAYMZ) **OTT.**

Center. Shoots right. 6'2", 184 lbs. Born, Maplewood, MN, January 29, 1989.
(Ottawa's 1st choice, 29th overall, in 2007 Entry Draft).

			Regular Season					Playoffs				
Season	Club	League	GP	G	A	Pts	PIM	GP	G	A	Pts	PIM
2003-04	Det. Caesars	MWEHL	68	19	24	43	72	....	....	....	....	....
2004-05	USNTDP	U-17	13	6	6	12	10	....	....	....	....	....
	USNTDP	NAHL	40	10	12	22	41	1	0	0	0	0
2005-06	USNTDP	U-18	38	11	14	25	62	....	....	....	....	....
	USNTDP	NAHL	13	6	10	16	14	....	....	....	....	....
2006-07	U. of Minnesota	WCHA	43	7	8	15	51	....	....	....	....	....

O'BYRNE, Ryan (oh-BUHRN, RIGH-uhn) **MTL.**

Defense. Shoots right. 6'5", 234 lbs. Born, Victoria, B.C., July 19, 1984.
(Montreal's 4th choice, 79th overall, in 2003 Entry Draft).

			Regular Season					Playoffs				
Season	Club	League	GP	G	A	Pts	PIM	GP	G	A	Pts	PIM
2001-02	Victoria Salsa	BCHL	52	2	9	11	91	....	....	....	....	....
2002-03	Victoria Salsa	BCHL	32	3	6	9	94	....	....	....	....	....
	Nanaimo Clippers	BCHL	9	2	4	6	24	....	....	....	....	....
2003-04	Cornell Big Red	ECAC	31	0	2	2	71	....	....	....	....	....
2004-05	Cornell Big Red	ECACHL	33	3	7	10	68	....	....	....	....	....
2005-06	Cornell Big Red	ECACHL	28	7	6	13	69	....	....	....	....	....
2006-07	Hamilton Bulldogs	AHL	80	0	12	12	129	22	2	5	7	32

OGORODNIKOV, Sergei (oh-goh-RAWD-nee-kawf, SAIR-gay) NYI

Center. Shoots left. 6', 178 lbs. Born, Irkutsk, USSR, January 21, 1986.
(NY Islanders' 3rd choice, 82nd overall, in 2004 Entry Draft).

			Regular Season					Playoffs				
Season	Club	League	GP	G	A	Pts	PIM	GP	G	A	Pts	PIM
2002-03	Dyn'o Moscow 2	Russia-3	STATISTICS NOT AVAILABLE									
2003-04	Dyn'o Moscow 2	Russia-3	STATISTICS NOT AVAILABLE									
	THK Tver	Russia-2	21	8	3	11	14	....	....	....	....	....
2004-05	CSKA Moscow	Russia	18	2	4	6	2	....	....	....	....	....
2005-06	CSKA Moscow	Russia	3	0	0	0	2	....	....	....	....	....
	Ufa	Russia	14	0	3	3	8	6	0	0	0	4
	CSKA Moscow 2	Russia-3	STATISTICS NOT AVAILABLE									
2006-07	Bridgeport	AHL	27	3	3	6	10	....	....	....	....	....
	Pensacola	ECHL	42	18	22	40	30	....	....	....	....	....

O'HANLEY, Brian (oh-HAN-lee, BRIGH-uhn) S.J.

Defense. Shoots left. 6', 190 lbs. Born, Quincy, MA, December 18, 1984.
(San Jose's 10th choice, 267th overall, in 2003 Entry Draft).

			Regular Season					Playoffs				
Season	Club	League	GP	G	A	Pts	PIM	GP	G	A	Pts	PIM
2001-02	Bos. College High	High-MA	24	22	13	35	20	....	....	....	....	....
2002-03	Bos. College High	High-MA	23	22	21	43	12	....	....	....	....	....
2003-04	Salisbury School	High-CT	26	11	28	39	....	....	....	....	....	....
2004-05	Boston College	H-East	35	2	11	13	18	....	....	....	....	....
2005-06	Boston College	H-East	40	2	4	6	14	....	....	....	....	....
2006-07	Boston College	H-East	36	2	3	5	12	....	....	....	....	....

OKPOSO, Kyle (awk-POH-soh, KIGHL) NYI

Right wing. Shoots right. 6', 195 lbs. Born, St. Paul, MN, April 16, 1988.
(NY Islanders' 1st choice, 7th overall, in 2006 Entry Draft).

			Regular Season					Playoffs				
Season	Club	League	GP	G	A	Pts	PIM	GP	G	A	Pts	PIM
2004-05	Shat.-St. Mary's	High-MN	65	47	45	92	72	....	....	....	....	....
2005-06	Des Moines	USHL	50	27	31	58	56	11	5	11	*16	8
2006-07	U. of Minnesota	WCHA	40	19	21	40	34	....	....	....	....	....

USHL All-Rookie Team (2006) • USHL First All-Star Team (2006) • USHL Rookie of the Year (2006) • WCHA All-Rookie Team (2007) • WCHA Second All-Star Team (2007)

OLVECKY, Peter (ohl-VEHT-skee, PEE-tuhr) MIN.

Center. Shoots left. 6'2", 214 lbs. Born, Trencin, Czech., October 11, 1985.
(Minnesota's 3rd choice, 78th overall, in 2004 Entry Draft).

			Regular Season					Playoffs				
Season	Club	League	GP	G	A	Pts	PIM	GP	G	A	Pts	PIM
2003-04	Dukla Trencin Jr.	Slovak-Jr.	40	16	20	36	74	2	0	0	0	12
	Dukla Trencin	Slovakia	16	0	0	0	18	....	....	....	....	....
	Dukla Trencin U18	Svk-U18	2	0	0	0	0	....	....	....	....	....
2004-05	SHK 37 Piestany	Slovak-2	1	0	0	0	10	....	....	....	....	....
	Dukla Trencin Jr.	Slovak-Jr.	8	1	3	4	10	2	1	4	5	4
	Dukla Trencin	Slovakia	45	10	9	19	49	12	1	0	1	6
2005-06	Houston Aeros	AHL	67	14	18	32	56	7	1	3	4	4
2006-07	Houston Aeros	AHL	69	12	15	27	46	....	....	....	....	....

OLVER, Darin (AWL-vuhr, DAIR-ehn)

Center. Shoots left. 6', 170 lbs. Born, Burnaby, B.C., March 5, 1985.
(NY Rangers' 3rd choice, 36th overall, in 2004 Entry Draft).

			Regular Season					Playoffs				
Season	Club	League	GP	G	A	Pts	PIM	GP	G	A	Pts	PIM
2002-03	Chilliwack Chiefs	BCHL	59	34	55	89	57	....	....	....	....	....
2003-04	Northern Mich.	CCHA	41	13	21	34	26	....	....	....	....	....
2004-05	Northern Mich.	CCHA	40	9	*34	43	30	....	....	....	....	....
2005-06	Northern Mich.	CCHA	36	15	20	35	32	....	....	....	....	....
2006-07	Northern Mich.	CCHA	41	14	20	34	47	....	....	....	....	....
	Hartford Wolf Pack	AHL	6	1	0	1	8	....	....	....	....	....

OMARK, Linus (OH-mahrk, LIH-nuhs) EDM.

Left wing. Shoots left. 5'9", 168 lbs. Born, Overtornea, Sweden, February 5, 1987.
(Edmonton's 4th choice, 97th overall, in 2007 Entry Draft).

			Regular Season					Playoffs				
Season	Club	League	GP	G	A	Pts	PIM	GP	G	A	Pts	PIM
2003-04	Lulea HF U18	Swe-U18	14	14	8	22	18	7	3	4	7	0
	Lulea HF Jr.	Swe-Jr.	1	0	0	0	0	....	....	....	....	....
2004-05	Lulea HF U18	Swe-U18	1	2	0	2	0	....	....	....	....	....
	Lulea HF Jr.	Swe-Jr.	32	8	9	17	44	7	4	2	6	2
2005-06	Lulea HF Jr.	Swe-Jr.	32	22	21	43	56	5	1	2	3	28
	Lulea HF	Sweden	19	0	1	1	10	3	0	0	0	0
2006-07	Lulea HF	Sweden	50	8	9	17	32	4	1	0	1	2

O'MARRA, Ryan (oh-MAHR-ah, RIGH-uhn) EDM.

Center. Shoots right. 6'2", 193 lbs. Born, Tokyo, Japan, June 9, 1987.
(NY Islanders' 1st choice, 15th overall, in 2005 Entry Draft).

			Regular Season					Playoffs				
Season	Club	League	GP	G	A	Pts	PIM	GP	G	A	Pts	PIM
2002-03	Miss. Senators	GTHL	76	51	60	111	83	....	....	....	....	....
	Georgetown	OPJHL	3	0	2	2	0	....	....	....	....	....
	Streetsville Derbys	OPJHL	6	0	1	1	2	....	....	....	....	....
2003-04	Erie Otters	OHL	63	16	16	32	33	9	5	5	10	6
2004-05	Erie Otters	OHL	64	25	38	63	60	6	4	1	5	0
2005-06	Erie Otters	OHL	61	27	50	77	134	....	....	....	....	....
	Bridgeport	AHL	8	4	1	5	4	3	0	1	1	2
2006-07	Erie Otters	OHL	13	8	6	14	26	....	....	....	....	....
	Saginaw Spirit	OHL	33	18	19	37	48	3	2	1	3	4

Traded to **Edmonton** by **NY Islanders** with Robert Nilsson and NY Islanders' 1st round choice (Alex Plante) in 2007 Entry Draft for Ryan Smyth, February 27, 2007.

O'NEILL, Wes (oh-NEEL, WEHS)

Defense. Shoots left. 6'4", 200 lbs. Born, Windsor, Ont., March 3, 1986.
(NY Islanders' 4th choice, 115th overall, in 2004 Entry Draft).

			Regular Season					Playoffs				
Season	Club	League	GP	G	A	Pts	PIM	GP	G	A	Pts	PIM
2000-01	Chatham Maroons	OHA-B	51	6	9	15	50	....	....	....	....	....
2001-02	Chatham Maroons	OHA-B	51	9	36	45	....	....	....	....	....	....
2002-03	Green Bay	USHL	50	2	15	17	79	....	....	....	....	....
2003-04	U. of Notre Dame	CCHA	39	2	10	12	28	....	....	....	....	....
2004-05	U. of Notre Dame	CCHA	38	6	14	20	52	....	....	....	....	....
2005-06	U. of Notre Dame	CCHA	35	6	19	25	40	....	....	....	....	....
2006-07	U. of Notre Dame	CCHA	42	3	18	21	40	....	....	....	....	....

O'NEILL, Will (oh-NEEL, WIHL) ATL.

Defense. Shoots left. 6', 195 lbs. Born, Boston, MA, April 28, 1988.
(Atlanta's 8th choice, 210th overall, in 2006 Entry Draft).

			Regular Season					Playoffs				
Season	Club	League	GP	G	A	Pts	PIM	GP	G	A	Pts	PIM
2004-05	Tabor	High-MA	....	1	16	17	....	....	....	....	....	....
2005-06	Tabor	High-MA	28	5	25	30	38	....	....	....	....	....
2006-07	Omaha Lancers	USHL	57	4	9	13	73	5	0	0	0	8

O'REILLY, Cal (oh-RIGH-lee, KAL) NSH.

Center. Shoots left. 6', 187 lbs. Born, Toronto, Ont., September 30, 1986.
(Nashville's 4th choice, 150th overall, in 2005 Entry Draft).

			Regular Season					Playoffs				
Season	Club	League	GP	G	A	Pts	PIM	GP	G	A	Pts	PIM
2002-03	St. Mary's Lincolns	OJHL-B	46	11	19	30	2	....	....	....	....	....
2003-04	Windsor Spitfires	OHL	61	3	18	21	2	3	0	1	1	0
2004-05	Windsor Spitfires	OHL	68	24	50	74	16	11	4	5	9	4
2005-06	Windsor Spitfires	OHL	68	18	81	99	8	7	3	8	11	0
	Milwaukee	AHL	2	0	0	0	0	10	0	1	1	0
2006-07	Milwaukee	AHL	78	18	47	65	20	4	1	2	3	0

ORESKOVIC, Phil (oh-rehs-KOH-vihch, FIHL) TOR.

Defense. Shoots right. 6'3", 217 lbs. Born, North York, Ont., January 26, 1987.
(Toronto's 2nd choice, 82nd overall, in 2005 Entry Draft).

			Regular Season					Playoffs				
Season	Club	League	GP	G	A	Pts	PIM	GP	G	A	Pts	PIM
2003-04	Brampton	OHL	66	0	7	7	64	12	0	2	2	16
2004-05	Brampton	OHL	61	1	6	7	147	6	0	0	0	4
2005-06	Brampton	OHL	65	3	9	12	202	11	0	0	0	34
2006-07	Brampton	OHL	36	2	12	14	113	....	....	....	....	....
	Owen Sound	OHL	26	1	7	8	66	4	0	0	0	2
	Toronto Marlies	AHL	3	0	1	1	2	....	....	....	....	....

ORESKOVICH, Victor (oh-rehs-KOH-vihch, VIHK-tohr) COL.

Right wing. Shoots right. 6'3", 215 lbs. Born, Whitby, Ont., August 15, 1986.
(Colorado's 2nd choice, 55th overall, in 2004 Entry Draft).

			Regular Season					Playoffs				
Season	Club	League	GP	G	A	Pts	PIM	GP	G	A	Pts	PIM
2002-03	Milton IceHawks	OPJHL	49	28	46	74	51	....	....	....	....	....
2003-04	Green Bay	USHL	58	11	26	37	33	....	....	....	....	....
2004-05	U. of Notre Dame	CCHA	37	1	2	3	69	....	....	....	....	....
2005-06	U. of Notre Dame	CCHA	10	2	1	3	8	....	....	....	....	....
	Kitchener Rangers	OHL	19	6	10	16	16	5	0	2	2	4
2006-07	Kitchener Rangers	OHL	62	28	32	60	48	5	2	0	2	4

ORLOV, Maxim (ohr-LAHF, max-EEM) WSH.

Center. Shoots left. 6', 176 lbs. Born, Moscow, USSR, March 31, 1981.
(Washington's 9th choice, 219th overall, in 1999 Entry Draft).

			Regular Season					Playoffs				
Season	Club	League	GP	G	A	Pts	PIM	GP	G	A	Pts	PIM
1998-99	CSKA Moscow	Russia	2	0	0	0	2	1	0	0	0	0
99-2000	CSKA Moscow	Russia	25	0	0	0	2	2	0	0	0	2
2000-01	CSKA Moscow	Russia	41	5	4	9	14	....	....	....	....	....
2001-02	CSKA Moscow 2	Russia-3	7	7	4	11	4	....	....	....	....	....
	CSKA Moscow	Russia	35	3	5	8	14	....	....	....	....	....
2002-03	MGU Moscow	Russia-3	2	0	0	0	0	....	....	....	....	....
	Leninogorsk	Russia-2	25	3	8	11	24	....	....	....	....	....
2003-04	Leninogorsk	Russia-2	35	5	9	14	39	2	0	0	0	0
2004-05	Kristall Saratov	Russia-2	47	13	23	36	46	4	0	0	0	2
2005-06	Ufa 2	Russia-3	20	8	8	16	10	....	....	....	....	....
	Ufa	Russia	5	0	0	0	0	....	....	....	....	....
2006-07	Toros Neftekamsk	Russia-2	55	5	22	27	46	....	....	....	....	....

ORPIK, Andrew (OHR-pihk, AN-droo) BUF.

Defense. Shoots right. 6'3", 200 lbs. Born, East Amherst, NY, March 12, 1986.
(Buffalo's 9th choice, 227th overall, in 2005 Entry Draft).

			Regular Season					Playoffs				
Season	Club	League	GP	G	A	Pts	PIM	GP	G	A	Pts	PIM
2003-04	Thayer Academy	High-MA	32	9	8	17	18	....	....	....	....	....
2004-05	Thayer Academy	High-MA	31	8	12	20	24	....	....	....	....	....
2005-06	Boston College	H-East	40	3	5	8	32	....	....	....	....	....
2006-07	Boston College	H-East	38	3	6	9	22	....	....	....	....	....

OSHIE, T.J. (OH-shee, TEE-JAY) ST.L.

Center. Shoots right. 5'10", 170 lbs. Born, Mt. Vernon, WA, December 23, 1986.
(St. Louis' 1st choice, 24th overall, in 2005 Entry Draft).

			Regular Season					Playoffs				
Season	Club	League	GP	G	A	Pts	PIM	GP	G	A	Pts	PIM
2004-05	Warroad Warriors	High-MN	31	37	62	99	22	....	....	....	....	....
	Sioux Falls	USHL	11	3	2	5	6	....	....	....	....	....
2005-06	North Dakota	WCHA	44	24	21	45	33	....	....	....	....	....
2006-07	North Dakota	WCHA	43	17	*35	52	30	....	....	....	....	....

WCHA All-Rookie Team (2006)

OSLUND, Nick (OZ-luhnd, NIHK) DET.

Right wing. Shoots right. 6'3", 195 lbs. Born, Burnsville, MN, November 15, 1987.
(Detroit's 6th choice, 191st overall, in 2006 Entry Draft).

			Regular Season					Playoffs				
Season	Club	League	GP	G	A	Pts	PIM	GP	G	A	Pts	PIM
2004-05	Burnsville	High-MN	27	29	18	47	28	....	....	....	....	....
2005-06	Burnsville	High-MN	26	22	30	52	30	....	....	....	....	....
2006-07	Tri-City Storm	USHL	56	7	14	21	24	9	0	1	1	0

OSTRCIL, Radim (AWS-tuhr-chihl, RA-dihm) BOS.

Defense. Shoots left. 5'11", 200 lbs. Born, Vsetin, Czech., January 15, 1989.
(Boston's 5th choice, 169th overall, in 2007 Entry Draft).

			Regular Season					Playoffs				
Season	Club	League	GP	G	A	Pts	PIM	GP	G	A	Pts	PIM
2002-03	HC Vsetin U17	CzR-U17	33	1	2	3	8	11	1	1	2	2
2003-04	HC Vsetin U17	CzR-U17	43	0	12	12	44	2	0	0	0	0
2004-05	HC Vsetin U17	CzR-U17	31	8	15	23	85	3	1	3	4	4
	HC Vsetin Jr.	CzRep-Jr.	19	0	3	3	14	3	0	0	0	2
2005-06	HC Vsetin U17	CzR-U17	1	1	1	2	0	3	2	2	4	0
	HC Vsetin Jr.	CzRep-Jr.	41	6	8	14	50	5	1	1	2	6
	Hr. Kralove	CzRep-2	1	0	0	0	0	1	0	0	0	0
	HC Vsetin	CzRep	3	0	0	0	6	....	....	....	....	....
2006-07	HC Vsetin Jr.	CzRep-Jr.	25	8	13	21	69	8	4	4	8	6
	HC Vsetin	CzRep	37	1	1	2	20	....	....	....	....	....

OULAHEN, Ryan (OO-la-hehn, RIGH-uhn) DET.

Center. Shoots left. 6', 180 lbs. Born, Newmarket, Ont., March 26, 1985.
(Detroit's 3rd choice, 164th overall, in 2003 Entry Draft).

			Regular Season					Playoffs				
Season	Club	League	GP	G	A	Pts	PIM	GP	G	A	Pts	PIM
2000-01	Wexford Raiders	Minor-ON	66	38	58	96	18	....	....	....	....	....
2001-02	Newmarket	OPJHL	48	18	17	35	4	....	....	....	....	....
2002-03	Brampton	OHL	61	21	22	43	6	11	2	1	3	2
2003-04	Brampton	OHL	57	17	18	35	26	12	3	7	10	6
2004-05	Brampton	OHL	64	27	31	58	22	5	1	4	5	4
2005-06	Grand Rapids	AHL	75	9	10	19	20	16	0	0	0	2
2006-07	Grand Rapids	AHL	79	11	16	27	42	7	0	2	2	4

OYSTRICK, Nathan (OI-strihk, NAY-thuhn) ATL.

Defense. Shoots left. 6', 215 lbs. Born, Regina, Sask., December 17, 1982.
(Atlanta's 7th choice, 198th overall, in 2002 Entry Draft).

			Regular Season					Playoffs				
Season	Club	League	GP	G	A	Pts	PIM	GP	G	A	Pts	PIM
99-2000	Reg. Pat Cdns.	SMHL	43	6	22	28	214	....	....	....	....	....
2000-01	South Surrey	BCHL	STATISTICS NOT AVAILABLE									
2001-02	South Surrey	BCHL	50	15	42	57	142	....	....	....	....	....
2002-03	Northern Mich.	CCHA	34	2	10	12	26	....	....	....	....	....
2003-04	Northern Mich.	CCHA	39	8	20	28	98	....	....	....	....	....
2004-05	Northern Mich.	CCHA	40	7	13	20	87	....	....	....	....	....
2005-06	Northern Mich.	CCHA	38	9	20	29	58	....	....	....	....	....
	Chicago Wolves	AHL	2	0	1	1	4	....	....	....	....	....
2006-07	Chicago Wolves	AHL	80	15	32	47	105	15	0	6	6	16

CCHA Second All-Star Team (2004) • CCHA First All-Star Team (2005, 2006) • NCAA West Second All-American Team (2006) • AHL All-Rookie Team (2007) • AHL Second All-Star Team (2007)

PACIORETTY, Max (pahk-OHR-eht-tee, MAX) MTL.

Left wing. Shoots left. 6'1", 209 lbs. Born, New Canaan, CT, November 20, 1988.
(Montreal's 2nd choice, 22nd overall, in 2007 Entry Draft).

			Regular Season					Playoffs				
Season	Club	League	GP	G	A	Pts	PIM	GP	G	A	Pts	PIM
2004-05	Taft Rhinos	High-CT	23	5	14	19	....	....	....	....	....	....
2005-06	Taft Rhinos	High-CT	26	7	26	33	....	....	....	....	....	....
2006-07	Sioux City	USHL	60	21	42	63	119	7	4	6	10	10

PACKARD, Dennis (PA-kuhrd, DEH-nihs)

Left wing. Shoots left. 6'4", 235 lbs. Born, St. Catherines, Ont., February 9, 1982.
(Tampa Bay's 8th choice, 219th overall, in 2001 Entry Draft).

			Regular Season					Playoffs				
Season	Club	League	GP	G	A	Pts	PIM	GP	G	A	Pts	PIM
99-2000	USNTDP	U-18	6	0	1	1	2	....	....	....	....	....
	USNTDP	USHL	55	11	14	25	85	....	....	....	....	....
2000-01	Harvard Crimson	ECAC	33	4	4	8	28	....	....	....	....	....
2001-02	Harvard Crimson	ECAC	32	9	10	19	34	....	....	....	....	....
2002-03	Harvard Crimson	ECAC	30	8	8	16	32	....	....	....	....	....
2003-04	Harvard Crimson	ECAC	36	11	11	22	16	....	....	....	....	....
2004-05	Springfield Falcons	AHL	47	2	8	10	25	....	....	....	....	....
	Johnstown Chiefs	ECHL	15	3	4	7	6	....	....	....	....	....
2005-06	Springfield Falcons	AHL	46	3	6	9	34	....	....	....	....	....
	Johnstown Chiefs	ECHL	16	2	9	11	12	5	0	1	1	4
2006-07	Providence Bruins	AHL	68	6	12	18	55	13	1	1	2	2

Signed as a free agent by **Boston**, July 17, 2006.

PAGE, Rob (PAYJ, RAWB) CBJ

Defense. Shoots right. 6'1", 188 lbs. Born, Edina, MN, July 9, 1985.
(Columbus' 7th choice, 167th overall, in 2004 Entry Draft).

			Regular Season					Playoffs				
Season	Club	League	GP	G	A	Pts	PIM	GP	G	A	Pts	PIM
2003-04	Blake Bears	High-MN	28	8	21	29	18	....	....	....	....	....
2004-05	Yale	ECACHL	32	2	9	11	68	....	....	....	....	....
2005-06	Yale	ECACHL	25	0	6	6	36	....	....	....	....	....
2006-07	Yale	ECACHL	31	3	10	13	52	....	....	....	....	....

PAINCHAUD, Chad (PAYN-show, CHAD) ATL.

Left wing. Shoots left. 6'1", 185 lbs. Born, Mississauga, Ont., May 27, 1986.
(Atlanta's 4th choice, 106th overall, in 2004 Entry Draft).

			Regular Season					Playoffs				
Season	Club	League	GP	G	A	Pts	PIM	GP	G	A	Pts	PIM
2002-03	Mississauga Reps	GTHL	52	47	47	94	....	....	....	....	....	....
2003-04	Mississauga	OHL	68	17	25	42	25	24	4	6	10	23
2004-05	Mississauga	OHL	8	3	3	6	11	....	....	....	....	....
	Sarnia Sting	OHL	49	18	16	34	22	....	....	....	....	....
2005-06	Sarnia Sting	OHL	49	31	34	65	65	....	....	....	....	....
2006-07	Gwinnett	ECHL	72	22	32	54	71	4	0	5	5	4

PALIN, Brett (PAY-lihn, BREHT) CGY.

Defense. Shoots right. 6'2", 200 lbs. Born, Nanaimo, B.C., June 23, 1984.

			Regular Season					Playoffs				
Season	Club	League	GP	G	A	Pts	PIM	GP	G	A	Pts	PIM
2000-01	Kelowna Rockets	WHL	39	0	0	0	25	....	....	....	....	....
2001-02	Kelowna Rockets	WHL	70	0	1	1	88	15	0	0	0	4
2002-03	Kelowna Rockets	WHL	71	1	17	18	118	19	0	4	4	12
2003-04	Kelowna Rockets	WHL	72	1	16	17	106	17	0	5	5	24
2004-05	Kelowna Rockets	WHL	72	4	21	25	71	24	4	6	10	52
2005-06	Omaha	AHL	64	0	5	5	46	....	....	....	....	....
2006-07	Omaha	AHL	78	1	9	10	71	6	1	0	1	0

Signed as a free agent by **Calgary**, August 5, 2005.

PALMIERI, Nick (pawl-mee-AIR-ee, NIHK) N.J.

Right wing. Shoots right. 6'3", 215 lbs. Born, Utica, NY, July 12, 1989.
(New Jersey's 2nd choice, 79th overall, in 2007 Entry Draft).

			Regular Season					Playoffs				
Season	Club	League	GP	G	A	Pts	PIM	GP	G	A	Pts	PIM
2004-05	Northwood	High-NY	STATISTICS NOT AVAILABLE									
2005-06	Erie Otters	OHL	68	13	10	23	79	....	....	....	....	....
2006-07	Erie Otters	OHL	56	24	21	45	99	....	....	....	....	....

PALUSHAJ, Aaron (puh-LOO-shigh, AIR-ruhn) ST.L.

Right wing. Shoots right. 5'11", 187 lbs. Born, Livonia, MI, September 7, 1989.
(St. Louis' 5th choice, 44th overall, in 2007 Entry Draft).

			Regular Season					Playoffs				
Season	Club	League	GP	G	A	Pts	PIM	GP	G	A	Pts	PIM
2005-06	Des Moines	USHL	58	10	23	33	53	11	2	4	6	15
2006-07	Des Moines	USHL	56	22	45	67	62	8	6	5	11	6

PANOV, Konstantin (PAN-ahv, KAWN-stan-tihn) NSH.

Left wing. Shoots left. 6', 195 lbs. Born, Chelyabinsk, USSR, June 29, 1980.
(Nashville's 10th choice, 131st overall, in 1999 Entry Draft).

			Regular Season					Playoffs				
Season	Club	League	GP	G	A	Pts	PIM	GP	G	A	Pts	PIM
1996-97	Yunior-T Kurgan	Russia-3	25	18	30	48	22	....	....	....	....	....
1997-98	Yunior-T Kurgan	Russia-3	20	7	3	10	6	....	....	....	....	....
	Chelyabinsk	Russia	6	2	0	2	4	2	0	0	0	0
1998-99	Kamloops Blazers	WHL	62	33	30	63	62	13	5	3	8	10
99-2000	Kamloops Blazers	WHL	64	43	30	73	47	....	....	....	....	....
2000-01	Kamloops Blazers	WHL	69	44	56	100	54	4	1	0	1	2
2001-02	Milwaukee	AHL	15	1	5	6	2	....	....	....	....	....
2002-03	Milwaukee	AHL	67	11	20	31	30	2	0	0	0	0
	Toledo Storm	ECHL	2	1	0	1	0	....	....	....	....	....
2003-04	Amur Khabarovsk	Russia	29	0	1	1	10	....	....	....	....	....
	Khabarovsk 2	Russia-3	8	8	6	14	5	....	....	....	....	....
2004-05	Chelyabinsk	Russia-2	51	13	22	35	32	8	2	1	3	12
2005-06	Chelyabinsk	Russia-2	40	15	12	27	62	14	8	5	13	37
2006-07	Lada Togliatti	Russia	45	3	7	10	32	3	1	1	2	0

WHL West Second All-Star Team (2000) • WHL West First All-Star Team (2001)

PAQUET, Philippe (pa-KEHT, fihl-EEP) MTL.

Defense. Shoots right. 6'3", 212 lbs. Born, Quebec City, Que., March 12, 1987.
(Montreal's 7th choice, 229th overall, in 2005 Entry Draft).

			Regular Season					Playoffs				
Season	Club	League	GP	G	A	Pts	PIM	GP	G	A	Pts	PIM
2003-04	St-Francois	QAAA	39	6	14	20	136	7	0	3	3	10
2004-05	Salisbury School	High-CT	26	1	4	5	10	....	....	....	....	....
2005-06	Clarkson Knights	ECACHL	37	2	5	7	91	....	....	....	....	....
2006-07	Clarkson Knights	ECACHL	37	3	4	7	*116	....	....	....	....	....

PARDY, Adam (PAHR-dee, A-duhm) CGY.

Defense. Shoots left. 6'4", 220 lbs. Born, Bonavista, Nfld., March 29, 1984.
(Calgary's 6th choice, 173rd overall, in 2004 Entry Draft).

			Regular Season					Playoffs				
Season	Club	League	GP	G	A	Pts	PIM	GP	G	A	Pts	PIM
2002-03	Yarmouth	MJrHL	1	0	0	0	2	....	....	....	....	....
	Antigonish	MJrHL	31	5	16	21	42	....	....	....	....	....
	Cape Breton	QMJHL	7	0	1	1	2	2	0	0	0	0
2003-04	Cape Breton	QMJHL	68	4	12	16	137	5	0	1	1	8
2004-05	Cape Breton	QMJHL	69	12	27	39	163	5	2	2	4	8
2005-06	Omaha	AHL	24	0	0	0	18	....	....	....	....	....
	Las Vegas	ECHL	41	1	11	12	55	10	2	1	3	12
2006-07	Omaha	AHL	70	2	6	8	60	6	1	1	2	0

PAROULEK, Martin (PAHR-oh-lehk, MAHR-tihn) CBJ

Right wing. Shoots right. 6'2", 193 lbs. Born, Uherske Hradiste, Czech., November 4, 1979.
(Columbus' 9th choice, 278th overall, in 2000 Entry Draft).

			Regular Season					Playoffs				
Season	Club	League	GP	G	A	Pts	PIM	GP	G	A	Pts	PIM
1998-99	HC Vsetin Jr.	CzRep-Jr.	45	25	19	44	....	....	....	....	....	....
	HC Slovnaft Vsetin	CzRep	11	1	1	2	....	7	0	1	1	0
99-2000	Vsetin	CzRep	48	11	14	25	24	8	1	1	2	4
2000-01	HC Draci Sumperk	CzRep-2	14	0	1	1	27	....	....	....	....	....
	HC Slovnaft Vsetin	CzRep	28	10	4	14	16	14	3	3	6	10
2001-02	Syracuse Crunch	AHL	59	11	14	25	31	9	1	1	2	4
2002-03	Syracuse Crunch	AHL	9	0	1	1	6	....	....	....	....	....
	HC Sparta Praha	CzRep	16	1	4	5	16	9	1	1	2	8
2003-04	HC Sparta Praha	CzRep	17	2	1	3	4	....	....	....	....	....
	Plzen	CzRep	19	7	10	17	16	12	1	3	4	12
2004-05	Beroun	CzRep-2	1	0	0	0	0	....	....	....	....	....
	Plzen	CzRep	38	7	11	18	49	....	....	....	....	....
2005-06	Plzen	CzRep	4	0	0	0	6	....	....	....	....	....
	HC Ocelari Trinec	CzRep	36	3	7	10	20	....	....	....	....	....
2006-07	BK Mlada Boleslav	CzRep-2	48	16	17	33	79	8	1	2	3	12
	HC Sparta Praha	CzRep	1	0	0	0	0	....	....	....	....	....

• Released by **Syracuse** (AHL) and signed as a free agent by **Sparta Praha** (CzRep) with Columbus retaining NHL rights, January 13, 2003.

PARSE, Scott (PARS, SKAWT) L.A.

Forward. Shoots right. 6'1", 185 lbs. Born, Kalamazoo, MI, September 5, 1984.
(Los Angeles' 5th choice, 174th overall, in 2004 Entry Draft).

			Regular Season					Playoffs				
Season	Club	League	GP	G	A	Pts	PIM	GP	G	A	Pts	PIM
2002-03	Tri-City Storm	USHL	48	21	23	44	32	3	2	1	3	8
2003-04	Nebraska-Omaha	CCHA	39	16	19	35	52	....	....	....	....	....
2004-05	Nebraska-Omaha	CCHA	39	19	30	49	32	....	....	....	....	....
2005-06	Nebraska-Omaha	CCHA	41	20	*41	*61	40	....	....	....	....	....
2006-07	Nebraska-Omaha	CCHA	40	24	28	52	36	....	....	....	....	....
	Grand Rapids	AHL	10	2	5	7	6	7	1	0	1	8

USHL All-Rookie Team (2003) • CCHA First All-Star Team (2005, 2007) • CCHA Player of the Year (2006) • NCAA West First All-American Team (2006) • NCAA West Second All-American Team (2007)

PARSHIN, Denis (PAHR-shihn, DEH-nihs) COL.

Right wing. Shoots left. 5'10", 165 lbs. Born, Rybinsk, USSR, February 1, 1986.
(Colorado's 3rd choice, 72nd overall, in 2004 Entry Draft).

			Regular Season					Playoffs				
Season	Club	League	GP	G	A	Pts	PIM	GP	G	A	Pts	PIM
2002-03	CSKA Moscow 2	Russia-3	4	1	0	1	2	....	....	....	....	....
2003-04	CSKA Moscow	Russia	27	2	4	6	4	....	....	....	....	....
	CSKA Moscow 2	Russia-3	STATISTICS NOT AVAILABLE									
2004-05	CSKA Moscow	Russia	42	3	4	7	18	....	....	....	....	....
2005-06	CSKA Moscow 2	Russia-3	STATISTICS NOT AVAILABLE									
	CSKA Moscow	Russia	37	2	8	10	22	6	0	2	2	2
2006-07	CSKA Moscow	Russia	54	18	14	32	24	12	2	2	4	8

PAUKOVICH, Geoff (paw-KOH-vihch, JEHF) **EDM.**

Left wing. Shoots left. 6'4", 208 lbs. Born, Englewood, CO, April 24, 1986.
(Edmonton's 4th choice, 57th overall, in 2004 Entry Draft).

			Regular Season					Playoffs				
Season	Club	League	GP	G	A	Pts	PIM	GP	G	A	Pts	PIM
2002-03	Tri-City Storm	USHL	31	1	3	4	29	....	....	....	....	....
2003-04	USNTDP	U-18	44	6	9	15	46	....	....	....	....	....
	USNTDP	NAHL	11	4	2	6	31	....	....	....	....	....
2004-05	U. of Denver	WCHA	41	12	10	22	120	....	....	....	....	....
2005-06	U. of Denver	WCHA	37	4	6	10	72	....	....	....	....	....
2006-07	U. of Denver	WCHA	39	8	9	17	65	....	....	....	....	....

PECKER, Cory (PEH-kuhr, KOH-ree)

Center. Shoots right. 5'11", 192 lbs. Born, Montreal, Que., March 20, 1981.
(Calgary's 7th choice, 166th overall, in 1999 Entry Draft).

			Regular Season					Playoffs				
Season	Club	League	GP	G	A	Pts	PIM	GP	G	A	Pts	PIM
1996-97	Lac St-Louis Lions	QAAA	40	30	40	70	....	7	4	2	6	....
1997-98	Sault Ste. Marie	OHL	29	3	4	7	15	....	....	....	....	....
1998-99	Sault Ste. Marie	OHL	68	25	34	59	24	5	1	2	3	2
99-2000	Sault Ste. Marie	OHL	65	33	36	69	38	12	6	8	14	8
2000-01	Sault Ste. Marie	OHL	31	24	16	40	37	....	....	....	....	....
	Erie Otters	OHL	30	17	22	39	32	15	14	9	23	16
2001-02	Erie Otters	OHL	56	*53	46	99	108	21	*25	17	*42	36
2002-03	Cincinnati	AHL	77	20	13	33	66	....	....	....	....	....
2003-04	Cincinnati	AHL	54	6	10	16	32	....	....	....	....	....
	Binghamton	AHL	14	3	5	8	27	1	0	0	0	0
2004-05	Cincinnati	AHL	49	4	8	12	51	....	....	....	....	....
	San Diego Gulls	ECHL	3	1	0	1	0	....	....	....	....	....
	Manitoba Moose	AHL	12	1	1	2	8	5	1	0	1	4
2005-06	San Antonio	AHL	3	0	1	1	2	....	....	....	....	....
	Binghamton	AHL	24	9	14	23	20	....	....	....	....	....
	Phoenix	ECHL	18	11	12	23	39	....	....	....	....	....
2006-07	Binghamton	AHL	78	17	30	47	81	....	....	....	....	....

OHL Second All-Star Team (2001) • OHL First All-Star Team (2002) • Memorial Cup Tournament All-Star Team (2002)

• Missed majority of 1997-98 season after being diagnosed with Chron's Disease. Signed as a free agent by **Anaheim**, July 8, 2002. Loaned to **Manitoba** (AHL) by **Anaheim** (Cincinnati-AHL) for cash, March 17, 2005. Signed to a PTO (tryout) contract by **Binghamton** (AHL), December 15, 2005. Signed as a free agent by **Ottawa**, July 26, 2006. Signed as a free agent by **Lausanne** (Swiss), May 30, 2007.

PECKHAM, Theo (PEHK-uhm, THEE-oh) **EDM.**

Defense. Shoots left. 6'2", 216 lbs. Born, Richmond Hill, Ont., November 10, 1987.
(Edmonton's 2nd choice, 75th overall, in 2006 Entry Draft).

			Regular Season					Playoffs				
Season	Club	League	GP	G	A	Pts	PIM	GP	G	A	Pts	PIM
2003-04	North York	OPJHL	29	1	4	5	46	....	....	....	....	....
2004-05	Owen Sound	OHL	61	1	9	10	209	8	0	0	0	8
2005-06	Owen Sound	OHL	67	6	9	15	236	11	1	6	7	32
2006-07	Owen Sound	OHL	53	10	25	35	173	4	0	1	1	0

PELECH, Matt (PEH-lihk, MAT) **CGY.**

Defense. Shoots right. 6'4", 224 lbs. Born, Toronto, Ont., September 4, 1987.
(Calgary's 1st choice, 26th overall, in 2005 Entry Draft).

			Regular Season					Playoffs				
Season	Club	League	GP	G	A	Pts	PIM	GP	G	A	Pts	PIM
2002-03	Vaughan	GTHL	44	3	13	16	113	....	....	....	....	....
2003-04	Sarnia Sting	OHL	62	4	6	10	39	5	0	1	1	12
2004-05	Sarnia Sting	OHL	31	1	5	6	74	....	....	....	....	....
2005-06	Sarnia Sting	OHL	18	0	2	2	59	....	....	....	....	....
	London Knights	OHL	34	1	7	8	80	19	0	0	0	48
2006-07	Belleville Bulls	OHL	58	5	30	35	171	12	0	3	3	22

PELLETIER, Pascal (PEHL-tyay, pas-KAL) **BOS.**

Right wing. Shoots right. 5'11", 197 lbs. Born, Labrador City, Nfld., June 16, 1983.

			Regular Season					Playoffs				
Season	Club	League	GP	G	A	Pts	PIM	GP	G	A	Pts	PIM
2000-01	Baie-Comeau	QMJHL	70	15	44	59	176	11	2	11	13	6
2001-02	Baie-Comeau	QMJHL	56	12	25	37	115	5	3	4	7	0
2002-03	Baie-Comeau	QMJHL	67	46	55	101	113	12	5	7	12	14
2003-04	Shawinigan	QMJHL	64	39	52	91	85	11	3	9	12	20
2004-05	Louisiana	ECHL	61	10	28	38	75	....	....	....	....	....
	Gwinnett	ECHL	6	0	1	1	2	5	0	2	2	2
2005-06	Providence Bruins	AHL	53	20	26	46	42	6	2	4	6	23
	Gwinnett	ECHL	21	18	12	30	18	....	....	....	....	....
2006-07	Providence Bruins	AHL	80	14	35	49	60	13	5	4	9	16

Signed as a free agent by **Boston**, August 7, 2006.

PELTIER, Derek (PEHL-tyay, DAIR-ihk) **COL.**

Defense. Shoots left. 5'11", 190 lbs. Born, Plymouth, MN, March 14, 1985.
(Colorado's 5th choice, 184th overall, in 2004 Entry Draft).

			Regular Season					Playoffs				
Season	Club	League	GP	G	A	Pts	PIM	GP	G	A	Pts	PIM
2003-04	Cedar Rapids	USHL	55	7	26	33	34	4	0	0	0	4
2004-05	U. of Minnesota	WCHA	43	6	13	19	22	....	....	....	....	....
2005-06	U. of Minnesota	WCHA	41	1	17	18	30	....	....	....	....	....
2006-07	U. of Minnesota	WCHA	44	4	11	15	28	....	....	....	....	....

PELUSO, Anthony (puh-LOO-soh, AN-toh-nee) **ST.L.**

Defense. Shoots right. 6'3", 222 lbs. Born, North York, Ont., April 18, 1989.
(St. Louis' 9th choice, 160th overall, in 2007 Entry Draft).

			Regular Season					Playoffs				
Season	Club	League	GP	G	A	Pts	PIM	GP	G	A	Pts	PIM
2004-05	Richmond Hill	Minor-ON	30	22	20	42	80	....	....	....	....	....
2005-06	Erie Otters	OHL	68	5	3	8	66	....	....	....	....	....
2006-07	Erie Otters	OHL	52	7	3	10	176	....	....	....	....	....

PELUSO, Chris (puh-LOO-soh, KRIHS) **PIT.**

Defense. Shoots left. 5'11", 180 lbs. Born, Wadena, MN, August 21, 1986.
(Pittsburgh's 9th choice, 194th overall, in 2004 Entry Draft).

			Regular Season					Playoffs				
Season	Club	League	GP	G	A	Pts	PIM	GP	G	A	Pts	PIM
2003-04	Brainerd	High-MN	25	10	33	43	....	....	....	....	....	....
2004-05	Sioux Falls	USHL	53	1	7	8	54	....	....	....	....	....
2005-06	Sioux Falls	USHL	57	5	19	24	49	14	0	4	4	8
2006-07	Bemidji State	CHA	26	0	6	6	24	....	....	....	....	....

PERKOVICH, Nathan (puhr-KOH-vihch, NAY-thuhn) **N.J.**

Right wing. Shoots right. 6'5", 195 lbs. Born, Canton, MI, October 15, 1985.
(New Jersey's 6th choice, 250th overall, in 2004 Entry Draft).

			Regular Season					Playoffs				
Season	Club	League	GP	G	A	Pts	PIM	GP	G	A	Pts	PIM
2003-04	Cedar Rapids	USHL	35	1	7	8	23	4	1	0	1	0
2004-05	Chicago Steel	USHL	37	6	2	8	55	7	2	2	4	4
2005-06	Chicago Steel	USHL	56	28	24	52	121	....	....	....	....	....
2006-07	Lake Superior	CCHA	42	15	7	22	59	....	....	....	....	....

PERREAULT, Mathieu (pair-OH, MA-tyew) **WSH.**

Center. Shoots left. 5'9", 151 lbs. Born, Drummondville, Que., January 5, 1988.
(Washington's 10th choice, 177th overall, in 2006 Entry Draft).

			Regular Season					Playoffs				
Season	Club	League	GP	G	A	Pts	PIM	GP	G	A	Pts	PIM
2004-05	Magog Catonniers	QAAA	41	25	47	72	68	9	5	10	15	12
2005-06	Acadie-Bathurst	QMJHL	62	18	34	52	42	17	10	11	21	8
2006-07	Acadie-Bathurst	QMJHL	67	41	78	119	66	12	6	8	14	8

QMJHL First All-Star Team (2007) • QMJHL Player of the Year (2007)

PERRON, David (peh-RAWN, DAY-vihd) **ST.L.**

Left wing. Shoots right. 6', 180 lbs. Born, Sherbrooke, Que., May 28, 1988.
(St. Louis' 3rd choice, 26th overall, in 2007 Entry Draft).

			Regular Season					Playoffs				
Season	Club	League	GP	G	A	Pts	PIM	GP	G	A	Pts	PIM
2005-06	St-Jerome	QJHL	51	24	45	69	92	8	4	5	9	8
2006-07	Lewiston	QMJHL	70	39	44	83	75	17	12	16	28	22

PERSSON, Dennis (PAIR-suhn, DEH-nihs) **BUF.**

Defense. Shoots left. 6'1", 181 lbs. Born, Nykoping, Sweden, June 2, 1988.
(Buffalo's 1st choice, 24th overall, in 2006 Entry Draft).

			Regular Season					Playoffs				
Season	Club	League	GP	G	A	Pts	PIM	GP	G	A	Pts	PIM
2004-05	Vasteras U18	Swe-U18	3	0	1	1	2	4	0	1	1	0
	Vasteras Jr.	Swe-Jr.	27	3	3	6	24	....	....	....	....	....
2005-06	Vasteras Jr.	Swe-Jr.	28	11	15	26	22	....	....	....	....	....
	VIK Vasteras HK	Sweden-2	19	0	2	2	6	....	....	....	....	....
2006-07	Djurgarden	Sweden	9	0	0	0	2	....	....	....	....	....
	Almtuna	Sweden-2	3	0	0	0	2	....	....	....	....	....
	Nykoping	Sweden-2	29	4	4	8	38	....	....	....	....	....
	Djurgarden Jr.	Swe-Jr.	11	1	3	4	8	5	2	3	5	2

PERVYSHIN, Andrei (pair-VIHSH-ihn, AWN-dray) **ST.L.**

Defense. Shoots left. 5'8", 156 lbs. Born, Arkhangelsk, USSR, February 2, 1985.
(St. Louis' 11th choice, 253rd overall, in 2003 Entry Draft).

			Regular Season					Playoffs				
Season	Club	League	GP	G	A	Pts	PIM	GP	G	A	Pts	PIM
2003-04	Spartak Moscow	Russia-2	59	3	6	9	14	13	0	1	1	4
2004-05	Ak Bars Kazan 2	Russia-3	....	0	1	1	....	....	....	....	....	....
	Ak Bars Kazan	Russia	52	0	3	3	10	2	0	0	0	0
2005-06	Ak Bars Kazan	Russia	48	3	7	10	22	13	0	3	3	14
2006-07	Ak Bars Kazan	Russia	45	5	8	13	71	12	2	3	5	8

PESONEN, Janne (PEHS-oh-nihn, YAH-nee) **ANA.**

Left wing. Shoots left. 5'11", 180 lbs. Born, Suomussalmi, Finland, May 11, 1982.
(Anaheim's 8th choice, 269th overall, in 2004 Entry Draft).

			Regular Season					Playoffs				
Season	Club	League	GP	G	A	Pts	PIM	GP	G	A	Pts	PIM
1998-99	Hokki Kajaani	Finland-3	2	0	0	0	0	....	....	....	....	....
99-2000	Karpat Oulu U18	Fin-U18	33	6	12	18	30	3	0	1	1	0
2000-01	Karpat Oulu Jr.	Fin-Jr.	41	9	22	31	18	6	1	1	2	0
2001-02	Karpat Oulu Jr.	Fin-Jr.	42	12	19	31	18	3	2	0	2	2
	Karpat Oulu	Finland	9	2	0	2	0	1	0	0	0	0
2002-03	Hokki Kajaani	Finland-2	40	15	21	36	62	3	2	0	2	4
2003-04	Karpat Oulu	Finland	56	17	13	30	28	15	1	1	2	4
2004-05	Karpat Oulu	Finland	55	11	18	29	42	12	2	0	2	0
2005-06	Karpat Oulu	Finland	53	8	14	22	34	11	4	0	4	8
2006-07	Karpat Oulu	Finland	56	22	33	55	38	9	4	3	7	10

PESTUNOV, Dmitri (pehs-too-NAWF, dih-MEE-tree) **PHX.**

Center. Shoots left. 5'9", 196 lbs. Born, Ust-Kamenogorsk, USSR, January 22, 1985.
(Phoenix's 2nd choice, 80th overall, in 2003 Entry Draft).

			Regular Season					Playoffs				
Season	Club	League	GP	G	A	Pts	PIM	GP	G	A	Pts	PIM
2002-03	Magnitogorsk	Russia	32	4	0	4	0	....	....	....	....	....
2003-04	Magnitogorsk	Russia	51	6	7	13	40	14	0	3	3	25
	Magnitogorsk 2	Russia-3	6	3	15	18	2	3	0	2	2	4
2004-05	Magnitogorsk	Russia	37	4	4	8	46	....	....	....	....	....
	Spartak Moscow	Russia	12	1	1	2	14	....	....	....	....	....
2005-06	Magnitogorsk	Russia	48	6	13	19	58	4	0	1	1	0
2006-07	Magnitogorsk	Russia	53	5	18	23	26	11	0	0	0	8

Signed as a free agent by **Spartak Moscow** (Russia), February 16, 2005.

PETERS, Geoff (PEE-tuhrz, JEHF) **ANA.**

Center. Shoots left. 6'1", 205 lbs. Born, Hamilton, Ont., April 30, 1978.
(Chicago's 3rd choice, 46th overall, in 1996 Entry Draft).

			Regular Season					Playoffs				
Season	Club	League	GP	G	A	Pts	PIM	GP	G	A	Pts	PIM
1993-94	Wexford Raiders	MTHL	34	39	26	65	26	....	....	....	....	....
	Wexford Raiders	MTJHL	1	0	0	0	0	....	....	....	....	....
1994-95	Niagara Falls	OHL	57	11	9	20	37	6	2	0	2	4
1995-96	Niagara Falls	OHL	64	25	34	59	51	10	4	4	8	8
1996-97	Erie Otters	OHL	28	12	10	22	39	5	1	3	4	7
1997-98	Erie Otters	OHL	31	15	11	26	36	....	....	....	....	....
	North Bay	OHL	20	11	14	25	22	....	....	....	....	....
	Indianapolis Ice	IHL	2	0	0	0	10	....	....	....	....	....
1998-99	Canada	Nat-Tm	38	9	4	13	50	....	....	....	....	....
	Portland Pirates	AHL	4	1	1	2	9	....	....	....	....	....
99-2000	Cleveland	IHL	68	10	4	14	87	7	0	3	3	4
2000-01	Norfolk Admirals	AHL	73	11	10	21	48	6	0	1	1	6
2001-02	Rochester	AHL	10	1	4	5	18	2	0	1	1	0
	Trenton Titans	ECHL	43	13	21	34	55	....	....	....	....	....
	Columbus	ECHL	22	5	13	18	7	....	....	....	....	....
2002-03	Manchester	Britain	4	0	1	1	4	....	....	....	....	....
	Reading Royals	ECHL	40	15	13	28	40	....	....	....	....	....
	Milwaukee	AHL	8	0	0	0	7	....	....	....	....	....
2003-04	Rochester	AHL	46	7	4	11	109	16	0	4	4	27
2004-05	Rochester	AHL	57	9	8	17	125	9	0	2	2	18
2005-06	Portland Pirates	AHL	64	23	22	45	89	19	4	6	10	30
2006-07	Portland Pirates	AHL	34	7	6	13	65	....	....	....	....	....

Signed as a free agent by **Manchester** (Britain), August 22, 2002. Signed as a free agent by **Reading** (ECHL) after **Manchester** (Britain) folded, November 11, 2002. Signed as a free agent by **Anaheim**, August 30, 2005.

PETERS, Warren (PEE-tuhrz, WAHR-ihn) **CGY.**

Center. Shoots left. 6', 200 lbs. Born, Saskatoon, Sask., July 10, 1982.

			Regular Season					Playoffs				
Season	Club	League	GP	G	A	Pts	PIM	GP	G	A	Pts	PIM
1998-99	Saskatoon Blades	WHL	53	8	6	14	111	....	....	....	....	....
99-2000	Saskatoon Blades	WHL	70	11	17	28	97	10	1	2	3	13
2000-01	Saskatoon Blades	WHL	63	27	14	41	111	....	....	....	....	....
2001-02	Saskatoon Blades	WHL	72	34	26	60	115	7	1	4	5	13
2002-03	Saskatoon Blades	WHL	71	31	44	75	108	6	1	6	7	6
	Portland Pirates	AHL	1	0	0	0	0	....	....	....	....	....
2003-04	Utah Grizzlies	AHL	55	4	4	8	63	....	....	....	....	....
	Idaho Steelheads	ECHL	21	6	7	13	33	....	....	....	....	....
2004-05	Idaho Steelheads	ECHL	69	23	23	46	131	4	0	1	1	12
2005-06	Omaha	AHL	77	15	10	25	133	....	....	....	....	....
2006-07	Omaha	AHL	79	17	16	33	95	6	2	1	3	4

Signed as a free agent by **Calgary**, August 5, 2005. Signed as a free agent by **Rauma** (Finland), June 4, 2007.

PETRECKI, Nicholas (peh-TREH-kee, NIHK-oh-las) **S.J.**

Defense. Shoots left. 6'3", 215 lbs. Born, Schenectady, NY, July 11, 1989.
(San Jose's 2nd choice, 28th overall, in 2007 Entry Draft).

			Regular Season					Playoffs				
Season	Club	League	GP	G	A	Pts	PIM	GP	G	A	Pts	PIM
2004-05	Capital District	EmJHL	53	5	18	23	159	....	....	....	....	....
2005-06	Omaha Lancers	USHL	53	0	3	3	110	5	0	0	0	0
2006-07	Omaha Lancers	USHL	54	11	14	25	177	5	0	0	0	10

PETRELL, Lennart (peh-TREHL, LEH-nahrt) **CBJ**

Center. Shoots left. 6'3", 198 lbs. Born, Helsinki, Finland, April 13, 1984.
(Columbus' 8th choice, 190th overall, in 2004 Entry Draft).

			Regular Season					Playoffs				
Season	Club	League	GP	G	A	Pts	PIM	GP	G	A	Pts	PIM
2000-01	K-Kissat Jr.	Fin-Jr.	4	3	2	5	0	....	....	....	....	....
	K-Kissat	Finland-4	1	0	0	0	0	....	....	....	....	....
2001-02	HIFK Helsinki U18	Fin-U18	18	10	8	18	12	8	2	0	2	2
	HIFK Helsinki Jr.	Fin-Jr.	5	0	0	0	0	....	....	....	....	....
2002-03	HIFK Helsinki Jr.	Fin-Jr.	28	2	2	4	35	7	3	1	4	29
2003-04	Suomi U20	Finland-2	7	1	0	1	0	....	....	....	....	....
	HIFK Helsinki Jr.	Fin-Jr.	33	11	17	28	28	10	6	7	13	2
	HIFK Helsinki	Finland	8	0	0	0	2	1	0	0	0	0
2004-05	HIFK Helsinki Jr.	Fin-Jr.	12	5	5	10	10	2	0	1	1	0
	HIFK Helsinki	Finland	35	3	2	5	35	4	0	1	1	2
2005-06	HIFK Helsinki	Finland	51	12	8	20	88	10	1	2	3	20
2006-07	HIFK Helsinki	Finland	53	19	11	30	74	5	0	0	0	2

PETROCHININ, Evgeny (peht-roh-CHIH-nihn, ehv-GEH-nee) **CBJ**

Defense. Shoots left. 6'2", 190 lbs. Born, Murmansk, USSR, February 7, 1976.
(Dallas' 5th choice, 150th overall, in 1994 Entry Draft).

			Regular Season					Playoffs				
Season	Club	League	GP	G	A	Pts	PIM	GP	G	A	Pts	PIM
1993-94	Spartak Moscow	CIS	2	0	0	0	0	....	....	....	....	....
1994-95	Spartak Moscow	CIS	45	0	2	2	14	....	....	....	....	....
1995-96	Spartak Moscow	CIS	50	5	17	22	18	5	3	0	3	0
1996-97	Spartak Moscow	Russia	32	5	6	11	52	....	....	....	....	....
1997-98	Spartak Moscow	Russia	46	12	6	18	100	....	....	....	....	....
1998-99	Spartak Moscow	Russia	21	4	6	10	14	....	....	....	....	....
	Ak Bars Kazan	Russia	6	0	2	2	2	9	1	1	2	24
99-2000	Magnitogorsk	Russia	33	7	10	17	38	14	2	1	3	26
2000-01	Cherepovets	Russia	40	8	7	15	38	9	2	0	2	40
2001-02	Cherepovets	Russia	35	35	2	8	10	1	0	0	0	0
2002-03	Cherepovets	Russia	29	3	6	9	14	10	1	0	1	0
2003-04	Cherepovets	Russia	43	4	9	13	85	....	....	....	....	....
	Cherepovets 2	Russia-3	1	0	2	2	0	....	....	....	....	....
2004-05	Magnitogorsk	Russia	48	3	4	7	14	3	0	0	0	2
2005-06	Magnitogorsk 2	Russia-3	1	0	0	0	0	....	....	....	....	....
	Vityaz Chekhov	Russia	18	0	3	3	6	....	....	....	....	....
2006-07	HK Dmitrov	Russia-2	9	3	1	4	32	....	....	....	....	....
	Nizhny Novgorod	Russia-2	1	0	0	0	0	....	....	....	....	....

Rights traded to **Columbus** by **Dallas** for Kirk Muller, September 28, 2001.

PETRUIC, Neil (peh-TROO-ihk, NEEL)

Defense. Shoots left. 6'1", 194 lbs. Born, Regina, Sask., July 30, 1982.
(Ottawa's 10th choice, 235th overall, in 2001 Entry Draft).

			Regular Season					Playoffs				
Season	Club	League	GP	G	A	Pts	PIM	GP	G	A	Pts	PIM
99-2000	Kindersley Klippers	SJHL	68	5	25	30	....	....	....	....	....	....
2000-01	Kindersley Klippers	SJHL	68	18	24	42	123	....	....	....	....	....
2001-02	U. Minn-Duluth	WCHA	40	3	6	9	54	....	....	....	....	....
2002-03	U. Minn-Duluth	WCHA	40	6	8	14	78	....	....	....	....	....
2003-04	U. Minn-Duluth	WCHA	45	4	10	14	56	....	....	....	....	....
2004-05	U. Minn-Duluth	WCHA	32	1	8	9	63	....	....	....	....	....
2005-06	Binghamton	AHL	51	1	3	4	31	....	....	....	....	....
	Charlotte	ECHL	10	2	4	6	6	....	....	....	....	....
2006-07	Binghamton	AHL	74	1	12	13	89	....	....	....	....	....

SJHL First All-Star Team (2001)

PETRUZALEK, Jakub (peh-troo-ZAL-ehk, YA-kuhb) **CAR.**

Center/Right wing. Shoots right. 5'10", 176 lbs. Born, Most, Czech., April 24, 1985.
(NY Rangers' 13th choice, 266th overall, in 2004 Entry Draft).

			Regular Season					Playoffs				
Season	Club	League	GP	G	A	Pts	PIM	GP	G	A	Pts	PIM
2002-03	Litvinov Jr.	CzRep-Jr.	21	17	13	30	10	....	....	....	....	....
	Litvinov	CzRep	5	0	0	0	0	....	....	....	....	....
2003-04	Litvinov Jr.	CzRep-Jr.	53	38	51	89	110	2	0	0	0	2
	Litvinov	CzRep	7	0	0	0	2	....	....	....	....	....
	SK HC Banik Most	CzRep-3	1	0	0	0	0	....	....	....	....	....
2004-05	Ottawa 67's	OHL	59	23	40	63	64	21	8	10	18	30
2005-06	Litvinov Jr.	CzRep-Jr.	3	4	2	6	4	....	....	....	....	....
	Litvinov	CzRep	19	1	1	2	6	....	....	....	....	....
	Barrie Colts	OHL	24	11	20	31	28	14	8	11	19	14
2006-07	Hartford Wolf Pack	AHL	6	0	2	2	0	....	....	....	....	....
	Charlotte	ECHL	7	1	9	10	4	....	....	....	....	....
	Albany River Rats	AHL	54	10	18	28	16	5	2	2	4	10

Traded to **Carolina** by **NY Rangers** with future considerations for Brad Isbister, November 21, 2006.

PETRY, Jeff (PEH-tree, JEHF) **EDM.**

Defense. Shoots right. 6'3", 176 lbs. Born, Ann Arbor, MI, December 9, 1987.
(Edmonton's 1st choice, 45th overall, in 2006 Entry Draft).

			Regular Season					Playoffs				
Season	Club	League	GP	G	A	Pts	PIM	GP	G	A	Pts	PIM
2004-05	St. Mary's Prep	High-MI	23	2	8	10	....	6	2	5	7	....
2005-06	Det. Caesers	MWEHL	33	7	21	28	24	....	....	....	....	....
	Des Moines	USHL	48	1	14	15	68	11	2	5	7	8
2006-07	Des Moines	USHL	55	18	27	45	71	8	0	6	6	10

PIERRO-ZABOTEL, Casey (PEE-air-oh-ZA-boh-tuhl, KAY-see) **PIT.**

Center. Shoots left. 6'1", 205 lbs. Born, Ashcroft, B.C., November 8, 1988.
(Pittsburgh's 4th choice, 80th overall, in 2007 Entry Draft).

			Regular Season					Playoffs				
Season	Club	League	GP	G	A	Pts	PIM	GP	G	A	Pts	PIM
2004-05	Merritt	BCHL	58	6	6	12	19	5	0	0	0	0
2005-06	Merritt	BCHL	60	20	35	55	29	9	9	4	13	10
2006-07	Merritt	BCHL	55	51	65	116	42	7	8	3	11	13

PIHLSTROM, Antti (PIHL-stuhm, AN-tee) **NSH.**

Left wing. Shoots left. 5'10", 181 lbs. Born, Vanntaa, Finland, October 22, 1984.

			Regular Season					Playoffs				
Season	Club	League	GP	G	A	Pts	PIM	GP	G	A	Pts	PIM
2001-02	Jokerit U18	Fin-U18	26	15	14	29	41	8	0	5	5	18
	Jokerit Helsinki Jr.	Fin-Jr.	1	0	0	0	0	....	....	....	....	....
2002-03	Blues Espoo Jr.	Fin-Jr.	36	10	16	26	38	10	1	1	2	8
2003-04	Blues Espoo Jr.	Fin-Jr.	23	9	19	28	42	1	0	2	2	0
	Suomi U20	Finland-2	4	0	1	1	2	....	....	....	....	....
	Blues Espoo	Finland	49	1	3	4	18	9	0	0	0	0
2004-05	Blues Espoo	Finland	53	4	3	7	30	....	....	....	....	....
	Blues Espoo Jr.	Fin-Jr.	11	7	3	10	36	7	0	2	2	26
2005-06	SaiPa	Finland	54	10	11	21	60	8	1	0	1	2
2006-07	HPK Hameenlinna	Finland	56	16	23	39	63	9	3	5	8	4

Signed as a free agent by **Nashville**, June 1, 2007.

PIKKARAINEN, Ilkka (pih-kar-AY-nihn, IHL-kah) **N.J.**

Right wing. Shoots right. 6'2", 200 lbs. Born, Sonkajarvi, Finland, April 19, 1981.
(New Jersey's 9th choice, 218th overall, in 2002 Entry Draft).

			Regular Season					Playoffs				
Season	Club	League	GP	G	A	Pts	PIM	GP	G	A	Pts	PIM
1998-99	HIFK Helsinki U18	Fin-U18	24	6	12	18	26	2	1	0	1	27
	HIFK Helsinki Jr.	Fin-Jr.	13	6	1	7	12	....	....	....	....	....
99-2000	HIFK Helsinki Jr.	Fin-Jr.	28	3	2	5	14	3	1	1	2	2
2000-01	HIFK Helsinki Jr.	Fin-Jr.	38	27	31	58	186	9	2	5	7	26
	HIFK Helsinki	Finland	4	0	0	0	8	2	0	0	0	0
2001-02	HIFK Helsinki	Finland	54	9	9	18	111	....	....	....	....	....
2002-03	HIFK Helsinki	Finland	47	11	12	23	40	....	....	....	....	....
2003-04	Albany River Rats	AHL	63	8	10	18	118	....	....	....	....	....
2004-05	Albany River Rats	AHL	71	12	12	24	102	....	....	....	....	....
2005-06	Albany River Rats	AHL	62	9	11	20	85	....	....	....	....	....
2006-07	HIFK Helsinki	Finland	53	17	20	37	140	5	0	1	1	2

PINEAULT, Adam (pih-NOH, A-duhm) **CBJ**

Right wing. Shoots right. 6'1", 201 lbs. Born, Holyoke, MA, May 23, 1986.
(Columbus' 2nd choice, 46th overall, in 2004 Entry Draft).

			Regular Season					Playoffs				
Season	Club	League	GP	G	A	Pts	PIM	GP	G	A	Pts	PIM
2000-01	Junior Bruins	EJHL	57	30	35	65	56	....	....	....	....	....
2001-02	USNTDP	U-17	20	5	4	9	14	....	....	....	....	....
	USNTDP	NAHL	38	11	4	15	11	....	....	....	....	....
2002-03	USNTDP	U-17	43	13	15	28	76	....	....	....	....	....
	USNTDP	U-18	4	4	3	7	6	....	....	....	....	....
	USNTDP	NAHL	9	5	4	9	13	....	....	....	....	....
2003-04	Boston College	H-East	30	4	4	8	32	....	....	....	....	....
2004-05	Moncton Wildcats	QMJHL	61	26	20	46	64	12	2	6	8	18
2005-06	Moncton Wildcats	QMJHL	55	29	30	59	94	21	14	8	22	25
2006-07	Syracuse Crunch	AHL	57	12	16	28	66	....	....	....	....	....

Memorial Cup Tournament All-Star Team (2006)

PINIZZOTTO, Steve (pih-nih-ZAW-toh, STEEV) WSH.

Center. Shoots right. 6'2", lbs. Born, Mississauga, Ont., April 26, 1984.

			Regular Season					Playoffs				
Season	Club	League	GP	G	A	Pts	PIM	GP	G	A	Pts	PIM
2002-03	Oakville Blades	OPJHL	44	16	24	40	152	2	0	0	0	2
2003-04	Oakville Blades	OPJHL	39	17	34	51	177	....	....	....	....	....
2004-05	Oakville Blades	OPJHL	STATISTICS NOT AVAILABLE									
2005-06	RIT Tigers	NCAA	20	7	6	13	32	....	....	....	....	....
2006-07	RIT Tigers	AH	34	13	31	44	76	....	....	....	....	....
	Hershey Bears	AHL	5	0	0	0	4	....	....	....	....	....

Signed as a free agent by **Washington**, March 16, 2007.

PISELLINI, Gino (pih-sehl-EE-nee, JEE-noh) PHI.

Right wing. Shoots right. 6', 210 lbs. Born, Melrose Park, IL, August 5, 1986.
(Philadelphia's 5th choice, 149th overall, in 2004 Entry Draft).

			Regular Season					Playoffs				
Season	Club	League	GP	G	A	Pts	PIM	GP	G	A	Pts	PIM
2003-04	Plymouth Whalers	OHL	68	15	15	30	214	9	0	3	3	23
2004-05	Plymouth Whalers	OHL	59	4	6	10	137	4	0	1	1	9
2005-06	Plymouth Whalers	OHL	63	15	16	31	194	13	0	3	3	28
2006-07	Philadelphia	AHL	32	1	1	2	53	....	....	....	....	....
	Trenton Titans	ECHL	23	1	3	4	65	5	0	1	1	11

PITTON, Jason (PIH-tuhn, JAY-suhn) NYI

Left wing. Shoots left. 6'3", 216 lbs. Born, Mississauga, Ont., May 23, 1986.
(NY Islanders' 9th choice, 244th overall, in 2004 Entry Draft).

			Regular Season					Playoffs				
Season	Club	League	GP	G	A	Pts	PIM	GP	G	A	Pts	PIM
2002-03	Brampton Capitals	OPJHL	47	23	18	41	46	....	....	....	....	....
	Sault Ste. Marie	OHL	1	0	0	0	0	....	....	....	....	....
2003-04	Sault Ste. Marie	OHL	67	9	11	20	37	....	....	....	....	....
2004-05	Sault Ste. Marie	OHL	68	23	19	42	35	7	2	2	4	4
2005-06	Sault Ste. Marie	OHL	37	18	9	27	29	....	....	....	....	....
	Guelph Storm	OHL	31	10	5	15	21	15	5	3	8	18
2006-07	Bridgeport	AHL	76	9	10	19	65	....	....	....	....	....

PLANTE, Alex (PLAWNT, AL-ehx) EDM.

Defense. Shoots right. 6'4", 225 lbs. Born, Brandon, Man., May 9, 1989.
(Edmonton's 2nd choice, 15th overall, in 2007 Entry Draft).

			Regular Season					Playoffs				
Season	Club	League	GP	G	A	Pts	PIM	GP	G	A	Pts	PIM
2004-05	Brandon	MMHL	37	5	21	26	120	....	....	....	....	....
	Calgary Hitmen	WHL	8	0	0	0	6	11	0	0	0	17
2005-06	Calgary Hitmen	WHL	54	1	3	4	72	13	0	0	0	6
2006-07	Calgary Hitmen	WHL	58	8	30	38	81	13	5	6	11	14

PLATONOV, Denis (PLAH-tah-nahv, DEH-nihs) NSH.

Right wing. Shoots left. 6'3", 205 lbs. Born, Saratov, USSR, November 6, 1981.
(Nashville's 4th choice, 75th overall, in 2001 Entry Draft).

			Regular Season					Playoffs				
Season	Club	League	GP	G	A	Pts	PIM	GP	G	A	Pts	PIM
1997-98	Kristall Saratov 2	Russia-3	20	4	2	6	34	....	....	....	....	....
1998-99	Kristall Saratov	Russia-2	14	1	0	1	61	....	....	....	....	....
99-2000	Kristall Saratov 2	Russia-3	5	0	0	0	37	....	....	....	....	....
	Kristall Saratov	Russia-2	32	9	4	13	60	....	....	....	....	....
2000-01	Kristall Saratov	Russia-2	51	14	6	20	75	....	....	....	....	....
2001-02	Kristall Saratov	Russia-2	50	18	14	32	96	....	....	....	....	....
2002-03	Ak Bars Kazan	Russia	47	8	9	17	49	5	0	0	0	2
2003-04	Milwaukee	AHL	3	0	0	0	0	....	....	....	....	....
	Ak Bars Kazan	Russia	28	5	3	8	18	8	1	0	1	2
	Ak Bars Kazan 2	Russia-3	STATISTICS NOT AVAILABLE									
2004-05	Ak Bars Kazan	Russia	38	3	7	10	10	....	....	....	....	....
	Nizhnekamsk	Russia	11	3	1	4	34	3	0	1	1	2
2005-06	Magnitogorsk	Russia	49	11	8	19	60	8	4	0	4	6
2006-07	Magnitogorsk	Russia	53	17	8	25	87	14	5	3	8	14

Assigned to **Kazan** (Russia) by **Nashville**, October 29, 2003.

PLEHANOV, Andrei (pleh-HAN-awf, AWN-dray) CBJ

Defense. Shoots right. 6'1", 187 lbs. Born, Nizhnekamsk, USSR, July 12, 1986.
(Columbus' 5th choice, 96th overall, in 2004 Entry Draft).

			Regular Season					Playoffs				
Season	Club	League	GP	G	A	Pts	PIM	GP	G	A	Pts	PIM
2003-04	Nizhnekamsk 2	Russia-3	STATISTICS NOT AVAILABLE									
2004-05	Nizhnekamsk	Russia	2	0	0	0	2	....	....	....	....	....
	Leninogorsk	Russia-2	1	0	0	0	4	....	....	....	....	....
	Perm 2	Russia-3	2	0	0	0	4	....	....	....	....	....
2005-06	Nizhnekamsk	Russia	45	1	2	33	22	5	0	0	0	0
2006-07	Nizhnekamsk	Russia	16	1	2	3	28	....	....	....	....	....

POHL, Petr (PAWL, PEE-tuhr) CBJ

Right wing. Shoots right. 5'11", 188 lbs. Born, Prostejov, Czech., August 28, 1986.
(Columbus' 6th choice, 133rd overall, in 2004 Entry Draft).

			Regular Season					Playoffs				
Season	Club	League	GP	G	A	Pts	PIM	GP	G	A	Pts	PIM
2001-02	HC Vitkovice U17	CzR-U17	38	34	19	53	65	2	1	0	1	4
	HC Vitkovice Jr.	CzRep-Jr.	10	0	2	2	2	....	....	....	....	....
2002-03	HC Vitkovice Jr.	CzRep-Jr.	36	13	22	35	30	2	1	0	1	6
2003-04	Gatineau	QMJHL	70	23	27	50	16	8	0	2	2	2
2004-05	Gatineau	QMJHL	62	27	32	59	16	10	6	4	10	4
2005-06	Acadie-Bathurst	QMJHL	62	27	43	70	44	17	6	10	16	12
2006-07	Syracuse Crunch	AHL	1	0	0	0	0	....	....	....	....	....
	Dayton Bombers	ECHL	65	8	16	24	18	18	3	3	6	10

POKULOK, Sasha (poh-KUH-lawk, SA-shuh) WSH.

Defense. Shoots left. 6'5", 220 lbs. Born, Montreal, Que., May 25, 1986.
(Washington's 1st choice, 14th overall, in 2005 Entry Draft).

			Regular Season					Playoffs				
Season	Club	League	GP	G	A	Pts	PIM	GP	G	A	Pts	PIM
2003-04	Notre Dame	SJHL	39	7	16	23	34	....	....	....	....	....
2004-05	Cornell Big Red	ECACHL	26	3	7	10	33	....	....	....	....	....
2005-06	Cornell Big Red	ECACHL	27	4	9	13	49	....	....	....	....	....
2006-07	Hershey Bears	AHL	1	0	0	0	0	....	....	....	....	....
	South Carolina	ECHL	16	3	6	9	22	....	....	....	....	....

ECACHL All-Rookie Team (2005)

POLUSHIN, Alexander (puh-LOOSH-ihn, al-EHX-AN-duhr) T.B.

Center. Shoots left. 6'3", 198 lbs. Born, Kirovo-Chepetsk, USSR, May 8, 1983.
(Tampa Bay's 2nd choice, 47th overall, in 2001 Entry Draft).

			Regular Season					Playoffs				
Season	Club	League	GP	G	A	Pts	PIM	GP	G	A	Pts	PIM
99-2000	Dyn'o Moscow 2	Russia-3	18	4	3	7	14	....	....	....	....	....
	Spartak Moscow	Russia-2	14	1	0	1	2	....	....	....	....	....
2000-01	THK Tver	Russia-2	38	10	5	15	10	....	....	....	....	....
2001-02	HK CSKA Moscow	Russia-2	55	28	21	49	18	....	....	....	....	....
2002-03	CSKA Moscow	Russia	47	5	6	11	22	....	....	....	....	....
2003-04	CSKA Moscow	Russia	13	5	2	7	4	....	....	....	....	....
2004-05	CSKA Moscow	Russia	17	3	4	7	4	....	....	....	....	....
2005-06	Cherepovets	Russia	42	8	5	13	14	1	0	0	0	0
2006-07	Mytischi	Russia	DID NOT PLAY									

POPOV, Andrei (PAH-pawv, AWN-dray) PHI.

Right wing. Shoots left. 6', 187 lbs. Born, Chelyabinsk, USSR, July 15, 1988.
(Philadelphia's 10th choice, 205th overall, in 2006 Entry Draft).

			Regular Season					Playoffs				
Season	Club	League	GP	G	A	Pts	PIM	GP	G	A	Pts	PIM
2003-04	Chelyabinsk 2	Russia-3	6	3	0	3	4	....	....	....	....	....
2004-05	Chelyabinsk 2	Russia-3	17	7	1	8	4	....	....	....	....	....
2005-06	Chelyabinsk 2	Russia-3	2	1	4	5	0	....	....	....	....	....
	Chelyabinsk	Russia-2	37	8	8	16	26	5	2	0	2	2
2006-07	Chelyabinsk 2	Russia-3	2	1	1	2	0	....	....	....	....	....
	Chelyabinsk	Russia	44	2	10	12	36	....	....	....	....	....

PORTER, Chris (POHR-tuhr, KRIHS) CHI.

Center. Shoots left. 6'1", 203 lbs. Born, Toronto, Ont., May 29, 1984.
(Chicago's 10th choice, 282nd overall, in 2003 Entry Draft).

			Regular Season					Playoffs				
Season	Club	League	GP	G	A	Pts	PIM	GP	G	A	Pts	PIM
2001-02	Shat.-St. Mary's	High-MN	75	10	25	35	32	....	....	....	....	....
2002-03	Lincoln Stars	USHL	59	13	22	35	74	10	4	3	7	10
2003-04	North Dakota	WCHA	41	10	15	25	46	....	....	....	....	....
2004-05	North Dakota	WCHA	45	12	3	15	36	....	....	....	....	....
2005-06	North Dakota	WCHA	46	7	16	23	40	....	....	....	....	....
2006-07	North Dakota	WCHA	43	13	17	30	38	....	....	....	....	....

PORTER, Kevin (POHR-tuhr, KEH-vihn) PHX.

Left wing. Shoots left. 5'11", 194 lbs. Born, Detroit, MI, March 12, 1986.
(Phoenix's 5th choice, 119th overall, in 2004 Entry Draft).

			Regular Season					Playoffs				
Season	Club	League	GP	G	A	Pts	PIM	GP	G	A	Pts	PIM
2002-03	USNTDP	U-17	19	9	11	20	8	....	....	....	....	....
	USNTDP	U-18	13	1	2	3	2	....	....	....	....	....
	USNTDP	NAHL	40	19	9	28	17	....	....	....	....	....
2003-04	USNTDP	U-18	44	5	21	26	26	....	....	....	....	....
	USNTDP	NAHL	11	3	8	11	4	....	....	....	....	....
2004-05	U. of Michigan	CCHA	39	11	13	24	51	....	....	....	....	....
2005-06	U. of Michigan	CCHA	39	17	21	38	30	....	....	....	....	....
2006-07	U. of Michigan	CCHA	41	24	34	58	16	....	....	....	....	....

CCHA Second All-Star Team (2007)

POSPISIL, Tomas (PAWS-pih-shihl, TAW-mahsh) ATL.

Right wing. Shoots right. 6', 185 lbs. Born, Sumperk, Czech., August 25, 1987.
(Atlanta's 6th choice, 135th overall, in 2005 Entry Draft).

			Regular Season					Playoffs				
Season	Club	League	GP	G	A	Pts	PIM	GP	G	A	Pts	PIM
2002-03	HC Trinec U17	CzR-U17	41	24	28	52	44	2	0	1	1	2
	HC Trinec Jr.	CzRep-Jr.	2	0	0	0	0	2	0	0	0	0
2003-04	HC Trinec U17	CzR-U17	3	3	3	6	14	5	5	2	7	26
	HC Trinec Jr.	CzRep-Jr.	45	14	11	25	40	2	1	1	2	0
2004-05	HC Ocelari Trinec	CzRep	14	0	0	0	0	....	....	....	....	....
	HC Trinec Jr.	CzRep-Jr.	38	19	18	37	44	5	4	1	5	27
2005-06	Sarnia Sting	OHL	60	25	30	55	61	....	....	....	....	....
2006-07	Sarnia Sting	OHL	55	29	38	67	38	4	1	5	6	4

POSTMA, Paul (POHST-muh, PAWL) ATL.

Defense. Shoots right. 6'2", 180 lbs. Born, Red Deer, Alta., February 22, 1989.
(Atlanta's 4th choice, 205th overall, in 2007 Entry Draft).

			Regular Season					Playoffs				
Season	Club	League	GP	G	A	Pts	PIM	GP	G	A	Pts	PIM
2004-05	Red Deer	AMHL	36	6	5	11	24	....	....	....	....	....
	Swift Current	WHL	4	0	0	0	0	....	....	....	....	....
2005-06	Swift Current	WHL	58	2	9	11	6	4	0	0	0	0
2006-07	Swift Current	WHL	70	5	19	24	42	6	0	1	1	0

POTTER, Corey (PAW-tuhr, KOHR-ee) NYR

Defense. Shoots right. 6'3", 205 lbs. Born, Lansing, MI, January 5, 1984.
(NY Rangers' 4th choice, 122nd overall, in 2003 Entry Draft).

			Regular Season					Playoffs				
Season	Club	League	GP	G	A	Pts	PIM	GP	G	A	Pts	PIM
99-2000	Det. Honeybaked	MWEHL	58	10	38	48	....	....	....	....	....	....
2000-01	USNTDP	U-17	13	0	0	0	6	....	....	....	....	....
	USNTDP	NAHL	53	4	4	8	20	....	....	....	....	....
2001-02	USNTDP	U-18	38	4	6	10	49	....	....	....	....	....
	USNTDP	USHL	13	2	2	4	12	....	....	....	....	....
	USNTDP	NAHL	10	0	3	3	4	....	....	....	....	....
2002-03	Michigan State	CCHA	35	4	4	8	30	....	....	....	....	....
2003-04	Michigan State	CCHA	38	0	8	8	63	....	....	....	....	....
2004-05	Michigan State	CCHA	32	0	6	6	73	....	....	....	....	....
2005-06	Michigan State	CCHA	45	4	18	22	117	....	....	....	....	....
2006-07	Hartford Wolf Pack	AHL	30	2	8	10	21	7	1	4	5	12
	Charlotte	ECHL	43	6	13	19	56	....	....	....	....	....

POTULNY, Grant (poh-TUHL-nee, GRANT)

Center. Shoots left. 6'3", 205 lbs. Born, Grand Forks, ND, March 4, 1980.
(Ottawa's 7th choice, 157th overall, in 2000 Entry Draft).

			Regular Season					Playoffs				
Season	Club	League	GP	G	A	Pts	PIM	GP	G	A	Pts	PIM
1998-99	Lincoln Stars	USHL	46	7	11	18	76	10	2	1	3	7
99-2000	Lincoln Stars	USHL	56	25	30	55	85	10	3	4	7	4
2000-01	U. of Minnesota	WCHA	42	22	11	33	38	....	....	....	....	....
2001-02	U. of Minnesota	WCHA	43	15	19	34	38	....	....	....	....	....
2002-03	U. of Minnesota	WCHA	23	15	8	23	12	....	....	....	....	....
2003-04	U. of Minnesota	WCHA	38	16	10	26	28	....	....	....	....	....
	Binghamton	AHL	3	0	1	1	0	2	0	0	0	0
2004-05	Binghamton	AHL	50	4	6	10	104	6	0	0	0	2
2005-06	Binghamton	AHL	78	23	23	46	122	....	....	....	....	....
2006-07	Binghamton	AHL	47	10	10	20	85	....	....	....	....	....

NCAA Championship All-Tournament Team (2002) • NCAA Championship Tournament MVP (2002)

PRUDDEN, Josh (PROO-dehn, JAWSH)

Left wing. Shoots left. 5'11", 190 lbs. Born, Andover, MA, January 10, 1980.

			Regular Season					Playoffs				
Season	Club	League	GP	G	A	Pts	PIM	GP	G	A	Pts	PIM
99-2000	New Hampshire	H-East	16	2	3	5	12	....	....	....	....	....
2000-01	New Hampshire	H-East	37	8	8	16	28	....	....	....	....	....
2001-02	New Hampshire	H-East	36	14	16	30	32	....	....	....	....	....
2002-03	New Hampshire	H-East	42	9	13	22	52	....	....	....	....	....
2003-04	Atlantic City	ECHL	60	18	34	52	54	4	0	0	0	2
2004-05	Cleveland Barons	AHL	73	14	8	22	54	....	....	....	....	....
2005-06	Cleveland Barons	AHL	76	9	12	21	46	....	....	....	....	....
2006-07	Worcester Sharks	AHL	56	9	22	31	34	6	0	1	1	9
	Fresno Falcons	ECHL	18	7	10	17	26	....	....	....	....	....

Signed as a free agent by **San Jose**, August 15, 2005.

PSURNY, Roman (P'SHUHR-nee, ROH-muhn) NYR

Left wing. Shoots left. 6'1", 179 lbs. Born, Gottwaldov/Zlin, Czech., February 23, 1986.
(NY Rangers' 10th choice, 135th overall, in 2004 Entry Draft).

			Regular Season					Playoffs				
Season	Club	League	GP	G	A	Pts	PIM	GP	G	A	Pts	PIM
2000-01	HC Zlin U17	CzR-U17	42	19	36	55	57	6	3	3	6	6
2002-03	HC Zlin U17	CzR-U17	22	17	27	44	20	3	1	1	2	4
	HC Zlin Jr.	CzRep-Jr.	15	3	7	10	0	....	....	....	....	....
2003-04	HC Zlin Jr.	CzRep-Jr.	52	18	33	51	104	5	0	0	0	2
	HC Hame Zlin	CzRep	9	0	0	0	0	....	....	....	....	....
2004-05	Medicine Hat	WHL	69	21	28	49	64	13	1	4	5	16
2005-06	Medicine Hat	WHL	66	24	30	54	54	13	4	7	11	10
2006-07	HC Hame Zlin	CzRep	45	4	2	6	20	....	....	....	....	....
	Trebic	CzRep-2	7	2	1	3	8	....	....	....	....	....

PURCELL, Teddy (puhr-SHEL, THE-dee) L.A.

Right wing. Shoots right. 6'3", 177 lbs. Born, St. Johns, Nfld., September 8, 1985.

			Regular Season					Playoffs				
Season	Club	League	GP	G	A	Pts	PIM	GP	G	A	Pts	PIM
2003-04	Notre Dame	SJHL	51	21	25	46	8	....	....	....	....	....
2004-05	Cedar Rapids	USHL	58	20	47	67	22	11	5	9	14	4
2005-06	Cedar Rapids	USHL	55	19	52	71	14	8	3	8	11	4
2006-07	U. of Maine	H-East	40	16	27	43	34	....	....	....	....	....

Signed as a free agent by **Los Angeles**, April 27, 2007.

PUUSTINEN, Juuso (POOS-tih-nehn, YUH-soh) CGY.

Right wing. Shoots right. 6'2", 188 lbs. Born, Kuopio, Finland, April 5, 1988.
(Calgary's 5th choice, 149th overall, in 2006 Entry Draft).

			Regular Season					Playoffs				
Season	Club	League	GP	G	A	Pts	PIM	GP	G	A	Pts	PIM
2004-05	KalPa Kuopio U18	Fin-U18	26	14	15	29	81	6	1	2	3	4
	KalPa Kuopio Jr.	Fin-Jr.	1	0	0	0	0	....	....	....	....	....
2005-06	KalPa Kuopio U18	Fin-U18	7	8	7	15	18	1	0	0	0	2
	KalPa Kuopio Jr.	Fin-Jr.	29	9	5	14	46	5	0	0	0	0
2006-07	Kamloops Blazers	WHL	64	32	39	71	52	4	0	3	3	4
	Suomi U20	Finland-2	2	0	1	1	2	....	....	....	....	....

PYATT, Tom (PIGH-at, TAWM) NYR

Center. Shoots left. 6', 185 lbs. Born, Thunder Bay, Ont., February 14, 1987.
(NY Rangers' 6th choice, 107th overall, in 2005 Entry Draft).

			Regular Season					Playoffs				
Season	Club	League	GP	G	A	Pts	PIM	GP	G	A	Pts	PIM
2003-04	Saginaw Spirit	OHL	67	9	9	18	21	....	....	....	....	....
2004-05	Saginaw Spirit	OHL	57	18	30	48	14	....	....	....	....	....
2005-06	Saginaw Spirit	OHL	58	24	29	53	29	4	1	2	3	4
2006-07	Saginaw Spirit	OHL	58	43	38	81	18	6	3	5	8	0
	Hartford Wolf Pack	AHL	1	0	0	0	0	....	....	....	....	....

PYETT, Logan (PIGH-eht, LOH-guhn) DET.

Defense. Shoots right. 5'10", 199 lbs. Born, Regina, Sask., May 26, 1988.
(Detroit's 7th choice, 212th overall, in 2006 Entry Draft).

			Regular Season					Playoffs				
Season	Club	League	GP	G	A	Pts	PIM	GP	G	A	Pts	PIM
2003-04	Regina Pat Cdns.	SMHL	44	18	27	45	34	....	....	....	....	....
	Regina Pats	WHL	2	0	1	1	0	3	0	0	0	0
2004-05	Regina Pats	WHL	67	5	19	24	67	....	....	....	....	....
2005-06	Regina Pats	WHL	71	10	35	45	89	6	1	6	7	12
2006-07	Regina Pats	WHL	71	14	48	62	84	10	3	6	9	4

QUICK, Kevin (KWIHK, KEH-vihn) T.B.

Defense. Shoots left. 6', 175 lbs. Born, Buffalo, NY, March 29, 1988.
(Tampa Bay's 2nd choice, 78th overall, in 2006 Entry Draft).

			Regular Season					Playoffs				
Season	Club	League	GP	G	A	Pts	PIM	GP	G	A	Pts	PIM
2004-05	Salisbury School	High-CT	27	3	9	12	3	....	....	....	....	....
2005-06	Salisbury School	High-CT	28	3	20	23	6	....	....	....	....	....
2006-07	Salisbury School	High-CT	25	1	10	11	10	....	....	....	....	....

• Signed Letter of Intent to attend **University of Michigan** (CCHA) in fall of 2007.

QUIST, William (KVIHST, WILL-yuhm) EDM.

Left wing. Shoots left. 6'3", 185 lbs. Born, Nybro, Sweden, July 31, 1989.
(Edmonton's 6th choice, 157th overall, in 2007 Entry Draft).

			Regular Season					Playoffs				
Season	Club	League	GP	G	A	Pts	PIM	GP	G	A	Pts	PIM
2005-06	Tingsryds AIF U18	Swe-U18	12	6	3	9	12	....	....	....	....	....
	Tingsryds AIF Jr.	Swe-Jr.	10	0	4	4	14	....	....	....	....	....
2006-07	Tingsryds AIF U18	Swe-U18	16	8	10	18	18	....	....	....	....	....
	Tingsryds AIF Jr.	Swe-Jr.	22	10	15	25	86	....	....	....	....	....
	Tingsryds AIF	Sweden-3	7	0	0	0	0	1	0	0	0	0

RABBIT, Wacey (RA-biht, WAY-see) BOS.

Center. Shoots left. 5'10", 171 lbs. Born, Lethbridge, Alta., November 16, 1986.
(Boston's 6th choice, 154th overall, in 2005 Entry Draft).

			Regular Season					Playoffs				
Season	Club	League	GP	G	A	Pts	PIM	GP	G	A	Pts	PIM
2001-02	Cgy. North Stars	AMHL	35	24	28	52	....	....	....	....	....	....
	Saskatoon Blades	WHL	3	0	1	1	0	....	....	....	....	....
2002-03	Saskatoon Blades	WHL	62	21	24	45	33	5	1	3	4	6
2003-04	Saskatoon Blades	WHL	60	9	8	17	51	....	....	....	....	....
2004-05	Saskatoon Blades	WHL	70	22	45	67	70	4	1	2	3	0
2005-06	Saskatoon Blades	WHL	64	28	28	56	45	10	5	3	8	4
2006-07	Providence Bruins	AHL	22	1	2	3	25	....	....	....	....	....
	Vancouver Giants	WHL	30	11	25	36	34	22	*11	9	20	16

RADUNSKE, Brock (ra-DOON-skee, BRAWK)

Left wing. Shoots left. 6'4", 187 lbs. Born, Kitchener, Ont., April 5, 1983.
(Edmonton's 5th choice, 79th overall, in 2002 Entry Draft).

			Regular Season					Playoffs				
Season	Club	League	GP	G	A	Pts	PIM	GP	G	A	Pts	PIM
99-2000	Aurora Tigers	OPJHL	42	6	14	20	23	4	4	8	12	2
2000-01	Newmarket	OPJHL	48	30	39	69	65	....	....	....	....	....
2001-02	Michigan State	CCHA	41	4	9	13	28	....	....	....	....	....
2002-03	Michigan State	CCHA	36	11	18	29	30	....	....	....	....	....
2003-04	Michigan State	CCHA	42	12	10	22	60	....	....	....	....	....
2004-05	Edmonton	AHL	8	1	1	2	2	....	....	....	....	....
	Greenville Grrrowl	ECHL	39	12	17	29	52	....	....	....	....	....
2005-06	Greenville Grrrowl	ECHL	63	38	16	54	58	6	1	2	3	14
2006-07	Grand Rapids	AHL	20	2	0	2	12	....	....	....	....	....
	HC Davos	Swiss	3	0	1	1	2	....	....	....	....	....
	Stockton Thunder	ECHL	16	14	19	33	12	3	0	0	0	2

Signed as a free agent by **Augsburger** (Germany), June 22, 2007.

RAHIMI, Daniel (RA-hih-mee, DAN-yehl) VAN.

Defense. Shoots left. 6'3", 221 lbs. Born, Umea, Sweden, April 28, 1987.
(Vancouver's 2nd choice, 82nd overall, in 2006 Entry Draft).

			Regular Season					Playoffs				
Season	Club	League	GP	G	A	Pts	PIM	GP	G	A	Pts	PIM
2003-04	Bjorkloven U18	Swe-U18	10	0	3	3	14	....	....	....	....	....
2004-05	Bjorkloven U18	Swe-U18	STATISTICS NOT AVAILABLE									
	Bjorkloven Jr.	Swe-Jr.	3	1	0	1	8	....	....	....	....	....
2005-06	Bjorkloven Jr.	Swe-Jr.	40	3	10	13	78	6	3	2	5	37
	IF Bjorkloven Umea	Sweden-2	6	0	0	0	4	....	....	....	....	....
2006-07	Bjorkloven Jr.	Swe-Jr.	8	0	2	2	18	....	....	....	....	....
	Manitoba Moose	AHL	1	0	0	0	0	4	0	0	0	2
	IF Bjorkloven Umea	Sweden-2	43	0	3	3	112	6	0	0	0	6

RAKHSHANI, Rhett (rahk-SHAH-nee, REHT) NYI

Right wing. Shoots right. 5'10", 170 lbs. Born, Orange, CA, March 6, 1988.
(NY Islanders' 4th choice, 100th overall, in 2006 Entry Draft).

			Regular Season					Playoffs				
Season	Club	League	GP	G	A	Pts	PIM	GP	G	A	Pts	PIM
2003-04	California Wave	Cal-Am	56	54	67	121	....	....	....	....	....	....
2004-05	USNTDP	U-17	14	6	5	11	32	....	....	....	....	....
	USNTDP	NAHL	40	12	15	27	21	9	1	4	5	2
2005-06	USNTDP	U-18	43	11	12	23	30	....	....	....	....	....
	USNTDP	NAHL	16	13	13	26	35	....	....	....	....	....
2006-07	U. of Denver	WCHA	40	10	26	36	38	....	....	....	....	....

RAMHOLT, Tim (RAM-hohlt, TIHM) CGY.

Defense. Shoots left. 6'2", 193 lbs. Born, Zurich, Switz., November 2, 1984.
(Calgary's 2nd choice, 39th overall, in 2003 Entry Draft).

			Regular Season					Playoffs				
Season	Club	League	GP	G	A	Pts	PIM	GP	G	A	Pts	PIM
99-2000	Zurich/Kusn Jr.	Swiss-Jr.	35	2	9	11	26	4	0	2	2	4
	Grasshopper	Swiss-2	2	0	0	0	0	....	....	....	....	....
2000-01	GC Zurich	Swiss-2	37	0	2	2	38	3	0	0	0	4
	GC Zurich Jr.	Swiss-Jr.	17	3	6	9	10	....	....	....	....	....
2001-02	ZSC Lions Zurich	Swiss	37	3	0	3	14	17	0	3	3	2
	GCK/ZSC Zurich Jr.	Swiss-Jr.	5	2	2	4	4	....	....	....	....	....
	GC Zurich	Swiss-2	3	0	0	0	0	....	....	....	....	....
2002-03	ZSC Lions Zurich	Swiss	30	2	0	2	12	9	0	1	1	0
	GC Zurich	Swiss-2	12	0	4	4	6	....	....	....	....	....
2003-04	Cape Breton	QMJHL	51	9	27	36	26	5	0	1	1	4
2004-05	ZSC Lions Zurich	Swiss	41	1	3	4	38	15	0	0	0	10
2005-06	Kloten Flyers	Swiss	42	0	1	1	48	11	0	1	1	8
2006-07	Omaha	AHL	67	2	10	12	61	6	0	1	1	10

RATCHUK, Michael (RAT-chuhk, MIGH-kuhl) PHI.

Defense. Shoots left. 5'10", 180 lbs. Born, Buffalo, NY, February 20, 1988.
(Philadelphia's 3rd choice, 42nd overall, in 2006 Entry Draft).

			Regular Season					Playoffs				
Season	Club	League	GP	G	A	Pts	PIM	GP	G	A	Pts	PIM
2004-05	USNTDP	U-17	15	1	4	5	16	....	....	....	....	....
	USNTDP	NAHL	33	3	6	9	14	10	1	1	2	2
2005-06	USNTDP	U-18	39	8	14	22	52	....	....	....	....	....
	USNTDP	NAHL	16	4	4	8	4	....	....	....	....	....
2006-07	Michigan State	CCHA	40	4	8	12	28	....	....	....	....	....

RAU, Chad (ROW, CHAD) TOR.

Center. Shoots right. 5'11", 185 lbs. Born, Eden Prairie, MN, January 18, 1987.
(Toronto's 6th choice, 228th overall, in 2005 Entry Draft).

			Regular Season					Playoffs				
Season	Club	League	GP	G	A	Pts	PIM	GP	G	A	Pts	PIM
2004-05	Des Moines	USHL	57	31	40	71	32	....	....	....	....	....
2005-06	Colorado College	WCHA	42	13	17	30	8	....	....	....	....	....
2006-07	Colorado College	WCHA	39	14	17	31	4	....	....	....	....	....

USHL All-Rookie Team (2005) • USHL First All-Star Team (2005) • USHL Rookie of the Year (2005)

RAYMOND, Mason (RAY-muhnd, MAY-sohn) VAN.

Left wing. Shoots left. 6', 165 lbs. Born, Cochrane, Alta., September 17, 1985.
(Vancouver's 2nd choice, 51st overall, in 2005 Entry Draft).

			Regular Season					Playoffs				
Season	Club	League	GP	G	A	Pts	PIM	GP	G	A	Pts	PIM
2003-04	Camrose Kodiaks	AJHL	....	27	35	62	....	....	....	....	....	....
2004-05	Camrose Kodiaks	AJHL	55	*41	41	82	80	15	8	*12	20	....
2005-06	U. Minn-Duluth	WCHA	40	11	17	28	30	....	....	....	....	....
2006-07	U. Minn-Duluth	WCHA	39	14	32	46	45	....	....	....	....	....
	Manitoba Moose	AHL	11	2	2	4	6	13	0	1	1	0

AJHL MVP (2005) • WCHA All-Rookie Team (2006) • WCHA First All-Star Team (2007)

REAVES, Ryan (REEVZ, RIGH-uhn) ST.L.

Right wing. Shoots right. 6'1", 193 lbs. Born, Winnipeg, Man., January 20, 1987.
(St. Louis' 4th choice, 156th overall, in 2005 Entry Draft).

			Regular Season					Playoffs				
Season	Club	League	GP	G	A	Pts	PIM	GP	G	A	Pts	PIM
2004-05	Brandon	WHL	64	7	9	16	79	23	2	4	6	43
2005-06	Brandon	WHL	68	14	14	28	91	6	0	1	1	8
2006-07	Brandon	WHL	69	15	20	35	76	11	1	4	5	19

REDDOX, Liam (REH-dawks, LEE-uhm) EDM.

Left wing. Shoots left. 5'10", 177 lbs. Born, East York, Ont., January 27, 1986.
(Edmonton's 5th choice, 112th overall, in 2004 Entry Draft).

			Regular Season					Playoffs				
Season	Club	League	GP	G	A	Pts	PIM	GP	G	A	Pts	PIM
2002-03	Wellington Dukes	OPJHL	45	32	32	64	29	....	....	....	....	....
	Peterborough	OHL	4	0	0	0	0	....	....	....	....	....
2003-04	Peterborough	OHL	68	31	33	64	24					
2004-05	Peterborough	OHL	68	36	46	82	38	14	3	10	13	10
2005-06	Peterborough	OHL	68	19	45	64	74	19	5	9	14	20
2006-07	Stockton Thunder	ECHL	70	8	18	26	49	6	2	1	3	4

OHL All-Rookie Team (2004)

REDENBACH, Tyler (REH-dehn-bak, TIGH-luhr) PHX.

Center. Shoots left. 6', 195 lbs. Born, Melville, Sask., September 25, 1984.
(Phoenix's 1st choice, 77th overall, in 2003 Entry Draft).

			Regular Season					Playoffs				
Season	Club	League	GP	G	A	Pts	PIM	GP	G	A	Pts	PIM
2000-01	North Kamloops	BCAHA	49	60	66	126	22	....	....	....	....	....
2001-02	Prince George	WHL	65	3	18	21	30	7	0	1	1	2
2002-03	Prince George	WHL	36	8	34	42	29	....	....	....	....	....
	Swift Current	WHL	24	9	17	26	6	4	0	4	4	4
2003-04	Swift Current	WHL	71	31	*74	*105	52	5	1	1	2	14
2004-05	Swift Current	WHL	42	14	23	37	49	....	....	....	....	....
	Lethbridge	WHL	23	5	21	26	14	5	0	2	2	6
2005-06	Providence Bruins	AHL	78	26	32	58	42	6	1	2	3	37
2006-07	Providence Bruins	AHL	13	0	5	5	6	....	....	....	....	....
	San Antonio	AHL	30	6	14	20	12	....	....	....	....	....
	Phoenix	ECHL	7	0	4	4	0	....	....	....	....	....

WHL East Second All-Star Team (2004)

Signed as a free agent by **Boston**, September 7, 2005. Traded to **Phoenix** by **Boston** for Philippe Sauve, November 14, 2006.

REDLIHS, Jekabs (REHD-lihs, YEH-kabs)

Defense. Shoots left. 6'2", 185 lbs. Born, Riga, USSR, March 29, 1982.
(Columbus' 6th choice, 119th overall, in 2002 Entry Draft).

			Regular Season					Playoffs				
Season	Club	League	GP	G	A	Pts	PIM	GP	G	A	Pts	PIM
1998-99	Dynamo Riga 18	Latvia-Jr.	STATISTICS NOT AVAILABLE									
99-2000	HC Essamika Jr.	EEHL	16	1	4	5	6	....	....	....	....	....
	Metalurgs Liepaja	Latvia	1	0	0	0	0	....	....	....	....	....
	Metalurgs Liepaja	EEHL	11	0	0	0	2	....	....	....	....	....
2000-01	Metalurgs Liepaja	EEHL	31	1	3	4	....	....	....	....	....	....
	Metalurgs Liepaja	Latvia	23	4	5	9	....	....	....	....	....	....
2001-02	NY Apple Core	EJHL	38	3	16	19	24	....	....	....	....	....
2002-03	Boston University	H-East	40	4	12	16	12	....	....	....	....	....
2003-04	Boston University	H-East	23	2	4	6	53	....	....	....	....	....
2004-05	Boston University	H-East	40	1	0	1	32	....	....	....	....	....
2005-06	Boston University	H-East	27	1	5	6	34	....	....	....	....	....
	Syracuse Crunch	AHL	4	0	0	0	6	....	....	....	....	....
2006-07	Syracuse Crunch	AHL	46	3	9	12	42	....	....	....	....	....
	Dayton Bombers	ECHL	7	0	1	1	4	....	....	....	....	....

Hockey East All-Rookie Team (2003)

REED, Harrison (REED, HAIR-rih-suhn) CAR.

Center/Right wing. Shoots right. 6'1", 185 lbs. Born, Newmarket, Ont., January 18, 1988.
(Carolina's 2nd choice, 93rd overall, in 2006 Entry Draft).

			Regular Season					Playoffs				
Season	Club	League	GP	G	A	Pts	PIM	GP	G	A	Pts	PIM
2004-05	Petrolia Jets	OJHL-B	43	11	18	29	43	....	....	....	....	....
	London Knights	OHL	6	0	0	0	0	4	0	1	1	0
2005-06	Sarnia Sting	OHL	68	26	24	50	50	....	....	....	....	....
2006-07	Sarnia Sting	OHL	67	29	52	81	30	4	0	4	4	8

REESE, Dylan (REES, DIH-luhn)

Defense. Shoots right. 6', 205 lbs. Born, Pittsburgh, PA, August 29, 1984.
(NY Rangers' 9th choice, 209th overall, in 2003 Entry Draft).

			Regular Season					Playoffs				
Season	Club	League	GP	G	A	Pts	PIM	GP	G	A	Pts	PIM
2000-01	Pittsburgh Hornets	MWEHL	66	14	42	66	....	....	....	....	....	....
2001-02	Pittsburgh Forge	NAHL	48	7	16	23	70	7	0	2	2	4
2002-03	Pittsburgh Forge	NAHL	56	11	30	41	98	5	2	3	5	6
2003-04	Harvard Crimson	ECAC	21	1	4	5	18	....	....	....	....	....
2004-05	Harvard Crimson	ECACHL	34	7	12	19	44	....	....	....	....	....
2005-06	Harvard Crimson	ECACHL	33	4	15	19	36	....	....	....	....	....
2006-07	Harvard Crimson	ECACHL	33	9	9	18	26	....	....	....	....	....
	Hartford Wolf Pack	AHL	10	0	4	4	12	2	0	0	0	2

ECACHL Second All-Star Team (2006, 2007)

REGIN, Peter (REE-gihn, PEE-tuhr) OTT.

Center. Shoots left. 6'1", 185 lbs. Born, Herning, Denmark, April 16, 1986.
(Ottawa's 4th choice, 87th overall, in 2004 Entry Draft).

			Regular Season					Playoffs				
Season	Club	League	GP	G	A	Pts	PIM	GP	G	A	Pts	PIM
2002-03	Herning IK	Denmark	24	0	1	1	4	10	1	3	4	4
2003-04	Herning IK	Denmark	33	9	11	20	14	....	....	....	....	....
2004-05	Herning Blue Fox	Denmark	36	19	27	46	43	16	5	8	13	2
2005-06	Timra IK	Sweden	44	4	7	11	14	....	....	....	....	....
2006-07	Timra IK	Sweden	51	9	7	16	16	7	2	2	4	2

RENAUD, Mickey (RAY-noh, MIH-kee) CGY.

Center. Shoots left. 6'2", 217 lbs. Born, Tecumseh, Ont., October 5, 1988.
(Calgary's 4th choice, 143rd overall, in 2007 Entry Draft).

			Regular Season					Playoffs				
Season	Club	League	GP	G	A	Pts	PIM	GP	G	A	Pts	PIM
2004-05	Tecumseh Chiefs	OJHL-B	39	9	14	23	8	....	....	....	....	....
2005-06	Windsor Spitfires	OHL	68	8	18	26	70	7	0	3	3	12
2006-07	Windsor Spitfires	OHL	68	22	32	54	76	....	....	....	....	....

REPIK, Michal (REH-pihk, MEE-khahl) FLA.

Right wing. Shoots right. 5'10", 180 lbs. Born, Vlasim, Czech., December 31, 1988.
(Florida's 2nd choice, 40th overall, in 2007 Entry Draft).

			Regular Season					Playoffs				
Season	Club	League	GP	G	A	Pts	PIM	GP	G	A	Pts	PIM
2002-03	Sparta U17	CzR-U17	18	7	10	17	6	2	0	0	0	0
2003-04	Sparta U17	CzR-U17	33	25	17	42	42	3	0	0	0	0
	Sparta Jr.	CzRep-Jr.	23	12	5	17	10	....	....	....	....	....
2004-05	Sparta U17	CzR-U17	2	2	3	5	6	....	....	....	....	....
	Sparta Jr.	CzRep-Jr.	45	26	31	57	24	8	2	4	6	10
2005-06	Vancouver Giants	WHL	69	24	28	52	55	14	3	3	6	19
2006-07	Vancouver Giants	WHL	56	24	31	55	56	22	10	*16	*26	24

Memorial Cup Tournament All-Star Team (2007) • Ed Chynoweth Trophy (Memorial Cup Tournament Leading Scorer) (2007)

REUL, Denis (ROIL, DEH-nihs) BOS.

Defense. Shoots right. 6'5", 215 lbs. Born, Marktredwitz, West Germany, June 29, 1989.
(Boston's 3rd choice, 130th overall, in 2007 Entry Draft).

			Regular Season					Playoffs				
Season	Club	League	GP	G	A	Pts	PIM	GP	G	A	Pts	PIM
2004-05	Mannheimer ERC	German-5	1	0	0	0	0	....	....	....	....	....
	Mannheim Jr.	Ger-Jr.	34	0	3	3	18	7	1	0	1	12
2005-06	Mannheim Jr.	Ger-Jr.	36	6	13	19	40	5	0	1	1	4
2006-07	Heilbronner Falken	German-3	16	0	1	1	16	....	....	....	....	....
	Heil./Mann. Jr.	Ger-Jr.	34	9	17	26	82	6	0	1	1	16

REYNOLDS, T.J. EDM.

Defense. Shoots right. 6'2", 225 lbs. Born, Kitchener, Ont., March 26, 1981.

			Regular Season					Playoffs				
Season	Club	League	GP	G	A	Pts	PIM	GP	G	A	Pts	PIM
1998-99	Oshawa Generals	OHL	17	0	1	1	27	1	0	0	0	5
99-2000	Oshawa Generals	OHL	59	1	6	7	115	5	0	1	1	16
2000-01	Oshawa Generals	OHL	2	0	1	1	5	....	....	....	....	....
	St. Michael's	OHL	50	1	3	4	163	18	0	3	3	70
2001-02	St. Michael's	OHL	8	0	1	1	27	....	....	....	....	....
	Mississauga	OHL	38	1	8	9	113	....	....	....	....	....
2002-03	Wheeling Nailers	ECHL	71	2	8	10	371	....	....	....	....	....
2003-04	Wilkes-Barre	AHL	4	0	0	0	7	....	....	....	....	....
	Wheeling Nailers	ECHL	66	4	16	20	247	5	0	1	1	4
2004-05	San Antonio	AHL	32	0	1	1	191	....	....	....	....	....
	Wheeling Nailers	ECHL	14	1	1	2	51	....	....	....	....	....
2005-06	Milwaukee	AHL	50	0	2	2	130	....	....	....	....	....
	Rockford IceHogs	UHL	3	1	2	3	26	....	....	....	....	....
2006-07	Milwaukee	AHL	42	0	1	1	93	3	0	0	0	0
	Rockford IceHogs	UHL	2	0	0	0	2	....	....	....	....	....

Signed as a free agent by **Milwaukee** (AHL), August 25, 2005. Signed as a free agent by **Edmonton**, July 17, 2007.

RHEAULT, Jonathan (RAY-oh, JAWN-ah-thuhn) PHI.

Right wing. Shoots right. 5'10", 190 lbs. Born, Arlington, TX, August 1, 1986.
(Philadelphia's 8th choice, 145th overall, in 2006 Entry Draft).

			Regular Season					Playoffs				
Season	Club	League	GP	G	A	Pts	PIM	GP	G	A	Pts	PIM
2003-04	N.H. Jr. Monarchs	EJHL	....	49	46	*95	....	....	....	....	....	....
2004-05	Providence College	H-East	36	11	8	19	36	....	....	....	....	....
2005-06	Providence College	H-East	35	16	14	30	29	....	....	....	....	....
2006-07	Providence College	H-East	35	12	13	25	38	....	....	....	....	....

RICHTER, Martin (RIHKH-tuhr, MAHR-tihn)

Defense. Shoots right. 6'1", 205 lbs. Born, Prostejov, Czech., December 6, 1977.
(NY Rangers' 9th choice, 269th overall, in 2000 Entry Draft).

			Regular Season					Playoffs				
Season	Club	League	GP	G	A	Pts	PIM	GP	G	A	Pts	PIM
1995-96	HC Olomouc	CzRep	3	0	0	0	0	1	0	0	0	0
1996-97	HC Olomouc	CzRep	27	1	0	1	26	....	....	....	....	....
1997-98	Karlovy Vary	CzRep	42	1	2	3	32	....	....	....	....	....
1998-99	Karlovy Vary	CzRep	51	3	6	9	44	....	....	....	....	....
99-2000	Karlovy Vary	CzRep	24	0	5	5	18	....	....	....	....	....
	SaiPa	Finland	26	1	3	4	54	....	....	....	....	....
2000-01	SaiPa	Finland	41	4	5	9	80	....	....	....	....	....
	Hartford Wolf Pack	AHL	1	0	0	0	0	....	....	....	....	....
2001-02	Hartford Wolf Pack	AHL	29	1	1	2	36	....	....	....	....	....
	HC Sparta Praha	CzRep	8	0	0	0	14	13	0	0	0	10
2002-03	HC Sparta Praha	CzRep	34	2	7	9	77	8	0	0	0	10
2003-04	HC Sparta Praha	CzRep	16	2	2	4	16	....	....	....	....	....
	CSKA Moscow	Russia	14	0	0	0	33	....	....	....	....	....
2004-05	HC Sparta Praha	CzRep	44	4	9	13	32	5	1	1	2	4
2005-06	Liberec	CzRep	47	6	20	26	64	5	0	1	1	8
2006-07	Hartford Wolf Pack	AHL	52	2	6	8	46	....	....	....	....	....

RIDDLE, Troy (RIH-duhl, TROI)

Center. Shoots right. 5'10", 175 lbs. Born, Minneapolis, MN, August 24, 1981.
(St. Louis' 5th choice, 129th overall, in 2000 Entry Draft).

			Regular Season					Playoffs				
Season	Club	League	GP	G	A	Pts	PIM	GP	G	A	Pts	PIM
1997-98	St. Margaret's	High-MN	29	33	35	68	....	....	....	....	....	....
1998-99	St. Margaret's	High-MN	29	54	45	99	....	....	....	....	....	....
99-2000	Des Moines	USHL	53	36	30	66	95	8	2	2	4	31
2000-01	U. of Minnesota	WCHA	38	16	14	30	49	....	....	....	....	....
2001-02	U. of Minnesota	WCHA	44	16	31	47	46	....	....	....	....	....
2002-03	U. of Minnesota	WCHA	45	26	26	52	50	....	....	....	....	....
2003-04	U. of Minnesota	WCHA	44	24	25	49	52	....	....	....	....	....
2004-05	Worcester IceCats	AHL	42	9	6	15	35	....	....	....	....	....
	Peoria Rivermen	ECHL	14	4	8	12	16	....	....	....	....	....
2005-06	Peoria Rivermen	AHL	55	11	11	22	47	....	....	....	....	....
	Alaska Aces	ECHL	7	2	2	4	6	21	4	3	7	28
2006-07	Philadelphia	AHL	3	0	0	0	0	....	....	....	....	....
	Trenton Titans	ECHL	68	28	37	65	60	5	3	2	5	10

USHL Second All-Star Team (2000) • USHL Rookie of the Year (2000)

RITOLA, Mattias (RIH-toh-lah, mat-TEE-uhs) DET.

Right wing. Shoots left. 6', 192 lbs. Born, Borlange, Sweden, March 14, 1987.
(Detroit's 4th choice, 103rd overall, in 2005 Entry Draft).

			Regular Season					Playoffs				
Season	Club	League	GP	G	A	Pts	PIM	GP	G	A	Pts	PIM
2003-04	V.Frolunda U18	Swe-U18	11	4	11	15	35	7	2	7	9	12
	V.Frolunda Jr.	Swe-Jr.	24	7	4	11	8	5	0	1	1	0
2004-05	Frolunda Jr.	Swe-Jr.	9	2	6	8	6	....	....	....	....	....
	Leksands IF U18	Swe-U18	STATISTICS NOT AVAILABLE									
	Leksands IF Jr.	Swe-Jr.	18	8	10	18	14	5	1	1	2	2
2005-06	Leksands IF Jr.	Swe-Jr.	14	4	2	6	16	....	....	....	....	....
	Leksands IF	Sweden	30	0	3	3	10	....	....	....	....	....
	Leksands IF	Sweden-Q	8	0	0	0	4	....	....	....	....	....
2006-07	Leksands IF Jr.	Swe-Jr.	12	5	7	12	16	....	....	....	....	....
	Leksands IF	Sweden-2	23	1	4	5	4	....	....	....	....	....
	IFK Arboga IK	Sweden-2	3	1	0	1	2	....	....	....	....	....
	Borlange HF	Sweden-3	11	4	6	10	14	....	....	....	....	....

ROBERTSON, Josh (RAW-buhrt-suhn, JAWSH) WSH.

Center. Shoots right. 5'11", 186 lbs. Born, Whitman, MA, August 25, 1984.
(Washington's 4th choice, 155th overall, in 2003 Entry Draft).

			Regular Season					Playoffs				
Season	Club	League	GP	G	A	Pts	PIM	GP	G	A	Pts	PIM
2000-01	Whitman-Hanson	High-MA	28	30	28	58	....	....	....	....	....	....
2001-02	Whitman-Hanson	High-MA	30	50	55	105	....	....	....	....	....	....
2002-03	Proctor	High-NH	34	37	44	81	....	....	....	....	....	....
2003-04	Proctor	High-NH	20	23	37	60	....	....	....	....	....	....
2004-05	Northeastern	H-East	22	4	3	7	0	....	....	....	....	....
2005-06	Northeastern	H-East	21	1	9	10	0	....	....	....	....	....
2006-07	Northeastern	H-East	DID NOT PLAY									

ROBINS, Bobby (RAW-bihns, BAW-bee)

Right wing. Shoots right. 6'1", 220 lbs. Born, Peshtigo, WI, October 17, 1981.

			Regular Season					Playoffs				
Season	Club	League	GP	G	A	Pts	PIM	GP	G	A	Pts	PIM
2001-02	Tri-City Storm	USHL	60	16	14	30	176	....	....	....	....	....
2002-03	U. Mass-Lowell	H-East	26	5	3	8	24	....	....	....	....	....
2003-04	U. Mass-Lowell	H-East	32	5	7	12	49	....	....	....	....	....
2004-05	U. Mass-Lowell	H-East	34	9	9	18	86	....	....	....	....	....
2005-06	U. Mass-Lowell	H-East	35	13	18	31	*94	....	....	....	....	....
	Binghamton	AHL	16	4	3	7	19	....	....	....	....	....
2006-07	Binghamton	AHL	80	7	8	15	110	....	....	....	....	....

Signed as a free agent by **Ottawa**, July 13, 2006.

ROGERS, Andy (RAW-juhrs, AN-dee) T.B.

Defense. Shoots left. 6'5", 206 lbs. Born, Calgary, Alta., August 25, 1986.
(Tampa Bay's 1st choice, 30th overall, in 2004 Entry Draft).

			Regular Season					Playoffs				
Season	Club	League	GP	G	A	Pts	PIM	GP	G	A	Pts	PIM
2000-01	Calgary AA Gold	CMHA	32	2	7	9	32	....	....	....	....	....
2001-02	Calgary AAA Gold	CBHL	30	1	13	14	80	....	....	....	....	....
2002-03	Calgary Hitmen	WHL	25	0	3	3	17	....	....	....	....	....
2003-04	Calgary Hitmen	WHL	64	1	3	4	89	7	0	0	0	11
2004-05	Calgary Hitmen	WHL	18	1	4	5	36	....	....	....	....	....
	Prince George	WHL	30	1	5	6	49	....	....	....	....	....
2005-06	Prince George	WHL	21	0	3	3	51	....	....	....	....	....
2006-07	Springfield Falcons	AHL	48	0	7	7	39	....	....	....	....	....

ROGERS, Doug (RAW-juhrs, DUHG) NYI

Center. Shoots right. 6', 175 lbs. Born, Watertown, MA, January 20, 1988.
(NY Islanders' 7th choice, 119th overall, in 2006 Entry Draft).

			Regular Season					Playoffs				
Season	Club	League	GP	G	A	Pts	PIM	GP	G	A	Pts	PIM
2003-04	St. Sebastian's	High-MA	28	24	24	48	....	....	....	....	....	....
2004-05	St. Sebastian's	High-MA	28	17	26	43	....	....	....	....	....	....
2005-06	St. Sebastian's	High-MA	28	24	38	62	20	....	....	....	....	....
2006-07	Harvard Crimson	ECACHL	33	7	17	24	18	....	....	....	....	....

ROHLFS, David (ROHLFS, DAY-vihd) EDM.

Right wing. Shoots right. 6'3", 219 lbs. Born, Ann Arbor, MI, June 4, 1984.
(Edmonton's 7th choice, 154th overall, in 2003 Entry Draft).

			Regular Season					Playoffs				
Season	Club	League	GP	G	A	Pts	PIM	GP	G	A	Pts	PIM
2000-01	Det. Compuware	MWEHL	70	35	21	56	....	....	....	....	....	....
	Det. Compuware	NAHL	4	0	1	1	0	....	....	....	....	....
2001-02	Det. Compuware	NAHL	60	13	10	23	36	....	....	....	....	....
2002-03	Det. Compuware	NAHL	53	30	14	44	36	5	2	1	3	8
2003-04	U. of Michigan	CCHA	43	7	6	13	26	....	....	....	....	....
2004-05	U. of Michigan	CCHA	34	5	5	10	14	....	....	....	....	....
2005-06	U. of Michigan	CCHA	40	2	10	12	43	....	....	....	....	....
2006-07	U. of Michigan	CCHA	41	17	17	34	30	....	....	....	....	....

ROMAN, Ondrej (ROH-mahn, AWN-dray) DAL.

Center. Shoots left. 6', 168 lbs. Born, Ostrava, Czech., April 8, 1989.
(Dallas' 6th choice, 136th overall, in 2007 Entry Draft).

			Regular Season					Playoffs				
Season	Club	League	GP	G	A	Pts	PIM	GP	G	A	Pts	PIM
2002-03	HC Ostrava U17	CzR-U17	6	1	1	2	0	....	....	....	....	....
2003-04	HC Ostrava U17	CzR-U17	55	38	27	65	61	....	....	....	....	....
2004-05	HC Ostrava U17	CzR-U17	8	8	16	24	22	....	....	....	....	....
	HC Ostrava Jr.	CzRep-Jr.	7	2	2	4	6	....	....	....	....	....
	HC Vitkovice U17	CzR-U17	2	0	3	3	2	....	....	....	....	....
	HC Vitkovice Jr.	CzRep-Jr.	30	8	3	11	12	....	....	....	....	....
2005-06	HC Vitkovice U17	CzR-U17	....	....	....	....	....	4	1	8	9	0
	HC Vitkovice Jr.	CzRep-Jr.	46	17	27	44	42	5	0	3	3	4
	HC Vitkovice Steel	CzRep	1	0	0	0	0	....	....	....	....	....
2006-07	Spokane Chiefs	WHL	70	4	44	48	42	6	1	4	5	0

ROMANO, Tony (roh-MAHN-oh, TOH-nee) N.J.

Center. Shoots right. 5'11", 185 lbs. Born, Smithtown, NY, January 5, 1988.
(New Jersey's 7th choice, 178th overall, in 2006 Entry Draft).

			Regular Season					Playoffs				
Season	Club	League	GP	G	A	Pts	PIM	GP	G	A	Pts	PIM
2004-05	New York Bobcats	AtJHL	....	47	54	101	....	....	....	....	....	....
2005-06	New York Bobcats	AtJHL	40	*50	52	*102	38	....	....	....	....	....
2006-07	Cornell Big Red	ECACHL	29	9	10	19	18	....	....	....	....	....

ROME, Ashton (ROHM, ASH-tuhn) S.J.

Right wing. Shoots right. 6'1", 205 lbs. Born, Nesbitt, Man., December 31, 1985.
(San Jose's 4th choice, 143rd overall, in 2006 Entry Draft).

			Regular Season					Playoffs				
Season	Club	League	GP	G	A	Pts	PIM	GP	G	A	Pts	PIM
2002-03	Moose Jaw	WHL	61	5	10	15	103	13	1	1	2	6
2003-04	Moose Jaw	WHL	72	15	22	37	139	10	6	2	8	18
2004-05	Moose Jaw	WHL	41	10	17	27	84	....	....	....	....	....
	Red Deer Rebels	WHL	31	9	10	19	39	7	3	1	4	14
2005-06	Red Deer Rebels	WHL	14	11	6	17	27	....	....	....	....	....
	Kamloops Blazers	WHL	51	19	28	47	103	....	....	....	....	....
2006-07	Worcester Sharks	AHL	65	8	3	11	63	6	1	0	1	2

• Re-entered NHL Entry Draft. Originally Boston's 3rd choice, 108th overall, in 2004 Entry Draft.

ROSEHILL, Jay (ROHZ-hihl, JAY) T.B.

Defense. Shoots left. 6'3", 195 lbs. Born, Olds, Alta., July 16, 1985.
(Tampa Bay's 6th choice, 227th overall, in 2003 Entry Draft).

			Regular Season					Playoffs				
Season	Club	League	GP	G	A	Pts	PIM	GP	G	A	Pts	PIM
2002-03	Olds Grizzlys	AJHL	59	1	4	5	219	....	....	....	....	....
2003-04	Olds Grizzlys	AJHL	42	4	12	16	172	14	2	2	4	....
2004-05	U. Minn-Duluth	WCHA	34	0	5	5	103	....	....	....	....	....
2005-06	Springfield Falcons	AHL	45	1	2	3	68	....	....	....	....	....
	Johnstown Chiefs	ECHL	5	0	0	0	13	5	0	0	0	4
2006-07	Springfield Falcons	AHL	64	0	6	6	85	....	....	....	....	....
	Johnstown Chiefs	ECHL	1	0	0	0	2	....	....	....	....	....

ROSS, Nick (RAWS, NIHK) PHX.

Defense. Shoots left. 6'1", 188 lbs. Born, Edmonton, Alta., February 10, 1989.
(Phoenix's 2nd choice, 30th overall, in 2007 Entry Draft).

			Regular Season					Playoffs				
Season	Club	League	GP	G	A	Pts	PIM	GP	G	A	Pts	PIM
2004-05	Lethbridge	AMHL	33	8	20	28	123	....	....	....	....	....
	Regina Pats	WHL	10	0	1	1	2	....	....	....	....	....
2005-06	Regina Pats	WHL	62	7	16	23	38	6	0	1	1	2
2006-07	Regina Pats	WHL	70	7	24	31	87	10	1	5	6	14

ROUSSIN, Dany (roo-SEH, DA-nee) L.A.

Center. Shoots left. 6'2", 190 lbs. Born, Quebec City, Que., January 9, 1985.
(Los Angeles' 2nd choice, 50th overall, in 2005 Entry Draft).

			Regular Season					Playoffs				
Season	Club	League	GP	G	A	Pts	PIM	GP	G	A	Pts	PIM
2000-01	Ste-Foy	QAAA	38	27	27	54	42	16	8	13	21	16
2001-02	Sherbrooke	QMJHL	66	10	14	24	38	....	....	....	....	....
2002-03	Sherbrooke	QMJHL	33	8	8	16	18	....	....	....	....	....
	Rimouski Oceanic	QMJHL	38	12	26	38	69	....	....	....	....	....
2003-04	Rimouski Oceanic	QMJHL	66	*59	58	117	70	9	2	10	12	12
2004-05	Rimouski Oceanic	QMJHL	69	54	62	116	66	13	11	9	20	8
2005-06	Manchester	AHL	29	4	2	6	24	3	1	1	2	0
	Reading Royals	ECHL	41	22	23	45	14	1	0	1	1	0
2006-07	Manchester	AHL	15	4	2	6	9	....	....	....	....	....
	Reading Royals	ECHL	47	8	17	25	24	....	....	....	....	....

• Re-entered NHL Entry Draft. Originally Florida's 10th choice, 223rd overall, in 2003 Entry Draft.
QMJHL First All-Star Team (2004) • QMJHL Second All-Star Team (2005)

RUDENKO, Konstantin (roo-DEHN-koh, KAWN-stan-tihn) PHI.

Left wing. Shoots right. 5'11", 180 lbs. Born, Ust-Kamenogorsk, USSR, July 23, 1981.
(Philadelphia's 3rd choice, 160th overall, in 1999 Entry Draft).

			Regular Season					Playoffs				
Season	Club	League	GP	G	A	Pts	PIM	GP	G	A	Pts	PIM
1997-98	Omsk 2	Russia-3	22	7	8	15	4	....	....	....	....	....
1998-99	Cherepovets	Russia	28	15	9	24	67	....	....	....	....	....
	Cherepovets 2	Russia-3	3	0	1	1	4	....	....	....	....	....
99-2000	St. Petersburg 2	Russia-3	7	2	4	6	2	....	....	....	....	....
	SKA St. Petersburg	Russia	19	1	1	2	10	1	0	0	0	0
2000-01	Yaroslavl	Russia	18	2	3	5	28	9	2	1	3	8
2001-02	Yaroslavl 2	Russia-3	2	1	1	2	2	....	....	....	....	....
	Yaroslavl	Russia	8	0	2	2	12	1	0	0	0	0
2002-03	Yaroslavl	Russia	20	3	4	7	20	2	0	0	0	0
2003-04	Yaroslavl 2	Russia-3	4	4	2	6	4	....	....	....	....	....
	Yaroslavl	Russia	43	10	12	22	18	3	0	0	0	0
2004-05	Yaroslavl 2	Russia-3	20	13	14	27	42	....	....	....	....	....
	Yaroslavl	Russia	21	1	0	1	8	2	0	0	0	0
2005-06	Yaroslavl	Russia	49	11	17	28	55	11	1	2	3	0
2006-07	Yaroslavl	Russia	35	11	8	19	30	7	2	2	4	6

RUEGSEGGER, Tyler (ROOG-suh-guhr, TIGH-luhr) **TOR.**

Center. Shoots right. 5'11", 170 lbs. Born, Denver, CO, January 19, 1988.
(Toronto's 6th choice, 166th overall, in 2006 Entry Draft).

			Regular Season					Playoffs				
Season	Club	League	GP	G	A	Pts	PIM	GP	G	A	Pts	PIM
2004-05	Shat.-St. Mary's	High-MN	69	26	54	80	30	....	....	....	....	....
2005-06	Shat.-St. Mary's	High-MN	60	38	51	89	70	....	....	....	....	....
2006-07	U. of Denver	WCHA	40	15	19	34	25	....	....	....	....	....

RUFENACH, Bryan (RUHF-ehn-ak, BRIGH-uhn) **DET.**

Defense. Shoots left. 5'11", 184 lbs. Born, Cameron, Ont., April 15, 1989.
(Detroit's 5th choice, 208th overall, in 2007 Entry Draft).

			Regular Season					Playoffs				
Season	Club	League	GP	G	A	Pts	PIM	GP	G	A	Pts	PIM
2005-06	Lindsay Muskies	OPJHL	48	11	15	26	50	4	1	1	2	6
2006-07	Lindsay Muskies	OPJHL	31	11	21	32	28	5	1	2	3	8

RUGGERI, Rosario (ROO-zhee-AIR-ee, roh-ZAHR-ee-oh)

Defense. Shoots left. 6'1", 202 lbs. Born, Montreal, Que., June 8, 1984.
(Philadelphia's 2nd choice, 105th overall, in 2002 Entry Draft).

			Regular Season					Playoffs				
Season	Club	League	GP	G	A	Pts	PIM	GP	G	A	Pts	PIM
99-2000	Lac St-Louis Lions	QAAA	40	0	7	7	70	....	....	....	....	....
2000-01	Lac St-Louis Lions	QAAA	24	6	11	17	117	5	1	3	4	4
	Montreal Rocket	QMJHL	9	0	0	0	8	....	....	....	....	....
2001-02	Chicoutimi	QMJHL	60	2	15	17	131	4	1	1	2	10
2002-03	Chicoutimi	QMJHL	70	10	37	47	64	3	0	0	0	21
2003-04	Chicoutimi	QMJHL	65	12	36	48	98	18	2	2	4	28
2004-05	Philadelphia	AHL	5	0	0	0	0	....	....	....	....	....
	Trenton Titans	ECHL	49	2	12	14	77	20	0	2	2	26
2005-06	Philadelphia	AHL	2	0	0	0	2	....	....	....	....	....
	Trenton Titans	ECHL	32	2	8	10	28	....	....	....	....	....
2006-07	Philadelphia	AHL	15	0	2	2	0	....	....	....	....	....
	Trenton Titans	ECHL	49	4	25	29	46	5	0	0	0	6

RULLIER, Joe (ROO-yay, JOH)

Defense. Shoots right. 6'3", 230 lbs. Born, Montreal, Que., January 28, 1980.
(Los Angeles' 5th choice, 133rd overall, in 1998 Entry Draft).

			Regular Season					Playoffs				
Season	Club	League	GP	G	A	Pts	PIM	GP	G	A	Pts	PIM
1996-97	Montreal-Bourassa	QAAA	24	5	10	15	....	....	....	....	....	....
	Rimouski Oceanic	QMJHL	23	0	3	3	87	4	0	0	0	11
1997-98	Rimouski Oceanic	QMJHL	55	1	10	11	176	16	1	4	5	34
1998-99	Rimouski Oceanic	QMJHL	54	7	32	39	202	11	2	3	5	26
99-2000	Rimouski Oceanic	QMJHL	49	3	32	35	161	14	1	8	9	34
2000-01	Lowell	AHL	63	1	1	2	162	4	0	1	1	2
2001-02	Manchester	AHL	62	2	2	4	133	3	0	0	0	5
2002-03	Manchester	AHL	62	3	6	9	166	3	0	0	0	2
2003-04	Manchester	AHL	73	3	12	15	186	6	0	0	0	4
2004-05	Manchester	AHL	71	3	13	16	322	6	0	2	2	27
2005-06	Hartford Wolf Pack	AHL	51	6	22	28	123	....	....	....	....	....
	Manchester	AHL	16	2	1	3	37	7	0	3	3	14
2006-07	Manitoba Moose	AHL	24	2	6	8	62	....	....	....	....	....
	Portland Pirates	AHL	6	0	1	1	14	....	....	....	....	....
	Springfield Falcons	AHL	10	0	5	5	18	....	....	....	....	....

Signed as a free agent by **NY Rangers**, August 10, 2005. Signed as a free agent by **Vancouver**, July 24, 2006. Traded to **Anaheim** by **Vancouver** for Colby Genoway, January 24, 2007. Traded to **Tampa Bay** by **Anaheim** for Doug O'Brien, February 27, 2007.

RUSSELL, Kris (RUH-sehl, KRIHS) **CBJ**

Defense. Shoots left. 5'10", 167 lbs. Born, Caroline, Alta., May 2, 1987.
(Columbus' 3rd choice, 67th overall, in 2005 Entry Draft).

			Regular Season					Playoffs				
Season	Club	League	GP	G	A	Pts	PIM	GP	G	A	Pts	PIM
2003-04	Medicine Hat	WHL	55	4	15	19	30	20	3	2	5	4
2004-05	Medicine Hat	WHL	72	26	35	61	37	10	2	1	3	4
2005-06	Medicine Hat	WHL	55	14	33	47	18	13	4	8	12	11
2006-07	Medicine Hat	WHL	59	32	37	69	56	23	4	15	19	24

WHL East Second All-Star Team (2005) • WHL East First All-Star Team (2006, 2007) • WHL Defenseman of the Year (2006) • Canadian Major Junior Sportsman of the Year (2006) • WHL Player of the Year (2007) • Canadian Major Junior Defenseman of the Year (2007)

RUSSELL, Ryan (RUH-sehl, RIGH-uhn) **MTL.**

Center. Shoots left. 5'10", 171 lbs. Born, Caroline, Alta., May 2, 1987.
(NY Rangers' 9th choice, 211th overall, in 2005 Entry Draft).

			Regular Season					Playoffs				
Season	Club	League	GP	G	A	Pts	PIM	GP	G	A	Pts	PIM
2003-04	Kootenay Ice	WHL	67	3	9	12	27	4	0	0	0	0
2004-05	Kootenay Ice	WHL	66	32	21	53	18	16	6	7	13	12
2005-06	Kootenay Ice	WHL	72	33	42	75	30	6	3	5	8	2
2006-07	Kootenay Ice	WHL	58	30	46	76	40	7	3	6	9	2

Traded to **Montreal** by **NY Rangers** for Montreal's 7th round choice (David Skokan) in 2007 Entry Draft, May 31, 2007.

RUST, Matt (RUHST, MAT) **FLA.**

Center. Shoots left. 5'10", 192 lbs. Born, Bloomfield Hills, MI, March 23, 1989.
(Florida's 4th choice, 101st overall, in 2007 Entry Draft).

			Regular Season					Playoffs				
Season	Club	League	GP	G	A	Pts	PIM	GP	G	A	Pts	PIM
2004-05	Det. Honeybaked	MWEHL	50	16	24	40	....	....	....	....	....	....
2005-06	USNTDP	U-17	20	5	5	10	22	....	....	....	....	....
	USNTDP	NAHL	36	9	8	17	36	12	2	0	2	0
2006-07	USNTDP	U-18	36	3	16	19	34	....	....	....	....	....
	USNTDP	NAHL	15	9	6	15	31	....	....	....	....	....

RUTH, Theo (ROOTH, THEE-oh) **WSH.**

Defense. Shoots right. 6'1", 199 lbs. Born, Naperville, IL, February 14, 1989.
(Washington's 3rd choice, 46th overall, in 2007 Entry Draft).

			Regular Season					Playoffs				
Season	Club	League	GP	G	A	Pts	PIM	GP	G	A	Pts	PIM
2004-05	Chicago Mission	MAHL	46	8	8	16	....	....	....	....	....	....
2005-06	USNTDP	U-17	18	2	3	5	22	....	....	....	....	....
	USNTDP	NAHL	36	1	2	3	33	12	0	2	2	8
2006-07	USNTDP	U-18	39	2	6	8	52	....	....	....	....	....
	USNTDP	NAHL	9	3	6	9	14	....	....	....	....	....

RUZICKA, Vladimir (roo-ZHEECH-kuh, vla-DIH-meer) **PHX.**

Center. Shoots left. 6'1", 196 lbs. Born, Most, Czech., February 17, 1989.
(Phoenix's 5th choice, 103rd overall, in 2007 Entry Draft).

			Regular Season					Playoffs				
Season	Club	League	GP	G	A	Pts	PIM	GP	G	A	Pts	PIM
2002-03	Slavia U17	CzR-U17	20	1	5	6	2	1	0	0	0	0
2003-04	Slavia U17	CzR-U17	51	18	35	53	24	7	5	8	13	4
2004-05	Slavia U17	CzR-U17	38	22	39	61	38	6	4	4	8	10
2005-06	Slavia U17	CzR-U17	3	3	6	9	22	6	5	7	12	14
	HC Slavia Praha Jr.	CzRep-Jr.	37	15	26	41	42	1	0	1	1	0
	HC Slavia Praha	CzRep	13	1	1	2	4	....	....	....	....	....
2006-07	HC Slavia Praha Jr.	CzRep-Jr.	37	24	34	58	54	4	1	2	3	4
	HC Slavia Praha	CzRep	3	0	0	0	0	....	....	....	....	....

RYAN, Ben (RIGH-uhn, BEHN) **NSH.**

Center. Shoots right. 5'11", 191 lbs. Born, Detroit, MI, October 16, 1988.
(Nashville's 5th choice, 114th overall, in 2007 Entry Draft).

			Regular Season					Playoffs				
Season	Club	League	GP	G	A	Pts	PIM	GP	G	A	Pts	PIM
2005-06	Des Moines	USHL	60	14	23	37	38	11	4	1	5	4
2006-07	Des Moines	USHL	59	22	42	64	66	8	3	5	8	8

RYAN, Billy (RIGH-uhn, BIHL-lee) **NYR**

Center. Shoots left. 6', 171 lbs. Born, Boston, MA, October 23, 1985.
(NY Rangers' 8th choice, 80th overall, in 2004 Entry Draft).

			Regular Season					Playoffs				
Season	Club	League	GP	G	A	Pts	PIM	GP	G	A	Pts	PIM
2002-03	Cushing	High-MA	29	14	33	47	10	....	....	....	....	....
2003-04	Cushing	High-MA	37	35	55	90	40	....	....	....	....	....
2004-05	U. of Maine	H-East	34	6	9	15	30	....	....	....	....	....
2005-06	U. of Maine	H-East	36	10	18	28	46	....	....	....	....	....
2006-07	U. of Maine	H-East	40	13	20	33	20	....	....	....	....	....

RYAN, Bobby (RIGH-uhn, BAW-bee) **ANA.**

Right wing. Shoots right. 6'1", 213 lbs. Born, Cherry Hill, NJ, March 17, 1987.
(Anaheim's 1st choice, 2nd overall, in 2005 Entry Draft).

			Regular Season					Playoffs				
Season	Club	League	GP	G	A	Pts	PIM	GP	G	A	Pts	PIM
2003-04	Owen Sound	OHL	65	22	17	39	52	7	1	2	3	2
2004-05	Owen Sound	OHL	62	37	52	89	51	8	2	7	9	8
2005-06	Owen Sound	OHL	59	31	64	95	44	11	5	7	12	14
	Portland Pirates	AHL	....	....	....	....	....	19	1	7	8	22
2006-07	Owen Sound	OHL	63	43	59	102	63	4	1	1	2	2
	Portland Pirates	AHL	8	3	6	9	6	....	....	....	....	....

OHL First All-Star Team (2005)

RYAN, Joe (RIGH-uhn, JOH) **L.A.**

Defense. Shoots right. 6'2", 189 lbs. Born, Winchester, MA, October 19, 1987.
(Los Angeles' 3rd choice, 48th overall, in 2006 Entry Draft).

			Regular Season					Playoffs				
Season	Club	League	GP	G	A	Pts	PIM	GP	G	A	Pts	PIM
2003-04	Quebec Remparts	QMJHL	57	0	9	9	98	5	0	0	0	8
2004-05	Quebec Remparts	QMJHL	63	4	9	13	134	13	0	2	2	28
2005-06	Quebec Remparts	QMJHL	61	6	18	24	202	23	2	8	10	29
2006-07	Quebec Remparts	QMJHL	59	5	17	22	125	3	0	0	0	4

RYAZANTSEV, Alexander (ree-ZAHNT-sehv, al-EHX-AN-duhr) **WSH.**

Defense. Shoots right. 6', 210 lbs. Born, Moscow, USSR, March 15, 1980.
(Colorado's 10th choice, 167th overall, in 1998 Entry Draft).

			Regular Season					Playoffs				
Season	Club	League	GP	G	A	Pts	PIM	GP	G	A	Pts	PIM
1996-97	SAK Moscow	Russia-3	18	0	0	0	8	....	....	....	....	....
	Spartak Moscow	Russia	20	1	2	3	4	....	....	....	....	....
1997-98	Spartak Moscow 2	Russia-3	31	3	8	11	26	....	....	....	....	....
	Victoriaville Tigres	QMJHL	22	6	9	15	14	4	0	0	0	0
1998-99	Victoriaville Tigres	QMJHL	64	17	40	57	57	6	0	3	3	10
	Hershey Bears	AHL	2	0	0	0	0	....	....	....	....	....
99-2000	Victoriaville Tigres	QMJHL	48	17	45	62	45	6	2	5	7	20
	Hershey Bears	AHL	2	0	1	1	2	6	1	1	2	0
2000-01	Hershey Bears	AHL	66	5	18	23	26	11	0	0	0	2
2001-02	Hershey Bears	AHL	76	5	19	24	28	5	0	1	1	4
2002-03	Hershey Bears	AHL	57	5	10	15	65	....	....	....	....	....
	Milwaukee	AHL	14	3	4	7	9	5	0	4	4	2
2003-04	Yaroslavl 2	Russia-3	1	0	0	0	0	....	....	....	....	....
	Yaroslavl	Russia	41	3	8	11	60	....	....	....	....	....
2004-05	Yaroslavl	Russia	53	4	15	19	32	4	0	1	1	4
2005-06	Dynamo Moscow	Russia	39	3	7	10	34	4	0	1	1	29
2006-07	SKA St. Petersburg	Russia	53	6	10	16	20	3	0	0	0	0

Traded to **Nashville** by **Colorado** for Nashville's 7th round choice (Linus Videll) in 2003 Entry Draft, March 11, 2003. Traded to **Washington** by **Nashville** for Mike Farrell, July 14, 2003.

RYDER, Dan (RIGH-duhr, DAN) **CGY.**

Center. Shoots right. 5'11", 191 lbs. Born, Bonavista, Nfld., January 12, 1987.
(Calgary's 3rd choice, 74th overall, in 2005 Entry Draft).

			Regular Season					Playoffs				
Season	Club	League	GP	G	A	Pts	PIM	GP	G	A	Pts	PIM
2003-04	Peterborough	OHL	63	20	32	52	16	....	....	....	....	....
2004-05	Peterborough	OHL	68	29	53	82	55	....	....	....	....	....
2005-06	Peterborough	OHL	65	38	44	82	57	19	*15	16	31	22
2006-07	Peterborough	OHL	29	24	35	59	21	....	....	....	....	....
	Plymouth Whalers	OHL	28	16	17	33	4	20	8	9	17	10

RYNO, Johan (RYUH-noh, YOH-han) **DET.**

Right wing. Shoots left. 6'4", 198 lbs. Born, Orebro, Sweden, June 5, 1986.
(Detroit's 6th choice, 137th overall, in 2005 Entry Draft).

			Regular Season					Playoffs				
Season	Club	League	GP	G	A	Pts	PIM	GP	G	A	Pts	PIM
2003-04	IFK Hallsberg	Sweden-3	28	9	18	27	30	....	....	....	....	....
2004-05	IFK Arboga IK	Sweden-2	2	0	0	0	0	....	....	....	....	....
	IFK Kumla Jr.	Swe-Jr.	29	20	18	38	14	....	....	....	....	....
2005-06	IK Oskarshamn	Sweden-2	34	13	10	23	64	....	....	....	....	....
2006-07	Frolunda Jr.	Swe-Jr.	2	1	0	1	2	....	....	....	....	....
	Frolunda	Sweden	14	0	0	0	14	....	....	....	....	....
	AIK IF Solna	Sweden-2	14	2	7	9	14	....	....	....	....	....
	Timra IK	Sweden	25	5	6	11	8	5	0	1	1	0

SACCHETTI, Nico (SA-sheh-tee, NEE-koh) DAL.

Center. Shoots right. 5'11", 189 lbs. Born, Virginia, MN, August 21, 1989.
(Dallas' 1st choice, 50th overall, in 2007 Entry Draft).

			Regular Season					Playoffs				
Season	Club	League	GP	G	A	Pts	PIM	GP	G	A	Pts	PIM
2004-05	Virginia Blue Devils	High-MN	29	25	29	54	....	....	....	....	....	....
2005-06	Virginia Blue Devils	High-MN	27	29	45	74	....	....	....	....	....	....
2006-07	Virginia Blue Devils	High-MN	25	38	52	90	22	....	....	....	....	....

SACKRISON, Andy (sak-RIH-suhn, AN-dee) ST.L.

Center. Shoots left. 6'1", 178 lbs. Born, St. Louis Park, MN, November 12, 1987.
(St. Louis' 7th choice, 124th overall, in 2006 Entry Draft).

			Regular Season					Playoffs				
Season	Club	League	GP	G	A	Pts	PIM	GP	G	A	Pts	PIM
2004-05	St. Louis Park	High-MN	26	18	15	33	....	....	....	....	....	....
2005-06	St. Louis Park	High-MN	25	42	27	69	....	....	....	....	....	....
2006-07	Tri-City Storm	USHL	59	12	15	27	19	9	2	0	2	6

Signed Letter of Intent to attend **Minnesota State University** (WCHA) in fall of 2007.

SAGAT, Martin (SHA-gat, MAHR-tehn)

Left wing. Shoots right. 6'3", 191 lbs. Born, Handlova, Czech., November 11, 1984.
(Toronto's 2nd choice, 91st overall, in 2003 Entry Draft).

			Regular Season					Playoffs				
Season	Club	League	GP	G	A	Pts	PIM	GP	G	A	Pts	PIM
2002-03	Dukla Trencin Jr.	Slovak-Jr.	37	18	20	38	49	3	1	3	4	4
	Dukla Trencin	Slovakia	17	0	0	0	0	2	0	0	0	0
2003-04	Kootenay Ice	WHL	57	11	32	43	39	4	0	2	2	2
2004-05	Kootenay Ice	WHL	72	17	46	63	51	16	8	14	22	18
2005-06	Toronto Marlies	AHL	60	13	8	21	22	5	0	0	0	8
2006-07	Toronto Marlies	AHL	71	4	11	15	43	....	....	....	....	....

ST. JACQUES, Chris (SAINT ZHAWK, KRIHS)

Center. Shoots right. 5'8", 181 lbs. Born, Edmonton, Alta., January 22, 1983.

			Regular Season					Playoffs				
Season	Club	League	GP	G	A	Pts	PIM	GP	G	A	Pts	PIM
99-2000	Medicine Hat	WHL	61	21	18	39	65	....	....	....	....	....
2000-01	Medicine Hat	WHL	70	37	36	73	84	....	....	....	....	....
2001-02	Medicine Hat	WHL	45	30	38	68	50	....	....	....	....	....
2002-03	Medicine Hat	WHL	70	31	*65	96	78	11	2	14	16	17
2003-04	Medicine Hat	WHL	64	33	59	92	80	20	12	*15	*27	18
2004-05	St. John's	AHL	4	0	0	0	2	....	....	....	....	....
	Pensacola	ECHL	66	18	29	47	74	3	0	1	1	6
2005-06	Toronto Marlies	AHL	20	1	3	4	12	....	....	....	....	....
	Pensacola	ECHL	34	10	17	27	45	....	....	....	....	....
2006-07	Toronto Marlies	AHL	16	0	1	1	12	....	....	....	....	....
	Columbia Inferno	ECHL	52	6	14	20	72	....	....	....	....	....

Signed as a free agent by **Toronto**, June 2, 2004.

SALCIDO, Brian (sal-SEE-doh, BRIGH-uhn) ANA.

Defense. Shoots left. 6'2", 198 lbs. Born, Los Angeles, CA, April 14, 1985.
(Anaheim's 5th choice, 141st overall, in 2005 Entry Draft).

			Regular Season					Playoffs				
Season	Club	League	GP	G	A	Pts	PIM	GP	G	A	Pts	PIM
2002-03	Shat.-St. Mary's	High-MN	53	8	35	43	....	....	....	....	....	....
2003-04	Colorado College	WCHA	12	1	0	1	48	....	....	....	....	....
2004-05	Colorado College	WCHA	38	7	23	30	52	....	....	....	....	....
2005-06	Colorado College	WCHA	42	8	32	40	69	....	....	....	....	....
2006-07	Portland Pirates	AHL	76	7	20	27	80	....	....	....	....	....

WCHA Second All-Star Team (2006)

SALMONSSON, Johannes (sal-MUHN-suhn, yoh-HA-nuhs) PIT.

Left wing. Shoots left. 6'2", 183 lbs. Born, Uppsala, Sweden, February 7, 1986.
(Pittsburgh's 2nd choice, 31st overall, in 2004 Entry Draft).

			Regular Season					Playoffs				
Season	Club	League	GP	G	A	Pts	PIM	GP	G	A	Pts	PIM
2002-03	Almtuna	Sweden-2	26	10	14	24	4	....	....	....	....	....
2003-04	Djurgarden Jr.	Swe-Jr.	6	4	9	13	6	....	....	....	....	....
	Djurgarden	Sweden	25	0	3	3	4	....	....	....	....	....
	Almtuna	Sweden-2	2	0	0	0	0	....	....	....	....	....
2004-05	Almtuna	Sweden-2	8	0	2	2	6	....	....	....	....	....
	Djurgarden Jr.	Swe-Jr.	4	2	0	2	4	....	....	....	....	....
	Djurgarden	Sweden	30	2	2	4	6	9	0	0	0	0
2005-06	Spokane Chiefs	WHL	54	12	15	27	30	....	....	....	....	....
2006-07	Brynas IF Gavle Jr.	Swe-Jr.	2	0	7	7	0	....	....	....	....	....
	Brynas IF Gavle	Sweden	45	8	3	11	28	....	....	....	....	....

Signed as a free agent by **Brynas**, September 18, 2006.

SALONEN, Pasi (SAH-loh-nehn, PA-see) WSH.

Left wing. Shoots left. 5'11", 187 lbs. Born, Helsinki, Finland, December 18, 1985.
(Washington's 9th choice, 138th overall, in 2004 Entry Draft).

			Regular Season					Playoffs				
Season	Club	League	GP	G	A	Pts	PIM	GP	G	A	Pts	PIM
2000-01	HIFK Helsinki U18	Fin-U18	28	6	8	14	4	....	....	....	....	....
2001-02	HIFK Helsinki U18	Fin-U18	16	10	14	24	39	8	6	4	10	4
	HIFK Helsinki Jr.	Fin-Jr.	19	5	6	11	2	....	....	....	....	....
2002-03	HIFK Helsinki Jr.	Fin-Jr.	32	16	11	27	10	10	8	3	11	2
2003-04	Suomi U20	Finland-2	3	0	0	0	0	....	....	....	....	....
	HIFK Helsinki Jr.	Fin-Jr.	30	12	10	22	60	9	4	4	8	8
	HIFK Helsinki	Finland	3	0	0	0	0	....	....	....	....	....
2004-05			DID NOT PLAY – INJURED									
2005-06	HIFK Helsinki Jr.	Fin-Jr.	10	4	2	6	4	....	....	....	....	....
	HIFK Helsinki	Finland	49	5	9	14	6	8	0	0	0	0
2006-07	HIFK Helsinki	Finland	51	5	7	12	55	2	0	0	0	0

SAMSON, Jerome CAR.

Right wing. Shoots right. 5'11", 175 lbs. Born, Greenfield Park, Que., September 4, 1987.

			Regular Season					Playoffs				
Season	Club	League	GP	G	A	Pts	PIM	GP	G	A	Pts	PIM
2004-05	Moncton Wildcats	QMJHL	63	6	11	17	22	12	1	4	5	8
2005-06	Moncton Wildcats	QMJHL	62	20	32	52	46	21	6	12	18	15
2006-07	Moncton Wildcats	QMJHL	38	19	33	52	20	....	....	....	....	....
	Val-d'Or Foreurs	QMJHL	33	25	22	47	16	20	14	12	26	10

Signed as a free agent by **Carolina**, July 2, 2007.

SANFORD, James (SAN-fohrd, JAYMZ)

Defense. Shoots left. 5'9", 190 lbs. Born, Alma, N.B., June 18, 1984.

			Regular Season					Playoffs				
Season	Club	League	GP	G	A	Pts	PIM	GP	G	A	Pts	PIM
2000-01	Victoriaville Tigres	QMJHL	41	0	6	6	60	....	....	....	....	....
	Moncton Wildcats	QMJHL	26	4	5	9	40	....	....	....	....	....
2001-02	Moncton Wildcats	QMJHL	72	19	39	58	151	....	....	....	....	....
2002-03	Moncton Wildcats	QMJHL	72	16	45	61	139	6	4	5	9	15
2003-04	Moncton Wildcats	QMJHL	61	16	37	53	126	20	5	11	16	18
2004-05	Hamilton Bulldogs	AHL	31	2	8	10	20	....	....	....	....	....
	Peoria Rivermen	ECHL	24	2	9	11	16	....	....	....	....	....
2005-06	Hamilton Bulldogs	AHL	54	10	18	28	39	....	....	....	....	....
	Long Beach	ECHL	8	0	4	4	12	4	2	4	6	17
2006-07	Milwaukee	AHL	7	0	1	1	4	1	0	0	0	2
	Texas Wildcatters	ECHL	18	2	9	11	18	....	....	....	....	....
	Utah Grizzlies	ECHL	3	1	2	3	2	....	....	....	....	....

Signed as a free agent by **Hamilton** (AHL), October 10, 2004. Signed as a free agent by **Montreal**, March 2, 2006.

SANGUINETTI, Bobby (san-GIH-neh-tee, BAW-bee) NYR

Defense. Shoots right. 6'3", 190 lbs. Born, Trenton, NJ, February 29, 1988.
(NY Rangers' 1st choice, 21st overall, in 2006 Entry Draft).

			Regular Season					Playoffs				
Season	Club	League	GP	G	A	Pts	PIM	GP	G	A	Pts	PIM
2003-04	Lawrenceville	High-NJ	26	4	17	21	....	....	....	....	....	....
2004-05	Owen Sound	OHL	67	4	20	24	12	5	0	2	2	0
2005-06	Owen Sound	OHL	68	14	51	65	44	11	5	10	15	4
2006-07	Owen Sound	OHL	67	23	30	53	48	4	3	3	6	2
	Hartford Wolf Pack	AHL	5	0	3	3	2	7	0	1	1	2

SANNITZ, Raffaele (ZAH-nihts, ra-FIGH-ehl-lay) CBJ

Center. Shoots left. 6'1", 212 lbs. Born, Mendrisio, Switz., May 18, 1983.
(Columbus' 9th choice, 204th overall, in 2001 Entry Draft).

			Regular Season					Playoffs				
Season	Club	League	GP	G	A	Pts	PIM	GP	G	A	Pts	PIM
1997-98	HC Lugano Jr.	Swiss-Jr.	33	7	12	19	54	....	....	....	....	....
1998-99	HC Lugano Jr.	Swiss-Jr.	38	5	12	17	62	....	....	....	....	....
	HC Lugano	Swiss	8	0	1	1	0	....	....	....	....	....
99-2000	HC Lugano Jr.	Swiss-Jr.	33	13	16	29	47	....	....	....	....	....
	HC Lugano	Swiss	1	0	0	0	2	....	....	....	....	....
2000-01	HC Sierre	Swiss-2	2	0	0	0	0	....	....	....	....	....
	HC Lugano Jr.	Swiss-Jr.	35	22	30	52	152	2	0	0	0	0
	HC Lugano	Swiss	13	1	0	1	0	2	0	0	0	0
2001-02	HC Lugano Jr.	Swiss-Jr.	14	14	13	27	18	3	3	2	5	4
	HC Lugano	Swiss	38	3	4	7	37	12	1	1	2	2
2002-03	HC Lugano	Swiss	14	1	1	2	37	....	....	....	....	....
2003-04	HC Lugano	Swiss	48	7	9	16	20	16	2	1	3	8
	EHC Chur	Swiss-2	2	2	1	3	2	....	....	....	....	....
2004-05	Syracuse Crunch	AHL	53	6	3	9	38	....	....	....	....	....
	Dayton Bombers	ECHL	2	0	3	3	0	....	....	....	....	....
2005-06	HC Lugano	Swiss	33	5	9	14	85	17	4	8	12	16
2006-07	HC Lugano	Swiss	38	6	20	26	50	6	3	3	6	41

• Missed majority of 2002-03 season recovering from shoulder injury suffered in game vs. Kloten (Swiss), October 12, 2002.

SANTORELLI, Mark (san-toh-REHL-ee, MAHRK) NSH.

Center. Shoots right. 6'1", 189 lbs. Born, Burnaby, B.C., August 6, 1988.
(Nashville's 6th choice, 119th overall, in 2007 Entry Draft).

			Regular Season					Playoffs				
Season	Club	League	GP	G	A	Pts	PIM	GP	G	A	Pts	PIM
2003-04	Abbotsford Pilots	PIJHL	40	12	19	31	33	....	....	....	....	....
	Chilliwack Chiefs	BCHL	1	0	1	1	0	....	....	....	....	....
2004-05	Salmon Arm	BCHL	59	9	16	25	10	11	2	3	5	6
2005-06	Salmon Arm	BCHL	20	2	10	12	11	....	....	....	....	....
	Burnaby Express	BCHL	39	15	28	43	16	20	2	14	16	14
2006-07	Chilliwack Bruins	WHL	72	29	53	82	46	5	2	3	5	2

SANTORELLI, Mike (san-toh-REHL-ee, MIGHK) NSH.

Center. Shoots right. 6', 194 lbs. Born, Vancouver, B.C., December 14, 1985.
(Nashville's 6th choice, 178th overall, in 2004 Entry Draft).

			Regular Season					Playoffs				
Season	Club	League	GP	G	A	Pts	PIM	GP	G	A	Pts	PIM
2003-04	Vernon Vipers	BCHL	60	43	53	96	26	5	0	2	2	0
2004-05	Northern Mich.	CCHA	40	16	14	30	22	....	....	....	....	....
2005-06	Northern Mich.	CCHA	40	15	18	33	24	....	....	....	....	....
2006-07	Northern Mich.	CCHA	41	*30	17	47	28	....	....	....	....	....

CCHA All-Rookie Team (2005) • CCHA First All-Star Team (2007) • NCAA West Second All-American Team (2007)

SARAUER, Andrew (suh-ROW-uhr, AN-droo) VAN.

Left wing. Shoots left. 6'4", 205 lbs. Born, Saskatoon, Sask., November 17, 1984.
(Vancouver's 3rd choice, 125th overall, in 2004 Entry Draft).

			Regular Season					Playoffs				
Season	Club	League	GP	G	A	Pts	PIM	GP	G	A	Pts	PIM
2002-03	Victoria Salsa	BCHL	57	11	17	28	73	....	....	....	....	....
2003-04	Langley Hornets	BCHL	57	43	32	75	71	....	....	....	....	....
2004-05	Northern Mich.	CCHA	25	3	4	7	10	....	....	....	....	....
2005-06	Northern Mich.	CCHA	18	2	3	5	8	....	....	....	....	....
2006-07	Northern Mich.	CCHA	30	5	5	10	10	....	....	....	....	....

SAUER, Michael (SAW-uhr, MIGH-kuhl) NYR

Defense. Shoots right. 6'3", 206 lbs. Born, St. Cloud, MN, August 7, 1987.
(NY Rangers' 2nd choice, 40th overall, in 2005 Entry Draft).

			Regular Season					Playoffs				
Season	Club	League	GP	G	A	Pts	PIM	GP	G	A	Pts	PIM
2003-04	St. Cloud Tech	High-MN	18	12	16	28	34	....	....	....	....	....
2004-05	Portland	WHL	32	2	11	13	10	....	....	....	....	....
2005-06	Portland	WHL	59	8	23	31	68	12	4	2	6	8
2006-07	Portland	WHL	33	4	8	12	46	....	....	....	....	....
	Medicine Hat	WHL	32	1	10	11	29	23	1	5	6	34

• Missed majority of 2004-05 season due to hip injury.

SAUNDERS, Nathan (SAWN-duhrz, NAY-thun) **ANA.**

Defense. Shoots right. 6'4", 220 lbs. Born, Charlottetown, PEI, April 25, 1985.
(Anaheim's 5th choice, 119th overall, in 2003 Entry Draft).

			Regular Season					Playoffs				
Season	Club	League	GP	G	A	Pts	PIM	GP	G	A	Pts	PIM
2001-02	Moncton Wildcats	QMJHL	54	4	11	15	88	....	....	....	....	....
2002-03	Moncton Wildcats	QMJHL	69	1	13	14	241	6	2	3	5	12
2003-04	Moncton Wildcats	QMJHL	68	4	26	30	267	20	1	1	2	34
2004-05	Moncton Wildcats	QMJHL	70	5	23	28	198	12	2	2	4	24
2005-06	Portland Pirates	AHL	20	1	0	1	75	9	0	0	0	19
2006-07	Portland Pirates	AHL	16	0	3	3	13	....	....	....	....	....
	Augusta Lynx	ECHL	59	1	13	14	107	2	0	0	0	0

SAWADA, Raymond (suh-WAW-duh, RAY-muhnd) **DAL.**

Right wing. Shoots right. 6'2", 195 lbs. Born, Richmond, B.C., February 19, 1985.
(Dallas' 3rd choice, 52nd overall, in 2004 Entry Draft).

			Regular Season					Playoffs				
Season	Club	League	GP	G	A	Pts	PIM	GP	G	A	Pts	PIM
2002-03	Richmond	PIJHL	36	7	17	24	155	....	....	....	....	....
2003-04	Nanaimo Clippers	BCHL	54	20	32	52	93	25	6	16	22	22
2004-05	Cornell Big Red	ECACHL	35	4	5	9	48	....	....	....	....	....
2005-06	Cornell Big Red	ECACHL	35	7	13	20	20	....	....	....	....	....
2006-07	Cornell Big Red	ECACHL	31	10	11	21	29	....	....	....	....	....

SAWYER, Jean-Claude (SOI-uhr, ZHAWN-KLOHD) **CHI.**

Defense. Shoots left. 6'3", 194 lbs. Born, Saint John, N.B., August 12, 1986.
(Minnesota's 8th choice, 161st overall, in 2004 Entry Draft).

			Regular Season					Playoffs				
Season	Club	League	GP	G	A	Pts	PIM	GP	G	A	Pts	PIM
2002-03	Cape Breton	QMJHL	31	3	2	5	44	3	0	0	0	2
2003-04	Cape Breton	QMJHL	56	5	13	18	48	2	0	0	0	2
2004-05	Cape Breton	QMJHL	58	10	22	32	53	5	2	2	4	4
2005-06	Cape Breton	QMJHL	69	12	41	53	108	9	4	0	4	15
2006-07	Cape Breton	QMJHL	68	15	62	77	87	16	3	16	19	6

QMJHL Second All-Star Team (2007)

Signed as a free agent by **Chicago**, July 2, 2007.

SCALZO, Mario (SKAL-zoh, MAHR-ee-oh) **DAL.**

Defense. Shoots left. 5'9", 187 lbs. Born, St-Hubert, Que., November 11, 1984.

			Regular Season					Playoffs				
Season	Club	League	GP	G	A	Pts	PIM	GP	G	A	Pts	PIM
2001-02	Antoine-Girouard	QAAA	40	8	27	35	50	....	....	....	....	....
	Victoriaville Tigres	QMJHL	1	0	1	1	0	1	0	0	0	0
2002-03	Victoriaville Tigres	QMJHL	72	10	34	44	134	4	0	3	3	6
2003-04	Victoriaville Tigres	QMJHL	68	16	52	68	113	....	....	....	....	....
2004-05	Victoriaville Tigres	QMJHL	39	11	19	30	73	....	....	....	....	....
	Rimouski Oceanic	QMJHL	23	13	31	44	31	13	7	14	21	10
2005-06	Iowa Stars	AHL	74	4	29	33	42	7	0	2	2	8
2006-07	Iowa Stars	AHL	73	4	21	25	89	9	0	3	3	10

QMJHL All-Rookie Team (2003) • QMJHL Second All-Star Team (2004) • QMJHL First All-Star Team (2005) • Memorial Cup All-Star Team (2005)

Signed as a free agent by **Dallas**, August 5, 2005.

SCEVIOUR, Colton (SEE-vee-yuhr, KOHL-tuhn) **DAL.**

Center/Right wing. Shoots right. 6', 201 lbs. Born, Red Deer, Alta., April 20, 1989.
(Dallas' 3rd choice, 112th overall, in 2007 Entry Draft).

			Regular Season					Playoffs				
Season	Club	League	GP	G	A	Pts	PIM	GP	G	A	Pts	PIM
2004-05	Red Deer	AMHL	36	15	22	37	32	....	....	....	....	....
	Portland	WHL	6	1	0	1	6	4	0	0	0	0
2005-06	Portland	WHL	58	3	6	9	25	12	0	1	1	4
2006-07	Portland	WHL	49	12	26	38	38	....	....	....	....	....

SCHAEFFER, Kevin (SHAY-fuhr, KEH-vihn) **NSH.**

Defense. Shoots right. 6', 203 lbs. Born, Huntington, NY, October 16, 1984.
(Nashville's 7th choice, 193rd overall, in 2004 Entry Draft).

			Regular Season					Playoffs				
Season	Club	League	GP	G	A	Pts	PIM	GP	G	A	Pts	PIM
2002-03	NY Apple Core	EJHL	65	20	38	58	60	....	....	....	....	....
2003-04	Boston University	H-East	38	5	12	17	20	....	....	....	....	....
2004-05	Boston University	H-East	41	2	12	14	26	....	....	....	....	....
2005-06	Boston University	H-East	40	4	9	13	18	....	....	....	....	....
2006-07	Boston University	H-East	33	6	4	10	22	....	....	....	....	....

Hockey East All-Rookie Team (2004)

SCHELL, Brad (SHEHL, BRAD)

Center. Shoots left. 6'1", 190 lbs. Born, Scott, Sask., August 5, 1984.
(Atlanta's 6th choice, 167th overall, in 2002 Entry Draft).

			Regular Season					Playoffs				
Season	Club	League	GP	G	A	Pts	PIM	GP	G	A	Pts	PIM
99-2000	North Battleford	SMHL	62	38	42	80	28	....	....	....	....	....
	Spokane Chiefs	WHL	1	0	0	0	0	....	....	....	....	....
2000-01	Spokane Chiefs	WHL	60	7	6	13	10	12	0	2	2	2
2001-02	Spokane Chiefs	WHL	70	20	36	56	16	11	0	8	8	6
2002-03	Spokane Chiefs	WHL	37	8	13	21	26	10	0	5	5	2
2003-04	Spokane Chiefs	WHL	71	35	57	92	47	4	1	0	1	0
2004-05	Gwinnett	ECHL	72	14	39	53	28	8	2	4	6	4
2005-06	Chicago Wolves	AHL	10	1	2	3	2	....	....	....	....	....
	Gwinnett	ECHL	59	23	56	79	30	17	1	12	13	8
2006-07	Chicago Wolves	AHL	12	2	2	4	0	15	0	2	2	4
	Gwinnett	ECHL	63	25	*85	*110	60	....	....	....	....	....

WHL West Second All-Star Team (2004) • ECHL First All-Star Team (2007) • ECHL Player of the Year (2007)

• Missed majority of 2002-03 season recovering from off-season back surgery.

SCHEVJEV, Maxim (shehv-YAWF-yehv, MAX-ihm) **BUF.**

Center. Shoots left. 6', 178 lbs. Born, Noginsk, USSR, July 5, 1984.
(Buffalo's 7th choice, 178th overall, in 2002 Entry Draft).

			Regular Season					Playoffs				
Season	Club	League	GP	G	A	Pts	PIM	GP	G	A	Pts	PIM
99-2000	Elektrostal 2	Russia-3	11	0	1	1	2	....	....	....	....	....
2000-01	Elektrostal	Russia-2	7	0	0	0	6	....	....	....	....	....
2001-02	Elektrostal 2	Russia-3	6	1	2	3	2	....	....	....	....	....
	Elektrostal	Russia-2	49	6	9	15	34	....	....	....	....	....
2002-03	Amur Khabarovsk	Russia	21	0	0	0	10	....	....	....	....	....
	Khabarovsk 2	Russia-3	5	2	1	3	4	....	....	....	....	....
2003-04	Kristall Elektrostal	Russia-2	26	4	5	9	20	....	....	....	....	....
	Voskresensk	Russia	18	1	0	1	2	....	....	....	....	....
2004-05	Kristall Elektrostal	Russia-2	48	4	7	11	109	....	....	....	....	....
2005-06	Yuzhny Ural Orsk	Russia-2	38	3	10	13	38	....	....	....	....	....
	Yuzhny Ural Orsk 2	Russia-3	3	1	3	4	0	....	....	....	....	....
	Kristall Elektrostal	Russia-3	STATISTICS NOT AVAILABLE									
2006-07	Kristall Elektrostal	Russia-2	47	4	7	11	52	....	....	....	....	....

SCHIESTEL, Drew (SHIGHS-tuhl, DROO) **BUF.**

Defense. Shoots right. 6'1", 180 lbs. Born, Hamilton, Ont., March 9, 1989.
(Buffalo's 2nd choice, 59th overall, in 2007 Entry Draft).

			Regular Season					Playoffs				
Season	Club	League	GP	G	A	Pts	PIM	GP	G	A	Pts	PIM
2004-05	Hamilton Reps	Minor-ON	68	21	27	46	....	....	....	....	....	....
2005-06	Mississauga	OHL	40	1	4	5	42	....	....	....	....	....
2006-07	Mississauga	OHL	66	6	15	21	40	5	0	6	6	2

SCHLEMKO, David (SHLEHM-koh, DAY-vihd) **PHX.**

Defense. Shoots left. 6'1", 195 lbs. Born, Edmonton, Alta., May 7, 1987.

			Regular Season					Playoffs				
Season	Club	League	GP	G	A	Pts	PIM	GP	G	A	Pts	PIM
2004-05	Medicine Hat	WHL	65	5	24	29	23	13	0	3	3	10
2005-06	Medicine Hat	WHL	69	9	35	44	44	13	2	5	7	15
2006-07	Medicine Hat	WHL	64	8	50	58	78	23	3	13	16	12

Signed as a free agent by **Phoenix**, July 19, 2007.

SCHNEIDER, David (SHNIGH-duhr, DAY-vihd) **T.B.**

Defense. Shoots left. 5'9", 190 lbs. Born, Melrose Park, IL, August 24, 1979.

			Regular Season					Playoffs				
Season	Club	League	GP	G	A	Pts	PIM	GP	G	A	Pts	PIM
1998-99	Princeton	ECAC	21	1	0	1	24	....	....	....	....	....
99-2000	Princeton	ECAC	30	5	11	16	22	....	....	....	....	....
2000-01	Princeton	ECAC	23	8	7	15	22	....	....	....	....	....
2001-02	Princeton	ECAC	24	4	14	18	20	....	....	....	....	....
	Trenton Titans	ECHL	2	0	1	1	5	....	....	....	....	....
2002-03	Trenton Titans	ECHL	26	5	11	16	22	....	....	....	....	....
2003-04	TPS Turku	Finland	54	8	11	19	72	13	2	3	5	20
2004-05	TPS Turku	Finland	26	2	3	5	49	6	0	1	1	25
2005-06	HPK Hameenlinna	Finland	51	8	18	26	98	13	1	3	4	16
2006-07	HPK Hameenlinna	Finland	53	8	17	25	72	9	3	2	5	16

Signed as a free agent by **Tampa Bay**, July 3, 2007.

SCHUTZ, Felix (SCHUTZ, FEEL-ihx) **BUF.**

Center. Shoots left. 5'11", 187 lbs. Born, Erding, West Germany, November 3, 1987.
(Buffalo's 4th choice, 117th overall, in 2006 Entry Draft).

			Regular Season					Playoffs				
Season	Club	League	GP	G	A	Pts	PIM	GP	G	A	Pts	PIM
2003-04	Mannheim Jr.	Ger-Jr.	30	22	22	44	12	....	....	....	....	....
2004-05	EV Landshut Jr.	Ger-Jr.	9	6	8	14	33	2	2	3	5	0
	Landshut Cann.	German-2	24	1	2	3	8	5	0	0	0	2
2005-06	Saint John	QMJHL	65	21	31	52	61	....	....	....	....	....
2006-07	Saint John	QMJHL	18	4	7	11	16	....	....	....	....	....
	Val-d'Or Foreurs	QMJHL	27	15	18	33	28	20	5	10	15	22

QMJHL All-Rookie Team (2006)

SCOTT, John (SKAWT, JAWN) **MIN.**

Defense. Shoots left. 6'8", 247 lbs. Born, St. Catharines, Ont., September 26, 1982.

			Regular Season					Playoffs				
Season	Club	League	GP	G	A	Pts	PIM	GP	G	A	Pts	PIM
2002-03	Michigan Tech	WCHA	31	1	3	4	64	....	....	....	....	....
2003-04	Michigan Tech	WCHA	35	1	3	4	100	....	....	....	....	....
2004-05	Michigan Tech	WCHA	36	2	3	5	101	....	....	....	....	....
2005-06	Michigan Tech	WCHA	24	3	2	5	87	....	....	....	....	....
2006-07	Houston Aeros	AHL	65	1	5	6	107	....	....	....	....	....

Signed as a free agent by **Houston** (AHL), September 26, 2006. Signed as a free agent by **Minnesota**, December 31, 2006.

SEABROOK, Keith (SEE-bruk, KEETH) **WSH.**

Defense. Shoots right. 6', 198 lbs. Born, Delta, B.C., August 2, 1988.
(Washington's 5th choice, 52nd overall, in 2006 Entry Draft).

			Regular Season					Playoffs				
Season	Club	League	GP	G	A	Pts	PIM	GP	G	A	Pts	PIM
2003-04	Coquitlam Express	BCHL	58	8	20	28	70	....	....	....	....	....
2005-06	Burnaby Express	BCHL	57	10	24	34	81	....	....	....	....	....
2006-07	U. of Denver	WCHA	37	2	11	13	24	....	....	....	....	....

• Left University of Denver (WCHA) and signed with Calgary (WHL), July 30, 2007.

SEDOV, Pavel (se-DAHF, PAH-vehl) **T.B.**

Right wing. Shoots left. 6'3", 200 lbs. Born, Voskresensk, USSR, January 12, 1982.
(Tampa Bay's 5th choice, 161st overall, in 2000 Entry Draft).

			Regular Season					Playoffs				
Season	Club	League	GP	G	A	Pts	PIM	GP	G	A	Pts	PIM
99-2000	Voskresensk	Russia-2	10	0	0	0	2	....	....	....	....	....
	Voskresensk 2	Russia-3	21	5	5	-10	26	....	....	....	....	....
2000-01	Voskresensk	Russia-2	38	2	1	3	10	....	....	....	....	....
2001-02	Voskresensk 2	Russia-3	12	4	1	5	0	....	....	....	....	....
	Voskresensk	Russia-2	18	3	1	4	0	....	....	....	....	....
2002-03	Voskresensk	Russia-2	25	1	5	6	6	....	....	....	....	....
	Voskresensk 2	Russia-3	7	2	4	6	4	....	....	....	....	....
2003-04	THK Tver	Russia-2	26	2	6	8	6	....	....	....	....	....
	Voskresensk	Russia	10	1	0	1	2	....	....	....	....	....
	Voskresensk 2	Russia-3	STATISTICS NOT AVAILABLE									
2004-05	HK Tver	Russia-3	STATISTICS NOT AVAILABLE									
	HK Dmitrov	Russia-3	STATISTICS NOT AVAILABLE									
	HK Ryazan	Russia-4	STATISTICS NOT AVAILABLE									
2005-06			DID NOT PLAY									
2006-07	HK Ryazan	Russia-3	70	24	29	53	16	....	....	....	....	....

SEGAL, Brandon (SEE-guhl, BRAN-duhn) ANA.

Right wing. Shoots right. 6'3", 213 lbs. Born, Richmond, B.C., July 12, 1983.
(Nashville's 2nd choice, 102nd overall, in 2002 Entry Draft).

			Regular Season					Playoffs				
Season	Club	League	GP	G	A	Pts	PIM	GP	G	A	Pts	PIM
99-2000	Calgary Hitmen	WHL	44	2	6	8	76	13	1	1	2	13
	Delta Ice Hawks	PIJHL	....	....	....	....	....	3	0	1	1	2
2000-01	Calgary Hitmen	WHL	72	16	11	27	103	12	1	1	2	17
2001-02	Calgary Hitmen	WHL	71	43	40	83	122	7	1	4	5	16
2002-03	Calgary Hitmen	WHL	71	31	27	58	104	5	2	2	4	4
2003-04	Calgary Hitmen	WHL	28	18	12	30	29	....	....	....	....	....
	Milwaukee	AHL	44	11	10	21	54	13	2	1	3	21
2004-05	Milwaukee	AHL	59	7	8	15	45	3	1	0	1	11
	Rockford IceHogs	UHL	10	5	4	9	27	11	11	5	16	10
2005-06	Milwaukee	AHL	79	18	15	33	126	21	1	2	3	16
2006-07	Milwaukee	AHL	77	20	9	29	84	4	1	0	1	2

Traded to **Anaheim** by **Nashville** for future considerations, June 25, 2007.

SEITSONEN, Aki (SIGHT-soh-nehn, AH-kee) CGY.

Center. Shoots right. 6'3", 203 lbs. Born, Riihimaki, Finland, February 5, 1986.
(Calgary's 4th choice, 118th overall, in 2004 Entry Draft).

			Regular Season					Playoffs				
Season	Club	League	GP	G	A	Pts	PIM	GP	G	A	Pts	PIM
2002-03	HPK U18	Fin-U18	28	15	18	33	6	2	1	1	2	0
	HPK Jr.	Fin-Jr.	1	1	0	1	0	....	....	....	....	....
2003-04	Prince Albert	WHL	71	16	24	40	18	5	0	0	0	0
2004-05	Prince Albert	WHL	67	24	28	52	14	17	5	9	14	10
2005-06	Prince Albert	WHL	66	20	15	35	22	....	....	....	....	....
	Omaha	AHL	7	0	0	0	2	....	....	....	....	....
2006-07	Omaha	AHL	13	1	3	4	0	....	....	....	....	....
	Las Vegas	ECHL	59	14	18	32	16	5	0	2	2	2

SEMENOV, Maxim (seh-MEH-nahv, max-EEM) TOR.

Defense. Shoots left. 6', 180 lbs. Born, Kamenogorsk, USSR, February 9, 1984.
(Toronto's 5th choice, 220th overall, in 2004 Entry Draft).

			Regular Season					Playoffs				
Season	Club	League	GP	G	A	Pts	PIM	GP	G	A	Pts	PIM
2002-03	Lada Togliatti 2	Russia-3	18	0	4	4	26	....	....	....	....	....
	Lada Togliatti	Russia	23	0	0	0	16	6	0	1	1	10
2003-04	Lada Togliatti	Russia	59	2	5	7	50	6	0	0	0	0
	Lada Togliatti 2	Russia-3	....	....	....	....	....	4	0	1	1	29
2004-05	Lada Togliatti	Russia	59	2	4	6	79	9	0	0	0	6
2005-06	Lada Togliatti	Russia	23	0	2	2	24	....	....	....	....	....
	Mytischi	Russia	28	2	8	10	76	9	1	0	1	8
2006-07	Mytischi	Russia	52	3	7	10	58	9	0	2	2	14

SEMIN, Dmitri (SEH-min, dih-MEE-tree) ST.L.

Center. Shoots left. 5'10", 185 lbs. Born, Moscow, USSR, August 14, 1983.
(St. Louis' 4th choice, 159th overall, in 2001 Entry Draft).

			Regular Season					Playoffs				
Season	Club	League	GP	G	A	Pts	PIM	GP	G	A	Pts	PIM
99-2000	Spartak Moscow 2	Russia-3	27	9	10	19	10	....	....	....	....	....
	Spartak Moscow	Russia-2	1	0	0	0	0	....	....	....	....	....
2000-01	Spartak Moscow	Russia	21	6	3	9	4	11	2	3	5	4
2001-02	Spartak Moscow 2	Russia-3	4	5	0	5	4	....	....	....	....	....
	Spartak Moscow	Russia	44	2	6	8	14	....	....	....	....	....
2002-03	Spartak Moscow	Russia	51	9	13	22	30	....	....	....	....	....
2003-04	Spartak Moscow	Russia-2	60	15	23	38	34	13	2	2	4	2
2004-05	Spartak Moscow	Russia	53	7	7	14	34	....	....	....	....	....
2005-06	Spartak Moscow	Russia	51	12	14	26	38	3	0	1	1	0
2006-07	Yaroslavl	Russia	41	13	13	26	30	7	3	2	5	2

SEPPANEN, Timo (SEH-pah-nehn, TEE-moh) PIT.

Defense. Shoots left. 6'1", 209 lbs. Born, Helsinki, Finland, July 22, 1987.
(Pittsburgh's 5th choice, 185th overall, in 2006 Entry Draft).

			Regular Season					Playoffs				
Season	Club	League	GP	G	A	Pts	PIM	GP	G	A	Pts	PIM
2002-03	HIFK Helsinki U18	Fin-U18	24	2	5	7	12	2	2	0	2	0
2003-04	HIFK Helsinki U18	Fin-U18	7	2	5	7	32	4	0	2	2	6
	HIFK Helsinki Jr.	Fin-Jr.	29	0	4	4	6	7	0	0	0	2
2004-05	HIFK Helsinki U18	Fin-U18	....	....	....	....	....	7	2	3	5	26
	HIFK Helsinki Jr.	Fin-Jr.	39	3	4	7	32	3	0	0	0	4
2005-06	Suomi U20	Finland-2	6	2	2	4	10	....	....	....	....	....
	HIFK Helsinki Jr.	Fin-Jr.	30	7	11	18	65	....	....	....	....	....
	HIFK Helsinki	Finland	21	0	0	0	2	5	0	1	1	0
2006-07	HIFK Helsinki Jr.	Fin-Jr.	12	2	2	4	10	....	....	....	....	....
	Suomi U20	Finland-2	6	1	0	1	6	....	....	....	....	....
	HIFK Helsinki	Finland	12	0	0	0	10	....	....	....	....	....
	HPK Jr.	Fin-Jr.	9	1	4	5	8	3	1	2	3	0
	HPK Hameenlinna	Finland	16	2	1	3	10	....	....	....	....	....

SERSEN, Michal (suhr-SEHN, MEE-khahl) PIT.

Defense. Shoots left. 6'2", 200 lbs. Born, Celnica, Czech., December 28, 1985.
(Pittsburgh's 7th choice, 130th overall, in 2004 Entry Draft).

			Regular Season					Playoffs				
Season	Club	League	GP	G	A	Pts	PIM	GP	G	A	Pts	PIM
2002-03	Bratislava Jr.	Slovak-Jr.	33	5	4	9	51	....	....	....	....	....
	Bratislava	Slovakia	17	0	0	0	0	....	....	....	....	....
2003-04	Rimouski Oceanic	QMJHL	45	7	18	25	30	9	1	5	6	6
2004-05	Rimouski Oceanic	QMJHL	67	9	33	42	74	13	0	8	8	18
2005-06	Quebec Remparts	QMJHL	63	22	57	79	76	23	3	18	21	36
2006-07	Bratislava	Slovakia	42	1	4	5	28	14	0	1	1	2

QMJHL Second All-Star Team (2006) • Memorial Cup Tournament All-Star Team (2006)

Signed as a free agent by **Bratislava** (Slovakia), October 14, 2006.

SERTICH, Andrew (SUHR-tihch, AN-droo)

Left wing. Shoots left. 6', 175 lbs. Born, Coleraine, MN, May 6, 1983.
(Pittsburgh's 5th choice, 136th overall, in 2002 Entry Draft).

			Regular Season					Playoffs				
Season	Club	League	GP	G	A	Pts	PIM	GP	G	A	Pts	PIM
1998/00	Greenway Raiders	High-MN	47	39	58	97	....	....	....	....	....	....
2000-01	Greenway Raiders	High-MN	31	35	45	80	14	....	....	....	....	....
2001-02	Greenway Raiders	High-MN	26	24	48	72	35	....	....	....	....	....
	Sioux Falls	USHL	13	2	4	6	0	2	0	0	0	2
2002-03	U. of Minnesota	WCHA	44	5	9	14	12	....	....	....	....	....
2003-04	U. of Minnesota	WCHA	43	8	14	22	14	....	....	....	....	....
2004-05	U. of Minnesota	WCHA	44	6	9	15	8	....	....	....	....	....
2005-06	U. of Minnesota	WCHA	41	8	8	16	22	....	....	....	....	....
2006-07	Utah Grizzlies	ECHL	72	7	40	47	41	....	....	....	....	....

• Statistics for 1998/00 **Greenway** (High-MN) are totals for 1998-2000 seasons.

SERTICH, Marty (SUHR-tihch, MAHR-tee) DAL.

Center. Shoots left. 5'9", 165 lbs. Born, Roseville, MN, October 13, 1982.

			Regular Season					Playoffs				
Season	Club	League	GP	G	A	Pts	PIM	GP	G	A	Pts	PIM
2001-02	Sioux Falls	USHL	61	19	33	52	30	3	1	0	1	0
2002-03	Colorado College	WCHA	42	9	20	29	26	....	....	....	....	....
2003-04	Colorado College	WCHA	39	11	28	39	12	....	....	....	....	....
2004-05	Colorado College	WCHA	42	27	37	*64	26	....	....	....	....	....
2005-06	Colorado College	WCHA	42	14	36	50	55	....	....	....	....	....
2006-07	Iowa Stars	AHL	44	13	20	33	24	2	0	1	1	0

WCHA Second All-Star Team (2006)

Signed as a free agent by **Dallas**, July 10, 2006.

SESTITO, Tim (sehs-TEE-toh, TIHM) EDM.

Center. Shoots left. 5'11", 195 lbs. Born, Rome, NY, August 28, 1984.

			Regular Season					Playoffs				
Season	Club	League	GP	G	A	Pts	PIM	GP	G	A	Pts	PIM
2001-02	Plymouth Whalers	OHL	51	10	11	21	40	6	0	0	0	0
2002-03	Plymouth Whalers	OHL	61	11	7	18	49	18	2	3	5	4
2003-04	Plymouth Whalers	OHL	57	10	20	30	68	9	4	1	5	14
2004-05	Plymouth Whalers	OHL	67	14	18	32	93	4	0	0	0	14
	Bridgeport	AHL	9	2	1	3	12	....	....	....	....	....
2005-06	Greenville Grrrowl	ECHL	72	21	23	44	127	6	2	2	4	24
2006-07	Wilkes-Barre	AHL	4	0	0	0	6	....	....	....	....	....
	Stockton Thunder	ECHL	66	13	13	26	132	6	2	1	3	6

Signed as a free agent by **Edmonton**, August 28, 2006.

SESTITO, Tommy (sehs-TEE-toh, TAW-mee) CBJ

Left wing. Shoots left. 6'4", 209 lbs. Born, Utica, NY, September 28, 1987.
(Columbus' 3rd choice, 85th overall, in 2006 Entry Draft).

			Regular Season					Playoffs				
Season	Club	League	GP	G	A	Pts	PIM	GP	G	A	Pts	PIM
2003-04	Syracuse Jr. Stars	EmJHL	31	13	16	29	137	6	5	6	11	32
2004-05	Plymouth Whalers	OHL	35	1	3	4	88	....	....	....	....	....
2005-06	Plymouth Whalers	OHL	57	10	10	20	176	13	5	2	7	29
2006-07	Plymouth Whalers	OHL	60	42	22	64	135	19	11	6	17	57

SETOGUCHI, Devin (SEHT-oh-GOO-chee, DEH-vihn) S.J.

Right wing. Shoots right. 6', 200 lbs. Born, Taber, Alta., January 1, 1987.
(San Jose's 1st choice, 8th overall, in 2005 Entry Draft).

			Regular Season					Playoffs				
Season	Club	League	GP	G	A	Pts	PIM	GP	G	A	Pts	PIM
2003-04	Saskatoon Blades	WHL	66	13	18	31	53	....	....	....	....	....
2004-05	Saskatoon Blades	WHL	69	33	31	64	34	4	0	1	1	0
2005-06	Saskatoon Blades	WHL	65	36	47	83	69	10	8	4	12	8
2006-07	Prince George	WHL	55	36	29	65	55	15	*11	10	21	24

WHL East Second All-Star Team (2006)

SETZINGER, Oliver (SEHT-zihn-guhr, AW-lih-vuhr) NSH.

Center. Shoots left. 6', 180 lbs. Born, Horn, Austria, July 11, 1983.
(Nashville's 5th choice, 76th overall, in 2001 Entry Draft).

			Regular Season					Playoffs				
Season	Club	League	GP	G	A	Pts	PIM	GP	G	A	Pts	PIM
1998-99	Wiener EV Jr.	Austria-Jr.	30	25	27	52	30	....	....	....	....	....
99-2000	Ilves Tampere Jr.	Fin-Jr.	35	6	4	10	65	....	....	....	....	....
	Ilves Tampere U18	Fin-U18	18	16	9	25	38	....	....	....	....	....
	Ilves Tampere	Finland	1	0	0	0	2	....	....	....	....	....
2000-01	Ilves Tampere Jr.	Fin-Jr.	31	8	12	20	74	....	....	....	....	....
	Ilves Tampere	Finland	14	0	1	1	10	....	....	....	....	....
2001-02	Ilves Tampere Jr.	Fin-Jr.	1	0	0	0	2	....	....	....	....	....
	Ilves Tampere	Finland	10	1	0	1	4	....	....	....	....	....
	Sport Vaasa	Finland-2	8	5	2	7	6	....	....	....	....	....
	Austria	Olympics	4	1	0	1	2	....	....	....	....	....
	EHC Linz	Austria	8	6	7	13	4	13	4	14	18	14
2002-03	Pelicans Lahti	Finland	56	7	14	21	54	....	....	....	....	....
2003-04	Pelicans Lahti	Finland	20	2	4	6	22	....	....	....	....	....
	KalPa Kuopio	Finland-2	8	4	7	11	20	....	....	....	....	....
	HPK Hameenlinna	Finland	14	6	3	9	10	8	4	2	6	4
2004-05	HPK Hameenlinna	Finland	53	11	17	28	67	10	0	1	1	2
2005-06	EV Vienna Capitals	Austria	45	32	38	70	98	5	4	2	6	8
2006-07	EV Vienna Capitals	Austria	56	26	50	76	62	3	2	4	6	16

SEVERYN, C.J. (SEH-vuhr-ihn, SEE-JAY) CGY.

Left wing. Shoots left. 6', 185 lbs. Born, Beaver, PA, June 2, 1989.
(Calgary's 5th choice, 186th overall, in 2007 Entry Draft).

			Regular Season					Playoffs				
Season	Club	League	GP	G	A	Pts	PIM	GP	G	A	Pts	PIM
2004-05	Pittsburgh Hornets	MWEHL	65	27	44	71	....	....	....	....	....	....
2005-06	USNTDP	U-17	19	2	3	5	40	....	....	....	....	....
	USNTDP	NAHL	32	2	13	15	77	12	1	0	1	12
2006-07	USNTDP	U-18	42	8	8	16	32	....	....	....	....	....
	USNTDP	NAHL	15	0	3	3	22	....	....	....	....	....

SEYDOUX, Philippe (SAY-doo, fihl-EEP) OTT.

Defense. Shoots left. 6'2", 185 lbs. Born, Bern, Switz., February 23, 1985.
(Ottawa's 3rd choice, 100th overall, in 2003 Entry Draft).

			Regular Season					Playoffs				
Season	Club	League	GP	G	A	Pts	PIM	GP	G	A	Pts	PIM
2000-01	SC Bern Jr.	Swiss-Jr.	30	1	3	4	8	4	1	2	0	6
2001-02	SC Bern Jr.	Swiss-Jr.	35	8	17	25	94	7	3	5	0	24
	SC Bern	Swiss	7	0	0	0	0	2	0	0	0	0
2002-03	Kloten Flyers Jr.	Swiss-Jr.	14	2	10	12	50	....	....	....	....	....
	Kloten Flyers	Swiss	14	0	1	1	4	5	0	0	0	6
2003-04	Kloten Flyers	Swiss	24	2	3	5	20	....	....	....	....	....
2004-05	Kloten Flyers	Swiss	28	1	8	9	22	5	0	0	0	2
2005-06	Kloten Flyers	Swiss	44	1	7	8	48	11	0	0	0	4
2006-07	HPK Hameenlinna	Finland	6	0	0	0	4	....	....	....	....	....
	Kloten Flyers	Swiss	7	0	2	2	4	....	....	....	....	....
	Fribourg	Swiss	21	2	7	9	38	4	0	1	1	4

SHADILOV, Igor (sha-DEE-lahf, EE-gohr) WSH.

Defense. Shoots left. 6'2", 189 lbs. Born, Moscow, USSR, June 7, 1980.
(Washington's 10th choice, 249th overall, in 1999 Entry Draft).

			Regular Season					Playoffs				
Season	Club	League	GP	G	A	Pts	PIM	GP	G	A	Pts	PIM
1996-97	Dyn'o Moscow 2	Russia-3	30	3	7	10	30	....	....	....	....	....
1997-98	Dynamo Moscow	Russia	38	1	0	1	6	....	....	....	....	....
1998-99	Dyn'o Moscow 2	Russia-3	28	2	9	11	15	....	....	....	....	....
	Dynamo Moscow	Russia	2	0	0	0	0	....	....	....	....	....
	Krylja Sovetov	Russia	9	0	0	0	0	....	....	....	....	....
99-2000	THK Tver	Russia-2	14	0	3	3	6	....	....	....	....	....
	Dynamo Moscow	Russia	26	0	2	2	8	16	0	0	0	2
2000-01	Dynamo Moscow	Russia	34	1	5	6	12	....	....	....	....	....
2001-02	Cherepovets	Russia	33	7	3	10	10	4	0	0	0	2
2002-03	Cherepovets	Russia	32	3	3	6	28	12	1	3	4	4
2003-04	Dynamo Moscow	Russia	56	4	8	12	16	3	0	1	1	2
2004-05	Dynamo Moscow	Russia	34	0	5	5	12	....	....	....	....	....
2005-06	Ak Bars Kazan	Russia	49	3	9	12	20	13	1	1	2	6
2006-07	Ak Bars Kazan	Russia	49	5	10	15	32	16	1	1	2	41

SHAFIGULIN, Grigory (sha-fih-GOO-lihn, grih-GOH-ree) NSH.

Center. Shoots left. 6'2", 185 lbs. Born, Chelyabinsk, USSR, January 13, 1985.
(Nashville's 8th choice, 98th overall, in 2003 Entry Draft).

			Regular Season					Playoffs				
Season	Club	League	GP	G	A	Pts	PIM	GP	G	A	Pts	PIM
2000-01	Chelyabinsk 2	Russia-3	6	3	2	5	8	....	....	....	....	....
2001-02	Yaroslavl 2	Russia-3	19	2	2	4	12	....	....	....	....	....
2002-03	Yaroslavl 2	Russia-3	33	18	12	30	46	7	0	4	4	31
	Yaroslavl	Russia	11	0	1	1	4	8	0	0	0	4
2003-04	Yaroslavl	Russia	29	3	0	3	4	2	0	0	0	0
	Yaroslavl 2	Russia-3	11	3	8	11	22	....	....	....	....	....
2004-05	Yaroslavl 2	Russia-3	1	0	2	2	0	....	....	....	....	....
	Yaroslavl	Russia	46	5	6	11	49	9	0	0	0	10
2005-06	Yaroslavl	Russia	32	3	6	9	20	3	0	0	0	6
	Yaroslavl 2	Russia-3	7	1	3	4	18	....	....	....	....	....
2006-07	Yaroslavl	Russia	54	5	16	21	46	7	3	0	3	14

SHARROW, Jim (SHA-row, JIHM) VAN.

Defense. Shoots right. 6'2", 198 lbs. Born, Framingham, MA, January 31, 1985.
(Atlanta's 2nd choice, 110th overall, in 2003 Entry Draft).

			Regular Season					Playoffs				
Season	Club	League	GP	G	A	Pts	PIM	GP	G	A	Pts	PIM
2001-02	USNTDP	U-17	17	2	11	13	2	....	....	....	....	....
	USNTDP	NAHL	44	3	5	8	28	....	....	....	....	....
2002-03	Halifax	QMJHL	70	2	14	16	54	25	2	4	6	24
2003-04	Halifax	QMJHL	52	12	26	38	67	....	....	....	....	....
2004-05	Halifax	QMJHL	69	16	31	47	76	13	5	6	11	6
2005-06	Chicago Wolves	AHL	47	2	17	19	17	....	....	....	....	....
	Gwinnett	ECHL	23	3	7	10	12	....	....	....	....	....
2006-07	Chicago Wolves	AHL	42	4	14	18	38	....	....	....	....	....

QMJHL All-Rookie Team (2003)

Traded to **Vancouver** by **Atlanta** for Jesse Schultz, June 23, 2007.

SHATTENKIRK, Kevin (SHAH-tehn-kuhrk, KEH-vihn) COL.

Defense. Shoots right. 5'11", 193 lbs. Born, Greenwich, CT, January 29, 1989.
(Colorado's 1st choice, 14th overall, in 2007 Entry Draft).

			Regular Season					Playoffs				
Season	Club	League	GP	G	A	Pts	PIM	GP	G	A	Pts	PIM
2004-05	Brunswick Bruins	High-CT	22	10	18	28	....	....	....	....	....	....
2005-06	USNTDP	U-17	13	4	4	8	4	....	....	....	....	....
	USNTDP	NAHL	28	6	9	15	17	12	3	7	10	10
2006-07	USNTDP	U-18	43	8	19	27	36	....	....	....	....	....
	USNTDP	NAHL	14	5	8	13	26	....	....	....	....	....

SHEFER, Andrei (SHEH-fuhr, AWN-dray) L.A.

Left wing. Shoots left. 6'1", 194 lbs. Born, Yekaterinburg, USSR, July 26, 1981.
(Los Angeles' 1st choice, 43rd overall, in 1999 Entry Draft).

			Regular Season					Playoffs				
Season	Club	League	GP	G	A	Pts	PIM	GP	G	A	Pts	PIM
1997-98	Yekaterinburg 2	Russia-3	16	3	3	6	18	....	....	....	....	....
1998-99	Cherepovets 3	Russia-4	6	2	2	4	18	....	....	....	....	....
	Cherepovets 2	Russia-3	21	6	5	11	20	....	....	....	....	....
	Cherepovets	Russia	8	1	0	1	4	....	....	....	....	....
99-2000	Halifax	QMJHL	72	34	42	76	30	10	0	5	5	4
2000-01	SKA St. Petersburg	Russia	11	6	1	7	4	....	....	....	....	....
	Cherepovets	Russia	20	1	1	2	10	6	1	0	1	0
2001-02	Cherepovets 2	Russia-3	3	1	2	3	2	....	....	....	....	....
	Cherepovets	Russia	8	0	0	0	6	....	....	....	....	....
	SKA St. Petersburg	Russia	28	4	4	8	10	....	....	....	....	....
2002-03	Cherepovets	Russia	37	2	4	6	10	10	0	0	0	0
	Cherepovets 2	Russia-3	3	1	2	3	2	....	....	....	....	....
2003-04	Cherepovets	Russia	55	4	6	10	46	....	....	....	....	....
2004-05	Cherepovets	Russia	46	1	11	12	18	....	....	....	....	....
2005-06	Cherepovets	Russia	45	2	1	3	32	4	0	1	1	0
2006-07	CSKA Moscow	Russia	45	7	7	14	48	2	0	0	0	2

SHEPPARD, James (sheh-PUHRD, JAYMZ) MIN.

Center. Shoots left. 6'2", 210 lbs. Born, Halifax, N.S., April 25, 1988.
(Minnesota's 1st choice, 9th overall, in 2006 Entry Draft).

			Regular Season					Playoffs				
Season	Club	League	GP	G	A	Pts	PIM	GP	G	A	Pts	PIM
2003-04	Dartmouth	NSMHL	61	38	54	92	46	....	....	....	....	....
2004-05	Cape Breton	QMJHL	65	14	31	45	40	5	1	3	4	2
2005-06	Cape Breton	QMJHL	66	30	54	84	78	9	2	5	7	12
2006-07	Cape Breton	QMJHL	56	33	63	96	62	16	8	12	20	14

QMJHL Second All-Star Team (2007)

SHINKAR, Alexander (shihn-KAHR, al-EHX-AN-duhr) TOR.

Right wing. Shoots left. 6'2", 192 lbs. Born, Ufa, USSR, July 3, 1981.
(Toronto's 9th choice, 254th overall, in 2000 Entry Draft).

			Regular Season					Playoffs				
Season	Club	League	GP	G	A	Pts	PIM	GP	G	A	Pts	PIM
1997-98	Novoil Ufa	Russia-3	22	6	2	8	4	....	....	....	....	....
1998-99	Cherepovets 2	Russia-3	25	7	2	9	8	....	....	....	....	....
	Cherepovets 3	Russia-4	8	0	4	4	4	....	....	....	....	....
99-2000	Cherepovets	Russia	18	1	1	2	2	8	0	0	0	0
2000-01	SKA St. Petersburg	Russia	43	7	4	11	50	....	....	....	....	....
2001-02	Ufa	Russia	27	3	3	6	8	....	....	....	....	....
	SKA St. Petersburg	Russia	18	3	4	7	10	....	....	....	....	....
2002-03	Cherepovets	Russia	32	3	1	4	12	11	0	1	1	6
2003-04	Ufa	Russia	15	2	0	2	16	....	....	....	....	....
	SKA St. Petersburg	Russia	12	4	1	5	0	....	....	....	....	....
2004-05	SKA St. Petersburg	Russia	57	16	14	30	22	....	....	....	....	....
2005-06	SKA St. Petersburg	Russia	44	5	8	13	26	2	0	0	0	2
	St. Petersburg 2	Russia-3	1	0	1	1	0	....	....	....	....	....
2006-07	SKA St. Petersburg	Russia	16	2	0	2	12	....	....	....	....	....
	St. Petersburg 2	Russia-3	6	7	2	9	6	....	....	....	....	....

SHIROKOV, Sergei (sheer-OH-kawv, SAIR-gay) VAN.

Wing. Shoots right. 5'10", 176 lbs. Born, Moscow, USSR, March 10, 1986.
(Vancouver's 3rd choice, 163rd overall, in 2006 Entry Draft).

			Regular Season					Playoffs				
Season	Club	League	GP	G	A	Pts	PIM	GP	G	A	Pts	PIM
2001-02	HK CSKA 2	Russia-3	18	2	3	5	0	....	....	....	....	....
2002-03	CSKA Moscow 2	Russia-3	2	0	0	0	0	....	....	....	....	....
2003-04	CSKA Moscow 2	Russia-3	66	39	41	80	66	....	....	....	....	....
2004-05	CSKA Moscow 2	Russia-3	25	16	13	29	47	....	....	....	....	....
	CSKA Moscow	Russia	8	0	0	0	0	....	....	....	....	....
	CSKA Moscow	Russia	8	0	0	0	0	....	....	....	....	....
2005-06	CSKA Moscow	Russia	39	7	7	14	26	4	0	0	0	0
2006-07	CSKA Moscow	Russia	52	16	19	35	36	12	4	6	10	4

SHUTRON, Ben (SHOO-trawn, BEHN) CHI.

Defense. Shoots right. 5'11", 186 lbs. Born, Ottawa, Ont., June 14, 1988.
(Chicago's 5th choice, 95th overall, in 2006 Entry Draft).

			Regular Season					Playoffs				
Season	Club	League	GP	G	A	Pts	PIM	GP	G	A	Pts	PIM
2004-05	Kingston	OHL	63	7	20	27	28	....	....	....	....	....
2005-06	Kingston	OHL	67	10	29	39	134	6	0	2	2	14
2006-07	Kingston	OHL	68	5	42	47	81	5	1	3	4	8

SIDDALL, Matt (sih-DUHL, MAT) ATL.

Right wing. Shoots right. 6'1", 210 lbs. Born, North Vancouver, B.C., September 26, 1984.
(Atlanta's 9th choice, 270th overall, in 2004 Entry Draft).

			Regular Season					Playoffs				
Season	Club	League	GP	G	A	Pts	PIM	GP	G	A	Pts	PIM
2003-04	Powell River Kings	BCHL	45	25	36	61	216	7	4	2	6	10
2004-05	Northern Mich.	CCHA	33	4	4	8	62	....	....	....	....	....
2005-06	Northern Mich.	CCHA	36	6	6	12	72	....	....	....	....	....
2006-07	Northern Mich.	CCHA	37	4	16	20	107	....	....	....	....	....

SIDORENKO, Kirill (sih-dohr-EHN-koh, kih-RIHL) DAL.

Center. Shoots left. 6'3", 187 lbs. Born, Omsk, USSR, March 30, 1983.
(Dallas' 9th choice, 180th overall, in 2002 Entry Draft).

			Regular Season					Playoffs				
Season	Club	League	GP	G	A	Pts	PIM	GP	G	A	Pts	PIM
1998-99	Omsk 2	Russia-4	2	0	0	0	2	....	....	....	....	....
99-2000	Omsk 2	Russia-3	26	2	11	13	14	....	....	....	....	....
2000-01	Omsk 2	Russia-3	30	8	7	15	44	....	....	....	....	....
2001-02	Mostovik Kurgan	Russia-2	50	11	6	17	64	....	....	....	....	....
2002-03	Sibir Novosibirsk	Russia	30	1	1	2	2	....	....	....	....	....
2003-04	Energiya Kemerovo	Russia-2	14	1	1	2	6	....	....	....	....	....
	Zauralje Kurgan	Russia-2	32	3	3	6	6	4	0	0	0	27
2004-05	Omsk 2	Russia-3	18	7	4	11	12	....	....	....	....	....
	CSK VVS Samara	Russia-2	16	2	2	4	0	....	....	....	....	....
2005-06	CSK VVS Samara	Russia-2	47	8	11	19	62	....	....	....	....	....
	Krylja Sovetov	Russia-2	6	3	3	6	8	17	1	3	4	4
2006-07	Krylja Sovetov 2	Russia-3	4	2	1	3	6	....	....	....	....	....
	Krylja Sovetov	Russia	35	5	4	9	22	....	....	....	....	....

SIDYAKIN, Andrei (sihd-YA-kihn, AWN-dray) MTL.

Right wing. Shoots left. 5'11", 169 lbs. Born, Ufa, USSR, January 20, 1979.
(Montreal's 10th choice, 202nd overall, in 1997 Entry Draft).

			Regular Season					Playoffs				
Season	Club	League	GP	G	A	Pts	PIM	GP	G	A	Pts	PIM
1994-95	Ufa	CIS	7	0	1	1	0	....	....	....	....	....
1995-96	Ufa	CIS	25	1	0	1	4	3	0	0	0	2
1996-97	Ufa	Russia	29	3	5	8	4	....	....	....	....	....
1997-98	Ufa	Russia	42	5	4	9	32	....	....	....	....	....
1998-99	Ufa	Russia	36	6	4	10	14	2	0	0	0	2
99-2000	Ufa	Russia	38	7	2	9	32	....	....	....	....	....
2000-01	Ufa	Russia	44	10	13	23	42	....	....	....	....	....
2001-02	Ufa	Russia	43	9	7	16	20	....	....	....	....	....
2002-03	Cherepovets	Russia	38	8	8	16	20	2	0	0	0	4
2003-04	Cherepovets	Russia	19	1	2	3	12	....	....	....	....	....
	Cherepovets 2	Russia-3	4	2	3	5	0	....	....	....	....	....
	Ufa	Russia	29	8	8	16	28	....	....	....	....	....
2004-05	Ufa	Russia	57	8	20	28	54	....	....	....	....	....
2005-06	Ufa	Russia	51	18	20	38	54	6	4	0	4	8
2006-07	Ufa	Russia	54	19	13	32	44	8	3	2	5	6

SIFERS, Jaime (SIH-fuhrs, JAY-mee) TOR.

Defense. Shoots right. 5'11", 210 lbs. Born, Stratford, CT, January 18, 1983.

			Regular Season					Playoffs				
Season	Club	League	GP	G	A	Pts	PIM	GP	G	A	Pts	PIM
2002-03	U. of Vermont	ECAC	34	4	14	18	66					
2003-04	U. of Vermont	ECAC	35	4	14	18	93					
2004-05	U. of Vermont	ECACHL	36	4	12	16	57					
2005-06	U. of Vermont	H-East	38	3	15	18	60					
	Toronto Marlies	AHL	2	0	0	0	2					
2006-07	Toronto Marlies	AHL	80	7	18	25	75					

ECACHL Second All-Star Team (2005)

Signed as a free agent by **Toronto**, July 20, 2006.

SIMEK, Juraj (SEE-mehk, YUHR-ay) VAN.

Wing. Shoots left. 6'1", 189 lbs. Born, Presov, Czech., September 29, 1987.
(Vancouver's 4th choice, 167th overall, in 2006 Entry Draft).

			Regular Season					Playoffs				
Season	Club	League	GP	G	A	Pts	PIM	GP	G	A	Pts	PIM
2002-03	SC Bern Jr.	Swiss-Jr.	2	1	0	1	0	2	0	0	0	0
2003-04	Kloten Flyers Jr.	Swiss-Jr.	36	8	6	14	28					
2004-05	Kloten Flyers Jr.	Swiss-Jr.	39	17	13	30	62	9	2	3	5	10
	Kloten Flyers	Swiss	18	0	0	0	0					
	Kloten Flyers	Swiss	18	0	0	0	0					
2005-06	Kloten Flyers Jr.	Swiss-Jr.	45	24	44	68	202					
	Kloten Flyers	Swiss	8	0	1	1	4					
	EHC Biel-Bienne	Swiss-2	3	0	0	0	2					
2006-07	Brandon	WHL	58	28	29	57	41	9	1	5	6	6

SIMMONDS, Wayne (SIH-muhnz, WAYN) L.A.

Right wing. Shoots right. 6'2", 162 lbs. Born, Scarborough, Ont., August 26, 1988.
(Los Angeles' 3rd choice, 61st overall, in 2007 Entry Draft).

			Regular Season					Playoffs				
Season	Club	League	GP	G	A	Pts	PIM	GP	G	A	Pts	PIM
2004-05	Tor. Jr. Canadiens	GTHL	67	32	40	72	97					
2005-06	Brockville Braves	CJHL	49	24	19	43	127	7	4	2	6	12
2006-07	Owen Sound	OHL	66	23	26	49	112	4	1	1	2	4

SIMS, Shane (SIHMZ, SHAYN) NYI

Defense. Shoots right. 6', 192 lbs. Born, East Amherst, NY, April 30, 1988.
(NY Islanders' 8th choice, 126th overall, in 2006 Entry Draft).

			Regular Season					Playoffs				
Season	Club	League	GP	G	A	Pts	PIM	GP	G	A	Pts	PIM
2004-05	Buffalo Lightning	OPJHL	48	14	26	40	47					
2005-06	Des Moines	USHL	59	10	12	22	80	11	2	0	2	12
2006-07	Des Moines	USHL	59	10	19	29	137	8	1	3	4	8

USHL All-Rookie Team (2006)

SINDEL, Jakub (SHIHN-dehl, YA-kuhb) CHI.

Center. Shoots right. 6', 172 lbs. Born, Jihlava, Czech., January 24, 1986.
(Chicago's 5th choice, 54th overall, in 2004 Entry Draft).

			Regular Season					Playoffs				
Season	Club	League	GP	G	A	Pts	PIM	GP	G	A	Pts	PIM
99-2000	Slavia U17	CzR-U17	32	10	6	16	6					
2000-01	Slavia U17	CzR-U17	26	12	15	27	2	6	1	0	1	0
2001-02	Slavia U17	CzR-U17	34	32	14	46	34	2	0	1	1	2
	HC Slavia Praha Jr.	CzRep-Jr.	14	7	4	11	10					
2002-03	HC Slavia Praha Jr.	CzRep-Jr.	35	12	11	23	39	2	0	1	1	0
2003-04	HC Sparta Praha	CzRep	34	5	1	6	14	13	1	1	2	2
	Sparta Jr.	CzRep-Jr.	13	8	14	22	4					
	HC Dukla Jihlava	CzRep-2	1	0	0	0	0					
2004-05	Sparta Jr.	CzRep-Jr.	9	5	16	21	16					
	HC Sparta Praha	CzRep	10	0	2	2	0					
	Trebic	CzRep-2	5	0	0	0	0					
	Brandon	WHL	35	16	13	29	12	24	7	4	11	22
2005-06	HC Sparta Praha	CzRep	12	1	1	2	6					
	Plzen	CzRep	31	11	8	19	18					
2006-07	Plzen	CzRep	50	16	10	26	30					
	BK Mlada Boleslav	CzRep-2	4	1	0	1	4	8	5	5	10	20

SIPOTZ, Brian (SIHP-awtz, BRIGH-uhn)

Defense. Shoots right. 6'7", 235 lbs. Born, South Bend, IN, September 16, 1981.
(Atlanta's 3rd choice, 100th overall, in 2001 Entry Draft).

			Regular Season					Playoffs				
Season	Club	League	GP	G	A	Pts	PIM	GP	G	A	Pts	PIM
99-2000	Culver Academy	High-IN	45	14	22	36	56					
2000-01	Miami U.	CCHA	32	0	1	1	48					
2001-02	Miami U.	CCHA	25	0	1	1	28					
2002-03	Miami U.	CCHA	26	0	0	0	24					
2003-04	Miami U.	CCHA	36	0	3	3	39					
2004-05	Chicago Wolves	AHL	75	2	6	8	31	18	1	2	3	6
	Gwinnett	ECHL	2	0	0	0	0					
2005-06	Chicago Wolves	AHL	57	2	12	14	41					
2006-07	Chicago Wolves	AHL	73	2	10	12	36	8	0	0	0	2

SJODIN, Viktor (shoh-DEEN, VIHK-tohr) NSH.

Wing. Shoots right. 6', 230 lbs. Born, Uppsala, Sweden, April 21, 1988.
(Nashville's 5th choice, 206th overall, in 2006 Entry Draft).

			Regular Season					Playoffs				
Season	Club	League	GP	G	A	Pts	PIM	GP	G	A	Pts	PIM
2004-05	Vasteras U18	Swe-U18	6	2	2	4	10	4	1	2	3	2
	Vasteras Jr.	Swe-Jr.	18	3	6	9	20					
2005-06	Vasteras Jr.	Swe-Jr.	31	12	5	17	79					
2006-07	Portland	WHL	68	13	12	25	79					

SKACHKOV, Evgeny (skatch-KAWF, yehv-GEH-nee) ST.L.

Left wing. Shoots right. 6', 187 lbs. Born, Penza, USSR, July 14, 1984.
(St. Louis' 10th choice, 221st overall, in 2003 Entry Draft).

			Regular Season					Playoffs				
Season	Club	League	GP	G	A	Pts	PIM	GP	G	A	Pts	PIM
2000-01	Dizelist Penza	Russia-2	9	0	0	0	0					
2001-02	Kapitan Stupino	Russia-3	STATISTICS NOT AVAILABLE									
2002-03	Stupino	Russia-3	STATISTICS NOT AVAILABLE									
	Kapitan Stupino	EEHL	34	4	4	8	2					
2003-04	CSKA Moscow 2	Russia-3	DID NOT PLAY – INJURED									
	CSKA Moscow	Russia	1	0	0	0	2					
2004-05	Spartak Moscow	Russia	9	0	2	2	0					
2005-06	Spartak Moscow 2	Russia-3	55	25	31	56	98					
	Spartak Moscow	Russia	2	0	0	0	6					
2006-07	Chelyabinsk	Russia	52	13	9	22	52					

SKILLE, Jack (SKIH-lee, JAK) CHI.

Right wing. Shoots right. 6'1", 198 lbs. Born, Madison, WI, May 19, 1987.
(Chicago's 1st choice, 7th overall, in 2005 Entry Draft).

			Regular Season					Playoffs				
Season	Club	League	GP	G	A	Pts	PIM	GP	G	A	Pts	PIM
2003-04	USNTDP	U-17	33	14	10	24	30					
	USNTDP	NAHL	28	11	9	20	31					
2004-05	USNTDP	U-18	26	9	11	20	36					
	USNTDP	NAHL	16	6	11	17	20					
2005-06	U. of Wisconsin	WCHA	41	13	8	21	37					
2006-07	U. of Wisconsin	WCHA	26	8	10	18	12					
	Norfolk Admirals	AHL	9	4	4	8	0	3	0	0	0	2

SKINNER, Brett (SKIH-nuhr, BREHT) ANA.

Defense. Shoots left. 6'1", 195 lbs. Born, Brandon, Man., June 28, 1983.
(Vancouver's 3rd choice, 68th overall, in 2002 Entry Draft).

			Regular Season					Playoffs				
Season	Club	League	GP	G	A	Pts	PIM	GP	G	A	Pts	PIM
1998-99	Brandon Kings	MMBHL	29	3	18	21	20					
99-2000	Brandon Kings	MMMHL	40	8	27	35	48					
2000-01	Trail Smoke Eaters	BCHL	59	11	24	35	43					
2001-02	Des Moines	USHL	44	9	38	47	25	3	0	1	1	0
2002-03	U. of Denver	WCHA	37	4	13	17	27					
2003-04	U. of Denver	WCHA	44	7	23	30	32					
2004-05	U. of Denver	WCHA	43	4	36	40	30					
2005-06	Manitoba Moose	AHL	65	4	21	25	33	13	0	4	4	19
2006-07	Portland Pirates	AHL	41	6	12	18	24					
	Augusta Lynx	ECHL	5	1	3	4	8					
	Omaha	AHL	21	0	6	6	2	5	0	3	3	2

USHL First All-Star Team (2002) • USHL Defenseman of the Year (2002) • WCHA First All-Star Team (2005) • NCAA West Second All-American Team (2005) • NCAA Championship All-Tournament Team (2005)

Traded to **Anaheim** by **Vancouver** with NY Islanders' 2nd round choice (previously acquired, Anaheim selected Bryce Swan) in 2006 Entry Draft for Keith Carney and Juha Alen, March 9, 2006.

SKOKAN, David (SKOH-kahn, DAY-vihd) NYR

Center. Shoots left. 6', 191 lbs. Born, Poprad, Czech., December 6, 1988.
(NY Rangers' 5th choice, 193rd overall, in 2007 Entry Draft).

			Regular Season					Playoffs				
Season	Club	League	GP	G	A	Pts	PIM	GP	G	A	Pts	PIM
2003-04	Poprad U18	Svk-U18	38	17	28	45	110	6	1	5	6	37
	HK SKP Poprad Jr.	Slovak-Jr.	7	2	0	2	7					
2004-05	Poprad U18	Svk-U18	4	4	6	10	37					
	HK SKP Poprad Jr.	Slovak-Jr.	24	5	19	24	52					
	HK SKP Poprad	Slovakia	8	0	0	0	6	2	0	0	0	25
2005-06	Rimouski Oceanic	QMJHL	53	6	15	21	143					
2006-07	Rimouski Oceanic	QMJHL	52	14	21	35	62					

SMABY, Matt (SMA-bee, MAT) T.B.

Defense. Shoots left. 6'6", 239 lbs. Born, Minneapolis, MN, October 14, 1984.
(Tampa Bay's 2nd choice, 41st overall, in 2003 Entry Draft).

			Regular Season					Playoffs				
Season	Club	League	GP	G	A	Pts	PIM	GP	G	A	Pts	PIM
2001-02	Shat.-St. Mary's	High-MN	65	7	18	25	134					
2002-03	Shat.-St. Mary's	High-MN	57	3	20	23	114					
2003-04	North Dakota	WCHA	39	1	6	7	81					
2004-05	North Dakota	WCHA	44	1	2	3	86					
2005-06	North Dakota	WCHA	46	4	15	19	*113					
2006-07	Springfield Falcons	AHL	66	2	14	16	43					

SMITH, Austin (SMIHTH, AUZ-tihn) DAL.

Right wing. Shoots right. 5'11", 160 lbs. Born, Dallas, TX, November 7, 1988.
(Dallas' 4th choice, 128th overall, in 2007 Entry Draft).

			Regular Season					Playoffs				
Season	Club	League	GP	G	A	Pts	PIM	GP	G	A	Pts	PIM
2003-04	Dallas Jesuit Prep	High-TX	STATISTICS NOT AVAILABLE									
2004-05	Dallas Jesuit Prep	High-TX	STATISTICS NOT AVAILABLE									
	Alliance Bulldogs	NTHL	53	29	46	75	24					
2005-06	The Gunnery	High-CT	31	23	20	43	22					
2006-07	The Gunnery	High-CT	30	25	38	63	36					

• Signed Letter of Intent to attend **Colgate University** (ECACHL) in fall of 2008.

SMITH, Brendan (SMIHTH, BREHN-duhn) DET.

Defense. Shoots left. 6'1", 170 lbs. Born, Toronto, Ont., February 8, 1989.
(Detroit's 1st choice, 27th overall, in 2007 Entry Draft).

			Regular Season					Playoffs				
Season	Club	League	GP	G	A	Pts	PIM	GP	G	A	Pts	PIM
2004-05	Toronto Marlboros	GTHL	66	22	63	85	120					
2005-06	St. Michael's	OPJHL	39	5	21	26	55	17	1	5	6	44
2006-07	St. Michael's	OPJHL	39	12	24	36	90	16	6	14	20	30

SMITH, Derek (SMIHTH, dair-IHK) OTT.

Defense. Shoots left. 6', 180 lbs. Born, Belleville, Ont., October 13, 1984.

			Regular Season					Playoffs				
Season	Club	League	GP	G	A	Pts	PIM	GP	G	A	Pts	PIM
2002-03	Wellington Dukes	OPJHL	21	6	10	16	26					
2003-04	Wellington Dukes	OPJHL	44	8	26	34	34					
2004-05	Lake Superior	CCHA	38	1	4	5	28					
2005-06	Lake Superior	CCHA	36	2	8	10	18					
2006-07	Lake Superior	CCHA	43	10	20	30	10					

Signed as a free agent by **Ottawa**, April 12, 2007.

SMITH, Trevor (SMIHTH, TREH-vuhr) **NYI**

Left wing. Shoots left. 6'1", 195 lbs. Born, North Vancouver, B.C., February 8, 1985.

			Regular Season					Playoffs				
Season	Club	League	GP	G	A	Pts	PIM	GP	G	A	Pts	PIM
2003-04	Quesnel	BCHL	44	28	19	47	50	....	....	....	....	....
2004-05	Omaha Lancers	USHL	60	29	39	68	78	5	3	1	4	2
2005-06	New Hampshire	H-East	39	10	10	20	34	....	....	....	....	....
2006-07	New Hampshire	H-East	39	21	22	43	39	....	....	....	....	....
	Bridgeport	AHL	8	1	2	3	2	....	....	....	....	....

NCAA East Second All-American Team (2007)

Signed as a free agent by **NY Islanders**, April 2, 2007.

SMOLENAK, Radek (SMOH-lehn-ahk, RA-dehk) **T.B.**

Left wing. Shoots left. 6'3", 180 lbs. Born, Prague, Czech., December 3, 1986.
(Tampa Bay's 2nd choice, 73rd overall, in 2005 Entry Draft).

			Regular Season					Playoffs				
Season	Club	League	GP	G	A	Pts	PIM	GP	G	A	Pts	PIM
2001-02	HC Kladno U17	CzR-U17	47	29	20	49	38	....	....	....	....	....
2002-03	HC Kladno U17	CzR-U17	41	39	27	66	50	9	7	3	10	18
	HC Kladno Jr.	CzRep-Jr.	4	2	0	2	6	....	....	....	....	....
2003-04	HC Kladno Jr.	CzRep-Jr.	54	27	25	52	51	7	3	4	7	0
2004-05	Kingston	OHL	67	32	28	60	58	....	....	....	....	....
2005-06	Kingston	OHL	65	42	42	84	109	6	1	3	4	20
2006-07	Springfield Falcons	AHL	20	0	1	1	8	....	....	....	....	....
	Johnstown Chiefs	ECHL	43	15	20	35	35	1	0	0	0	0

SMOLYANINOV, Vitali **T.B.**

Left wing. Shoots left. 6'3", 205 lbs. Born, Nizhnekamsk, USSR, August 5, 1983.
(Tampa Bay's 12th choice, 261st overall, in 2001 Entry Draft).

			Regular Season					Playoffs				
Season	Club	League	GP	G	A	Pts	PIM	GP	G	A	Pts	PIM
1998-99	Nizhnekamsk 2	Russia-4	12	1	0	1	0	....	....	....	....	....
99-2000	Nizhnekamsk 2	Russia-3	54	7	7	14	28	....	....	....	....	....
2000-01	Nizhnekamsk 2	Russia-3	STATISTICS NOT AVAILABLE									
2001-02	Nizhnekamsk	Russia	1	0	0	0	0	....	....	....	....	....
2002-03	HK Voronezh	Russia-2	14	1	1	2	12	....	....	....	....	....
2003-04	Karaganda	Kazakh.	9	2	3	5	0	....	....	....	....	....
	Karaganda	Russia-2	19	0	1	1	32	....	....	....	....	....
2004-05	Karaganda	Kazakh.	7	5	3	8	2	....	....	....	....	....
	Karaganda	Russia-2	20	1	5	6	10	....	....	....	....	....
2005-06	Irtysh Pavlodar	Kazakh.	14	8	6	14	12	....	....	....	....	....
	Irtysh Pavlodar	Russia-3	STATISTICS NOT AVAILABLE									
2006-07	Barys Astana	Russia-3	42	8	19	27	36	....	....	....	....	....
	Barys Astana	Kazakh.	22	10	6	16	52	....	....	....	....	....

SNEEP, Carl (SNEEP, KAHRL) **PIT.**

Defense. Shoots right. 6'4", 210 lbs. Born, St. Louis Park, MN, November 5, 1987.
(Pittsburgh's 2nd choice, 32nd overall, in 2006 Entry Draft).

			Regular Season					Playoffs				
Season	Club	League	GP	G	A	Pts	PIM	GP	G	A	Pts	PIM
2004-05	Brainerd	High-MN	26	20	21	41	25	....	....	....	....	....
2005-06	Brainerd	High-MN	26	14	23	37	34	....	....	....	....	....
	Lincoln Stars	USHL	13	1	3	4	9	9	0	1	1	6
2006-07	Boston College	H-East	38	1	9	10	8	....	....	....	....	....

SNELLMAN , Niko (SNEHL-mahn, NEE-KOH) **NSH.**

Left wing. Shoots left. 6'3", 208 lbs. Born, Tampere, Finland, March 12, 1988.
(Nashville's 2nd choice, 105th overall, in 2006 Entry Draft).

			Regular Season					Playoffs				
Season	Club	League	GP	G	A	Pts	PIM	GP	G	A	Pts	PIM
2004-05	Ilves Tampere U18	Fin-U18	22	5	1	6	44	5	0	0	0	2
2005-06	Ilves Tampere U18	Fin-U18	6	3	8	11	28	6	2	5	7	64
	Ilves Tampere Jr.	Fin-Jr.	23	4	4	8	74	3	0	0	0	4
2006-07	Regina Pats	WHL	32	5	5	10	65	....	....	....	....	....

SNOW, Aaron (SNOH, AIR-ruhn) **DAL.**

Left wing. Shoots left. 6', 199 lbs. Born, Windsor, Ont., May 20, 1988.
(Dallas' 2nd choice, 90th overall, in 2006 Entry Draft).

			Regular Season					Playoffs				
Season	Club	League	GP	G	A	Pts	PIM	GP	G	A	Pts	PIM
2003-04	Tecumseh Chiefs	OJHL-B	53	19	21	40	64	....	....	....	....	....
2004-05	Brampton	OHL	61	8	7	15	35	6	1	0	1	2
2005-06	Brampton	OHL	68	30	38	68	107	11	4	4	8	22
2006-07	Brampton	OHL	12	5	3	8	18	....	....	....	....	....
	Belleville Bulls	OHL	48	13	20	33	64	13	1	2	3	4

SOBOTKA, Vladimir (soh-BAWT-kah, vla-DIH-meer) **BOS.**

Center. Shoots left. 5'11", 194 lbs. Born, Trebic, Czech., July 2, 1987.
(Boston's 5th choice, 106th overall, in 2005 Entry Draft).

			Regular Season					Playoffs				
Season	Club	League	GP	G	A	Pts	PIM	GP	G	A	Pts	PIM
2002-03	Slavia U17	CzR-U17	46	16	24	40	48	8	1	1	2	29
2003-04	Slavia U17	CzR-U17	35	24	41	65	109	7	7	12	19	8
	HC Slavia Praha Jr.	CzRep-Jr.	18	6	6	12	16	....	....	....	....	....
	HC Slavia Praha	CzRep	1	0	0	0	0	....	....	....	....	....
2004-05	HC Slavia Praha Jr.	CzRep-Jr.	27	12	21	33	93	....	....	....	....	....
	HC Slavia Praha	CzRep	18	0	1	1	8	....	....	....	....	....
	Havl. Brod	CzRep-3	7	3	0	3	31	7	1	5	6	0
2005-06	HC Slavia Praha Jr.	CzRep-Jr.	8	10	4	14	42	....	....	....	....	....
	HC Slavia Praha	CzRep	33	1	9	10	28	11	2	3	5	10
2006-07	HC Slavia Praha	CzRep	33	7	6	13	38	....	....	....	....	....

SODERBERG, Carl (SOH-dehr-buhrg, KAHRL) **BOS.**

Center. Shoots left. 6'3", 198 lbs. Born, Malmo, Sweden, October 12, 1985.
(St. Louis' 2nd choice, 49th overall, in 2004 Entry Draft).

			Regular Season					Playoffs				
Season	Club	League	GP	G	A	Pts	PIM	GP	G	A	Pts	PIM
2000-01	Skane	Exhib.	8	1	2	3	2	....	....	....	....	....
	Malmo U18	Swe-U18	3	1	1	2	0	....	....	....	....	....
2001-02	Malmo U18	Swe-U18	13	9	20	29	18	....	....	....	....	....
	Malmo Jr.	Swe-Jr.	4	0	2	2	2	7	0	2	2	4
2002-03	Malmo U18	Swe-U18	4	6	3	9	25	....	....	....	....	....
	Malmo Jr.	Swe-Jr.	28	17	18	35	22	6	2	4	6	8
2003-04	Malmo U18	Swe-U18	27	23	25	48	30	6	1	2	3	10
	Malmo	Sweden	24	1	1	2	8	....	....	....	....	....
	Malmo	Sweden-Q	8	1	1	2	4	....	....	....	....	....
2004-05	Morrums GoIS IK	Sweden-2	14	5	6	11	8	....	....	....	....	....
	Malmo Jr.	Swe-Jr.	12	13	6	19	43	3	2	1	3	12
	Malmo	Sweden	38	0	5	5	8	....	....	....	....	....
	Malmo	Sweden-Q	7	0	0	0	0	....	....	....	....	....
2005-06	Malmo	Sweden-2	49	20	27	47	47	....	....	....	....	....
2006-07	Malmo	Sweden	31	12	18	30	14	....	....	....	....	....

Traded to **Boston** by **St. Louis** for Hannu Toivonen, July 23, 2007.

SOIN, Sergei (SOY-ihn, SAIR-gay) **NSH.**

Center/Left wing. Shoots left. 6', 185 lbs. Born, Moscow, USSR, March 31, 1982.
(Colorado's 3rd choice, 50th overall, in 2000 Entry Draft).

			Regular Season					Playoffs				
Season	Club	League	GP	G	A	Pts	PIM	GP	G	A	Pts	PIM
1997-98	Krylja Sovetov 2	Russia-3	2	0	0	0	0	....	....	....	....	....
1998-99	Krylja Sovetov	Russia	34	1	4	5	12	....	....	....	....	....
99-2000	Krylja Sovetov 2	Russia-3	8	2	3	5	12	....	....	....	....	....
	Krylja Sovetov	Russia-2	32	8	8	16	28	14	0	2	2	6
2000-01	Krylja Sovetov 2	Russia-3	8	2	3	5	12	....	....	....	....	....
	Krylja Sovetov	Russia-2	19	6	3	9	8	11	2	2	4	2
2001-02	Krylja Sovetov 2	Russia-3	5	2	6	8	20	....	....	....	....	....
	Krylja Sovetov	Russia	41	5	7	12	8	....	....	....	....	....
2002-03	Krylja Sovetov	Russia	49	8	6	14	40	....	....	....	....	....
2003-04	CSKA Moscow	Russia	49	1	6	7	32	....	....	....	....	....
2004-05	CSKA Moscow	Russia	19	3	3	6	10	....	....	....	....	....
2005-06	Cherepovets	Russia	48	5	12	17	36	4	1	1	2	0
2006-07	Cherepovets	Russia	52	12	12	24	78	5	2	1	3	0

Traded to **Nashville** by **Colorado** for Tomas Slovak, June 21, 2003.

SOLAREV, Ilja (SOH-luh-rehv, IHL-yuh) **T.B.**

Left wing. Shoots left. 6'3", 176 lbs. Born, Perm, USSR, August 2, 1982.
(Tampa Bay's 13th choice, 281st overall, in 2001 Entry Draft).

			Regular Season					Playoffs				
Season	Club	League	GP	G	A	Pts	PIM	GP	G	A	Pts	PIM
1997-98	Perm 2	Russia-3	4	1	0	1	0	....	....	....	....	....
1998-99	Perm 2	Russia-4	20	2	6	8	10	....	....	....	....	....
99-2000	Perm 2	Russia-3	35	3	2	5	24	....	....	....	....	....
2000-01	Perm 2	Russia-3	STATISTICS NOT AVAILABLE									
	Perm	Russia	5	0	1	1	0	....	....	....	....	....
2001-02	Leninogorsk	Russia-2	31	3	5	8	20	....	....	....	....	....
	HK Tambov	Russia-3	2	0	0	0	0	....	....	....	....	....
2002-03	Perm 2	Russia-3	STATISTICS NOT AVAILABLE									
	HK Brest	Belarus	STATISTICS NOT AVAILABLE									
2003-04	Motor Barnaul	Russia-2	34	6	6	12	20	1	0	0	0	0
2005-06	HK Lipetsk	Russia-2	49	4	6	10	30	3	0	0	0	0
2006-07	Satpayev	Russia-2	44	17	16	33	24	....	....	....	....	....
	Satpayev	Kazakh.	21	7	2	9	12	....	....	....	....	....

SONNE, Brett (SOHNE, BREHT) **ST.L.**

Center/Left wing. Shoots left. 5'11", 200 lbs. Born, Chilliwack, B.C., March 16, 1989.
(St. Louis' 6th choice, 85th overall, in 2007 Entry Draft).

			Regular Season					Playoffs				
Season	Club	League	GP	G	A	Pts	PIM	GP	G	A	Pts	PIM
2004-05	Port Coquitlam	PIJHL	47	21	34	55	125	....	....	....	....	....
	Calgary Hitmen	WHL	6	0	0	0	2	....	....	....	....	....
2005-06	Calgary Hitmen	WHL	64	12	9	21	38	13	1	2	3	8
2006-07	Calgary Hitmen	WHL	71	21	9	30	65	18	5	1	6	22

SOPANEN, Vili (SOH-puh-nehn, VIHL-ee) **N.J.**

Right wing. Shoots right. 6'4", 210 lbs. Born, Valkeala, Finland, October 21, 1987.
(New Jersey's 5th choice, 177th overall, in 2007 Entry Draft).

			Regular Season					Playoffs				
Season	Club	League	GP	G	A	Pts	PIM	GP	G	A	Pts	PIM
2003-04	K-Reipas U18	Fin-U18	20	1	2	3	14	....	....	....	....	....
2004-05	K-Reipas U18	Fin-U18	25	11	15	26	4	3	0	2	2	22
2005-06	Pelicans Lahti Jr.	Fin-Jr.	38	15	17	32	22	....	....	....	....	....
	Pelicans Lahti	Finland	3	0	0	0	0	....	....	....	....	....
2006-07	Pelicans Lahti Jr.	Fin-Jr.	33	18	21	39	40	15	5	13	18	18
	Suomi U20	Finland-2	6	1	1	2	4	....	....	....	....	....
	Pelicans Lahti	Finland	7	1	0	1	0	....	....	....	....	....

SPALING, Nick (SPAHL-ihng, NIHK) **NSH.**

Center. Shoots left. 6'1", 182 lbs. Born, Palmerston, Ont., September 19, 1988.
(Nashville's 3rd choice, 58th overall, in 2007 Entry Draft).

			Regular Season					Playoffs				
Season	Club	League	GP	G	A	Pts	PIM	GP	G	A	Pts	PIM
2004-05	Listowel Cyclones	OJHL-B	61	25	27	52	58	....	....	....	....	....
2005-06	Kitchener Rangers	OHL	62	10	15	25	22	5	0	3	3	0
2006-07	Kitchener Rangers	OHL	61	23	36	59	41	9	2	3	5	4

SPANG, Dan (SPANG, DAN) **S.J.**

Defense. Shoots left. 6', 205 lbs. Born, Winchester, MA, August 18, 1983.
(San Jose's 2nd choice, 52nd overall, in 2002 Entry Draft).

			Regular Season					Playoffs				
Season	Club	League	GP	G	A	Pts	PIM	GP	G	A	Pts	PIM
2000-01	Winchester High	High-MA	24	8	37	45	14	....	....	....	....	....
2001-02	Winchester High	High-MA	6	9	8	17	14	....	....	....	....	....
2002-03	Boston University	H-East	27	3	6	9	14	....	....	....	....	....
2003-04	Boston University	H-East	38	5	9	14	12	....	....	....	....	....
2004-05	Boston University	H-East	41	3	13	16	22	....	....	....	....	....
2005-06	Boston University	H-East	40	9	22	31	14	....	....	....	....	....
	Cleveland Barons	AHL	8	0	0	0	8	....	....	....	....	....
2006-07	Worcester Sharks	AHL	48	4	21	25	18	....	....	....	....	....

Hockey East First All-Star Team (2006) • NCAA East First All-American Team (2006)

• Missed majority of 2001-02 season recovering from head injuries suffered in automobile accident, October, 2001.

SPRUNGER, Julien (SRUHN-guhr, JEW-lee-ehn) MIN.

Right wing. Shoots right. 6'4", 197 lbs. Born, Fribourg, Switz., January 4, 1986.
(Minnesota's 7th choice, 117th overall, in 2004 Entry Draft).

			Regular Season					Playoffs				
Season	Club	League	GP	G	A	Pts	PIM	GP	G	A	Pts	PIM
2002-03	Fribourg Jr.	Swiss-Jr.	24	21	19	40	32	....	....	....	....	....
	Fribourg	Swiss	2	0	0	0	0	....	....	....	....	....
	HC Dudingen	Swiss-3	9	7	1	8	....	2	1	1	2	....
2003-04	Fribourg	Swiss	42	2	3	5	14	4	0	0	0	4
2004-05	Fribourg Jr.	Swiss-Jr.	4	3	4	7	4	....	....	....	....	....
	Chaux-de-Fonds	Swiss-2	1	0	0	0	0	....	....	....	....	....
	Fribourg	Swiss	41	9	7	16	35	11	2	1	3	14
2005-06	Fribourg Jr.	Swiss-Jr.	2	2	1	3	6	....	....	....	....	....
	Fribourg	Swiss	38	19	14	33	36	10	5	2	7	25
	Fribourg	Swiss-Q	....	....	....	....	....	5	2	1	3	4
2006-07	Fribourg	Swiss	34	10	10	20	46	....	....	....	....	....

SPURGEON, Tyler (SPUHR-juhn, TIGH-luhr) EDM.

Center. Shoots left. 5'10", 188 lbs. Born, Edmonton, Alta., April 10, 1986.
(Edmonton's 9th choice, 242nd overall, in 2004 Entry Draft).

			Regular Season					Playoffs				
Season	Club	League	GP	G	A	Pts	PIM	GP	G	A	Pts	PIM
2001-02	Edmonton MLAC	AMHL	35	39	36	75	12	....	....	....	....	....
	Kelowna Rockets	WHL	2	0	1	1	0	....	....	....	....	....
2002-03	Kelowna Rockets	WHL	50	7	6	13	21	19	2	5	7	6
2003-04	Kelowna Rockets	WHL	49	8	16	24	24	17	4	5	9	9
2004-05	Kelowna Rockets	WHL	72	21	41	62	32	24	11	6	17	12
2005-06	Kelowna Rockets	WHL	39	7	17	24	22	12	0	3	3	14
2006-07	Wilkes-Barre	AHL	34	5	10	15	10	6	1	0	1	4
	Stockton Thunder	ECHL	39	12	17	29	26	....	....	....	....	....

STAAL, Marc (STAHL, MAHRK) NYR

Defense. Shoots left. 6'4", 205 lbs. Born, Thunder Bay, Ont., January 13, 1987.
(NY Rangers' 1st choice, 12th overall, in 2005 Entry Draft).

			Regular Season					Playoffs				
Season	Club	League	GP	G	A	Pts	PIM	GP	G	A	Pts	PIM
2003-04	Sudbury Wolves	OHL	61	1	13	14	34	7	1	2	3	2
2004-05	Sudbury Wolves	OHL	65	6	20	26	53	12	0	4	4	15
2005-06	Sudbury Wolves	OHL	57	11	38	49	60	10	0	8	8	8
	Hartford Wolf Pack	AHL	....	....	....	....	....	12	0	2	2	8
2006-07	Sudbury Wolves	OHL	53	5	29	34	68	21	5	15	20	22

OHL First All-Star Team (2006, 2007)

STAFFORD, Garrett (STA-fuhrd, GAIR-reht) DET.

Defense. Shoots right. 6', 200 lbs. Born, Los Angeles, CA, January 28, 1980.

			Regular Season					Playoffs				
Season	Club	League	GP	G	A	Pts	PIM	GP	G	A	Pts	PIM
1996-97	Des Moines	USHL	37	1	10	11	40	5	0	0	0	0
1997-98	Des Moines	USHL	53	6	17	23	89	12	1	3	4	42
1998-99	Des Moines	USHL	56	8	33	41	54	13	2	2	4	18
99-2000	New Hampshire	H-East	38	3	9	12	28	....	....	....	....	....
2000-01	New Hampshire	H-East	37	5	21	26	44	....	....	....	....	....
2001-02	New Hampshire	H-East	36	5	22	27	42	....	....	....	....	....
2002-03	New Hampshire	H-East	23	1	15	16	24	....	....	....	....	....
2003-04	Cleveland Barons	AHL	73	12	34	46	71	6	0	0	0	6
2004-05	Cleveland Barons	AHL	68	6	18	24	55	....	....	....	....	....
2005-06	Cleveland Barons	AHL	80	11	28	39	86	....	....	....	....	....
2006-07	Worcester Sharks	AHL	77	11	30	41	58	6	0	3	3	2

Hockey East Second All-Star Team (2002) • AHL All-Rookie Team (2004) • AHL Second All-Star Team (2004)

Signed as a free agent by **Cleveland** (AHL), October 10, 2003. Signed as a free agent by **San Jose**, December 9, 2003. Signed as a free agent by **Detroit**, July 16, 2007.

STAHLBERG, Viktor (STAHL-buhrg, VIHK-tohr) TOR.

Left wing. Shoots left. 6'3", 196 lbs. Born, Stockholm, Sweden, January 17, 1986.
(Toronto's 5th choice, 161st overall, in 2006 Entry Draft).

			Regular Season					Playoffs				
Season	Club	League	GP	G	A	Pts	PIM	GP	G	A	Pts	PIM
2003-04	Molndal U18	Swe-U18	13	14	13	27	....	....	....	....	....	....
	Molndal Jr.	Swe-Jr.	18	25	10	35	....	....	....	....	....	....
	IF Molndal Hockey	Sweden-4	....	11	9	20	....	....	....	....	....	....
2004-05	Molndal Jr.	Swe-Jr.	11	16	7	23	....	....	....	....	....	....
	IF Molndal Hockey	Sweden-3	29	6	9	15	54	....	....	....	....	....
2005-06	Frolunda Jr.	Swe-Jr.	41	27	26	53	89	7	6	5	11	6
2006-07	U. of Vermont	H-East	39	7	8	15	53	....	....	....	....	....

STAMLER, Bretton (STAM-lehr, BREH-tuhn)

Defense. Shoots right. 6'1", 201 lbs. Born, Calgary, Alta., March 10, 1987.
(Detroit's 9th choice, 214th overall, in 2005 Entry Draft).

			Regular Season					Playoffs				
Season	Club	League	GP	G	A	Pts	PIM	GP	G	A	Pts	PIM
2002-03	Sherwood Park	AMHL	34	3	8	11	22	....	....	....	....	....
2003-04	Seattle	WHL	61	0	9	9	27	....	....	....	....	....
2004-05	Seattle	WHL	72	4	9	13	106	1	0	0	0	0
2005-06	Seattle	WHL	56	5	10	15	102	7	0	4	4	8
2006-07	Seattle	WHL	72	8	24	32	135	11	0	1	1	14

STARKOV, Kirill (stahr-KAWF, kih-RIHL) CBJ

Center. Shoots left. 6', 194 lbs. Born, Sverdlovsk, USSR, March 31, 1987.
(Columbus' 7th choice, 189th overall, in 2005 Entry Draft).

			Regular Season					Playoffs				
Season	Club	League	GP	G	A	Pts	PIM	GP	G	A	Pts	PIM
2002-03	Esbjerg Oilers	Denmark	28	2	4	6	6	14	0	0	0	0
2003-04	V.Frolunda U18	Swe-U18	9	6	6	12	2	7	2	3	5	2
	V.Frolunda Jr.	Swe-Jr.	25	3	10	13	4	5	2	0	2	0
2004-05	Frolunda U18	Swe-U18	1	0	0	0	4	3	2	1	3	0
	Frolunda Jr.	Swe-Jr.	34	18	12	30	6	3	2	2	4	2
2005-06	Frolunda Jr.	Swe-Jr.	19	8	16	24	16	6	3	4	7	2
	Frolunda	Sweden	34	1	2	3	4					
2006-07	Red Deer Rebels	WHL	72	34	37	71	41	7	2	4	6	4

STASYUK, Denis (stah-S'YUHK, DEH-nihs) FLA.

Center. Shoots left. 6'1", 165 lbs. Born, Novokuznetsk, USSR, September 2, 1985.
(Florida's 9th choice, 171st overall, in 2003 Entry Draft).

			Regular Season					Playoffs				
Season	Club	League	GP	G	A	Pts	PIM	GP	G	A	Pts	PIM
2002-03	Novokuznetsk 2	Russia-3	STATISTICS NOT AVAILABLE									
	Novokuznetsk	Russia	11	1	0	1	0	....	....	....	....	....
2003-04	Novokuznetsk	Russia	5	0	0	0	0	....	....	....	....	....
	Novokuznetsk 2	Russia-3	STATISTICS NOT AVAILABLE									
2004-05	Amur Khabarovsk	Russia-2	44	11	10	21	12	10	1	2	3	6
2005-06	Novokuznetsk	Russia	41	7	2	9	18	3	0	0	0	0
2006-07	Novokuznetsk	Russia	26	0	1	1	16	3	0	0	0	0

STAUBITZ, Brad (STAW-bihtz, BRAD) S.J.

Defense. Shoots right. 6'1", 215 lbs. Born, Bright's Grove, Ont., July 28, 1984.

			Regular Season					Playoffs				
Season	Club	League	GP	G	A	Pts	PIM	GP	G	A	Pts	PIM
2001-02	Sault Ste. Marie	OHL	45	0	3	3	46	3	0	0	0	2
2002-03	Sault Ste. Marie	OHL	55	2	6	8	116	4	0	0	0	7
2003-04	Sault Ste. Marie	OHL	66	6	18	24	140	....	....	....	....	....
2004-05	Sault Ste. Marie	OHL	40	2	11	13	101	....	....	....	....	....
	Ottawa 67's	OHL	30	5	8	13	80	21	4	16	20	70
2005-06	Cleveland Barons	AHL	71	0	6	6	245	....	....	....	....	....
2006-07	Worcester Sharks	AHL	51	1	4	5	137	5	0	0	0	13

Signed as a free agent by **San Jose**, September 19, 2005.

STEFANISHION, Matt (steh-fan-IHSH-yuhn, MAT)

Right wing. Shoots right. 6'3", 210 lbs. Born, Daysland, Alta., October 5, 1983.

			Regular Season					Playoffs				
Season	Club	League	GP	G	A	Pts	PIM	GP	G	A	Pts	PIM
2002-03	Melville	SJHL	60	21	30	51	235	....	....	....	....	....
2003-04	Estevan Bruins	SJHL	52	32	45	77	175	....	....	....	....	....
2004-05	Ferris State	CCHA	34	12	9	21	75	....	....	....	....	....
2005-06	Ferris State	CCHA	23	9	4	13	50	....	....	....	....	....
2006-07	Hershey Bears	AHL	3	0	0	0	0	....	....	....	....	....
	South Carolina	ECHL	56	16	24	40	90	....	....	....	....	....

Signed as a free agent by **Washington**, April 1, 2006.

STEHLIK, Richard (SHTEH-lihk, RIH-chuhrd) NSH.

Defense. Shoots left. 6'4", 248 lbs. Born, Skalica, Czech., June 22, 1984.
(Nashville's 5th choice, 76th overall, in 2003 Entry Draft).

			Regular Season					Playoffs				
Season	Club	League	GP	G	A	Pts	PIM	GP	G	A	Pts	PIM
99-2000	HK 36 Skalica Jr.	Slovak-Jr.	50	10	5	15	....	....	....	....	....	....
2000-01	HK 36 Skalica	Slovakia	45	1	1	2	14	3	0	0	0	2
2001-02	HK 36 Skalica	Slovakia	35	1	0	1	12	....	....	....	....	....
2002-03	Sherbrooke	QMJHL	43	8	16	24	105	12	1	5	6	20
2003-04	Lewiston	QMJHL	44	11	25	36	109	7	0	1	1	12
2004-05	HK 36 Skalica	Slovakia	40	8	3	11	28	....	....	....	....	....
	Dukla Trencin	Slovakia	13	1	5	6	33	12	3	3	6	62
2005-06	HC Sparta Praha	CzRep	42	3	7	10	79	17	0	2	2	18
2006-07	HC Sparta Praha	CzRep	42	8	1	9	75	16	0	0	0	22

STEJSKAL, Joe (STAY-kuhl, JOH) MTL.

Defense. Shoots right. 6'2", 187 lbs. Born, Grand Rapids, MN, April 30, 1988.
(Montreal's 6th choice, 133rd overall, in 2007 Entry Draft).

			Regular Season					Playoffs				
Season	Club	League	GP	G	A	Pts	PIM	GP	G	A	Pts	PIM
2003-04	Grand Rapids	High-MN	....	1	7	8	....	....	....	....	....	....
2004-05	Grand Rapids	High-MN	....	2	8	10	....	....	....	....	....	....
2005-06	Grand Rapids	High-MN	....	7	18	25	....	....	....	....	....	....
2006-07	Grand Rapids	High-MN	24	11	17	28	42	....	....	....	....	....

• Signed Letter of Intent to attend **Dartmouth College** (ECACHL) in fall of 2007.

STEPHENSON, Logan (STEE-vehn-suhn, LOH-guhn) PHX.

Defense. Shoots left. 6'3", 197 lbs. Born, Saskatoon, Sask., February 19, 1986.
(Phoenix's 2nd choice, 35th overall, in 2004 Entry Draft).

			Regular Season					Playoffs				
Season	Club	League	GP	G	A	Pts	PIM	GP	G	A	Pts	PIM
2001-02	Notre Dame	SMHL	37	4	2	6	74	....	....	....	....	....
	Tri-City Americans	WHL	....	....	....	....	....	3	0	0	0	0
2002-03	Tri-City Americans	WHL	50	0	6	6	121	....	....	....	....	....
2003-04	Tri-City Americans	WHL	69	3	8	11	112	11	1	1	2	10
2004-05	Tri-City Americans	WHL	59	6	9	15	86	5	0	0	0	2
2005-06	Tri-City Americans	WHL	71	10	43	53	162	5	1	0	1	18
2006-07	San Antonio	AHL	73	3	5	8	90	....	....	....	....	....

WHL West Second All-Star Team (2006)

STERLING, Brett (STUHR-lihng, BREHT) ATL.

Left wing. Shoots left. 5'8", 180 lbs. Born, Los Angeles, CA, April 24, 1984.
(Atlanta's 5th choice, 145th overall, in 2003 Entry Draft).

			Regular Season					Playoffs				
Season	Club	League	GP	G	A	Pts	PIM	GP	G	A	Pts	PIM
99-2000	L.A. Jr. Kings	SCAHA	35	45	25	70	....	....	....	....	....	....
2000-01	USNTDP	U-17	13	....	....	....	....	....	....	....	....	....
	USNTDP	NAHL	47	29	15	44	72	....	....	....	....	....
2001-02	USNTDP	U-18	31	21	15	36	18	....	....	....	....	....
	USNTDP	USHL	10	6	3	9	8	....	....	....	....	....
	USNTDP	NAHL	9	2	1	3	10	....	....	....	....	....
2002-03	Colorado College	WCHA	36	27	11	38	30	....	....	....	....	....
2003-04	Colorado College	WCHA	30	16	12	28	40	....	....	....	....	....
2004-05	Colorado College	WCHA	43	*34	29	63	74	....	....	....	....	....
2005-06	Colorado College	WCHA	42	31	24	55	66	....	....	....	....	....
2006-07	Chicago Wolves	AHL	77	*55	42	97	96	15	7	5	12	24

WCHA All-Rookie Team (2003) • WCHA First All-Star Team (2005, 2006) • NCAA West First All-American Team (2005, 2006) • AHL All-Rookie Team (2007) • AHL First All-Star Team (2007) • Dudley "Red" Garrett Memorial Award (Rookie of the Year • AHL) (2007) • Willie Marshall Award (Top Goal-scorer - AHL) (2007)

STEWART, Chris (STEW-ahrt, KRIHS) COL.

Right wing. Shoots right. 6'2", 228 lbs. Born, Toronto, Ont., October 30, 1987.
(Colorado's 1st choice, 18th overall, in 2006 Entry Draft).

			Regular Season					Playoffs				
Season	Club	League	GP	G	A	Pts	PIM	GP	G	A	Pts	PIM
2004-05	Kingston	OHL	64	18	12	30	45	....	....	....	....	....
2005-06	Kingston	OHL	62	37	50	87	118	6	2	0	2	13
2006-07	Kingston	OHL	61	36	46	82	108	5	4	2	6	6
	Albany River Rats	AHL	5	1	2	3	2	1	0	0	0	0

STEWART, Greg (STEW-ahrt, GREHG) MTL.

Left wing. Shoots left. 6'2", 200 lbs. Born, Kitchener, Ont., May 21, 1986.
(Montreal's 7th choice, 246th overall, in 2004 Entry Draft).

			Regular Season					Playoffs				
Season	Club	League	GP	G	A	Pts	PIM	GP	G	A	Pts	PIM
2003-04	Peterborough	OHL	58	4	6	10	76	....	....	....	....	....
2004-05	Peterborough	OHL	68	16	18	34	111	14	3	3	6	20
2005-06	Peterborough	OHL	60	24	15	39	83	19	1	6	7	30
2006-07	Cincinnati	ECHL	62	8	15	23	126	10	5	2	7	36

STOA, Ryan (STOH-ah, RIGH-uhn) COL.

Center. Shoots left. 6'3", 200 lbs. Born, Bloomington, MN, April 13, 1987.
(Colorado's 1st choice, 34th overall, in 2005 Entry Draft).

			Regular Season					Playoffs				
Season	Club	League	GP	G	A	Pts	PIM	GP	G	A	Pts	PIM
2003-04	USNTDP	U-17	18	9	8	17	....	....	....	....	....	....
	USNTDP	NAHL	42	10	12	22	26	7	7	1	8	2
2004-05	USNTDP	U-18	23	4	11	15	16	....	....	....	....	....
	USNTDP	NAHL	15	10	13	23	20	....	....	....	....	....
2005-06	U. of Minnesota	WCHA	41	10	15	25	43	....	....	....	....	....
2006-07	U. of Minnesota	WCHA	41	12	12	24	44	....	....	....	....	....

STOESZ, Myles (STOHZ, MIGH-uhlz) ATL.

Right wing. Shoots right. 6'2", 215 lbs. Born, Steinbach, Man., February 15, 1987.
(Atlanta's 8th choice, 207th overall, in 2005 Entry Draft).

			Regular Season					Playoffs				
Season	Club	League	GP	G	A	Pts	PIM	GP	G	A	Pts	PIM
2003-04	Spokane Chiefs	WHL	43	1	1	2	133	0	0	0	0	0
2004-05	Spokane Chiefs	WHL	67	1	8	9	238	....	....	....	....	....
2005-06	Spokane Chiefs	WHL	56	0	2	2	260	....	....	....	....	....
2006-07	Chilliwack Bruins	WHL	40	3	2	5	135	....	....	....	....	....
	Regina Pats	WHL	29	4	2	6	89	9	0	0	0	21

STOKES, Ryan (STOHKS, RIGH-uhn)

Defense. Shoots left. 6'4", 220 lbs. Born, Sarnia, Ont., June 23, 1983.

			Regular Season					Playoffs				
Season	Club	League	GP	G	A	Pts	PIM	GP	G	A	Pts	PIM
2001-02	Barrie Colts	OHL	53	0	5	5	31	20	0	0	0	16
2002-03	Mississauga	OHL	59	2	7	9	139	5	0	1	1	22
2003-04	Mississauga	OHL	66	4	20	24	179	24	2	9	11	74
2004-05	Houston Aeros	AHL	7	0	0	0	7	....	....	....	....	....
	Pensacola	ECHL	59	1	15	16	119	....	....	....	....	....
2005-06	Houston Aeros	AHL	75	2	3	5	164	6	0	1	1	10
2006-07	Houston Aeros	AHL	72	2	8	10	158	....	....	....	....	....

Signed as a free agent by **Minnesota**, May 25, 2004.

STOLYAROV, Gennady (stohl-yah-RAWF, gehn-AH-dee) DET.

Right wing. Shoots left. 6'4", 187 lbs. Born, Moscow, USSR, August 20, 1986.
(Detroit's 7th choice, 257th overall, in 2004 Entry Draft).

			Regular Season					Playoffs				
Season	Club	League	GP	G	A	Pts	PIM	GP	G	A	Pts	PIM
2003-04	Dyn'o Moscow 2	Russia-3	STATISTICS NOT AVAILABLE									
	THK Tver	Russia-2	24	3	1	4	4	....	....	....	....	....
2004-05	Vityaz Chekhov	Russia-2	25	0	1	1	2	....	....	....	....	....
2005-06	Kapitan Stupino	Russia-2	17	3	5	8	20	5	1	2	3	36
	Dynamo Moscow	Russia	12	0	0	0	4	3	0	1	1	0
2006-07	Dynamo Moscow	Russia	37	6	3	9	39	2	0	0	0	0

STONE, Ryan (STOHN, RIGH-uhn) PIT.

Center. Shoots left. 6'2", 207 lbs. Born, Calgary, Alta., March 20, 1985.
(Pittsburgh's 2nd choice, 32nd overall, in 2003 Entry Draft).

			Regular Season					Playoffs				
Season	Club	League	GP	G	A	Pts	PIM	GP	G	A	Pts	PIM
2000-01	Cgy. North Stars	AMHL	34	37	28	55	90	....	....	....	....	....
2001-02	Brandon	WHL	65	11	27	38	128	19	0	3	3	39
2002-03	Brandon	WHL	54	14	31	45	158	12	4	2	6	20
2003-04	Brandon	WHL	50	20	38	58	125	11	1	3	4	24
2004-05	Brandon	WHL	70	33	*66	99	127	24	4	*23	27	48
2005-06	Wilkes-Barre	AHL	75	14	22	36	109	11	4	7	11	12
2006-07	Wilkes-Barre	AHL	41	7	26	33	86	10	2	3	5	21

WHL East First All-Star Team (2005)

STONER, Clayton (STOH-nuhr, KLAY-tuhn) MIN.

Defense. Shoots left. 6'4", 215 lbs. Born, Port McNeill, B.C., February 19, 1985.
(Minnesota's 4th choice, 79th overall, in 2004 Entry Draft).

			Regular Season					Playoffs				
Season	Club	League	GP	G	A	Pts	PIM	GP	G	A	Pts	PIM
2000-01	Campbell River	VIJHL	47	4	16	20	57	....	....	....	....	....
2001-02	Campbell River	VIJHL	42	12	35	47	199	....	....	....	....	....
2002-03	Tri-City Americans	WHL	58	4	12	16	85	....	....	....	....	....
2003-04	Tri-City Americans	WHL	71	7	24	31	109	11	1	1	2	8
2004-05	Tri-City Americans	WHL	60	12	34	46	81	4	0	3	3	2
2005-06	Houston Aeros	AHL	73	6	18	24	92	3	1	1	2	7
2006-07	Houston Aeros	AHL	65	1	6	7	104	....	....	....	....	....

WHL West Second All-Star Team (2005)

STRACHAN, Tyson (STRAWN, TIGH-suhn)

Defense. Shoots right. 6'3", 205 lbs. Born, Melfort, Sask., October 30, 1984.
(Carolina's 6th choice, 137th overall, in 2003 Entry Draft).

			Regular Season					Playoffs				
Season	Club	League	GP	G	A	Pts	PIM	GP	G	A	Pts	PIM
2001-02	Tisdale Trojans	SMHL	42	5	18	23	70	....	....	....	....	....
	Melville	SJHL	2	0	0	0	0	....	....	....	....	....
2002-03	Vernon Vipers	BCHL	56	6	22	28	99	....	....	....	....	....
2003-04	Ohio State	CCHA	30	2	5	7	8	....	....	....	....	....
2004-05	Ohio State	CCHA	31	1	4	5	32	....	....	....	....	....
2005-06	Ohio State	CCHA	23	3	2	5	37	....	....	....	....	....
2006-07	Ohio State	CCHA	35	7	11	18	55	....	....	....	....	....
	Albany River Rats	AHL	1	0	0	0	0	....	....	....	....	....

STRAIT, Brian (STRAYT, BRIGH-uhn) PIT.

Defense. Shoots left. 6'1", 200 lbs. Born, Boston, MA, January 4, 1988.
(Pittsburgh's 3rd choice, 65th overall, in 2006 Entry Draft).

			Regular Season					Playoffs				
Season	Club	League	GP	G	A	Pts	PIM	GP	G	A	Pts	PIM
2003-04	NMH School	High-MA	30	5	15	20	....	....	....	....	....	....
2004-05	USNTDP	U-17	18	1	5	6	8	....	....	....	....	....
	USNTDP	NAHL	42	4	8	12	42	10	0	2	2	2
2005-06	USNTDP	U-18	40	2	7	9	31	....	....	....	....	....
	USNTDP	NAHL	15	0	5	5	41	....	....	....	....	....
2006-07	Boston University	H-East	36	3	3	6	47	....	....	....	....	....

STRALMAN, Anton (STROHL-muhn, AN-tawn) TOR.

Defense. Shoots right. 6'1", 180 lbs. Born, Tibro, Sweden , August 1, 1986.
(Toronto's 5th choice, 216th overall, in 2005 Entry Draft).

			Regular Season					Playoffs				
Season	Club	League	GP	G	A	Pts	PIM	GP	G	A	Pts	PIM
2002-03	Skovde IK Jr.	Swe-Jr.	46	20	9	29	38	....	....	....	....	....
2003-04	Skovde IK	Sweden-3	27	4	8	12	18	....	....	....	....	....
2004-05	Skovde IK	Sweden-2	50	10	11	21	40	....	....	....	....	....
2005-06	Timra IK	Sweden	45	1	4	5	28	....	....	....	....	....
	Timra IK Jr.	Swe-Jr.	....	....	....	....	....	3	0	0	0	4
2006-07	Timra IK	Sweden	53	10	11	21	34	7	1	3	4	10

STUART, Colin (STEW-ahrt, KAW-lihn) ATL.

Left wing. Shoots left. 6'2", 205 lbs. Born, Rochester, MN, July 8, 1982.
(Atlanta's 5th choice, 135th overall, in 2001 Entry Draft).

			Regular Season					Playoffs				
Season	Club	League	GP	G	A	Pts	PIM	GP	G	A	Pts	PIM
1998-99	Roch. Lourdes	High-MN	23	22	32	54	....	....	....	....	....	....
99-2000	Lincoln Stars	USHL	53	18	19	37	38	9	1	3	4	2
2000-01	Colorado College	WCHA	41	2	7	9	26	....	....	....	....	....
2001-02	Colorado College	WCHA	43	13	9	22	34	....	....	....	....	....
2002-03	Colorado College	WCHA	43	13	11	24	56	....	....	....	....	....
2003-04	Colorado College	WCHA	30	10	12	22	38	....	....	....	....	....
2004-05	Chicago Wolves	AHL	39	3	2	5	12	....	....	....	....	....
	Gwinnett	ECHL	5	1	3	4	4	....	....	....	....	....
2005-06	Chicago Wolves	AHL	78	13	14	27	65	....	....	....	....	....
2006-07	Chicago Wolves	AHL	67	18	11	29	75	15	2	5	7	10

SUBBAN, P.K. (soo-BAHN, PEE-KAY) MTL.

Defense. Shoots right. 5'11", 203 lbs. Born, Toronto, Ont., May 13, 1989.
(Montreal's 3rd choice, 43rd overall, in 2007 Entry Draft).

			Regular Season					Playoffs				
Season	Club	League	GP	G	A	Pts	PIM	GP	G	A	Pts	PIM
2004-05	Markham	GTHL	67	15	28	43	179	....	....	....	....	....
2005-06	Belleville Bulls	OHL	52	5	7	12	70	3	0	0	0	2
2006-07	Belleville Bulls	OHL	68	15	41	56	89	15	5	8	13	26

SUBBOTIN, Dmitri (soo-BOH-tihn, dih-MEE-tree) CBJ

Left wing. Shoots left. 6'1", 183 lbs. Born, Tomsk, USSR, October 20, 1977.
(NY Rangers' 3rd choice, 76th overall, in 1996 Entry Draft).

			Regular Season					Playoffs				
Season	Club	League	GP	G	A	Pts	PIM	GP	G	A	Pts	PIM
1993-94	Yekaterinburg	CIS	12	0	3	3	4	....	....	....	....	....
1994-95	Yekaterinburg	CIS	52	9	6	15	75	2	0	0	0	2
1995-96	CSKA Moscow	CIS	41	6	5	11	62	3	0	0	0	0
1996-97	CSKA Moscow	Russia-2	8	1	0	1	8	....	....	....	....	....
	HK CSKA Moscow	Russia	17	5	3	8	22	2	0	0	0	2
1997-98	HK CSKA Moscow	Russia	16	1	1	2	47	....	....	....	....	....
1998-99	Dynamo Moscow	Russia	1	0	1	1	0	....	....	....	....	....
	Lada Togliatti	Russia	31	8	3	11	47	7	0	0	0	4
99-2000	Lada Togliatti	Russia	27	10	4	14	26	7	1	1	2	4
	Lada Togliatti 2	Russia-3	2	0	1	1	0	....	....	....	....	....
2000-01	Dynamo Moscow	Russia	39	11	15	26	48	....	....	....	....	....
2001-02	Magnitogorsk	Russia	38	8	3	11	18	9	0	2	2	10
2002-03	Cherepovets	Russia	10	0	1	1	31	....	....	....	....	....
	CSKA Moscow	Russia	20	3	9	12	6	....	....	....	....	....
2003-04	CSKA Moscow	Russia	20	0	3	3	14	....	....	....	....	....
	Avangard Omsk	Russia	26	6	6	12	36	11	2	3	5	6
2004-05	Avangard Omsk	Russia	55	5	6	11	66	7	0	0	0	10
2005-06	Ufa	Russia	5	0	1	1	8	....	....	....	....	....
	MVD	Russia	27	6	8	14	52	4	1	3	4	4
2006-07	MVD	Russia	51	16	20	36	96	2	0	1	1	6

Claimed by **Columbus** from **NY Rangers** in Expansion Draft, June 23, 2000.

SUCHARSKI, Nick (soo-CHAR-skee, NIHK) CBJ

Left wing. Shoots left. 6'1", 165 lbs. Born, Toronto, Ont., November 15, 1987.
(Columbus' 6th choice, 136th overall, in 2006 Entry Draft).

			Regular Season					Playoffs				
Season	Club	League	GP	G	A	Pts	PIM	GP	G	A	Pts	PIM
2003-04	Wexford Raiders	OPJHL	43	15	29	44	48	....	....	....	....	....
2004-05	Wexford Raiders	OPJHL	46	26	27	53	78	13	6	10	16	20
2005-06	Michigan State	CCHA	36	2	5	7	18	....	....	....	....	....
2006-07	Michigan State	CCHA	41	9	15	24	32	....	....	....	....	....

SULLIVAN, Mike (SUHL-ih-vuhn, MIGHK) L.A.

Center. Shoots left. 6'4", 190 lbs. Born, Scarborough, Ont., September 14, 1984.
(Los Angeles' 9th choice, 244th overall, in 2003 Entry Draft).

			Regular Season					Playoffs				
Season	Club	League	GP	G	A	Pts	PIM	GP	G	A	Pts	PIM
2001-02	Uxbridge Bruins	OHA-C	42	22	27	49	20	....	....	....	....	....
2002-03	Stouffville Spirit	OPJHL	42	24	39	64	14	....	....	....	....	....
2003-04	Clarkson Knights	ECAC	40	8	11	19	14	....	....	....	....	....
2004-05	Clarkson Knights	ECACHL	37	8	9	17	20	....	....	....	....	....
2005-06	Clarkson Knights	ECACHL	36	15	11	26	30	....	....	....	....	....
2006-07	Clarkson Knights	ECACHL	39	8	9	17	16	....	....	....	....	....

SULLIVAN, Sean (SUHL-ih-vuhn, SHAWN) **PHX.**

Defense. Shoots left. 6', 188 lbs. Born, Boston, MA, March 29, 1984.
(Phoenix's 7th choice, 272nd overall, in 2003 Entry Draft).

			Regular Season					Playoffs				
Season	Club	League	GP	G	A	Pts	PIM	GP	G	A	Pts	PIM
2001-02	St. Sebastian's	High-MA	31	3	11	14	4	....	....	....	....	....
2002-03	St. Sebastian's	High-MA	41	9	30	39	59	....	....	....	....	....
2003-04	Boston University	H-East	36	2	5	7	14	....	....	....	....	....
2004-05	Boston University	H-East	41	1	3	4	10	....	....	....	....	....
2005-06	Boston University	H-East	40	3	14	17	32	....	....	....	....	....
2006-07	Boston University	H-East	38	3	12	15	12	....	....	....	....	....
	San Antonio	AHL	7	0	0	0	0	....	....	....	....	....

NCAA East Second All-American Team (2007)

SULZER, Alexander (ZUHLT-suhr, al-EHX-AN-duhr) **NSH.**

Defense. Shoots left. 6'1", 207 lbs. Born, Kaufbeuren, West Germany, May 30, 1984.
(Nashville's 7th choice, 92nd overall, in 2003 Entry Draft).

			Regular Season					Playoffs				
Season	Club	League	GP	G	A	Pts	PIM	GP	G	A	Pts	PIM
2000-01	ESV Kaufbeuren	German-3	38	3	6	9	20	....	....	....	....	....
	Kaufbeuren Jr.	Ger-Jr.	1	0	2	2	2	....	....	....	....	....
2001-02	ESV Kaufbeuren	German-3	19	1	9	10	14	....	....	....	....	....
	Kaufbeuren Jr.	Ger-Jr.	1	0	0	0	4	....	....	....	....	....
2002-03	ESV Kaufbeuren	German-2	26	5	3	8	38	1	0	1	1	4
	Hamburg Freezers	Germany	18	0	1	1	18	5	0	0	0	12
2003-04	Dusseldorf	Germany	46	4	1	5	56	4	0	0	0	8
2004-05	Dusseldorf	Germany	42	5	6	11	68	....	....	....	....	....
	EV Duisburg	German-2	....	....	....	....	....	7	0	3	3	6
2005-06	Dusseldorf	Germany	48	3	15	18	82	13	3	6	9	22
	Germany	Olympics	5	0	1	1	2	....	....	....	....	....
2006-07	Dusseldorf	Germany	44	4	11	15	82	9	2	1	3	20

SUMMERS, Chris (SUHM-mehrs, KRIHS) **PHX.**

Defense. Shoots left. 6'2", 180 lbs. Born, Ann Arbor, MI, February 5, 1988.
(Phoenix's 2nd choice, 29th overall, in 2006 Entry Draft).

			Regular Season					Playoffs				
Season	Club	League	GP	G	A	Pts	PIM	GP	G	A	Pts	PIM
2004-05	USNTDP	U-17	13	2	2	4	10	....	....	....	....	....
	USNTDP	NAHL	31	2	5	7	20	7	1	0	1	0
2005-06	USNTDP	U-18	42	4	9	13	67	....	....	....	....	....
	USNTDP	NAHL	17	2	2	4	20	....	....	....	....	....
2006-07	U. of Michigan	CCHA	41	6	8	14	58	....	....	....	....	....

SUTTER, Brandon (SUH-tuhr, BRAN-duhn) **CAR.**

Center/Right wing. Shoots right. 6'3", 170 lbs. Born, Huntington, NY, February 14, 1989.
(Carolina's 1st choice, 11th overall, in 2007 Entry Draft).

			Regular Season					Playoffs				
Season	Club	League	GP	G	A	Pts	PIM	GP	G	A	Pts	PIM
2003-04	Red Deer Chiefs	AMBHL	35	25	34	59	28	11	5	4	9	....
2004-05	Red Deer	AMHL	34	4	16	20	28	....	....	....	....	....
	Red Deer Rebels	WHL	7	0	2	2	8	7	1	4	5	2
2005-06	Red Deer Rebels	WHL	68	22	24	46	36	....	....	....	....	....
2006-07	Red Deer Rebels	WHL	71	20	37	57	54	7	0	3	3	14

SUTTER, Brett (SUH-tuhr, BREHT) **CGY.**

Center/Left wing. Shoots left. 6', 191 lbs. Born, Viking, Alta., June 2, 1987.
(Calgary's 7th choice, 179th overall, in 2005 Entry Draft).

			Regular Season					Playoffs				
Season	Club	League	GP	G	A	Pts	PIM	GP	G	A	Pts	PIM
2003-04	Kootenay Ice	WHL	44	5	7	12	26	4	0	0	0	4
2004-05	Kootenay Ice	WHL	70	8	11	19	70	16	1	2	3	16
2005-06	Kootenay Ice	WHL	16	8	7	15	21	....	....	....	....	....
	Red Deer Rebels	WHL	57	9	26	35	80	....	....	....	....	....
2006-07	Red Deer Rebels	WHL	67	28	29	57	77	7	3	4	7	11

SWAN, Bryce (SWAWN, BRIGHS) **ANA.**

Center. Shoots right. 6'2", 196 lbs. Born, Alderpoint, N.S., October 6, 1987.
(Anaheim's 2nd choice, 38th overall, in 2006 Entry Draft).

			Regular Season					Playoffs				
Season	Club	League	GP	G	A	Pts	PIM	GP	G	A	Pts	PIM
2004-05	Halifax	QMJHL	36	3	3	6	39	11	2	0	2	10
2005-06	Halifax	QMJHL	34	14	11	25	54	11	2	5	7	8
2006-07	Halifax	QMJHL	61	35	19	54	70	12	6	3	9	23

SWANSON, Jeremy (SWAWN-suhn, JAIR-eh-mee)

Defense. Shoots left. 6', 199 lbs. Born, Nipigon, Ont., June 21, 1984.
(Florida's choice, 169th overall, in 2002 Entry Draft).

			Regular Season					Playoffs				
Season	Club	League	GP	G	A	Pts	PIM	GP	G	A	Pts	PIM
99-2000	Thunder Bay Kings	TBMHL	48	8	16	24	19	....	....	....	....	....
2000-01	Sault Ste. Marie	OHL	54	1	6	7	60	....	....	....	....	....
2001-02	Barrie Colts	OHL	67	8	16	24	78	20	1	4	5	12
2002-03	Barrie Colts	OHL	68	7	34	41	129	....	....	....	....	....
2003-04	Barrie Colts	OHL	66	6	28	34	120	12	0	5	5	16
2004-05	San Antonio	AHL	21	1	3	4	22	....	....	....	....	....
	Texas Wildcatters	ECHL	44	1	6	7	62	....	....	....	....	....
2005-06	Rochester	AHL	11	0	0	0	23	....	....	....	....	....
	Florida Everblades	ECHL	14	1	3	4	12	....	....	....	....	....
2006-07	Rochester	AHL	47	0	2	2	47	6	0	4	4	14
	Florida Everblades	ECHL	16	0	3	3	41	....	....	....	....	....

OHL Second All-Star Team (2004)

SWEATT, Bill (SWEHT, BIHL) **CHI.**

Left wing. Shoots left. 6', 180 lbs. Born, Elburn, IL, September 21, 1988.
(Chicago's 2nd choice, 38th overall, in 2007 Entry Draft).

			Regular Season					Playoffs				
Season	Club	League	GP	G	A	Pts	PIM	GP	G	A	Pts	PIM
2003-04	Team Illinois	MWEHL	74	33	37	70	....	....	....	....	....	....
2004-05	USNTDP	U-17	11	5	10	15	54	....	....	....	....	....
	USNTDP	NAHL	41	7	9	16	12	10	4	3	7	6
2005-06	USNTDP	U-18	42	19	11	30	24	....	....	....	....	....
	USNTDP	NAHL	17	10	15	25	4	....	....	....	....	....
2006-07	Colorado College	WCHA	30	9	17	26	18	....	....	....	....	....

SWITZER, Craig (SWIHT-zuhr, KRAYG) **NSH.**

Defense. Shoots left. 6'1", 195 lbs. Born, Calgary, Alta., October 16, 1984.
(Nashville's 11th choice, 275th overall, in 2004 Entry Draft).

			Regular Season					Playoffs				
Season	Club	League	GP	G	A	Pts	PIM	GP	G	A	Pts	PIM
2003-04	Salmon Arm	BCHL	57	14	40	54	117	14	0	12	12	16
2004-05	New Hampshire	H-East	41	1	13	14	22	....	....	....	....	....
2005-06	New Hampshire	H-East	40	2	14	16	54	....	....	....	....	....
2006-07	New Hampshire	H-East	39	3	14	17	50	....	....	....	....	....

SYVRET, Corey (SIHV-reht, KOHR-ee) **FLA.**

Defense. Shoots left. 6'2", 193 lbs. Born, Millgrove, Ont., February 12, 1989.
(Florida's 6th choice, 181st overall, in 2007 Entry Draft).

			Regular Season					Playoffs				
Season	Club	League	GP	G	A	Pts	PIM	GP	G	A	Pts	PIM
2004-05	Cambridge	OJHL-B	46	2	3	5	56	....	....	....	....	....
2005-06	London Knights	OHL	59	0	5	5	35	11	0	1	1	6
2006-07	London Knights	OHL	34	0	2	2	29	....	....	....	....	....
	Guelph Storm	OHL	27	5	9	14	32	4	0	0	0	2

TANGRADI, Eric (tan-GRAY-dee, AIR-ihk) **ANA.**

Center. Shoots left. 6'3", 214 lbs. Born, Philadelphia, PA, February 10, 1989.
(Anaheim's 2nd choice, 42nd overall, in 2007 Entry Draft).

			Regular Season					Playoffs				
Season	Club	League	GP	G	A	Pts	PIM	GP	G	A	Pts	PIM
2005-06	Wyoming Prep	High-PA	38	21	23	44	120	....	....	....	....	....
2006-07	Belleville Bulls	OHL	65	5	15	20	32	15	8	9	17	14

TANGUAY, Maxime (TAN-guay, mahx-EEM) **CHI.**

Center. Shoots left. 5'11", 175 lbs. Born, Ste-Justine, Que., November 16, 1988.
(Chicago's 4th choice, 69th overall, in 2007 Entry Draft).

			Regular Season					Playoffs				
Season	Club	League	GP	G	A	Pts	PIM	GP	G	A	Pts	PIM
2004-05	Levis	QAAA	36	19	29	48	50	....	....	....	....	....
	Chicoutimi	QMJHL	23	1	1	2	6	11	2	3	5	2
2005-06	Chicoutimi	QMJHL	36	2	9	11	28	....	....	....	....	....
	Rimouski Oceanic	QMJHL	29	3	13	16	22	....	....	....	....	....
2006-07	Rimouski Oceanic	QMJHL	54	24	36	60	32	....	....	....	....	....

TARATUKHIN, Andrei (tahr-a-TOO-khin, AWN-dray) **CGY.**

Center. Shoots left. 6', 211 lbs. Born, Omsk, USSR, February 22, 1983.
(Calgary's 2nd choice, 41st overall, in 2001 Entry Draft).

			Regular Season					Playoffs				
Season	Club	League	GP	G	A	Pts	PIM	GP	G	A	Pts	PIM
99-2000	Omsk 2	Russia-3	27	10	6	16	16	....	....	....	....	....
	Avangard Omsk	Russia	....	....	....	....	....	1	1	0	1	0
2000-01	Omsk 2	Russia-3	41	19	28	47	69	....	....	....	....	....
2001-02	Mostovik Kurgan	Russia-2	44	13	22	35	30	....	....	....	....	....
	Yaroslavl 2	Russia-3	5	5	2	7	12	....	....	....	....	....
2002-03	Avangard Omsk	Russia	21	0	1	1	4	7	1	0	1	18
	Omsk 2	Russia-3	15	4	13	17	20	....	....	....	....	....
2003-04	Avangard Omsk	Russia	8	0	0	0	4	....	....	....	....	....
	Omsk 2	Russia-3	9	6	5	11	6	....	....	....	....	....
	Mechel	Russia-2	15	3	12	15	12	12	1	4	5	6
2004-05	Ufa 2	Russia-3	1	0	1	1	0	....	....	....	....	....
	Ufa	Russia	54	7	5	12	73	....	....	....	....	....
2005-06	Yaroslavl	Russia	40	9	15	24	85	11	2	2	4	24
	Russia	Olympics	5	0	0	0	2	....	....	....	....	....
2006-07	Omaha	AHL	80	17	43	60	80	....	....	....	....	....

TARKIR, Zach (TAHR-kihr, ZAK) **N.J.**

Defense. Shoots right. 6', 185 lbs. Born, Fresno, CA, June 28, 1984.
(New Jersey's 4th choice, 167th overall, in 2003 Entry Draft).

			Regular Season					Playoffs				
Season	Club	League	GP	G	A	Pts	PIM	GP	G	A	Pts	PIM
2001-02	Great Falls	AWHL	24	3	5	8	....	8	0	3	3	....
2002-03	Chilliwack Chiefs	BCHL	53	5	28	33	86	....	....	....	....	....
2003-04	Northern Mich.	CCHA	36	2	3	5	40	....	....	....	....	....
2004-05	Northern Mich.	CCHA	35	2	8	10	51	....	....	....	....	....
2005-06	Northern Mich.	CCHA	39	3	11	14	57	....	....	....	....	....
2006-07	Northern Mich.	CCHA	41	7	13	20	46	....	....	....	....	....
	Lowell Devils	AHL	2	0	0	0	0	....	....	....	....	....

TAYLOR, Adam (TAY-lohr, A-duhm) **FLA.**

Center. Shoots right. 6', 190 lbs. Born, Courtenay, B.C., June 24, 1984.
(Carolina's 4th choice, 224th overall, in 2002 Entry Draft).

			Regular Season					Playoffs				
Season	Club	League	GP	G	A	Pts	PIM	GP	G	A	Pts	PIM
2000-01	Burnaby Bulldogs	BCHL	59	6	14	20	179	....	....	....	....	....
	Kootenay Ice	WHL	36	1	2	3	17	1	0	0	0	0
2001-02	Kootenay Ice	WHL	72	11	23	34	119	19	3	4	7	15
2002-03	Kootenay Ice	WHL	72	14	28	42	69	11	3	2	5	14
2003-04	Kootenay Ice	WHL	72	19	33	52	54	4	0	1	1	4
2004-05	Kootenay Ice	WHL	72	20	32	52	95	16	4	12	16	20
2005-06	Victoria	ECHL	72	19	38	57	54	....	....	....	....	....
2006-07	Rochester	AHL	5	0	0	0	2	....	....	....	....	....
	Victoria	ECHL	15	1	5	6	12	....	....	....	....	....
	Pensacola	ECHL	15	3	8	11	12	....	....	....	....	....
	Florida Everblades	ECHL	37	21	20	41	38	16	3	9	12	18

Signed as a free agent by **Florida**, September 24, 2006.

TAYLOR, Justin (TAY-luhr, JUHS-tihn) **WSH.**

Center. Shoots left. 5'11", 180 lbs. Born, London, Ont., February 8, 1989.
(Washington's 8th choice, 180th overall, in 2007 Entry Draft).

			Regular Season					Playoffs				
Season	Club	League	GP	G	A	Pts	PIM	GP	G	A	Pts	PIM
2005-06	Wellington Dukes	OPJHL	48	18	13	31	12	12	0	3	3	8
2006-07	Wellington Dukes	OPJHL	37	20	32	52	36	....	....	....	....	....
	London Knights	OHL	31	6	12	18	18	16	4	6	10	17

TAYLOR, Justin (TAY-luhr, JUHS-tihn)

Left wing. Shoots left. 6'4", 200 lbs. Born, Edmonton, Alta., January 1, 1983.

			Regular Season					Playoffs				
Season	Club	League	GP	G	A	Pts	PIM	GP	G	A	Pts	PIM
99-2000	Medicine Hat	WHL	39	1	5	6	11	....	....	....	....	....
2000-01	Sherwood Park	AJHL	21	6	8	14	19	....	....	....	....	....
2001-02	Sherwood Park	AJHL	55	13	15	28	49	7	2	3	5	14
2002-03	Camrose Kodiaks	AJHL	45	11	24	35	71	17	7	11	18	34
2003-04	Red Deer Rebels	WHL	57	16	22	38	39	19	6	10	16	13
2004-05	Lowell	AHL	62	8	3	11	35	....	....	....	....	....
2005-06	Omaha	AHL	73	16	19	35	48	....	....	....	....	....
2006-07	Omaha	AHL	51	8	12	20	30	6	2	0	2	0

Signed as a free agent by **Calgary**, July 6, 2004.

TENKANEN, Valtteri (TEHN-kah-nehn, vahl-TEH-ree) L.A.

Center. Shoots left. 5'11", 183 lbs. Born, Jamsa, Finland, March 27, 1985.
(Los Angeles' 10th choice, 264th overall, in 2004 Entry Draft).

			Regular Season					Playoffs				
Season	Club	League	GP	G	A	Pts	PIM	GP	G	A	Pts	PIM
2001-02	JYP Jyvaskyla U18	Fin-U18	25	14	12	26	2	7	1	0	1	0
	JYP Jyvaskyla Jr.	Fin-Jr.	3	0	1	1	0	....	....	....	....	....
2002-03	JYP Jyvaskyla U18	Fin-U18	1	2	1	3	0	....	....	....	....	....
	JYP Jyvaskyla Jr.	Fin-Jr.	30	8	7	15	14	4	1	1	2	0
2003-04	Suomi U20	Finland-2	2	0	1	1	0	....	....	....	....	....
	JYP Jyvaskyla Jr.	Fin-Jr.	10	3	2	5	2	9	2	3	5	0
	JYP Jyvaskyla	Finland	25	1	3	4	2	2	0	0	0	0
2004-05	JYP Jyvaskyla Jr.	Fin-Jr.	12	1	5	6	14	6	2	1	3	25
	JYP Jyvaskyla	Finland	10	0	1	1	0	....	....	....	....	....
2005-06	JYP Jyvaskyla	Finland	35	0	6	6	4	3	0	1	1	0
2006-07	JYP Jyvaskyla	Finland	34	4	9	13	4	....	....	....	....	....

TERESCHENKO, Alexei (teh-reh-SHEHN-koh, al-EHX-ay) DAL.

Center. Shoots left. 5'11", 176 lbs. Born, Mozhaisk, USSR, December 16, 1980.
(Dallas' 4th choice, 91st overall, in 2000 Entry Draft).

			Regular Season					Playoffs				
Season	Club	League	GP	G	A	Pts	PIM	GP	G	A	Pts	PIM
1996-97	Dyn'o Moscow 2	Russia-3	9	0	0	0	2	....	....	....	....	....
1997-98	Dynamo Moscow	Russia	26	6	7	13	30	....	....	....	....	....
1998-99	Dyn'o Moscow 2	Russia-3	28	4	17	21	20	....	....	....	....	....
	THK Tver	Russia-2	12	3	4	7	4	....	....	....	....	....
	Dynamo Moscow	Russia	1	0	1	1	0	2	0	0	0	0
99-2000	Dynamo Moscow	Russia	27	1	1	2	10	17	1	1	2	8
2000-01	Dynamo Moscow	Russia	39	3	2	5	18	....	....	....	....	....
2001-02	Yaroslavl 2	Russia-3	1	0	0	0	0	....	....	....	....	....
	Dynamo Moscow	Russia	40	3	6	9	20	3	0	0	0	0
2002-03	Dynamo Moscow	Russia	40	7	9	16	14	5	1	0	1	2
2003-04	Dynamo Moscow	Russia	47	8	12	20	26	3	0	0	0	4
2004-05	Dynamo Moscow	Russia	31	3	6	9	8	10	0	1	1	2
2005-06	Ak Bars Kazan	Russia	36	3	12	15	12	10	0	4	4	12
2006-07	Ak Bars Kazan	Russia	53	8	22	30	38	16	3	6	9	6

TERNAVSKY, Artem (tuhr-NAV-skee, AHR-tehm) WSH.

Defense. Shoots left. 6'2", 208 lbs. Born, Magnitogorsk, USSR, June 2, 1983.
(Washington's 4th choice, 160th overall, in 2001 Entry Draft).

			Regular Season					Playoffs				
Season	Club	League	GP	G	A	Pts	PIM	GP	G	A	Pts	PIM
99-2000	CSKA Moscow 2	Russia-3	2	0	1	1	0	....	....	....	....	....
	HK Moscow 2	Russia-3	25	0	4	4	42	....	....	....	....	....
2000-01	Sherbrooke	QMJHL	65	3	15	18	143	....	....	....	....	....
2001-02	Mostovik Kurgan	Russia-2	25	0	0	0	46	....	....	....	....	....
2002-03	Sibir Novosibirsk	Russia	42	1	1	2	20	....	....	....	....	....
2003-04	Ufa	Russia	12	0	0	0	4	....	....	....	....	....
	Magnitogorsk 2	Russia-3	7	1	0	1	0	....	....	....	....	....
2004-05	Nizhny Novgorod	Russia-2	16	0	1	1	18	....	....	....	....	....
	Motor Barnaul	Russia-2	8	0	1	1	14	....	....	....	....	....
2005-06	Karaganda	Kazakh.	17	1	1	2	12	....	....	....	....	....
	Karaganda	Russia-2	39	3	2	5	26	6	0	1	1	2
2006-07	Gazovik Tyumen	Russia-2	56	3	12	15	78	3	1	0	1	4
	Ust-Kamenogorsk	Kazakh.	14	3	2	5	12	....	....	....	....	....

TERRY, Chris (TAIR-ee, KRIHS) CAR.

Left wing. Shoots left. 5'10", 195 lbs. Born, Brampton, Ont., April 7, 1989.
(Carolina's 4th choice, 132nd overall, in 2007 Entry Draft).

			Regular Season					Playoffs				
Season	Club	League	GP	G	A	Pts	PIM	GP	G	A	Pts	PIM
2003-04	Markham	GTHL	66	39	50	89	....	....	....	....	....	....
2004-05	Markham	GTHL	60	42	53	95	113	9	0	9	9	14
2005-06	Plymouth Whalers	OHL	64	9	19	28	72	11	3	2	5	4
2006-07	Plymouth Whalers	OHL	68	22	44	66	98	20	8	10	18	21

TESLIUK, Roman (tehs-L'YUHK, ROH-muhn)

Defense. Shoots right. 6'1", 195 lbs. Born, Severomorsk, USSR, January 21, 1986.
(Edmonton's 3rd choice, 44th overall, in 2004 Entry Draft).

			Regular Season					Playoffs				
Season	Club	League	GP	G	A	Pts	PIM	GP	G	A	Pts	PIM
2001-02	HK CSKA 2	Russia-3	1	0	0	0	4	....	....	....	....	....
2002-03	CSKA Moscow 2	Russia-3	6	0	2	2	6	....	....	....	....	....
2003-04	Kamloops Blazers	WHL	70	5	9	14	118	5	0	1	1	2
2004-05	Kamloops Blazers	WHL	70	9	20	29	109	6	4	1	5	6
2005-06	Kamloops Blazers	WHL	72	14	16	30	109	....	....	....	....	....
2006-07	Tri-City Americans	WHL	32	8	9	17	70	6	0	1	1	12
	Reading Royals	ECHL	24	4	2	6	32	....	....	....	....	....

THANG, Ryan (THAYNG, RIGH-uhn) NSH.

Left wing. Shoots right. 5'11", 186 lbs. Born, Chicago, IL, May 11, 1987.
(Nashville's 4th choice, 81st overall, in 2007 Entry Draft).

			Regular Season					Playoffs				
Season	Club	League	GP	G	A	Pts	PIM	GP	G	A	Pts	PIM
2004-05	Sioux Falls	USHL	58	9	22	31	45	....	....	....	....	....
2005-06	Sioux Falls	USHL	32	8	14	22	52	....	....	....	....	....
	Omaha Lancers	USHL	25	15	15	30	26	5	2	1	3	2
2006-07	U. of Notre Dame	CCHA	42	20	21	41	22	....	....	....	....	....

CCHA All-Rookie Team (2007)

THOMAS, Andrew (TAW-mas, AN-droo) WSH.

Defense. Shoots right. 6'2", 196 lbs. Born, West Bend, WI, November 14, 1985.
(Washington's 3rd choice, 109th overall, in 2005 Entry Draft).

			Regular Season					Playoffs				
Season	Club	League	GP	G	A	Pts	PIM	GP	G	A	Pts	PIM
2003-04	Waterloo	USHL	57	1	6	7	86	12	0	2	2	28
2004-05	U. of Denver	WCHA	42	2	5	7	78	....	....	....	....	....
2005-06	U. of Denver	WCHA	38	1	3	4	65	....	....	....	....	....
2006-07	U. of Denver	WCHA	40	2	5	7	71	....	....	....	....	....

THURESSON, Andreas (THUR-reh-suhn, an-DRAY-uhs) NSH.

Center. Shoots right. 6'1", 204 lbs. Born, Kristianstad, Sweden, November 18, 1987.
(Nashville's 7th choice, 144th overall, in 2007 Entry Draft).

			Regular Season					Playoffs				
Season	Club	League	GP	G	A	Pts	PIM	GP	G	A	Pts	PIM
2003-04	Malmo U18	Swe-U18	3	0	0	0	4	....	....	....	....	....
	Tyringe SoSS	Sweden-3	12	0	1	1	0	....	....	....	....	....
	Malmo Jr.	Swe-Jr.	19	2	2	4	16	8	0	0	0	6
2004-05	Malmo U18	Swe-U18	3	1	1	2	4	....	....	....	....	....
	Malmo Jr.	Swe-Jr.	30	4	4	8	28	3	2	1	3	2
2005-06	Malmo U18	Swe-U18	2	1	0	1	4	....	....	....	....	....
	Malmo Jr.	Swe-Jr.	38	15	18	33	71	....	....	....	....	....
	Malmo	Sweden-2	20	0	2	2	10	....	....	....	....	....
2006-07	Malmo	Sweden	48	10	5	15	26	....	....	....	....	....
	Malmo	Sweden-Q	10	2	2	4	2	....	....	....	....	....

TIMKIN, Alexei (TIHM-kihn, al-EHX-ay) DAL.

Right wing. Shoots left. 6'2", 194 lbs. Born, Kirov, USSR, April 21, 1979.
(Dallas' 6th choice, 160th overall, in 1997 Entry Draft).

			Regular Season					Playoffs				
Season	Club	League	GP	G	A	Pts	PIM	GP	G	A	Pts	PIM
1996-97	Yaroslavl 2	Russia-3	47	16	6	22	54	....	....	....	....	....
	Torpedo Yaroslavl	Russia	3	0	1	1	0	....	....	....	....	....
1997-98	Torpedo Yaroslavl	Russia	16	4	5	9	14	....	....	....	....	....
1998-99	Kirovo-Chepetsk	Russia-3	30	4	3	7	36	....	....	....	....	....
	St. Petersburg 2	Russia-4	1	0	0	0	2	....	....	....	....	....
99-2000	Kirovo-Chepetsk	Russia-3	49	29	13	42	26	....	....	....	....	....
2000-01	Kirovo-Chepetsk	Russia-3	STATISTICS NOT AVAILABLE									
2003-04	Kirovo-Chepetsk	Russia-2	3	0	1	1	4	....	....	....	....	....
	Karaganda	Russia-2	11	0	1	1	6	....	....	....	....	....
2005-06	Kirovo-Chepetsk	Russia-2	37	6	6	12	22	3	0	1	1	4
	HK Dmitrov	Russia-2	2	0	0	0	2	....	....	....	....	....
2006-07	Kirovo-Chepetsk	Russia-2	47	7	11	18	44	....	....	....	....	....

TKACHENKO, Ivan (t'kuh-CHEHN-koh, ee-VAHN) CBJ

Left wing. Shoots left. 5'10", 183 lbs. Born, Yaroslavl, USSR, November 9, 1979.
(Columbus' 5th choice, 98th overall, in 2002 Entry Draft).

			Regular Season					Playoffs				
Season	Club	League	GP	G	A	Pts	PIM	GP	G	A	Pts	PIM
1997-98	Yaroslavl 2	Russia-2	STATISTICS NOT AVAILABLE									
	Torpedo Yaroslavl	Russia	....	....	....	....	....	1	0	0	0	0
1998-99	Yaroslavl 2	Russia-3	28	15	13	28	26	....	....	....	....	....
99-2000	Yaroslavl 2	Russia-3	1	1	0	1	0	....	....	....	....	....
	Motor Zavolzhje	Russia-2	43	15	14	29	22	....	....	....	....	....
	Nizhnekamsk 2	Russia-3	8	6	3	9	24	....	....	....	....	....
	Nizhnekamsk	Russia	5	1	0	1	0	4	0	1	1	0
2000-01	Nizhnekamsk	Russia	28	2	2	4	14	4	0	1	1	0
2001-02	Yaroslavl 2	Russia-3	1	0	1	1	2	....	....	....	....	....
	Yaroslavl	Russia	44	13	20	33	57	9	5	2	7	4
2002-03	Yaroslavl	Russia	44	11	6	17	57	10	2	3	5	6
2003-04	Yaroslavl	Russia	56	7	11	18	22	3	0	0	0	0
2004-05	Yaroslavl	Russia	59	15	15	30	30	9	2	3	5	8
2005-06	Yaroslavl	Russia	45	10	21	31	30	11	1	2	3	16
	Yaroslavl 2	Russia-3	1	0	1	1	2	....	....	....	....	....
2006-07	Yaroslavl	Russia	52	9	24	33	30	7	1	2	3	6

TLUSTY, Jiri (T'LOO-stee, YIH-ree) TOR.

Center. Shoots left. 6', 209 lbs. Born, Slany, Czech., March 16, 1988.
(Toronto's 1st choice, 13th overall, in 2006 Entry Draft).

			Regular Season					Playoffs				
Season	Club	League	GP	G	A	Pts	PIM	GP	G	A	Pts	PIM
2001-02	HC Kladno U17	CzR-U17	1	0	0	0	0	....	....	....	....	....
2002-03	HC Kladno U17	CzR-U17	48	28	17	45	22	10	5	4	9	12
2003-04	HC Kladno U17	CzR-U17	1	0	0	0	2	1	0	0	0	2
	HC Kladno Jr.	CzRep-Jr.	51	10	3	13	12	1	0	0	0	0
2004-05	HC Kladno Jr.	CzRep-Jr.	42	15	12	27	54	10	2	2	4	8
2005-06	HC Kladno Jr.	CzRep-Jr.	6	4	2	6	2	6	7	6	13	6
	HC Rabat Kladno	CzRep	44	7	3	10	51	....	....	....	....	....
2006-07	Sault Ste. Marie	OHL	37	13	21	34	28	13	9	8	17	14
	Toronto Marlies	AHL	6	3	1	4	4	....	....	....	....	....

TOEWS, Jonathan (TAYVES, JAWN-ah-thuhn) CHI.

Center. Shoots left. 6'1", 203 lbs. Born, Winnipeg, Man., April 29, 1988.
(Chicago's 1st choice, 3rd overall, in 2006 Entry Draft).

			Regular Season					Playoffs				
Season	Club	League	GP	G	A	Pts	PIM	GP	G	A	Pts	PIM
2004-05	Shat.-St. Mary's	High-MN	64	48	62	110	38	....	....	....	....	....
2005-06	North Dakota	WCHA	42	22	17	39	22	....	....	....	....	....
2006-07	North Dakota	WCHA	34	18	28	46	10	....	....	....	....	....

WCHA Second All-Star Team (2007) • NCAA West First All-American Team (2007)

TOLPEKO, Denis (tohl-PEH-koh, DEH-nihs) PHI.

Right wing. Shoots left. 6', 190 lbs. Born, Moscow, USSR, January 29, 1985.

			Regular Season					Playoffs				
Season	Club	League	GP	G	A	Pts	PIM	GP	G	A	Pts	PIM
2003-04	Seattle	WHL	72	13	16	29	63	....	....	....	....	....
2004-05	Seattle	WHL	54	13	18	31	48	12	1	0	1	10
2005-06	Regina Pats	WHL	53	20	31	51	66	6	0	4	4	16
2006-07	Philadelphia	AHL	58	11	19	30	58	....	....	....	....	....

Signed as a free agent by **Philadelphia**, July 5, 2006.

TOPOL, Sergei (TOH-puhl, SAIR-gay) VAN.

Center. Shoots left. 6'2", 183 lbs. Born, Omsk, USSR, February 15, 1985.
(Vancouver's 8th choice, 252nd overall, in 2003 Entry Draft).

			Regular Season					Playoffs				
Season	Club	League	GP	G	A	Pts	PIM	GP	G	A	Pts	PIM
2002-03	Omsk 2	Russia-3	45	16	5	21	18	....	....	....	....	....
2003-04	Avangard Omsk	Russia	9	0	0	0	2	....	....	....	....	....
	Omsk 2	Russia-3	39	25	14	39	10	....	....	....	....	....
2004-05	Mechel	Russia-2	19	1	0	1	6	....	....	....	....	....
	Mechel 2	Russia-3	5	2	1	3	8	....	....	....	....	....
	Omsk 2	Russia-3	18	6	4	10	4	....	....	....	....	....
	Avangard Omsk	Russia	2	1	0	1	0	....	....	....	....	....
2005-06	Omsk 2	Russia-3	33	24	15	39	26	....	....	....	....	....
	Avangard Omsk	Russia	17	1	0	1	12	....	....	....	....	....
2006-07	Avangard Omsk 2	Russia-3	26	18	14	32	30	....	....	....	....	....
	Avangard Omsk	Russia	27	0	1	1	12	1	0	0	0	2

TORP, Nichlas (TOHRP, NIHK-luhs) MTL.

Defense. Shoots left. 5'10", 196 lbs. Born, Jonkoping, Sweden, April 10, 1989.
(Montreal's 8th choice, 163rd overall, in 2007 Entry Draft).

			Regular Season					Playoffs				
Season	Club	League	GP	G	A	Pts	PIM	GP	G	A	Pts	PIM
2004-05	HV 71 U18	Swe-U18	11	5	2	7	20	....	....	....	....	....
2005-06	HV 71 U18	Swe-U18	8	3	1	4	45	5	1	1	2	12
	HV 71 Jr.	Swe-Jr.	7	0	0	0	34	....	....	....	....	....
2006-07	HV 71 U18	Swe-U18	1	0	0	0	2	3	1	0	1	43
	HV 71 Jr.	Swe-Jr.	17	3	1	4	42	4	0	2	2	10

TORQUATO, Zack (tohr-KAH-toh, ZAK) DET.

Center. Shoots right. 6', 195 lbs. Born, Sault Ste Marie, Ont., June 8, 1989.
(Detroit's 4th choice, 178th overall, in 2007 Entry Draft).

			Regular Season					Playoffs				
Season	Club	League	GP	G	A	Pts	PIM	GP	G	A	Pts	PIM
2004-05	Stratford Cullitons	OJHL-B	47	34	41	75	52	....	....	....	....	....
2005-06	Saginaw Spirit	OHL	65	19	18	37	56	4	1	0	1	6
2006-07	Saginaw Spirit	OHL	22	10	13	23	24	....	....	....	....	....
	Erie Otters	OHL	43	20	26	46	69	....	....	....	....	....

TREMBLAY, Jonathan (TRAHM-blay, JAWN-ah-thuhn) S.J.

Right wing. Shoots right. 6'3", 240 lbs. Born, Fauquier, Ont., March 3, 1984.
(San Jose's 6th choice, 201st overall, in 2003 Entry Draft).

			Regular Season					Playoffs				
Season	Club	League	GP	G	A	Pts	PIM	GP	G	A	Pts	PIM
2001-02	Timmins Majors	GNML	STATISTICS NOT AVAILABLE									
	Acadie-Bathurst	QMJHL	2	0	0	0	5	1	0	0	0	0
2002-03	Acadie-Bathurst	QMJHL	62	0	1	1	232	9	0	0	0	45
2003-04	Acadie-Bathurst	QMJHL	60	3	0	3	*316	....	....	....	....	....
2004-05	Cleveland Barons	AHL	1	0	0	0	0	....	....	....	....	....
	Johnstown Chiefs	ECHL	46	2	3	5	136	....	....	....	....	....
2005-06	Toledo Storm	ECHL	1	0	0	0	0	....	....	....	....	....
	Kalamazoo Wings	UHL	8	0	0	0	20	....	....	....	....	....
	Quad City	UHL	37	0	2	2	62	....	....	....	....	....
2006-07	Worcester Sharks	AHL	3	0	0	0	5	....	....	....	....	....
	Fresno Falcons	ECHL	63	0	2	2	133	....	....	....	....	....

TREVELYAN, T.J. (truh-VEHL-yuhn, TEE-JAY) BOS.

Left wing. Shoots left. 5'10", 187 lbs. Born, Mississauga, Ont., March 6, 1984.

			Regular Season					Playoffs				
Season	Club	League	GP	G	A	Pts	PIM	GP	G	A	Pts	PIM
2002-03	St. Lawrence	ECAC	34	10	12	22	38	....	....	....	....	....
2003-04	St. Lawrence	ECAC	38	*23	16	39	62	....	....	....	....	....
2004-05	St. Lawrence	ECACHL	38	*25	20	45	61	....	....	....	....	....
2005-06	St. Lawrence	ECACHL	40	20	28	*48	43	....	....	....	....	....
2006-07	Providence Bruins	AHL	60	28	24	52	41	13	3	6	9	12
	Long Beach	ECHL	15	9	8	17	16	....	....	....	....	....

ECACHL First All-Star Team (2005, 2006) • ECACHL Player of the Year (2006) • NCAA East First All-American Team (2006)

Signed as a free agent by **Boston**, August 17, 2006.

TROPP, Corey (TROHP, KOHR-ee) BUF.

Right wing. Shoots right. 5'11", 183 lbs. Born, Grosse Pointe, MI, July 25, 1989.
(Buffalo's 3rd choice, 89th overall, in 2007 Entry Draft).

			Regular Season					Playoffs				
Season	Club	League	GP	G	A	Pts	PIM	GP	G	A	Pts	PIM
2005-06	Sioux Falls	USHL	46	7	8	15	21	14	2	3	5	8
2006-07	Sioux Falls	USHL	54	26	36	62	76	8	4	9	*13	0

TRUKHNO, Vyacheslav (trookh-NOH, V'YTACH-ih-slav) EDM.

Left wing. Shoots left. 6'1", 197 lbs. Born, Khimki, USSR, February 22, 1987.
(Edmonton's 6th choice, 120th overall, in 2005 Entry Draft).

			Regular Season					Playoffs				
Season	Club	League	GP	G	A	Pts	PIM	GP	G	A	Pts	PIM
2002-03	Rungstead IK	Denmark-2	1	2	3	5	0	....	....	....	....	....
	Rungstead	Denmark	27	7	4	11	8	12	0	1	1	8
2003-04	Rungstead	Denmark	35	12	11	23	18	7	0	0	0	8
2004-05	PEI Rocket	QMJHL	64	25	34	59	57	....	....	....	....	....
2005-06	PEI Rocket	QMJHL	60	28	68	96	81	3	2	2	4	0
2006-07	Gatineau	QMJHL	60	25	77	102	67	5	0	6	6	19

QMJHL All-Rookie Team (2005) • Canadian Major Junior All-Rookie Team (2005) • QMJHL First All-Star Team (2007)

TULUPOV, Kirill (too-LOO-pawv, kih-RIHL) N.J.

Defense. Shoots right. 6'3", 210 lbs. Born, Moscow, USSR, April 23, 1988.
(New Jersey's 3rd choice, 67th overall, in 2006 Entry Draft).

			Regular Season					Playoffs				
Season	Club	League	GP	G	A	Pts	PIM	GP	G	A	Pts	PIM
2004-05	Toronto Rattlers	Exhib.	57	7	16	23	33	....	....	....	....	....
2005-06	Toronto Rattlers	Exhib.	40	16	28	44	30	....	....	....	....	....
	Leninogorsk	Russia-2	8	1	1	2	14	3	0	2	2	8
2006-07	Chicoutimi	QMJHL	54	8	20	28	88	2	1	1	2	2

TUMA, Martin (TOO-ma, MAHR-tehn) FLA.

Defense. Shoots left. 6'4", 209 lbs. Born, Most, Czech., September 14, 1985.
(Florida's 8th choice, 162nd overall, in 2003 Entry Draft).

			Regular Season					Playoffs				
Season	Club	League	GP	G	A	Pts	PIM	GP	G	A	Pts	PIM
2000-01	Litvinov Jr.	CzRep-Jr.	45	4	12	16	62	6	0	3	3	8
2001-02	Litvinov Jr.	CzRep-Jr.	39	2	1	3	104	2	0	0	0	0
	Litvinov	CzRep	1	0	0	0	2	....	....	....	....	....
2002-03	Litvinov Jr.	CzRep-Jr.	34	1	3	4	123	....	....	....	....	....
2003-04	Sault Ste. Marie	OHL	57	0	5	5	48	....	....	....	....	....
2004-05	Sault Ste. Marie	OHL	61	10	13	23	107	7	0	3	3	6
	San Antonio	AHL	5	0	1	1	0	....	....	....	....	....
2005-06	Rochester	AHL	12	0	2	2	38	....	....	....	....	....
	Florida Everblades	ECHL	48	0	6	6	75	1	0	0	0	0
2006-07	Rochester	AHL	23	0	0	0	33	1	0	0	0	0
	Florida Everblades	ECHL	32	0	9	9	77	3	0	0	0	6

TUOMAINEN, Miikka (too-oh-MAY-nehn, MEE-kah) ATL.

Left wing. Shoots left. 6'3", 250 lbs. Born, Turku, Finland, May 22, 1986.
(Atlanta's 7th choice, 204th overall, in 2004 Entry Draft).

			Regular Season					Playoffs				
Season	Club	League	GP	G	A	Pts	PIM	GP	G	A	Pts	PIM
2001-02	TuTo Turku U18	Fin-U18	14	8	5	13	14	....	....	....	....	....
	TuTo Turku Jr.	Fin-Jr.	1	1	0	1	0	....	....	....	....	....
2002-03	TuTo Turku U18	Fin-U18	24	3	4	7	52	4	0	0	0	0
	TuTo Turku Jr.	Fin-Jr.	2	0	0	0	4	....	....	....	....	....
	TuTo Turku	Finland-2	6	0	0	0	0	....	....	....	....	....
2003-04	TuTo Turku Jr.	Fin-Jr.	20	10	7	17	6	....	....	....	....	....
	TuTo Turku U18	Fin-U18	20	10	7	17	6	....	....	....	....	....
	TuTo Turku	Finland-2	30	4	3	7	2	....	....	....	....	....
2004-05	TuTo Turku Jr.	Fin-Jr.	5	1	4	5	0	....	....	....	....	....
	TuTo Turku	Finland-2	42	4	4	8	22	7	1	0	1	2
2005-06	Lukko Rauma Jr.	Fin-Jr.	16	5	3	8	4	9	5	3	8	8
	Suomi U20	Finland-2	2	0	0	0	2	....	....	....	....	....
	Lukko Rauma	Finland	33	2	2	4	12	....	....	....	....	....
2006-07	Lukko Rauma Jr.	Fin-Jr.	5	0	1	1	0	....	....	....	....	....
	Lukko Rauma	Finland	54	6	8	14	77	3	1	0	1	0

TUREK, Ryan (TOOR-ehk, RIGH-uhn) ST.L.

Center. Shoots right. 5'11", 170 lbs. Born, Southfield, MI, September 22, 1987.
(St. Louis' 5th choice, 94th overall, in 2006 Entry Draft).

			Regular Season					Playoffs				
Season	Club	League	GP	G	A	Pts	PIM	GP	G	A	Pts	PIM
2004-05	Omaha Lancers	USHL	45	3	8	11	52	4	1	0	1	2
2005-06	Omaha Lancers	USHL	52	17	11	28	71	5	1	1	2	2
2006-07	Michigan State	CCHA	31	0	2	2	18	....	....	....	....	....

TURNBULL, Joshua (TUHRN-buhl, JAWSH-oo-uh) L.A.

Center. Shoots right. 5'10", 172 lbs. Born, Hayward, WI, July 12, 1988.
(Los Angeles' 8th choice, 137th overall, in 2007 Entry Draft).

			Regular Season					Playoffs				
Season	Club	League	GP	G	A	Pts	PIM	GP	G	A	Pts	PIM
2005-06	Duluth East	High-MN	STATISTICS NOT AVAILABLE									
2006-07	Waterloo	USHL	60	25	29	54	66	9	3	1	4	12

TURNER, Brennan (TUHR-nuhr, BREH-nuhn) CHI.

Defense. Shoots left. 6'3", 221 lbs. Born, Winnipeg, Man., December 5, 1986.
(Chicago's 8th choice, 134th overall, in 2005 Entry Draft).

			Regular Season					Playoffs				
Season	Club	League	GP	G	A	Pts	PIM	GP	G	A	Pts	PIM
2003-04	Notre Dame	SJHL	35	2	8	10	110	....	....	....	....	....
2004-05	Notre Dame	SJHL	41	5	12	17	207	8	0	1	1	25
2005-06	Yale	ECACHL	16	0	2	2	53	....	....	....	....	....
2006-07	Yale	ECACHL	27	0	0	0	71	....	....	....	....	....

TURRIS, Kyle (TUH-rihs, KIGHL) PHX.

Center. Shoots right. 6'1", 170 lbs. Born, New Westminster, B.C., August 14, 1989.
(Phoenix's 1st choice, 3rd overall, in 2007 Entry Draft).

			Regular Season					Playoffs				
Season	Club	League	GP	G	A	Pts	PIM	GP	G	A	Pts	PIM
2004-05	Grandview	BCAHA	30	13	20	33	....	....	....	....	....	....
2005-06	Burnaby Express	BCHL	57	36	36	72	32	20	10	13	23	6
2006-07	Burnaby Express	BCHL	53	66	55	121	83	14	12	14	26	16

• Signed Letter of Intent to attend **University of Wisconsin** (WCHA) in fall of 2007.

TYRELL, Dana (TIH-rehl, DAY-nuh) T.B.

Center/Right wing. Shoots left. 5'10", 185 lbs. Born, Airdrie, Alta., April 23, 1989.
(Tampa Bay's 1st choice, 47th overall, in 2007 Entry Draft).

			Regular Season					Playoffs				
Season	Club	League	GP	G	A	Pts	PIM	GP	G	A	Pts	PIM
2003-04	Airdrie Xtreme	AMBHL	35	21	47	68	28	7	6	4	10	....
2004-05	Strathmore	AMHL	34	16	23	39	20	16	8	9	*17	....
	Prince George	WHL	1	0	0	0	2	....	....	....	....	....
2005-06	Prince George	WHL	69	7	11	18	44	5	0	0	0	2
2006-07	Prince George	WHL	72	30	26	56	51	15	1	6	7	4

URQUHART, Cory (UHRK-hahrt, KOHR-ee) MTL.

Center. Shoots left. 6'3", 200 lbs. Born, Halifax, N.S., October 1, 1984.
(Montreal's 2nd choice, 40th overall, in 2003 Entry Draft).

			Regular Season					Playoffs				
Season	Club	League	GP	G	A	Pts	PIM	GP	G	A	Pts	PIM
1997-98	East Hants	NSBHL	60	35	46	81	24	....	....	....	....	....
1998-99	East Hants	NSBHL	62	54	60	114	74	....	....	....	....	....
99-2000	Dalhousie	NSMHL	21	15	14	29	12	....	....	....	....	....
2000-01	Quebec Remparts	QMJHL	60	25	24	49	32	2	0	0	0	2
2001-02	Quebec Remparts	QMJHL	36	8	10	18	4	....	....	....	....	....
	Montreal Rocket	QMJHL	34	9	9	18	6	7	3	2	5	0
2002-03	Montreal Rocket	QMJHL	71	35	43	78	28	7	9	6	15	6
2003-04	PEI Rocket	QMJHL	67	35	44	79	52	10	6	7	13	14
2004-05	Hamilton Bulldogs	AHL	1	0	0	0	0	....	....	....	....	....
	Long Beach	ECHL	63	16	15	31	14	6	0	0	0	2
2005-06	Hamilton Bulldogs	AHL	2	0	1	1	2	....	....	....	....	....
	Long Beach	ECHL	67	26	26	52	42	7	4	0	4	8
2006-07	Cincinnati	ECHL	43	22	18	40	47	....	....	....	....	....
	Hamilton Bulldogs	AHL	30	5	12	17	12	18	2	2	4	0

UTKIN, Dmitri (OOT-kihn, dih-MEE-tree) BOS.

Left wing. Shoots left. 6', 170 lbs. Born, Yaroslavl, USSR, June 10, 1984.
(Boston's 5th choice, 228th overall, in 2002 Entry Draft).

			Regular Season					Playoffs				
Season	Club	League	GP	G	A	Pts	PIM	GP	G	A	Pts	PIM
2000-01	Yaroslavl 2	Russia-3	49	12	1	13	10	....	....	....	....	....
2001-02	Yaroslavl 2	Russia-3	32	15	7	22	33	....	....	....	....	....
2002-03	Yaroslavl	Russia	4	0	1	1	0	....	....	....	....	....
2003-04	Spartak Moscow	Russia-2	57	10	10	20	8	13	3	3	6	2
2004-05	Keramin Minsk	BelOpen	8	2	0	2	31	....	....	....	....	....
	HK Brest	BelOpen	20	4	12	16	4	....	....	....	....	....
	HK Riga 2000	BelOpen	....	....	....	....	....	3	0	0	0	0
	HK Riga 2000	Latvia	....	....	....	....	....	6	3	2	5	0
2005-06	Spartak Moscow	Russia	33	3	1	4	4	2	0	0	0	0
	Spartak Moscow 2	Russia-3	10	5	2	7	8	....	....	....	....	....
2006-07	Chelyabinsk	Russia	50	6	8	14	20	....	....	....	....	....

VAGNER, Martin (VAHG-nuhr, MAHR-tihn) CAR.

Defense. Shoots left. 6'1", 214 lbs. Born, Jaromer, Czech., March 16, 1984.
(Carolina's 8th choice, 268th overall, in 2004 Entry Draft).

			Regular Season					Playoffs				
Season	Club	League	GP	G	A	Pts	PIM	GP	G	A	Pts	PIM
99-2000	Sparta Jr.	CzRep-Jr.	46	2	8	10	34	....	....	....	....	....
2000-01	HC Pardubice Jr.	CzRep-Jr.	53	2	12	14	46	....	....	....	....	....
2001-02	Hull Olympiques	QMJHL	64	6	28	34	81	8	0	1	1	10
2002-03	Hull Olympiques	QMJHL	53	1	12	13	98	20	1	4	5	38
2003-04	Gatineau	QMJHL	38	6	12	18	85	13	0	3	3	16
2004-05	Acadie-Bathurst	QMJHL	48	3	10	13	84	....	....	....	....	....
2005-06	Pardubice	CzRep	36	0	0	0	14	....	....	....	....	....
	Hr. Kralove	CzRep-2	12	0	1	1	12	....	....	....	....	....
2006-07	C. Budejovice	CzRep	40	0	0	0	20	3	0	0	0	0

• Re-entered NHL Entry Draft. Originally Dallas' 1st choice, 26th overall, in 2002 Entry Draft.

QMJHL All-Rookie Team (2002)

VAIVE, Justin (VIGHV, JUHS-tihn) ANA.

Left wing. Shoots left. 6'5", 210 lbs. Born, Buffalo, NY, July 8, 1989.
(Anaheim's 4th choice, 92nd overall, in 2007 Entry Draft).

			Regular Season					Playoffs				
Season	Club	League	GP	G	A	Pts	PIM	GP	G	A	Pts	PIM
2004-05	Toronto Marlboros	GTHL	72	38	64	102	....	....	....	....	....	....
2005-06	USNTDP	U-17	13	3	5	8	18	....	....	....	....	....
	USNTDP	NAHL	24	4	8	12	34	5	1	1	2	6
2006-07	USNTDP	U-18	43	7	8	15	49	....	....	....	....	....
	USNTDP	NAHL	15	4	1	5	22	....	....	....	....	....

VALABIK, Boris (vuh-LA-bihk, BOHR-ihs) ATL.

Defense. Shoots left. 6'7", 230 lbs. Born, Nitra, Czech., February 14, 1986.
(Atlanta's 1st choice, 10th overall, in 2004 Entry Draft).

			Regular Season					Playoffs				
Season	Club	League	GP	G	A	Pts	PIM	GP	G	A	Pts	PIM
2002-03	HKM Nitra Jr.	Slovak-Jr.	46	2	12	14	145	....	....	....	....	....
2003-04	Kitchener Rangers	OHL	68	3	13	16	278	5	0	0	0	8
2004-05	Kitchener Rangers	OHL	43	0	4	4	231	15	0	0	0	56
2005-06	Kitchener Rangers	OHL	52	1	9	10	216	5	0	2	2	14
2006-07	Chicago Wolves	AHL	50	2	7	9	184	8	0	1	1	37

OHL All-Rookie Team (2004) • Canadian Major Junior All-Rookie Team (2004)

VALENTENKO, Pavel (val-ehn-TEHN-koh, PAH-vehl) MTL.

Defense. Shoots left. 6'2", 214 lbs. Born, Nizhnekamsk, USSR, October 20, 1987.
(Montreal's 5th choice, 139th overall, in 2006 Entry Draft).

			Regular Season					Playoffs				
Season	Club	League	GP	G	A	Pts	PIM	GP	G	A	Pts	PIM
2002-03	Lada Togliatti 2	Russia-3	6	0	0	0	4	....	....	....	....	....
2003-04	Nizhnekamsk 2	Russia-3	26	0	1	1	28	....	....	....	....	....
2004-05	Nizhnekamsk 2	Russia-3	STATISTICS NOT AVAILABLE									
2005-06	Nizhnekamsk 2	Russia-3	STATISTICS NOT AVAILABLE									
	Nizhnekamsk	Russia	2	0	0	0	2	....	....	....	....	....
2006-07	Nizhnekamsk	Russia	50	0	2	2	62	4	0	0	0	2

VALETTE, Craig (va-LEHT, KRAIG) S.J.

Center. Shoots left. 6', 200 lbs. Born, Shellbrook, Sask., October 7, 1982.

			Regular Season					Playoffs				
Season	Club	League	GP	G	A	Pts	PIM	GP	G	A	Pts	PIM
1998-99	Sask. Contacts	SMHL	36	19	22	41	....	....	....	....	....	....
99-2000	Saskatoon Blades	WHL	47	2	1	3	25	3	0	0	0	0
2000-01	Saskatoon Blades	WHL	24	2	0	2	19	....	....	....	....	....
	Portland	WHL	39	8	6	14	39	16	0	2	2	27
2001-02	Portland	WHL	67	8	14	22	160	7	2	1	3	6
2002-03	Portland	WHL	71	30	26	56	192	7	5	4	9	18
2003-04	Cleveland Barons	AHL	56	6	10	16	77	5	0	0	0	2
2004-05	Cleveland Barons	AHL	79	6	6	12	94	....	....	....	....	....
2005-06	Cleveland Barons	AHL	69	5	6	11	95	....	....	....	....	....
2006-07	Worcester Sharks	AHL	55	15	11	26	77	1	0	0	0	0

Signed as a free agent by **San Jose**, April 4, 2003.

VALLIN, Ari (VAHL-ihn, AH-ree)

Defense. Shoots left. 5'11", 194 lbs. Born, Ylojarvi, Finland, March 21, 1978.

			Regular Season					Playoffs				
Season	Club	League	GP	G	A	Pts	PIM	GP	G	A	Pts	PIM
1996-97	Tappara Tampere	Finland	21	0	0	0	8	3	0	0	0	0
1997-98	Tappara Tampere	Finland	44	2	2	4	16	4	0	3	3	0
1998-99	HPK Hameenlinna	Finland	49	6	3	9	24	8	0	1	1	8
99-2000	Tappara Tampere	Finland	54	4	8	12	36	4	0	0	0	8
2000-01	HPK Hameenlinna	Finland	53	5	7	12	34	....	....	....	....	....
2001-02	Jokerit Helsinki	Finland	45	4	20	24	24	12	1	4	5	2
2002-03	Jokerit Helsinki	Finland	53	5	11	16	34	8	0	1	1	4
2003-04	Karpat Oulu	Finland	54	7	10	17	36	15	3	2	5	8
2004-05	Karpat Oulu	Finland	55	2	15	17	40	12	2	2	4	10
2005-06	Karpat Oulu	Finland	50	7	23	30	84	....	....	....	....	....
2006-07	Rochester	AHL	24	0	7	7	20	....	....	....	....	....
	Frolunda	Sweden	23	3	6	9	20	....	....	....	....	....

Signed as a free agent by **Florida**, July 6, 2006. Re-assigned to **Frolunda** by **Florida**, December 20, 2006.

VAN DER GULIK, David (VAN DUHR-GOO-lihk, DAY-vihd) CGY.

Right wing. Shoots left. 5'11", 183 lbs. Born, Abbotsford, B.C., April 20, 1983.
(Calgary's 10th choice, 206th overall, in 2002 Entry Draft).

			Regular Season					Playoffs				
Season	Club	League	GP	G	A	Pts	PIM	GP	G	A	Pts	PIM
99-2000	Chilliwack Chiefs	BCHL	41	35	46	81	....	....	....	....	....	....
2000-01	Chilliwack Chiefs	BCHL	60	42	38	80	....	....	....	....	....	....
2001-02	Chilliwack Chiefs	BCHL	56	38	62	100	90	13	8	11	19	....
2002-03	Boston University	H-East	40	10	10	20	56	....	....	....	....	....
2003-04	Boston University	H-East	35	13	7	20	74	....	....	....	....	....
2004-05	Boston University	H-East	41	18	13	31	48	....	....	....	....	....
2005-06	Boston University	H-East	25	11	11	22	26	....	....	....	....	....
2006-07	Omaha	AHL	80	16	27	43	69	6	0	2	2	4

Hockey East All-Rookie Team (2003)

VANDE VELDE, Chris (VAN-deh VEHLD, KRIHS) EDM.

Center. Shoots left. 6'2", 190 lbs. Born, Moorhead, MN, March 15, 1987.
(Edmonton's 5th choice, 97th overall, in 2005 Entry Draft).

			Regular Season					Playoffs				
Season	Club	League	GP	G	A	Pts	PIM	GP	G	A	Pts	PIM
2003-04	Moorhead Spuds	High-MN	29	19	24	43	....	....	....	....	....	....
2004-05	Moorhead Spuds	High-MN	30	35	32	67	28	....	....	....	....	....
	Lincoln Stars	USHL	7	1	4	5	0	4	0	2	2	0
2005-06	Lincoln Stars	USHL	56	16	20	36	70	9	1	3	4	10
2006-07	North Dakota	WCHA	38	3	6	9	37	....	....	....	....	....

VANDERMEER, Peter (VAN-duhr-meer, PEE-tuhr)

Left wing. Shoots left. 6', 210 lbs. Born, Carolina, Alta., October 14, 1975.

			Regular Season					Playoffs				
Season	Club	League	GP	G	A	Pts	PIM	GP	G	A	Pts	PIM
1992-93	Red Deer	AMHL	34	26	30	56	172	....	....	....	....	....
	Red Deer Rebels	WHL	2	0	0	0	2	....	....	....	....	....
1993-94	Red Deer Rebels	WHL	54	4	9	13	170	....	....	....	....	....
1994-95	Red Deer Rebels	WHL	61	16	16	32	218	....	....	....	....	....
1995-96	Red Deer Rebels	WHL	63	21	40	61	207	....	....	....	....	....
1996-97	Columbus Chill	ECHL	30	6	11	17	195	7	2	1	3	26
1997-98	Columbus Chill	ECHL	20	4	7	11	78	....	....	....	....	....
	Richmond	ECHL	18	2	5	7	165	....	....	....	....	....
	Rochester	AHL	30	4	2	6	140	4	1	0	1	13
1998-99	Rochester	AHL	2	1	0	1	16	16	1	0	1	38
	Binghamton	UHL	62	15	21	36	*390	5	2	2	4	0
99-2000	Wilkes-Barre	AHL	4	0	0	0	7	....	....	....	....	....
	Richmond	ECHL	58	31	25	56	*457	3	0	1	1	20
	Providence Bruins	AHL	....	....	....	....	....	9	0	3	3	2
2000-01	Providence Bruins	AHL	62	19	18	37	240	4	0	0	0	16
2001-02	Philadelphia	AHL	61	5	1	6	313	5	0	0	0	8
	Trenton Titans	ECHL	2	0	1	1	2	....	....	....	....	....
2002-03	Philadelphia	AHL	77	5	8	13	335	....	....	....	....	....
2003-04	Philadelphia	AHL	71	5	8	13	*398	12	1	0	1	29
2004-05	Grand Rapids	AHL	73	4	13	17	310	....	....	....	....	....
2005-06	Hamilton Bulldogs	AHL	67	6	6	12	276	....	....	....	....	....
2006-07	Hershey Bears	AHL	26	2	5	7	129	2	0	0	0	0

Signed as a free agent by **Philadelphia**, July 6, 2001. Signed as a free agent by **Detroit**, August 16, 2004. Signed as a free agent by **Montreal**, August 2, 2005. Signed as a free agent by **Washington**, July 21, 2006.

VANNELLI, Michael (vuh-NEHL-ee, MIGH-kuhl) ATL.

Defense. Shoots right. 6'2", 190 lbs. Born, St. Paul, MN, October 2, 1983.
(Atlanta's 4th choice, 136th overall, in 2003 Entry Draft).

			Regular Season					Playoffs				
Season	Club	League	GP	G	A	Pts	PIM	GP	G	A	Pts	PIM
2001-02	Cretin-Derham	High-MN	28	0	5	5	16	....	....	....	....	....
	Sioux Falls	USHL	37	0	5	5	24	....	....	....	....	....
2002-03	Sioux Falls	USHL	60	13	34	47	88	....	....	....	....	....
2003-04	U. of Minnesota	WCHA	27	2	9	11	10	....	....	....	....	....
2004-05	U. of Minnesota	WCHA	40	4	12	16	33	....	....	....	....	....
2005-06	U. of Minnesota	WCHA	40	7	10	17	44	....	....	....	....	....
2006-07	U. of Minnesota	WCHA	44	10	29	39	42	....	....	....	....	....

USHL First All-Star Team (2003) • WCHA Second All-Star Team (2007)

vanRIEMSDYK, James (VAN REEMZ-dighk, JAYMZ) PHI.

Left wing. Shoots left. 6'3", 205 lbs. Born, Middletown, NJ, May 4, 1989.
(Philadelphia's 1st choice, 2nd overall, in 2007 Entry Draft).

			Regular Season					Playoffs				
Season	Club	League	GP	G	A	Pts	PIM	GP	G	A	Pts	PIM
2004-05	Christian Bros.	High-NJ	30	36	24	60	....	....	....	....	....	....
2005-06	USNTDP	U-17	11	7	5	12	18	....	....	....	....	....
	USNTDP	U-18	14	1	3	4	6	....	....	....	....	....
	USNTDP	NAHL	37	18	11	29	36	7	1	0	1	8
2006-07	USNTDP	U-18	39	25	28	53	48	....	....	....	....	....
	USNTDP	NAHL	12	13	12	25	37	....	....	....	....	....

• Signed Letter of Intent to attend **University of New Hampshire** (Hockey East) in fall of 2007.

VAS, Janos (VAHSH, YAH-nohsh) DAL.

Left wing. Shoots left. 6'1", 205 lbs. Born, Dunaujvaros, Hungary, January 29, 1984.
(Dallas' 2nd choice, 32nd overall, in 2002 Entry Draft).

			Regular Season					Playoffs				
Season	Club	League	GP	G	A	Pts	PIM	GP	G	A	Pts	PIM
99-2000	Dunaferr SE	Hungary	2	2	0	0	0	....	....	....	....	....
2000-01	Malmo Jr.	Swe-Jr.	23	4	4	8	12	....	....	....	....	....
	Malmo U18	Swe-U18	3	2	0	2	4	....	....	....	....	....
2001-02	Malmo Jr.	Swe-Jr.	36	15	19	34	52	7	8	2	10	4
2002-03	Malmo Jr.	Swe-Jr.	17	5	12	17	14	....	....	....	....	....
	IK Pantern Malmo	Sweden-3	STATISTICS NOT AVAILABLE									
	IF Troja-Ljungby	Sweden-2	17	2	2	4	20	....	....	....	....	....
	Malmo	Sweden	14	1	0	1	2	....	....	....	....	....
2003-04	Malmo U18	Swe-U18	15	5	3	8	14	8	5	2	7	33
	Malmo	Sweden	6	0	0	0	0	....	....	....	....	....
	IK Pantern Malmo	Sweden-3	3	0	2	2	....	....	....	....	....	....
	Malmo	Sweden-Q	1	0	0	0	0	....	....	....	....	....
2004-05	Halmstad	Sweden-2	39	9	8	17	10	2	0	1	1	2
2005-06	Iowa Stars	AHL	35	2	9	11	18	7	1	1	2	2
	Idaho Steelheads	ECHL	10	4	5	9	15	....	....	....	....	....
2006-07	Iowa Stars	AHL	72	13	13	26	42	10	1	1	2	2

VASYUNOV, Alexander (vahs-YUH-nawv, al-EHX-AN-duhr) **N.J.**

Left wing. Shoots right. 6', 190 lbs. Born, Yaroslavl, USSR, April 22, 1988.
(New Jersey's 2nd choice, 58th overall, in 2006 Entry Draft).

			Regular Season					Playoffs				
Season	Club	League	GP	G	A	Pts	PIM	GP	G	A	Pts	PIM
2004-05	Yaroslavl 2	Russia-3	28	10	2	12	6	....	....	....	....	....
2005-06	Yaroslavl 2	Russia-3	29	29	6	35	14	....	....	....	....	....
	Yaroslavl	Russia	2	0	0	0	2	....	....	....	....	....
2006-07	Yaroslavl	Russia	17	0	0	0	4	....	....	....	....	....
	Yaroslavl 2	Russia-3	30	16	9	25	52	....	....	....	....	....

VEILLEUX, Keven (VAY-oo, KEH-vihn) **PIT.**

Center. Shoots right. 6'5", 202 lbs. Born, Saint-Renee, Que., June 27, 1989.
(Pittsburgh's 2nd choice, 51st overall, in 2007 Entry Draft).

			Regular Season					Playoffs				
Season	Club	League	GP	G	A	Pts	PIM	GP	G	A	Pts	PIM
2004-05	Levis	QAAA	11	1	0	1	0	2	0	1	1	0
2005-06	Levis	QAAA	26	12	23	35	53	....	....	....	....	....
	Victoriaville Tigres	QMJHL	33	2	13	15	4	5	0	1	1	2
2006-07	Victoriaville Tigres	QMJHL	70	20	35	55	53	6	1	5	6	4

VERNACE, Michael (vuhr-NAYS, MIGH-kuhl) **COL.**

Defense. Shoots left. 6'2", 200 lbs. Born, Toronto, Ont., May 26, 1986.
(San Jose's 6th choice, 201st overall, in 2004 Entry Draft).

			Regular Season					Playoffs				
Season	Club	League	GP	G	A	Pts	PIM	GP	G	A	Pts	PIM
2003-04	Bramalea Blues	OPJHL	33	3	12	15	16	....	....	....	....	....
	Brampton	OHL	2	1	1	2	0	11	2	3	5	8
2004-05	Brampton	OHL	68	12	38	50	42	6	2	2	4	0
2005-06	Brampton	OHL	68	10	62	72	54	11	1	5	6	6
2006-07	Albany River Rats	AHL	30	1	11	12	35	....	....	....	....	....
	Arizona Sundogs	CHL	24	3	11	14	20	....	....	....	....	....

OHL All-Rookie Team (2005)

Rights traded to **Colorado** by **San Jose** for Colorado's 6th round choice (Patrick Zackrisson) in 2007 Entry Draft, June 1, 2006.

VERSTEEG, Kris (vuhr-STEEG, KRIHS) **CHI.**

Right wing. Shoots right. 5'10", 179 lbs. Born, Lethbridge, Alta., May 13, 1986.
(Boston's 4th choice, 134th overall, in 2004 Entry Draft).

			Regular Season					Playoffs				
Season	Club	League	GP	G	A	Pts	PIM	GP	G	A	Pts	PIM
2002-03	Lethbridge	WHL	57	8	10	18	32	....	....	....	....	....
2003-04	Lethbridge	WHL	68	16	33	49	85	....	....	....	....	....
2004-05	Lethbridge	WHL	68	22	30	52	68	5	0	1	1	4
2005-06	Kamloops Blazers	WHL	14	6	6	12	24	....	....	....	....	....
	Red Deer Rebels	WHL	57	10	26	36	103	....	....	....	....	....
	Providence Bruins	AHL	13	2	4	6	13	3	0	0	0	6
2006-07	Providence Bruins	AHL	43	22	27	49	19	....	....	....	....	....
	Norfolk Admirals	AHL	27	4	19	23	20	2	0	0	0	2

Traded to **Chicago** by **Boston** with future considerations for Brandon Bochenski, February 3, 2007.

VESCE, Ryan (veks-KEE, RIGH-uhn)

Center. Shoots right. 5'8", 165 lbs. Born, Lloyd Harbor, NY, April 7, 1982.

			Regular Season					Playoffs				
Season	Club	League	GP	G	A	Pts	PIM	GP	G	A	Pts	PIM
2000-01	Cornell Big Red	ECAC	33	7	20	27	10	....	....	....	....	....
2001-02	Cornell Big Red	ECAC	35	10	20	30	10	....	....	....	....	....
2002-03	Cornell Big Red	ECAC	36	19	26	45	16	....	....	....	....	....
2003-04	Cornell Big Red	ECAC	27	10	16	26	14	....	....	....	....	....
2004-05	Rogle	Sweden-2	43	20	25	45	51	....	....	....	....	....
2005-06	Springfield Falcons	AHL	80	18	49	67	50	....	....	....	....	....
2006-07	Binghamton	AHL	80	16	35	51	51	....	....	....	....	....

Signed as a free agent by **Ottawa**, July 17, 2006. Signed as a free agent by **HIFK Helsinki** (Finland), July 17, 2007.

VIGILANTE, John (vih-jih-LAN-tee, JAWN) **NSH.**

Left wing. Shoots left. 6', 190 lbs. Born, Dearborn, MI, May 24, 1985.

			Regular Season					Playoffs				
Season	Club	League	GP	G	A	Pts	PIM	GP	G	A	Pts	PIM
2002-03	Plymouth Whalers	OHL	65	15	24	39	31	18	6	3	9	8
2003-04	Plymouth Whalers	OHL	66	30	38	68	25	9	1	7	8	8
2004-05	Plymouth Whalers	OHL	68	24	38	62	17	4	0	0	0	0
2005-06	Plymouth Whalers	OHL	55	24	53	77	34	13	4	12	16	0
2006-07	Milwaukee	AHL	62	8	19	27	10	2	0	0	0	2

Signed as a free agent by **Nashville**. December 7, 2005.

VISHNEVSKIY, Ivan (vihsh-NEHV-skee, ee-VAHN) **DAL.**

Defense. Shoots left. 5'11", 176 lbs. Born, Barnaul, USSR, February 18, 1988.
(Dallas' 1st choice, 27th overall, in 2006 Entry Draft).

			Regular Season					Playoffs				
Season	Club	League	GP	G	A	Pts	PIM	GP	G	A	Pts	PIM
2003-04	Lada Togliatti 2	Russia-3	16	0	0	0	10	....	....	....	....	....
2004-05	Lada Togliatti 2	Russia-3	STATISTICS NOT AVAILABLE									
2005-06	Rouyn-Noranda	QMJHL	54	13	35	48	57	5	2	1	3	2
2006-07	Rouyn-Noranda	QMJHL	60	14	37	51	90	16	5	8	13	8

QMJHL All-Rookie Team (2006)

VISHNYAKOV, Albert (vihsh-nyeh-KAWF, al-BAIRT) **T.B.**

Left wing. Shoots right. 6', 185 lbs. Born, Almyetevsk, USSR, December 30, 1983.
(Tampa Bay's 9th choice, 273rd overall, in 2003 Entry Draft).

			Regular Season					Playoffs				
Season	Club	League	GP	G	A	Pts	PIM	GP	G	A	Pts	PIM
99-2000	Almetjevsk 2	Russia-3	41	11	5	16	68	....	....	....	....	....
2000-01	Almetjevsk	Russia-2	29	0	0	0	2	....	....	....	....	....
2001-02	Ak Bars Kazan	Russia	9	0	1	1	2	....	....	....	....	....
	Nizhny Novgorod	Russia	6	1	0	1	0	....	....	....	....	....
	Nizh. Novgorod 2	Russia-3	4	2	2	4	10	....	....	....	....	....
2002-03	Ak Bars Kazan	Russia	47	7	6	13	47	5	1	0	1	0
2003-04	Nizhnekamsk	Russia	10	2	3	5	10	....	....	....	....	....
	Ak Bars Kazan 2	Russia-3	STATISTICS NOT AVAILABLE									
	Ak Bars Kazan	Russia	10	1	1	2	8	....	....	....	....	....
2004-05	Dynamo Moscow	Russia	28	1	2	3	10	....	....	....	....	....
2005-06	Dynamo Moscow	Russia	48	9	3	12	78	3	0	0	0	0
2006-07	Dynamo Moscow	Russia	33	9	6	15	36	1	0	0	0	0

VITALE, Joe (vih-TA-lee, JOH) **PIT.**

Center. Shoots right. 6', 205 lbs. Born, St. Louis, MO, August 20, 1985.
(Pittsburgh's 7th choice, 195th overall, in 2005 Entry Draft).

			Regular Season					Playoffs				
Season	Club	League	GP	G	A	Pts	PIM	GP	G	A	Pts	PIM
2003-04	St. Louis Jr. Blues	CSJHL	43	21	29	50	42	....	....	....	....	....
2004-05	Sioux Falls	USHL	53	11	20	31	62	....	....	....	....	....
2005-06	Northeastern	H-East	31	8	8	16	71	....	....	....	....	....
2006-07	Northeastern	H-East	35	7	9	16	54	....	....	....	....	....

VIUHKOLA, Jari (VEW-koh-lak, YA-ree) **N.J.**

Center. Shoots left. 6', 200 lbs. Born, Oulu, Finland, February 27, 1980.
(Chicago's 4th choice, 158th overall, in 1998 Entry Draft).

			Regular Season					Playoffs				
Season	Club	League	GP	G	A	Pts	PIM	GP	G	A	Pts	PIM
1995-96	Karpat Oulu U18	Fin-U18	11	8	8	16	20	....	....	....	....	....
	Karpat Oulu Jr.	Fin-Jr.	7	2	1	3	4	....	....	....	....	....
1996-97	Karpat Oulu U18	Fin-U18	8	3	5	8	37	....	....	....	....	....
	Karpat Oulu Jr.	Fin-Jr.	27	5	7	12	43	....	....	....	....	....
1997-98	Karpat Oulu U18	Fin-U18	7	4	5	9	18	....	....	....	....	....
	Karpat Oulu Jr.	Fin-Jr.	28	8	18	26	57	....	....	....	....	....
1998-99	Karpat Oulu Jr.	Fin-Jr.	30	12	24	36	22	....	....	....	....	....
	Karpat Oulu	Finland-2	14	5	5	10	6	4	0	1	1	0
99-2000	Karpat Oulu	Finland-2	31	6	15	21	59	7	1	0	1	2
	Karpat Oulu Jr.	Fin-Jr.	5	4	9	13	0	....	....	....	....	....
2000-01	Karpat Oulu	Finland	54	5	8	13	32	9	0	1	1	6
2001-02	Karpat Oulu	Finland	46	8	14	22	24	4	1	0	1	6
2002-03	Karpat Oulu	Finland	49	15	17	32	56	15	4	8	12	10
2003-04	Karpat Oulu	Finland	53	25	31	56	34	14	3	5	8	4
2004-05	Karpat Oulu	Finland	44	15	16	31	30	12	5	10	15	6
2005-06	Karpat Oulu	Finland	46	12	27	39	40	11	2	8	10	4
2006-07	Karpat Oulu	Finland	37	7	38	45	40	10	4	6	10	6

Signed as a free agent by **New Jersey**, May 27, 2007.

VOCE, Tony (VOHS, TOH-nee)

Center. Shoots left. 5'8", 185 lbs. Born, Philadelphia, PA, October 30, 1980.

			Regular Season					Playoffs				
Season	Club	League	GP	G	A	Pts	PIM	GP	G	A	Pts	PIM
1998-99	Lawrence	High-MA	....	39	30	*69	....	....	....	....	....	....
99-2000	Lawrence	High-MA	....	26	33	*59	....	....	....	....	....	....
2000-01	Boston College	H-East	42	12	14	26	40	....	....	....	....	....
2001-02	Boston College	H-East	38	26	22	48	65	....	....	....	....	....
2002-03	Boston College	H-East	37	*23	23	46	56	....	....	....	....	....
2003-04	Boston College	H-East	42	*29	18	47	48	....	....	....	....	....
2004-05	Philadelphia	AHL	73	22	17	39	85	4	0	0	0	4
2005-06	Philadelphia	AHL	67	28	27	55	87	....	....	....	....	....
2006-07	Philadelphia	AHL	41	8	13	21	44	....	....	....	....	....
	Grand Rapids	AHL	25	4	6	10	37	7	3	2	5	6

Hockey East First All-Star Team (2002, 2004) • NCAA East First All-American Team (2004)

Signed as a free agent by **Philadelphia**, July 13, 2004.

VOGELHUBER, Trent (VOH-guhl-hew-buhr, TREHNT) **CBJ**

Right wing. Shoots right. 6'2", 185 lbs. Born, Cleveland, OH, July 13, 1988.
(Columbus' 7th choice, 211th overall, in 2007 Entry Draft).

			Regular Season					Playoffs				
Season	Club	League	GP	G	A	Pts	PIM	GP	G	A	Pts	PIM
2004-05	Ohio AAA	Ind.	67	32	30	62	77	....	....	....	....	....
2005-06	Ohio AAA	GLHL	44	27	52	79	28	....	....	....	....	....
2006-07	St. Louis Bandits	NAHL	31	10	16	26	24	....	....	....	....	....

• Signed Letter of Intent to attend **Miami University** (CCHA) in fall of 2008.

VOLKOV, Konstantin (VOHL-kawf, KAWN-stan-tihn) **TOR.**

Right wing. Shoots left. 6', 176 lbs. Born, Kolpino, USSR, February 7, 1985.
(Toronto's 3rd choice, 125th overall, in 2003 Entry Draft).

			Regular Season					Playoffs				
Season	Club	League	GP	G	A	Pts	PIM	GP	G	A	Pts	PIM
2000-01	SKA St. Petersburg	Russia	2	0	1	1	0	....	....	....	....	....
2001-02	Dyn'o Moscow 2	Russia-3	21	3	7	10	10	....	....	....	....	....
2002-03	Dyn'o Moscow 2	Russia-3	29	13	17	30	2	....	....	....	....	....
2003-04	THK Tver	Russia-2	18	0	6	6	6	....	....	....	....	....
	CSK VVS Samara	Russia-2	22	6	6	12	16	....	....	....	....	....
	Lada Togliatti 2	Russia-3	10	2	7	9	10	11	0	10	10	4
2004-05	Lada Togliatti	Russia	1	0	0	0	0	....	....	....	....	....
2005-06	Vityaz Chekhov	Russia	28	3	2	5	8	....	....	....	....	....
2006-07	Vityaz Chekhov	Russia	32	7	3	10	10	2	0	0	0	4

VOLOSHENKO, Roman (voh-loh-SHEHN-koh, ROH-muhn) **MIN.**

Left wing. Shoots right. 6'1", 207 lbs. Born, Brest, USSR, May 12, 1986.
(Minnesota's 2nd choice, 42nd overall, in 2004 Entry Draft).

			Regular Season					Playoffs				
Season	Club	League	GP	G	A	Pts	PIM	GP	G	A	Pts	PIM
2001-02	Krylja Sovetov 2	Russia-3	8	2	3	5	0	....	....	....	....	....
2002-03	Krylja Sovetov	Russia	5	0	1	1	2	....	....	....	....	....
	Krylja Sovetov 2	Russia-3	6	3	1	4	2	....	....	....	....	....
2003-04	Krylja Sovetov	Russia-2	46	7	8	15	40	4	1	1	2	4
2004-05	Krylja Sovetov 2	Russia-3	1	0	0	0	2	....	....	....	....	....
	Krylja Sovetov	Russia-2	38	16	13	29	22	3	0	1	1	2
2005-06	Houston Aeros	AHL	69	33	27	60	36	7	0	1	1	0
2006-07	Houston Aeros	AHL	76	11	19	30	22	....	....	....	....	....

VOMELA, Lukas (voh-MEH-luh, LOO-kahsh) DAL.

Defense. Shoots left. 6'3", 189 lbs. Born, Ceske Budejovice, Czech., September 25, 1985.
(Dallas' 9th choice, 248th overall, in 2004 Entry Draft).

			Regular Season					Playoffs				
Season	Club	League	GP	G	A	Pts	PIM	GP	G	A	Pts	PIM
2000-01	C. Budejovice U17	CzR-U17	39	1	1	2	8	....	....	....	....	....
2001-02	C. Budejovice U17	CzR-U17	47	9	9	18	87	....	....	....	....	....
	C. Budejovice Jr.	CzRep-Jr.	1	0	0	0	0	....	....	....	....	....
2002-03	C. Budejovice Jr.	CzRep-Jr.	36	2	2	4	24	....	....	....	....	....
	C. Budejovice	CzRep	1	0	0	0	4	....	....	....	....	....
2003-04	C. Budejovice	CzRep	15	0	1	1	8	....	....	....	....	....
	C. Budejovice Jr.	CzRep-Jr.	21	1	7	8	45	....	....	....	....	....
2004-05	C. Budejovice	CzRep-2	2	0	0	0	0	....	....	....	....	....
	Jind. Hradec	CzRep-3	5	0	3	3	0	....	....	....	....	....
	C. Budejovice Jr.	CzRep-Jr.	30	3	10	13	68	2	0	1	1	4
2005-06	C. Budejovice	CzRep	1	0	0	0	0	....	....	....	....	....
	Jind. Hradec	CzRep-2	49	1	4	5	42	....	....	....	....	....
2006-07	HC Slavia Praha	CzRep	5	0	0	0	2	....	....	....	....	....
	HC Sparta Praha	CzRep	1	0	0	0	0	....	....	....	....	....
	Trebic	CzRep-2	36	2	5	7	91	2	0	0	0	2

VORACEK, Jakub (voh-RA-chehk, YA-kuhb) CBJ

Right wing. Shoots left. 6'1", 187 lbs. Born, Kladno, Czech., August 15, 1989.
(Columbus' 1st choice, 7th overall, in 2007 Entry Draft).

			Regular Season					Playoffs				
Season	Club	League	GP	G	A	Pts	PIM	GP	G	A	Pts	PIM
2002-03	HC Kladno U17	CzR-U17	2	1	1	2	2	2	1	1	2	0
2003-04	HC Kladno U17	CzR-U17	52	30	24	54	26	2	0	0	0	2
2004-05	HC Kladno U17	CzR-U17	30	23	39	62	44	7	5	4	9	14
	HC Kladno Jr.	CzRep-Jr.	16	5	7	12	6	1	1	0	1	2
2005-06	HC Kladno U17	CzR-U17	....	....	....	....	....	2	1	3	4	31
	HC Kladno Jr.	CzRep-Jr.	46	21	38	59	54	6	7	4	11	2
	HC Rabat Kladno	CzRep	1	0	0	0	0	....	....	....	....	....
2006-07	Halifax	QMJHL	59	23	63	86	26	12	7	17	24	6

QMJHL All-Rookie Team (2007) • QMJHL Rookie of the Year (2007)

VOROBIEV, Dmitri (voh-roh-BEE-ehf, dih-MEE-tree) TOR.

Defense. Shoots left. 6'2", 211 lbs. Born, Togliatti, USSR, October 18, 1985.
(Toronto's 3rd choice, 157th overall, in 2004 Entry Draft).

			Regular Season					Playoffs				
Season	Club	League	GP	G	A	Pts	PIM	GP	G	A	Pts	PIM
2002-03	Lada Togliatti 2	Russia-3	31	3	5	8	12	....	....	....	....	....
2003-04	Lada Togliatti 2	Russia-3	10	1	1	2	4	....	....	....	....	....
	Lada Togliatti	Russia	23	1	0	1	12	4	0	0	0	4
2004-05	Lada Togliatti	Russia	53	2	6	8	30	10	0	0	0	8
2005-06	Lada Togliatti	Russia	42	1	7	8	73	8	0	0	0	8
2006-07	Lada Togliatti	Russia	54	10	7	17	48	3	0	0	0	6

VOROS, Aaron (VOH-ruhs, AIR-ruhn) MIN.

Center. Shoots left. 6'3", 178 lbs. Born, Vancouver, B.C., July 2, 1981.
(New Jersey's 10th choice, 229th overall, in 2001 Entry Draft).

			Regular Season					Playoffs				
Season	Club	League	GP	G	A	Pts	PIM	GP	G	A	Pts	PIM
99-2000	Victoria Salsa	BCHL	58	14	21	35	285	....	....	....	....	....
2000-01	Victoria Salsa	BCHL	57	34	34	68	196	30	16	15	31	....
2001-02	Alaska	CCHA	37	18	12	30	*101	....	....	....	....	....
2002-03	Alaska	CCHA	16	2	5	7	42	....	....	....	....	....
2003-04	Alaska	CCHA	36	16	8	24	*132	....	....	....	....	....
	Albany River Rats	AHL	9	2	1	3	14	....	....	....	....	....
2004-05	Albany River Rats	AHL	71	11	17	28	220	....	....	....	....	....
2005-06	Albany River Rats	AHL	73	16	14	30	180	....	....	....	....	....
2006-07	Lowell Devils	AHL	39	9	8	17	111	....	....	....	....	....
	Houston Aeros	AHL	19	2	3	5	58	....	....	....	....	....

CCHA All-Rookie Team (2002)

• Missed majority of 2002-03 season recovering from leg surgery, January 30, 2003. Traded to **Minnesota** by **New Jersey** for Minnesota's 7th round choice in 2008 Entry Draft, February 28, 2007.

VOROSHNIN, Pavel (vo-rohsh-NIHN, PAH-vehl) BUF.

Defense. Shoots left. 6'3", 175 lbs. Born, Chelyabinsk, USSR, March 23, 1984.
(Buffalo's 7th choice, 172nd overall, in 2003 Entry Draft).

			Regular Season					Playoffs				
Season	Club	League	GP	G	A	Pts	PIM	GP	G	A	Pts	PIM
2001-02	Chelyabinsk	Russia-2	32	0	2	2	10	....	....	....	....	....
2002-03	Mississauga	OHL	68	9	27	36	81	1	0	0	0	2
2003-04	Mississauga	OHL	18	0	4	4	6	....	....	....	....	....
	Owen Sound	OHL	40	3	18	21	36	7	0	2	2	4
2004-05	Metallurg Serov	Russia-2	34	0	1	1	12	....	....	....	....	....
2005-06	Lada Togliatti	Russia	33	0	1	1	18	8	0	1	1	0
2006-07	Lada Togliatti	Russia	3	0	0	0	2	....	....	....	....	....
	Mytischi	Russia	9	0	1	1	0	....	....	....	....	....

VRANA, Petr (vuh-RA-nuh, PEE-tuhr) N.J.

Center. Shoots left. 5'10", 190 lbs. Born, Sternberk, Czech., March 29, 1985.
(New Jersey's 2nd choice, 42nd overall, in 2003 Entry Draft).

			Regular Season					Playoffs				
Season	Club	League	GP	G	A	Pts	PIM	GP	G	A	Pts	PIM
2001-02	HC Havirov Jr.	CzRep-Jr.	38	11	12	23	....	....	....	....	....	....
	HC Femax Havirov	CzRep	6	0	0	0	4	....	....	....	....	....
2002-03	Halifax	QMJHL	72	37	46	83	32	24	5	15	20	12
2003-04	Halifax	QMJHL	48	13	25	38	56	....	....	....	....	....
2004-05	Halifax	QMJHL	60	16	35	51	77	12	10	4	14	12
2005-06	Albany River Rats	AHL	74	12	23	35	91	....	....	....	....	....
2006-07	Lowell Devils	AHL	61	13	19	32	44	....	....	....	....	....

QMJHL All-Rookie Team (2003) • QMJHL Rookie of the Year (2003)

WAGNER, Steve (WAG-nuhr, STEEV) ST.L.

Defense. Shoots left. 6'2", 190 lbs. Born, Grand Rapids, MN, March 6, 1984.

			Regular Season					Playoffs				
Season	Club	League	GP	G	A	Pts	PIM	GP	G	A	Pts	PIM
2002-03	Des Moines	USHL	14	0	1	1	17	....	....	....	....	....
	Tri-City Storm	USHL	27	0	5	5	52	3	1	0	1	0
2003-04	Tri-City Storm	USHL	43	3	19	22	52	9	0	4	4	13
2004-05	Minnesota State	WCHA	37	1	9	10	40	....	....	....	....	....
2005-06	Minnesota State	WCHA	38	5	11	16	53	....	....	....	....	....
2006-07	Minnesota State	WCHA	38	6	23	29	63	....	....	....	....	....
	Peoria Rivermen	AHL	14	1	2	3	8	....	....	....	....	....

Signed as a free agent by **St. Louis**, March 20, 2007.

WALKER, Julian (WAH-kuhr, JEW-lee-ehn) MIN.

Wing. Shoots right. 6'2", 209 lbs. Born, Bern, Switz., September 10, 1986.
(Minnesota's 6th choice, 162nd overall, in 2006 Entry Draft).

			Regular Season					Playoffs				
Season	Club	League	GP	G	A	Pts	PIM	GP	G	A	Pts	PIM
2001-02	SC Bern Jr.	Swiss-Jr.	....	....	....	....	....	1	0	0	0	0
2002-03	SC Bern Jr.	Swiss-Jr.	34	2	5	7	14	3	0	0	0	4
2003-04	SC Bern Jr.	Swiss-Jr.	35	15	15	30	91	7	2	3	5	8
2004-05	SC Bern Jr.	Swiss-Jr.	42	25	32	57	84	9	1	11	12	10
	SC Langenthal	Swiss-2	3	0	0	0	0	....	....	....	....	....
2005-06	EHC Basel Jr.	Swiss-Jr.	6	3	2	5	6	....	....	....	....	....
	EHC Olten	Swiss-2	2	0	0	0	2	....	....	....	....	....
	EHC Basel	Swiss	36	2	0	2	41	5	1	0	1	6
2006-07	EHC Basel	Swiss	40	4	4	8	16	13	0	1	1	6
	EHC Olten	Swiss-2	8	8	4	12	0	....	....	....	....	....

WALLACE, Tim (WAHL-las, TIHM) PIT.

Right wing. Shoots right. 6'1", 207 lbs. Born, Anchorage, AK, August 6, 1984.

			Regular Season					Playoffs				
Season	Club	League	GP	G	A	Pts	PIM	GP	G	A	Pts	PIM
2002-03	U. of Notre Dame	CCHA	40	6	5	11	28	....	....	....	....	....
2003-04	U. of Notre Dame	CCHA	39	3	8	11	10	....	....	....	....	....
2004-05	U. of Notre Dame	CCHA	38	5	9	14	20	....	....	....	....	....
2005-06	U. of Notre Dame	CCHA	36	11	12	23	28	....	....	....	....	....
2006-07	Wilkes-Barre	AHL	32	5	9	14	39	11	1	1	2	2
	Wheeling Nailers	ECHL	19	6	11	17	23	....	....	....	....	....

Signed as a free agent by **Pittsburgh**, May 29, 2007.

WANDELL, Tom (VAHN-dehl, TAWM) DAL.

Center. Shoots left. 6'1", 183 lbs. Born, Sodertalje, Sweden, January 29, 1987.
(Dallas' 5th choice, 146th overall, in 2005 Entry Draft).

			Regular Season					Playoffs				
Season	Club	League	GP	G	A	Pts	PIM	GP	G	A	Pts	PIM
2002-03	Sodertalje SK U18	Swe-U18	13	8	7	15	6	....	....	....	....	....
2003-04	Sodertalje SK U18	Swe-U18	6	5	7	12	6	2	0	0	0	0
	Sodertalje SK Jr.	Swe-Jr.	33	7	15	22	14	2	0	0	0	0
2004-05	Sodertalje SK Jr.	Swe-Jr.	5	1	2	3	4	....	....	....	....	....
2005-06	Sodertalje SK Jr.	Swe-Jr.	41	19	20	39	45	4	1	0	1	2
	Sodertalje SK	Sweden	6	0	0	0	0	....	....	....	....	....
	Sodertalje SK	Sweden-Q	1	1	0	1	0	....	....	....	....	....
2006-07	Assat Pori Jr.	Fin-Jr.	4	1	1	2	0	....	....	....	....	....
	Assat Pori	Finland	50	6	6	12	20	....	....	....	....	....

WARD, Michael (WOHRD, MIGH-kuhl) T.B.

Defense. Shoots left. 6'2", 180 lbs. Born, Shippagan, N.B., August 13, 1989.
(Tampa Bay's 8th choice, 197th overall, in 2007 Entry Draft).

			Regular Season					Playoffs				
Season	Club	League	GP	G	A	Pts	PIM	GP	G	A	Pts	PIM
2005-06	Miramichi	NBPEI	34	6	17	23	24	....	....	....	....	....
2006-07	Lewiston	QMJHL	58	0	7	7	39	11	0	1	1	16

WARN, Max (VAHRN, MAX) DAL.

Left wing. Shoots left. 6'2", 194 lbs. Born, Helsinki, Finland, June 10, 1988.
(Dallas' 5th choice, 150th overall, in 2006 Entry Draft).

			Regular Season					Playoffs				
Season	Club	League	GP	G	A	Pts	PIM	GP	G	A	Pts	PIM
2004-05	HIFK Helsinki U18	Fin-U18	22	6	9	15	30	7	1	3	4	4
	HIFK Helsinki Jr.	Fin-Jr.	4	0	0	0	0	2	0	0	0	0
2005-06	HIFK Helsinki U18	Fin-U18	7	5	4	9	6	7	4	2	6	6
	HIFK Helsinki Jr.	Fin-Jr.	24	3	10	13	39	....	....	....	....	....
2006-07	HIFK Helsinki Jr.	Fin-Jr.	13	5	6	11	10	10	4	6	10	6
	HIFK Helsinki	Finland	1	0	0	0	0	....	....	....	....	....

WATHIER, Francis (waw-TEE-ay, FRAN-sihs) DAL.

Left wing. Shoots left. 6'3", 198 lbs. Born, St Isidore, Ont., December 7, 1984.
(Dallas' 8th choice, 185th overall, in 2003 Entry Draft).

			Regular Season					Playoffs				
Season	Club	League	GP	G	A	Pts	PIM	GP	G	A	Pts	PIM
2001-02	Hull Olympiques	QMJHL	63	1	3	4	68	12	1	2	3	30
2002-03	Hull Olympiques	QMJHL	72	9	18	27	143	20	1	6	7	20
2003-04	Gatineau	QMJHL	51	9	16	25	127	15	0	2	2	23
2004-05	Gatineau	QMJHL	67	15	20	35	96	10	0	2	2	8
2005-06	Iowa Stars	AHL	11	0	1	1	26	....	....	....	....	....
2006-07	Iowa Stars	AHL	57	14	3	17	78	12	0	4	4	25
	Idaho Steelheads	ECHL	17	4	9	13	31	7	1	1	2	4

• Missed majority of 2005-06 season recovering from two shoulder injuries.

WATKINS, Matt (WAHT-kihns, MAT) DAL.

Right wing. Shoots left. 5'10", 180 lbs. Born, Aylesbury, Sask., November 22, 1986.
(Dallas' 6th choice, 160th overall, in 2005 Entry Draft).

			Regular Season					Playoffs				
Season	Club	League	GP	G	A	Pts	PIM	GP	G	A	Pts	PIM
2003-04	Tisdale Trojans	SMHL	44	34	37	71	52	....	....	....	....	....
2004-05	Vernon Vipers	BCHL	60	36	38	74	53	....	....	....	....	....
2005-06	North Dakota	WCHA	46	5	4	9	45	....	....	....	....	....
2006-07	North Dakota	WCHA	38	6	11	17	31	....	....	....	....	....

WATSON, Ryan (WAWT-suhn , RIGH-uhn) FLA.

Left wing. Shoots left. 6'1", 175 lbs. Born, Cambridge, Ont., March 1, 1988.
(Florida's 7th choice, 191st overall, in 2007 Entry Draft).

			Regular Season					Playoffs				
Season	Club	League	GP	G	A	Pts	PIM	GP	G	A	Pts	PIM
2005-06	Cambridge	OJHL-B	46	7	19	26	58	16	5	5	10	14
2006-07	Cambridge	OJHL-B	37	27	29	56	55	9	2	7	9	18

• Signed Letter of Intent to attend **University of Western Michigan** (CCHA) in fall of 2007.

WATT, J.D. (WAHT , JAY-DEE) CGY.

Right wing. Shoots right. 6'2", 203 lbs. Born, Calgary, Alta., May 25, 1987.
(Calgary's 4th choice, 111th overall, in 2005 Entry Draft).

			Regular Season					Playoffs				
Season	Club	League	GP	G	A	Pts	PIM	GP	G	A	Pts	PIM
2003-04	Drumheller	AJHL	59	20	17	37	245	....	....	....	....	....
	Vancouver Giants	WHL	3	1	0	1	0	10	0	3	3	14
2004-05	Vancouver Giants	WHL	66	6	7	13	213	....	....	....	....	....
2005-06	Vancouver Giants	WHL	58	8	29	37	199	18	4	3	7	42
2006-07	Vancouver Giants	WHL	70	34	19	53	182	21	2	3	5	72

WEBER, Mike (WEH-buhr, MIGHK) BUF.

Defense. Shoots left. 6'2", 199 lbs. Born, Pittsburgh, PA, December 16, 1987.
(Buffalo's 3rd choice, 57th overall, in 2006 Entry Draft).

			Regular Season					Playoffs				
Season	Club	League	GP	G	A	Pts	PIM	GP	G	A	Pts	PIM
2002-03	Jr. Penguins	EmJHL	28	4	11	15	109	3	0	0	0	20
2003-04	Windsor Spitfires	OHL	65	0	2	2	49	....	....	....	....	....
2004-05	Windsor Spitfires	OHL	68	2	6	8	132	11	0	1	1	18
2005-06	Windsor Spitfires	OHL	68	5	21	26	181	7	0	0	0	12
2006-07	Windsor Spitfires	OHL	30	3	16	19	86	....	....	....	....	....
	Barrie Colts	OHL	30	3	12	15	86	7	0	6	6	10

WEBER, Will (WEH-buhr, WIHL) CBJ

Defense. Shoots left. 6'4", 205 lbs. Born, Gaylord, MI, October 28, 1988.
(Columbus' 3rd choice, 53rd overall, in 2007 Entry Draft).

			Regular Season					Playoffs				
Season	Club	League	GP	G	A	Pts	PIM	GP	G	A	Pts	PIM
2003-04	Gaylord	High-MI	STATISTICS NOT AVAILABLE									
2004-05	Gaylord	High-MI	STATISTICS NOT AVAILABLE									
2005-06	Gaylord	High-MI	STATISTICS NOT AVAILABLE									
2006-07	Gaylord	High-MI	25	18	20	38	104	....	....	....	....	....

• Signed Letter of Intent to attend **Miami University** (CCHA) in fall of 2008.

WEBER, Yannick (WEH-buhr, YAH-nihk) MTL.

Defense. Shoots right. 5'10", 193 lbs. Born, Morges, Switz., September 23, 1988.
(Montreal's 5th choice, 73rd overall, in 2007 Entry Draft).

			Regular Season					Playoffs				
Season	Club	League	GP	G	A	Pts	PIM	GP	G	A	Pts	PIM
2003-04	SC Bern Jr.	Swiss-Jr.	32	2	3	5	39	8	2	0	2	8
2004-05	SC Bern Jr.	Swiss-Jr.	37	5	4	9	62	5	0	0	0	22
2005-06	SC Bern Future Jr.	Swiss-Jr.	17	1	6	7	46	....	....	....	....	....
	SC Langenthal	Swiss-2	28	3	0	3	8	....	....	....	....	....
2006-07	SC Bern Future Jr.	Swiss-Jr.	1	0	0	0	2	....	....	....	....	....
	Kitchener Rangers	OHL	51	13	28	41	42	9	3	6	9	8

WELLAR, Patrick (WEHL-uhr, PAT-rihk)

Defense. Shoots left. 6'3", 210 lbs. Born, Carrot River, Sask., December 4, 1983.
(Washington's 5th choice, 77th overall, in 2002 Entry Draft).

			Regular Season					Playoffs				
Season	Club	League	GP	G	A	Pts	PIM	GP	G	A	Pts	PIM
99-2000	Sask. Contacts	SMHL	44	5	15	20	120	....	....	....	....	....
	Portland	WHL	1	0	0	0	0	....	....	....	....	....
2000-01	Portland	WHL	57	2	7	9	65	10	0	1	1	13
2001-02	Portland	WHL	61	3	10	13	125	7	0	2	2	4
2002-03	Portland	WHL	11	1	4	5	31	....	....	....	....	....
	Calgary Hitmen	WHL	49	3	11	14	88	5	0	0	0	15
2003-04	Calgary Hitmen	WHL	68	7	10	17	132	7	1	1	2	10
2004-05	Worcester IceCats	AHL	2	0	1	1	0	....	....	....	....	....
	Peoria Rivermen	ECHL	62	2	10	12	91	....	....	....	....	....
2005-06	Peoria Rivermen	AHL	5	0	0	0	2	....	....	....	....	....
	Alaska Aces	ECHL	53	6	13	19	89	22	2	2	4	30
2006-07	Peoria Rivermen	AHL	21	0	1	1	9	....	....	....	....	....
	Alaska Aces	ECHL	53	7	7	14	101	15	1	3	4	20

Signed as a free agent by **St. Louis**, June 30, 2004.

WELLER, Craig (WEHL-uhr, KRAIG) PHX.

Right wing. Shoots right. 6'3", 195 lbs. Born, Calgary, Alta., January 17, 1981.
(St. Louis' 6th choice, 167th overall, in 2000 Entry Draft).

			Regular Season					Playoffs				
Season	Club	League	GP	G	A	Pts	PIM	GP	G	A	Pts	PIM
1997-98	Cgy. AAA Flames	AMHL	33	2	10	12	65	3	0	1	1	2
1998-99	Calgary Canucks	AJHL	49	4	14	18	80	13	0	1	1	10
99-2000	Calgary Canucks	AJHL	53	3	14	17	100	4	0	0	0	4
2000-01	U. Minn-Duluth	WCHA	6	0	1	1	0	....	....	....	....	....
	Kootenay Ice	WHL	30	1	5	6	40	11	0	2	2	26
2001-02	Kootenay Ice	WHL	69	5	13	18	127	22	3	7	10	27
2002-03	Charlotte	ECHL	48	3	11	14	84	....	....	....	....	....
	Hartford Wolf Pack	AHL	11	0	0	0	8	2	0	0	0	0
2003-04	Hartford Wolf Pack	AHL	68	5	9	14	86	16	2	2	4	30
2004-05	Hartford Wolf Pack	AHL	76	10	9	19	182	6	0	1	1	6
2005-06	Hartford Wolf Pack	AHL	80	12	21	33	152	13	2	3	5	44
2006-07	Hartford Wolf Pack	AHL	56	11	6	17	96	4	0	0	0	4

WHL West Second All-Star Team (2002)

• Left **University of Minnesota-Duluth** (WCHA) and signed as a free agent by **Kootenay** (WHL), January 7, 2001. Signed as a free agent by **NY Rangers**, July 11, 2002. Signed as a free agent by **Phoenix**, July 19, 2007.

WELLER, Shawn (WEHL-uhr, SHAWN) OTT.

Left wing. Shoots left. 6'1", 188 lbs. Born, Glens Falls, NY, July 8, 1986.
(Ottawa's 3rd choice, 77th overall, in 2004 Entry Draft).

			Regular Season					Playoffs				
Season	Club	League	GP	G	A	Pts	PIM	GP	G	A	Pts	PIM
2001-02	South Glen Falls	High-NY	25	32	21	53	....	....	....	....	....	....
2002-03	Capital District	EJHL	STATISTICS NOT AVAILABLE									
2003-04	Capital District	EJHL	37	18	25	43	110	3	3	3	6	6
	Capital District	Exhib.	30	16	19	35	78	....	....	....	....	....
2004-05	Clarkson Knights	ECACHL	33	3	11	14	72	....	....	....	....	....
2005-06	Clarkson Knights	ECACHL	37	14	10	24	*103	....	....	....	....	....
2006-07	Clarkson Knights	ECACHL	39	19	21	40	62	....	....	....	....	....
	Binghamton	AHL	5	0	0	0	4	....	....	....	....	....

WERNER, Steve (WUHR-nuhr, STEEV) WSH.

Right wing. Shoots right. 6'1", 200 lbs. Born, Washington, DC, August 8, 1984.
(Washington's 2nd choice, 83rd overall, in 2003 Entry Draft).

			Regular Season					Playoffs				
Season	Club	League	GP	G	A	Pts	PIM	GP	G	A	Pts	PIM
99-2000	Wsh. Jr. Capitals	MetroHL	42	32	45	77	....	....	....	....	....	....
2000-01	USNTDP	U-17	13	5	2	7	2	....	....	....	....	....
	USNTDP	NAHL	56	7	21	28	24	....	....	....	....	....
2001-02	USNTDP	U-18	34	10	16	26	10	....	....	....	....	....
	USNTDP	USHL	10	2	3	5	9	....	....	....	....	....
	USNTDP	NAHL	10	4	1	5	23	....	....	....	....	....
2002-03	Massachusetts	H-East	37	16	22	38	4	....	....	....	....	....
2003-04	Massachusetts	H-East	33	7	17	24	18	....	....	....	....	....
2004-05	Massachusetts	H-East	38	14	13	27	12	....	....	....	....	....
2005-06	Massachusetts	H-East	35	13	14	27	26	....	....	....	....	....
	Hershey Bears	AHL	4	0	3	3	2	....	....	....	....	....
2006-07	Hershey Bears	AHL	26	3	3	6	26	....	....	....	....	....
	South Carolina	ECHL	26	10	7	17	14	....	....	....	....	....

Hockey East All-Rookie Team (2003)

WESSBECKER, John (WEHS-beh-kuhr, JAWN) T.B.

Defense. Shoots right. 6'1", 180 lbs. Born, Edina, MN, September 15, 1986.
(Tampa Bay's 9th choice, 225th overall, in 2005 Entry Draft).

			Regular Season					Playoffs				
Season	Club	League	GP	G	A	Pts	PIM	GP	G	A	Pts	PIM
2004-05	Blake Bears	High-MN	16	6	16	22	38	....	....	....	....	....
2005-06	Massachusetts	H-East	36	0	3	3	30	....	....	....	....	....
2006-07	Massachusetts	H-East	38	1	0	1	14	....	....	....	....	....

WESTGARTH, Kevin (WEHST-garth, KEH-vihn) L.A.

Right wing. Shoots right. 6'5", 242 lbs. Born, Amherstburg, Ont., February 7, 1984.

			Regular Season					Playoffs				
Season	Club	League	GP	G	A	Pts	PIM	GP	G	A	Pts	PIM
2003-04	Princeton	ECAC	25	3	3	6	48	....	....	....	....	....
2004-05	Princeton	ECACHL	29	4	3	7	36	....	....	....	....	....
2005-06	Princeton	ECACHL	29	10	13	23	36	....	....	....	....	....
2006-07	Princeton	ECACHL	33	8	16	24	40	....	....	....	....	....
	Manchester	AHL	14	1	2	3	44	....	....	....	....	....

Signed as a free agent by **Los Angeles**, March 15, 2007.

WHARTON, Kyle (WAWR-tuhn, KIGHL) CBJ

Defense. Shoots left. 6'3", 192 lbs. Born, Ottawa, Ont., March 3, 1986.
(Columbus' 3rd choice, 59th overall, in 2004 Entry Draft).

			Regular Season					Playoffs				
Season	Club	League	GP	G	A	Pts	PIM	GP	G	A	Pts	PIM
2001-02	Ottawa Valley	Minor-ON	34	18	24	42	....	....	....	....	....	....
2002-03	Ottawa 67's	OHL	39	3	5	8	16	....	....	....	....	....
2003-04	Ottawa 67's	OHL	43	4	10	14	50	7	2	3	5	4
2004-05	Ottawa 67's	OHL	29	1	12	13	23	....	....	....	....	....
	Sault Ste. Marie	OHL	28	4	12	16	22	7	1	5	6	4
2005-06	Sault Ste. Marie	OHL	34	6	16	22	62	....	....	....	....	....
	Guelph Storm	OHL	24	2	14	16	34	15	4	8	12	20
2006-07	Syracuse Crunch	AHL	2	0	0	0	4	....	....	....	....	....
	Eisbaren Berlin	Germany	30	2	6	8	36	3	0	0	0	14

• Assigned to **Berlin** (Germany) by **Columbus**, October 25, 2006.

WHEELER, Blake (WEE-luhr, BLAYK) PHX.

Right wing. Shoots right. 6'5", 214 lbs. Born, Robbinsdale, MN, August 31, 1986.
(Phoenix's 1st choice, 5th overall, in 2004 Entry Draft).

			Regular Season					Playoffs				
Season	Club	League	GP	G	A	Pts	PIM	GP	G	A	Pts	PIM
2002-03	Breck Mustangs	High-MN	26	15	27	42	....	....	....	....	....	....
2003-04	Team Northwest	UMEHL	24	5	6	11	....	....	....	....	....	....
	Breck Mustangs	High-MN	27	39	50	89	34	3	6	5	11	0
2004-05	Green Bay	USHL	58	19	28	47	43	....	....	....	....	....
2005-06	U. of Minnesota	WCHA	39	9	14	23	41	....	....	....	....	....
2006-07	U. of Minnesota	WCHA	44	18	20	38	42	....	....	....	....	....

USHL All-Rookie Team (2005)

WHITE, Patrick (WIGHT, PAT-rihk) VAN.

Center. Shoots right. 6'1", 186 lbs. Born, Grand Rapids, MN, January 20, 1989.
(Vancouver's 1st choice, 25th overall, in 2007 Entry Draft).

			Regular Season					Playoffs				
Season	Club	League	GP	G	A	Pts	PIM	GP	G	A	Pts	PIM
2003-04	Grand Rapids	High-MN	....	3	6	9	....	....	....	....	....	....
2004-05	Grand Rapids	High-MN	....	17	15	32	....	....	....	....	....	....
2005-06	Grand Rapids	High-MN	....	24	28	52	....	....	....	....	....	....
2006-07	Grand Rapids	High-MN	....	19	35	54	....	....	....	....	....	....
	Tri-City Storm	USHL	12	8	1	9	4	....	....	....	....	....

• Signed Letter of Intent to attend **University of Minnesota** (WCHA) in fall of 2007.

WHITE, Ryan (WIGHT, RIGH-uhn) MTL.

Center. Shoots right. 6', 212 lbs. Born, Brandon, Man., March 17, 1988.
(Montreal's 4th choice, 66th overall, in 2006 Entry Draft).

			Regular Season					Playoffs				
Season	Club	League	GP	G	A	Pts	PIM	GP	G	A	Pts	PIM
2003-04	Brandon	MMHL	39	21	41	62	90	11	7	7	14	22
2004-05	Calgary Hitmen	WHL	63	9	14	23	95	12	2	1	3	26
2005-06	Calgary Hitmen	WHL	72	20	33	53	121	13	3	4	7	18
2006-07	Calgary Hitmen	WHL	72	34	55	89	97	18	6	8	14	36

WHL East First All-Star Team (2007)

WICK, Roman (WIHK, ROH-muhn) **OTT.**

Right wing. Shoots left. 6'1", 187 lbs. Born, Kloten, Switz., December 30, 1985.
(Ottawa's 8th choice, 156th overall, in 2004 Entry Draft).

			Regular Season					Playoffs				
Season	Club	League	GP	G	A	Pts	PIM	GP	G	A	Pts	PIM
2000-01	Kloten Flyers Jr.	Swiss-Jr.	26	4	1	5	6	5	1	0	1	2
2001-02	Kloten Flyers Jr.	Swiss-Jr.	34	19	27	46	32	8	1	2	3	4
2002-03	Kloten Flyers	Swiss	9	1	0	1	4	1	0	0	0	0
	Kloten Flyers Jr.	Swiss-Jr.	28	29	22	51	68	2	0	1	1	0
2003-04	Kloten Flyers	Swiss	20	1	1	2	6	....	....	....	....	....
	Kloten Flyers	Swiss-Q	7	3	1	4	0	....	....	....	....	....
	GCK Lions Zurich	Swiss-2	6	4	0	4	6	....	....	....	....	....
2004-05	Red Deer Rebels	WHL	66	32	38	70	25	7	1	2	3	6
2005-06	Red Deer Rebels	WHL	23	7	10	17	8	....	....	....	....	....
	Lethbridge	WHL	38	14	17	31	20	6	4	3	7	6
2006-07	Kloten Flyers	Swiss	44	12	11	23	20	11	1	1	2	2

WIKNER, John (WIHK-nuhr, JAWN) **OTT.**

Left wing. Shoots left. 6'1", 179 lbs. Born, Molndal, Sweden, January 1, 1986.
(Ottawa's 11th choice, 284th overall, in 2004 Entry Draft).

			Regular Season					Playoffs				
Season	Club	League	GP	G	A	Pts	PIM	GP	G	A	Pts	PIM
2002-03	V.Frolunda Jr.	Swe-Jr.	19	3	6	9	41	6	0	0	0	10
2003-04	V.Frolunda Jr.	Swe-Jr.	31	6	3	9	22	9	0	0	0	6
2004-05	IF Molndal Hockey	Sweden-3	5	2	2	4	6	....	....	....	....	....
	Frolunda Jr.	Swe-Jr.	32	10	14	24	56	6	0	2	2	0
2005-06	Brandon	WHL	60	9	13	22	32	6	0	0	0	4
2006-07	AIK IF Solna Jr.	Swe-Jr.	8	0	1	1	20	....	....	....	....	....
	AIK IF Solna	Sweden-2	13	0	0	0	14	....	....	....	....	....
	Trangsunds IF	Sweden-3	21	10	6	16	26	....	....	....	....	....

WILD, Cody (WIGHLD, KOH-dee) **EDM.**

Defense. Shoots left. 6'1", 183 lbs. Born, Limestone, ME, June 5, 1987.
(Edmonton's 4th choice, 140th overall, in 2006 Entry Draft).

			Regular Season					Playoffs				
Season	Club	League	GP	G	A	Pts	PIM	GP	G	A	Pts	PIM
2003-04	Junior Bruins	EJHL	53	5	24	29	12	....	....	....	....	....
2004-05	Junior Bruins	EJHL	64	16	36	52	44	....	....	....	....	....
2005-06	Providence College	H-East	36	6	15	21	24	....	....	....	....	....
2006-07	Providence College	H-East	32	6	8	14	28	....	....	....	....	....

Hockey East All-Rookie Team (2006)

WILFORD, Marty (WIHL-fohrd, MAHR-tee)

Defense. Shoots left. 6'1", 212 lbs. Born, Cobourg, Ont., April 17, 1977.
(Chicago's 7th choice, 149th overall, in 1995 Entry Draft).

			Regular Season					Playoffs				
Season	Club	League	GP	G	A	Pts	PIM	GP	G	A	Pts	PIM
1993-94	Peterborough	OPJHL	40	3	19	22	*107	....	....	....	....	....
1994-95	Oshawa Generals	OHL	63	1	6	7	95	7	1	1	2	4
1995-96	Oshawa Generals	OHL	65	3	24	27	107	5	0	1	1	4
1996-97	Oshawa Generals	OHL	62	19	43	62	126	16	2	18	20	28
1997-98	Indianapolis Ice	IHL	26	0	4	4	16	....	....	....	....	....
	Columbus Chill	ECHL	46	8	27	35	123	....	....	....	....	....
1998-99	Indianapolis Ice	IHL	80	3	13	16	116	7	0	1	1	16
99-2000	Cleveland	IHL	7	0	3	3	24	....	....	....	....	....
	Houston Aeros	IHL	45	0	9	9	30	11	2	2	4	18
2000-01	Norfolk Admirals	AHL	80	7	41	48	102	9	1	5	6	8
2001-02	St. John's	AHL	60	4	21	25	70	....	....	....	....	....
	Milwaukee	AHL	8	1	3	4	12	....	....	....	....	....
	Hartford Wolf Pack	AHL	9	0	2	2	2	10	3	3	6	4
2002-03	Norfolk Admirals	AHL	80	13	35	48	87	9	0	3	3	16
2003-04	Norfolk Admirals	AHL	80	5	35	40	67	8	0	3	3	18
2004-05	Norfolk Admirals	AHL	78	7	30	37	80	6	0	4	4	15
2005-06	Manchester	AHL	79	5	36	41	81	7	0	3	3	19
2006-07	Iowa Stars	AHL	65	5	25	30	72	12	0	2	2	18

OHL Second All-Star Team (1997)

Traded to **Toronto** by **Chicago** for Shawn Thornton, September 30, 2001. Traded to **Nashville** by **Toronto** with D.J. Smith for Marc Moro, March 1, 2002. Signed as a free agent by **Chicago**, July 8, 2003. Signed as a free agent by **Los Angeles**, August 10, 2005. Signed as a free agent by **Iowa** (AHL), July 25, 2006. Signed as a free agent by **Hamburg** (Germany), July 8, 2007.

WILLIAMS, Nigel (WIHL-yuhms, NIGH-juhl) **COL.**

Defense. Shoots left. 6'4", 226 lbs. Born, Aurora, IL, April 18, 1988.
(Colorado's 2nd choice, 51st overall, in 2006 Entry Draft).

			Regular Season					Playoffs				
Season	Club	League	GP	G	A	Pts	PIM	GP	G	A	Pts	PIM
2004-05	Team Illinois	MWEHL	60	14	18	32	....	....	....	....	....	....
	USNTDP	U-17	3	2	1	3	4	....	....	....	....	....
2005-06	USNTDP	U-18	40	3	6	9	40	....	....	....	....	....
	USNTDP	NAHL	19	3	4	7	23	....	....	....	....	....
2006-07	U. of Wisconsin	WCHA	1	0	0	0	2	....	....	....	....	....
	Saginaw Spirit	OHL	46	17	19	36	92	6	2	1	3	10

WILSON, Clay (WIHL-suhn, KLAY) **ANA.**

Defense. Shoots left. 6', 195 lbs. Born, Sturgeon Lake, MN, April 5, 1983.

			Regular Season					Playoffs				
Season	Club	League	GP	G	A	Pts	PIM	GP	G	A	Pts	PIM
2001-02	Michigan Tech	WCHA	38	4	8	12	18	....	....	....	....	....
2002-03	Michigan Tech	WCHA	38	8	17	25	37	....	....	....	....	....
2003-04	Michigan Tech	WCHA	37	2	11	13	22	....	....	....	....	....
2004-05	Michigan Tech	WCHA	35	3	4	7	42	....	....	....	....	....
	Muskegon Fury	UHL	14	3	3	6	2	17	0	2	2	8
2005-06	Muskegon Fury	UHL	13	3	9	12	9	....	....	....	....	....
	Grand Rapids	AHL	60	10	27	37	40	16	0	3	3	8
2006-07	Portland Pirates	AHL	79	9	34	43	52	....	....	....	....	....

Signed as a free agent by **Anaheim**, July 11, 2006.

WILSON, Kelsey (WIHL-suhn, KEHL-see) **NSH.**

Left wing. Shoots left. 6'1", 218 lbs. Born, Sault Ste. Marie, Ont., January 22, 1986.

			Regular Season					Playoffs				
Season	Club	League	GP	G	A	Pts	PIM	GP	G	A	Pts	PIM
2003-04	Sarnia Sting	OHL	62	5	11	16	106	5	0	0	0	4
2004-05	Sarnia Sting	OHL	37	0	3	3	118	....	....	....	....	....
	Guelph Storm	OHL	23	7	4	11	78	4	0	0	0	9
2005-06	Guelph Storm	OHL	67	38	31	69	196	15	12	6	18	33
2006-07	Milwaukee	AHL	74	9	10	19	215	4	0	0	0	6

Signed as a free agent by **Nashville**, October 6, 2006.

WILSON, Kyle (WIHL-suhn, KIGHL) **WSH.**

Center. Shoots right. 6', 200 lbs. Born, Oakville, Ont., December 15, 1984.
(Minnesota's 12th choice, 272nd overall, in 2004 Entry Draft).

			Regular Season					Playoffs				
Season	Club	League	GP	G	A	Pts	PIM	GP	G	A	Pts	PIM
2000-01	Strathroy Rockets	OHA-B	33	12	17	29	15	5	2	2	4	2
2001-02	Strathroy Rockets	OHA-B	53	42	25	67	16	....	....	....	....	....
2002-03	Colgate	ECAC	33	4	2	6	15	....	....	....	....	....
2003-04	Colgate	ECAC	37	14	17	31	23	....	....	....	....	....
2004-05	Colgate	ECACHL	30	5	18	23	12	....	....	....	....	....
2005-06	Colgate	ECACHL	39	*23	18	41	22	....	....	....	....	....
2006-07	San Antonio	AHL	7	1	0	1	2	....	....	....	....	....
	South Carolina	ECHL	5	3	2	5	4	....	....	....	....	....
	Hershey Bears	AHL	54	24	30	54	26	19	7	9	16	8

ECACHL Second All-Star Team (2006)

Signed as a free agent by **San Antonio** (AHL), October 6, 2006. Signed as a free agent by **Washington**, July 5, 2007.

WINNETT, Ben (wih-NEHT, BEHN) **TOR.**

Left wing. Shoots right. 5'11", 173 lbs. Born, New Westminster, B.C., April 3, 1989.
(Toronto's 3rd choice, 104th overall, in 2007 Entry Draft).

			Regular Season					Playoffs				
Season	Club	League	GP	G	A	Pts	PIM	GP	G	A	Pts	PIM
2005-06	Salmon Arm	BCHL	60	18	31	49	31	1	1	1	2	6
2006-07	Salmon Arm	BCHL	39	27	30	57	58	11	3	7	10	12

WINNIK, Daniel (WIHN-ihk, DAN-yehl) **PHX.**

Center/Left wing. Shoots right. 6'2", 218 lbs. Born, Toronto, Ont., March 6, 1985.
(Phoenix's 10th choice, 265th overall, in 2004 Entry Draft).

			Regular Season					Playoffs				
Season	Club	League	GP	G	A	Pts	PIM	GP	G	A	Pts	PIM
2002-03	Wexford	OPJHL	47	20	33	53	70	18	11	11	22	24
2003-04	New Hampshire	H-East	38	4	10	14	12	....	....	....	....	....
2004-05	New Hampshire	H-East	42	18	22	40	26	....	....	....	....	....
2005-06	New Hampshire	H-East	39	15	26	41	44	....	....	....	....	....
	San Antonio	AHL	7	1	1	2	8	....	....	....	....	....
2006-07	San Antonio	AHL	66	9	12	21	34	....	....	....	....	....
	Phoenix	ECHL	5	0	6	6	9	....	....	....	....	....

Hockey East Second All-Star Team (2006)

WIRTANEN, Petteri (WEER-tah-nehn, PEH-tur-ree) **ANA.**

Center. Shoots left. 6'1", 202 lbs. Born, Hyvinkaa, Finland, May 28, 1986.
(Anaheim's 5th choice, 172nd overall, in 2006 Entry Draft).

			Regular Season					Playoffs				
Season	Club	League	GP	G	A	Pts	PIM	GP	G	A	Pts	PIM
2001-02	Ahmat Jr.	Fin-Jr.	1	1	0	1	2	....	....	....	....	....
2002-03	HPK U18	Fin-U18	27	17	12	29	36	2	0	0	0	2
	HPK Jr.	Fin-Jr.	2	1	0	1	0	....	....	....	....	....
2003-04	HPK U18	Fin-U18	7	2	3	5	10	2	0	0	0	0
	HPK Jr.	Fin-Jr.	40	7	11	18	26	....	....	....	....	....
2004-05	HPK Jr.	Fin-Jr.	43	14	25	39	42	2	0	0	0	10
	HPK Hameenlinna	Finland	8	0	0	0	0	....	....	....	....	....
2005-06	Suomi U20	Finland-2	2	0	2	2	2	....	....	....	....	....
	HPK Jr.	Fin-Jr.	3	4	2	6	4	....	....	....	....	....
	HPK Hameenlinna	Finland	50	8	3	11	24	13	1	0	1	12
2006-07	Portland Pirates	AHL	67	7	11	18	40	....	....	....	....	....

WISHART, Ty (wih-SHAHRT, TIGH) **S.J.**

Defense. Shoots left. 6'4", 205 lbs. Born, Belleville, Ont., May 19, 1988.
(San Jose's 1st choice, 16th overall, in 2006 Entry Draft).

			Regular Season					Playoffs				
Season	Club	League	GP	G	A	Pts	PIM	GP	G	A	Pts	PIM
2004-05	Prince George	WHL	58	1	7	8	41	....	....	....	....	....
2005-06	Prince George	WHL	70	5	32	37	68	5	0	0	0	4
2006-07	Prince George	WHL	62	11	38	49	59	15	3	8	11	6

WHL West Second All-Star Team (2007)

WOOD, Dustin (WUD, DUHS-tihn)

Defense. Shoots left. 6'1", 208 lbs. Born, Scarborough, Ont., May 21, 1981.

			Regular Season					Playoffs				
Season	Club	League	GP	G	A	Pts	PIM	GP	G	A	Pts	PIM
1998-99	Peterborough	OHL	62	1	8	9	14	5	0	0	0	0
99-2000	Peterborough	OHL	66	2	13	15	29	5	0	1	1	0
2000-01	Peterborough	OHL	64	5	20	25	41	7	0	3	3	11
2001-02	Peterborough	OHL	68	13	38	51	57	6	2	1	3	4
2002-03	Bridgeport	AHL	6	0	0	0	2	....	....	....	....	....
	Trenton Titans	ECHL	63	4	23	27	28	3	0	1	1	2
2003-04	Springfield Falcons	AHL	75	2	6	8	22	....	....	....	....	....
	Adirondack	UHL	1	0	0	0	0	....	....	....	....	....
2004-05	Utah Grizzlies	AHL	80	2	8	10	39	....	....	....	....	....
2005-06	Houston Aeros	AHL	64	1	6	7	48	....	....	....	....	....
	Syracuse Crunch	AHL	14	0	3	3	14	6	0	0	0	8
2006-07	Manitoba Moose	AHL	62	4	12	16	36	13	0	1	1	0

Signed as a free agent by **Phoenix**, June 2, 2004. Traded to **Minnesota** by **Phoenix** with Erik Westrum for Zbynek Michalek, August 26, 2005. Signed as a free agent by **Ingolstadt** (Germany), July 27, 2007.

WOOD, Stephen (WUD, STEE-vehn)

Defense. Shoots right. 6'3", 210 lbs. Born, Sudbury, MA, August 18, 1981.

			Regular Season					Playoffs				
Season	Club	League	GP	G	A	Pts	PIM	GP	G	A	Pts	PIM
2000-01	Providence College	H-East	36	3	4	7	68	....	....	....	....	....
2001-02	Providence College	H-East	36	5	18	23	78	....	....	....	....	....
2002-03	Providence College	H-East	34	9	20	29	48	....	....	....	....	....
2003-04	Providence College	H-East	37	11	18	29	66	....	....	....	....	....
	Philadelphia	AHL	4	0	0	0	0	....	....	....	....	....
2004-05	Philadelphia	AHL	24	0	2	2	14	....	....	....	....	....
	Trenton Titans	ECHL	42	4	13	17	83	20	4	6	10	39
2005-06	Philadelphia	AHL	28	2	9	11	22	....	....	....	....	....
	Trenton Titans	ECHL	38	7	21	28	67	2	2	0	2	2
2006-07	Bridgeport	AHL	12	1	4	5	6	....	....	....	....	....
	Peoria Rivermen	AHL	16	0	2	2	10	....	....	....	....	....
	Alaska Aces	ECHL	25	8	6	14	52	13	0	2	2	26

Hockey East Second All-Star Team (2003) • Hockey East First All-Star Team (2004) • NCAA East Second All-American Team (2004)

Signed as a free agent by **Philadelphia**, March 21, 2004.

WRIGHT, Ben (RIGHT, BEHN) **CBJ**

Defense. Shoots right. 6'2", 189 lbs. Born, Foremost, Alta., March 18, 1988.
(Columbus' 4th choice, 113th overall, in 2006 Entry Draft).

			Regular Season					Playoffs				
Season	Club	League	GP	G	A	Pts	PIM	GP	G	A	Pts	PIM
2003-04	Lethbridge Y	AMHL	36	9	24	33	28	....	....	....	....	....
	Lethbridge	WHL	3	0	0	0	4	....	....	....	....	....
2004-05	Brooks Bandits	AJHL	38	8	13	21	78	11	0	2	2	6
	Lethbridge	WHL	4	0	0	0	0	....	....	....	....	....
2005-06	Lethbridge	WHL	55	5	13	18	79	6	3	5	8	12
2006-07	Lethbridge	WHL	64	10	37	47	108	....	....	....	....	....

WYMAN, James (WIGH-muhn, JAYMZ) **MTL.**

Right wing. Shoots right. 6'2", 208 lbs. Born, Edina, MN, February 27, 1986.
(Montreal's 3rd choice, 100th overall, in 2004 Entry Draft).

			Regular Season					Playoffs				
Season	Club	League	GP	G	A	Pts	PIM	GP	G	A	Pts	PIM
2001-02	Blake Bears	High-MN	26	7	5	12	....	....	....	....	....	....
2002-03	Blake Bears	High-MN	28	17	23	40	12	....	....	....	....	....
2003-04	Blake Bears	High-MN	27	31	24	55	4	....	....	....	....	....
	Team Southwest	UMEHL	24	8	8	16	....	....	....	....	....	....
2004-05	Dartmouth	ECACHL	33	5	6	11	4	....	....	....	....	....
2005-06	Dartmouth	ECACHL	28	8	12	20	6	....	....	....	....	....
2006-07	Dartmouth	ECACHL	33	13	11	24	20	....	....	....	....	....

YACHMENEV, Denis (YATCH-muh-nehv, DEH-nihs) **FLA.**

Left wing. Shoots left. 6'1", 185 lbs. Born, Chelyabinsk, USSR, June 4, 1984.
(Florida's 9th choice, 200th overall, in 2002 Entry Draft).

			Regular Season					Playoffs				
Season	Club	League	GP	G	A	Pts	PIM	GP	G	A	Pts	PIM
2000-01	Chelyabinsk 2	Russia-3	36	40	27	67	....	....	....	....	....	....
2001-02	North Bay	OHL	65	17	12	29	32	5	2	0	2	0
2002-03	Saginaw Spirit	OHL	68	17	28	45	69	....	....	....	....	....
2003-04	Omsk 2	Russia-3	13	12	4	16	10	....	....	....	....	....
	Amur Khabarovsk	Russia	25	0	1	1	4	....	....	....	....	....
2004-05	Amur Khabarovsk	Russia-2	42	7	14	21	28	13	3	1	4	8
2005-06	Amur Khabarovsk	Russia-2	46	9	14	23	43	11	2	3	5	6
2006-07	Sibir Novosibirsk	Russia	16	0	0	0	8	1	0	0	0	0
	Sibir Novosibirsk 2	Russia-3	6	0	3	3	8					

YEMELIN, Alexei (yeh-MUH-lehn, al-EHX-ay) **MTL.**

Defense. Shoots left. 6', 187 lbs. Born, Togliatti, USSR, April 25, 1986.
(Montreal's 2nd choice, 84th overall, in 2004 Entry Draft).

			Regular Season					Playoffs				
Season	Club	League	GP	G	A	Pts	PIM	GP	G	A	Pts	PIM
2002-03	Lada Togliatti 2	Russia-3	31	1	1	2	20	....	....	....	....	....
2003-04	Lada Togliatti 2	Russia-3	2	0	0	0	10	....	....	....	....	....
	CSK VVS Samara	Russia-2	52	2	4	6	180	1	0	0	0	18
2004-05	Lada Togliatti	Russia	12	0	1	1	24	2	0	0	0	2
2005-06	Lada Togliatti	Russia	44	6	6	12	131	6	0	1	1	*47
2006-07	Lada Togliatti	Russia	43	2	5	7	74	3	0	0	0	4

YIP, Brandon (YIHP, BRAN-duhn) **COL.**

Right wing. Shoots right. 6'1", 180 lbs. Born, Vancouver, B.C., April 25, 1985.
(Colorado's 7th choice, 239th overall, in 2004 Entry Draft).

			Regular Season					Playoffs				
Season	Club	League	GP	G	A	Pts	PIM	GP	G	A	Pts	PIM
2003-04	Coquitlam Express	BCHL	56	31	38	69	87	4	1	2	3	14
2004-05	Coquitlam Express	BCHL	43	20	42	62	92	7	6	1	7	12
2005-06	Boston University	H-East	39	9	22	31	59	....	....	....	....	....
2006-07	Boston University	H-East	18	5	6	11	29	....	....	....	....	....

Hockey East All-Rookie Team (2006) • Hockey East Rookie of the Year (2006)

YUNKOV , Mikhail (yuhn-KAWF, mih-kigh-EHL) **WSH.**

Center. Shoots left. 6', 180 lbs. Born, Voskresensk, USSR, February 16, 1986.
(Washington's 5th choice, 62nd overall, in 2004 Entry Draft).

			Regular Season					Playoffs				
Season	Club	League	GP	G	A	Pts	PIM	GP	G	A	Pts	PIM
2001-02	Krylja Sovetov 2	Russia-3	4	0	1	1	0	....	....	....	....	....
2002-03	Krylja Sovetov 2	Russia-3	3	0	1	1	0	....	....	....	....	....
	Krylja Sovetov	Russia	7	1	0	1	2	....	....	....	....	....
2003-04	Krylja Sovetov	Russia-2	38	5	10	15	12	4	0	1	1	0
	Krylja Sovetov 2	Russia-3	STATISTICS NOT AVAILABLE									
2004-05	Krylja Sovetov 2	Russia-3	1	0	0	0	0	....	....	....	....	....
	Krylja Sovetov	Russia-2	38	9	14	23	22	3	0	1	1	4
2005-06	Ak Bars Kazan	Russia	33	3	4	7	35	11	0	1	1	6
2006-07	Ak Bars Kazan	Russia	47	3	6	9	12	16	1	2	3	8

ZABORSKY, Tomas (za-BOHR-skee, TAW-mahsh) **NYR**

Wing. Shoots left. 6'1", 180 lbs. Born, Banska Bystrica, Czech., November 14, 1987.
(NY Rangers' 5th choice, 137th overall, in 2006 Entry Draft).

			Regular Season					Playoffs				
Season	Club	League	GP	G	A	Pts	PIM	GP	G	A	Pts	PIM
2003-04	Dukla Trencin U18	Svk-U18	46	20	12	32	8	7	4	2	6	4
2004-05	Dukla Trencin U18	Svk-U18	46	44	25	69	53	7	4	4	8	39
	Dukla Trencin Jr.	Slovak-Jr.	7	1	2	3	0	1	0	1	1	0
2005-06	Dukla Trencin Jr.	Slovak-Jr.	42	39	22	61	18	7	10	5	15	2
	Dukla Trencin	Slovakia	4	0	0	0	2	....	....	....	....	....
	P. Bystrica	Slovak-2	5	0	1	1	2	....	....	....	....	....
2006-07	Saginaw Spirit	OHL	59	19	24	43	18	6	1	2	3	4

ZACKRISSON, Patrik (ZAK-rihs-suhn, PAT-rihk) **S.J.**

Right wing. Shoots right. 5'11", 190 lbs. Born, Ekero, Sweden, March 27, 1987.
(San Jose's 5th choice, 165th overall, in 2007 Entry Draft).

			Regular Season					Playoffs				
Season	Club	League	GP	G	A	Pts	PIM	GP	G	A	Pts	PIM
2002-03	Ska IK	Sweden-3	17	3	6	9	4	....	....	....	....	....
2003-04	V.Frolunda U18	Swe-U18	14	5	9	14	4	7	2	3	5	0
	V.Frolunda Jr.	Swe-Jr.	2	0	1	1	0	....	....	....	....	....
2004-05	Frolunda U18	Swe-U18	2	2	1	3	29	6	3	3	6	4
	Frolunda Jr.	Swe-Jr.	32	16	9	25	22	6	1	2	3	0
2005-06	Frolunda Jr.	Swe-Jr.	39	26	19	45	34	7	4	5	9	4
	Frolunda	Sweden	10	0	1	1	0	....	....	....	....	....
2006-07	Rogle	Sweden-2	38	17	23	40	32	....	....	....	....	....

ZAGRAPAN, Marek (ZAG-rah-pahn, MAIR-ehk) **BUF.**

Center. Shoots left. 6'1", 198 lbs. Born, Presov, Czech., December 6, 1986.
(Buffalo's 1st choice, 13th overall, in 2005 Entry Draft).

			Regular Season					Playoffs				
Season	Club	League	GP	G	A	Pts	PIM	GP	G	A	Pts	PIM
2001-02	HC Zlin U17	CzR-U17	48	23	14	37	24	6	1	0	1	2
2002-03	HC Zlin U17	CzR-U17	15	18	16	34	14	3	1	0	1	6
	HC Zlin Jr.	CzRep-Jr.	25	9	13	22	10	....	....	....	....	....
	HC Hame Zlin	CzRep	13	1	1	2	10	....	....	....	....	....
2003-04	HC Zlin Jr.	CzRep-Jr.	42	23	12	35	40	7	1	3	4	4
	HC Hame Zlin	CzRep	5	0	0	0	0	....	....	....	....	....
	HC Kometa Brno	CzRep-2	5	0	1	1	0	....	....	....	....	....
2004-05	Chicoutimi	QMJHL	59	32	50	82	50	17	11	6	17	28
2005-06	Chicoutimi	QMJHL	59	35	52	87	63	8	4	6	10	4
2006-07	Rochester	AHL	71	17	21	38	39	6	1	0	1	2

ZALEWSKI, Steven (zuh-LOO-skee, STEE-vehn) **S.J.**

Center. Shoots left. 6', 190 lbs. Born, Utica, NY, August 20, 1986.
(San Jose's 5th choice, 153rd overall, in 2004 Entry Draft).

			Regular Season					Playoffs				
Season	Club	League	GP	G	A	Pts	PIM	GP	G	A	Pts	PIM
2003-04	Northwood	High-NY	40	32	34	66	22	....	....	....	....	....
2004-05	Clarkson Knights	ECACHL	39	12	7	19	60	....	....	....	....	....
2005-06	Clarkson Knights	ECACHL	35	9	13	22	50	....	....	....	....	....
2006-07	Clarkson Knights	ECACHL	39	16	18	34	44	....	....	....	....	....

ZAPLETAL, Jan (ZAH-pleht-tuhl, YAHN) **T.B.**

Defense. Shoots right. 6'3", 190 lbs. Born, Brno, Czech., August 21, 1986.
(Tampa Bay's 6th choice, 188th overall, in 2004 Entry Draft).

			Regular Season					Playoffs				
Season	Club	League	GP	G	A	Pts	PIM	GP	G	A	Pts	PIM
2001-02	HC Ytong Brno Jr.	CzRep-Jr.	27	3	0	3	8	....	....	....	....	....
2002-03	HC Vsetin Jr.	CzRep-Jr.	27	4	3	7	8	10	0	0	0	2
2003-04	HC Vsetin Jr.	CzRep-Jr.	51	2	4	6	26	4	0	0	0	0
2004-05	Regina Pats	WHL	55	3	2	5	20	....	....	....	....	....
2005-06	HC Vsetin Jr.	CzRep-Jr.	9	0	3	3	2	....	....	....	....	....
	HC Vsetin	CzRep	16	0	0	0	10	....	....	....	....	....
	Jind. Hradec	CzRep-2	20	0	0	0	16	....	....	....	....	....
2006-07	VSK Technika Brno	CzRep-3	22	1	5	6	32	....	....	....	....	....

ZARB, Chris (ZAHRB, KRIHS) **PHI.**

Defense. Shoots right. 6'4", 210 lbs. Born, San Diego, CA, January 11, 1985.
(Philadelphia's 4th choice, 144th overall, in 2004 Entry Draft).

			Regular Season					Playoffs				
Season	Club	League	GP	G	A	Pts	PIM	GP	G	A	Pts	PIM
2002-03	Det. Caesars	MWEHL	60	15	35	50	60	....	....	....	....	....
2003-04	Tri-City Storm	USHL	43	4	20	24	78	11	0	4	4	17
2004-05	Tri-City Storm	USHL	48	9	14	23	147	....	....	....	....	....
2005-06	Ferris State	CCHA	29	0	10	10	35	....	....	....	....	....
2006-07	Ferris State	CCHA	29	1	13	14	75	....	....	....	....	....

ZELISKA, Lukas (zeh-LIHS-kah, LOO-kahsh) **NYR**

Center. Shoots right. 5'11", 175 lbs. Born, Martin, Czech., January 8, 1988.
(NY Rangers' 7th choice, 204th overall, in 2006 Entry Draft).

			Regular Season					Playoffs				
Season	Club	League	GP	G	A	Pts	PIM	GP	G	A	Pts	PIM
2003-04	HC Trinec U17	CzR-U17	48	39	41	80	166	5	2	2	4	4
	HC Trinec Jr.	CzRep-Jr.	7	1	1	2	2	....	....	....	....	....
2004-05	HC Trinec U17	CzR-U17	11	7	11	18	40	....	....	....	....	....
	HC Trinec Jr.	CzRep-Jr.	13	1	2	3	6	....	....	....	....	....
2005-06	HC Trinec Jr.	CzRep-Jr.	29	8	3	11	81	7	4	1	5	22
	HC Ocelari Trinec	CzRep	1	0	0	0	0	....	....	....	....	....
2006-07	Prince Albert	WHL	61	4	25	29	77	5	1	4	5	4

ZHARKOV, Vladimir (zhar-KAWV, vla-DIH-meer) **N.J.**

Right wing. Shoots left. 6', 185 lbs. Born, Pavlovsky Posad, USSR, January 10, 1988.
(New Jersey's 4th choice, 77th overall, in 2006 Entry Draft).

			Regular Season					Playoffs				
Season	Club	League	GP	G	A	Pts	PIM	GP	G	A	Pts	PIM
2004-05	CSKA Moscow 2	Russia-3	STATISTICS NOT AVAILABLE									
2005-06	CSKA Moscow	Russia	4	0	1	1	4	1	0	0	0	0
	CSKA Moscow 2	Russia-3	48	17	22	39	86	....	....	....	....	....
2006-07	CSKA Moscow	Russia	47	4	1	5	18	12	0	1	1	2

ZIMAKOV, Sergei (zih-MAH-kahv, SAIR-gay) **WSH.**

Defense. Shoots left. 6'1", 194 lbs. Born, Moscow, USSR, January 15, 1978.
(Washington's 4th choice, 58th overall, in 1996 Entry Draft).

			Regular Season					Playoffs				
Season	Club	League	GP	G	A	Pts	PIM	GP	G	A	Pts	PIM
1994-95	Omaha Lancers	USHL	48	14	46	60	22	....	....	....	....	....
1995-96	Krylja Sovetov	CIS	49	2	7	9	36	....	....	....	....	....
1996-97	Krylja Sovetov	Russia	39	4	3	7	57	2	0	0	0	0
1997-98	Krylja Sovetov	Russia	42	4	1	5	48	....	....	....	....	....
1998-99	Ak Bars Kazan	Russia	28	1	0	1	6	8	0	1	1	6
99-2000	Perm	Russia	31	1	2	3	34	3	0	1	1	0
2000-01	CSKA Moscow 2	Russia-3	3	2	2	4	2	....	....	....	....	....
	CSKA Moscow	Russia	26	1	5	6	28	....	....	....	....	....
2001-02	CSKA Moscow	Russia	42	3	10	13	74	....	....	....	....	....
2002-03	Ufa	Russia	11	0	0	0	8	....	....	....	....	....
	Ufa 2	Russia-3	STATISTICS NOT AVAILABLE									
2003-04	Spartak Moscow	Russia-2	60	11	17	28	38	12	0	1	1	10
2004-05	Spartak Moscow	Russia	23	2	2	4	20	....	....	....	....	....
2005-06	Spartak Moscow	Russia	46	3	11	14	55	3	0	0	0	4
2006-07	Vityaz Chekhov	Russia	36	3	2	5	38	3	0	0	0	0

ZIMMERMAN, Sean (ZIH-mehr-man, SHAWN) **N.J.**

Defense. Shoots right. 6'3", 205 lbs. Born, Denver, CO, May 24, 1987.
(New Jersey's 6th choice, 170th overall, in 2005 Entry Draft).

			Regular Season					Playoffs				
Season	Club	League	GP	G	A	Pts	PIM	GP	G	A	Pts	PIM
2002-03	Spokane Braves	KIJHL	45	3	5	8	70	....	....	....	....	....
2003-04	Spokane Chiefs	WHL	67	4	4	8	16	4	0	0	0	0
2004-05	Spokane Chiefs	WHL	71	2	14	16	36	....	....	....	....	....
2005-06	Spokane Chiefs	WHL	72	2	19	21	44	....	....	....	....	....
	Albany River Rats	AHL	6	0	0	0	4	....	....	....	....	....
2006-07	Spokane Chiefs	WHL	60	2	12	14	69	6	0	2	2	2
	Lowell Devils	AHL	1	0	0	0	2	....	....	....	....	....

ZUBAREV, Andrei (ZOO-bah-rehv, AWN-dray) **ATL.**

Defense. Shoots left. 6'1", 200 lbs. Born, Ufa, USSR, March 3, 1987.
(Atlanta's 7th choice, 187th overall, in 2005 Entry Draft).

			Regular Season					Playoffs				
Season	Club	League	GP	G	A	Pts	PIM	GP	G	A	Pts	PIM
2003-04	Ufa 2	Russia-3	STATISTICS NOT AVAILABLE									
	Ufa	Russia	6	0	1	1	4	....	....	....	....	....
2004-05	Ufa 2	Russia-3	28	2	4	6	32	....	....	....	....	....
	Ufa	Russia	5	0	0	0	4	....	....	....	....	....
2005-06	Ak Bars Kazan	Russia	40	2	11	13	40	....	....	....	....	....
2006-07	Ak Bars Kazan	Russia	20	0	0	0	32	....	....	....	....	....

ZUBOV, Ilja (ZOO-bahf, IHL-yah) **OTT.**

Center. Shoots left. 6', 176 lbs. Born, Chelyabinsk, USSR, February 14, 1987.
(Ottawa's 4th choice, 98th overall, in 2005 Entry Draft).

			Regular Season					Playoffs				
Season	Club	League	GP	G	A	Pts	PIM	GP	G	A	Pts	PIM
2003-04	Chelyabinsk	Russia-2	33	7	7	14	16	8	2	1	3	2
2004-05	Chelyabinsk	Russia-2	40	9	8	17	36	....	....	....	....	....
	Chelyabinsk 2	Russia-3	1	0	0	0	0	....	....	....	....	....
2005-06	Spartak Moscow 2	Russia-3	1	0	1	1	4	....	....	....	....	....
	Spartak Moscow	Russia	43	4	8	12	12	3	2	2	4	0
2006-07	Mytischi	Russia	16	1	1	2	4	....	....	....	....	....
	Ufa	Russia	26	3	7	10	4	8	2	3	5	2

Recently Retired 1,000-Game Players

Tie Domi

Tom Fitzgerald

Brian Leetch

Scott Mellanby

Joe Nieuwendyk

Mike Ricci

Tie Domi, Tom Fitzgerald, Brian Leetch, Scott Mellanby, Joe Nieuwendyk and Mike Ricci each announced their retirement in 2006-07. All had played at least 1,000 games in the NHL. Together, these six players combined for 7,109 games played in the regular season, plus 675 more in the playoffs, for 19 different NHL teams. They totaled 1,661 goals and 2,512 assists for 4,173 points.

2007-08 NHL Player Register

Note: The 2007-08 NHL Player Register lists forwards and defensemen only. Goaltenders are listed separately. The NHL Player Register lists every active skater who played in the NHL in 2006-07 plus additional players with NHL experience. Trades and roster changes are current as of August 14, 2007.

Abbreviations: A – assists; **F%** – faceoff winning percentage; **G** – goals; **GP** – games played; **GW** – game-winning goals scored; **Min** – average time on ice; **PIM** – penalties in minutes; **+/–** – plus/minus rating; **PP** – powerplay goals scored; **Pts** – points; **S** – shots on goal; **%** – shooting percentage; **SH** – shorthand goal scored; **TF** – Total faceoffs taken;
***** – league-leading total; **♦** – member of Stanley Cup-winning team.

Prospect Register begins on page 271.

Goaltender Register begins on page 581.

League abbreviations are listed on page 654.

ABID, Ramzi (a-BIHD, RAM-zee)

Left wing. Shoots left. 6'2", 210 lbs. Born, Montreal, Que., March 24, 1980. Phoenix's 3rd choice, 85th overall, in 2000 Entry Draft.

			Regular Season														Playoffs								
Season	Club	League	GP	G	A	Pts	PIM	PP	SH	GW	S	%	+/-	TF	F%	Min	GP	G	A	Pts	PIM	PP	SH	GW	Min
1995-96	Richelieu Riverains	QAAA	42	10	14	24	18	....	....	....	....	....	....	....	....	....	4	1	2	3	2	....	....	....	....
1996-97	Chicoutimi	QMJHL	65	13	24	37	141	....	....	....	....	....	....	....	....	....	21	2	12	14	28	....	....	....	....
1997-98	Chicoutimi	QMJHL	68	50	*85	*135	266	....	....	....	....	....	....	....	....	....	6	3	4	7	10	....	....	....	....
1998-99	Chicoutimi	QMJHL	21	11	15	26	97	....	....	....	....	....	....	....	....	....	....	....	....	....	....	....	....	....	....
	Acadie-Bathurst	QMJHL	24	14	22	36	102	....	....	....	....	....	....	....	....	....	23	14	20	34	*84	....	....	....	....
99-2000	Acadie-Bathurst	QMJHL	13	10	11	21	61	....	....	....	....	....	....	....	....	....	....	....	....	....	....	....	....	....	....
	Halifax	QMJHL	59	57	80	137	148	....	....	....	....	....	....	....	....	....	10	10	13	23	18	....	....	....	....
2000-01	Springfield	AHL	17	6	4	10	38	....	....	....	....	....	....	....	....	....	....	....	....	....	....	....	....	....	....
2001-02	Springfield	AHL	66	18	25	43	214	....	....	....	....	....	....	....	....	....	....	....	....	....	....	....	....	....	....
2002-03	**Phoenix**	**NHL**	**30**	**10**	**8**	**18**	**30**	**4**	**0**	**3**	**52**	**19.2**	**1**	**1**	**100.0**	**12:30**	....	....	....	....	....	....	....	....	....
	Springfield	AHL	27	15	10	25	50	....	....	....	....	....	....	....	....	....	....	....	....	....	....	....	....	....	....
	Pittsburgh	**NHL**	**3**	**0**	**0**	**0**	**2**	**0**	**0**	**0**	**7**	**0.0**	**–5**	**1**	**0.0**	**17:33**	....	....	....	....	....	....	....	....	....
2003-04	**Pittsburgh**	**NHL**	**16**	**3**	**2**	**5**	**27**	**2**	**0**	**1**	**35**	**8.6**	**–5**	**2**	**0.0**	**12:56**	....	....	....	....	....	....	....	....	....
2004-05	Wilkes-Barre	AHL	78	26	29	55	119	....	....	....	....	....	....	....	....	....	7	0	2	2	18	....	....	....	....
2005-06	**Atlanta**	**NHL**	**6**	**0**	**2**	**2**	**6**	**0**	**0**	**0**	**6**	**0.0**	**1**	**0**	**0.0**	**8:10**	....	....	....	....	....	....	....	....	....
	Chicago Wolves	AHL	75	34	42	76	165	....	....	....	....	....	....	....	....	....	....	....	....	....	....	....	....	....	....
2006-07	**Nashville**	**NHL**	**13**	**1**	**4**	**5**	**13**	**0**	**0**	**0**	**12**	**8.3**	**–3**	**1**	**0.0**	**10:51**	**2**	**0**	**0**	**0**	**0**	**0**	**0**	**0**	**5:18**
	Milwaukee	AHL	57	19	30	49	70	....	....	....	....	....	....	....	....	....	2	0	1	1	6	....	....	....	....
	NHL Totals		**68**	**14**	**16**	**30**	**78**	**6**	**0**	**4**	**112**	**12.5**		**5**	**20.0**	**12:08**	**2**	**0**	**0**	**0**	**0**	**0**	**0**	**0**	**5:18**

• Re-entered NHL Entry Draft. Originally Colorado's 5th choice, 28th overall, in 1998 Entry Draft.

QMJHL First All-Star Team (1998, 2000) • Jean Beliveau Trophy (QMJHL Leading Scorer) (1998) • Michel Briere Trophy (QMJHL MVP) (1998) • Canadian Major Junior First All-Star Team (2000) • Ed Chynoweth Trophy (Memorial Cup Tournament Leading Scorer) (2000)

• Missed majority of 2000-01 season recovering from wrist injury suffered in game vs. Louisville (AHL), October 27, 2000. Traded to **Pittsburgh** by **Phoenix** with Dan Focht and Guillaume Lefebvre for Jan Hrdina and Francois Leroux, March 11, 2003. • Missed majority of 2003-04 season recovering from knee injury suffered in game vs. Edmonton, December 6, 2003. Signed as a free agent by **Atlanta**, August 8, 2005. Signed as a free agent by **Nashville**, July 21, 2006. Signed as a free agent by **Bern** (Swiss), July 10, 2007.

ADAMS, Craig (A-duhms, KRAYG) CAR.

Right wing. Shoots right. 6', 200 lbs. Born, Seria, Brunei, April 26, 1977. Hartford's 9th choice, 223rd overall, in 1996 Entry Draft.

			Regular Season														Playoffs								
Season	Club	League	GP	G	A	Pts	PIM	PP	SH	GW	S	%	+/-	TF	F%	Min	GP	G	A	Pts	PIM	PP	SH	GW	Min
1995-96	Harvard Crimson	ECAC	34	8	9	17	56	....	....	....	....	....	....	....	....	....	....	....	....	....	....	....	....	....	....
1996-97	Harvard Crimson	ECAC	32	6	4	10	36	....	....	....	....	....	....	....	....	....	....	....	....	....	....	....	....	....	....
1997-98	Harvard Crimson	ECAC	12	6	6	12	12	....	....	....	....	....	....	....	....	....	....	....	....	....	....	....	....	....	....
1998-99	Harvard Crimson	ECAC	31	9	14	23	53	....	....	....	....	....	....	....	....	....	....	....	....	....	....	....	....	....	....
99-2000	Cincinnati	IHL	73	12	12	24	124	....	....	....	....	....	....	....	....	....	8	0	1	1	14	....	....	....	....
2000-01	**Carolina**	**NHL**	**44**	**1**	**0**	**1**	**20**	**0**	**0**	**0**	**15**	**6.7**	**–7**	**4**	**25.0**	**4:30**	**3**	**0**	**0**	**0**	**0**	**0**	**0**	**0**	**3:45**
	Cincinnati	IHL	4	0	1	1	9	....	....	....	....	....	....	....	....	....	1	0	0	0	2	....	....	....	....
2001-02	**Carolina**	**NHL**	**33**	**0**	**1**	**1**	**38**	**0**	**0**	**0**	**17**	**0.0**	**2**	**9**	**33.3**	**5:54**	**1**	**0**	**0**	**0**	**0**	**0**	**0**	**0**	**7:41**
	Lowell	AHL	22	5	4	9	51	....	....	....	....	....	....	....	....	....	....	....	....	....	....	....	....	....	....
2002-03	**Carolina**	**NHL**	**81**	**6**	**12**	**18**	**71**	**1**	**0**	**1**	**107**	**5.6**	**–11**	**20**	**35.0**	**12:12**	....	....	....	....	....	....	....	....	....
2003-04	**Carolina**	**NHL**	**80**	**7**	**10**	**17**	**69**	**0**	**1**	**0**	**110**	**6.4**	**–5**	**20**	**45.0**	**13:41**	....	....	....	....	....	....	....	....	....
2004-05	Milano Vipers	Italy	30	15	14	29	57	....	....	....	....	....	....	....	....	....	15	4	7	11	26	....	....	....	....
2005-06♦	**Carolina**	**NHL**	**67**	**10**	**11**	**21**	**51**	**1**	**1**	**2**	**68**	**14.7**	**1**	**13**	**53.9**	**12:18**	**25**	**0**	**0**	**0**	**10**	**0**	**0**	**0**	**8:16**
	Lowell	AHL	13	4	3	7	20	....	....	....	....	....	....	....	....	....	....	....	....	....	....	....	....	....	....
2006-07	**Carolina**	**NHL**	**82**	**7**	**7**	**14**	**54**	**0**	**1**	**1**	**71**	**9.9**	**–9**	**36**	**30.6**	**10:04**	....	....	....	....	....	....	....	....	....
	NHL Totals		**387**	**31**	**41**	**72**	**303**	**2**	**3**	**4**	**388**	**8.0**		**102**	**37.3**	**10:40**	**29**	**0**	**0**	**0**	**10**	**0**	**0**	**0**	**7:46**

Rights transferred to **Carolina** after **Hartford** franchise relocated, June 25, 1997. • Missed majority of 1997-98 season recovering from shoulder injury suffered in game vs. University of Wisconsin (WCHA), December 27, 1997. Signed as a free agent by **Milano**, (Italy), July 28, 2004. Signed as a free agent by **Anaheim**, August 25, 2005. Traded to **Carolina** by **Anaheim** for Bruno St. Jacques, October 3, 2005.

ADAMS, Kevyn (A-duhms, KEH-vihn) CHI.

Center. Shoots right. 6'1", 200 lbs. Born, Washington, DC, October 8, 1974. Boston's 1st choice, 25th overall, in 1993 Entry Draft.

			Regular Season														Playoffs								
Season	Club	League	GP	G	A	Pts	PIM	PP	SH	GW	S	%	+/-	TF	F%	Min	GP	G	A	Pts	PIM	PP	SH	GW	Min
1990-91	Niagara Scenics	NAHL	55	17	20	37	24	....	....	....	....	....	....	....	....	....	....	....	....	....	....	....	....	....	....
1991-92	Niagara Scenics	NAHL	40	25	33	58	51	....	....	....	....	....	....	....	....	....	....	....	....	....	....	....	....	....	....
1992-93	Miami U.	CCHA	40	17	15	32	18	....	....	....	....	....	....	....	....	....	....	....	....	....	....	....	....	....	....
1993-94	Miami U.	CCHA	36	15	28	43	24	....	....	....	....	....	....	....	....	....	....	....	....	....	....	....	....	....	....
1994-95	Miami U.	CCHA	38	20	29	49	30	....	....	....	....	....	....	....	....	....	....	....	....	....	....	....	....	....	....
1995-96	Miami U.	CCHA	36	17	30	47	30	....	....	....	....	....	....	....	....	....	....	....	....	....	....	....	....	....	....
1996-97	Grand Rapids	IHL	82	22	25	47	47	....	....	....	....	....	....	....	....	....	5	1	1	2	4	....	....	....	....
1997-98	**Toronto**	**NHL**	**5**	**0**	**0**	**0**	**7**	**0**	**0**	**0**	**3**	**0.0**	**0**	....	....	....	....	....	....	....	....	....	....	....	....
	St. John's	AHL	59	17	20	37	99	....	....	....	....	....	....	....	....	....	4	0	0	0	4	....	....	....	....
1998-99	**Toronto**	**NHL**	**1**	**0**	**0**	**0**	**0**	**0**	**0**	**0**	**1**	**0.0**	**0**	**9**	**44.4**	**7:56**	**7**	**0**	**2**	**2**	**14**	**0**	**0**	**0**	**11:18**
	St. John's	AHL	80	15	35	50	85	....	....	....	....	....	....	....	....	....	5	2	0	2	4	....	....	....	....
99-2000	**Toronto**	**NHL**	**52**	**5**	**8**	**13**	**39**	**0**	**0**	**0**	**70**	**7.1**	**–7**	**604**	**56.5**	**12:23**	**12**	**1**	**0**	**1**	**7**	**0**	**1**	**0**	**11:06**
	St. John's	AHL	23	6	11	17	24	....	....	....	....	....	....	....	....	....	....	....	....	....	....	....	....	....	....
2000-01	**Columbus**	**NHL**	**66**	**8**	**12**	**20**	**52**	**0**	**0**	**1**	**84**	**9.5**	**–4**	**1152**	**57.4**	**15:18**	....	....	....	....	....	....	....	....	....
	Florida	**NHL**	**12**	**3**	**6**	**9**	**2**	**0**	**0**	**2**	**21**	**14.3**	**7**	**198**	**47.5**	**17:25**	....	....	....	....	....	....	....	....	....

			Regular Season														Playoffs								
Season	Club	League	GP	G	A	Pts	PIM	PP	SH	GW	S	%	+/-	TF	F%	Min	GP	G	A	Pts	PIM	PP	SH	GW	Min
2001-02	**Florida**	**NHL**	**44**	**4**	**8**	**12**	**28**	**0**	**0**	**1**	**71**	**5.6**	**–3**	**572**	**57.9**	**13:21**	....	....	....	....	....	....	....	....	....
	Carolina	**NHL**	**33**	**2**	**3**	**5**	**15**	**0**	**0**	**1**	**37**	**5.4**	**–2**	**187**	**58.8**	**9:05**	**23**	**1**	**0**	**1**	**4**	**0**	**0**	**0**	**7:29**
2002-03	**Carolina**	**NHL**	**77**	**9**	**9**	**18**	**57**	**0**	**0**	**0**	**169**	**5.3**	**–8**	**1018**	**53.1**	**14:39**	....	....	....	....	....	....	....	....	....
2003-04	**Carolina**	**NHL**	**73**	**10**	**12**	**22**	**43**	**0**	**5**	**1**	**141**	**7.1**	**6**	**722**	**51.9**	**13:17**	....	....	....	....	....	....	....	....	....
2004-05	Dusseldorf	Germany	9	1	2	3	4	....	....	....	....	....	....	....	....	....	....	....	....	....	....	....	....	....	....
2005-06 ♦	**Carolina**	**NHL**	**82**	**15**	**8**	**23**	**36**	**0**	**2**	**2**	**160**	**9.4**	**0**	**633**	**49.1**	**12:53**	**25**	**0**	**0**	**0**	**14**	**0**	**0**	**0**	**11:44**
2006-07	**Carolina**	**NHL**	**35**	**2**	**2**	**4**	**17**	**0**	**1**	**0**	**36**	**5.6**	**–10**	**206**	**45.2**	**8:39**	....	....	....	....	....	....	....	....	....
	Phoenix	**NHL**	**33**	**1**	**7**	**8**	**8**	**0**	**0**	**0**	**51**	**2.0**	**–10**	**106**	**45.3**	**13:20**	....	....	....	....	....	....	....	....	....
	NHL Totals		**513**	**59**	**75**	**134**	**304**	**0**	**8**	**8**	**844**	**7.0**		**5407**	**53.8**	**13:06**	**67**	**2**	**2**	**4**	**39**	**0**	**1**	**0**	**10:07**

CCHA Second All-Star Team (1995)

Signed as a free agent by **Toronto**, August 7, 1997. Claimed by **Columbus** from **Toronto** in Expansion Draft, June 23, 2000. Traded to **Florida** by **Columbus** with Columbus's 4th round choice (Mike Woodford) in 2001 Entry Draft for Ray Whitney and future considerations, March 13, 2001. Traded to **Carolina** by **Florida** with Bret Hedican and Tomas Malec for Sandis Ozolinsh and Byron Ritchie, January 16, 2002. Signed as a free agent by **Dusseldorf** (Germany), February 13, 2005. Traded to **Phoenix** by **Carolina** for Dennis Seidenberg, January 8, 2007. Traded to **Chicago** by **Phoenix** for Radim Vrbata, August 11, 2007.

AFANASENKOV, Dmitry

(a-fahn-A-sehn-kahv, dih-MEE-tree)

Left wing. Shoots right. 6'2", 209 lbs. Born, Arkhangelsk, USSR, May 12, 1980. Tampa Bay's 3rd choice, 72nd overall, in 1998 Entry Draft.

Season	Club	League	GP	G	A	Pts	PIM	PP	SH	GW	S	%	+/-	TF	F%	Min	GP	G	A	Pts	PIM	PP	SH	GW	Min
1995-96	Yaroslavl 2	CIS-2	25	10	5	15	10	....	....	....	....	....	....	....	....	....	....	....	....	....	....	....	....	....	....
1996-97	Yaroslavl 2	Russia-3	45	20	15	35	14	....	....	....	....	....	....	....	....	....	....	....	....	....	....	....	....	....	....
1997-98	Yaroslavl 2	Russia-2	48	14	7	21	20	....	....	....	....	....	....	....	....	....	....	....	....	....	....	....	....	....	....
1998-99	Moncton Wildcats	QMJHL	15	5	5	10	12	....	....	....	....	....	....	....	....	....	....	....	....	....	....	....	....	....	....
	Sherbrooke	QMJHL	51	23	30	53	22	....	....	....	....	....	....	....	....	....	13	10	6	16	6	....	....	....	....
99-2000	Sherbrooke	QMJHL	60	56	43	99	70	....	....	....	....	....	....	....	....	....	5	3	2	5	4	....	....	....	....
2000-01	**Tampa Bay**	**NHL**	**9**	**1**	**1**	**2**	**4**	**0**	**0**	**0**	**8**	**12.5**	**1**	**7**	**28.6**	**11:24**	....	....	....	....	....	....	....	....	....
	Detroit Vipers	IHL	65	15	22	37	26	....	....	....	....	....	....	....	....	....	....	....	....	....	....	....	....	....	....
2001-02	**Tampa Bay**	**NHL**	**5**	**0**	**0**	**0**	**0**	**0**	**0**	**0**	**1**	**0.0**	**–1**	**0**	**0.0**	**4:54**	....	....	....	....	....	....	....	....	....
	Springfield	AHL	28	4	5	9	4	....	....	....	....	....	....	....	....	....	....	....	....	....	....	....	....	....	....
	Grand Rapids	AHL	18	1	2	3	2	....	....	....	....	....	....	....	....	....	....	....	....	....	....	....	....	....	....
2002-03	Springfield	AHL	41	4	9	13	25	....	....	....	....	....	....	....	....	....	....	....	....	....	....	....	....	....	....
	Kloten Flyers	Swiss	....	....	....	....	....	....	....	....	....	....	....	....	....	....	5	1	1	2	0	....	....	....	....
2003-04 ♦	**Tampa Bay**	**NHL**	**71**	**6**	**10**	**16**	**12**	**0**	**0**	**1**	**98**	**6.1**	**–4**	**2**	**0.0**	**12:21**	**23**	**1**	**2**	**3**	**6**	**0**	**0**	**0**	**13:06**
2004-05	Lada Togliatti	Russia	30	2	9	11	12	....	....	....	....	....	....	....	....	....	9	0	0	0	4	....	....	....	....
2005-06	**Tampa Bay**	**NHL**	**68**	**9**	**6**	**15**	**16**	**1**	**0**	**0**	**78**	**11.5**	**–7**	**17**	**29.4**	**9:44**	**5**	**0**	**1**	**1**	**2**	**0**	**0**	**0**	**15:46**
2006-07	**Tampa Bay**	**NHL**	**33**	**3**	**3**	**6**	**8**	**0**	**0**	**0**	**31**	**9.7**	**–6**	**12**	**33.3**	**9:02**	....	....	....	....	....	....	....	....	....
	Philadelphia	**NHL**	**41**	**8**	**7**	**15**	**12**	**0**	**0**	**0**	**65**	**12.3**	**–19**	**7**	**14.3**	**11:44**	....	....	....	....	....	....	....	....	....
	NHL Totals		**227**	**27**	**27**	**54**	**52**	**1**	**0**	**1**	**281**	**9.6**		**45**	**26.7**	**10:46**	**28**	**1**	**3**	**4**	**8**	**0**	**0**	**0**	**13:34**

• Assigned to **Kloten** (Swiss) by **Tampa Bay**, February 19, 2003. Signed as a free agent by **Togliatti** (Russia), September 28, 2004. Claimed on waivers by **Philadelphia** from **Tampa Bay**, December 30, 2006. Signed as a free agent by **Dynamo Moscow** (Russia), August 1, 2007.

AFINOGENOV, Maxim

(ah-fihn-ah-GEHN-ahf, max-EEM) **BUF.**

Right wing. Shoots left. 6', 191 lbs. Born, Moscow, USSR, September 4, 1979. Buffalo's 3rd choice, 69th overall, in 1997 Entry Draft.

Season	Club	League	GP	G	A	Pts	PIM	PP	SH	GW	S	%	+/-	TF	F%	Min	GP	G	A	Pts	PIM	PP	SH	GW	Min
1996-97	Dynamo Moscow	Russia	29	6	5	11	10	....	....	....	....	....	....	....	....	....	4	0	2	2	0	....	....	....	....
	Dynamo Moscow	EuroHL	3	0	0	0	0	....	....	....	....	....	....	....	....	....	3	1	0	1	4	....	....	....	....
1997-98	Dynamo Moscow	Russia	35	10	5	15	53	....	....	....	....	....	....	....	....	....	....	....	....	....	....	....	....	....	....
	Dynamo Moscow	EuroHL	6	3	1	4	27	....	....	....	....	....	....	....	....	....	....	....	....	....	....	....	....	....	....
1998-99	Dynamo Moscow	Russia	38	8	13	21	24	....	....	....	....	....	....	....	....	....	16	*10	6	*16	14	....	....	....	....
	Dynamo Moscow	EuroHL	5	3	5	8	29	....	....	....	....	....	....	....	....	....	4	2	1	3	27	....	....	....	....
99-2000	**Buffalo**	**NHL**	**65**	**16**	**18**	**34**	**41**	**2**	**0**	**2**	**128**	**12.5**	**–4**	**0**	**0.0**	**13:09**	**5**	**0**	**1**	**1**	**2**	**0**	**0**	**0**	**12:53**
	Rochester	AHL	15	6	12	18	8	....	....	....	....	....	....	....	....	....	8	3	1	4	4	....	....	....	....
2000-01	**Buffalo**	**NHL**	**78**	**14**	**22**	**36**	**40**	**3**	**0**	**5**	**190**	**7.4**	**1**	**2**	**0.0**	**14:32**	**11**	**2**	**3**	**5**	**4**	**0**	**0**	**0**	**10:56**
2001-02	**Buffalo**	**NHL**	**81**	**21**	**19**	**40**	**69**	**3**	**1**	**0**	**234**	**9.0**	**–9**	**1**	**100.0**	**15:22**	....	....	....	....	....	....	....	....	....
	Russia	Olympics	6	2	2	4	4	....	....	....	....	....	....	....	....	....	....	....	....	....	....	....	....	....	....
2002-03	**Buffalo**	**NHL**	**35**	**5**	**6**	**11**	**21**	**2**	**0**	**2**	**77**	**6.5**	**–12**	**4**	**50.0**	**13:24**	....	....	....	....	....	....	....	....	....
2003-04	**Buffalo**	**NHL**	**73**	**17**	**14**	**31**	**57**	**3**	**0**	**4**	**148**	**11.5**	**–4**	**9**	**22.2**	**13:46**	....	....	....	....	....	....	....	....	....
2004-05	Dynamo Moscow	Russia	36	13	14	27	91	....	....	....	....	....	....	....	....	....	10	4	4	8	8	....	....	....	....
2005-06	**Buffalo**	**NHL**	**77**	**22**	**51**	**73**	**84**	**11**	**0**	**3**	**241**	**9.1**	**6**	**17**	**17.7**	**16:20**	**18**	**3**	**5**	**8**	**10**	**0**	**0**	**0**	**16:53**
	Russia	Olympics	8	0	1	1	10	....	....	....	....	....	....	....	....	....	....	....	....	....	....	....	....	....	....
2006-07	**Buffalo**	**NHL**	**56**	**23**	**38**	**61**	**66**	**7**	**0**	**3**	**151**	**15.2**	**19**	**3**	**66.7**	**17:03**	**15**	**5**	**4**	**9**	**6**	**3**	**0**	**2**	**15:24**
	NHL Totals		**465**	**118**	**168**	**286**	**378**	**31**	**1**	**19**	**1169**	**10.1**		**36**	**27.8**	**14:53**	**49**	**10**	**13**	**23**	**22**	**3**	**0**	**2**	**14:41**

• Missed majority of 2002-03 season recovering from head injury suffered prior to training camp, August, 2002. Signed as a free agent by **Dynamo Moscow** (Russia), June 19, 2004.

ALBERTS, Andrew

(AL-buhrts, AN-droo) **BOS.**

Defense. Shoots left. 6'4", 216 lbs. Born, Minneapolis, MN, June 30, 1981. Boston's 5th choice, 179th overall, in 2001 Entry Draft.

Season	Club	League	GP	G	A	Pts	PIM	PP	SH	GW	S	%	+/-	TF	F%	Min	GP	G	A	Pts	PIM	PP	SH	GW	Min
1998-99	Benide	High-MN	26	10	25	35		....	....	....	....	....	....	....	....	....	....	....	....	....	....	....	....	....	....
99-2000	Waterloo	USHL	49	2	2	4	55	....	....	....	....	....	....	....	....	....	4	0	0	0	12	....	....	....	....
2000-01	Waterloo	USHL	54	4	10	14	128	....	....	....	....	....	....	....	....	....	....	....	....	....	....	....	....	....	....
2001-02	Boston College	H-East	38	2	10	12	52	....	....	....	....	....	....	....	....	....	....	....	....	....	....	....	....	....	....
2002-03	Boston College	H-East	39	6	16	22	60	....	....	....	....	....	....	....	....	....	....	....	....	....	....	....	....	....	....
2003-04	Boston College	H-East	42	4	12	16	64	....	....	....	....	....	....	....	....	....	....	....	....	....	....	....	....	....	....
2004-05	Boston College	H-East	30	4	12	16	67	....	....	....	....	....	....	....	....	....	....	....	....	....	....	....	....	....	....
	Providence Bruins	AHL	8	0	0	0	16	....	....	....	....	....	....	....	....	....	16	1	4	5	40	....	....	....	....
2005-06	**Boston**	**NHL**	**73**	**1**	**6**	**7**	**68**	**0**	**1**	**0**	**30**	**3.3**	**3**	**2**	**50.0**	**12:50**	....	....	....	....	....	....	....	....	....
	Providence Bruins	AHL	6	0	1	1	7	....	....	....	....	....	....	....	....	....	....	....	....	....	....	....	....	....	....
2006-07	**Boston**	**NHL**	**76**	**0**	**10**	**10**	**124**	**0**	**0**	**0**	**41**	**0.0**	**–15**	**1**	**0.0**	**19:40**	....	....	....	....	....	....	....	....	....
	NHL Totals		**149**	**1**	**16**	**17**	**192**	**0**	**1**	**0**	**71**	**1.4**		**3**	**33.3**	**16:19**	....	....	....	....	....	....	....	....	....

Hockey East Second All-Star Team (2004) • NCAA East First All-American Team (2004, 2005) • Hockey East First All-Star Team (2005)

ALEXEEV, Nikita

(uh-LEHX-ee-ehv, nih-KEE-tuh)

Right wing. Shoots left. 6'5", 227 lbs. Born, Murmansk, USSR, December 27, 1981. Tampa Bay's 1st choice, 8th overall, in 2000 Entry Draft.

Season	Club	League	GP	G	A	Pts	PIM	PP	SH	GW	S	%	+/-	TF	F%	Min	GP	G	A	Pts	PIM	PP	SH	GW	Min
1996-97	Krylja Sovetov 2	Russia-3	45	4	6	10	8	....	....	....	....	....	....	....	....	....	....	....	....	....	....	....	....	....	....
1997-98	Krylja Sovetov 2	Russia-3	61	11	4	15	36	....	....	....	....	....	....	....	....	....	....	....	....	....	....	....	....	....	....
1998-99	Erie Otters	OHL	61	17	18	35	14	....	....	....	....	....	....	....	....	....	5	1	1	2	4	....	....	....	....
99-2000	Erie Otters	OHL	64	24	29	53	42	....	....	....	....	....	....	....	....	....	13	4	3	7	6	....	....	....	....
2000-01	Erie Otters	OHL	64	31	41	72	45	....	....	....	....	....	....	....	....	....	12	7	7	14	12	....	....	....	....
2001-02	**Tampa Bay**	**NHL**	**44**	**4**	**4**	**8**	**8**	**1**	**0**	**1**	**47**	**8.5**	**–9**	**0**	**0.0**	**11:26**	....	....	....	....	....	....	....	....	....
	Springfield	AHL	35	5	9	14	16	....	....	....	....	....	....	....	....	....	....	....	....	....	....	....	....	....	....
2002-03	**Tampa Bay**	**NHL**	**37**	**4**	**2**	**6**	**8**	**1**	**0**	**1**	**52**	**7.7**	**–6**	**3**	**33.3**	**11:31**	**11**	**1**	**0**	**1**	**0**	**0**	**0**	**0**	**10:12**
	Springfield	AHL	36	7	5	12	8	....	....	....	....	....	....	....	....	....	....	....	....	....	....	....	....	....	....
2003-04	Hershey Bears	AHL	14	0	1	1	8	....	....	....	....	....	....	....	....	....	....	....	....	....	....	....	....	....	....
2004-05	Springfield	AHL	72	13	9	22	16	....	....	....	....	....	....	....	....	....	....	....	....	....	....	....	....	....	....
2005-06	Avangard Omsk	Russia	40	6	3	9	14	....	....	....	....	....	....	....	....	....	5	0	0	0	2	....	....	....	....
2006-07	**Tampa Bay**	**NHL**	**63**	**10**	**11**	**21**	**12**	**2**	**0**	**2**	**102**	**9.8**	**10**	**12**	**16.7**	**14:19**	....	....	....	....	....	....	....	....	....
	Chicago	**NHL**	**15**	**2**	**0**	**2**	**0**	**0**	**0**	**0**	**15**	**13.3**	**–3**	**1**	**100.0**	**11:33**	....	....	....	....	....	....	....	....	....
	NHL Totals		**159**	**20**	**17**	**37**	**28**	**4**	**0**	**4**	**216**	**9.3**		**16**	**25.0**	**12:36**	**11**	**1**	**0**	**1**	**0**	**0**	**0**	**0**	**10:12**

• Missed majority of 2003-04 season recovering from shoulder injury suffered in game vs. Philadelphia (AHL) on November 2, 2003. Traded to **Chicago** by **Tampa Bay** for Karl Stewart and Florida's 6th round choice (previously acquired) in 2008 Entry Draft, February 27, 2007.

			Regular Season														Playoffs								
Season	Club	League	GP	G	A	Pts	PIM	PP	SH	GW	S	%	+/-	TF	F%	Min	GP	G	A	Pts	PIM	PP	SH	GW	Min

ALFREDSSON, Daniel

(AHL-frehd-suhn, DAN-yehl) **OTT.**

Right wing. Shoots right. 5'11", 207 lbs. Born, Goteborg, Sweden, December 11, 1972. Ottawa's 5th choice, 133rd overall, in 1994 Entry Draft.

Season	Club	League	GP	G	A	Pts	PIM	PP	SH	GW	S	%	+/-	TF	F%	Min	GP	G	A	Pts	PIM	PP	SH	GW	Min
1990-91	Molndal Hockey	Sweden-2	3	0	0	0	2	....	....	....	....	....	....	....	....	....	8	4	4	8	4	....	....	....	....
1991-92	Molndal	Sweden-2	32	12	8	20	43	....	....	....	....	....	....	....	....	....	....	....	....	....	....	....	....	....	....
1992-93	V.Frolunda	Sweden	20	1	5	6	8	....	....	....	....	....	....	....	....	....	....	....	....	....	....	....	....	....	....
1993-94	V.Frolunda	Sweden	39	20	10	30	18	....	....	....	....	....	....	....	....	....	4	1	1	2	....	....	....	....	....
1994-95	V.Frolunda	Sweden	22	7	11	18	22	....	....	....	....	....	....	....	....	....	....	....	....	....	....	....	....	....	....
1995-96	**Ottawa**	**NHL**	**82**	**26**	**35**	**61**	**28**	**8**	**2**	**3**	**212**	**12.3**	**−18**	....	....	....	....	....	....	....	....	....	....	....	....
1996-97	**Ottawa**	**NHL**	**76**	**24**	**47**	**71**	**30**	**11**	**1**	**1**	**247**	**9.7**	**5**	....	....	....	**7**	**5**	**2**	**7**	**6**	**3**	**0**	**2**	....
1997-98	**Ottawa**	**NHL**	**55**	**17**	**28**	**45**	**18**	**7**	**0**	**7**	**149**	**11.4**	**7**	....	....	....	**11**	**7**	**2**	**9**	**20**	**2**	**1**	**1**	....
	Sweden	Olympics	4	2	3	5	2	....	....	....	....	....	....	....	....	....	....	....	....	....	....	....	....	....	....
1998-99	**Ottawa**	**NHL**	**58**	**11**	**22**	**33**	**14**	**3**	**0**	**5**	**163**	**6.7**	**8**	**7**	**57.1**	**17:22**	**4**	**1**	**2**	**3**	**4**	**1**	**0**	**0**	**22:23**
99-2000	**Ottawa**	**NHL**	**57**	**21**	**38**	**59**	**28**	**4**	**2**	**0**	**164**	**12.8**	**11**	**3**	**66.7**	**18:45**	**6**	**1**	**3**	**4**	**2**	**1**	**0**	**0**	**20:22**
2000-01	**Ottawa**	**NHL**	**68**	**24**	**46**	**70**	**30**	**10**	**0**	**3**	**206**	**11.7**	**11**	**8**	**50.0**	**18:47**	**4**	**1**	**0**	**1**	**2**	**0**	**0**	**0**	**21:20**
2001-02	**Ottawa**	**NHL**	**78**	**37**	**34**	**71**	**45**	**9**	**1**	**4**	**243**	**15.2**	**3**	**30**	**30.0**	**20:19**	**12**	**7**	**6**	**13**	**4**	**3**	**0**	**3**	**21:43**
	Sweden	Olympics	4	1	4	5	2	....	....	....	....	....	....	....	....	....	....	....	....	....	....	....	....	....	....
2002-03	**Ottawa**	**NHL**	**78**	**27**	**51**	**78**	**42**	**9**	**0**	**6**	**240**	**11.3**	**15**	**40**	**40.0**	**19:32**	**18**	**4**	**4**	**8**	**12**	**4**	**0**	**1**	**18:00**
2003-04	**Ottawa**	**NHL**	**77**	**32**	**48**	**80**	**24**	**9**	**0**	**5**	**230**	**13.9**	**12**	**33**	**24.2**	**19:24**	**7**	**1**	**2**	**3**	**2**	**0**	**0**	**0**	**20:03**
2004-05	Frolunda	Sweden	15	8	9	17	10	....	....	....	....	....	....	....	....	....	14	*12	6	*18	8	....	....	....	....
2005-06	**Ottawa**	**NHL**	**77**	**43**	**60**	**103**	**50**	**16**	**5**	**8**	**249**	**17.3**	**29**	**44**	**20.5**	**21:41**	**10**	**2**	**8**	**10**	**4**	**1**	**0**	**0**	**21:10**
	Sweden	Olympics	8	5	5	10	4	....	....	....	....	....	....	....	....	....	....	....	....	....	....	....	....	....	....
2006-07	**Ottawa**	**NHL**	**77**	**29**	**58**	**87**	**42**	**7**	**2**	**7**	**240**	**12.1**	**42**	**43**	**34.9**	**21:35**	**20**	***14**	**8**	***22**	**10**	**6**	**1**	**4**	**23:20**
	NHL Totals		**783**	**291**	**467**	**758**	**351**	**93**	**13**	**49**	**2343**	**12.4**		**208**	**32.2**	**19:48**	**99**	**43**	**37**	**80**	**66**	**21**	**2**	**11**	**20:59**

NHL All-Rookie Team (1996) • Calder Memorial Trophy (1996) • NHL Second All-Star Team (2006)
Played in NHL All-Star Game (1996, 1997, 1998, 2004)
Signed as a free agent by **Frolunda** (Sweden), November 10, 2004.

ALLEN, Bobby

(AHL-lehn, BAW-bee) **BOS.**

Defense. Shoots left. 6'1", 215 lbs. Born, Weymouth, MA, November 14, 1978. Boston's 2nd choice, 52nd overall, in 1998 Entry Draft.

Season	Club	League	GP	G	A	Pts	PIM	PP	SH	GW	S	%	+/-	TF	F%	Min	GP	G	A	Pts	PIM	PP	SH	GW	Min
1996-97	Cushing	High-MA	36	11	33	44	28	....	....	....	....	....	....	....	....	....	....	....	....	....	....	....	....	....	....
1997-98	Boston College	H-East	40	7	21	28	49	....	....	....	....	....	....	....	....	....	....	....	....	....	....	....	....	....	....
1998-99	Boston College	H-East	43	9	23	32	34	....	....	....	....	....	....	....	....	....	....	....	....	....	....	....	....	....	....
99-2000	Boston College	H-East	42	4	23	27	40	....	....	....	....	....	....	....	....	....	....	....	....	....	....	....	....	....	....
2000-01	Boston College	H-East	42	5	18	23	28	....	....	....	....	....	....	....	....	....	....	....	....	....	....	....	....	....	....
2001-02	Providence Bruins	AHL	49	5	10	15	18	....	....	....	....	....	....	....	....	....	....	....	....	....	....	....	....	....	....
	Hamilton	AHL	10	1	6	7	0	....	....	....	....	....	....	....	....	....	14	0	3	3	6	....	....	....	....
2002-03	**Edmonton**	**NHL**	**1**	**0**	**0**	**0**	**0**	**0**	**0**	**0**	**0**	**0.0**	**0**	**0**	**0.0**	**2:53**	....	....	....	....	....	....	....	....	....
	Hamilton	AHL	56	1	12	13	24	....	....	....	....	....	....	....	....	....	23	0	5	5	10	....	....	....	....
2003-04	Toronto	AHL	56	5	10	15	18	....	....	....	....	....	....	....	....	....	3	0	2	2	4	....	....	....	....
2004-05	Albany River Rats	AHL	66	5	11	16	20	....	....	....	....	....	....	....	....	....	....	....	....	....	....	....	....	....	....
2005-06	Albany River Rats	AHL	68	4	14	18	28	....	....	....	....	....	....	....	....	....	....	....	....	....	....	....	....	....	....
2006-07	**Boston**	**NHL**	**31**	**0**	**3**	**3**	**10**	**0**	**0**	**0**	**14**	**0.0**	**−1**	**0**	**0.0**	**13:02**	....	....	....	....	....	....	....	....	....
	Providence Bruins	AHL	31	5	13	18	14	....	....	....	....	....	....	....	....	....	....	....	....	....	....	....	....	....	....
	NHL Totals		**32**	**0**	**3**	**3**	**10**	**0**	**0**	**0**	**14**	**0.0**		**0**	**0.0**	**12:43**	....	....	....	....	....	....	....	....	....

Hockey East Second All-Star Team (2000) • Hockey East First All-Star Team (2001) • NCAA East First All-American Team (2001)
Traded to **Edmonton** by **Boston** for Sean Brown, March 19, 2002. Signed as a free agent by **New Jersey**, July 22, 2004. Signed as a free agent by **Boston**, July 17, 2006.

ALLEN, Bryan

(AHL-lehn, BRIGH-uhn) **FLA.**

Defense. Shoots left. 6'4", 220 lbs. Born, Kingston, Ont., August 21, 1980. Vancouver's 1st choice, 4th overall, in 1998 Entry Draft.

Season	Club	League	GP	G	A	Pts	PIM	PP	SH	GW	S	%	+/-	TF	F%	Min	GP	G	A	Pts	PIM	PP	SH	GW	Min
1995-96	Ernestown Jets	OHA-C	36	1	16	17	71	....	....	....	....	....	....	....	....	....	....	....	....	....	....	....	....	....	....
1996-97	Oshawa Generals	OHL	60	2	4	6	76	....	....	....	....	....	....	....	....	....	18	1	3	4	26	....	....	....	....
1997-98	Oshawa Generals	OHL	48	6	13	19	126	....	....	....	....	....	....	....	....	....	5	0	5	5	18	....	....	....	....
1998-99	Oshawa Generals	OHL	37	7	15	22	77	....	....	....	....	....	....	....	....	....	15	0	3	3	26	....	....	....	....
99-2000	Oshawa Generals	OHL	3	0	2	2	12	....	....	....	....	....	....	....	....	....	3	0	0	0	13	....	....	....	....
	Syracuse Crunch	AHL	9	1	1	2	11	....	....	....	....	....	....	....	....	....	2	0	0	0	2	....	....	....	....
2000-01	**Vancouver**	**NHL**	**6**	**0**	**0**	**0**	**0**	**0**	**0**	**0**	**2**	**0.0**	**0**	**0**	**0.0**	**9:20**	**2**	**0**	**0**	**0**	**2**	**0**	**0**	**0**	**13:47**
	Kansas City	IHL	75	5	20	25	99	....	....	....	....	....	....	....	....	....	....	....	....	....	....	....	....	....	....
2001-02	**Vancouver**	**NHL**	**11**	**0**	**0**	**0**	**6**	**0**	**0**	**0**	**4**	**0.0**	**1**	**0**	**0.0**	**10:47**	....	....	....	....	....	....	....	....	....
	Manitoba Moose	AHL	68	7	18	25	121	....	....	....	....	....	....	....	....	....	5	0	1	1	8	....	....	....	....
2002-03	**Vancouver**	**NHL**	**48**	**5**	**3**	**8**	**73**	**0**	**0**	**1**	**43**	**11.6**	**8**	**0**	**0.0**	**12:56**	**1**	**0**	**0**	**0**	**2**	**0**	**0**	**0**	**10:35**
	Manitoba Moose	AHL	7	0	1	1	4	....	....	....	....	....	....	....	....	....	....	....	....	....	....	....	....	....	....
2003-04	**Vancouver**	**NHL**	**74**	**2**	**5**	**7**	**94**	**0**	**0**	**0**	**70**	**2.9**	**−10**	**0**	**0.0**	**16:51**	**4**	**0**	**0**	**0**	**2**	**0**	**0**	**0**	**14:37**
2004-05	Voskresensk	Russia	19	0	3	3	34	....	....	....	....	....	....	....	....	....	....	....	....	....	....	....	....	....	....
2005-06	**Vancouver**	**NHL**	**77**	**7**	**10**	**17**	**115**	**1**	**0**	**0**	**88**	**8.0**	**4**	**0**	**0.0**	**20:27**	....	....	....	....	....	....	....	....	....
2006-07	**Florida**	**NHL**	**82**	**4**	**21**	**25**	**112**	**0**	**0**	**0**	**99**	**4.0**	**7**	**1**	**0.0**	**21:36**	....	....	....	....	....	....	....	....	....
	NHL Totals		**298**	**18**	**39**	**57**	**400**	**1**	**0**	**1**	**306**	**5.9**		**1**	**0.0**	**18:05**	**7**	**0**	**0**	**0**	**6**	**0**	**0**	**0**	**13:48**

OHL First All-Star Team (1999)
• Missed majority of 1999-2000 season recovering from knee injury suffered in training camp, September 21, 1999. Signed as a free agent by **Voskresensk** (Russia), December 20, 2004. Traded to **Florida** by **Vancouver** with Todd Bertuzzi and Alex Auld for Roberto Luongo, Lukas Krajicek and Florida's 6th round choice (Sergei Shirokov) in 2006 Entry Draft, June 23, 2006.

ALLISON, Jamie

(AL-lih-suhn, JAY-mee)

Defense. Shoots left. 6'1", 210 lbs. Born, Lindsay, Ont., May 13, 1975. Calgary's 2nd choice, 44th overall, in 1993 Entry Draft.

Season	Club	League	GP	G	A	Pts	PIM	PP	SH	GW	S	%	+/-	TF	F%	Min	GP	G	A	Pts	PIM	PP	SH	GW	Min
1990-91	Waterloo Siskins	OHA-B	38	3	8	11	91	....	....	....	....	....	....	....	....	....	....	....	....	....	....	....	....	....	....
1991-92	Windsor Spitfires	OHL	59	4	8	12	70	....	....	....	....	....	....	....	....	....	4	1	1	2	2	....	....	....	....
1992-93	Detroit	OHL	61	0	13	13	64	....	....	....	....	....	....	....	....	....	15	2	5	7	23	....	....	....	....
1993-94	Detroit	OHL	40	2	22	24	69	....	....	....	....	....	....	....	....	....	17	2	9	11	35	....	....	....	....
1994-95	Detroit	OHL	50	1	14	15	119	....	....	....	....	....	....	....	....	....	18	2	7	9	35	....	....	....	....
	Calgary	**NHL**	**1**	**0**	**0**	**0**	**0**	**0**	**0**	**0**	**0**	**0.0**	**0**	....	....	....	....	....	....	....	....	....	....	....	....
1995-96	Saint John Flames	AHL	71	3	16	19	223	....	....	....	....	....	....	....	....	....	14	0	2	2	16	....	....	....	....
1996-97	**Calgary**	**NHL**	**20**	**0**	**0**	**0**	**35**	**0**	**0**	**0**	**8**	**0.0**	**−4**	....	....	....	....	....	....	....	....	....	....	....	....
	Saint John Flames	AHL	46	3	6	9	139	....	....	....	....	....	....	....	....	....	5	0	1	1	4	....	....	....	....
1997-98	**Calgary**	**NHL**	**43**	**3**	**8**	**11**	**104**	**0**	**0**	**1**	**27**	**11.1**	**3**	....	....	....	....	....	....	....	....	....	....	....	....
	Saint John Flames	AHL	16	0	5	5	49	....	....	....	....	....	....	....	....	....	....	....	....	....	....	....	....	....	....
1998-99	Saint John Flames	AHL	5	0	0	0	23	....	....	....	....	....	....	....	....	....	....	....	....	....	....	....	....	....	....
	Chicago	**NHL**	**39**	**2**	**2**	**4**	**62**	**0**	**0**	**0**	**24**	**8.3**	**0**	**0**	**0.0**	**14:01**	....	....	....	....	....	....	....	....	....
	Indianapolis Ice	IHL	3	1	0	1	10	....	....	....	....	....	....	....	....	....	....	....	....	....	....	....	....	....	....
99-2000	**Chicago**	**NHL**	**59**	**1**	**3**	**4**	**102**	**0**	**0**	**0**	**24**	**4.2**	**−5**	**0**	**0.0**	**14:14**	....	....	....	....	....	....	....	....	....
2000-01	**Chicago**	**NHL**	**44**	**1**	**3**	**4**	**53**	**0**	**0**	**0**	**16**	**6.3**	**7**	**1**	**100.0**	**14:33**	....	....	....	....	....	....	....	....	....
2001-02	**Calgary**	**NHL**	**37**	**0**	**2**	**2**	**24**	**0**	**0**	**0**	**14**	**0.0**	**−3**	**2**	**0.0**	**7:44**	....	....	....	....	....	....	....	....	....
	Columbus	**NHL**	**7**	**0**	**0**	**0**	**28**	**0**	**0**	**0**	**2**	**0.0**	**−4**	**0**	**0.0**	**11:23**	....	....	....	....	....	....	....	....	....
2002-03	**Columbus**	**NHL**	**48**	**0**	**1**	**1**	**99**	**0**	**0**	**0**	**23**	**0.0**	**−15**	**1**	**100.0**	**11:57**	....	....	....	....	....	....	....	....	....
2003-04	**Nashville**	**NHL**	**47**	**0**	**3**	**3**	**76**	**0**	**0**	**0**	**19**	**0.0**	**−7**	**0**	**0.0**	**13:04**	....	....	....	....	....	....	....	....	....
2004-05	Cambridge	OHA-Sr.	5	0	3	3	4	....	....	....	....	....	....	....	....	....	....	....	....	....	....	....	....	....	....
2005-06	**Nashville**	**NHL**	**20**	**0**	**1**	**1**	**45**	**0**	**0**	**0**	**3**	**0.0**	**−6**	**3**	**66.7**	**8:00**	....	....	....	....	....	....	....	....	....
	Florida	**NHL**	**7**	**0**	**0**	**0**	**11**	**0**	**0**	**0**	**4**	**0.0**	**0**	**0**	**0.0**	**11:48**	....	....	....	....	....	....	....	....	....
2006-07	Binghamton	AHL	47	2	5	7	97	....	....	....	....	....	....	....	....	....	....	....	....	....	....	....	....	....	....
	NHL Totals		**372**	**7**	**23**	**30**	**639**	**0**	**0**	**1**	**164**	**4.3**		**7**	**57.1**	**12:25**	....	....	....	....	....	....	....	....	....

Traded to **Chicago** by **Calgary** with Marty McInnis and Erik Andersson for Jeff Shantz and Steve Dubinsky, October 27, 1998. Claimed by **Calgary** from **Chicago** in Waiver Draft, September 28, 2001. Traded to **Columbus** by **Calgary** for Blake Sloan, March 19, 2002. Signed as a free agent by **Nashville**, September 10, 2003. Claimed on waivers by **Florida** from **Nashville**, February 13, 2006. Signed as a free agent by **Ottawa**, July 26, 2006.

AMONTE, Tony
(uh-MAHN-tee, TOH-nee)

Right wing. Shoots left. 6', 200 lbs. Born, Hingham, MA, August 2, 1970. NY Rangers' 3rd choice, 68th overall, in 1988 Entry Draft.

			Regular Season														Playoffs								
Season	Club	League	GP	G	A	Pts	PIM	PP	SH	GW	S	%	+/-	TF	F%	Min	GP	G	A	Pts	PIM	PP	SH	GW	Min
1985-86	Thayer Academy	High-MA	2	0	0	0	0																		
1986-87	Thayer Academy	High-MA	25	25	32	57																			
1987-88	Thayer Academy	High-MA	28	30	38	68																			
1988-89	Thayer Academy	High-MA	25	35	38	73																			
1989-90	Boston University	H-East	41	25	33	58	52																		
1990-91	Boston University	H-East	38	31	37	68	82																		
	NY Rangers	**NHL**															2	0	2	2	0	0	0	0	
1991-92	**NY Rangers**	**NHL**	79	35	34	69	55	9	0	4	234	15.0	12				13	3	6	9	2	2	0	0	
1992-93	**NY Rangers**	**NHL**	83	33	43	76	49	13	0	4	270	12.2	0												
1993-94	**NY Rangers**	**NHL**	72	16	22	38	31	3	0	4	179	8.9	5												
	Chicago	**NHL**	7	1	3	4	6	1	0	0	16	6.3	–5				6	4	2	6	4	1	0	1	
1994-95	HC Fassa Canazei	Euroliga	14	22	16	38	10																		
	HC Fassa Canazei	EuroHL	2	5	1	6	0																		
	Chicago	**NHL**	48	15	20	35	41	6	1	3	105	14.3	7				16	3	3	6	10	0	0	0	
1995-96	**Chicago**	**NHL**	81	31	32	63	62	5	4	5	216	14.4	10				7	2	4	6	6	1	0	0	
1996-97	**Chicago**	**NHL**	81	41	36	77	64	9	2	4	266	15.4	35				6	4	2	6	8	0	0	0	
1997-98	**Chicago**	**NHL**	82	31	42	73	66	7	3	5	296	10.5	21												
	United States	Olympics	4	0	1	1	4																		
1998-99	**Chicago**	**NHL**	82	44	31	75	60	14	3	8	256	17.2	0	8	12.5	22:12									
99-2000	**Chicago**	**NHL**	82	43	41	84	48	11	5	2	260	16.5	10	22	22.7	21:54									
2000-01	**Chicago**	**NHL**	82	35	29	64	54	9	1	3	256	13.7	–22	27	40.7	22:09									
2001-02	**Chicago**	**NHL**	82	27	39	66	67	6	1	4	232	11.6	11	30	43.3	21:18	5	0	1	1	4	0	0	0	18:43
	United States	Olympics	6	2	2	4	0																		
2002-03	**Phoenix**	**NHL**	59	13	23	36	26	6	0	3	170	7.6	–12	53	35.9	19:27									
	Philadelphia	**NHL**	13	7	8	15	2	1	1	2	37	18.9	12	3	33.3	17:39	13	1	6	7	4	0	0	0	19:16
2003-04	**Philadelphia**	**NHL**	80	20	33	53	38	4	0	3	173	11.6	13	8	37.5	15:14	18	3	5	8	6	2	0	0	14:41
2004-05		Did not play																							
2005-06	**Calgary**	**NHL**	80	14	28	42	43	3	1	3	155	9.0	3	66	31.8	17:07	7	2	1	3	10	0	1	0	17:28
2006-07	**Calgary**	**NHL**	81	10	20	30	40	1	1	1	139	7.2	–4	18	33.3	14:09	6	0	1	1	0	0	0	0	9:34
	NHL Totals		1174	416	484	900	752	108	23	58	3260	12.8		235	34.0	19:10	99	22	33	55	56	6	1	1	16:05

Hockey East Second All-Star Team (1991) • NCAA Championship All-Tournament Team (1991) • NHL All-Rookie Team (1992)

Played in NHL All-Star Game (1997, 1998, 1999, 2000, 2001)

• Missed majority of 1985-86 season recovering from knee injury, October, 1985. Traded to **Chicago** by **NY Rangers** with the rights to Matt Oates for Stephane Matteau and Brian Noonan, March 21, 1994. Signed as a free agent by **Phoenix**, July 12, 2002. Traded to **Philadelphia** by **Phoenix** for Guillaume Lefebvre, Atlanta's 3rd round choice (previously acquired, Phoenix selected Tyler Redenbach) in 2003 Entry Draft and Philadelphia's 2nd round choice (later traded to NY Rangers – NY Rangers selected Brandon Dubinsky) in 2004 Entry Draft, March 10, 2003. Signed as a free agent by **Calgary**, August 2, 2005.

ANDERSSON, Jonas
(AN-duhr-suhn, YOH-nuhs) **NSH.**

Right wing. Shoots left. 6'2", 202 lbs. Born, Stockholm, Sweden, February 24, 1981. Nashville's 2nd choice, 33rd overall, in 1999 Entry Draft.

Season	Club	League	GP	G	A	Pts	PIM	PP	SH	GW	S	%	+/-	TF	F%	Min	GP	G	A	Pts	PIM	PP	SH	GW	Min
1997-98	AIK Solna Jr.	Swe-Jr.	33	14	16	30	32																		
1998-99	AIK Solna Jr.	Swe-Jr.	16	3	7	10	18																		
	London Knights	Britain	12	2	3	5	0																		
99-2000	North Bay	OHL	67	31	36	67	27										6	2	2	4	2				
	Milwaukee	IHL	2	1	0	1	0										2	0	0	0	2				
2000-01	Milwaukee	IHL	52	6	7	13	44										5	0	0	0	2				
2001-02	**Nashville**	**NHL**	5	0	0	0	2	0	0	0	4	0.0	–2	0	0.0	9:06									
	Milwaukee	AHL	71	13	17	30	19																		
2002-03	Milwaukee	AHL	49	7	4	11	12										5	0	1	1	4				
2003-04		Did not play – injured																							
2004-05	Sodertalje SK	Sweden	34	0	4	4	8																		
	Brynas IF Gavle	Sweden	7	2	0	2	2																		
2005-06	Ilves Tampere	Finland	48	8	10	18	26										4	2	0	2	0				
2006-07	HPK Hameenlinna	Finland	23	6	7	13	20										9	0	1	1	8				
	NHL Totals		5	0	0	0	2	0	0	0	4	0.0		0	0.0	9:06									

• Missed entire 2003-04 season recovering from wrist injury suffered in training camp, September 30, 2003. Signed as a free agent by **Sodertalje** (Sweden), April 28, 2004. Signed as a free agent by **Gavle** (Sweden), January 22, 2005.

ANTROPOV, Nik
(an-TROH-pahv, NIHK) **TOR.**

Center. Shoots left. 6'6", 230 lbs. Born, Ust-Kamenogorsk, USSR, February 18, 1980. Toronto's 1st choice, 10th overall, in 1998 Entry Draft.

Season	Club	League	GP	G	A	Pts	PIM	PP	SH	GW	S	%	+/-	TF	F%	Min	GP	G	A	Pts	PIM	PP	SH	GW	Min
1996-97	Ust-Kamenogorsk	Russia-2	8	2	1	3	6																		
1997-98	Ust-Kamenogorsk	Russia-2	42	15	24	39	62																		
1998-99	Dynamo Moscow	Russia	30	5	9	14	30										11	0	1	1	4				
99-2000	**Toronto**	**NHL**	66	12	18	30	41	0	0	2	89	13.5	14	501	46.3	12:48	3	0	0	0	4	0	0	0	10:14
	St. John's	AHL	2	0	0	0	4																		
2000-01	**Toronto**	**NHL**	52	6	11	17	30	0	0	1	71	8.5	5	431	44.3	10:02	9	2	1	3	12	1	0	1	11:04
2001-02	**Toronto**	**NHL**	11	1	1	2	4	0	0	0	12	8.3	–1	31	38.7	8:57									
	St. John's	AHL	34	11	24	35	47																		
2002-03	**Toronto**	**NHL**	72	16	29	45	124	2	1	6	102	15.7	11	621	40.1	15:00	3	0	0	0	0	0	0	0	19:17
2003-04	**Toronto**	**NHL**	62	13	18	31	62	1	1	2	89	14.6	7	309	40.8	15:18	13	0	2	2	18	0	0	0	15:56
2004-05	Ak Bars Kazan	Russia	10	2	3	5	6																		
	Yaroslavl	Russia	26	4	15	19	44										9	3	4	7	18				
2005-06	**Toronto**	**NHL**	57	12	19	31	56	2	1	0	113	10.6	13	172	34.3	15:34									
	Kazakhstan	Olympics	5	1	0	1	4																		
2006-07	**Toronto**	**NHL**	54	18	15	33	44	4	0	4	125	14.4	8	34	35.3	16:36									
	NHL Totals		374	78	111	189	361	9	3	15	601	13.0		2099	42.0	14:06	28	2	3	5	34	1	0	1	14:07

Signed as a free agent by **Kazan** (Russia), October 27, 2004. Signed as a free agent by **Yaroslavl** (Russia), December 20, 2004.

ARKHIPOV, Denis
(AHR-kih-pahv, DEH-nihs)

Center. Shoots left. 6'3", 214 lbs. Born, Kazan, USSR, May 19, 1979. Nashville's 2nd choice, 60th overall, in 1998 Entry Draft.

Season	Club	League	GP	G	A	Pts	PIM	PP	SH	GW	S	%	+/-	TF	F%	Min	GP	G	A	Pts	PIM	PP	SH	GW	Min
1994-95	Itil Kazan 2	CIS-2	40	20	12	32	10																		
1995-96	Ak Bars Kazan	CIS	15	10	8	18	10																		
1996-97	Ak Bars Kazan 2	Russia-3	50	17	23	40	20																		
	Ak Bars Kazan	Russia	1	1	0	1	0																		
1997-98	Ak Bars Kazan	Russia	29	2	2	4	2																		
1998-99	Ak Bars Kazan	Russia	34	12	1	13	22										9	2	3	5	6				
	Ak Bars Kazan	EuroHL	4	0	0	0	0										1	0	0	0	0				
99-2000	Ak Bars Kazan	Russia	32	7	9	16	14										18	5	5	10	6				
2000-01	**Nashville**	**NHL**	40	6	7	13	4	0	0	0	42	14.3	0	299	43.8	9:56									
	Milwaukee	IHL	40	9	8	17	11																		
2001-02	**Nashville**	**NHL**	82	20	22	42	16	7	0	6	118	16.9	–18	1108	44.8	15:43									
2002-03	**Nashville**	**NHL**	79	11	24	35	32	3	0	1	148	7.4	–18	1069	46.7	15:09									
2003-04	**Nashville**	**NHL**	72	9	12	21	22	3	0	3	91	9.9	–2	926	44.7	13:58									
2004-05	Ak Bars Kazan	Russia	45	9	8	17	28										4	0	0	0	0				
2005-06	Mytischi	Russia	50	8	8	16	28										9	2	1	3	0				
2006-07	**Chicago**	**NHL**	79	10	17	27	54	2	1	1	112	8.9	–13	981	49.2	15:43									
	NHL Totals		352	56	82	138	128	15	1	11	511	11.0		4383	46.2	14:34									

Signed as a free agent by **Kazan** (Russia), July 27, 2004. Signed as a free agent by **Chicago**, July 6, 2006. Signed as a free agent by **Kazan** (Russia), June 4, 2007.

ARMSTRONG, Colby

(AHRM-stawng, KOHL-bee) **PIT.**

Right wing. Shoots right. 6'2", 188 lbs. Born, Lloydminster, Sask., November 23, 1982. Pittsburgh's 1st choice, 21st overall, in 2001 Entry Draft.

			Regular Season														Playoffs								
Season	Club	League	GP	G	A	Pts	PIM	PP	SH	GW	S	%	+/-	TF	F%	Min	GP	G	A	Pts	PIM	PP	SH	GW	Min
1998-99	Sask. Contacts	SMHL	33	21	19	40	103																		
	Red Deer Rebels	WHL	1	0	1	1	0																		
99-2000	Red Deer Rebels	WHL	68	13	25	38	122										2	0	1	1	11				
2000-01	Red Deer Rebels	WHL	72	36	42	78	156										21	6	6	12	29				
2001-02	Red Deer Rebels	WHL	64	27	41	68	115										23	6	10	16	32				
2002-03	Wilkes-Barre	AHL	73	7	11	18	76										3	0	0	0	4				
2003-04	Wilkes-Barre	AHL	67	10	17	27	71										24	3	1	4	45				
2004-05	Wilkes-Barre	AHL	80	18	37	55	89										10	4	2	6	14				
2005-06	**Pittsburgh**	**NHL**	47	16	24	40	58	7	2	3	86	18.6	15	44	27.3	19:04									
	Wilkes-Barre	AHL	31	11	18	29	44																		
2006-07	**Pittsburgh**	**NHL**	80	12	22	34	67	1	1	3	145	8.3	2	13	15.4	16:50	5	0	1	1	11	0	0	0	15:18
	NHL Totals		127	28	46	74	125	8	3	6	231	12.1		57	24.6	17:39	5	0	1	1	11	0	0	0	15:18

ARMSTRONG, Derek

(AHRM-stawng, DAIR-ihk) **L.A.**

Center. Shoots right. 6', 190 lbs. Born, Ottawa, Ont., April 23, 1973. NY Islanders' 5th choice, 128th overall, in 1992 Entry Draft.

Season	Club	League	GP	G	A	Pts	PIM	PP	SH	GW	S	%	+/-	TF	F%	Min	GP	G	A	Pts	PIM	PP	SH	GW	Min
1989-90	Hawkesbury	CJHL	48	8	10	18	30																		
1990-91	Hawkesbury	CJHL	54	27	45	72	49																		
	Sudbury Wolves	OHL	2	0	2	2	0																		
1991-92	Sudbury Wolves	OHL	66	31	54	85	22										9	2	2	4	2				
1992-93	Sudbury Wolves	OHL	66	44	62	106	56										14	9	10	19	26				
1993-94	**NY Islanders**	**NHL**	1	0	0	0	0	0	0	0	2	0.0	0												
	Salt Lake	IHL	76	23	35	58	61																		
1994-95	Denver Grizzlies	IHL	59	13	18	31	65										6	0	2	2	0				
1995-96	**NY Islanders**	**NHL**	19	1	3	4	14	0	0	0	23	4.3	–6												
	Worcester IceCats	AHL	51	11	15	26	33										4	2	1	3	0				
1996-97	**NY Islanders**	**NHL**	50	6	7	13	33	0	0	2	36	16.7	–8												
	Utah Grizzlies	IHL	17	4	8	12	10										6	0	4	4	4				
1997-98	**Ottawa**	**NHL**	9	2	0	2	9	0	0	1	8	25.0	1												
	Detroit Vipers	IHL	10	0	1	1	2																		
	Hartford	AHL	54	16	30	46	40										15	2	6	8	22				
1998-99	**NY Rangers**	**NHL**	3	0	0	0	0	0	0	0	1	0.0	0	0	0.0	2:50									
	Hartford	AHL	59	29	51	80	73										7	5	4	9	10				
99-2000	**NY Rangers**	**NHL**	1	0	0	0	0	0	0	0	1	0.0	0	3	33.3	3:10									
	Hartford	AHL	77	28	54	82	101										23	7	16	23	24				
2000-01	**NY Rangers**	**NHL**	3	0	0	0	0	0	0	0	6	0.0	0	30	50.0	11:22									
	Hartford	AHL	75	32	*69	*101	73										5	0	6	6	6				
2001-02	SC Bern	Swiss	44	17	36	53	62										6	3	5	8	8				
2002-03	**Los Angeles**	**NHL**	66	12	26	38	30	2	0	1	106	11.3	5	708	50.0	15:40									
	Manchester	AHL	2	3	0	3	4																		
2003-04	**Los Angeles**	**NHL**	57	14	21	35	33	5	0	1	101	13.9	4	912	52.0	17:00									
2004-05	Geneve	Swiss	9	6	7	13	18																		
	Rapperswil	Swiss	3	1	3	4	4																		
2005-06	**Los Angeles**	**NHL**	62	13	28	41	46	7	0	1	100	13.0	–2	546	50.7	15:31									
2006-07	**Los Angeles**	**NHL**	67	11	33	44	62	3	0	0	109	10.1	13	842	47.9	15:04									
	NHL Totals		338	59	118	177	227	17	0	6	493	12.0		3041	50.1	15:31									

AHL Second All-Star Team (2000) • Jack A. Butterfield Trophy (Playoff MVP – AHL) (2000) • AHL First All-Star Team (2001) • John P. Sollenberger Trophy (Leading Scorer – AHL) (2001) • Les Cunningham Award (MVP – AHL) (2001)

Signed as a free agent by **Ottawa**, July 28, 1997. Loaned to **Hartford** (AHL) by **Ottawa**, October 28, 1997. Signed as a free agent by **NY Rangers**, August 10, 1998. Signed as a free agent by **Bern** (Swiss) with NY Rangers retaining NHL rights, July 18, 2001. Traded to **Los Angeles** by **NY Rangers** for Los Angeles' 6th round choice (Chris Holt) in 2003 Entry Draft, July 16, 2002. Signed as a free agent by **Geneve** (Swiss), October 12, 2004. Signed as a free agent by **Rapperswil** (Swiss), February 13, 2005.

ARNASON, Tyler

(AHR-na-suhn, TIGH-luhr) **COL.**

Center. Shoots left. 5'11", 204 lbs. Born, Oklahoma City, OK, March 16, 1979. Chicago's 6th choice, 183rd overall, in 1998 Entry Draft.

Season	Club	League	GP	G	A	Pts	PIM	PP	SH	GW	S	%	+/-	TF	F%	Min	GP	G	A	Pts	PIM	PP	SH	GW	Min
1996-97	Winnipeg South	MJHL	50	35	50	85	15										6	3	3	6	18				
1997-98	Fargo-Moorhead	USHL	52	37	45	82	16										4	1	1	2	2				
1998-99	St. Cloud State	WCHA	38	14	17	31	16																		
99-2000	St. Cloud State	WCHA	39	19	30	49	18																		
2000-01	St. Cloud State	WCHA	41	28	28	56	14																		
2001-02	**Chicago**	**NHL**	21	3	1	4	4	0	0	0	19	15.8	–3	112	41.1	9:28	3	0	0	0	0	0	0	0	7:43
	Norfolk Admirals	AHL	60	26	30	56	42																		
2002-03	**Chicago**	**NHL**	82	19	20	39	20	3	0	6	178	10.7	7	626	40.3	14:30									
2003-04	**Chicago**	**NHL**	82	22	33	55	16	6	0	2	222	9.9	–13	904	43.1	16:34									
2004-05	Brynas IF Gavle	Sweden	4	0	0	0	0																		
2005-06	**Chicago**	**NHL**	60	13	28	41	40	5	0	1	161	8.1	5	492	44.7	14:58									
	Ottawa	**NHL**	19	0	4	4	4	0	0	0	42	0.0	–4	172	51.7	12:19									
2006-07	**Colorado**	**NHL**	82	16	33	49	26	1	0	3	211	7.6	–8	422	43.8	14:20									
	NHL Totals		346	73	119	192	110	15	0	12	833	8.8		2728	43.3	14:36	3	0	0	0	0	0	0	0	7:43

USHL First All-Star Team (1998) • WCHA All-Rookie Team (1999) • WCHA Second All-Star Team (2000) • AHL All-Rookie Team (2002) • Dudley "Red" Garrett Memorial Award (Rookie of the Year – AHL) (2002) • NHL All-Rookie Team (2003)

Signed as a free agent by **Gavle** (Sweden), October 29, 2004. Traded to **Ottawa** by **Chicago** for Brandon Bochenski and Ottawa's 2nd round choice (Simon Danis-Pepin) in 2006 Entry Draft, March 9, 2006. Signed as a free agent by **Colorado**, July 1, 2006.

ARNOTT, Jason

(AHR-niht, JAY-suhn) **NSH.**

Center. Shoots right. 6'4", 220 lbs. Born, Collingwood, Ont., October 11, 1974. Edmonton's 1st choice, 7th overall, in 1993 Entry Draft.

Season	Club	League	GP	G	A	Pts	PIM	PP	SH	GW	S	%	+/-	TF	F%	Min	GP	G	A	Pts	PIM	PP	SH	GW	Min
1989-90	Stayner Siskins	OHA-C	34	21	31	52	12																		
1990-91	Lindsay Bears	OHA-B	42	17	44	61	10										8	9	8	17	6				
1991-92	Oshawa Generals	OHL	57	9	15	24	12																		
1992-93	Oshawa Generals	OHL	56	41	57	98	74										13	9	9	18	20				
1993-94	**Edmonton**	**NHL**	78	33	35	68	104	10	0	4	194	17.0	1												
1994-95	**Edmonton**	**NHL**	42	15	22	37	128	7	0	1	156	9.6	–14												
1995-96	**Edmonton**	**NHL**	64	28	31	59	87	8	0	5	244	11.5	–6												
1996-97	**Edmonton**	**NHL**	67	19	38	57	92	10	1	2	248	7.7	–21				12	3	6	9	18	1	0	0	
1997-98	**Edmonton**	**NHL**	35	5	13	18	78	1	0	0	100	5.0	–16												
	New Jersey	**NHL**	35	5	10	15	21	3	0	2	99	5.1	–8				5	0	2	2	0	0	0	0	
1998-99	**New Jersey**	**NHL**	74	27	27	54	79	8	0	3	200	13.5	10	872	49.3	15:24	7	2	2	4	4	1	0	0	16:48
99-2000♦	**New Jersey**	**NHL**	76	22	34	56	51	7	0	4	244	9.0	22	1172	46.9	17:05	23	8	12	20	18	3	0	1	16:29
2000-01	**New Jersey**	**NHL**	54	21	34	55	75	8	0	3	138	15.2	23	760	49.6	16:12	23	8	7	15	16	5	0	0	15:49
2001-02	**New Jersey**	**NHL**	63	22	19	41	59	8	0	1	169	13.0	3	934	47.8	17:13									
	Dallas	**NHL**	10	3	1	4	6	2	0	2	28	10.7	–1	77	52.0	18:13									
2002-03	**Dallas**	**NHL**	72	23	24	47	51	7	0	6	169	13.6	9	1130	53.3	16:12	11	3	2	5	6	1	0	0	15:35
2003-04	**Dallas**	**NHL**	73	21	36	57	66	5	0	5	143	14.7	23	1203	53.0	17:00	5	1	1	2	2	1	0	0	17:23
2004-05			DID NOT PLAY																						
2005-06	**Dallas**	**NHL**	81	32	44	76	102	11	1	5	167	19.2	13	1306	51.2	17:12	5	0	3	3	4	0	0	0	20:04
2006-07	**Nashville**	**NHL**	68	27	27	54	48	12	0	6	190	14.2	15	1145	50.6	17:59	5	2	1	3	2	1	0	0	19:17
	NHL Totals		892	303	395	698	1047	107	2	49	2489	12.2		8599	50.4	16:49	96	27	36	63	70	13	0	1	16:39

NHL All-Rookie Team (1994)

Played in NHL All-Star Game (1997)

Traded to **New Jersey** by **Edmonton** with Bryan Muir for Valeri Zelepukin and Bill Guerin, January 4, 1998. Traded to **Dallas** by **New Jersey** with Randy McKay and New Jersey's 1st round choice (later traded to Columbus – later traded to Buffalo – Buffalo selected Dan Paille) in 2002 Entry Draft for Joe Nieuwendyk and Jamie Langenbrunner, March 19, 2002. Signed as a free agent by **Nashville**, July 2, 2006.

ARTYUKHIN, Evgeny

(ahr-TYEW-khin, ehv-GEH-nee) **T.B.**

Right wing. Shoots left. 6'5", 254 lbs. Born, Moscow, USSR, April 4, 1983. Tampa Bay's 4th choice, 94th overall, in 2001 Entry Draft.

Season	Club	League	Regular Season														Playoffs								
			GP	G	A	Pts	PIM	PP	SH	GW	S	%	+/-	TF	F%	Min	GP	G	A	Pts	PIM	PP	SH	GW	Min
99-2000	Vityaz Podolsk 2	Russia-3	26	9	8	17	46	....	....	....	....	....	....	....	....	....	....	....	....	....	....	....	....	....	....
	Vityaz Podolsk	Russia-2	3	0	0	0	2	....	....	....	....	....	....	....	....	....	....	....	....	....	....	....	....	....	....
2000-01	Vityaz Podolsk	Russia	24	0	1	1	14	....	....	....	....	....	....	....	....	....	....	....	....	....	....	....	....	....	....
2001-02	Vityaz Podolsk 2	Russia-3	4	3	1	4	6	....	....	....	....	....	....	....	....	....	....	....	....	....	....	....	....	....	....
	Vityaz Podolsk	Russia-2	49	15	7	22	94	....	....	....	....	....	....	....	....	....	12	0	1	1	18	....	....	....	....
2002-03	Moncton Wildcats	QMJHL	53	13	27	40	204	....	....	....	....	....	....	....	....	....	6	1	2	3	29	....	....	....	....
2003-04	Hershey Bears	AHL	36	3	3	6	111	....	....	....	....	....	....	....	....	....	....	....	....	....	....	....	....	....	....
	Pensacola	ECHL	6	1	0	1	14	....	....	....	....	....	....	....	....	....	....	....	....	....	....	....	....	....	....
2004-05	Springfield	AHL	62	9	19	28	142	....	....	....	....	....	....	....	....	....	....	....	....	....	....	....	....	....	....
2005-06	**Tampa Bay**	**NHL**	**72**	**4**	**13**	**17**	**90**	**1**	**0**	**0**	**79**	**5.1**	**-4**	**0**	**0.0**	**8:43**	**5**	**1**	**0**	**1**	**6**	**0**	**0**	**0**	**8:14**
2006-07	Yaroslavl	Russia	44	5	8	13	183	....	....	....	....	....	....	....	....	....	1	0	0	0	0	....	....	....	....
	NHL Totals		**72**	**4**	**13**	**17**	**90**	**1**	**0**	**0**	**79**	**5.1**		**0**	**0.0**	**8:43**	**5**	**1**	**0**	**1**	**6**	**0**	**0**	**0**	**8:14**

Signed as a free agent by **Yaroslavl** (Russia), August 5, 2006.

ASHAM, Arron

(ASH-uhm, AIR-ruhn) **N.J.**

Right wing. Shoots right. 5'11", 210 lbs. Born, Portage La Prairie, Man., April 13, 1978. Montreal's 3rd choice, 71st overall, in 1996 Entry Draft.

Season	Club	League	GP	G	A	Pts	PIM	PP	SH	GW	S	%	+/-	TF	F%	Min	GP	G	A	Pts	PIM	PP	SH	GW	Min
1993-94	Portage	MAHA	21	18	19	37	82	....	....	....	....	....	....	....	....	....	....	....	....	....	....	....	....	....	....
1994-95	Red Deer Rebels	WHL	62	11	16	27	126	....	....	....	....	....	....	....	....	....	....	....	....	....	....	....	....	....	....
1995-96	Red Deer Rebels	WHL	70	32	45	77	174	....	....	....	....	....	....	....	....	....	10	6	3	9	20	....	....	....	....
1996-97	Red Deer Rebels	WHL	67	45	51	96	149	....	....	....	....	....	....	....	....	....	16	12	14	26	36	....	....	....	....
1997-98	Red Deer Rebels	WHL	67	43	49	92	153	....	....	....	....	....	....	....	....	....	5	0	2	2	8	....	....	....	....
	Fredericton	AHL	2	1	1	2	0	....	....	....	....	....	....	....	....	....	2	0	1	1	0	....	....	....	....
1998-99	**Montreal**	**NHL**	**7**	**0**	**0**	**0**	**0**	**0**	**0**	**0**	**5**	**0.0**	**-4**	**0**	**0.0**	**7:27**	....	....	....	....	....	....	....	....	....
	Fredericton	AHL	60	16	18	34	118	....	....	....	....	....	....	....	....	....	13	8	6	14	11	....	....	....	....
99-2000	**Montreal**	**NHL**	**33**	**4**	**2**	**6**	**24**	**0**	**1**	**1**	**29**	**13.8**	**-7**	**1**	**0.0**	**10:14**	....	....	....	....	....	....	....	....	....
	Quebec Citadelles	AHL	13	4	5	9	32	....	....	....	....	....	....	....	....	....	2	0	0	0	2	....	....	....	....
2000-01	**Montreal**	**NHL**	**46**	**2**	**3**	**5**	**59**	**0**	**0**	**0**	**32**	**6.3**	**-9**	**3**	**100.0**	**8:28**	....	....	....	....	....	....	....	....	....
	Quebec Citadelles	AHL	15	7	9	16	51	....	....	....	....	....	....	....	....	....	7	1	2	3	2	....	....	....	....
2001-02	**Montreal**	**NHL**	**35**	**5**	**4**	**9**	**55**	**0**	**0**	**0**	**30**	**16.7**	**7**	**4**	**25.0**	**8:13**	**3**	**0**	**1**	**1**	**0**	**0**	**0**	**0**	**5:39**
	Quebec Citadelles	AHL	24	9	14	23	35	....	....	....	....	....	....	....	....	....	....	....	....	....	....	....	....	....	....
2002-03	**NY Islanders**	**NHL**	**78**	**15**	**19**	**34**	**57**	**4**	**0**	**1**	**114**	**13.2**	**1**	**17**	**41.2**	**12:13**	**5**	**0**	**0**	**0**	**16**	**0**	**0**	**0**	**15:09**
2003-04	**NY Islanders**	**NHL**	**79**	**12**	**12**	**24**	**92**	**1**	**0**	**0**	**108**	**11.1**	**-12**	**23**	**34.8**	**13:13**	**5**	**0**	**1**	**1**	**4**	**0**	**0**	**0**	**8:44**
2004-05	EHC Visp	Swiss-2	5	2	4	6	6	....	....	....	....	....	....	....	....	....	4	1	1	2	8	....	....	....	....
2005-06	**NY Islanders**	**NHL**	**63**	**9**	**15**	**24**	**103**	**2**	**1**	**0**	**99**	**9.1**	**-5**	**63**	**41.3**	**13:33**	....	....	....	....	....	....	....	....	....
2006-07	**NY Islanders**	**NHL**	**80**	**11**	**12**	**23**	**63**	**0**	**0**	**2**	**85**	**12.9**	**3**	**10**	**60.0**	**9:20**	**5**	**1**	**0**	**1**	**0**	**0**	**0**	**0**	**10:08**
	NHL Totals		**421**	**58**	**67**	**125**	**453**	**7**	**2**	**4**	**502**	**11.6**		**121**	**42.1**	**11:04**	**18**	**1**	**2**	**3**	**20**	**0**	**0**	**0**	**10:23**

Traded to **NY Islanders** by **Montreal** with Montreal's 5th round choice (Marcus Paulsson) in 2002 Entry Draft for Mariusz Czerkawski, June 22, 2002. Signed as a free agent by **Visp** (Swiss-2), January 19, 2005. Signed as a free agent by **New Jersey**, August 7, 2007.

AUBIN, Serge

(oh-BEHN, SAIRZH)

Left wing. Shoots left. 6'1", 200 lbs. Born, Val-d'Or, Que., February 15, 1975. Pittsburgh's 9th choice, 161st overall, in 1994 Entry Draft.

Season	Club	League	GP	G	A	Pts	PIM	PP	SH	GW	S	%	+/-	TF	F%	Min	GP	G	A	Pts	PIM	PP	SH	GW	Min
1990-91	Abitibi Forestiers	QAAA	27	2	4	6	10	....	....	....	....	....	....	....	....	....	....	....	....	....	....	....	....	....	....
1991-92	Abitibi Forestiers	QAAA	42	28	32	60	36	....	....	....	....	....	....	....	....	....	1	0	1	1	0	....	....	....	....
1992-93	Drummondville	QMJHL	65	16	34	50	30	....	....	....	....	....	....	....	....	....	8	0	1	1	16	....	....	....	....
1993-94	Granby Bisons	QMJHL	63	42	32	74	80	....	....	....	....	....	....	....	....	....	7	2	3	5	8	....	....	....	....
1994-95	Granby Bisons	QMJHL	60	37	73	110	55	....	....	....	....	....	....	....	....	....	11	8	15	23	4	....	....	....	....
1995-96	Hampton Roads	ECHL	62	24	62	86	74	....	....	....	....	....	....	....	....	....	3	1	4	5	10	....	....	....	....
	Cleveland	IHL	2	0	0	0	0	....	....	....	....	....	....	....	....	....	2	0	0	0	0	....	....	....	....
1996-97	Cleveland	IHL	57	9	16	25	38	....	....	....	....	....	....	....	....	....	2	0	0	0	0	....	....	....	....
1997-98	Syracuse Crunch	AHL	55	6	14	20	57	....	....	....	....	....	....	....	....	....	....	....	....	....	....	....	....	....	....
	Hershey Bears	AHL	5	2	1	3	0	....	....	....	....	....	....	....	....	....	7	1	3	4	6	....	....	....	....
1998-99	Hershey Bears	AHL	64	30	39	69	58	....	....	....	....	....	....	....	....	....	3	0	1	1	2	....	....	....	....
	Colorado	**NHL**	**1**	**0**	**0**	**0**	**0**	**0**	**0**	**0**	**1**	**0.0**	**0**	**1**	**0.0**	**4:16**	....	....	....	....	....	....	....	....	....
99-2000	**Colorado**	**NHL**	**15**	**2**	**1**	**3**	**6**	**0**	**0**	**1**	**14**	**14.3**	**1**	**79**	**50.6**	**6:37**	**17**	**0**	**1**	**1**	**6**	**0**	**0**	**0**	**5:06**
	Hershey Bears	AHL	58	42	38	80	56	....	....	....	....	....	....	....	....	....	....	....	....	....	....	....	....	....	....
2000-01	**Columbus**	**NHL**	**81**	**13**	**17**	**30**	**107**	**0**	**0**	**2**	**110**	**11.8**	**-20**	**1346**	**51.3**	**16:20**	....	....	....	....	....	....	....	....	....
2001-02	**Columbus**	**NHL**	**71**	**8**	**8**	**16**	**32**	**1**	**0**	**1**	**86**	**9.3**	**-20**	**780**	**50.5**	**15:30**	....	....	....	....	....	....	....	....	....
2002-03	**Colorado**	**NHL**	**66**	**4**	**6**	**10**	**64**	**0**	**0**	**1**	**62**	**6.5**	**-2**	**613**	**50.2**	**11:58**	**5**	**0**	**0**	**0**	**4**	**0**	**0**	**0**	**5:25**
2003-04	**Atlanta**	**NHL**	**66**	**10**	**15**	**25**	**73**	**1**	**0**	**2**	**97**	**10.3**	**0**	**668**	**49.1**	**16:00**	....	....	....	....	....	....	....	....	....
2004-05	Geneve	Swiss	6	2	1	3	8	....	....	....	....	....	....	....	....	....	3	1	2	3	2	....	....	....	....
2005-06	**Atlanta**	**NHL**	**74**	**7**	**17**	**24**	**79**	**1**	**0**	**0**	**82**	**8.5**	**-4**	**468**	**45.9**	**11:06**	....	....	....	....	....	....	....	....	....
2006-07	Geneve	Swiss	40	21	29	50	50	....	....	....	....	....	....	....	....	....	5	1	2	3	8	....	....	....	....
	NHL Totals		**374**	**44**	**64**	**108**	**361**	**3**	**0**	**7**	**452**	**9.7**		**3955**	**50.0**	**13:53**	**22**	**0**	**1**	**1**	**10**	**0**	**0**	**0**	**5:10**

AHL First All-Star Team (2000)

Signed as a free agent by **Hershey** (AHL), July 24, 1998. Signed as a free agent by **Colorado**, December 22, 1998. Signed as a free agent by **Columbus**, July 11, 2000. Signed as a free agent by **Colorado**, August 27, 2002. Claimed by **Atlanta** from **Colorado** in Waiver Draft, October 3, 2003. Signed as a free agent by **Geneve** (Swiss), July 31, 2006.

AUCOIN, Adrian

(oh-KOIN, AY-dree-uhn) **CGY.**

Defense. Shoots right. 6'2", 215 lbs. Born, Ottawa, Ont., July 3, 1973. Vancouver's 7th choice, 117th overall, in 1992 Entry Draft.

Season	Club	League	GP	G	A	Pts	PIM	PP	SH	GW	S	%	+/-	TF	F%	Min	GP	G	A	Pts	PIM	PP	SH	GW	Min
1989-90	Nepean Raiders	CJHL	54	2	14	16	95	....	....	....	....	....	....	....	....	....	4	0	1	1	....	....	....	....	....
1990-91	Nepean Raiders	CJHL	56	17	33	50	125	....	....	....	....	....	....	....	....	....	....	....	....	....	....	....	....	....	....
1991-92	Boston University	H-East	32	2	10	12	60	....	....	....	....	....	....	....	....	....	....	....	....	....	....	....	....	....	....
1992-93	Canada	Nat-Tm	42	8	10	18	71	....	....	....	....	....	....	....	....	....	....	....	....	....	....	....	....	....	....
1993-94	Canada	Nat-Tm	59	5	12	17	80	....	....	....	....	....	....	....	....	....	....	....	....	....	....	....	....	....	....
	Canada	Olympics	4	0	0	0	2	....	....	....	....	....	....	....	....	....	....	....	....	....	....	....	....	....	....
	Hamilton	AHL	13	1	2	3	19	....	....	....	....	....	....	....	....	....	4	0	2	2	6	....	....	....	....
1994-95	Syracuse Crunch	AHL	71	13	18	31	52	....	....	....	....	....	....	....	....	....	....	....	....	....	....	....	....	....	....
	Vancouver	**NHL**	**1**	**1**	**0**	**1**	**0**	**0**	**0**	**0**	**2**	**50.0**	**1**	....	....	....	**4**	**1**	**0**	**1**	**0**	**1**	**0**	**0**	....
1995-96	**Vancouver**	**NHL**	**49**	**4**	**14**	**18**	**34**	**2**	**0**	**0**	**85**	**4.7**	**8**	....	....	....	**6**	**0**	**0**	**0**	**2**	**0**	**0**	**0**	....
	Syracuse Crunch	AHL	29	5	13	18	47	....	....	....	....	....	....	....	....	....	....	....	....	....	....	....	....	....	....
1996-97	**• Vancouver**	**NHL**	**70**	**5**	**16**	**21**	**63**	**1**	**0**	**0**	**116**	**4.3**	**0**	....	....	....	....	....	....	....	....	....	....	....	....
1997-98	**Vancouver**	**NHL**	**35**	**3**	**3**	**6**	**21**	**1**	**0**	**1**	**44**	**6.8**	**-4**	....	....	....	....	....	....	....	....	....	....	....	....
1998-99	**Vancouver**	**NHL**	**82**	**23**	**11**	**34**	**77**	**18**	**2**	**3**	**174**	**13.2**	**-14**	**1**	**100.0**	**23:52**	....	....	....	....	....	....	....	....	....
99-2000	**Vancouver**	**NHL**	**57**	**10**	**14**	**24**	**30**	**4**	**0**	**1**	**126**	**7.9**	**7**	**0**	**0.0**	**23:06**	....	....	....	....	....	....	....	....	....
2000-01	**Vancouver**	**NHL**	**47**	**3**	**13**	**16**	**20**	**1**	**0**	**0**	**99**	**3.0**	**13**	**0**	**0.0**	**18:21**	....	....	....	....	....	....	....	....	....
	Tampa Bay	**NHL**	**26**	**1**	**11**	**12**	**25**	**1**	**0**	**0**	**60**	**1.7**	**-8**	**0**	**0.0**	**23:34**	....	....	....	....	....	....	....	....	....
2001-02	**NY Islanders**	**NHL**	**81**	**12**	**22**	**34**	**62**	**7**	**0**	**1**	**232**	**5.2**	**23**	**0**	**0.0**	**28:54**	**7**	**2**	**5**	**7**	**4**	**2**	**0**	**0**	**32:19**
2002-03	**NY Islanders**	**NHL**	**73**	**8**	**27**	**35**	**70**	**5**	**0**	**1**	**175**	**4.6**	**-5**	**0**	**0.0**	**29:01**	**5**	**1**	**2**	**3**	**4**	**0**	**0**	**0**	**31:43**
2003-04	**NY Islanders**	**NHL**	**81**	**13**	**31**	**44**	**54**	**4**	**0**	**2**	**213**	**6.1**	**29**	**0**	**0.0**	**26:38**	**5**	**0**	**0**	**0**	**6**	**0**	**0**	**0**	**28:21**
2004-05	MODO	Sweden	14	2	4	6	32	....	....	....	....	....	....	....	....	....	6	1	0	1	16	....	....	....	....
2005-06	**Chicago**	**NHL**	**33**	**1**	**5**	**6**	**38**	**1**	**0**	**0**	**59**	**1.7**	**-13**	**0**	**0.0**	**22:58**	....	....	....	....	....	....	....	....	....
2006-07	**Chicago**	**NHL**	**59**	**4**	**12**	**16**	**50**	**2**	**0**	**3**	**96**	**4.2**	**-22**	**0**	**0.0**	**20:50**	....	....	....	....	....	....	....	....	....
	NHL Totals		**694**	**88**	**179**	**267**	**544**	**47**	**2**	**12**	**1481**	**5.9**		**1**	**100.0**	**24:46**	**27**	**4**	**7**	**11**	**16**	**3**	**0**	**0**	**30:58**

Played in NHL All-Star Game (2004)

• Missed majority of 1997-98 season recovering from ankle (October 4, 1997 vs. Anaheim) and groin (November 1, 1997 vs. Pittsburgh) injuries. Traded to **Tampa Bay** by **Vancouver** with Vancouver's 2nd round choice (Alexander Polushin) in 2001 Entry Draft for Dan Cloutier, February 7, 2001. Traded to **NY Islanders** by **Tampa Bay** with Alexander Kharitonov for Mathieu Biron and NY Islanders' 2nd round choice (later traded to Washington – later traded to Vancouver – Vancouver selected Denis Grot) in 2002 Entry Draft, June 22, 2001. Signed as a free agent by **MODO** (Sweden), December 21, 2004. Signed as a free agent by **Chicago**, August 2, 2005. Traded to **Calgary** by **Chicago** with Chicago's 7th round choice (C.J. Severyn) in 2007 Entry Draft for Andrei Zyuzin and Steve Marr, June 22, 2007.

AUCOIN, Keith

(oh-KOIN, KEETH) **CAR.**

Center. Shoots right. 5'9", 187 lbs. Born, Waltham, MA, November 6, 1978.

			Regular Season														Playoffs								
Season	Club	League	GP	G	A	Pts	PIM	PP	SH	GW	S	%	+/-	TF	F%	Min	GP	G	A	Pts	PIM	PP	SH	GW	Min
1997-98	Norwich U.	ECAC-3	26	19	14	33	....	....	....	....	....	....	....	....	....	....	....	....	....	....	....	....	....	....	....
1998-99	Norwich U.	ECAC-3	31	33	39	72	....	....	....	....	....	....	....	....	....	....	....	....	....	....	....	....	....	....	....
99-2000	Norwich U.	ECAC-3	31	36	41	77	14	....	....	....	....	....	....	....	....	....	....	....	....	....	....	....	....	....	....
2000-01	Norwich U.	ECAC-3	28	26	30	56	26	....	....	....	....	....	....	....	....	....	....	....	....	....	....	....	....	....	....
2001-02	Lowell	AHL	30	6	10	16	8	....	....	....	....	....	....	....	....	....	....	....	....	....	....	....	....	....	....
	Florida Everblades	ECHL	1	0	2	2	0	....	....	....	....	....	....	....	....	....	....	....	....	....	....	....	....	....	....
	BC Icemen	UHL	44	23	35	58	42	....	....	....	....	....	....	....	....	....	10	3	5	8	4	....	....	....	....
2002-03	Providence Bruins	AHL	78	25	49	74	71	....	....	....	....	....	....	....	....	....	4	0	1	1	6	....	....	....	....
2003-04	Cincinnati	AHL	80	18	30	48	64	....	....	....	....	....	....	....	....	....	9	0	3	3	4	....	....	....	....
2004-05	Memphis	CHL	5	4	5	9	10	....	....	....	....	....	....	....	....	....	....	....	....	....	....	....	....	....	....
	Providence Bruins	AHL	72	21	45	66	49	....	....	....	....	....	....	....	....	....	17	4	*14	18	18	....	....	....	....
2005-06	**Carolina**	**NHL**	**7**	**0**	**1**	**1**	**4**	**0**	**0**	**0**	**3**	**0.0**	**–4**	**4**	**100.0**	**5:19**	....	....	....	....	....	....	....	....	....
	Lowell	AHL	72	29	56	85	68	....	....	....	....	....	....	....	....	....	....	....	....	....	....	....	....	....	....
2006-07	**Carolina**	**NHL**	**8**	**0**	**1**	**1**	**0**	**0**	**0**	**0**	**6**	**0.0**	**1**	**29**	**65.5**	**6:17**	....	....	....	....	....	....	....	....	....
	Albany River Rats	AHL	65	27	72	99	108	....	....	....	....	....	....	....	....	....	5	1	3	4	7	....	....	....	....
	NHL Totals		**15**	**0**	**2**	**2**	**4**	**0**	**0**	**0**	**9**	**0.0**		**33**	**69.7**	**5:50**	....	....	....	....	....	....	....	....	....

ECAC-3 First All-Star Team (2000, 2001) • ECAC-3 Player of the Year (2000, 2001) • AHL Second All-Star Team (2006, 2007)

Signed as a free agent by **Lowell** (AHL), June 19, 2001. Signed as a free agent by **Providence** (AHL), August 2, 2002. Signed as a free agent by **Anaheim**, August 29, 2003. Signed to a PTO (tryout) contract by **Providence** (AHL), November 4, 2004, Signed as a free agent by **Providence** (AHL), December 9, 2004. Signed as a free agent by **Carolina**, August 4, 2005.

AVERY, Sean

(AY-vuhr-ee, SHAWN) **NYR**

Center. Shoots left. 5'10", 195 lbs. Born, Pickering, Ont., April 10, 1980.

Season	Club	League	GP	G	A	Pts	PIM	PP	SH	GW	S	%	+/-	TF	F%	Min	GP	G	A	Pts	PIM	PP	SH	GW	Min
1995-96	Markham	Minor-ON	70	34	81	115	180	....	....	....	....	....	....	....	....	....	....	....	....	....	....	....	....	....	....
	Markham Waxers	MTJHL	1	0	0	0	4	....	....	....	....	....	....	....	....	....	....	....	....	....	....	....	....	....	....
1996-97	Owen Sound	OHL	58	10	21	31	86	....	....	....	....	....	....	....	....	....	4	1	0	1	4	....	....	....	....
1997-98	Owen Sound	OHL	47	13	41	54	105	....	....	....	....	....	....	....	....	....	....	....	....	....	....	....	....	....	....
1998-99	Owen Sound	OHL	28	22	23	45	70	....	....	....	....	....	....	....	....	....	....	....	....	....	....	....	....	....	....
	Kingston	OHL	33	14	25	39	88	....	....	....	....	....	....	....	....	....	5	1	3	4	13	....	....	....	....
99-2000	Kingston	OHL	55	28	56	84	215	....	....	....	....	....	....	....	....	....	5	2	2	4	26	....	....	....	....
2000-01	Cincinnati	AHL	58	8	15	23	304	....	....	....	....	....	....	....	....	....	4	1	0	1	19	....	....	....	....
2001-02	**Detroit**	**NHL**	**36**	**2**	**2**	**4**	**68**	**0**	**0**	**1**	**30**	**6.7**	**1**	**299**	**51.8**	**7:51**	....	....	....	....	....	....	....	....	....
	Cincinnati	AHL	36	14	7	21	106	....	....	....	....	....	....	....	....	....	....	....	....	....	....	....	....	....	....
2002-03	**Detroit**	**NHL**	**39**	**5**	**6**	**11**	**120**	**0**	**0**	**2**	**40**	**12.5**	**7**	**224**	**58.0**	**7:03**	....	....	....	....	....	....	....	....	....
	Grand Rapids	AHL	15	6	6	12	82	....	....	....	....	....	....	....	....	....	....	....	....	....	....	....	....	....	....
	Los Angeles	**NHL**	**12**	**1**	**3**	**4**	**33**	**0**	**0**	**0**	**19**	**5.3**	**0**	**49**	**46.9**	**13:50**	....	....	....	....	....	....	....	....	....
	Manchester	AHL	....	....	....	....	....	....	....	....	....	....	....	....	....	....	3	2	1	3	8	....	....	....	....
2003-04	**Los Angeles**	**NHL**	**76**	**9**	**19**	**28**	***261**	**0**	**0**	**2**	**125**	**7.2**	**2**	**124**	**54.8**	**11:41**	....	....	....	....	....	....	....	....	....
2004-05	Pelicans Lahti	Finland	2	3	0	3	26	....	....	....	....	....	....	....	....	....	....	....	....	....	....	....	....	....	....
	Motor City	UHL	16	15	11	26	149	....	....	....	....	....	....	....	....	....	....	....	....	....	....	....	....	....	....
2005-06	**Los Angeles**	**NHL**	**75**	**15**	**24**	**39**	***257**	**1**	**3**	**1**	**189**	**7.9**	**–5**	**226**	**44.3**	**13:37**	....	....	....	....	....	....	....	....	....
2006-07	**Los Angeles**	**NHL**	**55**	**10**	**18**	**28**	**116**	**1**	**1**	**2**	**160**	**6.3**	**–10**	**180**	**47.2**	**16:52**	....	....	....	....	....	....	....	....	....
	NY Rangers	**NHL**	**29**	**8**	**12**	**20**	**58**	**1**	**0**	**0**	**89**	**9.0**	**11**	**110**	**52.7**	**17:49**	**10**	**1**	**4**	**5**	**27**	**0**	**0**	**0**	**19:27**
	NHL Totals		**322**	**50**	**84**	**134**	**913**	**3**	**4**	**8**	**652**	**7.7**		**1212**	**51.1**	**12:40**	**10**	**1**	**4**	**5**	**27**	**0**	**0**	**0**	**19:27**

Signed as a free agent by **Detroit**, September 21, 1999. Traded to **Los Angeles** by **Detroit** with Maxim Kuznetsov, Detroit's 1st round choice (Jeff Tambellini) in 2003 Entry Draft and Detroit's 2nd round choice (later traded to Boston – Boston selected Martins Karsums) in 2004 Entry Draft for Mathieu Schneider, March 11, 2003. Signed as a free agent by **Lahti** (Finland), November 24, 2004. Signed as a free agent by **Motor City** (UHL), February 11, 2005. Traded to **NY Rangers** by **Los Angeles** with John Seymour and future considerations for Jason Ward, Jan Marek, Marc-Andre Cliche and future considerations, February 5, 2007.

AXELSSON, P.J.

(AHX-ehl-suhn, PEE-JAY) **BOS.**

Left wing. Shoots left. 6'1", 175 lbs. Born, Kungalv, Sweden, February 26, 1975. Boston's 7th choice, 177th overall, in 1995 Entry Draft.

Season	Club	League	GP	G	A	Pts	PIM	PP	SH	GW	S	%	+/-	TF	F%	Min	GP	G	A	Pts	PIM	PP	SH	GW	Min
1992-93	V.Frolunda Jr.	Swe-Jr.	16	9	5	14	12	....	....	....	....	....	....	....	....	....	....	....	....	....	....	....	....	....	....
	V.Frolunda	Sweden	1	0	0	0	0	....	....	....	....	....	....	....	....	....	....	....	....	....	....	....	....	....	....
1993-94	V.Frolunda	Sweden	11	0	0	0	4	....	....	....	....	....	....	....	....	....	4	0	0	0	0	....	....	....	....
1994-95	V.Frolunda Jr.	Swe-Jr.	19	16	9	25	22	....	....	....	....	....	....	....	....	....	....	....	....	....	....	....	....	....	....
	V.Frolunda	Sweden	11	2	1	3	6	....	....	....	....	....	....	....	....	....	5	0	0	0	0	....	....	....	....
1995-96	V.Frolunda	Sweden	36	15	5	20	10	....	....	....	....	....	....	....	....	....	13	3	0	3	10	....	....	....	....
1996-97	V.Frolunda	Sweden	50	19	15	34	34	....	....	....	....	....	....	....	....	....	3	0	2	2	0	....	....	....	....
	V.Frolunda	EuroHL	3	1	1	2	0	....	....	....	....	....	....	....	....	....	3	0	0	0	2	....	....	....	....
1997-98	**Boston**	**NHL**	**82**	**8**	**19**	**27**	**38**	**2**	**0**	**1**	**144**	**5.6**	**–14**	....	....	....	**6**	**1**	**0**	**1**	**0**	**0**	**0**	**0**	....
1998-99	**Boston**	**NHL**	**77**	**7**	**10**	**17**	**18**	**0**	**0**	**2**	**146**	**4.8**	**–14**	**8**	**75.0**	**16:38**	**12**	**1**	**1**	**2**	**4**	**0**	**0**	**0**	**15:11**
99-2000	**Boston**	**NHL**	**81**	**10**	**16**	**26**	**24**	**0**	**0**	**4**	**186**	**5.4**	**1**	**22**	**27.3**	**16:43**	....	....	....	....	....	....	....	....	....
2000-01	**Boston**	**NHL**	**81**	**8**	**15**	**23**	**27**	**0**	**0**	**2**	**146**	**5.5**	**–12**	**41**	**36.6**	**12:30**	....	....	....	....	....	....	....	....	....
2001-02	**Boston**	**NHL**	**78**	**7**	**17**	**24**	**16**	**0**	**2**	**0**	**127**	**5.5**	**6**	**17**	**35.3**	**14:42**	**6**	**2**	**1**	**3**	**6**	**0**	**1**	**1**	**16:48**
	Sweden	Olympics	4	0	0	0	2	....	....	....	....	....	....	....	....	....	....	....	....	....	....	....	....	....	....
2002-03	**Boston**	**NHL**	**66**	**17**	**19**	**36**	**24**	**2**	**2**	**1**	**122**	**13.9**	**8**	**17**	**23.5**	**16:37**	**5**	**0**	**0**	**0**	**6**	**0**	**0**	**0**	**13:23**
2003-04	**Boston**	**NHL**	**68**	**6**	**14**	**20**	**42**	**0**	**0**	**1**	**107**	**5.6**	**2**	**13**	**15.4**	**16:19**	**7**	**0**	**0**	**0**	**4**	**0**	**0**	**0**	**14:43**
2004-05	Frolunda	Sweden	45	8	9	17	95	....	....	....	....	....	....	....	....	....	14	1	*10	11	18	....	....	....	....
2005-06	**Boston**	**NHL**	**59**	**10**	**18**	**28**	**4**	**1**	**2**	**1**	**113**	**8.8**	**–3**	**27**	**40.7**	**17:36**	....	....	....	....	....	....	....	....	....
	Sweden	Olympics	8	3	3	6	0	....	....	....	....	....	....	....	....	....	....	....	....	....	....	....	....	....	....
2006-07	**Boston**	**NHL**	**55**	**11**	**16**	**27**	**52**	**3**	**2**	**0**	**81**	**13.6**	**–10**	**38**	**34.2**	**19:34**	....	....	....	....	....	....	....	....	....
	NHL Totals		**647**	**84**	**144**	**228**	**245**	**8**	**8**	**12**	**1172**	**7.2**		**183**	**34.4**	**16:08**	**36**	**4**	**2**	**6**	**20**	**0**	**1**	**1**	**15:06**

Signed as a free agent by **Frolunda** (Sweden), September 15, 2004.

BABCHUK, Anton

(bab-CHUHK, AN-tawn) **CAR.**

Defense. Shoots right. 6'5", 212 lbs. Born, Kiev, USSR, May 6, 1984. Chicago's 1st choice, 21st overall, in 2002 Entry Draft.

Season	Club	League	GP	G	A	Pts	PIM	PP	SH	GW	S	%	+/-	TF	F%	Min	GP	G	A	Pts	PIM	PP	SH	GW	Min
99-2000	Elektrostal 2	Russia-3	6	0	0	0	8	....	....	....	....	....	....	....	....	....	....	....	....	....	....	....	....	....	....
	Elektrostal 2	Russia-3	18	0	1	1	18	....	....	....	....	....	....	....	....	....	....	....	....	....	....	....	....	....	....
2000-01	Elektrostal	Russia-2	7	0	0	0	12	....	....	....	....	....	....	....	....	....	....	....	....	....	....	....	....	....	....
	Russia 17	Nat-Tm	15	1	3	4	12	....	....	....	....	....	....	....	....	....	....	....	....	....	....	....	....	....	....
2001-02	Elektrostal	Russia-2	40	7	8	15	90	....	....	....	....	....	....	....	....	....	....	....	....	....	....	....	....	....	....
	Elektrostal 2	Russia-3	3	0	0	0	8	....	....	....	....	....	....	....	....	....	....	....	....	....	....	....	....	....	....
2002-03	Ak Bars Kazan	Russia	10	0	0	0	4	....	....	....	....	....	....	....	....	....	....	....	....	....	....	....	....	....	....
	St. Petersburg	Russia	20	3	0	3	10	....	....	....	....	....	....	....	....	....	....	....	....	....	....	....	....	....	....
	Spartak St. Pet.	Russia-2	1	1	0	1	0	....	....	....	....	....	....	....	....	....	....	....	....	....	....	....	....	....	....
2003-04	**Chicago**	**NHL**	**5**	**0**	**2**	**2**	**2**	**0**	**0**	**0**	**11**	**0.0**	**–1**	**0**	**0.0**	**12:43**	....	....	....	....	....	....	....	....	....
	Norfolk Admirals	AHL	73	8	14	22	89	....	....	....	....	....	....	....	....	....	8	0	2	2	6	....	....	....	....
2004-05	Norfolk Admirals	AHL	66	8	16	24	88	....	....	....	....	....	....	....	....	....	2	0	0	0	2	....	....	....	....
2005-06	**Chicago**	**NHL**	**17**	**2**	**3**	**5**	**16**	**1**	**0**	**0**	**24**	**8.3**	**–5**	**0**	**0.0**	**16:38**	....	....	....	....	....	....	....	....	....
	Norfolk Admirals	AHL	24	5	7	12	22	....	....	....	....	....	....	....	....	....	....	....	....	....	....	....	....	....	....
	♦ **Carolina**	**NHL**	**22**	**3**	**2**	**5**	**6**	**2**	**0**	**0**	**32**	**9.4**	**–2**	**0**	**0.0**	**13:22**	....	....	....	....	....	....	....	....	....
	Lowell	AHL	5	1	3	4	0	....	....	....	....	....	....	....	....	....	....	....	....	....	....	....	....	....	....
2006-07	**Carolina**	**NHL**	**52**	**2**	**12**	**14**	**30**	**0**	**0**	**2**	**63**	**3.2**	**–6**	**0**	**0.0**	**17:26**	....	....	....	....	....	....	....	....	....
	Albany River Rats	AHL	9	1	6	7	2	....	....	....	....	....	....	....	....	....	....	....	....	....	....	....	....	....	....
	NHL Totals		**96**	**7**	**19**	**26**	**54**	**3**	**0**	**2**	**130**	**5.4**		**0**	**0.0**	**16:07**	....	....	....	....	....	....	....	....	....

Traded to **Carolina** by **Chicago** for Danny Richmond and Columbus' 4th round choice (previously acquired, later traded to Toronto - Toronto selected James Reimer) in 2006 Entry Draft, January 20, 2006.

BACKES, David

(BA-kuhs, DAY-vihd) **ST.L.**

Center. Shoots right. 6'3", 200 lbs. Born, Blaine, MN, May 1, 1984. St. Louis' 2nd choice, 62nd overall, in 2003 Entry Draft.

			Regular Season														Playoffs								
Season	Club	League	GP	G	A	Pts	PIM	PP	SH	GW	S	%	+/-	TF	F%	Min	GP	G	A	Pts	PIM	PP	SH	GW	Min
99-2000	Spring Lake Park	High-MN	24	17	20	37	....	....	....	....	....	....	....	....	....	....	....	....	....	....	....	....	....	....	....
2000-01	Spring Lake Park	High-MN	24	29	46	75	....	....	....	....	....	....	....	....	....	....	....	....	....	....	....	....	....	....	....
2001-02	Chicago Steel	USHL	25	31	36	67	....	....	....	....	....	....	....	....	....	....	2	1	1	2	....	....	....	....	....
	Lincoln Stars	USHL	30	11	10	21	54	....	....	....	....	....	....	....	....	....	3	0	0	0	2	....	....	....	....
2002-03	Lincoln Stars	USHL	57	28	41	69	126	....	....	....	....	....	....	....	....	....	7	4	1	5	17	....	....	....	....
2003-04	Minnesota State	WCHA	39	16	21	37	66	....	....	....	....	....	....	....	....	....	....	....	....	....	....	....	....	....	....
2004-05	Minnesota State	WCHA	38	17	23	40	55	....	....	....	....	....	....	....	....	....	....	....	....	....	....	....	....	....	....
2005-06	Minnesota State	WCHA	38	13	29	42	91	....	....	....	....	....	....	....	....	....	....	....	....	....	....	....	....	....	....
	Peoria Rivermen	AHL	12	5	5	10	10	....	....	....	....	....	....	....	....	....	3	1	1	2	8	....	....	....	....
2006-07	**St. Louis**	**NHL**	**49**	**10**	**13**	**23**	**37**	**2**	**0**	**2**	**89**	**11.2**	**6**	**26**	**46.2**	**13:25**	....	....	....	....	....	....	....	....	....
	Peoria Rivermen	AHL	31	10	3	13	47	....	....	....	....	....	....	....	....	....	....	....	....	....	....	....	....	....	....
	NHL Totals		**49**	**10**	**13**	**23**	**37**	**2**	**0**	**2**	**89**	**11.2**		**26**	**46.2**	**13:25**	....	....	....	....	....	....	....	....	....

USHL First All-Star Team (2003) • WCHA All-Rookie Team (2004) • WCHA Second All-Star Team (2006) • NCAA West Second All-American Team (2006)

BACKMAN, Christian

(BAK-man, KRIH-stan) **ST.L.**

Defense. Shoots left. 6'4", 206 lbs. Born, Alingsas, Sweden, April 28, 1980. St. Louis' 1st choice, 24th overall, in 1998 Entry Draft.

Season	Club	League	GP	G	A	Pts	PIM	PP	SH	GW	S	%	+/-	TF	F%	Min	GP	G	A	Pts	PIM	PP	SH	GW	Min
1996-97	V.Frolunda Jr.	Swe-Jr.	26	2	5	7	16	....	....	....	....	....	....	....	....	....	....	....	....	....	....	....	....	....	....
1997-98	V.Frolunda U18	Swe-U18	4	4	1	5	2	....	....	....	....	....	....	....	....	....	5	2	2	4	2	....	....	....	....
	V.Frolunda Jr.	Swe-Jr.	28	5	14	19	12	....	....	....	....	....	....	....	....	....	2	0	1	1	4	....	....	....	....
1998-99	V.Frolunda Jr.	Swe-Jr.	4	0	2	2	4	....	....	....	....	....	....	....	....	....	....	....	....	....	....	....	....	....	....
	V.Frolunda	Sweden	49	0	4	4	4	....	....	....	....	....	....	....	....	....	4	0	0	0	0	....	....	....	....
99-2000	V.Frolunda Jr.	Swe-Jr.	5	1	1	2	0	....	....	....	....	....	....	....	....	....	3	1	1	2	0	....	....	....	....
	Gislaveds SK	Sweden-2	21	5	2	7	8	....	....	....	....	....	....	....	....	....	....	....	....	....	....	....	....	....	....
	V.Frolunda	Sweden	27	1	0	1	14	....	....	....	....	....	....	....	....	....	5	0	0	0	0	....	....	....	....
2000-01	V.Frolunda	Sweden	50	1	10	11	32	....	....	....	....	....	....	....	....	....	3	0	2	2	2	....	....	....	....
2001-02	V.Frolunda	Sweden	44	7	4	11	38	....	....	....	....	....	....	....	....	....	10	0	0	0	8	....	....	....	....
2002-03	**St. Louis**	**NHL**	**4**	**0**	**0**	**0**	**0**	**0**	**0**	**0**	**4**	**0.0**	**–3**	**0**	**0.0**	**12:22**	....	....	....	....	....	....	....	....	....
	Worcester IceCats	AHL	72	8	19	27	66	....	....	....	....	....	....	....	....	....	3	0	1	1	5	....	....	....	....
2003-04	**St. Louis**	**NHL**	**66**	**5**	**13**	**18**	**16**	**1**	**0**	**0**	**92**	**5.4**	**3**	**0**	**0.0**	**19:20**	**5**	**0**	**2**	**2**	**4**	**0**	**0**	**0**	**23:06**
	Worcester IceCats	AHL	4	1	2	3	2	....	....	....	....	....	....	....	....	....	....	....	....	....	....	....	....	....	....
2004-05	Frolunda	Sweden	50	4	15	19	40	....	....	....	....	....	....	....	....	....	14	2	7	9	10	....	....	....	....
2005-06	**St. Louis**	**NHL**	**52**	**6**	**12**	**18**	**48**	**3**	**0**	**1**	**70**	**8.6**	**–15**	**0**	**0.0**	**24:49**	....	....	....	....	....	....	....	....	....
	Sweden	Olympics	8	1	2	3	6	....	....	....	....	....	....	....	....	....	....	....	....	....	....	....	....	....	....
2006-07	**St. Louis**	**NHL**	**61**	**7**	**11**	**18**	**36**	**1**	**0**	**0**	**80**	**8.8**	**13**	**0**	**0.0**	**22:10**	....	....	....	....	....	....	....	....	....
	NHL Totals		**183**	**18**	**36**	**54**	**100**	**5**	**0**	**1**	**246**	**7.3**		**0**	**0.0**	**21:41**	**5**	**0**	**2**	**2**	**4**	**0**	**0**	**0**	**23:06**

Signed as a free agent by **Frolunda** (Sweden), September 15, 2004.

BALASTIK, Jaroslav

(ba-LASH-tihk, YAHR-roh-slav)

Right wing. Shoots left. 6'2", 205 lbs. Born, Gottwaldov, Czech., November 28, 1979. Columbus' 9th choice, 184th overall, in 2002 Entry Draft.

Season	Club	League	GP	G	A	Pts	PIM	PP	SH	GW	S	%	+/-	TF	F%	Min	GP	G	A	Pts	PIM	PP	SH	GW	Min
1996-97	AC ZPS Zlin Jr.	CzRep-Jr.	45	27	24	51	....	....	....	....	....	....	....	....	....	....	....	....	....	....	....	....	....	....	....
1997-98	HC ZPS Zlin Jr.	CzRep-Jr.	36	21	35	56	....	....	....	....	....	....	....	....	....	....	7	2	3	5	....	....	....	....	....
	Zlin	CzRep	6	0	2	2	....	....	....	....	....	....	....	....	....	....	....	....	....	....	....	....	....	....	....
1998-99	HC ZPS Zlin Jr.	CzRep-Jr.	....	....	....	....	....	....	....	....	....	....	....	....	....	....	2	0	0	0	....	....	....	....	....
	Zlin	CzRep	41	4	8	12	12	....	....	....	....	....	....	....	....	....	9	1	0	1	27	....	....	....	....
99-2000	HC Zlin Jr.	CzRep-Jr.	4	5	5	10	2	....	....	....	....	....	....	....	....	....	....	....	....	....	....	....	....	....	....
	Zlin	CzRep	48	7	10	17	0	....	....	....	....	....	....	....	....	....	4	0	1	1	2	....	....	....	....
2000-01	Zlin	CzRep	52	8	17	25	32	....	....	....	....	....	....	....	....	....	6	1	1	2	6	....	....	....	....
2001-02	Zlin	CzRep	50	25	19	44	32	....	....	....	....	....	....	....	....	....	11	3	5	8	14	....	....	....	....
2002-03	HC Hame Zlin	CzRep	31	14	8	22	26	....	....	....	....	....	....	....	....	....	....	....	....	....	....	....	....	....	....
	HPK Hameenlinna	Finland	13	5	7	12	2	....	....	....	....	....	....	....	....	....	13	4	3	7	6	....	....	....	....
2003-04	HC Hame Zlin	CzRep	51	*29	18	47	54	....	....	....	....	....	....	....	....	....	17	*9	9	*18	32	....	....	....	....
2004-05	HC Hame Zlin	CzRep	52	*30	16	46	74	....	....	....	....	....	....	....	....	....	17	4	9	13	*52	....	....	....	....
2005-06	**Columbus**	**NHL**	**66**	**12**	**10**	**22**	**26**	**7**	**0**	**2**	**158**	**7.6**	**–1**	**5**	**20.0**	**12:50**	....	....	....	....	....	....	....	....	....
	Syracuse Crunch	AHL	14	3	3	6	6	....	....	....	....	....	....	....	....	....	....	....	....	....	....	....	....	....	....
2006-07	**Columbus**	**NHL**	**8**	**1**	**1**	**2**	**4**	**1**	**0**	**0**	**6**	**16.7**	**–3**	**0**	**0.0**	**8:10**	....	....	....	....	....	....	....	....	....
	Syracuse Crunch	AHL	6	2	3	5	6	....	....	....	....	....	....	....	....	....	....	....	....	....	....	....	....	....	....
	HV 71 Jonkoping	Sweden	25	3	10	13	4	....	....	....	....	....	....	....	....	....	14	5	2	7	34	....	....	....	....
	NHL Totals		**74**	**13**	**11**	**24**	**30**	**8**	**0**	**2**	**164**	**7.9**		**5**	**20.0**	**12:20**	....	....	....	....	....	....	....	....	....

• Assigned to **Jonkoping** (Finland) by **Columbus**, December 13, 2006.

BALEJ, Jozef

(BAH-lay, YOH-zehf) **VAN.**

Right wing. Shoots right. 6'1", 195 lbs. Born, Myjava, Czech., February 22, 1982. Montreal's 3rd choice, 78th overall, in 2000 Entry Draft.

Season	Club	League	GP	G	A	Pts	PIM	PP	SH	GW	S	%	+/-	TF	F%	Min	GP	G	A	Pts	PIM	PP	SH	GW	Min
1996-97	Dukla Trencin Jr.	Slovak-Jr.	51	31	25	56	36	....	....	....	....	....	....	....	....	....	....	....	....	....	....	....	....	....	....
1997-98	Dukla Trencin Jr.	Slovak-Jr.	52	57	40	97	60	....	....	....	....	....	....	....	....	....	....	....	....	....	....	....	....	....	....
1998-99	Thunder Bay	USHL	38	8	7	15	9	....	....	....	....	....	....	....	....	....	....	....	....	....	....	....	....	....	....
	Rochester	USHL	17	0	1	1	2	....	....	....	....	....	....	....	....	....	....	....	....	....	....	....	....	....	....
99-2000	Portland	WHL	65	22	23	45	33	....	....	....	....	....	....	....	....	....	....	....	....	....	....	....	....	....	....
2000-01	Portland	WHL	46	32	21	53	18	....	....	....	....	....	....	....	....	....	16	9	6	15	6	....	....	....	....
2001-02	Portland	WHL	65	51	41	92	52	....	....	....	....	....	....	....	....	....	7	0	2	2	6	....	....	....	....
2002-03	Hamilton	AHL	56	5	15	20	29	....	....	....	....	....	....	....	....	....	....	....	....	....	....	....	....	....	....
2003-04	**Montreal**	**NHL**	**4**	**0**	**0**	**0**	**0**	**0**	**0**	**0**	**4**	**0.0**	**–1**	**2**	**50.0**	**12:38**	....	....	....	....	....	....	....	....	....
	Hamilton	AHL	55	25	33	58	32	....	....	....	....	....	....	....	....	....	....	....	....	....	....	....	....	....	....
	NY Rangers	**NHL**	**13**	**1**	**4**	**5**	**4**	**0**	**0**	**0**	**25**	**4.0**	**0**	**1**	**0.0**	**13:06**	....	....	....	....	....	....	....	....	....
	Hartford	AHL	5	1	3	4	21	....	....	....	....	....	....	....	....	....	16	9	7	16	10	....	....	....	....
2004-05	Hartford	AHL	69	20	22	42	46	....	....	....	....	....	....	....	....	....	6	0	0	0	4	....	....	....	....
2005-06	**Vancouver**	**NHL**	**1**	**0**	**1**	**1**	**0**	**0**	**0**	**0**	**3**	**0.0**	**1**	**0**	**0.0**	**7:56**	....	....	....	....	....	....	....	....	....
	Manitoba Moose	AHL	39	14	15	29	20	....	....	....	....	....	....	....	....	....	4	1	0	1	4	....	....	....	....
2006-07	Fribourg	Swiss	37	13	17	30	44	....	....	....	....	....	....	....	....	....	4	4	1	5	2	....	....	....	....
	NHL Totals		**18**	**1**	**5**	**6**	**4**	**0**	**0**	**0**	**32**	**3.1**		**3**	**33.3**	**12:43**	....	....	....	....	....	....	....	....	....

WHL West First All-Star Team (2002)

Traded to **NY Rangers** by **Montreal** with Montreal's 2nd round choice (Bruce Graham) in 2004 Entry Draft for Alex Kovalev, March 2, 2004. Traded to **Vancouver** by **NY Rangers** with future consdierations for Fedor Fedorov, October 7, 2005. Signed as a free agent by **Fribourg** (Austria), July 24, 2006.

BALLARD, Keith

(BAL-uhrd, KEETH) **PHX.**

Defense. Shoots left. 5'11", 208 lbs. Born, Baudette, MN, November 26, 1982. Buffalo's 1st choice, 11th overall, in 2002 Entry Draft.

Season	Club	League	GP	G	A	Pts	PIM	PP	SH	GW	S	%	+/-	TF	F%	Min	GP	G	A	Pts	PIM	PP	SH	GW	Min
99-2000	USNTDP	U-18	6	1	1	2	4	....	....	....	....	....	....	....	....	....	....	....	....	....	....	....	....	....	....
	USNTDP	USHL	58	12	21	33	119	....	....	....	....	....	....	....	....	....	....	....	....	....	....	....	....	....	....
2000-01	Omaha Lancers	USHL	56	22	29	51	168	....	....	....	....	....	....	....	....	....	10	1	6	7	8	....	....	....	....
2001-02	U. of Minnesota	WCHA	41	10	13	23	42	....	....	....	....	....	....	....	....	....	....	....	....	....	....	....	....	....	....
2002-03	U. of Minnesota	WCHA	41	12	29	41	78	....	....	....	....	....	....	....	....	....	....	....	....	....	....	....	....	....	....
2003-04	U. of Minnesota	WCHA	37	11	25	36	83	....	....	....	....	....	....	....	....	....	....	....	....	....	....	....	....	....	....
2004-05	Utah Grizzlies	AHL	60	2	18	20	88	....	....	....	....	....	....	....	....	....	....	....	....	....	....	....	....	....	....
2005-06	**Phoenix**	**NHL**	**82**	**8**	**31**	**39**	**99**	**1**	**3**	**1**	**102**	**7.8**	**–18**	**0**	**0.0**	**19:59**	....	....	....	....	....	....	....	....	....
2006-07	**Phoenix**	**NHL**	**69**	**5**	**22**	**27**	**59**	**2**	**0**	**0**	**79**	**6.3**	**–7**	**0**	**0.0**	**22:00**	....	....	....	....	....	....	....	....	....
	NHL Totals		**151**	**13**	**53**	**66**	**158**	**3**	**3**	**1**	**181**	**7.2**		**0**	**0.0**	**20:54**	....	....	....	....	....	....	....	....	....

USHL First All-Star Team (2001) • WCHA All-Rookie Team (2002) • WCHA First All-Star Team (2003, 2004) • NCAA West First All-American Team (2004)

Traded to **Colorado** by **Buffalo** for Steve Reinprecht, July 3, 2003. Traded to **Phoenix** by **Colorado** with Derek Morris for Ossi Vaananen, Chris Gratton and Phoenix's 2nd round choice (Paul Stastny) in 2005 Entry Draft, March 9, 2004.

BARCH, Krys

(BAHRCH, KRIHS) **DAL.**

Right wing. Shoots left. 6'2", 200 lbs. Born, Hamilton, Ont., March 26, 1980. Washington's 3rd choice, 106th overall, in 1998 Entry Draft.

			Regular Season														Playoffs								
Season	Club	League	GP	G	A	Pts	PIM	PP	SH	GW	S	%	+/-	TF	F%	Min	GP	G	A	Pts	PIM	PP	SH	GW	Min
1995-96	Georgetown	OPJHL	41	6	8	14	10	....	....	....	....	....	....	....	....	....	....	....	....	....	....	....	....	....	....
1996-97	Georgetown	OPJHL	51	18	26	44	58	....	....	....	....	....	....	....	....	....	....	....	....	....	....	....	....	....	....
1997-98	London Knights	OHL	65	9	27	36	62	....	....	....	....	....	....	....	....	....	16	4	3	7	16	....	....	....	....
1998-99	London Knights	OHL	66	18	20	38	66	....	....	....	....	....	....	....	....	....	25	9	17	26	15	....	....	....	....
99-2000	London Knights	OHL	56	23	26	49	78	....	....	....	....	....	....	....	....	....	....	....	....	....	....	....	....	....	....
	Portland Pirates	AHL	....	....	....	....	....	....	....	....	....	....	....	....	....	....	4	0	2	2	2	....	....	....	....
2000-01	Portland Pirates	AHL	76	10	15	25	91	....	....	....	....	....	....	....	....	....	2	0	0	0	0	....	....	....	....
2001-02	Portland Pirates	AHL	29	3	8	11	28	....	....	....	....	....	....	....	....	....	....	....	....	....	....	....	....	....	....
	Richmond	ECHL	25	6	4	10	43	....	....	....	....	....	....	....	....	....	....	....	....	....	....	....	....	....	....
2002-03	Portland Pirates	AHL	36	1	7	8	49	....	....	....	....	....	....	....	....	....	....	....	....	....	....	....	....	....	....
2003-04			DID NOT PLAY																						
2004-05	Norfolk Admirals	AHL	9	1	0	1	37	....	....	....	....	....	....	....	....	....	....	....	....	....	....	....	....	....	....
	Greenville	ECHL	55	11	19	30	154	....	....	....	....	....	....	....	....	....	3	0	0	0	36	....	....	....	....
2005-06	Iowa Stars	AHL	43	7	6	13	129	....	....	....	....	....	....	....	....	....	7	0	1	1	37	....	....	....	....
	Greenville	ECHL	14	10	4	14	75	....	....	....	....	....	....	....	....	....	....	....	....	....	....	....	....	....	....
2006-07	**Dallas**	**NHL**	26	3	2	5	107	0	0	2	12	25.0	2	1	0.0	5:38	....	....	....	....	....	....	....	....	....
	Iowa Stars	AHL	31	3	5	8	110	....	....	....	....	....	....	....	....	....	....	....	....	....	....	....	....	....	....
	NHL Totals		26	3	2	5	107	0	0	2	12	25.0		1	0.0	5:38	....	....	....	....	....	....	....	....	....

Signed as a free agent by **Dallas**, July 18, 2006.

BARINKA, Michal

(ba-RIHN-kuh, MIGH-kuhl)

Defense. Shoots left. 6'3", 217 lbs. Born, Vyskov, Czech., June 12, 1984. Chicago's 3rd choice, 59th overall, in 2003 Entry Draft.

Season	Club	League	GP	G	A	Pts	PIM	PP	SH	GW	S	%	+/-	TF	F%	Min	GP	G	A	Pts	PIM	PP	SH	GW	Min
99-2000	C. Budejovice U17	CzR-U17	48	1	12	13	26	....	....	....	....	....	....	....	....	....	6	0	2	2	4	....	....	....	....
2000-01	C. Budejovice Jr.	CzRep-Jr.	26	1	8	9	14	....	....	....	....	....	....	....	....	....	3	0	0	0	0	....	....	....	....
	C. Budejovice U17	CzR-U17	7	0	1	1	6	....	....	....	....	....	....	....	....	....	....	....	....	....	....	....	....	....	....
2001-02	C. Budejovice Jr.	CzRep-Jr.	31	3	13	16	60	....	....	....	....	....	....	....	....	....	7	3	4	7	35	....	....	....	....
	C. Budejovice	CzRep	3	0	0	0	0	....	....	....	....	....	....	....	....	....	....	....	....	....	....	....	....	....	....
2002-03	C. Budejovice Jr.	CzRep-Jr.	14	1	5	6	34	....	....	....	....	....	....	....	....	....	....	....	....	....	....	....	....	....	....
	C. Budejovice	CzRep	31	0	1	1	14	....	....	....	....	....	....	....	....	....	4	0	0	0	2	....	....	....	....
2003-04	**Chicago**	**NHL**	9	0	1	1	6	0	0	0	15	0.0	–5	0	0.0	13:48	....	....	....	....	....	....	....	....	....
	Norfolk Admirals	AHL	40	4	2	6	80	....	....	....	....	....	....	....	....	....	....	....	....	....	....	....	....	....	....
2004-05	Norfolk Admirals	AHL	59	1	10	11	77	....	....	....	....	....	....	....	....	....	....	....	....	....	....	....	....	....	....
2005-06	**Chicago**	**NHL**	25	0	1	1	20	0	0	0	19	0.0	–7	1	0.0	14:38	....	....	....	....	....	....	....	....	....
	Norfolk Admirals	AHL	54	1	11	12	86	....	....	....	....	....	....	....	....	....	4	0	0	0	11	....	....	....	....
2006-07	Binghamton	AHL	17	0	2	2	22	....	....	....	....	....	....	....	....	....	....	....	....	....	....	....	....	....	....
	Vitkovice	CzRep	15	3	3	6	18	....	....	....	....	....	....	....	....	....	....	....	....	....	....	....	....	....	....
	NHL Totals		34	0	2	2	26	0	0	0	34	0.0		1	0.0	14:25	....	....	....	....	....	....	....	....	....

Traded to **Ottawa** by **Chicago** with Tom Preissing, Josh Hennessy and Chicago's 2nd round choice in 2008 Entry Draft for Martin Havlat and Bryan Smolinski, July 10, 2006.

BARKER, Cam

(BAR-kuhr, KAM) **CHI.**

Defense. Shoots left. 6'3", 222 lbs. Born, Winnipeg, Man., April 4, 1986. Chicago's 1st choice, 3rd overall, in 2004 Entry Draft.

Season	Club	League	GP	G	A	Pts	PIM	PP	SH	GW	S	%	+/-	TF	F%	Min	GP	G	A	Pts	PIM	PP	SH	GW	Min
2001-02	Cornwall Colts	CJHL	72	6	23	29	132	....	....	....	....	....	....	....	....	....	....	....	....	....	....	....	....	....	....
	Medicine Hat	WHL	3	0	1	1	0	....	....	....	....	....	....	....	....	....	....	....	....	....	....	....	....	....	....
2002-03	Medicine Hat	WHL	64	10	37	47	79	....	....	....	....	....	....	....	....	....	11	3	4	7	17	....	....	....	....
2003-04	Medicine Hat	WHL	69	21	44	65	105	....	....	....	....	....	....	....	....	....	20	3	9	12	18	....	....	....	....
2004-05	Medicine Hat	WHL	52	15	33	48	99	....	....	....	....	....	....	....	....	....	12	3	3	6	16	....	....	....	....
2005-06	Medicine Hat	WHL	26	5	13	18	63	....	....	....	....	....	....	....	....	....	13	4	8	12	*59	....	....	....	....
	Chicago	**NHL**	1	0	0	0	0	0	0	0	1	0.0	0	0	0.0	11:02	....	....	....	....	....	....	....	....	....
2006-07	**Chicago**	**NHL**	35	1	7	8	44	1	0	0	38	2.6	–12	0	0.0	19:19	....	....	....	....	....	....	....	....	....
	Norfolk Admirals	AHL	34	5	10	15	53	....	....	....	....	....	....	....	....	....	6	1	3	4	13	....	....	....	....
	NHL Totals		36	1	7	8	44	1	0	0	39	2.6		0	0.0	19:05	....	....	....	....	....	....	....	....	....

BARNABY, Matthew

(BAHR-na-BEE, MA-thew)

Right wing. Shoots left. 6', 189 lbs. Born, Ottawa, Ont., May 4, 1973. Buffalo's 5th choice, 83rd overall, in 1992 Entry Draft.

Season	Club	League	GP	G	A	Pts	PIM	PP	SH	GW	S	%	+/-	TF	F%	Min	GP	G	A	Pts	PIM	PP	SH	GW	Min
1989-90	Hull Frontaliers	QAHA	50	43	50	93	149	....	....	....	....	....	....	....	....	....	....	....	....	....	....	....	....	....	....
	L'Outaouais	QAAA	2	0	0	0	0	....	....	....	....	....	....	....	....	....	....	....	....	....	....	....	....	....	....
1990-91	Beauport	QMJHL	52	9	5	14	262	....	....	....	....	....	....	....	....	....	....	....	....	....	....	....	....	....	....
1991-92	Beauport	QMJHL	63	29	37	66	*476	....	....	....	....	....	....	....	....	....	....	....	....	....	....	....	....	....	....
1992-93	Victoriaville Tigres	QMJHL	65	44	67	111	*448	....	....	....	....	....	....	....	....	....	6	2	4	6	44	....	....	....	....
	Buffalo	**NHL**	2	1	0	1	10	1	0	0	8	12.5	0	....	....	....	1	0	1	1	4	0	0	0	....
1993-94	**Buffalo**	**NHL**	35	2	4	6	106	1	0	0	13	15.4	–7	....	....	....	3	0	0	0	17	0	0	0	....
	Rochester	AHL	42	10	32	42	153	....	....	....	....	....	....	....	....	....	....	....	....	....	....	....	....	....	....
1994-95	Rochester	AHL	56	21	29	50	274	....	....	....	....	....	....	....	....	....	....	....	....	....	....	....	....	....	....
	Buffalo	**NHL**	23	1	1	2	116	0	0	0	27	3.7	–2	....	....	....	....	....	....	....	....	....	....	....	....
1995-96	**Buffalo**	**NHL**	73	15	16	31	*335	0	0	0	131	11.5	–2	....	....	....	....	....	....	....	....	....	....	....	....
1996-97	**Buffalo**	**NHL**	68	19	24	43	249	2	0	1	121	15.7	16	....	....	....	8	0	4	4	36	0	0	0	....
1997-98	**Buffalo**	**NHL**	72	5	20	25	289	0	0	2	96	5.2	8	....	....	....	15	7	6	13	22	3	0	1	....
1998-99	**Buffalo**	**NHL**	44	4	14	18	143	0	0	3	52	7.7	–2	6	16.7	13:56	....	....	....	....	....	....	....	....	....
	Pittsburgh	**NHL**	18	2	2	4	34	1	0	0	27	7.4	–10	3	66.7	13:33	13	0	0	0	35	0	0	0	10:27
99-2000	**Pittsburgh**	**NHL**	64	12	12	24	197	0	0	3	80	15.0	3	75	44.0	12:38	11	0	2	2	29	0	0	0	13:41
2000-01	**Pittsburgh**	**NHL**	47	1	4	5	*168	0	0	0	38	2.6	–7	15	33.3	7:49	....	....	....	....	....	....	....	....	....
	Tampa Bay	**NHL**	29	4	4	8	*97	1	0	0	29	13.8	–3	1	100.0	12:34	....	....	....	....	....	....	....	....	....
2001-02	**Tampa Bay**	**NHL**	29	0	0	0	70	0	0	0	13	0.0	–7	1	0.0	7:54	....	....	....	....	....	....	....	....	....
	NY Rangers	**NHL**	48	8	13	21	144	0	0	1	56	14.3	–3	12	33.3	11:24	....	....	....	....	....	....	....	....	....
2002-03	**NY Rangers**	**NHL**	79	14	22	36	142	1	0	1	104	13.5	9	5	40.0	13:00	....	....	....	....	....	....	....	....	....
2003-04	**NY Rangers**	**NHL**	69	12	20	32	120	0	0	1	80	15.0	15	23	43.5	11:49	....	....	....	....	....	....	....	....	....
	Colorado	**NHL**	13	4	5	9	37	1	0	2	24	16.7	3	1	100.0	15:25	11	0	2	2	27	0	0	0	12:22
2004-05			DID NOT PLAY																						
2005-06	**Chicago**	**NHL**	82	8	20	28	178	0	0	1	85	9.4	–11	11	45.5	13:26	....	....	....	....	....	....	....	....	....
2006-07	**Dallas**	**NHL**	39	1	6	7	127	0	0	0	22	4.5	5	1	0.0	8:07	....	....	....	....	....	....	....	....	....
	NHL Totals		834	113	187	300	2562	8	0	15	1006	11.2		154	41.6	11:50	62	7	15	22	170	3	0	1	12:04

Traded to **Pittsburgh** by **Buffalo** for Stu Barnes, March 11, 1999. Traded to **Tampa Bay** by **Pittsburgh** for Wayne Primeau, February 1, 2001. Traded to **NY Rangers** by **Tampa Bay** for Zdeno Ciger, December 12, 2001. Traded to **Colorado** by **NY Rangers** with NY Rangers' 3rd round choice (Denis Parshin) in 2004 Entry Draft for Chris McAllister, David Liffiton and Florida's 2nd round choice (previously acquired, later traded back to Florida – Florida selected David Shantz) in 2004 Entry Draft, March 8, 2004. Signed as a free agent by **Chicago**, July 2, 2004. Signed as a free agent by **Dallas**, July 5, 2006. • Missed remainder of 2006-07 season after sufffering a concussion in game vs. Phoenix, January 9, 2007.

BARNES, Stu

(BAHRNZ, STEW) **DAL.**

Center. Shoots right. 5'11", 180 lbs. Born, Spruce Grove, Alta., December 25, 1970. Winnipeg's 1st choice, 4th overall, in 1989 Entry Draft.

Season	Club	League	GP	G	A	Pts	PIM	PP	SH	GW	S	%	+/-	TF	F%	Min	GP	G	A	Pts	PIM	PP	SH	GW	Min
1986-87	St. Albert Saints	AJHL	53	41	34	*75	103	....	....	....	....	....	....	....	....	....	19	7	15	22	....	....	....	....	....
1987-88	New Westminster	WHL	71	37	64	101	88	....	....	....	....	....	....	....	....	....	5	2	3	5	6	....	....	....	....
1988-89	Tri-City	WHL	70	59	82	141	117	....	....	....	....	....	....	....	....	....	7	6	5	11	10	....	....	....	....
1989-90	Tri-City	WHL	63	52	92	144	165	....	....	....	....	....	....	....	....	....	7	1	5	6	26	....	....	....	....
1990-91	Canada	Nat-Tm	53	22	27	49	68	....	....	....	....	....	....	....	....	....	....	....	....	....	....	....	....	....	....
1991-92	**Winnipeg**	**NHL**	46	8	9	17	26	4	0	0	75	10.7	–2	....	....	....	....	....	....	....	....	....	....	....	....
	Moncton Hawks	AHL	30	13	19	32	10	....	....	....	....	....	....	....	....	....	11	3	9	12	6	....	....	....	....
1992-93	**Winnipeg**	**NHL**	38	12	10	22	10	3	0	3	73	16.4	–3	....	....	....	6	1	3	4	2	0	0	0	....
	Moncton Hawks	AHL	42	23	31	54	58	....	....	....	....	....	....	....	....	....	....	....	....	....	....	....	....	....	....
1993-94	**Winnipeg**	**NHL**	18	5	4	9	8	2	0	0	24	20.8	–1	....	....	....	....	....	....	....	....	....	....	....	....
	Florida	**NHL**	59	18	20	38	30	6	1	3	148	12.2	5	....	....	....	....	....	....	....	....	....	....	....	....
1994-95	**Florida**	**NHL**	41	10	19	29	8	1	0	2	93	10.8	7	....	....	....	....	....	....	....	....	....	....	....	....
1995-96	**Florida**	**NHL**	72	19	25	44	46	8	0	5	158	12.0	–12	....	....	....	22	6	10	16	4	2	0	2	....
1996-97	**Florida**	**NHL**	19	2	8	10	10	1	0	0	44	4.5	–3	....	....	....	....	....	....	....	....	....	....	....	....
	Pittsburgh	**NHL**	62	17	22	39	16	4	0	3	132	12.9	–20	....	....	....	5	0	1	1	0	0	0	0	....
1997-98	**Pittsburgh**	**NHL**	78	30	35	65	30	15	1	5	196	15.3	15	....	....	....	6	3	3	6	2	0	0	1	....

			Regular Season														Playoffs								
Season	Club	League	GP	G	A	Pts	PIM	PP	SH	GW	S	%	+/-	TF	F%	Min	GP	G	A	Pts	PIM	PP	SH	GW	Min
1998-99	**Pittsburgh**	**NHL**	64	20	12	32	20	13	0	3	155	12.9	–12	720	51.9	17:52	....	....	....	....	....	....	....	....	....
	Buffalo	**NHL**	17	0	4	4	10	0	0	0	25	0.0	1	236	51.3	18:20	21	7	3	10	6	4	0	1	14:40
99-2000	**Buffalo**	**NHL**	82	20	25	45	16	8	2	2	137	14.6	–3	778	48.5	17:23	5	3	0	3	2	2	0	1	17:02
2000-01	**Buffalo**	**NHL**	75	19	24	43	26	3	2	5	160	11.9	–2	1470	48.3	19:06	13	4	4	8	2	2	0	2	18:30
2001-02	**Buffalo**	**NHL**	68	17	31	48	26	5	0	4	127	13.4	6	984	47.2	18:35	....	....	....	....	....	....	....	....	....
2002-03	**Buffalo**	**NHL**	68	11	21	32	20	2	1	2	124	8.9	–13	923	49.0	18:29	....	....	....	....	....	....	....	....	....
	Dallas	**NHL**	13	2	5	7	8	2	0	1	25	8.0	2	76	44.7	17:23	12	2	3	5	0	0	0	2	19:06
2003-04	**Dallas**	**NHL**	77	11	18	29	18	0	1	4	135	8.1	7	879	52.9	18:05	5	0	0	0	0	0	0	0	14:59
2004-05				DID NOT PLAY																					
2005-06	**Dallas**	**NHL**	78	15	21	36	44	0	1	2	123	12.2	9	649	50.1	16:29	5	1	1	2	0	0	1	0	17:33
2006-07	**Dallas**	**NHL**	82	13	12	25	40	1	0	2	118	11.0	–2	734	48.6	16:06	7	1	3	4	4	1	0	0	18:45
	NHL Totals		1057	249	325	574	412	78	9	46	2072	12.0		7449	49.4	17:43	107	28	31	59	22	11	1	9	17:01

WHL West Second All-Star Team (1988, 1989) • WHL Rookie of the Year (1988) • WHL Player of the Year (1989)

Traded to **Florida** by **Winnipeg** with St. Louis' 6th round choice (previously acquired, later traded to Edmonton – later traded back to Winnipeg – Winnipeg selected Chris Kibermanis) in 1994 Entry Draft for Randy Gilhen, November 25, 1993. Traded to **Pittsburgh** by **Florida** with Jason Woolley for Chris Wells, November 19, 1996. Traded to **Buffalo** by **Pittsburgh** for Matthew Barnaby, March 11, 1999. Traded to **Dallas** by **Buffalo** for Michael Ryan and Dallas's 2nd round choice (Branislav Fabry) in 2003 Entry Draft, March 10, 2003.

BARNEY, Scott

(BAHR-nee, SKAWT)

Center. Shoots right. 6'4", 210 lbs. Born, Oshawa, Ont., March 27, 1979. Los Angeles' 3rd choice, 29th overall, in 1997 Entry Draft.

Season	Club	League	GP	G	A	Pts	PIM	PP	SH	GW	S	%	+/-	TF	F%	Min	GP	G	A	Pts	PIM	PP	SH	GW	Min
1994-95	North York	MTJHL	41	16	19	35	88	....	....	....	....	....	....	....	....	....	....	....	....	....	....	....	....	....	....
1995-96	Peterborough	OHL	60	22	24	46	52	....	....	....	....	....	....	....	....	....	24	6	8	14	38	....	....	....	....
1996-97	Peterborough	OHL	64	21	33	54	110	....	....	....	....	....	....	....	....	....	9	0	3	3	16	....	....	....	....
1997-98	Peterborough	OHL	62	44	32	76	60	....	....	....	....	....	....	....	....	....	4	1	0	1	6	....	....	....	....
1998-99	Peterborough	OHL	44	41	26	67	80	....	....	....	....	....	....	....	....	....	5	4	1	5	4	....	....	....	....
	Springfield	AHL	5	0	0	0	2	....	....	....	....	....	....	....	....	....	1	0	0	0	2	....	....	....	....
99-2000				DID NOT PLAY – INJURED																					
2000-01				DID NOT PLAY – INJURED																					
2001-02				DID NOT PLAY – INJURED																					
2002-03	**Los Angeles**	**NHL**	5	0	0	0	0	0	0	0	5	0.0	–1	0	0.0	9:04	....	....	....	....	....	....	....	....	....
	Manchester	AHL	57	13	5	18	74	....	....	....	....	....	....	....	....	....	....	....	....	....	....	....	....	....	....
2003-04	**Los Angeles**	**NHL**	19	5	6	11	4	2	0	0	31	16.1	3	7	14.3	11:12	....	....	....	....	....	....	....	....	....
	Manchester	AHL	44	20	14	34	28	....	....	....	....	....	....	....	....	....	6	2	3	5	8	....	....	....	....
2004-05				DID NOT PLAY																					
2005-06	**Atlanta**	**NHL**	3	0	0	0	0	0	0	0	4	0.0	–1	0	0.0	6:45	....	....	....	....	....	....	....	....	....
	Chicago Wolves	AHL	53	32	19	51	56	....	....	....	....	....	....	....	....	....	....	....	....	....	....	....	....	....	....
2006-07	Grand Rapids	AHL	40	4	8	12	26	....	....	....	....	....	....	....	....	....	....	....	....	....	....	....	....	....	....
	Hershey Bears	AHL	11	6	4	10	6	....	....	....	....	....	....	....	....	....	19	*10	9	19	14	....	....	....	....
	NHL Totals		27	5	6	11	4	2	0	0	40	12.5		7	14.3	10:19	....	....	....	....	....	....	....	....	....

• Missed entire 1999-2000, 2000-01 and 2001-02 seasons recovering from back injury suffered in training camp, September 28, 1999. Signed as a free agent by **Atlanta**, August 8, 2005.

BARTOVIC, Milan

(BAHR-tuh-vihch, MIH-lan) **ATL.**

Right wing. Shoots left. 5'11", 200 lbs. Born, Trencin, Czech., April 9, 1981. Buffalo's 2nd choice, 35th overall, in 1999 Entry Draft.

Season	Club	League	GP	G	A	Pts	PIM	PP	SH	GW	S	%	+/-	TF	F%	Min	GP	G	A	Pts	PIM	PP	SH	GW	Min
1997-98	Dukla Trencin Jr.	Slovak-Jr.	26	2	6	8	27	....	....	....	....	....	....	....	....	....	....	....	....	....	....	....	....	....	....
1998-99	Dukla Trencin Jr.	Slovak-Jr.	46	36	35	71	62	....	....	....	....	....	....	....	....	....	6	9	3	12	10	....	....	....	....
99-2000	Tri-City	WHL	18	8	9	17	12	....	....	....	....	....	....	....	....	....	....	....	....	....	....	....	....	....	....
	Brandon	WHL	38	18	22	40	28	....	....	....	....	....	....	....	....	....	....	....	....	....	....	....	....	....	....
2000-01	Brandon	WHL	34	15	25	40	40	....	....	....	....	....	....	....	....	....	6	1	2	3	8	....	....	....	....
	Rochester	AHL	2	1	1	2	0	....	....	....	....	....	....	....	....	....	4	0	1	1	2	....	....	....	....
2001-02	Rochester	AHL	73	15	11	26	56	....	....	....	....	....	....	....	....	....	2	0	0	0	0	....	....	....	....
2002-03	**Buffalo**	**NHL**	3	1	0	1	0	0	0	0	5	20.0	0	1	100.0	9:52	....	....	....	....	....	....	....	....	....
	Rochester	AHL	74	18	10	28	84	....	....	....	....	....	....	....	....	....	3	0	0	0	0	....	....	....	....
2003-04	**Buffalo**	**NHL**	23	1	8	9	18	0	0	0	30	3.3	1	2	100.0	12:53	....	....	....	....	....	....	....	....	....
	Rochester	AHL	52	18	11	29	52	....	....	....	....	....	....	....	....	....	2	0	0	0	2	....	....	....	....
2004-05	Rochester	AHL	69	10	18	28	83	....	....	....	....	....	....	....	....	....	9	0	3	3	22	....	....	....	....
2005-06	**Chicago**	**NHL**	24	1	6	7	8	0	0	0	35	2.9	0	1	0.0	8:50	....	....	....	....	....	....	....	....	....
	Norfolk Admirals	AHL	49	10	14	24	34	....	....	....	....	....	....	....	....	....	3	0	0	0	8	....	....	....	....
2006-07	Malmo	Sweden	24	1	4	5	26	....	....	....	....	....	....	....	....	....	....	....	....	....	....	....	....	....	....
	ZSC Lions Zurich	Swiss	12	2	3	5	2	....	....	....	....	....	....	....	....	....	3	0	1	1	0	....	....	....	....
	NHL Totals		50	3	14	17	26	0	0	0	70	4.3		4	75.0	10:45	....	....	....	....	....	....	....	....	....

• Missed majority of 2000-01 season recovering from shoulder injury suffered in game vs. Red Deer (WHL), October 10, 2000. Traded to **Chicago** by **Buffalo** for Michael Leighton, October 4, 2005. Signed as a free agent by **Malmo** (Sweden), August 31, 2006. Signed as a free agent by **Zurich** (Swiss), December 26, 2006. Signed as a free agent by **Atlanta**, August 8, 2007.

BATES, Shawn

(BAYTS, SHAWN) **NYI**

Center. Shoots right. 6', 210 lbs. Born, Melrose, MA, April 3, 1975. Boston's 4th choice, 103rd overall, in 1993 Entry Draft.

Season	Club	League	GP	G	A	Pts	PIM	PP	SH	GW	S	%	+/-	TF	F%	Min	GP	G	A	Pts	PIM	PP	SH	GW	Min
1990-91	Medford	High-MA	22	18	43	61	6	....	....	....	....	....	....	....	....	....	....	....	....	....	....	....	....	....	....
1991-92	Medford	High-MA	22	38	41	79	10	....	....	....	....	....	....	....	....	....	....	....	....	....	....	....	....	....	....
1992-93	Medford	High-MA	25	49	46	95	20	....	....	....	....	....	....	....	....	....	....	....	....	....	....	....	....	....	....
1993-94	Boston University	H-East	41	10	19	29	24	....	....	....	....	....	....	....	....	....	....	....	....	....	....	....	....	....	....
1994-95	Boston University	H-East	38	18	12	30	48	....	....	....	....	....	....	....	....	....	....	....	....	....	....	....	....	....	....
1995-96	Boston University	H-East	40	28	22	50	54	....	....	....	....	....	....	....	....	....	....	....	....	....	....	....	....	....	....
1996-97	Boston University	H-East	41	17	18	35	64	....	....	....	....	....	....	....	....	....	....	....	....	....	....	....	....	....	....
1997-98	**Boston**	**NHL**	13	2	0	2	2	0	0	0	12	16.7	–3	....	....	....	....	....	....	....	....	....	....	....	....
	Providence Bruins	AHL	50	15	19	34	22	....	....	....	....	....	....	....	....	....	....	....	....	....	....	....	....	....	....
1998-99	**Boston**	**NHL**	33	5	4	9	2	0	0	0	30	16.7	3	178	51.1	8:35	12	0	0	0	4	0	0	0	5:12
	Providence Bruins	AHL	37	25	21	46	39	....	....	....	....	....	....	....	....	....	....	....	....	....	....	....	....	....	....
99-2000	**Boston**	**NHL**	44	5	7	12	14	0	0	1	65	7.7	–17	460	47.0	10:52	....	....	....	....	....	....	....	....	....
2000-01	**Boston**	**NHL**	45	2	3	5	26	0	0	0	59	3.4	–12	413	50.6	9:19	....	....	....	....	....	....	....	....	....
	Providence Bruins	AHL	11	5	8	13	12	....	....	....	....	....	....	....	....	....	8	2	6	8	8	....	....	....	....
2001-02	**NY Islanders**	**NHL**	71	17	35	52	30	1	4	4	150	11.3	18	306	49.4	18:45	7	2	4	6	11	1	0	1	20:27
2002-03	**NY Islanders**	**NHL**	74	13	29	42	52	1	6	1	126	10.3	–9	398	57.0	18:26	5	1	0	1	0	1	0	0	18:36
2003-04	**NY Islanders**	**NHL**	69	9	23	32	46	0	1	1	115	7.8	–8	603	55.9	18:26	5	0	0	0	4	0	0	0	17:14
2004-05				DID NOT PLAY																					
2005-06	**NY Islanders**	**NHL**	66	15	19	34	60	1	1	4	95	15.8	–11	1063	51.3	17:12	....	....	....	....	....	....	....	....	....
2006-07	**NY Islanders**	**NHL**	48	4	6	10	34	0	1	0	50	8.0	13	455	53.2	12:32	....	....	....	....	....	....	....	....	....
	NHL Totals		463	72	126	198	266	3	13	11	702	10.3		3876	52.1	15:18	29	3	4	7	19	2	0	1	13:16

NCAA Championship All-Tournament Team (1995)

Signed as a free agent by **NY Islanders**, July 8, 2001.

BATTAGLIA, Bates

(buh-TAG-lee-ah, BAYTS) **TOR.**

Left wing. Shoots left. 6'2", 205 lbs. Born, Chicago, IL, December 13, 1975. Anaheim's 6th choice, 132nd overall, in 1994 Entry Draft.

Season	Club	League	GP	G	A	Pts	PIM	PP	SH	GW	S	%	+/-	TF	F%	Min	GP	G	A	Pts	PIM	PP	SH	GW	Min
1992-93	Team Illinois	MEHL	60	42	42	84	68	....	....	....	....	....	....	....	....	....	....	....	....	....	....	....	....	....	....
1993-94	Caledon	MTJHL	44	15	33	48	104	....	....	....	....	....	....	....	....	....	....	....	....	....	....	....	....	....	....
1994-95	Lake Superior	CCHA	38	6	14	20	34	....	....	....	....	....	....	....	....	....	....	....	....	....	....	....	....	....	....
1995-96	Lake Superior	CCHA	40	13	22	35	48	....	....	....	....	....	....	....	....	....	....	....	....	....	....	....	....	....	....
1996-97	Lake Superior	CCHA	38	12	27	39	80	....	....	....	....	....	....	....	....	....	....	....	....	....	....	....	....	....	....
1997-98	**Carolina**	**NHL**	33	2	4	6	10	0	0	1	21	9.5	–1	....	....	....	....	....	....	....	....	....	....	....	....
	New Haven	AHL	48	15	21	36	48	....	....	....	....	....	....	....	....	....	1	0	0	0	0	....	....	....	....
1998-99	**Carolina**	**NHL**	60	7	11	18	97	0	0	0	52	13.5	7	144	39.6	9:53	6	0	3	3	8	0	0	0	15:22
99-2000	**Carolina**	**NHL**	77	16	18	34	39	3	0	3	86	18.6	20	23	26.1	15:12	....	....	....	....	....	....	....	....	....
2000-01	**Carolina**	**NHL**	80	12	15	27	76	2	0	3	133	9.0	–14	5	60.0	14:28	6	0	2	2	2	0	0	0	11:25
2001-02	**Carolina**	**NHL**	82	21	25	46	44	5	1	2	167	12.6	–6	12	33.3	19:05	23	5	9	14	14	1	0	1	20:42
2002-03	**Carolina**	**NHL**	70	5	14	19	90	0	1	1	96	5.2	–17	16	25.0	18:39	....	....	....	....	....	....	....	....	....
	Colorado	**NHL**	13	1	5	6	10	1	0	1	27	3.7	–2	3	0.0	15:19	7	0	2	2	4	0	0	0	14:39
2003-04	**Colorado**	**NHL**	4	0	1	1	4	0	0	0	1	0.0	–1	1	100.0	11:04	....	....	....	....	....	....	....	....	....
	Washington	**NHL**	66	4	6	10	38	0	0	1	69	5.8	–23	116	32.8	13:37	....	....	....	....	....	....	....	....	....
2004-05	Mississippi	ECHL	25	6	11	17	24	....	....	....	....	....	....	....	....	....	4	0	0	0	10	....	....	....	....

Season	Club	League	GP	G	A	Pts	PIM	PP	SH	GW	S	%	+/-	TF	F%	Min	GP	G	A	Pts	PIM	PP	SH	GW	Min
			Regular Season														Playoffs								
2005-06	Toronto Marlies	AHL	79	20	47	67	86	....	....	....	....	....	....	....	....	....	5	1	1	2	6	....	....	....	....
2006-07	**Toronto**	**NHL**	**82**	**12**	**19**	**31**	**45**	**0**	**0**	**0**	**94**	**12.8**	**9**	**4**	**0.0**	**12:27**	....	....	....	....	....	....	....	....	....
	NHL Totals		**567**	**80**	**118**	**198**	**453**	**11**	**2**	**12**	**746**	**10.7**		**324**	**34.9**	**14:54**	**42**	**5**	**16**	**21**	**28**	**1**	**0**	**1**	**17:36**

Traded to **Hartford** by **Anaheim** with Anaheim's 4th round choice (Josef Vasicek) in 1998 Entry Draft for Mark Janssens, March 18, 1997. Rights transferred to **Carolina** after **Hartford** franchise relocated, June 25, 1997. Traded to **Colorado** by **Carolina** for Radim Vrbata, March 11, 2003. Traded to **Washington** by **Colorado** with Jonas Johansson for Steve Konowalchuk and Washington's 3rd round choice (later traded to Carolina – Carolina selected Casey Borer) in 2004 Entry Draft, October 22, 2003. Signed as a free agent by **Mississippi** (ECHL), February 21, 2005. Signed to a PTO (tryout) contract by **Toronto** (AHL), October 2, 2005. Signed as a free agent by **Toronto**, July 8, 2006.

BAUMGARTNER, Nolan

(BAWM-gahrt-nuhr, NOH-luhn) **DAL.**

Defense. Shoots right. 6'2", 205 lbs. Born, Calgary, Alta., March 23, 1976. Washington's 1st choice, 10th overall, in 1994 Entry Draft.

Season	Club	League	GP	G	A	Pts	PIM	PP	SH	GW	S	%	+/-	TF	F%	Min	GP	G	A	Pts	PIM	PP	SH	GW	Min
1991-92	Cgy. AAA Flames	AMHL	39	11	29	40	40	....	....	....	....	....	....	....	....	....	....	....	....	....	....	....	....	....	....
1992-93	Kamloops Blazers	WHL	43	0	5	5	30	....	....	....	....	....	....	....	....	....	11	1	1	2	0	....	....	....	....
1993-94	Kamloops Blazers	WHL	69	13	42	55	109	....	....	....	....	....	....	....	....	....	19	3	14	17	33	....	....	....	....
1994-95	Kamloops Blazers	WHL	62	8	36	44	71	....	....	....	....	....	....	....	....	....	21	4	13	17	16	....	....	....	....
1995-96	Kamloops Blazers	WHL	28	13	15	28	45	....	....	....	....	....	....	....	....	....	16	1	9	10	26	....	....	....	....
	Washington	**NHL**	**1**	**0**	**0**	**0**	**0**	**0**	**0**	**0**	**0**	**0.0**	**–1**	....	....	....	**1**	**0**	**0**	**0**	**10**	**0**	**0**	**0**	....
1996-97	Portland Pirates	AHL	8	2	2	4	4	....	....	....	....	....	....	....	....	....	....	....	....	....	....	....	....	....	....
1997-98	**Washington**	**NHL**	**4**	**0**	**1**	**1**	**0**	**0**	**0**	**0**	**4**	**0.0**	**0**	....	....	....	....	....	....	....	....	....	....	....	....
	Portland Pirates	AHL	70	2	24	26	70	....	....	....	....	....	....	....	....	....	10	1	4	5	10	....	....	....	....
1998-99	**Washington**	**NHL**	**5**	**0**	**0**	**0**	**0**	**0**	**0**	**0**	**1**	**0.0**	**–3**	**0**	**0.0**	**8:41**	....	....	....	....	....	....	....	....	....
	Portland Pirates	AHL	38	5	14	19	62	....	....	....	....	....	....	....	....	....	....	....	....	....	....	....	....	....	....
99-2000	**Washington**	**NHL**	**8**	**0**	**1**	**1**	**2**	**0**	**0**	**0**	**6**	**0.0**	**1**	**0**	**0.0**	**10:31**	....	....	....	....	....	....	....	....	....
	Portland Pirates	AHL	71	5	18	23	56	....	....	....	....	....	....	....	....	....	4	1	2	3	10	....	....	....	....
2000-01	**Chicago**	**NHL**	**8**	**0**	**0**	**0**	**6**	**0**	**0**	**0**	**7**	**0.0**	**–4**	**2**	**50.0**	**12:40**	....	....	....	....	....	....	....	....	....
	Norfolk Admirals	AHL	63	5	28	33	75	....	....	....	....	....	....	....	....	....	9	2	3	5	11	....	....	....	....
2001-02	Norfolk Admirals	AHL	76	10	24	34	72	....	....	....	....	....	....	....	....	....	4	0	1	1	2	....	....	....	....
2002-03	**Vancouver**	**NHL**	**8**	**1**	**2**	**3**	**4**	**1**	**0**	**0**	**7**	**14.3**	**4**	**0**	**0.0**	**11:36**	**2**	**0**	**0**	**0**	**0**	**0**	**0**	**0**	**11:07**
	Manitoba Moose	AHL	59	8	31	39	82	....	....	....	....	....	....	....	....	....	1	0	0	0	4	....	....	....	....
2003-04	**Pittsburgh**	**NHL**	**5**	**0**	**0**	**0**	**2**	**0**	**0**	**0**	**6**	**0.0**	**–7**	**0**	**0.0**	**19:20**	....	....	....	....	....	....	....	....	....
	Vancouver	**NHL**	**9**	**0**	**3**	**3**	**2**	**0**	**0**	**0**	**9**	**0.0**	**3**	**0**	**0.0**	**11:52**	....	....	....	....	....	....	....	....	....
	Manitoba Moose	AHL	55	6	21	27	101	....	....	....	....	....	....	....	....	....	....	....	....	....	....	....	....	....	....
2004-05	Manitoba Moose	AHL	78	9	30	39	51	....	....	....	....	....	....	....	....	....	14	0	4	4	10	....	....	....	....
2005-06	**Vancouver**	**NHL**	**70**	**5**	**29**	**34**	**30**	**4**	**1**	**1**	**73**	**6.8**	**11**	**1**	**0.0**	**16:29**	....	....	....	....	....	....	....	....	....
2006-07	**Philadelphia**	**NHL**	**6**	**0**	**1**	**1**	**21**	**0**	**0**	**0**	**4**	**0.0**	**0**	**0**	**0.0**	**15:00**	....	....	....	....	....	....	....	....	....
	Philadelphia	AHL	51	6	20	26	46	....	....	....	....	....	....	....	....	....	....	....	....	....	....	....	....	....	....
	Dallas	**NHL**	**7**	**0**	**2**	**2**	**0**	**0**	**0**	**0**	**4**	**0.0**	**0**	**0**	**0.0**	**12:14**	....	....	....	....	....	....	....	....	....
	NHL Totals		**131**	**6**	**39**	**45**	**67**	**5**	**1**	**1**	**121**	**5.0**		**3**	**33.3**	**14:43**	**3**	**0**	**0**	**0**	**10**	**0**	**0**	**0**	**11:06**

Memorial Cup Tournement All-Star Team (1994, 1995) • WHL West First All-Star Team (1995, 1996) • Canadian Major Junior First All-Star Team (1995) • Canadian Major Junior Defenseman of the Year (1995)

Traded to **Chicago** by **Washington** for Remi Royer, July 20, 2000. Signed as a free agent by **Vancouver**, July 11, 2002. Claimed by **Pittsburgh** from **Vancouver** in Waiver Draft, October 3, 2003. Claimed on waivers by **Vancouver** from **Pittsburgh**, November 1, 2003. Signed as a free agent by **Philadelphia**, July 1, 2006. Claimed on waivers by **Dallas** from **Philadelphia**, February 24, 2007.

BAYDA, Ryan

(BAY-duh, RIGH-uhn) **CAR.**

Left wing. Shoots left. 5'11", 185 lbs. Born, Saskatoon, Sask., December 9, 1980. Carolina's 2nd choice, 80th overall, in 2000 Entry Draft.

Season	Club	League	GP	G	A	Pts	PIM	PP	SH	GW	S	%	+/-	TF	F%	Min	GP	G	A	Pts	PIM	PP	SH	GW	Min
1995-96	Saskatoon Flyers	SMHL	60	85	74	159	85	....	....	....	....	....	....	....	....	....	....	....	....	....	....	....	....	....	....
1996-97	Sask. Contacts	SMHL	44	22	23	45	18	....	....	....	....	....	....	....	....	....	....	....	....	....	....	....	....	....	....
1997-98	Sask. Contacts	SMHL	41	29	49	78	103	....	....	....	....	....	....	....	....	....	....	....	....	....	....	....	....	....	....
1998-99	Vernon Vipers	BCHL	45	24	58	82	15	....	....	....	....	....	....	....	....	....	....	....	....	....	....	....	....	....	....
99-2000	North Dakota	WCHA	44	17	23	40	30	....	....	....	....	....	....	....	....	....	....	....	....	....	....	....	....	....	....
2000-01	North Dakota	WCHA	46	25	34	59	48	....	....	....	....	....	....	....	....	....	....	....	....	....	....	....	....	....	....
2001-02	North Dakota	WCHA	37	19	28	47	52	....	....	....	....	....	....	....	....	....	....	....	....	....	....	....	....	....	....
	Lowell	AHL	3	1	1	2	0	....	....	....	....	....	....	....	....	....	5	3	0	3	0	....	....	....	....
2002-03	**Carolina**	**NHL**	**25**	**4**	**10**	**14**	**16**	**0**	**0**	**1**	**49**	**8.2**	**–5**	**2**	**100.0**	**17:15**	....	....	....	....	....	....	....	....	....
	Lowell	AHL	53	11	32	43	32	....	....	....	....	....	....	....	....	....	....	....	....	....	....	....	....	....	....
2003-04	**Carolina**	**NHL**	**44**	**3**	**3**	**6**	**22**	**0**	**0**	**1**	**65**	**4.6**	**–14**	**4**	**0.0**	**10:57**	....	....	....	....	....	....	....	....	....
	Lowell	AHL	34	7	15	22	28	....	....	....	....	....	....	....	....	....	....	....	....	....	....	....	....	....	....
2004-05	Lowell	AHL	80	13	27	40	91	....	....	....	....	....	....	....	....	....	9	3	3	6	4	....	....	....	....
2005-06	Manitoba Moose	AHL	59	13	25	38	52	....	....	....	....	....	....	....	....	....	13	1	6	7	27	....	....	....	....
2006-07	**Carolina**	**NHL**	**9**	**1**	**1**	**2**	**2**	**0**	**0**	**0**	**10**	**10.0**	**–1**	**0**	**0.0**	**8:41**	....	....	....	....	....	....	....	....	....
	Albany River Rats	AHL	55	29	25	54	66	....	....	....	....	....	....	....	....	....	5	3	2	5	4	....	....	....	....
	NHL Totals		**78**	**8**	**14**	**22**	**40**	**0**	**0**	**2**	**124**	**6.5**		**6**	**33.3**	**12:42**	....	....	....	....	....	....	....	....	....

BCHL Rookie of the Year (1999) • WCHA All-Rookie Team (2000) • WCHA Second All-Star Team (2001, 2002)

BEAUCHEMIN, Francois

(boh-sheh-MEH, frahn-SWUH) **ANA.**

Defense. Shoots left. 6', 210 lbs. Born, Sorel, Que., June 4, 1980. Montreal's 3rd choice, 75th overall, in 1998 Entry Draft.

Season	Club	League	GP	G	A	Pts	PIM	PP	SH	GW	S	%	+/-	TF	F%	Min	GP	G	A	Pts	PIM	PP	SH	GW	Min
1995-96	Richelieu Riverains	QAAA	40	9	23	32	59	....	....	....	....	....	....	....	....	....	....	....	....	....	....	....	....	....	....
1996-97	Laval Titan	QMJHL	66	7	21	28	132	....	....	....	....	....	....	....	....	....	3	0	0	0	2	....	....	....	....
1997-98	Laval Titan	QMJHL	70	12	35	47	132	....	....	....	....	....	....	....	....	....	16	1	3	4	23	....	....	....	....
1998-99	Acadie-Bathurst	QMJHL	31	4	17	21	53	....	....	....	....	....	....	....	....	....	23	2	16	18	55	....	....	....	....
99-2000	Acadie-Bathurst	QMJHL	38	11	36	47	64	....	....	....	....	....	....	....	....	....	....	....	....	....	....	....	....	....	....
	Moncton Wildcats	QMJHL	33	8	31	39	35	....	....	....	....	....	....	....	....	....	16	2	11	13	14	....	....	....	....
2000-01	Quebec Citadelles	AHL	56	3	6	9	44	....	....	....	....	....	....	....	....	....	....	....	....	....	....	....	....	....	....
2001-02	Quebec Citadelles	AHL	56	8	11	19	88	....	....	....	....	....	....	....	....	....	3	0	1	1	0	....	....	....	....
	Mississippi	ECHL	7	1	3	4	2	....	....	....	....	....	....	....	....	....	....	....	....	....	....	....	....	....	....
2002-03	**Montreal**	**NHL**	**1**	**0**	**0**	**0**	**0**	**0**	**0**	**0**	**1**	**0.0**	**–1**	**0**	**0.0**	**17:11**	....	....	....	....	....	....	....	....	....
	Hamilton	AHL	75	7	21	28	92	....	....	....	....	....	....	....	....	....	23	1	9	10	16	....	....	....	....
2003-04	Hamilton	AHL	77	9	27	36	57	....	....	....	....	....	....	....	....	....	10	2	4	6	18	....	....	....	....
2004-05	Syracuse Crunch	AHL	72	3	27	30	55	....	....	....	....	....	....	....	....	....	....	....	....	....	....	....	....	....	....
2005-06	**Columbus**	**NHL**	**11**	**0**	**2**	**2**	**11**	**0**	**0**	**0**	**16**	**0.0**	**–6**	**0**	**0.0**	**17:16**	....	....	....	....	....	....	....	....	....
	Anaheim	**NHL**	**61**	**8**	**26**	**34**	**41**	**4**	**0**	**3**	**121**	**6.6**	**8**	**1**	**0.0**	**24:14**	**16**	**3**	**6**	**9**	**11**	**3**	**0**	**0**	**27:26**
2006-07 ♦	**Anaheim**	**NHL**	**71**	**7**	**21**	**28**	**49**	**2**	**0**	**0**	**128**	**5.5**	**7**	**1**	**0.0**	**25:28**	**20**	**4**	**4**	**8**	**16**	**4**	**0**	**0**	**30:33**
	NHL Totals		**144**	**15**	**49**	**64**	**101**	**6**	**0**	**3**	**266**	**5.6**		**2**	**0.0**	**24:16**	**36**	**7**	**10**	**17**	**27**	**7**	**0**	**0**	**29:10**

QMJHL All-Rookie Team (1997) • QMJHL Second All-Star Team (2000)

Claimed on waivers by **Columbus** from **Montreal**, September 15, 2004. Traded to **Anaheim** by **Columbus** with Tyler Wright for Sergei Fedorov and Anaheim's 5th round choice (Maxime Frechette) in 2006 Entry Draft, November 15, 2005.

BEECH, Kris

(BEECH, KRIHS) **CBJ**

Center. Shoots left. 6'3", 211 lbs. Born, Salmon Arm, B.C., February 5, 1981. Washington's 1st choice, 7th overall, in 1999 Entry Draft.

Season	Club	League	GP	G	A	Pts	PIM	PP	SH	GW	S	%	+/-	TF	F%	Min	GP	G	A	Pts	PIM	PP	SH	GW	Min
1996-97	Sicamous Eagles	KIJHL	49	34	36	70	80	....	....	....	....	....	....	....	....	....	....	....	....	....	....	....	....	....	....
	Calgary Hitmen	WHL	8	1	1	2	0	....	....	....	....	....	....	....	....	....	....	....	....	....	....	....	....	....	....
1997-98	Calgary Hitmen	WHL	58	10	25	35	24	....	....	....	....	....	....	....	....	....	12	4	5	9	32	....	....	....	....
1998-99	Calgary Hitmen	WHL	68	26	41	67	103	....	....	....	....	....	....	....	....	....	6	1	4	5	8	....	....	....	....
99-2000	Calgary Hitmen	WHL	66	32	54	86	99	....	....	....	....	....	....	....	....	....	5	3	5	8	16	....	....	....	....
2000-01	**Washington**	**NHL**	**4**	**0**	**0**	**0**	**2**	**0**	**0**	**0**	**0**	**0.0**	**–2**	**25**	**36.0**	**7:29**	....	....	....	....	....	....	....	....	....
	Calgary Hitmen	WHL	40	22	44	66	103	....	....	....	....	....	....	....	....	....	10	2	8	10	26	....	....	....	....
2001-02	**Pittsburgh**	**NHL**	**79**	**10**	**15**	**25**	**45**	**2**	**0**	**0**	**126**	**7.9**	**–25**	**604**	**45.2**	**13:33**	....	....	....	....	....	....	....	....	....
2002-03	**Pittsburgh**	**NHL**	**12**	**0**	**1**	**1**	**6**	**0**	**0**	**0**	**6**	**0.0**	**–3**	**96**	**42.7**	**10:34**	....	....	....	....	....	....	....	....	....
	Wilkes-Barre	AHL	50	19	24	43	76	....	....	....	....	....	....	....	....	....	5	1	1	2	0	....	....	....	....
2003-04	**Pittsburgh**	**NHL**	**4**	**0**	**1**	**1**	**6**	**0**	**0**	**0**	**6**	**0.0**	**0**	**45**	**40.0**	**12:32**	....	....	....	....	....	....	....	....	....
	Wilkes-Barre	AHL	53	20	25	45	97	....	....	....	....	....	....	....	....	....	22	9	6	15	22	....	....	....	....
2004-05	Wilkes-Barre	AHL	68	14	48	62	146	....	....	....	....	....	....	....	....	....	11	4	6	10	14	....	....	....	....

			Regular Season														Playoffs								
Season	Club	League	GP	G	A	Pts	PIM	PP	SH	GW	S	%	+/-	TF	F%	Min	GP	G	A	Pts	PIM	PP	SH	GW	Min
2005-06	Nashville	NHL	5	1	2	3	0	0	0	0	6	16.7	1	81	54.3	14:40									
	Milwaukee	AHL	48	18	32	50	48																		
	Washington	NHL	5	0	0	0	4	0	0	0	6	0.0	0	36	50.0	9:24									
	Hershey Bears	AHL	10	8	6	14	6										21	14	14	28	30				
2006-07	Washington	NHL	64	8	18	26	46	3	0	0	77	10.4	-11	744	48.4	12:28									
	NHL Totals		173	19	37	56	109	5	0	0	227	8.4		1631	46.8	12:42									

Traded to **Pittsburgh** by **Washington** with Michal Sivek, Ross Lupaschuk and future considerations for Jaromir Jagr and Frantisek Kucera, July 11, 2001. Traded to **Nashville** by **Pittsburgh** for Nashville's 4th round choice (later traded to Florida - Florida selected Derrick Lapoint) in 2006 Entry Draft, September 9, 2005. Traded to **Washington** by **Nashville** with Nashville's 1st round choice (Simeon Varlamov) in 2006 Entry Draft for Brendan Witt, March 9, 2006. Signed as a free agent by **Columbus**, August 7, 2007.

BEGIN, Steve
(bay-ZHIN, STEEV) **MTL.**

Center. Shoots left. 6', 193 lbs. Born, Trois-Rivieres, Que., June 14, 1978. Calgary's 3rd choice, 40th overall, in 1996 Entry Draft.

Season	Club	League	GP	G	A	Pts	PIM	PP	SH	GW	S	%	+/-	TF	F%	Min	GP	G	A	Pts	PIM	PP	SH	GW	Min
1993-94	Cap-d-Madelaine	QAAA	8	0	1	1	6										2	0	0	0	0				
1994-95	Cap-d-Madelaine	QAAA	35	9	15	24	48										3	0	0	0	2				
1995-96	Val-d'Or Foreurs	QMJHL	64	13	23	36	218										13	1	3	4	33				
1996-97	Val-d'Or Foreurs	QMJHL	58	13	33	46	229										10	0	3	3	8				
	Saint John Flames	AHL															4	0	2	2	6				
1997-98	Calgary	NHL	5	0	0	0	23	0	0	0	2	0.0	0												
	Val-d'Or Foreurs	QMJHL	35	18	17	35	73										15	2	12	14	34				
1998-99	Saint John Flames	AHL	73	11	9	20	156										7	2	0	2	18				
99-2000	Calgary	NHL	13	1	1	2	18	0	0	0	3	33.3	-3	19	47.4	7:13									
	Saint John Flames	AHL	47	13	12	25	99																		
2000-01	Calgary	NHL	4	0	0	0	21	0	0	0	3	0.0	0	0	0.0	6:04									
	Saint John Flames	AHL	58	14	14	28	109										19	10	7	17	18				
2001-02	Calgary	NHL	51	7	5	12	79	1	0	0	65	10.8	-3	129	53.5	9:25									
2002-03	Calgary	NHL	50	3	1	4	51	0	0	1	59	5.1	-7	50	60.0	9:13									
2003-04	Montreal	NHL	52	10	5	15	41	0	1	1	91	11.0	6	436	48.6	12:32	9	0	1	1	10	0	0	0	12:26
2004-05	Hamilton	AHL	21	10	3	13	20										4	0	2	2	8				
2005-06	Montreal	NHL	76	11	12	23	113	1	2	2	134	8.2	9	573	50.1	14:19	2	0	0	0	2	0	0	0	13:42
2006-07	Montreal	NHL	52	5	5	10	46	0	0	0	64	7.8	-6	159	49.7	11:55									
	NHL Totals		303	37	29	66	392	2	3	4	421	8.8		1366	50.2	11:28	11	0	1	1	12	0	0	0	12:40

Jack A. Butterfield Trophy (Playoff MVP – AHL) (2001)

Traded to **Buffalo** by **Calgary** with Chris Drury for Steve Reinprecht and Rhett Warrener, July 3, 2003. Claimed by **Montreal** from **Buffalo** in Waiver Draft, October 3, 2003.

BELAK, Wade
(BEE-lak, WAYD) **TOR.**

Defense. Shoots right. 6'5", 221 lbs. Born, Saskatoon, Sask., July 3, 1976. Quebec's 1st choice, 12th overall, in 1994 Entry Draft.

Season	Club	League	GP	G	A	Pts	PIM	PP	SH	GW	S	%	+/-	TF	F%	Min	GP	G	A	Pts	PIM	PP	SH	GW	Min
1991-92	North Battleford	SMBHL	57	6	20	26	186																		
1992-93	North Battleford	SJHL	50	5	15	20	146																		
	Saskatoon Blades	WHL	7	0	0	0	23										7	0	0	0	0				
1993-94	Saskatoon Blades	WHL	69	4	13	17	226										16	2	2	4	43				
1994-95	Saskatoon Blades	WHL	72	4	14	18	290										9	0	0	0	36				
	Cornwall Aces	AHL															11	1	2	3	40				
1995-96	Saskatoon Blades	WHL	63	3	15	18	207										4	0	0	0	9				
	Cornwall Aces	AHL	5	0	0	0	18										2	0	0	0	2				
1996-97	Colorado	NHL	5	0	0	0	11	0	0	0	1	0.0	-1												
	Hershey Bears	AHL	65	1	7	8	320										16	0	1	1	61				
1997-98	Colorado	NHL	8	1	1	2	27	0	0	1	2	50.0	-3												
	Hershey Bears	AHL	11	0	0	0	30																		
1998-99	Colorado	NHL	22	0	0	0	71	0	0	0	5	0.0	-2	0	0.0	6:48									
	Hershey Bears	AHL	17	0	1	1	49																		
	Calgary	NHL	9	0	1	1	23	0	0	0	2	0.0	3	0	0.0	10:46									
	Saint John Flames	AHL	12	0	2	2	43										6	0	1	1	23				
99-2000	Calgary	NHL	40	0	2	2	122	0	0	0	11	0.0	-4	1	0.0	7:33									
2000-01	Calgary	NHL	23	0	0	0	79	0	0	0	8	0.0	-2	0	0.0	6:54									
	Toronto	NHL	16	1	1	2	31	0	0	0	8	12.5	-4	0	0.0	13:38									
2001-02	Toronto	NHL	63	1	3	4	142	0	0	0	47	2.1	2	0	0.0	9:14	16	1	0	1	18	0	0	0	7:28
2002-03	Toronto	NHL	55	3	6	9	196	0	0	0	33	9.1	-2	0	0.0	10:50	2	0	0	0	4	0	0	0	8:22
2003-04	Toronto	NHL	34	1	1	2	109	0	0	0	15	6.7	0	0	0.0	7:00	4	0	0	0	14	0	0	0	9:59
2004-05	Coventry Blaze	Britain	20	3	5	8	109										8	1	1	2	16				
2005-06	Toronto	NHL	55	0	3	3	109	0	0	0	16	0.0	-13	0	0.0	9:59									
2006-07	Toronto	NHL	65	0	3	3	110	0	0	0	16	0.0	-8	0	0.0	5:02									
	NHL Totals		395	7	21	28	1030	0	0	1	164	4.3		1	0.0	8:25	22	1	0	1	36	0	0	0	8:00

Rights transferred to **Colorado** after **Quebec** franchise relocated, June 21, 1995. Traded to **Calgary** by **Colorado** with Rene Corbet, Robyn Regehr and Colorado's 2nd round compensatory choice (Jarret Stoll) in 2000 Entry Draft for Theoren Fleury and Chris Dingman, February 28, 1999. • Missed majority of 1999-2000 and 2000-01 seasons recovering from shoulder injury suffered in game vs. Colorado, February 10, 2000. Claimed on waivers by **Toronto** from **Calgary**, February 16, 2001. • Missed majority of 2003-04 season recovering from abdomen (November 20, 2003 vs. Edmonton) and knee (January 6, 2004 vs. Nashville) injuries. Signed as a free agent by **Coventry** (Britain), November 8, 2004.

BELANGER, Eric
(buh-LAWN-zhay, AIR-ihk) **MIN.**

Center. Shoots left. 6', 188 lbs. Born, Sherbrooke, Que., December 16, 1977. Los Angeles' 5th choice, 96th overall, in 1996 Entry Draft.

Season	Club	League	GP	G	A	Pts	PIM	PP	SH	GW	S	%	+/-	TF	F%	Min	GP	G	A	Pts	PIM	PP	SH	GW	Min
1993-94	Magog	QAAA	32	19	24	43	24										13	5	6	11	36				
1994-95	Beauport	QMJHL	71	12	28	40	24										18	5	9	14	25				
1995-96	Beauport	QMJHL	59	35	48	83	18										20	13	14	27	6				
1996-97	Beauport	QMJHL	31	13	37	50	30																		
	Rimouski Oceanic	QMJHL	31	26	41	67	36										4	2	3	5	10				
1997-98	Fredericton	AHL	56	17	34	51	28										4	2	1	3	2				
1998-99	Springfield	AHL	33	8	18	26	10										3	0	1	1	2				
	Long Beach	IHL	1	0	0	0	0																		
99-2000	Lowell	AHL	65	15	25	40	20										7	3	3	6	2				
2000-01	Los Angeles	NHL	62	9	12	21	16	1	2	1	80	11.3	14	849	56.4	13:25	13	1	4	5	2	0	0	1	13:47
	Lowell	AHL	13	8	10	18	4																		
2001-02	Los Angeles	NHL	53	8	16	24	21	2	1	1	67	11.9	2	882	57.7	14:33	7	0	0	0	4	0	0	0	12:57
2002-03	Los Angeles	NHL	62	16	19	35	26	0	3	1	114	14.0	-5	1143	51.8	17:42									
2003-04	Los Angeles	NHL	81	13	20	33	44	0	1	2	132	9.8	-16	1418	53.7	17:01									
2004-05	HC Forst Bolzano	Italy	12	13	10	23	20										9	3	7	10	33				
2005-06	Los Angeles	NHL	65	17	20	37	62	5	0	1	119	14.3	-5	1179	49.0	17:33									
2006-07	Carolina	NHL	56	8	12	20	14	3	0	0	100	8.0	-2	689	53.4	14:51									
	Atlanta	NHL	24	9	6	15	12	1	0	0	49	18.4	0	517	52.6	19:29	4	1	0	1	12	1	0	0	16:47
	NHL Totals		403	80	105	185	195	12	7	7	661	12.1		6677	53.3	16:11	24	2	4	6	18	1	0	1	14:03

Signed as a free agent by **Bolzano** (Italy), December 22, 2004. Traded to **Carolina** by **Los Angeles** with Tim Gleason for Oleg Tverdovsky and Jack Johnson, September 29, 2006. Traded to **Nashville** by **Carolina** for Josef Vasicek, February 9, 2007. Traded to **Atlanta** by **Nashville** for Vitaly Vishnevski, February 10, 2007. Signed as a free agent by **Minnesota**, July 3, 2007.

BELL, Brendan
(BEHL, BREHN-duhn) **PHX.**

Defense. Shoots left. 6'1", 205 lbs. Born, Ottawa, Ont., March 31, 1983. Toronto's 3rd choice, 65th overall, in 2001 Entry Draft.

Season	Club	League	GP	G	A	Pts	PIM	PP	SH	GW	S	%	+/-	TF	F%	Min	GP	G	A	Pts	PIM	PP	SH	GW	Min
1998-99	Ott. Jr. Senators	CJHL	54	7	20	27	46																		
99-2000	Ottawa 67's	OHL	48	1	32	33	34										5	0	1	1	4				
2000-01	Ottawa 67's	OHL	68	7	32	39	59										20	1	11	12	22				
2001-02	Ottawa 67's	OHL	67	10	36	46	56										13	2	5	7	25				
2002-03	Ottawa 67's	OHL	55	14	39	53	46										23	8	19	27	25				
2003-04	St. John's	AHL	74	7	18	25	72																		
2004-05	St. John's	AHL	75	6	25	31	57										5	0	1	1	2				
2005-06	Toronto	NHL	1	0	0	0	0	0	0	0	2	0.0	0	0	0.0	14:00									
	Toronto Marlies	AHL	70	6	37	43	99										5	0	4	4	10				

			Regular Season														Playoffs								
Season	Club	League	GP	G	A	Pts	PIM	PP	SH	GW	S	%	+/-	TF	F%	Min	GP	G	A	Pts	PIM	PP	SH	GW	Min
2006-07	**Toronto**	**NHL**	**31**	**1**	**4**	**5**	**19**	**1**	**0**	**0**	**29**	**3.4**	**–3**	**1**	**0.0**	**12:08**									
	Phoenix	**NHL**	**14**	**0**	**2**	**2**	**8**	**0**	**0**	**0**	**18**	**0.0**	**–8**	**0**	**0.0**	**17:07**									
	NHL Totals		**46**	**1**	**6**	**7**	**27**	**1**	**0**	**0**	**49**	**2.0**		**1**	**0.0**	**13:42**									

OHL First All-Star Team (2003) • Canadian Major Junior First All-Star Team (2003) • Canadian Major Junior Defenseman of the Year (2003)

Traded to **Phoenix** by **Toronto** with Toronto's 2nd round choice in 2008 Entry Draft for Yanic Perreault and Phoenix's 5th round choice in 2008 Entry Draft, February 27, 2007.

BELL, Mark

(BEHL, MAHRK) **TOR.**

Center. Shoots left. 6'4", 220 lbs. Born, St. Paul's, Ont., August 5, 1980. Chicago's 1st choice, 8th overall, in 1998 Entry Draft.

Season	Club	League	GP	G	A	Pts	PIM	PP	SH	GW	S	%	+/-	TF	F%	Min	GP	G	A	Pts	PIM	PP	SH	GW	Min
1995-96	Stratford Cullitons	OHA-B	47	8	15	23	32																		
1996-97	Ottawa 67's	OHL	65	8	12	20	40										24	4	7	11	13				
1997-98	Ottawa 67's	OHL	55	34	26	60	87										13	6	5	11	14				
1998-99	Ottawa 67's	OHL	44	29	26	55	69										9	6	5	11	8				
99-2000	Ottawa 67's	OHL	48	34	38	72	95										2	0	1	1	0				
2000-01	**Chicago**	**NHL**	**13**	**0**	**1**	**1**	**4**	**0**	**0**	**0**	**14**	**0.0**	**0**	**141**	**48.9**	**12:00**									
	Norfolk Admirals	AHL	61	15	27	42	126										9	4	3	7	10				
2001-02	**Chicago**	**NHL**	**80**	**12**	**16**	**28**	**124**	**1**	**0**	**1**	**120**	**10.0**	**–6**	**47**	**42.6**	**12:39**	**5**	**0**	**0**	**0**	**8**	**0**	**0**	**0**	**9:18**
2002-03	**Chicago**	**NHL**	**82**	**14**	**15**	**29**	**113**	**0**	**2**	**0**	**127**	**11.0**	**0**	**377**	**52.5**	**14:04**									
2003-04	**Chicago**	**NHL**	**82**	**21**	**24**	**45**	**106**	**2**	**0**	**1**	**202**	**10.4**	**–14**	**387**	**48.3**	**17:37**									
2004-05	Trondheim IK	Norway	25	10	17	27	87										11	6	6	12	44				
2005-06	**Chicago**	**NHL**	**82**	**25**	**23**	**48**	**107**	**11**	**1**	**1**	**227**	**11.0**	**–14**	**1034**	**48.5**	**17:37**									
2006-07	**San Jose**	**NHL**	**71**	**11**	**10**	**21**	**83**	**3**	**0**	**2**	**116**	**9.5**	**–9**	**108**	**48.2**	**12:57**	**4**	**0**	**0**	**0**	**2**	**0**	**0**	**0**	**10:16**
	NHL Totals		**410**	**83**	**89**	**172**	**537**	**17**	**3**	**5**	**806**	**10.3**		**2094**	**49.0**	**14:57**	**9**	**0**	**0**	**0**	**10**	**0**	**0**	**0**	**9:44**

Signed as a free agent by **Trondheim** (Norway), November 6, 2004. Traded to **San Jose** by **Chicago** for Tom Preissing and Josh Hennessy, July 10, 2006. Traded to **Toronto** by **San Jose** with Vesa Toskala for Toronto's 1st (later traded to St. Louis - St. Louis selected Lars Eller) and 2nd (later traded to St. Louis - St. Louis selected Aaron Palushaj) round choices in 2007 Entry Draft and Toronto's 4th round choice in 2009 Entry Draft, June 22, 2007.

BELLE, Shawn

(BEHL, SHAWN) **MIN.**

Defense. Shoots left. 6'1", 232 lbs. Born, Edmonton, Alta., January 3, 1985. St. Louis' 1st choice, 30th overall, in 2003 Entry Draft.

Season	Club	League	GP	G	A	Pts	PIM	PP	SH	GW	S	%	+/-	TF	F%	Min	GP	G	A	Pts	PIM	PP	SH	GW	Min
99-2000	K of C Squires	AMBHL	34	7	20	27	36																		
2000-01	K of C Squires	AMBHL	39	18	30	48	69																		
	Regina Pats	WHL	4	0	3	3	0																		
	Tri-City	WHL	2	0	1	1	0																		
2001-02	Tri-City	WHL	64	1	17	18	51										5	2	1	3	2				
2002-03	Tri-City	WHL	66	7	14	21	79																		
2003-04	Tri-City	WHL	55	9	20	29	68										11	3	5	8	15				
2004-05	Tri-City	WHL	62	13	32	45	76										5	1	1	2	6				
2005-06	Iowa Stars	AHL	45	1	2	3	63																		
	Houston Aeros	AHL	16	1	1	2	18										8	1	0	1	4				
2006-07	**Minnesota**	**NHL**	**9**	**0**	**1**	**1**	**0**	**0**	**0**	**0**	**3**	**0.0**	**4**	**0**	**0.0**	**9:56**									
	Houston Aeros	AHL	57	4	14	18	73																		
	NHL Totals		**9**	**0**	**1**	**1**	**0**	**0**	**0**	**0**	**3**	**0.0**		**0**	**0.0**	**9:56**									

Rights traded to **Dallas** by **St. Louis** for Jason Bacashihua, June 25, 2004. Traded to **Minnesota** by **Dallas** with Martin Skoula for Willie Mitchell and Minnesota's 2nd round choice (Nico Saccheti) in 2007 Entry Draft, March 9, 2006.

BERARD, Bryan

(buh-RAHRD, BRIGH-uhn)

Defense. Shoots left. 6'2", 220 lbs. Born, Woonsocket, RI, March 5, 1977. Ottawa's 1st choice, 1st overall, in 1995 Entry Draft.

Season	Club	League	GP	G	A	Pts	PIM	PP	SH	GW	S	%	+/-	TF	F%	Min	GP	G	A	Pts	PIM	PP	SH	GW	Min
1991-92	Mount St. Charles	High-RI	15	3	15	18	4																		
1992-93	Mount St. Charles	High-RI	15	8	12	20	18																		
1993-94	Mount St. Charles	High-RI	15	11	26	37	4.5										4	3	3	6	6				
1994-95	Detroit	OHL	58	20	55	75	97										21	4	20	24	38				
1995-96	Detroit	OHL	56	31	58	89	116										17	7	18	25	41				
1996-97	**NY Islanders**	**NHL**	**82**	**8**	**40**	**48**	**86**	**3**	**0**	**1**	**172**	**4.7**	**1**												
1997-98	**NY Islanders**	**NHL**	**75**	**14**	**32**	**46**	**59**	**8**	**1**	**2**	**192**	**7.3**	**–32**												
	United States	Olympics	2	0	0	0	0																		
1998-99	**NY Islanders**	**NHL**	**31**	**4**	**11**	**15**	**26**	**2**	**0**	**3**	**72**	**5.6**	**–6**	**0**	**0.0**	**24:45**									
	Toronto	**NHL**	**38**	**5**	**14**	**19**	**22**	**2**	**0**	**2**	**63**	**7.9**	**7**	**0**	**0.0**	**22:38**	**17**	**1**	**8**	**9**	**8**	**1**	**0**	**0**	**21:11**
99-2000	**Toronto**	**NHL**	**64**	**3**	**27**	**30**	**42**	**1**	**0**	**0**	**98**	**3.1**	**11**	**0**	**0.0**	**19:34**									
2000-01	**Toronto**	**NHL**	DID NOT PLAY – INJURED																						
2001-02	**NY Rangers**	**NHL**	**82**	**2**	**21**	**23**	**60**	**0**	**0**	**0**	**132**	**1.5**	**–1**	**0**	**0.0**	**19:38**									
2002-03	**Boston**	**NHL**	**80**	**10**	**28**	**38**	**64**	**4**	**0**	**1**	**205**	**4.9**	**–4**	**0**	**0.0**	**21:21**	**3**	**1**	**0**	**1**	**2**	**0**	**0**	**0**	**21:50**
2003-04	**Chicago**	**NHL**	**58**	**13**	**34**	**47**	**53**	**6**	**0**	**0**	**203**	**6.4**	**–24**	**0**	**0.0**	**21:46**									
2004-05			DID NOT PLAY																						
2005-06	**Columbus**	**NHL**	**44**	**12**	**20**	**32**	**32**	**11**	**0**	**2**	**126**	**9.5**	**–29**	**0**	**0.0**	**22:40**									
2006-07	**Columbus**	**NHL**	**11**	**0**	**3**	**3**	**8**	**0**	**0**	**0**	**22**	**0.0**	**–4**	**0**	**0.0**	**18:58**									
	NHL Totals		**565**	**71**	**230**	**301**	**452**	**37**	**1**	**11**	**1285**	**5.5**		**0**	**0.0**	**21:15**	**20**	**2**	**8**	**10**	**10**	**1**	**0**	**0**	**21:17**

OHL All-Rookie Team (1995) • OHL First All-Star Team (1995, 1996) • OHL Rookie of the Year (1995) • Canadian Major Junior First All-Star Team (1995, 1996) • Canadian Major Junior Rookie of the Year (1995) • Canadian Major Junior Defenseman of the Year (1996) • NHL All-Rookie Team (1997) • Calder Memorial Trophy (1997) • Bill Masterton Memorial Trophy (2004)

Traded to **NY Islanders** by **Ottawa** with Don Beaupre and Martin Straka for Damian Rhodes and Wade Redden, January 23, 1996. Traded to **Toronto** by **NY Islanders** with NY Islanders' 6th round choice (Jan Sochor) in 1999 Entry Draft for Felix Potvin and Toronto's 6th round choice (later traded to Tampa Bay – Tampa Bay selected Fedor Fedorov) in 1999 Entry Draft, January 9, 1999. • Missed remainder of 1999-2000 season and entire 2000-01 season recovering from eye injury suffered in game vs. Ottawa, March 11, 2000. Signed as a free agent by **NY Rangers**, October 5, 2001. Signed as a free agent by **Boston**, August 13, 2002. Signed as a free agent by **Chicago**, October 31, 2003. Signed as a free agent by **Columbus**, August 3, 2005. • Missed majority of 2006-07 season due to a recurring back injury.

BERG, Aki

(BUHRG, AH-kee)

Defense. Shoots left. 6'3", 213 lbs. Born, Turku, Finland, July 28, 1977. Los Angeles' 1st choice, 3rd overall, in 1995 Entry Draft.

Season	Club	League	GP	G	A	Pts	PIM	PP	SH	GW	S	%	+/-	TF	F%	Min	GP	G	A	Pts	PIM	PP	SH	GW	Min
1992-93	TPS Turku Jr.	Fin-Jr.	39	18	24	42	24																		
1993-94	TPS Turku U18	Fin-U18	3	2	1	3	6																		
	TPS Turku Jr.	Fin-Jr.	21	3	11	14	24										7	0	0	0	10				
	TPS Turku	Finland	6	0	3	3	4																		
	Kiekko-67 Turku	Finland-2	12	1	1	2	16																		
1994-95	TPS Turku Jr.	Fin-Jr.	8	1	0	1	30																		
	TPS Turku U18	Fin-U18	6	2	8	10	42										3	1	1	2	6				
	Kiekko-67 Turku	Finland-2	20	3	9	12	34																		
	TPS Turku	Finland	5	0	0	0	4																		
1995-96	**Los Angeles**	**NHL**	**51**	**0**	**7**	**7**	**29**	**0**	**0**	**0**	**56**	**0.0**	**–13**												
	Phoenix	IHL	20	0	3	3	18										2	0	0	0	4				
1996-97	**Los Angeles**	**NHL**	**41**	**2**	**6**	**8**	**24**	**2**	**0**	**0**	**65**	**3.1**	**–9**												
	Phoenix	IHL	23	1	3	4	21																		
1997-98	**Los Angeles**	**NHL**	**72**	**0**	**8**	**8**	**61**	**0**	**0**	**0**	**58**	**0.0**	**3**				**4**	**0**	**3**	**3**	**0**	**0**	**0**	**0**	
	Finland	Olympics	6	0	0	0	6																		
1998-99	TPS Turku	Finland	48	8	7	15	137										9	1	1	2	45				
99-2000	**Los Angeles**	**NHL**	**70**	**3**	**13**	**16**	**45**	**0**	**0**	**0**	**70**	**4.3**	**–1**	**0**	**0.0**	**16:39**	**2**	**0**	**0**	**0**	**2**	**0**	**0**	**0**	**15:03**
2000-01	**Los Angeles**	**NHL**	**47**	**0**	**4**	**4**	**43**	**0**	**0**	**0**	**31**	**0.0**	**3**	**0**	**0.0**	**14:54**									
	Toronto	**NHL**	**12**	**3**	**0**	**3**	**2**	**3**	**0**	**1**	**12**	**25.0**	**–6**	**0**	**0.0**	**18:13**	**11**	**0**	**2**	**2**	**4**	**0**	**0**	**0**	**16:31**
2001-02	**Toronto**	**NHL**	**81**	**1**	**10**	**11**	**46**	**0**	**0**	**0**	**66**	**1.5**	**14**	**1**	**100.0**	**18:43**	**20**	**0**	**1**	**1**	**37**	**0**	**0**	**0**	**18:25**
	Finland	Olympics	4	1	0	1	2																		
2002-03	**Toronto**	**NHL**	**78**	**4**	**7**	**11**	**28**	**0**	**0**	**2**	**49**	**8.2**	**3**	**0**	**0.0**	**15:02**	**7**	**1**	**1**	**2**	**2**	**0**	**0**	**0**	**19:45**
2003-04	**Toronto**	**NHL**	**79**	**2**	**7**	**9**	**40**	**0**	**0**	**0**	**69**	**2.9**	**–1**	**1**	**0.0**	**18:18**	**10**	**0**	**0**	**0**	**2**	**0**	**0**	**0**	**14:52**
2004-05	Timra IK	Sweden	47	6	14	20	46										7	0	0	0	6				
2005-06	**Toronto**	**NHL**	**75**	**0**	**8**	**8**	**56**	**0**	**0**	**0**	**42**	**0.0**	**–5**	**1**	**100.0**	**15:58**									
	Finland	Olympics	8	0	0	0	4																		
2006-07	TPS Turku	Finland	54	5	19	24	62										2	0	0	0	0				
	NHL Totals		**606**	**15**	**70**	**85**	**374**	**5**	**0**	**3**	**518**	**2.9**		**3**	**66.7**	**16:47**	**54**	**1**	**7**	**8**	**47**	**0**	**0**	**0**	**17:20**

Traded to **Toronto** by **Los Angeles** for Adam Mair and Toronto's 2nd round choice (Mike Cammalleri) in 2001 Entry Draft, March 13, 2001. Signed as a free agent by **Timra** (Sweden), September 22, 2004. Signed as a free agent by **Turku** (Finland), April 26, 2006.

BERGENHEIM, Sean
(BUHR-gehn-highm, SHAWN) **NYI**

Left wing. Shoots left. 5'10", 194 lbs. Born, Helsinki, Finland, February 8, 1984. NY Islanders' 1st choice, 22nd overall, in 2002 Entry Draft.

			Regular Season														Playoffs								
Season	Club	League	GP	G	A	Pts	PIM	PP	SH	GW	S	%	+/-	TF	F%	Min	GP	G	A	Pts	PIM	PP	SH	GW	Min
99-2000	Jokerit U18	Fin-U18	30	22	11	33	34	....	....	....	....	....	....	....	....	....	3	1	0	1	0	....	....	....	....
	Jokerit U18	Fin-U18	17	10	8	18	14	....	....	....	....	....	....	....	....	....	3	1	0	1	2	....	....	....	....
2000-01	Jokerit U18	Fin-U18	1	1	0	1	4	....	....	....	....	....	....	....	....	....	6	9	5	14	8	....	....	....	....
	Jokerit Helsinki Jr.	Fin-Jr.	18	6	4	10	26	....	....	....	....	....	....	....	....	....	2	0	0	0	4	....	....	....	....
2001-02	Jokerit U18	Fin-U18	....	....	....	....	....	....	....	....	....	....	....	....	....	....	5	6	2	8	18	....	....	....	....
	Jokerit Helsinki Jr.	Fin-Jr.	23	11	19	30	36	....	....	....	....	....	....	....	....	....	1	0	0	0	2	....	....	....	....
	Kiekko-Vantaa	Finland-2	4	0	0	0	52	....	....	....	....	....	....	....	....	....	....	....	....	....	....	....	....	....	....
	Jokerit Helsinki	Finland	28	2	2	4	4	....	....	....	....	....	....	....	....	....	....	....	....	....	....	....	....	....	....
2002-03	Jokerit Helsinki Jr.	Fin-Jr.	2	3	0	3	2	....	....	....	....	....	....	....	....	....	....	....	....	....	....	....	....	....	....
	Jokerit Helsinki	Finland	38	3	3	6	4	....	....	....	....	....	....	....	....	....	2	0	0	0	0	....	....	....	....
2003-04	**NY Islanders**	**NHL**	**18**	**1**	**1**	**2**	**4**	**0**	**1**	**0**	**12**	**8.3**	**–4**	**2**	**50.0**	**8:55**	....	....	....	....	....	....	....	....	....
	Jokerit Helsinki	Finland	20	2	2	4	18	....	....	....	....	....	....	....	....	....	3	1	1	2	0	....	....	....	....
	Bridgeport	AHL	....	....	....	....	....	....	....	....	....	....	....	....	....	....	7	2	3	5	10	....	....	....	....
2004-05	Bridgeport	AHL	61	15	14	29	69	....	....	....	....	....	....	....	....	....	....	....	....	....	....	....	....	....	....
2005-06	**NY Islanders**	**NHL**	**28**	**4**	**5**	**9**	**20**	**0**	**0**	**1**	**63**	**6.3**	**–11**	**14**	**28.6**	**13:17**	....	....	....	....	....	....	....	....	....
	Bridgeport	AHL	55	25	22	47	112	....	....	....	....	....	....	....	....	....	7	0	2	2	24	....	....	....	....
2006-07	Yaroslavl	Russia	9	1	4	5	26	....	....	....	....	....	....	....	....	....	....	....	....	....	....	....	....	....	....
	Frolunda	Sweden	36	16	17	33	80	....	....	....	....	....	....	....	....	....	....	....	....	....	....	....	....	....	....
	NHL Totals		**46**	**5**	**6**	**11**	**24**	**0**	**1**	**1**	**75**	**6.7**		**16**	**31.3**	**11:34**	....	....	....	....	....	....	....	....	....

Signed as a free agent by **Yaroslavl** (Russia), August 5, 2006. Signed as a free agent by **Frolunda** (Sweden), November 3, 2006.

BERGERON, Marc-Andre
(BAIR-zhur-uhn, MAHRK-AWN-dray) **NYI**

Defense. Shoots left. 5'10", 197 lbs. Born, St-Louis-de-France, Que., October 13, 1980.

Season	Club	League	GP	G	A	Pts	PIM	PP	SH	GW	S	%	+/-	TF	F%	Min	GP	G	A	Pts	PIM	PP	SH	GW	Min
1996-97	Cap-d-Madeleine	QAAA	4	0	1	1	0	....	....	....	....	....	....	....	....	....	2	0	0	0	0	....	....	....	....
1997-98	Baie-Comeau	QMJHL	40	6	14	20	48	....	....	....	....	....	....	....	....	....	....	....	....	....	....	....	....	....	....
1998-99	Baie-Comeau	QMJHL	46	8	14	22	57	....	....	....	....	....	....	....	....	....	....	....	....	....	....	....	....	....	....
	Shawinigan	QMJHL	24	6	7	13	66	....	....	....	....	....	....	....	....	....	5	2	2	4	24	....	....	....	....
99-2000	Shawinigan	QMJHL	70	24	50	74	173	....	....	....	....	....	....	....	....	....	13	4	7	11	45	....	....	....	....
2000-01	Shawinigan	QMJHL	69	42	59	101	185	....	....	....	....	....	....	....	....	....	10	4	11	15	24	....	....	....	....
2001-02	Hamilton	AHL	50	2	13	15	61	....	....	....	....	....	....	....	....	....	9	1	4	5	8	....	....	....	....
2002-03	**Edmonton**	**NHL**	**5**	**1**	**1**	**2**	**9**	**0**	**0**	**0**	**5**	**20.0**	**2**	**0**	**0.0**	**16:30**	**1**	**0**	**1**	**1**	**0**	**0**	**0**	**0**	**19:20**
	Hamilton	AHL	66	8	31	39	73	....	....	....	....	....	....	....	....	....	20	0	7	7	25	....	....	....	....
2003-04	**Edmonton**	**NHL**	**54**	**9**	**17**	**26**	**26**	**3**	**0**	**0**	**105**	**8.6**	**13**	**0**	**0.0**	**17:39**	....	....	....	....	....	....	....	....	....
	Toronto	AHL	17	4	3	7	23	....	....	....	....	....	....	....	....	....	....	....	....	....	....	....	....	....	....
2004-05	Brynas IF Gavle	Sweden	10	3	2	5	72	....	....	....	....	....	....	....	....	....	....	....	....	....	....	....	....	....	....
	Brynas IF Gavle	Sweden-Q	9	1	2	3	8	....	....	....	....	....	....	....	....	....	....	....	....	....	....	....	....	....	....
2005-06	**Edmonton**	**NHL**	**75**	**15**	**20**	**35**	**38**	**8**	**0**	**1**	**144**	**10.4**	**3**	**0**	**0.0**	**21:14**	**18**	**2**	**1**	**3**	**14**	**2**	**0**	**0**	**14:56**
2006-07	**Edmonton**	**NHL**	**55**	**8**	**17**	**25**	**28**	**6**	**0**	**3**	**111**	**7.2**	**–9**	**0**	**0.0**	**17:27**	....	....	....	....	....	....	....	....	....
	NY Islanders	**NHL**	**23**	**6**	**15**	**21**	**10**	**4**	**0**	**1**	**55**	**10.9**	**5**	**0**	**0.0**	**23:07**	**5**	**1**	**1**	**2**	**6**	**1**	**0**	**1**	**27:21**
	NHL Totals		**212**	**39**	**70**	**109**	**111**	**21**	**0**	**5**	**420**	**9.3**		**0**	**0.0**	**19:26**	**24**	**3**	**3**	**6**	**20**	**3**	**0**	**1**	**17:42**

QMJHL First All-Star Team (2001) • Canadian Major Junior First All-Star Team (2001) • Canadian Major Junior Defenseman of the Year (2001) • AHL Second All-Star Team (2003)

Signed as a free agent by **Edmonton**, July 20, 2001. Signed as a free agent by **Gavle** (Sweden), January 23, 2005. Traded to **NY Islanders** by **Edmonton** with Edmonton's 3rd round choice in 2008 Entry Draft for Denis Grebeshkov, February 18, 2007.

BERGERON, Patrice
(BAIR-zhuhr-uhn, pa-TREEZ) **BOS.**

Center. Shoots right. 6', 186 lbs. Born, Ancienne-Lorette, Que., July 24, 1985. Boston's 2nd choice, 45th overall, in 2003 Entry Draft.

Season	Club	League	GP	G	A	Pts	PIM	PP	SH	GW	S	%	+/-	TF	F%	Min	GP	G	A	Pts	PIM	PP	SH	GW	Min
2000-01	Ste-Foy	QAAA	5	1	2	3	0	....	....	....	....	....	....	....	....	....	....	....	....	....	....	....	....	....	....
2001-02	St-Francois	QAAA	38	25	37	62	18	....	....	....	....	....	....	....	....	....	8	6	4	10	10	....	....	....	....
	Acadie-Bathurst	QMJHL	4	0	1	1	0	....	....	....	....	....	....	....	....	....	....	....	....	....	....	....	....	....	....
2002-03	Acadie-Bathurst	QMJHL	70	23	50	73	62	....	....	....	....	....	....	....	....	....	11	6	9	15	6	....	....	....	....
2003-04	**Boston**	**NHL**	**71**	**16**	**23**	**39**	**22**	**7**	**0**	**2**	**133**	**12.0**	**5**	**699**	**49.4**	**16:21**	**7**	**1**	**3**	**4**	**0**	**0**	**0**	**1**	**17:13**
2004-05	Providence Bruins	AHL	68	21	40	61	59	....	....	....	....	....	....	....	....	....	16	5	7	12	4	....	....	....	....
2005-06	**Boston**	**NHL**	**81**	**31**	**42**	**73**	**22**	**12**	**1**	**6**	**310**	**10.0**	**3**	**1447**	**54.7**	**20:36**	....	....	....	....	....	....	....	....	....
2006-07	**Boston**	**NHL**	**77**	**22**	**48**	**70**	**26**	**14**	**0**	**6**	**224**	**9.8**	**–28**	**1560**	**51.2**	**20:49**	....	....	....	....	....	....	....	....	....
	NHL Totals		**229**	**69**	**113**	**182**	**70**	**33**	**1**	**14**	**667**	**10.3**		**3706**	**52.2**	**19:21**	**7**	**1**	**3**	**4**	**0**	**0**	**0**	**1**	**17:13**

BERGLUND, Christian
(BUHRG-luhnd, KRIH-stan) **FLA.**

Left wing. Shoots left. 5'11", 195 lbs. Born, Orebro, Sweden, March 12, 1980. New Jersey's 3rd choice, 37th overall, in 1998 Entry Draft.

Season	Club	League	GP	G	A	Pts	PIM	PP	SH	GW	S	%	+/-	TF	F%	Min	GP	G	A	Pts	PIM	PP	SH	GW	Min
1994-95	Kariskoga IK	Sweden-4	20	14	13	27	....	....	....	....	....	....	....	....	....	....	....	....	....	....	....	....	....	....	....
1995-96	Kristinehamn SK	Sweden-3	23	8	8	16	12	....	....	....	....	....	....	....	....	....	....	....	....	....	....	....	....	....	....
1996-97	Farjestad Jr.	Swe-Jr.	21	2	3	5	24	....	....	....	....	....	....	....	....	....	....	....	....	....	....	....	....	....	....
1997-98	Farjestad Jr.	Swe-Jr.	29	23	19	42	88	....	....	....	....	....	....	....	....	....	2	0	0	0	0	....	....	....	....
	Farjestad	Sweden	1	0	0	0	0	....	....	....	....	....	....	....	....	....	....	....	....	....	....	....	....	....	....
1998-99	Farjestad Jr.	Swe-Jr.	5	3	4	7	22	....	....	....	....	....	....	....	....	....	....	....	....	....	....	....	....	....	....
	Farjestad	Sweden	37	2	4	6	37	....	....	....	....	....	....	....	....	....	4	1	0	1	4	....	....	....	....
99-2000	Farjestad Jr.	Swe-Jr.	5	3	5	8	8	....	....	....	....	....	....	....	....	....	....	....	....	....	....	....	....	....	....
	Bofors	Sweden-2	6	2	0	2	12	....	....	....	....	....	....	....	....	....	....	....	....	....	....	....	....	....	....
	Farjestad	Sweden	43	8	6	14	44	....	....	....	....	....	....	....	....	....	7	2	1	3	10	....	....	....	....
2000-01	Farjestad	Sweden	49	17	20	37	*142	....	....	....	....	....	....	....	....	....	16	7	7	14	22	....	....	....	....
2001-02	**New Jersey**	**NHL**	**15**	**2**	**7**	**9**	**8**	**0**	**0**	**0**	**22**	**9.1**	**–3**	**2**	**50.0**	**12:26**	**3**	**0**	**0**	**0**	**2**	**0**	**0**	**0**	**11:31**
	Albany River Rats	AHL	60	21	26	47	69	....	....	....	....	....	....	....	....	....	....	....	....	....	....	....	....	....	....
2002-03	**New Jersey**	**NHL**	**38**	**4**	**5**	**9**	**20**	**0**	**0**	**0**	**50**	**8.0**	**3**	**11**	**9.1**	**10:11**	....	....	....	....	....	....	....	....	....
	Albany River Rats	AHL	26	6	14	20	57	....	....	....	....	....	....	....	....	....	....	....	....	....	....	....	....	....	....
2003-04	**New Jersey**	**NHL**	**23**	**2**	**3**	**5**	**4**	**0**	**0**	**0**	**33**	**6.1**	**–4**	**2**	**50.0**	**11:22**	....	....	....	....	....	....	....	....	....
	Florida	**NHL**	**10**	**3**	**1**	**4**	**10**	**0**	**0**	**0**	**17**	**17.6**	**–2**	**14**	**28.6**	**12:01**	....	....	....	....	....	....	....	....	....
2004-05	Farjestad	Sweden	48	7	13	20	97	....	....	....	....	....	....	....	....	....	14	2	3	5	56	....	....	....	....
2005-06	Rapperswil	Swiss	44	24	20	44	124	....	....	....	....	....	....	....	....	....	11	4	8	12	*63	....	....	....	....
2006-07	SC Bern	Swiss	42	17	25	42	97	....	....	....	....	....	....	....	....	....	16	5	5	10	18	....	....	....	....
	NHL Totals		**86**	**11**	**16**	**27**	**42**	**0**	**0**	**0**	**122**	**9.0**		**29**	**24.1**	**11:06**	**3**	**0**	**0**	**0**	**2**	**0**	**0**	**0**	**11:31**

• Missed majority of 2003-04 season recovering from hip injury suffered in game vs. Philadelphia, December 12, 2003. Traded to **Florida** by **New Jersey** with Victor Uchevatov for Viktor Kozlov, March 1, 2004. Signed as a free agent by **Farjestad** (Sweden), October 7, 2004. Signed as a free agent by **Rapperswil** (Swiss), August 26, 2005. Signed as a free agent by **Bern** (Swiss), May 19, 2006.

BERNIER, Steve
(BAIRN-yay, STEEV) **S.J.**

Right wing. Shoots right. 6'2", 235 lbs. Born, Quebec City, Que., March 31, 1985. San Jose's 2nd choice, 16th overall, in 2003 Entry Draft.

Season	Club	League	GP	G	A	Pts	PIM	PP	SH	GW	S	%	+/-	TF	F%	Min	GP	G	A	Pts	PIM	PP	SH	GW	Min
1998-99	Quebec AA Aces	QAHA	28	33	23	56	24	....	....	....	....	....	....	....	....	....	....	....	....	....	....	....	....	....	....
99-2000	Quebec AA Aces	QAHA	26	12	23	35	42	....	....	....	....	....	....	....	....	....	....	....	....	....	....	....	....	....	....
2000-01	Ste-Foy	QAAA	39	17	35	52	48	....	....	....	....	....	....	....	....	....	16	9	17	26	8	....	....	....	....
2001-02	Moncton Wildcats	QMJHL	66	31	28	59	51	....	....	....	....	....	....	....	....	....	....	....	....	....	....	....	....	....	....
2002-03	Moncton Wildcats	QMJHL	71	49	52	101	90	....	....	....	....	....	....	....	....	....	2	1	0	1	2	....	....	....	....
2003-04	Moncton Wildcats	QMJHL	66	36	46	82	80	....	....	....	....	....	....	....	....	....	20	7	10	17	17	....	....	....	....
2004-05	Moncton Wildcats	QMJHL	68	35	36	71	114	....	....	....	....	....	....	....	....	....	12	6	13	19	22	....	....	....	....
2005-06	**San Jose**	**NHL**	**39**	**14**	**13**	**27**	**35**	**2**	**1**	**1**	**75**	**18.7**	**4**	**8**	**62.5**	**14:08**	**11**	**1**	**5**	**6**	**8**	**1**	**0**	**1**	**15:17**
	Cleveland Barons	AHL	49	20	23	43	33	....	....	....	....	....	....	....	....	....	....	....	....	....	....	....	....	....	....
2006-07	**San Jose**	**NHL**	**62**	**15**	**16**	**31**	**29**	**6**	**0**	**4**	**104**	**14.4**	**5**	**18**	**27.8**	**13:35**	**11**	**0**	**1**	**1**	**2**	**0**	**0**	**0**	**10:39**
	Worcester Sharks	AHL	10	3	4	7	2	....	....	....	....	....	....	....	....	....	....	....	....	....	....	....	....	....	....
	NHL Totals		**101**	**29**	**29**	**58**	**64**	**8**	**1**	**5**	**179**	**16.2**		**26**	**38.5**	**13:48**	**22**	**1**	**6**	**7**	**10**	**1**	**0**	**1**	**12:58**

QMJHL All-Rookie Team (2002) • QMJHL Second All-Star Team (2003, 2004)

BERRY, Rick
(BAIR-ee, RIHK)

Defense. Shoots left. 6'2", 210 lbs. Born, Birtle, Man., November 4, 1978. Colorado's 3rd choice, 55th overall, in 1997 Entry Draft.

			Regular Season														Playoffs								
Season	Club	League	GP	G	A	Pts	PIM	PP	SH	GW	S	%	+/-	TF	F%	Min	GP	G	A	Pts	PIM	PP	SH	GW	Min
1994-95	Yellowhead	MMMHL	33	12	19	31	90																		
1995-96	Seattle	WHL	59	4	9	13	103	....	....	....	....	....	....	....	....	....	1	0	0	0	0	....	....	....	....
1996-97	Seattle	WHL	72	12	21	33	125	....	....	....	....	....	....	....	....	....	15	3	7	10	23	....	....	....	....
1997-98	Seattle	WHL	37	5	12	17	100	....	....	....	....	....	....	....	....	....	....	....	....	....	....	....	....	....	....
	Spokane Chiefs	WHL	22	4	9	13	31	....	....	....	....	....	....	....	....	....	17	1	4	5	26	....	....	....	....
1998-99	Hershey Bears	AHL	62	2	6	8	153	....	....	....	....	....	....	....	....	....	....	....	....	....	....	....	....	....	....
99-2000	Hershey Bears	AHL	64	9	16	25	148	....	....	....	....	....	....	....	....	....	13	2	3	5	24	....	....	....	....
2000-01	**Colorado**	**NHL**	**19**	**0**	**4**	**4**	**38**	**0**	**0**	**0**	**10**	**0.0**	**5**	**0**	**0.0**	**12:08**	....	....	....	....	....	....	....	....	....
	Hershey Bears	AHL	48	6	17	23	87	....	....	....	....	....	....	....	....	....	12	2	2	4	18	....	....	....	....
2001-02	**Colorado**	**NHL**	**57**	**0**	**0**	**0**	**60**	**0**	**0**	**0**	**29**	**0.0**	**1**	**0**	**0.0**	**9:29**	....	....	....	....	....	....	....	....	....
	Pittsburgh	**NHL**	**13**	**0**	**2**	**2**	**21**	**0**	**0**	**0**	**20**	**0.0**	**–4**	**0**	**0.0**	**19:39**	....	....	....	....	....	....	....	....	....
2002-03	**Washington**	**NHL**	**43**	**2**	**1**	**3**	**87**	**0**	**0**	**1**	**40**	**5.0**	**–3**	**0**	**0.0**	**12:58**	....	....	....	....	....	....	....	....	....
2003-04	**Washington**	**NHL**	**65**	**0**	**6**	**6**	**108**	**0**	**0**	**0**	**43**	**0.0**	**–5**	**2**	**50.0**	**12:11**	....	....	....	....	....	....	....	....	....
	Portland Pirates	AHL	10	2	1	3	12	....	....	....	....	....	....	....	....	....	....	....	....	....	....	....	....	....	....
2004-05	Utah Grizzlies	AHL	45	2	6	8	83	....	....	....	....	....	....	....	....	....	....	....	....	....	....	....	....	....	....
2005-06	San Antonio	AHL	5	0	0	0	4	....	....	....	....	....	....	....	....	....	....	....	....	....	....	....	....	....	....
	Milwaukee	AHL	64	1	11	12	121	....	....	....	....	....	....	....	....	....	7	0	0	0	15	....	....	....	....
2006-07	Bridgeport	AHL	76	3	15	18	155	....	....	....	....	....	....	....	....	....	....	....	....	....	....	....	....	....	....
	NHL Totals		**197**	**2**	**13**	**15**	**314**	**0**	**0**	**1**	**142**	**1.4**		**2**	**50.0**	**12:04**	....	....	....	....	....	....	....	....	....

Traded to **Pittsburgh** by **Colorado** with Ville Nieminen for Darius Kasparaitis, March 19, 2002. Claimed by **Washington** from **Pittsburgh** in Waiver Draft, October 4, 2002. Signed as a free agent by **Phoenix**, September 2, 2004. Traded to **Nashville** by **Phoenix** for future considerations, October 24, 2005. Signed as a free agent by **NY Islanders**, July 20, 2006. Signed as a free agent by **Springfield** (AHL), July 26, 2007.

BERTUZZI, Todd
(buhr-TOO-zee, TAWD) **ANA.**

Right wing. Shoots left. 6'3", 242 lbs. Born, Sudbury, Ont., February 2, 1975. NY Islanders' 1st choice, 23rd overall, in 1993 Entry Draft.

			Regular Season														Playoffs								
Season	Club	League	GP	G	A	Pts	PIM	PP	SH	GW	S	%	+/-	TF	F%	Min	GP	G	A	Pts	PIM	PP	SH	GW	Min
1990-91	Sudbury Legion	NOHA	48	25	46	71	247	....	....	....	....	....	....	....	....	....	....	....	....	....	....	....	....	....	....
	Sudbury Cubs	NOJHA	3	3	2	5	10	....	....	....	....	....	....	....	....	....	....	....	....	....	....	....	....	....	....
1991-92	Guelph Storm	OHL	47	7	14	21	145	....	....	....	....	....	....	....	....	....	....	....	....	....	....	....	....	....	....
1992-93	Guelph Storm	OHL	59	27	32	59	164	....	....	....	....	....	....	....	....	....	5	2	2	4	6	....	....	....	....
1993-94	Guelph Storm	OHL	61	28	54	82	165	....	....	....	....	....	....	....	....	....	9	2	6	8	30	....	....	....	....
1994-95	Guelph Storm	OHL	62	54	65	119	58	....	....	....	....	....	....	....	....	....	14	*15	18	33	41	....	....	....	....
1995-96	**NY Islanders**	**NHL**	**76**	**18**	**21**	**39**	**83**	**4**	**0**	**2**	**127**	**14.2**	**–14**	....	....	....	....	....	....	....	....	....	....	....	....
1996-97	**NY Islanders**	**NHL**	**64**	**10**	**13**	**23**	**68**	**3**	**0**	**1**	**79**	**12.7**	**–3**	....	....	....	....	....	....	....	....	....	....	....	....
	Utah Grizzlies	IHL	13	5	5	10	16	....	....	....	....	....	....	....	....	....	....	....	....	....	....	....	....	....	....
1997-98	**NY Islanders**	**NHL**	**52**	**7**	**11**	**18**	**58**	**1**	**0**	**1**	**63**	**11.1**	**–19**	....	....	....	....	....	....	....	....	....	....	....	....
	Vancouver	**NHL**	**22**	**6**	**9**	**15**	**63**	**1**	**1**	**1**	**39**	**15.4**	**2**	....	....	....	....	....	....	....	....	....	....	....	....
1998-99	**Vancouver**	**NHL**	**32**	**8**	**8**	**16**	**44**	**1**	**0**	**3**	**72**	**11.1**	**–6**	**191**	**43.5**	**18:28**	....	....	....	....	....	....	....	....	....
99-2000	**Vancouver**	**NHL**	**80**	**25**	**25**	**50**	**126**	**4**	**0**	**2**	**173**	**14.5**	**–2**	**476**	**46.6**	**15:24**	....	....	....	....	....	....	....	....	....
2000-01	**Vancouver**	**NHL**	**79**	**25**	**30**	**55**	**93**	**14**	**0**	**3**	**203**	**12.3**	**–18**	**84**	**45.2**	**17:13**	**4**	**2**	**2**	**4**	**8**	**0**	**0**	**0**	**19:01**
2001-02	**Vancouver**	**NHL**	**72**	**36**	**49**	**85**	**110**	**14**	**0**	**3**	**203**	**17.7**	**21**	**151**	**49.0**	**19:40**	**6**	**2**	**2**	**4**	**14**	**1**	**0**	**0**	**21:50**
2002-03	**Vancouver**	**NHL**	**82**	**46**	**51**	**97**	**144**	**25**	**0**	**7**	**243**	**18.9**	**2**	**208**	**47.1**	**20:34**	**14**	**2**	**4**	**6**	***60**	**1**	**0**	**0**	**21:05**
2003-04	**Vancouver**	**NHL**	**69**	**17**	**43**	**60**	**122**	**8**	**0**	**2**	**156**	**10.9**	**21**	**111**	**45.1**	**21:00**	....	....	....	....	....	....	....	....	....
2004-05			DID NOT PLAY – SUSPENDED																						
2005-06	**Vancouver**	**NHL**	**82**	**25**	**46**	**71**	**120**	**12**	**0**	**3**	**200**	**12.5**	**–17**	**363**	**43.8**	**19:08**	....	....	....	....	....	....	....	....	....
	Canada	Olympics	6	0	3	3	6	....	....	....	....	....	....	....	....	....	....	....	....	....	....	....	....	....	....
2006-07	**Florida**	**NHL**	**7**	**1**	**6**	**7**	**13**	**1**	**0**	**0**	**8**	**12.5**	**–4**	**0**	**0.0**	**16:32**	....	....	....	....	....	....	....	....	....
	Detroit	**NHL**	**8**	**2**	**2**	**4**	**6**	**0**	**0**	**0**	**15**	**13.3**	**3**	**2**	**50.0**	**15:32**	**16**	**3**	**4**	**7**	**15**	**1**	**0**	**0**	**14:25**
	NHL Totals		**725**	**226**	**314**	**540**	**1050**	**88**	**1**	**28**	**1581**	**14.3**		**1586**	**45.7**	**18:40**	**40**	**9**	**12**	**21**	**97**	**2**	**0**	**0**	**18:19**

OHL Second All-Star Team (1995) • NHL First All-Star Team (2003)

Played in NHL All-Star Game (2003, 2004)

Traded to **Vancouver** by **NY Islanders** with Bryan McCabe and NY Islanders' 3rd round choice (Jarkko Ruutu) in 1998 Entry Draft for Trevor Linden, February 6, 1998. • Missed majority of 1998-99 season recovering from leg injury suffered in game vs. Washington, November 1, 1998. • Suspended indefinitely by NHL for deliberate injury to Steve Moore in game vs. Colorado, March 8, 2004. Reinstated by NHL on August 8, 2005. Traded to **Florida** by **Vancouver** with Bryan Allen and Alex Auld for Roberto Luongo, Lukas Krajicek and Florida's 6th round choice (Sergei Shirokov) in 2006 Entry Draft, June 23, 2006. Traded to **Detroit** by **Florida** for Shawn Matthias and Detroit's 2nd round choice (later traded to Nashville - Nashville selected Nick Spaling) in 2007 Entry Draft, February 27, 2007. • Missed majority of 2006-07 season recovering from a recurring back injury. Signed as a free agent by **Anaheim**, July 2, 2007.

BETTS, Blair
(BEHTS, BLAIR) **NYR**

Center. Shoots left. 6'3", 210 lbs. Born, Edmonton, Alta., February 16, 1980. Calgary's 2nd choice, 33rd overall, in 1998 Entry Draft.

			Regular Season														Playoffs								
Season	Club	League	GP	G	A	Pts	PIM	PP	SH	GW	S	%	+/-	TF	F%	Min	GP	G	A	Pts	PIM	PP	SH	GW	Min
1995-96	Sherwood Park	AMHL	34	22	19	41	69	....	....	....	....	....	....	....	....	....	....	....	....	....	....	....	....	....	....
1996-97	Prince George	WHL	58	12	18	30	19	....	....	....	....	....	....	....	....	....	15	2	2	4	6	....	....	....	....
1997-98	Prince George	WHL	71	35	41	76	38	....	....	....	....	....	....	....	....	....	11	4	6	10	8	....	....	....	....
1998-99	Prince George	WHL	42	20	22	42	39	....	....	....	....	....	....	....	....	....	7	3	2	5	8	....	....	....	....
99-2000	Prince George	WHL	44	24	35	59	38	....	....	....	....	....	....	....	....	....	13	11	11	22	6	....	....	....	....
2000-01	Saint John Flames	AHL	75	13	15	28	28	....	....	....	....	....	....	....	....	....	19	2	3	5	4	....	....	....	....
2001-02	**Calgary**	**NHL**	**6**	**1**	**0**	**1**	**2**	**0**	**0**	**1**	**4**	**25.0**	**–1**	**39**	**48.7**	**7:05**	....	....	....	....	....	....	....	....	....
	Saint John Flames	AHL	67	20	29	49	10	....	....	....	....	....	....	....	....	....	....	....	....	....	....	....	....	....	....
2002-03	**Calgary**	**NHL**	**9**	**1**	**3**	**4**	**0**	**0**	**0**	**0**	**16**	**6.3**	**3**	**71**	**53.5**	**11:33**	....	....	....	....	....	....	....	....	....
	Saint John Flames	AHL	19	6	7	13	6	....	....	....	....	....	....	....	....	....	....	....	....	....	....	....	....	....	....
2003-04	**Calgary**	**NHL**	**20**	**1**	**2**	**3**	**10**	**1**	**0**	**1**	**21**	**4.8**	**–1**	**248**	**54.0**	**12:46**	....	....	....	....	....	....	....	....	....
2004-05	Hartford	AHL	16	5	4	9	4	....	....	....	....	....	....	....	....	....	....	....	....	....	....	....	....	....	....
2005-06	**NY Rangers**	**NHL**	**66**	**8**	**2**	**10**	**24**	**0**	**1**	**0**	**94**	**8.5**	**–10**	**817**	**53.4**	**12:55**	**4**	**1**	**1**	**2**	**2**	**0**	**0**	**0**	**16:12**
2006-07	**NY Rangers**	**NHL**	**82**	**9**	**4**	**13**	**24**	**1**	**1**	**0**	**120**	**7.5**	**–4**	**1186**	**52.3**	**14:02**	**10**	**0**	**0**	**0**	**4**	**0**	**0**	**0**	**11:15**
	NHL Totals		**183**	**20**	**11**	**31**	**60**	**2**	**2**	**2**	**255**	**7.8**		**2361**	**52.8**	**13:09**	**14**	**1**	**1**	**2**	**6**	**0**	**0**	**0**	**12:40**

• Missed majority of 2002-03 season recovering from shoulder injury suffered in training camp, September 27, 2002. • Missed majority of 2003-04 season recovering from shoulder injuries suffered in games vs. Chicago (November 22, 2003) and Colorado (December 31, 2003). Traded to **NY Rangers** by **Calgary** with Jamie McLennan and Greg Moore for Chris Simon and NY Rangers' 7th round choice (Matt Schneider) in 2004 Entry Draft, March 6, 2004.

BICKELL, Bryan
(bih-KEHL, BRIGH-uhn) **CHI.**

Left wing. Shoots left. 6'4", 223 lbs. Born, Bowmanville, Ont., March 9, 1986. Chicago's 3rd choice, 41st overall, in 2004 Entry Draft.

			Regular Season														Playoffs								
Season	Club	League	GP	G	A	Pts	PIM	PP	SH	GW	S	%	+/-	TF	F%	Min	GP	G	A	Pts	PIM	PP	SH	GW	Min
2000-01	Tor. Red Wings	GTHL	68	24	26	50	20	....	....	....	....	....	....	....	....	....	5	3	1	4	4	....	....	....	....
2001-02	Tor. Red Wings	GTHL	65	31	41	72	76	....	....	....	....	....	....	....	....	....	2	2	2	4	0	....	....	....	....
2002-03	Ottawa 67's	OHL	50	7	10	17	4	....	....	....	....	....	....	....	....	....	20	5	3	8	12	....	....	....	....
2003-04	Ottawa 67's	OHL	59	20	16	36	76	....	....	....	....	....	....	....	....	....	7	3	0	3	11	....	....	....	....
2004-05	Ottawa 67's	OHL	66	22	32	54	95	....	....	....	....	....	....	....	....	....	21	5	12	17	32	....	....	....	....
2005-06	Ottawa 67's	OHL	41	28	22	50	41	....	....	....	....	....	....	....	....	....	....	....	....	....	....	....	....	....	....
	Windsor Spitfires	OHL	26	17	16	33	19	....	....	....	....	....	....	....	....	....	7	5	5	10	10	....	....	....	....
2006-07	**Chicago**	**NHL**	**3**	**2**	**0**	**2**	**0**	**0**	**0**	**0**	**10**	**20.0**	**1**	**0**	**0.0**	**11:49**	....	....	....	....	....	....	....	....	....
	Norfolk Admirals	AHL	48	10	15	25	66	....	....	....	....	....	....	....	....	....	2	0	0	0	0	....	....	....	....
	NHL Totals		**3**	**2**	**0**	**2**	**0**	**0**	**0**	**0**	**10**	**20.0**		**0**	**0.0**	**11:49**	....	....	....	....	....	....	....	....	....

BIEKSA, Kevin
(BEEKS-ah, KEH-vihn) **VAN.**

Defense. Shoots right. 6'1", 205 lbs. Born, Grimsby, Ont., June 16, 1981. Vancouver's 4th choice, 151st overall, in 2001 Entry Draft.

			Regular Season														Playoffs								
Season	Club	League	GP	G	A	Pts	PIM	PP	SH	GW	S	%	+/-	TF	F%	Min	GP	G	A	Pts	PIM	PP	SH	GW	Min
1997-98	Burlington	OPJHL	27	0	3	3	10	....	....	....	....	....	....	....	....	....	....	....	....	....	....	....	....	....	....
1998-99	Burlington	OPJHL	49	8	29	37	83	....	....	....	....	....	....	....	....	....	....	....	....	....	....	....	....	....	....
99-2000	Burlington	OPJHL	49	6	27	33	139	....	....	....	....	....	....	....	....	....	....	....	....	....	....	....	....	....	....
2000-01	Bowling Green	CCHA	35	4	9	13	90	....	....	....	....	....	....	....	....	....	....	....	....	....	....	....	....	....	....
2001-02	Bowling Green	CCHA	40	5	10	15	68	....	....	....	....	....	....	....	....	....	....	....	....	....	....	....	....	....	....
2002-03	Bowling Green	CCHA	34	8	17	25	92	....	....	....	....	....	....	....	....	....	....	....	....	....	....	....	....	....	....
2003-04	Bowling Green	CCHA	38	7	15	22	66	....	....	....	....	....	....	....	....	....	....	....	....	....	....	....	....	....	....
	Manitoba Moose	AHL	4	0	2	2	2	....	....	....	....	....	....	....	....	....	....	....	....	....	....	....	....	....	....
2004-05	Manitoba Moose	AHL	80	12	27	39	192	....	....	....	....	....	....	....	....	....	14	1	1	2	52	....	....	....	....

Season	Club	League	GP	G	A	Pts	PIM	PP	SH	GW	S	%	+/-	TF	F%	Min	GP	G	A	Pts	PIM	PP	SH	GW	Min
			Regular Season														Playoffs								
2005-06	**Vancouver**	**NHL**	**39**	**0**	**6**	**6**	**77**	**0**	**0**	**0**	**38**	**0.0**	**–1**	**0**	**0.0**	**16:06**									
	Manitoba Moose	AHL	23	3	17	20	71										13	0	10	10	38				
2006-07	**Vancouver**	**NHL**	**81**	**12**	**30**	**42**	**134**	**6**	**0**	**2**	**203**	**5.9**	**1**	**0**	**0.0**	**24:16**	**9**	**0**	**0**	**0**	**20**	**0**	**0**	**0**	**28:01**
	NHL Totals		**120**	**12**	**36**	**48**	**211**	**6**	**0**	**2**	**241**	**5.0**		**0**	**0.0**	**21:37**	**9**	**0**	**0**	**0**	**20**	**0**	**0**	**0**	**28:01**

AHL All-Rookie Team (2005)

BIRON, Mathieu (BEE-rawn, MA-tyew) **MTL.**

Defense. Shoots right. 6'6", 230 lbs. Born, Lac-St-Charles, Que., April 29, 1980. Los Angeles' 1st choice, 21st overall, in 1998 Entry Draft.

Season	Club	League	GP	G	A	Pts	PIM	PP	SH	GW	S	%	+/-	TF	F%	Min	GP	G	A	Pts	PIM	PP	SH	GW	Min
1996-97	Ste-Foy	QAAA	40	4	22	26	49										10	3	4	7					
1997-98	Shawinigan	QMJHL	59	8	28	36	60										6	0	1	1	10				
1998-99	Shawinigan	QMJHL	69	13	32	45	116										6	0	2	2	6				
99-2000	**NY Islanders**	**NHL**	**60**	**4**	**4**	**8**	**38**	**2**	**0**	**2**	**70**	**5.7**	**–13**	**2**	**0.0**	**15:02**									
2000-01	**NY Islanders**	**NHL**	**14**	**0**	**1**	**1**	**12**	**0**	**0**	**0**	**10**	**0.0**	**2**	**0**	**0.0**	**12:21**									
	Lowell	AHL	22	1	3	4	17																		
	Springfield	AHL	34	0	6	6	18																		
2001-02	**Tampa Bay**	**NHL**	**36**	**0**	**0**	**0**	**12**	**0**	**0**	**0**	**35**	**0.0**	**–16**	**0**	**0.0**	**14:47**									
	Springfield	AHL	35	4	9	13	16																		
2002-03	**Florida**	**NHL**	**34**	**1**	**8**	**9**	**14**	**0**	**1**	**0**	**52**	**1.9**	**–18**	**0**	**0.0**	**21:08**									
	San Antonio	AHL	43	3	8	11	58																		
2003-04	**Florida**	**NHL**	**57**	**3**	**10**	**13**	**51**	**0**	**0**	**1**	**75**	**4.0**	**–13**	**0**	**0.0**	**18:13**									
2004-05			DID NOT PLAY																						
2005-06	**Washington**	**NHL**	**52**	**4**	**9**	**13**	**50**	**3**	**0**	**0**	**61**	**6.6**	**–11**	**0**	**0.0**	**12:14**									
2006-07	Worcester Sharks	AHL	24	3	15	18	42																		
	Hamilton	AHL	53	7	14	21	52										22	2	6	8	33				
	NHL Totals		**253**	**12**	**32**	**44**	**177**	**5**	**1**	**3**	**303**	**4.0**		**2**	**0.0**	**15:49**									

Traded to **NY Islanders** by **Los Angeles** with Olli Jokinen, Josh Green and Los Angeles' 1st round choice (Taylor Pyatt) in 1999 Entry Draft for Ziggy Palffy, Brian Smolinski, Marcel Cousineau and New Jersey's 4th round choice (previously acquired, Los Angeles selected Daniel Johansson) in 1999 Entry Draft, June 20, 1999. Traded to **Tampa Bay** by **NY Islanders** with NY Islanders' 2nd round choice (later traded to Washington – later traded to Vancouver – Vancouver selected Denis Grot) in 2002 Entry Draft for Adrian Aucoin and Alexander Kharitonov, June 22, 2001. Claimed by **Columbus** from **Tampa Bay** in Waiver Draft, October 4, 2002. Traded to **Florida** by **Columbus** for Petr Tenkrat, October 4, 2002. Signed as a free agent by **Washington**, August 10, 2005. Signed as a free agent by **San Jose**, August 9, 2006. Traded to **Montreal** by **San Jose** for Patrick Traverse, December 15, 2006.

BISAILLON, Sebastien (BIH-sigh-awn, suh-BAS-tee-yeh) **EDM.**

Defense. Shoots right. 6', 205 lbs. Born, Mont-Laurier, Que., December 8, 1986.

Season	Club	League	GP	G	A	Pts	PIM	PP	SH	GW	S	%	+/-	TF	F%	Min	GP	G	A	Pts	PIM	PP	SH	GW	Min
2002-03	Val-d'Or Foreurs	QMJHL	1	0	0	0	0																		
2003-04	Val-d'Or Foreurs	QMJHL	67	4	14	18	39										7	2	0	2	2				
2004-05	Val-d'Or Foreurs	QMJHL	69	15	33	48	39																		
2005-06	Val-d'Or Foreurs	QMJHL	63	35	36	71	56										5	0	4	4	2				
2006-07	**Edmonton**	**NHL**	**2**	**0**	**0**	**0**	**0**	**0**	**0**	**0**	**3**	**0.0**	**–1**	**0**	**0.0**	**14:12**									
	Val-d'Or Foreurs	QMJHL	63	12	40	52	30										20	2	10	12	12				
	NHL Totals		**2**	**0**	**0**	**0**	**0**	**0**	**0**	**0**	**3**	**0.0**		**0**	**0.0**	**14:12**									

Signed as a free agent by **Edmonton**, September 27, 2006.

BLAKE, Jason (BLAYK, JAY-suhn) **TOR.**

Center. Shoots left. 5'10", 180 lbs. Born, Moorhead, MN, September 2, 1973.

Season	Club	League	GP	G	A	Pts	PIM	PP	SH	GW	S	%	+/-	TF	F%	Min	GP	G	A	Pts	PIM	PP	SH	GW	Min
1991-92	Moorhead Spuds	High-MN	25	30	30	60																			
1992-93	Waterloo	USHL	45	24	27	51	107																		
1993-94	Waterloo	USHL	47	50	50	100	76																		
1994-95	Ferris State	CCHA	36	16	16	32	46																		
1995-96	North Dakota	WCHA	DID NOT PLAY – TRANSFERRED COLLEGES																						
1996-97	North Dakota	WCHA	43	19	32	51	44																		
1997-98	North Dakota	WCHA	38	24	27	51	62																		
1998-99	North Dakota	WCHA	38	*28	*41	*69	49																		
	Los Angeles	**NHL**	**1**	**1**	**0**	**1**	**0**	**0**	**0**	**0**	**5**	**20.0**	**1**	**14**	**35.7**	**17:13**									
	Orlando	IHL	5	3	5	8	6										13	3	4	7	20				
99-2000	**Los Angeles**	**NHL**	**64**	**5**	**18**	**23**	**26**	**0**	**0**	**1**	**131**	**3.8**	**4**	**269**	**43.9**	**11:17**	**3**	**0**	**0**	**0**	**0**	**0**	**0**	**0**	**9:35**
	Long Beach	IHL	7	3	6	9	2																		
2000-01	**Los Angeles**	**NHL**	**17**	**1**	**3**	**4**	**10**	**0**	**0**	**0**	**27**	**3.7**	**–8**	**13**	**61.5**	**10:03**									
	Lowell	AHL	2	0	1	1	2																		
	NY Islanders	**NHL**	**30**	**4**	**8**	**12**	**24**	**1**	**1**	**0**	**73**	**5.5**	**–12**	**118**	**44.1**	**15:43**									
2001-02	**NY Islanders**	**NHL**	**82**	**8**	**10**	**18**	**36**	**0**	**0**	**1**	**136**	**5.9**	**–11**	**23**	**43.5**	**12:54**	**7**	**0**	**1**	**1**	**13**	**0**	**0**	**0**	**12:13**
2002-03	**NY Islanders**	**NHL**	**81**	**25**	**30**	**55**	**58**	**3**	**1**	**4**	**253**	**9.9**	**16**	**22**	**18.2**	**17:38**	**5**	**0**	**1**	**1**	**2**	**0**	**0**	**0**	**19:39**
2003-04	**NY Islanders**	**NHL**	**75**	**22**	**25**	**47**	**56**	**1**	**4**	**3**	**243**	**9.1**	**11**	**70**	**41.4**	**18:49**	**4**	**2**	**0**	**2**	**2**	**0**	**0**	**0**	**18:09**
2004-05	HC Lugano	Swiss	7	2	2	4	4																		
2005-06	**NY Islanders**	**NHL**	**76**	**28**	**29**	**57**	**60**	**12**	**2**	**2**	**304**	**9.2**	**0**	**152**	**42.8**	**18:47**									
	United States	Olympics	6	0	0	0	2																		
2006-07	**NY Islanders**	**NHL**	**82**	**40**	**29**	**69**	**34**	**14**	**0**	**7**	**305**	**13.1**	**1**	**117**	**57.3**	**18:09**	**5**	**1**	**2**	**3**	**2**	**0**	**0**	**0**	**17:04**
	NHL Totals		**508**	**134**	**152**	**286**	**304**	**31**	**8**	**18**	**1477**	**9.1**		**798**	**44.9**	**16:08**	**24**	**3**	**4**	**7**	**19**	**0**	**0**	**0**	**15:26**

WCHA First All-Star Team (1997, 1998, 1999) • NCAA West Second All-American Team (1998) • WCHA Player of the Year (1999) • NCAA West First All-American Team (1999)

Played in NHL All-Star Game (2007)

Signed as a free agent by **Los Angeles**, April 20, 1999. Traded to **NY Islanders** by **Los Angeles** for NY Islanders' 5th round choice (Joel Andresen) in 2002 Entry Draft, January 3, 2001. Signed as a free agent by **Lugano** (Swiss), December 1, 2004. Signed as a free agent by **Toronto**, July 1, 2007.

BLAKE, Rob (BLAYK, RAWB) **L.A.**

Defense. Shoots right. 6'4", 225 lbs. Born, Simcoe, Ont., December 10, 1969. Los Angeles' 4th choice, 70th overall, in 1988 Entry Draft.

Season	Club	League	GP	G	A	Pts	PIM	PP	SH	GW	S	%	+/-	TF	F%	Min	GP	G	A	Pts	PIM	PP	SH	GW	Min
1985-86	Brantford Classics	OHA-B	39	3	13	16	43																		
1986-87	Stratford Cullitons	OHA-B	31	11	20	31	115																		
1987-88	Bowling Green	CCHA	43	5	8	13	88																		
1988-89	Bowling Green	CCHA	46	11	21	32	140																		
1989-90	Bowling Green	CCHA	42	23	36	59	140																		
	Los Angeles	**NHL**	**4**	**0**	**0**	**0**	**4**	**0**	**0**	**0**	**3**	**0.0**	**0**				**8**	**1**	**3**	**4**	**4**	**1**	**0**	**0**	
1990-91	**Los Angeles**	**NHL**	**75**	**12**	**34**	**46**	**125**	**9**	**0**	**2**	**150**	**8.0**	**3**				**12**	**1**	**4**	**5**	**26**	**1**	**0**	**0**	
1991-92	**Los Angeles**	**NHL**	**57**	**7**	**13**	**20**	**102**	**5**	**0**	**0**	**131**	**5.3**	**–5**				**6**	**2**	**1**	**3**	**12**	**0**	**0**	**0**	
1992-93	**Los Angeles**	**NHL**	**76**	**16**	**43**	**59**	**152**	**10**	**0**	**4**	**243**	**6.6**	**18**				**23**	**4**	**6**	**10**	**46**	**1**	**1**	**0**	
1993-94	**Los Angeles**	**NHL**	**84**	**20**	**48**	**68**	**137**	**7**	**0**	**6**	**304**	**6.6**	**–7**												
1994-95	**Los Angeles**	**NHL**	**24**	**4**	**7**	**11**	**38**	**4**	**0**	**1**	**76**	**5.3**	**–16**												
1995-96	**Los Angeles**	**NHL**	**6**	**1**	**2**	**3**	**8**	**0**	**0**	**0**	**13**	**7.7**	**0**												
1996-97	**Los Angeles**	**NHL**	**62**	**8**	**23**	**31**	**82**	**4**	**0**	**1**	**169**	**4.7**	**–28**												
1997-98	**Los Angeles**	**NHL**	**81**	**23**	**27**	**50**	**94**	**11**	**0**	**4**	**261**	**8.8**	**–3**				**4**	**0**	**0**	**0**	**6**	**0**	**0**	**0**	
	Canada	Olympics	6	1	1	2	2																		
1998-99	**Los Angeles**	**NHL**	**62**	**12**	**23**	**35**	**128**	**5**	**1**	**2**	**216**	**5.6**	**–7**	**0**	**0.0**	**24:52**									
99-2000	**Los Angeles**	**NHL**	**77**	**18**	**39**	**57**	**112**	**12**	**0**	**5**	**327**	**5.5**	**10**	**0**	**0.0**	**28:30**	**4**	**0**	**2**	**2**	**4**	**0**	**0**	**0**	**30:10**
2000-01	**Los Angeles**	**NHL**	**54**	**17**	**32**	**49**	**69**	**9**	**0**	**1**	**223**	**7.6**	**–8**	**0**	**0.0**	**28:11**									
	♦ Colorado	**NHL**	**13**	**2**	**8**	**10**	**8**	**1**	**0**	**1**	**44**	**4.5**	**11**	**0**	**0.0**	**26:03**	**23**	**6**	**13**	**19**	**16**	**3**	**0**	**0**	**29:26**
2001-02	**Colorado**	**NHL**	**75**	**16**	**40**	**56**	**58**	**10**	**0**	**2**	**229**	**7.0**	**16**	**0**	**0.0**	**27:35**	**20**	**6**	**6**	**12**	**16**	**1**	**0**	**0**	**26:38**
	Canada	Olympics	6	1	2	3	2																		
2002-03	**Colorado**	**NHL**	**79**	**17**	**28**	**45**	**57**	**8**	**2**	**3**	**269**	**6.3**	**20**	**0**	**0.0**	**26:21**	**7**	**1**	**2**	**3**	**8**	**0**	**0**	**0**	**27:28**
2003-04	**Colorado**	**NHL**	**74**	**13**	**33**	**46**	**61**	**8**	**0**	**3**	**242**	**5.4**	**6**	**1**	**0.0**	**24:23**	**9**	**0**	**5**	**5**	**6**	**0**	**0**	**0**	**20:17**

			Regular Season														Playoffs								
Season	Club	League	GP	G	A	Pts	PIM	PP	SH	GW	S	%	+/-	TF	F%	Min	GP	G	A	Pts	PIM	PP	SH	GW	Min
2004-05				DID NOT PLAY																					
2005-06	**Colorado**	**NHL**	**81**	**14**	**37**	**51**	**94**	**7**	**1**	**1**	**264**	**5.3**	**2**	**2**	**0.0**	**24:22**	**9**	**3**	**1**	**4**	**8**	**2**	**0**	**1**	**28:19**
	Canada	Olympics	6	0	1	1	2	....	....	....	....	....	....	....	....	....	....	....	....	....	....	....	....	....	....
2006-07	**Los Angeles**	**NHL**	**72**	**14**	**20**	**34**	**82**	**11**	**0**	**1**	**208**	**6.7**	**–26**	**3**	**33.3**	**24:24**	....	....	....	....	....	....	....	....	....
	NHL Totals		**1056**	**214**	**457**	**671**	**1411**	**121**	**4**	**37**	**3372**	**6.3**		**6**	**16.7**	**26:02**	**125**	**24**	**43**	**67**	**152**	**9**	**1**	**1**	**27:13**

CCHA Second All-Star Team (1989) • CCHA First All-Star Team (1990) • NCAA West First All-American Team (1990) • NHL All-Rookie Team (1991) • NHL First All-Star Team (1998) • James Norris Memorial Trophy (1998) • NHL Second All-Star Team (2000, 2001, 2002)

Played in NHL All-Star Game (1994, 1999, 2000, 2001, 2002, 2003, 2004)

• Missed majority of 1995-96 season recovering from knee injury suffered in game vs. Washington, October 20, 1995. Traded to **Colorado** by **Los Angeles** with Steve Reinprecht for Adam Deadmarsh, Aaron Miller, a player to be named later (Jared Aulin, March 22, 2001) and Colorado's 1st round choices in 2001 (Dave Steckel) and 2003 (Brian Boyle) Entry Drafts, February 21, 2001. Signed as a free agent by **Los Angeles**, July 1, 2006.

BLATNY, Zdenek

(BLAT-nee, z'DEHN-ehk)

Left wing. Shoots left. 6'1", 190 lbs. Born, Brno, Czech., January 14, 1981. Atlanta's 3rd choice, 68th overall, in 1999 Entry Draft.

Season	Club	League	GP	G	A	Pts	PIM	PP	SH	GW	S	%	+/-	TF	F%	Min	GP	G	A	Pts	PIM	PP	SH	GW	Min
1997-98	Brno Jr.	CzRep-Jr.	42	22	21	43	40	....	....	....	....	....	....	....	....	....	....	....	....	....	....	....	....	....	....
1998-99	Seattle	WHL	44	18	15	33	25	....	....	....	....	....	....	....	....	....	11	4	0	4	24	....	....	....	....
99-2000	Seattle	WHL	7	4	5	9	12	....	....	....	....	....	....	....	....	....	....	....	....	....	....	....	....	....	....
	Kootenay Ice	WHL	61	43	39	82	119	....	....	....	....	....	....	....	....	....	21	10	*17	27	46	....	....	....	....
2000-01	Kootenay Ice	WHL	58	37	48	85	120	....	....	....	....	....	....	....	....	....	11	8	10	18	24	....	....	....	....
2001-02	Greenville	ECHL	12	5	5	10	17	....	....	....	....	....	....	....	....	....	9	2	8	10	14	....	....	....	....
	Chicago Wolves	AHL	41	4	3	7	30	....	....	....	....	....	....	....	....	....	3	2	0	2	0	....	....	....	....
2002-03	**Atlanta**	**NHL**	**4**	**0**	**0**	**0**	**0**	**0**	**0**	**0**	**2**	**0.0**	**–1**	**0**	**0.0**	**10:31**	....	....	....	....	....	....	....	....	....
	Chicago Wolves	AHL	72	12	9	21	62	....	....	....	....	....	....	....	....	....	9	0	2	2	20	....	....	....	....
2003-04	**Atlanta**	**NHL**	**16**	**3**	**0**	**3**	**6**	**0**	**0**	**0**	**17**	**17.6**	**0**	**13**	**38.5**	**10:27**	....	....	....	....	....	....	....	....	....
	Chicago Wolves	AHL	61	11	23	34	115	....	....	....	....	....	....	....	....	....	10	0	4	4	24	....	....	....	....
2004-05	Pelicans Lahti	Finland	9	1	1	2	32	....	....	....	....	....	....	....	....	....	....	....	....	....	....	....	....	....	....
	Znojmo	CzRep	15	3	4	7	28	....	....	....	....	....	....	....	....	....	....	....	....	....	....	....	....	....	....
2005-06	**Boston**	**NHL**	**5**	**0**	**0**	**0**	**2**	**0**	**0**	**0**	**3**	**0.0**	**–2**	**0**	**0.0**	**5:08**	....	....	....	....	....	....	....	....	....
	Providence Bruins	AHL	35	8	22	30	21	....	....	....	....	....	....	....	....	....	....	....	....	....	....	....	....	....	....
	Springfield	AHL	31	14	15	29	20	....	....	....	....	....	....	....	....	....	....	....	....	....	....	....	....	....	....
2006-07	MODO	Sweden	16	2	1	3	44	....	....	....	....	....	....	....	....	....	20	3	4	7	34	....	....	....	....
	Springfield	AHL	19	5	8	13	18	....	....	....	....	....	....	....	....	....	....	....	....	....	....	....	....	....	....
	NHL Totals		**25**	**3**	**0**	**3**	**8**	**0**	**0**	**0**	**22**	**13.6**		**13**	**38.5**	**9:24**	....	....	....	....	....	....	....	....	....

WHL East Second All-Star Team (2000)

Signed as a free agent by **Lahti** (Finland), November 19, 2004. Signed as a free agent by **Znojmo** (CzRep), January 6, 2005. Signed as a free agent by **Boston**, September 29, 2005. Traded to **Tampa Bay** by **Boston** for Brian Eklund, February 8, 2006. Signed as a free agent by **MODO** (Sweden), January 12, 2007.

BLUNDEN, Michael

(BLUHN-dehn, MIGH-kuhl) **CHI.**

Right wing. Shoots right. 6'3", 207 lbs. Born, Toronto, Ont., December 15, 1986. Chicago's 2nd choice, 43rd overall, in 2005 Entry Draft.

Season	Club	League	GP	G	A	Pts	PIM	PP	SH	GW	S	%	+/-	TF	F%	Min	GP	G	A	Pts	PIM	PP	SH	GW	Min
2002-03	Erie Otters	OHL	63	10	7	17	55	....	....	....	....	....	....	....	....	....	....	....	....	....	....	....	....	....	....
2003-04	Erie Otters	OHL	52	22	17	39	53	....	....	....	....	....	....	....	....	....	3	0	0	0	0	....	....	....	....
2004-05	Erie Otters	OHL	61	22	19	41	75	....	....	....	....	....	....	....	....	....	2	0	0	0	2	....	....	....	....
2005-06	Erie Otters	OHL	60	46	38	84	63	....	....	....	....	....	....	....	....	....	....	....	....	....	....	....	....	....	....
	Norfolk Admirals	AHL	11	1	5	6	2	....	....	....	....	....	....	....	....	....	1	0	0	0	0	....	....	....	....
2006-07	**Chicago**	**NHL**	**9**	**0**	**0**	**0**	**10**	**0**	**0**	**0**	**10**	**0.0**	**–5**	**1**	**0.0**	**11:23**	....	....	....	....	....	....	....	....	....
	Norfolk Admirals	AHL	17	4	5	9	15	....	....	....	....	....	....	....	....	....	....	....	....	....	....	....	....	....	....
	NHL Totals		**9**	**0**	**0**	**0**	**10**	**0**	**0**	**0**	**10**	**0.0**		**1**	**0.0**	**11:23**	....	....	....	....	....	....	....	....	....

• Missed remainder of 2006-07 season after sufffering a shoulder injury in game vs. Hershey (AHL), December 10, 2006.

BOCHENSKI, Brandon

(boh-CHEHN-skee, BRAN-duhn) **BOS.**

Right wing. Shoots right. 6'1", 187 lbs. Born, Blaine, MN, April 4, 1982. Ottawa's 9th choice, 223rd overall, in 2001 Entry Draft.

Season	Club	League	GP	G	A	Pts	PIM	PP	SH	GW	S	%	+/-	TF	F%	Min	GP	G	A	Pts	PIM	PP	SH	GW	Min
99-2000	Blaine Bengals	High-MN	28	32	30	62	....	....	....	....	....	....	....	....	....	....	....	....	....	....	....	....	....	....	....
2000-01	Lincoln Stars	USHL	55	*47	33	80	22	....	....	....	....	....	....	....	....	....	11	5	7	12	4	....	....	....	....
2001-02	North Dakota	WCHA	36	17	15	32	36	....	....	....	....	....	....	....	....	....	....	....	....	....	....	....	....	....	....
2002-03	North Dakota	WCHA	43	35	27	62	42	....	....	....	....	....	....	....	....	....	....	....	....	....	....	....	....	....	....
2003-04	North Dakota	WCHA	41	27	33	60	40	....	....	....	....	....	....	....	....	....	....	....	....	....	....	....	....	....	....
2004-05	Binghamton	AHL	75	34	36	70	16	....	....	....	....	....	....	....	....	....	6	1	0	1	2	....	....	....	....
2005-06	**Ottawa**	**NHL**	**20**	**6**	**7**	**13**	**14**	**2**	**0**	**0**	**39**	**15.4**	**7**	**4**	**50.0**	**12:17**	....	....	....	....	....	....	....	....	....
	Binghamton	AHL	33	22	24	46	36	....	....	....	....	....	....	....	....	....	....	....	....	....	....	....	....	....	....
	Chicago	**NHL**	**20**	**2**	**2**	**4**	**8**	**0**	**0**	**0**	**23**	**8.7**	**–9**	**8**	**37.5**	**8:53**	....	....	....	....	....	....	....	....	....
	Norfolk Admirals	AHL	....	....	....	....	....	....	....	....	....	....	....	....	....	....	3	1	1	2	0	....	....	....	....
2006-07	**Chicago**	**NHL**	**10**	**2**	**0**	**2**	**2**	**0**	**0**	**0**	**20**	**10.0**	**–2**	**1**	**0.0**	**9:59**	....	....	....	....	....	....	....	....	....
	Norfolk Admirals	AHL	35	33	33	66	31	....	....	....	....	....	....	....	....	....	....	....	....	....	....	....	....	....	....
	Boston	**NHL**	**31**	**11**	**11**	**22**	**14**	**3**	**0**	**2**	**72**	**15.3**	**3**	**4**	**25.0**	**14:59**	....	....	....	....	....	....	....	....	....
	NHL Totals		**81**	**21**	**20**	**41**	**38**	**5**	**0**	**2**	**154**	**13.6**		**17**	**35.3**	**12:11**	....	....	....	....	....	....	....	....	....

USHL First All-Star Team (2001) • USHL Rookie of the Year (2001) • WCHA All-Rookie Team (2002) • WCHA Rookie of the Year (2002) • WCHA Second All-Star Team (2003) • WCHA First All-Star Team (2004) • NCAA West First All-American Team (2004) • AHL All-Rookie Team (2005)

Traded to **Chicago** by **Ottawa** with Ottawa's 2nd round choice (Simon Danis-Pepin) in 2006 Entry Draft for Tyler Arnason, March 9, 2006. Traded to **Boston** by **Chicago** for Kris Versteeg and future considerations, February 3, 2007.

BOGUNIECKI, Eric

(BOH-guhn-ih-kee, AIR-ihk)

Center. Shoots right. 5'8", 192 lbs. Born, New Haven, CT, May 6, 1975. St. Louis' 6th choice, 193rd overall, in 1993 Entry Draft.

Season	Club	League	GP	G	A	Pts	PIM	PP	SH	GW	S	%	+/-	TF	F%	Min	GP	G	A	Pts	PIM	PP	SH	GW	Min
1992-93	Westminster	High-CT	24	30	24	54	55	....	....	....	....	....	....	....	....	....	....	....	....	....	....	....	....	....	....
1993-94	New Hampshire	H-East	40	17	16	33	66	....	....	....	....	....	....	....	....	....	....	....	....	....	....	....	....	....	....
1994-95	New Hampshire	H-East	34	12	16	28	62	....	....	....	....	....	....	....	....	....	....	....	....	....	....	....	....	....	....
1995-96	New Hampshire	H-East	32	23	28	51	46	....	....	....	....	....	....	....	....	....	....	....	....	....	....	....	....	....	....
1996-97	New Hampshire	H-East	36	26	31	57	58	....	....	....	....	....	....	....	....	....	....	....	....	....	....	....	....	....	....
1997-98	Dayton Bombers	ECHL	26	19	18	37	36	....	....	....	....	....	....	....	....	....	....	....	....	....	....	....	....	....	....
	Fort Wayne	IHL	35	4	8	12	29	....	....	....	....	....	....	....	....	....	4	1	2	3	10	....	....	....	....
1998-99	Fort Wayne	IHL	72	32	34	66	100	....	....	....	....	....	....	....	....	....	2	0	1	1	2	....	....	....	....
99-2000	**Florida**	**NHL**	**4**	**0**	**0**	**0**	**2**	**0**	**0**	**0**	**5**	**0.0**	**–1**	**25**	**36.0**	**8:35**	....	....	....	....	....	....	....	....	....
	Louisville Panthers	AHL	57	33	42	75	148	....	....	....	....	....	....	....	....	....	4	3	2	5	20	....	....	....	....
2000-01	Louisville Panthers	AHL	28	13	12	25	56	....	....	....	....	....	....	....	....	....	....	....	....	....	....	....	....	....	....
	St. Louis	**NHL**	**1**	**0**	**0**	**0**	**0**	**0**	**0**	**0**	**1**	**0.0**	**–1**	**0**	**0.0**	**13:44**	....	....	....	....	....	....	....	....	....
	Worcester IceCats	AHL	45	17	28	45	100	....	....	....	....	....	....	....	....	....	9	3	2	5	10	....	....	....	....
2001-02	**St. Louis**	**NHL**	**8**	**0**	**1**	**1**	**4**	**0**	**0**	**0**	**10**	**0.0**	**–2**	**21**	**38.1**	**11:42**	**1**	**0**	**1**	**1**	**0**	**0**	**0**	**0**	**8:01**
	Worcester IceCats	AHL	63	*38	46	84	181	....	....	....	....	....	....	....	....	....	3	2	0	2	4	....	....	....	....
2002-03	**St. Louis**	**NHL**	**80**	**22**	**27**	**49**	**38**	**3**	**1**	**5**	**117**	**18.8**	**22**	**5**	**40.0**	**14:00**	**7**	**1**	**2**	**3**	**2**	**1**	**0**	**0**	**13:09**
2003-04	**St. Louis**	**NHL**	**27**	**6**	**4**	**10**	**20**	**2**	**0**	**2**	**40**	**15.0**	**–1**	**1**	**0.0**	**14:42**	**1**	**0**	**0**	**0**	**0**	**0**	**0**	**0**	**12:52**
	Worcester IceCats	AHL	3	0	1	1	0	....	....	....	....	....	....	....	....	....	....	....	....	....	....	....	....	....	....
2004-05	Worcester IceCats	AHL	30	14	11	25	46	....	....	....	....	....	....	....	....	....	....	....	....	....	....	....	....	....	....
	SC Langenthal	Swiss-2	10	5	3	8	47	....	....	....	....	....	....	....	....	....	....	....	....	....	....	....	....	....	....
2005-06	**St. Louis**	**NHL**	**9**	**1**	**4**	**5**	**4**	**1**	**0**	**0**	**12**	**8.3**	**–1**	**1**	**100.0**	**12:15**									
	Peoria Rivermen	AHL	2	0	0	0	4	....	....	....	....	....	....	....	....	....									
	Pittsburgh	**NHL**	**38**	**5**	**6**	**11**	**29**	**1**	**0**	**0**	**36**	**13.9**	**–2**	**74**	**48.7**	**10:50**									
2006-07	Syracuse Crunch	AHL	6	0	0	0	8	....	....	....	....	....	....	....	....	....									
	NY Islanders	**NHL**	**11**	**0**	**0**	**0**	**8**	**0**	**0**	**0**	**2**	**0.0**	**0**	**0**	**0.0**	**4:54**									
	Bridgeport	AHL	48	22	32	54	48	....	....	....	....	....	....	....	....	....									
	NHL Totals		**178**	**34**	**42**	**76**	**105**	**7**	**1**	**7**	**223**	**15.2**		**127**	**44.1**	**12:33**	**9**	**1**	**3**	**4**	**2**	**1**	**0**	**0**	**12:33**

Hockey East Second All-Star Team (1997) • AHL First All-Star Team (2002) • Les Cunningham Award (MVP – AHL) (2002)

Signed as a free agent by **Florida**, July 7, 1999. Traded to **St. Louis** by **Florida** for Andrei Podkonicky, December 17, 2000. • Missed majority of 2003-04 season recovering from shoulder (September 23, 2003 in training camp) and head (February 28, 2004 vs. Vancouver) injuries. Signed as a free agent by **Langenthal** (Swiss-2), October 4, 2004. Traded to **Pittsburgh** by **St. Louis** for Steve Poapst, December 9, 2005. Signed as a free agent by **Columbus**, August 22, 2006. Traded to **NY Islanders** by **Columbus** for Ryan Caldwell, October 25, 2006. Signed as a free agent by **Ingolstadt** (Germany), June 29, 2007.

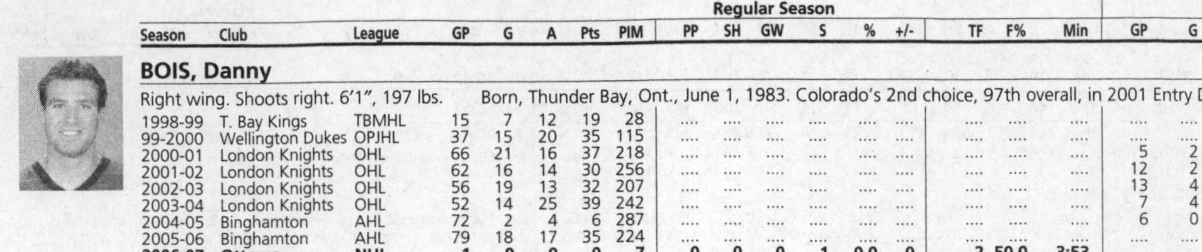

BOIS, Danny

(BOIZ, DA-nee) **OTT.**

Right wing. Shoots right. 6'1", 197 lbs. Born, Thunder Bay, Ont., June 1, 1983. Colorado's 2nd choice, 97th overall, in 2001 Entry Draft.

Season	Club	League	GP	G	A	Pts	PIM	PP	SH	GW	S	%	+/-	TF	F%	Min	GP	G	A	Pts	PIM	PP	SH	GW	Min
						Regular Season														Playoffs					
1998-99	T. Bay Kings	TBMHL	15	7	12	19	28																		
99-2000	Wellington Dukes	OPJHL	37	15	20	35	115																		
2000-01	London Knights	OHL	66	21	16	37	218										5	2	1	3	19				
2001-02	London Knights	OHL	62	16	14	30	256										12	2	2	4	47				
2002-03	London Knights	OHL	56	19	13	32	207										13	4	6	10	38				
2003-04	London Knights	OHL	52	14	25	39	242										7	4	4	8	29				
2004-05	Binghamton	AHL	72	2	4	6	287										6	0	1	1	2				
2005-06	Binghamton	AHL	79	18	17	35	224																		
2006-07	**Ottawa**	**NHL**	**1**	**0**	**0**	**0**	**7**	**0**	**0**	**0**	**1**	**0.0**	**0**	**2**	**50.0**	**3:53**									
	Binghamton	AHL	65	14	13	27	153																		
	NHL Totals		**1**	**0**	**0**	**0**	**7**	**0**	**0**	**0**	**1**	**0.0**		**2**	**50.0**	**3:53**									

Signed as a free agent by **Ottawa**, April 30, 2004.

BOLLAND, Dave

(BOHL-uhnd, DAYV) **CHI.**

Center. Shoots right. 6', 176 lbs. Born, Toronto, Ont., June 5, 1986. Chicago's 2nd choice, 32nd overall, in 2004 Entry Draft.

Season	Club	League	GP	G	A	Pts	PIM	PP	SH	GW	S	%	+/-	TF	F%	Min	GP	G	A	Pts	PIM	PP	SH	GW	Min
2000-01	Tor. Red Wings	GTHL	95	79	67	146																			
2001-02	Tor. Red Wings	GTHL	36	35	35	70	40																		
2002-03	London Knights	OHL	64	7	10	17	21										14	2	1	3	2				
2003-04	London Knights	OHL	65	37	30	67	58										15	3	10	13	18				
2004-05	London Knights	OHL	66	34	51	85	97										18	11	14	25	30				
2005-06	London Knights	OHL	59	*57	73	130	104										15	*15	9	24	41				
2006-07	**Chicago**	**NHL**	**1**	**0**	**0**	**0**	**0**	**0**	**0**	**0**	**1**	**0.0**	**–1**	**11**	**36.4**	**11:17**									
	Norfolk Admirals	AHL	65	17	32	49	53										6	0	4	4	17				
	NHL Totals		**1**	**0**	**0**	**0**	**0**	**0**	**0**	**0**	**1**	**0.0**		**11**	**36.4**	**11:17**									

OHL First All-Star Team (2006)

BONDRA, Peter

(BAWN-druh, PEE-tuhr)

Right wing. Shoots left. 6', 200 lbs. Born, Luck, USSR, February 7, 1968. Washington's 9th choice, 156th overall, in 1990 Entry Draft.

Season	Club	League	GP	G	A	Pts	PIM	PP	SH	GW	S	%	+/-	TF	F%	Min	GP	G	A	Pts	PIM	PP	SH	GW	Min
1986-87	VSZ Kosice	Czech	32	4	5	9	24																		
1987-88	VSZ Kosice	Czech	45	27	11	38	20																		
1988-89	VSZ Kosice	Czech	40	30	10	40	20																		
1989-90	VSZ Kosice	Czech	44	29	17	46											5	7	2	9					
1990-91	**Washington**	**NHL**	**54**	**12**	**16**	**28**	**47**	**4**	**0**	**1**	**95**	**12.6**	**–10**				**4**	**0**	**1**	**1**	**2**	**0**	**0**	**0**	
1991-92	**Washington**	**NHL**	**71**	**28**	**28**	**56**	**42**	**4**	**0**	**3**	**158**	**17.7**	**16**				**7**	**6**	**2**	**8**	**4**	**1**	**0**	**0**	
1992-93	**Washington**	**NHL**	**83**	**37**	**48**	**85**	**70**	**10**	**0**	**7**	**239**	**15.5**	**8**				**6**	**0**	**6**	**6**	**0**	**0**	**0**	**0**	
1993-94	**Washington**	**NHL**	**69**	**24**	**19**	**43**	**40**	**4**	**0**	**2**	**200**	**12.0**	**22**				**9**	**2**	**4**	**6**	**4**	**0**	**0**	**1**	
1994-95	HC Kosice	Slovakia	2	1	0	1	0																		
	Washington	**NHL**	**47**	***34**	**9**	**43**	**24**	**12**	**6**	**3**	**177**	**19.2**	**9**				**7**	**5**	**3**	**8**	**10**	**2**	**0**	**1**	
1995-96	Detroit Vipers	IHL	7	8	1	9	0																		
	Washington	**NHL**	**67**	**52**	**28**	**80**	**40**	**11**	**4**	**7**	**322**	**16.1**	**18**				**6**	**3**	**2**	**5**	**8**	**2**	**0**	**1**	
1996-97	**Washington**	**NHL**	**77**	**46**	**31**	**77**	**72**	**10**	**4**	**3**	**314**	**14.6**	**7**												
1997-98	**Washington**	**NHL**	**76**	***52**	**26**	**78**	**44**	**11**	**5**	**13**	**284**	**18.3**	**14**				**17**	**7**	**5**	**12**	**12**	**3**	**0**	**2**	
	Slovakia	Olympics	2	1	0	1	25																		
1998-99	**Washington**	**NHL**	**66**	**31**	**24**	**55**	**56**	**6**	**3**	**5**	**284**	**10.9**	**–1**	**1**	**0.0**	**20:35**									
99-2000	**Washington**	**NHL**	**62**	**21**	**17**	**38**	**30**	**5**	**3**	**5**	**187**	**11.2**	**5**	**2**	**50.0**	**18:48**	**5**	**1**	**1**	**2**	**4**	**1**	**0**	**0**	**17:30**
2000-01	**Washington**	**NHL**	**82**	**45**	**36**	**81**	**60**	**22**	**4**	**8**	**305**	**14.8**	**8**	**2**	**50.0**	**20:48**	**6**	**2**	**0**	**2**	**2**	**2**	**0**	**1**	**24:55**
2001-02	**Washington**	**NHL**	**77**	**39**	**31**	**70**	**80**	**17**	**1**	**8**	**333**	**11.7**	**–2**	**2**	**50.0**	**21:43**									
2002-03	**Washington**	**NHL**	**76**	**30**	**26**	**56**	**52**	**9**	**2**	**4**	**256**	**11.7**	**–3**	**13**	**30.8**	**18:53**	**6**	**4**	**2**	**6**	**8**	**2**	**0**	**0**	**22:39**
2003-04	**Washington**	**NHL**	**54**	**21**	**14**	**35**	**22**	**12**	**0**	**4**	**136**	**15.4**	**–17**	**2**	**50.0**	**18:43**									
	Ottawa	**NHL**	**23**	**5**	**9**	**14**	**16**	**2**	**0**	**1**	**52**	**9.6**	**1**	**4**	**0.0**	**18:21**	**7**	**0**	**0**	**0**	**6**	**0**	**0**	**0**	**16:36**
2004-05	HK SKP Poprad	Slovakia	6	4	2	6	4																		
2005-06	**Atlanta**	**NHL**	**60**	**21**	**18**	**39**	**40**	**8**	**0**	**1**	**143**	**14.7**	**–3**	**5**	**20.0**	**15:56**									
	Slovakia	Olympics	6	4	0	4	2																		
2006-07	**Chicago**	**NHL**	**37**	**5**	**9**	**14**	**26**	**2**	**0**	**3**	**46**	**10.9**	**2**	**1**	**0.0**	**12:01**									
	NHL Totals		**1081**	**503**	**389**	**892**	**761**	**149**	**32**	**78**	**3531**	**14.2**		**32**	**28.1**	**18:56**	**80**	**30**	**26**	**56**	**60**	**13**	**0**	**6**	**20:23**

Played in NHL All-Star Game (1993, 1996, 1997, 1998, 1999)

Traded to **Ottawa** by **Washington** for Brooks Laich and Ottawa's 2nd round choice (later traded to Colorado - Colorado selected Chris Durand) in 2005 Entry Draft, February 18, 2004. Signed as a free agent by **Poprad** (Slovakia), January 17, 2005. Signed as a free agent by **Atlanta**, September 18, 2005. Signed as a free agent by **Chicago**, December 10, 2006.

BONK, Radek

(BOHNK, RA-dehk) **NSH.**

Center. Shoots left. 6'3", 213 lbs. Born, Krnov, Czech., January 9, 1976. Ottawa's 1st choice, 3rd overall, in 1994 Entry Draft.

Season	Club	League	GP	G	A	Pts	PIM	PP	SH	GW	S	%	+/-	TF	F%	Min	GP	G	A	Pts	PIM	PP	SH	GW	Min
1990-91	Opava Jr.	Czech-Jr.	35	47	42	89	25																		
1991-92	AC ZPS Zlin Jr.	Czech-Jr.	45	47	36	83	30																		
1992-93	AC ZPS Zlin	Czech	30	5	5	10	10																		
1993-94	Las Vegas	IHL	76	42	45	87	208										5	1	2	3	10				
1994-95	Las Vegas	IHL	33	7	13	20	62																		
	Ottawa	**NHL**	**42**	**3**	**8**	**11**	**28**	**1**	**0**	**0**	**40**	**7.5**	**–5**												
	P.E.I. Senators	AHL															1	0	0	0	0				
1995-96	**Ottawa**	**NHL**	**76**	**16**	**19**	**35**	**36**	**5**	**0**	**1**	**161**	**9.9**	**–5**												
1996-97	**Ottawa**	**NHL**	**53**	**5**	**13**	**18**	**14**	**0**	**1**	**0**	**82**	**6.1**	**–4**				**7**	**0**	**1**	**1**	**4**	**0**	**0**	**0**	
1997-98	**Ottawa**	**NHL**	**65**	**7**	**9**	**16**	**16**	**1**	**0**	**0**	**93**	**7.5**	**–13**				**5**	**0**	**0**	**0**	**2**	**0**	**0**	**0**	
1998-99	**Ottawa**	**NHL**	**81**	**16**	**16**	**32**	**48**	**0**	**1**	**6**	**110**	**14.5**	**15**	**1184**	**50.1**	**13:44**	**4**	**0**	**0**	**0**	**6**	**0**	**0**	**0**	**16:16**
99-2000	Pardubice	CzRep	3	1	0	1	4																		
	Ottawa	**NHL**	**80**	**23**	**37**	**60**	**53**	**10**	**0**	**5**	**167**	**13.8**	**–2**	**1654**	**52.0**	**18:14**	**6**	**0**	**0**	**0**	**8**	**0**	**0**	**0**	**15:37**
2000-01	**Ottawa**	**NHL**	**74**	**23**	**36**	**59**	**52**	**5**	**2**	**3**	**139**	**16.5**	**27**	**1506**	**51.2**	**18:16**	**2**	**0**	**0**	**0**	**2**	**0**	**0**	**0**	**14:32**
2001-02	**Ottawa**	**NHL**	**82**	**25**	**45**	**70**	**52**	**6**	**2**	**5**	**170**	**14.7**	**3**	**1530**	**51.0**	**17:57**	**12**	**3**	**7**	**10**	**6**	**2**	**0**	**1**	**18:53**
2002-03	**Ottawa**	**NHL**	**70**	**22**	**32**	**54**	**36**	**11**	**0**	**4**	**146**	**15.1**	**6**	**1218**	**46.2**	**17:32**	**18**	**6**	**5**	**11**	**10**	**2**	**0**	**0**	**17:43**
2003-04	**Ottawa**	**NHL**	**66**	**12**	**32**	**44**	**66**	**6**	**0**	**1**	**98**	**12.2**	**2**	**1184**	**44.9**	**17:38**	**7**	**0**	**2**	**2**	**0**	**0**	**0**	**0**	**18:29**
2004-05	HC Ocelari Trinec	CzRep	27	6	10	16	44																		
	HC Hame Zlin	CzRep	6	3	2	5	4										6	0	2	2	8				
2005-06	**Montreal**	**NHL**	**61**	**6**	**15**	**21**	**52**	**0**	**2**	**1**	**76**	**7.9**	**–3**	**963**	**47.4**	**15:10**	**6**	**2**	**0**	**2**	**2**	**0**	**0**	**1**	**15:36**
2006-07	**Montreal**	**NHL**	**74**	**13**	**10**	**23**	**54**	**1**	**2**	**1**	**111**	**11.7**	**0**	**1198**	**49.8**	**15:52**									
	NHL Totals		**824**	**171**	**272**	**443**	**507**	**46**	**10**	**27**	**1393**	**12.3**		**10437**	**49.4**	**16:49**	**67**	**11**	**15**	**26**	**40**	**4**	**0**	**2**	**17:23**

Garry F. Longman Memorial Trophy (Rookie of the Year – IHL) (1994)

Played in NHL All-Star Game (2000, 2001)

Traded to **Los Angeles** by **Ottawa** for Los Angeles' 3rd round choice (Shawn Weller) in 2004 Entry Draft, June 26, 2004. Traded to **Montreal** by **Los Angeles** with Cristobal Huet for Mathieu Garon and San Jose's 3rd round choice (previously acquired, Los Angeles selected Paul Baier) in 2004 Entry Draft, June 26, 2004. Signed as a free agent by **Trinec** (CzRep), September 17, 2004. Signed as a free agent by **Zlin** (CzRep), January 31, 2005. Signed as a free agent by **Nashville**, July 2, 2007.

BOOGAARD, Derek

(BOO-gard, DAIR-ihk) **MIN.**

Left wing. Shoots right. 6'7", 254 lbs. Born, Saskatoon, Sask., June 23, 1982. Minnesota's 6th choice, 202nd overall, in 2001 Entry Draft.

Season	Club	League	GP	G	A	Pts	PIM	PP	SH	GW	S	%	+/-	TF	F%	Min	GP	G	A	Pts	PIM	PP	SH	GW	Min
1998-99	Regina Caps	SJHL	35	2	3	5	166																		
99-2000	Regina Pats	WHL	5	0	0	0	17																		
	Prince George	WHL	33	0	0	0	149																		
2000-01	Prince George	WHL	61	1	8	9	245										6	1	0	1	31				
2001-02	Prince George	WHL	2	0	0	0	16																		
	Medicine Hat	WHL	46	1	8	9	178																		
2002-03	Medicine Hat	WHL	27	1	2	3	65																		
	Louisiana	ECHL	33	1	2	3	240										2	0	0	0	0				
2003-04	Houston Aeros	AHL	53	0	4	4	207										2	0	1	1	16				
2004-05	Houston Aeros	AHL	56	1	4	5	259										5	0	0	0	38				

			Regular Season														Playoffs								
Season	Club	League	GP	G	A	Pts	PIM	PP	SH	GW	S	%	+/-	TF	F%	Min	GP	G	A	Pts	PIM	PP	SH	GW	Min
2005-06	Minnesota	NHL	65	2	4	6	158	0	0	1	15	13.3	2	0	0.0	5:23									
2006-07	Minnesota	NHL	48	0	1	1	120	0	0	0	11	0.0	0	0	0.0	4:38	4	0	1	1	20	0	0	0	5:59
	NHL Totals		113	2	5	7	278	0	0	1	26	7.7		0	0.0	5:04	4	0	1	1	20	0	0	0	5:59

BOOTH, David

(BOOTH, DAY-vihd) **FLA.**

Left wing. Shoots left. 6', 212 lbs. Born, Detroit, MI, November 24, 1984. Florida's 3rd choice, 53rd overall, in 2004 Entry Draft.

Season	Club	League	GP	G	A	Pts	PIM	PP	SH	GW	S	%	+/-	TF	F%	Min	GP	G	A	Pts	PIM	PP	SH	GW	Min
2000-01	Det. Compuware	NAHL	42	17	13	30	44										2	1	0	1	2				
2001-02	USNTDP	U-18	40	12	6	18	17																		
	USNTDP	USHL	12	4	3	7	6																		
	USNTDP	NAHL	6	1	3	4	18																		
2002-03	Michigan State	CCHA	39	17	19	36	53																		
2003-04	Michigan State	CCHA	30	8	10	18	30																		
2004-05	Michigan State	CCHA	29	7	9	16	30																		
2005-06	Michigan State	CCHA	37	13	22	35	50																		
2006-07	**Florida**	**NHL**	**48**	**3**	**7**	**10**	**12**	**0**	**0**	**1**	**86**	**3.5**	**0**	**11**	**36.4**	**9:34**									
	Rochester	AHL	25	7	7	14	26										6	0	2	2	4				
	NHL Totals		**48**	**3**	**7**	**10**	**12**	**0**	**0**	**1**	**86**	**3.5**		**11**	**36.4**	**9:34**									

CCHA All-Rookie Team (2003)

BOOTLAND, Darryl

(BOOT-land, DAIR-uhl) **NYI**

Right wing. Shoots right. 6'1", 197 lbs. Born, Toronto, Ont., November 2, 1981. Colorado's 12th choice, 252nd overall, in 2000 Entry Draft.

Season	Club	League	GP	G	A	Pts	PIM	PP	SH	GW	S	%	+/-	TF	F%	Min	GP	G	A	Pts	PIM	PP	SH	GW	Min
1997-98	Orangeville	OHA-B	44	22	26	48	177																		
1998-99	Barrie Colts	OHL	38	18	11	29	89																		
	St. Michael's	OHL	28	12	6	18	80																		
99-2000	St. Michael's	OHL	65	24	30	54	166																		
2000-01	St. Michael's	OHL	56	32	33	65	136										11	3	1	4	20				
2001-02	St. Michael's	OHL	61	41	56	97	137										15	8	10	18	50				
2002-03	Toledo Storm	ECHL	54	17	19	36	322																		
	Grand Rapids	AHL	16	1	4	5	41										15	3	2	5	46				
2003-04	**Detroit**	**NHL**	**22**	**1**	**1**	**2**	**74**	**0**	**0**	**1**	**13**	**7.7**	**–3**	**1**	**100.0**	**6:07**									
	Grand Rapids	AHL	54	12	2	14	175										4	0	1	1	2				
2004-05	Grand Rapids	AHL	78	14	20	34	336																		
2005-06	Grand Rapids	AHL	77	27	29	56	392										16	5	7	12	50				
2006-07	**Detroit**	**NHL**	**6**	**0**	**0**	**0**	**9**	**0**	**0**	**0**	**4**	**0.0**	**0**	**2**	**100.0**	**4:08**									
	Grand Rapids	AHL	68	18	13	31	222										6	1	0	1	32				
	NHL Totals		**28**	**1**	**1**	**2**	**83**	**0**	**0**	**1**	**17**	**5.9**		**3**	**100.0**	**5:41**									

Signed as a free agent by **Detroit**, July 25, 2002. Signed as a free agent by **NY Islanders**, July 9, 2007.

BOUCHARD, Joel

(BOO-shahrd, JOHL)

Defense. Shoots left. 6'1", 209 lbs. Born, Montreal, Que., January 23, 1974. Calgary's 7th choice, 129th overall, in 1992 Entry Draft.

Season	Club	League	GP	G	A	Pts	PIM	PP	SH	GW	S	%	+/-	TF	F%	Min	GP	G	A	Pts	PIM	PP	SH	GW	Min
1989-90	Mtl-Bourassa	QAAA	41	7	17	24	10										1	1	0	1	0				
1990-91	Longueuil	QMJHL	53	3	19	22	34										8	1	0	1	11				
1991-92	Verdun	QMJHL	70	9	20	29	55										19	1	7	8	20				
1992-93	Verdun	QMJHL	60	10	49	59	126										4	0	2	2	4				
1993-94	Verdun	QMJHL	60	15	55	70	62										4	1	0	1	6				
	Saint John Flames	AHL	1	0	0	0	0										2	0	0	0	0				
1994-95	Saint John Flames	AHL	77	6	25	31	63										5	1	0	1	4				
	Calgary	**NHL**	**2**	**0**	**0**	**0**	**0**	**0**	**0**	**0**	**0**	**0.0**	**0**												
1995-96	**Calgary**	**NHL**	**4**	**0**	**0**	**0**	**4**	**0**	**0**	**0**	**0**	**0.0**	**0**												
	Saint John Flames	AHL	74	8	25	33	104										16	1	4	5	10				
1996-97	**Calgary**	**NHL**	**76**	**4**	**5**	**9**	**49**	**0**	**1**	**0**	**61**	**6.6**	**–23**												
1997-98	**Calgary**	**NHL**	**44**	**5**	**7**	**12**	**57**	**0**	**1**	**1**	**51**	**9.8**	**0**												
	Saint John Flames	AHL	3	2	1	3	6																		
1998-99	**Nashville**	**NHL**	**64**	**4**	**11**	**15**	**60**	**0**	**0**	**0**	**78**	**5.1**	**–10**	**0**	**0.0**	**22:34**									
99-2000	**Nashville**	**NHL**	**52**	**1**	**4**	**5**	**23**	**0**	**0**	**0**	**60**	**1.7**	**–11**	**0**	**0.0**	**18:41**									
	Dallas	**NHL**	**2**	**0**	**0**	**0**	**2**	**0**	**0**	**0**	**1**	**0.0**	**1**	**0**	**0.0**	**9:45**									
2000-01	Grand Rapids	IHL	19	3	9	12	8																		
	Phoenix	**NHL**	**32**	**1**	**2**	**3**	**22**	**0**	**0**	**0**	**26**	**3.8**	**–8**	**0**	**0.0**	**14:28**									
2001-02	**New Jersey**	**NHL**	**1**	**0**	**1**	**1**	**0**	**0**	**0**	**0**	**0**	**0.0**	**1**	**0**	**0.0**	**19:26**									
	Albany River Rats	AHL	70	9	22	31	28																		
2002-03	**NY Rangers**	**NHL**	**27**	**5**	**7**	**12**	**14**	**1**	**0**	**2**	**41**	**12.2**	**6**	**0**	**0.0**	**20:07**									
	Hartford	AHL	22	6	14	20	22																		
	Pittsburgh	**NHL**	**7**	**0**	**1**	**1**	**0**	**0**	**0**	**0**	**6**	**0.0**	**–6**	**0**	**0.0**	**21:49**									
2003-04	**NY Rangers**	**NHL**	**28**	**1**	**7**	**8**	**10**	**0**	**0**	**0**	**34**	**2.9**	**2**	**0**	**0.0**	**16:42**									
2004-05	Hartford	AHL	7	1	2	3	6										6	0	2	2	20				
2005-06	**NY Islanders**	**NHL**	**25**	**1**	**8**	**9**	**23**	**0**	**0**	**0**	**45**	**2.2**	**5**	**0**	**0.0**	**21:56**									
	Bridgeport	AHL	15	4	9	13	10																		
2006-07	Bridgeport	AHL	4	0	3	3	0																		
	NHL Totals		**364**	**22**	**53**	**75**	**264**	**1**	**2**	**3**	**403**	**5.5**		**0**	**0.0**	**19:27**									

QMJHL First All-Star Team (1994)

Claimed by **Nashville** from **Calgary** in Expansion Draft, June 26, 1998. Claimed on waivers by **Dallas** from **Nashville**, March 14, 2000. Signed as a free agent by **Phoenix**, August 31, 2000. Signed as a free agent by **New Jersey**, October 25, 2001. Signed as a free agent by **NY Rangers**, August 5, 2002. Traded to **Pittsburgh** by **NY Rangers** with Richard Lintner, Rico Fata and Mikael Samuelsson for Mike Wilson, Alex Kovalev, Janne Laukkanen and Dan LaCouture, February 10, 2003. Signed as a free agent by **Buffalo**, July 14, 2003. Claimed by **NY Rangers** from **Buffalo** in Waiver Draft, October 3, 2003. • Spent majority of 2003-04 season as a healthy reserve. Signed as a free agent by **Hartford** (AHL), March 17, 2005. Signed as a free agent by **NY Islanders**, August 18, 2005. • Missed majority of 2006-07 season recovering from a recurring hamstring injury.

BOUCHARD, Pierre-Marc

(BOO-shahrd, PEE-air- MAHRK) **MIN.**

Center. Shoots left. 5'10", 172 lbs. Born, Sherbrooke, Que., April 27, 1984. Minnesota's 1st choice, 8th overall, in 2002 Entry Draft.

Season	Club	League	GP	G	A	Pts	PIM	PP	SH	GW	S	%	+/-	TF	F%	Min	GP	G	A	Pts	PIM	PP	SH	GW	Min
1998-99	Mtl.-Bourassa	QAHA	28	23	41	64																			
99-2000	Charles-Lemoyne	QAAA	42	28	*45	*74	20										9	4	8	12	6				
2000-01	Chicoutimi	QMJHL	67	38	57	95	20										6	5	8	13	0				
2001-02	Chicoutimi	QMJHL	69	46	*94	*140	54										4	2	3	5	4				
2002-03	**Minnesota**	**NHL**	**50**	**7**	**13**	**20**	**18**	**5**	**0**	**1**	**53**	**13.2**	**1**	**474**	**40.7**	**13:16**	**5**	**0**	**1**	**1**	**2**	**0**	**0**	**0**	**13:15**
2003-04	**Minnesota**	**NHL**	**61**	**4**	**18**	**22**	**22**	**2**	**0**	**0**	**60**	**6.7**	**–7**	**60**	**50.0**	**14:00**									
2004-05	Houston Aeros	AHL	67	12	42	54	46										5	0	1	1	0				
2005-06	**Minnesota**	**NHL**	**80**	**17**	**42**	**59**	**28**	**7**	**0**	**3**	**118**	**14.4**	**3**	**15**	**46.7**	**15:15**									
2006-07	**Minnesota**	**NHL**	**82**	**20**	**37**	**57**	**14**	**5**	**0**	**3**	**173**	**11.6**	**13**	**18**	**33.3**	**15:59**	**5**	**1**	**1**	**2**	**0**	**0**	**0**	**0**	**14:48**
	NHL Totals		**273**	**48**	**110**	**158**	**82**	**19**	**0**	**7**	**404**	**11.9**		**567**	**41.6**	**14:50**	**10**	**1**	**2**	**3**	**2**	**0**	**0**	**0**	**14:02**

QMJHL Rookie of the Year (2001) • QMJHL First All-Star Team (2002) • Canadian Major Junior First All-Star Team (2002) • Canadian Major Junior Player of the Year (2002)

BOUCHER, Philippe

(boo-SHAY, fihl-EEP) **DAL.**

Defense. Shoots right. 6'3", 221 lbs. Born, Ste-Apollinaire, Que., March 24, 1973. Buffalo's 1st choice, 13th overall, in 1991 Entry Draft.

Season	Club	League	GP	G	A	Pts	PIM	PP	SH	GW	S	%	+/-	TF	F%	Min	GP	G	A	Pts	PIM	PP	SH	GW	Min
1988-89	Ste-Foy	QAAA	5	0	0	0	2																		
1989-90	Ste-Foy	QAAA	42	26	60	86	76										12	6	*19	25	16				
1990-91	Granby Bisons	QMJHL	69	21	46	67	92																		
1991-92	Granby Bisons	QMJHL	49	22	37	59	47																		
	Laval Titan	QMJHL	16	7	11	18	36										10	5	6	11	8				
1992-93	Laval Titan	QMJHL	16	12	15	27	37										13	6	15	21	12				
	Buffalo	**NHL**	**18**	**0**	**4**	**4**	**14**	**0**	**0**	**0**	**28**	**0.0**	**1**												
	Rochester	AHL	5	4	3	7	8										3	0	1	1	2				
1993-94	**Buffalo**	**NHL**	**38**	**6**	**8**	**14**	**29**	**4**	**0**	**1**	**67**	**9.0**	**–1**				**7**	**1**	**1**	**2**	**2**	**1**	**0**	**0**	
	Rochester	AHL	31	10	22	32	51																		
1994-95	Rochester	AHL	43	14	27	41	26																		
	Buffalo	**NHL**	**9**	**1**	**4**	**5**	**0**	**0**	**0**	**0**	**15**	**6.7**	**6**												
	Los Angeles	**NHL**	**6**	**1**	**0**	**1**	**4**	**0**	**0**	**0**	**15**	**6.7**	**–3**												

			Regular Season														Playoffs								
Season	Club	League	GP	G	A	Pts	PIM	PP	SH	GW	S	%	+/-	TF	F%	Min	GP	G	A	Pts	PIM	PP	SH	GW	Min
1995-96	Los Angeles	NHL	53	7	16	23	31	5	0	1	145	4.8	-26												
	Phoenix	IHL	10	4	3	7	4																		
1996-97	Los Angeles	NHL	60	7	18	25	25	2	0	1	159	4.4	0												
1997-98	Los Angeles	NHL	45	6	10	16	49	1	0	0	80	7.5	6												
	Long Beach	IHL	2	0	1	1	4																		
1998-99	Los Angeles	NHL	45	2	6	8	32	1	0	0	87	2.3	-12	0	0.0	17:51									
99-2000	Los Angeles	NHL	1	0	0	0	0	0	0	0	3	0.0	0	0	0.0	17:04									
	Long Beach	IHL	14	4	11	15	8										6	0	9	9	8				
2000-01	Los Angeles	NHL	22	2	4	6	20	2	0	0	40	5.0	4	0	0.0	18:25	13	0	1	1	2	0	0	0	15:48
	Manitoba Moose	IHL	45	10	22	32	39																		
2001-02	Los Angeles	NHL	80	7	23	30	94	4	0	2	198	3.5	0	0	0.0	21:36	5	0	1	1	2	0	0	0	19:31
2002-03	Dallas	NHL	80	7	20	27	94	1	1	3	137	5.1	28	1	0.0	20:29	11	1	2	3	11	0	0	0	21:28
2003-04	Dallas	NHL	70	8	16	24	64	2	0	2	134	6.0	15	0	0.0	22:24	5	1	0	1	6	0	0	0	23:57
2004-05			DID NOT PLAY																						
2005-06	Dallas	NHL	66	16	27	43	77	8	0	3	174	9.2	28	1	100.0	23:25	5	0	1	1	2	0	0	0	21:35
2006-07	Dallas	NHL	76	19	32	51	104	12	0	4	222	8.6	2	1	0.0	22:54	7	0	1	1	6	0	0	0	27:22
	NHL Totals		669	89	188	277	637	42	1	17	1504	5.9		3	33.3	21:28	53	3	7	10	31	1	0	0	20:50

QMJHL Second All-Star Team (1991, 1992) • QMJHL Defensive Rookie of the Year (1991) • Canadian Major Junior Rookie of the Year (1991)

Played in NHL All-Star Game (2007)

Traded to **Los Angeles** by **Buffalo** with Denis Tsygurov and Grant Fuhr for Alexei Zhitnik, Robb Stauber, Charlie Huddy and Los Angeles' 5th round choice (Marian Menhart) in 1995 Entry Draft, February 14, 1995. • Missed majority of 1999-2000 season recovering from foot injury suffered in training camp, September, 1999. Signed as a free agent by **Dallas**, July 2, 2002.

BOUCK, Tyler

(BOWK, TIGH-luhr)

Center. Shoots left. 6', 196 lbs. Born, Camrose, Alta., January 13, 1980. Dallas' 2nd choice, 57th overall, in 1998 Entry Draft.

Season	Club	League	GP	G	A	Pts	PIM	PP	SH	GW	S	%	+/-	TF	F%	Min	GP	G	A	Pts	PIM	PP	SH	GW	Min
1995-96	Sherwood Park	AMHL	22	10	21	31	58																		
1996-97	Prince George	WHL	12	0	2	2	11																		
1997-98	Prince George	WHL	65	11	26	37	90										11	1	0	1	21				
1998-99	Prince George	WHL	56	22	25	47	178										2	0	2	2	10				
99-2000	Prince George	WHL	57	30	33	63	183										13	6	13	19	36				
2000-01	Dallas	NHL	48	2	5	7	29	0	0	1	41	4.9	-3	1	0.0	8:59	1	0	0	0	0	0	0	0	9:02
	Utah Grizzlies	IHL	24	2	6	8	39																		
2001-02	Phoenix	NHL	7	0	0	0	4	0	0	0	3	0.0	-1	0	0.0	6:54									
	Springfield	AHL	21	1	2	3	33																		
	Manitoba Moose	AHL	20	4	4	8	25																		
2002-03	Manitoba Moose	AHL	76	10	28	38	103										14	2	2	4	10				
2003-04	Vancouver	NHL	18	1	2	3	23	0	1	0	12	8.3	-4	0	0.0	9:18	1	0	0	0	0	0	0	0	5:15
	Manitoba Moose	AHL	49	11	14	25	100																		
2004-05	TPS Turku	Finland	40	3	7	10	100										6	1	0	1	12				
2005-06	Vancouver	NHL	12	1	1	2	21	0	0	0	6	16.7	0	0	0.0	6:22									
	Manitoba Moose	AHL	8	0	1	1	8																		
2006-07	Vancouver	NHL	6	0	0	0	16	0	0	0	7	0.0	-1	0	0.0	7:55									
	Manitoba Moose	AHL	24	1	3	4	36																		
	NHL Totals		91	4	8	12	93	0	1	1	69	5.8		1	0.0	8:28	2	0	0	0	0	0	0	0	7:09

WHL West First All-Star Team (2000)

Traded to **Phoenix** by **Dallas** for Jyrki Lumme, June 23, 2001. Traded to **Vancouver** by **Phoenix** with Todd Warriner, Trevor Letowski and Phoenix's 3rd round choice (later traded back to Phoenix – Phoenix selected Dimitri Pestunov) in 2003 Entry Draft for Drake Berehowsky and Denis Pederson, December 28, 2001. Signed as a free agent by **Turku** (Finland), October 22, 2004. • Missed majority of 2005-06 season recovering from a groin injury suffered in training camp (October 4, 2005) and as a healthy reserve. • Missed majority of 2006-07 season after suffering a shoulder injury in game vs. Hamilton (AHL), December 27, 2006.

BOUILLON, Francis

(BOO-liawn, FRAN-sihs) **MTL.**

Defense. Shoots left. 5'8", 201 lbs. Born, New York, NY, October 17, 1975.

Season	Club	League	GP	G	A	Pts	PIM	PP	SH	GW	S	%	+/-	TF	F%	Min	GP	G	A	Pts	PIM	PP	SH	GW	Min
1991-92	Mtl-Bourassa	QAAA	42	2	5	7	28										9	1	0	1	6				
1992-93	Laval Titan	QMJHL	46	0	7	7	45																		
1993-94	Laval Titan	QMJHL	68	3	15	18	129										19	2	9	11	48				
1994-95	Laval Titan	QMJHL	72	8	25	33	115										20	3	11	14	21				
1995-96	Granby	QMJHL	68	11	35	46	156										21	2	12	14	30				
1996-97	Wheeling Nailers	ECHL	69	10	32	42	77										3	0	2	2	10				
1997-98	Quebec Rafales	IHL	71	8	27	35	76																		
1998-99	Fredericton	AHL	79	19	36	55	174										5	2	1	3	0				
99-2000	Montreal	NHL	74	3	13	16	38	2	0	1	76	3.9	-7	1	0.0	15:52									
2000-01	Montreal	NHL	29	0	6	6	26	0	0	0	24	0.0	3	0	0.0	13:24									
	Quebec Citadelles	AHL	4	0	0	0	0																		
2001-02	Montreal	NHL	28	0	5	5	33	0	0	0	24	0.0	-5	0	0.0	18:47									
	Quebec Citadelles	AHL	38	8	14	22	30																		
2002-03	Nashville	NHL	4	0	0	0	2	0	0	0	0	0.0	-1	0	0.0	12:52									
	Montreal	NHL	20	3	1	4	2	0	1	0	30	10.0	-1	0	0.0	20:24									
	Hamilton	AHL	29	1	12	13	31																		
2003-04	Montreal	NHL	73	2	16	18	70	0	0	0	86	2.3	1	0	0.0	19:39	11	0	0	0	7	0	0	0	18:00
2004-05	Leksands IF	Sweden-2	31	10	21	31	46																		
2005-06	Montreal	NHL	67	3	19	22	34	3	0	1	75	4.0	-6	0	0.0	20:47	6	1	2	3	10	1	0	0	22:24
2006-07	Montreal	NHL	62	3	11	14	52	1	0	1	56	5.4	-10	0	0.0	18:19									
	NHL Totals		357	14	71	85	257	6	1	3	371	3.8		1	0.0	18:14	17	1	2	3	17	1	0	0	19:33

Signed as a free agent by **Montreal**, August 18, 1998. • Missed majority of 2000-01 season recovering from ankle injury suffered in game vs. Calgary, December 31, 2000. Claimed by **Nashville** from **Montreal** in Waiver Draft, October 4, 2002. Claimed on waivers by **Montreal** from **Nashville**, October 25, 2002. Signed as a free agent by **Leksands** (Sweden-2), November 15, 2004.

BOULERICE, Jesse

(BOO-luhr-ighs, JEH-see)

Right wing. Shoots right. 6'2", 215 lbs. Born, Plattsburgh, NY, August 10, 1978. Philadelphia's 4th choice, 133rd overall, in 1996 Entry Draft.

Season	Club	League	GP	G	A	Pts	PIM	PP	SH	GW	S	%	+/-	TF	F%	Min	GP	G	A	Pts	PIM	PP	SH	GW	Min
1994-95	Hawkesbury	CJHL	46	1	8	9	160																		
1995-96	Detroit	OHL	64	2	5	7	150										16	0	0	0	12				
1996-97	Detroit	OHL	33	10	14	24	209																		
1997-98	Plymouth Whalers	OHL	53	20	23	43	170										13	2	4	6	35				
1998-99	Philadelphia	AHL	24	1	2	3	82																		
	New Orleans	ECHL	12	0	1	1	38																		
99-2000	Philadelphia	AHL	40	3	4	7	85										4	0	2	2	4				
	Trenton Titans	ECHL	25	8	8	16	90																		
2000-01	Philadelphia	AHL	60	3	4	7	256										10	1	1	2	28				
2001-02	Philadelphia	NHL	3	0	0	0	5	0	0	0	1	0.0	-1	0	0.0	4:18									
	Philadelphia	AHL	41	2	5	7	204																		
	Lowell	AHL	15	2	4	6	80										5	0	2	2	6				
2002-03	Carolina	NHL	48	2	1	3	108	0	0	0	12	16.7	-2	0	0.0	3:54									
2003-04	Carolina	NHL	76	6	1	7	127	0	0	0	46	13.0	-5	0	0.0	6:32									
2004-05			DID NOT PLAY																						
2005-06	Carolina	NHL	26	0	0	0	51	0	0	0	3	0.0	-3	0	0.0	2:30									
	St. Louis	NHL	12	0	0	0	13	0	0	0	2	0.0	-4	0	0.0	2:39									
2006-07	Albany River Rats	AHL	16	4	3	7	36																		
	NHL Totals		165	8	2	10	304	0	0	0	64	12.5		0	0.0	4:49									

Traded to **Carolina** by **Philadelphia** for Greg Koehler, February 13, 2002. Traded to **St. Louis** by **Carolina** with Mike Zigomanis, the rights to Magnus Kahnberg, Carolina's 1st round choice (later traded to New Jersey - New Jersey selected Matthew Corrente) in 2006 Entry Draft, Toronto's 4th round choice (previously acquired, St. Louis selected Reto Berra) in 2006 Entry Draft and Chicago's 4th round choice (previously acquired, St. Louis selected Cade Fairchild) in 2007 Entry Draft for Doug Weight and Erkki Rajamaki, January 30, 2006. Signed as a free agent by **Carolina**, August 2, 2006.

			Regular Season														Playoffs								
Season	Club	League	GP	G	A	Pts	PIM	PP	SH	GW	S	%	+/-	TF	F%	Min	GP	G	A	Pts	PIM	PP	SH	GW	Min

BOULTON, Eric

(BOHL-tuhn, AIR-ihk)

Left wing. Shoots left. 6'1", 220 lbs. Born, Halifax, N.S., August 17, 1976. NY Rangers' 12th choice, 234th overall, in 1994 Entry Draft.

Season	Club	League	GP	G	A	Pts	PIM	PP	SH	GW	S	%	+/-	TF	F%	Min	GP	G	A	Pts	PIM	PP	SH	GW	Min
1992-93	Cole Harbour	MJrHL	44	12	15	27	212	....	....	....	....	....	....	....	....	....	....	....	....	....	....	....	....	....	....
1993-94	Oshawa Generals	OHL	45	4	3	7	149	....	....	....	....	....	....	....	....	....	5	0	0	0	16	....	....	....	....
1994-95	Oshawa Generals	OHL	27	7	5	12	125	....	....	....	....	....	....	....	....	....	....	....	....	....	....	....	....	....	....
	Sarnia Sting	OHL	24	3	7	10	134	....	....	....	....	....	....	....	....	....	4	0	1	1	10	....	....	....	....
1995-96	Sarnia Sting	OHL	66	14	29	43	243	....	....	....	....	....	....	....	....	....	9	0	3	3	29	....	....	....	....
1996-97	Binghamton	AHL	23	2	3	5	67	....	....	....	....	....	....	....	....	....	3	0	0	0	4	....	....	....	....
	Charlotte	ECHL	44	14	11	25	325	....	....	....	....	....	....	....	....	....	3	0	1	1	6	....	....	....	....
1997-98	Charlotte	ECHL	53	11	16	27	202	....	....	....	....	....	....	....	....	....	4	1	0	1	0	....	....	....	....
	Fort Wayne	IHL	8	0	2	2	42	....	....	....	....	....	....	....	....	....	....	....	....	....	....	....	....	....	....
1998-99	Kentucky	AHL	34	3	3	6	154	....	....	....	....	....	....	....	....	....	10	0	1	1	36	....	....	....	....
	Florida Everblades	ECHL	26	9	13	22	143	....	....	....	....	....	....	....	....	....	....	....	....	....	....	....	....	....	....
	Houston Aeros	IHL	7	1	0	1	41	....	....	....	....	....	....	....	....	....	....	....	....	....	....	....	....	....	....
99-2000	Rochester	AHL	76	2	2	4	276	....	....	....	....	....	....	....	....	....	18	2	1	3	53	....	....	....	....
2000-01	**Buffalo**	**NHL**	**35**	**1**	**2**	**3**	**94**	**0**	**0**	**0**	**20**	**5.0**	**–1**	**2**	**0.0**	**5:42**	....	....	....	....	....	....	....	....	....
2001-02	**Buffalo**	**NHL**	**35**	**2**	**3**	**5**	**129**	**0**	**0**	**1**	**21**	**9.5**	**–1**	**0**	**0.0**	**6:08**	....	....	....	....	....	....	....	....	....
2002-03	**Buffalo**	**NHL**	**58**	**1**	**5**	**6**	**178**	**0**	**0**	**0**	**33**	**3.0**	**1**	**6**	**33.3**	**6:35**	....	....	....	....	....	....	....	....	....
2003-04	**Buffalo**	**NHL**	**44**	**1**	**2**	**3**	**110**	**0**	**0**	**0**	**20**	**5.0**	**–2**	**1**	**0.0**	**4:52**	....	....	....	....	....	....	....	....	....
2004-05	Columbia Inferno	ECHL	48	23	16	39	124	....	....	....	....	....	....	....	....	....	4	2	3	5	8	....	....	....	....
2005-06	**Atlanta**	**NHL**	**51**	**4**	**5**	**9**	**87**	**0**	**0**	**0**	**28**	**14.3**	**–4**	**2**	**50.0**	**4:54**	....	....	....	....	....	....	....	....	....
2006-07	**Atlanta**	**NHL**	**45**	**3**	**4**	**7**	**49**	**0**	**0**	**0**	**42**	**7.1**	**2**	**2**	**50.0**	**6:16**	**4**	**0**	**0**	**0**	**24**	**0**	**0**	**0**	**5:04**
	NHL Totals		**268**	**12**	**21**	**33**	**647**	**0**	**0**	**1**	**164**	**7.3**		**13**	**30.8**	**5:45**	**4**	**0**	**0**	**0**	**24**	**0**	**0**	**0**	**5:04**

Signed as a free agent by **Buffalo**, September 14, 1999. Signed as a free agent by **Columbia** (ECHL), November 24, 2004. Signed as a free agent by **Atlanta**, August 8, 2005.

BOURDON, Luc

(BOOR-duhn, LEWK) **VAN.**

Defense. Shoots left. 6'3", 211 lbs. Born, Shippagan, N.B., February 16, 1987. Vancouver's 1st choice, 10th overall, in 2005 Entry Draft.

Season	Club	League	GP	G	A	Pts	PIM	PP	SH	GW	S	%	+/-	TF	F%	Min	GP	G	A	Pts	PIM	PP	SH	GW	Min
2002-03	Miramichi	NBMHL	20	2	12	14	106	....	....	....	....	....	....	....	....	....	....	....	....	....	....	....	....	....	....
2003-04	Val-d'Or Foreurs	QMJHL	64	2	6	8	58	....	....	....	....	....	....	....	....	....	7	1	0	1	4	....	....	....	....
2004-05	Val-d'Or Foreurs	QMJHL	70	13	19	32	117	....	....	....	....	....	....	....	....	....	....	....	....	....	....	....	....	....	....
2005-06	Val-d'Or Foreurs	QMJHL	20	2	18	20	54	....	....	....	....	....	....	....	....	....	....	....	....	....	....	....	....	....	....
	Moncton Wildcats	QMJHL	10	1	7	8	8	....	....	....	....	....	....	....	....	....	16	0	3	3	22	....	....	....	....
2006-07	**Vancouver**	**NHL**	**9**	**0**	**0**	**0**	**4**	**0**	**0**	**0**	**3**	**0.0**	**–1**	**0**	**0.0**	**8:50**	....	....	....	....	....	....	....	....	....
	Moncton Wildcats	QMJHL	13	3	11	14	28	....	....	....	....	....	....	....	....	....	....	....	....	....	....	....	....	....	....
	Cape Breton	QMJHL	23	1	5	6	45	....	....	....	....	....	....	....	....	....	16	2	11	13	28	....	....	....	....
	Manitoba Moose	AHL	....	....	....	....	....	....	....	....	....	....	....	....	....	....	5	0	0	0	2	....	....	....	....
	NHL Totals		**9**	**0**	**0**	**0**	**4**	**0**	**0**	**0**	**3**	**0.0**		**0**	**0.0**	**8:50**	....	....	....	....	....	....	....	....	....

BOURQUE, Rene

(BOHRK, reh-NAY) **CHI.**

Left wing. Shoots left. 6'2", 213 lbs. Born, Lac La Biche, Alta., December 10, 1981.

Season	Club	League	GP	G	A	Pts	PIM	PP	SH	GW	S	%	+/-	TF	F%	Min	GP	G	A	Pts	PIM	PP	SH	GW	Min
2000-01	U. of Wisconsin	WCHA	32	10	5	15	18	....	....	....	....	....	....	....	....	....	....	....	....	....	....	....	....	....	....
2001-02	U. of Wisconsin	WCHA	38	12	7	19	26	....	....	....	....	....	....	....	....	....	....	....	....	....	....	....	....	....	....
2002-03	U. of Wisconsin	WCHA	40	19	8	27	54	....	....	....	....	....	....	....	....	....	....	....	....	....	....	....	....	....	....
2003-04	U. of Wisconsin	WCHA	42	16	20	36	74	....	....	....	....	....	....	....	....	....	....	....	....	....	....	....	....	....	....
2004-05	Norfolk Admirals	AHL	78	33	27	60	105	....	....	....	....	....	....	....	....	....	6	1	0	1	8	....	....	....	....
2005-06	**Chicago**	**NHL**	**77**	**16**	**18**	**34**	**56**	**4**	**0**	**2**	**180**	**8.9**	**3**	**11**	**36.4**	**15:20**	....	....	....	....	....	....	....	....	....
2006-07	**Chicago**	**NHL**	**44**	**7**	**10**	**17**	**38**	**2**	**1**	**1**	**82**	**8.5**	**–4**	**9**	**22.2**	**16:01**	....	....	....	....	....	....	....	....	....
	Norfolk Admirals	AHL	1	0	0	0	0	....	....	....	....	....	....	....	....	....	....	....	....	....	....	....	....	....	....
	NHL Totals		**121**	**23**	**28**	**51**	**94**	**6**	**1**	**3**	**262**	**8.8**		**20**	**30.0**	**15:35**	....	....	....	....	....	....	....	....	....

AHL All-Rookie Team (2005) • Dudley "Red" Garrett Memorial Trophy (Top Rookie - AHL) (2005)

Signed as a free agent by **Chicago**, July 29, 2004.

BOUWMEESTER, Jay

(BOW-mee-stuhr, JAY) **FLA.**

Defense. Shoots left. 6'4", 212 lbs. Born, Edmonton, Alta., September 27, 1983. Florida's 1st choice, 3rd overall, in 2002 Entry Draft.

Season	Club	League	GP	G	A	Pts	PIM	PP	SH	GW	S	%	+/-	TF	F%	Min	GP	G	A	Pts	PIM	PP	SH	GW	Min
1998-99	Edmonton SSAC	AMHL	32	14	29	43	36	....	....	....	....	....	....	....	....	....	....	....	....	....	....	....	....	....	....
	Medicine Hat	WHL	8	2	1	3	2	....	....	....	....	....	....	....	....	....	....	....	....	....	....	....	....	....	....
99-2000	Medicine Hat	WHL	64	13	21	34	26	....	....	....	....	....	....	....	....	....	....	....	....	....	....	....	....	....	....
2000-01	Medicine Hat	WHL	61	14	39	53	44	....	....	....	....	....	....	....	....	....	....	....	....	....	....	....	....	....	....
2001-02	Medicine Hat	WHL	61	11	50	61	42	....	....	....	....	....	....	....	....	....	....	....	....	....	....	....	....	....	....
2002-03	**Florida**	**NHL**	**82**	**4**	**12**	**16**	**14**	**2**	**0**	**0**	**110**	**3.6**	**–29**	**0**	**0.0**	**20:09**	....	....	....	....	....	....	....	....	....
2003-04	**Florida**	**NHL**	**61**	**2**	**18**	**20**	**30**	**0**	**0**	**0**	**85**	**2.4**	**–15**	**0**	**0.0**	**23:02**	....	....	....	....	....	....	....	....	....
	San Antonio	AHL	2	0	1	1	2	....	....	....	....	....	....	....	....	....	....	....	....	....	....	....	....	....	....
2004-05	San Antonio	AHL	64	4	13	17	50	....	....	....	....	....	....	....	....	....	....	....	....	....	....	....	....	....	....
	Chicago Wolves	AHL	18	6	3	9	12	....	....	....	....	....	....	....	....	....	18	0	0	0	14	....	....	....	....
2005-06	**Florida**	**NHL**	**82**	**5**	**41**	**46**	**79**	**0**	**0**	**0**	**189**	**2.6**	**1**	**1**	**0.0**	**25:29**	....	....	....	....	....	....	....	....	....
	Canada	Olympics	6	0	0	0	0	....	....	....	....	....	....	....	....	....	....	....	....	....	....	....	....	....	....
2006-07	**Florida**	**NHL**	**82**	**12**	**30**	**42**	**66**	**3**	**0**	**3**	**174**	**6.9**	**23**	**0**	**0.0**	**26:09**	....	....	....	....	....	....	....	....	....
	NHL Totals		**307**	**23**	**101**	**124**	**189**	**5**	**0**	**3**	**558**	**4.1**		**1**	**0.0**	**23:45**	....	....	....	....	....	....	....	....	....

WHL East First All-Star Team (2002) • NHL All-Rookie Team (2003)

Played in NHL All-Star Game (2007)

Loaned to **Chicago** (AHL) by **Florida** (San Antonio-AHL) for cash, March 8, 2005.

BOYD, Dustin

(BOID, DUHS-tihn) **CGY.**

Center. Shoots left. 6', 192 lbs. Born, Winnipeg, Man., July 16, 1986. Calgary's 3rd choice, 98th overall, in 2004 Entry Draft.

Season	Club	League	GP	G	A	Pts	PIM	PP	SH	GW	S	%	+/-	TF	F%	Min	GP	G	A	Pts	PIM	PP	SH	GW	Min
2001-02	Wpg. Warriors	MMMHL	40	50	57	107	16	....	....	....	....	....	....	....	....	....	....	....	....	....	....	....	....	....	....
2002-03	Moose Jaw	WHL	63	11	17	28	15	....	....	....	....	....	....	....	....	....	13	0	3	3	2	....	....	....	....
2003-04	Moose Jaw	WHL	72	18	20	38	40	....	....	....	....	....	....	....	....	....	10	2	2	4	8	....	....	....	....
2004-05	Moose Jaw	WHL	66	26	35	61	57	....	....	....	....	....	....	....	....	....	5	1	2	3	2	....	....	....	....
2005-06	Moose Jaw	WHL	64	48	42	90	34	....	....	....	....	....	....	....	....	....	22	7	11	18	10	....	....	....	....
2006-07	**Calgary**	**NHL**	**13**	**2**	**2**	**4**	**4**	**0**	**0**	**1**	**8**	**25.0**	**5**	**16**	**50.0**	**10:09**	....	....	....	....	....	....	....	....	....
	Omaha	AHL	66	27	33	60	34	....	....	....	....	....	....	....	....	....	6	1	1	2	0	....	....	....	....
	NHL Totals		**13**	**2**	**2**	**4**	**4**	**0**	**0**	**1**	**8**	**25.0**		**16**	**50.0**	**10:09**	....	....	....	....	....	....	....	....	....

WHL East First All-Star Team (2006)

BOYES, Brad

(BOIZ, BRAD) **ST.L.**

Center. Shoots right. 6'1", 197 lbs. Born, Mississauga, Ont., April 17, 1982. Toronto's 1st choice, 24th overall, in 2000 Entry Draft.

Season	Club	League	GP	G	A	Pts	PIM	PP	SH	GW	S	%	+/-	TF	F%	Min	GP	G	A	Pts	PIM	PP	SH	GW	Min
1997-98	Mississauga Reps	MTHL	44	27	50	77	....	....	....	....	....	....	....	....	....	....	....	....	....	....	....	....	....	....	....
1998-99	Erie Otters	OHL	59	24	36	60	30	....	....	....	....	....	....	....	....	....	5	1	2	3	10	....	....	....	....
99-2000	Erie Otters	OHL	68	36	46	82	38	....	....	....	....	....	....	....	....	....	13	6	8	14	10	....	....	....	....
2000-01	Erie Otters	OHL	59	45	45	90	42	....	....	....	....	....	....	....	....	....	15	10	13	23	8	....	....	....	....
2001-02	Erie Otters	OHL	47	36	41	77	42	....	....	....	....	....	....	....	....	....	21	22	*19	41	27	....	....	....	....
2002-03	St. John's	AHL	65	23	28	51	45	....	....	....	....	....	....	....	....	....	....	....	....	....	....	....	....	....	....
	Cleveland Barons	AHL	15	7	6	13	21	....	....	....	....	....	....	....	....	....	....	....	....	....	....	....	....	....	....
2003-04	**San Jose**	**NHL**	**1**	**0**	**0**	**0**	**2**	**0**	**0**	**0**	**0**	**0.0**	**–2**	**0**	**0.0**	**13:03**	....	....	....	....	....	....	....	....	....
	Cleveland Barons	AHL	61	25	35	60	38	....	....	....	....	....	....	....	....	....	....	....	....	....	....	....	....	....	....
	Providence Bruins	AHL	17	6	6	12	13	....	....	....	....	....	....	....	....	....	2	1	0	1	0	....	....	....	....
2004-05	Providence Bruins	AHL	80	33	42	75	58	....	....	....	....	....	....	....	....	....	16	8	7	15	23	....	....	....	....
2005-06	**Boston**	**NHL**	**82**	**26**	**43**	**69**	**30**	**8**	**0**	**3**	**203**	**12.8**	**11**	**265**	**53.6**	**15:46**	....	....	....	....	....	....	....	....	....

			Regular Season														Playoffs								
Season	Club	League	GP	G	A	Pts	PIM	PP	SH	GW	S	%	+/-	TF	F%	Min	GP	G	A	Pts	PIM	PP	SH	GW	Min
2006-07	**Boston**	**NHL**	**62**	**13**	**21**	**34**	**25**	**1**	**1**	**1**	**139**	**9.4**	**–17**	**220**	**44.1**	**16:04**	....	....	....	....	....	....	....	....	....
	St. Louis	**NHL**	**19**	**4**	**8**	**12**	**4**	**0**	**0**	**1**	**43**	**9.3**	**0**	**93**	**58.1**	**17:25**	....	....	....	....	....	....	....	....	....
	NHL Totals		**164**	**43**	**72**	**115**	**61**	**9**	**1**	**5**	**385**	**11.2**		**578**	**50.7**	**16:03**	....	....	....	....	....	....	....	....	....

Canadian Major Junior Scholastic Player of the Year (2000) • OHL Second All-Star Team (2001) • OHL First All-Star Team (2002) • Canadian Major Junior Sportsman of the Year (2002) • AHL All-Rookie Team (2003) • AHL Second All-Star Team (2004) • NHL All-Rookie Team (2006)

Traded to **San Jose** by **Toronto** with Alyn McCauley and Toronto's 1st round choice (later traded to Boston – Boston selected Mark Stuart) in 2003 Entry Draft for Owen Nolan, March 5, 2003. Traded to **Boston** by **San Jose** for Jeff Jillson, March 9, 2004. Traded to **St. Louis** by **Boston** for Dennis Wideman, February 27, 2007.

BOYLE, Dan

(BOIL, DAN) **T.B.**

Defense. Shoots right. 5'11", 190 lbs. Born, Ottawa, Ont., July 12, 1976.

Season	Club	League	GP	G	A	Pts	PIM	PP	SH	GW	S	%	+/-	TF	F%	Min	GP	G	A	Pts	PIM	PP	SH	GW	Min
1992-93	Gloucester	CJHL	55	22	51	73	60	....	....	....	....	....	....	....	....	....	....	....	....	....	....	....	....	....	....
1993-94	Gloucester	CJHL	53	27	54	81	155	....	....	....	....	....	....	....	....	....	....	....	....	....	....	....	....	....	....
1994-95	Miami U.	CCHA	35	8	18	26	24	....	....	....	....	....	....	....	....	....	....	....	....	....	....	....	....	....	....
1995-96	Miami U.	CCHA	36	7	20	27	70	....	....	....	....	....	....	....	....	....	....	....	....	....	....	....	....	....	....
1996-97	Miami U.	CCHA	40	11	43	54	52	....	....	....	....	....	....	....	....	....	....	....	....	....	....	....	....	....	....
1997-98	Miami U.	CCHA	37	14	26	40	58	....	....	....	....	....	....	....	....	....	....	....	....	....	....	....	....	....	....
1998-99	**Florida**	**NHL**	**22**	**3**	**5**	**8**	**6**	**1**	**0**	**1**	**31**	**9.7**	**0**	**1**	**100.0**	**18:50**	....	....	....	....	....	....	....	....	....
	Kentucky	AHL	53	8	34	42	87	....	....	....	....	....	....	....	....	....	12	3	5	8	16	....	....	....	....
99-2000	**Florida**	**NHL**	**13**	**0**	**3**	**3**	**4**	**0**	**0**	**0**	**9**	**0.0**	**–2**	**0**	**0.0**	**16:57**	....	....	....	....	....	....	....	....	....
	Louisville Panthers	AHL	58	14	38	52	75	....	....	....	....	....	....	....	....	....	4	0	2	2	8	....	....	....	....
2000-01	**Florida**	**NHL**	**69**	**4**	**18**	**22**	**28**	**1**	**0**	**0**	**83**	**4.8**	**–14**	**0**	**0.0**	**16:56**	....	....	....	....	....	....	....	....	....
	Louisville Panthers	AHL	6	0	5	5	12	....	....	....	....	....	....	....	....	....	....	....	....	....	....	....	....	....	....
2001-02	**Florida**	**NHL**	**25**	**3**	**3**	**6**	**12**	**1**	**0**	**0**	**31**	**9.7**	**–1**	**2**	**50.0**	**15:40**	....	....	....	....	....	....	....	....	....
	Tampa Bay	**NHL**	**41**	**5**	**15**	**20**	**27**	**2**	**0**	**1**	**68**	**7.4**	**–15**	**0**	**0.0**	**22:28**	....	....	....	....	....	....	....	....	....
2002-03	**Tampa Bay**	**NHL**	**77**	**13**	**40**	**53**	**44**	**8**	**0**	**1**	**136**	**9.6**	**9**	**2**	**0.0**	**24:31**	**11**	**0**	**7**	**7**	**6**	**0**	**0**	**0**	**27:45**
2003-04♦	**Tampa Bay**	**NHL**	**78**	**9**	**30**	**39**	**60**	**3**	**0**	**2**	**137**	**6.6**	**23**	**0**	**0.0**	**22:46**	**23**	**2**	**8**	**10**	**16**	**1**	**0**	**0**	**21:27**
2004-05	Djurgarden	Sweden	32	9	9	18	47	....	....	....	....	....	....	....	....	....	12	2	3	5	26	....	....	....	....
2005-06	**Tampa Bay**	**NHL**	**79**	**15**	**38**	**53**	**38**	**6**	**0**	**4**	**153**	**9.8**	**–8**	**1**	**0.0**	**23:26**	**5**	**1**	**3**	**4**	**6**	**0**	**0**	**0**	**25:54**
	Canada	Olympics	DID NOT PLAY																						
2006-07	**Tampa Bay**	**NHL**	**82**	**20**	**43**	**63**	**62**	**10**	**1**	**4**	**203**	**9.9**	**–5**	**1**	**0.0**	**27:03**	**6**	**0**	**1**	**1**	**2**	**0**	**0**	**0**	**28:03**
	NHL Totals		**486**	**72**	**195**	**267**	**281**	**32**	**1**	**13**	**851**	**8.5**		**7**	**28.6**	**22:19**	**45**	**3**	**19**	**22**	**30**	**1**	**0**	**0**	**24:22**

CCHA First All-Star Team (1997, 1998) • NCAA West First All-American Team (1997, 1998) • AHL All-Rookie Team (1999 • AHL Second All-Star Team (1999, 2000) • NHL Second All-Star Team (2007)

Signed as a free agent by **Florida**, March 30, 1998. Traded to **Tampa Bay** by **Florida** for Tampa Bay's 5th round choice (Martin Tuma) in 2003 Entry Draft, January 7, 2002. Signed as a free agent by **Djurgarden** (Sweden), November 14, 2004.

BOYNTON, Nick

(BOIN-tuhn, NIHK) **PHX.**

Defense. Shoots right. 6'2", 211 lbs. Born, Nobleton, Ont., January 14, 1979. Boston's 1st choice, 21st overall, in 1999 Entry Draft.

Season	Club	League	GP	G	A	Pts	PIM	PP	SH	GW	S	%	+/-	TF	F%	Min	GP	G	A	Pts	PIM	PP	SH	GW	Min
1993-94	Caledon	MTJHL	4	0	1	1	0	....	....	....	....	....	....	....	....	....	....	....	....	....	....	....	....	....	....
1994-95	Caledon	MTJHL	44	10	35	45	139	....	....	....	....	....	....	....	....	....	....	....	....	....	....	....	....	....	....
1995-96	Ottawa 67's	OHL	64	10	14	24	90	....	....	....	....	....	....	....	....	....	4	0	3	3	10	....	....	....	....
1996-97	Ottawa 67's	OHL	63	13	51	64	143	....	....	....	....	....	....	....	....	....	24	4	*24	28	38	....	....	....	....
1997-98	Ottawa 67's	OHL	40	7	31	38	94	....	....	....	....	....	....	....	....	....	13	0	4	4	24	....	....	....	....
1998-99	Ottawa 67's	OHL	51	11	48	59	83	....	....	....	....	....	....	....	....	....	9	1	9	10	18	....	....	....	....
99-2000	**Boston**	**NHL**	**5**	**0**	**0**	**0**	**0**	**0**	**0**	**0**	**6**	**0.0**	**–5**	**0**	**0.0**	**21:21**	....	....	....	....	....	....	....	....	....
	Providence Bruins	AHL	53	5	14	19	66	....	....	....	....	....	....	....	....	....	12	1	0	1	6	....	....	....	....
2000-01	**Boston**	**NHL**	**1**	**0**	**0**	**0**	**0**	**0**	**0**	**0**	**1**	**0.0**	**–1**	**0**	**0.0**	**14:27**	....	....	....	....	....	....	....	....	....
	Providence Bruins	AHL	78	6	27	33	105	....	....	....	....	....	....	....	....	....	17	0	2	2	35	....	....	....	....
2001-02	**Boston**	**NHL**	**80**	**4**	**14**	**18**	**107**	**0**	**0**	**1**	**136**	**2.9**	**18**	**0**	**0.0**	**18:30**	**6**	**1**	**2**	**3**	**8**	**0**	**0**	**0**	**21:30**
2002-03	**Boston**	**NHL**	**78**	**7**	**17**	**24**	**99**	**0**	**1**	**2**	**160**	**4.4**	**8**	**1**	**0.0**	**22:41**	**5**	**0**	**1**	**1**	**4**	**0**	**0**	**0**	**23:22**
2003-04	**Boston**	**NHL**	**81**	**6**	**24**	**30**	**98**	**1**	**1**	**1**	**178**	**3.4**	**17**	**0**	**0.0**	**22:32**	**7**	**0**	**2**	**2**	**2**	**0**	**0**	**0**	**24:44**
2004-05	Nottingham	Britain	9	1	3	4	4	....	....	....	....	....	....	....	....	....	6	1	2	3	22	....	....	....	....
2005-06	**Boston**	**NHL**	**54**	**5**	**7**	**12**	**93**	**1**	**1**	**0**	**89**	**5.6**	**–7**	**1**	**100.0**	**20:39**	....	....	....	....	....	....	....	....	....
2006-07	**Phoenix**	**NHL**	**59**	**2**	**9**	**11**	**138**	**1**	**0**	**0**	**53**	**3.8**	**–13**	**1**	**0.0**	**16:48**	....	....	....	....	....	....	....	....	....
	NHL Totals		**358**	**24**	**71**	**95**	**535**	**3**	**3**	**4**	**623**	**3.9**		**3**	**33.3**	**20:24**	**18**	**1**	**5**	**6**	**14**	**0**	**0**	**0**	**23:16**

• Re-entered NHL Entry Draft. Originally Washington's 1st choice, 9th overall, in 1997 Entry Draft.

OHL All-Rookie Team (1996) • Memorial Cup Tournament All-Star Team (1999) • Stafford Smythe Memorial Trophy (Memorial Cup Tournament MVP) (1999) • NHL All-Rookie Team (2002)

Played in NHL All-Star Game (2004)

Signed as a free agent by **Nottingham** (Britain), January 26, 2005. Traded to **Phoenix** by **Boston** with Boston's 4th round choice (later traded to Toronto - Toronto selected Matt Frattin) in 2007 Entry Draft for Paul Mara and Phoenix's 3rd round choice (later traded to Anaheim - Anaheim selected Maxime Macenauer) in 2007 Entry Draft, June 26, 2006.

BRADLEY, Matt

(BRAD-lee, MAT) **WSH.**

Right wing. Shoots right. 6'3", 201 lbs. Born, Stittsville, Ont., June 13, 1978. San Jose's 4th choice, 102nd overall, in 1996 Entry Draft.

Season	Club	League	GP	G	A	Pts	PIM	PP	SH	GW	S	%	+/-	TF	F%	Min	GP	G	A	Pts	PIM	PP	SH	GW	Min
1994-95	Cumberland	CJHL	49	13	20	33	18	....	....	....	....	....	....	....	....	....	....	....	....	....	....	....	....	....	....
1995-96	Kingston	OHL	55	10	14	24	17	....	....	....	....	....	....	....	....	....	6	0	1	1	6	....	....	....	....
1996-97	Kingston	OHL	65	24	24	48	41	....	....	....	....	....	....	....	....	....	5	0	4	4	2	....	....	....	....
	Kentucky	AHL	1	0	1	1	0	....	....	....	....	....	....	....	....	....	....	....	....	....	....	....	....	....	....
1997-98	Kingston	OHL	55	33	50	83	24	....	....	....	....	....	....	....	....	....	8	3	4	7	7	....	....	....	....
1998-99	Kentucky	AHL	79	23	20	43	57	....	....	....	....	....	....	....	....	....	10	1	4	5	4	....	....	....	....
99-2000	Kentucky	AHL	80	22	19	41	81	....	....	....	....	....	....	....	....	....	9	6	3	9	9	....	....	....	....
2000-01	**San Jose**	**NHL**	**21**	**1**	**1**	**2**	**19**	**0**	**0**	**0**	**16**	**6.3**	**0**	**0**	**0.0**	**6:58**	....	....	....	....	....	....	....	....	....
	Kentucky	AHL	22	5	8	13	16	....	....	....	....	....	....	....	....	....	1	1	0	1	5	....	....	....	....
2001-02	**San Jose**	**NHL**	**54**	**9**	**13**	**22**	**43**	**0**	**0**	**2**	**63**	**14.3**	**22**	**2**	**0.0**	**8:27**	**10**	**0**	**0**	**0**	**0**	**0**	**0**	**0**	**5:16**
2002-03	**San Jose**	**NHL**	**46**	**2**	**3**	**5**	**37**	**0**	**0**	**0**	**21**	**9.5**	**–1**	**1**	**0.0**	**7:54**	....	....	....	....	....	....	....	....	....
2003-04	**Pittsburgh**	**NHL**	**82**	**7**	**9**	**16**	**65**	**0**	**0**	**1**	**85**	**8.2**	**–27**	**29**	**41.4**	**12:48**	....	....	....	....	....	....	....	....	....
2004-05	Bulldogs Dornbirn	Austria-2	6	5	2	7	18	....	....	....	....	....	....	....	....	....	....	....	....	....	....	....	....	....	....
2005-06	**Washington**	**NHL**	**74**	**7**	**12**	**19**	**72**	**0**	**0**	**1**	**87**	**8.0**	**–8**	**25**	**52.0**	**12:36**	....	....	....	....	....	....	....	....	....
2006-07	**Washington**	**NHL**	**57**	**4**	**9**	**13**	**47**	**0**	**0**	**0**	**77**	**5.2**	**–5**	**20**	**45.0**	**11:55**	....	....	....	....	....	....	....	....	....
	NHL Totals		**334**	**30**	**47**	**77**	**283**	**0**	**0**	**4**	**349**	**8.6**		**77**	**44.2**	**10:51**	**10**	**0**	**0**	**0**	**0**	**0**	**0**	**0**	**5:16**

Traded to **Pittsburgh** by **San Jose** for Wayne Primeau, March 11, 2003. Signed as a free agent by **Dornbirn** (Austria-2), November 14, 2004. Signed as a free agent by **Washington**, August 18, 2005.

BRASHEAR, Donald

(bra-SHEER, DAWN-uohld) **WSH.**

Left wing. Shoots left. 6'2", 235 lbs. Born, Bedford, IN, January 7, 1972.

Season	Club	League	GP	G	A	Pts	PIM	PP	SH	GW	S	%	+/-	TF	F%	Min	GP	G	A	Pts	PIM	PP	SH	GW	Min
1988-89	Ste-Foy	QAAA	10	1	2	3	10	....	....	....	....	....	....	....	....	....	....	....	....	....	....	....	....	....	....
1989-90	Longueuil	QMJHL	64	12	14	26	169	....	....	....	....	....	....	....	....	....	7	0	0	0	11	....	....	....	....
1990-91	Longueuil	QMJHL	68	12	26	38	195	....	....	....	....	....	....	....	....	....	8	0	3	3	33	....	....	....	....
1991-92	Verdun	QMJHL	65	18	24	42	283	....	....	....	....	....	....	....	....	....	18	4	2	6	98	....	....	....	....
1992-93	Fredericton	AHL	76	11	3	14	261	....	....	....	....	....	....	....	....	....	5	0	0	0	8	....	....	....	....
1993-94	**Montreal**	**NHL**	**14**	**2**	**2**	**4**	**34**	**0**	**0**	**0**	**15**	**13.3**	**0**	....	....	....	**2**	**0**	**0**	**0**	**0**	**0**	**0**	**0**	....
	Fredericton	AHL	62	38	28	66	250	....	....	....	....	....	....	....	....	....	....	....	....	....	....	....	....	....	....
1994-95	Fredericton	AHL	29	10	9	19	182	....	....	....	....	....	....	....	....	....	17	7	5	12	77	....	....	....	....
	Montreal	**NHL**	**20**	**1**	**1**	**2**	**63**	**0**	**0**	**1**	**10**	**10.0**	**–5**	....	....	....	....	....	....	....	....	....	....	....	....
1995-96	**Montreal**	**NHL**	**67**	**0**	**4**	**4**	**223**	**0**	**0**	**0**	**25**	**0.0**	**–10**	....	....	....	**6**	**0**	**0**	**0**	**2**	**0**	**0**	**0**	....
1996-97	**Montreal**	**NHL**	**10**	**0**	**0**	**0**	**38**	**0**	**0**	**0**	**6**	**0.0**	**–2**	....	....	....	....	....	....	....	....	....	....	....	....
	Vancouver	**NHL**	**59**	**8**	**5**	**13**	**207**	**0**	**0**	**2**	**55**	**14.5**	**–6**	....	....	....	....	....	....	....	....	....	....	....	....
1997-98	**Vancouver**	**NHL**	**77**	**9**	**9**	**18**	***372**	**0**	**0**	**1**	**64**	**14.1**	**–9**	....	....	....	....	....	....	....	....	....	....	....	....
1998-99	**Vancouver**	**NHL**	**82**	**8**	**10**	**18**	**209**	**2**	**0**	**1**	**112**	**7.1**	**–25**	**6**	**16.7**	**13:25**	....	....	....	....	....	....	....	....	....
99-2000	**Vancouver**	**NHL**	**60**	**11**	**2**	**13**	**136**	**1**	**0**	**3**	**83**	**13.3**	**–9**	**11**	**36.4**	**13:07**	....	....	....	....	....	....	....	....	....
2000-01	**Vancouver**	**NHL**	**79**	**9**	**19**	**28**	**145**	**0**	**0**	**1**	**127**	**7.1**	**0**	**6**	**16.7**	**13:27**	**4**	**0**	**0**	**0**	**0**	**0**	**0**	**0**	**14:47**
2001-02	**Vancouver**	**NHL**	**31**	**5**	**8**	**13**	**90**	**1**	**0**	**0**	**45**	**11.1**	**–8**	**4**	**25.0**	**13:58**	....	....	....	....	....	....	....	....	....
	Philadelphia	**NHL**	**50**	**4**	**15**	**19**	**109**	**0**	**0**	**2**	**62**	**6.5**	**0**	**1**	**0.0**	**13:00**	**5**	**0**	**0**	**0**	**19**	**0**	**0**	**0**	**9:55**
2002-03	**Philadelphia**	**NHL**	**80**	**8**	**17**	**25**	**161**	**0**	**0**	**1**	**99**	**8.1**	**5**	**27**	**33.3**	**13:23**	**13**	**1**	**2**	**3**	**21**	**0**	**0**	**0**	**11:09**
2003-04	**Philadelphia**	**NHL**	**64**	**6**	**7**	**13**	**212**	**0**	**0**	**0**	**72**	**8.3**	**–1**	**18**	**38.9**	**11:02**	**18**	**1**	**3**	**4**	**61**	**1**	**0**	**0**	**8:56**
2004-05	Quebec RadioX	QNAHL	47	18	32	50	260	....	....	....	....	....	....	....	....	....	8	4	6	10	42	....	....	....	....

			Regular Season														Playoffs								
Season	Club	League	GP	G	A	Pts	PIM	PP	SH	GW	S	%	+/-	TF	F%	Min	GP	G	A	Pts	PIM	PP	SH	GW	Min
2005-06	**Philadelphia**	**NHL**	**76**	**4**	**5**	**9**	**166**	**0**	**0**	**0**	**73**	**5.5**	**–2**	**7**	**28.6**	**8:36**	**1**	**0**	**0**	**0**	**0**	**0**	**0**	**0**	**4:20**
2006-07	**Washington**	**NHL**	**77**	**4**	**9**	**13**	**156**	**0**	**0**	**0**	**47**	**8.5**	**1**	**8**	**25.0**	**7:58**	....	....	....	....	....	....	....	....	....
	NHL Totals		**846**	**79**	**113**	**192**	**2321**	**4**	**0**	**12**	**895**	**8.8**		**88**	**30.7**	**11:49**	**49**	**2**	**5**	**7**	**103**	**0**	**0**	**0**	**10:13**

Signed as a free agent by **Montreal**, July 28, 1992. Traded to **Vancouver** by **Montreal** for Jassen Cullimore, November 13, 1996. Traded to **Philadelphia** by **Vancouver** with Vancouver's 6th round choice (later traded to Columbus – Columbus selected Jaroslav Balastik) in 2002 Entry Draft for Jan Hlavac and Tampa Bay's 3rd round choice (previously acquired, Vancouver selected Brett Skinner) in 2002 Entry Draft, December 17, 2001. Signed as a free agent by **Quebec** (QNAHL), September 21, 2004. Signed as a free agent by **Washington**, July 14, 2006.

BRENDL, Pavel

(BREHN-duhl, PAH-vehl)

Right wing. Shoots right. 6'1", 204 lbs. Born, Opocno, Czech., March 23, 1981. NY Rangers' 1st choice, 4th overall, in 1999 Entry Draft.

Season	Club	League	GP	G	A	Pts	PIM	PP	SH	GW	S	%	+/-	TF	F%	Min	GP	G	A	Pts	PIM	PP	SH	GW	Min
1996-97	HC Olomouc Jr.	CzRep-Jr.	40	35	17	52	....	....	....	....	....	....	....	....	....	....	....	....	....	....	....	....	....	....	....
1997-98	HC Olomouc Jr.	CzRep-Jr.	38	29	23	52	....	....	....	....	....	....	....	....	....	....	....	....	....	....	....	....	....	....	....
	HC Olomouc	CzRep-2	12	1	1	2	....	....	....	....	....	....	....	....	....	....	....	....	....	....	....	....	....	....	....
1998-99	Calgary Hitmen	WHL	68	*73	61	*134	40	....	....	....	....	....	....	....	....	....	20	*21	*25	*46	18	....	....	....	....
99-2000	Calgary Hitmen	WHL	61	*59	52	111	94	....	....	....	....	....	....	....	....	....	10	7	12	19	8	....	....	....	....
	Hartford	AHL	....	....	....	....	....	....	....	....	....	....	....	....	....	....	2	0	0	0	0	....	....	....	....
2000-01	Calgary Hitmen	WHL	49	40	35	75	66	....	....	....	....	....	....	....	....	....	10	7	6	13	6	....	....	....	....
2001-02	**Philadelphia**	**NHL**	**8**	**1**	**0**	**1**	**2**	**0**	**0**	**0**	**6**	**16.7**	**–1**	**21**	**19.1**	**8:59**	**2**	**0**	**0**	**0**	**0**	**0**	**0**	**0**	**11:28**
	Philadelphia	AHL	64	15	22	37	22	....	....	....	....	....	....	....	....	....	5	4	1	5	0	....	....	....	....
2002-03	**Philadelphia**	**NHL**	**42**	**5**	**7**	**12**	**4**	**1**	**0**	**1**	**80**	**6.3**	**8**	**9**	**22.2**	**10:19**	....	....	....	....	....	....	....	....	....
	Carolina	**NHL**	**8**	**0**	**1**	**1**	**2**	**0**	**0**	**0**	**14**	**0.0**	**–3**	**2**	**50.0**	**15:05**	....	....	....	....	....	....	....	....	....
2003-04	**Carolina**	**NHL**	**18**	**5**	**3**	**8**	**8**	**1**	**0**	**1**	**27**	**18.5**	**0**	**1**	**0.0**	**14:48**	....	....	....	....	....	....	....	....	....
	Lowell	AHL	33	17	16	33	34	....	....	....	....	....	....	....	....	....	....	....	....	....	....	....	....	....	....
2004-05	HC Ocelari Trinec	CzRep	2	0	0	0	0	....	....	....	....	....	....	....	....	....	....	....	....	....	....	....	....	....	....
	HC Olomouc	CzRep-2	3	0	0	0	12	....	....	....	....	....	....	....	....	....	....	....	....	....	....	....	....	....	....
	Jokipojat Joensuu	Finland-2	21	9	10	19	48	....	....	....	....	....	....	....	....	....	....	....	....	....	....	....	....	....	....
	HC Thurgau	Swiss-2	4	3	0	3	4	....	....	....	....	....	....	....	....	....	....	....	....	....	....	....	....	....	....
2005-06	Lowell	AHL	25	6	7	13	10	....	....	....	....	....	....	....	....	....	....	....	....	....	....	....	....	....	....
	Phoenix	**NHL**	**2**	**0**	**0**	**0**	**0**	**0**	**0**	**0**	**3**	**0.0**	**–3**	**1**	**0.0**	**8:54**	....	....	....	....	....	....	....	....	....
	San Antonio	AHL	38	13	11	24	8	....	....	....	....	....	....	....	....	....	....	....	....	....	....	....	....	....	....
2006-07	Mora IK	Sweden	54	*34	23	57	34	....	....	....	....	....	....	....	....	....	4	1	1	2	16	....	....	....	....
	NHL Totals		**78**	**11**	**11**	**22**	**16**	**2**	**0**	**2**	**130**	**8.5**		**34**	**20.6**	**11:40**	**2**	**0**	**0**	**0**	**0**	**0**	**0**	**0**	**11:28**

WHL East First All-Star Team (1999) • WHL Rookie of the Year (1999) • Canadian Major Junior First All-Star Team (1999) • Canadian Major Junior Rookie of the Year (1999) • Memorial Cup Tournament All-Star Team (1999) • WHL East Second All-Star Team (2000)

Traded to **Philadelphia** by **NY Rangers** with Jan Hlavac, Kim Johnsson and NY Rangers' 3rd round choice (Stefan Ruzicka) in 2003 Entry Draft for Eric Lindros, August 20, 2001. Traded to **Carolina** by **Philadelphia** with Bruno St. Jacques for Sami Kapanen and Ryan Bast, February 7, 2003. Signed as a free agent by **Trinec** (CzRep), September 17, 2004. Signed as a free agent by **Olomouc** (CzRep-2), October 14, 2004. Signed as a free agent by **Joensuu** (Finland-2), November 15, 2004. Signed as a free agent by **Thurgau** (Swiss-2), December 21, 2004. Signed as a free agent by **Joensuu** (Finland-2), January 13, 2005. Traded to **Phoenix** by **Carolina** for Krys Kolanos, December 28, 2005. Signed as a free agent by **Mora** (Sweden), May 4, 2006.

BRENNAN, Kip

(BREH-nan, KIHP) **NYI**

Left wing. Shoots left. 6'4", 230 lbs. Born, Kingston, Ont., August 27, 1980. Los Angeles' 4th choice, 103rd overall, in 1998 Entry Draft.

Season	Club	League	GP	G	A	Pts	PIM	PP	SH	GW	S	%	+/-	TF	F%	Min	GP	G	A	Pts	PIM	PP	SH	GW	Min
1995-96	St. Mike's B's	OPJHL	40	0	11	11	155	....	....	....	....	....	....	....	....	....	7	0	1	1	20	....	....	....	....
1996-97	Windsor Spitfires	OHL	42	0	10	10	156	....	....	....	....	....	....	....	....	....	5	0	1	1	16	....	....	....	....
1997-98	Windsor Spitfires	OHL	24	0	7	7	103	....	....	....	....	....	....	....	....	....	....	....	....	....	....	....	....	....	....
	Sudbury Wolves	OHL	24	0	3	3	85	....	....	....	....	....	....	....	....	....	....	....	....	....	....	....	....	....	....
1998-99	Sudbury Wolves	OHL	38	9	12	21	160	....	....	....	....	....	....	....	....	....	....	....	....	....	....	....	....	....	....
99-2000	Sudbury Wolves	OHL	55	16	16	32	228	....	....	....	....	....	....	....	....	....	12	3	3	6	67	....	....	....	....
2000-01	Lowell	AHL	23	2	3	5	117	....	....	....	....	....	....	....	....	....	....	....	....	....	....	....	....	....	....
	Sudbury Wolves	OHL	27	7	14	21	94	....	....	....	....	....	....	....	....	....	12	5	6	11	*92	....	....	....	....
2001-02	Manchester	AHL	44	4	1	5	269	....	....	....	....	....	....	....	....	....	4	0	1	1	26	....	....	....	....
	Los Angeles	**NHL**	**4**	**0**	**0**	**0**	**22**	**0**	**0**	**0**	**0**	**0.0**	**1**	**0**	**0.0**	**4:40**	....	....	....	....	....	....	....	....	....
2002-03	Manchester	AHL	35	3	2	5	195	....	....	....	....	....	....	....	....	....	3	0	0	0	0	....	....	....	....
	Los Angeles	**NHL**	**19**	**0**	**0**	**0**	**57**	**0**	**0**	**0**	**6**	**0.0**	**0**	**2**	**0.0**	**4:52**	....	....	....	....	....	....	....	....	....
2003-04	**Los Angeles**	**NHL**	**18**	**1**	**0**	**1**	**79**	**0**	**0**	**0**	**6**	**16.7**	**–1**	**0**	**0.0**	**5:01**	....	....	....	....	....	....	....	....	....
	Manchester	AHL	2	0	0	0	6	....	....	....	....	....	....	....	....	....	....	....	....	....	....	....	....	....	....
	Atlanta	**NHL**	**5**	**0**	**0**	**0**	**17**	**0**	**0**	**0**	**2**	**0.0**	**0**	**0**	**0.0**	**3:37**	....	....	....	....	....	....	....	....	....
2004-05	Chicago Wolves	AHL	48	7	6	13	267	....	....	....	....	....	....	....	....	....	18	1	1	2	*105	....	....	....	....
2005-06	**Anaheim**	**NHL**	**12**	**0**	**1**	**1**	**35**	**0**	**0**	**0**	**5**	**0.0**	**–2**	**1**	**0.0**	**4:16**	....	....	....	....	....	....	....	....	....
	Portland Pirates	AHL	9	2	1	3	22	....	....	....	....	....	....	....	....	....	....	....	....	....	....	....	....	....	....
2006-07	Hershey Bears	AHL	26	4	2	6	67	....	....	....	....	....	....	....	....	....	6	0	1	1	30	....	....	....	....
	Toronto Marlies	AHL	1	0	0	0	6	....	....	....	....	....	....	....	....	....	....	....	....	....	....	....	....	....	....
	Long Beach	ECHL	11	2	3	5	74	....	....	....	....	....	....	....	....	....	....	....	....	....	....	....	....	....	....
	NHL Totals		**58**	**1**	**1**	**2**	**210**	**0**	**0**	**0**	**19**	**5.3**		**3**	**0.0**	**4:40**									

Traded to **Atlanta** by **Los Angeles** for Jeff Cowan, March 9, 2004. • Spent the majority of the 2003-04 season as a healthy reserve. Signed as a free agent by **Chicago** (AHL), September 27, 2004. Traded to **Anaheim** by **Atlanta** for Mark Popovic, August 23, 2005. Signed as a free agent by **NY Islanders**, July 3, 2007.

BRENT, Tim

(BREHNT, TIHM) **PIT.**

Center. Shoots right. 6', 188 lbs. Born, Cambridge, Ont., March 10, 1984. Anaheim's 3rd choice, 75th overall, in 2004 Entry Draft.

Season	Club	League	GP	G	A	Pts	PIM	PP	SH	GW	S	%	+/-	TF	F%	Min	GP	G	A	Pts	PIM	PP	SH	GW	Min
99-2000	Cambridge	OHA-B	40	19	16	35	42	....	....	....	....	....	....	....	....	....	....	....	....	....	....	....	....	....	....
2000-01	St. Michael's	OHL	64	9	19	28	31	....	....	....	....	....	....	....	....	....	18	2	8	10	6	....	....	....	....
2001-02	St. Michael's	OHL	61	19	40	59	52	....	....	....	....	....	....	....	....	....	14	7	12	19	20	....	....	....	....
2002-03	St. Michael's	OHL	60	24	42	66	74	....	....	....	....	....	....	....	....	....	19	7	17	24	14	....	....	....	....
2003-04	St. Michael's	OHL	53	26	41	67	105	....	....	....	....	....	....	....	....	....	18	4	13	17	24	....	....	....	....
2004-05	Cincinnati	AHL	46	5	13	18	42	....	....	....	....	....	....	....	....	....	12	0	1	1	6	....	....	....	....
2005-06	Portland Pirates	AHL	37	15	9	24	32	....	....	....	....	....	....	....	....	....	15	4	4	8	16	....	....	....	....
2006-07	**Anaheim**	**NHL**	**15**	**1**	**0**	**1**	**6**	**0**	**0**	**0**	**14**	**7.1**	**–5**	**86**	**48.8**	**6:55**	....	....	....	....	....	....	....	....	....
	Portland Pirates	AHL	48	16	14	30	40	....	....	....	....	....	....	....	....	....	....	....	....	....	....	....	....	....	....
	NHL Totals		**15**	**1**	**0**	**1**	**6**	**0**	**0**	**0**	**14**	**7.1**		**86**	**48.8**	**6:55**	....	....	....	....	....	....	....	....	....

• Re-entered NHL Entry Draft. Originally Anaheim's 2nd choice, 37th overall, in 2002 Entry Draft.

Traded to **Pittsburgh** by **Anaheim** for Stephen Dixon, June 23, 2007.

BREWER, Eric

(BREW-uhr, AIR-ihk) **ST.L.**

Defense. Shoots left. 6'4", 229 lbs. Born, Vernon, B.C., April 17, 1979. NY Islanders' 2nd choice, 5th overall, in 1997 Entry Draft.

Season	Club	League	GP	G	A	Pts	PIM	PP	SH	GW	S	%	+/-	TF	F%	Min	GP	G	A	Pts	PIM	PP	SH	GW	Min
1994-95	Kamloops	BCAHA	40	19	19	38	62	....	....	....	....	....	....	....	....	....	....	....	....	....	....	....	....	....	....
1995-96	Prince George	WHL	63	4	10	14	25	....	....	....	....	....	....	....	....	....	....	....	....	....	....	....	....	....	....
1996-97	Prince George	WHL	71	5	24	29	81	....	....	....	....	....	....	....	....	....	15	2	4	6	16	....	....	....	....
1997-98	Prince George	WHL	34	5	28	33	45	....	....	....	....	....	....	....	....	....	11	4	2	6	19	....	....	....	....
1998-99	**NY Islanders**	**NHL**	**63**	**5**	**6**	**11**	**32**	**2**	**0**	**0**	**63**	**7.9**	**–14**	**0**	**0.0**	**15:28**	....	....	....	....	....	....	....	....	....
99-2000	**NY Islanders**	**NHL**	**26**	**0**	**2**	**2**	**20**	**0**	**0**	**0**	**30**	**0.0**	**–11**	**0**	**0.0**	**18:33**	....	....	....	....	....	....	....	....	....
	Lowell	AHL	25	2	2	4	26	....	....	....	....	....	....	....	....	....	7	0	0	0	0	....	....	....	....
2000-01	**Edmonton**	**NHL**	**77**	**7**	**14**	**21**	**53**	**2**	**0**	**2**	**91**	**7.7**	**15**	**0**	**0.0**	**18:31**	**6**	**1**	**5**	**6**	**2**	**1**	**0**	**0**	**28:12**
2001-02	**Edmonton**	**NHL**	**81**	**7**	**18**	**25**	**45**	**6**	**0**	**2**	**165**	**4.2**	**–5**	**0**	**0.0**	**23:56**	....	....	....	....	....	....	....	....	....
	Canada	Olympics	6	2	0	2	0	....	....	....	....	....	....	....	....	....	....	....	....	....	....	....	....	....	....
2002-03	**Edmonton**	**NHL**	**80**	**8**	**21**	**29**	**45**	**1**	**0**	**1**	**147**	**5.4**	**–11**	**1**	**100.0**	**24:56**	**6**	**1**	**3**	**4**	**6**	**0**	**0**	**0**	**25:31**
2003-04	**Edmonton**	**NHL**	**77**	**7**	**18**	**25**	**67**	**3**	**0**	**1**	**135**	**5.2**	**–6**	**0**	**0.0**	**24:40**	....	....	....	....	....	....	....	....	....
2004-05			DID NOT PLAY																						
2005-06	**St. Louis**	**NHL**	**32**	**6**	**3**	**9**	**45**	**1**	**0**	**1**	**64**	**9.4**	**–17**	**0**	**0.0**	**23:28**	....	....	....	....	....	....	....	....	....
2006-07	**St. Louis**	**NHL**	**82**	**6**	**23**	**29**	**69**	**2**	**0**	**1**	**111**	**5.4**	**–10**	**0**	**0.0**	**24:32**	....	....	....	....	....	....	....	....	....
	NHL Totals		**518**	**46**	**105**	**151**	**376**	**17**	**0**	**8**	**806**	**5.7**		**1**	**100.0**	**22:09**	**12**	**2**	**8**	**10**	**8**	**1**	**0**	**0**	**26:51**

WHL West Second All-Star Team (1998)

Played in NHL All-Star Game (2003)

Traded to **Edmonton** by **NY Islanders** with Josh Green and NY Islanders' 2nd round choice (Brad Winchester) in 2000 Entry Draft for Roman Hamrlik, June 24, 2000. Traded to **St. Louis** by **Edmonton** with Doug Lynch and Jeff Woywitka for Chris Pronger, August 2, 2005. • Missed majority of 2005-06 season recovering from shoulder injuries suffered in games at Columbus (November 16, 2005) and Atlanta (January 13, 2006).

BRIERE, Daniel
(bree-AIR, DAN-yehl) **PHI.**

Center. Shoots right. 5'10", 179 lbs. Born, Gatineau, Que., October 6, 1977. Phoenix's 2nd choice, 24th overall, in 1996 Entry Draft.

			Regular Season														Playoffs								
Season	Club	League	GP	G	A	Pts	PIM	PP	SH	GW	S	%	+/-	TF	F%	Min	GP	G	A	Pts	PIM	PP	SH	GW	Min
1992-93	Abitibi Regents	QAAA	42	24	30	54	28	....	....	....	....	....	....	....	....	....	3	0	3	3	8	....	....	....	....
1993-94	Gatineau	QAAA	44	56	47	103	56	....	....	....	....	....	....	....	....	....	....	....	....	....	....	....	....	....	....
1994-95	Drummondville	QMJHL	72	51	72	123	54	....	....	....	....	....	....	....	....	....	4	2	3	5	2	....	....	....	....
1995-96	Drummondville	QMJHL	67	*67	*96	*163	84	....	....	....	....	....	....	....	....	....	6	6	12	18	8	....	....	....	....
1996-97	Drummondville	QMJHL	59	52	78	130	94	....	....	....	....	....	....	....	....	....	8	7	7	14	14	....	....	....	....
1997-98	**Phoenix**	**NHL**	**5**	**1**	**0**	**1**	**2**	**0**	**0**	**0**	**4**	**25.0**	**1**	....	....	....	....	....	....	....	....	....	....	....	....
	Springfield	AHL	68	36	56	92	42	....	....	....	....	....	....	....	....	....	4	1	2	3	4	....	....	....	....
1998-99	**Phoenix**	**NHL**	**64**	**8**	**14**	**22**	**30**	**2**	**0**	**2**	**90**	**8.9**	**-3**	**484**	**47.5**	**11:13**	....	....	....	....	....	....	....	....	....
	Las Vegas	IHL	1	1	1	2	0	....	....	....	....	....	....	....	....	....	....	....	....	....	....	....	....	....	....
	Springfield	AHL	13	2	6	8	20	....	....	....	....	....	....	....	....	....	3	0	1	1	2	....	....	....	....
99-2000	**Phoenix**	**NHL**	**13**	**1**	**1**	**2**	**0**	**0**	**0**	**0**	**9**	**11.1**	**0**	**65**	**49.2**	**7:41**	**1**	**0**	**0**	**0**	**0**	**0**	**0**	**0**	**6:16**
	Springfield	AHL	58	29	42	71	56	....	....	....	....	....	....	....	....	....	....	....	....	....	....	....	....	....	....
2000-01	**Phoenix**	**NHL**	**30**	**11**	**4**	**15**	**12**	**9**	**0**	**1**	**43**	**25.6**	**-2**	**210**	**50.0**	**10:50**	....	....	....	....	....	....	....	....	....
	Springfield	AHL	30	21	25	46	30	....	....	....	....	....	....	....	....	....	....	....	....	....	....	....	....	....	....
2001-02	**Phoenix**	**NHL**	**78**	**32**	**28**	**60**	**52**	**12**	**0**	**5**	**149**	**21.5**	**6**	**951**	**51.8**	**15:44**	**5**	**2**	**1**	**3**	**2**	**1**	**0**	**1**	**16:25**
2002-03	**Phoenix**	**NHL**	**68**	**17**	**29**	**46**	**50**	**4**	**0**	**3**	**142**	**12.0**	**-21**	**1108**	**52.5**	**17:02**	....	....	....	....	....	....	....	....	....
	Buffalo	**NHL**	**14**	**7**	**5**	**12**	**12**	**5**	**0**	**1**	**39**	**17.9**	**1**	**206**	**50.0**	**17:49**	....	....	....	....	....	....	....	....	....
2003-04	**Buffalo**	**NHL**	**82**	**28**	**37**	**65**	**70**	**11**	**0**	**3**	**194**	**14.4**	**-7**	**1066**	**47.1**	**18:20**	....	....	....	....	....	....	....	....	....
2004-05	SC Bern	Swiss	36	16	29	45	26	....	....	....	....	....	....	....	....	....	11	1	6	7	2	....	....	....	....
2005-06	**Buffalo**	**NHL**	**48**	**25**	**33**	**58**	**48**	**11**	**0**	**4**	**147**	**17.0**	**3**	**517**	**50.7**	**19:04**	**18**	**8**	**11**	**19**	**12**	**3**	**0**	**2**	**18:48**
2006-07	**Buffalo**	**NHL**	**81**	**32**	**63**	**95**	**89**	**9**	**0**	**6**	**234**	**13.7**	**17**	**1089**	**49.6**	**19:19**	**16**	**3**	**12**	**15**	**16**	**2**	**0**	**1**	**20:53**
	NHL Totals		**483**	**162**	**214**	**376**	**365**	**63**	**0**	**25**	**1051**	**15.4**		**5696**	**50.0**	**16:14**	**40**	**13**	**24**	**37**	**30**	**6**	**0**	**4**	**19:01**

QMJHL All-Rookie Team (1995) • QMJHL Offensive Rookie of the Year (1995) • QMJHL Second All-Star Team (1996, 1997) • AHL All-Rookie Team (1998) • AHL First All-Star Team (1998) • Dudley "Red" Garrett Memorial Award (Rookie of the Year – AHL) (1998)

Played in NHL All-Star Game (2007)

Traded to **Buffalo** by **Phoenix** with Phoenix's 3rd round choice (Andrej Sekera) in 2004 Entry Draft for Chris Gratton and Buffalo's 4th round choice (later traded to Edmonton – Edmonton selected Liam Reddox) in 2004 Entry Draft, March 10, 2003. Signed as a free agent by **Bern** (Swiss), September 28, 2004. Signed as a free agent by **Philadelphia**, July 1, 2007.

BRIND'AMOUR, Rod
(BRIHND-uh-MOHR, RAWD) **CAR.**

Center. Shoots left. 6'1", 205 lbs. Born, Ottawa, Ont., August 9, 1970. St. Louis' 1st choice, 9th overall, in 1988 Entry Draft.

Season	Club	League	GP	G	A	Pts	PIM	PP	SH	GW	S	%	+/-	TF	F%	Min	GP	G	A	Pts	PIM	PP	SH	GW	Min
1986-87	Notre Dame	SMHL	33	38	50	88	66	....	....	....	....	....	....	....	....	....	....	....	....	....	....	....	....	....	....
1987-88	Notre Dame	SJHL	56	46	61	107	136	....	....	....	....	....	....	....	....	....	....	....	....	....	....	....	....	....	....
1988-89	Michigan State	CCHA	42	27	32	59	63	....	....	....	....	....	....	....	....	....	....	....	....	....	....	....	....	....	....
	St. Louis	**NHL**	....	....	....	....	....	....	....	....	....	....	....	....	....	....	**5**	**2**	**0**	**2**	**4**	**0**	**0**	**0**	....
1989-90	**St. Louis**	**NHL**	**79**	**26**	**35**	**61**	**46**	**10**	**0**	**1**	**160**	**16.3**	**23**	....	....	....	**12**	**5**	**8**	**13**	**6**	**1**	**0**	**0**	....
1990-91	**St. Louis**	**NHL**	**78**	**17**	**32**	**49**	**93**	**4**	**0**	**3**	**169**	**10.1**	**2**	....	....	....	**13**	**2**	**5**	**7**	**10**	**1**	**0**	**0**	....
1991-92	**Philadelphia**	**NHL**	**80**	**33**	**44**	**77**	**100**	**8**	**4**	**5**	**202**	**16.3**	**-3**	....	....	....	....	....	....	....	....	....	....	....	....
1992-93	**Philadelphia**	**NHL**	**81**	**37**	**49**	**86**	**89**	**13**	**4**	**4**	**206**	**18.0**	**-8**	....	....	....	....	....	....	....	....	....	....	....	....
1993-94	**Philadelphia**	**NHL**	**84**	**35**	**62**	**97**	**85**	**14**	**1**	**4**	**230**	**15.2**	**-9**	....	....	....	....	....	....	....	....	....	....	....	....
1994-95	**Philadelphia**	**NHL**	**48**	**12**	**27**	**39**	**33**	**4**	**1**	**2**	**86**	**14.0**	**-4**	....	....	....	**15**	**6**	**9**	**15**	**8**	**2**	**1**	**1**	....
1995-96	**Philadelphia**	**NHL**	**82**	**26**	**61**	**87**	**110**	**4**	**4**	**5**	**213**	**12.2**	**20**	....	....	....	**12**	**2**	**5**	**7**	**6**	**1**	**0**	**0**	....
1996-97	**Philadelphia**	**NHL**	**82**	**27**	**32**	**59**	**41**	**8**	**2**	**3**	**205**	**13.2**	**2**	....	....	....	**19**	***13**	**8**	**21**	**10**	**4**	**2**	**1**	....
1997-98	**Philadelphia**	**NHL**	**82**	**36**	**38**	**74**	**54**	**10**	**2**	**8**	**205**	**17.6**	**-2**	....	....	....	**5**	**2**	**2**	**4**	**7**	**0**	**0**	**0**	....
	Canada	Olympics	6	1	2	3	0	....	....	....	....	....	....	....	....	....	....	....	....	....	....	....	....	....	....
1998-99	**Philadelphia**	**NHL**	**82**	**24**	**50**	**74**	**47**	**10**	**0**	**3**	**191**	**12.6**	**3**	**1773**	**56.5**	**21:29**	**6**	**1**	**3**	**4**	**0**	**0**	**0**	**0**	**25:08**
99-2000	**Philadelphia**	**NHL**	**12**	**5**	**3**	**8**	**4**	**4**	**0**	**0**	**26**	**19.2**	**-1**	**291**	**60.5**	**20:50**	....	....	....	....	....	....	....	....	....
	Carolina	**NHL**	**33**	**4**	**10**	**14**	**22**	**0**	**1**	**1**	**61**	**6.6**	**-12**	**704**	**55.5**	**20:35**	....	....	....	....	....	....	....	....	....
2000-01	**Carolina**	**NHL**	**79**	**20**	**36**	**56**	**47**	**5**	**1**	**5**	**163**	**12.3**	**-7**	**1907**	**60.4**	**22:07**	**6**	**1**	**3**	**4**	**6**	**0**	**0**	**1**	**23:27**
2001-02	**Carolina**	**NHL**	**81**	**23**	**32**	**55**	**40**	**5**	**2**	**5**	**162**	**14.2**	**3**	**2058**	**59.2**	**22:07**	**23**	**4**	**8**	**12**	**16**	**2**	**1**	**1**	**24:52**
2002-03	**Carolina**	**NHL**	**48**	**14**	**23**	**37**	**37**	**7**	**1**	**0**	**110**	**12.7**	**-9**	**1242**	**56.5**	**23:46**	....	....	....	....	....	....	....	....	....
2003-04	**Carolina**	**NHL**	**78**	**12**	**26**	**38**	**28**	**1**	**0**	**1**	**141**	**8.5**	**0**	**1817**	**61.1**	**21:23**	....	....	....	....	....	....	....	....	....
2004-05	Kloten Flyers	Swiss	2	2	1	3	0	....	....	....	....	....	....	....	....	....	5	2	4	6	6	....	....	....	....
2005-06♦	**Carolina**	**NHL**	**78**	**31**	**39**	**70**	**68**	**19**	**2**	**5**	**198**	**15.7**	**8**	**2145**	**59.1**	**24:18**	**25**	**12**	**6**	**18**	**16**	**6**	**0**	**4**	**23:52**
2006-07	**Carolina**	**NHL**	**78**	**26**	**56**	**82**	**46**	**9**	**2**	**5**	**181**	**14.4**	**7**	**2047**	**59.3**	**23:19**	....	....	....	....	....	....	....	....	....
	NHL Totals		**1265**	**408**	**655**	**1063**	**990**	**135**	**27**	**60**	**2909**	**14.0**		**13984**	**58.9**	**22:25**	**141**	**50**	**57**	**107**	**89**	**17**	**4**	**8**	**24:20**

CCHA Rookie of the Year (1989) • NHL All-Rookie Team (1990) • Frank J. Selke Trophy (2006, 2007)

Played in NHL All-Star Game (1992)

Traded to **Philadelphia** by **St. Louis** with Dan Quinn for Ron Sutter and Murray Baron, September 22, 1991. Traded to **Carolina** by **Philadelphia** with Jean-Marc Pelletier and Philadelphia's 2nd round choice (later traded to Colorado – Colorado selected Agris Saviels) in 2000 Entry Draft for Keith Primeau and Carolina's 5th round choice (later traded to NY Islanders – NY Islanders selected Kristofer Ottosson) in 2000 Entry Draft, January 23, 2000. Signed as a free agent by **Kloten** (Swiss), February 16, 2005.

BRISEBOIS, Patrice
(BREES-bwah, pa-TREEZ) **MTL.**

Defense. Shoots right. 6'2", 203 lbs. Born, Montreal, Que., January 27, 1971. Montreal's 2nd choice, 30th overall, in 1989 Entry Draft.

Season	Club	League	GP	G	A	Pts	PIM	PP	SH	GW	S	%	+/-	TF	F%	Min	GP	G	A	Pts	PIM	PP	SH	GW	Min
1986-87	Mtl-Bourassa	QAAA	39	15	19	34	66	....	....	....	....	....	....	....	....	....	....	....	....	....	....	....	....	....	....
1987-88	Laval Titan	QMJHL	48	10	34	44	95	....	....	....	....	....	....	....	....	....	6	0	2	2	2	....	....	....	....
1988-89	Laval Titan	QMJHL	50	20	45	65	95	....	....	....	....	....	....	....	....	....	17	8	14	22	45	....	....	....	....
1989-90	Laval Titan	QMJHL	56	18	70	88	108	....	....	....	....	....	....	....	....	....	13	7	9	16	26	....	....	....	....
1990-91	Drummondville	QMJHL	54	17	44	61	72	....	....	....	....	....	....	....	....	....	14	6	18	24	49	....	....	....	....
	Montreal	**NHL**	**10**	**0**	**2**	**2**	**4**	**0**	**0**	**0**	**11**	**0.0**	**1**	....	....	....	....	....	....	....	....	....	....	....	....
1991-92	**Montreal**	**NHL**	**26**	**2**	**8**	**10**	**20**	**0**	**0**	**1**	**37**	**5.4**	**9**	....	....	....	**11**	**2**	**4**	**6**	**6**	**1**	**0**	**1**	....
	Fredericton	AHL	53	12	27	39	51	....	....	....	....	....	....	....	....	....	....	....	....	....	....	....	....	....	....
1992-93♦	**Montreal**	**NHL**	**70**	**10**	**21**	**31**	**79**	**4**	**0**	**2**	**123**	**8.1**	**6**	....	....	....	**20**	**0**	**4**	**4**	**18**	**0**	**0**	**0**	....
1993-94	**Montreal**	**NHL**	**53**	**2**	**21**	**23**	**63**	**1**	**0**	**0**	**71**	**2.8**	**5**	....	....	....	**7**	**0**	**4**	**4**	**6**	**0**	**0**	**0**	....
1994-95	**Montreal**	**NHL**	**35**	**4**	**8**	**12**	**26**	**0**	**0**	**2**	**67**	**6.0**	**-2**	....	....	....	....	....	....	....	....	....	....	....	....
1995-96	**Montreal**	**NHL**	**69**	**9**	**27**	**36**	**65**	**3**	**0**	**1**	**127**	**7.1**	**10**	....	....	....	**6**	**1**	**2**	**3**	**6**	**0**	**0**	**0**	....
1996-97	**Montreal**	**NHL**	**49**	**2**	**13**	**15**	**24**	**0**	**0**	**1**	**72**	**2.8**	**-7**	....	....	....	**3**	**1**	**1**	**2**	**24**	**0**	**0**	**1**	....
1997-98	**Montreal**	**NHL**	**79**	**10**	**27**	**37**	**67**	**5**	**0**	**1**	**125**	**8.0**	**16**	....	....	....	**10**	**1**	**0**	**1**	**0**	**0**	**0**	**0**	....
1998-99	**Montreal**	**NHL**	**54**	**3**	**9**	**12**	**28**	**1**	**0**	**1**	**90**	**3.3**	**-8**	**0**	**0.0**	**22:26**	....	....	....	....	....	....	....	....	....
99-2000	**Montreal**	**NHL**	**54**	**10**	**25**	**35**	**18**	**5**	**0**	**2**	**88**	**11.4**	**-1**	**0**	**0.0**	**23:14**	....	....	....	....	....	....	....	....	....
2000-01	**Montreal**	**NHL**	**77**	**15**	**21**	**36**	**28**	**11**	**0**	**4**	**178**	**8.4**	**-31**	**1**	**100.0**	**24:43**	....	....	....	....	....	....	....	....	....
2001-02	**Montreal**	**NHL**	**71**	**4**	**29**	**33**	**25**	**2**	**1**	**1**	**95**	**4.2**	**9**	**0**	**0.0**	**23:53**	**10**	**1**	**1**	**2**	**2**	**0**	**0**	**0**	**22:05**
2002-03	**Montreal**	**NHL**	**73**	**4**	**25**	**29**	**32**	**1**	**0**	**1**	**105**	**3.8**	**-14**	**0**	**0.0**	**23:23**	....	....	....	....	....	....	....	....	....
2003-04	**Montreal**	**NHL**	**71**	**4**	**27**	**31**	**22**	**2**	**0**	**0**	**96**	**4.2**	**17**	**0**	**0.0**	**21:20**	**11**	**2**	**1**	**3**	**4**	**1**	**0**	**0**	**22:30**
2004-05	Kloten Flyers	Swiss	10	3	1	4	2	....	....	....	....	....	....	....	....	....	....	....	....	....	....	....	....	....	....
2005-06	**Colorado**	**NHL**	**80**	**10**	**28**	**38**	**55**	**4**	**0**	**2**	**107**	**9.3**	**1**	**2**	**0.0**	**22:19**	**9**	**0**	**1**	**1**	**4**	**0**	**0**	**0**	**22:19**
2006-07	**Colorado**	**NHL**	**33**	**1**	**10**	**11**	**22**	**1**	**0**	**0**	**36**	**2.8**	**-5**	**0**	**0.0**	**19:23**	....	....	....	....	....	....	....	....	....
	NHL Totals		**904**	**90**	**301**	**391**	**578**	**40**	**1**	**19**	**1428**	**6.3**		**3**	**33.3**	**22:50**	**87**	**8**	**18**	**26**	**70**	**2**	**0**	**2**	**22:18**

QMJHL Second All-Star Team (1990) • QMJHL First All-Star Team (1991) • Canadian Major Junior Defenseman of the Year (1991) • Memorial Cup Tournament All-Star Team (1991)

Signed as a free agent by **Kloten** (Swiss), October 13, 2004. Signed as a free agent by **Colorado**, August 3, 2005. • Missed remainder of 2006-07 season after suffering a back injury in game vs. **Dallas**, December 27, 2006. Signed as a free agent by **Montreal**, August 3, 2007.

BRODZIAK, Kyle
(brohd-ZEE-ak, KIGHL) **EDM.**

Center. Shoots right. 6'2", 198 lbs. Born, St. Paul, Alta., May 25, 1984. Edmonton's 9th choice, 214th overall, in 2003 Entry Draft.

Season	Club	League	GP	G	A	Pts	PIM	PP	SH	GW	S	%	+/-	TF	F%	Min	GP	G	A	Pts	PIM	PP	SH	GW	Min
99-2000	Ft. Saskatchewan	AMBHL	36	23	33	56	57	....	....	....	....	....	....	....	....	....	....	....	....	....	....	....	....	....	....
	Moose Jaw	WHL	2	0	0	0	0	....	....	....	....	....	....	....	....	....	....	....	....	....	....	....	....	....	....
2000-01	Moose Jaw	WHL	57	2	8	10	49	....	....	....	....	....	....	....	....	....	3	0	0	0	0	....	....	....	....
2001-02	Moose Jaw	WHL	72	8	12	20	56	....	....	....	....	....	....	....	....	....	12	0	3	3	11	....	....	....	....
2002-03	Moose Jaw	WHL	72	32	30	62	84	....	....	....	....	....	....	....	....	....	13	5	3	8	16	....	....	....	....
2003-04	Moose Jaw	WHL	70	39	54	93	58	....	....	....	....	....	....	....	....	....	10	5	4	9	10	....	....	....	....
2004-05	Edmonton	AHL	56	6	26	32	49	....	....	....	....	....	....	....	....	....	....	....	....	....	....	....	....	....	....
2005-06	**Edmonton**	**NHL**	**10**	**0**	**0**	**0**	**4**	**0**	**0**	**0**	**7**	**0.0**	**-4**	**75**	**52.0**	**11:02**	....	....	....	....	....	....	....	....	....
	Iowa Stars	AHL	55	12	19	31	41	....	....	....	....	....	....	....	....	....	7	1	3	4	2	....	....	....	....

			Regular Season														Playoffs								
Season	Club	League	GP	G	A	Pts	PIM	PP	SH	GW	S	%	+/-	TF	F%	Min	GP	G	A	Pts	PIM	PP	SH	GW	Min
2006-07	**Edmonton**	**NHL**	**6**	**1**	**0**	**1**	**2**	**0**	**0**	**0**	**11**	**9.1**	**0**	**48**	**52.1**	**17:08**	....	....	....	....	....	....	....	....	....
	Wilkes-Barre	AHL	62	24	32	56	44	....	....	....	....	....	....	....	....	....	11	1	5	6	14	....	....	....	....
	NHL Totals		**16**	**1**	**0**	**1**	**6**	**0**	**0**	**0**	**18**	**5.6**		**123**	**52.0**	**13:19**	....	....	....	....	....	....	....	....	....

WHL East First All-Star Team (2004)

BROOKBANK, Sheldon

(BRUK-bank, SHEHL-duhn) **CBJ**

Defense. Shoots right. 6'2", 215 lbs. Born, Lanigan, Sask., October 3, 1980.

Season	Club	League	GP	G	A	Pts	PIM	PP	SH	GW	S	%	+/-	TF	F%	Min	GP	G	A	Pts	PIM	PP	SH	GW	Min
2000-01	Humboldt	SJHL	59	14	35	49	281	....	....	....	....	....	....	....	....	....	....	....	....	....	....	....	....	....	....
2001-02	Grand Rapids	AHL	6	0	1	1	24	....	....	....	....	....	....	....	....	....	....	....	....	....	....	....	....	....	....
	Mississippi	ECHL	62	8	21	29	137	....	....	....	....	....	....	....	....	....	10	1	4	5	27	....	....	....	....
2002-03	Grand Rapids	AHL	69	2	11	13	136	....	....	....	....	....	....	....	....	....	15	1	3	4	28	....	....	....	....
2003-04	Cincinnati	AHL	74	2	9	11	216	....	....	....	....	....	....	....	....	....	9	0	2	2	20	....	....	....	....
2004-05	Cincinnati	AHL	60	1	11	12	181	....	....	....	....	....	....	....	....	....	11	0	0	0	40	....	....	....	....
2005-06	Milwaukee	AHL	73	9	26	35	232	....	....	....	....	....	....	....	....	....	21	1	8	9	49	....	....	....	....
2006-07	**Nashville**	**NHL**	**3**	**0**	**1**	**1**	**12**	**0**	**0**	**0**	**3**	**0.0**	**0**	**0**	**0.0**	**8:16**	....	....	....	....	....	....	....	....	....
	Milwaukee	AHL	78	15	38	53	176	....	....	....	....	....	....	....	....	....	4	0	0	0	6	....	....	....	....
	NHL Totals		**3**	**0**	**1**	**1**	**12**	**0**	**0**	**0**	**3**	**0.0**		**0**	**0.0**	**8:16**	....	....	....	....	....	....	....	....	....

AHL First All-Star Team (2007) • Eddie Shore Award (Outstanding Defenseman - AHL) (2007)

Signed as a free agent by **Anaheim**, July 21, 2003. Signed as a free agent by **Nashville**, August 4, 2005. Signed as a free agent by **Columbus**, July 1, 2007.

BROOKBANK, Wade

(BRUK-bank, WAYD) **CAR.**

Defense. Shoots left. 6'4", 227 lbs. Born, Lanigan, Sask., September 29, 1977.

Season	Club	League	GP	G	A	Pts	PIM	PP	SH	GW	S	%	+/-	TF	F%	Min	GP	G	A	Pts	PIM	PP	SH	GW	Min
1997-98	Melville	SJHL	58	8	21	29	330	....	....	....	....	....	....	....	....	....	....	....	....	....	....	....	....	....	....
	Anchorage Aces	WCHL	7	0	0	0	46	....	....	....	....	....	....	....	....	....	4	0	0	0	20	....	....	....	....
1998-99	Anchorage Aces	WCHL	56	0	4	4	337	....	....	....	....	....	....	....	....	....	....	....	....	....	....	....	....	....	....
99-2000	Oklahoma City	CHL	68	3	9	12	354	....	....	....	....	....	....	....	....	....	7	1	1	2	29	....	....	....	....
2000-01	Orlando	IHL	29	0	1	1	122	....	....	....	....	....	....	....	....	....	4	0	0	0	6	....	....	....	....
	Oklahoma City	CHL	46	1	13	14	267	....	....	....	....	....	....	....	....	....	5	0	0	0	24	....	....	....	....
2001-02	Grand Rapids	AHL	73	1	6	7	337	....	....	....	....	....	....	....	....	....	3	0	1	1	14	....	....	....	....
2002-03	Binghamton	AHL	8	0	0	0	28	....	....	....	....	....	....	....	....	....	....	....	....	....	....	....	....	....	....
2003-04	**Nashville**	**NHL**	**9**	**0**	**0**	**0**	**38**	**0**	**0**	**0**	**1**	**0.0**	**–4**	**0**	**0.0**	**3:28**	....	....	....	....	....	....	....	....	....
	Milwaukee	AHL	6	0	0	0	6	....	....	....	....	....	....	....	....	....	....	....	....	....	....	....	....	....	....
	Binghamton	AHL	4	0	0	0	31	....	....	....	....	....	....	....	....	....	....	....	....	....	....	....	....	....	....
	Vancouver	**NHL**	**20**	**2**	**0**	**2**	**95**	**0**	**0**	**1**	**6**	**33.3**	**3**	**0**	**0.0**	**3:50**	....	....	....	....	....	....	....	....	....
	Manitoba Moose	AHL	4	0	0	0	12	....	....	....	....	....	....	....	....	....	....	....	....	....	....	....	....	....	....
2004-05	Manitoba Moose	AHL	68	0	10	10	285	....	....	....	....	....	....	....	....	....	9	0	0	0	10	....	....	....	....
2005-06	**Vancouver**	**NHL**	**32**	**1**	**2**	**3**	**81**	**0**	**0**	**0**	**10**	**10.0**	**3**	**0**	**0.0**	**4:56**	....	....	....	....	....	....	....	....	....
2006-07	**Boston**	**NHL**	**7**	**1**	**0**	**1**	**15**	**0**	**0**	**0**	**1**	**100.0**	**–1**	**1**	**0.0**	**4:25**	....	....	....	....	....	....	....	....	....
	Providence Bruins	AHL	4	0	0	0	15	....	....	....	....	....	....	....	....	....	....	....	....	....	....	....	....	....	....
	Wilkes-Barre	AHL	39	1	0	1	116	....	....	....	....	....	....	....	....	....	5	0	0	0	6	....	....	....	....
	NHL Totals		**68**	**4**	**2**	**6**	**229**	**0**	**0**	**1**	**18**	**22.2**		**1**	**0.0**	**4:22**	....	....	....	....	....	....	....	....	....

Signed as a free agent by **Orlando** (IHL), September 1, 2000. Signed as a free agent by **Ottawa**, July 27, 2001. • Missed majority of 2002-03 season recovering from knee injury suffered in game vs. Wilkes-Barre (AHL), November 2, 2002. Claimed by **Nashville** from **Ottawa** in Waiver Draft, October 3, 2003. Traded to **Vancouver** by **Nashville** for future considerations, December 17, 2003. Claimed on waivers by **Ottawa** from **Vancouver**, December 19, 2003. Traded to **Florida** by **Ottawa** for future considerations, December 29, 2003. Claimed on waivers by **Vancouver** from **Florida**, January 3, 2004. • Missed majority of 2005-06 season recovering from two head injuries suffered during the season and as a healthy reserve. Signed as a free agent by **Boston**, July 21, 2006. Traded to **Pittsburgh** by **Boston** for future considerations, December 19, 2006. Signed as a free agent by **Carolina**, July 3, 2007.

BROOKS, Alex

(BROOKS, AL-ehx) **ST.L.**

Defense. Shoots right. 6'1", 195 lbs. Born, Madison, WI, August 21, 1976.

Season	Club	League	GP	G	A	Pts	PIM	PP	SH	GW	S	%	+/-	TF	F%	Min	GP	G	A	Pts	PIM	PP	SH	GW	Min
1993-94	Madison Capitols	USHL	13	3	11	14	....	....	....	....	....	....	....	....	....	....	....	....	....	....	....	....	....	....	....
1994-95	Madison West	High-WI	24	13	28	41	....	....	....	....	....	....	....	....	....	....	....	....	....	....	....	....	....	....	....
1995-96	Green Bay	USHL	46	3	22	25	....	....	....	....	....	....	....	....	....	....	....	....	....	....	....	....	....	....	....
1996-97	U. of Wisconsin	WCHA	DID NOT PLAY – INJURED					....	....	....	....	....	....	....	....	....	....	....	....	....	....	....	....	....	....
1997-98	U. of Wisconsin	WCHA	40	1	4	5	72	....	....	....	....	....	....	....	....	....	....	....	....	....	....	....	....	....	....
1998-99	U. of Wisconsin	WCHA	37	0	3	3	73	....	....	....	....	....	....	....	....	....	....	....	....	....	....	....	....	....	....
99-2000	U. of Wisconsin	WCHA	41	4	10	14	78	....	....	....	....	....	....	....	....	....	....	....	....	....	....	....	....	....	....
2000-01	U. of Wisconsin	WCHA	41	3	16	19	76	....	....	....	....	....	....	....	....	....	....	....	....	....	....	....	....	....	....
2001-02	Jokerit Helsinki	Finland	53	1	3	4	109	....	....	....	....	....	....	....	....	....	12	0	0	0	11	....	....	....	....
2002-03	Albany River Rats	AHL	66	0	7	7	56	....	....	....	....	....	....	....	....	....	....	....	....	....	....	....	....	....	....
2003-04	Albany River Rats	AHL	77	2	6	8	100	....	....	....	....	....	....	....	....	....	....	....	....	....	....	....	....	....	....
2004-05	Albany River Rats	AHL	63	0	6	6	83	....	....	....	....	....	....	....	....	....	....	....	....	....	....	....	....	....	....
2005-06	Albany River Rats	AHL	58	1	4	5	81	....	....	....	....	....	....	....	....	....	....	....	....	....	....	....	....	....	....
2006-07	**New Jersey**	**NHL**	**19**	**0**	**1**	**1**	**4**	**0**	**0**	**0**	**4**	**0.0**	**–1**	**0**	**0.0**	**8:39**	....	....	....	....	....	....	....	....	....
	Lowell Devils	AHL	21	0	2	2	6	....	....	....	....	....	....	....	....	....	....	....	....	....	....	....	....	....	....
	NHL Totals		**19**	**0**	**1**	**1**	**4**	**0**	**0**	**0**	**4**	**0.0**		**0**	**0.0**	**8:39**	....	....	....	....	....	....	....	....	....

• Missed entire 1996-97 season recovering from back injury suffered during off-season training, August, 1996. Signed as a free agent by **New Jersey**, July 12, 2002. Signed as a free agent by **St. Louis**, July 19, 2007.

BROUWER, Troy

(BROW-uhr, TROI) **CHI.**

Right wing. Shoots right. 6'3", 220 lbs. Born, Vancouver, B.C., August 17, 1985. Chicago's 13th choice, 214th overall, in 2004 Entry Draft.

Season	Club	League	GP	G	A	Pts	PIM	PP	SH	GW	S	%	+/-	TF	F%	Min	GP	G	A	Pts	PIM	PP	SH	GW	Min
2001-02	Moose Jaw	WHL	13	0	0	0	7	....	....	....	....	....	....	....	....	....	....	....	....	....	....	....	....	....	....
2002-03	Moose Jaw	WHL	59	9	12	21	54	....	....	....	....	....	....	....	....	....	13	1	2	3	14	....	....	....	....
2003-04	Moose Jaw	WHL	72	23	26	49	111	....	....	....	....	....	....	....	....	....	10	3	0	3	12	....	....	....	....
2004-05	Moose Jaw	WHL	71	22	25	47	132	....	....	....	....	....	....	....	....	....	5	1	2	3	8	....	....	....	....
2005-06	Moose Jaw	WHL	72	49	53	*102	122	....	....	....	....	....	....	....	....	....	17	10	4	14	34	....	....	....	....
2006-07	**Chicago**	**NHL**	**10**	**0**	**0**	**0**	**7**	**0**	**0**	**0**	**7**	**0.0**	**–7**	**0**	**0.0**	**9:55**	....	....	....	....	....	....	....	....	....
	Norfolk Admirals	AHL	66	41	38	79	70	....	....	....	....	....	....	....	....	....	6	1	0	1	4	....	....	....	....
	NHL Totals		**10**	**0**	**0**	**0**	**7**	**0**	**0**	**0**	**7**	**0.0**		**0**	**0.0**	**9:55**	....	....	....	....	....	....	....	....	....

WHL East First All-Star Team (2006) • AHL All-Rookie Team (2007) • AHL Second All-Star Team (2007)

BROWN, Brad

(BROWN, BRAD)

Defense. Shoots right. 6'4", 220 lbs. Born, Baie Verte, Nfld., December 27, 1975. Montreal's 1st choice, 18th overall, in 1994 Entry Draft.

Season	Club	League	GP	G	A	Pts	PIM	PP	SH	GW	S	%	+/-	TF	F%	Min	GP	G	A	Pts	PIM	PP	SH	GW	Min
1990-91	Tor. Red Wings	MTHL	80	15	45	60	105	....	....	....	....	....	....	....	....	....	....	....	....	....	....	....	....	....	....
	St. Mike's B's	OHA-B	2	0	0	0	0	....	....	....	....	....	....	....	....	....	....	....	....	....	....	....	....	....	....
1991-92	North Bay	OHL	49	2	9	11	170	....	....	....	....	....	....	....	....	....	18	0	6	6	43	....	....	....	....
1992-93	North Bay	OHL	61	4	9	13	228	....	....	....	....	....	....	....	....	....	2	0	2	2	13	....	....	....	....
1993-94	North Bay	OHL	66	8	24	32	196	....	....	....	....	....	....	....	....	....	18	3	12	15	33	....	....	....	....
1994-95	North Bay	OHL	64	8	38	46	172	....	....	....	....	....	....	....	....	....	6	1	4	5	8	....	....	....	....
1995-96	Barrie Colts	OHL	27	3	13	16	82	....	....	....	....	....	....	....	....	....	....	....	....	....	....	....	....	....	....
	Fredericton	AHL	38	0	3	3	148	....	....	....	....	....	....	....	....	....	10	2	1	3	6	....	....	....	....
1996-97	**Montreal**	**NHL**	**8**	**0**	**0**	**0**	**22**	**0**	**0**	**0**	**0**	**0.0**	**–1**	....	....	....	....	....	....	....	....	....	....	....	....
	Fredericton	AHL	64	3	7	10	368	....	....	....	....	....	....	....	....	....	....	....	....	....	....	....	....	....	....
1997-98	Fredericton	AHL	64	1	8	9	297	....	....	....	....	....	....	....	....	....	4	0	0	0	29	....	....	....	....
1998-99	**Montreal**	**NHL**	**5**	**0**	**0**	**0**	**21**	**0**	**0**	**0**	**0**	**0.0**	**0**	**0**	**0.0**	**6:02**	....	....	....	....	....	....	....	....	....
	Chicago	**NHL**	**61**	**1**	**7**	**8**	**184**	**0**	**0**	**0**	**26**	**3.8**	**–4**	**0**	**0.0**	**15:08**	....	....	....	....	....	....	....	....	....
99-2000	**Chicago**	**NHL**	**57**	**0**	**9**	**9**	**134**	**0**	**0**	**0**	**15**	**0.0**	**–1**	**0**	**0.0**	**14:12**	....	....	....	....	....	....	....	....	....
2000-01	**NY Rangers**	**NHL**	**48**	**1**	**3**	**4**	**107**	**0**	**0**	**0**	**14**	**7.1**	**0**	**0**	**0.0**	**14:31**	....	....	....	....	....	....	....	....	....
2001-02	**Minnesota**	**NHL**	**51**	**0**	**4**	**4**	**123**	**0**	**0**	**0**	**23**	**0.0**	**–11**	**0**	**0.0**	**15:54**	....	....	....	....	....	....	....	....	....
2002-03	**Minnesota**	**NHL**	**57**	**0**	**1**	**1**	**90**	**0**	**0**	**0**	**10**	**0.0**	**–1**	**0**	**0.0**	**9:14**	**11**	**0**	**0**	**0**	**16**	**0**	**0**	**0**	**8:23**
2003-04	**Minnesota**	**NHL**	**30**	**0**	**1**	**1**	**54**	**0**	**0**	**0**	**14**	**0.0**	**–1**	**0**	**0.0**	**9:41**	....	....	....	....	....	....	....	....	....
	Buffalo	**NHL**	**13**	**0**	**2**	**2**	**12**	**0**	**0**	**0**	**6**	**0.0**	**3**	**0**	**0.0**	**16:33**	....	....	....	....	....	....	....	....	....

			Regular Season														Playoffs								
Season	Club	League	GP	G	A	Pts	PIM	PP	SH	GW	S	%	+/-	TF	F%	Min	GP	G	A	Pts	PIM	PP	SH	GW	Min
2004-05			DID NOT PLAY																						
2005-06	Toronto Marlies	AHL	38	2	2	4	93	....	....	....	....	....	....	....	....	....	2	0	0	0	0	....	....	....	....
2006-07	Toronto Marlies	AHL	36	0	3	3	62	....	....	....	....	....	....	....	....	....	....	....	....	....	....	....	....	....	....
	NHL Totals		**330**	**2**	**27**	**29**	**747**	**0**	**0**	**0**	**108**	**1.9**		**0**	**0.0**	**13:22**	**11**	**0**	**0**	**0**	**16**	**0**	**0**	**0**	**8:23**

OHL All-Rookie Team (1992)

Traded to **Chicago** by **Montreal** with Jocelyn Thibault and Dave Manson for Jeff Hackett, Eric Weinrich, Alain Nasreddine and Tampa Bay's 4th round choice (previously acquired, Montreal selected Chris Dyment) in 1999 Entry Draft, November 16, 1998. Traded to **NY Rangers** by **Chicago** with Michal Grosek for future considerations, October 5, 2000. Signed as a free agent by **Minnesota**, July 31, 2001. Traded to **Buffalo** by **Minnesota** with Minnesota's 6th round choice (Vjateslav Buravchikov) in 2005 Entry Draft for Buffalo's 4th round choice (Kyle Bailey) in 2005 Entry Draft, March 8, 2004. Signed as a free agent by **Toronto**, September 10, 2005.

BROWN, Curtis

(BROWN, KUHR-tihs) **S.J.**

Center/Left wing. Shoots left. 6', 195 lbs. Born, Unity, Sask., February 12, 1976. Buffalo's 2nd choice, 43rd overall, in 1994 Entry Draft.

Season	Club	League	GP	G	A	Pts	PIM	PP	SH	GW	S	%	+/-	TF	F%	Min	GP	G	A	Pts	PIM	PP	SH	GW	Min
1990-91	Unity Bantams	SBHL	60	93	104	197	55	....	....	....	....	....	....	....	....	....	....	....	....	....	....	....	....	....	....
1991-92	Moose Jaw	SMHL	36	35	30	65	44	....	....	....	....	....	....	....	....	....	....	....	....	....	....	....	....	....	....
1992-93	Moose Jaw	WHL	71	13	16	29	30	....	....	....	....	....	....	....	....	....	....	....	....	....	....	....	....	....	....
1993-94	Moose Jaw	WHL	72	27	38	65	82	....	....	....	....	....	....	....	....	....	....	....	....	....	....	....	....	....	....
1994-95	Moose Jaw	WHL	70	51	53	104	63	....	....	....	....	....	....	....	....	....	10	8	7	15	20	....	....	....	....
	Buffalo	**NHL**	**1**	**1**	**1**	**2**	**2**	**0**	**0**	**0**	**4**	**25.0**	**2**	....	....	....	....	....	....	....	....	....	....	....	....
1995-96	Moose Jaw	WHL	25	20	18	38	30	....	....	....	....	....	....	....	....	....	....	....	....	....	....	....	....	....	....
	Prince Albert	WHL	19	12	21	33	8	....	....	....	....	....	....	....	....	....	18	10	15	25	18	....	....	....	....
	Buffalo	**NHL**	**4**	**0**	**0**	**0**	**0**	**0**	**0**	**0**	**1**	**0.0**	**0**	....	....	....	....	....	....	....	....	....	....	....	....
	Rochester	AHL	....	....	....	....	....	....	....	....	....	....	....	....	....	....	12	0	1	1	2	....	....	....	....
1996-97	**Buffalo**	**NHL**	**28**	**4**	**3**	**7**	**18**	**0**	**0**	**1**	**31**	**12.9**	**4**	....	....	....	....	....	....	....	....	....	....	....	....
	Rochester	AHL	51	22	21	43	30	....	....	....	....	....	....	....	....	....	10	4	6	10	4	....	....	....	....
1997-98	**Buffalo**	**NHL**	**63**	**12**	**12**	**24**	**34**	**1**	**1**	**2**	**91**	**13.2**	**11**	....	....	....	**13**	**1**	**2**	**3**	**10**	**1**	**0**	**0**	....
1998-99	**Buffalo**	**NHL**	**78**	**16**	**31**	**47**	**56**	**5**	**1**	**3**	**128**	**12.5**	**23**	**1198**	**45.0**	**17:30**	**21**	**7**	**6**	**13**	**10**	**3**	**0**	**3**	**18:51**
99-2000	**Buffalo**	**NHL**	**74**	**22**	**29**	**51**	**42**	**5**	**0**	**4**	**149**	**14.8**	**19**	**1318**	**48.6**	**18:11**	**5**	**1**	**3**	**4**	**6**	**1**	**0**	**0**	**17:11**
2000-01	**Buffalo**	**NHL**	**70**	**10**	**22**	**32**	**34**	**2**	**1**	**0**	**105**	**9.5**	**15**	**1159**	**50.4**	**16:34**	**13**	**5**	**0**	**5**	**8**	**0**	**2**	**1**	**18:14**
2001-02	**Buffalo**	**NHL**	**82**	**20**	**17**	**37**	**32**	**4**	**1**	**5**	**171**	**11.7**	**–4**	**1608**	**49.0**	**17:48**	....	....	....	....	....	....	....	....	....
2002-03	**Buffalo**	**NHL**	**74**	**15**	**16**	**31**	**40**	**3**	**4**	**4**	**144**	**10.4**	**4**	**1387**	**49.5**	**16:53**	....	....	....	....	....	....	....	....	....
2003-04	**Buffalo**	**NHL**	**68**	**9**	**12**	**21**	**30**	**2**	**1**	**2**	**117**	**7.7**	**2**	**1182**	**51.5**	**16:36**	....	....	....	....	....	....	....	....	....
	San Jose	**NHL**	**12**	**2**	**2**	**4**	**6**	**0**	**0**	**0**	**21**	**9.5**	**1**	**105**	**47.6**	**16:26**	**17**	**0**	**2**	**2**	**18**	**0**	**0**	**0**	**14:37**
2004-05	San Diego Gulls	ECHL	47	9	29	38	24	....	....	....	....	....	....	....	....	....	....	....	....	....	....	....	....	....	....
2005-06	**Chicago**	**NHL**	**71**	**5**	**10**	**15**	**38**	**0**	**1**	**0**	**84**	**6.0**	**–9**	**881**	**50.6**	**13:39**	....	....	....	....	....	....	....	....	....
2006-07	**San Jose**	**NHL**	**78**	**8**	**12**	**20**	**56**	**0**	**2**	**3**	**84**	**9.5**	**–2**	**881**	**51.4**	**13:10**	**11**	**0**	**2**	**2**	**2**	**0**	**0**	**0**	**12:10**
	NHL Totals		**703**	**124**	**167**	**291**	**388**	**22**	**12**	**24**	**1130**	**11.0**		**9719**	**49.3**	**16:19**	**80**	**14**	**15**	**29**	**54**	**5**	**2**	**4**	**16:26**

WHL East First All-Star Team (1995) • WHL East Second All-Star Team (1996)

Traded to **San Jose** by **Buffalo** with Andy Delmore for Jeff Jillson and San Jose's compensatory 7th round choice (Andrew Orpik) in 2005 Entry Draft, March 9, 2004. Signed as a free agent by **Chicago**, July 2, 2004. Signed as a free agent by **San Diego** (ECHL), November 16, 2004. Signed as a free agent by **San Jose**, July 3, 2006.

BROWN, Dustin

(BROWN, DUHS-tihn) **L.A.**

Right wing. Shoots right. 6', 200 lbs. Born, Ithaca, NY, November 4, 1984. Los Angeles' 1st choice, 13th overall, in 2003 Entry Draft.

Season	Club	League	GP	G	A	Pts	PIM	PP	SH	GW	S	%	+/-	TF	F%	Min	GP	G	A	Pts	PIM	PP	SH	GW	Min
1998-99	Ithaca	High-NY	18	4	13	17	....	....	....	....	....	....	....	....	....	....	....	....	....	....	....	....	....	....	....
99-2000	Ithaca	High-NY	24	33	21	53	....	....	....	....	....	....	....	....	....	....	....	....	....	....	....	....	....	....	....
2000-01	Guelph Storm	OHL	53	23	22	45	45	....	....	....	....	....	....	....	....	....	4	0	0	0	10	....	....	....	....
2001-02	Guelph Storm	OHL	63	41	32	73	56	....	....	....	....	....	....	....	....	....	9	8	5	13	14	....	....	....	....
2002-03	Guelph Storm	OHL	58	34	42	76	89	....	....	....	....	....	....	....	....	....	11	7	8	15	6	....	....	....	....
2003-04	**Los Angeles**	**NHL**	**31**	**1**	**4**	**5**	**16**	**0**	**0**	**0**	**40**	**2.5**	**0**	**1**	**0.0**	**10:29**	....	....	....	....	....	....	....	....	....
2004-05	Manchester	AHL	79	29	45	74	96	....	....	....	....	....	....	....	....	....	6	5	2	7	10	....	....	....	....
2005-06	**Los Angeles**	**NHL**	**79**	**14**	**14**	**28**	**80**	**6**	**0**	**2**	**159**	**8.8**	**–10**	**15**	**66.7**	**13:59**	....	....	....	....	....	....	....	....	....
2006-07	**Los Angeles**	**NHL**	**81**	**17**	**29**	**46**	**54**	**13**	**0**	**1**	**195**	**8.7**	**–21**	**77**	**49.4**	**18:43**	....	....	....	....	....	....	....	....	....
	NHL Totals		**191**	**32**	**47**	**79**	**150**	**19**	**0**	**3**	**394**	**8.1**		**93**	**51.6**	**15:25**	....	....	....	....	....	....	....	....	....

OHL All-Rookie Team (2001) • Canadian Major Junior Scholastic Player of the Year (2003)

• Missed majority of 2003-04 season recovering from ankle injury suffered in game vs. Chicago, November 29, 2003.

BROWN, Sean

(BROWN, SHAWN)

Defense. Shoots left. 6'3", 215 lbs. Born, Oshawa, Ont., November 5, 1976. Boston's 2nd choice, 21st overall, in 1995 Entry Draft.

Season	Club	League	GP	G	A	Pts	PIM	PP	SH	GW	S	%	+/-	TF	F%	Min	GP	G	A	Pts	PIM	PP	SH	GW	Min
1992-93	Oshawa	MTJHL	15	0	1	1	9	....	....	....	....	....	....	....	....	....	....	....	....	....	....	....	....	....	....
1993-94	Wellington Dukes	MTJHL	32	5	14	19	165	....	....	....	....	....	....	....	....	....	....	....	....	....	....	....	....	....	....
	Belleville Bulls	OHL	28	1	2	3	53	....	....	....	....	....	....	....	....	....	8	0	0	0	17	....	....	....	....
1994-95	Belleville Bulls	OHL	58	2	16	18	200	....	....	....	....	....	....	....	....	....	16	4	2	6	*67	....	....	....	....
1995-96	Belleville Bulls	OHL	37	10	23	33	150	....	....	....	....	....	....	....	....	....	....	....	....	....	....	....	....	....	....
	Sarnia Sting	OHL	26	8	17	25	112	....	....	....	....	....	....	....	....	....	10	1	0	1	38	....	....	....	....
1996-97	**Edmonton**	**NHL**	**5**	**0**	**0**	**0**	**4**	**0**	**0**	**0**	**2**	**0.0**	**–1**	....	....	....	....	....	....	....	....	....	....	....	....
	Hamilton	AHL	61	1	7	8	238	....	....	....	....	....	....	....	....	....	19	1	0	1	47	....	....	....	....
1997-98	**Edmonton**	**NHL**	**18**	**0**	**1**	**1**	**43**	**0**	**0**	**0**	**9**	**0.0**	**–1**	....	....	....	....	....	....	....	....	....	....	....	....
	Hamilton	AHL	43	4	6	10	166	....	....	....	....	....	....	....	....	....	6	0	2	2	38	....	....	....	....
1998-99	**Edmonton**	**NHL**	**51**	**0**	**7**	**7**	**188**	**0**	**0**	**0**	**27**	**0.0**	**1**	**0**	**0.0**	**12:14**	**1**	**0**	**0**	**0**	**10**	**0**	**0**	**0**	**7:33**
99-2000	**Edmonton**	**NHL**	**72**	**4**	**8**	**12**	**192**	**0**	**0**	**2**	**36**	**11.1**	**1**	**0**	**0.0**	**12:41**	**3**	**0**	**0**	**0**	**23**	**0**	**0**	**0**	**6:12**
2000-01	**Edmonton**	**NHL**	**62**	**2**	**3**	**5**	**110**	**0**	**0**	**0**	**30**	**6.7**	**2**	**0**	**0.0**	**11:07**	....	....	....	....	....	....	....	....	....
2001-02	**Edmonton**	**NHL**	**61**	**6**	**4**	**10**	**127**	**3**	**0**	**1**	**58**	**10.3**	**8**	**0**	**0.0**	**12:36**	....	....	....	....	....	....	....	....	....
	Boston	**NHL**	**12**	**0**	**1**	**1**	**47**	**0**	**0**	**0**	**6**	**0.0**	**–1**	**0**	**0.0**	**16:22**	**4**	**0**	**0**	**0**	**2**	**0**	**0**	**0**	**5:49**
2002-03	**Boston**	**NHL**	**69**	**1**	**5**	**6**	**117**	**0**	**0**	**0**	**39**	**2.6**	**–6**	**2**	**50.0**	**6:26**	....	....	....	....	....	....	....	....	....
2003-04	**New Jersey**	**NHL**	**39**	**0**	**3**	**3**	**44**	**0**	**0**	**0**	**25**	**0.0**	**5**	**0**	**0.0**	**13:56**	**1**	**0**	**0**	**0**	**2**	**0**	**0**	**0**	**11:20**
	Albany River Rats	AHL	21	1	6	7	56	....	....	....	....	....	....	....	....	....	....	....	....	....	....	....	....	....	....
2004-05			DID NOT PLAY																						
2005-06	**New Jersey**	**NHL**	**35**	**1**	**11**	**12**	**27**	**0**	**0**	**0**	**37**	**2.7**	**–14**	**1**	**0.0**	**15:22**	....	....	....	....	....	....	....	....	....
	Vancouver	**NHL**	**12**	**0**	**0**	**0**	**8**	**0**	**0**	**0**	**12**	**0.0**	**–3**	**1**	**0.0**	**14:15**	....	....	....	....	....	....	....	....	....
2006-07	Dusseldorf	Germany	28	2	6	8	100	....	....	....	....	....	....	....	....	....	3	0	0	0	*64	....	....	....	....
	NHL Totals		**436**	**14**	**43**	**57**	**907**	**3**	**0**	**3**	**281**	**5.0**		**4**	**25.0**	**11:50**	**9**	**0**	**0**	**0**	**37**	**0**	**0**	**0**	**6:45**

OHL Second All-Star Team (1996)

Rights traded to **Edmonton** by **Boston** with Mariusz Czerkawski and Boston's 1st round choice (Matthieu Descoteaux) in 1996 Entry Draft for Bill Ranford, January 11, 1996. Traded to **Boston** by **Edmonton** for Bobby Allen, March 19, 2002. Signed as a free agent by **New Jersey**, July 24, 2003. Traded to **Vancouver** by **New Jersey** for Vancouver's 4th round choice (T. J. Miller) in 2006 Entry Draft, March 9, 2006. Signed as a free agent by **Dusseldorf** (Germany), July 28, 2006.

BRULE, Gilbert

(broo-LAY, zhihl-BAIR) **CBJ**

Center. Shoots right. 5'10", 180 lbs. Born, Edmonton, Alta., January 1, 1987. Columbus' 1st choice, 6th overall, in 2005 Entry Draft.

Season	Club	League	GP	G	A	Pts	PIM	PP	SH	GW	S	%	+/-	TF	F%	Min	GP	G	A	Pts	PIM	PP	SH	GW	Min
2002-03	Quesnel	BCHL	48	32	25	57	71	....	....	....	....	....	....	....	....	....	....	....	....	....	....	....	....	....	....
	Vancouver Giants	WHL	1	0	0	0	0	....	....	....	....	....	....	....	....	....	4	1	0	1	0	....	....	....	....
2003-04	Vancouver Giants	WHL	67	25	35	60	100	....	....	....	....	....	....	....	....	....	11	4	5	9	10	....	....	....	....
2004-05	Vancouver Giants	WHL	70	39	48	87	169	....	....	....	....	....	....	....	....	....	6	1	3	4	8	....	....	....	....
2005-06	**Columbus**	**NHL**	**7**	**2**	**2**	**4**	**0**	**0**	**0**	**0**	**11**	**18.2**	**–2**	**60**	**43.3**	**13:11**	....	....	....	....	....	....	....	....	....
	Vancouver Giants	WHL	27	23	15	38	40	....	....	....	....	....	....	....	....	....	18	*16	14	*30	44	....	....	....	....
2006-07	**Columbus**	**NHL**	**78**	**9**	**10**	**19**	**28**	**3**	**0**	**0**	**98**	**9.2**	**–21**	**268**	**45.9**	**10:39**	....	....	....	....	....	....	....	....	....
	NHL Totals		**85**	**11**	**12**	**23**	**28**	**3**	**0**	**0**	**109**	**10.1**		**328**	**45.4**	**10:51**	....	....	....	....	....	....	....	....	....

WHL West First All-Star Team (2005) • Canadian Major Junior Scholastic Player of the Year (2005) • WHL West Second All-Star Team (2006) • Memorial Cup Tournament All-Star Team (2006) • Ed Chynoweth Trophy (Memorial Cup Tournament Leading Scorer) (2006)

• Missed majority of 2005-06 season recovering from sternum (October 7, 2005 vs. Calgary) and leg (November 30, 2005 at Minnesota) injuries.

BRUNETTE, Andrew (broo-NEHT, AN-droo) **COL.**

Left wing. Shoots left. 6'1", 212 lbs. Born, Sudbury, Ont., August 24, 1973. Washington's 6th choice, 174th overall, in 1993 Entry Draft.

Season	Club	League	GP	G	A	Pts	PIM	PP	SH	GW	S	%	+/-	TF	F%	Min	GP	G	A	Pts	PIM	PP	SH	GW	Min
			Regular Season														Playoffs								
1989-90	Rayside-Balfour	NOHA	32	38	*65	*103	....	....	....	....	....	....	....	....	....	....	....	....	....	....	....	....	....	....	....
	Rayside-Balfour	NOJHA	4	1	1	2	0	....	....	....	....	....	....	....	....	....	....	....	....	....	....	....	....	....	....
1990-91	Owen Sound	OHL	63	15	20	35	15	....	....	....	....	....	....	....	....	....	....	....	....	....	....	....	....	....	....
1991-92	Owen Sound	OHL	66	51	47	98	42	....	....	....	....	....	....	....	....	....	5	5	0	5	8	....	....	....	....
1992-93	Owen Sound	OHL	66	*62	*100	*162	91	....	....	....	....	....	....	....	....	....	8	8	6	14	16	....	....	....	....
1993-94	Portland Pirates	AHL	23	9	11	20	10	....	....	....	....	....	....	....	....	....	2	0	1	1	0	....	....	....	....
	Providence Bruins	AHL	3	0	0	0	0	....	....	....	....	....	....	....	....	....	....	....	....	....	....	....	....	....	....
	Hampton Roads	ECHL	20	12	18	30	32	....	....	....	....	....	....	....	....	....	7	7	6	13	18	....	....	....	....
1994-95	Portland Pirates	AHL	79	30	50	80	53	....	....	....	....	....	....	....	....	....	7	3	3	6	10	....	....	....	....
1995-96	**Washington**	**NHL**	**11**	**3**	**3**	**6**	**0**	**0**	**0**	**1**	**16**	**18.8**	**5**	....	....	....	**6**	**1**	**3**	**4**	**0**	**0**	**0**	**0**	....
	Portland Pirates	AHL	69	28	66	94	125	....	....	....	....	....	....	....	....	....	20	11	18	29	15	....	....	....	....
1996-97	**Washington**	**NHL**	**23**	**4**	**7**	**11**	**12**	**2**	**0**	**0**	**23**	**17.4**	**–3**	....	....	....	....	....	....	....	....	....	....	....	....
	Portland Pirates	AHL	50	22	51	73	48	....	....	....	....	....	....	....	....	....	5	1	2	3	0	....	....	....	....
1997-98	**Washington**	**NHL**	**28**	**11**	**12**	**23**	**12**	**4**	**0**	**2**	**42**	**26.2**	**2**	....	....	....	....	....	....	....	....	....	....	....	....
	Portland Pirates	AHL	43	21	46	67	64	....	....	....	....	....	....	....	....	....	10	1	11	12	12	....	....	....	....
1998-99	**Nashville**	**NHL**	**77**	**11**	**20**	**31**	**26**	**7**	**0**	**1**	**65**	**16.9**	**–10**	**8**	**50.0**	**13:13**	....	....	....	....	....	....	....	....	....
99-2000	**Atlanta**	**NHL**	**81**	**23**	**27**	**50**	**30**	**9**	**0**	**2**	**107**	**21.5**	**–32**	**8**	**25.0**	**15:42**	....	....	....	....	....	....	....	....	....
2000-01	**Atlanta**	**NHL**	**77**	**15**	**44**	**59**	**26**	**6**	**0**	**4**	**104**	**14.4**	**–5**	**11**	**54.6**	**16:58**	....	....	....	....	....	....	....	....	....
2001-02	**Minnesota**	**NHL**	**81**	**21**	**48**	**69**	**18**	**10**	**0**	**2**	**106**	**19.8**	**–4**	**111**	**58.6**	**16:02**	....	....	....	....	....	....	....	....	....
2002-03	**Minnesota**	**NHL**	**82**	**18**	**28**	**46**	**30**	**9**	**0**	**2**	**97**	**18.6**	**–10**	**59**	**44.1**	**14:29**	**18**	**7**	**6**	**13**	**4**	**4**	**0**	**1**	**15:00**
2003-04	**Minnesota**	**NHL**	**82**	**15**	**34**	**49**	**12**	**7**	**0**	**3**	**90**	**16.7**	**3**	**49**	**46.9**	**15:32**	....	....	....	....	....	....	....	....	....
2004-05			Did not play																						
2005-06	**Colorado**	**NHL**	**82**	**24**	**39**	**63**	**48**	**11**	**0**	**2**	**129**	**18.6**	**9**	**18**	**33.3**	**15:01**	**9**	**3**	**6**	**9**	**8**	**1**	**0**	**1**	**17:47**
2006-07	**Colorado**	**NHL**	**82**	**27**	**56**	**83**	**36**	**9**	**0**	**2**	**173**	**15.6**	**–8**	**8**	**62.5**	**17:31**	....	....	....	....	....	....	....	....	....
	NHL Totals		**706**	**172**	**318**	**490**	**250**	**74**	**0**	**21**	**952**	**18.1**		**272**	**50.4**	**15:34**	**33**	**11**	**15**	**26**	**12**	**5**	**0**	**2**	**15:55**

OHL First All-Star Team (1993) • Canadian Major Junior Second All-Star Team (1993) • AHL Second All-Star Team (1995)

Claimed by **Nashville** from **Washington** in Expansion Draft, June 26, 1998. Traded to **Atlanta** by **Nashville** for Atlanta's 5th round choice (Matt Hendricks) in 2000 Entry Draft, June 21, 1999. Signed as a free agent by **Minnesota**, July 17, 2001. Signed as a free agent by **Colorado**, August 6, 2005.

BRYLIN, Sergei (BRIH-lin, SAIR-gay) **N.J.**

Left wing. Shoots left. 5'10", 190 lbs. Born, Moscow, USSR, January 13, 1974. New Jersey's 2nd choice, 42nd overall, in 1992 Entry Draft.

Season	Club	League	GP	G	A	Pts	PIM	PP	SH	GW	S	%	+/-	TF	F%	Min	GP	G	A	Pts	PIM	PP	SH	GW	Min
1991-92	CSKA Moscow	CIS	44	1	6	7	4	....	....	....	....	....	....	....	....	....	....	....	....	....	....	....	....	....	....
	CSKA Moscow 2	CIS-3	1	0	0	0	0	....	....	....	....	....	....	....	....	....	....	....	....	....	....	....	....	....	....
1992-93	CSKA Moscow	CIS	42	5	4	9	36	....	....	....	....	....	....	....	....	....	....	....	....	....	....	....	....	....	....
1993-94	CSKA Moscow	CIS	39	4	6	10	36	....	....	....	....	....	....	....	....	....	....	....	....	....	....	....	....	....	....
	Russian Penguins	IHL	13	4	5	9	18	....	....	....	....	....	....	....	....	....	....	....	....	....	....	....	....	....	....
1994-95	Albany River Rats	AHL	63	19	35	54	78	....	....	....	....	....	....	....	....	....	....	....	....	....	....	....	....	....	....
	◆ New Jersey	**NHL**	**26**	**6**	**8**	**14**	**8**	**0**	**0**	**0**	**41**	**14.6**	**12**	....	....	....	**12**	**1**	**2**	**3**	**4**	**0**	**0**	**0**	....
1995-96	**New Jersey**	**NHL**	**50**	**4**	**5**	**9**	**26**	**0**	**0**	**1**	**51**	**7.8**	**–2**	....	....	....	....	....	....	....	....	....	....	....	....
1996-97	**New Jersey**	**NHL**	**29**	**2**	**2**	**4**	**20**	**0**	**0**	**0**	**34**	**5.9**	**–13**	....	....	....	....	....	....	....	....	....	....	....	....
	Albany River Rats	AHL	43	17	24	41	38	....	....	....	....	....	....	....	....	....	16	4	8	12	12	....	....	....	....
1997-98	**New Jersey**	**NHL**	**18**	**2**	**3**	**5**	**0**	**0**	**0**	**0**	**20**	**10.0**	**4**	....	....	....	....	....	....	....	....	....	....	....	....
	Albany River Rats	AHL	44	21	22	43	60	....	....	....	....	....	....	....	....	....	....	....	....	....	....	....	....	....	....
1998-99	**New Jersey**	**NHL**	**47**	**5**	**10**	**15**	**28**	**3**	**0**	**1**	**51**	**9.8**	**8**	**184**	**50.5**	**12:55**	**5**	**3**	**1**	**4**	**4**	**1**	**0**	**1**	**18:21**
99-2000◆	**New Jersey**	**NHL**	**64**	**9**	**11**	**20**	**20**	**1**	**0**	**1**	**84**	**10.7**	**0**	**72**	**41.7**	**13:23**	**17**	**3**	**5**	**8**	**0**	**0**	**0**	**0**	**13:02**
2000-01	**New Jersey**	**NHL**	**75**	**23**	**29**	**52**	**24**	**3**	**1**	**0**	**130**	**17.7**	**25**	**43**	**44.2**	**15:31**	**20**	**3**	**4**	**7**	**6**	**1**	**0**	**1**	**13:07**
2001-02	**New Jersey**	**NHL**	**76**	**16**	**28**	**44**	**10**	**5**	**0**	**3**	**133**	**12.0**	**21**	**17**	**47.1**	**17:11**	**6**	**0**	**2**	**2**	**2**	**0**	**0**	**0**	**19:05**
2002-03◆	**New Jersey**	**NHL**	**52**	**11**	**8**	**19**	**16**	**3**	**1**	**1**	**86**	**12.8**	**–2**	**90**	**32.2**	**16:11**	**19**	**1**	**3**	**4**	**8**	**0**	**0**	**1**	**17:03**
2003-04	**New Jersey**	**NHL**	**82**	**14**	**19**	**33**	**20**	**7**	**0**	**1**	**98**	**14.3**	**10**	**695**	**46.6**	**16:25**	**5**	**0**	**0**	**0**	**0**	**0**	**0**	**0**	**15:02**
2004-05	Voskresensk	Russia	35	8	19	27	40	....	....	....	....	....	....	....	....	....	....	....	....	....	....	....	....	....	....
2005-06	**New Jersey**	**NHL**	**82**	**15**	**22**	**37**	**46**	**4**	**0**	**3**	**126**	**11.9**	**–4**	**807**	**48.7**	**15:44**	**9**	**2**	**0**	**2**	**2**	**0**	**0**	**0**	**16:34**
2006-07	**New Jersey**	**NHL**	**82**	**16**	**24**	**40**	**35**	**8**	**0**	**2**	**97**	**16.5**	**–5**	**277**	**45.5**	**17:45**	**11**	**1**	**2**	**3**	**6**	**1**	**0**	**0**	**18:12**
	NHL Totals		**683**	**123**	**169**	**292**	**253**	**34**	**2**	**13**	**951**	**12.9**		**2185**	**46.8**	**15:50**	**104**	**14**	**19**	**33**	**32**	**3**	**0**	**3**	**15:38**

Signed as a free agent by **Voskresensk** (Russia), November 4, 2004.

BULIS, Jan (BOO-lihs, YAHN)

Center. Shoots left. 6'1", 208 lbs. Born, Pardubice, Czech., March 18, 1978. Washington's 3rd choice, 43rd overall, in 1996 Entry Draft.

Season	Club	League	GP	G	A	Pts	PIM	PP	SH	GW	S	%	+/-	TF	F%	Min	GP	G	A	Pts	PIM	PP	SH	GW	Min
1993-94	HC Pardubice Jr.	CzRep-Jr.	25	16	11	27	....	....	....	....	....	....	....	....	....	....	....	....	....	....	....	....	....	....	....
1994-95	Kelowna Spartans	BCJHL	51	23	25	48	36	....	....	....	....	....	....	....	....	....	17	7	9	16	0	....	....	....	....
1995-96	Barrie Colts	OHL	59	29	30	59	22	....	....	....	....	....	....	....	....	....	7	2	3	5	2	....	....	....	....
1996-97	Barrie Colts	OHL	64	42	61	103	42	....	....	....	....	....	....	....	....	....	9	3	7	10	10	....	....	....	....
1997-98	Kingston	OHL	2	0	1	1	0	....	....	....	....	....	....	....	....	....	12	8	10	18	12	....	....	....	....
	Washington	**NHL**	**48**	**5**	**11**	**16**	**18**	**0**	**0**	**0**	**37**	**13.5**	**–5**	....	....	....	....	....	....	....	....	....	....	....	....
	Portland Pirates	AHL	3	1	4	5	12	....	....	....	....	....	....	....	....	....	....	....	....	....	....	....	....	....	....
1998-99	**Washington**	**NHL**	**38**	**7**	**16**	**23**	**6**	**3**	**0**	**3**	**57**	**12.3**	**3**	**599**	**48.9**	**14:27**	....	....	....	....	....	....	....	....	....
	Cincinnati	IHL	10	2	2	4	14	....	....	....	....	....	....	....	....	....	....	....	....	....	....	....	....	....	....
99-2000	**Washington**	**NHL**	**56**	**9**	**22**	**31**	**30**	**0**	**0**	**1**	**92**	**9.8**	**7**	**609**	**45.5**	**13:55**	....	....	....	....	....	....	....	....	....
2000-01	**Washington**	**NHL**	**39**	**5**	**13**	**18**	**26**	**1**	**0**	**0**	**41**	**12.2**	**0**	**224**	**46.9**	**11:53**	....	....	....	....	....	....	....	....	....
	Portland Pirates	AHL	4	0	2	2	0	....	....	....	....	....	....	....	....	....	....	....	....	....	....	....	....	....	....
	Montreal	**NHL**	**12**	**0**	**5**	**5**	**0**	**0**	**0**	**0**	**20**	**0.0**	**–1**	**230**	**48.3**	**18:25**	....	....	....	....	....	....	....	....	....
2001-02	**Montreal**	**NHL**	**53**	**9**	**10**	**19**	**8**	**1**	**0**	**3**	**87**	**10.3**	**–2**	**156**	**43.0**	**13:34**	**6**	**0**	**0**	**0**	**6**	**0**	**0**	**0**	**12:25**
2002-03	**Montreal**	**NHL**	**82**	**16**	**24**	**40**	**30**	**0**	**0**	**2**	**160**	**10.0**	**9**	**153**	**42.5**	**15:42**	....	....	....	....	....	....	....	....	....
2003-04	**Montreal**	**NHL**	**72**	**13**	**17**	**30**	**30**	**1**	**1**	**4**	**147**	**8.8**	**–8**	**103**	**46.6**	**17:07**	**11**	**1**	**1**	**2**	**4**	**0**	**0**	**0**	**17:23**
2004-05	Pardubice	CzRep	45	24	25	49	113	....	....	....	....	....	....	....	....	....	16	7	4	11	43	....	....	....	....
2005-06	**Montreal**	**NHL**	**73**	**20**	**20**	**40**	**50**	**6**	**1**	**3**	**131**	**15.3**	**2**	**129**	**44.2**	**15:37**	**6**	**1**	**1**	**2**	**2**	**0**	**0**	**0**	**16:42**
	Czech Republic	Olympics	8	0	0	0	10	....	....	....	....	....	....	....	....	....	....	....	....	....	....	....	....	....	....
2006-07	**Vancouver**	**NHL**	**79**	**12**	**11**	**23**	**70**	**1**	**1**	**2**	**122**	**9.8**	**–8**	**132**	**38.6**	**14:23**	**12**	**1**	**1**	**2**	**2**	**0**	**0**	**0**	**19:46**
	NHL Totals		**552**	**96**	**149**	**245**	**268**	**13**	**3**	**18**	**894**	**10.7**		**2335**	**46.0**	**14:56**	**35**	**3**	**3**	**6**	**14**	**0**	**0**	**0**	**17:14**

Traded to **Montreal** by **Washington** with Richard Zednik and Washington's 1st round choice (Alexander Perezhogin) in 2001 Entry Draft for Trevor Linden, Dainius Zubrus and New Jersey's 2nd round choice (previously acquired, later traded to Tampa Bay – Tampa Bay selected Andreas Holmqvist) in 2001 Entry Draft, March 13, 2001. Signed as a free agent by **Pardubice** (CzRep), September 17, 2004. Signed as a free agent by **Vancouver**, July 25, 2006.

BURISH, Adam (BUHR-ish, A-duhm) **CHI.**

Right wing. Shoots right. 6'1", 189 lbs. Born, Madison, WI, January 6, 1983. Chicago's 9th choice, 282nd overall, in 2002 Entry Draft.

Season	Club	League	GP	G	A	Pts	PIM	PP	SH	GW	S	%	+/-	TF	F%	Min	GP	G	A	Pts	PIM	PP	SH	GW	Min
2000-01	Edgewood	High-WI	22	25	30	55	22	....	....	....	....	....	....	....	....	....	....	....	....	....	....	....	....	....	....
2001-02	Green Bay	USHL	61	24	33	57	122	....	....	....	....	....	....	....	....	....	1	0	0	0	0	....	....	....	....
2002-03	U. of Wisconsin	WCHA	19	0	6	6	32	....	....	....	....	....	....	....	....	....	....	....	....	....	....	....	....	....	....
2003-04	U. of Wisconsin	WCHA	43	6	13	19	63	....	....	....	....	....	....	....	....	....	....	....	....	....	....	....	....	....	....
2004-05	U. of Wisconsin	WCHA	41	13	7	20	41	....	....	....	....	....	....	....	....	....	....	....	....	....	....	....	....	....	....
2005-06	U. of Wisconsin	WCHA	42	9	24	33	67	....	....	....	....	....	....	....	....	....	....	....	....	....	....	....	....	....	....
2006-07	**Chicago**	**NHL**	**9**	**0**	**0**	**0**	**2**	**0**	**0**	**0**	**12**	**0.0**	**–4**	**6**	**50.0**	**11:08**	....	....	....	....	....	....	....	....	....
	Norfolk Admirals	AHL	64	11	10	21	146	....	....	....	....	....	....	....	....	....	6	1	1	2	4	....	....	....	....
	NHL Totals		**9**	**0**	**0**	**0**	**2**	**0**	**0**	**0**	**12**	**0.0**		**6**	**50.0**	**11:08**	....	....	....	....	....	....	....	....	....

NCAA Championship All-Tournament Team (2006)

BURNS, Brent (BUHRNZ, BREHNT) **MIN.**

Defense. Shoots right. 6'4", 207 lbs. Born, Ajax, Ont., March 9, 1985. Minnesota's 1st choice, 20th overall, in 2003 Entry Draft.

Season	Club	League	GP	G	A	Pts	PIM	PP	SH	GW	S	%	+/-	TF	F%	Min	GP	G	A	Pts	PIM	PP	SH	GW	Min
2000-01	North York	MTHL	46	4	7	11	16	....	....	....	....	....	....	....	....	....	....	....	....	....	....	....	....	....	....
2001-02	Couchiching	OPJHL	68	15	25	40	14	....	....	....	....	....	....	....	....	....	....	....	....	....	....	....	....	....	....
2002-03	Brampton	OHL	68	15	25	40	14	....	....	....	....	....	....	....	....	....	11	5	6	11	6	....	....	....	....
2003-04	**Minnesota**	**NHL**	**36**	**1**	**5**	**6**	**12**	**0**	**0**	**0**	**34**	**2.9**	**–10**	**7**	**28.6**	**13:29**	....	....	....	....	....	....	....	....	....
	Houston Aeros	AHL	1	0	1	1	2	....	....	....	....	....	....	....	....	....	....	....	....	....	....	....	....	....	....
2004-05	Houston Aeros	AHL	73	11	16	27	57	....	....	....	....	....	....	....	....	....	5	0	0	0	4	....	....	....	....

Season	Club	League	GP	G	A	Pts	PIM	PP	SH	GW	S	%	+/-	TF	F%	Min	GP	G	A	Pts	PIM	PP	SH	GW	Min
					Regular Season												Playoffs								
2005-06	**Minnesota**	**NHL**	**72**	**4**	**12**	**16**	**32**	**1**	**0**	**1**	**73**	**5.5**	**-7**	**11**	**54.6**	**14:07**	....	....	....	....	....	....	....	....	....
2006-07	**Minnesota**	**NHL**	**77**	**7**	**18**	**25**	**26**	**3**	**0**	**3**	**108**	**6.5**	**16**	**4**	**25.0**	**15:48**	**5**	**0**	**1**	**1**	**14**	**0**	**0**	**0**	**18:59**
	NHL Totals		**185**	**12**	**35**	**47**	**70**	**4**	**0**	**4**	**215**	**5.6**		**22**	**40.9**	**14:42**	**5**	**0**	**1**	**1**	**14**	**0**	**0**	**0**	**18:59**

• Spent majority of 2003-04 season on assignment to Team Canada and as a healthy reserve.

BURROWS, Alexandre

(BUHR-ohz, al-ehx-AHN-druh) **VAN.**

Left wing. Shoots left. 6'1", 190 lbs. Born, Pincourt, Que., April 11, 1981.

Season	Club	League	GP	G	A	Pts	PIM	PP	SH	GW	S	%	+/-	TF	F%	Min	GP	G	A	Pts	PIM	PP	SH	GW	Min
2000-01	Shawinigan	QMJHL	63	16	14	30	105	....	....	....	....	....	....	....	....	....	10	2	1	3	8	....	....	....	....
2001-02	Shawinigan	QMJHL	64	35	35	70	184	....	....	....	....	....	....	....	....	....	10	9	10	19	20	....	....	....	....
2002-03	Greenville	ECHL	53	9	17	26	201	....	....	....	....	....	....	....	....	....	....	....	....	....	....	....	....	....	....
	Baton Rouge	ECHL	13	4	2	6	64	....	....	....	....	....	....	....	....	....	....	....	....	....	....	....	....	....	....
2003-04	Manitoba Moose	AHL	2	0	0	0	0	....	....	....	....	....	....	....	....	....	....	....	....	....	....	....	....	....	....
	Columbia Inferno	ECHL	64	29	44	73	194	....	....	....	....	....	....	....	....	....	4	2	0	2	28	....	....	....	....
2004-05	Manitoba Moose	AHL	72	9	17	26	107	....	....	....	....	....	....	....	....	....	14	0	3	3	37	....	....	....	....
	Columbia Inferno	ECHL	4	5	1	6	4	....	....	....	....	....	....	....	....	....	....	....	....	....	....	....	....	....	....
2005-06	**Vancouver**	**NHL**	**43**	**7**	**5**	**12**	**61**	**0**	**1**	**1**	**49**	**14.3**	**5**	**19**	**47.4**	**10:24**	....	....	....	....	....	....	....	....	....
	Manitoba Moose	AHL	33	12	18	30	57	....	....	....	....	....	....	....	....	....	13	6	7	13	27	....	....	....	....
2006-07	**Vancouver**	**NHL**	**81**	**3**	**6**	**9**	**93**	**0**	**0**	**1**	**70**	**4.3**	**-7**	**16**	**43.8**	**11:26**	**11**	**1**	**0**	**1**	**14**	**0**	**0**	**0**	**10:34**
	NHL Totals		**124**	**10**	**11**	**21**	**154**	**0**	**1**	**2**	**119**	**8.4**		**35**	**45.7**	**11:05**	**11**	**1**	**0**	**1**	**14**	**0**	**0**	**0**	**10:34**

Signed as a free agent by **Manitoba** (AHL), October 21, 2003. Signed as a free agent by **Vancouver**, November 8, 2005.

BUTENSCHON, Sven

(BUH-tehn-shohn, SVEHN)

Defense. Shoots left. 6'4", 215 lbs. Born, Itzehoe, West Germany, March 22, 1976. Pittsburgh's 3rd choice, 57th overall, in 1994 Entry Draft.

Season	Club	League	GP	G	A	Pts	PIM	PP	SH	GW	S	%	+/-	TF	F%	Min	GP	G	A	Pts	PIM	PP	SH	GW	Min
1991-92	Eastman Selects	MMMHL	36	2	10	12	110	....	....	....	....	....	....	....	....	....	....	....	....	....	....	....	....	....	....
1992-93	Eastman Selects	MMMHL	35	14	22	36	101	....	....	....	....	....	....	....	....	....	....	....	....	....	....	....	....	....	....
1993-94	Brandon	WHL	70	3	19	22	51	....	....	....	....	....	....	....	....	....	4	0	0	0	6	....	....	....	....
1994-95	Brandon	WHL	21	1	5	6	44	....	....	....	....	....	....	....	....	....	18	1	2	3	11	....	....	....	....
1995-96	Brandon	WHL	70	4	37	41	99	....	....	....	....	....	....	....	....	....	19	1	12	13	18	....	....	....	....
1996-97	Cleveland	IHL	75	3	12	15	68	....	....	....	....	....	....	....	....	....	10	0	1	1	4	....	....	....	....
1997-98	**Pittsburgh**	**NHL**	**8**	**0**	**0**	**0**	**6**	**0**	**0**	**0**	**4**	**0.0**	**-1**	....	....	....	....	....	....	....	....	....	....	....	....
	Syracuse Crunch	AHL	65	14	23	37	66	....	....	....	....	....	....	....	....	....	5	1	2	3	0	....	....	....	....
1998-99	**Pittsburgh**	**NHL**	**17**	**0**	**0**	**0**	**6**	**0**	**0**	**0**	**8**	**0.0**	**-7**	**0**	**0.0**	**13:08**	....	....	....	....	....	....	....	....	....
	Houston Aeros	IHL	57	1	4	5	81	....	....	....	....	....	....	....	....	....	....	....	....	....	....	....	....	....	....
99-2000	**Pittsburgh**	**NHL**	**3**	**0**	**0**	**0**	**0**	**0**	**0**	**0**	**2**	**0.0**	**3**	**0**	**0.0**	**16:25**	....	....	....	....	....	....	....	....	....
	Wilkes-Barre	AHL	75	19	21	40	101	....	....	....	....	....	....	....	....	....	....	....	....	....	....	....	....	....	....
2000-01	**Pittsburgh**	**NHL**	**5**	**0**	**1**	**1**	**2**	**0**	**0**	**0**	**6**	**0.0**	**1**	**0**	**0.0**	**17:51**	....	....	....	....	....	....	....	....	....
	Wilkes-Barre	AHL	55	7	28	35	85	....	....	....	....	....	....	....	....	....	....	....	....	....	....	....	....	....	....
	Edmonton	**NHL**	**7**	**1**	**1**	**2**	**2**	**0**	**0**	**0**	**3**	**33.3**	**2**	**0**	**0.0**	**11:07**	....	....	....	....	....	....	....	....	....
2001-02	**Edmonton**	**NHL**	**14**	**0**	**0**	**0**	**4**	**0**	**0**	**0**	**8**	**0.0**	**0**	**0**	**0.0**	**9:39**	....	....	....	....	....	....	....	....	....
	Hamilton	AHL	61	9	35	44	88	....	....	....	....	....	....	....	....	....	....	....	....	....	....	....	....	....	....
2002-03	**NY Islanders**	**NHL**	**37**	**0**	**4**	**4**	**26**	**0**	**0**	**0**	**19**	**0.0**	**-6**	**0**	**0.0**	**12:26**	....	....	....	....	....	....	....	....	....
	Bridgeport	AHL	36	3	13	16	58	....	....	....	....	....	....	....	....	....	9	3	6	9	6	....	....	....	....
2003-04	**NY Islanders**	**NHL**	**41**	**1**	**6**	**7**	**30**	**0**	**0**	**0**	**17**	**5.9**	**-3**	**0**	**0.0**	**11:15**	**4**	**0**	**0**	**0**	**0**	**0**	**0**	**0**	**7:42**
	Bridgeport	AHL	5	0	1	1	4	....	....	....	....	....	....	....	....	....	....	....	....	....	....	....	....	....	....
2004-05	Adler Mannheim	Germany	50	1	5	6	54	....	....	....	....	....	....	....	....	....	14	0	1	1	16	....	....	....	....
2005-06	**Vancouver**	**NHL**	**8**	**0**	**0**	**0**	**10**	**0**	**0**	**0**	**4**	**0.0**	**1**	**1**	**0.0**	**14:05**	....	....	....	....	....	....	....	....	....
	Manitoba Moose	AHL	60	15	22	37	30	....	....	....	....	....	....	....	....	....	13	0	6	6	12	....	....	....	....
2006-07	Adler Mannheim	Germany	42	3	3	6	34	....	....	....	....	....	....	....	....	....	11	1	3	4	12	....	....	....	....
	NHL Totals		**140**	**2**	**12**	**14**	**86**	**0**	**0**	**0**	**71**	**2.8**		**1**	**0.0**	**12:11**	**4**	**0**	**0**	**0**	**0**	**0**	**0**	**0**	**7:42**

Traded to **Edmonton** by **Pittsburgh** for Dan LaCouture, March 13, 2001. Signed as a free agent by **Florida**, July 9, 2002. Traded to **NY Islanders** by **Florida** for Juraj Kolnik and NY Islanders' 9th round choice (later traded to San Jose – San Jose selected Carter Lee) in 2003 Entry Draft, October 11, 2003. Signed as a free agent by **Mannheim** (Germany), August 2, 2004. Signed as a free agent by **Vancouver**, August 22, 2005.

BYFUGLIEN, Dustin

(bigh-FEWG-lehn, DUHS-tihn) **CHI.**

Defense. Shoots right. 6'3", 246 lbs. Born, Minneapolis, MN, March 27, 1985. Chicago's 8th choice, 245th overall, in 2003 Entry Draft.

Season	Club	League	GP	G	A	Pts	PIM	PP	SH	GW	S	%	+/-	TF	F%	Min	GP	G	A	Pts	PIM	PP	SH	GW	Min
2001-02	Chicago Mission	MAHL	52	32	30	62	40	....	....	....	....	....	....	....	....	....	....	....	....	....	....	....	....	....	....
	Brandon	WHL	3	0	0	0	0	....	....	....	....	....	....	....	....	....	....	....	....	....	....	....	....	....	....
2002-03	Brandon	WHL	8	1	1	2	4	....	....	....	....	....	....	....	....	....	....	....	....	....	....	....	....	....	....
	Prince George	WHL	48	9	28	37	74	....	....	....	....	....	....	....	....	....	5	1	3	4	12	....	....	....	....
2003-04	Prince George	WHL	66	16	29	45	137	....	....	....	....	....	....	....	....	....	....	....	....	....	....	....	....	....	....
2004-05	Prince George	WHL	64	22	36	58	184	....	....	....	....	....	....	....	....	....	....	....	....	....	....	....	....	....	....
2005-06	**Chicago**	**NHL**	**25**	**3**	**2**	**5**	**24**	**0**	**0**	**1**	**45**	**6.7**	**-6**	**0**	**0.0**	**17:19**	....	....	....	....	....	....	....	....	....
	Norfolk Admirals	AHL	53	8	15	23	75	....	....	....	....	....	....	....	....	....	4	1	2	3	4	....	....	....	....
2006-07	**Chicago**	**NHL**	**9**	**1**	**2**	**3**	**10**	**0**	**0**	**0**	**18**	**5.6**	**-2**	**0**	**0.0**	**17:18**	....	....	....	....	....	....	....	....	....
	Norfolk Admirals	AHL	63	16	28	44	146	....	....	....	....	....	....	....	....	....	6	0	2	2	18	....	....	....	....
	NHL Totals		**34**	**4**	**4**	**8**	**34**	**0**	**0**	**1**	**63**	**6.3**		**0**	**0.0**	**17:19**	....	....	....	....	....	....	....	....	....

AHL Second All-Star Team (2007)

CAIRNS, Eric

(KAIRNZ, AIR-ihk)

Defense. Shoots left. 6'6", 230 lbs. Born, Oakville, Ont., June 27, 1974. NY Rangers' 3rd choice, 72nd overall, in 1992 Entry Draft.

Season	Club	League	GP	G	A	Pts	PIM	PP	SH	GW	S	%	+/-	TF	F%	Min	GP	G	A	Pts	PIM	PP	SH	GW	Min
1990-91	Burlington	OHA-B	37	5	16	21	120	....	....	....	....	....	....	....	....	....	....	....	....	....	....	....	....	....	....
1991-92	Detroit	OHL	64	1	11	12	237	....	....	....	....	....	....	....	....	....	7	0	0	0	31	....	....	....	....
1992-93	Detroit	OHL	64	3	13	16	194	....	....	....	....	....	....	....	....	....	15	0	3	3	24	....	....	....	....
1993-94	Detroit	OHL	59	7	35	42	204	....	....	....	....	....	....	....	....	....	17	0	4	4	46	....	....	....	....
1994-95	Birmingham Bulls	ECHL	11	1	3	4	49	....	....	....	....	....	....	....	....	....	....	....	....	....	....	....	....	....	....
	Binghamton	AHL	27	0	3	3	134	....	....	....	....	....	....	....	....	....	9	1	1	2	28	....	....	....	....
1995-96	Binghamton	AHL	46	1	13	14	192	....	....	....	....	....	....	....	....	....	4	0	0	0	37	....	....	....	....
	Charlotte	ECHL	6	0	1	1	34	....	....	....	....	....	....	....	....	....	....	....	....	....	....	....	....	....	....
1996-97	**NY Rangers**	**NHL**	**40**	**0**	**1**	**1**	**147**	**0**	**0**	**0**	**17**	**0.0**	**-7**	....	....	....	**3**	**0**	**0**	**0**	**0**	**0**	**0**	**0**	....
	Binghamton	AHL	10	1	1	2	96	....	....	....	....	....	....	....	....	....	....	....	....	....	....	....	....	....	....
1997-98	**NY Rangers**	**NHL**	**39**	**0**	**3**	**3**	**92**	**0**	**0**	**0**	**17**	**0.0**	**-3**	....	....	....	....	....	....	....	....	....	....	....	....
	Hartford	AHL	7	1	2	3	43	....	....	....	....	....	....	....	....	....	....	....	....	....	....	....	....	....	....
1998-99	Hartford	AHL	11	0	2	2	49	....	....	....	....	....	....	....	....	....	....	....	....	....	....	....	....	....	....
	NY Islanders	**NHL**	**9**	**0**	**3**	**3**	**23**	**0**	**0**	**0**	**2**	**0.0**	**1**	**0**	**0.0**	**10:15**	....	....	....	....	....	....	....	....	....
	Lowell	AHL	24	0	0	0	91	....	....	....	....	....	....	....	....	....	3	1	0	1	32	....	....	....	....
99-2000	**NY Islanders**	**NHL**	**67**	**2**	**7**	**9**	**196**	**0**	**0**	**0**	**55**	**3.6**	**-5**	**0**	**0.0**	**17:43**	....	....	....	....	....	....	....	....	....
	Providence Bruins	AHL	4	1	1	2	14	....	....	....	....	....	....	....	....	....	....	....	....	....	....	....	....	....	....
2000-01	**NY Islanders**	**NHL**	**45**	**2**	**2**	**4**	**106**	**0**	**0**	**0**	**21**	**9.5**	**-18**	**1**	**0.0**	**16:24**	....	....	....	....	....	....	....	....	....
2001-02	**NY Islanders**	**NHL**	**74**	**2**	**5**	**7**	**176**	**0**	**0**	**1**	**34**	**5.9**	**-2**	**0**	**0.0**	**11:09**	**7**	**0**	**0**	**0**	**15**	**0**	**0**	**0**	**13:54**
2002-03	**NY Islanders**	**NHL**	**60**	**1**	**4**	**5**	**124**	**0**	**0**	**0**	**31**	**3.2**	**-7**	**0**	**0.0**	**11:50**	**5**	**0**	**0**	**0**	**13**	**0**	**0**	**0**	**6:02**
2003-04	**NY Islanders**	**NHL**	**72**	**2**	**6**	**8**	**189**	**0**	**0**	**0**	**24**	**8.3**	**-5**	**0**	**0.0**	**11:44**	**1**	**0**	**0**	**0**	**0**	**0**	**0**	**0**	**3:53**
2004-05	London Racers	Britain	22	2	6	8	85	....	....	....	....	....	....	....	....	....	....	....	....	....	....	....	....	....	....
2005-06	**Florida**	**NHL**	**23**	**0**	**1**	**1**	**37**	**0**	**0**	**0**	**11**	**0.0**	**1**	**0**	**0.0**	**7:48**	....	....	....	....	....	....	....	....	....
	Pittsburgh	**NHL**	**27**	**1**	**0**	**1**	**87**	**0**	**0**	**0**	**8**	**12.5**	**0**	**0**	**0.0**	**5:28**	....	....	....	....	....	....	....	....	....
2006-07	**Pittsburgh**	**NHL**	**1**	**0**	**0**	**0**	**5**	**0**	**0**	**0**	**0**	**0.0**	**0**	**0**	**0.0**	**0:42**	....	....	....	....	....	....	....	....	....
	Wilkes-Barre	AHL	2	0	0	0	10	....	....	....	....	....	....	....	....	....	....	....	....	....	....	....	....	....	....
	NHL Totals		**457**	**10**	**32**	**42**	**1182**	**0**	**0**	**1**	**220**	**4.5**		**1**	**0.0**	**12:30**	**16**	**0**	**0**	**0**	**28**	**0**	**0**	**0**	**10:06**

Claimed on waivers by **NY Islanders** from **NY Rangers**, December 22, 1998. Signed as a free agent by **Florida**, July 5, 2004. Signed as a free agent by **London** (Britain), November 1, 2004. Traded to **Pittsburgh** by **Florida** for Pittsburgh's 6th round choice (Peter Aston) in 2006 Entry Draft, January 18, 2006. • Missed majority of 2006-07 season recovering from post-concussion symptoms.

CAJANEK, Petr

(chuh-YA-nihk, PEE-tuhr) **ST.L.**

Right wing. Shoots left. 5'11", 193 lbs. Born, Gottwaldov/Zlin, Czech., August 18, 1975. St. Louis' 6th choice, 253rd overall, in 2001 Entry Draft.

			Regular Season														Playoffs								
Season	Club	League	GP	G	A	Pts	PIM	PP	SH	GW	S	%	+/-	TF	F%	Min	GP	G	A	Pts	PIM	PP	SH	GW	Min
1993-94	AC ZPS Zlin	CzRep	34	5	4	9	....	....	....	....	....	....	....	....	....	....	3	0	0	0	....	....	....	....	....
1994-95	AC ZPS Zlin	CzRep	35	7	9	16	8	....	....	....	....	....	....	....	....	....	12	2	6	8	4	....	....	....	....
1995-96	AC ZPS Zlin	CzRep	36	8	11	19	32	....	....	....	....	....	....	....	....	....	8	2	6	8	8	....	....	....	....
1996-97	AC ZPS Zlin	CzRep	50	9	30	39	46	....	....	....	....	....	....	....	....	....	....	....	....	....	....	....	....	....	....
1997-98	Zlin	CzRep	46	19	27	46	117	....	....	....	....	....	....	....	....	....	....	....	....	....	....	....	....	....	....
1998-99	Zlin	CzRep	49	15	33	48	123	....	....	....	....	....	....	....	....	....	11	5	7	12	12	....	....	....	....
99-2000	Zlin	CzRep	50	23	34	57	66	....	....	....	....	....	....	....	....	....	4	1	0	1	0	....	....	....	....
2000-01	Zlin	CzRep	52	18	31	49	105	....	....	....	....	....	....	....	....	....	6	0	4	4	22	....	....	....	....
2001-02	Zlin	CzRep	49	20	44	64	64	....	....	....	....	....	....	....	....	....	11	5	7	12	10	....	....	....	....
	Czech Republic	Olympics	4	0	0	0	0	....	....	....	....	....	....	....	....	....	....	....	....	....	....	....	....	....	....
2002-03	**St. Louis**	**NHL**	**51**	**9**	**29**	**38**	**20**	**2**	**2**	**1**	**90**	**10.0**	**16**	**793**	**48.4**	**15:56**	**2**	**0**	**0**	**0**	**2**	**0**	**0**	**0**	**11:07**
2003-04	**St. Louis**	**NHL**	**70**	**12**	**14**	**26**	**16**	**3**	**0**	**4**	**126**	**9.5**	**12**	**1000**	**47.6**	**17:48**	**5**	**0**	**2**	**2**	**2**	**0**	**0**	**0**	**19:27**
2004-05	HC Hame Zlin	CzRep	49	10	15	25	91	....	....	....	....	....	....	....	....	....	17	5	4	9	24	....	....	....	....
2005-06	**St. Louis**	**NHL**	**71**	**10**	**31**	**41**	**54**	**3**	**0**	**0**	**150**	**6.7**	**-22**	**888**	**49.7**	**18:53**	....	....	....	....	....	....	....	....	....
	Czech Republic	Olympics	7	1	0	1	4	....	....	....	....	....	....	....	....	....	....	....	....	....	....	....	....	....	....
2006-07	**St. Louis**	**NHL**	**77**	**15**	**33**	**48**	**54**	**1**	**0**	**1**	**167**	**9.0**	**9**	**539**	**50.3**	**16:15**	....	....	....	....	....	....	....	....	....
	NHL Totals		**269**	**46**	**107**	**153**	**144**	**9**	**2**	**6**	**533**	**8.6**		**3220**	**48.8**	**17:17**	**7**	**0**	**2**	**2**	**4**	**0**	**0**	**0**	**17:04**

Signed as a free agent by **Zlin** (CzRep), September 5, 2004.

CALDER, Kyle

(KAWL-dehr, KIGHL) **L.A.**

Left wing. Shoots left. 5'11", 180 lbs. Born, Mannville, Alta., January 5, 1979. Chicago's 7th choice, 130th overall, in 1997 Entry Draft.

			Regular Season														Playoffs								
Season	Club	League	GP	G	A	Pts	PIM	PP	SH	GW	S	%	+/-	TF	F%	Min	GP	G	A	Pts	PIM	PP	SH	GW	Min
1994-95	Leduc Oil Barons	AMHL	27	25	32	57	22	....	....	....	....	....	....	....	....	....	....	....	....	....	....	....	....	....	....
1995-96	Regina Pats	WHL	27	1	7	8	10	....	....	....	....	....	....	....	....	....	11	0	0	0	0	....	....	....	....
1996-97	Regina Pats	WHL	62	25	34	59	17	....	....	....	....	....	....	....	....	....	5	3	0	3	6	....	....	....	....
1997-98	Regina Pats	WHL	62	27	50	77	58	....	....	....	....	....	....	....	....	....	2	0	1	1	0	....	....	....	....
1998-99	Regina Pats	WHL	34	23	28	51	29	....	....	....	....	....	....	....	....	....	....	....	....	....	....	....	....	....	....
	Kamloops Blazers	WHL	27	19	18	37	30	....	....	....	....	....	....	....	....	....	15	6	10	16	6	....	....	....	....
99-2000	**Chicago**	**NHL**	**8**	**1**	**1**	**2**	**2**	**0**	**0**	**0**	**5**	**20.0**	**-3**	**2**	**0.0**	**9:59**	....	....	....	....	....	....	....	....	....
	Cleveland	IHL	74	14	22	36	43	....	....	....	....	....	....	....	....	....	9	2	2	4	14	....	....	....	....
2000-01	**Chicago**	**NHL**	**43**	**5**	**10**	**15**	**14**	**0**	**0**	**1**	**63**	**7.9**	**-4**	**2**	**0.0**	**12:43**	....	....	....	....	....	....	....	....	....
	Norfolk Admirals	AHL	37	12	15	27	21	....	....	....	....	....	....	....	....	....	9	2	6	8	2	....	....	....	....
2001-02	**Chicago**	**NHL**	**81**	**17**	**36**	**53**	**47**	**6**	**0**	**3**	**133**	**12.8**	**8**	**0**	**0.0**	**16:33**	**5**	**2**	**0**	**2**	**2**	**1**	**0**	**0**	**16:45**
2002-03	**Chicago**	**NHL**	**82**	**15**	**27**	**42**	**40**	**7**	**0**	**2**	**164**	**9.1**	**-6**	**4**	**25.0**	**16:43**	....	....	....	....	....	....	....	....	....
2003-04	**Chicago**	**NHL**	**66**	**21**	**18**	**39**	**29**	**10**	**0**	**1**	**144**	**14.6**	**-18**	**13**	**30.8**	**17:08**	....	....	....	....	....	....	....	....	....
2004-05	Sodertalje SK	Sweden	12	5	1	6	6	....	....	....	....	....	....	....	....	....	10	5	1	6	2	....	....	....	....
2005-06	**Chicago**	**NHL**	**79**	**26**	**33**	**59**	**52**	**6**	**2**	**6**	**183**	**14.2**	**-4**	**13**	**46.2**	**18:23**	....	....	....	....	....	....	....	....	....
2006-07	**Philadelphia**	**NHL**	**59**	**9**	**12**	**21**	**36**	**2**	**2**	**0**	**88**	**10.2**	**-31**	**10**	**30.0**	**15:02**	....	....	....	....	....	....	....	....	....
	Detroit	**NHL**	**19**	**5**	**9**	**14**	**22**	**1**	**0**	**2**	**42**	**11.9**	**6**	**2**	**50.0**	**17:05**	**13**	**0**	**1**	**1**	**8**	**0**	**0**	**0**	**8:59**
	NHL Totals		**437**	**99**	**146**	**245**	**242**	**32**	**4**	**15**	**822**	**12.0**		**46**	**32.6**	**16:19**	**18**	**2**	**1**	**3**	**10**	**1**	**0**	**0**	**11:09**

Signed as a free agent by **Sodertalje** (Sweden), January 20, 2005. Traded to **Philadelphia** by **Chicago** for Michael Handzus, August 4, 2006. Traded to **Chicago** by **Philadelphia** for Lasse Kukkonen and Chicago's 3rd round choice (Garrett Klotz) in 2007 Entry Draft, February 26, 2007. Traded to **Detroit** by **Chicago** for Jason Williams, February 26, 2007. Signed as a free agent by **Los Angeles**, July 2, 2007.

CALDWELL, Ryan

(KAWLD-wehl, RIGH-uhn) **PHX.**

Defense. Shoots left. 6'2", 174 lbs. Born, Deloraine, Man., June 15, 1981. NY Islanders' 7th choice, 202nd overall, in 2000 Entry Draft.

			Regular Season														Playoffs								
Season	Club	League	GP	G	A	Pts	PIM	PP	SH	GW	S	%	+/-	TF	F%	Min	GP	G	A	Pts	PIM	PP	SH	GW	Min
1998-99	Shat.-St. Mary's	High-MN	29	24	55	79	22	....	....	....	....	....	....	....	....	....	....	....	....	....	....	....	....	....	....
99-2000	Thunder Bay	USHL	46	3	20	23	152	....	....	....	....	....	....	....	....	....	....	....	....	....	....	....	....	....	....
2000-01	U. of Denver	WCHA	36	3	20	23	76	....	....	....	....	....	....	....	....	....	....	....	....	....	....	....	....	....	....
2001-02	U. of Denver	WCHA	40	3	16	19	76	....	....	....	....	....	....	....	....	....	....	....	....	....	....	....	....	....	....
2002-03	U. of Denver	WCHA	38	5	14	19	58	....	....	....	....	....	....	....	....	....	....	....	....	....	....	....	....	....	....
2003-04	U. of Denver	WCHA	42	15	12	27	96	....	....	....	....	....	....	....	....	....	....	....	....	....	....	....	....	....	....
2004-05	Bridgeport	AHL	73	2	19	21	65	....	....	....	....	....	....	....	....	....	....	....	....	....	....	....	....	....	....
2005-06	**NY Islanders**	**NHL**	**2**	**0**	**0**	**0**	**2**	**0**	**0**	**0**	**2**	**0.0**	**-2**	**0**	**0.0**	**16:33**	....	....	....	....	....	....	....	....	....
	Bridgeport	AHL	61	2	13	15	38	....	....	....	....	....	....	....	....	....	7	1	1	2	2	....	....	....	....
2006-07	Syracuse Crunch	AHL	61	7	23	30	94	....	....	....	....	....	....	....	....	....	....	....	....	....	....	....	....	....	....
	NHL Totals		**2**	**0**	**0**	**0**	**2**	**0**	**0**	**0**	**2**	**0.0**		**0**	**0.0**	**16:33**	....	....	....	....	....	....	....	....	....

WCHA All-Rookie Team (2001) • WCHA Second All-Star Team (2004) • NCAA West First All-American Team (2004) • NCAA Championship All-Tournament Team (2004)

Traded to **Columbus** by **NY Islanders** for Eric Boguniecki, October 25, 2006. Signed as a free agent by **Phoenix**, July 23, 2007.

CALLAHAN, Ryan

(kal-AH-han, RIGH-uhn) **NYR**

Right wing. Shoots right. 5'11", 185 lbs. Born, Rochester, NY, March 21, 1985. NY Rangers' 9th choice, 127th overall, in 2004 Entry Draft.

			Regular Season														Playoffs								
Season	Club	League	GP	G	A	Pts	PIM	PP	SH	GW	S	%	+/-	TF	F%	Min	GP	G	A	Pts	PIM	PP	SH	GW	Min
2002-03	Guelph Storm	OHL	59	14	17	31	47	....	....	....	....	....	....	....	....	....	11	0	3	3	2	....	....	....	....
2003-04	Guelph Storm	OHL	68	36	32	68	86	....	....	....	....	....	....	....	....	....	22	*13	8	21	20	....	....	....	....
2004-05	Guelph Storm	OHL	60	28	26	54	108	....	....	....	....	....	....	....	....	....	4	1	1	2	6	....	....	....	....
2005-06	Guelph Storm	OHL	62	52	32	84	126	....	....	....	....	....	....	....	....	....	13	7	17	24	20	....	....	....	....
2006-07	**NY Rangers**	**NHL**	**14**	**4**	**2**	**6**	**9**	**0**	**0**	**1**	**40**	**10.0**	**5**	**3**	**66.7**	**10:31**	**10**	**2**	**1**	**3**	**6**	**1**	**0**	**0**	**12:19**
	Hartford	AHL	60	35	20	55	74	....	....	....	....	....	....	....	....	....	....	....	....	....	....	....	....	....	....
	NHL Totals		**14**	**4**	**2**	**6**	**9**	**0**	**0**	**1**	**40**	**10.0**		**3**	**66.7**	**10:31**	**10**	**2**	**1**	**3**	**6**	**1**	**0**	**0**	**12:19**

OHL Second All-Star Team (2006) • AHL All-Rookie Team (2007)

CAMMALLERI, Michael

(kam-UH-LAIR-ee, MIGH-kuhl) **L.A.**

Center. Shoots left. 5'9", 185 lbs. Born, Richmond Hill, Ont., June 8, 1982. Los Angeles' 3rd choice, 49th overall, in 2001 Entry Draft.

			Regular Season														Playoffs								
Season	Club	League	GP	G	A	Pts	PIM	PP	SH	GW	S	%	+/-	TF	F%	Min	GP	G	A	Pts	PIM	PP	SH	GW	Min
1997-98	Bramalea Blues	OPJHL	46	36	52	88	30	....	....	....	....	....	....	....	....	....	....	....	....	....	....	....	....	....	....
1998-99	Bramalea Blues	OPJHL	41	31	72	103	51	....	....	....	....	....	....	....	....	....	....	....	....	....	....	....	....	....	....
99-2000	U. of Michigan	CCHA	39	13	13	26	32	....	....	....	....	....	....	....	....	....	....	....	....	....	....	....	....	....	....
2000-01	U. of Michigan	CCHA	42	*29	32	61	24	....	....	....	....	....	....	....	....	....	....	....	....	....	....	....	....	....	....
2001-02	U. of Michigan	CCHA	29	23	21	44	28	....	....	....	....	....	....	....	....	....	....	....	....	....	....	....	....	....	....
2002-03	**Los Angeles**	**NHL**	**28**	**5**	**3**	**8**	**22**	**2**	**0**	**2**	**40**	**12.5**	**-4**	**253**	**51.4**	**14:05**	....	....	....	....	....	....	....	....	....
	Manchester	AHL	13	5	15	20	12	....	....	....	....	....	....	....	....	....	....	....	....	....	....	....	....	....	....
2003-04	**Los Angeles**	**NHL**	**31**	**9**	**6**	**15**	**20**	**2**	**0**	**2**	**53**	**17.0**	**1**	**280**	**53.6**	**13:18**	....	....	....	....	....	....	....	....	....
	Manchester	AHL	41	20	19	39	28	....	....	....	....	....	....	....	....	....	1	0	1	1	0	....	....	....	....
2004-05	Manchester	AHL	79	*46	63	109	60	....	....	....	....	....	....	....	....	....	6	1	5	6	0	....	....	....	....
2005-06	**Los Angeles**	**NHL**	**80**	**26**	**29**	**55**	**50**	**15**	**0**	**4**	**206**	**12.6**	**-14**	**578**	**53.5**	**16:45**	....	....	....	....	....	....	....	....	....
2006-07	**Los Angeles**	**NHL**	**81**	**34**	**46**	**80**	**48**	**16**	**0**	**5**	**299**	**11.4**	**5**	**301**	**54.2**	**18:03**	....	....	....	....	....	....	....	....	....
	NHL Totals		**220**	**74**	**84**	**158**	**140**	**35**	**0**	**13**	**598**	**12.4**		**1412**	**53.3**	**16:24**	....	....	....	....	....	....	....	....	....

CCHA First All-Star Team (2001) • NCAA West Second All-American Team (2001) • CCHA Second All-Star Team (2002) • NCAA West First All-American Team (2002) • AHL Second All-Star Team (2005) • Willie Marshall Award (Top Goal-scorer - AHL) (2005)

• Missed majority of 2002-03 season recovering from head injury suffered in game vs. San Jose, January 28, 2003.

CAMPBELL, Brian

(KAM-behl, BRIGH-uhn) **BUF.**

Defense. Shoots left. 6', 190 lbs. Born, Strathroy, Ont., May 23, 1979. Buffalo's 7th choice, 156th overall, in 1997 Entry Draft.

			Regular Season														Playoffs								
Season	Club	League	GP	G	A	Pts	PIM	PP	SH	GW	S	%	+/-	TF	F%	Min	GP	G	A	Pts	PIM	PP	SH	GW	Min
1994-95	Petrolia Oil Barons	OHA-B	49	11	27	38	43	....	....	....	....	....	....	....	....	....	....	....	....	....	....	....	....	....	....
1995-96	Ottawa 67's	OHL	66	5	22	27	23	....	....	....	....	....	....	....	....	....	4	0	1	1	2	....	....	....	....
1996-97	Ottawa 67's	OHL	66	7	36	43	12	....	....	....	....	....	....	....	....	....	24	2	11	13	8	....	....	....	....
1997-98	Ottawa 67's	OHL	66	14	39	53	31	....	....	....	....	....	....	....	....	....	13	1	14	15	0	....	....	....	....
1998-99	Ottawa 67's	OHL	62	12	75	87	27	....	....	....	....	....	....	....	....	....	9	2	10	12	6	....	....	....	....
	Rochester	AHL															2	0	0	0	0	....	....	....	....
99-2000	**Buffalo**	**NHL**	**12**	**1**	**4**	**5**	**4**	**0**	**0**	**0**	**10**	**10.0**	**-2**	**0**	**0.0**	**15:48**	....	....	....	....	....	....	....	....	....
	Rochester	AHL	67	2	24	26	22	....	....	....	....	....	....	....	....	....	21	0	3	3	0	....	....	....	....
2000-01	**Buffalo**	**NHL**	**8**	**0**	**0**	**0**	**2**	**0**	**0**	**0**	**7**	**0.0**	**-2**	**0**	**0.0**	**15:40**	....	....	....	....	....	....	....	....	....
	Rochester	AHL	65	7	25	32	24	....	....	....	....	....	....	....	....	....	4	0	1	1	0	....	....	....	....

			Regular Season														Playoffs								
Season	Club	League	GP	G	A	Pts	PIM	PP	SH	GW	S	%	+/-	TF	F%	Min	GP	G	A	Pts	PIM	PP	SH	GW	Min
2001-02	**Buffalo**	**NHL**	**29**	**3**	**3**	**6**	**12**	**0**	**0**	**0**	**30**	**10.0**	**0**	**1**	**0.0**	**15:18**	....	....	....	....	....	....	....	....	....
	Rochester	AHL	45	2	35	37	13	....	....	....	....	....	....	....	....	....	....	....	....	....	....	....	....	....	....
2002-03	**Buffalo**	**NHL**	**65**	**2**	**17**	**19**	**20**	**0**	**0**	**1**	**90**	**2.2**	**-8**	**1**	**0.0**	**18:40**	....	....	....	....	....	....	....	....	....
2003-04	**Buffalo**	**NHL**	**53**	**3**	**8**	**11**	**12**	**0**	**0**	**0**	**45**	**6.7**	**-8**	**0**	**0.0**	**16:02**	....	....	....	....	....	....	....	....	....
2004-05	Jokerit Helsinki	Finland	44	12	13	25	12	....	....	....	....	....	....	....	....	....	12	3	4	7	6	....	....	....	....
2005-06	**Buffalo**	**NHL**	**79**	**12**	**32**	**44**	**16**	**5**	**0**	**5**	**105**	**11.4**	**-14**	**0**	**0.0**	**17:43**	**18**	**0**	**6**	**6**	**12**	**0**	**0**	**0**	**20:29**
2006-07	**Buffalo**	**NHL**	**82**	**6**	**42**	**48**	**35**	**1**	**0**	**1**	**92**	**6.5**	**28**	**0**	**0.0**	**21:53**	**16**	**3**	**4**	**7**	**14**	**2**	**0**	**0**	**21:39**
	NHL Totals		**328**	**27**	**106**	**133**	**101**	**6**	**0**	**7**	**379**	**7.1**		**2**	**0.0**	**18:20**	**34**	**3**	**10**	**13**	**26**	**2**	**0**	**0**	**21:02**

OHL First All-Star Team (1999) • OHL MVP (1999) • Canadian Major Junior First All-Star Team (1999) • Canadian Major Junior Player of the Year (1999) • George Parsons Trophy (Memorial Cup Tournament Most Sportsmanlike Player) (1999)

Played in NHL All-Star Game (2007)

Signed as a free agent by **Jokerit Helsinki** (Finland), October 19, 2004.

CAMPBELL, Darcy (KAM-behl, DAHR-see) CBJ

Defense. Shoots left. 6'1", 180 lbs. Born, Airdrie, Alta., May 12, 1984.

Season	Club	League	GP	G	A	Pts	PIM	PP	SH	GW	S	%	+/-	TF	F%	Min	GP	G	A	Pts	PIM	PP	SH	GW	Min
2002-03	Canmore Eagles	AJHL	62	10	37	47	112	....	....	....	....	....	....	....	....	....	9	2	2	4	6	....	....	....	....
2003-04	Canmore Eagles	AJHL	24	6	15	21	25	....	....	....	....	....	....	....	....	....	14	2	7	9	2	....	....	....	....
	Olds Grizzlys	AJHL	36	9	19	28	40	....	....	....	....	....	....	....	....	....	....	....	....	....	....	....	....	....	....
2004-05	Alaska	CCHA	37	2	10	12	56	....	....	....	....	....	....	....	....	....	....	....	....	....	....	....	....	....	....
2005-06	Alaska	CCHA	38	5	9	14	67	....	....	....	....	....	....	....	....	....	....	....	....	....	....	....	....	....	....
2006-07	Alaska	CCHA	39	4	20	24	54	....	....	....	....	....	....	....	....	....	....	....	....	....	....	....	....	....	....
	Columbus	**NHL**	**1**	**0**	**0**	**0**	**0**	**0**	**0**	**0**	**0**	**0.0**	**0**	**0**	**0.0**	**5:41**	....	....	....	....	....	....	....	....	....
	NHL Totals		**1**	**0**	**0**	**0**	**0**	**0**	**0**	**0**	**0**	**0.0**		**0**	**0.0**	**5:41**	....	....	....	....	....	....	....	....	....

AJHL South All-Rookie Team (2003) • AJHL South First All-Star Team (2004)

Signed as a free agent by **Columbus**, March 24, 2007.

CAMPBELL, Gregory (KAM-behl, GREH-goh-ree) FLA.

Left wing. Shoots left. 6', 194 lbs. Born, London, Ont., December 17, 1983. Florida's 4th choice, 67th overall, in 2002 Entry Draft.

Season	Club	League	GP	G	A	Pts	PIM	PP	SH	GW	S	%	+/-	TF	F%	Min	GP	G	A	Pts	PIM	PP	SH	GW	Min
1998-99	Aylmer Aces	OHA-B	49	5	9	14	44	....	....	....	....	....	....	....	....	....	....	....	....	....	....	....	....	....	....
99-2000	St. Thomas Stars	OHA-B	51	12	8	20	51	....	....	....	....	....	....	....	....	....	....	....	....	....	....	....	....	....	....
2000-01	Plymouth Whalers	OHL	65	2	12	14	40	....	....	....	....	....	....	....	....	....	10	0	0	0	7	....	....	....	....
2001-02	Plymouth Whalers	OHL	65	17	36	53	105	....	....	....	....	....	....	....	....	....	6	0	2	2	13	....	....	....	....
2002-03	Kitchener Rangers	OHL	55	23	33	56	116	....	....	....	....	....	....	....	....	....	21	15	4	19	34	....	....	....	....
2003-04	**Florida**	**NHL**	**2**	**0**	**0**	**0**	**5**	**0**	**0**	**0**	**0**	**0.0**	**-1**	**1**	**0.0**	**9:09**	....	....	....	....	....	....	....	....	....
	San Antonio	AHL	76	13	16	29	73	....	....	....	....	....	....	....	....	....	....	....	....	....	....	....	....	....	....
2004-05	San Antonio	AHL	70	12	16	28	113	....	....	....	....	....	....	....	....	....	....	....	....	....	....	....	....	....	....
2005-06	**Florida**	**NHL**	**64**	**3**	**6**	**9**	**40**	**0**	**0**	**0**	**59**	**5.1**	**-11**	**38**	**34.2**	**8:38**	....	....	....	....	....	....	....	....	....
	Rochester	AHL	11	3	3	6	30	....	....	....	....	....	....	....	....	....	....	....	....	....	....	....	....	....	....
2006-07	**Florida**	**NHL**	**79**	**6**	**3**	**9**	**66**	**0**	**1**	**0**	**103**	**5.8**	**-10**	**588**	**45.2**	**10:34**	....	....	....	....	....	....	....	....	....
	NHL Totals		**145**	**9**	**9**	**18**	**111**	**0**	**1**	**0**	**162**	**5.6**		**627**	**44.5**	**9:42**	....	....	....	....	....	....	....	....	....

Memorial Cup Tournament All-Star Team (2003) • George Parsons Trophy (Memorial Cup Tournament Most Sportsmanlike Player) (2003) • Ed Chynoweth Trophy (Memorial Cup Tournament Leading Scorer) (2003)

CAMPOLI, Chris (kam-POH-lee, KRIHS) NYI

Defense. Shoots left. 5'11", 190 lbs. Born, North York, Ont., July 9, 1984. NY Islanders' 8th choice, 227th overall, in 2004 Entry Draft.

Season	Club	League	GP	G	A	Pts	PIM	PP	SH	GW	S	%	+/-	TF	F%	Min	GP	G	A	Pts	PIM	PP	SH	GW	Min
2001-02	Erie Otters	OHL	68	2	24	26	117	....	....	....	....	....	....	....	....	....	20	0	5	5	18	....	....	....	....
2002-03	Erie Otters	OHL	60	8	40	48	82	....	....	....	....	....	....	....	....	....	....	....	....	....	....	....	....	....	....
2003-04	Erie Otters	OHL	67	20	46	66	66	....	....	....	....	....	....	....	....	....	8	0	6	6	16	....	....	....	....
2004-05	Bridgeport	AHL	79	15	34	49	78	....	....	....	....	....	....	....	....	....	....	....	....	....	....	....	....	....	....
2005-06	**NY Islanders**	**NHL**	**80**	**9**	**25**	**34**	**46**	**2**	**0**	**2**	**123**	**7.3**	**-16**	**0**	**0.0**	**18:32**	....	....	....	....	....	....	....	....	....
2006-07	**NY Islanders**	**NHL**	**51**	**1**	**13**	**14**	**23**	**0**	**0**	**0**	**41**	**2.4**	**-3**	**0**	**0.0**	**14:50**	**5**	**1**	**1**	**2**	**2**	**0**	**0**	**0**	**13:30**
	Bridgeport	AHL	15	3	3	6	8	....	....	....	....	....	....	....	....	....	....	....	....	....	....	....	....	....	....
	NHL Totals		**131**	**10**	**38**	**48**	**69**	**2**	**0**	**2**	**164**	**6.1**		**0**	**0.0**	**17:06**	**5**	**1**	**1**	**2**	**2**	**0**	**0**	**0**	**13:30**

OHL Humanitarian Player of the Year (2004) • Canadian Major Junior Humanitarian Player of the Year (2004) • AHL All-Rookie Team (2005)

CARCILLO, Daniel (KAR-sihl-oh, DAN-yuhl) PHX.

Left wing. Shoots left. 5'11", 202 lbs. Born, King City, Ont., January 28, 1985. Pittsburgh's 4th choice, 73rd overall, in 2003 Entry Draft.

Season	Club	League	GP	G	A	Pts	PIM	PP	SH	GW	S	%	+/-	TF	F%	Min	GP	G	A	Pts	PIM	PP	SH	GW	Min
2001-02	Milton Merchants	OHA-B	47	15	16	31	162	....	....	....	....	....	....	....	....	....	....	....	....	....	....	....	....	....	....
2002-03	Sarnia Sting	OHL	68	29	37	66	157	....	....	....	....	....	....	....	....	....	6	0	4	4	14	....	....	....	....
2003-04	Sarnia Sting	OHL	61	30	29	59	148	....	....	....	....	....	....	....	....	....	4	1	2	3	12	....	....	....	....
2004-05	Sarnia Sting	OHL	12	2	7	9	40	....	....	....	....	....	....	....	....	....	....	....	....	....	....	....	....	....	....
	Mississauga	OHL	20	8	10	18	75	....	....	....	....	....	....	....	....	....	5	3	1	4	18	....	....	....	....
2005-06	Wilkes-Barre	AHL	51	11	13	24	311	....	....	....	....	....	....	....	....	....	11	1	0	1	47	....	....	....	....
	Wheeling Nailers	ECHL	6	3	2	5	32	....	....	....	....	....	....	....	....	....	....	....	....	....	....	....	....	....	....
2006-07	Wilkes-Barre	AHL	52	21	9	30	183	....	....	....	....	....	....	....	....	....	....	....	....	....	....	....	....	....	....
	Phoenix	**NHL**	**18**	**4**	**3**	**7**	**74**	**3**	**0**	**0**	**32**	**12.5**	**-7**	**0**	**0.0**	**14:56**	....	....	....	....	....	....	....	....	....
	NHL Totals		**18**	**4**	**3**	**7**	**74**	**3**	**0**	**0**	**32**	**12.5**		**0**	**0.0**	**14:56**	....	....	....	....	....	....	....	....	....

Traded to **Phoenix** by **Pittsburgh** with Pittsburgh's 3rd round choice in 2008 Entry Draft for Georges Laraque, February 27, 2007.

CARD, Mike (KARD, MIGHK) BUF.

Defense. Shoots right. 6', 189 lbs. Born, Kitchener, Ont., February 18, 1986. Buffalo's 7th choice, 241st overall, in 2004 Entry Draft.

Season	Club	League	GP	G	A	Pts	PIM	PP	SH	GW	S	%	+/-	TF	F%	Min	GP	G	A	Pts	PIM	PP	SH	GW	Min
2002-03	Kelowna Rockets	WHL	61	7	22	29	41	....	....	....	....	....	....	....	....	....	19	2	6	8	12	....	....	....	....
2003-04	Kelowna Rockets	WHL	72	6	12	18	47	....	....	....	....	....	....	....	....	....	17	2	4	6	20	....	....	....	....
2004-05	Kelowna Rockets	WHL	72	10	35	45	85	....	....	....	....	....	....	....	....	....	24	2	5	7	38	....	....	....	....
2005-06	Kelowna Rockets	WHL	64	12	43	55	103	....	....	....	....	....	....	....	....	....	12	0	3	3	8	....	....	....	....
2006-07	**Buffalo**	**NHL**	**4**	**0**	**0**	**0**	**0**	**0**	**0**	**0**	**0**	**0.0**	**0**	**0**	**0.0**	**4:34**	....	....	....	....	....	....	....	....	....
	Rochester	AHL	50	1	8	9	38	....	....	....	....	....	....	....	....	....	6	0	0	0	8	....	....	....	....
	Florida Everblades	ECHL	6	1	3	4	2	....	....	....	....	....	....	....	....	....	9	1	4	5	14	....	....	....	....
	NHL Totals		**4**	**0**	**0**	**0**	**0**	**0**	**0**	**0**	**0**	**0.0**		**0**	**0.0**	**4:34**	....	....	....	....	....	....	....	....	....

CARKNER, Matt (KARK-nehr, MAT) OTT.

Defense. Shoots right. 6'4", 230 lbs. Born, Winchester, Ont., November 3, 1980. Montreal's 2nd choice, 58th overall, in 1999 Entry Draft.

Season	Club	League	GP	G	A	Pts	PIM	PP	SH	GW	S	%	+/-	TF	F%	Min	GP	G	A	Pts	PIM	PP	SH	GW	Min
1996-97	Winchester	OHA-B	29	1	18	19		....	....	....	....	....	....	....	....	....	....	....	....	....	....	....	....	....	....
1997-98	Peterborough	OHL	57	0	6	6	121	....	....	....	....	....	....	....	....	....	4	0	0	0	2	....	....	....	....
1998-99	Peterborough	OHL	60	2	16	18	173	....	....	....	....	....	....	....	....	....	5	0	0	0	20	....	....	....	....
99-2000	Peterborough	OHL	62	3	13	16	177	....	....	....	....	....	....	....	....	....	5	0	1	1	6	....	....	....	....
2000-01	Peterborough	OHL	53	8	8	16	128	....	....	....	....	....	....	....	....	....	7	0	3	3	25	....	....	....	....
2001-02	Cleveland Barons	AHL	74	0	3	3	335	....	....	....	....	....	....	....	....	....	....	....	....	....	....	....	....	....	....
2002-03	Cleveland Barons	AHL	39	1	4	5	104	....	....	....	....	....	....	....	....	....	....	....	....	....	....	....	....	....	....
2003-04	Cleveland Barons	AHL	60	2	11	13	115	....	....	....	....	....	....	....	....	....	9	0	3	3	39	....	....	....	....
2004-05	Cleveland Barons	AHL	73	0	10	10	192	....	....	....	....	....	....	....	....	....	....	....	....	....	....	....	....	....	....
2005-06	**San Jose**	**NHL**	**1**	**0**	**1**	**1**	**2**	**0**	**0**	**0**	**0**	**0.0**	**0**	**0**	**0.0**	**6:01**	....	....	....	....	....	....	....	....	....
	Cleveland Barons	AHL	69	10	21	31	202	....	....	....	....	....	....	....	....	....	....	....	....	....	....	....	....	....	....
2006-07	Wilkes-Barre	AHL	75	6	24	30	167	....	....	....	....	....	....	....	....	....	8	1	0	1	19	....	....	....	....
	NHL Totals		**1**	**0**	**1**	**1**	**2**	**0**	**0**	**0**	**0**	**0.0**		**0**	**0.0**	**6:01**	....	....	....	....	....	....	....	....	....

Yanick Dupre Memorial Award (Outstanding Humanitarian Contribution - AHL) (2007)

Signed as a free agent by **San Jose**, June 6, 2001. • Missed majority of 2002-03 season recovering from knee injury suffered in game vs. Utah (AHL), January 4, 2003. Signed as a free agent by **Pittsburgh**, July 23, 2006. Signed as a free agent by **Ottawa**, July 3, 2007.

Season	Club	League	Regular Season														Playoffs								
			GP	G	A	Pts	PIM	PP	SH	GW	S	%	+/-	TF	F%	Min	GP	G	A	Pts	PIM	PP	SH	GW	Min

CARLE, Matt

(KAHRL, MAT) **S.J.**

Defense. Shoots left. 6', 205 lbs. Born, Anchorage, AK, September 25, 1984. San Jose's 4th choice, 47th overall, in 2003 Entry Draft.

Season	Club	League	GP	G	A	Pts	PIM	PP	SH	GW	S	%	+/-	TF	F%	Min	GP	G	A	Pts	PIM	PP	SH	GW	Min
99-2000	Alaska All-Stars	AASHA	42	14	28	42	....	....	....	....	....	....	....	....	....	....	....	....	....	....	....	....	....	....	....
2000-01	USNTDP	U-17	13	0	1	1	....	....	....	....	....	....	....	....	....	....	....	....	....	....	....	....	....	....	....
	USNTDP	NAHL	55	1	4	5	33	....	....	....	....	....	....	....	....	....	....	....	....	....	....	....	....	....	....
2001-02	USNTDP	U-18	45	3	13	16	30	....	....	....	....	....	....	....	....	....	....	....	....	....	....	....	....	....	....
	USNTDP	USHL	12	0	0	0	21	....	....	....	....	....	....	....	....	....	....	....	....	....	....	....	....	....	....
	USNTDP	NAHL	7	1	2	3	0	....	....	....	....	....	....	....	....	....	....	....	....	....	....	....	....	....	....
2002-03	River City Lancers	USHL	59	12	30	42	98	....	....	....	....	....	....	....	....	....	11	2	2	4	20	....	....	....	....
2003-04	U. of Denver	WCHA	30	5	20	25	33	....	....	....	....	....	....	....	....	....	....	....	....	....	....	....	....	....	....
2004-05	U. of Denver	WCHA	43	13	31	44	68	....	....	....	....	....	....	....	....	....	....	....	....	....	....	....	....	....	....
2005-06	U. of Denver	WCHA	39	11	*42	53	58	....	....	....	....	....	....	....	....	....	....	....	....	....	....	....	....	....	....
	San Jose	**NHL**	**12**	**3**	**3**	**6**	**14**	**2**	**0**	**1**	**11**	**27.3**	**–2**	**0**	**0.0**	**16:07**	**11**	**0**	**3**	**3**	**4**	**0**	**0**	**0**	**15:17**
2006-07	**San Jose**	**NHL**	**77**	**11**	**31**	**42**	**30**	**8**	**0**	**1**	**111**	**9.9**	**9**	**1**	**0.0**	**18:08**	**11**	**2**	**3**	**5**	**0**	**1**	**0**	**1**	**14:51**
	Worcester Sharks	AHL	3	0	2	2	0	....	....	....	....	....	....	....	....	....	....	....	....	....	....	....	....	....	....
	NHL Totals		**89**	**14**	**34**	**48**	**44**	**10**	**0**	**2**	**122**	**11.5**		**1**	**0.0**	**17:52**	**22**	**2**	**6**	**8**	**4**	**1**	**0**	**1**	**15:04**

USHL First All-Star Team (2003) • USHL Defenseman of the Year (2003) • WCHA All-Rookie Team (2004) • WCHA First All-Star Team (2005, 2006) • NCAA West First All-American Team (2005, 2006) • NCAA Championship All-Tournament Team (2005) • WCHA Player of the Year (2006) • Hobey Baker Memorial Award (Top U.S. Collegiate Player) (2006) • NHL All-Rookie Team (2007)

CARNEY, Keith

(KAHRN-nee, KEETH) **MIN.**

Defense. Shoots left. 6'2", 204 lbs. Born, Providence, RI, February 3, 1970. Buffalo's 3rd choice, 76th overall, in 1988 Entry Draft.

Season	Club	League	GP	G	A	Pts	PIM	PP	SH	GW	S	%	+/-	TF	F%	Min	GP	G	A	Pts	PIM	PP	SH	GW	Min
1987-88	Mount St. Charles	High-RI	23	12	43	55	....	....	....	....	....	....	....	....	....	....	....	....	....	....	....	....	....	....	....
1988-89	U. of Maine	H-East	40	4	22	26	24	....	....	....	....	....	....	....	....	....	....	....	....	....	....	....	....	....	....
1989-90	U. of Maine	H-East	41	3	41	44	43	....	....	....	....	....	....	....	....	....	....	....	....	....	....	....	....	....	....
1990-91	U. of Maine	H-East	40	7	49	56	38	....	....	....	....	....	....	....	....	....	....	....	....	....	....	....	....	....	....
1991-92	United States	Nat-Tm	49	2	17	19	16	....	....	....	....	....	....	....	....	....	....	....	....	....	....	....	....	....	....
	Buffalo	**NHL**	**14**	**1**	**2**	**3**	**18**	**1**	**0**	**0**	**17**	**5.9**	**–3**	....	....	....	**7**	**0**	**3**	**3**	**0**	**0**	**0**	**0**	....
	Rochester	AHL	24	1	10	11	2	....	....	....	....	....	....	....	....	....	2	0	2	2	0	....	....	....	....
1992-93	**Buffalo**	**NHL**	**30**	**2**	**4**	**6**	**55**	**0**	**0**	**1**	**26**	**7.7**	**3**	....	....	....	**8**	**0**	**3**	**3**	**6**	**0**	**0**	**0**	....
	Rochester	AHL	41	5	21	26	32	....	....	....	....	....	....	....	....	....	....	....	....	....	....	....	....	....	....
1993-94	**Buffalo**	**NHL**	**7**	**1**	**3**	**4**	**4**	**0**	**0**	**0**	**6**	**16.7**	**–1**	....	....	....	....	....	....	....	....	....	....	....	....
	Chicago	**NHL**	**30**	**3**	**5**	**8**	**35**	**0**	**0**	**0**	**31**	**9.7**	**15**	....	....	....	**6**	**0**	**1**	**1**	**4**	**0**	**0**	**0**	....
	Indianapolis Ice	IHL	28	0	14	14	20	....	....	....	....	....	....	....	....	....	....	....	....	....	....	....	....	....	....
1994-95	**Chicago**	**NHL**	**18**	**1**	**0**	**1**	**11**	**0**	**0**	**1**	**14**	**7.1**	**–1**	....	....	....	**4**	**0**	**1**	**1**	**0**	**0**	**0**	**0**	....
1995-96	**Chicago**	**NHL**	**82**	**5**	**14**	**19**	**94**	**1**	**0**	**1**	**69**	**7.2**	**31**	....	....	....	**10**	**0**	**3**	**3**	**4**	**0**	**0**	**0**	....
1996-97	**Chicago**	**NHL**	**81**	**3**	**15**	**18**	**62**	**0**	**0**	**1**	**77**	**3.9**	**26**	....	....	....	**6**	**1**	**1**	**2**	**2**	**0**	**0**	**0**	....
1997-98	**Chicago**	**NHL**	**60**	**2**	**13**	**15**	**73**	**0**	**1**	**0**	**53**	**3.8**	**–7**	....	....	....	....	....	....	....	....	....	....	....	....
	United States	Olympics	4	0	0	0	2	....	....	....	....	....	....	....	....	....	....	....	....	....	....	....	....	....	....
	Phoenix	**NHL**	**20**	**1**	**6**	**7**	**18**	**1**	**0**	**0**	**18**	**5.6**	**5**	....	....	....	**6**	**0**	**0**	**0**	**4**	**0**	**0**	**0**	....
1998-99	**Phoenix**	**NHL**	**82**	**2**	**14**	**16**	**62**	**0**	**2**	**0**	**62**	**3.2**	**15**	**0**	**0.0**	**22:46**	**7**	**1**	**2**	**3**	**10**	**0**	**0**	**0**	**23:59**
99-2000	**Phoenix**	**NHL**	**82**	**4**	**20**	**24**	**87**	**0**	**0**	**1**	**73**	**5.5**	**11**	**0**	**0.0**	**21:12**	**5**	**0**	**0**	**0**	**17**	**0**	**0**	**0**	**22:38**
2000-01	**Phoenix**	**NHL**	**82**	**2**	**14**	**16**	**86**	**0**	**0**	**0**	**65**	**3.1**	**15**	**0**	**0.0**	**20:53**	....	....	....	....	....	....	....	....	....
2001-02	**Anaheim**	**NHL**	**60**	**5**	**9**	**14**	**30**	**0**	**0**	**1**	**66**	**7.6**	**14**	**0**	**0.0**	**20:47**	....	....	....	....	....	....	....	....	....
2002-03	**Anaheim**	**NHL**	**81**	**4**	**18**	**22**	**65**	**0**	**0**	**1**	**87**	**4.6**	**8**	**0**	**0.0**	**22:34**	**21**	**0**	**4**	**4**	**16**	**0**	**0**	**0**	**26:40**
2003-04	**Anaheim**	**NHL**	**69**	**2**	**5**	**7**	**42**	**1**	**0**	**0**	**58**	**3.4**	**–5**	**0**	**0.0**	**21:43**	....	....	....	....	....	....	....	....	....
2004-05			DID NOT PLAY																						
2005-06	**Anaheim**	**NHL**	**61**	**2**	**16**	**18**	**48**	**1**	**0**	**1**	**71**	**2.8**	**13**	**1**	**0.0**	**19:19**	....	....	....	....	....	....	....	....	....
	Vancouver	**NHL**	**18**	**0**	**2**	**2**	**14**	**0**	**0**	**0**	**14**	**0.0**	**–5**	**0**	**0.0**	**24:30**	....	....	....	....	....	....	....	....	....
2006-07	**Minnesota**	**NHL**	**80**	**4**	**13**	**17**	**58**	**0**	**0**	**1**	**31**	**12.9**	**22**	**2**	**100.0**	**15:31**	**5**	**0**	**0**	**0**	**4**	**0**	**0**	**0**	**13:57**
	NHL Totals		**957**	**44**	**173**	**217**	**862**	**5**	**3**	**9**	**838**	**5.3**		**3**	**66.7**	**20:44**	**85**	**2**	**18**	**20**	**67**	**0**	**0**	**0**	**23:58**

Hockey East Second All-Star Team (1990) • NCAA East Second All-American Team (1990) • Hockey East First All-Star Team (1991) • NCAA East First All-American Team (1991)

Traded to **Chicago** by **Buffalo** with Buffalo's 6th round choice (Marc Magliarditi) in 1995 Entry Draft for Craig Muni and Chicago's 5th round choice (Daniel Bienvenue) in 1995 Entry Draft, October 26, 1993. Traded to **Phoenix** by **Chicago** with Jim Cummins for Chad Kilger and Jayson More, March 4, 1998. Traded to **Anaheim** by **Phoenix** for Calgary's 2nd round choice (previously acquired, later traded back to Calgary – Calgary selected Andrei Taratukhin) in 2001 Entry Draft, June 19, 2001. Traded to **Vancouver** by **Anaheim** with Juha Alen for Brett Skinner and NY Islanders' 2nd round choice (previously acquired, Anaheim selected Bryce Swan) in 2006 Entry Draft, March 9, 2006. Signed as a free agent by **Minnesota**, July 1, 2006.

CARTER, Anson

(KAHR-tuhr, AN-sohn)

Right wing. Shoots right. 6'1", 210 lbs. Born, Toronto, Ont., June 6, 1974. Quebec's 11th choice, 220th overall, in 1992 Entry Draft.

Season	Club	League	GP	G	A	Pts	PIM	PP	SH	GW	S	%	+/-	TF	F%	Min	GP	G	A	Pts	PIM	PP	SH	GW	Min
1989-90	Don Mills Flyers	MTHL	40	15	47	62	105	....	....	....	....	....	....	....	....	....	....	....	....	....	....	....	....	....	....
1990-91	Don Mills Flyers	MTHL	67	69	73	142	43	....	....	....	....	....	....	....	....	....	....	....	....	....	....	....	....	....	....
1991-92	Wexford Raiders	MTJHL	42	18	22	40	24	....	....	....	....	....	....	....	....	....	....	....	....	....	....	....	....	....	....
1992-93	Michigan State	CCHA	34	15	7	22	20	....	....	....	....	....	....	....	....	....	....	....	....	....	....	....	....	....	....
1993-94	Michigan State	CCHA	39	30	24	54	36	....	....	....	....	....	....	....	....	....	....	....	....	....	....	....	....	....	....
1994-95	Michigan State	CCHA	39	34	17	51	40	....	....	....	....	....	....	....	....	....	....	....	....	....	....	....	....	....	....
1995-96	Michigan State	CCHA	42	23	20	43	36	....	....	....	....	....	....	....	....	....	....	....	....	....	....	....	....	....	....
1996-97	**Washington**	**NHL**	**19**	**3**	**2**	**5**	**7**	**1**	**0**	**1**	**28**	**10.7**	**0**	....	....	....	....	....	....	....	....	....	....	....	....
	Portland Pirates	AHL	27	19	19	38	11	....	....	....	....	....	....	....	....	....	....	....	....	....	....	....	....	....	....
	Boston	**NHL**	**19**	**8**	**5**	**13**	**2**	**1**	**1**	**1**	**51**	**15.7**	**–7**	....	....	....	....	....	....	....	....	....	....	....	....
1997-98	**Boston**	**NHL**	**78**	**16**	**27**	**43**	**31**	**6**	**0**	**4**	**179**	**8.9**	**7**	....	....	....	**6**	**1**	**1**	**2**	**0**	**0**	**0**	**0**	....
1998-99	Utah Grizzlies	IHL	6	1	1	2	0	....	....	....	....	....	....	....	....	....	....	....	....	....	....	....	....	....	....
	Boston	**NHL**	**55**	**24**	**16**	**40**	**22**	**6**	**0**	**6**	**123**	**19.5**	**7**	**172**	**43.0**	**18:44**	**12**	**4**	**3**	**7**	**0**	**1**	**0**	**1**	**21:31**
99-2000	**Boston**	**NHL**	**59**	**22**	**25**	**47**	**14**	**4**	**0**	**1**	**144**	**15.3**	**8**	**793**	**48.2**	**20:31**	....	....	....	....	....	....	....	....	....
2000-01	**Edmonton**	**NHL**	**61**	**16**	**26**	**42**	**23**	**7**	**1**	**4**	**102**	**15.7**	**1**	**80**	**47.5**	**18:13**	**6**	**3**	**1**	**4**	**4**	**1**	**0**	**1**	**19:42**
2001-02	**Edmonton**	**NHL**	**82**	**28**	**32**	**60**	**25**	**12**	**0**	**6**	**181**	**15.5**	**3**	**316**	**46.5**	**19:18**	....	....	....	....	....	....	....	....	....
2002-03	**Edmonton**	**NHL**	**68**	**25**	**30**	**55**	**20**	**10**	**0**	**1**	**176**	**14.2**	**–11**	**217**	**43.8**	**19:39**	....	....	....	....	....	....	....	....	....
	NY Rangers	**NHL**	**11**	**1**	**4**	**5**	**6**	**0**	**0**	**0**	**17**	**5.9**	**0**	**5**	**20.0**	**17:49**	....	....	....	....	....	....	....	....	....
2003-04	**NY Rangers**	**NHL**	**43**	**10**	**7**	**17**	**14**	**4**	**1**	**2**	**63**	**15.9**	**–12**	**21**	**28.6**	**15:35**	....	....	....	....	....	....	....	....	....
	Washington	**NHL**	**19**	**5**	**5**	**10**	**6**	**2**	**0**	**2**	**33**	**15.2**	**2**	**9**	**44.4**	**19:33**	....	....	....	....	....	....	....	....	....
	Los Angeles	**NHL**	**15**	**0**	**1**	**1**	**0**	**0**	**0**	**0**	**18**	**0.0**	**–5**	**58**	**29.3**	**16:43**	....	....	....	....	....	....	....	....	....
2004-05			DID NOT PLAY																						
2005-06	**Vancouver**	**NHL**	**81**	**33**	**22**	**55**	**41**	**15**	**0**	**7**	**146**	**22.6**	**–1**	**28**	**39.3**	**14:34**	....	....	....	....	....	....	....	....	....
2006-07	**Columbus**	**NHL**	**54**	**10**	**17**	**27**	**16**	**3**	**0**	**1**	**62**	**16.1**	**–1**	**83**	**50.6**	**14:49**	....	....	....	....	....	....	....	....	....
	Carolina	**NHL**	**10**	**1**	**0**	**1**	**2**	**1**	**0**	**0**	**8**	**12.5**	**–3**	**1**	**100.0**	**10:03**	....	....	....	....	....	....	....	....	....
	NHL Totals		**674**	**202**	**219**	**421**	**229**	**72**	**3**	**36**	**1331**	**15.2**		**1783**	**45.9**	**17:38**	**24**	**8**	**5**	**13**	**4**	**2**	**0**	**2**	**20:54**

CCHA First All-Star Team (1994, 1995) • NCAA West Second All-American Team (1995) • CCHA Second All-Star Team (1996)

Rights transferred to **Colorado** after **Quebec** franchise relocated, June 21, 1995. Traded to **Washington** by **Colorado** for Washington's 4th round choice (Ben Storey) in 1996 Entry Draft, April 3, 1996. Traded to **Boston** by **Washington** with Jim Carey, Jason Allison and Washington's 3rd round choice (Lee Goren) in 1997 Entry Draft for Bill Ranford, Adam Oates and Rick Tocchet, March 1, 1997. Signed as a free agent by **Utah** (IHL) with Boston retaining NHL rights, October 20, 1998. Traded to **Edmonton** by **Boston** with Boston's 1st (Ales Hemsky) and 2nd (Doug Lynch) round choices in 2001 Entry Draft for Bill Guerin and future considerations, November 15, 2000. Traded to **NY Rangers** by **Edmonton** with Ales Pisa for Radek Dvorak and Cory Cross, March 11, 2003. Traded to **Washington** by **NY Rangers** for Jaromir Jagr, January 23, 2004. Traded to **Los Angeles** by **Washington** for Jared Aulin, March 8, 2004. Signed as a free agent by **Vancouver**, August 17, 2005. Signed as a free agent by **Columbus**, September 13, 2006. Traded to **Carolina** by **Columbus** for Carolina's 5th round choice in 2008 Entry Draft, February 23, 2007.

CARTER, Jeff

(KAHR-tuhr, JEHF) **PHI.**

Center. Shoots right. 6'3", 200 lbs. Born, London, Ont., January 1, 1985. Philadelphia's 1st choice, 11th overall, in 2003 Entry Draft.

Season	Club	League	GP	G	A	Pts	PIM	PP	SH	GW	S	%	+/-	TF	F%	Min	GP	G	A	Pts	PIM	PP	SH	GW	Min
2000-01	Strathroy Rockets	OHA-B	49	27	20	47	10	....	....	....	....	....	....	....	....	....	....	....	....	....	....	....	....	....	....
2001-02	Sault Ste. Marie	OHL	63	18	17	35	12	....	....	....	....	....	....	....	....	....	4	0	0	0	2	....	....	....	....
2002-03	Sault Ste. Marie	OHL	61	35	36	71	55	....	....	....	....	....	....	....	....	....	4	0	2	2	2	....	....	....	....
2003-04	Sault Ste. Marie	OHL	57	36	30	66	26	....	....	....	....	....	....	....	....	....	....	....	....	....	....	....	....	....	....
	Philadelphia	AHL	....	....	....	....	....	....	....	....	....	....	....	....	....	....	12	4	1	5	0	....	....	....	....
2004-05	Sault Ste. Marie	OHL	55	34	40	74	40	....	....	....	....	....	....	....	....	....	7	5	5	10	6	....	....	....	....
	Philadelphia	AHL	3	0	1	1	4	....	....	....	....	....	....	....	....	....	21	12	11	23	12	....	....	....	....
2005-06	**Philadelphia**	**NHL**	**81**	**23**	**19**	**42**	**40**	**6**	**2**	**7**	**189**	**12.2**	**10**	**683**	**48.2**	**12:04**	**6**	**0**	**0**	**0**	**10**	**0**	**0**	**0**	**13:04**
2006-07	**Philadelphia**	**NHL**	**62**	**14**	**23**	**37**	**48**	**3**	**2**	**1**	**215**	**6.5**	**–17**	**1062**	**45.4**	**19:00**	....	....	....	....	....	....	....	....	....
	NHL Totals		**143**	**37**	**42**	**79**	**88**	**9**	**4**	**8**	**404**	**9.2**		**1745**	**46.5**	**15:04**	**6**	**0**	**0**	**0**	**10**	**0**	**0**	**0**	**13:04**

OHL Second All-Star Team (2004) • OHL First All-Star Team (2005) • Canadian Major Junior Sportsman of the Year (2005) • Canadian Major Junior First All-Star Team (2005)

CARTER, Ryan
(KAHR-tuhr, RIGH-uhn) **ANA.**

Left wing. Shoots left. 6'1", 205 lbs. Born, White Bear Lake, MN, August 3, 1983.

			Regular Season														Playoffs								
Season	Club	League	GP	G	A	Pts	PIM	PP	SH	GW	S	%	+/-	TF	F%	Min	GP	G	A	Pts	PIM	PP	SH	GW	Min
2002-03	Green Bay	USHL	55	19	17	36	94	....	....	....	....	....	....	....	....	....	....	....	....	....	....	....	....	....	....
2003-04	Green Bay	USHL	59	22	23	45	131	....	....	....	....	....	....	....	....	....	....	....	....	....	....	....	....	....	....
2004-05	Minnesota State	WCHA	37	15	8	23	44	....	....	....	....	....	....	....	....	....	....	....	....	....	....	....	....	....	....
2005-06	Minnesota State	WCHA	39	19	16	35	71	....	....	....	....	....	....	....	....	....	....	....	....	....	....	....	....	....	....
2006-07	Portland Pirates	AHL	76	16	20	36	85	....	....	....	....	....	....	....	....	....	....	....	....	....	....	....	....	....	....
	◆ **Anaheim**	**NHL**	....	....	....	....	....	....	....	....	....	....	....	....	....	....	**4**	**0**	**0**	**0**	**0**	**0**	**0**	**0**	**3:12**
	NHL Totals		....	....	....	....	....	....	....	....	....	....	....	....	....	....	**4**	**0**	**0**	**0**	**0**	**0**	**0**	**0**	**3:12**

Signed as a free agent by **Anaheim**, July 12, 2006.

CHARA, Zdeno
(CHAH-rah, z'DEHN-oh) **BOS.**

Defense. Shoots left. 6'9", 251 lbs. Born, Trencin, Czech., March 18, 1977. NY Islanders' 3rd choice, 56th overall, in 1996 Entry Draft.

			Regular Season														Playoffs								
Season	Club	League	GP	G	A	Pts	PIM	PP	SH	GW	S	%	+/-	TF	F%	Min	GP	G	A	Pts	PIM	PP	SH	GW	Min
1994-95	Dukla Trencin U18	Svk-U18	30	22	22	44	113	....	....	....	....	....	....	....	....	....	....	....	....	....	....	....	....	....	....
	Dukla Trencin Jr.	Slovak-Jr.	2	0	0	0	0	....	....	....	....	....	....	....	....	....	....	....	....	....	....	....	....	....	....
1995-96	Dukla Trencin Jr.	Slovak-Jr.	22	1	13	14	80	....	....	....	....	....	....	....	....	....	....	....	....	....	....	....	....	....	....
	HK VTJ Piestany	Slovak-2	10	1	3	4	10	....	....	....	....	....	....	....	....	....	....	....	....	....	....	....	....	....	....
	Sparta Jr.	CzRep-Jr.	15	1	2	3	42	....	....	....	....	....	....	....	....	....	....	....	....	....	....	....	....	....	....
	HC Sparta Praha	CzRep	1	0	0	0	0	....	....	....	....	....	....	....	....	....	....	....	....	....	....	....	....	....	....
1996-97	Prince George	WHL	49	3	19	22	120	....	....	....	....	....	....	....	....	....	15	1	7	8	45	....	....	....	....
1997-98	**NY Islanders**	**NHL**	**25**	**0**	**1**	**1**	**50**	**0**	**0**	**0**	**10**	**0.0**	**1**	....	....	....	....	....	....	....	....	....	....	....	....
	Kentucky	AHL	48	4	9	13	125	....	....	....	....	....	....	....	....	....	1	0	0	0	4	....	....	....	....
1998-99	**NY Islanders**	**NHL**	**59**	**2**	**6**	**8**	**83**	**0**	**1**	**0**	**56**	**3.6**	**–8**	**0**	**0.0**	**18:54**	....	....	....	....	....	....	....	....	....
	Lowell	AHL	23	2	2	4	47	....	....	....	....	....	....	....	....	....	....	....	....	....	....	....	....	....	....
99-2000	**NY Islanders**	**NHL**	**65**	**2**	**9**	**11**	**57**	**0**	**0**	**1**	**47**	**4.3**	**–27**	**0**	**0.0**	**22:52**	....	....	....	....	....	....	....	....	....
2000-01	**NY Islanders**	**NHL**	**82**	**2**	**7**	**9**	**157**	**0**	**1**	**0**	**83**	**2.4**	**–27**	**0**	**0.0**	**22:20**	....	....	....	....	....	....	....	....	....
2001-02	Dukla Trencin	Slovakia	8	2	2	4	32	....	....	....	....	....	....	....	....	....	....	....	....	....	....	....	....	....	....
	Ottawa	**NHL**	**75**	**10**	**13**	**23**	**156**	**4**	**1**	**2**	**105**	**9.5**	**30**	**0**	**0.0**	**22:16**	**10**	**0**	**1**	**1**	**12**	**0**	**0**	**0**	**26:07**
2002-03	**Ottawa**	**NHL**	**74**	**9**	**30**	**39**	**116**	**3**	**0**	**2**	**168**	**5.4**	**29**	**0**	**0.0**	**24:57**	**18**	**1**	**6**	**7**	**14**	**0**	**0**	**0**	**25:07**
2003-04	**Ottawa**	**NHL**	**79**	**16**	**25**	**41**	**147**	**7**	**0**	**3**	**185**	**8.6**	**33**	**0**	**0.0**	**24:38**	**7**	**1**	**1**	**2**	**8**	**0**	**0**	**0**	**24:38**
2004-05	Farjestad	Sweden	33	10	15	25	132	....	....	....	....	....	....	....	....	....	13	3	5	8	82	....	....	....	....
2005-06	**Ottawa**	**NHL**	**71**	**16**	**27**	**43**	**135**	**10**	**1**	**3**	**212**	**7.5**	**17**	**24**	**41.7**	**27:11**	**10**	**1**	**3**	**4**	**23**	**1**	**0**	**0**	**27:32**
	Slovakia	Olympics	6	1	1	2	2	....	....	....	....	....	....	....	....	....	....	....	....	....	....	....	....	....	....
2006-07	**Boston**	**NHL**	**80**	**11**	**32**	**43**	**100**	**9**	**0**	**3**	**204**	**5.4**	**–21**	**1**	**0.0**	**27:58**	....	....	....	....	....	....	....	....	....
	NHL Totals		**610**	**68**	**150**	**218**	**1001**	**33**	**4**	**14**	**1070**	**6.4**		**25**	**40.0**	**24:02**	**45**	**3**	**11**	**14**	**57**	**1**	**0**	**0**	**25:48**

AHL All-Rookie Team (1998) • NHL First All-Star Team (2004) • NHL Second All-Star Team (2006)

Played in NHL All-Star Game (2003, 2007)

Traded to **Ottawa** by **NY Islanders** with Bill Muckalt and NY Islanders' 1st round choice (Jason Spezza) in 2001 Entry Draft for Alexei Yashin, June 23, 2001. Signed as a free agent by **Farjestad** (Sweden), September 24, 2004. Signed as a free agent by **Boston**, July 1, 2006.

CHEECHOO, Jonathan
(CHEE-choo, JAWN-ah-thuhn) **S.J.**

Right wing. Shoots right. 6'1", 200 lbs. Born, Moose Factory, Ont., July 15, 1980. San Jose's 2nd choice, 29th overall, in 1998 Entry Draft.

			Regular Season														Playoffs								
Season	Club	League	GP	G	A	Pts	PIM	PP	SH	GW	S	%	+/-	TF	F%	Min	GP	G	A	Pts	PIM	PP	SH	GW	Min
1996-97	Kitchener	OHA-B	43	35	41	76	33	....	....	....	....	....	....	....	....	....	....	....	....	....	....	....	....	....	....
1997-98	Belleville Bulls	OHL	64	31	45	76	62	....	....	....	....	....	....	....	....	....	10	4	2	6	10	....	....	....	....
1998-99	Belleville Bulls	OHL	63	35	47	82	74	....	....	....	....	....	....	....	....	....	21	15	15	30	27	....	....	....	....
99-2000	Belleville Bulls	OHL	66	45	46	91	102	....	....	....	....	....	....	....	....	....	16	5	12	17	16	....	....	....	....
2000-01	Kentucky	AHL	75	32	34	66	63	....	....	....	....	....	....	....	....	....	3	0	0	0	0	....	....	....	....
2001-02	Cleveland Barons	AHL	53	21	25	46	54	....	....	....	....	....	....	....	....	....	....	....	....	....	....	....	....	....	....
2002-03	**San Jose**	**NHL**	**66**	**9**	**7**	**16**	**39**	**0**	**0**	**3**	**94**	**9.6**	**–5**	**8**	**37.5**	**10:43**	....	....	....	....	....	....	....	....	....
	Cleveland Barons	AHL	9	3	4	7	16	....	....	....	....	....	....	....	....	....	....	....	....	....	....	....	....	....	....
2003-04	**San Jose**	**NHL**	**81**	**28**	**19**	**47**	**33**	**8**	**0**	**9**	**175**	**16.0**	**5**	**7**	**14.3**	**16:12**	**17**	**4**	**6**	**10**	**10**	**1**	**0**	**0**	**17:37**
2004-05	HV 71 Jonkoping	Sweden	20	5	0	5	10	....	....	....	....	....	....	....	....	....	....	....	....	....	....	....	....	....	....
2005-06	**San Jose**	**NHL**	**82**	***56**	**37**	**93**	**58**	**24**	**2**	**11**	**317**	**17.7**	**23**	**20**	**20.0**	**19:57**	**11**	**4**	**5**	**9**	**8**	**1**	**0**	**1**	**24:00**
2006-07	**San Jose**	**NHL**	**76**	**37**	**32**	**69**	**69**	**15**	**0**	**5**	**250**	**14.8**	**11**	**32**	**31.3**	**17:34**	**11**	**3**	**3**	**6**	**6**	**1**	**0**	**1**	**16:25**
	NHL Totals		**305**	**130**	**95**	**225**	**199**	**47**	**2**	**28**	**836**	**15.6**		**67**	**26.9**	**16:22**	**39**	**11**	**14**	**25**	**24**	**3**	**0**	**2**	**19:05**

OHL All-Rookie Team (1998) • AHL All-Rookie Team (2001) • Maurice "Rocket" Richard Trophy (2006)

Played in NHL All-Star Game (2007)

Signed as a free agent by **Jonkoping** (Sweden), December 21, 2004.

CHELIOS, Chris
(CHELL-EE-ohs, KRIHS) **DET.**

Defense. Shoots right. 5'11", 191 lbs. Born, Chicago, IL, January 25, 1962. Montreal's 5th choice, 40th overall, in 1981 Entry Draft.

			Regular Season														Playoffs								
Season	Club	League	GP	G	A	Pts	PIM	PP	SH	GW	S	%	+/-	TF	F%	Min	GP	G	A	Pts	PIM	PP	SH	GW	Min
1979-80	Moose Jaw	SJHL	53	12	31	43	118	....	....	....	....	....	....	....	....	....	....	....	....	....	....	....	....	....	....
1980-81	Moose Jaw	SJHL	54	23	64	87	175	....	....	....	....	....	....	....	....	....	....	....	....	....	....	....	....	....	....
1981-82	U. of Wisconsin	WCHA	43	6	43	49	50	....	....	....	....	....	....	....	....	....	....	....	....	....	....	....	....	....	....
1982-83	U. of Wisconsin	WCHA	26	9	17	26	50	....	....	....	....	....	....	....	....	....	....	....	....	....	....	....	....	....	....
1983-84	United States	Nat-Tm	60	14	35	49	58	....	....	....	....	....	....	....	....	....	....	....	....	....	....	....	....	....	....
	United States	Olympics	6	0	4	4	8	....	....	....	....	....	....	....	....	....	....	....	....	....	....	....	....	....	....
	Montreal	**NHL**	**12**	**0**	**2**	**2**	**12**	**0**	**0**	**0**	**23**	**0.0**	**–5**	....	....	....	**15**	**1**	**9**	**10**	**17**	**1**	**0**	**0**	....
1984-85	**Montreal**	**NHL**	**74**	**9**	**55**	**64**	**87**	**2**	**1**	**0**	**199**	**4.5**	**11**	....	....	....	**9**	**2**	**8**	**10**	**17**	**2**	**0**	**0**	....
1985-86 ◆	**Montreal**	**NHL**	**41**	**8**	**26**	**34**	**67**	**2**	**0**	**0**	**101**	**7.9**	**4**	....	....	....	**20**	**2**	**9**	**11**	**49**	**1**	**0**	**0**	....
1986-87	**Montreal**	**NHL**	**71**	**11**	**33**	**44**	**124**	**6**	**0**	**2**	**141**	**7.8**	**–5**	....	....	....	**17**	**4**	**9**	**13**	**38**	**2**	**1**	**0**	....
1987-88	**Montreal**	**NHL**	**71**	**20**	**41**	**61**	**172**	**10**	**1**	**5**	**199**	**10.1**	**14**	....	....	....	**11**	**3**	**1**	**4**	**29**	**1**	**0**	**0**	....
1988-89	**Montreal**	**NHL**	**80**	**15**	**58**	**73**	**185**	**8**	**0**	**6**	**206**	**7.3**	**35**	....	....	....	**21**	**4**	**15**	**19**	**28**	**1**	**0**	**2**	....
1989-90	**Montreal**	**NHL**	**53**	**9**	**22**	**31**	**136**	**1**	**2**	**1**	**123**	**7.3**	**20**	....	....	....	**5**	**0**	**1**	**1**	**8**	**0**	**0**	**0**	....
1990-91	**Chicago**	**NHL**	**77**	**12**	**52**	**64**	**192**	**5**	**2**	**2**	**187**	**6.4**	**23**	....	....	....	**6**	**1**	**7**	**8**	**46**	**1**	**0**	**0**	....
1991-92	**Chicago**	**NHL**	**80**	**9**	**47**	**56**	**245**	**2**	**2**	**2**	**239**	**3.8**	**24**	....	....	....	**18**	**6**	**15**	**21**	**37**	**3**	**0**	**1**	....
1992-93	**Chicago**	**NHL**	**84**	**15**	**58**	**73**	**282**	**8**	**0**	**2**	**290**	**5.2**	**14**	....	....	....	**4**	**0**	**2**	**2**	**14**	**0**	**0**	**0**	....
1993-94	**Chicago**	**NHL**	**76**	**16**	**44**	**60**	**212**	**7**	**1**	**2**	**219**	**7.3**	**12**	....	....	....	**6**	**1**	**1**	**2**	**8**	**1**	**0**	**0**	....
1994-95	EHC Biel-Bienne	Swiss	3	0	3	3	4	....	....	....	....	....	....	....	....	....	....	....	....	....	....	....	....	....	....
	Chicago	**NHL**	**48**	**5**	**33**	**38**	**72**	**3**	**1**	**0**	**166**	**3.0**	**17**	....	....	....	**16**	**4**	**7**	**11**	**12**	**0**	**1**	**3**	....
1995-96	**Chicago**	**NHL**	**81**	**14**	**58**	**72**	**140**	**7**	**0**	**3**	**219**	**6.4**	**25**	....	....	....	**9**	**0**	**3**	**3**	**8**	**0**	**0**	**0**	....
1996-97	**Chicago**	**NHL**	**72**	**10**	**38**	**48**	**112**	**2**	**0**	**2**	**194**	**5.2**	**16**	....	....	....	**6**	**0**	**1**	**1**	**8**	**0**	**0**	**0**	....
1997-98	**Chicago**	**NHL**	**81**	**3**	**39**	**42**	**151**	**1**	**0**	**0**	**205**	**1.5**	**–7**	....	....	....	....	....	....	....	....	....	....	....	....
	United States	Olympics	4	2	0	2	2	....	....	....	....	....	....	....	....	....	....	....	....	....	....	....	....	....	....
1998-99	**Chicago**	**NHL**	**65**	**8**	**26**	**34**	**89**	**2**	**1**	**0**	**172**	**4.7**	**–4**	**4**	**25.0**	**27:19**	....	....	....	....	....	....	....	....	....
	Detroit	**NHL**	**10**	**1**	**1**	**2**	**4**	**1**	**0**	**1**	**15**	**6.7**	**5**	**0**	**0.0**	**22:21**	**10**	**0**	**4**	**4**	**14**	**0**	**0**	**0**	**27:15**
99-2000	**Detroit**	**NHL**	**81**	**3**	**31**	**34**	**103**	**0**	**0**	**0**	**135**	**2.2**	**48**	**0**	**0.0**	**25:16**	**9**	**0**	**1**	**1**	**8**	**0**	**0**	**0**	**24:06**
2000-01	**Detroit**	**NHL**	**24**	**0**	**3**	**3**	**45**	**0**	**0**	**0**	**26**	**0.0**	**4**	**0**	**0.0**	**22:51**	**5**	**1**	**0**	**1**	**2**	**0**	**0**	**0**	**19:41**
2001-02 ◆	**Detroit**	**NHL**	**79**	**6**	**33**	**39**	**126**	**1**	**0**	**1**	**128**	**4.7**	**40**	**0**	**0.0**	**25:18**	**23**	**1**	**13**	**14**	**44**	**1**	**0**	**0**	**26:22**
	United States	Olympics	6	1	0	1	4	....	....	....	....	....	....	....	....	....	....	....	....	....	....	....	....	....	....
2002-03	**Detroit**	**NHL**	**66**	**2**	**17**	**19**	**78**	**0**	**1**	**1**	**92**	**2.2**	**4**	**0**	**0.0**	**24:15**	**4**	**0**	**0**	**0**	**2**	**0**	**0**	**0**	**25:43**
2003-04	**Detroit**	**NHL**	**69**	**2**	**19**	**21**	**61**	**0**	**0**	**0**	**113**	**1.8**	**12**	**0**	**0.0**	**21:21**	**8**	**0**	**1**	**1**	**4**	**0**	**0**	**0**	**21:13**
2004-05	Motor City	UHL	23	5	19	24	25	....	....	....	....	....	....	....	....	....	....	....	....	....	....	....	....	....	....
2005-06	**Detroit**	**NHL**	**81**	**4**	**7**	**11**	**108**	**1**	**1**	**0**	**83**	**4.8**	**22**	**4**	**25.0**	**18:29**	**6**	**0**	**0**	**0**	**6**	**0**	**0**	**0**	**19:25**
	United States	Olympics	6	0	1	1	2	....	....	....	....	....	....	....	....	....	....	....	....	....	....	....	....	....	....
2006-07	**Detroit**	**NHL**	**71**	**0**	**11**	**11**	**34**	**0**	**0**	**0**	**72**	**0.0**	**11**	**1**	**0.0**	**18:08**	**18**	**1**	**6**	**7**	**12**	**0**	**1**	**0**	**20:07**
	NHL Totals		**1547**	**182**	**754**	**936**	**2837**	**69**	**13**	**30**	**3547**	**5.1**		**9**	**22.2**	**22:48**	**246**	**31**	**113**	**144**	**411**	**14**	**3**	**6**	**23:26**

WCHA Second All-Star Team (1983) • NCAA Championship All-Tournament Team (1983) • NHL All-Rookie Team (1985) • NHL First All-Star Team (1989, 1993, 1995, 1996, 2002) • James Norris Memorial Trophy (1989, 1993, 1996) • NHL Second All-Star Team (1991, 1997) • Bud Light Plus/Minus Award (2002)

Played in NHL All-Star Game (1985, 1990, 1991, 1992, 1993, 1994, 1996, 1997, 1998, 2000, 2002)

Traded to **Chicago** by **Montreal** with Montreal's 2nd round choice (Michael Pomichter) in 1991 Entry Draft for Denis Savard, June 29, 1990. Traded to **Detroit** by **Chicago** for Anders Eriksson and Detroit's 1st round choices in 1999 (Steve McCarthy) and 2001 (Adam Munro) Entry Drafts, March 23, 1999. • Missed majority of 2000-01 season recovering from knee injury suffered in game vs. Dallas, November 17, 2000. Signed as a free agent by **Motor City** (UHL), February 1, 2005.

CHIMERA, Jason
(chihm-AIR-a, JAY-suhn) **CBJ**

Left wing. Shoots left. 6'2", 206 lbs. Born, Edmonton, Alta., May 2, 1979. Edmonton's 5th choice, 121st overall, in 1997 Entry Draft.

			Regular Season														Playoffs								
Season	Club	League	GP	G	A	Pts	PIM	PP	SH	GW	S	%	+/-	TF	F%	Min	GP	G	A	Pts	PIM	PP	SH	GW	Min
1994-95	Edmonton Pats	AMHL	33	27	31	58	42	....	....	....	....	....	....	....	....	....	....	....	....	....	....	....	....	....	....
1995-96	Edmonton Pats	AMHL	34	23	24	47	44	....	....	....	....	....	....	....	....	....	....	....	....	....	....	....	....	....	....
1996-97	Medicine Hat	WHL	71	16	23	39	64	....	....	....	....	....	....	....	....	....	4	0	1	1	4	....	....	....	....
1997-98	Medicine Hat	WHL	72	34	32	66	93	....	....	....	....	....	....	....	....	....	....	....	....	....	....	....	....	....	....
	Hamilton	AHL	4	0	0	0	8	....	....	....	....	....	....	....	....	....	....	....	....	....	....	....	....	....	....
1998-99	Medicine Hat	WHL	37	18	22	40	84	....	....	....	....	....	....	....	....	....	....	....	....	....	....	....	....	....	....
	Brandon	WHL	21	14	12	26	32	....	....	....	....	....	....	....	....	....	5	4	1	5	8	....	....	....	....
99-2000	Hamilton	AHL	78	15	13	28	77	....	....	....	....	....	....	....	....	....	10	0	2	2	12	....	....	....	....
2000-01	**Edmonton**	**NHL**	**1**	**0**	**0**	**0**	**0**	**0**	**0**	**0**	**0**	**0.0**	**0**	**0**	**0.0**	**6:58**	....	....	....	....	....	....	....	....	....
	Hamilton	AHL	78	29	25	54	93	....	....	....	....	....	....	....	....	....	....	....	....	....	....	....	....	....	....
2001-02	**Edmonton**	**NHL**	**3**	**1**	**0**	**1**	**0**	**0**	**0**	**0**	**3**	**33.3**	**–3**	**0**	**0.0**	**12:44**	....	....	....	....	....	....	....	....	....
	Hamilton	AHL	77	26	51	77	158	....	....	....	....	....	....	....	....	....	15	4	6	10	10	....	....	....	....
2002-03	**Edmonton**	**NHL**	**66**	**14**	**9**	**23**	**36**	**0**	**1**	**4**	**90**	**15.6**	**–2**	**11**	**54.6**	**10:46**	**2**	**0**	**2**	**2**	**0**	**0**	**0**	**0**	**10:55**
2003-04	**Edmonton**	**NHL**	**60**	**4**	**8**	**12**	**57**	**0**	**0**	**1**	**79**	**5.1**	**–1**	**22**	**31.8**	**10:07**	....	....	....	....	....	....	....	....	....
2004-05	AS Varese Hockey	Italy	15	7	3	10	34	....	....	....	....	....	....	....	....	....	5	2	1	3	31	....	....	....	....
2005-06	**Columbus**	**NHL**	**80**	**17**	**13**	**30**	**95**	**1**	**1**	**5**	**127**	**13.4**	**–10**	**16**	**50.0**	**12:41**	....	....	....	....	....	....	....	....	....
2006-07	**Columbus**	**NHL**	**82**	**15**	**21**	**36**	**91**	**2**	**2**	**2**	**151**	**9.9**	**2**	**38**	**36.8**	**15:22**	....	....	....	....	....	....	....	....	....
	NHL Totals		**292**	**51**	**51**	**102**	**279**	**3**	**4**	**12**	**450**	**11.3**		**87**	**40.2**	**12:27**	**2**	**0**	**2**	**2**	**0**	**0**	**0**	**0**	**10:55**

AHL First All-Star Team (2002)

Traded to **Phoenix** by **Edmonton** with Edmonton's 3rd round choice (later traded to Carolina – later traded to NY Rangers – NY Rangers selected Billy Ryan) in 2004 Entry Draft for New Jersey's 2nd round choice (previously acquired, Edmonton selected Geoff Paukovich) in 2004 Entry Draft and Buffalo's 4th round choice (previously acquired, Edmonton selected Liam Reddox) in 2004 Entry Draft, June 26, 2004. Signed as a free agent by **Varese** (Italy), December 15, 2004. Traded to **Columbus** by **Phoenix** with Cale Hulse and Mike Rupp for Geoff Sanderson and Tim Jackman, October 8, 2005.

CHISTOV, Stanislav
(chihs-TAHV, STAN-ihs-lahv) **BOS.**

Left wing. Shoots right. 5'10", 200 lbs. Born, Chelyabinsk, USSR, April 17, 1983. Anaheim's 1st choice, 5th overall, in 2001 Entry Draft.

Season	Club	League	GP	G	A	Pts	PIM	PP	SH	GW	S	%	+/-	TF	F%	Min	GP	G	A	Pts	PIM	PP	SH	GW	Min
1998-99	Chelyabinsk 2	Russia-4	1	0	0	0	0	....	....	....	....	....	....	....	....	....	....	....	....	....	....	....	....	....	....
	Georgetown	OPJHL	14	10	7	17	21	....	....	....	....	....	....	....	....	....	....	....	....	....	....	....	....	....	....
99-2000	Omsk 2	Russia-3	5	4	3	7	8	....	....	....	....	....	....	....	....	....	....	....	....	....	....	....	....	....	....
	Omsk 2	Russia-3	18	12	4	16	24	....	....	....	....	....	....	....	....	....	....	....	....	....	....	....	....	....	....
	Novokuznetsk	Russia	9	7	4	11	18	....	....	....	....	....	....	....	....	....	....	....	....	....	....	....	....	....	....
	Avangard Omsk	Russia	3	1	0	1	2	....	....	....	....	....	....	....	....	....	....	....	....	....	....	....	....	....	....
2000-01	Omsk 2	Russia-3	8	5	4	9	2	....	....	....	....	....	....	....	....	....	....	....	....	....	....	....	....	....	....
	Avangard Omsk	Russia	24	4	8	12	12	....	....	....	....	....	....	....	....	....	5	0	0	0	2	....	....	....	....
2001-02	Avangard Omsk	Russia	9	0	0	0	4	....	....	....	....	....	....	....	....	....	....	....	....	....	....	....	....	....	....
	CSKA Moscow 2	Russia-3	1	1	2	3	0	....	....	....	....	....	....	....	....	....	....	....	....	....	....	....	....	....	....
2002-03	**Anaheim**	**NHL**	**79**	**12**	**18**	**30**	**54**	**3**	**0**	**2**	**114**	**10.5**	**4**	**3**	**0.0**	**13:35**	**21**	**4**	**2**	**6**	**8**	**0**	**0**	**1**	**13:22**
2003-04	**Anaheim**	**NHL**	**56**	**2**	**16**	**18**	**26**	**2**	**0**	**0**	**70**	**2.9**	**–16**	**4**	**0.0**	**12:20**	....	....	....	....	....	....	....	....	....
	Cincinnati	AHL	23	5	8	13	45	....	....	....	....	....	....	....	....	....	9	6	2	8	4	....	....	....	....
2004-05	Cincinnati	AHL	79	15	23	38	141	....	....	....	....	....	....	....	....	....	9	2	1	3	6	....	....	....	....
2005-06	Magnitogorsk	Russia	47	11	21	32	97	....	....	....	....	....	....	....	....	....	11	4	4	8	14	....	....	....	....
2006-07	**Anaheim**	**NHL**	**1**	**0**	**0**	**0**	**0**	**0**	**0**	**0**	**0**	**0.0**	**0**	**0**	**0.0**	**4:09**	....	....	....	....	....	....	....	....	....
	Portland Pirates	AHL	3	1	0	1	0	....	....	....	....	....	....	....	....	....	....	....	....	....	....	....	....	....	....
	Boston	**NHL**	**60**	**5**	**8**	**13**	**36**	**1**	**0**	**1**	**49**	**10.2**	**–8**	**34**	**29.4**	**8:35**	....	....	....	....	....	....	....	....	....
	NHL Totals		**196**	**19**	**42**	**61**	**116**	**6**	**0**	**3**	**233**	**8.2**		**41**	**24.4**	**11:39**	**21**	**4**	**2**	**6**	**8**	**0**	**0**	**1**	**13:22**

Traded to **Boston** by **Anaheim** for Phoenix's 3rd round choice (previously acquired, Anaheim selected Maxime Macenauer) in 2007 Entry Draft and future considerations, November 13, 2006. Signed as a free agent by **Ufa** (Russia), August 9, 2007.

CHOUINARD, Eric
(shwee-NAHR, AIR-ihk)

Left wing. Shoots left. 6'3", 215 lbs. Born, Atlanta, GA, July 8, 1980. Montreal's 1st choice, 16th overall, in 1998 Entry Draft.

Season	Club	League	GP	G	A	Pts	PIM	PP	SH	GW	S	%	+/-	TF	F%	Min	GP	G	A	Pts	PIM	PP	SH	GW	Min
1995-96	Magog	QAHA	22	12	14	26	12	....	....	....	....	....	....	....	....	....	....	....	....	....	....	....	....	....	....
	Ste-Foy	QAAA	17	2	5	7	....	....	....	....	....	....	....	....	....	....	15	7	12	19	12	....	....	....	....
1996-97	Ste-Foy	QAAA	40	29	41	70	40	....	....	....	....	....	....	....	....	....	10	14	9	23	....	....	....	....	....
1997-98	Quebec Remparts	QMJHL	68	41	42	83	18	....	....	....	....	....	....	....	....	....	14	7	10	17	6	....	....	....	....
1998-99	Quebec Remparts	QMJHL	62	50	59	109	56	....	....	....	....	....	....	....	....	....	13	8	10	18	8	....	....	....	....
	Fredericton	AHL	....	....	....	....	....	....	....	....	....	....	....	....	....	....	6	3	2	5	0	....	....	....	....
99-2000	Quebec Remparts	QMJHL	50	57	47	104	105	....	....	....	....	....	....	....	....	....	11	14	4	18	8	....	....	....	....
2000-01	**Montreal**	**NHL**	**13**	**1**	**3**	**4**	**0**	**1**	**0**	**0**	**11**	**9.1**	**0**	**31**	**54.8**	**10:59**	....	....	....	....	....	....	....	....	....
	Quebec Citadelles	AHL	48	12	21	33	6	....	....	....	....	....	....	....	....	....	9	2	0	2	2	....	....	....	....
2001-02	Quebec Citadelles	AHL	65	19	23	42	18	....	....	....	....	....	....	....	....	....	2	0	0	0	0	....	....	....	....
2002-03	Utah Grizzlies	AHL	32	12	12	24	16	....	....	....	....	....	....	....	....	....	....	....	....	....	....	....	....	....	....
	Philadelphia	**NHL**	**28**	**4**	**4**	**8**	**8**	**1**	**0**	**0**	**45**	**8.9**	**2**	**12**	**33.3**	**9:38**	....	....	....	....	....	....	....	....	....
2003-04	**Philadelphia**	**NHL**	**17**	**3**	**0**	**3**	**0**	**0**	**0**	**0**	**15**	**20.0**	**–3**	**24**	**50.0**	**7:59**	....	....	....	....	....	....	....	....	....
	Minnesota	**NHL**	**31**	**3**	**4**	**7**	**6**	**0**	**0**	**1**	**45**	**6.7**	**–7**	**261**	**44.8**	**13:36**	....	....	....	....	....	....	....	....	....
	Philadelphia	AHL	1	0	0	0	0	....	....	....	....	....	....	....	....	....	....	....	....	....	....	....	....	....	....
2004-05	Salzburg	Austria	16	5	5	10	42	....	....	....	....	....	....	....	....	....	....	....	....	....	....	....	....	....	....
2005-06	**Philadelphia**	**NHL**	**1**	**0**	**0**	**0**	**2**	**0**	**0**	**0**	**0**	**0.0**	**0**	**2**	**50.0**	**4:30**	....	....	....	....	....	....	....	....	....
	Philadelphia	AHL	24	7	7	14	4	....	....	....	....	....	....	....	....	....	....	....	....	....	....	....	....	....	....
	San Antonio	AHL	47	8	12	20	22	....	....	....	....	....	....	....	....	....	....	....	....	....	....	....	....	....	....
2006-07	Straubing Tigers	Germany	27	6	17	23	32	....	....	....	....	....	....	....	....	....	....	....	....	....	....	....	....	....	....
	NHL Totals		**90**	**11**	**11**	**22**	**16**	**2**	**0**	**1**	**116**	**9.5**		**330**	**45.8**	**10:49**	....	....	....	....	....	....	....	....	....

Traded to **Philadelphia** by **Montreal** for Philadelphia's 2nd round choice (Maxim Lapierre) in 2003 Entry Draft, January 29, 2003. Traded to **Minnesota** by **Philadelphia** for Minnesota's 5th round choice (Chris Zarb) in 2004 Entry Draft, December 17, 2003. Signed as a free agent by **Salzburg** (Austria), October 14, 2004. Signed as a free agent by **Philadelphia**, August 22, 2005. Traded to **Phoenix** by **Philadelphia** for Kiel McLeod, December 28, 2005. Signed as a free agent by **Yaroslavl** (Russia), August 5, 2006. Signed as a free agent by **Straubing** (Germany), December 1, 2006.

CHOUINARD, Marc
(shwee-NAHR, MAHRK)

Center. Shoots right. 6'5", 218 lbs. Born, Charlesbourg, Que., May 6, 1977. Winnipeg's 2nd choice, 32nd overall, in 1995 Entry Draft.

Season	Club	League	GP	G	A	Pts	PIM	PP	SH	GW	S	%	+/-	TF	F%	Min	GP	G	A	Pts	PIM	PP	SH	GW	Min
1992-93	Ste-Foy	QAAA	3	1	1	2	2	....	....	....	....	....	....	....	....	....	....	....	....	....	....	....	....	....	....
	Beauboury Selects	QAHA	28	26	45	71	42	....	....	....	....	....	....	....	....	....	....	....	....	....	....	....	....	....	....
1993-94	Beauport	QMJHL	62	11	19	30	23	....	....	....	....	....	....	....	....	....	13	2	5	7	2	....	....	....	....
1994-95	Beauport	QMJHL	68	24	40	64	32	....	....	....	....	....	....	....	....	....	18	1	6	7	4	....	....	....	....
1995-96	Beauport	QMJHL	30	14	21	35	19	....	....	....	....	....	....	....	....	....	....	....	....	....	....	....	....	....	....
	Halifax	QMJHL	24	6	12	18	17	....	....	....	....	....	....	....	....	....	6	2	1	3	2	....	....	....	....
1996-97	Halifax	QMJHL	63	24	49	73	74	....	....	....	....	....	....	....	....	....	18	9	16	25	12	....	....	....	....
1997-98	Cincinnati	AHL	8	1	2	3	4	....	....	....	....	....	....	....	....	....	....	....	....	....	....	....	....	....	....
1998-99	Cincinnati	AHL	69	7	8	15	20	....	....	....	....	....	....	....	....	....	3	0	0	0	4	....	....	....	....
99-2000	Cincinnati	AHL	70	17	16	33	29	....	....	....	....	....	....	....	....	....	....	....	....	....	....	....	....	....	....
2000-01	**Anaheim**	**NHL**	**44**	**3**	**4**	**7**	**12**	**0**	**0**	**1**	**26**	**11.5**	**–5**	**414**	**60.9**	**7:50**	....	....	....	....	....	....	....	....	....
	Cincinnati	AHL	32	10	9	19	4	....	....	....	....	....	....	....	....	....	....	....	....	....	....	....	....	....	....
2001-02	**Anaheim**	**NHL**	**45**	**4**	**5**	**9**	**10**	**0**	**0**	**0**	**40**	**10.0**	**2**	**581**	**54.9**	**10:36**	....	....	....	....	....	....	....	....	....
2002-03	**Anaheim**	**NHL**	**70**	**3**	**4**	**7**	**40**	**0**	**1**	**0**	**52**	**5.8**	**–9**	**662**	**54.5**	**9:25**	**15**	**1**	**0**	**1**	**0**	**0**	**0**	**0**	**7:16**
2003-04	**Minnesota**	**NHL**	**45**	**11**	**10**	**21**	**17**	**3**	**1**	**2**	**70**	**15.7**	**4**	**809**	**53.7**	**15:58**	....	....	....	....	....	....	....	....	....
2004-05	Frisk-Asker IF	Norway	16	9	8	17	26	....	....	....	....	....	....	....	....	....	3	5	2	7	29	....	....	....	....
2005-06	**Minnesota**	**NHL**	**74**	**14**	**16**	**30**	**34**	**6**	**2**	**3**	**112**	**12.5**	**1**	**1089**	**52.7**	**16:29**	....	....	....	....	....	....	....	....	....
2006-07	**Vancouver**	**NHL**	**42**	**2**	**2**	**4**	**10**	**1**	**0**	**0**	**15**	**13.3**	**–2**	**392**	**48.7**	**9:26**	....	....	....	....	....	....	....	....	....
	Manitoba Moose	AHL	13	3	1	4	5	....	....	....	....	....	....	....	....	....	4	0	0	0	4	....	....	....	....
	NHL Totals		**320**	**37**	**41**	**78**	**123**	**10**	**4**	**6**	**315**	**11.7**		**3947**	**54.0**	**11:55**	**15**	**1**	**0**	**1**	**0**	**0**	**0**	**0**	**7:16**

Traded to **Anaheim** by **Winnipeg** with Teemu Selanne and Winnipeg's 4th round choice (later traded to Toronto – later traded to Montreal – Montreal selected Kim Staal) in 1996 Entry Draft for Chad Kilger, Oleg Tverdovsky and Anaheim's 3rd round choice (Per-Anton Lundstrom) in 1996 Entry Draft, February 7, 1996. Signed as a free agent by **Minnesota**, July 28, 2003. Signed as a free agent by **Frisk-Asker** (Norway), January 1, 2005. Signed as a free agent by **Vancouver**, July 20, 2006.

CHRISTENSEN, Erik (KRIHS-tehn-suhn, AIR-ihk) PIT.

Center. Shoots left. 6'1", 208 lbs. Born, Edmonton, Alta., December 17, 1983. Pittsburgh's 3rd choice, 69th overall, in 2002 Entry Draft.

			Regular Season														Playoffs								
Season	Club	League	GP	G	A	Pts	PIM	PP	SH	GW	S	%	+/-	TF	F%	Min	GP	G	A	Pts	PIM	PP	SH	GW	Min
1998-99	Leduc Oil Kings	AMBHL	36	34	42	76	70	....	....	....	....	....	....	....	....	....	....	....	....	....	....	....	....	....	....
99-2000	Kamloops Blazers	WHL	66	9	5	14	41	....	....	....	....	....	....	....	....	....	4	0	0	0	2	....	....	....	....
2000-01	Kamloops Blazers	WHL	72	21	23	44	36	....	....	....	....	....	....	....	....	....	4	1	1	2	0	....	....	....	....
2001-02	Kamloops Blazers	WHL	70	22	36	58	68	....	....	....	....	....	....	....	....	....	4	0	0	0	4	....	....	....	....
2002-03	Kamloops Blazers	WHL	67	*54	54	*108	60	....	....	....	....	....	....	....	....	....	6	1	7	8	14	....	....	....	....
2003-04	Kamloops Blazers	WHL	29	10	14	24	40	....	....	....	....	....	....	....	....	....	....	....	....	....	....	....	....	....	....
	Brandon	WHL	34	17	21	38	20	....	....	....	....	....	....	....	....	....	11	8	4	12	8	....	....	....	....
2004-05	Wilkes-Barre	AHL	77	14	13	27	33	....	....	....	....	....	....	....	....	....	11	1	6	7	4	....	....	....	....
2005-06	**Pittsburgh**	**NHL**	**33**	**6**	**7**	**13**	**34**	**2**	**0**	**0**	**85**	**7.1**	**–3**	**381**	**53.0**	**14:17**	....	....	....	....	....	....	....	....	....
	Wilkes-Barre	AHL	48	24	22	46	50	....	....	....	....	....	....	....	....	....	11	2	2	4	2	....	....	....	....
2006-07	**Pittsburgh**	**NHL**	**61**	**18**	**15**	**33**	**26**	**6**	**0**	**1**	**133**	**13.5**	**–3**	**240**	**56.3**	**11:38**	**4**	**0**	**0**	**0**	**6**	**0**	**0**	**0**	**8:15**
	Wilkes-Barre	AHL	16	12	12	24	8	....	....	....	....	....	....	....	....	....	....	....	....	....	....	....	....	....	....
	NHL Totals		**94**	**24**	**22**	**46**	**60**	**8**	**0**	**1**	**218**	**11.0**		**621**	**54.3**	**12:34**	**4**	**0**	**0**	**0**	**6**	**0**	**0**	**0**	**8:15**

WHL West First All-Star Team (2003)

CHUBAROV, Artem (choo-BAH-rahf, AHR-tehm) VAN.

Center. Shoots left. 6'1", 205 lbs. Born, Gorky, USSR, December 13, 1979. Vancouver's 2nd choice, 31st overall, in 1998 Entry Draft.

			Regular Season														Playoffs								
Season	Club	League	GP	G	A	Pts	PIM	PP	SH	GW	S	%	+/-	TF	F%	Min	GP	G	A	Pts	PIM	PP	SH	GW	Min
1994-95	Nizh. Novgorod 2	CIS-2	60	20	30	50	20	....	....	....	....	....	....	....	....	....	....	....	....	....	....	....	....	....	....
1995-96	Niz. Novgorod Jr.	CIS-Jr.	60	22	25	47	20	....	....	....	....	....	....	....	....	....	....	....	....	....	....	....	....	....	....
1996-97	Nizhny Novgorod	Russia	15	1	1	2	8	....	....	....	....	....	....	....	....	....	....	....	....	....	....	....	....	....	....
1997-98	Dynamo Moscow	Russia	30	1	4	5	4	....	....	....	....	....	....	....	....	....	....	....	....	....	....	....	....	....	....
1998-99	Dynamo Moscow	Russia	34	8	2	10	10	....	....	....	....	....	....	....	....	....	12	0	0	0	4	....	....	....	....
99-2000	**Vancouver**	**NHL**	**49**	**1**	**8**	**9**	**10**	**0**	**0**	**1**	**53**	**1.9**	**–4**	**488**	**48.0**	**11:43**	....	....	....	....	....	....	....	....	....
	Syracuse Crunch	AHL	14	7	6	13	4	....	....	....	....	....	....	....	....	....	1	0	0	0	0	....	....	....	....
2000-01	**Vancouver**	**NHL**	**1**	**0**	**0**	**0**	**0**	**0**	**0**	**0**	**0**	**0.0**	**–1**	**17**	**52.9**	**15:08**	....	....	....	....	....	....	....	....	....
	Kansas City	IHL	10	7	4	11	12	....	....	....	....	....	....	....	....	....	....	....	....	....	....	....	....	....	....
2001-02	**Vancouver**	**NHL**	**51**	**5**	**5**	**10**	**10**	**0**	**0**	**3**	**73**	**6.8**	**–3**	**517**	**53.6**	**12:37**	**6**	**0**	**1**	**1**	**0**	**0**	**0**	**0**	**14:44**
	Manitoba Moose	AHL	19	7	12	19	4	....	....	....	....	....	....	....	....	....	....	....	....	....	....	....	....	....	....
2002-03	**Vancouver**	**NHL**	**62**	**7**	**13**	**20**	**6**	**1**	**0**	**1**	**78**	**9.0**	**4**	**862**	**50.8**	**14:21**	**14**	**0**	**2**	**2**	**4**	**0**	**0**	**0**	**14:56**
2003-04	**Vancouver**	**NHL**	**65**	**12**	**7**	**19**	**14**	**1**	**1**	**3**	**93**	**12.9**	**1**	**963**	**53.3**	**14:05**	**7**	**0**	**1**	**1**	**0**	**0**	**0**	**0**	**19:07**
2004-05	Dynamo Moscow	Russia	27	4	9	13	10	....	....	....	....	....	....	....	....	....	....	....	....	....	....	....	....	....	....
2005-06	Avangard Omsk	Russia	47	10	15	25	36	....	....	....	....	....	....	....	....	....	11	5	3	8	10	....	....	....	....
2006-07	Avangard Omsk	Russia	40	9	27	36	4	....	....	....	....	....	....	....	....	....	9	2	6	8	2	....	....	....	....
	NHL Totals		**228**	**25**	**33**	**58**	**40**	**2**	**1**	**8**	**297**	**8.4**		**2847**	**51.7**	**13:19**	**27**	**0**	**4**	**4**	**4**	**0**	**0**	**0**	**15:59**

• Missed majority of 2000-01 season recovering from shoulder injury suffered in game vs. Manitoba (IHL), November 15, 2000. Signed as a free agent by **Dynamo Moscow** (Russia), June 19, 2004. Signed as a free agent by **Omsk** (Russia), August 22, 2005.

CIBAK, Martin (TSEE-bak, MAHR-tihn)

Center. Shoots left. 6'1", 196 lbs. Born, Liptovsky Mikulas, Czech., May 17, 1980. Tampa Bay's 11th choice, 252nd overall, in 1998 Entry Draft.

			Regular Season														Playoffs								
Season	Club	League	GP	G	A	Pts	PIM	PP	SH	GW	S	%	+/-	TF	F%	Min	GP	G	A	Pts	PIM	PP	SH	GW	Min
1995-96	L. Mikulas Jr.	Slovak-Jr.	48	38	35	73	....	....	....	....	....	....	....	....	....	....	....	....	....	....	....	....	....	....	....
1996-97	L. Mikulas Jr.	Slovak-Jr.	45	22	18	40	....	....	....	....	....	....	....	....	....	....	....	....	....	....	....	....	....	....	....
1997-98	L. Mikulas Jr.	Slovak-Jr.	42	31	21	52	....	....	....	....	....	....	....	....	....	....	....	....	....	....	....	....	....	....	....
	L. Mikulas	Slovakia	28	1	3	4	10	....	....	....	....	....	....	....	....	....	....	....	....	....	....	....	....	....	....
1998-99	Medicine Hat	WHL	66	21	26	47	72	....	....	....	....	....	....	....	....	....	....	....	....	....	....	....	....	....	....
99-2000	Medicine Hat	WHL	58	16	29	45	77	....	....	....	....	....	....	....	....	....	....	....	....	....	....	....	....	....	....
2000-01	Detroit Vipers	IHL	79	10	28	38	88	....	....	....	....	....	....	....	....	....	....	....	....	....	....	....	....	....	....
2001-02	**Tampa Bay**	**NHL**	**26**	**1**	**5**	**6**	**8**	**0**	**0**	**0**	**22**	**4.5**	**–6**	**85**	**34.1**	**11:08**	....	....	....	....	....	....	....	....	....
	Springfield	AHL	52	5	9	14	44	....	....	....	....	....	....	....	....	....	....	....	....	....	....	....	....	....	....
2002-03	Springfield	AHL	62	5	15	20	78	....	....	....	....	....	....	....	....	....	6	1	2	3	4	....	....	....	....
2003-04◆	**Tampa Bay**	**NHL**	**63**	**2**	**7**	**9**	**30**	**0**	**0**	**0**	**44**	**4.5**	**–1**	**321**	**45.2**	**7:35**	**6**	**0**	**1**	**1**	**0**	**0**	**0**	**0**	**7:35**
	Hershey Bears	AHL	1	0	0	0	2	....	....	....	....	....	....	....	....	....	....	....	....	....	....	....	....	....	....
2004-05	L. Mikulas	Slovakia	4	0	0	0	6	....	....	....	....	....	....	....	....	....	....	....	....	....	....	....	....	....	....
	Plzen	CzRep	30	4	11	15	52	....	....	....	....	....	....	....	....	....	....	....	....	....	....	....	....	....	....
	HC Kosice	Slovakia	6	1	3	4	8	....	....	....	....	....	....	....	....	....	10	2	5	7	36	....	....	....	....
2005-06	**Tampa Bay**	**NHL**	**65**	**2**	**6**	**8**	**22**	**0**	**0**	**0**	**50**	**4.0**	**–9**	**175**	**32.6**	**6:36**	**5**	**0**	**0**	**0**	**0**	**0**	**0**	**0**	**3:56**
2006-07	Frolunda	Sweden	55	10	13	23	94	....	....	....	....	....	....	....	....	....	....	....	....	....	....	....	....	....	....
	NHL Totals		**154**	**5**	**18**	**23**	**60**	**0**	**0**	**0**	**116**	**4.3**		**581**	**39.8**	**7:46**	**11**	**0**	**1**	**1**	**0**	**0**	**0**	**0**	**5:56**

Signed as a free agent by **Liptovsky Mikulas** (Slovakia), September 17, 2004. Signed as a free agent by **Plzen** (CzRep), October 18, 2004. Signed as a free agent by **Kosice** (Slovakia), January 31, 2005. Signed as a free agent by **Frolunda** (Sweden), August 16, 2006.

CLARK, Brett (KLAHRK, BREHT) COL.

Defense. Shoots left. 6', 195 lbs. Born, Wapella, Sask., December 23, 1976. Montreal's 7th choice, 154th overall, in 1996 Entry Draft.

			Regular Season														Playoffs								
Season	Club	League	GP	G	A	Pts	PIM	PP	SH	GW	S	%	+/-	TF	F%	Min	GP	G	A	Pts	PIM	PP	SH	GW	Min
1994-95	Melville	SJHL	62	19	32	51	77	....	....	....	....	....	....	....	....	....	....	....	....	....	....	....	....	....	....
1995-96	U. of Maine	H-East	39	7	31	38	22	....	....	....	....	....	....	....	....	....	....	....	....	....	....	....	....	....	....
1996-97	Canada	Nat-Tm	57	6	21	27	52	....	....	....	....	....	....	....	....	....	....	....	....	....	....	....	....	....	....
1997-98	**Montreal**	**NHL**	**41**	**1**	**0**	**1**	**20**	**0**	**0**	**0**	**26**	**3.8**	**–3**	....	....	....	....	....	....	....	....	....	....	....	....
	Fredericton	AHL	20	0	6	6	6	....	....	....	....	....	....	....	....	....	4	0	1	1	17	....	....	....	....
1998-99	**Montreal**	**NHL**	**61**	**2**	**2**	**4**	**16**	**0**	**0**	**0**	**36**	**5.6**	**–3**	**0**	**0.0**	**13:11**	....	....	....	....	....	....	....	....	....
	Fredericton	AHL	3	1	0	1	0	....	....	....	....	....	....	....	....	....	....	....	....	....	....	....	....	....	....
99-2000	**Atlanta**	**NHL**	**14**	**0**	**1**	**1**	**4**	**0**	**0**	**0**	**13**	**0.0**	**–12**	**0**	**0.0**	**16:51**	....	....	....	....	....	....	....	....	....
	Orlando	IHL	63	9	17	26	31	....	....	....	....	....	....	....	....	....	6	0	1	1	0	....	....	....	....
2000-01	**Atlanta**	**NHL**	**28**	**1**	**2**	**3**	**14**	**0**	**0**	**0**	**35**	**2.9**	**–12**	**0**	**0.0**	**18:02**	....	....	....	....	....	....	....	....	....
	Orlando	IHL	43	2	9	11	32	....	....	....	....	....	....	....	....	....	15	1	6	7	2	....	....	....	....
2001-02	**Atlanta**	**NHL**	**2**	**0**	**0**	**0**	**0**	**0**	**0**	**0**	**0**	**0.0**	**–3**	**1**	**100.0**	**15:32**	....	....	....	....	....	....	....	....	....
	Chicago Wolves	AHL	42	3	17	20	18	....	....	....	....	....	....	....	....	....	....	....	....	....	....	....	....	....	....
	Hershey Bears	AHL	32	7	9	16	12	....	....	....	....	....	....	....	....	....	8	0	2	2	6	....	....	....	....
2002-03	Hershey Bears	AHL	80	8	27	35	26	....	....	....	....	....	....	....	....	....	5	0	4	4	4	....	....	....	....
2003-04	**Colorado**	**NHL**	**12**	**1**	**1**	**2**	**6**	**0**	**0**	**0**	**14**	**7.1**	**3**	**0**	**0.0**	**10:26**	....	....	....	....	....	....	....	....	....
	Hershey Bears	AHL	64	11	21	32	37	....	....	....	....	....	....	....	....	....	....	....	....	....	....	....	....	....	....
2004-05	Hershey Bears	AHL	67	7	37	44	54	....	....	....	....	....	....	....	....	....	....	....	....	....	....	....	....	....	....
2005-06	**Colorado**	**NHL**	**80**	**9**	**27**	**36**	**56**	**4**	**0**	**1**	**148**	**6.1**	**3**	**1**	**0.0**	**19:39**	**9**	**2**	**2**	**4**	**2**	**0**	**1**	**0**	**24:17**
2006-07	**Colorado**	**NHL**	**82**	**10**	**29**	**39**	**50**	**4**	**0**	**1**	**140**	**7.1**	**5**	**1**	**100.0**	**23:41**	....	....	....	....	....	....	....	....	....
	NHL Totals		**320**	**24**	**62**	**86**	**166**	**8**	**0**	**2**	**412**	**5.8**		**3**	**66.7**	**18:41**	**9**	**2**	**2**	**4**	**2**	**0**	**1**	**0**	**24:17**

Claimed by **Atlanta** from **Montreal** in Expansion Draft, June 25, 1999. Traded to **Colorado** by **Atlanta** for Frederic Cassivi, January 24, 2002.

CLARK, Chris (KLAHRK, KRIHS) WSH.

Right wing. Shoots right. 6', 196 lbs. Born, South Windsor, CT, March 8, 1976. Calgary's 3rd choice, 77th overall, in 1994 Entry Draft.

			Regular Season														Playoffs								
Season	Club	League	GP	G	A	Pts	PIM	PP	SH	GW	S	%	+/-	TF	F%	Min	GP	G	A	Pts	PIM	PP	SH	GW	Min
1990-91	South Windsor	High-CT	23	16	15	31	24	....	....	....	....	....	....	....	....	....	....	....	....	....	....	....	....	....	....
1991-92	Spring. Olympics	NEJHL	49	21	29	50	56	....	....	....	....	....	....	....	....	....	....	....	....	....	....	....	....	....	....
1992-93	Spring. Olympics	NEJHL	43	17	60	77	120	....	....	....	....	....	....	....	....	....	....	....	....	....	....	....	....	....	....
1993-94	Spring. Olympics	NEJHL	35	31	26	57	185	....	....	....	....	....	....	....	....	....	....	....	....	....	....	....	....	....	....
1994-95	Clarkson Knights	ECAC	32	12	11	23	92	....	....	....	....	....	....	....	....	....	....	....	....	....	....	....	....	....	....
1995-96	Clarkson Knights	ECAC	38	10	8	18	108	....	....	....	....	....	....	....	....	....	....	....	....	....	....	....	....	....	....
1996-97	Clarkson Knights	ECAC	37	23	25	48	*86	....	....	....	....	....	....	....	....	....	....	....	....	....	....	....	....	....	....
1997-98	Clarkson Knights	ECAC	35	18	21	39	*106	....	....	....	....	....	....	....	....	....	....	....	....	....	....	....	....	....	....
1998-99	Saint John Flames	AHL	73	13	27	40	123	....	....	....	....	....	....	....	....	....	7	2	4	6	15	....	....	....	....
99-2000	**Calgary**	**NHL**	**22**	**0**	**1**	**1**	**14**	**0**	**0**	**0**	**17**	**0.0**	**–3**	**0**	**0.0**	**9:02**	....	....	....	....	....	....	....	....	....
	Saint John Flames	AHL	48	16	17	33	134	....	....	....	....	....	....	....	....	....	....	....	....	....	....	....	....	....	....
2000-01	**Calgary**	**NHL**	**29**	**5**	**1**	**6**	**38**	**1**	**0**	**0**	**43**	**11.6**	**0**	**3**	**33.3**	**11:56**	....	....	....	....	....	....	....	....	....
	Saint John Flames	AHL	48	18	17	35	131	....	....	....	....	....	....	....	....	....	18	4	10	14	49	....	....	....	....
2001-02	**Calgary**	**NHL**	**64**	**10**	**7**	**17**	**79**	**2**	**1**	**4**	**109**	**9.2**	**–12**	**21**	**33.3**	**13:57**	....	....	....	....	....	....	....	....	....
2002-03	**Calgary**	**NHL**	**81**	**10**	**12**	**22**	**126**	**2**	**0**	**2**	**156**	**6.4**	**–11**	**40**	**32.5**	**14:24**	....	....	....	....	....	....	....	....	....
2003-04	**Calgary**	**NHL**	**82**	**10**	**15**	**25**	**106**	**4**	**0**	**2**	**137**	**7.3**	**–3**	**97**	**36.1**	**14:05**	**26**	**3**	**3**	**6**	**30**	**1**	**0**	**0**	**14:34**

			Regular Season														Playoffs								
Season	Club	League	GP	G	A	Pts	PIM	PP	SH	GW	S	%	+/-	TF	F%	Min	GP	G	A	Pts	PIM	PP	SH	GW	Min
2004-05	SC Bern	Swiss	3	0	0	0	6	....	....	....	....	....	....	....	....	....	....	....	....	....	....	....	....	....	....
	Storhamar	Norway	15	10	4	14	86	....	....	....	....	....	....	....	....	....	7	4	4	8	14	....	....	....	....
2005-06	**Washington**	**NHL**	**78**	**20**	**19**	**39**	**110**	**1**	**3**	**0**	**144**	**13.9**	**9**	**209**	**49.3**	**15:24**	....	....	....	....	....	....	....	....	....
2006-07	**Washington**	**NHL**	**74**	**30**	**24**	**54**	**66**	**9**	**4**	**2**	**164**	**18.3**	**–10**	**118**	**50.9**	**18:25**	....	....	....	....	....	....	....	....	....
	NHL Totals		**430**	**85**	**79**	**164**	**539**	**19**	**8**	**10**	**770**	**11.0**		**488**	**44.9**	**14:42**	**26**	**3**	**3**	**6**	**30**	**1**	**0**	**0**	**14:34**

ECAC Second All-Star Team (1998)

Signed as a free agent by **Bern** (Swiss), October 3, 2004. Signed as a free agent by **Storhamar** (Norway), December 29, 2004. Traded to **Washington** by **Calgary** with Calgary's 7th round choice (Andrew Glass) in 2007 Entry Draft for Washington's 7th round choice (Devin Didiomete) in 2006 Entry Draft and Washington's 6th round choice (later traded to Colorado - Colorado selected Jens Hellgren) in 2007 Entry Draft, August 4, 2005.

CLARKE, Noah
(KLAHRK, NOH-uh) **N.J.**

Left wing. Shoots left. 5'9", 190 lbs. Born, La Verne, CA, June 11, 1979. Los Angeles' 10th choice, 250th overall, in 1999 Entry Draft.

Season	Club	League	GP	G	A	Pts	PIM	PP	SH	GW	S	%	+/-	TF	F%	Min	GP	G	A	Pts	PIM	PP	SH	GW	Min
1996-97	Shat.-St. Mary's	High-MN	30	33	44	77	....	....	....	....	....	....	....	....	....	....	....	....	....	....	....	....	....	....	....
1997-98	Des Moines	USHL	54	19	30	49	29	....	....	....	....	....	....	....	....	....	12	2	9	11	23	....	....	....	....
1998-99	Des Moines	USHL	52	31	32	63	47	....	....	....	....	....	....	....	....	....	13	8	2	10	16	....	....	....	....
99-2000	Colorado College	WCHA	39	17	20	37	30	....	....	....	....	....	....	....	....	....	....	....	....	....	....	....	....	....	....
2000-01	Colorado College	WCHA	41	12	20	32	22	....	....	....	....	....	....	....	....	....	....	....	....	....	....	....	....	....	....
2001-02	Colorado College	WCHA	42	13	24	37	32	....	....	....	....	....	....	....	....	....	....	....	....	....	....	....	....	....	....
2002-03	Colorado College	WCHA	42	21	*49	70	15	....	....	....	....	....	....	....	....	....	....	....	....	....	....	....	....	....	....
	Manchester	AHL	3	1	1	2	0	....	....	....	....	....	....	....	....	....	....	....	....	....	....	....	....	....	....
2003-04	**Los Angeles**	**NHL**	**2**	**0**	**1**	**1**	**0**	**0**	**0**	**0**	**3**	**0.0**	**1**	**0**	**0.0**	**9:39**	....	....	....	....	....	....	....	....	....
	Manchester	AHL	71	25	26	51	24	....	....	....	....	....	....	....	....	....	6	3	1	4	4	....	....	....	....
2004-05	Manchester	AHL	61	21	24	45	24	....	....	....	....	....	....	....	....	....	6	1	0	1	4	....	....	....	....
2005-06	**Los Angeles**	**NHL**	**5**	**0**	**0**	**0**	**0**	**0**	**0**	**0**	**3**	**0.0**	**0**	**3**	**33.3**	**7:23**	....	....	....	....	....	....	....	....	....
	Manchester	AHL	69	14	30	44	33	....	....	....	....	....	....	....	....	....	7	4	4	8	2	....	....	....	....
2006-07	**Los Angeles**	**NHL**	**13**	**2**	**0**	**2**	**4**	**0**	**1**	**0**	**11**	**18.2**	**–6**	**43**	**39.5**	**8:36**	....	....	....	....	....	....	....	....	....
	Manchester	AHL	63	24	33	57	27	....	....	....	....	....	....	....	....	....	16	1	3	4	4	....	....	....	....
	NHL Totals		**20**	**2**	**1**	**3**	**4**	**0**	**1**	**0**	**17**	**11.8**		**46**	**39.1**	**8:24**	....	....	....	....	....	....	....	....	....

USHL All-Rookie Team (1998) • USHL First All-Star Team (1999) • Curt Hammer Award (Most Gentlemanly Player - USHL) (1999) • WCHA All-Rookie Team (2000) • WCHA Second All-Star Team (2003) • NCAA West First All-American Team (2003) • AHL All-Rookie Team (2004)

Signed as a free agent by **New Jersey**, July 24, 2007.

CLARKSON, David
(KLAHRK-suhn, DAYV-ihd) **N.J.**

Right wing. Shoots right. 6'1", 205 lbs. Born, Toronto, Ont., March 31, 1984.

Season	Club	League	GP	G	A	Pts	PIM	PP	SH	GW	S	%	+/-	TF	F%	Min	GP	G	A	Pts	PIM	PP	SH	GW	Min
2001-02	Belleville Bulls	OHL	22	2	7	9	34	....	....	....	....	....	....	....	....	....	8	1	1	2	6	....	....	....	....
2002-03	Belleville Bulls	OHL	3	0	0	0	11	....	....	....	....	....	....	....	....	....	....	....	....	....	....	....	....	....	....
	Kitchener Rangers	OHL	54	17	11	28	122	....	....	....	....	....	....	....	....	....	21	4	3	7	23	....	....	....	....
2003-04	Kitchener Rangers	OHL	55	22	17	39	173	....	....	....	....	....	....	....	....	....	....	....	....	....	....	....	....	....	....
2004-05	Kitchener Rangers	OHL	51	33	21	54	145	....	....	....	....	....	....	....	....	....	15	6	2	8	40	....	....	....	....
2005-06	Albany River Rats	AHL	56	13	21	34	233	....	....	....	....	....	....	....	....	....	....	....	....	....	....	....	....	....	....
2006-07	**New Jersey**	**NHL**	**7**	**3**	**1**	**4**	**6**	**2**	**0**	**1**	**18**	**16.7**	**–1**	**1**	**0.0**	**17:02**	**3**	**0**	**0**	**0**	**2**	**0**	**0**	**0**	**6:42**
	Lowell Devils	AHL	67	20	18	38	150	....	....	....	....	....	....	....	....	....	....	....	....	....	....	....	....	....	....
	NHL Totals		**7**	**3**	**1**	**4**	**6**	**2**	**0**	**1**	**18**	**16.7**		**1**	**0.0**	**17:02**	**3**	**0**	**0**	**0**	**2**	**0**	**0**	**0**	**6:42**

Signed as a free agent by **New Jersey**, August 12, 2005.

CLASSEN, Greg
(KLAW-sehn, GREHG) **VAN.**

Center. Shoots left. 6'1", 200 lbs. Born, Aylsham, Sask., August 24, 1977.

Season	Club	League	GP	G	A	Pts	PIM	PP	SH	GW	S	%	+/-	TF	F%	Min	GP	G	A	Pts	PIM	PP	SH	GW	Min
1997-98	Nipawin Hawks	SJHL	59	32	50	82	50	....	....	....	....	....	....	....	....	....	14	8	13	21	6	....	....	....	....
1998-99	Merrimack	H-East	36	14	11	25	28	....	....	....	....	....	....	....	....	....	....	....	....	....	....	....	....	....	....
99-2000	Merrimack	H-East	36	14	16	30	16	....	....	....	....	....	....	....	....	....	....	....	....	....	....	....	....	....	....
	Milwaukee	IHL	11	1	0	1	2	....	....	....	....	....	....	....	....	....	2	0	0	0	2	....	....	....	....
2000-01	**Nashville**	**NHL**	**27**	**2**	**4**	**6**	**14**	**1**	**0**	**0**	**18**	**11.1**	**–4**	**195**	**42.1**	**10:16**	....	....	....	....	....	....	....	....	....
	Milwaukee	IHL	23	5	10	15	31	....	....	....	....	....	....	....	....	....	5	0	0	0	0	....	....	....	....
2001-02	**Nashville**	**NHL**	**55**	**5**	**6**	**11**	**30**	**0**	**1**	**0**	**32**	**15.6**	**1**	**389**	**43.2**	**10:09**	....	....	....	....	....	....	....	....	....
	Milwaukee	AHL	8	2	4	6	12	....	....	....	....	....	....	....	....	....	....	....	....	....	....	....	....	....	....
2002-03	**Nashville**	**NHL**	**8**	**0**	**0**	**0**	**4**	**0**	**0**	**0**	**2**	**0.0**	**–3**	**65**	**52.3**	**10:02**	....	....	....	....	....	....	....	....	....
	Milwaukee	AHL	72	20	28	48	61	....	....	....	....	....	....	....	....	....	6	1	1	2	4	....	....	....	....
2003-04	Milwaukee	AHL	68	18	29	47	95	....	....	....	....	....	....	....	....	....	20	4	3	7	12	....	....	....	....
2004-05	Assat Pori	Finland	42	8	10	18	74	....	....	....	....	....	....	....	....	....	2	0	0	0	0	....	....	....	....
2005-06	Milwaukee	AHL	76	24	26	50	67	....	....	....	....	....	....	....	....	....	21	1	15	16	18	....	....	....	....
2006-07	Hamburg Freezers	Germany	50	9	26	35	70	....	....	....	....	....	....	....	....	....	7	1	0	1	14	....	....	....	....
	NHL Totals		**90**	**7**	**10**	**17**	**48**	**1**	**1**	**0**	**52**	**13.5**		**649**	**43.8**	**10:10**	....	....	....	....	....	....	....	....	....

Hockey East All-Rookie Team (1999)

Signed as a free agent by **Nashville**, March 27, 2000. Signed as a free agent by **Pori** (Finland), July 25, 2004. Signed as a free agent by **Hamburg** (Germany), August 2, 2006. Signed as a free agent by **Vancouver**, July 3, 2007.

CLEARY, Daniel
(KLIH-ree, DAN-yehl) **DET.**

Right wing. Shoots left. 6', 210 lbs. Born, Carbonear, Nfld., December 18, 1978. Chicago's 1st choice, 13th overall, in 1997 Entry Draft.

Season	Club	League	GP	G	A	Pts	PIM	PP	SH	GW	S	%	+/-	TF	F%	Min	GP	G	A	Pts	PIM	PP	SH	GW	Min
1993-94	Kingston	MTJHL	41	18	28	46	33	....	....	....	....	....	....	....	....	....	2	0	1	1	0	....	....	....	....
1994-95	Belleville Bulls	OHL	62	26	55	81	62	....	....	....	....	....	....	....	....	....	16	7	10	17	23	....	....	....	....
1995-96	Belleville Bulls	OHL	64	53	62	115	74	....	....	....	....	....	....	....	....	....	14	10	17	27	40	....	....	....	....
1996-97	Belleville Bulls	OHL	64	32	48	80	88	....	....	....	....	....	....	....	....	....	6	3	4	7	6	....	....	....	....
1997-98	**Chicago**	**NHL**	**6**	**0**	**0**	**0**	**0**	**0**	**0**	**0**	**4**	**0.0**	**–2**	....	....	....	....	....	....	....	....	....	....	....	....
	Belleville Bulls	OHL	30	16	31	47	14	....	....	....	....	....	....	....	....	....	10	6	*17	*23	10	....	....	....	....
	Indianapolis Ice	IHL	4	2	1	3	6	....	....	....	....	....	....	....	....	....	....	....	....	....	....	....	....	....	....
1998-99	**Chicago**	**NHL**	**35**	**4**	**5**	**9**	**24**	**0**	**0**	**0**	**49**	**8.2**	**–1**	**13**	**46.2**	**14:21**	....	....	....	....	....	....	....	....	....
	Portland Pirates	AHL	30	9	17	26	74	....	....	....	....	....	....	....	....	....	....	....	....	....	....	....	....	....	....
	Hamilton	AHL	9	0	1	1	7	....	....	....	....	....	....	....	....	....	3	0	0	0	0	....	....	....	....
99-2000	**Edmonton**	**NHL**	**17**	**3**	**2**	**5**	**8**	**0**	**0**	**1**	**18**	**16.7**	**–1**	**1**	**100.0**	**9:44**	**4**	**0**	**1**	**1**	**2**	**0**	**0**	**0**	**8:40**
	Hamilton	AHL	58	22	52	74	108	....	....	....	....	....	....	....	....	....	5	2	3	5	18	....	....	....	....
2000-01	**Edmonton**	**NHL**	**81**	**14**	**21**	**35**	**37**	**2**	**0**	**2**	**107**	**13.1**	**5**	**13**	**23.1**	**12:58**	**6**	**1**	**1**	**2**	**8**	**1**	**0**	**0**	**14:09**
2001-02	**Edmonton**	**NHL**	**65**	**10**	**19**	**29**	**51**	**2**	**1**	**1**	**75**	**13.3**	**–1**	**5**	**60.0**	**12:43**	....	....	....	....	....	....	....	....	....
2002-03	**Edmonton**	**NHL**	**57**	**4**	**13**	**17**	**31**	**0**	**0**	**1**	**89**	**4.5**	**5**	**5**	**40.0**	**11:58**	....	....	....	....	....	....	....	....	....
2003-04	**Phoenix**	**NHL**	**68**	**6**	**11**	**17**	**42**	**0**	**3**	**0**	**83**	**7.2**	**–8**	**51**	**39.2**	**13:12**	....	....	....	....	....	....	....	....	....
2004-05	Mora IK	Sweden	47	11	26	37	138	....	....	....	....	....	....	....	....	....	....	....	....	....	....	....	....	....	....
2005-06	**Detroit**	**NHL**	**77**	**3**	**12**	**15**	**40**	**0**	**0**	**1**	**106**	**2.8**	**5**	**286**	**45.8**	**10:30**	**6**	**0**	**1**	**1**	**6**	**0**	**0**	**0**	**10:44**
2006-07	**Detroit**	**NHL**	**71**	**20**	**20**	**40**	**24**	**6**	**2**	**5**	**135**	**14.8**	**6**	**411**	**51.1**	**15:28**	**18**	**4**	**8**	**12**	**30**	**1**	**2**	**0**	**16:28**
	NHL Totals		**477**	**64**	**103**	**167**	**257**	**10**	**6**	**11**	**666**	**9.6**		**785**	**47.9**	**12:48**	**34**	**5**	**11**	**16**	**46**	**2**	**2**	**0**	**14:08**

OHL All-Rookie Team (1995) • OHL First All-Star Team (1996, 1997) • AHL Second All-Star Team (2000)

Traded to **Edmonton** by **Chicago** with Chad Kilger, Ethan Moreau and Christian Laflamme for Boris Mironov, Dean McAmmond and Jonas Elofsson, March 20, 1999. Signed as a free agent by **Phoenix**, July 15, 2003. Signed as a free agent by **Mora** (Sweden), September 6, 2004. Signed as a free agent by **Detroit**, October 4, 2005.

CLOWE, Ryane
(KLOH, RIGH-uhn) **S.J.**

Right wing. Shoots right. 6'2", 225 lbs. Born, St. John's, Nfld., September 30, 1982. San Jose's 5th choice, 175th overall, in 2001 Entry Draft.

Season	Club	League	GP	G	A	Pts	PIM	PP	SH	GW	S	%	+/-	TF	F%	Min	GP	G	A	Pts	PIM	PP	SH	GW	Min
2000-01	Rimouski Oceanic	QMJHL	32	15	10	25	43	....	....	....	....	....	....	....	....	....	11	8	1	9	12	....	....	....	....
2001-02	Rimouski Oceanic	QMJHL	53	28	45	73	120	....	....	....	....	....	....	....	....	....	7	1	6	7	2	....	....	....	....
2002-03	Rimouski Oceanic	QMJHL	17	8	19	27	44	....	....	....	....	....	....	....	....	....	....	....	....	....	....	....	....	....	....
	Montreal Rocket	QMJHL	43	18	30	48	60	....	....	....	....	....	....	....	....	....	7	3	7	10	6	....	....	....	....
2003-04	Cleveland Barons	AHL	72	11	29	40	97	....	....	....	....	....	....	....	....	....	8	3	1	4	9	....	....	....	....
2004-05	Cleveland Barons	AHL	74	27	35	62	101	....	....	....	....	....	....	....	....	....	....	....	....	....	....	....	....	....	....

			Regular Season														Playoffs								
Season	Club	League	GP	G	A	Pts	PIM	PP	SH	GW	S	%	+/-	TF	F%	Min	GP	G	A	Pts	PIM	PP	SH	GW	Min
2005-06	**San Jose**	**NHL**	**18**	**0**	**2**	**2**	**9**	**0**	**0**	**0**	**14**	**0.0**	**–2**	**2**	**0.0**	**9:40**	**1**	**0**	**0**	**0**	**0**	**0**	**0**	**0**	**5:06**
	Cleveland Barons	AHL	35	13	21	34	35	....	....	....	....	....	....	....	....	....	....	....	....	....	....	....	....	....	....
2006-07	**San Jose**	**NHL**	**58**	**16**	**18**	**34**	**78**	**4**	**0**	**3**	**93**	**17.2**	**4**	**5**	**60.0**	**13:11**	**11**	**4**	**2**	**6**	**17**	**0**	**0**	**1**	**15:19**
	NHL Totals		**76**	**16**	**20**	**36**	**87**	**4**	**0**	**3**	**107**	**15.0**		**7**	**42.9**	**12:21**	**12**	**4**	**2**	**6**	**17**	**0**	**0**	**1**	**14:28**

CLYMER, Ben

(KLIH-mehr, BEHN) **WSH.**

Right wing. Shoots right. 6'1", 200 lbs. Born, Bloomington, MN, April 11, 1978. Boston's 3rd choice, 27th overall, in 1997 Entry Draft.

Season	Club	League	GP	G	A	Pts	PIM	PP	SH	GW	S	%	+/-	TF	F%	Min	GP	G	A	Pts	PIM	PP	SH	GW	Min
1993-94	Jefferson Jaguars	High-MN	23	3	7	10	20	....	....	....	....	....	....	....	....	....	....	....	....	....	....	....	....	....	....
1994-95	Jefferson Jaguars	High-MN	28	11	22	33	36	....	....	....	....	....	....	....	....	....	....	....	....	....	....	....	....	....	....
1995-96	Jefferson Jaguars	High-MN	18	12	34	46	34	....	....	....	....	....	....	....	....	....	5	0	6	6	6	....	....	....	....
1996-97	U. of Minnesota	WCHA	29	7	13	20	64	....	....	....	....	....	....	....	....	....	....	....	....	....	....	....	....	....	....
1997-98	U. of Minnesota	WCHA	1	0	0	0	2	....	....	....	....	....	....	....	....	....	....	....	....	....	....	....	....	....	....
1998-99	Seattle	WHL	70	12	44	56	93	....	....	....	....	....	....	....	....	....	11	1	5	6	12	....	....	....	....
99-2000	**Tampa Bay**	**NHL**	**60**	**2**	**6**	**8**	**87**	**2**	**0**	**0**	**98**	**2.0**	**–26**	**3**	**66.7**	**19:37**	....	....	....	....	....	....	....	....	....
	Detroit Vipers	IHL	19	1	9	10	30	....	....	....	....	....	....	....	....	....	....	....	....	....	....	....	....	....	....
2000-01	**Tampa Bay**	**NHL**	**23**	**5**	**1**	**6**	**21**	**3**	**0**	**0**	**25**	**20.0**	**–7**	**8**	**25.0**	**13:03**	....	....	....	....	....	....	....	....	....
	Detroit Vipers	IHL	53	5	8	13	88	....	....	....	....	....	....	....	....	....	....	....	....	....	....	....	....	....	....
2001-02	**Tampa Bay**	**NHL**	**81**	**14**	**20**	**34**	**36**	**4**	**0**	**2**	**151**	**9.3**	**–10**	**14**	**28.6**	**17:26**	....	....	....	....	....	....	....	....	....
2002-03	**Tampa Bay**	**NHL**	**65**	**6**	**12**	**18**	**57**	**1**	**0**	**1**	**103**	**5.8**	**–2**	**15**	**0.0**	**13:39**	**11**	**0**	**2**	**2**	**6**	**0**	**0**	**0**	**13:30**
2003-04♦	**Tampa Bay**	**NHL**	**66**	**2**	**8**	**10**	**50**	**0**	**0**	**0**	**96**	**2.1**	**5**	**25**	**28.0**	**9:48**	**5**	**0**	**0**	**0**	**0**	**0**	**0**	**0**	**7:46**
2004-05	EHC Biel-Bienne	Swiss-2	19	11	12	23	30	....	....	....	....	....	....	....	....	....	11	6	11	17	24	....	....	....	....
2005-06	**Washington**	**NHL**	**77**	**16**	**17**	**33**	**72**	**3**	**0**	**3**	**149**	**10.7**	**–7**	**11**	**45.5**	**14:10**	....	....	....	....	....	....	....	....	....
2006-07	**Washington**	**NHL**	**66**	**7**	**13**	**20**	**44**	**0**	**0**	**0**	**78**	**9.0**	**–17**	**7**	**14.3**	**13:57**	....	....	....	....	....	....	....	....	....
	NHL Totals		**438**	**52**	**77**	**129**	**367**	**13**	**0**	**6**	**700**	**7.4**		**83**	**25.3**	**14:41**	**16**	**0**	**2**	**2**	**6**	**0**	**0**	**0**	**11:42**

• Missed majority of 1997-98 season recovering from shoulder injury suffered in game vs. University of Michigan (CCHA), October 10, 1997. Signed as a free agent by **Tampa Bay**, October 2, 1999. Signed as a free agent by **Biel-Bienne** (Swiss-2), December 2, 2004. Signed as a free agent by **Washington**, August 8, 2005.

COBURN, Braydon

(KOH-buhrn, BRAY-duhn) **PHI.**

Defense. Shoots left. 6'5", 220 lbs. Born, Calgary, Alta., February 27, 1985. Atlanta's 1st choice, 8th overall, in 2003 Entry Draft.

Season	Club	League	GP	G	A	Pts	PIM	PP	SH	GW	S	%	+/-	TF	F%	Min	GP	G	A	Pts	PIM	PP	SH	GW	Min
2000-01	Notre Dame	SMHL	32	3	19	22	70	....	....	....	....	....	....	....	....	....	....	....	....	....	....	....	....	....	....
	Portland	WHL	2	0	1	1	0	....	....	....	....	....	....	....	....	....	14	0	4	4	2	....	....	....	....
2001-02	Portland	WHL	68	4	33	37	100	....	....	....	....	....	....	....	....	....	7	1	1	2	9	....	....	....	....
2002-03	Portland	WHL	53	3	16	19	147	....	....	....	....	....	....	....	....	....	7	0	1	1	8	....	....	....	....
2003-04	Portland	WHL	55	10	20	30	92	....	....	....	....	....	....	....	....	....	5	0	1	1	10	....	....	....	....
2004-05	Portland	WHL	60	12	32	44	144	....	....	....	....	....	....	....	....	....	7	1	5	6	6	....	....	....	....
	Chicago Wolves	AHL	3	0	1	1	5	....	....	....	....	....	....	....	....	....	18	0	1	1	36	....	....	....	....
2005-06	**Atlanta**	**NHL**	**9**	**0**	**1**	**1**	**4**	**0**	**0**	**0**	**4**	**0.0**	**–2**	**0**	**0.0**	**7:43**	....	....	....	....	....	....	....	....	....
	Chicago Wolves	AHL	73	6	20	26	134	....	....	....	....	....	....	....	....	....	....	....	....	....	....	....	....	....	....
2006-07	**Atlanta**	**NHL**	**29**	**0**	**4**	**4**	**30**	**0**	**0**	**0**	**21**	**0.0**	**1**	**0**	**0.0**	**11:41**	....	....	....	....	....	....	....	....	....
	Chicago Wolves	AHL	15	1	10	11	36	....	....	....	....	....	....	....	....	....	....	....	....	....	....	....	....	....	....
	Philadelphia	**NHL**	**20**	**3**	**4**	**7**	**16**	**1**	**0**	**0**	**33**	**9.1**	**–2**	**0**	**0.0**	**20:58**	....	....	....	....	....	....	....	....	....
	NHL Totals		**58**	**3**	**9**	**12**	**50**	**1**	**0**	**0**	**58**	**5.2**		**0**	**0.0**	**14:16**	....	....	....	....	....	....	....	....	....

WHL Rookie of the Year (2002) • WHL West First All-Star Team (2004, 2005)

Traded to **Philadelphia** by **Atlanta** for Alexei Zhitnik, February 24, 2007.

COLAIACOVO, Carlo

(koh-lee-A-KOH-voh, KAHR-loh) **TOR.**

Defense. Shoots left. 6'1", 200 lbs. Born, Toronto, Ont., January 27, 1983. Toronto's 1st choice, 17th overall, in 2001 Entry Draft.

Season	Club	League	GP	G	A	Pts	PIM	PP	SH	GW	S	%	+/-	TF	F%	Min	GP	G	A	Pts	PIM	PP	SH	GW	Min
1998-99	Mississauga Reps	GTHL	44	10	12	23	28	....	....	....	....	....	....	....	....	....	....	....	....	....	....	....	....	....	....
99-2000	Erie Otters	OHL	52	4	18	22	12	....	....	....	....	....	....	....	....	....	13	2	4	6	9	....	....	....	....
2000-01	Erie Otters	OHL	62	12	27	39	59	....	....	....	....	....	....	....	....	....	14	4	7	11	16	....	....	....	....
2001-02	Erie Otters	OHL	60	13	27	40	49	....	....	....	....	....	....	....	....	....	21	7	10	17	20	....	....	....	....
2002-03	**Toronto**	**NHL**	**2**	**0**	**1**	**1**	**0**	**0**	**0**	**0**	**1**	**0.0**	**0**	**0**	**0.0**	**13:43**	....	....	....	....	....	....	....	....	....
	Erie Otters	OHL	35	14	21	35	12	....	....	....	....	....	....	....	....	....	....	....	....	....	....	....	....	....	....
2003-04	**Toronto**	**NHL**	**2**	**0**	**1**	**1**	**2**	**0**	**0**	**0**	**0**	**0.0**	**1**	**0**	**0.0**	**13:56**	....	....	....	....	....	....	....	....	....
	St. John's	AHL	62	6	25	31	50	....	....	....	....	....	....	....	....	....	....	....	....	....	....	....	....	....	....
2004-05	St. John's	AHL	49	4	20	24	59	....	....	....	....	....	....	....	....	....	5	0	1	1	2	....	....	....	....
2005-06	**Toronto**	**NHL**	**21**	**2**	**5**	**7**	**17**	**1**	**0**	**0**	**21**	**9.5**	**0**	**1**	**0.0**	**15:26**	....	....	....	....	....	....	....	....	....
	Toronto Marlies	AHL	14	5	6	11	14	....	....	....	....	....	....	....	....	....	....	....	....	....	....	....	....	....	....
2006-07	**Toronto**	**NHL**	**48**	**8**	**9**	**17**	**22**	**0**	**0**	**1**	**60**	**13.3**	**5**	**0**	**0.0**	**17:57**	....	....	....	....	....	....	....	....	....
	Toronto Marlies	AHL	5	1	5	6	4	....	....	....	....	....	....	....	....	....	....	....	....	....	....	....	....	....	....
	NHL Totals		**73**	**10**	**16**	**26**	**41**	**1**	**0**	**1**	**82**	**12.2**		**1**	**0.0**	**17:00**	....	....	....	....	....	....	....	....	....

OHL Second All-Star Team (2002, 2003)

• Missed remainder of 2005-06 season recovering from head injury suffered in game at Ottawa, January 23, 2006.

COLE, Erik

(KOHL, AIR-ihk) **CAR.**

Left wing. Shoots left. 6'2", 205 lbs. Born, Oswego, NY, November 6, 1978. Carolina's 3rd choice, 71st overall, in 1998 Entry Draft.

Season	Club	League	GP	G	A	Pts	PIM	PP	SH	GW	S	%	+/-	TF	F%	Min	GP	G	A	Pts	PIM	PP	SH	GW	Min
1995-96	Oswego	High-NY	40	49	41	90	....	....	....	....	....	....	....	....	....	....	....	....	....	....	....	....	....	....	....
1996-97	Des Moines	USHL	48	30	34	64	140	....	....	....	....	....	....	....	....	....	5	2	0	2	6	....	....	....	....
1997-98	Clarkson Knights	ECAC	34	11	20	31	55	....	....	....	....	....	....	....	....	....	....	....	....	....	....	....	....	....	....
1998-99	Clarkson Knights	ECAC	36	*22	20	42	50	....	....	....	....	....	....	....	....	....	....	....	....	....	....	....	....	....	....
99-2000	Clarkson Knights	ECAC	33	19	11	30	46	....	....	....	....	....	....	....	....	....	....	....	....	....	....	....	....	....	....
	Cincinnati	IHL	9	4	3	7	2	....	....	....	....	....	....	....	....	....	7	1	1	2	2	....	....	....	....
2000-01	Cincinnati	IHL	69	23	20	43	28	....	....	....	....	....	....	....	....	....	5	1	0	1	2	....	....	....	....
2001-02	**Carolina**	**NHL**	**81**	**16**	**24**	**40**	**35**	**3**	**0**	**2**	**159**	**10.1**	**–10**	**17**	**47.1**	**16:04**	**23**	**6**	**3**	**9**	**30**	**1**	**0**	**1**	**18:27**
2002-03	**Carolina**	**NHL**	**53**	**14**	**13**	**27**	**72**	**6**	**2**	**3**	**125**	**11.2**	**1**	**56**	**39.3**	**17:08**	....	....	....	....	....	....	....	....	....
2003-04	**Carolina**	**NHL**	**80**	**18**	**24**	**42**	**93**	**2**	**2**	**3**	**172**	**10.5**	**–4**	**15**	**46.7**	**18:06**	....	....	....	....	....	....	....	....	....
2004-05	Eisbaren Berlin	Germany	39	6	21	27	76	....	....	....	....	....	....	....	....	....	8	5	1	6	37	....	....	....	....
2005-06♦	**Carolina**	**NHL**	**60**	**30**	**29**	**59**	**54**	**3**	**3**	**8**	**164**	**18.3**	**19**	**19**	**36.8**	**19:18**	**2**	**0**	**0**	**0**	**0**	**0**	**0**	**0**	**15:29**
	United States	Olympics	6	1	2	3	0	....	....	....	....	....	....	....	....	....	....	....	....	....	....	....	....	....	....
2006-07	**Carolina**	**NHL**	**71**	**29**	**32**	**61**	**76**	**9**	**0**	**4**	**166**	**17.5**	**2**	**27**	**40.7**	**18:01**	....	....	....	....	....	....	....	....	....
	NHL Totals		**345**	**107**	**122**	**229**	**330**	**23**	**7**	**20**	**786**	**13.6**		**134**	**41.0**	**17:40**	**25**	**6**	**3**	**9**	**30**	**1**	**0**	**1**	**18:13**

ECAC Rookie of the Year (1998) (co-winner - Willie Mitchell) • ECAC First All-Star Team (1999) • NCAA East Second All-American Team (1999) • ECAC Second All-Star Team (2000)

Signed as a free agent by **Berlin** (Germany), October 24, 2004.

COLLEY, Kevin

(KAW-lee, KEH-vihn)

Center. Shoots right. 5'10", 175 lbs. Born, New Haven, CT, January 4, 1979.

Season	Club	League	GP	G	A	Pts	PIM	PP	SH	GW	S	%	+/-	TF	F%	Min	GP	G	A	Pts	PIM	PP	SH	GW	Min
1996-97	Oshawa Generals	OHL	64	19	17	36	46	....	....	....	....	....	....	....	....	....	16	2	4	6	25	....	....	....	....
1997-98	Oshawa Generals	OHL	57	27	41	68	107	....	....	....	....	....	....	....	....	....	7	1	5	6	14	....	....	....	....
1998-99	Oshawa Generals	OHL	63	39	62	101	68	....	....	....	....	....	....	....	....	....	14	7	13	20	32	....	....	....	....
99-2000	Hartford	AHL	5	0	0	0	2	....	....	....	....	....	....	....	....	....	....	....	....	....	....	....	....	....	....
	Charlotte	ECHL	5	2	1	3	10	....	....	....	....	....	....	....	....	....	....	....	....	....	....	....	....	....	....
	Dayton Bombers	ECHL	24	8	6	14	111	....	....	....	....	....	....	....	....	....	2	1	0	1	4	....	....	....	....
2000-01	Pensacola	ECHL	23	6	11	17	44	....	....	....	....	....	....	....	....	....	....	....	....	....	....	....	....	....	....
	New Orleans	ECHL	23	11	8	19	27	....	....	....	....	....	....	....	....	....	8	1	1	2	12	....	....	....	....
2001-02	Providence Bruins	AHL	4	0	1	1	27	....	....	....	....	....	....	....	....	....	....	....	....	....	....	....	....	....	....
	Atlantic City	ECHL	41	23	30	53	90	....	....	....	....	....	....	....	....	....	....	....	....	....	....	....	....	....	....
	Rochester	AHL	25	3	4	7	70	....	....	....	....	....	....	....	....	....	2	0	1	1	0	....	....	....	....
2002-03	Syracuse Crunch	AHL	16	2	3	5	6	....	....	....	....	....	....	....	....	....	....	....	....	....	....	....	....	....	....
	Atlantic City	ECHL	50	33	38	71	190	....	....	....	....	....	....	....	....	....	17	*13	7	20	27	....	....	....	....
	Worcester IceCats	AHL	6	1	1	2	27	....	....	....	....	....	....	....	....	....	....	....	....	....	....	....	....	....	....
2003-04	Bridgeport	AHL	78	12	19	31	122	....	....	....	....	....	....	....	....	....	3	1	0	1	12	....	....	....	....
2004-05	Bridgeport	AHL	59	11	13	24	212	....	....	....	....	....	....	....	....	....	....	....	....	....	....	....	....	....	....
2005-06	**NY Islanders**	**NHL**	**16**	**0**	**0**	**0**	**52**	**0**	**0**	**0**	**4**	**0.0**	**–2**	**55**	**63.6**	**4:44**	....	....	....	....	....	....	....	....	....
	Bridgeport	AHL	21	5	5	10	60	....	....	....	....	....	....	....	....	....	....	....	....	....	....	....	....	....	....

Season	Club	League	Regular Season														Playoffs								
			GP	G	A	Pts	PIM	PP	SH	GW	S	%	+/-	TF	F%	Min	GP	G	A	Pts	PIM	PP	SH	GW	Min
2006-07			DID NOT PLAY – INJURED																						
	NHL Totals		**16**	**0**	**0**	**0**	**52**	**0**	**0**	**0**	**4**	**0.0**		**55**	**63.6**	**4:44**	....	....	....	....	....	....	....	....	....

Signed as a free agent by **NY Islanders**, June 10, 2004. • Missed remainder of 2005-06 season and entire 2006-07 season recovering from broken neck suffered in game vs. Washington, January 31, 2006.

COLLINS, Rob

(KAW-lihns, RAWB)

Center. Shoots right. 5'10", 174 lbs. Born, Kitchener, Ont., March 15, 1978.

Season	Club	League	GP	G	A	Pts	PIM	PP	SH	GW	S	%	+/-	TF	F%	Min	GP	G	A	Pts	PIM	PP	SH	GW	Min
1998-99	Ferris State	CCHA	36	3	9	12	14	....	....	....	....	....	....	....	....	....	....	....	....	....	....	....	....	....	....
99-2000	Ferris State	CCHA	38	11	20	31	39	....	....	....	....	....	....	....	....	....	....	....	....	....	....	....	....	....	....
2000-01	Ferris State	CCHA	35	15	17	32	23	....	....	....	....	....	....	....	....	....	....	....	....	....	....	....	....	....	....
2001-02	Ferris State	CCHA	36	15	33	48	30	....	....	....	....	....	....	....	....	....	....	....	....	....	....	....	....	....	....
	Grand Rapids	AHL	5	0	2	2	0	....	....	....	....	....	....	....	....	....	....	....	....	....	....	....	....	....	....
2002-03	Grand Rapids	AHL	73	11	20	31	16	....	....	....	....	....	....	....	....	....	15	3	8	11	10	....	....	....	....
2003-04	Bridgeport	AHL	75	9	23	32	42	....	....	....	....	....	....	....	....	....	7	3	5	8	10	....	....	....	....
2004-05	Bridgeport	AHL	78	23	39	62	67	....	....	....	....	....	....	....	....	....	....	....	....	....	....	....	....	....	....
2005-06	**NY Islanders**	**NHL**	**8**	**1**	**1**	**2**	**0**	**1**	**0**	**0**	**8**	**12.5**	**1**	**2**	**0.0**	**6:27**	....	....	....	....	....	....	....	....	....
	Bridgeport	AHL	67	21	48	69	54	....	....	....	....	....	....	....	....	....	7	4	2	6	10	....	....	....	....
2006-07	Dusseldorf	Germany	52	21	22	43	30	....	....	....	....	....	....	....	....	....	4	1	2	3	4	....	....	....	....
	NHL Totals		**8**	**1**	**1**	**2**	**0**	**1**	**0**	**0**	**8**	**12.5**		**2**	**0.0**	**6:27**	....	....	....	....	....	....	....	....	....

CCHA First All-Star Team (2002) • NCAA West Second All-American Team (2002)

Signed as a free agent by **NY Islanders**, July 22, 2002. Signed as a free agent with **Dusseldorf** (Germany), July 12, 2006.

COLLITON, Jeremy

(KAW-lih-tuhn, JAIR-eh-mee) **NYI**

Center. Shoots right. 6'2", 195 lbs. Born, Blackie, Alta., January 13, 1985. NY Islanders' 4th choice, 58th overall, in 2003 Entry Draft.

Season	Club	League	GP	G	A	Pts	PIM	PP	SH	GW	S	%	+/-	TF	F%	Min	GP	G	A	Pts	PIM	PP	SH	GW	Min
99-2000	Airdrie Express	AMHL	33	16	25	41	28	....	....	....	....	....	....	....	....	....	....	....	....	....	....	....	....	....	....
2000-01	Crowsnest Pass	AJHL	63	18	30	48	98	....	....	....	....	....	....	....	....	....	....	....	....	....	....	....	....	....	....
2001-02	Prince Albert	WHL	68	11	21	32	53	....	....	....	....	....	....	....	....	....	....	....	....	....	....	....	....	....	....
2002-03	Prince Albert	WHL	58	20	28	48	76	....	....	....	....	....	....	....	....	....	....	....	....	....	....	....	....	....	....
2003-04	Prince Albert	WHL	62	24	26	50	73	....	....	....	....	....	....	....	....	....	6	5	5	10	8	....	....	....	....
2004-05	Prince Albert	WHL	41	16	30	46	25	....	....	....	....	....	....	....	....	....	17	3	4	7	21	....	....	....	....
2005-06	**NY Islanders**	**NHL**	**19**	**1**	**1**	**2**	**6**	**0**	**0**	**0**	**9**	**11.1**	**2**	**76**	**40.8**	**6:18**	....	....	....	....	....	....	....	....	....
	Bridgeport	AHL	66	20	32	52	44	....	....	....	....	....	....	....	....	....	6	0	1	1	2	....	....	....	....
2006-07	**NY Islanders**	**NHL**	**1**	**0**	**0**	**0**	**0**	**0**	**0**	**0**	**0**	**0.0**	**–1**	**0**	**0.0**	**4:40**	....	....	....	....	....	....	....	....	....
	Bridgeport	AHL	45	10	12	22	32	....	....	....	....	....	....	....	....	....	....	....	....	....	....	....	....	....	....
	NHL Totals		**20**	**1**	**1**	**2**	**6**	**0**	**0**	**0**	**9**	**11.1**		**76**	**40.8**	**6:14**	....	....	....	....	....	....	....	....	....

COMEAU, Blake

(KOH-moh, BLAYK) **NYI**

Right wing. Shoots right. 6'1", 207 lbs. Born, Meadow Lake, Sask., February 18, 1986. NY Islanders' 2nd choice, 47th overall, in 2004 Entry Draft.

Season	Club	League	GP	G	A	Pts	PIM	PP	SH	GW	S	%	+/-	TF	F%	Min	GP	G	A	Pts	PIM	PP	SH	GW	Min
2001-02	Sask. Contacts	SMHL	42	27	33	60	72	....	....	....	....	....	....	....	....	....	....	....	....	....	....	....	....	....	....
	Kelowna Rockets	WHL	3	0	0	0	4	....	....	....	....	....	....	....	....	....	....	....	....	....	....	....	....	....	....
2002-03	Kelowna Rockets	WHL	54	5	18	23	77	....	....	....	....	....	....	....	....	....	19	2	1	3	20	....	....	....	....
2003-04	Kelowna Rockets	WHL	71	10	23	33	123	....	....	....	....	....	....	....	....	....	17	4	2	6	23	....	....	....	....
2004-05	Kelowna Rockets	WHL	65	24	23	47	108	....	....	....	....	....	....	....	....	....	24	6	12	18	34	....	....	....	....
2005-06	Kelowna Rockets	WHL	60	21	53	74	85	....	....	....	....	....	....	....	....	....	12	4	9	13	22	....	....	....	....
	Bridgeport	AHL	....	....	....	....	....	....	....	....	....	....	....	....	....	....	7	0	3	3	0	....	....	....	....
2006-07	**NY Islanders**	**NHL**	**3**	**0**	**0**	**0**	**0**	**0**	**0**	**0**	**1**	**0.0**	**0**	**0**	**0.0**	**9:25**	....	....	....	....	....	....	....	....	....
	Bridgeport	AHL	61	12	31	43	46	....	....	....	....	....	....	....	....	....	....	....	....	....	....	....	....	....	....
	NHL Totals		**3**	**0**	**0**	**0**	**0**	**0**	**0**	**0**	**1**	**0.0**		**0**	**0.0**	**9:25**	....	....	....	....	....	....	....	....	....

WHL West First All-Star Team (2006)

COMMODORE, Mike

(KAWM-uh-dohr, MIGHK) **CAR.**

Defense. Shoots right. 6'5", 228 lbs. Born, Fort Saskatchewan, Alta., November 7, 1979. New Jersey's 2nd choice, 42nd overall, in 1999 Entry Draft.

Season	Club	League	GP	G	A	Pts	PIM	PP	SH	GW	S	%	+/-	TF	F%	Min	GP	G	A	Pts	PIM	PP	SH	GW	Min
1996-97	Ft. Saskatchewan	AJHL	51	3	8	11	244	....	....	....	....	....	....	....	....	....	....	....	....	....	....	....	....	....	....
1997-98	North Dakota	WCHA	29	0	5	5	74	....	....	....	....	....	....	....	....	....	....	....	....	....	....	....	....	....	....
1998-99	North Dakota	WCHA	39	5	8	13	154	....	....	....	....	....	....	....	....	....	....	....	....	....	....	....	....	....	....
99-2000	North Dakota	WCHA	38	5	7	12	*154	....	....	....	....	....	....	....	....	....	....	....	....	....	....	....	....	....	....
2000-01	**New Jersey**	**NHL**	**20**	**1**	**4**	**5**	**14**	**0**	**0**	**0**	**11**	**9.1**	**5**	**0**	**0.0**	**12:46**	....	....	....	....	....	....	....	....	....
	Albany River Rats	AHL	41	2	5	7	59	....	....	....	....	....	....	....	....	....	....	....	....	....	....	....	....	....	....
2001-02	**New Jersey**	**NHL**	**37**	**0**	**1**	**1**	**30**	**0**	**0**	**0**	**22**	**0.0**	**–12**	**0**	**0.0**	**12:37**	....	....	....	....	....	....	....	....	....
	Albany River Rats	AHL	14	0	3	3	31	....	....	....	....	....	....	....	....	....	....	....	....	....	....	....	....	....	....
2002-03	Cincinnati	AHL	61	2	9	11	210	....	....	....	....	....	....	....	....	....	....	....	....	....	....	....	....	....	....
	Calgary	**NHL**	**6**	**0**	**1**	**1**	**19**	**0**	**0**	**0**	**5**	**0.0**	**2**	**0**	**0.0**	**11:35**	....	....	....	....	....	....	....	....	....
	Saint John Flames	AHL	7	0	3	3	18	....	....	....	....	....	....	....	....	....	....	....	....	....	....	....	....	....	....
2003-04	**Calgary**	**NHL**	**12**	**0**	**0**	**0**	**25**	**0**	**0**	**0**	**10**	**0.0**	**–4**	**0**	**0.0**	**15:17**	**20**	**0**	**2**	**2**	**19**	**0**	**0**	**0**	**11:34**
	Lowell	AHL	37	5	11	16	75	....	....	....	....	....	....	....	....	....	....	....	....	....	....	....	....	....	....
2004-05	Lowell	AHL	73	6	29	35	175	....	....	....	....	....	....	....	....	....	11	1	2	3	18	....	....	....	....
2005-06♦	**Carolina**	**NHL**	**72**	**3**	**10**	**13**	**138**	**0**	**0**	**2**	**72**	**4.2**	**12**	**1**	**0.0**	**15:30**	**25**	**2**	**2**	**4**	**33**	**0**	**1**	**0**	**19:27**
2006-07	**Carolina**	**NHL**	**82**	**7**	**22**	**29**	**113**	**0**	**2**	**1**	**136**	**5.1**	**0**	**0**	**0.0**	**19:54**	....	....	....	....	....	....	....	....	....
	NHL Totals		**229**	**11**	**38**	**49**	**339**	**0**	**2**	**3**	**256**	**4.3**		**1**	**0.0**	**16:15**	**45**	**2**	**4**	**6**	**52**	**0**	**1**	**0**	**15:57**

NCAA Championship All-Tournament Team (2000)

Traded to **Anaheim** by **New Jersey** with Petr Sykora, Jean-Francois Damphousse and Igor Pohanka for Jeff Friesen, Oleg Tverdovsky and Maxim Balmochnykh, July 6, 2002. Traded to **Calgary** by **Anaheim** with Jean-Francois Damphousse for Rob Niedermayer, March 11, 2003. Traded to **Carolina** by **Calgary** for Atlanta's 3rd round choice (previously acquired, Calgary selected Gord Baldwin) in 2005 Entry Draft, July 29, 2005.

COMRIE, Mike

(KAWM-ree, MIGHK) **NYI**

Center. Shoots left. 5'10", 185 lbs. Born, Edmonton, Alta., September 11, 1980. Edmonton's 5th choice, 91st overall, in 1999 Entry Draft.

Season	Club	League	GP	G	A	Pts	PIM	PP	SH	GW	S	%	+/-	TF	F%	Min	GP	G	A	Pts	PIM	PP	SH	GW	Min
1995-96	Edmonton SSAC	AMHL	33	51	52	103	....	....	....	....	....	....	....	....	....	....	....	....	....	....	....	....	....	....	....
1996-97	St. Albert Saints	AJHL	63	37	41	78	44	....	....	....	....	....	....	....	....	....	....	....	....	....	....	....	....	....	....
1997-98	St. Albert Saints	AJHL	58	*60	*78	*138	134	....	....	....	....	....	....	....	....	....	19	*24	*24	*48	51	....	....	....	....
1998-99	U. of Michigan	CCHA	42	19	25	44	38	....	....	....	....	....	....	....	....	....	....	....	....	....	....	....	....	....	....
99-2000	U. of Michigan	CCHA	40	24	35	59	95	....	....	....	....	....	....	....	....	....	....	....	....	....	....	....	....	....	....
2000-01	Kootenay Ice	WHL	37	39	40	79	79	....	....	....	....	....	....	....	....	....	....	....	....	....	....	....	....	....	....
	Edmonton	**NHL**	**41**	**8**	**14**	**22**	**14**	**3**	**0**	**1**	**62**	**12.9**	**6**	**372**	**43.3**	**11:23**	**6**	**1**	**2**	**3**	**0**	**1**	**0**	**1**	**15:00**
2001-02	**Edmonton**	**NHL**	**82**	**33**	**27**	**60**	**45**	**8**	**0**	**5**	**170**	**19.4**	**16**	**1198**	**47.3**	**17:32**	....	....	....	....	....	....	....	....	....
2002-03	**Edmonton**	**NHL**	**69**	**20**	**31**	**51**	**90**	**8**	**0**	**6**	**170**	**11.8**	**–18**	**1069**	**47.1**	**17:51**	**6**	**1**	**0**	**1**	**10**	**0**	**0**	**0**	**13:07**
2003-04	**Philadelphia**	**NHL**	**21**	**4**	**5**	**9**	**12**	**0**	**0**	**1**	**36**	**11.1**	**2**	**165**	**50.9**	**12:51**	....	....	....	....	....	....	....	....	....
	Phoenix	**NHL**	**28**	**8**	**7**	**15**	**16**	**1**	**1**	**1**	**65**	**12.3**	**–8**	**304**	**50.3**	**17:50**	....	....	....	....	....	....	....	....	....
2004-05	Farjestad	Sweden	10	1	6	7	10	....	....	....	....	....	....	....	....	....	....	....	....	....	....	....	....	....	....
2005-06	**Phoenix**	**NHL**	**80**	**30**	**30**	**60**	**55**	**10**	**0**	**4**	**190**	**15.8**	**2**	**781**	**52.8**	**16:01**	....	....	....	....	....	....	....	....	....
2006-07	**Phoenix**	**NHL**	**24**	**7**	**13**	**20**	**20**	**4**	**0**	**1**	**38**	**18.4**	**1**	**210**	**48.6**	**16:36**	....	....	....	....	....	....	....	....	....
	Ottawa	**NHL**	**41**	**13**	**12**	**25**	**24**	**3**	**0**	**2**	**87**	**14.9**	**–1**	**244**	**50.0**	**14:27**	**20**	**2**	**4**	**6**	**17**	**0**	**0**	**0**	**12:41**
	NHL Totals		**386**	**123**	**139**	**262**	**276**	**37**	**1**	**21**	**818**	**15.0**		**4343**	**48.4**	**16:00**	**32**	**4**	**6**	**10**	**27**	**1**	**0**	**1**	**13:12**

CCHA All-Rookie Team (1999) • CCHA First All-Star Team (1999) • CCHA Rookie of the Year (1999) • CCHA First All-Star Team (2000) • NCAA West Second All-American Team (2000)

• Left **University of Michigan** (CCHA) and signed as a free agent by **Kootenay** (WHL), August 23, 2000. • Left **Kootenay** (WHL) and signed with **Edmonton**, December 30, 2000. Traded to **Philadelphia** by **Edmonton** for Jeff Woywitka, Philadelphia's 1st round choice (Rob Schremp) in 2004 Entry Draft and Philadelphia's 3rd round choice (Danny Syvret) in 2005 Entry Draft, December 16, 2003. Traded to **Phoenix** by **Philadelphia** for Sean Burke, Branko Radivojevic and Ben Eager, February 9, 2004. Signed as a free agent by **Farjestad** (Sweden), October 30, 2004. Traded to **Ottawa** by **Phoenix** for Alexei Kaigorodov, January 3, 2007. Signed as a free agent by **NY Islanders**, July 5, 2007.

CONNER, Chris
(KAWN-uhr, KRIHS) **DAL.**

Wing. Shoots left. 5'7", 180 lbs. Born, Westland, MI, December 23, 1983.

Season	Club	League	GP	G	A	Pts	PIM	PP	SH	GW	S	%	+/-	TF	F%	Min	GP	G	A	Pts	PIM	PP	SH	GW	Min
			Regular Season														Playoffs								
2002-03	Michigan Tech	WCHA	38	13	24	37	8	....	....	....	....	....	....	....	....	....	....	....	....	....	....	....	....	....	....
2003-04	Michigan Tech	WCHA	38	25	14	39	12	....	....	....	....	....	....	....	....	....	....	....	....	....	....	....	....	....	....
2004-05	Michigan Tech	WCHA	37	14	10	24	6	....	....	....	....	....	....	....	....	....	....	....	....	....	....	....	....	....	....
2005-06	Michigan Tech	WCHA	38	17	12	29	18	....	....	....	....	....	....	....	....	....	....	....	....	....	....	....	....	....	....
	Iowa Stars	AHL	15	2	3	5	0	....	....	....	....	....	....	....	....	....	7	1	1	2	2	....	....	....	....
2006-07	**Dallas**	**NHL**	**11**	**1**	**2**	**3**	**4**	**0**	**0**	**0**	**18**	**5.6**	**-3**	**1**	**100.0**	**11:15**	....	....	....	....	....	....	....	....	....
	Iowa Stars	AHL	48	19	18	37	24	....	....	....	....	....	....	....	....	....	12	2	5	7	2	....	....	....	....
	NHL Totals		**11**	**1**	**2**	**3**	**4**	**0**	**0**	**0**	**18**	**5.6**		**1**	**100.0**	**11:15**	....	....	....	....	....	....	....	....	....

WCHA Second All-Star Team (2004)

Signed as a free agent by **Dallas**, July 13, 2006.

CONNOLLY, Tim
(KAW-nuhl-lee, TIHM) **BUF.**

Center. Shoots right. 6'1", 195 lbs. Born, Syracuse, NY, May 7, 1981. NY Islanders' 1st choice, 5th overall, in 1999 Entry Draft.

Season	Club	League	GP	G	A	Pts	PIM	PP	SH	GW	S	%	+/-	TF	F%	Min	GP	G	A	Pts	PIM	PP	SH	GW	Min
1996-97	Syracuse	MTJHL	50	42	62	104	34	....	....	....	....	....	....	....	....	....	....	....	....	....	....	....	....	....	....
1997-98	Erie Otters	OHL	59	30	32	62	32	....	....	....	....	....	....	....	....	....	7	1	6	7	6	....	....	....	....
1998-99	Erie Otters	OHL	46	34	34	68	50	....	....	....	....	....	....	....	....	....	....	....	....	....	....	....	....	....	....
99-2000	**NY Islanders**	**NHL**	**81**	**14**	**20**	**34**	**44**	**2**	**1**	**1**	**114**	**12.3**	**-25**	**786**	**36.3**	**16:18**	....	....	....	....	....	....	....	....	....
2000-01	**NY Islanders**	**NHL**	**82**	**10**	**31**	**41**	**42**	**5**	**0**	**0**	**171**	**5.8**	**-14**	**989**	**41.7**	**20:02**	....	....	....	....	....	....	....	....	....
2001-02	**Buffalo**	**NHL**	**82**	**10**	**35**	**45**	**34**	**3**	**0**	**3**	**126**	**7.9**	**4**	**1074**	**39.6**	**16:58**	....	....	....	....	....	....	....	....	....
2002-03	**Buffalo**	**NHL**	**80**	**12**	**13**	**25**	**32**	**6**	**0**	**2**	**159**	**7.5**	**-28**	**845**	**42.8**	**16:00**	....	....	....	....	....	....	....	....	....
2003-04	**Buffalo**	**NHL**	DID NOT PLAY – INJURED																						
2004-05	Langnau	Swiss	16	7	3	10	14	....	....	....	....	....	....	....	....	....	....	....	....	....	....	....	....	....	....
2005-06	**Buffalo**	**NHL**	**63**	**16**	**39**	**55**	**28**	**7**	**0**	**3**	**99**	**16.2**	**5**	**844**	**42.5**	**18:00**	**8**	**5**	**6**	**11**	**0**	**1**	**1**	**1**	**17:29**
2006-07	**Buffalo**	**NHL**	**2**	**1**	**0**	**1**	**2**	**0**	**0**	**0**	**2**	**50.0**	**1**	**13**	**53.9**	**13:07**	**16**	**0**	**9**	**9**	**4**	**0**	**0**	**0**	**16:56**
	NHL Totals		**390**	**63**	**138**	**201**	**182**	**23**	**1**	**9**	**671**	**9.4**		**4551**	**40.7**	**17:25**	**24**	**5**	**15**	**20**	**4**	**1**	**1**	**1**	**17:07**

Traded to **Buffalo** by **NY Islanders** with Taylor Pyatt for Michael Peca, June 24, 2001. • Missed entire 2003-04 season recovering from head injury suffered in pre-season game vs. Chicago, October 2, 2003. Signed as a free agent by **Langnau** (Swiss), October 10, 2004. • Missed majority of 2006-07 season recovering from concussion suffered in game vs. Carolina, May 22, 2006.

CONROY, Craig
(KAWN-roi, KRAYG) **CGY.**

Center. Shoots right. 6'2", 197 lbs. Born, Potsdam, NY, September 4, 1971. Montreal's 7th choice, 123rd overall, in 1990 Entry Draft.

Season	Club	League	GP	G	A	Pts	PIM	PP	SH	GW	S	%	+/-	TF	F%	Min	GP	G	A	Pts	PIM	PP	SH	GW	Min
1989-90	Northwood	High-NY	31	33	43	76		....	....	....	....	....	....	....	....	....	....	....	....	....	....	....	....	....	....
1990-91	Clarkson Knights	ECAC	40	8	21	29	24	....	....	....	....	....	....	....	....	....	....	....	....	....	....	....	....	....	....
1991-92	Clarkson Knights	ECAC	31	19	17	36	36	....	....	....	....	....	....	....	....	....	....	....	....	....	....	....	....	....	....
1992-93	Clarkson Knights	ECAC	35	10	23	33	26	....	....	....	....	....	....	....	....	....	....	....	....	....	....	....	....	....	....
1993-94	Clarkson Knights	ECAC	34	26	*40	*66	46	....	....	....	....	....	....	....	....	....	....	....	....	....	....	....	....	....	....
1994-95	Fredericton	AHL	55	26	18	44	29	....	....	....	....	....	....	....	....	....	11	7	3	10	6	....	....	....	....
	Montreal	**NHL**	**6**	**1**	**0**	**1**	**0**	**0**	**0**	**0**	**4**	**25.0**	**-1**	....	....	....	....	....	....	....	....	....	....	....	....
1995-96	**Montreal**	**NHL**	**7**	**0**	**0**	**0**	**2**	**0**	**0**	**0**	**1**	**0.0**	**-4**	....	....	....	....	....	....	....	....	....	....	....	....
	Fredericton	AHL	67	31	38	69	65	....	....	....	....	....	....	....	....	....	10	5	7	12	6	....	....	....	....
1996-97	Fredericton	AHL	9	10	6	16	10	....	....	....	....	....	....	....	....	....	....	....	....	....	....	....	....	....	....
	St. Louis	**NHL**	**61**	**6**	**11**	**17**	**43**	**0**	**0**	**1**	**74**	**8.1**	**0**	....	....	....	**6**	**0**	**0**	**0**	**8**	**0**	**0**	**0**	....
	Worcester IceCats	AHL	5	5	6	11	2	....	....	....	....	....	....	....	....	....	....	....	....	....	....	....	....	....	....
1997-98	**St. Louis**	**NHL**	**81**	**14**	**29**	**43**	**46**	**0**	**3**	**1**	**118**	**11.9**	**20**	....	....	....	**10**	**1**	**2**	**3**	**8**	**0**	**0**	**1**	....
1998-99	**St. Louis**	**NHL**	**69**	**14**	**25**	**39**	**38**	**0**	**1**	**1**	**134**	**10.4**	**14**	**1190**	**54.6**	**16:39**	**13**	**2**	**1**	**3**	**6**	**0**	**0**	**0**	**15:09**
99-2000	**St. Louis**	**NHL**	**79**	**12**	**15**	**27**	**36**	**1**	**2**	**3**	**98**	**12.2**	**5**	**1339**	**53.6**	**14:48**	**7**	**0**	**2**	**2**	**2**	**0**	**0**	**0**	**13:13**
2000-01	**St. Louis**	**NHL**	**69**	**11**	**14**	**25**	**46**	**0**	**3**	**2**	**101**	**10.9**	**2**	**729**	**55.1**	**14:01**	....	....	....	....	....	....	....	....	....
	Calgary	**NHL**	**14**	**3**	**4**	**7**	**14**	**0**	**1**	**0**	**32**	**9.4**	**0**	**264**	**52.7**	**18:08**	....	....	....	....	....	....	....	....	....
2001-02	**Calgary**	**NHL**	**81**	**27**	**48**	**75**	**32**	**7**	**2**	**4**	**146**	**18.5**	**24**	**1654**	**54.3**	**20:56**	....	....	....	....	....	....	....	....	....
2002-03	**Calgary**	**NHL**	**79**	**22**	**37**	**59**	**36**	**5**	**0**	**2**	**143**	**15.4**	**-4**	**1579**	**57.0**	**19:47**	....	....	....	....	....	....	....	....	....
2003-04	**Calgary**	**NHL**	**63**	**8**	**39**	**47**	**44**	**2**	**0**	**0**	**112**	**7.1**	**13**	**1402**	**53.9**	**19:13**	**26**	**6**	**11**	**17**	**12**	**2**	**0**	**1**	**20:23**
2004-05			DID NOT PLAY																						
2005-06	**Los Angeles**	**NHL**	**78**	**22**	**44**	**66**	**78**	**5**	**3**	**3**	**154**	**14.3**	**13**	**1429**	**51.2**	**19:13**	....	....	....	....	....	....	....	....	....
	United States	Olympics	6	1	4	5	2	....	....	....	....	....	....	....	....	....	....	....	....	....	....	....	....	....	....
2006-07	**Los Angeles**	**NHL**	**52**	**5**	**11**	**16**	**38**	**4**	**0**	**2**	**73**	**6.8**	**-13**	**802**	**51.5**	**15:29**	....	....	....	....	....	....	....	....	....
	Calgary	**NHL**	**28**	**8**	**13**	**21**	**18**	**0**	**1**	**0**	**39**	**20.5**	**10**	**443**	**50.3**	**16:00**	**6**	**1**	**1**	**2**	**8**	**0**	**0**	**0**	**15:33**
	NHL Totals		**767**	**153**	**290**	**443**	**471**	**24**	**16**	**19**	**1229**	**12.4**		**10831**	**53.8**	**17:35**	**68**	**10**	**17**	**27**	**44**	**2**	**0**	**2**	**17:33**

ECAC First All-Star Team (1994) • NCAA East First All-American Team (1994) • NCAA Final Four All-Tournament Team (1994)

Traded to **St. Louis** by **Montreal** with Pierre Turgeon and Rory Fitzpatrick for Murray Baron, Shayne Corson and St. Louis' 5th round choice (Gennady Razin) in 1997 Entry Draft, October 29, 1996. Traded to **Calgary** by **St. Louis** with St. Louis' 7th round choice (David Moss) in 2001 Entry Draft for Cory Stillman, March 13, 2001. Signed as a free agent by **Los Angeles**, July 6, 2004. Traded to **Calgary** by **Los Angeles** for Jamie Lundmark, Calgary's 4th round choice (Dwight King) in 2007 Entry Draft and Calgary's 2nd round choice in 2008 Entry Draft, January 29, 2007.

COOKE, Matt
(KUK, MAT) **VAN.**

Center. Shoots left. 5'11", 205 lbs. Born, Belleville, Ont., September 7, 1978. Vancouver's 8th choice, 144th overall, in 1997 Entry Draft.

Season	Club	League	GP	G	A	Pts	PIM	PP	SH	GW	S	%	+/-	TF	F%	Min	GP	G	A	Pts	PIM	PP	SH	GW	Min
1994-95	Wellington Dukes	MTJHL	46	9	23	32	62	....	....	....	....	....	....	....	....	....	....	....	....	....	....	....	....	....	....
1995-96	Windsor Spitfires	OHL	61	8	11	19	102	....	....	....	....	....	....	....	....	....	7	1	3	4	6	....	....	....	....
1996-97	Windsor Spitfires	OHL	65	45	50	95	146	....	....	....	....	....	....	....	....	....	5	5	5	10	10	....	....	....	....
1997-98	Windsor Spitfires	OHL	23	14	19	33	50	....	....	....	....	....	....	....	....	....	....	....	....	....	....	....	....	....	....
	Kingston	OHL	25	8	13	21	49	....	....	....	....	....	....	....	....	....	12	8	8	16	20	....	....	....	....
1998-99	**Vancouver**	**NHL**	**30**	**0**	**2**	**2**	**27**	**0**	**0**	**0**	**22**	**0.0**	**-12**	**189**	**40.2**	**8:07**	....	....	....	....	....	....	....	....	....
	Syracuse Crunch	AHL	37	15	18	33	119	....	....	....	....	....	....	....	....	....	....	....	....	....	....	....	....	....	....
99-2000	**Vancouver**	**NHL**	**51**	**5**	**7**	**12**	**39**	**0**	**1**	**1**	**58**	**8.6**	**3**	**71**	**39.4**	**11:48**	....	....	....	....	....	....	....	....	....
	Syracuse Crunch	AHL	18	5	8	13	27	....	....	....	....	....	....	....	....	....	....	....	....	....	....	....	....	....	....
2000-01	**Vancouver**	**NHL**	**81**	**14**	**13**	**27**	**94**	**0**	**2**	**0**	**121**	**11.6**	**5**	**321**	**43.0**	**14:35**	**4**	**0**	**0**	**0**	**4**	**0**	**0**	**0**	**12:04**
2001-02	**Vancouver**	**NHL**	**82**	**13**	**20**	**33**	**111**	**1**	**0**	**2**	**103**	**12.6**	**4**	**28**	**32.1**	**14:03**	**6**	**3**	**2**	**5**	**0**	**1**	**0**	**0**	**15:09**
2002-03	**Vancouver**	**NHL**	**82**	**15**	**27**	**42**	**82**	**1**	**4**	**0**	**118**	**12.7**	**21**	**31**	**35.5**	**13:24**	**14**	**2**	**1**	**3**	**12**	**0**	**0**	**0**	**14:07**
2003-04	**Vancouver**	**NHL**	**53**	**11**	**12**	**23**	**73**	**1**	**1**	**4**	**79**	**13.9**	**5**	**34**	**52.9**	**14:06**	**7**	**3**	**1**	**4**	**12**	**0**	**0**	**1**	**18:23**
2004-05			DID NOT PLAY																						
2005-06	**Vancouver**	**NHL**	**45**	**8**	**10**	**18**	**71**	**0**	**0**	**2**	**67**	**11.9**	**-8**	**25**	**24.0**	**13:57**	....	....	....	....	....	....	....	....	....
2006-07	**Vancouver**	**NHL**	**81**	**10**	**20**	**30**	**64**	**1**	**0**	**3**	**133**	**7.5**	**0**	**19**	**47.4**	**15:37**	**1**	**0**	**0**	**0**	**2**	**0**	**0**	**0**	**9:51**
	NHL Totals		**505**	**76**	**111**	**187**	**561**	**4**	**8**	**12**	**701**	**10.8**		**718**	**41.1**	**13:42**	**32**	**8**	**4**	**12**	**30**	**1**	**0**	**1**	**14:51**

CORAZZINI, Carl
(koh-ra-ZEE-nee, KAHRL) **DET.**

Center. Shoots right. 5'10", 182 lbs. Born, Framingham, MA, April 21, 1979.

Season	Club	League	GP	G	A	Pts	PIM	PP	SH	GW	S	%	+/-	TF	F%	Min	GP	G	A	Pts	PIM	PP	SH	GW	Min
1996-97	St. Sebastian's	High-MA	25	29	31	60		....	....	....	....	....	....	....	....	....	....	....	....	....	....	....	....	....	....
1997-98	Boston University	H-East	36	9	6	15	4	....	....	....	....	....	....	....	....	....	....	....	....	....	....	....	....	....	....
1998-99	Boston University	H-East	37	15	9	24	12	....	....	....	....	....	....	....	....	....	....	....	....	....	....	....	....	....	....
99-2000	Boston University	H-East	42	22	20	42	44	....	....	....	....	....	....	....	....	....	....	....	....	....	....	....	....	....	....
2000-01	Boston University	H-East	35	16	20	36	48	....	....	....	....	....	....	....	....	....	....	....	....	....	....	....	....	....	....
2001-02	Providence Bruins	AHL	61	7	8	15	10	....	....	....	....	....	....	....	....	....	....	....	....	....	....	....	....	....	....
2002-03	Providence Bruins	AHL	33	7	6	13	4	....	....	....	....	....	....	....	....	....	4	0	0	0	0	....	....	....	....
	Atlantic City	ECHL	27	13	8	21	14	....	....	....	....	....	....	....	....	....	....	....	....	....	....	....	....	....	....
2003-04	**Boston**	**NHL**	**12**	**2**	**0**	**2**	**0**	**0**	**1**	**0**	**16**	**12.5**	**2**	**6**	**33.3**	**10:41**	....	....	....	....	....	....	....	....	....
	Providence Bruins	AHL	62	16	9	25	6	....	....	....	....	....	....	....	....	....	2	1	0	1	2	....	....	....	....
2004-05	Providence Bruins	AHL	8	0	0	0	0	....	....	....	....	....	....	....	....	....	....	....	....	....	....	....	....	....	....
	Hershey Bears	AHL	52	10	13	23	6	....	....	....	....	....	....	....	....	....	....	....	....	....	....	....	....	....	....
2005-06	Norfolk Admirals	AHL	75	26	29	55	16	....	....	....	....	....	....	....	....	....	4	2	2	4	0	....	....	....	....
2006-07	**Chicago**	**NHL**	**7**	**0**	**1**	**1**	**2**	**0**	**0**	**0**	**5**	**0.0**	**0**	**1**	**0.0**	**10:47**	....	....	....	....	....	....	....	....	....
	Norfolk Admirals	AHL	68	28	29	57	18	....	....	....	....	....	....	....	....	....	6	4	1	5	2	....	....	....	....
	NHL Totals		**19**	**2**	**1**	**3**	**2**	**0**	**1**	**0**	**21**	**9.5**		**7**	**28.6**	**10:44**	....	....	....	....	....	....	....	....	....

Hockey East All-Rookie Team (1998) • Hockey East First All-Star Team (2001) • NCAA East Second All-American Team (2001)

Signed as a free agent by **Boston**, August 8, 2001. Signed as a free agent by **Providence** (AHL), October 1. 2004. Traded to **Hershey** (AHL) by **Providence** (AHL) for Darrel Scoville, November 15, 2004. Signed as a free agent by **Norfolk** (AHL), October 18, 2005. Signed as a free agent by **Chicago**, July 17, 2006. Signed as a free agent by **Detroit**, July 16, 2007.

CORSO, Daniel
(KOHR-soh, DAN-yehl)

Center. Shoots left. 5'10", 187 lbs. Born, Montreal, Que., April 3, 1978. St. Louis' 6th choice, 169th overall, in 1996 Entry Draft.

			Regular Season														Playoffs								
Season	Club	League	GP	G	A	Pts	PIM	PP	SH	GW	S	%	+/-	TF	F%	Min	GP	G	A	Pts	PIM	PP	SH	GW	Min
1993-94	Magog	QAAA	36	17	22	39	....	....	....	....	....	....	....	....	....	....	12	10	12	22	....	....	....	....	....
1994-95	Victoriaville Tigres	QMJHL	65	27	26	53	6	....	....	....	....	....	....	....	....	....	4	2	5	7	2	....	....	....	....
1995-96	Victoriaville Tigres	QMJHL	65	49	65	114	77	....	....	....	....	....	....	....	....	....	12	6	7	13	4	....	....	....	....
1996-97	Victoriaville Tigres	QMJHL	54	51	68	119	50	....	....	....	....	....	....	....	....	....	....	....	....	....	....	....	....	....	....
1997-98	Victoriaville Tigres	QMJHL	35	24	51	75	20	....	....	....	....	....	....	....	....	....	3	1	1	2	2	....	....	....	....
1998-99	Worcester IceCats	AHL	63	14	14	28	26	....	....	....	....	....	....	....	....	....	....	....	....	....	....	....	....	....	....
99-2000	Worcester IceCats	AHL	71	21	34	55	19	....	....	....	....	....	....	....	....	....	9	2	3	5	10	....	....	....	....
2000-01	**St. Louis**	**NHL**	**28**	**10**	**3**	**13**	**14**	**5**	**0**	**4**	**42**	**23.8**	**0**	**296**	**56.1**	**13:56**	**12**	**0**	**1**	**1**	**0**	**0**	**0**	**0**	**8:52**
	Worcester IceCats	AHL	52	19	37	56	47	....	....	....	....	....	....	....	....	....	....	....	....	....	....	....	....	....	....
2001-02	**St. Louis**	**NHL**	**41**	**4**	**7**	**11**	**6**	**1**	**0**	**2**	**25**	**16.0**	**3**	**423**	**54.9**	**11:13**	**2**	**0**	**0**	**0**	**0**	**0**	**0**	**0**	**8:51**
2002-03	**St. Louis**	**NHL**	**1**	**0**	**0**	**0**	**0**	**0**	**0**	**0**	**0**	**0.0**	**–1**	**8**	**50.0**	**7:44**	....	....	....	....	....	....	....	....	....
	Worcester IceCats	AHL	1	0	0	0	0	....	....	....	....	....	....	....	....	....	....	....	....	....	....	....	....	....	....
2003-04	Binghamton	AHL	32	7	11	18	16	....	....	....	....	....	....	....	....	....	....	....	....	....	....	....	....	....	....
	Atlanta	**NHL**	**7**	**0**	**1**	**1**	**0**	**0**	**0**	**0**	**2**	**0.0**	**–2**	**105**	**47.6**	**12:59**	....	....	....	....	....	....	....	....	....
	Chicago Wolves	AHL	29	8	18	26	15	....	....	....	....	....	....	....	....	....	10	1	5	6	0	....	....	....	....
2004-05	Kassel Huskies	Germany	45	8	30	38	32	....	....	....	....	....	....	....	....	....	7	1	5	6	20	....	....	....	....
2005-06	Frankfurt Lions	Germany	29	11	17	28	57	....	....	....	....	....	....	....	....	....	....	....	....	....	....	....	....	....	....
2006-07	Philadelphia	AHL	6	2	4	6	4	....	....	....	....	....	....	....	....	....	....	....	....	....	....	....	....	....	....
	Springfield	AHL	58	13	33	46	35	....	....	....	....	....	....	....	....	....	....	....	....	....	....	....	....	....	....
	NHL Totals		**77**	**14**	**11**	**25**	**20**	**6**	**0**	**6**	**69**	**20.3**		**832**	**54.3**	**12:19**	**14**	**0**	**1**	**1**	**0**	**0**	**0**	**0**	**8:52**

QMJHL All-Rookie Team (1995) • QMJHL First All-Star Team (1997) • QMJHL MVP (1997)

• Spent majority of 2001-02 season on practice roster, October 22, 2001. • Missed majority of 2002-03 season recovering from shoulder injury suffered in game vs. Anaheim, October 10, 2003. Signed as a free agent by **Ottawa**, September 2, 2003. Traded to **Atlanta** by **Ottawa** for Brad Tapper, January 6, 2004. Signed as a free agent by **Kassel** (Germany), August 7, 2004. Signed as a free agent by **Frankfurt** (Germany), June 9, 2005. Signed as a free agent by **Philadelphia**, July 13, 2006. Traded to **Tampa Bay** by **Philadelphia** for Darren Reid, November 9, 2006.

CORVO, Joe
(KOHR-voh, JOH) **OTT.**

Defense. Shoots right. 6', 205 lbs. Born, Oak Park, IL, June 20, 1977. Los Angeles' 4th choice, 83rd overall, in 1997 Entry Draft.

			Regular Season														Playoffs								
Season	Club	League	GP	G	A	Pts	PIM	PP	SH	GW	S	%	+/-	TF	F%	Min	GP	G	A	Pts	PIM	PP	SH	GW	Min
1995-96	Western Mich.	CCHA	41	5	25	30	38	....	....	....	....	....	....	....	....	....	....	....	....	....	....	....	....	....	....
1996-97	Western Mich.	CCHA	32	12	21	33	85	....	....	....	....	....	....	....	....	....	....	....	....	....	....	....	....	....	....
1997-98	Western Mich.	CCHA	32	5	12	17	93	....	....	....	....	....	....	....	....	....	....	....	....	....	....	....	....	....	....
1998-99	Springfield	AHL	50	5	15	20	32	....	....	....	....	....	....	....	....	....	....	....	....	....	....	....	....	....	....
	Hampton Roads	ECHL	5	0	0	0	15	....	....	....	....	....	....	....	....	....	4	0	1	1	0	....	....	....	....
99-2000			DID NOT PLAY																						
2000-01	Lowell	AHL	77	10	23	33	31	....	....	....	....	....	....	....	....	....	4	3	1	4	0	....	....	....	....
2001-02	Manchester	AHL	80	13	37	50	30	....	....	....	....	....	....	....	....	....	5	0	5	5	0	....	....	....	....
2002-03	**Los Angeles**	**NHL**	**50**	**5**	**7**	**12**	**14**	**2**	**0**	**0**	**84**	**6.0**	**2**	**0**	**0.0**	**18:37**	....	....	....	....	....	....	....	....	....
	Manchester	AHL	26	8	18	26	8	....	....	....	....	....	....	....	....	....	3	0	0	0	0	....	....	....	....
2003-04	**Los Angeles**	**NHL**	**72**	**8**	**17**	**25**	**36**	**0**	**0**	**3**	**150**	**5.3**	**7**	**1**	**0.0**	**21:09**	....	....	....	....	....	....	....	....	....
2004-05	Chicago Wolves	AHL	23	7	7	14	14	....	....	....	....	....	....	....	....	....	18	4	5	9	12	....	....	....	....
2005-06	**Los Angeles**	**NHL**	**81**	**14**	**26**	**40**	**38**	**7**	**0**	**3**	**190**	**7.4**	**16**	**0**	**0.0**	**19:59**	....	....	....	....	....	....	....	....	....
2006-07	**Ottawa**	**NHL**	**76**	**8**	**29**	**37**	**42**	**3**	**0**	**2**	**160**	**5.0**	**8**	**0**	**0.0**	**18:04**	**20**	**2**	**7**	**9**	**6**	**1**	**0**	**1**	**17:18**
	NHL Totals		**279**	**35**	**79**	**114**	**130**	**12**	**0**	**8**	**584**	**6.0**		**1**	**0.0**	**19:31**	**20**	**2**	**7**	**9**	**6**	**1**	**0**	**1**	**17:18**

CCHA All-Rookie Team (1996) • CCHA Second All-Star Team (1997)

• Missed entire 1999-2000 season after failing to come to contract terms with **Los Angeles.** Signed as a free agent by **Chicago** (AHL), February 24, 2005. Signed as a free agent by **Ottawa**, July 1, 2006.

COTE, Jean-Philippe
(KOH-tay, ZHAWN-fihl-EEP) **MTL.**

Defense. Shoots left. 6'3", 213 lbs. Born, Charlesbourg, Que., April 22, 1982. Toronto's 10th choice, 265th overall, in 2000 Entry Draft.

			Regular Season														Playoffs								
Season	Club	League	GP	G	A	Pts	PIM	PP	SH	GW	S	%	+/-	TF	F%	Min	GP	G	A	Pts	PIM	PP	SH	GW	Min
1998-99	Ste-Foy	QAAA	38	10	24	34	34	....	....	....	....	....	....	....	....	....	17	1	8	9	17	....	....	....	....
	Quebec Remparts	QMJHL	8	0	0	0	2	....	....	....	....	....	....	....	....	....	....	....	....	....	....	....	....	....	....
99-2000	Quebec Remparts	QMJHL	34	0	10	10	15	....	....	....	....	....	....	....	....	....	....	....	....	....	....	....	....	....	....
	Cape Breton	QMJHL	28	0	4	4	21	....	....	....	....	....	....	....	....	....	4	0	1	1	4	....	....	....	....
2000-01	Cape Breton	QMJHL	71	6	29	35	90	....	....	....	....	....	....	....	....	....	12	0	0	0	18	....	....	....	....
2001-02	Cape Breton	QMJHL	61	4	20	24	72	....	....	....	....	....	....	....	....	....	16	1	6	7	38	....	....	....	....
2002-03	Cape Breton	QMJHL	16	1	3	4	12	....	....	....	....	....	....	....	....	....	....	....	....	....	....	....	....	....	....
	Acadie-Bathurst	QMJHL	48	8	18	26	87	....	....	....	....	....	....	....	....	....	11	2	3	5	20	....	....	....	....
2003-04	Hamilton	AHL	75	2	7	9	79	....	....	....	....	....	....	....	....	....	10	0	4	4	24	....	....	....	....
2004-05	Hamilton	AHL	51	1	8	9	58	....	....	....	....	....	....	....	....	....	4	0	1	1	0	....	....	....	....
2005-06	**Montreal**	**NHL**	**8**	**0**	**0**	**0**	**4**	**0**	**0**	**0**	**2**	**0.0**	**2**	**0**	**0.0**	**11:02**	....	....	....	....	....	....	....	....	....
	Hamilton	AHL	61	3	8	11	113	....	....	....	....	....	....	....	....	....	....	....	....	....	....	....	....	....	....
2006-07	Hamilton	AHL	68	3	9	12	115	....	....	....	....	....	....	....	....	....	6	0	0	0	2	....	....	....	....
	NHL Totals		**8**	**0**	**0**	**0**	**4**	**0**	**0**	**0**	**2**	**0.0**		**0**	**0.0**	**11:02**	....	....	....	....	....	....	....	....	....

Signed as a free agent by **Montreal**, August 19, 2004.

COTE, Riley
(KOH-tay, RIGH-lee) **PHI.**

Right wing. Shoots left. 6'1", 210 lbs. Born, Winnipeg, Man., March 16, 1982.

			Regular Season														Playoffs								
Season	Club	League	GP	G	A	Pts	PIM	PP	SH	GW	S	%	+/-	TF	F%	Min	GP	G	A	Pts	PIM	PP	SH	GW	Min
1998-99	Prince Albert	WHL	37	3	2	5	63	....	....	....	....	....	....	....	....	....	9	0	0	0	9	....	....	....	....
99-2000	Prince Albert	WHL	67	6	7	13	71	....	....	....	....	....	....	....	....	....	3	1	0	1	2	....	....	....	....
2000-01	Prince Albert	WHL	64	17	35	52	114	....	....	....	....	....	....	....	....	....	....	....	....	....	....	....	....	....	....
2001-02	Prince Albert	WHL	67	28	23	51	134	....	....	....	....	....	....	....	....	....	....	....	....	....	....	....	....	....	....
2002-03	St. John's	AHL	6	0	0	0	5	....	....	....	....	....	....	....	....	....	....	....	....	....	....	....	....	....	....
	Memphis	CHL	51	8	6	14	241	....	....	....	....	....	....	....	....	....	14	1	0	1	54	....	....	....	....
2003-04	Syracuse Crunch	AHL	9	0	0	0	19	....	....	....	....	....	....	....	....	....	....	....	....	....	....	....	....	....	....
	Dayton Bombers	ECHL	57	6	11	17	258	....	....	....	....	....	....	....	....	....	....	....	....	....	....	....	....	....	....
2004-05	Philadelphia	AHL	61	4	7	11	280	....	....	....	....	....	....	....	....	....	13	0	0	0	6	....	....	....	....
2005-06	Philadelphia	AHL	70	3	1	4	259	....	....	....	....	....	....	....	....	....	....	....	....	....	....	....	....	....	....
2006-07	**Philadelphia**	**NHL**	**8**	**0**	**0**	**0**	**11**	**0**	**0**	**0**	**3**	**0.0**	**0**	**0**	**0.0**	**4:30**	....	....	....	....	....	....	....	....	....
	Philadelphia	AHL	37	1	4	5	125	....	....	....	....	....	....	....	....	....	....	....	....	....	....	....	....	....	....
	NHL Totals		**8**	**0**	**0**	**0**	**11**	**0**	**0**	**0**	**3**	**0.0**		**0**	**0.0**	**4:30**	....	....	....	....	....	....	....	....	....

Signed as a free agent by **Philadelphia**, August 23, 2005.

COULOMBE, Patrick
(KOO-lawmb, PAT-rihk) **VAN.**

Defense. Shoots left. 5'11", 185 lbs. Born, St-Fabien, Que., April 23, 1985.

			Regular Season														Playoffs								
Season	Club	League	GP	G	A	Pts	PIM	PP	SH	GW	S	%	+/-	TF	F%	Min	GP	G	A	Pts	PIM	PP	SH	GW	Min
2001-02	Rimouski Oceanic	QMJHL	34	0	8	8	30	....	....	....	....	....	....	....	....	....	7	0	3	3	2	....	....	....	....
2002-03	Rimouski Oceanic	QMJHL	72	6	25	31	48	....	....	....	....	....	....	....	....	....	....	....	....	....	....	....	....	....	....
2003-04	Rimouski Oceanic	QMJHL	59	7	38	45	32	....	....	....	....	....	....	....	....	....	9	0	5	5	0	....	....	....	....
2004-05	Rimouski Oceanic	QMJHL	70	8	60	68	46	....	....	....	....	....	....	....	....	....	13	2	17	19	6	....	....	....	....
2005-06	Rimouski Oceanic	QMJHL	29	5	23	28	18	....	....	....	....	....	....	....	....	....	....	....	....	....	....	....	....	....	....
	Chicoutimi	QMJHL	33	18	31	49	22	....	....	....	....	....	....	....	....	....	9	2	10	12	6	....	....	....	....
2006-07	**Vancouver**	**NHL**	**7**	**0**	**1**	**1**	**4**	**0**	**0**	**0**	**11**	**0.0**	**–6**	**0**	**0.0**	**13:38**	....	....	....	....	....	....	....	....	....
	Manitoba Moose	AHL	44	3	6	9	22	....	....	....	....	....	....	....	....	....	1	0	0	0	0	....	....	....	....
	Victoria	ECHL	6	0	3	3	2	....	....	....	....	....	....	....	....	....	6	0	2	2	0	....	....	....	....
	NHL Totals		**7**	**0**	**1**	**1**	**4**	**0**	**0**	**0**	**11**	**0.0**		**0**	**0.0**	**13:38**	....	....	....	....	....	....	....	....	....

Signed as a free agent by **Vancouver**, November 3, 2006.

COWAN, Jeff

(KOW-an, JEHF) **VAN.**

Left wing. Shoots left. 6'2", 205 lbs. Born, Scarborough, Ont., September 27, 1976.

			Regular Season														Playoffs								
Season	Club	League	GP	G	A	Pts	PIM	PP	SH	GW	S	%	+/-	TF	F%	Min	GP	G	A	Pts	PIM	PP	SH	GW	Min
1992-93	Guelph Platers	OHA-B	45	8	8	16	22																		
1993-94	Guelph Platers	OHA-B	43	30	26	56	96																		
	Guelph Storm	OHL	17	1	0	1	5																		
1994-95	Guelph Storm	OHL	51	10	7	17	14										14	1	1	2	0				
1995-96	Barrie Colts	OHL	66	38	14	52	29										5	1	2	3	6				
1996-97	Saint John Flames	AHL	22	5	5	10	8																		
	Roanoke Express	ECHL	47	21	13	34	42																		
1997-98	Saint John Flames	AHL	69	15	13	28	23										13	4	1	5	14				
1998-99	Saint John Flames	AHL	71	7	12	19	117										4	0	1	1	10				
99-2000	Calgary	NHL	13	4	1	5	16	0	0	0	26	15.4	2	0	0.0	10:22									
	Saint John Flames	AHL	47	15	10	25	77																		
2000-01	Calgary	NHL	51	9	4	13	74	2	0	1	48	18.8	–8	5	20.0	9:06									
2001-02	Calgary	NHL	19	1	0	1	40	0	0	1	13	7.7	–3	2	50.0	7:44									
	Atlanta	NHL	38	4	1	5	50	0	0	1	51	7.8	–11	5	20.0	12:27									
2002-03	Atlanta	NHL	66	3	5	8	115	0	0	0	52	5.8	–15	10	30.0	8:24									
2003-04	Atlanta	NHL	58	9	15	24	68	1	0	1	74	12.2	2	9	22.2	10:04									
	Los Angeles	NHL	13	2	1	3	24	1	0	0	15	13.3	–1	2	50.0	11:43									
2004-05		DID NOT PLAY																							
2005-06	Los Angeles	NHL	46	8	1	9	73	0	0	0	53	15.1	–8	4	25.0	8:26									
2006-07	Los Angeles	NHL	21	0	2	2	32	0	0	0	28	0.0	–1	1	0.0	7:37									
	Vancouver	NHL	42	7	3	10	93	0	1	0	46	15.2	4	0	0.0	8:15	10	2	0	2	22	0	0	1	11:38
	NHL Totals		367	47	33	80	585	4	1	4	406	11.6		38	26.3	9:17	10	2	0	2	22	0	0	1	11:38

Signed as a free agent by **Calgary**, October 2, 1995. Traded to **Atlanta** by **Calgary** with the rights to Kurtis Foster for Petr Buzek and Atlanta's 6th round choice (Adam Pardy) in 2004 Entry Draft, December 18, 2001. Traded to **Los Angeles** by **Atlanta** for Kip Brennan, March 9, 2004. Claimed on waivers by **Vancouver** from **Los Angeles**, December 30, 2006.

CRAIG, Ryan

(KRAIG, RIGH-uhn) **T.B.**

Center. Shoots left. 6'2", 220 lbs. Born, Abbotsford, B.C., January 6, 1982. Tampa Bay's 10th choice, 255th overall, in 2002 Entry Draft.

			Regular Season														Playoffs								
Season	Club	League	GP	G	A	Pts	PIM	PP	SH	GW	S	%	+/-	TF	F%	Min	GP	G	A	Pts	PIM	PP	SH	GW	Min
1997-98	Abbotsford	BCAHA	80	118	120	238	110																		
	Brandon	WHL	1	0	0	0	0																		
1998-99	Brandon	WHL	54	11	12	23	46										5	0	0	0	4				
99-2000	Brandon	WHL	65	17	19	36	40																		
2000-01	Brandon	WHL	70	38	33	71	49										6	3	0	3	7				
2001-02	Brandon	WHL	52	29	35	64	52										19	11	10	21	13				
2002-03	Brandon	WHL	60	42	32	74	69										17	5	8	13	29				
2003-04	Hershey Bears	AHL	61	4	8	12	24																		
	Pensacola	ECHL	5	3	5	8	0										2	0	1	1	0				
2004-05	Springfield	AHL	80	27	14	41	50																		
2005-06	Tampa Bay	NHL	48	15	13	28	6	6	0	0	81	18.5	–4	95	46.3	15:21	5	0	0	0	10	0	0	0	12:59
	Springfield	AHL	28	12	10	22	14																		
2006-07	Tampa Bay	NHL	72	14	13	27	55	4	0	2	130	10.8	–11	110	40.0	15:20	6	0	0	0	12	0	0	0	7:02
	NHL Totals		120	29	26	55	61	10	0	2	211	13.7		205	42.9	15:21	11	0	0	0	22	0	0	0	9:44

WHL East First All-Star Team (2003) • Canadian Major Junior Humanitarian Player of the Year (2003)

CROSBY, Sidney

(KRAWZ-bee, SIHD-nee) **PIT.**

Center. Shoots left. 5'11", 200 lbs. Born, Cole Harbour, N.S., August 7, 1987. Pittsburgh's 1st choice, 1st overall, in 2005 Entry Draft.

			Regular Season														Playoffs								
Season	Club	League	GP	G	A	Pts	PIM	PP	SH	GW	S	%	+/-	TF	F%	Min	GP	G	A	Pts	PIM	PP	SH	GW	Min
2001-02	Dartmouth	NSMHL	74	95	98	193	114																		
2002-03	Shat.-St. Mary's	High-MN	57	72	90	162	....																		
2003-04	Rimouski Oceanic	QMJHL	59	54	*81	*135	74										9	7	9	16	10				
2004-05	Rimouski Oceanic	QMJHL	62	*66	*102	*168	84										13	*14	*17	*31	16				
2005-06	Pittsburgh	NHL	81	39	63	102	110	16	0	5	278	14.0	–1	1174	45.5	20:08									
2006-07	Pittsburgh	NHL	79	36	84	*120	60	13	0	4	250	14.4	10	1686	49.8	20:46	5	3	2	5	4	1	0	1	21:40
	NHL Totals		160	75	147	222	170	29	0	9	528	14.2		2860	48.0	20:26	5	3	2	5	4	1	0	1	21:40

QMJHL All-Rookie Team (2004) • QMJHL First All-Star Team (2004, 2005) • QMJHL Player of the Year (2004, 2005) • Canadian Major Junior First All-Star Team (2004, 2005) • Canadian Major Junior Rookie of the Year (2004) • Canadian Major Junior Player of the Year (2004, 2005) • Memorial Cup All-Star Team (2005) • Ed Chynoweth Trophy (Memorial Cup Tournament Leading Scorer) (2005) • NHL All-Rookie Team (2006) • NHL First All-Star Team (2007) • Art Ross Trophy (2007) • Lester B. Pearson Award (2007) • Hart Memorial Trophy (2007)

Played in NHL All-Star Game (2007)

CROSS, Cory

(KRAWS, KOH-ree)

Defense. Shoots left. 6'5", 225 lbs. Born, Lloydminster, Alta., January 3, 1971. Tampa Bay's 1st choice, 1st overall, in 1992 Supplemental Draft.

			Regular Season														Playoffs								
Season	Club	League	GP	G	A	Pts	PIM	PP	SH	GW	S	%	+/-	TF	F%	Min	GP	G	A	Pts	PIM	PP	SH	GW	Min
1990-91	U. of Alberta	CWUAA	20	2	5	7	16																		
1991-92	U. of Alberta	CWUAA	41	4	11	15	82																		
1992-93	U. of Alberta	CWUAA	43	11	28	39	107																		
	Atlanta Knights	IHL	7	0	1	1	2										4	0	0	0	6				
1993-94	Tampa Bay	NHL	5	0	0	0	6	0	0	0	5	0.0	–3												
	Atlanta Knights	IHL	70	4	14	18	72										9	1	2	3	14				
1994-95	Atlanta Knights	IHL	41	5	10	15	67																		
	Tampa Bay	NHL	43	1	5	6	41	0	0	1	35	2.9	–6												
1995-96	Tampa Bay	NHL	75	2	14	16	66	0	0	0	57	3.5	4				6	0	0	0	22	0	0	0	
1996-97	Tampa Bay	NHL	72	4	5	9	95	0	0	2	75	5.3	6												
1997-98	Tampa Bay	NHL	74	3	6	9	77	0	1	0	72	4.2	–24												
1998-99	Tampa Bay	NHL	67	2	16	18	92	0	0	0	96	2.1	–25	0	0.0	22:38									
99-2000	Toronto	NHL	71	4	11	15	64	0	0	1	60	6.7	13	0	0.0	15:59	12	0	2	2	2	0	0	0	15:21
2000-01	Toronto	NHL	41	3	5	8	50	1	0	1	34	8.8	7	0	0.0	18:00	11	2	1	3	10	0	0	1	16:05
2001-02	Toronto	NHL	50	3	9	12	54	0	0	1	39	7.7	11	0	0.0	15:18	12	0	0	0	8	0	0	0	17:00
2002-03	NY Rangers	NHL	26	0	4	4	16	0	0	0	18	0.0	13	1	0.0	17:12									
	Hartford	AHL	2	0	0	0	2																		
	Edmonton	NHL	11	2	3	5	8	1	0	1	11	18.2	3	0	0.0	17:51	6	0	1	1	20	0	0	0	20:37
2003-04	Edmonton	NHL	68	7	14	21	56	1	0	1	83	8.4	9	0	0.0	19:14									
2004-05		DID NOT PLAY																							
2005-06	Edmonton	NHL	34	2	3	5	38	0	1	0	20	10.0	–5	0	0.0	12:46									
	Pittsburgh	NHL	6	0	1	1	6	0	0	0	1	0.0	–1	0	0.0	13:13									
	Detroit	NHL	16	1	1	2	15	0	0	0	11	9.1	3	0	0.0	12:44									
2006-07	Hamburg Freezers	Germany	48	2	7	9	190										7	2	2	4	32				
	NHL Totals		659	34	97	131	684	3	2	8	617	5.5		1	0.0	17:30	47	2	4	6	62	0	0	1	16:48

Traded to **Toronto** by **Tampa Bay** with Tampa Bay's 7th round choice (Ivan Kolozvary) in 2001 Entry Draft for Fredrik Modin, October 1, 1999. Signed as a free agent by **NY Rangers**, December 17, 2002. Traded to **Edmonton** by **NY Rangers** with Radek Dvorak for Anson Carter and Ales Pisa, March 11, 2003. Traded to **Pittsburgh** by **Edmonton** with Jani Rita for Dick Tarnstrom, January 26, 2006. Traded to **Detroit** by **Pittsburgh** for Detroit's 4th round choice (Alex Grant) in 2007 Entry Draft, March 8, 2006. Signed as a free agent by **Hamburg** (Germany), July 25, 2006.

CULLEN, Mark

(KUH-lehn, MAHRK) **DET.**

Center. Shoots left. 5'11", 190 lbs. Born, Moorhead, MN, October 28, 1978.

			Regular Season														Playoffs								
Season	Club	League	GP	G	A	Pts	PIM	PP	SH	GW	S	%	+/-	TF	F%	Min	GP	G	A	Pts	PIM	PP	SH	GW	Min
1996-97	Fargo High	High-ND	30	20	45	65	....																		
1997-98	Fargo-Moorhead	USHL	30	17	37	54	16										4	3	0	3	25				
1998-99	Colorado College	WCHA	42	8	25	33	22																		
99-2000	Colorado College	WCHA	37	11	20	31	22																		
2000-01	Colorado College	WCHA	31	20	33	53	26																		
2001-02	Colorado College	WCHA	43	14	36	50	14																		
2002-03	Houston Aeros	AHL	72	22	25	47	20										15	3	7	10	4				
2003-04	Houston Aeros	AHL	53	10	28	38	28										2	0	0	0	0				
2004-05	Houston Aeros	AHL	64	10	24	34	26										5	1	1	2	0				
2005-06	Chicago	NHL	29	7	9	16	2	0	0	0	45	15.6	7	281	48.8	13:15									
	Norfolk Admirals	AHL	54	29	39	68	48										4	2	2	4	0				

			Regular Season														Playoffs								
Season	Club	League	GP	G	A	Pts	PIM	PP	SH	GW	S	%	+/-	TF	F%	Min	GP	G	A	Pts	PIM	PP	SH	GW	Min
2006-07	Philadelphia	NHL	3	0	0	0	0	0	0	0	4	0.0	–3	14	50.0	6:15	....	....	....	....	....	....	....	....	....
	Philadelphia	AHL	56	16	36	52	34	....	....	....	....	....	....	....	....	....	....	....	....	....	....	....	....	....	....
	NHL Totals		32	7	9	16	2	0	0	0	49	14.3		295	48.8	12:36	....	....	....	....	....	....	....	....	....

USHL All-Rookie Team (1998) • USHL Rookie of the Year (1998) • WCHA First All-Star Team (2001, 2002) • NCAA West Second All-American Team (2001) • Fred Hunt Memorial Trophy (Sportsmanship - AHL) (2006)

Signed as a free agent by **Minnesota**, April 8, 2002. Signed as a free agent by **Chicago**, August 4, 2005. Signed as a free agent by **Philadelphia**, July 5, 2006. Signed as a free agent by **Detroit**, July 16, 2007.

CULLEN, Matt

(KUH-lehn, MAT) **CAR.**

Center. Shoots left. 6'1", 205 lbs. Born, Virginia, MN, November 2, 1976. Anaheim's 2nd choice, 35th overall, in 1996 Entry Draft.

Season	Club	League	GP	G	A	Pts	PIM	PP	SH	GW	S	%	+/-	TF	F%	Min	GP	G	A	Pts	PIM	PP	SH	GW	Min
1994-95	Moorhead Spuds	High-MN	28	47	42	89	78	....	....	....	....	....	....	....	....	....	....	....	....	....	....	....	....	....	....
1995-96	St. Cloud State	WCHA	39	12	29	41	28	....	....	....	....	....	....	....	....	....	....	....	....	....	....	....	....	....	....
1996-97	St. Cloud State	WCHA	36	15	30	45	70	....	....	....	....	....	....	....	....	....	....	....	....	....	....	....	....	....	....
	Baltimore Bandits	AHL	6	3	3	6	7	....	....	....	....	....	....	....	....	....	3	0	2	2	0	....	....	....	....
1997-98	Anaheim	NHL	61	6	21	27	23	2	0	0	75	8.0	–4	....	....	....	....	....	....	....	....	....	....	....	....
	Cincinnati	AHL	18	15	12	27	2	....	....	....	....	....	....	....	....	....	....	....	....	....	....	....	....	....	....
1998-99	Anaheim	NHL	75	11	14	25	47	5	1	1	112	9.8	–12	1047	47.7	15:31	4	0	0	0	0	0	0	0	15:30
	Cincinnati	AHL	3	1	2	3	8	....	....	....	....	....	....	....	....	....	....	....	....	....	....	....	....	....	....
99-2000	Anaheim	NHL	80	13	26	39	24	1	0	1	137	9.5	5	1247	44.6	16:54	....	....	....	....	....	....	....	....	....
2000-01	Anaheim	NHL	82	10	30	40	38	4	0	1	159	6.3	–23	1478	48.0	18:15	....	....	....	....	....	....	....	....	....
2001-02	Anaheim	NHL	79	18	30	48	24	3	1	4	164	11.0	–1	1283	51.4	17:01	....	....	....	....	....	....	....	....	....
2002-03	Anaheim	NHL	50	7	14	21	12	1	0	1	77	9.1	–4	271	50.6	14:18	....	....	....	....	....	....	....	....	....
	Florida	NHL	30	6	6	12	22	2	1	1	54	11.1	–4	423	47.3	14:43	....	....	....	....	....	....	....	....	....
2003-04	Florida	NHL	56	6	13	19	24	1	0	2	75	8.0	–2	735	50.6	14:12	....	....	....	....	....	....	....	....	....
2004-05	SG Cortina	Italy	36	*27	33	60	64	....	....	....	....	....	....	....	....	....	18	8	14	22	32	....	....	....	....
2005-06 ♦	Carolina	NHL	78	25	24	49	40	8	0	5	214	11.7	4	583	52.1	16:26	25	4	14	18	12	2	0	1	15:37
2006-07	NY Rangers	NHL	80	16	25	41	52	2	3	2	217	7.4	0	1134	54.6	17:10	10	1	3	4	6	0	0	1	16:55
	NHL Totals		671	118	203	321	306	29	6	18	1284	9.2		8201	49.5	16:20	39	5	17	22	18	2	0	2	15:57

WCHA Second All-Star Team (1997)

Traded to **Florida** by **Anaheim** with Pavel Trnka and Anaheim's 4th round choice (James Pemberton) in 2003 Entry Draft for Sandis Ozolinsh and Lance Ward, January 30, 2003. Signed as a free agent by **Carolina**, August 5, 2004. Signed as a free agent by **Cortina** (Italy), September 18, 2004. Signed as a free agent by **NY Rangers**, July 1, 2006. Traded to **Carolina** by **NY Rangers** for Andrew Hutchinson, Joe Barnes and Carolina's 3rd round choice in 2008 Entry Draft, July 17, 2007.

CULLIMORE, Jassen

(KUHL-ih-mohr, JAY-suhn)

Defense. Shoots left. 6'5", 244 lbs. Born, Simcoe, Ont., December 4, 1972. Vancouver's 2nd choice, 29th overall, in 1991 Entry Draft.

Season	Club	League	GP	G	A	Pts	PIM	PP	SH	GW	S	%	+/-	TF	F%	Min	GP	G	A	Pts	PIM	PP	SH	GW	Min
1986-87	Caledonia	OHA-C	18	2	0	2	9	....	....	....	....	....	....	....	....	....	....	....	....	....	....	....	....	....	....
1987-88	Simcoe Rams	OHA-C	35	11	14	25	92	....	....	....	....	....	....	....	....	....	....	....	....	....	....	....	....	....	....
1988-89	Peterborough	OHA-B	29	11	17	28	88	....	....	....	....	....	....	....	....	....	....	....	....	....	....	....	....	....	....
	Peterborough	OHL	20	2	1	3	6	....	....	....	....	....	....	....	....	....	....	....	....	....	....	....	....	....	....
1989-90	Peterborough	OHL	59	2	6	8	61	....	....	....	....	....	....	....	....	....	11	0	2	2	8	....	....	....	....
1990-91	Peterborough	OHL	62	8	16	24	74	....	....	....	....	....	....	....	....	....	4	1	0	1	7	....	....	....	....
1991-92	Peterborough	OHL	54	9	37	46	65	....	....	....	....	....	....	....	....	....	10	3	6	9	8	....	....	....	....
1992-93	Hamilton	AHL	56	5	7	12	60	....	....	....	....	....	....	....	....	....	....	....	....	....	....	....	....	....	....
1993-94	Hamilton	AHL	71	8	20	28	86	....	....	....	....	....	....	....	....	....	3	0	1	1	2	....	....	....	....
1994-95	Syracuse Crunch	AHL	33	2	7	9	66	....	....	....	....	....	....	....	....	....	....	....	....	....	....	....	....	....	....
	Vancouver	NHL	34	1	2	3	39	0	0	0	30	3.3	–2	....	....	....	11	0	0	0	12	0	0	0	....
1995-96	Vancouver	NHL	27	1	1	2	21	0	0	1	12	8.3	4	....	....	....	....	....	....	....	....	....	....	....	....
1996-97	Vancouver	NHL	3	0	0	0	2	0	0	0	2	0.0	–2	....	....	....	....	....	....	....	....	....	....	....	....
	Montreal	NHL	49	2	6	8	42	0	1	1	52	3.8	4	....	....	....	2	0	0	0	2	0	0	0	....
1997-98	Montreal	NHL	3	0	0	0	4	0	0	0	1	0.0	0	....	....	....	....	....	....	....	....	....	....	....	....
	Fredericton	AHL	5	1	0	1	8	....	....	....	....	....	....	....	....	....	....	....	....	....	....	....	....	....	....
	Tampa Bay	NHL	25	1	2	3	22	1	0	0	17	5.9	–4	....	....	....	....	....	....	....	....	....	....	....	....
1998-99	Tampa Bay	NHL	78	5	12	17	81	1	1	1	73	6.8	–22	0	0.0	20:14	....	....	....	....	....	....	....	....	....
99-2000	Providence Bruins	AHL	16	5	10	15	31	....	....	....	....	....	....	....	....	....	....	....	....	....	....	....	....	....	....
	Tampa Bay	NHL	46	1	1	2	66	0	0	0	23	4.3	–12	2	0.0	15:38	....	....	....	....	....	....	....	....	....
2000-01	Tampa Bay	NHL	74	1	6	7	80	0	0	0	56	1.8	–6	0	0.0	19:43	....	....	....	....	....	....	....	....	....
2001-02	Tampa Bay	NHL	78	4	9	13	58	0	0	1	84	4.8	–1	0	0.0	20:07	....	....	....	....	....	....	....	....	....
2002-03	Tampa Bay	NHL	28	1	3	4	31	0	0	0	23	4.3	3	0	0.0	18:25	11	1	1	2	4	0	0	0	22:11
2003-04 ♦	Tampa Bay	NHL	79	2	5	7	58	0	0	1	78	2.6	8	0	0.0	19:02	11	0	2	2	6	0	0	0	15:15
2004-05			DID NOT PLAY																						
2005-06	Chicago	NHL	54	1	6	7	53	1	0	1	23	4.3	–24	0	0.0	16:58	....	....	....	....	....	....	....	....	....
2006-07	Chicago	NHL	65	1	6	7	64	0	0	0	17	5.9	–6	0	0.0	16:17	....	....	....	....	....	....	....	....	....
	NHL Totals		643	21	59	80	621	3	2	6	491	4.3		2	0.0	18:34	35	1	3	4	24	0	0	0	18:43

OHL Second All-Star Team (1992)

Traded to **Montreal** by **Vancouver** for Donald Brashear, November 13, 1996. Claimed on waivers by **Tampa Bay** from **Montreal**, January 22, 1998. Loaned to **Providence** (AHL) by **Tampa Bay**, October 1, 1999. • Missed majority of 2002-03 season recovering from elbow injury suffered in game vs. Vancouver, November 29, 2002. Signed as a free agent by **Chicago**, July 22, 2004. Traded to **Montreal** by **Chicago** with Tony Salmelainen for Sergei Samsonov, June 16, 2007.

CUMISKEY, Kyle

(kuh-MIHS-kee, KIGHL) **COL.**

Defense. Shoots left. 5'10", 185 lbs. Born, Abbotsford, B.C., December 2, 1986. Colorado's 9th choice, 222nd overall, in 2005 Entry Draft.

Season	Club	League	GP	G	A	Pts	PIM	PP	SH	GW	S	%	+/-	TF	F%	Min	GP	G	A	Pts	PIM	PP	SH	GW	Min
2002-03	Penticton	BCHL	59	10	11	21	36	....	....	....	....	....	....	....	....	....	....	....	....	....	....	....	....	....	....
2003-04	Kelowna Rockets	WHL	54	2	7	9	20	....	....	....	....	....	....	....	....	....	17	0	0	0	0	....	....	....	....
2004-05	Kelowna Rockets	WHL	72	4	36	40	47	....	....	....	....	....	....	....	....	....	24	0	13	13	12	....	....	....	....
2005-06	Kelowna Rockets	WHL	51	6	24	30	52	....	....	....	....	....	....	....	....	....	12	0	6	6	8	....	....	....	....
2006-07	Colorado	NHL	9	1	1	2	2	0	0	0	8	12.5	0	0	0.0	13:28	....	....	....	....	....	....	....	....	....
	Albany River Rats	AHL	63	7	26	33	32	....	....	....	....	....	....	....	....	....	5	0	2	2	6	....	....	....	....
	NHL Totals		9	1	1	2	2	0	0	0	8	12.5		0	0.0	13:28	....	....	....	....	....	....	....	....	....

CUTTA, Jakub

(KOO-tuh, YA-kuhb) **WSH.**

Defense. Shoots left. 6'3", 214 lbs. Born, Jablonec nad Nisou, Czech., December 29, 1981. Washington's 3rd choice, 61st overall, in 2000 Entry Draft.

Season	Club	League	GP	G	A	Pts	PIM	PP	SH	GW	S	%	+/-	TF	F%	Min	GP	G	A	Pts	PIM	PP	SH	GW	Min
1997-98	Liberec Jr.	CzRep-Jr.	29	3	13	16	70	....	....	....	....	....	....	....	....	....	....	....	....	....	....	....	....	....	....
1998-99	Swift Current	WHL	59	3	3	6	63	....	....	....	....	....	....	....	....	....	....	....	....	....	....	....	....	....	....
99-2000	Swift Current	WHL	71	2	12	14	114	....	....	....	....	....	....	....	....	....	12	0	2	2	24	....	....	....	....
2000-01	Washington	NHL	3	0	0	0	0	0	0	0	1	0.0	–1	0	0.0	11:33	....	....	....	....	....	....	....	....	....
	Swift Current	WHL	47	5	8	13	102	....	....	....	....	....	....	....	....	....	16	1	3	4	32	....	....	....	....
2001-02	Washington	NHL	2	0	0	0	0	0	0	0	2	0.0	–3	0	0.0	16:02	....	....	....	....	....	....	....	....	....
	Portland Pirates	AHL	56	1	3	4	69	....	....	....	....	....	....	....	....	....	....	....	....	....	....	....	....	....	....
2002-03	Portland Pirates	AHL	66	3	12	15	106	....	....	....	....	....	....	....	....	....	3	0	0	0	2	....	....	....	....
2003-04	Washington	NHL	3	0	0	0	0	0	0	0	1	0.0	–1	0	0.0	13:54	....	....	....	....	....	....	....	....	....
	Portland Pirates	AHL	59	1	5	6	58	....	....	....	....	....	....	....	....	....	7	2	0	2	7	....	....	....	....
2004-05	Portland Pirates	AHL	63	0	5	5	100	....	....	....	....	....	....	....	....	....	....	....	....	....	....	....	....	....	....
2005-06	Hershey Bears	AHL	51	1	2	3	84	....	....	....	....	....	....	....	....	....	21	2	3	5	38	....	....	....	....
2006-07	Liberec	CzRep	37	0	2	2	99	....	....	....	....	....	....	....	....	....	6	0	1	1	16	....	....	....	....
	NHL Totals		8	0	0	0	0	0	0	0	4	0.0		0	0.0	13:33	....	....	....	....	....	....	....	....	....

Signed as a free agent by **Liberec** (CzRep), August 22, 2006.

CZERKAWSKI, Mariusz

(chehr-KAWV-skee, MAIR-ee-UHZ)

Right wing. Shoots left. 6', 200 lbs. Born, Radomsko, Poland, April 13, 1972. Boston's 5th choice, 106th overall, in 1991 Entry Draft.

Season	Club	League	GP	G	A	Pts	PIM	PP	SH	GW	S	%	+/-	TF	F%	Min	GP	G	A	Pts	PIM	PP	SH	GW	Min
1990-91	GKS Tychy	Poland	24	25	15	40	....	....	....	....	....	....	....	....	....	....	....	....	....	....	....	....	....	....	....
1991-92	Djurgarden	Sweden	39	8	5	13	4	....	....	....	....	....	....	....	....	....	3	0	0	0	2	....	....	....	....
	Poland	Olympics	5	0	1	1	4	....	....	....	....	....	....	....	....	....	....	....	....	....	....	....	....	....	....
1992-93	Hammarby	Sweden-2	32	*39	30	*69	74	....	....	....	....	....	....	....	....	....	13	*16	7	*23	34	....	....	....	....
1993-94	Djurgarden	Sweden	39	13	21	34	20	....	....	....	....	....	....	....	....	....	6	3	1	4	2	....	....	....	....
	Boston	NHL	4	2	1	3	0	1	0	0	11	18.2	–2	....	....	....	13	3	3	6	4	1	0	0	....

			Regular Season														Playoffs								
Season	Club	League	GP	G	A	Pts	PIM	PP	SH	GW	S	%	+/-	TF	F%	Min	GP	G	A	Pts	PIM	PP	SH	GW	Min
1994-95	Kiekko-Espoo	Finland	7	9	3	12	10	....	....	....	....	....	....	....	....	....	....	....	....	....	....	....	....	....	....
	Boston	NHL	47	12	14	26	31	1	0	2	126	9.5	4	....	....	....	5	1	0	1	0	0	0	0	....
1995-96	Boston	NHL	33	5	6	11	10	1	0	0	63	7.9	−11	....	....	....	....	....	....	....	....	....	....	....	....
	Edmonton	NHL	37	12	17	29	8	2	0	1	79	15.2	7	....	....	....	....	....	....	....	....	....	....	....	....
1996-97	Edmonton	NHL	76	26	21	47	16	4	0	3	182	14.3	0	....	....	....	12	2	1	3	10	0	0	0	....
1997-98	NY Islanders	NHL	68	12	13	25	23	2	0	1	136	8.8	11	....	....	....	....	....	....	....	....	....	....	....	....
1998-99	NY Islanders	NHL	78	21	17	38	14	4	0	1	205	10.2	−10	2	0.0	14:18	....	....	....	....	....	....	....	....	....
99-2000	NY Islanders	NHL	79	35	35	70	34	16	0	4	276	12.7	−16	4	25.0	17:45	....	....	....	....	....	....	....	....	....
2000-01	NY Islanders	NHL	82	30	32	62	48	10	1	0	287	10.5	−24	8	50.0	18:44	....	....	....	....	....	....	....	....	....
2001-02	NY Islanders	NHL	82	22	29	51	48	6	0	6	169	13.0	−8	10	10.0	15:58	7	2	2	4	4	1	0	0	12:58
2002-03	Montreal	NHL	43	5	9	14	16	1	0	0	77	6.5	−7	2	0.0	13:10	....	....	....	....	....	....	....	....	....
	Hamilton	AHL	20	8	12	20	12	....	....	....	....	....	....	....	....	....	6	1	3	4	6	....	....	....	....
2003-04	NY Islanders	NHL	81	25	24	49	16	9	0	2	157	15.9	8	6	16.7	13:02	5	0	1	1	0	0	0	0	10:43
2004-05	Djurgarden	Sweden	46	15	9	24	20	....	....	....	....	....	....	....	....	....	5	1	0	1	2	....	....	....	....
2005-06	Toronto	NHL	19	4	1	5	6	1	0	0	41	9.8	−2	0	0.0	13:30	....	....	....	....	....	....	....	....	....
	Boston	NHL	16	4	1	5	4	0	0	0	31	12.9	−4	0	0.0	12:01	....	....	....	....	....	....	....	....	....
2006-07	Rapperswil	Swiss	43	21	20	41	70	....	....	....	....	....	....	....	....	....	7	6	6	12	16	....	....	....	....
	NHL Totals		745	215	220	435	274	58	1	20	1840	11.7		32	21.9	15:29	42	8	7	15	18	2	0	0	12:02

Played in NHL All-Star Game (2000)

Traded to **Edmonton** by **Boston** with Sean Brown and Boston's 1st round choice (Matthieu Descoteaux) in 1996 Entry Draft for Bill Ranford, January 11, 1996. Traded to **NY Islanders** by **Edmonton** for Dan LaCouture, August 25, 1997. Traded to **Montreal** by **NY Islanders** for Arron Asham and Montreal's 5th round choice (Marcus Paulsson) in 2002 Entry Draft, June 22, 2002. Signed as a free agent by **NY Islanders**, July 17, 2003. Signed as a free agent by **Djurgarden** (Sweden), September 9, 2004. Signed as a free agent by **Toronto**, September 10, 2005. Claimed on waivers by **Boston** from **Toronto**, March 8, 2006. Signed as a free agent by **Rapperswil** (Swiss), July 21, 2006.

DAGENAIS, Pierre

(da-ZHUH-nay, PEE-air)

Right wing. Shoots left. 6'4", 217 lbs. Born, Blainville, Que., March 4, 1978. New Jersey's 6th choice, 105th overall, in 1998 Entry Draft.

Season	Club	League	GP	G	A	Pts	PIM	PP	SH	GW	S	%	+/-	TF	F%	Min	GP	G	A	Pts	PIM	PP	SH	GW	Min
1994-95	Laval-Laurentides	QAAA	34	28	14	42	68	....	....	....	....	....	....	....	....	....	13	10	9	19	32	....	....	....	....
1995-96	Moncton Alpines	QMJHL	67	43	25	68	59	....	....	....	....	....	....	....	....	....	....	....	....	....	....	....	....	....	....
1996-97	Moncton Wildcats	QMJHL	6	4	2	6	0	....	....	....	....	....	....	....	....	....	....	....	....	....	....	....	....	....	....
	Laval Titan	QMJHL	37	16	14	30	40	....	....	....	....	....	....	....	....	....	....	....	....	....	....	....	....	....	....
	Rouyn-Noranda	QMJHL	27	21	8	29	22	....	....	....	....	....	....	....	....	....	....	....	....	....	....	....	....	....	....
1997-98	Rouyn-Noranda	QMJHL	60	*66	67	133	50	....	....	....	....	....	....	....	....	....	6	6	2	8	2	....	....	....	....
1998-99	Albany River Rats	AHL	69	17	13	30	37	....	....	....	....	....	....	....	....	....	4	0	0	0	0	....	....	....	....
99-2000	Albany River Rats	AHL	80	35	30	65	47	....	....	....	....	....	....	....	....	....	5	1	0	1	14	....	....	....	....
2000-01	New Jersey	NHL	9	3	2	5	6	1	0	1	20	15.0	1	8	37.5	12:22	....	....	....	....	....	....	....	....	....
	Albany River Rats	AHL	69	34	28	62	52	....	....	....	....	....	....	....	....	....	....	....	....	....	....	....	....	....	....
2001-02	New Jersey	NHL	16	3	3	6	4	1	0	1	30	10.0	−5	5	40.0	10:54	....	....	....	....	....	....	....	....	....
	Albany River Rats	AHL	6	0	2	2	2	....	....	....	....	....	....	....	....	....	....	....	....	....	....	....	....	....	....
	Florida	NHL	26	7	1	8	4	2	0	0	47	14.9	−5	4	75.0	11:04	....	....	....	....	....	....	....	....	....
	Utah Grizzlies	AHL	4	1	1	2	2	....	....	....	....	....	....	....	....	....	....	....	....	....	....	....	....	....	....
2002-03	Florida	NHL	9	0	0	0	4	0	0	0	5	0.0	−1	0	0.0	6:01	....	....	....	....	....	....	....	....	....
	San Antonio	AHL	49	21	14	35	28	....	....	....	....	....	....	....	....	....	3	2	0	2	2	....	....	....	....
2003-04	Montreal	NHL	50	17	10	27	24	4	0	3	149	11.4	15	121	42.2	13:53	8	0	1	1	6	0	0	0	12:06
	Hamilton	AHL	20	12	9	21	19	....	....	....	....	....	....	....	....	....	....	....	....	....	....	....	....	....	....
2004-05	HC Ajoie	Swiss-2	7	5	5	10	12	....	....	....	....	....	....	....	....	....	6	7	7	14	6	....	....	....	....
2005-06	Montreal	NHL	32	5	7	12	16	2	0	1	74	6.8	−5	81	53.1	9:55	....	....	....	....	....	....	....	....	....
	Hamilton	AHL	38	12	13	25	23	....	....	....	....	....	....	....	....	....	....	....	....	....	....	....	....	....	....
2006-07	Jokerit Helsinki	Finland	16	2	7	9	12	....	....	....	....	....	....	....	....	....	....	....	....	....	....	....	....	....	....
	NHL Totals		142	35	23	58	58	10	0	6	325	10.8		219	46.6	11:33	8	0	1	1	6	0	0	0	12:06

• Re-entered NHL Entry Draft. Originally New Jersey's 4th choice, 47th overall, in 1996 Entry Draft.

QMJHL All-Rookie Team (1996) • QMJHL Second All-Star Team (1998) • AHL Second All-Star Team (2001)

Claimed on waivers by **Florida** from **New Jersey**, January 12, 2002. Signed as a free agent by **Montreal**, July 4, 2003. Signed as a free agent by **Ajoie** (Swiss-2), January 10, 2005. Signed as a free agent by **Jokerit Helsinki** (Finland), October 18, 2006.

DAIGLE, Alexandre

(DAYG, al-ehx-AHN-druh)

Center. Shoots left. 6', 195 lbs. Born, Montreal, Que., February 7, 1975. Ottawa's 1st choice, 1st overall, in 1993 Entry Draft.

Season	Club	League	GP	G	A	Pts	PIM	PP	SH	GW	S	%	+/-	TF	F%	Min	GP	G	A	Pts	PIM	PP	SH	GW	Min
1990-91	Laval-Laurentides	QAAA	42	*50	*60	*110	98	....	....	....	....	....	....	....	....	....	13	5	9	14	23	....	....	....	....
1991-92	Victoriaville Tigres	QMJHL	66	35	75	110	63	....	....	....	....	....	....	....	....	....	....	....	....	....	....	....	....	....	....
1992-93	Victoriaville Tigres	QMJHL	53	45	92	137	85	....	....	....	....	....	....	....	....	....	6	5	6	11	4	....	....	....	....
1993-94	Ottawa	NHL	84	20	31	51	40	4	0	2	168	11.9	−45	....	....	....	....	....	....	....	....	....	....	....	....
1994-95	Victoriaville Tigres	QMJHL	18	14	20	34	16	....	....	....	....	....	....	....	....	....	....	....	....	....	....	....	....	....	....
	Ottawa	NHL	47	16	21	37	14	4	1	2	105	15.2	−22	....	....	....	....	....	....	....	....	....	....	....	....
1995-96	Ottawa	NHL	50	5	12	17	24	1	0	0	77	6.5	−30	....	....	....	....	....	....	....	....	....	....	....	....
1996-97	Ottawa	NHL	82	26	25	51	33	4	0	5	203	12.8	−33	....	....	....	7	0	0	0	2	0	0	0	....
1997-98	Ottawa	NHL	38	7	9	16	8	4	0	2	68	10.3	−7	....	....	....	....	....	....	....	....	....	....	....	....
	Philadelphia	NHL	37	9	17	26	6	4	0	3	78	11.5	−1	....	....	....	5	0	2	2	0	0	0	0	....
1998-99	Philadelphia	NHL	31	3	2	5	2	1	0	1	26	11.5	−1	53	39.6	7:59	....	....	....	....	....	....	....	....	....
	Tampa Bay	NHL	32	6	6	12	2	3	0	0	56	10.7	−12	4	50.0	13:59	....	....	....	....	....	....	....	....	....
99-2000	NY Rangers	NHL	58	8	18	26	23	1	0	1	52	15.4	−5	339	53.1	10:59	....	....	....	....	....	....	....	....	....
	Hartford	AHL	16	6	13	19	4	....	....	....	....	....	....	....	....	....	....	....	....	....	....	....	....	....	....
2000-01			OUT OF HOCKEY – RETIRED																						
2001-02			OUT OF HOCKEY – RETIRED																						
2002-03	Pittsburgh	NHL	33	4	3	7	8	1	0	0	48	8.3	−10	24	33.3	10:57	....	....	....	....	....	....	....	....	....
	Wilkes-Barre	AHL	40	9	29	38	18	....	....	....	....	....	....	....	....	....	4	0	1	1	0	....	....	....	....
2003-04	Minnesota	NHL	78	20	31	51	14	6	0	3	145	13.8	−4	72	51.4	15:10	....	....	....	....	....	....	....	....	....
2004-05	Morges	Swiss-2	....	....	....	....	....	....	....	....	....	....	....	....	....	....	2	1	1	2	0	....	....	....	....
2005-06	Minnesota	NHL	46	5	23	28	12	2	0	1	59	8.5	−6	12	41.7	13:00	....	....	....	....	....	....	....	....	....
	Manchester	AHL	16	6	8	14	4	....	....	....	....	....	....	....	....	....	7	4	7	11	6	....	....	....	....
2006-07	HC Davos	Swiss	44	22	39	61	44	....	....	....	....	....	....	....	....	....	18	4	9	13	6	....	....	....	....
	NHL Totals		616	129	198	327	186	35	1	20	1085	11.9		504	50.2	12:30	12	0	2	2	2	0	0	0	....

QMJHL Second All-Star Team (1992) • QMJHL Offensive Rookie of the Year (1992) • Canadian Major Junior Rookie of the Year (1992) • QMJHL First All-Star Team (1993)

Traded to **Philadelphia** by **Ottawa** for Vaclav Prospal, Pat Falloon and Dallas' 2nd round choice (previously acquired, Ottawa selected Chris Bala) in 1998 Entry Draft, January 17, 1998. Traded to **Edmonton** by **Philadelphia** for Andrei Kovalenko, January 29, 1999. Traded to **Tampa Bay** by **Edmonton** for Alexander Selivanov, January 29, 1999. Traded to **NY Rangers** by **Tampa Bay** for cash, October 3, 1999. Signed as a free agent by **Pittsburgh**, August 13, 2002. Signed as a free agent by **Minnesota**, September 30, 2003. Signed as a free agent by **Morges** (Swiss-2), February 5, 2005. Signed as a free agent by **Davos** (Swiss), May 13, 2006.

DALEY, Trevor

(DAY-lee, TREH-vuhr) **DAL.**

Defense. Shoots left. 5'11", 207 lbs. Born, Toronto, Ont., October 9, 1983. Dallas' 5th choice, 43rd overall, in 2002 Entry Draft.

Season	Club	League	GP	G	A	Pts	PIM	PP	SH	GW	S	%	+/-	TF	F%	Min	GP	G	A	Pts	PIM	PP	SH	GW	Min
1998-99	Vaughan Vipers	OPJHL	44	10	36	46	79	....	....	....	....	....	....	....	....	....	....	....	....	....	....	....	....	....	....
99-2000	Sault Ste. Marie	OHL	54	16	30	46	77	....	....	....	....	....	....	....	....	....	15	3	7	10	12	....	....	....	....
2000-01	Sault Ste. Marie	OHL	58	14	27	41	105	....	....	....	....	....	....	....	....	....	....	....	....	....	....	....	....	....	....
2001-02	Sault Ste. Marie	OHL	47	9	39	48	38	....	....	....	....	....	....	....	....	....	6	2	2	4	4	....	....	....	....
2002-03	Sault Ste. Marie	OHL	57	20	33	53	128	....	....	....	....	....	....	....	....	....	1	0	0	0	2	....	....	....	....
2003-04	Dallas	NHL	27	1	5	6	14	1	0	0	34	2.9	−6	0	0.0	16:02	1	0	0	0	0	0	0	0	10:21
	Utah Grizzlies	AHL	40	8	6	14	76	....	....	....	....	....	....	....	....	....	....	....	....	....	....	....	....	....	....
2004-05	Hamilton	AHL	78	7	27	34	109	....	....	....	....	....	....	....	....	....	4	0	1	1	2	....	....	....	....
2005-06	Dallas	NHL	81	3	11	14	87	0	0	1	91	3.3	−2	0	0.0	18:40	3	0	0	0	0	0	0	0	11:30
2006-07	Dallas	NHL	74	4	8	12	63	0	0	1	68	5.9	2	0	0.0	19:23	7	1	0	1	4	0	0	0	22:26
	NHL Totals		182	8	24	32	164	1	0	2	193	4.1		0	0.0	18:34	11	1	0	1	4	0	0	0	18:21

DALLMAN, Kevin
(DAL-mahn, KEH-vihn) **L.A.**

Defense. Shoots right. 5'11", 195 lbs. Born, Niagara Falls, Ont., February 26, 1981.

Season	Club	League	GP	G	A	Pts	PIM	PP	SH	GW	S	%	+/-	TF	F%	Min	GP	G	A	Pts	PIM	PP	SH	GW	Min
1996-97	Niagara Falls	OHA-B	3	0	1	1	2	....	....	....	....	....	....	....	....	....	....	....	....	....	....	....	....	....	....
1997-98	Niagara Falls	OHA-B	47	13	25	38	42	....	....	....	....	....	....	....	....	....	....	....	....	....	....	....	....	....	....
1998-99	Guelph Storm	OHL	68	8	30	38	52	....	....	....	....	....	....	....	....	....	11	1	4	5	2	....	....	....	....
99-2000	Guelph Storm	OHL	67	13	46	59	38	....	....	....	....	....	....	....	....	....	6	0	2	2	11	....	....	....	....
2000-01	Guelph Storm	OHL	66	25	52	77	88	....	....	....	....	....	....	....	....	....	1	0	0	0	0	....	....	....	....
2001-02	Guelph Storm	OHL	67	23	63	86	68	....	....	....	....	....	....	....	....	....	9	8	8	16	22	....	....	....	....
2002-03	Providence Bruins	AHL	72	2	19	21	53	....	....	....	....	....	....	....	....	....	....	....	....	....	....	....	....	....	....
2003-04	Providence Bruins	AHL	65	6	23	29	44	....	....	....	....	....	....	....	....	....	2	0	0	0	0	....	....	....	....
2004-05	Providence Bruins	AHL	71	8	26	34	48	....	....	....	....	....	....	....	....	....	17	4	6	10	20	....	....	....	....
2005-06	**Boston**	**NHL**	**21**	**0**	**1**	**1**	**8**	**0**	**0**	**0**	**42**	**0.0**	**1**	**0**	**0.0**	**19:24**	....	....	....	....	....	....	....	....	....
	St. Louis	**NHL**	**46**	**4**	**9**	**13**	**21**	**3**	**0**	**0**	**89**	**4.5**	**–15**	**11**	**18.2**	**18:49**	....	....	....	....	....	....	....	....	....
2006-07	**Los Angeles**	**NHL**	**53**	**1**	**9**	**10**	**12**	**0**	**0**	**0**	**76**	**1.3**	**–13**	**20**	**20.0**	**12:48**	....	....	....	....	....	....	....	....	....
	Manchester	AHL	3	4	0	4	4	....	....	....	....	....	....	....	....	....	....	....	....	....	....	....	....	....	....
	NHL Totals		**120**	**5**	**19**	**24**	**41**	**3**	**0**	**0**	**207**	**2.4**		**31**	**19.4**	**16:16**	....	....	....	....	....	....	....	....	....

Memorial Cup Tournament All-Star Team (2002)

Signed as a free agent by **Boston**, July 18, 2002. Claimed on waivers by **St. Louis** from **Boston**, December 3, 2005. Signed as a free agent by **Los Angeles**, July 10, 2006.

DANDENAULT, Mathieu
(DAHN-deh-noh, MA-tyew) **MTL.**

Defense. Shoots right. 6', 215 lbs. Born, Sherbrooke, Que., February 3, 1976. Detroit's 2nd choice, 49th overall, in 1994 Entry Draft.

Season	Club	League	GP	G	A	Pts	PIM	PP	SH	GW	S	%	+/-	TF	F%	Min	GP	G	A	Pts	PIM	PP	SH	GW	Min
1990-91	Gloucester	Minor-ON	44	52	50	102	30	....	....	....	....	....	....	....	....	....	....	....	....	....	....	....	....	....	....
1991-92	Vanier Voyageurs	OHA-B	33	27	31	58	20	....	....	....	....	....	....	....	....	....	....	....	....	....	....	....	....	....	....
	Gloucester	CJHL	6	3	4	7	0	....	....	....	....	....	....	....	....	....	....	....	....	....	....	....	....	....	....
1992-93	Gloucester	CJHL	55	11	26	37	64	....	....	....	....	....	....	....	....	....	....	....	....	....	....	....	....	....	....
1993-94	Sherbrooke	QMJHL	67	17	36	53	67	....	....	....	....	....	....	....	....	....	12	4	10	14	12	....	....	....	....
1994-95	Sherbrooke	QMJHL	67	37	70	107	76	....	....	....	....	....	....	....	....	....	7	1	7	8	10	....	....	....	....
1995-96	**Detroit**	**NHL**	**34**	**5**	**7**	**12**	**6**	**1**	**0**	**0**	**32**	**15.6**	**6**	....	....	....	....	....	....	....	....	....	....	....	....
	Adirondack	AHL	4	0	0	0	0	....	....	....	....	....	....	....	....	....	....	....	....	....	....	....	....	....	....
1996-97 ♦	**Detroit**	**NHL**	**65**	**3**	**9**	**12**	**28**	**0**	**0**	**0**	**81**	**3.7**	**–10**	....	....	....	....	....	....	....	....	....	....	....	....
1997-98 ♦	**Detroit**	**NHL**	**68**	**5**	**12**	**17**	**43**	**0**	**0**	**0**	**75**	**6.7**	**5**	....	....	....	**3**	**1**	**0**	**1**	**0**	**1**	**0**	**0**	....
1998-99	**Detroit**	**NHL**	**75**	**4**	**10**	**14**	**59**	**0**	**0**	**0**	**94**	**4.3**	**17**	**3**	**0.0**	**15:10**	**10**	**0**	**1**	**1**	**0**	**0**	**0**	**0**	**11:51**
99-2000	**Detroit**	**NHL**	**81**	**6**	**12**	**18**	**20**	**0**	**0**	**0**	**98**	**6.1**	**–12**	**1**	**100.0**	**12:10**	**6**	**0**	**0**	**0**	**2**	**0**	**0**	**0**	**8:31**
2000-01	**Detroit**	**NHL**	**73**	**10**	**15**	**25**	**38**	**2**	**0**	**2**	**95**	**10.5**	**11**	**0**	**0.0**	**16:06**	**6**	**0**	**1**	**1**	**0**	**0**	**0**	**0**	**14:11**
2001-02 ♦	**Detroit**	**NHL**	**81**	**8**	**12**	**20**	**44**	**2**	**0**	**3**	**97**	**8.2**	**–5**	**1**	**0.0**	**16:43**	**23**	**1**	**2**	**3**	**8**	**0**	**1**	**0**	**13:29**
2002-03	**Detroit**	**NHL**	**74**	**4**	**15**	**19**	**64**	**1**	**0**	**0**	**74**	**5.4**	**25**	**0**	**0.0**	**19:08**	**4**	**0**	**0**	**0**	**2**	**0**	**0**	**0**	**25:51**
2003-04	**Detroit**	**NHL**	**65**	**3**	**9**	**12**	**40**	**0**	**1**	**0**	**68**	**4.4**	**9**	**1**	**0.0**	**13:47**	**12**	**1**	**1**	**2**	**6**	**0**	**0**	**1**	**13:33**
2004-05	Asiago	Italy	10	0	2	2	2	....	....	....	....	....	....	....	....	....	9	1	6	7	4	....	....	....	....
2005-06	**Montreal**	**NHL**	**82**	**5**	**15**	**20**	**83**	**0**	**0**	**1**	**101**	**5.0**	**8**	**0**	**0.0**	**18:38**	**6**	**0**	**3**	**3**	**4**	**0**	**0**	**0**	**19:48**
2006-07	**Montreal**	**NHL**	**68**	**2**	**6**	**8**	**40**	**0**	**0**	**0**	**54**	**3.7**	**–8**	**3**	**0.0**	**16:07**	....	....	....	....	....	....	....	....	....
	NHL Totals		**766**	**55**	**122**	**177**	**465**	**6**	**1**	**6**	**869**	**6.3**		**9**	**11.1**	**16:00**	**70**	**3**	**8**	**11**	**22**	**1**	**1**	**1**	**14:10**

Signed as a free agent by **Asiago** (Italy), December 27, 2004. Signed as a free agent by **Montreal**, August 3, 2005.

DARCHE, Mathieu
(DAHRSH, MA-thew) **T.B.**

Left wing. Shoots left. 6'1", 220 lbs. Born, St. Laurent, Que., November 26, 1976.

Season	Club	League	GP	G	A	Pts	PIM	PP	SH	GW	S	%	+/-	TF	F%	Min	GP	G	A	Pts	PIM	PP	SH	GW	Min
1995-96	Choate-Rosemary	High-CT	STATISTICS NOT AVAILABLE																						
1996-97	McGill Redmen	OUAA	23	1	2	3	27	....	....	....	....	....	....	....	....	....	....	....	....	....	....	....	....	....	....
1997-98	McGill Redmen	OUAA	40	28	17	45	69	....	....	....	....	....	....	....	....	....	....	....	....	....	....	....	....	....	....
1998-99	McGill Redmen	OUAA	32	16	24	40	60	....	....	....	....	....	....	....	....	....	....	....	....	....	....	....	....	....	....
99-2000	McGill Redmen	OUAA	33	31	41	*72	38	....	....	....	....	....	....	....	....	....	5	2	8	10	16	....	....	....	....
2000-01	**Columbus**	**NHL**	**9**	**0**	**0**	**0**	**0**	**0**	**0**	**0**	**9**	**0.0**	**–4**	**1**	**0.0**	**10:07**	....	....	....	....	....	....	....	....	....
	Syracuse Crunch	AHL	66	16	24	40	21	....	....	....	....	....	....	....	....	....	5	0	1	1	4	....	....	....	....
2001-02	**Columbus**	**NHL**	**14**	**1**	**1**	**2**	**6**	**0**	**0**	**0**	**15**	**6.7**	**–5**	**3**	**33.3**	**9:49**	....	....	....	....	....	....	....	....	....
	Syracuse Crunch	AHL	63	22	23	45	26	....	....	....	....	....	....	....	....	....	10	2	5	7	2	....	....	....	....
2002-03	**Columbus**	**NHL**	**1**	**0**	**0**	**0**	**0**	**0**	**0**	**0**	**0**	**0.0**	**–1**	**0**	**0.0**	**6:57**	....	....	....	....	....	....	....	....	....
	Syracuse Crunch	AHL	76	32	32	64	38	....	....	....	....	....	....	....	....	....	....	....	....	....	....	....	....	....	....
2003-04	**Nashville**	**NHL**	**2**	**0**	**0**	**0**	**0**	**0**	**0**	**0**	**1**	**0.0**	**–1**	**0**	**0.0**	**6:39**	....	....	....	....	....	....	....	....	....
	Milwaukee	AHL	76	28	31	59	41	....	....	....	....	....	....	....	....	....	22	6	8	14	8	....	....	....	....
2004-05	Hershey Bears	AHL	79	29	25	54	49	....	....	....	....	....	....	....	....	....	....	....	....	....	....	....	....	....	....
2005-06	Fuchse Duisburg	Germany	52	12	13	25	88	....	....	....	....	....	....	....	....	....	5	1	3	4	4	....	....	....	....
2006-07	**San Jose**	**NHL**	**2**	**0**	**0**	**0**	**0**	**0**	**0**	**0**	**3**	**0.0**	**0**	**0**	**0.0**	**9:13**	....	....	....	....	....	....	....	....	....
	Worcester Sharks	AHL	76	35	45	80	72	....	....	....	....	....	....	....	....	....	5	2	2	4	2	....	....	....	....
	NHL Totals		**28**	**1**	**1**	**2**	**6**	**0**	**0**	**0**	**28**	**3.6**		**4**	**25.0**	**9:33**	....	....	....	....	....	....	....	....	....

OUAA East Second All-Star Team (1998) • OUAA East First All-Star Team (1999) • OUAA First All-Star Team (2000) • CIAU All-Canadian Team (2000)

Signed as a free agent by **Columbus**, May 16, 2000. Signed as a free agent by **Nashville**, September 10, 2003. Signed as a free agent by **Colorado**, July 26, 2004. Signed as a free agent by **San Jose**, July 10, 2006. Signed as a free agent by **Tampa Bay**, July 2, 2007.

DATSYUK, Pavel
(daht-SOOK, PAH-vehl) **DET.**

Center. Shoots left. 5'11", 197 lbs. Born, Sverdlovsk, USSR, July 20, 1978. Detroit's 8th choice, 171st overall, in 1998 Entry Draft.

Season	Club	League	GP	G	A	Pts	PIM	PP	SH	GW	S	%	+/-	TF	F%	Min	GP	G	A	Pts	PIM	PP	SH	GW	Min
1996-97	Yekaterinburg 2	Russia-3	18	2	2	4	4	....	....	....	....	....	....	....	....	....	....	....	....	....	....	....	....	....	....
	Yekaterinburg	Russia	36	12	10	22	12	....	....	....	....	....	....	....	....	....	....	....	....	....	....	....	....	....	....
1997-98	Yekaterinburg	Russia	24	3	5	8	4	....	....	....	....	....	....	....	....	....	....	....	....	....	....	....	....	....	....
	Yekaterinburg	Russia	22	7	8	15	4	....	....	....	....	....	....	....	....	....	....	....	....	....	....	....	....	....	....
1998-99	Yekaterinburg 2	Russia-4	10	14	14	28	4	....	....	....	....	....	....	....	....	....	....	....	....	....	....	....	....	....	....
	Yekaterinburg	Russia-2	35	21	23	44	14	....	....	....	....	....	....	....	....	....	9	3	7	10	10	....	....	....	....
99-2000	Yekaterinburg	Russia	15	1	3	4	4	....	....	....	....	....	....	....	....	....	....	....	....	....	....	....	....	....	....
2000-01	Ak Bars Kazan	Russia	42	9	18	27	10	....	....	....	....	....	....	....	....	....	4	0	1	1	2	....	....	....	....
2001-02 ♦	**Detroit**	**NHL**	**70**	**11**	**24**	**35**	**4**	**2**	**0**	**1**	**79**	**13.9**	**4**	**794**	**47.7**	**13:39**	**21**	**3**	**3**	**6**	**2**	**1**	**0**	**1**	**10:40**
	Russia	Olympics	6	1	2	3	0	....	....	....	....	....	....	....	....	....	....	....	....	....	....	....	....	....	....
2002-03	**Detroit**	**NHL**	**64**	**12**	**39**	**51**	**16**	**1**	**0**	**1**	**82**	**14.6**	**20**	**778**	**48.2**	**15:28**	**4**	**0**	**0**	**0**	**0**	**0**	**0**	**0**	**18:48**
2003-04	**Detroit**	**NHL**	**75**	**30**	**38**	**68**	**35**	**8**	**1**	**4**	**136**	**22.1**	**–2**	**1314**	**54.0**	**18:16**	**12**	**0**	**6**	**6**	**2**	**0**	**0**	**0**	**17:23**
2004-05	Dynamo Moscow	Russia	47	15	17	32	16	....	....	....	....	....	....	....	....	....	10	*6	3	9	4	....	....	....	....
2005-06	**Detroit**	**NHL**	**75**	**28**	**59**	**87**	**22**	**11**	**0**	**4**	**145**	**19.3**	**26**	**1059**	**53.1**	**17:53**	**5**	**0**	**3**	**3**	**0**	**0**	**0**	**0**	**20:05**
	Russia	Olympics	8	1	7	8	10	....	....	....	....	....	....	....	....	....	....	....	....	....	....	....	....	....	....
2006-07	**Detroit**	**NHL**	**79**	**27**	**60**	**87**	**20**	**5**	**2**	**5**	**207**	**13.0**	**36**	**845**	**56.2**	**19:57**	**18**	**8**	**8**	**16**	**8**	**4**	**0**	**2**	**22:03**
	NHL Totals		**363**	**108**	**220**	**328**	**97**	**27**	**3**	**15**	**649**	**16.6**		**4790**	**52.2**	**17:10**	**60**	**11**	**20**	**31**	**12**	**5**	**0**	**3**	**16:45**

Played in NHL All-Star Game (2004) • Lady Byng Memorial Trophy (2006, 2007)

• Spent majority of 1999-2000 season on **Kazan** (Russia) reserve squad. Signed as a free agent by **Dynamo Moscow** (Russia), June 19, 2004.

DAVISON, Rob
(DAY-vihs-ohn, RAWB) **S.J.**

Defense. Shoots left. 6'3", 220 lbs. Born, St. Catharines, Ont., May 1, 1980. San Jose's 4th choice, 98th overall, in 1998 Entry Draft.

Season	Club	League	GP	G	A	Pts	PIM	PP	SH	GW	S	%	+/-	TF	F%	Min	GP	G	A	Pts	PIM	PP	SH	GW	Min
1996-97	St. Mike's B's	OPJHL	45	2	6	8	93	....	....	....	....	....	....	....	....	....	6	0	0	0	9	....	....	....	....
1997-98	North Bay	OHL	59	0	11	11	200	....	....	....	....	....	....	....	....	....	....	....	....	....	....	....	....	....	....
1998-99	North Bay	OHL	59	2	17	19	150	....	....	....	....	....	....	....	....	....	4	0	1	1	12	....	....	....	....
99-2000	North Bay	OHL	67	4	6	10	194	....	....	....	....	....	....	....	....	....	6	0	1	1	8	....	....	....	....
2000-01	Kentucky	AHL	72	0	4	4	230	....	....	....	....	....	....	....	....	....	3	0	0	0	0	....	....	....	....
2001-02	Cleveland Barons	AHL	70	1	3	4	206	....	....	....	....	....	....	....	....	....	....	....	....	....	....	....	....	....	....
2002-03	**San Jose**	**NHL**	**15**	**1**	**2**	**3**	**22**	**0**	**0**	**0**	**15**	**6.7**	**4**	**0**	**0.0**	**17:53**	....	....	....	....	....	....	....	....	....
	Cleveland Barons	AHL	42	1	3	4	82	....	....	....	....	....	....	....	....	....	....	....	....	....	....	....	....	....	....
2003-04	**San Jose**	**NHL**	**55**	**0**	**3**	**3**	**92**	**0**	**0**	**0**	**33**	**0.0**	**–3**	**0**	**0.0**	**14:22**	**5**	**0**	**2**	**2**	**4**	**0**	**0**	**0**	**9:01**
2004-05	Cardiff Devils	Britain	24	2	3	5	114	....	....	....	....	....	....	....	....	....	8	0	1	1	12	....	....	....	....

			Regular Season														Playoffs								
Season	Club	League	GP	G	A	Pts	PIM	PP	SH	GW	S	%	+/-	TF	F%	Min	GP	G	A	Pts	PIM	PP	SH	GW	Min
2005-06	San Jose	NHL	69	1	5	6	76	0	0	0	36	2.8	6	0	0.0	13:50	1	0	0	0	0	0	0	0	8:00
2006-07	San Jose	NHL	22	0	2	2	27	0	0	0	14	0.0	–2	0	0.0	9:19									
	NHL Totals		161	2	12	14	217	0	0	0	98	2.0		0	0.0	13:47	6	0	2	2	4	0	0	0	8:51

Signed as a free agent by **Cardiff** (Britain), October 5, 2004.

DAWES, Nigel

(DAWZ, NIGH-juhl) **NYR**

Left wing. Shoots left. 5'8", 190 lbs. Born, Winnipeg, Man., February 9, 1985. NY Rangers' 5th choice, 149th overall, in 2003 Entry Draft.

Season	Club	League	GP	G	A	Pts	PIM	PP	SH	GW	S	%	+/-	TF	F%	Min	GP	G	A	Pts	PIM	PP	SH	GW	Min
2000-01	Wpg. Warriors	MMMHL	36	55	41	96	74																		
2001-02	Kootenay Ice	WHL	54	15	19	34	14										22	9	6	15	8				
2002-03	Kootenay Ice	WHL	72	47	45	92	54										11	4	8	12	6				
2003-04	Hartford	AHL	4	0	0	0	0																		
	Kootenay Ice	WHL	56	47	23	70	31										4	1	2	3	10				
2004-05	Kootenay Ice	WHL	63	50	26	76	30										12	5	10	15	5				
2005-06	Hartford	AHL	77	35	31	66	21										13	6	6	12	9				
2006-07	NY Rangers	NHL	8	1	0	1	0	0	0	0	7	14.3	–4	1	0.0	6:44	1	0	0	0	0	0	0	0	9:02
	Hartford	AHL	65	27	33	60	29										7	5	6	11	9				
	NHL Totals		8	1	0	1	0	0	0	0	7	14.3		1	0.0	6:44	1	0	0	0	0	0	0	0	9:02

WHL West Second All-Star Team (2003) • WHL West First All-Star Team (2004, 2005)

DELMORE, Andy

(DEHL-mohr, AN-dee)

Defense. Shoots right. 6', 200 lbs. Born, LaSalle, Ont., December 26, 1976.

Season	Club	League	GP	G	A	Pts	PIM	PP	SH	GW	S	%	+/-	TF	F%	Min	GP	G	A	Pts	PIM	PP	SH	GW	Min
1992-93	Chatham	OHA-B	47	4	21	25	38																		
1993-94	North Bay	OHL	45	2	7	9	33										17	0	0	0	2				
1994-95	North Bay	OHL	40	2	14	16	21																		
	Sarnia Sting	OHL	27	5	13	18	27										3	0	0	0	2				
1995-96	Sarnia Sting	OHL	64	21	38	59	45										10	3	7	10	2				
1996-97	Sarnia Sting	OHL	64	18	60	78	39										12	2	10	12	10				
	Fredericton	AHL	4	0	1	1	0																		
1997-98	Philadelphia	AHL	73	9	30	39	46										18	4	4	8	21				
1998-99	Philadelphia	NHL	2	0	1	1	0	0	0	0	2	0.0	–1	0	0.0	20:42									
	Philadelphia	AHL	70	5	18	23	51										15	1	4	5	6				
99-2000	Philadelphia	NHL	27	2	5	7	8	0	0	1	55	3.6	–1	0	0.0	17:17	18	5	2	7	14	1	0	1	17:33
	Philadelphia	AHL	39	12	14	26	31																		
2000-01	Philadelphia	NHL	66	5	9	14	16	2	0	0	119	4.2	2	0	0.0	17:39	2	1	0	1	2	0	0	1	15:20
2001-02	Nashville	NHL	73	16	22	38	22	11	0	3	175	9.1	–13	0	0.0	19:40									
2002-03	Nashville	NHL	71	18	16	34	28	14	0	6	149	12.1	–17	0	0.0	17:05									
2003-04	Buffalo	NHL	37	2	5	7	29	2	0	0	40	5.0	–5	0	0.0	15:11									
	Rochester	AHL	8	0	2	2	2																		
2004-05	Adler Mannheim	Germany	50	7	16	23	59										14	1	6	7	12				
2005-06	Columbus	NHL	7	0	0	0	2	0	0	0	7	0.0	–1	0	0.0	15:24									
	Syracuse Crunch	AHL	66	17	55	72	46										6	0	1	1	19				
2006-07	Springfield	AHL	47	12	12	24	22																		
	Chicago Wolves	AHL	28	5	11	16	10										15	0	6	6	2				
	NHL Totals		283	43	58	101	105	29	0	10	547	7.9		0	0.0	17:38	20	6	2	8	16	1	0	2	17:19

OHL First All-Star Team (1997) • AHL First All-Star Team (2006) • Eddie Shore Award (Outstanding Defenseman - AHL) (2006)

Signed as a free agent by **Philadelphia**, June 9, 1997. Traded to **Nashville** by **Philadelphia** for Nashville's 3rd round choice (later traded to Phoenix – Phoenix selected Joe Callahan) in 2002 Entry Draft, July 31, 2001. Traded to **Buffalo** by **Nashville** for Buffalo's 3rd round choice (later traded to Minnesota – Minnesota selected Clayton Stoner) in 2004 Entry Draft, June 27, 2003. Traded to **San Jose** by **Buffalo** with Curtis Brown for Jeff Jillson and San Jose's compensatory 7th round choice (Andrew Orpik) in 2005 Entry Draft, March 9, 2004. Traded to **Boston** by **San Jose** for future considerations, March 9, 2004. Signed as a free agent by **Mannheim** (Germany), July 21, 2004. Signed as a free agent by **Detroit**, August 16, 2005. Claimed on waivers by **Columbus** from **Detroit**, October 4, 2005. Signed as a free agent by **Tampa Bay**, July 1, 2006. Traded to **Atlanta** by **Tampa Bay** with Andre Deveaux for Stephen Baby and Kyle Wanvig, February 1, 2007. Signed as a free agent by **Hamburg** (Germany), June 13, 2007.

DEMITRA, Pavol

(deh-MEET-rah, PAH-vohl) **MIN.**

Left wing. Shoots left. 6', 202 lbs. Born, Dubnica, Czech., November 29, 1974. Ottawa's 9th choice, 227th overall, in 1993 Entry Draft.

Season	Club	League	GP	G	A	Pts	PIM	PP	SH	GW	S	%	+/-	TF	F%	Min	GP	G	A	Pts	PIM	PP	SH	GW	Min
1991-92	Dubnica	Czech-2	28	13	10	23	12																		
1992-93	Dubnica	Czech-2	4	3	0	3																			
	Dukla Trencin	Czech	46	11	17	28	0																		
1993-94	Ottawa	NHL	12	1	1	2	4	1	0	0	10	10.0	–7												
	P.E.I. Senators	AHL	41	18	23	41	8																		
1994-95	P.E.I. Senators	AHL	61	26	48	74	23										5	0	7	7	0				
	Ottawa	NHL	16	4	3	7	0	1	0	0	21	19.0	–4												
1995-96	Ottawa	NHL	31	7	10	17	6	2	0	1	66	10.6	–3												
	P.E.I. Senators	AHL	48	28	53	81	44																		
1996-97	Dukla Trencin	Slovakia	1	1	1	2																			
	Las Vegas	IHL	22	8	13	21	10																		
	St. Louis	NHL	8	3	0	3	2	2	0	1	15	20.0	0				6	1	3	4	6	0	0	0	
	Grand Rapids	IHL	42	20	30	50	24																		
1997-98	St. Louis	NHL	61	22	30	52	22	4	4	6	147	15.0	11				10	3	3	6	2	0	0	0	
1998-99	St. Louis	NHL	82	37	52	89	16	14	0	10	259	14.3	13	250	44.0	20:10	13	5	4	9	4	3	0	1	19:10
99-2000	St. Louis	NHL	71	28	47	75	8	8	0	4	241	11.6	34	41	39.0	19:13									
2000-01	St. Louis	NHL	44	20	25	45	16	5	0	5	124	16.1	27	8	37.5	18:03	15	2	4	6	2	0	0	1	18:13
2001-02	St. Louis	NHL	82	35	43	78	46	11	0	10	212	16.5	13	1224	48.1	19:11	10	4	7	11	6	2	1	1	19:45
	Slovakia	Olympics	2	1	2	3	2																		
2002-03	St. Louis	NHL	78	36	57	93	32	11	0	4	205	17.6	0	1253	46.1	19:47	7	2	4	6	2	1	0	0	18:20
2003-04	St. Louis	NHL	68	23	35	58	18	8	0	5	179	12.8	1	770	47.3	20:30	5	1	0	1	4	0	0	0	18:07
2004-05	Dukla Trencin	Slovakia	54	*28	*54	*82	39										12	4	13	17	14				
2005-06	Los Angeles	NHL	58	25	37	62	42	7	5	7	184	13.6	21	114	49.1	21:04									
	Slovakia	Olympics	6	2	5	7	2																		
2006-07	Minnesota	NHL	71	25	39	64	28	9	1	4	175	14.3	0	513	47.8	20:39	5	1	3	4	0	0	0	0	19:47
	NHL Totals		682	266	379	645	240	83	10	57	1838	14.5		4173	47.0	19:53	71	19	28	47	26	6	1	3	18:52

Lady Byng Memorial Trophy (2000)

Played in NHL All-Star Game (1999, 2000, 2002)

Traded to **St. Louis** by **Ottawa** for Christer Olsson, November 27, 1996. Signed as a free agent by **Trencin** (Slovakia), September 17, 2004. Signed as a free agent by **Los Angeles**, August 2, 2005. Traded to **Minnesota** by **Los Angeles** for Patrick O'Sullivan and Edmonton's 1st round choice (previously acquired, Los Angeles selected Trevor Lewis) in 2006 Entry Draft, June 24, 2006.

DEMPSEY, Nathan

(DEHMP-see, NAY-thuhn)

Defense. Shoots right. 6', 190 lbs. Born, Spruce Grove, Alta., July 14, 1974. Toronto's 12th choice, 245th overall, in 1992 Entry Draft.

Season	Club	League	GP	G	A	Pts	PIM	PP	SH	GW	S	%	+/-	TF	F%	Min	GP	G	A	Pts	PIM	PP	SH	GW	Min
1990-91	St. Albert Saints	AMHL	34	11	20	31	73																		
1991-92	Regina Pats	WHL	70	4	22	26	72																		
1992-93	Regina Pats	WHL	72	12	29	41	95										13	3	8	11	14				
	St. John's	AHL															2	0	0	0	0				
1993-94	Regina Pats	WHL	56	14	36	50	100										4	0	0	0	4				
1994-95	St. John's	AHL	74	7	30	37	91										5	1	0	1	11				
1995-96	St. John's	AHL	73	5	15	20	103										4	1	0	1	9				
1996-97	Toronto	NHL	14	1	1	2	2	0	0	0	11	9.1	–2												
	St. John's	AHL	52	8	18	26	108										6	1	0	1	4				
1997-98	St. John's	AHL	68	12	16	28	85										4	0	0	0	0				
1998-99	St. John's	AHL	67	2	29	31	70										5	0	1	1	2				
99-2000	Toronto	NHL	6	0	2	2	2	0	0	0	3	0.0	2	1	0.0	13:40									
	St. John's	AHL	44	15	12	27	40																		
2000-01	Toronto	NHL	25	1	9	10	4	1	0	0	31	3.2	13	0	0.0	15:53									
	St. John's	AHL	55	11	28	39	60										4	0	4	4	8				
2001-02	Toronto	NHL	3	0	0	0	0	0	0	0	3	0.0	1	0	0.0	14:00	6	0	2	2	0	0	0	0	14:31
	St. John's	AHL	75	13	48	61	66										11	1	5	6	8				
2002-03	Chicago	NHL	67	5	23	28	26	1	0	2	124	4.0	–7	0	0.0	20:55									

			Regular Season														Playoffs								
Season	**Club**	**League**	**GP**	**G**	**A**	**Pts**	**PIM**	**PP**	**SH**	**GW**	**S**	**%**	**+/-**	**TF**	**F%**	**Min**	**GP**	**G**	**A**	**Pts**	**PIM**	**PP**	**SH**	**GW**	**Min**
2003-04	**Chicago**	**NHL**	**58**	**8**	**17**	**25**	**30**	**2**	**0**	**1**	**155**	**5.2**	**–5**	**1**	**0.0**	**23:48**	....	....	....	....	....	....	....	....	....
	Los Angeles	**NHL**	**17**	**4**	**3**	**7**	**2**	**1**	**0**	**0**	**28**	**14.3**	**–7**	**0**	**0.0**	**20:23**	....	....	....	....	....	....	....	....	....
2004-05	Eisbaren Berlin	Germany	10	2	3	5	26	....	....	....	....	....	....	....	....	....	12	0	3	3	14	....	....	....	....
2005-06	**Los Angeles**	**NHL**	**53**	**2**	**11**	**13**	**48**	**0**	**0**	**0**	**58**	**3.4**	**0**	**0**	**0.0**	**19:09**	....	....	....	....	....	....	....	....	....
2006-07	**Boston**	**NHL**	**17**	**0**	**1**	**1**	**6**	**0**	**0**	**0**	**4**	**0.0**	**–2**	**0**	**0.0**	**9:57**	....	....	....	....	....	....	....	....	....
	Providence Bruins	AHL	46	4	17	21	40	....	....	....	....	....	....	....	....	....	3	0	0	0	2	....	....	....	....
	NHL Totals		**260**	**21**	**67**	**88**	**120**	**5**	**0**	**3**	**417**	**5.0**		**2**	**0.0**	**19:39**	**6**	**0**	**2**	**2**	**0**	**0**	**0**	**0**	**14:31**

WHL East Second All-Star Team (1994) • AHL Second All-Star Team (2002) • Fred T. Hunt Memorial Award (Sportsmanship – AHL) (2002)

Signed as a free agent by **Chicago**, July 12, 2002. Traded to **Los Angeles** by **Chicago** for Los Angeles' 4th round choice (Nathan Davis) in 2005 Entry Draft, March 2, 2004. Signed as a free agent by **Berlin** (Germany), February 9, 2005. Signed as a free agent by **Boston**, August 7, 2006. Signed as a free agent by **Bern** (Swiss), June 10, 2007.

DEVEREAUX, Boyd

(DEH-vuhr-oh, BOID) **TOR.**

Center. Shoots left. 6'2", 195 lbs. Born, Seaforth, Ont., April 16, 1978. Edmonton's 1st choice, 6th overall, in 1996 Entry Draft.

Season	Club	League	GP	G	A	Pts	PIM	PP	SH	GW	S	%	+/-	TF	F%	Min	GP	G	A	Pts	PIM	PP	SH	GW	Min
1992-93	Seaforth Sailors	OHA-D	34	7	20	27	13	....	....	....	....	....	....	....	....	....	....	....	....	....	....	....	....	....	....
1993-94	Stratford Cullitons	OHA-B	46	12	27	39	8	....	....	....	....	....	....	....	....	....	....	....	....	....	....	....	....	....	....
1994-95	Stratford Cullitons	OHA-B	45	31	74	105	21	....	....	....	....	....	....	....	....	....	....	....	....	....	....	....	....	....	....
1995-96	Kitchener Rangers	OHL	66	20	38	58	35	....	....	....	....	....	....	....	....	....	12	3	7	10	4	....	....	....	....
1996-97	Kitchener Rangers	OHL	54	28	41	69	37	....	....	....	....	....	....	....	....	....	13	4	11	15	8	....	....	....	....
	Hamilton	AHL	....	....	....	....	....	....	....	....	....	....	....	....	....	....	1	0	1	1	0	....	....	....	....
1997-98	**Edmonton**	**NHL**	**38**	**1**	**4**	**5**	**6**	**0**	**0**	**0**	**27**	**3.7**	**–5**	....	....	....	....	....	....	....	....	....	....	....	....
	Hamilton	AHL	14	5	6	11	6	....	....	....	....	....	....	....	....	....	9	1	1	2	8	....	....	....	....
1998-99	**Edmonton**	**NHL**	**61**	**6**	**8**	**14**	**23**	**0**	**1**	**4**	**39**	**15.4**	**2**	**409**	**42.8**	**10:09**	**1**	**0**	**0**	**0**	**0**	**0**	**0**	**0**	**32:46**
	Hamilton	AHL	7	4	6	10	2	....	....	....	....	....	....	....	....	....	8	0	3	3	4	....	....	....	....
99-2000	**Edmonton**	**NHL**	**76**	**8**	**19**	**27**	**20**	**0**	**1**	**2**	**108**	**7.4**	**7**	**241**	**34.9**	**12:36**	....	....	....	....	....	....	....	....	....
2000-01	**Detroit**	**NHL**	**55**	**5**	**6**	**11**	**14**	**0**	**0**	**0**	**66**	**7.6**	**1**	**124**	**37.1**	**10:08**	**2**	**0**	**0**	**0**	**0**	**0**	**0**	**0**	**10:39**
2001-02◆	**Detroit**	**NHL**	**79**	**9**	**16**	**25**	**24**	**0**	**0**	**2**	**116**	**7.8**	**9**	**12**	**33.3**	**11:30**	**21**	**2**	**4**	**6**	**4**	**0**	**0**	**0**	**10:58**
2002-03	**Detroit**	**NHL**	**61**	**3**	**9**	**12**	**16**	**0**	**0**	**1**	**72**	**4.2**	**4**	**7**	**42.9**	**9:26**	....	....	....	....	....	....	....	....	....
2003-04	**Detroit**	**NHL**	**61**	**6**	**9**	**15**	**20**	**0**	**0**	**2**	**62**	**9.7**	**–1**	**14**	**50.0**	**9:58**	**3**	**1**	**0**	**1**	**0**	**0**	**0**	**0**	**6:36**
2004-05			DID NOT PLAY																						
2005-06	**Phoenix**	**NHL**	**78**	**8**	**14**	**22**	**44**	**1**	**0**	**1**	**76**	**10.5**	**–13**	**281**	**36.7**	**12:47**	....	....	....	....	....	....	....	....	....
2006-07	**Toronto**	**NHL**	**33**	**8**	**11**	**19**	**12**	**0**	**0**	**0**	**57**	**14.0**	**4**	**42**	**26.2**	**15:17**	....	....	....	....	....	....	....	....	....
	Toronto Marlies	AHL	30	6	8	14	14	....	....	....	....	....	....	....	....	....	....	....	....	....	....	....	....	....	....
	NHL Totals		**542**	**54**	**96**	**150**	**179**	**1**	**2**	**12**	**623**	**8.7**		**1130**	**38.3**	**11:22**	**27**	**3**	**4**	**7**	**4**	**0**	**0**	**0**	**11:16**

Canadian Major Junior Scholastic Player of the Year (1996)

Signed as a free agent by **Detroit**, August 23, 2000. Signed as a free agent by **Phoenix**, July 5, 2004. Signed as a free agent by **Toronto**, October 7, 2006.

de VRIES, Greg

(deh-VREES, GREHG) **NSH.**

Defense. Shoots left. 6'2", 215 lbs. Born, Sundridge, Ont., January 4, 1973.

Season	Club	League	GP	G	A	Pts	PIM	PP	SH	GW	S	%	+/-	TF	F%	Min	GP	G	A	Pts	PIM	PP	SH	GW	Min
1988-89	Cortina Astros	Minor-ON	35	28	40	68	....	....	....	....	....	....	....	....	....	....	....	....	....	....	....	....	....	....	....
1989-90	Aurora Eagles	OHA-B	42	1	16	17	32	....	....	....	....	....	....	....	....	....	....	....	....	....	....	....	....	....	....
1990-91	Stratford Cullitons	OHA-B	40	8	32	40	120	....	....	....	....	....	....	....	....	....	3	2	1	3	20	....	....	....	....
1991-92	Thorold	OHA-B	3	0	0	0	0	....	....	....	....	....	....	....	....	....	....	....	....	....	....	....	....	....	....
	Bowling Green	CCHA	24	0	3	3	20	....	....	....	....	....	....	....	....	....	....	....	....	....	....	....	....	....	....
1992-93	Niagara Falls	OHL	62	3	23	26	86	....	....	....	....	....	....	....	....	....	4	0	1	1	6	....	....	....	....
1993-94	Niagara Falls	OHL	64	5	40	45	135	....	....	....	....	....	....	....	....	....	....	....	....	....	....	....	....	....	....
	Cape Breton	AHL	9	0	0	0	11	....	....	....	....	....	....	....	....	....	1	0	0	0	0	....	....	....	....
1994-95	Cape Breton	AHL	77	5	19	24	68	....	....	....	....	....	....	....	....	....	....	....	....	....	....	....	....	....	....
1995-96	**Edmonton**	**NHL**	**13**	**1**	**1**	**2**	**12**	**0**	**0**	**0**	**8**	**12.5**	**–2**	....	....	....	....	....	....	....	....	....	....	....	....
	Cape Breton	AHL	58	9	30	39	174	....	....	....	....	....	....	....	....	....	....	....	....	....	....	....	....	....	....
1996-97	**Edmonton**	**NHL**	**37**	**0**	**4**	**4**	**52**	**0**	**0**	**0**	**31**	**0.0**	**–2**	....	....	....	**12**	**0**	**1**	**1**	**8**	**0**	**0**	**0**	....
	Hamilton	AHL	34	4	14	18	26	....	....	....	....	....	....	....	....	....	....	....	....	....	....	....	....	....	....
1997-98	**Edmonton**	**NHL**	**65**	**7**	**4**	**11**	**80**	**1**	**0**	**0**	**53**	**13.2**	**–17**	....	....	....	**7**	**0**	**0**	**0**	**21**	**0**	**0**	**0**	....
1998-99	**Nashville**	**NHL**	**6**	**0**	**0**	**0**	**4**	**0**	**0**	**0**	**1**	**1.0**	**–4**	**0**	**0.0**	**18:11**	....	....	....	....	....	....	....	....	....
	Colorado	**NHL**	**67**	**1**	**3**	**4**	**60**	**0**	**0**	**0**	**56**	**56.0**	**–3**	**1**	**100.0**	**16:23**	**19**	**0**	**2**	**2**	**22**	**0**	**0**	**0**	**12:09**
99-2000	**Colorado**	**NHL**	**69**	**2**	**7**	**9**	**73**	**0**	**0**	**0**	**40**	**5.0**	**–7**	**0**	**0.0**	**14:59**	**5**	**0**	**0**	**0**	**4**	**0**	**0**	**0**	**8:09**
2000-01◆	**Colorado**	**NHL**	**79**	**5**	**12**	**17**	**51**	**0**	**0**	**0**	**76**	**6.6**	**23**	**0**	**0.0**	**17:06**	**23**	**0**	**1**	**1**	**20**	**0**	**0**	**0**	**14:17**
2001-02	**Colorado**	**NHL**	**82**	**8**	**12**	**20**	**57**	**1**	**1**	**3**	**148**	**5.4**	**18**	**1**	**0.0**	**23:03**	**21**	**4**	**9**	**13**	**2**	**0**	**0**	**1**	**24:12**
2002-03	**Colorado**	**NHL**	**82**	**6**	**26**	**32**	**70**	**0**	**0**	**2**	**112**	**5.4**	**15**	**1**	**100.0**	**22:15**	**7**	**2**	**0**	**2**	**0**	**0**	**0**	**0**	**22:11**
2003-04	**NY Rangers**	**NHL**	**53**	**3**	**12**	**15**	**37**	**0**	**0**	**0**	**58**	**5.2**	**12**	**0**	**0.0**	**19:01**	....	....	....	....	....	....	....	....	....
	Ottawa	**NHL**	**13**	**0**	**1**	**1**	**6**	**0**	**0**	**0**	**12**	**0.0**	**0**	**0**	**0.0**	**17:51**	**7**	**0**	**1**	**1**	**8**	**0**	**0**	**0**	**17:51**
2004-05			DID NOT PLAY																						
2005-06	**Atlanta**	**NHL**	**82**	**7**	**28**	**35**	**76**	**3**	**0**	**2**	**111**	**6.3**	**1**	**1**	**100.0**	**22:01**	....	....	....	....	....	....	....	....	....
2006-07	**Atlanta**	**NHL**	**82**	**3**	**21**	**24**	**66**	**0**	**0**	**0**	**102**	**2.9**	**–3**	**0**	**0.0**	**22:14**	**4**	**1**	**0**	**1**	**4**	**0**	**0**	**0**	**19:17**
	NHL Totals		**730**	**43**	**131**	**174**	**644**	**5**	**1**	**7**	**808**	**5.3**		**4**	**75.0**	**19:48**	**105**	**7**	**14**	**21**	**89**	**0**	**0**	**1**	**17:02**

Signed as a free agent by **Edmonton**, March 20, 1994. Traded to **Nashville** by **Edmonton** with Eric Fichaud and Drake Berehowsky for Mikhail Shtalenkov and Jim Dowd, October 1, 1998. Traded to **Colorado** by **Nashville** for Colorado's 2nd round choice (Ed Hill) in 1999 Entry Draft, October 24, 1998. Signed as a free agent by **NY Rangers**, July 14, 2003. Traded to **Ottawa** by **NY Rangers** for Karel Rachunek and Alexandre Giroux, March 9, 2004. Traded to **Atlanta** by **Ottawa** with Marian Hossa for Dany Heatley, August 23, 2005. Signed as a free agent by **Nashville**, July 2, 2007.

DIMITRAKOS, Niko

(DIH-mih-tra-kohs, NEE-KOH) **OTT.**

Right wing. Shoots right. 5'11", 205 lbs. Born, Somerville, MA, May 21, 1979. San Jose's 4th choice, 155th overall, in 1999 Entry Draft.

Season	Club	League	GP	G	A	Pts	PIM	PP	SH	GW	S	%	+/-	TF	F%	Min	GP	G	A	Pts	PIM	PP	SH	GW	Min
1994-95	Matignon	High-MA	23	10	12	22	....	....	....	....	....	....	....	....	....	....	....	....	....	....	....	....	....	....	....
1995-96	Matignon	High-MA	25	12	28	40	....	....	....	....	....	....	....	....	....	....	....	....	....	....	....	....	....	....	....
1996-97	Matignon	High-MA	25	23	32	55	....	....	....	....	....	....	....	....	....	....	....	....	....	....	....	....	....	....	....
1997-98	Avon Old Farms	High-CT	26	27	28	55	....	....	....	....	....	....	....	....	....	....	....	....	....	....	....	....	....	....	....
1998-99	U. of Maine	H-East	35	8	19	27	33	....	....	....	....	....	....	....	....	....	....	....	....	....	....	....	....	....	....
99-2000	U. of Maine	H-East	32	11	16	27	16	....	....	....	....	....	....	....	....	....	....	....	....	....	....	....	....	....	....
2000-01	U. of Maine	H-East	29	11	14	25	43	....	....	....	....	....	....	....	....	....	....	....	....	....	....	....	....	....	....
2001-02	U. of Maine	H-East	43	20	31	51	44	....	....	....	....	....	....	....	....	....	....	....	....	....	....	....	....	....	....
2002-03	**San Jose**	**NHL**	**21**	**6**	**7**	**13**	**8**	**3**	**0**	**0**	**34**	**17.6**	**–7**	**2**	**50.0**	**14:15**	....	....	....	....	....	....	....	....	....
	Cleveland Barons	AHL	55	15	29	44	30	....	....	....	....	....	....	....	....	....	....	....	....	....	....	....	....	....	....
2003-04	**San Jose**	**NHL**	**68**	**9**	**15**	**24**	**49**	**2**	**0**	**4**	**116**	**7.8**	**6**	**4**	**50.0**	**13:20**	**15**	**1**	**8**	**9**	**8**	**0**	**0**	**1**	**14:31**
	Cleveland Barons	AHL	7	4	4	8	4	....	....	....	....	....	....	....	....	....	....	....	....	....	....	....	....	....	....
2004-05	Langnau	Swiss	3	0	1	1	2	....	....	....	....	....	....	....	....	....	6	3	3	6	16	....	....	....	....
2005-06	**San Jose**	**NHL**	**45**	**4**	**12**	**16**	**26**	**0**	**0**	**0**	**66**	**6.1**	**0**	**8**	**25.0**	**11:54**	....	....	....	....	....	....	....	....	....
	Philadelphia	**NHL**	**19**	**5**	**4**	**9**	**6**	**1**	**0**	**1**	**27**	**18.5**	**4**	**2**	**50.0**	**10:52**	**5**	**0**	**0**	**0**	**2**	**0**	**0**	**0**	**10:07**
2006-07	**Philadelphia**	**NHL**	**5**	**0**	**0**	**0**	**6**	**0**	**0**	**0**	**4**	**0.0**	**–4**	**0**	**0.0**	**8:32**	....	....	....	....	....	....	....	....	....
	Philadelphia	AHL	45	15	13	28	34	....	....	....	....	....	....	....	....	....	....	....	....	....	....	....	....	....	....
	Chicago Wolves	AHL	17	4	10	14	20	....	....	....	....	....	....	....	....	....	15	3	7	10	8	....	....	....	....
	NHL Totals		**158**	**24**	**38**	**62**	**95**	**6**	**0**	**5**	**247**	**9.7**		**16**	**37.5**	**12:36**	**20**	**1**	**8**	**9**	**10**	**0**	**0**	**1**	**13:25**

NCAA Championship All-Tournament Team (1999) • Hockey East Second All-Star Team (2002)

Signed as a free agent by **Langnau** (Swiss), February 2, 2005. Traded to **Philadelphia** by **San Jose** for Philadelphia's 3rd round choice (later traded to Columbus - Columbus selected Tommy Sestito) in 2006 Entry Draft, March 9, 2006. Signed as a free agent by **Ottawa**, July 13, 2007.

DiPENTA, Joe

(DIH-pehn-tah, JOH)

Defense. Shoots left. 6'2", 200 lbs. Born, Barrie, Ont., February 25, 1979. Florida's 2nd choice, 61st overall, in 1998 Entry Draft.

Season	Club	League	GP	G	A	Pts	PIM	PP	SH	GW	S	%	+/-	TF	F%	Min	GP	G	A	Pts	PIM	PP	SH	GW	Min
1996-97	Smiths Falls Bears	CJHL	54	13	22	35	92	....	....	....	....	....	....	....	....	....	....	....	....	....	....	....	....	....	....
1997-98	Boston University	H-East	38	2	16	18	50	....	....	....	....	....	....	....	....	....	....	....	....	....	....	....	....	....	....
1998-99	Boston University	H-East	36	2	15	17	72	....	....	....	....	....	....	....	....	....	....	....	....	....	....	....	....	....	....
99-2000	Halifax	QMJHL	63	13	43	56	83	....	....	....	....	....	....	....	....	....	10	3	4	7	26	....	....	....	....
2000-01	Philadelphia	AHL	71	3	5	8	65	....	....	....	....	....	....	....	....	....	10	1	2	3	15	....	....	....	....
2001-02	Philadelphia	AHL	61	2	4	6	71	....	....	....	....	....	....	....	....	....	....	....	....	....	....	....	....	....	....
	Chicago Wolves	AHL	15	0	2	2	15	....	....	....	....	....	....	....	....	....	25	1	3	4	22	....	....	....	....
2002-03	**Atlanta**	**NHL**	**3**	**1**	**1**	**2**	**0**	**0**	**0**	**0**	**2**	**50.0**	**3**	**0**	**0.0**	**15:47**	....	....	....	....	....	....	....	....	....
	Chicago Wolves	AHL	76	2	17	19	107	....	....	....	....	....	....	....	....	....	9	0	1	1	7	....	....	....	....
2003-04	Chicago Wolves	AHL	73	0	6	6	105	....	....	....	....	....	....	....	....	....	10	1	0	1	13	....	....	....	....
2004-05	Manitoba Moose	AHL	73	2	10	12	48	....	....	....	....	....	....	....	....	....	14	0	5	5	2	....	....	....	....

Season	Club	League	GP	G	A	Pts	PIM	PP	SH	GW	S	%	+/-	TF	F%	Min	GP	G	A	Pts	PIM	PP	SH	GW	Min
			Regular Season														Playoffs								
2005-06	**Anaheim**	**NHL**	**72**	**2**	**6**	**8**	**46**	**0**	**0**	**0**	**27**	**7.4**	**8**	**0**	**0.0**	**13:31**	**16**	**0**	**0**	**0**	**13**	**0**	**0**	**0**	**11:34**
2006-07♦	**Anaheim**	**NHL**	**76**	**2**	**6**	**8**	**48**	**0**	**0**	**1**	**33**	**6.1**	**1**	**1**	**0.0**	**12:09**	**16**	**0**	**0**	**0**	**4**	**0**	**0**	**0**	**8:12**
	NHL Totals		**151**	**5**	**13**	**18**	**94**	**0**	**0**	**1**	**62**	**8.1**		**1**	**0.0**	**12:53**	**32**	**0**	**0**	**0**	**17**	**0**	**0**	**0**	**9:53**

• Left **Boston University** (Hockey East) and signed with **Halifax** (QMJHL), May 2, 1999. Signed as a free agent by **Philadelphia**, July 12, 2000. Traded to **Atlanta** by **Philadelphia** for Jarrod Skalde, March 5, 2002. Signed as a free agent by **Vancouver**, August 19, 2004. Signed as a free agent by **Anaheim**, August 11, 2005.

DISALVATORE, Jon

(dih-sal-vuh-TOH-ray, JAWN) **PHX.**

Right wing. Shoots right. 6'1", 200 lbs. Born, Bangor, ME, March 30, 1981. San Jose's 2nd choice, 104th overall, in 2000 Entry Draft.

Season	Club	League	GP	G	A	Pts	PIM	PP	SH	GW	S	%	+/-	TF	F%	Min	GP	G	A	Pts	PIM	PP	SH	GW	Min
1997-98	N.E. Jr. Coyotes	EJHL	38	24	41	65	....	....	....	....	....	....	....	....	....	....	....	....	....	....	....	....	....	....	....
1998-99	N.E. Jr. Coyotes	EJHL	48	44	76	*120	38	....	....	....	....	....	....	....	....	....	....	....	....	....	....	....	....	....	....
99-2000	Providence	H-East	38	15	12	27	12	....	....	....	....	....	....	....	....	....	....	....	....	....	....	....	....	....	....
2000-01	Providence	H-East	36	9	16	25	29	....	....	....	....	....	....	....	....	....	....	....	....	....	....	....	....	....	....
2001-02	Providence	H-East	38	16	26	42	6	....	....	....	....	....	....	....	....	....	....	....	....	....	....	....	....	....	....
2002-03	Providence	H-East	36	19	29	48	12	....	....	....	....	....	....	....	....	....	....	....	....	....	....	....	....	....	....
2003-04	Cleveland Barons	AHL	74	22	24	46	30	....	....	....	....	....	....	....	....	....	8	1	1	2	2	....	....	....	....
2004-05	Worcester IceCats	AHL	79	22	23	45	42	....	....	....	....	....	....	....	....	....	....	....	....	....	....	....	....	....	....
2005-06	**St. Louis**	**NHL**	**5**	**0**	**0**	**0**	**2**	**0**	**0**	**0**	**3**	**0.0**	**–1**	**0**	**0.0**	**8:27**	....	....	....	....	....	....	....	....	....
	Peoria Rivermen	AHL	72	22	45	67	42	....	....	....	....	....	....	....	....	....	4	0	0	0	0	....	....	....	....
2006-07	Peoria Rivermen	AHL	76	21	39	60	50	....	....	....	....	....	....	....	....	....	....	....	....	....	....	....	....	....	....
	NHL Totals		**5**	**0**	**0**	**0**	**2**	**0**	**0**	**0**	**3**	**0.0**		**0**	**0.0**	**8:27**	....	....	....	....	....	....	....	....	....

Signed as a free agent by **St. Louis**, June 30, 2004. Signed as a free agent by **Phoenix**, July 9, 2007.

DOAN, Shane

(DOHN, SHAYN) **PHX.**

Right wing. Shoots right. 6'2", 216 lbs. Born, Halkirk, Alta., October 10, 1976. Winnipeg's 1st choice, 7th overall, in 1995 Entry Draft.

Season	Club	League	GP	G	A	Pts	PIM	PP	SH	GW	S	%	+/-	TF	F%	Min	GP	G	A	Pts	PIM	PP	SH	GW	Min
1991-92	Killam Selects	AAHA	56	80	84	164	74	....	....	....	....	....	....	....	....	....	....	....	....	....	....	....	....	....	....
1992-93	Kamloops Blazers	WHL	51	7	12	19	65	....	....	....	....	....	....	....	....	....	13	0	1	1	8	....	....	....	....
1993-94	Kamloops Blazers	WHL	52	24	24	48	88	....	....	....	....	....	....	....	....	....	....	....	....	....	....	....	....	....	....
1994-95	Kamloops Blazers	WHL	71	37	57	94	106	....	....	....	....	....	....	....	....	....	21	6	10	16	16	....	....	....	....
1995-96	**Winnipeg**	**NHL**	**74**	**7**	**10**	**17**	**101**	**1**	**0**	**3**	**106**	**6.6**	**–9**	....	....	....	**6**	**0**	**0**	**0**	**6**	**0**	**0**	**0**	....
1996-97	**Phoenix**	**NHL**	**63**	**4**	**8**	**12**	**49**	**0**	**0**	**0**	**100**	**4.0**	**–3**	....	....	....	**4**	**0**	**0**	**0**	**2**	**0**	**0**	**0**	....
1997-98	**Phoenix**	**NHL**	**33**	**5**	**6**	**11**	**35**	**0**	**0**	**3**	**42**	**11.9**	**–3**	....	....	....	**6**	**1**	**0**	**1**	**6**	**0**	**0**	**0**	....
	Springfield	AHL	39	21	21	42	64	....	....	....	....	....	....	....	....	....	....	....	....	....	....	....	....	....	....
1998-99	**Phoenix**	**NHL**	**79**	**6**	**16**	**22**	**54**	**0**	**0**	**0**	**156**	**3.8**	**–5**	**6**	**16.7**	**12:42**	**7**	**2**	**2**	**4**	**6**	**0**	**0**	**2**	**17:58**
99-2000	**Phoenix**	**NHL**	**81**	**26**	**25**	**51**	**66**	**1**	**1**	**4**	**221**	**11.8**	**6**	**25**	**36.0**	**16:51**	**4**	**1**	**2**	**3**	**8**	**1**	**0**	**0**	**18:11**
2000-01	**Phoenix**	**NHL**	**76**	**26**	**37**	**63**	**89**	**6**	**1**	**6**	**220**	**11.8**	**0**	**15**	**40.0**	**19:32**	....	....	....	....	....	....	....	....	....
2001-02	**Phoenix**	**NHL**	**81**	**20**	**29**	**49**	**61**	**6**	**0**	**2**	**205**	**9.8**	**11**	**52**	**44.2**	**18:10**	**5**	**2**	**2**	**4**	**6**	**0**	**0**	**0**	**17:21**
2002-03	**Phoenix**	**NHL**	**82**	**21**	**37**	**58**	**86**	**7**	**0**	**2**	**225**	**9.3**	**3**	**623**	**39.8**	**18:47**	....	....	....	....	....	....	....	....	....
2003-04	**Phoenix**	**NHL**	**79**	**27**	**41**	**68**	**47**	**9**	**2**	**1**	**254**	**10.6**	**–11**	**55**	**40.0**	**21:46**	....	....	....	....	....	....	....	....	....
2004-05			DID NOT PLAY																						
2005-06	**Phoenix**	**NHL**	**82**	**30**	**36**	**66**	**123**	**17**	**0**	**7**	**254**	**11.8**	**–9**	**126**	**43.7**	**19:08**	....	....	....	....	....	....	....	....	....
	Canada	Olympics	6	2	1	3	2	....	....	....	....	....	....	....	....	....	....	....	....	....	....	....	....	....	....
2006-07	**Phoenix**	**NHL**	**73**	**27**	**28**	**55**	**73**	**11**	**0**	**7**	**209**	**12.9**	**–14**	**174**	**39.1**	**20:27**	....	....	....	....	....	....	....	....	....
	NHL Totals		**803**	**199**	**273**	**472**	**784**	**58**	**4**	**35**	**1992**	**10.0**		**1076**	**40.1**	**18:24**	**32**	**6**	**6**	**12**	**34**	**1**	**0**	**2**	**17:50**

Memorial Cup Tournament All-Star Team (1995) • Stafford Smythe Memorial Trophy (Memorial Cup Tournament MVP) (1995)
Played in NHL All-Star Game (2004)
Transferred to **Phoenix** after **Winnipeg** franchise relocated, July 1, 1996.

DONOVAN, Shean

(DAW-nuh-vuhn, SHAWN) **OTT.**

Right wing. Shoots right. 6'2", 209 lbs. Born, Timmins, Ont., January 22, 1975. San Jose's 2nd choice, 28th overall, in 1993 Entry Draft.

Season	Club	League	GP	G	A	Pts	PIM	PP	SH	GW	S	%	+/-	TF	F%	Min	GP	G	A	Pts	PIM	PP	SH	GW	Min
1990-91	Kanata Valley	CJHL	44	8	5	13	8	....	....	....	....	....	....	....	....	....	....	....	....	....	....	....	....	....	....
1991-92	Ottawa 67's	OHL	58	11	8	19	14	....	....	....	....	....	....	....	....	....	11	1	0	1	5	....	....	....	....
1992-93	Ottawa 67's	OHL	66	29	23	52	33	....	....	....	....	....	....	....	....	....	....	....	....	....	....	....	....	....	....
1993-94	Ottawa 67's	OHL	62	35	49	84	63	....	....	....	....	....	....	....	....	....	17	10	11	21	14	....	....	....	....
1994-95	Ottawa 67's	OHL	29	22	19	41	41	....	....	....	....	....	....	....	....	....	....	....	....	....	....	....	....	....	....
	San Jose	**NHL**	**14**	**0**	**0**	**0**	**6**	**0**	**0**	**0**	**13**	**0.0**	**–6**	....	....	....	**7**	**0**	**1**	**1**	**6**	**0**	**0**	**0**	....
	Kansas City	IHL	5	0	2	2	7	....	....	....	....	....	....	....	....	....	14	5	3	8	23	....	....	....	....
1995-96	**San Jose**	**NHL**	**74**	**13**	**8**	**21**	**39**	**0**	**1**	**2**	**73**	**17.8**	**–17**	....	....	....	....	....	....	....	....	....	....	....	....
	Kansas City	IHL	4	0	0	0	8	....	....	....	....	....	....	....	....	....	5	0	0	0	8	....	....	....	....
1996-97	**San Jose**	**NHL**	**73**	**9**	**6**	**15**	**42**	**0**	**1**	**0**	**115**	**7.8**	**–18**	....	....	....	....	....	....	....	....	....	....	....	....
	Kentucky	AHL	3	1	3	4	18	....	....	....	....	....	....	....	....	....	....	....	....	....	....	....	....	....	....
1997-98	**San Jose**	**NHL**	**20**	**3**	**3**	**6**	**22**	**0**	**0**	**0**	**24**	**12.5**	**3**	....	....	....	....	....	....	....	....	....	....	....	....
	Colorado	**NHL**	**47**	**5**	**7**	**12**	**48**	**0**	**0**	**0**	**57**	**8.8**	**3**	....	....	....	....	....	....	....	....	....	....	....	....
1998-99	**Colorado**	**NHL**	**68**	**7**	**12**	**19**	**37**	**1**	**0**	**1**	**81**	**8.6**	**4**	**9**	**22.2**	**8:46**	**5**	**0**	**0**	**0**	**2**	**0**	**0**	**0**	**4:55**
99-2000	**Colorado**	**NHL**	**18**	**1**	**0**	**1**	**8**	**0**	**0**	**0**	**13**	**7.7**	**–4**	**1**	**0.0**	**5:20**	....	....	....	....	....	....	....	....	....
	Atlanta	**NHL**	**33**	**4**	**7**	**11**	**18**	**1**	**0**	**1**	**53**	**7.5**	**–13**	**22**	**31.8**	**14:19**	....	....	....	....	....	....	....	....	....
2000-01	**Atlanta**	**NHL**	**63**	**12**	**11**	**23**	**47**	**1**	**3**	**1**	**93**	**12.9**	**–14**	**218**	**45.9**	**14:03**	....	....	....	....	....	....	....	....	....
2001-02	**Atlanta**	**NHL**	**48**	**6**	**6**	**12**	**40**	**1**	**0**	**2**	**64**	**9.4**	**–16**	**12**	**50.0**	**13:30**	....	....	....	....	....	....	....	....	....
	Pittsburgh	**NHL**	**13**	**2**	**1**	**3**	**4**	**0**	**0**	**0**	**18**	**11.1**	**–5**	**4**	**0.0**	**14:34**	....	....	....	....	....	....	....	....	....
2002-03	**Pittsburgh**	**NHL**	**52**	**4**	**5**	**9**	**30**	**0**	**1**	**0**	**66**	**6.1**	**–6**	**37**	**24.3**	**13:01**	....	....	....	....	....	....	....	....	....
	Calgary	**NHL**	**13**	**1**	**2**	**3**	**7**	**0**	**0**	**1**	**22**	**4.5**	**–2**	**3**	**66.7**	**15:39**	....	....	....	....	....	....	....	....	....
2003-04	**Calgary**	**NHL**	**82**	**18**	**24**	**42**	**72**	**3**	**3**	**8**	**138**	**13.0**	**14**	**53**	**39.6**	**14:55**	**24**	**5**	**5**	**10**	**23**	**0**	**0**	**2**	**15:27**
2004-05	Geneve	Swiss	12	5	3	8	30	....	....	....	....	....	....	....	....	....	....	....	....	....	....	....	....	....	....
2005-06	**Calgary**	**NHL**	**80**	**9**	**11**	**20**	**82**	**0**	**1**	**0**	**132**	**6.8**	**9**	**26**	**30.8**	**11:47**	**7**	**0**	**0**	**0**	**6**	**0**	**0**	**0**	**11:24**
2006-07	**Boston**	**NHL**	**76**	**6**	**11**	**17**	**56**	**0**	**0**	**0**	**108**	**5.6**	**–13**	**41**	**43.9**	**14:09**	....	....	....	....	....	....	....	....	....
	NHL Totals		**774**	**100**	**114**	**214**	**558**	**7**	**10**	**16**	**1070**	**9.3**		**426**	**40.6**	**12:50**	**43**	**5**	**6**	**11**	**37**	**0**	**0**	**2**	**13:12**

Traded to **Colorado** by **San Jose** with San Jose's 1st round choice (Alex Tanguay) in 1998 Entry Draft for Mike Ricci and Colorado's 2nd round choice (later traded to Buffalo – Buffalo selected Jaroslav Kristek), in 1998 Entry Draft, November 21, 1997. Traded to **Atlanta** by **Colorado** for Rick Tabaracci, December 8, 1999. Claimed on waivers by **Pittsburgh** from **Atlanta**, March 15, 2002. Traded to **Calgary** by **Pittsburgh** for Micki Dupont and Mathias Johansson, March 11, 2003. Signed as a free agent by **Geneve** (Swiss), November 13, 2004. Signed as a free agent by **Boston**, July 2, 2006. Traded to **Ottawa** by **Boston** for Peter Schaefer, July 17, 2007.

DOWD, Jim

(DOWD, JIHM)

Center. Shoots right. 6'1", 190 lbs. Born, Brick, NJ, December 25, 1968. New Jersey's 7th choice, 149th overall, in 1987 Entry Draft.

Season	Club	League	GP	G	A	Pts	PIM	PP	SH	GW	S	%	+/-	TF	F%	Min	GP	G	A	Pts	PIM	PP	SH	GW	Min
1983-84	Brick Township	High-NJ	20	19	30	49	....	....	....	....	....	....	....	....	....	....	....	....	....	....	....	....	....	....	....
1984-85	Brick Township	High-NJ	24	58	55	113	....	....	....	....	....	....	....	....	....	....	....	....	....	....	....	....	....	....	....
1985-86	Brick Township	High-NJ	24	47	51	98	....	....	....	....	....	....	....	....	....	....	....	....	....	....	....	....	....	....	....
1986-87	Brick Township	High-NJ	24	22	33	55	....	....	....	....	....	....	....	....	....	....	....	....	....	....	....	....	....	....	....
1987-88	Lake Superior	CCHA	45	18	27	45	16	....	....	....	....	....	....	....	....	....	....	....	....	....	....	....	....	....	....
1988-89	Lake Superior	CCHA	46	24	35	59	40	....	....	....	....	....	....	....	....	....	....	....	....	....	....	....	....	....	....
1989-90	Lake Superior	CCHA	46	25	*67	92	30	....	....	....	....	....	....	....	....	....	....	....	....	....	....	....	....	....	....
1990-91	Lake Superior	CCHA	44	24	*54	*78	53	....	....	....	....	....	....	....	....	....	....	....	....	....	....	....	....	....	....
1991-92	**New Jersey**	**NHL**	**1**	**0**	**0**	**0**	**0**	**0**	**0**	**0**	**0**	**0.0**	**0**	....	....	....	....	....	....	....	....	....	....	....	....
	Utica Devils	AHL	78	17	42	59	47	....	....	....	....	....	....	....	....	....	4	2	2	4	4	....	....	....	....
1992-93	**New Jersey**	**NHL**	**1**	**0**	**0**	**0**	**0**	**0**	**0**	**0**	**1**	**0.0**	**–1**	....	....	....	....	....	....	....	....	....	....	....	....
	Utica Devils	AHL	78	27	45	72	62	....	....	....	....	....	....	....	....	....	5	1	7	8	10	....	....	....	....
1993-94	**New Jersey**	**NHL**	**15**	**5**	**10**	**15**	**0**	**2**	**0**	**0**	**26**	**19.2**	**8**	....	....	....	**19**	**2**	**6**	**8**	**8**	**0**	**0**	**0**	....
	Albany River Rats	AHL	58	26	37	63	76	....	....	....	....	....	....	....	....	....	....	....	....	....	....	....	....	....	....
1994-95♦	**New Jersey**	**NHL**	**10**	**1**	**4**	**5**	**0**	**1**	**0**	**0**	**14**	**7.1**	**–5**	....	....	....	**11**	**2**	**1**	**3**	**8**	**0**	**0**	**1**	....
1995-96	**New Jersey**	**NHL**	**28**	**4**	**9**	**13**	**17**	**0**	**0**	**0**	**41**	**9.8**	**–1**	....	....	....	....	....	....	....	....	....	....	....	....
	Vancouver	**NHL**	**38**	**1**	**6**	**7**	**6**	**0**	**0**	**0**	**35**	**2.9**	**–8**	....	....	....	**1**	**0**	**0**	**0**	**0**	**0**	**0**	**0**	....
1996-97	**NY Islanders**	**NHL**	**3**	**0**	**0**	**0**	**0**	**0**	**0**	**0**	**0**	**0.0**	**–1**	....	....	....	....	....	....	....	....	....	....	....	....
	Utah Grizzlies	IHL	48	10	21	31	27	....	....	....	....	....	....	....	....	....	....	....	....	....	....	....	....	....	....
	Saint John Flames	AHL	24	5	11	16	18	....	....	....	....	....	....	....	....	....	5	1	2	3	0	....	....	....	....
1997-98	**Calgary**	**NHL**	**48**	**6**	**8**	**14**	**12**	**0**	**1**	**0**	**58**	**10.3**	**10**	....	....	....	....	....	....	....	....	....	....	....	....
	Saint John Flames	AHL	35	8	30	38	20	....	....	....	....	....	....	....	....	....	19	3	13	16	10	....	....	....	....
1998-99	**Edmonton**	**NHL**	**1**	**0**	**0**	**0**	**0**	**0**	**0**	**0**	**1**	**0.0**	**0**	**7**	**14.3**	**9:47**	....	....	....	....	....	....	....	....	....
	Hamilton	AHL	51	15	29	44	82	....	....	....	....	....	....	....	....	....	11	3	6	9	8	....	....	....	....

			Regular Season														Playoffs								
Season	Club	League	GP	G	A	Pts	PIM	PP	SH	GW	S	%	+/-	TF	F%	Min	GP	G	A	Pts	PIM	PP	SH	GW	Min
99-2000	**Edmonton**	**NHL**	69	5	18	23	45	2	0	1	103	4.9	10	720	54.0	13:08	5	2	1	3	4	0	0	0	15:22
2000-01	**Minnesota**	**NHL**	68	7	22	29	80	0	0	0	92	7.6	–6	1154	50.7	17:50	....	....	....	....	....	....	....	....	....
2001-02	**Minnesota**	**NHL**	82	13	30	43	54	5	0	1	111	11.7	–14	1243	52.9	15:34	....	....	....	....	....	....	....	....	....
2002-03	**Minnesota**	**NHL**	78	8	17	25	31	3	1	2	78	10.3	–1	930	47.9	13:03	15	0	2	2	0	0	0	0	12:58
2003-04	**Minnesota**	**NHL**	55	4	20	24	38	2	0	2	41	9.8	6	712	48.5	14:07	....	....	....	....	....	....	....	....	....
	Montreal	**NHL**	14	3	2	5	6	0	1	0	13	23.1	6	167	47.3	13:30	11	0	2	2	2	0	0	0	15:34
2004-05	Hamburg Freezers	Germany	20	4	9	13	12	....	....	....	....	....	....	....	....	....	....	....	....	....	....	....	....	....	....
2005-06	**Chicago**	**NHL**	60	3	12	15	38	0	0	0	55	5.5	–5	664	51.7	12:43	....	....	....	....	....	....	....	....	....
	Colorado	**NHL**	18	2	1	3	2	0	1	0	12	16.7	–6	180	51.7	12:04	9	2	3	5	20	0	1	0	14:11
2006-07	**New Jersey**	**NHL**	66	4	4	8	20	0	1	1	44	9.1	–5	274	51.8	8:17	11	0	0	0	4	0	0	0	4:33
	NHL Totals		**655**	**66**	**163**	**229**	**349**	**15**	**5**	**7**	**725**	**9.1**		**6051**	**50.9**	**13:32**	**82**	**8**	**15**	**23**	**46**	**0**	**1**	**1**	**12:10**

CCHA Second All-Star Team (1990) • NCAA West Second All-American Team (1990) • CCHA First All-Star Team (1991) • CCHA Player of the Year (1991) • NCAA West First All-American Team (1991)

• Missed majority of 1994-95 season recovering from shoulder injury suffered in game vs. Quebec, February 2, 1995. Traded to **Hartford** by **New Jersey** with New Jersey's 2nd round choice (later traded to Calgary – Calgary selected Dmitri Kokorev) in 1997 Entry Draft for Jocelyn Lemieux and Hartford's 2nd round choice (later traded to Dallas – Dallas selected John Erskine) in 1998 Entry Draft, December 19, 1995. Traded to **Vancouver** by **Hartford** with Frantisek Kucera and Hartford's 2nd round choice (Ryan Bonni) in 1997 Entry Draft for Jeff Brown and Vancouver's 3rd round choice (later traded to Calgary – Calgary selected Paul Manning) in 1998 Entry Draft, December 19, 1995. Claimed by **NY Islanders** from **Vancouver** in Waiver Draft, September 30, 1996. Signed as a free agent by **Calgary**, August, 1997. Traded to **Nashville** by **Calgary** for future considerations, June 26, 1998. Traded to **Edmonton** by **Nashville** with Mikhail Shtalenkov for Eric Fichaud, Drake Berehowsky and Greg de Vries, October 1, 1998. Claimed by **Minnesota** from **Edmonton** in Expansion Draft, June 23, 2000. Traded to **Montreal** by **Minnesota** for Montreal's 4th round choice (Julien Sprunger) in 2004 Entry Draft, March 4, 2004. Signed as a free agent by **Hamburg** (Germany), October 1, 2004. Signed as a free agent by **Chicago**, August 5, 2005. Traded to **Colorado** by **Chicago** for Colorado's 4th round choice (later traded to Toronto - Toronto selected James Reimer) in 2006 Entry Draft, March 9, 2006. Signed as a free agent by **New Jersey**, November 2, 2006.

DOWNEY, Aaron

(DOW-nee, AIR-ruhn)

Right wing. Shoots right. 6'1", 215 lbs. Born, Shelburne, Ont., August 27, 1974.

Season	Club	League	GP	G	A	Pts	PIM	PP	SH	GW	S	%	+/-	TF	F%	Min	GP	G	A	Pts	PIM	PP	SH	GW	Min
1990-91	Grand Valley	OHA-C	27	6	8	14	57	....	....	....	....	....	....	....	....	....	....	....	....	....	....	....	....	....	....
1991-92	Collingwood	OHA-B	40	9	8	17	111	....	....	....	....	....	....	....	....	....	....	....	....	....	....	....	....	....	....
1992-93	Guelph Storm	OHL	53	3	3	6	88	....	....	....	....	....	....	....	....	....	5	1	0	1	0	....	....	....	....
1993-94	Cole Harbour	NSMHL	35	8	20	28	210	....	....	....	....	....	....	....	....	....	....	....	....	....	....	....	....	....	....
1994-95	Cole Harbour	NSMHL	40	10	31	41	320	....	....	....	....	....	....	....	....	....	....	....	....	....	....	....	....	....	....
1995-96	Hampton Roads	ECHL	65	12	11	23	354	....	....	....	....	....	....	....	....	....	....	....	....	....	....	....	....	....	....
1996-97	Manitoba Moose	IHL	2	0	0	0	17	....	....	....	....	....	....	....	....	....	....	....	....	....	....	....	....	....	....
	Portland Pirates	AHL	3	0	0	0	19	....	....	....	....	....	....	....	....	....	....	....	....	....	....	....	....	....	....
	Hampton Roads	ECHL	64	8	8	16	338	....	....	....	....	....	....	....	....	....	9	0	3	3	26	....	....	....	....
1997-98	Providence Bruins	AHL	78	5	10	15	*407	....	....	....	....	....	....	....	....	....	....	....	....	....	....	....	....	....	....
1998-99	Providence Bruins	AHL	75	10	12	22	*401	....	....	....	....	....	....	....	....	....	19	1	1	2	46	....	....	....	....
99-2000	**Boston**	**NHL**	1	0	0	0	0	0	0	0	0	0.0	0	0	0.0	8:31	....	....	....	....	....	....	....	....	....
	Providence Bruins	AHL	47	6	4	10	221	....	....	....	....	....	....	....	....	....	14	1	0	1	24	....	....	....	....
2000-01	**Chicago**	**NHL**	3	0	0	0	6	0	0	0	2	0.0	–1	0	0.0	5:30	....	....	....	....	....	....	....	....	....
	Norfolk Admirals	AHL	67	6	15	21	234	....	....	....	....	....	....	....	....	....	9	0	0	0	4	....	....	....	....
2001-02	**Chicago**	**NHL**	36	1	0	1	76	0	0	1	10	10.0	–2	0	0.0	5:06	4	0	0	0	8	0	0	0	6:29
	Norfolk Admirals	AHL	12	0	2	2	21	....	....	....	....	....	....	....	....	....	....	....	....	....	....	....	....	....	....
2002-03	**Dallas**	**NHL**	43	1	1	2	69	0	0	0	14	7.1	1	0	0.0	4:47	....	....	....	....	....	....	....	....	....
2003-04	**Dallas**	**NHL**	37	1	1	2	77	0	0	1	11	9.1	2	0	0.0	4:30	....	....	....	....	....	....	....	....	....
2004-05			DID NOT PLAY																						
2005-06	**St. Louis**	**NHL**	17	2	0	2	45	0	0	0	11	18.2	0	0	0.0	3:56	....	....	....	....	....	....	....	....	....
	Montreal	**NHL**	25	1	4	5	50	0	0	0	10	10.0	2	1	0.0	6:43	1	0	0	0	0	0	0	0	6:17
2006-07	**Montreal**	**NHL**	21	1	0	1	48	0	0	1	10	10.0	–6	0	0.0	4:59	....	....	....	....	....	....	....	....	....
	Providence Bruins	AHL	15	0	0	0	30	....	....	....	....	....	....	....	....	....	1	0	0	0	12	....	....	....	....
	NHL Totals		**183**	**7**	**6**	**13**	**371**	**0**	**0**	**3**	**68**	**10.3**		**1**	**0.0**	**5:02**	**5**	**0**	**0**	**0**	**8**	**0**	**0**	**0**	**6:27**

Signed as a free agent by **Boston**, January 20, 1998. Signed as a free agent by **Chicago**, August 13, 2000. Signed as a free agent by **Dallas**, July 3, 2002. • Spent majority of 2003-04 season as a healthy reserve. Signed as a free agent by **St. Louis**, August 1, 2005. Claimed on waivers by **Montreal** from **St. Louis**, January 23, 2006.

DRAKE, Dallas

(DRAYK, DAL-uhs) **DET.**

Right wing. Shoots left. 6'1", 195 lbs. Born, Trail, B.C., February 4, 1969. Detroit's 6th choice, 116th overall, in 1989 Entry Draft.

Season	Club	League	GP	G	A	Pts	PIM	PP	SH	GW	S	%	+/-	TF	F%	Min	GP	G	A	Pts	PIM	PP	SH	GW	Min
1984-85	Rossland	KIJHL	30	13	37	50	....	....	....	....	....	....	....	....	....	....	....	....	....	....	....	....	....	....	....
1985-86	Rossland	KIJHL	41	53	73	126	....	....	....	....	....	....	....	....	....	....	....	....	....	....	....	....	....	....	....
1986-87	Rossland	KIJHL	40	55	80	135	....	....	....	....	....	....	....	....	....	....	....	....	....	....	....	....	....	....	....
1987-88	Vernon Lakers	BCJHL	47	39	85	124	50	....	....	....	....	....	....	....	....	....	11	9	17	26	30	....	....	....	....
1988-89	Northern Mich.	WCHA	38	17	22	39	22	....	....	....	....	....	....	....	....	....	7	1	2	3	4	....	....	....	....
1989-90	Northern Mich.	WCHA	36	13	24	37	42	....	....	....	....	....	....	....	....	....	....	....	....	....	....	....	....	....	....
1990-91	Northern Mich.	WCHA	44	22	36	58	89	....	....	....	....	....	....	....	....	....	....	....	....	....	....	....	....	....	....
1991-92	Northern Mich.	WCHA	38	*39	41	*80	46	....	....	....	....	....	....	....	....	....	....	....	....	....	....	....	....	....	....
1992-93	**Detroit**	**NHL**	72	18	26	44	93	3	2	5	89	20.2	15	....	....	....	7	3	3	6	6	1	0	0	....
1993-94	**Detroit**	**NHL**	47	10	22	32	37	0	1	2	78	12.8	5	....	....	....	....	....	....	....	....	....	....	....	....
	Adirondack	AHL	1	2	0	2	0	....	....	....	....	....	....	....	....	....	....	....	....	....	....	....	....	....	....
	Winnipeg	**NHL**	15	3	5	8	12	1	1	1	34	8.8	–6	....	....	....	....	....	....	....	....	....	....	....	....
1994-95	**Winnipeg**	**NHL**	43	8	18	26	30	0	0	1	66	12.1	–6	....	....	....	....	....	....	....	....	....	....	....	....
1995-96	**Winnipeg**	**NHL**	69	19	20	39	36	4	4	2	121	15.7	–7	....	....	....	3	0	0	0	0	0	0	0	....
1996-97	**Phoenix**	**NHL**	63	17	19	36	52	5	1	1	113	15.0	–11	....	....	....	7	0	1	1	2	0	0	0	....
1997-98	**Phoenix**	**NHL**	60	11	29	40	71	3	0	2	112	9.8	17	....	....	....	4	0	1	1	2	0	0	0	....
1998-99	**Phoenix**	**NHL**	53	9	22	31	65	0	0	3	105	8.6	17	5	60.0	15:38	7	4	3	7	4	2	0	1	19:51
99-2000	**Phoenix**	**NHL**	79	15	30	45	62	0	2	5	127	11.8	11	4	25.0	15:48	5	0	1	1	4	0	0	0	15:30
2000-01	**St. Louis**	**NHL**	82	12	29	41	71	2	0	3	142	8.5	18	11	45.5	14:44	15	4	2	6	16	0	1	1	14:08
2001-02	**St. Louis**	**NHL**	80	11	15	26	87	1	3	2	116	9.5	8	92	32.6	13:26	8	0	0	0	8	0	0	0	11:59
2002-03	**St. Louis**	**NHL**	80	20	10	30	66	4	1	2	113	17.7	–7	56	39.3	14:48	7	1	4	5	23	0	0	1	13:04
2003-04	**St. Louis**	**NHL**	79	13	22	35	65	3	2	1	121	10.7	10	92	45.7	16:57	5	1	1	2	2	0	0	1	16:45
2004-05			DID NOT PLAY																						
2005-06	**St. Louis**	**NHL**	62	2	24	26	59	1	0	1	88	2.3	–13	122	45.9	16:55	....	....	....	....	....	....	....	....	....
2006-07	**St. Louis**	**NHL**	60	6	6	12	38	0	2	2	74	8.1	–14	202	53.0	12:53	....	....	....	....	....	....	....	....	....
	NHL Totals		**944**	**174**	**297**	**471**	**844**	**27**	**19**	**33**	**1499**	**11.6**		**584**	**45.5**	**15:08**	**68**	**13**	**16**	**29**	**67**	**3**	**1**	**4**	**14:53**

WCHA First All-Star Team (1992) • NCAA West First All-American Team (1992)

Traded to **Winnipeg** by **Detroit** with Tim Cheveldae for Bob Essensa and Sergei Bautin, March 8, 1994. Transferred to **Phoenix** after **Winnipeg** franchise relocated, July 1, 1996. Claimed by **Minnesota** from **Phoenix** in Expansion Draft, June 23, 2000. Signed as a free agent by **St. Louis**, July 1, 2000. Signed as a free agent by **Detroit**, July 9, 2007.

DRAPER, Kris

(DRAY-puhr, KRIHS) **DET.**

Center. Shoots left. 5'10", 188 lbs. Born, Toronto, Ont., May 24, 1971. Winnipeg's 4th choice, 62nd overall, in 1989 Entry Draft.

Season	Club	League	GP	G	A	Pts	PIM	PP	SH	GW	S	%	+/-	TF	F%	Min	GP	G	A	Pts	PIM	PP	SH	GW	Min
1987-88	Don Mills Flyers	MTHL	40	35	32	67	46	....	....	....	....	....	....	....	....	....	....	....	....	....	....	....	....	....	....
1988-89	Canada	Nat-Tm	60	11	15	26	16	....	....	....	....	....	....	....	....	....	....	....	....	....	....	....	....	....	....
1989-90	Canada	Nat-Tm	61	12	22	34	44	....	....	....	....	....	....	....	....	....	....	....	....	....	....	....	....	....	....
1990-91	Ottawa 67's	OHL	39	19	42	61	35	....	....	....	....	....	....	....	....	....	17	8	11	19	20	....	....	....	....
	Winnipeg	**NHL**	3	1	0	1	5	0	0	0	1	100.0	0	....	....	....	....	....	....	....	....	....	....	....	....
	Moncton Hawks	AHL	7	2	1	3	2	....	....	....	....	....	....	....	....	....	....	....	....	....	....	....	....	....	....
1991-92	**Winnipeg**	**NHL**	10	2	0	2	2	0	0	0	19	10.5	0	....	....	....	2	0	0	0	0	0	0	0	....
	Moncton Hawks	AHL	61	11	18	29	113	....	....	....	....	....	....	....	....	....	4	0	1	1	6	....	....	....	....
1992-93	**Winnipeg**	**NHL**	7	0	0	0	2	0	0	0	5	0.0	–6	....	....	....	....	....	....	....	....	....	....	....	....
	Moncton Hawks	AHL	67	12	23	35	40	....	....	....	....	....	....	....	....	....	5	2	2	4	18	....	....	....	....
1993-94	**Detroit**	**NHL**	39	5	8	13	31	0	1	0	55	9.1	11	....	....	....	7	2	2	4	4	0	1	0	....
	Adirondack	AHL	46	20	23	43	49	....	....	....	....	....	....	....	....	....	....	....	....	....	....	....	....	....	....
1994-95	**Detroit**	**NHL**	36	2	6	8	22	0	0	0	44	4.5	1	....	....	....	18	4	1	5	12	0	1	1	....
1995-96	**Detroit**	**NHL**	52	7	9	16	32	0	1	0	51	13.7	2	....	....	....	18	4	2	6	18	0	1	0	....
1996-97♦	**Detroit**	**NHL**	76	8	5	13	73	1	0	1	85	9.4	–11	....	....	....	20	2	4	6	12	0	1	0	....
1997-98♦	**Detroit**	**NHL**	64	13	10	23	45	1	0	4	96	13.5	5	....	....	....	19	1	3	4	12	0	0	1	....
1998-99	**Detroit**	**NHL**	80	4	14	18	79	0	1	1	78	5.1	2	887	54.6	12:43	10	0	1	1	6	0	0	0	11:35
99-2000	**Detroit**	**NHL**	51	5	7	12	28	0	0	3	76	6.6	3	380	57.6	13:33	9	2	0	2	6	0	0	0	12:26
2000-01	**Detroit**	**NHL**	75	8	17	25	38	0	1	1	123	6.5	17	997	56.5	13:26	6	0	1	1	2	0	0	0	16:08
2001-02♦	**Detroit**	**NHL**	82	15	15	30	56	0	2	3	137	10.9	26	756	53.2	15:35	23	2	3	5	20	0	0	0	17:00
2002-03	**Detroit**	**NHL**	82	14	21	35	82	0	1	2	142	9.9	6	1059	56.9	16:12	4	0	0	0	4	0	0	0	17:29
2003-04	**Detroit**	**NHL**	67	24	16	40	31	2	5	1	149	16.1	22	1058	56.9	17:44	12	1	3	4	6	0	0	0	18:29

Season	Club	League	GP	G	A	Pts	PIM	PP	SH	GW	S	%	+/-	TF	F%	Min	GP	G	A	Pts	PIM	PP	SH	GW	Min
			Regular Season														Playoffs								
2004-05			DID NOT PLAY																						
2005-06	**Detroit**	**NHL**	**80**	**10**	**22**	**32**	**58**	**0**	**1**	**1**	**153**	**6.5**	**3**	**1287**	**57.7**	**17:46**	**6**	**0**	**0**	**0**	**6**	**0**	**0**	**0**	**19:58**
	Canada	Olympics	6	0	0	0	0																		
2006-07	**Detroit**	**NHL**	**81**	**14**	**15**	**29**	**58**	**0**	**5**	**1**	**157**	**8.9**	**7**	**1242**	**57.3**	**16:45**	**18**	**2**	**0**	**2**	**24**	**0**	**0**	**0**	**16:36**
	NHL Totals		**885**	**132**	**165**	**297**	**642**	**4**	**18**	**18**	**1371**	**9.6**		**7666**	**56.5**	**15:32**	**172**	**20**	**20**	**40**	**132**	**0**	**4**	**2**	**16:12**

Frank J. Selke Trophy (2004)

Traded to **Detroit** by **Winnipeg** for future considerations, June 30, 1993.

DRURY, Chris

(DROO-ree, KRIHS) **NYR**

Center. Shoots right. 5'10", 200 lbs. Born, Trumbull, CT, August 20, 1976. Quebec's 5th choice, 72nd overall, in 1994 Entry Draft.

Season	Club	League	GP	G	A	Pts	PIM	PP	SH	GW	S	%	+/-	TF	F%	Min	GP	G	A	Pts	PIM	PP	SH	GW	Min
1991-92	Fairfield Prep	High-CT	25	22	27	49																			
1992-93	Fairfield Prep	High-CT	24	25	32	57	15																		
1993-94	Fairfield Prep	High-CT	24	37	18	55																			
1994-95	Boston University	H-East	39	12	15	27	38																		
1995-96	Boston University	H-East	37	35	33	*68	46																		
1996-97	Boston University	H-East	41	*38	24	62	64																		
1997-98	Boston University	H-East	38	28	29	57	88																		
1998-99	**Colorado**	**NHL**	**79**	**20**	**24**	**44**	**62**	**6**	**0**	**3**	**138**	**14.5**	**9**	**418**	**46.9**	**13:15**	**19**	**6**	**2**	**8**	**4**	**0**	**0**	**4**	**11:28**
99-2000	**Colorado**	**NHL**	**82**	**20**	**47**	**67**	**42**	**7**	**0**	**2**	**213**	**9.4**	**8**	**1321**	**53.1**	**18:33**	**17**	**4**	**10**	**14**	**4**	**1**	**0**	**2**	**18:30**
2000-01♦	**Colorado**	**NHL**	**71**	**24**	**41**	**65**	**47**	**11**	**0**	**5**	**204**	**11.8**	**6**	**552**	**55.1**	**18:03**	**23**	**11**	**5**	**16**	**4**	**2**	**0**	**2**	**19:06**
2001-02	**Colorado**	**NHL**	**82**	**21**	**25**	**46**	**38**	**5**	**0**	**6**	**236**	**8.9**	**1**	**1139**	**53.2**	**17:57**	**21**	**5**	**7**	**12**	**10**	**1**	**0**	**3**	**17:01**
	United States	Olympics	6	0	0	0	0																		
2002-03	**Calgary**	**NHL**	**80**	**23**	**30**	**53**	**33**	**5**	**1**	**5**	**224**	**10.3**	**-9**	**942**	**53.8**	**18:33**									
2003-04	**Buffalo**	**NHL**	**76**	**18**	**35**	**53**	**68**	**5**	**1**	**2**	**152**	**11.8**	**8**	**1491**	**54.9**	**18:04**									
2004-05			DID NOT PLAY																						
2005-06	**Buffalo**	**NHL**	**81**	**30**	**37**	**67**	**32**	**16**	**2**	**5**	**172**	**17.4**	**-11**	**1641**	**55.5**	**18:06**	**18**	**9**	**9**	**18**	**10**	**5**	**1**	**1**	**19:20**
	United States	Olympics	6	0	3	3	2																		
2006-07	**Buffalo**	**NHL**	**77**	**37**	**32**	**69**	**30**	**17**	**3**	**9**	**199**	**18.6**	**1**	**1613**	**58.8**	**18:47**	**16**	**8**	**5**	**13**	**2**	**3**	**0**	**3**	**20:45**
	NHL Totals		**628**	**193**	**271**	**464**	**352**	**72**	**7**	**37**	**1538**	**12.5**		**9117**	**54.8**	**17:40**	**114**	**43**	**38**	**81**	**34**	**12**	**1**	**15**	**17:37**

Hockey East Second All-Star Team (1996, 1997) • NCAA East Second All-American Team (1996) • Hockey East Player of the Year (1997, 1998) • NCAA East First All-American Team (1997, 1998) • NCAA Championship All-Tournament Team (1997) • Hockey East First All-Star Team (1998) • Hobey Baker Memorial Award (Top U.S. Collegiate Player) (1998) • NHL All-Rookie Team (1999) • Calder Memorial Trophy (1999)

Rights transferred to **Colorado** after **Quebec** franchise relocated, June 21, 1995. Traded to **Calgary** by **Colorado** with Stephane Yelle for Derek Morris, Jeff Shantz and Dean McAmmond, October 1, 2002. Traded to **Buffalo** by **Calgary** with Steve Begin for Steve Reinprecht and Rhett Warrener, July 3, 2003. Signed as a free agent by **NY Rangers**, July 1, 2007.

DUBINSKY, Brandon

(DOO-bihn-skee, BRAN-duhn) **NYR**

Center. Shoots left. 6'1", 210 lbs. Born, Anchorage, AK, April 29, 1986. NY Rangers' 6th choice, 60th overall, in 2004 Entry Draft.

Season	Club	League	GP	G	A	Pts	PIM	PP	SH	GW	S	%	+/-	TF	F%	Min	GP	G	A	Pts	PIM	PP	SH	GW	Min
2001-02	Alaska All-Stars	AASHA	37	14	24	38																			
2002-03	Portland	WHL	44	8	18	26	35										7	2	2	4	10				
2003-04	Portland	WHL	71	30	48	78	137										5	0	2	2	6				
2004-05	Portland	WHL	68	23	36	59	160										7	4	5	9	8				
2005-06	Portland	WHL	51	21	46	67	98										12	5	10	15	24				
	Hartford	AHL															11	5	5	10	14				
2006-07	**NY Rangers**	**NHL**	**6**	**0**	**0**	**0**	**2**	**0**	**0**	**0**	**9**	**0.0**	**0**	**26**	**46.2**	**8:10**									
	Hartford	AHL	71	21	22	43	115										7	1	3	4	12				
	NHL Totals		**6**	**0**	**0**	**0**	**2**	**0**	**0**	**0**	**9**	**0.0**		**26**	**46.2**	**8:10**									

WHL West Second All-Star Team (2004, 2006)

DUMONT, J.P.

(DOO-mawnt, JAY-pee) **NSH.**

Right wing. Shoots left. 6'1", 205 lbs. Born, Montreal, Que., April 1, 1978. NY Islanders' 1st choice, 3rd overall, in 1996 Entry Draft.

Season	Club	League	GP	G	A	Pts	PIM	PP	SH	GW	S	%	+/-	TF	F%	Min	GP	G	A	Pts	PIM	PP	SH	GW	Min
1993-94	Mtl-Bourassa	QAAA	44	27	20	47	44										4	2	3	5	4				
1994-95	Mtl-Bourassa	QAAA	10	2	7	9	12																		
	Val-d'Or Foreurs	QMJHL	48	5	14	19	24																		
1995-96	Val-d'Or Foreurs	QMJHL	66	48	57	105	109										13	12	8	20	22				
1996-97	Val-d'Or Foreurs	QMJHL	62	44	64	108	86										13	9	7	16	12				
1997-98	Val-d'Or Foreurs	QMJHL	55	57	42	99	63										19	31	15	46	18				
1998-99	**Chicago**	**NHL**	**25**	**9**	**6**	**15**	**10**	**0**	**0**	**2**	**42**	**21.4**	**7**	**10**	**50.0**	**14:14**									
	Portland Pirates	AHL	50	32	14	46	39																		
	Chicago Wolves	IHL															10	4	1	5	6				
99-2000	**Chicago**	**NHL**	**47**	**10**	**8**	**18**	**18**	**0**	**0**	**1**	**86**	**11.6**	**-6**	**12**	**33.3**	**12:54**									
	Cleveland	IHL	7	5	2	7	8																		
	Rochester	AHL	13	7	10	17	18										21	14	7	21	32				
2000-01	**Buffalo**	**NHL**	**79**	**23**	**28**	**51**	**54**	**9**	**0**	**5**	**156**	**14.7**	**1**	**3**	**33.3**	**15:01**	**13**	**4**	**3**	**7**	**8**	**0**	**0**	**0**	**14:32**
2001-02	**Buffalo**	**NHL**	**76**	**23**	**21**	**44**	**42**	**7**	**0**	**3**	**154**	**14.9**	**-10**	**4**	**50.0**	**15:14**									
2002-03	**Buffalo**	**NHL**	**76**	**14**	**21**	**35**	**44**	**2**	**0**	**2**	**135**	**10.4**	**-14**	**15**	**20.0**	**15:04**									
2003-04	**Buffalo**	**NHL**	**77**	**22**	**31**	**53**	**40**	**10**	**0**	**1**	**156**	**14.1**	**-9**	**32**	**43.8**	**17:00**									
2004-05	SC Bern	Swiss	3	2	2	4	6										10	4	1	5	16				
2005-06	**Buffalo**	**NHL**	**54**	**20**	**20**	**40**	**38**	**9**	**0**	**4**	**116**	**17.2**	**-1**	**9**	**11.1**	**16:00**	**18**	**7**	**7**	**14**	**14**	**3**	**0**	**1**	**16:39**
2006-07	**Nashville**	**NHL**	**82**	**21**	**45**	**66**	**28**	**5**	**0**	**3**	**143**	**14.7**	**14**	**6**	**16.7**	**16:12**	**5**	**4**	**2**	**6**	**0**	**1**	**1**	**1**	**21:03**
	NHL Totals		**516**	**142**	**180**	**322**	**274**	**42**	**0**	**21**	**988**	**14.4**		**91**	**34.1**	**15:25**	**36**	**15**	**12**	**27**	**22**	**4**	**1**	**2**	**16:30**

QMJHL Second All-Star Team (1997) • AHL All-Rookie Team (1999)

Rights traded to **Chicago** by **NY Islanders** with NY Islanders' 5th round choice (later traded to Philadelphia – Philadelphia selected Francis Belanger) in 1998 Entry Draft for Dmitri Nabokov, May 30, 1998. Traded to **Buffalo** by **Chicago** with Doug Gilmour for Michal Grosek, March 10, 2000. Signed as a free agent by **Bern** (Swiss), February 9, 2005. Signed as a free agent by **Nashville**, August 29, 2006.

DuPONT, Micki

(DOO-pawnt, MIH-kee) **ST.L.**

Defense. Shoots right. 5'10", 186 lbs. Born, Calgary, Alta., April 15, 1980. Calgary's 9th choice, 270th overall, in 2000 Entry Draft.

Season	Club	League	GP	G	A	Pts	PIM	PP	SH	GW	S	%	+/-	TF	F%	Min	GP	G	A	Pts	PIM	PP	SH	GW	Min
1995-96	Calgary Blazers	AMHL	35	10	35	45	68																		
1996-97	Kamloops Blazers	WHL	59	8	27	35	39										5	0	4	4	8				
1997-98	Kamloops Blazers	WHL	71	13	41	54	91										7	0	1	1	10				
1998-99	Kamloops Blazers	WHL	59	8	27	35	110										15	2	8	10	22				
99-2000	Kamloops Blazers	WHL	70	26	62	88	156										4	0	2	2	17				
	Long Beach	IHL	1	0	0	0	0																		
	San Diego Gulls	WCHL															7	2	2	4	0				
2000-01	Saint John Flames	AHL	67	8	21	29	28										19	1	9	10	14				
2001-02	**Calgary**	**NHL**	**2**	**0**	**0**	**0**	**2**	**0**	**0**	**0**	**2**	**0.0**	**0**	**0**	**0.0**	**14:44**									
	Saint John Flames	AHL	77	7	33	40	77																		
2002-03	**Calgary**	**NHL**	**16**	**1**	**2**	**3**	**4**	**0**	**0**	**0**	**27**	**3.7**	**-5**	**0**	**0.0**	**16:45**									
	Saint John Flames	AHL	44	12	21	33	73																		
	Wilkes-Barre	AHL	14	1	4	5	16										6	3	0	3	21				
2003-04	Eisbaren Berlin	Germany	45	10	22	32	76										10	3	6	9	35				
2004-05	Eisbaren Berlin	Germany	51	11	22	33	93										11	2	5	7	41				
2005-06	Eisbaren Berlin	Germany	52	11	21	32	78										11	4	10	*14	10				
2006-07	**Pittsburgh**	**NHL**	**3**	**0**	**1**	**1**	**4**	**0**	**0**	**0**	**6**	**0.0**	**-3**	**0**	**0.0**	**13:48**									
	Wilkes-Barre	AHL	78	18	33	51	101										11	5	9	14	16				
	NHL Totals		**21**	**1**	**3**	**4**	**10**	**0**	**0**	**0**	**35**	**2.9**		**0**	**0.0**	**16:08**									

AHL All-Rookie Team (2001) • AHL First All-Star Team (2007)

Traded to **Pittsburgh** by **Calgary** with Mathias Johansson for Shean Donovan, March 11, 2003. Signed as a free agent by **Berlin** (Germany), August 6, 2003. Signed as a free agent by **St. Louis**, July 3, 2007.

DUPUIS, Pascal
(doo-PWEE, pas-KAL) **ATL.**

Left wing. Shoots left. 6', 200 lbs. Born, Laval, Que., April 7, 1979.

			Regular Season														Playoffs								
Season	Club	League	GP	G	A	Pts	PIM	PP	SH	GW	S	%	+/-	TF	F%	Min	GP	G	A	Pts	PIM	PP	SH	GW	Min
1995-96	Laval-Laurentides	QAAA	41	10	15	25											14	11	11	22					
1996-97	Rouyn-Noranda	QMJHL	44	9	15	24	20																		
1997-98	Rouyn-Noranda	QMJHL	39	9	17	26	36																		
	Shawinigan	QMJHL	28	7	13	20	10										6	2	0	2	4				
1998-99	Shawinigan	QMJHL	57	30	42	72	118										6	1	8	9	18				
99-2000	Shawinigan	QMJHL	61	50	55	105	99										13	*15	7	22	4				
2000-01	**Minnesota**	**NHL**	**4**	**1**	**0**	**1**	**4**	**1**	**0**	**0**	**8**	**12.5**	**0**	**0**	**0.0**	**15:36**									
	Cleveland	IHL	70	19	24	43	37										4	0	0	0	0				
2001-02	**Minnesota**	**NHL**	**76**	**15**	**12**	**27**	**16**	**3**	**2**	**0**	**154**	**9.7**	**-10**	**40**	**32.5**	**15:08**									
2002-03	**Minnesota**	**NHL**	**80**	**20**	**28**	**48**	**44**	**6**	**0**	**4**	**183**	**10.9**	**17**	**186**	**40.9**	**17:30**	**16**	**4**	**4**	**8**	**8**	**2**	**0**	**1**	**16:58**
2003-04	**Minnesota**	**NHL**	**59**	**11**	**15**	**26**	**20**	**2**	**0**	**1**	**127**	**8.7**	**5**	**129**	**45.7**	**15:48**									
2004-05	HC Ajoie	Swiss-2	8	5	5	10	26										6	6	8	14	8				
2005-06	**Minnesota**	**NHL**	**67**	**10**	**16**	**26**	**40**	**4**	**0**	**2**	**151**	**6.6**	**-10**	**93**	**29.0**	**16:30**									
2006-07	**Minnesota**	**NHL**	**48**	**10**	**3**	**13**	**38**	**2**	**2**	**0**	**106**	**9.4**	**-7**	**110**	**27.3**	**15:07**									
	NY Rangers	**NHL**	**6**	**1**	**0**	**1**	**0**	**0**	**0**	**0**	**10**	**10.0**	**-4**	**2**	**50.0**	**15:30**									
	Atlanta	**NHL**	**17**	**3**	**2**	**5**	**4**	**0**	**0**	**1**	**40**	**7.5**	**-6**	**19**	**52.6**	**16:44**	**4**	**1**	**2**	**3**	**4**	**0**	**0**	**0**	**20:28**
	NHL Totals		**357**	**71**	**76**	**147**	**166**	**18**	**4**	**8**	**779**	**9.1**		**579**	**37.3**	**16:07**	**20**	**5**	**6**	**11**	**12**	**2**	**0**	**1**	**17:40**

Signed as a free agent by **Minnesota**, August 18, 2000. Signed as a free agent by **Ajoie** (Swiss-2), January 14, 2005. Traded to **NY Rangers** by **Minnesota** for Adam Hall, February 9, 2007. Traded to **Atlanta** by **NY Rangers** with NY Rangers' 3rd round choice (later traded to Pittsburgh - Pittsburgh selected Robert Bortuzzo) in 2007 Entry Draft for Alex Bourret, February 27, 2007.

DVORAK, Radek
(duh-VOHR-ak, RA-dehk) **FLA.**

Right wing. Shoots right. 6'2", 200 lbs. Born, Tabor, Czech., March 9, 1977. Florida's 1st choice, 10th overall, in 1995 Entry Draft.

			Regular Season														Playoffs								
Season	Club	League	GP	G	A	Pts	PIM	PP	SH	GW	S	%	+/-	TF	F%	Min	GP	G	A	Pts	PIM	PP	SH	GW	Min
1992-93	C. Budejovice Jr.	Czech-Jr.	35	44	46	90																			
1993-94	C. Budejovice Jr.	CzRep-Jr.	20	17	18	35																			
	C. Budejovice	CzRep	8	0	0	0	0																		
1994-95	C. Budejovice	CzRep	10	3	5	8	2										9	5	1	6					
1995-96	**Florida**	**NHL**	**77**	**13**	**14**	**27**	**20**	**0**	**0**	**4**	**126**	**10.3**	**5**				**16**	**1**	**3**	**4**	**0**	**0**	**0**	**0**	
1996-97	**Florida**	**NHL**	**78**	**18**	**21**	**39**	**30**	**2**	**0**	**1**	**139**	**12.9**	**-2**				**3**	**0**	**0**	**0**	**0**	**0**	**0**	**0**	
1997-98	**Florida**	**NHL**	**64**	**12**	**24**	**36**	**33**	**2**	**3**	**0**	**112**	**10.7**	**-1**												
1998-99	**Florida**	**NHL**	**82**	**19**	**24**	**43**	**29**	**0**	**4**	**0**	**182**	**10.4**	**7**	**98**	**46.9**	**16:13**									
99-2000	**Florida**	**NHL**	**35**	**7**	**10**	**17**	**6**	**0**	**0**	**1**	**67**	**10.4**	**5**	**16**	**37.5**	**15:25**									
	NY Rangers	**NHL**	**46**	**11**	**22**	**33**	**10**	**2**	**1**	**0**	**90**	**12.2**	**0**	**34**	**35.3**	**18:24**									
2000-01	**NY Rangers**	**NHL**	**82**	**31**	**36**	**67**	**20**	**5**	**2**	**3**	**230**	**13.5**	**9**	**20**	**30.0**	**19:04**									
2001-02	**NY Rangers**	**NHL**	**65**	**17**	**20**	**37**	**14**	**3**	**3**	**1**	**210**	**8.1**	**-20**	**5**	**0.0**	**19:44**									
	Czech Republic	Olympics	4	0	0	0	0																		
2002-03	**NY Rangers**	**NHL**	**63**	**6**	**21**	**27**	**16**	**2**	**0**	**0**	**134**	**4.5**	**-3**	**9**	**44.4**	**15:42**									
	Edmonton	**NHL**	**12**	**4**	**4**	**8**	**14**	**1**	**0**	**0**	**32**	**12.5**	**-3**	**1**	**0.0**	**16:07**	**4**	**1**	**0**	**1**	**0**	**0**	**0**	**1**	**15:05**
2003-04	**Edmonton**	**NHL**	**78**	**15**	**35**	**50**	**26**	**6**	**0**	**0**	**188**	**8.0**	**18**	**24**	**29.2**	**16:56**									
2004-05	C. Budejovice	CzRep-2	32	23	35	58	18										16	5	13	18	20				
2005-06	**Edmonton**	**NHL**	**64**	**8**	**20**	**28**	**26**	**2**	**0**	**2**	**131**	**6.1**	**-2**	**14**	**28.6**	**16:34**	**16**	**0**	**2**	**2**	**4**	**0**	**0**	**0**	**13:29**
2006-07	**St. Louis**	**NHL**	**82**	**10**	**27**	**37**	**48**	**1**	**1**	**1**	**139**	**7.2**	**-6**	**26**	**38.5**	**15:38**									
	NHL Totals		**828**	**171**	**278**	**449**	**292**	**26**	**14**	**13**	**1780**	**9.6**		**247**	**38.5**	**17:05**	**39**	**2**	**5**	**7**	**4**	**0**	**0**	**1**	**13:48**

Traded to **San Jose** by **Florida** for Mike Vernon and San Jose's 3rd round choice (Sean O'Connor) in 2000 Entry Draft, December 30, 1999. Traded to **NY Rangers** by **San Jose** for Todd Harvey and NY Rangers' 4th round choice (Dimitri Patzold) in 2001 Entry Draft, December 30, 1999. Traded to **Edmonton** by **NY Rangers** with Cory Cross for Anson Carter and Ales Pisa, March 11, 2003. Signed as a free agent by **Ceske Budejovice** (CzRep-2), September 15, 2004. Signed as a free agent by **St. Louis**, September 14, 2006. Signed as a free agent by **Florida**, July 1, 2007.

EAGER, Ben
(EE-guhr, BEHN) **PHI.**

Left wing. Shoots left. 6'3", 225 lbs. Born, Ottawa, Ont., January 22, 1984. Phoenix's 2nd choice, 23rd overall, in 2002 Entry Draft.

			Regular Season														Playoffs								
Season	Club	League	GP	G	A	Pts	PIM	PP	SH	GW	S	%	+/-	TF	F%	Min	GP	G	A	Pts	PIM	PP	SH	GW	Min
99-2000	Ott. Jr. Senators	CJHL	50	8	11	19	119																		
2000-01	Oshawa Generals	OHL	61	4	6	10	120																		
2001-02	Oshawa Generals	OHL	63	14	23	37	255										5	0	1	1	13				
2002-03	Oshawa Generals	OHL	58	16	24	40	216										8	0	4	4	8				
2003-04	Oshawa Generals	OHL	61	25	27	52	204										7	2	3	5	31				
	Philadelphia	AHL	5	0	0	0	0										3	0	1	1	8				
2004-05	Philadelphia	AHL	66	7	10	17	232										16	1	1	2	71				
2005-06	**Philadelphia**	**NHL**	**25**	**3**	**5**	**8**	**18**	**0**	**0**	**0**	**21**	**14.3**	**0**	**0**	**0.0**	**7:24**	**2**	**0**	**0**	**0**	**26**	**0**	**0**	**0**	**7:06**
	Philadelphia	AHL	49	6	12	18	256																		
2006-07	**Philadelphia**	**NHL**	**63**	**6**	**5**	**11**	***233**	**0**	**0**	**0**	**48**	**12.5**	**-13**	**1**	**100.0**	**8:14**									
	Philadelphia	AHL	3	0	0	0	21																		
	NHL Totals		**88**	**9**	**10**	**19**	**251**	**0**	**0**	**0**	**69**	**13.0**		**1**	**100.0**	**8:00**	**2**	**0**	**0**	**0**	**26**	**0**	**0**	**0**	**7:06**

Traded to **Philadelphia** by **Phoenix** with Sean Burke and Branko Radivojevic for Mike Comrie, February 9, 2004.

EATON, Mark
(EE-tohn, MAHRK) **PIT.**

Defense. Shoots left. 6'2", 204 lbs. Born, Wilmington, DE, May 6, 1977.

			Regular Season														Playoffs								
Season	Club	League	GP	G	A	Pts	PIM	PP	SH	GW	S	%	+/-	TF	F%	Min	GP	G	A	Pts	PIM	PP	SH	GW	Min
1995-96	Waterloo	USHL	50	4	21	25																			
1996-97	Waterloo	USHL	50	6	32	38	62																		
1997-98	U. of Notre Dame	CCHA	41	12	17	29	32																		
1998-99	Philadelphia	AHL	74	9	27	36	38										16	4	8	12	0				
99-2000	**Philadelphia**	**NHL**	**27**	**1**	**1**	**2**	**8**	**0**	**0**	**1**	**25**	**4.0**	**1**	**0**	**0.0**	**18:17**	**7**	**0**	**0**	**0**	**0**	**0**	**0**	**0**	**13:36**
	Philadelphia	AHL	47	9	17	26	6																		
2000-01	**Nashville**	**NHL**	**34**	**3**	**8**	**11**	**14**	**1**	**0**	**1**	**32**	**9.4**	**7**	**0**	**0.0**	**17:13**									
	Milwaukee	IHL	34	3	12	15	27																		
2001-02	**Nashville**	**NHL**	**58**	**3**	**5**	**8**	**24**	**0**	**0**	**0**	**52**	**5.8**	**-12**	**0**	**0.0**	**17:12**									
2002-03	**Nashville**	**NHL**	**50**	**2**	**7**	**9**	**22**	**0**	**0**	**0**	**52**	**3.8**	**1**	**0**	**0.0**	**15:45**									
	Milwaukee	AHL	3	1	0	1	2																		
2003-04	**Nashville**	**NHL**	**75**	**4**	**9**	**13**	**26**	**0**	**0**	**1**	**82**	**4.9**	**16**	**0**	**0.0**	**20:56**	**6**	**0**	**0**	**0**	**2**	**0**	**0**	**0**	**19:51**
2004-05	Grand Rapids	AHL	29	3	3	6	21																		
2005-06	**Nashville**	**NHL**	**69**	**3**	**1**	**4**	**44**	**0**	**0**	**0**	**28**	**10.7**	**-2**	**0**	**0.0**	**19:43**	**5**	**0**	**0**	**0**	**8**	**0**	**0**	**0**	**17:49**
2006-07	**Pittsburgh**	**NHL**	**35**	**0**	**3**	**3**	**16**	**0**	**0**	**0**	**22**	**0.0**	**-6**	**0**	**0.0**	**19:12**	**5**	**0**	**0**	**0**	**0**	**0**	**0**	**0**	**18:31**
	NHL Totals		**348**	**16**	**34**	**50**	**154**	**1**	**0**	**3**	**293**	**5.5**		**0**	**0.0**	**18:35**	**23**	**0**	**0**	**0**	**10**	**0**	**0**	**0**	**17:13**

USHL Second All-Star Team (1997) • Curt Hammer Award (Most Gentlemanly Player – USHL) (1997) • CCHA Rookie of the Year (1998)

Signed as a free agent by **Philadelphia**, August 4, 1998. Traded to **Nashville** by **Philadelphia** for Detroit's 3rd round choice (previously acquired, Philadelphia selected Patrick Sharp) in 2001 Entry Draft, September 29, 2000. Signed as a free agent by **Grand Rapids** (AHL), February 16, 2005. Signed as a free agent by **Pittsburgh**, July 3, 2006.

EAVES, Patrick
(EEVZ, PAT-rihk) **OTT.**

Right wing. Shoots right. 6', 188 lbs. Born, Calgary, Alta., May 1, 1984. Ottawa's 1st choice, 29th overall, in 2003 Entry Draft.

			Regular Season														Playoffs								
Season	Club	League	GP	G	A	Pts	PIM	PP	SH	GW	S	%	+/-	TF	F%	Min	GP	G	A	Pts	PIM	PP	SH	GW	Min
99-2000	Shat.-St. Mary's	High-MN	50	23	24	47																			
2000-01	USNTDP	U-17	13	7	8	15	3																		
	USNTDP	NAHL	34	12	11	23	75																		
2001-02	USNTDP	U-18	32	19	21	40	87																		
	USNTDP	USHL	9	1	4	5	18																		
	USNTDP	NAHL	8	5	3	8	37																		
2002-03	Boston College	H-East	14	10	8	18	61																		
2003-04	Boston College	H-East	34	18	23	41	66																		
2004-05	Boston College	H-East	36	19	29	48	36																		
2005-06	**Ottawa**	**NHL**	**58**	**20**	**9**	**29**	**22**	**5**	**1**	**4**	**100**	**20.0**	**7**	**14**	**21.4**	**12:29**	**10**	**1**	**0**	**1**	**10**	**0**	**0**	**0**	**11:40**
	Binghamton	AHL	18	5	8	13	10																		
2006-07	**Ottawa**	**NHL**	**73**	**14**	**18**	**32**	**36**	**3**	**1**	**1**	**130**	**10.8**	**1**	**9**	**11.1**	**12:13**	**7**	**0**	**2**	**2**	**2**	**0**	**0**	**0**	**7:23**
	NHL Totals		**131**	**34**	**27**	**61**	**58**	**8**	**2**	**5**	**230**	**14.8**		**23**	**17.4**	**12:20**	**17**	**1**	**2**	**3**	**12**	**0**	**0**	**0**	**9:54**

Hockey East Second All-Star Team (2004) • NCAA East Second All-American Team (2004) • Hockey East First All-Star Team (2005) • NCAA East First All-American Team (2005)

• Missed majority of 2002-03 season recovering from neck injury suffered in game vs. Maine (Hockey East), December 7, 2002.

EDLER, Alexander
(EHD-luhr, al-EHX-AN-duhr) **VAN.**

Defense. Shoots left. 6'3", 220 lbs. Born, Ostersund, Sweden, April 21, 1986. Vancouver's 2nd choice, 91st overall, in 2004 Entry Draft.

Season	Club	League	GP	G	A	Pts	PIM	PP	SH	GW	S	%	+/-	TF	F%	Min	Playoffs GP	G	A	Pts	PIM	PP	SH	GW	Min
2001-02	Jamtland	Exhib.	8	0	1	1	2	....	....	....	....	....	....	....	....	....	....	....	....	....	....	....	....	....	....
2002-03	Jamtland	Exhib.	8	2	1	3	0	....	....	....	....	....	....	....	....	....	....	....	....	....	....	....	....	....	....
2003-04	Jamtland Jr.	Swe-Jr.	6	0	3	3	6	....	....	....	....	....	....	....	....	....	....	....	....	....	....	....	....	....	....
	Jamtland	Sweden-3	24	3	6	9	20	....	....	....	....	....	....	....	....	....	....	....	....	....	....	....	....	....	....
2004-05	MODO Jr.	Swe-Jr.	33	8	15	23	40	....	....	....	....	....	....	....	....	....	5	1	0	1	6	....	....	....	....
2005-06	Kelowna Rockets	WHL	62	13	40	53	44	....	....	....	....	....	....	....	....	....	12	3	5	8	12	....	....	....	....
2006-07	**Vancouver**	**NHL**	**22**	**1**	**2**	**3**	**6**	**0**	**0**	**0**	**10**	**10.0**	**3**	**0**	**0.0**	**11:27**	**3**	**0**	**0**	**0**	**2**	**0**	**0**	**0**	**11:51**
	Manitoba Moose	AHL	49	5	21	26	28	....	....	....	....	....	....	....	....	....	8	0	0	0	2	....	....	....	....
	NHL Totals		**22**	**1**	**2**	**3**	**6**	**0**	**0**	**0**	**10**	**10.0**		**0**	**0.0**	**11:27**	**3**	**0**	**0**	**0**	**2**	**0**	**0**	**0**	**11:51**

EHRHOFF, Christian
(AIR-hawf, KRIHS-tyehn) **S.J.**

Defense. Shoots left. 6'2", 200 lbs. Born, Moers, West Germany, July 6, 1982. San Jose's 2nd choice, 106th overall, in 2001 Entry Draft.

Season	Club	League	GP	G	A	Pts	PIM	PP	SH	GW	S	%	+/-	TF	F%	Min	Playoffs GP	G	A	Pts	PIM	PP	SH	GW	Min
1998-99	Krefelder EV Jr.	Ger-Jr.	22	10	14	24	46	....	....	....	....	....	....	....	....	....	....	....	....	....	....	....	....	....	....
99-2000	EV Duisburg	German-3	41	3	12	15	50	....	....	....	....	....	....	....	....	....	....	....	....	....	....	....	....	....	....
	Krefeld Pinguine	Germany	9	1	0	1	6	....	....	....	....	....	....	....	....	....	3	0	0	0	0	....	....	....	....
2000-01	EV Duisburg	German-3	6	1	2	3	12	....	....	....	....	....	....	....	....	....	....	....	....	....	....	....	....	....	....
	Krefeld Pinguine	Germany	58	3	11	14	73	....	....	....	....	....	....	....	....	....	....	....	....	....	....	....	....	....	....
2001-02	Krefeld Pinguine	Germany	46	7	17	24	81	....	....	....	....	....	....	....	....	....	3	0	0	0	2	....	....	....	....
	Germany	Olympics	7	0	0	0	8	....	....	....	....	....	....	....	....	....	....	....	....	....	....	....	....	....	....
2002-03	Krefeld Pinguine	Germany	48	10	17	27	54	....	....	....	....	....	....	....	....	....	14	3	6	9	24	....	....	....	....
2003-04	**San Jose**	**NHL**	**41**	**1**	**11**	**12**	**14**	**0**	**0**	**1**	**58**	**1.7**	**4**	**0**	**0.0**	**15:23**	....	....	....	....	....	....	....	....	....
	Cleveland Barons	AHL	27	4	10	14	43	....	....	....	....	....	....	....	....	....	9	2	6	8	11	....	....	....	....
2004-05	Cleveland Barons	AHL	79	12	23	35	103	....	....	....	....	....	....	....	....	....	....	....	....	....	....	....	....	....	....
2005-06	**San Jose**	**NHL**	**64**	**5**	**18**	**23**	**32**	**2**	**0**	**2**	**124**	**4.0**	**10**	**0**	**0.0**	**17:48**	**11**	**2**	**6**	**8**	**18**	**1**	**0**	**1**	**19:47**
	Germany	Olympics	5	1	1	2	4	....	....	....	....	....	....	....	....	....	....	....	....	....	....	....	....	....	....
2006-07	**San Jose**	**NHL**	**82**	**10**	**23**	**33**	**63**	**6**	**0**	**2**	**164**	**6.1**	**8**	**1**	**0.0**	**18:34**	**11**	**0**	**2**	**2**	**6**	**0**	**0**	**0**	**17:47**
	NHL Totals		**187**	**16**	**52**	**68**	**109**	**8**	**0**	**5**	**346**	**4.6**		**1**	**0.0**	**17:37**	**22**	**2**	**8**	**10**	**24**	**1**	**0**	**1**	**18:47**

EKMAN, Nils
(EHK-mahn, NIHLZ)

Left wing. Shoots left. 6', 185 lbs. Born, Stockholm, Sweden, March 11, 1976. Calgary's 6th choice, 107th overall, in 1994 Entry Draft.

Season	Club	League	GP	G	A	Pts	PIM	PP	SH	GW	S	%	+/-	TF	F%	Min	Playoffs GP	G	A	Pts	PIM	PP	SH	GW	Min
1993-94	Hammarby Jr.	Swe-Jr.	11	4	5	9	14	....	....	....	....	....	....	....	....	....	....	....	....	....	....	....	....	....	....
	Hammarby	Sweden-2	18	7	2	9	4	....	....	....	....	....	....	....	....	....	....	....	....	....	....	....	....	....	....
1994-95	Hammarby Jr.	Swe-Jr.	2	2	1	3	0	....	....	....	....	....	....	....	....	....	....	....	....	....	....	....	....	....	....
	Hammarby	Sweden-2	32	10	8	18	18	....	....	....	....	....	....	....	....	....	....	....	....	....	....	....	....	....	....
1995-96	Hammarby	Sweden-2	26	9	7	16	53	....	....	....	....	....	....	....	....	....	1	0	0	0	0	....	....	....	....
1996-97	Kiekko-Espoo	Finland	50	24	19	43	60	....	....	....	....	....	....	....	....	....	4	2	0	2	4	....	....	....	....
1997-98	Kiekko-Espoo	Finland	43	14	14	28	86	....	....	....	....	....	....	....	....	....	7	2	2	4	27	....	....	....	....
	Saint John Flames	AHL	....	....	....	....	....	....	....	....	....	....	....	....	....	....	1	0	0	0	2	....	....	....	....
1998-99	Blues Espoo	Finland	52	20	14	34	96	....	....	....	....	....	....	....	....	....	3	1	1	2	6	....	....	....	....
99-2000	Detroit Vipers	IHL	10	7	2	9	8	....	....	....	....	....	....	....	....	....	....	....	....	....	....	....	....	....	....
	Tampa Bay	**NHL**	**28**	**2**	**2**	**4**	**36**	**1**	**0**	**0**	**42**	**4.8**	**–8**	**3**	**0.0**	**11:12**	....	....	....	....	....	....	....	....	....
	Long Beach	IHL	27	11	12	23	26	....	....	....	....	....	....	....	....	....	5	3	3	6	4	....	....	....	....
2000-01	**Tampa Bay**	**NHL**	**43**	**9**	**11**	**20**	**40**	**2**	**1**	**1**	**72**	**12.5**	**–15**	**16**	**37.5**	**15:45**	....	....	....	....	....	....	....	....	....
	Detroit Vipers	IHL	33	22	14	36	63	....	....	....	....	....	....	....	....	....	....	....	....	....	....	....	....	....	....
2001-02	Djurgarden	Sweden	38	16	15	31	57	....	....	....	....	....	....	....	....	....	4	1	0	1	32	....	....	....	....
2002-03	Hartford	AHL	57	30	36	66	73	....	....	....	....	....	....	....	....	....	2	0	2	2	4	....	....	....	....
2003-04	**San Jose**	**NHL**	**82**	**22**	**33**	**55**	**34**	**1**	**4**	**5**	**147**	**15.0**	**30**	**23**	**21.7**	**14:54**	**16**	**0**	**3**	**3**	**8**	**0**	**0**	**0**	**13:02**
2004-05	Djurgarden	Sweden	44	18	27	45	106	....	....	....	....	....	....	....	....	....	12	4	5	9	20	....	....	....	....
2005-06	**San Jose**	**NHL**	**77**	**21**	**36**	**57**	**54**	**5**	**0**	**2**	**176**	**11.9**	**20**	**39**	**46.2**	**15:12**	**11**	**2**	**2**	**4**	**8**	**1**	**0**	**0**	**15:14**
2006-07	**Pittsburgh**	**NHL**	**34**	**6**	**9**	**15**	**24**	**2**	**0**	**0**	**69**	**8.7**	**–14**	**6**	**0.0**	**13:49**	**1**	**0**	**0**	**0**	**0**	**0**	**0**	**0**	**10:03**
	NHL Totals		**264**	**60**	**91**	**151**	**188**	**11**	**5**	**8**	**506**	**11.9**		**87**	**33.3**	**14:36**	**28**	**2**	**5**	**7**	**16**	**1**	**0**	**0**	**13:48**

Garry F. Longman Memorial Trophy (Rookie of the Year – IHL) (2000)

Traded to **Tampa Bay** by **Calgary** with Calgary's 4th round choice (later traded to NY Islanders – NY Islanders selected Vladimir Gorbunov) in 2000 Entry Draft for Andreas Johansson, November 20, 1999. Traded to **NY Rangers** by **Tampa Bay** with Kyle Freadrich for Tim Taylor, June 30, 2001. Traded to **San Jose** by **NY Rangers** for Chad Wiseman, August 12, 2003. Signed as a free agent by **Djurgarden** (Sweden), September 16, 2004. Traded to **Pittsburgh** by **San Jose** with Patrick Ehelechner for Carolina's 2nd round choice (previously acquired, later traded to Philadelphia - Philadelphia selected Kevin Marshall) in 2007 Entry Draft, July 20, 2006. • Missed majority of 2006-07 season recovering from elbow injury suffered in game vs. Toronto, December 29, 2006. Signed as a free agent by **Khimik** (Russia), August 12, 2007.

ELIAS, Patrik
(ehl-EE-ahsh, PAT-rihk) **N.J.**

Left wing. Shoots left. 6'1", 195 lbs. Born, Trebic, Czech., April 13, 1976. New Jersey's 2nd choice, 51st overall, in 1994 Entry Draft.

Season	Club	League	GP	G	A	Pts	PIM	PP	SH	GW	S	%	+/-	TF	F%	Min	Playoffs GP	G	A	Pts	PIM	PP	SH	GW	Min
1992-93	Poldi Kladno	Czech	2	0	0	0	....	....	....	....	....	....	....	....	....	....	....	....	....	....	....	....	....	....	....
1993-94	HC Kladno	CzRep	15	1	2	3	....	....	....	....	....	....	....	....	....	....	11	2	2	4	....	....	....	....	....
1994-95	HC Kladno	CzRep	28	4	3	7	37	....	....	....	....	....	....	....	....	....	7	1	2	3	12	....	....	....	....
1995-96	**New Jersey**	**NHL**	**1**	**0**	**0**	**0**	**0**	**0**	**0**	**0**	**2**	**0.0**	**–1**	....	....	....	....	....	....	....	....	....	....	....	....
	Albany River Rats	AHL	74	27	36	63	83	....	....	....	....	....	....	....	....	....	4	1	1	2	2	....	....	....	....
1996-97	**New Jersey**	**NHL**	**17**	**2**	**3**	**5**	**2**	**0**	**0**	**0**	**23**	**8.7**	**–4**	....	....	....	**8**	**2**	**3**	**5**	**4**	**1**	**0**	**0**	....
	Albany River Rats	AHL	57	24	43	67	76	....	....	....	....	....	....	....	....	....	6	1	2	3	8	....	....	....	....
1997-98	**New Jersey**	**NHL**	**74**	**18**	**19**	**37**	**28**	**5**	**0**	**6**	**147**	**12.2**	**18**	....	....	....	**4**	**0**	**1**	**1**	**0**	**0**	**0**	**0**	....
	Albany River Rats	AHL	3	3	0	3	2	....	....	....	....	....	....	....	....	....	....	....	....	....	....	....	....	....	....
1998-99	**New Jersey**	**NHL**	**74**	**17**	**33**	**50**	**34**	**3**	**0**	**2**	**157**	**10.8**	**19**	**99**	**38.4**	**15:50**	**7**	**0**	**5**	**5**	**6**	**0**	**0**	**0**	**18:07**
99-2000	Trebic	CzRep-2	2	2	1	3	2	....	....	....	....	....	....	....	....	....	....	....	....	....	....	....	....	....	....
	Pardubice	CzRep	5	1	4	5	31	....	....	....	....	....	....	....	....	....	....	....	....	....	....	....	....	....	....
	♦ New Jersey	**NHL**	**72**	**35**	**37**	**72**	**58**	**9**	**0**	**9**	**183**	**19.1**	**16**	**134**	**45.5**	**17:28**	**23**	**7**	***13**	**20**	**9**	**2**	**1**	**1**	**17:44**
2000-01	**New Jersey**	**NHL**	**82**	**40**	**56**	**96**	**51**	**8**	**3**	**6**	**220**	**18.2**	**45**	**155**	**41.3**	**18:44**	**25**	**9**	**14**	**23**	**10**	**3**	**1**	**2**	**18:14**
2001-02	**New Jersey**	**NHL**	**75**	**29**	**32**	**61**	**36**	**8**	**1**	**8**	**199**	**14.6**	**4**	**128**	**45.3**	**18:57**	**6**	**2**	**4**	**6**	**6**	**2**	**0**	**0**	**20:33**
	Czech Republic	Olympics	4	1	1	2	0	....	....	....	....	....	....	....	....	....	....	....	....	....	....	....	....	....	....
2002-03 ♦	**New Jersey**	**NHL**	**81**	**28**	**29**	**57**	**22**	**6**	**0**	**4**	**255**	**11.0**	**17**	**427**	**43.8**	**18:05**	**24**	**5**	**8**	**13**	**26**	**2**	**0**	**2**	**17:14**
2003-04	**New Jersey**	**NHL**	**82**	**38**	**43**	**81**	**44**	**9**	**3**	**9**	**300**	**12.7**	**26**	**49**	**36.7**	**18:46**	**5**	**3**	**2**	**5**	**2**	**1**	**0**	**1**	**18:59**
2004-05	Znojmo	CzRep	28	8	20	28	65	....	....	....	....	....	....	....	....	....	....	....	....	....	....	....	....	....	....
	Magnitogorsk	Russia	17	5	9	14	28	....	....	....	....	....	....	....	....	....	....	....	....	....	....	....	....	....	....
2005-06	**New Jersey**	**NHL**	**38**	**16**	**29**	**45**	**20**	**6**	**0**	**3**	**142**	**11.3**	**11**	**10**	**20.0**	**18:34**	**9**	**6**	**10**	**16**	**4**	**4**	**0**	**0**	**18:43**
	Czech Republic	Olympics	1	0	0	0	2	....	....	....	....	....	....	....	....	....	....	....	....	....	....	....	....	....	....
2006-07	**New Jersey**	**NHL**	**75**	**21**	**48**	**69**	**38**	**8**	**0**	**5**	**267**	**7.9**	**1**	**18**	**38.9**	**18:37**	**10**	**1**	**9**	**10**	**4**	**1**	**0**	**0**	**19:13**
	NHL Totals		**671**	**244**	**329**	**573**	**333**	**62**	**7**	**52**	**1895**	**12.9**		**1020**	**42.6**	**18:07**	**121**	**35**	**69**	**104**	**71**	**16**	**2**	**6**	**18:11**

NHL All-Rookie Team (1998) • NHL First All-Star Team (2001) • Bud Light Plus/Minus Award (2001) (tied with Joe Sakic)

Played in NHL All-Star Game (2000, 2002)

Signed as a free agent by **Znojmo** (CzRep), September 6, 2004. Signed as a free agent by **Magnitogorsk** (Russia), December 9, 2004. • Missed majority of 2005-06 season recovering from hepatitis-A.

ELLIS, Matt
(EHL-ihs, MAT) **DET.**

Left wing. Shoots left. 6', 188 lbs. Born, Welland, Ont., August 31, 1981.

Season	Club	League	GP	G	A	Pts	PIM	PP	SH	GW	S	%	+/-	TF	F%	Min	Playoffs GP	G	A	Pts	PIM	PP	SH	GW	Min
1998-99	St. Michael's	OHL	47	10	8	18	6	....	....	....	....	....	....	....	....	....	....	....	....	....	....	....	....	....	....
99-2000	St. Michael's	OHL	59	15	20	35	20	....	....	....	....	....	....	....	....	....	....	....	....	....	....	....	....	....	....
2000-01	St. Michael's	OHL	68	21	24	45	19	....	....	....	....	....	....	....	....	....	18	4	8	12	6	....	....	....	....
2001-02	St. Michael's	OHL	66	38	51	89	20	....	....	....	....	....	....	....	....	....	15	8	6	14	6	....	....	....	....
2002-03	Toledo Storm	ECHL	71	27	32	59	34	....	....	....	....	....	....	....	....	....	7	3	5	8	0	....	....	....	....
2003-04	Grand Rapids	AHL	64	5	10	15	23	....	....	....	....	....	....	....	....	....	4	0	0	0	2	....	....	....	....
2004-05	Grand Rapids	AHL	79	18	23	41	59	....	....	....	....	....	....	....	....	....	....	....	....	....	....	....	....	....	....
2005-06	Grand Rapids	AHL	74	20	28	48	61	....	....	....	....	....	....	....	....	....	16	4	1	5	20	....	....	....	....
2006-07	**Detroit**	**NHL**	**16**	**0**	**0**	**0**	**6**	**0**	**0**	**0**	**22**	**0.0**	**–1**	**48**	**47.9**	**5:35**	....	....	....	....	....	....	....	....	....
	Grand Rapids	AHL	65	26	23	49	44	....	....	....	....	....	....	....	....	....	7	4	3	7	4	....	....	....	....
	NHL Totals		**16**	**0**	**0**	**0**	**6**	**0**	**0**	**0**	**22**	**0.0**		**48**	**47.9**	**5:35**	....	....	....	....	....	....	....	....	....

Signed as a free agent by **Detroit**, May 10, 2002.

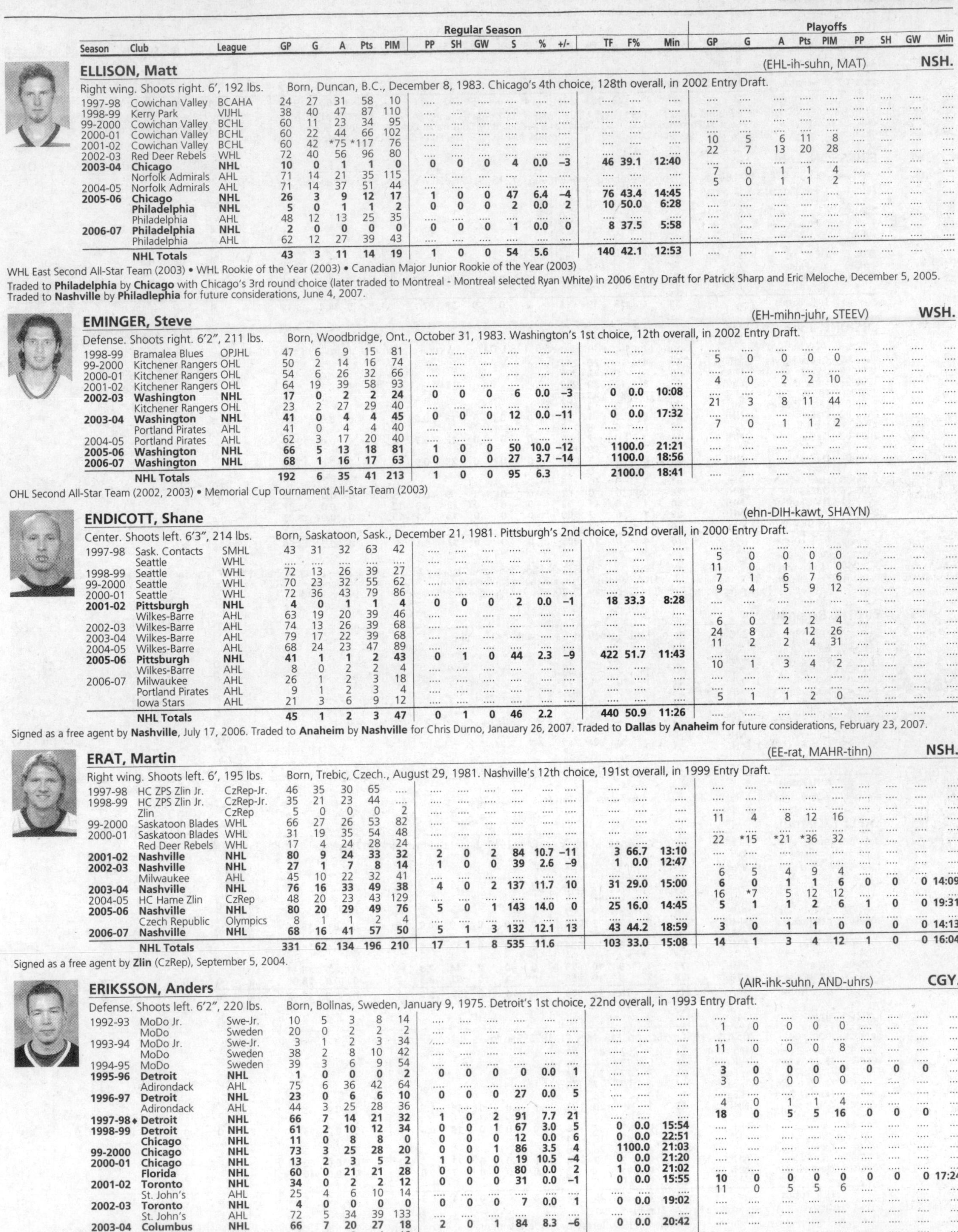

ELLISON, Matt

(EHL-ih-suhn, MAT) **NSH.**

Right wing. Shoots right. 6', 192 lbs. Born, Duncan, B.C., December 8, 1983. Chicago's 4th choice, 128th overall, in 2002 Entry Draft.

			Regular Season														Playoffs								
Season	Club	League	GP	G	A	Pts	PIM	PP	SH	GW	S	%	+/-	TF	F%	Min	GP	G	A	Pts	PIM	PP	SH	GW	Min
1997-98	Cowichan Valley	BCAHA	24	27	31	58	10	....	....	....	....	....	....	....	....	....	....	....	....	....	....	....	....	....	....
1998-99	Kerry Park	VIJHL	38	40	47	87	110	....	....	....	....	....	....	....	....	....	....	....	....	....	....	....	....	....	....
99-2000	Cowichan Valley	BCHL	60	11	23	34	95	....	....	....	....	....	....	....	....	....	....	....	....	....	....	....	....	....	....
2000-01	Cowichan Valley	BCHL	60	22	44	66	102	....	....	....	....	....	....	....	....	....	....	....	....	....	....	....	....	....	....
2001-02	Cowichan Valley	BCHL	60	42	*75	*117	76	....	....	....	....	....	....	....	....	....	10	5	6	11	8	....	....	....	....
2002-03	Red Deer Rebels	WHL	72	40	56	96	80	....	....	....	....	....	....	....	....	....	22	7	13	20	28	....	....	....	....
2003-04	**Chicago**	**NHL**	**10**	**0**	**1**	**1**	**0**	**0**	**0**	**0**	**4**	**0.0**	**–3**	**46**	**39.1**	**12:40**	....	....	....	....	....	....	....	....	....
	Norfolk Admirals	AHL	71	14	21	35	115	....	....	....	....	....	....	....	....	....	7	0	1	1	4	....	....	....	....
2004-05	Norfolk Admirals	AHL	71	14	37	51	44	....	....	....	....	....	....	....	....	....	5	0	1	1	2	....	....	....	....
2005-06	**Chicago**	**NHL**	**26**	**3**	**9**	**12**	**17**	**1**	**0**	**0**	**47**	**6.4**	**–4**	**76**	**43.4**	**14:45**	....	....	....	....	....	....	....	....	....
	Philadelphia	**NHL**	**5**	**0**	**1**	**1**	**2**	**0**	**0**	**0**	**2**	**0.0**	**2**	**10**	**50.0**	**6:28**	....	....	....	....	....	....	....	....	....
	Philadelphia	AHL	48	12	13	25	35	....	....	....	....	....	....	....	....	....	....	....	....	....	....	....	....	....	....
2006-07	**Philadelphia**	**NHL**	**2**	**0**	**0**	**0**	**0**	**0**	**0**	**0**	**1**	**0.0**	**0**	**8**	**37.5**	**5:58**	....	....	....	....	....	....	....	....	....
	Philadelphia	AHL	62	12	27	39	43	....	....	....	....	....	....	....	....	....	....	....	....	....	....	....	....	....	....
	NHL Totals		**43**	**3**	**11**	**14**	**19**	**1**	**0**	**0**	**54**	**5.6**		**140**	**42.1**	**12:53**	....	....	....	....	....	....	....	....	....

WHL East Second All-Star Team (2003) • WHL Rookie of the Year (2003) • Canadian Major Junior Rookie of the Year (2003)

Traded to **Philadelphia** by **Chicago** with Chicago's 3rd round choice (later traded to Montreal - Montreal selected Ryan White) in 2006 Entry Draft for Patrick Sharp and Eric Meloche, December 5, 2005. Traded to **Nashville** by **Philadlephia** for future considerations, June 4, 2007.

EMINGER, Steve

(EH-mihn-juhr, STEEV) **WSH.**

Defense. Shoots right. 6'2", 211 lbs. Born, Woodbridge, Ont., October 31, 1983. Washington's 1st choice, 12th overall, in 2002 Entry Draft.

			Regular Season														Playoffs								
Season	Club	League	GP	G	A	Pts	PIM	PP	SH	GW	S	%	+/-	TF	F%	Min	GP	G	A	Pts	PIM	PP	SH	GW	Min
1998-99	Bramalea Blues	OPJHL	47	6	9	15	81	....	....	....	....	....	....	....	....	....	....	....	....	....	....	....	....	....	....
99-2000	Kitchener Rangers	OHL	50	2	14	16	74	....	....	....	....	....	....	....	....	....	5	0	0	0	0	....	....	....	....
2000-01	Kitchener Rangers	OHL	54	6	26	32	66	....	....	....	....	....	....	....	....	....	....	....	....	....	....	....	....	....	....
2001-02	Kitchener Rangers	OHL	64	19	39	58	93	....	....	....	....	....	....	....	....	....	4	0	2	2	10	....	....	....	....
2002-03	**Washington**	**NHL**	**17**	**0**	**2**	**2**	**24**	**0**	**0**	**0**	**6**	**0.0**	**–3**	**0**	**0.0**	**10:08**	....	....	....	....	....	....	....	....	....
	Kitchener Rangers	OHL	23	2	27	29	40	....	....	....	....	....	....	....	....	....	21	3	8	11	44	....	....	....	....
2003-04	**Washington**	**NHL**	**41**	**0**	**4**	**4**	**45**	**0**	**0**	**0**	**12**	**0.0**	**–11**	**0**	**0.0**	**17:32**	....	....	....	....	....	....	....	....	....
	Portland Pirates	AHL	41	0	4	4	40	....	....	....	....	....	....	....	....	....	7	0	1	1	2	....	....	....	....
2004-05	Portland Pirates	AHL	62	3	17	20	40	....	....	....	....	....	....	....	....	....	....	....	....	....	....	....	....	....	....
2005-06	**Washington**	**NHL**	**66**	**5**	**13**	**18**	**81**	**1**	**0**	**0**	**50**	**10.0**	**–12**	**1**	**100.0**	**21:21**	....	....	....	....	....	....	....	....	....
2006-07	**Washington**	**NHL**	**68**	**1**	**16**	**17**	**63**	**0**	**0**	**0**	**27**	**3.7**	**–14**	**1**	**100.0**	**18:56**	....	....	....	....	....	....	....	....	....
	NHL Totals		**192**	**6**	**35**	**41**	**213**	**1**	**0**	**0**	**95**	**6.3**		**2**	**100.0**	**18:41**	....	....	....	....	....	....	....	....	....

OHL Second All-Star Team (2002, 2003) • Memorial Cup Tournament All-Star Team (2003)

ENDICOTT, Shane

(ehn-DIH-kawt, SHAYN)

Center. Shoots left. 6'3", 214 lbs. Born, Saskatoon, Sask., December 21, 1981. Pittsburgh's 2nd choice, 52nd overall, in 2000 Entry Draft.

			Regular Season														Playoffs								
Season	Club	League	GP	G	A	Pts	PIM	PP	SH	GW	S	%	+/-	TF	F%	Min	GP	G	A	Pts	PIM	PP	SH	GW	Min
1997-98	Sask. Contacts	SMHL	43	31	32	63	42	....	....	....	....	....	....	....	....	....	....	....	....	....	....	....	....	....	....
	Seattle	WHL	....	....	....	....	....	....	....	....	....	....	....	....	....	....	5	0	0	0	0	....	....	....	....
1998-99	Seattle	WHL	72	13	26	39	27	....	....	....	....	....	....	....	....	....	11	0	1	1	0	....	....	....	....
99-2000	Seattle	WHL	70	23	32	55	62	....	....	....	....	....	....	....	....	....	7	1	6	7	6	....	....	....	....
2000-01	Seattle	WHL	72	36	43	79	86	....	....	....	....	....	....	....	....	....	9	4	5	9	12	....	....	....	....
2001-02	**Pittsburgh**	**NHL**	**4**	**0**	**1**	**1**	**4**	**0**	**0**	**0**	**2**	**0.0**	**–1**	**18**	**33.3**	**8:28**	....	....	....	....	....	....	....	....	....
	Wilkes-Barre	AHL	63	19	20	39	46	....	....	....	....	....	....	....	....	....	....	....	....	....	....	....	....	....	....
2002-03	Wilkes-Barre	AHL	74	13	26	39	68	....	....	....	....	....	....	....	....	....	6	0	2	2	4	....	....	....	....
2003-04	Wilkes-Barre	AHL	79	17	22	39	68	....	....	....	....	....	....	....	....	....	24	8	4	12	26	....	....	....	....
2004-05	Wilkes-Barre	AHL	68	24	23	47	89	....	....	....	....	....	....	....	....	....	11	2	2	4	31	....	....	....	....
2005-06	**Pittsburgh**	**NHL**	**41**	**1**	**1**	**2**	**43**	**0**	**1**	**0**	**44**	**2.3**	**–9**	**422**	**51.7**	**11:43**	....	....	....	....	....	....	....	....	....
	Wilkes-Barre	AHL	8	0	2	2	4	....	....	....	....	....	....	....	....	....	10	1	3	4	2	....	....	....	....
2006-07	Milwaukee	AHL	26	1	2	3	18	....	....	....	....	....	....	....	....	....	....	....	....	....	....	....	....	....	....
	Portland Pirates	AHL	9	1	2	3	4	....	....	....	....	....	....	....	....	....	....	....	....	....	....	....	....	....	....
	Iowa Stars	AHL	21	3	6	9	12	....	....	....	....	....	....	....	....	....	5	1	1	2	0	....	....	....	....
	NHL Totals		**45**	**1**	**2**	**3**	**47**	**0**	**1**	**0**	**46**	**2.2**		**440**	**50.9**	**11:26**	....	....	....	....	....	....	....	....	....

Signed as a free agent by **Nashville**, July 17, 2006. Traded to **Anaheim** by **Nashville** for Chris Durno, Janauary 26, 2007. Traded to **Dallas** by **Anaheim** for future considerations, February 23, 2007.

ERAT, Martin

(EE-rat, MAHR-tihn) **NSH.**

Right wing. Shoots left. 6', 195 lbs. Born, Trebic, Czech., August 29, 1981. Nashville's 12th choice, 191st overall, in 1999 Entry Draft.

			Regular Season														Playoffs								
Season	Club	League	GP	G	A	Pts	PIM	PP	SH	GW	S	%	+/-	TF	F%	Min	GP	G	A	Pts	PIM	PP	SH	GW	Min
1997-98	HC ZPS Zlin Jr.	CzRep-Jr.	46	35	30	65	....	....	....	....	....	....	....	....	....	....	....	....	....	....	....	....	....	....	....
1998-99	HC ZPS Zlin Jr.	CzRep-Jr.	35	21	23	44	....	....	....	....	....	....	....	....	....	....	....	....	....	....	....	....	....	....	....
	Zlin	CzRep	5	0	0	0	2	....	....	....	....	....	....	....	....	....	....	....	....	....	....	....	....	....	....
99-2000	Saskatoon Blades	WHL	66	27	26	53	82	....	....	....	....	....	....	....	....	....	11	4	8	12	16	....	....	....	....
2000-01	Saskatoon Blades	WHL	31	19	35	54	48	....	....	....	....	....	....	....	....	....	....	....	....	....	....	....	....	....	....
	Red Deer Rebels	WHL	17	4	24	28	24	....	....	....	....	....	....	....	....	....	22	*15	*21	*36	32	....	....	....	....
2001-02	**Nashville**	**NHL**	**80**	**9**	**24**	**33**	**32**	**2**	**0**	**2**	**84**	**10.7**	**–11**	**3**	**66.7**	**13:10**	....	....	....	....	....	....	....	....	....
2002-03	**Nashville**	**NHL**	**27**	**1**	**7**	**8**	**14**	**1**	**0**	**0**	**39**	**2.6**	**–9**	**1**	**0.0**	**12:47**	....	....	....	....	....	....	....	....	....
	Milwaukee	AHL	45	10	22	32	41	....	....	....	....	....	....	....	....	....	6	5	4	9	4	....	....	....	....
2003-04	**Nashville**	**NHL**	**76**	**16**	**33**	**49**	**38**	**4**	**0**	**2**	**137**	**11.7**	**10**	**31**	**29.0**	**15:00**	**6**	**0**	**1**	**1**	**6**	**0**	**0**	**0**	**14:09**
2004-05	HC Hame Zlin	CzRep	48	20	23	43	129	....	....	....	....	....	....	....	....	....	16	*7	5	12	12	....	....	....	....
2005-06	**Nashville**	**NHL**	**80**	**20**	**29**	**49**	**76**	**5**	**0**	**1**	**143**	**14.0**	**0**	**25**	**16.0**	**14:45**	**5**	**1**	**1**	**2**	**6**	**1**	**0**	**0**	**19:31**
	Czech Republic	Olympics	8	1	1	2	4	....	....	....	....	....	....	....	....	....	....	....	....	....	....	....	....	....	....
2006-07	**Nashville**	**NHL**	**68**	**16**	**41**	**57**	**50**	**5**	**1**	**3**	**132**	**12.1**	**13**	**43**	**44.2**	**18:59**	**3**	**0**	**1**	**1**	**0**	**0**	**0**	**0**	**14:13**
	NHL Totals		**331**	**62**	**134**	**196**	**210**	**17**	**1**	**8**	**535**	**11.6**		**103**	**33.0**	**15:08**	**14**	**1**	**3**	**4**	**12**	**1**	**0**	**0**	**16:04**

Signed as a free agent by **Zlin** (CzRep), September 5, 2004.

ERIKSSON, Anders

(AIR-ihk-suhn, AND-uhrs) **CGY.**

Defense. Shoots left. 6'2", 220 lbs. Born, Bollnas, Sweden, January 9, 1975. Detroit's 1st choice, 22nd overall, in 1993 Entry Draft.

			Regular Season														Playoffs								
Season	Club	League	GP	G	A	Pts	PIM	PP	SH	GW	S	%	+/-	TF	F%	Min	GP	G	A	Pts	PIM	PP	SH	GW	Min
1992-93	MoDo Jr.	Swe-Jr.	10	5	3	8	14	....	....	....	....	....	....	....	....	....	....	....	....	....	....	....	....	....	....
	MoDo	Sweden	20	0	2	2	2	....	....	....	....	....	....	....	....	....	1	0	0	0	0	....	....	....	....
1993-94	MoDo Jr.	Swe-Jr.	3	1	2	3	34	....	....	....	....	....	....	....	....	....	....	....	....	....	....	....	....	....	....
	MoDo	Sweden	38	2	8	10	42	....	....	....	....	....	....	....	....	....	11	0	0	0	8	....	....	....	....
1994-95	MoDo	Sweden	39	3	6	9	54	....	....	....	....	....	....	....	....	....	....	....	....	....	....	....	....	....	....
1995-96	**Detroit**	**NHL**	**1**	**0**	**0**	**0**	**2**	**0**	**0**	**0**	**0**	**0.0**	**1**	....	....	....	**3**	**0**	**0**	**0**	**0**	**0**	**0**	**0**	....
	Adirondack	AHL	75	6	36	42	64	....	....	....	....	....	....	....	....	....	3	0	0	0	0	....	....	....	....
1996-97	**Detroit**	**NHL**	**23**	**0**	**6**	**6**	**10**	**0**	**0**	**0**	**27**	**0.0**	**5**	....	....	....	....	....	....	....	....	....	....	....	....
	Adirondack	AHL	44	3	25	28	36	....	....	....	....	....	....	....	....	....	4	0	1	1	4	....	....	....	....
1997-98♦	**Detroit**	**NHL**	**66**	**7**	**14**	**21**	**32**	**1**	**0**	**2**	**91**	**7.7**	**21**	....	....	....	**18**	**0**	**5**	**5**	**16**	**0**	**0**	**0**	....
1998-99	**Detroit**	**NHL**	**61**	**2**	**10**	**12**	**34**	**0**	**0**	**1**	**67**	**3.0**	**5**	**0**	**0.0**	**15:54**	....	....	....	....	....	....	....	....	....
	Chicago	**NHL**	**11**	**0**	**8**	**8**	**0**	**0**	**0**	**0**	**12**	**0.0**	**6**	**0**	**0.0**	**22:51**	....	....	....	....	....	....	....	....	....
99-2000	**Chicago**	**NHL**	**73**	**3**	**25**	**28**	**20**	**0**	**0**	**1**	**86**	**3.5**	**4**	**1**	**100.0**	**21:03**	....	....	....	....	....	....	....	....	....
2000-01	**Chicago**	**NHL**	**13**	**2**	**3**	**5**	**2**	**1**	**0**	**0**	**19**	**10.5**	**–4**	**0**	**0.0**	**21:20**	....	....	....	....	....	....	....	....	....
	Florida	**NHL**	**60**	**0**	**21**	**21**	**28**	**0**	**0**	**0**	**80**	**0.0**	**2**	**1**	**0.0**	**21:02**	....	....	....	....	....	....	....	....	....
2001-02	**Toronto**	**NHL**	**34**	**0**	**2**	**2**	**12**	**0**	**0**	**0**	**31**	**0.0**	**–1**	**0**	**0.0**	**15:55**	**10**	**0**	**0**	**0**	**0**	**0**	**0**	**0**	**17:24**
	St. John's	AHL	25	4	6	10	14	....	....	....	....	....	....	....	....	....	11	0	5	5	6	....	....	....	....
2002-03	**Toronto**	**NHL**	**4**	**0**	**0**	**0**	**0**	**0**	**0**	**0**	**7**	**0.0**	**1**	**0**	**0.0**	**19:02**	....	....	....	....	....	....	....	....	....
	St. John's	AHL	72	5	34	39	133	....	....	....	....	....	....	....	....	....	....	....	....	....	....	....	....	....	....
2003-04	**Columbus**	**NHL**	**66**	**7**	**20**	**27**	**18**	**2**	**0**	**1**	**84**	**8.3**	**–6**	**0**	**0.0**	**20:42**	....	....	....	....	....	....	....	....	....
	Syracuse Crunch	AHL	9	1	3	4	12	....	....	....	....	....	....	....	....	....	....	....	....	....	....	....	....	....	....
2004-05	HV 71 Jonkoping	Sweden	32	1	9	10	54	....	....	....	....	....	....	....	....	....	....	....	....	....	....	....	....	....	....

Season	Club	League	Regular Season														Playoffs								
Season	Club	League	GP	G	A	Pts	PIM	PP	SH	GW	S	%	+/-	TF	F%	Min	GP	G	A	Pts	PIM	PP	SH	GW	Min
2005-06	Magnitogorsk	Russia	17	2	7	9	10	....	....	....	....	....	....	....	....	....	11	3	2	5	16	....	....	....	....
	Springfield	AHL	12	1	8	9	10	....	....	....	....	....	....	....	....	....	....	....	....	....	....	....	....	....	....
2006-07	**Columbus**	**NHL**	**79**	**0**	**23**	**23**	**46**	**0**	**0**	**0**	**78**	**0.0**	**12**	**1**	**100.0**	**20:12**	....	....	....	....	....	....	....	....	....
	NHL Totals		**491**	**21**	**132**	**153**	**204**	**4**	**0**	**5**	**582**	**3.6**		**3**	**66.7**	**19:39**	**31**	**0**	**5**	**5**	**16**	**0**	**0**	**0**	**17:24**

Traded to **Chicago** by **Detroit** with Detroit's 1st round choices in 1999 (Steve McCarthy) and 2001 (Adam Munro) Entry Drafts for Chris Chelios, March 23, 1999. Traded to **Florida** by **Chicago** for Jaroslav Spacek, November 6, 2000. Signed as a free agent by **Toronto**, July 9, 2001. Signed as a free agent by **Columbus**, October 10, 2003. Signed as a free agent by **Calgary**, September 16, 2004. Signed as a free agent by **Jonkoping** (Sweden), October 29, 2004. Signed as a fee agent by **Columbus**, July 1, 2006. Signed as a free agent by **Calgary**, July 5, 2007.

ERIKSSON, Loui

(AIR-ihk-suhn, LOO-ee) **DAL.**

Left wing. Shoots left. 6'1", 183 lbs. Born, Goteborg, Sweden, July 17, 1985. Dallas' 1st choice, 33rd overall, in 2003 Entry Draft.

Season	Club	League	GP	G	A	Pts	PIM	PP	SH	GW	S	%	+/-	TF	F%	Min	GP	G	A	Pts	PIM	PP	SH	GW	Min
2000-01	V.Frolunda U18	Swe-U18	9	5	3	8	4	....	....	....	....	....	....	....	....	....	....	....	....	....	....	....	....	....	....
	V.Frolunda Jr.	Swe-Jr.	1	0	0	0	0	....	....	....	....	....	....	....	....	....	....	....	....	....	....	....	....	....	....
2001-02	V.Frolunda U18	Swe-U18	1	1	0	1	0	....	....	....	....	....	....	....	....	....	....	....	....	....	....	....	....	....	....
	V.Frolunda Jr.	Swe-Jr.	35	7	15	22	2	....	....	....	....	....	....	....	....	....	8	2	3	5	2	....	....	....	....
2002-03	V.Frolunda Jr.	Swe-Jr.	30	16	15	31	10	....	....	....	....	....	....	....	....	....	8	4	6	10	4	....	....	....	....
2003-04	V.Frolunda	Sweden	46	8	5	13	4	....	....	....	....	....	....	....	....	....	10	1	5	6	0	....	....	....	....
2004-05	Frolunda	Sweden	39	5	9	14	4	....	....	....	....	....	....	....	....	....	12	0	0	0	0	....	....	....	....
2005-06	Iowa Stars	AHL	78	31	29	60	27	....	....	....	....	....	....	....	....	....	7	2	5	7	0	....	....	....	....
2006-07	**Dallas**	**NHL**	**59**	**6**	**13**	**19**	**18**	**2**	**0**	**0**	**78**	**7.7**	**–3**	**9**	**44.4**	**13:11**	**4**	**0**	**1**	**1**	**0**	**0**	**0**	**0**	**15:47**
	Iowa Stars	AHL	15	5	3	8	13	....	....	....	....	....	....	....	....	....	9	2	5	7	0	....	....	....	....
	NHL Totals		**59**	**6**	**13**	**19**	**18**	**2**	**0**	**0**	**78**	**7.7**		**9**	**44.4**	**13:11**	**4**	**0**	**1**	**1**	**0**	**0**	**0**	**0**	**15:47**

ERSKINE, John

(AIR-skign, JAWN) **WSH.**

Defense. Shoots left. 6'4", 216 lbs. Born, Kingston, Ont., June 26, 1980. Dallas' 1st choice, 39th overall, in 1998 Entry Draft.

Season	Club	League	GP	G	A	Pts	PIM	PP	SH	GW	S	%	+/-	TF	F%	Min	GP	G	A	Pts	PIM	PP	SH	GW	Min
1996-97	Quinte Hawks	MTJHL	48	4	16	20	241	....	....	....	....	....	....	....	....	....	....	....	....	....	....	....	....	....	....
1997-98	London Knights	OHL	55	0	9	9	205	....	....	....	....	....	....	....	....	....	16	0	5	5	25	....	....	....	....
1998-99	London Knights	OHL	57	8	12	20	208	....	....	....	....	....	....	....	....	....	25	5	10	15	38	....	....	....	....
99-2000	London Knights	OHL	58	12	31	43	177	....	....	....	....	....	....	....	....	....	....	....	....	....	....	....	....	....	....
2000-01	Utah Grizzlies	IHL	77	1	8	9	284	....	....	....	....	....	....	....	....	....	....	....	....	....	....	....	....	....	....
2001-02	**Dallas**	**NHL**	**33**	**0**	**1**	**1**	**62**	**0**	**0**	**0**	**16**	**0.0**	**–8**	**0**	**0.0**	**10:44**	....	....	....	....	....	....	....	....	....
	Utah Grizzlies	AHL	39	2	6	8	118	....	....	....	....	....	....	....	....	....	3	0	0	0	10	....	....	....	....
2002-03	**Dallas**	**NHL**	**16**	**2**	**0**	**2**	**29**	**0**	**0**	**0**	**12**	**16.7**	**1**	**0**	**0.0**	**10:45**	....	....	....	....	....	....	....	....	....
	Utah Grizzlies	AHL	52	2	8	10	274	....	....	....	....	....	....	....	....	....	1	0	1	1	15	....	....	....	....
2003-04	**Dallas**	**NHL**	**32**	**0**	**1**	**1**	**84**	**0**	**0**	**0**	**23**	**0.0**	**–9**	**0**	**0.0**	**12:36**	....	....	....	....	....	....	....	....	....
	Utah Grizzlies	AHL	5	0	0	0	18	....	....	....	....	....	....	....	....	....	....	....	....	....	....	....	....	....	....
2004-05	Houston Aeros	AHL	61	3	7	10	238	....	....	....	....	....	....	....	....	....	5	0	1	1	20	....	....	....	....
2005-06	**Dallas**	**NHL**	**26**	**0**	**0**	**0**	**62**	**0**	**0**	**0**	**9**	**0.0**	**–3**	**0**	**0.0**	**11:00**	....	....	....	....	....	....	....	....	....
	NY Islanders	**NHL**	**34**	**1**	**0**	**1**	**99**	**0**	**0**	**0**	**23**	**4.3**	**–12**	**0**	**0.0**	**14:37**	....	....	....	....	....	....	....	....	....
2006-07	**Washington**	**NHL**	**29**	**1**	**6**	**7**	**69**	**0**	**0**	**0**	**14**	**7.1**	**–13**	**0**	**0.0**	**18:03**	....	....	....	....	....	....	....	....	....
	Hershey Bears	AHL	4	0	2	2	9	....	....	....	....	....	....	....	....	....	....	....	....	....	....	....	....	....	....
	NHL Totals		**170**	**4**	**8**	**12**	**405**	**0**	**0**	**0**	**97**	**4.1**		**0**	**0.0**	**13:09**	....	....	....	....	....	....	....	....	....

OHL First All-Star Team (2000)

• Missed majority of 2003-04 season recovering from ankle (December 27, 2003 vs. Columbus) and hernia (January 24, 2004 vs. St. Louis) injuries. Traded to **NY Islanders** by **Dallas** with Dallas' 2nd round choice (Jesse Joensuu) in 2006 Entry Draft for Janne Niinimaa and NY Islanders' 5th round choice (Ondrej Roman) in 2007 Entry Draft, January 10, 2005. Signed as a free agent by **Washington**, September 14, 2006. • Missed majority of 2006-07 season recovering from foot (December 16, 2006 vs. Philadelphia) and thumb (March 9, 2007 vs. Carolina) injuries.

EVANS, Brennan

(EH-vans, BREH-nuhn) **S.J.**

Defense. Shoots left. 6'3", 220 lbs. Born, North Battleford, Sask., January 16, 1982.

Season	Club	League	GP	G	A	Pts	PIM	PP	SH	GW	S	%	+/-	TF	F%	Min	GP	G	A	Pts	PIM	PP	SH	GW	Min
1998-99	Camrose Kodiaks	AJHL	47	1	6	7	98	....	....	....	....	....	....	....	....	....	5	0	2	2	0	....	....	....	....
	Seattle	WHL	....	....	....	....	....	....	....	....	....	....	....	....	....	....	1	0	0	0	0	....	....	....	....
99-2000	Seattle	WHL	52	1	2	3	40	....	....	....	....	....	....	....	....	....	1	0	0	0	0	....	....	....	....
2000-01	Seattle	WHL	11	1	0	1	25	....	....	....	....	....	....	....	....	....	....	....	....	....	....	....	....	....	....
	Kootenay Ice	WHL	55	2	7	9	105	....	....	....	....	....	....	....	....	....	11	0	0	0	25	....	....	....	....
2001-02	Kootenay Ice	WHL	72	2	3	5	121	....	....	....	....	....	....	....	....	....	22	0	6	6	38	....	....	....	....
2002-03	Kootenay Ice	WHL	67	6	17	23	182	....	....	....	....	....	....	....	....	....	11	1	1	2	24	....	....	....	....
2003-04	Lowell	AHL	64	1	9	10	65	....	....	....	....	....	....	....	....	....	....	....	....	....	....	....	....	....	....
	Calgary	**NHL**	....	....	....	....	....	....	....	....	....	....	....	....	....	....	**2**	**0**	**0**	**0**	**0**	**0**	**0**	**0**	**2:52**
2004-05	Lowell	AHL	51	0	7	7	79	....	....	....	....	....	....	....	....	....	5	0	0	0	2	....	....	....	....
2005-06	Binghamton	AHL	70	3	6	9	198	....	....	....	....	....	....	....	....	....	....	....	....	....	....	....	....	....	....
2006-07	Worcester Sharks	AHL	75	2	14	16	170	....	....	....	....	....	....	....	....	....	5	0	1	1	21	....	....	....	....
	NHL Totals		....	....	....	....	....	....	....	....	....	....	....	....	....	....	**2**	**0**	**0**	**0**	**0**	**0**	**0**	**0**	**2:52**

Signed as a free agent by **Calgary**, September 30, 2003. Signed as a free agent by **San Jose**, July 18, 2007.

EXELBY, Garnet

(EHX-uhl-bee, GAHR-neht) **ATL.**

Defense. Shoots left. 6'1", 215 lbs. Born, Ste. Anne, Man., August 16, 1981. Atlanta's 9th choice, 217th overall, in 1999 Entry Draft.

Season	Club	League	GP	G	A	Pts	PIM	PP	SH	GW	S	%	+/-	TF	F%	Min	GP	G	A	Pts	PIM	PP	SH	GW	Min
1997-98	Winnipeg South	MJHL	46	5	11	16	110	....	....	....	....	....	....	....	....	....	....	....	....	....	....	....	....	....	....
1998-99	Saskatoon Blades	WHL	61	5	3	8	91	....	....	....	....	....	....	....	....	....	....	....	....	....	....	....	....	....	....
99-2000	Saskatoon Blades	WHL	63	1	8	9	79	....	....	....	....	....	....	....	....	....	11	0	2	2	21	....	....	....	....
2000-01	Saskatoon Blades	WHL	43	5	10	15	110	....	....	....	....	....	....	....	....	....	....	....	....	....	....	....	....	....	....
	Regina Pats	WHL	22	2	8	10	51	....	....	....	....	....	....	....	....	....	6	0	2	2	2	....	....	....	....
2001-02	Chicago Wolves	AHL	75	3	4	7	257	....	....	....	....	....	....	....	....	....	25	0	4	4	49	....	....	....	....
2002-03	**Atlanta**	**NHL**	**15**	**0**	**2**	**2**	**41**	**0**	**0**	**0**	**9**	**0.0**	**0**	**0**	**0.0**	**18:04**	....	....	....	....	....	....	....	....	....
	Chicago Wolves	AHL	53	3	6	9	140	....	....	....	....	....	....	....	....	....	9	0	1	1	27	....	....	....	....
2003-04	**Atlanta**	**NHL**	**71**	**1**	**9**	**10**	**134**	**0**	**0**	**0**	**42**	**2.4**	**–10**	**0**	**0.0**	**19:32**	....	....	....	....	....	....	....	....	....
2004-05			DID NOT PLAY																						
2005-06	**Atlanta**	**NHL**	**75**	**1**	**9**	**10**	**75**	**0**	**0**	**0**	**44**	**2.3**	**11**	**0**	**0.0**	**15:41**	....	....	....	....	....	....	....	....	....
2006-07	**Atlanta**	**NHL**	**58**	**2**	**8**	**10**	**56**	**0**	**1**	**0**	**57**	**3.5**	**2**	**0**	**0.0**	**18:00**	**4**	**0**	**0**	**0**	**6**	**0**	**0**	**0**	**15:38**
	NHL Totals		**219**	**4**	**28**	**32**	**306**	**0**	**1**	**0**	**152**	**2.6**		**0**	**0.0**	**17:42**	**4**	**0**	**0**	**0**	**6**	**0**	**0**	**0**	**15:38**

FAHEY, Jim

(FA-hee, JIHM) **CHI.**

Defense. Shoots right. 6', 205 lbs. Born, Boston, MA, May 11, 1979. San Jose's 9th choice, 212th overall, in 1998 Entry Draft.

Season	Club	League	GP	G	A	Pts	PIM	PP	SH	GW	S	%	+/-	TF	F%	Min	GP	G	A	Pts	PIM	PP	SH	GW	Min
1997-98	Catholic Memorial	High-MA	24	12	32	44	28	....	....	....	....	....	....	....	....	....	....	....	....	....	....	....	....	....	....
1998-99	Northeastern	H-East	32	5	13	18	34	....	....	....	....	....	....	....	....	....	....	....	....	....	....	....	....	....	....
99-2000	Northeastern	H-East	36	3	17	20	62	....	....	....	....	....	....	....	....	....	....	....	....	....	....	....	....	....	....
2000-01	Northeastern	H-East	36	4	23	27	48	....	....	....	....	....	....	....	....	....	....	....	....	....	....	....	....	....	....
2001-02	Northeastern	H-East	39	14	32	46	50	....	....	....	....	....	....	....	....	....	....	....	....	....	....	....	....	....	....
2002-03	**San Jose**	**NHL**	**43**	**1**	**19**	**20**	**33**	**0**	**0**	**0**	**66**	**1.5**	**–3**	**1**	**100.0**	**18:20**	....	....	....	....	....	....	....	....	....
	Cleveland Barons	AHL	25	3	14	17	42	....	....	....	....	....	....	....	....	....	....	....	....	....	....	....	....	....	....
2003-04	**San Jose**	**NHL**	**15**	**0**	**2**	**2**	**18**	**0**	**0**	**0**	**19**	**0.0**	**–2**	**0**	**0.0**	**16:54**	**2**	**0**	**0**	**0**	**0**	**0**	**0**	**0**	**4:41**
	Cleveland Barons	AHL	32	1	18	19	64	....	....	....	....	....	....	....	....	....	....	....	....	....	....	....	....	....	....
2004-05	Cleveland Barons	AHL	69	4	22	26	146	....	....	....	....	....	....	....	....	....	....	....	....	....	....	....	....	....	....
2005-06	**San Jose**	**NHL**	**21**	**0**	**2**	**2**	**14**	**0**	**0**	**0**	**22**	**0.0**	**–11**	**0**	**0.0**	**12:39**	....	....	....	....	....	....	....	....	....
2006-07	**New Jersey**	**NHL**	**13**	**0**	**1**	**1**	**2**	**0**	**0**	**0**	**7**	**0.0**	**0**	**0**	**0.0**	**10:47**	....	....	....	....	....	....	....	....	....
	Lowell Devils	AHL	28	0	9	9	37	....	....	....	....	....	....	....	....	....	....	....	....	....	....	....	....	....	....
	NHL Totals		**92**	**1**	**24**	**25**	**67**	**0**	**0**	**0**	**114**	**0.9**		**1**	**100.0**	**15:44**	**2**	**0**	**0**	**0**	**0**	**0**	**0**	**0**	**4:41**

Hockey East Second All-Star Team (2001) • Hockey East First All-Star Team (2002)

• Spent majority of the 2005-06 season as a healthy reserve. Traded to **New Jersey** by **San Jose** with Alexander Korolyuk for Vladimir Malakhov and New Jersey's 1st round choice (later traded to St. Louis - St. Louis selected David Perron) in 2007 Entry Draft, October 1, 2006. Signed as a free agent by **Chicago**, July 27, 2007.

FATA, Drew
(FA-tuh, DROO) **NYI**

Defense. Shoots left. 6'1", 211 lbs. Born, Sault Ste. Marie, Ont., July 28, 1983. Pittsburgh's 3rd choice, 86th overall, in 2001 Entry Draft.

Season	Club	League	GP	G	A	Pts	PIM	PP	SH	GW	S	%	+/-	TF	F%	Min	Playoffs GP	G	A	Pts	PIM	PP	SH	GW	Min
1998-99	S.S. Marie AA	NOHA	46	4	16	20	55	....	....	....	....	....	....	....	....	....	....	....	....	....	....	....	....	....	....
99-2000	St. Mike's B's	OPJHL	49	9	18	27	144	....	....	....	....	....	....	....	....	....	....	....	....	....	....	....	....	....	....
2000-01	St. Michael's	OHL	58	5	15	20	134	....	....	....	....	....	....	....	....	....	18	1	3	4	26	....	....	....	....
2001-02	St. Michael's	OHL	67	7	21	28	175	....	....	....	....	....	....	....	....	....	15	1	9	10	38	....	....	....	....
2002-03	St. Michael's	OHL	35	6	13	19	66	....	....	....	....	....	....	....	....	....	....	....	....	....	....	....	....	....	....
	Kingston	OHL	34	2	17	19	64	....	....	....	....	....	....	....	....	....	....	....	....	....	....	....	....	....	....
2003-04	Wilkes-Barre	AHL	23	1	2	3	26	....	....	....	....	....	....	....	....	....	....	....	....	....	....	....	....	....	....
	Wheeling Nailers	ECHL	28	6	10	16	61	....	....	....	....	....	....	....	....	....	4	0	0	0	8	....	....	....	....
2004-05	Wilkes-Barre	AHL	32	1	1	2	88	....	....	....	....	....	....	....	....	....	5	0	1	1	37	....	....	....	....
	Wheeling Nailers	ECHL	22	0	1	1	55	....	....	....	....	....	....	....	....	....	....	....	....	....	....	....	....	....	....
2005-06	Wilkes-Barre	AHL	28	1	12	13	98	....	....	....	....	....	....	....	....	....	11	0	0	0	16	....	....	....	....
	Wheeling Nailers	ECHL	34	10	8	18	145	....	....	....	....	....	....	....	....	....	....	....	....	....	....	....	....	....	....
2006-07	**NY Islanders**	**NHL**	**3**	**1**	**0**	**1**	**5**	**0**	**0**	**0**	**1**	**100.0**	**–2**	**0**	**0.0**	**10:17**	**1**	**0**	**0**	**0**	**0**	**0**	**0**	**0**	**6:04**
	Bridgeport	AHL	64	3	7	10	185	....	....	....	....	....	....	....	....	....	....	....	....	....	....	....	....	....	....
	NHL Totals		**3**	**1**	**0**	**1**	**5**	**0**	**0**	**0**	**1**	**100.0**	....	**0**	**0.0**	**10:17**	**1**	**0**	**0**	**0**	**0**	**0**	**0**	**0**	**6:04**

Signed as a free agent by **NY Islanders**, December 21, 2006.

FATA, Rico
(FA-tuh, REE-koh)

Right wing. Shoots left. 6', 205 lbs. Born, Sault Ste. Marie, Ont., February 12, 1980. Calgary's 1st choice, 6th overall, in 1998 Entry Draft.

Season	Club	League	GP	G	A	Pts	PIM	PP	SH	GW	S	%	+/-	TF	F%	Min	Playoffs GP	G	A	Pts	PIM	PP	SH	GW	Min
1994-95	Soo Legion	NOHA	51	52	51	103	....	....	....	....	....	....	....	....	....	....	....	....	....	....	....	....	....	....	....
1995-96	Sault Ste. Marie	OHL	62	11	15	26	52	....	....	....	....	....	....	....	....	....	4	0	0	0	0	....	....	....	....
1996-97	London Knights	OHL	59	19	34	53	76	....	....	....	....	....	....	....	....	....	....	....	....	....	....	....	....	....	....
1997-98	London Knights	OHL	64	43	33	76	110	....	....	....	....	....	....	....	....	....	16	9	5	14	*49	....	....	....	....
1998-99	**Calgary**	**NHL**	**20**	**0**	**1**	**1**	**4**	**0**	**0**	**0**	**13**	**0.0**	**0**	**2**	**50.0**	**7:36**	....	....	....	....	....	....	....	....	....
	London Knights	OHL	23	15	18	33	41	....	....	....	....	....	....	....	....	....	25	10	12	22	42	....	....	....	....
99-2000	**Calgary**	**NHL**	**2**	**0**	**0**	**0**	**0**	**0**	**0**	**0**	**0**	**0.0**	**–1**	**0**	**0.0**	**10:06**	....	....	....	....	....	....	....	....	....
	Saint John Flames	AHL	76	29	29	58	65	....	....	....	....	....	....	....	....	....	3	0	0	0	4	....	....	....	....
2000-01	**Calgary**	**NHL**	**5**	**0**	**0**	**0**	**6**	**0**	**0**	**0**	**6**	**0.0**	**–3**	**0**	**0.0**	**9:25**	....	....	....	....	....	....	....	....	....
	Saint John Flames	AHL	70	23	29	52	129	....	....	....	....	....	....	....	....	....	19	2	3	5	22	....	....	....	....
2001-02	**NY Rangers**	**NHL**	**10**	**0**	**0**	**0**	**0**	**0**	**0**	**0**	**8**	**0.0**	**–2**	**55**	**47.3**	**8:31**	....	....	....	....	....	....	....	....	....
	Hartford	AHL	61	35	36	71	36	....	....	....	....	....	....	....	....	....	10	2	5	7	4	....	....	....	....
2002-03	**NY Rangers**	**NHL**	**36**	**2**	**4**	**6**	**6**	**0**	**0**	**0**	**30**	**6.7**	**–1**	**30**	**50.0**	**7:16**	....	....	....	....	....	....	....	....	....
	Hartford	AHL	9	8	6	14	6	....	....	....	....	....	....	....	....	....	....	....	....	....	....	....	....	....	....
	Pittsburgh	**NHL**	**27**	**5**	**8**	**13**	**10**	**0**	**0**	**0**	**49**	**10.2**	**–6**	**87**	**49.4**	**17:46**	....	....	....	....	....	....	....	....	....
2003-04	**Pittsburgh**	**NHL**	**73**	**16**	**18**	**34**	**54**	**6**	**2**	**1**	**163**	**9.8**	**–46**	**1205**	**47.1**	**17:58**	....	....	....	....	....	....	....	....	....
2004-05	Asiago	Italy	35	18	20	38	36	....	....	....	....	....	....	....	....	....	9	7	5	12	10	....	....	....	....
2005-06	**Pittsburgh**	**NHL**	**20**	**0**	**0**	**0**	**10**	**0**	**0**	**0**	**18**	**0.0**	**–5**	**204**	**41.7**	**13:06**	....	....	....	....	....	....	....	....	....
	Wilkes-Barre	AHL	25	8	10	18	39	....	....	....	....	....	....	....	....	....	....	....	....	....	....	....	....	....	....
	Atlanta	**NHL**	**6**	**0**	**1**	**1**	**4**	**0**	**0**	**0**	**1**	**0.0**	**–2**	**20**	**55.0**	**7:18**	....	....	....	....	....	....	....	....	....
	Washington	**NHL**	**21**	**3**	**3**	**6**	**8**	**1**	**0**	**0**	**31**	**9.7**	**3**	**3**	**33.3**	**8:11**	....	....	....	....	....	....	....	....	....
2006-07	**Washington**	**NHL**	**10**	**1**	**1**	**2**	**2**	**0**	**0**	**0**	**15**	**6.7**	**3**	**7**	**57.1**	**10:26**	....	....	....	....	....	....	....	....	....
	Adler Mannheim	Germany	29	8	10	18	12	....	....	....	....	....	....	....	....	....	11	2	4	6	8	....	....	....	....
	NHL Totals		**230**	**27**	**36**	**63**	**104**	**7**	**2**	**1**	**334**	**8.1**	....	**1613**	**46.7**	**12:47**	....	....	....	....	....	....	....	....	....

AHL All-Rookie Team (2000) • AHL Second All-Star Team (2002)

Claimed on waivers by **NY Rangers** from **Calgary**, October 3, 2001. Traded to **Pittsburgh** by **NY Rangers** with Joel Bouchard, Richard Lintner and Mikael Samuelsson for Mike Wilson, Alex Kovalev, Janne Laukkanen and Dan LaCouture, February 10, 2003. Signed as a free agent by **Asiago** (Italy), August 15, 2004. Claimed on waivers by **Atlanta** from **Pittsburgh**, January 31, 2006. Claimed on waivers by **Washington** from **Atlanta**, March 9, 2006.

FEDOROV, Fedor
(FEH-duh-rahf, feh-DUHR)

Center. Shoots left. 6'3", 230 lbs. Born, Appatity, USSR, June 11, 1981. Vancouver's 2nd choice, 66th overall, in 2001 Entry Draft.

Season	Club	League	GP	G	A	Pts	PIM	PP	SH	GW	S	%	+/-	TF	F%	Min	Playoffs GP	G	A	Pts	PIM	PP	SH	GW	Min
1997-98	Det. Caesars	MNHL	13	3	7	10	18	....	....	....	....	....	....	....	....	....	....	....	....	....	....	....	....	....	....
1998-99	Port Huron	UHL	42	2	5	7	20	....	....	....	....	....	....	....	....	....	....	....	....	....	....	....	....	....	....
99-2000	Windsor Spitfires	OHL	60	7	10	17	115	....	....	....	....	....	....	....	....	....	12	1	0	1	4	....	....	....	....
2000-01	Sudbury Wolves	OHL	67	33	45	78	88	....	....	....	....	....	....	....	....	....	12	4	6	10	36	....	....	....	....
2001-02	Columbia Inferno	ECHL	2	0	2	2	0	....	....	....	....	....	....	....	....	....	....	....	....	....	....	....	....	....	....
	Manitoba Moose	AHL	8	2	1	3	6	....	....	....	....	....	....	....	....	....	....	....	....	....	....	....	....	....	....
2002-03	**Vancouver**	**NHL**	**7**	**0**	**1**	**1**	**4**	**0**	**0**	**0**	**2**	**0.0**	**0**	**26**	**46.2**	**9:10**	....	....	....	....	....	....	....	....	....
	Manitoba Moose	AHL	50	10	13	23	61	....	....	....	....	....	....	....	....	....	3	1	2	3	0	....	....	....	....
2003-04	**Vancouver**	**NHL**	**8**	**0**	**1**	**1**	**4**	**0**	**0**	**0**	**10**	**0.0**	**0**	**4**	**50.0**	**10:59**	....	....	....	....	....	....	....	....	....
	Manitoba Moose	AHL	58	23	16	39	52	....	....	....	....	....	....	....	....	....	....	....	....	....	....	....	....	....	....
2004-05	Spartak Moscow	Russia	19	4	7	11	52	....	....	....	....	....	....	....	....	....	....	....	....	....	....	....	....	....	....
	Magnitogorsk	Russia	10	3	0	3	22	....	....	....	....	....	....	....	....	....	5	2	0	2	30	....	....	....	....
2005-06	**NY Rangers**	**NHL**	**3**	**0**	**0**	**0**	**6**	**0**	**0**	**0**	**2**	**0.0**	**0**	**1**	**0.0**	**9:49**	....	....	....	....	....	....	....	....	....
	Hartford	AHL	38	2	15	17	80	....	....	....	....	....	....	....	....	....	....	....	....	....	....	....	....	....	....
	Syracuse Crunch	AHL	12	2	3	5	22	....	....	....	....	....	....	....	....	....	3	0	0	0	2	....	....	....	....
2006-07	Yaroslavl	Russia	20	4	3	7	32	....	....	....	....	....	....	....	....	....	....	....	....	....	....	....	....	....	....
	Malmo	Sweden	8	2	4	6	51	....	....	....	....	....	....	....	....	....	....	....	....	....	....	....	....	....	....
	Malmo	Sweden-Q	10	4	10	14	55	....	....	....	....	....	....	....	....	....	....	....	....	....	....	....	....	....	....
	NHL Totals		**18**	**0**	**2**	**2**	**14**	**0**	**0**	**0**	**14**	**0.0**	....	**31**	**45.2**	**10:05**	....	....	....	....	....	....	....	....	....

• Re-entered NHL Entry Draft. Originally Tampa Bay's 7th choice, 182nd overall, in 1999 Entry Draft.

Signed as an underage free agent by **Detroit** (IHL), August 5, 1998. Released by **Detroit** (IHL), September 30, 1998. Signed as an underage free agent by **Port Huron** (UHL), October 1, 1998. • Missed majority of 2001-02 season recovering from eye injury suffered in game vs. Macon (ECHL), November 17, 2001. Signed as a free agent by **Spartak Moscow** (Russia), November 15, 2004. Signed as a free agent by **Magnitogorsk** (Russia), February 16, 2005. Traded to **NY Rangers** by **Vancouver** for Jozef Balej and future considerations, October 7, 2005. Loaned to **Syracuse** (AHL) by **NY Rangers** (Hartford-AHL) for cash, March 11, 2006. Signed as a free agent by **Yaroslavl** (Russia), July 25, 2006. Signed as a free agent by **Malmo** (Sweden), January 30, 2007.

FEDOROV, Sergei
(FEH-duh-rahf, SAIR-gay) **CBJ**

Center. Shoots left. 6'2", 205 lbs. Born, Pskov, USSR, December 13, 1969. Detroit's 4th choice, 74th overall, in 1989 Entry Draft.

Season	Club	League	GP	G	A	Pts	PIM	PP	SH	GW	S	%	+/-	TF	F%	Min	Playoffs GP	G	A	Pts	PIM	PP	SH	GW	Min
1985-86	Dynamo Minsk	USSR-2	15	6	1	7	10	....	....	....	....	....	....	....	....	....	....	....	....	....	....	....	....	....	....
1986-87	CSKA Moscow	USSR	29	6	6	12	12	....	....	....	....	....	....	....	....	....	....	....	....	....	....	....	....	....	....
1987-88	CSKA Moscow	USSR	48	7	9	16	20	....	....	....	....	....	....	....	....	....	....	....	....	....	....	....	....	....	....
1988-89	CSKA Moscow	USSR	44	9	8	17	35	....	....	....	....	....	....	....	....	....	....	....	....	....	....	....	....	....	....
1989-90	CSKA Moscow	USSR	48	19	10	29	22	....	....	....	....	....	....	....	....	....	....	....	....	....	....	....	....	....	....
	CSKA Moscow	Super-S	5	2	2	4	11	....	....	....	....	....	....	....	....	....	....	....	....	....	....	....	....	....	....
1990-91	**Detroit**	**NHL**	**77**	**31**	**48**	**79**	**66**	**11**	**3**	**5**	**259**	**12.0**	**11**	....	....	....	**7**	**1**	**5**	**6**	**4**	**0**	**0**	**1**	....
1991-92	**Detroit**	**NHL**	**80**	**32**	**54**	**86**	**72**	**7**	**2**	**5**	**249**	**12.9**	**26**	....	....	....	**11**	**5**	**5**	**10**	**8**	**1**	**2**	**1**	....
1992-93	**Detroit**	**NHL**	**73**	**34**	**53**	**87**	**72**	**13**	**4**	**3**	**217**	**15.7**	**33**	....	....	....	**7**	**3**	**6**	**9**	**23**	**1**	**1**	**0**	....
1993-94	**Detroit**	**NHL**	**82**	**56**	**64**	**120**	**34**	**13**	**4**	**10**	**337**	**16.6**	**48**	....	....	....	**7**	**1**	**7**	**8**	**6**	**0**	**0**	**0**	....
1994-95	**Detroit**	**NHL**	**42**	**20**	**30**	**50**	**24**	**7**	**3**	**5**	**147**	**13.6**	**6**	....	....	....	**17**	**7**	***17**	***24**	**6**	**3**	**0**	**0**	....
1995-96	**Detroit**	**NHL**	**78**	**39**	**68**	**107**	**48**	**11**	**3**	**11**	**306**	**12.7**	**49**	....	....	....	**19**	**2**	***18**	**20**	**10**	**0**	**0**	**2**	....
1996-97♦	**Detroit**	**NHL**	**74**	**30**	**33**	**63**	**30**	**9**	**2**	**4**	**273**	**11.0**	**29**	....	....	....	**20**	**8**	**12**	**20**	**12**	**3**	**0**	**4**	....
1997-98	Russia	Olympics	6	1	5	6	8	....	....	....	....	....	....	....	....	....	....	....	....	....	....	....	....	....	....
	♦ Detroit	**NHL**	**21**	**6**	**11**	**17**	**25**	**2**	**0**	**2**	**68**	**8.8**	**10**	....	....	....	**22**	***10**	**10**	**20**	**12**	**2**	**1**	**1**	....
1998-99	**Detroit**	**NHL**	**77**	**26**	**37**	**63**	**66**	**6**	**2**	**3**	**224**	**11.6**	**9**	**1414**	**51.7**	**19:21**	**10**	**1**	**8**	**9**	**8**	**0**	**0**	**0**	**19:54**
99-2000	**Detroit**	**NHL**	**68**	**27**	**35**	**62**	**22**	**4**	**4**	**7**	**263**	**10.3**	**8**	**1274**	**53.8**	**20:05**	**9**	**4**	**4**	**8**	**4**	**2**	**0**	**1**	**20:48**
2000-01	**Detroit**	**NHL**	**75**	**32**	**37**	**69**	**40**	**14**	**2**	**7**	**268**	**11.9**	**12**	**1601**	**55.8**	**21:05**	**6**	**2**	**5**	**7**	**0**	**1**	**0**	**1**	**22:19**
2001-02♦	**Detroit**	**NHL**	**81**	**31**	**37**	**68**	**36**	**10**	**0**	**6**	**256**	**12.1**	**20**	**1160**	**51.7**	**19:33**	**23**	**5**	**14**	**19**	**20**	**2**	**1**	**0**	**22:20**
	Russia	Olympics	6	2	2	4	4	....	....	....	....	....	....	....	....	....	....	....	....	....	....	....	....	....	....
2002-03	**Detroit**	**NHL**	**80**	**36**	**47**	**83**	**52**	**10**	**2**	**11**	**281**	**12.8**	**15**	**1580**	**53.4**	**21:11**	**4**	**1**	**2**	**3**	**0**	**0**	**0**	**0**	**22:07**
2003-04	**Anaheim**	**NHL**	**80**	**31**	**34**	**65**	**42**	**9**	**2**	**6**	**268**	**11.6**	**–5**	**1558**	**56.6**	**21:05**	....	....	....	....	....	....	....	....	....

Season	Club	League	GP	G	A	Pts	PIM	PP	SH	GW	S	%	+/-	TF	F%	Min	GP	G	A	Pts	PIM	PP	SH	GW	Min
			Regular Season														**Playoffs**								
2004-05			DID NOT PLAY																						
2005-06	**Anaheim**	**NHL**	5	0	1	1	2	0	0	0	18	0.0	-1	80	55.0	20:17	....	....	....	....	....	....	....	....	....
	Columbus	**NHL**	62	12	31	43	64	3	1	2	142	8.5	-1	1169	51.8	21:06	....	....	....	....	....	....	....	....	....
2006-07	**Columbus**	**NHL**	73	18	24	42	56	7	2	2	163	11.0	-7	680	52.4	19:56	....	....	....	....	....	....	....	....	....
	NHL Totals		1128	461	644	1105	751	136	36	89	3739	12.3		10516	53.6	20:25	162	50	113	163	113	15	5	11	21:35

NHL All-Rookie Team (1991) • NHL First All-Star Team (1994) • Frank J. Selke Trophy (1994, 1996) • Lester B. Pearson Award (1994) • Hart Memorial Trophy (1994)

Played in NHL All-Star Game (1992, 1994, 1996, 2001, 2002, 2003)

• Missed majority of 1997-98 season after failing to come to contract terms with **Detroit**. Signed as a free agent by **Anaheim**, July 19, 2003. Traded to **Columbus** by **Anaheim** with Anaheim's 5th round choice (Maxime Frechette) in 2006 Entry Draft for Tyler Wright and Francois Beauchemin, November 15, 2005.

FEDORUK, Todd

(FEH-duh-ruhk, TAWD) **DAL.**

Left wing. Shoots left. 6'2", 235 lbs. Born, Redwater, Alta., February 13, 1979. Philadelphia's 6th choice, 164th overall, in 1997 Entry Draft.

Season	Club	League	GP	G	A	Pts	PIM	PP	SH	GW	S	%	+/-	TF	F%	Min	GP	G	A	Pts	PIM	PP	SH	GW	Min
1994-95	Ft. Saskatchewan	AMHL	STATISTICS NOT AVAILABLE																						
1995-96	Kelowna Rockets	WHL	44	1	1	2	83	....	....	....	....	....	....	....	....	....	4	0	0	0	6	....	....	....	....
1996-97	Kelowna Rockets	WHL	31	1	5	6	87	....	....	....	....	....	....	....	....	....	6	0	0	0	13	....	....	....	....
1997-98	Kelowna Rockets	WHL	31	3	5	8	120	....	....	....	....	....	....	....	....	....	....	....	....	....	....	....	....	....	....
	Regina Pats	WHL	21	4	3	7	80	....	....	....	....	....	....	....	....	....	9	1	2	3	23	....	....	....	....
1998-99	Regina Pats	WHL	39	12	12	24	107	....	....	....	....	....	....	....	....	....	....	....	....	....	....	....	....	....	....
	Prince Albert	WHL	28	6	4	10	75	....	....	....	....	....	....	....	....	....	13	1	6	7	49	....	....	....	....
99-2000	Trenton Titans	ECHL	18	2	5	7	118	....	....	....	....	....	....	....	....	....	....	....	....	....	....	....	....	....	....
	Philadelphia	AHL	19	1	2	3	40	....	....	....	....	....	....	....	....	....	5	0	1	1	2	....	....	....	....
2000-01	**Philadelphia**	**NHL**	53	5	5	10	109	0	0	0	28	17.9	0	0	0.0	7:02	2	0	0	0	20	0	0	0	5:57
	Philadelphia	AHL	14	0	1	1	49	....	....	....	....	....	....	....	....	....	....	....	....	....	....	....	....	....	....
2001-02	**Philadelphia**	**NHL**	55	3	4	7	141	0	0	0	21	14.3	-2	5	0.0	6:21	3	0	0	0	0	0	0	0	2:46
	Philadelphia	AHL	7	0	1	1	54	....	....	....	....	....	....	....	....	....	....	....	....	....	....	....	....	....	....
2002-03	**Philadelphia**	**NHL**	63	1	5	6	105	0	0	0	33	3.0	1	1	0.0	6:30	1	0	0	0	0	0	0	0	4:52
2003-04	**Philadelphia**	**NHL**	49	1	4	5	136	0	0	1	33	3.0	-4	0	0.0	6:47	1	0	0	0	2	0	0	0	6:42
	Philadelphia	AHL	2	0	2	2	2	....	....	....	....	....	....	....	....	....	....	....	....	....	....	....	....	....	....
2004-05	Philadelphia	AHL	42	4	12	16	142	....	....	....	....	....	....	....	....	....	16	2	2	4	33	....	....	....	....
2005-06	**Anaheim**	**NHL**	76	4	19	23	174	0	0	1	69	5.8	6	8	37.5	8:24	12	0	0	0	16	0	0	0	8:19
2006-07	**Anaheim**	**NHL**	10	0	3	3	36	0	0	0	2	0.0	2	1	0.0	7:30	....	....	....	....	....	....	....	....	....
	Philadelphia	**NHL**	48	3	8	11	84	0	0	0	28	10.7	-11	2	0.0	9:03	....	....	....	....	....	....	....	....	....
	NHL Totals		354	17	48	65	785	0	0	2	214	7.9		17	17.6	7:23	19	0	0	0	38	0	0	0	6:56

Traded to **Anaheim** by **Philadelphia** for Anaheim's 2nd round choice (later traded to Phoenix - Phoenix selected Pier-Olivier Pelletier) in 2005 Entry Draft, July 29, 2005. Traded to **Philadelphia** by **Anaheim** for Philadelphia's 4th round choice (Justin Vaive) in 2007 Entry Draft, November 13, 2006. Signed as a free agent by **Dallas**, July 9, 2007.

FEDOTENKO, Ruslan

(feh-doh-TEHN-koh, roos-LAHN) **NYI**

Left wing. Shoots left. 6'2", 195 lbs. Born, Kiev, USSR, January 18, 1979.

Season	Club	League	GP	G	A	Pts	PIM	PP	SH	GW	S	%	+/-	TF	F%	Min	GP	G	A	Pts	PIM	PP	SH	GW	Min
1995-96	Kiev 2	EEHL	33	9	11	20	12	....	....	....	....	....	....	....	....	....	....	....	....	....	....	....	....	....	....
	Sokol Kiev	CIS	2	0	0	0	0	....	....	....	....	....	....	....	....	....	....	....	....	....	....	....	....	....	....
1996-97	TPS Turku U18	Fin-U18	3	3	2	5	2	....	....	....	....	....	....	....	....	....	....	....	....	....	....	....	....	....	....
	TPS Turku Jr.	Fin-Jr.	11	1	1	2	2	....	....	....	....	....	....	....	....	....	....	....	....	....	....	....	....	....	....
	Kiekko-67 Turku	Finland-2	22	4	3	7	16	....	....	....	....	....	....	....	....	....	....	....	....	....	....	....	....	....	....
	Kiekko Turku	Finland-3	....	....	....	....	....	....	....	....	....	....	....	....	....	....	3	1	0	1	2	....	....	....	....
1997-98	Melfort Mustangs	SJHL	68	35	31	66	55	....	....	....	....	....	....	....	....	....	....	....	....	....	....	....	....	....	....
1998-99	Sioux City	USHL	55	43	34	77	139	....	....	....	....	....	....	....	....	....	5	5	1	6	9	....	....	....	....
99-2000	Trenton Titans	ECHL	8	5	3	8	9	....	....	....	....	....	....	....	....	....	....	....	....	....	....	....	....	....	....
	Philadelphia	AHL	67	16	34	50	42	....	....	....	....	....	....	....	....	....	2	0	0	0	0	....	....	....	....
2000-01	**Philadelphia**	**NHL**	74	16	20	36	72	3	0	4	119	13.4	8	7	71.4	14:38	6	0	1	1	4	0	0	0	11:18
	Philadelphia	AHL	8	1	0	1	8	....	....	....	....	....	....	....	....	....	....	....	....	....	....	....	....	....	....
2001-02	**Philadelphia**	**NHL**	78	17	9	26	43	0	1	3	121	14.0	15	41	43.9	13:56	5	1	0	1	2	0	0	1	14:11
	Ukraine	Olympics	1	1	0	1	4	....	....	....	....	....	....	....	....	....	....	....	....	....	....	....	....	....	....
2002-03	**Tampa Bay**	**NHL**	76	19	13	32	44	6	0	6	114	16.7	-7	90	48.9	16:01	11	0	1	1	2	0	0	0	13:58
2003-04♦	**Tampa Bay**	**NHL**	77	17	22	39	30	0	0	3	116	14.7	14	58	55.2	14:39	22	12	2	14	14	5	0	3	16:40
2004-05			DID NOT PLAY																						
2005-06	**Tampa Bay**	**NHL**	80	26	15	41	44	4	0	6	164	15.9	-4	28	42.9	15:21	5	0	0	0	20	0	0	0	14:38
2006-07	**Tampa Bay**	**NHL**	80	12	20	32	52	2	0	1	154	7.8	-3	8	25.0	16:15	4	0	0	0	4	0	0	0	17:27
	NHL Totals		465	107	99	206	285	15	1	23	788	13.6		232	48.7	15:09	53	13	4	17	46	5	0	4	15:08

Signed as a free agent by **Philadelphia**, August 3, 1999. Traded to **Tampa Bay** by **Philadelphia** with Tampa Bay's 2nd round choice (previously acquired, later traded to Dallas – Dallas selected Tobias Stephan) in 2002 Entry Draft and Phoenix's 2nd round choice (previously acquired, later traded to San Jose – San Jose selected Dan Spang) in 2002 Entry Draft for Tampa Bay's 1st round choice (Joni Pitkanen) in 2002 Entry Draft, June 21, 2002. Signed as a free agent by **NY Islanders**, July 4, 2007.

FEHR, Eric

(FAIR, AIR-ihk) **WSH.**

Right wing. Shoots right. 6'4", 212 lbs. Born, Winkler, Man., September 7, 1985. Washington's 1st choice, 18th overall, in 2003 Entry Draft.

Season	Club	League	GP	G	A	Pts	PIM	PP	SH	GW	S	%	+/-	TF	F%	Min	GP	G	A	Pts	PIM	PP	SH	GW	Min
2000-01	Pembina Valley	MMMHL	36	45	13	58	30	....	....	....	....	....	....	....	....	....	....	....	....	....	....	....	....	....	....
	Brandon	WHL	4	0	0	0	0	....	....	....	....	....	....	....	....	....	....	....	....	....	....	....	....	....	....
2001-02	Brandon	WHL	63	11	16	27	29	....	....	....	....	....	....	....	....	....	12	1	1	2	0	....	....	....	....
2002-03	Brandon	WHL	70	26	29	55	76	....	....	....	....	....	....	....	....	....	17	4	8	12	26	....	....	....	....
2003-04	Brandon	WHL	71	50	34	84	129	....	....	....	....	....	....	....	....	....	7	5	0	5	16	....	....	....	....
2004-05	Brandon	WHL	71	*59	52	*111	91	....	....	....	....	....	....	....	....	....	24	16	16	*32	47	....	....	....	....
2005-06	**Washington**	**NHL**	11	0	0	0	2	0	0	0	10	0.0	0	4	25.0	5:45	....	....	....	....	....	....	....	....	....
	Hershey Bears	AHL	70	25	28	53	70	....	....	....	....	....	....	....	....	....	19	8	3	11	8	....	....	....	....
2006-07	**Washington**	**NHL**	14	2	1	3	8	0	0	1	25	8.0	3	6	16.7	10:43	....	....	....	....	....	....	....	....	....
	Hershey Bears	AHL	40	22	19	41	63	....	....	....	....	....	....	....	....	....	....	....	....	....	....	....	....	....	....
	NHL Totals		25	2	1	3	10	0	0	1	35	5.7		10	20.0	8:32	....	....	....	....	....	....	....	....	....

WHL East First All-Star Team (2005) • WHL Player of the Year (2005)

FERENCE, Andrew

(FAIR-ehns, AN-droo) **BOS.**

Defense. Shoots left. 5'10", 191 lbs. Born, Edmonton, Alta., March 17, 1979. Pittsburgh's 8th choice, 208th overall, in 1997 Entry Draft.

Season	Club	League	GP	G	A	Pts	PIM	PP	SH	GW	S	%	+/-	TF	F%	Min	GP	G	A	Pts	PIM	PP	SH	GW	Min
1994-95	Sherwood Park	AMHL	31	4	14	18	74	....	....	....	....	....	....	....	....	....	....	....	....	....	....	....	....	....	....
	Portland	WHL	2	0	0	0	4	....	....	....	....	....	....	....	....	....	....	....	....	....	....	....	....	....	....
1995-96	Portland	WHL	72	9	31	40	159	....	....	....	....	....	....	....	....	....	7	1	3	4	12	....	....	....	....
1996-97	Portland	WHL	72	12	32	44	163	....	....	....	....	....	....	....	....	....	6	1	2	3	12	....	....	....	....
1997-98	Portland	WHL	72	11	57	68	142	....	....	....	....	....	....	....	....	....	16	2	18	20	28	....	....	....	....
1998-99	Portland	WHL	40	11	21	32	104	....	....	....	....	....	....	....	....	....	4	1	4	5	10	....	....	....	....
	Kansas City	IHL	5	1	2	3	4	....	....	....	....	....	....	....	....	....	3	0	0	0	9	....	....	....	....
99-2000	**Pittsburgh**	**NHL**	30	2	4	6	20	0	0	1	26	7.7	3	0	0.0	16:19	....	....	....	....	....	....	....	....	....
	Wilkes-Barre	AHL	44	8	20	28	58	....	....	....	....	....	....	....	....	....	....	....	....	....	....	....	....	....	....
2000-01	**Pittsburgh**	**NHL**	36	4	11	15	28	1	0	1	47	8.5	6	0	0.0	18:51	18	3	7	10	16	1	0	1	22:02
	Wilkes-Barre	AHL	43	6	18	24	95	....	....	....	....	....	....	....	....	....	3	1	0	1	12	....	....	....	....
2001-02	**Pittsburgh**	**NHL**	75	4	7	11	73	1	0	0	82	4.9	-12	2	0.0	18:34	....	....	....	....	....	....	....	....	....
2002-03	**Pittsburgh**	**NHL**	22	1	3	4	36	1	0	0	22	4.5	-16	1	100.0	19:33	....	....	....	....	....	....	....	....	....
	Wilkes-Barre	AHL	1	0	0	0	2	....	....	....	....	....	....	....	....	....	....	....	....	....	....	....	....	....	....
	Calgary	**NHL**	16	0	4	4	6	0	0	0	17	0.0	1	0	0.0	17:38	....	....	....	....	....	....	....	....	....
2003-04	**Calgary**	**NHL**	72	4	12	16	53	1	0	0	86	4.7	5	0	0.0	18:40	26	0	3	3	25	0	0	0	24:13
2004-05	C. Budejovice	CzRep-2	19	5	6	11	45	....	....	....	....	....	....	....	....	....	12	2	7	9	10	....	....	....	....
2005-06	**Calgary**	**NHL**	82	4	27	31	85	2	0	0	111	3.6	-12	1	0.0	20:08	7	0	4	4	12	0	0	0	23:09
2006-07	**Calgary**	**NHL**	54	2	10	12	66	1	0	0	51	3.9	7	3	33.3	18:29	....	....	....	....	....	....	....	....	....
	Boston	**NHL**	26	1	2	3	31	0	0	0	29	3.4	-2	0	0.0	22:22	....	....	....	....	....	....	....	....	....
	NHL Totals		413	22	80	102	398	7	0	2	471	4.7		7	28.6	19:00	51	3	14	17	53	1	0	1	23:18

WHL West First All-Star Team (1998) • WHL West Second All-Star Team (1999)

• Missed majority of 2002-03 season recovering from groin (November 18, 2002 vs. Montreal) and ankle (March 20, 2003 vs. Los Angeles) injuries. Traded to **Calgary** by **Pittsburgh** for Calgary's 3rd round choice (Brian Gifford) in 2004 Entry Draft, February 9, 2003. Signed as a free agent by **Ceske Budejovice** (CzRep-2), December 1, 2004. Traded to **Boston** by **Calgary** with Chuck Kobasew for Brad Stuart and Wayne Primeau, February 10, 2007.

FERENCE, Brad (FAIR-ehns, BRAD) DET.

Defense. Shoots right. 6'3", 218 lbs. Born, Calgary, Alta., April 2, 1979. Vancouver's 1st choice, 10th overall, in 1997 Entry Draft.

			Regular Season														Playoffs								
Season	Club	League	GP	G	A	Pts	PIM	PP	SH	GW	S	%	+/-	TF	F%	Min	GP	G	A	Pts	PIM	PP	SH	GW	Min
1994-95	Calgary Royals	ABHL	60	19	47	66	220	....	....	....	....	....	....	....	....	....	....	....	....	....	....	....	....	....	....
1995-96	Calgary Royals	ABHL	22	7	21	28	140	....	....	....	....	....	....	....	....	....	....	....	....	....	....	....	....	....	....
	Spokane Chiefs	WHL	5	0	2	2	18	....	....	....	....	....	....	....	....	....	....	....	....	....	....	....	....	....	....
1996-97	Spokane Chiefs	WHL	67	6	20	26	324	....	....	....	....	....	....	....	....	....	9	0	4	4	21	....	....	....	....
1997-98	Spokane Chiefs	WHL	54	9	30	39	213	....	....	....	....	....	....	....	....	....	18	0	7	7	59	....	....	....	....
1998-99	Spokane Chiefs	WHL	31	3	22	25	125	....	....	....	....	....	....	....	....	....	....	....	....	....	....	....	....	....	....
	Tri-City	WHL	20	6	15	21	116	....	....	....	....	....	....	....	....	....	12	1	9	10	63	....	....	....	....
99-2000	**Florida**	**NHL**	**13**	**0**	**2**	**2**	**46**	**0**	**0**	**0**	**10**	**0.0**	**2**	**0**	**0.0**	**13:40**	....	....	....	....	....	....	....	....	....
	Louisville Panthers	AHL	58	2	7	9	231	....	....	....	....	....	....	....	....	....	2	0	0	0	2	....	....	....	....
2000-01	**Florida**	**NHL**	**14**	**0**	**1**	**1**	**14**	**0**	**0**	**0**	**5**	**0.0**	**-10**	**0**	**0.0**	**13:03**	....	....	....	....	....	....	....	....	....
	Louisville Panthers	AHL	52	3	21	24	200	....	....	....	....	....	....	....	....	....	....	....	....	....	....	....	....	....	....
2001-02	**Florida**	**NHL**	**80**	**2**	**15**	**17**	**254**	**0**	**0**	**0**	**65**	**3.1**	**-13**	**1**	**0.0**	**19:44**	....	....	....	....	....	....	....	....	....
2002-03	**Florida**	**NHL**	**60**	**2**	**6**	**8**	**118**	**0**	**0**	**0**	**41**	**4.9**	**2**	**0**	**0.0**	**15:58**	....	....	....	....	....	....	....	....	....
	Phoenix	**NHL**	**15**	**0**	**1**	**1**	**28**	**0**	**0**	**0**	**8**	**0.0**	**-5**	**0**	**0.0**	**16:33**	....	....	....	....	....	....	....	....	....
2003-04	**Phoenix**	**NHL**	**63**	**0**	**5**	**5**	**103**	**0**	**0**	**0**	**39**	**0.0**	**-19**	**0**	**0.0**	**14:03**	....	....	....	....	....	....	....	....	....
2004-05	Morzine-Avoriaz	France	17	2	10	12	138	....	....	....	....	....	....	....	....	....	4	1	4	5	10	....	....	....	....
2005-06	San Antonio	AHL	19	2	9	11	39	....	....	....	....	....	....	....	....	....	....	....	....	....	....	....	....	....	....
	Albany River Rats	AHL	43	3	8	11	96	....	....	....	....	....	....	....	....	....	....	....	....	....	....	....	....	....	....
2006-07	**Calgary**	**NHL**	**5**	**0**	**0**	**0**	**2**	**0**	**0**	**0**	**1**	**0.0**	**-1**	**0**	**0.0**	**11:46**	....	....	....	....	....	....	....	....	....
	Omaha	AHL	73	3	23	26	210	....	....	....	....	....	....	....	....	....	6	0	0	0	6	....	....	....	....
	NHL Totals		**250**	**4**	**30**	**34**	**565**	**0**	**0**	**0**	**169**	**2.4**		**1**	**0.0**	**16:21**	....	....	....	....	....	....	....	....	....

Memorial Cup Tournament All-Star Team (1998)

Traded to **Florida** by **Vancouver** with Pavel Bure, Bret Hedican and Vancouver's 3rd round choice (Robert Fried) in 2000 Entry Draft for Ed Jovanovski, Dave Gagner, Mike Brown, Kevin Weekes and Florida's 1st round choice (Nathan Smith) in 2000 Entry Draft, January 17, 1999. Traded to **Phoenix** by **Florida** for Darcy Hordichuk and Phoenix's 2nd round choice (later traded to Tampa Bay – Tampa Bay selected Matt Smaby) in 2003 Entry Draft, March 8, 2003. Signed as a free agent by **Morzine-Avoriaz** (France), October 28, 2004. Traded to **New Jersey** by **Phoenix** for Pascal Rheaume, Ray Schultz and Steven Spencer, November 25, 2005. Signed as a free agent by **Calgary**, July 27, 2006. Signed as a free agent by **Detroit**, July 3, 2007.

FERGUSON, Scott (fuhr-GUH-sohn, SKAWT)

Defense. Shoots left. 6'1", 195 lbs. Born, Camrose, Alta., January 6, 1973.

			Regular Season														Playoffs								
Season	Club	League	GP	G	A	Pts	PIM	PP	SH	GW	S	%	+/-	TF	F%	Min	GP	G	A	Pts	PIM	PP	SH	GW	Min
1990-91	Sherwood Park	AJHL	32	2	9	11	91	....	....	....	....	....	....	....	....	....	....	....	....	....	....	....	....	....	....
	Kamloops Blazers	WHL	4	0	0	0	0	....	....	....	....	....	....	....	....	....	....	....	....	....	....	....	....	....	....
1991-92	Kamloops Blazers	WHL	62	4	10	14	138	....	....	....	....	....	....	....	....	....	12	0	2	2	21	....	....	....	....
1992-93	Kamloops Blazers	WHL	71	4	19	23	206	....	....	....	....	....	....	....	....	....	13	0	2	2	24	....	....	....	....
1993-94	Kamloops Blazers	WHL	68	5	49	54	180	....	....	....	....	....	....	....	....	....	19	5	11	16	48	....	....	....	....
1994-95	Cape Breton	AHL	58	4	6	10	103	....	....	....	....	....	....	....	....	....	....	....	....	....	....	....	....	....	....
	Wheeling	ECHL	5	1	5	6	16	....	....	....	....	....	....	....	....	....	....	....	....	....	....	....	....	....	....
1995-96	Cape Breton	AHL	80	5	16	21	196	....	....	....	....	....	....	....	....	....	....	....	....	....	....	....	....	....	....
1996-97	Hamilton	AHL	74	6	14	20	115	....	....	....	....	....	....	....	....	....	21	5	7	12	59	....	....	....	....
1997-98	**Edmonton**	**NHL**	**1**	**0**	**0**	**0**	**0**	**0**	**0**	**0**	**0**	**0.0**	**1**	....	....	....	....	....	....	....	....	....	....	....	....
	Hamilton	AHL	77	7	17	24	150	....	....	....	....	....	....	....	....	....	9	0	3	3	16	....	....	....	....
1998-99	**Anaheim**	**NHL**	**2**	**0**	**1**	**1**	**0**	**0**	**0**	**0**	**1**	**0.0**	**0**	**0**	**0.0**	**15:09**	....	....	....	....	....	....	....	....	....
	Cincinnati	AHL	78	4	31	35	59	....	....	....	....	....	....	....	....	....	3	0	0	0	4	....	....	....	....
99-2000	Cincinnati	AHL	77	7	25	32	166	....	....	....	....	....	....	....	....	....	....	....	....	....	....	....	....	....	....
2000-01	**Edmonton**	**NHL**	**20**	**0**	**1**	**1**	**13**	**0**	**0**	**0**	**8**	**0.0**	**2**	**0**	**0.0**	**10:55**	**6**	**0**	**0**	**0**	**0**	**0**	**0**	**0**	**8:21**
	Hamilton	AHL	42	3	18	21	79	....	....	....	....	....	....	....	....	....	....	....	....	....	....	....	....	....	....
2001-02	**Edmonton**	**NHL**	**50**	**3**	**2**	**5**	**75**	**0**	**0**	**0**	**27**	**11.1**	**11**	**0**	**0.0**	**13:40**	....	....	....	....	....	....	....	....	....
2002-03	**Edmonton**	**NHL**	**78**	**3**	**5**	**8**	**120**	**0**	**0**	**0**	**45**	**6.7**	**11**	**1**	**100.0**	**12:18**	**5**	**0**	**0**	**0**	**8**	**0**	**0**	**0**	**11:44**
2003-04	**Edmonton**	**NHL**	**52**	**1**	**5**	**6**	**80**	**0**	**0**	**1**	**38**	**2.6**	**-5**	**0**	**0.0**	**13:21**	....	....	....	....	....	....	....	....	....
2004-05			DID NOT PLAY																						
2005-06	**Minnesota**	**NHL**	**15**	**0**	**0**	**0**	**22**	**0**	**0**	**0**	**6**	**0.0**	**-3**	**1**	**100.0**	**9:11**	....	....	....	....	....	....	....	....	....
	Houston Aeros	AHL	46	5	8	13	105	....	....	....	....	....	....	....	....	....	8	0	2	2	21	....	....	....	....
2006-07	Worcester Sharks	AHL	79	4	19	23	101	....	....	....	....	....	....	....	....	....	6	0	0	0	6	....	....	....	....
	NHL Totals		**218**	**7**	**14**	**21**	**310**	**0**	**0**	**1**	**125**	**5.6**		**2**	**50.0**	**12:33**	**11**	**0**	**0**	**0**	**8**	**0**	**0**	**0**	**9:53**

WHL West Second All-Star Team (1994)

Signed as a free agent by **Edmonton**, June 2, 1994. Traded to **Ottawa** by **Edmonton** for Frantisek Musil, March 9, 1998. Signed as a free agent by **Anaheim**, July 27, 1998. Signed as a free agent by **Edmonton**, July 5, 2000. Signed as a free agent by **Minnesota**, August 4, 2005. Signed as a free agent by **San Jose**, July 14, 2006. Signed as a free agent by **Ingolstadt** (Germany), July 11, 2007.

FERLAND, Jonathan (fair-LAWN, JAWN-ah-thuhn) MTL.

Right wing. Shoots right. 6'2", 212 lbs. Born, Ste-Marie-de-Beauce, Que., February 9, 1983. Montreal's 5th choice, 212th overall, in 2002 Entry Draft.

			Regular Season														Playoffs								
Season	Club	League	GP	G	A	Pts	PIM	PP	SH	GW	S	%	+/-	TF	F%	Min	GP	G	A	Pts	PIM	PP	SH	GW	Min
1998-99	Laval-Laurentides	QAAA	42	18	17	35	50	....	....	....	....	....	....	....	....	....	....	....	....	....	....	....	....	....	....
99-2000	Moncton Wildcats	QMJHL	52	3	6	9	21	....	....	....	....	....	....	....	....	....	11	0	1	1	0	....	....	....	....
2000-01	Acadie-Bathurst	QMJHL	70	17	11	28	135	....	....	....	....	....	....	....	....	....	13	0	4	4	47	....	....	....	....
2001-02	Acadie-Bathurst	QMJHL	55	28	46	74	104	....	....	....	....	....	....	....	....	....	16	5	12	17	16	....	....	....	....
2002-03	Acadie-Bathurst	QMJHL	68	45	44	89	94	....	....	....	....	....	....	....	....	....	11	4	5	9	16	....	....	....	....
2003-04	Hamilton	AHL	70	5	10	15	43	....	....	....	....	....	....	....	....	....	10	0	0	0	6	....	....	....	....
2004-05	Hamilton	AHL	62	6	8	14	24	....	....	....	....	....	....	....	....	....	4	0	0	0	4	....	....	....	....
2005-06	**Montreal**	**NHL**	**7**	**1**	**0**	**1**	**2**	**0**	**0**	**0**	**9**	**11.1**	**-2**	**2**	**0.0**	**6:37**	....	....	....	....	....	....	....	....	....
	Hamilton	AHL	39	7	8	15	65	....	....	....	....	....	....	....	....	....	....	....	....	....	....	....	....	....	....
2006-07	Hamilton	AHL	78	23	14	37	87	....	....	....	....	....	....	....	....	....	22	3	6	9	19	....	....	....	....
	NHL Totals		**7**	**1**	**0**	**1**	**2**	**0**	**0**	**0**	**9**	**11.1**		**2**	**0.0**	**6:37**	....	....	....	....	....	....	....	....	....

FIDDLER, Vern (FIHD-luhr, VUHRN) NSH.

Center. Shoots left. 5'11", 204 lbs. Born, Edmonton, Alta., May 9, 1980.

			Regular Season														Playoffs								
Season	Club	League	GP	G	A	Pts	PIM	PP	SH	GW	S	%	+/-	TF	F%	Min	GP	G	A	Pts	PIM	PP	SH	GW	Min
1997-98	Kelowna Rockets	WHL	65	10	11	21	31	....	....	....	....	....	....	....	....	....	7	0	1	1	4	....	....	....	....
1998-99	Kelowna Rockets	WHL	68	22	21	43	82	....	....	....	....	....	....	....	....	....	6	2	0	2	8	....	....	....	....
99-2000	Kelowna Rockets	WHL	64	20	28	48	60	....	....	....	....	....	....	....	....	....	5	1	3	4	4	....	....	....	....
2000-01	Kelowna Rockets	WHL	3	0	2	2	0	....	....	....	....	....	....	....	....	....	....	....	....	....	....	....	....	....	....
	Medicine Hat	WHL	67	33	38	71	100	....	....	....	....	....	....	....	....	....	....	....	....	....	....	....	....	....	....
	Arkansas	ECHL	3	0	1	1	2	....	....	....	....	....	....	....	....	....	5	3	0	3	5	....	....	....	....
2001-02	Norfolk Admirals	AHL	38	8	5	13	28	....	....	....	....	....	....	....	....	....	4	1	3	4	2	....	....	....	....
	Roanoke Express	ECHL	44	27	28	55	71	....	....	....	....	....	....	....	....	....	....	....	....	....	....	....	....	....	....
2002-03	**Nashville**	**NHL**	**19**	**4**	**2**	**6**	**14**	**0**	**0**	**1**	**20**	**20.0**	**2**	**171**	**53.8**	**9:40**	....	....	....	....	....	....	....	....	....
	Milwaukee	AHL	54	8	16	24	70	....	....	....	....	....	....	....	....	....	6	1	2	3	14	....	....	....	....
2003-04	**Nashville**	**NHL**	**17**	**0**	**0**	**0**	**23**	**0**	**0**	**0**	**8**	**0.0**	**-6**	**123**	**49.6**	**8:06**	....	....	....	....	....	....	....	....	....
	Milwaukee	AHL	47	9	15	24	72	....	....	....	....	....	....	....	....	....	22	5	3	8	36	....	....	....	....
2004-05	Milwaukee	AHL	73	20	22	42	70	....	....	....	....	....	....	....	....	....	7	0	0	0	18	....	....	....	....
2005-06	**Nashville**	**NHL**	**40**	**8**	**4**	**12**	**42**	**3**	**0**	**2**	**46**	**17.4**	**-2**	**464**	**52.6**	**13:49**	**2**	**0**	**1**	**1**	**0**	**0**	**0**	**0**	**8:48**
	Milwaukee	AHL	11	1	6	7	20	....	....	....	....	....	....	....	....	....	....	....	....	....	....	....	....	....	....
2006-07	**Nashville**	**NHL**	**72**	**11**	**15**	**26**	**40**	**0**	**1**	**1**	**90**	**12.2**	**11**	**680**	**51.6**	**13:38**	**5**	**1**	**1**	**2**	**4**	**0**	**0**	**0**	**12:21**
	NHL Totals		**148**	**23**	**21**	**44**	**119**	**3**	**1**	**4**	**164**	**14.0**		**1438**	**52.0**	**12:32**	**7**	**1**	**2**	**3**	**4**	**0**	**0**	**0**	**11:20**

ECHL All-Rookie Team (2002)

Signed as a free agent by **Arkansas** (ECHL), March 31, 2001. Traded to **Roanoke** (ECHL) by **Arkansas** (ECHL) for Calvin Elfring, August 11, 2001. Signed as a free agent by **Nashville**, May 6, 2002.

FILPPULA, Valtteri (FIHL-poo-luh, VAL-tuhr-ee) DET.

Center. Shoots left. 6', 189 lbs. Born, Vantaa, Finland, March 20, 1984. Detroit's 3rd choice, 95th overall, in 2002 Entry Draft.

			Regular Season														Playoffs								
Season	Club	League	GP	G	A	Pts	PIM	PP	SH	GW	S	%	+/-	TF	F%	Min	GP	G	A	Pts	PIM	PP	SH	GW	Min
2000-01	Jokerit U18	Fin-U18	31	18	29	47	4	....	....	....	....	....	....	....	....	....	6	4	4	8	0	....	....	....	....
	Jokerit Helsinki Jr.	Fin-Jr.	1	0	1	1	0	....	....	....	....	....	....	....	....	....	....	....	....	....	....	....	....	....	....
2001-02	Jokerit U18	Fin-U18	1	0	1	1	0	....	....	....	....	....	....	....	....	....	8	4	9	13	2	....	....	....	....
	Jokerit Helsinki Jr.	Fin-Jr.	40	8	15	23	14	....	....	....	....	....	....	....	....	....	1	0	0	0	0	....	....	....	....
2002-03	Jokerit Helsinki Jr.	Fin-Jr.	35	16	37	53	14	....	....	....	....	....	....	....	....	....	11	4	10	14	4	....	....	....	....
2003-04	Suomi U20	Finland-2	1	0	0	0	2	....	....	....	....	....	....	....	....	....	....	....	....	....	....	....	....	....	....
	Jokerit Helsinki	Finland	49	5	13	18	6	....	....	....	....	....	....	....	....	....	....	....	....	....	....	....	....	....	....
2004-05	Jokerit Helsinki	Finland	55	10	20	30	20	....	....	....	....	....	....	....	....	....	12	5	6	11	2	....	....	....	....

			Regular Season														Playoffs								
Season	Club	League	GP	G	A	Pts	PIM	PP	SH	GW	S	%	+/-	TF	F%	Min	GP	G	A	Pts	PIM	PP	SH	GW	Min
2005-06	**Detroit**	**NHL**	**4**	**0**	**1**	**1**	**2**	**0**	**0**	**0**	**1**	**0.0**	**1**	**21**	**47.6**	**7:19**	....	....	....	....	....	....	....	....	....
	Grand Rapids	AHL	74	20	51	71	30	....	....	....	....	....	....	....	....	....	16	7	9	16	4	....	....	....	....
2006-07	**Detroit**	**NHL**	**73**	**10**	**7**	**17**	**20**	**0**	**0**	**1**	**76**	**13.2**	**8**	**267**	**55.8**	**11:16**	**18**	**3**	**2**	**5**	**2**	**0**	**0**	**0**	**12:12**
	Grand Rapids	AHL	3	2	2	4	2	....	....	....	....	....	....	....	....	....	....	....	....	....	....	....	....	....	....
	NHL Totals		**77**	**10**	**8**	**18**	**22**	**0**	**0**	**1**	**77**	**13.0**		**288**	**55.2**	**11:03**	**18**	**3**	**2**	**5**	**2**	**0**	**0**	**0**	**12:12**

FINGER, Jeff

(FIHN-guhr, JEHF) **COL.**

Defense. Shoots right. 6'1", 205 lbs. Born, Hancock, MI, December 18, 1979. Colorado's 11th choice, 240th overall, in 1999 Entry Draft.

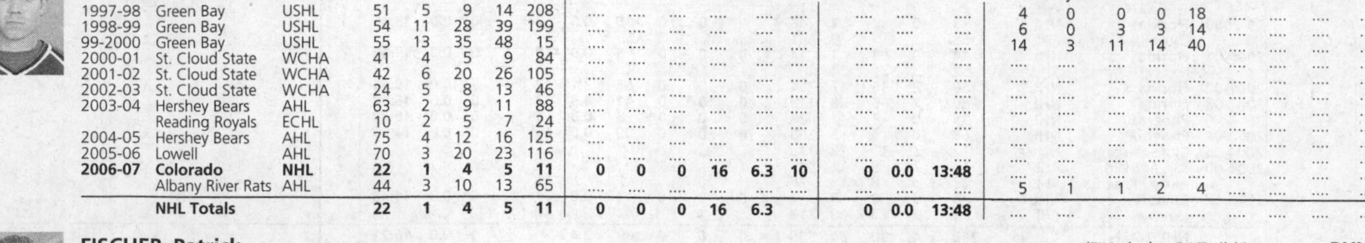

Season	Club	League	GP	G	A	Pts	PIM	PP	SH	GW	S	%	+/-	TF	F%	Min	GP	G	A	Pts	PIM	PP	SH	GW	Min
1997-98	Green Bay	USHL	51	5	9	14	208	....	....	....	....	....	....	....	....	....	4	0	0	0	18	....	....	....	....
1998-99	Green Bay	USHL	54	11	28	39	199	....	....	....	....	....	....	....	....	....	6	0	3	3	14	....	....	....	....
99-2000	Green Bay	USHL	55	13	35	48	15	....	....	....	....	....	....	....	....	....	14	3	11	14	40	....	....	....	....
2000-01	St. Cloud State	WCHA	41	4	5	9	84	....	....	....	....	....	....	....	....	....	....	....	....	....	....	....	....	....	....
2001-02	St. Cloud State	WCHA	42	6	20	26	105	....	....	....	....	....	....	....	....	....	....	....	....	....	....	....	....	....	....
2002-03	St. Cloud State	WCHA	24	5	8	13	46	....	....	....	....	....	....	....	....	....	....	....	....	....	....	....	....	....	....
2003-04	Hershey Bears	AHL	63	2	9	11	88	....	....	....	....	....	....	....	....	....	....	....	....	....	....	....	....	....	....
	Reading Royals	ECHL	10	2	5	7	24	....	....	....	....	....	....	....	....	....	....	....	....	....	....	....	....	....	....
2004-05	Hershey Bears	AHL	75	4	12	16	125	....	....	....	....	....	....	....	....	....	....	....	....	....	....	....	....	....	....
2005-06	Lowell	AHL	70	3	20	23	116	....	....	....	....	....	....	....	....	....	....	....	....	....	....	....	....	....	....
2006-07	**Colorado**	**NHL**	**22**	**1**	**4**	**5**	**11**	**0**	**0**	**0**	**16**	**6.3**	**10**	**0**	**0.0**	**13:48**	....	....	....	....	....	....	....	....	....
	Albany River Rats	AHL	44	3	10	13	65	....	....	....	....	....	....	....	....	....	5	1	1	2	4	....	....	....	....
	NHL Totals		**22**	**1**	**4**	**5**	**11**	**0**	**0**	**0**	**16**	**6.3**		**0**	**0.0**	**13:48**	....	....	....	....	....	....	....	....	....

FISCHER, Patrick

(FIH-shuhr, PAT-rihk) **PHX.**

Center. Shoots left. 5'11", 194 lbs. Born, Zug, Switz., September 6, 1975.

Season	Club	League	GP	G	A	Pts	PIM	PP	SH	GW	S	%	+/-	TF	F%	Min	GP	G	A	Pts	PIM	PP	SH	GW	Min
1993-94	EV Zug	Swiss	32	3	5	8	14	....	....	....	....	....	....	....	....	....	9	0	2	2	6	....	....	....	....
1994-95	EV Zug	Swiss	36	10	18	28	30	....	....	....	....	....	....	....	....	....	12	2	3	5	14	....	....	....	....
1995-96	EV Zug	Swiss	36	10	17	27	24	....	....	....	....	....	....	....	....	....	....	....	....	....	....	....	....	....	....
1996-97	EV Zug	Swiss	43	20	18	38	26	....	....	....	....	....	....	....	....	....	....	....	....	....	....	....	....	....	....
1997-98	HC Lugano	Swiss	40	15	28	43	38	....	....	....	....	....	....	....	....	....	....	....	....	....	....	....	....	....	....
1998-99	HC Lugano	Swiss	45	11	17	28	73	....	....	....	....	....	....	....	....	....	....	....	....	....	....	....	....	....	....
99-2000	HC Davos	Swiss	44	19	17	36	107	....	....	....	....	....	....	....	....	....	5	2	2	4	0	....	....	....	....
2000-01	HC Davos	Swiss	42	13	27	40	54	....	....	....	....	....	....	....	....	....	....	....	....	....	....	....	....	....	....
2001-02	HC Davos	Swiss	38	8	22	30	36	....	....	....	....	....	....	....	....	....	....	....	....	....	....	....	....	....	....
2002-03	HC Davos	Swiss	44	17	21	38	87	....	....	....	....	....	....	....	....	....	....	....	....	....	....	....	....	....	....
2003-04	EV Zug	Swiss	46	12	23	35	70	....	....	....	....	....	....	....	....	....	5	1	4	5	0	....	....	....	....
2004-05	EV Zug	Swiss	44	17	18	35	64	....	....	....	....	....	....	....	....	....	9	2	5	7	12	....	....	....	....
2005-06	EV Zug	Swiss	44	21	32	53	72	....	....	....	....	....	....	....	....	....	....	....	....	....	....	....	....	....	....
	Switzerland	Olympics	6	1	1	2	4	....	....	....	....	....	....	....	....	....	....	....	....	....	....	....	....	....	....
2006-07	**Phoenix**	**NHL**	**27**	**4**	**6**	**10**	**24**	**0**	**0**	**1**	**32**	**12.5**	**0**	**67**	**40.3**	**10:51**	....	....	....	....	....	....	....	....	....
	San Antonio	AHL	4	0	1	1	6	....	....	....	....	....	....	....	....	....	....	....	....	....	....	....	....	....	....
	Rapperswil	Swiss	44	7	11	18	68	....	....	....	....	....	....	....	....	....	7	1	0	1	8	....	....	....	....
	NHL Totals		**27**	**4**	**6**	**10**	**24**	**0**	**0**	**1**	**32**	**12.5**		**67**	**40.3**	**10:51**	....	....	....	....	....	....	....	....	....

Signed as a free agent by **Phoenix**, May 5, 2006.

FISHER, Mike

(FIH-shuhr, MIGHK) **OTT.**

Center. Shoots right. 6'1", 213 lbs. Born, Peterborough, Ont., June 5, 1980. Ottawa's 2nd choice, 44th overall, in 1998 Entry Draft.

Season	Club	League	GP	G	A	Pts	PIM	PP	SH	GW	S	%	+/-	TF	F%	Min	GP	G	A	Pts	PIM	PP	SH	GW	Min
1996-97	Peterborough	OPJHL	51	26	30	56	35	....	....	....	....	....	....	....	....	....	....	....	....	....	....	....	....	....	....
1997-98	Sudbury Wolves	OHL	66	24	25	49	65	....	....	....	....	....	....	....	....	....	9	2	2	4	13	....	....	....	....
1998-99	Sudbury Wolves	OHL	68	41	65	106	55	....	....	....	....	....	....	....	....	....	4	2	1	3	4	....	....	....	....
99-2000	**Ottawa**	**NHL**	**32**	**4**	**5**	**9**	**15**	**0**	**0**	**1**	**49**	**8.2**	**–6**	**356**	**47.8**	**12:57**	....	....	....	....	....	....	....	....	....
2000-01	**Ottawa**	**NHL**	**60**	**7**	**12**	**19**	**46**	**0**	**0**	**3**	**83**	**8.4**	**–1**	**709**	**50.2**	**11:38**	**4**	**0**	**1**	**1**	**4**	**0**	**0**	**0**	**13:41**
2001-02	**Ottawa**	**NHL**	**58**	**15**	**9**	**24**	**55**	**0**	**3**	**4**	**123**	**12.2**	**8**	**848**	**48.7**	**14:05**	**10**	**2**	**1**	**3**	**0**	**0**	**0**	**0**	**16:17**
2002-03	**Ottawa**	**NHL**	**74**	**18**	**20**	**38**	**54**	**5**	**1**	**3**	**142**	**12.7**	**13**	**1077**	**48.1**	**15:59**	**18**	**2**	**2**	**4**	**16**	**0**	**1**	**1**	**16:58**
2003-04	**Ottawa**	**NHL**	**24**	**4**	**6**	**10**	**39**	**1**	**0**	**0**	**47**	**8.5**	**–3**	**357**	**42.0**	**17:26**	**7**	**1**	**0**	**1**	**4**	**0**	**0**	**1**	**16:11**
2004-05	EV Zug	Swiss	21	9	18	27	34	....	....	....	....	....	....	....	....	....	9	2	3	5	10	....	....	....	....
2005-06	**Ottawa**	**NHL**	**68**	**22**	**22**	**44**	**64**	**2**	**4**	**3**	**150**	**14.7**	**23**	**883**	**50.3**	**17:09**	**10**	**2**	**2**	**4**	**12**	**0**	**1**	**0**	**18:50**
2006-07	**Ottawa**	**NHL**	**68**	**22**	**26**	**48**	**41**	**7**	**2**	**3**	**193**	**11.4**	**15**	**1191**	**52.1**	**18:25**	**20**	**5**	**5**	**10**	**24**	**2**	**1**	**1**	**17:43**
	NHL Totals		**384**	**92**	**100**	**192**	**314**	**15**	**10**	**17**	**787**	**11.7**		**5421**	**49.3**	**15:30**	**69**	**12**	**11**	**23**	**60**	**2**	**3**	**3**	**17:05**

• Missed majority of 1999-2000 season recovering from knee injury suffered in game vs. Boston, December 30, 1999. • Missed majority of 2003-04 season recovering from elbow injury suffered in practice, October 4, 2003. Signed as a free agent by **Zug** (Swiss), November 1, 2004.

FITZPATRICK, Rory

(FIHTZ-pa-trihk, ROHR-ee)

Defense. Shoots right. 6'2", 208 lbs. Born, Rochester, NY, January 11, 1975. Montreal's 2nd choice, 47th overall, in 1993 Entry Draft.

Season	Club	League	GP	G	A	Pts	PIM	PP	SH	GW	S	%	+/-	TF	F%	Min	GP	G	A	Pts	PIM	PP	SH	GW	Min
1990-91	Rochester	EmJHL	40	0	5	5	....	....	....	....	....	....	....	....	....	....	....	....	....	....	....	....	....	....	....
1991-92	Rochester	EmJHL	28	8	28	36	141	....	....	....	....	....	....	....	....	....	....	....	....	....	....	....	....	....	....
1992-93	Sudbury Wolves	OHL	58	4	20	24	68	....	....	....	....	....	....	....	....	....	14	0	0	0	17	....	....	....	....
1993-94	Sudbury Wolves	OHL	65	12	34	46	112	....	....	....	....	....	....	....	....	....	10	2	5	7	10	....	....	....	....
1994-95	Sudbury Wolves	OHL	56	12	36	48	72	....	....	....	....	....	....	....	....	....	18	3	15	18	21	....	....	....	....
	Fredericton	AHL	....	....	....	....	....	....	....	....	....	....	....	....	....	....	10	1	2	3	5	....	....	....	....
1995-96	**Montreal**	**NHL**	**42**	**0**	**2**	**2**	**18**	**0**	**0**	**0**	**31**	**0.0**	**–7**	....	....	....	**6**	**1**	**1**	**2**	**0**	**0**	**0**	**0**	....
	Fredericton	AHL	18	4	6	10	36	....	....	....	....	....	....	....	....	....	....	....	....	....	....	....	....	....	....
1996-97	**Montreal**	**NHL**	**6**	**0**	**1**	**1**	**6**	**0**	**0**	**0**	**5**	**0.0**	**–2**	....	....	....	....	....	....	....	....	....	....	....	....
	St. Louis	**NHL**	**2**	**0**	**0**	**0**	**2**	**0**	**0**	**0**	**1**	**0.0**	**–2**	....	....	....	....	....	....	....	....	....	....	....	....
	Worcester IceCats	AHL	49	4	13	17	78	....	....	....	....	....	....	....	....	....	5	1	2	3	0	....	....	....	....
1997-98	Worcester IceCats	AHL	62	8	22	30	111	....	....	....	....	....	....	....	....	....	11	0	3	3	26	....	....	....	....
1998-99	**St. Louis**	**NHL**	**1**	**0**	**0**	**0**	**2**	**0**	**0**	**0**	**0**	**0.0**	**–3**	**0**	**0.0**	**4:49**	....	....	....	....	....	....	....	....	....
	Worcester IceCats	AHL	53	5	16	21	82	....	....	....	....	....	....	....	....	....	4	0	1	1	17	....	....	....	....
99-2000	Worcester IceCats	AHL	28	0	5	5	48	....	....	....	....	....	....	....	....	....	....	....	....	....	....	....	....	....	....
	Milwaukee	IHL	27	2	1	3	27	....	....	....	....	....	....	....	....	....	3	0	2	2	2	....	....	....	....
2000-01	**Nashville**	**NHL**	**2**	**0**	**0**	**0**	**2**	**0**	**0**	**0**	**0**	**0.0**	**–2**	**0**	**0.0**	**9:47**	....	....	....	....	....	....	....	....	....
	Milwaukee	IHL	22	0	2	2	32	....	....	....	....	....	....	....	....	....	....	....	....	....	....	....	....	....	....
	Hamilton	AHL	34	3	17	20	29	....	....	....	....	....	....	....	....	....	....	....	....	....	....	....	....	....	....
2001-02	**Buffalo**	**NHL**	**5**	**0**	**0**	**0**	**4**	**0**	**0**	**0**	**2**	**0.0**	**–2**	**0**	**0.0**	**11:54**	....	....	....	....	....	....	....	....	....
	Rochester	AHL	60	4	8	12	83	....	....	....	....	....	....	....	....	....	2	0	1	1	0	....	....	....	....
2002-03	**Buffalo**	**NHL**	**36**	**1**	**3**	**4**	**16**	**0**	**0**	**0**	**29**	**3.4**	**–7**	**0**	**0.0**	**17:02**	....	....	....	....	....	....	....	....	....
	Rochester	AHL	41	5	11	16	65	....	....	....	....	....	....	....	....	....	....	....	....	....	....	....	....	....	....
2003-04	**Buffalo**	**NHL**	**60**	**4**	**7**	**11**	**44**	**2**	**0**	**2**	**78**	**5.1**	**–5**	**1**	**100.0**	**19:02**	....	....	....	....	....	....	....	....	....
2004-05	Rochester	AHL	20	1	1	2	18	....	....	....	....	....	....	....	....	....	9	0	1	1	12	....	....	....	....
2005-06	**Buffalo**	**NHL**	**56**	**4**	**5**	**9**	**50**	**2**	**0**	**1**	**45**	**8.9**	**–18**	**1**	**0.0**	**16:22**	**11**	**0**	**4**	**4**	**16**	**0**	**0**	**0**	**17:12**
2006-07	**Vancouver**	**NHL**	**58**	**1**	**6**	**7**	**46**	**0**	**0**	**1**	**41**	**2.4**	**12**	**1**	**100.0**	**14:06**	**3**	**0**	**0**	**0**	**6**	**0**	**0**	**0**	**21:08**
	NHL Totals		**268**	**10**	**24**	**34**	**190**	**4**	**0**	**4**	**232**	**4.3**		**3**	**66.7**	**16:23**	**20**	**1**	**5**	**6**	**22**	**0**	**0**	**0**	**18:02**

OHL All-Rookie Team (1993)

Traded to **St. Louis** by **Montreal** with Pierre Turgeon and Craig Conroy for Murray Baron, Shayne Corson and St. Louis' 5th round choice (Gennady Razin) in 1997 Entry Draft, October 29, 1996. Claimed by **Boston** from **St. Louis** in Waiver Draft, October 5, 1998. Claimed on waivers by **St. Louis** from **Boston**, October 7, 1998. Traded to **Nashville** by **St. Louis** for Dan Keczmer, February 9, 2000. Traded to **Edmonton** by **Nashville** for future considerations, January 12, 2001. Signed as a free agent by **Buffalo**, August 14, 2001. Signed as a free agent by **Rochester** (AHL), March 2, 2005. Signed as a free agent by **Vancouver**, August 18, 2006.

FLEISCHMANN, Tomas

(FLIGHSH-muhn, TAW-mahsh) **WSH.**

Left wing. Shoots left. 6'1", 190 lbs. Born, Koprivnice, Czech., May 16, 1984. Detroit's 2nd choice, 63rd overall, in 2002 Entry Draft.

Season	Club	League	GP	G	A	Pts	PIM	PP	SH	GW	S	%	+/-	TF	F%	Min	GP	G	A	Pts	PIM	PP	SH	GW	Min
99-2000	HC Vitkovice Jr.	CzRep-Jr.	46	9	13	22	6	....	....	....	....	....	....	....	....	....	....	....	....	....	....	....	....	....	....
2000-01	HC Vitkovice U17	CzR-U17	30	28	34	62	8	....	....	....	....	....	....	....	....	....	....	....	....	....	....	....	....	....	....
	HC Vitkovice Jr.	CzRep-Jr.	21	4	9	13	8	....	....	....	....	....	....	....	....	....	....	....	....	....	....	....	....	....	....
2001-02	HC Vitkovice Jr.	CzRep-Jr.	46	26	35	51	16	....	....	....	....	....	....	....	....	....	....	....	....	....	....	....	....	....	....
	TJ Novy Jicin	CzRep-3	8	3	2	5	8	....	....	....	....	....	....	....	....	....	7	3	4	7	35	....	....	....	....
2002-03	Moose Jaw	WHL	65	21	50	71	36	....	....	....	....	....	....	....	....	....	12	4	11	15	6	....	....	....	....

			Regular Season														Playoffs								
Season	Club	League	GP	G	A	Pts	PIM	PP	SH	GW	S	%	+/-	TF	F%	Min	GP	G	A	Pts	PIM	PP	SH	GW	Min
2003-04	Moose Jaw	WHL	60	33	42	75	32	....	....	....	....	....	....	....	....	....	10	3	4	7	10	....	....	....	....
2004-05	Portland Pirates	AHL	53	7	12	19	14	....	....	....	....	....	....	....	....	....	....	....	....	....	....	....	....	....	....
2005-06	**Washington**	**NHL**	**14**	**0**	**2**	**2**	**0**	**0**	**0**	**0**	**11**	**0.0**	**-7**	**5**	**40.0**	**6:45**	....	....	....	....	....	....	....	....	....
	Hershey Bears	AHL	57	30	33	63	32	....	....	....	....	....	....	....	....	....	20	11	*21	32	15	....	....	....	....
2006-07	**Washington**	**NHL**	**29**	**4**	**4**	**8**	**8**	**1**	**0**	**1**	**52**	**7.7**	**-6**	**14**	**35.7**	**11:38**	....	....	....	....	....	....	....	....	....
	Hershey Bears	AHL	45	22	29	51	22	....	....	....	....	....	....	....	....	....	19	5	16	21	10	....	....	....	....
	NHL Totals		**43**	**4**	**6**	**10**	**8**	**1**	**0**	**1**	**63**	**6.3**		**19**	**36.8**	**10:03**	....	....	....	....	....	....	....	....	....

WHL East Second All-Star Team (2004)

Traded to **Washington** by **Detroit** with Detroit's 1st round choice (Mike Green) in 2004 Entry Draft and Detroit's 4th round choice (Luke Lynes) in 2006 Entry Draft for Robert Lang, February 27, 2004.

FLINN, Ryan

(FLIHN, RIGH-yan) **EDM.**

Left wing. Shoots left. 6'5", 248 lbs. Born, Halifax, N.S., April 20, 1980. New Jersey's 8th choice, 143rd overall, in 1998 Entry Draft.

Season	Club	League	GP	G	A	Pts	PIM	PP	SH	GW	S	%	+/-	TF	F%	Min	GP	G	A	Pts	PIM	PP	SH	GW	Min
1996-97	Laval Titan	QMJHL	23	3	2	5	56	....	....	....	....	....	....	....	....	....	2	0	0	0	0	....	....	....	....
1997-98	Laval Titan	QMJHL	59	4	12	16	217	....	....	....	....	....	....	....	....	....	15	1	0	1	63	....	....	....	....
1998-99	Acadie-Bathurst	QMJHL	44	3	4	7	195	....	....	....	....	....	....	....	....	....	23	2	0	2	37	....	....	....	....
99-2000	Halifax	QMJHL	67	14	19	33	365	....	....	....	....	....	....	....	....	....	....	....	....	....	....	....	....	....	....
2000-01	Cape Breton	QMJHL	57	16	17	33	280	....	....	....	....	....	....	....	....	....	9	1	1	2	43	....	....	....	....
2001-02	Reading Royals	ECHL	20	1	3	4	130	....	....	....	....	....	....	....	....	....	....	....	....	....	....	....	....	....	....
	Los Angeles	**NHL**	**10**	**0**	**0**	**0**	**51**	**0**	**0**	**0**	**2**	**0.0**	**0**	**0**	**0.0**	**3:29**	....	....	....	....	....	....	....	....	....
	Manchester	AHL	37	0	1	1	113	....	....	....	....	....	....	....	....	....	1	0	0	0	0	....	....	....	....
2002-03	**Los Angeles**	**NHL**	**19**	**1**	**0**	**1**	**28**	**0**	**0**	**0**	**13**	**7.7**	**0**	**0**	**0.0**	**5:28**	....	....	....	....	....	....	....	....	....
	Manchester	AHL	27	2	2	4	95	....	....	....	....	....	....	....	....	....	....	....	....	....	....	....	....	....	....
2003-04	Manchester	AHL	59	3	5	8	164	....	....	....	....	....	....	....	....	....	6	0	0	0	4	....	....	....	....
2004-05	Manchester	AHL	14	1	1	2	112	....	....	....	....	....	....	....	....	....	....	....	....	....	....	....	....	....	....
2005-06	**Los Angeles**	**NHL**	**2**	**0**	**0**	**0**	**5**	**0**	**0**	**0**	**0**	**0.0**	**0**	**0**	**0.0**	**0:25**	....	....	....	....	....	....	....	....	....
	Manchester	AHL	6	0	1	1	38	....	....	....	....	....	....	....	....	....	....	....	....	....	....	....	....	....	....
2006-07	San Antonio	AHL	61	2	4	6	166	....	....	....	....	....	....	....	....	....	....	....	....	....	....	....	....	....	....
	NHL Totals		**31**	**1**	**0**	**1**	**84**	**0**	**0**	**0**	**15**	**6.7**		**0**	**0.0**	**4:30**	....	....	....	....	....	....	....	....	....

Signed as a free agent by **Los Angeles**, January 8, 2002. • Missed majority of 2004-05 season recovering from foot and leg injuries. • Missed majority of 2005-06 season recovering from head injury suffered in game vs. Chicago, November 26, 2005. Signed as a free agent by **Edmonton**, July 17, 2007.

FOOTE, Adam

(FUT, A-duhm) **CBJ**

Defense. Shoots right. 6'2", 224 lbs. Born, Toronto, Ont., July 10, 1971. Quebec's 2nd choice, 22nd overall, in 1989 Entry Draft.

Season	Club	League	GP	G	A	Pts	PIM	PP	SH	GW	S	%	+/-	TF	F%	Min	GP	G	A	Pts	PIM	PP	SH	GW	Min
1987-88	Whitby Midgets	Minor-ON	65	25	43	68	108	....	....	....	....	....	....	....	....	....	....	....	....	....	....	....	....	....	....
1988-89	Sault Ste. Marie	OHL	66	7	32	39	120	....	....	....	....	....	....	....	....	....	....	....	....	....	....	....	....	....	....
1989-90	Sault Ste. Marie	OHL	61	12	43	55	199	....	....	....	....	....	....	....	....	....	....	....	....	....	....	....	....	....	....
1990-91	Sault Ste. Marie	OHL	59	18	51	69	93	....	....	....	....	....	....	....	....	....	14	5	12	17	28	....	....	....	....
1991-92	**Quebec**	**NHL**	**46**	**2**	**5**	**7**	**44**	**0**	**0**	**0**	**55**	**3.6**	**-4**	....	....	....	....	....	....	....	....	....	....	....	....
	Halifax Citadels	AHL	6	0	1	1	2	....	....	....	....	....	....	....	....	....	....	....	....	....	....	....	....	....	....
1992-93	**Quebec**	**NHL**	**81**	**4**	**12**	**16**	**168**	**0**	**1**	**0**	**54**	**7.4**	**6**	....	....	....	**6**	**0**	**1**	**1**	**2**	**0**	**0**	**0**	....
1993-94	**Quebec**	**NHL**	**45**	**2**	**6**	**8**	**67**	**0**	**0**	**0**	**42**	**4.8**	**3**	....	....	....	....	....	....	....	....	....	....	....	....
1994-95	**Quebec**	**NHL**	**35**	**0**	**7**	**7**	**52**	**0**	**0**	**0**	**24**	**0.0**	**17**	....	....	....	**6**	**0**	**1**	**1**	**14**	**0**	**0**	**0**	....
1995-96♦	**Colorado**	**NHL**	**73**	**5**	**11**	**16**	**88**	**1**	**0**	**1**	**49**	**10.2**	**27**	....	....	....	**22**	**1**	**3**	**4**	**36**	**0**	**0**	**0**	....
1996-97	**Colorado**	**NHL**	**78**	**2**	**19**	**21**	**135**	**0**	**0**	**0**	**60**	**3.3**	**16**	....	....	....	**17**	**0**	**4**	**4**	**62**	**0**	**0**	**0**	....
1997-98	**Colorado**	**NHL**	**77**	**3**	**14**	**17**	**124**	**0**	**0**	**1**	**64**	**4.7**	**-3**	....	....	....	**7**	**0**	**0**	**0**	**23**	**0**	**0**	**0**	....
	Canada	Olympics	6	0	1	1	4	....	....	....	....	....	....	....	....	....	....	....	....	....	....	....	....	....	....
1998-99	**Colorado**	**NHL**	**64**	**5**	**16**	**21**	**92**	**3**	**0**	**0**	**83**	**6.0**	**20**	**0**	**0.0**	**24:50**	**19**	**2**	**3**	**5**	**24**	**1**	**0**	**0**	**28:34**
99-2000	**Colorado**	**NHL**	**59**	**5**	**13**	**18**	**98**	**1**	**0**	**2**	**63**	**7.9**	**5**	**0**	**0.0**	**25:51**	**16**	**0**	**7**	**7**	**28**	**0**	**0**	**0**	**26:05**
2000-01♦	**Colorado**	**NHL**	**35**	**3**	**12**	**15**	**42**	**1**	**1**	**1**	**59**	**5.1**	**6**	**0**	**0.0**	**25:22**	**23**	**3**	**4**	**7**	***47**	**1**	**0**	**1**	**28:22**
2001-02	**Colorado**	**NHL**	**55**	**5**	**22**	**27**	**55**	**1**	**1**	**0**	**85**	**5.9**	**7**	**0**	**0.0**	**25:59**	**21**	**1**	**6**	**7**	**28**	**0**	**0**	**0**	**27:46**
	Canada	Olympics	6	1	0	1	2	....	....	....	....	....	....	....	....	....	....	....	....	....	....	....	....	....	....
2002-03	**Colorado**	**NHL**	**78**	**11**	**20**	**31**	**88**	**3**	**0**	**2**	**106**	**10.4**	**30**	**0**	**0.0**	**25:43**	**6**	**0**	**1**	**1**	**8**	**0**	**0**	**0**	**24:12**
2003-04	**Colorado**	**NHL**	**73**	**8**	**22**	**30**	**87**	**5**	**0**	**1**	**105**	**7.6**	**13**	**0**	**0.0**	**24:03**	**11**	**0**	**4**	**4**	**10**	**0**	**0**	**0**	**25:06**
2004-05			DID NOT PLAY																						
2005-06	**Columbus**	**NHL**	**65**	**6**	**16**	**22**	**89**	**2**	**2**	**1**	**67**	**9.0**	**-16**	**0**	**0.0**	**24:34**	....	....	....	....	....	....	....	....	....
	Canada	Olympics	6	0	1	1	6	....	....	....	....	....	....	....	....	....	....	....	....	....	....	....	....	....	....
2006-07	**Columbus**	**NHL**	**59**	**3**	**9**	**12**	**71**	**2**	**0**	**0**	**78**	**3.8**	**-17**	**0**	**0.0**	**24:44**	....	....	....	....	....	....	....	....	....
	NHL Totals		**923**	**64**	**204**	**268**	**1300**	**19**	**5**	**9**	**994**	**6.4**		**0**	**0.0**	**25:06**	**154**	**7**	**34**	**41**	**282**	**2**	**0**	**1**	**27:15**

OHL First All-Star Team (1991)

Transferred to **Colorado** after **Quebec** franchise relocated, June 21, 1995. • Missed majority of 2000-01 season recovering from shoulder injury suffered in game vs. Carolina, January 6, 2001. Signed as a free agent by **Columbus**, August 2, 2005.

FORBES, Colin

(FOHRBS, KAW-lihn)

Center. Shoots left. 6'3", 215 lbs. Born, New Westminster, B.C., February 16, 1976. Philadelphia's 5th choice, 166th overall, in 1994 Entry Draft.

Season	Club	League	GP	G	A	Pts	PIM	PP	SH	GW	S	%	+/-	TF	F%	Min	GP	G	A	Pts	PIM	PP	SH	GW	Min
1993-94	Sherwood Park	AJHL	47	18	22	40	76	....	....	....	....	....	....	....	....	....	....	....	....	....	....	....	....	....	....
1994-95	Portland	WHL	72	24	31	55	108	....	....	....	....	....	....	....	....	....	9	1	3	4	10	....	....	....	....
1995-96	Portland	WHL	72	33	44	77	137	....	....	....	....	....	....	....	....	....	7	2	5	7	14	....	....	....	....
	Hershey Bears	AHL	2	1	0	1	2	....	....	....	....	....	....	....	....	....	4	0	2	2	2	....	....	....	....
1996-97	**Philadelphia**	**NHL**	**3**	**1**	**0**	**1**	**0**	**0**	**0**	**0**	**3**	**33.3**	**0**	....	....	....	**3**	**0**	**0**	**0**	**0**	**0**	**0**	**0**	....
	Philadelphia	AHL	74	21	28	49	108	....	....	....	....	....	....	....	....	....	10	5	5	10	33	....	....	....	....
1997-98	**Philadelphia**	**NHL**	**63**	**12**	**7**	**19**	**59**	**2**	**0**	**2**	**93**	**12.9**	**2**	....	....	....	**5**	**0**	**0**	**0**	**2**	**0**	**0**	**0**	....
	Philadelphia	AHL	13	7	4	11	22	....	....	....	....	....	....	....	....	....	....	....	....	....	....	....	....	....	....
1998-99	**Philadelphia**	**NHL**	**66**	**9**	**7**	**16**	**51**	**0**	**0**	**4**	**92**	**9.8**	**0**	**2**	**50.0**	**12:35**	....	....	....	....	....	....	....	....	....
	Tampa Bay	**NHL**	**14**	**3**	**1**	**4**	**10**	**0**	**1**	**0**	**25**	**12.0**	**-5**	**0**	**0.0**	**17:30**	....	....	....	....	....	....	....	....	....
99-2000	**Tampa Bay**	**NHL**	**8**	**0**	**0**	**0**	**18**	**0**	**0**	**0**	**3**	**0.0**	**-4**	**1**	**0.0**	**8:53**	....	....	....	....	....	....	....	....	....
	Ottawa	**NHL**	**45**	**2**	**5**	**7**	**12**	**0**	**0**	**0**	**54**	**3.7**	**-1**	**82**	**47.6**	**8:34**	**5**	**1**	**0**	**1**	**14**	**0**	**0**	**0**	**6:48**
2000-01	**Ottawa**	**NHL**	**39**	**0**	**1**	**1**	**31**	**0**	**0**	**0**	**26**	**0.0**	**-3**	**10**	**40.0**	**6:10**	....	....	....	....	....	....	....	....	....
	NY Rangers	**NHL**	**19**	**1**	**4**	**5**	**15**	**0**	**0**	**0**	**20**	**5.0**	**-3**	**1**	**0.0**	**7:52**	....	....	....	....	....	....	....	....	....
2001-02	Utah Grizzlies	AHL	4	0	0	0	21	....	....	....	....	....	....	....	....	....	....	....	....	....	....	....	....	....	....
	Washington	**NHL**	**38**	**5**	**3**	**8**	**15**	**0**	**1**	**1**	**49**	**10.2**	**-2**	**253**	**44.7**	**11:01**	....	....	....	....	....	....	....	....	....
	Portland Pirates	AHL	14	4	5	9	18	....	....	....	....	....	....	....	....	....	....	....	....	....	....	....	....	....	....
2002-03	**Washington**	**NHL**	**5**	**0**	**0**	**0**	**0**	**0**	**0**	**0**	**3**	**0.0**	**-2**	**12**	**50.0**	**9:38**	....	....	....	....	....	....	....	....	....
	Portland Pirates	AHL	69	22	38	60	73	....	....	....	....	....	....	....	....	....	3	2	2	4	4	....	....	....	....
2003-04	**Washington**	**NHL**	**2**	**0**	**0**	**0**	**0**	**0**	**0**	**0**	**2**	**0.0**	**-2**	**3**	**33.3**	**8:53**	....	....	....	....	....	....	....	....	....
	Portland Pirates	AHL	69	16	32	48	59	....	....	....	....	....	....	....	....	....	7	0	6	6	16	....	....	....	....
2004-05	Lowell	AHL	76	27	37	64	80	....	....	....	....	....	....	....	....	....	11	3	1	4	20	....	....	....	....
2005-06	Lowell	AHL	34	10	18	28	24	....	....	....	....	....	....	....	....	....	....	....	....	....	....	....	....	....	....
	Washington	**NHL**	**9**	**0**	**0**	**0**	**2**	**0**	**0**	**0**	**10**	**0.0**	**-2**	**7**	**42.9**	**8:16**	....	....	....	....	....	....	....	....	....
	Hershey Bears	AHL	36	11	12	23	16	....	....	....	....	....	....	....	....	....	21	5	9	14	16	....	....	....	....
2006-07	Adler Mannheim	Germany	51	11	29	40	50	....	....	....	....	....	....	....	....	....	11	4	*10	*14	24	....	....	....	....
	NHL Totals		**311**	**33**	**28**	**61**	**213**	**2**	**2**	**7**	**380**	**8.7**		**371**	**45.0**	**10:08**	**13**	**1**	**0**	**1**	**16**	**0**	**0**	**0**	**6:48**

Traded to **Tampa Bay** by **Philadelphia** with Philadelphia's 4th round choice (Michal Lanicek) in 1999 Entry Draft for Mikael Andersson and Sandy McCarthy, March 20, 1999. Traded to **Ottawa** by **Tampa Bay** for Bruce Gardiner, November 11, 1999. Traded to **NY Rangers** by **Ottawa** for Eric Lacroix, March 1, 2001. Signed as a free agent by **Washington**, January 8, 2002. Signed as a free agent by **Colorado** , September 11, 2003. . Signed as a free agent by **Washington**, November 4, 2003. Signed as a free agent by **Carolina**, August 11, 2004. Traded to **Washington** by **Carolina** for Stephen Peat, December 28, 2005. Signed as a free agent by **Mannheim** (Germany), August 10, 2006.

FORSBERG, Peter

(FOHRS-buhrg, PEE-tuhr)

Center. Shoots left. 6', 205 lbs. Born, Ornskoldsvik, Sweden, July 20, 1973. Philadelphia's 1st choice, 6th overall, in 1991 Entry Draft.

Season	Club	League	GP	G	A	Pts	PIM	PP	SH	GW	S	%	+/-	TF	F%	Min	GP	G	A	Pts	PIM	PP	SH	GW	Min
1989-90	MoDo Jr.	Swe-Jr.	30	15	12	27	42	....	....	....	....	....	....	....	....	....	....	....	....	....	....	....	....	....	....
	MoDo	Sweden	1	0	1	1	4	....	....	....	....	....	....	....	....	....	....	....	....	....	....	....	....	....	....
1990-91	MoDo Jr.	Swe-Jr.	39	38	64	102	56	....	....	....	....	....	....	....	....	....	....	....	....	....	....	....	....	....	....
	MoDo	Sweden	23	7	10	17	22	....	....	....	....	....	....	....	....	....	....	....	....	....	....	....	....	....	....
1991-92	MoDo	Sweden	39	9	18	27	78	....	....	....	....	....	....	....	....	....	....	....	....	....	....	....	....	....	....
1992-93	MoDo Jr.	Swe-Jr.	2	0	3	3	4	....	....	....	....	....	....	....	....	....	....	....	....	....	....	....	....	....	....
	MoDo	Sweden	39	23	24	47	92	....	....	....	....	....	....	....	....	....	3	4	1	5	0	....	....	....	....

			Regular Season														Playoffs								
Season	Club	League	GP	G	A	Pts	PIM	PP	SH	GW	S	%	+/-	TF	F%	Min	GP	G	A	Pts	PIM	PP	SH	GW	Min
1993-94	MoDo	Sweden	39	18	26	44	82	....	....	....	....	....	....	....	....	....	11	9	7	16	14	....	....	....	....
	Sweden	Olympics	8	2	6	8	6	....	....	....	....	....	....	....	....	....	....	....	....	....	....	....	....	....	....
1994 95	MoDo	Sweden	11	5	9	14	20	....	....	....	....	....	....	....	....	....	....	....	....	....	....	....	....	....	....
	Quebec	NHL	47	15	35	50	16	3	0	3	86	17.4	17	....	....	....	6	2	4	6	4	1	0	0	....
1995-96 ♦	Colorado	NHL	82	30	86	116	47	7	3	3	217	13.8	26	....	....	....	22	10	11	21	18	3	0	1	....
1996-97	Colorado	NHL	65	28	58	86	73	5	4	4	188	14.9	31	....	....	....	14	5	12	17	10	3	0	0	....
1997-98	Colorado	NHL	72	25	66	91	94	7	3	7	202	12.4	6	....	....	....	7	6	5	11	12	2	0	0	....
	Sweden	Olympics	4	1	4	5	6	....	....	....	....	....	....	....	....	....	....	....	....	....	....	....	....	....	....
1998-99	Colorado	NHL	78	30	67	97	108	9	2	7	217	13.8	27	895	54.4	23:29	19	8	16	*24	31	1	1	0	21:39
99-2000	Colorado	NHL	49	14	37	51	52	3	0	2	105	13.3	9	519	46.6	20:55	16	7	8	15	12	2	1	4	20:59
2000-01 ♦	Colorado	NHL	73	27	62	89	54	12	2	5	178	15.2	23	755	46.6	20:48	11	4	10	14	6	1	0	2	21:55
2001-02	Colorado	NHL	....	....	....	....	....	....	....	....	....	....	....	....	....	....	20	9	*18	*27	20	0	0	4	18:10
2002-03	Colorado	NHL	75	29	*77	*106	70	8	0	2	166	17.5	52	709	47.0	19:20	7	2	6	8	6	1	0	0	20:01
2003-04	Colorado	NHL	39	18	37	55	30	3	1	5	85	21.2	16	549	42.3	19:12	11	4	7	11	12	1	0	1	19:02
2004-05	MODO	Sweden	33	13	26	39	88	....	....	....	....	....	....	....	....	....	1	0	0	0	2	....	....	....	....
2005-06	Philadelphia	NHL	60	19	56	75	46	8	1	2	132	14.4	21	941	50.6	18:47	6	4	4	8	6	1	0	2	18:55
	Sweden	Olympics	6	0	6	6	0	....	....	....	....	....	....	....	....	....	....	....	....	....	....	....	....	....	....
2006-07	Philadelphia	NHL	40	11	29	40	72	5	0	2	63	17.5	2	690	50.9	17:44	....	....	....	....	....	....	....	....	....
	Nashville	NHL	17	2	13	15	16	1	0	1	36	5.6	5	267	47.6	19:36	5	2	2	4	12	0	0	0	20:57
	NHL Totals		697	248	623	871	678	71	16	43	1675	14.8		5325	48.8	20:17	144	63	103	166	149	16	2	14	20:12

NHL All-Rookie Team (1995) • Calder Memorial Trophy (1995) • NHL First All-Star Team (1998, 1999, 2003) • Bud Light Plus/Minus Award (2003) (tied with Milan Hejduk) • Art Ross Trophy (2003) • Hart Memorial Trophy (2003).

Played in NHL All-Star Game (1996, 1998, 1999, 2001, 2003)

Traded to **Quebec** by **Philadelphia** with Steve Duchesne, Kerry Huffman, Mike Ricci, Ron Hextall, Philadelphia's 1st round choice (Jocelyn Thibault) in 1993 Entry Draft, $15,000,000 and future considerations (Chris Simon and Philadelphia's 1st round choice (later traded to Toronto – later traded to Washington – Washington selected Nolan Baumgartner) in 1994 Entry Draft, July 21, 1992) for Eric Lindros, June 30, 1992. Transferred to **Colorado** after **Quebec** franchise relocated, June 21, 1995. • Missed entire 2001-02 regular season recovering from spleen (May 9, 2001 vs. Los Angeles) and ankle (January 10, 2002 in practice) injuries. • Missed majority of 2003-04 season recovering from groin (October 28, 2003 vs. Calgary) and hip (February 16, 2004 vs. Vancouver) injuries. Signed as a free agent by **MODO** (Sweden), September 18, 2004. Signed as a free agent by **Philadelphia**, August 3, 2005. Traded to **Nashville** by **Philadelphia** for Scottie Upshall, Ryan Parent and Nashville's 1st (later traded back to Nashville - Nashville selected Jonathon Blum) and 3rd (later traded to Washington - Washington selected Phil Desimone) round choices in 2007 Entry Draft, February 15, 2007.

FOSTER, Kurtis
(FAW-stuhr, KUHR-this) **MIN.**

Defense. Shoots right. 6'5", 218 lbs. Born, Carp, Ont., November 24, 1981. Calgary's 2nd choice, 40th overall, in 2000 Entry Draft.

Season	Club	League	GP	G	A	Pts	PIM	PP	SH	GW	S	%	+/-	TF	F%	Min	GP	G	A	Pts	PIM	PP	SH	GW	Min
1996-97	Ottawa Valley	ODMHA	36	7	18	25	88	....	....	....	....	....	....	....	....	....	....	....	....	....	....	....	....	....	....
1997-98	Peterborough	OHL	39	1	1	2	45	....	....	....	....	....	....	....	....	....	4	0	0	0	2	....	....	....	....
1998-99	Peterborough	OHL	54	2	13	15	59	....	....	....	....	....	....	....	....	....	5	0	0	0	6	....	....	....	....
99-2000	Peterborough	OHL	68	6	18	24	116	....	....	....	....	....	....	....	....	....	5	1	2	3	4	....	....	....	....
2000-01	Peterborough	OHL	62	17	24	41	78	....	....	....	....	....	....	....	....	....	7	1	1	2	10	....	....	....	....
2001-02	Peterborough	OHL	33	10	4	14	58	....	....	....	....	....	....	....	....	....	....	....	....	....	....	....	....	....	....
	Chicago Wolves	AHL	39	6	9	15	59	....	....	....	....	....	....	....	....	....	14	1	1	2	21	....	....	....	....
2002-03	Atlanta	NHL	2	0	0	0	0	0	0	0	1	0.0	–2	0	0.0	11:06	....	....	....	....	....	....	....	....	....
	Chicago Wolves	AHL	75	15	27	42	159	....	....	....	....	....	....	....	....	....	9	1	3	4	14	....	....	....	....
2003-04	Atlanta	NHL	3	0	1	1	0	0	0	0	1	0.0	0	0	0.0	6:58	....	....	....	....	....	....	....	....	....
	Chicago Wolves	AHL	67	11	19	30	95	....	....	....	....	....	....	....	....	....	10	0	3	3	12	....	....	....	....
2004-05	Cincinnati	AHL	78	17	25	42	71	....	....	....	....	....	....	....	....	....	9	2	3	5	28	....	....	....	....
2005-06	Minnesota	NHL	58	10	18	28	60	6	0	2	124	8.1	–3	0	0.0	19:13	....	....	....	....	....	....	....	....	....
	Houston Aeros	AHL	19	4	11	15	32	....	....	....	....	....	....	....	....	....	....	....	....	....	....	....	....	....	....
2006-07	Minnesota	NHL	57	3	20	23	52	0	0	0	135	2.2	–3	1	100.0	17:59	3	0	2	2	0	0	0	0	18:38
	NHL Totals		120	13	39	52	112	6	0	2	261	5.0		1	100.0	18:11	3	0	2	2	0	0	0	0	18:38

Yanick Dupre Memorial Award (Outstanding Humanitarian Contribution - AHL) (2004)

Rights traded to **Atlanta** by **Calgary** with Jeff Cowan for Petr Buzek and Atlanta's 6th round choice (Adam Pardy) in 2004 Entry Draft, December 18, 2001. Traded to **Anaheim** by **Atlanta** for Niclas Havelid, June 26, 2004. Signed as a free agent by **Minnesota**, August 4, 2005.

FOY, Matt
(FOI, MAT) **MIN.**

Right wing. Shoots right. 6'2", 219 lbs. Born, Oakville, Ont., May 18, 1983. Minnesota's 6th choice, 175th overall, in 2002 Entry Draft.

Season	Club	League	GP	G	A	Pts	PIM	PP	SH	GW	S	%	+/-	TF	F%	Min	GP	G	A	Pts	PIM	PP	SH	GW	Min
2000-01	Wexford Raiders	OPJHL	47	43	49	92	30	....	....	....	....	....	....	....	....	....	....	....	....	....	....	....	....	....	....
2001-02	Merrimack	H-East	31	7	17	24	48	....	....	....	....	....	....	....	....	....	....	....	....	....	....	....	....	....	....
2002-03	Ottawa 67's	OHL	68	61	71	132	112	....	....	....	....	....	....	....	....	....	21	11	20	31	47	....	....	....	....
2003-04	Houston Aeros	AHL	51	11	13	24	74	....	....	....	....	....	....	....	....	....	1	0	0	0	0	....	....	....	....
2004-05	Houston Aeros	AHL	69	12	13	25	78	....	....	....	....	....	....	....	....	....	5	1	2	3	6	....	....	....	....
2005-06	Minnesota	NHL	19	2	3	5	16	1	0	0	21	9.5	–4	1	0.0	10:59	....	....	....	....	....	....	....	....	....
	Houston Aeros	AHL	51	15	25	40	122	....	....	....	....	....	....	....	....	....	8	5	3	8	29	....	....	....	....
2006-07	Minnesota	NHL	9	0	0	0	4	0	0	0	6	0.0	–1	0	0.0	7:11	....	....	....	....	....	....	....	....	....
	Houston Aeros	AHL	62	27	23	50	121	....	....	....	....	....	....	....	....	....	....	....	....	....	....	....	....	....	....
	NHL Totals		28	2	3	5	20	1	0	0	27	7.4		1	0.0	9:46	....	....	....	....	....	....	....	....	....

OHL First All-Star Team (2003)

• Officially announced intention to withdraw from **Merrimack College** (Hockey East) for academic reasons, May 30, 2002.

FRANZEN, Johan
(FRAN-zehn, YOH-han) **DET.**

Left wing. Shoots left. 6'3", 218 lbs. Born, Landsbro, Sweden, December 23, 1979. Detroit's 1st choice, 97th overall, in 2004 Entry Draft.

Season	Club	League	GP	G	A	Pts	PIM	PP	SH	GW	S	%	+/-	TF	F%	Min	GP	G	A	Pts	PIM	PP	SH	GW	Min
2001-02	Linkopings HC	Sweden	36	2	6	8	64	....	....	....	....	....	....	....	....	....	....	....	....	....	....	....	....	....	....
2002-03	Linkopings HC	Sweden	37	2	4	6	14	....	....	....	....	....	....	....	....	....	....	....	....	....	....	....	....	....	....
2003-04	Linkopings HC	Sweden	49	12	18	30	26	....	....	....	....	....	....	....	....	....	5	0	1	1	8	....	....	....	....
2004-05	Linkopings HC	Sweden	43	7	7	14	45	....	....	....	....	....	....	....	....	....	6	2	0	2	16	....	....	....	....
2005-06	Detroit	NHL	80	12	4	16	36	0	2	2	119	10.1	4	171	41.5	12:27	6	1	2	3	4	0	0	0	12:00
2006-07	Detroit	NHL	69	10	20	30	37	0	1	2	151	6.6	20	45	40.0	15:35	18	3	4	7	10	0	0	2	16:47
	NHL Totals		149	22	24	46	73	0	3	4	270	8.1		216	41.2	13:54	24	4	6	10	14	0	0	2	15:35

FRASER, Colin
(FRAY-zuhr, KAW-lihn) **CHI.**

Center. Shoots left. 6'1", 190 lbs. Born, Surrey, B.C., January 28, 1985. Philadelphia's 3rd choice, 69th overall, in 2003 Entry Draft.

Season	Club	League	GP	G	A	Pts	PIM	PP	SH	GW	S	%	+/-	TF	F%	Min	GP	G	A	Pts	PIM	PP	SH	GW	Min
2000-01	Port Coquitlam	PIJHL	38	16	24	40	90	....	....	....	....	....	....	....	....	....	8	2	2	4	21	....	....	....	....
2001-02	Red Deer Rebels	WHL	67	11	31	42	126	....	....	....	....	....	....	....	....	....	23	2	1	3	39	....	....	....	....
2002-03	Red Deer Rebels	WHL	69	15	37	52	192	....	....	....	....	....	....	....	....	....	22	7	6	13	40	....	....	....	....
2003-04	Red Deer Rebels	WHL	70	24	29	53	174	....	....	....	....	....	....	....	....	....	19	5	9	14	24	....	....	....	....
2004-05	Red Deer Rebels	WHL	63	24	43	67	148	....	....	....	....	....	....	....	....	....	7	2	5	7	8	....	....	....	....
	Norfolk Admirals	AHL	3	0	0	0	20	....	....	....	....	....	....	....	....	....	6	1	0	1	2	....	....	....	....
2005-06	Norfolk Admirals	AHL	75	12	13	25	145	....	....	....	....	....	....	....	....	....	4	0	0	0	7	....	....	....	....
2006-07	Chicago	NHL	1	0	0	0	2	0	0	0	0	0.0	–1	2	0.0	3:18	....	....	....	....	....	....	....	....	....
	Norfolk Admirals	AHL	67	12	24	36	158	....	....	....	....	....	....	....	....	....	6	1	0	1	21	....	....	....	....
	NHL Totals		1	0	0	0	2	0	0	0	0	0.0		2	0.0	3:18	....	....	....	....	....	....	....	....	....

Canadian Major Junior Humanitarian Player of the Year (2005)

Traded to **Chicago** by **Philadelphia** with Jim Vandermeer and Los Angeles' 2nd round choice (previously acquired, Chicago selected Bryan Bickell) in 2004 Entry Draft for Alex Zhamnov and Washington's 4th round choice (previously acquired, Philadelphia selected R.J. Anderson) in 2004 Entry Draft, February 19, 2004.

FRASER, Mark
(FRAY-zuhr, MAHRK) **N.J.**

Defense. Shoots left. 6'4", 210 lbs. Born, Ottawa, Ont., September 29, 1986. New Jersey's 3rd choice, 84th overall, in 2005 Entry Draft.

Season	Club	League	GP	G	A	Pts	PIM	PP	SH	GW	S	%	+/-	TF	F%	Min	GP	G	A	Pts	PIM	PP	SH	GW	Min
2004-05	Gloucester	CJHL	STATISTICS NOT AVAILABLE																						
	Kitchener Rangers	OHL	58	0	8	8	96	....	....	....	....	....	....	....	....	....	15	0	3	3	26	....	....	....	....
2005-06	Kitchener Rangers	OHL	59	0	5	5	129	....	....	....	....	....	....	....	....	....	5	0	1	1	4	....	....	....	....
	Albany River Rats	AHL	4	0	0	0	2	....	....	....	....	....	....	....	....	....	....	....	....	....	....	....	....	....	....
2006-07	New Jersey	NHL	7	0	0	0	7	0	0	0	1	0.0	–1	0	0.0	3:34	....	....	....	....	....	....	....	....	....
	Lowell Devils	AHL	71	1	8	9	73	....	....	....	....	....	....	....	....	....	....	....	....	....	....	....	....	....	....
	NHL Totals		7	0	0	0	7	0	0	0	1	0.0		0	0.0	3:34	....	....	....	....	....	....	....	....	....

FRIESEN, Jeff
(FREE-zuhn, JEHF)

Left wing. Shoots left. 6'1", 205 lbs. Born, Meadow Lake, Sask., August 5, 1976. San Jose's 1st choice, 11th overall, in 1994 Entry Draft.

			Regular Season														Playoffs								
Season	Club	League	GP	G	A	Pts	PIM	PP	SH	GW	S	%	+/-	TF	F%	Min	GP	G	A	Pts	PIM	PP	SH	GW	Min
1991-92	Sask. Contacts	SMHL	35	37	51	88	75	....	....	....	....	....	....	....	....	....	....	....	....	....	....	....	....	....	....
	Regina Pats	WHL	4	3	1	4	2	....	....	....	....	....	....	....	....	....	....	....	....	....	....	....	....	....	....
1992-93	Regina Pats	WHL	70	45	38	83	23	....	....	....	....	....	....	....	....	....	13	7	10	17	8	....	....	....	....
1993-94	Regina Pats	WHL	66	51	67	118	48	....	....	....	....	....	....	....	....	....	4	3	2	5	2	....	....	....	....
1994-95	Regina Pats	WHL	25	21	23	44	22	....	....	....	....	....	....	....	....	....	....	....	....	....	....	....	....	....	....
	San Jose	**NHL**	**48**	**15**	**10**	**25**	**14**	**5**	**1**	**2**	**86**	**17.4**	**–8**	....	....	....	**11**	**1**	**5**	**6**	**4**	**0**	**0**	**0**	....
1995-96	**San Jose**	**NHL**	**79**	**15**	**31**	**46**	**42**	**2**	**0**	**0**	**123**	**12.2**	**–19**	....	....	....	....	....	....	....	....	....	....	....	....
1996-97	**San Jose**	**NHL**	**82**	**28**	**34**	**62**	**75**	**6**	**2**	**5**	**200**	**14.0**	**–8**	....	....	....	....	....	....	....	....	....	....	....	....
1997-98	**San Jose**	**NHL**	**79**	**31**	**32**	**63**	**40**	**7**	**6**	**7**	**186**	**16.7**	**8**	....	....	....	**6**	**0**	**1**	**1**	**2**	**0**	**0**	**0**	....
1998-99	**San Jose**	**NHL**	**78**	**22**	**35**	**57**	**42**	**10**	**1**	**3**	**215**	**10.2**	**3**	**24**	**33.3**	**19:25**	**6**	**2**	**2**	**4**	**14**	**1**	**0**	**0**	**22:22**
99-2000	**San Jose**	**NHL**	**82**	**26**	**35**	**61**	**47**	**11**	**3**	**7**	**191**	**13.6**	**–2**	**3**	**66.7**	**19:48**	**11**	**2**	**2**	**4**	**10**	**0**	**0**	**0**	**17:21**
2000-01	**San Jose**	**NHL**	**64**	**12**	**24**	**36**	**56**	**2**	**0**	**1**	**120**	**10.0**	**7**	**7**	**28.6**	**18:51**	....	....	....	....	....	....	....	....	....
	Anaheim	**NHL**	**15**	**2**	**10**	**12**	**10**	**2**	**0**	**0**	**29**	**6.9**	**–2**	**43**	**55.8**	**21:28**	....	....	....	....	....	....	....	....	....
2001-02	**Anaheim**	**NHL**	**81**	**17**	**26**	**43**	**44**	**1**	**1**	**0**	**161**	**10.6**	**–1**	**45**	**48.9**	**17:59**	....	....	....	....	....	....	....	....	....
2002-03 ♦	**New Jersey**	**NHL**	**81**	**23**	**28**	**51**	**26**	**3**	**0**	**4**	**179**	**12.8**	**23**	**11**	**45.5**	**15:33**	**24**	**10**	**4**	**14**	**6**	**1**	**0**	**4**	**16:02**
2003-04	**New Jersey**	**NHL**	**81**	**17**	**20**	**37**	**26**	**5**	**0**	**4**	**177**	**9.6**	**8**	**31**	**45.2**	**15:08**	**5**	**0**	**0**	**0**	**4**	**0**	**0**	**0**	**12:55**
2004-05		DID NOT PLAY																							
2005-06	**Washington**	**NHL**	**33**	**3**	**4**	**7**	**24**	**0**	**0**	**0**	**64**	**4.7**	**–11**	**13**	**46.2**	**14:45**	....	....	....	....	....	....	....	....	....
	Anaheim	**NHL**	**18**	**1**	**3**	**4**	**8**	**0**	**0**	**1**	**11**	**9.1**	**–4**	**0**	**0.0**	**10:53**	**16**	**3**	**1**	**4**	**6**	**0**	**0**	**0**	**11:14**
2006-07	**Calgary**	**NHL**	**72**	**6**	**6**	**12**	**34**	**0**	**1**	**0**	**55**	**10.9**	**–2**	**21**	**38.1**	**12:11**	**5**	**0**	**0**	**0**	**2**	**0**	**0**	**0**	**10:50**
	NHL Totals		**893**	**218**	**298**	**516**	**488**	**54**	**15**	**34**	**1797**	**12.1**		**198**	**46.0**	**16:48**	**84**	**18**	**15**	**33**	**48**	**2**	**0**	**4**	**15:03**

WHL Rookie of the Year (1993) • Canadian Major Junior Rookie of the Year (1993) • NHL All-Rookie Team (1995)

Traded to **Anaheim** by **San Jose** with Steve Shields and San Jose's 2nd round choice (later traded to Dallas – Dallas selected Vojtech Polak) in 2003 Entry Draft for Teemu Selanne, March 5, 2001. Traded to **New Jersey** by **Anaheim** with Oleg Tverdovsky and Maxim Balmochnykh for Petr Sykora, Mike Commodore, Jean-Francois Damphousse and Igor Pohanka, July 6, 2002. Traded to **Washington** by **New Jersey** for Washington's 3rd round choice (Kirill Tulupov) in 2006 Entry Draft, September 26, 2005. Traded to **Anaheim** by **Washington** for Anaheim's 2nd round choice (Keith Seabrook) in 2006 Entry Draft, March 9, 2006. Signed as a free agent by **Calgary**, July 5, 2006.

FRITSCHE, Dan
(FRIH-tchee, DAN) **CBJ**

Center. Shoots right. 6'1", 202 lbs. Born, Parma, OH, July 13, 1985. Columbus' 2nd choice, 46th overall, in 2003 Entry Draft.

Season	Club	League	GP	G	A	Pts	PIM	PP	SH	GW	S	%	+/-	TF	F%	Min	GP	G	A	Pts	PIM	PP	SH	GW	Min
2000-01	Cleveland Barons	NAHL	49	23	29	52	47	....	....	....	....	....	....	....	....	....	1	1	1	2	0	....	....	....	....
2001-02	Sarnia Sting	OHL	17	5	13	18	20	....	....	....	....	....	....	....	....	....	....	....	....	....	....	....	....	....	....
2002-03	Sarnia Sting	OHL	61	32	39	71	79	....	....	....	....	....	....	....	....	....	5	2	2	4	4	....	....	....	....
2003-04	Sarnia Sting	OHL	27	16	13	29	26	....	....	....	....	....	....	....	....	....	5	1	5	6	0	....	....	....	....
	Columbus	**NHL**	**19**	**1**	**0**	**1**	**12**	**0**	**0**	**0**	**19**	**5.3**	**–5**	**139**	**38.1**	**8:24**	....	....	....	....	....	....	....	....	....
	Syracuse Crunch	AHL	4	2	0	2	0	....	....	....	....	....	....	....	....	....	4	0	1	1	4	....	....	....	....
2004-05	Sarnia Sting	OHL	2	1	1	2	0	....	....	....	....	....	....	....	....	....	....	....	....	....	....	....	....	....	....
	London Knights	OHL	28	17	18	35	18	....	....	....	....	....	....	....	....	....	17	9	13	22	12	....	....	....	....
2005-06	**Columbus**	**NHL**	**59**	**6**	**7**	**13**	**22**	**0**	**0**	**0**	**93**	**6.5**	**–14**	**270**	**48.9**	**10:17**	....	....	....	....	....	....	....	....	....
	Syracuse Crunch	AHL	19	5	4	9	12	....	....	....	....	....	....	....	....	....	6	2	2	4	8	....	....	....	....
2006-07	**Columbus**	**NHL**	**59**	**12**	**15**	**27**	**35**	**5**	**1**	**4**	**81**	**14.8**	**3**	**296**	**49.3**	**14:02**	....	....	....	....	....	....	....	....	....
	NHL Totals		**137**	**19**	**22**	**41**	**69**	**5**	**1**	**4**	**193**	**9.8**		**705**	**47.0**	**11:38**	....	....	....	....	....	....	....	....	....

Memorial Cup Tournament All-Star Team (2005)

• Missed majority of 2001-02 season recovering from shoulder surgery, December 12, 2001.

FROLOV, Alexander
(froh-LAHF, al-EHX-AN-duhr) **L.A.**

Left wing. Shoots right. 6'2", 210 lbs. Born, Moscow, USSR, June 19, 1982. Los Angeles' 1st choice, 20th overall, in 2000 Entry Draft.

Season	Club	League	GP	G	A	Pts	PIM	PP	SH	GW	S	%	+/-	TF	F%	Min	GP	G	A	Pts	PIM	PP	SH	GW	Min
1998-99	Spartak Moscow	Russia	1	0	0	0	0	....	....	....	....	....	....	....	....	....	....	....	....	....	....	....	....	....	....
99-2000	Yaroslavl 2	Russia-3	36	27	13	40	30	....	....	....	....	....	....	....	....	....	....	....	....	....	....	....	....	....	....
2001-02	Spartak Moscow	Russia	44	20	19	39	8	....	....	....	....	....	....	....	....	....	....	....	....	....	....	....	....	....	....
	Krylja Sovetov 2	Russia-3	2	0	0	0	4	....	....	....	....	....	....	....	....	....	....	....	....	....	....	....	....	....	....
	Krylja Sovetov	Russia	43	18	12	30	16	....	....	....	....	....	....	....	....	....	3	1	0	1	0	....	....	....	....
2002-03	**Los Angeles**	**NHL**	**79**	**14**	**17**	**31**	**34**	**1**	**0**	**3**	**141**	**9.9**	**12**	**9**	**22.2**	**14:23**	....	....	....	....	....	....	....	....	....
2003-04	**Los Angeles**	**NHL**	**77**	**24**	**24**	**48**	**24**	**5**	**2**	**3**	**168**	**14.3**	**8**	**34**	**32.4**	**17:13**	....	....	....	....	....	....	....	....	....
	Nizhny Novgorod	Russia	1	0	0	0	0	....	....	....	....	....	....	....	....	....	....	....	....	....	....	....	....	....	....
2004-05	CSKA Moscow	Russia	42	20	17	37	10	....	....	....	....	....	....	....	....	....	....	....	....	....	....	....	....	....	....
	Dynamo Moscow	Russia	6	2	1	3	2	....	....	....	....	....	....	....	....	....	6	2	1	3	0	....	....	....	....
2005-06	**Los Angeles**	**NHL**	**69**	**21**	**33**	**54**	**40**	**4**	**3**	**4**	**174**	**12.1**	**17**	**4**	**50.0**	**19:18**	....	....	....	....	....	....	....	....	....
	Russia	Olympics	3	0	1	1	0	....	....	....	....	....	....	....	....	....	....	....	....	....	....	....	....	....	....
2006-07	**Los Angeles**	**NHL**	**82**	**35**	**36**	**71**	**34**	**10**	**1**	**6**	**195**	**17.9**	**–8**	**19**	**36.8**	**19:56**	....	....	....	....	....	....	....	....	....
	NHL Totals		**307**	**94**	**110**	**204**	**132**	**20**	**6**	**16**	**678**	**13.9**		**66**	**33.3**	**17:41**	....	....	....	....	....	....	....	....	....

Signed as a free agent by **CSKA Moscow** (Russia), July 14, 2004. Signed as a free agent by **Dynamo Moscow** (Russia), February 17, 2005.

FUNK, Michael
(FUHNK, MIGH-kuhl) **BUF.**

Defense. Shoots left. 6'4", 213 lbs. Born, Abbotsford, B.C., August 15, 1986. Buffalo's 2nd choice, 43rd overall, in 2004 Entry Draft.

Season	Club	League	GP	G	A	Pts	PIM	PP	SH	GW	S	%	+/-	TF	F%	Min	GP	G	A	Pts	PIM	PP	SH	GW	Min
2001-02	Abbotsford	BCAHA	72	9	24	33	84	....	....	....	....	....	....	....	....	....	....	....	....	....	....	....	....	....	....
2002-03	Portland	WHL	68	1	15	16	54	....	....	....	....	....	....	....	....	....	7	0	1	1	15	....	....	....	....
2003-04	Portland	WHL	71	3	25	28	86	....	....	....	....	....	....	....	....	....	5	0	1	1	6	....	....	....	....
2004-05	Portland	WHL	71	8	22	30	84	....	....	....	....	....	....	....	....	....	7	1	1	2	4	....	....	....	....
2005-06	Portland	WHL	70	11	36	47	88	....	....	....	....	....	....	....	....	....	5	0	0	0	8	....	....	....	....
2006-07	**Buffalo**	**NHL**	**5**	**0**	**2**	**2**	**0**	**0**	**0**	**0**	**1**	**0.0**	**2**	**0**	**0.0**	**3:26**	....	....	....	....	....	....	....	....	....
	Rochester	AHL	61	2	5	7	57	....	....	....	....	....	....	....	....	....	6	0	1	1	4	....	....	....	....
	NHL Totals		**5**	**0**	**2**	**2**	**0**	**0**	**0**	**0**	**1**	**0.0**		**0**	**0.0**	**3:26**	....	....	....	....	....	....	....	....	....

FUSSEY, Owen
(FOO-see, OH-wehn)

Right wing. Shoots left. 6', 195 lbs. Born, Winnipeg, Man., April 2, 1983. Washington's 2nd choice, 90th overall, in 2001 Entry Draft.

Season	Club	League	GP	G	A	Pts	PIM	PP	SH	GW	S	%	+/-	TF	F%	Min	GP	G	A	Pts	PIM	PP	SH	GW	Min
1998-99	Wpg. Warriors	MMMHL	40	38	33	71	24	....	....	....	....	....	....	....	....	....	....	....	....	....	....	....	....	....	....
99-2000	Calgary Hitmen	WHL	51	7	6	13	35	....	....	....	....	....	....	....	....	....	12	3	4	7	2	....	....	....	....
2000-01	Calgary Hitmen	WHL	48	15	10	25	33	....	....	....	....	....	....	....	....	....	12	2	1	3	6	....	....	....	....
2001-02	Calgary Hitmen	WHL	72	43	27	70	61	....	....	....	....	....	....	....	....	....	7	3	1	4	4	....	....	....	....
2002-03	Calgary Hitmen	WHL	39	17	18	35	31	....	....	....	....	....	....	....	....	....	....	....	....	....	....	....	....	....	....
	Moose Jaw	WHL	27	24	12	36	20	....	....	....	....	....	....	....	....	....	13	6	6	12	10	....	....	....	....
2003-04	**Washington**	**NHL**	**4**	**0**	**1**	**1**	**0**	**0**	**0**	**0**	**6**	**0.0**	**–1**	**0**	**0.0**	**8:16**	....	....	....	....	....	....	....	....	....
	Portland Pirates	AHL	69	6	7	13	23	....	....	....	....	....	....	....	....	....	7	0	0	0	5	....	....	....	....
2004-05	Portland Pirates	AHL	71	14	12	26	26	....	....	....	....	....	....	....	....	....	....	....	....	....	....	....	....	....	....
2005-06	Hershey Bears	AHL	50	2	10	12	38	....	....	....	....	....	....	....	....	....	1	0	0	0	0	....	....	....	....
2006-07	Toronto Marlies	AHL	14	1	1	2	4	....	....	....	....	....	....	....	....	....	....	....	....	....	....	....	....	....	....
	Columbia Inferno	ECHL	53	25	20	45	32	....	....	....	....	....	....	....	....	....	....	....	....	....	....	....	....	....	....
	NHL Totals		**4**	**0**	**1**	**1**	**0**	**0**	**0**	**0**	**6**	**0.0**		**0**	**0.0**	**8:16**	....	....	....	....	....	....	....	....	....

GABORIK, Marian
(GAB-rihk, MAIR-ee-uhn) **MIN.**

Right wing. Shoots left. 6'1", 193 lbs. Born, Trencin, Czech., February 14, 1982. Minnesota's 1st choice, 3rd overall, in 2000 Entry Draft.

Season	Club	League	GP	G	A	Pts	PIM	PP	SH	GW	S	%	+/-	TF	F%	Min	GP	G	A	Pts	PIM	PP	SH	GW	Min
1997-98	Dukla Trencin Jr.	Slovak-Jr.	36	37	22	59	28	....	....	....	....	....	....	....	....	....	....	....	....	....	....	....	....	....	....
	Dukla Trencin	Slovakia	1	1	0	1	0	....	....	....	....	....	....	....	....	....	....	....	....	....	....	....	....	....	....
1998-99	Dukla Trencin	Slovakia	33	11	9	20	6	....	....	....	....	....	....	....	....	....	3	1	0	1	2	....	....	....	....
99-2000	Dukla Trencin	Slovakia	50	25	21	46	34	....	....	....	....	....	....	....	....	....	5	1	2	3	2	....	....	....	....
2000-01	**Minnesota**	**NHL**	**71**	**18**	**18**	**36**	**32**	**6**	**0**	**3**	**179**	**10.1**	**–6**	**3**	**33.3**	**15:26**	....	....	....	....	....	....	....	....	....
2001-02	**Minnesota**	**NHL**	**78**	**30**	**37**	**67**	**34**	**10**	**0**	**4**	**221**	**13.6**	**0**	**4**	**25.0**	**16:47**	....	....	....	....	....	....	....	....	....
2002-03	**Minnesota**	**NHL**	**81**	**30**	**35**	**65**	**46**	**5**	**1**	**8**	**280**	**10.7**	**12**	**16**	**25.0**	**17:24**	**18**	**9**	**8**	**17**	**6**	**4**	**0**	**0**	**18:12**
2003-04	Dukla Trencin	Slovakia	9	10	3	13	10	....	....	....	....	....	....	....	....	....	....	....	....	....	....	....	....	....	....
	Minnesota	**NHL**	**65**	**18**	**22**	**40**	**20**	**3**	**0**	**4**	**220**	**8.2**	**10**	**11**	**45.5**	**18:17**	....	....	....	....	....	....	....	....	....

Season	Club	League	Regular Season GP	G	A	Pts	PIM	PP	SH	GW	S	%	+/-	TF	F%	Min	Playoffs GP	G	A	Pts	PIM	PP	SH	GW	Min
2004-05	Dukla Trencin	Slovakia	29	25	27	52	46	....	....	....	....	....	....	....	....	....	12	8	9	17	26	....	....	....	....
	Farjestad	Sweden	12	6	4	10	45	....	....	....	....	....	....	....	....	....	....	....	....	....	....	....	....	....	....
2005-06	**Minnesota**	**NHL**	**65**	**38**	**28**	**66**	**64**	**10**	**2**	**7**	**252**	**15.1**	**6**	**11**	**27.3**	**18:26**	....	....	....	....	....	....	....	....	....
	Slovakia	Olympics	6	3	4	7	4	....	....	....	....	....	....	....	....	....	....	....	....	....	....	....	....	....	....
2006-07	**Minnesota**	**NHL**	**48**	**30**	**27**	**57**	**40**	**12**	**1**	**7**	**196**	**15.3**	**12**	**4**	**0.0**	**19:38**	**5**	**3**	**1**	**4**	**8**	**1**	**1**	**1**	**19:32**
	NHL Totals		**408**	**164**	**167**	**331**	**236**	**46**	**4**	**33**	**1348**	**12.2**		**49**	**28.6**	**17:30**	**23**	**12**	**9**	**21**	**14**	**5**	**1**	**1**	**18:29**

Played in NHL All-Star Game (2003)

Signed as a free agent by **Trencin** (Slovakia), July 5, 2004. Signed as a free agent by **Farjestad** (Sweden), December 21, 2004.

GAGNE, Simon

(gah-N'YAY, see-MOHN) **PHI.**

Left wing. Shoots left. 6', 195 lbs. Born, Ste-Foy, Que., February 29, 1980. Philadelphia's 1st choice, 22nd overall, in 1998 Entry Draft.

Season	Club	League	GP	G	A	Pts	PIM	PP	SH	GW	S	%	+/-	TF	F%	Min	GP	G	A	Pts	PIM	PP	SH	GW	Min
1995-96	Ste-Foy	QAAA	27	13	9	22	18	....	....	....	....	....	....	....	....	....	15	7	8	15	8	....	....	....	....
1996-97	Beauport	QMJHL	51	9	22	31	49	....	....	....	....	....	....	....	....	....	....	....	....	....	....	....	....	....	....
1997-98	Quebec Remparts	QMJHL	53	30	39	69	26	....	....	....	....	....	....	....	....	....	12	11	5	16	23	....	....	....	....
1998-99	Quebec Remparts	QMJHL	61	50	*70	*120	42	....	....	....	....	....	....	....	....	....	13	9	8	17	4	....	....	....	....
99-2000	**Philadelphia**	**NHL**	**80**	**20**	**28**	**48**	**22**	**8**	**1**	**4**	**159**	**12.6**	**11**	**443**	**42.2**	**14:59**	**17**	**5**	**5**	**10**	**2**	**2**	**0**	**1**	**16:46**
2000-01	**Philadelphia**	**NHL**	**69**	**27**	**32**	**59**	**18**	**6**	**0**	**7**	**191**	**14.1**	**24**	**21**	**28.6**	**18:05**	**6**	**3**	**0**	**3**	**0**	**2**	**0**	**0**	**19:09**
2001-02	**Philadelphia**	**NHL**	**79**	**33**	**33**	**66**	**32**	**4**	**1**	**7**	**199**	**16.6**	**31**	**6**	**83.3**	**18:09**	**5**	**0**	**0**	**0**	**2**	**0**	**0**	**0**	**19:16**
	Canada	Olympics	6	1	3	4	0	....	....	....	....	....	....	....	....	....	....	....	....	....	....	....	....	....	....
2002-03	**Philadelphia**	**NHL**	**46**	**9**	**18**	**27**	**16**	**1**	**1**	**3**	**115**	**7.8**	**20**	**70**	**42.9**	**17:24**	**13**	**4**	**1**	**5**	**6**	**0**	**1**	**1**	**18:13**
2003-04	**Philadelphia**	**NHL**	**80**	**24**	**21**	**45**	**29**	**6**	**0**	**6**	**211**	**11.4**	**12**	**104**	**39.4**	**16:27**	**18**	**5**	**4**	**9**	**12**	**0**	**0**	**1**	**16:48**
2004-05			DID NOT PLAY																						
2005-06	**Philadelphia**	**NHL**	**72**	**47**	**32**	**79**	**38**	**12**	**2**	**7**	**334**	**14.1**	**31**	**18**	**38.9**	**20:46**	**6**	**3**	**1**	**4**	**2**	**1**	**0**	**0**	**21:45**
	Canada	Olympics	6	1	2	3	6	....	....	....	....	....	....	....	....	....	....	....	....	....	....	....	....	....	....
2006-07	**Philadelphia**	**NHL**	**76**	**41**	**27**	**68**	**30**	**13**	**2**	**4**	**291**	**14.1**	**2**	**49**	**42.9**	**21:02**	....	....	....	....	....	....	....	....	....
	NHL Totals		**502**	**201**	**191**	**392**	**185**	**50**	**7**	**38**	**1500**	**13.4**		**711**	**41.8**	**18:06**	**65**	**20**	**11**	**31**	**24**	**5**	**1**	**3**	**17:56**

QMJHL Second All-Star Team (1999) • NHL All-Rookie Team (2000)

Played in NHL ALL-Star Game (2001, 2007)

GAMACHE, Simon

(ga-MOHSH, see-MOHN) **TOR.**

Center. Shoots left. 5'10", 186 lbs. Born, Thetford Mines, Que., January 3, 1981. Atlanta's 14th choice, 290th overall, in 2000 Entry Draft.

Season	Club	League	GP	G	A	Pts	PIM	PP	SH	GW	S	%	+/-	TF	F%	Min	GP	G	A	Pts	PIM	PP	SH	GW	Min
1997-98	Levis-Lauzon	QAAA	42	28	26	54		....	....	....	....	....	....	....	....	....	4	1	1	2		....	....	....	....
1998-99	Val-d'Or Foreurs	QMJHL	70	19	43	62	54	....	....	....	....	....	....	....	....	....	6	1	2	3	4	....	....	....	....
99-2000	Val-d'Or Foreurs	QMJHL	72	64	79	143	74	....	....	....	....	....	....	....	....	....	....	....	....	....	....	....	....	....	....
2000-01	Val-d'Or Foreurs	QMJHL	72	*74	*110	*184	70	....	....	....	....	....	....	....	....	....	21	*22	*35	*57	18	....	....	....	....
2001-02	Chicago Wolves	AHL	26	2	4	6	11	....	....	....	....	....	....	....	....	....	....	....	....	....	....	....	....	....	....
	Greenville	ECHL	31	19	19	38	35	....	....	....	....	....	....	....	....	....	17	*15	9	*24	22	....	....	....	....
2002-03	**Atlanta**	**NHL**	**2**	**0**	**0**	**0**	**2**	**0**	**0**	**0**	**3**	**0.0**	**–1**	**0**	**0.0**	**12:37**	....	....	....	....	....	....	....	....	....
	Chicago Wolves	AHL	76	35	42	77	37	....	....	....	....	....	....	....	....	....	9	7	2	9	4	....	....	....	....
2003-04	**Atlanta**	**NHL**	**2**	**0**	**1**	**1**	**0**	**0**	**0**	**0**	**1**	**0.0**	**0**	**0**	**0.0**	**6:39**	....	....	....	....	....	....	....	....	....
	Chicago Wolves	AHL	16	5	6	11	4	....	....	....	....	....	....	....	....	....	....	....	....	....	....	....	....	....	....
	Nashville	**NHL**	**7**	**1**	**0**	**1**	**0**	**1**	**0**	**0**	**4**	**25.0**	**–3**	**18**	**55.6**	**7:35**	....	....	....	....	....	....	....	....	....
	Milwaukee	AHL	52	18	27	45	26	....	....	....	....	....	....	....	....	....	22	6	*18	24	14	....	....	....	....
2004-05	Milwaukee	AHL	80	29	57	86	93	....	....	....	....	....	....	....	....	....	7	6	4	10	18	....	....	....	....
2005-06	**Nashville**	**NHL**	**11**	**0**	**0**	**0**	**0**	**0**	**0**	**0**	**4**	**0.0**	**–6**	**2**	**50.0**	**8:16**	....	....	....	....	....	....	....	....	....
	Milwaukee	AHL	39	18	19	37	46	....	....	....	....	....	....	....	....	....	21	12	16	28	22	....	....	....	....
	St. Louis	**NHL**	**15**	**3**	**4**	**7**	**10**	**0**	**0**	**0**	**32**	**9.4**	**1**	**4**	**50.0**	**13:53**	....	....	....	....	....	....	....	....	....
2006-07	SC Bern	Swiss	44	20	*46	*66	40	....	....	....	....	....	....	....	....	....	16	7	9	*16	10	....	....	....	....
	NHL Totals		**37**	**4**	**5**	**9**	**12**	**1**	**0**	**0**	**44**	**9.1**		**24**	**54.2**	**10:34**	....	....	....	....	....	....	....	....	....

Canadian Major Junior Second All-Star Team (2000) • QMJHL First All-Star Team (2001) • Michel Briere Trophy (MVP – QMJHL) (2001) • Canadian Major Junior First All-Star Team (2001) • Canadian Major Junior Player of the Year (2001) • Memorial Cup Tournament All-Star Team (2001) • Ed Chynoweth Trophy (Memorial Cup Tournament Leading Scorer) (2001) • ECHL All-Rookie Team (2002) • ECHL Playoff MVP (2002) (co-winner - Tyrone Garner) • AHL First All-Star Team (2005)

Traded to **Nashville** by **Atlanta** with Kirill Safronov for Ben Simon and Tomas Kloucek, December 2, 2003. Claimed on waivers by **St. Louis** from **Nashville**, November 29, 2005. Signed as a free agent by **Toronto**, June 25, 2007.

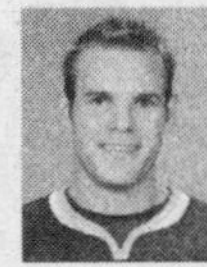

GAUSTAD, Paul

(GAW-stad, PAWL) **BUF.**

Center. Shoots left. 6'4", 222 lbs. Born, Fargo, ND, February 3, 1982. Buffalo's 6th choice, 220th overall, in 2000 Entry Draft.

Season	Club	League	GP	G	A	Pts	PIM	PP	SH	GW	S	%	+/-	TF	F%	Min	GP	G	A	Pts	PIM	PP	SH	GW	Min
1998-99	Portland Hawks	USAHA	45	47	53	100	81	....	....	....	....	....	....	....	....	....	....	....	....	....	....	....	....	....	....
99-2000	Portland	WHL	56	6	8	14	110	....	....	....	....	....	....	....	....	....	....	....	....	....	....	....	....	....	....
2000-01	Portland	WHL	70	11	30	41	168	....	....	....	....	....	....	....	....	....	16	10	6	16	59	....	....	....	....
2001-02	Portland	WHL	72	36	44	80	202	....	....	....	....	....	....	....	....	....	6	3	1	4	16	....	....	....	....
2002-03	**Buffalo**	**NHL**	**1**	**0**	**0**	**0**	**0**	**0**	**0**	**0**	**0**	**0.0**	**0**	**7**	**42.9**	**5:48**	....	....	....	....	....	....	....	....	....
	Rochester	AHL	80	14	39	53	137	....	....	....	....	....	....	....	....	....	3	0	0	0	4	....	....	....	....
2003-04	Rochester	AHL	78	9	22	31	169	....	....	....	....	....	....	....	....	....	16	3	10	13	30	....	....	....	....
2004-05	Rochester	AHL	76	18	25	43	192	....	....	....	....	....	....	....	....	....	9	6	5	11	16	....	....	....	....
2005-06	**Buffalo**	**NHL**	**78**	**9**	**15**	**24**	**65**	**0**	**0**	**0**	**113**	**8.0**	**4**	**829**	**52.2**	**12:08**	**18**	**0**	**4**	**4**	**14**	**0**	**0**	**0**	**12:21**
2006-07	**Buffalo**	**NHL**	**54**	**9**	**13**	**22**	**74**	**3**	**0**	**0**	**75**	**12.0**	**11**	**386**	**52.9**	**13:19**	**7**	**0**	**1**	**1**	**2**	**0**	**0**	**0**	**11:00**
	NHL Totals		**133**	**18**	**28**	**46**	**139**	**3**	**0**	**0**	**188**	**9.6**		**1222**	**52.4**	**12:34**	**25**	**0**	**5**	**5**	**16**	**0**	**0**	**0**	**11:58**

GAUTHIER, Denis

(GOH-tyay, DEH-nihs) **PHI.**

Defense. Shoots left. 6'3", 224 lbs. Born, Montreal, Que., October 1, 1976. Calgary's 1st choice, 20th overall, in 1995 Entry Draft.

Season	Club	League	GP	G	A	Pts	PIM	PP	SH	GW	S	%	+/-	TF	F%	Min	GP	G	A	Pts	PIM	PP	SH	GW	Min
1991-92	Richelieu AA	QAHA	STATISTICS NOT AVAILABLE																						
1992-93	Drummondville	QMJHL	61	1	7	8	136	....	....	....	....	....	....	....	....	....	10	0	5	5	40	....	....	....	....
1993-94	Drummondville	QMJHL	60	0	7	7	176	....	....	....	....	....	....	....	....	....	9	2	0	2	41	....	....	....	....
1994-95	Drummondville	QMJHL	64	9	31	40	190	....	....	....	....	....	....	....	....	....	4	0	5	5	12	....	....	....	....
1995-96	Drummondville	QMJHL	53	25	49	74	140	....	....	....	....	....	....	....	....	....	6	4	4	8	32	....	....	....	....
	Saint John Flames	AHL	5	2	0	2	8	....	....	....	....	....	....	....	....	....	16	1	6	7	20	....	....	....	....
1996-97	Saint John Flames	AHL	73	3	28	31	74	....	....	....	....	....	....	....	....	....	5	0	0	0	6	....	....	....	....
1997-98	**Calgary**	**NHL**	**10**	**0**	**0**	**0**	**16**	**0**	**0**	**0**	**3**	**0.0**	**–5**	....	....	....	....	....	....	....	....	....	....	....	....
	Saint John Flames	AHL	68	4	20	24	154	....	....	....	....	....	....	....	....	....	21	0	4	4	83	....	....	....	....
1998-99	**Calgary**	**NHL**	**55**	**3**	**4**	**7**	**68**	**0**	**0**	**0**	**40**	**7.5**	**3**	**0**	**0.0**	**12:41**	....	....	....	....	....	....	....	....	....
	Saint John Flames	AHL	16	0	3	3	31	....	....	....	....	....	....	....	....	....	....	....	....	....	....	....	....	....	....
99-2000	**Calgary**	**NHL**	**39**	**1**	**1**	**2**	**50**	**0**	**0**	**0**	**29**	**3.4**	**–4**	**0**	**0.0**	**19:21**	....	....	....	....	....	....	....	....	....
2000-01	**Calgary**	**NHL**	**62**	**2**	**6**	**8**	**78**	**0**	**0**	**0**	**33**	**6.1**	**3**	**0**	**0.0**	**16:37**	....	....	....	....	....	....	....	....	....
2001-02	**Calgary**	**NHL**	**66**	**5**	**8**	**13**	**91**	**0**	**1**	**2**	**76**	**6.6**	**9**	**0**	**0.0**	**19:19**	....	....	....	....	....	....	....	....	....
2002-03	**Calgary**	**NHL**	**72**	**1**	**11**	**12**	**99**	**0**	**0**	**1**	**50**	**2.0**	**5**	**0**	**0.0**	**19:52**	....	....	....	....	....	....	....	....	....
2003-04	**Calgary**	**NHL**	**80**	**1**	**15**	**16**	**113**	**0**	**0**	**0**	**90**	**1.1**	**4**	**0**	**0.0**	**18:43**	**6**	**0**	**1**	**1**	**4**	**0**	**0**	**0**	**18:33**
2004-05			DID NOT PLAY																						
2005-06	**Phoenix**	**NHL**	**45**	**2**	**9**	**11**	**61**	**0**	**0**	**0**	**43**	**4.7**	**–4**	**0**	**0.0**	**16:58**	....	....	....	....	....	....	....	....	....
	Philadelphia	**NHL**	**17**	**0**	**0**	**0**	**37**	**0**	**0**	**0**	**13**	**0.0**	**6**	**0**	**0.0**	**15:21**	**6**	**0**	**1**	**1**	**19**	**0**	**0**	**0**	**18:21**
2006-07	**Philadelphia**	**NHL**	**43**	**0**	**4**	**4**	**45**	**0**	**0**	**0**	**23**	**0.0**	**–11**	**0**	**0.0**	**16:39**	....	....	....	....	....	....	....	....	....
	NHL Totals		**489**	**15**	**58**	**73**	**658**	**0**	**1**	**3**	**400**	**3.8**		**0**	**0.0**	**17:35**	**12**	**0**	**2**	**2**	**23**	**0**	**0**	**0**	**18:27**

QMJHL First All-Star Team (1996) • Canadian Major Junior First All-Star Team (1996)

• Missed majority of 1999-2000 season recovering from hip injury suffered in game vs. St. Louis, February 1, 2000. Traded to **Phoenix** by **Calgary** with Oleg Saprykin for Daymond Langkow, August 26, 2004. Traded to **Philadelphia** by **Phoenix** for Josh Gratton, Florida's 2nd round choice (previously acquired, later traded to Detroit - Detroit selected Cory Emerton) in 2006 Entry Draft and Tampa Bay's 2nd round choice (previously acquired, later traded to Detroit - Detroit selected Shawn Matthias) in 2006 Entry Draft, March 9, 2006.

GAUTHIER, Gabe

(GOH-tyay, GAYB) **L.A.**

Left wing. Shoots left. 5'9", 205 lbs. Born, Torrance, CA, January 20, 1984.

Season	Club	League	GP	G	A	Pts	PIM	PP	SH	GW	S	%	+/-	TF	F%	Min	Playoffs GP	G	A	Pts	PIM	PP	SH	GW	Min
2002-03	U. of Denver	WCHA	41	8	8	16	30																		
2003-04	U. of Denver	WCHA	42	18	25	43	32																		
2004-05	U. of Denver	WCHA	41	23	29	52	44																		
2005-06	U. of Denver	WCHA	38	15	24	39	35																		
2006-07	**Los Angeles**	**NHL**	**5**	**0**	**0**	**0**	**2**	**0**	**0**	**0**	**6**	**0.0**	**-1**	**23**	**47.8**	**9:57**									
	Manchester	AHL	69	14	28	42	54										16	1	4	5	14				
	NHL Totals		**5**	**0**	**0**	**0**	**2**	**0**	**0**	**0**	**6**	**0.0**		**23**	**47.8**	**9:57**									

NCAA Championship All-Tournament Team (2005)

Signed as a free agent by **Los Angeles**, July 7, 2006.

GAVEY, Aaron

(GAY-vee, AIR-ruhn)

Center. Shoots left. 6'2", 189 lbs. Born, Sudbury, Ont., February 22, 1974. Tampa Bay's 4th choice, 74th overall, in 1992 Entry Draft.

Season	Club	League	GP	G	A	Pts	PIM	PP	SH	GW	S	%	+/-	TF	F%	Min	Playoffs GP	G	A	Pts	PIM	PP	SH	GW	Min
1990-91	Peterborough	OHA-B	42	26	30	56	68																		
1991-92	Sault Ste. Marie	OHL	48	7	11	18	27										19	5	1	6	10				
1992-93	Sault Ste. Marie	OHL	62	45	39	84	116										18	5	9	14	36				
1993-94	Sault Ste. Marie	OHL	60	42	60	102	116										14	11	10	21	22				
1994-95	Atlanta Knights	IHL	66	18	17	35	85										5	0	1	1	9				
1995-96	**Tampa Bay**	**NHL**	**73**	**8**	**4**	**12**	**56**	**1**	**1**	**2**	**65**	**12.3**	**-6**				**6**	**0**	**0**	**0**	**4**	**0**	**0**	**0**	
1996-97	**Tampa Bay**	**NHL**	**16**	**1**	**2**	**3**	**12**	**0**	**0**	**0**	**8**	**12.5**	**-1**												
	Calgary	**NHL**	**41**	**7**	**9**	**16**	**34**	**3**	**0**	**1**	**54**	**13.0**	**-11**												
1997-98	**Calgary**	**NHL**	**26**	**2**	**3**	**5**	**24**	**0**	**0**	**1**	**27**	**7.4**	**-5**												
	Saint John Flames	AHL	8	4	3	7	28																		
1998-99	**Dallas**	**NHL**	**7**	**0**	**0**	**0**	**10**	**0**	**0**	**0**	**4**	**0.0**	**-1**	**43**	**48.8**	**8:09**									
	Michigan	IHL	67	24	33	57	128										5	2	3	5	4				
99-2000	**Dallas**	**NHL**	**41**	**7**	**6**	**13**	**44**	**1**	**0**	**2**	**39**	**17.9**	**0**	**263**	**51.7**	**9:55**	**13**	**1**	**2**	**3**	**10**	**0**	**0**	**1**	**6:09**
	Michigan	IHL	28	14	15	29	73																		
2000-01	**Minnesota**	**NHL**	**75**	**10**	**14**	**24**	**52**	**1**	**0**	**2**	**100**	**10.0**	**-8**	**584**	**43.5**	**14:00**									
2001-02	**Minnesota**	**NHL**	**71**	**6**	**11**	**17**	**38**	**1**	**0**	**0**	**75**	**8.0**	**-21**	**254**	**42.5**	**11:55**									
2002-03	**Toronto**	**NHL**	**5**	**0**	**1**	**1**	**0**	**0**	**0**	**0**	**8**	**0.0**	**1**	**31**	**48.4**	**11:19**									
	St. John's	AHL	70	14	29	43	83																		
2003-04	St. John's	AHL	75	22	45	67	100																		
2004-05	Storhamar	Norway	1	0	0	0	0																		
	Utah Grizzlies	AHL	60	5	14	19	58																		
2005-06	**Anaheim**	**NHL**	**5**	**0**	**0**	**0**	**2**	**0**	**0**	**0**	**2**	**0.0**	**0**	**12**	**50.0**	**4:03**									
	Portland Pirates	AHL	72	16	31	47	106										19	1	3	4	43				
2006-07	Kolner Haie	Germany	39	7	4	11	91										9	5	3	8	20				
	NHL Totals		**360**	**41**	**50**	**91**	**272**	**7**	**1**	**8**	**382**	**10.7**		**1187**	**45.5**	**11:57**	**19**	**1**	**2**	**3**	**14**	**0**	**0**	**1**	**6:09**

Traded to **Calgary** by **Tampa Bay** for Rick Tabaracci, November 19, 1996. Traded to **Dallas** by **Calgary** for Bob Bassen, July 14, 1998. Traded to **Minnesota** by **Dallas** with Pavel Patera, Dallas' 8th round choice (Eric Johansson) in 2000 Entry Draft and Minnesota's 4th round choice (previously acquired, later traded to Los Angeles – Los Angeles selected Aaron Rome) in 2002 Entry Draft for Brad Lukowich and Minnesota's 3rd (Yared Hagos) and 9th (Dale Sullivan) round choices in 2001 Entry Draft, June 25, 2000. Signed as a free agent by **Toronto**, July 24, 2002. Signed as a free agent by **Storhamar** (Norway), November 2, 2004. Signed as a free agent by **Phoenix**, November 29, 2004. Signed as a free agent by **Anaheim**, September 12, 2005. Signed as a free agent by **Koln** (Germany), September 12, 2006.

GELINAS, Martin

(ZHEHL-in-nuh, MAHR-tihn) **NSH.**

Left wing. Shoots left. 5'11", 195 lbs. Born, Shawinigan, Que., June 5, 1970. Los Angeles' 1st choice, 7th overall, in 1988 Entry Draft.

Season	Club	League	GP	G	A	Pts	PIM	PP	SH	GW	S	%	+/-	TF	F%	Min	Playoffs GP	G	A	Pts	PIM	PP	SH	GW	Min
1985-86	Noranda Aces	NOHA	5	1	1	2	0																		
1986-87	Montreal L'est	QAAA	41	36	42	78	36										7	7	5	12	2				
1987-88	Hull Olympiques	QMJHL	65	63	68	131	74										17	15	18	33	32				
1988-89	Hull Olympiques	QMJHL	41	38	39	77	31										9	5	4	9	14				
	Edmonton	**NHL**	**6**	**1**	**2**	**3**	**0**	**0**	**0**	**0**	**14**	**7.1**	**-1**												
1989-90 ♦	**Edmonton**	**NHL**	**46**	**17**	**8**	**25**	**30**	**5**	**0**	**2**	**71**	**23.9**	**0**				**20**	**2**	**3**	**5**	**6**	**0**	**0**	**0**	
1990-91	**Edmonton**	**NHL**	**73**	**20**	**20**	**40**	**34**	**4**	**0**	**2**	**124**	**16.1**	**-7**				**18**	**3**	**6**	**9**	**25**	**0**	**0**	**1**	
1991-92	**Edmonton**	**NHL**	**68**	**11**	**18**	**29**	**62**	**1**	**0**	**0**	**94**	**11.7**	**14**				**15**	**1**	**3**	**4**	**10**	**0**	**0**	**0**	
1992-93	**Edmonton**	**NHL**	**65**	**11**	**12**	**23**	**30**	**0**	**0**	**1**	**93**	**11.8**	**3**												
1993-94	**Quebec**	**NHL**	**31**	**6**	**6**	**12**	**8**	**0**	**0**	**0**	**53**	**11.3**	**-2**												
	Vancouver	**NHL**	**33**	**8**	**8**	**16**	**26**	**3**	**0**	**1**	**54**	**14.8**	**-6**				**24**	**5**	**4**	**9**	**14**	**2**	**0**	**1**	
1994-95	**Vancouver**	**NHL**	**46**	**13**	**10**	**23**	**36**	**1**	**0**	**4**	**75**	**17.3**	**8**				**3**	**0**	**1**	**1**	**0**	**0**	**0**	**0**	
1995-96	**Vancouver**	**NHL**	**81**	**30**	**26**	**56**	**59**	**3**	**4**	**5**	**181**	**16.6**	**8**				**6**	**1**	**1**	**2**	**12**	**1**	**0**	**0**	
1996-97	**Vancouver**	**NHL**	**74**	**35**	**33**	**68**	**42**	**6**	**1**	**3**	**177**	**19.8**	**6**												
1997-98	**Vancouver**	**NHL**	**24**	**4**	**4**	**8**	**10**	**1**	**1**	**1**	**49**	**8.2**	**-6**												
	Carolina	**NHL**	**40**	**12**	**14**	**26**	**30**	**2**	**1**	**4**	**98**	**12.2**	**1**												
1998-99	**Carolina**	**NHL**	**76**	**13**	**15**	**28**	**67**	**0**	**0**	**2**	**111**	**11.7**	**3**	**6**	**50.0**	**13:13**	**6**	**0**	**3**	**3**	**2**	**0**	**0**	**0**	**19:33**
99-2000	**Carolina**	**NHL**	**81**	**14**	**16**	**30**	**40**	**3**	**0**	**0**	**139**	**10.1**	**-10**	**5**	**40.0**	**13:39**									
2000-01	**Carolina**	**NHL**	**79**	**23**	**29**	**52**	**59**	**6**	**1**	**4**	**170**	**13.5**	**-4**	**6**	**0.0**	**17:54**	**6**	**0**	**1**	**1**	**6**	**0**	**0**	**0**	**17:51**
2001-02	**Carolina**	**NHL**	**72**	**13**	**16**	**29**	**30**	**3**	**0**	**1**	**121**	**10.7**	**-1**	**13**	**23.1**	**16:05**	**23**	**3**	**4**	**7**	**10**	**0**	**0**	**1**	**14:16**
2002-03	**Calgary**	**NHL**	**81**	**21**	**31**	**52**	**51**	**6**	**0**	**3**	**152**	**13.8**	**-3**	**96**	**51.0**	**16:33**									
2003-04	**Calgary**	**NHL**	**76**	**17**	**18**	**35**	**70**	**5**	**0**	**3**	**139**	**12.2**	**10**	**27**	**48.2**	**14:50**	**26**	**8**	**7**	**15**	**35**	**2**	**0**	**3**	**15:58**
2004-05	Morges	Swiss-2	41	37	21	58	81										4	2	2	4	24				
	HC Lugano	Swiss	1	0	0	0	0										5	0	1	1	2				
2005-06	**Florida**	**NHL**	**82**	**17**	**24**	**41**	**80**	**4**	**0**	**3**	**186**	**9.1**	**27**	**24**	**41.7**	**15:59**									
2006-07	**Florida**	**NHL**	**82**	**14**	**30**	**44**	**36**	**7**	**0**	**1**	**171**	**8.2**	**7**	**27**	**40.7**	**13:26**									
	NHL Totals		**1216**	**300**	**340**	**640**	**800**	**60**	**8**	**40**	**2272**	**13.2**		**204**	**44.6**	**15:12**	**147**	**23**	**33**	**56**	**120**	**5**	**0**	**6**	**15:51**

QMJHL First All-Star Team (1988) • QMJHL Offensive Rookie of the Year (1988) • Canadian Major Junior Rookie of the Year (1988) • George Parsons Trophy (Memorial Cup Tournament Most Sportsmanlike Player) (1988)

Traded to **Edmonton** by **Los Angeles** with Jimmy Carson and Los Angeles' 1st round choices in 1989 (later traded to New Jersey – New Jersey selected Jason Miller), 1991 (Martin Rucinsky) and 1993 (Nick Stajduhar) Entry Drafts and cash for Wayne Gretzky, Mike Krushelnyski and Marty McSorley, August 9, 1988. Traded to **Quebec** by **Edmonton** with Edmonton's 6th round choice (Nicholas Checco) in 1993 Entry Draft for Scott Pearson, June 20, 1993. Claimed on waivers by **Vancouver** from **Quebec**, January 15, 1994. Traded to **Carolina** by **Vancouver** with Kirk McLean for Sean Burke, Geoff Sanderson and Enrico Ciccone, January 3, 1998. Signed as a free agent by **Calgary**, July 2, 2002. Signed as a free agent by **Morges** (Swiss-2), September 23, 2004. Signed as a free agent by **Lugano** (Swiss), February 17, 2005. Signed as a free agent by **Florida**, August 2, 2005. Signed as a free agent by **Nashville**, July 26, 2007.

GERMYN, Carsen

(JUHR-mihn, KAHR-sehn) **CGY.**

Right wing. Shoots right. 5'10", 185 lbs. Born, Campbell River, B.C., February 22, 1982.

Season	Club	League	GP	G	A	Pts	PIM	PP	SH	GW	S	%	+/-	TF	F%	Min	Playoffs GP	G	A	Pts	PIM	PP	SH	GW	Min
1998-99	Kelowna Rockets	WHL	59	6	10	16	61										5	0	0	0	2				
99-2000	Kelowna Rockets	WHL	71	16	29	45	111										5	3	3	6	4				
2000-01	Kelowna Rockets	WHL	71	35	52	87	102										6	2	6	8	10				
2001-02	Kelowna Rockets	WHL	23	10	18	28	43																		
	Red Deer Rebels	WHL	37	23	25	48	83										23	4	12	16	24				
2002-03	Red Deer Rebels	WHL	63	26	33	59	108										23	4	9	13	25				
2003-04	Norfolk Admirals	AHL	77	11	16	27	104										6	1	0	1	2				
2004-05	Lowell	AHL	60	9	11	20	115										10	0	0	0	25				
2005-06	**Calgary**	**NHL**	**2**	**0**	**0**	**0**	**0**	**0**	**0**	**0**	**2**	**0.0**	**-1**	**0**	**0.0**	**5:00**									
	Omaha	AHL	77	24	31	55	127																		
2006-07	**Calgary**	**NHL**	**2**	**0**	**0**	**0**	**0**	**0**	**0**	**0**	**3**	**0.0**	**0**	**2**	**50.0**	**8:26**									
	Omaha	AHL	77	28	32	60	124										6	1	1	2	2				
	NHL Totals		**4**	**0**	**0**	**0**	**0**	**0**	**0**	**0**	**5**	**0.0**		**2**	**50.0**	**6:43**									

Signed as a free agent by **Calgary**, July 6, 2004.

GERVAIS, Bruno
(ZHUR-vay, BROO-noh) **NYI**

Defense. Shoots right. 6', 188 lbs. Born, Longueuil, Que., October 3, 1984. NY Islanders' 6th choice, 182nd overall, in 2003 Entry Draft.

			Regular Season														Playoffs								
Season	Club	League	GP	G	A	Pts	PIM	PP	SH	GW	S	%	+/-	TF	F%	Min	GP	G	A	Pts	PIM	PP	SH	GW	Min
99-2000	Antoine-Girouard	QAAA	6	0	0	0	0	....	....	....	....	....	....	....	....	....	4	0	0	0	0	....	....	....	....
2000-01	Antoine-Girouard	QAAA	40	8	27	35	46	....	....	....	....	....	....	....	....	....	7	4	2	6	8	....	....	....	....
2001-02	Acadie-Bathurst	QMJHL	65	4	12	16	42	....	....	....	....	....	....	....	....	....	16	3	1	4	8	....	....	....	....
2002-03	Acadie-Bathurst	QMJHL	72	22	28	50	73	....	....	....	....	....	....	....	....	....	11	3	5	8	14	....	....	....	....
2003-04	Acadie-Bathurst	QMJHL	23	4	6	10	28	....	....	....	....	....	....	....	....	....	....	....	....	....	....	....	....	....	....
2004-05	Bridgeport	AHL	76	8	22	30	58	....	....	....	....	....	....	....	....	....	....	....	....	....	....	....	....	....	....
2005-06	**NY Islanders**	**NHL**	**27**	**3**	**4**	**7**	**8**	**1**	**0**	**0**	**21**	**14.3**	**–1**	**0**	**0.0**	**16:47**	....	....	....	....	....	....	....	....	....
	Bridgeport	AHL	55	17	25	42	70	....	....	....	....	....	....	....	....	....	7	1	2	3	0	....	....	....	....
2006-07	**NY Islanders**	**NHL**	**51**	**0**	**6**	**6**	**28**	**0**	**0**	**0**	**47**	**0.0**	**–10**	**0**	**0.0**	**15:23**	**5**	**1**	**1**	**2**	**2**	**0**	**0**	**0**	**15:36**
	Bridgeport	AHL	3	0	0	0	6	....	....	....	....	....	....	....	....	....	....	....	....	....	....	....	....	....	....
	NHL Totals		**78**	**3**	**10**	**13**	**36**	**1**	**0**	**0**	**68**	**4.4**		**0**	**0.0**	**15:52**	**5**	**1**	**1**	**2**	**2**	**0**	**0**	**0**	**15:36**

QMJHL Second All-Star Team (2003)
• Missed majority of 2003-04 season recovering from knee injury suffered during Team Canada Jr. training camp, December 12, 2003.

GETZLAF, Ryan
(GEHTZ-laf, RIGH-uhn) **ANA.**

Center. Shoots right. 6'3", 211 lbs. Born, Regina, Sask., May 10, 1985. Anaheim's 1st choice, 19th overall, in 2003 Entry Draft.

			Regular Season														Playoffs								
Season	Club	League	GP	G	A	Pts	PIM	PP	SH	GW	S	%	+/-	TF	F%	Min	GP	G	A	Pts	PIM	PP	SH	GW	Min
2000-01	Regina Rangers	SBHL	41	33	41	74	189	....	....	....	....	....	....	....	....	....	....	....	....	....	....	....	....	....	....
	Reg. Pat Cdns.	SMHL	8	4	3	7	8	....	....	....	....	....	....	....	....	....	....	....	....	....	....	....	....	....	....
2001-02	Calgary Hitmen	WHL	63	9	9	18	34	....	....	....	....	....	....	....	....	....	7	2	1	3	4	....	....	....	....
2002-03	Calgary Hitmen	WHL	70	29	39	68	121	....	....	....	....	....	....	....	....	....	5	1	1	2	6	....	....	....	....
2003-04	Calgary Hitmen	WHL	49	28	47	75	97	....	....	....	....	....	....	....	....	....	7	5	1	6	12	....	....	....	....
2004-05	Calgary Hitmen	WHL	51	29	25	54	102	....	....	....	....	....	....	....	....	....	12	4	13	17	18	....	....	....	....
	Cincinnati	AHL	....	....	....	....	....	....	....	....	....	....	....	....	....	....	10	1	4	5	4	....	....	....	....
2005-06	**Anaheim**	**NHL**	**57**	**14**	**25**	**39**	**22**	**10**	**0**	**1**	**116**	**12.1**	**6**	**534**	**44.0**	**12:35**	**16**	**3**	**4**	**7**	**13**	**2**	**0**	**1**	**15:49**
	Portland Pirates	AHL	17	8	25	33	36	....	....	....	....	....	....	....	....	....	1	0	0	0	4	....	....	....	....
2006-07 ♦	**Anaheim**	**NHL**	**82**	**25**	**33**	**58**	**66**	**11**	**1**	**6**	**203**	**12.3**	**17**	**888**	**49.4**	**15:04**	**21**	**7**	**10**	**17**	**32**	**3**	**1**	**3**	**21:43**
	NHL Totals		**139**	**39**	**58**	**97**	**88**	**21**	**1**	**7**	**319**	**12.2**		**1422**	**47.4**	**14:02**	**37**	**10**	**14**	**24**	**45**	**5**	**1**	**4**	**19:10**

WHL East First All-Star Team (2004) • WHL East Second All-Star Team (2005)

GILBERT, Tom
(GIHL-buhrt, TAWM) **EDM.**

Defense. Shoots right. 6'3", 210 lbs. Born, Minneapolis, MN, January 10, 1983. Colorado's 5th choice, 129th overall, in 2002 Entry Draft.

			Regular Season														Playoffs								
Season	Club	League	GP	G	A	Pts	PIM	PP	SH	GW	S	%	+/-	TF	F%	Min	GP	G	A	Pts	PIM	PP	SH	GW	Min
99-2000	Bloomington-Jeff.	High-MN	18	7	18	25	....	....	....	....	....	....	....	....	....	....	....	....	....	....	....	....	....	....	....
2000-01	Bloomington-Jeff.	High-MN	23	20	18	38	....	....	....	....	....	....	....	....	....	....	....	....	....	....	....	....	....	....	....
	Chicago Steel	USHL	1	0	0	0	0	....	....	....	....	....	....	....	....	....	....	....	....	....	....	....	....	....	....
2001-02	Chicago Steel	USHL	57	13	15	28	62	....	....	....	....	....	....	....	....	....	4	0	0	0	4	....	....	....	....
2002-03	U. of Wisconsin	WCHA	39	7	13	20	36	....	....	....	....	....	....	....	....	....	....	....	....	....	....	....	....	....	....
2003-04	U. of Wisconsin	WCHA	39	6	15	21	36	....	....	....	....	....	....	....	....	....	....	....	....	....	....	....	....	....	....
2004-05	U. of Wisconsin	WCHA	41	8	9	17	48	....	....	....	....	....	....	....	....	....	....	....	....	....	....	....	....	....	....
2005-06	U. of Wisconsin	WCHA	43	12	19	31	32	....	....	....	....	....	....	....	....	....	....	....	....	....	....	....	....	....	....
2006-07	**Edmonton**	**NHL**	**12**	**1**	**5**	**6**	**0**	**0**	**0**	**0**	**13**	**7.7**	**–1**	**0**	**0.0**	**20:05**	....	....	....	....	....	....	....	....	....
	Wilkes-Barre	AHL	48	4	26	30	32	....	....	....	....	....	....	....	....	....	10	1	7	8	10	....	....	....	....
	NHL Totals		**12**	**1**	**5**	**6**	**0**	**0**	**0**	**0**	**13**	**7.7**		**0**	**0.0**	**20:05**	....	....	....	....	....	....	....	....	....

WCHA First All-Star Team (2006) • NCAA West Second All-American Team (2006) • NCAA Championship All-Tournament Team (2006)
Traded to **Edmonton** by **Colorado** for Tommy Salo and Edmonton's 6th round choice (Justin Mercier) in 2005 Entry Draft, March 8, 2004.

GILL, Hal
(GIHL, HAL) **TOR.**

Defense. Shoots left. 6'7", 250 lbs. Born, Concord, MA, April 6, 1975. Boston's 8th choice, 207th overall, in 1993 Entry Draft.

			Regular Season														Playoffs								
Season	Club	League	GP	G	A	Pts	PIM	PP	SH	GW	S	%	+/-	TF	F%	Min	GP	G	A	Pts	PIM	PP	SH	GW	Min
1992-93	Nashoba	High-MA	20	25	25	50	....	....	....	....	....	....	....	....	....	....	....	....	....	....	....	....	....	....	....
1993-94	Providence	H-East	31	1	2	3	26	....	....	....	....	....	....	....	....	....	....	....	....	....	....	....	....	....	....
1994-95	Providence	H-East	26	1	3	4	22	....	....	....	....	....	....	....	....	....	....	....	....	....	....	....	....	....	....
1995-96	Providence	H-East	39	5	12	17	54	....	....	....	....	....	....	....	....	....	....	....	....	....	....	....	....	....	....
1996-97	Providence	H-East	35	5	16	21	52	....	....	....	....	....	....	....	....	....	....	....	....	....	....	....	....	....	....
1997-98	**Boston**	**NHL**	**68**	**2**	**4**	**6**	**47**	**0**	**0**	**0**	**56**	**3.6**	**4**	....	....	....	**6**	**0**	**0**	**0**	**4**	**0**	**0**	**0**	....
	Providence Bruins	AHL	4	1	0	1	23	....	....	....	....	....	....	....	....	....	....	....	....	....	....	....	....	....	....
1998-99	**Boston**	**NHL**	**80**	**3**	**7**	**10**	**63**	**0**	**0**	**2**	**102**	**2.9**	**–10**	**1**	**100.0**	**20:54**	**12**	**0**	**0**	**0**	**14**	**0**	**0**	**0**	**20:41**
99-2000	**Boston**	**NHL**	**81**	**3**	**9**	**12**	**51**	**0**	**0**	**0**	**120**	**2.5**	**0**	**0**	**0.0**	**17:15**	....	....	....	....	....	....	....	....	....
2000-01	**Boston**	**NHL**	**80**	**1**	**10**	**11**	**71**	**0**	**0**	**0**	**79**	**1.3**	**–2**	**0**	**0.0**	**18:21**	....	....	....	....	....	....	....	....	....
2001-02	**Boston**	**NHL**	**79**	**4**	**18**	**22**	**77**	**0**	**0**	**0**	**137**	**2.9**	**16**	**0**	**0.0**	**24:13**	**6**	**0**	**1**	**1**	**2**	**0**	**0**	**0**	**23:04**
2002-03	**Boston**	**NHL**	**76**	**4**	**13**	**17**	**56**	**0**	**0**	**0**	**114**	**3.5**	**21**	**0**	**0.0**	**20:42**	**5**	**0**	**0**	**0**	**4**	**0**	**0**	**0**	**20:19**
2003-04	**Boston**	**NHL**	**82**	**2**	**7**	**9**	**99**	**0**	**0**	**0**	**104**	**1.9**	**16**	**0**	**0.0**	**18:24**	**7**	**0**	**1**	**1**	**4**	**0**	**0**	**0**	**19:03**
2004-05	Lukko Rauma	Finland	31	2	8	10	110	....	....	....	....	....	....	....	....	....	8	0	0	0	*57	....	....	....	....
2005-06	**Boston**	**NHL**	**80**	**1**	**9**	**10**	**124**	**0**	**0**	**0**	**68**	**1.5**	**–4**	**0**	**0.0**	**18:37**	....	....	....	....	....	....	....	....	....
2006-07	**Toronto**	**NHL**	**82**	**6**	**14**	**20**	**91**	**0**	**0**	**1**	**79**	**7.6**	**11**	**1**	**0.0**	**18:53**	....	....	....	....	....	....	....	....	....
	NHL Totals		**708**	**26**	**91**	**117**	**679**	**0**	**0**	**3**	**859**	**3.0**		**2**	**50.0**	**19:38**	**36**	**0**	**2**	**2**	**28**	**0**	**0**	**0**	**20:43**

Signed as a free agent by **Rauma** (Finland), November 25, 2004. Signed as a free agent by **Toronto**, July 1, 2006.

GILLIES, Trevor
(GIHL-eez, TREH-vuhr) **CAR.**

Left wing. Shoots left. 6'3", 215 lbs. Born, Cambridge, Ont., January 30, 1979.

			Regular Season														Playoffs								
Season	Club	League	GP	G	A	Pts	PIM	PP	SH	GW	S	%	+/-	TF	F%	Min	GP	G	A	Pts	PIM	PP	SH	GW	Min
1996-97	North Bay	OHL	26	0	3	3	72	....	....	....	....	....	....	....	....	....	....	....	....	....	....	....	....	....	....
1997-98	North Bay	OHL	2	0	0	0	4	....	....	....	....	....	....	....	....	....	....	....	....	....	....	....	....	....	....
	Sarnia Sting	OHL	17	0	1	1	33	....	....	....	....	....	....	....	....	....	....	....	....	....	....	....	....	....	....
	Oshawa Generals	OHL	45	1	2	3	184	....	....	....	....	....	....	....	....	....	7	0	1	1	12	....	....	....	....
1998-99	Oshawa Generals	OHL	66	6	9	15	270	....	....	....	....	....	....	....	....	....	11	0	2	2	28	....	....	....	....
99-2000	Lowell	AHL	8	0	0	0	38	....	....	....	....	....	....	....	....	....	....	....	....	....	....	....	....	....	....
	Mississippi	ECHL	53	0	6	6	202	....	....	....	....	....	....	....	....	....	....	....	....	....	....	....	....	....	....
2000-01	Greensboro	ECHL	63	1	6	7	303	....	....	....	....	....	....	....	....	....	....	....	....	....	....	....	....	....	....
	Worcester IceCats	AHL	....	....	....	....	....	....	....	....	....	....	....	....	....	....	6	0	0	0	24	....	....	....	....
2001-02	Providence Bruins	AHL	5	0	0	0	21	....	....	....	....	....	....	....	....	....	....	....	....	....	....	....	....	....	....
	Augusta Lynx	ECHL	46	0	1	1	*269	....	....	....	....	....	....	....	....	....	....	....	....	....	....	....	....	....	....
	Richmond	ECHL	18	0	1	1	*51	....	....	....	....	....	....	....	....	....	....	....	....	....	....	....	....	....	....
2002-03	Lowell	AHL	25	0	1	1	132	....	....	....	....	....	....	....	....	....	....	....	....	....	....	....	....	....	....
	Richmond	ECHL	6	0	0	0	20	....	....	....	....	....	....	....	....	....	....	....	....	....	....	....	....	....	....
	Peoria Rivermen	ECHL	24	0	1	1	180	....	....	....	....	....	....	....	....	....	....	....	....	....	....	....	....	....	....
2003-04	Springfield	AHL	61	2	1	3	277	....	....	....	....	....	....	....	....	....	....	....	....	....	....	....	....	....	....
2004-05	Hartford	AHL	49	0	2	2	277	....	....	....	....	....	....	....	....	....	....	....	....	....	....	....	....	....	....
2005-06	**Anaheim**	**NHL**	**1**	**0**	**0**	**0**	**21**	**0**	**0**	**0**	**1**	**0.0**	**0**	**0**	**0.0**	**2:40**	....	....	....	....	....	....	....	....	....
	Portland Pirates	AHL	50	2	3	5	169	....	....	....	....	....	....	....	....	....	4	0	0	0	0	....	....	....	....
2006-07	Portland Pirates	AHL	51	1	6	7	151	....	....	....	....	....	....	....	....	....	....	....	....	....	....	....	....	....	....
	Augusta Lynx	ECHL	7	0	2	2	23	....	....	....	....	....	....	....	....	....	....	....	....	....	....	....	....	....	....
	NHL Totals		**1**	**0**	**0**	**0**	**21**	**0**	**0**	**0**	**1**	**0.0**		**0**	**0.0**	**2:40**	....	....	....	....	....	....	....	....	....

Signed as a free agent by **NY Rangers**, July 20, 2004. Traded to **Anaheim** by **NY Rangers** with NY Rangers' 4th round choice (later traded back to NY Rangers - later traded to Washington - Washington selected Brett Bruneteau) in 2007 Entry Draft for Steve Rucchin, August 23, 2005. Signed as a free agent by **Carolina**, July 2, 2007.

GIONTA, Brian
(jee-OHN-tuh, BRIGH-uhn) **N.J.**

Right wing. Shoots right. 5'7", 175 lbs. Born, Rochester, NY, January 18, 1979. New Jersey's 4th choice, 82nd overall, in 1998 Entry Draft.

			Regular Season														Playoffs								
Season	Club	League	GP	G	A	Pts	PIM	PP	SH	GW	S	%	+/-	TF	F%	Min	GP	G	A	Pts	PIM	PP	SH	GW	Min
1994-95	Rochester	EmJHL	28	*52	37	*89	....	....	....	....	....	....	....	....	....	....	....	....	....	....	....	....	....	....	....
1995-96	Niagara Scenic	MTJHL	51	47	44	91	59	....	....	....	....	....	....	....	....	....	....	....	....	....	....	....	....	....	....
1996-97	Niagara Scenic	MTJHL	50	57	70	127	101	....	....	....	....	....	....	....	....	....	6	6	11	17	21	....	....	....	....
1997-98	Boston College	H-East	40	30	32	62	44	....	....	....	....	....	....	....	....	....	....	....	....	....	....	....	....	....	....
1998-99	Boston College	H-East	39	27	33	60	46	....	....	....	....	....	....	....	....	....	....	....	....	....	....	....	....	....	....
99-2000	Boston College	H-East	42	*33	23	56	66	....	....	....	....	....	....	....	....	....	....	....	....	....	....	....	....	....	....

			Regular Season														Playoffs								
Season	Club	League	GP	G	A	Pts	PIM	PP	SH	GW	S	%	+/-	TF	F%	Min	GP	G	A	Pts	PIM	PP	SH	GW	Min
2000-01	Boston College	H-East	43	*33	21	*54	47	....	....	....	....	....	....	....	....	....	....	....	....	....	....	....	....	....	....
2001-02	**New Jersey**	**NHL**	**33**	**4**	**7**	**11**	**8**	**0**	**0**	**0**	**58**	**6.9**	**10**	**36**	**44.4**	**13:25**	**6**	**2**	**2**	**4**	**0**	**0**	**1**	**2**	**17:08**
	Albany River Rats	AHL	37	9	16	25	18	....	....	....	....	....	....	....	....	....	....	....	....	....	....	....	....	....	....
2002-03 ♦	**New Jersey**	**NHL**	**58**	**12**	**13**	**25**	**23**	**2**	**0**	**3**	**129**	**9.3**	**5**	**14**	**57.1**	**14:48**	**24**	**1**	**8**	**9**	**6**	**0**	**0**	**0**	**14:31**
2003-04	**New Jersey**	**NHL**	**75**	**21**	**8**	**29**	**36**	**0**	**0**	**8**	**174**	**12.1**	**19**	**60**	**58.3**	**14:44**	**5**	**2**	**3**	**5**	**0**	**1**	**0**	**0**	**15:41**
2004-05	Albany River Rats	AHL	15	5	7	12	10	....	....	....	....	....	....	....	....	....	....	....	....	....	....	....	....	....	....
2005-06	**New Jersey**	**NHL**	**82**	**48**	**41**	**89**	**46**	**24**	**1**	**10**	**291**	**16.5**	**18**	**73**	**38.4**	**19:49**	**9**	**3**	**4**	**7**	**2**	**1**	**1**	**2**	**20:06**
	United States	Olympics	6	4	0	4	2	....	....	....	....	....	....	....	....	....	....	....	....	....	....	....	....	....	....
2006-07	**New Jersey**	**NHL**	**62**	**25**	**20**	**45**	**36**	**11**	**0**	**4**	**194**	**12.9**	**–3**	**31**	**38.7**	**18:49**	**11**	**8**	**1**	**9**	**4**	**3**	**0**	**1**	**19:15**
	NHL Totals		**310**	**110**	**89**	**199**	**149**	**37**	**1**	**25**	**846**	**13.0**		**214**	**46.3**	**16:46**	**55**	**16**	**18**	**34**	**12**	**5**	**2**	**5**	**16:46**

Hockey East Rookie of the Year (1998) • Hockey East Second All-Star Team (1998) • NCAA East Second All-American Team (1998) • Hockey East First All-Star Team (1999, 2000, 2001) • NCAA East First All-American Team (1999, 2000, 2001) • Hockey East Player of the Year (2001)

GIORDANO, Mark

(jee-ohr-DAN-oh, MAHRK) **CGY.**

Defense. Shoots left. 6', 203 lbs. Born, Toronto, Ont., October 3, 1983.

Season	Club	League	GP	G	A	Pts	PIM	PP	SH	GW	S	%	+/-	TF	F%	Min	GP	G	A	Pts	PIM	PP	SH	GW	Min
2002-03	Owen Sound	OHL	68	18	30	48	109	....	....	....	....	....	....	....	....	....	4	1	3	4	2	....	....	....	....
2003-04	Owen Sound	OHL	65	14	35	49	72	....	....	....	....	....	....	....	....	....	7	1	3	4	5	....	....	....	....
2004-05	Lowell	AHL	66	6	10	16	85	....	....	....	....	....	....	....	....	....	11	0	1	1	41	....	....	....	....
2005-06	**Calgary**	**NHL**	**7**	**0**	**1**	**1**	**8**	**0**	**0**	**0**	**5**	**0.0**	**2**	**0**	**0.0**	**12:05**	....	....	....	....	....	....	....	....	....
	Omaha	AHL	73	16	42	58	141	....	....	....	....	....	....	....	....	....	....	....	....	....	....	....	....	....	....
2006-07	**Calgary**	**NHL**	**48**	**7**	**8**	**15**	**36**	**3**	**0**	**2**	**49**	**14.3**	**7**	**0**	**0.0**	**13:27**	**4**	**1**	**0**	**1**	**0**	**1**	**0**	**0**	**12:16**
	Omaha	AHL	5	0	2	2	8	....	....	....	....	....	....	....	....	....	3	0	1	1	2	....	....	....	....
	NHL Totals		**55**	**7**	**9**	**16**	**44**	**3**	**0**	**2**	**54**	**13.0**		**0**	**0.0**	**13:16**	**4**	**1**	**0**	**1**	**0**	**1**	**0**	**0**	**12:16**

Signed as a free agent by **Calgary**, July 6, 2004.

GIRARDI, Dan

(jih-RAHR-dee, DAN) **NYR**

Defense. Shoots right. 6'2", 205 lbs. Born, Welland, Ont., April 29, 1984.

Season	Club	League	GP	G	A	Pts	PIM	PP	SH	GW	S	%	+/-	TF	F%	Min	GP	G	A	Pts	PIM	PP	SH	GW	Min
2000-01	Barrie Colts	OHL	6	0	0	0	0	....	....	....	....	....	....	....	....	....	....	....	....	....	....	....	....	....	....
2001-02	Barrie Colts	OHL	21	0	1	1	0	....	....	....	....	....	....	....	....	....	20	0	0	0	0	....	....	....	....
2002-03	Barrie Colts	OHL	31	3	13	16	24	....	....	....	....	....	....	....	....	....	....	....	....	....	....	....	....	....	....
	Guelph Storm	OHL	36	1	13	14	20	....	....	....	....	....	....	....	....	....	11	0	9	9	14	....	....	....	....
2003-04	Guelph Storm	OHL	68	8	39	47	55	....	....	....	....	....	....	....	....	....	22	2	17	19	10	....	....	....	....
2004-05	Guelph Storm	OHL	38	5	20	25	24	....	....	....	....	....	....	....	....	....	....	....	....	....	....	....	....	....	....
	London Knights	OHL	31	4	10	14	14	....	....	....	....	....	....	....	....	....	18	0	6	6	10	....	....	....	....
2005-06	Hartford	AHL	66	8	31	39	44	....	....	....	....	....	....	....	....	....	13	4	5	9	8	....	....	....	....
	Charlotte	ECHL	7	1	4	5	6	....	....	....	....	....	....	....	....	....	....	....	....	....	....	....	....	....	....
2006-07	**NY Rangers**	**NHL**	**34**	**0**	**6**	**6**	**8**	**0**	**0**	**0**	**33**	**0.0**	**7**	**0**	**0.0**	**15:50**	**10**	**0**	**0**	**0**	**4**	**0**	**0**	**0**	**19:52**
	Hartford	AHL	45	2	22	24	16	....	....	....	....	....	....	....	....	....	....	....	....	....	....	....	....	....	....
	NHL Totals		**34**	**0**	**6**	**6**	**8**	**0**	**0**	**0**	**33**	**0.0**		**0**	**0.0**	**15:50**	**10**	**0**	**0**	**0**	**4**	**0**	**0**	**0**	**19:52**

AHL All-Rookie Team (2006)

Signed as a free agent by **NY Rangers**, July 1, 2006.

GIROUX, Alexandre

(ZHIH-roo, al-ehx-AHN-druh) **ATL.**

Center/Left wing. Shoots left. 6'3", 190 lbs. Born, Quebec City, Que., June 16, 1981. Ottawa's 9th choice, 213th overall, in 1999 Entry Draft.

Season	Club	League	GP	G	A	Pts	PIM	PP	SH	GW	S	%	+/-	TF	F%	Min	GP	G	A	Pts	PIM	PP	SH	GW	Min
1997-98	Ste-Foy	QAAA	42	28	30	58	96	....	....	....	....	....	....	....	....	....	....	....	....	....	....	....	....	....	....
1998-99	Hull Olympiques	QMJHL	67	15	22	37	124	....	....	....	....	....	....	....	....	....	22	2	2	4	8	....	....	....	....
99-2000	Hull Olympiques	QMJHL	72	52	47	99	117	....	....	....	....	....	....	....	....	....	15	12	6	18	30	....	....	....	....
2000-01	Hull Olympiques	QMJHL	38	31	32	63	62	....	....	....	....	....	....	....	....	....	....	....	....	....	....	....	....	....	....
	Rouyn-Noranda	QMJHL	25	13	14	27	56	....	....	....	....	....	....	....	....	....	9	2	6	8	22	....	....	....	....
2001-02	Grand Rapids	AHL	70	11	16	27	74	....	....	....	....	....	....	....	....	....	....	....	....	....	....	....	....	....	....
2002-03	Binghamton	AHL	67	19	16	35	101	....	....	....	....	....	....	....	....	....	10	1	0	1	10	....	....	....	....
2003-04	Binghamton	AHL	59	19	23	42	79	....	....	....	....	....	....	....	....	....	....	....	....	....	....	....	....	....	....
	Hartford	AHL	16	6	3	9	13	....	....	....	....	....	....	....	....	....	16	3	4	7	28	....	....	....	....
2004-05	Hartford	AHL	78	32	22	54	128	....	....	....	....	....	....	....	....	....	6	3	3	6	23	....	....	....	....
2005-06	**NY Rangers**	**NHL**	**1**	**0**	**0**	**0**	**0**	**0**	**0**	**0**	**0**	**0.0**	**–1**	**0**	**0.0**	**2:50**	....	....	....	....	....	....	....	....	....
	Hartford	AHL	73	36	31	67	102	....	....	....	....	....	....	....	....	....	13	7	9	16	17	....	....	....	....
2006-07	**Washington**	**NHL**	**9**	**2**	**2**	**4**	**2**	**0**	**0**	**0**	**11**	**18.2**	**–4**	**2**	**50.0**	**10:11**	....	....	....	....	....	....	....	....	....
	Hershey Bears	AHL	67	42	28	70	82	....	....	....	....	....	....	....	....	....	19	4	7	11	27	....	....	....	....
	NHL Totals		**10**	**2**	**2**	**4**	**2**	**0**	**0**	**0**	**11**	**18.2**		**2**	**50.0**	**9:27**	....	....	....	....	....	....	....	....	....

Traded to **NY Rangers** by **Ottawa** with Karel Rachunek for Greg De Vries, March 9, 2004. Signed as a free agent by **Washington**, July 14, 2006. Signed as a free agent by **Atlanta**, July 13, 2007.

GIROUX, Raymond

(zhih-ROO, ray-MAWN)

Defense. Shoots left. 6'1", 190 lbs. Born, North Bay, Ont., July 20, 1976. Philadelphia's 7th choice, 202nd overall, in 1994 Entry Draft.

Season	Club	League	GP	G	A	Pts	PIM	PP	SH	GW	S	%	+/-	TF	F%	Min	GP	G	A	Pts	PIM	PP	SH	GW	Min
1992-93	Powassan Hawks	NOHA	45	8	18	26	117	....	....	....	....	....	....	....	....	....	....	....	....	....	....	....	....	....	....
1993-94	Powassan Hawks	NOJHA	36	10	40	50	42	....	....	....	....	....	....	....	....	....	....	....	....	....	....	....	....	....	....
1994-95	Yale	ECAC	27	1	3	4	8	....	....	....	....	....	....	....	....	....	....	....	....	....	....	....	....	....	....
1995-96	Yale	ECAC	30	3	16	19	36	....	....	....	....	....	....	....	....	....	....	....	....	....	....	....	....	....	....
1996-97	Yale	ECAC	32	9	12	21	38	....	....	....	....	....	....	....	....	....	....	....	....	....	....	....	....	....	....
1997-98	Yale	ECAC	35	9	*30	39	62	....	....	....	....	....	....	....	....	....	....	....	....	....	....	....	....	....	....
1998-99	Lowell	AHL	59	13	19	32	92	....	....	....	....	....	....	....	....	....	3	1	1	2	0	....	....	....	....
99-2000	**NY Islanders**	**NHL**	**14**	**0**	**9**	**9**	**10**	**0**	**0**	**0**	**24**	**0.0**	**0**	**9**	**22.2**	**14:40**	....	....	....	....	....	....	....	....	....
	Lowell	AHL	49	12	21	33	34	....	....	....	....	....	....	....	....	....	7	0	0	0	2	....	....	....	....
2000-01	HIFK Helsinki	Finland	22	3	9	12	34	....	....	....	....	....	....	....	....	....	....	....	....	....	....	....	....	....	....
	AIK Solna	Sweden	9	0	1	1	16	....	....	....	....	....	....	....	....	....	....	....	....	....	....	....	....	....	....
	Jokerit Helsinki	Finland	24	4	9	13	16	....	....	....	....	....	....	....	....	....	5	0	0	0	0	....	....	....	....
2001-02	**NY Islanders**	**NHL**	**2**	**0**	**0**	**0**	**2**	**0**	**0**	**0**	**2**	**0.0**	**–1**	**0**	**0.0**	**12:18**	....	....	....	....	....	....	....	....	....
	Bridgeport	AHL	79	13	40	53	73	....	....	....	....	....	....	....	....	....	19	1	7	8	20	....	....	....	....
2002-03	**New Jersey**	**NHL**	**11**	**0**	**1**	**1**	**6**	**0**	**0**	**0**	**20**	**0.0**	**–2**	**0**	**0.0**	**18:18**	....	....	....	....	....	....	....	....	....
	Albany River Rats	AHL	67	11	38	49	49	....	....	....	....	....	....	....	....	....	....	....	....	....	....	....	....	....	....
2003-04	**New Jersey**	**NHL**	**11**	**0**	**3**	**3**	**4**	**0**	**0**	**0**	**17**	**0.0**	**–3**	**0**	**0.0**	**20:55**	**4**	**0**	**0**	**0**	**0**	**0**	**0**	**0**	**15:15**
	Albany River Rats	AHL	65	11	17	28	34	....	....	....	....	....	....	....	....	....	....	....	....	....	....	....	....	....	....
2004-05	Houston Aeros	AHL	70	13	20	33	54	....	....	....	....	....	....	....	....	....	5	0	0	0	13	....	....	....	....
2005-06	Ak Bars Kazan	Russia	46	9	11	20	56	....	....	....	....	....	....	....	....	....	13	3	8	11	14	....	....	....	....
2006-07	Ak Bars Kazan	Russia	50	13	27	40	83	....	....	....	....	....	....	....	....	....	16	3	5	8	22	....	....	....	....
	NHL Totals		**38**	**0**	**13**	**13**	**22**	**0**	**0**	**0**	**63**	**0.0**		**9**	**22.2**	**17:24**	**4**	**0**	**0**	**0**	**0**	**0**	**0**	**0**	**15:15**

ECAC First All-Star Team (1998) • ECAC Player of the Year (1998) • NCAA East First All-American Team (1998) • AHL First All-Star Team (2003)

Rights traded to **NY Islanders** by **Philadelphia** for NY Islanders' 6th round choice (later traded to Montreal – Montreal selected Scott Selig) in 2000 Entry Draft, August 25, 1998. Signed as a free agent by **New Jersey**, July 12, 2002. Signed as a free agent by **Minnesota**, July 7, 2004. Signed as a free agent by **Kazan** (Russia), September 11, 2005.

GIULIANO, Jeff

(JOO-lee-A-noh, JEHF) **L.A.**

Left wing. Shoots left. 5'9", 205 lbs. Born, Nashua, NH, June 20, 1979.

Season	Club	League	GP	G	A	Pts	PIM	PP	SH	GW	S	%	+/-	TF	F%	Min	GP	G	A	Pts	PIM	PP	SH	GW	Min
1998-99	Boston College	H-East	43	5	15	20	10	....	....	....	....	....	....	....	....	....	....	....	....	....	....	....	....	....	....
99-2000	Boston College	H-East	42	10	13	23	16	....	....	....	....	....	....	....	....	....	....	....	....	....	....	....	....	....	....
2000-01	Boston College	H-East	43	14	22	36	28	....	....	....	....	....	....	....	....	....	....	....	....	....	....	....	....	....	....
2001-02	Boston College	H-East	38	11	24	35	14	....	....	....	....	....	....	....	....	....	....	....	....	....	....	....	....	....	....
2002-03	Manchester	AHL	47	4	11	15	8	....	....	....	....	....	....	....	....	....	3	1	0	1	0	....	....	....	....
	Reading Royals	ECHL	38	7	23	30	6	....	....	....	....	....	....	....	....	....	....	....	....	....	....	....	....	....	....
2003-04	Manchester	AHL	80	6	14	20	16	....	....	....	....	....	....	....	....	....	1	0	0	0	0	....	....	....	....
2004-05	Manchester	AHL	69	8	16	24	21	....	....	....	....	....	....	....	....	....	2	0	0	0	0	....	....	....	....

			Regular Season														Playoffs								
Season	Club	League	GP	G	A	Pts	PIM	PP	SH	GW	S	%	+/-	TF	F%	Min	GP	G	A	Pts	PIM	PP	SH	GW	Min
2005-06	Los Angeles	NHL	48	3	4	7	26	0	0	2	32	9.4	0	252	46.0	9:45	....	....	....	....	....	....	....	....	....
	Manchester	AHL	19	5	6	11	17	....	....	....	....	....	....	....	....	....	7	3	1	4	2	....	....	....	....
2006-07	Manchester	AHL	35	4	10	14	27	....	....	....	....	....	....	....	....	....	16	3	3	6	12	....	....	....	....
	NHL Totals		48	3	4	7	26	0	0	2	32	9.4		252	46.0	9:45	....	....	....	....	....	....	....	....	....

Signed as a free agent by **Los Angeles**, August 12, 2005. • Missed majority of 2006-07 season recovering from a recurring abdominal injury.

GLEASON, Tim

(GLEE-suhn, TIHM) **CAR.**

Defense. Shoots left. 6', 217 lbs. Born, Clawson, MI, January 29, 1983. Ottawa's 2nd choice, 23rd overall, in 2001 Entry Draft.

Season	Club	League	GP	G	A	Pts	PIM	PP	SH	GW	S	%	+/-	TF	F%	Min	GP	G	A	Pts	PIM	PP	SH	GW	Min
1998-99	Leamington Flyers	OHA-B	52	5	26	31	76	....	....	....	....	....	....	....	....	....	....	....	....	....	....	....	....	....	....
99-2000	Windsor Spitfires	OHL	55	5	13	18	101	....	....	....	....	....	....	....	....	....	12	2	4	6	14	....	....	....	....
2000-01	Windsor Spitfires	OHL	47	8	28	36	124	....	....	....	....	....	....	....	....	....	9	1	2	3	23	....	....	....	....
2001-02	Windsor Spitfires	OHL	67	17	42	59	109	....	....	....	....	....	....	....	....	....	16	7	13	20	40	....	....	....	....
2002-03	Windsor Spitfires	OHL	45	7	31	38	75	....	....	....	....	....	....	....	....	....	7	5	2	7	17	....	....	....	....
2003-04	Los Angeles	NHL	47	0	7	7	21	0	0	0	45	0.0	1	0	0.0	14:59	....	....	....	....	....	....	....	....	....
	Manchester	AHL	22	0	8	8	19	....	....	....	....	....	....	....	....	....	6	0	1	1	4	....	....	....	....
2004-05	Manchester	AHL	67	10	14	24	112	....	....	....	....	....	....	....	....	....	5	0	0	0	4	....	....	....	....
2005-06	Los Angeles	NHL	78	2	19	21	77	0	0	0	72	2.8	0	0	0.0	17:41	....	....	....	....	....	....	....	....	....
2006-07	Carolina	NHL	57	2	4	6	57	1	0	0	72	2.8	−10	0	0.0	18:53	....	....	....	....	....	....	....	....	....
	NHL Totals		182	4	30	34	155	1	0	0	189	2.1		0	0.0	17:22	....	....	....	....	....	....	....	....	....

Rights traded to **Los Angeles** by **Ottawa** for Bryan Smolinski, March 11, 2003. Traded to **Carolina** by **Los Angeles** with Eric Belanger for Oleg Tverdovsky and Jack Johnson, September 29, 2006.

GLENCROSS, Curtis

(GLEHN-kraws, KUHR-tihs) **CBJ**

Center. Shoots left. 6'1", 195 lbs. Born, Kindersley, Sask., December 28, 1982.

Season	Club	League	GP	G	A	Pts	PIM	PP	SH	GW	S	%	+/-	TF	F%	Min	GP	G	A	Pts	PIM	PP	SH	GW	Min
2001-02	Brooks Bandits	AJHL	....	42	26	68		....	....	....	....	....	....	....	....	....	....	....	....	....	....	....	....	....	....
2002-03	Alaska Anchorage	WCHA	35	11	12	23	79	....	....	....	....	....	....	....	....	....	....	....	....	....	....	....	....	....	....
2003-04	Alaska Anchorage	WCHA	37	21	13	34	79	....	....	....	....	....	....	....	....	....	....	....	....	....	....	....	....	....	....
	Cincinnati	AHL	7	2	1	3	6	....	....	....	....	....	....	....	....	....	9	1	6	7	10	....	....	....	....
2004-05	Cincinnati	AHL	51	6	3	9	63	....	....	....	....	....	....	....	....	....	12	2	0	2	10	....	....	....	....
2005-06	Portland Pirates	AHL	41	15	10	25	85	....	....	....	....	....	....	....	....	....	19	4	6	10	37	....	....	....	....
2006-07	Anaheim	NHL	2	1	0	1	2	0	0	0	5	20.0	−1	0	0.0	10:43	....	....	....	....	....	....	....	....	....
	Portland Pirates	AHL	31	6	10	16	74	....	....	....	....	....	....	....	....	....	....	....	....	....	....	....	....	....	....
	Columbus	NHL	7	0	0	0	0	0	0	0	3	0.0	−4	2	0.0	8:43	....	....	....	....	....	....	....	....	....
	Syracuse Crunch	AHL	29	19	16	35	53	....	....	....	....	....	....	....	....	....	....	....	....	....	....	....	....	....	....
	NHL Totals		9	1	0	1	2	0	0	0	8	12.5		2	0.0	9:09	....	....	....	....	....	....	....	....	....

Signed as a free agent by **Anaheim**, March 25, 2004. Traded to **Columbus** by **Anaheim** with Zenon Konopka and Anaheim's 7th round choice (Trent Vogelhuber) in 2007 Entry Draft for Mark Hartigan, Joe Motzko and Columbus' 4th round choice (Sebastian Stefaniszin) in 2007 Entry Draft, January 26, 2007.

GLOBKE, Rob

(GLAWB-kee, RAWB) **FLA.**

Center. Shoots right. 6'2", 208 lbs. Born, Farmington, MI, October 24, 1982. Florida's 3rd choice, 40th overall, in 2002 Entry Draft.

Season	Club	League	GP	G	A	Pts	PIM	PP	SH	GW	S	%	+/-	TF	F%	Min	GP	G	A	Pts	PIM	PP	SH	GW	Min
1998-99	Det. Compuware	NAHL	55	8	14	22	111	....	....	....	....	....	....	....	....	....	7	1	2	3	2	....	....	....	....
99-2000	USNTDP	U-18	6	4	2	6	6	....	....	....	....	....	....	....	....	....	....	....	....	....	....	....	....	....	....
	USNTDP	USHL	54	15	21	36	68	....	....	....	....	....	....	....	....	....	....	....	....	....	....	....	....	....	....
2000-01	U. of Notre Dame	CCHA	33	17	9	26	74	....	....	....	....	....	....	....	....	....	....	....	....	....	....	....	....	....	....
2001-02	U. of Notre Dame	CCHA	33	11	11	22	79	....	....	....	....	....	....	....	....	....	....	....	....	....	....	....	....	....	....
2002-03	U. of Notre Dame	CCHA	40	21	15	36	44	....	....	....	....	....	....	....	....	....	....	....	....	....	....	....	....	....	....
2003-04	U. of Notre Dame	CCHA	39	19	21	40	42	....	....	....	....	....	....	....	....	....	....	....	....	....	....	....	....	....	....
2004-05	San Antonio	AHL	63	6	6	12	21	....	....	....	....	....	....	....	....	....	....	....	....	....	....	....	....	....	....
	Texas Wildcatters	ECHL	10	8	4	12	13	....	....	....	....	....	....	....	....	....	....	....	....	....	....	....	....	....	....
2005-06	Florida	NHL	18	1	0	1	6	0	0	0	18	5.6	0	1	0.0	7:17	....	....	....	....	....	....	....	....	....
	Rochester	AHL	52	6	9	15	54	....	....	....	....	....	....	....	....	....	....	....	....	....	....	....	....	....	....
2006-07	Florida	NHL	19	0	1	1	0	0	0	0	15	0.0	−3	0	0.0	6:04	....	....	....	....	....	....	....	....	....
	Rochester	AHL	48	7	11	18	37	....	....	....	....	....	....	....	....	....	4	0	0	0	0	....	....	....	....
	NHL Totals		37	1	1	2	6	0	0	0	33	3.0		1	0.0	6:40	....	....	....	....	....	....	....	....	....

CCHA Second All-Star Team (2004)

GLUMAC, Mike

(GLOO-kmak, MIGHK) **ST.L.**

Right wing. Shoots right. 6'2", 200 lbs. Born, Niagara Falls, Ont., April 5, 1980.

Season	Club	League	GP	G	A	Pts	PIM	PP	SH	GW	S	%	+/-	TF	F%	Min	GP	G	A	Pts	PIM	PP	SH	GW	Min
1996-97	St. Mike's B's	OPJHL	50	13	25	38	33	....	....	....	....	....	....	....	....	....	6	1	0	1	2	....	....	....	....
1997-98	Newmarket	OPJHL	36	16	16	32	57	....	....	....	....	....	....	....	....	....	....	....	....	....	....	....	....	....	....
1998-99	Miami U.	CCHA	35	2	0	2	44	....	....	....	....	....	....	....	....	....	....	....	....	....	....	....	....	....	....
99-2000	Miami U.	CCHA	36	8	5	13	52	....	....	....	....	....	....	....	....	....	....	....	....	....	....	....	....	....	....
2000-01	Miami U.	CCHA	37	9	10	19	46	....	....	....	....	....	....	....	....	....	....	....	....	....	....	....	....	....	....
2001-02	Miami U.	CCHA	36	15	8	23	28	....	....	....	....	....	....	....	....	....	....	....	....	....	....	....	....	....	....
2002-03	Pee Dee Pride	ECHL	69	37	32	69	49	....	....	....	....	....	....	....	....	....	....	....	....	....	....	....	....	....	....
	Cleveland Barons	AHL	2	0	0	0	0	....	....	....	....	....	....	....	....	....	....	....	....	....	....	....	....	....	....
2003-04	Worcester IceCats	AHL	80	28	24	52	74	....	....	....	....	....	....	....	....	....	10	3	3	6	11	....	....	....	....
2004-05	Worcester IceCats	AHL	45	12	17	29	27	....	....	....	....	....	....	....	....	....	....	....	....	....	....	....	....	....	....
2005-06	St. Louis	NHL	33	7	5	12	33	5	0	0	55	12.7	−8	5	40.0	12:25	....	....	....	....	....	....	....	....	....
	Peoria Rivermen	AHL	49	25	32	57	64	....	....	....	....	....	....	....	....	....	4	1	1	2	5	....	....	....	....
2006-07	St. Louis	NHL	3	0	1	1	0	0	0	0	4	0.0	1	0	0.0	8:24	....	....	....	....	....	....	....	....	....
	Peoria Rivermen	AHL	72	27	30	57	115	....	....	....	....	....	....	....	....	....	....	....	....	....	....	....	....	....	....
	NHL Totals		36	7	6	13	33	5	0	0	59	11.9		5	40.0	12:05	....	....	....	....	....	....	....	....	....

ECHL All-Rookie Team (2003)

Signed as a free agent by **Pee Dee** (ECHL), August 28, 2002. Signed as a free agent by **Worcester** (AHL), October 6, 2003. Signed as a free agent by **St. Louis**, June 29, 2004.

GOC, Marcel

(GAWCH, MAHR-sehl) **S.J.**

Center. Shoots left. 6'1", 195 lbs. Born, Calw, West Germany, August 24, 1983. San Jose's 1st choice, 20th overall, in 2001 Entry Draft.

Season	Club	League	GP	G	A	Pts	PIM	PP	SH	GW	S	%	+/-	TF	F%	Min	GP	G	A	Pts	PIM	PP	SH	GW	Min
1998-99	Schwenningen Jr.	Ger-Jr.	12	23	10	33	12	....	....	....	....	....	....	....	....	....	....	....	....	....	....	....	....	....	....
99-2000	Schwenningen	Germany	51	0	3	3	4	....	....	....	....	....	....	....	....	....	11	1	1	2	2	....	....	....	....
2000-01	Schwenningen	Germany	58	13	28	41	12	....	....	....	....	....	....	....	....	....	....	....	....	....	....	....	....	....	....
2001-02	Schwenningen	Germany	45	8	9	17	24	....	....	....	....	....	....	....	....	....	....	....	....	....	....	....	....	....	....
	Adler Mannheim	Germany	8	0	2	2	0	....	....	....	....	....	....	....	....	....	....	....	....	....	....	....	....	....	....
2002-03	Adler Mannheim	Germany	36	6	14	20	16	....	....	....	....	....	....	....	....	....	8	1	2	3	0	....	....	....	....
2003-04	Cleveland Barons	AHL	78	16	21	37	24	....	....	....	....	....	....	....	....	....	....	....	....	....	....	....	....	....	....
	San Jose	NHL	....	....	....	....	....	....	....	....	....	....	....	....	....	....	5	1	1	2	0	0	0	1	7:08
2004-05	Cleveland Barons	AHL	76	16	34	50	28	....	....	....	....	....	....	....	....	....	....	....	....	....	....	....	....	....	....
2005-06	San Jose	NHL	81	8	14	22	22	2	0	2	96	8.3	−7	808	47.9	11:42	11	0	3	3	0	0	0	0	12:38
	Germany	Olympics	5	1	0	1	0	....	....	....	....	....	....	....	....	....	....	....	....	....	....	....	....	....	....
2006-07	San Jose	NHL	78	5	8	13	24	0	1	0	96	5.2	−2	659	55.2	12:01	11	2	1	3	4	0	0	0	14:49
	NHL Totals		159	13	22	35	46	2	1	2	192	6.8		1467	51.2	11:51	27	3	5	8	4	0	0	1	12:30

GODARD, Eric

(GAW-duhrd, AIR-ihk) **CGY.**

Right wing. Shoots right. 6'4", 220 lbs. Born, Vernon, B.C., March 7, 1980.

Season	Club	League	GP	G	A	Pts	PIM	PP	SH	GW	S	%	+/-	TF	F%	Min	GP	G	A	Pts	PIM	PP	SH	GW	Min
1997-98	Lethbridge	WHL	7	0	0	0	26	....	....	....	....	....	....	....	....	....	2	0	0	0	0	....	....	....	....
1998-99	Lethbridge	WHL	66	2	5	7	213	....	....	....	....	....	....	....	....	....	4	0	0	0	14	....	....	....	....
99-2000	Lethbridge	WHL	60	3	5	8	*310	....	....	....	....	....	....	....	....	....	....	....	....	....	....	....	....	....	....
	Louisville Panthers	AHL	4	0	1	1	16	....	....	....	....	....	....	....	....	....	....	....	....	....	....	....	....	....	....
2000-01	Louisville Panthers	AHL	45	0	0	0	132	....	....	....	....	....	....	....	....	....	....	....	....	....	....	....	....	....	....
2001-02	Bridgeport	AHL	67	1	4	5	198	....	....	....	....	....	....	....	....	....	20	0	4	4	30	....	....	....	....
2002-03	NY Islanders	NHL	19	0	0	0	48	0	0	0	6	0.0	−3	0	0.0	4:32	2	0	1	1	4	0	0	0	1:09
	Bridgeport	AHL	46	2	2	4	199	....	....	....	....	....	....	....	....	....	6	0	0	0	16	....	....	....	....
2003-04	NY Islanders	NHL	31	0	1	1	97	0	0	0	5	0.0	−2	1	0.0	3:46	....	....	....	....	....	....	....	....	....
	Bridgeport	AHL	7	0	0	0	13	....	....	....	....	....	....	....	....	....	....	....	....	....	....	....	....	....	....

			Regular Season														Playoffs								
Season	**Club**	**League**	**GP**	**G**	**A**	**Pts**	**PIM**	**PP**	**SH**	**GW**	**S**	**%**	**+/-**	**TF**	**F%**	**Min**	**GP**	**G**	**A**	**Pts**	**PIM**	**PP**	**SH**	**GW**	**Min**
2004-05	Bridgeport	AHL	75	7	11	18	295	....	....	....	....	....	....	....	....	....	....	....	....	....	....	....	....	....	....
2005-06	**NY Islanders**	**NHL**	**57**	**2**	**2**	**4**	**115**	**0**	**0**	**0**	**17**	**11.8**	**–2**	**1**	**0.0**	**3:34**	....	....	....	....	....	....	....	....	....
2006-07	**Calgary**	**NHL**	**19**	**0**	**1**	**1**	**50**	**0**	**0**	**0**	**3**	**0.0**	**0**	**0**	**0.0**	**3:47**	....	....	....	....	....	....	....	....	....
	Omaha	AHL	36	5	4	9	94	....	....	....	....	....	....	....	....	....	....	....	....	....	....	....	....	....	....
	NHL Totals		**126**	**2**	**4**	**6**	**310**	**0**	**0**	**0**	**31**	**6.5**		**2**	**0.0**	**3:48**	**2**	**0**	**1**	**1**	**4**	**0**	**0**	**0**	**1:09**

Signed as a free agent by **Florida**, September 24, 1999. Traded to **NY Islanders** by **Florida** for Florida's 3rd round choice (previously acquired, Florida selected Gregory Campbell) in 2002 Entry Draft, June 22, 2002. • Spent majority of 2003-04 season as a healthy reserve. Signed as a free agent by **Calgary**, August 14, 2006.

GOERTZEN, Steven

(GUHRT-sehn, STEE-vehn) **CBJ**

Right wing. Shoots right. 6'2", 216 lbs. Born, Stony Plain, Alta., May 26, 1984. Columbus' 11th choice, 225th overall, in 2002 Entry Draft.

Season	Club	League	GP	G	A	Pts	PIM	PP	SH	GW	S	%	+/-	TF	F%	Min	GP	G	A	Pts	PIM	PP	SH	GW	Min
99-2000	Spruce Grove	AMBHL	36	16	17	33	30	....	....	....	....	....	....	....	....	....	....	....	....	....	....	....	....	....	....
2000-01	St. Albert Raiders	AMHL	34	11	19	30	70	....	....	....	....	....	....	....	....	....	....	....	....	....	....	....	....	....	....
	St. Albert Saints	AJHL	1	0	0	0	0	....	....	....	....	....	....	....	....	....	....	....	....	....	....	....	....	....	....
2001-02	Seattle	WHL	66	6	9	15	45	....	....	....	....	....	....	....	....	....	11	2	0	2	4	....	....	....	....
2002-03	Seattle	WHL	71	12	19	31	95	....	....	....	....	....	....	....	....	....	14	4	3	7	9	....	....	....	....
2003-04	Seattle	WHL	69	15	18	33	115	....	....	....	....	....	....	....	....	....	....	....	....	....	....	....	....	....	....
	Syracuse Crunch	AHL	8	0	3	3	4	....	....	....	....	....	....	....	....	....	1	0	0	0	0	....	....	....	....
2004-05	Syracuse Crunch	AHL	57	2	7	9	100	....	....	....	....	....	....	....	....	....	....	....	....	....	....	....	....	....	....
2005-06	**Columbus**	**NHL**	**39**	**0**	**0**	**0**	**44**	**0**	**0**	**0**	**23**	**0.0**	**–17**	**11**	**54.6**	**8:32**	....	....	....	....	....	....	....	....	....
	Syracuse Crunch	AHL	40	7	8	15	55	....	....	....	....	....	....	....	....	....	6	0	1	1	34	....	....	....	....
2006-07	**Columbus**	**NHL**	**7**	**0**	**0**	**0**	**10**	**0**	**0**	**0**	**1**	**0.0**	**0**	**0**	**0.0**	**5:21**	....	....	....	....	....	....	....	....	....
	Syracuse Crunch	AHL	60	9	7	16	120	....	....	....	....	....	....	....	....	....	....	....	....	....	....	....	....	....	....
	NHL Totals		**46**	**0**	**0**	**0**	**54**	**0**	**0**	**0**	**24**	**0.0**		**11**	**54.5**	**8:03**	....	....	....	....	....	....	....	....	....

GOMEZ, Scott

(GOH-mehz, SKAWT) **NYR**

Center. Shoots left. 5'11", 200 lbs. Born, Anchorage, AK, December 23, 1979. New Jersey's 2nd choice, 27th overall, in 1998 Entry Draft.

Season	Club	League	GP	G	A	Pts	PIM	PP	SH	GW	S	%	+/-	TF	F%	Min	GP	G	A	Pts	PIM	PP	SH	GW	Min
1994-95	East High	High-AK	28	30	48	78	....	....	....	....	....	....	....	....	....	....	....	....	....	....	....	....	....	....	....
1995-96	East High	High-AK	27	*56	49	*101	....	....	....	....	....	....	....	....	....	....	....	....	....	....	....	....	....	....	....
	Anchorage	AAHL	40	*70	*67	*137	44	....	....	....	....	....	....	....	....	....	....	....	....	....	....	....	....	....	....
1996-97	South Surrey	BCHL	56	48	76	124	94	....	....	....	....	....	....	....	....	....	21	18	23	41	57	....	....	....	....
1997-98	Tri-City	WHL	45	12	37	49	57	....	....	....	....	....	....	....	....	....	....	....	....	....	....	....	....	....	....
1998-99	Tri-City	WHL	58	30	*78	108	55	....	....	....	....	....	....	....	....	....	10	6	13	19	31	....	....	....	....
99-2000♦	**New Jersey**	**NHL**	**82**	**19**	**51**	**70**	**78**	**7**	**0**	**1**	**204**	**9.3**	**14**	**341**	**44.6**	**16:21**	**23**	**4**	**6**	**10**	**4**	**1**	**0**	**2**	**14:08**
2000-01	**New Jersey**	**NHL**	**76**	**14**	**49**	**63**	**46**	**2**	**0**	**4**	**155**	**9.0**	**–1**	**1010**	**44.6**	**15:46**	**25**	**5**	**9**	**14**	**24**	**0**	**0**	**0**	**16:06**
2001-02	**New Jersey**	**NHL**	**76**	**10**	**38**	**48**	**36**	**1**	**0**	**1**	**156**	**6.4**	**–4**	**628**	**48.7**	**16:46**	....	....	....	....	....	....	....	....	....
2002-03♦	**New Jersey**	**NHL**	**80**	**13**	**42**	**55**	**48**	**2**	**0**	**4**	**205**	**6.3**	**17**	**864**	**47.5**	**16:01**	**24**	**3**	**9**	**12**	**2**	**0**	**0**	**0**	**13:45**
2003-04	**New Jersey**	**NHL**	**80**	**14**	***56**	**70**	**70**	**3**	**0**	**1**	**189**	**7.4**	**18**	**1129**	**46.2**	**16:00**	**5**	**0**	**6**	**6**	**0**	**0**	**0**	**0**	**17:14**
2004-05	Alaska Aces	ECHL	61	13	*73	*86	69	....	....	....	....	....	....	....	....	....	4	1	3	4	4	....	....	....	....
2005-06	**New Jersey**	**NHL**	**82**	**33**	**51**	**84**	**42**	**9**	**0**	**5**	**244**	**13.5**	**8**	**1434**	**52.6**	**18:47**	**9**	**5**	**4**	**9**	**6**	**4**	**0**	**1**	**18:14**
	United States	Olympics	6	1	4	5	10	....	....	....	....	....	....	....	....	....	....	....	....	....	....	....	....	....	....
2006-07	**New Jersey**	**NHL**	**72**	**13**	**47**	**60**	**42**	**4**	**0**	**1**	**248**	**5.2**	**7**	**1204**	**52.2**	**18:56**	**11**	**4**	**10**	**14**	**14**	**0**	**0**	**1**	**20:01**
	NHL Totals		**548**	**116**	**334**	**450**	**362**	**28**	**0**	**17**	**1401**	**8.3**		**6610**	**48.7**	**16:56**	**97**	**21**	**44**	**65**	**50**	**5**	**0**	**4**	**15:45**

WHL West First All-Star Team (1999) • NHL All-Rookie Team (2000) • Calder Memorial Trophy (2000) • ECHL First All-Star Team (2005) • ECHL MVP (2005)

Played in NHL All-Star Game (2000)

Signed as a free agent by **Alaska** (ECHL), October 25, 2004. Signed as a free agent by **NY Rangers**, July 1, 2007.

GONCHAR, Sergei

(gohn-CHAR, SAIR-gay) **PIT.**

Defense. Shoots left. 6'2", 211 lbs. Born, Chelyabinsk, USSR, April 13, 1974. Washington's 1st choice, 14th overall, in 1992 Entry Draft.

Season	Club	League	GP	G	A	Pts	PIM	PP	SH	GW	S	%	+/-	TF	F%	Min	GP	G	A	Pts	PIM	PP	SH	GW	Min
1990-91	Mechel	USSR-2	2	0	0	0	0	....	....	....	....	....	....	....	....	....	....	....	....	....	....	....	....	....	....
	Chelyabinsk	USSR-Q	11	0	0	0	4	....	....	....	....	....	....	....	....	....	....	....	....	....	....	....	....	....	....
1991-92	Chelyabinsk	CIS	31	1	0	1	6	....	....	....	....	....	....	....	....	....	....	....	....	....	....	....	....	....	....
1992-93	Dynamo Moscow	CIS	31	1	3	4	70	....	....	....	....	....	....	....	....	....	10	0	0	0	12	....	....	....	....
1993-94	Dynamo Moscow	CIS	44	4	5	9	36	....	....	....	....	....	....	....	....	....	....	....	....	....	....	....	....	....	....
	Portland Pirates	AHL	....	....	....	....	....	....	....	....	....	....	....	....	....	....	2	0	0	0	0	....	....	....	....
1994-95	Portland Pirates	AHL	61	10	32	42	67	....	....	....	....	....	....	....	....	....	....	....	....	....	....	....	....	....	....
	Washington	**NHL**	**31**	**2**	**5**	**7**	**22**	**0**	**0**	**0**	**38**	**5.3**	**4**	....	....	....	**7**	**2**	**2**	**4**	**2**	**0**	**0**	**1**	....
1995-96	**Washington**	**NHL**	**78**	**15**	**26**	**41**	**60**	**4**	**0**	**4**	**139**	**10.8**	**25**	....	....	....	**6**	**2**	**4**	**6**	**4**	**1**	**0**	**0**	....
1996-97	**Washington**	**NHL**	**57**	**13**	**17**	**30**	**36**	**3**	**0**	**3**	**129**	**10.1**	**–11**	....	....	....	....	....	....	....	....	....	....	....	....
1997-98	Lada Togliatti	Russia	7	3	2	5	4	....	....	....	....	....	....	....	....	....	....	....	....	....	....	....	....	....	....
	Russia	Olympics	6	0	2	2	0	....	....	....	....	....	....	....	....	....	....	....	....	....	....	....	....	....	....
	Washington	**NHL**	**72**	**5**	**16**	**21**	**66**	**2**	**0**	**0**	**134**	**3.7**	**2**	....	....	....	**21**	**7**	**4**	**11**	**30**	**3**	**1**	**2**	....
1998-99	**Washington**	**NHL**	**53**	**21**	**10**	**31**	**57**	**13**	**1**	**3**	**180**	**11.7**	**1**	**0**	**0.0**	**23:55**	....	....	....	....	....	....	....	....	....
99-2000	**Washington**	**NHL**	**73**	**18**	**36**	**54**	**52**	**5**	**0**	**3**	**181**	**9.9**	**26**	**0**	**0.0**	**21:46**	**5**	**1**	**0**	**1**	**6**	**0**	**0**	**0**	**19:58**
2000-01	**Washington**	**NHL**	**76**	**19**	**38**	**57**	**70**	**8**	**0**	**2**	**241**	**7.9**	**12**	**1**	**100.0**	**22:26**	**6**	**1**	**3**	**4**	**2**	**1**	**0**	**0**	**19:45**
2001-02	**Washington**	**NHL**	**76**	**26**	**33**	**59**	**58**	**7**	**0**	**2**	**216**	**12.0**	**–1**	**1**	**100.0**	**23:51**	....	....	....	....	....	....	....	....	....
	Russia	Olympics	6	0	0	0	2	....	....	....	....	....	....	....	....	....	....	....	....	....	....	....	....	....	....
2002-03	**Washington**	**NHL**	**82**	**18**	**49**	**67**	**52**	**7**	**0**	**2**	**224**	**8.0**	**13**	**0**	**0.0**	**26:35**	**6**	**0**	**5**	**5**	**4**	**0**	**0**	**0**	**29:00**
2003-04	**Washington**	**NHL**	**56**	**7**	**42**	**49**	**44**	**4**	**0**	**0**	**127**	**5.5**	**–20**	**0**	**0.0**	**27:57**	....	....	....	....	....	....	....	....	....
	Boston	**NHL**	**15**	**4**	**5**	**9**	**12**	**2**	**0**	**0**	**34**	**11.8**	**6**	**0**	**0.0**	**25:32**	**7**	**1**	**4**	**5**	**4**	**1**	**0**	**1**	**27:51**
2004-05	Magnitogorsk	Russia	40	2	17	19	54	....	....	....	....	....	....	....	....	....	4	1	1	2	6	....	....	....	....
2005-06	**Pittsburgh**	**NHL**	**75**	**12**	**46**	**58**	**100**	**8**	**0**	**2**	**192**	**6.3**	**–13**	**0**	**0.0**	**24:40**	....	....	....	....	....	....	....	....	....
	Russia	Olympics	8	0	2	2	8	....	....	....	....	....	....	....	....	....	....	....	....	....	....	....	....	....	....
2006-07	**Pittsburgh**	**NHL**	**82**	**13**	**54**	**67**	**72**	**10**	**1**	**3**	**191**	**6.8**	**–5**	**0**	**0.0**	**26:34**	**5**	**1**	**3**	**4**	**2**	**1**	**0**	**0**	**26:53**
	NHL Totals		**826**	**173**	**377**	**550**	**701**	**73**	**2**	**24**	**2026**	**8.5**		**2**	**100.0**	**24:43**	**63**	**15**	**25**	**40**	**54**	**7**	**1**	**4**	**24:53**

NHL Second All-Star Team (2002, 2003)

Played in NHL All-Star Game (2001, 2002, 2003)

Traded to **Boston** by **Washington** for Shaonne Morrisonn and Boston's 1st (Jeff Schultz) and 2nd (Michail Yunkov) round choices in 2004 Entry Draft, March 3, 2004. Signed as a free agent by **Magnitogorsk** (Russia), September 21, 2004. Signed as a free agent by **Pittsburgh**, August 3, 2005.

GORDON, Boyd

(GOHR-duhn, BOID) **WSH.**

Center. Shoots right. 6'1", 201 lbs. Born, Unity, Sask., October 19, 1983. Washington's 3rd choice, 17th overall, in 2002 Entry Draft.

Season	Club	League	GP	G	A	Pts	PIM	PP	SH	GW	S	%	+/-	TF	F%	Min	GP	G	A	Pts	PIM	PP	SH	GW	Min
1997-98	Regina Flyers	SMHA	60	70	102	172	53	....	....	....	....	....	....	....	....	....	....	....	....	....	....	....	....	....	....
1998-99	Regina Rangers	SMBHL	60	70	102	172	53	....	....	....	....	....	....	....	....	....	....	....	....	....	....	....	....	....	....
99-2000	Red Deer Rebels	WHL	66	10	26	36	24	....	....	....	....	....	....	....	....	....	4	0	1	1	16	....	....	....	....
2000-01	Red Deer Rebels	WHL	72	12	27	39	39	....	....	....	....	....	....	....	....	....	22	3	6	9	2	....	....	....	....
2001-02	Red Deer Rebels	WHL	66	22	29	51	19	....	....	....	....	....	....	....	....	....	23	10	12	22	8	....	....	....	....
2002-03	Red Deer Rebels	WHL	56	33	48	81	28	....	....	....	....	....	....	....	....	....	23	8	12	20	14	....	....	....	....
2003-04	**Washington**	**NHL**	**41**	**1**	**5**	**6**	**8**	**0**	**0**	**0**	**42**	**2.4**	**–9**	**328**	**43.0**	**13:11**	....	....	....	....	....	....	....	....	....
	Portland Pirates	AHL	43	5	17	22	16	....	....	....	....	....	....	....	....	....	7	2	1	3	0	....	....	....	....
2004-05	Portland Pirates	AHL	80	17	22	39	35	....	....	....	....	....	....	....	....	....	....	....	....	....	....	....	....	....	....
2005-06	**Washington**	**NHL**	**25**	**0**	**1**	**1**	**4**	**0**	**0**	**0**	**12**	**0.0**	**–4**	**216**	**46.3**	**11:40**	....	....	....	....	....	....	....	....	....
	Hershey Bears	AHL	58	16	22	38	23	....	....	....	....	....	....	....	....	....	21	3	5	8	10	....	....	....	....
2006-07	**Washington**	**NHL**	**71**	**7**	**22**	**29**	**14**	**0**	**2**	**0**	**104**	**6.7**	**10**	**1214**	**52.1**	**15:53**	....	....	....	....	....	....	....	....	....
	NHL Totals		**137**	**8**	**28**	**36**	**26**	**0**	**2**	**0**	**158**	**5.1**		**1758**	**49.7**	**14:18**	....	....	....	....	....	....	....	....	....

WHL East First All-Star Team (2003)

GOREN, Lee

(GOH-rehn, LEE)

Right wing. Shoots right. 6'3", 205 lbs. Born, Winnipeg, Man., December 26, 1977. Boston's 5th choice, 63rd overall, in 1997 Entry Draft.

Season	Club	League	GP	G	A	Pts	PIM	PP	SH	GW	S	%	+/-	TF	F%	Min	GP	G	A	Pts	PIM	PP	SH	GW	Min
			Regular Season														Playoffs								
1994-95	Wpg. Warriors	MMMHL	31	19	31	50	50	....	....	....	....	....	....	....	....	....	....	....	....	....	....	....	....	....	....
1995-96	Minot Top Guns	SJHL	56	25	35	61	....	....	....	....	....	....	....	....	....	....	12	5	20	25	....	....	....	....	....
	Saskatoon Blades	WHL	2	0	0	0	2	....	....	....	....	....	....	....	....	....	....	....	....	....	....	....	....	....	....
1996-97	North Dakota	WCHA	DID NOT PLAY																						
1997-98	North Dakota	WCHA	29	3	13	16	26	....	....	....	....	....	....	....	....	....	....	....	....	....	....	....	....	....	....
1998-99	North Dakota	WCHA	38	26	19	45	20	....	....	....	....	....	....	....	....	....	....	....	....	....	....	....	....	....	....
99-2000	North Dakota	WCHA	44	*34	29	63	42	....	....	....	....	....	....	....	....	....	....	....	....	....	....	....	....	....	....
2000-01	**Boston**	**NHL**	**21**	**2**	**0**	**2**	**7**	**1**	**0**	**0**	**9**	**22.2**	**–3**	**21**	**38.1**	**4:24**	....	....	....	....	....	....	....	....	....
	Providence Bruins	AHL	54	15	18	33	72	....	....	....	....	....	....	....	....	....	17	5	2	7	11	....	....	....	....
2001-02	Providence Bruins	AHL	71	11	26	37	121	....	....	....	....	....	....	....	....	....	2	0	0	0	0	....	....	....	....
2002-03	Providence Bruins	AHL	65	32	37	69	106	....	....	....	....	....	....	....	....	....	3	0	1	1	0	....	....	....	....
	Boston	**NHL**	**14**	**2**	**1**	**3**	**7**	**2**	**0**	**0**	**15**	**13.3**	**–2**	**0**	**0.0**	**8:15**	**5**	**0**	**0**	**0**	**5**	**0**	**0**	**0**	**6:29**
2003-04	**Florida**	**NHL**	**2**	**0**	**1**	**1**	**0**	**0**	**0**	**0**	**1**	**0.0**	**–4**	**1**	**100.0**	**13:20**	....	....	....	....	....	....	....	....	....
	San Antonio	AHL	65	27	22	49	72	....	....	....	....	....	....	....	....	....	....	....	....	....	....	....	....	....	....
2004-05	Manitoba Moose	AHL	79	32	30	62	117	....	....	....	....	....	....	....	....	....	14	*10	3	13	23	....	....	....	....
2005-06	**Vancouver**	**NHL**	**28**	**1**	**2**	**3**	**30**	**0**	**0**	**1**	**37**	**2.7**	**–6**	**9**	**22.2**	**7:25**	....	....	....	....	....	....	....	....	....
	Manitoba Moose	AHL	42	22	19	41	84	....	....	....	....	....	....	....	....	....	13	3	7	10	27	....	....	....	....
2006-07	**Vancouver**	**NHL**	**2**	**0**	**0**	**0**	**0**	**0**	**0**	**0**	**2**	**0.0**	**–1**	**0**	**0.0**	**11:21**	....	....	....	....	....	....	....	....	....
	Manitoba Moose	AHL	72	26	42	68	86	....	....	....	....	....	....	....	....	....	13	4	5	9	16	....	....	....	....
	NHL Totals		**67**	**5**	**4**	**9**	**44**	**3**	**0**	**1**	**64**	**7.8**		**31**	**35.5**	**6:56**	**5**	**0**	**0**	**0**	**5**	**0**	**0**	**0**	**6:29**

WCHA Second All-Star Team (2000) • NCAA West Second All-American Team (2000) • NCAA Championship All-Tournament Team (2000) • NCAA Championship Tournament MVP (2000)

• Ruled ineligible to play during 1996-97 season by NCAA due to appearance with **Saskatoon** (WHL) in 1995-96 season. Signed as a free agent by **Florida**, July 24, 2003. Signed as a free agent by **Vancouver**, July 7, 2004. Signed as a free agent by **Skelleftea** (Sweden), June 8, 2007.

GORGES, Josh

(GOHR-juhz, JAWSH) **MTL.**

Defense. Shoots left. 6'1", 195 lbs. Born, Kelowna, B.C., August 14, 1984.

Season	Club	League	GP	G	A	Pts	PIM	PP	SH	GW	S	%	+/-	TF	F%	Min	GP	G	A	Pts	PIM	PP	SH	GW	Min
2000-01	Kelowna Rockets	WHL	57	4	6	10	24	....	....	....	....	....	....	....	....	....	6	1	1	2	4	....	....	....	....
2001-02	Kelowna Rockets	WHL	72	7	34	41	74	....	....	....	....	....	....	....	....	....	15	1	7	8	8	....	....	....	....
2002-03	Kelowna Rockets	WHL	54	11	48	59	76	....	....	....	....	....	....	....	....	....	19	3	17	20	16	....	....	....	....
2003-04	Kelowna Rockets	WHL	62	11	31	42	38	....	....	....	....	....	....	....	....	....	17	2	13	15	6	....	....	....	....
2004-05	Cleveland Barons	AHL	74	4	8	12	37	....	....	....	....	....	....	....	....	....	....	....	....	....	....	....	....	....	....
2005-06	**San Jose**	**NHL**	**49**	**0**	**6**	**6**	**31**	**0**	**0**	**0**	**25**	**0.0**	**5**	**0**	**0.0**	**17:38**	**11**	**0**	**1**	**1**	**4**	**0**	**0**	**0**	**18:56**
	Cleveland Barons	AHL	18	2	3	5	12	....	....	....	....	....	....	....	....	....	....	....	....	....	....	....	....	....	....
2006-07	**San Jose**	**NHL**	**47**	**1**	**3**	**4**	**26**	**0**	**0**	**0**	**37**	**2.7**	**–3**	**0**	**0.0**	**17:48**	....	....	....	....	....	....	....	....	....
	Worcester Sharks	AHL	7	0	1	1	2	....	....	....	....	....	....	....	....	....	....	....	....	....	....	....	....	....	....
	Montreal	**NHL**	**7**	**0**	**0**	**0**	**0**	**0**	**0**	**0**	**3**	**0.0**	**–1**	**0**	**0.0**	**12:28**	....	....	....	....	....	....	....	....	....
	NHL Totals		**103**	**1**	**9**	**10**	**57**	**0**	**0**	**0**	**65**	**1.5**		**0**	**0.0**	**17:21**	**11**	**0**	**1**	**1**	**4**	**0**	**0**	**0**	**18:56**

WHL West Second All-Star Team (2003) • WHL West First All-Star Team (2004) • George Parsons Trophy (Memorial Cup Tournament Most Sportsmanlike Player) (2004)

Signed as a free agent by **San Jose**, September 20, 2002. Traded to **Montreal** by **San Jose** with San Jose's 1st round choice (Max Pacioretty) in 2007 Entry Draft for Craig Rivet and Montreal's 5th round choice in 2008 Entry Draft, February 25, 2007.

GOVE, David

(GOHV, DAY-vihd) **CAR.**

Center/Right wing. Shoots left. 5'9", 190 lbs. Born, Centerville, MA, May 4, 1978.

Season	Club	League	GP	G	A	Pts	PIM	PP	SH	GW	S	%	+/-	TF	F%	Min	GP	G	A	Pts	PIM	PP	SH	GW	Min
1997-98	Western Mich.	CCHA	36	8	7	15	8	....	....	....	....	....	....	....	....	....	....	....	....	....	....	....	....	....	....
1998-99	Western Mich.	CCHA	33	9	14	23	12	....	....	....	....	....	....	....	....	....	....	....	....	....	....	....	....	....	....
99-2000	Western Mich.	CCHA	36	18	28	46	22	....	....	....	....	....	....	....	....	....	....	....	....	....	....	....	....	....	....
2000-01	Western Mich.	CCHA	39	22	37	59	16	....	....	....	....	....	....	....	....	....	....	....	....	....	....	....	....	....	....
	Orlando	IHL	9	1	1	2	2	....	....	....	....	....	....	....	....	....	1	0	0	0	0	....	....	....	....
2001-02	Grand Rapids	AHL	17	2	4	6	8	....	....	....	....	....	....	....	....	....	....	....	....	....	....	....	....	....	....
	Johnstown Chiefs	ECHL	54	17	32	49	32	....	....	....	....	....	....	....	....	....	8	1	3	4	4	....	....	....	....
2002-03	San Antonio	AHL	72	15	20	35	30	....	....	....	....	....	....	....	....	....	3	0	1	1	0	....	....	....	....
	Laredo Bucks	CHL	8	4	12	16	15	....	....	....	....	....	....	....	....	....	....	....	....	....	....	....	....	....	....
2003-04	Utah Grizzlies	AHL	75	14	22	36	28	....	....	....	....	....	....	....	....	....	....	....	....	....	....	....	....	....	....
2004-05	Providence Bruins	AHL	70	13	18	31	30	....	....	....	....	....	....	....	....	....	17	3	3	6	14	....	....	....	....
2005-06	**Carolina**	**NHL**	**1**	**0**	**1**	**1**	**0**	**0**	**0**	**0**	**0**	**0.0**	**2**	**0**	**0.0**	**7:12**	....	....	....	....	....	....	....	....	....
	Lowell	AHL	65	20	26	46	50	....	....	....	....	....	....	....	....	....	....	....	....	....	....	....	....	....	....
2006-07	**Carolina**	**NHL**	**1**	**0**	**0**	**0**	**0**	**0**	**0**	**0**	**0**	**0.0**	**0**	**0**	**0.0**	**3:16**	....	....	....	....	....	....	....	....	....
	Albany River Rats	AHL	49	8	13	21	27	....	....	....	....	....	....	....	....	....	4	0	2	2	4	....	....	....	....
	NHL Totals		**2**	**0**	**1**	**1**	**0**	**0**	**0**	**0**	**0**	**0.0**		**0**	**0.0**	**5:14**	....	....	....	....	....	....	....	....	....

Signed as a free agent by **Carolina**, August 4, 2005.

GRABOVSKI, Mikhail

(gra-BAWV-skee, mih-kigh-EHL) **MTL.**

Center. Shoots left. 5'9", 172 lbs. Born, Potsdam, East Germany, January 31, 1984. Montreal's 4th choice, 150th overall, in 2004 Entry Draft.

Season	Club	League	GP	G	A	Pts	PIM	PP	SH	GW	S	%	+/-	TF	F%	Min	GP	G	A	Pts	PIM	PP	SH	GW	Min
2001-02	HC Minsk	Belarus	26	10	7	17	16	....	....	....	....	....	....	....	....	....	....	....	....	....	....	....	....	....	....
2002-03	HC Minsk	Belarus	STATISTICS NOT AVAILABLE																						
2003-04	Nizhnekamsk	Russia	45	6	11	17	26	....	....	....	....	....	....	....	....	....	5	0	0	0	4	....	....	....	....
2004-05	Nizhnekamsk	Russia	60	16	20	36	32	....	....	....	....	....	....	....	....	....	3	2	0	2	2	....	....	....	....
	Yunost-Minsk	BelOpen	....	....	....	....	....	....	....	....	....	....	....	....	....	....	5	2	4	6	6	....	....	....	....
2005-06	Dynamo Moscow	Russia	48	10	17	27	28	....	....	....	....	....	....	....	....	....	4	0	0	0	4	....	....	....	....
	Yunost-Minsk	BelOpen	8	6	8	14	10	....	....	....	....	....	....	....	....	....	....	....	....	....	....	....	....	....	....
2006-07	**Montreal**	**NHL**	**3**	**0**	**0**	**0**	**0**	**0**	**0**	**0**	**5**	**0.0**	**–2**	**31**	**41.9**	**13:18**	....	....	....	....	....	....	....	....	....
	Hamilton	AHL	66	17	37	54	34	....	....	....	....	....	....	....	....	....	20	4	7	11	21	....	....	....	....
	NHL Totals		**3**	**0**	**0**	**0**	**0**	**0**	**0**	**0**	**5**	**0.0**		**31**	**41.9**	**13:18**	....	....	....	....	....	....	....	....	....

GRAND-PIERRE, Jean-Luc

(GRAHN pee-AIR, ZHAWN-LOOK) **N.J.**

Defense. Shoots right. 6'3", 225 lbs. Born, Montreal, Que., February 2, 1977. St. Louis' 6th choice, 179th overall, in 1995 Entry Draft.

Season	Club	League	GP	G	A	Pts	PIM	PP	SH	GW	S	%	+/-	TF	F%	Min	GP	G	A	Pts	PIM	PP	SH	GW	Min
1992-93	Lac St-Louis Lions	QAAA	1	0	0	0	2	....	....	....	....	....	....	....	....	....	....	....	....	....	....	....	....	....	....
1993-94	Beauport	QMJHL	46	1	4	5	27	....	....	....	....	....	....	....	....	....	1	0	0	0	0	....	....	....	....
1994-95	Val-d'Or Foreurs	QMJHL	59	10	13	23	126	....	....	....	....	....	....	....	....	....	....	....	....	....	....	....	....	....	....
1995-96	Val-d'Or Foreurs	QMJHL	67	13	21	34	209	....	....	....	....	....	....	....	....	....	13	1	4	5	47	....	....	....	....
1996-97	Val-d'Or Foreurs	QMJHL	58	9	24	33	186	....	....	....	....	....	....	....	....	....	13	5	8	13	46	....	....	....	....
1997-98	Rochester	AHL	75	4	6	10	211	....	....	....	....	....	....	....	....	....	4	0	0	0	2	....	....	....	....
1998-99	**Buffalo**	**NHL**	**16**	**0**	**1**	**1**	**17**	**0**	**0**	**0**	**11**	**0.0**	**0**	**0**	**0.0**	**13:36**	....	....	....	....	....	....	....	....	....
	Rochester	AHL	55	5	4	9	90	....	....	....	....	....	....	....	....	....	....	....	....	....	....	....	....	....	....
99-2000	**Buffalo**	**NHL**	**11**	**0**	**0**	**0**	**15**	**0**	**0**	**0**	**11**	**0.0**	**–1**	**0**	**0.0**	**15:11**	**4**	**0**	**0**	**0**	**4**	**0**	**0**	**0**	**17:34**
	Rochester	AHL	62	5	8	13	124	....	....	....	....	....	....	....	....	....	17	0	1	1	40	....	....	....	....
2000-01	**Columbus**	**NHL**	**64**	**1**	**4**	**5**	**73**	**0**	**0**	**0**	**33**	**3.0**	**–6**	**0**	**0.0**	**12:51**	....	....	....	....	....	....	....	....	....
2001-02	**Columbus**	**NHL**	**81**	**2**	**6**	**8**	**90**	**0**	**0**	**0**	**62**	**3.2**	**–28**	**3**	**0.0**	**15:20**	....	....	....	....	....	....	....	....	....
2002-03	**Columbus**	**NHL**	**41**	**1**	**0**	**1**	**64**	**0**	**0**	**0**	**32**	**3.1**	**–6**	**0**	**0.0**	**13:38**	....	....	....	....	....	....	....	....	....
	Syracuse Crunch	AHL	2	1	0	1	6	....	....	....	....	....	....	....	....	....	....	....	....	....	....	....	....	....	....
2003-04	**Columbus**	**NHL**	**16**	**0**	**0**	**0**	**12**	**0**	**0**	**0**	**15**	**0.0**	**–3**	**2**	**100.0**	**7:25**	....	....	....	....	....	....	....	....	....
	Atlanta	**NHL**	**27**	**2**	**2**	**4**	**26**	**0**	**1**	**0**	**19**	**10.5**	**–7**	**1**	**0.0**	**15:25**	....	....	....	....	....	....	....	....	....
	Washington	**NHL**	**13**	**1**	**0**	**1**	**14**	**0**	**0**	**0**	**19**	**5.3**	**–2**	**2**	**0.0**	**11:34**	....	....	....	....	....	....	....	....	....
2004-05	IF Troja-Ljungby	Sweden-2	21	2	3	5	69	....	....	....	....	....	....	....	....	....	....	....	....	....	....	....	....	....	....

Season	Club	League	GP	G	A	Pts	PIM	PP	SH	GW	S	%	+/-	TF	F%	Min	GP	G	A	Pts	PIM	PP	SH	GW	Min
			Regular Season														Playoffs								
2005-06	Fuchse Duisburg	Germany	45	10	9	19	176										5	2	2	4	8				
2006-07	Dusseldorf	Germany	44	9	14	23	63										9	1	1	2	10				
	NHL Totals		**269**	**7**	**13**	**20**	**311**	**0**	**1**	**0**	**202**	**3.5**		**8**	**25.0**	**13:44**	**4**	**0**	**0**	**0**	**4**	**0**	**0**	**0**	**17:34**

Traded to **Buffalo** by **St. Louis** with Ottawa's 2nd round choice (previously acquired, Buffalo selected Cory Sarich) in 1996 Entry Draft and St. Louis' 3rd round choice (Maxim Afinogenov) in 1997 Entry Draft for Yuri Khmylev and Buffalo's 8th round choice (Andrei Podkonicky) in 1996 Entry Draft, March 20, 1996. Traded to **Columbus** by **Buffalo** with Matt Davidson, San Jose's 5th round choice (previously acquired, Columbus selected Tyler Kolarik) in 2000 Entry Draft and Buffalo's 5th round choice (later traded to Calgary – later traded to Detroit – Detroit selected Andreas Jamtin) in 2001 Entry Draft to complete Expansion Draft agreement which had Columbus select Geoff Sanderson and Dwayne Roloson from Buffalo, June 23, 2000. Traded to **Atlanta** by **Columbus** for future considerations, December 31, 2003. Claimed on waivers by **Washington** from **Atlanta**, March 9, 2004. Signed as a free agent by **Troja-Ljungby** (Sweden-2), December 10, 2004. Signed as a free agent by **Duisburg** (Germany), September 2, 2005. Signed as a free agent by **Dusseldorf** (Germany), July 28, 2006. Signed as a free agent by **New Jersey**, July 24, 2007.

GRANT, Triston

(GRANT, TRIHS-tuhn) **PHI.**

Left wing. Shoots left. 6'1", 215 lbs. Born, Brandon, Man., February 2, 1984. Philadelphia's 10th choice, 286th overall, in 2004 Entry Draft.

Season	Club	League	GP	G	A	Pts	PIM	PP	SH	GW	S	%	+/-	TF	F%	Min	GP	G	A	Pts	PIM	PP	SH	GW	Min
2000-01	Neepawa Natives	MJHL	STATISTICS NOT AVAILABLE																						
	Lethbridge	WHL	23	2	0	2	75										5	0	0	0	11				
2001-02	Lethbridge	WHL	36	8	1	9	110																		
	Vancouver Giants	WHL	21	2	4	6	53																		
2002-03	Vancouver Giants	WHL	72	10	10	20	200										4	0	0	0	10				
2003-04	Vancouver Giants	WHL	69	10	8	18	267										11	1	1	2	33				
2004-05	Vancouver Giants	WHL	70	20	12	32	193										6	1	0	1	8				
2005-06	Philadelphia	AHL	64	2	3	5	190																		
2006-07	**Philadelphia**	**NHL**	**8**	**0**	**1**	**1**	**10**	**0**	**0**	**0**	**3**	**0.0**	**–1**	**0**	**0.0**	**4:32**									
	Philadelphia	AHL	61	5	6	11	199																		
	NHL Totals		**8**	**0**	**1**	**1**	**10**	**0**	**0**	**0**	**3**	**0.0**		**0**	**0.0**	**4:32**									

GRATTON, Chris

(GRAHT-uhn, KRIHS) **T.B.**

Center. Shoots left. 6'4", 231 lbs. Born, Brantford, Ont., July 5, 1975. Tampa Bay's 1st choice, 3rd overall, in 1993 Entry Draft.

Season	Club	League	GP	G	A	Pts	PIM	PP	SH	GW	S	%	+/-	TF	F%	Min	GP	G	A	Pts	PIM	PP	SH	GW	Min
1989-90	Brantford Classics	OHA-B	1	0	2	2	2																		
1990-91	Brantford Classics	OHA-B	31	30	30	60	28																		
1991-92	Kingston	OHL	62	27	39	66	37																		
1992-93	Kingston	OHL	58	55	54	109	125										16	11	18	29	42				
1993-94	**Tampa Bay**	**NHL**	**84**	**13**	**29**	**42**	**123**	**5**	**1**	**2**	**161**	**8.1**	**–25**												
1994-95	**Tampa Bay**	**NHL**	**46**	**7**	**20**	**27**	**89**	**2**	**0**	**0**	**91**	**7.7**	**–2**												
1995-96	**Tampa Bay**	**NHL**	**82**	**17**	**21**	**38**	**105**	**7**	**0**	**3**	**183**	**9.3**	**–13**				**6**	**0**	**2**	**2**	**27**	**0**	**0**	**0**	
1996-97	**Tampa Bay**	**NHL**	**82**	**30**	**32**	**62**	**201**	**9**	**0**	**4**	**230**	**13.0**	**–28**												
1997-98	**Philadelphia**	**NHL**	**82**	**22**	**40**	**62**	**159**	**5**	**0**	**2**	**182**	**12.1**	**11**				**5**	**2**	**0**	**2**	**10**	**0**	**0**	**0**	
1998-99	**Philadelphia**	**NHL**	**26**	**1**	**7**	**8**	**41**	**0**	**0**	**0**	**54**	**1.9**	**–8**	**38**	**42.1**	**14:25**									
	Tampa Bay	**NHL**	**52**	**7**	**19**	**26**	**102**	**1**	**0**	**1**	**127**	**5.5**	**–20**	**1032**	**53.9**	**18:20**									
99-2000	**Tampa Bay**	**NHL**	**58**	**14**	**27**	**41**	**121**	**4**	**0**	**1**	**168**	**8.3**	**–24**	**1341**	**55.9**	**20:03**									
	Buffalo	**NHL**	**14**	**1**	**7**	**8**	**15**	**0**	**0**	**0**	**34**	**2.9**	**1**	**256**	**54.3**	**16:40**	**5**	**0**	**1**	**1**	**4**	**0**	**0**	**1**	**14:56**
2000-01	**Buffalo**	**NHL**	**82**	**19**	**21**	**40**	**102**	**5**	**0**	**5**	**156**	**12.2**	**0**	**1161**	**57.3**	**14:37**	**13**	**6**	**4**	**10**	**14**	**2**	**0**	**1**	**12:33**
2001-02	**Buffalo**	**NHL**	**82**	**15**	**24**	**39**	**75**	**1**	**0**	**5**	**139**	**10.8**	**0**	**1297**	**53.8**	**14:57**									
2002-03	**Buffalo**	**NHL**	**66**	**15**	**29**	**44**	**86**	**4**	**0**	**2**	**187**	**8.0**	**–5**	**1099**	**58.9**	**16:26**									
	Phoenix	**NHL**	**14**	**0**	**1**	**1**	**21**	**0**	**0**	**0**	**28**	**0.0**	**–11**	**231**	**57.1**	**17:12**									
2003-04	**Phoenix**	**NHL**	**68**	**11**	**18**	**29**	**93**	**3**	**0**	**1**	**122**	**9.0**	**–19**	**1090**	**55.3**	**14:40**									
	Colorado	**NHL**	**13**	**2**	**1**	**3**	**18**	**0**	**0**	**0**	**28**	**7.1**	**1**	**252**	**57.5**	**16:55**	**11**	**0**	**0**	**0**	**27**	**0**	**0**	**0**	**12:14**
2004-05			DID NOT PLAY																						
2005-06	**Florida**	**NHL**	**76**	**17**	**22**	**39**	**104**	**4**	**1**	**2**	**135**	**12.6**	**6**	**960**	**51.3**	**15:43**									
2006-07	**Florida**	**NHL**	**81**	**13**	**22**	**35**	**94**	**1**	**0**	**1**	**131**	**9.9**	**1**	**517**	**56.7**	**12:06**									
	NHL Totals		**1008**	**204**	**340**	**544**	**1549**	**51**	**2**	**29**	**2156**	**9.5**		**9274**	**55.4**	**15:37**	**40**	**8**	**7**	**15**	**82**	**2**	**0**	**1**	**12:50**

OHL All-Rookie Team (1992) • OHL Rookie of the Year (1992)

Signed as a free agent by **Philadelphia**, August 14, 1997. Traded to **Tampa Bay** by **Philadelphia** with Mike Sillinger for Mikael Renberg and Daymond Langkow, December 12, 1998. Traded to **Buffalo** by **Tampa Bay** with Tampa Bay's 2nd round choice (Derek Roy) in 2001 Entry Draft for Cory Sarich, Wayne Primeau, Brian Holzinger and Buffalo's 3rd round choice (Alexander Kharitonov) in 2000 Entry Draft, March 9, 2000. Traded to **Phoenix** by **Buffalo** with Buffalo's 4th round choice (later traded to Edmonton – Edmonton selected Liam Reddox) in 2004 Entry Draft for Daniel Briere and Phoenix's 3rd round choice (Andrej Sekera) in 2004 Entry Draft, March 10, 2003. Traded to **Colorado** by **Phoenix** with Ossi Vaananen and Phoenix's 2nd round choice (Paul Stastny) in 2005 Entry Draft for Derek Morris and Keith Ballard, March 9, 2004. Signed as a free agent by **Florida**, August 12, 2005. Traded to **Tampa Bay** by **Florida** for Tampa Bay's 2nd round choice in 2008 Entry Draft, June 13, 2007.

GRATTON, Josh

(GRAHT-uhn, JAWSH) **PHX.**

Left wing. Shoots left. 6'2", 214 lbs. Born, Brantford, Ont., September 9, 1982.

Season	Club	League	GP	G	A	Pts	PIM	PP	SH	GW	S	%	+/-	TF	F%	Min	GP	G	A	Pts	PIM	PP	SH	GW	Min
2000-01	Sudbury Wolves	OHL	44	5	13	18	110										9	1	1	2	25				
2001-02	Sudbury Wolves	OHL	14	5	4	9	47																		
	Kingston	OHL	46	14	14	28	140										1	1	0	1	7				
2002-03	Windsor Spitfires	OHL	62	26	30	56	192										6	2	1	3	8				
2003-04	Cincinnati	AHL	21	2	2	4	69										8	0	0	0	35				
	San Diego Gulls	ECHL	30	4	6	10	239																		
2004-05	Philadelphia	AHL	57	9	5	14	246										21	3	3	6	78				
	Trenton Titans	ECHL	1	0	0	0	0																		
2005-06	**Philadelphia**	**NHL**	**3**	**0**	**0**	**0**	**14**	**0**	**0**	**0**	**3**	**0.0**	**0**	**0**	**0.0**	**5:00**									
	Philadelphia	AHL	53	9	10	19	265																		
	Phoenix	**NHL**	**11**	**1**	**0**	**1**	**30**	**0**	**0**	**0**	**14**	**7.1**	**–3**	**0**	**0.0**	**8:00**									
2006-07	**Phoenix**	**NHL**	**52**	**1**	**1**	**2**	**188**	**0**	**0**	**0**	**29**	**3.4**	**–9**	**1**	**0.0**	**5:54**									
	San Antonio	AHL	3	1	1	2	8																		
	NHL Totals		**66**	**2**	**1**	**3**	**232**	**0**	**0**	**0**	**46**	**4.3**		**1**	**0.0**	**6:13**									

Signed as a free agent by **Philadelphia**, July 27, 2004. Traded to **Phoenix** by **Philadelphia** with Florida's 2nd round choice (previously acquired, later traded to Detroit - Detroit selected Cory Emerton) in 2006 Entry Draft and Tampa Bay's 2nd round choice (previously acquired, later traded to Detroit - Detroit selected Shawn Matthias) in 2006 Entry Draft for Denis Gauthier, March 9, 2006.

GREBESHKOV, Denis

(greh-behsh-KAHV, DEH-nihs) **EDM.**

Defense. Shoots left. 6', 190 lbs. Born, Yaroslavl, USSR, October 11, 1983. Los Angeles' 1st choice, 18th overall, in 2002 Entry Draft.

Season	Club	League	GP	G	A	Pts	PIM	PP	SH	GW	S	%	+/-	TF	F%	Min	GP	G	A	Pts	PIM	PP	SH	GW	Min
99-2000	Yaroslavl 2	Russia-3	42	2	1	3	12										6	0	0	0	2				
2000-01	Yaroslavl 2	Russia-3	34	7	2	9	20																		
2001-02	Yaroslavl 2	Russia-3	7	1	1	2	2																		
	Yaroslavl	Russia	27	1	2	3	10																		
2002-03	Yaroslavl	Russia	48	0	7	7	26										10	0	1	1	2				
2003-04	**Los Angeles**	**NHL**	**4**	**0**	**1**	**1**	**0**	**0**	**0**	**0**	**5**	**0.0**	**–4**	**0**	**0.0**	**18:29**									
	Manchester	AHL	43	2	7	9	34										6	0	1	1	6				
2004-05	Manchester	AHL	75	5	44	49	87										6	0	4	4	2				
2005-06	**Los Angeles**	**NHL**	**8**	**0**	**2**	**2**	**12**	**0**	**0**	**0**	**10**	**0.0**	**–4**	**0**	**0.0**	**15:16**									
	Manchester	AHL	48	2	25	27	59																		
	NY Islanders	**NHL**	**21**	**0**	**3**	**3**	**8**	**0**	**0**	**0**	**14**	**0.0**	**–8**	**0**	**0.0**	**17:11**									
	Bridgeport	AHL															7	1	1	2	8				
2006-07	Yaroslavl	Russia	47	8	9	17	79										7	0	2	2	6				
	NHL Totals		**33**	**0**	**6**	**6**	**20**	**0**	**0**	**0**	**29**	**0.0**		**0**	**0.0**	**16:53**									

Traded to **NY Islanders** by **Los Angeles** with Jeff Tambellini for Mark Parrish and Brent Sopel, March 8, 2006. Signed as a free agent by **Yaroslavl** (Russia), July 10, 2006. Traded to **Edmonton** by **NY Islanders** for Marc-Andre Bergeron and Edmonton's 3rd round choice in 2008 Entry Draft, February 18, 2007.

GREEN, Josh

(GREEN, JAWSH)

Left wing. Shoots left. 6'3", 215 lbs. Born, Camrose, Alta., November 16, 1977. Los Angeles' 1st choice, 30th overall, in 1996 Entry Draft.

Season	Club	League	GP	G	A	Pts	PIM	PP	SH	GW	S	%	+/-	TF	F%	Min	GP	G	A	Pts	PIM	PP	SH	GW	Min
1992-93	Camrose Kodiaks	ABHL	60	55	45	100	80																		
1993-94	Medicine Hat	WHL	63	22	22	44	43										3	0	0	0	4				
1994-95	Medicine Hat	WHL	68	32	23	55	64										5	5	1	6	2				
1995-96	Medicine Hat	WHL	46	18	25	43	55										5	2	2	4	4				
1996-97	Medicine Hat	WHL	51	25	32	57	61																		
	Swift Current	WHL	23	10	15	25	33										10	9	7	16	19				
1997-98	Swift Current	WHL	5	9	1	10	9																		
	Portland	WHL	26	26	18	44	27																		
	Fredericton	AHL	43	16	15	31	14										4	1	3	4	6				

			Regular Season														Playoffs								
Season	Club	League	GP	G	A	Pts	PIM	PP	SH	GW	S	%	+/-	TF	F%	Min	GP	G	A	Pts	PIM	PP	SH	GW	Min
1998-99	Los Angeles	NHL	27	1	3	4	8	1	0	0	35	2.9	–5	2	50.0	11:44	....	....	....	....	....	....	....	....	....
	Springfield	AHL	41	15	15	30	29	....	....	....	....	....	....	....	....	....	....	....	....	....	....	....	....	....	....
99-2000	NY Islanders	NHL	49	12	14	26	41	2	0	3	109	11.0	–7	12	50.0	13:36	....	....	....	....	....	....	....	....	....
	Lowell	AHL	17	6	2	8	19	....	....	....	....	....	....	....	....	....	....	....	....	....	....	....	....	....	....
2000-01	Hamilton	AHL	2	2	0	2	2	....	....	....	....	....	....	....	....	....	....	....	....	....	....	....	....	....	....
	Edmonton	NHL	....	....	....	....	....	....	....	....	....	....	....	....	....	....	3	0	0	0	0	0	0	0	7:55
2001-02	Edmonton	NHL	61	10	5	15	52	1	0	1	78	12.8	9	18	38.9	10:05	....	....	....	....	....	....	....	....	....
2002-03	Edmonton	NHL	20	0	2	2	12	0	0	0	20	0.0	–3	5	0.0	10:22	....	....	....	....	....	....	....	....	....
	NY Rangers	NHL	4	0	0	0	2	0	0	0	3	0.0	–1	0	0.0	9:07	....	....	....	....	....	....	....	....	....
	Washington	NHL	21	1	2	3	7	0	0	0	20	5.0	1	3	0.0	8:07	....	....	....	....	....	....	....	....	....
2003-04	Calgary	NHL	36	2	4	6	24	0	0	0	47	4.3	–3	39	30.8	11:18	....	....	....	....	....	....	....	....	....
	Lowell	AHL	22	6	9	15	46	....	....	....	....	....	....	....	....	....	....	....	....	....	....	....	....	....	....
	NY Rangers	NHL	14	3	2	5	8	0	0	1	29	10.3	0	9	55.6	14:16	....	....	....	....	....	....	....	....	....
2004-05	Manitoba Moose	AHL	67	21	19	40	72	....	....	....	....	....	....	....	....	....	14	9	5	14	26	....	....	....	....
2005-06	Vancouver	NHL	33	4	2	6	14	0	0	0	35	11.4	2	146	40.4	8:35	....	....	....	....	....	....	....	....	....
	Manitoba Moose	AHL	35	7	24	31	33	....	....	....	....	....	....	....	....	....	10	5	5	10	23	....	....	....	....
2006-07	Vancouver	NHL	57	2	5	7	25	0	0	2	74	2.7	0	266	40.6	11:25	9	0	1	1	12	0	0	0	10:13
	NHL Totals		322	35	39	74	193	4	0	7	450	7.8		500	39.6	11:02	12	0	1	1	12	0	0	0	9:38

Traded to **NY Islanders** by **Los Angeles** with Olli Jokinen, Mathieu Biron and Los Angeles' 1st round choice (Taylor Pyatt) in 1999 Entry Draft for Ziggy Palffy, Brian Smolinski, Marcel Cousineau and New Jersey's 4th round choice (previously acquired, Los Angeles selected Daniel Johansson) in 1999 Entry Draft, June 20, 1999. Traded to **Edmonton** by **NY Islanders** with Eric Brewer and NY Islanders' 2nd round choice (Brad Winchester) in 2000 Entry Draft for Roman Hamrlik, June 24, 2000. • Missed majority of 2000-01 season recovering from shoulder injury suffered in game vs. Detroit, October 10, 2000. Traded to **NY Rangers** by **Edmonton** for future considerations, December 12, 2002. Claimed on waivers by **Washington** from **NY Rangers**, January 15, 2003. Signed as a free agent by **Calgary**, July 17, 2003. Claimed on waivers by **NY Rangers** from **Calgary**, March 6, 2004. Signed to a PTO (tryout) contract by **Manitoba** (AHL), September 27, 2004. Signed as a free agent by **Vancouver**, August 23, 2005. Signed as a free agent by **Salzburg** (Austria), July 30, 2007.

GREEN, Mike

(GREEN, MIGHK)

Center. Shoots right. 5'11", 192 lbs. Born, Calgary, Alta., August 23, 1979.

1996-97	Cgy. North Stars	AMHL	35	34	27	61	78	....	....	....	....	....	....	....	....	....	....	....	....	....	....	....	....	....	....
	Edmonton Ice	WHL	7	0	2	2	0	....	....	....	....	....	....	....	....	....	....	....	....	....	....	....	....	....	....
1997-98	Edmonton Ice	WHL	71	15	26	41	16	....	....	....	....	....	....	....	....	....	....	....	....	....	....	....	....	....	....
1998-99	Kootenay Ice	WHL	71	35	45	80	37	....	....	....	....	....	....	....	....	....	7	2	2	4	4	....	....	....	....
99-2000	Kootenay Ice	WHL	69	43	49	92	63	....	....	....	....	....	....	....	....	....	21	9	16	25	20	....	....	....	....
2000-01	Port Huron	UHL	11	1	5	6	6	....	....	....	....	....	....	....	....	....	....	....	....	....	....	....	....	....	....
	Louisville Panthers	AHL	24	2	1	3	4	....	....	....	....	....	....	....	....	....	....	....	....	....	....	....	....	....	....
	Knoxville Speed	UHL	48	18	24	42	35	....	....	....	....	....	....	....	....	....	1	0	0	0	0	....	....	....	....
2001-02	Macon Whoopee	ECHL	54	27	35	62	18	....	....	....	....	....	....	....	....	....	....	....	....	....	....	....	....	....	....
	Cincinnati	AHL	22	2	9	11	4	....	....	....	....	....	....	....	....	....	3	0	0	0	0	....	....	....	....
2002-03	San Antonio	AHL	80	26	34	60	25	....	....	....	....	....	....	....	....	....	3	0	2	2	0	....	....	....	....
2003-04	Florida	NHL	11	0	1	1	2	0	0	0	7	0.0	0	42	47.6	8:16	....	....	....	....	....	....	....	....	....
	San Antonio	AHL	45	12	23	35	16	....	....	....	....	....	....	....	....	....	....	....	....	....	....	....	....	....	....
	NY Rangers	NHL	13	1	2	3	2	0	0	0	13	7.7	0	98	39.8	9:53	....	....	....	....	....	....	....	....	....
2004-05	Nurnberg	Germany	44	11	17	28	38	....	....	....	....	....	....	....	....	....	6	1	3	4	0	....	....	....	....
2005-06	Hannover	Germany	50	17	26	43	122	....	....	....	....	....	....	....	....	....	9	3	0	3	14	....	....	....	....
2006-07	Iowa Stars	AHL	23	8	9	17	16	....	....	....	....	....	....	....	....	....	....	....	....	....	....	....	....	....	....
	Hershey Bears	AHL	12	3	5	8	26	....	....	....	....	....	....	....	....	....	19	7	9	16	38	....	....	....	....
	NHL Totals		24	1	3	4	4	0	0	0	20	5.0		140	42.1	9:08	....	....	....	....	....	....	....	....	....

WHL East Second All-Star Team (2000)

Signed as a free agent by **Florida**, April 7, 2000. Claimed on waivers by **NY Rangers** from **Florida**, March 9, 2004. Signed as a free agent by **Nurnberg** (Germany), August 2, 2004. Traded to **Dallas** by **NY Rangers** for future considerations, June 14, 2006. Signed as a free agent by **Hannover** (Germany), July 30, 2007.

GREEN, Mike

(GREEN, MIGHK) **WSH.**

Defense. Shoots right. 6'1", 208 lbs. Born, Calgary, Alta., October 12, 1985. Washington's 3rd choice, 29th overall, in 2004 Entry Draft.

2000-01	Cgy. North Stars	AMHL	36	4	23	27	34	....	....	....	....	....	....	....	....	....	....	....	....	....	....	....	....	....	....
	Saskatoon Blades	WHL	7	0	2	2	0	....	....	....	....	....	....	....	....	....	....	....	....	....	....	....	....	....	....
2001-02	Saskatoon Blades	WHL	62	3	20	23	57	....	....	....	....	....	....	....	....	....	7	0	1	1	2	....	....	....	....
2002-03	Saskatoon Blades	WHL	72	6	36	42	70	....	....	....	....	....	....	....	....	....	6	0	2	2	6	....	....	....	....
2003-04	Saskatoon Blades	WHL	59	14	25	39	92	....	....	....	....	....	....	....	....	....	....	....	....	....	....	....	....	....	....
2004-05	Saskatoon Blades	WHL	67	14	52	66	105	....	....	....	....	....	....	....	....	....	4	0	0	0	6	....	....	....	....
2005-06	Washington	NHL	22	1	2	3	18	0	0	0	13	7.7	–8	0	0.0	14:54	....	....	....	....	....	....	....	....	....
	Hershey Bears	AHL	56	9	34	43	79	....	....	....	....	....	....	....	....	....	21	3	15	18	30	....	....	....	....
2006-07	Washington	NHL	70	2	10	12	36	0	0	0	68	2.9	–10	0	0.0	15:29	....	....	....	....	....	....	....	....	....
	NHL Totals		92	3	12	15	54	0	0	0	81	3.7		0	0.0	15:21	....	....	....	....	....	....	....	....	....

WHL East First All-Star Team (2005) • AHL All-Rookie Team (2006)

GREEN, Travis

(GREEN, TRA-vihs)

Center. Shoots right. 6'1", 204 lbs. Born, Castlegar, B.C., December 20, 1970. NY Islanders' 2nd choice, 23rd overall, in 1989 Entry Draft.

1985-86	Castlegar Rebels	KIJHL	35	30	40	70	41	....	....	....	....	....	....	....	....	....	....	....	....	....	....	....	....	....	....
1986-87	Spokane Chiefs	WHL	64	8	17	25	27	....	....	....	....	....	....	....	....	....	3	0	0	0	0	....	....	....	....
1987-88	Spokane Chiefs	WHL	72	33	54	87	42	....	....	....	....	....	....	....	....	....	15	10	10	20	13	....	....	....	....
1988-89	Spokane Chiefs	WHL	75	51	51	102	79	....	....	....	....	....	....	....	....	....	....	....	....	....	....	....	....	....	....
1989-90	Spokane Chiefs	WHL	50	45	44	89	80	....	....	....	....	....	....	....	....	....	....	....	....	....	....	....	....	....	....
	Medicine Hat	WHL	25	15	24	39	19	....	....	....	....	....	....	....	....	....	3	0	0	0	2	....	....	....	....
1990-91	Capital District	AHL	73	21	34	55	26	....	....	....	....	....	....	....	....	....	....	....	....	....	....	....	....	....	....
1991-92	Capital District	AHL	71	23	27	50	10	....	....	....	....	....	....	....	....	....	7	0	4	4	21	....	....	....	....
1992-93	NY Islanders	NHL	61	7	18	25	43	1	0	0	115	6.1	4	....	....	....	12	3	1	4	6	0	0	0	....
	Capital District	AHL	20	12	11	23	39	....	....	....	....	....	....	....	....	....	....	....	....	....	....	....	....	....	....
1993-94	NY Islanders	NHL	83	18	22	40	44	1	0	2	164	11.0	16	....	....	....	4	0	0	0	2	0	0	0	....
1994-95	NY Islanders	NHL	42	5	7	12	25	0	0	0	59	8.5	–10	....	....	....	....	....	....	....	....	....	....	....	....
1995-96	NY Islanders	NHL	69	25	45	70	42	14	1	2	186	13.4	–20	....	....	....	....	....	....	....	....	....	....	....	....
1996-97	NY Islanders	NHL	79	23	41	64	38	10	0	3	177	13.0	–5	....	....	....	....	....	....	....	....	....	....	....	....
1997-98	NY Islanders	NHL	54	14	12	26	66	8	0	2	99	14.1	–19	....	....	....	....	....	....	....	....	....	....	....	....
	Anaheim	NHL	22	5	11	16	16	1	0	0	42	11.9	–10	....	....	....	....	....	....	....	....	....	....	....	....
1998-99	Anaheim	NHL	79	13	17	30	81	3	1	2	165	7.9	–7	1325	52.8	17:17	4	0	1	1	4	0	0	0	15:02
99-2000	Phoenix	NHL	78	25	21	46	45	6	0	2	157	15.9	–4	1322	55.6	16:36	5	2	1	3	2	0	0	0	17:23
2000-01	Phoenix	NHL	69	13	15	28	63	3	0	0	113	11.5	–11	1135	54.9	16:05	....	....	....	....	....	....	....	....	....
2001-02	Toronto	NHL	82	11	23	34	61	3	0	2	119	9.2	13	647	54.1	14:32	20	3	6	9	34	0	0	1	20:34
2002-03	Toronto	NHL	75	12	12	24	67	2	1	3	86	14.0	2	802	53.5	12:57	4	2	1	3	4	0	1	1	18:09
2003-04	Boston	NHL	64	11	5	16	67	2	0	2	104	10.6	–6	845	55.6	15:17	7	0	1	1	8	0	0	0	15:37
2004-05			DID NOT PLAY																						
2005-06	Boston	NHL	82	10	12	22	79	0	2	1	118	8.5	–2	976	54.4	15:04	....	....	....	....	....	....	....	....	....
2006-07	Anaheim	NHL	7	1	1	2	6	0	0	0	3	33.3	3	29	41.4	7:58	....	....	....	....	....	....	....	....	....
	Toronto	NHL	24	0	0	0	21	0	0	0	19	0.0	1	168	54.8	9:10	....	....	....	....	....	....	....	....	....
	NHL Totals		970	193	262	455	764	54	5	21	1726	11.2		7249	54.4	15:02	56	10	11	21	60	0	1	2	18:30

Traded to **Anaheim** by **NY Islanders** with Doug Houda and Tony Tuzzolino for Joe Sacco, J.J. Daigneault and Mark Janssens, February 6, 1998. Traded to **Phoenix** by **Anaheim** with Anaheim's 1st round choice (Scott Kelman) in 1999 Entry Draft for Oleg Tverdovsky, June 26, 1999. Traded to **Toronto** by **Phoenix** with Robert Reichel and Craig Mills for Danny Markov, June 12, 2001. Claimed by **Columbus** from **Toronto** in Waiver Draft, October 3, 2003. Traded to **Boston** by **Columbus** for Boston's 6th round choice (Lennart Petrell) in 2004 Entry Draft, October 3, 2003. Signed as a free agent by **Anaheim**, August 10, 2006. Claimed on waivers by **Toronto** from **Anaheim**, January 10, 2007. • Missed majority of 2006-07 season as a healthy scratch.

GREENE, Andy

(GREEN, AN-dee) **N.J.**

Defense. Shoots left. 5'11", 195 lbs. Born, Trenton, MI, October 30, 1982.

2002-03	Miami U.	CCHA	41	4	19	23	64	....	....	....	....	....	....	....	....	....	....	....	....	....	....	....	....	....	....
2003-04	Miami U.	CCHA	41	7	19	26	78	....	....	....	....	....	....	....	....	....	....	....	....	....	....	....	....	....	....
2004-05	Miami U.	CCHA	38	7	27	34	66	....	....	....	....	....	....	....	....	....	....	....	....	....	....	....	....	....	....
2005-06	Miami U.	CCHA	39	9	22	31	48	....	....	....	....	....	....	....	....	....	....	....	....	....	....	....	....	....	....

			Regular Season														Playoffs								
Season	Club	League	GP	G	A	Pts	PIM	PP	SH	GW	S	%	+/-	TF	F%	Min	GP	G	A	Pts	PIM	PP	SH	GW	Min
2006-07	**New Jersey**	**NHL**	**23**	**1**	**5**	**6**	**6**	**1**	**0**	**0**	**23**	**4.3**	**−1**	**0**	**0.0**	**14:15**	**11**	**2**	**1**	**3**	**2**	**0**	**0**	**1**	**17:04**
	Lowell Devils	AHL	52	5	16	21	28	....	....	....	....	....	....	....	....	....	....	....	....	....	....	....	....	....	....
	NHL Totals		**23**	**1**	**5**	**6**	**6**	**1**	**0**	**0**	**23**	**4.3**		**0**	**0.0**	**14:15**	**11**	**2**	**1**	**3**	**2**	**0**	**0**	**1**	**17:04**

CCHA All-Rookie Team (2003) • CCHA First All-Star Team (2004, 2005, 2006) • NCAA West First All-American Team (2006)

Signed as a free agent by **New Jersey**, April 4, 2006.

GREENE, Matt
(GREEN, MAT) **EDM.**

Defense. Shoots right. 6'3", 223 lbs. Born, Grand Ledge, MI, May 13, 1983. Edmonton's 4th choice, 44th overall, in 2002 Entry Draft.

Season	Club	League	GP	G	A	Pts	PIM	PP	SH	GW	S	%	+/-	TF	F%	Min	GP	G	A	Pts	PIM	PP	SH	GW	Min
2000-01	USNTDP	U-18	34	0	9	9	8	....	....	....	....	....	....	....	....	....	....	....	....	....	....	....	....	....	....
	USNTDP	USHL	20	0	1	1	51	....	....	....	....	....	....	....	....	....	....	....	....	....	....	....	....	....	....
2001-02	Green Bay	USHL	55	4	20	24	150	....	....	....	....	....	....	....	....	....	7	0	1	1	31	....	....	....	....
2002-03	North Dakota	WCHA	39	0	4	4	*135	....	....	....	....	....	....	....	....	....	....	....	....	....	....	....	....	....	....
2003-04	North Dakota	WCHA	40	1	16	17	86	....	....	....	....	....	....	....	....	....	....	....	....	....	....	....	....	....	....
2004-05	North Dakota	WCHA	43	2	8	10	*126	....	....	....	....	....	....	....	....	....	....	....	....	....	....	....	....	....	....
2005-06	**Edmonton**	**NHL**	**27**	**0**	**2**	**2**	**43**	**0**	**0**	**0**	**10**	**0.0**	**−6**	**0**	**0.0**	**11:13**	**18**	**0**	**1**	**1**	**34**	**0**	**0**	**0**	**10:03**
	Iowa Stars	AHL	26	2	5	7	47	....	....	....	....	....	....	....	....	....	....	....	....	....	....	....	....	....	....
2006-07	**Edmonton**	**NHL**	**78**	**1**	**9**	**10**	**109**	**0**	**0**	**0**	**52**	**1.9**	**−22**	**0**	**0.0**	**17:36**	....	....	....	....	....	....	....	....	....
	NHL Totals		**105**	**1**	**11**	**12**	**152**	**0**	**0**	**0**	**62**	**1.6**		**0**	**0.0**	**15:58**	**18**	**0**	**1**	**1**	**34**	**0**	**0**	**0**	**10:03**

USHL Second All-Star Team (2002)

GRENIER, Martin
(GREH-n'yay, MAHR-tihn) **PHI.**

Defense. Shoots left. 6'5", 245 lbs. Born, Laval, Que., November 2, 1980. Colorado's 2nd choice, 45th overall, in 1999 Entry Draft.

Season	Club	League	GP	G	A	Pts	PIM	PP	SH	GW	S	%	+/-	TF	F%	Min	GP	G	A	Pts	PIM	PP	SH	GW	Min
1996-97	Laval-Laurentides	QAAA	34	3	16	19	117	....	....	....	....	....	....	....	....	....	13	0	4	4	....	....	....	....	....
1997-98	Quebec Remparts	QMJHL	61	4	11	15	202	....	....	....	....	....	....	....	....	....	14	0	2	2	36	....	....	....	....
1998-99	Quebec Remparts	QMJHL	60	7	18	25	*479	....	....	....	....	....	....	....	....	....	13	0	4	4	29	....	....	....	....
99-2000	Quebec Remparts	QMJHL	67	11	35	46	302	....	....	....	....	....	....	....	....	....	7	1	4	5	27	....	....	....	....
2000-01	Quebec Remparts	QMJHL	26	5	16	21	82	....	....	....	....	....	....	....	....	....	....	....	....	....	....	....	....	....	....
	Victoriaville Tigres	QMJHL	28	9	19	28	108	....	....	....	....	....	....	....	....	....	13	2	8	10	51	....	....	....	....
2001-02	**Phoenix**	**NHL**	**5**	**0**	**0**	**0**	**5**	**0**	**0**	**0**	**1**	**0.0**	**0**	**1**	**100.0**	**5:56**	....	....	....	....	....	....	....	....	....
	Springfield	AHL	69	2	6	8	241	....	....	....	....	....	....	....	....	....	....	....	....	....	....	....	....	....	....
2002-03	**Phoenix**	**NHL**	**3**	**0**	**0**	**0**	**0**	**0**	**0**	**0**	**0**	**0.0**	**−1**	**0**	**0.0**	**6:11**	....	....	....	....	....	....	....	....	....
	Springfield	AHL	73	2	10	12	232	....	....	....	....	....	....	....	....	....	6	0	1	1	12	....	....	....	....
2003-04	**Vancouver**	**NHL**	**7**	**1**	**0**	**1**	**9**	**0**	**0**	**0**	**6**	**16.7**	**3**	**0**	**0.0**	**6:50**	....	....	....	....	....	....	....	....	....
	Manitoba Moose	AHL	38	5	4	9	145	....	....	....	....	....	....	....	....	....	....	....	....	....	....	....	....	....	....
	Hartford	AHL	12	0	2	2	105	....	....	....	....	....	....	....	....	....	9	0	1	1	32	....	....	....	....
2004-05	Hartford	AHL	23	2	5	7	136	....	....	....	....	....	....	....	....	....	5	0	0	0	32	....	....	....	....
	Charlotte	ECHL	4	0	2	2	10	....	....	....	....	....	....	....	....	....	....	....	....	....	....	....	....	....	....
2005-06	Hartford	AHL	76	4	8	12	278	....	....	....	....	....	....	....	....	....	11	0	0	0	33	....	....	....	....
2006-07	**Philadelphia**	**NHL**	**3**	**0**	**0**	**0**	**0**	**0**	**0**	**0**	**0**	**0.0**	**−3**	**0**	**0.0**	**4:40**	....	....	....	....	....	....	....	....	....
	Philadelphia	AHL	57	2	1	3	156	....	....	....	....	....	....	....	....	....	....	....	....	....	....	....	....	....	....
	NHL Totals		**18**	**1**	**0**	**1**	**14**	**0**	**0**	**0**	**7**	**14.3**		**1**	**100.0**	**6:07**	....	....	....	....	....	....	....	....	....

Traded to **Boston** by **Colorado** with Brian Rolston, Samuel Pahlsson and New Jersey's 1st round choice (previously acquired, Boston selected Martin Samuelsson) in 2000 Entry Draft for Raymond Bourque and Dave Andreychuk, March 6, 2000. Signed as a free agent by **Phoenix**, June 27, 2001. Traded to **Vancouver** by **Phoenix** for Bryan Helmer, July 25, 2003. Traded to **NY Rangers** by **Vancouver** with R.J. Umberger for Martin Rucinsky, March 9, 2004. Signed as a free agent by **Philadelphia**, July 13, 2006.

GRIER, Mike
(GREER, MIGHK) **S.J.**

Right wing. Shoots right. 6'1", 225 lbs. Born, Detroit, MI, January 5, 1975. St. Louis' 7th choice, 219th overall, in 1993 Entry Draft.

Season	Club	League	GP	G	A	Pts	PIM	PP	SH	GW	S	%	+/-	TF	F%	Min	GP	G	A	Pts	PIM	PP	SH	GW	Min
1992-93	St. Sebastian's	High-MA	22	16	27	43	32	....	....	....	....	....	....	....	....	....	....	....	....	....	....	....	....	....	....
1993-94	Boston University	H-East	39	9	9	18	56	....	....	....	....	....	....	....	....	....	....	....	....	....	....	....	....	....	....
1994-95	Boston University	H-East	37	*29	26	55	85	....	....	....	....	....	....	....	....	....	....	....	....	....	....	....	....	....	....
1995-96	Boston University	H-East	38	21	25	46	82	....	....	....	....	....	....	....	....	....	....	....	....	....	....	....	....	....	....
1996-97	**Edmonton**	**NHL**	**79**	**15**	**17**	**32**	**45**	**4**	**0**	**2**	**89**	**16.9**	**7**	....	....	....	**12**	**3**	**1**	**4**	**4**	**1**	**0**	**1**	....
1997-98	**Edmonton**	**NHL**	**66**	**9**	**6**	**15**	**73**	**1**	**0**	**1**	**90**	**10.0**	**−3**	....	....	....	**12**	**2**	**2**	**4**	**13**	**0**	**0**	**1**	....
1998-99	**Edmonton**	**NHL**	**82**	**20**	**24**	**44**	**54**	**3**	**2**	**1**	**143**	**14.0**	**5**	**34**	**20.6**	**15:57**	**4**	**1**	**1**	**2**	**6**	**0**	**0**	**0**	**23:26**
99-2000	**Edmonton**	**NHL**	**65**	**9**	**22**	**31**	**68**	**0**	**3**	**2**	**115**	**7.8**	**9**	**32**	**46.8**	**15:45**	....	....	....	....	....	....	....	....	....
2000-01	**Edmonton**	**NHL**	**74**	**20**	**16**	**36**	**20**	**2**	**3**	**2**	**124**	**16.1**	**11**	**36**	**38.9**	**16:44**	**6**	**0**	**0**	**0**	**8**	**0**	**0**	**0**	**21:23**
2001-02	**Edmonton**	**NHL**	**82**	**8**	**17**	**25**	**32**	**0**	**2**	**3**	**112**	**7.1**	**1**	**38**	**47.4**	**15:01**	....	....	....	....	....	....	....	....	....
2002-03	**Washington**	**NHL**	**82**	**15**	**17**	**32**	**36**	**2**	**2**	**2**	**133**	**11.3**	**−14**	**98**	**43.9**	**17:48**	**6**	**1**	**1**	**2**	**2**	**0**	**0**	**0**	**17:59**
2003-04	**Washington**	**NHL**	**68**	**8**	**12**	**20**	**32**	**1**	**1**	**0**	**115**	**7.0**	**−19**	**54**	**44.4**	**17:25**	....	....	....	....	....	....	....	....	....
	Buffalo	**NHL**	**14**	**1**	**8**	**9**	**4**	**0**	**0**	**0**	**18**	**5.6**	**10**	**11**	**63.6**	**17:29**	....	....	....	....	....	....	....	....	....
2004-05			DID NOT PLAY																						
2005-06	**Buffalo**	**NHL**	**81**	**7**	**16**	**23**	**28**	**0**	**0**	**4**	**109**	**6.4**	**−7**	**9**	**22.2**	**14:22**	**18**	**3**	**5**	**8**	**2**	**0**	**1**	**0**	**16:17**
2006-07	**San Jose**	**NHL**	**81**	**16**	**17**	**33**	**43**	**2**	**3**	**1**	**125**	**12.8**	**−5**	**46**	**41.3**	**16:26**	**11**	**2**	**2**	**4**	**27**	**0**	**0**	**0**	**17:16**
	NHL Totals		**774**	**128**	**172**	**300**	**435**	**15**	**16**	**18**	**1173**	**10.9**		**358**	**41.6**	**16:12**	**69**	**12**	**12**	**24**	**62**	**1**	**1**	**2**	**18:04**

Hockey East First All-Star Team (1995) • NCAA East First All-American Team (1995)

Rights traded to **Edmonton** by **St. Louis** with Curtis Joseph for St. Louis' 1st round choices in 1996 (previously acquired, St. Louis selected Marty Reasoner) and 1997 (previously acquired, later traded to Los Angeles – Los Angeles selected Matt Zultek) Entry Drafts, August 4, 1995. Traded to **Washington** by **Edmonton** for Washington's 2nd round choice (later traded to NY Islanders – NY Islanders selected Evgeni Tunik) in 2003 Entry Draft and Vancouver's 3rd round choice (previously acquired, Edmonton selected Zachery Stortini) in 2003 Entry Draft, October 7, 2002. Traded to **Buffalo** by **Washington** for Jakub Klepis, March 9, 2004. Signed as a free agent by **San Jose**, July 3, 2006.

GROSSMAN, Nicklas
(GROHS-man, NIHK-luhs) **DAL.**

Defense. Shoots left. 6'3", 206 lbs. Born, Stockholm, Sweden, January 22, 1985. Dallas' 4th choice, 56th overall, in 2004 Entry Draft.

Season	Club	League	GP	G	A	Pts	PIM	PP	SH	GW	S	%	+/-	TF	F%	Min	GP	G	A	Pts	PIM	PP	SH	GW	Min
2002-03	Sodertalje SK Jr.	Swe-Jr.	34	1	1	2	32	....	....	....	....	....	....	....	....	....	....	....	....	....	....	....	....	....	....
2003-04	Sodertalje SK Jr.	Swe-Jr.	33	1	2	3	32	....	....	....	....	....	....	....	....	....	2	0	0	0	0	....	....	....	....
	Sodertalje SK	Sweden	1	0	0	0	0	....	....	....	....	....	....	....	....	....	....	....	....	....	....	....	....	....	....
2004-05	Sodertalje SK Jr.	Swe-Jr.	12	3	6	9	8	....	....	....	....	....	....	....	....	....	1	0	0	0	0	....	....	....	....
	Sodertalje SK	Sweden	31	0	2	2	14	....	....	....	....	....	....	....	....	....	9	0	0	0	0	....	....	....	....
2005-06	Iowa Stars	AHL	61	2	3	5	49	....	....	....	....	....	....	....	....	....	7	0	1	1	4	....	....	....	....
2006-07	**Dallas**	**NHL**	**8**	**0**	**0**	**0**	**4**	**0**	**0**	**0**	**8**	**0.0**	**−1**	**0**	**0.0**	**12:49**	....	....	....	....	....	....	....	....	....
	Iowa Stars	AHL	67	2	8	10	40	....	....	....	....	....	....	....	....	....	8	0	0	0	10	....	....	....	....
	NHL Totals		**8**	**0**	**0**	**0**	**4**	**0**	**0**	**0**	**8**	**0.0**		**0**	**0.0**	**12:49**	....	....	....	....	....	....	....	....	....

GUENIN, Nate
(GEH-nihn, NAYT) **PHI.**

Defense. Shoots right. 6'2", 210 lbs. Born, Sewickley, PA, December 10, 1982. NY Rangers' 3rd choice, 127th overall, in 2002 Entry Draft.

Season	Club	League	GP	G	A	Pts	PIM	PP	SH	GW	S	%	+/-	TF	F%	Min	GP	G	A	Pts	PIM	PP	SH	GW	Min
99-2000	Pittsburgh	AAHA	40	3	10	13	122	....	....	....	....	....	....	....	....	....	....	....	....	....	....	....	....	....	....
2000-01	Green Bay	USHL	54	2	11	13	70	....	....	....	....	....	....	....	....	....	4	1	1	2	6	....	....	....	....
2001-02	Green Bay	USHL	56	4	11	15	150	....	....	....	....	....	....	....	....	....	7	3	3	6	10	....	....	....	....
2002-03	Ohio State	CCHA	42	2	9	11	85	....	....	....	....	....	....	....	....	....	....	....	....	....	....	....	....	....	....
2003-04	Ohio State	CCHA	29	2	15	17	92	....	....	....	....	....	....	....	....	....	....	....	....	....	....	....	....	....	....
2004-05	Ohio State	CCHA	41	2	12	14	136	....	....	....	....	....	....	....	....	....	....	....	....	....	....	....	....	....	....
2005-06	Ohio State	CCHA	39	0	11	11	87	....	....	....	....	....	....	....	....	....	....	....	....	....	....	....	....	....	....
2006-07	**Philadelphia**	**NHL**	**9**	**0**	**2**	**2**	**4**	**0**	**0**	**0**	**0**	**0.0**	**0**	**0**	**0.0**	**8:40**	....	....	....	....	....	....	....	....	....
	Philadelphia	AHL	68	3	9	12	92	....	....	....	....	....	....	....	....	....	....	....	....	....	....	....	....	....	....
	NHL Totals		**9**	**0**	**2**	**2**	**4**	**0**	**0**	**0**	**0**	**0.0**		**0**	**0.0**	**8:40**	....	....	....	....	....	....	....	....	....

USHL All-Rookie Team (2001) • CCHA Second All-Star Team (2005)

Signed as a free agent by **Philadelphia**, August 16, 2006.

GUERIN, Bill

(GAIR-ihn, BIHL) **NYI**

Right wing. Shoots right. 6'2", 220 lbs. Born, Worcester, MA, November 9, 1970. New Jersey's 1st choice, 5th overall, in 1989 Entry Draft.

			Regular Season														Playoffs								
Season	Club	League	GP	G	A	Pts	PIM	PP	SH	GW	S	%	+/-	TF	F%	Min	GP	G	A	Pts	PIM	PP	SH	GW	Min
1985-86	Spring. Olympics	NEJHL	48	26	19	45	71																		
1986-87	Spring. Olympics	NEJHL	32	34	20	54	40																		
1987-88	Spring. Olympics	NEJHL	38	31	44	75	146																		
1988-89	Spring. Olympics	NEJHL	31	32	35	67	90																		
1989-90	Boston College	H-East	39	14	11	25	54																		
1990-91	Boston College	H-East	38	26	19	45	102																		
1991-92	United States	Nat-Tm	46	12	15	27	67																		
	New Jersey	**NHL**	**5**	**0**	**1**	**1**	**9**	**0**	**0**	**0**	**8**	**0.0**	**1**				**6**	**3**	**0**	**3**	**4**	**0**	**0**	**0**	
	Utica Devils	AHL	22	13	10	23	6										4	1	3	4	14				
1992-93	**New Jersey**	**NHL**	**65**	**14**	**20**	**34**	**63**	**0**	**0**	**2**	**123**	**11.4**	**14**				**5**	**1**	**1**	**2**	**4**	**0**	**0**	**0**	
	Utica Devils	AHL	18	10	7	17	47																		
1993-94	**New Jersey**	**NHL**	**81**	**25**	**19**	**44**	**101**	**2**	**0**	**3**	**195**	**12.8**	**14**				**17**	**2**	**1**	**3**	**35**	**0**	**0**	**1**	
1994-95♦	**New Jersey**	**NHL**	**48**	**12**	**13**	**25**	**72**	**4**	**0**	**3**	**96**	**12.5**	**6**				**20**	**3**	**8**	**11**	**30**	**1**	**0**	**0**	
1995-96	**New Jersey**	**NHL**	**80**	**23**	**30**	**53**	**116**	**8**	**0**	**6**	**216**	**10.6**	**7**												
1996-97	**New Jersey**	**NHL**	**82**	**29**	**18**	**47**	**95**	**7**	**0**	**9**	**177**	**16.4**	**–2**				**8**	**2**	**1**	**3**	**18**	**1**	**0**	**1**	
1997-98	**New Jersey**	**NHL**	**19**	**5**	**5**	**10**	**13**	**1**	**0**	**2**	**48**	**10.4**	**0**												
	Edmonton	**NHL**	**40**	**13**	**16**	**29**	**80**	**8**	**0**	**2**	**130**	**10.0**	**1**				**12**	**7**	**1**	**8**	**17**	**4**	**0**	**0**	
	United States	Olympics	4	0	3	3	2																		
1998-99	**Edmonton**	**NHL**	**80**	**30**	**34**	**64**	**133**	**13**	**0**	**2**	**261**	**11.5**	**7**	**74**	**40.5**	**19:42**	**3**	**0**	**2**	**2**	**2**	**0**	**0**	**0**	**26:14**
99-2000	**Edmonton**	**NHL**	**70**	**24**	**22**	**46**	**123**	**11**	**0**	**2**	**188**	**12.8**	**4**	**13**	**46.2**	**18:01**	**5**	**3**	**2**	**5**	**9**	**1**	**0**	**0**	**17:55**
2000-01	**Edmonton**	**NHL**	**21**	**12**	**10**	**22**	**18**	**4**	**0**	**1**	**64**	**18.8**	**11**	**0**	**0.0**	**19:49**									
	Boston	**NHL**	**64**	**28**	**35**	**63**	**122**	**7**	**1**	**4**	**225**	**12.4**	**–4**	**36**	**41.7**	**22:43**									
2001-02	**Boston**	**NHL**	**78**	**41**	**25**	**66**	**91**	**10**	**1**	**7**	**355**	**11.5**	**–1**	**17**	**52.9**	**20:45**	**6**	**4**	**2**	**6**	**6**	**3**	**0**	**0**	**21:17**
	United States	Olympics	6	4	0	4	4																		
2002-03	**Dallas**	**NHL**	**64**	**25**	**25**	**50**	**113**	**11**	**0**	**2**	**229**	**10.9**	**5**	**20**	**25.0**	**18:33**	**4**	**0**	**0**	**0**	**4**	**0**	**0**	**0**	**8:34**
2003-04	**Dallas**	**NHL**	**82**	**34**	**35**	**69**	**109**	**9**	**0**	**10**	**263**	**12.9**	**14**	**16**	**18.8**	**18:42**	**5**	**0**	**1**	**1**	**4**	**0**	**0**	**0**	**20:09**
2004-05			DID NOT PLAY																						
2005-06	**Dallas**	**NHL**	**70**	**13**	**27**	**40**	**115**	**3**	**0**	**2**	**210**	**6.2**	**0**	**16**	**50.0**	**16:25**	**5**	**3**	**1**	**4**	**0**	**1**	**0**	**0**	**16:14**
	United States	Olympics	6	1	0	1	0																		
2006-07	**St. Louis**	**NHL**	**61**	**28**	**19**	**47**	**52**	**7**	**0**	**6**	**189**	**14.8**	**8**	**10**	**50.0**	**17:26**									
	San Jose	**NHL**	**16**	**8**	**1**	**9**	**14**	**2**	**0**	**1**	**36**	**22.2**	**2**	**2**	**50.0**	**15:22**	**9**	**0**	**2**	**2**	**12**	**0**	**0**	**0**	**17:06**
	NHL Totals		**1026**	**364**	**355**	**719**	**1439**	**107**	**2**	**64**	**3013**	**12.1**		**204**	**40.2**	**18:59**	**105**	**28**	**22**	**50**	**145**	**11**	**0**	**2**	**18:00**

NHL Second All-Star Team (2002)

Played in NHL All-Star Game (2001, 2003, 2004, 2007)

Traded to **Edmonton** by **New Jersey** with Valeri Zelepukin for Jason Arnott and Bryan Muir, January 4, 1998. Traded to **Boston** by **Edmonton** for Anson Carter, Boston's 1st (Ales Hemsky) and 2nd (Doug Lynch) round choices in 2001 Entry Draft and future considerations, November 15, 2000. Signed as a free agent by **Dallas**, July 3, 2002. Signed as a free agent by **St. Louis**, July 3, 2006. Traded to **San Jose** by **St. Louis** for Ville Nieminen, Jay Barriball and New Jersey's 1st round choice (previously acquired, St. Louis selected David Perron) in 2007 Entry Draft, February 27, 2007. Signed as a free agent by **NY Islanders**, July 5, 2007.

GUITE, Ben

(GEE-tay, BEHN) **COL.**

Right wing. Shoots right. 6'1", 211 lbs. Born, Montreal, Que., July 17, 1978. Montreal's 8th choice, 172nd overall, in 1997 Entry Draft.

			Regular Season														Playoffs								
Season	Club	League	GP	G	A	Pts	PIM	PP	SH	GW	S	%	+/-	TF	F%	Min	GP	G	A	Pts	PIM	PP	SH	GW	Min
1994-95	Lac St-Louis Lions	QAAA	40	9	12	21											4	0	0	0	0				
1995-96	Capital District	Exhib.	STATISTICS NOT AVAILABLE																						
1996-97	U. of Maine	H-East	34	7	7	14	21																		
1997-98	U. of Maine	H-East	32	6	12	18	20																		
1998-99	U. of Maine	H-East	40	12	16	28	30																		
99-2000	U. of Maine	H-East	40	22	14	36	36																		
2000-01	Tallahassee	ECHL	68	11	18	29	34																		
2001-02	Bridgeport	AHL	68	12	18	30	39																		
	Cincinnati	AHL	10	2	5	7	4										3	0	0	0	2				
2002-03	Cincinnati	AHL	80	13	16	29	44																		
2003-04	Bridgeport	AHL	79	6	18	24	73										7	0	0	0	6				
2004-05	Providence Bruins	AHL	77	9	15	24	69										17	3	4	7	34				
2005-06	**Boston**	**NHL**	**1**	**0**	**0**	**0**	**0**	**0**	**0**	**0**	**2**	**0.0**	**0**	**11**	**18.2**	**8:53**									
	Providence Bruins	AHL	73	22	30	52	87										6	1	3	4	14				
2006-07	**Colorado**	**NHL**	**39**	**3**	**8**	**11**	**16**	**0**	**1**	**1**	**63**	**4.8**	**–4**	**388**	**49.5**	**12:17**									
	Albany River Rats	AHL	36	10	19	29	22																		
	NHL Totals		**40**	**3**	**8**	**11**	**16**	**0**	**1**	**1**	**65**	**4.6**		**399**	**48.6**	**12:12**									

Signed as a free agent by **NY Islanders**, August, 2001. Traded to **Anaheim** by **NY Islanders** with the rights to Bjorn Mellin for Dave Roche, March 19, 2002. Signed as a free agent by **NY Rangers**, September 16, 2003. Signed as a free agent by **Bridgeport** (AHL), October 10, 2003. Signed to a PTO (tryout) contract by **Providence** (AHL), September 28, 2004. Signed as a free agent by **Boston**, August 15, 2005. Signed as a free agent by **Colorado**, July 12, 2006.

HAGMAN, Niklas

(HAG-muhn, NIHK-luhs) **DAL.**

Left wing. Shoots left. 6', 205 lbs. Born, Espoo, Finland, December 5, 1979. Florida's 3rd choice, 70th overall, in 1999 Entry Draft.

			Regular Season														Playoffs								
Season	Club	League	GP	G	A	Pts	PIM	PP	SH	GW	S	%	+/-	TF	F%	Min	GP	G	A	Pts	PIM	PP	SH	GW	Min
1995-96	HIFK Helsinki U18	Fin-U18	26	12	21	33	32										4	3	0	3	2				
	HIFK Helsinki Jr.	Fin-Jr.	12	3	1	4	0																		
1996-97	HIFK Helsinki Jr.	Fin-Jr.	30	13	12	25	30																		
	HIFK Helsinki U18	Fin-U18	21	19	12	31	46										4	1	1	2	0				
1997-98	HIFK Helsinki U18	Fin-U18	1	0	1	1	0																		
	HIFK Helsinki Jr.	Fin-Jr.	26	9	5	14	16																		
	HIFK Helsinki	Finland	8	1	0	1	0																		
1998-99	HIFK Helsinki Jr.	Fin-Jr.	15	4	10	14	43																		
	HIFK Helsinki	Finland	17	1	1	2	14																		
	HIFK Helsinki	EuroHL	1	0	1	1	0																		
	Blues Espoo	Finland	14	1	1	2	2										4	1	0	1	0				
99-2000	Karpat Oulu Jr.	Fin-Jr.	4	7	3	10	0																		
	Karpat Oulu	Finland-2	41	17	18	35	12										7	4	2	6	0				
2000-01	Karpat Oulu	Finland	56	28	18	46	32										8	3	1	4	0				
2001-02	**Florida**	**NHL**	**78**	**10**	**18**	**28**	**8**	**0**	**1**	**2**	**134**	**7.5**	**–6**	**32**	**28.1**	**13:50**									
	Finland	Olympics	4	1	2	3	0																		
2002-03	**Florida**	**NHL**	**80**	**8**	**15**	**23**	**20**	**2**	**0**	**0**	**132**	**6.1**	**–8**	**17**	**11.8**	**13:31**									
2003-04	**Florida**	**NHL**	**75**	**10**	**13**	**23**	**22**	**0**	**1**	**2**	**122**	**8.2**	**–5**	**19**	**21.1**	**14:47**									
2004-05	HC Davos	Swiss	44	17	22	39	20										15	10	7	17	6				
2005-06	**Florida**	**NHL**	**30**	**2**	**4**	**6**	**2**	**0**	**0**	**0**	**52**	**3.8**	**–8**	**10**	**10.0**	**14:00**									
	Dallas	**NHL**	**54**	**6**	**9**	**15**	**16**	**0**	**1**	**0**	**74**	**8.1**	**–2**	**6**	**66.7**	**11:17**	**5**	**2**	**1**	**3**	**4**	**0**	**0**	**1**	**10:50**
	Finland	Olympics	8	0	1	1	2																		
2006-07	**Dallas**	**NHL**	**82**	**17**	**12**	**29**	**34**	**2**	**1**	**2**	**152**	**11.2**	**3**	**15**	**20.0**	**14:26**	**7**	**0**	**1**	**1**	**10**	**0**	**0**	**0**	**16:26**
	NHL Totals		**399**	**53**	**71**	**124**	**102**	**4**	**4**	**6**	**666**	**8.0**		**99**	**23.2**	**13:44**	**12**	**2**	**2**	**4**	**14**	**0**	**0**	**1**	**14:06**

Signed as a free agent by **Davos** (Swiss), July 23, 2004. Traded to **Dallas** by **Florida** for Dallas' 7th round choice (Sergei Gayduchenko) in 2007 Entry Draft, December 12, 2005.

HAHL, Riku

(HAHL, REE-koo) **COL.**

Center. Shoots left. 6'1", 205 lbs. Born, Hameenlinna, Finland, November 1, 1980. Colorado's 9th choice, 183rd overall, in 1999 Entry Draft.

			Regular Season														Playoffs								
Season	Club	League	GP	G	A	Pts	PIM	PP	SH	GW	S	%	+/-	TF	F%	Min	GP	G	A	Pts	PIM	PP	SH	GW	Min
1996-97	HPK U18	Fin-U18	32	19	24	43	22																		
	HPK Jr.	Fin-Jr.	2	0	1	1	2										6	2	0	2	2				
1997-98	HPK U18	Fin-U18	10	5	14	19	6																		
	HPK Jr.	Fin-Jr.	35	13	6	19	12																		
1998-99	HPK Jr.	Fin-Jr.	7	0	2	2	6										2	0	3	3	0				
	HPK Hameenlinna	Finland	28	0	1	1	0										8	0	0	0	2				
99-2000	HPK Jr.	Fin-Jr.	19	6	10	16	24																		
	HPK Hameenlinna	Finland	50	4	3	7	18										8	0	0	0	2				
2000-01	HPK Jr.	Fin-Jr.	2	1	3	4	0																		
	HPK Hameenlinna	Finland	55	3	9	12	32																		
2001-02	**Colorado**	**NHL**	**22**	**2**	**3**	**5**	**14**	**0**	**0**	**1**	**17**	**11.8**	**1**	**94**	**35.1**	**9:26**	**21**	**1**	**2**	**3**	**0**	**0**	**0**	**0**	**7:31**
	Hershey Bears	AHL	52	6	17	23	16																		

Season	Club	League	GP	G	A	Pts	PIM	PP	SH	GW	S	%	+/-	TF	F%	Min	GP	G	A	Pts	PIM	PP	SH	GW	Min
								Regular Season									Playoffs								
2002-03	Hershey Bears	AHL	28	7	7	14	17	....	....	....	....	....	....	....	....	....	....	....	....	....	....	....	....	....	....
	Colorado	NHL	42	3	4	7	12	0	0	0	61	4.9	3	69	37.7	11:03	6	0	2	2	2	0	0	0	13:49
2003-04	Colorado	NHL	28	0	1	1	12	0	0	0	40	0.0	-7	107	41.1	12:17	7	1	0	1	2	0	0	0	12:08
2004-05	HPK Hameenlinna	Finland	44	8	13	21	12	....	....	....	....	....	....	....	....	....	10	2	6	8	2	....	....	....	....
2005-06	HC Davos	Swiss	41	8	17	25	22	....	....	....	....	....	....	....	....	....	14	2	9	11	20	....	....	....	....
2006-07	Timra IK	Sweden	31	4	13	17	16	....	....	....	....	....	....	....	....	....	1	0	0	0	0	....	....	....	....
	NHL Totals		92	5	8	13	38	0	0	1	118	4.2		270	38.1	11:02	34	2	4	6	4	0	0	0	9:35

• Missed majority of 2003-04 season recovering from shoulder injury suffered in game vs. Edmonton, October 23, 2003. Signed as a free agent by **Hameenlinna** (Finland), September 15, 2004. Signed as a free agent by **Davos** (Swiss), September 5, 2005. Signed as a free agent by **Timra** (Sweden), May 15, 2006.

HAINSEY, Ron (HAYN-zee, RAWN) CBJ

Defense. Shoots left. 6'3", 211 lbs. Born, Bolton, CT, March 24, 1981. Montreal's 1st choice, 13th overall, in 2000 Entry Draft.

Season	Club	League	GP	G	A	Pts	PIM	PP	SH	GW	S	%	+/-	TF	F%	Min	GP	G	A	Pts	PIM	PP	SH	GW	Min
1997-98	USNTDP	U-17	18	2	7	9	28	....	....	....	....	....	....	....	....	....	....	....	....	....	....	....	....	....	....
	USNTDP	USHL	3	0	0	0	0	....	....	....	....	....	....	....	....	....	....	....	....	....	....	....	....	....	....
	USNTDP	NAHL	40	4	7	11	16	....	....	....	....	....	....	....	....	....	5	0	1	1	0	....	....	....	....
1998-99	USNTDP	U-18	6	2	1	3	8	....	....	....	....	....	....	....	....	....	....	....	....	....	....	....	....	....	....
	USNTDP	USHL	48	5	12	17	45	....	....	....	....	....	....	....	....	....	....	....	....	....	....	....	....	....	....
99-2000	U. Mass-Lowell	H-East	30	3	8	11	20	....	....	....	....	....	....	....	....	....	....	....	....	....	....	....	....	....	....
2000-01	U. Mass-Lowell	H-East	33	10	26	36	51	....	....	....	....	....	....	....	....	....	....	....	....	....	....	....	....	....	....
	Quebec Citadelles	AHL	4	1	0	1	0	....	....	....	....	....	....	....	....	....	1	0	0	0	0	....	....	....	....
2001-02	Quebec Citadelles	AHL	63	7	24	31	26	....	....	....	....	....	....	....	....	....	3	0	0	0	0	....	....	....	....
2002-03	Montreal	NHL	21	0	0	0	2	0	0	0	12	0.0	-1	0	0.0	12:25	....	....	....	....	....	....	....	....	....
	Hamilton	AHL	33	2	11	13	26	....	....	....	....	....	....	....	....	....	23	1	10	11	20	....	....	....	....
2003-04	Montreal	NHL	11	1	1	2	4	0	0	0	11	9.1	3	0	0.0	13:15	....	....	....	....	....	....	....	....	....
	Hamilton	AHL	54	7	24	31	35	....	....	....	....	....	....	....	....	....	10	0	5	5	6	....	....	....	....
2004-05	Hamilton	AHL	68	9	14	23	45	....	....	....	....	....	....	....	....	....	4	1	1	2	0	....	....	....	....
2005-06	Hamilton	AHL	22	3	14	17	19	....	....	....	....	....	....	....	....	....	....	....	....	....	....	....	....	....	....
	Columbus	NHL	55	2	15	17	43	1	0	0	81	2.5	13	1	0.0	17:47	....	....	....	....	....	....	....	....	....
2006-07	Columbus	NHL	80	9	25	34	69	7	0	0	136	6.6	-19	2	50.0	22:53	....	....	....	....	....	....	....	....	....
	NHL Totals		167	12	41	53	118	8	0	0	240	5.0		3	33.3	19:15	....	....	....	....	....	....	....	....	....

Hockey East First All-Star Team (2001) • NCAA East Second All-American Team (2001) • AHL All-Rookie Team (2002)

Claimed on waivers by **Columbus** from **Montreal**, November 29, 2005.

HALE, David (HAYL, DAY-vihd) CGY.

Defense. Shoots left. 6'2", 215 lbs. Born, Colorado Springs, CO, June 18, 1981. New Jersey's 1st choice, 22nd overall, in 2000 Entry Draft.

Season	Club	League	GP	G	A	Pts	PIM	PP	SH	GW	S	%	+/-	TF	F%	Min	GP	G	A	Pts	PIM	PP	SH	GW	Min
1997-98	Colorado North	High-CO	25	11	33	44	154	....	....	....	....	....	....	....	....	....	....	....	....	....	....	....	....	....	....
1998-99	Sioux City	USHL	56	3	15	18	127	....	....	....	....	....	....	....	....	....	5	0	0	0	18	....	....	....	....
99-2000	Sioux City	USHL	54	6	18	24	187	....	....	....	....	....	....	....	....	....	5	0	2	2	6	....	....	....	....
2000-01	North Dakota	WCHA	44	4	5	9	79	....	....	....	....	....	....	....	....	....	....	....	....	....	....	....	....	....	....
2001-02	North Dakota	WCHA	34	4	5	9	63	....	....	....	....	....	....	....	....	....	....	....	....	....	....	....	....	....	....
2002-03	North Dakota	WCHA	26	2	6	8	49	....	....	....	....	....	....	....	....	....	....	....	....	....	....	....	....	....	....
2003-04	New Jersey	NHL	65	0	4	4	72	0	0	0	45	0.0	12	0	0.0	15:01	1	0	0	0	0	0	0	0	8:59
2004-05	Albany River Rats	AHL	30	2	3	5	39	....	....	....	....	....	....	....	....	....	....	....	....	....	....	....	....	....	....
2005-06	New Jersey	NHL	38	0	4	4	21	0	0	0	19	0.0	5	0	0.0	12:03	8	0	2	2	12	0	0	0	12:06
	Albany River Rats	AHL	30	2	5	7	64	....	....	....	....	....	....	....	....	....	....	....	....	....	....	....	....	....	....
2006-07	New Jersey	NHL	43	0	1	1	26	0	0	0	21	0.0	2	0	0.0	9:41	....	....	....	....	....	....	....	....	....
	Lowell Devils	AHL	2	0	1	1	0	....	....	....	....	....	....	....	....	....	....	....	....	....	....	....	....	....	....
	Calgary	NHL	11	0	0	0	10	0	0	0	12	0.0	-2	0	0.0	15:47	2	0	0	0	6	0	0	0	12:42
	NHL Totals		157	0	9	9	129	0	0	0	97	0.0		0	0.0	12:53	11	0	2	2	18	0	0	0	11:56

USHL First All-Star Team (2000)

Traded to **Calgary** by **New Jersey** with New Jersey's 5th round choice (later traded to Buffalo - Buffalo selected Jean-Simon Allard) in 2007 Entry Draft for Calgary's 3rd round choice (Nick Palmieri) in 2007 Entry Draft, February 27, 2007.

HALL, Adam (HAWL, A-duhm)

Right wing. Shoots right. 6'3", 210 lbs. Born, Kalamazoo, MI, August 14, 1980. Nashville's 3rd choice, 52nd overall, in 1999 Entry Draft.

Season	Club	League	GP	G	A	Pts	PIM	PP	SH	GW	S	%	+/-	TF	F%	Min	GP	G	A	Pts	PIM	PP	SH	GW	Min
1996-97	Bramalea Blues	OPJHL	43	9	14	23	92	....	....	....	....	....	....	....	....	....	....	....	....	....	....	....	....	....	....
1997-98	USNTDP	U-18	29	18	9	27	19	....	....	....	....	....	....	....	....	....	....	....	....	....	....	....	....	....	....
	USNTDP	USHL	21	9	11	20	20	....	....	....	....	....	....	....	....	....	....	....	....	....	....	....	....	....	....
	USNTDP	NAHL	15	12	1	13	20	....	....	....	....	....	....	....	....	....	6	3	2	5	4	....	....	....	....
1998-99	Michigan State	CCHA	36	16	7	23	74	....	....	....	....	....	....	....	....	....	....	....	....	....	....	....	....	....	....
99-2000	Michigan State	CCHA	40	*26	13	39	38	....	....	....	....	....	....	....	....	....	....	....	....	....	....	....	....	....	....
2000-01	Michigan State	CCHA	42	18	12	30	42	....	....	....	....	....	....	....	....	....	....	....	....	....	....	....	....	....	....
2001-02	Michigan State	CCHA	41	19	15	34	36	....	....	....	....	....	....	....	....	....	....	....	....	....	....	....	....	....	....
	Nashville	NHL	1	0	1	1	0	0	0	0	2	0.0	0	0	0.0	14:04	....	....	....	....	....	....	....	....	....
	Milwaukee	AHL	6	2	2	4	4	....	....	....	....	....	....	....	....	....	....	....	....	....	....	....	....	....	....
2002-03	Nashville	NHL	79	16	12	28	31	8	0	2	146	11.0	-8	17	52.9	14:09	....	....	....	....	....	....	....	....	....
	Milwaukee	AHL	1	0	0	0	2	....	....	....	....	....	....	....	....	....	....	....	....	....	....	....	....	....	....
2003-04	Nashville	NHL	79	13	14	27	37	6	0	1	151	8.6	-8	348	56.3	16:14	6	2	1	3	2	0	0	1	18:29
2004-05	KalPa Kuopio	Finland-2	36	23	17	40	28	....	....	....	....	....	....	....	....	....	9	2	3	5	4	....	....	....	....
2005-06	Nashville	NHL	75	14	15	29	40	10	0	5	122	11.5	0	470	48.9	16:47	5	1	0	1	0	1	0	1	12:10
2006-07	NY Rangers	NHL	49	4	8	12	18	3	0	0	61	6.6	-13	59	45.8	12:27	....	....	....	....	....	....	....	....	....
	Minnesota	NHL	23	2	3	5	8	0	0	0	42	4.8	2	11	72.7	12:13	3	0	0	0	7	0	0	0	10:06
	NHL Totals		306	49	53	102	134	27	0	8	524	9.4		905	51.9	14:55	14	3	1	4	9	1	0	2	14:26

CCHA Second All-Star Team (2000)

Signed as a free agent by **Kuopio** (Finland-2), October 11, 2004. Traded to **NY Rangers** by **Nashville** for Dominic Moore, July 19, 2006. Traded to **Minnesota** by **NY Rangers** for Pascal Dupuis, February 9, 2007.

HALPERN, Jeff (HAL-pehrn, JEHF) DAL.

Center. Shoots right. 6', 203 lbs. Born, Potomac, MD, May 3, 1976.

Season	Club	League	GP	G	A	Pts	PIM	PP	SH	GW	S	%	+/-	TF	F%	Min	GP	G	A	Pts	PIM	PP	SH	GW	Min
1994-95	Stratford Cullitons	OHA-B	44	29	54	83	43	....	....	....	....	....	....	....	....	....	....	....	....	....	....	....	....	....	....
1995-96	Princeton	ECAC	29	3	11	14	30	....	....	....	....	....	....	....	....	....	....	....	....	....	....	....	....	....	....
1996-97	Princeton	ECAC	33	7	24	31	35	....	....	....	....	....	....	....	....	....	....	....	....	....	....	....	....	....	....
1997-98	Princeton	ECAC	36	*28	25	*53	46	....	....	....	....	....	....	....	....	....	....	....	....	....	....	....	....	....	....
1998-99	Princeton	ECAC	33	*22	22	44	32	....	....	....	....	....	....	....	....	....	....	....	....	....	....	....	....	....	....
	Portland Pirates	AHL	6	2	1	3	4	....	....	....	....	....	....	....	....	....	....	....	....	....	....	....	....	....	....
99-2000	Washington	NHL	79	18	11	29	39	4	4	1	108	16.7	21	812	51.1	13:14	5	2	1	3	0	1	0	1	15:16
2000-01	Washington	NHL	80	21	21	42	60	2	1	5	110	19.1	13	1293	52.4	16:08	6	2	3	5	17	1	0	1	20:02
2001-02	Washington	NHL	48	5	14	19	29	0	0	4	74	6.8	-9	661	56.0	15:19	....	....	....	....	....	....	....	....	....
2002-03	Washington	NHL	82	13	21	34	88	1	2	2	126	10.3	6	1492	54.1	17:25	6	0	1	1	2	0	0	0	19:59
2003-04	Washington	NHL	79	19	27	46	56	7	0	2	114	16.7	-21	1509	54.3	19:03	....	....	....	....	....	....	....	....	....
2004-05	HC Ajoie	Swiss-2	15	5	12	17	52	....	....	....	....	....	....	....	....	....	....	....	....	....	....	....	....	....	....
	Kloten Flyers	Swiss	9	7	4	11	6	....	....	....	....	....	....	....	....	....	....	....	....	....	....	....	....	....	....
2005-06	Washington	NHL	70	11	33	44	79	6	0	1	151	7.3	-8	1454	55.2	20:00	....	....	....	....	....	....	....	....	....
2006-07	Dallas	NHL	76	8	17	25	78	1	0	4	106	7.5	-7	1135	51.8	16:48	7	2	1	3	4	0	0	1	18:57
	NHL Totals		514	95	144	239	429	21	7	19	789	12.0		8356	53.6	16:54	24	6	6	12	23	2	0	3	18:43

ECAC Second All-Star Team (1998, 1999)

Signed as a free agent by **Washington**, March 29, 1999. Signed as a free agent by **Ajoie** (Swiss-2), October 8, 2004. Signed as a free agent by **Kloten** (Swiss), December 30, 2004. Signed as a free agent by **Dallas**, July 5, 2006.

HAMEL, Denis

(ha-MEHL, deh-NEE) **OTT.**

Left wing. Shoots left. 6'1", 201 lbs. Born, Lachute, Que., May 10, 1977. St. Louis' 5th choice, 153rd overall, in 1995 Entry Draft.

			Regular Season														Playoffs								
Season	Club	League	GP	G	A	Pts	PIM	PP	SH	GW	S	%	+/-	TF	F%	Min	GP	G	A	Pts	PIM	PP	SH	GW	Min
1992-93	Lachute Regents	QAAA	32	18	24	42	....	....	....	....	....	....	....	....	....	....	....	....	....	....	....	....	....	....	....
1993-94	Lac St-Louis Lions	QAAA	28	10	11	21	50	....	....	....	....	....	....	....	....	....	....	....	....	....	....	....	....	....	....
	Abitibi Forestiers	QAAA	15	5	7	12	29	....	....	....	....	....	....	....	....	....	5	0	3	3	16	....	....	....	....
1994-95	Chicoutimi	QMJHL	66	15	12	27	155	....	....	....	....	....	....	....	....	....	12	2	0	2	27	....	....	....	....
1995-96	Chicoutimi	QMJHL	65	40	49	89	199	....	....	....	....	....	....	....	....	....	17	10	14	24	64	....	....	....	....
1996-97	Chicoutimi	QMJHL	70	50	50	100	357	....	....	....	....	....	....	....	....	....	20	15	10	25	58	....	....	....	....
1997-98	Rochester	AHL	74	10	15	25	98	....	....	....	....	....	....	....	....	....	4	1	2	3	0	....	....	....	....
1998-99	Rochester	AHL	74	16	17	33	121	....	....	....	....	....	....	....	....	....	20	3	4	7	10	....	....	....	....
99-2000	**Buffalo**	**NHL**	**3**	**1**	**0**	**1**	**0**	**0**	**0**	**0**	**3**	**33.3**	**–1**	**0**	**0.0**	**9:45**	....	....	....	....	....	....	....	....	....
	Rochester	AHL	76	34	24	58	122	....	....	....	....	....	....	....	....	....	21	6	7	13	49	....	....	....	....
2000-01	**Buffalo**	**NHL**	**41**	**8**	**3**	**11**	**22**	**1**	**1**	**3**	**55**	**14.5**	**–2**	**171**	**33.9**	**10:58**	....	....	....	....	....	....	....	....	....
2001-02	**Buffalo**	**NHL**	**61**	**2**	**6**	**8**	**28**	**0**	**0**	**0**	**80**	**2.5**	**–1**	**94**	**39.4**	**11:00**	....	....	....	....	....	....	....	....	....
2002-03	**Buffalo**	**NHL**	**25**	**2**	**0**	**2**	**17**	**0**	**0**	**1**	**41**	**4.9**	**–4**	**4**	**25.0**	**12:40**	....	....	....	....	....	....	....	....	....
	Rochester	AHL	48	27	20	47	64	....	....	....	....	....	....	....	....	....	3	3	2	5	4	....	....	....	....
2003-04	**Ottawa**	**NHL**	**5**	**0**	**0**	**0**	**0**	**0**	**0**	**0**	**6**	**0.0**	**–3**	**1**	**100.0**	**6:16**	....	....	....	....	....	....	....	....	....
	Binghamton	AHL	78	29	38	67	116	....	....	....	....	....	....	....	....	....	2	0	0	0	2	....	....	....	....
2004-05	Binghamton	AHL	80	39	39	78	75	....	....	....	....	....	....	....	....	....	5	1	0	1	4	....	....	....	....
2005-06	**Ottawa**	**NHL**	**4**	**1**	**0**	**1**	**0**	**0**	**0**	**0**	**9**	**11.1**	**1**	**1**	**0.0**	**9:10**	....	....	....	....	....	....	....	....	....
	Binghamton	AHL	77	*56	35	91	65	....	....	....	....	....	....	....	....	....	....	....	....	....	....	....	....	....	....
2006-07	**Ottawa**	**NHL**	**43**	**4**	**3**	**7**	**10**	**0**	**0**	**0**	**36**	**11.1**	**4**	**9**	**33.3**	**5:38**	....	....	....	....	....	....	....	....	....
	Atlanta	**NHL**	**3**	**1**	**0**	**1**	**0**	**0**	**0**	**0**	**3**	**33.3**	**0**	**2**	**0.0**	**10:25**	....	....	....	....	....	....	....	....	....
	Philadelphia	**NHL**	**7**	**0**	**0**	**0**	**0**	**0**	**0**	**0**	**3**	**0.0**	**–4**	**0**	**0.0**	**6:58**	....	....	....	....	....	....	....	....	....
	NHL Totals		**192**	**19**	**12**	**31**	**77**	**1**	**1**	**4**	**236**	**8.1**		**282**	**35.5**	**9:40**	....	....	....	....	....	....	....	....	....

QMJHL All-Rookie Team (1995) • AHL First All-Star Team (2004) • Willie Marshall Award (Top Goal-scorer - AHL) (2006) (tied with Don MacLean)

Traded to **Buffalo** by **St. Louis** for Charlie Huddy and Buffalo's 7th round choice (Daniel Corso) in 1996 Entry Draft, March 19, 1996. • Missed majority of 2000-01 season recovering from knee injury suffered in game vs. NY Islanders, January 27, 2001. Signed as a free agent by **Ottawa**, July 5, 2003. Claimed by **Washington** from **Ottawa** in Waiver Draft, October 3, 2003. Traded to **Ottawa** by **Washington** for future considerations, October 5, 2003. Claimed on waivers by **Atlanta** from **Ottawa**, February 10, 2007. Claimed on waivers by **Philadelphia** from **Atlanta**, February 27, 2007. Signed as a free agent by **Ottawa** , July 6, 2007.

HAMHUIS, Dan

(HAM-HOOS, DAN) **NSH.**

Defense. Shoots left. 6'1", 200 lbs. Born, Smithers, B.C., December 13, 1982. Nashville's 1st choice, 12th overall, in 2001 Entry Draft.

Season	Club	League	GP	G	A	Pts	PIM	PP	SH	GW	S	%	+/-	TF	F%	Min	GP	G	A	Pts	PIM	PP	SH	GW	Min
1997-98	Smithers A's	BCAHA	59	59	72	131	59	....	....	....	....	....	....	....	....	....	....	....	....	....	....	....	....	....	....
1998-99	Prince George	WHL	56	1	3	4	45	....	....	....	....	....	....	....	....	....	7	1	2	3	8	....	....	....	....
99-2000	Prince George	WHL	70	10	23	33	140	....	....	....	....	....	....	....	....	....	13	2	3	5	35	....	....	....	....
2000-01	Prince George	WHL	62	13	47	60	125	....	....	....	....	....	....	....	....	....	6	2	3	5	15	....	....	....	....
2001-02	Prince George	WHL	59	10	50	60	135	....	....	....	....	....	....	....	....	....	7	0	5	5	16	....	....	....	....
2002-03	Milwaukee	AHL	68	6	21	27	81	....	....	....	....	....	....	....	....	....	6	0	3	3	2	....	....	....	....
2003-04	**Nashville**	**NHL**	**80**	**7**	**19**	**26**	**57**	**2**	**0**	**4**	**115**	**6.1**	**–12**	**0**	**0.0**	**22:08**	**6**	**0**	**2**	**2**	**6**	**0**	**0**	**0**	**20:29**
2004-05	Milwaukee	AHL	76	13	38	51	85	....	....	....	....	....	....	....	....	....	7	0	2	2	10	....	....	....	....
2005-06	**Nashville**	**NHL**	**82**	**7**	**31**	**38**	**70**	**4**	**1**	**1**	**135**	**5.2**	**11**	**0**	**0.0**	**22:34**	**5**	**0**	**2**	**2**	**2**	**0**	**0**	**0**	**19:41**
2006-07	**Nashville**	**NHL**	**81**	**6**	**14**	**20**	**66**	**0**	**0**	**1**	**84**	**7.1**	**8**	**1**	**0.0**	**21:20**	**5**	**0**	**1**	**1**	**2**	**0**	**0**	**0**	**21:36**
	NHL Totals		**243**	**20**	**64**	**84**	**193**	**6**	**1**	**6**	**334**	**6.0**		**1**	**0.0**	**22:01**	**16**	**0**	**5**	**5**	**10**	**0**	**0**	**0**	**20:35**

WHL West First All-Star Team (2001, 2002) • WHL Player of the Year (2002) • Canadian Major Junior First All-Star Team (2002) • Canadian Major Junior Defenseman of the Year (2002) • AHL Second All-Star Team (2005)

HAMILTON, Jeff

(HAM-ihl-tuhn, JEHF) **CAR.**

Center. Shoots right. 5'10", 185 lbs. Born, Englewood, OH, September 4, 1977.

Season	Club	League	GP	G	A	Pts	PIM	PP	SH	GW	S	%	+/-	TF	F%	Min	GP	G	A	Pts	PIM	PP	SH	GW	Min
1995-96	Avon Old Farms	High-CT	24	29	23	52	....	....	....	....	....	....	....	....	....	....	....	....	....	....	....	....	....	....	....
1996-97	Yale	ECAC	31	10	13	23	26	....	....	....	....	....	....	....	....	....	....	....	....	....	....	....	....	....	....
1997-98	Yale	ECAC	33	27	20	47	28	....	....	....	....	....	....	....	....	....	....	....	....	....	....	....	....	....	....
1998-99	Yale	ECAC	30	20	28	48	51	....	....	....	....	....	....	....	....	....	....	....	....	....	....	....	....	....	....
99-2000	Yale	ECAC	2	0	1	1	0	....	....	....	....	....	....	....	....	....	....	....	....	....	....	....	....	....	....
2000-01	Yale	ECAC	31	23	32	55	39	....	....	....	....	....	....	....	....	....	....	....	....	....	....	....	....	....	....
2001-02	Karpat Oulu	Finland	39	18	15	33	16	....	....	....	....	....	....	....	....	....	3	0	0	0	0	....	....	....	....
2002-03	Bridgeport	AHL	67	22	16	38	35	....	....	....	....	....	....	....	....	....	9	3	3	6	0	....	....	....	....
2003-04	**NY Islanders**	**NHL**	**1**	**0**	**0**	**0**	**0**	**0**	**0**	**0**	**1**	**0.0**	**0**	**0**	**0.0**	**10:00**	....	....	....	....	....	....	....	....	....
	Bridgeport	AHL	67	*43	25	68	26	....	....	....	....	....	....	....	....	....	7	4	0	4	4	....	....	....	....
2004-05	Hartford	AHL	60	23	30	53	32	....	....	....	....	....	....	....	....	....	6	4	3	7	0	....	....	....	....
2005-06	Ak Bars Kazan	Russia	8	0	1	1	16	....	....	....	....	....	....	....	....	....	....	....	....	....	....	....	....	....	....
	NY Islanders	**NHL**	**13**	**2**	**6**	**8**	**8**	**1**	**0**	**0**	**29**	**6.9**	**0**	**6**	**16.7**	**10:33**	....	....	....	....	....	....	....	....	....
	Bridgeport	AHL	39	24	26	50	28	....	....	....	....	....	....	....	....	....	....	....	....	....	....	....	....	....	....
2006-07	**Chicago**	**NHL**	**70**	**18**	**21**	**39**	**22**	**3**	**0**	**4**	**138**	**13.0**	**–4**	**55**	**36.4**	**12:56**	....	....	....	....	....	....	....	....	....
	NHL Totals		**84**	**20**	**27**	**47**	**30**	**4**	**0**	**4**	**168**	**11.9**		**61**	**34.4**	**12:31**	....	....	....	....	....	....	....	....	....

ECAC All-Rookie Team (1997) • ECAC First All-Star Team (1998, 1999, 2001) • NCAA East Second All-American Team (1998, 1999) • NCAA East First All-American Team (2001) • AHL First All-Star Team (2004) • Willie Marshall Award (Top Goal-scorer - AHL) (2004)

• Missed majority of 1999-2000 season recovering from abdominal injury originally suffered in game vs. University of Michigan (CCHA), October 30, 1999. Signed as a free agent by **Oulu** (Finland), October 4, 2001. Signed as a free agent by **NY Islanders**, August 6, 2002. Signed as a free agent by **Hartford** (AHL), October 10, 2004. Signed as a free agent by **Kazan** (Russia), September 5, 2005. Signed as a free agent by **Chicago**, September 29, 2006. Signed as a free agent by **Carolina**, July 1, 2007.

HAMRLIK, Roman

(HAHM-reh-lik, ROH-muhn) **MTL.**

Defense. Shoots left. 6'2", 208 lbs. Born, Gottwaldov/Zlin, Czech., April 12, 1974. Tampa Bay's 1st choice, 1st overall, in 1992 Entry Draft.

Season	Club	League	GP	G	A	Pts	PIM	PP	SH	GW	S	%	+/-	TF	F%	Min	GP	G	A	Pts	PIM	PP	SH	GW	Min
1990-91	AC ZPS Zlin	Czech	14	2	2	4	18	....	....	....	....	....	....	....	....	....	....	....	....	....	....	....	....	....	....
1991-92	AC ZPS Zlin	Czech	34	5	5	10	50	....	....	....	....	....	....	....	....	....	....	....	....	....	....	....	....	....	....
1992-93	**Tampa Bay**	**NHL**	**67**	**6**	**15**	**21**	**71**	**1**	**0**	**1**	**113**	**5.3**	**–21**	....	....	....	....	....	....	....	....	....	....	....	....
	Atlanta Knights	IHL	2	1	1	2	2	....	....	....	....	....	....	....	....	....	....	....	....	....	....	....	....	....	....
1993-94	**Tampa Bay**	**NHL**	**64**	**3**	**18**	**21**	**135**	**0**	**0**	**0**	**158**	**1.9**	**–14**	....	....	....	....	....	....	....	....	....	....	....	....
1994-95	AC ZPS Zlin	CzRep	2	1	0	1	10	....	....	....	....	....	....	....	....	....	....	....	....	....	....	....	....	....	....
	Tampa Bay	**NHL**	**48**	**12**	**11**	**23**	**86**	**7**	**1**	**2**	**134**	**9.0**	**–18**	....	....	....	....	....	....	....	....	....	....	....	....
1995-96	**Tampa Bay**	**NHL**	**82**	**16**	**49**	**65**	**103**	**12**	**0**	**2**	**281**	**5.7**	**–24**	....	....	....	**5**	**0**	**1**	**1**	**4**	**0**	**0**	**0**	....
1996-97	**Tampa Bay**	**NHL**	**79**	**12**	**28**	**40**	**57**	**6**	**0**	**0**	**238**	**5.0**	**–29**	....	....	....	....	....	....	....	....	....	....	....	....
1997-98	**Tampa Bay**	**NHL**	**37**	**3**	**12**	**15**	**22**	**1**	**0**	**0**	**86**	**3.5**	**–18**	....	....	....	....	....	....	....	....	....	....	....	....
	Edmonton	**NHL**	**41**	**6**	**20**	**26**	**48**	**4**	**1**	**3**	**112**	**5.4**	**3**	....	....	....	**12**	**0**	**6**	**6**	**12**	**0**	**0**	**0**	....
	Czech Republic	Olympics	6	1	0	1	2	....	....	....	....	....	....	....	....	....	....	....	....	....	....	....	....	....	....
1998-99	**Edmonton**	**NHL**	**75**	**8**	**24**	**32**	**70**	**3**	**0**	**0**	**172**	**4.7**	**9**	**0**	**0.0**	**23:49**	**3**	**0**	**0**	**0**	**2**	**0**	**0**	**0**	**16:23**
99-2000	Zlin	CzRep	6	0	3	3	4	....	....	....	....	....	....	....	....	....	....	....	....	....	....	....	....	....	....
	Edmonton	**NHL**	**80**	**8**	**37**	**45**	**68**	**5**	**0**	**0**	**180**	**4.4**	**1**	**0**	**0.0**	**25:18**	**5**	**0**	**1**	**1**	**4**	**0**	**0**	**0**	**24:44**
2000-01	**NY Islanders**	**NHL**	**76**	**16**	**30**	**46**	**92**	**5**	**1**	**4**	**232**	**6.9**	**–20**	**1**	**100.0**	**25:12**	....	....	....	....	....	....	....	....	....
2001-02	**NY Islanders**	**NHL**	**70**	**11**	**26**	**37**	**78**	**4**	**1**	**1**	**169**	**6.5**	**7**	**1**	**0.0**	**25:32**	**7**	**1**	**6**	**7**	**6**	**0**	**0**	**0**	**29:09**
	Czech Republic	Olympics	4	0	1	1	2	....	....	....	....	....	....	....	....	....	....	....	....	....	....	....	....	....	....
2002-03	**NY Islanders**	**NHL**	**73**	**9**	**32**	**41**	**87**	**3**	**0**	**2**	**151**	**6.0**	**21**	**0**	**0.0**	**26:34**	**5**	**0**	**2**	**2**	**2**	**0**	**0**	**0**	**29:24**
2003-04	**NY Islanders**	**NHL**	**81**	**7**	**22**	**29**	**68**	**2**	**0**	**2**	**182**	**3.8**	**2**	**0**	**0.0**	**24:35**	**5**	**0**	**1**	**1**	**2**	**0**	**0**	**0**	**25:30**
2004-05	HC Hame Zlin	CzRep	45	2	14	16	70	....	....	....	....	....	....	....	....	....	17	1	3	4	24	....	....	....	....
2005-06	**Calgary**	**NHL**	**51**	**7**	**19**	**26**	**56**	**1**	**1**	**0**	**89**	**7.9**	**8**	**0**	**0.0**	**21:51**	**7**	**0**	**2**	**2**	**2**	**0**	**0**	**0**	**19:44**
2006-07	**Calgary**	**NHL**	**75**	**7**	**31**	**38**	**88**	**1**	**0**	**1**	**125**	**5.6**	**22**	**0**	**0.0**	**24:52**	**6**	**0**	**1**	**1**	**8**	**0**	**0**	**0**	**26:53**
	NHL Totals		**999**	**131**	**374**	**505**	**1129**	**55**	**5**	**18**	**2422**	**5.4**		**2**	**50.0**	**24:49**	**55**	**1**	**20**	**21**	**42**	**0**	**0**	**0**	**25:01**

Played in NHL All-Star Game (1996, 1999, 2003)

Traded to **Edmonton** by **Tampa Bay** with Paul Comrie for Bryan Marchment, Steve Kelly and Jason Bonsignore, December 30, 1997. Traded to **NY Islanders** by **Edmonton** for Eric Brewer, Josh Green and NY Islanders' 2nd round choice (Brad Winchester) in 2000 Entry Draft, June 24, 2000. Signed as a free agent by **Zlin** (CzRep), August 4, 2004. Signed as a free agent by **Calgary**, August 14, 2005 Signed as a free agent by **Montreal**, July 2, 2007.

			Regular Season														Playoffs								
Season	Club	League	GP	G	A	Pts	PIM	PP	SH	GW	S	%	+/-	TF	F%	Min	GP	G	A	Pts	PIM	PP	SH	GW	Min

HANDZUS, Michal

(HAHND-zuhs, MIGH-kuhl) **L.A.**

Center. Shoots left. 6'5", 217 lbs. Born, Banska Bystrica, Czech., March 11, 1977. St. Louis' 3rd choice, 101st overall, in 1995 Entry Draft.

Season	Club	League	GP	G	A	Pts	PIM	PP	SH	GW	S	%	+/-	TF	F%	Min	GP	G	A	Pts	PIM	PP	SH	GW	Min
1993-94	B. Bystrica Jr.	Slovak-Jr.	40	23	36	59	....	....	....	....	....	....	....	....	....	....	....	....	....	....	....	....	....	....	....
1994-95	B. Bystrica	Slovak-2	22	15	14	29	10	....	....	....	....	....	....	....	....	....	....	....	....	....	....	....	....	....	....
1995-96	B. Bystrica	Slovakia	19	3	1	4	8	....	....	....	....	....	....	....	....	....	....	....	....	....	....	....	....	....	....
1996-97	HC SKP PS Poprad	Slovakia	44	15	18	33	....	....	....	....	....	....	....	....	....	....	....	....	....	....	....	....	....	....	....
1997-98	Worcester IceCats	AHL	69	27	36	63	54	....	....	....	....	....	....	....	....	....	11	2	6	8	10	....	....	....	....
1998-99	**St. Louis**	**NHL**	**66**	**4**	**12**	**16**	**30**	**0**	**0**	**0**	**78**	**5.1**	**-9**	**794**	**49.9**	**14:48**	**11**	**0**	**2**	**2**	**8**	**0**	**0**	**0**	**16:52**
99-2000	**St. Louis**	**NHL**	**81**	**25**	**28**	**53**	**44**	**3**	**4**	**5**	**166**	**15.1**	**19**	**1243**	**51.5**	**17:43**	**7**	**0**	**3**	**3**	**6**	**0**	**0**	**0**	**16:35**
2000-01	**St. Louis**	**NHL**	**36**	**10**	**14**	**24**	**12**	**3**	**2**	**2**	**58**	**17.2**	**11**	**581**	**50.6**	**18:00**	....	....	....	....	....	....	....	....	....
	Phoenix	**NHL**	**10**	**4**	**4**	**8**	**21**	**0**	**1**	**0**	**14**	**28.6**	**5**	**111**	**60.4**	**15:26**	....	....	....	....	....	....	....	....	....
2001-02	**Phoenix**	**NHL**	**79**	**15**	**30**	**45**	**34**	**3**	**1**	**1**	**94**	**16.0**	**-8**	**1227**	**48.7**	**16:09**	**5**	**0**	**0**	**0**	**2**	**0**	**0**	**0**	**15:01**
	Slovakia	Olympics	2	1	0	1	6	....	....	....	....	....	....	....	....	....	....	....	....	....	....	....	....	....	....
2002-03	**Philadelphia**	**NHL**	**82**	**23**	**21**	**44**	**46**	**1**	**1**	**9**	**133**	**17.3**	**13**	**1350**	**52.3**	**17:33**	**13**	**2**	**6**	**8**	**6**	**0**	**0**	**1**	**18:23**
2003-04	**Philadelphia**	**NHL**	**82**	**20**	**38**	**58**	**82**	**7**	**1**	**2**	**135**	**14.8**	**18**	**1457**	**49.9**	**18:43**	**18**	**5**	**5**	**10**	**10**	**0**	**0**	**1**	**18:33**
2004-05	HKm Zvolen	Slovakia	33	14	24	38	34	....	....	....	....	....	....	....	....	....	17	5	10	15	6	....	....	....	....
2005-06	**Philadelphia**	**NHL**	**73**	**11**	**33**	**44**	**38**	**2**	**1**	**1**	**113**	**9.7**	**-2**	**1143**	**53.2**	**18:28**	**6**	**0**	**2**	**2**	**2**	**0**	**0**	**0**	**15:56**
2006-07	**Chicago**	**NHL**	**8**	**3**	**5**	**8**	**6**	**1**	**0**	**0**	**9**	**33.3**	**4**	**173**	**51.5**	**20:59**	....	....	....	....	....	....	....	....	....
	NHL Totals		**517**	**115**	**185**	**300**	**313**	**20**	**11**	**20**	**800**	**14.4**		**8079**	**51.0**	**17:22**	**60**	**7**	**18**	**25**	**34**	**0**	**0**	**1**	**17:25**

Traded to **Phoenix** by **St. Louis** with Ladislav Nagy, the rights to Jeff Taffe and St. Louis' 1st round choice (Ben Eager) in 2002 Entry Draft for Keith Tkachuk, March 13, 2001. Traded to **Philadelphia** by **Phoenix** with Robert Esche for Brian Boucher and Nashville's 3rd round choice (previously acquired, Phoenix selected Joe Callahan) in 2002 Entry Draft, June 12, 2002. Signed as a free agent by **Zvolen** (Slovakia), October 27, 2004. Traded to **Chicago** by **Philadelphia** for Kyle Calder, August 4, 2006. • Missed remainder of 2006-07 season recovering from knee injury suffered in game vs. St. Louis, October 21, 2006. Signed as a free agent by **Los Angeles**, July 2, 2007.

HANNAN, Scott

(HAN-nan, SKAWT) **COL.**

Defense. Shoots left. 6'1", 225 lbs. Born, Richmond, B.C., January 23, 1979. San Jose's 2nd choice, 23rd overall, in 1997 Entry Draft.

Season	Club	League	GP	G	A	Pts	PIM	PP	SH	GW	S	%	+/-	TF	F%	Min	GP	G	A	Pts	PIM	PP	SH	GW	Min
1994-95	Surrey Wolves	BCAHA	70	54	54	108	200	....	....	....	....	....	....	....	....	....	....	....	....	....	....	....	....	....	....
	Tacoma Rockets	WHL	2	0	0	0	0	....	....	....	....	....	....	....	....	....	....	....	....	....	....	....	....	....	....
1995-96	Kelowna Rockets	WHL	69	4	5	9	76	....	....	....	....	....	....	....	....	....	6	0	1	1	4	....	....	....	....
1996-97	Kelowna Rockets	WHL	70	17	26	43	101	....	....	....	....	....	....	....	....	....	6	0	0	0	8	....	....	....	....
1997-98	Kelowna Rockets	WHL	47	10	30	40	70	....	....	....	....	....	....	....	....	....	7	2	7	9	14	....	....	....	....
1998-99	**San Jose**	**NHL**	**5**	**0**	**2**	**2**	**6**	**0**	**0**	**0**	**4**	**0.0**	**0**	**0**	**0.0**	**7:15**	....	....	....	....	....	....	....	....	....
	Kelowna Rockets	WHL	47	15	30	45	92	....	....	....	....	....	....	....	....	....	6	1	2	3	14	....	....	....	....
	Kentucky	AHL	2	0	0	0	2	....	....	....	....	....	....	....	....	....	12	0	2	2	10	....	....	....	....
99-2000	**San Jose**	**NHL**	**30**	**1**	**2**	**3**	**10**	**0**	**0**	**0**	**28**	**3.6**	**7**	**1**	**0.0**	**17:09**	**1**	**0**	**1**	**1**	**0**	**0**	**0**	**0**	**18:14**
	Kentucky	AHL	41	5	12	17	40	....	....	....	....	....	....	....	....	....	....	....	....	....	....	....	....	....	....
2000-01	**San Jose**	**NHL**	**75**	**3**	**14**	**17**	**51**	**0**	**0**	**1**	**96**	**3.1**	**10**	**0**	**0.0**	**19:02**	**6**	**0**	**1**	**1**	**6**	**0**	**0**	**0**	**25:10**
2001-02	**San Jose**	**NHL**	**75**	**2**	**12**	**14**	**57**	**0**	**0**	**1**	**68**	**2.9**	**10**	**1**	**100.0**	**20:19**	**12**	**0**	**2**	**2**	**12**	**0**	**0**	**0**	**20:46**
2002-03	**San Jose**	**NHL**	**81**	**3**	**19**	**22**	**61**	**1**	**0**	**0**	**103**	**2.9**	**0**	**3**	**33.3**	**24:16**	....	....	....	....	....	....	....	....	....
2003-04	**San Jose**	**NHL**	**82**	**6**	**15**	**21**	**48**	**0**	**0**	**0**	**114**	**5.3**	**10**	**0**	**0.0**	**23:41**	**17**	**1**	**5**	**6**	**22**	**1**	**0**	**1**	**26:38**
2004-05			DID NOT PLAY																						
2005-06	**San Jose**	**NHL**	**81**	**6**	**18**	**24**	**58**	**2**	**0**	**1**	**104**	**5.8**	**7**	**0**	**0.0**	**24:34**	**11**	**0**	**1**	**1**	**6**	**0**	**0**	**0**	**25:16**
2006-07	**San Jose**	**NHL**	**79**	**4**	**20**	**24**	**38**	**0**	**1**	**1**	**79**	**5.1**	**1**	**0**	**0.0**	**22:49**	**11**	**0**	**2**	**2**	**33**	**0**	**0**	**0**	**21:42**
	NHL Totals		**508**	**25**	**102**	**127**	**329**	**3**	**1**	**4**	**596**	**4.2**		**5**	**40.0**	**22:03**	**58**	**1**	**12**	**13**	**79**	**1**	**0**	**1**	**23:56**

WHL West First All-Star Team (1999)

Signed as a free agent by **Colorado**, July 1, 2007.

HANSEN, Jannik

(HAHN-suhn, YAH-nihk) **VAN.**

Left wing. Shoots right. 6'1", 201 lbs. Born, Herlev, Denmark, March 15, 1986. Vancouver's 7th choice, 287th overall, in 2004 Entry Draft.

Season	Club	League	GP	G	A	Pts	PIM	PP	SH	GW	S	%	+/-	TF	F%	Min	GP	G	A	Pts	PIM	PP	SH	GW	Min
2002-03	Rodovre	Denmark	15	0	0	0	0	....	....	....	....	....	....	....	....	....	....	....	....	....	....	....	....	....	....
	Malmo U18	Swe-U18	12	8	7	15	2	....	....	....	....	....	....	....	....	....	3	2	0	2	0	....	....	....	....
2003-04	Rodovre	Denmark	35	12	7	19	48	....	....	....	....	....	....	....	....	....	....	....	....	....	....	....	....	....	....
2004-05	Rodovre	Denmark	32	17	17	34	40	....	....	....	....	....	....	....	....	....	5	3	1	4	24	....	....	....	....
2005-06	Portland	WHL	64	24	40	64	67	....	....	....	....	....	....	....	....	....	12	7	6	13	16	....	....	....	....
2006-07	Manitoba Moose	AHL	72	12	22	34	38	....	....	....	....	....	....	....	....	....	6	0	0	0	2	....	....	....	....
	Vancouver	**NHL**	....	....	....	....	....	....	....	....	....	....	....	....	....	....	**10**	**0**	**1**	**1**	**4**	**0**	**0**	**0**	**12:41**
	NHL Totals		....	....	....	....	....	....	....	....	....	....	....	....	....	....	**10**	**0**	**1**	**1**	**4**	**0**	**0**	**0**	**12:41**

HARRISON, Jay

(HAIR-ih-suhn, JAY) **TOR.**

Defense. Shoots left. 6'4", 211 lbs. Born, Oshawa, Ont., November 3, 1982. Toronto's 4th choice, 82nd overall, in 2001 Entry Draft.

Season	Club	League	GP	G	A	Pts	PIM	PP	SH	GW	S	%	+/-	TF	F%	Min	GP	G	A	Pts	PIM	PP	SH	GW	Min
1997-98	Oshawa	OHA-B	42	1	11	12	143	....	....	....	....	....	....	....	....	....	....	....	....	....	....	....	....	....	....
1998-99	Brampton	OHL	63	1	14	15	108	....	....	....	....	....	....	....	....	....	....	....	....	....	....	....	....	....	....
99-2000	Brampton	OHL	68	2	18	20	139	....	....	....	....	....	....	....	....	....	6	0	2	2	15	....	....	....	....
2000-01	Brampton	OHL	53	4	15	19	112	....	....	....	....	....	....	....	....	....	9	1	1	2	17	....	....	....	....
2001-02	Brampton	OHL	61	12	31	43	116	....	....	....	....	....	....	....	....	....	....	....	....	....	....	....	....	....	....
	St. John's	AHL	7	0	1	1	2	....	....	....	....	....	....	....	....	....	10	0	0	0	4	....	....	....	....
	Memphis	CHL	....	....	....	....	....	....	....	....	....	....	....	....	....	....	1	0	0	0	2	....	....	....	....
2002-03	St. John's	AHL	72	2	8	10	72	....	....	....	....	....	....	....	....	....	....	....	....	....	....	....	....	....	....
2003-04	St. John's	AHL	70	4	5	9	141	....	....	....	....	....	....	....	....	....	....	....	....	....	....	....	....	....	....
2004-05	St. John's	AHL	60	0	4	4	108	....	....	....	....	....	....	....	....	....	4	0	1	1	14	....	....	....	....
2005-06	**Toronto**	**NHL**	**8**	**0**	**1**	**1**	**2**	**0**	**0**	**0**	**7**	**0.0**	**5**	**0**	**0.0**	**18:50**	....	....	....	....	....	....	....	....	....
	Toronto Marlies	AHL	57	9	20	29	100	....	....	....	....	....	....	....	....	....	5	1	3	4	8	....	....	....	....
2006-07	**Toronto**	**NHL**	**5**	**0**	**0**	**0**	**6**	**0**	**0**	**0**	**3**	**0.0**	**-5**	**0**	**0.0**	**8:22**	....	....	....	....	....	....	....	....	....
	Toronto Marlies	AHL	41	4	14	18	68	....	....	....	....	....	....	....	....	....	....	....	....	....	....	....	....	....	....
	NHL Totals		**13**	**0**	**1**	**1**	**8**	**0**	**0**	**0**	**10**	**0.0**		**0**	**0.0**	**14:48**	....	....	....	....	....	....	....	....	....

OHL All-Rookie Team (1999)

HARROLD, Peter

(HAIR-ohld, PEE-tuhr) **L.A.**

Defense. Shoots right. 5'11", 195 lbs. Born, Kirtland Hills, OH, June 8, 1983.

Season	Club	League	GP	G	A	Pts	PIM	PP	SH	GW	S	%	+/-	TF	F%	Min	GP	G	A	Pts	PIM	PP	SH	GW	Min
2003-04	Boston College	H-East	40	2	12	14	12	....	....	....	....	....	....	....	....	....	....	....	....	....	....	....	....	....	....
2004-05	Boston College	H-East	35	4	10	14	22	....	....	....	....	....	....	....	....	....	....	....	....	....	....	....	....	....	....
2005-06	Boston College	H-East	42	7	23	30	32	....	....	....	....	....	....	....	....	....	....	....	....	....	....	....	....	....	....
2006-07	**Los Angeles**	**NHL**	**12**	**0**	**2**	**2**	**8**	**0**	**0**	**0**	**11**	**0.0**	**0**	**1**	**0.0**	**15:12**	....	....	....	....	....	....	....	....	....
	Manchester	AHL	62	7	27	34	43	....	....	....	....	....	....	....	....	....	16	3	8	11	18	....	....	....	....
	NHL Totals		**12**	**0**	**2**	**2**	**8**	**0**	**0**	**0**	**11**	**0.0**		**1**	**0.0**	**15:12**	....	....	....	....	....	....	....	....	....

Hockey East First All-Star Team (2006) • NCAA East First All-American Team (2006)

Signed as a free agent by **Los Angeles**. April 12, 2006.

HARTIGAN, Mark

(HAHR-tih-guhn, MAHRK) **DET.**

Center. Shoots left. 6', 200 lbs. Born, Fort St. John, B.C., October 15, 1977.

Season	Club	League	GP	G	A	Pts	PIM	PP	SH	GW	S	%	+/-	TF	F%	Min	GP	G	A	Pts	PIM	PP	SH	GW	Min
1996-97	Weyburn	SJHL	52	44	32	76	....	....	....	....	....	....	....	....	....	....	....	....	....	....	....	....	....	....	....
1997-98	Weyburn	SJHL	62	*59	46	*105	81	....	....	....	....	....	....	....	....	....	23	17	21	38	10	....	....	....	....
1998-99	St. Cloud State	WCHA	DID NOT PLAY – FRESHMAN																						
99-2000	St. Cloud State	WCHA	37	22	20	42	24	....	....	....	....	....	....	....	....	....	....	....	....	....	....	....	....	....	....
2000-01	St. Cloud State	WCHA	40	27	21	48	20	....	....	....	....	....	....	....	....	....	....	....	....	....	....	....	....	....	....
2001-02	St. Cloud State	WCHA	42	*37	38	75	42	....	....	....	....	....	....	....	....	....	....	....	....	....	....	....	....	....	....
	Atlanta	**NHL**	**2**	**0**	**0**	**0**	**2**	**0**	**0**	**0**	**3**	**0.0**	**-2**	**18**	**38.9**	**13:16**	....	....	....	....	....	....	....	....	....
2002-03	Chicago Wolves	AHL	55	15	31	46	43	....	....	....	....	....	....	....	....	....	9	1	2	3	10	....	....	....	....
	Atlanta	**NHL**	**23**	**5**	**2**	**7**	**6**	**1**	**0**	**0**	**25**	**20.0**	**-8**	**220**	**47.3**	**10:52**	....	....	....	....	....	....	....	....	....
2003-04	**Columbus**	**NHL**	**9**	**1**	**3**	**4**	**6**	**1**	**0**	**0**	**15**	**6.7**	**-2**	**138**	**40.6**	**16:19**	....	....	....	....	....	....	....	....	....
	Syracuse Crunch	AHL	69	23	23	46	86	....	....	....	....	....	....	....	....	....	7	1	4	5	8	....	....	....	....
2004-05	Syracuse Crunch	AHL	69	31	28	59	105	....	....	....	....	....	....	....	....	....	....	....	....	....	....	....	....	....	....

Season	Club	League	Regular Season GP	G	A	Pts	PIM	PP	SH	GW	S	%	+/-	TF	F%	Min	Playoffs GP	G	A	Pts	PIM	PP	SH	GW	Min
2005-06	Columbus	NHL	33	9	3	12	22	3	0	1	54	16.7	–1	194	44.9	11:39	....	....	....	....	....	....	....	....	....
	Syracuse Crunch	AHL	49	34	41	75	48	....	....	....	....	....	....	....	....	....	6	1	2	3	33	....	....	....	....
2006-07	Columbus	NHL	6	1	2	3	2	1	0	0	11	9.1	2	83	45.8	13:51	....	....	....	....	....	....	....	....	....
	Syracuse Crunch	AHL	34	19	13	32	51	....	....	....	....	....	....	....	....	....	....	....	....	....	....	....	....	....	....
	♦ Anaheim	NHL	6	0	0	0	4	0	0	0	4	0.0	–1	23	26.1	7:41	1	0	0	0	0	0	0	0	3:34
	Portland Pirates	AHL	25	9	16	25	20	....	....	....	....	....	....	....	....	....	....	....	....	....	....	....	....	....	....
	NHL Totals		79	16	10	26	42	6	0	1	112	14.3		676	44.1	11:51	1	0	0	0	0	0	0	0	3:34

WCHA First All-Star Team (2002) • WCHA Player of the Year (2002)

Signed as a free agent by **Atlanta**, March 27, 2002. Signed as a free agent by **Columbus**, July 15, 2003. Traded to **Anaheim** by **Columbus** with Joe Motzko and Columbus'4th round choice (Sebastian Stefaniszin) in 2007 Entry Draft for Zenon Konopka, Curtis Glencross and Anaheim's 7th round choice (Trent Vogelhuber) in 2007 Entry Draft, January 26, 2007. Signed as a free agent by **Detroit**, July 16, 2007.

HARTNELL, Scott

(HAHRT-nuhl, SKAWT) **PHI.**

Left wing. Shoots left. 6'2", 210 lbs. Born, Regina, Sask., April 18, 1982. Nashville's 1st choice, 6th overall, in 2000 Entry Draft.

Season	Club	League	GP	G	A	Pts	PIM	PP	SH	GW	S	%	+/-	TF	F%	Min	GP	G	A	Pts	PIM	PP	SH	GW	Min
1997-98	Lloydminster	AJHL	56	9	25	34	82	....	....	....	....	....	....	....	....	....	4	2	1	3	8	....	....	....	....
	Prince Albert	WHL	1	0	1	1	2	....	....	....	....	....	....	....	....	....	....	....	....	....	....	....	....	....	....
1998-99	Prince Albert	WHL	65	10	34	44	104	....	....	....	....	....	....	....	....	....	14	0	5	5	22	....	....	....	....
99-2000	Prince Albert	WHL	62	27	55	82	124	....	....	....	....	....	....	....	....	....	6	3	2	5	6	....	....	....	....
2000-01	Nashville	NHL	75	2	14	16	48	0	0	0	92	2.2	–8	3	33.3	10:54	....	....	....	....	....	....	....	....	....
2001-02	Nashville	NHL	75	14	27	41	111	3	0	4	162	8.6	5	12	25.0	16:58	....	....	....	....	....	....	....	....	....
2002-03	Nashville	NHL	82	12	22	34	101	2	0	2	221	5.4	–3	23	30.4	15:17	....	....	....	....	....	....	....	....	....
2003-04	Nashville	NHL	59	18	15	33	87	5	0	3	154	11.7	–5	48	37.5	16:16	6	1	2	3	2	0	0	0	15:37
2004-05	Valerengen IF Oslo	Norway	28	17	12	29	103	....	....	....	....	....	....	....	....	....	11	12	7	19	24	....	....	....	....
2005-06	Nashville	NHL	81	25	23	48	101	10	2	8	211	11.8	8	58	37.9	16:05	5	1	0	1	4	0	0	0	12:12
2006-07	Nashville	NHL	64	22	17	39	96	10	0	2	150	14.7	19	134	47.0	15:43	5	1	1	2	28	1	0	0	14:23
	NHL Totals		436	93	118	211	544	30	2	19	990	9.4		278	41.0	15:10	16	3	3	6	34	1	0	0	14:10

Signed as a free agent by **Oslo** (Norway), October 21, 2004. Traded to **Philadelphia** by **Nashville** with Kimmo Timmonen for Nashville's 1st round choice (previously acquired, Nashville selected Jonathon Blum) in 2007 Entry Draft, June 18, 2007.

HATCHER, Derian

(HAT-chuhr, DAIR-ee-an) **PHI.**

Defense. Shoots left. 6'5", 235 lbs. Born, Sterling Hts., MI, June 4, 1972. Minnesota's 1st choice, 8th overall, in 1990 Entry Draft.

Season	Club	League	GP	G	A	Pts	PIM	PP	SH	GW	S	%	+/-	TF	F%	Min	GP	G	A	Pts	PIM	PP	SH	GW	Min
1987-88	Detroit GPD	MNHL	25	5	13	18	52	....	....	....	....	....	....	....	....	....	....	....	....	....	....	....	....	....	....
1988-89	Detroit GPD	MNHL	51	19	35	54	100	....	....	....	....	....	....	....	....	....	....	....	....	....	....	....	....	....	....
1989-90	North Bay	OHL	64	14	38	52	81	....	....	....	....	....	....	....	....	....	5	2	3	5	8	....	....	....	....
1990-91	North Bay	OHL	64	13	49	62	163	....	....	....	....	....	....	....	....	....	10	2	10	12	28	....	....	....	....
1991-92	Minnesota	NHL	43	8	4	12	88	0	0	2	51	15.7	7	....	....	....	5	0	2	2	8	0	0	0	....
1992-93	Minnesota	NHL	67	4	15	19	178	0	0	1	73	5.5	–27	....	....	....	....	....	....	....	....	....	....	....	....
	Kalamazoo Wings	IHL	2	1	2	3	21	....	....	....	....	....	....	....	....	....	....	....	....	....	....	....	....	....	....
1993-94	Dallas	NHL	83	12	19	31	211	2	1	2	132	9.1	19	....	....	....	9	0	2	2	14	0	0	0	....
1994-95	Dallas	NHL	43	5	11	16	105	2	0	2	74	6.8	3	....	....	....	....	....	....	....	....	....	....	....	....
1995-96	Dallas	NHL	79	8	23	31	129	2	0	1	125	6.4	–12	....	....	....	....	....	....	....	....	....	....	....	....
1996-97	Dallas	NHL	63	3	19	22	97	0	0	0	96	3.1	8	....	....	....	7	0	2	2	20	0	0	0	....
1997-98	Dallas	NHL	70	6	25	31	132	3	0	2	74	8.1	9	....	....	....	17	3	3	6	39	2	0	0	....
	United States	Olympics	4	0	0	0	0	....	....	....	....	....	....	....	....	....	....	....	....	....	....	....	....	....	....
1998-99 ♦	Dallas	NHL	80	9	21	30	102	3	0	2	125	7.2	21	0	0.0	24:44	18	1	6	7	24	0	0	0	29:06
99-2000	Dallas	NHL	57	2	22	24	68	0	0	0	90	2.2	6	0	0.0	27:33	23	1	3	4	29	0	0	0	27:40
2000-01	Dallas	NHL	80	2	21	23	77	1	0	2	97	2.1	5	0	0.0	25:53	10	0	1	1	16	0	0	0	28:53
2001-02	Dallas	NHL	80	4	21	25	87	1	0	0	111	3.6	12	0	0.0	26:40	....	....	....	....	....	....	....	....	....
2002-03	Dallas	NHL	82	8	22	30	106	1	1	2	159	5.0	37	0	0.0	25:51	11	1	2	3	33	0	0	0	30:02
2003-04	Detroit	NHL	15	0	4	4	8	0	0	0	18	0.0	4	0	0.0	19:38	12	0	1	1	15	0	0	0	22:54
2004-05	Motor City	UHL	24	5	12	17	27	....	....	....	....	....	....	....	....	....	....	....	....	....	....	....	....	....	....
2005-06	Philadelphia	NHL	77	4	13	17	93	1	1	0	98	4.1	2	0	0.0	23:30	6	0	2	2	10	0	0	0	21:36
	United States	Olympics	6	0	0	0	12	....	....	....	....	....	....	....	....	....	....	....	....	....	....	....	....	....	....
2006-07	Philadelphia	NHL	82	3	6	9	67	3	0	1	81	3.7	–24	0	0.0	23:40	....	....	....	....	....	....	....	....	....
	NHL Totals		1001	78	246	324	1548	19	3	17	1404	5.6		0	0.0	25:10	118	6	24	30	208	2	0	0	27:18

NHL Second All-Star Team (2003)

Played in NHL All-Star Game (1997)

Transferred to **Dallas** after **Minnesota** franchise relocated, June 9, 1993. Signed as a free agent by **Detroit**, July 3, 2003. • Missed majority of 2003-04 season recovering from knee injury suffered in game vs. Vancouver, October 16, 2003. Signed as a free agent by **Motor City** (UHL), February 1, 2005. Signed as a free agent by **Philadelphia**, August 2, 2005.

HAVELID, Niclas

(HAHV-lihd, NIHK-luhs) **ATL.**

Defense. Shoots left. 6', 200 lbs. Born, Stockholm, Sweden, April 12, 1973. Anaheim's 2nd choice, 83rd overall, in 1999 Entry Draft.

Season	Club	League	GP	G	A	Pts	PIM	PP	SH	GW	S	%	+/-	TF	F%	Min	GP	G	A	Pts	PIM	PP	SH	GW	Min
1988-89	Enkopings SK	Sweden-3	7	0	1	1	0	....	....	....	....	....	....	....	....	....	....	....	....	....	....	....	....	....	....
1989-90	Enkopings SK	Sweden-3	24	1	2	3	28	....	....	....	....	....	....	....	....	....	....	....	....	....	....	....	....	....	....
1990-91	Arlanda	Sweden-2	30	2	3	5	22	....	....	....	....	....	....	....	....	....	....	....	....	....	....	....	....	....	....
1991-92	AIK Solna	Sweden	10	0	0	0	2	....	....	....	....	....	....	....	....	....	....	....	....	....	....	....	....	....	....
1992-93	AIK Solna	Sweden	30	1	2	3	22	....	....	....	....	....	....	....	....	....	3	0	0	0	2	....	....	....	....
1993-94	AIK Solna	Sweden-2	22	3	9	12	14	....	....	....	....	....	....	....	....	....	....	....	....	....	....	....	....	....	....
1994-95	AIK Solna	Sweden	40	3	7	10	38	....	....	....	....	....	....	....	....	....	....	....	....	....	....	....	....	....	....
1995-96	AIK Solna	Sweden	40	5	6	11	30	....	....	....	....	....	....	....	....	....	....	....	....	....	....	....	....	....	....
1996-97	AIK Solna	Sweden	49	3	6	9	42	....	....	....	....	....	....	....	....	....	7	1	2	3	8	....	....	....	....
1997-98	AIK Solna	Sweden	43	8	4	12	42	....	....	....	....	....	....	....	....	....	10	1	3	4	39	....	....	....	....
1998-99	Malmo	Sweden	50	10	12	22	42	....	....	....	....	....	....	....	....	....	8	0	4	4	10	....	....	....	....
99-2000	Anaheim	NHL	50	2	7	9	20	0	0	2	70	2.9	0	1	0.0	19:10	....	....	....	....	....	....	....	....	....
	Cincinnati	AHL	2	0	0	0	0	....	....	....	....	....	....	....	....	....	....	....	....	....	....	....	....	....	....
2000-01	Anaheim	NHL	47	4	10	14	34	2	0	1	69	5.8	–6	4	0.0	21:51	....	....	....	....	....	....	....	....	....
2001-02	Anaheim	NHL	52	1	2	3	40	0	0	0	45	2.2	–13	1	0.0	17:01	....	....	....	....	....	....	....	....	....
2002-03	Anaheim	NHL	82	11	22	33	30	4	0	5	169	6.5	5	3	0.0	22:30	21	0	4	4	2	0	0	0	25:41
2003-04	Anaheim	NHL	79	6	20	26	28	5	0	3	122	4.9	–28	0	0.0	22:39	....	....	....	....	....	....	....	....	....
2004-05	Sodertalje SK	Sweden	46	2	2	4	60	....	....	....	....	....	....	....	....	....	10	1	1	2	18	....	....	....	....
2005-06	Atlanta	NHL	82	4	28	32	48	2	0	0	84	4.8	9	0	0.0	24:25	....	....	....	....	....	....	....	....	....
	Sweden	Olympics	7	0	0	0	4	....	....	....	....	....	....	....	....	....	....	....	....	....	....	....	....	....	....
2006-07	Atlanta	NHL	77	3	18	21	52	1	0	1	82	3.7	–2	1	0.0	25:16	4	0	2	2	0	0	0	0	24:14
	NHL Totals		469	31	107	138	252	14	0	12	641	4.8		10	0.0	22:17	25	0	6	6	2	0	0	0	25:27

Traded to **Atlanta** by **Anaheim** for Kurtis Foster, June 26, 2004. Signed as a free agent by **Sodertalje** (Sweden), August 9, 2004.

HAVLAT, Martin

(HAHV-lat, MAHR-tihn) **CHI.**

Right wing. Shoots left. 6'1", 204 lbs. Born, Mlada Boleslav, Czech., April 19, 1981. Ottawa's 1st choice, 26th overall, in 1999 Entry Draft.

Season	Club	League	GP	G	A	Pts	PIM	PP	SH	GW	S	%	+/-	TF	F%	Min	GP	G	A	Pts	PIM	PP	SH	GW	Min
1997-98	Ytong Brno Jr.	CzRep-Jr.	32	38	29	67	....	....	....	....	....	....	....	....	....	....	....	....	....	....	....	....	....	....	....
1998-99	HC Trinec Jr.	CzRep-Jr.	31	28	23	51	....	....	....	....	....	....	....	....	....	....	....	....	....	....	....	....	....	....	....
	Trinec	CzRep	24	2	3	5	4	....	....	....	....	....	....	....	....	....	8	0	0	0	....	....	....	....	....
99-2000	HC Ocelari Trinec	CzRep	46	13	29	42	42	....	....	....	....	....	....	....	....	....	4	0	2	2	8	....	....	....	....
2000-01	Ottawa	NHL	73	19	23	42	20	7	0	5	133	14.3	8	40	30.0	13:47	4	0	0	0	2	0	0	0	14:04
2001-02	Ottawa	NHL	72	22	28	50	66	9	0	6	145	15.2	–7	15	40.0	14:46	12	2	5	7	14	2	0	2	16:19
	Czech Republic	Olympics	4	3	1	4	27	....	....	....	....	....	....	....	....	....	....	....	....	....	....	....	....	....	....
2002-03	Ottawa	NHL	67	24	35	59	30	9	0	4	179	13.4	20	7	14.3	16:27	18	5	6	11	14	1	0	2	16:27
2003-04	HC Sparta Praha	CzRep	5	1	3	4	8	....	....	....	....	....	....	....	....	....	....	....	....	....	....	....	....	....	....
	Ottawa	NHL	68	31	37	68	46	13	0	7	175	17.7	12	11	36.4	16:44	7	0	3	3	2	0	0	0	16:10
2004-05	Znojmo	CzRep	12	10	4	14	16	....	....	....	....	....	....	....	....	....	....	....	....	....	....	....	....	....	....
	Dynamo Moscow	Russia	10	2	0	2	14	....	....	....	....	....	....	....	....	....	....	....	....	....	....	....	....	....	....
	HC Sparta Praha	CzRep	9	5	4	9	37	....	....	....	....	....	....	....	....	....	5	0	0	0	20	....	....	....	....

Season	Club	League	GP	G	A	Pts	PIM	PP	SH	GW	S	%	+/-	TF	F%	Min	GP	G	A	Pts	PIM	PP	SH	GW	Min
			Regular Season														Playoffs								
2005-06	**Ottawa**	**NHL**	**18**	**9**	**7**	**16**	**4**	**2**	**1**	**1**	**57**	**15.8**	**6**	**25**	**36.0**	**18:11**	**10**	**7**	**6**	**13**	**4**	**3**	**0**	**1**	**17:13**
2006-07	**Chicago**	**NHL**	**56**	**25**	**32**	**57**	**28**	**5**	**0**	**1**	**176**	**14.2**	**15**	**12**	**33.3**	**21:24**	....	....	....	....	....	....	....	....	....
	NHL Totals		**354**	**130**	**162**	**292**	**194**	**45**	**1**	**24**	**865**	**15.0**		**110**	**32.7**	**16:29**	**51**	**14**	**20**	**34**	**36**	**6**	**0**	**5**	**16:21**

NHL All-Rookie Team (2001)

Played in NHL All-Star Game (2007)

Signed as a free agent by **Znojmo** (CzRep), September 24, 2004. Signed as a free agent by **Dynamo Moscow** (Russia), November 10, 2004. Signed as a free agent by **Znojmo** (CzRep), January 18, 2005. Signed as a free agent by **Sparta Praha** (CzRep), January 31, 2005. • Missed majority of 2005-06 season recovering from shoulder injury suffered in game vs. Montreal, November 29, 2005. Traded to **Chicago** by **Ottawa** with Bryan Smolinski for Tom Preissing, Josh Hennessy, Michal Barinka and Chicago's 2nd round choice in 2008 Entry Draft, July 10, 2006.

HAYDAR, Darren (HAY-duhr, DAIR-ehn) ATL.

Right wing. Shoots right. 5'9", 170 lbs. Born, Toronto, Ont., October 22, 1979. Nashville's 14th choice, 248th overall, in 1999 Entry Draft.

Season	Club	League	GP	G	A	Pts	PIM	PP	SH	GW	S	%	+/-	TF	F%	Min	GP	G	A	Pts	PIM	PP	SH	GW	Min
1995-96	Milton Merchants	OPJHL	6	1	2	3	4	....	....	....	....	....	....	....	....	....	....	....	....	....	....	....	....	....	....
1996-97	Milton Merchants	OPJHL	51	32	68	100	68	....	....	....	....	....	....	....	....	....	....	....	....	....	....	....	....	....	....
1997-98	Milton Merchants	OPJHL	51	*71	*69	*140	65	....	....	....	....	....	....	....	....	....	....	....	....	....	....	....	....	....	....
1998-99	New Hampshire	H-East	41	31	30	61	34	....	....	....	....	....	....	....	....	....	....	....	....	....	....	....	....	....	....
99-2000	New Hampshire	H-East	38	22	19	41	42	....	....	....	....	....	....	....	....	....	....	....	....	....	....	....	....	....	....
2000-01	New Hampshire	H-East	39	18	23	41	38	....	....	....	....	....	....	....	....	....	....	....	....	....	....	....	....	....	....
2001-02	New Hampshire	H-East	40	31	*45	*76	28	....	....	....	....	....	....	....	....	....	....	....	....	....	....	....	....	....	....
2002-03	**Nashville**	**NHL**	**2**	**0**	**0**	**0**	**0**	**0**	**0**	**0**	**1**	**0.0**	**–1**	**0**	**0.0**	**8:54**	....	....	....	....	....	....	....	....	....
	Milwaukee	AHL	75	29	46	75	36	....	....	....	....	....	....	....	....	....	6	1	4	5	2	....	....	....	....
2003-04	Milwaukee	AHL	79	22	37	59	35	....	....	....	....	....	....	....	....	....	22	*11	15	*26	10	....	....	....	....
2004-05	Milwaukee	AHL	59	24	26	50	42	....	....	....	....	....	....	....	....	....	7	3	4	7	14	....	....	....	....
2005-06	Milwaukee	AHL	80	35	57	92	50	....	....	....	....	....	....	....	....	....	21	*18	17	*35	18	....	....	....	....
2006-07	**Atlanta**	**NHL**	**4**	**0**	**0**	**0**	**0**	**0**	**0**	**0**	**4**	**0.0**	**0**	**3**	**66.7**	**8:01**	....	....	....	....	....	....	....	....	....
	Chicago Wolves	AHL	73	41	*81	*122	55	....	....	....	....	....	....	....	....	....	15	*10	*14	*24	14	....	....	....	....
	NHL Totals		**6**	**0**	**0**	**0**	**0**	**0**	**0**	**0**	**5**	**0.0**		**3**	**66.7**	**8:19**	....	....	....	....	....	....	....	....	....

Hockey East Second All-Star Team (1999, 2000) • Hockey East Rookie of the Year (1999) • Hockey East First All-Star Team (2002) • Hockey East Player of the Year (2002) • AHL All-Rookie Team (2003) • Dudley "Red" Garrett Memorial Award (Rookie of the Year – AHL) (2003) • AHL First All-Star Team (2007) • John P. Sollenberger Trophy (Top Scorer - AHL) (2007) • Les Cunningham Award (MVP - AHL) (2007)

Signed as a free agent by **Atlanta**, July 4, 2006.

HEALEY, Eric (HEE-lee, AIR-ihk) COL.

Left wing. Shoots left. 5'11", 201 lbs. Born, Hull, MA, January 20, 1975.

Season	Club	League	GP	G	A	Pts	PIM	PP	SH	GW	S	%	+/-	TF	F%	Min	GP	G	A	Pts	PIM	PP	SH	GW	Min
1993-94	New England	NEJHL	37	61	76	137	....	....	....	....	....	....	....	....	....	....	....	....	....	....	....	....	....	....	....
1994-95	RPI Engineers	ECAC	37	13	11	24	35	....	....	....	....	....	....	....	....	....	....	....	....	....	....	....	....	....	....
1995-96	RPI Engineers	ECAC	35	18	22	40	57	....	....	....	....	....	....	....	....	....	....	....	....	....	....	....	....	....	....
1996-97	RPI Engineers	ECAC	36	30	26	56	63	....	....	....	....	....	....	....	....	....	....	....	....	....	....	....	....	....	....
1997-98	RPI Engineers	ECAC	35	21	27	48	42	....	....	....	....	....	....	....	....	....	....	....	....	....	....	....	....	....	....
1998-99	Saint John Flames	AHL	64	14	24	38	77	....	....	....	....	....	....	....	....	....	....	....	....	....	....	....	....	....	....
	Orlando	IHL	13	5	4	9	13	....	....	....	....	....	....	....	....	....	8	1	0	1	12	....	....	....	....
99-2000	Springfield	AHL	32	14	15	29	51	....	....	....	....	....	....	....	....	....	1	0	0	0	2	....	....	....	....
2000-01	Springfield	AHL	66	16	17	33	53	....	....	....	....	....	....	....	....	....	....	....	....	....	....	....	....	....	....
2001-02	Manchester	AHL	65	24	34	58	45	....	....	....	....	....	....	....	....	....	5	2	2	4	8	....	....	....	....
	Jackson Bandits	ECHL	2	1	1	2	0	....	....	....	....	....	....	....	....	....	....	....	....	....	....	....	....	....	....
2002-03	Manchester	AHL	75	*42	31	73	47	....	....	....	....	....	....	....	....	....	3	1	0	1	2	....	....	....	....
2003-04	Chicago Wolves	AHL	71	31	20	51	52	....	....	....	....	....	....	....	....	....	10	3	6	9	10	....	....	....	....
2004-05	Adler Mannheim	Germany	50	16	13	29	54	....	....	....	....	....	....	....	....	....	13	2	4	6	12	....	....	....	....
2005-06	**Boston**	**NHL**	**2**	**0**	**0**	**0**	**2**	**0**	**0**	**0**	**1**	**0.0**	**0**	**0**	**0.0**	**8:28**	....	....	....	....	....	....	....	....	....
	Providence Bruins	AHL	66	29	42	71	49	....	....	....	....	....	....	....	....	....	5	2	3	5	0	....	....	....	....
2006-07	Springfield	AHL	80	27	48	75	51	....	....	....	....	....	....	....	....	....	....	....	....	....	....	....	....	....	....
	NHL Totals		**2**	**0**	**0**	**0**	**2**	**0**	**0**	**0**	**1**	**0.0**		**0**	**0.0**	**8:28**	....	....	....	....	....	....	....	....	....

ECAC Second All-Star Team (1997) • NCAA East Second All-American Team (1997, 1998) • ECAC First All-Star Team (1998) • Fred T. Hunt Memorial Award (Sportsmanship – AHL) (2003) (co-winner - Chris Ferraro)

Signed as a free agent by **Calgary**, September 22, 1998. Signed as a free agent by **Phoenix**, July 26, 1999. Signed to a PTO (tryout) contract by **Manchester** (AHL), September 30, 2001. Signed as a free agent by **Atlanta**, August 12, 2003. Signed as a free agent by **Mannheim** (Germany), July 9, 2004. Signed as a free agent by **Boston**, August 15, 2005. Signed as a free agent by **Tampa Bay**, July 15, 2006. Signed as a free agent by **Colorado**, July 13, 2007.

HEALEY, Paul (HEE-lee, PAWL)

Left wing. Shoots right. 6'2", 198 lbs. Born, Edmonton, Alta., March 20, 1975. Philadelphia's 7th choice, 192nd overall, in 1993 Entry Draft.

Season	Club	League	GP	G	A	Pts	PIM	PP	SH	GW	S	%	+/-	TF	F%	Min	GP	G	A	Pts	PIM	PP	SH	GW	Min
1991-92	Ft. Saskatchewan	AJHL	52	11	19	30	40	....	....	....	....	....	....	....	....	....	....	....	....	....	....	....	....	....	....
1992-93	Prince Albert	WHL	72	12	20	32	66	....	....	....	....	....	....	....	....	....	....	....	....	....	....	....	....	....	....
1993-94	Prince Albert	WHL	63	23	26	49	70	....	....	....	....	....	....	....	....	....	....	....	....	....	....	....	....	....	....
1994-95	Prince Albert	WHL	71	43	50	93	67	....	....	....	....	....	....	....	....	....	12	3	4	7	2	....	....	....	....
1995-96	Hershey Bears	AHL	60	7	15	22	35	....	....	....	....	....	....	....	....	....	....	....	....	....	....	....	....	....	....
1996-97	**Philadelphia**	**NHL**	**2**	**0**	**0**	**0**	**0**	**0**	**0**	**0**	**0**	**0.0**	**0**	....	....	....	....	....	....	....	....	....	....	....	....
	Philadelphia	AHL	64	21	19	40	56	....	....	....	....	....	....	....	....	....	10	4	1	5	10	....	....	....	....
1997-98	**Philadelphia**	**NHL**	**4**	**0**	**0**	**0**	**12**	**0**	**0**	**0**	**0**	**0.0**	**0**	....	....	....	....	....	....	....	....	....	....	....	....
	Philadelphia	AHL	71	34	18	52	48	....	....	....	....	....	....	....	....	....	20	6	2	8	4	....	....	....	....
1998-99	Philadelphia	AHL	72	26	20	46	39	....	....	....	....	....	....	....	....	....	15	4	6	10	11	....	....	....	....
99-2000	Milwaukee	IHL	76	21	18	39	28	....	....	....	....	....	....	....	....	....	3	1	2	3	0	....	....	....	....
2000-01	Hamilton	AHL	79	39	32	71	34	....	....	....	....	....	....	....	....	....	....	....	....	....	....	....	....	....	....
2001-02	**Toronto**	**NHL**	**21**	**3**	**7**	**10**	**2**	**0**	**0**	**0**	**29**	**10.3**	**7**	**5**	**60.0**	**11:03**	**18**	**0**	**1**	**1**	**2**	**0**	**0**	**0**	**9:01**
	St. John's	AHL	58	27	29	56	30	....	....	....	....	....	....	....	....	....	2	1	1	2	8	....	....	....	....
2002-03	**Toronto**	**NHL**	**44**	**3**	**7**	**10**	**16**	**1**	**0**	**0**	**43**	**7.0**	**8**	**13**	**38.5**	**12:00**	**4**	**0**	**1**	**1**	**2**	**0**	**0**	**0**	**9:14**
	St. John's	AHL	17	6	10	16	12	....	....	....	....	....	....	....	....	....	....	....	....	....	....	....	....	....	....
2003-04	**NY Rangers**	**NHL**	**4**	**0**	**0**	**0**	**0**	**0**	**0**	**0**	**0**	**0.0**	**0**	**1**	**0.0**	**4:50**	....	....	....	....	....	....	....	....	....
	Hartford	AHL	50	11	10	21	37	....	....	....	....	....	....	....	....	....	....	....	....	....	....	....	....	....	....
	San Antonio	AHL	18	5	5	10	20	....	....	....	....	....	....	....	....	....	....	....	....	....	....	....	....	....	....
2004-05	San Antonio	AHL	62	6	17	23	50	....	....	....	....	....	....	....	....	....	....	....	....	....	....	....	....	....	....
	Edmonton	AHL	17	3	6	9	29	....	....	....	....	....	....	....	....	....	....	....	....	....	....	....	....	....	....
2005-06	**Colorado**	**NHL**	**2**	**0**	**0**	**0**	**14**	**0**	**0**	**0**	**0**	**0.0**	**0**	**0**	**0.0**	**5:33**	....	....	....	....	....	....	....	....	....
	Lowell	AHL	59	19	21	40	51	....	....	....	....	....	....	....	....	....	....	....	....	....	....	....	....	....	....
2006-07	Linkopings HC	Sweden	24	0	2	2	22	....	....	....	....	....	....	....	....	....	....	....	....	....	....	....	....	....	....
	Assat Pori	Finland	25	3	2	5	39	....	....	....	....	....	....	....	....	....	....	....	....	....	....	....	....	....	....
	NHL Totals		**77**	**6**	**14**	**20**	**44**	**1**	**0**	**0**	**72**	**8.3**		**19**	**42.1**	**11:08**	**22**	**0**	**2**	**2**	**4**	**0**	**0**	**0**	**9:03**

WHL East Second All-Star Team (1995)

Traded to **Nashville** by **Philadelphia** for Matt Henderson, September 27, 1999. Signed as a free agent by **Edmonton**, August 31, 2000. Signed as a free agent by **Toronto**, July 24, 2001. Signed as a free agent by **NY Rangers**, July 28, 2003. Traded to **Florida** by **NY Rangers** for Jeff Paul, March 9, 2004. Loaned to **Edmonton** (AHL) by **Florida** (San Antonio-AHL) for cash, March 12, 2005. Signed as a free agent by **Colorado**, August 16, 2005. Signed as a free agent by **Assat Pori** (Finland), December 1, 2006. Signed as a free agent by **Jesenice** (Slovakia), June 28, 2007.

HEATLEY, Dany (HEET-lee, DA-nee) OTT.

Left wing. Shoots left. 6'3", 216 lbs. Born, Freiburg, West Germany, January 21, 1981. Atlanta's 1st choice, 2nd overall, in 2000 Entry Draft.

Season	Club	League	GP	G	A	Pts	PIM	PP	SH	GW	S	%	+/-	TF	F%	Min	GP	G	A	Pts	PIM	PP	SH	GW	Min
1996-97	Calgary Blazers	AMHL	25	30	42	72	26	....	....	....	....	....	....	....	....	....	....	....	....	....	....	....	....	....	....
1997-98	Calgary Buffaloes	AMHL	36	39	42	*81	34	....	....	....	....	....	....	....	....	....	10	10	12	*22	30	....	....	....	....
1998-99	Calgary Canucks	AJHL	60	*70	56	*126	91	....	....	....	....	....	....	....	....	....	13	*22	13	*35	6	....	....	....	....
99-2000	U. of Wisconsin	WCHA	38	28	28	56	32	....	....	....	....	....	....	....	....	....	....	....	....	....	....	....	....	....	....
2000-01	U. of Wisconsin	WCHA	39	24	33	57	74	....	....	....	....	....	....	....	....	....	....	....	....	....	....	....	....	....	....
2001-02	**Atlanta**	**NHL**	**82**	**26**	**41**	**67**	**56**	**7**	**0**	**4**	**202**	**12.9**	**–19**	**116**	**32.8**	**19:53**	....	....	....	....	....	....	....	....	....
2002-03	**Atlanta**	**NHL**	**77**	**41**	**48**	**89**	**58**	**19**	**1**	**6**	**252**	**16.3**	**–8**	**49**	**36.7**	**21:57**	....	....	....	....	....	....	....	....	....
2003-04	**Atlanta**	**NHL**	**31**	**13**	**12**	**25**	**18**	**5**	**0**	**3**	**83**	**15.7**	**–8**	**41**	**24.4**	**19:53**	....	....	....	....	....	....	....	....	....
2004-05	SC Bern	Swiss	16	14	10	24	58	....	....	....	....	....	....	....	....	....	....	....	....	....	....	....	....	....	....
	Ak Bars Kazan	Russia	11	3	1	4	22	....	....	....	....	....	....	....	....	....	4	2	1	3	4	....	....	....	....

			Regular Season														Playoffs								
Season	Club	League	GP	G	A	Pts	PIM	PP	SH	GW	S	%	+/-	TF	F%	Min	GP	G	A	Pts	PIM	PP	SH	GW	Min
2005-06	**Ottawa**	**NHL**	**82**	**50**	**53**	**103**	**86**	**23**	**2**	**7**	**300**	**16.7**	**29**	**166**	**53.6**	**21:09**	**10**	**3**	**9**	**12**	**11**	**3**	**0**	**1**	**18:56**
	Canada	Olympics	6	2	1	3	8	....	....	....	....	....	....	....	....	....	....	....	....	....	....	....	....	....	....
2006-07	**Ottawa**	**NHL**	**82**	**50**	**55**	**105**	**74**	**17**	**3**	**10**	**310**	**16.1**	**31**	**60**	**38.3**	**21:02**	**20**	**7**	***15**	***22**	**14**	**2**	**0**	**2**	**21:18**
	NHL Totals		**354**	**180**	**209**	**389**	**292**	**71**	**6**	**30**	**1147**	**15.7**		**432**	**41.2**	**20:54**	**30**	**10**	**24**	**34**	**25**	**5**	**0**	**3**	**20:31**

WCHA First All-Star Team (2000) • WCHA Rookie of the Year (2000) • NCAA West Second All-American Team (2000) • WCHA Second All-Star Team (2001) • NCAA West First All-American Team (2001) • NHL All-Rookie Team (2002) • Calder Memorial Trophy (2002) • NHL Second All-Star Team (2006) • NHL First All-Star Team (2007)

Played in NHL All-Star Game (2003, 2007)

• Missed majority of 2003-04 season recovering from injuries suffered in automobile accident, September 29, 2003. Signed as a free agent by **Bern** (Swiss), October 13, 2004. Signed as a free agent by **Kazan** (Russia), February 9, 2005. Traded to **Ottawa** by **Atlanta** for Marian Hossa and Greg de Vries, August 23, 2005.

HECHT, Jochen

(HEHKHT, YOH-khehn) **BUF.**

Left wing. Shoots left. 6'1", 195 lbs. Born, Mannheim, West Germany, June 21, 1977. St. Louis' 1st choice, 49th overall, in 1995 Entry Draft.

Season	Club	League	GP	G	A	Pts	PIM	PP	SH	GW	S	%	+/-	TF	F%	Min	GP	G	A	Pts	PIM	PP	SH	GW	Min
1993-94	Mannheim Jr.	Ger-Jr.	28	27	13	40	103	....	....	....	....	....	....	....	....	....	....	....	....	....	....	....	....	....	....
1994-95	Adler Mannheim	Germany	43	11	12	23	68	....	....	....	....	....	....	....	....	....	10	5	4	9	12	....	....	....	....
1995-96	Adler Mannheim	Germany	44	12	16	28	68	....	....	....	....	....	....	....	....	....	8	3	2	5	6	....	....	....	....
1996-97	Adler Mannheim	Germany	46	21	21	42	36	....	....	....	....	....	....	....	....	....	9	3	3	6	4	....	....	....	....
1997-98	Adler Mannheim	Germany	44	7	19	26	42	....	....	....	....	....	....	....	....	....	10	1	1	2	14	....	....	....	....
	Adler Mannheim	EuroHL	5	0	4	4	8	....	....	....	....	....	....	....	....	....	....	....	....	....	....	....	....	....	....
	Germany	Olympics	4	1	0	1	6	....	....	....	....	....	....	....	....	....	....	....	....	....	....	....	....	....	....
1998-99	**St. Louis**	**NHL**	**3**	**0**	**0**	**0**	**0**	**0**	**0**	**0**	**4**	**0.0**	**-2**	**19**	**21.1**	**13:16**	**5**	**2**	**0**	**2**	**0**	**0**	**0**	**0**	**16:40**
	Worcester IceCats	AHL	74	21	35	56	48	....	....	....	....	....	....	....	....	....	4	1	1	2	2	....	....	....	....
99-2000	**St. Louis**	**NHL**	**63**	**13**	**21**	**34**	**28**	**5**	**0**	**1**	**140**	**9.3**	**20**	**75**	**49.3**	**15:25**	**7**	**4**	**6**	**10**	**2**	**1**	**0**	**1**	**17:02**
2000-01	**St. Louis**	**NHL**	**72**	**19**	**25**	**44**	**48**	**8**	**3**	**1**	**208**	**9.1**	**11**	**160**	**43.8**	**17:56**	**15**	**2**	**4**	**6**	**4**	**0**	**0**	**0**	**17:19**
2001-02	**Edmonton**	**NHL**	**82**	**16**	**24**	**40**	**60**	**5**	**0**	**3**	**211**	**7.6**	**4**	**26**	**53.9**	**15:00**	....	....	....	....	....	....	....	....	....
	Germany	Olympics	4	1	1	2	2	....	....	....	....	....	....	....	....	....	....	....	....	....	....	....	....	....	....
2002-03	**Buffalo**	**NHL**	**49**	**10**	**16**	**26**	**30**	**2**	**0**	**2**	**145**	**6.9**	**4**	**33**	**30.3**	**17:55**	....	....	....	....	....	....	....	....	....
2003-04	**Buffalo**	**NHL**	**64**	**15**	**37**	**52**	**49**	**2**	**1**	**0**	**174**	**8.6**	**17**	**141**	**43.3**	**19:00**	....	....	....	....	....	....	....	....	....
2004-05	Adler Mannheim	Germany	48	16	34	50	151	....	....	....	....	....	....	....	....	....	14	10	10	*20	14	....	....	....	....
2005-06	**Buffalo**	**NHL**	**64**	**18**	**24**	**42**	**34**	**4**	**2**	**4**	**179**	**10.1**	**10**	**156**	**39.7**	**18:07**	**15**	**2**	**6**	**8**	**8**	**0**	**0**	**1**	**17:29**
2006-07	**Buffalo**	**NHL**	**76**	**19**	**37**	**56**	**39**	**3**	**0**	**1**	**197**	**9.6**	**19**	**145**	**39.3**	**18:51**	**16**	**4**	**1**	**5**	**10**	**0**	**0**	**1**	**17:41**
	NHL Totals		**473**	**110**	**184**	**294**	**288**	**29**	**6**	**12**	**1258**	**8.7**		**755**	**41.7**	**17:22**	**58**	**14**	**17**	**31**	**24**	**1**	**0**	**3**	**17:22**

Traded to **Edmonton** by **St. Louis** with Marty Reasoner and Jan Horacek for Doug Weight and Michel Riesen, July 1, 2001. Traded to **Buffalo** by **Edmonton** for Atlanta's 2nd round choice (previously acquired, Edmonton selected Jeff Deslauriers) in 2002 Entry Draft and Nashville's 2nd round choice (previously acquired, Edmonton selected Jarret Stoll) in 2002 Entry Draft, June 22, 2002. Signed as a free agent by **Mannheim** (Germany), August 2, 2004.

HEDICAN, Bret

(HEH-dih-kan, BREHT) **CAR.**

Defense. Shoots left. 6'2", 210 lbs. Born, St. Paul, MN, August 10, 1970. St. Louis' 10th choice, 198th overall, in 1988 Entry Draft.

Season	Club	League	GP	G	A	Pts	PIM	PP	SH	GW	S	%	+/-	TF	F%	Min	GP	G	A	Pts	PIM	PP	SH	GW	Min
1987-88	North St. Paul	High-MN	23	15	19	34	16	....	....	....	....	....	....	....	....	....	....	....	....	....	....	....	....	....	....
1988-89	St. Cloud State	NCAA-3	28	5	3	8	28	....	....	....	....	....	....	....	....	....	....	....	....	....	....	....	....	....	....
1989-90	St. Cloud State	NCAA-3	36	4	17	21	37	....	....	....	....	....	....	....	....	....	....	....	....	....	....	....	....	....	....
1990-91	St. Cloud State	WCHA	41	21	26	47	26	....	....	....	....	....	....	....	....	....	....	....	....	....	....	....	....	....	....
1991-92	United States	Nat-Tm	54	1	8	9	59	....	....	....	....	....	....	....	....	....	....	....	....	....	....	....	....	....	....
	United States	Olympics	8	0	0	0	4	....	....	....	....	....	....	....	....	....	....	....	....	....	....	....	....	....	....
	St. Louis	**NHL**	**4**	**1**	**0**	**1**	**0**	**0**	**0**	**0**	**1**	**100.0**	**1**	....	....	....	**5**	**0**	**0**	**0**	**0**	**0**	**0**	**0**	....
1992-93	**St. Louis**	**NHL**	**42**	**0**	**8**	**8**	**30**	**0**	**0**	**0**	**40**	**0.0**	**-2**	....	....	....	**10**	**0**	**0**	**0**	**14**	**0**	**0**	**0**	....
	Peoria Rivermen	IHL	19	0	8	8	10	....	....	....	....	....	....	....	....	....	....	....	....	....	....	....	....	....	....
1993-94	**St. Louis**	**NHL**	**61**	**0**	**11**	**11**	**64**	**0**	**0**	**0**	**78**	**0.0**	**-8**	....	....	....	....	....	....	....	....	....	....	....	....
	Vancouver	**NHL**	**8**	**0**	**1**	**1**	**0**	**0**	**0**	**0**	**10**	**0.0**	**1**	....	....	....	**24**	**1**	**6**	**7**	**16**	**0**	**0**	**0**	....
1994-95	**Vancouver**	**NHL**	**45**	**2**	**11**	**13**	**34**	**0**	**0**	**0**	**56**	**3.6**	**-3**	....	....	....	**11**	**0**	**2**	**2**	**6**	**0**	**0**	**0**	....
1995-96	**Vancouver**	**NHL**	**77**	**6**	**23**	**29**	**83**	**1**	**0**	**0**	**113**	**5.3**	**8**	....	....	....	**6**	**0**	**1**	**1**	**10**	**0**	**0**	**0**	....
1996-97	**Vancouver**	**NHL**	**67**	**4**	**15**	**19**	**51**	**2**	**0**	**1**	**93**	**4.3**	**-3**	....	....	....	....	....	....	....	....	....	....	....	....
1997-98	**Vancouver**	**NHL**	**71**	**3**	**24**	**27**	**79**	**1**	**0**	**0**	**84**	**3.6**	**3**	....	....	....	....	....	....	....	....	....	....	....	....
1998-99	**Vancouver**	**NHL**	**42**	**2**	**11**	**13**	**34**	**0**	**2**	**0**	**52**	**3.8**	**7**	**0**	**0.0**	**18:40**	....	....	....	....	....	....	....	....	....
	Florida	**NHL**	**25**	**3**	**7**	**10**	**17**	**0**	**0**	**1**	**38**	**7.9**	**-2**	**0**	**0.0**	**22:24**	....	....	....	....	....	....	....	....	....
99-2000	**Florida**	**NHL**	**76**	**6**	**19**	**25**	**68**	**2**	**0**	**1**	**58**	**10.3**	**4**	**0**	**0.0**	**19:36**	**4**	**0**	**0**	**0**	**0**	**0**	**0**	**0**	**20:42**
2000-01	**Florida**	**NHL**	**70**	**5**	**15**	**20**	**72**	**4**	**0**	**1**	**104**	**4.8**	**-7**	**0**	**0.0**	**21:49**	....	....	....	....	....	....	....	....	....
2001-02	**Florida**	**NHL**	**31**	**3**	**7**	**10**	**12**	**0**	**0**	**0**	**46**	**6.5**	**-4**	**0**	**0.0**	**24:27**	....	....	....	....	....	....	....	....	....
	Carolina	**NHL**	**26**	**2**	**4**	**6**	**10**	**0**	**0**	**1**	**39**	**5.1**	**3**	**0**	**0.0**	**22:56**	**23**	**1**	**4**	**5**	**20**	**0**	**0**	**0**	**23:52**
2002-03	**Carolina**	**NHL**	**72**	**3**	**14**	**17**	**75**	**1**	**0**	**1**	**113**	**2.7**	**-24**	**0**	**0.0**	**23:02**	....	....	....	....	....	....	....	....	....
2003-04	**Carolina**	**NHL**	**81**	**7**	**17**	**24**	**64**	**2**	**0**	**3**	**112**	**6.3**	**-10**	**0**	**0.0**	**22:35**	....	....	....	....	....	....	....	....	....
2004-05			DID NOT PLAY																						
2005-06♦	**Carolina**	**NHL**	**74**	**5**	**22**	**27**	**58**	**2**	**1**	**1**	**73**	**6.8**	**11**	**0**	**0.0**	**20:19**	**25**	**2**	**9**	**11**	**42**	**0**	**0**	**0**	**22:40**
	United States	Olympics	6	0	1	1	6	....	....	....	....	....	....	....	....	....	....	....	....	....	....	....	....	....	....
2006-07	**Carolina**	**NHL**	**50**	**0**	**10**	**10**	**36**	**0**	**0**	**0**	**44**	**0.0**	**-8**	**0**	**0.0**	**19:58**	....	....	....	....	....	....	....	....	....
	NHL Totals		**922**	**52**	**219**	**271**	**787**	**15**	**3**	**10**	**1154**	**4.5**		**0**	**0.0**	**21:24**	**108**	**4**	**22**	**26**	**108**	**0**	**0**	**0**	**23:03**

WCHA First All-Star Team (1991)

Traded to **Vancouver** by **St. Louis** with Jeff Brown and Nathan LaFayette for Craig Janney, March 21, 1994. Traded to **Florida** by **Vancouver** with Pavel Bure, Brad Ference and Vancouver's 3rd round choice (Robert Fried) in 2000 Entry Draft for Ed Jovanovski, Dave Gagner, Mike Brown, Kevin Weekes and Florida's 1st round choice (Nathan Smith) in 2000 Entry Draft, January 17, 1999. Traded to **Carolina** by **Florida** with Kevyn Adams and Tomas Malec for Sandis Ozolinsh and Byron Ritchie, January 16, 2002.

HEDSTROM, Jonathan

(HEHD-struhm, JAWN-ah-thuhn)

Right wing. Shoots left. 6', 200 lbs. Born, Skelleftea, Sweden, December 27, 1977. Toronto's 8th choice, 221st overall, in 1997 Entry Draft.

Season	Club	League	GP	G	A	Pts	PIM	PP	SH	GW	S	%	+/-	TF	F%	Min	GP	G	A	Pts	PIM	PP	SH	GW	Min
1995-96	Skelleftea AIK HK	Sweden-2	7	0	0	0	0	....	....	....	....	....	....	....	....	....	....	....	....	....	....	....	....	....	....
1996-97	Skelleftea Jr.	Swe-Jr.	9	4	4	8	....	....	....	....	....	....	....	....	....	....	....	....	....	....	....	....	....	....	....
	Skelleftea AIK HK	Sweden-2	12	1	1	2	10	....	....	....	....	....	....	....	....	....	6	0	0	0	2	....	....	....	....
1997-98	Skelleftea Jr.	Swe-Jr.	1	0	0	0	2	....	....	....	....	....	....	....	....	....	....	....	....	....	....	....	....	....	....
	Skelleftea AIK HK	Sweden-2	16	2	3	5	....	....	....	....	....	....	....	....	....	....	....	....	....	....	....	....	....	....	....
1998-99	Skelleftea AIK HK	Sweden-2	36	15	28	43	74	....	....	....	....	....	....	....	....	....	....	....	....	....	....	....	....	....	....
99-2000	Lulea HF	Sweden	48	9	17	26	46	....	....	....	....	....	....	....	....	....	9	2	1	3	12	....	....	....	....
2000-01	Lulea HF	Sweden	46	9	19	28	68	....	....	....	....	....	....	....	....	....	12	1	6	7	16	....	....	....	....
2001-02	Lulea HF	Sweden	47	11	7	18	38	....	....	....	....	....	....	....	....	....	4	2	1	3	6	....	....	....	....
2002-03	**Anaheim**	**NHL**	**4**	**0**	**0**	**0**	**0**	**0**	**0**	**0**	**3**	**0.0**	**-1**	**1**	**0.0**	**7:51**	....	....	....	....	....	....	....	....	....
	Cincinnati	AHL	50	14	21	35	62	....	....	....	....	....	....	....	....	....	....	....	....	....	....	....	....	....	....
2003-04	Djurgarden	Sweden	48	12	22	34	94	....	....	....	....	....	....	....	....	....	3	0	2	2	12	....	....	....	....
2004-05	Timra IK	Sweden	46	14	21	35	92	....	....	....	....	....	....	....	....	....	7	3	5	8	16	....	....	....	....
2005-06	**Anaheim**	**NHL**	**79**	**13**	**14**	**27**	**48**	**2**	**2**	**5**	**99**	**13.1**	**2**	**26**	**26.9**	**16:17**	**3**	**0**	**1**	**1**	**2**	**0**	**0**	**0**	**16:58**
2006-07	Timra IK	Sweden	54	13	25	38	74	....	....	....	....	....	....	....	....	....	7	2	3	5	14	....	....	....	....
	NHL Totals		**83**	**13**	**14**	**27**	**48**	**2**	**2**	**5**	**102**	**12.7**		**27**	**25.9**	**15:52**	**3**	**0**	**1**	**1**	**2**	**0**	**0**	**0**	**16:58**

Rights traded to **Anaheim** by **Toronto** for Anaheim's 6th (Vadim Sozinov) and 7th (Markus Seikola) round choices in 2000 Entry Draft, June 25, 2000. Signed as a free agent by **Djurgarden** (Sweden), September 1, 2003. Signed as a free agent by **Timra** (Sweden), August, 2004. Signed as a free agent by **Timra** (Sweden), August 15, 2006.

HEEREMA, Jeff

(HEER-eh-muh, JEHF)

Right wing. Shoots right. 6'2", 212 lbs. Born, Thunder Bay, Ont., January 17, 1980. Carolina's 1st choice, 11th overall, in 1998 Entry Draft.

Season	Club	League	GP	G	A	Pts	PIM	PP	SH	GW	S	%	+/-	TF	F%	Min	GP	G	A	Pts	PIM	PP	SH	GW	Min
1996-97	T. Bay Kings	TBMHL	54	42	29	71	112	....	....	....	....	....	....	....	....	....	....	....	....	....	....	....	....	....	....
1997-98	Sarnia Sting	OHL	63	32	40	72	88	....	....	....	....	....	....	....	....	....	5	4	1	5	10	....	....	....	....
1998-99	Sarnia Sting	OHL	62	31	39	70	113	....	....	....	....	....	....	....	....	....	6	5	1	6	0	....	....	....	....
99-2000	Sarnia Sting	OHL	67	36	41	77	62	....	....	....	....	....	....	....	....	....	7	4	2	6	10	....	....	....	....
2000-01	Cincinnati	IHL	73	17	16	33	42	....	....	....	....	....	....	....	....	....	4	0	0	0	0	....	....	....	....
2001-02	Lowell	AHL	76	33	37	70	90	....	....	....	....	....	....	....	....	....	5	2	3	5	2	....	....	....	....
2002-03	**Carolina**	**NHL**	**10**	**3**	**0**	**3**	**2**	**1**	**0**	**0**	**16**	**18.8**	**-2**	**0**	**0.0**	**9:37**	....	....	....	....	....	....	....	....	....
	Lowell	AHL	36	15	17	32	25	....	....	....	....	....	....	....	....	....	....	....	....	....	....	....	....	....	....
2003-04	**St. Louis**	**NHL**	**22**	**1**	**2**	**3**	**4**	**0**	**0**	**1**	**28**	**3.6**	**-5**	**2**	**50.0**	**10:26**	....	....	....	....	....	....	....	....	....
	Worcester IceCats	AHL	1	0	0	0	2	....	....	....	....	....	....	....	....	....	....	....	....	....	....	....	....	....	....
	Hartford	AHL	41	12	15	27	25	....	....	....	....	....	....	....	....	....	4	0	0	0	9	....	....	....	....
2004-05	Manitoba Moose	AHL	80	14	31	45	67	....	....	....	....	....	....	....	....	....	14	4	6	10	12	....	....	....	....

			Regular Season														Playoffs								
Season	Club	League	GP	G	A	Pts	PIM	PP	SH	GW	S	%	+/-	TF	F%	Min	GP	G	A	Pts	PIM	PP	SH	GW	Min
2005-06	Binghamton	AHL	77	27	47	74	69	....	....	....	....	....	....	....	....	....	....	....	....	....	....	....	....	....	....
2006-07	Binghamton	AHL	78	36	31	67	75	....	....	....	....	....	....	....	....	....	....	....	....	....	....	....	....	....	....
	NHL Totals		**32**	**4**	**2**	**6**	**6**	**1**	**0**	**1**	**44**	**9.1**		**2**	**50.0**	**10:11**	....	....	....	....	....	....	....	....	....

Claimed on waivers by **NY Rangers** from **Carolina**, September 30, 2003. Claimed by **St. Louis** from **NY Rangers** in Waiver Draft, October 3, 2003. Claimed on waivers by **NY Rangers** from **St. Louis**, January 10, 2004. Signed as a free agent by **Vancouver**, August 19, 2004. Signed as a free agent by **Ottawa**, August 26, 2005.

HEJDA, Jan (HAY-dah, YAHN) CBJ

Defense. Shoots left. 6'3", 209 lbs. Born, Prague, Czech., June 18, 1978. Buffalo's 4th choice, 106th overall, in 2003 Entry Draft.

Season	Club	League	GP	G	A	Pts	PIM	PP	SH	GW	S	%	+/-	TF	F%	Min	GP	G	A	Pts	PIM	PP	SH	GW	Min
1997-98	HC Slavia Praha	CzRep	44	2	5	7	51	....	....	....	....	....	....	....	....	....	5	0	0	0	6	....	....	....	....
1998-99	HC Slavia Praha	CzRep	34	1	2	3	38	....	....	....	....	....	....	....	....	....	....	....	....	....	....	....	....	....	....
99-2000	HC Slavia Praha	CzRep	26	1	2	3	14	....	....	....	....	....	....	....	....	....	....	....	....	....	....	....	....	....	....
	HC Femax Havirov	CzRep	7	0	2	2	6	....	....	....	....	....	....	....	....	....	....	....	....	....	....	....	....	....	....
	Liberec	CzRep-2	1	0	0	0	4	....	....	....	....	....	....	....	....	....	....	....	....	....	....	....	....	....	....
2000-01	HC Slavia Praha	CzRep	38	2	6	8	70	....	....	....	....	....	....	....	....	....	11	3	0	3	12	....	....	....	....
	SK Kadan	CzRep-2	8	1	0	1	6	....	....	....	....	....	....	....	....	....	....	....	....	....	....	....	....	....	....
2001-02	HC Slavia Praha	CzRep	42	9	8	17	52	....	....	....	....	....	....	....	....	....	9	1	1	2	14	....	....	....	....
2002-03	HC Slavia Praha	CzRep	52	6	11	17	44	....	....	....	....	....	....	....	....	....	17	5	8	13	12	....	....	....	....
2003-04	CSKA Moscow	Russia	60	1	5	6	26	....	....	....	....	....	....	....	....	....	....	....	....	....	....	....	....	....	....
2004-05	CSKA Moscow	Russia	60	2	11	13	59	....	....	....	....	....	....	....	....	....	....	....	....	....	....	....	....	....	....
2005-06	Mytischi	Russia	50	3	12	15	56	....	....	....	....	....	....	....	....	....	9	2	3	5	24	....	....	....	....
2006-07	**Edmonton**	**NHL**	**39**	**1**	**8**	**9**	**20**	**0**	**0**	**1**	**33**	**3.0**	**–6**	**0**	**0.0**	**20:23**	....	....	....	....	....	....	....	....	....
	Hamilton	AHL	5	0	3	3	21	....	....	....	....	....	....	....	....	....	....	....	....	....	....	....	....	....	....
	NHL Totals		**39**	**1**	**8**	**9**	**20**	**0**	**0**	**1**	**33**	**3.0**		**0**	**0.0**	**20:23**	....	....	....	....	....	....	....	....	....

Rights traded to **Edmonton** by **Buffalo** for Edmonton's 7th round choice (Nick Eno) in 2007 Entry Draft, July 10, 2006. Signed as a free agent by **Columbus**, July 5, 2007.

HEJDUK, Milan (HAY-dook, MEE-lan) COL.

Right wing. Shoots right. 6', 190 lbs. Born, Usti nad Labem, Czech., February 14, 1976. Quebec's 6th choice, 87th overall, in 1994 Entry Draft.

Season	Club	League	GP	G	A	Pts	PIM	PP	SH	GW	S	%	+/-	TF	F%	Min	GP	G	A	Pts	PIM	PP	SH	GW	Min
1993-94	HC Pardubice	CzRep	22	6	3	9	....	....	....	....	....	....	....	....	....	....	10	5	1	6	....	....	....	....	....
1994-95	HC Pardubice	CzRep	43	11	13	24	6	....	....	....	....	....	....	....	....	....	6	3	1	4	0	....	....	....	....
1995-96	Pardubice	CzRep	37	13	7	20	....	....	....	....	....	....	....	....	....	....	....	....	....	....	....	....	....	....	....
1996-97	Pardubice	CzRep	51	27	11	38	10	....	....	....	....	....	....	....	....	....	10	6	0	6	27	....	....	....	....
1997-98	Pardubice	CzRep	48	26	19	45	20	....	....	....	....	....	....	....	....	....	3	0	0	0	2	....	....	....	....
	Czech Republic	Olympics	4	0	0	0	2	....	....	....	....	....	....	....	....	....	....	....	....	....	....	....	....	....	....
1998-99	**Colorado**	**NHL**	**82**	**14**	**34**	**48**	**26**	**4**	**0**	**5**	**178**	**7.9**	**8**	**2**	**50.0**	**15:45**	**16**	**6**	**6**	**12**	**4**	**1**	**0**	**3**	**15:53**
99-2000	**Colorado**	**NHL**	**82**	**36**	**36**	**72**	**16**	**13**	**0**	**9**	**228**	**15.8**	**14**	**3**	**100.0**	**19:58**	**17**	**5**	**4**	**9**	**6**	**3**	**0**	**1**	**19:56**
2000-01 ♦	**Colorado**	**NHL**	**80**	**41**	**38**	**79**	**36**	**12**	**1**	**9**	**213**	**19.2**	**32**	**3**	**33.3**	**19:52**	**23**	**7**	***16**	**23**	**6**	**4**	**0**	**1**	**21:33**
2001-02	**Colorado**	**NHL**	**62**	**21**	**23**	**44**	**24**	**7**	**1**	**5**	**139**	**15.1**	**0**	**5**	**40.0**	**20:11**	**16**	**3**	**3**	**6**	**4**	**1**	**0**	**0**	**18:24**
	Czech Republic	Olympics	4	1	0	1	0	....	....	....	....	....	....	....	....	....	....	....	....	....	....	....	....	....	....
2002-03	**Colorado**	**NHL**	**82**	***50**	**48**	**98**	**32**	**18**	**0**	**4**	**244**	**20.5**	**52**	**43**	**44.2**	**19:50**	**7**	**2**	**2**	**4**	**2**	**1**	**0**	**0**	**20:42**
2003-04	**Colorado**	**NHL**	**82**	**35**	**40**	**75**	**20**	**16**	**0**	**6**	**237**	**14.8**	**19**	**69**	**47.8**	**18:46**	**11**	**5**	**2**	**7**	**0**	**2**	**0**	**0**	**18:40**
2004-05	Pardubice	CzRep	48	25	26	51	14	....	....	....	....	....	....	....	....	....	16	6	2	8	6	....	....	....	....
2005-06	**Colorado**	**NHL**	**74**	**24**	**34**	**58**	**24**	**14**	**1**	**2**	**221**	**10.9**	**13**	**23**	**17.4**	**18:33**	**9**	**2**	**6**	**8**	**2**	**0**	**0**	**0**	**20:56**
	Czech Republic	Olympics	8	2	1	3	2	....	....	....	....	....	....	....	....	....	....	....	....	....	....	....	....	....	....
2006-07	**Colorado**	**NHL**	**80**	**35**	**35**	**70**	**44**	**12**	**1**	**6**	**257**	**13.6**	**10**	**109**	**45.0**	**17:53**	....	....	....	....	....	....	....	....	....
	NHL Totals		**624**	**256**	**288**	**544**	**222**	**96**	**4**	**46**	**1717**	**14.9**		**257**	**43.6**	**18:49**	**99**	**30**	**39**	**69**	**24**	**12**	**0**	**5**	**19:25**

NHL All-Rookie Team (1999) • NHL Second All-Star Team (2003) • Bud Light Plus/Minus Award (2003) (tied with Peter Forsberg) • Maurice "Rocket" Richard Trophy (2003)

Played in NHL All-Star Game (2000, 2001)

Rights transferred to **Colorado** after **Quebec** franchise relocated, June 21, 1995. Signed as a free agent by **Pardubice** (CzRep), September 18, 2004.

HELBLING, Timo (HEHL-blihng, TEE-moh)

Defense. Shoots right. 6'3", 209 lbs. Born, Basel, Switz., July 21, 1981. Nashville's 11th choice, 162nd overall, in 1999 Entry Draft.

Season	Club	League	GP	G	A	Pts	PIM	PP	SH	GW	S	%	+/-	TF	F%	Min	GP	G	A	Pts	PIM	PP	SH	GW	Min
1997-98	HC Davos Jr.	Swiss-Jr.	34	6	6	12	38	....	....	....	....	....	....	....	....	....	....	....	....	....	....	....	....	....	....
1998-99	HC Davos Jr.	Swiss-Jr.	28	5	10	15	116	....	....	....	....	....	....	....	....	....	2	1	3	4	35	....	....	....	....
	HC Davos	Swiss	44	0	0	0	8	....	....	....	....	....	....	....	....	....	4	0	0	0	0	....	....	....	....
99-2000	HC Davos	Swiss	44	0	0	0	49	....	....	....	....	....	....	....	....	....	5	0	0	0	0	....	....	....	....
2000-01	Windsor Spitfires	OHL	54	7	14	21	90	....	....	....	....	....	....	....	....	....	7	0	2	2	11	....	....	....	....
	Milwaukee	IHL	....	....	....	....	....	....	....	....	....	....	....	....	....	....	1	0	0	0	0	....	....	....	....
2001-02	Milwaukee	AHL	67	2	6	8	59	....	....	....	....	....	....	....	....	....	....	....	....	....	....	....	....	....	....
2002-03	Milwaukee	AHL	23	0	1	1	37	....	....	....	....	....	....	....	....	....	....	....	....	....	....	....	....	....	....
	Toledo Storm	ECHL	35	3	8	11	75	....	....	....	....	....	....	....	....	....	7	0	1	1	2	....	....	....	....
2003-04	Milwaukee	AHL	37	0	2	2	46	....	....	....	....	....	....	....	....	....	....	....	....	....	....	....	....	....	....
	Utah Grizzlies	AHL	23	3	2	5	47	....	....	....	....	....	....	....	....	....	....	....	....	....	....	....	....	....	....
2004-05	Kloten Flyers	Swiss	44	2	9	11	120	....	....	....	....	....	....	....	....	....	5	1	3	4	8	....	....	....	....
2005-06	**Tampa Bay**	**NHL**	**9**	**0**	**1**	**1**	**6**	**0**	**0**	**0**	**2**	**0.0**	**–3**	**0**	**0.0**	**10:19**	....	....	....	....	....	....	....	....	....
	Springfield	AHL	60	7	14	21	56	....	....	....	....	....	....	....	....	....	....	....	....	....	....	....	....	....	....
2006-07	**Washington**	**NHL**	**2**	**0**	**0**	**0**	**2**	**0**	**0**	**0**	**0**	**0.0**	**–1**	**0**	**0.0**	**12:00**	....	....	....	....	....	....	....	....	....
	Hershey Bears	AHL	49	1	16	17	106	....	....	....	....	....	....	....	....	....	....	....	....	....	....	....	....	....	....
	Rochester	AHL	20	0	8	8	50	....	....	....	....	....	....	....	....	....	6	2	0	2	6	....	....	....	....
	NHL Totals		**11**	**0**	**1**	**1**	**8**	**0**	**0**	**0**	**2**	**0.0**		**0**	**0.0**	**10:37**	....	....	....	....	....	....	....	....	....

Traded to **Tampa Bay** by **Nashville** for Tampa Bay's 8th round choice (Pekka Rinne) in 2004 Entry Draft, February 25, 2004. Signed as a free agent by **Kloten** (Swiss), June 17, 2004. Signed as a free agent by **Washington**, August 9, 2006. Traded to **Buffalo** by **Washington** with Dainius Zubrus for Jiri Novotny and Buffalo's 1st round choice (later traded to San Jose - San Jose selected Nicholas Petrecki) in 2007 Entry Draft, February 27, 2007. Signed as a free agent by **Lugano** (Swiss), June 4, 2007.

HELMER, Bryan (HEHL-muhr, BRIGH-uhn) PHX.

Defense. Shoots right. 6'1", 208 lbs. Born, Sault Ste. Marie, Ont., July 15, 1972.

Season	Club	League	GP	G	A	Pts	PIM	PP	SH	GW	S	%	+/-	TF	F%	Min	GP	G	A	Pts	PIM	PP	SH	GW	Min
1989-90	Wellington Dukes	OHA-B	44	4	20	24	204	....	....	....	....	....	....	....	....	....	....	....	....	....	....	....	....	....	....
	Belleville Bulls	OHL	6	0	1	1	0	....	....	....	....	....	....	....	....	....	....	....	....	....	....	....	....	....	....
1990-91	Wellington Dukes	OHA-B	50	11	14	25	109	....	....	....	....	....	....	....	....	....	....	....	....	....	....	....	....	....	....
1991-92	Wellington Dukes	MTJHL	42	17	31	48	66	....	....	....	....	....	....	....	....	....	3	2	1	3	0	....	....	....	....
1992-93	Wellington Dukes	MTJHL	48	21	54	75	84	....	....	....	....	....	....	....	....	....	9	4	8	12	22	....	....	....	....
1993-94	Albany River Rats	AHL	65	4	19	23	79	....	....	....	....	....	....	....	....	....	5	0	0	0	9	....	....	....	....
1994-95	Albany River Rats	AHL	77	7	36	43	101	....	....	....	....	....	....	....	....	....	7	1	0	1	0	....	....	....	....
1995-96	Albany River Rats	AHL	80	14	30	44	107	....	....	....	....	....	....	....	....	....	4	2	0	2	6	....	....	....	....
1996-97	Albany River Rats	AHL	77	12	27	39	113	....	....	....	....	....	....	....	....	....	16	1	7	8	10	....	....	....	....
1997-98	Albany River Rats	AHL	80	14	49	63	101	....	....	....	....	....	....	....	....	....	13	4	9	13	18	....	....	....	....
1998-99	**Phoenix**	**NHL**	**11**	**0**	**0**	**0**	**23**	**0**	**0**	**0**	**11**	**0.0**	**2**	**0**	**0.0**	**7:43**	....	....	....	....	....	....	....	....	....
	Las Vegas	IHL	8	1	3	4	28	....	....	....	....	....	....	....	....	....	....	....	....	....	....	....	....	....	....
	St. Louis	**NHL**	**29**	**0**	**4**	**4**	**19**	**0**	**0**	**0**	**38**	**0.0**	**3**	**1**	**100.0**	**19:08**	....	....	....	....	....	....	....	....	....
	Worcester IceCats	AHL	16	7	8	15	18	....	....	....	....	....	....	....	....	....	4	0	0	0	12	....	....	....	....
99-2000	**St. Louis**	**NHL**	**15**	**1**	**1**	**2**	**10**	**1**	**0**	**1**	**19**	**5.3**	**–3**	**0**	**0.0**	**16:15**	....	....	....	....	....	....	....	....	....
	Worcester IceCats	AHL	54	10	25	35	124	....	....	....	....	....	....	....	....	....	9	1	4	5	10	....	....	....	....
2000-01	**Vancouver**	**NHL**	**20**	**2**	**4**	**6**	**18**	**0**	**0**	**0**	**28**	**7.1**	**0**	**0**	**0.0**	**16:51**	....	....	....	....	....	....	....	....	....
	Kansas City	IHL	42	4	15	19	76	....	....	....	....	....	....	....	....	....	....	....	....	....	....	....	....	....	....
2001-02	**Vancouver**	**NHL**	**40**	**5**	**5**	**10**	**53**	**2**	**0**	**1**	**43**	**11.6**	**10**	**0**	**0.0**	**12:04**	**6**	**0**	**0**	**0**	**0**	**0**	**0**	**0**	**9:09**
	Manitoba Moose	AHL	34	6	18	24	69	....	....	....	....	....	....	....	....	....	....	....	....	....	....	....	....	....	....
2002-03	**Vancouver**	**NHL**	**2**	**0**	**0**	**0**	**0**	**0**	**0**	**0**	**2**	**0.0**	**1**	**0**	**0.0**	**13:24**	....	....	....	....	....	....	....	....	....
	Manitoba Moose	AHL	60	7	24	31	82	....	....	....	....	....	....	....	....	....	14	0	4	4	20	....	....	....	....
2003-04	**Phoenix**	**NHL**	**17**	**0**	**1**	**1**	**10**	**0**	**0**	**0**	**10**	**0.0**	**–5**	**0**	**0.0**	**12:46**	....	....	....	....	....	....	....	....	....
	Springfield	AHL	9	1	6	7	6	....	....	....	....	....	....	....	....	....	....	....	....	....	....	....	....	....	....
2004-05	Grand Rapids	AHL	80	7	18	25	64	....	....	....	....	....	....	....	....	....	....	....	....	....	....	....	....	....	....

			Regular Season														Playoffs								
Season	Club	League	GP	G	A	Pts	PIM	PP	SH	GW	S	%	+/-	TF	F%	Min	GP	G	A	Pts	PIM	PP	SH	GW	Min
2005-06	Grand Rapids	AHL	80	12	44	56	138	....	....	....	....	....	....	....	....	....	16	1	8	9	24	....	....	....	....
2006-07	San Antonio	AHL	70	6	23	29	81	....	....	....	....	....	....	....	....	....	....	....	....	....	....	....	....	....	....
	NHL Totals		**134**	**8**	**15**	**23**	**133**	**3**	**0**	**2**	**151**	**5.3**		**1**	**100.0**	**14:32**	**6**	**0**	**0**	**0**	**0**	**0**	**0**	**0**	**9:09**

AHL First All-Star Team (1998) • AHL Second All-Star Team (2006)

Signed as a free agent by **New Jersey**, July 10, 1994. Signed as a free agent by **Phoenix**, July 17, 1998. Claimed on waivers by **St. Louis** from **Phoenix**, December 19, 1998. Signed as a free agent by **Vancouver**, August 21, 2000. Traded to **Phoenix** by **Vancouver** for Martin Grenier, July 25, 2003. • Missed majority of 2003-04 season recovering from shoulder injury suffered in training camp, September 29, 2003. Signed as a free agent by **Detroit**, July 21, 2004. Signed as a free agent by **Phoenix**, July 19, 2006.

HEMSKY, Ales

(HEHM-skee, ahl-EHSH) **EDM.**

Right wing. Shoots right. 6', 192 lbs. Born, Pardubice, Czech., August 13, 1983. Edmonton's 1st choice, 13th overall, in 2001 Entry Draft.

Season	Club	League	GP	G	A	Pts	PIM	PP	SH	GW	S	%	+/-	TF	F%	Min	GP	G	A	Pts	PIM	PP	SH	GW	Min
99-2000	HC Pardubice Jr.	CzRep-Jr.	45	20	36	56	54	....	....	....	....	....	....	....	....	....	7	4	14	18	36	....	....	....	....
	Pardubice	CzRep	4	0	1	1	0	....	....	....	....	....	....	....	....	....	....	....	....	....	....	....	....	....	....
2000-01	Hull Olympiques	QMJHL	68	36	64	100	67	....	....	....	....	....	....	....	....	....	5	2	3	5	2	....	....	....	....
2001-02	Hull Olympiques	QMJHL	53	27	70	97	86	....	....	....	....	....	....	....	....	....	10	6	10	16	6	....	....	....	....
2002-03	**Edmonton**	**NHL**	**59**	**6**	**24**	**30**	**14**	**0**	**0**	**1**	**50**	**12.0**	**5**	**3**	**33.3**	**12:04**	**6**	**0**	**0**	**0**	**0**	**0**	**0**	**0**	**12:46**
2003-04	**Edmonton**	**NHL**	**71**	**12**	**22**	**34**	**14**	**4**	**0**	**3**	**87**	**13.8**	**-7**	**3**	**33.3**	**14:26**	....	....	....	....	....	....	....	....	....
2004-05	Pardubice	CzRep	47	13	18	31	28	....	....	....	....	....	....	....	....	....	16	4	*10	*14	26	....	....	....	....
2005-06	**Edmonton**	**NHL**	**81**	**19**	**58**	**77**	**64**	**7**	**1**	**4**	**178**	**10.7**	**-5**	**7**	**42.9**	**16:59**	**24**	**6**	**11**	**17**	**14**	**4**	**0**	**2**	**16:06**
	Czech Republic	Olympics	8	1	2	3	2	....	....	....	....	....	....	....	....	....	....	....	....	....	....	....	....	....	....
2006-07	**Edmonton**	**NHL**	**64**	**13**	**40**	**53**	**40**	**5**	**0**	**1**	**122**	**10.7**	**-7**	**10**	**30.0**	**16:59**	....	....	....	....	....	....	....	....	....
	NHL Totals		**275**	**50**	**144**	**194**	**132**	**16**	**1**	**9**	**437**	**11.4**		**23**	**34.8**	**15:16**	**30**	**6**	**11**	**17**	**14**	**4**	**0**	**2**	**15:26**

QMJHL Second All-Star Team (2002)

Signed as a free agent by **Pardubice** (CzRep), September 18, 2004.

HENNESSY, Josh

(HEHN-eh-see, JAWSH) **OTT.**

Center. Shoots left. 6', 198 lbs. Born, Brockton, MA, February 7, 1985. San Jose's 3rd choice, 43rd overall, in 2003 Entry Draft.

Season	Club	League	GP	G	A	Pts	PIM	PP	SH	GW	S	%	+/-	TF	F%	Min	GP	G	A	Pts	PIM	PP	SH	GW	Min
2000-01	Milton Academy	High-MA	28	20	30	50	20	....	....	....	....	....	....	....	....	....	....	....	....	....	....	....	....	....	....
2001-02	Quebec Remparts	QMJHL	70	20	20	40	24	....	....	....	....	....	....	....	....	....	9	3	9	12	8	....	....	....	....
2002-03	Quebec Remparts	QMJHL	72	33	51	84	44	....	....	....	....	....	....	....	....	....	11	6	9	15	10	....	....	....	....
2003-04	Quebec Remparts	QMJHL	59	40	42	82	55	....	....	....	....	....	....	....	....	....	....	....	....	....	....	....	....	....	....
2004-05	Quebec Remparts	QMJHL	68	35	50	85	39	....	....	....	....	....	....	....	....	....	12	2	9	11	6	....	....	....	....
2005-06	Cleveland Barons	AHL	80	24	39	63	60	....	....	....	....	....	....	....	....	....	....	....	....	....	....	....	....	....	....
2006-07	**Ottawa**	**NHL**	**10**	**1**	**0**	**1**	**4**	**0**	**0**	**0**	**6**	**16.7**	**0**	**43**	**37.2**	**5:39**	....	....	....	....	....	....	....	....	....
	Binghamton	AHL	76	27	30	57	54	....	....	....	....	....	....	....	....	....	....	....	....	....	....	....	....	....	....
	NHL Totals		**10**	**1**	**0**	**1**	**4**	**0**	**0**	**0**	**6**	**16.7**		**43**	**37.2**	**5:39**	....	....	....	....	....	....	....	....	....

Traded to **Chicago** by **San Jose** with Tom Preissing for Mark Bell, July 9, 2006. Traded to **Ottawa** by **Chicago** with Tom Preissing, Michal Barinka and Chicago's 2nd round choice in 2008 Entry Draft for Martin Havlat and Bryan Smolinski, July 10, 2006.

HENRY, Alex

(HEHN-ree, AL-ehx) **NSH.**

Defense. Shoots left. 6'5", 220 lbs. Born, Elliot Lake, Ont., October 18, 1979. Edmonton's 2nd choice, 67th overall, in 1998 Entry Draft.

Season	Club	League	GP	G	A	Pts	PIM	PP	SH	GW	S	%	+/-	TF	F%	Min	GP	G	A	Pts	PIM	PP	SH	GW	Min
1995-96	Timmins Majors	NOHA	30	4	11	15	6	....	....	....	....	....	....	....	....	....	....	....	....	....	....	....	....	....	....
	Timmins	NOJHA	2	0	0	0	0	....	....	....	....	....	....	....	....	....	....	....	....	....	....	....	....	....	....
1996-97	London Knights	OHL	61	1	10	11	65	....	....	....	....	....	....	....	....	....	....	....	....	....	....	....	....	....	....
1997-98	London Knights	OHL	62	5	9	14	97	....	....	....	....	....	....	....	....	....	16	0	3	3	14	....	....	....	....
1998-99	London Knights	OHL	68	5	23	28	105	....	....	....	....	....	....	....	....	....	25	3	10	13	22	....	....	....	....
99-2000	Hamilton	AHL	60	1	0	1	69	....	....	....	....	....	....	....	....	....	....	....	....	....	....	....	....	....	....
2000-01	Hamilton	AHL	56	2	3	5	87	....	....	....	....	....	....	....	....	....	....	....	....	....	....	....	....	....	....
2001-02	Hamilton	AHL	69	4	8	12	143	....	....	....	....	....	....	....	....	....	15	1	2	3	16	....	....	....	....
2002-03	**Edmonton**	**NHL**	**3**	**0**	**0**	**0**	**0**	**0**	**0**	**0**	**0**	**0.0**	**-1**	**0**	**0.0**	**7:02**	....	....	....	....	....	....	....	....	....
	Washington	**NHL**	**38**	**0**	**0**	**0**	**80**	**0**	**0**	**0**	**8**	**0.0**	**-4**	**1**	**0.0**	**3:39**	....	....	....	....	....	....	....	....	....
	Portland Pirates	AHL	3	0	1	1	0	....	....	....	....	....	....	....	....	....	....	....	....	....	....	....	....	....	....
2003-04	**Minnesota**	**NHL**	**71**	**2**	**4**	**6**	**106**	**0**	**0**	**0**	**37**	**5.4**	**4**	**2**	**0.0**	**14:53**	....	....	....	....	....	....	....	....	....
2004-05	ESV Kaufbeuren	German-2	26	6	6	12	32	....	....	....	....	....	....	....	....	....	....	....	....	....	....	....	....	....	....
2005-06	**Minnesota**	**NHL**	**63**	**0**	**5**	**5**	**73**	**0**	**0**	**0**	**41**	**0.0**	**-4**	**2**	**50.0**	**11:26**	....	....	....	....	....	....	....	....	....
2006-07	Milwaukee	AHL	64	1	6	7	66	....	....	....	....	....	....	....	....	....	2	0	0	0	7	....	....	....	....
	NHL Totals		**175**	**2**	**9**	**11**	**259**	**0**	**0**	**0**	**86**	**2.3**		**5**	**20.0**	**11:04**	....	....	....	....	....	....	....	....	....

Claimed on waivers by **Washington** from **Edmonton**, October 24, 2002. Claimed on waivers by **Minnesota** from **Washington**, October 9, 2003. Signed as a free agent by **Kaufbeuren** (German-2), January 15, 2005. Signed as a free agent by **Nashville**, August 22, 2006.

HEWARD, Jamie

(HEW-uhrd, JAY-mee)

Defense. Shoots right. 6'2", 215 lbs. Born, Regina, Sask., March 30, 1971. Pittsburgh's 1st choice, 16th overall, in 1989 Entry Draft.

Season	Club	League	GP	G	A	Pts	PIM	PP	SH	GW	S	%	+/-	TF	F%	Min	GP	G	A	Pts	PIM	PP	SH	GW	Min
1987-88	Regina Pats	WHL	68	10	17	27	17	....	....	....	....	....	....	....	....	....	4	1	1	2	2	....	....	....	....
1988-89	Regina Pats	WHL	52	31	28	59	29	....	....	....	....	....	....	....	....	....	....	....	....	....	....	....	....	....	....
1989-90	Regina Pats	WHL	72	14	44	58	42	....	....	....	....	....	....	....	....	....	11	2	2	4	10	....	....	....	....
1990-91	Regina Pats	WHL	71	23	61	84	41	....	....	....	....	....	....	....	....	....	8	2	9	11	6	....	....	....	....
1991-92	Muskegon	IHL	54	6	21	27	37	....	....	....	....	....	....	....	....	....	14	1	4	5	4	....	....	....	....
1992-93	Cleveland	IHL	58	9	18	27	64	....	....	....	....	....	....	....	....	....	....	....	....	....	....	....	....	....	....
1993-94	Cleveland	IHL	73	8	16	24	72	....	....	....	....	....	....	....	....	....	....	....	....	....	....	....	....	....	....
1994-95	Canada	Nat-Tm	51	11	35	46	32	....	....	....	....	....	....	....	....	....	....	....	....	....	....	....	....	....	....
1995-96	**Toronto**	**NHL**	**5**	**0**	**0**	**0**	**0**	**0**	**0**	**0**	**8**	**0.0**	**-1**	....	....	....	....	....	....	....	....	....	....	....	....
	St. John's	AHL	73	22	34	56	33	....	....	....	....	....	....	....	....	....	3	1	1	2	6	....	....	....	....
1996-97	**Toronto**	**NHL**	**20**	**1**	**4**	**5**	**6**	**0**	**0**	**0**	**23**	**4.3**	**-6**	....	....	....	....	....	....	....	....	....	....	....	....
	St. John's	AHL	27	8	19	27	26	....	....	....	....	....	....	....	....	....	9	1	3	4	6	....	....	....	....
1997-98	Philadelphia	AHL	72	17	48	65	54	....	....	....	....	....	....	....	....	....	20	3	16	19	10	....	....	....	....
1998-99	**Nashville**	**NHL**	**63**	**6**	**12**	**18**	**44**	**4**	**0**	**1**	**124**	**4.8**	**-24**	**0**	**0.0**	**16:12**	....	....	....	....	....	....	....	....	....
99-2000	**NY Islanders**	**NHL**	**54**	**6**	**11**	**17**	**26**	**2**	**0**	**1**	**92**	**6.5**	**-9**	**0**	**0.0**	**19:58**	....	....	....	....	....	....	....	....	....
2000-01	**Columbus**	**NHL**	**69**	**11**	**16**	**27**	**33**	**9**	**0**	**1**	**108**	**10.2**	**3**	**0**	**0.0**	**14:21**	....	....	....	....	....	....	....	....	....
2001-02	**Columbus**	**NHL**	**28**	**1**	**2**	**3**	**7**	**0**	**0**	**0**	**38**	**2.6**	**-9**	**1**	**100.0**	**14:04**	....	....	....	....	....	....	....	....	....
	Syracuse Crunch	AHL	14	3	10	13	6	....	....	....	....	....	....	....	....	....	10	0	4	4	6	....	....	....	....
2002-03	Geneve	Swiss	40	8	23	31	60	....	....	....	....	....	....	....	....	....	6	1	1	2	22	....	....	....	....
2003-04	ZSC Lions Zurich	Swiss	25	5	9	14	57	....	....	....	....	....	....	....	....	....	6	0	1	1	24	....	....	....	....
2004-05	Langnau	Swiss	44	3	14	17	91	....	....	....	....	....	....	....	....	....	5	0	0	0	40	....	....	....	....
2005-06	**Washington**	**NHL**	**71**	**7**	**21**	**28**	**54**	**4**	**0**	**2**	**140**	**5.0**	**-5**	**1**	**0.0**	**21:52**	....	....	....	....	....	....	....	....	....
2006-07	**Washington**	**NHL**	**52**	**4**	**12**	**16**	**27**	**2**	**0**	**1**	**50**	**8.0**	**4**	**0**	**0.0**	**16:22**	....	....	....	....	....	....	....	....	....
	Los Angeles	**NHL**	**19**	**2**	**6**	**8**	**20**	**1**	**0**	**0**	**25**	**8.0**	**-2**	**0**	**0.0**	**19:44**	....	....	....	....	....	....	....	....	....
	NHL Totals		**381**	**38**	**84**	**122**	**217**	**22**	**0**	**6**	**608**	**6.3**		**2**	**50.0**	**17:35**	....	....	....	....	....	....	....	....	....

WHL East First All-Star Team (1991) • AHL First All-Star Team (1996, 1998) • Eddie Shore Award (Outstanding Defenseman – AHL) (1998)

Signed as a free agent by **Toronto**, May 4, 1995. Signed as a free agent by **Philadelphia**, July 31, 1997. Signed as a free agent by **Nashville**, August 10, 1998. Signed as a free agent by **NY Islanders**, July 27, 1999. Claimed on waivers by **Columbus** from **NY Islanders**, May 26, 2000. Signed as a free agent by **Geneve**, (Swiss), April 17, 2000. Signed as a free agent by **Washington**, August 12, 2005. Traded to **Los Angeles** by **Washington** for future considerations, February 27, 2007. Signed as a free agent by **St. Petersburg** (Russia), August 13, 2007.

HIGGINS, Christopher

(HIH-gihns, KRIHS-toh-fuhr) **MTL.**

Center. Shoots left. 6', 202 lbs. Born, Smithtown, NY, June 2, 1983. Montreal's 1st choice, 14th overall, in 2002 Entry Draft.

Season	Club	League	GP	G	A	Pts	PIM	PP	SH	GW	S	%	+/-	TF	F%	Min	GP	G	A	Pts	PIM	PP	SH	GW	Min
99-2000	Avon Old Farms	High-CT	27	19	20	39	10	....	....	....	....	....	....	....	....	....	....	....	....	....	....	....	....	....	....
2000-01	Avon Old Farms	High-CT	24	22	14	36	29	....	....	....	....	....	....	....	....	....	....	....	....	....	....	....	....	....	....
2001-02	Yale	ECAC	27	14	17	31	32	....	....	....	....	....	....	....	....	....	....	....	....	....	....	....	....	....	....
2002-03	Yale	ECAC	28	20	21	41	41	....	....	....	....	....	....	....	....	....	....	....	....	....	....	....	....	....	....
2003-04	**Montreal**	**NHL**	**2**	**0**	**0**	**0**	**0**	**0**	**0**	**0**	**0**	**0.0**	**0**	**9**	**22.2**	**6:18**	....	....	....	....	....	....	....	....	....
	Hamilton	AHL	67	21	27	48	18	....	....	....	....	....	....	....	....	....	10	3	2	5	0	....	....	....	....
2004-05	Hamilton	AHL	76	28	23	51	33	....	....	....	....	....	....	....	....	....	4	3	3	6	4	....	....	....	....

			Regular Season														Playoffs								
Season	Club	League	GP	G	A	Pts	PIM	PP	SH	GW	S	%	+/-	TF	F%	Min	GP	G	A	Pts	PIM	PP	SH	GW	Min
2005-06	**Montreal**	**NHL**	**80**	**23**	**15**	**38**	**26**	**7**	**3**	**3**	**148**	**15.5**	**–1**	**45**	**51.1**	**14:25**	**6**	**1**	**3**	**4**	**0**	**0**	**0**	**0**	**17:04**
2006-07	**Montreal**	**NHL**	**61**	**22**	**16**	**38**	**26**	**8**	**3**	**3**	**159**	**13.8**	**–11**	**53**	**34.0**	**17:54**	....	....	....	....	....	....	....	....	....
	NHL Totals		**143**	**45**	**31**	**76**	**52**	**15**	**6**	**6**	**307**	**14.7**		**107**	**40.2**	**15:47**	**6**	**1**	**3**	**4**	**0**	**0**	**0**	**0**	**17:04**

ECAC All-Rookie Team (2002) • ECAC Second All-Star Team (2002) • ECAC Rookie of the Year (2002) • ECAC First All-Star Team (2003) • ECAC Player of the Year (2003) (co-winner - David LeNeveu) • NCAA East First All-American Team (2003)

HILBERT, Andy

(HIHL-buhrt, AN-dee) **NYI**

Center/Left wing. Shoots left. 5'11", 194 lbs. Born, Lansing, MI, February 6, 1981. Boston's 3rd choice, 37th overall, in 2000 Entry Draft.

Season	Club	League	GP	G	A	Pts	PIM	PP	SH	GW	S	%	+/-	TF	F%	Min	GP	G	A	Pts	PIM	PP	SH	GW	Min
1997-98	USNTDP	U-17	29	14	10	24	34	....	....	....	....	....	....	....	....	....	....	....	....	....	....	....	....	....	....
	USNTDP	NAHL	39	19	16	35	102	....	....	....	....	....	....	....	....	....	7	1	4	5	12	....	....	....	....
1998-99	USNTDP	U-18	6	6	1	7	4	....	....	....	....	....	....	....	....	....	....	....	....	....	....	....	....	....	....
	USNTDP	USHL	46	23	35	58	140	....	....	....	....	....	....	....	....	....	....	....	....	....	....	....	....	....	....
99-2000	U. of Michigan	CCHA	35	17	15	32	39	....	....	....	....	....	....	....	....	....	....	....	....	....	....	....	....	....	....
2000-01	U. of Michigan	CCHA	42	26	38	64	72	....	....	....	....	....	....	....	....	....	....	....	....	....	....	....	....	....	....
2001-02	**Boston**	**NHL**	**6**	**1**	**0**	**1**	**2**	**0**	**0**	**0**	**11**	**9.1**	**–2**	**4**	**50.0**	**11:34**	....	....	....	....	....	....	....	....	....
	Providence Bruins	AHL	72	26	27	53	74	....	....	....	....	....	....	....	....	....	2	0	0	0	2	....	....	....	....
2002-03	Providence Bruins	AHL	64	35	35	70	119	....	....	....	....	....	....	....	....	....	4	0	1	1	4	....	....	....	....
	Boston	**NHL**	**14**	**0**	**3**	**3**	**7**	**0**	**0**	**0**	**22**	**0.0**	**–1**	**34**	**44.1**	**11:30**	....	....	....	....	....	....	....	....	....
2003-04	**Boston**	**NHL**	**18**	**2**	**0**	**2**	**9**	**0**	**0**	**0**	**27**	**7.4**	**1**	**11**	**54.6**	**8:57**	**5**	**1**	**0**	**1**	**0**	**0**	**0**	**0**	**5:32**
	Providence Bruins	AHL	19	3	5	8	20	....	....	....	....	....	....	....	....	....	....	....	....	....	....	....	....	....	....
2004-05	Providence Bruins	AHL	79	37	42	79	83	....	....	....	....	....	....	....	....	....	17	7	*14	*21	27	....	....	....	....
2005-06	**Chicago**	**NHL**	**28**	**5**	**4**	**9**	**22**	**0**	**0**	**1**	**50**	**10.0**	**–4**	**21**	**38.1**	**10:05**	....	....	....	....	....	....	....	....	....
	Norfolk Admirals	AHL	5	3	4	7	2	....	....	....	....	....	....	....	....	....	....	....	....	....	....	....	....	....	....
	Pittsburgh	**NHL**	**19**	**7**	**11**	**18**	**16**	**3**	**0**	**1**	**51**	**13.7**	**8**	**146**	**38.4**	**17:27**	....	....	....	....	....	....	....	....	....
2006-07	**NY Islanders**	**NHL**	**81**	**8**	**20**	**28**	**34**	**0**	**0**	**1**	**164**	**4.9**	**10**	**128**	**52.3**	**11:30**	**5**	**0**	**0**	**0**	**2**	**0**	**0**	**0**	**8:08**
	NHL Totals		**166**	**23**	**38**	**61**	**90**	**3**	**0**	**3**	**325**	**7.1**		**344**	**44.8**	**11:40**	**10**	**1**	**0**	**1**	**2**	**0**	**0**	**0**	**6:50**

CCHA First All-Star Team (2001) • NCAA West First All-American Team (2001) • AHL All-Rookie Team (2002) • AHL Second All-Star Team (2005)

• Missed majority of 2003-04 season recovering from groin injury suffered in pre-season game vs. Detroit, September 15, 2003. Traded to **Chicago** by **Boston** for Chicago's 5th round choice (later traded to NY Islanders - NY Islanders selected Shane Sims) in 2006 Entry Draft, November 6, 2005. Claimed on waivers by **Pittsburgh** from **Chicago**, March 9, 2006. Signed as a free agent by **NY Islanders**, July 4, 2006.

HILL, Sean

(HIHL, SHAWN) **MIN.**

Defense. Shoots right. 6', 211 lbs. Born, Duluth, MN, February 14, 1970. Montreal's 9th choice, 167th overall, in 1988 Entry Draft.

Season	Club	League	GP	G	A	Pts	PIM	PP	SH	GW	S	%	+/-	TF	F%	Min	GP	G	A	Pts	PIM	PP	SH	GW	Min
1986-87	Lakefield Chiefs	OHA-C	3	1	1	2	14	....	....	....	....	....	....	....	....	....	....	....	....	....	....	....	....	....	....
1987-88	Duluth East	High-MN	24	10	17	27	....	....	....	....	....	....	....	....	....	....	....	....	....	....	....	....	....	....	....
1988-89	U. of Wisconsin	WCHA	45	2	23	25	69	....	....	....	....	....	....	....	....	....	....	....	....	....	....	....	....	....	....
1989-90	U. of Wisconsin	WCHA	42	14	39	53	78	....	....	....	....	....	....	....	....	....	....	....	....	....	....	....	....	....	....
1990-91	U. of Wisconsin	WCHA	37	19	32	51	122	....	....	....	....	....	....	....	....	....	....	....	....	....	....	....	....	....	....
	Montreal	**NHL**	....	....	....	....	....	....	....	....	....	....	....	....	....	....	**1**	**0**	**0**	**0**	**0**	**0**	**0**	**0**	....
	Fredericton	AHL	....	....	....	....	....	....	....	....	....	....	....	....	....	....	3	0	2	2	2	....	....	....	....
1991-92	Fredericton	AHL	42	7	20	27	65	....	....	....	....	....	....	....	....	....	7	1	3	4	6	....	....	....	....
	United States	Nat-Tm	12	4	3	7	16	....	....	....	....	....	....	....	....	....	....	....	....	....	....	....	....	....	....
	United States	Olympics	8	2	0	2	6	....	....	....	....	....	....	....	....	....	....	....	....	....	....	....	....	....	....
	Montreal	**NHL**	....	....	....	....	....	....	....	....	....	....	....	....	....	....	**4**	**1**	**0**	**1**	**2**	**0**	**0**	**0**	....
1992-93 ♦	**Montreal**	**NHL**	**31**	**2**	**6**	**8**	**54**	**1**	**0**	**1**	**37**	**5.4**	**–5**	....	....	....	**3**	**0**	**0**	**0**	**4**	**0**	**0**	**0**	....
	Fredericton	AHL	6	1	3	4	10	....	....	....	....	....	....	....	....	....	....	....	....	....	....	....	....	....	....
1993-94	**Anaheim**	**NHL**	**68**	**7**	**20**	**27**	**78**	**2**	**1**	**1**	**165**	**4.2**	**–12**	....	....	....	....	....	....	....	....	....	....	....	....
1994-95	**Ottawa**	**NHL**	**45**	**1**	**14**	**15**	**30**	**0**	**0**	**0**	**107**	**0.9**	**–11**	....	....	....	....	....	....	....	....	....	....	....	....
1995-96	**Ottawa**	**NHL**	**80**	**7**	**14**	**21**	**94**	**2**	**0**	**2**	**157**	**4.5**	**–26**	....	....	....	....	....	....	....	....	....	....	....	....
1996-97	**Ottawa**	**NHL**	**5**	**0**	**0**	**0**	**4**	**0**	**0**	**0**	**9**	**0.0**	**1**	....	....	....	....	....	....	....	....	....	....	....	....
1997-98	**Ottawa**	**NHL**	**13**	**1**	**1**	**2**	**6**	**0**	**0**	**0**	**16**	**6.3**	**–3**	....	....	....	....	....	....	....	....	....	....	....	....
	Carolina	**NHL**	**42**	**0**	**5**	**5**	**48**	**0**	**0**	**0**	**37**	**0.0**	**–2**	....	....	....	....	....	....	....	....	....	....	....	....
1998-99	**Carolina**	**NHL**	**54**	**0**	**10**	**10**	**48**	**0**	**0**	**0**	**44**	**0.0**	**9**	**0**	**0.0**	**19:02**	....	....	....	....	....	....	....	....	....
99-2000	**Carolina**	**NHL**	**62**	**13**	**31**	**44**	**59**	**8**	**0**	**2**	**150**	**8.7**	**3**	**1**	**0.0**	**24:31**	....	....	....	....	....	....	....	....	....
2000-01	**St. Louis**	**NHL**	**48**	**1**	**10**	**11**	**51**	**0**	**0**	**0**	**47**	**2.1**	**5**	**1**	**0.0**	**17:23**	**15**	**0**	**1**	**1**	**12**	**0**	**0**	**0**	**13:46**
2001-02	**St. Louis**	**NHL**	**23**	**0**	**3**	**3**	**28**	**0**	**0**	**0**	**29**	**0.0**	**1**	**0**	**0.0**	**15:56**	....	....	....	....	....	....	....	....	....
	Carolina	**NHL**	**49**	**7**	**23**	**30**	**61**	**4**	**0**	**2**	**116**	**6.0**	**–1**	**1**	**0.0**	**23:58**	**23**	**4**	**4**	**8**	**20**	**4**	**0**	**1**	**25:55**
2002-03	**Carolina**	**NHL**	**82**	**5**	**24**	**29**	**141**	**1**	**0**	**0**	**188**	**2.7**	**4**	**1**	**0.0**	**24:21**	....	....	....	....	....	....	....	....	....
2003-04	**Carolina**	**NHL**	**80**	**13**	**26**	**39**	**84**	**6**	**0**	**1**	**228**	**5.7**	**–2**	**2**	**50.0**	**25:24**	....	....	....	....	....	....	....	....	....
2004-05			DID NOT PLAY																						
2005-06	**Florida**	**NHL**	**78**	**2**	**18**	**20**	**80**	**1**	**0**	**0**	**110**	**1.8**	**3**	**0**	**0.0**	**20:09**	....	....	....	....	....	....	....	....	....
2006-07	**NY Islanders**	**NHL**	**81**	**1**	**24**	**25**	**110**	**0**	**0**	**0**	**88**	**1.1**	**6**	**0**	**0.0**	**22:33**	**4**	**0**	**0**	**0**	**0**	**0**	**0**	**0**	**18:38**
	NHL Totals		**841**	**60**	**229**	**289**	**976**	**25**	**1**	**9**	**1528**	**3.9**		**6**	**16.7**	**22:10**	**50**	**5**	**5**	**10**	**38**	**4**	**0**	**1**	**20:53**

WCHA Second All-Star Team (1990, 1991) • NCAA West Second All-American Team (1991)

Claimed by **Anaheim** from **Montreal** in Expansion Draft, June 24, 1993. Traded to **Ottawa** by **Anaheim** with Anaheim's 9th round choice (Frederic Cassivi) in 1994 Entry Draft for Ottawa's 3rd round choice (later traded to Tampa Bay – Tampa Bay selected Vadim Epanchintsev) in 1994 Entry Draft, June 29, 1994. • Missed remainder of 1996-97 season recovering from knee injury suffered in game vs. New Jersey, October 18, 1996. Traded to **Carolina** by **Ottawa** for Chris Murray, November 18, 1997. Signed as a free agent by **St. Louis**, July 1, 2000. Traded to **Carolina** by **St. Louis** for Steve Halko and Carolina's 4th round choice (later traded to Atlanta – Atlanta selected Lane Manson) in 2002 Entry Draft, December 5, 2001. Signed as a free agent by **Florida**, July 15, 2004. Signed as a free agent by **NY Islanders**, August 15, 2006. Signed as a free agent by **Minnesota**, July 6, 2007.

HINOTE, Dan

(HIGH-noht, DAN) **ST.L.**

Right wing. Shoots right. 6', 190 lbs. Born, Leesburg, FL, January 30, 1977. Colorado's 9th choice, 167th overall, in 1996 Entry Draft.

Season	Club	League	GP	G	A	Pts	PIM	PP	SH	GW	S	%	+/-	TF	F%	Min	GP	G	A	Pts	PIM	PP	SH	GW	Min
1993-94	Elk River Elks	High-MN	STATISTICS NOT AVAILABLE																						
1994-95	Army	NCAA	33	20	24	44	20	....	....	....	....	....	....	....	....	....	....	....	....	....	....	....	....	....	....
1995-96	Army	NCAA	34	21	24	45	22	....	....	....	....	....	....	....	....	....	....	....	....	....	....	....	....	....	....
1996-97	Oshawa Generals	OHL	60	15	13	28	58	....	....	....	....	....	....	....	....	....	18	4	5	9	8	....	....	....	....
1997-98	Oshawa Generals	OHL	35	12	15	27	39	....	....	....	....	....	....	....	....	....	5	2	2	4	7	....	....	....	....
	Hershey Bears	AHL	24	1	4	5	25	....	....	....	....	....	....	....	....	....	....	....	....	....	....	....	....	....	....
1998-99	Hershey Bears	AHL	65	4	16	20	95	....	....	....	....	....	....	....	....	....	5	3	1	4	6	....	....	....	....
99-2000	**Colorado**	**NHL**	**27**	**1**	**3**	**4**	**10**	**0**	**0**	**0**	**14**	**7.1**	**0**	**132**	**51.5**	**7:51**	....	....	....	....	....	....	....	....	....
	Hershey Bears	AHL	55	28	31	59	96	....	....	....	....	....	....	....	....	....	14	4	5	9	19	....	....	....	....
2000-01 ♦	**Colorado**	**NHL**	**76**	**5**	**10**	**15**	**51**	**1**	**0**	**1**	**69**	**7.2**	**1**	**506**	**49.8**	**10:21**	**23**	**2**	**4**	**6**	**21**	**0**	**0**	**0**	**8:22**
2001-02	**Colorado**	**NHL**	**58**	**6**	**6**	**12**	**39**	**0**	**1**	**3**	**75**	**8.0**	**8**	**267**	**51.3**	**12:27**	**19**	**1**	**2**	**3**	**9**	**0**	**0**	**0**	**10:46**
2002-03	**Colorado**	**NHL**	**60**	**6**	**4**	**10**	**49**	**0**	**0**	**3**	**65**	**9.2**	**4**	**218**	**46.8**	**10:36**	**7**	**1**	**2**	**3**	**2**	**0**	**0**	**0**	**14:19**
2003-04	**Colorado**	**NHL**	**59**	**4**	**7**	**11**	**57**	**0**	**2**	**0**	**53**	**7.5**	**–6**	**151**	**48.3**	**12:42**	**11**	**1**	**0**	**1**	**0**	**0**	**1**	**0**	**13:04**
2004-05	MODO	Sweden	18	2	1	3	106	....	....	....	....	....	....	....	....	....	5	0	0	0	56	....	....	....	....
2005-06	**Colorado**	**NHL**	**73**	**5**	**8**	**13**	**48**	**0**	**1**	**2**	**70**	**7.1**	**–5**	**335**	**42.1**	**10:41**	**9**	**1**	**1**	**2**	**31**	**0**	**0**	**0**	**13:27**
2006-07	**St. Louis**	**NHL**	**41**	**5**	**5**	**10**	**23**	**0**	**0**	**1**	**37**	**13.5**	**–8**	**173**	**49.1**	**13:04**	....	....	....	....	....	....	....	....	....
	NHL Totals		**394**	**32**	**43**	**75**	**277**	**1**	**4**	**10**	**383**	**8.4**		**1782**	**48.1**	**11:14**	**69**	**6**	**9**	**15**	**63**	**0**	**1**	**0**	**11:02**

Signed as a free agent by **MODO** (Sweden), December 22, 2004. Signed as a free agent by **St. Louis**, July 3, 2006.

HLAVAC, Jan

(huh-LAH-vahch, YAHN) **T.B.**

Left wing. Shoots left. 6', 185 lbs. Born, Prague, Czech., September 20, 1976. NY Islanders' 2nd choice, 28th overall, in 1995 Entry Draft.

Season	Club	League	GP	G	A	Pts	PIM	PP	SH	GW	S	%	+/-	TF	F%	Min	GP	G	A	Pts	PIM	PP	SH	GW	Min
1993-94	Sparta Jr.	CzRep-Jr.	27	12	15	27	....	....	....	....	....	....	....	....	....	....	....	....	....	....	....	....	....	....	....
	HC Sparta Praha	CzRep	9	1	1	2	....	....	....	....	....	....	....	....	....	....	....	....	....	....	....	....	....	....	....
1994-95	HC Sparta Praha	CzRep	38	7	6	13	18	....	....	....	....	....	....	....	....	....	5	0	2	2	0	....	....	....	....
1995-96	HC Sparta Praha	CzRep	34	8	5	13	....	....	....	....	....	....	....	....	....	....	12	1	2	3	....	....	....	....	....
1996-97	HC Sparta Praha	CzRep	38	8	13	21	24	....	....	....	....	....	....	....	....	....	10	5	2	7	2	....	....	....	....
	HC Sparta Praha	EuroHL	3	4	0	4	6	....	....	....	....	....	....	....	....	....	....	....	....	....	....	....	....	....	....
1997-98	HC Sparta Praha	CzRep	48	17	30	47	40	....	....	....	....	....	....	....	....	....	5	1	0	1	2	....	....	....	....
	HC Sparta Praha	EuroHL	5	0	3	3	4	....	....	....	....	....	....	....	....	....	....	....	....	....	....	....	....	....	....
1998-99	HC Sparta Praha	CzRep	49	*33	20	53	52	....	....	....	....	....	....	....	....	....	6	1	3	4	....	....	....	....	....
	HC Sparta Praha	EuroHL	5	4	2	6	0	....	....	....	....	....	....	....	....	....	1	1	1	2	0	....	....	....	....
99-2000	**NY Rangers**	**NHL**	**67**	**19**	**23**	**42**	**16**	**6**	**0**	**2**	**134**	**14.2**	**3**	**6**	**33.3**	**15:09**	....	....	....	....	....	....	....	....	....
	Hartford	AHL	3	1	0	1	0	....	....	....	....	....	....	....	....	....	....	....	....	....	....	....	....	....	....
2000-01	**NY Rangers**	**NHL**	**79**	**28**	**36**	**64**	**20**	**5**	**0**	**6**	**195**	**14.4**	**3**	**0**	**0.0**	**16:38**	....	....	....	....	....	....	....	....	....

			Regular Season														Playoffs								
Season	Club	League	GP	G	A	Pts	PIM	PP	SH	GW	S	%	+/-	TF	F%	Min	GP	G	A	Pts	PIM	PP	SH	GW	Min
2001-02	**Philadelphia**	**NHL**	**31**	**7**	**3**	**10**	**8**	**0**	**0**	**1**	**62**	**11.3**	**5**	**0**	**0.0**	**12:36**	....	....	....	....	....	....	....	....	....
	Vancouver	**NHL**	**46**	**9**	**12**	**21**	**10**	**1**	**0**	**2**	**70**	**12.9**	**4**	**2**	**100.0**	**14:46**	**5**	**0**	**1**	**1**	**0**	**0**	**0**	**0**	**9:38**
2002-03	**Vancouver**	**NHL**	**9**	**1**	**1**	**2**	**6**	**0**	**0**	**0**	**7**	**14.3**	**–1**	**0**	**0.0**	**10:51**	....	....	....	....	....	....	....	....	....
	Carolina	**NHL**	**52**	**9**	**15**	**24**	**22**	**6**	**0**	**1**	**116**	**7.8**	**–9**	**21**	**38.1**	**17:10**	....	....	....	....	....	....	....	....	....
2003-04	**NY Rangers**	**NHL**	**72**	**5**	**21**	**26**	**16**	**2**	**0**	**0**	**125**	**4.0**	**–8**	**7**	**42.9**	**13:52**	....	....	....	....	....	....	....	....	....
2004-05	HC Sparta Praha	CzRep	48	10	28	38	34	....	....	....	....	....	....	....	....	....	5	2	0	2	6	....	....	....	....
2005-06	Geneve	Swiss	42	12	22	34	28	....	....	....	....	....	....	....	....	....	4	1	0	1	2	....	....	....	....
2006-07	HC Sparta Praha	CzRep	41	20	11	31	85	....	....	....	....	....	....	....	....	....	16	8	2	10	16	....	....	....	....
	NHL Totals		**356**	**78**	**111**	**189**	**98**	**20**	**0**	**12**	**709**	**11.0**		**36**	**41.7**	**15:08**	**5**	**0**	**1**	**1**	**0**	**0**	**0**	**0**	**9:38**

Traded to **Calgary** by **NY Islanders** for Jorgen Jonsson, July 14, 1998. Rights traded to **NY Rangers** by **Calgary** with Calgary's 1st (Jamie Lundmark) and 3rd (later traded back to Calgary – Calgary selected Craig Andersson) round choices in 1999 Entry Draft for Marc Savard and NY Rangers' 1st round choice (Oleg Saprykin) in 1999 Entry Draft, June 26, 1999. Traded to **Philadelphia** by **NY Rangers** with Kim Johnsson, Pavel Brendl and NY Rangers' 3rd round choice (Stefan Ruzicka) in 2003 Entry Draft for Eric Lindros, August 20, 2001. Traded to **Vancouver** by **Philadelphia** with Tampa Bay's 3rd round choice (previously acquired, Vancouver selected Brett Skinner) in 2002 Entry Draft for Donald Brashear and Vancouver's 6th round choice (later traded to Columbus – Columbus selected Jaroslav Balastik) in 2002 Entry Draft, December 17, 2001. Traded to **Carolina** by **Vancouver** with Harold Druken for Darren Langdon and Marek Malik, November 1, 2002. Signed as a free agent by **NY Rangers**, August 28, 2003. Signed as a free agent by **Sparta Praha** (CzRep), August 9, 2004. Signed as a free agent by **Geneve** (Swiss), September, 2005. Signed as a free agent by **Sparta Praha** (CzRep), May 24, 2006. Signed as a free agent by **Tampa Bay**, June 14, 2007.

HNIDY, Shane

(NIGH-dee, SHAYN) **ANA.**

Defense. Shoots right. 6'2", 210 lbs. Born, Neepawa, Man., November 8, 1975. Buffalo's 7th choice, 173rd overall, in 1994 Entry Draft.

Season	Club	League	GP	G	A	Pts	PIM	PP	SH	GW	S	%	+/-	TF	F%	Min	GP	G	A	Pts	PIM	PP	SH	GW	Min
1990-91	Yellowhead	MMMHL	36	9	11	20	92	....	....	....	....	....	....	....	....	....	....	....	....	....	....	....	....	....	....
1991-92	Swift Current	WHL	56	1	3	4	11	....	....	....	....	....	....	....	....	....	4	0	0	0	0	....	....	....	....
1992-93	Swift Current	WHL	45	5	12	17	62	....	....	....	....	....	....	....	....	....	....	....	....	....	....	....	....	....	....
	Prince Albert	WHL	27	2	10	12	43	....	....	....	....	....	....	....	....	....	....	....	....	....	....	....	....	....	....
1993-94	Prince Albert	WHL	69	7	26	33	113	....	....	....	....	....	....	....	....	....	....	....	....	....	....	....	....	....	....
1994-95	Prince Albert	WHL	72	5	29	34	169	....	....	....	....	....	....	....	....	....	15	4	7	11	29	....	....	....	....
1995-96	Prince Albert	WHL	58	11	42	53	100	....	....	....	....	....	....	....	....	....	18	4	11	15	34	....	....	....	....
1996-97	Baton Rouge	ECHL	21	3	10	13	50	....	....	....	....	....	....	....	....	....	....	....	....	....	....	....	....	....	....
	Saint John Flames	AHL	44	2	12	14	112	....	....	....	....	....	....	....	....	....	....	....	....	....	....	....	....	....	....
1997-98	Grand Rapids	IHL	77	6	12	18	210	....	....	....	....	....	....	....	....	....	3	0	2	2	23	....	....	....	....
1998-99	Adirondack	AHL	68	9	20	29	121	....	....	....	....	....	....	....	....	....	3	0	1	1	0	....	....	....	....
99-2000	Cincinnati	AHL	68	9	19	28	153	....	....	....	....	....	....	....	....	....	....	....	....	....	....	....	....	....	....
2000-01	**Ottawa**	**NHL**	**52**	**3**	**2**	**5**	**84**	**0**	**0**	**1**	**47**	**6.4**	**8**	**0**	**0.0**	**13:05**	**1**	**0**	**0**	**0**	**0**	**0**	**0**	**0**	**13:23**
	Grand Rapids	IHL	2	0	0	0	2	....	....	....	....	....	....	....	....	....	....	....	....	....	....	....	....	....	....
2001-02	**Ottawa**	**NHL**	**33**	**1**	**1**	**2**	**57**	**0**	**0**	**0**	**34**	**2.9**	**–10**	**0**	**0.0**	**16:56**	**12**	**1**	**1**	**2**	**12**	**0**	**0**	**0**	**16:00**
2002-03	**Ottawa**	**NHL**	**67**	**0**	**8**	**8**	**130**	**0**	**0**	**0**	**58**	**0.0**	**–1**	**1**	**0.0**	**13:55**	**1**	**0**	**0**	**0**	**0**	**0**	**0**	**0**	**9:38**
2003-04	**Ottawa**	**NHL**	**37**	**0**	**5**	**5**	**72**	**0**	**0**	**0**	**16**	**0.0**	**2**	**0**	**0.0**	**11:19**	....	....	....	....	....	....	....	....	....
	Nashville	**NHL**	**9**	**0**	**2**	**2**	**10**	**0**	**0**	**0**	**12**	**0.0**	**3**	**0**	**0.0**	**18:11**	**5**	**0**	**0**	**0**	**6**	**0**	**0**	**0**	**12:31**
2004-05	Florida Everblades	ECHL	19	1	4	5	56	....	....	....	....	....	....	....	....	....	17	0	4	4	6	....	....	....	....
2005-06	**Atlanta**	**NHL**	**66**	**0**	**3**	**3**	**33**	**0**	**0**	**0**	**50**	**0.0**	**1**	**0**	**0.0**	**10:14**	....	....	....	....	....	....	....	....	....
2006-07	**Atlanta**	**NHL**	**72**	**5**	**7**	**12**	**63**	**0**	**1**	**1**	**86**	**5.8**	**15**	**0**	**0.0**	**15:38**	**4**	**1**	**0**	**1**	**0**	**0**	**0**	**0**	**15:48**
	NHL Totals		**336**	**9**	**28**	**37**	**449**	**0**	**1**	**2**	**303**	**3.0**		**1**	**0.0**	**13:33**	**23**	**2**	**1**	**3**	**18**	**0**	**0**	**0**	**14:49**

Signed as a free agent by **Detroit**, August 6, 1998. Traded to **Ottawa** by **Detroit** for Ottawa's 8th round choice (Todd Jackson) in 2000 Entry Draft, June 25, 2000. • Missed majority of 2001-02 season recovering from ankle injury suffered in game vs. Boston, December 26, 2001. Traded to **Nashville** by **Ottawa** for Colorado's 3rd round choice (previously acquired, Ottawa selected Peter Regin) in 2004 Entry Draft, March 9, 2004. Signed as a free agent by **Florida** (ECHL), December 6, 2004. Traded to **Atlanta** by **Nashville** for Atlanta's 4th round choice (Niko Snellman) in 2006 Entry Draft, July 30, 2005. Signed as a free agent by **Anaheim**, July 5, 2007.

HOGGAN, Jeff

(HOH-guhn, JEHF) **BOS.**

Right wing. Shoots left. 6'1", 188 lbs. Born, Hope, B.C., February 1, 1978.

Season	Club	League	GP	G	A	Pts	PIM	PP	SH	GW	S	%	+/-	TF	F%	Min	GP	G	A	Pts	PIM	PP	SH	GW	Min
1998-99	Powell River Kings	BCHL	STATISTICS NOT AVAILABLE																						
99-2000	Nebraska-Omaha	CCHA	34	16	9	25	82	....	....	....	....	....	....	....	....	....	....	....	....	....	....	....	....	....	....
2000-01	Nebraska-Omaha	CCHA	42	12	17	29	78	....	....	....	....	....	....	....	....	....	....	....	....	....	....	....	....	....	....
2001-02	Nebraska-Omaha	CCHA	41	24	21	45	92	....	....	....	....	....	....	....	....	....	....	....	....	....	....	....	....	....	....
	Houston Aeros	AHL	....	....	....	....	....	....	....	....	....	....	....	....	....	....	4	0	0	0	2	....	....	....	....
2002-03	Houston Aeros	AHL	65	6	5	11	45	....	....	....	....	....	....	....	....	....	14	1	2	3	23	....	....	....	....
2003-04	Houston Aeros	AHL	77	21	15	36	88	....	....	....	....	....	....	....	....	....	2	0	1	1	4	....	....	....	....
2004-05	Worcester IceCats	AHL	47	16	9	25	55	....	....	....	....	....	....	....	....	....	....	....	....	....	....	....	....	....	....
2005-06	**St. Louis**	**NHL**	**52**	**2**	**6**	**8**	**34**	**0**	**0**	**0**	**60**	**3.3**	**–16**	**4**	**25.0**	**8:47**	....	....	....	....	....	....	....	....	....
2006-07	**Boston**	**NHL**	**46**	**0**	**2**	**2**	**33**	**0**	**0**	**0**	**53**	**0.0**	**–8**	**3**	**33.3**	**7:04**	....	....	....	....	....	....	....	....	....
	Providence Bruins	AHL	22	4	7	11	27	....	....	....	....	....	....	....	....	....	13	4	3	7	17	....	....	....	....
	NHL Totals		**98**	**2**	**8**	**10**	**67**	**0**	**0**	**0**	**113**	**1.8**		**7**	**28.6**	**7:59**	....	....	....	....	....	....	....	....	....

CCHA First All-Star Team (2002) • NCAA West Second All-American Team (2002)

Signed to a PTO (tryout) contract by **Houston** (AHL), April 4, 2002. Signed as a free agent by **Minnesota**, August 20, 2002. Signed as a free agent by **Worcester** (AHL), September, 2004. Signed as a free agent by **St. Louis**, August 2, 2005. Signed as a free agent by **Boston**, July 21, 2006.

HOLIK, Bobby

(HOH-leek, BAW-bee) **ATL.**

Center. Shoots right. 6'4", 230 lbs. Born, Jihlava, Czech., January 1, 1971. Hartford's 1st choice, 10th overall, in 1989 Entry Draft.

Season	Club	League	GP	G	A	Pts	PIM	PP	SH	GW	S	%	+/-	TF	F%	Min	GP	G	A	Pts	PIM	PP	SH	GW	Min
1987-88	Dukla Jihlava	Czech	31	5	9	14	16	....	....	....	....	....	....	....	....	....	....	....	....	....	....	....	....	....	....
1988-89	Dukla Jihlava	Czech	24	7	10	17	32	....	....	....	....	....	....	....	....	....	....	....	....	....	....	....	....	....	....
1989-90	Dukla Jihlava	Czech	42	15	26	41	....	....	....	....	....	....	....	....	....	....	....	....	....	....	....	....	....	....	....
1990-91	**Hartford**	**NHL**	**78**	**21**	**22**	**43**	**113**	**8**	**0**	**3**	**173**	**12.1**	**–3**	....	....	....	**6**	**0**	**0**	**0**	**7**	**0**	**0**	**0**	....
1991-92	**Hartford**	**NHL**	**76**	**21**	**24**	**45**	**44**	**1**	**0**	**2**	**207**	**10.1**	**4**	....	....	....	**7**	**0**	**1**	**1**	**6**	**0**	**0**	**0**	....
1992-93	**New Jersey**	**NHL**	**61**	**20**	**19**	**39**	**76**	**7**	**0**	**4**	**180**	**11.1**	**–6**	....	....	....	**5**	**1**	**1**	**2**	**6**	**0**	**0**	**0**	....
	Utica Devils	AHL	1	0	0	0	2	....	....	....	....	....	....	....	....	....	....	....	....	....	....	....	....	....	....
1993-94	**New Jersey**	**NHL**	**70**	**13**	**20**	**33**	**72**	**2**	**0**	**3**	**130**	**10.0**	**28**	....	....	....	**20**	**0**	**3**	**3**	**6**	**0**	**0**	**0**	....
1994-95 ♦	**New Jersey**	**NHL**	**48**	**10**	**10**	**20**	**18**	**0**	**0**	**2**	**84**	**11.9**	**9**	....	....	....	**20**	**4**	**4**	**8**	**22**	**2**	**0**	**1**	....
1995-96	**New Jersey**	**NHL**	**63**	**13**	**17**	**30**	**58**	**1**	**0**	**1**	**157**	**8.3**	**9**	....	....	....	....	....	....	....	....	....	....	....	....
1996-97	**New Jersey**	**NHL**	**82**	**23**	**39**	**62**	**54**	**5**	**0**	**6**	**192**	**12.0**	**24**	....	....	....	**10**	**2**	**3**	**5**	**4**	**1**	**0**	**0**	....
1997-98	**New Jersey**	**NHL**	**82**	**29**	**36**	**65**	**100**	**8**	**0**	**8**	**238**	**12.2**	**23**	....	....	....	**5**	**0**	**0**	**0**	**8**	**0**	**0**	**0**	....
1998-99	**New Jersey**	**NHL**	**78**	**27**	**37**	**64**	**119**	**5**	**0**	**8**	**253**	**10.7**	**16**	**1350**	**53.6**	**17:34**	**7**	**0**	**7**	**7**	**6**	**0**	**0**	**0**	**18:14**
99-2000 ♦	**New Jersey**	**NHL**	**79**	**23**	**23**	**46**	**106**	**7**	**0**	**4**	**257**	**8.9**	**7**	**1390**	**55.6**	**16:53**	**23**	**3**	**7**	**10**	**14**	**0**	**0**	**1**	**17:29**
2000-01	**New Jersey**	**NHL**	**80**	**15**	**35**	**50**	**97**	**3**	**0**	**3**	**206**	**7.3**	**19**	**1365**	**56.0**	**15:49**	**25**	**6**	**10**	**16**	**37**	**1**	**0**	**3**	**16:05**
2001-02	**New Jersey**	**NHL**	**81**	**25**	**29**	**54**	**97**	**6**	**0**	**3**	**270**	**9.3**	**7**	**1594**	**54.5**	**17:42**	**6**	**4**	**1**	**5**	**2**	**1**	**0**	**0**	**17:53**
2002-03	**NY Rangers**	**NHL**	**64**	**16**	**19**	**35**	**52**	**3**	**0**	**2**	**213**	**7.5**	**–1**	**1390**	**58.2**	**18:07**	....	....	....	....	....	....	....	....	....
2003-04	**NY Rangers**	**NHL**	**82**	**25**	**31**	**56**	**96**	**8**	**0**	**4**	**225**	**11.1**	**4**	**1664**	**54.2**	**18:34**	....	....	....	....	....	....	....	....	....
2004-05			DID NOT PLAY																						
2005-06	**Atlanta**	**NHL**	**64**	**15**	**18**	**33**	**79**	**5**	**0**	**0**	**151**	**9.9**	**–6**	**1385**	**55.7**	**17:31**	....	....	....	....	....	....	....	....	....
2006-07	**Atlanta**	**NHL**	**82**	**11**	**18**	**29**	**86**	**2**	**1**	**1**	**190**	**5.8**	**–3**	**1427**	**57.5**	**15:56**	**4**	**0**	**1**	**1**	**0**	**0**	**0**	**0**	**15:24**
	NHL Totals		**1170**	**307**	**397**	**704**	**1267**	**71**	**1**	**54**	**3126**	**9.8**		**11565**	**55.6**	**17:14**	**138**	**20**	**38**	**58**	**118**	**5**	**0**	**5**	**16:56**

Played in NHL All-Star Game (1998, 1999)

Traded to **New Jersey** by **Hartford** with Hartford's 2nd round choice (Jay Pandolfo) in 1993 Entry Draft for Sean Burke and Eric Weinrich, August 28, 1992. Signed as a free agent by **NY Rangers**, July 1, 2002. Signed as a free agent by **Atlanta**, August 2, 2005.

HOLLWEG, Ryan

(HOHL-wehg, RIGH-uhn) **NYR**

Center. Shoots left. 5'11", 210 lbs. Born, Downey, CA, April 23, 1983. NY Rangers' 10th choice, 238th overall, in 2001 Entry Draft.

Season	Club	League	GP	G	A	Pts	PIM	PP	SH	GW	S	%	+/-	TF	F%	Min	GP	G	A	Pts	PIM	PP	SH	GW	Min
1998-99	Grandview	PIJHL	41	23	27	50	135	....	....	....	....	....	....	....	....	....	....	....	....	....	....	....	....	....	....
	Langley Hornets	BCHL	58	14	40	54	187	....	....	....	....	....	....	....	....	....	....	....	....	....	....	....	....	....	....
99-2000	Medicine Hat	WHL	54	19	27	46	107	....	....	....	....	....	....	....	....	....	....	....	....	....	....	....	....	....	....
2000-01	Medicine Hat	WHL	65	19	39	58	125	....	....	....	....	....	....	....	....	....	....	....	....	....	....	....	....	....	....
2001-02	Medicine Hat	WHL	58	30	40	70	121	....	....	....	....	....	....	....	....	....	....	....	....	....	....	....	....	....	....
	Hartford	AHL	8	1	1	2	2	....	....	....	....	....	....	....	....	....	9	0	2	2	19	....	....	....	....
2002-03	Medicine Hat	WHL	4	1	1	2	8	....	....	....	....	....	....	....	....	....	....	....	....	....	....	....	....	....	....
2003-04	Medicine Hat	WHL	52	25	32	57	117	....	....	....	....	....	....	....	....	....	20	6	9	15	22	....	....	....	....
2004-05	Hartford	AHL	73	8	6	14	239	....	....	....	....	....	....	....	....	....	6	1	0	1	9	....	....	....	....

			Regular Season														Playoffs								
Season	Club	League	GP	G	A	Pts	PIM	PP	SH	GW	S	%	+/-	TF	F%	Min	GP	G	A	Pts	PIM	PP	SH	GW	Min
2005-06	**NY Rangers**	**NHL**	**52**	**2**	**3**	**5**	**84**	**0**	**0**	**0**	**32**	**6.3**	**-3**	**19**	**57.9**	**7:15**	**4**	**0**	**1**	**1**	**19**	**0**	**0**	**0**	**10:26**
	Hartford	AHL	7	2	1	3	11	....	....	....	....	....	....	....	....	....	....	....	....	....	....	....	....	....	....
2006-07	**NY Rangers**	**NHL**	**78**	**1**	**2**	**3**	**131**	**0**	**0**	**0**	**63**	**1.6**	**-11**	**86**	**39.5**	**8:14**	**2**	**0**	**0**	**0**	**2**	**0**	**0**	**0**	**5:19**
	NHL Totals		**130**	**3**	**5**	**8**	**215**	**0**	**0**	**0**	**95**	**3.2**		**105**	**42.9**	**7:50**	**6**	**0**	**1**	**1**	**21**	**0**	**0**	**0**	**8:44**

• Missed majority of 2002-03 season recovering from head injury suffered in game vs. Vancouver (WHL), October 8, 2002.

HOLMQVIST, Michael

(HOHLM-kvihst, MIGH-kuhl)

Center. Shoots left. 6'3", 205 lbs. Born, Stockholm, Sweden, June 8, 1979. Anaheim's 1st choice, 18th overall, in 1997 Entry Draft.

Season	Club	League	GP	G	A	Pts	PIM	PP	SH	GW	S	%	+/-	TF	F%	Min	GP	G	A	Pts	PIM	PP	SH	GW	Min
1995-96	Djurgarden Jr.	Swe-Jr.	24	7	2	9	4	....	....	....	....	....	....	....	....	....	....	....	....	....	....	....	....	....	....
1996-97	Djurgarden Jr.	Swe-Jr.	39	29	35	64	110	....	....	....	....	....	....	....	....	....	....	....	....	....	....	....	....	....	....
	Djurgarden	Sweden	9	0	0	0	0	....	....	....	....	....	....	....	....	....	....	....	....	....	....	....	....	....	....
1997-98	Farjestad	Sweden	41	2	3	5	6	....	....	....	....	....	....	....	....	....	7	0	0	0	0	....	....	....	....
	Farjestad	EuroHL	5	2	2	4	2	....	....	....	....	....	....	....	....	....	....	....	....	....	....	....	....	....	....
1998-99	Farjestad Jr.	Swe-Jr.	2	2	2	4	2	....	....	....	....	....	....	....	....	....	....	....	....	....	....	....	....	....	....
	Farjestad	EuroHL	3	0	0	0	0	....	....	....	....	....	....	....	....	....	....	....	....	....	....	....	....	....	....
	Farjestad	Sweden	15	0	0	0	6	....	....	....	....	....	....	....	....	....	1	0	0	0	0	....	....	....	....
	Hammarby	Sweden-2	3	2	0	2	0	....	....	....	....	....	....	....	....	....	....	....	....	....	....	....	....	....	....
99-2000	TPS Turku	Finland	54	12	3	15	14	....	....	....	....	....	....	....	....	....	11	2	3	5	4	....	....	....	....
2000-01	TPS Turku	Finland	46	4	5	9	8	....	....	....	....	....	....	....	....	....	10	1	3	4	2	....	....	....	....
2001-02	TPS Turku	Finland	56	9	13	22	16	....	....	....	....	....	....	....	....	....	8	1	0	1	12	....	....	....	....
2002-03	TPS Turku	Finland	56	15	25	40	36	....	....	....	....	....	....	....	....	....	7	0	0	0	4	....	....	....	....
2003-04	**Anaheim**	**NHL**	**21**	**2**	**0**	**2**	**25**	**0**	**0**	**0**	**18**	**11.1**	**-6**	**16**	**31.3**	**8:24**	....	....	....	....	....	....	....	....	....
	Cincinnati	AHL	24	7	7	14	20	....	....	....	....	....	....	....	....	....	....	....	....	....	....	....	....	....	....
2004-05	Cincinnati	AHL	79	14	32	46	111	....	....	....	....	....	....	....	....	....	11	2	2	4	10	....	....	....	....
2005-06	**Chicago**	**NHL**	**72**	**10**	**10**	**20**	**16**	**2**	**0**	**1**	**106**	**9.4**	**-14**	**85**	**36.5**	**13:32**	....	....	....	....	....	....	....	....	....
2006-07	**Chicago**	**NHL**	**63**	**6**	**7**	**13**	**31**	**1**	**0**	**0**	**80**	**7.5**	**-5**	**161**	**44.7**	**13:47**	....	....	....	....	....	....	....	....	....
	NHL Totals		**156**	**18**	**17**	**35**	**72**	**3**	**0**	**1**	**204**	**8.8**		**262**	**41.2**	**12:57**	....	....	....	....	....	....	....	....	....

Traded to **Chicago** by **Anaheim** for Travis Moen, July 30, 2005.

HOLMSTROM, Tomas

(HOHLM-struhm, TAW-mas) **DET.**

Left wing. Shoots left. 6', 202 lbs. Born, Pitea, Sweden, January 23, 1973. Detroit's 9th choice, 257th overall, in 1994 Entry Draft.

Season	Club	League	GP	G	A	Pts	PIM	PP	SH	GW	S	%	+/-	TF	F%	Min	GP	G	A	Pts	PIM	PP	SH	GW	Min
1989-90	Pitea HC	Sweden-2	9	1	0	1	4	....	....	....	....	....	....	....	....	....	....	....	....	....	....	....	....	....	....
1990-91	Pitea HC	Sweden-2	26	5	4	9	16	....	....	....	....	....	....	....	....	....	....	....	....	....	....	....	....	....	....
1991-92	Pitea HC	Sweden-2	31	15	12	27	44	....	....	....	....	....	....	....	....	....	....	....	....	....	....	....	....	....	....
1992-93	Pitea HC	Sweden-2	32	17	15	32	30	....	....	....	....	....	....	....	....	....	....	....	....	....	....	....	....	....	....
1993-94	Bodens IK	Sweden-2	34	23	16	39	86	....	....	....	....	....	....	....	....	....	9	3	3	6	24	....	....	....	....
1994-95	Lulea HF	Sweden	40	14	14	28	56	....	....	....	....	....	....	....	....	....	8	1	2	3	20	....	....	....	....
1995-96	Lulea HF	Sweden	34	12	11	23	78	....	....	....	....	....	....	....	....	....	11	6	2	8	22	....	....	....	....
1996-97♦	**Detroit**	**NHL**	**47**	**6**	**3**	**9**	**33**	**3**	**0**	**0**	**53**	**11.3**	**-10**	....	....	....	**1**	**0**	**0**	**0**	**0**	**0**	**0**	**0**	....
	Adirondack	AHL	6	3	1	4	7	....	....	....	....	....	....	....	....	....	....	....	....	....	....	....	....	....	....
1997-98♦	**Detroit**	**NHL**	**57**	**5**	**17**	**22**	**44**	**1**	**0**	**1**	**48**	**10.4**	**6**	....	....	....	**22**	**7**	**12**	**19**	**16**	**2**	**0**	**0**	....
1998-99	**Detroit**	**NHL**	**82**	**13**	**21**	**34**	**69**	**5**	**0**	**4**	**100**	**13.0**	**-11**	**0**	**0.0**	**12:22**	**10**	**4**	**3**	**7**	**4**	**2**	**0**	**1**	**12:32**
99-2000	**Detroit**	**NHL**	**72**	**13**	**22**	**35**	**43**	**4**	**0**	**1**	**71**	**18.3**	**4**	**0**	**0.0**	**12:06**	**9**	**3**	**1**	**4**	**16**	**1**	**0**	**1**	**11:42**
2000-01	**Detroit**	**NHL**	**73**	**16**	**24**	**40**	**40**	**9**	**0**	**2**	**74**	**21.6**	**-12**	**2**	**50.0**	**11:41**	**6**	**1**	**3**	**4**	**8**	**1**	**0**	**0**	**14:23**
2001-02♦	**Detroit**	**NHL**	**69**	**8**	**18**	**26**	**58**	**6**	**0**	**1**	**79**	**10.1**	**-12**	**2**	**0.0**	**12:23**	**23**	**8**	**3**	**11**	**8**	**3**	**0**	**2**	**11:31**
	Sweden	Olympics	4	1	0	1	0	....	....	....	....	....	....	....	....	....	....	....	....	....	....	....	....	....	....
2002-03	**Detroit**	**NHL**	**74**	**20**	**20**	**40**	**62**	**12**	**0**	**2**	**109**	**18.3**	**11**	**2**	**0.0**	**12:28**	**4**	**1**	**1**	**2**	**4**	**1**	**0**	**0**	**14:37**
2003-04	**Detroit**	**NHL**	**67**	**15**	**15**	**30**	**38**	**6**	**0**	**0**	**74**	**20.3**	**8**	**3**	**0.0**	**12:23**	**12**	**2**	**2**	**4**	**10**	**1**	**0**	**1**	**11:27**
2004-05	Lulea HF	Sweden	47	14	16	30	50	....	....	....	....	....	....	....	....	....	4	0	0	0	18	....	....	....	....
2005-06	**Detroit**	**NHL**	**81**	**29**	**30**	**59**	**66**	**11**	**0**	**8**	**140**	**20.7**	**14**	**0**	**0.0**	**13:59**	**6**	**1**	**2**	**3**	**12**	**1**	**0**	**0**	**17:04**
	Sweden	Olympics	8	1	3	4	10	....	....	....	....	....	....	....	....	....	....	....	....	....	....	....	....	....	....
2006-07	**Detroit**	**NHL**	**77**	**30**	**22**	**52**	**58**	**13**	**0**	**5**	**176**	**17.0**	**13**	**0**	**0.0**	**15:13**	**15**	**5**	**3**	**8**	**14**	**4**	**0**	**1**	**16:15**
	NHL Totals		**699**	**155**	**192**	**347**	**511**	**70**	**0**	**24**	**924**	**16.8**		**9**	**11.1**	**12:51**	**108**	**32**	**30**	**62**	**92**	**16**	**0**	**6**	**13:13**

Signed as a free agent by **Lulea** (Sweden), September 16, 2004.

HORCOFF, Shawn

(hohr-KAWF, SHAWN) **EDM.**

Center. Shoots left. 6'1", 204 lbs. Born, Trail, B.C., September 17, 1978. Edmonton's 3rd choice, 99th overall, in 1998 Entry Draft.

Season	Club	League	GP	G	A	Pts	PIM	PP	SH	GW	S	%	+/-	TF	F%	Min	GP	G	A	Pts	PIM	PP	SH	GW	Min
1994-95	Trail Smokies	RMJHL	47	50	46	96	26	....	....	....	....	....	....	....	....	....	....	....	....	....	....	....	....	....	....
1995-96	Chilliwack Chiefs	BCHL	58	49	96	*145	44	....	....	....	....	....	....	....	....	....	9	5	19	24	12	....	....	....	....
1996-97	Michigan State	CCHA	40	10	13	23	20	....	....	....	....	....	....	....	....	....	....	....	....	....	....	....	....	....	....
1997-98	Michigan State	CCHA	34	14	13	27	50	....	....	....	....	....	....	....	....	....	....	....	....	....	....	....	....	....	....
1998-99	Michigan State	CCHA	39	12	25	37	70	....	....	....	....	....	....	....	....	....	....	....	....	....	....	....	....	....	....
99-2000	Michigan State	CCHA	42	14	*51	*65	50	....	....	....	....	....	....	....	....	....	....	....	....	....	....	....	....	....	....
2000-01	**Edmonton**	**NHL**	**49**	**9**	**7**	**16**	**10**	**0**	**0**	**2**	**42**	**21.4**	**8**	**122**	**41.8**	**9:14**	**5**	**0**	**0**	**0**	**0**	**0**	**0**	**0**	**6:31**
	Hamilton	AHL	24	10	18	28	19	....	....	....	....	....	....	....	....	....	....	....	....	....	....	....	....	....	....
2001-02	**Edmonton**	**NHL**	**61**	**8**	**14**	**22**	**18**	**0**	**0**	**0**	**57**	**14.0**	**3**	**454**	**46.3**	**11:20**	....	....	....	....	....	....	....	....	....
	Hamilton	AHL	2	1	2	3	6	....	....	....	....	....	....	....	....	....	....	....	....	....	....	....	....	....	....
2002-03	**Edmonton**	**NHL**	**78**	**12**	**21**	**33**	**55**	**2**	**0**	**3**	**98**	**12.2**	**10**	**301**	**42.9**	**13:30**	**6**	**3**	**1**	**4**	**6**	**0**	**0**	**1**	**15:27**
2003-04	**Edmonton**	**NHL**	**80**	**15**	**25**	**40**	**73**	**0**	**2**	**3**	**110**	**13.6**	**0**	**1378**	**50.7**	**17:31**	....	....	....	....	....	....	....	....	....
2004-05	Mora IK	Sweden	50	19	27	46	117	....	....	....	....	....	....	....	....	....	....	....	....	....	....	....	....	....	....
2005-06	**Edmonton**	**NHL**	**79**	**22**	**51**	**73**	**85**	**3**	**3**	**5**	**167**	**13.2**	**0**	**1421**	**52.7**	**19:59**	**24**	**7**	**12**	**19**	**12**	**1**	**1**	**2**	**21:37**
2006-07	**Edmonton**	**NHL**	**80**	**16**	**35**	**51**	**56**	**5**	**0**	**5**	**168**	**9.5**	**-22**	**1422**	**50.6**	**20:50**	....	....	....	....	....	....	....	....	....
	NHL Totals		**427**	**82**	**153**	**235**	**297**	**10**	**5**	**18**	**642**	**12.8**		**5098**	**50.2**	**16:01**	**35**	**10**	**13**	**23**	**18**	**1**	**1**	**3**	**18:24**

CCHA First All-Star Team (2000) • CCHA Player of the Year (2000) • NCAA West First All-American Team (2000)

Signed as a free agent by **Mora** (Sweden), September 6, 2004.

HORDICHUK, Darcy

(HOHR-dih-chuhk, DAHR-see) **NSH.**

Left wing. Shoots left. 6'1", 215 lbs. Born, Kamsack, Sask., August 10, 1980. Atlanta's 9th choice, 180th overall, in 2000 Entry Draft.

Season	Club	League	GP	G	A	Pts	PIM	PP	SH	GW	S	%	+/-	TF	F%	Min	GP	G	A	Pts	PIM	PP	SH	GW	Min
1996-97	Yorkton Mallers	SMHL	57	6	15	21	230	....	....	....	....	....	....	....	....	....	....	....	....	....	....	....	....	....	....
	Calgary Hitmen	WHL	3	0	0	0	2	....	....	....	....	....	....	....	....	....	....	....	....	....	....	....	....	....	....
1997-98	Dauphin Kings	MJHL	58	12	21	33	279	....	....	....	....	....	....	....	....	....	....	....	....	....	....	....	....	....	....
1998-99	Saskatoon Blades	WHL	66	3	2	5	246	....	....	....	....	....	....	....	....	....	....	....	....	....	....	....	....	....	....
99-2000	Saskatoon Blades	WHL	63	6	8	14	269	....	....	....	....	....	....	....	....	....	11	4	2	6	43	....	....	....	....
2000-01	**Atlanta**	**NHL**	**11**	**0**	**0**	**0**	**38**	**0**	**0**	**0**	**6**	**0.0**	**-3**	**0**	**0.0**	**7:18**	....	....	....	....	....	....	....	....	....
	Orlando	IHL	69	7	3	10	*369	....	....	....	....	....	....	....	....	....	16	3	3	6	*41	....	....	....	....
2001-02	**Atlanta**	**NHL**	**33**	**1**	**1**	**2**	**127**	**0**	**0**	**0**	**8**	**12.5**	**-5**	**4**	**25.0**	**6:03**	....	....	....	....	....	....	....	....	....
	Chicago Wolves	AHL	34	5	4	9	127	....	....	....	....	....	....	....	....	....	....	....	....	....	....	....	....	....	....
	Phoenix	**NHL**	**1**	**0**	**0**	**0**	**14**	**0**	**0**	**0**	**0**	**0.0**	**0**	**0**	**0.0**	**7:18**	....	....	....	....	....	....	....	....	....
2002-03	**Phoenix**	**NHL**	**25**	**0**	**0**	**0**	**82**	**0**	**0**	**0**	**5**	**0.0**	**-1**	**0**	**0.0**	**4:47**	....	....	....	....	....	....	....	....	....
	Springfield	AHL	22	1	3	4	38	....	....	....	....	....	....	....	....	....	....	....	....	....	....	....	....	....	....
	Florida	**NHL**	**3**	**0**	**0**	**0**	**15**	**0**	**0**	**0**	**2**	**0.0**	**-1**	**0**	**0.0**	**9:45**	....	....	....	....	....	....	....	....	....
2003-04	**Florida**	**NHL**	**57**	**3**	**1**	**4**	**158**	**0**	**0**	**1**	**27**	**11.1**	**-10**	**4**	**50.0**	**6:46**	....	....	....	....	....	....	....	....	....
2004-05			DID NOT PLAY																						
2005-06	**Nashville**	**NHL**	**74**	**7**	**6**	**13**	**163**	**0**	**0**	**1**	**52**	**13.5**	**9**	**1**	**0.0**	**6:09**	....	....	....	....	....	....	....	....	....
2006-07	**Nashville**	**NHL**	**53**	**1**	**3**	**4**	**90**	**0**	**0**	**0**	**22**	**4.5**	**-2**	**0**	**0.0**	**4:48**	**2**	**0**	**0**	**0**	**0**	**0**	**0**	**0**	**3:38**
	NHL Totals		**257**	**12**	**11**	**23**	**687**	**0**	**0**	**2**	**122**	**9.8**		**9**	**33.3**	**5:57**	**2**	**0**	**0**	**0**	**0**	**0**	**0**	**0**	**3:38**

Traded to **Phoenix** by **Atlanta** with Atlanta's 4th (Lance Monych) and 5th (John Zeiler) round choices in 2002 Entry Draft for Kiril Safronov, the rights to Ruslan Zainullin and Phoenix's 4th round choice (Patrick Dwyer) in 2002 Entry Draft, March 19, 2002. Traded to **Florida** by **Phoenix** with Phoenix's 2nd round choice (later traded to Tampa Bay – Tampa Bay selected Matt Smaby) in 2003 Entry Draft for Brad Ference, March 8, 2003. Traded to **Nashville** by **Florida** for Nashville's 4th round choice (Matt Duffy) in 2005 Entry Draft, July 27, 2005.

HORTON, Nathan
(HOHR-tuhn, NAY-thuhn) **FLA.**

Center. Shoots right. 6'2", 229 lbs. Born, Welland, Ont., May 29, 1985. Florida's 1st choice, 3rd overall, in 2003 Entry Draft.

			Regular Season														Playoffs								
Season	Club	League	GP	G	A	Pts	PIM	PP	SH	GW	S	%	+/-	TF	F%	Min	GP	G	A	Pts	PIM	PP	SH	GW	Min
2000-01	Thorold	OHA-B	41	16	31	47	75																		
2001-02	Oshawa Generals	OHL	64	31	36	67	84										5	1	2	3	10				
2002-03	Oshawa Generals	OHL	54	33	35	68	111										13	9	6	15	10				
2003-04	**Florida**	**NHL**	**55**	**14**	**8**	**22**	**57**	**6**	**1**	**0**	**81**	**17.3**	**–5**	**270**	**41.9**	**13:20**									
2004-05	San Antonio	AHL	21	5	4	9	21																		
2005-06	**Florida**	**NHL**	**71**	**28**	**19**	**47**	**89**	**3**	**0**	**1**	**162**	**17.3**	**8**	**24**	**45.8**	**16:53**									
2006-07	**Florida**	**NHL**	**82**	**31**	**31**	**62**	**61**	**7**	**1**	**3**	**217**	**14.3**	**15**	**31**	**48.4**	**18:04**									
	NHL Totals		**208**	**73**	**58**	**131**	**207**	**16**	**2**	**4**	**460**	**15.9**		**325**	**42.8**	**16:25**									

OHL All-Rookie Team (2002)

Signed as a free agent by **San Antonio** (AHL), October 28, 2004.

HOSSA, Marcel
(HOH-sa, MAHR-sehl) **NYR**

Left wing. Shoots left. 6'3", 220 lbs. Born, Ilava, Czech., October 12, 1981. Montreal's 2nd choice, 16th overall, in 2000 Entry Draft.

			Regular Season														Playoffs								
Season	Club	League	GP	G	A	Pts	PIM	PP	SH	GW	S	%	+/-	TF	F%	Min	GP	G	A	Pts	PIM	PP	SH	GW	Min
1996-97	Dukla Trencin Jr.	Slovak-Jr.	45	30	21	51	30																		
1997-98	Dukla Trencin Jr.	Slovak-Jr.	39	11	38	49	44																		
1998-99	Portland	WHL	70	7	14	21	66										2	0	0	0	2				
99-2000	Portland	WHL	60	24	29	53	58																		
2000-01	Portland	WHL	58	34	56	90	58										16	5	7	12	14				
2001-02	**Montreal**	**NHL**	**10**	**3**	**1**	**4**	**2**	**0**	**0**	**0**	**20**	**15.0**	**2**	**0**	**0.0**	**11:09**									
	Quebec Citadelles	AHL	50	17	15	32	24										3	0	0	0	4				
2002-03	Hamilton	AHL	37	19	13	32	18										21	4	7	11	12				
	Montreal	**NHL**	**34**	**6**	**7**	**13**	**14**	**2**	**0**	**1**	**51**	**11.8**	**3**	**4**	**50.0**	**13:58**									
2003-04	**Montreal**	**NHL**	**15**	**1**	**1**	**2**	**8**	**0**	**0**	**0**	**19**	**5.3**	**–3**	**5**	**40.0**	**14:50**									
	Hamilton	AHL	57	18	22	40	45										10	2	3	5	8				
2004-05	Mora IK	Sweden	48	18	6	24	69																		
2005-06	**NY Rangers**	**NHL**	**64**	**10**	**6**	**16**	**28**	**3**	**0**	**0**	**105**	**9.5**	**–6**	**7**	**28.6**	**10:45**	**4**	**0**	**0**	**0**	**6**	**0**	**0**	**0**	**13:18**
	Slovakia	Olympics	6	0	0	0	0																		
2006-07	**NY Rangers**	**NHL**	**64**	**10**	**8**	**18**	**26**	**3**	**0**	**2**	**83**	**12.0**	**–4**	**18**	**16.7**	**12:27**	**10**	**2**	**2**	**4**	**4**	**0**	**0**	**0**	**15:58**
	NHL Totals		**187**	**30**	**23**	**53**	**78**	**8**	**0**	**3**	**278**	**10.8**		**34**	**26.5**	**12:16**	**14**	**2**	**2**	**4**	**10**	**0**	**0**	**0**	**15:12**

WHL West Second All-Star Team (2001)

Signed as a free agent by **Mora** (Sweden), September 25, 2004. Traded to **NY Rangers** by **Montreal** for Garth Murray, September 30, 2005.

HOSSA, Marian
(HOH-sa, MAIR-ee-uhn) **ATL.**

Right wing. Shoots left. 6'1", 210 lbs. Born, Stara Lubovna, Czech., January 12, 1979. Ottawa's 1st choice, 12th overall, in 1997 Entry Draft.

			Regular Season														Playoffs								
Season	Club	League	GP	G	A	Pts	PIM	PP	SH	GW	S	%	+/-	TF	F%	Min	GP	G	A	Pts	PIM	PP	SH	GW	Min
1995-96	Dukla Trencin Jr.	Slovak-Jr.	53	42	49	91	26																		
1996-97	Dukla Trencin	Slovakia	46	25	19	44	33										7	5	5	10					
1997-98	Portland	WHL	53	45	40	85	50										16	13	6	19	6				
	Ottawa	**NHL**	**7**	**0**	**1**	**1**	**0**	**0**	**0**	**0**	**10**	**0.0**	**–1**												
1998-99	**Ottawa**	**NHL**	**60**	**15**	**15**	**30**	**37**	**1**	**0**	**2**	**124**	**12.1**	**18**	**4**	**25.0**	**13:59**	**4**	**0**	**2**	**2**	**4**	**0**	**0**	**0**	**16:46**
99-2000	**Ottawa**	**NHL**	**78**	**29**	**27**	**56**	**32**	**5**	**0**	**4**	**240**	**12.1**	**5**	**7**	**57.1**	**17:12**	**6**	**0**	**0**	**0**	**2**	**0**	**0**	**0**	**15:22**
2000-01	**Ottawa**	**NHL**	**81**	**32**	**43**	**75**	**44**	**11**	**2**	**7**	**249**	**12.9**	**19**	**14**	**42.9**	**18:01**	**4**	**1**	**1**	**2**	**4**	**0**	**0**	**0**	**19:02**
2001-02	Dukla Trencin	Slovakia	8	3	4	7	16																		
	Ottawa	**NHL**	**80**	**31**	**35**	**66**	**50**	**9**	**1**	**4**	**278**	**11.2**	**11**	**12**	**33.3**	**18:29**	**12**	**4**	**6**	**10**	**2**	**1**	**0**	**0**	**19:04**
	Slovakia	Olympics	2	4	2	6	0																		
2002-03	**Ottawa**	**NHL**	**80**	**45**	**35**	**80**	**34**	**14**	**0**	**10**	**229**	**19.7**	**8**	**19**	**36.8**	**18:31**	**18**	**5**	**11**	**16**	**6**	**3**	**0**	**1**	**18:41**
2003-04	**Ottawa**	**NHL**	**81**	**36**	**46**	**82**	**46**	**14**	**1**	**5**	**233**	**15.5**	**4**	**25**	**40.0**	**18:37**	**7**	**3**	**1**	**4**	**0**	**1**	**0**	**2**	**21:24**
2004-05	Mora IK	Sweden	24	18	14	32	22																		
	Dukla Trencin	Slovakia	25	22	20	42	38										5	4	5	9	14				
2005-06	**Atlanta**	**NHL**	**80**	**39**	**53**	**92**	**67**	**14**	**7**	**7**	**341**	**11.4**	**17**	**15**	**26.7**	**21:41**									
	Slovakia	Olympics	6	5	5	10	4																		
2006-07	**Atlanta**	**NHL**	**82**	**43**	**57**	**100**	**49**	**17**	**3**	**5**	**340**	**12.6**	**18**	**18**	**22.2**	**21:41**	**4**	**0**	**1**	**1**	**6**	**0**	**0**	**0**	**18:55**
	NHL Totals		**629**	**270**	**312**	**582**	**359**	**85**	**14**	**44**	**2044**	**13.2**		**114**	**35.1**	**18:41**	**55**	**13**	**22**	**35**	**24**	**5**	**0**	**3**	**18:39**

WHL West First All-Star Team (1998) • WHL Rookie of the Year (1998) • Canadian Major Junior First All-Star Team (1998) • Memorial Cup Tournament All-Star Team (1998) • NHL All-Rookie Team (1999)

Played in NHL All-Star Game (2001, 2003, 2007)

Signed as a free agent by **Trencin** (Slovakia), September 16, 2004. Signed as a free agent by **Mora** (Sweden), November 11, 2004. Signed as a free agent by **Trencin** (Slovakia), January 31, 2005. Traded to **Atlanta** by **Ottawa** with Greg de Vries for Dany Heatley, August 23, 2005.

HRDINA, Jan
(huhr-DEE-nah, YAHN)

Center. Shoots right. 6', 205 lbs. Born, Hradec Kralove, Czech., February 5, 1976. Pittsburgh's 4th choice, 128th overall, in 1995 Entry Draft.

			Regular Season														Playoffs								
Season	Club	League	GP	G	A	Pts	PIM	PP	SH	GW	S	%	+/-	TF	F%	Min	GP	G	A	Pts	PIM	PP	SH	GW	Min
1993-94	Hr. Kralove Jr.	CzRep-Jr.	10	1	6	7	0																		
	Hr. Kralove	CzRep	23	1	5	6											4	0	1	1					
1994-95	Seattle	WHL	69	41	59	100	79										4	0	1	1	8				
1995-96	Seattle	WHL	30	19	28	47	37																		
	Spokane Chiefs	WHL	18	10	16	26	25										18	5	14	19	49				
1996-97	Cleveland	IHL	68	23	31	54	82										13	1	2	3	8				
1997-98	Syracuse Crunch	AHL	72	20	24	44	82										5	1	3	4	10				
1998-99	**Pittsburgh**	**NHL**	**82**	**13**	**29**	**42**	**40**	**3**	**0**	**2**	**94**	**13.8**	**–2**	**1461**	**56.7**	**16:26**	**13**	**4**	**1**	**5**	**12**	**1**	**0**	**1**	**21:03**
99-2000	**Pittsburgh**	**NHL**	**70**	**13**	**33**	**46**	**43**	**3**	**0**	**1**	**84**	**15.5**	**13**	**1392**	**53.7**	**18:47**	**9**	**4**	**8**	**12**	**2**	**1**	**0**	**0**	**22:04**
2000-01	**Pittsburgh**	**NHL**	**78**	**15**	**28**	**43**	**48**	**3**	**0**	**1**	**89**	**16.9**	**19**	**1067**	**53.8**	**15:56**	**18**	**2**	**5**	**7**	**8**	**0**	**0**	**0**	**15:04**
2001-02	**Pittsburgh**	**NHL**	**79**	**24**	**33**	**57**	**50**	**6**	**0**	**6**	**115**	**20.9**	**–7**	**667**	**50.4**	**19:51**									
	Czech Republic	Olympics	4	0	0	0	0																		
2002-03	**Pittsburgh**	**NHL**	**57**	**14**	**25**	**39**	**34**	**11**	**0**	**4**	**84**	**16.7**	**1**	**984**	**56.0**	**19:45**									
	Phoenix	**NHL**	**4**	**0**	**4**	**4**	**8**	**0**	**0**	**0**	**2**	**0.0**	**3**	**70**	**60.0**	**18:12**									
2003-04	**Phoenix**	**NHL**	**55**	**11**	**15**	**26**	**30**	**5**	**0**	**1**	**62**	**17.7**	**–10**	**677**	**50.7**	**17:57**									
	New Jersey	**NHL**	**13**	**1**	**6**	**7**	**10**	**0**	**0**	**0**	**11**	**9.1**	**4**	**148**	**55.4**	**12:51**	**5**	**2**	**0**	**2**	**2**	**0**	**0**	**0**	**13:22**
2004-05	HC Rabat Kladno	CzRep	23	4	3	7	38										7	3	3	6	4				
2005-06	**Columbus**	**NHL**	**75**	**10**	**23**	**33**	**78**	**4**	**1**	**0**	**78**	**12.8**	**–8**	**1086**	**51.9**	**16:58**									
2006-07	HIFK Helsinki	Finland	10	2	6	8	22																		
	HV 71 Jonkoping	Sweden	41	7	19	26	66										14	2	8	10	82				
	NHL Totals		**513**	**101**	**196**	**297**	**341**	**35**	**1**	**15**	**619**	**16.3**		**7552**	**53.9**	**17:44**	**45**	**12**	**14**	**26**	**24**	**2**	**0**	**1**	**18:00**

Traded to **Phoenix** by **Pittsburgh** with Francois Leroux for Ramzi Abid, Dan Focht and Guillaume Lefebvre, March 11, 2003. Traded to **New Jersey** by **Phoenix** for Mike Rupp and New Jersey's 2nd round choice (later traded to Edmonton – Edmonton selected Geoff Paukovich) in 2004 Entry Draft, March 5, 2004. Signed as a free agent by **Kladno** (CzRep), October 4, 2004. Signed as a free agent by **Columbus**, August 10, 2005. Signed as a free agent by **Jonkoping** (Sweden), August 28, 2006. Loaned to **HIFK Helsinki** (Finland) by **Jonkoping** (Sweden), September 5, 2006.

HUBACEK, Petr
(HOO-buh-chehk, PEE-tuhr) **NSH.**

Center. Shoots right. 6'2", 185 lbs. Born, Brno, Czech., September 2, 1979. Philadelphia's 11th choice, 243rd overall, in 1998 Entry Draft.

			Regular Season														Playoffs								
Season	Club	League	GP	G	A	Pts	PIM	PP	SH	GW	S	%	+/-	TF	F%	Min	GP	G	A	Pts	PIM	PP	SH	GW	Min
1997-98	Brno Jr.	CzRep-Jr.	17	9	5	14																			
	Brno	CzRep-2	48	6	10	16																			
1998-99	HC Vitkovice	CzRep	25	0	4	4	2										4	0	0	0					
99-2000	HC Vitkovice	CzRep	48	11	12	23	81																		
2000-01	**Philadelphia**	**NHL**	**6**	**1**	**0**	**1**	**2**	**0**	**0**	**0**	**5**	**20.0**	**–1**	**39**	**25.6**	**11:20**									
	Philadelphia	AHL	62	3	9	12	29										9	0	1	1	6				
2001-02	Philadelphia	AHL	22	1	6	7	8																		
	Milwaukee	AHL	14	2	0	2	0																		
2002-03	HC Hame Zlin	CzRep	44	4	15	19	14																		
	HC Vitkovice	CzRep	7	1	4	5	10										6	1	0	1	16				
2003-04	HC Vitkovice	CzRep	46	7	14	21	26										6	1	0	1	*53				
2004-05	Vitkovice	CzRep	51	13	11	24	38										9	0	1	1	33				

Season	Club	League	GP	G	A	Pts	PIM	PP	SH	GW	S	%	+/-	TF	F%	Min	GP	G	A	Pts	PIM	PP	SH	GW	Min
			Regular Season														Playoffs								
2005-06	Vitkovice	CzRep	52	17	23	40	46	....	....	....	....	....	....	....	....	....	6	1	0	1	2	....	....	....	....
2006-07	Vitkovice	CzRep	49	17	19	36	62	....	....	....	....	....	....	....	....	....	....	....	....	....	....	....	....	....	....
	NHL Totals		**6**	**1**	**0**	**1**	**2**	**0**	**0**	**0**	**5**	**20.0**		**39**	**25.6**	**11:20**	....	....	....	....	....	....	....	....	....

Traded to **Nashville** by **Philadelphia** with Jason Beckett for Yves Sarault, January 11, 2002. Signed as a free agent by **Zlin** (CzRep) with Nashville retaining NHL rights, August 4, 2002.

HUDLER, Jiri

(HOOD-luhr, YIH-ree) **DET.**

Center. Shoots left. 5'9", 178 lbs. Born, Olomouc, Czech., January 4, 1984. Detroit's 1st choice, 58th overall, in 2002 Entry Draft.

Season	Club	League	GP	G	A	Pts	PIM	PP	SH	GW	S	%	+/-	TF	F%	Min	GP	G	A	Pts	PIM	PP	SH	GW	Min
1998-99	HC Vsetin U17	CzR-U17	46	57	57	114	....	....	....	....	....	....	....	....	....	....	....	....	....	....	....	....	....	....	....
99-2000	HC Vsetin Jr.	CzRep-Jr.	53	29	31	60	75	....	....	....	....	....	....	....	....	....	....	....	....	....	....	....	....	....	....
	Vsetin	CzRep	2	0	1	1	0	....	....	....	....	....	....	....	....	....	....	....	....	....	....	....	....	....	....
2000-01	HC Vsetin Jr.	CzRep-Jr.	16	8	14	22	16	....	....	....	....	....	....	....	....	....	....	....	....	....	....	....	....	....	....
	HC Slovnaft Vsetin	CzRep	22	1	4	5	10	....	....	....	....	....	....	....	....	....	....	....	....	....	....	....	....	....	....
	HC Femax Havirov	CzRep	15	5	1	6	12	....	....	....	....	....	....	....	....	....	....	....	....	....	....	....	....	....	....
2001-02	HC Vsetin	CzRep	46	15	31	46	54	....	....	....	....	....	....	....	....	....	....	....	....	....	....	....	....	....	....
	Liberec	CzRep-2	13	9	7	16	10	....	....	....	....	....	....	....	....	....	....	....	....	....	....	....	....	....	....
	HC Olomouc	CzRep-3	1	0	2	2	4	....	....	....	....	....	....	....	....	....	....	....	....	....	....	....	....	....	....
2002-03	HC Vsetin	CzRep	30	19	27	46	22	....	....	....	....	....	....	....	....	....	....	....	....	....	....	....	....	....	....
	Ak Bars Kazan	Russia	11	1	5	6	12	....	....	....	....	....	....	....	....	....	1	0	0	0	0	....	....	....	....
2003-04	**Detroit**	**NHL**	**12**	**1**	**2**	**3**	**10**	**1**	**0**	**0**	**8**	**12.5**	**–1**	**50**	**30.0**	**8:10**	....	....	....	....	....	....	....	....	....
	Grand Rapids	AHL	57	17	32	49	46	....	....	....	....	....	....	....	....	....	4	1	5	6	2	....	....	....	....
2004-05	Grand Rapids	AHL	52	12	22	34	10	....	....	....	....	....	....	....	....	....	....	....	....	....	....	....	....	....	....
	HC Vsetin	CzRep	7	5	2	7	10	....	....	....	....	....	....	....	....	....	....	....	....	....	....	....	....	....	....
2005-06	**Detroit**	**NHL**	**4**	**0**	**0**	**0**	**2**	**0**	**0**	**0**	**3**	**0.0**	**0**	**0**	**0.0**	**7:13**	....	....	....	....	....	....	....	....	....
	Grand Rapids	AHL	76	36	61	97	56	....	....	....	....	....	....	....	....	....	16	6	16	22	20	....	....	....	....
2006-07	**Detroit**	**NHL**	**76**	**15**	**10**	**25**	**36**	**3**	**0**	**4**	**107**	**14.0**	**16**	**20**	**30.0**	**10:02**	**6**	**0**	**2**	**2**	**4**	**0**	**0**	**0**	**9:09**
	NHL Totals		**92**	**16**	**12**	**28**	**48**	**4**	**0**	**4**	**118**	**13.6**		**70**	**30.0**	**9:40**	**6**	**0**	**2**	**2**	**4**	**0**	**0**	**0**	**9:09**

AHL Second All-Star Team (2006)

Signed as a free agent by **Vsetin** (CzRep), December 2, 2004.

HUNT, Jamie

(HUHNT, JAY-mee) **WSH.**

Defense. Shoots left. 6'2", 200 lbs. Born, Calgary, Alta., April 20, 1984.

Season	Club	League	GP	G	A	Pts	PIM	PP	SH	GW	S	%	+/-	TF	F%	Min	GP	G	A	Pts	PIM	PP	SH	GW	Min
2002-03	Calgary Canucks	AJHL	63	8	20	28	35	....	....	....	....	....	....	....	....	....	....	....	....	....	....	....	....	....	....
2003-04	Mercyhurst	AH	27	3	16	19	4	....	....	....	....	....	....	....	....	....	....	....	....	....	....	....	....	....	....
2004-05	Mercyhurst	AH	38	5	12	17	36	....	....	....	....	....	....	....	....	....	....	....	....	....	....	....	....	....	....
2005-06	Mercyhurst	AH	33	12	33	45	49	....	....	....	....	....	....	....	....	....	....	....	....	....	....	....	....	....	....
2006-07	**Washington**	**NHL**	**1**	**0**	**0**	**0**	**0**	**0**	**0**	**0**	**0**	**0.0**	**–1**	**0**	**0.0**	**6:01**	....	....	....	....	....	....	....	....	....
	Hershey Bears	AHL	36	2	10	12	33	....	....	....	....	....	....	....	....	....	....	....	....	....	....	....	....	....	....
	NHL Totals		**1**	**0**	**0**	**0**	**0**	**0**	**0**	**0**	**0**	**0.0**		**0**	**0.0**	**6:01**	....	....	....	....	....	....	....	....	....

AH All-Rookie Team (2004) • AH First All-Star Team (2006)

Signed as a free agent by **Washington**, March 31, 2006. • Missed majority of 2006-07 season recovering from wrist injury suffered in game vs. Philadelphia (AHL), January 24, 2007.

HUNTER, Trent

(HUHN-tuhr, TREHNT) **NYI**

Right wing. Shoots right. 6'3", 210 lbs. Born, Red Deer, Alta., July 5, 1980. Anaheim's 4th choice, 150th overall, in 1998 Entry Draft.

Season	Club	League	GP	G	A	Pts	PIM	PP	SH	GW	S	%	+/-	TF	F%	Min	GP	G	A	Pts	PIM	PP	SH	GW	Min
1996-97	Red Deer	AMHL	42	30	25	55	50	....	....	....	....	....	....	....	....	....	....	....	....	....	....	....	....	....	....
1997-98	Prince George	WHL	60	13	14	27	34	....	....	....	....	....	....	....	....	....	8	1	0	1	4	....	....	....	....
1998-99	Prince George	WHL	50	18	20	38	34	....	....	....	....	....	....	....	....	....	7	2	5	7	2	....	....	....	....
99-2000	Prince George	WHL	67	46	49	95	47	....	....	....	....	....	....	....	....	....	13	7	15	22	6	....	....	....	....
2000-01	Springfield	AHL	57	18	17	35	14	....	....	....	....	....	....	....	....	....	....	....	....	....	....	....	....	....	....
2001-02	Bridgeport	AHL	80	30	35	65	30	....	....	....	....	....	....	....	....	....	17	8	11	19	6	....	....	....	....
	NY Islanders	**NHL**	....	....	....	....	....	....	....	....	....	....	....	....	....	....	**4**	**1**	**1**	**2**	**2**	**0**	**0**	**0**	**11:13**
2002-03	Bridgeport	AHL	70	30	41	71	39	....	....	....	....	....	....	....	....	....	9	7	4	11	10	....	....	....	....
	NY Islanders	**NHL**	**8**	**0**	**4**	**4**	**4**	**0**	**0**	**0**	**19**	**0.0**	**5**	**1**	**0.0**	**12:13**	....	....	....	....	....	....	....	....	....
2003-04	**NY Islanders**	**NHL**	**77**	**25**	**26**	**51**	**16**	**4**	**0**	**7**	**187**	**13.4**	**23**	**19**	**36.8**	**15:39**	**5**	**0**	**0**	**0**	**4**	**0**	**0**	**0**	**11:38**
2004-05	Nykoping	Sweden-2	33	13	12	25	73	....	....	....	....	....	....	....	....	....	4	5	3	8	2	....	....	....	....
2005-06	**NY Islanders**	**NHL**	**82**	**16**	**19**	**35**	**34**	**5**	**0**	**3**	**221**	**7.2**	**–9**	**32**	**28.1**	**17:50**	....	....	....	....	....	....	....	....	....
2006-07	**NY Islanders**	**NHL**	**77**	**20**	**15**	**35**	**22**	**5**	**1**	**2**	**168**	**11.9**	**5**	**14**	**42.9**	**16:00**	**5**	**3**	**0**	**3**	**0**	**0**	**0**	**0**	**15:05**
	NHL Totals		**244**	**61**	**64**	**125**	**76**	**14**	**1**	**12**	**595**	**10.3**		**66**	**33.3**	**16:23**	**14**	**4**	**1**	**5**	**6**	**0**	**0**	**0**	**12:45**

WHL West First All-Star Team (2000) • NHL All-Rookie Team (2004)

Traded to **NY Islanders** by **Anaheim** for Columbus' 4th round choice (previously acquired, Anaheim selected Jonas Ronnqvist) in 2000 Entry Draft, May 23, 2000. Signed as a free agent by **Nykoping** (Sweden-2), November 8, 2004.

HUSELIUS, Kristian

(hoo-SAY-lee-uhs, KRIHST-yan) **CGY.**

Left wing. Shoots left. 6'1", 184 lbs. Born, Osterhaninge, Sweden, November 10, 1978. Florida's 2nd choice, 47th overall, in 1997 Entry Draft.

Season	Club	League	GP	G	A	Pts	PIM	PP	SH	GW	S	%	+/-	TF	F%	Min	GP	G	A	Pts	PIM	PP	SH	GW	Min
1994-95	Hammarby Jr.	Swe-Jr.	17	6	2	8	2	....	....	....	....	....	....	....	....	....	....	....	....	....	....	....	....	....	....
1995-96	Hammarby Jr.	Swe-Jr.	25	13	8	21	14	....	....	....	....	....	....	....	....	....	....	....	....	....	....	....	....	....	....
	Hammarby	Sweden-2	6	1	0	1	0	....	....	....	....	....	....	....	....	....	....	....	....	....	....	....	....	....	....
1996-97	Farjestad	Sweden	13	2	0	2	4	....	....	....	....	....	....	....	....	....	5	1	0	1	0	....	....	....	....
1997-98	Farjestad	Sweden	34	2	1	3	2	....	....	....	....	....	....	....	....	....	11	0	0	0	0	....	....	....	....
	Farjestad	EuroHL	5	2	3	5	0	....	....	....	....	....	....	....	....	....	....	....	....	....	....	....	....	....	....
1998-99	Farjestad	Sweden	28	4	4	8	4	....	....	....	....	....	....	....	....	....	....	....	....	....	....	....	....	....	....
	Farjestad	EuroHL	6	2	2	4	8	....	....	....	....	....	....	....	....	....	1	0	0	0	0	....	....	....	....
	V.Frolunda	Sweden	20	2	2	4	2	....	....	....	....	....	....	....	....	....	4	1	0	1	0	....	....	....	....
99-2000	V.Frolunda	Sweden	50	21	23	44	20	....	....	....	....	....	....	....	....	....	5	2	2	4	8	....	....	....	....
2000-01	V.Frolunda	Sweden	49	*32	*35	*67	26	....	....	....	....	....	....	....	....	....	5	4	5	9	14	....	....	....	....
2001-02	**Florida**	**NHL**	**79**	**23**	**22**	**45**	**14**	**6**	**1**	**3**	**169**	**13.6**	**–4**	**14**	**21.4**	**16:55**	....	....	....	....	....	....	....	....	....
2002-03	**Florida**	**NHL**	**78**	**20**	**23**	**43**	**20**	**3**	**0**	**3**	**187**	**10.7**	**–6**	**6**	**33.3**	**17:20**	....	....	....	....	....	....	....	....	....
2003-04	**Florida**	**NHL**	**76**	**10**	**21**	**31**	**24**	**2**	**0**	**2**	**168**	**6.0**	**–6**	**185**	**37.8**	**14:14**	....	....	....	....	....	....	....	....	....
2004-05	Linkopings HC	Sweden	34	14	*35	49	10	....	....	....	....	....	....	....	....	....	....	....	....	....	....	....	....	....	....
	Rapperswil	Swiss	....	....	....	....	....	....	....	....	....	....	....	....	....	....	4	1	3	4	2	....	....	....	....
2005-06	**Florida**	**NHL**	**24**	**5**	**3**	**8**	**4**	**2**	**0**	**0**	**57**	**8.8**	**–11**	**3**	**66.7**	**14:44**	....	....	....	....	....	....	....	....	....
	Calgary	**NHL**	**54**	**15**	**24**	**39**	**36**	**6**	**0**	**4**	**107**	**14.0**	**2**	**3**	**33.3**	**14:55**	**7**	**2**	**4**	**6**	**4**	**2**	**0**	**0**	**15:35**
2006-07	**Calgary**	**NHL**	**81**	**34**	**43**	**77**	**26**	**14**	**2**	**6**	**173**	**19.7**	**21**	**14**	**28.6**	**17:23**	**6**	**0**	**2**	**2**	**4**	**0**	**0**	**0**	**15:08**
	NHL Totals		**392**	**107**	**136**	**243**	**124**	**33**	**3**	**18**	**861**	**12.4**		**225**	**36.4**	**16:10**	**13**	**2**	**6**	**8**	**8**	**2**	**0**	**0**	**15:23**

NHL All-Rookie Team (2002)

Signed as a free agent by **Linkopings** (Sweden), July 29, 2004. Signed as a free agent by **Rapperswil** (Swiss), February 23, 2005. Traded to **Calgary** by **Florida** for Steve Montador and Dustin Johner, December 2, 2005.

HUSKINS, Kent

(HUHS-kihnz, KEHNT) **ANA.**

Defense. Shoots left. 6'3", 217 lbs. Born, Ottawa, Ont., May 4, 1979. Chicago's 3rd choice, 156th overall, in 1998 Entry Draft.

Season	Club	League	GP	G	A	Pts	PIM	PP	SH	GW	S	%	+/-	TF	F%	Min	GP	G	A	Pts	PIM	PP	SH	GW	Min
1995-96	Kanata Valley	CJHL	49	6	21	27	18	....	....	....	....	....	....	....	....	....	....	....	....	....	....	....	....	....	....
1996-97	Kanata Valley	CJHL	53	11	36	47	89	....	....	....	....	....	....	....	....	....	....	....	....	....	....	....	....	....	....
1997-98	Clarkson Knights	ECAC	35	2	8	10	46	....	....	....	....	....	....	....	....	....	....	....	....	....	....	....	....	....	....
1998-99	Clarkson Knights	ECAC	37	5	11	16	28	....	....	....	....	....	....	....	....	....	....	....	....	....	....	....	....	....	....
99-2000	Clarkson Knights	ECAC	28	2	16	18	30	....	....	....	....	....	....	....	....	....	....	....	....	....	....	....	....	....	....
2000-01	Clarkson Knights	ECAC	35	6	28	34	22	....	....	....	....	....	....	....	....	....	....	....	....	....	....	....	....	....	....
2001-02	Norfolk Admirals	AHL	65	4	11	15	44	....	....	....	....	....	....	....	....	....	4	0	1	1	0	....	....	....	....
2002-03	Norfolk Admirals	AHL	80	5	22	27	48	....	....	....	....	....	....	....	....	....	9	2	2	4	4	....	....	....	....
2003-04	San Antonio	AHL	79	5	14	19	42	....	....	....	....	....	....	....	....	....	....	....	....	....	....	....	....	....	....
2004-05	Manitoba Moose	AHL	65	5	11	16	41	....	....	....	....	....	....	....	....	....	14	0	2	2	12	....	....	....	....
2005-06	Portland Pirates	AHL	80	8	23	31	64	....	....	....	....	....	....	....	....	....	18	3	6	9	14	....	....	....	....

			Regular Season														Playoffs								
Season	Club	League	GP	G	A	Pts	PIM	PP	SH	GW	S	%	+/-	TF	F%	Min	GP	G	A	Pts	PIM	PP	SH	GW	Min
2006-07 ♦	**Anaheim**	**NHL**	**33**	**0**	**3**	**3**	**14**	**0**	**0**	**0**	**16**	**0.0**	**–3**	**0**	**0.0**	**14:04**	**21**	**0**	**1**	**1**	**11**	**0**	**0**	**0**	**11:45**
	Portland Pirates	AHL	39	3	12	15	23																		
	NHL Totals		**33**	**0**	**3**	**3**	**14**	**0**	**0**	**0**	**16**	**0.0**		**0**	**0.0**	**14:04**	**21**	**0**	**1**	**1**	**11**	**0**	**0**	**0**	**11:45**

ECAC First All-Star Team (2000, 2001) • NCAA East First All-American Team (2001)

Signed as a free agent by **Florida**, August 14, 2003. Signed as a free agent by **Manitoba** (AHL), September 16, 2004. Signed as a free agent by **Anaheim**, August 30, 2005.

HUSSEY, Matt

(HUH-see, MAT) **COL.**

Center. Shoots left. 6'2", 212 lbs. Born, New Haven, CT, May 28, 1979. Pittsburgh's 10th choice, 254th overall, in 1998 Entry Draft.

Season	Club	League	GP	G	A	Pts	PIM	PP	SH	GW	S	%	+/-	TF	F%	Min	GP	G	A	Pts	PIM	PP	SH	GW	Min
1996-97	Wayzata	High-MN	48	34	31	65																			
1997-98	Avon Old Farms	High-CT	26	26	23	49	20																		
1998-99	U. of Wisconsin	WCHA	37	10	5	15	18																		
99-2000	U. of Wisconsin	WCHA	35	5	11	16	8																		
2000-01	U. of Wisconsin	WCHA	40	9	11	20	24																		
2001-02	U. of Wisconsin	WCHA	39	18	15	33	16																		
2002-03	Wilkes-Barre	AHL	69	12	11	23	28										2	0	0	0	0				
2003-04	**Pittsburgh**	**NHL**	**3**	**2**	**1**	**3**	**0**	**2**	**0**	**0**	**8**	**25.0**	**–1**	**0**	**0.0**	**13:35**									
	Wilkes-Barre	AHL	55	2	1	3	6										6	2	2	4	0				
2004-05	Wilkes-Barre	AHL	80	16	14	30	19										10	1	2	3	2				
2005-06	**Pittsburgh**	**NHL**	**13**	**0**	**1**	**1**	**0**	**0**	**0**	**0**	**17**	**0.0**	**–5**	**63**	**38.1**	**10:17**									
	Wilkes-Barre	AHL	65	21	30	51	34										9	1	0	1	0				
2006-07	**Detroit**	**NHL**	**5**	**0**	**0**	**0**	**2**	**0**	**0**	**0**	**6**	**0.0**	**0**	**0**	**0.0**	**5:38**									
	Grand Rapids	AHL	75	15	29	44	36										6	1	1	2	2				
	NHL Totals		**21**	**2**	**2**	**4**	**2**	**2**	**0**	**0**	**31**	**6.5**		**63**	**38.1**	**9:39**									

Signed as a free agent by **Detroit**, July 13, 2006. Signed as a free agent by **Colorado**, July 13, 2007.

HUTCHINSON, Andrew

(HUHT-chihn-suhn, AN-droo) **NYR**

Defense. Shoots right. 6'2", 206 lbs. Born, Evanston, IL, March 24, 1980. Nashville's 4th choice, 54th overall, in 1999 Entry Draft.

Season	Club	League	GP	G	A	Pts	PIM	PP	SH	GW	S	%	+/-	TF	F%	Min	GP	G	A	Pts	PIM	PP	SH	GW	Min
1996-97	Det. Caesars	MNHL	82	15	41	56																			
1997-98	USNTDP	U-18	27	3	11	14	35																		
	USNTDP	USHL	15	0	7	7	8																		
	USNTDP	NAHL	12	2	0	2	8										5	2	3	5	2				
1998-99	Michigan State	CCHA	37	3	12	15	26																		
99-2000	Michigan State	CCHA	42	5	12	17	64																		
2000-01	Michigan State	CCHA	42	5	19	24	46																		
2001-02	Milwaukee	AHL	5	0	1	1	0																		
	Michigan State	CCHA	39	6	16	22	24																		
2002-03	Milwaukee	AHL	63	9	17	26	40										3	1	0	1	0				
	Toledo Storm	ECHL	10	2	5	7	4																		
2003-04	**Nashville**	**NHL**	**18**	**4**	**4**	**8**	**4**	**2**	**0**	**1**	**24**	**16.7**	**1**	**0**	**0.0**	**16:43**									
	Milwaukee	AHL	46	12	12	24	39										22	5	11	16	33				
2004-05	Milwaukee	AHL	76	10	35	45	79										7	1	3	4	8				
2005-06 ♦	**Carolina**	**NHL**	**36**	**3**	**8**	**11**	**18**	**2**	**0**	**0**	**33**	**9.1**	**–2**	**0**	**0.0**	**10:22**									
2006-07	**Carolina**	**NHL**	**41**	**3**	**11**	**14**	**30**	**2**	**0**	**0**	**45**	**6.7**	**0**	**0**	**0.0**	**12:13**									
	NHL Totals		**95**	**10**	**23**	**33**	**52**	**6**	**0**	**1**	**102**	**9.8**		**0**	**0.0**	**12:22**									

CCHA Second All-Star Team (2001, 2002) • NCAA West Second All-American Team (2002)

Traded to **Carolina** by **Nashville** for Phoenix's 3rd round choice (previously acquired, Nashville selected Teemu Laakso) in 2005 Entry Draft, July 29, 2005. Traded to **NY Rangers** by **Carolina** with Joe Barnes and Carolina's 3rd round choice in 2008 Entry Draft for Matt Cullen, July 17, 2007.

IGINLA, Jarome

(ih-GIHN-lah, jah-ROHM) **CGY.**

Right wing. Shoots right. 6'1", 204 lbs. Born, Edmonton, Alta., July 1, 1977. Dallas' 1st choice, 11th overall, in 1995 Entry Draft.

Season	Club	League	GP	G	A	Pts	PIM	PP	SH	GW	S	%	+/-	TF	F%	Min	GP	G	A	Pts	PIM	PP	SH	GW	Min
1991-92	St. Albert Raiders	AMHL	36	26	30	56	22																		
1992-93	St. Albert Raiders	AMHL	36	34	53	*87	20																		
1993-94	Kamloops Blazers	WHL	48	6	23	29	33										19	3	6	9	10				
1994-95	Kamloops Blazers	WHL	72	33	38	71	111										21	7	11	18	34				
1995-96	Kamloops Blazers	WHL	63	63	73	136	120										16	16	13	29	44				
	Calgary	**NHL**															**2**	**1**	**1**	**2**	**0**	**0**	**0**	**0**	
1996-97	**Calgary**	**NHL**	**82**	**21**	**29**	**50**	**37**	**8**	**1**	**3**	**169**	**12.4**	**–4**												
1997-98	**Calgary**	**NHL**	**70**	**13**	**19**	**32**	**29**	**0**	**2**	**1**	**154**	**8.4**	**–10**												
1998-99	**Calgary**	**NHL**	**82**	**28**	**23**	**51**	**58**	**7**	**0**	**4**	**211**	**13.3**	**1**	**111**	**51.4**	**16:30**									
99-2000	**Calgary**	**NHL**	**77**	**29**	**34**	**63**	**26**	**12**	**0**	**4**	**256**	**11.3**	**0**	**278**	**52.9**	**18:24**									
2000-01	**Calgary**	**NHL**	**77**	**31**	**40**	**71**	**62**	**10**	**0**	**4**	**229**	**13.5**	**–2**	**638**	**51.7**	**19:58**									
2001-02	**Calgary**	**NHL**	**82**	***52**	**44**	***96**	**77**	**16**	**1**	**7**	**311**	**16.7**	**27**	**308**	**55.2**	**22:22**									
	Canada	Olympics	6	3	1	4	0																		
2002-03	**Calgary**	**NHL**	**75**	**35**	**32**	**67**	**49**	**11**	**3**	**6**	**316**	**11.1**	**–10**	**90**	**43.3**	**21:26**									
2003-04	**Calgary**	**NHL**	**81**	***41**	**32**	**73**	**84**	**8**	**4**	**10**	**265**	**15.5**	**21**	**305**	**54.4**	**21:18**	**26**	***13**	**9**	**22**	**45**	**4**	**2**	**3**	**23:18**
2004-05			DID NOT PLAY																						
2005-06	**Calgary**	**NHL**	**82**	**35**	**32**	**67**	**86**	**17**	**1**	**6**	**293**	**11.9**	**5**	**541**	**54.2**	**21:42**	**7**	**5**	**3**	**8**	**11**	**1**	**1**	**1**	**24:14**
	Canada	Olympics	6	2	1	3	4																		
2006-07	**Calgary**	**NHL**	**70**	**39**	**55**	**94**	**40**	**13**	**1**	**7**	**264**	**14.8**	**12**	**406**	**53.0**	**22:04**	**6**	**2**	**2**	**4**	**12**	**0**	**0**	**1**	**23:45**
	NHL Totals		**778**	**324**	**340**	**664**	**548**	**102**	**13**	**52**	**2468**	**13.1**		**2677**	**52.9**	**20:27**	**41**	**21**	**15**	**36**	**68**	**5**	**3**	**5**	**23:32**

George Parsons Trophy (Memorial Cup Tournament Most Sportsmanlike Player) (1995) • WHL West First All-Star Team (1996) • WHL Player of the Year (1996) • Canadian Major Junior First All-Star Team (1996) • NHL All-Rookie Team (1997) • NHL First All-Star Team (2002) • Maurice "Rocket" Richard Trophy (2002) • Art Ross Trophy (2002) • Lester B. Pearson Award (2002) • NHL Second All-Star Team (2004) • King Clancy Memorial Trophy (2004) • Maurice "Rocket" Richard Trophy (2004) (tied with Ilya Kovalchuk and Rick Nash)

Played in NHL All-Star Game (2002, 2003, 2004)

Traded to **Calgary** by **Dallas** with Corey Millen for Joe Nieuwendyk, December 19, 1995.

IMMONEN, Jarkko

(IH-moh-nihn, YAHR-koh) **NYR**

Center. Shoots right. 6', 210 lbs. Born, Rantasalmi, Finland, April 19, 1982. Toronto's 8th choice, 254th overall, in 2002 Entry Draft.

Season	Club	League	GP	G	A	Pts	PIM	PP	SH	GW	S	%	+/-	TF	F%	Min	GP	G	A	Pts	PIM	PP	SH	GW	Min
1997-98	SaPKo Jr.	Fin-Jr.	14	8	12	20	0																		
1998-99	SaPKo Jr.	Fin-Jr.	12	6	10	16	14																		
	SaPKo Savonlinna	Finland-2	36	2	2	4	6																		
99-2000	SaPKo Jr.	Fin-Jr.															2	0	4	4	4				
	SaPKo Savonlinna	Finland-2	42	18	16	34	34																		
2000-01	TuTo Turku Jr.	Fin-Jr.	1	0	1	1	0										1	0	0	0	2				
	TuTo Turku	Finland-2	41	20	20	40	22										11	5	7	12	10				
2001-02	Assat Pori	Finland	44	0	2	2	6																		
	Assat Pori Jr.	Fin-Jr.															8	5	1	6	10				
2002-03	JYP Jyvaskyla	Finland	56	10	23	33	34										7	1	1	2	8				
2003-04	JYP Jyvaskyla	Finland	52	23	26	49	28										2	0	0	0	0				
2004-05	JYP Jyvaskyla	Finland	54	19	28	47	24										3	0	2	2	2				
2005-06	**NY Rangers**	**NHL**	**6**	**2**	**0**	**2**	**0**	**1**	**0**	**0**	**8**	**25.0**	**–1**	**51**	**56.9**	**10:15**									
	Hartford	AHL	74	30	40	70	34										6	2	3	5	2				
2006-07	**NY Rangers**	**NHL**	**14**	**1**	**5**	**6**	**4**	**0**	**0**	**1**	**14**	**7.1**	**–2**	**108**	**56.5**	**10:22**									
	Hartford	AHL	54	20	26	46	30										7	2	6	8	2				
	NHL Totals		**20**	**3**	**5**	**8**	**4**	**1**	**0**	**1**	**22**	**13.6**		**159**	**56.6**	**10:20**									

Traded to **NY Rangers** by **Toronto** with Maxim Kondratiev, Toronto's 1st round choice (later traded to Calgary - Calgary selected Kris Chucko) in 2004 Entry Draft and Toronto's 2nd round choice (Michael Sauer) in 2005 Entry Draft for Brian Leetch and Edmonton's 4th round choice (previously acquired, Toronto selected Roman Kukumberg) in 2004 Entry Draft, March 3, 2004.

ISBISTER, Brad
(IHZ-bihs-tuhr, BRAD) **VAN.**

Left wing. Shoots right. 6'4", 231 lbs. Born, Edmonton, Alta., May 7, 1977. Winnipeg's 4th choice, 67th overall, in 1995 Entry Draft.

			Regular Season														Playoffs								
Season	Club	League	GP	G	A	Pts	PIM	PP	SH	GW	S	%	+/-	TF	F%	Min	GP	G	A	Pts	PIM	PP	SH	GW	Min
1992-93	Calgary Canucks	ABHL	35	24	25	49	74	....	....	....	....	....	....	....	....	....	....	....	....	....	....	....	....	....	....
1993-94	Portland	WHL	64	7	10	17	45	....	....	....	....	....	....	....	....	....	10	0	2	2	0	....	....	....	....
1994-95	Portland	WHL	67	16	20	36	123	....	....	....	....	....	....	....	....	....	....	....	....	....	....	....	....	....	....
1995-96	Portland	WHL	71	45	44	89	184	....	....	....	....	....	....	....	....	....	7	2	4	6	20	....	....	....	....
1996-97	Portland	WHL	24	15	18	33	45	....	....	....	....	....	....	....	....	....	6	2	1	3	16	....	....	....	....
	Springfield	AHL	7	3	1	4	14	....	....	....	....	....	....	....	....	....	9	1	2	3	10	....	....	....	....
1997-98	**Phoenix**	**NHL**	**66**	**9**	**8**	**17**	**102**	**1**	**0**	**1**	**115**	**7.8**	**4**	....	....	....	**5**	**0**	**0**	**0**	**2**	**0**	**0**	**0**	....
	Springfield	AHL	9	8	2	10	36	....	....	....	....	....	....	....	....	....	....	....	....	....	....	....	....	....	....
1998-99	**Phoenix**	**NHL**	**32**	**4**	**4**	**8**	**46**	**0**	**0**	**2**	**48**	**8.3**	**1**	**3**	**0.0**	**11:33**	....	....	....	....	....	....	....	....	....
	Springfield	AHL	4	1	1	2	12	....	....	....	....	....	....	....	....	....	....	....	....	....	....	....	....	....	....
	Las Vegas	IHL	2	0	0	0	9	....	....	....	....	....	....	....	....	....	....	....	....	....	....	....	....	....	....
99-2000	**NY Islanders**	**NHL**	**64**	**22**	**20**	**42**	**100**	**9**	**0**	**1**	**135**	**16.3**	**–18**	**55**	**54.6**	**16:58**	....	....	....	....	....	....	....	....	....
2000-01	**NY Islanders**	**NHL**	**51**	**18**	**14**	**32**	**59**	**7**	**1**	**4**	**129**	**14.0**	**–19**	**255**	**45.9**	**19:26**	....	....	....	....	....	....	....	....	....
2001-02	**NY Islanders**	**NHL**	**79**	**17**	**21**	**38**	**113**	**4**	**0**	**2**	**142**	**12.0**	**1**	**71**	**45.1**	**15:18**	**3**	**1**	**1**	**2**	**17**	**1**	**0**	**1**	**12:33**
2002-03	**NY Islanders**	**NHL**	**53**	**10**	**13**	**23**	**34**	**2**	**0**	**2**	**90**	**11.1**	**–9**	**13**	**46.2**	**13:54**	....	....	....	....	....	....	....	....	....
	Edmonton	**NHL**	**13**	**3**	**2**	**5**	**9**	**0**	**0**	**1**	**29**	**10.3**	**0**	**10**	**50.0**	**13:14**	**6**	**0**	**1**	**1**	**12**	**0**	**0**	**0**	**10:04**
2003-04	**Edmonton**	**NHL**	**51**	**10**	**8**	**18**	**54**	**1**	**0**	**2**	**80**	**12.5**	**–2**	**55**	**56.4**	**12:46**	....	....	....	....	....	....	....	....	....
2004-05	Innsbruck	Austria	11	7	4	11	41	....	....	....	....	....	....	....	....	....	5	3	1	4	6	....	....	....	....
2005-06	**Boston**	**NHL**	**58**	**6**	**17**	**23**	**46**	**1**	**0**	**0**	**112**	**5.4**	**–2**	**10**	**60.0**	**13:55**	....	....	....	....	....	....	....	....	....
2006-07	Albany River Rats	AHL	9	3	5	8	54	....	....	....	....	....	....	....	....	....	....	....	....	....	....	....	....	....	....
	NY Rangers	**NHL**	**19**	**1**	**4**	**5**	**14**	**1**	**0**	**0**	**36**	**2.8**	**5**	**12**	**33.3**	**13:36**	**4**	**0**	**0**	**0**	**2**	**0**	**0**	**0**	**9:58**
	Hartford	AHL	34	12	8	20	22	....	....	....	....	....	....	....	....	....	....	....	....	....	....	....	....	....	....
	NHL Totals		**486**	**100**	**111**	**211**	**577**	**26**	**1**	**15**	**916**	**10.9**		**484**	**47.7**	**14:57**	**18**	**1**	**2**	**3**	**33**	**1**	**0**	**1**	**10:36**

WHL West Second All-Star Team (1997)

Rights transferred to **Phoenix** after **Winnipeg** franchise relocated, July 1, 1996. Traded to **NY Islanders** by **Phoenix** with Phoenix's 3rd round choice (Brian Collins) in 1999 Entry Draft for Robert Reichel, NY Islanders' 3rd round choice (Jason Jaspers) in 1999 Entry Draft and Ottawa's 4th round choice (previously acquired, Phoenix selected Preston Mizzi) in 1999 Entry Draft, March 20, 1999. Traded to **Edmonton** by **NY Islanders** with Raffi Torres for Janne Niinimaa and Washington's 2nd round choice (previously acquired, NY Islanders selected Evgeni Tunik) in 2003 Entry Draft , March 11, 2003. Signed as a free agent by **Innsbruck** (Austria), February 12, 2005. Traded to **Boston** by **Edmonton** for Boston's 4th round choice (later traded back to Boston - later traded to San Jose - San Jose selected James Delory) in 2006 Entry Draft, August 1, 2005. Signed as a free agent by **Carolina**, August 30, 2006. Traded to **NY Rangers** by **Carolina** for Jakub Petruzalek and future considerations, November 21, 2006. Signed as a free agent by **Vancouver**, July 3, 2007.

IVANANS, Raitis
(ih-VAH-nehns, RIGH-this) **L.A.**

Left wing. Shoots left. 6'3", 263 lbs. Born, Riga, USSR, January 1, 1979.

Season	Club	League	GP	G	A	Pts	PIM	PP	SH	GW	S	%	+/-	TF	F%	Min	GP	G	A	Pts	PIM	PP	SH	GW	Min
1997-98	Flint Generals	UHL	18	0	1	1	20	....	....	....	....	....	....	....	....	....	....	....	....	....	....	....	....	....	....
1998-99	Macon Whoopee	CHL	16	1	1	2	20	....	....	....	....	....	....	....	....	....	....	....	....	....	....	....	....	....	....
	Tulsa Oilers	CHL	32	2	7	9	39	....	....	....	....	....	....	....	....	....	....	....	....	....	....	....	....	....	....
99-2000	Pensacola	ECHL	59	3	7	10	146	....	....	....	....	....	....	....	....	....	2	0	0	0	0	....	....	....	....
2000-01	Hershey Bears	AHL	2	0	0	0	0	....	....	....	....	....	....	....	....	....	....	....	....	....	....	....	....	....	....
	New Haven	UHL	66	4	10	14	270	....	....	....	....	....	....	....	....	....	8	1	0	1	4	....	....	....	....
2001-02	Toledo Storm	ECHL	16	2	2	4	59	....	....	....	....	....	....	....	....	....	....	....	....	....	....	....	....	....	....
	Baton Rouge	ECHL	40	4	5	9	180	....	....	....	....	....	....	....	....	....	....	....	....	....	....	....	....	....	....
2002-03	Milwaukee	AHL	17	0	0	0	38	....	....	....	....	....	....	....	....	....	1	0	0	0	15	....	....	....	....
	Rockford IceHogs	UHL	50	4	2	6	208	....	....	....	....	....	....	....	....	....	....	....	....	....	....	....	....	....	....
2003-04	Milwaukee	AHL	54	1	7	8	166	....	....	....	....	....	....	....	....	....	7	0	1	1	17	....	....	....	....
	Rockford IceHogs	UHL	1	0	0	0	0	....	....	....	....	....	....	....	....	....	....	....	....	....	....	....	....	....	....
2004-05	Hamilton	AHL	75	2	5	7	259	....	....	....	....	....	....	....	....	....	2	0	1	1	0	....	....	....	....
2005-06	**Montreal**	**NHL**	**4**	**0**	**0**	**0**	**9**	**0**	**0**	**0**	**0**	**0.0**	**–1**	**0**	**0.0**	**2:58**	....	....	....	....	....	....	....	....	....
	Hamilton	AHL	43	2	0	2	120	....	....	....	....	....	....	....	....	....	....	....	....	....	....	....	....	....	....
2006-07	**Los Angeles**	**NHL**	**66**	**4**	**4**	**8**	**140**	**0**	**0**	**0**	**37**	**10.8**	**–12**	**1**	**0.0**	**6:59**	....	....	....	....	....	....	....	....	....
	NHL Totals		**70**	**4**	**4**	**8**	**149**	**0**	**0**	**0**	**37**	**10.8**		**1**	**0.0**	**6:45**	....	....	....	....	....	....	....	....	....

Signed as a free agent by **Montreal**, July 16, 2004 Signed as a free agent by **Los Angeles**, July 13, 2006.

JACINA, Greg
(ja-SEE-nah, GREHG)

Left wing. Shoots right. 6', 203 lbs. Born, Guelph, Ont., May 22, 1982.

Season	Club	League	GP	G	A	Pts	PIM	PP	SH	GW	S	%	+/-	TF	F%	Min	GP	G	A	Pts	PIM	PP	SH	GW	Min
99-2000	Owen Sound	OHL	66	12	29	41	62	....	....	....	....	....	....	....	....	....	....	....	....	....	....	....	....	....	....
2000-01	Owen Sound	OHL	57	25	26	51	101	....	....	....	....	....	....	....	....	....	4	0	1	1	15	....	....	....	....
2001-02	Owen Sound	OHL	33	15	20	35	64	....	....	....	....	....	....	....	....	....	....	....	....	....	....	....	....	....	....
	Mississauga	OHL	28	14	26	40	43	....	....	....	....	....	....	....	....	....	....	....	....	....	....	....	....	....	....
2002-03	Mississauga	OHL	56	19	47	66	114	....	....	....	....	....	....	....	....	....	5	6	5	11	17	....	....	....	....
2003-04	San Antonio	AHL	13	0	4	4	22	....	....	....	....	....	....	....	....	....	....	....	....	....	....	....	....	....	....
	Augusta Lynx	ECHL	58	15	23	38	170	....	....	....	....	....	....	....	....	....	....	....	....	....	....	....	....	....	....
2004-05	San Antonio	AHL	78	11	20	31	150	....	....	....	....	....	....	....	....	....	....	....	....	....	....	....	....	....	....
2005-06	**Florida**	**NHL**	**11**	**0**	**1**	**1**	**4**	**0**	**0**	**0**	**10**	**0.0**	**–1**	**2**	**0.0**	**5:50**	....	....	....	....	....	....	....	....	....
	Rochester	AHL	35	7	4	11	152	....	....	....	....	....	....	....	....	....	....	....	....	....	....	....	....	....	....
2006-07	**Florida**	**NHL**	**3**	**0**	**0**	**0**	**2**	**0**	**0**	**0**	**2**	**0.0**	**–1**	**0**	**0.0**	**6:52**	....	....	....	....	....	....	....	....	....
	Rochester	AHL	61	15	20	35	96	....	....	....	....	....	....	....	....	....	3	0	1	1	4	....	....	....	....
	NHL Totals		**14**	**0**	**1**	**1**	**6**	**0**	**0**	**0**	**12**	**0.0**		**2**	**0.0**	**6:04**	....	....	....	....	....	....	....	....	....

Signed as a free agent by **Florida**, August 12, 2003. Signed as a free agent by **Rauma** (Finland), July 13, 2007.

JACKMAN, Barret
(JAK-man, BAIR-reht) **ST.L.**

Defense. Shoots left. 6', 213 lbs. Born, Trail, B.C., March 5, 1981. St. Louis' 1st choice, 17th overall, in 1999 Entry Draft.

Season	Club	League	GP	G	A	Pts	PIM	PP	SH	GW	S	%	+/-	TF	F%	Min	GP	G	A	Pts	PIM	PP	SH	GW	Min
1996-97	Beaver Valley	VIJHL	32	22	25	47	180	....	....	....	....	....	....	....	....	....	....	....	....	....	....	....	....	....	....
1997-98	Regina Pats	WHL	68	2	11	13	224	....	....	....	....	....	....	....	....	....	9	0	3	3	32	....	....	....	....
1998-99	Regina Pats	WHL	70	8	36	44	259	....	....	....	....	....	....	....	....	....	....	....	....	....	....	....	....	....	....
99-2000	Regina Pats	WHL	53	9	37	46	175	....	....	....	....	....	....	....	....	....	6	1	1	2	19	....	....	....	....
	Worcester IceCats	AHL	....	....	....	....	....	....	....	....	....	....	....	....	....	....	2	0	0	0	13	....	....	....	....
2000-01	Regina Pats	WHL	43	9	27	36	138	....	....	....	....	....	....	....	....	....	6	0	3	3	8	....	....	....	....
2001-02	**St. Louis**	**NHL**	**1**	**0**	**0**	**0**	**0**	**0**	**0**	**0**	**1**	**0.0**	**0**	**0**	**0.0**	**18:56**	**1**	**0**	**0**	**0**	**2**	**0**	**0**	**0**	**18:24**
	Worcester IceCats	AHL	75	2	12	14	266	....	....	....	....	....	....	....	....	....	3	0	1	1	4	....	....	....	....
2002-03	**St. Louis**	**NHL**	**82**	**3**	**16**	**19**	**190**	**0**	**0**	**0**	**66**	**4.5**	**23**	**0**	**0.0**	**20:03**	**7**	**0**	**0**	**0**	**14**	**0**	**0**	**0**	**21:59**
2003-04	**St. Louis**	**NHL**	**15**	**1**	**2**	**3**	**41**	**0**	**0**	**0**	**11**	**9.1**	**–1**	**0**	**0.0**	**18:16**	....	....	....	....	....	....	....	....	....
2004-05	Missouri	UHL	28	3	17	20	61	....	....	....	....	....	....	....	....	....	3	0	0	0	4	....	....	....	....
2005-06	**St. Louis**	**NHL**	**63**	**4**	**6**	**10**	**156**	**0**	**0**	**2**	**56**	**7.1**	**–6**	**0**	**0.0**	**18:46**	....	....	....	....	....	....	....	....	....
2006-07	**St. Louis**	**NHL**	**70**	**3**	**24**	**27**	**82**	**1**	**0**	**1**	**86**	**3.5**	**20**	**0**	**0.0**	**21:30**	....	....	....	....	....	....	....	....	....
	Peoria Rivermen	AHL	1	0	0	0	0	....	....	....	....	....	....	....	....	....	....	....	....	....	....	....	....	....	....
	NHL Totals		**231**	**11**	**48**	**59**	**469**	**1**	**0**	**3**	**220**	**5.0**		**0**	**0.0**	**20:01**	**8**	**0**	**0**	**0**	**16**	**0**	**0**	**0**	**21:32**

WHL East Second All-Star Team (2000) • AHL All-Rookie Team (2002) • NHL All-Rookie Team (2003) • Calder Memorial Trophy (2003)

• Missed majority of 2003-04 season recovering from shoulder injury suffered in game vs. Vancouver, October 22, 2003. Signed as a free agent by **Missouri** (UHL), February 3, 2005.

JACKMAN, Ric
(JAK-man, RIHK)

Defense. Shoots right. 6'2", 214 lbs. Born, Toronto, Ont., June 28, 1978. Dallas' 1st choice, 5th overall, in 1996 Entry Draft.

Season	Club	League	GP	G	A	Pts	PIM	PP	SH	GW	S	%	+/-	TF	F%	Min	GP	G	A	Pts	PIM	PP	SH	GW	Min
1993-94	Miss. Sens	MTHL	81	35	53	88	156	....	....	....	....	....	....	....	....	....	....	....	....	....	....	....	....	....	....
1994-95	Miss. Sens	MTHL	53	20	37	57	120	....	....	....	....	....	....	....	....	....	....	....	....	....	....	....	....	....	....
	Richmond Hill	MTJHL	10	2	9	11	16	....	....	....	....	....	....	....	....	....	....	....	....	....	....	....	....	....	....
1995-96	Sault Ste. Marie	OHL	66	13	29	42	97	....	....	....	....	....	....	....	....	....	4	1	0	1	15	....	....	....	....
1996-97	Sault Ste. Marie	OHL	53	13	34	47	116	....	....	....	....	....	....	....	....	....	10	2	6	8	24	....	....	....	....
1997-98	Sault Ste. Marie	OHL	60	33	40	73	111	....	....	....	....	....	....	....	....	....	....	....	....	....	....	....	....	....	....
	Michigan	IHL	14	1	5	6	10	....	....	....	....	....	....	....	....	....	4	0	0	0	10	....	....	....	....
1998-99	Michigan	IHL	71	13	17	30	106	....	....	....	....	....	....	....	....	....	5	0	4	4	6	....	....	....	....
99-2000	**Dallas**	**NHL**	**22**	**1**	**2**	**3**	**6**	**1**	**0**	**0**	**16**	**6.3**	**–1**	**0**	**0.0**	**8:06**	....	....	....	....	....	....	....	....	....
	Michigan	IHL	50	3	16	19	51	....	....	....	....	....	....	....	....	....	....	....	....	....	....	....	....	....	....
2000-01	**Dallas**	**NHL**	**16**	**0**	**0**	**0**	**18**	**0**	**0**	**0**	**10**	**0.0**	**–6**	**0**	**0.0**	**8:51**	....	....	....	....	....	....	....	....	....
	Utah Grizzlies	IHL	57	9	19	28	24	....	....	....	....	....	....	....	....	....	....	....	....	....	....	....	....	....	....

			Regular Season														Playoffs								
Season	Club	League	GP	G	A	Pts	PIM	PP	SH	GW	S	%	+/-	TF	F%	Min	GP	G	A	Pts	PIM	PP	SH	GW	Min
2001-02	**Boston**	**NHL**	**2**	**0**	**0**	**0**	**2**	**0**	**0**	**0**	**4**	**0.0**	**–1**	**0**	**0.0**	**13:26**	....	....	....	....	....	....	....	....	....
	Providence Bruins	AHL	9	0	1	1	8	....	....	....	....	....	....	....	....	....	2	0	0	0	2	....	....	....	....
2002-03	**Toronto**	**NHL**	**42**	**0**	**2**	**2**	**41**	**0**	**0**	**0**	**35**	**0.0**	**–10**	**0**	**0.0**	**13:59**	....	....	....	....	....	....	....	....	....
	St. John's	AHL	8	2	6	8	24	....	....	....	....	....	....	....	....	....	....	....	....	....	....	....	....	....	....
2003-04	**Toronto**	**NHL**	**29**	**2**	**4**	**6**	**13**	**1**	**0**	**1**	**35**	**5.7**	**–11**	**0**	**0.0**	**18:00**	....	....	....	....	....	....	....	....	....
	Pittsburgh	**NHL**	**25**	**7**	**17**	**24**	**14**	**6**	**0**	**1**	**56**	**12.5**	**–5**	**0**	**0.0**	**24:14**	....	....	....	....	....	....	....	....	....
2004-05	Bjorkloven	Sweden-2	46	13	26	39	209	....	....	....	....	....	....	....	....	....	....	....	....	....	....	....	....	....	....
2005-06	**Pittsburgh**	**NHL**	**49**	**6**	**22**	**28**	**46**	**3**	**0**	**1**	**95**	**6.3**	**–20**	**0**	**0.0**	**18:21**	....	....	....	....	....	....	....	....	....
	Florida	**NHL**	**15**	**1**	**1**	**2**	**6**	**0**	**0**	**0**	**25**	**4.0**	**0**	**0**	**0.0**	**14:04**	....	....	....	....	....	....	....	....	....
2006-07	**Florida**	**NHL**	**7**	**1**	**0**	**1**	**10**	**0**	**0**	**1**	**13**	**7.7**	**–3**	**0**	**0.0**	**10:31**	....	....	....	....	....	....	....	....	....
	♦ Anaheim	**NHL**	**24**	**1**	**10**	**11**	**10**	**1**	**0**	**0**	**23**	**4.3**	**3**	**0**	**0.0**	**14:38**	**7**	**1**	**1**	**2**	**2**	**1**	**0**	**0**	**6:04**
	NHL Totals		**231**	**19**	**58**	**77**	**166**	**12**	**0**	**4**	**312**	**6.1**		**0**	**0.0**	**15:34**	**7**	**1**	**1**	**2**	**2**	**1**	**0**	**0**	**6:04**

OHL All-Rookie Team (1996) • OHL Second All-Star Team (1998)

Traded to **Boston** by **Dallas** for Cameron Mann, June 23, 2001. • Missed majority of 2001-02 season recovering from shoulder injury suffered in game vs. St. Louis, October 21, 2001. Traded to **Toronto** by **Boston** for the rights to Kris Vernarsky, May 13, 2002. Traded to **Pittsburgh** by **Toronto** for Drake Berehowsky, February 11, 2004. Signed as a free agent by **Bjorkloven** (Sweden-2), September 17, 2004. Traded to **Florida** by **Pittsburgh** for Petr Taticek, March 9, 2006. Traded to **Anaheim** by **Florida** for Anaheim's 6th round choice (Corey Syvret) in 2007 Entry Draft, January 3, 2007. Signed as a free agent by **Salzburg** (Austria), August 2, 2007.

JACKMAN, Tim

(JAK-man, TIHM) **NYI**

Right wing. Shoots right. 6'4", 210 lbs. Born, Minot, ND, November 14, 1981. Columbus' 2nd choice, 38th overall, in 2001 Entry Draft.

Season	Club	League	GP	G	A	Pts	PIM	PP	SH	GW	S	%	+/-	TF	F%	Min	GP	G	A	Pts	PIM	PP	SH	GW	Min
1998-99	Park Center	High-MN	22	22	22	44	....	....	....	....	....	....	....	....	....	....	....	....	....	....	....	....	....	....	....
99-2000	Park Center	High-MN	19	34	22	56	....	....	....	....	....	....	....	....	....	....	....	....	....	....	....	....	....	....	....
	Twin Cities	USHL	25	11	9	20	58	....	....	....	....	....	....	....	....	....	13	8	5	13	12	....	....	....	....
2000-01	Minnesota State	WCHA	37	11	14	25	92	....	....	....	....	....	....	....	....	....	....	....	....	....	....	....	....	....	....
2001-02	Minnesota State	WCHA	36	14	14	28	86	....	....	....	....	....	....	....	....	....	....	....	....	....	....	....	....	....	....
2002-03	Syracuse Crunch	AHL	77	9	7	16	48	....	....	....	....	....	....	....	....	....	....	....	....	....	....	....	....	....	....
2003-04	**Columbus**	**NHL**	**19**	**1**	**2**	**3**	**16**	**0**	**0**	**0**	**18**	**5.6**	**–7**	**1**	**100.0**	**9:56**	....	....	....	....	....	....	....	....	....
	Syracuse Crunch	AHL	64	23	13	36	61	....	....	....	....	....	....	....	....	....	7	2	3	5	12	....	....	....	....
2004-05	Syracuse Crunch	AHL	73	14	21	35	98	....	....	....	....	....	....	....	....	....	....	....	....	....	....	....	....	....	....
2005-06	**Phoenix**	**NHL**	**8**	**0**	**0**	**0**	**21**	**0**	**0**	**0**	**4**	**0.0**	**1**	**1**	**0.0**	**7:13**	....	....	....	....	....	....	....	....	....
	San Antonio	AHL	50	7	13	20	127	....	....	....	....	....	....	....	....	....	....	....	....	....	....	....	....	....	....
	Manchester	AHL	18	2	3	5	33	....	....	....	....	....	....	....	....	....	7	0	3	3	20	....	....	....	....
2006-07	**Los Angeles**	**NHL**	**5**	**0**	**0**	**0**	**10**	**0**	**0**	**0**	**3**	**0.0**	**–1**	**0**	**0.0**	**6:36**	....	....	....	....	....	....	....	....	....
	Manchester	AHL	69	19	14	33	143	....	....	....	....	....	....	....	....	....	16	3	3	6	26	....	....	....	....
	NHL Totals		**32**	**1**	**2**	**3**	**47**	**0**	**0**	**0**	**25**	**4.0**		**2**	**50.0**	**8:44**	....	....	....	....	....	....	....	....	....

Traded to **Phoenix** by **Columbus** with Geoff Sanderson for Cale Hulse, Mike Rupp and Jason Chimera, October 8, 2005. Traded to **Los Angeles** by **Phoenix** for Yanick Lehoux, March 9, 2006. Signed as a free agent by **NY Islanders**, July 5, 2007.

JACQUES, Jean-Francois

(ZHAWK, ZHAWN-fran-SWUH) **EDM.**

Left wing. Shoots left. 6'4", 217 lbs. Born, Montreal, Que., April 29, 1985. Edmonton's 3rd choice, 68th overall, in 2003 Entry Draft.

Season	Club	League	GP	G	A	Pts	PIM	PP	SH	GW	S	%	+/-	TF	F%	Min	GP	G	A	Pts	PIM	PP	SH	GW	Min
2000-01	Cap-d-Madeleine	QAAA	39	22	13	35	28	....	....	....	....	....	....	....	....	....	10	5	8	13	14	....	....	....	....
2001-02	Baie-Comeau	QMJHL	66	10	14	24	136	....	....	....	....	....	....	....	....	....	5	1	0	1	2	....	....	....	....
2002-03	Baie-Comeau	QMJHL	67	12	21	33	123	....	....	....	....	....	....	....	....	....	12	4	2	6	13	....	....	....	....
2003-04	Baie-Comeau	QMJHL	59	20	24	44	70	....	....	....	....	....	....	....	....	....	4	1	0	1	4	....	....	....	....
2004-05	Baie-Comeau	QMJHL	69	36	42	78	56	....	....	....	....	....	....	....	....	....	6	3	5	8	6	....	....	....	....
	Edmonton	AHL	6	0	0	0	5	....	....	....	....	....	....	....	....	....	....	....	....	....	....	....	....	....	....
2005-06	**Edmonton**	**NHL**	**7**	**0**	**0**	**0**	**0**	**0**	**0**	**0**	**8**	**0.0**	**–3**	**0**	**0.0**	**6:43**	....	....	....	....	....	....	....	....	....
	Hamilton	AHL	65	24	19	43	131	....	....	....	....	....	....	....	....	....	....	....	....	....	....	....	....	....	....
2006-07	**Edmonton**	**NHL**	**37**	**0**	**0**	**0**	**33**	**0**	**0**	**0**	**23**	**0.0**	**–11**	**2**	**0.0**	**7:55**	....	....	....	....	....	....	....	....	....
	Wilkes-Barre	AHL	29	10	17	27	53	....	....	....	....	....	....	....	....	....	11	1	2	3	43	....	....	....	....
	NHL Totals		**44**	**0**	**0**	**0**	**33**	**0**	**0**	**0**	**31**	**0.0**		**2**	**0.0**	**7:43**	....	....	....	....	....	....	....	....	....

JAGR, Jaromir

(YAH-guhr, YAIR-oh-MEER) **NYR**

Right wing. Shoots left. 6'3", 240 lbs. Born, Kladno, Czech., February 15, 1972. Pittsburgh's 1st choice, 5th overall, in 1990 Entry Draft.

Season	Club	League	GP	G	A	Pts	PIM	PP	SH	GW	S	%	+/-	TF	F%	Min	GP	G	A	Pts	PIM	PP	SH	GW	Min
1984-85	Kladno Jr.	Czech-Jr.	34	24	17	41	....	....	....	....	....	....	....	....	....	....	....	....	....	....	....	....	....	....	....
1985-86	Kladno Jr.	Czech-Jr.	36	41	29	70	....	....	....	....	....	....	....	....	....	....	....	....	....	....	....	....	....	....	....
1986-87	Kladno Jr.	Czech-Jr.	30	35	35	70	....	....	....	....	....	....	....	....	....	....	....	....	....	....	....	....	....	....	....
1987-88	Kladno Jr.	Czech-Jr.	35	57	27	84	....	....	....	....	....	....	....	....	....	....	....	....	....	....	....	....	....	....	....
1988-89	Kladno	Czech	29	3	3	6	4	....	....	....	....	....	....	....	....	....	10	5	7	12	0	....	....	....	....
1989-90	Poldi Kladno	Czech	42	22	28	50	....	....	....	....	....	....	....	....	....	....	9	*8	2	10	....	....	....	....	....
1990-91♦	**Pittsburgh**	**NHL**	**80**	**27**	**30**	**57**	**42**	**7**	**0**	**4**	**136**	**19.9**	**–4**	....	....	....	**24**	**3**	**10**	**13**	**6**	**1**	**0**	**1**	....
1991-92♦	**Pittsburgh**	**NHL**	**70**	**32**	**37**	**69**	**34**	**4**	**0**	**4**	**194**	**16.5**	**12**	....	....	....	**21**	**11**	**13**	**24**	**6**	**2**	**0**	**4**	....
1992-93	**Pittsburgh**	**NHL**	**81**	**34**	**60**	**94**	**61**	**10**	**1**	**9**	**242**	**14.0**	**30**	....	....	....	**12**	**5**	**4**	**9**	**23**	**1**	**0**	**1**	....
1993-94	**Pittsburgh**	**NHL**	**80**	**32**	**67**	**99**	**61**	**9**	**0**	**6**	**298**	**10.7**	**15**	....	....	....	**6**	**2**	**4**	**6**	**16**	**0**	**0**	**1**	....
1994-95	HC Kladno	CzRep	11	8	14	22	10	....	....	....	....	....	....	....	....	....	....	....	....	....	....	....	....	....	....
	HC Bolzano	Euroliga	5	8	8	16	4	....	....	....	....	....	....	....	....	....	....	....	....	....	....	....	....	....	....
	HC Bolzano	Italy	1	0	0	0	0	....	....	....	....	....	....	....	....	....	....	....	....	....	....	....	....	....	....
	Schalke	German-2	1	1	10	11	0	....	....	....	....	....	....	....	....	....	....	....	....	....	....	....	....	....	....
	Pittsburgh	**NHL**	**48**	**32**	**38**	***70**	**37**	**8**	**3**	**7**	**192**	**16.7**	**23**	....	....	....	**12**	**10**	**5**	**15**	**6**	**2**	**1**	**1**	....
1995-96	**Pittsburgh**	**NHL**	**82**	**62**	**87**	**149**	**96**	**20**	**1**	**12**	**403**	**15.4**	**31**	....	....	....	**18**	**11**	**12**	**23**	**18**	**5**	**1**	**1**	....
1996-97	**Pittsburgh**	**NHL**	**63**	**47**	**48**	**95**	**40**	**11**	**2**	**6**	**234**	**20.1**	**22**	....	....	....	**5**	**4**	**4**	**8**	**4**	**2**	**0**	**0**	....
1997-98	**Pittsburgh**	**NHL**	**77**	**35**	***67**	***102**	**64**	**7**	**0**	**8**	**262**	**13.4**	**17**	....	....	....	**6**	**4**	**5**	**9**	**2**	**1**	**0**	**0**	....
	Czech Republic	Olympics	6	1	4	5	2	....	....	....	....	....	....	....	....	....	....	....	....	....	....	....	....	....	....
1998-99	**Pittsburgh**	**NHL**	**81**	**44**	***83**	***127**	**66**	**10**	**1**	**7**	**343**	**12.8**	**17**	**4**	**50.0**	**25:51**	**9**	**5**	**7**	**12**	**16**	**1**	**0**	**1**	**25:32**
99-2000	**Pittsburgh**	**NHL**	**63**	**42**	**54**	***96**	**50**	**10**	**0**	**5**	**290**	**14.5**	**25**	**9**	**22.2**	**23:12**	**11**	**8**	**8**	**16**	**6**	**2**	**0**	**4**	**24:32**
2000-01	**Pittsburgh**	**NHL**	**81**	**52**	***69**	***121**	**42**	**14**	**1**	**10**	**317**	**16.4**	**19**	**2**	**0.0**	**23:19**	**16**	**2**	**10**	**12**	**18**	**2**	**0**	**0**	**22:15**
2001-02	**Washington**	**NHL**	**69**	**31**	**48**	**79**	**30**	**10**	**0**	**3**	**197**	**15.7**	**0**	**2**	**50.0**	**21:43**	....	....	....	....	....	....	....	....	....
	Czech Republic	Olympics	4	2	3	5	4	....	....	....	....	....	....	....	....	....	....	....	....	....	....	....	....	....	....
2002-03	**Washington**	**NHL**	**75**	**36**	**41**	**77**	**38**	**13**	**2**	**9**	**290**	**12.4**	**5**	**5**	**20.0**	**21:18**	**6**	**2**	**5**	**7**	**2**	**1**	**0**	**0**	**25:13**
2003-04	**Washington**	**NHL**	**46**	**16**	**29**	**45**	**26**	**6**	**0**	**1**	**159**	**10.1**	**–4**	**1**	**0.0**	**21:05**	....	....	....	....	....	....	....	....	....
	NY Rangers	**NHL**	**31**	**15**	**14**	**29**	**12**	**4**	**0**	**2**	**98**	**15.3**	**–1**	**0**	**0.0**	**20:45**	....	....	....	....	....	....	....	....	....
2004-05	HC Rabat Kladno	CzRep	17	11	17	28	16	....	....	....	....	....	....	....	....	....	....	....	....	....	....	....	....	....	....
	Avangard Omsk	Russia	32	16	22	38	63	....	....	....	....	....	....	....	....	....	11	4	*10	*14	22	....	....	....	....
2005-06	**NY Rangers**	**NHL**	**82**	**54**	**69**	**123**	**72**	**24**	**0**	**9**	**368**	**14.7**	**34**	**6**	**16.7**	**22:05**	**3**	**0**	**1**	**1**	**2**	**0**	**0**	**0**	**13:47**
	Czech Republic	Olympics	8	2	5	7	6	....	....	....	....	....	....	....	....	....	....	....	....	....	....	....	....	....	....
2006-07	**NY Rangers**	**NHL**	**82**	**30**	**66**	**96**	**78**	**7**	**0**	**5**	**324**	**9.3**	**26**	**6**	**16.7**	**21:46**	**10**	**5**	**6**	**11**	**12**	**2**	**0**	**0**	**22:07**
	NHL Totals		**1191**	**621**	**907**	**1528**	**849**	**174**	**11**	**107**	**4347**	**14.3**		**35**	**22.9**	**22:32**	**159**	**72**	**94**	**166**	**137**	**22**	**2**	**14**	**23:05**

NHL All-Rookie Team (1991) • NHL First All-Star Team (1995, 1996, 1998, 1999, 2000, 2001, 2006) • Art Ross Trophy (1995, 1998, 1999, 2000, 2001) • NHL Second All-Star Team (1997) • Lester B. Pearson Award (1999, 2000, 2006) • Hart Memorial Trophy (1999)

Played in NHL All-Star Game (1992, 1993, 1996, 1998, 1999, 2000, 2002, 2003, 2004)

Traded to **Washington** by **Pittsburgh** with Frantisek Kucera for Kris Beech, Michal Sivek, Ross Lupaschuk and future considerations, July 11, 2001. Traded to **NY Rangers** by **Washington** for Anson Carter, January 23, 2004. Signed as a free agent by **Kladno** (CzRep), September 17, 2004. Signed as a free agent by **Omsk** (Russia), November 7, 2004.

JAMES, Connor

(JAYMZ, KAW-nuhr) **PIT.**

Right wing. Shoots right. 5'10", 180 lbs. Born, Calgary, Alta., August 25, 1982. Los Angeles' 11th choice, 279th overall, in 2002 Entry Draft.

Season	Club	League	GP	G	A	Pts	PIM	PP	SH	GW	S	%	+/-	TF	F%	Min	GP	G	A	Pts	PIM	PP	SH	GW	Min
1998-99	Calgary Buffaloes	AMHL	36	33	53	86	20	....	....	....	....	....	....	....	....	....	....	....	....	....	....	....	....	....	....
99-2000	Calgary Royals	AJHL	64	36	57	93	41	....	....	....	....	....	....	....	....	....	....	....	....	....	....	....	....	....	....
2000-01	U. of Denver	WCHA	38	8	19	27	14	....	....	....	....	....	....	....	....	....	....	....	....	....	....	....	....	....	....
2001-02	U. of Denver	WCHA	41	16	26	42	18	....	....	....	....	....	....	....	....	....	....	....	....	....	....	....	....	....	....
2002-03	U. of Denver	WCHA	41	20	23	43	12	....	....	....	....	....	....	....	....	....	....	....	....	....	....	....	....	....	....
2003-04	U. of Denver	WCHA	40	13	25	38	16	....	....	....	....	....	....	....	....	....	....	....	....	....	....	....	....	....	....
2004-05	Bakersfield	ECHL	51	21	25	46	34	....	....	....	....	....	....	....	....	....	5	3	1	4	0	....	....	....	....
	Manchester	AHL	14	2	1	3	10	....	....	....	....	....	....	....	....	....	3	0	0	0	0	....	....	....	....

			Regular Season														Playoffs								
Season	Club	League	GP	G	A	Pts	PIM	PP	SH	GW	S	%	+/-	TF	F%	Min	GP	G	A	Pts	PIM	PP	SH	GW	Min
2005-06	**Los Angeles**	**NHL**	**2**	**0**	**0**	**0**	**0**	**0**	**0**	**0**	**1**	**0.0**	**–1**	**6**	**33.3**	**7:19**									
	Manchester	AHL	77	17	25	42	43										7	0	0	0	2				
2006-07	Wilkes-Barre	AHL	70	12	20	32	29										11	4	4	8	8				
	NHL Totals		**2**	**0**	**0**	**0**	**0**	**0**	**0**	**0**	**1**	**0.0**		**6**	**33.3**	**7:19**									

NCAA Championship All-Tournament Team (2004)
Signed as a free agent by **Pittsburgh**, August 9, 2006.

JANCEVSKI, Dan

(jan-SEHV-skee, DAN) **T.B.**

Defense. Shoots left. 6'3", 220 lbs. Born, Windsor, Ont., June 15, 1981. Dallas' 2nd choice, 66th overall, in 1999 Entry Draft.

Season	Club	League	GP	G	A	Pts	PIM	PP	SH	GW	S	%	+/-	TF	F%	Min	GP	G	A	Pts	PIM	PP	SH	GW	Min
1995-96	Riverside Selects	Minor-ON	59	9	22	31	67																		
1996-97	Windsor Lions	Minor-ON	47	6	20	26	99																		
1997-98	Tecumseh	OHA-B	49	3	11	14	145																		
1998-99	London Knights	OHL	68	2	12	14	115										25	1	7	8	24				
99-2000	London Knights	OHL	59	8	15	23	138																		
2000-01	London Knights	OHL	39	4	23	27	95																		
	Sudbury Wolves	OHL	31	3	14	17	42										12	0	9	9	17				
2001-02	Utah Grizzlies	AHL	77	0	13	13	147										5	0	0	0	4				
2002-03	Utah Grizzlies	AHL	76	1	10	11	172										2	0	1	1	12				
2003-04	Utah Grizzlies	AHL	80	5	17	22	171																		
2004-05	Hamilton	AHL	80	6	20	26	163										4	0	0	0	2				
2005-06	**Dallas**	**NHL**	**2**	**0**	**0**	**0**	**0**	**0**	**0**	**0**	**0**	**0.0**	**1**	**0**	**0.0**	**9:13**									
	Iowa Stars	AHL	77	9	29	38	91										7	1	1	2	6				
2006-07	Hamilton	AHL	80	7	24	31	87										22	3	11	14	16				
	NHL Totals		**2**	**0**	**0**	**0**	**0**	**0**	**0**	**0**	**0**	**0.0**		**0**	**0.0**	**9:13**									

Signed as a free agent by **Montreal**, July 13, 2006. Signed as a free agent by **Tampa Bay**, July 6, 2007.

JANIK, Doug

(JAN-nihk, DUHG) **T.B.**

Defense. Shoots left. 6'2", 209 lbs. Born, Agawam, MA, March 26, 1980. Buffalo's 3rd choice, 55th overall, in 1999 Entry Draft.

Season	Club	League	GP	G	A	Pts	PIM	PP	SH	GW	S	%	+/-	TF	F%	Min	GP	G	A	Pts	PIM	PP	SH	GW	Min
1995-96	N.E. Jr. Whalers	EJHL	48	16	38	54																			
1996-97	N.E. Jr. Whalers	EJHL	39	12	24	36	22										11	5	9	14	10				
1997-98	USNTDP	U-18	29	6	13	19	43																		
	USNTDP	USHL	19	1	6	7	34																		
	USNTDP	NAHL	10	0	4	4	10										7	1	3	4	18				
1998-99	U. of Maine	H-East	35	3	13	16	44																		
99-2000	U. of Maine	H-East	36	6	14	20	54																		
2000-01	U. of Maine	H-East	39	3	15	18	52																		
2001-02	Rochester	AHL	80	6	17	23	100										2	0	0	0	0				
2002-03	**Buffalo**	**NHL**	**6**	**0**	**0**	**0**	**2**	**0**	**0**	**0**	**1**	**0.0**	**1**	**0**	**0.0**	**7:42**									
	Rochester	AHL	75	3	13	16	120										3	0	0	0	6				
2003-04	**Buffalo**	**NHL**	**4**	**0**	**0**	**0**	**19**	**0**	**0**	**0**	**3**	**0.0**	**0**	**0**	**0.0**	**8:26**									
	Rochester	AHL	74	2	14	16	109										16	1	2	3	22				
2004-05	Rochester	AHL	76	2	10	12	196										9	0	2	2	10				
2005-06	Rochester	AHL	71	5	19	24	161																		
	Buffalo	**NHL**															**5**	**1**	**0**	**1**	**2**	**0**	**0**	**0**	**10:30**
2006-07	**Tampa Bay**	**NHL**	**75**	**2**	**9**	**11**	**53**	**0**	**0**	**0**	**49**	**4.1**	**–11**	**0**	**0.0**	**14:28**	**1**	**0**	**0**	**0**	**0**	**0**	**0**	**0**	**3:42**
	NHL Totals		**85**	**2**	**9**	**11**	**74**	**0**	**0**	**0**	**53**	**3.8**		**0**	**0.0**	**13:43**	**6**	**1**	**0**	**1**	**2**	**0**	**0**	**0**	**9:22**

Signed as a free agent by **Tampa Bay**, July 6, 2006.

JANSSEN, Cam

(JAN-suhn, KAM) **N.J.**

Right wing. Shoots right. 6', 210 lbs. Born, St. Louis, MO, April 15, 1984. New Jersey's 6th choice, 117th overall, in 2002 Entry Draft.

Season	Club	League	GP	G	A	Pts	PIM	PP	SH	GW	S	%	+/-	TF	F%	Min	GP	G	A	Pts	PIM	PP	SH	GW	Min
2000-01	St. Louis Jr. Blues	CSJHL	45	1	2	3	244																		
2001-02	Windsor Spitfires	OHL	64	5	17	22	*268										10	0	0	0	13				
2002-03	Windsor Spitfires	OHL	50	1	12	13	211										7	0	1	1	22				
2003-04	Windsor Spitfires	OHL	35	4	9	13	144																		
	Guelph Storm	OHL	29	7	4	11	125										22	3	3	6	49				
2004-05	Albany River Rats	AHL	70	1	3	4	337																		
2005-06	**New Jersey**	**NHL**	**47**	**0**	**0**	**0**	**91**	**0**	**0**	**0**	**10**	**0.0**	**–3**	**2**	**100.0**	**4:44**	**9**	**0**	**0**	**0**	**26**	**0**	**0**	**0**	**3:43**
	Albany River Rats	AHL	26	1	3	4	117																		
2006-07	**New Jersey**	**NHL**	**48**	**1**	**0**	**1**	**114**	**0**	**0**	**0**	**9**	**11.1**	**–2**	**1**	**100.0**	**4:06**									
	Lowell Devils	AHL	9	0	1	1	29																		
	NHL Totals		**95**	**1**	**0**	**1**	**205**	**0**	**0**	**0**	**19**	**5.3**		**3**	**100.0**	**4:24**	**9**	**0**	**0**	**0**	**26**	**0**	**0**	**0**	**3:43**

JARRETT, Cole

(JAIR-reht, KOHL)

Wing. Shoots left. 6', 195 lbs. Born, Sault Ste. Marie, Ont., January 4, 1983. Columbus' 6th choice, 141st overall, in 2001 Entry Draft.

Season	Club	League	GP	G	A	Pts	PIM	PP	SH	GW	S	%	+/-	TF	F%	Min	GP	G	A	Pts	PIM	PP	SH	GW	Min
1998-99	Waterloo Siskins	OHA-B	44	6	10	16	43										4	2	2	4	5				
99-2000	Plymouth Whalers	OHL	57	3	7	10	47										23	3	7	10	19				
2000-01	Plymouth Whalers	OHL	60	12	36	48	98										19	6	12	18	29				
2001-02	Plymouth Whalers	OHL	51	14	24	38	92										6	1	1	2	18				
2002-03	Plymouth Whalers	OHL	58	14	41	55	138										14	5	6	11	29				
2003-04	Bridgeport	AHL	59	2	14	16	38																		
2004-05	Bridgeport	AHL	61	7	13	20	65																		
2005-06	**NY Islanders**	**NHL**	**1**	**0**	**0**	**0**	**0**	**0**	**0**	**0**	**1**	**0.0**	**1**	**0**	**0.0**	**13:48**									
	Bridgeport	AHL	78	3	20	23	88										7	0	0	0	13				
2006-07	Eisbaren Berlin	Germany	50	7	17	24	99										3	1	0	1	8				
	NHL Totals		**1**	**0**	**0**	**0**	**0**	**0**	**0**	**0**	**1**	**0.0**		**0**	**0.0**	**13:48**									

Signed as a free agent by **NY Islanders**, September 9, 2003. Signed as a free agent by **Berlin** (Germany), June 21, 2006.

JASPERS, Jason

(JAS-puhrs, JAY-suhn)

Center. Shoots left. 5'11", 207 lbs. Born, Thunder Bay, Ont., April 8, 1981. Phoenix's 4th choice, 71st overall, in 1999 Entry Draft.

Season	Club	League	GP	G	A	Pts	PIM	PP	SH	GW	S	%	+/-	TF	F%	Min	GP	G	A	Pts	PIM	PP	SH	GW	Min
1996-97	Thunder Bay	TBAHA	70	51	69	120	67																		
1997-98	Thunder Bay	TBAHA	72	45	75	120	90																		
1998-99	Sudbury Wolves	OHL	68	28	33	61	81										4	2	1	3	13				
99-2000	Sudbury Wolves	OHL	68	46	61	107	107										12	4	6	10	27				
2000-01	Sudbury Wolves	OHL	63	42	42	84	77										12	3	16	19	18				
2001-02	**Phoenix**	**NHL**	**4**	**0**	**1**	**1**	**4**	**0**	**0**	**0**	**1**	**0.0**	**–1**	**14**	**35.7**	**8:07**									
	Springfield	AHL	71	25	23	48	55																		
2002-03	**Phoenix**	**NHL**	**2**	**0**	**0**	**0**	**0**	**0**	**0**	**0**	**0**	**0.0**	**–1**	**14**	**57.1**	**7:17**									
	Springfield	AHL	63	4	15	19	57										6	0	0	0	4				
2003-04	**Phoenix**	**NHL**	**3**	**0**	**0**	**0**	**2**	**0**	**0**	**0**	**3**	**0.0**	**–1**	**19**	**57.9**	**11:24**									
	Springfield	AHL	58	16	22	38	56																		
2004-05	Utah Grizzlies	AHL	11	0	3	3	6																		
	Springfield	AHL	48	12	17	29	45																		
2005-06	Springfield	AHL	77	29	37	66	86																		
2006-07	Adler Mannheim	Germany	48	14	15	29	102										11	6	7	13	6				
	NHL Totals		**9**	**0**	**1**	**1**	**6**	**0**	**0**	**0**	**4**	**0.0**		**47**	**51.1**	**9:01**									

OHL Second All-Star Team (2000)
Loaned to **Springfield** (AHL) by **Utah** (AHL) for cash, November 20, 2004. Signed as a free agent by **Tampa Bay**, August 18, 2005. Signed as a free agent by **Mannheim** (Germany), July 18, 2006.

JILLSON, Jeff
(JIHL-suhn, JEHF) **COL.**

Defense. Shoots right. 6'3", 215 lbs. Born, North Smithfield, RI, July 24, 1980. San Jose's 1st choice, 14th overall, in 1999 Entry Draft.

			Regular Season														Playoffs								
Season	Club	League	GP	G	A	Pts	PIM	PP	SH	GW	S	%	+/-	TF	F%	Min	GP	G	A	Pts	PIM	PP	SH	GW	Min
1995-96	Mount St. Charles	High-RI	15	8	7	15	15	....	....	....	....	....	....	....	....	....	5	1	1	2	4	....	....	....	....
1996-97	Mount St. Charles	High-RI	15	16	14	30	20	....	....	....	....	....	....	....	....	....	4	0	4	4	6	....	....	....	....
1997-98	Mount St. Charles	High-RI	15	10	13	23	32	....	....	....	....	....	....	....	....	....	5	4	5	9	6	....	....	....	....
1998-99	U. of Michigan	CCHA	38	5	19	24	71	....	....	....	....	....	....	....	....	....	....	....	....	....	....	....	....	....	....
99-2000	U. of Michigan	CCHA	38	8	26	34	115	....	....	....	....	....	....	....	....	....	....	....	....	....	....	....	....	....	....
2000-01	U. of Michigan	CCHA	43	10	20	30	74	....	....	....	....	....	....	....	....	....	....	....	....	....	....	....	....	....	....
2001-02	San Jose	NHL	48	5	13	18	29	3	0	2	47	10.6	2	0	0.0	14:36	4	0	0	0	0	0	0	0	5:45
	Cleveland Barons	AHL	27	2	13	15	45	....	....	....	....	....	....	....	....	....	....	....	....	....	....	....	....	....	....
2002-03	San Jose	NHL	26	0	6	6	9	0	0	0	22	0.0	–7	0	0.0	13:45	....	....	....	....	....	....	....	....	....
	Cleveland Barons	AHL	19	3	5	8	12	....	....	....	....	....	....	....	....	....	....	....	....	....	....	....	....	....	....
	Providence Bruins	AHL	30	4	11	15	26	....	....	....	....	....	....	....	....	....	4	0	2	2	8	....	....	....	....
2003-04	Boston	NHL	50	4	10	14	35	1	0	1	80	5.0	–1	0	0.0	17:53	....	....	....	....	....	....	....	....	....
	Buffalo	NHL	14	0	3	3	19	0	0	0	35	0.0	–3	0	0.0	18:21	....	....	....	....	....	....	....	....	....
2004-05	Rochester	AHL	78	12	17	29	46	....	....	....	....	....	....	....	....	....	9	1	1	2	12	....	....	....	....
2005-06	Buffalo	NHL	2	0	0	0	4	0	0	0	1	0.0	0	0	0.0	14:40	4	0	0	0	0	0	0	0	11:41
	Rochester	AHL	73	10	20	30	94	....	....	....	....	....	....	....	....	....	....	....	....	....	....	....	....	....	....
2006-07	Eisbaren Berlin	Germany	30	2	9	11	48	....	....	....	....	....	....	....	....	....	1	0	0	0	2	....	....	....	....
	NHL Totals		140	9	32	41	96	4	0	3	185	4.9		0	0.0	15:59	8	0	0	0	0	0	0	0	8:43

CCHA All-Rookie Team (1999) • CCHA First All-Star Team (2000, 2001) • NCAA West First All-American Team (2000) • NCAA West Second All-American Team (2001)

Traded to **Boston** by **San Jose** with Jeff Hackett for Kyle McLaren and Boston's 4th round choice (Torrey Mitchell) in 2004 Entry Draft, January 23, 2003. Traded to **San Jose** by **Boston** for Brad Boyes, March 9, 2004. Traded to **Buffalo** by **San Jose** with San Jose's compensatory 7th round choice (Andrew Orpik) in 2005 Entry Draft for Curtis Brown and Andy Delmore, March 9, 2004. Signed as a free agent by **Berlin** (Germany), October 25, 2006. Signed as a free agent by **Colorado**, July 17, 2007.

JOHANSSON, Jonas
(yoh-HAHN-suhn, YOH-nuhs)

Right wing. Shoots right. 6'3", 215 lbs. Born, Jonkoping, Sweden, March 18, 1984. Colorado's 1st choice, 28th overall, in 2002 Entry Draft.

Season	Club	League	GP	G	A	Pts	PIM	PP	SH	GW	S	%	+/-	TF	F%	Min	GP	G	A	Pts	PIM	PP	SH	GW	Min
99-2000	HV 71 Jr.	Swe-Jr.	9	6	3	9	2	....	....	....	....	....	....	....	....	....	2	0	0	0	4	....	....	....	....
2000-01	HV 71 Jr.	Swe-Jr.	27	13	8	21	14	....	....	....	....	....	....	....	....	....	2	1	0	1	0	....	....	....	....
2001-02	HV 71 Jr.	Swe-Jr.	26	15	19	34	20	....	....	....	....	....	....	....	....	....	....	....	....	....	....	....	....	....	....
	HV 71 Jonkoping	Sweden	5	0	0	0	0	....	....	....	....	....	....	....	....	....	2	0	0	0	0	....	....	....	....
2002-03	Kamloops Blazers	WHL	26	10	25	35	8	....	....	....	....	....	....	....	....	....	6	1	2	3	4	....	....	....	....
2003-04	Kamloops Blazers	WHL	72	18	19	37	70	....	....	....	....	....	....	....	....	....	5	2	2	4	4	....	....	....	....
2004-05	Portland Pirates	AHL	50	3	6	9	8	....	....	....	....	....	....	....	....	....	....	....	....	....	....	....	....	....	....
	South Carolina	ECHL	5	4	2	6	10	....	....	....	....	....	....	....	....	....	....	....	....	....	....	....	....	....	....
2005-06	Washington	NHL	1	0	0	0	2	0	0	0	0	0.0	0	0	0.0	4:14	....	....	....	....	....	....	....	....	....
	Lulea HF	Sweden	10	0	0	0	0	....	....	....	....	....	....	....	....	....	....	....	....	....	....	....	....	....	....
	Hershey Bears	AHL	37	5	5	10	24	....	....	....	....	....	....	....	....	....	2	1	0	1	4	....	....	....	....
	South Carolina	ECHL	5	5	3	8	2	....	....	....	....	....	....	....	....	....	....	....	....	....	....	....	....	....	....
2006-07	Hershey Bears	AHL	44	5	19	24	48	....	....	....	....	....	....	....	....	....	....	....	....	....	....	....	....	....	....
	Grand Rapids	AHL	12	3	2	5	10	....	....	....	....	....	....	....	....	....	....	....	....	....	....	....	....	....	....
	NHL Totals		1	0	0	0	2	0	0	0	0	0.0		0	0.0	4:14	....	....	....	....	....	....	....	....	....

Traded to **Washington** by **Colorado** with Bates Battaglia for Steve Konowalchuk and Washington's 3rd round choice (later traded to Carolina – Carolina selected Casey Borer) in 2004 Entry Draft, October 22, 2003.

JOHNSON, Aaron
(JAWN-suhn, AIR-ruhn) **NYI**

Defense. Shoots left. 6'2", 211 lbs. Born, Port Hawkesbury, N.S., April 30, 1983. Columbus' 4th choice, 85th overall, in 2001 Entry Draft.

Season	Club	League	GP	G	A	Pts	PIM	PP	SH	GW	S	%	+/-	TF	F%	Min	GP	G	A	Pts	PIM	PP	SH	GW	Min
1998-99	Cape Breton	NSAHA	56	28	42	70	98	....	....	....	....	....	....	....	....	....	....	....	....	....	....	....	....	....	....
99-2000	Rimouski Oceanic	QMJHL	63	1	14	15	57	....	....	....	....	....	....	....	....	....	8	0	0	0	0	....	....	....	....
2000-01	Rimouski Oceanic	QMJHL	64	12	41	53	128	....	....	....	....	....	....	....	....	....	11	2	4	6	35	....	....	....	....
2001-02	Rimouski Oceanic	QMJHL	68	17	49	66	172	....	....	....	....	....	....	....	....	....	7	1	2	3	12	....	....	....	....
2002-03	Rimouski Oceanic	QMJHL	25	4	20	24	41	....	....	....	....	....	....	....	....	....	....	....	....	....	....	....	....	....	....
	Quebec Remparts	QMJHL	32	6	31	37	41	....	....	....	....	....	....	....	....	....	11	4	4	8	25	....	....	....	....
2003-04	Columbus	NHL	29	2	6	8	32	0	0	1	33	6.1	–2	0	0.0	15:02	....	....	....	....	....	....	....	....	....
	Syracuse Crunch	AHL	49	6	15	21	83	....	....	....	....	....	....	....	....	....	7	2	3	5	27	....	....	....	....
2004-05	Syracuse Crunch	AHL	77	6	17	23	140	....	....	....	....	....	....	....	....	....	....	....	....	....	....	....	....	....	....
2005-06	Columbus	NHL	26	2	6	8	23	1	0	1	28	7.1	9	0	0.0	14:12	....	....	....	....	....	....	....	....	....
	Syracuse Crunch	AHL	49	5	24	29	122	....	....	....	....	....	....	....	....	....	6	1	3	4	19	....	....	....	....
2006-07	Columbus	NHL	61	3	7	10	38	0	0	0	52	5.8	–9	0	0.0	12:44	....	....	....	....	....	....	....	....	....
	NHL Totals		116	7	19	26	93	1	0	2	113	6.2		0	0.0	13:38	....	....	....	....	....	....	....	....	....

Signed as a free agent by **NY Islanders**, July 12, 2007.

JOHNSON, Jack
(JAWN-suhn, JAK) **L.A.**

Defense. Shoots left. 6'1", 201 lbs. Born, Indianapolis, IN, January 13, 1987. Carolina's 1st choice, 3rd overall, in 2005 Entry Draft.

Season	Club	League	GP	G	A	Pts	PIM	PP	SH	GW	S	%	+/-	TF	F%	Min	GP	G	A	Pts	PIM	PP	SH	GW	Min
2002-03	Shat.-St. Mary's	High-MN	48	15	27	42	....	....	....	....	....	....	....	....	....	....	....	....	....	....	....	....	....	....	....
2003-04	USNTDP	U-17	31	12	9	21	78	....	....	....	....	....	....	....	....	....	....	....	....	....	....	....	....	....	....
	USNTDP	NAHL	29	3	12	15	93	....	....	....	....	....	....	....	....	....	....	....	....	....	....	....	....	....	....
2004-05	USNTDP	U-18	26	5	9	14	86	....	....	....	....	....	....	....	....	....	....	....	....	....	....	....	....	....	....
	USNTDP	NAHL	12	7	10	17	57	....	....	....	....	....	....	....	....	....	....	....	....	....	....	....	....	....	....
2005-06	U. of Michigan	CCHA	38	10	22	32	*149	....	....	....	....	....	....	....	....	....	....	....	....	....	....	....	....	....	....
2006-07	U. of Michigan	CCHA	36	16	23	39	87	....	....	....	....	....	....	....	....	....	....	....	....	....	....	....	....	....	....
	Los Angeles	NHL	5	0	0	0	18	0	0	0	5	0.0	–5	0	0.0	21:23	....	....	....	....	....	....	....	....	....
	NHL Totals		5	0	0	0	18	0	0	0	5	0.0		0	0.0	21:23	....	....	....	....	....	....	....	....	....

CCHA All-Rookie Team (2006) • CCHA First All-Star Team (2007) • NCAA West First All-American Team (2007)

Traded to **Los Angeles** by **Carolina** with Oleg Tverdovsky for Eric Belanger and Tim Gleason, September 29, 2006.

JOHNSON, Mike
(JAWN-suhn, MIGHK)

Right wing. Shoots right. 6'2", 202 lbs. Born, Scarborough, Ont., October 3, 1974.

Season	Club	League	GP	G	A	Pts	PIM	PP	SH	GW	S	%	+/-	TF	F%	Min	GP	G	A	Pts	PIM	PP	SH	GW	Min
1991-92	Hillcrest Summits	MTHL	45	43	66	109	....	....	....	....	....	....	....	....	....	....	20	10	19	29	....	....	....	....	....
1992-93	Aurora Eagles	MTJHL	48	25	40	65	18	....	....	....	....	....	....	....	....	....	7	7	15	22	....	....	....	....	....
1993-94	Bowling Green	CCHA	38	6	14	20	18	....	....	....	....	....	....	....	....	....	....	....	....	....	....	....	....	....	....
1994-95	Bowling Green	CCHA	37	16	33	49	35	....	....	....	....	....	....	....	....	....	....	....	....	....	....	....	....	....	....
1995-96	Bowling Green	CCHA	30	12	19	31	22	....	....	....	....	....	....	....	....	....	....	....	....	....	....	....	....	....	....
1996-97	Bowling Green	CCHA	38	30	32	62	46	....	....	....	....	....	....	....	....	....	....	....	....	....	....	....	....	....	....
	Toronto	NHL	13	2	2	4	4	0	1	1	27	7.4	–2	....	....	....	....	....	....	....	....	....	....	....	....
1997-98	Toronto	NHL	82	15	32	47	24	5	0	0	143	10.5	–4	....	....	....	....	....	....	....	....	....	....	....	....
1998-99	Toronto	NHL	79	20	24	44	35	5	3	2	149	13.4	13	15	53.3	16:16	17	3	2	5	4	0	0	1	16:28
99-2000	Toronto	NHL	52	11	14	25	23	2	1	3	89	12.4	8	2	50.0	15:22	....	....	....	....	....	....	....	....	....
	Tampa Bay	NHL	28	10	12	22	4	4	0	0	43	23.3	–2	5	60.0	20:33	....	....	....	....	....	....	....	....	....
2000-01	Tampa Bay	NHL	64	11	27	38	38	3	1	0	107	10.3	–10	2	0.0	18:13	....	....	....	....	....	....	....	....	....
	Phoenix	NHL	12	2	3	5	4	1	0	0	17	11.8	0	0	0.0	12:12	....	....	....	....	....	....	....	....	....
2001-02	Phoenix	NHL	57	5	22	27	28	1	2	0	73	6.8	14	13	30.8	15:49	5	1	1	2	6	0	0	0	14:45
2002-03	Phoenix	NHL	82	23	40	63	47	8	0	3	178	12.9	9	34	50.0	19:39	....	....	....	....	....	....	....	....	....
2003-04	Phoenix	NHL	11	1	9	10	10	1	0	0	17	5.9	–1	2	50.0	19:50	....	....	....	....	....	....	....	....	....
2004-05	Farjestad	Sweden	8	1	2	3	4	....	....	....	....	....	....	....	....	....	6	0	2	2	4	....	....	....	....
2005-06	Phoenix	NHL	80	16	38	54	50	6	1	3	145	11.0	7	234	44.4	16:34	....	....	....	....	....	....	....	....	....
2006-07	Montreal	NHL	80	11	20	31	40	1	2	1	131	8.4	6	38	31.6	15:23	....	....	....	....	....	....	....	....	....
	NHL Totals		640	127	243	370	307	37	11	13	1119	11.3		345	43.5	16:59	22	4	3	7	10	0	0	1	16:05

NHL All-Rookie Team (1998)

Signed as a free agent by **Toronto**, March 16, 1997. Traded to **Tampa Bay** by **Toronto** with Marek Posmyk and Toronto's 5th (Pavel Sedov) and 6th (Aaron Gionet) round choices in 2000 Entry Draft for Darcy Tucker and Tampa Bay's 4th round choice (Miguel Delisle) in 2000 Entry Draft, February 9, 2000. Traded to **Phoenix** by **Tampa Bay** with Paul Mara, Ruslan Zainullin and NY Islanders' 2nd round choice (previously acquired, Phoenix selected Matthew Spiller) in 2001 Entry Draft for Nikolai Khabibulin and Stan Neckar, March 5, 2001. • Missed majority of 2003-04 season recovering from shoulder injury suffered in game vs. Los Angeles, November 1, 2003. Signed as a free agent by **Farjestad** (Sweden), January 31, 2005. Traded to **Montreal** by **Phoenix** for Montreal's 4th round choice (Vladimir Ruzicka) in 2007 Entry Draft, July 12, 2006.

JOHNSON, Ryan

(JAWN-suhn, RIGH-uhn) **ST.L.**

Center. Shoots left. 6'1", 211 lbs. Born, Thunder Bay, Ont., June 14, 1976. Florida's 4th choice, 36th overall, in 1994 Entry Draft.

			Regular Season														Playoffs								
Season	Club	League	GP	G	A	Pts	PIM	PP	SH	GW	S	%	+/-	TF	F%	Min	GP	G	A	Pts	PIM	PP	SH	GW	Min
1992-93	Thunder Bay	TBAHA	60	25	33	58	....	....	....	....	....	....	....	....	....	....	....	....	....	....	....	....	....	....	....
1993-94	Thunder Bay	USHL	48	14	36	50	28	....	....	....	....	....	....	....	....	....	....	....	....	....	....	....	....	....	....
1994-95	North Dakota	WCHA	38	6	22	28	39	....	....	....	....	....	....	....	....	....	....	....	....	....	....	....	....	....	....
1995-96	North Dakota	WCHA	21	2	17	19	14	....	....	....	....	....	....	....	....	....	....	....	....	....	....	....	....	....	....
	Canada	Nat-Tm	28	5	12	17	14	....	....	....	....	....	....	....	....	....	....	....	....	....	....	....	....	....	....
1996-97	Carolina	AHL	79	18	24	42	28	....	....	....	....	....	....	....	....	....	....	....	....	....	....	....	....	....	....
1997-98	**Florida**	**NHL**	**10**	**0**	**2**	**2**	**0**	**0**	**0**	**0**	**6**	**0.0**	**-4**	....	....	....	....	....	....	....	....	....	....	....	....
	New Haven	AHL	64	19	48	67	12	....	....	....	....	....	....	....	....	....	3	0	1	1	0	....	....	....	....
1998-99	**Florida**	**NHL**	**1**	**1**	**0**	**1**	**0**	**0**	**0**	**0**	**1**	**100.0**	**0**	**16**	**37.5**	**15:26**	....	....	....	....	....	....	....	....	....
	New Haven	AHL	37	8	19	27	18	....	....	....	....	....	....	....	....	....	....	....	....	....	....	....	....	....	....
99-2000	**Florida**	**NHL**	**66**	**4**	**12**	**16**	**14**	**0**	**0**	**0**	**44**	**9.1**	**1**	**684**	**51.8**	**11:47**	....	....	....	....	....	....	....	....	....
	Tampa Bay	**NHL**	**14**	**0**	**2**	**2**	**2**	**0**	**0**	**0**	**5**	**0.0**	**-9**	**117**	**53.0**	**11:02**	....	....	....	....	....	....	....	....	....
2000-01	**Tampa Bay**	**NHL**	**80**	**7**	**14**	**21**	**44**	**1**	**0**	**0**	**71**	**9.9**	**-20**	**951**	**48.9**	**15:47**	....	....	....	....	....	....	....	....	....
2001-02	**Florida**	**NHL**	**29**	**1**	**3**	**4**	**10**	**0**	**0**	**0**	**24**	**4.2**	**-5**	**336**	**47.9**	**13:00**	....	....	....	....	....	....	....	....	....
2002-03	**Florida**	**NHL**	**58**	**2**	**5**	**7**	**26**	**0**	**0**	**0**	**54**	**3.7**	**-13**	**689**	**48.0**	**10:40**	....	....	....	....	....	....	....	....	....
	St. Louis	**NHL**	**17**	**0**	**0**	**0**	**12**	**0**	**0**	**0**	**13**	**0.0**	**0**	**180**	**51.7**	**10:34**	**6**	**0**	**2**	**2**	**6**	**0**	**0**	**0**	**8:14**
2003-04	**St. Louis**	**NHL**	**69**	**4**	**7**	**11**	**8**	**0**	**1**	**1**	**36**	**11.1**	**-2**	**537**	**53.6**	**9:54**	**3**	**0**	**0**	**0**	**0**	**0**	**0**	**0**	**6:11**
2004-05	Missouri	UHL	29	7	14	21	12	....	....	....	....	....	....	....	....	....	6	1	0	1	13	....	....	....	....
2005-06	**St. Louis**	**NHL**	**65**	**3**	**6**	**9**	**33**	**1**	**1**	**0**	**57**	**5.3**	**-21**	**569**	**55.9**	**11:24**	....	....	....	....	....	....	....	....	....
2006-07	**St. Louis**	**NHL**	**59**	**7**	**4**	**11**	**47**	**0**	**2**	**0**	**50**	**14.0**	**-7**	**525**	**55.4**	**12:21**	....	....	....	....	....	....	....	....	....
	NHL Totals		**468**	**29**	**55**	**84**	**196**	**2**	**4**	**1**	**361**	**8.0**		**4604**	**51.5**	**12:05**	**9**	**0**	**2**	**2**	**6**	**0**	**0**	**0**	**7:33**

Traded to **Tampa Bay** by **Florida** with Dwayne Hay for Mike Sillinger, March 14, 2000. Traded to **Florida** by **Tampa Bay** with Tampa Bay's 6th round choice (later traded back to Tampa Bay – Tampa Bay selected Doug O'Brien) in 2003 Entry Draft for Vaclav Prospal, July 10, 2001. • Missed majority of 2001-02 season recovering from head injury suffered in game vs. St. Louis, December 22, 2001. Claimed on waivers by **St. Louis** from **Florida**, February 19, 2003. Signed as a free agent by **Missouri** (UHL), February 3, 2005.

JOHNSSON, Kim

(YAWN-suhn, KIHM) **MIN.**

Defense. Shoots left. 6'1", 200 lbs. Born, Malmo, Sweden, March 16, 1976. NY Rangers' 15th choice, 286th overall, in 1994 Entry Draft.

			Regular Season														Playoffs								
Season	Club	League	GP	G	A	Pts	PIM	PP	SH	GW	S	%	+/-	TF	F%	Min	GP	G	A	Pts	PIM	PP	SH	GW	Min
1993-94	Malmo IF Jr.	Swe-Jr.	14	5	3	8	14	....	....	....	....	....	....	....	....	....	....	....	....	....	....	....	....	....	....
	Malmo IF	Sweden	2	0	0	0	0	....	....	....	....	....	....	....	....	....	....	....	....	....	....	....	....	....	....
1994-95	Malmo IF Jr.	Swe-Jr.	29	6	15	21	40	....	....	....	....	....	....	....	....	....	....	....	....	....	....	....	....	....	....
	Malmo IF	Sweden	13	0	0	0	4	....	....	....	....	....	....	....	....	....	1	0	0	0	0	....	....	....	....
1995-96	Malmo IF	Sweden	38	2	0	2	30	....	....	....	....	....	....	....	....	....	4	0	1	1	8	....	....	....	....
1996-97	Malmo	Sweden	49	4	9	13	42	....	....	....	....	....	....	....	....	....	4	0	0	0	2	....	....	....	....
1997-98	Malmo	Sweden	45	5	9	14	29	....	....	....	....	....	....	....	....	....	....	....	....	....	....	....	....	....	....
1998-99	Malmo	Sweden	49	9	8	17	76	....	....	....	....	....	....	....	....	....	8	2	3	5	12	....	....	....	....
99-2000	**NY Rangers**	**NHL**	**76**	**6**	**15**	**21**	**46**	**1**	**0**	**1**	**101**	**5.9**	**-13**	**0**	**0.0**	**18:06**	....	....	....	....	....	....	....	....	....
2000-01	**NY Rangers**	**NHL**	**75**	**5**	**21**	**26**	**40**	**4**	**0**	**0**	**104**	**4.8**	**-3**	**0**	**0.0**	**21:16**	....	....	....	....	....	....	....	....	....
2001-02	**Philadelphia**	**NHL**	**82**	**11**	**30**	**41**	**42**	**5**	**0**	**1**	**150**	**7.3**	**12**	**0**	**0.0**	**23:02**	**5**	**0**	**0**	**0**	**2**	**0**	**0**	**0**	**22:48**
	Sweden	Olympics	4	1	1	2	0	....	....	....	....	....	....	....	....	....	....	....	....	....	....	....	....	....	....
2002-03	**Philadelphia**	**NHL**	**82**	**10**	**29**	**39**	**38**	**5**	**0**	**2**	**159**	**6.3**	**11**	**0**	**0.0**	**24:05**	**13**	**0**	**3**	**3**	**8**	**0**	**0**	**0**	**26:07**
2003-04	**Philadelphia**	**NHL**	**80**	**13**	**29**	**42**	**26**	**4**	**0**	**3**	**189**	**6.9**	**16**	**0**	**0.0**	**24:27**	**15**	**2**	**6**	**8**	**8**	**0**	**0**	**1**	**26:11**
2004-05	HC Ambri-Piotta	Swiss	24	4	10	14	61	....	....	....	....	....	....	....	....	....	....	....	....	....	....	....	....	....	....
2005-06	**Philadelphia**	**NHL**	**47**	**6**	**19**	**25**	**34**	**3**	**0**	**0**	**97**	**6.2**	**5**	**0**	**0.0**	**23:17**	....	....	....	....	....	....	....	....	....
	Sweden	Olympics	DID NOT PLAY																						
2006-07	**Minnesota**	**NHL**	**76**	**3**	**19**	**22**	**64**	**3**	**0**	**0**	**98**	**3.1**	**-4**	**0**	**0.0**	**23:33**	**4**	**0**	**0**	**0**	**2**	**0**	**0**	**0**	**23:06**
	NHL Totals		**518**	**54**	**162**	**216**	**290**	**25**	**0**	**7**	**898**	**6.0**		**0**	**0.0**	**22:32**	**37**	**2**	**9**	**11**	**20**	**0**	**0**	**1**	**25:22**

Traded to **Philadelphia** by **NY Rangers** with Jan Hlavac, Pavel Brendl and NY Rangers' 3rd round choice (Stefan Ruzicka) in 2003 Entry Draft for Eric Lindros, August 20, 2001. Signed as a free agent by **Ambri-Piotta** (Swiss), September 18, 2004. Signed as a free agent by **Minnesota**, July 1, 2006.

JOKELA, Mikko

(YOH-kih-lah, MEE-koh) **VAN.**

Defense. Shoots right. 6'1", 212 lbs. Born, Lappeenranta, Finland, March 4, 1980. New Jersey's 5th choice, 96th overall, in 1998 Entry Draft.

			Regular Season														Playoffs								
Season	Club	League	GP	G	A	Pts	PIM	PP	SH	GW	S	%	+/-	TF	F%	Min	GP	G	A	Pts	PIM	PP	SH	GW	Min
1995-96	KalPa Kuopio U18	Fin-U18	9	2	1	3	20	....	....	....	....	....	....	....	....	....	....	....	....	....	....	....	....	....	....
	KalPa Kuopio Jr.	Fin-Jr.	2	0	0	0	0	....	....	....	....	....	....	....	....	....	....	....	....	....	....	....	....	....	....
1996-97	KalPa Kuopio U18	Fin-U18	11	3	2	5	8	....	....	....	....	....	....	....	....	....	5	1	1	2	4	....	....	....	....
	KalPa Kuopio Jr.	Fin-Jr.	34	2	5	7	18	....	....	....	....	....	....	....	....	....	....	....	....	....	....	....	....	....	....
1997-98	HIFK Helsinki U18	Fin-U18	4	5	1	6	2	....	....	....	....	....	....	....	....	....	....	....	....	....	....	....	....	....	....
	HIFK Helsinki Jr.	Fin-Jr.	22	2	5	7	14	....	....	....	....	....	....	....	....	....	....	....	....	....	....	....	....	....	....
	HIFK Helsinki	Finland	16	0	0	0	0	....	....	....	....	....	....	....	....	....	....	....	....	....	....	....	....	....	....
	Hermes Kokkola	Finland-2	6	0	1	1	2	....	....	....	....	....	....	....	....	....	....	....	....	....	....	....	....	....	....
1998-99	HIFK Helsinki	Finland	3	0	0	0	2	....	....	....	....	....	....	....	....	....	....	....	....	....	....	....	....	....	....
	KalPa Kuopio Jr.	Fin-Jr.	8	7	4	11	8	....	....	....	....	....	....	....	....	....	....	....	....	....	....	....	....	....	....
	KalPa Kuopio	Finland	42	1	2	3	18	....	....	....	....	....	....	....	....	....	....	....	....	....	....	....	....	....	....
	KalPa Kuopio	Finland-Q	....	....	....	....	....	....	....	....	....	....	....	....	....	....	6	0	0	0	2	....	....	....	....
99-2000	SaiPa Jr.	Fin-Jr.	1	0	0	0	0	....	....	....	....	....	....	....	....	....	....	....	....	....	....	....	....	....	....
	SaiPa	Finland	48	0	5	5	50	....	....	....	....	....	....	....	....	....	....	....	....	....	....	....	....	....	....
2000-01	SaiPa Jr.	Fin-Jr.	4	2	2	4	2	....	....	....	....	....	....	....	....	....	2	0	0	0	2	....	....	....	....
	KooKoo Kouvola	Finland-2	5	3	0	3	0	....	....	....	....	....	....	....	....	....	....	....	....	....	....	....	....	....	....
	SaiPa	Finland	50	1	0	1	26	....	....	....	....	....	....	....	....	....	....	....	....	....	....	....	....	....	....
2001-02	Albany River Rats	AHL	56	5	13	18	28	....	....	....	....	....	....	....	....	....	....	....	....	....	....	....	....	....	....
2002-03	Albany River Rats	AHL	44	8	11	19	35	....	....	....	....	....	....	....	....	....	....	....	....	....	....	....	....	....	....
	Vancouver	**NHL**	**1**	**0**	**0**	**0**	**0**	**0**	**0**	**0**	**3**	**0.0**	**0**	**0**	**0.0**	**5:09**	....	....	....	....	....	....	....	....	....
	Manitoba Moose	AHL	32	3	7	10	17	....	....	....	....	....	....	....	....	....	14	1	4	5	2	....	....	....	....
2003-04	Manitoba Moose	AHL	78	5	10	15	52	....	....	....	....	....	....	....	....	....	....	....	....	....	....	....	....	....	....
2004-05	HPK Hameenlinna	Finland	55	4	12	16	102	....	....	....	....	....	....	....	....	....	10	2	1	3	12	....	....	....	....
2005-06	HPK Hameenlinna	Finland	25	6	2	8	65	....	....	....	....	....	....	....	....	....	11	2	3	5	43	....	....	....	....
2006-07	HPK Hameenlinna	Finland	29	5	12	17	40	....	....	....	....	....	....	....	....	....	9	1	3	4	12	....	....	....	....
	NHL Totals		**1**	**0**	**0**	**0**	**0**	**0**	**0**	**0**	**3**	**0.0**		**0**	**0.0**	**5:09**	....	....	....	....	....	....	....	....	....

Traded to **Vancouver** by **New Jersey** for Steve Kariya, January 24, 2003. Signed as a free agent by **Hameenlinna** (Finland), April 17, 2004.

JOKINEN, Jussi

(YOH-kih-nihn, YEW-see) **DAL.**

Center. Shoots left. 5'11", 190 lbs. Born, Kalajoki, Finland, April 1, 1983. Dallas' 7th choice, 192nd overall, in 2001 Entry Draft.

			Regular Season														Playoffs								
Season	Club	League	GP	G	A	Pts	PIM	PP	SH	GW	S	%	+/-	TF	F%	Min	GP	G	A	Pts	PIM	PP	SH	GW	Min
99-2000	Karpat Oulu U18	Fin-U18	15	6	25	31	14	....	....	....	....	....	....	....	....	....	6	2	3	5	0	....	....	....	....
	Karpat Oulu Jr.	Fin-Jr.	28	4	7	11	14	....	....	....	....	....	....	....	....	....	....	....	....	....	....	....	....	....	....
2000-01	Karpat Oulu U18	Fin-U18	1	2	1	3	0	....	....	....	....	....	....	....	....	....	....	....	....	....	....	....	....	....	....
	Karpat Oulu Jr.	Fin-Jr.	41	18	31	49	69	....	....	....	....	....	....	....	....	....	6	2	1	3	0	....	....	....	....
2001-02	Karpat Oulu Jr.	Fin-Jr.	2	4	1	5	2	....	....	....	....	....	....	....	....	....	1	1	1	2	0	....	....	....	....
	Karpat Oulu	Finland	54	10	6	16	38	....	....	....	....	....	....	....	....	....	4	1	0	1	0	....	....	....	....
2002-03	Karpat Oulu	Finland	51	14	23	37	10	....	....	....	....	....	....	....	....	....	15	2	1	3	33	....	....	....	....
2003-04	Karpat Oulu	Finland	55	15	23	38	20	....	....	....	....	....	....	....	....	....	15	3	4	7	6	....	....	....	....
2004-05	Karpat Oulu	Finland	56	23	24	47	24	....	....	....	....	....	....	....	....	....	12	3	4	7	2	....	....	....	....
2005-06	**Dallas**	**NHL**	**81**	**17**	**38**	**55**	**30**	**8**	**0**	**2**	**107**	**15.9**	**2**	**23**	**30.4**	**13:34**	**5**	**2**	**1**	**3**	**0**	**1**	**0**	**0**	**13:40**
	Finland	Olympics	8	1	3	4	2	....	....	....	....	....	....	....	....	....	....	....	....	....	....	....	....	....	....
2006-07	**Dallas**	**NHL**	**82**	**14**	**34**	**48**	**18**	**6**	**0**	**1**	**121**	**11.6**	**8**	**278**	**52.2**	**13:54**	**4**	**0**	**1**	**1**	**0**	**0**	**0**	**0**	**13:22**
	NHL Totals		**163**	**31**	**72**	**103**	**48**	**14**	**0**	**3**	**228**	**13.6**		**301**	**50.5**	**13:44**	**9**	**2**	**2**	**4**	**0**	**1**	**0**	**0**	**13:32**

JOKINEN, Olli

(YOH-kih-nihn, OH-lee) **FLA.**

Center. Shoots left. 6'3", 218 lbs. Born, Kuopio, Finland, December 5, 1978. Los Angeles' 1st choice, 3rd overall, in 1997 Entry Draft.

			Regular Season														Playoffs								
Season	Club	League	GP	G	A	Pts	PIM	PP	SH	GW	S	%	+/-	TF	F%	Min	GP	G	A	Pts	PIM	PP	SH	GW	Min
1994-95	KalPa Kuopio U18	Fin-U18	30	22	28	50	92	....	....	....	....	....	....	....	....	....	....	....	....	....	....	....	....	....	....
	KalPa Kuopio Jr.	Fin-Jr.	6	0	1	1	6	....	....	....	....	....	....	....	....	....	....	....	....	....	....	....	....	....	....
1995-96	KalPa Kuopio U18	Fin-U18	9	9	13	22	4	....	....	....	....	....	....	....	....	....	....	....	....	....	....	....	....	....	....
	KalPa Kuopio Jr.	Fin-Jr.	25	20	14	34	47	....	....	....	....	....	....	....	....	....	7	4	4	8	20	....	....	....	....
	KalPa Kuopio	Finland	15	1	1	2	2	....	....	....	....	....	....	....	....	....	....	....	....	....	....	....	....	....	....
1996-97	HIFK Helsinki Jr.	Fin-Jr.	2	1	0	1	6	....	....	....	....	....	....	....	....	....	....	....	....	....	....	....	....	....	....
	HIFK Helsinki	Finland	50	14	27	41	88	....	....	....	....	....	....	....	....	....	....	....	....	....	....	....	....	....	....

			Regular Season														Playoffs								
Season	Club	League	GP	G	A	Pts	PIM	PP	SH	GW	S	%	+/-	TF	F%	Min	GP	G	A	Pts	PIM	PP	SH	GW	Min
1997-98	**Los Angeles**	**NHL**	**8**	**0**	**0**	**0**	**6**	**0**	**0**	**0**	**12**	**0.0**	**-5**	....	....	....	....	....	....	....	....	....	....	....	....
	HIFK Helsinki	Finland	30	11	28	39	32	....	....	....	....	....	....	....	....	....	9	7	2	9	2	....	....	....	....
1998-99	**Los Angeles**	**NHL**	**66**	**9**	**12**	**21**	**44**	**3**	**1**	**1**	**87**	**10.3**	**-10**	**779**	**43.9**	**14:42**	....	....	....	....	....	....	....	....	....
	Springfield	AHL	9	3	6	9	6	....	....	....	....	....	....	....	....	....	....	....	....	....	....	....	....	....	....
99-2000	**NY Islanders**	**NHL**	**82**	**11**	**10**	**21**	**80**	**1**	**2**	**3**	**138**	**8.0**	**0**	**841**	**46.1**	**16:15**	....	....	....	....	....	....	....	....	....
2000-01	**Florida**	**NHL**	**78**	**6**	**10**	**16**	**106**	**0**	**0**	**0**	**121**	**5.0**	**-22**	**638**	**42.3**	**13:23**	....	....	....	....	....	....	....	....	....
2001-02	**Florida**	**NHL**	**80**	**9**	**20**	**29**	**98**	**3**	**1**	**0**	**153**	**5.9**	**-16**	**1222**	**45.2**	**18:05**	....	....	....	....	....	....	....	....	....
	Finland	Olympics	4	2	1	3	0	....	....	....	....	....	....	....	....	....	....	....	....	....	....	....	....	....	....
2002-03	**Florida**	**NHL**	**81**	**36**	**29**	**65**	**79**	**13**	**3**	**6**	**240**	**15.0**	**-17**	**1925**	**46.7**	**22:02**	....	....	....	....	....	....	....	....	....
2003-04	**Florida**	**NHL**	**82**	**26**	**32**	**58**	**81**	**8**	**2**	**8**	**280**	**9.3**	**-16**	**1986**	**47.1**	**22:35**	....	....	....	....	....	....	....	....	....
2004-05	Kloten Flyers	Swiss	8	6	1	7	14	....	....	....	....	....	....	....	....	....	....	....	....	....	....	....	....	....	....
	Sodertalje SK	Sweden	23	13	9	22	52	....	....	....	....	....	....	....	....	....	....	....	....	....	....	....	....	....	....
	HIFK Helsinki	Finland	14	9	8	17	10	....	....	....	....	....	....	....	....	....	5	2	0	2	24	....	....	....	....
2005-06	**Florida**	**NHL**	**82**	**38**	**51**	**89**	**88**	**14**	**1**	**9**	**351**	**10.8**	**14**	**955**	**46.9**	**20:29**	....	....	....	....	....	....	....	....	....
	Finland	Olympics	8	6	2	8	2	....	....	....	....	....	....	....	....	....	....	....	....	....	....	....	....	....	....
2006-07	**Florida**	**NHL**	**82**	**39**	**52**	**91**	**78**	**9**	**1**	**8**	**351**	**11.1**	**18**	**1074**	**44.3**	**20:32**	....	....	....	....	....	....	....	....	....
	NHL Totals		**641**	**174**	**216**	**390**	**660**	**51**	**11**	**35**	**1733**	**10.0**		**9420**	**45.7**	**18:38**	....	....	....	....	....	....	....	....	....

Played in NHL All-Star Game (2003)

Traded to **NY Islanders** by **Los Angeles** with Josh Green, Mathieu Biron and Los Angeles' 1st round choice (Taylor Pyatt) in 1999 Entry Draft for Ziggy Palffy, Bryan Smolinski, Marcel Cousineau and New Jersey's 4th round choice (previously acquired, Los Angeles selected Daniel Johansson) in 1999 Entry Draft, June 20, 1999. Traded to **Florida** by **NY Islanders** with Roberto Luongo for Mark Parrish and Oleg Kvasha, June 24, 2000. Signed as a free agent by **Kloten** (Swiss), September 15, 2004. Signed as a free agent by **Sodertalje** (Sweden), November, 2004. Signed as a free agent by **HIFK Helsinki** (Finland), January 30, 2005.

JONES, Blair (JOHNZ, BLAYR) T.B.

Center. Shoots right. 6'3", 210 lbs. Born, Central Butte, Sask., September 27, 1986. Tampa Bay's 5th choice, 102nd overall, in 2005 Entry Draft.

Season	Club	League	GP	G	A	Pts	PIM	PP	SH	GW	S	%	+/-	TF	F%	Min	GP	G	A	Pts	PIM	PP	SH	GW	Min
2002-03	Bethune	SBHL	STATISTICS NOT AVAILABLE																						
	Red Deer Rebels	WHL	37	3	4	7	17	....	....	....	....	....	....	....	....	....	10	1	0	1	0	....	....	....	....
2003-04	Red Deer Rebels	WHL	72	9	22	31	55	....	....	....	....	....	....	....	....	....	19	1	5	6	24	....	....	....	....
2004-05	Red Deer Rebels	WHL	39	7	18	25	48	....	....	....	....	....	....	....	....	....	....	....	....	....	....	....	....	....	....
	Moose Jaw	WHL	29	7	18	25	30	....	....	....	....	....	....	....	....	....	5	2	5	7	8	....	....	....	....
2005-06	Moose Jaw	WHL	72	35	50	85	85	....	....	....	....	....	....	....	....	....	22	9	12	21	45	....	....	....	....
2006-07	**Tampa Bay**	**NHL**	**20**	**1**	**2**	**3**	**2**	**0**	**0**	**0**	**6**	**16.7**	**0**	**65**	**41.5**	**5:46**	....	....	....	....	....	....	....	....	....
	Springfield	AHL	45	5	16	21	36	....	....	....	....	....	....	....	....	....	....	....	....	....	....	....	....	....	....
	NHL Totals		**20**	**1**	**2**	**3**	**2**	**0**	**0**	**0**	**6**	**16.7**		**65**	**41.5**	**5:46**	....	....	....	....	....	....	....	....	....

WHL East Second All-Star Team (2006)

JONES, Matt (JOHNZ, MAT) PHX.

Defense. Shoots left. 6', 215 lbs. Born, Downers Grove, IL, August 8, 1983. Phoenix's 5th choice, 80th overall, in 2002 Entry Draft.

Season	Club	League	GP	G	A	Pts	PIM	PP	SH	GW	S	%	+/-	TF	F%	Min	GP	G	A	Pts	PIM	PP	SH	GW	Min
99-2000	Green Bay	USHL	54	1	4	5	59	....	....	....	....	....	....	....	....	....	13	0	0	0	2	....	....	....	....
2000-01	Green Bay	USHL	52	3	10	13	58	....	....	....	....	....	....	....	....	....	4	0	0	0	2	....	....	....	....
2001-02	North Dakota	WCHA	37	2	5	7	20	....	....	....	....	....	....	....	....	....	....	....	....	....	....	....	....	....	....
2002-03	North Dakota	WCHA	39	1	6	7	26	....	....	....	....	....	....	....	....	....	....	....	....	....	....	....	....	....	....
2003-04	North Dakota	WCHA	41	7	14	21	40	....	....	....	....	....	....	....	....	....	....	....	....	....	....	....	....	....	....
2004-05	North Dakota	WCHA	45	6	11	17	66	....	....	....	....	....	....	....	....	....	....	....	....	....	....	....	....	....	....
2005-06	**Phoenix**	**NHL**	**16**	**0**	**2**	**2**	**14**	**0**	**0**	**0**	**10**	**0.0**	**-2**	**0**	**0.0**	**11:35**	....	....	....	....	....	....	....	....	....
	San Antonio	AHL	59	2	11	13	46	....	....	....	....	....	....	....	....	....	....	....	....	....	....	....	....	....	....
2006-07	**Phoenix**	**NHL**	**45**	**1**	**6**	**7**	**39**	**0**	**0**	**0**	**20**	**5.0**	**-12**	**0**	**0.0**	**16:23**	....	....	....	....	....	....	....	....	....
	San Antonio	AHL	24	0	2	2	23	....	....	....	....	....	....	....	....	....	....	....	....	....	....	....	....	....	....
	NHL Totals		**61**	**1**	**8**	**9**	**53**	**0**	**0**	**0**	**30**	**3.3**		**0**	**0.0**	**15:07**	....	....	....	....	....	....	....	....	....

WCHA Second All-Star Team (2004)

JONES, Randy (JOHNZ, RAN-dee) PHI.

Defense. Shoots left. 6'2", 200 lbs. Born, Quispamsis, N.B., July 23, 1981.

Season	Club	League	GP	G	A	Pts	PIM	PP	SH	GW	S	%	+/-	TF	F%	Min	GP	G	A	Pts	PIM	PP	SH	GW	Min
99-2000	Cobourg Cougars	OPJHL	44	20	36	56	51	....	....	....	....	....	....	....	....	....	....	....	....	....	....	....	....	....	....
2000-01	Cobourg Cougars	OPJHL	28	15	21	36	46	....	....	....	....	....	....	....	....	....	....	....	....	....	....	....	....	....	....
2001-02	Clarkson Knights	ECAC	34	9	11	20	32	....	....	....	....	....	....	....	....	....	....	....	....	....	....	....	....	....	....
2002-03	Clarkson Knights	ECAC	33	13	20	33	65	....	....	....	....	....	....	....	....	....	....	....	....	....	....	....	....	....	....
2003-04	**Philadelphia**	**NHL**	**5**	**0**	**0**	**0**	**0**	**0**	**0**	**0**	**5**	**0.0**	**1**	**0**	**0.0**	**12:00**	....	....	....	....	....	....	....	....	....
	Philadelphia	AHL	55	8	24	32	63	....	....	....	....	....	....	....	....	....	12	0	1	1	17	....	....	....	....
2004-05	Philadelphia	AHL	69	5	19	24	32	....	....	....	....	....	....	....	....	....	18	0	5	5	10	....	....	....	....
2005-06	**Philadelphia**	**NHL**	**28**	**0**	**8**	**8**	**16**	**0**	**0**	**0**	**21**	**0.0**	**-6**	**1**	**100.0**	**14:58**	....	....	....	....	....	....	....	....	....
	Philadelphia	AHL	21	2	3	5	53	....	....	....	....	....	....	....	....	....	....	....	....	....	....	....	....	....	....
2006-07	**Philadelphia**	**NHL**	**66**	**4**	**18**	**22**	**38**	**0**	**0**	**0**	**67**	**6.0**	**-14**	**1**	**0.0**	**16:06**	....	....	....	....	....	....	....	....	....
	NHL Totals		**99**	**4**	**26**	**30**	**54**	**0**	**0**	**0**	**93**	**4.3**		**2**	**50.0**	**15:34**	....	....	....	....	....	....	....	....	....

ECAC First All-Star Team (2003)

Signed as a free agent by **Philadelphia**, July 24, 2003.

JONSSON, Lars (YAWN-suhn, LARZ) PHI.

Defense. Shoots left. 6'1", 205 lbs. Born, Borlange, Sweden, January 2, 1982. Boston's 1st choice, 7th overall, in 2000 Entry Draft.

Season	Club	League	GP	G	A	Pts	PIM	PP	SH	GW	S	%	+/-	TF	F%	Min	GP	G	A	Pts	PIM	PP	SH	GW	Min
1998-99	Leksands IF Jr.	Swe-Jr.	40	4	8	12	42	....	....	....	....	....	....	....	....	....	....	....	....	....	....	....	....	....	....
99-2000	Leksands IF Jr.	Swe-Jr.	34	16	22	38	50	....	....	....	....	....	....	....	....	....	2	0	0	0	0	....	....	....	....
	Leksands IF	Sweden	5	0	0	0	4	....	....	....	....	....	....	....	....	....	....	....	....	....	....	....	....	....	....
2000-01	Leksands IF Jr.	Swe-Jr.	7	1	3	4	6	....	....	....	....	....	....	....	....	....	....	....	....	....	....	....	....	....	....
	Leksands IF	Sweden	31	2	1	3	12	....	....	....	....	....	....	....	....	....	....	....	....	....	....	....	....	....	....
2001-02	Leksands IF Jr.	Swe-Jr.	3	2	1	3	4	....	....	....	....	....	....	....	....	....	1	0	0	0	0	....	....	....	....
	Leksands IF	Sweden-2	28	1	7	8	59	....	....	....	....	....	....	....	....	....	....	....	....	....	....	....	....	....	....
2002-03	Leksands IF	Sweden	21	0	0	0	12	....	....	....	....	....	....	....	....	....	5	0	0	0	2	....	....	....	....
	Bjorkloven	Sweden-2	9	3	4	7	10	....	....	....	....	....	....	....	....	....	....	....	....	....	....	....	....	....	....
	IFK Arboga IK	Sweden-2	4	0	0	0	4	....	....	....	....	....	....	....	....	....	....	....	....	....	....	....	....	....	....
2003-04	Leksands IF	Sweden	50	3	9	12	30	....	....	....	....	....	....	....	....	....	....	....	....	....	....	....	....	....	....
	Leksands IF	Sweden-Q	4	1	0	1	2	....	....	....	....	....	....	....	....	....	....	....	....	....	....	....	....	....	....
2004-05	Timra IK	Sweden	50	5	6	11	32	....	....	....	....	....	....	....	....	....	7	0	0	0	2	....	....	....	....
2005-06	HV 71 Jonkoping	Sweden	50	11	16	27	46	....	....	....	....	....	....	....	....	....	11	2	3	5	14	....	....	....	....
2006-07	**Philadelphia**	**NHL**	**8**	**0**	**2**	**2**	**6**	**0**	**0**	**0**	**4**	**0.0**	**-4**	**0**	**0.0**	**12:25**	....	....	....	....	....	....	....	....	....
	Philadelphia	AHL	40	4	11	15	26	....	....	....	....	....	....	....	....	....	....	....	....	....	....	....	....	....	....
	NHL Totals		**8**	**0**	**2**	**2**	**6**	**0**	**0**	**0**	**4**	**0.0**		**0**	**0.0**	**12:25**	....	....	....	....	....	....	....	....	....

Signed as a free agent by **Philadephia**, July 1, 2006.

JOVANOVSKI, Ed (joh-van-OHV-skee, EHD) PHX.

Defense. Shoots left. 6'2", 210 lbs. Born, Windsor, Ont., June 26, 1976. Florida's 1st choice, 1st overall, in 1994 Entry Draft.

Season	Club	League	GP	G	A	Pts	PIM	PP	SH	GW	S	%	+/-	TF	F%	Min	GP	G	A	Pts	PIM	PP	SH	GW	Min
1991-92	Windsor	Minor-ON	50	25	40	65	88	....	....	....	....	....	....	....	....	....	....	....	....	....	....	....	....	....	....
1992-93	Windsor Bulldogs	OHA-B	48	7	46	53	88	....	....	....	....	....	....	....	....	....	....	....	....	....	....	....	....	....	....
1993-94	Windsor Spitfires	OHL	62	15	36	51	221	....	....	....	....	....	....	....	....	....	4	0	0	0	15	....	....	....	....
1994-95	Windsor Spitfires	OHL	50	23	42	65	198	....	....	....	....	....	....	....	....	....	9	2	7	9	39	....	....	....	....
1995-96	**Florida**	**NHL**	**70**	**10**	**11**	**21**	**137**	**2**	**0**	**2**	**116**	**8.6**	**-3**	....	....	....	**22**	**1**	**8**	**9**	**52**	**0**	**0**	**0**	....
1996-97	**Florida**	**NHL**	**61**	**7**	**16**	**23**	**172**	**3**	**0**	**1**	**80**	**8.8**	**-1**	....	....	....	**5**	**0**	**0**	**0**	**4**	**0**	**0**	**0**	....
1997-98	**Florida**	**NHL**	**81**	**9**	**14**	**23**	**158**	**2**	**1**	**3**	**142**	**6.3**	**-12**	....	....	....	....	....	....	....	....	....	....	....	....
1998-99	**Florida**	**NHL**	**41**	**3**	**13**	**16**	**82**	**1**	**0**	**1**	**68**	**4.4**	**-4**	**0**	**0.0**	**22:35**	....	....	....	....	....	....	....	....	....
	Vancouver	**NHL**	**31**	**2**	**9**	**11**	**44**	**0**	**0**	**0**	**41**	**4.9**	**-5**	**0**	**0.0**	**21:16**	....	....	....	....	....	....	....	....	....
99-2000	**Vancouver**	**NHL**	**75**	**5**	**21**	**26**	**54**	**1**	**0**	**1**	**109**	**4.6**	**-3**	**0**	**0.0**	**24:03**	....	....	....	....	....	....	....	....	....
2000-01	**Vancouver**	**NHL**	**79**	**12**	**35**	**47**	**102**	**4**	**0**	**2**	**193**	**6.2**	**-1**	**0**	**0.0**	**24:57**	**4**	**1**	**1**	**2**	**0**	**0**	**0**	**0**	**25:54**
2001-02	**Vancouver**	**NHL**	**82**	**17**	**31**	**48**	**101**	**7**	**1**	**3**	**202**	**8.4**	**-7**	**0**	**0.0**	**25:11**	**6**	**1**	**4**	**5**	**8**	**1**	**0**	**0**	**25:48**
	Canada	Olympics	6	0	3	3	4	....	....	....	....	....	....	....	....	....	....	....	....	....	....	....	....	....	....
2002-03	**Vancouver**	**NHL**	**67**	**6**	**40**	**46**	**113**	**2**	**0**	**1**	**145**	**4.1**	**19**	**0**	**0.0**	**24:15**	**14**	**7**	**1**	**8**	**22**	**4**	**1**	**2**	**23:40**

Season	Club	League	Regular Season GP	G	A	Pts	PIM	PP	SH	GW	S	%	+/-	TF	F%	Min	Playoffs GP	G	A	Pts	PIM	PP	SH	GW	Min
2003-04	**Vancouver**	**NHL**	**56**	**7**	**16**	**23**	**64**	**2**	**0**	**1**	**143**	**4.9**	**2**	**0**	**0.0**	**23:11**	**7**	**0**	**4**	**4**	**6**	**0**	**0**	**0**	**26:36**
2004-05			DID NOT PLAY																						
2005-06	**Vancouver**	**NHL**	**44**	**8**	**25**	**33**	**58**	**6**	**0**	**2**	**87**	**9.2**	**–8**	**0**	**0.0**	**24:26**	....	....	....	....	....	....	....	....	....
	Canada	Olympics	DID NOT PLAY – INJURED																						
2006-07	**Phoenix**	**NHL**	**54**	**11**	**18**	**29**	**63**	**6**	**0**	**1**	**135**	**8.1**	**–6**	**0**	**0.0**	**23:09**	....	....	....	....	....	....	....	....	....
	NHL Totals		**741**	**97**	**249**	**346**	**1148**	**36**	**2**	**18**	**1461**	**6.6**		**0**	**0.0**	**23:57**	**58**	**10**	**18**	**28**	**92**	**5**	**1**	**2**	**25:02**

OHL All-Rookie Team (1994) • OHL Second All-Star Team (1994) • OHL First All-Star Team (1995) • NHL All-Rookie Team (1996)

Played in NHL All-Star Game (2001, 2002, 2003, 2007)

Traded to **Vancouver** by **Florida** with Dave Gagner, Mike Brown, Kevin Weekes and Florida's 1st round choice (Nathan Smith) in 2000 Entry Draft for Pavel Bure, Bret Hedican, Brad Ference and Vancouver's 3rd round choice (Robert Fried) in 2000 Entry Draft, January 17, 1999. Signed as a free agent by **Phoenix**, July 1, 2006.

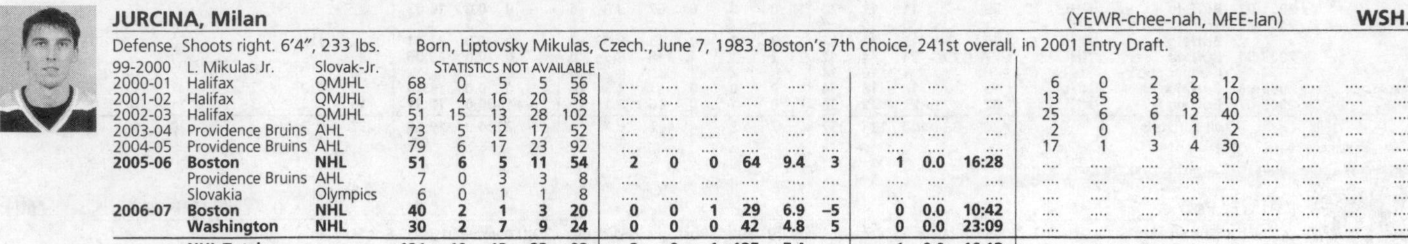

JURCINA, Milan (YEWR-chee-nah, MEE-lan) WSH.

Defense. Shoots right. 6'4", 233 lbs. Born, Liptovsky Mikulas, Czech., June 7, 1983. Boston's 7th choice, 241st overall, in 2001 Entry Draft.

Season	Club	League	GP	G	A	Pts	PIM	PP	SH	GW	S	%	+/-	TF	F%	Min	GP	G	A	Pts	PIM	PP	SH	GW	Min
99-2000	L. Mikulas Jr.	Slovak-Jr.	STATISTICS NOT AVAILABLE																						
2000-01	Halifax	QMJHL	68	0	5	5	56	....	....	....	....	....	....	....	....	....	6	0	2	2	12	....	....	....	....
2001-02	Halifax	QMJHL	61	4	16	20	58	....	....	....	....	....	....	....	....	....	13	5	3	8	10	....	....	....	....
2002-03	Halifax	QMJHL	51	15	13	28	102	....	....	....	....	....	....	....	....	....	25	6	6	12	40	....	....	....	....
2003-04	Providence Bruins	AHL	73	5	12	17	52	....	....	....	....	....	....	....	....	....	2	0	1	1	2	....	....	....	....
2004-05	Providence Bruins	AHL	79	6	17	23	92	....	....	....	....	....	....	....	....	....	17	1	3	4	30	....	....	....	....
2005-06	**Boston**	**NHL**	**51**	**6**	**5**	**11**	**54**	**2**	**0**	**0**	**64**	**9.4**	**3**	**1**	**0.0**	**16:28**	....	....	....	....	....	....	....	....	....
	Providence Bruins	AHL	7	0	3	3	8	....	....	....	....	....	....	....	....	....	....	....	....	....	....	....	....	....	....
	Slovakia	Olympics	6	0	1	1	8	....	....	....	....	....	....	....	....	....	....	....	....	....	....	....	....	....	....
2006-07	**Boston**	**NHL**	**40**	**2**	**1**	**3**	**20**	**0**	**0**	**1**	**29**	**6.9**	**–5**	**0**	**0.0**	**10:42**	....	....	....	....	....	....	....	....	....
	Washington	**NHL**	**30**	**2**	**7**	**9**	**24**	**0**	**0**	**0**	**42**	**4.8**	**5**	**0**	**0.0**	**23:09**	....	....	....	....	....	....	....	....	....
	NHL Totals		**121**	**10**	**13**	**23**	**98**	**2**	**0**	**1**	**135**	**7.4**		**1**	**0.0**	**16:13**	....	....	....	....	....	....	....	....	....

Traded to **Washington** by **Boston** for Washington's 4th round choice in 2008 Entry Draft, February 1, 2007.

KABERLE, Frantisek (KA-buhr-lay, FRAN-tih-sehk) CAR.

Defense. Shoots left. 6', 190 lbs. Born, Kladno, Czech., November 8, 1973. Los Angeles' 3rd choice, 76th overall, in 1999 Entry Draft.

Season	Club	League	GP	G	A	Pts	PIM	PP	SH	GW	S	%	+/-	TF	F%	Min	GP	G	A	Pts	PIM	PP	SH	GW	Min
1991-92	Poldi Kladno	Czech	37	1	4	5	8	....	....	....	....	....	....	....	....	....	8	0	1	1	0	....	....	....	....
1992-93	Poldi Kladno	Czech	40	4	5	9	....	....	....	....	....	....	....	....	....	....	9	2	4	6	....	....	....	....	....
1993-94	HC Kladno	CzRep	41	4	16	20	....	....	....	....	....	....	....	....	....	....	11	1	1	2	....	....	....	....	....
1994-95	HC Kladno	CzRep	40	7	17	24	20	....	....	....	....	....	....	....	....	....	8	0	3	3	12	....	....	....	....
1995-96	MoDo	Sweden	40	5	7	12	34	....	....	....	....	....	....	....	....	....	8	0	1	1	0	....	....	....	....
1996-97	MoDo	Sweden	50	3	11	14	28	....	....	....	....	....	....	....	....	....	....	....	....	....	....	....	....	....	....
1997-98	MoDo	Sweden	46	5	4	9	22	....	....	....	....	....	....	....	....	....	9	1	1	2	4	....	....	....	....
1998-99	MoDo	Sweden	45	15	18	33	4	....	....	....	....	....	....	....	....	....	13	2	5	7	8	....	....	....	....
99-2000	**Los Angeles**	**NHL**	**37**	**0**	**9**	**9**	**4**	**0**	**0**	**0**	**41**	**0.0**	**3**	**0**	**0.0**	**17:04**	....	....	....	....	....	....	....	....	....
	Long Beach	IHL	18	2	8	10	8	....	....	....	....	....	....	....	....	....	....	....	....	....	....	....	....	....	....
	Atlanta	**NHL**	**14**	**1**	**6**	**7**	**6**	**0**	**1**	**0**	**35**	**2.9**	**–13**	**0**	**0.0**	**24:39**	....	....	....	....	....	....	....	....	....
	Lowell	AHL	4	0	2	2	0	....	....	....	....	....	....	....	....	....	....	....	....	....	....	....	....	....	....
2000-01	**Atlanta**	**NHL**	**51**	**4**	**11**	**15**	**18**	**1**	**0**	**1**	**99**	**4.0**	**11**	**1**	**0.0**	**22:17**	....	....	....	....	....	....	....	....	....
2001-02	**Atlanta**	**NHL**	**61**	**5**	**20**	**25**	**24**	**1**	**0**	**0**	**82**	**6.1**	**–11**	**0**	**0.0**	**21:35**	....	....	....	....	....	....	....	....	....
2002-03	**Atlanta**	**NHL**	**79**	**7**	**19**	**26**	**32**	**3**	**1**	**2**	**105**	**6.7**	**–19**	**0**	**0.0**	**21:57**	....	....	....	....	....	....	....	....	....
2003-04	**Atlanta**	**NHL**	**67**	**3**	**26**	**29**	**30**	**2**	**0**	**1**	**94**	**3.2**	**2**	**2**	**50.0**	**23:20**	....	....	....	....	....	....	....	....	....
2004-05	HC Rabat Kladno	CzRep	22	5	11	16	34	....	....	....	....	....	....	....	....	....	....	....	....	....	....	....	....	....	....
	MODO	Sweden	8	2	2	4	0	....	....	....	....	....	....	....	....	....	6	1	0	1	27	....	....	....	....
2005-06♦	**Carolina**	**NHL**	**77**	**6**	**38**	**44**	**46**	**1**	**0**	**3**	**126**	**4.8**	**8**	**0**	**0.0**	**19:37**	**25**	**4**	**9**	**13**	**8**	**3**	**0**	**1**	**18:25**
	Czech Republic	Olympics	8	0	1	1	6	....	....	....	....	....	....	....	....	....	....	....	....	....	....	....	....	....	....
2006-07	**Carolina**	**NHL**	**27**	**2**	**6**	**8**	**20**	**1**	**0**	**1**	**33**	**6.1**	**8**	**0**	**0.0**	**15:32**	....	....	....	....	....	....	....	....	....
	NHL Totals		**413**	**28**	**135**	**163**	**180**	**9**	**2**	**8**	**615**	**4.6**		**3**	**33.3**	**20:57**	**25**	**4**	**9**	**13**	**8**	**3**	**0**	**1**	**18:25**

Traded to **Atlanta** by **Los Angeles** with Donald Audette for Kelly Buchberger and Nelson Emerson, March 13, 2000. Signed as a free agent by **Carolina**, July 15, 2004. Signed as a free agent by **Kladno** (CzRep), September 17, 2004. Signed as a free agent by **MODO** (Sweden), January 31, 2005. • Missed majority of 2006-07 season recovering from off-season shoulder surgery.

KABERLE, Tomas (KA-buhr-lay, TAW-mas) TOR.

Defense. Shoots left. 6'1", 198 lbs. Born, Rakovnik, Czech., March 2, 1978. Toronto's 13th choice, 204th overall, in 1996 Entry Draft.

Season	Club	League	GP	G	A	Pts	PIM	PP	SH	GW	S	%	+/-	TF	F%	Min	GP	G	A	Pts	PIM	PP	SH	GW	Min
1994-95	HC Kladno Jr.	CzRep-Jr.	37	7	10	17	....	....	....	....	....	....	....	....	....	....	....	....	....	....	....	....	....	....	....
	HC Kladno	CzRep	4	0	1	1	0	....	....	....	....	....	....	....	....	....	....	....	....	....	....	....	....	....	....
1995-96	Kladno Jr.	CzRep-Jr.	23	6	13	19	....	....	....	....	....	....	....	....	....	....	....	....	....	....	....	....	....	....	....
	HC Poldi Kladno	CzRep	23	0	1	1	2	....	....	....	....	....	....	....	....	....	2	0	0	0	0	....	....	....	....
1996-97	HC Poldi Kladno	CzRep	49	0	5	5	26	....	....	....	....	....	....	....	....	....	3	0	0	0	0	....	....	....	....
1997-98	Kladno	CzRep	47	4	19	23	12	....	....	....	....	....	....	....	....	....	....	....	....	....	....	....	....	....	....
	St. John's	AHL	2	0	0	0	0	....	....	....	....	....	....	....	....	....	....	....	....	....	....	....	....	....	....
1998-99	**Toronto**	**NHL**	**57**	**4**	**18**	**22**	**12**	**0**	**0**	**2**	**71**	**5.6**	**3**	**0**	**0.0**	**18:42**	**14**	**0**	**3**	**3**	**2**	**0**	**0**	**0**	**17:10**
99-2000	**Toronto**	**NHL**	**82**	**7**	**33**	**40**	**24**	**2**	**0**	**0**	**82**	**8.5**	**3**	**0**	**0.0**	**22:55**	**12**	**1**	**4**	**5**	**0**	**0**	**0**	**1**	**23:01**
2000-01	**Toronto**	**NHL**	**82**	**6**	**39**	**45**	**24**	**0**	**0**	**1**	**96**	**6.3**	**10**	**2**	**0.0**	**22:41**	**11**	**1**	**3**	**4**	**0**	**0**	**0**	**1**	**21:33**
2001-02	Kladno	CzRep	9	1	7	8	4	....	....	....	....	....	....	....	....	....	....	....	....	....	....	....	....	....	....
	Toronto	**NHL**	**69**	**10**	**29**	**39**	**2**	**5**	**0**	**3**	**85**	**11.8**	**5**	**2**	**100.0**	**25:00**	**20**	**2**	**8**	**10**	**16**	**0**	**0**	**0**	**28:40**
	Czech Republic	Olympics	4	0	1	1	2	....	....	....	....	....	....	....	....	....	....	....	....	....	....	....	....	....	....
2002-03	**Toronto**	**NHL**	**82**	**11**	**36**	**47**	**30**	**4**	**1**	**2**	**119**	**9.2**	**20**	**3**	**66.7**	**24:50**	**7**	**2**	**1**	**3**	**0**	**1**	**0**	**1**	**30:04**
2003-04	**Toronto**	**NHL**	**71**	**3**	**28**	**31**	**18**	**0**	**0**	**1**	**88**	**3.4**	**16**	**2**	**0.0**	**23:12**	**13**	**0**	**3**	**3**	**6**	**0**	**0**	**0**	**20:16**
2004-05	HC Rabat Kladno	CzRep	49	8	31	39	38	....	....	....	....	....	....	....	....	....	7	1	0	1	0	....	....	....	....
2005-06	**Toronto**	**NHL**	**82**	**9**	**58**	**67**	**46**	**6**	**0**	**2**	**163**	**5.5**	**–1**	**0**	**0.0**	**28:10**	....	....	....	....	....	....	....	....	....
	Czech Republic	Olympics	8	2	2	4	2	....	....	....	....	....	....	....	....	....	....	....	....	....	....	....	....	....	....
2006-07	**Toronto**	**NHL**	**74**	**11**	**47**	**58**	**20**	**2**	**0**	**1**	**128**	**8.6**	**3**	**0**	**0.0**	**25:52**	....	....	....	....	....	....	....	....	....
	NHL Totals		**599**	**61**	**288**	**349**	**176**	**19**	**1**	**12**	**832**	**7.3**		**9**	**44.4**	**24:06**	**77**	**6**	**22**	**28**	**24**	**1**	**0**	**3**	**23:23**

Played in NHL All-Star Game (2002, 2007)

Signed as a restricted free agent by **Kladno** (CzRep) with **Toronto** retaining NHL rights, September 29, 2001. Signed as a free agent by **Kladno** (CzRep), September 17, 2004.

KAIGORODOV, Alexei (kay-goh-ROH-dahv, al-EHX-ay) PHX.

Center. Shoots left. 6'1", 183 lbs. Born, Chelyabinsk, USSR, July 29, 1983. Ottawa's 2nd choice, 47th overall, in 2002 Entry Draft.

Season	Club	League	GP	G	A	Pts	PIM	PP	SH	GW	S	%	+/-	TF	F%	Min	GP	G	A	Pts	PIM	PP	SH	GW	Min
1998-99	Magnitogorsk 2	Russia-4	10	6	4	10	2	....	....	....	....	....	....	....	....	....	....	....	....	....	....	....	....	....	....
99-2000	Magnitogorsk 2	Russia-3	19	2	3	5	8	....	....	....	....	....	....	....	....	....	....	....	....	....	....	....	....	....	....
2000-01	Magnitogorsk 2	Russia-3	45	12	30	42	26	....	....	....	....	....	....	....	....	....	....	....	....	....	....	....	....	....	....
2001-02	Magnitogorsk	Russia	46	4	12	16	20	....	....	....	....	....	....	....	....	....	9	0	3	3	2	....	....	....	....
2002-03	Magnitogorsk	Russia	46	8	14	22	20	....	....	....	....	....	....	....	....	....	3	0	1	1	0	....	....	....	....
2003-04	Magnitogorsk	Russia	49	4	12	16	24	....	....	....	....	....	....	....	....	....	14	2	2	4	4	....	....	....	....
2004-05	Magnitogorsk	Russia	57	15	34	49	40	....	....	....	....	....	....	....	....	....	5	0	3	3	2	....	....	....	....
2005-06	Magnitogorsk	Russia	50	9	21	30	42	....	....	....	....	....	....	....	....	....	11	0	1	1	6	....	....	....	....
2006-07	**Ottawa**	**NHL**	**6**	**0**	**1**	**1**	**0**	**0**	**0**	**0**	**3**	**0.0**	**1**	**24**	**20.8**	**4:53**	....	....	....	....	....	....	....	....	....
	Magnitogorsk	Russia	32	6	12	18	18	....	....	....	....	....	....	....	....	....	15	2	8	10	14	....	....	....	....
	NHL Totals		**6**	**0**	**1**	**1**	**0**	**0**	**0**	**0**	**3**	**0.0**		**24**	**20.8**	**4:53**	....	....	....	....	....	....	....	....	....

Traded to **Phoenix** by **Ottawa** for Mike Comrie, January 3, 2007.

KALETA, Patrick (ka-LEH-tuh, PAT-rihk) BUF.

Right wing. Shoots right. 5'11", 202 lbs. Born, Buffalo, NY, June 8, 1986. Buffalo's 5th choice, 176th overall, in 2004 Entry Draft.

Season	Club	League	GP	G	A	Pts	PIM	PP	SH	GW	S	%	+/-	TF	F%	Min	GP	G	A	Pts	PIM	PP	SH	GW	Min
2002-03	Peterborough	OHL	67	7	9	16	67	....	....	....	....	....	....	....	....	....	7	0	0	0	6	....	....	....	....
2003-04	Peterborough	OHL	67	14	14	28	124	....	....	....	....	....	....	....	....	....	....	....	....	....	....	....	....	....	....
2004-05	Peterborough	OHL	62	24	28	52	146	....	....	....	....	....	....	....	....	....	14	3	3	6	30	....	....	....	....
2005-06	Peterborough	OHL	68	16	35	51	121	....	....	....	....	....	....	....	....	....	19	8	10	18	43	....	....	....	....
2006-07	**Buffalo**	**NHL**	**7**	**0**	**2**	**2**	**21**	**0**	**0**	**0**	**6**	**0.0**	**3**	**0**	**0.0**	**6:49**	....	....	....	....	....	....	....	....	....
	Rochester	AHL	58	5	10	15	133	....	....	....	....	....	....	....	....	....	5	0	0	0	12	....	....	....	....
	NHL Totals		**7**	**0**	**2**	**2**	**21**	**0**	**0**	**0**	**6**	**0.0**		**0**	**0.0**	**6:49**	....	....	....	....	....	....	....	....	....

KALININ, Dmitri

(kah-LIHN-ihn, dih-MEE-tree) **BUF.**

Defense. Shoots left. 6'3", 212 lbs. Born, Chelyabinsk, USSR, July 22, 1980. Buffalo's 1st choice, 18th overall, in 1998 Entry Draft.

Season	Club	League	Regular Season GP	G	A	Pts	PIM	PP	SH	GW	S	%	+/-	TF	F%	Min	Playoffs GP	G	A	Pts	PIM	PP	SH	GW	Min
1995-96	Chelyabinsk	CIS	20	0	3	3	10																		
1996-97	Yunior-T Kurgan	Russia-3	20	0	0	0	10																		
	Chelyabinsk	Russia	2	0	0	0	0										2	0	0	0	0				
1997-98	Chelyabinsk	Russia	26	0	2	2	24																		
1998-99	Moncton Wildcats	QMJHL	39	7	18	25	44										4	1	1	2	0				
	Rochester	AHL	3	0	1	1	14										7	0	0	0	6				
99-2000	**Buffalo**	**NHL**	**4**	**0**	**0**	**0**	**4**	**0**	**0**	**0**	**3**	**0.0**	**0**	**0**	**0.0**	**16:53**									
	Rochester	AHL	75	2	19	21	52										21	2	9	11	8				
2000-01	**Buffalo**	**NHL**	**79**	**4**	**18**	**22**	**38**	**2**	**0**	**0**	**88**	**4.5**	**-2**	**1**	**100.0**	**19:50**	**13**	**0**	**2**	**2**	**4**	**0**	**0**	**0**	**20:05**
2001-02	**Buffalo**	**NHL**	**58**	**2**	**11**	**13**	**26**	**0**	**0**	**0**	**67**	**3.0**	**-6**	**0**	**0.0**	**18:03**									
2002-03	Rochester	AHL	1	0	0	0	0																		
	Buffalo	**NHL**	**65**	**8**	**13**	**21**	**57**	**3**	**1**	**0**	**83**	**9.6**	**-7**	**0**	**0.0**	**21:41**									
2003-04	**Buffalo**	**NHL**	**77**	**10**	**24**	**34**	**42**	**2**	**1**	**4**	**118**	**8.5**	**0**	**0**	**0.0**	**23:06**									
2004-05	Magnitogorsk	Russia	48	2	8	10	14										5	0	0	0	2				
2005-06	**Buffalo**	**NHL**	**55**	**2**	**16**	**18**	**54**	**0**	**0**	**0**	**47**	**4.3**	**14**	**0**	**0.0**	**16:45**	**8**	**0**	**2**	**2**	**2**	**0**	**0**	**0**	**16:53**
2006-07	**Buffalo**	**NHL**	**82**	**7**	**22**	**29**	**36**	**0**	**1**	**0**	**86**	**8.1**	**19**	**1**	**100.0**	**19:31**	**16**	**2**	**3**	**5**	**14**	**0**	**0**	**0**	**18:11**
	NHL Totals		**420**	**33**	**104**	**137**	**257**	**7**	**3**	**4**	**492**	**6.7**		**2**	**100.0**	**19:59**	**37**	**2**	**7**	**9**	**20**	**0**	**0**	**0**	**18:34**

AHL All-Rookie Team (2000)

Signed as a free agent by **Magnitogorsk** (Russia), September 25, 2004.

KALUS, Petr

(KAY-lihs, PEE-tuhr) **MIN.**

Left wing. Shoots left. 6'1", 201 lbs. Born, Ostrava, Czech., June 29, 1987. Boston's 2nd choice, 39th overall, in 2005 Entry Draft.

Season	Club	League	Regular Season GP	G	A	Pts	PIM	PP	SH	GW	S	%	+/-	TF	F%	Min	Playoffs GP	G	A	Pts	PIM	PP	SH	GW	Min
2002-03	HC Ostrava U17	CzR-U17	18	3	19	22	14																		
	HC Vitkovice U17	CzR-U17	10	3	1	4	37																		
	HC Vitkovice Jr.	CzRep-Jr.	11	0	0	0	4																		
2003-04	HC Vitkovice U17	CzR-U17	9	7	5	12	60										7	3	5	8	2				
	HC Vitkovice Jr.	CzRep-Jr.	41	8	8	16	67																		
2004-05	HC Vitkovice Jr.	CzRep-Jr.	39	20	11	31	161										2	2	0	2	25				
	Vitkovice	CzRep	1	0	0	0	0																		
2005-06	Regina Pats	WHL	60	36	22	58	87										6	4	1	5	6				
2006-07	**Boston**	**NHL**	**9**	**4**	**1**	**5**	**6**	**1**	**0**	**0**	**8**	**50.0**	**0**	**0**	**0.0**	**11:16**									
	Providence Bruins	AHL	43	13	17	30	110										9	1	0	1	12				
	NHL Totals		**9**	**4**	**1**	**5**	**6**	**1**	**0**	**0**	**8**	**50.0**		**0**	**0.0**	**11:16**									

Traded to **Minnesota** by **Boston** with Boston's 4th round choice in 2009 Entry Draft for Manny Fernandez, July 1, 2007.

KANE, Boyd

(KAYN, BOID) **PHI.**

Left wing. Shoots left. 6'2", 220 lbs. Born, Swift Current, Sask., April 18, 1978. NY Rangers' 4th choice, 114th overall, in 1998 Entry Draft.

Season	Club	League	Regular Season GP	G	A	Pts	PIM	PP	SH	GW	S	%	+/-	TF	F%	Min	Playoffs GP	G	A	Pts	PIM	PP	SH	GW	Min
1994-95	Regina Pats	WHL	25	6	5	11	6										4	0	0	0	0				
1995-96	Regina Pats	WHL	72	21	42	63	155										11	5	7	12	12				
1996-97	Regina Pats	WHL	66	25	50	75	154										5	1	1	2	15				
1997-98	Regina Pats	WHL	68	48	45	93	133										9	5	7	12	29				
1998-99	Hartford	AHL	56	3	5	8	23																		
	Charlotte	ECHL	12	5	6	11	14																		
99-2000	Hartford	AHL	8	0	0	0	9																		
	Charlotte	ECHL	47	10	19	29	110																		
	Binghamton	UHL	3	0	2	2	4										1	0	0	0	0				
2000-01	Charlotte	ECHL	12	9	8	17	6																		
	Hartford	AHL	56	11	17	28	81										5	2	0	2	2				
2001-02	Hartford	AHL	78	17	22	39	193										10	1	2	3	50				
2002-03	Springfield	AHL	72	15	22	37	121										6	3	1	4	8				
2003-04	**Philadelphia**	**NHL**	**7**	**0**	**0**	**0**	**7**	**0**	**0**	**0**	**6**	**0.0**	**-4**	**3**	**33.3**	**9:56**									
	Philadelphia	AHL	73	13	22	35	177										12	0	1	1	39				
2004-05	Philadelphia	AHL	58	9	15	24	112										21	0	7	7	28				
2005-06	**Washington**	**NHL**	**5**	**0**	**1**	**1**	**2**	**0**	**0**	**0**	**1**	**0.0**	**1**	**0**	**0.0**	**4:04**									
	Hershey Bears	AHL	74	20	29	49	185										21	4	9	13	14				
2006-07	**Philadelphia**	**NHL**	**15**	**0**	**2**	**2**	**28**	**0**	**0**	**0**	**7**	**0.0**	**-4**	**4**	**25.0**	**6:58**									
	Philadelphia	AHL	57	10	22	32	98																		
	NHL Totals		**27**	**0**	**3**	**3**	**37**	**0**	**0**	**0**	**14**	**0.0**		**7**	**28.6**	**7:12**									

• Re-entered NHL Entry Draft. Originally Pittsburgh's 3rd choice, 72nd overall, in 1996 Entry Draft.

Traded to **Tampa Bay** by **NY Rangers** for Gordie Dwyer, October 10, 2002. Signed as a free agent by **Philadelphia**, July 14, 2003. Signed as a free agent by **Washington**, August 12, 2005. Signed as a free agent by **Philadelphia**, July 13, 2006.

KANKO, Petr

(KAN-koh, PEE-tuhr) **L.A.**

Right wing. Shoots left. 5'10", 195 lbs. Born, Pribram, Czech., February 7, 1984. Los Angeles' 3rd choice, 66th overall, in 2002 Entry Draft.

Season	Club	League	Regular Season GP	G	A	Pts	PIM	PP	SH	GW	S	%	+/-	TF	F%	Min	Playoffs GP	G	A	Pts	PIM	PP	SH	GW	Min
2000-01	Sparta Jr.	CzRep-Jr.	43	27	10	37	80																		
	HC Sparta Praha	CzRep	6	1	0	1	0																		
2001-02	Kitchener Rangers	OHL	61	28	32	60	54										4	0	2	2	0				
2002-03	Kitchener Rangers	OHL	60	33	34	67	123										20	11	16	27	17				
2003-04	Kitchener Rangers	OHL	55	26	42	68	97										5	2	2	4	10				
	Manchester	AHL	6	1	3	4	0										6	1	3	4	2				
2004-05	Manchester	AHL	60	4	14	18	118										6	0	0	0	18				
2005-06	**Los Angeles**	**NHL**	**10**	**1**	**0**	**1**	**0**	**0**	**0**	**0**	**7**	**14.3**	**1**	**0**	**0.0**	**4:42**									
	Manchester	AHL	60	15	12	27	52										7	1	1	2	5				
2006-07	Manchester	AHL	58	11	8	19	57										11	1	1	2	12				
	NHL Totals		**10**	**1**	**0**	**1**	**0**	**0**	**0**	**0**	**7**	**14.3**		**0**	**0.0**	**4:42**									

KAPANEN, Niko

(KA-pah-nehn, NEE-KOH) **PHX.**

Center. Shoots left. 5'9", 180 lbs. Born, Hameenlinna, Finland, April 29, 1978. Dallas' 5th choice, 173rd overall, in 1998 Entry Draft.

Season	Club	League	Regular Season GP	G	A	Pts	PIM	PP	SH	GW	S	%	+/-	TF	F%	Min	Playoffs GP	G	A	Pts	PIM	PP	SH	GW	Min
1993-94	HPK U18	Fin-U18	31	17	33	50	34																		
1994-95	HPK U18	Fin-U18	31	16	39	55	40																		
	HPK Jr.	Fin-Jr.	6	3	5	8	0																		
1995-96	HPK U18	Fin-U18	10	6	6	12	8																		
	HPK Jr.	Fin-Jr.	26	15	22	37	34																		
	HPK Hameenlinna	Finland	7	1	0	1	0																		
1996-97	HPK Jr.	Fin-Jr.	5	1	7	8	2										2	0	1	1	2				
	HPK Hameenlinna	Finland	41	6	9	15	12										10	4	5	9	2				
	HPK Hameenlinna	EuroHL	6	3	0	3	4										1	0	0	0	0				
1997-98	HPK Jr.	Fin-Jr.	2	1	1	2	0																		
	HPK Hameenlinna	Finland	48	8	18	26	44																		
1998-99	HPK Jr.	Fin-Jr.	5	3	1	4	0										1	0	2	2	0				
	HPK Hameenlinna	Finland	53	14	29	43	49										8	3	4	7	4				
99-2000	HPK Hameenlinna	Finland	53	20	28	48	38										8	1	9	10	4				
2000-01	TPS Turku	Finland	56	11	22	33	20										10	2	1	3	4				
2001-02	**Dallas**	**NHL**	**9**	**0**	**1**	**1**	**2**	**0**	**0**	**0**	**3**	**0.0**	**-1**	**59**	**40.7**	**9:44**									
	Utah Grizzlies	AHL	59	13	28	41	40										5	2	1	3	0				
2002-03	**Dallas**	**NHL**	**82**	**5**	**29**	**34**	**44**	**0**	**1**	**1**	**80**	**6.3**	**25**	**1111**	**47.5**	**14:39**	**12**	**4**	**3**	**7**	**12**	**0**	**1**	**0**	**16:03**
2003-04	**Dallas**	**NHL**	**67**	**1**	**5**	**6**	**16**	**0**	**0**	**0**	**57**	**1.8**	**-15**	**619**	**47.7**	**11:30**	**1**	**1**	**0**	**1**	**0**	**0**	**0**	**0**	**6:51**
2004-05	EV Zug	Swiss	44	10	33	43	24										9	2	5	7	35				
2005-06	**Dallas**	**NHL**	**81**	**14**	**21**	**35**	**36**	**5**	**2**	**4**	**97**	**14.4**	**-10**	**798**	**49.9**	**14:13**	**5**	**0**	**1**	**1**	**10**	**0**	**0**	**0**	**14:52**
	Finland	Olympics	8	2	1	3	2																		

			Regular Season														Playoffs								
Season	Club	League	GP	G	A	Pts	PIM	PP	SH	GW	S	%	+/-	TF	F%	Min	GP	G	A	Pts	PIM	PP	SH	GW	Min
2006-07	**Atlanta**	**NHL**	**60**	**4**	**9**	**13**	**20**	**1**	**0**	**0**	**51**	**7.8**	**–12**	**527**	**54.1**	**10:45**									
	Phoenix	**NHL**	**19**	**2**	**7**	**9**	**8**	**1**	**0**	**1**	**28**	**7.1**	**–11**	**279**	**54.1**	**17:36**									
	NHL Totals		**318**	**26**	**72**	**98**	**126**	**7**	**3**	**6**	**316**	**8.2**		**3393**	**49.5**	**13:11**	**18**	**5**	**4**	**9**	**22**	**0**	**1**	**0**	**15:13**

Signed as a free agent by **Zug** (Swiss), June 9, 2004. Traded to **Atlanta** by **Dallas** with Dallas' 7th round choice (Will O'Neill) in 2006 Entry Draft for Patrik Stefan and Jaroslav Modry, June 24, 2006. Claimed on waivers by **Phoenix** from **Atlanta**, February 27, 2007.

KAPANEN, Sami (KA-pah-nehn, SA-mee) PHI.

Right wing. Shoots left. 5'10", 185 lbs. Born, Vantaa, Finland, June 14, 1973. Hartford's 4th choice, 87th overall, in 1995 Entry Draft.

Season	Club	League	GP	G	A	Pts	PIM	PP	SH	GW	S	%	+/-	TF	F%	Min	GP	G	A	Pts	PIM	PP	SH	GW	Min
1989-90	KalPa Kuopio Jr.	Fin-Jr.	30	14	13	27	4																		
1990-91	KalPa Kuopio Jr.	Fin-Jr.	31	9	27	36	10																		
	KalPa Kuopio	Finland	14	1	2	3	2										8	2	1	3	2				
1991-92	KalPa Kuopio Jr.	Fin-Jr.	8	1	3	4	12																		
	KalPa Kuopio	Finland	42	15	10	25	8																		
1992-93	KalPa Kuopio Jr.	Fin-Jr.	8	11	16	27	2																		
	KalPa Kuopio	Finland	37	4	17	21	12																		
1993-94	KalPa Kuopio	Finland	48	23	32	55	16																		
	Finland	Olympics	8	1	0	1	2																		
1994-95	HIFK Helsinki	Finland	49	14	28	42	42										3	0	0	0	0				
1995-96	**Hartford**	**NHL**	**35**	**5**	**4**	**9**	**6**	**0**	**0**	**0**	**46**	**10.9**	**0**												
	Springfield	AHL	28	14	17	31	4										3	1	2	3	0				
1996-97	**Hartford**	**NHL**	**45**	**13**	**12**	**25**	**2**	**3**	**0**	**2**	**82**	**15.9**	**6**												
1997-98	**Carolina**	**NHL**	**81**	**26**	**37**	**63**	**16**	**4**	**0**	**5**	**190**	**13.7**	**9**												
	Finland	Olympics	6	0	1	1	0																		
1998-99	**Carolina**	**NHL**	**81**	**24**	**35**	**59**	**10**	**5**	**0**	**7**	**254**	**9.4**	**–1**	**10**	**50.0**	**19:25**	**5**	**1**	**1**	**2**	**0**	**0**	**0**	**0**	**19:09**
99-2000	**Carolina**	**NHL**	**76**	**24**	**24**	**48**	**12**	**7**	**0**	**5**	**229**	**10.5**	**10**	**2**	**50.0**	**19:53**									
2000-01	**Carolina**	**NHL**	**82**	**20**	**37**	**57**	**24**	**7**	**0**	**4**	**223**	**9.0**	**–12**	**6**	**16.7**	**18:56**	**6**	**2**	**3**	**5**	**0**	**1**	**0**	**0**	**20:13**
2001-02	**Carolina**	**NHL**	**77**	**27**	**42**	**69**	**23**	**11**	**0**	**4**	**248**	**10.9**	**9**	**7**	**14.3**	**20:38**	**23**	**1**	**8**	**9**	**6**	**0**	**0**	**0**	**20:03**
	Finland	Olympics	4	1	2	3	4																		
2002-03	**Carolina**	**NHL**	**43**	**6**	**12**	**18**	**12**	**3**	**0**	**1**	**108**	**5.6**	**–17**	**16**	**31.3**	**18:37**									
	Philadelphia	**NHL**	**28**	**4**	**9**	**13**	**6**	**2**	**0**	**1**	**81**	**4.9**	**–1**	**5**	**40.0**	**19:21**	**13**	**4**	**3**	**7**	**6**	**2**	**0**	**0**	**20:12**
2003-04	**Philadelphia**	**NHL**	**74**	**12**	**18**	**30**	**14**	**0**	**1**	**2**	**149**	**8.1**	**9**	**18**	**44.4**	**16:31**	**18**	**3**	**7**	**10**	**6**	**0**	**1**	**1**	**17:41**
2004-05	KalPa Kuopio	Finland-2	10	6	3	9	2										9	5	3	8	4				
2005-06	**Philadelphia**	**NHL**	**58**	**12**	**22**	**34**	**12**	**3**	**4**	**2**	**123**	**9.8**	**–9**	**43**	**39.5**	**18:04**	**6**	**0**	**0**	**0**	**2**	**0**	**0**	**0**	**20:19**
2006-07	**Philadelphia**	**NHL**	**77**	**11**	**14**	**25**	**22**	**1**	**2**	**1**	**129**	**8.5**	**–21**	**39**	**33.3**	**16:58**									
	NHL Totals		**757**	**184**	**266**	**450**	**159**	**46**	**7**	**34**	**1862**	**9.9**		**146**	**36.3**	**18:42**	**71**	**11**	**22**	**33**	**20**	**3**	**1**	**1**	**19:27**

Played in NHL All-Star Game (2000, 2002)

Transferred to **Carolina** after **Hartford** franchise relocated, June 25, 1997. Traded to **Philadelphia** by **Carolina** with Ryan Bast for Pavel Brendl and Bruno St. Jacques, February 7, 2003. Signed as a free agent by **Kuopio** (Finland-2), November 17, 2004.

KARIYA, Paul (kah-REE-ah, PAWL) ST.L.

Left wing. Shoots left. 5'10", 176 lbs. Born, Vancouver, B.C., October 16, 1974. Anaheim's 1st choice, 4th overall, in 1993 Entry Draft.

Season	Club	League	GP	G	A	Pts	PIM	PP	SH	GW	S	%	+/-	TF	F%	Min	GP	G	A	Pts	PIM	PP	SH	GW	Min
1990-91	Penticton	BCJHL	54	45	67	112	8																		
1991-92	Penticton	BCJHL	40	46	86	132	18																		
1992-93	U. of Maine	H-East	39	25	*75	*100	12																		
1993-94	U. of Maine	H-East	12	8	16	24	4																		
	Canada	Nat-Tm	23	7	34	41	2																		
	Canada	Olympics	8	3	4	7	2																		
1994-95	**Anaheim**	**NHL**	**47**	**18**	**21**	**39**	**4**	**7**	**1**	**3**	**134**	**13.4**	**–17**												
1995-96	**Anaheim**	**NHL**	**82**	**50**	**58**	**108**	**20**	**20**	**3**	**9**	**349**	**14.3**	**9**												
1996-97	**Anaheim**	**NHL**	**69**	**44**	**55**	**99**	**6**	**15**	**3**	**10**	**340**	**12.9**	**36**				**11**	**7**	**6**	**13**	**4**	**4**	**0**	**1**	
1997-98	**Anaheim**	**NHL**	**22**	**17**	**14**	**31**	**23**	**3**	**0**	**2**	**103**	**16.5**	**12**												
1998-99	**Anaheim**	**NHL**	**82**	**39**	**62**	**101**	**40**	**11**	**2**	**4**	**429**	**9.1**	**17**	**91**	**48.4**	**25:32**	**3**	**1**	**3**	**4**	**0**	**0**	**0**	**0**	**26:03**
99-2000	**Anaheim**	**NHL**	**74**	**42**	**44**	**86**	**24**	**11**	**3**	**3**	**324**	**13.0**	**22**	**99**	**39.4**	**24:22**									
2000-01	**Anaheim**	**NHL**	**66**	**33**	**34**	**67**	**20**	**18**	**3**	**3**	**230**	**14.3**	**–9**	**149**	**44.3**	**23:02**									
2001-02	**Anaheim**	**NHL**	**82**	**32**	**25**	**57**	**28**	**11**	**0**	**8**	**289**	**11.1**	**–15**	**94**	**41.5**	**22:13**									
	Canada	Olympics	6	3	1	4	0																		
2002-03	**Anaheim**	**NHL**	**82**	**25**	**56**	**81**	**48**	**11**	**1**	**2**	**257**	**9.7**	**–3**	**39**	**30.8**	**20:17**	**21**	**6**	**6**	**12**	**6**	**0**	**0**	**1**	**21:15**
2003-04	**Colorado**	**NHL**	**51**	**11**	**25**	**36**	**22**	**5**	**1**	**1**	**110**	**10.0**	**–5**	**18**	**27.8**	**18:37**	**1**	**0**	**1**	**1**	**0**	**0**	**0**	**0**	**16:00**
2004-05			DID NOT PLAY																						
2005-06	**Nashville**	**NHL**	**82**	**31**	**54**	**85**	**40**	**14**	**0**	**3**	**245**	**12.7**	**–6**	**9**	**11.1**	**19:05**	**5**	**2**	**5**	**7**	**0**	**2**	**0**	**0**	**20:47**
2006-07	**Nashville**	**NHL**	**82**	**24**	**52**	**76**	**36**	**5**	**0**	**2**	**224**	**10.7**	**6**	**3**	**0.0**	**20:23**	**5**	**0**	**2**	**2**	**2**	**0**	**0**	**0**	**19:36**
	NHL Totals		**821**	**366**	**500**	**866**	**311**	**131**	**17**	**50**	**3034**	**12.1**		**502**	**41.0**	**21:47**	**46**	**16**	**23**	**39**	**12**	**6**	**0**	**2**	**21:12**

Hockey East First All-Star Team (1993) • Hockey East Rookie of the Year (1993) • Hockey East Player of the Year (1993) • NCAA East First All-American Team (1993) • NCAA Championship All-Tournament Team (1993) • Hobey Baker Memorial Award (Top U.S. Collegiate Player) (1993) • NHL All-Rookie Team (1995) • Lady Byng Memorial Trophy (1996, 1997) • NHL First All-Star Team (1996, 1997, 1999) • NHL Second All-Star Team (2000, 2003)

Played in NHL All-Star Game (1996, 1997, 1999, 2000, 2001, 2002, 2003)

• Missed majority of 1997-98 season after failing to come to contract terms with **Anaheim** and recovering from head injury suffered in game vs. San Jose, February 1, 1998. Signed as a free agent by **Colorado**, July 3, 2003. Signed as a free agent by **Nashville**, August 5, 2005. Signed as a free agent by **St. Louis**, July 1, 2007.

KARLSSON, Andreas (KARL-suhn, awn-DRAY-uhs) T.B.

Center. Shoots left. 6'4", 205 lbs. Born, Ludvika, Sweden, August 19, 1975. Calgary's 8th choice, 148th overall, in 1993 Entry Draft.

Season	Club	League	GP	G	A	Pts	PIM	PP	SH	GW	S	%	+/-	TF	F%	Min	GP	G	A	Pts	PIM	PP	SH	GW	Min
1992-93	Leksands IF	Sweden	13	0	0	0	6																		
1993-94	Leksands IF	Sweden	21	0	0	0	10										3	0	0	0	0				
1994-95	Leksands IF Jr.	Swe-Jr.	3	3	3	6	0																		
	Leksands IF	Sweden	24	7	8	15	0										4	0	1	1	0				
1995-96	Leksands IF Jr.	Swe-Jr.	2	4	1	5	6																		
	Leksands IF	Sweden	40	10	13	23	10																		
1996-97	Leksands IF	Sweden	49	13	11	24	39										9	2	0	2	2				
1997-98	Leksands IF	Sweden	33	9	14	23	20										4	1	0	1	0				
	Leksands IF	EuroHL	6	2	3	5	2																		
1998-99	Leksands IF	Sweden	49	18	15	33	18										4	1	0	1	6				
	Leksands IF	EuroHL	6	1	3	4	2										2	1	1	2	2				
99-2000	**Atlanta**	**NHL**	**51**	**5**	**9**	**14**	**14**	**1**	**0**	**0**	**74**	**6.8**	**–17**	**552**	**46.7**	**13:00**									
	Orlando	IHL	18	5	5	10	6																		
2000-01	**Atlanta**	**NHL**	**60**	**5**	**11**	**16**	**16**	**0**	**1**	**0**	**83**	**6.0**	**–2**	**743**	**48.6**	**12:54**									
2001-02	**Atlanta**	**NHL**	**42**	**1**	**7**	**8**	**20**	**0**	**0**	**0**	**41**	**2.4**	**–8**	**386**	**45.1**	**12:30**									
	Chicago Wolves	AHL	16	6	14	20	11										23	7	14	21	6				
2002-03	Chicago Wolves	AHL	41	12	20	32	16										9	1	3	4	4				
2003-04	EHC Basel	Swiss	40	7	21	28	30																		
2004-05	HV 71 Jonkoping	Sweden	39	11	13	24	12																		
2005-06	HV 71 Jonkoping	Sweden	50	*26	29	*55	30										12	5	8	13	8				
2006-07	**Tampa Bay**	**NHL**	**53**	**3**	**6**	**9**	**12**	**0**	**0**	**1**	**25**	**12.0**	**–4**	**286**	**45.1**	**8:25**	**6**	**0**	**0**	**0**	**0**	**0**	**0**	**0**	**7:07**
	NHL Totals		**206**	**14**	**33**	**47**	**62**	**1**	**1**	**1**	**223**	**6.3**		**1967**	**46.9**	**11:41**	**6**	**0**	**0**	**0**	**0**	**0**	**0**	**0**	**7:07**

Traded to **Atlanta** by **Calgary** for future considerations, June 25, 1999. Signed as a free agent by **Basel** (Swiss), July 18, 2003. Signed as a free agent by **Tampa Bay**, July 1, 2006.

KASPARAITIS, Darius (KAZ-puhr-IGH-tihz, DAIR-ee-uhs) NYR

Defense. Shoots left. 5'11", 215 lbs. Born, Elektrenai, USSR, October 16, 1972. NY Islanders' 1st choice, 5th overall, in 1992 Entry Draft.

Season	Club	League	GP	G	A	Pts	PIM	PP	SH	GW	S	%	+/-	TF	F%	Min	GP	G	A	Pts	PIM	PP	SH	GW	Min
1988-89	Dynamo Moscow	USSR	3	0	0	0	0																		
1989-90	Dynamo Moscow	USSR	1	0	0	0	0																		
1990-91	Dyn'o Moscow 2	USSR-3	16	3	....	....																			
	Dynamo Moscow	USSR	17	0	1	1	10																		
1991-92	Dynamo Moscow	CIS	31	2	10	12	14																		
	Dyn'o Moscow 2	CIS-3	8	2	1	3	8																		
	Russia	Olympics	8	0	2	2	2																		
1992-93	Dynamo Moscow	CIS	7	1	3	4	8																		
	NY Islanders	**NHL**	**79**	**4**	**17**	**21**	**166**	**0**	**0**	**0**	**92**	**4.3**	**15**				**18**	**0**	**5**	**5**	**31**	**0**	**0**	**0**	

Season	Club	League	GP	G	A	Pts	PIM	PP	SH	GW	S	%	+/-	TF	F%	Min	GP	G	A	Pts	PIM	PP	SH	GW	Min
			Regular Season														Playoffs								
1993-94	**NY Islanders**	**NHL**	**76**	**1**	**10**	**11**	**142**	**0**	**0**	**0**	**81**	**1.2**	**-6**	....	....	....	**4**	**0**	**0**	**0**	**8**	**0**	**0**	**0**	....
1994-95	**NY Islanders**	**NHL**	**13**	**0**	**1**	**1**	**22**	**0**	**0**	**0**	**8**	**0.0**	**-11**	....	....	....	....	....	....	....	....	....	....	....	....
1995-96	**NY Islanders**	**NHL**	**46**	**1**	**7**	**8**	**93**	**0**	**0**	**0**	**34**	**2.9**	**-12**	....	....	....	....	....	....	....	....	....	....	....	....
1996-97	**NY Islanders**	**NHL**	**18**	**0**	**5**	**5**	**16**	**0**	**0**	**0**	**12**	**0.0**	**-7**	....	....	....	....	....	....	....	....	....	....	....	....
	Pittsburgh	**NHL**	**57**	**2**	**16**	**18**	**84**	**0**	**0**	**0**	**46**	**4.3**	**24**	....	....	....	**5**	**0**	**0**	**0**	**6**	**0**	**0**	**0**	....
1997-98	**Pittsburgh**	**NHL**	**81**	**4**	**8**	**12**	**127**	**0**	**2**	**0**	**71**	**5.6**	**3**	....	....	....	**5**	**0**	**0**	**0**	**8**	**0**	**0**	**0**	....
	Russia	Olympics	6	0	2	2	6	....	....	....	....	....	....	....	....	....	....	....	....	....	....	....	....	....	....
1998-99	**Pittsburgh**	**NHL**	**48**	**1**	**4**	**5**	**70**	**0**	**0**	**0**	**32**	**3.1**	**12**	**0**	**0.0**	**16:01**	....	....	....	....	....	....	....	....	....
99-2000	**Pittsburgh**	**NHL**	**73**	**3**	**12**	**15**	**146**	**1**	**0**	**1**	**76**	**3.9**	**-12**	**0**	**0.0**	**18:07**	**11**	**1**	**1**	**2**	**10**	**0**	**0**	**0**	**21:39**
2000-01	**Pittsburgh**	**NHL**	**77**	**3**	**16**	**19**	**111**	**1**	**0**	**0**	**81**	**3.7**	**11**	**0**	**0.0**	**19:14**	**17**	**1**	**1**	**2**	**26**	**0**	**0**	**1**	**19:52**
2001-02	**Pittsburgh**	**NHL**	**69**	**2**	**12**	**14**	**123**	**0**	**0**	**0**	**75**	**2.7**	**-1**	**1**	**0.0**	**20:32**	....	....	....	....	....	....	....	....	....
	Russia	Olympics	6	1	0	1	4	....	....	....	....	....	....	....	....	....	....	....	....	....	....	....	....	....	....
	Colorado	**NHL**	**11**	**0**	**0**	**0**	**19**	**0**	**0**	**0**	**6**	**0.0**	**1**	**0**	**0.0**	**19:44**	**21**	**0**	**3**	**3**	**18**	**0**	**0**	**0**	**20:46**
2002-03	**NY Rangers**	**NHL**	**80**	**3**	**11**	**14**	**85**	**0**	**0**	**1**	**84**	**3.6**	**5**	**0**	**0.0**	**18:54**	....	....	....	....	....	....	....	....	....
2003-04	**NY Rangers**	**NHL**	**44**	**1**	**9**	**10**	**48**	**0**	**0**	**0**	**29**	**3.4**	**11**	**0**	**0.0**	**16:23**	....	....	....	....	....	....	....	....	....
2004-05	Ak Bars Kazan	Russia	28	1	3	4	118	....	....	....	....	....	....	....	....	....	3	0	0	0	6	....	....	....	....
2005-06	**NY Rangers**	**NHL**	**67**	**0**	**6**	**6**	**97**	**0**	**0**	**0**	**48**	**0.0**	**7**	**0**	**0.0**	**17:28**	**2**	**0**	**0**	**0**	**0**	**0**	**0**	**0**	**16:23**
	Russia	Olympics	8	0	2	2	8	....	....	....	....	....	....	....	....	....	....	....	....	....	....	....	....	....	....
2006-07	**NY Rangers**	**NHL**	**24**	**2**	**2**	**4**	**30**	**0**	**0**	**0**	**9**	**22.2**	**-1**	**0**	**0.0**	**14:52**	....	....	....	....	....	....	....	....	....
	Hartford	AHL	12	0	3	3	8	....	....	....	....	....	....	....	....	....	....	....	....	....	....	....	....	....	....
	NHL Totals		**863**	**27**	**136**	**163**	**1379**	**2**	**2**	**2**	**784**	**3.4**		**1**	**0.0**	**18:11**	**83**	**2**	**10**	**12**	**107**	**0**	**0**	**1**	**20:29**

Traded to **Pittsburgh** by **NY Islanders** with Andreas Johansson for Bryan Smolinski, November 17, 1996. Traded to **Colorado** by **Pittsburgh** for Ville Niemenen and Rick Berry, March 19, 2002. Signed as a free agent by **NY Rangers**, July 2, 2002. Signed as a free agent by **Kazan** (Russia), October 22, 2004.

KAVANAGH, Pat

(KA-vuh-naw, PAT)

Right wing. Shoots right. 6'3", 192 lbs. Born, Ottawa, Ont., March 14, 1979. Philadelphia's 2nd choice, 50th overall, in 1997 Entry Draft.

Season	Club	League	GP	G	A	Pts	PIM	PP	SH	GW	S	%	+/-	TF	F%	Min	GP	G	A	Pts	PIM	PP	SH	GW	Min
1995-96	Kanata Valley	CJHL	54	19	16	35	99	....	....	....	....	....	....	....	....	....	....	....	....	....	....	....	....	....	....
1996-97	Peterborough	OHL	43	6	8	14	53	....	....	....	....	....	....	....	....	....	11	1	1	2	12	....	....	....	....
1997-98	Peterborough	OHL	66	10	16	26	85	....	....	....	....	....	....	....	....	....	4	1	0	1	6	....	....	....	....
1998-99	Peterborough	OHL	68	26	43	69	118	....	....	....	....	....	....	....	....	....	5	0	5	5	10	....	....	....	....
99-2000	Syracuse Crunch	AHL	68	12	8	20	56	....	....	....	....	....	....	....	....	....	4	0	0	0	0	....	....	....	....
2000-01	Kansas City	IHL	78	26	15	41	86	....	....	....	....	....	....	....	....	....	....	....	....	....	....	....	....	....	....
	Vancouver	**NHL**	....	....	....	....	....	....	....	....	....	....	....	....	....	....	**3**	**0**	**0**	**0**	**2**	**0**	**0**	**0**	**8:27**
2001-02	Manitoba Moose	AHL	70	13	19	32	100	....	....	....	....	....	....	....	....	....	7	1	0	1	6	....	....	....	....
2002-03	**Vancouver**	**NHL**	**3**	**1**	**0**	**1**	**2**	**0**	**0**	**1**	**4**	**25.0**	**2**	**27**	**37.0**	**10:23**	....	....	....	....	....	....	....	....	....
	Manitoba Moose	AHL	63	15	15	30	96	....	....	....	....	....	....	....	....	....	14	7	4	11	20	....	....	....	....
2003-04	**Vancouver**	**NHL**	**3**	**1**	**0**	**1**	**0**	**0**	**0**	**0**	**1**	**100.0**	**0**	**21**	**52.4**	**7:58**	....	....	....	....	....	....	....	....	....
	Manitoba Moose	AHL	73	23	22	45	69	....	....	....	....	....	....	....	....	....	....	....	....	....	....	....	....	....	....
2004-05	Binghamton	AHL	80	14	17	31	87	....	....	....	....	....	....	....	....	....	6	0	1	1	10	....	....	....	....
2005-06	**Philadelphia**	**NHL**	**8**	**0**	**0**	**0**	**2**	**0**	**0**	**0**	**1**	**0.0**	**-2**	**35**	**68.6**	**5:14**	....	....	....	....	....	....	....	....	....
	Philadelphia	AHL	73	20	23	43	81	....	....	....	....	....	....	....	....	....	....	....	....	....	....	....	....	....	....
2006-07	Portland Pirates	AHL	2	0	0	0	4	....	....	....	....	....	....	....	....	....	....	....	....	....	....	....	....	....	....
	SaiPa	Finland	23	3	5	8	24	....	....	....	....	....	....	....	....	....	....	....	....	....	....	....	....	....	....
	HV 71 Jonkoping	Sweden	10	1	2	3	6	....	....	....	....	....	....	....	....	....	14	1	1	2	62	....	....	....	....
	NHL Totals		**14**	**2**	**0**	**2**	**4**	**0**	**0**	**1**	**6**	**33.3**		**83**	**54.2**	**6:55**	**3**	**0**	**0**	**0**	**2**	**0**	**0**	**0**	**8:27**

Traded to **Vancouver** by **Philadelphia** for Vancouver's 6th round choice (Konstantin Rudenko) in 1999 Entry Draft, June 1, 1999. Signed as a free agent by **Ottawa**, July 27, 2004. Signed as a free agent by **Philadelphia**, August 22, 2005. Signed as a free agent by **Portland** (AHL), October 11, 2006. Signed as a free agent by **SaiPa** (Finland), December 12, 2006. Signed as a free agent by **Jonkoping** (Sweden), January 31, 2007.

KEITH, Duncan

(KEETH, DUHN-kuhn) **CHI.**

Defense. Shoots left. 6', 187 lbs. Born, Winnipeg, Man., July 16, 1983. Chicago's 2nd choice, 54th overall, in 2002 Entry Draft.

Season	Club	League	GP	G	A	Pts	PIM	PP	SH	GW	S	%	+/-	TF	F%	Min	GP	G	A	Pts	PIM	PP	SH	GW	Min
1998-99	Penticton	BCAHA	44	51	57	108	45	....	....	....	....	....	....	....	....	....	....	....	....	....	....	....	....	....	....
99-2000	Penticton	BCHL	59	9	27	36	37	....	....	....	....	....	....	....	....	....	....	....	....	....	....	....	....	....	....
2000-01	Penticton	BCHL	60	18	64	82	61	....	....	....	....	....	....	....	....	....	9	4	6	10	18	....	....	....	....
2001-02	Michigan State	CCHA	41	3	12	15	18	....	....	....	....	....	....	....	....	....	....	....	....	....	....	....	....	....	....
2002-03	Michigan State	CCHA	15	3	6	9	8	....	....	....	....	....	....	....	....	....	....	....	....	....	....	....	....	....	....
	Kelowna Rockets	WHL	37	11	35	46	60	....	....	....	....	....	....	....	....	....	19	3	11	14	12	....	....	....	....
2003-04	Norfolk Admirals	AHL	75	7	18	25	44	....	....	....	....	....	....	....	....	....	8	1	1	2	6	....	....	....	....
2004-05	Norfolk Admirals	AHL	79	9	17	26	78	....	....	....	....	....	....	....	....	....	6	0	0	0	14	....	....	....	....
2005-06	**Chicago**	**NHL**	**81**	**9**	**12**	**21**	**79**	**1**	**1**	**0**	**134**	**6.7**	**-11**	**0**	**0.0**	**23:26**	....	....	....	....	....	....	....	....	....
2006-07	**Chicago**	**NHL**	**82**	**2**	**29**	**31**	**76**	**0**	**0**	**0**	**122**	**1.6**	**0**	**0**	**0.0**	**23:36**	....	....	....	....	....	....	....	....	....
	NHL Totals		**163**	**11**	**41**	**52**	**155**	**1**	**1**	**0**	**256**	**4.3**		**0**	**0.0**	**23:31**	....	....	....	....	....	....	....	....	....

• Left **Michigan State University** (CCHA) and signed as a free agent by **Kelowna** (WHL), December 27, 2002.

KEITH, Matt

(KEETH, MAT) **ANA.**

Right wing. Shoots right. 6'2", 200 lbs. Born, Edmonton, Alta., April 11, 1983. Chicago's 3rd choice, 59th overall, in 2001 Entry Draft.

Season	Club	League	GP	G	A	Pts	PIM	PP	SH	GW	S	%	+/-	TF	F%	Min	GP	G	A	Pts	PIM	PP	SH	GW	Min
1998-99	Banff Icemen	HJHL	STATISTICS NOT AVAILABLE																						
	Spokane Chiefs	WHL	7	1	0	1	4	....	....	....	....	....	....	....	....	....	....	....	....	....	....	....	....	....	....
99-2000	Spokane Chiefs	WHL	39	1	3	4	37	....	....	....	....	....	....	....	....	....	15	1	2	3	11	....	....	....	....
2000-01	Spokane Chiefs	WHL	33	13	14	27	63	....	....	....	....	....	....	....	....	....	12	1	3	4	14	....	....	....	....
2001-02	Spokane Chiefs	WHL	68	34	33	67	71	....	....	....	....	....	....	....	....	....	11	5	5	10	16	....	....	....	....
2002-03	Spokane Chiefs	WHL	7	2	2	4	11	....	....	....	....	....	....	....	....	....	....	....	....	....	....	....	....	....	....
	Red Deer Rebels	WHL	49	25	26	51	32	....	....	....	....	....	....	....	....	....	23	6	7	13	30	....	....	....	....
2003-04	**Chicago**	**NHL**	**20**	**2**	**3**	**5**	**10**	**1**	**0**	**0**	**21**	**9.5**	**-5**	**2**	**100.0**	**11:58**	....	....	....	....	....	....	....	....	....
	Norfolk Admirals	AHL	66	13	13	26	57	....	....	....	....	....	....	....	....	....	8	1	2	3	10	....	....	....	....
2004-05	Norfolk Admirals	AHL	80	18	31	49	74	....	....	....	....	....	....	....	....	....	6	0	1	1	0	....	....	....	....
2005-06	**Chicago**	**NHL**	**2**	**0**	**0**	**0**	**0**	**0**	**0**	**0**	**6**	**0.0**	**0**	**0**	**0.0**	**11:42**	....	....	....	....	....	....	....	....	....
	Norfolk Admirals	AHL	72	26	19	45	61	....	....	....	....	....	....	....	....	....	3	0	1	1	0	....	....	....	....
2006-07	**Chicago**	**NHL**	**2**	**0**	**0**	**0**	**4**	**0**	**0**	**0**	**0**	**0.0**	**-2**	**0**	**0.0**	**9:33**	....	....	....	....	....	....	....	....	....
	Norfolk Admirals	AHL	19	2	8	10	15	....	....	....	....	....	....	....	....	....	....	....	....	....	....	....	....	....	....
	Portland Pirates	AHL	44	10	12	22	22	....	....	....	....	....	....	....	....	....	....	....	....	....	....	....	....	....	....
	NHL Totals		**24**	**2**	**3**	**5**	**14**	**1**	**0**	**0**	**27**	**7.4**		**2**	**100.0**	**11:44**	....	....	....	....	....	....	....	....	....

• Missed majority of 2000-01 season recovering from shoulder injury suffered in game vs. Tri-City (WHL), September 22, 2000. Traded to **Anaheim** by **Chicago** with Sebastien Caron and Chris Durno for Pierre Parenteau and Bruno St. Jacques, December 28, 2006.

KELLY, Chris

(KEHL-lee, KRIHS) **OTT.**

Center/Left wing. Shoots left. 6', 199 lbs. Born, Toronto, Ont., November 11, 1980. Ottawa's 4th choice, 94th overall, in 1999 Entry Draft.

Season	Club	League	GP	G	A	Pts	PIM	PP	SH	GW	S	%	+/-	TF	F%	Min	GP	G	A	Pts	PIM	PP	SH	GW	Min
1995-96	Toronto Marlies	MTHL	42	25	45	70	25	....	....	....	....	....	....	....	....	....	....	....	....	....	....	....	....	....	....
1996-97	Aurora Tigers	MTJHL	49	14	20	34	11	....	....	....	....	....	....	....	....	....	....	....	....	....	....	....	....	....	....
1997-98	London Knights	OHL	54	15	14	29	4	....	....	....	....	....	....	....	....	....	16	4	5	9	12	....	....	....	....
1998-99	London Knights	OHL	68	36	41	77	60	....	....	....	....	....	....	....	....	....	25	9	17	26	22	....	....	....	....
99-2000	London Knights	OHL	63	29	43	72	57	....	....	....	....	....	....	....	....	....	....	....	....	....	....	....	....	....	....
2000-01	London Knights	OHL	31	21	34	55	46	....	....	....	....	....	....	....	....	....	....	....	....	....	....	....	....	....	....
	Sudbury Wolves	OHL	19	5	16	21	17	....	....	....	....	....	....	....	....	....	12	11	5	16	14	....	....	....	....
2001-02	Grand Rapids	AHL	31	3	3	6	20	....	....	....	....	....	....	....	....	....	5	1	1	2	5	....	....	....	....
	Muskegon Fury	UHL	4	1	2	3	0	....	....	....	....	....	....	....	....	....	....	....	....	....	....	....	....	....	....
2002-03	Binghamton	AHL	77	17	14	31	73	....	....	....	....	....	....	....	....	....	14	2	3	5	8	....	....	....	....
2003-04	**Ottawa**	**NHL**	**4**	**0**	**0**	**0**	**0**	**0**	**0**	**0**	**4**	**0.0**	**-2**	**5**	**40.0**	**9:29**	....	....	....	....	....	....	....	....	....
	Binghamton	AHL	54	15	19	34	40	....	....	....	....	....	....	....	....	....	2	0	0	0	4	....	....	....	....
2004-05	Binghamton	AHL	77	24	36	60	57	....	....	....	....	....	....	....	....	....	6	1	2	3	11	....	....	....	....
2005-06	**Ottawa**	**NHL**	**82**	**10**	**20**	**30**	**76**	**1**	**0**	**2**	**112**	**8.9**	**21**	**808**	**45.8**	**12:20**	**10**	**0**	**0**	**0**	**2**	**0**	**0**	**0**	**11:49**
2006-07	**Ottawa**	**NHL**	**82**	**15**	**23**	**38**	**40**	**1**	**2**	**0**	**131**	**11.5**	**28**	**564**	**49.8**	**15:18**	**20**	**3**	**4**	**7**	**4**	**0**	**0**	**0**	**15:28**
	NHL Totals		**168**	**25**	**43**	**68**	**116**	**2**	**2**	**2**	**247**	**10.1**		**1377**	**47.4**	**13:43**	**30**	**3**	**4**	**7**	**6**	**0**	**0**	**0**	**14:15**

KELLY, Steve
(KEHL-lee, STEEV) **MIN.**

Center. Shoots left. 6'2", 205 lbs. Born, Vancouver, B.C., October 26, 1976. Edmonton's 1st choice, 6th overall, in 1995 Entry Draft.

Season	Club	League	GP	G	A	Pts	PIM	PP	SH	GW	S	%	+/-	TF	F%	Min	Playoffs GP	G	A	Pts	PIM	PP	SH	GW	Min
1991-92	Westbank	BCAHA	30	25	60	85	75																		
1992-93	Prince Albert	WHL	65	11	9	20	75																		
1993-94	Prince Albert	WHL	65	19	42	61	106																		
1994-95	Prince Albert	WHL	68	31	41	72	153										15	7	9	16	35				
1995-96	Prince Albert	WHL	70	27	74	101	203										18	13	18	31	47				
1996-97	**Edmonton**	**NHL**	**8**	**1**	**0**	**1**	**6**	**0**	**0**	**1**	**6**	**16.7**	**–1**				**6**	**0**	**0**	**0**	**2**	**0**	**0**	**0**	
	Hamilton	AHL	48	9	29	38	111										11	3	3	6	24				
1997-98	**Edmonton**	**NHL**	**19**	**0**	**2**	**2**	**8**	**0**	**0**	**0**	**5**	**0.0**	**–4**												
	Hamilton	AHL	11	2	8	10	18																		
	Tampa Bay	**NHL**	**24**	**2**	**1**	**3**	**15**	**1**	**0**	**0**	**17**	**11.8**	**–9**												
	Milwaukee	IHL	5	0	1	1	19																		
	Cleveland	IHL	5	1	1	2	29										1	0	1	1	0				
1998-99	**Tampa Bay**	**NHL**	**34**	**1**	**3**	**4**	**27**	**0**	**0**	**1**	**15**	**6.7**	**–15**	**11**	**54.5**	**10:51**									
	Cleveland	IHL	18	6	7	13	36																		
99-2000	Detroit Vipers	IHL	1	0	0	0	4																		
	♦ **New Jersey**	**NHL**	**1**	**0**	**0**	**0**	**0**	**0**	**0**	**0**	**0**	**0.0**	**0**	**0**	**0.0**	**4:28**	**10**	**0**	**0**	**0**	**4**	**0**	**0**	**0**	**11:32**
	Albany River Rats	AHL	76	21	36	57	131										3	1	1	2	2				
2000-01	**New Jersey**	**NHL**	**24**	**2**	**2**	**4**	**21**	**0**	**0**	**0**	**18**	**11.1**	**0**	**87**	**48.3**	**9:58**									
	Los Angeles	**NHL**	**11**	**1**	**0**	**1**	**4**	**0**	**0**	**0**	**4**	**25.0**	**0**	**51**	**39.2**	**6:44**	**8**	**0**	**0**	**0**	**2**	**0**	**0**	**0**	**5:23**
2001-02	**Los Angeles**	**NHL**	**8**	**0**	**1**	**1**	**2**	**0**	**0**	**0**	**0**	**0.0**	**–1**	**44**	**36.4**	**6:52**	**1**	**0**	**0**	**0**	**0**	**0**	**0**	**0**	**5:54**
	Manchester	AHL	49	10	21	31	88										5	1	8	9	4				
2002-03	Manchester	AHL	54	19	44	63	144										3	0	1	1	0				
	Los Angeles	**NHL**	**15**	**2**	**3**	**5**	**0**	**0**	**0**	**1**	**14**	**14.3**	**–6**	**133**	**42.9**	**12:29**									
2003-04	**Los Angeles**	**NHL**	**3**	**0**	**0**	**0**	**0**	**0**	**0**	**0**	**5**	**0.0**	**0**	**30**	**43.3**	**10:30**									
	Manchester	AHL	59	21	49	70	117										1	0	0	0	2				
2004-05	Adler Mannheim	Germany	46	11	22	33	*210										12	1	4	5	*72				
2005-06	Adler Mannheim	Germany	19	4	17	21	44																		
	Frankfurt Lions	Germany	22	6	14	20	119																		
2006-07	Frankfurt Lions	Germany	47	9	29	38	209										8	2	8	10	30				
	NHL Totals		**147**	**9**	**12**	**21**	**83**	**1**	**0**	**3**	**84**	**10.7**		**356**	**43.3**	**10:00**	**25**	**0**	**0**	**0**	**8**	**0**	**0**	**0**	**8:39**

Traded to **Tampa Bay** by **Edmonton** with Bryan Marchment and Jason Bonsignore for Roman Hamrlik and Paul Comrie, December 30, 1997. Traded to **New Jersey** by **Tampa Bay** for New Jersey's 7th round choice (Brian Eklund) in 2000 Entry Draft, October 7, 1999. Traded to **Los Angeles** by **New Jersey** to complete transaction that sent Bob Corkum to New Jersey (February 23, 2001), February 27, 2001. • Spent majority of 2000-01 season with New Jersey and Los Angeles as a healthy reserve. Signed as a free agent by **Mannheim** (Germany), May 4, 2004. Signed as a free agent by **Minnesota**, July 2, 2007.

KESLER, Ryan
(KEHZ-luhr, RIGH-uhn) **VAN.**

Center. Shoots right. 6'2", 205 lbs. Born, Livonia, MI, August 31, 1984. Vancouver's 1st choice, 23rd overall, in 2003 Entry Draft.

Season	Club	League	GP	G	A	Pts	PIM	PP	SH	GW	S	%	+/-	TF	F%	Min	Playoffs GP	G	A	Pts	PIM	PP	SH	GW	Min
99-2000	Det. Honeybaked	MWEHL	72	44	73	117																			
2000-01	USNTDP	U-18	26	8	20	28	24																		
	USNTDP	NAHL	56	7	21	28	40																		
2001-02	USNTDP	U-18	46	11	33	44	23																		
	USNTDP	USHL	13	5	5	10	10																		
	USNTDP	NAHL	10	5	6	11	4																		
2002-03	Ohio State	CCHA	40	11	20	31	44																		
2003-04	**Vancouver**	**NHL**	**28**	**2**	**3**	**5**	**16**	**0**	**0**	**0**	**23**	**8.7**	**–2**	**194**	**40.2**	**10:42**									
	Manitoba Moose	AHL	33	3	8	11	29																		
2004-05	Manitoba Moose	AHL	78	30	27	57	105										14	4	5	9	8				
2005-06	**Vancouver**	**NHL**	**82**	**10**	**13**	**23**	**79**	**1**	**0**	**2**	**119**	**8.4**	**1**	**984**	**46.8**	**14:03**									
2006-07	**Vancouver**	**NHL**	**48**	**6**	**10**	**16**	**40**	**0**	**0**	**0**	**88**	**6.8**	**1**	**690**	**46.1**	**16:26**	**1**	**0**	**0**	**0**	**0**	**0**	**0**	**0**	**27:51**
	NHL Totals		**158**	**18**	**26**	**44**	**135**	**1**	**0**	**2**	**230**	**7.8**		**1868**	**45.8**	**14:11**	**1**	**0**	**0**	**0**	**0**	**0**	**0**	**0**	**27:51**

KESSEL, Phil
(KEH-suhl, FIHL) **BOS.**

Center. Shoots right. 6', 193 lbs. Born, Madison, WI, October 2, 1987. Boston's 1st choice, 5th overall, in 2006 Entry Draft.

Season	Club	League	GP	G	A	Pts	PIM	PP	SH	GW	S	%	+/-	TF	F%	Min	Playoffs GP	G	A	Pts	PIM	PP	SH	GW	Min
2003-04	USNTDP	U-17	32	31	18	49	8																		
	USNTDP	NAHL	30	21	12	33	18																		
2004-05	USNTDP	U-18	31	41	32	73	16																		
	USNTDP	NAHL	14	11	14	25	21																		
2005-06	U. of Minnesota	WCHA	39	18	33	51	28																		
2006-07	**Boston**	**NHL**	**70**	**11**	**18**	**29**	**12**	**1**	**0**	**0**	**170**	**6.5**	**–12**	**373**	**40.8**	**14:04**									
	Providence Bruins	AHL	2	1	0	1	2																		
	NHL Totals		**70**	**11**	**18**	**29**	**12**	**1**	**0**	**0**	**170**	**6.5**		**373**	**40.8**	**14:04**									

WCHA All-Rookie Team (2006) • WCHA Rookie of the Year (2006) • Bill Masterton Memorial Trophy (2007)

KHAVANOV, Alexander
(khuh-VAN-ahf, al-EHX-AN-duhr)

Defense. Shoots left. 6'2", 205 lbs. Born, Moscow, USSR, January 30, 1972. St. Louis' 8th choice, 232nd overall, in 1999 Entry Draft.

Season	Club	League	GP	G	A	Pts	PIM	PP	SH	GW	S	%	+/-	TF	F%	Min	Playoffs GP	G	A	Pts	PIM	PP	SH	GW	Min
1992-93	Birmingham Bulls	ECHL	19	0	3	3	14																		
	Raleigh IceCaps	ECHL	17	0	6	6	8																		
1993-94	St. Petersburg	CIS	41	1	2	3	24																		
1994-95	St. Petersburg	CIS	49	7	0	7	32										3	0	0	0	0				
1995-96	St. Petersburg	CIS	32	1	5	6	41																		
	HPK Hameenlinna	Finland	16	0	2	2	4										9	0	0	0	0				
1996-97	Cherepovets	Russia	39	3	8	11	56										3	1	0	1	4				
1997-98	Cherepovets	Russia	44	3	5	8	46																		
1998-99	Dynamo Moscow	Russia	40	2	7	9	14										16	1	5	6	35				
	Dynamo Moscow	EuroHL	5	0	1	1	2										6	0	0	0	4				
99-2000	Dynamo Moscow	Russia	38	5	12	17	49										17	0	3	3	4				
	Dynamo Moscow	EuroHL	6	2	0	2	0																		
2000-01	**St. Louis**	**NHL**	**74**	**7**	**16**	**23**	**52**	**2**	**0**	**0**	**92**	**7.6**	**16**	**0**	**0.0**	**20:54**	**15**	**3**	**2**	**5**	**14**	**1**	**0**	**0**	**21:16**
2001-02	**St. Louis**	**NHL**	**81**	**3**	**21**	**24**	**55**	**0**	**0**	**0**	**87**	**3.4**	**9**	**0**	**0.0**	**17:13**	**4**	**0**	**0**	**0**	**2**	**0**	**0**	**0**	**15:08**
2002-03	**St. Louis**	**NHL**	**81**	**8**	**25**	**33**	**48**	**2**	**1**	**2**	**90**	**8.9**	**–1**	**2**	**50.0**	**21:57**	**7**	**2**	**3**	**5**	**2**	**1**	**0**	**0**	**19:05**
2003-04	**St. Louis**	**NHL**	**48**	**3**	**7**	**10**	**18**	**2**	**0**	**0**	**62**	**4.8**	**2**	**1**	**0.0**	**19:20**									
2004-05	St. Petersburg	Russia	3	0	0	0	27																		
2005-06	**Toronto**	**NHL**	**64**	**6**	**6**	**12**	**60**	**2**	**1**	**0**	**44**	**13.6**	**–11**	**0**	**0.0**	**17:08**									
2006-07	HC Davos	Swiss	34	1	19	20	72																		
	NHL Totals		**348**	**27**	**75**	**102**	**233**	**8**	**2**	**2**	**375**	**7.2**		**3**	**33.3**	**19:23**	**26**	**5**	**5**	**10**	**18**	**2**	**0**	**0**	**19:44**

Signed as a free agent by **St. Petersburg** (Russia), September 25, 2004. Signed as a free agent by **Toronto**, August 9, 2005. Signed as a free agent by **Davos** (Swiss), September 17, 2006.

KILGER, Chad
(KIHL-guhr, CHAD) **TOR.**

Left wing. Shoots left. 6'4", 224 lbs. Born, Cornwall, Ont., November 27, 1976. Anaheim's 1st choice, 4th overall, in 1995 Entry Draft.

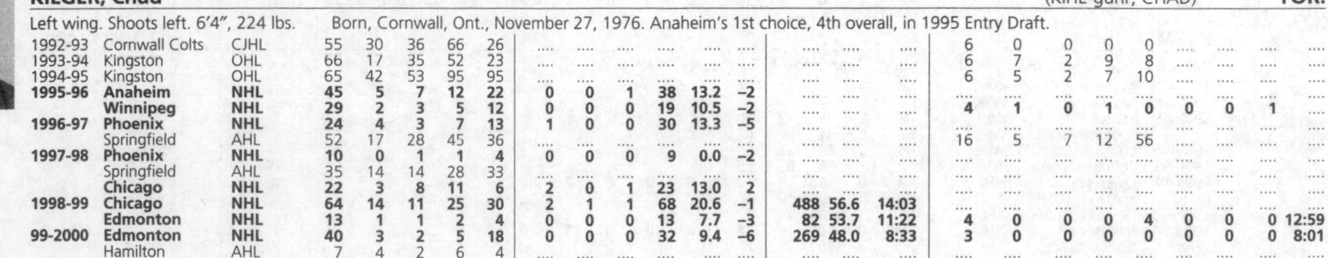

Season	Club	League	GP	G	A	Pts	PIM	PP	SH	GW	S	%	+/-	TF	F%	Min	Playoffs GP	G	A	Pts	PIM	PP	SH	GW	Min
1992-93	Cornwall Colts	CJHL	55	30	36	66	26										6	0	0	0	0				
1993-94	Kingston	OHL	66	17	35	52	23										6	7	2	9	8				
1994-95	Kingston	OHL	65	42	53	95	95										6	5	2	7	10				
1995-96	**Anaheim**	**NHL**	**45**	**5**	**7**	**12**	**22**	**0**	**0**	**1**	**38**	**13.2**	**–2**												
	Winnipeg	**NHL**	**29**	**2**	**3**	**5**	**12**	**0**	**0**	**0**	**19**	**10.5**	**–2**				**4**	**1**	**0**	**1**	**0**	**0**	**0**	**1**	
1996-97	**Phoenix**	**NHL**	**24**	**4**	**3**	**7**	**13**	**1**	**0**	**0**	**30**	**13.3**	**–5**												
	Springfield	AHL	52	17	28	45	36										16	5	7	12	56				
1997-98	**Phoenix**	**NHL**	**10**	**0**	**1**	**1**	**4**	**0**	**0**	**0**	**9**	**0.0**	**–2**												
	Springfield	AHL	35	14	14	28	33																		
	Chicago	**NHL**	**22**	**3**	**8**	**11**	**6**	**2**	**0**	**1**	**23**	**13.0**	**2**												
1998-99	**Chicago**	**NHL**	**64**	**14**	**11**	**25**	**30**	**2**	**1**	**1**	**68**	**20.6**	**–1**	**488**	**56.6**	**14:03**									
	Edmonton	**NHL**	**13**	**1**	**1**	**2**	**4**	**0**	**0**	**0**	**13**	**7.7**	**–3**	**82**	**53.7**	**11:22**	**4**	**0**	**0**	**0**	**4**	**0**	**0**	**0**	**12:59**
99-2000	**Edmonton**	**NHL**	**40**	**3**	**2**	**5**	**18**	**0**	**0**	**0**	**32**	**9.4**	**–6**	**269**	**48.0**	**8:33**	**3**	**0**	**0**	**0**	**0**	**0**	**0**	**0**	**8:01**
	Hamilton	AHL	7	4	2	6	4																		

			Regular Season														Playoffs								
Season	Club	League	GP	G	A	Pts	PIM	PP	SH	GW	S	%	+/-	TF	F%	Min	GP	G	A	Pts	PIM	PP	SH	GW	Min
2000-01	**Edmonton**	**NHL**	**34**	**5**	**2**	**7**	**17**	**1**	**0**	**0**	**28**	**17.9**	**−7**	**391**	**53.5**	**8:18**	....	....	....	....	....	....	....	....	....
	Montreal	**NHL**	**43**	**9**	**16**	**25**	**34**	**1**	**1**	**1**	**75**	**12.0**	**−1**	**319**	**52.4**	**17:57**	....	....	....	....	....	....	....	....	....
2001-02	**Montreal**	**NHL**	**75**	**8**	**15**	**23**	**27**	**0**	**1**	**2**	**87**	**9.2**	**−7**	**357**	**53.8**	**13:14**	**12**	**0**	**1**	**1**	**9**	**0**	**0**	**0**	**14:00**
2002-03	**Montreal**	**NHL**	**60**	**9**	**7**	**16**	**21**	**0**	**0**	**1**	**60**	**15.0**	**−4**	**208**	**46.6**	**10:42**	....	....	....	....	....	....	....	....	....
2003-04	**Montreal**	**NHL**	**36**	**2**	**2**	**4**	**14**	**0**	**0**	**0**	**29**	**6.9**	**2**	**95**	**48.4**	**10:26**	....	....	....	....	....	....	....	....	....
	Hamilton	AHL	2	1	0	1	0	....	....	....	....	....	....	....	....	....	....	....	....	....	....	....	....	....	....
	Toronto	**NHL**	**5**	**1**	**1**	**2**	**2**	**0**	**0**	**1**	**6**	**16.7**	**2**	**2**	**0.0**	**12:14**	**13**	**2**	**1**	**3**	**0**	**0**	**0**	**0**	**11:41**
2004-05			DID NOT PLAY																						
2005-06	**Toronto**	**NHL**	**79**	**17**	**11**	**28**	**63**	**1**	**1**	**2**	**103**	**16.5**	**−6**	**89**	**51.7**	**12:25**	....	....	....	....	....	....	....	....	....
2006-07	**Toronto**	**NHL**	**82**	**14**	**14**	**28**	**58**	**0**	**1**	**2**	**141**	**9.9**	**−5**	**198**	**46.0**	**14:30**	....	....	....	....	....	....	....	....	....
	NHL Totals		**661**	**97**	**104**	**201**	**345**	**8**	**5**	**12**	**761**	**12.7**		**2498**	**51.9**	**12:35**	**36**	**3**	**2**	**5**	**13**	**0**	**0**	**1**	**12:22**

Traded to **Winnipeg** by **Anaheim** with Oleg Tverdovsky and Anaheim's 3rd round choice (Per-Anton Lundstrom) in 1996 Entry Draft for Teemu Selanne, Marc Chouinard and Winnipeg's 4th round choice (later traded to Toronto – later traded to Montreal – Montreal selected Kim Staal) in 1996 Entry Draft, February 7, 1996. Transferred to **Phoenix** after **Winnipeg** franchise relocated, July 1, 1996. Traded to **Chicago** by **Phoenix** with Jayson More for Keith Carney and Jim Cummins, March 4, 1998. Traded to **Edmonton** by **Chicago** with Daniel Cleary, Ethan Moreau and Christian Laflamme for Boris Mironov, Dean McAmmond and Jonas Elofsson, March 20, 1999. Traded to **Montreal** by **Edmonton** for Sergei Zholtok, December 18, 2000. Claimed on waivers by **Toronto** from **Montreal**, March 9, 2004.

KING, D.J. (KIHNG, DEE-JAY) ST.L.

Center. Shoots left. 6'3", 225 lbs. Born, Meadow Lake, Sask., January 27, 1984. St. Louis' 6th choice, 191st overall, in 2002 Entry Draft.

Season	Club	League	GP	G	A	Pts	PIM	PP	SH	GW	S	%	+/-	TF	F%	Min	GP	G	A	Pts	PIM	PP	SH	GW	Min
2000-01	Beardy's	SMHL	52	30	28	58	120	....	....	....	....	....	....	....	....	....	....	....	....	....	....	....	....	....	....
2001-02	Lethbridge	WHL	65	10	14	24	104	....	....	....	....	....	....	....	....	....	....	....	....	....	....	....	....	....	....
2002-03	Lethbridge	WHL	55	15	17	32	139	....	....	....	....	....	....	....	....	....	....	....	....	....	....	....	....	....	....
2003-04	Lethbridge	WHL	35	8	15	23	102	....	....	....	....	....	....	....	....	....	....	....	....	....	....	....	....	....	....
	Kelowna Rockets	WHL	28	5	2	7	80	....	....	....	....	....	....	....	....	....	17	1	6	7	16	....	....	....	....
2004-05	Worcester IceCats	AHL	74	6	8	14	178	....	....	....	....	....	....	....	....	....	....	....	....	....	....	....	....	....	....
2005-06	Peoria Rivermen	AHL	67	5	6	11	160	....	....	....	....	....	....	....	....	....	2	0	0	0	2	....	....	....	....
	Alaska Aces	ECHL	5	0	4	4	4	....	....	....	....	....	....	....	....	....	....	....	....	....	....	....	....	....	....
2006-07	**St. Louis**	**NHL**	**27**	**1**	**1**	**2**	**52**	**0**	**0**	**0**	**12**	**8.3**	**−3**	**2**	**50.0**	**5:31**	....	....	....	....	....	....	....	....	....
	Peoria Rivermen	AHL	38	5	4	9	102	....	....	....	....	....	....	....	....	....	....	....	....	....	....	....	....	....	....
	NHL Totals		**27**	**1**	**1**	**2**	**52**	**0**	**0**	**0**	**12**	**8.3**		**2**	**50.0**	**5:31**	....	....	....	....	....	....	....	....	....

KING, Jason (KIHNG, JAY-suhn) ANA.

Center. Shoots left. 6'1", 195 lbs. Born, Corner Brook, Nfld., September 14, 1981. Vancouver's 5th choice, 212th overall, in 2001 Entry Draft.

Season	Club	League	GP	G	A	Pts	PIM	PP	SH	GW	S	%	+/-	TF	F%	Min	GP	G	A	Pts	PIM	PP	SH	GW	Min
99-2000	Halifax	QMJHL	53	3	7	10	8	....	....	....	....	....	....	....	....	....	10	0	0	0	2	....	....	....	....
2000-01	Halifax	QMJHL	72	48	41	89	78	....	....	....	....	....	....	....	....	....	6	3	2	5	16	....	....	....	....
2001-02	Halifax	QMJHL	61	*63	36	99	39	....	....	....	....	....	....	....	....	....	13	9	8	17	13	....	....	....	....
2002-03	**Vancouver**	**NHL**	**8**	**0**	**2**	**2**	**0**	**0**	**0**	**0**	**12**	**0.0**	**0**	**0**	**0.0**	**11:17**	....	....	....	....	....	....	....	....	....
	Manitoba Moose	AHL	67	20	20	40	15	....	....	....	....	....	....	....	....	....	14	4	3	7	14	....	....	....	....
2003-04	**Vancouver**	**NHL**	**47**	**12**	**9**	**21**	**8**	**6**	**0**	**1**	**107**	**11.2**	**0**	**3**	**66.7**	**12:43**	**1**	**0**	**0**	**0**	**0**	**0**	**0**	**0**	**6:21**
	Manitoba Moose	AHL	29	12	11	23	6	....	....	....	....	....	....	....	....	....	....	....	....	....	....	....	....	....	....
2004-05	Manitoba Moose	AHL	59	26	27	53	22	....	....	....	....	....	....	....	....	....	....	....	....	....	....	....	....	....	....
2005-06	Manitoba Moose	AHL	36	20	14	34	34	....	....	....	....	....	....	....	....	....	13	3	4	7	8	....	....	....	....
2006-07	Skelleftea AIK HK	Sweden	55	15	4	19	20	....	....	....	....	....	....	....	....	....	....	....	....	....	....	....	....	....	....
	Skelleftea AIK HK	Sweden-Q	9	3	2	5	6	....	....	....	....	....	....	....	....	....	....	....	....	....	....	....	....	....	....
	NHL Totals		**55**	**12**	**11**	**23**	**8**	**6**	**0**	**1**	**119**	**10.1**		**3**	**66.7**	**12:30**	**1**	**0**	**0**	**0**	**0**	**0**	**0**	**0**	**6:21**

QMJHL Second All-Star Team (2001)

• Missed majority of 2005-06 season recovering from head injury suffered near the end of the 2004-05 season. Traded to **Anaheim** by **Vancouver** for Ryan Shannon and future considerations, June 23, 2007. Signed as a free agent by **Skelleftea** (Sweden), September 13, 2006.

KLEE, Ken (KLEE, KEHN) ATL.

Defense. Shoots right. 6', 215 lbs. Born, Indianapolis, IN, April 24, 1971. Washington's 11th choice, 177th overall, in 1990 Entry Draft.

Season	Club	League	GP	G	A	Pts	PIM	PP	SH	GW	S	%	+/-	TF	F%	Min	GP	G	A	Pts	PIM	PP	SH	GW	Min
1988-89	St. Mike's B's	OHA-B	40	9	23	32	64	....	....	....	....	....	....	....	....	....	27	5	12	17	54	....	....	....	....
1989-90	Bowling Green	CCHA	39	0	5	5	52	....	....	....	....	....	....	....	....	....	....	....	....	....	....	....	....	....	....
1990-91	Bowling Green	CCHA	37	7	28	35	50	....	....	....	....	....	....	....	....	....	....	....	....	....	....	....	....	....	....
1991-92	Bowling Green	CCHA	10	0	1	1	14	....	....	....	....	....	....	....	....	....	....	....	....	....	....	....	....	....	....
1992-93	Baltimore	AHL	77	4	14	18	93	....	....	....	....	....	....	....	....	....	7	0	1	1	15	....	....	....	....
1993-94	Portland Pirates	AHL	65	2	9	11	87	....	....	....	....	....	....	....	....	....	17	1	2	3	14	....	....	....	....
1994-95	Portland Pirates	AHL	49	5	7	12	89	....	....	....	....	....	....	....	....	....	....	....	....	....	....	....	....	....	....
	Washington	**NHL**	**23**	**3**	**1**	**4**	**41**	**0**	**0**	**0**	**18**	**16.7**	**2**	....	....	....	**7**	**0**	**0**	**0**	**4**	**0**	**0**	**0**	....
1995-96	**Washington**	**NHL**	**66**	**8**	**3**	**11**	**60**	**0**	**1**	**2**	**76**	**10.5**	**−1**	....	....	....	**1**	**0**	**0**	**0**	**0**	**0**	**0**	**0**	....
1996-97	**Washington**	**NHL**	**80**	**3**	**8**	**11**	**115**	**0**	**0**	**2**	**108**	**2.8**	**−5**	....	....	....	....	....	....	....	....	....	....	....	....
1997-98	**Washington**	**NHL**	**51**	**4**	**2**	**6**	**46**	**0**	**0**	**1**	**44**	**9.1**	**−3**	....	....	....	**9**	**1**	**0**	**1**	**10**	**0**	**0**	**0**	....
1998-99	**Washington**	**NHL**	**78**	**7**	**13**	**20**	**80**	**0**	**0**	**1**	**132**	**5.3**	**−9**	**0**	**0.0**	**19:07**	....	....	....	....	....	....	....	....	....
99-2000	**Washington**	**NHL**	**80**	**7**	**13**	**20**	**79**	**0**	**0**	**2**	**113**	**6.2**	**8**	**0**	**0.0**	**20:29**	**5**	**0**	**1**	**1**	**10**	**0**	**0**	**0**	**21:38**
2000-01	**Washington**	**NHL**	**54**	**2**	**4**	**6**	**60**	**0**	**0**	**0**	**58**	**3.4**	**−5**	**0**	**0.0**	**17:15**	**6**	**0**	**1**	**1**	**8**	**0**	**0**	**0**	**13:47**
2001-02	**Washington**	**NHL**	**68**	**8**	**8**	**16**	**38**	**2**	**0**	**3**	**85**	**9.4**	**4**	**2**	**0.0**	**19:24**	....	....	....	....	....	....	....	....	....
2002-03	**Washington**	**NHL**	**70**	**1**	**16**	**17**	**89**	**0**	**0**	**0**	**67**	**1.5**	**22**	**0**	**0.0**	**21:49**	**6**	**0**	**0**	**0**	**6**	**0**	**0**	**0**	**23:11**
2003-04	**Toronto**	**NHL**	**66**	**4**	**25**	**29**	**36**	**3**	**0**	**1**	**85**	**4.7**	**−1**	**1**	**100.0**	**22:08**	**11**	**0**	**0**	**0**	**6**	**0**	**0**	**0**	**18:45**
2004-05			DID NOT PLAY																						
2005-06	**Toronto**	**NHL**	**56**	**3**	**12**	**15**	**66**	**1**	**0**	**1**	**65**	**4.6**	**−1**	**0**	**0.0**	**20:02**	....	....	....	....	....	....	....	....	....
	New Jersey	**NHL**	**18**	**0**	**0**	**0**	**14**	**0**	**0**	**0**	**5**	**0.0**	**−3**	**0**	**0.0**	**15:03**	**6**	**1**	**0**	**1**	**6**	**0**	**0**	**0**	**12:05**
2006-07	**Colorado**	**NHL**	**81**	**3**	**16**	**19**	**68**	**0**	**0**	**0**	**90**	**3.3**	**18**	**0**	**0.0**	**20:38**	....	....	....	....	....	....	....	....	....
	NHL Totals		**791**	**53**	**121**	**174**	**792**	**6**	**1**	**13**	**946**	**5.6**		**3**	**33.3**	**20:01**	**51**	**2**	**2**	**4**	**50**	**0**	**0**	**0**	**17:54**

Signed as a free agent by **Toronto**, September 27, 2003. Traded to **New Jersey** by **Toronto** for Aleksander Suglobov, March 8, 2006. Signed as a free agent by **Colorado**, July 24, 2006. Signed as a free agent by **Atlanta**, July 2, 2007.

KLEIN, Kevin (KLIGHN, KEH-vihn) NSH.

Defense. Shoots right. 6'1", 195 lbs. Born, Kitchener, Ont., December 13, 1984. Nashville's 3rd choice, 37th overall, in 2003 Entry Draft.

Season	Club	League	GP	G	A	Pts	PIM	PP	SH	GW	S	%	+/-	TF	F%	Min	GP	G	A	Pts	PIM	PP	SH	GW	Min
99-2000	Kitchener Midgets	Minor-ON	54	12	29	41	40	....	....	....	....	....	....	....	....	....	....	....	....	....	....	....	....	....	....
2000-01	St. Michael's	OHL	58	3	16	19	21	....	....	....	....	....	....	....	....	....	18	0	5	5	17	....	....	....	....
2001-02	St. Michael's	OHL	68	5	22	27	35	....	....	....	....	....	....	....	....	....	15	2	7	9	12	....	....	....	....
2002-03	St. Michael's	OHL	67	11	33	44	88	....	....	....	....	....	....	....	....	....	17	1	9	10	8	....	....	....	....
2003-04	St. Michael's	OHL	5	0	1	1	2	....	....	....	....	....	....	....	....	....	....	....	....	....	....	....	....	....	....
	Guelph Storm	OHL	46	6	23	29	40	....	....	....	....	....	....	....	....	....	22	10	11	21	12	....	....	....	....
2004-05	Milwaukee	AHL	65	4	12	16	22	....	....	....	....	....	....	....	....	....	7	0	0	0	11	....	....	....	....
	Rockford IceHogs	UHL	3	2	1	3	0	....	....	....	....	....	....	....	....	....	....	....	....	....	....	....	....	....	....
2005-06	**Nashville**	**NHL**	**2**	**0**	**0**	**0**	**0**	**0**	**0**	**0**	**0**	**0.0**	**−1**	**0**	**0.0**	**13:40**	....	....	....	....	....	....	....	....	....
	Milwaukee	AHL	76	10	33	43	31	....	....	....	....	....	....	....	....	....	21	3	7	10	31	....	....	....	....
2006-07	**Nashville**	**NHL**	**3**	**1**	**0**	**1**	**0**	**0**	**0**	**0**	**2**	**50.0**	**3**	**0**	**0.0**	**16:37**	....	....	....	....	....	....	....	....	....
	Milwaukee	AHL	70	5	15	20	67	....	....	....	....	....	....	....	....	....	4	1	0	1	0	....	....	....	....
	NHL Totals		**5**	**1**	**0**	**1**	**0**	**0**	**0**	**0**	**2**	**50.0**		**0**	**0.0**	**15:26**	....	....	....	....	....	....	....	....	....

KLEMM, Jon (KLEHM, JAWN)

Defense. Shoots right. 6'2", 200 lbs. Born, Cranbrook, B.C., January 8, 1970.

Season	Club	League	GP	G	A	Pts	PIM	PP	SH	GW	S	%	+/-	TF	F%	Min	GP	G	A	Pts	PIM	PP	SH	GW	Min
1986-87	Cranbrook Colts	KIJHL	59	20	51	71	54	....	....	....	....	....	....	....	....	....	....	....	....	....	....	....	....	....	....
1987-88	Seattle	WHL	68	6	7	13	24	....	....	....	....	....	....	....	....	....	....	....	....	....	....	....	....	....	....
1988-89	Seattle	WHL	2	1	1	2	0	....	....	....	....	....	....	....	....	....	....	....	....	....	....	....	....	....	....
	Spokane Chiefs	WHL	66	6	34	40	42	....	....	....	....	....	....	....	....	....	....	....	....	....	....	....	....	....	....
1989-90	Spokane Chiefs	WHL	66	3	28	31	100	....	....	....	....	....	....	....	....	....	6	1	1	2	5	....	....	....	....
1990-91	Spokane Chiefs	WHL	72	7	58	65	65	....	....	....	....	....	....	....	....	....	15	3	6	9	8	....	....	....	....
1991-92	**Quebec**	**NHL**	**4**	**0**	**1**	**1**	**0**	**0**	**0**	**0**	**2**	**0.0**	**2**	....	....	....	....	....	....	....	....	....	....	....	....
	Halifax Citadels	AHL	70	6	13	19	40	....	....	....	....	....	....	....	....	....	....	....	....	....	....	....	....	....	....
1992-93	Halifax Citadels	AHL	80	3	20	23	32	....	....	....	....	....	....	....	....	....	....	....	....	....	....	....	....	....	....
1993-94	**Quebec**	**NHL**	**7**	**0**	**0**	**0**	**4**	**0**	**0**	**0**	**11**	**0.0**	**−1**	....	....	....	....	....	....	....	....	....	....	....	....
	Cornwall Aces	AHL	66	4	26	30	78	....	....	....	....	....	....	....	....	....	13	1	2	3	6	....	....	....	....

Season	Club	League	GP	G	A	Pts	PIM	PP	SH	GW	S	%	+/-	TF	F%	Min	GP	G	A	Pts	PIM	PP	SH	GW	Min
			Regular Season														Playoffs								
1994-95	Cornwall Aces	AHL	65	6	13	19	84	....	....	....	....	....	....	....	....	....	....	....	....	....	....	....	....	....	....
	Quebec	**NHL**	**4**	**1**	**0**	**1**	**2**	**0**	**0**	**0**	**5**	**20.0**	**3**	....	....	....	....	....	....	....	....	....	....	....	....
1995-96♦	**Colorado**	**NHL**	**56**	**3**	**12**	**15**	**20**	**0**	**1**	**1**	**61**	**4.9**	**12**	....	....	....	**15**	**2**	**1**	**3**	**0**	**1**	**0**	**0**	....
1996-97	**Colorado**	**NHL**	**80**	**9**	**15**	**24**	**37**	**1**	**2**	**1**	**103**	**8.7**	**12**	....	....	....	**17**	**1**	**1**	**2**	**6**	**0**	**0**	**0**	....
1997-98	**Colorado**	**NHL**	**67**	**6**	**8**	**14**	**30**	**0**	**0**	**0**	**64**	**10.0**	**-3**	....	....	....	**4**	**0**	**0**	**0**	**0**	**0**	**0**	**0**	....
1998-99	**Colorado**	**NHL**	**39**	**1**	**2**	**3**	**31**	**0**	**0**	**0**	**28**	**3.6**	**4**	**14**	**35.7**	**13:43**	**19**	**0**	**1**	**1**	**10**	**0**	**0**	**0**	**8:32**
99-2000	**Colorado**	**NHL**	**73**	**5**	**7**	**12**	**34**	**0**	**0**	**0**	**64**	**7.8**	**26**	**17**	**47.1**	**17:22**	**17**	**2**	**1**	**3**	**9**	**0**	**0**	**1**	**14:25**
2000-01♦	**Colorado**	**NHL**	**78**	**4**	**11**	**15**	**54**	**2**	**0**	**2**	**97**	**4.1**	**22**	**1**	**100.0**	**19:56**	**22**	**1**	**2**	**3**	**16**	**0**	**0**	**1**	**16:15**
2001-02	**Chicago**	**NHL**	**82**	**4**	**16**	**20**	**42**	**2**	**0**	**1**	**111**	**3.6**	**-3**	**1**	**0.0**	**23:50**	**5**	**0**	**1**	**1**	**4**	**0**	**0**	**0**	**21:58**
2002-03	**Chicago**	**NHL**	**70**	**2**	**14**	**16**	**44**	**1**	**0**	**1**	**74**	**2.7**	**-9**	**2**	**0.0**	**21:57**	....	....	....	....	....	....	....	....	....
2003-04	**Chicago**	**NHL**	**19**	**0**	**1**	**1**	**20**	**0**	**0**	**0**	**19**	**0.0**	**6**	**0**	**0.0**	**21:21**	....	....	....	....	....	....	....	....	....
	Dallas	**NHL**	**58**	**2**	**4**	**6**	**24**	**0**	**0**	**1**	**52**	**3.8**	**10**	**1**	**0.0**	**16:00**	....	....	....	....	....	....	....	....	....
2004-05			DID NOT PLAY																						
2005-06	**Dallas**	**NHL**	**76**	**4**	**7**	**11**	**60**	**1**	**0**	**1**	**57**	**7.0**	**-3**	**2**	**50.0**	**16:56**	**5**	**1**	**0**	**1**	**0**	**0**	**0**	**0**	**15:44**
2006-07	**Dallas**	**NHL**	**38**	**1**	**2**	**3**	**24**	**0**	**0**	**0**	**25**	**4.0**	**0**	**0**	**0.0**	**13:03**	**1**	**0**	**0**	**0**	**2**	**0**	**0**	**0**	**13:47**
	NHL Totals		**751**	**42**	**100**	**142**	**426**	**7**	**3**	**8**	**769**	**5.5**		**38**	**39.5**	**18:42**	**105**	**7**	**7**	**14**	**47**	**1**	**0**	**1**	**14:01**

WHL West Second All-Star Team (1991)

Signed as a free agent by **Quebec**, May 14, 1991. Transferred to **Colorado** after **Quebec** franchise relocated, June 21, 1995. • Missed majority of 1998-99 season recovering from knee injury suffered in game vs. Phoenix, November 10, 1998. Signed as a free agent by **Chicago**, July 1, 2001. Traded to **Dallas** by **Chicago** with NY Rangers' 4th round choice (previously acquired, Dallas selected Fredrik Naslund) in 2004 Entry Draft for Stephane Robidas and Dallas' 2nd round choice (Jakub Sindel) in 2004 Entry Draft, November 17, 2003. • Missed majority of 2006-07 season as a healthy scratch.

KLEPIS, Jakub (KLEH-pihsh, YA-kuhb) WSH.

Center. Shoots right. 6'1", 198 lbs. Born, Prague, Czech., June 5, 1984. Ottawa's 1st choice, 16th overall, in 2002 Entry Draft.

Season	Club	League	GP	G	A	Pts	PIM	PP	SH	GW	S	%	+/-	TF	F%	Min	GP	G	A	Pts	PIM	PP	SH	GW	Min
99-2000	Slavia Jr.	CzRep-Jr.	48	14	26	40	30	....	....	....	....	....	....	....	....	....	....	....	....	....	....	....	....	....	....
2000-01	Slavia Jr.	CzRep-Jr.	52	21	25	46	82	....	....	....	....	....	....	....	....	....	....	....	....	....	....	....	....	....	....
2001-02	Portland	WHL	70	14	50	64	111	....	....	....	....	....	....	....	....	....	7	0	3	3	22	....	....	....	....
2002-03	HC Slavia Praha	CzRep	38	2	6	8	22	....	....	....	....	....	....	....	....	....	4	0	0	0	6	....	....	....	....
	Slavia Jr.	CzRep-Jr.	11	4	5	9	59	....	....	....	....	....	....	....	....	....	3	0	3	3	4	....	....	....	....
2003-04	HC Slavia Praha	CzRep	44	4	9	13	43	....	....	....	....	....	....	....	....	....	17	5	3	8	10	....	....	....	....
2004-05	Portland Pirates	AHL	78	13	14	27	76	....	....	....	....	....	....	....	....	....	....	....	....	....	....	....	....	....	....
2005-06	**Washington**	**NHL**	**25**	**1**	**3**	**4**	**8**	**0**	**0**	**0**	**26**	**3.8**	**-11**	**22**	**40.9**	**7:25**	....	....	....	....	....	....	....	....	....
	Hershey Bears	AHL	54	11	20	31	49	....	....	....	....	....	....	....	....	....	15	2	6	8	4	....	....	....	....
2006-07	**Washington**	**NHL**	**41**	**3**	**7**	**10**	**28**	**0**	**0**	**0**	**38**	**7.9**	**-2**	**184**	**41.3**	**9:58**	....	....	....	....	....	....	....	....	....
	Hershey Bears	AHL	31	6	26	32	24	....	....	....	....	....	....	....	....	....	19	7	7	14	14	....	....	....	....
	NHL Totals		**66**	**4**	**10**	**14**	**36**	**0**	**0**	**0**	**64**	**6.3**		**206**	**41.3**	**9:00**	....	....	....	....	....	....	....	....	....

Traded to **Buffalo** by **Ottawa** for Vaclav Varada and Buffalo's 5th round choice (Tim Cook) in 2003 Entry Draft, February 25, 2003. Traded to **Washington** by **Buffalo** for Mike Grier, March 9, 2004.

KLESLA, Rostislav (KLEHS-luh, RAHS-tih-slav) CBJ

Defense. Shoots left. 6'3", 216 lbs. Born, Novy Jicin, Czech., March 21, 1982. Columbus' 1st choice, 4th overall, in 2000 Entry Draft.

Season	Club	League	GP	G	A	Pts	PIM	PP	SH	GW	S	%	+/-	TF	F%	Min	GP	G	A	Pts	PIM	PP	SH	GW	Min
1997-98	HC Opava Jr.	CzRep-Jr.	38	11	18	29	87	....	....	....	....	....	....	....	....	....	8	2	2	4	0	....	....	....	....
1998-99	Sioux City	USHL	54	4	12	16	100	....	....	....	....	....	....	....	....	....	5	2	0	2	2	....	....	....	....
99-2000	Brampton	OHL	67	16	29	45	174	....	....	....	....	....	....	....	....	....	6	1	1	2	21	....	....	....	....
2000-01	**Columbus**	**NHL**	**8**	**2**	**0**	**2**	**6**	**0**	**0**	**0**	**10**	**20.0**	**-1**	**0**	**0.0**	**18:25**	....	....	....	....	....	....	....	....	....
	Brampton	OHL	45	18	36	54	59	....	....	....	....	....	....	....	....	....	9	2	9	11	26	....	....	....	....
2001-02	**Columbus**	**NHL**	**75**	**8**	**8**	**16**	**74**	**1**	**0**	**0**	**102**	**7.8**	**-6**	**0**	**0.0**	**18:52**	....	....	....	....	....	....	....	....	....
2002-03	**Columbus**	**NHL**	**72**	**2**	**14**	**16**	**71**	**0**	**0**	**0**	**89**	**2.2**	**-22**	**0**	**0.0**	**18:45**	....	....	....	....	....	....	....	....	....
2003-04	**Columbus**	**NHL**	**47**	**2**	**11**	**13**	**27**	**0**	**0**	**1**	**74**	**2.7**	**-16**	**0**	**0.0**	**18:19**	....	....	....	....	....	....	....	....	....
2004-05	HC Vsetin	CzRep	41	7	17	24	136	....	....	....	....	....	....	....	....	....	....	....	....	....	....	....	....	....	....
	HPK Hameenlinna	Finland	9	1	2	3	12	....	....	....	....	....	....	....	....	....	10	0	2	2	12	....	....	....	....
2005-06	**Columbus**	**NHL**	**51**	**6**	**13**	**19**	**75**	**2**	**0**	**1**	**84**	**7.1**	**-4**	**2**	**100.0**	**21:27**	....	....	....	....	....	....	....	....	....
2006-07	**Columbus**	**NHL**	**75**	**9**	**13**	**22**	**105**	**2**	**0**	**0**	**159**	**5.7**	**-13**	**0**	**0.0**	**22:54**	....	....	....	....	....	....	....	....	....
	NHL Totals		**328**	**29**	**59**	**88**	**358**	**5**	**0**	**2**	**518**	**5.6**		**2**	**100.0**	**20:05**	....	....	....	....	....	....	....	....	....

OHL All-Rookie Team (2000) • Canadian Major Junior All-Rookie Team (2000) • OHL First All-Star Team (2001) • NHL All-Rookie Team (2002)

Returned to **Brampton** (OHL) by **Columbus**, October 28, 2000. Signed as a free agent by **Vsetin** (CzRep), September 17, 2004. Signed as a free agent by **Hameenlinna** (Finland), January 29, 2005.

KLOUCEK, Tomas (KLOH-chehk, TAW-mahsh)

Defense. Shoots left. 6'3", 235 lbs. Born, Prague, Czech., March 7, 1980. NY Rangers' 6th choice, 131st overall, in 1998 Entry Draft.

Season	Club	League	GP	G	A	Pts	PIM	PP	SH	GW	S	%	+/-	TF	F%	Min	GP	G	A	Pts	PIM	PP	SH	GW	Min
1995-96	Slavia Jr.	CzRep-Jr.	40	2	8	10	....	....	....	....	....	....	....	....	....	....	....	....	....	....	....	....	....	....	....
1996-97	Slavia Jr.	CzRep-Jr.	43	4	14	18	44	....	....	....	....	....	....	....	....	....	....	....	....	....	....	....	....	....	....
1997-98	Slavia Jr.	CzRep-Jr.	43	1	9	10	....	....	....	....	....	....	....	....	....	....	....	....	....	....	....	....	....	....	....
1998-99	Cape Breton	QMJHL	59	4	17	21	162	....	....	....	....	....	....	....	....	....	2	0	0	0	4	....	....	....	....
99-2000	Hartford	AHL	73	2	8	10	113	....	....	....	....	....	....	....	....	....	23	0	4	4	18	....	....	....	....
2000-01	**NY Rangers**	**NHL**	**43**	**1**	**4**	**5**	**74**	**0**	**0**	**0**	**22**	**4.5**	**-3**	**0**	**0.0**	**16:43**	....	....	....	....	....	....	....	....	....
	Hartford	AHL	21	0	2	2	44	....	....	....	....	....	....	....	....	....	....	....	....	....	....	....	....	....	....
2001-02	**NY Rangers**	**NHL**	**52**	**1**	**3**	**4**	**137**	**0**	**0**	**0**	**21**	**4.8**	**-2**	**1**	**0.0**	**11:58**	....	....	....	....	....	....	....	....	....
	Hartford	AHL	9	0	2	2	27	....	....	....	....	....	....	....	....	....	10	1	1	2	8	....	....	....	....
2002-03	Hartford	AHL	20	3	4	7	102	....	....	....	....	....	....	....	....	....	....	....	....	....	....	....	....	....	....
	Nashville	**NHL**	**3**	**0**	**0**	**0**	**2**	**0**	**0**	**0**	**1**	**0.0**	**1**	**0**	**0.0**	**9:45**	....	....	....	....	....	....	....	....	....
	Milwaukee	AHL	34	0	6	6	80	....	....	....	....	....	....	....	....	....	....	....	....	....	....	....	....	....	....
2003-04	**Nashville**	**NHL**	**5**	**0**	**1**	**1**	**10**	**0**	**0**	**0**	**0**	**0.0**	**3**	**0**	**0.0**	**11:34**	....	....	....	....	....	....	....	....	....
	Atlanta	**NHL**	**37**	**0**	**0**	**0**	**25**	**0**	**0**	**0**	**12**	**0.0**	**-8**	**0**	**0.0**	**8:00**	....	....	....	....	....	....	....	....	....
2004-05	HC Slavia Praha	CzRep	29	1	1	2	28	....	....	....	....	....	....	....	....	....	....	....	....	....	....	....	....	....	....
	HC Ocelari Trinec	CzRep	11	1	2	3	24	....	....	....	....	....	....	....	....	....	....	....	....	....	....	....	....	....	....
	Liberec	CzRep	8	1	0	1	12	....	....	....	....	....	....	....	....	....	9	0	1	1	35	....	....	....	....
2005-06	**Atlanta**	**NHL**	**1**	**0**	**0**	**0**	**2**	**0**	**0**	**0**	**0**	**0.0**	**0**	**0**	**0.0**	**3:14**	....	....	....	....	....	....	....	....	....
	Chicago Wolves	AHL	33	0	1	1	94	....	....	....	....	....	....	....	....	....	....	....	....	....	....	....	....	....	....
2006-07	Syracuse Crunch	AHL	68	2	9	11	133	....	....	....	....	....	....	....	....	....	....	....	....	....	....	....	....	....	....
	NHL Totals		**141**	**2**	**8**	**10**	**250**	**0**	**0**	**0**	**56**	**3.6**		**1**	**0.0**	**12:15**	....	....	....	....	....	....	....	....	....

AHL All-Rookie Team (2000)

Traded to **Nashville** by **NY Rangers** with Rem Murray and Marek Zidlicky for Mike Dunham, December 12, 2002. Traded to **Atlanta** by **Nashville** with Ben Simon for Simon Gamache and Kirill Safronov, December 2, 2003. Signed as a free agent by **Slavia Praha** (CzRep), September 17, 2004. Signed as a free agent by **Trinec** (CzRep), December, 2004. Signed as a free agent by **Liberec** (CzRep), January 31, 2005. • Missed majority of 2005-06 season recovering from ankle injury suffered in game vs. Cleveland (AHL), January 15, 2006. Signed as a free agent by **Columbus**, July 6, 2006.

KNUBLE, Mike (kuh-NOO-buhl, MIGHK) PHI.

Right wing. Shoots right. 6'3", 230 lbs. Born, Toronto, Ont., July 4, 1972. Detroit's 4th choice, 76th overall, in 1991 Entry Draft.

Season	Club	League	GP	G	A	Pts	PIM	PP	SH	GW	S	%	+/-	TF	F%	Min	GP	G	A	Pts	PIM	PP	SH	GW	Min
1988-89	East Kentwood	High-MI	28	52	37	89	60	....	....	....	....	....	....	....	....	....	....	....	....	....	....	....	....	....	....
1989-90	East Kentwood	High-MI	29	63	40	103	40	....	....	....	....	....	....	....	....	....	....	....	....	....	....	....	....	....	....
1990-91	Kalamazoo	NAHL	36	18	24	42	30	....	....	....	....	....	....	....	....	....	....	....	....	....	....	....	....	....	....
1991-92	U. of Michigan	CCHA	43	7	8	15	48	....	....	....	....	....	....	....	....	....	....	....	....	....	....	....	....	....	....
1992-93	U. of Michigan	CCHA	39	26	16	42	57	....	....	....	....	....	....	....	....	....	....	....	....	....	....	....	....	....	....
1993-94	U. of Michigan	CCHA	41	32	26	58	71	....	....	....	....	....	....	....	....	....	....	....	....	....	....	....	....	....	....
1994-95	U. of Michigan	CCHA	34	*38	22	60	62	....	....	....	....	....	....	....	....	....	....	....	....	....	....	....	....	....	....
	Adirondack	AHL	....	....	....	....	....	....	....	....	....	....	....	....	....	....	3	0	0	0	0	....	....	....	....
1995-96	Adirondack	AHL	80	22	23	45	59	....	....	....	....	....	....	....	....	....	3	1	0	1	0	....	....	....	....
1996-97	**Detroit**	**NHL**	**9**	**1**	**0**	**1**	**0**	**0**	**0**	**0**	**10**	**10.0**	**-1**	....	....	....	....	....	....	....	....	....	....	....	....
	Adirondack	AHL	68	28	35	63	54	....	....	....	....	....	....	....	....	....	....	....	....	....	....	....	....	....	....
1997-98♦	**Detroit**	**NHL**	**53**	**7**	**6**	**13**	**16**	**0**	**0**	**0**	**54**	**13.0**	**2**	....	....	....	**3**	**0**	**1**	**1**	**0**	**0**	**0**	**0**	....
1998-99	**NY Rangers**	**NHL**	**82**	**15**	**20**	**35**	**26**	**3**	**0**	**1**	**113**	**13.3**	**-7**	**1**	**100.0**	**14:52**	....	....	....	....	....	....	....	....	....
99-2000	**NY Rangers**	**NHL**	**59**	**9**	**5**	**14**	**18**	**1**	**0**	**1**	**50**	**18.0**	**-5**	**9**	**55.6**	**10:39**	....	....	....	....	....	....	....	....	....
	Boston	**NHL**	**14**	**3**	**3**	**6**	**8**	**1**	**0**	**1**	**28**	**10.7**	**-2**	**3**	**0.0**	**19:29**	....	....	....	....	....	....	....	....	....
2000-01	**Boston**	**NHL**	**82**	**7**	**13**	**20**	**37**	**0**	**1**	**1**	**92**	**7.6**	**0**	**115**	**31.3**	**10:34**	....	....	....	....	....	....	....	....	....
2001-02	**Boston**	**NHL**	**54**	**8**	**6**	**14**	**42**	**0**	**0**	**2**	**77**	**10.4**	**9**	**27**	**44.4**	**9:45**	**2**	**0**	**0**	**0**	**0**	**0**	**0**	**0**	**3:30**
2002-03	**Boston**	**NHL**	**75**	**30**	**29**	**59**	**45**	**9**	**0**	**4**	**185**	**16.2**	**18**	**34**	**44.1**	**17:24**	**5**	**0**	**2**	**2**	**2**	**0**	**0**	**0**	**17:35**
2003-04	**Boston**	**NHL**	**82**	**21**	**25**	**46**	**32**	**4**	**0**	**3**	**192**	**10.9**	**19**	**54**	**31.5**	**18:47**	**7**	**2**	**0**	**2**	**0**	**1**	**0**	**0**	**19:45**
2004-05	Linkopings HC	Sweden	49	*26	13	39	40	....	....	....	....	....	....	....	....	....	6	0	1	1	2	....	....	....	....

			Regular Season														Playoffs								
Season	Club	League	GP	G	A	Pts	PIM	PP	SH	GW	S	%	+/-	TF	F%	Min	GP	G	A	Pts	PIM	PP	SH	GW	Min
2005-06	**Philadelphia**	**NHL**	**82**	**34**	**31**	**65**	**80**	**13**	**2**	**6**	**217**	**15.7**	**25**	**161**	**32.3**	**20:21**	**6**	**1**	**3**	**4**	**8**	**0**	**0**	**0**	**19:17**
	United States	Olympics	6	1	1	2	4																		
2006-07	**Philadelphia**	**NHL**	**64**	**24**	**30**	**54**	**56**	**10**	**0**	**1**	**160**	**15.0**	**2**	**62**	**37.1**	**19:38**									
	NHL Totals		**656**	**159**	**168**	**327**	**360**	**41**	**3**	**20**	**1178**	**13.5**		**466**	**34.5**	**15:38**	**23**	**3**	**6**	**9**	**10**	**1**	**0**	**0**	**17:27**

CCHA Second All-Star Team (1994, 1995) • NCAA West Second All-American Team (1995)

Traded to **NY Rangers** by **Detroit** for NY Rangers' 2nd round choice (Tomas Kopecky) in 2000 Entry Draft, October 1, 1998. Traded to **Boston** by **NY Rangers** for Rob DiMaio, March 10, 2000. Signed as a free agent by **Philadelphia**, July 3, 2004. Signed as a free agent by **Linkopings** (Sweden), August 2, 2004.

KOALSKA, Matt

(KOHL-skuh, MAT)

Center. Shoots left. 6'1", 196 lbs. Born, St. Paul, MN, May 16, 1980. Nashville's 7th choice, 154th overall, in 2000 Entry Draft.

Season	Club	League	GP	G	A	Pts	PIM	PP	SH	GW	S	%	+/-	TF	F%	Min	GP	G	A	Pts	PIM	PP	SH	GW	Min
1998-99	Hill-Murray	High-MN	26	20	50	70	18																		
99-2000	Twin Cities	USHL	57	24	34	58	19										13	5	5	10	4				
2000-01	U. of Minnesota	WCHA	42	10	24	34	36																		
2001-02	U. of Minnesota	WCHA	44	10	23	33	34																		
2002-03	U. of Minnesota	WCHA	41	9	31	40	26																		
2003-04	U. of Minnesota	WCHA	44	13	26	39	44																		
2004-05	Bridgeport	AHL	60	7	8	15	22																		
2005-06	**NY Islanders**	**NHL**	**3**	**0**	**0**	**0**	**2**	**0**	**0**	**0**	**3**	**0.0**	**–1**	**13**	**53.9**	**5:44**									
	Bridgeport	AHL	75	19	30	49	82										7	2	1	3	0				
2006-07	Bridgeport	AHL	3	0	0	0	0																		
	Hershey Bears	AHL	11	3	2	5	4																		
	Binghamton	AHL	37	5	6	11	22																		
	NHL Totals		**3**	**0**	**0**	**0**	**2**	**0**	**0**	**0**	**3**	**0.0**		**13**	**53.8**	**5:44**									

Signed as a free agent by **NY Islanders**, August 11, 2004. Traded to **Ottawa** by **NY Islanders** for Tomas Malec, January 5, 2007. Signed as a free agent by **Bolzano** (Italy), August 9, 2007.

KOBASEW, Chuck

(KOH-buh-soo, CHUHK) **BOS.**

Center. Shoots left. 6', 193 lbs. Born, Vancouver, B.C., April 17, 1982. Calgary's 1st choice, 14th overall, in 2001 Entry Draft.

Season	Club	League	GP	G	A	Pts	PIM	PP	SH	GW	S	%	+/-	TF	F%	Min	GP	G	A	Pts	PIM	PP	SH	GW	Min
1997-98	Osoyoos Heat	KIJHL	6	2	2	4	2																		
1998-99	Osoyoos Heat	KIJHL	23	25	24	49																			
	Penticton	BCHL	30	11	17	28	18																		
99-2000	Penticton	BCHL	58	*54	52	106	83																		
2000-01	Boston College	H-East	43	27	22	49	38																		
2001-02	Kelowna Rockets	WHL	55	41	21	62	114										15	10	5	15	22				
2002-03	**Calgary**	**NHL**	**23**	**4**	**2**	**6**	**8**	**1**	**0**	**1**	**29**	**13.8**	**–3**	**5**	**0.0**	**11:48**									
	Saint John Flames	AHL	48	21	12	33	61																		
2003-04	**Calgary**	**NHL**	**70**	**6**	**11**	**17**	**51**	**3**	**0**	**0**	**78**	**7.7**	**–12**	**91**	**42.9**	**10:22**	**26**	**0**	**1**	**1**	**24**	**0**	**0**	**0**	**9:02**
2004-05	Lowell	AHL	79	38	37	75	110										11	6	3	9	27				
2005-06	**Calgary**	**NHL**	**77**	**20**	**11**	**31**	**64**	**10**	**0**	**4**	**143**	**14.0**	**–10**	**47**	**25.5**	**12:16**	**7**	**1**	**0**	**1**	**0**	**0**	**0**	**1**	**12:29**
2006-07	**Calgary**	**NHL**	**40**	**4**	**13**	**17**	**37**	**1**	**0**	**1**	**69**	**5.8**	**7**	**26**	**30.8**	**13:13**									
	Boston	**NHL**	**10**	**1**	**1**	**2**	**25**	**1**	**0**	**0**	**24**	**4.2**	**–6**	**6**	**16.7**	**18:51**									
	NHL Totals		**220**	**35**	**38**	**73**	**185**	**16**	**0**	**6**	**343**	**10.2**		**175**	**34.3**	**12:05**	**33**	**1**	**1**	**2**	**24**	**0**	**0**	**1**	**9:45**

Hockey East Second All-Star Team (2001) • Hockey East Rookie of the Year (2001) • NCAA Championship All-Tournament Team (2001) • NCAA Championship Tournament MVP (2001) • AHL First All-Star Team (2005)

• Left **Boston College** (Hockey East) and signed with **Kelowna** (WHL), August 13, 2001. Traded to **Boston** by **Calgary** with Andrew Ference for Brad Stuart and Wayne Primeau, February 10, 2007.

KOCI, David

(KOH-chee, DAY-vihd) **CHI.**

Left wing. Shoots left. 6'6", 238 lbs. Born, Prague, Czech., May 12, 1981. Pittsburgh's 5th choice, 146th overall, in 2000 Entry Draft.

Season	Club	League	GP	G	A	Pts	PIM	PP	SH	GW	S	%	+/-	TF	F%	Min	GP	G	A	Pts	PIM	PP	SH	GW	Min
1997-98	Sparta Jr.	CzRep-Jr.	41	2	9	11	105																		
1998-99	Hvezda Praha Jr.	CzRep-Jr.	22	1	3	4	36																		
	Sparta Jr.	CzRep-Jr.	7	0	0	0	4																		
99-2000	Sparta Jr.	CzRep-Jr.	47	0	6	6	124																		
2000-01	Prince George	WHL	70	2	7	9	155										6	0	0	0	20				
2001-02	Wilkes-Barre	AHL	26	1	3	4	98																		
	Wheeling Nailers	ECHL	33	2	4	6	105																		
2002-03	Wilkes-Barre	AHL	9	0	0	0	4																		
	Wheeling Nailers	ECHL	48	0	1	1	103																		
2003-04	Wilkes-Barre	AHL	78	1	7	8	298										10	0	0	0	24				
2004-05	Wilkes-Barre	AHL	68	1	8	9	311																		
2005-06	Wilkes-Barre	AHL	13	0	0	0	59																		
2006-07	**Chicago**	**NHL**	**9**	**0**	**0**	**0**	**88**	**0**	**0**	**0**	**3**	**0.0**	**–3**	**0**	**0.0**	**4:44**									
	Norfolk Admirals	AHL	44	0	1	1	223																		
	NHL Totals		**9**	**0**	**0**	**0**	**88**	**0**	**0**	**0**	**3**	**0.0**		**0**	**0.0**	**4:44**									

• Missed majority of 2005-06 season recovering from a knee injury, November, 2006. Signed as a free agent by **Chicago**, July 17, 2006.

KOIVU, Mikko

(KOI-voo, MEE-koh) **MIN.**

Center. Shoots left. 6'3", 207 lbs. Born, Turku, Finland, March 12, 1983. Minnesota's 1st choice, 6th overall, in 2001 Entry Draft.

Season	Club	League	GP	G	A	Pts	PIM	PP	SH	GW	S	%	+/-	TF	F%	Min	GP	G	A	Pts	PIM	PP	SH	GW	Min
99-2000	TPS Turku U18	Fin-U18	11	4	9	13	18																		
	TPS Turku Jr.	Fin-Jr.	30	4	8	12	22										13	1	4	5	8				
2000-01	TPS Turku U18	Fin-U18															7	2	10	12	2				
	TPS Turku Jr.	Fin-Jr.	26	9	36	45	26										3	1	1	2	6				
	TPS Turku	Finland	21	0	1	1	2																		
2001-02	TPS Turku Jr.	Fin-Jr.	2	0	1	1	12																		
	TPS Turku	Finland	48	4	3	7	34										8	0	3	3	4				
2002-03	TPS Turku	Finland	37	7	13	20	20										7	2	2	4	6				
2003-04	TPS Turku	Finland	45	6	24	30	36										13	1	7	8	8				
2004-05	Houston Aeros	AHL	67	20	28	48	47										5	1	0	1	2				
2005-06	**Minnesota**	**NHL**	**64**	**6**	**15**	**21**	**40**	**3**	**0**	**0**	**96**	**6.3**	**–9**	**724**	**47.4**	**13:17**									
	Finland	Olympics	8	0	0	0	6																		
2006-07	**Minnesota**	**NHL**	**82**	**20**	**34**	**54**	**58**	**9**	**2**	**2**	**162**	**12.3**	**6**	**1165**	**50.9**	**17:29**	**5**	**1**	**0**	**1**	**4**	**0**	**0**	**0**	**17:43**
	NHL Totals		**146**	**26**	**49**	**75**	**98**	**12**	**2**	**2**	**258**	**10.1**		**1889**	**49.6**	**15:38**	**5**	**1**	**0**	**1**	**4**	**0**	**0**	**0**	**17:43**

KOIVU, Saku

(KOI-voo, SA-koo) **MTL.**

Center. Shoots left. 5'10", 187 lbs. Born, Turku, Finland, November 23, 1974. Montreal's 1st choice, 21st overall, in 1993 Entry Draft.

Season	Club	League	GP	G	A	Pts	PIM	PP	SH	GW	S	%	+/-	TF	F%	Min	GP	G	A	Pts	PIM	PP	SH	GW	Min
1990-91	TPS Turku U18	Fin-U18	24	20	28	48	26																		
	TPS Turku Jr.	Fin-Jr.	13	3	7	10	6																		
1991-92	TPS Turku U18	Fin-U18	12	3	7	10	6																		
	TPS Turku Jr.	Fin-Jr.	34	25	28	53	57										8	5	9	14	6				
1992-93	TPS Turku	Finland	46	3	7	10	28										11	3	2	5	2				
1993-94	TPS Turku	Finland	47	23	30	53	42										11	4	8	12	16				
	Finland	Olympics	8	4	3	7	12																		
1994-95	TPS Turku	Finland	45	27	47	74	73										13	7	10	17	16				
1995-96	**Montreal**	**NHL**	**82**	**20**	**25**	**45**	**40**	**8**	**3**	**2**	**136**	**14.7**	**–7**				**6**	**3**	**1**	**4**	**8**	**0**	**0**	**0**	
1996-97	**Montreal**	**NHL**	**50**	**17**	**39**	**56**	**38**	**5**	**0**	**3**	**135**	**12.6**	**7**				**5**	**1**	**3**	**4**	**10**	**0**	**0**	**0**	
1997-98	**Montreal**	**NHL**	**69**	**14**	**43**	**57**	**48**	**2**	**2**	**3**	**145**	**9.7**	**8**				**6**	**2**	**3**	**5**	**2**	**1**	**0**	**0**	
	Finland	Olympics	6	2	8	10	4																		
1998-99	**Montreal**	**NHL**	**65**	**14**	**30**	**44**	**38**	**4**	**2**	**0**	**145**	**9.7**	**–7**	**1427**	**52.6**	**20:02**									
99-2000	**Montreal**	**NHL**	**24**	**3**	**18**	**21**	**14**	**1**	**0**	**0**	**53**	**5.7**	**7**	**495**	**52.9**	**19:13**									
2000-01	**Montreal**	**NHL**	**54**	**17**	**30**	**47**	**40**	**7**	**0**	**3**	**113**	**15.0**	**2**	**1092**	**47.6**	**21:23**									
2001-02	**Montreal**	**NHL**	**3**	**0**	**2**	**2**	**0**	**0**	**0**	**0**	**2**	**0.0**	**0**	**13**	**61.5**	**13:57**	**12**	**4**	**6**	**10**	**4**	**1**	**0**	**1**	**15:54**
2002-03	**Montreal**	**NHL**	**82**	**21**	**50**	**71**	**72**	**5**	**1**	**5**	**147**	**14.3**	**5**	**1566**	**49.6**	**19:14**									
2003-04	**Montreal**	**NHL**	**68**	**14**	**41**	**55**	**52**	**5**	**0**	**3**	**112**	**12.5**	**–5**	**1194**	**53.9**	**19:18**	**11**	**3**	**8**	**11**	**10**	**2**	**0**	**0**	**20:34**
2004-05	TPS Turku	Finland	20	8	8	16	28										6	3	2	5	30				

			Regular Season															Playoffs								
Season	Club	League	GP	G	A	Pts	PIM	PP	SH	GW	S	%	+/-	TF	F%	Min	GP	G	A	Pts	PIM	PP	SH	GW	Min
2005-06	**Montreal**	**NHL**	**72**	**17**	**45**	**62**	**70**	**5**	**0**	**4**	**138**	**12.3**	**1**	**1412**	**53.8**	**18:31**	**3**	**0**	**2**	**2**	**2**	**0**	**0**	**0**	**14:24**
	Finland	Olympics	8	3	8	11	12	....	....	....	....	....	....	....	....	....	....	....	....	....	....	....	....	....	....
2006-07	**Montreal**	**NHL**	**81**	**22**	**53**	**75**	**74**	**11**	**1**	**4**	**154**	**14.3**	**−21**	**1453**	**54.9**	**18:07**	....	....	....	....	....	....	....	....	....
	NHL Totals		**650**	**159**	**376**	**535**	**486**	**53**	**9**	**27**	**1280**	**12.4**		**8652**	**52.2**	**19:16**	**43**	**13**	**23**	**36**	**36**	**4**	**0**	**1**	**17:42**

Bill Masterton Memorial Trophy (2002) • Olympic Tournament All-Star Team (2006) • King Clancy Memorial Trophy (2007)

Played in NHL All-Star Game (1998)

Missed majority of 1999-2000 season recovering from shoulder injury suffered in game vs. NY Rangers, October 30, 1999. • Missed majority of 2001-02 season recovering from non-Hodgkin 's lymphoma, September 6, 2001. Signed as a free agent by **Turku** (Finland), October 21, 2004.

KOLANOS, Krys

(koh-LA-nohs, KRIHS)

Center. Shoots right. 6'3", 206 lbs. Born, Calgary, Alta., July 27, 1981. Phoenix's 1st choice, 19th overall, in 2000 Entry Draft.

Season	Club	League	GP	G	A	Pts	PIM	PP	SH	GW	S	%	+/-	TF	F%	Min	GP	G	A	Pts	PIM	PP	SH	GW	Min
1996-97	Calgary Flames	AAHA	24	24	35	59	....	....	....	....	....	....	....	....	....	....	....	....	....	....	....	....	....	....	....
1997-98	Calgary Buffaloes	AMHL	34	34	43	77	29	....	....	....	....	....	....	....	....	....	....	....	....	....	....	....	....	....	....
1998-99	Calgary Royals	AJHL	58	43	67	110	98	....	....	....	....	....	....	....	....	....	....	....	....	....	....	....	....	....	....
99-2000	Boston College	H-East	42	16	16	32	48	....	....	....	....	....	....	....	....	....	....	....	....	....	....	....	....	....	....
2000-01	Boston College	H-East	41	25	25	50	54	....	....	....	....	....	....	....	....	....	....	....	....	....	....	....	....	....	....
2001-02	**Phoenix**	**NHL**	**57**	**11**	**11**	**22**	**48**	**0**	**0**	**5**	**81**	**13.6**	**6**	**703**	**46.4**	**13:05**	**2**	**0**	**0**	**0**	**6**	**0**	**0**	**0**	**11:12**
2002-03	**Phoenix**	**NHL**	**2**	**0**	**0**	**0**	**0**	**0**	**0**	**0**	**8**	**0.0**	**0**	**16**	**31.3**	**14:06**	....	....	....	....	....	....	....	....	....
2003-04	**Phoenix**	**NHL**	**41**	**4**	**6**	**10**	**24**	**1**	**0**	**1**	**61**	**6.6**	**−9**	**283**	**43.8**	**13:31**	....	....	....	....	....	....	....	....	....
	Springfield	AHL	32	10	11	21	38	....	....	....	....	....	....	....	....	....	....	....	....	....	....	....	....	....	....
2004-05	Blues Espoo	Finland	15	7	9	16	40	....	....	....	....	....	....	....	....	....	....	....	....	....	....	....	....	....	....
	Krefeld Pinguine	Germany	7	3	2	5	16	....	....	....	....	....	....	....	....	....	....	....	....	....	....	....	....	....	....
2005-06	**Phoenix**	**NHL**	**9**	**2**	**1**	**3**	**2**	**1**	**0**	**0**	**15**	**13.3**	**2**	**75**	**53.3**	**11:30**	....	....	....	....	....	....	....	....	....
	San Antonio	AHL	3	0	1	1	0	....	....	....	....	....	....	....	....	....	....	....	....	....	....	....	....	....	....
	Edmonton	**NHL**	**6**	**0**	**0**	**0**	**2**	**0**	**0**	**0**	**7**	**0.0**	**−1**	**32**	**50.0**	**7:39**	....	....	....	....	....	....	....	....	....
	Lowell	AHL	19	10	11	21	40	....	....	....	....	....	....	....	....	....	....	....	....	....	....	....	....	....	....
	Wilkes-Barre	AHL	18	10	8	18	19	....	....	....	....	....	....	....	....	....	11	2	0	2	16	....	....	....	....
2006-07	Grand Rapids	AHL	17	6	6	12	8	....	....	....	....	....	....	....	....	....	....	....	....	....	....	....	....	....	....
	Langnau	Swiss	14	2	9	11	48	....	....	....	....	....	....	....	....	....	....	....	....	....	....	....	....	....	....
	EV Zug	Swiss	....	....	....	....	....	....	....	....	....	....	....	....	....	....	8	6	0	6	8	....	....	....	....
	NHL Totals		**115**	**17**	**18**	**35**	**76**	**2**	**0**	**6**	**172**	**9.9**		**1109**	**46.1**	**12:51**	**2**	**0**	**0**	**0**	**6**	**0**	**0**	**0**	**11:12**

Hockey East All-Rookie Team (2000) • Hockey East Second All-Star Team (2001) • NCAA East Second All-American Team (2001) • NCAA Championship All-Tournament Team (2001)

• Missed majority of 2002-03 season recovering from head injury suffered in game vs. Pittsburgh, March 20, 2002. Signed as a free agent by **Espoo** (Finland), October 25, 2004. Signed as a free agent by **Krefeld** (Germany), February 16, 2005. Claimed on waivers by **Edmonton** from **Phoenix**, November 11, 2005. Claimed on waivers by **Phoenix** from **Edmonton**, December 19, 2005. Traded to **Carolina** by **Phoenix** for Pavel Brendl, December 28, 2005. Traded to **Pittsburgh** by **Carolina** with Niklas Nordgren and Carolina's 2nd round choice (later traded to San Jose - later traded to Philadelphia - Philadelphia selected Kevin Marshall) in 2007 Entry Draft for Mark Recchi, March 9, 2006. Signed as a free agent by **Detroit**, July 15, 2006.

KOLNIK, Juraj

(KOHL-nihk, YUHR-ay)

Right wing. Shoots right. 5'10", 190 lbs. Born, Nitra, Czech., November 13, 1980. NY Islanders' 7th choice, 101st overall, in 1999 Entry Draft.

Season	Club	League	GP	G	A	Pts	PIM	PP	SH	GW	S	%	+/-	TF	F%	Min	GP	G	A	Pts	PIM	PP	SH	GW	Min
1997-98	Nitra Jr.	Slovak-Jr.	26	28	16	44	50	....	....	....	....	....	....	....	....	....	....	....	....	....	....	....	....	....	....
	Nitra	Slovakia	28	1	3	4	6	....	....	....	....	....	....	....	....	....	....	....	....	....	....	....	....	....	....
1998-99	Quebec Remparts	QMJHL	12	6	5	11	6	....	....	....	....	....	....	....	....	....	....	....	....	....	....	....	....	....	....
	Rimouski Oceanic	QMJHL	50	36	37	73	34	....	....	....	....	....	....	....	....	....	11	9	6	15	6	....	....	....	....
99-2000	Rimouski Oceanic	QMJHL	47	53	53	106	53	....	....	....	....	....	....	....	....	....	14	10	17	27	16	....	....	....	....
2000-01	**NY Islanders**	**NHL**	**29**	**4**	**3**	**7**	**12**	**0**	**0**	**0**	**38**	**10.5**	**−8**	**1**	**100.0**	**10:28**	....	....	....	....	....	....	....	....	....
	Lowell	AHL	25	2	6	8	18	....	....	....	....	....	....	....	....	....	....	....	....	....	....	....	....	....	....
	Springfield	AHL	29	15	20	35	20	....	....	....	....	....	....	....	....	....	....	....	....	....	....	....	....	....	....
2001-02	**NY Islanders**	**NHL**	**7**	**2**	**0**	**2**	**0**	**1**	**0**	**0**	**10**	**20.0**	**−2**	**1**	**0.0**	**7:57**	....	....	....	....	....	....	....	....	....
	Bridgeport	AHL	67	18	30	48	40	....	....	....	....	....	....	....	....	....	20	7	14	21	17	....	....	....	....
2002-03	**Florida**	**NHL**	**10**	**0**	**1**	**1**	**0**	**0**	**0**	**0**	**14**	**0.0**	**1**	**1**	**0.0**	**10:33**	....	....	....	....	....	....	....	....	....
	San Antonio	AHL	65	25	15	40	36	....	....	....	....	....	....	....	....	....	3	0	1	1	4	....	....	....	....
2003-04	**Florida**	**NHL**	**53**	**14**	**11**	**25**	**14**	**2**	**0**	**1**	**100**	**14.0**	**−7**	**25**	**64.0**	**16:05**	....	....	....	....	....	....	....	....	....
	San Antonio	AHL	15	2	14	16	21	....	....	....	....	....	....	....	....	....	....	....	....	....	....	....	....	....	....
2004-05	San Antonio	AHL	74	13	16	29	24	....	....	....	....	....	....	....	....	....	....	....	....	....	....	....	....	....	....
2005-06	**Florida**	**NHL**	**77**	**15**	**20**	**35**	**40**	**4**	**1**	**3**	**145**	**10.3**	**1**	**28**	**28.6**	**14:19**	....	....	....	....	....	....	....	....	....
2006-07	**Florida**	**NHL**	**64**	**11**	**14**	**25**	**18**	**0**	**0**	**1**	**113**	**9.7**	**2**	**5**	**40.0**	**12:05**	....	....	....	....	....	....	....	....	....
	NHL Totals		**240**	**46**	**49**	**95**	**84**	**7**	**1**	**5**	**420**	**11.0**		**61**	**44.3**	**13:18**	....	....	....	....	....	....	....	....	....

Memorial Cup Tournament All-Star Team (2000)

Traded to **Florida** by **NY Islanders** with NY Islanders' 9th round choice (later traded to San Jose – San Jose selected Carter Lee) in 2003 Entry Draft for Sven Butenschon, October 11, 2002. Signed as a free agent by **Geneve-Servette** (Swiss), August 6, 2007.

KOLTSOV, Konstantin

(kohlt-SAHV, KAWN-stan-tihn)

Right wing. Shoots left. 6', 206 lbs. Born, Minsk, USSR, April 17, 1981. Pittsburgh's 1st choice, 18th overall, in 1999 Entry Draft.

Season	Club	League	GP	G	A	Pts	PIM	PP	SH	GW	S	%	+/-	TF	F%	Min	GP	G	A	Pts	PIM	PP	SH	GW	Min
1997-98	Cherepovets 2	Russia-3	44	11	12	23	16	....	....	....	....	....	....	....	....	....	....	....	....	....	....	....	....	....	....
	Cherepovets	Russia	2	0	0	0	2	....	....	....	....	....	....	....	....	....	....	....	....	....	....	....	....	....	....
1998-99	Cherepovets 3	Russia-4	2	0	1	1	2	....	....	....	....	....	....	....	....	....	....	....	....	....	....	....	....	....	....
	Cherepovets 2	Russia-3	11	1	4	5	18	....	....	....	....	....	....	....	....	....	....	....	....	....	....	....	....	....	....
	Cherepovets	Russia	33	3	0	3	8	....	....	....	....	....	....	....	....	....	1	0	0	0	2	....	....	....	....
99-2000	Magnitogorsk	Russia	30	3	4	7	12	....	....	....	....	....	....	....	....	....	11	1	1	2	6	....	....	....	....
2000-01	Ak Bars Kazan	Russia	24	7	8	15	10	....	....	....	....	....	....	....	....	....	2	0	0	0	4	....	....	....	....
	Spartak 2	Russia-3	2	0	1	1	0	....	....	....	....	....	....	....	....	....	....	....	....	....	....	....	....	....	....
2001-02	Ak Bars Kazan	Russia	10	1	2	3	2	....	....	....	....	....	....	....	....	....	....	....	....	....	....	....	....	....	....
	Spartak Moscow	Russia	23	1	0	1	12	....	....	....	....	....	....	....	....	....	....	....	....	....	....	....	....	....	....
	Belarus	Olympics	2	0	0	0	0	....	....	....	....	....	....	....	....	....	....	....	....	....	....	....	....	....	....
2002-03	**Pittsburgh**	**NHL**	**2**	**0**	**0**	**0**	**0**	**0**	**0**	**0**	**4**	**0.0**	**−2**	**0**	**0.0**	**13:06**	....	....	....	....	....	....	....	....	....
	Wilkes-Barre	AHL	65	9	21	30	41	....	....	....	....	....	....	....	....	....	6	2	4	6	4	....	....	....	....
2003-04	**Pittsburgh**	**NHL**	**82**	**9**	**20**	**29**	**30**	**2**	**0**	**3**	**123**	**7.3**	**−30**	**12**	**33.3**	**15:21**	....	....	....	....	....	....	....	....	....
	Wilkes-Barre	AHL	....	....	....	....	....	....	....	....	....	....	....	....	....	....	24	6	11	17	18	....	....	....	....
2004-05	Dynamo Minsk	BelOpen	11	6	2	8	38	....	....	....	....	....	....	....	....	....	....	....	....	....	....	....	....	....	....
	Spartak Moscow	Russia	31	6	10	16	48	....	....	....	....	....	....	....	....	....	....	....	....	....	....	....	....	....	....
2005-06	**Pittsburgh**	**NHL**	**60**	**3**	**6**	**9**	**20**	**0**	**1**	**0**	**72**	**4.2**	**−10**	**14**	**21.4**	**13:15**	....	....	....	....	....	....	....	....	....
	Wilkes-Barre	AHL	18	7	5	12	13	....	....	....	....	....	....	....	....	....	....	....	....	....	....	....	....	....	....
2006-07	Ufa	Russia	54	15	11	26	45	....	....	....	....	....	....	....	....	....	8	1	1	2	2	....	....	....	....
	NHL Totals		**144**	**12**	**26**	**38**	**50**	**2**	**1**	**3**	**199**	**6.0**		**26**	**26.9**	**14:27**	....	....	....	....	....	....	....	....	....

Signed as a free agent by **Minsk** (BelOpen), September 15, 2004. Signed as a free agent by **Spartak Moscow** (Russia), November, 2004. Signed as a free agent by **Ufa** (Russia), August 17, 2006.

KOMISAREK, Mike

(koh-mih-SAIR-ehk, MIGHK) **MTL.**

Defense. Shoots right. 6'4", 242 lbs. Born, West Islip, NY, January 19, 1982. Montreal's 1st choice, 7th overall, in 2001 Entry Draft.

Season	Club	League	GP	G	A	Pts	PIM	PP	SH	GW	S	%	+/-	TF	F%	Min	GP	G	A	Pts	PIM	PP	SH	GW	Min
1998-99	N.E. Jr. Coyotes	EJHL	53	17	24	51	....	....	....	....	....	....	....	....	....	....	....	....	....	....	....	....	....	....	....
99-2000	USNTDP	U-18	6	0	0	0	12	....	....	....	....	....	....	....	....	....	....	....	....	....	....	....	....	....	....
	USNTDP	USHL	51	5	8	13	124	....	....	....	....	....	....	....	....	....	....	....	....	....	....	....	....	....	....
	USNTDP	NAHL	1	0	0	0	16	....	....	....	....	....	....	....	....	....	....	....	....	....	....	....	....	....	....
2000-01	U. of Michigan	CCHA	41	4	12	16	77	....	....	....	....	....	....	....	....	....	....	....	....	....	....	....	....	....	....
2001-02	U. of Michigan	CCHA	40	11	19	30	70	....	....	....	....	....	....	....	....	....	....	....	....	....	....	....	....	....	....
2002-03	**Montreal**	**NHL**	**21**	**0**	**1**	**1**	**28**	**0**	**0**	**0**	**26**	**0.0**	**−6**	**0**	**0.0**	**16:42**	....	....	....	....	....	....	....	....	....
	Hamilton	AHL	56	5	25	30	79	....	....	....	....	....	....	....	....	....	23	1	5	6	60	....	....	....	....
2003-04	**Montreal**	**NHL**	**46**	**0**	**4**	**4**	**34**	**0**	**0**	**0**	**40**	**0.0**	**4**	**0**	**0.0**	**12:00**	**7**	**0**	**0**	**0**	**8**	**0**	**0**	**0**	**14:09**
	Hamilton	AHL	18	2	7	9	47	....	....	....	....	....	....	....	....	....	....	....	....	....	....	....	....	....	....
2004-05	Hamilton	AHL	20	1	4	5	49	....	....	....	....	....	....	....	....	....	4	0	1	1	8	....	....	....	....
2005-06	**Montreal**	**NHL**	**71**	**2**	**4**	**6**	**116**	**0**	**0**	**0**	**66**	**3.0**	**−1**	**0**	**0.0**	**14:40**	**6**	**0**	**0**	**0**	**10**	**0**	**0**	**0**	**18:35**
2006-07	**Montreal**	**NHL**	**82**	**4**	**15**	**19**	**96**	**0**	**1**	**1**	**78**	**5.1**	**7**	**0**	**0.0**	**19:16**	....	....	....	....	....	....	....	....	....
	NHL Totals		**220**	**6**	**24**	**30**	**274**	**0**	**2**	**1**	**210**	**2.9**		**0**	**0.0**	**16:01**	**13**	**0**	**0**	**0**	**18**	**0**	**0**	**0**	**16:11**

CCHA First All-Star Team (2002) • NCAA West First All-American Team (2002) • AHL All-Rookie Team (2003)

KONDRATIEV, Maxim
(kohn-DRAT-yehv, max-EEM) **ANA.**

Defense. Shoots left. 6'1", 194 lbs. Born, Togliatti, USSR, January 20, 1983. Toronto's 7th choice, 168th overall, in 2001 Entry Draft.

Season	Club	League	GP	G	A	Pts	PIM	PP	SH	GW	S	%	+/-	TF	F%	Min	GP	G	A	Pts	PIM	PP	SH	GW	Min
			Regular Season														Playoffs								
99-2000	Lada Togliatti 2	Russia-3	16	0	2	2	6	....	....	....	....	....	....	....	....	....	....	....	....	....	....	....	....	....	....
	Lada Togliatti	Russia	20	1	1	2	....	....	....	....	....	....	....	....	....	....	....	....	....	....	....	....	....	....	....
2000-01	Lada Togliatti 2	Russia-3	STATISTICS NOT AVAILABLE																						
	CSK VVS Samara	Russia-2	18	2	1	3	24	....	....	....	....	....	....	....	....	....	....	....	....	....	....	....	....	....	....
2001-02	Lada Togliatti	Russia	43	3	3	6	32	....	....	....	....	....	....	....	....	....	4	0	0	0	0	....	....	....	....
2002-03	Lada Togliatti	Russia	47	2	3	5	56	....	....	....	....	....	....	....	....	....	10	0	0	0	6	....	....	....	....
2003-04	**Toronto**	**NHL**	**7**	**0**	**0**	**0**	**2**	**0**	**0**	**0**	**6**	**0.0**	**0**	**0**	**0.0**	**15:36**	....	....	....	....	....	....	....	....	....
	St. John's	AHL	18	3	5	8	10	....	....	....	....	....	....	....	....	....	....	....	....	....	....	....	....	....	....
	Lada Togliatti	Russia	29	2	3	5	85	....	....	....	....	....	....	....	....	....	6	0	0	0	16	....	....	....	....
2004-05	Hartford	AHL	13	1	4	5	8	....	....	....	....	....	....	....	....	....	....	....	....	....	....	....	....	....	....
	Lada Togliatti	Russia	32	2	4	6	65	....	....	....	....	....	....	....	....	....	5	0	2	2	0	....	....	....	....
2005-06	**NY Rangers**	**NHL**	**29**	**1**	**2**	**3**	**22**	**1**	**0**	**0**	**16**	**6.3**	**-2**	**0**	**0.0**	**16:17**	....	....	....	....	....	....	....	....	....
	Hartford	AHL	4	0	0	0	0	....	....	....	....	....	....	....	....	....	....	....	....	....	....	....	....	....	....
	Portland Pirates	AHL	37	4	13	17	19	....	....	....	....	....	....	....	....	....	13	5	9	14	12	....	....	....	....
2006-07	Lada Togliatti	Russia	51	3	16	19	144	....	....	....	....	....	....	....	....	....	3	1	0	1	2	....	....	....	....
	NHL Totals		**36**	**1**	**2**	**3**	**24**	**1**	**0**	**0**	**22**	**4.5**		**0**	**0.0**	**16:09**	....	....	....	....	....	....	....	....	....

Assigned to **Togliatti** (Russia) by **Toronto**, December 16, 2003. Traded to **NY Rangers** by **Toronto** with Jarkko Immonen, Toronto's 1st round choice (later traded to Calgary - Calgary selected Kris Chucko) in 2004 Entry Draft and Toronto's 2nd round choice (Michael Sauer) in 2005 Entry Draft for Brian Leetch and Edmonton's 4th round choice (previously acquired, Toronto selected Roman Kukumberg) in 2004 Entry Draft, March 3, 2004. Signed as a free agent by **Togliatti** (Russia), November 11, 2004. Traded to **Anaheim** by **NY Rangers** for Petr Sykora and NY Rangers' 4th round choice (previously acquired, later traded to Washington - Washington selected Brett Bruneteau) in 2007 Entry Draft, January 8, 2006. Signed as a free agent by **Togliatti** (Russia), August 18, 2006.

KONOPKA, Zenon
(kuh-NOHP-kah, ZEH-nohn) **CBJ**

Center. Shoots left. 6'1", 213 lbs. Born, Niagara Falls, Ont., January 2, 1981.

Season	Club	League	GP	G	A	Pts	PIM	PP	SH	GW	S	%	+/-	TF	F%	Min	GP	G	A	Pts	PIM	PP	SH	GW	Min
1998-99	Ottawa 67's	OHL	56	7	8	15	62	....	....	....	....	....	....	....	....	....	7	0	0	0	2	....	....	....	....
99-2000	Ottawa 67's	OHL	59	8	11	19	107	....	....	....	....	....	....	....	....	....	11	1	2	3	8	....	....	....	....
2000-01	Ottawa 67's	OHL	66	20	45	65	120	....	....	....	....	....	....	....	....	....	20	7	13	20	47	....	....	....	....
2001-02	Ottawa 67's	OHL	61	18	68	86	100	....	....	....	....	....	....	....	....	....	13	8	6	14	49	....	....	....	....
2002-03	Wilkes-Barre	AHL	4	0	1	1	9	....	....	....	....	....	....	....	....	....	....	....	....	....	....	....	....	....	....
	Wheeling Nailers	ECHL	68	22	48	70	231	....	....	....	....	....	....	....	....	....	....	....	....	....	....	....	....	....	....
2003-04	Utah Grizzlies	AHL	43	7	4	11	198	....	....	....	....	....	....	....	....	....	....	....	....	....	....	....	....	....	....
	Idaho Steelheads	ECHL	23	6	22	28	82	....	....	....	....	....	....	....	....	....	17	9	8	17	30	....	....	....	....
2004-05	Cincinnati	AHL	75	17	29	46	212	....	....	....	....	....	....	....	....	....	12	3	3	6	26	....	....	....	....
2005-06	**Anaheim**	**NHL**	**23**	**4**	**3**	**7**	**48**	**2**	**0**	**0**	**18**	**22.2**	**-4**	**142**	**53.5**	**7:19**	....	....	....	....	....	....	....	....	....
	Portland Pirates	AHL	34	18	26	44	57	....	....	....	....	....	....	....	....	....	19	11	18	29	46	....	....	....	....
2006-07	Lada Togliatti	Russia	4	0	0	0	8	....	....	....	....	....	....	....	....	....	....	....	....	....	....	....	....	....	....
	Columbus	**NHL**	**6**	**0**	**0**	**0**	**20**	**0**	**0**	**0**	**2**	**0.0**	**-2**	**22**	**63.6**	**5:00**	....	....	....	....	....	....	....	....	....
	Portland Pirates	AHL	42	11	24	35	97	....	....	....	....	....	....	....	....	....	....	....	....	....	....	....	....	....	....
	Syracuse Crunch	AHL	20	9	11	20	70	....	....	....	....	....	....	....	....	....	....	....	....	....	....	....	....	....	....
	NHL Totals		**29**	**4**	**3**	**7**	**68**	**2**	**0**	**0**	**20**	**20.0**		**164**	**54.9**	**6:50**	....	....	....	....	....	....	....	....	....

ECHL All-Rookie Team (2003)

Signed as a free agent by **Utah** (AHL), September 10, 2003. Signed as a free agent by **Anaheim**, September 1, 2004. Signed as a free agent by **Togliatti** (Russia), July 26, 2006. Traded to **Columbus** by **Anaheim** with Curtis Glencross and Anaheim's 7th round choice (Trent Vogelhuber) in 2007 Entry Draft for Mark Hartigan, Joe Motzko and Columbus' 4th round choice (Sebastian Stefaniszin) in 2007 Entry Draft, January 26, 2007.

KOPECKY, Tomas
(koh-PEHTS-kee, TAW-mahsh) **DET.**

Center. Shoots left. 6'3", 199 lbs. Born, Ilava, Czech., February 5, 1982. Detroit's 2nd choice, 38th overall, in 2000 Entry Draft.

Season	Club	League	GP	G	A	Pts	PIM	PP	SH	GW	S	%	+/-	TF	F%	Min	GP	G	A	Pts	PIM	PP	SH	GW	Min
1997-98	Dukla Trencin Jr.	Slovak-Jr.	41	19	22	41	....	....	....	....	....	....	....	....	....	....	....	....	....	....	....	....	....	....	....
1998-99	Dukla Trencin Jr.	Slovak-Jr.	44	13	16	29	18	....	....	....	....	....	....	....	....	....	....	....	....	....	....	....	....	....	....
99-2000	Dukla Trencin Jr.	Slovak-Jr.	14	8	9	17	36	....	....	....	....	....	....	....	....	....	....	....	....	....	....	....	....	....	....
	Dukla Trencin	Slovakia	52	3	4	7	24	....	....	....	....	....	....	....	....	....	5	0	0	0	0	....	....	....	....
2000-01	Lethbridge	WHL	49	22	28	50	52	....	....	....	....	....	....	....	....	....	5	1	1	2	6	....	....	....	....
	Cincinnati	AHL	1	0	0	0	0	....	....	....	....	....	....	....	....	....	....	....	....	....	....	....	....	....	....
2001-02	Lethbridge	WHL	60	34	42	76	94	....	....	....	....	....	....	....	....	....	4	2	1	3	15	....	....	....	....
	Cincinnati	AHL	2	1	1	2	6	....	....	....	....	....	....	....	....	....	2	0	0	0	0	....	....	....	....
2002-03	Grand Rapids	AHL	70	17	21	38	32	....	....	....	....	....	....	....	....	....	14	0	0	0	6	....	....	....	....
2003-04	Grand Rapids	AHL	48	6	6	12	28	....	....	....	....	....	....	....	....	....	1	0	0	0	2	....	....	....	....
2004-05	Grand Rapids	AHL	48	8	8	16	35	....	....	....	....	....	....	....	....	....	....	....	....	....	....	....	....	....	....
2005-06	**Detroit**	**NHL**	**1**	**0**	**0**	**0**	**2**	**0**	**0**	**0**	**1**	**0.0**	**1**	**0**	**0.0**	**9:41**	....	....	....	....	....	....	....	....	....
	Grand Rapids	AHL	77	32	37	69	108	....	....	....	....	....	....	....	....	....	16	3	4	7	25	....	....	....	....
2006-07	**Detroit**	**NHL**	**26**	**1**	**0**	**1**	**22**	**0**	**0**	**0**	**27**	**3.7**	**-2**	**5**	**40.0**	**7:15**	**4**	**0**	**0**	**0**	**6**	**0**	**0**	**0**	**3:38**
	NHL Totals		**27**	**1**	**0**	**1**	**24**	**0**	**0**	**0**	**28**	**3.6**		**5**	**40.0**	**7:20**	**4**	**0**	**0**	**0**	**6**	**0**	**0**	**0**	**3:38**

• Missed majority of 2006-07 season recovering from broken collarbone suffered in game vs. Chicago, December 14, 2006.

KOPITAR, Anze
(KOH-pih-tahr, AN-zheh) **L.A.**

Center. Shoots left. 6'4", 220 lbs. Born, Jesenice, Yugoslavia, August 24, 1987. Los Angeles' 1st choice, 11th overall, in 2005 Entry Draft.

Season	Club	League	GP	G	A	Pts	PIM	PP	SH	GW	S	%	+/-	TF	F%	Min	GP	G	A	Pts	PIM	PP	SH	GW	Min
2002-03	Jesenice U18	Sloven-U18	14	38	38	76	10	....	....	....	....	....	....	....	....	....	....	....	....	....	....	....	....	....	....
	Jesenice Jr.	Sloven-Jr.	20	15	12	27	8	....	....	....	....	....	....	....	....	....	....	....	....	....	....	....	....	....	....
	Kranjska Gora	Slovenia	11	4	4	8	4	....	....	....	....	....	....	....	....	....	....	....	....	....	....	....	....	....	....
2003-04	Jesenice Jr.	Sloven-Jr.	25	32	28	60	16	....	....	....	....	....	....	....	....	....	....	....	....	....	....	....	....	....	....
	Kranjska Gora	Slovenia	21	14	11	25	10	....	....	....	....	....	....	....	....	....	4	1	1	2	0	....	....	....	....
2004-05	Sodertalje SK U18	Swe-U18	1	1	2	3	0	....	....	....	....	....	....	....	....	....	1	0	0	0	2	....	....	....	....
	Sodertalje SK Jr.	Swe-Jr.	30	28	21	49	26	....	....	....	....	....	....	....	....	....	2	1	1	2	0	....	....	....	....
	Sodertalje SK	Sweden	5	0	0	0	0	....	....	....	....	....	....	....	....	....	10	0	0	0	0	....	....	....	....
2005-06	Sodertalje SK	Sweden	47	8	12	20	28	....	....	....	....	....	....	....	....	....	....	....	....	....	....	....	....	....	....
	Sodertalje SK	Sweden-Q	10	7	4	11	6	....	....	....	....	....	....	....	....	....	....	....	....	....	....	....	....	....	....
2006-07	**Los Angeles**	**NHL**	**72**	**20**	**41**	**61**	**24**	**7**	**2**	**1**	**193**	**10.4**	**-12**	**1204**	**46.1**	**20:32**	....	....	....	....	....	....	....	....	....
	NHL Totals		**72**	**20**	**41**	**61**	**24**	**7**	**2**	**1**	**193**	**10.4**		**1204**	**46.1**	**20:32**	....	....	....	....	....	....	....	....	....

KOROLYUK, Alexander
(koh-roh-LYUHK, al-EHX-AN-duhr) **N.J.**

Left wing. Shoots left. 5'9", 190 lbs. Born, Moscow, USSR, January 15, 1976. San Jose's 6th choice, 141st overall, in 1994 Entry Draft.

Season	Club	League	GP	G	A	Pts	PIM	PP	SH	GW	S	%	+/-	TF	F%	Min	GP	G	A	Pts	PIM	PP	SH	GW	Min
1993-94	Krylja Sovetov	CIS	22	4	4	8	20	....	....	....	....	....	....	....	....	....	3	1	0	1	4	....	....	....	....
1994-95	Krylja Sovetov	CIS	52	16	13	29	62	....	....	....	....	....	....	....	....	....	4	1	2	3	4	....	....	....	....
1995-96	Krylja Sovetov	CIS	50	30	19	49	77	....	....	....	....	....	....	....	....	....	....	....	....	....	....	....	....	....	....
1996-97	Krylja Sovetov	Russia	17	8	5	13	46	....	....	....	....	....	....	....	....	....	....	....	....	....	....	....	....	....	....
	Manitoba Moose	IHL	42	20	16	36	71	....	....	....	....	....	....	....	....	....	....	....	....	....	....	....	....	....	....
1997-98	**San Jose**	**NHL**	**19**	**2**	**3**	**5**	**6**	**1**	**0**	**0**	**23**	**8.7**	**-5**	....	....	....	....	....	....	....	....	....	....	....	....
	Kentucky	AHL	44	16	23	39	96	....	....	....	....	....	....	....	....	....	3	0	0	0	0	....	....	....	....
1998-99	**San Jose**	**NHL**	**55**	**12**	**18**	**30**	**26**	**2**	**0**	**0**	**96**	**12.5**	**3**	**4**	**50.0**	**13:53**	**6**	**1**	**3**	**4**	**2**	**0**	**0**	**1**	**11:01**
	Kentucky	AHL	23	9	13	22	16	....	....	....	....	....	....	....	....	....	....	....	....	....	....	....	....	....	....
99-2000	**San Jose**	**NHL**	**57**	**14**	**21**	**35**	**35**	**3**	**0**	**1**	**124**	**11.3**	**4**	**1**	**100.0**	**13:36**	**9**	**0**	**3**	**3**	**6**	**0**	**0**	**0**	**11:37**
2000-01	Ak Bars Kazan	Russia	6	0	5	5	4	....	....	....	....	....	....	....	....	....	....	....	....	....	....	....	....	....	....
	San Jose	**NHL**	**70**	**12**	**13**	**25**	**41**	**3**	**0**	**1**	**140**	**8.6**	**2**	**30**	**33.3**	**11:56**	**2**	**0**	**0**	**0**	**0**	**0**	**0**	**0**	**8:11**
2001-02	**San Jose**	**NHL**	**32**	**3**	**7**	**10**	**14**	**0**	**0**	**1**	**49**	**6.1**	**2**	**10**	**30.0**	**12:16**	....	....	....	....	....	....	....	....	....
2002-03	Ak Bars Kazan	Russia	45	14	17	31	46	....	....	....	....	....	....	....	....	....	4	0	0	0	0	....	....	....	....
2003-04	**San Jose**	**NHL**	**63**	**19**	**18**	**37**	**18**	**4**	**0**	**2**	**108**	**17.6**	**20**	**14**	**50.0**	**14:55**	**17**	**5**	**2**	**7**	**10**	**2**	**0**	**1**	**16:40**
2004-05	Vityaz Chekhov	Russia-2	42	24	28	52	54	....	....	....	....	....	....	....	....	....	....	....	....	....	....	....	....	....	....
	Voskresensk	Russia	10	4	3	7	14	....	....	....	....	....	....	....	....	....	....	....	....	....	....	....	....	....	....

			Regular Season														Playoffs								
Season	Club	League	GP	G	A	Pts	PIM	PP	SH	GW	S	%	+/-	TF	F%	Min	GP	G	A	Pts	PIM	PP	SH	GW	Min
2005-06	Vityaz Chekhov	Russia	45	19	15	34	86																		
	Russia	Olympics	6	1	1	2	6																		
2006-07	Vityaz Chekhov	Russia	48	17	28	45	76										3	0	0	0	8				
	NHL Totals		**296**	**62**	**80**	**142**	**140**	**13**	**0**	**5**	**540**	**11.5**		**59**	**39.0**	**13:23**	**34**	**6**	**8**	**14**	**18**	**2**	**0**	**2**	**13:50**

• Spent majority of 2001-02 season on practice roster. Signed as a free agent by **Kazan** (Russia), July 9, 2002. Signed as a free agent by **Chekhov** (Russia-2), September 25, 2004. Signed as a free agent by **Voskresensk** (Russia), February 14, 2005. Traded to **New Jersey** by **San Jose** with Jim Fahey for Vladimir Malakhov and New Jersey's 1st round choice (later traded to St. Louis - St. Louis selected David Perron) in 2007 Entry Draft, October 1, 2006.

KOSTITSYN, Andrei

(kaws-TIHT-sihn, AWN-dray) **MTL.**

Wing. Shoots left. 6', 200 lbs. Born, Novopolotsk, USSR, February 3, 1985. Montreal's 1st choice, 10th overall, in 2003 Entry Draft.

Season	Club	League	GP	G	A	Pts	PIM	PP	SH	GW	S	%	+/-	TF	F%	Min	GP	G	A	Pts	PIM	PP	SH	GW	Min
2000-01	Novopolotsk	Belarus	1	2	1	3	2																		
	Novopolotsk	EEHL	5	1	0	1	0																		
	Yunost Minsk	Belarus	3	1	4	5	8																		
	HC Vitebsk	Belarus	17	17	6	23	42																		
2001-02	Novopolotsk	Belarus	17	9	6	15	28																		
	Novopolotsk	EEHL	29	9	8	17	16																		
	Yunost Minsk	Belarus	6	2	0	2	8																		
2002-03	CSKA Moscow	Russia	6	0	0	0	2																		
	Voskresensk	Russia-2	2	1	1	2	0																		
	Yunost Minsk	Belarus	4	6	4	10	43																		
	CSKA Moscow 2	Russia-3	3	2	2	4	25																		
2003-04	CSKA Moscow 2	Russia-3	STATISTICS NOT AVAILABLE																						
	CSKA Moscow	Russia	12	0	1	1	2																		
	Yunost Minsk	Belarus	STATISTICS NOT AVAILABLE																						
2004-05	Hamilton	AHL	66	12	11	23	24										3	0	0	0	0				
2005-06	**Montreal**	**NHL**	**12**	**2**	**1**	**3**	**2**	**0**	**0**	**0**	**9**	**22.2**	**1**	**1**	**0.0**	**7:32**									
	Hamilton	AHL	64	18	29	47	76																		
2006-07	**Montreal**	**NHL**	**22**	**1**	**10**	**11**	**6**	**0**	**0**	**0**	**38**	**2.6**	**3**	**1**	**0.0**	**13:17**									
	Hamilton	AHL	50	21	31	52	50																		
	NHL Totals		**34**	**3**	**11**	**14**	**8**	**0**	**0**	**0**	**47**	**6.4**		**2**	**0.0**	**11:15**									

KOSTOPOULOS, Tom

(kaw-STAWP-oh-lihs, TAWM) **MTL.**

Right wing. Shoots right. 6', 205 lbs. Born, Mississauga, Ont., January 24, 1979. Pittsburgh's 9th choice, 204th overall, in 1999 Entry Draft.

Season	Club	League	GP	G	A	Pts	PIM	PP	SH	GW	S	%	+/-	TF	F%	Min	GP	G	A	Pts	PIM	PP	SH	GW	Min
1995-96	Brampton	OPJHL	24	9	9	18	28																		
1996-97	London Knights	OHL	64	13	12	25	67																		
1997-98	London Knights	OHL	66	24	26	50	108										16	6	4	10	26				
1998-99	London Knights	OHL	66	27	60	87	114										25	19	16	35	32				
99-2000	Wilkes-Barre	AHL	76	26	32	58	121																		
2000-01	Wilkes-Barre	AHL	80	16	36	52	120										21	3	9	12	6				
2001-02	**Pittsburgh**	**NHL**	**11**	**1**	**2**	**3**	**9**	**0**	**0**	**0**	**8**	**12.5**	**–1**	**0**	**0.0**	**12:03**									
	Wilkes-Barre	AHL	70	27	26	53	112																		
2002-03	**Pittsburgh**	**NHL**	**8**	**0**	**1**	**1**	**0**	**0**	**0**	**0**	**6**	**0.0**	**–4**	**2**	**0.0**	**4:33**									
	Wilkes-Barre	AHL	71	21	42	63	131										6	1	2	3	7				
2003-04	**Pittsburgh**	**NHL**	**60**	**9**	**13**	**22**	**67**	**2**	**1**	**1**	**101**	**8.9**	**–14**	**10**	**30.0**	**14:26**									
	Wilkes-Barre	AHL	21	7	13	20	43										24	7	16	23	32				
2004-05	Manchester	AHL	64	25	46	71	99										6	0	7	7	10				
2005-06	**Los Angeles**	**NHL**	**76**	**8**	**14**	**22**	**100**	**0**	**0**	**1**	**74**	**10.8**	**–8**	**30**	**36.7**	**12:56**									
2006-07	**Los Angeles**	**NHL**	**76**	**7**	**15**	**22**	**73**	**0**	**0**	**0**	**90**	**7.8**	**–2**	**62**	**29.0**	**11:34**									
	NHL Totals		**231**	**25**	**45**	**70**	**249**	**2**	**1**	**2**	**279**	**9.0**		**104**	**30.8**	**12:32**									

Signed as a free agent by **Manchester** (AHL), July 12, 2004. Signed as a free agent by **Los Angeles**, August 1, 2005. Signed as a free agent by **Montreal**, July 4, 2007.

KOTALIK, Ales

(KOH-tahl-eek, ahl-EHSH) **BUF.**

Right wing. Shoots right. 6'1", 227 lbs. Born, Jindrichuv Hradec, Czech., December 23, 1978. Buffalo's 7th choice, 164th overall, in 1998 Entry Draft.

Season	Club	League	GP	G	A	Pts	PIM	PP	SH	GW	S	%	+/-	TF	F%	Min	GP	G	A	Pts	PIM	PP	SH	GW	Min
1993-94	C. Budejovice Jr.	CzRep-Jr.	28	12	12	24																			
1994-95	C. Budejovice Jr.	CzRep-Jr.	36	26	17	43																			
1995-96	C. Budejovice Jr.	CzRep-Jr.	28	6	7	13																			
1996-97	C. Budejovice Jr.	CzRep-Jr.	36	15	16	31	24																		
1997-98	C. Budejovice	CzRep	47	9	7	16	14																		
1998-99	C. Budejovice	CzRep	41	8	13	21	16										3	0	0	0					
99-2000	C. Budejovice	CzRep	43	7	12	19	34										3	0	1	1	6				
2000-01	C. Budejovice	CzRep	52	19	29	48	54																		
2001-02	**Buffalo**	**NHL**	**13**	**1**	**3**	**4**	**2**	**0**	**0**	**0**	**21**	**4.8**	**–1**	**11**	**27.3**	**12:35**									
	Rochester	AHL	68	18	25	43	55										1	0	0	0	0				
2002-03	**Buffalo**	**NHL**	**68**	**21**	**14**	**35**	**30**	**4**	**0**	**2**	**138**	**15.2**	**–2**	**37**	**51.4**	**15:15**									
	Rochester	AHL	8	0	2	2	4																		
2003-04	**Buffalo**	**NHL**	**62**	**15**	**11**	**26**	**41**	**2**	**0**	**3**	**142**	**10.6**	**–1**	**14**	**50.0**	**15:11**									
2004-05	Liberec	CzRep	25	8	8	16	46										12	2	5	7	12				
2005-06	**Buffalo**	**NHL**	**82**	**25**	**37**	**62**	**62**	**10**	**0**	**5**	**261**	**9.6**	**–3**	**29**	**41.4**	**15:34**	**18**	**4**	**7**	**11**	**8**	**0**	**0**	**3**	**15:15**
	Czech Republic	Olympics	4	0	0	0	0																		
2006-07	**Buffalo**	**NHL**	**66**	**16**	**22**	**38**	**46**	**3**	**0**	**4**	**162**	**9.9**	**–5**	**35**	**48.6**	**14:31**	**16**	**2**	**2**	**4**	**8**	**0**	**0**	**0**	**12:29**
	NHL Totals		**291**	**78**	**87**	**165**	**181**	**19**	**0**	**14**	**724**	**10.8**		**126**	**46.0**	**15:02**	**34**	**6**	**9**	**15**	**16**	**0**	**0**	**3**	**13:57**

Signed as a free agent by **Liberec** (CzRep), September 6, 2004.

KOVALCHUK, Ilya

(koh-vuhl-CHUHK, IHL-yah) **ATL.**

Left wing. Shoots right. 6'1", 225 lbs. Born, Tver, USSR, April 15, 1983. Atlanta's 1st choice, 1st overall, in 2001 Entry Draft.

Season	Club	League	GP	G	A	Pts	PIM	PP	SH	GW	S	%	+/-	TF	F%	Min	GP	G	A	Pts	PIM	PP	SH	GW	Min
99-2000	Spartak Moscow	Russia-2	49	12	5	17	75																		
	Spartak 2	Russia-3	2	2	1	3	14																		
2000-01	Spartak Moscow	Russia	40	28	18	46	78										12	14	4	18	38				
2001-02	**Atlanta**	**NHL**	**65**	**29**	**22**	**51**	**28**	**7**	**0**	**4**	**184**	**15.8**	**–19**	**6**	**16.7**	**18:32**									
	Russia	Olympics	6	1	2	3	14																		
2002-03	**Atlanta**	**NHL**	**81**	**38**	**29**	**67**	**57**	**9**	**0**	**3**	**257**	**14.8**	**–24**	**15**	**40.0**	**19:27**									
2003-04	**Atlanta**	**NHL**	**81**	***41**	**46**	**87**	**63**	**16**	**1**	**6**	**341**	**12.0**	**–10**	**28**	**32.1**	**23:41**									
2004-05	Ak Bars Kazan	Russia	53	19	23	42	72										4	0	1	1	0				
2005-06	**Atlanta**	**NHL**	**78**	**52**	**46**	**98**	**68**	**27**	**0**	**7**	**323**	**16.1**	**–6**	**47**	**40.4**	**22:23**									
	Russia	Olympics	8	4	1	5	31																		
2006-07	**Atlanta**	**NHL**	**82**	**42**	**34**	**76**	**66**	**18**	**0**	**7**	**336**	**12.5**	**–2**	**66**	**39.4**	**21:32**	**4**	**1**	**1**	**2**	**19**	**0**	**0**	**0**	**18:42**
	NHL Totals		**387**	**202**	**177**	**379**	**282**	**77**	**1**	**27**	**1441**	**14.0**		**162**	**37.7**	**21:13**	**4**	**1**	**1**	**2**	**19**	**0**	**0**	**0**	**18:42**

NHL All-Rookie Team (2002) • NHL Second All-Star Team (2004) • Maurice "Rocket" Richard Trophy (2004) (tied with Jarome Iginla and Rick Nash)
Played in NHL All-Star Game (2004)
Signed as a free agent by **Kazan** (Russia) August 22, 2004.

KOVALEV, Alex

(koh-VAH-lehv, AL-ehx) **MTL.**

Right wing. Shoots left. 6'1", 222 lbs. Born, Togliatti, USSR, February 24, 1973. NY Rangers' 1st choice, 15th overall, in 1991 Entry Draft.

Season	Club	League	GP	G	A	Pts	PIM	PP	SH	GW	S	%	+/-	TF	F%	Min	GP	G	A	Pts	PIM	PP	SH	GW	Min
1989-90	Dynamo Moscow	USSR	1	0	0	0	0																		
1990-91	Dyn'o Moscow 2	USSR-3	21	16																					
	Dynamo Moscow	USSR	18	1	2	3	4																		
	Dynamo Moscow	Super-S	1	0	0	0	0																		
1991-92	Dynamo Moscow	CIS	33	16	9	25	20																		
	Dyn'o Moscow 2	CIS-3	4	5	0	5	12																		
	Russia	Olympics	8	1	2	3	14																		
1992-93	**NY Rangers**	**NHL**	**65**	**20**	**18**	**38**	**79**	**3**	**0**	**3**	**134**	**14.9**	**–10**												
	Binghamton	AHL	13	13	11	24	35										9	3	5	8	14				
1993-94♦	**NY Rangers**	**NHL**	**76**	**23**	**33**	**56**	**154**	**7**	**0**	**3**	**184**	**12.5**	**18**				**23**	**9**	**12**	**21**	**18**	**5**	**0**	**2**	

			Regular Season														Playoffs								
Season	Club	League	GP	G	A	Pts	PIM	PP	SH	GW	S	%	+/-	TF	F%	Min	GP	G	A	Pts	PIM	PP	SH	GW	Min
1994-95	Lada Togliatti	CIS	12	8	8	16	49	....	....	....	....	....	....	....	....	....	....	....	....	....	....	....	....	....	....
	NY Rangers	NHL	48	13	15	28	30	1	1	1	103	12.6	–6	....	....	....	10	4	7	11	10	0	0	0	....
1995-96	NY Rangers	NHL	81	24	34	58	98	8	1	7	206	11.7	5	....	....	....	11	3	4	7	14	0	0	1	....
1996-97	NY Rangers	NHL	45	13	22	35	42	1	0	0	110	11.8	11	....	....	....	....	....	....	....	....	....	....	....	....
1997-98	NY Rangers	NHL	73	23	30	53	44	8	0	3	173	13.3	–22	....	....	....	....	....	....	....	....	....	....	....	....
1998-99	NY Rangers	NHL	14	3	4	7	12	1	0	1	35	8.6	–6	18	44.4	19:53	....	....	....	....	....	....	....	....	....
	Pittsburgh	NHL	63	20	26	46	37	5	1	4	156	12.8	8	226	43.4	20:30	10	5	7	12	14	0	0	1	20:24
99-2000	Pittsburgh	NHL	82	26	40	66	94	9	2	4	254	10.2	–3	306	47.4	22:53	11	1	5	6	10	0	0	0	26:35
2000-01	Pittsburgh	NHL	79	44	51	95	96	12	2	9	307	14.3	12	255	40.0	23:35	18	5	5	10	16	1	0	0	20:57
2001-02	Pittsburgh	NHL	67	32	44	76	80	8	1	3	266	12.0	2	179	45.3	24:03	....	....	....	....	....	....	....	....	....
	Russia	Olympics	6	3	1	4	4	....	....	....	....	....	....	....	....	....	....	....	....	....	....	....	....	....	....
2002-03	Pittsburgh	NHL	54	27	37	64	50	8	0	1	212	12.7	–11	19	31.6	24:03	....	....	....	....	....	....	....	....	....
	NY Rangers	NHL	24	10	3	13	20	3	0	2	59	16.9	2	19	42.1	20:09	....	....	....	....	....	....	....	....	....
2003-04	NY Rangers	NHL	66	13	29	42	54	3	0	0	178	7.3	–5	29	48.3	19:37	....	....	....	....	....	....	....	....	....
	Montreal	NHL	12	1	2	3	12	0	0	1	29	3.4	–4	2	50.0	15:36	11	6	4	10	8	1	0	1	20:11
2004-05	Ak Bars Kazan	Russia	35	10	12	22	80	....	....	....	....	....	....	....	....	....	4	0	0	0	8	....	....	....	....
2005-06	Montreal	NHL	69	23	42	65	76	9	0	5	206	11.2	–1	47	48.9	19:28	6	4	3	7	4	1	0	0	19:21
	Russia	Olympics	8	4	2	6	4	....	....	....	....	....	....	....	....	....	....	....	....	....	....	....	....	....	....
2006-07	Montreal	NHL	73	18	29	47	78	8	0	5	197	9.1	–19	162	46.3	18:15	....	....	....	....	....	....	....	....	....
	NHL Totals		991	333	459	792	1056	94	8	52	2809	11.9		1262	44.5	21:20	100	37	47	84	94	8	0	5	21:38

Played in NHL All-Star Game (2001, 2003)

Traded to **Pittsburgh** by **NY Rangers** with Harry York for Petr Nedved, Chris Tamer and Sean Pronger, November 25, 1998. Traded to **NY Rangers** by **Pittsburgh** with Mike Wilson, Janne Laukkanen and Dan LaCouture for Joel Bouchard, Richard Lintner, Rico Fata and Mikael Samuelsson, February 10, 2003. Traded to **Montreal** by **NY Rangers** for Jozef Balej and Montreal's 2nd round choice (Bruce Graham) in 2004 Entry Draft, March 2, 2004. Signed as a free agent by **Kazan** (Russia), November 3, 2004.

KOZLOV, Viktor

(KAWZ-lahf, VIHK-tohr) **WSH.**

Center. Shoots right. 6'5", 235 lbs. Born, Togliatti, USSR, February 14, 1975. San Jose's 1st choice, 6th overall, in 1993 Entry Draft.

Season	Club	League	GP	G	A	Pts	PIM	PP	SH	GW	S	%	+/-	TF	F%	Min	GP	G	A	Pts	PIM	PP	SH	GW	Min
1990-91	Lada Togliatti	USSR-2	2	2	0	2	0	....	....	....	....	....	....	....	....	....	....	....	....	....	....	....	....	....	....
1991-92	Lada Togliatti	CIS	3	0	0	0	0	....	....	....	....	....	....	....	....	....	....	....	....	....	....	....	....	....	....
1992-93	Dynamo Moscow	CIS	30	6	5	11	4	....	....	....	....	....	....	....	....	....	10	3	0	3	0	....	....	....	....
1993-94	Dynamo Moscow	CIS	42	16	9	25	14	....	....	....	....	....	....	....	....	....	....	....	....	....	....	....	....	....	....
1994-95	Dynamo Moscow	CIS	3	1	1	2	2	....	....	....	....	....	....	....	....	....	....	....	....	....	....	....	....	....	....
	San Jose	NHL	16	2	0	2	2	0	0	0	23	8.7	–5	....	....	....	....	....	....	....	....	....	....	....	....
	Kansas City	IHL	4	1	1	2	0	....	....	....	....	....	....	....	....	....	13	4	5	9	12	....	....	....	....
1995-96	San Jose	NHL	62	6	13	19	6	1	0	0	107	5.6	–15	....	....	....	....	....	....	....	....	....	....	....	....
	Kansas City	IHL	15	4	7	11	12	....	....	....	....	....	....	....	....	....	....	....	....	....	....	....	....	....	....
1996-97	San Jose	NHL	78	16	25	41	40	4	0	4	184	8.7	–16	....	....	....	....	....	....	....	....	....	....	....	....
1997-98	San Jose	NHL	18	5	2	7	2	2	0	0	51	9.8	–2	....	....	....	....	....	....	....	....	....	....	....	....
	Florida	NHL	46	12	11	23	14	3	2	0	114	10.5	–1	....	....	....	....	....	....	....	....	....	....	....	....
1998-99	Florida	NHL	65	16	35	51	24	5	1	1	209	7.7	13	985	41.2	19:03	....	....	....	....	....	....	....	....	....
99-2000	Florida	NHL	80	17	53	70	16	6	0	2	223	7.6	24	1616	42.9	19:27	4	0	1	1	0	0	0	0	16:06
2000-01	Florida	NHL	51	14	23	37	10	6	0	2	139	10.1	–4	817	41.6	18:23	....	....	....	....	....	....	....	....	....
2001-02	Florida	NHL	50	9	18	27	20	6	0	1	143	6.3	–16	840	43.1	19:54	....	....	....	....	....	....	....	....	....
2002-03	Florida	NHL	74	22	34	56	18	7	1	1	232	9.5	–8	404	42.8	22:35	....	....	....	....	....	....	....	....	....
2003-04	Florida	NHL	48	11	16	27	16	3	1	1	117	9.4	–4	200	49.0	19:30	....	....	....	....	....	....	....	....	....
	New Jersey	NHL	11	2	4	6	2	0	0	0	26	7.7	0	112	56.3	13:26	2	0	0	0	0	0	0	0	8:55
2004-05	Lada Togliatti	Russia	52	15	22	37	22	....	....	....	....	....	....	....	....	....	10	3	3	6	6	....	....	....	....
2005-06	New Jersey	NHL	69	12	13	25	16	2	0	1	122	9.8	0	185	47.0	13:32	3	0	0	0	0	0	0	0	14:05
	Russia	Olympics	8	2	3	5	2	....	....	....	....	....	....	....	....	....	....	....	....	....	....	....	....	....	....
2006-07	NY Islanders	NHL	81	25	26	51	28	5	0	4	165	15.2	12	462	39.0	16:25	5	0	2	2	2	0	0	0	16:34
	NHL Totals		749	169	273	442	214	50	5	17	1855	9.1		5621	42.7	18:25	14	0	3	3	2	0	0	0	14:48

Played in NHL All-Star Game (2000)

Traded to **Florida** by **San Jose** with Florida's 5th round choice (previously acquired, Florida selected Jaroslav Spacek) in 1998 Entry Draft for Dave Lowry and Florida's 1st round choice (later traded to Tampa Bay – Tampa Bay selected Vincent Lecavalier) in 1998 Entry Draft, November 13, 1997. Traded to **New Jersey** by **Florida** for Christian Berglund and Victor Uchevatov, March 1, 2004. Signed as a free agent by **Togliatti** (Russia), July 11, 2004. Signed as a free agent by **NY Islanders**, September 13, 2006. Signed as a free agent by **Washington**, July 1, 2007.

KOZLOV, Vyacheslav

(KAWZ-lahf, V'YTACH-ih-slav) **ATL.**

Left wing. Shoots left. 5'10", 190 lbs. Born, Voskresensk, USSR, May 3, 1972. Detroit's 2nd choice, 45th overall, in 1990 Entry Draft.

Season	Club	League	GP	G	A	Pts	PIM	PP	SH	GW	S	%	+/-	TF	F%	Min	GP	G	A	Pts	PIM	PP	SH	GW	Min
1987-88	Voskresensk	USSR	2	0	0	0	0	....	....	....	....	....	....	....	....	....	....	....	....	....	....	....	....	....	....
1988-89	Voskresensk	USSR	14	0	1	1	2	....	....	....	....	....	....	....	....	....	....	....	....	....	....	....	....	....	....
1989-90	Voskresensk	USSR	45	14	12	26	38	....	....	....	....	....	....	....	....	....	....	....	....	....	....	....	....	....	....
1990-91	Voskresensk	USSR	45	11	13	24	46	....	....	....	....	....	....	....	....	....	....	....	....	....	....	....	....	....	....
1991-92	CSKA Moscow	CIS	11	6	5	11	12	....	....	....	....	....	....	....	....	....	....	....	....	....	....	....	....	....	....
	Detroit	NHL	7	0	2	2	2	0	0	0	9	0.0	–2	....	....	....	....	....	....	....	....	....	....	....	....
1992-93	Detroit	NHL	17	4	1	5	14	0	0	0	26	15.4	–1	....	....	....	4	0	2	2	2	0	0	0	....
	Adirondack	AHL	45	23	36	59	54	....	....	....	....	....	....	....	....	....	4	1	1	2	4	....	....	....	....
1993-94	Detroit	NHL	77	34	39	73	50	8	2	6	202	16.8	27	....	....	....	7	2	5	7	12	0	0	0	....
	Adirondack	AHL	3	0	1	1	15	....	....	....	....	....	....	....	....	....	....	....	....	....	....	....	....	....	....
1994-95	CSKA Moscow	CIS	10	3	4	7	14	....	....	....	....	....	....	....	....	....	....	....	....	....	....	....	....	....	....
	Detroit	NHL	46	13	20	33	45	5	0	3	97	13.4	12	....	....	....	18	9	7	16	10	1	0	4	....
1995-96	Detroit	NHL	82	36	37	73	70	9	0	7	237	15.2	33	....	....	....	19	5	7	12	10	2	0	1	....
1996-97♦	Detroit	NHL	75	23	22	45	46	3	0	6	211	10.9	21	....	....	....	20	8	5	13	14	4	0	2	....
1997-98♦	Detroit	NHL	80	25	27	52	46	6	0	1	221	11.3	14	....	....	....	22	6	8	14	10	1	0	4	....
1998-99	Detroit	NHL	79	29	29	58	45	6	1	4	209	13.9	10	38	36.8	16:02	10	6	1	7	4	3	0	0	14:44
99-2000	Detroit	NHL	72	18	18	36	28	4	0	3	165	10.9	11	28	35.7	15:30	8	2	1	3	12	1	0	1	12:20
2000-01	Detroit	NHL	72	20	18	38	30	4	0	5	187	10.7	9	51	47.1	14:43	6	4	1	5	2	2	0	0	16:27
2001-02	Buffalo	NHL	38	9	13	22	16	3	0	1	68	13.2	0	24	41.7	16:31	....	....	....	....	....	....	....	....	....
2002-03	Atlanta	NHL	79	21	49	70	66	9	1	2	185	11.4	–10	67	34.3	20:01	....	....	....	....	....	....	....	....	....
2003-04	Atlanta	NHL	76	20	32	52	74	6	0	1	191	10.5	–12	164	32.3	20:20	....	....	....	....	....	....	....	....	....
2004-05	Voskresensk	Russia	38	12	18	30	69	....	....	....	....	....	....	....	....	....	....	....	....	....	....	....	....	....	....
	Ak Bars Kazan	Russia	8	2	4	6	0	....	....	....	....	....	....	....	....	....	4	1	0	1	8	....	....	....	....
2005-06	Atlanta	NHL	82	25	46	71	33	8	0	1	206	12.1	14	317	39.8	17:47	....	....	....	....	....	....	....	....	....
2006-07	Atlanta	NHL	81	28	52	80	36	8	0	8	190	14.7	9	326	46.9	20:29	4	0	0	0	6	0	0	0	17:33
	NHL Totals		963	305	405	710	601	79	4	48	2404	12.7		1015	40.7	17:49	118	42	37	79	82	14	0	12	14:49

Traded to **Buffalo** by **Detroit** with Detroit's 1st round choice (later traded to Columbus – later traded to Atlanta – Atlanta selected Jim Slater) in 2002 Entry Draft for Dominik Hasek, July 1, 2001. • Missed majority of 2001-02 season recovering from Achilles tendon injury suffered in game vs. Columbus, December 31, 2001. Traded to **Atlanta** by **Buffalo** with Buffalo's 2nd round choice (later traded to Columbus – Columbus selected Joakim Lindstrom) in 2003 Entry Draft for Atlanta's 2nd round choice (later traded to Edmonton – Edmonton selected Jeff Deslauriers) in 2003 Entry Draft and Vancouver's 3rd round choice (previously acquired, Buffalo selected John Adams) in 2003 Entry Draft, June 22, 2002. Signed as a free agent by **Voskresensk** (Russia), September 15, 2004. Signed as a free agent by **Kazan** (Russia), February 17, 2005.

KRAFT, Milan

(KRAFT, MEE-lan) **PIT.**

Center. Shoots right. 6'4", 212 lbs. Born, Plzen, Czech., January 17, 1980. Pittsburgh's 1st choice, 23rd overall, in 1998 Entry Draft.

Season	Club	League	GP	G	A	Pts	PIM	PP	SH	GW	S	%	+/-	TF	F%	Min	GP	G	A	Pts	PIM	PP	SH	GW	Min
1995-96	HC Plzen Jr.	CzRep-Jr.	49	54	41	95	....	....	....	....	....	....	....	....	....	....	....	....	....	....	....	....	....	....	....
1996-97	HC Plzen Jr.	CzRep-Jr.	29	24	12	36	....	....	....	....	....	....	....	....	....	....	....	....	....	....	....	....	....	....	....
	HC ZKZ Plzen	CzRep	9	0	1	1	2	....	....	....	....	....	....	....	....	....	....	....	....	....	....	....	....	....	....
1997-98	HC Plzen Jr.	CzRep-Jr.	24	22	21	43	12	....	....	....	....	....	....	....	....	....	....	....	....	....	....	....	....	....	....
	Plzen	CzRep	16	0	5	5	0	....	....	....	....	....	....	....	....	....	1	0	0	0	0	....	....	....	....
1998-99	Prince Albert	WHL	68	40	46	86	32	....	....	....	....	....	....	....	....	....	14	7	13	20	6	....	....	....	....
99-2000	Prince Albert	WHL	56	34	35	69	42	....	....	....	....	....	....	....	....	....	6	4	1	5	4	....	....	....	....
2000-01	Pittsburgh	NHL	42	7	7	14	8	1	1	1	63	11.1	–6	427	37.9	11:41	8	0	0	0	2	0	0	0	12:13
	Wilkes-Barre	AHL	40	21	23	44	27	....	....	....	....	....	....	....	....	....	14	12	7	19	6	....	....	....	....
2001-02	Pittsburgh	NHL	68	8	8	16	16	1	0	2	103	7.8	–9	766	44.7	12:29	....	....	....	....	....	....	....	....	....
	Wilkes-Barre	AHL	8	4	4	8	10	....	....	....	....	....	....	....	....	....	....	....	....	....	....	....	....	....	....
2002-03	Wilkes-Barre	AHL	40	13	24	37	28	....	....	....	....	....	....	....	....	....	6	2	4	6	4	....	....	....	....
	Pittsburgh	NHL	31	7	5	12	10	0	0	1	50	14.0	–8	392	43.1	13:56	....	....	....	....	....	....	....	....	....
2003-04	Pittsburgh	NHL	66	19	21	40	18	6	0	1	134	14.2	–22	970	47.4	15:16	....	....	....	....	....	....	....	....	....
2004-05	Plzen	CzRep	17	2	4	6	6	....	....	....	....	....	....	....	....	....	....	....	....	....	....	....	....	....	....
	Karlovy Vary	CzRep	35	9	10	19	20	....	....	....	....	....	....	....	....	....	....	....	....	....	....	....	....	....	....

Season	Club	League	GP	G	A	Pts	PIM	PP	SH	GW	S	%	+/-	TF	F%	Min	GP	G	A	Pts	PIM	PP	SH	GW	Min
			Regular Season														Playoffs								
2005-06	Avangard Omsk	Russia	28	2	5	7	14	....	....	....	....	....	....	....	....	....	....	....	....	....	....	....	....	....	....
	Karlovy Vary	CzRep	19	7	5	12	16	....	....	....	....	....	....	....	....	....	....	....	....	....	....	....	....	....	....
2006-07	Karlovy Vary	CzRep	25	6	3	9	28	....	....	....	....	....	....	....	....	....	3	0	0	0	8	....	....	....	....
	NHL Totals		**207**	**41**	**41**	**82**	**52**	**8**	**1**	**5**	**350**	**11.7**		**2555**	**44.3**	**13:26**	**8**	**0**	**0**	**0**	**2**	**0**	**0**	**0**	**12:13**

Signed as a free agent by **Plzen** (CzRep), September 17, 2004. Signed as a free agent by **Karlovy Vary** (CzRep), October 27, 2004. Signed as a free agent by **Omsk** (Russia), August 26, 2005.

KRAJICEK, Lukas
(KRIGH-ee-chehk, LOO-kahsh) **VAN.**

Defense. Shoots left. 6'2", 196 lbs. Born, Prostejov, Czech., March 11, 1983. Florida's 2nd choice, 24th overall, in 2001 Entry Draft.

Season	Club	League	GP	G	A	Pts	PIM	PP	SH	GW	S	%	+/-	TF	F%	Min	GP	G	A	Pts	PIM	PP	SH	GW	Min
1998-99	HC ZPS Zlin Jr.	CzRep-Jr.	48	8	18	26	40	....	....	....	....	....	....	....	....	....	....	....	....	....	....	....	....	....	....
99-2000	Det. Compuware	NAHL	53	5	22	27	61	....	....	....	....	....	....	....	....	....	5	0	1	1	18	....	....	....	....
2000-01	Peterborough	OHL	61	8	27	35	53	....	....	....	....	....	....	....	....	....	7	0	5	5	0	....	....	....	....
2001-02	**Florida**	**NHL**	**5**	**0**	**0**	**0**	**0**	**0**	**0**	**0**	**3**	**0.0**	**0**	**0**	**0.0**	**13:23**	....	....	....	....	....	....	....	....	....
	Peterborough	OHL	55	10	32	42	56	....	....	....	....	....	....	....	....	....	6	0	5	5	6	....	....	....	....
2002-03	Peterborough	OHL	52	11	42	53	42	....	....	....	....	....	....	....	....	....	7	0	3	3	0	....	....	....	....
	San Antonio	AHL	3	0	1	1	0	....	....	....	....	....	....	....	....	....	3	0	0	0	0	....	....	....	....
2003-04	**Florida**	**NHL**	**18**	**1**	**6**	**7**	**12**	**1**	**0**	**0**	**16**	**6.3**	**–2**	**0**	**0.0**	**13:32**	....	....	....	....	....	....	....	....	....
	San Antonio	AHL	54	5	12	17	24	....	....	....	....	....	....	....	....	....	....	....	....	....	....	....	....	....	....
2004-05	San Antonio	AHL	78	2	22	24	57	....	....	....	....	....	....	....	....	....	....	....	....	....	....	....	....	....	....
2005-06	**Florida**	**NHL**	**67**	**2**	**14**	**16**	**50**	**2**	**0**	**0**	**89**	**2.2**	**1**	**0**	**0.0**	**18:30**	....	....	....	....	....	....	....	....	....
2006-07	**Vancouver**	**NHL**	**78**	**3**	**13**	**16**	**64**	**1**	**0**	**2**	**105**	**2.9**	**–4**	**0**	**0.0**	**18:31**	**12**	**0**	**2**	**2**	**12**	**0**	**0**	**0**	**18:50**
	NHL Totals		**168**	**6**	**33**	**39**	**126**	**4**	**0**	**2**	**213**	**2.8**		**0**	**0.0**	**17:49**	**12**	**0**	**2**	**2**	**12**	**0**	**0**	**0**	**18:50**

OHL All-Rookie Team (2001) • OHL First All-Star Team (2003)

• Returned to **Peterborough** (OHL) by **Florida**, October 28, 2001. Traded to **Vancouver** by **Florida** with Roberto Luongo and Florida's 6th round choice (Sergei Shirokov) in 2006 Entry Draft for Todd Bertuzzi, Bryan Allen and Alex Auld, June 23, 2006.

KREJCI, David
(KRIGH-chee, DAY-vihd) **BOS.**

Center. Shoots right. 6', 178 lbs. Born, Sternberk, Czech., April 28, 1986. Boston's 1st choice, 63rd overall, in 2004 Entry Draft.

Season	Club	League	GP	G	A	Pts	PIM	PP	SH	GW	S	%	+/-	TF	F%	Min	GP	G	A	Pts	PIM	PP	SH	GW	Min
2000-01	HC Olomouc U17	CzR-U17	26	2	6	8	4	....	....	....	....	....	....	....	....	....	3	1	1	2	0	....	....	....	....
2001-02	HC Trinec U17	CzR-U17	48	32	27	59	30	....	....	....	....	....	....	....	....	....	6	2	4	6	2	....	....	....	....
2002-03	HC Trinec U17	CzR-U17	22	12	24	36	42	....	....	....	....	....	....	....	....	....	....	....	....	....	....	....	....	....	....
	HC Trinec Jr.	CzRep-Jr.	12	4	5	9	2	....	....	....	....	....	....	....	....	....	12	5	5	10	8	....	....	....	....
2003-04	HC Kladno Jr.	CzRep-Jr.	50	23	37	60	37	....	....	....	....	....	....	....	....	....	7	3	6	9	4	....	....	....	....
2004-05	Gatineau	QMJHL	62	22	41	63	31	....	....	....	....	....	....	....	....	....	10	2	7	9	10	....	....	....	....
2005-06	Gatineau	QMJHL	55	27	54	81	54	....	....	....	....	....	....	....	....	....	17	10	22	32	24	....	....	....	....
2006-07	**Boston**	**NHL**	**6**	**0**	**0**	**0**	**2**	**0**	**0**	**0**	**2**	**0.0**	**–3**	**14**	**28.6**	**4:24**	....	....	....	....	....	....	....	....	....
	Providence Bruins	AHL	69	31	43	74	47	....	....	....	....	....	....	....	....	....	13	3	13	16	22	....	....	....	....
	NHL Totals		**6**	**0**	**0**	**0**	**2**	**0**	**0**	**0**	**2**	**0.0**		**14**	**28.6**	**4:24**	....	....	....	....	....	....	....	....	....

KREPS, Kamil
(KREHPS, KA-mihl) **FLA.**

Center. Shoots right. 6'2", 194 lbs. Born, Litomerice, Czech., November 18, 1984. Florida's 3rd choice, 38th overall, in 2003 Entry Draft.

Season	Club	League	GP	G	A	Pts	PIM	PP	SH	GW	S	%	+/-	TF	F%	Min	GP	G	A	Pts	PIM	PP	SH	GW	Min
99-2000	Litvinov Jr.	CzRep-Jr.	48	18	16	34	10	....	....	....	....	....	....	....	....	....	....	....	....	....	....	....	....	....	....
2000-01	Litvinov Jr.	CzRep-Jr.	47	16	23	39	6	....	....	....	....	....	....	....	....	....	6	2	6	8	10	....	....	....	....
2001-02	Brampton	OHL	68	19	24	43	14	....	....	....	....	....	....	....	....	....	....	....	....	....	....	....	....	....	....
2002-03	Brampton	OHL	53	19	42	61	12	....	....	....	....	....	....	....	....	....	11	3	5	8	4	....	....	....	....
2003-04	Brampton	OHL	57	19	27	46	19	....	....	....	....	....	....	....	....	....	12	7	8	15	2	....	....	....	....
2004-05	San Antonio	AHL	58	5	6	11	11	....	....	....	....	....	....	....	....	....	....	....	....	....	....	....	....	....	....
	Texas Wildcatters	ECHL	12	5	6	11	6	....	....	....	....	....	....	....	....	....	....	....	....	....	....	....	....	....	....
2005-06	Rochester	AHL	61	13	19	32	20	....	....	....	....	....	....	....	....	....	....	....	....	....	....	....	....	....	....
2006-07	**Florida**	**NHL**	**14**	**1**	**1**	**2**	**6**	**0**	**0**	**0**	**20**	**5.0**	**–1**	**113**	**48.7**	**11:13**	....	....	....	....	....	....	....	....	....
	Rochester	AHL	50	14	21	35	16	....	....	....	....	....	....	....	....	....	6	1	0	1	0	....	....	....	....
	NHL Totals		**14**	**1**	**1**	**2**	**6**	**0**	**0**	**0**	**20**	**5.0**		**113**	**48.7**	**11:13**	....	....	....	....	....	....	....	....	....

KROG, Jason
(KROHG, JAY-suhn) **ATL.**

Center. Shoots right. 5'11", 185 lbs. Born, Fernie, B.C., October 9, 1975.

Season	Club	League	GP	G	A	Pts	PIM	PP	SH	GW	S	%	+/-	TF	F%	Min	GP	G	A	Pts	PIM	PP	SH	GW	Min
1992-93	Chilliwack Chiefs	BCJHL	52	30	27	57	52	....	....	....	....	....	....	....	....	....	....	....	....	....	....	....	....	....	....
1993-94	Chilliwack Chiefs	BCJHL	42	19	36	55	20	....	....	....	....	....	....	....	....	....	....	....	....	....	....	....	....	....	....
1994-95	Chilliwack Chiefs	BCJHL	60	47	81	128	36	....	....	....	....	....	....	....	....	....	....	....	....	....	....	....	....	....	....
1995-96	New Hampshire	H-East	34	4	16	20	20	....	....	....	....	....	....	....	....	....	....	....	....	....	....	....	....	....	....
1996-97	New Hampshire	H-East	39	23	*44	*67	28	....	....	....	....	....	....	....	....	....	....	....	....	....	....	....	....	....	....
1997-98	New Hampshire	H-East	38	*33	33	66	44	....	....	....	....	....	....	....	....	....	....	....	....	....	....	....	....	....	....
1998-99	New Hampshire	H-East	41	*34	*51	*85	38	....	....	....	....	....	....	....	....	....	....	....	....	....	....	....	....	....	....
99-2000	**NY Islanders**	**NHL**	**17**	**2**	**4**	**6**	**6**	**1**	**0**	**0**	**22**	**9.1**	**–1**	**81**	**53.1**	**10:03**	....	....	....	....	....	....	....	....	....
	Lowell	AHL	45	6	21	27	22	....	....	....	....	....	....	....	....	....	....	....	....	....	....	....	....	....	....
	Providence Bruins	AHL	11	9	8	17	4	....	....	....	....	....	....	....	....	....	6	2	2	4	0	....	....	....	....
2000-01	**NY Islanders**	**NHL**	**9**	**0**	**3**	**3**	**0**	**0**	**0**	**0**	**7**	**0.0**	**4**	**60**	**48.3**	**10:32**	....	....	....	....	....	....	....	....	....
	Lowell	AHL	26	11	16	27	6	....	....	....	....	....	....	....	....	....	....	....	....	....	....	....	....	....	....
	Springfield	AHL	24	7	23	30	4	....	....	....	....	....	....	....	....	....	....	....	....	....	....	....	....	....	....
2001-02	**NY Islanders**	**NHL**	**2**	**0**	**0**	**0**	**0**	**0**	**0**	**0**	**0**	**0.0**	**0**	**13**	**46.2**	**6:40**	....	....	....	....	....	....	....	....	....
	Bridgeport	AHL	64	26	36	62	13	....	....	....	....	....	....	....	....	....	20	10	13	23	8	....	....	....	....
2002-03	**Anaheim**	**NHL**	**67**	**10**	**15**	**25**	**12**	**0**	**1**	**1**	**92**	**10.9**	**1**	**634**	**60.4**	**13:47**	**21**	**3**	**1**	**4**	**4**	**0**	**0**	**0**	**•12:10**
	Cincinnati	AHL	9	3	4	7	6	....	....	....	....	....	....	....	....	....	....	....	....	....	....	....	....	....	....
2003-04	**Anaheim**	**NHL**	**80**	**6**	**12**	**18**	**16**	**1**	**0**	**1**	**111**	**5.4**	**–4**	**769**	**58.5**	**11:58**	....	....	....	....	....	....	....	....	....
2004-05	EC Villacher SV	Austria	48	27	33	60	38	....	....	....	....	....	....	....	....	....	3	0	1	1	4	....	....	....	....
2005-06	Geneve	Swiss	29	15	14	29	32	....	....	....	....	....	....	....	....	....	....	....	....	....	....	....	....	....	....
	Frolunda	Sweden	7	5	1	6	6	....	....	....	....	....	....	....	....	....	17	5	3	8	10	....	....	....	....
2006-07	**Atlanta**	**NHL**	**14**	**1**	**3**	**4**	**6**	**0**	**0**	**0**	**14**	**7.1**	**3**	**165**	**55.2**	**13:58**	....	....	....	....	....	....	....	....	....
	Chicago Wolves	AHL	44	26	54	80	20	....	....	....	....	....	....	....	....	....	15	5	14	19	17	....	....	....	....
	NY Rangers	**NHL**	**9**	**2**	**0**	**2**	**4**	**0**	**0**	**1**	**8**	**25.0**	**2**	**66**	**56.1**	**9:58**	....	....	....	....	....	....	....	....	....
	NHL Totals		**198**	**21**	**37**	**58**	**44**	**2**	**1**	**3**	**254**	**8.3**		**1788**	**58.1**	**12:21**	**21**	**3**	**1**	**4**	**4**	**0**	**0**	**0**	**12:10**

Hockey East First All-Star Team (1997, 1998, 1999) • NCAA East Second All-American Team (1997) • Hockey East Player of the Year (1999) • NCAA East First All-American Team (1999) • NCAA Championship All-Tournament Team (1999) • Hobey Baker Memorial Award (Top U.S. Collegiate Player) (1999)

Signed as a free agent by **NY Islanders**, May 14, 1999. Loaned to **Providence** (AHL) by **NY Islanders**, March 1, 2000. Signed as a free agent by **Anaheim**, July 17, 2002. Signed as a free agent by **Villacher** (Austria), August 24, 2004. Signed as a free agent by **Geneve** (Swiss), May 19, 2005. Signed as a free agent by **Frolunda** (Sweden), January 31, 2006. Signed as a free agent by **Atlanta**, July 4, 2006. Claimed on waivers by **NY Rangers** from **Atlanta**, January 12, 2007. Claimed on waivers by **Atlanta** from **NY Rangers**, February 27, 2007.

KRONWALL, Niklas
(KRAWN-wahl, NIHK-luhs) **DET.**

Defense. Shoots left. 6', 189 lbs. Born, Stockholm, Sweden, January 12, 1981. Detroit's 1st choice, 29th overall, in 2000 Entry Draft.

Season	Club	League	GP	G	A	Pts	PIM	PP	SH	GW	S	%	+/-	TF	F%	Min	GP	G	A	Pts	PIM	PP	SH	GW	Min
1996-97	Djurgarden Jr.	Swe-Jr.	1	0	0	0	0	....	....	....	....	....	....	....	....	....	....	....	....	....	....	....	....	....	....
1997-98	Djurgarden Jr.	Swe-Jr.	27	4	3	7	71	....	....	....	....	....	....	....	....	....	2	0	0	0	2	....	....	....	....
1998-99	Huddinge IK	Sweden-2	14	0	1	1	10	....	....	....	....	....	....	....	....	....	....	....	....	....	....	....	....	....	....
	Huddinge IK Jr.	Swe-Jr.	2	0	0	0	6	....	....	....	....	....	....	....	....	....	....	....	....	....	....	....	....	....	....
99-2000	Djurgarden	Sweden	37	1	4	5	16	....	....	....	....	....	....	....	....	....	8	0	0	0	8	....	....	....	....
2000-01	Djurgarden	Sweden	31	1	9	10	32	....	....	....	....	....	....	....	....	....	15	0	1	1	8	....	....	....	....
2001-02	Djurgarden	Sweden	48	5	7	12	34	....	....	....	....	....	....	....	....	....	5	0	0	0	0	....	....	....	....
2002-03	Djurgarden	Sweden	50	5	13	18	46	....	....	....	....	....	....	....	....	....	12	3	2	5	18	....	....	....	....
2003-04	**Detroit**	**NHL**	**20**	**1**	**4**	**5**	**16**	**0**	**0**	**1**	**18**	**5.6**	**5**	**0**	**0.0**	**13:51**	....	....	....	....	....	....	....	....	....
	Grand Rapids	AHL	25	2	11	13	20	....	....	....	....	....	....	....	....	....	....	....	....	....	....	....	....	....	....
2004-05	Grand Rapids	AHL	76	13	40	53	53	....	....	....	....	....	....	....	....	....	....	....	....	....	....	....	....	....	....

			Regular Season														Playoffs								
Season	Club	League	GP	G	A	Pts	PIM	PP	SH	GW	S	%	+/-	TF	F%	Min	GP	G	A	Pts	PIM	PP	SH	GW	Min
2005-06	**Detroit**	**NHL**	**27**	**1**	**8**	**9**	**28**	**1**	**0**	**0**	**28**	**3.6**	**11**	**0**	**0.0**	**20:31**	**6**	**0**	**3**	**3**	**2**	**0**	**0**	**0**	**22:43**
	Grand Rapids	AHL	1	0	0	0	0	....	....	....	....	....	....	....	....	....	....	....	....	....	....	....	....	....	....
	Sweden	Olympics	2	1	1	2	8	....	....	....	....	....	....	....	....	....	....	....	....	....	....	....	....	....	....
2006-07	**Detroit**	**NHL**	**68**	**1**	**21**	**22**	**54**	**1**	**0**	**0**	**104**	**1.0**	**0**	**0**	**0.0**	**20:39**	....	....	....	....	....	....	....	....	....
	NHL Totals		**115**	**3**	**33**	**36**	**98**	**2**	**0**	**1**	**150**	**2.0**		**0**	**0.0**	**19:26**	**6**	**0**	**3**	**3**	**2**	**0**	**0**	**0**	**22:43**

AHL First All-Star Team (2005) • Eddie Shore Award (Outstanding Defenseman – AHL) (2005)
• Missed majority of 2005-06 season recovering from knee surgery.

KRONWALL, Staffan

(KRAWN-wahl, STAH-fuhn) **TOR.**

Defense. Shoots left. 6'3", 209 lbs. Born, Jarfalla, Sweden, September 10, 1982. Toronto's 9th choice, 285th overall, in 2002 Entry Draft.

Season	Club	League	GP	G	A	Pts	PIM	PP	SH	GW	S	%	+/-	TF	F%	Min	GP	G	A	Pts	PIM	PP	SH	GW	Min
99-2000	Huddinge IK Jr.	Swe-Jr.	34	2	0	2	38	....	....	....	....	....	....	....	....	....	....	....	....	....	....	....	....	....	....
	Huddinge IK U18	Swe-U18	7	0	3	3	0	....	....	....	....	....	....	....	....	....	....	....	....	....	....	....	....	....	....
2000-01	Huddinge IK Jr.	Swe-Jr.	23	6	1	7	16	....	....	....	....	....	....	....	....	....	....	....	....	....	....	....	....	....	....
	Huddinge IK	Sweden-3	1	0	0	0	0	....	....	....	....	....	....	....	....	....	....	....	....	....	....	....	....	....	....
2001-02	Huddinge IK	Sweden-2	42	4	7	11	30	....	....	....	....	....	....	....	....	....	....	....	....	....	....	....	....	....	....
	Huddinge IK Jr.	Swe-Jr.	1	0	0	0	0	....	....	....	....	....	....	....	....	....	4	2	1	3	27	....	....	....	....
2002-03	Djurgarden	Sweden	48	4	6	10	65	....	....	....	....	....	....	....	....	....	12	1	1	2	8	....	....	....	....
2003-04	Djurgarden	Sweden	44	1	5	6	54	....	....	....	....	....	....	....	....	....	4	0	1	1	2	....	....	....	....
2004-05	Brynas IF Gavle	Sweden	3	0	1	1	4	....	....	....	....	....	....	....	....	....	....	....	....	....	....	....	....	....	....
	Djurgarden Jr.	Swe-Jr.	5	2	4	6	0	....	....	....	....	....	....	....	....	....	....	....	....	....	....	....	....	....	....
	Djurgarden	Sweden	35	1	4	5	43	....	....	....	....	....	....	....	....	....	12	2	0	2	10	....	....	....	....
2005-06	**Toronto**	**NHL**	**34**	**0**	**1**	**1**	**14**	**0**	**0**	**0**	**18**	**0.0**	**–3**	**0**	**0.0**	**12:57**	....	....	....	....	....	....	....	....	....
	Toronto Marlies	AHL	16	1	10	11	12	....	....	....	....	....	....	....	....	....	4	0	2	2	2	....	....	....	....
2006-07	Toronto Marlies	AHL	47	3	14	17	32	....	....	....	....	....	....	....	....	....	....	....	....	....	....	....	....	....	....
	NHL Totals		**34**	**0**	**1**	**1**	**14**	**0**	**0**	**0**	**18**	**0.0**		**0**	**0.0**	**12:57**	....	....	....	....	....	....	....	....	....

KUBA, Filip

(KOO-bah, FIHL-ihp) **T.B.**

Defense. Shoots left. 6'3", 205 lbs. Born, Ostrava, Czech., December 29, 1976. Florida's 8th choice, 192nd overall, in 1995 Entry Draft.

Season	Club	League	GP	G	A	Pts	PIM	PP	SH	GW	S	%	+/-	TF	F%	Min	GP	G	A	Pts	PIM	PP	SH	GW	Min
1994-95	HC Vitkovice Jr.	CzRep-Jr.	35	10	15	25	....	....	....	....	....	....	....	....	....	....	....	....	....	....	....	....	....	....	....
	HC Vitkovice	CzRep	....	....	....	....	....	....	....	....	....	....	....	....	....	....	4	0	0	0	2	....	....	....	....
1995-96	HC Vitkovice	CzRep	19	0	1	1	....	....	....	....	....	....	....	....	....	....	....	....	....	....	....	....	....	....	....
1996-97	Carolina	AHL	51	0	12	12	38	....	....	....	....	....	....	....	....	....	....	....	....	....	....	....	....	....	....
1997-98	New Haven	AHL	77	4	13	17	58	....	....	....	....	....	....	....	....	....	3	1	1	2	0	....	....	....	....
1998-99	**Florida**	**NHL**	**5**	**0**	**1**	**1**	**0**	**0**	**0**	**0**	**5**	**0.0**	**2**	**0**	**0.0**	**22:29**	....	....	....	....	....	....	....	....	....
	Kentucky	AHL	45	2	8	10	33	....	....	....	....	....	....	....	....	....	10	0	1	1	4	....	....	....	....
99-2000	**Florida**	**NHL**	**13**	**1**	**5**	**6**	**2**	**1**	**0**	**1**	**16**	**6.3**	**–3**	**0**	**0.0**	**13:52**	....	....	....	....	....	....	....	....	....
	Houston Aeros	IHL	27	3	6	9	13	....	....	....	....	....	....	....	....	....	11	1	2	3	4	....	....	....	....
2000-01	**Minnesota**	**NHL**	**75**	**9**	**21**	**30**	**28**	**4**	**0**	**4**	**141**	**6.4**	**–6**	**1**	**0.0**	**24:16**	....	....	....	....	....	....	....	....	....
2001-02	**Minnesota**	**NHL**	**62**	**5**	**19**	**24**	**32**	**3**	**0**	**1**	**101**	**5.0**	**–6**	**0**	**0.0**	**25:30**	....	....	....	....	....	....	....	....	....
2002-03	**Minnesota**	**NHL**	**78**	**8**	**21**	**29**	**29**	**4**	**2**	**1**	**129**	**6.2**	**0**	**1**	**0.0**	**23:56**	**18**	**3**	**5**	**8**	**24**	**3**	**0**	**0**	**26:46**
2003-04	**Minnesota**	**NHL**	**77**	**5**	**19**	**24**	**28**	**2**	**1**	**2**	**114**	**4.4**	**–7**	**2**	**0.0**	**24:06**	....	....	....	....	....	....	....	....	....
2004-05			DID NOT PLAY																						
2005-06	**Minnesota**	**NHL**	**65**	**6**	**19**	**25**	**44**	**1**	**1**	**1**	**69**	**8.7**	**0**	**2**	**0.0**	**21:46**	....	....	....	....	....	....	....	....	....
	Czech Republic	Olympics	8	1	0	1	0	....	....	....	....	....	....	....	....	....	....	....	....	....	....	....	....	....	....
2006-07	**Tampa Bay**	**NHL**	**81**	**15**	**22**	**37**	**36**	**5**	**1**	**2**	**106**	**14.2**	**–9**	**0**	**0.0**	**20:12**	**6**	**1**	**4**	**5**	**4**	**0**	**1**	**0**	**20:47**
	NHL Totals		**456**	**49**	**127**	**176**	**199**	**20**	**5**	**12**	**681**	**7.2**		**6**	**0.0**	**22:57**	**24**	**4**	**9**	**13**	**28**	**3**	**1**	**0**	**25:16**

Played in NHL All-Star Game (2004)
Traded to **Calgary** by **Florida** for Rocky Thompson, March 16, 2000. Claimed by **Minnesota** from **Calgary** in Expansion Draft, June 23, 2000. Signed as a free agent by **Tampa Bay**, July 1, 2006.

KUBINA, Pavel

(koo-BEE-nuh, PAH-vehl) **TOR.**

Defense. Shoots right. 6'4", 244 lbs. Born, Celadna, Czech., April 15, 1977. Tampa Bay's 6th choice, 179th overall, in 1996 Entry Draft.

Season	Club	League	GP	G	A	Pts	PIM	PP	SH	GW	S	%	+/-	TF	F%	Min	GP	G	A	Pts	PIM	PP	SH	GW	Min
1993-94	HC Vitkovice Jr.	CzRep-Jr.	35	4	3	7	....	....	....	....	....	....	....	....	....	....	....	....	....	....	....	....	....	....	....
	HC Vitkovice	CzRep	1	0	0	0	....	....	....	....	....	....	....	....	....	....	....	....	....	....	....	....	....	....	....
1994-95	HC Vitkovice Jr.	CzRep-Jr.	20	6	10	16	....	....	....	....	....	....	....	....	....	....	....	....	....	....	....	....	....	....	....
	HC Vitkovice	CzRep	8	2	0	2	10	....	....	....	....	....	....	....	....	....	4	0	0	0	0	....	....	....	....
1995-96	HC Vitkovice Jr.	CzRep-Jr.	16	5	10	15	....	....	....	....	....	....	....	....	....	....	....	....	....	....	....	....	....	....	....
	HC Vitkovice	CzRep	33	3	4	7	32	....	....	....	....	....	....	....	....	....	4	0	0	0	0	....	....	....	....
1996-97	HC Vitkovice	CzRep	1	0	0	0	0	....	....	....	....	....	....	....	....	....	....	....	....	....	....	....	....	....	....
	Moose Jaw	WHL	61	12	32	44	116	....	....	....	....	....	....	....	....	....	11	2	5	7	27	....	....	....	....
1997-98	**Tampa Bay**	**NHL**	**10**	**1**	**2**	**3**	**22**	**0**	**0**	**0**	**8**	**12.5**	**–1**	....	....	....	....	....	....	....	....	....	....	....	....
	Adirondack	AHL	55	4	8	12	86	....	....	....	....	....	....	....	....	....	1	1	0	1	14	....	....	....	....
1998-99	**Tampa Bay**	**NHL**	**68**	**9**	**12**	**21**	**80**	**3**	**1**	**1**	**119**	**7.6**	**–33**	**2**	**0.0**	**22:47**	....	....	....	....	....	....	....	....	....
	Cleveland	IHL	6	2	2	4	16	....	....	....	....	....	....	....	....	....	....	....	....	....	....	....	....	....	....
99-2000	**Tampa Bay**	**NHL**	**69**	**8**	**18**	**26**	**93**	**6**	**0**	**3**	**128**	**6.3**	**–19**	**0**	**0.0**	**22:32**	....	....	....	....	....	....	....	....	....
2000-01	**Tampa Bay**	**NHL**	**70**	**11**	**19**	**30**	**103**	**6**	**1**	**1**	**128**	**8.6**	**–14**	**2**	**0.0**	**24:06**	....	....	....	....	....	....	....	....	....
2001-02	**Tampa Bay**	**NHL**	**82**	**11**	**23**	**34**	**106**	**5**	**2**	**3**	**189**	**5.8**	**–22**	**1**	**100.0**	**23:39**	....	....	....	....	....	....	....	....	....
	Czech Republic	Olympics	4	0	1	1	0	....	....	....	....	....	....	....	....	....	....	....	....	....	....	....	....	....	....
2002-03	**Tampa Bay**	**NHL**	**75**	**3**	**19**	**22**	**78**	**0**	**0**	**0**	**139**	**2.2**	**–7**	**1**	**0.0**	**21:24**	**11**	**0**	**0**	**0**	**12**	**0**	**0**	**0**	**24:52**
2003-04♦	**Tampa Bay**	**NHL**	**81**	**17**	**18**	**35**	**85**	**8**	**1**	**4**	**153**	**11.1**	**9**	**1**	**0.0**	**21:09**	**22**	**0**	**4**	**4**	**50**	**0**	**0**	**0**	**22:54**
2004-05	Vitkovice	CzRep	28	6	5	11	46	....	....	....	....	....	....	....	....	....	12	4	6	10	34	....	....	....	....
2005-06	**Tampa Bay**	**NHL**	**76**	**5**	**33**	**38**	**96**	**4**	**0**	**3**	**155**	**3.2**	**–12**	**2**	**0.0**	**22:25**	**5**	**1**	**1**	**2**	**26**	**1**	**0**	**0**	**20:09**
	Czech Republic	Olympics	8	1	1	2	12	....	....	....	....	....	....	....	....	....	....	....	....	....	....	....	....	....	....
2006-07	**Toronto**	**NHL**	**61**	**7**	**14**	**21**	**48**	**4**	**0**	**1**	**97**	**7.2**	**7**	**0**	**0.0**	**21:19**	....	....	....	....	....	....	....	....	....
	NHL Totals		**592**	**72**	**158**	**230**	**711**	**36**	**5**	**16**	**1116**	**6.5**		**9**	**11.1**	**22:26**	**38**	**1**	**5**	**6**	**88**	**1**	**0**	**0**	**23:06**

Played in NHL All-Star Game (2004)
Signed as a free agent by **Vitkovice** (CzRep), September 17, 2004. Signed as a free agent by **Toronto**, July 1, 2006.

KUKKONEN, Lasse

(koo-KOH-nuhn, LAH-say) **PHI.**

Defense. Shoots left. 6'1", 190 lbs. Born, Oulu, Finland, September 18, 1981. Chicago's 4th choice, 151st overall, in 2003 Entry Draft.

Season	Club	League	GP	G	A	Pts	PIM	PP	SH	GW	S	%	+/-	TF	F%	Min	GP	G	A	Pts	PIM	PP	SH	GW	Min
1997-98	Karpat Oulu U18	Fin-U18	36	5	16	21	46	....	....	....	....	....	....	....	....	....	....	....	....	....	....	....	....	....	....
1998-99	Karpat Oulu U18	Fin-U18	2	1	2	3	0	....	....	....	....	....	....	....	....	....	....	....	....	....	....	....	....	....	....
	Karpat Oulu Jr.	Fin-Jr.	34	2	13	15	24	....	....	....	....	....	....	....	....	....	....	....	....	....	....	....	....	....	....
99-2000	Karpat Oulu Jr.	Fin-Jr.	27	9	11	20	26	....	....	....	....	....	....	....	....	....	....	....	....	....	....	....	....	....	....
	Karpat Oulu	Finland-2	22	0	4	4	14	....	....	....	....	....	....	....	....	....	....	....	....	....	....	....	....	....	....
2000-01	Karpat Oulu	Finland	47	1	5	6	46	....	....	....	....	....	....	....	....	....	9	0	2	2	4	....	....	....	....
2001-02	Karpat Oulu	Finland	55	2	6	8	42	....	....	....	....	....	....	....	....	....	4	0	3	3	4	....	....	....	....
	Karpat Oulu Jr.	Fin-Jr.	....	....	....	....	....	....	....	....	....	....	....	....	....	....	1	1	0	1	0	....	....	....	....
2002-03	Karpat Oulu	Finland	56	6	12	18	67	....	....	....	....	....	....	....	....	....	15	1	4	5	16	....	....	....	....
2003-04	**Chicago**	**NHL**	**10**	**0**	**1**	**1**	**4**	**0**	**0**	**0**	**9**	**0.0**	**–2**	**0**	**0.0**	**13:37**	....	....	....	....	....	....	....	....	....
	Norfolk Admirals	AHL	59	3	11	14	58	....	....	....	....	....	....	....	....	....	8	0	0	0	8	....	....	....	....
2004-05	Karpat Oulu	Finland	55	5	13	18	68	....	....	....	....	....	....	....	....	....	12	0	2	2	6	....	....	....	....
2005-06	Karpat Oulu	Finland	56	11	16	27	38	....	....	....	....	....	....	....	....	....	11	5	7	12	8	....	....	....	....
	Finland	Olympics	2	0	0	0	0	....	....	....	....	....	....	....	....	....	....	....	....	....	....	....	....	....	....
2006-07	**Chicago**	**NHL**	**54**	**5**	**9**	**14**	**30**	**1**	**0**	**2**	**45**	**11.1**	**5**	**0**	**0.0**	**16:35**	....	....	....	....	....	....	....	....	....
	Philadelphia	**NHL**	**20**	**0**	**0**	**0**	**8**	**0**	**0**	**0**	**9**	**0.0**	**–1**	**0**	**0.0**	**18:29**	....	....	....	....	....	....	....	....	....
	NHL Totals		**84**	**5**	**10**	**15**	**42**	**1**	**0**	**2**	**63**	**7.9**		**0**	**0.0**	**16:41**	....	....	....	....	....	....	....	....	....

Signed as a free agent by **Oulu** (Finland), September 11, 2004. Traded to **Philadelphia** by **Chicago** with Chicago's 3rd round choice (Garrett Klotz) in 2007 Entry Draft for Kyle Calder, February 26, 2007.

KUNITZ, Chris
(KOO-nihtz, KRIHS) **ANA.**

Left wing. Shoots left. 5'11", 198 lbs. Born, Regina, Sask., September 26, 1979.

			Regular Season														Playoffs								
Season	Club	League	GP	G	A	Pts	PIM	PP	SH	GW	S	%	+/-	TF	F%	Min	GP	G	A	Pts	PIM	PP	SH	GW	Min
1996-97	Yorkton Mallers	SMHL	64	38	38	76	233																		
1997-98	Melville	SJHL	STATISTICS NOT AVAILABLE																						
1998-99	Melville	SJHL	63	57	32	89	222																		
99-2000	Ferris State	CCHA	38	20	9	29	70																		
2000-01	Ferris State	CCHA	37	16	13	29	81																		
2001-02	Ferris State	CCHA	35	*28	10	38	68																		
2002-03	Ferris State	CCHA	42	*35	*44	*79	56																		
2003-04	**Anaheim**	**NHL**	**21**	**0**	**6**	**6**	**12**	**0**	**0**	**0**	**31**	**0.0**	**1**	**7**	**14.3**	**9:07**									
	Cincinnati	AHL	59	19	25	44	101										9	3	2	5	24				
2004-05	Cincinnati	AHL	54	22	17	39	71										12	1	7	8	20				
2005-06	**Atlanta**	**NHL**	**2**	**0**	**0**	**0**	**2**	**0**	**0**	**0**	**0**	**0.0**	**–3**	**0**	**0.0**	**5:43**									
	Anaheim	**NHL**	**67**	**19**	**22**	**41**	**69**	**5**	**1**	**2**	**149**	**12.8**	**19**	**15**	**46.7**	**14:08**	**16**	**3**	**5**	**8**	**8**	**0**	**0**	**0**	**12:30**
	Portland Pirates	AHL	5	0	4	4	12																		
2006-07♦	**Anaheim**	**NHL**	**81**	**25**	**35**	**60**	**81**	**11**	**0**	**5**	**180**	**13.9**	**23**	**13**	**30.8**	**17:03**	**13**	**1**	**5**	**6**	**19**	**0**	**0**	**0**	**17:47**
	NHL Totals		**171**	**44**	**63**	**107**	**164**	**16**	**1**	**7**	**360**	**12.2**		**35**	**34.3**	**14:48**	**29**	**4**	**10**	**14**	**27**	**0**	**0**	**0**	**14:52**

CCHA First All-Star Team (2002, 2003) • CCHA Player of the Year (2003) • NCAA West First All-American Team (2003)

Signed as a free agent by **Anaheim**, April 1, 2003. Claimed on waivers by **Atlanta** from **Anaheim**, October 4, 2005. Claimed on waivers by **Anaheim** from **Atlanta**, October 18, 2005.

KUTLAK, Zdenek
(KUHT-lak, z'DEHN-ehk) **BOS.**

Defense. Shoots left. 6'3", 221 lbs. Born, Ceske Budejovice, Czech., February 13, 1980. Boston's 10th choice, 237th overall, in 2000 Entry Draft.

Season	Club	League	GP	G	A	Pts	PIM	PP	SH	GW	S	%	+/-	TF	F%	Min	GP	G	A	Pts	PIM	PP	SH	GW	Min
1996-97	C. Budejovice Jr.	CzRep-Jr.	45	8	11	19	20																		
1997-98	C. Budejovice Jr.	CzRep-Jr.	43	1	6	7	30																		
1998-99	C. Budejovice Jr.	CzRep-Jr.	31	6	14	20	20																		
	C. Budejovice	CzRep	22	1	3	4	4										3	0	0	0	0				
99-2000	C. Budejovice Jr.	CzRep-Jr.	8	4	2	6	26																		
	Jind. Hradec	CzRep-3	4	1	1	2	0																		
	IHC Pisek	CzRep-2	3	1	0	1	0										2	0	0	0	2				
	C. Budejovice	CzRep	28	1	0	1	2										1	0	0	0	0				
2000-01	**Boston**	**NHL**	**10**	**0**	**2**	**2**	**4**	**0**	**0**	**0**	**7**	**0.0**	**–3**	**0**	**0.0**	**16:05**									
	Providence Bruins	AHL	62	4	5	9	16																		
2001-02	Providence Bruins	AHL	80	5	15	20	73										2	0	0	0	0				
2002-03	**Boston**	**NHL**	**4**	**1**	**0**	**1**	**0**	**0**	**0**	**0**	**1**	**100.0**	**0**	**0**	**0.0**	**5:16**									
	Providence Bruins	AHL	68	4	12	16	52										4	1	0	1	2				
2003-04	**Boston**	**NHL**	**2**	**0**	**0**	**0**	**0**	**0**	**0**	**0**	**0**	**0.0**	**–1**	**0**	**0.0**	**11:33**									
	Providence Bruins	AHL	47	7	12	19	22										2	0	0	0	2				
2004-05	Karlovy Vary	CzRep	52	5	9	14	26																		
2005-06	C. Budejovice	CzRep	49	6	9	15	32										10	2	2	4	12				
2006-07	C. Budejovice	CzRep	46	5	10	15	50										11	0	0	0	49				
	NHL Totals		**16**	**1**	**2**	**3**	**4**	**0**	**0**	**0**	**8**	**12.5**		**0**	**0.0**	**12:49**									

Signed as a free agent by **Karlovy Vary** (CzRep), May 16, 2004.

KVASHA, Oleg
(kuh-VAH-shah, OH-lehg)

Left wing/Center. Shoots right. 6'5", 230 lbs. Born, Moscow, USSR, July 26, 1978. Florida's 3rd choice, 65th overall, in 1996 Entry Draft.

Season	Club	League	GP	G	A	Pts	PIM	PP	SH	GW	S	%	+/-	TF	F%	Min	GP	G	A	Pts	PIM	PP	SH	GW	Min
1995-96	CSKA Moscow	CIS	38	2	3	5	14										2	0	0	0	0				
1996-97	CSKA Moscow	Russia-2	44	20	22	42	115																		
1997-98	New Haven	AHL	57	13	16	29	46										3	2	1	3	0				
1998-99	**Florida**	**NHL**	**68**	**12**	**13**	**25**	**45**	**4**	**0**	**2**	**138**	**8.7**	**5**	**373**	**28.4**	**12:48**									
99-2000	**Florida**	**NHL**	**78**	**5**	**20**	**25**	**34**	**2**	**0**	**0**	**110**	**4.5**	**3**	**553**	**34.9**	**11:24**	**4**	**0**	**0**	**0**	**0**	**0**	**0**	**0**	**10:18**
2000-01	**NY Islanders**	**NHL**	**62**	**11**	**9**	**20**	**46**	**0**	**0**	**0**	**118**	**9.3**	**–15**	**627**	**43.7**	**14:56**									
2001-02	**NY Islanders**	**NHL**	**71**	**13**	**25**	**38**	**80**	**2**	**0**	**3**	**119**	**10.9**	**–4**	**456**	**47.4**	**14:12**	**7**	**0**	**1**	**1**	**6**	**0**	**0**	**0**	**15:17**
	Russia	Olympics	5	0	0	0	0																		
2002-03	**NY Islanders**	**NHL**	**69**	**12**	**14**	**26**	**44**	**0**	**1**	**2**	**121**	**9.9**	**4**	**256**	**43.0**	**13:03**	**5**	**0**	**1**	**1**	**2**	**0**	**0**	**0**	**16:26**
2003-04	**NY Islanders**	**NHL**	**81**	**15**	**36**	**51**	**48**	**5**	**3**	**3**	**147**	**10.2**	**4**	**656**	**38.3**	**17:52**	**5**	**1**	**0**	**1**	**0**	**1**	**0**	**0**	**16:05**
2004-05	Cherepovets	Russia	22	6	5	11	24																		
	CSKA Moscow	Russia	26	3	6	9	20																		
2005-06	**NY Islanders**	**NHL**	**49**	**9**	**12**	**21**	**32**	**1**	**0**	**1**	**104**	**8.7**	**–2**	**238**	**52.9**	**14:26**									
	Phoenix	**NHL**	**15**	**4**	**7**	**11**	**6**	**0**	**0**	**0**	**32**	**12.5**	**5**	**16**	**43.8**	**13:32**									
2006-07	Vityaz Chekhov	Russia	27	7	8	15	28										1	0	0	0	0				
	NHL Totals		**493**	**81**	**136**	**217**	**335**	**14**	**4**	**11**	**889**	**9.1**		**3175**	**40.4**	**14:06**	**21**	**1**	**2**	**3**	**8**	**1**	**0**	**0**	**14:48**

Traded to **NY Islanders** by **Florida** with Mark Parrish for Roberto Luongo and Olli Jokinen, June 24, 2000. Signed as a free agent by **Cherepovets** (Russia), September 25, 2004. Loaned to **CSKA Moscow** (Russia) by **Cherepovets** (Russia), December 20, 2004. Traded to **Phoenix** by **NY Islanders** for Phoenix's 3rd round choice (later traded to Boston - Boston selected Brad Marchand) in 2006 Entry Draft, March 9, 2006.

KWIATKOWSKI, Joel
(KWEE-at-KOW-skee, JOHL)

Defense. Shoots left. 6'2", 210 lbs. Born, Kindersley, Sask., March 22, 1977. Dallas' 7th choice, 194th overall, in 1996 Entry Draft.

Season	Club	League	GP	G	A	Pts	PIM	PP	SH	GW	S	%	+/-	TF	F%	Min	GP	G	A	Pts	PIM	PP	SH	GW	Min
1994-95	Tacoma Rockets	WHL	70	4	13	17	66										4	0	0	0	2				
1995-96	Kelowna Rockets	WHL	40	6	17	23	85																		
	Prince George	WHL	32	6	11	17	48																		
1996-97	Prince George	WHL	72	15	37	52	94										15	4	2	6	24				
1997-98	Prince George	WHL	62	21	43	64	65										11	3	6	9	6				
1998-99	Cincinnati	AHL	80	12	21	33	48										3	2	0	2	0				
99-2000	Cincinnati	AHL	70	4	22	26	28																		
2000-01	**Ottawa**	**NHL**	**4**	**1**	**0**	**1**	**0**	**0**	**0**	**0**	**2**	**50.0**	**1**	**0**	**0.0**	**12:04**									
	Grand Rapids	IHL	77	4	17	21	58										10	1	0	1	4				
2001-02	**Ottawa**	**NHL**	**11**	**0**	**0**	**0**	**12**	**0**	**0**	**0**	**9**	**0.0**	**5**	**0**	**0.0**	**13:41**									
	Grand Rapids	AHL	65	8	21	29	94										5	1	2	3	12				
2002-03	**Ottawa**	**NHL**	**20**	**0**	**2**	**2**	**6**	**0**	**0**	**0**	**28**	**0.0**	**2**	**2**	**0.0**	**12:13**									
	Binghamton	AHL	1	0	0	0	2																		
	Washington	**NHL**	**34**	**0**	**3**	**3**	**12**	**0**	**0**	**0**	**28**	**0.0**	**1**	**2**	**0.0**	**15:32**	**6**	**0**	**0**	**0**	**2**	**0**	**0**	**0**	**17:48**
2003-04	**Washington**	**NHL**	**80**	**6**	**6**	**12**	**89**	**2**	**0**	**0**	**90**	**6.7**	**–28**	**0**	**0.0**	**21:16**									
2004-05	San Antonio	AHL	64	13	19	32	76																		
	St. John's	AHL	17	7	6	13	16										5	0	4	4	23				
2005-06	**Florida**	**NHL**	**73**	**4**	**8**	**12**	**86**	**1**	**0**	**1**	**87**	**4.6**	**3**	**0**	**0.0**	**16:21**									
2006-07	**Florida**	**NHL**	**41**	**5**	**5**	**10**	**20**	**1**	**0**	**2**	**46**	**10.9**	**–5**	**1**	**100.0**	**9:46**									
	Pittsburgh	**NHL**	**1**	**0**	**0**	**0**	**0**	**0**	**0**	**0**	**0**	**0.0**	**–1**	**0**	**0.0**	**11:59**									
	NHL Totals		**264**	**16**	**24**	**40**	**225**	**4**	**0**	**3**	**290**	**5.5**		**5**	**20.0**	**16:12**	**6**	**0**	**0**	**0**	**2**	**0**	**0**	**0**	**17:48**

WHL West Second All-Star Team (1997) • WHL West First All-Star Team (1998)

Signed as a free agent by **Anaheim**, June 18, 1998. Traded to **Ottawa** by **Anaheim** for Patrick Traverse, June 12, 2000. Traded to **Washington** by **Ottawa** for Washington's 9th round choice (later traded back to Washington – Washington selected Mark Olafson) in 2003 Entry Draft, January 15, 2003. Signed as a free agent by **Florida**, July 16, 2004. Loaned to **St. John's** (AHL) by **Florida** (San Antonio-AHL) for cash, March 11, 2005. Traded to **Pittsburgh** by **Florida** for Florida's 4th round choice (previously acquired, Florida selected Matt Rust) in 2007 Entry Draft, February 27, 2007.

LAAKSONEN, Antti
(lah-AHK-soh-nehn, AN-tee)

Left wing. Shoots left. 6', 187 lbs. Born, Tammela, Finland, October 3, 1973. Boston's 10th choice, 191st overall, in 1997 Entry Draft.

Season	Club	League	GP	G	A	Pts	PIM	PP	SH	GW	S	%	+/-	TF	F%	Min	GP	G	A	Pts	PIM	PP	SH	GW	Min
1989-90	FoPS Forssa Jr.	Fin-Jr.	3	0	0	0	0																		
1990-91	FoPS Forssa Jr.	Fin-Jr.	STATISTICS NOT AVAILABLE																						
	FoPS Forssa	Finland-2	2	0	0	0	0																		
1991-92	FoPS Forssa Jr.	Fin-Jr.	24	19	23	42	22																		
	FoPS Forssa	Finland-2	41	16	15	31	8																		
1992-93	FoPS Forssa Jr.	Fin-Jr.	12	7	7	14	14																		
	FoPS Forssa	Finland-2	34	11	19	30	36																		
	HPK Jr.	Fin-Jr.	1	1	1	2	0																		
	HPK Hameenlinna	Finland	2	0	0	0	0																		
1993-94	U. of Denver	WCHA	36	12	9	21	38																		

			Regular Season														Playoffs								
Season	Club	League	GP	G	A	Pts	PIM	PP	SH	GW	S	%	+/-	TF	F%	Min	GP	G	A	Pts	PIM	PP	SH	GW	Min
1994-95	U. of Denver	WCHA	40	17	18	35	42	....	....	....	....	....	....	....	....	....	....	....	....	....	....	....	....	....	....
1995-96	U. of Denver	WCHA	39	25	28	53	71	....	....	....	....	....	....	....	....	....	....	....	....	....	....	....	....	....	....
1996-97	U. of Denver	WCHA	39	21	17	38	63	....	....	....	....	....	....	....	....	....	....	....	....	....	....	....	....	....	....
1997-98	Providence Bruins	AHL	38	3	2	5	14	....	....	....	....	....	....	....	....	....	....	....	....	....	....	....	....	....	....
	Charlotte	ECHL	15	4	3	7	12	....	....	....	....	....	....	....	....	....	6	0	3	3	0	....	....	....	....
1998-99	**Boston**	**NHL**	**11**	**1**	**2**	**3**	**2**	**0**	**0**	**0**	**8**	**12.5**	**–1**	**0**	**0.0**	**9:20**	....	....	....	....	....	....	....	....	....
	Providence Bruins	AHL	66	25	33	58	52	....	....	....	....	....	....	....	....	....	19	7	2	9	28	....	....	....	....
99-2000	**Boston**	**NHL**	**27**	**6**	**3**	**9**	**2**	**0**	**0**	**1**	**23**	**26.1**	**3**	**3**	**66.7**	**7:50**	....	....	....	....	....	....	....	....	....
	Providence Bruins	AHL	40	10	12	22	57	....	....	....	....	....	....	....	....	....	14	5	4	9	4	....	....	....	....
2000-01	**Minnesota**	**NHL**	**82**	**12**	**16**	**28**	**24**	**0**	**2**	**1**	**129**	**9.3**	**–7**	**15**	**26.7**	**16:27**	....	....	....	....	....	....	....	....	....
2001-02	**Minnesota**	**NHL**	**82**	**16**	**17**	**33**	**22**	**0**	**0**	**1**	**104**	**15.4**	**–5**	**19**	**42.1**	**16:20**	....	....	....	....	....	....	....	....	....
2002-03	**Minnesota**	**NHL**	**82**	**15**	**16**	**31**	**26**	**1**	**2**	**4**	**106**	**14.2**	**4**	**51**	**29.4**	**15:55**	**16**	**1**	**3**	**4**	**4**	**0**	**0**	**0**	**16:34**
2003-04	**Minnesota**	**NHL**	**77**	**12**	**14**	**26**	**20**	**0**	**1**	**1**	**100**	**12.0**	**0**	**144**	**36.1**	**16:03**	....	....	....	....	....	....	....	....	....
2004-05			DID NOT PLAY																						
2005-06	**Colorado**	**NHL**	**81**	**16**	**18**	**34**	**40**	**0**	**2**	**4**	**141**	**11.3**	**–2**	**46**	**28.3**	**16:00**	**9**	**0**	**2**	**2**	**2**	**0**	**0**	**0**	**15:23**
	Finland	Olympics	8	0	0	0	6	....	....	....	....	....	....	....	....	....	....	....	....	....	....	....	....	....	....
2006-07	**Colorado**	**NHL**	**41**	**3**	**1**	**4**	**16**	**0**	**1**	**0**	**43**	**7.0**	**–3**	**13**	**7.7**	**10:41**	....	....	....	....	....	....	....	....	....
	Albany River Rats	AHL	24	9	7	16	4	....	....	....	....	....	....	....	....	....	1	0	0	0	0	....	....	....	....
	NHL Totals		**483**	**81**	**87**	**168**	**152**	**1**	**8**	**12**	**654**	**12.4**		**291**	**32.6**	**15:04**	**25**	**1**	**5**	**6**	**6**	**0**	**0**	**0**	**16:09**

WCHA Second All-Star Team (1996)

Signed as a free agent by **Minnesota**, July 14, 2000. Signed as a free agent by **Colorado**, July 2, 2004. Signed as a free agent by **Fribourg-Gotteron** (Swiss), June 18, 2007.

LaCOUTURE, Dan

(LA-koo-TUHR, DAN) **ANA.**

Left wing. Shoots left. 6'2", 215 lbs. Born, Hyannis, MA, April 18, 1977. NY Islanders' 2nd choice, 29th overall, in 1996 Entry Draft.

Season	Club	League	GP	G	A	Pts	PIM	PP	SH	GW	S	%	+/-	TF	F%	Min	GP	G	A	Pts	PIM	PP	SH	GW	Min
1992-93	Natick Redmen	High-MA	20	38	34	72	46	....	....	....	....	....	....	....	....	....	....	....	....	....	....	....	....	....	....
1993-94	Natick Redmen	High-MA	21	52	49	101	58	....	....	....	....	....	....	....	....	....	....	....	....	....	....	....	....	....	....
1994-95	Spring. Olympics	NEJHL	52	44	56	100	98	....	....	....	....	....	....	....	....	....	....	....	....	....	....	....	....	....	....
1995-96	Spring. Olympics	NEJHL	29	24	35	59	79	....	....	....	....	....	....	....	....	....	13	12	13	25	23	....	....	....	....
1996-97	Boston University	H-East	31	13	12	25	18	....	....	....	....	....	....	....	....	....	....	....	....	....	....	....	....	....	....
1997-98	Hamilton	AHL	77	15	10	25	31	....	....	....	....	....	....	....	....	....	5	1	0	1	0	....	....	....	....
1998-99	**Edmonton**	**NHL**	**3**	**0**	**0**	**0**	**0**	**0**	**0**	**0**	**0**	**0.0**	**1**	**0**	**0.0**	**6:30**	....	....	....	....	....	....	....	....	....
	Hamilton	AHL	72	17	14	31	73	....	....	....	....	....	....	....	....	....	9	2	1	3	2	....	....	....	....
99-2000	**Edmonton**	**NHL**	**5**	**0**	**0**	**0**	**10**	**0**	**0**	**0**	**2**	**0.0**	**0**	**0**	**0.0**	**7:02**	**1**	**0**	**0**	**0**	**0**	**0**	**0**	**0**	**2:05**
	Hamilton	AHL	70	23	17	40	85	....	....	....	....	....	....	....	....	....	6	2	1	3	0	....	....	....	....
2000-01	**Edmonton**	**NHL**	**37**	**2**	**4**	**6**	**29**	**0**	**0**	**1**	**22**	**9.1**	**–2**	**5**	**20.0**	**7:06**	....	....	....	....	....	....	....	....	....
	Pittsburgh	**NHL**	**11**	**0**	**0**	**0**	**14**	**0**	**0**	**0**	**1**	**0.0**	**0**	**1**	**100.0**	**5:57**	**5**	**0**	**0**	**0**	**2**	**0**	**0**	**0**	**5:46**
2001-02	**Pittsburgh**	**NHL**	**82**	**6**	**11**	**17**	**71**	**0**	**1**	**0**	**77**	**7.8**	**–19**	**21**	**38.1**	**13:16**	....	....	....	....	....	....	....	....	....
2002-03	**Pittsburgh**	**NHL**	**44**	**2**	**2**	**4**	**72**	**0**	**0**	**0**	**30**	**6.7**	**–8**	**5**	**80.0**	**9:13**	....	....	....	....	....	....	....	....	....
	NY Rangers	**NHL**	**24**	**1**	**4**	**5**	**0**	**0**	**0**	**0**	**17**	**5.9**	**4**	**1**	**0.0**	**10:18**	....	....	....	....	....	....	....	....	....
2003-04	**NY Rangers**	**NHL**	**59**	**5**	**2**	**7**	**82**	**1**	**0**	**1**	**39**	**12.8**	**–13**	**8**	**50.0**	**9:29**	....	....	....	....	....	....	....	....	....
2004-05	Providence Bruins	AHL	64	12	15	27	52	....	....	....	....	....	....	....	....	....	6	1	1	2	4	....	....	....	....
2005-06	HC Davos	Swiss	4	2	1	3	4	....	....	....	....	....	....	....	....	....	....	....	....	....	....	....	....	....	....
	Boston	**NHL**	**55**	**2**	**2**	**4**	**53**	**0**	**1**	**0**	**37**	**5.4**	**–6**	**0**	**0.0**	**6:15**	....	....	....	....	....	....	....	....	....
2006-07	**New Jersey**	**NHL**	**6**	**0**	**0**	**0**	**7**	**0**	**0**	**0**	**0**	**0.0**	**0**	**0**	**0.0**	**4:57**	....	....	....	....	....	....	....	....	....
	Lowell Devils	AHL	39	8	3	11	33	....	....	....	....	....	....	....	....	....	....	....	....	....	....	....	....	....	....
	NHL Totals		**326**	**18**	**25**	**43**	**338**	**1**	**2**	**2**	**225**	**8.0**		**41**	**43.9**	**9:23**	**6**	**0**	**0**	**0**	**2**	**0**	**0**	**0**	**5:09**

Traded to **Edmonton** by **NY Islanders** for Mariusz Czerkawski, August 25, 1997. Traded to **Pittsburgh** by **Edmonton** for Sven Butenschon, March 13, 2001. Traded to **NY Rangers** by **Pittsburgh** with Mike Wilson, Alex Kovalev and Janne Laukkanen for Joel Bouchard, Richard Lintner, Rico Fata and Mikael Samuelsson, February 10, 2003. Signed to a PTO (tryout) contract by **Providence** (AHL), November 2, 2004. Signed as a free agent by **Boston**, November 24, 2005. Signed as a free agent by **New Jersey**, October 4, 2006. Signed as a free agent by **Anaheim**, July 18, 2007.

LADD, Andrew

(LAD, AN-droo) **CAR.**

Left wing. Shoots left. 6'2", 201 lbs. Born, Maple Ridge, B.C., December 12, 1985. Carolina's 1st choice, 4th overall, in 2004 Entry Draft.

Season	Club	League	GP	G	A	Pts	PIM	PP	SH	GW	S	%	+/-	TF	F%	Min	GP	G	A	Pts	PIM	PP	SH	GW	Min
2000-01	Okanagan Chiefs	BCAHA	6	4	8	12	10	....	....	....	....	....	....	....	....	....	....	....	....	....	....	....	....	....	....
2001-02	Port Coquitlam	BCAHA	50	50	41	91	49	....	....	....	....	....	....	....	....	....	....	....	....	....	....	....	....	....	....
	Vancouver Giants	WHL	1	0	0	0	0	....	....	....	....	....	....	....	....	....	....	....	....	....	....	....	....	....	....
2002-03	Coquitlam	BCHL	58	15	40	55	61	....	....	....	....	....	....	....	....	....	....	....	....	....	....	....	....	....	....
2003-04	Calgary Hitmen	WHL	71	30	45	75	119	....	....	....	....	....	....	....	....	....	7	1	6	7	10	....	....	....	....
2004-05	Calgary Hitmen	WHL	65	19	26	45	167	....	....	....	....	....	....	....	....	....	12	7	4	11	18	....	....	....	....
2005-06♦	**Carolina**	**NHL**	**29**	**6**	**5**	**11**	**4**	**3**	**0**	**0**	**43**	**14.0**	**0**	**0**	**0.0**	**11:10**	**17**	**2**	**3**	**5**	**4**	**0**	**0**	**1**	**9:27**
	Lowell	AHL	25	11	8	19	28	....	....	....	....	....	....	....	....	....	....	....	....	....	....	....	....	....	....
2006-07	**Carolina**	**NHL**	**65**	**11**	**10**	**21**	**46**	**2**	**0**	**3**	**109**	**10.1**	**1**	**1**	**0.0**	**11:12**	....	....	....	....	....	....	....	....	....
	NHL Totals		**94**	**17**	**15**	**32**	**50**	**5**	**0**	**3**	**152**	**11.2**		**1**	**0.0**	**11:11**	**17**	**2**	**3**	**5**	**4**	**0**	**0**	**1**	**9:27**

LAICH, Brooks

(LAYCH, BRUKS) **WSH.**

Center. Shoots left. 6'2", 210 lbs. Born, Wawota, Sask., June 23, 1983. Ottawa's 7th choice, 193rd overall, in 2001 Entry Draft.

Season	Club	League	GP	G	A	Pts	PIM	PP	SH	GW	S	%	+/-	TF	F%	Min	GP	G	A	Pts	PIM	PP	SH	GW	Min
99-2000	Tisdale Trojans	SMHL	57	51	52	103	....	....	....	....	....	....	....	....	....	....	....	....	....	....	....	....	....	....	....
2000-01	Moose Jaw	WHL	71	9	21	30	28	....	....	....	....	....	....	....	....	....	4	0	0	0	5	....	....	....	....
2001-02	Moose Jaw	WHL	28	6	14	20	12	....	....	....	....	....	....	....	....	....	....	....	....	....	....	....	....	....	....
	Seattle	WHL	47	22	36	58	42	....	....	....	....	....	....	....	....	....	11	5	3	8	11	....	....	....	....
2002-03	Seattle	WHL	60	41	53	94	65	....	....	....	....	....	....	....	....	....	15	5	14	19	24	....	....	....	....
2003-04	**Ottawa**	**NHL**	**1**	**0**	**0**	**0**	**2**	**0**	**0**	**0**	**1**	**0.0**	**0**	**7**	**42.9**	**9:34**	....	....	....	....	....	....	....	....	....
	Binghamton	AHL	44	15	18	33	16	....	....	....	....	....	....	....	....	....	....	....	....	....	....	....	....	....	....
	Washington	**NHL**	**4**	**0**	**1**	**1**	**0**	**0**	**0**	**0**	**2**	**0.0**	**–1**	**49**	**51.0**	**10:50**	....	....	....	....	....	....	....	....	....
	Portland Pirates	AHL	22	1	3	4	12	....	....	....	....	....	....	....	....	....	6	0	0	0	0	....	....	....	....
2004-05	Portland Pirates	AHL	68	16	10	26	33	....	....	....	....	....	....	....	....	....	....	....	....	....	....	....	....	....	....
2005-06	**Washington**	**NHL**	**73**	**7**	**14**	**21**	**26**	**1**	**0**	**1**	**118**	**5.9**	**–9**	**666**	**49.7**	**11:13**	....	....	....	....	....	....	....	....	....
	Hershey Bears	AHL	10	7	6	13	8	....	....	....	....	....	....	....	....	....	21	8	7	15	29	....	....	....	....
2006-07	**Washington**	**NHL**	**73**	**8**	**10**	**18**	**29**	**2**	**3**	**0**	**119**	**6.7**	**–2**	**563**	**51.9**	**13:36**	....	....	....	....	....	....	....	....	....
	NHL Totals		**151**	**15**	**25**	**40**	**57**	**3**	**3**	**1**	**240**	**6.3**		**1285**	**50.7**	**12:21**	....	....	....	....	....	....	....	....	....

WHL West First All-Star Team (2003)

Traded to **Washington** by **Ottawa** with Ottawa's 2nd round choice (later traded to Colorado - Colorado selected Chris Durand) in 2005 Entry Draft for Peter Bondra, February 18, 2004.

LAING, Quintin

(LANG, QUIHN-tihn)

Left wing. Shoots left. 6'2", 175 lbs. Born, Rosetown, Sask., June 8, 1979. Detroit's 3rd choice, 102nd overall, in 1997 Entry Draft.

Season	Club	League	GP	G	A	Pts	PIM	PP	SH	GW	S	%	+/-	TF	F%	Min	GP	G	A	Pts	PIM	PP	SH	GW	Min
1993-94	Delisle Contacts	SAHA	30	25	50	75	25	....	....	....	....	....	....	....	....	....	....	....	....	....	....	....	....	....	....
1994-95	Delisle Contacts	SAHA	30	30	45	75	15	....	....	....	....	....	....	....	....	....	....	....	....	....	....	....	....	....	....
1995-96	Sask. Contacts	SMHL	44	18	12	30	20	....	....	....	....	....	....	....	....	....	....	....	....	....	....	....	....	....	....
1996-97	Kelowna Rockets	WHL	63	13	24	37	54	....	....	....	....	....	....	....	....	....	1	0	0	0	0	....	....	....	....
1997-98	Kelowna Rockets	WHL	59	11	24	35	47	....	....	....	....	....	....	....	....	....	7	0	1	1	8	....	....	....	....
1998-99	Kelowna Rockets	WHL	70	11	10	21	107	....	....	....	....	....	....	....	....	....	6	3	0	3	0	....	....	....	....
99-2000	Kelowna Rockets	WHL	68	22	30	52	61	....	....	....	....	....	....	....	....	....	5	1	1	2	8	....	....	....	....
2000-01	Norfolk Admirals	AHL	10	0	1	1	10	....	....	....	....	....	....	....	....	....	....	....	....	....	....	....	....	....	....
	Jackson Bandits	ECHL	60	13	24	37	39	....	....	....	....	....	....	....	....	....	5	0	0	0	0	....	....	....	....
2001-02	Jackson Bandits	ECHL	16	4	6	10	12	....	....	....	....	....	....	....	....	....	....	....	....	....	....	....	....	....	....
	Norfolk Admirals	AHL	61	6	15	21	32	....	....	....	....	....	....	....	....	....	4	0	0	0	2	....	....	....	....
2002-03	Norfolk Admirals	AHL	69	5	12	17	33	....	....	....	....	....	....	....	....	....	8	2	2	4	0	....	....	....	....
2003-04	**Chicago**	**NHL**	**3**	**0**	**1**	**1**	**0**	**0**	**0**	**0**	**3**	**0.0**	**1**	**0**	**0.0**	**11:57**	....	....	....	....	....	....	....	....	....
	Norfolk Admirals	AHL	78	12	10	22	74	....	....	....	....	....	....	....	....	....	8	5	1	6	4	....	....	....	....
2004-05	Norfolk Admirals	AHL	66	10	13	23	54	....	....	....	....	....	....	....	....	....	4	0	0	0	0	....	....	....	....
2005-06	Norfolk Admirals	AHL	73	14	31	45	70	....	....	....	....	....	....	....	....	....	4	0	0	0	0	....	....	....	....
2006-07	Hershey Bears	AHL	75	15	28	43	44	....	....	....	....	....	....	....	....	....	19	2	5	7	21	....	....	....	....
	NHL Totals		**3**	**0**	**1**	**1**	**0**	**0**	**0**	**0**	**3**	**0.0**		**0**	**0.0**	**11:57**	....	....	....	....	....	....	....	....	....

Signed as a free agent by **Chicago**, June 4, 2003. Signed as a free agent by **Washington**, July 18, 2006.

LAMPMAN, Bryce

(LAMP-man, BRIGHS) **T.B.**

Defense. Shoots left. 6'1", 199 lbs. Born, Rochester, MN, August 31, 1982. NY Rangers' 4th choice, 113th overall, in 2001 Entry Draft.

			Regular Season														Playoffs								
Season	Club	League	GP	G	A	Pts	PIM	PP	SH	GW	S	%	+/-	TF	F%	Min	GP	G	A	Pts	PIM	PP	SH	GW	Min
1998-99	Rochester	USHL	53	3	8	11	33	....	....	....	....	....	....	....	....	....	....	....	....	....	....	....	....	....	....
99-2000	Rochester	USHL	10	0	0	0	14	....	....	....	....	....	....	....	....	....	....	....	....	....	....	....	....	....	....
	Omaha Lancers	USHL	11	1	2	3	38	....	....	....	....	....	....	....	....	....	4	0	0	0	0	....	....	....	....
2000-01	Omaha Lancers	USHL	55	10	11	21	77	....	....	....	....	....	....	....	....	....	12	1	4	5	12	....	....	....	....
2001-02	Nebraska-Omaha	CCHA	26	0	4	4	28	....	....	....	....	....	....	....	....	....	....	....	....	....	....	....	....	....	....
2002-03	Kamloops Blazers	WHL	29	1	17	18	32	....	....	....	....	....	....	....	....	....	....	....	....	....	....	....	....	....	....
	Hartford	AHL	45	0	6	6	32	....	....	....	....	....	....	....	....	....	2	0	1	1	0	....	....	....	....
2003-04	**NY Rangers**	**NHL**	**8**	**0**	**0**	**0**	**0**	**0**	**0**	**0**	**7**	**0.0**	**–4**	**0**	**0.0**	**19:34**	....	....	....	....	....	....	....	....	....
	Hartford	AHL	68	4	11	15	50	....	....	....	....	....	....	....	....	....	16	1	3	4	14	....	....	....	....
2004-05	Hartford	AHL	74	7	18	25	74	....	....	....	....	....	....	....	....	....	4	0	0	0	4	....	....	....	....
2005-06	**NY Rangers**	**NHL**	**1**	**0**	**0**	**0**	**2**	**0**	**0**	**0**	**1**	**0.0**	**–1**	**0**	**0.0**	**13:40**	....	....	....	....	....	....	....	....	....
	Hartford	AHL	11	2	3	5	16	....	....	....	....	....	....	....	....	....	....	....	....	....	....	....	....	....	....
2006-07	**NY Rangers**	**NHL**	**1**	**0**	**0**	**0**	**0**	**0**	**0**	**0**	**0**	**0.0**	**0**	**0**	**0.0**	**12:08**	....	....	....	....	....	....	....	....	....
	Hartford	AHL	60	6	19	25	62	....	....	....	....	....	....	....	....	....	7	2	0	2	2	....	....	....	....
	NHL Totals		**10**	**0**	**0**	**0**	**2**	**0**	**0**	**0**	**8**	**0.0**		**0**	**0.0**	**18:14**	....	....	....	....	....	....	....	....	....

• Left **University of Nebraska-Omaha** (CCHA) and signed as a free agent by **Kamloops** (WHL), August 1, 2002. • Missed majority of 2005-06 season recovering from a shoulder injury. Signed as a free agent by **Turku** (Finland), June 6, 2007. Rights traded to **Tampa Bay** by **NY Rangers** for the rights to Mitch Fritz, July 4, 2007.

LANG, Robert

(LANG, RAW-buhrt) **CHI.**

Center. Shoots right. 6'3", 216 lbs. Born, Teplice, Czech., December 19, 1970. Los Angeles' 6th choice, 133rd overall, in 1990 Entry Draft.

			Regular Season														Playoffs								
Season	Club	League	GP	G	A	Pts	PIM	PP	SH	GW	S	%	+/-	TF	F%	Min	GP	G	A	Pts	PIM	PP	SH	GW	Min
1988-89	CHZ Litvinov	Czech	7	3	2	5	0	....	....	....	....	....	....	....	....	....	....	....	....	....	....	....	....	....	....
1989-90	CHZ Litvinov	Czech	32	8	7	15	....	....	....	....	....	....	....	....	....	....	8	3	3	6	....	....	....	....	....
1990-91	HC CHZ Litvinov	Czech	56	26	26	52	38	....	....	....	....	....	....	....	....	....	....	....	....	....	....	....	....	....	....
1991-92	Litvinov	Czech	43	12	31	43	34	....	....	....	....	....	....	....	....	....	....	....	....	....	....	....	....	....	....
	Czechoslovakia	Olympics	8	5	8	13	8	....	....	....	....	....	....	....	....	....	....	....	....	....	....	....	....	....	....
1992-93	**Los Angeles**	**NHL**	**11**	**0**	**5**	**5**	**2**	**0**	**0**	**0**	**3**	**0.0**	**–3**	....	....	....	....	....	....	....	....	....	....	....	....
	Phoenix	IHL	38	9	21	30	20	....	....	....	....	....	....	....	....	....	....	....	....	....	....	....	....	....	....
1993-94	**Los Angeles**	**NHL**	**32**	**9**	**10**	**19**	**10**	**0**	**0**	**0**	**41**	**22.0**	**7**	....	....	....	....	....	....	....	....	....	....	....	....
	Phoenix	IHL	44	11	24	35	34	....	....	....	....	....	....	....	....	....	....	....	....	....	....	....	....	....	....
1994-95	Litvinov	CzRep	16	4	19	23	28	....	....	....	....	....	....	....	....	....	....	....	....	....	....	....	....	....	....
	Los Angeles	**NHL**	**36**	**4**	**8**	**12**	**4**	**0**	**0**	**0**	**38**	**10.5**	**–7**	....	....	....	....	....	....	....	....	....	....	....	....
1995-96	**Los Angeles**	**NHL**	**68**	**6**	**16**	**22**	**10**	**0**	**2**	**0**	**71**	**8.5**	**–15**	....	....	....	....	....	....	....	....	....	....	....	....
1996-97	HC Sparta Praha	CzRep	38	14	27	41	30	....	....	....	....	....	....	....	....	....	5	1	2	3	4	....	....	....	....
	HC Sparta Praha	EuroHL	4	2	2	4	0	....	....	....	....	....	....	....	....	....	4	2	1	3	2	....	....	....	....
1997-98	**Boston**	**NHL**	**3**	**0**	**0**	**0**	**2**	**0**	**0**	**0**	**2**	**0.0**	**1**	....	....	....	....	....	....	....	....	....	....	....	....
	Pittsburgh	**NHL**	**51**	**9**	**13**	**22**	**14**	**1**	**1**	**2**	**64**	**14.1**	**6**	....	....	....	**6**	**0**	**3**	**3**	**2**	**0**	**0**	**0**	....
	Czech Republic	Olympics	6	0	3	3	0	....	....	....	....	....	....	....	....	....	....	....	....	....	....	....	....	....	....
	Houston Aeros	IHL	9	1	7	8	4	....	....	....	....	....	....	....	....	....	....	....	....	....	....	....	....	....	....
1998-99	**Pittsburgh**	**NHL**	**72**	**21**	**23**	**44**	**24**	**7**	**0**	**3**	**137**	**15.3**	**–10**	**964**	**44.8**	**16:24**	**12**	**0**	**2**	**2**	**0**	**0**	**0**	**0**	**13:58**
99-2000	**Pittsburgh**	**NHL**	**78**	**23**	**42**	**65**	**14**	**13**	**0**	**5**	**142**	**16.2**	**–9**	**1433**	**50.7**	**19:22**	**11**	**3**	**3**	**6**	**0**	**2**	**0**	**0**	**21:42**
2000-01	**Pittsburgh**	**NHL**	**82**	**32**	**48**	**80**	**28**	**10**	**0**	**2**	**177**	**18.1**	**20**	**1348**	**43.9**	**20:24**	**16**	**4**	**4**	**8**	**4**	**0**	**0**	**0**	**19:21**
2001-02	**Pittsburgh**	**NHL**	**62**	**18**	**32**	**50**	**16**	**5**	**1**	**3**	**175**	**10.3**	**9**	**1172**	**46.3**	**22:56**	....	....	....	....	....	....	....	....	....
	Czech Republic	Olympics	4	1	2	3	2	....	....	....	....	....	....	....	....	....	....	....	....	....	....	....	....	....	....
2002-03	**Washington**	**NHL**	**82**	**22**	**47**	**69**	**22**	**10**	**0**	**2**	**146**	**15.1**	**12**	**1069**	**45.9**	**18:47**	**6**	**2**	**1**	**3**	**2**	**0**	**0**	**1**	**21:55**
2003-04	**Washington**	**NHL**	**63**	**29**	**45**	**74**	**24**	**10**	**0**	**2**	**149**	**19.5**	**2**	**744**	**44.1**	**21:46**	....	....	....	....	....	....	....	....	....
	Detroit	**NHL**	**6**	**1**	**4**	**5**	**0**	**0**	**0**	**1**	**14**	**7.1**	**2**	**96**	**57.3**	**16:20**	**12**	**4**	**5**	**9**	**6**	**0**	**0**	**0**	**18:10**
2004-05			DID NOT PLAY																						
2005-06	**Detroit**	**NHL**	**72**	**20**	**42**	**62**	**72**	**8**	**0**	**3**	**171**	**11.7**	**17**	**861**	**50.3**	**16:15**	**6**	**3**	**3**	**6**	**2**	**2**	**0**	**0**	**19:12**
	Czech Republic	Olympics	8	0	4	4	4	....	....	....	....	....	....	....	....	....	....	....	....	....	....	....	....	....	....
2006-07	**Detroit**	**NHL**	**81**	**19**	**33**	**52**	**66**	**6**	**0**	**4**	**166**	**11.4**	**12**	**812**	**49.4**	**16:49**	**18**	**2**	**6**	**8**	**8**	**0**	**0**	**0**	**15:10**
	NHL Totals		**799**	**213**	**368**	**581**	**308**	**70**	**4**	**27**	**1496**	**14.2**		**8499**	**47.1**	**18:56**	**87**	**18**	**27**	**45**	**24**	**4**	**0**	**1**	**17:57**

Played in NHL All-Star Game (2004)

Signed as a free agent by **Pittsburgh**, September 2, 1997. Claimed by **Boston** from **Pittsburgh** in Waiver Draft, September 28, 1997. Claimed on waivers by **Pittsburgh** from **Boston**, October 25, 1997. Signed as a free agent by **Washington**, July 1, 2002. Traded to **Detroit** by **Washington** for Tomas Fleischmann, Detroit's 1st round choice (Mike Green) in 2004 Entry Draft and Detroit's 4th round choice (Luke Lynes) in 2006 Entry Draft, February 27, 2004. Signed as a free agent by **Chicago**, July 2, 2007.

LANGENBRUNNER, Jamie

(lan-gehn-BRUH-nuhr, JAY-mee) **N.J.**

Right wing. Shoots right. 6'1", 200 lbs. Born, Cloquet, MN, July 24, 1975. Dallas' 2nd choice, 35th overall, in 1993 Entry Draft.

			Regular Season														Playoffs								
Season	Club	League	GP	G	A	Pts	PIM	PP	SH	GW	S	%	+/-	TF	F%	Min	GP	G	A	Pts	PIM	PP	SH	GW	Min
1990-91	Cloquet	High-MN	20	6	16	22	8	....	....	....	....	....	....	....	....	....	....	....	....	....	....	....	....	....	....
1991-92	Cloquet	High-MN	23	16	23	39	24	....	....	....	....	....	....	....	....	....	....	....	....	....	....	....	....	....	....
1992-93	Cloquet	High-MN	27	27	62	89	18	....	....	....	....	....	....	....	....	....	....	....	....	....	....	....	....	....	....
1993-94	Peterborough	OHL	62	33	58	91	53	....	....	....	....	....	....	....	....	....	7	4	6	10	2	....	....	....	....
1994-95	Peterborough	OHL	62	42	57	99	84	....	....	....	....	....	....	....	....	....	11	8	14	22	12	....	....	....	....
	Dallas	**NHL**	**2**	**0**	**0**	**0**	**2**	**0**	**0**	**0**	**1**	**0.0**	**0**	....	....	....	....	....	....	....	....	....	....	....	....
	Kalamazoo Wings	IHL	....	....	....	....	....	....	....	....	....	....	....	....	....	....	11	1	3	4	2	....	....	....	....
1995-96	**Dallas**	**NHL**	**12**	**2**	**2**	**4**	**6**	**1**	**0**	**0**	**15**	**13.3**	**–2**	....	....	....	....	....	....	....	....	....	....	....	....
	Michigan	IHL	59	25	40	65	129	....	....	....	....	....	....	....	....	....	10	3	10	13	8	....	....	....	....
1996-97	**Dallas**	**NHL**	**76**	**13**	**26**	**39**	**51**	**3**	**0**	**3**	**112**	**11.6**	**–2**	....	....	....	**5**	**1**	**1**	**2**	**14**	**0**	**0**	**1**	....
1997-98	**Dallas**	**NHL**	**81**	**23**	**29**	**52**	**61**	**8**	**0**	**6**	**159**	**14.5**	**9**	....	....	....	**16**	**1**	**4**	**5**	**14**	**0**	**0**	**1**	....
	United States	Olympics	3	0	0	0	4	....	....	....	....	....	....	....	....	....	....	....	....	....	....	....	....	....	....
1998-99 ♦	**Dallas**	**NHL**	**75**	**12**	**33**	**45**	**62**	**4**	**0**	**1**	**145**	**8.3**	**10**	**217**	**46.1**	**15:51**	**23**	**10**	**7**	**17**	**16**	**4**	**0**	**3**	**17:43**
99-2000	**Dallas**	**NHL**	**65**	**18**	**21**	**39**	**68**	**4**	**2**	**6**	**153**	**11.8**	**16**	**40**	**50.0**	**17:33**	**15**	**1**	**7**	**8**	**18**	**1**	**0**	**0**	**15:28**
2000-01	**Dallas**	**NHL**	**53**	**12**	**18**	**30**	**57**	**3**	**2**	**4**	**104**	**11.5**	**4**	**316**	**45.3**	**16:30**	**10**	**2**	**2**	**4**	**6**	**0**	**0**	**1**	**19:26**
2001-02	**Dallas**	**NHL**	**68**	**10**	**16**	**26**	**54**	**0**	**1**	**2**	**132**	**7.6**	**–11**	**120**	**45.0**	**15:45**	....	....	....	....	....	....	....	....	....
	New Jersey	**NHL**	**14**	**3**	**3**	**6**	**23**	**0**	**0**	**2**	**31**	**9.7**	**2**	**2**	**50.0**	**15:27**	**5**	**0**	**1**	**1**	**8**	**0**	**0**	**0**	**14:57**
2002-03 ♦	**New Jersey**	**NHL**	**78**	**22**	**33**	**55**	**65**	**5**	**1**	**5**	**197**	**11.2**	**17**	**72**	**47.2**	**17:48**	**24**	***11**	**7**	***18**	**16**	**1**	**0**	**4**	**17:34**
2003-04	**New Jersey**	**NHL**	**53**	**10**	**16**	**26**	**43**	**1**	**2**	**2**	**130**	**7.7**	**9**	**31**	**51.6**	**16:01**	**5**	**0**	**2**	**2**	**2**	**0**	**0**	**0**	**15:04**
2004-05	ERC Ingolstadt	Germany	11	2	2	4	22	....	....	....	....	....	....	....	....	....	11	1	6	7	6	....	....	....	....
2005-06	**New Jersey**	**NHL**	**80**	**19**	**34**	**53**	**74**	**8**	**1**	**1**	**243**	**7.8**	**–1**	**41**	**43.9**	**18:36**	**9**	**3**	**10**	**13**	**16**	**1**	**0**	**1**	**19:46**
2006-07	**New Jersey**	**NHL**	**82**	**23**	**37**	**60**	**64**	**12**	**0**	**7**	**243**	**9.5**	**–9**	**23**	**34.8**	**18:33**	**11**	**2**	**6**	**8**	**7**	**1**	**0**	**1**	**19:16**
	NHL Totals		**739**	**167**	**268**	**435**	**630**	**49**	**9**	**39**	**1665**	**10.0**		**862**	**45.7**	**17:09**	**123**	**31**	**47**	**78**	**117**	**8**	**0**	**12**	**17:36**

Traded to **New Jersey** by **Dallas** with Joe Nieuwendyk for Jason Arnott, Randy McKay and New Jersey's 1st round choice (later traded to Columbus – later traded to Buffalo – Buffalo selected Dan Paille) in 2002 Entry Draft, March 19, 2002. Signed as a free agent by **Ingolstadt** (Germany), January 24, 2005.

LANGFELD, Josh

(LANG-fehld, JAWSH)

Right wing. Shoots right. 6'3", 216 lbs. Born, Fridley, MN, July 17, 1977. Ottawa's 3rd choice, 66th overall, in 1997 Entry Draft.

			Regular Season														Playoffs								
Season	Club	League	GP	G	A	Pts	PIM	PP	SH	GW	S	%	+/-	TF	F%	Min	GP	G	A	Pts	PIM	PP	SH	GW	Min
1995-96	Great Falls	AFHL	45	45	40	85	105	....	....	....	....	....	....	....	....	....	....	....	....	....	....	....	....	....	....
1996-97	Lincoln Stars	USHL	38	35	23	58	100	....	....	....	....	....	....	....	....	....	14	8	*13	*21	42	....	....	....	....
1997-98	U. of Michigan	CCHA	46	19	17	36	66	....	....	....	....	....	....	....	....	....	....	....	....	....	....	....	....	....	....
1998-99	U. of Michigan	CCHA	41	21	14	35	84	....	....	....	....	....	....	....	....	....	....	....	....	....	....	....	....	....	....
99-2000	U. of Michigan	CCHA	39	9	21	30	56	....	....	....	....	....	....	....	....	....	....	....	....	....	....	....	....	....	....
2000-01	U. of Michigan	CCHA	42	16	12	28	44	....	....	....	....	....	....	....	....	....	....	....	....	....	....	....	....	....	....
2001-02	**Ottawa**	**NHL**	**1**	**0**	**0**	**0**	**2**	**0**	**0**	**0**	**5**	**0.0**	**0**	**0**	**0.0**	**8:15**	....	....	....	....	....	....	....	....	....
	Grand Rapids	AHL	68	21	16	37	29	....	....	....	....	....	....	....	....	....	5	2	0	2	0	....	....	....	....
2002-03	**Ottawa**	**NHL**	**12**	**0**	**1**	**1**	**4**	**0**	**0**	**0**	**16**	**0.0**	**2**	**0**	**0.0**	**11:11**	....	....	....	....	....	....	....	....	....
	Binghamton	AHL	59	14	21	35	38	....	....	....	....	....	....	....	....	....	13	5	3	8	8	....	....	....	....
2003-04	**Ottawa**	**NHL**	**38**	**7**	**10**	**17**	**16**	**2**	**0**	**2**	**59**	**11.9**	**6**	**5**	**80.0**	**10:53**	....	....	....	....	....	....	....	....	....
	Binghamton	AHL	30	13	14	27	25	....	....	....	....	....	....	....	....	....	2	0	0	0	0	....	....	....	....
2004-05	Binghamton	AHL	74	32	25	57	75	....	....	....	....	....	....	....	....	....	6	2	2	4	2	....	....	....	....
2005-06	**San Jose**	**NHL**	**39**	**2**	**9**	**11**	**16**	**0**	**1**	**0**	**53**	**3.8**	**4**	**8**	**12.5**	**11:46**	....	....	....	....	....	....	....	....	....
	Boston	**NHL**	**18**	**0**	**1**	**1**	**10**	**0**	**0**	**0**	**32**	**0.0**	**–6**	**6**	**16.7**	**9:24**	....	....	....	....	....	....	....	....	....

			Regular Season														Playoffs								
Season	Club	League	GP	G	A	Pts	PIM	PP	SH	GW	S	%	+/-	TF	F%	Min	GP	G	A	Pts	PIM	PP	SH	GW	Min
2006-07	Detroit	NHL	33	0	2	2	12	0	0	0	37	0.0	2	11	100.0	5:33	....	....	....	....	....	....	....	....	....
	Grand Rapids	AHL	38	13	19	32	44	....	....	....	....	....	....	....	....	....	....	....	....	....	....	....	....	....	....
	NHL Totals		141	9	23	32	60	2	1	2	202	4.5		20	35.0	9:42	....	....	....	....	....	....	....	....	....

NCAA Championship All-Tournament Team (1998)

Signed as a free agent by **San Jose**, September 12, 2005. Claimed on waivers by **Boston** from **San Jose**, January 31, 2006. Signed as a free agent by **Detroit**, July 14, 2006.

LANGKOW, Daymond

(LANG-kow, DAY-muhn) **CGY.**

Center. Shoots left. 5'10", 179 lbs. Born, Edmonton, Alta., September 27, 1976. Tampa Bay's 1st choice, 5th overall, in 1995 Entry Draft.

Season	Club	League	GP	G	A	Pts	PIM	PP	SH	GW	S	%	+/-	TF	F%	Min	GP	G	A	Pts	PIM	PP	SH	GW	Min
1991-92	Edmonton Pats	AMHL	35	36	45	81	100	....	....	....	....	....	....	....	....	....	....	....	....	....	....	....	....	....	....
	Tri-City	WHL	1	0	0	0	0	....	....	....	....	....	....	....	....	....	....	....	....	....	....	....	....	....	....
1992-93	Tri-City	WHL	64	22	42	64	100	....	....	....	....	....	....	....	....	....	4	1	0	1	4	....	....	....	....
1993-94	Tri-City	WHL	61	40	43	83	174	....	....	....	....	....	....	....	....	....	4	2	2	4	15	....	....	....	....
1994-95	Tri-City	WHL	72	*67	73	*140	142	....	....	....	....	....	....	....	....	....	17	12	15	27	52	....	....	....	....
1995-96	Tri-City	WHL	48	30	61	91	103	....	....	....	....	....	....	....	....	....	11	14	13	27	20	....	....	....	....
	Tampa Bay	NHL	4	0	1	1	0	0	0	0	4	0.0	–1	....	....	....	....	....	....	....	....	....	....	....	....
1996-97	Tampa Bay	NHL	79	15	13	28	35	3	1	1	170	8.8	1	....	....	....	....	....	....	....	....	....	....	....	....
	Adirondack	AHL	2	1	1	2	0	....	....	....	....	....	....	....	....	....	....	....	....	....	....	....	....	....	....
1997-98	Tampa Bay	NHL	68	8	14	22	62	2	0	1	156	5.1	–9	....	....	....	....	....	....	....	....	....	....	....	....
1998-99	Tampa Bay	NHL	22	4	6	10	15	1	0	1	40	10.0	0	399	48.4	17:10	....	....	....	....	....	....	....	....	....
	Cleveland	IHL	4	1	1	2	18	....	....	....	....	....	....	....	....	....	....	....	....	....	....	....	....	....	....
	Philadelphia	NHL	56	10	13	23	24	3	1	1	109	9.2	–8	738	48.0	15:12	6	0	2	2	2	0	0	0	16:50
99-2000	Philadelphia	NHL	82	18	32	50	56	5	0	7	222	8.1	1	1263	45.1	16:57	16	5	5	10	23	1	1	2	20:03
2000-01	Philadelphia	NHL	71	13	41	54	50	3	0	2	190	6.8	12	1181	47.2	18:38	6	2	4	6	2	1	0	0	20:17
2001-02	Phoenix	NHL	80	27	35	62	36	6	3	2	171	15.8	18	1379	46.2	19:11	5	1	0	1	0	0	0	0	21:06
2002-03	Phoenix	NHL	82	20	32	52	56	4	2	2	196	10.2	20	1972	46.5	21:00	....	....	....	....	....	....	....	....	....
2003-04	Phoenix	NHL	81	21	31	52	40	4	1	2	174	12.1	4	1472	43.1	21:07	....	....	....	....	....	....	....	....	....
2004-05				DID NOT PLAY																					
2005-06	Calgary	NHL	82	25	34	59	46	11	0	7	171	14.6	2	1130	47.4	18:07	7	1	5	6	6	1	0	0	19:42
2006-07	Calgary	NHL	81	33	44	77	44	10	1	6	247	13.4	23	1173	45.9	20:07	6	2	2	4	4	2	0	1	20:06
	NHL Totals		788	194	296	490	464	52	9	32	1850	10.5		10707	46.1	18:53	46	11	18	29	37	5	1	3	19:44

WHL West First All-Star Team (1995) • Canadian Major Junior First All-Star Team (1995) • WHL West Second All-Star Team (1996)

Traded to **Philadelphia** by **Tampa Bay** with Mikael Renberg for Chris Gratton and Mike Sillinger, December 12, 1998. Traded to **Phoenix** by **Philadelphia** for Phoenix's 2nd round choice (later traded to Tampa Bay – later traded to San Jose – San Jose selected Dan Spang) in 2002 Entry Draft and Phoenix's 1st round choice (Jeff Carter) in 2003 Entry Draft, July 2, 2001. Traded to **Calgary** by **Phoenix** for Denis Gauthier and Oleg Saprykin, August 26, 2004.

LAPERRIERE, Ian

(luh-PAIR-ee-YAIR, EE-an) **COL.**

Right wing. Shoots right. 6'1", 200 lbs. Born, Montreal, Que., January 19, 1974. St. Louis' 6th choice, 158th overall, in 1992 Entry Draft.

Season	Club	League	GP	G	A	Pts	PIM	PP	SH	GW	S	%	+/-	TF	F%	Min	GP	G	A	Pts	PIM	PP	SH	GW	Min
1989-90	Mtl-Bourassa	QAAA	22	4	10	14	10	....	....	....	....	....	....	....	....	....	3	0	1	1	6	....	....	....	....
1990-91	Drummondville	QMJHL	65	19	29	48	117	....	....	....	....	....	....	....	....	....	14	2	9	11	48	....	....	....	....
1991-92	Drummondville	QMJHL	70	28	49	77	160	....	....	....	....	....	....	....	....	....	4	2	2	4	9	....	....	....	....
1992-93	Drummondville	QMJHL	60	44	*96	140	188	....	....	....	....	....	....	....	....	....	10	6	13	19	20	....	....	....	....
1993-94	Drummondville	QMJHL	62	41	72	113	150	....	....	....	....	....	....	....	....	....	9	4	6	10	35	....	....	....	....
	St. Louis	NHL	1	0	0	0	0	0	0	0	1	0.0	0	....	....	....	....	....	....	....	....	....	....	....	....
	Peoria Rivermen	IHL	....	....	....	....	....	....	....	....	....	....	....	....	....	....	5	1	3	4	2	....	....	....	....
1994-95	Peoria Rivermen	IHL	51	16	32	48	111	....	....	....	....	....	....	....	....	....	....	....	....	....	....	....	....	....	....
	St. Louis	NHL	37	13	14	27	85	1	0	1	53	24.5	12	....	....	....	7	0	4	4	21	0	0	0	....
1995-96	St. Louis	NHL	33	3	6	9	87	1	0	1	31	9.7	–4	....	....	....	....	....	....	....	....	....	....	....	....
	Worcester IceCats	AHL	3	2	1	3	22	....	....	....	....	....	....	....	....	....	....	....	....	....	....	....	....	....	....
	NY Rangers	NHL	28	1	2	3	53	0	0	0	21	4.8	–5	....	....	....	....	....	....	....	....	....	....	....	....
	Los Angeles	NHL	10	2	3	5	15	0	0	0	18	11.1	–2	....	....	....	....	....	....	....	....	....	....	....	....
1996-97	Los Angeles	NHL	62	8	15	23	102	0	1	2	84	9.5	–25	....	....	....	....	....	....	....	....	....	....	....	....
1997-98	Los Angeles	NHL	77	6	15	21	131	0	1	1	74	8.1	0	....	....	....	4	1	0	1	6	0	0	0	....
1998-99	Los Angeles	NHL	72	3	10	13	138	0	0	1	62	4.8	–5	643	47.3	11:47	....	....	....	....	....	....	....	....	....
99-2000	Los Angeles	NHL	79	9	13	22	185	0	0	1	87	10.3	–14	1111	53.7	13:15	4	0	0	0	2	0	0	0	10:22
2000-01	Los Angeles	NHL	79	8	10	18	141	0	0	0	60	13.3	5	297	51.9	12:02	13	1	2	3	12	0	0	0	14:01
2001-02	Los Angeles	NHL	81	8	14	22	125	0	0	3	89	9.0	5	134	49.3	13:45	7	0	1	1	9	0	0	0	14:18
2002-03	Los Angeles	NHL	73	7	12	19	122	1	1	1	85	8.2	–9	317	49.2	15:46	....	....	....	....	....	....	....	....	....
2003-04	Los Angeles	NHL	62	10	12	22	58	1	0	3	59	16.9	–4	446	54.0	15:50	....	....	....	....	....	....	....	....	....
2004-05				DID NOT PLAY																					
2005-06	Colorado	NHL	82	21	24	45	116	1	1	3	133	15.8	3	963	45.9	17:10	9	0	1	1	27	0	0	0	13:40
2006-07	Colorado	NHL	81	8	21	29	133	0	0	0	118	6.8	5	389	46.8	13:51	....	....	....	....	....	....	....	....	....
	NHL Totals		857	107	171	278	1491	5	4	17	975	11.0		4300	49.8	14:09	44	2	8	10	77	0	0	0	13:32

QMJHL Second All-Star Team (1993)

Traded to **NY Rangers** by **St. Louis** for Stephane Matteau, December 28, 1995. Traded to **Los Angeles** by **NY Rangers** with Ray Ferraro, Mattias Norstrom, Nathan LaFayette and NY Rangers' 4th round choice (Sean Blanchard) in 1997 Entry Draft for Marty McSorley, Jari Kurri and Shane Churla, March 14, 1996. Signed as a free agent by **Colorado**, July 2, 2004.

LAPIERRE, Maxim

(la-PEE-air, MAX-ihm) **MTL.**

Center. Shoots right. 6'2", 196 lbs. Born, St. Leonard, Que., March 29, 1985. Montreal's 3rd choice, 61st overall, in 2003 Entry Draft.

Season	Club	League	GP	G	A	Pts	PIM	PP	SH	GW	S	%	+/-	TF	F%	Min	GP	G	A	Pts	PIM	PP	SH	GW	Min
2001-02	Cap-d-Madeleine	QAAA	42	14	27	41	44	....	....	....	....	....	....	....	....	....	10	3	5	8	16	....	....	....	....
	Montreal Rocket	QMJHL	9	2	0	2	2	....	....	....	....	....	....	....	....	....	....	....	....	....	....	....	....	....	....
2002-03	Montreal Rocket	QMJHL	72	22	21	43	55	....	....	....	....	....	....	....	....	....	7	1	3	4	6	....	....	....	....
2003-04	PEI Rocket	QMJHL	67	25	36	61	138	....	....	....	....	....	....	....	....	....	11	7	2	9	14	....	....	....	....
2004-05	PEI Rocket	QMJHL	69	25	27	52	139	....	....	....	....	....	....	....	....	....	....	....	....	....	....	....	....	....	....
2005-06	Montreal	NHL	1	0	0	0	0	0	0	0	0	0.0	–1	2	50.0	3:04	....	....	....	....	....	....	....	....	....
	Hamilton	AHL	73	13	23	36	214	....	....	....	....	....	....	....	....	....	....	....	....	....	....	....	....	....	....
2006-07	Montreal	NHL	46	6	6	12	24	0	1	2	82	7.3	–7	425	45.2	11:25	....	....	....	....	....	....	....	....	....
	Hamilton	AHL	37	11	13	24	59	....	....	....	....	....	....	....	....	....	22	6	6	12	41	....	....	....	....
	NHL Totals		47	6	6	12	24	0	1	2	82	7.3		427	45.2	11:14	....	....	....	....	....	....	....	....	....

LAPOINTE, Martin

(luh-POYNT, MAHR-tihn) **CHI.**

Right wing. Shoots right. 5'11", 215 lbs. Born, Ville St-Pierre, Que., September 12, 1973. Detroit's 1st choice, 10th overall, in 1991 Entry Draft.

Season	Club	League	GP	G	A	Pts	PIM	PP	SH	GW	S	%	+/-	TF	F%	Min	GP	G	A	Pts	PIM	PP	SH	GW	Min
1988-89	Lac St-Louis Lions	QAAA	42	39	45	84	46	....	....	....	....	....	....	....	....	....	3	6	2	8	4	....	....	....	....
1989-90	Laval Titan	QMJHL	65	42	54	96	77	....	....	....	....	....	....	....	....	....	14	8	17	25	54	....	....	....	....
1990-91	Laval Titan	QMJHL	64	44	54	98	66	....	....	....	....	....	....	....	....	....	13	7	14	21	26	....	....	....	....
1991-92	Laval Titan	QMJHL	31	25	30	55	84	....	....	....	....	....	....	....	....	....	10	4	10	14	32	....	....	....	....
	Detroit	NHL	4	0	1	1	5	0	0	0	2	0.0	2	....	....	....	3	0	1	1	4	0	0	0	....
	Adirondack	AHL	....	....	....	....	....	....	....	....	....	....	....	....	....	....	8	2	2	4	4	....	....	....	....
1992-93	Laval Titan	QMJHL	35	38	51	89	41	....	....	....	....	....	....	....	....	....	13	*13	*17	*30	22	....	....	....	....
	Detroit	NHL	3	0	0	0	0	0	0	0	2	0.0	–2	....	....	....	....	....	....	....	....	....	....	....	....
	Adirondack	AHL	8	1	2	3	9	....	....	....	....	....	....	....	....	....	....	....	....	....	....	....	....	....	....
1993-94	Detroit	NHL	50	8	8	16	55	2	0	0	45	17.8	7	....	....	....	4	0	0	0	6	0	0	0	....
	Adirondack	AHL	28	25	21	46	47	....	....	....	....	....	....	....	....	....	4	1	1	2	8	....	....	....	....
1994-95	Adirondack	AHL	39	29	16	45	80	....	....	....	....	....	....	....	....	....	....	....	....	....	....	....	....	....	....
	Detroit	NHL	39	4	6	10	73	0	0	1	46	8.7	1	....	....	....	2	0	1	1	8	0	0	0	....
1995-96	Detroit	NHL	58	6	3	9	93	1	0	0	76	7.9	0	....	....	....	11	1	2	3	12	0	0	0	....
1996-97♦	Detroit	NHL	78	16	17	33	167	5	1	1	149	10.7	–14	....	....	....	20	4	8	12	60	1	0	1	....
1997-98♦	Detroit	NHL	79	15	19	34	106	4	0	3	154	9.7	0	....	....	....	21	9	6	15	20	2	1	1	....
1998-99	Detroit	NHL	77	16	13	29	141	7	1	4	153	10.5	7	217	47.9	15:06	10	0	2	2	20	0	0	0	11:43
99-2000	Detroit	NHL	82	16	25	41	121	1	1	2	127	12.6	17	287	54.4	14:43	9	3	1	4	20	2	0	1	14:28
2000-01	Detroit	NHL	82	27	30	57	127	13	0	8	181	14.9	3	461	53.2	16:06	6	0	1	1	8	0	0	0	16:53
2001-02	Boston	NHL	68	17	23	40	101	4	0	2	141	12.1	12	222	53.6	17:22	6	1	2	3	12	1	0	1	16:58
2002-03	Boston	NHL	59	8	10	18	87	1	0	1	110	7.3	–19	52	48.1	15:22	5	1	0	1	14	0	0	0	14:39
2003-04	Boston	NHL	78	15	10	25	67	9	0	2	136	11.0	–5	101	51.5	14:26	7	0	0	0	14	0	0	0	15:21

			Regular Season														Playoffs								
Season	Club	League	GP	G	A	Pts	PIM	PP	SH	GW	S	%	+/-	TF	F%	Min	GP	G	A	Pts	PIM	PP	SH	GW	Min
2004-05			DID NOT PLAY																						
2005-06	**Chicago**	**NHL**	**82**	**14**	**17**	**31**	**106**	**6**	**0**	**3**	**135**	**10.4**	**–30**	**354**	**56.5**	**14:46**	....	....	....	....	....	....	....	....	....
2006-07	**Chicago**	**NHL**	**82**	**13**	**11**	**24**	**98**	**5**	**1**	**2**	**102**	**12.7**	**–14**	**341**	**52.8**	**13:59**	....	....	....	....	....	....	....	....	....
	NHL Totals		**921**	**175**	**193**	**368**	**1347**	**58**	**4**	**29**	**1559**	**11.2**		**2035**	**53.1**	**15:11**	**104**	**19**	**24**	**43**	**198**	**6**	**1**	**4**	**14:41**

QMJHL First All-Star Team (1990, 1993) • QMJHL Offensive Rookie of the Year (1990) • QMJHL Second All-Star Team (1991) • Memorial Cup Tournament All-Star Team (1993)

Signed as a free agent by **Boston**, July 2, 2001. Signed as a free agent by **Chicago**, August 3, 2005.

LARAQUE, Georges
(luh-RAK, ZHAWRZH) **PIT.**

Right wing. Shoots right. 6'3", 243 lbs. Born, Montreal, Que., December 7, 1976. Edmonton's 2nd choice, 31st overall, in 1995 Entry Draft.

Season	Club	League	GP	G	A	Pts	PIM	PP	SH	GW	S	%	+/-	TF	F%	Min	GP	G	A	Pts	PIM	PP	SH	GW	Min
1991-92	Mtl-Bourassa	QAHA	28	20	20	40	30	....	....	....	....	....	....	....	....	....	....	....	....	....	....	....	....	....	....
1992-93	Mtl-Bourassa	QAAA	37	8	20	28	50	....	....	....	....	....	....	....	....	....	3	1	2	3	2	....	....	....	....
1993-94	St-Jean Lynx	QMJHL	70	11	11	22	142	....	....	....	....	....	....	....	....	....	4	0	0	0	7	....	....	....	....
1994-95	St-Jean Lynx	QMJHL	62	19	22	41	259	....	....	....	....	....	....	....	....	....	7	1	1	2	42	....	....	....	....
1995-96	Laval Titan	QMJHL	11	8	13	21	76	....	....	....	....	....	....	....	....	....	....	....	....	....	....	....	....	....	....
	St-Hyacinthe	QMJHL	8	3	4	7	59	....	....	....	....	....	....	....	....	....	....	....	....	....	....	....	....	....	....
	Granby	QMJHL	22	9	7	16	125	....	....	....	....	....	....	....	....	....	18	7	6	13	104	....	....	....	....
1996-97	Hamilton	AHL	73	14	20	34	179	....	....	....	....	....	....	....	....	....	15	1	3	4	12	....	....	....	....
1997-98	**Edmonton**	**NHL**	**11**	**0**	**0**	**0**	**59**	**0**	**0**	**0**	**4**	**0.0**	**–4**	....	....	....	....	....	....	....	....	....	....	....	....
	Hamilton	AHL	46	10	20	30	154	....	....	....	....	....	....	....	....	....	3	0	0	0	11	....	....	....	....
1998-99	**Edmonton**	**NHL**	**39**	**3**	**2**	**5**	**57**	**0**	**0**	**0**	**17**	**17.6**	**–1**	**0**	**0.0**	**5:31**	**4**	**0**	**0**	**0**	**2**	**0**	**0**	**0**	**7:35**
	Hamilton	AHL	25	6	8	14	93	....	....	....	....	....	....	....	....	....	....	....	....	....	....	....	....	....	....
99-2000	**Edmonton**	**NHL**	**76**	**8**	**8**	**16**	**123**	**0**	**0**	**0**	**56**	**14.3**	**5**	**0**	**0.0**	**8:28**	**5**	**0**	**1**	**1**	**6**	**0**	**0**	**0**	**9:14**
2000-01	**Edmonton**	**NHL**	**82**	**13**	**16**	**29**	**148**	**1**	**0**	**1**	**73**	**17.8**	**5**	**0**	**0.0**	**9:03**	**6**	**1**	**1**	**2**	**8**	**0**	**0**	**0**	**9:54**
2001-02	**Edmonton**	**NHL**	**80**	**5**	**14**	**19**	**157**	**1**	**0**	**1**	**95**	**5.3**	**6**	**0**	**0.0**	**9:48**	....	....	....	....	....	....	....	....	....
2002-03	**Edmonton**	**NHL**	**64**	**6**	**7**	**13**	**110**	**0**	**0**	**2**	**46**	**13.0**	**–4**	**0**	**0.0**	**9:15**	**6**	**1**	**3**	**4**	**4**	**0**	**0**	**0**	**12:11**
2003-04	**Edmonton**	**NHL**	**66**	**6**	**11**	**17**	**99**	**1**	**0**	**1**	**54**	**11.1**	**7**	**0**	**0.0**	**9:22**	....	....	....	....	....	....	....	....	....
2004-05	AIK Solna	Sweden-3	16	11	5	16	24	....	....	....	....	....	....	....	....	....	....	....	....	....	....	....	....	....	....
2005-06	**Edmonton**	**NHL**	**72**	**2**	**10**	**12**	**73**	**0**	**0**	**0**	**50**	**4.0**	**–5**	**3**	**33.3**	**6:35**	**15**	**1**	**1**	**2**	***44**	**0**	**0**	**0**	**5:31**
2006-07	**Phoenix**	**NHL**	**56**	**5**	**17**	**22**	**52**	**1**	**0**	**0**	**34**	**14.7**	**7**	**14**	**28.6**	**10:17**	....	....	....	....	....	....	....	....	....
	Pittsburgh	**NHL**	**17**	**0**	**2**	**2**	**18**	**0**	**0**	**0**	**10**	**0.0**	**–3**	**3**	**33.3**	**7:34**	**2**	**0**	**0**	**0**	**0**	**0**	**0**	**0**	**4:25**
	NHL Totals		**563**	**48**	**87**	**135**	**896**	**4**	**0**	**5**	**439**	**10.9**		**20**	**30.0**	**8:39**	**38**	**3**	**6**	**9**	**64**	**0**	**0**	**0**	**7:55**

Signed as a free agent by **Solna** (Sweden-3), January 31, 2005. Signed as a free agent by **Phoenix**, July 5, 2006. Traded to **Pittsburgh** by **Phoenix** for Daniel Carcillo and Pittsburgh's 3rd round choice in 2008 Entry Draft, February 27, 2007.

LARMAN, Drew
(LAHR-man, DROO) **FLA.**

Center. Shoots right. 6'3", 195 lbs. Born, Canton, MI, May 15, 1985.

Season	Club	League	GP	G	A	Pts	PIM	PP	SH	GW	S	%	+/-	TF	F%	Min	GP	G	A	Pts	PIM	PP	SH	GW	Min
2002-03	Sarnia Sting	OHL	67	4	14	18	25	....	....	....	....	....	....	....	....	....	....	....	....	....	....	....	....	....	....
2003-04	Sarnia Sting	OHL	68	9	18	27	13	....	....	....	....	....	....	....	....	....	5	0	1	1	0	....	....	....	....
2004-05	Sarnia Sting	OHL	12	2	0	2	6	....	....	....	....	....	....	....	....	....	....	....	....	....	....	....	....	....	....
	London Knights	OHL	58	11	10	21	28	....	....	....	....	....	....	....	....	....	18	3	4	7	8	....	....	....	....
2005-06	Rochester	AHL	44	7	8	15	24	....	....	....	....	....	....	....	....	....	....	....	....	....	....	....	....	....	....
	Florida Everblades	ECHL	6	0	0	0	4	....	....	....	....	....	....	....	....	....	8	4	2	6	4	....	....	....	....
2006-07	**Florida**	**NHL**	**16**	**2**	**0**	**2**	**2**	**0**	**0**	**0**	**15**	**13.3**	**–3**	**97**	**46.4**	**7:23**	....	....	....	....	....	....	....	....	....
	Rochester	AHL	54	17	11	28	35	....	....	....	....	....	....	....	....	....	....	....	....	....	....	....	....	....	....
	NHL Totals		**16**	**2**	**0**	**2**	**2**	**0**	**0**	**0**	**15**	**13.3**		**97**	**46.4**	**7:23**	....	....	....	....	....	....	....	....	....

Signed as a free agent by **Florida**, September 28, 2005.

LaROSE, Chad
(lah-ROHZ, CHAD) **CAR.**

Right wing. Shoots right. 5'10", 181 lbs. Born, Fraser, MI, March 27, 1982.

Season	Club	League	GP	G	A	Pts	PIM	PP	SH	GW	S	%	+/-	TF	F%	Min	GP	G	A	Pts	PIM	PP	SH	GW	Min
99-2000	Sioux Falls	USHL	54	29	26	55	28	....	....	....	....	....	....	....	....	....	3	0	1	1	0	....	....	....	....
2000-01	Sioux Falls	USHL	24	11	22	33	50	....	....	....	....	....	....	....	....	....	....	....	....	....	....	....	....	....	....
	Plymouth Whalers	OHL	32	18	7	25	24	....	....	....	....	....	....	....	....	....	19	10	10	20	22	....	....	....	....
2001-02	Plymouth Whalers	OHL	53	32	27	59	40	....	....	....	....	....	....	....	....	....	6	3	4	7	16	....	....	....	....
2002-03	Plymouth Whalers	OHL	67	61	56	117	52	....	....	....	....	....	....	....	....	....	15	9	8	17	25	....	....	....	....
2003-04	Florida Everblades	ECHL	41	16	19	35	16	....	....	....	....	....	....	....	....	....	14	3	4	7	20	....	....	....	....
	Lowell	AHL	36	7	9	16	29	....	....	....	....	....	....	....	....	....	....	....	....	....	....	....	....	....	....
2004-05	Lowell	AHL	66	20	22	42	32	....	....	....	....	....	....	....	....	....	11	3	5	8	10	....	....	....	....
2005-06♦	**Carolina**	**NHL**	**49**	**1**	**12**	**13**	**35**	**0**	**0**	**1**	**62**	**1.6**	**7**	**5**	**40.0**	**10:35**	**21**	**0**	**1**	**1**	**10**	**0**	**0**	**0**	**8:58**
	Lowell	AHL	23	14	11	25	10	....	....	....	....	....	....	....	....	....	....	....	....	....	....	....	....	....	....
2006-07	**Carolina**	**NHL**	**80**	**6**	**12**	**18**	**10**	**0**	**2**	**0**	**94**	**6.4**	**–2**	**50**	**30.0**	**10:13**	....	....	....	....	....	....	....	....	....
	NHL Totals		**129**	**7**	**24**	**31**	**45**	**0**	**2**	**1**	**156**	**4.5**		**55**	**30.9**	**10:21**	**21**	**0**	**1**	**1**	**10**	**0**	**0**	**0**	**8:58**

OHL Second All-Star Team (2003)

Signed as a free agent by **Carolina**, August 6, 2003.

LAROSE, Cory
(lah-ROHZ, KOH-ree)

Center. Shoots left. 6', 191 lbs. Born, Campbellton, N.B., May 14, 1975.

Season	Club	League	GP	G	A	Pts	PIM	PP	SH	GW	S	%	+/-	TF	F%	Min	GP	G	A	Pts	PIM	PP	SH	GW	Min
1993-94	Kimball Union	High-NH	21	18	11	29	14	....	....	....	....	....	....	....	....	....	....	....	....	....	....	....	....	....	....
1994-95	Langley Thunder	BCJHL	STATISTICS NOT AVAILABLE																						
1995-96	Langley Thunder	BCJHL	54	28	46	74	61	....	....	....	....	....	....	....	....	....	....	....	....	....	....	....	....	....	....
1996-97	U. of Maine	H-East	35	10	27	37	32	....	....	....	....	....	....	....	....	....	....	....	....	....	....	....	....	....	....
1997-98	U. of Maine	H-East	34	15	25	40	22	....	....	....	....	....	....	....	....	....	....	....	....	....	....	....	....	....	....
1998-99	U. of Maine	H-East	38	21	31	52	34	....	....	....	....	....	....	....	....	....	....	....	....	....	....	....	....	....	....
99-2000	U. of Maine	H-East	39	15	*36	51	45	....	....	....	....	....	....	....	....	....	....	....	....	....	....	....	....	....	....
2000-01	Cleveland	IHL	4	1	1	2	6	....	....	....	....	....	....	....	....	....	....	....	....	....	....	....	....	....	....
	Jackson Bandits	ECHL	63	21	32	53	73	....	....	....	....	....	....	....	....	....	5	2	2	4	12	....	....	....	....
2001-02	Houston Aeros	AHL	78	32	32	64	73	....	....	....	....	....	....	....	....	....	14	6	8	14	15	....	....	....	....
2002-03	Houston Aeros	AHL	58	18	38	56	57	....	....	....	....	....	....	....	....	....	....	....	....	....	....	....	....	....	....
	Hartford	AHL	24	9	10	19	20	....	....	....	....	....	....	....	....	....	2	0	1	1	0	....	....	....	....
2003-04	**NY Rangers**	**NHL**	**7**	**0**	**1**	**1**	**4**	**0**	**0**	**0**	**10**	**0.0**	**–2**	**40**	**47.5**	**11:27**	....	....	....	....	....	....	....	....	....
	Hartford	AHL	69	13	36	49	66	....	....	....	....	....	....	....	....	....	14	4	6	10	24	....	....	....	....
2004-05	Chicago Wolves	AHL	80	26	37	63	44	....	....	....	....	....	....	....	....	....	18	6	6	12	29	....	....	....	....
2005-06	Langnau	Swiss	42	17	14	31	76	....	....	....	....	....	....	....	....	....	6	4	3	7	6	....	....	....	....
2006-07	Chicago Wolves	AHL	63	22	61	83	75	....	....	....	....	....	....	....	....	....	15	3	4	7	21	....	....	....	....
	NHL Totals		**7**	**0**	**1**	**1**	**4**	**0**	**0**	**0**	**10**	**0.0**		**40**	**47.5**	**11:27**	....	....	....	....	....	....	....	....	....

Hockey East First All-Star Team (2000) • NCAA East Second All-American Team (2000) • AHL All-Rookie Team (2002)

Signed as a free agent by **Minnesota**, May 10, 2000. Traded to **NY Rangers** by **Minnesota** for Jay Henderson, February 20, 2003. Signed as a free agent by **Atlanta**, July 14, 2004. Signed as a free agent by **Langnau** (Swiss), May 5, 2005. Signed as a free agent by **Atlanta**, June 21, 2006.

LARSEN, Brad
(LAR-suhn, BRAD) **ATL.**

Left wing. Shoots left. 6', 210 lbs. Born, Nakusp, B.C., June 28, 1977. Colorado's 5th choice, 87th overall, in 1997 Entry Draft.

Season	Club	League	GP	G	A	Pts	PIM	PP	SH	GW	S	%	+/-	TF	F%	Min	GP	G	A	Pts	PIM	PP	SH	GW	Min
1992-93	Nelson	RMJHL	42	31	37	68	164	....	....	....	....	....	....	....	....	....	....	....	....	....	....	....	....	....	....
1993-94	Swift Current	WHL	64	15	18	33	32	....	....	....	....	....	....	....	....	....	7	1	2	3	4	....	....	....	....
1994-95	Swift Current	WHL	62	24	33	57	73	....	....	....	....	....	....	....	....	....	6	0	1	1	2	....	....	....	....
1995-96	Swift Current	WHL	51	30	47	77	67	....	....	....	....	....	....	....	....	....	6	3	2	5	13	....	....	....	....
1996-97	Swift Current	WHL	61	36	46	82	61	....	....	....	....	....	....	....	....	....	....	....	....	....	....	....	....	....	....
1997-98	**Colorado**	**NHL**	**1**	**0**	**0**	**0**	**0**	**0**	**0**	**0**	**0**	**0.0**	**0**	....	....	....	....	....	....	....	....	....	....	....	....
	Hershey Bears	AHL	65	12	10	22	80	....	....	....	....	....	....	....	....	....	7	3	2	5	2	....	....	....	....
1998-99	Hershey Bears	AHL	18	3	4	7	11	....	....	....	....	....	....	....	....	....	5	0	1	1	6	....	....	....	....
99-2000	Hershey Bears	AHL	52	13	26	39	66	....	....	....	....	....	....	....	....	....	14	5	2	7	29	....	....	....	....
2000-01	**Colorado**	**NHL**	**9**	**0**	**0**	**0**	**0**	**0**	**0**	**0**	**3**	**0.0**	**1**	**14**	**57.1**	**9:17**	....	....	....	....	....	....	....	....	....
	Hershey Bears	AHL	67	21	25	46	93	....	....	....	....	....	....	....	....	....	10	1	3	4	6	....	....	....	....
2001-02	**Colorado**	**NHL**	**50**	**2**	**7**	**9**	**47**	**1**	**0**	**0**	**38**	**5.3**	**4**	**71**	**54.9**	**8:07**	**21**	**1**	**1**	**2**	**13**	**0**	**0**	**0**	**7:07**
2002-03	**Colorado**	**NHL**	**6**	**0**	**3**	**3**	**2**	**0**	**0**	**0**	**6**	**0.0**	**3**	**31**	**41.9**	**8:17**	....	....	....	....	....	....	....	....	....
	Hershey Bears	AHL	25	3	6	9	25	....	....	....	....	....	....	....	....	....	4	1	1	2	8	....	....	....	....

			Regular Season														Playoffs								
Season	Club	League	GP	G	A	Pts	PIM	PP	SH	GW	S	%	+/-	TF	F%	Min	GP	G	A	Pts	PIM	PP	SH	GW	Min
2003-04	**Colorado**	**NHL**	**26**	**2**	**2**	**4**	**11**	**0**	**0**	**0**	**17**	**11.8**	**2**	**9**	**44.4**	**7:41**	....	....	....	....	....	....	....	....	....
	Hershey Bears	AHL	21	4	13	17	40	....	....	....	....	....	....	....	....	....	....	....	....	....	....	....	....	....	....
	Atlanta	**NHL**	**6**	**0**	**0**	**0**	**2**	**0**	**0**	**0**	**6**	**0.0**	**–2**	**6**	**66.7**	**13:39**	....	....	....	....	....	....	....	....	....
2004-05	Chicago Wolves	AHL	75	26	23	49	112	....	....	....	....	....	....	....	....	....	18	4	7	11	22	....	....	....	....
2005-06	**Atlanta**	**NHL**	**62**	**7**	**8**	**15**	**21**	**0**	**3**	**1**	**48**	**14.6**	**–3**	**81**	**34.6**	**10:59**	....	....	....	....	....	....	....	....	....
	Chicago Wolves	AHL	6	1	0	1	8	....	....	....	....	....	....	....	....	....	....	....	....	....	....	....	....	....	....
2006-07	**Atlanta**	**NHL**	**72**	**7**	**6**	**13**	**39**	**0**	**2**	**0**	**61**	**11.5**	**–11**	**82**	**39.0**	**12:22**	**4**	**0**	**2**	**2**	**0**	**0**	**0**	**0**	**16:57**
	NHL Totals		**232**	**18**	**26**	**44**	**122**	**1**	**5**	**1**	**179**	**10.1**		**294**	**43.5**	**10:21**	**25**	**1**	**3**	**4**	**13**	**0**	**0**	**0**	**8:41**

• Re-entered NHL Entry Draft. Originally Ottawa's 3rd choice, 53rd overall, in 1995 Entry Draft.

WHL East Second All-Star Team (1997)

Rights traded to **Colorado** by **Ottawa** for Janne Laukkanen, January 26, 1996. • Missed majority of 1998-99 season recovering from abdominal injury suffered in game vs. Albany (AHL), November 20, 1998. • Missed majority of 2002-03 season recovering from groin (October 27, 2002 vs. Minnesota) and back (December 11, 2002 vs. Vancouver) injuries. Claimed on waivers by **Atlanta** from **Colorado**, February 25, 2004.

LASHOFF, Matt (LASH-awf, MAT) BOS.

Defense. Shoots left. 6'2", 204 lbs. Born, East Greenbush, NY, September 29, 1986. Boston's 1st choice, 22nd overall, in 2005 Entry Draft.

Season	Club	League	GP	G	A	Pts	PIM	PP	SH	GW	S	%	+/-	TF	F%	Min	GP	G	A	Pts	PIM	PP	SH	GW	Min
2002-03	USNTDP	U-17	16	1	3	4	14	....	....	....	....	....	....	....	....	....	....	....	....	....	....	....	....	....	....
	USNTDP	NAHL	46	2	5	7	53	....	....	....	....	....	....	....	....	....	....	....	....	....	....	....	....	....	....
2003-04	Kitchener Rangers	OHL	62	5	19	24	94	....	....	....	....	....	....	....	....	....	5	0	1	1	0	....	....	....	....
2004-05	Kitchener Rangers	OHL	44	4	18	22	44	....	....	....	....	....	....	....	....	....	13	0	3	3	18	....	....	....	....
2005-06	Kitchener Rangers	OHL	56	7	40	47	146	....	....	....	....	....	....	....	....	....	5	1	1	2	12	....	....	....	....
	Providence Bruins	AHL	7	1	1	2	6	....	....	....	....	....	....	....	....	....	6	0	0	0	6	....	....	....	....
2006-07	**Boston**	**NHL**	**12**	**0**	**2**	**2**	**12**	**0**	**0**	**0**	**8**	**0.0**	**–6**	**0**	**0.0**	**14:55**	....	....	....	....	....	....	....	....	....
	Providence Bruins	AHL	64	11	26	37	60	....	....	....	....	....	....	....	....	....	....	....	....	....	....	....	....	....	....
	NHL Totals		**12**	**0**	**2**	**2**	**12**	**0**	**0**	**0**	**8**	**0.0**		**0**	**0.0**	**14:55**	....	....	....	....	....	....	....	....	....

AHL All-Rookie Team (2007)

LATENDRESSE, Guillaume (lah-TEHN-drehs, GEE-OHM) MTL.

Right wing. Shoots left. 6'2", 229 lbs. Born, Ste-Catherine, Que., May 24, 1987. Montreal's 2nd choice, 45th overall, in 2005 Entry Draft.

Season	Club	League	GP	G	A	Pts	PIM	PP	SH	GW	S	%	+/-	TF	F%	Min	GP	G	A	Pts	PIM	PP	SH	GW	Min
2003-04	Drummondville	QMJHL	53	24	25	49	66	....	....	....	....	....	....	....	....	....	....	....	....	....	....	....	....	....	....
2004-05	Drummondville	QMJHL	65	29	49	78	76	....	....	....	....	....	....	....	....	....	6	6	4	10	7	....	....	....	....
2005-06	Drummondville	QMJHL	51	43	40	83	105	....	....	....	....	....	....	....	....	....	5	3	2	5	8	....	....	....	....
2006-07	**Montreal**	**NHL**	**80**	**16**	**13**	**29**	**47**	**5**	**0**	**3**	**121**	**13.2**	**–20**	**16**	**12.5**	**12:36**	....	....	....	....	....	....	....	....	....
	NHL Totals		**80**	**16**	**13**	**29**	**47**	**5**	**0**	**3**	**121**	**13.2**		**16**	**12.5**	**12:36**	....	....	....	....	....	....	....	....	....

QMJHL All-Rookie Team (2004)

LAW, Kirby (LAW, KUHR-bee)

Right wing. Shoots right. 6'1", 185 lbs. Born, McCreary, Man., March 11, 1977.

Season	Club	League	GP	G	A	Pts	PIM	PP	SH	GW	S	%	+/-	TF	F%	Min	GP	G	A	Pts	PIM	PP	SH	GW	Min
1991-92	McCreary	MAHA	60	89	103	192	60	....	....	....	....	....	....	....	....	....	....	....	....	....	....	....	....	....	....
1992-93	Dauphin Kings	MJHL	48	20	15	35	8	....	....	....	....	....	....	....	....	....	....	....	....	....	....	....	....	....	....
1993-94	Saskatoon Blades	WHL	66	9	11	20	39	....	....	....	....	....	....	....	....	....	16	0	0	0	6	....	....	....	....
1994-95	Saskatoon Blades	WHL	46	10	15	25	44	....	....	....	....	....	....	....	....	....	....	....	....	....	....	....	....	....	....
	Lethbridge	WHL	24	4	10	14	38	....	....	....	....	....	....	....	....	....	....	....	....	....	....	....	....	....	....
1995-96	Lethbridge	WHL	71	17	45	62	133	....	....	....	....	....	....	....	....	....	4	0	0	0	12	....	....	....	....
1996-97	Lethbridge	WHL	72	39	52	91	200	....	....	....	....	....	....	....	....	....	19	4	14	18	60	....	....	....	....
1997-98	Brandon	WHL	49	34	44	78	153	....	....	....	....	....	....	....	....	....	9	3	3	6	41	....	....	....	....
1998-99	Orlando	IHL	67	18	13	31	136	....	....	....	....	....	....	....	....	....	....	....	....	....	....	....	....	....	....
	Adirondack	AHL	11	2	3	5	40	....	....	....	....	....	....	....	....	....	3	1	0	1	2	....	....	....	....
99-2000	Louisville Panthers	AHL	66	31	21	52	173	....	....	....	....	....	....	....	....	....	....	....	....	....	....	....	....	....	....
	Orlando	IHL	1	1	0	1	0	....	....	....	....	....	....	....	....	....	....	....	....	....	....	....	....	....	....
	Philadelphia	AHL	12	1	4	5	6	....	....	....	....	....	....	....	....	....	5	2	0	2	2	....	....	....	....
2000-01	**Philadelphia**	**NHL**	**1**	**0**	**0**	**0**	**0**	**0**	**0**	**0**	**0**	**0.0**	**–1**	**0**	**0.0**	**3:23**	....	....	....	....	....	....	....	....	....
	Philadelphia	AHL	78	27	34	61	150	....	....	....	....	....	....	....	....	....	10	1	6	7	16	....	....	....	....
2001-02	Philadelphia	AHL	71	18	24	42	102	....	....	....	....	....	....	....	....	....	5	0	0	0	0	....	....	....	....
2002-03	**Philadelphia**	**NHL**	**2**	**0**	**0**	**0**	**2**	**0**	**0**	**0**	**0**	**0.0**	**0**	**0**	**0.0**	**1:41**	....	....	....	....	....	....	....	....	....
	Philadelphia	AHL	74	22	19	41	166	....	....	....	....	....	....	....	....	....	....	....	....	....	....	....	....	....	....
2003-04	**Philadelphia**	**NHL**	**6**	**0**	**1**	**1**	**2**	**0**	**0**	**0**	**1**	**0.0**	**0**	**0**	**0.0**	**8:10**	....	....	....	....	....	....	....	....	....
	Philadelphia	AHL	74	32	41	73	139	....	....	....	....	....	....	....	....	....	12	0	5	5	12	....	....	....	....
2004-05	Houston Aeros	AHL	80	25	24	49	134	....	....	....	....	....	....	....	....	....	5	0	1	1	4	....	....	....	....
2005-06	Houston Aeros	AHL	80	43	*67	*110	95	....	....	....	....	....	....	....	....	....	8	4	5	9	4	....	....	....	....
2006-07	Geneve	Swiss	44	17	32	49	40	....	....	....	....	....	....	....	....	....	5	1	3	4	0	....	....	....	....
	NHL Totals		**9**	**0**	**1**	**1**	**4**	**0**	**0**	**0**	**1**	**0.0**		**0**	**0.0**	**6:11**	....	....	....	....	....	....	....	....	....

AHL First All-Star Team (2006)

Signed as a free agent by **Atlanta**, July 27, 1999. Traded to **Philadelphia** by **Atlanta** for Vancouver's 6th round choice (previously acquired, Atlanta selected Jeff Dwyer) in 2000 Entry Draft and Philadelphia's 6th round choice (Pasi Nurminen) in 2001 Entry Draft, March 14, 2000. Signed as a free agent by **Minnesota**, July 6, 2004. Signed as a free agent by **Geneve** (Swiss), May 11, 2006.

LEACH, Jay T.B.

Defense. Shoots left. 6'4", 220 lbs. Born, Syracuse, NY, September 2, 1979. Phoenix's 5th choice, 115th overall, in 1998 Entry Draft.

Season	Club	League	GP	G	A	Pts	PIM	PP	SH	GW	S	%	+/-	TF	F%	Min	GP	G	A	Pts	PIM	PP	SH	GW	Min
1994-95	John Marshall	High-MN	10	0	0	0	14	....	....	....	....	....	....	....	....	....	....	....	....	....	....	....	....	....	....
1995-96	John Marshall	High-MN	11	1	2	3	8	....	....	....	....	....	....	....	....	....	4	0	0	0	0	....	....	....	....
	Capital District	Exhib.	53	3	8	11	33	....	....	....	....	....	....	....	....	....	....	....	....	....	....	....	....	....	....
1996-97	Capital District	Exhib.	57	8	50	58	140	....	....	....	....	....	....	....	....	....	....	....	....	....	....	....	....	....	....
1997-98	Providence	H-East	32	0	8	8	29	....	....	....	....	....	....	....	....	....	....	....	....	....	....	....	....	....	....
1998-99	Providence	H-East	33	1	8	9	42	....	....	....	....	....	....	....	....	....	....	....	....	....	....	....	....	....	....
99-2000	Providence	H-East	37	1	9	10	101	....	....	....	....	....	....	....	....	....	....	....	....	....	....	....	....	....	....
2000-01	Providence	H-East	40	4	21	25	104	....	....	....	....	....	....	....	....	....	....	....	....	....	....	....	....	....	....
2001-02	Mississippi	ECHL	70	3	13	16	116	....	....	....	....	....	....	....	....	....	10	1	1	2	8	....	....	....	....
2002-03	Springfield	AHL	9	0	0	0	0	....	....	....	....	....	....	....	....	....	....	....	....	....	....	....	....	....	....
	Augusta Lynx	ECHL	65	8	11	19	162	....	....	....	....	....	....	....	....	....	....	....	....	....	....	....	....	....	....
2003-04	Providence Bruins	AHL	3	0	0	0	4	....	....	....	....	....	....	....	....	....	....	....	....	....	....	....	....	....	....
	Long Beach	ECHL	3	0	1	1	4	....	....	....	....	....	....	....	....	....	....	....	....	....	....	....	....	....	....
	Bridgeport	AHL	23	0	1	1	33	....	....	....	....	....	....	....	....	....	7	0	1	1	10	....	....	....	....
	Trenton Titans	ECHL	31	2	11	13	45	....	....	....	....	....	....	....	....	....	....	....	....	....	....	....	....	....	....
2004-05	Providence Bruins	AHL	62	4	5	9	92	....	....	....	....	....	....	....	....	....	17	0	0	0	28	....	....	....	....
	Trenton Titans	ECHL	11	0	2	2	17	....	....	....	....	....	....	....	....	....	....	....	....	....	....	....	....	....	....
2005-06	**Boston**	**NHL**	**2**	**0**	**0**	**0**	**7**	**0**	**0**	**0**	**0**	**0.0**	**1**	**0**	**0.0**	**6:20**	....	....	....	....	....	....	....	....	....
	Providence Bruins	AHL	72	5	11	16	100	....	....	....	....	....	....	....	....	....	6	0	1	1	15	....	....	....	....
2006-07	Providence Bruins	AHL	73	2	5	7	128	....	....	....	....	....	....	....	....	....	13	0	4	4	13	....	....	....	....
	NHL Totals		**2**	**0**	**0**	**0**	**7**	**0**	**0**	**0**	**0**	**0.0**		**0**	**0.0**	**6:20**	....	....	....	....	....	....	....	....	....

Signed as a free agent by **Boston**, September 26, 2003. Signed as a free agent by **Tampa Bay**, July 3, 2007.

LEAHY, Patrick (LEH-hey, PAT-rihk)

Right wing. Shoots right. 6'3", 200 lbs. Born, Brighton, MA, June 9, 1979. NY Rangers' 5th choice, 122nd overall, in 1998 Entry Draft.

Season	Club	League	GP	G	A	Pts	PIM	PP	SH	GW	S	%	+/-	TF	F%	Min	GP	G	A	Pts	PIM	PP	SH	GW	Min
1996-97	Bos. College High	High-MA	25	24	24	48	....	....	....	....	....	....	....	....	....	....	....	....	....	....	....	....	....	....	....
1997-98	Miami U.	CCHA	28	0	1	1	24	....	....	....	....	....	....	....	....	....	....	....	....	....	....	....	....	....	....
1998-99	Miami U.	CCHA	34	10	20	30	40	....	....	....	....	....	....	....	....	....	....	....	....	....	....	....	....	....	....
99-2000	Miami U.	CCHA	36	16	22	38	89	....	....	....	....	....	....	....	....	....	....	....	....	....	....	....	....	....	....
2000-01	Miami U.	CCHA	37	13	19	32	14	....	....	....	....	....	....	....	....	....	....	....	....	....	....	....	....	....	....
2001-02	Trenton Titans	ECHL	41	20	21	41	64	....	....	....	....	....	....	....	....	....	....	....	....	....	....	....	....	....	....
	Hershey Bears	AHL	9	1	2	3	8	....	....	....	....	....	....	....	....	....	....	....	....	....	....	....	....	....	....
	Portland Pirates	AHL	9	1	1	2	8	....	....	....	....	....	....	....	....	....	....	....	....	....	....	....	....	....	....
	Bridgeport	AHL	14	2	2	4	2	....	....	....	....	....	....	....	....	....	20	3	4	7	4	....	....	....	....
2002-03	Providence Bruins	AHL	66	20	23	43	63	....	....	....	....	....	....	....	....	....	4	1	0	1	18	....	....	....	....

			Regular Season														Playoffs								
Season	Club	League	GP	G	A	Pts	PIM	PP	SH	GW	S	%	+/-	TF	F%	Min	GP	G	A	Pts	PIM	PP	SH	GW	Min
2003-04	**Boston**	**NHL**	**6**	**0**	**0**	**0**	**0**	**0**	**0**	**0**	**2**	**0.0**	**1**	**0**	**0.0**	**5:27**	....	....	....	....	....	....	....	....	....
	Providence Bruins	AHL	55	14	16	30	37	....	....	....	....	....	....	....	....	....	2	0	0	0	0	....	....	....	....
2004-05	Providence Bruins	AHL	38	1	14	15	18	....	....	....	....	....	....	....	....	....	17	4	6	10	20	....	....	....	....
2005-06	**Boston**	**NHL**	**43**	**4**	**4**	**8**	**19**	**0**	**0**	**0**	**46**	**8.7**	**–2**	**12**	**58.3**	**9:06**	....	....	....	....	....	....	....	....	....
	Providence Bruins	AHL	4	1	2	3	4	....	....	....	....	....	....	....	....	....	....	....	....	....	....	....	....	....	....
2006-07	**Nashville**	**NHL**	**1**	**0**	**0**	**0**	**0**	**0**	**0**	**0**	**0**	**0.0**	**0**	**0**	**0.0**	**5:46**	....	....	....	....	....	....	....	....	....
	Milwaukee	AHL	52	10	21	31	30	....	....	....	....	....	....	....	....	....	3	1	1	2	2	....	....	....	....
	NHL Totals		**50**	**4**	**4**	**8**	**19**	**0**	**0**	**0**	**48**	**8.3**		**12**	**58.3**	**8:35**	....	....	....	....	....	....	....	....	....

Signed as a free agent by **Boston**, July 28, 2003. Signed as a free agent by **Nashville**, July 17, 2006.

LEBDA, Brett

(LEHB-dah, BREHT) **DET.**

Defense. Shoots left. 5'9", 194 lbs. Born, Buffalo Grove, IL, January 15, 1982.

Season	Club	League	GP	G	A	Pts	PIM	PP	SH	GW	S	%	+/-	TF	F%	Min	GP	G	A	Pts	PIM	PP	SH	GW	Min
1998-99	USNTDP	U-17	11	1	7	8	4	....	....	....	....	....	....	....	....	....	....	....	....	....	....	....	....	....	....
	USNTDP	USHL	3	0	0	0	0	....	....	....	....	....	....	....	....	....	....	....	....	....	....	....	....	....	....
	USNTDP	NAHL	52	11	17	28	56	....	....	....	....	....	....	....	....	....	....	....	....	....	....	....	....	....	....
99-2000	USNTDP	U-18	4	0	0	0	6	....	....	....	....	....	....	....	....	....	....	....	....	....	....	....	....	....	....
	USNTDP	USHL	22	6	7	13	28	....	....	....	....	....	....	....	....	....	....	....	....	....	....	....	....	....	....
2000-01	U. of Notre Dame	CCHA	39	7	19	26	109	....	....	....	....	....	....	....	....	....	....	....	....	....	....	....	....	....	....
2001-02	U. of Notre Dame	CCHA	34	6	8	14	54	....	....	....	....	....	....	....	....	....	....	....	....	....	....	....	....	....	....
2002-03	U. of Notre Dame	CCHA	40	7	14	21	48	....	....	....	....	....	....	....	....	....	....	....	....	....	....	....	....	....	....
2003-04	U. of Notre Dame	CCHA	39	6	18	24	42	....	....	....	....	....	....	....	....	....	....	....	....	....	....	....	....	....	....
	Grand Rapids	AHL	6	0	1	1	0	....	....	....	....	....	....	....	....	....	4	0	0	0	2	....	....	....	....
2004-05	Grand Rapids	AHL	80	2	10	12	34	....	....	....	....	....	....	....	....	....	....	....	....	....	....	....	....	....	....
2005-06	**Detroit**	**NHL**	**46**	**3**	**9**	**12**	**20**	**1**	**0**	**1**	**50**	**6.0**	**9**	**2**	**0.0**	**12:38**	**6**	**0**	**0**	**0**	**4**	**0**	**0**	**0**	**13:09**
	Grand Rapids	AHL	25	4	14	18	42	....	....	....	....	....	....	....	....	....	11	1	4	5	8	....	....	....	....
2006-07	**Detroit**	**NHL**	**74**	**5**	**13**	**18**	**61**	**1**	**0**	**2**	**107**	**4.7**	**16**	**0**	**0.0**	**14:54**	**12**	**0**	**2**	**2**	**8**	**0**	**0**	**0**	**16:23**
	NHL Totals		**120**	**8**	**22**	**30**	**81**	**2**	**0**	**3**	**157**	**5.1**		**2**	**0.0**	**14:02**	**18**	**0**	**2**	**2**	**12**	**0**	**0**	**0**	**15:18**

CCHA All-Rookie Team (2001) • CCHA Second All-Star Team (2004)

Signed as a free agent by **Detroit**, April 1, 2004.

LECAVALIER, Vincent

(luh-KAV-uhl-YAY, VIHN-sihnt) **T.B.**

Center. Shoots left. 6'4", 223 lbs. Born, Ile Bizard, Que., April 21, 1980. Tampa Bay's 1st choice, 1st overall, in 1998 Entry Draft.

Season	Club	League	GP	G	A	Pts	PIM	PP	SH	GW	S	%	+/-	TF	F%	Min	GP	G	A	Pts	PIM	PP	SH	GW	Min
1995-96	Notre Dame	SMHL	22	52	52	104		....	....	....	....	....	....	....	....	....	....	....	....	....	....	....	....	....	....
1996-97	Rimouski Oceanic	QMJHL	64	42	61	103	38	....	....	....	....	....	....	....	....	....	4	4	3	7	2	....	....	....	....
1997-98	Rimouski Oceanic	QMJHL	58	44	71	115	117	....	....	....	....	....	....	....	....	....	18	*15	*26	*41	46	....	....	....	....
1998-99	**Tampa Bay**	**NHL**	**82**	**13**	**15**	**28**	**23**	**2**	**0**	**2**	**125**	**10.4**	**–19**	**953**	**40.3**	**13:40**	....	....	....	....	....	....	....	....	....
99-2000	**Tampa Bay**	**NHL**	**80**	**25**	**42**	**67**	**43**	**6**	**0**	**3**	**166**	**15.1**	**–25**	**1288**	**44.4**	**19:18**	....	....	....	....	....	....	....	....	....
2000-01	**Tampa Bay**	**NHL**	**68**	**23**	**28**	**51**	**66**	**7**	**0**	**3**	**165**	**13.9**	**–26**	**1278**	**44.9**	**19:57**	....	....	....	....	....	....	....	....	....
2001-02	**Tampa Bay**	**NHL**	**76**	**20**	**17**	**37**	**61**	**5**	**0**	**3**	**164**	**12.2**	**–18**	**931**	**41.5**	**17:09**	....	....	....	....	....	....	....	....	....
2002-03	**Tampa Bay**	**NHL**	**80**	**33**	**45**	**78**	**39**	**11**	**2**	**3**	**274**	**12.0**	**0**	**1200**	**43.9**	**19:33**	**11**	**3**	**3**	**6**	**22**	**1**	**0**	**1**	**22:36**
2003-04♦	**Tampa Bay**	**NHL**	**81**	**32**	**34**	**66**	**52**	**5**	**2**	**6**	**242**	**13.2**	**23**	**1119**	**41.4**	**18:04**	**23**	**9**	**7**	**16**	**25**	**2**	**0**	**0**	**19:39**
2004-05	Ak Bars Kazan	Russia	30	7	9	16	78	....	....	....	....	....	....	....	....	....	4	1	0	1	6	....	....	....	....
2005-06	**Tampa Bay**	**NHL**	**80**	**35**	**40**	**75**	**90**	**13**	**2**	**7**	**309**	**11.3**	**0**	**1366**	**51.2**	**20:08**	**5**	**1**	**3**	**4**	**7**	**1**	**0**	**0**	**22:17**
	Canada	Olympics	6	0	3	3	16	....	....	....	....	....	....	....	....	....	....	....	....	....	....	....	....	....	....
2006-07	**Tampa Bay**	**NHL**	**82**	***52**	**56**	**108**	**44**	**16**	**5**	**7**	**339**	**15.3**	**2**	**1653**	**46.6**	**22:36**	**6**	**5**	**2**	**7**	**10**	**1**	**0**	**1**	**26:29**
	NHL Totals		**629**	**233**	**277**	**510**	**418**	**65**	**11**	**34**	**1784**	**13.1**		**9788**	**44.7**	**18:47**	**45**	**18**	**15**	**33**	**64**	**5**	**0**	**2**	**21:34**

QMJHL All-Rookie Team (1997) • QMJHL Offensive Rookie of the Year (1997) • Canadian Major Junior Rookie of the Year (1997) • QMJHL First All-Star Team (1998) • Canadian Major Junior First All-Star Team (1998) • NHL Second All-Star Team (2007) • Maurice "Rocket" Richard Trophy (2007)

Played in NHL All-Star Game (2003, 2007)

Signed as a free agent by **Kazan** (Russia), November 4, 2004.

LeCLAIR, John

(luh-KLAIR, JAWN)

Left wing. Shoots left. 6'3", 226 lbs. Born, St. Albans, VT, July 5, 1969. Montreal's 2nd choice, 33rd overall, in 1987 Entry Draft.

Season	Club	League	GP	G	A	Pts	PIM	PP	SH	GW	S	%	+/-	TF	F%	Min	GP	G	A	Pts	PIM	PP	SH	GW	Min
1985-86	Bellows	High-VT	22	41	28	69	14	....	....	....	....	....	....	....	....	....	....	....	....	....	....	....	....	....	....
1986-87	Bellows	High-VT	23	44	40	84	14	....	....	....	....	....	....	....	....	....	....	....	....	....	....	....	....	....	....
1987-88	U. of Vermont	ECAC	31	12	22	34	62	....	....	....	....	....	....	....	....	....	....	....	....	....	....	....	....	....	....
1988-89	U. of Vermont	ECAC	18	9	12	21	40	....	....	....	....	....	....	....	....	....	....	....	....	....	....	....	....	....	....
1989-90	U. of Vermont	ECAC	10	10	6	16	38	....	....	....	....	....	....	....	....	....	....	....	....	....	....	....	....	....	....
1990-91	U. of Vermont	ECAC	33	25	20	45	58	....	....	....	....	....	....	....	....	....	....	....	....	....	....	....	....	....	....
	Montreal	**NHL**	**10**	**2**	**5**	**7**	**2**	**0**	**0**	**1**	**12**	**16.7**	**1**	....	....	....	**3**	**0**	**0**	**0**	**0**	**0**	**0**	**0**	....
1991-92	**Montreal**	**NHL**	**59**	**8**	**11**	**19**	**14**	**3**	**0**	**0**	**73**	**11.0**	**5**	....	....	....	**8**	**1**	**1**	**2**	**4**	**0**	**0**	**0**	....
	Fredericton	AHL	8	7	7	14	10	....	....	....	....	....	....	....	....	....	2	0	0	0	4	....	....	....	....
1992-93♦	**Montreal**	**NHL**	**72**	**19**	**25**	**44**	**33**	**2**	**0**	**2**	**139**	**13.7**	**11**	....	....	....	**20**	**4**	**6**	**10**	**14**	**0**	**0**	**3**	....
1993-94	**Montreal**	**NHL**	**74**	**19**	**24**	**43**	**32**	**1**	**0**	**1**	**153**	**12.4**	**17**	....	....	....	**7**	**2**	**1**	**3**	**8**	**1**	**0**	**0**	....
1994-95	**Montreal**	**NHL**	**9**	**1**	**4**	**5**	**10**	**1**	**0**	**0**	**18**	**5.6**	**–1**	....	....	....	....	....	....	....	....	....	....	....	....
	Philadelphia	**NHL**	**37**	**25**	**24**	**49**	**20**	**5**	**0**	**7**	**113**	**22.1**	**21**	....	....	....	**15**	**5**	**7**	**12**	**4**	**1**	**0**	**1**	....
1995-96	**Philadelphia**	**NHL**	**82**	**51**	**46**	**97**	**64**	**19**	**0**	**10**	**270**	**18.9**	**21**	....	....	....	**11**	**6**	**5**	**11**	**6**	**4**	**0**	**1**	....
1996-97	**Philadelphia**	**NHL**	**82**	**50**	**47**	**97**	**58**	**10**	**0**	**5**	**324**	**15.4**	**44**	....	....	....	**19**	**9**	**12**	**21**	**10**	**4**	**0**	**3**	....
1997-98	**Philadelphia**	**NHL**	**82**	**51**	**36**	**87**	**32**	**16**	**0**	**9**	**303**	**16.8**	**30**	....	....	....	**5**	**1**	**1**	**2**	**8**	**1**	**0**	**1**	....
	United States	Olympics	4	0	1	1	0	....	....	....	....	....	....	....	....	....	....	....	....	....	....	....	....	....	....
1998-99	**Philadelphia**	**NHL**	**76**	**43**	**47**	**90**	**30**	**16**	**0**	**7**	**246**	**17.5**	**36**	**7**	**14.3**	**21:03**	**6**	**3**	**0**	**3**	**12**	**2**	**0**	**0**	**20:14**
99-2000	**Philadelphia**	**NHL**	**82**	**40**	**37**	**77**	**36**	**13**	**0**	**7**	**249**	**16.1**	**8**	**7**	**28.6**	**20:18**	**18**	**6**	**7**	**13**	**6**	**4**	**0**	**2**	**21:16**
2000-01	**Philadelphia**	**NHL**	**16**	**7**	**5**	**12**	**0**	**3**	**0**	**2**	**48**	**14.6**	**2**	**0**	**0.0**	**19:06**	**6**	**1**	**2**	**3**	**2**	**0**	**0**	**0**	**19:34**
2001-02	**Philadelphia**	**NHL**	**82**	**25**	**26**	**51**	**30**	**4**	**0**	**6**	**220**	**11.4**	**5**	**4**	**75.0**	**17:30**	**5**	**0**	**0**	**0**	**2**	**0**	**0**	**0**	**17:18**
	United States	Olympics	6	*6	1	7	2	....	....	....	....	....	....	....	....	....	....	....	....	....	....	....	....	....	....
2002-03	**Philadelphia**	**NHL**	**35**	**18**	**10**	**28**	**16**	**8**	**0**	**4**	**99**	**18.2**	**10**	**3**	**66.7**	**16:09**	**13**	**2**	**3**	**5**	**10**	**1**	**0**	**0**	**17:09**
2003-04	**Philadelphia**	**NHL**	**75**	**23**	**32**	**55**	**51**	**8**	**0**	**4**	**182**	**12.6**	**20**	**9**	**33.3**	**16:06**	**18**	**2**	**2**	**4**	**8**	**0**	**0**	**0**	**15:57**
2004-05		DID NOT PLAY																							
2005-06	**Pittsburgh**	**NHL**	**73**	**22**	**29**	**51**	**61**	**8**	**1**	**0**	**135**	**16.3**	**–24**	**13**	**46.2**	**15:45**	....	....	....	....	....	....	....	....	....
2006-07	**Pittsburgh**	**NHL**	**21**	**2**	**5**	**7**	**12**	**1**	**0**	**0**	**27**	**7.4**	**–2**	**0**	**0.0**	**11:51**	....	....	....	....	....	....	....	....	....
	NHL Totals		**967**	**406**	**413**	**819**	**501**	**118**	**1**	**65**	**2611**	**15.5**		**43**	**39.5**	**17:46**	**154**	**42**	**47**	**89**	**94**	**18**	**0**	**11**	**18:28**

ECAC Second All-Star Team (1991) • NHL First All-Star Team (1995, 1998) • NHL Second All-Star Team (1996, 1997, 1999) • Bud Ice Plus/Minus Award (1997) • Bud Light Plus/Minus Award (1999)

Played in NHL All-Star Game (1996, 1997, 1998, 1999, 2000)

• Missed majority of 1989-90 season recovering from knee surgery, January 20, 1990. Traded to **Philadelphia** by **Montreal** with Eric Desjardins and Gilbert Dionne for Mark Recchi and Philadelphia's 3rd round choice (Martin Hohenberger) in 1995 Entry Draft, February 9, 1995. • Missed majority of 2000-01 season recovering from back injury suffered in game vs. Boston, October 7, 2000. • Missed majority of 2002-03 season recovering from shoulder injury suffered in game vs. St. Louis, November 27, 2002. Signed as a free agent by **Pittsburgh**, August 15, 2005. • Released by Pittsburgh, December 14, 2006.

LEEB, Brad

(LEEB, BRAD)

Right wing. Shoots right. 5'11", 187 lbs. Born, Red Deer, Alta., August 27, 1979.

Season	Club	League	GP	G	A	Pts	PIM	PP	SH	GW	S	%	+/-	TF	F%	Min	GP	G	A	Pts	PIM	PP	SH	GW	Min
1994-95	Red Deer Vipers	AMHL	36	31	14	45	93	....	....	....	....	....	....	....	....	....	....	....	....	....	....	....	....	....	....
	Red Deer Rebels	WHL	3	0	0	0	4	....	....	....	....	....	....	....	....	....	....	....	....	....	....	....	....	....	....
1995-96	Red Deer Rebels	WHL	38	3	6	9	30	....	....	....	....	....	....	....	....	....	10	2	0	2	11	....	....	....	....
1996-97	Red Deer Rebels	WHL	70	15	20	35	76	....	....	....	....	....	....	....	....	....	16	3	3	6	6	....	....	....	....
1997-98	Red Deer Rebels	WHL	63	23	23	46	88	....	....	....	....	....	....	....	....	....	3	2	0	2	2	....	....	....	....
1998-99	Red Deer Rebels	WHL	64	32	47	79	84	....	....	....	....	....	....	....	....	....	9	5	9	14	10	....	....	....	....
99-2000	**Vancouver**	**NHL**	**2**	**0**	**0**	**0**	**2**	**0**	**0**	**0**	**3**	**0.0**	**–2**	**0**	**0.0**	**12:07**	....	....	....	....	....	....	....	....	....
	Syracuse Crunch	AHL	61	19	18	37	50	....	....	....	....	....	....	....	....	....	4	0	0	0	6	....	....	....	....
2000-01	Kansas City	IHL	53	18	16	34	53	....	....	....	....	....	....	....	....	....	....	....	....	....	....	....	....	....	....
2001-02	**Vancouver**	**NHL**	**2**	**0**	**0**	**0**	**0**	**0**	**0**	**0**	**1**	**0.0**	**1**	**0**	**0.0**	**9:35**	....	....	....	....	....	....	....	....	....
	Manitoba Moose	AHL	60	17	15	32	45	....	....	....	....	....	....	....	....	....	....	....	....	....	....	....	....	....	....
2002-03	St. John's	AHL	79	35	26	61	78	....	....	....	....	....	....	....	....	....	....	....	....	....	....	....	....	....	....
2003-04	**Toronto**	**NHL**	**1**	**0**	**0**	**0**	**0**	**0**	**0**	**0**	**1**	**0.0**	**–1**	**0**	**0.0**	**10:31**	....	....	....	....	....	....	....	....	....
	St. John's	AHL	77	24	25	49	116	....	....	....	....	....	....	....	....	....	....	....	....	....	....	....	....	....	....
2004-05	St. John's	AHL	48	16	13	29	43	....	....	....	....	....	....	....	....	....	3	2	1	3	0	....	....	....	....

Season	Club	League	GP	G	A	Pts	PIM	PP	SH	GW	S	%	+/-	TF	F%	Min	GP	G	A	Pts	PIM	PP	SH	GW	Min
		Regular Season															Playoffs								
2005-06	Toronto Marlies	AHL	79	34	24	58	91	....	....	....	....	....	....	....	....	....	5	3	0	3	6	....	....	....	....
2006-07	Toronto Marlies	AHL	34	9	6	15	25	....	....	....	....	....	....	....	....	....	....	....	....	....	....	....	....	....	....
	NHL Totals		5	0	0	0	2	0	0	0	5	0.0		0	0.0	10:47	....	....	....	....	....	....	....	....	....

WHL East Second All-Star Team (1999)

Signed as a free agent by **Vancouver**, October 8, 1999. Traded to **Toronto** by **Vancouver** for Tomas Mojzis, September 4, 2002. • Missed majority of 2006-07 season recovering from back and foot injuries.

LEFEBVRE, Guillaume

(luh-FAYV, GEE-OHM)

Left wing. Shoots left. 6'1", 202 lbs. Born, Amos, Que., May 7, 1981. Philadelphia's 6th choice, 227th overall, in 2000 Entry Draft.

Season	Club	League	GP	G	A	Pts	PIM	PP	SH	GW	S	%	+/-	TF	F%	Min	GP	G	A	Pts	PIM	PP	SH	GW	Min
1996-97	Amos Forestiers	QAAA	40	7	12	19	14	....	....	....	....	....	....	....	....	....	....	....	....	....	....	....	....	....	....
1997-98	Amos Forestiers	QAAA	42	12	16	28	100	....	....	....	....	....	....	....	....	....	6	4	5	9	....	....	....	....	....
1998-99	Shawinigan	QMJHL	40	3	1	4	49	....	....	....	....	....	....	....	....	....	....	....	....	....	....	....	....	....	....
	Cape Breton	QMJHL	24	2	7	9	13	....	....	....	....	....	....	....	....	....	5	0	1	1	0	....	....	....	....
99-2000	Cape Breton	QMJHL	44	26	28	54	82	....	....	....	....	....	....	....	....	....	....	....	....	....	....	....	....	....	....
	Quebec Remparts	QMJHL	2	3	1	4	0	....	....	....	....	....	....	....	....	....	....	....	....	....	....	....	....	....	....
	Rouyn-Noranda	QMJHL	25	4	11	15	39	....	....	....	....	....	....	....	....	....	11	4	0	4	25	....	....	....	....
2000-01	Rouyn-Noranda	QMJHL	61	24	43	67	160	....	....	....	....	....	....	....	....	....	9	3	1	4	22	....	....	....	....
	Philadelphia	AHL	....	....	....	....	....	....	....	....	....	....	....	....	....	....	9	0	1	1	2	....	....	....	....
2001-02	**Philadelphia**	**NHL**	**3**	**0**	**0**	**0**	**0**	**0**	**0**	**0**	**3**	**0.0**	**–1**	**0**	**0.0**	**5:55**	....	....	....	....	....	....	....	....	....
	Philadelphia	AHL	78	19	15	34	111	....	....	....	....	....	....	....	....	....	5	0	0	0	4	....	....	....	....
2002-03	**Philadelphia**	**NHL**	**14**	**0**	**0**	**0**	**4**	**0**	**0**	**0**	**5**	**0.0**	**1**	**0**	**0.0**	**7:27**	....	....	....	....	....	....	....	....	....
	Philadelphia	AHL	47	7	6	13	113	....	....	....	....	....	....	....	....	....	....	....	....	....	....	....	....	....	....
	Pittsburgh	**NHL**	**12**	**2**	**4**	**6**	**0**	**0**	**0**	**0**	**14**	**14.3**	**1**	**1**	**100.0**	**17:30**	....	....	....	....	....	....	....	....	....
	Wilkes-Barre	AHL	1	1	0	1	0	....	....	....	....	....	....	....	....	....	5	0	0	0	6	....	....	....	....
2003-04	Wilkes-Barre	AHL	64	4	12	16	78	....	....	....	....	....	....	....	....	....	14	1	0	1	19	....	....	....	....
2004-05	Wilkes-Barre	AHL	34	3	3	6	76	....	....	....	....	....	....	....	....	....	11	1	0	1	23	....	....	....	....
2005-06	**Pittsburgh**	**NHL**	**9**	**0**	**0**	**0**	**9**	**0**	**0**	**0**	**3**	**0.0**	**–3**	**1**	**0.0**	**12:21**	....	....	....	....	....	....	....	....	....
	Wilkes-Barre	AHL	66	16	19	35	113	....	....	....	....	....	....	....	....	....	8	0	2	2	14	....	....	....	....
2006-07	St. Jean Chiefs	QNAHL	48	20	33	53	135	....	....	....	....	....	....	....	....	....	....	....	....	....	....	....	....	....	....
	NHL Totals		**38**	**2**	**4**	**6**	**13**	**0**	**0**	**0**	**25**	**8.0**		**2**	**50.0**	**11:40**	....	....	....	....	....	....	....	....	....

Traded to **Phoenix** by **Philadelphia** with Atlanta's 3rd round choice (previously acquired, Phoenix selected Tyler Redenbach) in 2003 Entry Draft and Philadelphia's 2nd round choice (later traded to NY Rangers – NY Rangers selected Brandon Dubinsky) in 2004 Entry Draft for Tony Amonte, March 10, 2003. Traded to **Pittsburgh** by **Phoenix** with Ramzi Abid and Dan Focht for Jan Hrdina and Francois Leroux, March 11, 2003.

LEGWAND, David

(LEHG-wawnd, DAY-vihd) **NSH.**

Center. Shoots left. 6'2", 190 lbs. Born, Detroit, MI, August 17, 1980. Nashville's 1st choice, 2nd overall, in 1998 Entry Draft.

Season	Club	League	GP	G	A	Pts	PIM	PP	SH	GW	S	%	+/-	TF	F%	Min	GP	G	A	Pts	PIM	PP	SH	GW	Min
1996-97	Det. Compuware	MNHL	44	21	41	62	58	....	....	....	....	....	....	....	....	....	....	....	....	....	....	....	....	....	....
1997-98	Plymouth Whalers	OHL	59	54	51	105	56	....	....	....	....	....	....	....	....	....	15	8	12	20	24	....	....	....	....
1998-99	Plymouth Whalers	OHL	55	31	49	80	65	....	....	....	....	....	....	....	....	....	11	3	8	11	8	....	....	....	....
	Nashville	**NHL**	**1**	**0**	**0**	**0**	**0**	**0**	**0**	**0**	**2**	**0.0**	**0**	**9**	**55.6**	**12:50**	....	....	....	....	....	....	....	....	....
99-2000	**Nashville**	**NHL**	**71**	**13**	**15**	**28**	**30**	**4**	**0**	**2**	**111**	**11.7**	**–6**	**637**	**41.6**	**14:43**	....	....	....	....	....	....	....	....	....
2000-01	**Nashville**	**NHL**	**81**	**13**	**28**	**41**	**38**	**3**	**0**	**3**	**172**	**7.6**	**1**	**888**	**40.3**	**15:14**	....	....	....	....	....	....	....	....	....
2001-02	**Nashville**	**NHL**	**63**	**11**	**19**	**30**	**54**	**1**	**1**	**1**	**121**	**9.1**	**1**	**843**	**40.5**	**16:25**	....	....	....	....	....	....	....	....	....
2002-03	**Nashville**	**NHL**	**64**	**17**	**31**	**48**	**34**	**3**	**1**	**4**	**167**	**10.2**	**–2**	**1095**	**46.6**	**19:14**	....	....	....	....	....	....	....	....	....
2003-04	**Nashville**	**NHL**	**82**	**18**	**29**	**47**	**46**	**5**	**1**	**5**	**165**	**10.9**	**9**	**1109**	**45.1**	**17:17**	**6**	**1**	**0**	**1**	**8**	**0**	**1**	**0**	**15:41**
2004-05	EHC Basel	Swiss-2	3	6	2	8	2	....	....	....	....	....	....	....	....	....	19	16	23	39	20	....	....	....	....
2005-06	**Nashville**	**NHL**	**44**	**7**	**19**	**26**	**34**	**0**	**0**	**5**	**109**	**6.4**	**3**	**580**	**44.7**	**16:50**	**5**	**0**	**1**	**1**	**8**	**0**	**0**	**0**	**17:21**
	Milwaukee	AHL	3	0	0	0	0	....	....	....	....	....	....	....	....	....	....	....	....	....	....	....	....	....	....
2006-07	**Nashville**	**NHL**	**78**	**27**	**36**	**63**	**44**	**3**	**1**	**7**	**153**	**17.6**	**23**	**1108**	**45.3**	**18:22**	**5**	**0**	**3**	**3**	**2**	**0**	**0**	**0**	**22:23**
	NHL Totals		**484**	**106**	**177**	**283**	**280**	**19**	**4**	**27**	**1000**	**10.6**		**6269**	**43.7**	**16:50**	**16**	**1**	**4**	**5**	**18**	**0**	**1**	**0**	**18:18**

OHL All-Rookie Team (1998) • OHL First All-Star Team (1998) • OHL Rookie of the Year (1998) • OHL MVP (1998) • Canadian Major Junior Rookie of the Year (1998)

Signed as a free agent by **Basel** (Swiss-2), January 27, 2005.

LEHOUX, Yanick

(luh-HOO, YAH-nihk) **PHX.**

Center. Shoots right. 6'1", 200 lbs. Born, Montreal, Que., April 8, 1982. Los Angeles' 3rd choice, 86th overall, in 2000 Entry Draft.

Season	Club	League	GP	G	A	Pts	PIM	PP	SH	GW	S	%	+/-	TF	F%	Min	GP	G	A	Pts	PIM	PP	SH	GW	Min
1997-98	Cap-d-Madeleine	QAAA	42	29	50	79	26	....	....	....	....	....	....	....	....	....	....	....	....	....	....	....	....	....	....
1998-99	Baie-Comeau	QMJHL	63	10	20	30	31	....	....	....	....	....	....	....	....	....	....	....	....	....	....	....	....	....	....
99-2000	Baie-Comeau	QMJHL	67	31	61	92	14	....	....	....	....	....	....	....	....	....	6	1	2	3	2	....	....	....	....
2000-01	Baie-Comeau	QMJHL	70	67	68	135	62	....	....	....	....	....	....	....	....	....	11	8	16	24	0	....	....	....	....
2001-02	Baie-Comeau	QMJHL	66	56	69	125	63	....	....	....	....	....	....	....	....	....	5	5	4	9	0	....	....	....	....
	Manchester	AHL	....	....	....	....	....	....	....	....	....	....	....	....	....	....	1	0	0	0	0	....	....	....	....
2002-03	Manchester	AHL	78	16	21	37	26	....	....	....	....	....	....	....	....	....	1	0	0	0	0	....	....	....	....
2003-04	Manchester	AHL	66	14	28	42	22	....	....	....	....	....	....	....	....	....	5	2	3	5	16	....	....	....	....
2004-05	Manchester	AHL	38	23	31	54	16	....	....	....	....	....	....	....	....	....	....	....	....	....	....	....	....	....	....
2005-06	Geneve	Swiss	7	5	2	7	6	....	....	....	....	....	....	....	....	....	....	....	....	....	....	....	....	....	....
	EHC Basel	Swiss	4	0	2	2	4	....	....	....	....	....	....	....	....	....	....	....	....	....	....	....	....	....	....
	Phoenix	**NHL**	**3**	**1**	**0**	**1**	**2**	**0**	**0**	**0**	**5**	**20.0**	**1**	**24**	**33.3**	**9:50**	....	....	....	....	....	....	....	....	....
	Manchester	AHL	31	10	6	16	23	....	....	....	....	....	....	....	....	....	....	....	....	....	....	....	....	....	....
	San Antonio	AHL	23	8	6	14	13	....	....	....	....	....	....	....	....	....	....	....	....	....	....	....	....	....	....
2006-07	**Phoenix**	**NHL**	**7**	**1**	**2**	**3**	**4**	**1**	**0**	**0**	**10**	**10.0**	**–1**	**10**	**60.0**	**12:32**	....	....	....	....	....	....	....	....	....
	San Antonio	AHL	72	31	42	73	26	....	....	....	....	....	....	....	....	....	....	....	....	....	....	....	....	....	....
	NHL Totals		**10**	**2**	**2**	**4**	**6**	**1**	**0**	**0**	**15**	**13.3**		**34**	**41.2**	**11:44**	....	....	....	....	....	....	....	....	....

QMJHL Second All-Star Team (2002)

Claimed on waivers by **Phoenix** from **Los Angeles**, November 5, 2005. Claimed on waivers by **Los Angeles** from **Phoenix**, November 25, 2005. Traded to **Phoenix** by **Los Angeles** for Tim Jackman, March 9, 2006.

LEHTINEN, Jere

(LEH-tih-nehn, YUH-ree) **DAL.**

Right wing. Shoots right. 6', 200 lbs. Born, Espoo, Finland, June 24, 1973. Minnesota's 3rd choice, 88th overall, in 1992 Entry Draft.

Season	Club	League	GP	G	A	Pts	PIM	PP	SH	GW	S	%	+/-	TF	F%	Min	GP	G	A	Pts	PIM	PP	SH	GW	Min
1989-90	Kiekko-Espoo Jr.	Fin-Jr.	32	23	23	46	6	....	....	....	....	....	....	....	....	....	5	0	3	3	0	....	....	....	....
1990-91	K-Espoo U18	Fin-U18	11	18	14	32	0	....	....	....	....	....	....	....	....	....	....	....	....	....	....	....	....	....	....
	Kiekko-Espoo Jr.	Fin-Jr.	10	8	6	14	4	....	....	....	....	....	....	....	....	....	....	....	....	....	....	....	....	....	....
	Kiekko-Espoo	Finland-2	32	15	9	24	12	....	....	....	....	....	....	....	....	....	....	....	....	....	....	....	....	....	....
1991-92	Kiekko-67 Jr.	Fin-Jr.	8	5	4	9	2	....	....	....	....	....	....	....	....	....	....	....	....	....	....	....	....	....	....
	Kiekko-Espoo Jr.	Fin-Jr.	8	5	4	9	2	....	....	....	....	....	....	....	....	....	....	....	....	....	....	....	....	....	....
	Kiekko-Espoo	Finland-2	43	32	17	49	6	....	....	....	....	....	....	....	....	....	5	2	4	6	2	....	....	....	....
1992-93	Kiekko-67 Jr.	Fin-Jr.	4	5	3	8	8	....	....	....	....	....	....	....	....	....	....	....	....	....	....	....	....	....	....
	Kiekko-Espoo Jr.	Fin-Jr.	4	5	3	8	8	....	....	....	....	....	....	....	....	....	....	....	....	....	....	....	....	....	....
	Kiekko-Espoo	Finland	45	13	14	27	6	....	....	....	....	....	....	....	....	....	....	....	....	....	....	....	....	....	....
1993-94	TPS Turku	Finland	42	19	20	39	6	....	....	....	....	....	....	....	....	....	11	11	2	13	2	....	....	....	....
	Finland	Olympics	8	3	0	3	0	....	....	....	....	....	....	....	....	....	....	....	....	....	....	....	....	....	....
1994-95	TPS Turku	Finland	39	19	23	42	33	....	....	....	....	....	....	....	....	....	13	8	6	14	4	....	....	....	....
1995-96	**Dallas**	**NHL**	**57**	**6**	**22**	**28**	**16**	**0**	**0**	**1**	**109**	**5.5**	**5**	....	....	....	....	....	....	....	....	....	....	....	....
	Michigan	IHL	1	1	0	1	0	....	....	....	....	....	....	....	....	....	....	....	....	....	....	....	....	....	....
1996-97	**Dallas**	**NHL**	**63**	**16**	**27**	**43**	**2**	**3**	**1**	**2**	**134**	**11.9**	**26**	....	....	....	**7**	**2**	**2**	**4**	**0**	**0**	**0**	**0**	....
1997-98	**Dallas**	**NHL**	**72**	**23**	**19**	**42**	**20**	**7**	**2**	**6**	**201**	**11.4**	**19**	....	....	....	**12**	**3**	**5**	**8**	**2**	**1**	**0**	**0**	....
	Finland	Olympics	6	4	2	6	2	....	....	....	....	....	....	....	....	....	....	....	....	....	....	....	....	....	....
1998-99♦	**Dallas**	**NHL**	**74**	**20**	**32**	**52**	**18**	**7**	**1**	**2**	**173**	**11.6**	**29**	**9**	**33.3**	**19:36**	**23**	**10**	**3**	**13**	**2**	**1**	**1**	**0**	**21:09**
99-2000	**Dallas**	**NHL**	**17**	**3**	**5**	**8**	**0**	**0**	**0**	**1**	**29**	**10.3**	**1**	**0**	**0.0**	**17:31**	**13**	**1**	**5**	**6**	**2**	**0**	**0**	**0**	**21:15**
2000-01	**Dallas**	**NHL**	**74**	**20**	**25**	**45**	**24**	**7**	**0**	**1**	**148**	**13.5**	**14**	**7**	**28.6**	**19:17**	**10**	**1**	**0**	**1**	**2**	**0**	**0**	**0**	**20:13**
2001-02	**Dallas**	**NHL**	**73**	**25**	**24**	**49**	**14**	**7**	**1**	**4**	**198**	**12.6**	**27**	**18**	**22.2**	**19:50**	....	....	....	....	....	....	....	....	....
	Finland	Olympics	4	1	2	3	2	....	....	....	....	....	....	....	....	....	....	....	....	....	....	....	....	....	....
2002-03	**Dallas**	**NHL**	**80**	**31**	**17**	**48**	**20**	**5**	**0**	**3**	**238**	**13.0**	**39**	**36**	**22.2**	**18:47**	**12**	**3**	**2**	**5**	**0**	**1**	**0**	**1**	**21:12**
2003-04	**Dallas**	**NHL**	**58**	**13**	**13**	**26**	**20**	**4**	**1**	**4**	**138**	**9.4**	**0**	**10**	**40.0**	**19:27**	**5**	**0**	**0**	**0**	**0**	**0**	**0**	**0**	**19:19**

Season	Club	League	GP	G	A	Pts	PIM	PP	SH	GW	S	%	+/-	TF	F%	Min	GP	G	A	Pts	PIM	PP	SH	GW	Min
			Regular Season														**Playoffs**								
2004-05			DID NOT PLAY																						
2005-06	**Dallas**	**NHL**	**80**	**33**	**19**	**52**	**30**	**14**	**1**	**6**	**216**	**15.3**	**9**	**28**	**21.4**	**18:42**	**5**	**3**	**1**	**4**	**0**	**1**	**0**	**0**	**22:10**
	Finland	Olympics	8	3	5	8	0	....	....	....	....	....	....	....	....	....	....	....	....	....	....	....	....	....	....
2006-07	**Dallas**	**NHL**	**73**	**26**	**17**	**43**	**16**	**11**	**1**	**5**	**194**	**13.4**	**5**	**36**	**13.9**	**19:26**	**7**	**0**	**0**	**0**	**2**	**0**	**0**	**0**	**24:02**
	NHL Totals		**721**	**216**	**220**	**436**	**180**	**65**	**8**	**35**	**1778**	**12.1**		**144**	**22.2**	**19:13**	**94**	**23**	**18**	**41**	**10**	**4**	**1**	**1**	**21:16**

Frank J. Selke Trophy (1998, 1999, 2003)

Played in NHL All-Star Game (1998)

Rights transferred to **Dallas** after **Minnesota** franchise relocated, June 9, 1993. • Missed majority of 1999-2000 season recovering from leg injury suffered in game vs. Nashville, October 16, 1999.

LEHTONEN, Mikko

(LEH-tuh-nehn, MEE-koh)

Defense. Shoots left. 6'1", 194 lbs. Born, Oulu, Finland, June 12, 1978. Nashville's 9th choice, 271st overall, in 2001 Entry Draft.

Season	Club	League	GP	G	A	Pts	PIM	PP	SH	GW	S	%	+/-	TF	F%	Min	GP	G	A	Pts	PIM	PP	SH	GW	Min
1995-96	Karpat Oulu U18	Fin-U18	15	4	5	9	30	....	....	....	....	....	....	....	....	....	....	....	....	....	....	....	....	....	....
1996-97	Karpat Oulu Jr.	Fin-Jr.	35	6	19	25	82	....	....	....	....	....	....	....	....	....	....	....	....	....	....	....	....	....	....
1997-98	Karpat Oulu Jr.	Fin-Jr.	34	8	12	20	56	....	....	....	....	....	....	....	....	....	....	....	....	....	....	....	....	....	....
	Karpat Oulu U18	Fin-U18	11	5	7	12	31	....	....	....	....	....	....	....	....	....	....	....	....	....	....	....	....	....	....
1998-99	Karpat Oulu Jr.	Fin-Jr.	35	13	22	35	65	....	....	....	....	....	....	....	....	....	....	....	....	....	....	....	....	....	....
	Karpat Oulu	Finland-2	2	0	0	0	0	....	....	....	....	....	....	....	....	....	....	....	....	....	....	....	....	....	....
	Karpat Oulu U18	Fin-U18	13	6	14	20	14	....	....	....	....	....	....	....	....	....	....	....	....	....	....	....	....	....	....
99-2000	Karpat Oulu	Finland-2	45	5	10	15	26	....	....	....	....	....	....	....	....	....	6	0	0	0	4	....	....	....	....
2000-01	Karpat Oulu	Finland	54	6	9	15	58	....	....	....	....	....	....	....	....	....	9	0	3	3	4	....	....	....	....
2001-02	Karpat Oulu	Finland	55	8	11	19	32	....	....	....	....	....	....	....	....	....	4	1	1	2	4	....	....	....	....
2002-03	Karpat Oulu	Finland	55	5	12	17	50	....	....	....	....	....	....	....	....	....	15	3	1	4	22	....	....	....	....
2003-04	Karpat Oulu	Finland	53	5	13	18	62	....	....	....	....	....	....	....	....	....	12	2	4	6	8	....	....	....	....
2004-05	Karpat Oulu	Finland	53	11	17	28	28	....	....	....	....	....	....	....	....	....	12	3	3	6	12	....	....	....	....
2005-06	Karpat Oulu	Finland	43	6	8	14	46	....	....	....	....	....	....	....	....	....	10	2	2	4	12	....	....	....	....
2006-07	**Nashville**	**NHL**	**15**	**1**	**2**	**3**	**8**	**0**	**0**	**0**	**14**	**7.1**	**0**	**0**	**0.0**	**14:36**	....	....	....	....	....	....	....	....	....
	Milwaukee	AHL	35	4	8	12	28	....	....	....	....	....	....	....	....	....	....	....	....	....	....	....	....	....	....
	Rochester	AHL	21	1	8	9	10	....	....	....	....	....	....	....	....	....	....	....	....	....	....	....	....	....	....
	NHL Totals		**15**	**1**	**2**	**3**	**8**	**0**	**0**	**0**	**14**	**7.1**		**0**	**0.0**	**14:36**	....	....	....	....	....	....	....	....	....

Traded to **Buffalo** by **Nashville** for Buffalo's 4th round choice (Mark Santorelli) in 2007 Entry Draft, February 27, 2007. Signed as a free agent by **Oulu** (Finland), July 30, 2007.

LEOPOLD, Jordan

(LEE-oh-pohld, JOHR-dahn) **COL.**

Defense. Shoots left. 6'1", 200 lbs. Born, Golden Valley, MN, August 3, 1980. Anaheim's 1st choice, 44th overall, in 1999 Entry Draft.

Season	Club	League	GP	G	A	Pts	PIM	PP	SH	GW	S	%	+/-	TF	F%	Min	GP	G	A	Pts	PIM	PP	SH	GW	Min
1995-96	Armstrong	High-MN	19	11	14	25	30	....	....	....	....	....	....	....	....	....	....	....	....	....	....	....	....	....	....
1996-97	Armstrong	High-MN	30	24	36	60	....	....	....	....	....	....	....	....	....	....	....	....	....	....	....	....	....	....	....
1997-98	USNTDP	U-18	25	7	3	10	2	....	....	....	....	....	....	....	....	....	....	....	....	....	....	....	....	....	....
	USNTDP	USHL	19	2	4	6	6	....	....	....	....	....	....	....	....	....	....	....	....	....	....	....	....	....	....
	USNTDP	NAHL	16	2	5	7	8	....	....	....	....	....	....	....	....	....	....	....	....	....	....	....	....	....	....
1998-99	U. of Minnesota	WCHA	39	7	16	23	20	....	....	....	....	....	....	....	....	....	....	....	....	....	....	....	....	....	....
99-2000	U. of Minnesota	WCHA	39	6	18	24	20	....	....	....	....	....	....	....	....	....	....	....	....	....	....	....	....	....	....
2000-01	U. of Minnesota	WCHA	42	12	37	49	38	....	....	....	....	....	....	....	....	....	....	....	....	....	....	....	....	....	....
2001-02	U. of Minnesota	WCHA	44	20	28	48	28	....	....	....	....	....	....	....	....	....	....	....	....	....	....	....	....	....	....
2002-03	**Calgary**	**NHL**	**58**	**4**	**10**	**14**	**12**	**3**	**0**	**0**	**78**	**5.1**	**-15**	**0**	**0.0**	**20:36**	....	....	....	....	....	....	....	....	....
	Saint John Flames	AHL	3	1	2	3	0	....	....	....	....	....	....	....	....	....	....	....	....	....	....	....	....	....	....
2003-04	**Calgary**	**NHL**	**82**	**9**	**24**	**33**	**24**	**6**	**0**	**1**	**138**	**6.5**	**8**	**0**	**0.0**	**22:14**	**26**	**0**	**10**	**10**	**6**	**0**	**0**	**0**	**25:41**
2004-05			DID NOT PLAY																						
2005-06	**Calgary**	**NHL**	**74**	**2**	**18**	**20**	**68**	**2**	**0**	**1**	**87**	**2.3**	**6**	**0**	**0.0**	**22:20**	**7**	**0**	**1**	**1**	**4**	**0**	**0**	**0**	**19:13**
	United States	Olympics	6	1	0	1	4	....	....	....	....	....	....	....	....	....	....	....	....	....	....	....	....	....	....
2006-07	**Colorado**	**NHL**	**15**	**2**	**3**	**5**	**14**	**1**	**1**	**0**	**19**	**10.5**	**-4**	**0**	**0.0**	**19:47**	....	....	....	....	....	....	....	....	....
	NHL Totals		**229**	**17**	**55**	**72**	**118**	**12**	**1**	**2**	**322**	**5.3**		**0**	**0.0**	**21:41**	**33**	**0**	**11**	**11**	**10**	**0**	**0**	**0**	**24:19**

WCHA All-Rookie Team (1999) • WCHA Second All-Star Team (2000) • WCHA First All-Star Team (2001, 2002) • NCAA West First All-American Team (2001) • Hobey Baker Memorial Award (Top U.S. Collegiate Player) (2002)

Traded to **Calgary** by **Anaheim** for Andrei Nazarov and Calgary's 2nd round choice (later traded to Phoenix – later traded back to Calgary – Calgary selected Andrei Taratukhin) in 2001 Entry Draft, September 26, 2000. Traded to **Colorado** by **Calgary** with Calgary's 2nd round choice (Codey Burki) in 2006 Entry Draft and Calgary's 2nd round choice (Trevor Cann) in 2007 Entry Draft for Alex Tanguay, June 24, 2006. • Missed majority of 2006-07 season recovering from off-season hernia surgery, groin injury and wrist injury suffered in game vs. Calgary (February 15, 2007).

LESSARD, Francis

(leh-SAHR, FRAN-sihs)

Right wing. Shoots right. 6'3", 225 lbs. Born, Montreal, Que., May 30, 1979. Carolina's 3rd choice, 80th overall, in 1997 Entry Draft.

Season	Club	League	GP	G	A	Pts	PIM	PP	SH	GW	S	%	+/-	TF	F%	Min	GP	G	A	Pts	PIM	PP	SH	GW	Min
1994-95	Laval-Laurentides	QAAA	1	0	0	0	0	....	....	....	....	....	....	....	....	....	....	....	....	....	....	....	....	....	....
1995-96	Laval-Laurentides	QAAA	41	5	7	12	73	....	....	....	....	....	....	....	....	....	13	1	3	4	....	....	....	....	....
1996-97	Val-d'Or Foreurs	QMJHL	66	1	9	10	287	....	....	....	....	....	....	....	....	....	....	....	....	....	....	....	....	....	....
1997-98	Val-d'Or Foreurs	QMJHL	63	3	20	23	338	....	....	....	....	....	....	....	....	....	19	1	6	7	*101	....	....	....	....
1998-99	Drummondville	QMJHL	53	12	36	48	295	....	....	....	....	....	....	....	....	....	....	....	....	....	....	....	....	....	....
99-2000	Philadelphia	AHL	78	4	8	12	416	....	....	....	....	....	....	....	....	....	5	0	1	1	7	....	....	....	....
2000-01	Philadelphia	AHL	64	3	7	10	330	....	....	....	....	....	....	....	....	....	10	0	0	0	33	....	....	....	....
2001-02	Philadelphia	AHL	60	0	6	6	251	....	....	....	....	....	....	....	....	....	....	....	....	....	....	....	....	....	....
	Atlanta	**NHL**	**5**	**0**	**0**	**0**	**26**	**0**	**0**	**0**	**2**	**0.0**	**0**	**0**	**0.0**	**12:45**	....	....	....	....	....	....	....	....	....
	Chicago Wolves	AHL	7	2	1	3	34	....	....	....	....	....	....	....	....	....	15	0	1	1	40	....	....	....	....
2002-03	**Atlanta**	**NHL**	**18**	**0**	**2**	**2**	**61**	**0**	**0**	**0**	**7**	**0.0**	**1**	**0**	**0.0**	**5:40**	....	....	....	....	....	....	....	....	....
	Chicago Wolves	AHL	50	2	5	7	194	....	....	....	....	....	....	....	....	....	1	0	0	0	0	....	....	....	....
2003-04	**Atlanta**	**NHL**	**62**	**1**	**1**	**2**	**181**	**0**	**0**	**0**	**19**	**5.3**	**-5**	**1**	**0.0**	**4:28**	....	....	....	....	....	....	....	....	....
2004-05			DID NOT PLAY																						
2005-06	**Atlanta**	**NHL**	**6**	**0**	**0**	**0**	**0**	**0**	**0**	**0**	**0**	**0.0**	**-2**	**0**	**0.0**	**2:33**	....	....	....	....	....	....	....	....	....
	Chicago Wolves	AHL	36	2	3	5	163	....	....	....	....	....	....	....	....	....	....	....	....	....	....	....	....	....	....
2006-07	Hartford	AHL	58	3	6	9	*309	....	....	....	....	....	....	....	....	....	....	....	....	....	....	....	....	....	....
	NHL Totals		**91**	**1**	**3**	**4**	**268**	**0**	**0**	**0**	**28**	**3.6**		**1**	**0.0**	**5:02**	....	....	....	....	....	....	....	....	....

Memorial Cup Tournament All-Star Team (1998)

Traded to **Philadelphia** by **Carolina** for Philadelphia's 8th round choice (Antti Jokella) in 1999 Entry Draft, May 25, 1999. Traded to **Atlanta** by **Philadelphia** for David Harlock and Atlanta's 3rd (later traded to Phoenix – Phoenix selected Tyler Redenbach) and 7th (later traded to San Jose – San Jose selected Joe Pavelski) round choices in 2003 Entry Draft, March 15, 2002.

LESSARD, Junior

(leh-SAHR, JEW-nyuhr) **DAL.**

Right wing/Center. Shoots right. 6', 195 lbs. Born, St-Joseph-de-Beauce, Que., May 26, 1980.

Season	Club	League	GP	G	A	Pts	PIM	PP	SH	GW	S	%	+/-	TF	F%	Min	GP	G	A	Pts	PIM	PP	SH	GW	Min
99-2000	Portage Terriers	MJHL	60	60	48	108	61	....	....	....	....	....	....	....	....	....	....	....	....	....	....	....	....	....	....
2000-01	U. Minn-Duluth	WCHA	36	4	8	12	12	....	....	....	....	....	....	....	....	....	....	....	....	....	....	....	....	....	....
2001-02	U. Minn-Duluth	WCHA	39	17	13	30	50	....	....	....	....	....	....	....	....	....	....	....	....	....	....	....	....	....	....
2002-03	U. Minn-Duluth	WCHA	40	21	16	37	20	....	....	....	....	....	....	....	....	....	....	....	....	....	....	....	....	....	....
2003-04	U. Minn-Duluth	WCHA	45	*32	31	*63	34	....	....	....	....	....	....	....	....	....	....	....	....	....	....	....	....	....	....
2004-05	Houston Aeros	AHL	71	11	11	22	25	....	....	....	....	....	....	....	....	....	5	1	0	1	0	....	....	....	....
2005-06	**Dallas**	**NHL**	**5**	**1**	**0**	**1**	**12**	**0**	**0**	**0**	**6**	**16.7**	**0**	**0**	**0.0**	**7:23**	....	....	....	....	....	....	....	....	....
	Iowa Stars	AHL	66	26	31	57	30	....	....	....	....	....	....	....	....	....	7	3	4	7	4	....	....	....	....
2006-07	**Dallas**	**NHL**	**1**	**1**	**0**	**1**	**0**	**1**	**0**	**0**	**3**	**33.3**	**1**	**0**	**0.0**	**11:56**	....	....	....	....	....	....	....	....	....
	Iowa Stars	AHL	65	27	25	52	32	....	....	....	....	....	....	....	....	....	12	4	5	9	4	....	....	....	....
	NHL Totals		**6**	**2**	**0**	**2**	**12**	**1**	**0**	**0**	**9**	**22.2**		**0**	**0.0**	**8:09**	....	....	....	....	....	....	....	....	....

WCHA First All-Star Team (2004) • WCHA Player of the Year (2004) • NCAA West First All-American Team (2004) • NCAA Championship All-Tournament Team (2004) • Hobey Baker Memorial Award (Top U.S. Collegiate Player) (2004)

Signed as a free agent by **Dallas**, April 15, 2004.

LETANG, Kris
(leh-TANG, KRIHS) **PIT.**

Defense. Shoots right. 6', 201 lbs. Born, Montreal, Que., April 24, 1987. Pittsburgh's 3rd choice, 62nd overall, in 2005 Entry Draft.

Season	Club	League	GP	G	A	Pts	PIM	PP	SH	GW	S	%	+/-	TF	F%	Min	Playoffs GP	G	A	Pts	PIM	PP	SH	GW	Min
2002-03	Antoine-Girouard	QAAA	42	2	10	12	34	....	....	....	....	....	....	....	....	....	....	....	....	....	....	....	....	....	....
2003-04	Antoine-Girouard	QAAA	39	12	41	53	94	....	....	....	....	....	....	....	....	....	13	7	9	16	38	....	....	....	....
2004-05	Val-d'Or Foreurs	QMJHL	70	13	19	32	79	....	....	....	....	....	....	....	....	....	....	....	....	....	....	....	....	....	....
2005-06	Val-d'Or Foreurs	QMJHL	60	25	43	68	156	....	....	....	....	....	....	....	....	....	5	1	5	6	20	....	....	....	....
2006-07	Val-d'Or Foreurs	QMJHL	40	14	38	52	74	....	....	....	....	....	....	....	....	....	19	12	19	31	48	....	....	....	....
	Pittsburgh	**NHL**	**7**	**2**	**0**	**2**	**4**	**2**	**0**	**0**	**8**	**25.0**	**-3**	**0**	**0.0**	**11:33**	....	....	....	....	....	....	....	....	....
	Wilkes-Barre	AHL	....	....	....	....	....	....	....	....	....	....	....	....	....	....	1	0	1	1	2	....	....	....	....
	NHL Totals		**7**	**2**	**0**	**2**	**4**	**2**	**0**	**0**	**8**	**25.0**		**0**	**0.0**	**11:33**	....	....	....	....	....	....	....	....	....

QMJHL All-Rookie Team (2005) • Canadian Major Junior All-Rookie Team (2005) • QMJHL First All-Star Team (2006, 2007)

LETOWSKI, Trevor
(leh-TOW-skee, TREH-vuhr) **CAR.**

Right wing. Shoots right. 5'10", 180 lbs. Born, Thunder Bay, Ont., April 5, 1977. Phoenix's 6th choice, 174th overall, in 1996 Entry Draft.

Season	Club	League	GP	G	A	Pts	PIM	PP	SH	GW	S	%	+/-	TF	F%	Min	Playoffs GP	G	A	Pts	PIM	PP	SH	GW	Min
1993-94	T. Bay Kings	TBMHL	64	41	60	101	48	....	....	....	....	....	....	....	....	....	....	....	....	....	....	....	....	....	....
1994-95	Sarnia Sting	OHL	66	22	19	41	33	....	....	....	....	....	....	....	....	....	4	0	1	1	9	....	....	....	....
1995-96	Sarnia Sting	OHL	66	36	63	99	66	....	....	....	....	....	....	....	....	....	10	9	5	14	10	....	....	....	....
1996-97	Sarnia Sting	OHL	55	35	73	108	51	....	....	....	....	....	....	....	....	....	12	9	12	21	20	....	....	....	....
1997-98	Springfield	AHL	75	11	20	31	26	....	....	....	....	....	....	....	....	....	4	1	0	1	2	....	....	....	....
1998-99	**Phoenix**	**NHL**	**14**	**2**	**2**	**4**	**2**	**0**	**0**	**0**	**8**	**25.0**	**1**	**49**	**55.1**	**6:01**	....	....	....	....	....	....	....	....	....
	Springfield	AHL	67	32	35	67	46	....	....	....	....	....	....	....	....	....	3	1	0	1	2	....	....	....	....
99-2000	**Phoenix**	**NHL**	**82**	**19**	**20**	**39**	**20**	**3**	**4**	**3**	**125**	**15.2**	**2**	**692**	**47.7**	**16:03**	**5**	**1**	**1**	**2**	**4**	**0**	**0**	**0**	**15:52**
2000-01	**Phoenix**	**NHL**	**77**	**7**	**15**	**22**	**32**	**0**	**1**	**3**	**110**	**6.4**	**-2**	**726**	**46.1**	**16:20**	....	....	....	....	....	....	....	....	....
2001-02	**Phoenix**	**NHL**	**33**	**2**	**6**	**8**	**4**	**0**	**0**	**0**	**43**	**4.7**	**2**	**250**	**52.4**	**14:27**	....	....	....	....	....	....	....	....	....
	Vancouver	**NHL**	**42**	**7**	**10**	**17**	**15**	**1**	**0**	**0**	**65**	**10.8**	**2**	**111**	**44.1**	**12:47**	**6**	**0**	**1**	**1**	**8**	**0**	**0**	**0**	**11:50**
2002-03	**Vancouver**	**NHL**	**78**	**11**	**14**	**25**	**36**	**1**	**1**	**2**	**136**	**8.1**	**8**	**70**	**41.4**	**12:26**	**6**	**0**	**1**	**1**	**0**	**0**	**0**	**0**	**9:40**
2003-04	**Columbus**	**NHL**	**73**	**15**	**17**	**32**	**16**	**4**	**0**	**1**	**126**	**11.9**	**-12**	**146**	**43.8**	**16:19**	....	....	....	....	....	....	....	....	....
2004-05	Fribourg	Swiss	9	4	5	9	6	....	....	....	....	....	....	....	....	....	11	7	9	16	8	....	....	....	....
2005-06	**Columbus**	**NHL**	**81**	**10**	**18**	**28**	**36**	**1**	**1**	**1**	**135**	**7.4**	**-2**	**284**	**45.8**	**16:32**	....	....	....	....	....	....	....	....	....
2006-07	**Carolina**	**NHL**	**61**	**2**	**6**	**8**	**18**	**0**	**0**	**0**	**69**	**2.9**	**-8**	**208**	**48.6**	**9:41**	....	....	....	....	....	....	....	....	....
	NHL Totals		**541**	**75**	**108**	**183**	**179**	**10**	**7**	**10**	**817**	**9.2**		**2536**	**47.2**	**14:21**	**17**	**1**	**3**	**4**	**12**	**0**	**0**	**0**	**12:15**

Traded to **Vancouver** by **Phoenix** with Todd Warriner, Tyler Bouck and Phoenix's 3rd round choice (later traded back to Phoenix – Phoenix selected Dimitri Pestunov) in 2003 Entry Draft for Drake Berehowsky and Denis Pederson, December 28, 2001. Signed as a free agent by **Columbus**, July 3, 2003. Signed as a free agent by **Fribourg** (Swiss), January 7, 2005. Signed as a free agent by **Carolina**, July 6, 2006.

LIDSTROM, Nicklas
(LID-struhm, NIHK-luhs) **DET.**

Defense. Shoots left. 6'1", 193 lbs. Born, Vasteras, Sweden, April 28, 1970. Detroit's 3rd choice, 53rd overall, in 1989 Entry Draft.

Season	Club	League	GP	G	A	Pts	PIM	PP	SH	GW	S	%	+/-	TF	F%	Min	Playoffs GP	G	A	Pts	PIM	PP	SH	GW	Min
1987-88	Vasteras	Sweden-2	3	0	0	0	0	....	....	....	....	....	....	....	....	....	5	0	0	0	6	....	....	....	....
1988-89	Vasteras IK	Sweden	34	1	6	7	4	....	....	....	....	....	....	....	....	....	5	0	2	2	0	....	....	....	....
1989-90	Vasteras IK	Sweden	39	8	8	16	14	....	....	....	....	....	....	....	....	....	2	0	1	1	2	....	....	....	....
1990-91	Vasteras IK	Sweden	38	4	19	23	2	....	....	....	....	....	....	....	....	....	4	0	0	0	4	....	....	....	....
1991-92	**Detroit**	**NHL**	**80**	**11**	**49**	**60**	**22**	**5**	**0**	**1**	**168**	**6.5**	**36**	....	....	....	**11**	**1**	**2**	**3**	**0**	**1**	**0**	**0**	....
1992-93	**Detroit**	**NHL**	**84**	**7**	**34**	**41**	**28**	**3**	**0**	**2**	**156**	**4.5**	**7**	....	....	....	**7**	**1**	**0**	**1**	**0**	**1**	**0**	**0**	....
1993-94	**Detroit**	**NHL**	**84**	**10**	**46**	**56**	**26**	**4**	**0**	**3**	**200**	**5.0**	**43**	....	....	....	**7**	**3**	**2**	**5**	**0**	**1**	**1**	**0**	....
1994-95	Vasteras IK	Sweden	13	2	10	12	4	....	....	....	....	....	....	....	....	....	....	....	....	....	....	....	....	....	....
	Detroit	**NHL**	**43**	**10**	**16**	**26**	**6**	**7**	**0**	**0**	**90**	**11.1**	**15**	....	....	....	**18**	**4**	**12**	**16**	**8**	**3**	**0**	**2**	....
1995-96	**Detroit**	**NHL**	**81**	**17**	**50**	**67**	**20**	**8**	**1**	**1**	**211**	**8.1**	**29**	....	....	....	**19**	**5**	**9**	**14**	**10**	**1**	**0**	**0**	....
1996-97♦	**Detroit**	**NHL**	**79**	**15**	**42**	**57**	**30**	**8**	**0**	**1**	**214**	**7.0**	**11**	....	....	....	**20**	**2**	**6**	**8**	**2**	**0**	**0**	**0**	....
1997-98♦	**Detroit**	**NHL**	**80**	**17**	**42**	**59**	**18**	**7**	**1**	**1**	**205**	**8.3**	**22**	....	....	....	**22**	**6**	**13**	**19**	**8**	**2**	**0**	**2**	....
	Sweden	Olympics	4	1	1	2	2	....	....	....	....	....	....	....	....	....	....	....	....	....	....	....	....	....	....
1998-99	**Detroit**	**NHL**	**81**	**14**	**43**	**57**	**14**	**6**	**2**	**3**	**205**	**6.8**	**14**	**0**	**0.0**	**26:31**	**10**	**2**	**9**	**11**	**4**	**2**	**0**	**0**	**30:21**
99-2000	**Detroit**	**NHL**	**81**	**20**	**53**	**73**	**18**	**9**	**4**	**3**	**218**	**9.2**	**19**	**0**	**0.0**	**28:45**	**9**	**2**	**4**	**6**	**4**	**1**	**0**	**0**	**30:28**
2000-01	**Detroit**	**NHL**	**82**	**15**	**56**	**71**	**18**	**8**	**0**	**0**	**272**	**5.5**	**9**	**0**	**0.0**	**28:27**	**6**	**1**	**7**	**8**	**0**	**0**	**0**	**0**	**29:17**
2001-02♦	**Detroit**	**NHL**	**78**	**9**	**50**	**59**	**20**	**6**	**0**	**0**	**215**	**4.2**	**13**	**0**	**0.0**	**28:49**	**23**	**5**	**11**	**16**	**2**	**2**	**1**	**2**	**31:10**
	Sweden	Olympics	4	1	5	6	0	....	....	....	....	....	....	....	....	....	....	....	....	....	....	....	....	....	....
2002-03	**Detroit**	**NHL**	**82**	**18**	**44**	**62**	**38**	**8**	**1**	**4**	**175**	**10.3**	**40**	**0**	**0.0**	**29:20**	**4**	**0**	**2**	**2**	**0**	**0**	**0**	**0**	**33:35**
2003-04	**Detroit**	**NHL**	**81**	**10**	**28**	**38**	**18**	**3**	**1**	**3**	**194**	**5.2**	**19**	**0**	**0.0**	**27:39**	**12**	**2**	**5**	**7**	**4**	**2**	**0**	**0**	**27:01**
2004-05			DID NOT PLAY																						
2005-06	**Detroit**	**NHL**	**80**	**16**	**64**	**80**	**50**	**9**	**0**	**2**	**243**	**6.6**	**21**	**0**	**0.0**	**28:07**	**6**	**1**	**1**	**2**	**2**	**1**	**0**	**1**	**31:55**
	Sweden	Olympics	8	2	4	6	2	....	....	....	....	....	....	....	....	....	....	....	....	....	....	....	....	....	....
2006-07	**Detroit**	**NHL**	**80**	**13**	**49**	**62**	**46**	**10**	**0**	**1**	**224**	**5.8**	**40**	**0**	**0.0**	**27:29**	**18**	**4**	**14**	**18**	**6**	**4**	**0**	**2**	**30:37**
	NHL Totals		**1176**	**202**	**666**	**868**	**372**	**101**	**10**	**25**	**2990**	**6.8**		**0**	**0.0**	**28:08**	**192**	**39**	**97**	**136**	**50**	**21**	**2**	**9**	**30:22**

NHL All-Rookie Team (1992) • NHL First All-Star Team (1998, 1999, 2000, 2001, 2002, 2003, 2006, 2007) • James Norris Memorial Trophy (2001, 2002, 2003, 2006, 2007) • Conn Smythe Trophy (2002) • Olympic Tournament All-Star Team (2006)

Played in NHL All-Star Game (1996, 1998, 1999, 2000, 2001, 2002, 2003, 2004, 2007)

LIFFITON, David
(LIH-fih-tuhn, DAY-vihd) **NYR**

Defense. Shoots left. 6'2", 210 lbs. Born, Windsor, Ont., October 18, 1984. Colorado's 1st choice, 63rd overall, in 2003 Entry Draft.

Season	Club	League	GP	G	A	Pts	PIM	PP	SH	GW	S	%	+/-	TF	F%	Min	Playoffs GP	G	A	Pts	PIM	PP	SH	GW	Min
2000-01	Aylmer Aces	OHA-B	51	1	9	10	51	....	....	....	....	....	....	....	....	....	....	....	....	....	....	....	....	....	....
2001-02	Plymouth Whalers	OHL	64	3	9	12	65	....	....	....	....	....	....	....	....	....	6	0	0	0	0	....	....	....	....
2002-03	Plymouth Whalers	OHL	64	5	11	16	139	....	....	....	....	....	....	....	....	....	18	1	3	4	29	....	....	....	....
2003-04	Plymouth Whalers	OHL	44	2	9	11	85	....	....	....	....	....	....	....	....	....	9	0	0	0	12	....	....	....	....
2004-05	Hartford	AHL	33	0	1	1	74	....	....	....	....	....	....	....	....	....	....	....	....	....	....	....	....	....	....
	Charlotte	ECHL	16	0	2	2	18	....	....	....	....	....	....	....	....	....	15	1	4	5	27	....	....	....	....
2005-06	**NY Rangers**	**NHL**	**1**	**0**	**0**	**0**	**2**	**0**	**0**	**0**	**0**	**0.0**	**0**	**0**	**0.0**	**8:42**	....	....	....	....	....	....	....	....	....
	Hartford	AHL	50	2	7	9	158	....	....	....	....	....	....	....	....	....	....	....	....	....	....	....	....	....	....
2006-07	**NY Rangers**	**NHL**	**2**	**0**	**0**	**0**	**7**	**0**	**0**	**0**	**2**	**0.0**	**1**	**0**	**0.0**	**11:31**	....	....	....	....	....	....	....	....	....
	Hartford	AHL	72	2	11	13	189	....	....	....	....	....	....	....	....	....	7	1	1	2	18	....	....	....	....
	NHL Totals		**3**	**0**	**0**	**0**	**9**	**0**	**0**	**0**	**2**	**0.0**		**0**	**0.0**	**10:35**	....	....	....	....	....	....	....	....	....

Traded to **NY Rangers** by **Colorado** with Chris McAllister and Florida's 2nd round choice (previously acquired, later traded back to Florida – Florida selected David Shantz) in 2004 Entry Draft for Matthew Barnaby and NY Rangers' 3rd round choice (Denis Parshin) in 2004 Entry Draft, March 8, 2004.

LILES, John-Michael
(LIGH-uhls, JAWN-MIGHK-uhl) **COL.**

Defense. Shoots left. 5'10", 185 lbs. Born, Zionsville, IN, November 25, 1980. Colorado's 8th choice, 159th overall, in 2000 Entry Draft.

Season	Club	League	GP	G	A	Pts	PIM	PP	SH	GW	S	%	+/-	TF	F%	Min	Playoffs GP	G	A	Pts	PIM	PP	SH	GW	Min
1997-98	USNTDP	U-17	15	0	6	6	4	....	....	....	....	....	....	....	....	....	....	....	....	....	....	....	....	....	....
	USNTDP	USHL	5	0	1	1	0	....	....	....	....	....	....	....	....	....	....	....	....	....	....	....	....	....	....
	USNTDP	NAHL	42	4	7	11	40	....	....	....	....	....	....	....	....	....	5	2	0	2	0	....	....	....	....
1998-99	USNTDP	USHL	46	4	14	18	47	....	....	....	....	....	....	....	....	....	....	....	....	....	....	....	....	....	....
	USNTDP	NAHL	13	2	5	7	6	....	....	....	....	....	....	....	....	....	....	....	....	....	....	....	....	....	....
99-2000	Michigan State	CCHA	40	8	20	28	26	....	....	....	....	....	....	....	....	....	....	....	....	....	....	....	....	....	....
2000-01	Michigan State	CCHA	42	7	18	25	28	....	....	....	....	....	....	....	....	....	....	....	....	....	....	....	....	....	....
2001-02	Michigan State	CCHA	41	13	22	35	18	....	....	....	....	....	....	....	....	....	....	....	....	....	....	....	....	....	....
2002-03	Michigan State	CCHA	39	16	34	50	46	....	....	....	....	....	....	....	....	....	....	....	....	....	....	....	....	....	....
	Hershey Bears	AHL	5	0	1	1	4	....	....	....	....	....	....	....	....	....	5	0	0	0	2	....	....	....	....
2003-04	**Colorado**	**NHL**	**79**	**10**	**24**	**34**	**28**	**2**	**0**	**1**	**115**	**8.7**	**7**	**0**	**0.0**	**16:14**	**11**	**0**	**1**	**1**	**4**	**0**	**0**	**0**	**16:41**
2004-05	Iserlohn Roosters	Germany	17	5	6	11	24	....	....	....	....	....	....	....	....	....	....	....	....	....	....	....	....	....	....
2005-06	**Colorado**	**NHL**	**82**	**14**	**35**	**49**	**44**	**6**	**0**	**1**	**154**	**9.1**	**5**	**1**	**100.0**	**18:31**	**9**	**1**	**2**	**3**	**6**	**1**	**0**	**0**	**17:35**
	United States	Olympics	6	0	2	2	2	....	....	....	....	....	....	....	....	....	....	....	....	....	....	....	....	....	....
2006-07	**Colorado**	**NHL**	**71**	**14**	**30**	**44**	**24**	**8**	**0**	**3**	**128**	**10.9**	**0**	**0**	**0.0**	**17:46**	....	....	....	....	....	....	....	....	....
	NHL Totals		**232**	**38**	**89**	**127**	**96**	**16**	**0**	**5**	**397**	**9.6**		**1**	**100.0**	**17:31**	**20**	**1**	**3**	**4**	**10**	**1**	**0**	**0**	**17:05**

CCHA Second All-Star Team (2001) • CCHA First All-Star Team (2002, 2003) • NCAA West Second All-American Team (2002) • NCAA West First All-American Team (2003) • NHL All-Rookie Team (2004)

Signed as a free agent by **Iserlohn** (Germany), December 29, 2004.

Season	Club	League	GP	G	A	Pts	PIM	PP	SH	GW	S	%	+/-	TF	F%	Min	GP	G	A	Pts	PIM	PP	SH	GW	Min
			Regular Season														Playoffs								

LILJA, Andreas

(LIHL-yuh, awn-DRAY-uhs) **DET.**

Defense. Shoots left. 6'3", 230 lbs. Born, Helsingborg, Sweden, July 13, 1975. Los Angeles' 2nd choice, 54th overall, in 2000 Entry Draft.

Season	Club	League	GP	G	A	Pts	PIM	PP	SH	GW	S	%	+/-	TF	F%	Min	GP	G	A	Pts	PIM	PP	SH	GW	Min
1993-94	Malmo IF Jr.	Swe-Jr.	14	3	7	10	38	....	....	....	....	....	....	....	....	....	....	....	....	....	....	....	....	....	....
1994-95	Malmo IF Jr.	Swe-Jr.	30	7	13	20	82	....	....	....	....	....	....	....	....	....	....	....	....	....	....	....	....	....	....
	Malmo IF	Sweden	3	0	0	0	2	....	....	....	....	....	....	....	....	....	....	....	....	....	....	....	....	....	....
1995-96	Malmo IF Jr.	Swe-Jr.	3	0	1	1	6	....	....	....	....	....	....	....	....	....	....	....	....	....	....	....	....	....	....
	Malmo IF	Sweden	40	1	5	6	63	....	....	....	....	....	....	....	....	....	5	0	1	1	2	....	....	....	....
1996-97	Malmo	Sweden	47	1	0	1	22	....	....	....	....	....	....	....	....	....	4	0	0	0	10	....	....	....	....
1997-98	Malmo	Sweden	10	0	0	0	0	....	....	....	....	....	....	....	....	....	....	....	....	....	....	....	....	....	....
	Mora IK	Sweden-2	13	1	4	5	30	....	....	....	....	....	....	....	....	....	4	1	0	1	14	....	....	....	....
1998-99	Malmo	Sweden	41	0	3	3	44	....	....	....	....	....	....	....	....	....	1	0	0	0	4	....	....	....	....
99-2000	Malmo	Sweden	49	8	11	19	88	....	....	....	....	....	....	....	....	....	6	0	0	0	8	....	....	....	....
2000-01	**Los Angeles**	**NHL**	**2**	**0**	**0**	**0**	**4**	**0**	**0**	**0**	**1**	**0.0**	**–2**	**0**	**0.0**	**12:22**	**1**	**0**	**0**	**0**	**0**	**0**	**0**	**0**	**6:56**
	Lowell	AHL	61	7	29	36	149	....	....	....	....	....	....	....	....	....	4	0	6	6	6	....	....	....	....
2001-02	**Los Angeles**	**NHL**	**26**	**1**	**4**	**5**	**22**	**1**	**0**	**0**	**12**	**8.3**	**3**	**0**	**0.0**	**11:27**	**5**	**0**	**0**	**0**	**6**	**0**	**0**	**0**	**10:26**
	Manchester	AHL	4	0	1	1	4	....	....	....	....	....	....	....	....	....	....	....	....	....	....	....	....	....	....
2002-03	**Los Angeles**	**NHL**	**17**	**0**	**3**	**3**	**14**	**0**	**0**	**0**	**13**	**0.0**	**5**	**0**	**0.0**	**20:04**	....	....	....	....	....	....	....	....	....
	Florida	**NHL**	**56**	**4**	**8**	**12**	**56**	**0**	**0**	**0**	**59**	**6.8**	**8**	**0**	**0.0**	**19:11**	....	....	....	....	....	....	....	....	....
2003-04	**Florida**	**NHL**	**79**	**3**	**4**	**7**	**90**	**0**	**0**	**0**	**79**	**3.8**	**–8**	**1**	**0.0**	**19:34**	....	....	....	....	....	....	....	....	....
2004-05	Mora IK	Sweden	44	3	8	11	67	....	....	....	....	....	....	....	....	....	....	....	....	....	....	....	....	....	....
	HC Ambri-Piotta	Swiss	....	....	....	....	....	....	....	....	....	....	....	....	....	....	5	0	2	2	6	....	....	....	....
2005-06	**Detroit**	**NHL**	**82**	**2**	**13**	**15**	**98**	**0**	**0**	**1**	**78**	**2.6**	**18**	**1**	**0.0**	**19:01**	**6**	**0**	**1**	**1**	**6**	**0**	**0**	**0**	**19:21**
2006-07	**Detroit**	**NHL**	**57**	**0**	**5**	**5**	**54**	**0**	**0**	**0**	**37**	**0.0**	**6**	**1**	**0.0**	**15:25**	**18**	**1**	**0**	**1**	**10**	**0**	**0**	**0**	**19:02**
	NHL Totals		**319**	**10**	**37**	**47**	**338**	**1**	**0**	**1**	**279**	**3.6**		**3**	**0.0**	**17:56**	**30**	**1**	**1**	**2**	**22**	**0**	**0**	**0**	**17:16**

• Spent majority of 2001-02 season as a healthy reserve. Traded to **Florida** by **Los Angeles** with Jaroslav Bednar for Dmitry Yushkevich and Florida's 5th round choice (previously acquired, Los Angeles selected Brady Murray) in 2003 Entry Draft, Novermber 26, 2002. Signed as a free agent by **Nashville**, July 26, 2004. Signed as a free agent by **Mora** (Sweden), September 15, 2004. Signed as a free agent by **Ambri-Piotta** (Swiss), February 25, 2005. Signed as a free agent by **Detroit**, August 24, 2005.

LINDEN, Trevor

(LIHND-duhn, TREH-vuhr)

Right wing. Shoots right. 6'4", 215 lbs. Born, Medicine Hat, Alta., April 11, 1970. Vancouver's 1st choice, 2nd overall, in 1988 Entry Draft.

Season	Club	League	GP	G	A	Pts	PIM	PP	SH	GW	S	%	+/-	TF	F%	Min	GP	G	A	Pts	PIM	PP	SH	GW	Min
1985-86	Medicine Hat	AMHL	40	14	22	36	14	....	....	....	....	....	....	....	....	....	....	....	....	....	....	....	....	....	....
	Medicine Hat	WHL	5	2	0	2	0	....	....	....	....	....	....	....	....	....	....	....	....	....	....	....	....	....	....
1986-87	Medicine Hat	WHL	72	14	22	36	59	....	....	....	....	....	....	....	....	....	20	5	4	9	17	....	....	....	....
1987-88	Medicine Hat	WHL	67	46	64	110	76	....	....	....	....	....	....	....	....	....	16	*13	12	25	19	....	....	....	....
1988-89	**Vancouver**	**NHL**	**80**	**30**	**29**	**59**	**41**	**10**	**1**	**2**	**186**	**16.1**	**–10**	....	....	....	**7**	**3**	**4**	**7**	**8**	**2**	**1**	**0**	....
1989-90	**Vancouver**	**NHL**	**73**	**21**	**30**	**51**	**43**	**6**	**2**	**3**	**171**	**12.3**	**–17**	....	....	....	....	....	....	....	....	....	....	....	....
1990-91	**Vancouver**	**NHL**	**80**	**33**	**37**	**70**	**65**	**16**	**2**	**4**	**229**	**14.4**	**–25**	....	....	....	**6**	**0**	**7**	**7**	**2**	**0**	**0**	**0**	....
1991-92	**Vancouver**	**NHL**	**80**	**31**	**44**	**75**	**101**	**6**	**1**	**6**	**201**	**15.4**	**3**	....	....	....	**13**	**4**	**8**	**12**	**6**	**2**	**0**	**1**	....
1992-93	**Vancouver**	**NHL**	**84**	**33**	**39**	**72**	**64**	**8**	**0**	**3**	**209**	**15.8**	**19**	....	....	....	**12**	**5**	**8**	**13**	**16**	**2**	**0**	**1**	....
1993-94	**Vancouver**	**NHL**	**84**	**32**	**29**	**61**	**73**	**10**	**2**	**3**	**234**	**13.7**	**6**	....	....	....	**24**	**12**	**13**	**25**	**18**	**5**	**1**	**1**	....
1994-95	**Vancouver**	**NHL**	**48**	**18**	**22**	**40**	**40**	**9**	**0**	**1**	**129**	**14.0**	**–5**	....	....	....	**11**	**2**	**6**	**8**	**12**	**1**	**0**	**0**	....
1995-96	**Vancouver**	**NHL**	**82**	**33**	**47**	**80**	**42**	**12**	**1**	**2**	**202**	**16.3**	**6**	....	....	....	**6**	**4**	**4**	**8**	**6**	**2**	**0**	**0**	....
1996-97	**Vancouver**	**NHL**	**49**	**9**	**31**	**40**	**27**	**2**	**2**	**2**	**84**	**10.7**	**5**	....	....	....	....	....	....	....	....	....	....	....	....
1997-98	**Vancouver**	**NHL**	**42**	**7**	**14**	**21**	**49**	**2**	**0**	**1**	**74**	**9.5**	**–13**	....	....	....	....	....	....	....	....	....	....	....	....
	NY Islanders	**NHL**	**25**	**10**	**7**	**17**	**33**	**3**	**2**	**1**	**59**	**16.9**	**–1**	....	....	....	....	....	....	....	....	....	....	....	....
	Canada	Olympics	6	1	0	1	10	....	....	....	....	....	....	....	....	....	....	....	....	....	....	....	....	....	....
1998-99	**NY Islanders**	**NHL**	**82**	**18**	**29**	**47**	**32**	**8**	**1**	**1**	**167**	**10.8**	**–14**	**261**	**50.2**	**21:29**	....	....	....	....	....	....	....	....	....
99-2000	**Montreal**	**NHL**	**50**	**13**	**17**	**30**	**34**	**4**	**0**	**3**	**87**	**14.9**	**–3**	**860**	**56.3**	**17:51**	....	....	....	....	....	....	....	....	....
2000-01	**Montreal**	**NHL**	**57**	**12**	**21**	**33**	**52**	**6**	**0**	**3**	**96**	**12.5**	**–2**	**1142**	**52.7**	**20:47**	....	....	....	....	....	....	....	....	....
	Washington	**NHL**	**12**	**3**	**1**	**4**	**8**	**0**	**0**	**0**	**30**	**10.0**	**2**	**75**	**60.0**	**18:03**	**6**	**0**	**4**	**4**	**14**	**0**	**0**	**0**	**22:41**
2001-02	**Washington**	**NHL**	**16**	**1**	**2**	**3**	**6**	**1**	**0**	**0**	**19**	**5.3**	**–2**	**71**	**49.3**	**16:06**	....	....	....	....	....	....	....	....	....
	Vancouver	**NHL**	**64**	**12**	**22**	**34**	**65**	**2**	**0**	**2**	**122**	**9.8**	**–3**	**1190**	**53.4**	**19:23**	**6**	**1**	**4**	**5**	**0**	**0**	**0**	**0**	**19:36**
2002-03	**Vancouver**	**NHL**	**71**	**19**	**22**	**41**	**30**	**4**	**1**	**1**	**116**	**16.4**	**–1**	**568**	**54.4**	**15:52**	**14**	**1**	**2**	**3**	**10**	**0**	**1**	**0**	**17:38**
2003-04	**Vancouver**	**NHL**	**82**	**14**	**22**	**36**	**26**	**4**	**0**	**1**	**97**	**14.4**	**–6**	**1285**	**55.8**	**16:17**	**7**	**0**	**0**	**0**	**6**	**0**	**0**	**0**	**18:29**
2004-05			DID NOT PLAY																						
2005-06	**Vancouver**	**NHL**	**82**	**7**	**9**	**16**	**15**	**1**	**1**	**0**	**55**	**12.7**	**3**	**668**	**49.6**	**11:20**	....	....	....	....	....	....	....	....	....
2006-07	**Vancouver**	**NHL**	**80**	**12**	**13**	**25**	**34**	**5**	**0**	**1**	**92**	**13.0**	**–6**	**211**	**50.7**	**12:20**	**12**	**2**	**5**	**7**	**6**	**1**	**0**	**2**	**17:15**
	NHL Totals		**1323**	**368**	**487**	**855**	**880**	**119**	**16**	**40**	**2659**	**13.8**		**6331**	**53.6**	**16:40**	**124**	**34**	**65**	**99**	**104**	**15**	**3**	**5**	**18:36**

WHL East Second All-Star Team (1988) • Memorial Cup Tournament All-Star Team (1988) • NHL All-Rookie Team (1989) • King Clancy Memorial Trophy (1997)

Played in NHL All-Star Game (1991, 1992)

Traded to **NY Islanders** by **Vancouver** for Todd Bertuzzi, Bryan McCabe and NY Islanders' 3rd round choice (Jarkko Ruutu) in 1998 Entry Draft, February 6, 1998. Traded to **Montreal** by **NY Islanders** for Montreal's 1st round choice (Branislav Mezei) in 1999 Entry Draft, May 29, 1999. Traded to **Washington** by **Montreal** with Dainius Zubrus and New Jersey's 2nd round choice (previously acquired, later traded to Tampa Bay – Tampa Bay selected Andreas Holmqvist) in 2001 Entry Draft for Richard Zednik, Jan Bulis and Washington's 1st round choice (Alexander Perezhogin) in 2001 Entry Draft, March 13, 2001. Traded to **Vancouver** by **Washington** with NY Islanders' 2nd round choice (previously acquired, Vancouver selected Denis Grot) in 2002 Entry Draft for Vancouver's 1st round choice (Boyd Gordon) in 2002 Entry Draft and Vancouver's 3rd round choice (later traded to Edmonton – Edmonton selected Zachery Stortini) in 2003 Entry Draft, November 10, 2001.

LINDROS, Eric

(LIHND-rahz, AIR-ihk)

Center. Shoots right. 6'4", 240 lbs. Born, London, Ont., February 28, 1973. Quebec's 1st choice, 1st overall, in 1991 Entry Draft.

Season	Club	League	GP	G	A	Pts	PIM	PP	SH	GW	S	%	+/-	TF	F%	Min	GP	G	A	Pts	PIM	PP	SH	GW	Min
1988-89	St. Mike's B's	OHA-B	37	24	43	67	193	....	....	....	....	....	....	....	....	....	27	23	25	48	155	....	....	....	....
1989-90	Det. Compuware	NAHL	14	23	29	52	123	....	....	....	....	....	....	....	....	....	....	....	....	....	....	....	....	....	....
	Oshawa Generals	OHL	25	17	19	36	61	....	....	....	....	....	....	....	....	....	17	18	18	36	76	....	....	....	....
1990-91	Oshawa Generals	OHL	57	*71	78	*149	189	....	....	....	....	....	....	....	....	....	16	*18	20	*38	*93	....	....	....	....
1991-92	Oshawa Generals	OHL	13	9	22	31	54	....	....	....	....	....	....	....	....	....	....	....	....	....	....	....	....	....	....
	Canada	Nat-Tm	24	19	16	35	34	....	....	....	....	....	....	....	....	....	....	....	....	....	....	....	....	....	....
	Canada	Olympics	8	5	6	11	5	....	....	....	....	....	....	....	....	....	....	....	....	....	....	....	....	....	....
1992-93	**Philadelphia**	**NHL**	**61**	**41**	**34**	**75**	**147**	**8**	**1**	**5**	**180**	**22.8**	**28**	....	....	....	....	....	....	....	....	....	....	....	....
1993-94	**Philadelphia**	**NHL**	**65**	**44**	**53**	**97**	**103**	**13**	**2**	**9**	**197**	**22.3**	**16**	....	....	....	....	....	....	....	....	....	....	....	....
1994-95	**Philadelphia**	**NHL**	**46**	**29**	**41**	***70**	**60**	**7**	**0**	**4**	**144**	**20.1**	**27**	....	....	....	**12**	**4**	**11**	**15**	**18**	**0**	**0**	**1**	....
1995-96	**Philadelphia**	**NHL**	**73**	**47**	**68**	**115**	**163**	**15**	**0**	**4**	**294**	**16.0**	**26**	....	....	....	**12**	**6**	**6**	**12**	**43**	**3**	**0**	**2**	....
1996-97	**Philadelphia**	**NHL**	**52**	**32**	**47**	**79**	**136**	**9**	**0**	**7**	**198**	**16.2**	**31**	....	....	....	**19**	**12**	**14**	***26**	**40**	**4**	**0**	**1**	....
1997-98	**Philadelphia**	**NHL**	**63**	**30**	**41**	**71**	**134**	**10**	**1**	**4**	**202**	**14.9**	**14**	....	....	....	**5**	**1**	**2**	**3**	**17**	**0**	**0**	**0**	....
	Canada	Olympics	6	2	3	5	2	....	....	....	....	....	....	....	....	....	....	....	....	....	....	....	....	....	....
1998-99	**Philadelphia**	**NHL**	**71**	**40**	**53**	**93**	**120**	**10**	**1**	**2**	**242**	**16.5**	**35**	**1529**	**60.0**	**22:56**	....	....	....	....	....	....	....	....	....
99-2000	**Philadelphia**	**NHL**	**55**	**27**	**32**	**59**	**83**	**10**	**1**	**2**	**187**	**14.4**	**11**	**1318**	**57.8**	**22:02**	**2**	**1**	**0**	**1**	**0**	**0**	**0**	**0**	**8:26**
2000-01	**Philadelphia**	**NHL**	DID NOT PLAY – INJURED																						
2001-02	**NY Rangers**	**NHL**	**72**	**37**	**36**	**73**	**138**	**12**	**1**	**4**	**196**	**18.9**	**19**	**1707**	**54.4**	**21:03**	....	....	....	....	....	....	....	....	....
	Canada	Olympics	6	1	0	1	8	....	....	....	....	....	....	....	....	....	....	....	....	....	....	....	....	....	....
2002-03	**NY Rangers**	**NHL**	**81**	**19**	**34**	**53**	**141**	**9**	**0**	**3**	**235**	**8.1**	**5**	**778**	**53.0**	**20:15**	....	....	....	....	....	....	....	....	....
2003-04	**NY Rangers**	**NHL**	**39**	**10**	**22**	**32**	**60**	**3**	**0**	**0**	**83**	**12.0**	**7**	**492**	**54.5**	**15:59**	....	....	....	....	....	....	....	....	....
2004-05			DID NOT PLAY																						
2005-06	**Toronto**	**NHL**	**33**	**11**	**11**	**22**	**43**	**4**	**0**	**2**	**59**	**18.6**	**–3**	**480**	**53.5**	**17:24**	....	....	....	....	....	....	....	....	....
2006-07	**Dallas**	**NHL**	**49**	**5**	**21**	**26**	**70**	**1**	**0**	**0**	**95**	**5.3**	**–1**	**241**	**53.9**	**14:39**	**3**	**0**	**0**	**0**	**4**	**0**	**0**	**0**	**9:46**
	NHL Totals		**760**	**372**	**493**	**865**	**1398**	**111**	**7**	**46**	**2312**	**16.1**		**6545**	**56.1**	**19:47**	**53**	**24**	**33**	**57**	**122**	**7**	**0**	**4**	**9:14**

Memorial Cup Tournament All-Star Team (1990) • OHL First All-Star Team (1991) • OHL MVP (1991) • Canadian Major Junior Player of the Year (1991) • NHL All-Rookie Team (1993) • NHL First All-Star Team (1995) • Lester B. Pearson Award (1995) • Hart Memorial Trophy (1995) • NHL Second All-Star Team (1996)

Played in NHL All-Star Game (1994, 1996, 1997, 1998, 1999, 2000)

Traded to **Philadelphia** by **Quebec** for Peter Forsberg, Steve Duchesne, Kerry Huffman, Mike Ricci, Ron Hextall, Philadelphia's 1st round choice (Jocelyn Thibault) in 1993 Entry Draft, $15,000,000 and future considerations (Chris Simon and Philadelphia's 1st round choice (later traded to Toronto – later traded to Washington – Washington selected Nolan Baumgartner) in 1994 Entry Draft, July 21, 1992), June 30, 1992. • Missed entire 2000-01 season recovering from head injury suffered in game vs. New Jersey, May 26, 2000 and due to contract dispute with Philadelphia Flyers. Traded to **NY Rangers** by **Philadelphia** for Kim Johnsson, Jan Havac, Pavel Brendl and NY Rangers' 3rd round choice (Stefan Ruzicka) in 2003 Entry Draft, August 20, 2001. • Missed majority of 2003-04 season recovering from shoulder (October 23, 2003 vs. Florida) and head (January 28, 2004 vs. Washington) injuries. Signed as a free agent by **Toronto**, August 11, 2005. Signed as a free agent by **Dallas**, July 17, 2006.

LINDSTROM, Joakim
(LIHND-struhm, YOH-ah-kihm) **CBJ**

Center. Shoots left. 6', 187 lbs. Born, Skelleftea, Sweden, December 5, 1983. Columbus' 2nd choice, 41st overall, in 2002 Entry Draft.

			Regular Season														Playoffs								
Season	Club	League	GP	G	A	Pts	PIM	PP	SH	GW	S	%	+/-	TF	F%	Min	GP	G	A	Pts	PIM	PP	SH	GW	Min
99-2000	MoDo U18	Swe-U18	17	6	*14	20	32	....	....	....	....	....	....	....	....	....	....	....	....	....	....	....	....	....	....
	Malmo Jr.	Swe-Jr.	10	4	4	8	2	....	....	....	....	....	....	....	....	....	....	....	....	....	....	....	....	....	....
2000-01	Malmo Jr.	Swe-Jr.	12	7	14	21	46	....	....	....	....	....	....	....	....	....	4	2	3	5	24	....	....	....	....
	MoDo	Sweden	10	2	3	5	2	....	....	....	....	....	....	....	....	....	7	0	1	1	0	....	....	....	....
2001-02	Malmo Jr.	Swe-Jr.	10	9	6	15	67	....	....	....	....	....	....	....	....	....	....	....	....	....	....	....	....	....	....
	IF Troja-Ljungby	Sweden-2	3	0	0	0	12	....	....	....	....	....	....	....	....	....	....	....	....	....	....	....	....	....	....
	MODO	Sweden	42	4	3	7	20	....	....	....	....	....	....	....	....	....	14	3	5	8	8	....	....	....	....
2002-03	MODO	Sweden	29	4	2	6	14	....	....	....	....	....	....	....	....	....	6	1	1	2	2	....	....	....	....
	Malmo Jr.	Swe-Jr.	2	5	1	6	8	....	....	....	....	....	....	....	....	....	....	....	....	....	....	....	....	....	....
	Ornskoldsviks SK	Sweden-2	2	1	1	2	4	....	....	....	....	....	....	....	....	....	....	....	....	....	....	....	....	....	....
2003-04	MODO	Sweden	15	0	2	2	0	....	....	....	....	....	....	....	....	....	....	....	....	....	....	....	....	....	....
	Sundsvall	Sweden-2	2	0	5	5	0	....	....	....	....	....	....	....	....	....	....	....	....	....	....	....	....	....	....
2004-05	MODO Jr.	Swe-Jr.	2	4	1	5	0	....	....	....	....	....	....	....	....	....	....	....	....	....	....	....	....	....	....
	MODO	Sweden	37	2	3	5	24	....	....	....	....	....	....	....	....	....	....	....	....	....	....	....	....	....	....
	Syracuse Crunch	AHL	13	4	4	8	0	....	....	....	....	....	....	....	....	....	....	....	....	....	....	....	....	....	....
2005-06	**Columbus**	**NHL**	**3**	**0**	**0**	**0**	**0**	**0**	**0**	**0**	**4**	**0.0**	**0**	**0**	**0.0**	**5:11**	....	....	....	....	....	....	....	....	....
	Syracuse Crunch	AHL	64	14	29	43	52	....	....	....	....	....	....	....	....	....	6	1	1	2	0	....	....	....	....
2006-07	**Columbus**	**NHL**	**9**	**1**	**0**	**1**	**4**	**0**	**0**	**0**	**9**	**11.1**	**–3**	**0**	**0.0**	**8:28**	....	....	....	....	....	....	....	....	....
	Syracuse Crunch	AHL	50	22	26	48	34	....	....	....	....	....	....	....	....	....	....	....	....	....	....	....	....	....	....
	NHL Totals		**12**	**1**	**0**	**1**	**4**	**0**	**0**	**0**	**13**	**7.7**		**0**	**0.0**	**7:39**	....	....	....	....	....	....	....	....	....

LING, David
(LIHNG, DAY-vihd) **TOR.**

Right wing. Shoots right. 5'10", 204 lbs. Born, Halifax, N.S., January 9, 1975. Quebec's 9th choice, 179th overall, in 1993 Entry Draft.

Season	Club	League	GP	G	A	Pts	PIM	PP	SH	GW	S	%	+/-	TF	F%	Min	GP	G	A	Pts	PIM	PP	SH	GW	Min
1991-92	Charlotwn Abbies	MJrHL	30	33	42	75	270	....	....	....	....	....	....	....	....	....	....	....	....	....	....	....	....	....	....
	St. Mike's B's	OHA-B	8	5	14	19	25	....	....	....	....	....	....	....	....	....	....	....	....	....	....	....	....	....	....
1992-93	Kingston	OHL	64	17	46	63	275	....	....	....	....	....	....	....	....	....	16	3	12	15	*72	....	....	....	....
1993-94	Kingston	OHL	61	37	40	77	*254	....	....	....	....	....	....	....	....	....	6	4	2	6	16	....	....	....	....
1994-95	Kingston	OHL	62	*61	74	135	136	....	....	....	....	....	....	....	....	....	6	7	8	15	12	....	....	....	....
1995-96	Saint John Flames	AHL	75	24	32	56	179	....	....	....	....	....	....	....	....	....	9	0	5	5	12	....	....	....	....
1996-97	Saint John Flames	AHL	5	0	2	2	19	....	....	....	....	....	....	....	....	....	....	....	....	....	....	....	....	....	....
	Montreal	**NHL**	**2**	**0**	**0**	**0**	**0**	**0**	**0**	**0**	**0**	**0.0**	**0**	....	....	....	....	....	....	....	....	....	....	....	....
	Fredericton	AHL	48	22	36	58	229	....	....	....	....	....	....	....	....	....	....	....	....	....	....	....	....	....	....
1997-98	**Montreal**	**NHL**	**1**	**0**	**0**	**0**	**0**	**0**	**0**	**0**	**1**	**0.0**	**–1**	....	....	....	....	....	....	....	....	....	....	....	....
	Fredericton	AHL	67	25	41	66	148	....	....	....	....	....	....	....	....	....	....	....	....	....	....	....	....	....	....
	Indianapolis Ice	IHL	12	8	6	14	30	....	....	....	....	....	....	....	....	....	5	4	1	5	31	....	....	....	....
1998-99	Kansas City	IHL	82	30	42	72	112	....	....	....	....	....	....	....	....	....	3	1	0	1	20	....	....	....	....
99-2000	Kansas City	IHL	82	35	48	83	210	....	....	....	....	....	....	....	....	....	....	....	....	....	....	....	....	....	....
2000-01	Utah Grizzlies	IHL	79	15	28	43	202	....	....	....	....	....	....	....	....	....	....	....	....	....	....	....	....	....	....
2001-02	**Columbus**	**NHL**	**5**	**0**	**0**	**0**	**7**	**0**	**0**	**0**	**5**	**0.0**	**–1**	**1**	**0.0**	**9:47**	....	....	....	....	....	....	....	....	....
	Syracuse Crunch	AHL	71	19	41	60	240	....	....	....	....	....	....	....	....	....	10	5	5	10	16	....	....	....	....
2002-03	**Columbus**	**NHL**	**35**	**3**	**2**	**5**	**86**	**0**	**0**	**0**	**37**	**8.1**	**–6**	**15**	**40.0**	**7:56**	....	....	....	....	....	....	....	....	....
	Syracuse Crunch	AHL	46	7	34	41	129	....	....	....	....	....	....	....	....	....	....	....	....	....	....	....	....	....	....
2003-04	**Columbus**	**NHL**	**50**	**1**	**2**	**3**	**98**	**0**	**0**	**0**	**45**	**2.2**	**–3**	**8**	**37.5**	**7:45**	....	....	....	....	....	....	....	....	....
	Syracuse Crunch	AHL	14	7	10	17	25	....	....	....	....	....	....	....	....	....	7	0	1	1	36	....	....	....	....
2004-05	St. John's	AHL	80	28	60	88	152	....	....	....	....	....	....	....	....	....	5	1	1	2	43	....	....	....	....
2005-06	Spartak Moscow	Russia	50	15	17	32	40	....	....	....	....	....	....	....	....	....	3	2	1	3	4	....	....	....	....
2006-07	Dynamo Moscow	Russia	42	10	16	26	91	....	....	....	....	....	....	....	....	....	3	1	1	2	4	....	....	....	....
	NHL Totals		**93**	**4**	**4**	**8**	**191**	**0**	**0**	**0**	**88**	**4.5**		**24**	**37.5**	**7:56**	....	....	....	....	....	....	....	....	....

OHL First All-Star Team (1995) • OHL MVP (1995) • Canadian Major Junior First All-Star Team (1995) • Canadian Major Junior Player of the Year (1995) • IHL First All-Star Team (2000)

Rights transferred to **Colorado** after **Quebec** franchise relocated, June 21, 1995. Traded to **Calgary** by **Colorado** with Colorado's 9th round choice (Steve Shirreffs) in 1995 Entry Draft for Calgary's 9th round choice (Chris George) in 1995 Entry Draft, July 7, 1995. Traded to **Montreal** by **Calgary** with Calgary's 6th round choice (Gordie Dwyer) in 1998 Entry Draft for Scott Fraser, October 24, 1996. Traded to **Chicago** by **Montreal** for Martin Gendron, March 14, 1998. Signed as a free agent by **Kansas City** (IHL) with Chicago retaining NHL rights, September 3, 1998. Traded to **Dallas** by **Chicago** for future considerations, August 11, 2000. Signed as a free agent by **Columbus**, July 7, 2001. Signed as a free agent by **Toronto**, July 29, 2004. Signed as a free agent by **Dynamo Moscow** (Russia), August 22, 2006. Signed as a free agent by **Toronto**, July 9, 2007.

LISIN, Enver
(LIH-sihn, EHN-vuhr)

Right wing. Shoots left. 6'2", 190 lbs. Born, Moscow, USSR, April 22, 1986. Phoenix's 3rd choice, 50th overall, in 2004 Entry Draft.

Season	Club	League	GP	G	A	Pts	PIM	PP	SH	GW	S	%	+/-	TF	F%	Min	GP	G	A	Pts	PIM	PP	SH	GW	Min
2001-02	Dyn'o Moscow 2	Russia-3	6	3	0	3	14	....	....	....	....	....	....	....	....	....	....	....	....	....	....	....	....	....	....
2002-03	Dyn'o Moscow 2	Russia-3	STATISTICS NOT AVAILABLE																						
2003-04	Dyn'o Moscow 2	Russia-3	STATISTICS NOT AVAILABLE																						
	Kristall Saratov	Russia-2	35	10	6	16	30	....	....	....	....	....	....	....	....	....	4	1	0	1	0	....	....	....	....
2004-05	Ak Bars Kazan 2	Russia-3	....	4	3	7	....	....	....	....	....	....	....	....	....	....	....	....	....	....	....	....	....	....	....
	Ak Bars Kazan	Russia	53	8	4	12	4	....	....	....	....	....	....	....	....	....	3	0	0	0	0	....	....	....	....
2005-06	Ak Bars Kazan	Russia	43	7	5	12	26	....	....	....	....	....	....	....	....	....	13	3	1	4	6	....	....	....	....
2006-07	**Phoenix**	**NHL**	**17**	**1**	**1**	**2**	**16**	**1**	**0**	**0**	**35**	**2.9**	**–18**	**7**	**28.6**	**15:02**	....	....	....	....	....	....	....	....	....
	San Antonio	AHL	2	2	0	2	4	....	....	....	....	....	....	....	....	....	....	....	....	....	....	....	....	....	....
	Ak Bars Kazan	Russia	20	6	2	8	18	....	....	....	....	....	....	....	....	....	1	0	0	0	0	....	....	....	....
	NHL Totals		**17**	**1**	**1**	**2**	**16**	**1**	**0**	**0**	**35**	**2.9**		**7**	**28.6**	**15:02**	....	....	....	....	....	....	....	....	....

Signed as a free agent by **Kazan** (Russia), December, 2006. Signed as a free agent by **Mytischy** (Russia), July 2, 2007.

LOJEK, Martin
(LOI-yehk, MAHR-tihn) **FLA.**

Defense. Shoots right. 6'4", 220 lbs. Born, Brno, Czech., August 19, 1985. Florida's 5th choice, 105th overall, in 2003 Entry Draft.

Season	Club	League	GP	G	A	Pts	PIM	PP	SH	GW	S	%	+/-	TF	F%	Min	GP	G	A	Pts	PIM	PP	SH	GW	Min
2000-01	HC Pardubice Jr.	CzRep-Jr.	48	2	2	4	42	....	....	....	....	....	....	....	....	....	7	0	0	0	6	....	....	....	....
2001-02	HC Pardubice Jr.	CzRep-Jr.	40	2	4	6	24	....	....	....	....	....	....	....	....	....	7	1	0	1	2	....	....	....	....
2002-03	Brampton	OHL	65	1	13	14	47	....	....	....	....	....	....	....	....	....	11	0	1	1	6	....	....	....	....
2003-04	Brampton	OHL	68	3	17	20	37	....	....	....	....	....	....	....	....	....	12	0	4	4	2	....	....	....	....
2004-05	Brampton	OHL	58	1	12	13	58	....	....	....	....	....	....	....	....	....	6	0	0	0	6	....	....	....	....
2005-06	Rochester	AHL	15	1	1	2	16	....	....	....	....	....	....	....	....	....	....	....	....	....	....	....	....	....	....
	Florida Everblades	ECHL	45	3	11	14	40	....	....	....	....	....	....	....	....	....	2	0	0	0	0	....	....	....	....
2006-07	**Florida**	**NHL**	**3**	**0**	**1**	**1**	**0**	**0**	**0**	**0**	**0**	**0.0**	**2**	**0**	**0.0**	**8:23**	....	....	....	....	....	....	....	....	....
	Rochester	AHL	69	6	13	19	87	....	....	....	....	....	....	....	....	....	....	....	....	....	....	....	....	....	....
	NHL Totals		**3**	**0**	**1**	**1**	**0**	**0**	**0**	**0**	**0**	**0.0**		**0**	**0.0**	**8:23**	....	....	....	....	....	....	....	....	....

LOMBARDI, Matthew
(lawm-BAHR-dee, MA-thew) **CGY.**

Center. Shoots left. 6', 193 lbs. Born, Montreal, Que., March 18, 1982. Calgary's 3rd choice, 90th overall, in 2002 Entry Draft.

Season	Club	League	GP	G	A	Pts	PIM	PP	SH	GW	S	%	+/-	TF	F%	Min	GP	G	A	Pts	PIM	PP	SH	GW	Min
1997-98	Gatineau	QAAA	42	10	13	23	....	....	....	....	....	....	....	....	....	....	13	4	7	11	....	....	....	....	....
1998-99	Victoriaville Tigres	QMJHL	47	6	10	16	8	....	....	....	....	....	....	....	....	....	5	0	0	0	0	....	....	....	....
99-2000	Victoriaville Tigres	QMJHL	65	18	26	44	28	....	....	....	....	....	....	....	....	....	6	0	0	0	6	....	....	....	....
2000-01	Victoriaville Tigres	QMJHL	72	28	39	67	66	....	....	....	....	....	....	....	....	....	13	12	6	18	10	....	....	....	....
2001-02	Victoriaville Tigres	QMJHL	66	57	73	130	70	....	....	....	....	....	....	....	....	....	22	*17	18	35	18	....	....	....	....
2002-03	Saint John Flames	AHL	76	25	21	46	41	....	....	....	....	....	....	....	....	....	....	....	....	....	....	....	....	....	....
2003-04	**Calgary**	**NHL**	**79**	**16**	**13**	**29**	**32**	**3**	**2**	**4**	**130**	**12.3**	**4**	**992**	**47.9**	**14:26**	**13**	**1**	**5**	**6**	**4**	**0**	**0**	**1**	**14:46**
2004-05	Lowell	AHL	9	3	1	4	9	....	....	....	....	....	....	....	....	....	11	0	3	3	16	....	....	....	....
2005-06	**Calgary**	**NHL**	**55**	**6**	**20**	**26**	**48**	**1**	**2**	**2**	**72**	**8.3**	**–1**	**499**	**52.9**	**14:09**	**7**	**0**	**2**	**2**	**2**	**0**	**0**	**0**	**15:51**
	Omaha	AHL	1	1	1	2	0	....	....	....	....	....	....	....	....	....	....	....	....	....	....	....	....	....	....
2006-07	**Calgary**	**NHL**	**81**	**20**	**26**	**46**	**48**	**5**	**4**	**5**	**176**	**11.4**	**10**	**965**	**49.1**	**16:22**	**6**	**1**	**1**	**2**	**0**	**1**	**0**	**0**	**15:19**
	NHL Totals		**215**	**42**	**59**	**101**	**128**	**9**	**8**	**11**	**378**	**11.1**		**2456**	**49.4**	**15:05**	**26**	**2**	**8**	**10**	**6**	**1**	**0**	**1**	**15:11**

• Re-entered NHL Entry Draft. Originally Edmonton's 7th choice, 215th overall, in 2000 Entry Draft.

Memorial Cup Tournament All-Star Team (2002) • Ed Chynoweth Trophy (Memorial Cup Tournament Leading Scorer) (2002)

LOW, Reed

(LOH, REED)

Right wing. Shoots right. 6'4", 220 lbs. Born, Moose Jaw, Sask., June 21, 1976. St. Louis' 7th choice, 177th overall, in 1996 Entry Draft.

			Regular Season														Playoffs								
Season	Club	League	GP	G	A	Pts	PIM	PP	SH	GW	S	%	+/-	TF	F%	Min	GP	G	A	Pts	PIM	PP	SH	GW	Min
1994-95	Minot Top Guns	SJHL	STATISTICS NOT AVAILABLE																						
	Regina Pats	WHL	2	0	0	0	5	....	....	....	....	....	....	....	....	....	....	....	....	....	....	....	....	....	....
1995-96	Moose Jaw	WHL	61	12	7	19	221	....	....	....	....	....	....	....	....	....	....	....	....	....	....	....	....	....	....
1996-97	Moose Jaw	WHL	62	16	11	27	228	....	....	....	....	....	....	....	....	....	12	2	1	3	50	....	....	....	....
1997-98	Worcester IceCats	AHL	17	1	1	2	75	....	....	....	....	....	....	....	....	....	3	0	0	0	0	....	....	....	....
	Baton Rouge	ECHL	39	4	2	6	145	....	....	....	....	....	....	....	....	....	....	....	....	....	....	....	....	....	....
1998-99	Worcester IceCats	AHL	77	5	6	11	239	....	....	....	....	....	....	....	....	....	4	0	0	0	2	....	....	....	....
99-2000	Worcester IceCats	AHL	80	12	16	28	203	....	....	....	....	....	....	....	....	....	9	1	3	4	16	....	....	....	....
2000-01	**St. Louis**	**NHL**	**56**	**1**	**5**	**6**	**159**	**0**	**0**	**0**	**31**	**3.2**	**4**	**2**	**50.0**	**6:17**	....	....	....	....	....	....	....	....	....
2001-02	**St. Louis**	**NHL**	**58**	**0**	**5**	**5**	**160**	**0**	**0**	**0**	**25**	**0.0**	**–3**	**0**	**0.0**	**5:22**	....	....	....	....	....	....	....	....	....
2002-03	**St. Louis**	**NHL**	**79**	**2**	**4**	**6**	**234**	**0**	**0**	**1**	**48**	**4.2**	**3**	**14**	**71.4**	**6:19**	....	....	....	....	....	....	....	....	....
2003-04	**St. Louis**	**NHL**	**57**	**0**	**2**	**2**	**141**	**0**	**0**	**0**	**28**	**0.0**	**–6**	**0**	**0.0**	**5:42**	....	....	....	....	....	....	....	....	....
2004-05			DID NOT PLAY																						
2005-06	Peoria Rivermen	AHL	20	3	5	8	40	....	....	....	....	....	....	....	....	....	....	....	....	....	....	....	....	....	....
	Missouri	UHL	4	2	1	3	13	....	....	....	....	....	....	....	....	....	....	....	....	....	....	....	....	....	....
2006-07	**Chicago**	**NHL**	**6**	**0**	**0**	**0**	**31**	**0**	**0**	**0**	**0**	**0.0**	**–1**	**0**	**0.0**	**3:33**	....	....	....	....	....	....	....	....	....
	Norfolk Admirals	AHL	58	4	6	10	172	....	....	....	....	....	....	....	....	....	5	1	0	1	6	....	....	....	....
	NHL Totals		**256**	**3**	**16**	**19**	**725**	**0**	**0**	**1**	**132**	**2.3**		**16**	**68.8**	**5:53**	....	....	....	....	....	....	....	....	....

Signed as a free agent by **Chicago**, July 27, 2006.

LOYNS, Lynn

(LOINZ, LIHN)

Left wing. Shoots left. 5'11", 205 lbs. Born, Naicam, Sask., February 21, 1981.

Season	Club	League	GP	G	A	Pts	PIM	PP	SH	GW	S	%	+/-	TF	F%	Min	GP	G	A	Pts	PIM	PP	SH	GW	Min
1996-97	Naicam Vikings	SAHA	41	90	70	160	58	....	....	....	....	....	....	....	....	....	....	....	....	....	....	....	....	....	....
1997-98	Spokane Chiefs	WHL	49	1	12	13	8	....	....	....	....	....	....	....	....	....	13	1	4	5	2	....	....	....	....
1998-99	Spokane Chiefs	WHL	72	20	30	50	43	....	....	....	....	....	....	....	....	....	....	....	....	....	....	....	....	....	....
99-2000	Spokane Chiefs	WHL	71	20	29	49	47	....	....	....	....	....	....	....	....	....	14	3	2	5	12	....	....	....	....
2000-01	Spokane Chiefs	WHL	66	31	42	73	81	....	....	....	....	....	....	....	....	....	....	....	....	....	....	....	....	....	....
2001-02	Cleveland Barons	AHL	76	9	9	18	81	....	....	....	....	....	....	....	....	....	....	....	....	....	....	....	....	....	....
2002-03	**San Jose**	**NHL**	**19**	**3**	**0**	**3**	**19**	**0**	**0**	**0**	**12**	**25.0**	**–4**	**1**	**0.0**	**7:50**	....	....	....	....	....	....	....	....	....
	Cleveland Barons	AHL	36	7	8	15	39	....	....	....	....	....	....	....	....	....	....	....	....	....	....	....	....	....	....
2003-04	**San Jose**	**NHL**	**2**	**0**	**0**	**0**	**0**	**0**	**0**	**0**	**0**	**0.0**	**–1**	**0**	**0.0**	**7:33**	....	....	....	....	....	....	....	....	....
	Cleveland Barons	AHL	30	5	9	14	40	....	....	....	....	....	....	....	....	....	....	....	....	....	....	....	....	....	....
	Calgary	**NHL**	**12**	**0**	**2**	**2**	**2**	**0**	**0**	**0**	**6**	**0.0**	**–2**	**86**	**44.2**	**11:13**	....	....	....	....	....	....	....	....	....
	Lowell	AHL	18	6	6	12	9	....	....	....	....	....	....	....	....	....	....	....	....	....	....	....	....	....	....
2004-05	Lowell	AHL	77	7	8	15	42	....	....	....	....	....	....	....	....	....	11	0	0	0	0	....	....	....	....
2005-06	**Calgary**	**NHL**	**1**	**0**	**0**	**0**	**0**	**0**	**0**	**0**	**0**	**0.0**	**0**	**0**	**0.0**	**6:15**	....	....	....	....	....	....	....	....	....
	Omaha	AHL	68	9	8	17	50	....	....	....	....	....	....	....	....	....	....	....	....	....	....	....	....	....	....
2006-07	Krefeld Pinguine	Germany	51	16	14	30	26	....	....	....	....	....	....	....	....	....	2	1	0	1	6	....	....	....	....
	NHL Totals		**34**	**3**	**2**	**5**	**21**	**0**	**0**	**0**	**18**	**16.7**		**87**	**43.7**	**8:58**	....	....	....	....	....	....	....	....	....

Signed as a free agent by **San Jose**, October 3, 2001. Traded to **Calgary** by **San Jose** for Calgary's 5th round choice (later traded to Florida – Florida selected Bret Nasby) in 2004 Entry Draft, January 9, 2004. Signed as a free agent by **Krefeld** (Germany), August 25, 2006.

LUKOWICH, Brad

(loo-KUH-which, BRAD) **T.B.**

Defense. Shoots left. 6'1", 205 lbs. Born, Cranbrook, B.C., August 12, 1976. NY Islanders' 4th choice, 90th overall, in 1994 Entry Draft.

Season	Club	League	GP	G	A	Pts	PIM	PP	SH	GW	S	%	+/-	TF	F%	Min	GP	G	A	Pts	PIM	PP	SH	GW	Min
1992-93	Cranbrook Colts	RMJHL	54	21	41	62	162	....	....	....	....	....	....	....	....	....	....	....	....	....	....	....	....	....	....
	Kamloops Blazers	WHL	1	0	0	0	0	....	....	....	....	....	....	....	....	....	....	....	....	....	....	....	....	....	....
1993-94	Kamloops Blazers	WHL	42	5	11	16	166	....	....	....	....	....	....	....	....	....	16	0	1	1	35	....	....	....	....
1994-95	Kamloops Blazers	WHL	63	10	35	45	125	....	....	....	....	....	....	....	....	....	18	0	7	7	21	....	....	....	....
1995-96	Kamloops Blazers	WHL	65	14	55	69	114	....	....	....	....	....	....	....	....	....	13	2	10	12	29	....	....	....	....
1996-97	Michigan	IHL	69	2	6	8	77	....	....	....	....	....	....	....	....	....	4	0	1	1	2	....	....	....	....
1997-98	**Dallas**	**NHL**	**4**	**0**	**1**	**1**	**2**	**0**	**0**	**0**	**2**	**0.0**	**–2**	....	....	....	....	....	....	....	....	....	....	....	....
	Michigan	IHL	60	6	27	33	104	....	....	....	....	....	....	....	....	....	4	0	4	4	14	....	....	....	....
1998-99	**Dallas**	**NHL**	**14**	**1**	**2**	**3**	**19**	**0**	**0**	**0**	**8**	**12.5**	**3**	**0**	**0.0**	**16:18**	**8**	**0**	**1**	**1**	**4**	**0**	**0**	**0**	**10:00**
	Michigan	IHL	67	8	21	29	95	....	....	....	....	....	....	....	....	....	....	....	....	....	....	....	....	....	....
99-2000	**Dallas**	**NHL**	**60**	**3**	**1**	**4**	**50**	**0**	**0**	**1**	**33**	**9.1**	**–14**	**1**	**0.0**	**11:44**	....	....	....	....	....	....	....	....	....
2000-01	**Dallas**	**NHL**	**80**	**4**	**10**	**14**	**76**	**0**	**0**	**2**	**43**	**9.3**	**28**	**1**	**100.0**	**14:48**	**10**	**1**	**0**	**1**	**4**	**0**	**0**	**0**	**17:28**
2001-02	**Dallas**	**NHL**	**66**	**1**	**6**	**7**	**40**	**0**	**0**	**0**	**56**	**1.8**	**–1**	**0**	**0.0**	**13:14**	....	....	....	....	....	....	....	....	....
2002-03	**Tampa Bay**	**NHL**	**70**	**1**	**14**	**15**	**46**	**0**	**0**	**0**	**52**	**1.9**	**4**	**1**	**0.0**	**17:34**	**9**	**0**	**1**	**1**	**2**	**0**	**0**	**0**	**17:48**
2003-04♦	**Tampa Bay**	**NHL**	**79**	**5**	**14**	**19**	**24**	**0**	**0**	**1**	**86**	**5.8**	**29**	**3**	**0.0**	**18:45**	**18**	**0**	**2**	**2**	**6**	**0**	**0**	**0**	**15:51**
2004-05	Fort Worth	CHL	16	3	5	8	33	....	....	....	....	....	....	....	....	....	....	....	....	....	....	....	....	....	....
2005-06	**NY Islanders**	**NHL**	**57**	**1**	**12**	**13**	**32**	**0**	**0**	**1**	**36**	**2.8**	**–3**	**0**	**0.0**	**19:15**	....	....	....	....	....	....	....	....	....
	New Jersey	**NHL**	**18**	**1**	**7**	**8**	**8**	**0**	**0**	**0**	**13**	**7.7**	**3**	**0**	**0.0**	**19:11**	**9**	**0**	**0**	**0**	**4**	**0**	**0**	**0**	**21:28**
2006-07	**New Jersey**	**NHL**	**75**	**4**	**8**	**12**	**36**	**0**	**1**	**2**	**50**	**8.0**	**1**	**0**	**0.0**	**20:13**	**11**	**0**	**1**	**1**	**2**	**0**	**0**	**0**	**19:57**
	NHL Totals		**523**	**21**	**75**	**96**	**333**	**0**	**1**	**7**	**379**	**5.5**		**6**	**16.7**	**16:41**	**65**	**1**	**5**	**6**	**22**	**0**	**0**	**0**	**17:07**

Traded to **Dallas** by **NY Islanders** for Dallas' 3rd round choice (Robert Schnabel) in 1997 Entry Draft, June 1, 1996. Traded to **Minnesota** by **Dallas** with Manny Fernandez for Minnesota's 3rd round choice (Joel Lundqvist) in 2000 Entry Draft and Minnesota's 4th round choice (later traded back to Minnesota – later traded to Los Angeles – Los Angeles selected Aaron Rome) in 2002 Entry Draft, June 12, 2000. Traded to **Dallas** by **Minnesota** with Minnesota's 3rd (Yared Hagos) and 9th (Dale Sullivan) round choices in 2001 Entry Draft for Aaron Gavey, Pavel Patera, Dallas' 8th round choice (Eric Johansson) in 2000 Entry Draft and Minnesota's 4th round choice (previously acquired, later traded to Los Angeles – Los Angeles selected Aaron Rome) in 2002 Entry Draft, June 25, 2000. Traded to **Tampa Bay** by **Dallas** with Dallas' 7th round choice (Jay Rosehill) in 2003 Entry Draft for Tampa Bay's 2nd round choice (previously acquired, later traded back to Tampa Bay – later traded to Dallas – Dallas selected Tobias Stephan) in 2002 Entry Draft, June 22, 2002. Signed as a free agent by **Fort Worth** (CHL), September 21, 2004. Signed as a free agent by **NY Islanders**, August 11, 2005. Traded to **New Jersey** by **NY Islanders** for New Jersey's 3rd round choice (later traded to Phoenix - Phoenix selected Jonas Ahnelov) in 2006 Entry Draft, March 9, 2006. Signed as a free agent by **Tampa Bay**, July 3, 2007.

LUNDMARK, Jamie

(LUHND-mahrk, JAY-mee)

Center. Shoots right. 6', 200 lbs. Born, Edmonton, Alta., January 16, 1981. NY Rangers' 2nd choice, 9th overall, in 1999 Entry Draft.

Season	Club	League	GP	G	A	Pts	PIM	PP	SH	GW	S	%	+/-	TF	F%	Min	GP	G	A	Pts	PIM	PP	SH	GW	Min
1996-97	St. Albert Saints	AJHL	35	10	9	19	8	....	....	....	....	....	....	....	....	....	....	....	....	....	....	....	....	....	....
1997-98	St. Albert Saints	AJHL	57	33	58	91	171	....	....	....	....	....	....	....	....	....	19	13	18	31	5	....	....	....	....
1998-99	Moose Jaw	WHL	70	40	51	91	121	....	....	....	....	....	....	....	....	....	11	5	4	9	24	....	....	....	....
99-2000	Moose Jaw	WHL	37	21	27	48	33	....	....	....	....	....	....	....	....	....	....	....	....	....	....	....	....	....	....
2000-01	Seattle	WHL	52	35	42	77	49	....	....	....	....	....	....	....	....	....	9	4	4	8	16	....	....	....	....
2001-02	Hartford	AHL	79	27	32	59	56	....	....	....	....	....	....	....	....	....	10	3	4	7	16	....	....	....	....
2002-03	**NY Rangers**	**NHL**	**55**	**8**	**11**	**19**	**16**	**0**	**0**	**0**	**78**	**10.3**	**–3**	**62**	**43.6**	**12:04**	....	....	....	....	....	....	....	....	....
	Hartford	AHL	22	9	9	18	18	....	....	....	....	....	....	....	....	....	2	0	0	0	0	....	....	....	....
2003-04	**NY Rangers**	**NHL**	**56**	**2**	**8**	**10**	**33**	**0**	**0**	**1**	**68**	**2.9**	**–8**	**379**	**40.4**	**12:46**	....	....	....	....	....	....	....	....	....
2004-05	HC Forst Bolzano	Italy	14	9	9	18	22	....	....	....	....	....	....	....	....	....	....	....	....	....	....	....	....	....	....
	Hartford	AHL	64	14	27	41	146	....	....	....	....	....	....	....	....	....	6	2	4	6	8	....	....	....	....
2005-06	**NY Rangers**	**NHL**	**3**	**1**	**0**	**1**	**6**	**0**	**0**	**0**	**1**	**100.0**	**–2**	**2**	**0.0**	**9:49**	....	....	....	....	....	....	....	....	....
	Phoenix	**NHL**	**38**	**5**	**13**	**18**	**36**	**1**	**0**	**0**	**61**	**8.2**	**–1**	**366**	**58.7**	**12:37**	....	....	....	....	....	....	....	....	....
	San Antonio	AHL	4	1	2	3	2	....	....	....	....	....	....	....	....	....	....	....	....	....	....	....	....	....	....
	Calgary	**NHL**	**12**	**4**	**6**	**10**	**20**	**1**	**0**	**1**	**16**	**25.0**	**2**	**103**	**53.4**	**12:32**	**4**	**0**	**1**	**1**	**7**	**0**	**0**	**0**	**9:44**
2006-07	**Calgary**	**NHL**	**39**	**0**	**4**	**4**	**31**	**0**	**0**	**0**	**28**	**0.0**	**–4**	**233**	**55.4**	**8:37**	....	....	....	....	....	....	....	....	....
	Los Angeles	**NHL**	**29**	**7**	**2**	**9**	**25**	**0**	**0**	**0**	**53**	**13.2**	**–8**	**410**	**47.6**	**16:03**	....	....	....	....	....	....	....	....	....
	NHL Totals		**232**	**27**	**44**	**71**	**167**	**2**	**0**	**2**	**305**	**8.9**		**1555**	**49.8**	**12:14**	**4**	**0**	**1**	**1**	**7**	**0**	**0**	**0**	**9:44**

WHL All-Rookie Team (1999) • WHL East Second All-Star Team (1999) • WHL West First All-Star Team (2001)

Signed as a free agent by **Bolzano** (Italy), September 21, 2004. Signed as a free agent by **Hartford** (AHL), November 16, 2004. Traded to **Phoenix** by **NY Rangers** for Jeff Taffe, October 18. 2005. Traded to **Calgary** by **Phoenix** for Calgary's 4th round choice (later traded to NY Islanders - NY Islanders selected Doug Rogers) in 2006 Entry Draft, March 9, 2006. Traded to **Los Angeles** by **Calgary** with Calgary's 4th round choice (Dwight King) in 2007 Entry Draft and Calgary's 2nd round choice in 2008 Entry Draft for Craig Conroy, January 29, 2007.

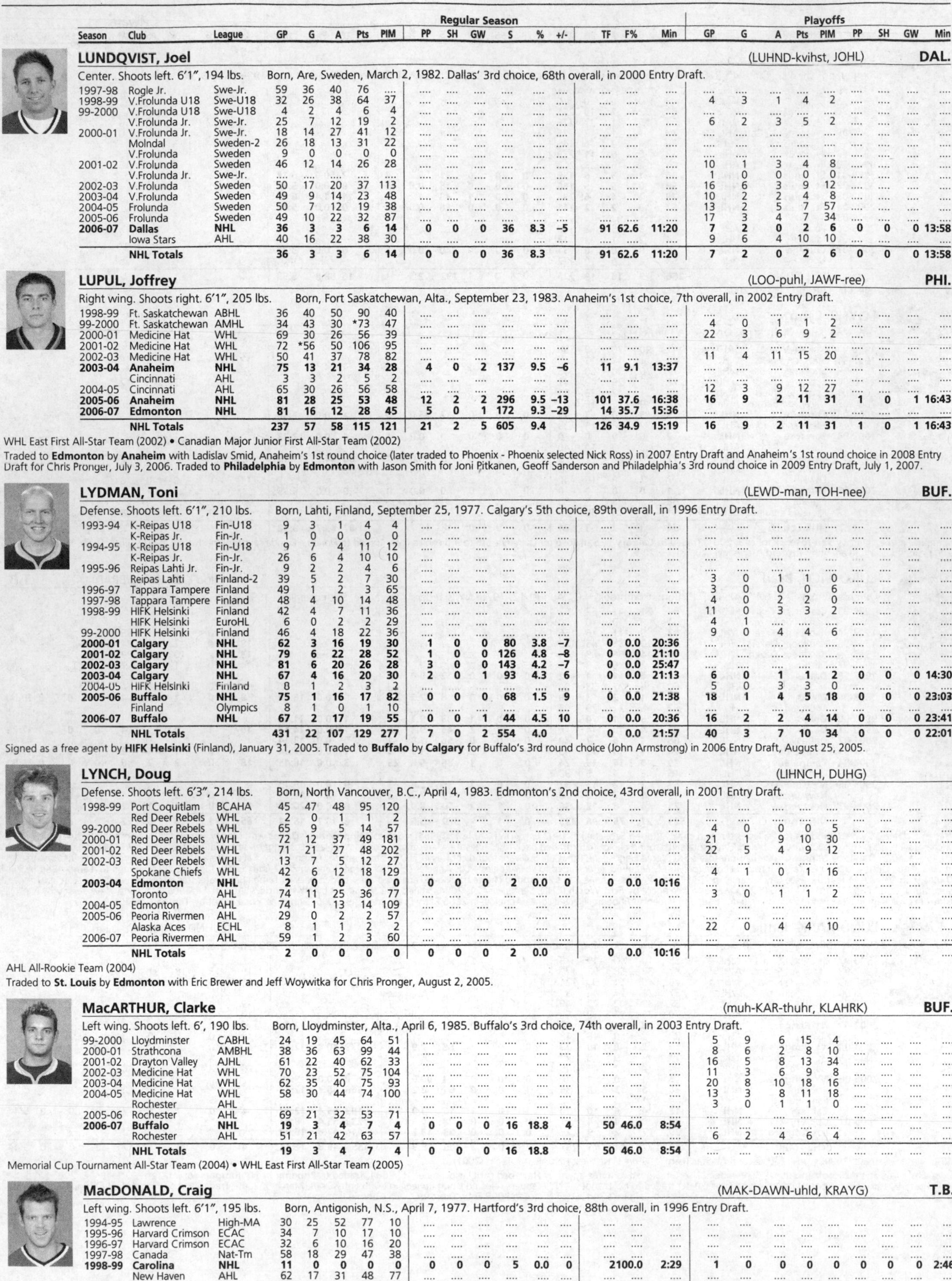

LUNDQVIST, Joel (LUHND-kvihst, JOHL) **DAL.**

Center. Shoots left. 6'1", 194 lbs. Born, Are, Sweden, March 2, 1982. Dallas' 3rd choice, 68th overall, in 2000 Entry Draft.

			Regular Season														Playoffs								
Season	Club	League	GP	G	A	Pts	PIM	PP	SH	GW	S	%	+/-	TF	F%	Min	GP	G	A	Pts	PIM	PP	SH	GW	Min
1997-98	Rogle Jr.	Swe-Jr.	59	36	40	76	....	....	....	....	....	....	....	....	....	....	....	....	....	....	....	....	....	....	....
1998-99	V.Frolunda U18	Swe-U18	32	26	38	64	37	....	....	....	....	....	....	....	....	....	4	3	1	4	2	....	....	....	....
99-2000	V.Frolunda U18	Swe-U18	4	2	4	6	4	....	....	....	....	....	....	....	....	....	....	....	....	....	....	....	....	....	....
	V.Frolunda Jr.	Swe-Jr.	25	7	12	19	2	....	....	....	....	....	....	....	....	....	6	2	3	5	2	....	....	....	....
2000-01	V.Frolunda Jr.	Swe-Jr.	18	14	27	41	12	....	....	....	....	....	....	....	....	....	....	....	....	....	....	....	....	....	....
	Molndal	Sweden-2	26	18	13	31	22	....	....	....	....	....	....	....	....	....	....	....	....	....	....	....	....	....	....
	V.Frolunda	Sweden	9	0	0	0	0	....	....	....	....	....	....	....	....	....	....	....	....	....	....	....	....	....	....
2001-02	V.Frolunda	Sweden	46	12	14	26	28	....	....	....	....	....	....	....	....	....	10	1	3	4	8	....	....	....	....
	V.Frolunda Jr.	Swe-Jr.	....	....	....	....	....	....	....	....	....	....	....	....	....	....	1	0	0	0	0	....	....	....	....
2002-03	V.Frolunda	Sweden	50	17	20	37	113	....	....	....	....	....	....	....	....	....	16	6	3	9	12	....	....	....	....
2003-04	V.Frolunda	Sweden	49	9	14	23	48	....	....	....	....	....	....	....	....	....	10	2	2	4	8	....	....	....	....
2004-05	Frolunda	Sweden	50	7	12	19	38	....	....	....	....	....	....	....	....	....	13	2	5	7	57	....	....	....	....
2005-06	Frolunda	Sweden	49	10	22	32	87	....	....	....	....	....	....	....	....	....	17	3	4	7	34	....	....	....	....
2006-07	**Dallas**	**NHL**	**36**	**3**	**3**	**6**	**14**	**0**	**0**	**0**	**36**	**8.3**	**–5**	**91**	**62.6**	**11:20**	**7**	**2**	**0**	**2**	**6**	**0**	**0**	**0**	**13:58**
	Iowa Stars	AHL	40	16	22	38	30	....	....	....	....	....	....	....	....	....	9	6	4	10	10	....	....	....	....
	NHL Totals		**36**	**3**	**3**	**6**	**14**	**0**	**0**	**0**	**36**	**8.3**		**91**	**62.6**	**11:20**	**7**	**2**	**0**	**2**	**6**	**0**	**0**	**0**	**13:58**

LUPUL, Joffrey (LOO-puhl, JAWF-ree) **PHI.**

Right wing. Shoots right. 6'1", 205 lbs. Born, Fort Saskatchewan, Alta., September 23, 1983. Anaheim's 1st choice, 7th overall, in 2002 Entry Draft.

Season	Club	League	GP	G	A	Pts	PIM	PP	SH	GW	S	%	+/-	TF	F%	Min	GP	G	A	Pts	PIM	PP	SH	GW	Min
1998-99	Ft. Saskatchewan	ABHL	36	40	50	90	40	....	....	....	....	....	....	....	....	....	....	....	....	....	....	....	....	....	....
99-2000	Ft. Saskatchewan	AMHL	34	43	30	*73	47	....	....	....	....	....	....	....	....	....	4	0	1	1	2	....	....	....	....
2000-01	Medicine Hat	WHL	69	30	26	56	39	....	....	....	....	....	....	....	....	....	22	3	6	9	2	....	....	....	....
2001-02	Medicine Hat	WHL	72	*56	50	106	95	....	....	....	....	....	....	....	....	....	....	....	....	....	....	....	....	....	....
2002-03	Medicine Hat	WHL	50	41	37	78	82	....	....	....	....	....	....	....	....	....	11	4	11	15	20	....	....	....	....
2003-04	**Anaheim**	**NHL**	**75**	**13**	**21**	**34**	**28**	**4**	**0**	**2**	**137**	**9.5**	**–6**	**11**	**9.1**	**13:37**	....	....	....	....	....	....	....	....	....
	Cincinnati	AHL	3	3	2	5	2	....	....	....	....	....	....	....	....	....	....	....	....	....	....	....	....	....	....
2004-05	Cincinnati	AHL	65	30	26	56	58	....	....	....	....	....	....	....	....	....	12	3	9	12	27	....	....	....	....
2005-06	**Anaheim**	**NHL**	**81**	**28**	**25**	**53**	**48**	**12**	**2**	**2**	**296**	**9.5**	**–13**	**101**	**37.6**	**16:38**	**16**	**9**	**2**	**11**	**31**	**1**	**0**	**1**	**16:43**
2006-07	**Edmonton**	**NHL**	**81**	**16**	**12**	**28**	**45**	**5**	**0**	**1**	**172**	**9.3**	**–29**	**14**	**35.7**	**15:36**	....	....	....	....	....	....	....	....	....
	NHL Totals		**237**	**57**	**58**	**115**	**121**	**21**	**2**	**5**	**605**	**9.4**		**126**	**34.9**	**15:19**	**16**	**9**	**2**	**11**	**31**	**1**	**0**	**1**	**16:43**

WHL East First All-Star Team (2002) • Canadian Major Junior First All-Star Team (2002)

Traded to **Edmonton** by **Anaheim** with Ladislav Smid, Anaheim's 1st round choice (later traded to Phoenix - Phoenix selected Nick Ross) in 2007 Entry Draft and Anaheim's 1st round choice in 2008 Entry Draft for Chris Pronger, July 3, 2006. Traded to **Philadelphia** by **Edmonton** with Jason Smith for Joni Pitkanen, Geoff Sanderson and Philadelphia's 3rd round choice in 2009 Entry Draft, July 1, 2007.

LYDMAN, Toni (LEWD-man, TOH-nee) **BUF.**

Defense. Shoots left. 6'1", 210 lbs. Born, Lahti, Finland, September 25, 1977. Calgary's 5th choice, 89th overall, in 1996 Entry Draft.

Season	Club	League	GP	G	A	Pts	PIM	PP	SH	GW	S	%	+/-	TF	F%	Min	GP	G	A	Pts	PIM	PP	SH	GW	Min
1993-94	K-Reipas U18	Fin-U18	9	3	1	4	4	....	....	....	....	....	....	....	....	....	....	....	....	....	....	....	....	....	....
	K-Reipas Jr.	Fin-Jr.	1	0	0	0	0	....	....	....	....	....	....	....	....	....	....	....	....	....	....	....	....	....	....
1994-95	K-Reipas U18	Fin-U18	9	7	4	11	12	....	....	....	....	....	....	....	....	....	....	....	....	....	....	....	....	....	....
	K-Reipas Jr.	Fin-Jr.	26	6	4	10	10	....	....	....	....	....	....	....	....	....	....	....	....	....	....	....	....	....	....
1995-96	Reipas Lahti Jr.	Fin-Jr.	9	2	2	4	6	....	....	....	....	....	....	....	....	....	....	....	....	....	....	....	....	....	....
	Reipas Lahti	Finland-2	39	5	2	7	30	....	....	....	....	....	....	....	....	....	3	0	1	1	0	....	....	....	....
1996-97	Tappara Tampere	Finland	49	1	2	3	65	....	....	....	....	....	....	....	....	....	3	0	0	0	6	....	....	....	....
1997-98	Tappara Tampere	Finland	48	4	10	14	48	....	....	....	....	....	....	....	....	....	4	0	2	2	0	....	....	....	....
1998-99	HIFK Helsinki	Finland	42	4	7	11	36	....	....	....	....	....	....	....	....	....	11	0	3	3	2	....	....	....	....
	HIFK Helsinki	EuroHL	6	0	2	2	29	....	....	....	....	....	....	....	....	....	4	1	....	....	....	....	....	....	....
99-2000	HIFK Helsinki	Finland	46	4	18	22	36	....	....	....	....	....	....	....	....	....	9	0	4	4	6	....	....	....	....
2000-01	**Calgary**	**NHL**	**62**	**3**	**16**	**19**	**30**	**1**	**0**	**0**	**80**	**3.8**	**–7**	**0**	**0.0**	**20:36**	....	....	....	....	....	....	....	....	....
2001-02	**Calgary**	**NHL**	**79**	**6**	**22**	**28**	**52**	**1**	**0**	**0**	**126**	**4.8**	**–8**	**0**	**0.0**	**21:10**	....	....	....	....	....	....	....	....	....
2002-03	**Calgary**	**NHL**	**81**	**6**	**20**	**26**	**28**	**3**	**0**	**0**	**143**	**4.2**	**–7**	**0**	**0.0**	**25:47**	....	....	....	....	....	....	....	....	....
2003-04	**Calgary**	**NHL**	**67**	**4**	**16**	**20**	**30**	**2**	**0**	**1**	**93**	**4.3**	**6**	**0**	**0.0**	**21:13**	**6**	**0**	**1**	**1**	**2**	**0**	**0**	**0**	**14:30**
2004-05	HIFK Helsinki	Finland	8	1	2	3	2	....	....	....	....	....	....	....	....	....	5	0	3	3	0	....	....	....	....
2005-06	**Buffalo**	**NHL**	**75**	**1**	**16**	**17**	**82**	**0**	**0**	**0**	**68**	**1.5**	**9**	**0**	**0.0**	**21:38**	**18**	**1**	**4**	**5**	**18**	**0**	**0**	**0**	**23:03**
	Finland	Olympics	8	1	0	1	10	....	....	....	....	....	....	....	....	....	....	....	....	....	....	....	....	....	....
2006-07	**Buffalo**	**NHL**	**67**	**2**	**17**	**19**	**55**	**0**	**0**	**1**	**44**	**4.5**	**10**	**0**	**0.0**	**20:36**	**16**	**2**	**2**	**4**	**14**	**0**	**0**	**0**	**23:41**
	NHL Totals		**431**	**22**	**107**	**129**	**277**	**7**	**0**	**2**	**554**	**4.0**		**0**	**0.0**	**21:57**	**40**	**3**	**7**	**10**	**34**	**0**	**0**	**0**	**22:01**

Signed as a free agent by **HIFK Helsinki** (Finland), January 31, 2005. Traded to **Buffalo** by **Calgary** for Buffalo's 3rd round choice (John Armstrong) in 2006 Entry Draft, August 25, 2005.

LYNCH, Doug (LIHNCH, DUHG)

Defense. Shoots left. 6'3", 214 lbs. Born, North Vancouver, B.C., April 4, 1983. Edmonton's 2nd choice, 43rd overall, in 2001 Entry Draft.

Season	Club	League	GP	G	A	Pts	PIM	PP	SH	GW	S	%	+/-	TF	F%	Min	GP	G	A	Pts	PIM	PP	SH	GW	Min
1998-99	Port Coquitlam	BCAHA	45	47	48	95	120	....	....	....	....	....	....	....	....	....	....	....	....	....	....	....	....	....	....
	Red Deer Rebels	WHL	2	0	1	1	2	....	....	....	....	....	....	....	....	....	....	....	....	....	....	....	....	....	....
99-2000	Red Deer Rebels	WHL	65	9	5	14	57	....	....	....	....	....	....	....	....	....	4	0	0	0	5	....	....	....	....
2000-01	Red Deer Rebels	WHL	72	12	37	49	181	....	....	....	....	....	....	....	....	....	21	1	9	10	30	....	....	....	....
2001-02	Red Deer Rebels	WHL	71	21	27	48	202	....	....	....	....	....	....	....	....	....	22	5	4	9	12	....	....	....	....
2002-03	Red Deer Rebels	WHL	13	7	5	12	27	....	....	....	....	....	....	....	....	....	....	....	....	....	....	....	....	....	....
	Spokane Chiefs	WHL	42	6	12	18	129	....	....	....	....	....	....	....	....	....	4	1	0	1	16	....	....	....	....
2003-04	**Edmonton**	**NHL**	**2**	**0**	**0**	**0**	**0**	**0**	**0**	**0**	**2**	**0.0**	**0**	**0**	**0.0**	**10:16**	....	....	....	....	....	....	....	....	....
	Toronto	AHL	74	11	25	36	77	....	....	....	....	....	....	....	....	....	3	0	1	1	2	....	....	....	....
2004-05	Edmonton	AHL	74	1	13	14	109	....	....	....	....	....	....	....	....	....	....	....	....	....	....	....	....	....	....
2005-06	Peoria Rivermen	AHL	29	0	2	2	57	....	....	....	....	....	....	....	....	....	....	....	....	....	....	....	....	....	....
	Alaska Aces	ECHL	8	1	1	2	2	....	....	....	....	....	....	....	....	....	22	0	4	4	10	....	....	....	....
2006-07	Peoria Rivermen	AHL	59	1	2	3	60	....	....	....	....	....	....	....	....	....	....	....	....	....	....	....	....	....	....
	NHL Totals		**2**	**0**	**0**	**0**	**0**	**0**	**0**	**0**	**2**	**0.0**		**0**	**0.0**	**10:16**	....	....	....	....	....	....	....	....	....

AHL All-Rookie Team (2004)

Traded to **St. Louis** by **Edmonton** with Eric Brewer and Jeff Woywitka for Chris Pronger, August 2, 2005.

MacARTHUR, Clarke (muh-KAR-thuhr, KLAHRK) **BUF.**

Left wing. Shoots left. 6', 190 lbs. Born, Lloydminster, Alta., April 6, 1985. Buffalo's 3rd choice, 74th overall, in 2003 Entry Draft.

Season	Club	League	GP	G	A	Pts	PIM	PP	SH	GW	S	%	+/-	TF	F%	Min	GP	G	A	Pts	PIM	PP	SH	GW	Min
99-2000	Lloydminster	CABHL	24	19	45	64	51	....	....	....	....	....	....	....	....	....	5	9	6	15	4	....	....	....	....
2000-01	Strathcona	AMBHL	38	36	63	99	44	....	....	....	....	....	....	....	....	....	8	6	2	8	10	....	....	....	....
2001-02	Drayton Valley	AJHL	61	22	40	62	33	....	....	....	....	....	....	....	....	....	16	5	8	13	34	....	....	....	....
2002-03	Medicine Hat	WHL	70	23	52	75	104	....	....	....	....	....	....	....	....	....	11	3	6	9	8	....	....	....	....
2003-04	Medicine Hat	WHL	62	35	40	75	93	....	....	....	....	....	....	....	....	....	20	8	10	18	16	....	....	....	....
2004-05	Medicine Hat	WHL	58	30	44	74	100	....	....	....	....	....	....	....	....	....	13	3	8	11	18	....	....	....	....
	Rochester	AHL	....	....	....	....	....	....	....	....	....	....	....	....	....	....	3	0	1	1	0	....	....	....	....
2005-06	Rochester	AHL	69	21	32	53	71	....	....	....	....	....	....	....	....	....	....	....	....	....	....	....	....	....	....
2006-07	**Buffalo**	**NHL**	**19**	**3**	**4**	**7**	**4**	**0**	**0**	**0**	**16**	**18.8**	**4**	**50**	**46.0**	**8:54**	....	....	....	....	....	....	....	....	....
	Rochester	AHL	51	21	42	63	57	....	....	....	....	....	....	....	....	....	6	2	4	6	4	....	....	....	....
	NHL Totals		**19**	**3**	**4**	**7**	**4**	**0**	**0**	**0**	**16**	**18.8**		**50**	**46.0**	**8:54**									

Memorial Cup Tournament All-Star Team (2004) • WHL East First All-Star Team (2005)

MacDONALD, Craig (MAK-DAWN-uhld, KRAYG) **T.B.**

Left wing. Shoots left. 6'1", 195 lbs. Born, Antigonish, N.S., April 7, 1977. Hartford's 3rd choice, 88th overall, in 1996 Entry Draft.

Season	Club	League	GP	G	A	Pts	PIM	PP	SH	GW	S	%	+/-	TF	F%	Min	GP	G	A	Pts	PIM	PP	SH	GW	Min
1994-95	Lawrence	High-MA	30	25	52	77	10	....	....	....	....	....	....	....	....	....	....	....	....	....	....	....	....	....	....
1995-96	Harvard Crimson	ECAC	34	7	10	17	10	....	....	....	....	....	....	....	....	....	....	....	....	....	....	....	....	....	....
1996-97	Harvard Crimson	ECAC	32	6	10	16	20	....	....	....	....	....	....	....	....	....	....	....	....	....	....	....	....	....	....
1997-98	Canada	Nat-Tm	58	18	29	47	38	....	....	....	....	....	....	....	....	....	....	....	....	....	....	....	....	....	....
1998-99	**Carolina**	**NHL**	**11**	**0**	**0**	**0**	**0**	**0**	**0**	**0**	**5**	**0.0**	**0**	**2**	**100.0**	**2:29**	**1**	**0**	**0**	**0**	**0**	**0**	**0**	**0**	**2:46**
	New Haven	AHL	62	17	31	48	77	....	....	....	....	....	....	....	....	....	....	....	....	....	....	....	....	....	....
99-2000	Cincinnati	IHL	78	12	24	36	76	....	....	....	....	....	....	....	....	....	11	4	1	5	8	....	....	....	....

Season	Club	League	GP	G	A	Pts	PIM	PP	SH	GW	S	%	+/-	TF	F%	Min	GP	G	A	Pts	PIM	PP	SH	GW	Min
			Regular Season														Playoffs								
2000-01	Cincinnati	IHL	82	20	28	48	104	....	....	....	....	....	....	....	....	....	5	0	1	1	6	....	....	....	....
2001-02	**Carolina**	**NHL**	**12**	**1**	**1**	**2**	**0**	**0**	**0**	**0**	**15**	**6.7**	**–1**	**19**	**47.4**	**10:11**	**4**	**0**	**0**	**0**	**2**	**0**	**0**	**0**	**4:42**
	Lowell	AHL	64	19	22	41	61	....	....	....	....	....	....	....	....	....	....	....	....	....	....	....	....	....	....
2002-03	**Carolina**	**NHL**	**35**	**1**	**3**	**4**	**20**	**0**	**0**	**0**	**43**	**2.3**	**–3**	**72**	**55.6**	**9:21**	....	....	....	....	....	....	....	....	....
	Lowell	AHL	27	7	20	27	38	....	....	....	....	....	....	....	....	....	....	....	....	....	....	....	....	....	....
2003-04	**Florida**	**NHL**	**34**	**0**	**3**	**3**	**25**	**0**	**0**	**0**	**42**	**0.0**	**–5**	**398**	**45.7**	**12:31**	....	....	....	....	....	....	....	....	....
	San Antonio	AHL	2	0	0	0	4	....	....	....	....	....	....	....	....	....	....	....	....	....	....	....	....	....	....
	Boston	**NHL**	**18**	**0**	**3**	**3**	**8**	**0**	**0**	**0**	**17**	**0.0**	**0**	**155**	**47.1**	**8:42**	**1**	**0**	**0**	**0**	**0**	**0**	**0**	**0**	**2:11**
2004-05	Lowell	AHL	71	10	18	28	104	....	....	....	....	....	....	....	....	....	2	0	0	0	0	....	....	....	....
2005-06	**Calgary**	**NHL**	**25**	**3**	**2**	**5**	**8**	**1**	**0**	**0**	**27**	**11.1**	**5**	**33**	**45.5**	**10:16**	**1**	**0**	**0**	**0**	**0**	**0**	**0**	**0**	**7:50**
	Omaha	AHL	37	8	19	27	57	....	....	....	....	....	....	....	....	....	....	....	....	....	....	....	....	....	....
2006-07	**Chicago**	**NHL**	**25**	**3**	**2**	**5**	**14**	**0**	**1**	**0**	**30**	**10.0**	**–2**	**178**	**47.8**	**11:12**	....	....	....	....	....	....	....	....	....
	Norfolk Admirals	AHL	50	15	25	40	45	....	....	....	....	....	....	....	....	....	6	2	3	5	8	....	....	....	....
	NHL Totals		**160**	**8**	**14**	**22**	**75**	**1**	**1**	**0**	**179**	**4.5**		**857**	**47.4**	**9:59**	**7**	**0**	**0**	**0**	**2**	**0**	**0**	**0**	**4:31**

Rights transferred to **Carolina** after **Hartford** franchise relocated, June 25, 1997. Signed as a free agent by **Florida**, August 14, 2003. Claimed on waivers by **Boston** from **Florida**, January 20, 2004. Signed as a free agent by **Calgary**, August 11, 2005. Signed as a free agent by **Chicago**, August 1, 2006. Signed as a free agent by **Tampa Bay**, July 2, 2007.

MacKENZIE, Derek

(muh-KEHN-zee, DAIR-ihk) **CBJ**

Center. Shoots left. 5'11", 185 lbs. Born, Sudbury, Ont., June 11, 1981. Atlanta's 6th choice, 128th overall, in 1999 Entry Draft.

Season	Club	League	GP	G	A	Pts	PIM	PP	SH	GW	S	%	+/-	TF	F%	Min	GP	G	A	Pts	PIM	PP	SH	GW	Min
1996-97	Rayside-Balfour	NOJHA	40	23	32	55	40	....	....	....	....	....	....	....	....	....	....	....	....	....	....	....	....	....	....
1997-98	Sudbury Wolves	OHL	59	9	11	20	26	....	....	....	....	....	....	....	....	....	....	....	....	....	....	....	....	....	....
1998-99	Sudbury Wolves	OHL	68	22	65	87	74	....	....	....	....	....	....	....	....	....	4	2	4	6	2	....	....	....	....
99-2000	Sudbury Wolves	OHL	68	24	33	57	110	....	....	....	....	....	....	....	....	....	12	5	9	14	16	....	....	....	....
2000-01	Sudbury Wolves	OHL	62	40	49	89	89	....	....	....	....	....	....	....	....	....	12	6	8	14	16	....	....	....	....
2001-02	**Atlanta**	**NHL**	**1**	**0**	**0**	**0**	**2**	**0**	**0**	**0**	**1**	**0.0**	**–1**	**16**	**56.3**	**13:51**	....	....	....	....	....	....	....	....	....
	Chicago Wolves	AHL	68	13	12	25	80	....	....	....	....	....	....	....	....	....	25	4	2	6	20	....	....	....	....
2002-03	Chicago Wolves	AHL	80	14	18	32	97	....	....	....	....	....	....	....	....	....	9	0	0	0	4	....	....	....	....
2003-04	**Atlanta**	**NHL**	**12**	**0**	**1**	**1**	**10**	**0**	**0**	**0**	**7**	**0.0**	**0**	**63**	**46.0**	**6:38**	....	....	....	....	....	....	....	....	....
	Chicago Wolves	AHL	63	19	16	35	67	....	....	....	....	....	....	....	....	....	10	7	1	8	13	....	....	....	....
2004-05	Chicago Wolves	AHL	78	13	20	33	87	....	....	....	....	....	....	....	....	....	18	5	6	11	33	....	....	....	....
2005-06	**Atlanta**	**NHL**	**11**	**0**	**1**	**1**	**8**	**0**	**0**	**0**	**11**	**0.0**	**0**	**59**	**55.9**	**6:33**	....	....	....	....	....	....	....	....	....
	Chicago Wolves	AHL	36	10	12	22	48	....	....	....	....	....	....	....	....	....	....	....	....	....	....	....	....	....	....
2006-07	**Atlanta**	**NHL**	**4**	**0**	**0**	**0**	**0**	**0**	**0**	**0**	**3**	**0.0**	**1**	**16**	**56.3**	**5:00**	....	....	....	....	....	....	....	....	....
	Chicago Wolves	AHL	52	14	23	37	62	....	....	....	....	....	....	....	....	....	....	....	....	....	....	....	....	....	....
	NHL Totals		**28**	**0**	**2**	**2**	**20**	**0**	**0**	**0**	**22**	**0.0**		**154**	**51.9**	**6:37**	....	....	....	....	....	....	....	....	....

Signed as a free agent by **Columbus**, July 11, 2007.

MacLEAN, Don

(muh-KLAIN, DAWN)

Center. Shoots left. 6'2", 199 lbs. Born, Sydney, N.S., January 14, 1977. Los Angeles' 2nd choice, 33rd overall, in 1995 Entry Draft.

Season	Club	League	GP	G	A	Pts	PIM	PP	SH	GW	S	%	+/-	TF	F%	Min	GP	G	A	Pts	PIM	PP	SH	GW	Min
1992-93	Halifax Hawks	NSMHL	27	15	25	40	34	....	....	....	....	....	....	....	....	....	....	....	....	....	....	....	....	....	....
1993-94	Halifax Hawks	NSMHL	25	35	35	70	151	....	....	....	....	....	....	....	....	....	....	....	....	....	....	....	....	....	....
1994-95	Beauport	QMJHL	64	15	27	42	37	....	....	....	....	....	....	....	....	....	17	4	4	8	6	....	....	....	....
1995-96	Beauport	QMJHL	1	0	1	1	0	....	....	....	....	....	....	....	....	....	....	....	....	....	....	....	....	....	....
	Laval Titan	QMJHL	21	17	11	28	29	....	....	....	....	....	....	....	....	....	....	....	....	....	....	....	....	....	....
	Hull Olympiques	QMJHL	39	26	34	60	44	....	....	....	....	....	....	....	....	....	17	6	7	13	14	....	....	....	....
1996-97	Hull Olympiques	QMJHL	69	34	47	81	67	....	....	....	....	....	....	....	....	....	14	11	10	21	39	....	....	....	....
1997-98	**Los Angeles**	**NHL**	**22**	**5**	**2**	**7**	**4**	**2**	**0**	**0**	**25**	**20.0**	**–1**	....	....	....	....	....	....	....	....	....	....	....	....
	Fredericton	AHL	39	9	5	14	32	....	....	....	....	....	....	....	....	....	4	1	3	4	2	....	....	....	....
1998-99	Springfield	AHL	41	5	14	19	31	....	....	....	....	....	....	....	....	....	....	....	....	....	....	....	....	....	....
	Grand Rapids	IHL	28	6	13	19	8	....	....	....	....	....	....	....	....	....	....	....	....	....	....	....	....	....	....
99-2000	Lowell	AHL	40	11	17	28	18	....	....	....	....	....	....	....	....	....	....	....	....	....	....	....	....	....	....
	St. John's	AHL	21	14	12	26	8	....	....	....	....	....	....	....	....	....	....	....	....	....	....	....	....	....	....
2000-01	**Toronto**	**NHL**	**3**	**0**	**1**	**1**	**2**	**0**	**0**	**0**	**2**	**0.0**	**–2**	**33**	**54.6**	**9:48**	....	....	....	....	....	....	....	....	....
	St. John's	AHL	61	26	34	60	48	....	....	....	....	....	....	....	....	....	4	2	1	3	2	....	....	....	....
2001-02	St. John's	AHL	75	33	*54	*87	49	....	....	....	....	....	....	....	....	....	9	5	5	10	6	....	....	....	....
	Toronto	**NHL**	....	....	....	....	....	....	....	....	....	....	....	....	....	....	**3**	**0**	**0**	**0**	**0**	**0**	**0**	**0**	**1:39**
2002-03	Syracuse Crunch	AHL	17	9	9	18	6	....	....	....	....	....	....	....	....	....	....	....	....	....	....	....	....	....	....
2003-04	**Columbus**	**NHL**	**4**	**1**	**0**	**1**	**0**	**0**	**0**	**0**	**10**	**10.0**	**–1**	**31**	**58.1**	**11:41**	....	....	....	....	....	....	....	....	....
	Syracuse Crunch	AHL	77	27	41	68	45	....	....	....	....	....	....	....	....	....	7	0	3	3	4	....	....	....	....
2004-05	Blues Espoo	Finland	51	22	21	43	46	....	....	....	....	....	....	....	....	....	....	....	....	....	....	....	....	....	....
2005-06	**Detroit**	**NHL**	**3**	**1**	**1**	**2**	**0**	**1**	**0**	**1**	**3**	**33.3**	**2**	**13**	**61.5**	**12:45**	....	....	....	....	....	....	....	....	....
	Grand Rapids	AHL	76	*56	32	88	63	....	....	....	....	....	....	....	....	....	14	6	2	8	8	....	....	....	....
2006-07	**Phoenix**	**NHL**	**9**	**1**	**1**	**2**	**0**	**0**	**0**	**0**	**12**	**8.3**	**–4**	**2**	**50.0**	**12:38**	....	....	....	....	....	....	....	....	....
	San Antonio	AHL	66	33	28	61	51	....	....	....	....	....	....	....	....	....	....	....	....	....	....	....	....	....	....
	NHL Totals		**41**	**8**	**5**	**13**	**6**	**3**	**0**	**1**	**52**	**15.4**		**79**	**57.0**	**12:00**	**3**	**0**	**0**	**0**	**0**	**0**	**0**	**0**	**1:39**

John P. Sollenberger Trophy (Leading Scorer – AHL) (2002) • AHL First All-Star Team (2006) • Willie Marshall Award (Top Goal-scorer - AHL) (2006) (tied with Denis Hamel) • Les Cunningham Plaque (MVP-AHL) (2006)

Traded to **Toronto** by **Los Angeles** for Craig Charron, February 23, 2000. Signed as a free agent by **Columbus**, July 17, 2002. • Missed majority of 2002-03 season recovering from neck surgery, September 16, 2002. Signed as a free agent by **Espoo** (Finland), July 2, 2004. Signed as a free agent by **Detroit**, August 24, 2005. Signed as a free agent by **Phoenix**, July 17, 2006. Signed as a free agent by **Zurich** (Swiss), July 16, 2007.

MADDEN, John

(MA-dehn, JAWN) **N.J.**

Center. Shoots left. 5'11", 190 lbs. Born, Barrie, Ont., May 4, 1973.

Season	Club	League	GP	G	A	Pts	PIM	PP	SH	GW	S	%	+/-	TF	F%	Min	GP	G	A	Pts	PIM	PP	SH	GW	Min
1989-90	Alliston Hornets	OHA-C	31	24	25	49	26	....	....	....	....	....	....	....	....	....	....	....	....	....	....	....	....	....	....
1990-91	Alliston Hornets	OHA-C	14	15	21	36	10	....	....	....	....	....	....	....	....	....	....	....	....	....	....	....	....	....	....
	Barrie Colts	OHA-B	1	0	0	0	0	....	....	....	....	....	....	....	....	....	....	....	....	....	....	....	....	....	....
1991-92	Barrie Colts	OHA-B	42	50	54	104	46	....	....	....	....	....	....	....	....	....	13	10	9	19	14	....	....	....	....
1992-93	Barrie Colts	COJHL	43	49	75	124	62	....	....	....	....	....	....	....	....	....	....	....	....	....	....	....	....	....	....
1993-94	U. of Michigan	CCHA	36	6	11	17	14	....	....	....	....	....	....	....	....	....	....	....	....	....	....	....	....	....	....
1994-95	U. of Michigan	CCHA	39	21	22	43	8	....	....	....	....	....	....	....	....	....	....	....	....	....	....	....	....	....	....
1995-96	U. of Michigan	CCHA	43	27	30	57	45	....	....	....	....	....	....	....	....	....	....	....	....	....	....	....	....	....	....
1996-97	U. of Michigan	CCHA	42	26	37	63	56	....	....	....	....	....	....	....	....	....	....	....	....	....	....	....	....	....	....
1997-98	Albany River Rats	AHL	74	20	36	56	40	....	....	....	....	....	....	....	....	....	13	3	13	16	14	....	....	....	....
1998-99	**New Jersey**	**NHL**	**4**	**0**	**1**	**1**	**0**	**0**	**0**	**0**	**4**	**0.0**	**–2**	**0**	**0.0**	**9:13**	....	....	....	....	....	....	....	....	....
	Albany River Rats	AHL	75	38	60	98	44	....	....	....	....	....	....	....	....	....	5	2	2	4	6	....	....	....	....
99-2000 ♦	**New Jersey**	**NHL**	**74**	**16**	**9**	**25**	**6**	**0**	**6**	**3**	**115**	**13.9**	**7**	**770**	**47.5**	**11:40**	**20**	**3**	**4**	**7**	**0**	**0**	**1**	**2**	**15:30**
2000-01	**New Jersey**	**NHL**	**80**	**23**	**15**	**38**	**12**	**0**	**3**	**4**	**163**	**14.1**	**24**	**974**	**46.6**	**15:35**	**25**	**4**	**3**	**7**	**6**	**0**	**0**	**0**	**15:15**
2001-02	**New Jersey**	**NHL**	**82**	**15**	**8**	**23**	**25**	**0**	**0**	**2**	**170**	**8.8**	**6**	**1001**	**47.0**	**15:36**	**6**	**0**	**0**	**0**	**0**	**0**	**0**	**0**	**17:25**
2002-03 ♦	**New Jersey**	**NHL**	**80**	**19**	**22**	**41**	**26**	**2**	**2**	**3**	**207**	**9.2**	**13**	**1502**	**50.9**	**18:18**	**24**	**6**	**10**	**16**	**2**	**2**	**1**	**1**	**19:38**
2003-04	**New Jersey**	**NHL**	**80**	**12**	**23**	**35**	**22**	**1**	**1**	**1**	**210**	**5.7**	**7**	**1377**	**53.3**	**17:17**	**5**	**0**	**0**	**0**	**0**	**0**	**0**	**0**	**14:51**
2004-05	HIFK Helsinki	Finland	3	0	0	0	0	....	....	....	....	....	....	....	....	....	....	....	....	....	....	....	....	....	....
2005-06	**New Jersey**	**NHL**	**82**	**16**	**20**	**36**	**36**	**0**	**1**	**0**	**194**	**8.2**	**–7**	**1613**	**51.5**	**18:59**	**9**	**4**	**1**	**5**	**8**	**0**	**2**	**0**	**18:56**
2006-07	**New Jersey**	**NHL**	**74**	**12**	**20**	**32**	**14**	**0**	**0**	**1**	**153**	**7.8**	**–7**	**1366**	**49.8**	**18:53**	**11**	**1**	**1**	**2**	**2**	**0**	**0**	**0**	**21:17**
	NHL Totals		**556**	**113**	**118**	**231**	**141**	**3**	**13**	**14**	**1216**	**9.3**		**8603**	**50.0**	**16:36**	**100**	**18**	**19**	**37**	**18**	**2**	**4**	**3**	**17:28**

CCHA First All-Star Team (1997) • NCAA West First All-American Team (1997) • Frank J. Selke Trophy (2001)

Signed as a free agent by **New Jersey**, June 26, 1997. Signed as a free agent by **HIFK Helsinki** (Finland), November 29, 2004.

MAIR, Adam

(MAIR, A-duhm) **BUF.**

Center. Shoots right. 6'1", 208 lbs. Born, Hamilton, Ont., February 15, 1979. Toronto's 2nd choice, 84th overall, in 1997 Entry Draft.

Season	Club	League	GP	G	A	Pts	PIM	PP	SH	GW	S	%	+/-	TF	F%	Min	GP	G	A	Pts	PIM	PP	SH	GW	Min
1994-95	Ohsweken	OHA-B	39	21	23	44	91	....	....	....	....	....	....	....	....	....	....	....	....	....	....	....	....	....	....
1995-96	Owen Sound	OHL	62	12	15	27	63	....	....	....	....	....	....	....	....	....	6	0	0	0	2	....	....	....	....
1996-97	Owen Sound	OHL	65	16	35	51	113	....	....	....	....	....	....	....	....	....	4	1	0	1	2	....	....	....	....
1997-98	Owen Sound	OHL	56	25	27	52	179	....	....	....	....	....	....	....	....	....	11	6	3	9	31	....	....	....	....
1998-99	Owen Sound	OHL	43	23	41	64	109	....	....	....	....	....	....	....	....	....	16	10	10	20	*47	....	....	....	....
	Toronto	**NHL**	....	....	....	....	....	....	....	....	....	....	....	....	....	....	**5**	**1**	**0**	**1**	**14**	**0**	**0**	**0**	**5:37**
	St. John's	AHL	....	....	....	....	....	....	....	....	....	....	....	....	....	....	3	1	0	1	6	....	....	....	....

			Regular Season														Playoffs								
Season	Club	League	GP	G	A	Pts	PIM	PP	SH	GW	S	%	+/-	TF	F%	Min	GP	G	A	Pts	PIM	PP	SH	GW	Min
99-2000	**Toronto**	NHL	8	1	0	1	6	0	0	0	7	14.3	–1	9	33.3	11:33	5	0	0	0	8	0	0	0	10:15
	St. John's	AHL	66	22	27	49	124																		
2000-01	**Toronto**	NHL	16	0	2	2	14	0	0	0	17	0.0	3	56	51.8	9:01									
	St. John's	AHL	47	18	27	45	69																		
	Los Angeles	NHL	10	0	0	0	6	0	0	0	5	0.0	–3	21	61.9	6:14									
2001-02	**Los Angeles**	NHL	18	1	1	2	57	0	0	0	10	10.0	1	31	58.1	7:11									
	Manchester	AHL	27	10	9	19	48										5	5	1	6	10				
2002-03	**Buffalo**	NHL	79	6	11	17	146	0	1	1	83	7.2	–4	572	51.2	10:37									
2003-04	**Buffalo**	NHL	81	6	14	20	146	1	0	1	82	7.3	–3	340	45.9	9:38									
2004-05		DID NOT PLAY																							
2005-06	**Buffalo**	NHL	40	2	5	7	47	0	0	0	40	5.0	–2	12	41.7	7:59	3	0	0	0	0	0	0	0	9:17
2006-07	**Buffalo**	NHL	82	2	9	11	128	0	0	0	73	2.7	–1	130	46.2	7:33	16	1	4	5	10	0	0	0	7:33
	NHL Totals		334	18	42	60	550	1	1	2	317	5.7		1171	49.3	8:56	29	2	4	6	32	0	0	0	7:52

Traded to **Los Angeles** by **Toronto** with Toronto's 2nd round choice (Mike Cammalleri) in 2001 Entry Draft for Aki Berg, March 13, 2001. Traded to **Buffalo** by **Los Angeles** with Los Angeles' 5th round choice (Thomas Morrow) in 2003 Entry Draft for Erik Rasmussen, July 24, 2002. • Missed majority of 2005-06 season recovering from groin (training camp) and head (January 12, 2006 vs. Phoenix) injuries.

MAJESKY, Ivan

(migh-EHV-skee, ee-VAHN)

Defense. Shoots right. 6'5", 230 lbs. Born, Banska Bystrica, Czech., September 2, 1976. Florida's 12th choice, 267th overall, in 2001 Entry Draft.

Season	Club	League	GP	G	A	Pts	PIM	PP	SH	GW	S	%	+/-	TF	F%	Min	GP	G	A	Pts	PIM	PP	SH	GW	Min
1995-96	B. Bystrica	Slovakia	17	0	0	0	18																		
1996-97	B. Bystrica	Slovakia	49	2	4	6																			
1997-98	B. Bystrica	Slovak-2	43	6	7	13	50																		
1998-99	B. Bystrica	Slovakia	48	7	7	14	68																		
	HKm Zvolen	Slovakia															6	0	2	2	2				
99-2000	HKm Zvolen	Slovakia	51	7	9	16	68										10	0	4	4	2				
2000-01	Ilves Tampere	Finland	54	2	14	16	99										9	0	1	1	6				
2001-02	Ilves Tampere	Finland	44	6	6	12	84																		
	Slovakia	Olympics	4	0	1	1	4																		
2002-03	**Florida**	NHL	82	4	8	12	92	0	0	2	52	7.7	–18	0	0.0	20:53									
2003-04	**Atlanta**	NHL	63	3	7	10	76	0	0	0	35	8.6	–7	2	50.0	14:28									
2004-05	HC Sparta Praha	CzRep	28	2	6	8	40										5	2	1	3	6				
2005-06	**Washington**	NHL	57	1	8	9	66	0	1	0	35	2.9	–2	0	0.0	17:19									
	Slovakia	Olympics	6	0	0	0	4																		
2006-07	Karpat Oulu	Finland	12	2	4	6	18																		
	Linkopings HC	Sweden	46	0	2	2	83										15	1	4	5	43				
	NHL Totals		202	8	23	31	234	0	1	2	122	6.6		2	50.0	17:53									

Traded to **Atlanta** by **Florida** for Atlanta's 2nd round choice (Kamil Kreps) in 2003 Entry Draft, June 21, 2003. Signed as a free agent by **Sparta Praha** (CzRep), November 12, 2004. Signed as a free agent by **Washington**, August 10, 2005.Signed as a free agent by **Karpat Oulu** (Finland), September 14, 2006. Signed as a free agent by **Linkopings** (Sweden), November, 2006

MAKI, Tomi

(MA-kee, TAW-mee) **CGY.**

Right wing. Shoots left. 5'11", 187 lbs. Born, Helsinki, Finland, August 19, 1983. Calgary's 4th choice, 108th overall, in 2001 Entry Draft.

Season	Club	League	GP	G	A	Pts	PIM	PP	SH	GW	S	%	+/-	TF	F%	Min	GP	G	A	Pts	PIM	PP	SH	GW	Min
99-2000	Jokerit Helsinki Jr.	Fin-Jr.	33	6	1	7	12										3	0	0	0	0				
2000-01	Jokerit U18	Fin-U18	10	4	10	14	4										6	4	3	7	0				
	Jokerit Helsinki Jr.	Fin-Jr.	39	7	8	15	10										2	0	0	0	2				
2001-02	Jokerit Helsinki Jr.	Fin-Jr.	29	12	13	25	12										1	0	0	0	2				
	Kiekko-Vantaa	Finland-2	5	0	0	0	0																		
	Jokerit Helsinki	Finland	8	0	1	1	2																		
2002-03	Jokerit Helsinki Jr.	Fin-Jr.	14	4	4	8	12										11	3	3	6	4				
	Kiekko-Vantaa	Finland-2	3	1	0	1	4																		
	Jokerit Helsinki	Finland	18	2	2	4	4										1	0	0	0	0				
2003-04	Jokerit Helsinki	Finland	50	5	5	10	14										8	0	0	0	0				
2004-05	Jokerit Helsinki	Finland	51	1	4	5	14										12	1	1	2	2				
2005-06	Omaha	AHL	80	12	17	29	33																		
2006-07	**Calgary**	NHL	1	0	0	0	0	0	0	0	0	0.0	0	0	0.0	10:56									
	Omaha	AHL	67	4	11	15	20										6	1	1	2	2				
	NHL Totals		1	0	0	0	0	0	0	0	0	0.0		0	0.0	10:56									

MALEC, Tomas

(MA-lehts, TAW-mahsh)

Defense. Shoots left. 6'2", 193 lbs. Born, Skalica, Czech., May 13, 1982. Florida's 4th choice, 64th overall, in 2001 Entry Draft.

Season	Club	League	GP	G	A	Pts	PIM	PP	SH	GW	S	%	+/-	TF	F%	Min	GP	G	A	Pts	PIM	PP	SH	GW	Min
99-2000	HK 36 Skalica Jr.	Slovak-Jr.	46	6	5	11	150																		
2000-01	Rimouski Oceanic	QMJHL	64	13	50	63	198										11	0	11	11	26				
2001-02	Rimouski Oceanic	QMJHL	51	14	32	46	164										7	3	1	4	10				
	Lowell	AHL															4	0	0	0	4				
2002-03	**Carolina**	NHL	41	0	2	2	43	0	0	0	30	0.0	–5	1	100.0	11:13									
	Lowell	AHL	30	0	4	4	50																		
2003-04	**Carolina**	NHL	2	0	0	0	2	0	0	0	1	0.0	–1	0	0.0	9:32									
	Lowell	AHL	74	7	13	20	101																		
2004-05	Cincinnati	AHL	66	4	14	18	104										6	0	2	2	10				
2005-06	**Ottawa**	NHL	2	0	0	0	2	0	0	0	1	0.0	4	0	0.0	11:44									
	Binghamton	AHL	79	1	27	28	118																		
2006-07	**Ottawa**	NHL	1	0	0	0	0	0	0	0	1	0.0	0	0	0.0	14:47									
	Binghamton	AHL	33	1	12	13	35																		
	Bridgeport	AHL	43	2	7	9	44																		
	NHL Totals		46	0	2	2	47	0	0	0	33	0.0		1	100.0	11:15									

Traded to **Carolina** by **Florida** with Bret Hedican and Kevyn Adams for Sandis Ozolinsh and Byron Ritchie, January 16, 2002. Traded to **Anaheim** by **Carolina** with Carolina's 3rd round choice (Kyle Klubertanz) in 2004 Entry Draft for Martin Gerber, June 18, 2004. Signed as a free agent by **Ottawa**, August 19, 2005. Traded to **NY Islanders** by **Ottawa** for Matt Koalska, January 5, 2007. Signed as a free agent by **Trinec** (CzRep), May 1, 2007.

MALHOTRA, Manny

(mal-HOH-truh, MAN-ee) **CBJ**

Center. Shoots left. 6'2", 215 lbs. Born, Mississauga, Ont., May 18, 1980. NY Rangers' 1st choice, 7th overall, in 1998 Entry Draft.

Season	Club	League	GP	G	A	Pts	PIM	PP	SH	GW	S	%	+/-	TF	F%	Min	GP	G	A	Pts	PIM	PP	SH	GW	Min
1995-96	Mississauga Reps	MTHL	54	27	44	71	62																		
1996-97	Guelph Storm	OHL	61	16	28	44	26										18	7	7	14	11				
1997-98	Guelph Storm	OHL	57	16	35	51	29										12	7	6	13	8				
1998-99	**NY Rangers**	NHL	73	8	8	16	13	1	0	2	61	13.1	–2	588	43.9	8:36									
99-2000	**NY Rangers**	NHL	27	0	0	0	4	0	0	0	18	0.0	–6	132	44.7	6:42									
	Guelph Storm	OHL	5	2	2	4	4										6	0	2	2	4				
	Hartford	AHL	12	1	5	6	2										23	1	2	3	10				
2000-01	**NY Rangers**	NHL	50	4	8	12	31	0	0	2	46	8.7	–10	248	44.4	9:03									
	Hartford	AHL	28	5	6	11	69										5	0	0	0	0				
2001-02	**NY Rangers**	NHL	56	7	6	13	42	0	1	1	41	17.1	–1	310	42.9	10:14									
	Dallas	NHL	16	1	0	1	5	0	0	0	19	5.3	–3	121	48.8	10:37									
2002-03	**Dallas**	NHL	59	3	7	10	42	0	0	1	62	4.8	–2	447	47.0	9:22	5	1	0	1	0	0	0	0	8:13
2003-04	**Dallas**	NHL	9	0	0	0	4	0	0	0	4	0.0	–2	13	61.5	7:48									
	Columbus	NHL	56	12	13	25	24	1	0	2	103	11.7	–5	840	53.8	14:47									
2004-05	Ljubljana	Slovenia	13	6	7	13	20																		
	Ljubljana	Interliga	13	7	7	14	16																		
	HV 71 Jonkoping	Sweden	20	5	2	7	16																		
2005-06	**Columbus**	NHL	58	10	21	31	41	1	1	0	102	9.8	1	827	56.4	16:21									
2006-07	**Columbus**	NHL	82	9	16	25	76	2	0	3	109	8.3	–8	1127	55.1	14:48									
	NHL Totals		486	54	79	133	282	5	2	11	565	9.6		4653	51.1	11:34	5	1	0	1	0	0	0	0	8:13

Memorial Cup Tournament All-Star Team (1998) • George Parsons Trophy (Memorial Cup Tournament Most Sportsmanlike Player) (1998)

Traded to **Dallas** by **NY Rangers** with Barrett Heisten for Martin Rucinsky and Roman Lyashenko, March 12, 2002. Claimed on waivers by **Columbus** from **Dallas**, November 21, 2003. Signed as a free agent by **Ljubljana** (Slovenia), October 8, 2004. Signed as a free agent by **Jonkoping** (Sweden), December 20, 2004.

MALIK, Marek
(MAW-leck, MAIR-ehk) **NYR**

Defense. Shoots left. 6'6", 240 lbs. Born, Ostrava, Czech., June 24, 1975. Hartford's 2nd choice, 72nd overall, in 1993 Entry Draft.

			Regular Season														Playoffs								
Season	Club	League	GP	G	A	Pts	PIM	PP	SH	GW	S	%	+/-	TF	F%	Min	GP	G	A	Pts	PIM	PP	SH	GW	Min
1992-93	TJ Vitkovice Jr.	Czech-Jr.	20	5	10	15	16	....	....	....	....	....	....	....	....	....	....	....	....	....	....	....	....	....	....
1993-94	HC Vitkovice	CzRep	38	3	3	6	0	....	....	....	....	....	....	....	....	....	3	0	1	1	0	....	....	....	....
1994-95	Springfield	AHL	58	11	30	41	91	....	....	....	....	....	....	....	....	....	....	....	....	....	....	....	....	....	....
	Hartford	**NHL**	**1**	**0**	**1**	**1**	**0**	**0**	**0**	**0**	**0**	**0.0**	**1**	....	....	....	....	....	....	....	....	....	....	....	....
1995-96	**Hartford**	**NHL**	**7**	**0**	**0**	**0**	**4**	**0**	**0**	**0**	**2**	**0.0**	**-3**	....	....	....	....	....	....	....	....	....	....	....	....
	Springfield	AHL	68	8	14	22	135	....	....	....	....	....	....	....	....	....	8	1	3	4	20	....	....	....	....
1996-97	**Hartford**	**NHL**	**47**	**1**	**5**	**6**	**50**	**0**	**0**	**1**	**33**	**3.0**	**5**	....	....	....	....	....	....	....	....	....	....	....	....
	Springfield	AHL	3	0	3	3	4	....	....	....	....	....	....	....	....	....	....	....	....	....	....	....	....	....	....
1997-98	Malmo	Sweden	37	1	5	6	21	....	....	....	....	....	....	....	....	....	....	....	....	....	....	....	....	....	....
1998-99	HC Vitkovice	CzRep	1	1	0	1	6	....	....	....	....	....	....	....	....	....	....	....	....	....	....	....	....	....	....
	Carolina	**NHL**	**52**	**2**	**9**	**11**	**36**	**1**	**0**	**0**	**36**	**5.6**	**-6**	**0**	**0.0**	**21:14**	**4**	**0**	**0**	**0**	**4**	**0**	**0**	**0**	**11:26**
	New Haven	AHL	21	2	8	10	28	....	....	....	....	....	....	....	....	....	....	....	....	....	....	....	....	....	....
99-2000	**Carolina**	**NHL**	**57**	**4**	**10**	**14**	**63**	**0**	**0**	**1**	**57**	**7.0**	**13**	**0**	**0.0**	**18:00**	....	....	....	....	....	....	....	....	....
2000-01	**Carolina**	**NHL**	**61**	**6**	**14**	**20**	**34**	**1**	**0**	**1**	**72**	**8.3**	**-4**	**0**	**0.0**	**19:36**	**3**	**0**	**0**	**0**	**6**	**0**	**0**	**0**	**19:37**
2001-02	**Carolina**	**NHL**	**82**	**4**	**19**	**23**	**88**	**0**	**0**	**0**	**91**	**4.4**	**8**	**0**	**0.0**	**20:29**	**23**	**0**	**3**	**3**	**18**	**0**	**0**	**0**	**18:09**
2002-03	**Carolina**	**NHL**	**10**	**0**	**2**	**2**	**16**	**0**	**0**	**0**	**9**	**0.0**	**-3**	**0**	**0.0**	**17:02**	....	....	....	....	....	....	....	....	....
	Vancouver	**NHL**	**69**	**7**	**11**	**18**	**52**	**1**	**1**	**2**	**68**	**10.3**	**23**	**1**	**0.0**	**18:06**	**14**	**1**	**1**	**2**	**10**	**1**	**0**	**0**	**16:06**
2003-04	**Vancouver**	**NHL**	**78**	**3**	**16**	**19**	**45**	**0**	**0**	**0**	**61**	**4.9**	**35**	**1**	**0.0**	**18:05**	**7**	**0**	**0**	**0**	**10**	**0**	**0**	**0**	**20:03**
2004-05	Vitkovice	CzRep	42	1	9	10	50	....	....	....	....	....	....	....	....	....	7	0	0	0	37	....	....	....	....
2005-06	**NY Rangers**	**NHL**	**74**	**2**	**16**	**18**	**78**	**0**	**0**	**2**	**70**	**2.9**	**28**	**0**	**0.0**	**20:26**	**4**	**0**	**1**	**1**	**6**	**0**	**0**	**0**	**20:43**
	Czech Republic	Olympics	8	0	0	0	8	....	....	....	....	....	....	....	....	....	....	....	....	....	....	....	....	....	....
2006-07	**NY Rangers**	**NHL**	**69**	**2**	**19**	**21**	**70**	**0**	**0**	**0**	**57**	**3.5**	**32**	**2**	**0.0**	**19:16**	**10**	**1**	**3**	**4**	**10**	**0**	**0**	**0**	**21:25**
	NHL Totals		**607**	**31**	**122**	**153**	**536**	**3**	**1**	**7**	**556**	**5.6**		**4**	**0.0**	**19:20**	**65**	**2**	**8**	**10**	**64**	**1**	**0**	**0**	**18:14**

Transferred to **Carolina** after **Hartford** franchise relocated, June 25, 1997. Traded to **Vancouver** by **Carolina** with Darren Langdon for Jan Hlavac and Harold Druken, November 1, 2002. Signed as a free agent by **Vitkovice** (CzRep), September 17, 2004. Signed as a free agent by **NY Rangers**, August 2, 2005.

MALKIN, Evgeni
(MAHL-kihn, ehv-GEH-nee) **PIT.**

Center. Shoots left. 6'3", 195 lbs. Born, Magnitogorsk, USSR, July 31, 1986. Pittsburgh's 1st choice, 2nd overall, in 2004 Entry Draft.

			Regular Season														Playoffs								
Season	Club	League	GP	G	A	Pts	PIM	PP	SH	GW	S	%	+/-	TF	F%	Min	GP	G	A	Pts	PIM	PP	SH	GW	Min
2003-04	Magnitogorsk 2	Russia-3	2	1	0	1	8	....	....	....	....	....	....	....	....	....	....	....	....	....	....	....	....	....	....
	Magnitogorsk	Russia	34	3	9	12	12	....	....	....	....	....	....	....	....	....	....	....	....	....	....	....	....	....	....
2004-05	Magnitogorsk 2	Russia-3	2	1	1	2	2	....	....	....	....	....	....	....	....	....	....	....	....	....	....	....	....	....	....
	Magnitogorsk	Russia	52	12	20	32	24	....	....	....	....	....	....	....	....	....	5	0	4	4	0	....	....	....	....
2005-06	Magnitogorsk	Russia	46	21	26	47	46	....	....	....	....	....	....	....	....	....	11	5	10	15	41	....	....	....	....
	Russia	Olympics	7	2	4	6	31	....	....	....	....	....	....	....	....	....	....	....	....	....	....	....	....	....	....
2006-07	**Pittsburgh**	**NHL**	**78**	**33**	**52**	**85**	**80**	**16**	**0**	**6**	**242**	**13.6**	**2**	**728**	**43.3**	**19:10**	**5**	**0**	**4**	**4**	**8**	**0**	**0**	**0**	**19:34**
	NHL Totals		**78**	**33**	**52**	**85**	**80**	**16**	**0**	**6**	**242**	**13.6**		**728**	**43.3**	**19:10**	**5**	**0**	**4**	**4**	**8**	**0**	**0**	**0**	**19:34**

NHL All-Rookie Team (2007) • Calder Memorial Trophy (2007)

MALONE, Ryan
(MA-lohn, RIGH-uhn) **PIT.**

Left wing. Shoots left. 6'4", 224 lbs. Born, Pittsburgh, PA, December 1, 1979. Pittsburgh's 5th choice, 115th overall, in 1999 Entry Draft.

			Regular Season														Playoffs								
Season	Club	League	GP	G	A	Pts	PIM	PP	SH	GW	S	%	+/-	TF	F%	Min	GP	G	A	Pts	PIM	PP	SH	GW	Min
1997-98	Shat.-St. Mary's	High-MN	50	41	44	85	69	....	....	....	....	....	....	....	....	....	....	....	....	....	....	....	....	....	....
1998-99	Omaha Lancers	USHL	51	14	22	36	81	....	....	....	....	....	....	....	....	....	12	2	4	6	23	....	....	....	....
99-2000	St. Cloud State	WCHA	38	9	21	30	68	....	....	....	....	....	....	....	....	....	....	....	....	....	....	....	....	....	....
2000-01	St. Cloud State	WCHA	36	7	18	25	52	....	....	....	....	....	....	....	....	....	....	....	....	....	....	....	....	....	....
2001-02	St. Cloud State	WCHA	41	24	25	49	76	....	....	....	....	....	....	....	....	....	....	....	....	....	....	....	....	....	....
2002-03	St. Cloud State	WCHA	27	16	20	36	85	....	....	....	....	....	....	....	....	....	....	....	....	....	....	....	....	....	....
	Wilkes-Barre	AHL	3	0	1	1	2	....	....	....	....	....	....	....	....	....	....	....	....	....	....	....	....	....	....
2003-04	**Pittsburgh**	**NHL**	**81**	**22**	**21**	**43**	**64**	**5**	**3**	**4**	**139**	**15.8**	**-23**	**230**	**27.4**	**18:54**	....	....	....	....	....	....	....	....	....
2004-05	Blues Espoo	Finland	9	2	1	3	36	....	....	....	....	....	....	....	....	....	....	....	....	....	....	....	....	....	....
	SV Renon	Italy	10	6	2	8	20	....	....	....	....	....	....	....	....	....	6	4	4	8	36	....	....	....	....
	HC Ambri-Piotta	Swiss	....	....	....	....	....	....	....	....	....	....	....	....	....	....	1	0	0	0	2	....	....	....	....
2005-06	**Pittsburgh**	**NHL**	**77**	**22**	**22**	**44**	**63**	**10**	**5**	**1**	**153**	**14.4**	**-22**	**728**	**39.6**	**18:06**	....	....	....	....	....	....	....	....	....
2006-07	**Pittsburgh**	**NHL**	**64**	**16**	**15**	**31**	**71**	**1**	**1**	**0**	**125**	**12.8**	**4**	**109**	**44.0**	**16:15**	**5**	**0**	**0**	**0**	**0**	**0**	**0**	**0**	**13:48**
	NHL Totals		**222**	**60**	**58**	**118**	**198**	**16**	**9**	**5**	**417**	**14.4**		**1067**	**37.4**	**17:51**	**5**	**0**	**0**	**0**	**0**	**0**	**0**	**0**	**13:48**

NHL All-Rookie Team (2004)

Signed as a free agent by **Espoo** (Finland), September 29, 2004. Signed as a free agent by **Renon** (Italy), January 3, 2005. Signed as a free agent by **Ambri-Piotta** (Swiss), February 25, 2005.

MALTBY, Kirk
(MAHLT-bee, KUHRK) **DET.**

Right wing. Shoots right. 5'11", 196 lbs. Born, Guelph, Ont., December 22, 1972. Edmonton's 4th choice, 65th overall, in 1992 Entry Draft.

			Regular Season														Playoffs								
Season	Club	League	GP	G	A	Pts	PIM	PP	SH	GW	S	%	+/-	TF	F%	Min	GP	G	A	Pts	PIM	PP	SH	GW	Min
1988-89	Cambridge	OHA-B	48	28	18	46	138	....	....	....	....	....	....	....	....	....	....	....	....	....	....	....	....	....	....
1989-90	Owen Sound	OHL	61	12	15	27	90	....	....	....	....	....	....	....	....	....	12	1	6	7	15	....	....	....	....
1990-91	Owen Sound	OHL	66	34	32	66	100	....	....	....	....	....	....	....	....	....	....	....	....	....	....	....	....	....	....
1991-92	Owen Sound	OHL	66	50	41	91	99	....	....	....	....	....	....	....	....	....	5	3	3	6	18	....	....	....	....
1992-93	Cape Breton	AHL	73	22	23	45	130	....	....	....	....	....	....	....	....	....	16	3	3	6	45	....	....	....	....
1993-94	**Edmonton**	**NHL**	**68**	**11**	**8**	**19**	**74**	**0**	**1**	**1**	**89**	**12.4**	**-2**	....	....	....	....	....	....	....	....	....	....	....	....
1994-95	**Edmonton**	**NHL**	**47**	**8**	**3**	**11**	**49**	**0**	**2**	**1**	**73**	**11.0**	**-11**	....	....	....	....	....	....	....	....	....	....	....	....
1995-96	**Edmonton**	**NHL**	**49**	**2**	**6**	**8**	**61**	**0**	**0**	**1**	**51**	**3.9**	**-16**	....	....	....	....	....	....	....	....	....	....	....	....
	Cape Breton	AHL	4	1	2	3	6	....	....	....	....	....	....	....	....	....	....	....	....	....	....	....	....	....	....
	Detroit	**NHL**	**6**	**1**	**0**	**1**	**6**	**0**	**0**	**0**	**4**	**25.0**	**0**	....	....	....	**8**	**0**	**1**	**1**	**4**	**0**	**0**	**0**	....
1996-97 ♦	**Detroit**	**NHL**	**66**	**3**	**5**	**8**	**75**	**0**	**0**	**0**	**62**	**4.8**	**3**	....	....	....	**20**	**5**	**2**	**7**	**24**	**0**	**1**	**1**	....
1997-98 ♦	**Detroit**	**NHL**	**65**	**14**	**9**	**23**	**89**	**2**	**1**	**3**	**106**	**13.2**	**11**	....	....	....	**22**	**3**	**1**	**4**	**30**	**0**	**1**	**0**	....
1998-99	**Detroit**	**NHL**	**53**	**8**	**6**	**14**	**34**	**0**	**1**	**2**	**76**	**10.5**	**-6**	**10**	**40.0**	**13:13**	**10**	**1**	**0**	**1**	**8**	**0**	**0**	**1**	**11:32**
99-2000	**Detroit**	**NHL**	**41**	**6**	**8**	**14**	**24**	**0**	**2**	**1**	**71**	**8.5**	**1**	**2**	**50.0**	**13:30**	**8**	**0**	**1**	**1**	**4**	**0**	**0**	**0**	**13:45**
2000-01	**Detroit**	**NHL**	**79**	**12**	**7**	**19**	**22**	**1**	**3**	**3**	**119**	**10.1**	**16**	**14**	**35.7**	**14:17**	**6**	**0**	**0**	**0**	**6**	**0**	**0**	**0**	**15:23**
2001-02 ♦	**Detroit**	**NHL**	**82**	**9**	**15**	**24**	**40**	**0**	**1**	**5**	**108**	**8.3**	**15**	**38**	**47.4**	**13:23**	**23**	**3**	**3**	**6**	**32**	**0**	**2**	**0**	**16:34**
2002-03	**Detroit**	**NHL**	**82**	**14**	**23**	**37**	**91**	**0**	**4**	**1**	**116**	**12.1**	**17**	**43**	**37.2**	**16:10**	**4**	**0**	**0**	**0**	**4**	**0**	**0**	**0**	**17:18**
2003-04	**Detroit**	**NHL**	**79**	**14**	**19**	**33**	**80**	**1**	**4**	**4**	**123**	**11.4**	**24**	**30**	**43.3**	**16:16**	**12**	**1**	**3**	**4**	**11**	**0**	**0**	**0**	**17:34**
2004-05			DID NOT PLAY																						
2005-06	**Detroit**	**NHL**	**82**	**5**	**6**	**11**	**80**	**0**	**1**	**0**	**115**	**4.3**	**-9**	**22**	**50.0**	**13:44**	**6**	**2**	**1**	**3**	**4**	**0**	**0**	**1**	**13:02**
2006-07	**Detroit**	**NHL**	**82**	**6**	**5**	**11**	**50**	**0**	**0**	**0**	**113**	**5.3**	**-9**	**14**	**28.6**	**13:11**	**18**	**1**	**1**	**2**	**10**	**0**	**1**	**0**	**10:46**
	NHL Totals		**881**	**113**	**120**	**233**	**775**	**4**	**20**	**22**	**1226**	**9.2**		**173**	**41.6**	**14:18**	**137**	**16**	**13**	**29**	**137**	**0**	**5**	**3**	**14:23**

Traded to **Detroit** by **Edmonton** for Dan McGillis, March 20, 1996. • Missed majority of 1999-2000 season recovering from hernia injury suffered in game vs. Dallas, October 5, 1999.

MANCARI, Mark
(man-KAH-ree, MAHRK) **BUF.**

Right wing. Shoots right. 6'3", 220 lbs. Born, London, Ont., July 11, 1985. Buffalo's 6th choice, 207th overall, in 2004 Entry Draft.

			Regular Season														Playoffs								
Season	Club	League	GP	G	A	Pts	PIM	PP	SH	GW	S	%	+/-	TF	F%	Min	GP	G	A	Pts	PIM	PP	SH	GW	Min
2001-02	Ottawa 67's	OHL	34	3	3	6	10	....	....	....	....	....	....	....	....	....	2	0	1	1	0	....	....	....	....
2002-03	Ottawa 67's	OHL	61	8	11	19	20	....	....	....	....	....	....	....	....	....	11	2	1	3	2	....	....	....	....
2003-04	Ottawa 67's	OHL	67	29	36	65	56	....	....	....	....	....	....	....	....	....	7	5	3	8	11	....	....	....	....
2004-05	Ottawa 67's	OHL	64	36	32	68	86	....	....	....	....	....	....	....	....	....	21	*14	10	24	24	....	....	....	....
2005-06	Rochester	AHL	71	18	24	42	80	....	....	....	....	....	....	....	....	....	....	....	....	....	....	....	....	....	....
2006-07	**Buffalo**	**NHL**	**3**	**0**	**1**	**1**	**2**	**0**	**0**	**0**	**1**	**0.0**	**-1**	**0**	**0.0**	**6:12**	....	....	....	....	....	....	....	....	....
	Rochester	AHL	64	23	34	57	49	....	....	....	....	....	....	....	....	....	6	1	5	6	6	....	....	....	....
	NHL Totals		**3**	**0**	**1**	**1**	**2**	**0**	**0**	**0**	**1**	**0.0**		**0**	**0.0**	**6:12**	....	....	....	....	....	....	....	....	....

MANLOW, Eric

(MAN-low, AIR-ihk)

Center. Shoots left. 6', 180 lbs. Born, Belleville, Ont., April 7, 1975. Chicago's 2nd choice, 50th overall, in 1993 Entry Draft.

			Regular Season														Playoffs								
Season	Club	League	GP	G	A	Pts	PIM	PP	SH	GW	S	%	+/-	TF	F%	Min	GP	G	A	Pts	PIM	PP	SH	GW	Min
1990-91	Peterborough	Minor-ON	59	67	51	118	90																		
	Peterborough	OHA-B	1	0	0	0	0																		
1991-92	Kitchener Rangers	OHL	59	12	20	32	17										14	2	5	7	10				
1992-93	Kitchener Rangers	OHL	53	26	21	47	31										4	0	1	1	2				
1993-94	Kitchener Rangers	OHL	49	28	32	60	25										3	0	1	1	4				
1994-95	Kitchener Rangers	OHL	44	25	29	54	26																		
	Detroit	OHL	16	4	16	20	11										21	11	10	21	18				
1995-96	Indianapolis Ice	IHL	75	6	11	17	32										4	0	1	1	4				
1996-97	Baltimore Bandits	AHL	36	6	6	12	13										3	0	0	0	0				
	Columbus Chill	ECHL	32	18	18	36	20																		
1997-98	Indianapolis Ice	IHL	60	8	11	19	25										3	1	0	1	0				
1998-99	Long Beach	IHL	51	9	19	28	30										8	0	0	0	8				
	Florida Everblades	ECHL	18	8	15	23	11																		
99-2000	Florida Everblades	ECHL	26	14	24	38	24																		
	Providence Bruins	AHL	46	17	16	33	14										14	6	8	14	8				
2000-01	**Boston**	**NHL**	**8**	**0**	**1**	**1**	**2**	**0**	**0**	**0**	**3**	**0.0**	**0**	**61**	**50.8**	**7:26**									
	Providence Bruins	AHL	60	16	51	67	18										17	6	7	13	6				
2001-02	**Boston**	**NHL**	**3**	**0**	**0**	**0**	**0**	**0**	**0**	**0**	**2**	**0.0**	**0**	**16**	**31.3**	**6:05**									
	Providence Bruins	AHL	70	13	35	48	30										2	0	0	0	2				
2002-03	**NY Islanders**	**NHL**	**8**	**2**	**1**	**3**	**4**	**1**	**0**	**0**	**7**	**28.6**	**2**	**84**	**54.8**	**12:27**									
	Bridgeport	AHL	62	19	40	59	58										9	0	6	6	2				
2003-04	**NY Islanders**	**NHL**	**18**	**0**	**2**	**2**	**2**	**0**	**0**	**0**	**10**	**0.0**	**–2**	**178**	**53.9**	**10:13**									
	Bridgeport	AHL	40	8	27	35	16										1	0	0	0	2				
2004-05	Grand Rapids	AHL	61	21	20	41	24																		
2005-06	Grand Rapids	AHL	80	25	47	72	44										16	3	3	6	12				
2006-07	Hamilton	AHL	60	5	13	18	28										22	6	5	11	10				
	NHL Totals		**37**	**2**	**4**	**6**	**8**	**1**	**0**	**0**	**22**	**9.1**		**339**	**52.5**	**9:46**									

Signed as a free agent by **Providence** (AHL), January 24, 2000. Signed as a free agent by **Boston**, July 11, 2000. Signed as a free agent by **NY Islanders**, July 21, 2002. Signed as a free agent by **Detroit**, July 21, 2004. Signed as a free agent by **Hamilton** (AHL), July 10, 2006.

MAPLETOFT, Justin

(MAP-uhl-tawft, JUHS-tihn) **OTT.**

Center. Shoots left. 6'1", 202 lbs. Born, Lloydminster, Sask., January 11, 1981. NY Islanders' 9th choice, 130th overall, in 1999 Entry Draft.

			Regular Season														Playoffs								
Season	Club	League	GP	G	A	Pts	PIM	PP	SH	GW	S	%	+/-	TF	F%	Min	GP	G	A	Pts	PIM	PP	SH	GW	Min
1996-97	Calgary Royals	AMHL	36	25	36	51																			
	Red Deer Rebels	WHL	2	0	0	0	0																		
1997-98	Red Deer Rebels	WHL	65	9	4	13	41																		
1998-99	Red Deer Rebels	WHL	72	24	22	46	81																		
99-2000	Red Deer Rebels	WHL	72	39	57	96	135										4	2	1	3	28				
2000-01	Red Deer Rebels	WHL	70	43	*77	*120	111										22	13	*21	34	59				
2001-02	Bridgeport	AHL	80	13	20	33	60										20	7	10	17	23				
2002-03	**NY Islanders**	**NHL**	**11**	**2**	**2**	**4**	**2**	**1**	**0**	**0**	**12**	**16.7**	**–1**	**138**	**41.3**	**12:17**	**2**	**0**	**0**	**0**	**0**	**0**	**0**	**0**	**7:23**
	Bridgeport	AHL	63	13	26	39	47										7	1	2	3	6				
2003-04	**NY Islanders**	**NHL**	**27**	**1**	**4**	**5**	**6**	**0**	**0**	**0**	**15**	**6.7**	**–1**	**134**	**48.5**	**6:09**									
	Bridgeport	AHL	36	10	13	23	59																		
2004-05	Bridgeport	AHL	61	11	24	35	51																		
2005-06	Jokerit Helsinki	Finland	18	1	3	4	8																		
	Sodertalje SK	Sweden	31	14	7	21	34																		
	Sodertalje SK	Sweden-Q	10	1	5	6	8																		
2006-07	Nurnberg	Germany	10	2	3	5	2										13	2	4	6	10				
	NHL Totals		**38**	**3**	**6**	**9**	**8**	**1**	**0**	**0**	**27**	**11.1**		**272**	**44.9**	**7:56**	**2**	**0**	**0**	**0**	**0**	**0**	**0**	**0**	**7:23**

WHL East First All-Star Team (2000, 2001) • WHL Player of the Year (2001) • Canadian Major Junior First All-Star Team (2001)

Signed as a free agent by **Jokerit Helsinki** (Finland), September 6, 2005. Signed as a free agent by **Sodertalje** (Sweden), November 8, 2005. Signed as a free agent by **Ottawa**, August 10, 2007. Signed as a free agent by **Nurnberg** (Germany), January 25, 2007.

MARA, Paul

(MAIR-uh, PAWL) **NYR**

Defense. Shoots left. 6'4", 219 lbs. Born, Ridgewood, NJ, September 7, 1979. Tampa Bay's 1st choice, 7th overall, in 1997 Entry Draft.

			Regular Season														Playoffs								
Season	Club	League	GP	G	A	Pts	PIM	PP	SH	GW	S	%	+/-	TF	F%	Min	GP	G	A	Pts	PIM	PP	SH	GW	Min
1994-95	Belmont Hill	High-MA	28	5	17	22	28																		
1995-96	Belmont Hill	High-MA	28	18	20	38	40																		
1996-97	Sudbury Wolves	OHL	44	9	34	43	61																		
1997-98	Sudbury Wolves	OHL	25	8	18	26	79																		
	Plymouth Whalers	OHL	25	8	15	23	30										15	3	14	17	30				
1998-99	Plymouth Whalers	OHL	52	13	41	54	95										11	5	7	12	28				
	Tampa Bay	**NHL**	**1**	**1**	**1**	**2**	**0**	**1**	**0**	**0**	**1**	**100.0**	**–3**	**0**	**0.0**	**19:34**									
99-2000	**Tampa Bay**	**NHL**	**54**	**7**	**11**	**18**	**73**	**4**	**0**	**1**	**78**	**9.0**	**–27**	**0**	**0.0**	**22:13**									
	Detroit Vipers	IHL	15	3	5	8	22																		
2000-01	**Tampa Bay**	**NHL**	**46**	**6**	**10**	**16**	**40**	**2**	**0**	**1**	**58**	**10.3**	**–17**	**0**	**0.0**	**23:06**									
	Detroit Vipers	IHL	10	3	3	6	22																		
	Phoenix	**NHL**	**16**	**0**	**4**	**4**	**14**	**0**	**0**	**0**	**20**	**0.0**	**1**	**0**	**0.0**	**19:22**									
2001-02	**Phoenix**	**NHL**	**75**	**7**	**17**	**24**	**58**	**2**	**0**	**0**	**112**	**6.3**	**–6**	**2**	**100.0**	**21:34**	**5**	**0**	**0**	**0**	**4**	**0**	**0**	**0**	**22:57**
2002-03	**Phoenix**	**NHL**	**73**	**10**	**15**	**25**	**78**	**1**	**0**	**0**	**95**	**10.5**	**–7**	**1**	**0.0**	**21:06**									
2003-04	**Phoenix**	**NHL**	**81**	**6**	**36**	**42**	**48**	**1**	**0**	**0**	**140**	**4.3**	**–11**	**2**	**0.0**	**23:37**									
2004-05	Hannover	Germany	35	5	13	18	89																		
2005-06	**Phoenix**	**NHL**	**78**	**15**	**32**	**47**	**70**	**8**	**0**	**0**	**157**	**9.6**	**–12**	**1**	**0.0**	**21:29**									
2006-07	**Boston**	**NHL**	**59**	**3**	**15**	**18**	**95**	**0**	**0**	**0**	**60**	**5.0**	**–22**	**0**	**0.0**	**21:53**									
	NY Rangers	**NHL**	**19**	**2**	**3**	**5**	**18**	**1**	**0**	**0**	**40**	**5.0**	**6**	**0**	**0.0**	**22:56**	**10**	**2**	**2**	**4**	**18**	**2**	**0**	**0**	**19:43**
	NHL Totals		**502**	**57**	**144**	**201**	**494**	**20**	**0**	**2**	**761**	**7.5**		**6**	**33.3**	**22:03**	**15**	**2**	**2**	**4**	**22**	**2**	**0**	**0**	**20:48**

Traded to **Phoenix** by **Tampa Bay** with Mike Johnson, Ruslan Zainullin and NY Islanders' 2nd round choice (previously acquired, Phoenix selected Matthew Spiller) in 2001 Entry Draft for Nikolai Khabibulin and Stan Neckar, March 5, 2001. Signed as a free agent by **Hannover** (Germany), October 29, 2004. Traded to **Boston** by **Phoenix** with Phoenix's 3rd round choice (later traded to Anaheim - Anaheim selected Maxime Macenauer) in 2007 Entry Draft for Nick Boynton and Boston's 4th round choice (later traded to Toronto - Toronto selected Matt Frattin) in 2007 Entry Draft, June 26, 2006. Traded to **NY Rangers** by **Boston** for Aaron Ward, February 27, 2007.

MARCHANT, Todd

(mahr-SHAHNT, TAWD) **ANA.**

Center. Shoots left. 5'10", 180 lbs. Born, Buffalo, NY, August 12, 1973. NY Rangers' 8th choice, 164th overall, in 1993 Entry Draft.

			Regular Season														Playoffs								
Season	Club	League	GP	G	A	Pts	PIM	PP	SH	GW	S	%	+/-	TF	F%	Min	GP	G	A	Pts	PIM	PP	SH	GW	Min
1990-91	Niagara Scenics	NAHL	37	31	47	78																			
1991-92	Clarkson Knights	ECAC	32	20	12	32	32																		
1992-93	Clarkson Knights	ECAC	33	18	28	46	38																		
1993-94	United States	Nat-Tm	59	28	39	67	48																		
	United States	Olympics	8	1	1	2	6																		
	NY Rangers	**NHL**	**1**	**0**	**0**	**0**	**0**	**0**	**0**	**0**	**1**	**0.0**	**–1**												
	Binghamton	AHL	8	2	7	9	6																		
	Edmonton	**NHL**	**3**	**0**	**1**	**1**	**2**	**0**	**0**	**0**	**5**	**0.0**	**–1**												
	Cape Breton	AHL	3	1	4	5	2										5	1	1	2	0				
1994-95	Cape Breton	AHL	38	22	25	47	25																		
	Edmonton	**NHL**	**45**	**13**	**14**	**27**	**32**	**3**	**2**	**2**	**95**	**13.7**	**–3**												
1995-96	**Edmonton**	**NHL**	**81**	**19**	**19**	**38**	**66**	**2**	**3**	**2**	**221**	**8.6**	**–19**												
1996-97	**Edmonton**	**NHL**	**79**	**14**	**19**	**33**	**44**	**0**	**4**	**3**	**202**	**6.9**	**11**				**12**	**4**	**2**	**6**	**12**	**0**	**3**	**1**	
1997-98	**Edmonton**	**NHL**	**76**	**14**	**21**	**35**	**71**	**2**	**1**	**3**	**194**	**7.2**	**9**				**12**	**1**	**1**	**2**	**10**	**0**	**0**	**0**	
1998-99	**Edmonton**	**NHL**	**82**	**14**	**22**	**36**	**65**	**3**	**1**	**2**	**183**	**7.7**	**3**	**1449**	**50.0**	**16:47**	**4**	**1**	**1**	**2**	**12**	**0**	**0**	**0**	**24:21**
99-2000	**Edmonton**	**NHL**	**82**	**17**	**23**	**40**	**70**	**0**	**1**	**0**	**170**	**10.0**	**7**	**1593**	**52.9**	**17:08**	**3**	**1**	**0**	**1**	**2**	**0**	**0**	**0**	**18:07**
2000-01	**Edmonton**	**NHL**	**71**	**13**	**26**	**39**	**51**	**0**	**4**	**2**	**113**	**11.5**	**1**	**1549**	**53.8**	**17:54**	**6**	**0**	**0**	**0**	**4**	**0**	**0**	**0**	**22:57**
2001-02	**Edmonton**	**NHL**	**82**	**12**	**22**	**34**	**41**	**0**	**3**	**1**	**124**	**9.7**	**7**	**1523**	**52.4**	**16:58**									
2002-03	**Edmonton**	**NHL**	**77**	**20**	**40**	**60**	**48**	**7**	**1**	**3**	**146**	**13.7**	**13**	**1336**	**58.0**	**19:54**	**6**	**0**	**2**	**2**	**2**	**0**	**0**	**0**	**20:03**
2003-04	**Columbus**	**NHL**	**77**	**9**	**25**	**34**	**34**	**4**	**0**	**2**	**163**	**5.5**	**–17**	**1412**	**50.9**	**20:39**									

			Regular Season														Playoffs								
Season	Club	League	GP	G	A	Pts	PIM	PP	SH	GW	S	%	+/-	TF	F%	Min	GP	G	A	Pts	PIM	PP	SH	GW	Min
2004-05			Did not play																						
2005-06	**Columbus**	**NHL**	**18**	**3**	**6**	**9**	**20**	**0**	**0**	**0**	**42**	**7.1**	**–1**	**289**	**50.2**	**20:05**	....	....	....	....	....	....	....	....	....
	Anaheim	**NHL**	**61**	**6**	**19**	**25**	**46**	**0**	**0**	**0**	**90**	**6.7**	**3**	**743**	**51.7**	**16:25**	**16**	**3**	**10**	**13**	**14**	**0**	**0**	**0**	**17:34**
2006-07 ♦	**Anaheim**	**NHL**	**56**	**8**	**15**	**23**	**44**	**0**	**3**	**2**	**115**	**7.0**	**7**	**647**	**54.3**	**15:10**	**11**	**0**	**3**	**3**	**12**	**0**	**0**	**0**	**15:44**
	NHL Totals		**891**	**162**	**272**	**434**	**634**	**21**	**23**	**22**	**1864**	**8.7**		**10541**	**52.9**	**17:47**	**70**	**10**	**19**	**29**	**68**	**0**	**3**	**1**	**18:47**

ECAC Second All-Star Team (1993)

Traded to **Edmonton** by **NY Rangers** for Craig MacTavish, March 21, 1994. Signed as a free agent by **Columbus**, July 3, 2003. Claimed on waivers by **Anaheim** from **Columbus**, November 21, 2005.

MARJAMAKI, Masi

(mahr-juh-MA-kee, MAH-see) **NYI**

Right wing. Shoots left. 6'2", 184 lbs. Born, Pori, Finland, January 16, 1985. NY Islanders' 4th choice, 144th overall, in 2005 Entry Draft.

Season	Club	League	GP	G	A	Pts	PIM	PP	SH	GW	S	%	+/-	TF	F%	Min	GP	G	A	Pts	PIM	PP	SH	GW	Min
2001-02	Assat Pori U18	Fin-U18	24	6	16	22	93	....	....	....	....	....	....	....	....	....	1	0	1	1	2	....	....	....	....
	Assat Pori Jr.	Fin-Jr.	1	0	0	0	0	....	....	....	....	....	....	....	....	....	6	3	2	5	2	....	....	....	....
2002-03	Red Deer Rebels	WHL	65	15	20	35	56	....	....	....	....	....	....	....	....	....	23	1	2	3	20	....	....	....	....
2003-04	Red Deer Rebels	WHL	28	6	8	14	46	....	....	....	....	....	....	....	....	....	....	....	....	....	....	....	....	....	....
	Moose Jaw	WHL	35	15	10	25	57	....	....	....	....	....	....	....	....	....	10	1	3	4	15	....	....	....	....
2004-05	Moose Jaw	WHL	51	14	32	46	49	....	....	....	....	....	....	....	....	....	5	1	2	3	5	....	....	....	....
2005-06	**NY Islanders**	**NHL**	**1**	**0**	**0**	**0**	**0**	**0**	**0**	**0**	**0**	**0.0**	**0**	**0**	**0.0**	**5:17**	....	....	....	....	....	....	....	....	....
	Bridgeport	AHL	75	9	22	31	77	....	....	....	....	....	....	....	....	....	7	3	0	3	4	....	....	....	....
2006-07	Bridgeport	AHL	78	6	11	17	80	....	....	....	....	....	....	....	....	....	....	....	....	....	....	....	....	....	....
	NHL Totals		**1**	**0**	**0**	**0**	**0**	**0**	**0**	**0**	**0**	**0.0**		**0**	**0.0**	**5:17**	....	....	....	....	....	....	....	....	....

• Re-entered NHL Entry Draft. Originally Boston's 3rd choice, 66th overall, in 2003 Entry Draft.

MARKOV, Andrei

(MAHR-kahf, AHN-dray) **MTL.**

Defense. Shoots left. 6', 203 lbs. Born, Voskresensk, USSR, December 20, 1978. Montreal's 6th choice, 162nd overall, in 1998 Entry Draft.

Season	Club	League	GP	G	A	Pts	PIM	PP	SH	GW	S	%	+/-	TF	F%	Min	GP	G	A	Pts	PIM	PP	SH	GW	Min
1995-96	Voskresensk	CIS	38	0	0	0	14	....	....	....	....	....	....	....	....	....	....	....	....	....	....	....	....	....	....
1996-97	Voskresensk	Russia	43	8	4	12	32	....	....	....	....	....	....	....	....	....	2	1	1	2	0	....	....	....	....
1997-98	Voskresensk	Russia	43	10	5	15	83	....	....	....	....	....	....	....	....	....	....	....	....	....	....	....	....	....	....
1998-99	Dynamo Moscow	Russia	38	10	11	21	32	....	....	....	....	....	....	....	....	....	16	3	6	9	6	....	....	....	....
	Dynamo Moscow	EuroHL	12	7	5	12	12	....	....	....	....	....	....	....	....	....	6	2	2	4	4	....	....	....	....
99-2000	Dynamo Moscow	Russia	29	11	12	23	28	....	....	....	....	....	....	....	....	....	17	4	3	7	8	....	....	....	....
2000-01	**Montreal**	**NHL**	**63**	**6**	**17**	**23**	**18**	**2**	**0**	**0**	**82**	**7.3**	**–6**	**2**	**50.0**	**16:53**	....	....	....	....	....	....	....	....	....
	Quebec Citadelles	AHL	14	0	5	5	4	....	....	....	....	....	....	....	....	....	7	1	1	2	2	....	....	....	....
2001-02	**Montreal**	**NHL**	**56**	**5**	**19**	**24**	**24**	**2**	**0**	**1**	**73**	**6.8**	**–1**	**0**	**0.0**	**17:15**	**12**	**1**	**3**	**4**	**8**	**0**	**0**	**1**	**15:53**
	Quebec Citadelles	AHL	12	4	6	10	7	....	....	....	....	....	....	....	....	....	....	....	....	....	....	....	....	....	....
2002-03	**Montreal**	**NHL**	**79**	**13**	**24**	**37**	**34**	**3**	**0**	**2**	**159**	**8.2**	**13**	**1**	**0.0**	**23:17**	....	....	....	....	....	....	....	....	....
2003-04	**Montreal**	**NHL**	**69**	**6**	**22**	**28**	**20**	**2**	**0**	**0**	**105**	**5.7**	**–2**	**2**	**50.0**	**21:29**	**11**	**1**	**4**	**5**	**8**	**0**	**0**	**1**	**22:52**
2004-05	Dynamo Moscow	Russia	42	7	16	23	76	....	....	....	....	....	....	....	....	....	10	2	0	2	22	....	....	....	....
2005-06	**Montreal**	**NHL**	**67**	**10**	**36**	**46**	**74**	**6**	**1**	**1**	**88**	**11.4**	**13**	**1**	**0.0**	**23:33**	**6**	**0**	**1**	**1**	**4**	**0**	**0**	**0**	**25:29**
	Russia	Olympics	8	1	2	3	6	....	....	....	....	....	....	....	....	....	....	....	....	....	....	....	....	....	....
2006-07	**Montreal**	**NHL**	**77**	**6**	**43**	**49**	**56**	**5**	**0**	**2**	**128**	**4.7**	**2**	**1**	**0.0**	**24:29**	....	....	....	....	....	....	....	....	....
	NHL Totals		**411**	**46**	**161**	**207**	**226**	**20**	**1**	**6**	**635**	**7.2**		**7**	**28.6**	**21:27**	**29**	**2**	**8**	**10**	**20**	**0**	**0**	**2**	**20:31**

Signed as a free agent by **Dynamo Moscow** (Russia), June 19, 2004.

MARKOV, Danny

(MAHR-kahf, DA-nee)

Defense. Shoots left. 6'1", 190 lbs. Born, Moscow, USSR, July 30, 1976. Toronto's 7th choice, 223rd overall, in 1995 Entry Draft.

Season	Club	League	GP	G	A	Pts	PIM	PP	SH	GW	S	%	+/-	TF	F%	Min	GP	G	A	Pts	PIM	PP	SH	GW	Min
1993-94	Spartak Moscow	CIS	13	1	0	1	6	....	....	....	....	....	....	....	....	....	1	0	0	0	0	....	....	....	....
1994-95	Spartak Moscow	CIS	39	0	1	1	36	....	....	....	....	....	....	....	....	....	....	....	....	....	....	....	....	....	....
1995-96	Spartak Moscow	CIS	38	2	0	2	12	....	....	....	....	....	....	....	....	....	2	0	0	0	2	....	....	....	....
1996-97	Spartak Moscow	Russia	39	3	6	9	41	....	....	....	....	....	....	....	....	....	....	....	....	....	....	....	....	....	....
	St. John's	AHL	10	2	4	6	18	....	....	....	....	....	....	....	....	....	11	2	6	8	14	....	....	....	....
1997-98	**Toronto**	**NHL**	**25**	**2**	**5**	**7**	**28**	**1**	**0**	**0**	**15**	**13.3**	**0**	....	....	....	....	....	....	....	....	....	....	....	....
	St. John's	AHL	52	3	23	26	124	....	....	....	....	....	....	....	....	....	2	0	1	1	0	....	....	....	....
1998-99	**Toronto**	**NHL**	**57**	**4**	**8**	**12**	**47**	**0**	**0**	**0**	**34**	**11.8**	**5**	**0**	**0.0**	**18:41**	**17**	**0**	**6**	**6**	**18**	**0**	**0**	**0**	**22:24**
99-2000	**Toronto**	**NHL**	**59**	**0**	**10**	**10**	**28**	**0**	**0**	**0**	**38**	**0.0**	**13**	**1**	**0.0**	**20:08**	**12**	**0**	**3**	**3**	**10**	**0**	**0**	**0**	**21:05**
2000-01	**Toronto**	**NHL**	**59**	**3**	**13**	**16**	**34**	**1**	**0**	**2**	**49**	**6.1**	**6**	**0**	**0.0**	**19:02**	**11**	**1**	**1**	**2**	**12**	**0**	**0**	**0**	**21:30**
2001-02	**Phoenix**	**NHL**	**72**	**6**	**30**	**36**	**67**	**4**	**0**	**1**	**103**	**5.8**	**–7**	**0**	**0.0**	**22:55**	....	....	....	....	....	....	....	....	....
	Russia	Olympics	5	0	1	1	0	....	....	....	....	....	....	....	....	....	....	....	....	....	....	....	....	....	....
2002-03	**Phoenix**	**NHL**	**64**	**4**	**16**	**20**	**36**	**2**	**0**	**0**	**105**	**3.8**	**2**	**0**	**0.0**	**23:16**	....	....	....	....	....	....	....	....	....
2003-04	**Carolina**	**NHL**	**44**	**4**	**10**	**14**	**37**	**2**	**0**	**1**	**73**	**5.5**	**–6**	**0**	**0.0**	**23:39**	....	....	....	....	....	....	....	....	....
	Philadelphia	**NHL**	**34**	**2**	**3**	**5**	**58**	**1**	**0**	**1**	**27**	**7.4**	**0**	**0**	**0.0**	**21:16**	**18**	**1**	**2**	**3**	**25**	**0**	**0**	**1**	**23:03**
2004-05	Vityaz Chekhov	Russia-2	26	5	7	12	16	....	....	....	....	....	....	....	....	....	12	0	3	3	6	....	....	....	....
2005-06	**Nashville**	**NHL**	**58**	**0**	**11**	**11**	**62**	**0**	**0**	**0**	**59**	**0.0**	**9**	**0**	**0.0**	**19:33**	**5**	**0**	**0**	**0**	**6**	**0**	**0**	**0**	**19:22**
	Russia	Olympics	8	0	2	2	4	....	....	....	....	....	....	....	....	....	....	....	....	....	....	....	....	....	....
2006-07	**Detroit**	**NHL**	**66**	**4**	**12**	**16**	**59**	**0**	**0**	**0**	**66**	**6.1**	**25**	**0**	**0.0**	**18:53**	**18**	**0**	**0**	**0**	**13**	**0**	**0**	**0**	**22:04**
	NHL Totals		**538**	**29**	**118**	**147**	**456**	**11**	**0**	**5**	**569**	**5.1**		**1**	**0.0**	**20:47**	**81**	**2**	**12**	**14**	**84**	**0**	**0**	**1**	**21:58**

Traded to **Phoenix** by **Toronto** for Robert Reichel, Travis Green and Craig Mills, June 12, 2001. Traded to **Carolina** by **Phoenix** with Edmonton's 3rd round choice (previously acquired, later traded to NY Rangers - NY Rangers selected Billy Ryan) in 2004 Entry Draft for David Tanabe and Igor Knyazev, June 21, 2003. Traded to **Philadelphia** by **Carolina** for Justin Williams, January 20, 2004. Signed as a free agent by **Chekhov** (Russia-2), November 15, 2004. Traded to **Nashville** by **Philadelphia** for Nashville's 3rd round choice (later traded to Los Angeles - Los Angeles selected Bud Holloway) in 2006 Entry Draft, August 2, 2005. Signed as a free agent by **Detroit**, July 26, 2006.

MARLEAU, Patrick

(mahr-LOH, PAT-rihk) **S.J.**

Center. Shoots left. 6'2", 220 lbs. Born, Aneroid, Sask., September 15, 1979. San Jose's 1st choice, 2nd overall, in 1997 Entry Draft.

Season	Club	League	GP	G	A	Pts	PIM	PP	SH	GW	S	%	+/-	TF	F%	Min	GP	G	A	Pts	PIM	PP	SH	GW	Min
1993-94	Swift Current	SMHL	53	72	95	167	....	....	....	....	....	....	....	....	....	....	....	....	....	....	....	....	....	....	....
1994-95	Swift Current	SMHL	31	30	22	52	18	....	....	....	....	....	....	....	....	....	....	....	....	....	....	....	....	....	....
1995-96	Seattle	WHL	72	32	42	74	22	....	....	....	....	....	....	....	....	....	5	3	4	7	4	....	....	....	....
1996-97	Seattle	WHL	71	51	74	125	37	....	....	....	....	....	....	....	....	....	15	7	16	23	12	....	....	....	....
1997-98	**San Jose**	**NHL**	**74**	**13**	**19**	**32**	**14**	**1**	**0**	**2**	**90**	**14.4**	**5**	....	....	....	**5**	**0**	**1**	**1**	**0**	**0**	**0**	**0**	....
1998-99	**San Jose**	**NHL**	**81**	**21**	**24**	**45**	**24**	**4**	**0**	**4**	**134**	**15.7**	**10**	**1121**	**43.4**	**15:11**	**6**	**2**	**1**	**3**	**4**	**2**	**0**	**0**	**11:08**
99-2000	**San Jose**	**NHL**	**81**	**17**	**23**	**40**	**36**	**3**	**0**	**3**	**161**	**10.6**	**–9**	**851**	**42.0**	**14:11**	**5**	**1**	**1**	**2**	**2**	**1**	**0**	**0**	**11:51**
2000-01	**San Jose**	**NHL**	**81**	**25**	**27**	**52**	**22**	**5**	**0**	**6**	**146**	**17.1**	**7**	**1088**	**44.8**	**16:17**	**6**	**2**	**0**	**2**	**4**	**0**	**0**	**0**	**14:50**
2001-02	**San Jose**	**NHL**	**79**	**21**	**23**	**44**	**40**	**3**	**0**	**5**	**121**	**17.4**	**9**	**897**	**47.3**	**14:04**	**12**	**6**	**5**	**11**	**6**	**1**	**0**	**3**	**15:50**
2002-03	**San Jose**	**NHL**	**82**	**28**	**29**	**57**	**33**	**8**	**1**	**3**	**172**	**16.3**	**–10**	**1403**	**47.3**	**18:31**	....	....	....	....	....	....	....	....	....
2003-04	**San Jose**	**NHL**	**80**	**28**	**29**	**57**	**24**	**9**	**0**	**5**	**220**	**12.7**	**–5**	**1014**	**41.6**	**18:12**	**17**	**8**	**4**	**12**	**6**	**4**	**1**	**2**	**19:16**
2004-05			Did not play																						
2005-06	**San Jose**	**NHL**	**82**	**34**	**52**	**86**	**26**	**20**	**1**	**4**	**260**	**13.1**	**–12**	**1216**	**46.8**	**19:56**	**11**	**9**	**5**	**14**	**8**	**4**	**0**	**2**	**21:07**
2006-07	**San Jose**	**NHL**	**77**	**32**	**46**	**78**	**33**	**14**	**0**	**9**	**180**	**17.8**	**9**	**693**	**50.5**	**18:34**	**11**	**3**	**3**	**6**	**2**	**1**	**0**	**1**	**18:59**
	NHL Totals		**717**	**219**	**272**	**491**	**252**	**67**	**2**	**41**	**1484**	**14.8**		**8283**	**45.4**	**16:52**	**73**	**31**	**20**	**51**	**32**	**13**	**1**	**8**	**17:16**

WHL West First All-Star Team (1997)

Played in NHL All-Star Game (2004, 2007)

MARSHALL, Grant

(MAR-shuhl, GRANT) **N.J.**

Right wing. Shoots right. 6'1", 200 lbs. Born, Mississauga, Ont., June 9, 1973. Toronto's 2nd choice, 23rd overall, in 1992 Entry Draft.

Season	Club	League	GP	G	A	Pts	PIM	PP	SH	GW	S	%	+/-	TF	F%	Min	GP	G	A	Pts	PIM	PP	SH	GW	Min
1989-90	Tor. Young Nats	MTHL	39	15	28	43	56	....	....	....	....	....	....	....	....	....	....	....	....	....	....	....	....	....	....
1990-91	Ottawa 67's	OHL	26	6	11	17	25	....	....	....	....	....	....	....	....	....	1	0	0	0	0	....	....	....	....
1991-92	Ottawa 67's	OHL	61	32	51	83	132	....	....	....	....	....	....	....	....	....	11	6	11	17	11	....	....	....	....
1992-93	Ottawa 67's	OHL	30	14	29	43	83	....	....	....	....	....	....	....	....	....	....	....	....	....	....	....	....	....	....
	Newmarket	OHL	31	11	25	36	89	....	....	....	....	....	....	....	....	....	7	4	7	11	20	....	....	....	....
	St. John's	AHL	2	0	0	0	0	....	....	....	....	....	....	....	....	....	2	0	0	0	2	....	....	....	....
1993-94	St. John's	AHL	67	11	29	40	155	....	....	....	....	....	....	....	....	....	11	1	5	6	17	....	....	....	....
1994-95	Kalamazoo Wings	IHL	61	17	29	46	96	....	....	....	....	....	....	....	....	....	16	9	3	12	27	....	....	....	....
	Dallas	**NHL**	**2**	**0**	**1**	**1**	**0**	**0**	**0**	**0**	**0**	**0.0**	**1**	....	....	....	....	....	....	....	....	....	....	....	....
1995-96	**Dallas**	**NHL**	**70**	**9**	**19**	**28**	**111**	**0**	**0**	**0**	**62**	**14.5**	**0**	....	....	....	....	....	....	....	....	....	....	....	....
1996-97	**Dallas**	**NHL**	**56**	**6**	**4**	**10**	**98**	**0**	**0**	**0**	**0**	**0.0**	**5**	....	....	....	**5**	**0**	**2**	**2**	**8**	**0**	**0**	**0**	....
1997-98	**Dallas**	**NHL**	**72**	**9**	**10**	**19**	**96**	**3**	**0**	**1**	**91**	**9.9**	**–2**	....	....	....	**17**	**0**	**2**	**2**	***47**	**0**	**0**	**0**	....

			Regular Season														Playoffs								
Season	Club	League	GP	G	A	Pts	PIM	PP	SH	GW	S	%	+/-	TF	F%	Min	GP	G	A	Pts	PIM	PP	SH	GW	Min
1998-99 ♦	**Dallas**	**NHL**	**82**	**13**	**18**	**31**	**85**	**2**	**0**	**4**	**112**	**11.6**	**1**	**2**	**50.0**	**12:39**	**14**	**0**	**3**	**3**	**20**	**0**	**0**	**0**	**11:42**
99-2000	**Dallas**	**NHL**	**45**	**2**	**6**	**8**	**38**	**1**	**0**	**0**	**43**	**4.7**	**–5**	**3**	**0.0**	**11:19**	**14**	**0**	**1**	**1**	**4**	**0**	**0**	**0**	**10:08**
2000-01	**Dallas**	**NHL**	**75**	**13**	**24**	**37**	**64**	**4**	**0**	**1**	**93**	**14.0**	**1**	**16**	**56.3**	**11:05**	**9**	**0**	**0**	**0**	**0**	**0**	**0**	**0**	**11:15**
2001-02	**Columbus**	**NHL**	**81**	**15**	**18**	**33**	**86**	**6**	**0**	**4**	**152**	**9.9**	**–20**	**28**	**39.3**	**15:27**	....	....	....	....	....	....	....	....	....
2002-03	**Columbus**	**NHL**	**66**	**8**	**20**	**28**	**71**	**3**	**0**	**2**	**96**	**8.3**	**–8**	**26**	**46.2**	**13:56**	....	....	....	....	....	....	....	....	....
	♦ New Jersey	**NHL**	**10**	**1**	**3**	**4**	**7**	**0**	**0**	**0**	**17**	**5.9**	**–3**	**1**	**100.0**	**11:38**	**24**	**6**	**2**	**8**	**8**	**2**	**0**	**1**	**14:30**
2003-04	**New Jersey**	**NHL**	**65**	**8**	**7**	**15**	**67**	**5**	**0**	**2**	**76**	**10.5**	**–9**	**5**	**40.0**	**12:53**	....	....	....	....	....	....	....	....	....
2004-05			DID NOT PLAY																						
2005-06	**New Jersey**	**NHL**	**76**	**8**	**17**	**25**	**70**	**4**	**0**	**3**	**89**	**9.0**	**–18**	**4**	**25.0**	**12:38**	**7**	**0**	**1**	**1**	**8**	**0**	**0**	**0**	**14:07**
2006-07	Lowell Devils	AHL	59	8	16	24	31	....	....	....	....	....	....	....	....	....	....	....	....	....	....	....	....	....	....
	NHL Totals		**700**	**92**	**147**	**239**	**793**	**28**	**0**	**17**	**831**	**11.1**		**85**	**43.5**	**12:56**	**90**	**6**	**11**	**17**	**95**	**2**	**0**	**1**	**12:33**

• Missed majority of 1990-91 season recovering from neck injury suffered in game vs. Sudbury (OHL), December 4, 1990. Awarded to **Dallas** from **Toronto** with Peter Zezel as compensation for Toronto's signing of free agent Mike Craig, August 10, 1994. Traded to **Columbus** by **Dallas** for Columbus' 2nd round choice (Loui Eriksson) in 2003 Entry Draft, August 29, 2001. Traded to **New Jersey** by **Columbus** for New Jersey's 4th round choice (later traded to Carolina – later traded to Calgary – Calgary selected Kristopher Hogg) in 2004 Entry Draft, March 10, 2003.

MARTENSSON, Tony

(MOHR-tehn-suhn, TOH-nee) **ANA.**

Center. Shoots left. 6', 189 lbs. Born, Upplands Vasby, Sweden, June 23, 1980. Anaheim's 9th choice, 224th overall, in 2001 Entry Draft.

Season	Club	League	GP	G	A	Pts	PIM	PP	SH	GW	S	%	+/-	TF	F%	Min	GP	G	A	Pts	PIM	PP	SH	GW	Min
1997-98	Arlanda	Sweden-2	12	2	4	6	0	....	....	....	....	....	....	....	....	....	2	0	0	0	0	....	....	....	....
1998-99	Arlanda	Sweden-2	37	8	22	30	8	....	....	....	....	....	....	....	....	....	2	0	0	0	0	....	....	....	....
99-2000	Arlanda	Sweden-2	44	21	28	49	14	....	....	....	....	....	....	....	....	....	....	....	....	....	....	....	....	....	....
2000-01	Brynas IF Gavle	Sweden	50	15	11	26	20	....	....	....	....	....	....	....	....	....	4	0	1	1	2	....	....	....	....
	Brynas IF Gavle Jr.	Swe-Jr.	1	1	0	1	0	....	....	....	....	....	....	....	....	....	....	....	....	....	....	....	....	....	....
2001-02	Brynas IF Gavle	Sweden	50	9	17	26	14	....	....	....	....	....	....	....	....	....	4	1	3	4	0	....	....	....	....
2002-03	Cincinnati	AHL	79	17	36	53	20	....	....	....	....	....	....	....	....	....	....	....	....	....	....	....	....	....	....
2003-04	**Anaheim**	**NHL**	**6**	**1**	**1**	**2**	**0**	**0**	**0**	**0**	**4**	**25.0**	**–2**	**18**	**44.4**	**6:58**	....	....	....	....	....	....	....	....	....
	Cincinnati	AHL	67	16	34	50	20	....	....	....	....	....	....	....	....	....	9	3	10	13	4	....	....	....	....
2004-05	Linkopings HC	Sweden	50	13	21	34	12	....	....	....	....	....	....	....	....	....	5	0	1	1	0	....	....	....	....
2005-06	Linkopings HC	Sweden	49	16	30	46	32	....	....	....	....	....	....	....	....	....	13	2	6	8	2	....	....	....	....
2006-07	Linkopings HC	Sweden	55	18	36	54	20	....	....	....	....	....	....	....	....	....	15	2	9	11	16	....	....	....	....
	NHL Totals		**6**	**1**	**1**	**2**	**0**	**0**	**0**	**0**	**4**	**25.0**		**18**	**44.4**	**6:58**	....	....	....	....	....	....	....	....	....

Signed as a free agent by **Linkopings** (Sweden), May 17, 2004.

MARTIN, Paul

(MAHR-tihn, PAWL) **N.J.**

Defense. Shoots left. 6'1", 190 lbs. Born, Minneapolis, MN, March 5, 1981. New Jersey's 5th choice, 62nd overall, in 2000 Entry Draft.

Season	Club	League	GP	G	A	Pts	PIM	PP	SH	GW	S	%	+/-	TF	F%	Min	GP	G	A	Pts	PIM	PP	SH	GW	Min
1998 99	Elk River Elks	High-MN	24	9	11	20	....	....	....	....	....	....	....	....	....	....	....	....	....	....	....	....	....	....	....
99-2000	Elk River Elks	High-MN	24	15	35	50	26	....	....	....	....	....	....	....	....	....	....	....	....	....	....	....	....	....	....
2000-01	U. of Minnesota	WCHA	38	3	17	20	8	....	....	....	....	....	....	....	....	....	....	....	....	....	....	....	....	....	....
2001-02	U. of Minnesota	WCHA	44	8	30	38	22	....	....	....	....	....	....	....	....	....	....	....	....	....	....	....	....	....	....
2002-03	U. of Minnesota	WCHA	45	9	30	39	32	....	....	....	....	....	....	....	....	....	....	....	....	....	....	....	....	....	....
2003-04	**New Jersey**	**NHL**	**70**	**6**	**18**	**24**	**4**	**2**	**0**	**2**	**82**	**7.3**	**12**	**0**	**0.0**	**20:08**	**5**	**1**	**1**	**2**	**4**	**1**	**0**	**0**	**23:40**
2004-05	Fribourg	Swiss	11	3	4	7	2	....	....	....	....	....	....	....	....	....	....	....	....	....	....	....	....	....	....
2005-06	**New Jersey**	**NHL**	**80**	**5**	**32**	**37**	**32**	**3**	**0**	**0**	**97**	**5.2**	**1**	**0**	**0.0**	**23:37**	**9**	**0**	**3**	**3**	**4**	**0**	**0**	**0**	**24:17**
	United States	Olympics	DID NOT PLAY																						
2006-07	**New Jersey**	**NHL**	**82**	**3**	**23**	**26**	**18**	**1**	**0**	**0**	**84**	**3.6**	**–9**	**0**	**0.0**	**25:13**	**11**	**0**	**4**	**4**	**6**	**0**	**0**	**0**	**25:09**
	NHL Totals		**232**	**14**	**73**	**87**	**54**	**6**	**0**	**2**	**263**	**5.3**		**0**	**0.0**	**23:08**	**25**	**1**	**8**	**9**	**14**	**1**	**0**	**0**	**24:32**

Minnesota High School Player of the Year (1999) • WCHA All-Rookie Team (2001) • WCHA Second All-Star Team (2002, 2003) • NCAA West Second All-American Team (2003) • NCAA Championship All-Tournament Team (2003)

Signed as a free agent by **Fribourg** (Swiss), November 4, 2004.

MARTINEK, Radek

(MAHR-tih-nehk, RA-dehk) **NYI**

Defense. Shoots right. 5'11", 200 lbs. Born, Havlickuv Brod, Czech., August 31, 1976. NY Islanders' 12th choice, 228th overall, in 1999 Entry Draft.

Season	Club	League	GP	G	A	Pts	PIM	PP	SH	GW	S	%	+/-	TF	F%	Min	GP	G	A	Pts	PIM	PP	SH	GW	Min
1996-97	C. Budejovice	CzRep	52	3	5	8	40	....	....	....	....	....	....	....	....	....	5	0	1	1	2	....	....	....	....
	C. Budejovice	EuroHL	6	0	0	0	0	....	....	....	....	....	....	....	....	....	2	0	0	0	0	....	....	....	....
1997-98	C. Budejovice	CzRep	42	2	7	9	36	....	....	....	....	....	....	....	....	....	....	....	....	....	....	....	....	....	....
1998-99	C. Budejovice	CzRep	52	12	13	25	50	....	....	....	....	....	....	....	....	....	3	0	2	2	....	....	....	....	....
99-2000	C. Budejovice	CzRep	45	5	18	23	24	....	....	....	....	....	....	....	....	....	3	0	0	0	6	....	....	....	....
2000-01	C. Budejovice	CzRep	44	8	10	18	45	....	....	....	....	....	....	....	....	....	....	....	....	....	....	....	....	....	....
2001-02	**NY Islanders**	**NHL**	**23**	**1**	**4**	**5**	**16**	**0**	**0**	**1**	**25**	**4.0**	**5**	**0**	**0.0**	**21:07**	....	....	....	....	....	....	....	....	....
2002-03	**NY Islanders**	**NHL**	**66**	**2**	**11**	**13**	**26**	**0**	**0**	**1**	**67**	**3.0**	**15**	**0**	**0.0**	**17:15**	**4**	**0**	**0**	**0**	**4**	**0**	**0**	**0**	**10:16**
	Bridgeport	AHL	3	0	3	3	2	....	....	....	....	....	....	....	....	....	....	....	....	....	....	....	....	....	....
2003-04	**NY Islanders**	**NHL**	**47**	**4**	**3**	**7**	**43**	**0**	**0**	**1**	**48**	**8.3**	**–9**	**0**	**0.0**	**13:03**	**5**	**0**	**1**	**1**	**0**	**0**	**0**	**0**	**12:12**
2004-05	C. Budejovice	CzRep-2	30	12	18	30	80	....	....	....	....	....	....	....	....	....	12	2	3	5	6	....	....	....	....
2005-06	**NY Islanders**	**NHL**	**74**	**1**	**16**	**17**	**32**	**0**	**0**	**0**	**79**	**1.3**	**–9**	**1**	**0.0**	**18:16**	....	....	....	....	....	....	....	....	....
2006-07	**NY Islanders**	**NHL**	**43**	**2**	**15**	**17**	**40**	**0**	**0**	**0**	**44**	**4.5**	**19**	**1**	**100.0**	**19:54**	....	....	....	....	....	....	....	....	....
	NHL Totals		**253**	**10**	**49**	**59**	**157**	**0**	**0**	**3**	**263**	**3.8**		**2**	**50.0**	**17:34**	**9**	**0**	**1**	**1**	**4**	**0**	**0**	**0**	**11:20**

• Missed majority of 2001-02 season recovering from knee injury suffered in game vs. NY Rangers, November 11, 2001. Signed as a free agent by **Ceske Budejovice** (CzRep-2), September 17, 2004.

MARTINS, Steve

(MAHR-tihns, STEEV)

Center. Shoots left. 5'9", 185 lbs. Born, Gatineau, Que., April 13, 1972. Hartford's 1st choice, 5th overall, in 1994 Supplemental Draft.

Season	Club	League	GP	G	A	Pts	PIM	PP	SH	GW	S	%	+/-	TF	F%	Min	GP	G	A	Pts	PIM	PP	SH	GW	Min
1988-89	L'Outaouais	QAAA	38	18	33	51	70	....	....	....	....	....	....	....	....	....	....	....	....	....	....	....	....	....	....
1989-90	Choate-Rosemary	High-CT	STATISTICS NOT AVAILABLE																						
1990-91	Choate-Rosemary	High-CT	STATISTICS NOT AVAILABLE																						
1991-92	Harvard Crimson	ECAC	20	13	14	27	26	....	....	....	....	....	....	....	....	....	....	....	....	....	....	....	....	....	....
1992-93	Harvard Crimson	ECAC	18	6	8	14	40	....	....	....	....	....	....	....	....	....	....	....	....	....	....	....	....	....	....
1993-94	Harvard Crimson	ECAC	32	25	35	60	*93	....	....	....	....	....	....	....	....	....	....	....	....	....	....	....	....	....	....
1994-95	Harvard Crimson	ECAC	28	15	23	38	93	....	....	....	....	....	....	....	....	....	....	....	....	....	....	....	....	....	....
1995-96	**Hartford**	**NHL**	**23**	**1**	**3**	**4**	**8**	**0**	**0**	**0**	**27**	**3.7**	**–3**	....	....	....	....	....	....	....	....	....	....	....	....
	Springfield	AHL	30	9	20	29	10	....	....	....	....	....	....	....	....	....	....	....	....	....	....	....	....	....	....
1996-97	**Hartford**	**NHL**	**2**	**0**	**1**	**1**	**0**	**0**	**0**	**0**	**2**	**0.0**	**0**	....	....	....	....	....	....	....	....	....	....	....	....
	Springfield	AHL	63	12	31	43	78	....	....	....	....	....	....	....	....	....	17	1	3	4	26	....	....	....	....
1997-98	**Carolina**	**NHL**	**3**	**0**	**0**	**0**	**0**	**0**	**0**	**0**	**0**	**0.0**	**0**	....	....	....	....	....	....	....	....	....	....	....	....
	Chicago Wolves	IHL	78	20	41	61	122	....	....	....	....	....	....	....	....	....	21	6	14	20	28	....	....	....	....
1998-99	**Ottawa**	**NHL**	**36**	**4**	**3**	**7**	**10**	**1**	**0**	**1**	**27**	**14.8**	**4**	**191**	**56.0**	**8:28**	....	....	....	....	....	....	....	....	....
	Detroit Vipers	IHL	4	1	6	7	16	....	....	....	....	....	....	....	....	....	....	....	....	....	....	....	....	....	....
99-2000	**Ottawa**	**NHL**	**2**	**1**	**0**	**1**	**0**	**0**	**0**	**0**	**3**	**33.3**	**–1**	**3**	**0.0**	**11:10**	....	....	....	....	....	....	....	....	....
	Tampa Bay	**NHL**	**57**	**5**	**7**	**12**	**37**	**0**	**1**	**1**	**62**	**8.1**	**–11**	**806**	**50.9**	**13:27**	....	....	....	....	....	....	....	....	....
2000-01	**Tampa Bay**	**NHL**	**20**	**1**	**1**	**2**	**13**	**0**	**0**	**0**	**18**	**5.6**	**–9**	**184**	**52.2**	**9:35**	....	....	....	....	....	....	....	....	....
	Detroit Vipers	IHL	8	5	4	9	4	....	....	....	....	....	....	....	....	....	....	....	....	....	....	....	....	....	....
	NY Islanders	**NHL**	**39**	**1**	**3**	**4**	**20**	**0**	**1**	**0**	**28**	**3.6**	**–7**	**302**	**58.0**	**9:41**	....	....	....	....	....	....	....	....	....
	Chicago Wolves	IHL	5	1	2	3	0	....	....	....	....	....	....	....	....	....	16	1	6	7	22	....	....	....	....
2001-02	**Ottawa**	**NHL**	**14**	**1**	**0**	**1**	**4**	**0**	**0**	**0**	**11**	**9.1**	**1**	**121**	**55.4**	**9:33**	**2**	**0**	**0**	**0**	**0**	**0**	**0**	**0**	**7:13**
	Grand Rapids	AHL	51	10	21	31	66	....	....	....	....	....	....	....	....	....	3	0	0	0	0	....	....	....	....
2002-03	**Ottawa**	**NHL**	**14**	**2**	**3**	**5**	**10**	**0**	**0**	**0**	**13**	**15.4**	**3**	**111**	**55.9**	**9:45**	....	....	....	....	....	....	....	....	....
	Binghamton	AHL	26	5	11	16	31	....	....	....	....	....	....	....	....	....	....	....	....	....	....	....	....	....	....
	St. Louis	**NHL**	**28**	**3**	**3**	**6**	**18**	**0**	**1**	**0**	**25**	**12.0**	**–8**	**369**	**54.7**	**13:38**	**2**	**0**	**1**	**1**	**0**	**0**	**0**	**0**	**9:23**
2003-04	**St. Louis**	**NHL**	**25**	**1**	**0**	**1**	**22**	**0**	**1**	**0**	**27**	**3.7**	**–7**	**172**	**61.1**	**10:29**	**1**	**0**	**0**	**0**	**0**	**0**	**0**	**0**	**5:29**
	Worcester IceCats	AHL	22	4	9	13	16	....	....	....	....	....	....	....	....	....	....	....	....	....	....	....	....	....	....
2004-05	JYP Jyvaskyla	Finland	54	13	12	25	66	....	....	....	....	....	....	....	....	....	3	0	0	0	4	....	....	....	....

			Regular Season														Playoffs								
Season	Club	League	GP	G	A	Pts	PIM	PP	SH	GW	S	%	+/-	TF	F%	Min	GP	G	A	Pts	PIM	PP	SH	GW	Min
2005-06	**Ottawa**	**NHL**	**4**	**1**	**1**	**2**	**0**	**0**	**0**	**0**	**6**	**16.7**	**2**	**23**	**47.8**	**7:50**	....	....	....	....	....	....	....	....	....
	Binghamton	AHL	76	22	58	80	80	....	....	....	....	....	....	....	....	....	....	....	....	....	....	....	....	....	....
2006-07	Chicago Wolves	AHL	48	13	26	39	49	....	....	....	....	....	....	....	....	....	....	....	....	....	....	....	....	....	....
	NHL Totals		**267**	**21**	**25**	**46**	**142**	**1**	**4**	**2**	**249**	**8.4**		**2282**	**54.1**	**10:55**	**5**	**0**	**1**	**1**	**0**	**0**	**0**	**0**	**7:44**

ECAC First All-Star Team (1994) • ECAC Player of the Year (1994) • NCAA East First All-American Team (1994) • NCAA Final Four All-Tournament Team (1994)

Transferred to **Carolina** after **Hartford** franchise relocated, June 25, 1997. Signed as a free agent by **Ottawa**, July 20, 1998. Claimed on waivers by **Tampa Bay** from **Ottawa**, October 29, 1999. Traded to **NY Islanders** by **Tampa Bay** for future considerations, January 3, 2001. Signed as a free agent by **Ottawa**, August 30, 2001. Claimed on waivers by **St. Louis** from **Ottawa**, January 15, 2003. Signed as a free agent by **Jyvaskyla** (Finland), September 7, 2004. Signed as a free agent by **Ottawa**, August 19, 2005.

MATVICHUK, Richard

(MAT-vih-chuhk, RIH-chuhrd) **N.J.**

Defense. Shoots left. 6'3", 215 lbs. Born, Edmonton, Alta., February 5, 1973. Minnesota's 1st choice, 8th overall, in 1991 Entry Draft.

Season	Club	League	GP	G	A	Pts	PIM	PP	SH	GW	S	%	+/-	TF	F%	Min	GP	G	A	Pts	PIM	PP	SH	GW	Min
1988-89	Ft. Saskatchewan	AJHL	58	7	36	43	147	....	....	....	....	....	....	....	....	....	....	....	....	....	....	....	....	....	....
1989-90	Saskatoon Blades	WHL	56	8	24	32	126	....	....	....	....	....	....	....	....	....	10	2	8	10	16	....	....	....	....
1990-91	Saskatoon Blades	WHL	68	13	36	49	117	....	....	....	....	....	....	....	....	....	....	....	....	....	....	....	....	....	....
1991-92	Saskatoon Blades	WHL	58	14	40	54	126	....	....	....	....	....	....	....	....	....	22	1	9	10	61	....	....	....	....
1992-93	**Minnesota**	**NHL**	**53**	**2**	**3**	**5**	**26**	**1**	**0**	**0**	**51**	**3.9**	**–8**	....	....	....	....	....	....	....	....	....	....	....	....
	Kalamazoo Wings	IHL	3	0	1	1	6	....	....	....	....	....	....	....	....	....	....	....	....	....	....	....	....	....	....
1993-94	**Dallas**	**NHL**	**25**	**0**	**3**	**3**	**22**	**0**	**0**	**0**	**18**	**0.0**	**1**	....	....	....	**7**	**1**	**1**	**2**	**12**	**1**	**0**	**0**	....
	Kalamazoo Wings	IHL	43	8	17	25	84	....	....	....	....	....	....	....	....	....	....	....	....	....	....	....	....	....	....
1994-95	**Dallas**	**NHL**	**14**	**0**	**2**	**2**	**14**	**0**	**0**	**0**	**21**	**0.0**	**–7**	....	....	....	**5**	**0**	**2**	**2**	**4**	**0**	**0**	**0**	....
	Kalamazoo Wings	IHL	17	0	6	6	16	....	....	....	....	....	....	....	....	....	....	....	....	....	....	....	....	....	....
1995-96	**Dallas**	**NHL**	**73**	**6**	**16**	**22**	**71**	**0**	**0**	**1**	**81**	**7.4**	**4**	....	....	....	....	....	....	....	....	....	....	....	....
1996-97	**Dallas**	**NHL**	**57**	**5**	**7**	**12**	**87**	**0**	**2**	**0**	**83**	**6.0**	**1**	....	....	....	**7**	**0**	**1**	**1**	**20**	**0**	**0**	**0**	....
1997-98	**Dallas**	**NHL**	**74**	**3**	**15**	**18**	**63**	**0**	**0**	**0**	**71**	**4.2**	**7**	....	....	....	**16**	**1**	**1**	**2**	**14**	**0**	**0**	**0**	....
1998-99♦	**Dallas**	**NHL**	**64**	**3**	**9**	**12**	**51**	**1**	**0**	**0**	**54**	**5.6**	**23**	**0**	**0.0**	**21:19**	**22**	**1**	**5**	**6**	**20**	**0**	**0**	**0**	**22:40**
99-2000	**Dallas**	**NHL**	**70**	**4**	**21**	**25**	**42**	**0**	**0**	**1**	**73**	**5.5**	**7**	**0**	**0.0**	**24:27**	**23**	**2**	**5**	**7**	**14**	**0**	**0**	**0**	**25:51**
2000-01	**Dallas**	**NHL**	**78**	**4**	**16**	**20**	**62**	**2**	**0**	**1**	**85**	**4.7**	**5**	**1**	**100.0**	**22:53**	**10**	**0**	**0**	**0**	**14**	**0**	**0**	**0**	**22:43**
2001-02	**Dallas**	**NHL**	**82**	**9**	**12**	**21**	**52**	**4**	**0**	**2**	**109**	**8.3**	**11**	**1**	**0.0**	**23:47**	....	....	....	....	....	....	....	....	....
2002-03	**Dallas**	**NHL**	**68**	**1**	**5**	**6**	**58**	**0**	**0**	**1**	**59**	**1.7**	**1**	**3**	**0.0**	**19:23**	**12**	**0**	**3**	**3**	**8**	**0**	**0**	**0**	**19:55**
2003-04	**Dallas**	**NHL**	**75**	**1**	**20**	**21**	**36**	**0**	**0**	**1**	**85**	**1.2**	**0**	**2**	**50.0**	**21:50**	**5**	**0**	**1**	**1**	**8**	**0**	**0**	**0**	**22:15**
2004-05			Did not play																						
2005-06	**New Jersey**	**NHL**	**62**	**1**	**10**	**11**	**40**	**0**	**0**	**0**	**43**	**2.3**	**2**	**0**	**0.0**	**18:13**	**7**	**0**	**0**	**0**	**4**	**0**	**0**	**0**	**16:41**
2006-07	**New Jersey**	**NHL**	**1**	**0**	**0**	**0**	**0**	**0**	**0**	**0**	**0**	**0.0**	**–1**	**0**	**0.0**	**12:45**	**9**	**0**	**0**	**0**	**10**	**0**	**0**	**0**	**19:11**
	NHL Totals		**796**	**39**	**139**	**178**	**624**	**8**	**2**	**7**	**833**	**4.7**		**7**	**28.6**	**21:49**	**123**	**5**	**19**	**24**	**128**	**1**	**0**	**0**	**22:17**

WHL East First All-Star Team (1992)

Transferred to **Dallas** after **Minnesota** franchise relocated, June 9, 1993. Signed as a free agent by **New Jersey**, July 12, 2004. • Missed majority of 2006-07 season recovering from a recurring back injury.

MAY, Brad

(MAY, BRAD) **ANA.**

Left wing. Shoots left. 6'1", 220 lbs. Born, Toronto, Ont., November 29, 1971. Buffalo's 1st choice, 14th overall, in 1990 Entry Draft.

Season	Club	League	GP	G	A	Pts	PIM	PP	SH	GW	S	%	+/-	TF	F%	Min	GP	G	A	Pts	PIM	PP	SH	GW	Min
1987-88	Markham	Minor-ON	31	22	37	59	58	....	....	....	....	....	....	....	....	....	....	....	....	....	....	....	....	....	....
	Markham	OHA-B	6	1	1	2	21	....	....	....	....	....	....	....	....	....	....	....	....	....	....	....	....	....	....
1988-89	Niagara Falls	OHL	65	8	14	22	304	....	....	....	....	....	....	....	....	....	17	0	1	1	55	....	....	....	....
1989-90	Niagara Falls	OHL	61	32	58	90	223	....	....	....	....	....	....	....	....	....	16	9	13	22	64	....	....	....	....
1990-91	Niagara Falls	OHL	34	37	32	69	93	....	....	....	....	....	....	....	....	....	14	11	14	25	53	....	....	....	....
1991-92	**Buffalo**	**NHL**	**69**	**11**	**6**	**17**	**309**	**1**	**0**	**3**	**82**	**13.4**	**–12**	....	....	....	**7**	**1**	**4**	**5**	**2**	**0**	**0**	**1**	....
1992-93	**Buffalo**	**NHL**	**82**	**13**	**13**	**26**	**242**	**0**	**0**	**1**	**114**	**11.4**	**3**	....	....	....	**8**	**1**	**1**	**2**	**14**	**0**	**0**	**1**	....
1993-94	**Buffalo**	**NHL**	**84**	**18**	**27**	**45**	**171**	**3**	**0**	**3**	**166**	**10.8**	**–6**	....	....	....	**7**	**0**	**2**	**2**	**9**	**0**	**0**	**0**	....
1994-95	**Buffalo**	**NHL**	**33**	**3**	**3**	**6**	**87**	**1**	**0**	**0**	**42**	**7.1**	**5**	....	....	....	**4**	**0**	**0**	**0**	**2**	**0**	**0**	**0**	....
1995-96	**Buffalo**	**NHL**	**79**	**15**	**29**	**44**	**295**	**3**	**0**	**4**	**168**	**8.9**	**6**	....	....	....	....	....	....	....	....	....	....	....	....
1996-97	**Buffalo**	**NHL**	**42**	**3**	**4**	**7**	**106**	**1**	**0**	**1**	**75**	**4.0**	**–8**	....	....	....	**10**	**1**	**1**	**2**	**32**	**0**	**0**	**0**	....
1997-98	**Buffalo**	**NHL**	**36**	**4**	**7**	**11**	**113**	**0**	**0**	**0**	**41**	**9.8**	**2**	....	....	....	....	....	....	....	....	....	....	....	....
	Vancouver	**NHL**	**27**	**9**	**3**	**12**	**41**	**4**	**0**	**2**	**56**	**16.1**	**0**	....	....	....	....	....	....	....	....	....	....	....	....
1998-99	**Vancouver**	**NHL**	**66**	**6**	**11**	**17**	**102**	**1**	**0**	**1**	**91**	**6.6**	**–14**	**8**	**12.5**	**13:04**	....	....	....	....	....	....	....	....	....
99-2000	**Vancouver**	**NHL**	**59**	**9**	**7**	**16**	**90**	**0**	**0**	**3**	**66**	**13.6**	**–2**	**3**	**0.0**	**10:24**	....	....	....	....	....	....	....	....	....
2000-01	**Phoenix**	**NHL**	**62**	**11**	**14**	**25**	**107**	**0**	**0**	**0**	**83**	**13.3**	**10**	**3**	**33.3**	**11:11**	....	....	....	....	....	....	....	....	....
2001-02	**Phoenix**	**NHL**	**72**	**10**	**12**	**22**	**95**	**1**	**0**	**3**	**105**	**9.5**	**11**	**3**	**0.0**	**12:04**	**5**	**0**	**0**	**0**	**0**	**0**	**0**	**0**	**10:19**
2002-03	**Phoenix**	**NHL**	**20**	**3**	**4**	**7**	**32**	**0**	**0**	**0**	**24**	**12.5**	**3**	**0**	**0.0**	**9:56**	....	....	....	....	....	....	....	....	....
	Vancouver	**NHL**	**3**	**0**	**0**	**0**	**10**	**0**	**0**	**0**	**1**	**0.0**	**1**	**0**	**0.0**	**7:48**	**14**	**0**	**0**	**0**	**15**	**0**	**0**	**0**	**7:25**
2003-04	**Vancouver**	**NHL**	**70**	**5**	**6**	**11**	**137**	**0**	**0**	**0**	**75**	**6.7**	**–2**	**8**	**50.0**	**8:56**	**6**	**1**	**0**	**1**	**6**	**0**	**0**	**0**	**7:07**
2004-05			Did not play																						
2005-06	**Colorado**	**NHL**	**54**	**3**	**3**	**6**	**82**	**0**	**0**	**0**	**55**	**5.5**	**–14**	**6**	**33.3**	**8:23**	**3**	**0**	**0**	**0**	**0**	**0**	**0**	**0**	**9:21**
2006-07	**Colorado**	**NHL**	**10**	**0**	**3**	**3**	**8**	**0**	**0**	**0**	**11**	**0.0**	**0**	**0**	**0.0**	**11:28**	....	....	....	....	....	....	....	....	....
	♦ **Anaheim**	**NHL**	**14**	**0**	**1**	**1**	**13**	**0**	**0**	**0**	**11**	**0.0**	**–1**	**0**	**0.0**	**8:39**	**18**	**0**	**1**	**1**	**28**	**0**	**0**	**0**	**7:21**
	NHL Totals		**882**	**123**	**153**	**276**	**2040**	**15**	**0**	**21**	**1266**	**9.7**		**31**	**25.8**	**10:38**	**82**	**4**	**9**	**13**	**108**	**0**	**0**	**2**	**7:48**

OHL Second All-Star Team (1990, 1991)

• Missed majority of 1990-91 season recovering from knee injury suffered at Team Canada Juniors evaluation camp, August 21, 1990. Traded to **Vancouver** by **Buffalo** with Buffalo's 3rd round choice (later traded to Tampa Bay – Tampa Bay selected Jimmie Olvestad) in 1999 Entry Draft for Geoff Sanderson, February 4, 1998. Traded to **Phoenix** by **Vancouver** for future considerations, June 24, 2000. • Missed majority of 2002-03 season recovering from shoulder injury suffered in pre-season game vs. Detroit, October 6, 2002. Traded to **Vancouver** by **Phoenix** for Phoenix's 3rd round choice (previously acquired, Phoenix selected Dimitri Pestunov) in 2003 Entry Draft, March 11, 2003. Signed as a free agent by **Colorado**, August 5, 2005. Traded to **Anaheim** by **Colorado** for Michael Wall, February 27, 2007. • Missed majority of 2006-07 season recovering from shoulder injury suffered in pre-season game vs. Detroit, September 25, 2006.

MAYERS, Jamal

(MAI-uhrz, JUH-MAHL) **ST.L.**

Right wing. Shoots right. 6'2", 220 lbs. Born, Toronto, Ont., October 24, 1974. St. Louis' 3rd choice, 89th overall, in 1993 Entry Draft.

Season	Club	League	GP	G	A	Pts	PIM	PP	SH	GW	S	%	+/-	TF	F%	Min	GP	G	A	Pts	PIM	PP	SH	GW	Min
1990-91	Thornhill	MTJHL	44	12	24	36	78	....	....	....	....	....	....	....	....	....	....	....	....	....	....	....	....	....	....
1991-92	Thornhill	MTJHL	56	38	69	107	36	....	....	....	....	....	....	....	....	....	....	....	....	....	....	....	....	....	....
1992-93	Western Mich.	CCHA	38	8	17	25	26	....	....	....	....	....	....	....	....	....	....	....	....	....	....	....	....	....	....
1993-94	Western Mich.	CCHA	40	17	32	49	40	....	....	....	....	....	....	....	....	....	....	....	....	....	....	....	....	....	....
1994-95	Western Mich.	CCHA	39	13	32	45	40	....	....	....	....	....	....	....	....	....	....	....	....	....	....	....	....	....	....
1995-96	Western Mich.	CCHA	38	17	22	39	75	....	....	....	....	....	....	....	....	....	....	....	....	....	....	....	....	....	....
1996-97	**St. Louis**	**NHL**	**6**	**0**	**1**	**1**	**2**	**0**	**0**	**0**	**7**	**0.0**	**–3**	....	....	....	....	....	....	....	....	....	....	....	....
	Worcester IceCats	AHL	62	12	14	26	104	....	....	....	....	....	....	....	....	....	5	4	5	9	4	....	....	....	....
1997-98	Worcester IceCats	AHL	61	19	24	43	117	....	....	....	....	....	....	....	....	....	11	3	4	7	10	....	....	....	....
1998-99	**St. Louis**	**NHL**	**34**	**4**	**5**	**9**	**40**	**0**	**0**	**0**	**48**	**8.3**	**–3**	**2**	**50.0**	**8:08**	**11**	**0**	**1**	**1**	**8**	**0**	**0**	**0**	**8:34**
	Worcester IceCats	AHL	20	9	7	16	34	....	....	....	....	....	....	....	....	....	....	....	....	....	....	....	....	....	....
99-2000	**St. Louis**	**NHL**	**79**	**7**	**10**	**17**	**90**	**0**	**0**	**0**	**99**	**7.1**	**0**	**77**	**52.0**	**9:46**	**7**	**0**	**4**	**4**	**2**	**0**	**0**	**0**	**10:42**
2000-01	**St. Louis**	**NHL**	**77**	**8**	**13**	**21**	**117**	**0**	**0**	**0**	**132**	**6.1**	**–3**	**273**	**51.3**	**11:04**	**15**	**2**	**3**	**5**	**8**	**0**	**0**	**0**	**11:28**
2001-02	**St. Louis**	**NHL**	**77**	**9**	**8**	**17**	**99**	**0**	**1**	**0**	**105**	**8.6**	**9**	**761**	**52.6**	**11:36**	**10**	**3**	**0**	**3**	**2**	**0**	**0**	**2**	**11:14**
2002-03	**St. Louis**	**NHL**	**15**	**2**	**5**	**7**	**8**	**0**	**0**	**0**	**26**	**7.7**	**1**	**111**	**51.4**	**14:21**	....	....	....	....	....	....	....	....	....
2003-04	**St. Louis**	**NHL**	**80**	**6**	**5**	**11**	**91**	**0**	**1**	**3**	**130**	**4.6**	**–19**	**681**	**48.6**	**13:01**	**5**	**0**	**0**	**0**	**0**	**0**	**0**	**0**	**12:55**
2004-05	Hammarby	Sweden-2	19	9	13	22	36	....	....	....	....	....	....	....	....	....	....	....	....	....	....	....	....	....	....
	Missouri	UHL	13	5	2	7	68	....	....	....	....	....	....	....	....	....	....	....	....	....	....	....	....	....	....
2005-06	**St. Louis**	**NHL**	**67**	**15**	**11**	**26**	**129**	**0**	**2**	**1**	**111**	**13.5**	**–22**	**363**	**48.5**	**15:07**	....	....	....	....	....	....	....	....	....
2006-07	**St. Louis**	**NHL**	**80**	**8**	**14**	**22**	**89**	**0**	**2**	**0**	**129**	**6.2**	**–19**	**432**	**57.4**	**14:37**	....	....	....	....	....	....	....	....	....
	NHL Totals		**515**	**59**	**72**	**131**	**665**	**0**	**6**	**4**	**787**	**7.5**		**2700**	**51.6**	**12:15**	**48**	**5**	**8**	**13**	**20**	**0**	**0**	**2**	**10:47**

• Missed majority of 2002-03 season recovering from knee injury suffered in game vs. Calgary, November 16, 2002. Signed as a free agent by **Hammarby** (Sweden-2), November 16, 2004. Signed as a free agent by **Missouri** (UHL), March 11, 2005.

McAMMOND, Dean

(muhK-AM-uhnd, DEEN) **OTT.**

Center. Shoots left. 5'11", 189 lbs. Born, Grand Cache, Alta., June 15, 1973. Chicago's 1st choice, 22nd overall, in 1991 Entry Draft.

Season	Club	League	GP	G	A	Pts	PIM	PP	SH	GW	S	%	+/-	TF	F%	Min	GP	G	A	Pts	PIM	PP	SH	GW	Min
1988-89	St. Albert Raiders	AMHL	36	33	44	77	132	....	....	....	....	....	....	....	....	....	....	....	....	....	....	....	....	....	....
1989-90	Prince Albert	WHL	53	11	11	22	49	....	....	....	....	....	....	....	....	....	14	2	3	5	18	....	....	....	....
1990-91	Prince Albert	WHL	71	33	35	68	108	....	....	....	....	....	....	....	....	....	2	0	1	1	6	....	....	....	....
1991-92	Prince Albert	WHL	63	37	54	91	189	....	....	....	....	....	....	....	....	....	10	12	11	23	26	....	....	....	....
	Chicago	**NHL**	**5**	**0**	**2**	**2**	**0**	**0**	**0**	**0**	**4**	**0.0**	**–2**	....	....	....	**3**	**0**	**0**	**0**	**2**	**0**	**0**	**0**	....
1992-93	Prince Albert	WHL	30	19	29	48	44	....	....	....	....	....	....	....	....	....	....	....	....	....	....	....	....	....	....
	Swift Current	WHL	18	10	13	23	24	....	....	....	....	....	....	....	....	....	17	*16	19	35	20	....	....	....	....

			Regular Season														Playoffs								
Season	Club	League	GP	G	A	Pts	PIM	PP	SH	GW	S	%	+/-	TF	F%	Min	GP	G	A	Pts	PIM	PP	SH	GW	Min
1993-94	Edmonton	NHL	45	6	21	27	16	2	0	0	52	11.5	12	....	....	....	....	....	....	....	....	....	....	....	....
	Cape Breton	AHL	28	9	12	21	38	....	....	....	....	....	....	....	....	....	....	....	....	....	....	....	....	....	....
1994-95	Edmonton	NHL	6	0	0	0	0	0	0	0	3	0.0	-1	....	....	....	....	....	....	....	....	....	....	....	....
1995-96	Edmonton	NHL	53	15	15	30	23	4	0	0	79	19.0	6	....	....	....	....	....	....	....	....	....	....	....	....
	Cape Breton	AHL	22	9	15	24	55	....	....	....	....	....	....	....	....	....	....	....	....	....	....	....	....	....	....
1996-97	Edmonton	NHL	57	12	17	29	28	4	0	6	106	11.3	-15	....	....	....	....	....	....	....	....	....	....	....	....
1997-98	Edmonton	NHL	77	19	31	50	46	8	0	3	128	14.8	9	....	....	....	12	1	4	5	12	0	0	0	....
1998-99	Edmonton	NHL	65	9	16	25	36	1	0	0	122	7.4	5	26	38.5	14:15	....	....	....	....	....	....	....	....	....
	Chicago	NHL	12	1	4	5	2	0	0	1	16	6.3	3	37	48.6	15:43	....	....	....	....	....	....	....	....	....
99-2000	Chicago	NHL	76	14	18	32	72	1	0	1	118	11.9	11	257	39.7	16:25	....	....	....	....	....	....	....	....	....
2000-01	Chicago	NHL	61	10	16	26	43	1	0	1	95	10.5	4	23	43.5	15:30	....	....	....	....	....	....	....	....	....
	Philadelphia	NHL	10	1	1	2	0	1	0	0	17	5.9	-1	65	46.2	12:00	4	0	0	0	2	0	0	0	9:25
2001-02	Calgary	NHL	73	21	30	51	60	7	0	4	152	13.8	2	143	55.2	18:56	....	....	....	....	....	....	....	....	....
2002-03	Colorado	NHL	41	10	8	18	10	2	0	2	72	13.9	1	9	55.6	14:24	....	....	....	....	....	....	....	....	....
2003-04	Calgary	NHL	64	17	13	30	18	4	1	5	101	16.8	9	768	49.1	16:52	....	....	....	....	....	....	....	....	....
2004-05	Albany River Rats	AHL	79	19	42	61	72	....	....	....	....	....	....	....	....	....	....	....	....	....	....	....	....	....	....
2005-06	St. Louis	NHL	78	15	22	37	32	4	0	0	116	12.9	-25	289	47.4	16:02	....	....	....	....	....	....	....	....	....
2006-07	Ottawa	NHL	81	14	15	29	28	0	2	1	86	16.3	11	677	44.2	11:08	18	5	3	8	11	0	1	1	11:27
	NHL Totals		804	164	229	393	414	39	3	24	1267	12.9		2294	46.5	15:23	37	6	7	13	27	0	1	1	11:05

Traded to **Edmonton** by **Chicago** with Igor Kravchuk for Joe Murphy, February 24, 1993. Traded to **Chicago** by **Edmonton** with Boris Mironov and Jonas Elofsson for Chad Kilger, Daniel Cleary, Ethan Moreau and Christian Laflamme, March 20, 1999. Traded to **Philadelphia** by **Chicago** for Philadelphia's 3rd round choice (later traded to Toronto – Toronto selected Nicolas Corbeil) in 2001 Entry Draft, March 13, 2001. Traded to **Calgary** by **Philadelphia** for Calgary's 4th round choice (Rosario Ruggeri) in 2002 Entry Draft, June 24, 2001. Traded to **Colorado** by **Calgary** with Derek Morris and Jeff Shantz for Chris Drury and Stephane Yelle, October 1, 2002. Traded to **Calgary** by **Colorado** for Calgary's 5th round choice (Mark McCutcheon) in 2003 Entry Draft, March 11, 2003. • Ruled ineligible to play remainder of 2002-03 season by NHL due to transaction violation by Calgary, March 15, 2003. Signed as a free agent by **New Jersey**, October 5, 2004. Signed as a free agent by **St. Louis**, August 9, 2005. Signed as a free agent by **Ottawa**, August 2, 2006.

McCABE, Bryan

(muh-KAYB, BRIGH-uhn) **TOR.**

Defense. Shoots left. 6'2", 220 lbs. Born, St. Catharines, Ont., June 8, 1975. NY Islanders' 2nd choice, 40th overall, in 1993 Entry Draft.

Season	Club	League	GP	G	A	Pts	PIM	PP	SH	GW	S	%	+/-	TF	F%	Min	GP	G	A	Pts	PIM	PP	SH	GW	Min
1990-91	Calgary Canucks	AMHL	33	14	34	48	55	....	....	....	....	....	....	....	....	....	....	....	....	....	....	....	....	....	....
1991-92	Medicine Hat	WHL	68	6	24	30	157	....	....	....	....	....	....	....	....	....	4	0	0	0	6	....	....	....	....
1992-93	Medicine Hat	WHL	14	0	13	13	83	....	....	....	....	....	....	....	....	....	....	....	....	....	....	....	....	....	....
	Spokane Chiefs	WHL	46	3	44	47	134	....	....	....	....	....	....	....	....	....	6	1	5	6	28	....	....	....	....
1993-94	Spokane Chiefs	WHL	64	22	62	84	218	....	....	....	....	....	....	....	....	....	3	0	4	4	4	....	....	....	....
1994-95	Spokane Chiefs	WHL	42	14	39	53	115	....	....	....	....	....	....	....	....	....	....	....	....	....	....	....	....	....	....
	Brandon	WHL	20	6	10	16	38	....	....	....	....	....	....	....	....	....	18	4	13	17	59	....	....	....	....
1995-96	NY Islanders	NHL	82	7	16	23	156	3	0	1	130	5.4	-24	....	....	....	....	....	....	....	....	....	....	....	....
1996-97	NY Islanders	NHL	82	8	20	28	165	2	1	2	117	6.8	-2	....	....	....	....	....	....	....	....	....	....	....	....
1997-98	NY Islanders	NHL	56	3	9	12	145	1	0	0	81	3.7	9	....	....	....	....	....	....	....	....	....	....	....	....
	Vancouver	NHL	26	1	11	12	64	0	1	0	42	2.4	10	....	....	....	....	....	....	....	....	....	....	....	....
1998-99	Vancouver	NHL	69	7	14	21	120	1	2	0	98	7.1	-11	1	0.0	24:13	....	....	....	....	....	....	....	....	....
99-2000	Chicago	NHL	79	6	19	25	139	2	0	2	119	5.0	-8	1	0.0	23:23	....	....	....	....	....	....	....	....	....
2000-01	Toronto	NHL	82	5	24	29	123	3	0	2	159	3.1	16	0	0.0	23:49	11	2	3	5	16	1	0	0	23:56
2001-02	Toronto	NHL	82	17	26	43	129	8	0	1	157	10.8	16	1	0.0	24:34	20	5	5	10	30	3	0	1	29:33
2002-03	Toronto	NHL	75	6	18	24	135	3	0	1	149	4.0	9	1	0.0	23:39	7	0	3	3	10	0	0	0	27:28
2003-04	Toronto	NHL	75	16	37	53	86	8	0	2	168	9.5	22	2	50.0	25:44	13	3	5	8	14	2	0	0	28:47
2004-05	HV 71 Jonkoping	Sweden	10	1	0	1	30	....	....	....	....	....	....	....	....	....	....	....	....	....	....	....	....	....	....
2005-06	Toronto	NHL	73	19	49	68	116	13	0	6	207	9.2	-1	1	0.0	28:18	....	....	....	....	....	....	....	....	....
	Canada	Olympics	6	0	0	0	18	....	....	....	....	....	....	....	....	....	....	....	....	....	....	....	....	....	....
2006-07	Toronto	NHL	82	15	42	57	115	11	0	1	207	7.2	3	0	0.0	26:50	....	....	....	....	....	....	....	....	....
	NHL Totals		863	110	285	395	1493	55	4	18	1634	6.7		7	14.3	25:03	51	10	16	26	70	6	0	1	27:51

WHL West Second All-Star Team (1993) • WHL West First All-Star Team (1994) • WHL East First All-Star Team (1995) • Memorial Cup Tournament All-Star Team (1995) • NHL Second All-Star Team (2004)

Traded to **Vancouver** by **NY Islanders** with Todd Bertuzzi and NY Islanders' 3rd round choice (Jarkko Ruutu) in 1998 Entry Draft for Trevor Linden, February 6, 1998. Traded to **Chicago** by **Vancouver** with Vancouver's 1st round choice (Pavel Vorobiev) in 2000 Entry Draft for Chicago's 1st round choice (later traded to Tampa Bay – later traded to NY Rangers – NY Rangers selected Pavel Brendl) in 1999 Entry Draft, June 25, 1999. Traded to **Toronto** by **Chicago** for Alexander Karpovtsev and Toronto's 4th round choice (Vladimir Gusev) in 2001 Entry Draft, October 2, 2000. Signed as a free agent by **Jonkoping** (Sweden), October 29, 2004.

McCARTHY, Steve

(muh-KAHR-thee, STEEV) **ATL.**

Defense. Shoots left. 6'1", 205 lbs. Born, Trail, B.C., February 3, 1981. Chicago's 1st choice, 23rd overall, in 1999 Entry Draft.

Season	Club	League	GP	G	A	Pts	PIM	PP	SH	GW	S	%	+/-	TF	F%	Min	GP	G	A	Pts	PIM	PP	SH	GW	Min
1996-97	Trail	BCHL	57	25	52	77	81	....	....	....	....	....	....	....	....	....	....	....	....	....	....	....	....	....	....
	Edmonton Ice	WHL	2	0	0	0	0	....	....	....	....	....	....	....	....	....	....	....	....	....	....	....	....	....	....
1997-98	Edmonton Ice	WHL	58	11	29	40	59	....	....	....	....	....	....	....	....	....	....	....	....	....	....	....	....	....	....
1998-99	Kootenay Ice	WHL	57	19	33	52	79	....	....	....	....	....	....	....	....	....	6	0	5	5	8	....	....	....	....
99-2000	Chicago	NHL	5	1	1	2	4	1	0	0	4	25.0	0	0	0.0	15:09	....	....	....	....	....	....	....	....	....
	Kootenay Ice	WHL	37	13	23	36	36	....	....	....	....	....	....	....	....	....	....	....	....	....	....	....	....	....	....
2000-01	Chicago	NHL	44	0	5	5	8	0	0	0	32	0.0	-7	0	0.0	14:47	....	....	....	....	....	....	....	....	....
	Norfolk Admirals	AHL	7	0	4	4	2	....	....	....	....	....	....	....	....	....	....	....	....	....	....	....	....	....	....
2001-02	Chicago	NHL	3	0	0	0	2	0	0	0	2	0.0	-1	0	0.0	11:48	....	....	....	....	....	....	....	....	....
	Norfolk Admirals	AHL	77	7	21	28	37	....	....	....	....	....	....	....	....	....	2	0	3	3	2	....	....	....	....
2002-03	Chicago	NHL	57	1	4	5	23	0	0	0	55	1.8	-1	0	0.0	16:25	....	....	....	....	....	....	....	....	....
	Norfolk Admirals	AHL	19	1	6	7	14	....	....	....	....	....	....	....	....	....	9	0	4	4	0	....	....	....	....
2003-04	Chicago	NHL	25	1	3	4	8	0	0	0	29	3.4	-9	0	0.0	19:21	....	....	....	....	....	....	....	....	....
2004-05			DID NOT PLAY																						
2005-06	Vancouver	NHL	51	2	4	6	43	0	0	0	46	4.3	3	0	0.0	13:17	....	....	....	....	....	....	....	....	....
	Atlanta	NHL	16	7	3	10	8	2	0	0	20	35.0	0	0	0.0	16:44	....	....	....	....	....	....	....	....	....
2006-07	Atlanta	NHL	46	4	12	16	24	3	0	0	51	7.8	4	0	0.0	15:17	....	....	....	....	....	....	....	....	....
	NHL Totals		247	16	32	48	120	6	0	0	239	6.7		0	0.0	15:30	....	....	....	....	....	....	....	....	....

• Missed majority of 2003-04 season recovering from groin injury suffered in game vs. Calgary, November 22, 2003. Traded to **Vancouver** by **Chicago** for Vancouver's 3rd round choice in 2007 Entry Draft, August 22, 2005. Traded to **Atlanta** by **Vancouver** for Vancouver's 3rd round choice (Josh Unice) in 2007 Entry Draft, March 9, 2006.

McCARTY, Darren

(muh-KAHR-tee, DAIR-ehn)

Right wing. Shoots right. 6'1", 210 lbs. Born, Burnaby, B.C., April 1, 1972. Detroit's 2nd choice, 46th overall, in 1992 Entry Draft.

Season	Club	League	GP	G	A	Pts	PIM	PP	SH	GW	S	%	+/-	TF	F%	Min	GP	G	A	Pts	PIM	PP	SH	GW	Min
1988-89	Peterborough	OHA-B	34	18	17	35	135	....	....	....	....	....	....	....	....	....	....	....	....	....	....	....	....	....	....
1989-90	Belleville Bulls	OHL	63	12	15	27	142	....	....	....	....	....	....	....	....	....	11	1	1	2	21	....	....	....	....
1990-91	Belleville Bulls	OHL	60	30	37	67	151	....	....	....	....	....	....	....	....	....	6	2	2	4	13	....	....	....	....
1991-92	Belleville Bulls	OHL	65	*55	72	127	177	....	....	....	....	....	....	....	....	....	5	1	4	5	13	....	....	....	....
1992-93	Adirondack	AHL	73	17	19	36	278	....	....	....	....	....	....	....	....	....	11	0	1	1	33	....	....	....	....
1993-94	Detroit	NHL	67	9	17	26	181	0	0	2	81	11.1	12	....	....	....	7	2	2	4	8	0	0	0	....
1994-95	Detroit	NHL	31	5	8	13	88	1	0	2	27	18.5	5	....	....	....	18	3	2	5	14	0	0	0	....
1995-96	Detroit	NHL	63	15	14	29	158	8	0	1	102	14.7	14	....	....	....	19	3	2	5	20	0	0	0	....
1996-97♦	Detroit	NHL	68	19	30	49	126	5	0	6	171	11.1	14	....	....	....	20	3	4	7	34	0	0	2	....
1997-98♦	Detroit	NHL	71	15	22	37	157	5	1	2	166	9.0	0	....	....	....	22	3	8	11	34	0	0	1	....
1998-99	Detroit	NHL	69	14	26	40	108	6	0	1	140	10.0	10	15	33.3	17:04	10	1	1	2	23	0	0	0	13:04
99-2000	Detroit	NHL	24	6	6	12	48	0	0	1	40	15.0	1	1	0.0	13:40	9	0	1	1	12	0	0	0	14:09
2000-01	Detroit	NHL	72	12	10	22	123	1	1	3	118	10.2	-5	26	53.9	13:26	6	1	0	1	2	0	0	0	13:11
2001-02♦	Detroit	NHL	62	5	7	12	98	0	0	1	74	6.8	2	26	38.5	11:47	23	4	4	8	34	0	0	1	13:33
2002-03	Detroit	NHL	73	13	9	22	138	1	0	2	129	10.1	10	320	57.8	13:18	4	0	0	0	6	0	0	0	15:45
2003-04	Detroit	NHL	43	6	5	11	50	1	0	0	61	9.8	2	141	50.4	12:20	12	0	1	1	7	0	0	0	11:30
2004-05			DID NOT PLAY																						
2005-06	Calgary	NHL	67	7	6	13	117	1	0	0	67	10.4	-1	234	50.0	11:43	7	2	0	2	15	0	0	1	9:50
2006-07	Calgary	NHL	32	0	0	0	58	0	0	0	15	0.0	-3	6	83.3	5:24	....	....	....	....	....	....	....	....	....
	NHL Totals		742	126	160	286	1450	29	2	21	1191	10.6		769	52.9	12:49	157	22	25	47	209	0	0	6	12:56

OHL First All-Star Team (1992)

• Missed majority of 1999-2000 season recovering from hernia injury suffered in game vs. Dallas, November 10, 1999. Signed as a free agent by **Calgary**, August 2, 2005. • Missed majority of 2006-07 season recovering from a hernia injury.

McCAULEY, Alyn

(muh-KAW-lee, AL-ihn)

Center. Shoots left. 5'11", 200 lbs. Born, Brockville, Ont., May 29, 1977. New Jersey's 5th choice, 79th overall, in 1995 Entry Draft.

			Regular Season														Playoffs								
Season	Club	League	GP	G	A	Pts	PIM	PP	SH	GW	S	%	+/-	TF	F%	Min	GP	G	A	Pts	PIM	PP	SH	GW	Min
1991-92	Kingston	MTJHL	37	5	17	22	6																		
1992-93	Kingston	MTJHL	38	31	29	60	18																		
1993-94	Ottawa 67's	OHL	38	13	23	36	10										13	5	14	19	4				
1994-95	Ottawa 67's	OHL	65	16	38	54	20																		
1995-96	Ottawa 67's	OHL	55	34	48	82	24										2	0	0	0	0				
1996-97	Ottawa 67's	OHL	50	*56	56	112	16										22	14	22	36	14				
	St. John's	AHL															3	0	1	1	0				
1997-98	**Toronto**	**NHL**	**60**	**6**	**10**	**16**	**6**	**0**	**0**	**1**	**77**	**7.8**	**–7**												
1998-99	**Toronto**	**NHL**	**39**	**9**	**15**	**24**	**2**	**1**	**0**	**1**	**76**	**11.8**	**7**	**591**	**46.4**	**15:10**									
99-2000	**Toronto**	**NHL**	**45**	**5**	**5**	**10**	**10**	**1**	**0**	**0**	**41**	**12.2**	**–6**	**450**	**47.8**	**10:46**	**5**	**0**	**0**	**0**	**6**	**0**	**0**	**0**	**7:51**
	St. John's	AHL	5	1	1	2	0																		
2000-01	**Toronto**	**NHL**	**14**	**1**	**0**	**1**	**0**	**0**	**0**	**0**	**13**	**7.7**	**0**	**139**	**46.8**	**10:28**	**10**	**0**	**0**	**0**	**2**	**0**	**0**	**0**	**9:34**
	St. John's	AHL	47	16	28	44	12																		
2001-02	**Toronto**	**NHL**	**82**	**6**	**10**	**16**	**18**	**0**	**1**	**1**	**95**	**6.3**	**10**	**951**	**48.1**	**11:24**	**20**	**5**	**10**	**15**	**4**	**1**	**0**	**2**	**19:12**
2002-03	**Toronto**	**NHL**	**64**	**6**	**9**	**15**	**16**	**0**	**0**	**0**	**79**	**7.6**	**3**	**515**	**44.5**	**12:54**									
	San Jose	**NHL**	**16**	**3**	**7**	**10**	**4**	**3**	**0**	**0**	**29**	**10.3**	**–2**	**81**	**50.6**	**17:29**									
2003-04	**San Jose**	**NHL**	**82**	**20**	**27**	**47**	**28**	**5**	**0**	**4**	**146**	**13.7**	**23**	**1216**	**47.7**	**16:51**	**11**	**2**	**1**	**3**	**2**	**0**	**0**	**0**	**14:17**
2004-05			DID NOT PLAY																						
2005-06	**San Jose**	**NHL**	**76**	**12**	**14**	**26**	**30**	**4**	**2**	**3**	**105**	**11.4**	**–3**	**692**	**49.1**	**14:14**	**6**	**0**	**1**	**1**	**4**	**0**	**0**	**0**	**11:17**
2006-07	**Los Angeles**	**NHL**	**10**	**1**	**0**	**1**	**2**	**0**	**0**	**0**	**4**	**25.0**	**0**	**96**	**43.8**	**9:43**									
	NHL Totals		**488**	**69**	**97**	**166**	**116**	**14**	**3**	**10**	**665**	**10.4**		**4731**	**47.4**	**13:36**	**52**	**7**	**12**	**19**	**18**	**1**	**0**	**2**	**14:18**

OHL First All-Star Team (1996, 1997) • OHL MVP (1996, 1997) • Canadian Major Junior First All-Star Team (1997) • Canadian Major Junior Player of the Year (1997)

Rights traded to **Toronto** by **New Jersey** with Jason Smith and Steve Sullivan for Doug Gilmour, Dave Ellett and New Jersey's 3rd round choice (previously acquired, New Jersey selected Andre Lakos) in 1999 Entry Draft, February 25, 1997. Traded to **San Jose** by **Toronto** with Brad Boyes and Toronto's 1st round choice (later traded to Boston – Boston selected Mark Stuart) in 2003 Entry Draft for Owen Nolan, March 5, 2003. Signed as a free agent by **Los Angeles**, July 2, 2006. • Missed majority of 2006-07 season recovering from a recurring knee injury.

McCLEMENT, Jay

(muh-KLEHM-ehnt, JAY) **ST.L.**

Center. Shoots left. 6'1", 199 lbs. Born, Kingston, Ont., March 2, 1983. St. Louis' 1st choice, 57th overall, in 2001 Entry Draft.

Season	Club	League	GP	G	A	Pts	PIM	PP	SH	GW	S	%	+/-	TF	F%	Min	GP	G	A	Pts	PIM	PP	SH	GW	Min
1997-98	Kingston	OPJHL	48	3	8	11	15																		
1998-99	Kingston	OPJHL	51	25	28	53	34																		
99-2000	Brampton	OHL	63	13	16	29	34										6	0	4	4	8				
2000-01	Brampton	OHL	66	30	19	49	61										9	4	2	6	10				
2001-02	Brampton	OHL	61	26	29	55	43																		
2002-03	Brampton	OHL	45	22	27	49	37										11	3	4	7	11				
	Worcester IceCats	AHL															1	0	0	0	0				
2003-04	Worcester IceCats	AHL	69	12	13	25	20										10	0	3	3	0				
2004-05	Worcester IceCats	AHL	79	17	34	51	45																		
2005-06	**St. Louis**	**NHL**	**67**	**6**	**21**	**27**	**30**	**1**	**0**	**2**	**76**	**7.9**	**–23**	**691**	**46.9**	**13:56**									
	Peoria Rivermen	AHL	11	4	5	9	4										4	0	2	2	2				
2006-07	**St. Louis**	**NHL**	**81**	**8**	**28**	**36**	**55**	**0**	**0**	**0**	**104**	**7.7**	**3**	**839**	**52.7**	**13:53**									
	NHL Totals		**148**	**14**	**49**	**63**	**85**	**1**	**0**	**2**	**180**	**7.8**		**1530**	**50.1**	**13:55**									

McCORMICK, Cody

(muh-KOHR-mihk, KOH-dee) **COL.**

Center/Right wing. Shoots right. 6'3", 215 lbs. Born, London, Ont., April 18, 1983. Colorado's 5th choice, 144th overall, in 2001 Entry Draft.

Season	Club	League	GP	G	A	Pts	PIM	PP	SH	GW	S	%	+/-	TF	F%	Min	GP	G	A	Pts	PIM	PP	SH	GW	Min
1998-99	Elgin-Middlesex	MHAO	58	22	40	62	81																		
99-2000	Belleville Bulls	OHL	45	3	4	7	42										9	1	0	1	10				
2000-01	Belleville Bulls	OHL	66	7	16	23	135										10	1	1	2	23				
2001-02	Belleville Bulls	OHL	63	10	17	27	118										11	2	4	6	24				
2002-03	Belleville Bulls	OHL	61	36	33	69	166										7	4	7	11	11				
2003-04	**Colorado**	**NHL**	**44**	**2**	**3**	**5**	**73**	**0**	**0**	**1**	**33**	**6.1**	**–4**	**110**	**32.7**	**8:07**									
	Hershey Bears	AHL	32	3	6	9	60																		
2004-05	Hershey Bears	AHL	40	5	6	11	68																		
2005-06	**Colorado**	**NHL**	**45**	**4**	**4**	**8**	**29**	**0**	**0**	**1**	**43**	**9.3**	**1**	**16**	**25.0**	**7:42**									
	Lowell	AHL	13	1	6	7	34																		
2006-07	**Colorado**	**NHL**	**6**	**0**	**1**	**1**	**6**	**0**	**0**	**0**	**6**	**0.0**	**1**	**3**	**33.3**	**6:44**									
	Albany River Rats	AHL	42	8	8	16	64										5	1	0	1	4				
	NHL Totals		**95**	**6**	**8**	**14**	**108**	**0**	**0**	**2**	**82**	**7.3**		**129**	**31.8**	**7:50**									

OHL First All-Star Team (2003)

McDONALD, Andy

(muhk-DAWN-uhld, AN-dee) **ANA.**

Center. Shoots left. 5'11", 185 lbs. Born, Strathroy, Ont., August 25, 1977.

Season	Club	League	GP	G	A	Pts	PIM	PP	SH	GW	S	%	+/-	TF	F%	Min	GP	G	A	Pts	PIM	PP	SH	GW	Min
1993-94	Strathroy Rockets	OHA-B	7	2	2	4	0																		
1994-95	Strathroy Rockets	OHA-B	50	32	41	73	24																		
1995-96	Strathroy Rockets	OHA-B	52	31	56	87	103																		
1996-97	Colgate	ECAC	33	9	10	19	16																		
1997-98	Colgate	ECAC	35	13	19	32	26																		
1998-99	Colgate	ECAC	35	20	26	46	42																		
99-2000	Colgate	ECAC	34	25	*33	*58	49																		
2000-01	**Anaheim**	**NHL**	**16**	**1**	**0**	**1**	**6**	**0**	**0**	**0**	**21**	**4.8**	**0**	**139**	**48.9**	**11:11**									
	Cincinnati	AHL	46	15	25	40	21										3	0	1	1	2				
2001-02	**Anaheim**	**NHL**	**53**	**7**	**21**	**28**	**10**	**2**	**0**	**3**	**79**	**8.9**	**2**	**818**	**53.7**	**15:59**									
	Cincinnati	AHL	21	7	25	32	6																		
2002-03	**Anaheim**	**NHL**	**46**	**10**	**11**	**21**	**14**	**3**	**0**	**1**	**92**	**10.9**	**–1**	**604**	**56.0**	**18:31**									
2003-04	**Anaheim**	**NHL**	**79**	**9**	**21**	**30**	**24**	**2**	**1**	**1**	**162**	**5.6**	**–13**	**282**	**54.3**	**16:34**									
2004-05	ERC Ingolstadt	Germany	36	13	17	30	26										10	5	2	7	35				
2005-06	**Anaheim**	**NHL**	**82**	**34**	**51**	**85**	**32**	**13**	**0**	**7**	**229**	**14.8**	**24**	**1095**	**56.3**	**16:48**	**16**	**2**	**7**	**9**	**10**	**2**	**0**	**0**	**16:33**
2006-07 ♦	**Anaheim**	**NHL**	**82**	**27**	**51**	**78**	**46**	**8**	**0**	**3**	**252**	**10.7**	**16**	**908**	**55.4**	**17:35**	**21**	**10**	**4**	**14**	**10**	**5**	**0**	**0**	**18:37**
	NHL Totals		**358**	**88**	**155**	**243**	**132**	**28**	**1**	**15**	**835**	**10.5**		**3846**	**55.0**	**16:47**	**37**	**12**	**11**	**23**	**20**	**7**	**0**	**0**	**17:44**

ECAC Second All-Star Team (1999) • ECAC First All-Star Team (2000) • ECAC Player of the Year (2000) • NCAA East First All-American Team (2000)

Played in NHL All-Star Game (2007)

Signed as a free agent by **Anaheim**, April 3, 2000. Signed as a free agent by **Ingolstadt** (Germany), September 17, 2004.

McDONELL, Kent

(MAHK-dah-NEHL, KEHNT)

Right wing. Shoots right. 6'2", 205 lbs. Born, Williamstown, Ont., March 1, 1979. Detroit's 3rd choice, 181st overall, in 1999 Entry Draft.

Season	Club	League	GP	G	A	Pts	PIM	PP	SH	GW	S	%	+/-	TF	F%	Min	GP	G	A	Pts	PIM	PP	SH	GW	Min
1995-96	Cornwall Colts	CJHL	33	21	14	35	64																		
1996-97	Guelph Storm	OHL	56	7	5	12	57										16	0	2	2	4				
1997-98	Guelph Storm	OHL	64	28	23	51	76										12	7	4	11	18				
1998-99	Guelph Storm	OHL	60	31	38	69	110										11	4	3	7	36				
99-2000	Guelph Storm	OHL	56	35	35	70	100										6	1	4	5	6				
2000-01	Dayton Bombers	ECHL	28	16	9	25	94										3	0	0	0	4				
	Syracuse Crunch	AHL	32	3	3	6	36										3	1	0	1	0				
2001-02	Syracuse Crunch	AHL	72	18	13	31	122										3	0	2	2	0				
2002-03	**Columbus**	**NHL**	**3**	**0**	**0**	**0**	**0**	**0**	**0**	**0**	**4**	**0.0**	**–1**	**0**	**0.0**	**8:40**									
	Syracuse Crunch	AHL	72	14	24	38	93																		
2003-04	**Columbus**	**NHL**	**29**	**1**	**2**	**3**	**36**	**0**	**0**	**0**	**23**	**4.3**	**–7**	**5**	**60.0**	**10:18**									
	Syracuse Crunch	AHL	51	17	31	48	102																		
2004-05	Aylmer Blues	OHA-Sr.	5	2	4	6	21										5	0	1	1	10				
	Bergen Flyers	Norway	11	12	3	15	75																		
	EV Duisburg	German-2	19	4	9	13	57										10	3	3	6	37				

Season	Club	League	GP	G	A	Pts	PIM	PP	SH	GW	S	%	+/-	TF	F%	Min	GP	G	A	Pts	PIM	PP	SH	GW	Min
			Regular Season														Playoffs								
2005-06	Grand Rapids	AHL	77	21	37	58	171	....	....	....	....	....	....	....	....	....	16	5	4	9	20	....	....	....	....
2006-07	TPS Turku	Finland	45	14	30	44	75	....	....	....	....	....	....	....	....	....	2	0	0	0	0	....	....	....	....
	NHL Totals		**32**	**1**	**2**	**3**	**36**	**0**	**0**	**0**	**27**	**3.7**		**5**	**60.0**	**10:09**	....	....	....	....	....	....	....	....	....

• Re-entered NHL Entry Draft. Originally Carolina's 9th choice, 225th overall, in 1997 Entry Draft.

Traded to **Columbus** by **Detroit** for Columbus's 6th round choice (Andreas Sundin) in 2003 Entry Draft, August 14, 2000. Signed as a free agent by **Aylmer** (OHA-Sr.), October, 2004. Signed as a free agent by **Bergen** (Norway), October 22, 2004. Signed as a free agent by **Duisburg** (German-2), December 30, 2004. Signed as a free agent by **Detroit**, August 12, 2005. Signed as a free agent by **Turku** (Finland), October 9, 2006.

McGILLIS, Dan

(MUHK-gihl-ihs, DAN)

Defense. Shoots left. 6'3", 220 lbs. Born, Hawkesbury, Ont., July 1, 1972. Detroit's 10th choice, 238th overall, in 1992 Entry Draft.

Season	Club	League	GP	G	A	Pts	PIM	PP	SH	GW	S	%	+/-	TF	F%	Min	GP	G	A	Pts	PIM	PP	SH	GW	Min
1989-90	Hawkesbury	CJHL	55	2	1	3	52	....	....	....	....	....	....	....	....	....	....	....	....	....	....	....	....	....	....
1990-91	Hawkesbury	CJHL	56	8	22	30	92	....	....	....	....	....	....	....	....	....	....	....	....	....	....	....	....	....	....
1991-92	Hawkesbury	CJHL	36	5	19	24	106	....	....	....	....	....	....	....	....	....	....	....	....	....	....	....	....	....	....
1992-93	Northeastern	H-East	35	5	12	17	42	....	....	....	....	....	....	....	....	....	....	....	....	....	....	....	....	....	....
1993-94	Northeastern	H-East	38	4	25	29	82	....	....	....	....	....	....	....	....	....	....	....	....	....	....	....	....	....	....
1994-95	Northeastern	H-East	34	9	22	31	70	....	....	....	....	....	....	....	....	....	....	....	....	....	....	....	....	....	....
1995-96	Northeastern	H-East	34	12	24	36	50	....	....	....	....	....	....	....	....	....	....	....	....	....	....	....	....	....	....
1996-97	**Edmonton**	**NHL**	**73**	**6**	**16**	**22**	**52**	**2**	**1**	**2**	**139**	**4.3**	**2**	....	....	....	**12**	**0**	**5**	**5**	**24**	**0**	**0**	**0**	....
1997-98	**Edmonton**	**NHL**	**67**	**10**	**15**	**25**	**74**	**5**	**0**	**3**	**119**	**8.4**	**−17**	....	....	....	....	....	....	....	....	....	....	....	....
	Philadelphia	**NHL**	**13**	**1**	**5**	**6**	**35**	**1**	**0**	**0**	**18**	**5.6**	**−4**	....	....	....	**5**	**1**	**2**	**3**	**10**	**1**	**0**	**0**	....
1998-99	**Philadelphia**	**NHL**	**78**	**8**	**37**	**45**	**61**	**6**	**0**	**4**	**164**	**4.9**	**16**	**0**	**0.0**	**21:41**	**6**	**0**	**1**	**1**	**12**	**0**	**0**	**0**	**19:36**
99-2000	**Philadelphia**	**NHL**	**68**	**4**	**14**	**18**	**55**	**3**	**0**	**1**	**128**	**3.1**	**16**	**0**	**0.0**	**20:04**	**18**	**2**	**6**	**8**	**12**	**0**	**0**	**0**	**24:42**
2000-01	**Philadelphia**	**NHL**	**82**	**14**	**35**	**49**	**86**	**4**	**0**	**4**	**207**	**6.8**	**13**	**1**	**0.0**	**23:23**	**6**	**1**	**0**	**1**	**6**	**0**	**1**	**0**	**24:12**
2001-02	**Philadelphia**	**NHL**	**75**	**5**	**14**	**19**	**46**	**2**	**0**	**1**	**147**	**3.4**	**17**	**0**	**0.0**	**21:04**	**5**	**1**	**0**	**1**	**8**	**1**	**0**	**0**	**20:27**
2002-03	**Philadelphia**	**NHL**	**24**	**0**	**3**	**3**	**20**	**0**	**0**	**0**	**41**	**0.0**	**7**	**0**	**0.0**	**18:13**	....	....	....	....	....	....	....	....	....
	San Jose	**NHL**	**37**	**3**	**13**	**16**	**30**	**2**	**0**	**0**	**71**	**4.2**	**−6**	**0**	**0.0**	**21:54**	....	....	....	....	....	....	....	....	....
	Boston	**NHL**	**10**	**0**	**1**	**1**	**10**	**0**	**0**	**0**	**18**	**0.0**	**2**	**0**	**0.0**	**21:15**	**5**	**3**	**0**	**3**	**2**	**2**	**0**	**1**	**18:54**
2003-04	**Boston**	**NHL**	**80**	**5**	**23**	**28**	**65**	**1**	**0**	**2**	**117**	**4.3**	**−1**	**1**	**0.0**	**19:43**	**7**	**0**	**0**	**0**	**2**	**0**	**0**	**0**	**18:38**
2004-05			DID NOT PLAY																						
2005-06	**New Jersey**	**NHL**	**27**	**0**	**6**	**6**	**36**	**0**	**0**	**0**	**32**	**0.0**	**−5**	**0**	**0.0**	**14:14**	....	....	....	....	....	....	....	....	....
	Albany River Rats	AHL	40	7	18	25	57	....	....	....	....	....	....	....	....	....	....	....	....	....	....	....	....	....	....
2006-07	Lowell Devils	AHL	68	10	31	41	62	....	....	....	....	....	....	....	....	....	....	....	....	....	....	....	....	....	....
	NHL Totals		**634**	**56**	**182**	**238**	**570**	**26**	**1**	**17**	**1201**	**4.7**		**2**	**0.0**	**20:44**	**64**	**8**	**14**	**22**	**76**	**4**	**1**	**1**	**22:01**

Hockey East First All-Star Team (1995, 1996) • NCAA East First All-American Team (1996)

Traded to **Edmonton** by **Detroit** for Kirk Maltby, March 20, 1996. Traded to **Philadelphia** by **Edmonton** with Edmonton's 2nd round choice (Jason Beckett) in 1998 Entry Draft for Janne Niinimaa, March 24, 1998. Traded to **San Jose** by **Philadelphia** for Marcus Ragnarsson, December 6, 2002. Traded to **Boston** by **San Jose** for Boston's 2nd round choice (later traded to NY Rangers – NY Rangers selected Ivan Baranka) in 2003 Entry Draft, March 11, 2003. Signed as a free agent by **New Jersey**, August 4, 2005.

McGRATTAN, Brian

(muh-GRA-tuhn, BRIGH-uhn) **OTT.**

Right wing. Shoots right. 6'4", 231 lbs. Born, Hamilton, Ont., September 2, 1981. Los Angeles' 5th choice, 104th overall, in 1999 Entry Draft.

Season	Club	League	GP	G	A	Pts	PIM	PP	SH	GW	S	%	+/-	TF	F%	Min	GP	G	A	Pts	PIM	PP	SH	GW	Min
1997-98	Guelph Fire	OHA-B	15	4	3	7	94	....	....	....	....	....	....	....	....	....	....	....	....	....	....	....	....	....	....
	Guelph Storm	OHL	25	3	2	5	11	....	....	....	....	....	....	....	....	....	....	....	....	....	....	....	....	....	....
1998-99	Guelph Storm	OHL	6	1	3	4	15	....	....	....	....	....	....	....	....	....	....	....	....	....	....	....	....	....	....
	Sudbury Wolves	OHL	53	7	10	17	153	....	....	....	....	....	....	....	....	....	4	0	0	0	8	....	....	....	....
99-2000	Sudbury Wolves	OHL	25	2	8	10	79	....	....	....	....	....	....	....	....	....	....	....	....	....	....	....	....	....	....
	Mississauga	OHL	42	9	13	22	166	....	....	....	....	....	....	....	....	....	....	....	....	....	....	....	....	....	....
2000-01	Mississauga	OHL	31	20	9	29	83	....	....	....	....	....	....	....	....	....	....	....	....	....	....	....	....	....	....
2001-02	Mississauga	OHL	7	2	3	5	16	....	....	....	....	....	....	....	....	....	....	....	....	....	....	....	....	....	....
	Owen Sound	OHL	2	0	0	0	0	....	....	....	....	....	....	....	....	....	....	....	....	....	....	....	....	....	....
	Oshawa Generals	OHL	25	10	5	15	72	....	....	....	....	....	....	....	....	....	....	....	....	....	....	....	....	....	....
	Sault Ste. Marie	OHL	26	8	7	15	71	....	....	....	....	....	....	....	....	....	6	2	0	2	20	....	....	....	....
2002-03	Binghamton	AHL	59	9	10	19	173	....	....	....	....	....	....	....	....	....	1	0	0	0	0	....	....	....	....
2003-04	Binghamton	AHL	66	9	11	20	327	....	....	....	....	....	....	....	....	....	1	0	0	0	0	....	....	....	....
2004-05	Binghamton	AHL	71	7	1	8	*551	....	....	....	....	....	....	....	....	....	6	0	2	2	28	....	....	....	....
2005-06	**Ottawa**	**NHL**	**60**	**2**	**3**	**5**	**141**	**0**	**0**	**0**	**36**	**5.6**	**0**	**0**	**0.0**	**4:14**	....	....	....	....	....	....	....	....	....
2006-07	**Ottawa**	**NHL**	**45**	**0**	**2**	**2**	**100**	**0**	**0**	**0**	**22**	**0.0**	**−1**	**1**	**100.0**	**3:51**	....	....	....	....	....	....	....	....	....
	NHL Totals		**105**	**2**	**5**	**7**	**241**	**0**	**0**	**0**	**58**	**3.4**		**1**	**100.0**	**4:04**	....	....	....	....	....	....	....	....	....

Signed as a free agent by **Ottawa**, June 2, 2002.

McIVER, Nathan

(muh-KEE-vuhr, NAY-thuhn) **VAN.**

Defense. Shoots left. 6'2", 206 lbs. Born, Summerside, P.E.I., January 6, 1985. Vancouver's 9th choice, 254th overall, in 2003 Entry Draft.

Season	Club	League	GP	G	A	Pts	PIM	PP	SH	GW	S	%	+/-	TF	F%	Min	GP	G	A	Pts	PIM	PP	SH	GW	Min
2001-02	Summerside	MJrHL	47	4	4	8	91	....	....	....	....	....	....	....	....	....	5	0	0	0	9	....	....	....	....
2002-03	St. Michael's	OHL	68	5	10	15	121	....	....	....	....	....	....	....	....	....	19	0	4	4	41	....	....	....	....
2003-04	St. Michael's	OHL	57	4	11	15	183	....	....	....	....	....	....	....	....	....	16	0	1	1	22	....	....	....	....
2004-05	St. Michael's	OHL	67	4	22	26	160	....	....	....	....	....	....	....	....	....	3	0	1	1	13	....	....	....	....
2005-06	Manitoba Moose	AHL	66	1	6	7	155	....	....	....	....	....	....	....	....	....	12	0	0	0	28	....	....	....	....
2006-07	**Vancouver**	**NHL**	**1**	**0**	**0**	**0**	**7**	**0**	**0**	**0**	**0**	**0.0**	**−3**	**0**	**0.0**	**11:20**	....	....	....	....	....	....	....	....	....
	Manitoba Moose	AHL	63	1	2	3	139	....	....	....	....	....	....	....	....	....	2	0	0	0	0	....	....	....	....
	NHL Totals		**1**	**0**	**0**	**0**	**7**	**0**	**0**	**0**	**0**	**0.0**		**0**	**0.0**	**11:20**	....	....	....	....	....	....	....	....	....

McKEE, Jay

(muh-KEE, JAY) **ST.L.**

Defense. Shoots left. 6'3", 199 lbs. Born, Kingston, Ont., September 8, 1977. Buffalo's 1st choice, 14th overall, in 1995 Entry Draft.

Season	Club	League	GP	G	A	Pts	PIM	PP	SH	GW	S	%	+/-	TF	F%	Min	GP	G	A	Pts	PIM	PP	SH	GW	Min
1992-93	Ernestown Jets	OHA-C	36	0	17	17	37	....	....	....	....	....	....	....	....	....	....	....	....	....	....	....	....	....	....
	Kingston	MTJHL	2	0	0	0	0	....	....	....	....	....	....	....	....	....	....	....	....	....	....	....	....	....	....
1993-94	Sudbury Wolves	OHL	51	0	1	1	51	....	....	....	....	....	....	....	....	....	3	0	0	0	0	....	....	....	....
1994-95	Sudbury Wolves	OHL	39	6	6	12	91	....	....	....	....	....	....	....	....	....	....	....	....	....	....	....	....	....	....
	Niagara Falls	OHL	26	3	13	16	60	....	....	....	....	....	....	....	....	....	6	2	3	5	10	....	....	....	....
1995-96	Niagara Falls	OHL	64	5	41	46	129	....	....	....	....	....	....	....	....	....	10	1	5	6	16	....	....	....	....
	Buffalo	**NHL**	**1**	**0**	**1**	**1**	**2**	**0**	**0**	**0**	**2**	**0.0**	**1**	....	....	....	....	....	....	....	....	....	....	....	....
	Rochester	AHL	4	0	1	1	15	....	....	....	....	....	....	....	....	....	....	....	....	....	....	....	....	....	....
1996-97	**Buffalo**	**NHL**	**43**	**1**	**9**	**10**	**35**	**0**	**0**	**0**	**29**	**3.4**	**3**	....	....	....	**3**	**0**	**0**	**0**	**0**	**0**	**0**	**0**	....
	Rochester	AHL	7	2	5	7	4	....	....	....	....	....	....	....	....	....	....	....	....	....	....	....	....	....	....
1997-98	**Buffalo**	**NHL**	**56**	**1**	**13**	**14**	**42**	**0**	**0**	**0**	**55**	**1.8**	**−1**	....	....	....	**1**	**0**	**0**	**0**	**0**	**0**	**0**	**0**	....
	Rochester	AHL	13	1	7	8	11	....	....	....	....	....	....	....	....	....	....	....	....	....	....	....	....	....	....
1998-99	**Buffalo**	**NHL**	**72**	**0**	**6**	**6**	**75**	**0**	**0**	**0**	**57**	**0.0**	**20**	**0**	**0.0**	**20:28**	**21**	**0**	**3**	**3**	**24**	**0**	**0**	**0**	**22:31**
99-2000	**Buffalo**	**NHL**	**78**	**5**	**12**	**17**	**50**	**1**	**0**	**1**	**84**	**6.0**	**5**	**0**	**0.0**	**20:58**	**1**	**0**	**0**	**0**	**0**	**0**	**0**	**0**	**17:57**
2000-01	**Buffalo**	**NHL**	**74**	**1**	**10**	**11**	**76**	**0**	**0**	**0**	**62**	**1.6**	**9**	**2**	**0.0**	**19:24**	**8**	**1**	**0**	**1**	**6**	**0**	**0**	**1**	**19:23**
2001-02	**Buffalo**	**NHL**	**81**	**2**	**11**	**13**	**43**	**0**	**0**	**1**	**50**	**4.0**	**18**	**0**	**0.0**	**19:26**	....	....	....	....	....	....	....	....	....
2002-03	**Buffalo**	**NHL**	**59**	**0**	**5**	**5**	**49**	**0**	**0**	**0**	**44**	**0.0**	**−16**	**0**	**0.0**	**18:45**	....	....	....	....	....	....	....	....	....
2003-04	**Buffalo**	**NHL**	**43**	**2**	**3**	**5**	**41**	**0**	**0**	**1**	**29**	**6.9**	**6**	**0**	**0.0**	**17:44**	....	....	....	....	....	....	....	....	....
2004-05			DID NOT PLAY																						
2005-06	**Buffalo**	**NHL**	**75**	**5**	**11**	**16**	**57**	**0**	**1**	**0**	**50**	**10.0**	**0**	**1**	**0.0**	**18:03**	**17**	**2**	**3**	**5**	**30**	**0**	**0**	**1**	**20:17**
2006-07	**St. Louis**	**NHL**	**23**	**0**	**0**	**0**	**12**	**0**	**0**	**0**	**19**	**0.0**	**−9**	**0**	**0.0**	**20:14**	....	....	....	....	....	....	....	....	....
	NHL Totals		**605**	**17**	**81**	**98**	**482**	**1**	**1**	**3**	**481**	**3.5**		**3**	**0.0**	**19:25**	**51**	**3**	**6**	**9**	**60**	**0**	**0**	**2**	**21:05**

OHL Second All-Star Team (1996)

Signed as a free agent by **St. Louis**, July 1, 2006. • Missed majority of 2006-07 season recovering from a hand injury suffered in game vs. Vancouver, October 20, 2006.

McLAREN, Kyle

(muh-KLAIR-uhn, KIGHL) **S.J.**

Defense. Shoots left. 6'5", 230 lbs. Born, Humboldt, Sask., June 18, 1977. Boston's 1st choice, 9th overall, in 1995 Entry Draft.

Season	Club	League	GP	G	A	Pts	PIM	PP	SH	GW	S	%	+/-	TF	F%	Min	GP	G	A	Pts	PIM	PP	SH	GW	Min
			Regular Season														Playoffs								
1992-93	Lethbridge	AMHL	60	28	28	56	84	....	....	....	....	....	....	....	....	....	....	....	....	....	....	....	....	....	....
1993-94	Tacoma Rockets	WHL	62	1	9	10	53	....	....	....	....	....	....	....	....	....	6	1	4	5	6	....	....	....	....
1994-95	Tacoma Rockets	WHL	47	13	19	32	68	....	....	....	....	....	....	....	....	....	4	1	1	2	4	....	....	....	....
1995-96	**Boston**	**NHL**	74	5	12	17	73	0	0	0	74	6.8	16	....	....	....	5	0	0	0	14	0	0	0	....
1996-97	**Boston**	**NHL**	58	5	9	14	54	0	0	1	68	7.4	–9	....	....	....	....	....	....	....	....	....	....	....	....
1997-98	**Boston**	**NHL**	66	5	20	25	56	2	0	0	101	5.0	13	....	....	....	6	1	0	1	4	1	0	0	....
1998-99	**Boston**	**NHL**	52	6	18	24	48	3	0	0	97	6.2	1	0	0.0	23:25	12	0	3	3	10	0	0	0	26:45
99-2000	**Boston**	**NHL**	71	8	11	19	67	2	0	3	142	5.6	–4	5	40.0	23:18	....	....	....	....	....	....	....	....	....
2000-01	**Boston**	**NHL**	58	5	12	17	53	2	0	0	91	5.5	–5	4	50.0	24:14	....	....	....	....	....	....	....	....	....
2001-02	**Boston**	**NHL**	38	0	8	8	19	0	0	0	57	0.0	–4	1	0.0	19:21	4	0	0	0	20	0	0	0	18:37
2002-03	**San Jose**	**NHL**	33	0	8	8	30	0	0	0	43	0.0	–10	0	0.0	22:40	....	....	....	....	....	....	....	....	....
2003-04	**San Jose**	**NHL**	64	2	22	24	60	0	1	0	67	3.0	10	1	0.0	21:01	16	0	3	3	10	0	0	0	24:09
2004-05			DID NOT PLAY																						
2005-06	**San Jose**	**NHL**	77	2	21	23	66	0	0	1	67	3.0	6	0	0.0	22:52	11	0	3	3	4	0	0	0	20:42
2006-07	**San Jose**	**NHL**	67	5	12	17	61	1	0	0	43	11.6	10	0	0.0	21:25	11	0	4	4	10	0	0	0	22:47
	NHL Totals		**658**	**43**	**153**	**196**	**587**	**10**	**1**	**5**	**850**	**5.1**		**11**	**36.4**	**22:24**	**65**	**1**	**13**	**14**	**72**	**1**	**0**	**0**	**23:20**

NHL All-Rookie Team (1996)

• Missed majority of 2001-02 season recovering from chest (October 10, 2001 vs. Minnesota) and wrist (December 26, 2001 vs. Ottawa) injuries. • Missed majority of 2002-03 season in contract dispute with Boston. Traded to **San Jose** by **Boston** with Boston's 4th round choice (Torrey Mitchell) in 2004 Entry Draft for Jeff Hackett and Jeff Jillson, January 23, 2003.

McLEAN, Brett

(muh-KLAYN, BREHT) **FLA.**

Center. Shoots left. 5'11", 185 lbs. Born, Comox, B.C., August 14, 1978. Dallas' 9th choice, 242nd overall, in 1997 Entry Draft.

Season	Club	League	GP	G	A	Pts	PIM	PP	SH	GW	S	%	+/-	TF	F%	Min	GP	G	A	Pts	PIM	PP	SH	GW	Min
1993-94	Notre Dame	SMBHL	71	109	124	233	70	....	....	....	....	....	....	....	....	....	....	....	....	....	....	....	....	....	....
1994-95	Tacoma Rockets	WHL	67	11	23	34	33	....	....	....	....	....	....	....	....	....	4	0	1	1	0	....	....	....	....
1995-96	Kelowna Rockets	WHL	71	37	42	79	60	....	....	....	....	....	....	....	....	....	6	2	2	4	6	....	....	....	....
1996-97	Kelowna Rockets	WHL	72	44	60	104	98	....	....	....	....	....	....	....	....	....	6	4	2	6	12	....	....	....	....
1997-98	Kelowna Rockets	WHL	54	42	45	87	91	....	....	....	....	....	....	....	....	....	7	4	5	9	17	....	....	....	....
1998-99	Kelowna Rockets	WHL	44	32	38	70	46	....	....	....	....	....	....	....	....	....	....	....	....	....	....	....	....	....	....
	Brandon	WHL	21	15	16	31	20	....	....	....	....	....	....	....	....	....	5	1	6	7	8	....	....	....	....
	Cincinnati	AHL	7	0	3	3	6	....	....	....	....	....	....	....	....	....	....	....	....	....	....	....	....	....	....
99-2000	Johnstown Chiefs	ECHL	8	4	7	11	6	....	....	....	....	....	....	....	....	....	....	....	....	....	....	....	....	....	....
	Saint John Flames	AHL	72	15	23	38	115	....	....	....	....	....	....	....	....	....	3	0	1	1	2	....	....	....	....
2000-01	Cleveland	IHL	74	20	24	44	54	....	....	....	....	....	....	....	....	....	4	0	0	0	18	....	....	....	....
2001-02	Houston Aeros	AHL	78	24	21	45	71	....	....	....	....	....	....	....	....	....	14	1	6	7	12	....	....	....	....
2002-03	**Chicago**	**NHL**	2	0	0	0	0	0	0	0	1	0.0	–1	19	26.3	10:47	....	....	....	....	....	....	....	....	....
	Norfolk Admirals	AHL	77	23	38	61	60	....	....	....	....	....	....	....	....	....	9	2	6	8	9	....	....	....	....
2003-04	**Chicago**	**NHL**	76	11	20	31	54	5	1	0	125	8.8	–11	1135	51.1	17:33	....	....	....	....	....	....	....	....	....
	Norfolk Admirals	AHL	4	3	3	6	6	....	....	....	....	....	....	....	....	....	....	....	....	....	....	....	....	....	....
2004-05	Malmo	Sweden	38	7	6	13	102	....	....	....	....	....	....	....	....	....	....	....	....	....	....	....	....	....	....
	Malmo	Sweden-Q	9	1	1	2	16	....	....	....	....	....	....	....	....	....	....	....	....	....	....	....	....	....	....
2005-06	**Colorado**	**NHL**	82	9	31	40	51	1	0	0	115	7.8	–7	770	50.7	12:12	8	0	1	1	4	0	0	0	10:40
2006-07	**Colorado**	**NHL**	78	15	20	35	36	0	0	3	134	11.2	8	413	50.1	13:38	....	....	....	....	....	....	....	....	....
	NHL Totals		**238**	**35**	**71**	**106**	**141**	**6**	**1**	**3**	**375**	**9.3**		**2337**	**50.6**	**14:22**	**8**	**0**	**1**	**1**	**4**	**0**	**0**	**0**	**10:40**

WHL West Second All-Star Team (1998)

Signed as a free agent by **Calgary**, September, 1999. Signed as a free agent by **Minnesota**, July 13, 2000. Signed as a free agent by **Chicago**, July 23, 2002. Signed as a free agent by **Colorado**, July 22, 2004. Signed as a free agent by **Malmo** (Sweden), September 24, 2004. Signed as a free agent by **Florida**, July 1, 2007.

MEECH, Derek

(MEECH, DAIR-ihk) **DET.**

Defense. Shoots left. 5'11", 197 lbs. Born, Winnipeg, Man., April 21, 1984. Detroit's 7th choice, 229th overall, in 2002 Entry Draft.

Season	Club	League	GP	G	A	Pts	PIM	PP	SH	GW	S	%	+/-	TF	F%	Min	GP	G	A	Pts	PIM	PP	SH	GW	Min
99-2000	Wpg. Warriors	MMMHL	36	15	40	55	24	....	....	....	....	....	....	....	....	....	....	....	....	....	....	....	....	....	....
	Red Deer Rebels	WHL	5	1	0	1	2	....	....	....	....	....	....	....	....	....	....	....	....	....	....	....	....	....	....
2000-01	Red Deer Rebels	WHL	60	2	7	9	40	....	....	....	....	....	....	....	....	....	22	0	0	0	9	....	....	....	....
2001-02	Red Deer Rebels	WHL	71	8	19	27	33	....	....	....	....	....	....	....	....	....	13	1	1	2	6	....	....	....	....
2002-03	Red Deer Rebels	WHL	65	6	16	22	53	....	....	....	....	....	....	....	....	....	12	1	1	2	12	....	....	....	....
2003-04	Red Deer Rebels	WHL	62	10	28	38	40	....	....	....	....	....	....	....	....	....	19	4	7	11	10	....	....	....	....
2004-05	Grand Rapids	AHL	78	6	8	14	40	....	....	....	....	....	....	....	....	....	....	....	....	....	....	....	....	....	....
2005-06	Grand Rapids	AHL	79	4	16	20	85	....	....	....	....	....	....	....	....	....	16	0	2	2	4	....	....	....	....
2006-07	**Detroit**	**NHL**	4	0	0	0	2	0	0	0	3	0.0	1	0	0.0	5:47	....	....	....	....	....	....	....	....	....
	Grand Rapids	AHL	67	6	23	29	40	....	....	....	....	....	....	....	....	....	7	0	1	1	4	....	....	....	....
	NHL Totals		**4**	**0**	**0**	**0**	**2**	**0**	**0**	**0**	**3**	**0.0**		**0**	**0.0**	**5:47**	....	....	....	....	....	....	....	....	....

WHL East Second All-Star Team (2004)

MELICHAR, Josef

(mehl-ee-KHAHR, YOH-sehf)

Defense. Shoots left. 6'2", 220 lbs. Born, Ceske Budejovice, Czech., January 20, 1979. Pittsburgh's 3rd choice, 71st overall, in 1997 Entry Draft.

Season	Club	League	GP	G	A	Pts	PIM	PP	SH	GW	S	%	+/-	TF	F%	Min	GP	G	A	Pts	PIM	PP	SH	GW	Min
1995-96	C. Budejovice Jr.	CzRep-Jr.	38	3	4	7	....	....	....	....	....	....	....	....	....	....	....	....	....	....	....	....	....	....	....
1996-97	C. Budejovice Jr.	CzRep-Jr.	41	2	3	5	10	....	....	....	....	....	....	....	....	....	....	....	....	....	....	....	....	....	....
1997-98	Tri-City	WHL	67	9	24	33	154	....	....	....	....	....	....	....	....	....	....	....	....	....	....	....	....	....	....
1998-99	Tri-City	WHL	65	8	28	36	125	....	....	....	....	....	....	....	....	....	11	1	0	1	15	....	....	....	....
99-2000	Wilkes-Barre	AHL	80	3	9	12	126	....	....	....	....	....	....	....	....	....	....	....	....	....	....	....	....	....	....
2000-01	**Pittsburgh**	**NHL**	18	0	2	2	21	0	0	0	9	0.0	–5	0	0.0	14:54	....	....	....	....	....	....	....	....	....
	Wilkes-Barre	AHL	46	2	5	7	69	....	....	....	....	....	....	....	....	....	21	0	5	5	6	....	....	....	....
2001-02	**Pittsburgh**	**NHL**	60	0	3	3	68	0	0	0	46	0.0	–1	0	0.0	16:46	....	....	....	....	....	....	....	....	....
2002-03	**Pittsburgh**	**NHL**	8	0	0	0	2	0	0	0	6	0.0	–2	0	0.0	15:19	....	....	....	....	....	....	....	....	....
2003-04	**Pittsburgh**	**NHL**	82	3	5	8	62	0	0	0	78	3.8	–17	0	0.0	19:01	....	....	....	....	....	....	....	....	....
2004-05	HC Sparta Praha	CzRep	13	0	4	4	8	....	....	....	....	....	....	....	....	....	5	0	0	0	6	....	....	....	....
2005-06	**Pittsburgh**	**NHL**	72	3	12	15	66	0	1	0	53	5.7	–2	0	0.0	17:26	....	....	....	....	....	....	....	....	....
2006-07	**Pittsburgh**	**NHL**	70	1	11	12	44	0	0	0	57	1.8	1	0	0.0	18:49	5	0	0	0	2	0	0	0	17:21
	NHL Totals		**310**	**7**	**33**	**40**	**263**	**0**	**1**	**0**	**249**	**2.8**		**0**	**0.0**	**17:50**	**5**	**0**	**0**	**0**	**2**	**0**	**0**	**0**	**17:21**

• Missed majority of 2002-03 season recovering from shoulder injury suffered in game vs. Boston, October 13, 2002. Signed as a free agent by **Sparta Praha** (CzRep), September 17, 2004.

MELIN, Bjorn

(MEH-lihn, b-YOHRN) **ANA.**

Right wing. Shoots right. 6'1", 205 lbs. Born, Jonkoping, Sweden, July 4, 1981. NY Islanders' 11th choice, 163rd overall, in 1999 Entry Draft.

Season	Club	League	GP	G	A	Pts	PIM	PP	SH	GW	S	%	+/-	TF	F%	Min	GP	G	A	Pts	PIM	PP	SH	GW	Min
1997-98	HV 71 Jr.	Swe-Jr.	8	0	3	3	2	....	....	....	....	....	....	....	....	....	....	....	....	....	....	....	....	....	....
1998-99	HV 71 Jr.	Swe-Jr.	30	12	7	19	50	....	....	....	....	....	....	....	....	....	....	....	....	....	....	....	....	....	....
99-2000	HV 71 Jr.	Swe-Jr.	24	19	16	35	70	....	....	....	....	....	....	....	....	....	....	....	....	....	....	....	....	....	....
	HV 71 Jonkoping	Sweden	23	3	0	3	2	....	....	....	....	....	....	....	....	....	5	0	0	0	0	....	....	....	....
2000-01	HV 71 Jr.	Swe-Jr.	10	6	5	11	66	....	....	....	....	....	....	....	....	....	....	....	....	....	....	....	....	....	....
	HV 71 Jonkoping	Sweden	43	2	1	3	26	....	....	....	....	....	....	....	....	....	....	....	....	....	....	....	....	....	....
2001-02	HV 71 Jonkoping	Sweden	50	7	9	16	40	....	....	....	....	....	....	....	....	....	8	0	0	0	6	....	....	....	....
2002-03	HV 71 Jonkoping	Sweden	48	7	9	16	44	....	....	....	....	....	....	....	....	....	7	0	2	2	6	....	....	....	....
2003-04	HV 71 Jonkoping	Sweden	47	7	11	18	28	....	....	....	....	....	....	....	....	....	19	4	8	12	10	....	....	....	....
2004-05	Malmo	Sweden	46	9	10	19	22	....	....	....	....	....	....	....	....	....	....	....	....	....	....	....	....	....	....
	Malmo	Sweden-Q	10	1	2	3	8	....	....	....	....	....	....	....	....	....	....	....	....	....	....	....	....	....	....
2005-06	HV 71 Jonkoping	Sweden	49	17	19	36	48	....	....	....	....	....	....	....	....	....	10	4	1	5	16	....	....	....	....
2006-07	**Anaheim**	**NHL**	3	1	0	1	0	0	0	0	1	100.0	–1	0	0.0	7:19	....	....	....	....	....	....	....	....	....
	Portland Pirates	AHL	59	8	14	22	28	....	....	....	....	....	....	....	....	....	....	....	....	....	....	....	....	....	....
	NHL Totals		**3**	**1**	**0**	**1**	**0**	**0**	**0**	**0**	**1**	**100.0**		**0**	**0.0**	**7:19**	....	....	....	....	....	....	....	....	....

Rights traded to **Anaheim** by **NY Islanders** with Ben Guite for Dave Roche, March 19, 2002.

MELLANBY, Scott

(MEH-lihn-bee, SKAWT)

Right wing. Shoots right. 6'1", 210 lbs. Born, Montreal, Que., June 11, 1966. Philadelphia's 2nd choice, 27th overall, in 1984 Entry Draft.

			Regular Season														Playoffs								
Season	Club	League	GP	G	A	Pts	PIM	PP	SH	GW	S	%	+/-	TF	F%	Min	GP	G	A	Pts	PIM	PP	SH	GW	Min
1982-83	Don Mills Flyers	MTHL	72	66	52	118	38	....	....	....	....	....	....	....	....	....	....	....	....	....	....	....	....	....	....
1983-84	Henry Carr	OHA-B	39	37	37	74	97	....	....	....	....	....	....	....	....	....	....	....	....	....	....	....	....	....	....
1984-85	U. of Wisconsin	WCHA	40	14	24	38	60	....	....	....	....	....	....	....	....	....	....	....	....	....	....	....	....	....	....
1985-86	U. of Wisconsin	WCHA	32	21	23	44	89	....	....	....	....	....	....	....	....	....	....	....	....	....	....	....	....	....	....
	Philadelphia	**NHL**	**2**	**0**	**0**	**0**	**0**	**0**	**0**	**0**	**0**	**0.0**	**–1**	....	....	....	....	....	....	....	....	....	....	....	....
1986-87	**Philadelphia**	**NHL**	**71**	**11**	**21**	**32**	**94**	**1**	**0**	**0**	**118**	**9.3**	**8**	....	....	....	**24**	**5**	**5**	**10**	**46**	**0**	**0**	**1**	....
1987-88	**Philadelphia**	**NHL**	**75**	**25**	**26**	**51**	**185**	**7**	**0**	**2**	**190**	**13.2**	**–7**	....	....	....	**7**	**0**	**1**	**1**	**16**	**0**	**0**	**0**	....
1988-89	**Philadelphia**	**NHL**	**76**	**21**	**29**	**50**	**183**	**11**	**0**	**3**	**202**	**10.4**	**–13**	....	....	....	**19**	**4**	**5**	**9**	**28**	**0**	**0**	**0**	....
1989-90	**Philadelphia**	**NHL**	**57**	**6**	**17**	**23**	**77**	**0**	**0**	**1**	**104**	**5.8**	**–4**	....	....	....	....	....	....	....	....	....	....	....	....
1990-91	**Philadelphia**	**NHL**	**74**	**20**	**21**	**41**	**155**	**5**	**0**	**6**	**165**	**12.1**	**8**	....	....	....	....	....	....	....	....	....	....	....	....
1991-92	**Edmonton**	**NHL**	**80**	**23**	**27**	**50**	**197**	**7**	**0**	**5**	**159**	**14.5**	**5**	....	....	....	**16**	**2**	**1**	**3**	**29**	**1**	**0**	**1**	....
1992-93	**Edmonton**	**NHL**	**69**	**15**	**17**	**32**	**147**	**6**	**0**	**3**	**114**	**13.2**	**–4**	....	....	....	....	....	....	....	....	....	....	....	....
1993-94	**Florida**	**NHL**	**80**	**30**	**30**	**60**	**149**	**17**	**0**	**4**	**204**	**14.7**	**0**	....	....	....	....	....	....	....	....	....	....	....	....
1994-95	**Florida**	**NHL**	**48**	**13**	**12**	**25**	**90**	**4**	**0**	**5**	**130**	**10.0**	**–16**	....	....	....	....	....	....	....	....	....	....	....	....
1995-96	**Florida**	**NHL**	**79**	**32**	**38**	**70**	**160**	**19**	**0**	**3**	**225**	**14.2**	**4**	....	....	....	**22**	**3**	**6**	**9**	**44**	**2**	**0**	**0**	....
1996-97	**Florida**	**NHL**	**82**	**27**	**29**	**56**	**170**	**9**	**1**	**4**	**221**	**12.2**	**7**	....	....	....	**5**	**0**	**2**	**2**	**4**	**0**	**0**	**0**	....
1997-98	**Florida**	**NHL**	**79**	**15**	**24**	**39**	**127**	**6**	**0**	**1**	**188**	**8.0**	**–14**	....	....	....	....	....	....	....	....	....	....	....	....
1998-99	**Florida**	**NHL**	**67**	**18**	**27**	**45**	**85**	**4**	**0**	**3**	**136**	**13.2**	**5**	**11**	**27.3**	**16:14**	....	....	....	....	....	....	....	....	....
99-2000	**Florida**	**NHL**	**77**	**18**	**28**	**46**	**126**	**6**	**0**	**2**	**134**	**13.4**	**14**	**20**	**60.0**	**14:51**	**4**	**0**	**1**	**1**	**2**	**0**	**0**	**0**	**13:09**
2000-01	**Florida**	**NHL**	**40**	**4**	**9**	**13**	**46**	**1**	**0**	**0**	**58**	**6.9**	**–13**	**4**	**50.0**	**14:59**	....	....	....	....	....	....	....	....	....
	St. Louis	**NHL**	**23**	**7**	**1**	**8**	**25**	**2**	**0**	**0**	**37**	**18.9**	**0**	**1**	**0.0**	**15:00**	**15**	**3**	**3**	**6**	**17**	**2**	**0**	**0**	**14:43**
2001-02	**St. Louis**	**NHL**	**64**	**15**	**26**	**41**	**93**	**8**	**0**	**2**	**137**	**10.9**	**–5**	**3**	**0.0**	**15:40**	**10**	**7**	**3**	**10**	**18**	**4**	**0**	**1**	**17:54**
2002-03	**St. Louis**	**NHL**	**80**	**26**	**31**	**57**	**176**	**13**	**0**	**4**	**132**	**19.7**	**1**	**11**	**45.5**	**16:39**	**6**	**0**	**1**	**1**	**10**	**0**	**0**	**0**	**16:18**
2003-04	**St. Louis**	**NHL**	**68**	**14**	**17**	**31**	**76**	**6**	**0**	**3**	**103**	**13.6**	**–7**	**4**	**50.0**	**15:29**	**4**	**0**	**1**	**1**	**2**	**0**	**0**	**0**	**14:16**
2004-05			DID NOT PLAY																						
2005-06	**Atlanta**	**NHL**	**71**	**12**	**22**	**34**	**55**	**3**	**0**	**3**	**100**	**12.0**	**5**	**37**	**43.2**	**13:25**	....	....	....	....	....	....	....	....	....
2006-07	**Atlanta**	**NHL**	**69**	**12**	**24**	**36**	**63**	**5**	**0**	**2**	**103**	**11.7**	**–9**	**35**	**45.7**	**13:43**	**4**	**0**	**0**	**0**	**4**	**0**	**0**	**0**	**13:34**
	NHL Totals		**1431**	**364**	**476**	**840**	**2479**	**140**	**1**	**56**	**2960**	**12.3**		**126**	**44.4**	**15:08**	**136**	**24**	**29**	**53**	**220**	**9**	**0**	**3**	**15:23**

Played in NHL All-Star Game (1996)

Traded to **Edmonton** by **Philadelphia** with Craig Fisher and Craig Berube for Dave Brown, Corey Foster and Jari Kurri, May 30, 1991. Claimed by **Florida** from **Edmonton** in Expansion Draft, June 24, 1993. Traded to **St. Louis** by **Florida** for the rights to Dave Morisset and St. Louis' 5th round choice (Vince Bellissimo) in 2002 Entry Draft, February 9, 2001. Signed as a free agent by **Atlanta**, July 26, 2004.

MELOCHE, Eric

(muh-LAWSH, AIR-ihk)

Right wing. Shoots right. 5'10", 202 lbs. Born, Montreal, Que., May 1, 1976. Pittsburgh's 7th choice, 186th overall, in 1996 Entry Draft.

Season	Club	League	GP	G	A	Pts	PIM	PP	SH	GW	S	%	+/-	TF	F%	Min	GP	G	A	Pts	PIM	PP	SH	GW	Min
1994-95	Cornwall Colts	CJHL	40	7	15	22	51	....	....	....	....	....	....	....	....	....	....	....	....	....	....	....	....	....	....
1995-96	Cornwall Colts	CJHL	64	68	53	121	162	....	....	....	....	....	....	....	....	....	....	....	....	....	....	....	....	....	....
1996-97	Ohio State	CCHA	39	12	11	23	78	....	....	....	....	....	....	....	....	....	....	....	....	....	....	....	....	....	....
1997-98	Ohio State	CCHA	42	26	22	48	86	....	....	....	....	....	....	....	....	....	....	....	....	....	....	....	....	....	....
1998-99	Ohio State	CCHA	35	11	16	27	87	....	....	....	....	....	....	....	....	....	....	....	....	....	....	....	....	....	....
99-2000	Ohio State	CCHA	36	20	11	31	*138	....	....	....	....	....	....	....	....	....	....	....	....	....	....	....	....	....	....
2000-01	Wilkes-Barre	AHL	79	20	20	40	72	....	....	....	....	....	....	....	....	....	21	6	10	16	17	....	....	....	....
2001-02	**Pittsburgh**	**NHL**	**23**	**0**	**1**	**1**	**8**	**0**	**0**	**0**	**29**	**0.0**	**–7**	**4**	**0.0**	**10:10**	....	....	....	....	....	....	....	....	....
	Wilkes-Barre	AHL	55	13	14	27	91	....	....	....	....	....	....	....	....	....	....	....	....	....	....	....	....	....	....
2002-03	**Pittsburgh**	**NHL**	**13**	**5**	**1**	**6**	**4**	**2**	**0**	**1**	**34**	**14.7**	**–2**	**27**	**55.6**	**16:52**	....	....	....	....	....	....	....	....	....
	Wilkes-Barre	AHL	59	12	17	29	95	....	....	....	....	....	....	....	....	....	6	1	0	1	20	....	....	....	....
2003-04	**Pittsburgh**	**NHL**	**25**	**3**	**7**	**10**	**20**	**0**	**0**	**0**	**28**	**10.7**	**–6**	**92**	**39.1**	**14:47**	....	....	....	....	....	....	....	....	....
	Wilkes-Barre	AHL	56	16	26	42	49	....	....	....	....	....	....	....	....	....	23	9	6	15	14	....	....	....	....
2004-05	Philadelphia	AHL	63	6	11	17	102	....	....	....	....	....	....	....	....	....	17	3	2	5	18	....	....	....	....
2005-06	Philadelphia	AHL	10	1	2	3	16	....	....	....	....	....	....	....	....	....	....	....	....	....	....	....	....	....	....
	Norfolk Admirals	AHL	47	7	14	21	81	....	....	....	....	....	....	....	....	....	4	0	0	0	11	....	....	....	....
2006-07	**Philadelphia**	**NHL**	**13**	**1**	**2**	**3**	**4**	**1**	**0**	**0**	**12**	**8.3**	**–6**	**28**	**46.4**	**8:21**	....	....	....	....	....	....	....	....	....
	Philadelphia	AHL	49	11	13	24	82	....	....	....	....	....	....	....	....	....	....	....	....	....	....	....	....	....	....
	NHL Totals		**74**	**9**	**11**	**20**	**36**	**3**	**0**	**1**	**103**	**8.7**		**151**	**42.4**	**12:35**	....	....	....	....	....	....	....	....	....

Signed as a free agent by **Philadelphia**, July 14, 2004. Traded to **Chicago** by **Philadelphia** with Patrick Sharp for Matt Ellison and Chicago's 3rd round choice (later traded to Montreal - Montereal selected Ryan White) in 2006 Entry Draft, December 5, 2005. Traded to **Philadelphia** by **Chicago** for Vaclav Pletka, August 2, 2006.

MESZAROS, Andrej

(MEHT-zahr-ohsh, AWN-dray) **OTT.**

Defense. Shoots left. 6'1", 220 lbs. Born, Povazska Bystrica, Czech., October 13, 1985. Ottawa's 1st choice, 23rd overall, in 2004 Entry Draft.

Season	Club	League	GP	G	A	Pts	PIM	PP	SH	GW	S	%	+/-	TF	F%	Min	GP	G	A	Pts	PIM	PP	SH	GW	Min
2002-03	Dukla Trencin Jr.	Slovak-Jr.	33	6	10	16	12	....	....	....	....	....	....	....	....	....	....	....	....	....	....	....	....	....	....
	Dukla Trencin	Slovakia	23	0	1	1	4	....	....	....	....	....	....	....	....	....	....	....	....	....	....	....	....	....	....
2003-04	Dukla Trencin Jr.	Slovak-Jr.	5	2	2	4	0	....	....	....	....	....	....	....	....	....	....	....	....	....	....	....	....	....	....
	Dukla Trencin	Slovakia	44	3	3	6	8	....	....	....	....	....	....	....	....	....	14	3	1	4	2	....	....	....	....
2004-05	Vancouver Giants	WHL	59	11	30	41	94	....	....	....	....	....	....	....	....	....	6	1	3	4	14	....	....	....	....
2005-06	**Ottawa**	**NHL**	**82**	**10**	**29**	**39**	**61**	**5**	**0**	**2**	**137**	**7.3**	**34**	**1**	**0.0**	**18:11**	**10**	**1**	**0**	**1**	**18**	**0**	**0**	**0**	**17:50**
	Slovakia	Olympics	6	0	2	2	4	....	....	....	....	....	....	....	....	....	....	....	....	....	....	....	....	....	....
2006-07	**Ottawa**	**NHL**	**82**	**7**	**28**	**35**	**102**	**0**	**0**	**1**	**147**	**4.8**	**–15**	**0**	**0.0**	**21:41**	**20**	**1**	**6**	**7**	**12**	**0**	**0**	**0**	**20:29**
	NHL Totals		**164**	**17**	**57**	**74**	**163**	**5**	**0**	**3**	**284**	**6.0**		**1**	**0.0**	**19:56**	**30**	**2**	**6**	**8**	**30**	**0**	**0**	**0**	**19:36**

WHL West Second All-Star Team (2005) • NHL All-Rookie Team (2006)

METHOT, Marc

(meh-TOH, MAHRK) **CBJ**

Defense. Shoots left. 6'3", 224 lbs. Born, Ottawa, Ont., June 21, 1985. Columbus' 7th choice, 168th overall, in 2003 Entry Draft.

Season	Club	League	GP	G	A	Pts	PIM	PP	SH	GW	S	%	+/-	TF	F%	Min	GP	G	A	Pts	PIM	PP	SH	GW	Min
2001-02	Kanata Laser	CJHL	50	3	10	13	22	....	....	....	....	....	....	....	....	....	....	....	....	....	....	....	....	....	....
2002-03	London Knights	OHL	68	2	13	15	46	....	....	....	....	....	....	....	....	....	14	2	4	6	6	....	....	....	....
2003-04	London Knights	OHL	63	2	9	11	66	....	....	....	....	....	....	....	....	....	15	0	3	3	18	....	....	....	....
2004-05	London Knights	OHL	67	4	12	16	88	....	....	....	....	....	....	....	....	....	18	2	1	3	32	....	....	....	....
2005-06	Syracuse Crunch	AHL	70	1	12	13	75	....	....	....	....	....	....	....	....	....	5	0	0	0	8	....	....	....	....
2006-07	**Columbus**	**NHL**	**20**	**0**	**4**	**4**	**12**	**0**	**0**	**0**	**11**	**0.0**	**5**	**0**	**0.0**	**14:38**	....	....	....	....	....	....	....	....	....
	Syracuse Crunch	AHL	59	1	15	16	58	....	....	....	....	....	....	....	....	....	....	....	....	....	....	....	....	....	....
	NHL Totals		**20**	**0**	**4**	**4**	**12**	**0**	**0**	**0**	**11**	**0.0**		**0**	**0.0**	**14:38**	....	....	....	....	....	....	....	....	....

METROPOLIT, Glen

(meh-troh-PAW-liht, GLEHN)

Center. Shoots right. 5'10", 195 lbs. Born, Toronto, Ont., June 25, 1974.

Season	Club	League	GP	G	A	Pts	PIM	PP	SH	GW	S	%	+/-	TF	F%	Min	GP	G	A	Pts	PIM	PP	SH	GW	Min
1992-93	Richmond Hill	MTJHL	43	27	36	63	36	....	....	....	....	....	....	....	....	....	....	....	....	....	....	....	....	....	....
1993-94	Richmond Hill	MTJHL	49	38	62	100	83	....	....	....	....	....	....	....	....	....	....	....	....	....	....	....	....	....	....
1994-95	Vernon Vipers	BCJHL	60	43	74	117	92	....	....	....	....	....	....	....	....	....	....	....	....	....	....	....	....	....	....
1995-96	Nashville Knights	ECHL	58	30	31	61	62	....	....	....	....	....	....	....	....	....	5	3	8	11	2	....	....	....	....
	Atlanta Knights	IHL	1	0	0	0	0	....	....	....	....	....	....	....	....	....	....	....	....	....	....	....	....	....	....
1996-97	Pensacola	ECHL	54	35	47	82	45	....	....	....	....	....	....	....	....	....	12	9	16	25	28	....	....	....	....
	Quebec Rafales	IHL	22	5	4	9	14	....	....	....	....	....	....	....	....	....	5	0	0	0	2	....	....	....	....
1997-98	Grand Rapids	IHL	79	20	35	55	90	....	....	....	....	....	....	....	....	....	3	1	1	2	0	....	....	....	....
1998-99	Grand Rapids	IHL	77	28	53	81	92	....	....	....	....	....	....	....	....	....	....	....	....	....	....	....	....	....	....
99-2000	**Washington**	**NHL**	**30**	**6**	**13**	**19**	**4**	**1**	**0**	**1**	**57**	**10.5**	**5**	**37**	**46.0**	**13:17**	**2**	**0**	**0**	**0**	**2**	**0**	**0**	**0**	**7:07**
	Portland Pirates	AHL	48	18	42	60	73	....	....	....	....	....	....	....	....	....	1	1	0	1	0	....	....	....	....
2000-01	**Washington**	**NHL**	**15**	**1**	**5**	**6**	**10**	**0**	**0**	**0**	**20**	**5.0**	**–2**	**3**	**33.3**	**11:50**	**1**	**0**	**0**	**0**	**0**	**0**	**0**	**0**	**7:03**
	Portland Pirates	AHL	51	25	42	67	59	....	....	....	....	....	....	....	....	....	....	....	....	....	....	....	....	....	....
2001-02	**Tampa Bay**	**NHL**	**2**	**0**	**0**	**0**	**0**	**0**	**0**	**0**	**1**	**0.0**	**–2**	**2**	**50.0**	**10:26**	....	....	....	....	....	....	....	....	....
	Washington	**NHL**	**33**	**1**	**16**	**17**	**6**	**0**	**0**	**0**	**51**	**2.0**	**3**	**145**	**49.7**	**14:24**	....	....	....	....	....	....	....	....	....
	Portland Pirates	AHL	32	17	22	39	20	....	....	....	....	....	....	....	....	....	....	....	....	....	....	....	....	....	....
2002-03	**Washington**	**NHL**	**23**	**2**	**3**	**5**	**6**	**0**	**0**	**1**	**22**	**9.1**	**4**	**99**	**49.5**	**10:07**	....	....	....	....	....	....	....	....	....
	Portland Pirates	AHL	33	7	23	30	23	....	....	....	....	....	....	....	....	....	3	1	1	2	0	....	....	....	....
2003-04	Jokerit Helsinki	Finland	55	15	35	50	77	....	....	....	....	....	....	....	....	....	7	6	1	7	33	....	....	....	....
2004-05	Jokerit Helsinki	Finland	51	16	31	47	42	....	....	....	....	....	....	....	....	....	12	5	6	11	20	....	....	....	....

			Regular Season														Playoffs								
Season	Club	League	GP	G	A	Pts	PIM	PP	SH	GW	S	%	+/-	TF	F%	Min	GP	G	A	Pts	PIM	PP	SH	GW	Min
2005-06	HC Lugano	Swiss	44	24	*39	*63	60	....	....	....	....	....	....	....	....	....	17	9	18	27	8	....	....	....	....
2006-07	**Atlanta**	**NHL**	57	12	16	28	20	4	0	2	92	13.0	9	206	49.0	11:47	....	....	....	....	....	....	....	....	....
	St. Louis	**NHL**	20	2	3	5	14	1	0	0	31	6.5	0	154	50.0	12:58	....	....	....	....	....	....	....	....	....
	NHL Totals		180	24	56	80	60	6	0	4	274	8.8		646	49.2	12:25	3	0	0	0	2	0	0	0	7:05

Signed as a free agent by **Washington**, July 19, 1999. Claimed by **Tampa Bay** from **Washington** in Waiver Draft, September 28, 2001. Claimed on waivers by **Washington** from **Tampa Bay**, October 20, 2001. Signed as a free agent by **Jokerit Helsinki** (Finland), April 22, 2003. Claimed by **Ottawa** from **Washington** in Waiver Draft, October 3, 2003. Signed as a free agent by **Atlanta**, July 3, 2006. Traded to **St. Louis** by **Atlanta** with Atlanta's 1st (later traded to Calgary - Calgary selected Mikael Backlund) and 3rd (Brett Sonne) round choices in 2007 Entry Draft, and Atlanta's 1st (later traded back to Atlanta) and 2nd round choices in 2008 Entry Draft for Keith Tkachuk, February 25, 2007.

MEYER, Freddy
(MAY-uhr, FREHD) **NYI**

Defense. Shoots left. 5'10", 192 lbs. Born, Sanbornville, NH, January 4, 1981.

Season	Club	League	GP	G	A	Pts	PIM	PP	SH	GW	S	%	+/-	TF	F%	Min	GP	G	A	Pts	PIM	PP	SH	GW	Min
1996-97	Cardigan Mtn.	High-NH	STATISTICS NOT AVAILABLE																						
1997-98	USNTDP	NAHL	....	....	....	....	....	....	....	....	....	....	....	....	....	....	2	1	0	1	37	....	....	....	....
1998-99	USNTDP	U-18	6	1	4	5	8	....	....	....	....	....	....	....	....	....	....	....	....	....	....	....	....	....	....
	USNTDP	USHL	54	10	23	33	151	....	....	....	....	....	....	....	....	....	....	....	....	....	....	....	....	....	....
99-2000	USNTDP	USHL	28	3	8	11	60	....	....	....	....	....	....	....	....	....	....	....	....	....	....	....	....	....	....
	USNTDP	NAHL	3	0	2	2	0	....	....	....	....	....	....	....	....	....	....	....	....	....	....	....	....	....	....
	Boston University	H-East	25	1	11	12	52	....	....	....	....	....	....	....	....	....	....	....	....	....	....	....	....	....	....
2000-01	Boston University	H-East	28	6	13	19	82	....	....	....	....	....	....	....	....	....	....	....	....	....	....	....	....	....	....
2001-02	Boston University	H-East	37	5	15	20	78	....	....	....	....	....	....	....	....	....	....	....	....	....	....	....	....	....	....
2002-03	Boston University	H-East	36	5	16	21	76	....	....	....	....	....	....	....	....	....	....	....	....	....	....	....	....	....	....
2003-04	**Philadelphia**	**NHL**	1	0	0	0	0	0	0	0	1	0.0	0	0	0.0	15:24	....	....	....	....	....	....	....	....	....
	Philadelphia	AHL	59	14	14	28	50	....	....	....	....	....	....	....	....	....	12	0	3	3	8	....	....	....	....
2004-05	Philadelphia	AHL	59	6	9	15	71	....	....	....	....	....	....	....	....	....	21	3	9	12	34	....	....	....	....
2005-06	**Philadelphia**	**NHL**	57	6	21	27	33	2	0	0	68	8.8	10	0	0.0	17:56	6	0	1	1	8	0	0	0	18:23
	Philadelphia	AHL	11	3	3	6	22	....	....	....	....	....	....	....	....	....	....	....	....	....	....	....	....	....	....
2006-07	**Philadelphia**	**NHL**	25	2	3	5	14	1	0	0	27	7.4	–4	0	0.0	18:36	....	....	....	....	....	....	....	....	....
	NY Islanders	**NHL**	35	0	3	3	24	0	0	0	14	0.0	0	0	0.0	16:39	....	....	....	....	....	....	....	....	....
	NHL Totals		118	8	27	35	71	3	0	0	110	7.3		0	0.0	17:41	6	0	1	1	8	0	0	0	18:23

Hockey East All-Rookie Team (2000) • Hockey East First All-Star Team (2003) • NCAA East First All-American Team (2003)

Signed as a free agent by **Philadelphia**, May 21, 2003. Traded to **NY Islanders** by **Philadelphia** with Philadelphia's 3rd round choice (Mark Katic) in 2007 Entry Draft for Alexei Zhitnik, December 16, 2006.

MEZEI, Branislav
(MEH-tzay, BRAN-ih-slav) **FLA.**

Defense. Shoots left. 6'4", 235 lbs. Born, Nitra, Czech., October 8, 1980. NY Islanders' 3rd choice, 10th overall, in 1999 Entry Draft.

Season	Club	League	GP	G	A	Pts	PIM	PP	SH	GW	S	%	+/-	TF	F%	Min	GP	G	A	Pts	PIM	PP	SH	GW	Min
1996-97	Nitra Jr.	Slovak-Jr.	40	8	17	25	42	....	....	....	....	....	....	....	....	....	....	....	....	....	....	....	....	....	....
1997-98	Belleville Bulls	OHL	53	3	5	8	58	....	....	....	....	....	....	....	....	....	8	0	2	2	8	....	....	....	....
1998-99	Belleville Bulls	OHL	60	5	18	23	90	....	....	....	....	....	....	....	....	....	18	0	4	4	29	....	....	....	....
99-2000	Belleville Bulls	OHL	58	7	21	28	99	....	....	....	....	....	....	....	....	....	6	0	3	3	10	....	....	....	....
2000-01	**NY Islanders**	**NHL**	42	1	4	5	53	0	0	0	29	3.4	–5	0	0.0	14:48	....	....	....	....	....	....	....	....	....
	Lowell	AHL	20	0	3	3	28	....	....	....	....	....	....	....	....	....	....	....	....	....	....	....	....	....	....
2001-02	**NY Islanders**	**NHL**	24	0	2	2	12	0	0	0	4	0.0	2	0	0.0	8:28	....	....	....	....	....	....	....	....	....
	Bridgeport	AHL	59	1	9	10	137	....	....	....	....	....	....	....	....	....	20	0	1	1	48	....	....	....	....
2002-03	**Florida**	**NHL**	11	2	0	2	10	0	0	1	10	20.0	–2	0	0.0	18:22	....	....	....	....	....	....	....	....	....
	San Antonio	AHL	1	0	0	0	0	....	....	....	....	....	....	....	....	....	3	0	0	0	0	....	....	....	....
2003-04	**Florida**	**NHL**	45	0	7	7	80	0	0	0	26	0.0	–4	0	0.0	17:43	....	....	....	....	....	....	....	....	....
2004-05	HC Ocelari Trinec	CzRep	41	1	2	3	68	....	....	....	....	....	....	....	....	....	....	....	....	....	....	....	....	....	....
	Dukla Trencin	Slovakia	10	1	1	2	16	....	....	....	....	....	....	....	....	....	12	1	2	3	38	....	....	....	....
2005-06	**Florida**	**NHL**	16	0	1	1	37	0	0	0	13	0.0	3	0	0.0	19:17	....	....	....	....	....	....	....	....	....
2006-07	**Florida**	**NHL**	45	0	3	3	55	0	0	0	24	0.0	5	1	100.0	15:58	....	....	....	....	....	....	....	....	....
	NHL Totals		183	3	17	20	247	0	0	1	106	2.8		1	100.0	15:35	....	....	....	....	....	....	....	....	....

OHL First All-Star Team (2000)

Traded to **Florida** by **NY Islanders** for Jason Wiemer, July 3, 2002. • Missed majority of 2002-03 season recovering from ankle (October 12, 2002 vs. Atlanta) and foot (January 1, 2003 vs. New Jersey) injuries. Signed as a free agent by **Trinec** (CzRep), September 25, 2004. Signed as a free agent by **Trencin** (Slovakia), January 30, 2005. • Missed remainder of 2005-06 season recovering from knee injury sufferd in game vs. NY Rangers, November 9, 2005.

MICHALEK, Milan
(mih-KHAL-ihk, MEE-lan) **S.J.**

Right wing. Shoots left. 6'2", 225 lbs. Born, Jindrichuv Hradec, Czech., December 7, 1984. San Jose's 1st choice, 6th overall, in 2003 Entry Draft.

Season	Club	League	GP	G	A	Pts	PIM	PP	SH	GW	S	%	+/-	TF	F%	Min	GP	G	A	Pts	PIM	PP	SH	GW	Min
99-2000	C. Budejovice Jr.	CzRep-Jr.	48	16	26	42	42	....	....	....	....	....	....	....	....	....	6	3	1	4	4	....	....	....	....
2000-01	C. Budejovice Jr.	CzRep-Jr.	30	10	13	23	30	....	....	....	....	....	....	....	....	....	4	1	3	4	2	....	....	....	....
	C. Budejovice	CzRep	5	0	0	0	0	....	....	....	....	....	....	....	....	....	....	....	....	....	....	....	....	....	....
2001-02	C. Budejovice	CzRep	47	6	11	17	12	....	....	....	....	....	....	....	....	....	....	....	....	....	....	....	....	....	....
	C. Budejovice Jr.	CzRep-Jr.	5	3	2	5	4	....	....	....	....	....	....	....	....	....	7	5	4	9	14	....	....	....	....
2002-03	C. Budejovice	CzRep	46	3	5	8	14	....	....	....	....	....	....	....	....	....	4	1	0	1	2	....	....	....	....
	Kladno	CzRep-2	....	....	....	....	....	....	....	....	....	....	....	....	....	....	6	2	2	4	16	....	....	....	....
2003-04	**San Jose**	**NHL**	2	1	0	1	4	0	0	0	1	100.0	1	0	0.0	9:05	....	....	....	....	....	....	....	....	....
	Cleveland Barons	AHL	7	2	2	4	4	....	....	....	....	....	....	....	....	....	....	....	....	....	....	....	....	....	....
2004-05			DID NOT PLAY																						
2005-06	**San Jose**	**NHL**	81	17	18	35	45	4	0	2	159	10.7	1	4	0.0	15:46	9	1	4	5	8	1	0	0	15:11
2006-07	**San Jose**	**NHL**	78	26	40	66	36	11	0	9	191	13.6	17	11	18.2	16:46	11	4	2	6	4	0	0	1	18:50
	NHL Totals		161	44	58	102	85	15	0	11	351	12.5		15	13.3	16:10	20	5	6	11	12	1	0	1	17:11

• Missed majority of 2003-04 season recovering from knee injury suffered in game vs. Calgary, October 11, 2003.

MICHALEK, Zbynek
(mih-KHAL-ihk, z'BIGH-nehk) **PHX.**

Defense. Shoots right. 6'1", 200 lbs. Born, Jindrichuv Hradec, Czech., December 23, 1982.

Season	Club	League	GP	G	A	Pts	PIM	PP	SH	GW	S	%	+/-	TF	F%	Min	GP	G	A	Pts	PIM	PP	SH	GW	Min
99-2000	Karlovy Vary Jr.	CzRep-Jr.	40	2	10	12	20	....	....	....	....	....	....	....	....	....	....	....	....	....	....	....	....	....	....
2000-01	Shawinigan	QMJHL	69	10	29	39	52	....	....	....	....	....	....	....	....	....	3	0	0	0	0	....	....	....	....
2001-02	Shawinigan	QMJHL	68	16	35	51	54	....	....	....	....	....	....	....	....	....	12	8	9	17	17	....	....	....	....
2002-03	Houston Aeros	AHL	62	4	10	14	26	....	....	....	....	....	....	....	....	....	23	1	1	2	6	....	....	....	....
2003-04	**Minnesota**	**NHL**	22	1	1	2	4	0	0	0	17	5.9	–7	0	0.0	14:13	....	....	....	....	....	....	....	....	....
	Houston Aeros	AHL	55	5	16	21	32	....	....	....	....	....	....	....	....	....	2	1	0	1	0	....	....	....	....
2004-05	Houston Aeros	AHL	76	7	17	24	48	....	....	....	....	....	....	....	....	....	5	1	2	3	4	....	....	....	....
2005-06	**Phoenix**	**NHL**	82	9	15	24	62	5	0	2	105	8.6	4	0	0.0	22:50	....	....	....	....	....	....	....	....	....
2006-07	**Phoenix**	**NHL**	82	4	24	28	34	3	0	0	144	2.8	–20	1	100.0	23:40	....	....	....	....	....	....	....	....	....
	NHL Totals		186	14	40	54	100	8	0	2	266	5.3		1	100.0	22:11	....	....	....	....	....	....	....	....	....

Signed as a free agent by **Minnesota**, September 29, 2001. Traded to **Phoenix** by **Minnesota** for Erik Westrum and Dustin Wood, August 26, 2005.

MIETTINEN, Antti
(mih-EHT-tih-nehn, AN-tee) **DAL.**

Right wing. Shoots right. 6', 190 lbs. Born, Hameenlinna, Finland, July 3, 1980. Dallas' 10th choice, 224th overall, in 2000 Entry Draft.

Season	Club	League	GP	G	A	Pts	PIM	PP	SH	GW	S	%	+/-	TF	F%	Min	GP	G	A	Pts	PIM	PP	SH	GW	Min
1996-97	HPK U18	Fin-U18	36	24	29	53	34	....	....	....	....	....	....	....	....	....	....	....	....	....	....	....	....	....	....
1997-98	HPK U18	Fin-U18	34	13	28	41	63	....	....	....	....	....	....	....	....	....	....	....	....	....	....	....	....	....	....
	HPK Jr.	Fin-Jr.	8	1	0	1	2	....	....	....	....	....	....	....	....	....	....	....	....	....	....	....	....	....	....
1998-99	HPK Jr.	Fin-Jr.	35	17	22	39	28	....	....	....	....	....	....	....	....	....	3	2	3	5	2	....	....	....	....
	FPS Forssa	Finland-2	4	3	1	4	6	....	....	....	....	....	....	....	....	....	....	....	....	....	....	....	....	....	....
	HPK Hameenlinna	Finland	13	0	0	0	2	....	....	....	....	....	....	....	....	....	4	0	0	0	0	....	....	....	....
99-2000	HPK Jr.	Fin-Jr.	31	24	53	77	28	....	....	....	....	....	....	....	....	....	2	1	6	7	2	....	....	....	....
	HPK Hameenlinna	Finland	39	2	1	3	8	....	....	....	....	....	....	....	....	....	7	1	0	1	0	....	....	....	....
2000-01	HPK Jr.	Fin-Jr.	4	3	10	13	2	....	....	....	....	....	....	....	....	....	....	....	....	....	....	....	....	....	....
	HPK Hameenlinna	Finland	55	13	11	24	20	....	....	....	....	....	....	....	....	....	....	....	....	....	....	....	....	....	....
2001-02	HPK Hameenlinna	Finland	56	19	37	56	50	....	....	....	....	....	....	....	....	....	8	2	4	6	8	....	....	....	....
2002-03	HPK Hameenlinna	Finland	53	25	25	50	54	....	....	....	....	....	....	....	....	....	10	1	7	8	29	....	....	....	....
2003-04	**Dallas**	**NHL**	16	1	0	1	0	0	0	1	17	5.9	–9	1	0.0	9:51	....	....	....	....	....	....	....	....	....
	Utah Grizzlies	AHL	48	7	23	30	20	....	....	....	....	....	....	....	....	....	....	....	....	....	....	....	....	....	....
2004-05	Hamilton	AHL	35	8	20	28	21	....	....	....	....	....	....	....	....	....	4	1	1	2	6	....	....	....	....

Season	Club	League	GP	G	A	Pts	PIM	PP	SH	GW	S	%	+/-	TF	F%	Min	GP	G	A	Pts	PIM	PP	SH	GW	Min
			Regular Season														**Playoffs**								
2005-06	**Dallas**	**NHL**	**79**	**11**	**20**	**31**	**46**	**4**	**0**	**1**	**107**	**10.3**	**0**	**1**	**100.0**	**12:06**	**5**	**0**	**1**	**1**	**8**	**0**	**0**	**0**	**12:10**
2006-07	**Dallas**	**NHL**	**74**	**11**	**14**	**25**	**38**	**6**	**0**	**1**	**141**	**7.8**	**–5**	**11**	**18.2**	**14:20**	**4**	**1**	**1**	**2**	**2**	**0**	**0**	**0**	**12:16**
	NHL Totals		**169**	**23**	**34**	**57**	**84**	**10**	**0**	**3**	**265**	**8.7**		**13**	**23.1**	**12:52**	**9**	**1**	**2**	**3**	**10**	**0**	**0**	**0**	**12:13**

MIKHNOV, Alexei

(MIHKH-nahf, al-EHX-ay) **EDM.**

Left wing. Shoots left. 6'5", 200 lbs. Born, Kiev, USSR, August 31, 1982. Edmonton's 1st choice, 17th overall, in 2000 Entry Draft.

Season	Club	League	GP	G	A	Pts	PIM	PP	SH	GW	S	%	+/-	TF	F%	Min	GP	G	A	Pts	PIM	PP	SH	GW	Min
1997-98	Yaroslavl	Russia	6	0	0	0	0	....	....	....	....	....	....	....	....	....	....	....	....	....	....	....	....	....	....
1998-99	Yaroslavl 2	Russia-3	14	2	2	4	4	....	....	....	....	....	....	....	....	....	....	....	....	....	....	....	....	....	....
99-2000	Yaroslavl 2	Russia-3	53	24	17	41	10	....	....	....	....	....	....	....	....	....	....	....	....	....	....	....	....	....	....
2000-01	HK Moscow	Russia-2	4	0	0	0	2	....	....	....	....	....	....	....	....	....	....	....	....	....	....	....	....	....	....
	THK Tver	Russia-2	22	5	11	16	6	....	....	....	....	....	....	....	....	....	....	....	....	....	....	....	....	....	....
2001-02	Dyn'o Moscow 2	Russia-3	8	8	6	14	0	....	....	....	....	....	....	....	....	....	....	....	....	....	....	....	....	....	....
	Dynamo Moscow	Russia	35	2	1	3	4	....	....	....	....	....	....	....	....	....	3	0	0	0	2	....	....	....	....
	Ufa	Russia	1	0	0	0	0	....	....	....	....	....	....	....	....	....	....	....	....	....	....	....	....	....	....
2002-03	Sibir Novosibirsk	Russia	51	7	9	16	10	....	....	....	....	....	....	....	....	....	....	....	....	....	....	....	....	....	....
2003-04	Sibir Novosibirsk	Russia	58	14	8	22	22	....	....	....	....	....	....	....	....	....	....	....	....	....	....	....	....	....	....
2004-05	Sibir Novosibirsk	Russia	26	2	3	5	12	....	....	....	....	....	....	....	....	....	....	....	....	....	....	....	....	....	....
	Yaroslavl 2	Russia-3	2	1	0	1	0	....	....	....	....	....	....	....	....	....	....	....	....	....	....	....	....	....	....
	Yaroslavl	Russia	18	0	9	9	4	....	....	....	....	....	....	....	....	....	7	0	0	0	4	....	....	....	....
2005-06	Yaroslavl	Russia	40	14	7	21	18	....	....	....	....	....	....	....	....	....	11	4	4	8	4	....	....	....	....
2006-07	**Edmonton**	**NHL**	**2**	**0**	**0**	**0**	**0**	**0**	**0**	**0**	**0**	**0.0**	**0**	**0**	**0.0**	**6:52**	....	....	....	....	....	....	....	....	....
	Wilkes-Barre	AHL	27	6	12	18	22	....	....	....	....	....	....	....	....	....	....	....	....	....	....	....	....	....	....
	Yaroslavl	Russia	11	5	3	8	6	....	....	....	....	....	....	....	....	....	7	2	3	5	4	....	....	....	....
	NHL Totals		**2**	**0**	**0**	**0**	**0**	**0**	**0**	**0**	**0**	**0.0**		**0**	**0.0**	**6:52**	....	....	....	....	....	....	....	....	....

MILLER, Aaron

(MIHL-luhr, AIR-ruhn) **VAN.**

Defense. Shoots right. 6'3", 218 lbs. Born, Buffalo, NY, August 11, 1971. NY Rangers' 6th choice, 88th overall, in 1989 Entry Draft.

Season	Club	League	GP	G	A	Pts	PIM	PP	SH	GW	S	%	+/-	TF	F%	Min	GP	G	A	Pts	PIM	PP	SH	GW	Min
1987-88	Niagara Scenics	NAHL	30	4	9	13	2	....	....	....	....	....	....	....	....	....	....	....	....	....	....	....	....	....	....
1988-89	Niagara Scenics	NAHL	59	24	38	62	60	....	....	....	....	....	....	....	....	....	....	....	....	....	....	....	....	....	....
1989-90	U. of Vermont	ECAC	31	1	15	16	24	....	....	....	....	....	....	....	....	....	....	....	....	....	....	....	....	....	....
1990-91	U. of Vermont	ECAC	30	3	7	10	22	....	....	....	....	....	....	....	....	....	....	....	....	....	....	....	....	....	....
1991-92	U. of Vermont	ECAC	31	3	16	19	28	....	....	....	....	....	....	....	....	....	....	....	....	....	....	....	....	....	....
1992-93	U. of Vermont	ECAC	30	4	13	17	16	....	....	....	....	....	....	....	....	....	....	....	....	....	....	....	....	....	....
1993-94	**Quebec**	**NHL**	**1**	**0**	**0**	**0**	**0**	**0**	**0**	**0**	**0**	**0.0**	**–1**	....	....	....	....	....	....	....	....	....	....	....	....
	Cornwall Aces	AHL	64	4	10	14	49	....	....	....	....	....	....	....	....	....	13	0	2	2	10	....	....	....	....
1994-95	Cornwall Aces	AHL	76	4	18	22	69	....	....	....	....	....	....	....	....	....	....	....	....	....	....	....	....	....	....
	Quebec	**NHL**	**9**	**0**	**3**	**3**	**6**	**0**	**0**	**0**	**12**	**0.0**	**2**	....	....	....	....	....	....	....	....	....	....	....	....
1995-96	**Colorado**	**NHL**	**5**	**0**	**0**	**0**	**0**	**0**	**0**	**0**	**2**	**0.0**	**0**	....	....	....	....	....	....	....	....	....	....	....	....
	Cornwall Aces	AHL	62	4	23	27	77	....	....	....	....	....	....	....	....	....	8	0	1	1	6	....	....	....	....
1996-97	**Colorado**	**NHL**	**56**	**5**	**12**	**17**	**15**	**0**	**0**	**3**	**47**	**10.6**	**15**	....	....	....	**17**	**1**	**2**	**3**	**10**	**0**	**0**	**0**	....
1997-98	**Colorado**	**NHL**	**55**	**2**	**2**	**4**	**51**	**0**	**0**	**0**	**29**	**6.9**	**0**	....	....	....	**7**	**0**	**0**	**0**	**8**	**0**	**0**	**0**	....
1998-99	**Colorado**	**NHL**	**76**	**5**	**13**	**18**	**42**	**1**	**0**	**2**	**87**	**5.7**	**3**	**0**	**0.0**	**21:49**	**19**	**1**	**5**	**6**	**10**	**0**	**0**	**0**	**21:13**
99-2000	**Colorado**	**NHL**	**53**	**1**	**7**	**8**	**36**	**0**	**0**	**0**	**44**	**2.3**	**3**	**0**	**0.0**	**19:05**	**17**	**1**	**1**	**2**	**6**	**0**	**0**	**0**	**19:12**
2000-01	**Colorado**	**NHL**	**56**	**4**	**9**	**13**	**29**	**0**	**0**	**0**	**49**	**8.2**	**19**	**0**	**0.0**	**18:25**	....	....	....	....	....	....	....	....	....
	Los Angeles	**NHL**	**13**	**0**	**5**	**5**	**14**	**0**	**0**	**0**	**10**	**0.0**	**3**	**1**	**0.0**	**22:44**	**13**	**0**	**1**	**1**	**6**	**0**	**0**	**0**	**22:02**
2001-02	**Los Angeles**	**NHL**	**74**	**5**	**12**	**17**	**54**	**0**	**1**	**3**	**75**	**6.7**	**14**	**0**	**0.0**	**22:21**	**7**	**0**	**0**	**0**	**0**	**0**	**0**	**0**	**26:28**
	United States	Olympics	6	0	0	0	4	....	....	....	....	....	....	....	....	....	....	....	....	....	....	....	....	....	....
2002-03	**Los Angeles**	**NHL**	**49**	**1**	**5**	**6**	**24**	**0**	**0**	**0**	**34**	**2.9**	**–7**	**1**	**100.0**	**21:30**	....	....	....	....	....	....	....	....	....
2003-04	**Los Angeles**	**NHL**	**35**	**1**	**2**	**3**	**32**	**0**	**0**	**0**	**26**	**3.8**	**–3**	**0**	**0.0**	**19:00**	....	....	....	....	....	....	....	....	....
2004-05			DID NOT PLAY																						
2005-06	**Los Angeles**	**NHL**	**56**	**0**	**8**	**8**	**27**	**0**	**0**	**0**	**32**	**0.0**	**–6**	**1**	**100.0**	**18:26**	....	....	....	....	....	....	....	....	....
2006-07	**Los Angeles**	**NHL**	**82**	**0**	**8**	**8**	**60**	**0**	**0**	**0**	**56**	**0.0**	**–14**	**1**	**0.0**	**19:36**	....	....	....	....	....	....	....	....	....
	NHL Totals		**620**	**24**	**86**	**110**	**390**	**1**	**1**	**8**	**503**	**4.8**		**4**	**50.0**	**20:16**	**80**	**3**	**9**	**12**	**40**	**0**	**0**	**0**	**21:27**

ECAC First All-Star Team (1993) • NCAA East Second All-American Team (1993)

Traded to **Quebec** by **NY Rangers** with NY Rangers' 5th round choice (Bill Lindsay) in 1991 Entry Draft for Joe Cirella, January 17, 1991. Transferred to **Colorado** after **Quebec** franchise relocated, June 21, 1995. Traded to **Los Angeles** by **Colorado** with Adam Deadmarsh, a player to be named later (Jared Aulin, March 22, 2001) and Colorado's 1st round choices in 2001 (Dave Steckel) and 2003 (Brian Boyle) Entry Drafts for Rob Blake and Steve Reinprecht, February 21, 2001. • Missed majority of 2003-04 season recovering from cervical injury suffered in game vs. Atlanta, December 10, 2003. Signed as a free agent by **Vancouver**, July 9, 2007.

MILLER, Drew

(MIHL-luhr, DROO) **ANA.**

Left wing. Shoots left. 6'2", 174 lbs. Born, Dover, NJ, February 17, 1984. Anaheim's 6th choice, 186th overall, in 2003 Entry Draft.

Season	Club	League	GP	G	A	Pts	PIM	PP	SH	GW	S	%	+/-	TF	F%	Min	GP	G	A	Pts	PIM	PP	SH	GW	Min
2000-01	Capital Centre	NAHL	37	4	3	7	22	....	....	....	....	....	....	....	....	....	....	....	....	....	....	....	....	....	....
2001-02	Capital Centre	NAHL	54	18	16	34	56	....	....	....	....	....	....	....	....	....	....	....	....	....	....	....	....	....	....
2002-03	Capital Centre	NAHL	11	10	9	19	....	....	....	....	....	....	....	....	....	....	....	....	....	....	....	....	....	....	....
	River City Lancers	USHL	49	14	11	25	22	....	....	....	....	....	....	....	....	....	11	5	4	9	6	....	....	....	....
2003-04	Michigan State	CCHA	41	4	6	10	39	....	....	....	....	....	....	....	....	....	....	....	....	....	....	....	....	....	....
2004-05	Michigan State	CCHA	40	17	16	33	20	....	....	....	....	....	....	....	....	....	....	....	....	....	....	....	....	....	....
2005-06	Michigan State	CCHA	44	18	25	43	30	....	....	....	....	....	....	....	....	....	....	....	....	....	....	....	....	....	....
2006-07	Portland Pirates	AHL	79	16	20	36	51	....	....	....	....	....	....	....	....	....	....	....	....	....	....	....	....	....	....
	♦ Anaheim	**NHL**	....	....	....	....	....	....	....	....	....	....	....	....	....	....	**3**	**0**	**0**	**0**	**2**	**0**	**0**	**0**	**7:00**
	NHL Totals		....	....	....	....	....	....	....	....	....	....	....	....	....	....	**3**	**0**	**0**	**0**	**2**	**0**	**0**	**0**	**7:00**

MILLEY, Norm

(MIHL-lee, NOHR-man) **T.B.**

Right wing. Shoots right. 6', 211 lbs. Born, Toronto, Ont., February 14, 1980. Buffalo's 3rd choice, 47th overall, in 1998 Entry Draft.

Season	Club	League	GP	G	A	Pts	PIM	PP	SH	GW	S	%	+/-	TF	F%	Min	GP	G	A	Pts	PIM	PP	SH	GW	Min
1995-96	Tor. Red Wings	MTHL	42	42	36	78	....	....	....	....	....	....	....	....	....	....	....	....	....	....	....	....	....	....	....
	St. Mike's B's	OPJHL	5	2	1	3	0	....	....	....	....	....	....	....	....	....	....	....	....	....	....	....	....	....	....
1996-97	Sudbury Wolves	OHL	61	30	32	62	15	....	....	....	....	....	....	....	....	....	....	....	....	....	....	....	....	....	....
1997-98	Sudbury Wolves	OHL	62	33	41	74	48	....	....	....	....	....	....	....	....	....	10	0	1	1	4	....	....	....	....
1998-99	Sudbury Wolves	OHL	68	52	68	120	47	....	....	....	....	....	....	....	....	....	4	2	3	5	4	....	....	....	....
99-2000	Sudbury Wolves	OHL	68	*52	60	112	47	....	....	....	....	....	....	....	....	....	12	8	11	19	6	....	....	....	....
2000-01	Rochester	AHL	77	20	27	47	56	....	....	....	....	....	....	....	....	....	4	0	0	0	2	....	....	....	....
2001-02	**Buffalo**	**NHL**	**5**	**0**	**1**	**1**	**0**	**0**	**0**	**0**	**10**	**0.0**	**0**	**1**	**0.0**	**13:12**	....	....	....	....	....	....	....	....	....
	Rochester	AHL	74	20	18	38	20	....	....	....	....	....	....	....	....	....	2	0	3	3	6	....	....	....	....
2002-03	Rochester	AHL	67	16	32	48	39	....	....	....	....	....	....	....	....	....	3	2	0	2	2	....	....	....	....
	Buffalo	**NHL**	**8**	**0**	**2**	**2**	**6**	**0**	**0**	**0**	**8**	**0.0**	**–2**	**2**	**50.0**	**10:41**	....	....	....	....	....	....	....	....	....
2003-04	**Buffalo**	**NHL**	**2**	**0**	**0**	**0**	**2**	**0**	**0**	**0**	**2**	**0.0**	**0**	**0**	**0.0**	**8:20**	....	....	....	....	....	....	....	....	....
	Rochester	AHL	77	18	19	37	60	....	....	....	....	....	....	....	....	....	16	7	6	13	10	....	....	....	....
2004-05	Rochester	AHL	72	12	21	33	46	....	....	....	....	....	....	....	....	....	9	1	2	3	4	....	....	....	....
2005-06	**Tampa Bay**	**NHL**	**14**	**2**	**1**	**3**	**4**	**1**	**0**	**0**	**12**	**16.7**	**–2**	**0**	**0.0**	**7:09**	....	....	....	....	....	....	....	....	....
	Springfield	AHL	53	19	29	48	34	....	....	....	....	....	....	....	....	....	....	....	....	....	....	....	....	....	....
2006-07	Springfield	AHL	73	26	34	60	46	....	....	....	....	....	....	....	....	....	....	....	....	....	....	....	....	....	....
	NHL Totals		**29**	**2**	**4**	**6**	**12**	**1**	**0**	**0**	**32**	**6.3**		**3**	**33.3**	**9:15**	....	....	....	....	....	....	....	....	....

OHL All-Rookie Team (1997) • OHL Second All-Star Team (1999) • OHL First All-Star Team (2000) • Canadian Major Junior First All-Star Team (2000)

Signed as a free agent by **Tampa Bay**, August 18, 2005.

MILROY, Duncan

(MIHL-roi, DUHN-kuhn) **MTL.**

Right wing. Shoots right. 6', 195 lbs. Born, Edmonton, Alta., February 8, 1983. Montreal's 3rd choice, 37th overall, in 2001 Entry Draft.

Season	Club	League	GP	G	A	Pts	PIM	PP	SH	GW	S	%	+/-	TF	F%	Min	GP	G	A	Pts	PIM	PP	SH	GW	Min
1998-99	Edm. Maple Leafs	AMHL	34	34	36	70	73	....	....	....	....	....	....	....	....	....	....	....	....	....	....	....	....	....	....
	Swift Current	WHL	3	0	0	0	0	....	....	....	....	....	....	....	....	....	....	....	....	....	....	....	....	....	....
99-2000	Swift Current	WHL	68	15	15	30	20	....	....	....	....	....	....	....	....	....	12	3	5	8	12	....	....	....	....
2000-01	Swift Current	WHL	68	38	54	92	51	....	....	....	....	....	....	....	....	....	19	9	12	21	6	....	....	....	....
2001-02	Swift Current	WHL	26	20	11	31	20	....	....	....	....	....	....	....	....	....	....	....	....	....	....	....	....	....	....
	Kootenay Ice	WHL	38	25	31	56	24	....	....	....	....	....	....	....	....	....	22	*17	*20	*37	26	....	....	....	....
2002-03	Kootenay Ice	WHL	61	34	44	78	40	....	....	....	....	....	....	....	....	....	11	5	3	8	8	....	....	....	....

			Regular Season														Playoffs								
Season	Club	League	GP	G	A	Pts	PIM	PP	SH	GW	S	%	+/-	TF	F%	Min	GP	G	A	Pts	PIM	PP	SH	GW	Min
2003-04	Hamilton	AHL	50	4	10	14	14	....	....	....	....	....	....	....	....	....	10	3	1	4	4	....	....	....	....
2004-05	Hamilton	AHL	76	15	18	33	18	....	....	....	....	....	....	....	....	....	3	0	0	0	2	....	....	....	....
2005-06	Hamilton	AHL	77	16	19	35	63	....	....	....	....	....	....	....	....	....	....	....	....	....	....	....	....	....	....
2006-07	**Montreal**	**NHL**	**5**	**0**	**1**	**1**	**0**	**0**	**0**	**0**	**6**	**0.0**	**–2**	**1**	**0.0**	**12:56**	....	....	....	....	....	....	....	....	....
	Hamilton	AHL	64	25	33	58	24	....	....	....	....	....	....	....	....	....	22	2	11	13	10	....	....	....	....
	NHL Totals		**5**	**0**	**1**	**1**	**0**	**0**	**0**	**0**	**6**	**0.0**		**1**	**0.0**	**12:56**	....	....	....	....	....	....	....	....	....

Yanick Dupre Memorial Award (Outstanding Humanitarian Contribution - AHL) (2005)

MINK, Graham
(MIHNK, GRAY-uhm) **S.J.**

Center. Shoots right. 6'3", 220 lbs. Born, Stowe, VT, May 21, 1979.

Season	Club	League	GP	G	A	Pts	PIM	PP	SH	GW	S	%	+/-	TF	F%	Min	GP	G	A	Pts	PIM	PP	SH	GW	Min
1997-98	NMH School	High-MA	25	17	25	42		....	....	....	....	....	....	....	....	....	....	....	....	....	....	....	....	....	....
1998-99	U. of Vermont	ECAC	27	4	2	6	34	....	....	....	....	....	....	....	....	....	....	....	....	....	....	....	....	....	....
99-2000	U. of Vermont	ECAC	17	7	4	11	14	....	....	....	....	....	....	....	....	....	....	....	....	....	....	....	....	....	....
2000-01	U. of Vermont	ECAC	32	17	12	29	52	....	....	....	....	....	....	....	....	....	....	....	....	....	....	....	....	....	....
2001-02	Richmond	ECHL	29	8	9	17	78	....	....	....	....	....	....	....	....	....	....	....	....	....	....	....	....	....	....
	Portland Pirates	AHL	56	17	17	34	50	....	....	....	....	....	....	....	....	....	....	....	....	....	....	....	....	....	....
2002-03	Portland Pirates	AHL	71	22	15	37	115	....	....	....	....	....	....	....	....	....	....	....	....	....	....	....	....	....	....
2003-04	**Washington**	**NHL**	**2**	**0**	**0**	**0**	**2**	**0**	**0**	**0**	**0**	**0.0**	**–1**	**1**	**0.0**	**5:32**	....	....	....	....	....	....	....	....	....
	Portland Pirates	AHL	68	18	19	37	74	....	....	....	....	....	....	....	....	....	3	0	1	1	4	....	....	....	....
2004-05	Portland Pirates	AHL	63	18	21	39	86	....	....	....	....	....	....	....	....	....	....	....	....	....	....	....	....	....	....
2005-06	**Washington**	**NHL**	**3**	**0**	**0**	**0**	**0**	**0**	**0**	**0**	**1**	**0.0**	**0**	**0**	**0.0**	**5:32**	....	....	....	....	....	....	....	....	....
	Hershey Bears	AHL	43	21	19	40	50	....	....	....	....	....	....	....	....	....	21	8	13	21	29	....	....	....	....
2006-07	Worcester Sharks	AHL	61	31	32	63	52	....	....	....	....	....	....	....	....	....	6	1	5	6	8	....	....	....	....
	NHL Totals		**5**	**0**	**0**	**0**	**2**	**0**	**0**	**0**	**1**	**0.0**		**1**	**0.0**	**5:32**	....	....	....	....	....	....	....	....	....

Signed as a free agent by **Portland** (AHL), September 30, 2001. Signed as a free agent by **Washington**, April 9, 2002. Signed as a free agent by **San Jose**, July 14, 2006.

MITCHELL, Willie
(MIH-chuhl, WIHL-lee) **VAN.**

Defense. Shoots left. 6'3", 205 lbs. Born, Port McNeill, B.C., April 23, 1977. New Jersey's 12th choice, 199th overall, in 1996 Entry Draft.

Season	Club	League	GP	G	A	Pts	PIM	PP	SH	GW	S	%	+/-	TF	F%	Min	GP	G	A	Pts	PIM	PP	SH	GW	Min
1993-94	Notre Dame	SMHL	31	4	11	15	81	....	....	....	....	....	....	....	....	....	....	....	....	....	....	....	....	....	....
1994-95	Kelowna Spartans	BCHL	42	3	8	11	71	....	....	....	....	....	....	....	....	....	....	....	....	....	....	....	....	....	....
1995-96	Melfort Mustangs	SJHL	19	2	6	8	....	....	....	....	....	....	....	....	....	....	14	0	2	2	12	....	....	....	....
1996-97	Melfort Mustangs	SJHL	64	14	42	56	227	....	....	....	....	....	....	....	....	....	4	0	1	1	23	....	....	....	....
1997-98	Clarkson Knights	ECAC	34	9	17	26	105	....	....	....	....	....	....	....	....	....	....	....	....	....	....	....	....	....	....
1998-99	Clarkson Knights	ECAC	34	10	19	29	40	....	....	....	....	....	....	....	....	....	....	....	....	....	....	....	....	....	....
	Albany River Rats	AHL	6	1	3	4	29	....	....	....	....	....	....	....	....	....	....	....	....	....	....	....	....	....	....
99-2000	**New Jersey**	**NHL**	**2**	**0**	**0**	**0**	**0**	**0**	**0**	**0**	**2**	**0.0**	**1**	**0**	**0.0**	**16:04**	....	....	....	....	....	....	....	....	....
	Albany River Rats	AHL	63	5	14	19	71	....	....	....	....	....	....	....	....	....	5	1	2	3	4	....	....	....	....
2000-01	**New Jersey**	**NHL**	**16**	**0**	**2**	**2**	**29**	**0**	**0**	**0**	**14**	**0.0**	**0**	**0**	**0.0**	**14:52**	....	....	....	....	....	....	....	....	....
	Albany River Rats	AHL	41	3	13	16	94	....	....	....	....	....	....	....	....	....	....	....	....	....	....	....	....	....	....
	Minnesota	**NHL**	**17**	**1**	**7**	**8**	**11**	**0**	**0**	**0**	**16**	**6.3**	**4**	**0**	**0.0**	**20:49**	....	....	....	....	....	....	....	....	....
2001-02	**Minnesota**	**NHL**	**68**	**3**	**10**	**13**	**68**	**0**	**0**	**1**	**67**	**4.5**	**–16**	**0**	**0.0**	**21:25**	....	....	....	....	....	....	....	....	....
2002-03	**Minnesota**	**NHL**	**69**	**2**	**12**	**14**	**84**	**0**	**1**	**1**	**67**	**3.0**	**13**	**0**	**0.0**	**21:28**	**18**	**1**	**3**	**4**	**14**	**0**	**0**	**0**	**24:48**
2003-04	**Minnesota**	**NHL**	**70**	**1**	**13**	**14**	**83**	**0**	**0**	**0**	**58**	**1.7**	**12**	**2**	**50.0**	**22:36**	....	....	....	....	....	....	....	....	....
2004-05		DID NOT PLAY																							
2005-06	**Minnesota**	**NHL**	**64**	**2**	**6**	**8**	**87**	**0**	**0**	**0**	**48**	**4.2**	**15**	**0**	**0.0**	**20:52**	....	....	....	....	....	....	....	....	....
	Dallas	**NHL**	**16**	**0**	**2**	**2**	**26**	**0**	**0**	**0**	**10**	**0.0**	**4**	**0**	**0.0**	**20:46**	**5**	**0**	**0**	**0**	**2**	**0**	**0**	**0**	**23:21**
2006-07	**Vancouver**	**NHL**	**62**	**1**	**10**	**11**	**45**	**0**	**0**	**0**	**54**	**1.9**	**1**	**0**	**0.0**	**22:13**	**12**	**0**	**1**	**1**	**12**	**0**	**0**	**0**	**27:14**
	NHL Totals		**384**	**10**	**62**	**72**	**433**	**0**	**1**	**2**	**336**	**3.0**		**2**	**50.0**	**21:19**	**35**	**1**	**4**	**5**	**28**	**0**	**0**	**0**	**25:26**

SJHL First All-Star Team (1997) • SJHL Top Defenseman Award (1997) • ECAC Second All-Star Team (1998) • ECAC Rookie of the Year (1998) (co-winner - Erik Cole) • ECAC First All-Star Team (1999) • NCAA East Second All-American Team (1999)

Traded to **Minnesota** by **New Jersey** for Sean O'Donnell, March 4, 2001. Traded to **Dallas** by **Minnesota** with Minnesota's 2nd round choice (Nico Saccheti) in 2007 Entry Draft for Martin Skoula and Shawn Belle, March 9, 2006. Signed as a free agent by **Vancouver**, July 1, 2006.

MODANO, Mike
(moh-DA-noh, MIGHK) **DAL.**

Center. Shoots left. 6'3", 205 lbs. Born, Livonia, MI, June 7, 1970. Minnesota's 1st choice, 1st overall, in 1988 Entry Draft.

Season	Club	League	GP	G	A	Pts	PIM	PP	SH	GW	S	%	+/-	TF	F%	Min	GP	G	A	Pts	PIM	PP	SH	GW	Min
1985-86	Det. Compuware	MNHL	69	66	65	131	32	....	....	....	....	....	....	....	....	....	....	....	....	....	....	....	....	....	....
1986-87	Prince Albert	WHL	70	32	30	62	96	....	....	....	....	....	....	....	....	....	8	1	4	5	4	....	....	....	....
1987-88	Prince Albert	WHL	65	47	80	127	80	....	....	....	....	....	....	....	....	....	9	7	11	18	18	....	....	....	....
1988-89	Prince Albert	WHL	41	39	66	105	74	....	....	....	....	....	....	....	....	....	....	....	....	....	....	....	....	....	....
	Minnesota	**NHL**	....	....	....	....	....	....	....	....	....	....	....	....	....	....	**2**	**0**	**0**	**0**	**0**	**0**	**0**	**0**	....
1989-90	**Minnesota**	**NHL**	**80**	**29**	**46**	**75**	**63**	**12**	**0**	**2**	**172**	**16.9**	**–7**	....	....	....	**7**	**1**	**1**	**2**	**12**	**0**	**0**	**0**	....
1990-91	**Minnesota**	**NHL**	**79**	**28**	**36**	**64**	**65**	**9**	**0**	**2**	**232**	**12.1**	**2**	....	....	....	**23**	**8**	**12**	**20**	**16**	**3**	**0**	**1**	....
1991-92	**Minnesota**	**NHL**	**76**	**33**	**44**	**77**	**46**	**5**	**0**	**8**	**256**	**12.9**	**–9**	....	....	....	**7**	**3**	**2**	**5**	**4**	**1**	**0**	**0**	....
1992-93	**Minnesota**	**NHL**	**82**	**33**	**60**	**93**	**83**	**9**	**0**	**7**	**307**	**10.7**	**–7**	....	....	....	....	....	....	....	....	....	....	....	....
1993-94	**Dallas**	**NHL**	**76**	**50**	**43**	**93**	**54**	**18**	**0**	**4**	**281**	**17.8**	**–8**	....	....	....	**9**	**7**	**3**	**10**	**16**	**2**	**0**	**2**	....
1994-95	**Dallas**	**NHL**	**30**	**12**	**17**	**29**	**8**	**4**	**1**	**0**	**100**	**12.0**	**7**	....	....	....	....	....	....	....	....	....	....	....	....
1995-96	**Dallas**	**NHL**	**78**	**36**	**45**	**81**	**63**	**8**	**4**	**4**	**320**	**11.3**	**–12**	....	....	....	....	....	....	....	....	....	....	....	....
1996-97	**Dallas**	**NHL**	**80**	**35**	**48**	**83**	**42**	**9**	**5**	**9**	**291**	**12.0**	**43**	....	....	....	**7**	**4**	**1**	**5**	**0**	**1**	**1**	**2**	....
1997-98	**Dallas**	**NHL**	**52**	**21**	**38**	**59**	**32**	**7**	**5**	**2**	**191**	**11.0**	**25**	....	....	....	**17**	**4**	**10**	**14**	**12**	**1**	**0**	**1**	....
	United States	Olympics	4	2	0	2	0	....	....	....	....	....	....	....	....	....	....	....	....	....	....	....	....	....	....
1998-99 ♦	**Dallas**	**NHL**	**77**	**34**	**47**	**81**	**44**	**6**	**4**	**7**	**224**	**15.2**	**29**	**1572**	**51.1**	**20:50**	**23**	**5**	***18**	**23**	**16**	**1**	**1**	**1**	**24:40**
99-2000	**Dallas**	**NHL**	**77**	**38**	**43**	**81**	**48**	**11**	**1**	**8**	**188**	**20.2**	**0**	**1763**	**51.4**	**22:55**	**23**	**10**	***13**	**23**	**10**	**4**	**0**	**2**	**25:26**
2000-01	**Dallas**	**NHL**	**81**	**33**	**51**	**84**	**52**	**8**	**3**	**7**	**208**	**15.9**	**26**	**1791**	**52.0**	**22:24**	**9**	**3**	**4**	**7**	**0**	**2**	**0**	**0**	**25:43**
2001-02	**Dallas**	**NHL**	**78**	**34**	**43**	**77**	**38**	**6**	**2**	**5**	**219**	**15.5**	**14**	**1710**	**53.7**	**22:27**	....	....	....	....	....	....	....	....	....
	United States	Olympics	6	0	*6	6	4	....	....	....	....	....	....	....	....	....	....	....	....	....	....	....	....	....	....
2002-03	**Dallas**	**NHL**	**79**	**28**	**57**	**85**	**30**	**5**	**2**	**6**	**193**	**14.5**	**34**	**1808**	**51.4**	**20:53**	**12**	**5**	**10**	**15**	**4**	**1**	**0**	**2**	**23:53**
2003-04	**Dallas**	**NHL**	**76**	**14**	**30**	**44**	**46**	**6**	**0**	**0**	**152**	**9.2**	**–21**	**1523**	**52.6**	**20:27**	**5**	**1**	**2**	**3**	**8**	**1**	**0**	**0**	**23:17**
2004-05		DID NOT PLAY																							
2005-06	**Dallas**	**NHL**	**78**	**27**	**50**	**77**	**58**	**12**	**1**	**4**	**207**	**13.0**	**23**	**1421**	**51.1**	**19:34**	**5**	**1**	**3**	**4**	**4**	**1**	**0**	**0**	**22:14**
	United States	Olympics	6	2	0	2	6	....	....	....	....	....	....	....	....	....	....	....	....	....	....	....	....	....	....
2006-07	**Dallas**	**NHL**	**59**	**22**	**21**	**43**	**34**	**9**	**0**	**7**	**141**	**15.6**	**9**	**918**	**52.2**	**18:24**	**7**	**1**	**1**	**2**	**4**	**1**	**0**	**1**	**26:14**
	NHL Totals		**1238**	**507**	**719**	**1226**	**806**	**144**	**28**	**82**	**3682**	**13.8**		**12506**	**51.9**	**21:05**	**156**	**53**	**80**	**133**	**106**	**19**	**2**	**12**	**24:47**

WHL East First All-Star Team (1989) • NHL All-Rookie Team (1990) • NHL Second All-Star Team (2000)

Played in NHL All-Star Game (1993, 1998, 1999, 2000, 2003, 2004)

Transferred to **Dallas** after **Minnesota** franchise relocated, June 9, 1993.

MODIN, Fredrik
(moh-DEEN, FREHD-rihk) **CBJ**

Left wing. Shoots left. 6'4", 220 lbs. Born, Sundsvall, Sweden, October 8, 1974. Toronto's 3rd choice, 64th overall, in 1994 Entry Draft.

Season	Club	League	GP	G	A	Pts	PIM	PP	SH	GW	S	%	+/-	TF	F%	Min	GP	G	A	Pts	PIM	PP	SH	GW	Min
1991-92	Sundsvall/Timra	Sweden-2	11	1	0	1	0	....	....	....	....	....	....	....	....	....	....	....	....	....	....	....	....	....	....
1992-93	Sundsvall/Timra	Sweden-2	30	5	7	12	12	....	....	....	....	....	....	....	....	....	5	1	0	1	0	....	....	....	....
1993-94	Sundsvall/Timra	Sweden-2	30	16	15	31	36	....	....	....	....	....	....	....	....	....	2	0	1	1	6	....	....	....	....
1994-95	Brynas IF Gavle	Sweden	38	9	10	19	33	....	....	....	....	....	....	....	....	....	14	4	4	8	6	....	....	....	....
1995-96	Brynas IF Gavle	Sweden	22	4	8	12	22	....	....	....	....	....	....	....	....	....	....	....	....	....	....	....	....	....	....
1996-97	**Toronto**	**NHL**	**76**	**6**	**7**	**13**	**24**	**0**	**0**	**0**	**85**	**7.1**	**–14**	....	....	....	....	....	....	....	....	....	....	....	....
1997-98	**Toronto**	**NHL**	**74**	**16**	**16**	**32**	**32**	**1**	**0**	**4**	**137**	**11.7**	**–5**	....	....	....	....	....	....	....	....	....	....	....	....
1998-99	**Toronto**	**NHL**	**67**	**16**	**15**	**31**	**35**	**1**	**0**	**3**	**108**	**14.8**	**14**	**2**	**50.0**	**13:34**	**8**	**0**	**0**	**0**	**6**	**0**	**0**	**0**	**9:50**
99-2000	**Tampa Bay**	**NHL**	**80**	**22**	**26**	**48**	**18**	**3**	**0**	**5**	**167**	**13.2**	**–26**	**6**	**50.0**	**15:32**	....	....	....	....	....	....	....	....	....
2000-01	**Tampa Bay**	**NHL**	**76**	**32**	**24**	**56**	**48**	**8**	**0**	**4**	**217**	**14.7**	**–1**	**21**	**42.9**	**17:15**	....	....	....	....	....	....	....	....	....
2001-02	**Tampa Bay**	**NHL**	**54**	**14**	**17**	**31**	**27**	**2**	**0**	**4**	**141**	**9.9**	**0**	**25**	**40.0**	**19:05**	....	....	....	....	....	....	....	....	....
2002-03	**Tampa Bay**	**NHL**	**76**	**17**	**23**	**40**	**43**	**2**	**1**	**4**	**179**	**9.5**	**7**	**35**	**28.6**	**17:35**	**11**	**2**	**0**	**2**	**18**	**0**	**0**	**0**	**19:18**
2003-04 ♦	**Tampa Bay**	**NHL**	**82**	**29**	**28**	**57**	**32**	**5**	**1**	**2**	**206**	**14.1**	**31**	**138**	**38.4**	**18:12**	**23**	**8**	**11**	**19**	**10**	**3**	**0**	**2**	**20:47**
2004-05	Timra IK	Sweden	43	12	24	36	58	....	....	....	....	....	....	....	....	....	7	1	1	2	8	....	....	....	....

Season	Club	League	GP	G	A	Pts	PIM	PP	SH	GW	S	%	+/-	TF	F%	Min	GP	G	A	Pts	PIM	PP	SH	GW	Min
			Regular Season														Playoffs								
2005-06	**Tampa Bay**	**NHL**	**77**	**31**	**23**	**54**	**56**	**12**	**1**	**4**	**221**	**14.0**	**5**	**171**	**51.5**	**19:35**	**5**	**0**	**0**	**0**	**6**	**0**	**0**	**0**	**18:46**
	Sweden	Olympics	8	2	1	3	6	....	....	....	....	....	....	....	....	....	....	....	....	....	....	....	....	....	....
2006-07	**Columbus**	**NHL**	**79**	**22**	**20**	**42**	**50**	**6**	**0**	**4**	**220**	**10.0**	**–3**	**508**	**46.5**	**19:07**	....	....	....	....	....	....	....	....	....
	NHL Totals		**741**	**205**	**199**	**404**	**365**	**40**	**3**	**34**	**1681**	**12.2**		**906**	**45.3**	**17:30**	**47**	**10**	**11**	**21**	**40**	**3**	**0**	**2**	**18:21**

Played in NHL All-Star Game (2001)

Traded to **Tampa Bay** by **Toronto** for Cory Cross and Tampa Bay's 7th round choice (Ivan Kolozvary) in 2001 Entry Draft, October 1, 1999. Signed as a free agent by **Timra** (Sweden), October 5, 2004. Traded to **Columbus** by **Tampa Bay** with Fredrik Norrena for Marc Denis, June 30, 2006.

MODRY, Jaroslav

(MOH-dree, YAHR-roh-slav) **L.A.**

Defense. Shoots left. 6'2", 220 lbs. Born, Ceske Budejovice, Czech., February 27, 1971. New Jersey's 11th choice, 179th overall, in 1990 Entry Draft.

Season	Club	League	GP	G	A	Pts	PIM	PP	SH	GW	S	%	+/-	TF	F%	Min	GP	G	A	Pts	PIM	PP	SH	GW	Min
1987-88	C. Budejovice	Czech	3	0	0	0	0	....	....	....	....	....	....	....	....	....	....	....	....	....	....	....	....	....	....
1988-89	C. Budejovice	Czech	28	0	1	1	8	....	....	....	....	....	....	....	....	....	....	....	....	....	....	....	....	....	....
1989-90	C. Budejovice	Czech	41	2	2	4	....	....	....	....	....	....	....	....	....	....	....	....	....	....	....	....	....	....	....
1990-91	Dukla Trencin	Czech	33	1	9	10	6	....	....	....	....	....	....	....	....	....	....	....	....	....	....	....	....	....	....
1991-92	C. Budejovice	Czech-2	14	4	10	14	....	....	....	....	....	....	....	....	....	....	....	....	....	....	....	....	....	....	....
	Dukla Trencin	Czech	18	0	4	4	6	....	....	....	....	....	....	....	....	....	....	....	....	....	....	....	....	....	....
1992-93	Utica Devils	AHL	80	7	35	42	62	....	....	....	....	....	....	....	....	....	5	0	2	2	2	....	....	....	....
1993-94	**New Jersey**	**NHL**	**41**	**2**	**15**	**17**	**18**	**2**	**0**	**0**	**35**	**5.7**	**10**	....	....	....	....	....	....	....	....	....	....	....	....
	Albany River Rats	AHL	19	1	5	6	25	....	....	....	....	....	....	....	....	....	....	....	....	....	....	....	....	....	....
1994-95	C. Budejovice	CzRep	19	1	3	4	30	....	....	....	....	....	....	....	....	....	....	....	....	....	....	....	....	....	....
	New Jersey	**NHL**	**11**	**0**	**0**	**0**	**0**	**0**	**0**	**0**	**10**	**0.0**	**–1**	....	....	....	....	....	....	....	....	....	....	....	....
	Albany River Rats	AHL	18	5	6	11	14	....	....	....	....	....	....	....	....	....	14	3	3	6	4	....	....	....	....
1995-96	**Ottawa**	**NHL**	**64**	**4**	**14**	**18**	**38**	**1**	**0**	**1**	**89**	**4.5**	**–17**	....	....	....	....	....	....	....	....	....	....	....	....
	Los Angeles	**NHL**	**9**	**0**	**3**	**3**	**6**	**0**	**0**	**0**	**17**	**0.0**	**–4**	....	....	....	....	....	....	....	....	....	....	....	....
1996-97	**Los Angeles**	**NHL**	**30**	**3**	**3**	**6**	**25**	**1**	**1**	**0**	**32**	**9.4**	**–13**	....	....	....	....	....	....	....	....	....	....	....	....
	Phoenix	IHL	23	3	12	15	17	....	....	....	....	....	....	....	....	....	....	....	....	....	....	....	....	....	....
	Utah Grizzlies	IHL	11	1	4	5	20	....	....	....	....	....	....	....	....	....	7	0	1	1	6	....	....	....	....
1997-98	Utah Grizzlies	IHL	74	12	21	33	72	....	....	....	....	....	....	....	....	....	4	0	2	2	6	....	....	....	....
1998-99	**Los Angeles**	**NHL**	**5**	**0**	**1**	**1**	**0**	**0**	**0**	**0**	**11**	**0.0**	**1**	**0**	**0.0**	**26:00**	....	....	....	....	....	....	....	....	....
	Long Beach	IHL	64	6	29	35	44	....	....	....	....	....	....	....	....	....	8	4	2	6	4	....	....	....	....
99-2000	**Los Angeles**	**NHL**	**26**	**5**	**4**	**9**	**18**	**5**	**0**	**1**	**32**	**15.6**	**–2**	**0**	**0.0**	**19:13**	**2**	**0**	**0**	**0**	**2**	**0**	**0**	**0**	**16:48**
	Long Beach	IHL	11	2	4	6	8	....	....	....	....	....	....	....	....	....	....	....	....	....	....	....	....	....	....
2000-01	**Los Angeles**	**NHL**	**63**	**4**	**15**	**19**	**48**	**0**	**0**	**0**	**72**	**5.6**	**16**	**0**	**0.0**	**18:22**	**10**	**1**	**0**	**1**	**4**	**1**	**0**	**1**	**16:08**
2001-02	**Los Angeles**	**NHL**	**80**	**4**	**38**	**42**	**65**	**4**	**0**	**0**	**119**	**3.4**	**–4**	**0**	**0.0**	**19:31**	**7**	**0**	**2**	**2**	**0**	**0**	**0**	**0**	**21:26**
2002-03	**Los Angeles**	**NHL**	**82**	**13**	**25**	**38**	**68**	**8**	**0**	**1**	**205**	**6.3**	**–13**	**1**	**0.0**	**22:39**	....	....	....	....	....	....	....	....	....
2003-04	**Los Angeles**	**NHL**	**79**	**5**	**27**	**32**	**44**	**1**	**0**	**1**	**196**	**2.6**	**11**	**1**	**0.0**	**24:24**	....	....	....	....	....	....	....	....	....
2004-05	Liberec	CzRep	19	3	7	10	24	....	....	....	....	....	....	....	....	....	12	0	4	4	22	....	....	....	....
2005-06	**Atlanta**	**NHL**	**79**	**7**	**31**	**38**	**76**	**5**	**0**	**2**	**143**	**4.9**	**–9**	**0**	**0.0**	**20:48**	....	....	....	....	....	....	....	....	....
2006-07	**Dallas**	**NHL**	**57**	**1**	**9**	**10**	**32**	**0**	**0**	**0**	**60**	**1.7**	**10**	**1**	**0.0**	**17:30**	....	....	....	....	....	....	....	....	....
	Los Angeles	**NHL**	**19**	**0**	**8**	**8**	**22**	**0**	**0**	**0**	**29**	**0.0**	**1**	**0**	**0.0**	**22:57**	....	....	....	....	....	....	....	....	....
	NHL Totals		**645**	**48**	**193**	**241**	**460**	**27**	**1**	**6**	**1050**	**4.6**		**3**	**0.0**	**20:50**	**19**	**1**	**2**	**3**	**6**	**1**	**0**	**1**	**18:09**

Played in NHL All-Star Game (2002)

Traded to **Ottawa** by **New Jersey** for Ottawa's 4th round choice (Alyn McCauley) in 1995 Entry Draft, July 8, 1995. Traded to **Los Angeles** by **Ottawa** with Ottawa's 8th round choice (Stephen Valiquette) in 1996 Entry Draft for Kevin Brown, March 20, 1996. Signed as a free agent by **Atlanta**, July 1, 2004. Signed as a free agent by **Liberec** (CzRep), October 20, 2004. Traded to **Dallas** by **Atlanta** with Patrik Stefan for Niko Kapanen and Dallas's 7th round choice (Will O'Neill) in 2006 Entry Draft, June 24, 2006. Traded to **Los Angeles** by **Dallas** with the rights to Johan Fransson, Dallas' 2nd (Oscar Moller) and 3rd (Bryan Cameron) round choices in 2007 Entry Draft and Dallas' 1st round choice in 2008 Entry Draft for Mattias Norstrom, Konstantin Pushkarev and Los Angeles' 3rd (Sergei Korostin) and 4th (later traded to Columbus - Columbus selected Maxim Mayorov) round choices in 2007 Entry Draft, February 27, 2007.

MOEN, Travis

(MOH-ehn, TRA-vihs) **ANA.**

Left wing. Shoots left. 6'2", 216 lbs. Born, Stewart Valley, Sask., April 6, 1982. Calgary's 6th choice, 155th overall, in 2000 Entry Draft.

Season	Club	League	GP	G	A	Pts	PIM	PP	SH	GW	S	%	+/-	TF	F%	Min	GP	G	A	Pts	PIM	PP	SH	GW	Min
1998-99	Swift Current	SMHL	STATISTICS NOT AVAILABLE																						
	Kelowna Rockets	WHL	4	0	0	0	0	....	....	....	....	....	....	....	....	....	....	....	....	....	....	....	....	....	....
99-2000	Kelowna Rockets	WHL	66	9	6	15	96	....	....	....	....	....	....	....	....	....	5	1	1	2	2	....	....	....	....
2000-01	Kelowna Rockets	WHL	40	8	8	16	106	....	....	....	....	....	....	....	....	....	....	....	....	....	....	....	....	....	....
2001-02	Kelowna Rockets	WHL	71	10	17	27	197	....	....	....	....	....	....	....	....	....	13	1	0	1	28	....	....	....	....
2002-03	Norfolk Admirals	AHL	42	1	2	3	62	....	....	....	....	....	....	....	....	....	9	0	0	0	20	....	....	....	....
2003-04	**Chicago**	**NHL**	**82**	**4**	**2**	**6**	**142**	**0**	**0**	**2**	**51**	**7.8**	**–17**	**19**	**15.8**	**10:57**	....	....	....	....	....	....	....	....	....
2004-05	Norfolk Admirals	AHL	79	8	12	20	187	....	....	....	....	....	....	....	....	....	6	0	1	1	6	....	....	....	....
2005-06	**Anaheim**	**NHL**	**39**	**4**	**1**	**5**	**72**	**0**	**0**	**0**	**28**	**14.3**	**–3**	**8**	**12.5**	**11:03**	**9**	**1**	**0**	**1**	**10**	**0**	**0**	**0**	**8:25**
2006-07 ♦	**Anaheim**	**NHL**	**82**	**11**	**10**	**21**	**101**	**0**	**0**	**0**	**124**	**8.9**	**–4**	**10**	**30.0**	**14:48**	**21**	**7**	**5**	**12**	**22**	**0**	**0**	**3**	**17:19**
	NHL Totals		**203**	**19**	**13**	**32**	**315**	**0**	**0**	**2**	**203**	**9.4**		**37**	**18.9**	**12:32**	**30**	**8**	**5**	**13**	**32**	**0**	**0**	**3**	**14:39**

Signed as a free agent by **Chicago**, October 21, 2002. Traded to **Anaheim** by **Chicago** for Michael Holmqvist, July 30, 2005. • Missed majority of the 2005-06 season recovering from knee and shoulder injuries and as a healthy reserve.

MOJZIS, Tomas

(MOI-shihsh, TAW-mash)

Defense. Shoots left. 6'1", 192 lbs. Born, Kolin, Czech., May 2, 1982. Toronto's 11th choice, 246th overall, in 2001 Entry Draft.

Season	Club	League	GP	G	A	Pts	PIM	PP	SH	GW	S	%	+/-	TF	F%	Min	GP	G	A	Pts	PIM	PP	SH	GW	Min
99-2000	HC Pardubice Jr.	CzRep-Jr.	40	7	1	8	....	....	....	....	....	....	....	....	....	....	....	....	....	....	....	....	....	....	....
2000-01	Moose Jaw	WHL	72	11	25	36	115	....	....	....	....	....	....	....	....	....	4	0	1	1	8	....	....	....	....
2001-02	Moose Jaw	WHL	28	2	11	13	43	....	....	....	....	....	....	....	....	....	....	....	....	....	....	....	....	....	....
	Seattle	WHL	36	8	15	23	66	....	....	....	....	....	....	....	....	....	11	1	3	4	20	....	....	....	....
2002-03	Seattle	WHL	62	21	49	70	126	....	....	....	....	....	....	....	....	....	15	1	6	7	36	....	....	....	....
2003-04	Manitoba Moose	AHL	63	5	13	18	50	....	....	....	....	....	....	....	....	....	....	....	....	....	....	....	....	....	....
2004-05	Manitoba Moose	AHL	80	7	23	30	62	....	....	....	....	....	....	....	....	....	14	0	2	2	28	....	....	....	....
2005-06	**Vancouver**	**NHL**	**7**	**0**	**1**	**1**	**12**	**0**	**0**	**0**	**7**	**0.0**	**2**	**0**	**0.0**	**13:57**	....	....	....	....	....	....	....	....	....
	Manitoba Moose	AHL	37	5	13	18	52	....	....	....	....	....	....	....	....	....	....	....	....	....	....	....	....	....	....
	Peoria Rivermen	AHL	12	3	4	7	14	....	....	....	....	....	....	....	....	....	1	0	0	0	0	....	....	....	....
2006-07	**St. Louis**	**NHL**	**6**	**1**	**0**	**1**	**0**	**0**	**0**	**0**	**7**	**14.3**	**0**	**0**	**0.0**	**10:03**	....	....	....	....	....	....	....	....	....
	Peoria Rivermen	AHL	69	2	24	26	112	....	....	....	....	....	....	....	....	....	....	....	....	....	....	....	....	....	....
	NHL Totals		**13**	**1**	**1**	**2**	**12**	**0**	**0**	**0**	**14**	**7.1**		**0**	**0.0**	**12:09**	....	....	....	....	....	....	....	....	....

WHL West First All-Star Team (2003) • Canadian Major Junior First All-Star Team (2003)

Traded to **Vancouver** by **Toronto** for Brad Leeb, September 4, 2002. Traded to **St. Louis** by **Vancouver** with Vancouver's 3rd round choice (later traded to New Jersey - New Jersey selected Vladimir Zharkov) in 2006 Entry Draft for Eric Weinrich, March 9, 2006. Signed as a free agent by **Sibir** (Russia), May 21, 2007.

MONTADOR, Steve

(MAWN-tuh-dohr, STEEV) **FLA.**

Defense. Shoots right. 6', 205 lbs. Born, Vancouver, B.C., December 21, 1979.

Season	Club	League	GP	G	A	Pts	PIM	PP	SH	GW	S	%	+/-	TF	F%	Min	GP	G	A	Pts	PIM	PP	SH	GW	Min
1995-96	St. Mike's B's	OPJHL	46	3	16	19	145	....	....	....	....	....	....	....	....	....	7	1	2	3	10	....	....	....	....
1996-97	North Bay	OHL	63	7	28	35	129	....	....	....	....	....	....	....	....	....	....	....	....	....	....	....	....	....	....
1997-98	North Bay	OHL	37	5	16	21	54	....	....	....	....	....	....	....	....	....	....	....	....	....	....	....	....	....	....
	Erie Otters	OHL	26	3	17	20	35	....	....	....	....	....	....	....	....	....	7	1	1	2	9	....	....	....	....
1998-99	Erie Otters	OHL	61	9	33	42	114	....	....	....	....	....	....	....	....	....	5	0	2	2	4	....	....	....	....
99-2000	Peterborough	OHL	64	14	42	56	97	....	....	....	....	....	....	....	....	....	5	0	2	2	4	....	....	....	....
	Saint John Flames	AHL	....	....	....	....	....	....	....	....	....	....	....	....	....	....	2	0	0	0	0	....	....	....	....
2000-01	Saint John Flames	AHL	58	1	6	7	95	....	....	....	....	....	....	....	....	....	19	0	8	8	13	....	....	....	....
2001-02	**Calgary**	**NHL**	**11**	**1**	**2**	**3**	**26**	**0**	**0**	**0**	**10**	**10.0**	**–2**	**0**	**0.0**	**12:12**	....	....	....	....	....	....	....	....	....
	Saint John Flames	AHL	67	9	16	25	107	....	....	....	....	....	....	....	....	....	....	....	....	....	....	....	....	....	....
2002-03	**Calgary**	**NHL**	**50**	**1**	**1**	**2**	**114**	**0**	**0**	**0**	**64**	**1.6**	**–9**	**0**	**0.0**	**15:11**	....	....	....	....	....	....	....	....	....
	Saint John Flames	AHL	11	1	7	8	20	....	....	....	....	....	....	....	....	....	....	....	....	....	....	....	....	....	....
2003-04	**Calgary**	**NHL**	**26**	**1**	**2**	**3**	**50**	**0**	**0**	**1**	**31**	**3.2**	**–1**	**1**	**0.0**	**11:46**	**20**	**1**	**2**	**3**	**6**	**0**	**0**	**1**	**17:43**
2004-05	HC Mulhouse	France	15	1	7	8	69	....	....	....	....	....	....	....	....	....	....	....	....	....	....	....	....	....	....
2005-06	**Calgary**	**NHL**	**7**	**1**	**0**	**1**	**11**	**0**	**0**	**0**	**13**	**7.7**	**0**	**0**	**0.0**	**11:49**	....	....	....	....	....	....	....	....	....
	Florida	**NHL**	**51**	**1**	**5**	**6**	**68**	**0**	**0**	**0**	**42**	**2.4**	**4**	**0**	**0.0**	**14:04**	....	....	....	....	....	....	....	....	....
2006-07	**Florida**	**NHL**	**72**	**1**	**8**	**9**	**119**	**0**	**0**	**0**	**88**	**1.1**	**1**	**0**	**0.0**	**13:08**	....	....	....	....	....	....	....	....	....
	NHL Totals		**217**	**6**	**18**	**24**	**388**	**0**	**0**	**1**	**248**	**2.4**		**1**	**0.0**	**13:35**	**20**	**1**	**2**	**3**	**6**	**0**	**0**	**1**	**17:43**

Signed as a free agent by **Calgary**, April 10, 2000. • Spent majority of 2003-04 season as a healthy reserve. Signed as a free agent by **Mulhouse** (France), September 17, 2004. Traded to **Florida** by **Calgary** with Dustin Johner for Kristian Huselius, December 2, 2005.

Season	Club	League	GP	G	A	Pts	PIM	PP	SH	GW	S	%	+/-	TF	F%	Min	GP	G	A	Pts	PIM	PP	SH	GW	Min
			Regular Season														Playoffs								

MOORE, Dominic

(MOOR, DOHM-ihn-ihk) **MIN.**

Center. Shoots left. 6', 193 lbs. Born, Thornhill, Ont., August 3, 1980. NY Rangers' 2nd choice, 95th overall, in 2000 Entry Draft.

Season	Club	League	GP	G	A	Pts	PIM	PP	SH	GW	S	%	+/-	TF	F%	Min	GP	G	A	Pts	PIM	PP	SH	GW	Min
1996-97	Thornhill Islanders	MTJHL	29	4	6	10	48	....	....	....	....	....	....	....	....	....	1	0	1	1	0	....	....	....	....
1997-98	Aurora Tigers	OPJHL	51	10	15	25	16	....	....	....	....	....	....	....	....	....	....	....	....	....	....	....	....	....	....
1998-99	Aurora Tigers	OPJHL	51	34	53	87	70	....	....	....	....	....	....	....	....	....	....	....	....	....	....	....	....	....	....
99-2000	Harvard Crimson	ECAC	30	12	24	28	16	....	....	....	....	....	....	....	....	....	....	....	....	....	....	....	....	....	....
2000-01	Harvard Crimson	ECAC	32	15	28	43	40	....	....	....	....	....	....	....	....	....	....	....	....	....	....	....	....	....	....
2001-02	Harvard Crimson	ECAC	32	13	16	29	37	....	....	....	....	....	....	....	....	....	....	....	....	....	....	....	....	....	....
2002-03	Harvard Crimson	ECAC	34	*24	27	*51	30	....	....	....	....	....	....	....	....	....	....	....	....	....	....	....	....	....	....
2003-04	**NY Rangers**	**NHL**	**5**	**0**	**3**	**3**	**0**	**0**	**0**	**0**	**3**	**0.0**	**0**	**36**	**30.6**	**9:18**	....	....	....	....	....	....	....	....	....
	Hartford	AHL	70	14	25	39	60	....	....	....	....	....	....	....	....	....	16	3	3	6	8	....	....	....	....
2004-05	Hartford	AHL	78	19	31	50	78	....	....	....	....	....	....	....	....	....	6	1	1	2	4	....	....	....	....
2005-06	**NY Rangers**	**NHL**	**82**	**9**	**9**	**18**	**28**	**2**	**0**	**1**	**139**	**6.5**	**4**	**814**	**46.3**	**12:28**	**4**	**0**	**0**	**0**	**2**	**0**	**0**	**0**	**11:21**
2006-07	**Pittsburgh**	**NHL**	**59**	**6**	**9**	**15**	**46**	**0**	**0**	**0**	**100**	**6.0**	**1**	**678**	**51.6**	**13:04**	....	....	....	....	....	....	....	....	....
	Minnesota	**NHL**	**10**	**2**	**0**	**2**	**10**	**0**	**0**	**1**	**11**	**18.2**	**3**	**66**	**62.1**	**10:12**	....	....	....	....	....	....	....	....	....
	NHL Totals		**156**	**17**	**21**	**38**	**84**	**2**	**0**	**2**	**253**	**6.7**		**1594**	**48.9**	**12:27**	**4**	**0**	**0**	**0**	**2**	**0**	**0**	**0**	**11:21**

ECAC All-Rookie Team (2000) • ECAC Second All-Star Team (2001) • ECAC First All-Star Team (2003) • NCAA East First All-American Team (2003)

Traded to **Nashville** by **NY Rangers** for Adam Hall, July 19, 2006. Traded to **Pittsburgh** by **Nashville** with Libor Pivko for Pittsburgh's 3rd round choice (Ryan Thang) in 2007 Entry Draft, July 19, 2006. Traded to **Minnesota** by **Pittsburgh** for Minnesota's 3rd round choice (Casey Pierro-Zabotel) in 2007 Entry Draft, February 27, 2007.

MORAN, Brad

(moh-RAN, BRAD) **VAN.**

Center. Shoots left. 5'11", 187 lbs. Born, Abbotsford, B.C., March 20, 1979. Buffalo's 8th choice, 191st overall, in 1998 Entry Draft.

Season	Club	League	GP	G	A	Pts	PIM	PP	SH	GW	S	%	+/-	TF	F%	Min	GP	G	A	Pts	PIM	PP	SH	GW	Min
1994-95	Abbotsford	BCAHA	56	66	93	159	40	....	....	....	....	....	....	....	....	....	....	....	....	....	....	....	....	....	....
1995-96	Calgary Hitmen	WHL	70	13	31	44	28	....	....	....	....	....	....	....	....	....	....	....	....	....	....	....	....	....	....
1996-97	Calgary Hitmen	WHL	72	30	36	66	61	....	....	....	....	....	....	....	....	....	....	....	....	....	....	....	....	....	....
1997-98	Calgary Hitmen	WHL	72	53	49	102	64	....	....	....	....	....	....	....	....	....	18	10	8	18	20	....	....	....	....
1998-99	Calgary Hitmen	WHL	71	60	58	118	96	....	....	....	....	....	....	....	....	....	21	17	*25	42	26	....	....	....	....
99-2000	Calgary Hitmen	WHL	72	48	*72	*120	84	....	....	....	....	....	....	....	....	....	13	7	15	22	18	....	....	....	....
2000-01	Syracuse Crunch	AHL	71	11	19	30	30	....	....	....	....	....	....	....	....	....	5	3	4	7	2	....	....	....	....
2001-02	**Columbus**	**NHL**	**3**	**0**	**0**	**0**	**0**	**0**	**0**	**0**	**2**	**0.0**	**0**	**22**	**40.9**	**7:39**	....	....	....	....	....	....	....	....	....
	Syracuse Crunch	AHL	64	25	24	49	51	....	....	....	....	....	....	....	....	....	10	5	8	13	2	....	....	....	....
2002-03	Syracuse Crunch	AHL	47	12	19	31	22	....	....	....	....	....	....	....	....	....	....	....	....	....	....	....	....	....	....
2003-04	**Columbus**	**NHL**	**2**	**1**	**1**	**2**	**2**	**0**	**0**	**0**	**4**	**25.0**	**–1**	**25**	**64.0**	**10:03**	....	....	....	....	....	....	....	....	....
	Syracuse Crunch	AHL	72	24	35	59	44	....	....	....	....	....	....	....	....	....	7	5	3	8	2	....	....	....	....
2004-05	Syracuse Crunch	AHL	80	26	46	72	70	....	....	....	....	....	....	....	....	....	....	....	....	....	....	....	....	....	....
2005-06	Langnau	Swiss	18	4	4	8	18	....	....	....	....	....	....	....	....	....	6	4	6	10	10	....	....	....	....
2006-07	**Vancouver**	**NHL**	**3**	**0**	**1**	**1**	**2**	**0**	**0**	**0**	**3**	**0.0**	**0**	**24**	**58.3**	**12:38**	....	....	....	....	....	....	....	....	....
	Manitoba Moose	AHL	69	25	47	72	52	....	....	....	....	....	....	....	....	....	13	5	6	11	12	....	....	....	....
	NHL Totals		**8**	**1**	**2**	**3**	**4**	**0**	**0**	**0**	**9**	**11.1**		**71**	**54.9**	**10:07**	....	....	....	....	....	....	....	....	....

WHL East First All-Star Team (1999, 2000) • WHL Player of the Year (2000)

Signed as a free agent by **Columbus**, June 5, 2000. Signed as a free agent by **Vancouver**, June 19, 2006.

MORAN, Ian

(moh-RAN, EE-an) **N.J.**

Defense. Shoots right. 6', 205 lbs. Born, Cleveland, OH, August 24, 1972. Pittsburgh's 5th choice, 107th overall, in 1990 Entry Draft.

Season	Club	League	GP	G	A	Pts	PIM	PP	SH	GW	S	%	+/-	TF	F%	Min	GP	G	A	Pts	PIM	PP	SH	GW	Min
1987-88	Belmont Hill	High-MA	25	3	13	16	15	....	....	....	....	....	....	....	....	....	....	....	....	....	....	....	....	....	....
1988-89	Belmont Hill	High-MA	23	7	25	32	8	....	....	....	....	....	....	....	....	....	....	....	....	....	....	....	....	....	....
1989-90	Belmont Hill	High-MA	23	10	36	46	....	....	....	....	....	....	....	....	....	....	....	....	....	....	....	....	....	....	....
1990-91	Belmont Hill	High-MA	23	7	44	51	12	....	....	....	....	....	....	....	....	....	....	....	....	....	....	....	....	....	....
1991-92	Boston College	H-East	30	2	16	18	44	....	....	....	....	....	....	....	....	....	....	....	....	....	....	....	....	....	....
1992-93	Boston College	H-East	31	8	12	20	32	....	....	....	....	....	....	....	....	....	....	....	....	....	....	....	....	....	....
1993-94	United States	Nat-Tm	50	8	15	23	69	....	....	....	....	....	....	....	....	....	....	....	....	....	....	....	....	....	....
	Cleveland	IHL	33	5	13	18	39	....	....	....	....	....	....	....	....	....	....	....	....	....	....	....	....	....	....
1994-95	Cleveland	IHL	64	7	31	38	94	....	....	....	....	....	....	....	....	....	4	0	1	1	2	....	....	....	....
	Pittsburgh	**NHL**	....	....	....	....	....	....	....	....	....	....	....	....	....	....	**8**	**0**	**0**	**0**	**0**	**0**	**0**	**0**	....
1995-96	**Pittsburgh**	**NHL**	**51**	**1**	**1**	**2**	**47**	**0**	**0**	**0**	**44**	**2.3**	**–1**	....	....	....	....	....	....	....	....	....	....	....	....
1996-97	**Pittsburgh**	**NHL**	**36**	**4**	**5**	**9**	**22**	**0**	**0**	**0**	**50**	**8.0**	**–11**	....	....	....	**5**	**1**	**2**	**3**	**4**	**0**	**0**	**0**	....
	Cleveland	IHL	36	6	23	29	26	....	....	....	....	....	....	....	....	....	....	....	....	....	....	....	....	....	....
1997-98	**Pittsburgh**	**NHL**	**37**	**1**	**6**	**7**	**19**	**0**	**0**	**1**	**33**	**3.0**	**0**	....	....	....	**6**	**0**	**0**	**0**	**2**	**0**	**0**	**0**	....
1998-99	**Pittsburgh**	**NHL**	**62**	**4**	**5**	**9**	**37**	**0**	**1**	**0**	**65**	**6.2**	**1**	**32**	**34.4**	**16:34**	**13**	**0**	**2**	**2**	**8**	**0**	**0**	**0**	**21:10**
99-2000	**Pittsburgh**	**NHL**	**73**	**4**	**8**	**12**	**28**	**0**	**0**	**0**	**58**	**6.9**	**–10**	**210**	**33.8**	**11:21**	**11**	**0**	**1**	**1**	**2**	**0**	**0**	**0**	**8:52**
2000-01	**Pittsburgh**	**NHL**	**40**	**3**	**4**	**7**	**28**	**0**	**0**	**1**	**73**	**4.1**	**5**	**4**	**25.0**	**17:43**	**18**	**0**	**1**	**1**	**4**	**0**	**0**	**0**	**15:54**
2001-02	**Pittsburgh**	**NHL**	**64**	**2**	**8**	**10**	**54**	**0**	**0**	**1**	**94**	**2.1**	**–11**	**2**	**100.0**	**20:00**	....	....	....	....	....	....	....	....	....
2002-03	**Pittsburgh**	**NHL**	**70**	**0**	**7**	**7**	**46**	**0**	**0**	**0**	**85**	**0.0**	**–17**	**4**	**75.0**	**18:37**	....	....	....	....	....	....	....	....	....
	Boston	**NHL**	**8**	**0**	**1**	**1**	**2**	**0**	**0**	**0**	**11**	**0.0**	**–1**	**1**	**100.0**	**16:22**	**5**	**0**	**1**	**1**	**4**	**0**	**0**	**0**	**18:24**
2003-04	**Boston**	**NHL**	**35**	**1**	**4**	**5**	**28**	**0**	**0**	**0**	**54**	**1.9**	**3**	**1**	**100.0**	**18:45**	....	....	....	....	....	....	....	....	....
2004-05	Bofors	Sweden-2	7	0	4	4	22	....	....	....	....	....	....	....	....	....	....	....	....	....	....	....	....	....	....
	Nottingham	Britain	9	0	4	4	8	....	....	....	....	....	....	....	....	....	5	0	1	1	2	....	....	....	....
2005-06	**Boston**	**NHL**	**12**	**1**	**1**	**2**	**10**	**0**	**0**	**0**	**7**	**14.3**	**0**	**1**	**0.0**	**14:25**	....	....	....	....	....	....	....	....	....
2006-07	**Anaheim**	**NHL**	**1**	**0**	**0**	**0**	**0**	**0**	**0**	**0**	**0**	**0.0**	**–1**	**0**	**0.0**	**6:06**	....	....	....	....	....	....	....	....	....
	Portland Pirates	AHL	18	1	4	5	10	....	....	....	....	....	....	....	....	....	....	....	....	....	....	....	....	....	....
	Eisbaren Berlin	Germany	9	1	4	5	8	....	....	....	....	....	....	....	....	....	3	0	0	0	2	....	....	....	....
	NHL Totals		**489**	**21**	**50**	**71**	**321**	**0**	**1**	**3**	**574**	**3.7**		**255**	**35.3**	**16:45**	**66**	**1**	**7**	**8**	**24**	**0**	**0**	**0**	**15:59**

Hockey East All-Rookie Team (1992) • Hockey East Rookie of the Year (1992) (co-winner - Craig Darby)

• Missed majority of 1997-98 season recovering from knee injury suffered in training camp, September 30, 1997. • Missed majority of 2000-01 season recovering from hand injury suffered in game vs. Edmonton, November 11, 2000. Traded to **Boston** by **Pittsburgh** for Boston's 4th round choice (Paul Bissonnette) in 2003 Entry Draft, March 11, 2003. • Missed majority of 2003-04 season recovering from ankle injury suffered in game vs. Tampa Bay, December 23, 2003. Signed as a free agent by **Bofors** (Sweden-2), November 3, 2004. Signed as a free agent by **Nottingham** (Britain), January 22, 2005. • Missed remainder of 2005-06 season after suffering knee injury in game vs. Toronto (October 27, 2005) and recovering from resulting knee surgery (November 3, 2005). Signed as a free agent by **Anaheim**, August 15, 2006. Signed as a free agent by **Berlin** (Gemany), January 25, 2007. Signed as a free agent by **New Jersey**, July 24, 2007.

MOREAU, Ethan

(moh-ROH, EE-than) **EDM.**

Left wing. Shoots left. 6'2", 220 lbs. Born, Huntsville, Ont., September 22, 1975. Chicago's 1st choice, 14th overall, in 1994 Entry Draft.

Season	Club	League	GP	G	A	Pts	PIM	PP	SH	GW	S	%	+/-	TF	F%	Min	GP	G	A	Pts	PIM	PP	SH	GW	Min
1990-91	Orillia Terriers	OHA-B	42	17	22	39	26	....	....	....	....	....	....	....	....	....	12	6	6	12	18	....	....	....	....
1991-92	Niagara Falls	OHL	62	20	35	55	39	....	....	....	....	....	....	....	....	....	17	4	6	10	4	....	....	....	....
1992-93	Niagara Falls	OHL	65	32	41	73	69	....	....	....	....	....	....	....	....	....	4	0	3	3	4	....	....	....	....
1993-94	Niagara Falls	OHL	59	44	54	98	100	....	....	....	....	....	....	....	....	....	....	....	....	....	....	....	....	....	....
1994-95	Niagara Falls	OHL	39	25	41	66	69	....	....	....	....	....	....	....	....	....	....	....	....	....	....	....	....	....	....
	Sudbury Wolves	OHL	23	13	17	30	22	....	....	....	....	....	....	....	....	....	18	6	12	18	26	....	....	....	....
1995-96	**Chicago**	**NHL**	**8**	**0**	**1**	**1**	**4**	**0**	**0**	**0**	**1**	**0.0**	**1**	....	....	....	....	....	....	....	....	....	....	....	....
	Indianapolis Ice	IHL	71	21	20	41	126	....	....	....	....	....	....	....	....	....	5	4	0	4	8	....	....	....	....
1996-97	**Chicago**	**NHL**	**82**	**15**	**16**	**31**	**123**	**0**	**0**	**1**	**114**	**13.2**	**13**	....	....	....	**6**	**1**	**0**	**1**	**9**	**0**	**0**	**0**	....
1997-98	**Chicago**	**NHL**	**54**	**9**	**9**	**18**	**73**	**2**	**0**	**0**	**87**	**10.3**	**0**	....	....	....	....	....	....	....	....	....	....	....	....
1998-99	**Chicago**	**NHL**	**66**	**9**	**6**	**15**	**84**	**0**	**0**	**1**	**80**	**11.3**	**–5**	**3**	**33.3**	**12:30**	....	....	....	....	....	....	....	....	....
	Edmonton	**NHL**	**14**	**1**	**5**	**6**	**8**	**0**	**0**	**1**	**16**	**6.3**	**2**	**1**	**0.0**	**11:47**	**4**	**0**	**3**	**3**	**6**	**0**	**0**	**0**	**17:26**
99-2000	**Edmonton**	**NHL**	**73**	**17**	**10**	**27**	**62**	**1**	**0**	**3**	**106**	**16.0**	**8**	**8**	**62.5**	**15:07**	**5**	**0**	**1**	**1**	**0**	**0**	**0**	**0**	**15:46**
2000-01	**Edmonton**	**NHL**	**68**	**9**	**10**	**19**	**90**	**0**	**1**	**3**	**97**	**9.3**	**–6**	**2**	**0.0**	**14:11**	**4**	**0**	**0**	**0**	**2**	**0**	**0**	**0**	**10:35**
2001-02	**Edmonton**	**NHL**	**80**	**11**	**5**	**16**	**81**	**0**	**2**	**1**	**129**	**8.5**	**4**	**11**	**54.6**	**12:43**	....	....	....	....	....	....	....	....	....
2002-03	**Edmonton**	**NHL**	**78**	**14**	**17**	**31**	**112**	**2**	**3**	**2**	**137**	**10.2**	**–7**	**25**	**12.0**	**13:30**	**6**	**0**	**1**	**1**	**16**	**0**	**0**	**0**	**12:23**
2003-04	**Edmonton**	**NHL**	**81**	**20**	**12**	**32**	**96**	**0**	**3**	**5**	**180**	**11.1**	**7**	**59**	**44.1**	**15:04**	....	....	....	....	....	....	....	....	....
2004-05	EC Villacher SV	Austria	16	10	6	16	73	....	....	....	....	....	....	....	....	....	3	4	0	4	0	....	....	....	....
2005-06	**Edmonton**	**NHL**	**74**	**11**	**16**	**27**	**87**	**2**	**4**	**4**	**151**	**7.3**	**6**	**29**	**48.3**	**15:59**	**21**	**2**	**1**	**3**	**19**	**0**	**0**	**0**	**14:35**
2006-07	**Edmonton**	**NHL**	**7**	**1**	**0**	**1**	**12**	**0**	**0**	**0**	**18**	**5.6**	**–4**	**20**	**50.0**	**15:08**	....	....	....	....	....	....	....	....	....
	NHL Totals		**685**	**117**	**107**	**224**	**832**	**7**	**13**	**21**	**1116**	**10.5**		**158**	**41.1**	**14:07**	**46**	**3**	**6**	**9**	**52**	**0**	**0**	**0**	**14:17**

OHL All-Rookie Team (1992)

Traded to **Edmonton** by **Chicago** with Daniel Cleary, Chad Kilger and Christian Laflamme for Boris Mironov, Dean McAmmond and Jonas Elofsson, March 20, 1999. Signed as a free agent by **Villacher** (Austria), December 20, 2004. • Missed majority of 2006-07 season recovering from a shoulder injury suffered in game vs. Detroit, October 21, 2006.

MORGAN, Gavin

(MOHR-guhn, GA-vihn)

Center. Shoots right. 5'11", 191 lbs. Born, Scarborough, Ont., July 9, 1976.

			Regular Season														Playoffs								
Season	Club	League	GP	G	A	Pts	PIM	PP	SH	GW	S	%	+/-	TF	F%	Min	GP	G	A	Pts	PIM	PP	SH	GW	Min
1992-93	Wexford Raiders	MTJHL	3	0	1	1	0	....	....	....	....	....	....	....	....	....	....	....	....	....	....	....	....	....	....
1993-94	Wexford Raiders	MTJHL	49	18	32	50	91	....	....	....	....	....	....	....	....	....	....	....	....	....	....	....	....	....	....
1994-95	Wexford Raiders	MTJHL	49	26	39	65	170	....	....	....	....	....	....	....	....	....	....	....	....	....	....	....	....	....	....
1995-96	U. of Denver	WCHA	28	2	9	11	47	....	....	....	....	....	....	....	....	....	....	....	....	....	....	....	....	....	....
1996-97	U. of Denver	WCHA	41	8	15	23	46	....	....	....	....	....	....	....	....	....	....	....	....	....	....	....	....	....	....
1997-98	U. of Denver	WCHA	37	9	8	17	42	....	....	....	....	....	....	....	....	....	....	....	....	....	....	....	....	....	....
1998-99	U. of Denver	WCHA	40	13	16	29	85	....	....	....	....	....	....	....	....	....	....	....	....	....	....	....	....	....	....
99-2000	Idaho Steelheads	WCHL	54	17	33	50	150	....	....	....	....	....	....	....	....	....	3	0	3	3	4	....	....	....	....
	Long Beach	IHL	7	0	1	1	10	....	....	....	....	....	....	....	....	....	....	....	....	....	....	....	....	....	....
	Utah Grizzlies	IHL	10	0	2	2	4	....	....	....	....	....	....	....	....	....	2	1	0	1	2	....	....	....	....
2000-01	Utah Grizzlies	IHL	79	7	14	21	187	....	....	....	....	....	....	....	....	....	....	....	....	....	....	....	....	....	....
2001-02	Utah Grizzlies	AHL	76	8	24	32	249	....	....	....	....	....	....	....	....	....	5	0	1	1	2	....	....	....	....
2002-03	Utah Grizzlies	AHL	73	15	24	39	244	....	....	....	....	....	....	....	....	....	2	0	1	1	17	....	....	....	....
2003-04	**Dallas**	**NHL**	**6**	**0**	**0**	**0**	**21**	**0**	**0**	**0**	**7**	**0.0**	**0**	**20**	**70.0**	**5:49**	....	....	....	....	....	....	....	....	....
	Hershey Bears	AHL	67	10	23	33	152	....	....	....	....	....	....	....	....	....	....	....	....	....	....	....	....	....	....
2004-05	Hamilton	AHL	76	10	23	33	147	....	....	....	....	....	....	....	....	....	4	0	0	0	6	....	....	....	....
2005-06	Peoria Rivermen	AHL	73	18	22	40	116	....	....	....	....	....	....	....	....	....	4	0	1	1	6	....	....	....	....
	EHC Basel	Swiss	10	1	3	4	38	....	....	....	....	....	....	....	....	....	....	....	....	....	....	....	....	....	....
2006-07	Peoria Rivermen	AHL	54	4	15	19	93	....	....	....	....	....	....	....	....	....	....	....	....	....	....	....	....	....	....
	NHL Totals		**6**	**0**	**0**	**0**	**21**	**0**	**0**	**0**	**7**	**0.0**		**20**	**70.0**	**5:49**	....	....	....	....	....	....	....	....	....

Signed as a free agent by **Idaho** (WCHL), August 25, 1999. Signed as a free agent by **Utah** (IHL), June 26, 2000. Signed as a free agent by **Dallas**, July 17, 2001. Signed as a free agent by **Montreal**, July 26, 2004. Signed as a free agent by **Basel** (Swiss), August 29, 2005.

MORGAN, Jason

(MOHR-guhn, JAY-suhn) **WSH.**

Center. Shoots left. 6'1", 200 lbs. Born, St. John's, Nfld., October 9, 1976. Los Angeles' 5th choice, 118th overall, in 1995 Entry Draft.

Season	Club	League	GP	G	A	Pts	PIM	PP	SH	GW	S	%	+/-	TF	F%	Min	GP	G	A	Pts	PIM	PP	SH	GW	Min
1992-93	Kitchener AA	Minor-ON	69	44	40	84	85	....	....	....	....	....	....	....	....	....	....	....	....	....	....	....	....	....	....
1993-94	Kitchener Rangers	OHL	65	6	15	21	16	....	....	....	....	....	....	....	....	....	5	1	0	1	0	....	....	....	....
1994-95	Kitchener Rangers	OHL	35	3	15	18	25	....	....	....	....	....	....	....	....	....	....	....	....	....	....	....	....	....	....
	Kingston	OHL	20	0	3	3	14	....	....	....	....	....	....	....	....	....	6	0	2	2	0	....	....	....	....
1995-96	Kingston	OHL	66	16	38	54	50	....	....	....	....	....	....	....	....	....	6	1	2	3	0	....	....	....	....
1996-97	**Los Angeles**	**NHL**	**3**	**0**	**0**	**0**	**0**	**0**	**0**	**0**	**4**	**0.0**	**–3**	....	....	....	....	....	....	....	....	....	....	....	....
	Phoenix	IHL	57	3	6	9	29	....	....	....	....	....	....	....	....	....	....	....	....	....	....	....	....	....	....
	Mississippi	ECHL	6	3	0	3	0	....	....	....	....	....	....	....	....	....	3	1	1	2	6	....	....	....	....
1997-98	**Los Angeles**	**NHL**	**11**	**1**	**0**	**1**	**4**	**0**	**0**	**0**	**5**	**20.0**	**–7**	....	....	....	....	....	....	....	....	....	....	....	....
	Springfield	AHL	58	13	22	35	66	....	....	....	....	....	....	....	....	....	3	1	0	1	18	....	....	....	....
1998-99	Long Beach	IHL	13	4	6	10	18	....	....	....	....	....	....	....	....	....	....	....	....	....	....	....	....	....	....
	Springfield	AHL	46	6	16	22	51	....	....	....	....	....	....	....	....	....	3	0	0	0	6	....	....	....	....
99-2000	Cincinnati	IHL	15	1	3	4	14	....	....	....	....	....	....	....	....	....	....	....	....	....	....	....	....	....	....
	Florida Everblades	ECHL	48	14	25	39	79	....	....	....	....	....	....	....	....	....	5	2	2	4	16	....	....	....	....
2000-01	Florida Everblades	ECHL	37	15	22	37	41	....	....	....	....	....	....	....	....	....	5	2	3	5	17	....	....	....	....
	Hamilton	AHL	11	2	0	2	10	....	....	....	....	....	....	....	....	....	....	....	....	....	....	....	....	....	....
	Springfield	AHL	16	1	4	5	19	....	....	....	....	....	....	....	....	....	....	....	....	....	....	....	....	....	....
	Saint John Flames	AHL	....	....	....	....	....	....	....	....	....	....	....	....	....	....	6	0	1	1	2	....	....	....	....
2001-02	Saint John Flames	AHL	76	17	20	37	69	....	....	....	....	....	....	....	....	....	....	....	....	....	....	....	....	....	....
2002-03	Saint John Flames	AHL	80	13	40	53	63	....	....	....	....	....	....	....	....	....	....	....	....	....	....	....	....	....	....
2003-04	**Calgary**	**NHL**	**13**	**0**	**2**	**2**	**2**	**0**	**0**	**0**	**14**	**0.0**	**1**	**98**	**44.9**	**9:45**	....	....	....	....	....	....	....	....	....
	Lowell	AHL	21	6	13	19	16	....	....	....	....	....	....	....	....	....	....	....	....	....	....	....	....	....	....
	Nashville	**NHL**	**6**	**0**	**2**	**2**	**2**	**0**	**0**	**0**	**6**	**0.0**	**0**	**15**	**73.3**	**10:06**	....	....	....	....	....	....	....	....	....
	Norfolk Admirals	AHL	19	6	8	14	16	....	....	....	....	....	....	....	....	....	8	0	1	1	10	....	....	....	....
2004-05	Norfolk Admirals	AHL	71	9	20	29	116	....	....	....	....	....	....	....	....	....	6	2	2	4	8	....	....	....	....
2005-06	**Chicago**	**NHL**	**7**	**1**	**1**	**2**	**6**	**0**	**0**	**0**	**6**	**16.7**	**1**	**52**	**55.8**	**10:06**	....	....	....	....	....	....	....	....	....
	Norfolk Admirals	AHL	51	8	31	39	58	....	....	....	....	....	....	....	....	....	....	....	....	....	....	....	....	....	....
2006-07	**Minnesota**	**NHL**	**4**	**0**	**0**	**0**	**4**	**0**	**0**	**0**	**0**	**0.0**	**–1**	**25**	**56.0**	**7:29**	....	....	....	....	....	....	....	....	....
	Houston Aeros	AHL	57	12	14	26	73	....	....	....	....	....	....	....	....	....	....	....	....	....	....	....	....	....	....
	NHL Totals		**44**	**2**	**5**	**7**	**18**	**0**	**0**	**0**	**35**	**5.7**		**190**	**51.6**	**9:36**	....	....	....	....	....	....	....	....	....

Signed to a PTO (tryout) contract by **Saint John** (AHL), April 22, 2001. Signed as a free agent by **Saint John** (AHL), August 28, 2001. Signed as a free agent by **Calgary**, July 11, 2002. Claimed on waivers by **Nashville** from **Calgary**, December 31, 2003. Claimed on waivers by **Calgary** from **Nashville**, February 19, 2004. Traded to **Chicago** by **Calgary** with Calgary's 6th round choice (Joseph Fallon) in 2005 Entry Draft for Ville Nieminen, February 24, 2004. Signed as a free agent by **Minnesota**, July 17, 2006. Signed as a free agent by **Washington**, July 17, 2007.

MORO, Marc

(MOH-roh, MAHRK)

Defense. Shoots left. 6'1", 218 lbs. Born, Toronto, Ont., July 17, 1977. Ottawa's 2nd choice, 27th overall, in 1995 Entry Draft.

Season	Club	League	GP	G	A	Pts	PIM	PP	SH	GW	S	%	+/-	TF	F%	Min	GP	G	A	Pts	PIM	PP	SH	GW	Min
1992-93	Miss. Sens	MTHL	42	9	18	27	56	....	....	....	....	....	....	....	....	....	....	....	....	....	....	....	....	....	....
	Miss. Sens	MTJHL	2	0	0	0	0	....	....	....	....	....	....	....	....	....	....	....	....	....	....	....	....	....	....
1993-94	Kingston	MTJHL	12	0	2	2	10	....	....	....	....	....	....	....	....	....	....	....	....	....	....	....	....	....	....
	Kingston	OHL	43	0	3	3	81	....	....	....	....	....	....	....	....	....	....	....	....	....	....	....	....	....	....
1994-95	Kingston	OHL	64	4	12	16	255	....	....	....	....	....	....	....	....	....	6	0	0	0	23	....	....	....	....
1995-96	Kingston	OHL	66	4	17	21	261	....	....	....	....	....	....	....	....	....	6	0	0	0	12	....	....	....	....
	P.E.I. Senators	AHL	2	0	0	0	7	....	....	....	....	....	....	....	....	....	2	0	0	0	4	....	....	....	....
1996-97	Kingston	OHL	37	4	8	12	97	....	....	....	....	....	....	....	....	....	....	....	....	....	....	....	....	....	....
	Sault Ste. Marie	OHL	26	0	5	5	74	....	....	....	....	....	....	....	....	....	11	1	6	7	38	....	....	....	....
1997-98	**Anaheim**	**NHL**	**1**	**0**	**0**	**0**	**0**	**0**	**0**	**0**	**0**	**0.0**	**0**	....	....	....	....	....	....	....	....	....	....	....	....
	Cincinnati	AHL	74	1	6	7	181	....	....	....	....	....	....	....	....	....	....	....	....	....	....	....	....	....	....
1998-99	Milwaukee	IHL	80	0	5	5	264	....	....	....	....	....	....	....	....	....	2	0	0	0	4	....	....	....	....
99-2000	**Nashville**	**NHL**	**8**	**0**	**0**	**0**	**40**	**0**	**0**	**0**	**3**	**0.0**	**–3**	**0**	**0.0**	**10:55**	....	....	....	....	....	....	....	....	....
	Milwaukee	IHL	64	5	5	10	203	....	....	....	....	....	....	....	....	....	....	....	....	....	....	....	....	....	....
2000-01	**Nashville**	**NHL**	**6**	**0**	**0**	**0**	**12**	**0**	**0**	**0**	**1**	**0.0**	**1**	**0**	**0.0**	**3:34**	....	....	....	....	....	....	....	....	....
	Milwaukee	IHL	68	2	9	11	190	....	....	....	....	....	....	....	....	....	5	1	0	1	10	....	....	....	....
2001-02	**Nashville**	**NHL**	**13**	**0**	**0**	**0**	**23**	**0**	**0**	**0**	**7**	**0.0**	**–3**	**0**	**0.0**	**12:02**	....	....	....	....	....	....	....	....	....
	Milwaukee	AHL	41	1	8	9	81	....	....	....	....	....	....	....	....	....	....	....	....	....	....	....	....	....	....
	Toronto	**NHL**	**2**	**0**	**0**	**0**	**2**	**0**	**0**	**0**	**0**	**0.0**	**0**	**0**	**0.0**	**11:23**	....	....	....	....	....	....	....	....	....
	St. John's	AHL	7	1	0	1	21	....	....	....	....	....	....	....	....	....	....	....	....	....	....	....	....	....	....
2002-03	St. John's	AHL	68	3	8	11	128	....	....	....	....	....	....	....	....	....	....	....	....	....	....	....	....	....	....
2003-04	St. John's	AHL	76	1	9	10	144	....	....	....	....	....	....	....	....	....	....	....	....	....	....	....	....	....	....
2004-05	St. John's	AHL	78	2	6	8	202	....	....	....	....	....	....	....	....	....	5	0	1	1	4	....	....	....	....
2005-06	Toronto Marlies	AHL	73	1	8	9	149	....	....	....	....	....	....	....	....	....	5	0	0	0	11	....	....	....	....
2006-07	Toronto Marlies	AHL	79	2	5	7	139	....	....	....	....	....	....	....	....	....	....	....	....	....	....	....	....	....	....
	NHL Totals		**30**	**0**	**0**	**0**	**77**	**0**	**0**	**0**	**11**	**0.0**		**0**	**0.0**	**9:56**	....	....	....	....	....	....	....	....	....

Rights traded to **Anaheim** by **Ottawa** with Ted Drury for Jason York and Shaun Van Allen, October 1, 1996. Traded to **Nashville** by **Anaheim** with Chris Mason for Dominic Roussel, October 5, 1998. Traded to **Toronto** by **Nashville** for D.J. Smith and Marty Wilford, March 1, 2002.

MORRIS, Derek

(MOH-rihs, DAIR-ihk) **PHX.**

Defense. Shoots right. 6', 220 lbs. Born, Edmonton, Alta., August 24, 1978. Calgary's 1st choice, 13th overall, in 1996 Entry Draft.

Season	Club	League	GP	G	A	Pts	PIM	PP	SH	GW	S	%	+/-	TF	F%	Min	GP	G	A	Pts	PIM	PP	SH	GW	Min
1994-95	Red Deer Vipers	AMHL	31	6	35	41	74																		
1995-96	Regina Pats	WHL	67	8	44	52	70	....	....	....	....	....	....	....	....	....	11	1	7	8	26	....	....	....	....
1996-97	Regina Pats	WHL	67	18	57	75	180	....	....	....	....	....	....	....	....	....	5	0	3	3	9	....	....	....	....
	Saint John Flames	AHL	7	0	3	3	7	....	....	....	....	....	....	....	....	....	5	0	3	3	7	....	....	....	....
1997-98	**Calgary**	**NHL**	**82**	**9**	**20**	**29**	**88**	**5**	**1**	**1**	**120**	**7.5**	**1**	....	....	....	....	....	....	....	....	....	....	....	....
1998-99	**Calgary**	**NHL**	**71**	**7**	**27**	**34**	**73**	**3**	**0**	**2**	**150**	**4.7**	**4**	**0**	**0.0**	**20:44**	....	....	....	....	....	....	....	....	....
99-2000	**Calgary**	**NHL**	**78**	**9**	**29**	**38**	**80**	**3**	**0**	**2**	**193**	**4.7**	**2**	**0**	**0.0**	**24:51**	....	....	....	....	....	....	....	....	....
2000-01	**Calgary**	**NHL**	**51**	**5**	**23**	**28**	**56**	**3**	**1**	**4**	**142**	**3.5**	**–15**	**0**	**0.0**	**25:51**	....	....	....	....	....	....	....	....	....
	Saint John Flames	AHL	3	1	2	3	2	....	....	....	....	....	....	....	....	....	....	....	....	....	....	....	....	....	....
2001-02	**Calgary**	**NHL**	**61**	**4**	**30**	**34**	**88**	**2**	**0**	**1**	**166**	**2.4**	**–4**	**1**	**100.0**	**24:40**	....	....	....	....	....	....	....	....	....
2002-03	**Colorado**	**NHL**	**75**	**11**	**37**	**48**	**68**	**9**	**0**	**7**	**191**	**5.8**	**16**	**0**	**0.0**	**23:49**	**7**	**0**	**3**	**3**	**6**	**0**	**0**	**0**	**22:44**
2003-04	**Colorado**	**NHL**	**69**	**6**	**22**	**28**	**47**	**2**	**0**	**1**	**139**	**4.3**	**4**	**0**	**0.0**	**20:53**	....	....	....	....	....	....	....	....	....
	Phoenix	**NHL**	**14**	**0**	**4**	**4**	**2**	**0**	**0**	**0**	**28**	**0.0**	**–5**	**0**	**0.0**	**25:02**	....	....	....	....	....	....	....	....	....

			Regular Season														Playoffs								
Season	Club	League	GP	G	A	Pts	PIM	PP	SH	GW	S	%	+/-	TF	F%	Min	GP	G	A	Pts	PIM	PP	SH	GW	Min
2004-05			DID NOT PLAY																						
2005-06	**Phoenix**	**NHL**	**53**	**6**	**21**	**27**	**54**	**4**	**1**	**2**	**91**	**6.6**	**-7**	**1**	**0.0**	**20:52**	....	....	....	....	....	....	....	....	....
2006-07	**Phoenix**	**NHL**	**82**	**6**	**19**	**25**	**115**	**2**	**0**	**1**	**129**	**4.7**	**-18**	**1**	**100.0**	**20:29**	....	....	....	....	....	....	....	....	....
	NHL Totals		**636**	**63**	**232**	**295**	**671**	**33**	**3**	**21**	**1349**	**4.7**		**3**	**66.7**	**22:44**	**7**	**0**	**3**	**3**	**6**	**0**	**0**	**0**	**22:44**

WHL East First All-Star Team (1997) • NHL All-Rookie Team (1998)

Traded to **Colorado** by **Calgary** with Jeff Shantz and Dean McAmmond for Chris Drury and Stephane Yelle, October 1, 2002. Traded to **Phoenix** by **Colorado** with Keith Ballard for Ossi Vaananen, Chris Gratton and Phoenix's 2nd round choice (Paul Stastny) in 2005 Entry Draft, March 9, 2004.

MORRISON, Brendan

(MOHR-ih-suhn, BREHN-duhn) **VAN.**

Center. Shoots left. 5'11", 181 lbs. Born, Pitt Meadows, B.C., August 15, 1975. New Jersey's 3rd choice, 39th overall, in 1993 Entry Draft.

Season	Club	League	GP	G	A	Pts	PIM	PP	SH	GW	S	%	+/-	TF	F%	Min	GP	G	A	Pts	PIM	PP	SH	GW	Min
1990-91	Ridge Meadows	BCAHA	77	126	127	253	88	....	....	....	....	....	....	....	....	....	....	....	....	....	....	....	....	....	....
1991-92	Ridge Meadows	BCAHA	55	56	111	167	56	....	....	....	....	....	....	....	....	....	....	....	....	....	....	....	....	....	....
1992-93	Penticton	BCJHL	56	35	59	94	45	....	....	....	....	....	....	....	....	....	....	....	....	....	....	....	....	....	....
1993-94	U. of Michigan	CCHA	38	20	28	48	24	....	....	....	....	....	....	....	....	....	5	2	7	9	2	....	....	....	....
1994-95	U. of Michigan	CCHA	39	23	*53	*76	42	....	....	....	....	....	....	....	....	....	5	1	11	12	6	....	....	....	....
1995-96	U. of Michigan	CCHA	35	28	44	*72	41	....	....	....	....	....	....	....	....	....	7	6	9	15	4	....	....	....	....
1996-97	U. of Michigan	CCHA	43	31	*57	*88	52	....	....	....	....	....	....	....	....	....	6	6	8	14	8	....	....	....	....
1997-98	**New Jersey**	**NHL**	**11**	**5**	**4**	**9**	**0**	**0**	**0**	**1**	**19**	**26.3**	**3**	....	....	....	**3**	**0**	**1**	**1**	**0**	**0**	**0**	**0**	....
	Albany River Rats	AHL	72	35	49	84	44	....	....	....	....	....	....	....	....	....	8	3	4	7	19	....	....	....	....
1998-99	**New Jersey**	**NHL**	**76**	**13**	**33**	**46**	**18**	**5**	**0**	**2**	**111**	**11.7**	**-4**	**920**	**51.1**	**13:55**	**7**	**0**	**2**	**2**	**0**	**0**	**0**	**0**	**13:04**
99-2000	Trebic	CzRep-2	2	0	0	0	0	....	....	....	....	....	....	....	....	....	....	....	....	....	....	....	....	....	....
	Pardubice	CzRep	6	5	2	7	2	....	....	....	....	....	....	....	....	....	....	....	....	....	....	....	....	....	....
	New Jersey	**NHL**	**44**	**5**	**21**	**26**	**8**	**2**	**0**	**1**	**79**	**6.3**	**8**	**572**	**51.1**	**16:09**	....	....	....	....	....	....	....	....	....
	Vancouver	**NHL**	**12**	**2**	**7**	**9**	**10**	**0**	**0**	**0**	**17**	**11.8**	**4**	**48**	**54.2**	**14:41**	....	....	....	....	....	....	....	....	....
2000-01	**Vancouver**	**NHL**	**82**	**16**	**38**	**54**	**42**	**3**	**2**	**3**	**179**	**8.9**	**2**	**1685**	**50.1**	**18:22**	**4**	**1**	**2**	**3**	**0**	**1**	**0**	**0**	**20:50**
2001-02	**Vancouver**	**NHL**	**82**	**23**	**44**	**67**	**26**	**6**	**0**	**4**	**183**	**12.6**	**18**	**1307**	**49.9**	**19:21**	**6**	**0**	**2**	**2**	**6**	**0**	**0**	**0**	**19:44**
2002-03	**Vancouver**	**NHL**	**82**	**25**	**46**	**71**	**36**	**6**	**2**	**8**	**167**	**15.0**	**18**	**1585**	**48.3**	**21:13**	**14**	**4**	**7**	**11**	**18**	**1**	**0**	**1**	**20:18**
2003-04	**Vancouver**	**NHL**	**82**	**22**	**38**	**60**	**50**	**5**	**1**	**4**	**161**	**13.7**	**16**	**1486**	**51.0**	**20:08**	**7**	**2**	**3**	**5**	**8**	**1**	**0**	**1**	**22:00**
2004-05	Linkopings HC	Sweden	45	16	28	44	50	....	....	....	....	....	....	....	....	....	6	0	2	2	10	....	....	....	....
2005-06	**Vancouver**	**NHL**	**82**	**19**	**37**	**56**	**84**	**8**	**0**	**5**	**156**	**12.2**	**-1**	**1328**	**50.5**	**19:31**	....	....	....	....	....	....	....	....	....
2006-07	**Vancouver**	**NHL**	**82**	**20**	**31**	**51**	**60**	**6**	**2**	**3**	**139**	**14.4**	**-9**	**1230**	**50.8**	**17:57**	**12**	**1**	**3**	**4**	**6**	**0**	**0**	**0**	**23:09**
	NHL Totals		**635**	**150**	**299**	**449**	**334**	**41**	**7**	**31**	**1211**	**12.4**		**10161**	**50.2**	**18:26**	**53**	**8**	**20**	**28**	**38**	**3**	**0**	**2**	**20:11**

CCHA Rookie of the Year (1994) • CCHA First All-Star Team (1995, 1996, 1997) • NCAA West First All-American Team (1995, 1996, 1997) • CCHA Player of the Year (1996, 1997) • NCAA Championship All-Tournament Team (1996) • NCAA Championship Tournament MVP (1996) • Hobey Baker Memorial Award (Top U.S. Collegiate Player) (1997) • AHL All-Rookie Team (1998)

Traded to **Vancouver** by **New Jersey** with Denis Pederson for Alexander Mogilny, March 14, 2000. Signed as a free agent by **Linkopings** (Sweden), September, 2004.

MORRISONN, Shaone

(MOHR-ih-suhn, SHAWN) **WSH.**

Defense. Shoots left. 6'4", 210 lbs. Born, Vancouver, B.C., December 23, 1982. Boston's 1st choice, 19th overall, in 2001 Entry Draft.

Season	Club	League	GP	G	A	Pts	PIM	PP	SH	GW	S	%	+/-	TF	F%	Min	GP	G	A	Pts	PIM	PP	SH	GW	Min
1997-98	Vancouver T-Birds	BCAHA	45	16	44	60	75	....	....	....	....	....	....	....	....	....	....	....	....	....	....	....	....	....	....
1998-99	South Surrey	BCHL	19	0	2	2	13	....	....	....	....	....	....	....	....	....	....	....	....	....	....	....	....	....	....
99-2000	Kamloops Blazers	WHL	57	1	6	7	80	....	....	....	....	....	....	....	....	....	4	0	0	0	6	....	....	....	....
2000-01	Kamloops Blazers	WHL	61	13	25	38	132	....	....	....	....	....	....	....	....	....	4	0	0	0	6	....	....	....	....
2001-02	Kamloops Blazers	WHL	61	11	26	37	106	....	....	....	....	....	....	....	....	....	4	0	2	2	2	....	....	....	....
2002-03	**Boston**	**NHL**	**11**	**0**	**0**	**0**	**8**	**0**	**0**	**0**	**4**	**0.0**	**0**	**0**	**0.0**	**8:57**	....	....	....	....	....	....	....	....	....
	Providence Bruins	AHL	60	5	16	21	103	....	....	....	....	....	....	....	....	....	4	0	0	0	6	....	....	....	....
2003-04	**Boston**	**NHL**	**30**	**1**	**7**	**8**	**10**	**0**	**0**	**0**	**13**	**7.7**	**10**	**0**	**0.0**	**18:11**	....	....	....	....	....	....	....	....	....
	Providence Bruins	AHL	18	0	2	2	16	....	....	....	....	....	....	....	....	....	....	....	....	....	....	....	....	....	....
	Washington	**NHL**	**3**	**0**	**0**	**0**	**0**	**0**	**0**	**0**	**1**	**0.0**	**0**	**0**	**0.0**	**18:52**	....	....	....	....	....	....	....	....	....
	Portland Pirates	AHL	13	1	4	5	10	....	....	....	....	....	....	....	....	....	7	0	1	1	4	....	....	....	....
2004-05	Portland Pirates	AHL	71	4	14	18	63	....	....	....	....	....	....	....	....	....	....	....	....	....	....	....	....	....	....
2005-06	**Washington**	**NHL**	**80**	**1**	**13**	**14**	**91**	**0**	**0**	**0**	**56**	**1.8**	**7**	**4**	**0.0**	**20:44**	....	....	....	....	....	....	....	....	....
2006-07	**Washington**	**NHL**	**78**	**3**	**10**	**13**	**106**	**0**	**0**	**0**	**46**	**6.5**	**3**	**2**	**0.0**	**20:57**	....	....	....	....	....	....	....	....	....
	NHL Totals		**202**	**5**	**30**	**35**	**215**	**0**	**0**	**0**	**120**	**4.2**		**6**	**0.0**	**19:46**	....	....	....	....	....	....	....	....	....

Traded to **Washington** by **Boston** with Boston's 1st (Jeff Schultz) and 2nd (Michail Yunkov) round choices in 2004 Entry Draft for Sergei Gonchar, March 3, 2004.

MORROW, Brenden

(MOHR-roh, BREHN-duhn) **DAL.**

Left wing. Shoots left. 5'11", 210 lbs. Born, Carlyle, Sask., January 16, 1979. Dallas' 1st choice, 25th overall, in 1997 Entry Draft.

Season	Club	League	GP	G	A	Pts	PIM	PP	SH	GW	S	%	+/-	TF	F%	Min	GP	G	A	Pts	PIM	PP	SH	GW	Min
1994-95	Estevan	SMBHL	60	117	72	189	45	....	....	....	....	....	....	....	....	....	....	....	....	....	....	....	....	....	....
1995-96	Portland	WHL	65	13	12	25	61	....	....	....	....	....	....	....	....	....	7	0	0	0	8	....	....	....	....
1996-97	Portland	WHL	71	39	49	88	178	....	....	....	....	....	....	....	....	....	6	2	1	3	4	....	....	....	....
1997-98	Portland	WHL	68	34	52	86	184	....	....	....	....	....	....	....	....	....	16	10	8	18	65	....	....	....	....
1998-99	Portland	WHL	61	41	44	85	248	....	....	....	....	....	....	....	....	....	4	0	4	4	18	....	....	....	....
99-2000	**Dallas**	**NHL**	**64**	**14**	**19**	**33**	**81**	**3**	**0**	**3**	**113**	**12.4**	**8**	**25**	**48.0**	**15:51**	**21**	**2**	**4**	**6**	**22**	**1**	**0**	**0**	**15:04**
	Michigan	IHL	9	2	0	2	18	....	....	....	....	....	....	....	....	....	....	....	....	....	....	....	....	....	....
2000-01	**Dallas**	**NHL**	**82**	**20**	**24**	**44**	**128**	**7**	**0**	**6**	**121**	**16.5**	**18**	**22**	**45.5**	**15:29**	**10**	**0**	**3**	**3**	**12**	**0**	**0**	**0**	**17:00**
2001-02	**Dallas**	**NHL**	**72**	**17**	**18**	**35**	**109**	**4**	**0**	**3**	**102**	**16.7**	**12**	**39**	**41.0**	**16:52**	....	....	....	....	....	....	....	....	....
2002-03	**Dallas**	**NHL**	**71**	**21**	**22**	**43**	**134**	**2**	**3**	**4**	**105**	**20.0**	**20**	**29**	**27.6**	**15:43**	**12**	**3**	**5**	**8**	**16**	**2**	**0**	**0**	**21:03**
2003-04	**Dallas**	**NHL**	**81**	**25**	**24**	**49**	**121**	**9**	**0**	**3**	**132**	**18.9**	**10**	**38**	**47.4**	**19:24**	**5**	**0**	**1**	**1**	**4**	**0**	**0**	**0**	**21:29**
2004-05	Oklahoma City	CHL	19	8	14	22	31	....	....	....	....	....	....	....	....	....	....	....	....	....	....	....	....	....	....
2005-06	**Dallas**	**NHL**	**81**	**23**	**42**	**65**	**183**	**8**	**1**	**4**	**146**	**15.8**	**30**	**32**	**37.5**	**19:15**	**5**	**1**	**5**	**6**	**6**	**0**	**0**	**0**	**21:57**
2006-07	**Dallas**	**NHL**	**40**	**16**	**15**	**31**	**33**	**8**	**0**	**3**	**101**	**15.8**	**-2**	**51**	**39.2**	**18:16**	**7**	**2**	**1**	**3**	**18**	**2**	**0**	**1**	**21:54**
	NHL Totals		**491**	**136**	**164**	**300**	**789**	**41**	**4**	**26**	**820**	**16.6**		**236**	**40.7**	**17:16**	**60**	**8**	**19**	**27**	**78**	**5**	**0**	**1**	**18:29**

WHL West First All-Star Team (1999)

Signed as a free agent by **Oklahoma City** (CHL), October 19, 2004. • Missed majority of 2006-07 season recovering from groin and wrist injuries.

MOSS, Dave

(MAWS, DAYV) **CGY.**

Left wing. Shoots left. 6'3", 203 lbs. Born, Dearborn, MI, December 28, 1981. Calgary's 9th choice, 220th overall, in 2001 Entry Draft.

Season	Club	League	GP	G	A	Pts	PIM	PP	SH	GW	S	%	+/-	TF	F%	Min	GP	G	A	Pts	PIM	PP	SH	GW	Min
99-2000	Catholic Central	High-MI	28	18	20	28	20	....	....	....	....	....	....	....	....	....	....	....	....	....	....	....	....	....	....
2000-01	St. Louis Jr. Blues	CSJHL	9	2	2	4	2	....	....	....	....	....	....	....	....	....	....	....	....	....	....	....	....	....	....
	Cedar Rapids	USHL	51	20	18	38	14	....	....	....	....	....	....	....	....	....	4	0	1	1	2	....	....	....	....
2001-02	U. of Michigan	CCHA	43	4	9	13	10	....	....	....	....	....	....	....	....	....	....	....	....	....	....	....	....	....	....
2002-03	U. of Michigan	CCHA	43	14	17	31	37	....	....	....	....	....	....	....	....	....	....	....	....	....	....	....	....	....	....
2003-04	U. of Michigan	CCHA	38	8	12	20	18	....	....	....	....	....	....	....	....	....	....	....	....	....	....	....	....	....	....
2004-05	U. of Michigan	CCHA	38	10	20	30	26	....	....	....	....	....	....	....	....	....	....	....	....	....	....	....	....	....	....
2005-06	Omaha	AHL	63	21	27	48	28	....	....	....	....	....	....	....	....	....	....	....	....	....	....	....	....	....	....
2006-07	**Calgary**	**NHL**	**41**	**10**	**8**	**18**	**12**	**3**	**0**	**1**	**70**	**14.3**	**5**	**11**	**36.4**	**11:13**	**6**	**0**	**1**	**1**	**0**	**0**	**0**	**0**	**10:30**
	Omaha	AHL	28	9	12	21	22	....	....	....	....	....	....	....	....	....	....	....	....	....	....	....	....	....	....
	NHL Totals		**41**	**10**	**8**	**18**	**12**	**3**	**0**	**1**	**70**	**14.3**		**11**	**36.4**	**11:13**	**6**	**0**	**1**	**1**	**0**	**0**	**0**	**0**	**10:30**

MOTTAU, Mike

(MAW-tuh, MIGHK) **N.J.**

Defense. Shoots left. 6', 190 lbs. Born, Quincy, MA, March 19, 1978. NY Rangers' 10th choice, 182nd overall, in 1997 Entry Draft.

Season	Club	League	GP	G	A	Pts	PIM	PP	SH	GW	S	%	+/-	TF	F%	Min	GP	G	A	Pts	PIM	PP	SH	GW	Min
1994-95	Thayer Academy	High-MA	29	7	19	26	....	....	....	....	....	....	....	....	....	....	....	....	....	....	....	....	....	....	....
1995-96	Thayer Academy	High-MA	31	6	20	26	14	....	....	....	....	....	....	....	....	....	....	....	....	....	....	....	....	....	....
1996-97	Boston College	H-East	38	5	18	23	77	....	....	....	....	....	....	....	....	....	....	....	....	....	....	....	....	....	....
1997-98	Boston College	H-East	40	13	36	49	50	....	....	....	....	....	....	....	....	....	....	....	....	....	....	....	....	....	....
1998-99	Boston College	H-East	43	3	39	42	44	....	....	....	....	....	....	....	....	....	....	....	....	....	....	....	....	....	....
99-2000	Boston College	H-East	42	6	37	43	61	....	....	....	....	....	....	....	....	....	....	....	....	....	....	....	....	....	....
2000-01	**NY Rangers**	**NHL**	**18**	**0**	**3**	**3**	**13**	**0**	**0**	**0**	**17**	**0.0**	**-6**	**0**	**0.0**	**15:18**	....	....	....	....	....	....	....	....	....
	Hartford	AHL	61	10	33	43	45	....	....	....	....	....	....	....	....	....	5	0	1	1	19	....	....	....	....
2001-02	**NY Rangers**	**NHL**	**1**	**0**	**0**	**0**	**0**	**0**	**0**	**0**	**0**	**0.0**	**0**	**0**	**0.0**	**6:20**	....	....	....	....	....	....	....	....	....
	Hartford	AHL	80	9	42	51	56	....	....	....	....	....	....	....	....	....	10	0	5	5	4	....	....	....	....
2002-03	Hartford	AHL	29	1	18	19	24	....	....	....	....	....	....	....	....	....	....	....	....	....	....	....	....	....	....
	Calgary	**NHL**	**4**	**0**	**0**	**0**	**0**	**0**	**0**	**0**	**0**	**0.0**	**-1**	**0**	**0.0**	**9:50**	....	....	....	....	....	....	....	....	....
	Saint John Flames	AHL	32	5	12	17	14	....	....	....	....	....	....	....	....	....	....	....	....	....	....	....	....	....	....

			Regular Season														Playoffs								
Season	Club	League	GP	G	A	Pts	PIM	PP	SH	GW	S	%	+/-	TF	F%	Min	GP	G	A	Pts	PIM	PP	SH	GW	Min
2003-04	Cincinnati	AHL	69	9	22	31	79	....	....	....	....	....	....	....	....	....	9	1	2	3	8	....	....	....	....
2004-05	Worcester IceCats	AHL	73	4	31	35	23	....	....	....	....	....	....	....	....	....	....	....	....	....	....	....	....	....	....
2005-06	Peoria Rivermen	AHL	76	8	48	56	81	....	....	....	....	....	....	....	....	....	4	0	1	1	6	....	....	....	....
2006-07	Lowell Devils	AHL	43	1	26	27	33	....	....	....	....	....	....	....	....	....	....	....	....	....	....	....	....	....	....
	NHL Totals		**23**	**0**	**3**	**3**	**13**	**0**	**0**	**0**	**17**	**0.0**		**0**	**0.0**	**13:57**	....	....	....	....	....	....	....	....	....

Hockey East First All-Star Team (1998, 2000) • NCAA East Second All-American Team (1998) • NCAA Championship All-Tournament Team (1998, 2000) • Hockey East Second All-Star Team (1999) • NCAA East First All-American Team (1999, 2000) • Hockey East Player of the Year (2000) (co-winner - Ty Conklin) • Hobey Baker Memorial Award (Top U.S. Collegiate Player) (2000) • AHL All-Rookie Team (2001)

Traded to **Calgary** by **NY Rangers** for Calgary's 6th round choice (Ivan Dornic) in 2003 Entry Draft and future considerations, January 22, 2003. Signed as a free agent by **Anaheim**, July 25, 2003. Signed as a free agent by **Worcester** (AHL), September 30, 2004. Signed as a free agent by **New Jersey**, July 17, 2006.

MOTZKO, Joe (MAWTS-koh, JOH) WSH.

Right wing. Shoots right. 6', 184 lbs. Born, Bemidji, MN, March 14, 1980.

Season	Club	League	GP	G	A	Pts	PIM	PP	SH	GW	S	%	+/-	TF	F%	Min	GP	G	A	Pts	PIM	PP	SH	GW	Min
1997-98	Bemidji Jacks	High-MN	25	24	28	52	....	....	....	....	....	....	....	....	....	....	....	....	....	....	....	....	....	....	....
1998-99	Omaha Lancers	USHL	51	15	21	36	60	....	....	....	....	....	....	....	....	....	12	7	3	10	12	....	....	....	....
99-2000	St. Cloud State	WCHA	36	9	15	24	52	....	....	....	....	....	....	....	....	....	....	....	....	....	....	....	....	....	....
2000-01	St. Cloud State	WCHA	41	17	20	37	54	....	....	....	....	....	....	....	....	....	....	....	....	....	....	....	....	....	....
2001-02	St. Cloud State	WCHA	39	9	30	39	34	....	....	....	....	....	....	....	....	....	....	....	....	....	....	....	....	....	....
2002-03	St. Cloud State	WCHA	38	17	25	42	59	....	....	....	....	....	....	....	....	....	....	....	....	....	....	....	....	....	....
	Syracuse Crunch	AHL	2	0	0	0	0	....	....	....	....	....	....	....	....	....	....	....	....	....	....	....	....	....	....
2003-04	**Columbus**	**NHL**	**2**	**0**	**0**	**0**	**0**	**0**	**0**	**0**	**1**	**0.0**	**0**	**0**	**0.0**	**7:16**	....	....	....	....	....	....	....	....	....
	Syracuse Crunch	AHL	70	17	24	41	38	....	....	....	....	....	....	....	....	....	7	2	2	4	6	....	....	....	....
2004-05	Syracuse Crunch	AHL	79	28	38	66	72	....	....	....	....	....	....	....	....	....	....	....	....	....	....	....	....	....	....
2005-06	**Columbus**	**NHL**	**2**	**0**	**0**	**0**	**0**	**0**	**0**	**0**	**3**	**0.0**	**–2**	**1**	**0.0**	**10:35**	....	....	....	....	....	....	....	....	....
	Syracuse Crunch	AHL	61	27	34	61	54	....	....	....	....	....	....	....	....	....	3	0	0	0	0	....	....	....	....
2006-07	**Columbus**	**NHL**	**7**	**1**	**0**	**1**	**0**	**0**	**0**	**0**	**10**	**10.0**	**0**	**1**	**0.0**	**6:27**	....	....	....	....	....	....	....	....	....
	Syracuse Crunch	AHL	33	13	23	36	29	....	....	....	....	....	....	....	....	....	....	....	....	....	....	....	....	....	....
	Portland Pirates	AHL	34	15	14	29	20	....	....	....	....	....	....	....	....	....	....	....	....	....	....	....	....	....	....
	♦ Anaheim	**NHL**	....	....	....	....	....	....	....	....	....	....	....	....	....	....	**3**	**0**	**0**	**0**	**2**	**0**	**0**	**0**	**3:55**
	NHL Totals		**11**	**1**	**0**	**1**	**0**	**0**	**0**	**0**	**14**	**7.1**		**2**	**0.0**	**7:21**	**3**	**0**	**0**	**0**	**2**	**0**	**0**	**0**	**3:55**

Signed as a free agent by **Columbus**, May 15, 2003. Traded to **Anaheim** by **Columbus** with Mark Hartigan and Columbus' 4th round choice (Sebastian Stefaniszin) in 2007 Entry Draft for Zenon Konopka, Curtis Glencross and Anaheim's 7th round choice (Trent Vogelhuber) in 2007 Entry Draft, January 26, 2007. Signed as a free agent by **Washington**, July 9, 2007.

MOWERS, Mark (MAH-wuhrs, MAHRK) BOS.

Center. Shoots right. 5'11", 174 lbs. Born, Decatur, GA, February 16, 1974.

Season	Club	League	GP	G	A	Pts	PIM	PP	SH	GW	S	%	+/-	TF	F%	Min	GP	G	A	Pts	PIM	PP	SH	GW	Min
1992-93	Saginaw Jr. Gears	NAHL	39	31	39	70	....	....	....	....	....	....	....	....	....	....	....	....	....	....	....	....	....	....	....
1993-94	Dubuque	USHL	47	51	31	82	80	....	....	....	....	....	....	....	....	....	....	....	....	....	....	....	....	....	....
1994-95	New Hampshire	H-East	36	13	23	36	16	....	....	....	....	....	....	....	....	....	....	....	....	....	....	....	....	....	....
1995-96	New Hampshire	H-East	34	21	26	47	18	....	....	....	....	....	....	....	....	....	....	....	....	....	....	....	....	....	....
1996-97	New Hampshire	H-East	39	26	32	58	52	....	....	....	....	....	....	....	....	....	....	....	....	....	....	....	....	....	....
1997-98	New Hampshire	H-East	35	25	31	56	32	....	....	....	....	....	....	....	....	....	....	....	....	....	....	....	....	....	....
1998-99	**Nashville**	**NHL**	**30**	**0**	**6**	**6**	**4**	**0**	**0**	**0**	**24**	**0.0**	**–4**	**241**	**49.0**	**9:22**	....	....	....	....	....	....	....	....	....
	Milwaukee	IHL	51	14	22	36	24	....	....	....	....	....	....	....	....	....	1	0	0	0	0	....	....	....	....
99-2000	**Nashville**	**NHL**	**41**	**4**	**5**	**9**	**10**	**0**	**0**	**0**	**50**	**8.0**	**0**	**312**	**45.2**	**10:58**	....	....	....	....	....	....	....	....	....
	Milwaukee	IHL	23	11	15	26	34	....	....	....	....	....	....	....	....	....	....	....	....	....	....	....	....	....	....
2000-01	Milwaukee	IHL	63	25	25	50	54	....	....	....	....	....	....	....	....	....	5	1	2	3	2	....	....	....	....
2001-02	**Nashville**	**NHL**	**14**	**1**	**2**	**3**	**2**	**0**	**0**	**0**	**5**	**20.0**	**–2**	**24**	**33.3**	**8:31**	....	....	....	....	....	....	....	....	....
	Milwaukee	AHL	45	19	20	39	34	....	....	....	....	....	....	....	....	....	....	....	....	....	....	....	....	....	....
2002-03	Grand Rapids	AHL	78	34	47	81	47	....	....	....	....	....	....	....	....	....	15	3	4	7	4	....	....	....	....
2003-04	**Detroit**	**NHL**	**52**	**3**	**8**	**11**	**4**	**1**	**0**	**1**	**48**	**6.3**	**3**	**400**	**47.8**	**10:27**	....	....	....	....	....	....	....	....	....
	Grand Rapids	AHL	16	8	6	14	4	....	....	....	....	....	....	....	....	....	....	....	....	....	....	....	....	....	....
2004-05	Malmo	Sweden	9	2	0	2	0	....	....	....	....	....	....	....	....	....	....	....	....	....	....	....	....	....	....
	Fribourg	Swiss	3	2	0	2	0	....	....	....	....	....	....	....	....	....	9	9	8	17	12	....	....	....	....
2005-06	**Detroit**	**NHL**	**46**	**4**	**11**	**15**	**16**	**0**	**0**	**0**	**65**	**6.2**	**13**	**100**	**52.0**	**8:18**	**3**	**0**	**0**	**0**	**0**	**0**	**0**	**0**	**9:27**
2006-07	**Boston**	**NHL**	**78**	**5**	**12**	**17**	**26**	**0**	**1**	**0**	**60**	**8.3**	**–10**	**593**	**45.0**	**12:00**	....	....	....	....	....	....	....	....	....
	NHL Totals		**261**	**17**	**44**	**61**	**62**	**1**	**1**	**1**	**252**	**6.7**		**1670**	**46.5**	**10:23**	**3**	**0**	**0**	**0**	**0**	**0**	**0**	**0**	**9:27**

Hockey East Rookie of the Year (1995) • Hockey East Second All-Star Team (1998) • NCAA East First All-American Team (1998) • Ken McKenzie Trophy (U.S. - Born Rookie of the Year – IHL) (1999) • AHL Second All-Star Team (2003)

Signed as a free agent by **Nashville**, June 11, 1998. Signed as a free agent by **Detroit**, August 5, 2002. Signed as a free agent by **Malmo** (Sweden), December 21, 2004. Signed as a free agent by **Fribourg** (Swiss), February 4, 2005. Signed as a free agent by **Boston**, July 6, 2006.

MUIR, Bryan (MEWR, BRIGH-uhn)

Defense. Shoots left. 6'3", 224 lbs. Born, Winnipeg, Man., June 8, 1973.

Season	Club	League	GP	G	A	Pts	PIM	PP	SH	GW	S	%	+/-	TF	F%	Min	GP	G	A	Pts	PIM	PP	SH	GW	Min
1991-92	Wexford Raiders	MTJHL	44	3	19	22	35	....	....	....	....	....	....	....	....	....	....	....	....	....	....	....	....	....	....
1992-93	New Hampshire	H-East	26	1	2	3	24	....	....	....	....	....	....	....	....	....	....	....	....	....	....	....	....	....	....
1993-94	New Hampshire	H-East	40	0	4	4	48	....	....	....	....	....	....	....	....	....	....	....	....	....	....	....	....	....	....
1994-95	New Hampshire	H-East	28	9	9	18	46	....	....	....	....	....	....	....	....	....	....	....	....	....	....	....	....	....	....
1995-96	Canada	Nat-Tm	42	6	12	18	38	....	....	....	....	....	....	....	....	....	....	....	....	....	....	....	....	....	....
	Edmonton	**NHL**	**5**	**0**	**0**	**0**	**6**	**0**	**0**	**0**	**4**	**0.0**	**–4**	....	....	....	....	....	....	....	....	....	....	....	....
1996-97	Hamilton	AHL	75	8	16	24	80	....	....	....	....	....	....	....	....	....	14	0	5	5	12	....	....	....	....
	Edmonton	**NHL**	....	....	....	....	....	....	....	....	....	....	....	....	....	....	**5**	**0**	**0**	**0**	**4**	**0**	**0**	**0**	....
1997-98	**Edmonton**	**NHL**	**7**	**0**	**0**	**0**	**17**	**0**	**0**	**0**	**6**	**0.0**	**0**	....	....	....	....	....	....	....	....	....	....	....	....
	Hamilton	AHL	28	3	10	13	62	....	....	....	....	....	....	....	....	....	....	....	....	....	....	....	....	....	....
	Albany River Rats	AHL	41	3	10	13	67	....	....	....	....	....	....	....	....	....	13	3	0	3	12	....	....	....	....
1998-99	**New Jersey**	**NHL**	**1**	**0**	**0**	**0**	**0**	**0**	**0**	**0**	**4**	**0.0**	**0**	**0**	**0.0**	**9:54**	....	....	....	....	....	....	....	....	....
	Albany River Rats	AHL	10	0	0	0	29	....	....	....	....	....	....	....	....	....	....	....	....	....	....	....	....	....	....
	Chicago	**NHL**	**53**	**1**	**4**	**5**	**50**	**0**	**0**	**0**	**78**	**1.3**	**1**	**0**	**0.0**	**18:49**	....	....	....	....	....	....	....	....	....
	Portland Pirates	AHL	2	1	1	2	2	....	....	....	....	....	....	....	....	....	....	....	....	....	....	....	....	....	....
99-2000	**Chicago**	**NHL**	**11**	**2**	**3**	**5**	**13**	**0**	**1**	**0**	**19**	**10.5**	**–1**	**0**	**0.0**	**17:54**	....	....	....	....	....	....	....	....	....
	Tampa Bay	**NHL**	**30**	**1**	**1**	**2**	**32**	**0**	**0**	**0**	**32**	**3.1**	**–8**	**1**	**100.0**	**19:29**	....	....	....	....	....	....	....	....	....
2000-01	**Tampa Bay**	**NHL**	**10**	**0**	**3**	**3**	**15**	**0**	**0**	**0**	**14**	**0.0**	**–7**	**1**	**0.0**	**18:34**	....	....	....	....	....	....	....	....	....
	Detroit Vipers	IHL	21	5	7	12	36	....	....	....	....	....	....	....	....	....	....	....	....	....	....	....	....	....	....
	♦ Colorado	**NHL**	**8**	**0**	**0**	**0**	**4**	**0**	**0**	**0**	**3**	**0.0**	**0**	**0**	**0.0**	**8:14**	**3**	**0**	**0**	**0**	**0**	**0**	**0**	**0**	**3:15**
	Hershey Bears	AHL	26	5	8	13	50	....	....	....	....	....	....	....	....	....	....	....	....	....	....	....	....	....	....
2001-02	**♦ Colorado**	**NHL**	**22**	**1**	**1**	**2**	**9**	**0**	**0**	**0**	**26**	**3.8**	**1**	**0**	**0.0**	**10:20**	**21**	**0**	**0**	**0**	**2**	**0**	**0**	**0**	**5:39**
	Hershey Bears	AHL	59	10	16	26	133	....	....	....	....	....	....	....	....	....	....	....	....	....	....	....	....	....	....
2002-03	**Colorado**	**NHL**	**32**	**0**	**2**	**2**	**19**	**0**	**0**	**0**	**9**	**0.0**	**3**	**0**	**0.0**	**6:33**	....	....	....	....	....	....	....	....	....
	Hershey Bears	AHL	36	9	12	21	75	....	....	....	....	....	....	....	....	....	5	2	6	8	6	....	....	....	....
2003-04	**Los Angeles**	**NHL**	**2**	**0**	**1**	**1**	**2**	**0**	**0**	**0**	**2**	**0.0**	**1**	**0**	**0.0**	**17:56**	....	....	....	....	....	....	....	....	....
	Manchester	AHL	73	13	37	50	141	....	....	....	....	....	....	....	....	....	6	2	3	5	12	....	....	....	....
2004-05	MODO	Sweden	26	1	5	6	36	....	....	....	....	....	....	....	....	....	....	....	....	....	....	....	....	....	....
	Blues Espoo	Finland	11	1	0	1	30	....	....	....	....	....	....	....	....	....	....	....	....	....	....	....	....	....	....
2005-06	**Washington**	**NHL**	**72**	**8**	**18**	**26**	**72**	**4**	**0**	**0**	**136**	**5.9**	**–9**	**1**	**100.0**	**21:10**	....	....	....	....	....	....	....	....	....
2006-07	**Washington**	**NHL**	**26**	**3**	**4**	**7**	**42**	**0**	**0**	**1**	**28**	**10.7**	**3**	**0**	**0.0**	**14:37**	....	....	....	....	....	....	....	....	....
	NHL Totals		**279**	**16**	**37**	**53**	**281**	**4**	**1**	**1**	**361**	**4.4**		**3**	**66.7**	**16:33**	**29**	**0**	**0**	**0**	**6**	**0**	**0**	**0**	**5:21**

AHL First All-Star Team (2004)

Signed to five-game ATO (tryout) contract by **Edmonton**, February 29, 1996. Signed as a free agent by **Edmonton**, April 30, 1996. Traded to **New Jersey** by **Edmonton** with Jason Arnott for Valeri Zelepukin and Bill Guerin, January 4, 1998. Traded to **Chicago** by **New Jersey** for Chicago's 3rd round choice (Mike Rupp) in 2000 Entry Draft. November 13, 1998. Traded to **Tampa Bay** by **Chicago** with Reid Simpson for Michael Nylander, November 12, 1999. • Missed majority of 1999-2000 season recovering from leg injury suffered in game vs. Atlanta, November 17, 1999. Traded to **Colorado** by **Tampa Bay** for Colorado's 8th round choice (Dmitri Bezrukov) in 2001 Entry Draft, January 23, 2001. Signed as a free agent by **Los Angeles**, July 31, 2003. Signed as a free agent by **MODO** (Sweden), July 26, 2004. Signed as a free agent by **Espoo** (Finland), January 31, 2005. Signed as a free agent by **Washington**, August 30, 2005. • Missed majority of 2006-07 season recovering from a foot injury.

			Regular Season														Playoffs								
Season	Club	League	GP	G	A	Pts	PIM	PP	SH	GW	S	%	+/-	TF	F%	Min	GP	G	A	Pts	PIM	PP	SH	GW	Min

MURLEY, Matt

(MUHR-lee, MAT) **PHX.**

Left wing. Shoots left. 6'1", 206 lbs. Born, Troy, NY, December 17, 1979. Pittsburgh's 2nd choice, 51st overall, in 1999 Entry Draft.

Season	Club	League	GP	G	A	Pts	PIM	PP	SH	GW	S	%	+/-	TF	F%	Min	GP	G	A	Pts	PIM	PP	SH	GW	Min
1996-97	Syracuse	MTJHL	48	52	58	110	111																		
1997-98	Syracuse	MTJHL	49	56	70	126	103																		
1998-99	RPI Engineers	ECAC	36	17	32	49	32																		
99-2000	RPI Engineers	ECAC	35	9	29	38	42																		
2000-01	RPI Engineers	ECAC	34	*24	18	42	34																		
2001-02	RPI Engineers	ECAC	32	*24	22	46	26																		
2002-03	Wilkes-Barre	AHL	73	21	37	58	45										6	0	2	2	15				
2003-04	**Pittsburgh**	**NHL**	**18**	**1**	**1**	**2**	**14**	**0**	**0**	**0**	**20**	**5.0**	**−6**	**2**	**50.0**	**11:49**									
	Wilkes-Barre	AHL	63	10	26	36	69										24	7	6	13	17				
2004-05	Wilkes-Barre	AHL	80	17	24	41	55										11	3	0	3	0				
2005-06	**Pittsburgh**	**NHL**	**41**	**1**	**5**	**6**	**24**	**0**	**0**	**0**	**48**	**2.1**	**−9**	**11**	**36.4**	**11:29**									
2006-07	Albany River Rats	AHL	61	23	32	55	18										5	1	5	6	8				
	NHL Totals		**59**	**2**	**6**	**8**	**38**	**0**	**0**	**0**	**68**	**2.9**		**13**	**38.5**	**11:35**									

ECAC First All-Star Team (2002)

Signed as a free agent by **Colorado**, July 12, 2006. Signed as a free agent by **Phoenix**, July 20, 2007.

MURPHY, Curtis

(MUHR-fee, KUHR-this)

Defense. Shoots right. 5'8", 185 lbs. Born, Kerrobert, Sask., December 3, 1975.

Season	Club	League	GP	G	A	Pts	PIM	PP	SH	GW	S	%	+/-	TF	F%	Min	GP	G	A	Pts	PIM	PP	SH	GW	Min
1993-94	Nipawin Hawks	SJHL	60	21	33	54																			
1994-95	North Dakota	WCHA	33	6	10	16	28																		
1995-96	North Dakota	WCHA	38	6	12	18	58																		
1996-97	North Dakota	WCHA	43	12	30	42	36																		
1997-98	North Dakota	WCHA	39	8	34	42	78																		
1998-99	Orlando	IHL	80	22	35	57	60										17	4	5	9	16				
99-2000	Orlando	IHL	81	8	43	51	59										6	0	2	2	6				
2000-01	Orlando	IHL	51	19	30	49	55										10	2	9	11	12				
2001-02	Houston Aeros	AHL	80	12	35	47	75										14	2	4	6	10				
2002-03	**Minnesota**	**NHL**	**1**	**0**	**0**	**0**	**0**	**0**	**0**	**0**	**0**	**0.0**	**0**	**0**	**0.0**	**8:56**									
	Houston Aeros	AHL	80	23	31	54	63										23	2	7	9	22				
2003-04	Milwaukee	AHL	79	17	36	53	51										22	4	8	12	12				
2004-05	Yaroslavl	Russia	60	6	6	12	50										9	1	1	2	6				
2005-06	Houston Aeros	AHL	80	14	53	67	76										8	0	4	4	4				
2006-07	Houston Aeros	AHL	75	10	35	45	52																		
	NHL Totals		**1**	**0**	**0**	**0**	**0**	**0**	**0**	**0**	**0**	**0.0**		**0**	**0.0**	**8:56**									

WCHA First All-Star Team (1997, 1998) • NCAA West Second All-American Team (1997) • WCHA Player of the Year (1998) • NCAA West First All-American Team (1998) • IHL First All-Star Team (2001) • AHL First All-Star Team (2003, 2004, 2006) • Eddie Shore Award (Outstanding Defenseman – AHL) (2003, 2004)

Signed as a free agent by **Minnesota**, June 18, 2001. Traded to **Nashville** by **Minnesota** for Chris Bala, June 26, 2003. Signed as a free agent by **Yaroslavl** (Russia), May 28, 2004.

MURRAY, Douglas

(MUHR-ree, DUHG-luhs) **S.J.**

Defense. Shoots left. 6'3", 240 lbs. Born, Bromma, Sweden, March 12, 1980. San Jose's 6th choice, 241st overall, in 1999 Entry Draft.

Season	Club	League	GP	G	A	Pts	PIM	PP	SH	GW	S	%	+/-	TF	F%	Min	GP	G	A	Pts	PIM	PP	SH	GW	Min
1998-99	NY Apple Core	EJHL	60	17	47	64	62																		
99-2000	Cornell Big Red	ECAC	32	3	6	9	38																		
2000-01	Cornell Big Red	ECAC	25	5	13	18	39																		
2001-02	Cornell Big Red	ECAC	35	11	21	32	67																		
2002-03	Cornell Big Red	ECAC	35	5	20	25	30																		
2003-04	Cleveland Barons	AHL	72	10	12	22	75										9	3	0	3	37				
2004-05	Cleveland Barons	AHL	54	6	17	23	56																		
2005-06	**San Jose**	**NHL**	**34**	**0**	**1**	**1**	**27**	**0**	**0**	**0**	**21**	**0.0**	**3**	**0**	**0.0**	**13:53**									
	Cleveland Barons	AHL	20	1	7	8	37																		
2006-07	**San Jose**	**NHL**	**35**	**0**	**3**	**3**	**31**	**0**	**0**	**0**	**18**	**0.0**	**0**	**0**	**0.0**	**10:46**									
	Worcester Sharks	AHL	5	2	1	3	8																		
	NHL Totals		**69**	**0**	**4**	**4**	**58**	**0**	**0**	**0**	**39**	**0.0**		**0**	**0.0**	**12:18**									

ECAC First All-Star Team (2002, 2003) • NCAA East First All-American Team (2003)

• Missed majority of 2006-07 season recovering from a respiratory infection.

MURRAY, Garth

(MUHR-ree, GARTH) **MTL.**

Center. Shoots left. 6'2", 208 lbs. Born, Regina, Sask., September 17, 1982. NY Rangers' 3rd choice, 79th overall, in 2001 Entry Draft.

Season	Club	League	GP	G	A	Pts	PIM	PP	SH	GW	S	%	+/-	TF	F%	Min	GP	G	A	Pts	PIM	PP	SH	GW	Min
1997-98	Calgary Buffaloes	AMHL	56	26	34	60	110																		
	Regina Pats	WHL	4	0	0	0	2										2	0	0	0	0				
1998-99	Regina Pats	WHL	60	3	5	8	101																		
99-2000	Regina Pats	WHL	68	14	26	40	155										7	1	1	2	7				
2000-01	Regina Pats	WHL	72	28	16	44	183										6	1	1	2	10				
2001-02	Regina Pats	WHL	62	33	30	63	154										6	2	3	5	9				
	Hartford	AHL	4	0	0	0	0										9	1	3	4	6				
2002-03	Hartford	AHL	64	10	14	24	121										2	0	0	0	6				
2003-04	**NY Rangers**	**NHL**	**20**	**1**	**0**	**1**	**24**	**0**	**0**	**0**	**18**	**5.6**	**−5**	**5**	**20.0**	**9:16**									
	Hartford	AHL	63	11	11	22	159										16	0	4	4	29				
2004-05	Hartford	AHL	55	4	5	9	182										5	1	0	1	8				
2005-06	**Montreal**	**NHL**	**36**	**5**	**1**	**6**	**44**	**0**	**0**	**1**	**25**	**20.0**	**−2**	**99**	**46.5**	**9:15**	**6**	**0**	**0**	**0**	**0**	**0**	**0**	**0**	**12:39**
	Hamilton	AHL	26	1	1	2	46																		
2006-07	**Montreal**	**NHL**	**43**	**2**	**1**	**3**	**32**	**0**	**0**	**0**	**28**	**7.1**	**−10**	**107**	**42.1**	**8:23**									
	NHL Totals		**99**	**8**	**2**	**10**	**100**	**0**	**0**	**1**	**71**	**11.3**		**211**	**43.6**	**8:53**	**6**	**0**	**0**	**0**	**0**	**0**	**0**	**0**	**12:39**

Traded to **Montreal** by **NY Rangers** for Marcel Hossa, September 30, 2005.

MURRAY, Glen

(MUHR-ree, GLEHN) **BOS.**

Right wing. Shoots right. 6'3", 215 lbs. Born, Halifax, N.S., November 1, 1972. Boston's 1st choice, 18th overall, in 1991 Entry Draft.

Season	Club	League	GP	G	A	Pts	PIM	PP	SH	GW	S	%	+/-	TF	F%	Min	GP	G	A	Pts	PIM	PP	SH	GW	Min
1988-89	Bridgewater	NSMHL	45	50	56	106	62																		
1989-90	Sudbury Wolves	OHL	62	8	28	36	17										7	0	0	0	4				
1990-91	Sudbury Wolves	OHL	66	27	38	65	82										5	8	4	12	10				
1991-92	Sudbury Wolves	OHL	54	37	47	84	93										11	7	4	11	18				
	Boston	**NHL**	**5**	**3**	**1**	**4**	**0**	**1**	**0**	**0**	**20**	**15.0**	**2**				**15**	**4**	**2**	**6**	**10**	**1**	**0**	**0**	
1992-93	**Boston**	**NHL**	**27**	**3**	**4**	**7**	**8**	**2**	**0**	**1**	**28**	**10.7**	**−6**												
	Providence Bruins	AHL	48	30	26	56	42										6	1	4	5	4				
1993-94	**Boston**	**NHL**	**81**	**18**	**13**	**31**	**48**	**0**	**0**	**4**	**114**	**15.8**	**−1**				**13**	**4**	**5**	**9**	**14**	**0**	**0**	**0**	
1994-95	**Boston**	**NHL**	**35**	**5**	**2**	**7**	**46**	**0**	**0**	**2**	**64**	**7.8**	**−11**				**2**	**0**	**0**	**0**	**2**	**0**	**0**	**0**	
1995-96	**Pittsburgh**	**NHL**	**69**	**14**	**15**	**29**	**57**	**0**	**0**	**2**	**100**	**14.0**	**4**				**18**	**2**	**6**	**8**	**10**	**0**	**0**	**1**	
1996-97	**Pittsburgh**	**NHL**	**66**	**11**	**11**	**22**	**24**	**3**	**0**	**1**	**127**	**8.7**	**−19**												
	Los Angeles	**NHL**	**11**	**5**	**3**	**8**	**8**	**0**	**0**	**0**	**26**	**19.2**	**−2**												
1997-98	**Los Angeles**	**NHL**	**81**	**29**	**31**	**60**	**54**	**7**	**3**	**7**	**193**	**15.0**	**6**				**4**	**2**	**0**	**2**	**6**	**0**	**0**	**0**	
1998-99	**Los Angeles**	**NHL**	**61**	**16**	**15**	**31**	**36**	**3**	**3**	**3**	**173**	**9.2**	**−14**	**12**	**25.0**	**20:33**									
99-2000	**Los Angeles**	**NHL**	**78**	**29**	**33**	**62**	**60**	**10**	**1**	**2**	**202**	**14.4**	**13**	**15**	**80.0**	**18:30**	**4**	**0**	**0**	**0**	**2**	**0**	**0**	**0**	**19:04**
2000-01	**Los Angeles**	**NHL**	**64**	**18**	**21**	**39**	**32**	**3**	**1**	**1**	**138**	**13.0**	**9**	**7**	**42.9**	**18:12**	**13**	**4**	**3**	**7**	**4**	**1**	**0**	**1**	**19:51**
2001-02	**Los Angeles**	**NHL**	**9**	**6**	**5**	**11**	**0**	**4**	**0**	**2**	**34**	**17.6**	**5**	**1**	**100.0**	**19:08**									
	Boston	**NHL**	**73**	**35**	**25**	**60**	**40**	**5**	**0**	**7**	**212**	**16.5**	**26**	**39**	**23.1**	**19:50**	**6**	**1**	**4**	**5**	**4**	**0**	**0**	**0**	**18:02**
2002-03	**Boston**	**NHL**	**82**	**44**	**48**	**92**	**64**	**12**	**0**	**5**	**331**	**13.3**	**9**	**32**	**37.5**	**22:36**	**5**	**1**	**1**	**2**	**4**	**0**	**0**	**0**	**19:36**
2003-04	**Boston**	**NHL**	**81**	**32**	**28**	**60**	**56**	**11**	**0**	**9**	**260**	**12.3**	**17**	**53**	**35.9**	**20:56**	**7**	**2**	**1**	**3**	**8**	**0**	**0**	**1**	**19:57**

Season	Club	League	GP	G	A	Pts	PIM	PP	SH	GW	S	%	+/-	TF	F%	Min	GP	G	A	Pts	PIM	PP	SH	GW	Min
			Regular Season														Playoffs								
2004-05			DID NOT PLAY																						
2005-06	**Boston**	**NHL**	**64**	**24**	**29**	**53**	**52**	**6**	**1**	**3**	**195**	**12.3**	**–8**	**14**	**28.6**	**20:12**	....	....	....	....	....	....	....	....	....
2006-07	**Boston**	**NHL**	**59**	**28**	**17**	**45**	**44**	**12**	**0**	**4**	**201**	**13.9**	**–12**	**19**	**52.6**	**18:45**	....	....	....	....	....	....	....	....	....
	NHL Totals		**946**	**320**	**301**	**621**	**629**	**79**	**9**	**53**	**2418**	**13.2**		**192**	**38.0**	**20:01**	**87**	**20**	**22**	**42**	**64**	**2**	**0**	**3**	**19:26**

Played in NHL All-Star Game (2003, 2004)

Traded to **Pittsburgh** by **Boston** with Bryan Smolinski and Boston's 3rd round choice (Boyd Kane) in 1996 Entry Draft for Kevin Stevens and Shawn McEachern, August 2, 1995. Traded to **Los Angeles** by **Pittsburgh** for Ed Olczyk, March 18, 1997. Traded to **Boston** by **Los Angeles** with Jozef Stumpel for Jason Allison and Mikko Eloranta, October 24, 2001.

MURRAY, Marty

(MUHR-ree, MAHR-tee)

Center. Shoots left. 5'9", 180 lbs. Born, Deloraine, Man., February 16, 1975. Calgary's 5th choice, 96th overall, in 1993 Entry Draft.

Season	Club	League	GP	G	A	Pts	PIM	PP	SH	GW	S	%	+/-	TF	F%	Min	GP	G	A	Pts	PIM	PP	SH	GW	Min
1990-91	S-W Cougars	MMMHL	36	46	47	93	50	....	....	....	....	....	....	....	....	....	....	....	....	....	....	....	....	....	....
1991-92	Brandon	WHL	68	20	36	56	22	....	....	....	....	....	....	....	....	....	....	....	....	....	....	....	....	....	....
1992-93	Brandon	WHL	67	29	65	94	50	....	....	....	....	....	....	....	....	....	4	1	3	4	0	....	....	....	....
1993-94	Brandon	WHL	64	43	71	114	33	....	....	....	....	....	....	....	....	....	14	6	14	20	14	....	....	....	....
1994-95	Brandon	WHL	65	40	*88	128	53	....	....	....	....	....	....	....	....	....	18	9	*20	29	16	....	....	....	....
1995-96	**Calgary**	**NHL**	**15**	**3**	**3**	**6**	**0**	**2**	**0**	**0**	**22**	**13.6**	**–4**	....	....	....	....	....	....	....	....	....	....	....	....
	Saint John Flames	AHL	58	25	31	56	20	....	....	....	....	....	....	....	....	....	14	2	4	6	4	....	....	....	....
1996-97	**Calgary**	**NHL**	**2**	**0**	**0**	**0**	**4**	**0**	**0**	**0**	**2**	**0.0**	**0**	....	....	....	....	....	....	....	....	....	....	....	....
	Saint John Flames	AHL	67	19	39	58	40	....	....	....	....	....	....	....	....	....	5	2	3	5	4	....	....	....	....
1997-98	**Calgary**	**NHL**	**2**	**0**	**0**	**0**	**2**	**0**	**0**	**0**	**2**	**0.0**	**1**	....	....	....	....	....	....	....	....	....	....	....	....
	Saint John Flames	AHL	41	10	30	40	16	....	....	....	....	....	....	....	....	....	21	10	10	20	12	....	....	....	....
1998-99	EC Villacher SV	Alpenliga	33	26	41	67	12	....	....	....	....	....	....	....	....	....	....	....	....	....	....	....	....	....	....
	EC Villacher SV	Austria	17	13	17	30	6	....	....	....	....	....	....	....	....	....	6	1	4	5	0	....	....	....	....
99-2000	Kolner Haie	Germany	56	12	47	59	28	....	....	....	....	....	....	....	....	....	10	4	3	7	2	....	....	....	....
2000-01	**Calgary**	**NHL**	**7**	**0**	**0**	**0**	**0**	**0**	**0**	**0**	**6**	**0.0**	**–2**	**88**	**55.7**	**14:28**	....	....	....	....	....	....	....	....	....
	Saint John Flames	AHL	56	24	52	76	36	....	....	....	....	....	....	....	....	....	19	4	16	20	18	....	....	....	....
2001-02	**Philadelphia**	**NHL**	**74**	**12**	**15**	**27**	**10**	**1**	**1**	**2**	**109**	**11.0**	**10**	**913**	**50.7**	**13:56**	**5**	**0**	**1**	**1**	**0**	**0**	**0**	**0**	**13:14**
	Philadelphia	AHL	3	0	3	3	2	....	....	....	....	....	....	....	....	....	....	....	....	....	....	....	....	....	....
2002-03	**Philadelphia**	**NHL**	**76**	**11**	**15**	**26**	**13**	**1**	**1**	**0**	**105**	**10.5**	**–1**	**472**	**55.1**	**12:22**	**4**	**0**	**0**	**0**	**4**	**0**	**0**	**0**	**11:01**
2003-04	**Carolina**	**NHL**	**66**	**5**	**7**	**12**	**8**	**0**	**0**	**0**	**56**	**8.9**	**6**	**229**	**52.8**	**11:49**	....	....	....	....	....	....	....	....	....
2004-05			DID NOT PLAY																						
2005-06	Hannover	Germany	24	7	15	22	16	....	....	....	....	....	....	....	....	....	9	4	3	7	35	....	....	....	....
2006-07	Philadelphia	AHL	11	2	13	15	4	....	....	....	....	....	....	....	....	....	....	....	....	....	....	....	....	....	....
	Los Angeles	**NHL**	**19**	**0**	**2**	**2**	**4**	**0**	**0**	**0**	**4**	**0.0**	**–5**	**139**	**46.8**	**9:32**	....	....	....	....	....	....	....	....	....
	Manchester	AHL	34	12	28	40	24	....	....	....	....	....	....	....	....	....	16	6	8	14	11	....	....	....	....
	NHL Totals		**261**	**31**	**42**	**73**	**41**	**4**	**2**	**2**	**306**	**10.1**		**1841**	**52.0**	**12:32**	**9**	**0**	**1**	**1**	**4**	**0**	**0**	**0**	**12:15**

WHL East First All-Star Team (1994, 1995) • Canadian Major Junior Second All-Star Team (1994) • WHL Player of the Year (1995)

Signed as a free agent by **Philadelphia**, July 9, 2001. Traded to **Carolina** by **Philadelphia** for Carolina's 6th round choice (Frederik Cabana) in 2004 Entry Draft, June 22, 2003. Signed as a free agent by **Hannover** (Germany), August 16, 2005. Signed as a free agent by **Philadelphia**, June 15, 2006. Claimed on waivers by **Los Angeles** from **Philadelphia**, November 11, 2006. Signed as a free agent by **Lugano** (Swiss), May 27, 2007.

MURRAY, Rem

(MUHR-ree, REHM)

Center/left wing. Shoots left. 6'2", 200 lbs. Born, Stratford, Ont., October 9, 1972. Los Angeles' 5th choice, 135th overall, in 1992 Entry Draft.

Season	Club	League	GP	G	A	Pts	PIM	PP	SH	GW	S	%	+/-	TF	F%	Min	GP	G	A	Pts	PIM	PP	SH	GW	Min
1989-90	Stratford Cullitons	OHA-B	46	19	32	51	48	....	....	....	....	....	....	....	....	....	....	....	....	....	....	....	....	....	....
1990-91	Stratford Cullitons	OHA-B	48	39	59	98	39	....	....	....	....	....	....	....	....	....	....	....	....	....	....	....	....	....	....
1991-92	Michigan State	CCHA	41	12	36	48	16	....	....	....	....	....	....	....	....	....	....	....	....	....	....	....	....	....	....
1992-93	Michigan State	CCHA	40	22	35	57	24	....	....	....	....	....	....	....	....	....	....	....	....	....	....	....	....	....	....
1993-94	Michigan State	CCHA	41	16	38	54	18	....	....	....	....	....	....	....	....	....	....	....	....	....	....	....	....	....	....
1994-95	Michigan State	CCHA	40	20	36	56	21	....	....	....	....	....	....	....	....	....	....	....	....	....	....	....	....	....	....
1995-96	Cape Breton	AHL	79	31	59	90	40	....	....	....	....	....	....	....	....	....	....	....	....	....	....	....	....	....	....
1996-97	**Edmonton**	**NHL**	**82**	**11**	**20**	**31**	**16**	**1**	**0**	**2**	**85**	**12.9**	**9**	....	....	....	**12**	**1**	**2**	**3**	**4**	**0**	**0**	**0**	....
1997-98	**Edmonton**	**NHL**	**61**	**9**	**9**	**18**	**39**	**2**	**2**	**0**	**59**	**15.3**	**–9**	....	....	....	**11**	**1**	**4**	**5**	**2**	**0**	**0**	**0**	....
1998-99	**Edmonton**	**NHL**	**78**	**21**	**18**	**39**	**20**	**4**	**1**	**4**	**116**	**18.1**	**4**	**1013**	**48.1**	**15:50**	**4**	**1**	**1**	**2**	**2**	**0**	**0**	**0**	**22:40**
99-2000	**Edmonton**	**NHL**	**44**	**9**	**5**	**14**	**8**	**2**	**0**	**3**	**65**	**13.8**	**–2**	**303**	**50.5**	**14:16**	**5**	**0**	**1**	**1**	**2**	**0**	**0**	**0**	**15:19**
2000-01	**Edmonton**	**NHL**	**82**	**15**	**21**	**36**	**24**	**1**	**3**	**3**	**122**	**12.3**	**5**	**694**	**49.3**	**15:21**	**6**	**2**	**0**	**2**	**6**	**1**	**0**	**0**	**18:10**
2001-02	**Edmonton**	**NHL**	**69**	**7**	**17**	**24**	**14**	**0**	**2**	**1**	**84**	**8.3**	**5**	**825**	**50.9**	**14:27**	....	....	....	....	....	....	....	....	....
	NY Rangers	**NHL**	**11**	**1**	**2**	**3**	**4**	**0**	**0**	**0**	**14**	**7.1**	**–9**	**151**	**51.7**	**15:51**	....	....	....	....	....	....	....	....	....
2002-03	**NY Rangers**	**NHL**	**32**	**6**	**6**	**12**	**4**	**1**	**1**	**1**	**62**	**9.7**	**–3**	**118**	**53.4**	**15:39**	....	....	....	....	....	....	....	....	....
	Nashville	**NHL**	**53**	**6**	**13**	**19**	**18**	**1**	**0**	**0**	**81**	**7.4**	**1**	**720**	**49.2**	**17:16**	....	....	....	....	....	....	....	....	....
2003-04	**Nashville**	**NHL**	**39**	**8**	**9**	**17**	**12**	**0**	**2**	**1**	**58**	**13.8**	**–1**	**169**	**46.2**	**16:37**	....	....	....	....	....	....	....	....	....
2004-05			DID NOT PLAY																						
2005-06	**Edmonton**	**NHL**	**9**	**1**	**1**	**2**	**2**	**0**	**0**	**0**	**6**	**16.7**	**1**	**40**	**50.0**	**7:49**	**24**	**0**	**4**	**4**	**2**	**0**	**0**	**0**	**8:37**
	Houston Aeros	AHL	54	11	24	35	8	....	....	....	....	....	....	....	....	....	....	....	....	....	....	....	....	....	....
2006-07	HIFK Helsinki	Finland	56	20	26	46	38	....	....	....	....	....	....	....	....	....	5	4	0	4	4	....	....	....	....
	NHL Totals		**560**	**94**	**121**	**215**	**161**	**12**	**11**	**15**	**752**	**12.5**		**4033**	**49.5**	**15:25**	**62**	**5**	**12**	**17**	**18**	**1**	**0**	**0**	**12:24**

CCHA Second All-Star Team (1995)

Signed as a free agent by **Edmonton**, September 19, 1995. Traded to **NY Rangers** by **Edmonton** with Tom Poti for Mike York and NY Rangers' 4th round choice (Ivan Koltsov) in 2002 Entry Draft, March 19, 2002. Traded to **Nashville** by **NY Rangers** with Tomas Kloucek and Marek Zidlicky for Mike Dunham, December 12, 2002. • Missed majority of 2003-04 season recovering from neck injury suffered in game vs. Detroit, January 5, 2004. Signed as a free agent by **HIFK Helsinki** (Finland), August 18, 2006.

NAGY, Ladislav

(NA-gee, LA-dih-slahv) **L.A.**

Left wing. Shoots left. 5'11", 192 lbs. Born, Saca, Czech., June 1, 1979. St. Louis' 6th choice, 177th overall, in 1997 Entry Draft.

Season	Club	League	GP	G	A	Pts	PIM	PP	SH	GW	S	%	+/-	TF	F%	Min	GP	G	A	Pts	PIM	PP	SH	GW	Min
1995-96	HK Dragon Presov	Slovakia	11	6	5	11	....	....	....	....	....	....	....	....	....	....	....	....	....	....	....	....	....	....	....
1996-97	HC Kosice Jr.	Slovak-Jr.	45	29	30	59	105	....	....	....	....	....	....	....	....	....	....	....	....	....	....	....	....	....	....
1997-98	HC Kosice	Slovakia	29	19	15	34	41	....	....	....	....	....	....	....	....	....	11	2	4	6	6	....	....	....	....
1998-99	Halifax	QMJHL	63	71	55	126	148	....	....	....	....	....	....	....	....	....	5	3	3	6	18	....	....	....	....
	Worcester IceCats	AHL	....	....	....	....	....	....	....	....	....	....	....	....	....	....	3	2	2	4	0	....	....	....	....
99-2000	**St. Louis**	**NHL**	**11**	**2**	**4**	**6**	**2**	**1**	**0**	**0**	**15**	**13.3**	**2**	**6**	**33.3**	**12:19**	**6**	**1**	**1**	**2**	**0**	**0**	**0**	**0**	**13:29**
	Worcester IceCats	AHL	69	23	28	51	67	....	....	....	....	....	....	....	....	....	2	1	0	1	0	....	....	....	....
2000-01	**St. Louis**	**NHL**	**40**	**8**	**8**	**16**	**20**	**2**	**0**	**2**	**59**	**13.6**	**–2**	**28**	**50.0**	**13:03**	....	....	....	....	....	....	....	....	....
	Worcester IceCats	AHL	20	6	14	20	36	....	....	....	....	....	....	....	....	....	....	....	....	....	....	....	....	....	....
	Phoenix	**NHL**	**6**	**0**	**1**	**1**	**2**	**0**	**0**	**0**	**5**	**0.0**	**0**	**0**	**0.0**	**12:38**	....	....	....	....	....	....	....	....	....
2001-02	**Phoenix**	**NHL**	**74**	**23**	**19**	**42**	**50**	**5**	**0**	**5**	**187**	**12.3**	**6**	**17**	**47.1**	**15:04**	**5**	**0**	**0**	**0**	**21**	**0**	**0**	**0**	**15:45**
2002-03	HC Kosice	Slovakia	1	2	1	3	0	....	....	....	....	....	....	....	....	....	....	....	....	....	....	....	....	....	....
	Phoenix	**NHL**	**80**	**22**	**35**	**57**	**92**	**8**	**0**	**6**	**209**	**10.5**	**17**	**41**	**34.2**	**17:28**	....	....	....	....	....	....	....	....	....
2003-04	**Phoenix**	**NHL**	**55**	**24**	**28**	**52**	**46**	**11**	**0**	**6**	**160**	**15.0**	**11**	**33**	**42.4**	**18:10**	....	....	....	....	....	....	....	....	....
2004-05	HC Kosice	Slovakia	18	9	7	16	40	....	....	....	....	....	....	....	....	....	....	....	....	....	....	....	....	....	....
	Mora IK	Sweden	19	4	4	8	22	....	....	....	....	....	....	....	....	....	....	....	....	....	....	....	....	....	....
2005-06	**Phoenix**	**NHL**	**51**	**15**	**41**	**56**	**74**	**7**	**1**	**4**	**132**	**11.4**	**8**	**72**	**40.3**	**18:53**	....	....	....	....	....	....	....	....	....
2006-07	**Phoenix**	**NHL**	**55**	**8**	**33**	**41**	**48**	**2**	**0**	**0**	**113**	**7.1**	**–2**	**43**	**30.2**	**17:52**	....	....	....	....	....	....	....	....	....
	Dallas	**NHL**	**25**	**4**	**10**	**14**	**6**	**2**	**0**	**1**	**33**	**12.1**	**–3**	**5**	**20.0**	**16:08**	**7**	**1**	**1**	**2**	**2**	**0**	**0**	**0**	**18:53**
	NHL Totals		**397**	**106**	**179**	**285**	**340**	**38**	**1**	**24**	**913**	**11.6**		**245**	**38.8**	**16:36**	**18**	**2**	**2**	**4**	**23**	**0**	**0**	**0**	**16:13**

Traded to **Phoenix** by **St. Louis** with Michal Handzus, the rights to Jeff Taffe and St. Louis' 1st round choice (Ben Eager) in 2002 Entry Draft for Keith Tkachuk, March 13, 2001. Signed as a free agent by **Kosice** (Slovakia), September 17, 2004. Signed as a free agent by **Mora** (Sweden), December 17, 2004. Traded to **Dallas** by **Phoenix** for Mathias Tjarnqvist and Dallas' 1st round choice (later traded to Edmonton - Edmonton selected Riley Nash) in 2007 Entry Draft, February 12, 2007. Signed as a free agent by **Los Angeles**, July 2, 2007.

NASH, Rick

(NASH, RIHK) **CBJ**

Left wing. Shoots left. 6'4", 215 lbs. Born, Brampton, Ont., June 16, 1984. Columbus' 1st choice, 1st overall, in 2002 Entry Draft.

Season	Club	League	GP	G	A	Pts	PIM	PP	SH	GW	S	%	+/-	TF	F%	Min	GP	G	A	Pts	PIM	PP	SH	GW	Min
99-2000	Tor. Marlboros	GTHL	34	61	54	115	34	....	....	....	....	....	....	....	....	....	....	....	....	....	....	....	....	....	....
2000-01	London Knights	OHL	58	31	35	66	56	....	....	....	....	....	....	....	....	....	4	3	3	6	8	....	....	....	....
2001-02	London Knights	OHL	54	32	40	72	88	....	....	....	....	....	....	....	....	....	12	10	9	19	21	....	....	....	....
2002-03	**Columbus**	**NHL**	**74**	**17**	**22**	**39**	**78**	**6**	**0**	**2**	**154**	**11.0**	**–27**	**14**	**35.7**	**13:57**	....	....	....	....	....	....	....	....	....
2003-04	**Columbus**	**NHL**	**80**	***41**	**16**	**57**	**87**	**19**	**0**	**7**	**269**	**15.2**	**–35**	**21**	**28.6**	**17:38**	....	....	....	....	....	....	....	....	....
2004-05	HC Davos	Swiss	44	26	20	46	83	....	....	....	....	....	....	....	....	....	15	9	2	11	26	....	....	....	....

			Regular Season														Playoffs								
Season	Club	League	GP	G	A	Pts	PIM	PP	SH	GW	S	%	+/-	TF	F%	Min	GP	G	A	Pts	PIM	PP	SH	GW	Min
2005-06	Columbus	NHL	54	31	23	54	51	11	0	4	170	18.2	5	38	50.0	18:16	....	....	....	....	....	....	....	....	....
	Canada	Olympics	6	0	1	1	10	....	....	....	....	....	....	....	....	....	....	....	....	....	....	....	....	....	....
2006-07	Columbus	NHL	75	27	30	57	73	9	1	5	228	11.8	–8	143	42.7	19:12	....	....	....	....	....	....	....	....	....
	NHL Totals		283	116	91	207	289	45	1	18	821	14.1		216	42.1	17:12	....	....	....	....	....	....	....	....	....

OHL All-Rookie Team (2001) • OHL Rookie of the Year (2001) • CHL All-Rookie Team (2001) • NHL All-Rookie Team (2003) • Maurice "Rocket" Richard Trophy (2004) (tied with Jarome Iginla and Ilya Kovalchuk)

Played in NHL All-Star Game (2004, 2007)

Signed as a free agent by **Davos** (Swiss), August 3, 2004.

NASH, Tyson

(NASH, TIGH-suhn)

Left wing. Shoots left. 5'11", 191 lbs. Born, Edmonton, Alta., March 11, 1975. Vancouver's 10th choice, 247th overall, in 1994 Entry Draft.

Season	Club	League	GP	G	A	Pts	PIM	PP	SH	GW	S	%	+/-	TF	F%	Min	GP	G	A	Pts	PIM	PP	SH	GW	Min
1990-91	Sherwood Park	AMHL	40	17	28	43	63	....	....	....	....	....	....	....	....	....	....	....	....	....	....	....	....	....	....
1991-92	Kamloops Blazers	WHL	33	1	6	7	62	....	....	....	....	....	....	....	....	....	4	0	0	0	0	....	....	....	....
1992-93	Kamloops Blazers	WHL	61	10	16	26	78	....	....	....	....	....	....	....	....	....	13	3	2	5	32	....	....	....	....
1993-94	Kamloops Blazers	WHL	65	20	36	56	135	....	....	....	....	....	....	....	....	....	16	3	4	7	12	....	....	....	....
1994-95	Kamloops Blazers	WHL	63	34	41	75	70	....	....	....	....	....	....	....	....	....	21	10	7	17	30	....	....	....	....
1995-96	Syracuse Crunch	AHL	50	4	7	11	58	....	....	....	....	....	....	....	....	....	4	0	0	0	11	....	....	....	....
	Raleigh IceCaps	ECHL	6	1	1	2	8	....	....	....	....	....	....	....	....	....	....	....	....	....	....	....	....	....	....
1996-97	Syracuse Crunch	AHL	77	17	17	34	105	....	....	....	....	....	....	....	....	....	3	0	2	2	0	....	....	....	....
1997-98	Syracuse Crunch	AHL	74	20	20	40	184	....	....	....	....	....	....	....	....	....	5	0	2	2	28	....	....	....	....
1998-99	St. Louis	NHL	2	0	0	0	5	0	0	0	1	0.0	–1	0	0.0	7:44	1	0	0	0	2	0	0	0	6:25
	Worcester IceCats	AHL	55	14	22	36	143	....	....	....	....	....	....	....	....	....	4	4	1	5	27	....	....	....	....
99-2000	St. Louis	NHL	66	4	9	13	150	0	1	1	68	5.9	6	0	0.0	8:35	6	1	0	1	24	0	0	0	8:36
2000-01	St. Louis	NHL	57	8	7	15	110	0	1	0	113	7.1	8	2	50.0	12:29	....	....	....	....	....	....	....	....	....
2001-02	St. Louis	NHL	64	6	7	13	100	0	0	1	66	9.1	2	14	35.7	10:03	9	0	1	1	20	0	0	0	8:03
2002-03	St. Louis	NHL	66	6	3	9	114	1	0	2	77	7.8	0	9	11.1	9:53	7	2	1	3	6	0	0	0	9:05
2003-04	Phoenix	NHL	69	3	5	8	110	0	0	0	83	3.6	–6	13	38.5	11:53	....	....	....	....	....	....	....	....	....
2004-05			DID NOT PLAY																						
2005-06	Phoenix	NHL	50	0	6	6	84	0	0	0	44	0.0	–7	20	55.0	10:03	....	....	....	....	....	....	....	....	....
2006-07	San Antonio	AHL	19	6	6	12	48	....	....	....	....	....	....	....	....	....	....	....	....	....	....	....	....	....	....
	Toronto Marlies	AHL	54	10	13	23	134	....	....	....	....	....	....	....	....	....	....	....	....	....	....	....	....	....	....
	NHL Totals		374	27	37	64	673	1	2	4	452	6.0		58	39.7	10:27	23	3	2	5	52	0	0	0	8:26

Signed as a free agent by **St. Louis**, July 14, 1998. Traded to **Phoenix** by **St. Louis** for Phoenix's 5th round choice (Lee Stempniak) in 2003 Entry Draft, June 21, 2003. Traded to **Toronto** by **Phoenix** with Boston's 4th round choice (previously acquired, Toronto selected Matt Frattin) in 2007 Entry Draft for Mikael Tellqvist, November 29. 2006.

NASLUND, Markus

(NAZ-luhnd, MAHR-kuhs) **VAN.**

Left wing. Shoots left. 5'11", 195 lbs. Born, Ornskoldsvik, Sweden, July 30, 1973. Pittsburgh's 1st choice, 16th overall, in 1991 Entry Draft.

Season	Club	League	GP	G	A	Pts	PIM	PP	SH	GW	S	%	+/-	TF	F%	Min	GP	G	A	Pts	PIM	PP	SH	GW	Min
1988-89	Ornskoldsviks IF	Sweden-3	14	7	6	13	....	....	....	....	....	....	....	....	....	....	....	....	....	....	....	....	....	....	....
1989-90	MoDo Jr.	Swe-Jr.	33	43	35	78	20	....	....	....	....	....	....	....	....	....	....	....	....	....	....	....	....	....	....
1990-91	MoDo	Sweden	32	10	9	19	14	....	....	....	....	....	....	....	....	....	....	....	....	....	....	....	....	....	....
1991-92	MoDo	Sweden	39	22	18	40	54	....	....	....	....	....	....	....	....	....	....	....	....	....	....	....	....	....	....
1992-93	MoDo Jr.	Swe-Jr.	2	4	1	5	2	....	....	....	....	....	....	....	....	....	....	....	....	....	....	....	....	....	....
	MoDo	Sweden	39	22	17	39	67	....	....	....	....	....	....	....	....	....	3	3	2	5	0	....	....	....	....
1993-94	Pittsburgh	NHL	71	4	7	11	27	1	0	0	80	5.0	–3	....	....	....	....	....	....	....	....	....	....	....	....
	Cleveland	IHL	5	1	6	7	4	....	....	....	....	....	....	....	....	....	....	....	....	....	....	....	....	....	....
1994-95	Pittsburgh	NHL	14	2	2	4	2	0	0	0	13	15.4	0	....	....	....	....	....	....	....	....	....	....	....	....
	Cleveland	IHL	7	3	4	7	6	....	....	....	....	....	....	....	....	....	4	1	3	4	8	....	....	....	....
1995-96	Pittsburgh	NHL	66	19	33	52	36	3	0	4	125	15.2	17	....	....	....	....	....	....	....	....	....	....	....	....
	Vancouver	NHL	10	3	0	3	6	1	0	1	19	15.8	3	....	....	....	6	1	2	3	8	1	0	0	....
1996-97	Vancouver	NHL	78	21	20	41	30	4	0	4	120	17.5	–15	....	....	....	....	....	....	....	....	....	....	....	....
1997-98	Vancouver	NHL	76	14	20	34	56	2	1	0	106	13.2	5	....	....	....	....	....	....	....	....	....	....	....	....
1998-99	Vancouver	NHL	80	36	30	66	74	15	2	3	205	17.6	–13	14	57.1	19:57	....	....	....	....	....	....	....	....	....
99-2000	Vancouver	NHL	82	27	38	65	64	6	2	3	271	10.0	–5	13	46.2	20:13	....	....	....	....	....	....	....	....	....
2000-01	Vancouver	NHL	72	41	34	75	58	18	1	5	277	14.8	–2	6	50.0	19:03	....	....	....	....	....	....	....	....	....
2001-02	Vancouver	NHL	81	40	50	90	50	8	0	6	302	13.2	22	5	20.0	19:31	6	1	1	2	2	0	0	0	18:54
	Sweden	Olympics	4	2	1	3	0	....	....	....	....	....	....	....	....	....	....	....	....	....	....	....	....	....	....
2002-03	Vancouver	NHL	82	48	56	104	52	24	0	12	294	16.3	6	6	33.3	19:54	14	5	9	14	18	2	0	1	18:14
2003-04	Vancouver	NHL	78	35	49	84	58	5	0	6	296	11.8	24	14	35.7	19:23	7	2	7	9	2	2	0	0	19:21
2004-05	MODO	Sweden	13	8	9	17	8	....	....	....	....	....	....	....	....	....	6	0	1	1	10	....	....	....	....
2005-06	Vancouver	NHL	81	32	47	79	66	13	0	2	264	12.1	–19	7	28.6	18:28	....	....	....	....	....	....	....	....	....
	Sweden	Olympics	DID NOT PLAY – INJURED																						
2006-07	Vancouver	NHL	82	24	36	60	54	9	0	5	222	10.8	3	6	50.0	17:44	12	4	1	5	16	1	0	0	21:36
	NHL Totals		953	346	422	768	633	109	6	51	2594	13.3		71	42.3	19:17	45	13	20	33	46	6	0	1	19:34

NHL First All-Star Team (2002, 2003, 2004) • Lester B. Pearson Award (2003)

Played in NHL All-Star Game (1999, 2001, 2002, 2003, 2004)

Traded to **Vancouver** by **Pittsburgh** for Alek Stojanov, March 20, 1996. Signed as a free agent by **MODO** (Sweden), December 20, 2004.

NASREDDINE, Alain

(NAS-ruh-deen, AL-eh) **PIT.**

Defense. Shoots left. 6'1", 204 lbs. Born, Montreal, Que., July 10, 1975. Florida's 8th choice, 135th overall, in 1993 Entry Draft.

Season	Club	League	GP	G	A	Pts	PIM	PP	SH	GW	S	%	+/-	TF	F%	Min	GP	G	A	Pts	PIM	PP	SH	GW	Min
1990-91	Mtl-Bourassa	QAAA	35	10	25	35	50	....	....	....	....	....	....	....	....	....	....	....	....	....	....	....	....	....	....
1991-92	Drummondville	QMJHL	61	1	9	10	78	....	....	....	....	....	....	....	....	....	4	0	0	0	17	....	....	....	....
1992-93	Drummondville	QMJHL	64	0	14	14	137	....	....	....	....	....	....	....	....	....	10	0	1	1	36	....	....	....	....
1993-94	Chicoutimi	QMJHL	60	3	24	27	218	....	....	....	....	....	....	....	....	....	26	2	10	12	118	....	....	....	....
1994-95	Chicoutimi	QMJHL	67	8	31	39	342	....	....	....	....	....	....	....	....	....	13	3	5	8	40	....	....	....	....
1995-96	Carolina Panthers	AHL	63	0	5	5	245	....	....	....	....	....	....	....	....	....	....	....	....	....	....	....	....	....	....
1996-97	Carolina	AHL	26	0	4	4	109	....	....	....	....	....	....	....	....	....	....	....	....	....	....	....	....	....	....
	Indianapolis Ice	IHL	49	0	2	2	248	....	....	....	....	....	....	....	....	....	4	1	1	2	27	....	....	....	....
1997-98	Indianapolis Ice	IHL	75	1	12	13	258	....	....	....	....	....	....	....	....	....	5	0	2	2	12	....	....	....	....
1998-99	Chicago	NHL	7	0	0	0	19	0	0	0	2	0.0	–2	0	0.0	12:11	....	....	....	....	....	....	....	....	....
	Portland Pirates	AHL	7	0	1	1	36	....	....	....	....	....	....	....	....	....	....	....	....	....	....	....	....	....	....
	Montreal	NHL	8	0	0	0	33	0	0	0	1	0.0	1	0	0.0	8:12	....	....	....	....	....	....	....	....	....
	Fredericton	AHL	38	0	10	10	108	....	....	....	....	....	....	....	....	....	15	0	3	3	39	....	....	....	....
99-2000	Quebec Citadelles	AHL	59	1	6	7	178	....	....	....	....	....	....	....	....	....	....	....	....	....	....	....	....	....	....
	Hamilton	AHL	11	0	0	0	12	....	....	....	....	....	....	....	....	....	10	1	1	2	14	....	....	....	....
2000-01	Hamilton	AHL	74	4	14	18	164	....	....	....	....	....	....	....	....	....	....	....	....	....	....	....	....	....	....
2001-02	Hamilton	AHL	79	7	10	17	154	....	....	....	....	....	....	....	....	....	12	1	3	4	22	....	....	....	....
2002-03	Bridgeport	AHL	67	3	9	12	114	....	....	....	....	....	....	....	....	....	9	0	0	0	27	....	....	....	....
	NY Islanders	NHL	3	0	0	0	2	0	0	0	0	0.0	0	0	0.0	12:11	....	....	....	....	....	....	....	....	....
2003-04	Bridgeport	AHL	53	1	6	7	70	....	....	....	....	....	....	....	....	....	....	....	....	....	....	....	....	....	....
	Wilkes-Barre	AHL	17	1	1	2	16	....	....	....	....	....	....	....	....	....	24	1	0	1	48	....	....	....	....
2004-05	Wilkes-Barre	AHL	75	3	15	18	129	....	....	....	....	....	....	....	....	....	11	0	1	1	18	....	....	....	....
2005-06	Pittsburgh	NHL	6	0	0	0	8	0	0	0	3	0.0	2	0	0.0	15:11	....	....	....	....	....	....	....	....	....
	Wilkes-Barre	AHL	71	0	12	12	71	....	....	....	....	....	....	....	....	....	....	....	....	....	....	....	....	....	....
2006-07	Pittsburgh	NHL	44	1	4	5	18	0	0	0	29	3.4	12	0	0.0	15:47	....	....	....	....	....	....	....	....	....
	Wilkes-Barre	AHL	19	3	5	8	25	....	....	....	....	....	....	....	....	....	....	....	....	....	....	....	....	....	....
	NHL Totals		68	1	4	5	80	0	0	0	35	2.9		0	0.0	14:18	....	....	....	....	....	....	....	....	....

QMJHL Second All-Star Team (1995)

Traded to **Chicago** by **Florida** for Ivan Droppa, December 18, 1996. Traded to **Montreal** by **Chicago** with Jeff Hackett, Eric Weinrich and Tampa Bay's 4th round choice (previously acquired, Montreal selected Chris Dyment) in 1999 Entry Draft for Jocelyn Thibault, Dave Manson and Brad Brown, November 16, 1998. Traded to **Edmonton** by **Montreal** with Igor Ulanov for Christian Laflamme and Matthieu Descoteaux, March 9, 2000. Signed as a free agent by **NY Islanders**, September 6, 2002. Traded to **Pittsburgh** by **NY Islanders** for Steve Webb, March 8, 2004.

			Regular Season														Playoffs								
Season	Club	League	GP	G	A	Pts	PIM	PP	SH	GW	S	%	+/-	TF	F%	Min	GP	G	A	Pts	PIM	PP	SH	GW	Min

NEDOROST, Andrej
(neh-DOHR-awst, AWN-dray) **CBJ**

Left wing. Shoots left. 6'1", 199 lbs. Born, Trencin, Czech., April 30, 1980. Columbus' 10th choice, 286th overall, in 2000 Entry Draft.

Season	Club	League	GP	G	A	Pts	PIM	PP	SH	GW	S	%	+/-	TF	F%	Min	GP	G	A	Pts	PIM	PP	SH	GW	Min
1995-96	Dukla Trencin Jr.	Slovak-Jr.	40	50	35	85	....	....	....	....	....	....	....	....	....	....	....	....	....	....	....	....	....	....	....
1996-97	Dukla Trencin Jr.	Slovak-Jr.	45	15	16	31	....	....	....	....	....	....	....	....	....	....	....	....	....	....	....	....	....	....	....
1997-98	Dukla Trencin Jr.	Slovak-Jr.	45	27	22	49	61	....	....	....	....	....	....	....	....	....	....	....	....	....	....	....	....	....	....
	Dukla Trencin	Slovakia	1	0	0	0	0	....	....	....	....	....	....	....	....	....	....	....	....	....	....	....	....	....	....
1998-99	Essen Jr.	Ger-Jr.	17	37	18	55	43	....	....	....	....	....	....	....	....	....	....	....	....	....	....	....	....	....	....
	Essen	German-2	30	3	5	8	22	....	....	....	....	....	....	....	....	....	....	....	....	....	....	....	....	....	....
99-2000	Essen	Germany	66	7	5	12	44	....	....	....	....	....	....	....	....	....	....	....	....	....	....	....	....	....	....
2000-01	Plzen	CzRep	33	10	8	18	22	....	....	....	....	....	....	....	....	....	....	....	....	....	....	....	....	....	....
2001-02	**Columbus**	**NHL**	**7**	**0**	**2**	**2**	**2**	**0**	**0**	**0**	**12**	**0.0**	**–3**	**11**	**100.0**	**12:56**	....	....	....	....	....	....	....	....	....
	Syracuse Crunch	AHL	37	5	13	18	28	....	....	....	....	....	....	....	....	....	10	1	3	4	4	....	....	....	....
2002-03	**Columbus**	**NHL**	**12**	**0**	**1**	**1**	**4**	**0**	**0**	**0**	**10**	**0.0**	**–6**	**30**	**36.7**	**9:15**	....	....	....	....	....	....	....	....	....
	Syracuse Crunch	AHL	63	14	19	33	85	....	....	....	....	....	....	....	....	....	....	....	....	....	....	....	....	....	....
2003-04	**Columbus**	**NHL**	**9**	**2**	**0**	**2**	**6**	**0**	**0**	**0**	**16**	**12.5**	**0**	**13**	**69.2**	**13:02**	....	....	....	....	....	....	....	....	....
	Syracuse Crunch	AHL	8	0	2	2	6	....	....	....	....	....	....	....	....	....	....	....	....	....	....	....	....	....	....
	Magnitogorsk	Russia	16	3	4	7	12	....	....	....	....	....	....	....	....	....	7	0	3	3	4	....	....	....	....
2004-05	Magnitogorsk	Russia	12	1	0	1	4	....	....	....	....	....	....	....	....	....	....	....	....	....	....	....	....	....	....
	Nizhnekamsk	Russia	7	0	0	0	4	....	....	....	....	....	....	....	....	....	....	....	....	....	....	....	....	....	....
	Karlovy Vary	CzRep	20	6	5	11	16	....	....	....	....	....	....	....	....	....	....	....	....	....	....	....	....	....	....
2005-06	Karlovy Vary	CzRep	36	7	11	18	26	....	....	....	....	....	....	....	....	....	....	....	....	....	....	....	....	....	....
	Hamburg Freezers	Germany	5	0	2	2	4	....	....	....	....	....	....	....	....	....	6	1	0	1	2	....	....	....	....
2006-07	Malmo	Sweden	21	2	6	8	20	....	....	....	....	....	....	....	....	....	....	....	....	....	....	....	....	....	....
	Skelleftea AIK HK	Sweden	14	4	2	6	10	....	....	....	....	....	....	....	....	....	....	....	....	....	....	....	....	....	....
	Skelleftea AIK HK	Sweden-Q	10	1	3	4	8	....	....	....	....	....	....	....	....	....	....	....	....	....	....	....	....	....	....
	NHL Totals		**28**	**2**	**3**	**5**	**12**	**0**	**0**	**0**	**38**	**5.3**		**44**	**47.7**	**11:23**	....	....	....	....	....	....	....	....	....

Assigned to **Magnitogorsk** (Russia) by **Columbus**, December 17, 2003. Signed as a free agent by **Karlovy Vary** (CzRep), January 22, 2005. Signed as a free agent by **Hamburg** (Germany), February 17, 2006. Signed as a free agent by **Malmo** (Sweden), August 15, 2006.

NEDOROST, Vaclav
(neh-DOHR-awst, VAT-slav) **FLA.**

Center. Shoots left. 6'1", 190 lbs. Born, Ceske Budejovice, Czech., March 16, 1982. Colorado's 1st choice, 14th overall, in 2000 Entry Draft.

Season	Club	League	GP	G	A	Pts	PIM	PP	SH	GW	S	%	+/-	TF	F%	Min	GP	G	A	Pts	PIM	PP	SH	GW	Min
1997-98	C. Budejovice Jr.	CzRep-Jr.	43	30	23	53	20	....	....	....	....	....	....	....	....	....	....	....	....	....	....	....	....	....	....
1998-99	C. Budejovice Jr.	CzRep-Jr.	39	6	15	21	20	....	....	....	....	....	....	....	....	....	....	....	....	....	....	....	....	....	....
	C. Budejovice	CzRep	7	0	2	2	0	....	....	....	....	....	....	....	....	....	....	....	....	....	....	....	....	....	....
99-2000	C. Budejovice Jr.	CzRep-Jr.	14	4	7	11	4	....	....	....	....	....	....	....	....	....	....	....	....	....	....	....	....	....	....
	C. Budejovice	CzRep	38	8	6	14	6	....	....	....	....	....	....	....	....	....	3	0	0	0	0	....	....	....	....
2000-01	C. Budejovice	CzRep	36	3	12	15	14	....	....	....	....	....	....	....	....	....	....	....	....	....	....	....	....	....	....
2001-02	**Colorado**	**NHL**	**25**	**2**	**2**	**4**	**2**	**1**	**0**	**0**	**22**	**9.1**	**–4**	**62**	**45.2**	**10:15**	....	....	....	....	....	....	....	....	....
	Hershey Bears	AHL	49	12	22	34	16	....	....	....	....	....	....	....	....	....	7	2	3	5	2	....	....	....	....
2002-03	**Colorado**	**NHL**	**42**	**4**	**5**	**9**	**20**	**1**	**0**	**0**	**35**	**11.4**	**8**	**151**	**44.4**	**10:29**	....	....	....	....	....	....	....	....	....
	Hershey Bears	AHL	5	3	2	5	0	....	....	....	....	....	....	....	....	....	5	2	2	4	0	....	....	....	....
2003-04	**Florida**	**NHL**	**32**	**4**	**3**	**7**	**12**	**2**	**0**	**0**	**38**	**10.5**	**–6**	**121**	**42.2**	**11:32**	....	....	....	....	....	....	....	....	....
	San Antonio	AHL	21	9	6	15	2	....	....	....	....	....	....	....	....	....	....	....	....	....	....	....	....	....	....
2004-05	Liberec	CzRep	48	15	18	33	20	....	....	....	....	....	....	....	....	....	6	0	1	1	12	....	....	....	....
2005-06			DID NOT PLAY – INJURED																						
2006-07	C. Budejovice	CzRep	30	3	7	10	36	....	....	....	....	....	....	....	....	....	....	....	....	....	....	....	....	....	....
	NHL Totals		**99**	**10**	**10**	**20**	**34**	**4**	**0**	**0**	**95**	**10.5**		**334**	**43.7**	**10:46**	....	....	....	....	....	....	....	....	....

Traded to **Florida** by **Colorado** with Eric Messier for Peter Worrell and Florida's 2nd round choice (later traded to NY Rangers – later traded back to Florida – Florida selected David Shantz) in 2004 Entry Draft, July 18, 2003. Signed as a free agent by **Liberec** (CzRep), September 4, 2004. Signed as a free agent by **Ceske Budejovice** (CzRep), April 28, 2005. • Missed entire 2005-06 season recovering from knee surgery.

NEDVED, Petr
(NEHD-VEHD, PEE-tuhr)

Center. Shoots left. 6'3", 196 lbs. Born, Liberec, Czech., December 9, 1971. Vancouver's 1st choice, 2nd overall, in 1990 Entry Draft.

Season	Club	League	GP	G	A	Pts	PIM	PP	SH	GW	S	%	+/-	TF	F%	Min	GP	G	A	Pts	PIM	PP	SH	GW	Min
1988-89	CHZ Litvinov Jr.	Czech-Jr.	20	32	19	51	12	....	....	....	....	....	....	....	....	....	....	....	....	....	....	....	....	....	....
1989-90	Seattle	WHL	71	65	80	145	80	....	....	....	....	....	....	....	....	....	11	4	9	13	2	....	....	....	....
1990-91	**Vancouver**	**NHL**	**61**	**10**	**6**	**16**	**20**	**1**	**0**	**0**	**97**	**10.3**	**–21**	....	....	....	**6**	**0**	**1**	**1**	**0**	**0**	**0**	**0**	....
1991-92	**Vancouver**	**NHL**	**77**	**15**	**22**	**37**	**36**	**5**	**0**	**1**	**99**	**15.2**	**–3**	....	....	....	**10**	**1**	**4**	**5**	**16**	**0**	**0**	**0**	....
1992-93	**Vancouver**	**NHL**	**84**	**38**	**33**	**71**	**96**	**2**	**1**	**3**	**149**	**25.5**	**20**	....	....	....	**12**	**2**	**3**	**5**	**2**	**0**	**0**	**0**	....
1993-94	Canada	Nat-Tm	17	19	12	31	16	....	....	....	....	....	....	....	....	....	....	....	....	....	....	....	....	....	....
	Canada	Olympics	8	5	1	6	6	....	....	....	....	....	....	....	....	....	....	....	....	....	....	....	....	....	....
	St. Louis	**NHL**	**19**	**6**	**14**	**20**	**8**	**2**	**0**	**0**	**63**	**9.5**	**2**	....	....	....	**4**	**0**	**1**	**1**	**4**	**0**	**0**	**0**	....
1994-95	**NY Rangers**	**NHL**	**46**	**11**	**12**	**23**	**26**	**1**	**0**	**3**	**123**	**8.9**	**–1**	....	....	....	**10**	**3**	**2**	**5**	**6**	**2**	**0**	**0**	....
1995-96	**Pittsburgh**	**NHL**	**80**	**45**	**54**	**99**	**68**	**8**	**1**	**5**	**204**	**22.1**	**37**	....	....	....	**18**	**10**	**10**	**20**	**16**	**4**	**0**	**2**	....
1996-97	**Pittsburgh**	**NHL**	**74**	**33**	**38**	**71**	**66**	**12**	**3**	**4**	**189**	**17.5**	**–2**	....	....	....	**5**	**1**	**2**	**3**	**12**	**0**	**1**	**0**	....
1997-98	Stadion Liberec	CzRep-2	2	0	3	3	....	....	....	....	....	....	....	....	....	....	....	....	....	....	....	....	....	....	....
	TJ Novy Jicin	CzRep-3	7	9	16	25	....	....	....	....	....	....	....	....	....	....	....	....	....	....	....	....	....	....	....
	HC Sparta Praha	CzRep	5	2	3	5	8	....	....	....	....	....	....	....	....	....	6	0	2	2	52	....	....	....	....
	Las Vegas	IHL	3	3	3	6	4	....	....	....	....	....	....	....	....	....	....	....	....	....	....	....	....	....	....
1998-99	Las Vegas	IHL	13	8	10	18	32	....	....	....	....	....	....	....	....	....	....	....	....	....	....	....	....	....	....
	NY Rangers	**NHL**	**56**	**20**	**27**	**47**	**50**	**9**	**1**	**3**	**153**	**13.1**	**–6**	**1069**	**52.5**	**20:31**	....	....	....	....	....	....	....	....	....
99-2000	**NY Rangers**	**NHL**	**76**	**24**	**44**	**68**	**40**	**6**	**2**	**4**	**201**	**11.9**	**2**	**1354**	**54.0**	**19:54**	....	....	....	....	....	....	....	....	....
2000-01	**NY Rangers**	**NHL**	**79**	**32**	**46**	**78**	**54**	**9**	**1**	**5**	**230**	**13.9**	**10**	**1349**	**49.7**	**20:16**	....	....	....	....	....	....	....	....	....
2001-02	Liberec	CzRep-2	1	3	0	3	2	....	....	....	....	....	....	....	....	....	....	....	....	....	....	....	....	....	....
	NY Rangers	**NHL**	**78**	**21**	**25**	**46**	**36**	**6**	**1**	**3**	**175**	**12.0**	**–8**	**1402**	**52.1**	**19:22**	....	....	....	....	....	....	....	....	....
2002-03	**NY Rangers**	**NHL**	**78**	**27**	**31**	**58**	**64**	**8**	**3**	**4**	**205**	**13.2**	**–4**	**1142**	**53.0**	**20:21**	....	....	....	....	....	....	....	....	....
2003-04	**NY Rangers**	**NHL**	**65**	**14**	**17**	**31**	**42**	**5**	**0**	**3**	**153**	**9.2**	**–9**	**929**	**48.6**	**18:51**	....	....	....	....	....	....	....	....	....
	Edmonton	**NHL**	**16**	**5**	**10**	**15**	**4**	**2**	**0**	**0**	**37**	**13.5**	**1**	**226**	**46.9**	**18:11**	....	....	....	....	....	....	....	....	....
2004-05	HC Sparta Praha	CzRep	46	22	13	35	44	....	....	....	....	....	....	....	....	....	5	2	3	5	10	....	....	....	....
2005-06	**Phoenix**	**NHL**	**25**	**2**	**9**	**11**	**34**	**1**	**0**	**1**	**43**	**4.7**	**–6**	**299**	**48.2**	**16:29**	....	....	....	....	....	....	....	....	....
	Philadelphia	**NHL**	**28**	**5**	**9**	**14**	**36**	**2**	**0**	**0**	**47**	**10.6**	**–8**	**416**	**53.4**	**17:05**	**6**	**2**	**0**	**2**	**8**	**1**	**0**	**0**	**17:28**
2006-07	**Philadelphia**	**NHL**	**21**	**1**	**6**	**7**	**18**	**0**	**0**	**0**	**18**	**5.6**	**–20**	**336**	**52.7**	**16:15**	....	....	....	....	....	....	....	....	....
	Philadelphia	AHL	14	4	7	11	10	....	....	....	....	....	....	....	....	....	....	....	....	....	....	....	....	....	....
	Edmonton	**NHL**	**19**	**1**	**4**	**5**	**10**	**1**	**0**	**0**	**21**	**4.8**	**–5**	**178**	**50.0**	**13:11**	....	....	....	....	....	....	....	....	....
	NHL Totals		**982**	**310**	**407**	**717**	**708**	**80**	**13**	**39**	**2207**	**14.0**		**8700**	**51.6**	**19:09**	**71**	**19**	**23**	**42**	**64**	**7**	**1**	**2**	**17:28**

WHL Rookie of the Year (1990) • Canadian Major Junior Rookie of the Year (1990)

Signed as a free agent by **St. Louis**, March 5, 1994. Traded to **NY Rangers** by **St. Louis** for Esa Tikkanen and Doug Lidster, July 24, 1994. Traded to **Pittsburgh** by **NY Rangers** with Sergei Zubov for Luc Robitaille and Ulf Samuelsson, August 31, 1995. Traded to **NY Rangers** by **Pittsburgh** with Chris Tamer and Sean Pronger for Alex Kovalev and Harry York, November 25, 1998. Traded to **Edmonton** by **NY Rangers** with Jussi Markkanen for Stephen Valiquette, Dwight Helminen and Edmonton's 2nd round compensatory choice (Dane Byers) in 2004 Entry Draft, March 3, 2004. Signed as a free agent by **Phoenix**, August 26, 2004. Signed as a free agent by **Sparta Praha** (CzRep), September 17, 2004. Traded to **Philadelphia** by **Phoenix** with Phoenix's 4th round choice (Joonas Lehtivuori) in 2006 Entry Draft for Dennis Seidenberg and Philadelphia's 4th round choice (later traded to NY Islanders - NY Islanders selected Tomas Marcinko) in 2006 Entry Draft, January 20, 2006. Claimed on waivers by **Edmonton** from **Philadelphia**, January 2, 2007. Signed as a free agent by **Sparta Praha** (CzRep), July 19, 2007.

NEIL, Chris
(NEEL, KRIHS) **OTT.**

Right wing. Shoots right. 6'1", 209 lbs. Born, Markdale, Ont., June 18, 1979. Ottawa's 7th choice, 161st overall, in 1998 Entry Draft.

Season	Club	League	GP	G	A	Pts	PIM	PP	SH	GW	S	%	+/-	TF	F%	Min	GP	G	A	Pts	PIM	PP	SH	GW	Min
1995-96	Orangeville	OHA-B	43	15	15	30	50	....	....	....	....	....	....	....	....	....	....	....	....	....	....	....	....	....	....
1996-97	North Bay	OHL	65	13	16	29	150	....	....	....	....	....	....	....	....	....	....	....	....	....	....	....	....	....	....
1997-98	North Bay	OHL	59	26	29	55	231	....	....	....	....	....	....	....	....	....	....	....	....	....	....	....	....	....	....
1998-99	North Bay	OHL	66	26	46	72	215	....	....	....	....	....	....	....	....	....	4	1	0	1	15	....	....	....	....
99-2000	Mobile Mysticks	ECHL	4	0	2	2	39	....	....	....	....	....	....	....	....	....	....	....	....	....	....	....	....	....	....
	Grand Rapids	IHL	51	9	10	19	301	....	....	....	....	....	....	....	....	....	8	0	2	2	24	....	....	....	....
2000-01	Grand Rapids	IHL	78	15	21	36	354	....	....	....	....	....	....	....	....	....	10	2	2	4	22	....	....	....	....
2001-02	**Ottawa**	**NHL**	**72**	**10**	**7**	**17**	**231**	**1**	**0**	**0**	**56**	**17.9**	**5**	**0**	**0.0**	**8:22**	**12**	**0**	**0**	**0**	**12**	**0**	**0**	**0**	**7:12**
2002-03	**Ottawa**	**NHL**	**68**	**6**	**4**	**10**	**147**	**0**	**0**	**0**	**62**	**9.7**	**8**	**5**	**60.0**	**7:40**	**15**	**1**	**0**	**1**	**24**	**0**	**0**	**0**	**7:57**
2003-04	**Ottawa**	**NHL**	**82**	**8**	**8**	**16**	**194**	**0**	**0**	**1**	**76**	**10.5**	**13**	**14**	**42.9**	**8:51**	**7**	**0**	**1**	**1**	**19**	**0**	**0**	**0**	**6:45**
2004-05	Binghamton	AHL	22	4	6	10	132										6	1	1	2	26				

			Regular Season														Playoffs								
Season	Club	League	GP	G	A	Pts	PIM	PP	SH	GW	S	%	+/-	TF	F%	Min	GP	G	A	Pts	PIM	PP	SH	GW	Min
2005-06	Ottawa	NHL	79	16	17	33	204	8	0	0	126	12.7	9	9	22.2	12:18	10	1	0	1	14	0	0	0	6:58
2006-07	Ottawa	NHL	82	12	16	28	177	3	0	3	139	8.6	6	13	38.5	13:08	20	2	2	4	20	0	0	0	10:40
	NHL Totals		383	52	52	104	953	12	0	4	459	11.3		41	39.0	10:11	64	4	3	7	89	0	0	0	8:23

Signed as a free agent by **Binghamton** (AHL), March 2, 2005.

NEWBURY, Kris

(new-BUHR-ee, KRIHS) **TOR.**

Center. Shoots left. 5'10", 205 lbs. Born, Brampton, Ont., February 19, 1982. San Jose's 4th choice, 139th overall, in 2002 Entry Draft.

Season	Club	League	GP	G	A	Pts	PIM	PP	SH	GW	S	%	+/-	TF	F%	Min	GP	G	A	Pts	PIM	PP	SH	GW	Min
1996-97	Brampton	OPJHL	28	9	4	13	36																		
1997-98	Brampton	OPJHL	46	11	21	32	161																		
1998-99	Belleville Bulls	OHL	51	6	8	14	89																		
99-2000	Belleville Bulls	OHL	34	6	18	24	72																		
	Sarnia Sting	OHL	27	6	8	14	44										7	0	3	3	16				
2000-01	Sarnia Sting	OHL	64	28	30	58	126										4	1	3	4	20				
2001-02	Sarnia Sting	OHL	66	42	62	104	141										5	1	3	4	15				
2002-03	Sarnia Sting	OHL	64	34	58	92	149										6	4	4	8	16				
2003-04	St. John's	AHL	72	5	15	20	153																		
2004-05	St. John's	AHL	55	4	9	13	103										5	0	0	0	36				
	Pensacola	ECHL	6	2	4	6	20																		
2005-06	Toronto Marlies	AHL	74	22	37	59	215										5	0	1	1	12				
2006-07	Toronto	NHL	15	2	2	4	26	0	0	0	30	6.7	4	20	45.0	7:42									
	Toronto Marlies	AHL	37	12	24	36	87																		
	NHL Totals		15	2	2	4	26	0	0	0	30	6.7		20	45.0	7:42									

OHL Second All-Star Team (2002)

Signed as a free agent by **St. John's** (AHL), October 2, 2003. Signed as a free agent by **Toronto**, July 17, 2006.

NICHOL, Scott

(NIH-KOHL, SKAWT) **NSH.**

Center. Shoots right. 5'9", 175 lbs. Born, Edmonton, Alta., December 31, 1974. Buffalo's 9th choice, 272nd overall, in 1993 Entry Draft.

Season	Club	League	GP	G	A	Pts	PIM	PP	SH	GW	S	%	+/-	TF	F%	Min	GP	G	A	Pts	PIM	PP	SH	GW	Min
1991-92	Cgy. AAA Flames	AMHL	23	26	16	42	132																		
1992-93	Portland	WHL	67	31	33	64	146										16	8	8	16	41				
1993-94	Portland	WHL	65	40	53	93	144										10	3	8	11	16				
1994-95	Rochester	AHL	71	11	16	27	136										5	0	3	3	14				
1995-96	Buffalo	NHL	2	0	0	0	10	0	0	0	4	0.0	0												
	Rochester	AHL	62	14	18	32	170										19	7	6	13	36				
1996-97	Rochester	AHL	68	22	21	43	133										10	2	1	3	26				
1997-98	Buffalo	NHL	3	0	0	0	4	0	0	0	5	0.0	0												
	Rochester	AHL	35	13	7	20	113										17	0	6	6	18				
1998-99	Rochester	AHL	52	13	20	33	120																		
99-2000	Rochester	AHL	37	7	11	18	141										12	0	3	3	10				
2000-01	Detroit Vipers	IHL	67	7	24	31	198										11	1	1	2	12				
2001-02	Calgary	NHL	60	8	9	17	107	2	1	0	49	16.3	-9	458	53.1	12:41									
2002-03	Calgary	NHL	68	5	5	10	149	0	1	0	66	7.6	-7	357	58.3	10:47									
2003-04	Chicago	NHL	75	7	11	18	145	0	0	1	112	6.3	-16	1178	57.4	15:46									
2004-05	London Racers	Britain	16	7	12	19	86																		
2005-06	Nashville	NHL	34	3	3	6	79	0	1	0	32	9.4	3	242	58.3	10:30	3	0	0	0	2	0	0	0	7:45
	Milwaukee	AHL	6	3	5	8	18																		
2006-07	Nashville	NHL	59	7	6	13	79	1	1	2	58	12.1	7	623	58.0	12:32	5	0	0	0	17	0	0	0	10:22
	NHL Totals		301	30	34	64	573	3	4	3	326	9.2		2858	57.0	12:45	8	0	0	0	19	0	0	0	9:23

• Missed majority of 1999-2000 season recovering from knee injury suffered in game vs. Saint John (AHL), February 16, 2000. Signed as a free agent by **Calgary**, July 1, 2001. Signed as a free agent by **Chicago**, July 1, 2003. Signed as a free agent by **London** (Britain), October 26, 2004. Signed as a free agent by **Nashville**, August 6, 2005.

NICKULAS, Eric

(NIHK-luhs, AIR-ihk)

Right wing. Shoots right. 5'11", 206 lbs. Born, Hyannis, MA, March 25, 1975. Boston's 3rd choice, 99th overall, in 1994 Entry Draft.

Season	Club	League	GP	G	A	Pts	PIM	PP	SH	GW	S	%	+/-	TF	F%	Min	GP	G	A	Pts	PIM	PP	SH	GW	Min
1991-92	Barnstable	High-MA	24	30	25	55																			
1992-93	Tabor	High-MA	28	25	25	50																			
1993-94	Cushing	High-MA	25	46	36	82																			
1994-95	New Hampshire	H-East	33	15	9	24	32																		
1995-96	New Hampshire	H-East	34	26	12	38	66																		
1996-97	New Hampshire	H-East	39	29	22	51	80																		
1997-98	Orlando	IHL	76	22	9	31	77										6	0	0	0	10				
1998-99	Boston	NHL	2	0	0	0	0	0	0	0	0	0.0	0	0	0.0	3:27	1	0	0	0	2	0	0	0	4:35
	Providence Bruins	AHL	75	31	27	58	83										18	8	12	20	33				
99-2000	Boston	NHL	20	5	6	11	12	1	0	0	28	17.9	-1	4	50.0	11:13									
	Providence Bruins	AHL	40	6	6	12	37										12	2	3	5	20				
2000-01	Boston	NHL	7	0	0	0	4	0	0	0	6	0.0	-2	1	100.0	7:07									
	Providence Bruins	AHL	62	20	23	43	100										12	4	4	8	24				
2001-02	Worcester IceCats	AHL	54	11	25	36	48										3	0	1	1	2				
2002-03	St. Louis	NHL	8	0	1	1	6	0	0	0	3	0.0	-2	0	0.0	9:31									
	Worcester IceCats	AHL	39	17	16	33	40										3	0	0	0	2				
2003-04	St. Louis	NHL	44	7	11	18	44	1	0	1	80	8.8	-2	10	30.0	12:50									
	Chicago	NHL	21	1	1	2	8	0	0	0	41	2.4	-6	11	45.5	13:46									
2004-05	Norfolk Admirals	AHL	53	11	11	22	32										6	0	3	3	8				
2005-06	Boston	NHL	16	2	4	6	8	0	0	0	14	14.3	2	8	25.0	8:08									
	Providence Bruins	AHL	38	10	16	26	46										5	1	1	2	4				
2006-07	Hannover Scorp.	Germany	48	13	17	30	129										4	2	0	2	6				
	NHL Totals		118	15	23	38	82	2	0	1	172	8.7		34	38.2	11:22	1	0	0	0	2	0	0	0	4:35

Ken McKenzie Trophy (U.S.- Born Rookie of the Year – IHL) (1998)

Signed as a free agent by **Worcester** (AHL), November 10, 2001. Signed as a free agent by **St. Louis**, July 16, 2002. Claimed on waivers by **Chicago** from **St. Louis**, February 24, 2004. Signed as a free agent by **Boston**, August 23, 2005. Signed as a free agent by **Hannover** (Germany), June 19, 2006.

NIEDERMAYER, Rob

(NEE-duhr-MIGH-uhr, RAWB) **ANA.**

Center. Shoots left. 6'2", 204 lbs. Born, Cassiar, B.C., December 28, 1974. Florida's 1st choice, 5th overall, in 1993 Entry Draft.

Season	Club	League	GP	G	A	Pts	PIM	PP	SH	GW	S	%	+/-	TF	F%	Min	GP	G	A	Pts	PIM	PP	SH	GW	Min
1989-90	Cranbrook Blazers	BCAHA	35	42	40	82	30																		
1990-91	Medicine Hat	WHL	71	24	26	50	8										12	3	7	10	2				
1991-92	Medicine Hat	WHL	71	32	46	78	77										4	2	3	5	2				
1992-93	Medicine Hat	WHL	52	43	34	77	67																		
1993-94	Florida	NHL	65	9	17	26	51	3	0	2	67	13.4	-11												
1994-95	Medicine Hat	WHL	13	9	15	24	14																		
	Florida	NHL	48	4	6	10	36	1	0	0	58	6.9	-13												
1995-96	Florida	NHL	82	26	35	61	107	11	0	6	155	16.8	1				22	5	3	8	12	2	0	2	
1996-97	Florida	NHL	60	14	24	38	54	3	0	2	136	10.3	4				5	2	1	3	6	1	0	0	
1997-98	Florida	NHL	33	8	7	15	41	5	0	2	64	12.5	-9												
1998-99	Florida	NHL	82	18	33	51	50	6	1	3	142	12.7	-13	1895	47.1	21:17									
99-2000	Florida	NHL	81	10	23	33	46	1	0	4	135	7.4	-5	1632	47.9	19:04	4	1	0	1	6	0	0	0	15:55
2000-01	Florida	NHL	67	12	20	32	50	3	1	0	115	10.4	-12	997	45.0	20:30									
2001-02	Calgary	NHL	57	6	14	20	49	1	2	1	87	6.9	-15	777	48.4	18:01									
2002-03	Calgary	NHL	54	8	10	18	42	2	0	1	104	7.7	-13	139	48.9	17:29									
	Anaheim	NHL	12	2	2	4	15	1	0	0	21	9.5	3	14	42.9	15:21	21	3	7	10	18	0	2	0	23:35
2003-04	Anaheim	NHL	55	12	16	28	34	6	0	2	111	10.8	-6	45	64.4	19:28									
2004-05	Ferencvaros	Hungary	5	2	1	3	14																		

Season	Club	League	GP	G	A	Pts	PIM	PP	SH	GW	S	%	+/-	TF	F%	Min	GP	G	A	Pts	PIM	PP	SH	GW	Min
			Regular Season														Playoffs								
2005-06	Anaheim	NHL	76	15	24	39	89	4	1	2	140	10.7	-5	447	45.6	17:52	16	1	3	4	10	1	0	0	19:36
2006-07♦	Anaheim	NHL	82	5	11	16	77	0	0	0	106	4.7	-8	76	40.8	16:39	21	5	5	10	39	0	1	1	18:35
	NHL Totals		854	149	242	391	741	47	5	25	1441	10.3		6022	47.1	18:45	89	17	19	36	91	4	3	3	20:22

WHL East First All-Star Team (1993)

• Missed majority of 1997-98 season recovering from thumb (November 26, 1997 vs. Boston) and head (March 19, 1998 vs. Buffalo) injuries. Traded to **Calgary** by **Florida** with Philadelphia's 2nd round choice (previously acquired, Calgary selected Andrei Medvedev) in 2001 Entry Draft for Valeri Bure and Jason Wiemer, June 23, 2001. Traded to **Anaheim** by **Calgary** for Mike Commodore and Jean-Francois Damphousse, March 11, 2003. Signed as a free agent by **Ferencvaros** (Hungary), January 17, 2005.

NIEDERMAYER, Scott

(NEE-duhr-MIGH-uhr, SKAWT) **ANA.**

Defense. Shoots left. 6'1", 200 lbs. Born, Edmonton, Alta., August 31, 1973. New Jersey's 1st choice, 3rd overall, in 1991 Entry Draft.

Season	Club	League	GP	G	A	Pts	PIM	PP	SH	GW	S	%	+/-	TF	F%	Min	GP	G	A	Pts	PIM	PP	SH	GW	Min
1988-89	Cranbrook Blazers	BCAHA	62	55	37	92	100	....	....	....	....	....	....	....	....	....	....	....	....	....	....	....	....	....	....
1989-90	Kamloops Blazers	WHL	64	14	55	69	64	....	....	....	....	....	....	....	....	....	17	2	14	16	35	....	....	....	....
1990-91	Kamloops Blazers	WHL	57	26	56	82	52	....	....	....	....	....	....	....	....	....	....	....	....	....	....	....	....	....	....
1991-92	Kamloops Blazers	WHL	35	7	32	39	61	....	....	....	....	....	....	....	....	....	17	9	14	23	28	....	....	....	....
	New Jersey	NHL	4	0	1	1	2	0	0	0	4	0.0	1	....	....	....	....	....	....	....	....	....	....	....	....
1992-93	New Jersey	NHL	80	11	29	40	47	5	0	0	131	8.4	8	....	....	....	5	0	3	3	2	0	0	0	....
1993-94	New Jersey	NHL	81	10	36	46	42	5	0	2	135	7.4	34	....	....	....	20	2	2	4	8	1	0	0	....
1994-95♦	New Jersey	NHL	48	4	15	19	18	4	0	0	52	7.7	19	....	....	....	20	4	7	11	10	2	0	1	....
1995-96	New Jersey	NHL	79	8	25	33	46	6	0	0	179	4.5	5	....	....	....	....	....	....	....	....	....	....	....	....
1996-97	New Jersey	NHL	81	5	30	35	64	3	0	3	159	3.1	-4	....	....	....	10	2	4	6	6	2	0	1	....
1997-98	New Jersey	NHL	81	14	43	57	27	11	0	1	175	8.0	5	....	....	....	6	0	2	2	4	0	0	0	....
1998-99	Utah Grizzlies	IHL	5	0	2	2	0	....	....	....	....	....	....	....	....	....	....	....	....	....	....	....	....	....	....
	New Jersey	NHL	72	11	35	46	26	1	1	3	161	6.8	16	13	15.4	24:40	7	1	3	4	18	1	0	0	25:30
99-2000♦	New Jersey	NHL	71	7	31	38	48	1	0	0	109	6.4	19	8	37.5	24:21	22	5	2	7	10	0	2	1	25:28
2000-01	New Jersey	NHL	57	6	29	35	22	1	0	5	87	6.9	14	5	0.0	23:19	21	0	6	6	14	0	0	0	23:53
2001-02	New Jersey	NHL	76	11	22	33	30	2	0	6	129	8.5	12	1	100.0	24:17	6	0	2	2	6	0	0	0	26:37
	Canada	Olympics	6	1	1	2	4	....	....	....	....	....	....	....	....	....	....	....	....	....	....	....	....	....	....
2002-03♦	New Jersey	NHL	81	11	28	39	62	3	0	3	164	6.7	23	1	0.0	24:30	24	2	*16	*18	16	1	0	0	26:07
2003-04	New Jersey	NHL	81	14	40	54	44	9	0	3	165	8.5	20	1	0.0	25:56	5	1	0	1	6	0	0	0	27:21
2004-05			DID NOT PLAY																						
2005-06	Anaheim	NHL	82	13	50	63	96	9	0	3	181	7.2	8	7	28.6	25:30	16	2	9	11	14	1	1	1	28:54
	Canada	Olympics	DID NOT PLAY – INJURED																						
2006-07♦	Anaheim	NHL	79	15	54	69	86	9	0	3	172	8.7	6	1	100.0	27:31	21	3	8	11	26	1	0	2	29:51
	NHL Totals		1053	140	468	608	660	69	1	32	2003	7.0		37	24.3	25:05	183	22	64	86	140	9	3	6	26:40

WHL West First All-Star Team (1991, 1992) • Canadian Major Junior Scholastic Player of the Year (1991) • Memorial Cup Tournament All-Star Team (1992) • Stafford Smythe Memorial Trophy (Memorial Cup Tournament MVP) (1992) • NHL All-Rookie Team (1993) • NHL Second All-Star Team (1998) • NHL First All-Star Team (2004, 2006, 2007) • James Norris Memorial Trophy (2004) • Conn Smythe Trophy (2007)

Played in NHL All-Star Game (1998, 2001, 2004, 2007)

Signed to PTO (tryout) contract by **Utah** (IHL) with **New Jersey** retaining NHL rights, October 19, 1998. Signed as a free agent by **Anaheim**, August 4, 2005.

NIELSEN, Frans

(NEEL-sehn, FRAHNZ) **NYI**

Center. Shoots left. 5'11", 172 lbs. Born, Herning, Denmark, April 24, 1984. NY Islanders' 2nd choice, 87th overall, in 2002 Entry Draft.

Season	Club	League	GP	G	A	Pts	PIM	PP	SH	GW	S	%	+/-	TF	F%	Min	GP	G	A	Pts	PIM	PP	SH	GW	Min
99-2000	Herning IK Jr.	Den-Jr.	36	18	16	34	6	....	....	....	....	....	....	....	....	....	....	....	....	....	....	....	....	....	....
2000-01	Herning IK	Denmark	38	18	19	37	6	....	....	....	....	....	....	....	....	....	....	....	....	....	....	....	....	....	....
2001-02	Malmo	Sweden	20	0	1	1	0	....	....	....	....	....	....	....	....	....	....	....	....	....	....	....	....	....	....
	Malmo Jr.	Swe-Jr.	29	15	27	42	8	....	....	....	....	....	....	....	....	....	7	3	7	10	2	....	....	....	....
2002-03	Malmo	Sweden	47	3	6	9	10	....	....	....	....	....	....	....	....	....	....	....	....	....	....	....	....	....	....
	Malmo Jr.	Swe-Jr.	2	1	3	4	0	....	....	....	....	....	....	....	....	....	....	....	....	....	....	....	....	....	....
2003-04	Malmo	Sweden	50	9	7	16	28	....	....	....	....	....	....	....	....	....	....	....	....	....	....	....	....	....	....
	Malmo	Sweden-Q	10	3	5	8	2	....	....	....	....	....	....	....	....	....	....	....	....	....	....	....	....	....	....
2004-05	Malmo	Sweden	49	8	7	15	6	....	....	....	....	....	....	....	....	....	....	....	....	....	....	....	....	....	....
	Malmo	Sweden-Q	10	7	2	9	0	....	....	....	....	....	....	....	....	....	....	....	....	....	....	....	....	....	....
2005-06	Timra IK	Sweden	50	5	13	18	22	....	....	....	....	....	....	....	....	....	....	....	....	....	....	....	....	....	....
2006-07	NY Islanders	NHL	15	1	1	2	0	0	0	1	16	6.3	-2	53	45.3	5:13	....	....	....	....	....	....	....	....	....
	Bridgeport	AHL	54	20	24	44	10	....	....	....	....	....	....	....	....	....	....	....	....	....	....	....	....	....	....
	NHL Totals		15	1	1	2	0	0	0	1	16	6.3		53	45.3	5:13	....	....	....	....	....	....	....	....	....

NIEMINEN, Ville

(nee-EHM-ih-nehn, VIHL-ee)

Left wing. Shoots left. 5'11", 200 lbs. Born, Tampere, Finland, April 6, 1977. Colorado's 4th choice, 78th overall, in 1997 Entry Draft.

Season	Club	League	GP	G	A	Pts	PIM	PP	SH	GW	S	%	+/-	TF	F%	Min	GP	G	A	Pts	PIM	PP	SH	GW	Min
1993-94	Tappara U18	Fin-U18	29	13	20	33	66	....	....	....	....	....	....	....	....	....	5	1	2	3	0	....	....	....	....
1994-95	Tappara U18	Fin-U18	15	14	18	32	68	....	....	....	....	....	....	....	....	....	7	2	16	18	22	....	....	....	....
	Tappara Jr.	Fin-Jr.	16	11	21	32	47	....	....	....	....	....	....	....	....	....	....	....	....	....	....	....	....	....	....
	Tappara Tampere	Finland	16	0	0	0	0	....	....	....	....	....	....	....	....	....	....	....	....	....	....	....	....	....	....
1995-96	Tappara Jr.	Fin-Jr.	20	20	23	43	63	....	....	....	....	....	....	....	....	....	....	....	....	....	....	....	....	....	....
	Tappara Tampere	Finland	4	0	1	1	8	....	....	....	....	....	....	....	....	....	....	....	....	....	....	....	....	....	....
	KooVee Tampere	Finland-2	7	2	1	3	4	....	....	....	....	....	....	....	....	....	....	....	....	....	....	....	....	....	....
1996-97	Tappara Jr.	Fin-Jr.	2	2	7	9	2	....	....	....	....	....	....	....	....	....	....	....	....	....	....	....	....	....	....
	Tappara Tampere	Finland	49	10	13	23	120	....	....	....	....	....	....	....	....	....	3	1	0	1	8	....	....	....	....
1997-98	Hershey Bears	AHL	74	14	22	36	85	....	....	....	....	....	....	....	....	....	....	....	....	....	....	....	....	....	....
1998-99	Hershey Bears	AHL	67	24	19	43	127	....	....	....	....	....	....	....	....	....	3	0	1	1	0	....	....	....	....
99-2000	Colorado	NHL	1	0	0	0	0	0	0	0	2	0.0	0	0	0.0	10:12	....	....	....	....	....	....	....	....	....
	Hershey Bears	AHL	74	21	30	51	54	....	....	....	....	....	....	....	....	....	9	2	4	6	6	....	....	....	....
2000-01♦	Colorado	NHL	50	14	8	22	38	2	0	3	68	20.6	8	3	33.3	12:26	23	4	6	10	20	3	0	1	14:10
	Hershey Bears	AHL	28	10	11	21	48	....	....	....	....	....	....	....	....	....	....	....	....	....	....	....	....	....	....
2001-02	Colorado	NHL	53	10	14	24	30	1	0	5	72	13.9	1	8	62.5	12:41	....	....	....	....	....	....	....	....	....
	Finland	Olympics	4	0	1	1	2	....	....	....	....	....	....	....	....	....	....	....	....	....	....	....	....	....	....
	Pittsburgh	NHL	13	1	2	3	8	0	0	0	11	9.1	-2	0	0.0	16:10	....	....	....	....	....	....	....	....	....
2002-03	Pittsburgh	NHL	75	9	12	21	93	0	2	1	86	10.5	-25	46	52.2	14:08	....	....	....	....	....	....	....	....	....
2003-04	Chicago	NHL	60	2	11	13	40	1	0	0	56	3.6	-15	4	25.0	11:46	....	....	....	....	....	....	....	....	....
	Calgary	NHL	19	3	5	8	18	0	0	1	27	11.1	6	5	0.0	14:36	24	4	4	8	55	1	0	0	16:17
2004-05	Tappara Tampere	Finland	26	14	13	27	32	....	....	....	....	....	....	....	....	....	8	2	4	6	12	....	....	....	....
2005-06	NY Rangers	NHL	48	5	12	17	53	0	0	2	73	6.8	10	6	33.3	11:38	....	....	....	....	....	....	....	....	....
	Finland	Olympics	8	0	1	1	4	....	....	....	....	....	....	....	....	....	....	....	....	....	....	....	....	....	....
	San Jose	NHL	22	3	4	7	10	0	1	0	41	7.3	-3	3	33.3	15:23	11	0	2	2	24	0	0	0	15:39
2006-07	San Jose	NHL	30	1	1	2	14	0	0	0	30	3.3	-7	0	0.0	8:38	....	....	....	....	....	....	....	....	....
	St. Louis	NHL	14	0	0	0	29	0	0	0	13	0.0	-1	0	0.0	9:09	....	....	....	....	....	....	....	....	....
	NHL Totals		385	48	69	117	333	4	3	12	479	10.0		75	45.3	12:35	58	8	12	20	99	4	0	1	15:19

Traded to **Pittsburgh** by **Colorado** with Rick Berry for Darius Kasparaitis, March 19, 2002. Signed as a free agent by **Chicago**, July 29, 2003. Traded to **Calgary** by **Chicago** for Jason Morgan and Calgary's 6th round choice (Joseph Fallon) in 2005 Entry Draft, February 24, 2004. Signed as a free agent by **Tappara Tampere** (Finland), July 22, 2004. Signed as a free agent by **NY Rangers**, August 4, 2005. Traded to **San Jose** by **NY Rangers** for San Jose's 3rd round choice (later traded to Anaheim - Anaheim selected John DeGray) in 2006 Entry Draft, March 8, 2006. Traded to **St. Louis** by **San Jose** with Jay Barriball and New Jersey's 1st round choice (previously acquired, St. Louis selected David Perron) in 2007 Entry Draft for Bill Guerin, February 27, 2007.

NIEUWENDYK, Joe

(NEW-ihn-DIGHK, JOH)

Center. Shoots left. 6'2", 205 lbs. Born, Oshawa, Ont., September 10, 1966. Calgary's 2nd choice, 27th overall, in 1985 Entry Draft.

Season	Club	League	GP	G	A	Pts	PIM	PP	SH	GW	S	%	+/-	TF	F%	Min	GP	G	A	Pts	PIM	PP	SH	GW	Min
1983-84	Pickering Panthers	OHA-B	38	30	28	58	35	....	....	....	....	....	....	....	....	....	....	....	....	....	....	....	....	....	....
1984-85	Cornell Big Red	ECAC	29	21	24	45	30	....	....	....	....	....	....	....	....	....	....	....	....	....	....	....	....	....	....
1985-86	Cornell Big Red	ECAC	29	26	28	54	67	....	....	....	....	....	....	....	....	....	....	....	....	....	....	....	....	....	....
1986-87	Cornell Big Red	ECAC	23	26	26	52	26	....	....	....	....	....	....	....	....	....	....	....	....	....	....	....	....	....	....
	Calgary	NHL	9	5	1	6	0	2	0	1	16	31.3	0	....	....	....	6	2	2	4	0	0	0	0	....
1987-88	Calgary	NHL	75	51	41	92	23	31	3	8	212	24.1	20	....	....	....	8	3	4	7	2	1	0	0	....
1988-89♦	Calgary	NHL	77	51	31	82	40	19	3	11	215	23.7	26	....	....	....	22	10	4	14	10	6	0	1	....
1989-90	Calgary	NHL	79	45	50	95	40	18	0	3	226	19.9	32	....	....	....	6	4	6	10	4	1	0	0	....
1990-91	Calgary	NHL	79	45	40	85	36	22	4	1	222	20.3	19	....	....	....	7	4	1	5	10	2	0	0	....
1991-92	Calgary	NHL	69	22	34	56	55	7	0	2	137	16.1	-1	....	....	....	....	....	....	....	....	....	....	....	....
1992-93	Calgary	NHL	79	38	37	75	52	14	0	6	208	18.3	9	....	....	....	6	3	6	9	10	1	0	0	....
1993-94	Calgary	NHL	64	36	39	75	51	14	1	7	191	18.8	19	....	....	....	6	2	2	4	0	1	0	0	....

Season	Club	League	GP	G	A	Pts	PIM	PP	SH	GW	S	%	+/-	TF	F%	Min	GP	G	A	Pts	PIM	PP	SH	GW	Min
			Regular Season														Playoffs								
1994-95	Calgary	NHL	46	21	29	50	33	3	0	4	122	17.2	11	....	....	....	5	4	3	7	0	2	0	1	....
1995-96	Dallas	NHL	52	14	18	32	41	8	0	3	138	10.1	–17	....	....	....	....	....	....	....	....	....	....	....	....
1996-97	Dallas	NHL	66	30	21	51	32	8	0	2	173	17.3	–5	....	....	....	7	2	2	4	6	0	0	0	....
1997-98	Dallas	NHL	73	39	30	69	30	14	0	11	203	19.2	16	....	....	....	1	1	0	1	0	0	0	0	....
	Canada	Olympics	6	2	3	5	2	....	....	....	....	....	....	....	....	....	....	....	....	....	....	....	....	....	....
1998-99♦	Dallas	NHL	67	28	27	55	34	8	0	8	157	17.8	11	1170	63.2	15:33	23	*11	10	21	19	3	0	6	18:27
99-2000	Dallas	NHL	48	15	19	34	26	7	0	2	110	13.6	–1	924	59.1	16:15	23	7	3	10	18	3	0	2	16:41
2000-01	Dallas	NHL	69	29	23	52	30	12	0	4	166	17.5	5	1262	57.2	16:11	7	4	0	4	4	1	0	1	15:50
2001-02	Dallas	NHL	67	23	24	47	18	6	0	5	157	14.6	–2	1345	59.6	16:59	....	....	....	....	....	....	....	....	....
	Canada	Olympics	6	1	1	2	0	....	....	....	....	....	....	....	....	....	....	....	....	....	....	....	....	....	....
	New Jersey	NHL	14	2	9	11	4	0	0	1	32	6.3	2	275	55.3	16:22	5	0	1	1	0	0	0	0	19:22
2002-03♦	New Jersey	NHL	80	17	28	45	56	3	0	4	201	8.5	10	1383	58.5	16:45	17	3	6	9	4	1	0	0	15:03
2003-04	Toronto	NHL	64	22	28	50	26	10	1	5	131	16.8	7	970	60.4	15:38	9	6	0	6	4	1	0	2	15:24
2004-05		DID NOT PLAY																							
2005-06	Florida	NHL	65	26	30	56	46	7	0	3	195	13.3	–2	1224	59.4	16:23	....	....	....	....	....	....	....	....	....
2006-07	Florida	NHL	15	5	3	8	4	2	0	2	30	16.7	–4	207	53.6	13:24	....	....	....	....	....	....	....	....	....
	NHL Totals		1257	564	562	1126	677	215	12	93	3242	17.4		8760	59.3	16:11	158	66	50	116	91	23	0	13	16:47

ECAC Rookie of the Year (1985) • ECAC First All-Star Team (1986, 1987) • NCAA East First All-American Team (1986, 1987) • ECAC Player of the Year (1987) • Calder Memorial Trophy (1988) • NHL All-Rookie Team (1988) • Dodge Ram Tough Award (1988) • King Clancy Memorial Trophy (1995) • Conn Smythe Trophy (1999)

Played in NHL All-Star Game (1988, 1989, 1990, 1994)

Traded to **Dallas** by **Calgary** for Corey Millen and Jarome Iginla, December 19, 1995. Traded to **New Jersey** by **Dallas** with Jamie Langenbrunner for Jason Arnott, Randy McKay and New Jersey's 1st round choice (later traded to Columbus – later traded to Buffalo – Buffalo selected Dan Paille) in 2002 Entry Draft, March 19, 2002. Signed as a free agent by **Toronto**, September 9, 2003. Signed as a free agent by **Florida**, August 1, 2005. • Officially announced retirement, December 7, 2006.

NIINIMAA, Janne

(nih-NEE-mah, YAH-nee)

Defense. Shoots left. 6'1", 220 lbs. Born, Raahe, Finland, May 22, 1975. Philadelphia's 1st choice, 36th overall, in 1993 Entry Draft.

Season	Club	League	GP	G	A	Pts	PIM	PP	SH	GW	S	%	+/-	TF	F%	Min	GP	G	A	Pts	PIM	PP	SH	GW	Min
1990-91	Karpat Oulu Jr.	Fin-Jr.	7	1	1	2	4	....	....	....	....	....	....	....	....	....	....	....	....	....	....	....	....	....	....
1991-92	Karpat Oulu Jr.	Fin-Jr.	3	0	0	0	4	....	....	....	....	....	....	....	....	....	....	....	....	....	....	....	....	....	....
	Karpat Oulu	Finland-2	41	2	11	13	49	....	....	....	....	....	....	....	....	....	4	0	0	0	0	....	....	....	....
1992-93	Karpat Oulu U18	Fin-U18	....	....	....	....	....	....	....	....	....	....	....	....	....	....	6	2	5	7	6	....	....	....	....
	Karpat Oulu Jr.	Fin-Jr.	10	3	9	12	16	....	....	....	....	....	....	....	....	....	....	....	....	....	....	....	....	....	....
	Karpat Oulu	Finland-2	29	2	3	5	14	....	....	....	....	....	....	....	....	....	....	....	....	....	....	....	....	....	....
	KKP Kiiminki	Finland-3	1	0	2	2	2	....	....	....	....	....	....	....	....	....	....	....	....	....	....	....	....	....	....
1993-94	Jokerit Helsinki Jr.	Fin-Jr.	10	2	6	8	41	....	....	....	....	....	....	....	....	....	....	....	....	....	....	....	....	....	....
	Jokerit Helsinki	Finland	45	3	8	11	24	....	....	....	....	....	....	....	....	....	12	1	1	2	4	....	....	....	....
1994-95	Jokerit Helsinki Jr.	Fin-Jr.	6	6	3	9	39	....	....	....	....	....	....	....	....	....	....	....	....	....	....	....	....	....	....
	Jokerit Helsinki	Finland	42	7	10	17	36	....	....	....	....	....	....	....	....	....	10	1	4	5	35	....	....	....	....
1995-96	Jokerit Helsinki Jr.	Fin-Jr.	....	....	....	....	....	....	....	....	....	....	....	....	....	....	2	3	4	7	6	....	....	....	....
	Jokerit Helsinki	Finland	49	5	15	20	79	....	....	....	....	....	....	....	....	....	11	0	2	2	12	....	....	....	....
1996-97	Philadelphia	NHL	77	4	40	44	58	1	0	2	141	2.8	12	....	....	....	19	1	12	13	16	1	0	1	....
1997-98	Philadelphia	NHL	66	3	31	34	56	2	0	1	115	2.6	6	....	....	....	....	....	....	....	....	....	....	....	....
	Edmonton	NHL	11	1	8	9	6	1	0	0	19	5.3	7	....	....	....	11	1	1	2	12	0	0	1	....
	Finland	Olympics	6	0	3	3	8	....	....	....	....	....	....	....	....	....	....	....	....	....	....	....	....	....	....
1998-99	Edmonton	NHL	81	4	24	28	88	2	0	1	142	2.8	7	1	0.0	23:54	4	0	0	0	2	0	0	0	28:16
99-2000	Edmonton	NHL	81	8	25	33	89	2	2	0	133	6.0	14	0	0.0	24:28	5	0	2	2	2	0	0	0	21:39
2000-01	Edmonton	NHL	82	12	34	46	90	8	0	1	122	9.8	6	0	0.0	25:20	6	0	2	2	6	0	0	0	28:33
2001-02	Edmonton	NHL	81	5	39	44	80	1	0	2	119	4.2	13	0	0.0	26:02	....	....	....	....	....	....	....	....	....
	Finland	Olympics	4	0	3	3	2	....	....	....	....	....	....	....	....	....	....	....	....	....	....	....	....	....	....
2002-03	Edmonton	NHL	63	4	24	28	66	2	0	0	90	4.4	–7	1	0.0	26:48	....	....	....	....	....	....	....	....	....
	NY Islanders	NHL	13	1	5	6	14	1	0	0	11	9.1	–2	0	0.0	23:02	5	0	1	1	12	0	0	0	23:32
2003-04	NY Islanders	NHL	82	9	19	28	64	4	0	2	97	9.3	12	0	0.0	23:15	5	1	2	3	2	1	0	1	24:31
2004-05	Malmo	Sweden	10	0	3	3	34	....	....	....	....	....	....	....	....	....	....	....	....	....	....	....	....	....	....
	Karpat Oulu	Finland	26	3	10	13	30	....	....	....	....	....	....	....	....	....	12	0	5	5	8	....	....	....	....
2005-06	NY Islanders	NHL	41	1	9	10	62	0	0	0	23	4.3	–7	1	0.0	20:30	....	....	....	....	....	....	....	....	....
	Dallas	NHL	22	2	4	6	24	1	1	1	26	7.7	–5	0	0.0	18:25	4	0	1	1	8	0	0	0	14:07
2006-07	Montreal	NHL	41	0	3	3	36	0	0	0	29	0.0	–13	0	0.0	14:51	....	....	....	....	....	....	....	....	....
	NHL Totals		741	54	265	319	733	25	3	10	1067	5.1		3	0.0	23:36	59	3	21	24	60	2	0	3	23:46

NHL All-Rookie Team (1997)

Played in NHL All-Star Game (2001)

Traded to **Edmonton** by **Philadelphia** for Dan McGillis and Edmonton's 2nd round choice (Jason Beckett) in 1998 Entry Draft, March 24, 1998. Traded to **NY Islanders** by **Edmonton** with Washington's 2nd round choice (previously acquired, NY Islanders selected Evgeni Tunik) in 2003 Entry Draft for Brad Isbister and Raffi Torres, March 11, 2003. Signed as a free agent by **Malmo** (Sweden), November 17, 2004. Signed as a free agent by **Oulu** (Finland), January 3, 2005. Traded to **Dallas** by **NY Islanders** with NY Islanders' 5th round choice (Ondrej Roman) in 2007 Entry Draft for John Erskine and Dallas' 2nd round choice (Jesse Joensuu) in 2006 Entry Draft, January 10, 2005. Traded to **Montreal** by **Dallas** with Dallas' 5th round choice (Andrew Conboy) in 2007 Entry Draft for Mike Ribeiro and Montreal's 6th round choice in 2008 Entry Draft, September 30, 2006.

NILSON, Marcus

(NIHL-suhn, MAHR-kuhs) **CGY.**

Left wing. Shoots right. 6'2", 193 lbs. Born, Balsta, Sweden, March 1, 1978. Florida's 1st choice, 20th overall, in 1996 Entry Draft.

Season	Club	League	GP	G	A	Pts	PIM	PP	SH	GW	S	%	+/-	TF	F%	Min	GP	G	A	Pts	PIM	PP	SH	GW	Min
1994-95	Djurgarden Jr.	Swe-Jr.	24	7	8	15	22	....	....	....	....	....	....	....	....	....	....	....	....	....	....	....	....	....	....
1995-96	Djurgarden Jr.	Swe-Jr.	25	19	17	36	46	....	....	....	....	....	....	....	....	....	2	1	1	2	12	....	....	....	....
	Djurgarden	Sweden	12	0	0	0	0	....	....	....	....	....	....	....	....	....	1	0	0	0	0	....	....	....	....
1996-97	Djurgarden	Sweden	37	0	3	3	33	....	....	....	....	....	....	....	....	....	4	0	0	0	0	....	....	....	....
1997-98	Djurgarden	Sweden	41	4	7	11	18	....	....	....	....	....	....	....	....	....	15	2	1	3	16	....	....	....	....
1998-99	Florida	NHL	8	1	1	2	5	0	0	1	7	14.3	2	6	50.0	12:24	....	....	....	....	....	....	....	....	....
	New Haven	AHL	69	8	25	33	10	....	....	....	....	....	....	....	....	....	....	....	....	....	....	....	....	....	....
99-2000	Florida	NHL	9	0	2	2	2	0	0	0	6	0.0	2	14	64.3	7:56	....	....	....	....	....	....	....	....	....
	Louisville Panthers	AHL	64	9	23	32	52	....	....	....	....	....	....	....	....	....	4	0	0	0	2	....	....	....	....
2000-01	Florida	NHL	78	12	24	36	74	0	0	2	141	8.5	–3	169	40.8	15:46	....	....	....	....	....	....	....	....	....
2001-02	Florida	NHL	81	14	19	33	55	6	1	2	147	9.5	–14	539	43.8	16:31	....	....	....	....	....	....	....	....	....
2002-03	Florida	NHL	82	15	19	34	31	7	1	0	187	8.0	2	469	46.7	15:31	....	....	....	....	....	....	....	....	....
2003-04	Florida	NHL	69	6	13	19	26	1	1	1	110	5.5	–9	151	44.4	15:30	....	....	....	....	....	....	....	....	....
	Calgary	NHL	14	5	0	5	14	1	0	2	23	21.7	3	173	45.1	16:43	26	4	7	11	12	0	0	1	19:25
2004-05	Djurgarden	Sweden	48	17	22	39	110	....	....	....	....	....	....	....	....	....	7	1	2	3	10	....	....	....	....
2005-06	Calgary	NHL	70	6	11	17	32	2	0	2	83	7.2	13	392	45.4	14:50	....	....	....	....	....	....	....	....	....
2006-07	Calgary	NHL	63	5	10	15	27	0	0	1	69	7.2	7	119	31.9	13:07	6	0	0	0	2	0	0	0	13:32
	NHL Totals		474	64	99	163	266	17	3	11	773	8.3		2032	44.1	15:09	32	4	7	11	14	0	0	1	18:19

Traded to **Calgary** by **Florida** for Calgary's 2nd round choice (David Booth) in 2004 Entry Draft, March 8, 2004. Signed as a free agent by **Djurgarden** (Sweden), September 16, 2004.

NILSSON, Robert

(NIHL-suhn, RAW-buhrt) **EDM.**

Center. Shoots left. 5'11", 185 lbs. Born, Calgary, Alta., January 10, 1985. NY Islanders' 1st choice, 15th overall, in 2003 Entry Draft.

Season	Club	League	GP	G	A	Pts	PIM	PP	SH	GW	S	%	+/-	TF	F%	Min	GP	G	A	Pts	PIM	PP	SH	GW	Min
2000-01	Leksands IF Jr.	Swe-Jr.	23	14	28	42	26	....	....	....	....	....	....	....	....	....	2	0	0	0	2	....	....	....	....
	Leksands IF U18	Swe-U18	4	6	3	9	6	....	....	....	....	....	....	....	....	....	2	0	2	2	2	....	....	....	....
2001-02	Leksands IF Jr.	Swe-Jr.	21	13	18	31	24	....	....	....	....	....	....	....	....	....	5	0	5	5	8	....	....	....	....
	Leksands IF	Sweden-2	14	1	4	5	8	....	....	....	....	....	....	....	....	....	....	....	....	....	....	....	....	....	....
2002-03	Leksands IF	Sweden	41	8	13	21	10	....	....	....	....	....	....	....	....	....	5	0	1	1	2	....	....	....	....
	Leksands IF Jr.	Swe-Jr.	....	....	....	....	....	....	....	....	....	....	....	....	....	....	2	1	1	2	2	....	....	....	....
2003-04	Leksands IF Jr.	Swe-Jr.	4	2	8	10	4	....	....	....	....	....	....	....	....	....	....	....	....	....	....	....	....	....	....
	Leksands IF	Sweden	34	2	4	6	6	....	....	....	....	....	....	....	....	....	....	....	....	....	....	....	....	....	....
	Fribourg	Swiss	7	1	3	4	2	....	....	....	....	....	....	....	....	....	4	1	0	1	2	....	....	....	....
2004-05	Almtuna	Sweden-2	3	0	1	1	2	....	....	....	....	....	....	....	....	....	....	....	....	....	....	....	....	....	....
	Hammarby	Sweden-2	7	0	4	4	4	....	....	....	....	....	....	....	....	....	....	....	....	....	....	....	....	....	....
	Djurgarden Jr.	Swe-Jr.	8	8	4	12	12	....	....	....	....	....	....	....	....	....	....	....	....	....	....	....	....	....	....
	Djurgarden	Sweden	23	2	4	6	6	....	....	....	....	....	....	....	....	....	3	0	0	0	0	....	....	....	....
2005-06	NY Islanders	NHL	53	6	14	20	26	1	0	1	70	8.6	–6	31	29.0	11:52	....	....	....	....	....	....	....	....	....
	Bridgeport	AHL	29	8	20	28	12	....	....	....	....	....	....	....	....	....	7	1	4	5	0	....	....	....	....

Season	Club	League	Regular Season														Playoffs								
Season	Club	League	GP	G	A	Pts	PIM	PP	SH	GW	S	%	+/-	TF	F%	Min	GP	G	A	Pts	PIM	PP	SH	GW	Min
2006-07	Bridgeport	AHL	50	12	34	46	34	....	....	....	....	....	....	....	....	....	....	....	....	....	....	....	....	....	....
	Edmonton	**NHL**	**4**	**1**	**0**	**1**	**4**	**0**	**0**	**0**	**8**	**12.5**	**–1**	**2**	**50.0**	**17:21**	....	....	....	....	....	....	....	....	....
	Wilkes-Barre	AHL	19	6	14	20	14	....	....	....	....	....	....	....	....	....	11	3	12	15	8	....	....	....	....
	NHL Totals		**57**	**7**	**14**	**21**	**30**	**1**	**0**	**1**	**78**	**9.0**		**33**	**30.3**	**12:15**	....	....	....	....	....	....	....	....	....

Traded to **Edmonton** by **NY Islanders** with Ryan O'Marra and NY Islanders' 1st round choice (Alex Plante) in 2007 Entry Draft for Ryan Smyth, February 27, 2007.

NOKELAINEN, Petteri

(noh-kuh-LAY-nehn, PEH-tuh-ree) **NYI**

Center. Shoots right. 6'1", 187 lbs. Born, Imatra, Finland, January 16, 1986. NY Islanders' 1st choice, 16th overall, in 2004 Entry Draft.

Season	Club	League	GP	G	A	Pts	PIM	PP	SH	GW	S	%	+/-	TF	F%	Min	GP	G	A	Pts	PIM	PP	SH	GW	Min
2001-02	SaiPa U18	Fin-U18	6	2	1	3	14	....	....	....	....	....	....	....	....	....	....	....	....	....	....	....	....	....	....
2002-03	SaiPa U18	Fin-U18	10	3	8	11	18	....	....	....	....	....	....	....	....	....	....	....	....	....	....	....	....	....	....
	SaiPa Jr.	Fin-Jr.	28	7	4	11	28	....	....	....	....	....	....	....	....	....	3	1	0	1	4	....	....	....	....
	SaiPa	Finland	2	1	0	1	2	....	....	....	....	....	....	....	....	....	....	....	....	....	....	....	....	....	....
2003-04	Suomi U20	Finland-2	3	0	1	1	0	....	....	....	....	....	....	....	....	....	....	....	....	....	....	....	....	....	....
	SaiPa Jr.	Fin-Jr.	10	5	3	8	4	....	....	....	....	....	....	....	....	....	4	0	1	1	0	....	....	....	....
	SaiPa	Finland	40	4	4	8	16	....	....	....	....	....	....	....	....	....	....	....	....	....	....	....	....	....	....
2004-05	SaiPa	Finland	52	15	5	20	34	....	....	....	....	....	....	....	....	....	....	....	....	....	....	....	....	....	....
2005-06	**NY Islanders**	**NHL**	**15**	**1**	**1**	**2**	**4**	**0**	**0**	**1**	**13**	**7.7**	**–1**	**82**	**48.8**	**7:47**	....	....	....	....	....	....	....	....	....
2006-07	Bridgeport	AHL	60	6	10	16	51	....	....	....	....	....	....	....	....	....	....	....	....	....	....	....	....	....	....
	NHL Totals		**15**	**1**	**1**	**2**	**4**	**0**	**0**	**1**	**13**	**7.7**		**82**	**48.8**	**7:47**	....	....	....	....	....	....	....	....	....

• Missed majority of 2005-06 season recovering from knee injury suffered in game vs. Pittsburgh, November 3, 2005.

NOLAN, Owen

(NOH-lan, OH-wehn) **CGY.**

Right wing. Shoots right. 6'1", 215 lbs. Born, Belfast, N.Ireland, February 12, 1972. Quebec's 1st choice, 1st overall, in 1990 Entry Draft.

Season	Club	League	GP	G	A	Pts	PIM	PP	SH	GW	S	%	+/-	TF	F%	Min	GP	G	A	Pts	PIM	PP	SH	GW	Min
1987-88	Thorold	Minor-ON	28	53	32	85	24	....	....	....	....	....	....	....	....	....	....	....	....	....	....	....	....	....	....
	Thorold	OHA-B	3	1	0	1	2	....	....	....	....	....	....	....	....	....	....	....	....	....	....	....	....	....	....
1988-89	Cornwall Royals	OHL	62	34	25	59	213	....	....	....	....	....	....	....	....	....	18	5	11	16	41	....	....	....	....
1989-90	Cornwall Royals	OHL	58	51	59	110	240	....	....	....	....	....	....	....	....	....	6	7	5	12	26	....	....	....	....
1990-91	**Quebec**	**NHL**	**59**	**3**	**10**	**13**	**109**	**0**	**0**	**0**	**54**	**5.6**	**–19**	....	....	....	....	....	....	....	....	....	....	....	....
	Halifax Citadels	AHL	6	4	4	8	11	....	....	....	....	....	....	....	....	....	....	....	....	....	....	....	....	....	....
1991-92	**Quebec**	**NHL**	**75**	**42**	**31**	**73**	**183**	**17**	**0**	**0**	**190**	**22.1**	**–9**	....	....	....	....	....	....	....	....	....	....	....	....
1992-93	**Quebec**	**NHL**	**73**	**36**	**41**	**77**	**185**	**15**	**0**	**4**	**241**	**14.9**	**–1**	....	....	....	**5**	**1**	**0**	**1**	**2**	**0**	**0**	**0**	....
1993-94	**Quebec**	**NHL**	**6**	**2**	**2**	**4**	**8**	**0**	**0**	**0**	**15**	**13.3**	**2**	....	....	....	....	....	....	....	....	....	....	....	....
1994-95	**Quebec**	**NHL**	**46**	**30**	**19**	**49**	**46**	**13**	**2**	**8**	**137**	**21.9**	**21**	....	....	....	**6**	**2**	**3**	**5**	**6**	**0**	**0**	**0**	....
1995-96	**Colorado**	**NHL**	**9**	**4**	**4**	**8**	**9**	**4**	**0**	**0**	**23**	**17.4**	**–3**	....	....	....	....	....	....	....	....	....	....	....	....
	San Jose	**NHL**	**72**	**29**	**32**	**61**	**137**	**12**	**1**	**2**	**184**	**15.8**	**–30**	....	....	....	....	....	....	....	....	....	....	....	....
1996-97	**San Jose**	**NHL**	**72**	**31**	**32**	**63**	**155**	**10**	**0**	**3**	**225**	**13.8**	**–19**	....	....	....	....	....	....	....	....	....	....	....	....
1997-98	**San Jose**	**NHL**	**75**	**14**	**27**	**41**	**144**	**3**	**1**	**1**	**192**	**7.3**	**–2**	....	....	....	**6**	**2**	**2**	**4**	**26**	**2**	**0**	**1**	....
1998-99	**San Jose**	**NHL**	**78**	**19**	**26**	**45**	**129**	**6**	**2**	**3**	**207**	**9.2**	**16**	**657**	**49.3**	**19:09**	**6**	**1**	**1**	**2**	**6**	**0**	**0**	**0**	**20:15**
99-2000	**San Jose**	**NHL**	**78**	**44**	**40**	**84**	**110**	**18**	**4**	**6**	**261**	**16.9**	**–1**	**357**	**50.7**	**21:07**	**10**	**8**	**2**	**10**	**6**	**2**	**2**	**3**	**22:14**
2000-01	**San Jose**	**NHL**	**57**	**24**	**25**	**49**	**75**	**10**	**1**	**4**	**191**	**12.6**	**0**	**407**	**46.9**	**21:49**	**6**	**1**	**1**	**2**	**8**	**0**	**0**	**1**	**22:45**
2001-02	**San Jose**	**NHL**	**75**	**23**	**43**	**66**	**93**	**8**	**2**	**2**	**217**	**10.6**	**7**	**545**	**47.0**	**19:23**	**12**	**3**	**6**	**9**	**8**	**0**	**0**	**0**	**19:46**
	Canada	Olympics	6	0	3	3	2	....	....	....	....	....	....	....	....	....	....	....	....	....	....	....	....	....	....
2002-03	**San Jose**	**NHL**	**61**	**22**	**20**	**42**	**91**	**8**	**3**	**4**	**192**	**11.5**	**–5**	**226**	**50.4**	**18:08**	....	....	....	....	....	....	....	....	....
	Toronto	**NHL**	**14**	**7**	**5**	**12**	**16**	**5**	**0**	**1**	**29**	**24.1**	**2**	**56**	**48.2**	**17:00**	**7**	**0**	**2**	**2**	**2**	**0**	**0**	**0**	**23:19**
2003-04	**Toronto**	**NHL**	**65**	**19**	**29**	**48**	**110**	**7**	**2**	**3**	**154**	**12.3**	**4**	**242**	**53.3**	**17:57**	....	....	....	....	....	....	....	....	....
2004-05		DID NOT PLAY																							
2006-07	**Phoenix**	**NHL**	**76**	**16**	**24**	**40**	**56**	**2**	**3**	**1**	**154**	**10.4**	**–2**	**238**	**52.5**	**15:25**	....	....	....	....	....	....	....	....	....
	NHL Totals		**991**	**365**	**410**	**775**	**1656**	**138**	**21**	**42**	**2666**	**13.7**		**2728**	**49.4**	**18:53**	**58**	**18**	**17**	**35**	**64**	**4**	**2**	**5**	**21:29**

OHL Rookie of the Year (1989) • OHL First All-Star Team (1990)

Played in NHL All-Star Game (1992, 1996, 1997, 2000, 2002)

• Missed majority of 1993-94 season recovering from shoulder injury suffered in game vs. Tampa Bay, November 13, 1993. Transferred to **Colorado** after **Quebec** franchise relocated, June 21, 1995. Traded to **San Jose** by **Colorado** for Sandis Ozolinsh, October 26, 1995. Traded to **Toronto** by **San Jose** for Alyn McCauley, Brad Boyes and Toronto's 1st round choice (later traded to Boston – Boston selected Mark Stuart) in 2003 Entry Draft, March 5, 2003. Signed as a free agent by **Phoenix**, August 16, 2006. Signed as a free agent by **Calgary**, July 3, 2007.

NORDGREN, Niklas

(NORHD-grehn, NIHK-luhs)

Left wing. Shoots right. 5'11", 185 lbs. Born, Ornskoldsvik, Sweden, June 28, 1979. Carolina's 7th choice, 195th overall, in 1997 Entry Draft.

Season	Club	League	GP	G	A	Pts	PIM	PP	SH	GW	S	%	+/-	TF	F%	Min	GP	G	A	Pts	PIM	PP	SH	GW	Min
1996-97	MoDo	Sweden	5	0	0	0	0	....	....	....	....	....	....	....	....	....	....	....	....	....	....	....	....	....	....
1997-98	MoDo Jr.	Swe-Jr.	22	14	6	20	....	....	....	....	....	....	....	....	....	....	....	....	....	....	....	....	....	....	....
	Malmo Jr.	Swe-Jr.	28	15	15	30	52	....	....	....	....	....	....	....	....	....	....	....	....	....	....	....	....	....	....
1998-99	MoDo	Sweden	7	0	0	0	2	....	....	....	....	....	....	....	....	....	....	....	....	....	....	....	....	....	....
	Malmo Jr.	Swe-Jr.	22	7	4	11	22	....	....	....	....	....	....	....	....	....	3	2	1	3	0	....	....	....	....
99-2000	Sundsvall	Sweden-2	27	21	11	32	58	....	....	....	....	....	....	....	....	....	....	....	....	....	....	....	....	....	....
	MoDo	EuroHL	1	0	0	0	0	....	....	....	....	....	....	....	....	....	1	0	0	0	0	....	....	....	....
2000-01	Sundsvall	Sweden-2	35	22	19	41	45	....	....	....	....	....	....	....	....	....	....	....	....	....	....	....	....	....	....
2001-02	Timra IK Jr.	Swe-Jr.	1	1	1	2	0	....	....	....	....	....	....	....	....	....	....	....	....	....	....	....	....	....	....
	Timra IK	Sweden	49	8	6	14	16	....	....	....	....	....	....	....	....	....	....	....	....	....	....	....	....	....	....
	Timra IK	Sweden-Q	10	3	3	5	4	....	....	....	....	....	....	....	....	....	....	....	....	....	....	....	....	....	....
2002-03	Timra IK	Sweden	47	20	23	43	40	....	....	....	....	....	....	....	....	....	10	1	4	5	4	....	....	....	....
2003-04	Timra IK	Sweden	46	13	15	28	44	....	....	....	....	....	....	....	....	....	10	4	1	5	32	....	....	....	....
2004-05	Timra IK	Sweden	46	19	17	36	71	....	....	....	....	....	....	....	....	....	7	0	2	2	6	....	....	....	....
2005-06	**Carolina**	**NHL**	**43**	**4**	**2**	**6**	**30**	**0**	**0**	**0**	**32**	**12.5**	**–4**	**4**	**25.0**	**7:28**	....	....	....	....	....	....	....	....	....
	Lowell	AHL	8	6	4	10	10	....	....	....	....	....	....	....	....	....	....	....	....	....	....	....	....	....	....
	Pittsburgh	**NHL**	**15**	**0**	**0**	**0**	**4**	**0**	**0**	**0**	**6**	**0.0**	**–4**	**1**	**0.0**	**5:59**	....	....	....	....	....	....	....	....	....
2006-07	Rapperswil	Swiss	41	17	13	30	74	....	....	....	....	....	....	....	....	....	6	1	1	2	10	....	....	....	....
	NHL Totals		**58**	**4**	**2**	**6**	**34**	**0**	**0**	**0**	**38**	**10.5**		**5**	**20.0**	**7:05**	....	....	....	....	....	....	....	....	....

Traded to **Pittsburgh** by **Carolina** with Krys Kolanos and Carolina's 2nd round choice (later traded to San Jose - later traded to Philadelphia - Philadelphia selected Kevin Marshall) in 2007 Entry Draft for Mark Recchi, March 9, 2006. Signed as a free agent by **Rapperswil** (Swiss), May 10, 2006.

NORDQVIST, Jonas

(NAWRD-kvihst, YOH-nuhs) **CHI.**

Center. Shoots left. 6'3", 202 lbs. Born, Leksand, Sweden, April 26, 1982. Chicago's 3rd choice, 49th overall, in 2000 Entry Draft.

Season	Club	League	GP	G	A	Pts	PIM	PP	SH	GW	S	%	+/-	TF	F%	Min	GP	G	A	Pts	PIM	PP	SH	GW	Min
1997-98	Leksands IF Jr.	Swe-Jr.	42	26	35	61	....	....	....	....	....	....	....	....	....	....	....	....	....	....	....	....	....	....	....
1998-99	Leksands IF Jr.	Swe-Jr.	32	14	25	39	....	....	....	....	....	....	....	....	....	....	....	....	....	....	....	....	....	....	....
99-2000	Leksands IF Jr.	Swe-Jr.	34	15	24	39	32	....	....	....	....	....	....	....	....	....	2	0	0	0	2	....	....	....	....
	Leksands IF	Sweden	3	0	0	0	0	....	....	....	....	....	....	....	....	....	....	....	....	....	....	....	....	....	....
	Leksands IF U18	Swe-U18	2	0	2	2	0	....	....	....	....	....	....	....	....	....	4	3	5	8	0	....	....	....	....
2000-01	Leksands IF Jr.	Swe-Jr.	10	6	13	19	6	....	....	....	....	....	....	....	....	....	5	1	6	7	2	....	....	....	....
	Leksands IF	Sweden	42	3	4	7	4	....	....	....	....	....	....	....	....	....	....	....	....	....	....	....	....	....	....
2001-02	Leksands IF Jr.	Swe-Jr.	8	14	7	21	6	....	....	....	....	....	....	....	....	....	1	0	1	1	0	....	....	....	....
	Leksands IF	Sweden-2	40	8	7	15	16	....	....	....	....	....	....	....	....	....	....	....	....	....	....	....	....	....	....
2002-03	Rogle	Sweden-2	27	12	19	32	4	....	....	....	....	....	....	....	....	....	....	....	....	....	....	....	....	....	....
2003-04	Lulea HF	Sweden	47	13	11	24	18	....	....	....	....	....	....	....	....	....	3	0	0	0	2	....	....	....	....
2004-05	Lulea HF	Sweden	49	16	16	32	12	....	....	....	....	....	....	....	....	....	4	1	1	2	0	....	....	....	....
2005-06	Lulea HF	Sweden	46	19	22	41	30	....	....	....	....	....	....	....	....	....	6	1	2	3	6	....	....	....	....
2006-07	**Chicago**	**NHL**	**3**	**0**	**2**	**2**	**2**	**0**	**0**	**0**	**2**	**0.0**	**1**	**27**	**29.6**	**13:55**	....	....	....	....	....	....	....	....	....
	Norfolk Admirals	AHL	65	15	26	41	18	....	....	....	....	....	....	....	....	....	6	3	4	7	0	....	....	....	....
	NHL Totals		**3**	**0**	**2**	**2**	**2**	**0**	**0**	**0**	**2**	**0.0**		**27**	**29.6**	**13:55**	....	....	....	....	....	....	....	....	....

NORSTROM, Mattias
(NOHR-struhm, mat-TEE-uhs) **DAL.**

Defense. Shoots left. 6'2", 210 lbs. Born, Stockholm, Sweden, January 2, 1972. NY Rangers' 2nd choice, 48th overall, in 1992 Entry Draft.

			Regular Season														Playoffs								
Season	Club	League	GP	G	A	Pts	PIM	PP	SH	GW	S	%	+/-	TF	F%	Min	GP	G	A	Pts	PIM	PP	SH	GW	Min
1990-91	Mora IK	Sweden-2	9	1	1	2	6	....	....	....	....	....	....	....	....	....	1	0	0	0	2	....	....	....	....
1991-92	AIK Solna	Sweden	39	4	3	7	28	....	....	....	....	....	....	....	....	....	3	0	2	2	2	....	....	....	....
1992-93	AIK Solna	Sweden	22	0	1	1	16	....	....	....	....	....	....	....	....	....	....	....	....	....	....	....	....	....	....
1993-94	**NY Rangers**	**NHL**	**9**	**0**	**2**	**2**	**6**	**0**	**0**	**0**	**3**	**0.0**	**0**	....	....	....	....	....	....	....	....	....	....	....	....
	Binghamton	AHL	55	1	9	10	70	....	....	....	....	....	....	....	....	....	....	....	....	....	....	....	....	....	....
1994-95	Binghamton	AHL	63	9	10	19	91	....	....	....	....	....	....	....	....	....	....	....	....	....	....	....	....	....	....
	NY Rangers	**NHL**	**9**	**0**	**3**	**3**	**2**	**0**	**0**	**0**	**4**	**0.0**	**2**	....	....	....	**3**	**0**	**0**	**0**	**0**	**0**	**0**	**0**	....
1995-96	**NY Rangers**	**NHL**	**25**	**2**	**1**	**3**	**22**	**0**	**0**	**0**	**17**	**11.8**	**5**	....	....	....	....	....	....	....	....	....	....	....	....
	Los Angeles	**NHL**	**11**	**0**	**1**	**1**	**18**	**0**	**0**	**0**	**17**	**0.0**	**–8**	....	....	....	....	....	....	....	....	....	....	....	....
1996-97	**Los Angeles**	**NHL**	**80**	**1**	**21**	**22**	**84**	**0**	**0**	**0**	**106**	**0.9**	**–4**	....	....	....	....	....	....	....	....	....	....	....	....
1997-98	**Los Angeles**	**NHL**	**73**	**1**	**12**	**13**	**90**	**0**	**0**	**0**	**61**	**1.6**	**14**	....	....	....	**4**	**0**	**0**	**0**	**2**	**0**	**0**	**0**	....
	Sweden	Olympics	4	0	1	1	2	....	....	....	....	....	....	....	....	....	....	....	....	....	....	....	....	....	....
1998-99	**Los Angeles**	**NHL**	**78**	**2**	**5**	**7**	**36**	**0**	**1**	**0**	**61**	**3.3**	**–10**	**1**	**0.0**	**20:20**	....	....	....	....	....	....	....	....	....
99-2000	**Los Angeles**	**NHL**	**82**	**1**	**13**	**14**	**66**	**0**	**0**	**0**	**62**	**1.6**	**22**	**0**	**0.0**	**21:49**	**4**	**0**	**0**	**0**	**6**	**0**	**0**	**0**	**21:36**
2000-01	**Los Angeles**	**NHL**	**82**	**0**	**18**	**18**	**60**	**0**	**0**	**0**	**59**	**0.0**	**10**	**2**	**0.0**	**21:50**	**13**	**0**	**2**	**2**	**18**	**0**	**0**	**0**	**23:16**
2001-02	**Los Angeles**	**NHL**	**79**	**2**	**9**	**11**	**38**	**0**	**0**	**0**	**42**	**4.8**	**–2**	**0**	**0.0**	**23:01**	**7**	**0**	**0**	**0**	**4**	**0**	**0**	**0**	**23:24**
	Sweden	Olympics	4	0	0	0	0	....	....	....	....	....	....	....	....	....	....	....	....	....	....	....	....	....	....
2002-03	**Los Angeles**	**NHL**	**82**	**0**	**6**	**6**	**49**	**0**	**0**	**0**	**63**	**0.0**	**0**	**1**	**100.0**	**21:30**	....	....	....	....	....	....	....	....	....
2003-04	**Los Angeles**	**NHL**	**74**	**1**	**13**	**14**	**44**	**0**	**0**	**0**	**65**	**1.5**	**–3**	**1**	**100.0**	**22:26**	....	....	....	....	....	....	....	....	....
2004-05	AIK Solna	Sweden-3	8	1	0	1	4	....	....	....	....	....	....	....	....	....	....	....	....	....	....	....	....	....	....
2005-06	**Los Angeles**	**NHL**	**77**	**4**	**23**	**27**	**58**	**2**	**1**	**1**	**83**	**4.8**	**–3**	**0**	**0.0**	**21:07**	....	....	....	....	....	....	....	....	....
2006-07	**Los Angeles**	**NHL**	**62**	**2**	**7**	**9**	**40**	**0**	**0**	**0**	**44**	**4.5**	**–20**	**4**	**25.0**	**20:55**	....	....	....	....	....	....	....	....	....
	Dallas	**NHL**	**14**	**0**	**2**	**2**	**8**	**0**	**0**	**0**	**16**	**0.0**	**2**	**0**	**0.0**	**18:54**	**7**	**0**	**0**	**0**	**8**	**0**	**0**	**0**	**23:36**
	NHL Totals		**837**	**16**	**136**	**152**	**621**	**2**	**2**	**1**	**703**	**2.3**		**9**	**33.3**	**21:35**	**38**	**0**	**2**	**2**	**38**	**0**	**0**	**0**	**23:09**

Played in NHL All-Star Game (1999, 2004)

Traded to **Los Angeles** by **NY Rangers** with Ray Ferraro, Ian Laperriere, Nathan Lafayette and NY Rangers' 4th round choice (Sean Blanchard) in 1997 Entry Draft for Marty McSorley, Jari Kurri and Shane Churla, March 14, 1996. Signed as a free agent by **Solna** (Sweden-3), January 11, 2005. Traded to **Dallas** by **Los Angeles** with Konstantin Pushkarev and Los Angeles' 3rd (Sergei Korostin) and 4th (later traded to Columbus - Columbus selected Maxim Mayorov) round choices in 2007 Entry Draft for Jaroslav Modry, the rights to Johan Fransson, Dallas' 2nd (Oscar Moller) and 3rd (Bryan Cameron) round choices in 2007 Entry Draft and Dallas' 1st round choice in 2008 Entry Draft , February 27, 2007.

NORTON, Brad
(NOHR-tuhn, BRAD) **S.J.**

Defense. Shoots left. 6'6", 235 lbs. Born, Cambridge, MA, February 13, 1975. Edmonton's 9th choice, 215th overall, in 1993 Entry Draft.

Season	Club	League	GP	G	A	Pts	PIM	PP	SH	GW	S	%	+/-	TF	F%	Min	GP	G	A	Pts	PIM	PP	SH	GW	Min
1992-93	Cushing	High-MA	31	10	26	36	....	....	....	....	....	....	....	....	....	....	....	....	....	....	....	....	....	....	....
1993-94	Cushing	High-MA	STATISTICS NOT AVAILABLE																						
1994-95	U. Mass-Amherst	H-East	30	0	6	6	89	....	....	....	....	....	....	....	....	....	....	....	....	....	....	....	....	....	....
1995-96	U. Mass-Amherst	H-East	34	4	12	16	99	....	....	....	....	....	....	....	....	....	....	....	....	....	....	....	....	....	....
1996-97	U. Mass-Amherst	H-East	35	2	16	18	88	....	....	....	....	....	....	....	....	....	....	....	....	....	....	....	....	....	....
1997-98	U. Mass-Amherst	H-East	20	2	13	15	28	....	....	....	....	....	....	....	....	....	....	....	....	....	....	....	....	....	....
	Detroit Vipers	IHL	33	1	4	5	56	....	....	....	....	....	....	....	....	....	22	0	2	2	87	....	....	....	....
1998-99	Hamilton	AHL	58	1	8	9	134	....	....	....	....	....	....	....	....	....	11	0	1	1	6	....	....	....	....
99-2000	Hamilton	AHL	40	5	12	17	104	....	....	....	....	....	....	....	....	....	10	1	4	5	26	....	....	....	....
2000-01	Hamilton	AHL	46	3	15	18	114	....	....	....	....	....	....	....	....	....	....	....	....	....	....	....	....	....	....
2001-02	**Florida**	**NHL**	**22**	**0**	**2**	**2**	**45**	**0**	**0**	**0**	**6**	**0.0**	**–2**	**1**	**0.0**	**9:15**	....	....	....	....	....	....	....	....	....
	Hershey Bears	AHL	40	0	10	10	62	....	....	....	....	....	....	....	....	....	2	0	0	0	6	....	....	....	....
2002-03	**Los Angeles**	**NHL**	**53**	**3**	**3**	**6**	**97**	**0**	**0**	**0**	**19**	**15.8**	**1**	**2**	**0.0**	**6:04**	....	....	....	....	....	....	....	....	....
2003-04	**Los Angeles**	**NHL**	**20**	**0**	**1**	**1**	**77**	**0**	**0**	**0**	**10**	**0.0**	**–1**	**0**	**0.0**	**8:34**	....	....	....	....	....	....	....	....	....
	Washington	**NHL**	**16**	**0**	**1**	**1**	**17**	**0**	**0**	**0**	**6**	**0.0**	**–4**	**0**	**0.0**	**12:50**	....	....	....	....	....	....	....	....	....
2004-05			DID NOT PLAY																						
2005-06	Jokerit Helsinki	Finland	20	2	2	4	91	....	....	....	....	....	....	....	....	....	....	....	....	....	....	....	....	....	....
	Ottawa	**NHL**	**7**	**0**	**0**	**0**	**31**	**0**	**0**	**0**	**3**	**0.0**	**1**	**0**	**0.0**	**10:10**	....	....	....	....	....	....	....	....	....
	Binghamton	AHL	36	0	4	4	102	....	....	....	....	....	....	....	....	....	....	....	....	....	....	....	....	....	....
2006-07	**Detroit**	**NHL**	**6**	**0**	**1**	**1**	**20**	**0**	**0**	**0**	**2**	**0.0**	**2**	**0**	**0.0**	**4:08**	....	....	....	....	....	....	....	....	....
	Grand Rapids	AHL	43	1	4	5	102	....	....	....	....	....	....	....	....	....	7	1	2	3	24	....	....	....	....
	NHL Totals		**124**	**3**	**8**	**11**	**287**	**0**	**0**	**0**	**46**	**6.5**		**3**	**0.0**	**8:03**									

Signed as a free agent by **Florida**, July 27, 2001. Signed as a free agent by **Los Angeles**, October, 8, 2002. Claimed on waivers by **Washington** from **Los Angeles**, March 4, 2004. • Missed majority of 2003-04 season recovering from arm injury suffered in pre-season game vs. Phoenix, September 20, 2003. Signed as a free agent by **Jokerit Helsinki** (Finland), October 11, 2005. Signed as a free agent by **Ottawa**, March 8, 2006. Signed as a free agent by **Detroit**, July 24, 2006. Signed as a free agent by **San Jose**, July 18, 2007.

NOVAK, Filip
(NOH-vak, FIHL-ihp)

Defense. Shoots left. 6'1", 198 lbs. Born, Ceske Budejovice, Czech., May 7, 1982. NY Rangers' 1st choice, 64th overall, in 2000 Entry Draft.

Season	Club	League	GP	G	A	Pts	PIM	PP	SH	GW	S	%	+/-	TF	F%	Min	GP	G	A	Pts	PIM	PP	SH	GW	Min
1998-99	C. Budejovice Jr.	CzRep-Jr.	68	8	10	18	34	....	....	....	....	....	....	....	....	....	....	....	....	....	....	....	....	....	....
99-2000	Regina Pats	WHL	47	7	32	39	70	....	....	....	....	....	....	....	....	....	7	1	4	5	5	....	....	....	....
2000-01	Regina Pats	WHL	64	17	50	67	75	....	....	....	....	....	....	....	....	....	6	1	4	5	6	....	....	....	....
2001-02	Regina Pats	WHL	60	12	46	58	125	....	....	....	....	....	....	....	....	....	6	2	2	4	19	....	....	....	....
2002-03	San Antonio	AHL	57	10	17	27	79	....	....	....	....	....	....	....	....	....	1	0	0	0	0	....	....	....	....
2003-04			DID NOT PLAY – INJURED																						
2004-05	San Antonio	AHL	71	1	12	13	84	....	....	....	....	....	....	....	....	....	....	....	....	....	....	....	....	....	....
2005-06	**Ottawa**	**NHL**	**11**	**0**	**0**	**0**	**4**	**0**	**0**	**0**	**5**	**0.0**	**–2**	**0**	**0.0**	**9:26**	....	....	....	....	....	....	....	....	....
	Binghamton	AHL	64	8	44	52	58	....	....	....	....	....	....	....	....	....	....	....	....	....	....	....	....	....	....
2006-07	**Columbus**	**NHL**	**6**	**0**	**0**	**0**	**2**	**0**	**0**	**0**	**3**	**0.0**	**1**	**0**	**0.0**	**9:55**	....	....	....	....	....	....	....	....	....
	Syracuse Crunch	AHL	67	5	32	37	92	....	....	....	....	....	....	....	....	....	....	....	....	....	....	....	....	....	....
	NHL Totals		**17**	**0**	**0**	**0**	**6**	**0**	**0**	**0**	**8**	**0.0**		**0**	**0.0**	**9:36**	....	....	....	....	....	....	....	....	....

WHL East Second All-Star Team (2001) • WHL East First All-Star Team (2002) • AHL All-Rookie Team (2003)

Traded to **Florida** by **NY Rangers** with Igor Ulanov, NY Rangers' 1st (later traded to Calgary – Calgary selected Eric Nystrom) and 2nd (Rob Globke) round choices in 2002 Entry Draft and NY Rangers' 4th round choice (later traded to Atlanta – Atlanta selected Guillaume Desbiens) in 2003 Entry Draft for Pavel Bure and Florida's 2nd round choice (Lee Falardeau) in 2002 Entry Draft, March 18, 2002. • Missed entire 2003-04 season recovering from ankle injury suffered in training camp, September 17, 2003. Traded to **Ottawa** by **Florida** for future considerations, October 5, 2005. Signed as a free agent by **Columbus**, August 13, 2006.

NOVOTNY, Jiri
(nuh-VAWT-nee, YIH-ree) **CBJ**

Center. Shoots right. 6'4", 194 lbs. Born, Pelhrimov, Czech., August 12, 1983. Buffalo's 1st choice, 22nd overall, in 2001 Entry Draft.

Season	Club	League	GP	G	A	Pts	PIM	PP	SH	GW	S	%	+/-	TF	F%	Min	GP	G	A	Pts	PIM	PP	SH	GW	Min
99-2000	C. Budejovice Jr.	CzRep-Jr.	36	11	10	21	6	....	....	....	....	....	....	....	....	....	....	....	....	....	....	....	....	....	....
	C. Budejovice U17	CzR-U17	11	5	7	12	4	....	....	....	....	....	....	....	....	....	....	....	....	....	....	....	....	....	....
	HC Slezan Opava	CzRep-2	17	2	2	4	6	....	....	....	....	....	....	....	....	....	....	....	....	....	....	....	....	....	....
2000-01	C. Budejovice Jr.	CzRep-Jr.	33	10	10	20	....	....	....	....	....	....	....	....	....	....	....	....	....	....	....	....	....	....	....
	Havl. Brod	CzRep-3	1	0	0	0	0	....	....	....	....	....	....	....	....	....	....	....	....	....	....	....	....	....	....
2001-02	C. Budejovice Jr.	CzRep-Jr.	7	4	4	8	4	....	....	....	....	....	....	....	....	....	....	....	....	....	....	....	....	....	....
	Jind. Hradec	CzRep-3	3	1	3	4	0	....	....	....	....	....	....	....	....	....	....	....	....	....	....	....	....	....	....
	C. Budejovice	CzRep	41	8	6	14	6	....	....	....	....	....	....	....	....	....	....	....	....	....	....	....	....	....	....
2002-03	Rochester	AHL	43	2	9	11	14	....	....	....	....	....	....	....	....	....	3	0	1	1	10	....	....	....	....
2003-04	Rochester	AHL	48	1	14	15	16	....	....	....	....	....	....	....	....	....	13	0	1	1	10	....	....	....	....
2004-05	Rochester	AHL	61	5	20	25	36	....	....	....	....	....	....	....	....	....	9	2	2	4	4	....	....	....	....
2005-06	**Buffalo**	**NHL**	**14**	**2**	**1**	**3**	**0**	**0**	**1**	**0**	**15**	**13.3**	**–5**	**139**	**45.3**	**12:15**	**4**	**0**	**0**	**0**	**0**	**0**	**0**	**0**	**10:27**
	Rochester	AHL	66	17	37	54	40	....	....	....	....	....	....	....	....	....	....	....	....	....	....	....	....	....	....
2006-07	**Buffalo**	**NHL**	**50**	**6**	**7**	**13**	**26**	**0**	**0**	**0**	**60**	**10.0**	**–2**	**324**	**44.1**	**12:19**	....	....	....	....	....	....	....	....	....
	Washington	**NHL**	**18**	**0**	**6**	**6**	**2**	**0**	**0**	**0**	**19**	**0.0**	**–2**	**202**	**51.5**	**14:36**	....	....	....	....	....	....	....	....	....
	NHL Totals		**82**	**8**	**14**	**22**	**28**	**0**	**1**	**0**	**94**	**8.5**		**665**	**46.6**	**12:49**	**4**	**0**	**0**	**0**	**0**	**0**	**0**	**0**	**10:27**

Traded to **Washington** by **Buffalo** with Buffalo's 1st round choice (later traded to San Jose - San Jose selected Nicholas Petrecki) in 2007 Entry Draft for Dainius Zubrus and Timo Helbling, February 27, 2007. Signed as a free agent by **Columbus**, July 3, 2007.

NUMMELIN, Petteri

(NOO-muh-lihn, PEH-tuh-ree) **MIN.**

Defense. Shoots left. 5'10", 191 lbs. Born, Turku, Finland, November 25, 1972. Columbus' 3rd choice, 133rd overall, in 2000 Entry Draft.

			Regular Season														Playoffs								
Season	Club	League	GP	G	A	Pts	PIM	PP	SH	GW	S	%	+/-	TF	F%	Min	GP	G	A	Pts	PIM	PP	SH	GW	Min
1988-89	TPS Turku U18	Fin-U18	9	4	10	14	12																		
	TPS Turku Jr.	Fin-Jr.	11	2	3	5	2																		
1989-90	TPS Turku Jr.	Fin-Jr.	33	6	14	20	45																		
1990-91	TPS Turku Jr.	Fin-Jr.	35	20	16	36	28																		
	Kiekko-67 Turku	Finland-2	2	0	2	2	4																		
1991-92	Kiekko-67 Jr.	Fin-Jr.	13	16	15	31	28																		
	Kiekko-67 Turku	Finland-2	41	12	24	36	36																		
1992-93	TPS Turku Jr.	Fin-Jr.	1	1	0	1	0																		
	TPS Turku	Finland	3	0	0	0	8																		
	Kiekko-67 Turku	Finland-2	28	14	15	29	18																		
	Reipas Lahti	Finland	14	3	4	7	18																		
	Reipas Lahti	Finland-Q	6	2	4	6	2																		
1993-94	TPS Turku	Finland	44	14	24	38	20										11	0	3	3	4				
1994-95	TPS Turku	Finland	48	10	17	27	32										11	4	3	7	0				
1995-96	V.Frolunda	Sweden	32	7	11	18	26										12	2	7	9	4				
1996-97	V.Frolunda	Sweden	44	20	14	34	39										2	0	1	1	0				
1997-98	HC Davos	Swiss	33	13	17	30	24										17	8	14	22	2				
1998-99	HC Davos	Swiss	44	11	42	53	22										4	0	2	2	2				
99-2000	HC Davos	Swiss	40	15	23	38	20										5	0	3	3	0				
2000-01	**Columbus**	**NHL**	**61**	**4**	**12**	**16**	**10**	**2**	**0**	**0**	**99**	**4.0**	**–11**	**1**	**0.0**	**17:14**									
2001-02	HC Lugano	Swiss	35	4	18	22	6										13	6	9	15	2				
2002-03	HC Lugano	Swiss	43	18	39	57	12										8	3	6	9	2				
2003-04	HC Lugano	Swiss	48	20	39	59	59										16	6	19	25	4				
2004-05	HC Lugano	Swiss	36	13	34	47	18										3	1	0	1	2				
2005-06	HC Lugano	Swiss	38	13	30	43	22										17	9	*20	*29	10				
	Finland	Olympics	8	0	2	2	2																		
2006-07	**Minnesota**	**NHL**	**51**	**3**	**17**	**20**	**22**	**0**	**0**	**0**	**69**	**4.3**	**–15**	**0**	**0.0**	**20:17**	**3**	**1**	**1**	**2**	**0**	**1**	**0**	**0**	**19:59**
	NHL Totals		**112**	**7**	**29**	**36**	**32**	**2**	**0**	**0**	**168**	**4.2**		**1**	**0.0**	**18:37**	**3**	**1**	**1**	**2**	**0**	**1**	**0**	**0**	**19:59**

Traded to **Atlanta** by **Columbus** with Chris Nielsen for Tomi Kallio and Pauli Levokari, December 2, 2002. Rights traded to **Minnesota** by **Atlanta** for Edmonton's 3rd round choice (previously acquired, Atlanta selected Spencer Machacek) in 2007 Entry Draft, June 14, 2006.

NUMMINEN, Teppo

(NOO-mih-nehn, TEH-poh) **BUF.**

Defense. Shoots right. 6'2", 198 lbs. Born, Tampere, Finland, July 3, 1968. Winnipeg's 2nd choice, 29th overall, in 1986 Entry Draft.

			Regular Season														Playoffs								
Season	Club	League	GP	G	A	Pts	PIM	PP	SH	GW	S	%	+/-	TF	F%	Min	GP	G	A	Pts	PIM	PP	SH	GW	Min
1984-85	Whitby Lawmen	OJHL	16	3	9	12	0																		
1985-86	Tappara Jr.	Fin-Jr.	2	0	0	0	0										3	0	1	1	2				
	Tappara Tampere	Finland	31	2	4	6	6										8	0	0	0	0				
1986-87	Tappara Tampere	Finland	44	9	9	18	16										9	4	1	5	4				
1987-88	Tappara Tampere	Finland	40	10	10	20	29										10	6	6	12	6				
	Finland	Olympics	6	1	4	5	0																		
1988-89	**Winnipeg**	**NHL**	**69**	**1**	**14**	**15**	**36**	**0**	**1**	**0**	**85**	**1.2**	**–11**												
1989-90	**Winnipeg**	**NHL**	**79**	**11**	**32**	**43**	**20**	**1**	**0**	**1**	**105**	**10.5**	**–4**				**7**	**1**	**2**	**3**	**10**	**0**	**0**	**0**	
1990-91	**Winnipeg**	**NHL**	**80**	**8**	**25**	**33**	**28**	**3**	**0**	**0**	**151**	**5.3**	**–15**												
1991-92	**Winnipeg**	**NHL**	**80**	**5**	**34**	**39**	**32**	**4**	**0**	**1**	**143**	**3.5**	**15**				**7**	**0**	**0**	**0**	**0**	**0**	**0**	**0**	
1992-93	**Winnipeg**	**NHL**	**66**	**7**	**30**	**37**	**33**	**3**	**1**	**0**	**103**	**6.8**	**4**				**6**	**1**	**1**	**2**	**2**	**1**	**0**	**0**	
1993-94	**Winnipeg**	**NHL**	**57**	**5**	**18**	**23**	**28**	**4**	**0**	**1**	**89**	**5.6**	**–23**												
1994-95	TuTo Turku	Finland	12	3	8	11	4																		
	Winnipeg	**NHL**	**42**	**5**	**16**	**21**	**16**	**2**	**0**	**0**	**86**	**5.8**	**12**												
1995-96	**Winnipeg**	**NHL**	**74**	**11**	**43**	**54**	**22**	**6**	**0**	**3**	**165**	**6.7**	**–4**				**6**	**0**	**0**	**0**	**2**	**0**	**0**	**0**	
1996-97	**Phoenix**	**NHL**	**82**	**2**	**25**	**27**	**28**	**0**	**0**	**0**	**135**	**1.5**	**–3**				**7**	**3**	**3**	**6**	**0**	**1**	**0**	**1**	
1997-98	**Phoenix**	**NHL**	**82**	**11**	**40**	**51**	**30**	**6**	**0**	**2**	**126**	**8.7**	**25**				**1**	**0**	**0**	**0**	**0**	**0**	**0**	**0**	
	Finland	Olympics	6	1	1	2	2																		
1998-99	**Phoenix**	**NHL**	**82**	**10**	**30**	**40**	**30**	**1**	**0**	**0**	**156**	**6.4**	**3**	**2**	**0.0**	**24:26**	**7**	**2**	**1**	**3**	**4**	**2**	**0**	**0**	**26:09**
99-2000	**Phoenix**	**NHL**	**79**	**8**	**34**	**42**	**16**	**2**	**0**	**2**	**126**	**6.3**	**21**	**1**	**0.0**	**23:37**	**5**	**1**	**1**	**2**	**0**	**0**	**0**	**0**	**23:11**
2000-01	**Phoenix**	**NHL**	**72**	**5**	**26**	**31**	**36**	**1**	**0**	**2**	**109**	**4.6**	**9**	**0**	**0.0**	**24:28**									
2001-02	**Phoenix**	**NHL**	**76**	**13**	**35**	**48**	**20**	**4**	**0**	**6**	**117**	**11.1**	**13**	**0**	**0.0**	**23:51**	**4**	**0**	**0**	**0**	**2**	**0**	**0**	**0**	**25:33**
	Finland	Olympics	4	0	1	1	0																		
2002-03	**Phoenix**	**NHL**	**78**	**6**	**24**	**30**	**30**	**2**	**0**	**1**	**108**	**5.6**	**0**	**0**	**0.0**	**23:51**									
2003-04	**Dallas**	**NHL**	**62**	**3**	**14**	**17**	**18**	**0**	**0**	**0**	**83**	**3.6**	**–5**	**1**	**100.0**	**21:40**	**4**	**0**	**1**	**1**	**0**	**0**	**0**	**0**	**19:13**
2004-05				DID NOT PLAY																					
2005-06	**Buffalo**	**NHL**	**75**	**2**	**38**	**40**	**36**	**0**	**0**	**0**	**60**	**3.3**	**6**	**1**	**100.0**	**19:30**	**12**	**1**	**1**	**2**	**4**	**1**	**0**	**0**	**18:45**
	Finland	Olympics	8	1	2	3	2																		
2006-07	**Buffalo**	**NHL**	**79**	**2**	**27**	**29**	**32**	**0**	**0**	**0**	**69**	**2.9**	**17**	**0**	**0.0**	**20:48**	**16**	**0**	**4**	**4**	**4**	**0**	**0**	**0**	**19:33**
	NHL Totals		**1314**	**115**	**505**	**620**	**491**	**39**	**2**	**19**	**2016**	**5.7**		**5**	**40.0**	**22:49**	**82**	**9**	**14**	**23**	**28**	**5**	**0**	**1**	**21:10**

Played in NHL All-Star Game (1999, 2000, 2001)

Transferred to **Phoenix** after **Winnipeg** franchise relocated, July 1, 1996. Traded to **Dallas** by **Phoenix** for Mike Sillinger, July 22, 2003. Signed as a free agent by **Buffalo**, August 4, 2005.

NYCHOLAT, Lawrence

(NIH-koh-lat, LAW-rehnts) **OTT.**

Defense. Shoots left. 5'11", 197 lbs. Born, Calgary, Alta., May 7, 1979.

			Regular Season														Playoffs								
Season	Club	League	GP	G	A	Pts	PIM	PP	SH	GW	S	%	+/-	TF	F%	Min	GP	G	A	Pts	PIM	PP	SH	GW	Min
1995-96	Notre Dame	SMHL	42	10	36	46	66																		
1996-97	Swift Current	WHL	67	8	13	21	82										10	0	0	0	24				
1997-98	Swift Current	WHL	71	13	35	48	108										1	0	0	0	0				
1998-99	Swift Current	WHL	72	16	44	60	125										6	2	2	4	12				
99-2000	Swift Current	WHL	70	22	58	80	92										2	0	0	0	0				
2000-01	Jackson Bandits	ECHL	5	1	2	3	5																		
	Cleveland	IHL	42	3	7	10	69										4	0	0	0	2				
2001-02	Houston Aeros	AHL	72	3	11	14	92										14	1	0	1	23				
2002-03	Houston Aeros	AHL	66	11	28	39	155																		
	Hartford	AHL	15	2	9	11	6										2	2	0	2	0				
2003-04	**NY Rangers**	**NHL**	**9**	**0**	**0**	**0**	**6**	**0**	**0**	**0**	**6**	**0.0**	**–2**	**0**	**0.0**	**17:09**									
	Hartford	AHL	72	6	26	32	130										16	0	5	5	28				
2004-05	Hartford	AHL	79	5	38	43	132										6	0	3	3	11				
2005-06	Hershey Bears	AHL	73	13	44	57	94										16	2	12	14	12				
2006-07	**Washington**	**NHL**	**18**	**2**	**6**	**8**	**12**	**0**	**0**	**0**	**22**	**9.1**	**–3**	**0**	**0.0**	**20:32**									
	Hershey Bears	AHL	29	3	25	28	39																		
	Ottawa	**NHL**	**1**	**0**	**0**	**0**	**0**	**0**	**0**	**0**	**3**	**0.0**	**0**	**0**	**0.0**	**12:48**									
	NHL Totals		**28**	**2**	**6**	**8**	**18**	**0**	**0**	**0**	**31**	**6.5**		**0**	**0.0**	**19:10**									

Signed as a free agent by **Minnesota**, August 31, 2000. Traded to **NY Rangers** by **Minnesota** for Johan Holmqvist, March 11, 2003. Signed as a free agent by **Washington**, August 9, 2005. Traded to **Ottawa** by **Washington** for Andy Hedlund and Ottawa's 6th round choice (Justin Taylor) in 2007 Entry Draft, February 26, 2007.

NYLANDER, Michael

(NEE-lan-duhr, MIGH-kuhl) **WSH.**

Center. Shoots left. 6'1", 195 lbs. Born, Stockholm, Sweden, October 3, 1972. Hartford's 4th choice, 59th overall, in 1991 Entry Draft.

			Regular Season														Playoffs								
Season	Club	League	GP	G	A	Pts	PIM	PP	SH	GW	S	%	+/-	TF	F%	Min	GP	G	A	Pts	PIM	PP	SH	GW	Min
1989-90	Huddinge IK	Sweden-2	31	7	15	22	4										5	3	0	3	0				
1990-91	Huddinge IK	Sweden-2	33	14	20	34	10										2	0	0	0	0				
1991-92	AIK Solna	Sweden	40	11	17	28	30										3	1	4	5	4				
1992-93	**Hartford**	**NHL**	**59**	**11**	**22**	**33**	**36**	**3**	**0**	**1**	**85**	**12.9**	**–7**												
	Springfield	AHL															3	3	3	6	2				
1993-94	**Hartford**	**NHL**	**58**	**11**	**33**	**44**	**24**	**4**	**0**	**1**	**74**	**14.9**	**–2**												
	Springfield	AHL	4	0	9	9	0																		
	Calgary	**NHL**	**15**	**2**	**9**	**11**	**6**	**0**	**0**	**0**	**21**	**9.5**	**10**				**3**	**0**	**0**	**0**	**0**	**0**	**0**	**0**	
1994-95	JYP HT Jyvaskyla	Finland	16	11	19	30	63																		
	Calgary	**NHL**	**6**	**0**	**1**	**1**	**2**	**0**	**0**	**0**	**2**	**0.0**	**1**				**6**	**0**	**6**	**6**	**2**	**0**	**0**	**0**	
1995-96	**Calgary**	**NHL**	**73**	**17**	**38**	**55**	**20**	**4**	**0**	**6**	**163**	**10.4**	**0**				**4**	**0**	**0**	**0**	**0**	**0**	**0**	**0**	
1996-97	HC Lugano	Swiss	36	12	43	55	28										8	3	8	11	8				
1997-98	**Calgary**	**NHL**	**65**	**13**	**23**	**36**	**24**	**0**	**0**	**2**	**117**	**11.1**	**10**												
	Sweden	Olympics	4	0	0	0	6																		

			Regular Season														Playoffs								
Season	Club	League	GP	G	A	Pts	PIM	PP	SH	GW	S	%	+/-	TF	F%	Min	GP	G	A	Pts	PIM	PP	SH	GW	Min
1998-99	**Calgary**	**NHL**	**9**	**2**	**3**	**5**	**2**	**1**	**0**	**0**	**7**	**28.6**	**1**	**25**	**60.0**	**11:10**									
	Tampa Bay	**NHL**	**24**	**2**	**7**	**9**	**6**	**0**	**0**	**0**	**26**	**7.7**	**–10**	**75**	**44.0**	**13:29**									
99-2000	**Tampa Bay**	**NHL**	**11**	**1**	**2**	**3**	**4**	**1**	**0**	**0**	**10**	**10.0**	**–3**	**35**	**57.1**	**10:32**									
	Chicago	**NHL**	**66**	**23**	**28**	**51**	**26**	**4**	**0**	**2**	**112**	**20.5**	**9**	**561**	**46.9**	**16:39**									
2000-01	**Chicago**	**NHL**	**82**	**25**	**39**	**64**	**32**	**4**	**0**	**5**	**176**	**14.2**	**7**	**1036**	**48.3**	**18:52**									
2001-02	**Chicago**	**NHL**	**82**	**15**	**46**	**61**	**50**	**6**	**0**	**2**	**158**	**9.5**	**28**	**974**	**50.2**	**15:33**	**5**	**0**	**3**	**3**	**2**	**0**	**0**	**0**	**15:20**
	Sweden	Olympics	4	1	2	3	0																		
2002-03	**Chicago**	**NHL**	**9**	**0**	**4**	**4**	**4**	**0**	**0**	**0**	**20**	**0.0**	**0**	**86**	**48.8**	**15:19**									
	Washington	**NHL**	**71**	**17**	**39**	**56**	**36**	**7**	**0**	**2**	**141**	**12.1**	**3**	**1005**	**47.4**	**18:41**	**6**	**3**	**2**	**5**	**8**	**1**	**0**	**1**	**16:45**
2003-04	**Washington**	**NHL**	**3**	**0**	**2**	**2**	**8**	**0**	**0**	**0**	**1**	**0.0**	**1**	**22**	**54.6**	**14:57**									
	Boston	**NHL**	**15**	**1**	**11**	**12**	**14**	**0**	**0**	**1**	**29**	**3.4**	**3**	**128**	**46.1**	**15:43**	**6**	**3**	**3**	**6**	**0**	**0**	**0**	**0**	**18:57**
2004-05	Karpat Oulu	Finland	23	5	15	20	22																		
	St. Petersburg	Russia	8	2	5	7	0																		
	Ak Bars Kazan	Russia	5	0	1	1	2																		
2005-06	**NY Rangers**	**NHL**	**81**	**23**	**56**	**79**	**76**	**6**	**0**	**4**	**172**	**13.4**	**31**	**1143**	**46.5**	**19:20**	**4**	**0**	**1**	**1**	**0**	**0**	**0**	**0**	**20:33**
2006-07	**NY Rangers**	**NHL**	**79**	**26**	**57**	**83**	**42**	**14**	**0**	**4**	**193**	**13.5**	**12**	**1054**	**47.5**	**20:23**	**10**	**6**	**7**	**13**	**0**	**2**	**0**	**2**	**21:50**
	NHL Totals		**808**	**189**	**420**	**609**	**412**	**54**	**0**	**30**	**1507**	**12.5**		**6144**	**47.9**	**17:38**	**44**	**12**	**22**	**34**	**12**	**3**	**0**	**3**	**19:04**

Traded to **Calgary** by **Hartford** with James Patrick and Zarley Zalapski for Gary Suter, Paul Ranheim and Ted Drury, March 10, 1994. • Missed majority of 1994-95 season recovering from wrist injury suffered in game vs. St. Louis, January 24, 1995. Traded to **Tampa Bay** by **Calgary** for Andrei Nazarov, January 19, 1999. Traded to **Chicago** by **Tampa Bay** for Bryan Muir and Reid Simpson, November 12, 1999. Traded to **Washington** by **Chicago** with Chicago's 3rd round choice (Stephen Werner) in 2003 Entry Draft and future considerations for Chris Simon and Andrei Nikolishin, November 1, 2002. • Missed majority of 2003-04 season recovering from leg injury suffered in practice, October 2, 2003. Traded to **Boston** by **Washington** for Boston's 4th round compensatory choice (Patrick McNeill) in 2005 Entry Draft and Boston's 2nd round choice (Francois Bouchard) in 2006 Entry Draft, March 4, 2004. Signed as a free agent by **NY Rangers**, August 10, 2004. Signed as a free agent by **Oulu** (Finland), September 25, 2004. Signed as a free agent by **St. Petersburg** (Russia), December 20, 2004. Signed as a free agent by **Kazan** (Russia), February 14, 2005. Signed as a free agent by **Washington**, July 2, 2007.

NYSTROM, Eric
(NIGH-stuhm, AIR-ihk) **CGY.**

Left wing. Shoots left. 6'1", 205 lbs. Born, Syosset, NY, February 14, 1983. Calgary's 1st choice, 10th overall, in 2002 Entry Draft.

Season	Club	League	GP	G	A	Pts	PIM	PP	SH	GW	S	%	+/-	TF	F%	Min	GP	G	A	Pts	PIM	PP	SH	GW	Min
99-2000	USNTDP	NAHL	55	7	16	23	57										3	0	0	0	0				
2000-01	USNTDP	U-18	43	10	12	22	52																		
	USNTDP	USHL	23	5	5	10	50																		
2001-02	U. of Michigan	CCHA	40	18	13	31	42																		
2002-03	U. of Michigan	CCHA	39	15	11	26	24																		
2003-04	U. of Michigan	CCHA	43	10	12	22	50																		
2004-05	U. of Michigan	CCHA	38	13	19	32	33																		
2005-06	**Calgary**	**NHL**	**2**	**0**	**0**	**0**	**0**	**0**	**0**	**0**	**0**	**0.0**	**–1**	**5**	**60.0**	**12:01**									
	Omaha	AHL	78	15	18	33	37																		
2006-07	Omaha	AHL	12	2	0	2	0										5	0	0	0	2				
	NHL Totals		**2**	**0**	**0**	**0**	**0**	**0**	**0**	**0**	**0**	**0.0**		**5**	**60.0**	**12:00**									

CCHA All-Rookie Team (2002)

• Missed majority of 2006-07 season recovering from a shoulder injury.

O'BRIEN, Doug
(oh-BRIGH-uhn, DUHG)

Defense. Shoots left. 6'1", 200 lbs. Born, St. John's, Nfld., February 16, 1984. Tampa Bay's 4th choice, 192nd overall, in 2003 Entry Draft.

Season	Club	League	GP	G	A	Pts	PIM	PP	SH	GW	S	%	+/-	TF	F%	Min	GP	G	A	Pts	PIM	PP	SH	GW	Min
2000-01	Hull Olympiques	QMJHL	47	1	6	7	16										5	0	1	1	0				
2001-02	Hull Olympiques	QMJHL	46	1	5	6	36										12	0	0	0	14				
2002-03	Hull Olympiques	QMJHL	71	10	34	44	102										19	3	12	15	18				
2003-04	Gatineau	QMJHL	66	17	46	63	146										15	1	8	9	16				
2004-05	Springfield	AHL	74	4	13	17	76																		
	Johnstown Chiefs	ECHL	3	0	0	0	2																		
2005-06	**Tampa Bay**	**NHL**	**5**	**0**	**0**	**0**	**2**	**0**	**0**	**0**	**2**	**0.0**	**0**	**0**	**0.0**	**7:44**									
	Springfield	AHL	74	7	25	32	70																		
2006-07	Springfield	AHL	53	6	13	19	34																		
	Portland Pirates	AHL	22	0	6	6	19																		
	NHL Totals		**5**	**0**	**0**	**0**	**2**	**0**	**0**	**0**	**2**	**0.0**		**0**	**0.0**	**7:44**									

QMJHL First All-Star Team (2004) • Memorial Cup Tournament All-Star Team (2003, 2004) • Ed Chynoweth Trophy (Memorial Cup Tournament Leading Scorer) (2004)

Traded to **Anaheim** by **Tampa Bay** for Joe Rullier, February 27, 2007.

O'BRIEN, Shane
(oh-BRIGH-uhn, SHAYN) **T.B.**

Defense. Shoots left. 6'2", 228 lbs. Born, Port Hope, Ont., August 9, 1983. Anaheim's 8th choice, 250th overall, in 2003 Entry Draft.

Season	Club	League	GP	G	A	Pts	PIM	PP	SH	GW	S	%	+/-	TF	F%	Min	GP	G	A	Pts	PIM	PP	SH	GW	Min
99-2000	Port Hope	OPJHL	47	6	27	33	110																		
2000-01	Kingston	OHL	61	2	12	14	89										4	0	1	1	6				
2001-02	Kingston	OHL	67	10	23	33	132										1	0	0	0	2				
2002-03	Kingston	OHL	28	8	15	23	100																		
	St. Michael's	OHL	34	8	11	19	108										19	4	10	14	*79				
2003-04	Cincinnati	AHL	60	2	8	10	163										9	0	2	2	20				
2004-05	Cincinnati	AHL	77	5	20	25	319										12	1	3	4	57				
2005-06	Portland Pirates	AHL	77	8	33	41	287										19	6	16	22	*81				
2006-07	**Anaheim**	**NHL**	**62**	**2**	**12**	**14**	**140**	**1**	**0**	**2**	**55**	**3.6**	**5**	**0**	**0.0**	**14:04**									
	Tampa Bay	**NHL**	**18**	**0**	**2**	**2**	**36**	**0**	**0**	**0**	**17**	**0.0**	**–8**	**0**	**0.0**	**18:08**	**6**	**0**	**0**	**0**	**12**	**0**	**0**	**0**	**17:12**
	NHL Totals		**80**	**2**	**14**	**16**	**176**	**1**	**0**	**2**	**72**	**2.8**		**0**	**0.0**	**14:59**	**6**	**0**	**0**	**0**	**12**	**0**	**0**	**0**	**17:12**

Traded to **Tampa Bay** by **Anaheim** with Colorado's 3rd round choice (previously acquired, Tampa Bay selected Luca Cunti) in 2007 Entry Draft for Gerald Coleman and Tampa Bay's 1st round choice (later traded to Minnesota - Minnesota selected Colton Gillies) in 2007 Entry Draft, February 24, 2007.

O'DONNELL, Sean
(oh-DOHN-uhl, SHAWN) **ANA.**

Defense. Shoots left. 6'3", 231 lbs. Born, Ottawa, Ont., October 13, 1971. Buffalo's 6th choice, 123rd overall, in 1991 Entry Draft.

Season	Club	League	GP	G	A	Pts	PIM	PP	SH	GW	S	%	+/-	TF	F%	Min	GP	G	A	Pts	PIM	PP	SH	GW	Min
1987-88	Kanata Valley	CJHL	54	4	25	29	96																		
1988-89	Sudbury Wolves	OHL	56	1	9	10	49																		
1989-90	Sudbury Wolves	OHL	64	7	19	26	84										7	1	2	3	8				
1990-91	Sudbury Wolves	OHL	66	8	23	31	114										5	1	4	5	10				
1991-92	Rochester	AHL	73	4	9	13	193										16	1	2	3	21				
1992-93	Rochester	AHL	74	3	18	21	203										17	1	6	7	38				
1993-94	Rochester	AHL	64	2	10	12	242										4	0	1	1	21				
1994-95	Phoenix	IHL	61	2	18	20	132										9	0	1	1	21				
	Los Angeles	**NHL**	**15**	**0**	**2**	**2**	**49**	**0**	**0**	**0**	**12**	**0.0**	**–2**												
1995-96	**Los Angeles**	**NHL**	**71**	**2**	**5**	**7**	**127**	**0**	**0**	**0**	**65**	**3.1**	**3**												
1996-97	**Los Angeles**	**NHL**	**55**	**5**	**12**	**17**	**144**	**2**	**0**	**0**	**68**	**7.4**	**–13**												
1997-98	**Los Angeles**	**NHL**	**80**	**2**	**15**	**17**	**179**	**0**	**0**	**1**	**71**	**2.8**	**7**				**4**	**1**	**0**	**1**	**36**	**0**	**0**	**0**	
1998-99	**Los Angeles**	**NHL**	**80**	**1**	**13**	**14**	**186**	**0**	**0**	**0**	**64**	**1.6**	**1**	**0**	**0.0**	**19:10**									
99-2000	**Los Angeles**	**NHL**	**80**	**2**	**12**	**14**	**114**	**0**	**0**	**1**	**51**	**3.9**	**4**	**0**	**0.0**	**17:41**	**4**	**1**	**0**	**1**	**4**	**0**	**0**	**0**	**16:26**
2000-01	**Minnesota**	**NHL**	**63**	**4**	**12**	**16**	**128**	**1**	**0**	**2**	**58**	**6.9**	**–2**	**12**	**50.0**	**23:00**									
	New Jersey	**NHL**	**17**	**0**	**1**	**1**	**33**	**0**	**0**	**0**	**9**	**0.0**	**2**	**0**	**0.0**	**16:27**	**23**	**1**	**2**	**3**	**41**	**0**	**0**	**0**	**16:21**
2001-02	**Boston**	**NHL**	**80**	**3**	**22**	**25**	**89**	**1**	**0**	**2**	**112**	**2.7**	**27**	**0**	**0.0**	**24:50**	**6**	**0**	**2**	**2**	**4**	**0**	**0**	**0**	**24:58**
2002-03	**Boston**	**NHL**	**70**	**1**	**15**	**16**	**76**	**0**	**0**	**1**	**61**	**1.6**	**8**	**1**	**0.0**	**22:05**									
2003-04	**Boston**	**NHL**	**82**	**1**	**10**	**11**	**110**	**0**	**0**	**0**	**72**	**1.4**	**10**	**3**	**33.3**	**20:36**	**7**	**0**	**0**	**0**	**0**	**0**	**0**	**0**	**19:53**
2004-05			DID NOT PLAY																						
2005-06	**Phoenix**	**NHL**	**57**	**1**	**7**	**8**	**121**	**0**	**0**	**0**	**23**	**4.3**	**3**	**0**	**0.0**	**16:18**									
	Anaheim	**NHL**	**21**	**1**	**2**	**3**	**26**	**0**	**0**	**0**	**10**	**10.0**	**3**	**0**	**0.0**	**17:13**	**16**	**2**	**3**	**5**	**23**	**0**	**0**	**1**	**16:44**
2006-07 •	**Anaheim**	**NHL**	**79**	**2**	**15**	**17**	**92**	**0**	**0**	**1**	**47**	**4.3**	**9**	**1**	**0.0**	**19:55**	**21**	**0**	**2**	**2**	**10**	**0**	**0**	**0**	**20:20**
	NHL Totals		**850**	**25**	**143**	**168**	**1474**	**4**	**0**	**8**	**723**	**3.5**		**17**	**41.2**	**20:17**	**81**	**5**	**9**	**14**	**118**	**0**	**0**	**1**	**18:31**

Traded to **Los Angeles** by **Buffalo** for Doug Houda, July 26, 1994. Claimed by **Minnesota** from **Los Angeles** in Expansion Draft, June 23, 2000. Traded to **New Jersey** by **Minnesota** for Willie Mitchell, March 4, 2001. Signed as a free agent by **Boston**, July 2, 2001. Signed as a free agent by **Phoenix**, July 6, 2004. Traded to **Anaheim** by **Phoenix** for Joel Perreault, March 9, 2006.

ODUYA, Johnny

(oh-DOO-yuh, JAW-nee) **N.J.**

Defense. Shoots left. 6', 200 lbs. Born, Stockholm, Sweden, October 1, 1981. Washington's 6th choice, 221st overall, in 2001 Entry Draft.

Season	Club	League	GP	G	A	Pts	PIM	PP	SH	GW	S	%	+/-	TF	F%	Min	GP	G	A	Pts	PIM	PP	SH	GW	Min
							Regular Season										Playoffs								
1996-97	Hammarby Jr.	Swe-Jr.	13	0	0	0	....																		
1997-98	Hammarby Jr.	Swe-Jr.	26	3	11	14	70																		
1998-99	Hammarby Jr.	Swe-Jr.	38	14	31	45	45																		
99-2000	Hammarby Jr.	Swe-Jr.	32	3	18	21	48										6	1	2	3	4				
	Hammarby	Sweden-2	1	0	0	0	0										1	0	0	0	0				
2000-01	Moncton Wildcats	QMJHL	44	11	38	49	147																		
	Victoriaville Tigres	QMJHL	24	3	16	19	112										13	4	9	13	10				
2001-02	Hammarby	Sweden-2	46	11	14	25	66										2	1	0	1	4				
2002-03	Hammarby	Sweden-2	48	15	25	40	200																		
2003-04	Djurgarden	Sweden	42	4	4	8	*173										4	0	0	0	6				
2004-05	Djurgarden	Sweden	49	2	4	6	139										12	0	2	2	39				
2005-06	Frolunda	Sweden	47	8	11	19	95										17	1	2	3	16				
2006-07	**New Jersey**	**NHL**	**76**	**2**	**9**	**11**	**61**	**0**	**0**	**0**	**55**	**3.6**	**–5**	**0**	**0.0**	**18:31**	**6**	**0**	**1**	**1**	**6**	**0**	**0**	**0**	**12:59**
	NHL Totals		**76**	**2**	**9**	**11**	**61**	**0**	**0**	**0**	**55**	**3.6**		**0**	**0.0**	**18:31**	**6**	**0**	**1**	**1**	**6**	**0**	**0**	**0**	**12:59**

Signed as a free agent by **New Jersey**, July 24, 2006.

OHLUND, Mattias

(OH-luhnd, mat-TEE-uhs) **VAN.**

Defense. Shoots left. 6'2", 220 lbs. Born, Pitea, Sweden, September 9, 1976. Vancouver's 1st choice, 13th overall, in 1994 Entry Draft.

Season	Club	League	GP	G	A	Pts	PIM	PP	SH	GW	S	%	+/-	TF	F%	Min	GP	G	A	Pts	PIM	PP	SH	GW	Min
1992-93	Pitea HC	Sweden-2	22	0	6	6	16																		
1993-94	Pitea HC	Sweden-2	28	7	10	17	62																		
1994-95	Lulea HF	Sweden	34	6	10	16	34										9	4	0	4	16				
1995-96	Lulea HF	Sweden	38	4	10	14	26										13	1	0	1	47				
1996-97	Lulea HF	Sweden	47	7	9	16	38										10	1	2	3	8				
	Lulea HF	EuroHL	6	0	3	3	0																		
1997-98	**Vancouver**	**NHL**	**77**	**7**	**23**	**30**	**76**	**1**	**0**	**0**	**172**	**4.1**	**3**												
	Sweden	Olympics	4	0	1	1	4																		
1998-99	**Vancouver**	**NHL**	**74**	**9**	**26**	**35**	**83**	**2**	**1**	**1**	**129**	**7.0**	**–19**	**0**	**0.0**	**26:04**									
99-2000	**Vancouver**	**NHL**	**42**	**4**	**16**	**20**	**24**	**2**	**1**	**1**	**63**	**6.3**	**6**	**0**	**0.0**	**27:41**									
2000-01	**Vancouver**	**NHL**	**65**	**8**	**20**	**28**	**46**	**1**	**1**	**4**	**136**	**5.9**	**–16**	**0**	**0.0**	**25:00**	**4**	**1**	**3**	**4**	**6**	**1**	**0**	**0**	**26:32**
2001-02	**Vancouver**	**NHL**	**81**	**10**	**26**	**36**	**56**	**4**	**1**	**3**	**193**	**5.2**	**16**	**0**	**0.0**	**25:17**	**6**	**1**	**1**	**2**	**6**	**0**	**0**	**0**	**28:48**
	Sweden	Olympics	4	0	2	2	2																		
2002-03	**Vancouver**	**NHL**	**59**	**2**	**27**	**29**	**42**	**0**	**0**	**0**	**100**	**2.0**	**1**	**0**	**0.0**	**25:23**	**13**	**3**	**4**	**7**	**12**	**0**	**0**	**0**	**24:01**
2003-04	**Vancouver**	**NHL**	**82**	**14**	**20**	**34**	**73**	**5**	**0**	**3**	**129**	**10.9**	**14**	**0**	**0.0**	**25:47**	**7**	**1**	**4**	**5**	**13**	**0**	**0**	**1**	**27:25**
2004-05	Lulea HF	Sweden	2	1	0	1	4																		
2005-06	**Vancouver**	**NHL**	**78**	**13**	**20**	**33**	**92**	**8**	**1**	**2**	**183**	**7.1**	**–6**	**1**	**0.0**	**25:40**									
	Sweden	Olympics	6	0	2	2	2																		
2006-07	**Vancouver**	**NHL**	**77**	**11**	**20**	**31**	**80**	**6**	**0**	**2**	**170**	**6.5**	**–3**	**1**	**0.0**	**24:47**	**12**	**2**	**5**	**7**	**12**	**1**	**0**	**0**	**28:18**
	NHL Totals		**635**	**78**	**198**	**276**	**572**	**29**	**5**	**16**	**1275**	**6.1**		**2**	**0.0**	**25:36**	**42**	**8**	**17**	**25**	**49**	**2**	**0**	**1**	**26:44**

NHL All-Rookie Team (1998)
Played in NHL All-Star Game (1999)
Signed as a free agent by **Lulea** (Sweden), December 21, 2004.

OLESZ, Rostislav

(OH-lehsh, RAHS-tih-slav) **FLA.**

Center. Shoots left. 6'1", 214 lbs. Born, Bilovec, Czech., October 10, 1985. Florida's 1st choice, 7th overall, in 2004 Entry Draft.

Season	Club	League	GP	G	A	Pts	PIM	PP	SH	GW	S	%	+/-	TF	F%	Min	GP	G	A	Pts	PIM	PP	SH	GW	Min
2000-01	HC Vitkovice Jr.	CzRep-Jr.	15	10	3	13	14																		
	HC Vitkovice	CzRep	3	0	1	1	0																		
2001-02	HC Vitkovice	CzRep	11	1	2	3	0																		
	HC Vitkovice Jr.	CzRep-Jr.	34	19	20	39	81										2	0	0	0	2				
2002-03	HC Vitkovice Jr.	CzRep-Jr.	7	1	1	2	12																		
	HC Vitkovice	CzRep	40	6	3	9	41										5	0	0	0	2				
	HC Slezan Opava	CzRep-2	1	0	0	0	0																		
2003-04	HC Vitkovice Jr.	CzRep-Jr.	3	2	0	2	0																		
	HC Vitkovice	CzRep	35	1	11	12	10										6	2	1	3	4				
	HC Dukla Jihlava	CzRep-2	2	1	0	1	0										1	0	0	0	0				
2004-05	HC Sparta Praha	CzRep	47	6	7	13	12										5	0	2	2	0				
	Sparta Jr.	CzRep-Jr															1	0	1	1	0				
2005-06	**Florida**	**NHL**	**59**	**8**	**13**	**21**	**24**	**0**	**1**	**3**	**105**	**7.6**	**–4**	**10**	**30.0**	**14:52**									
	Czech Republic	Olympics	8	0	0	0	2																		
2006-07	**Florida**	**NHL**	**75**	**11**	**19**	**30**	**28**	**2**	**0**	**2**	**164**	**6.7**	**2**	**12**	**58.3**	**15:30**									
	Rochester	AHL	4	1	2	3	4																		
	NHL Totals		**134**	**19**	**32**	**51**	**52**	**2**	**1**	**5**	**269**	**7.1**		**22**	**45.5**	**15:13**									

OLIVER, David

(AWL-ih-vuhr, DAY-vihd)

Right wing. Shoots right. 6', 190 lbs. Born, Sechelt, B.C., April 17, 1971. Edmonton's 7th choice, 144th overall, in 1991 Entry Draft.

Season	Club	League	GP	G	A	Pts	PIM	PP	SH	GW	S	%	+/-	TF	F%	Min	GP	G	A	Pts	PIM	PP	SH	GW	Min
1988-89	Vernon Lakers	BCJHL	58	41	38	79	38																		
1989-90	Vernon Lakers	BCJHL	58	51	48	99	22																		
1990-91	U. of Michigan	CCHA	27	13	11	24	34																		
1991-92	U. of Michigan	CCHA	44	31	27	58	32																		
1992-93	U. of Michigan	CCHA	40	35	20	55	18																		
1993-94	U. of Michigan	CCHA	41	28	40	68	16																		
1994-95	Cape Breton	AHL	32	11	18	29	8																		
	Edmonton	**NHL**	**44**	**16**	**14**	**30**	**20**	**10**	**0**	**0**	**79**	**20.3**	**–11**												
1995-96	**Edmonton**	**NHL**	**80**	**20**	**19**	**39**	**34**	**14**	**0**	**0**	**131**	**15.3**	**–22**												
1996-97	**Edmonton**	**NHL**	**17**	**1**	**2**	**3**	**4**	**0**	**0**	**0**	**22**	**4.5**	**–8**												
	NY Rangers	**NHL**	**14**	**2**	**1**	**3**	**4**	**0**	**0**	**0**	**13**	**15.4**	**3**				**3**	**0**	**0**	**0**	**0**	**0**	**0**	**0**	
1997-98	Houston Aeros	IHL	78	38	27	65	60										4	3	0	3	4				
1998-99	**Ottawa**	**NHL**	**17**	**2**	**5**	**7**	**4**	**0**	**0**	**0**	**18**	**11.1**	**1**	**3**	**33.3**	**10:34**									
	Houston Aeros	IHL	37	18	17	35	30										19	10	6	16	22				
99-2000	**Phoenix**	**NHL**	**9**	**1**	**0**	**1**	**2**	**1**	**0**	**0**	**6**	**16.7**	**0**	**0**	**0.0**	**7:38**									
	Houston Aeros	IHL	45	16	11	27	40										11	3	4	7	8				
2000-01	**Ottawa**	**NHL**	**7**	**0**	**0**	**0**	**2**	**0**	**0**	**0**	**2**	**0.0**	**0**	**0**	**0.0**	**5:37**									
	Grand Rapids	IHL	51	14	17	31	35										10	6	2	8	8				
2001-02	Munchen Barons	Germany	59	20	14	34	30										9	2	2	4	6				
2002-03	**Dallas**	**NHL**	**6**	**0**	**3**	**3**	**2**	**0**	**0**	**0**	**5**	**0.0**	**1**	**0**	**0.0**	**9:13**	**6**	**0**	**0**	**0**	**2**	**0**	**0**	**0**	**6:33**
	Utah Grizzlies	AHL	37	11	14	25	14																		
2003-04	**Dallas**	**NHL**	**36**	**7**	**5**	**12**	**12**	**3**	**0**	**1**	**30**	**23.3**	**6**	**1**	**100.0**	**9:51**	**1**	**0**	**0**	**0**	**0**	**0**	**0**	**0**	**7:31**
	Utah Grizzlies	AHL	31	5	12	17	12																		
2004-05	Guildford Flames	Britain-2	16	8	14	22	4										15	3	5	8	31				
2005-06	**Dallas**	**NHL**	**3**	**0**	**0**	**0**	**0**	**0**	**0**	**0**	**1**	**0.0**	**–1**	**0**	**0.0**	**7:37**									
	Iowa Stars	AHL	54	21	13	34	26										5	3	0	3	4				
2006-07	Rogle	Sweden-2	29	5	7	12	34																		
	NHL Totals		**233**	**49**	**49**	**98**	**84**	**28**	**0**	**1**	**307**	**16.0**		**4**	**50.0**	**9:14**	**10**	**0**	**0**	**0**	**2**	**0**	**0**	**0**	**6:41**

CCHA Second All-Star Team (1993) • CCHA First All-Star Team (1994) • CCHA Player of the Year (1994) • NCAA West First All-American Team (1994)

Claimed on waivers by **NY Rangers** from **Edmonton**, February 21, 1997. Signed as a free agent by **Ottawa**, July 2, 1998. Signed as a free agent by **Phoenix**, July 20, 1999. Signed as a free agent by **Ottawa**, August 2, 2000. Signed as a free agent by **Dallas**, July 30, 2002. Signed as a free agent by **Guildford** (Britain-2), January 13, 2005. Signed as a free agent by **Rogle** (Sweden-2), July 31, 2006.

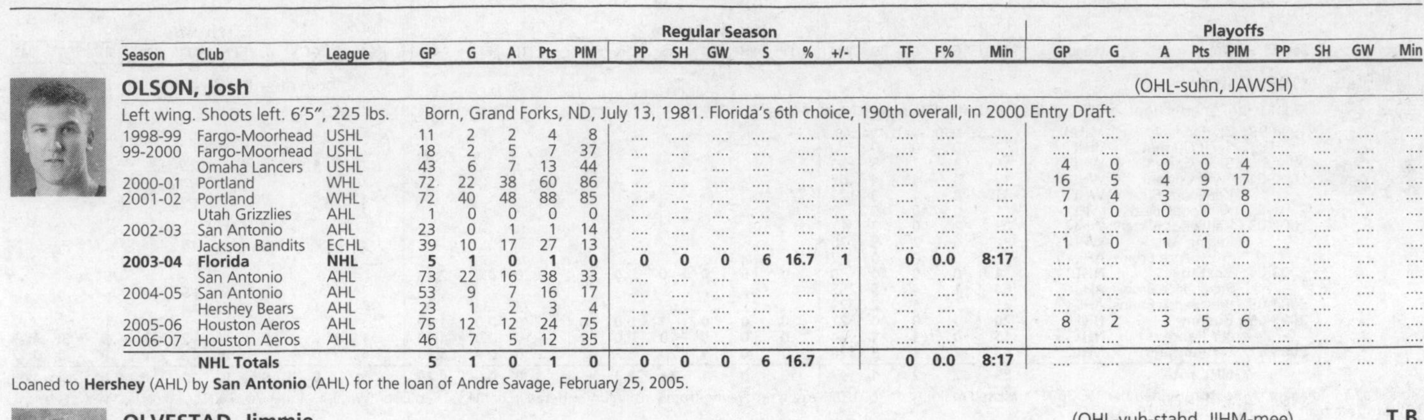

Season	Club	League	GP	G	A	Pts	PIM	PP	SH	GW	S	%	+/-	TF	F%	Min	GP	G	A	Pts	PIM	PP	SH	GW	Min
		Regular Season															Playoffs								

OLSON, Josh

(OHL-suhn, JAWSH)

Left wing. Shoots left. 6'5", 225 lbs. Born, Grand Forks, ND, July 13, 1981. Florida's 6th choice, 190th overall, in 2000 Entry Draft.

Season	Club	League	GP	G	A	Pts	PIM	PP	SH	GW	S	%	+/-	TF	F%	Min	GP	G	A	Pts	PIM	PP	SH	GW	Min
1998-99	Fargo-Moorhead	USHL	11	2	2	4	8																		
99-2000	Fargo-Moorhead	USHL	18	2	5	7	37																		
	Omaha Lancers	USHL	43	6	7	13	44										4	0	0	0	4				
2000-01	Portland	WHL	72	22	38	60	86										16	5	4	9	17				
2001-02	Portland	WHL	72	40	48	88	85										7	4	3	7	8				
	Utah Grizzlies	AHL	1	0	0	0	0										1	0	0	0	0				
2002-03	San Antonio	AHL	23	0	1	1	14																		
	Jackson Bandits	ECHL	39	10	17	27	13										1	0	1	1	0				
2003-04	**Florida**	**NHL**	**5**	**1**	**0**	**1**	**0**	**0**	**0**	**0**	**6**	**16.7**	**1**	**0**	**0.0**	**8:17**									
	San Antonio	AHL	73	22	16	38	33																		
2004-05	San Antonio	AHL	53	9	7	16	17																		
	Hershey Bears	AHL	23	1	2	3	4																		
2005-06	Houston Aeros	AHL	75	12	12	24	75										8	2	3	5	6				
2006-07	Houston Aeros	AHL	46	7	5	12	35																		
	NHL Totals		**5**	**1**	**0**	**1**	**0**	**0**	**0**	**0**	**6**	**16.7**		**0**	**0.0**	**8:17**									

Loaned to **Hershey** (AHL) by **San Antonio** (AHL) for the loan of Andre Savage, February 25, 2005.

OLVESTAD, Jimmie

(OHL-vuh-stahd, JIHM-mee) **T.B.**

Left wing. Shoots left. 6'1", 194 lbs. Born, Stockholm, Sweden, February 16, 1980. Tampa Bay's 4th choice, 88th overall, in 1999 Entry Draft.

Season	Club	League	GP	G	A	Pts	PIM	PP	SH	GW	S	%	+/-	TF	F%	Min	GP	G	A	Pts	PIM	PP	SH	GW	Min
1996-97	Huddinge IK Jr.	Swe-Jr.	40	15	16	31																			
1997-98	Djurgarden Jr.	Swe-Jr.	10	3	3	6	10																		
	Huddinge IK	Sweden-2	11	0	0	0	6																		
1998-99	Djurgarden	Sweden	44	2	4	6	18										4	0	0	0	8				
99-2000	Djurgarden	Sweden	50	6	3	9	34										13	1	2	3	12				
2000-01	Djurgarden	Sweden	50	7	8	15	79										16	7	2	9	14				
2001-02	**Tampa Bay**	**NHL**	**74**	**3**	**11**	**14**	**24**	**0**	**0**	**0**	**99**	**3.0**	**3**	**14**	**28.6**	**14:00**									
2002-03	**Tampa Bay**	**NHL**	**37**	**0**	**3**	**3**	**16**	**0**	**0**	**0**	**30**	**0.0**	**–2**	**12**	**33.3**	**10:28**									
	Springfield	AHL	6	0	1	1	13																		
2003-04	Hamilton	AHL	76	7	14	21	56										4	2	0	2	4				
2004-05	Djurgarden	Sweden	46	4	8	12	89										12	0	1	1	47				
2005-06	Djurgarden	Sweden	50	10	9	19	90																		
2006-07	Djurgarden	Sweden	54	9	13	22	104																		
	NHL Totals		**111**	**3**	**14**	**17**	**40**	**0**	**0**	**0**	**129**	**2.3**		**26**	**30.8**	**12:49**									

Signed as a free agent by **Djurgarden** (Sweden), April 27, 2004.

ONDRUS, Ben

(AWN-druhs, BEHN) **TOR.**

Right wing. Shoots right. 6', 194 lbs. Born, Sherwood Park, Alta., June 25, 1982.

Season	Club	League	GP	G	A	Pts	PIM	PP	SH	GW	S	%	+/-	TF	F%	Min	GP	G	A	Pts	PIM	PP	SH	GW	Min
1997-98	Sherwood Park	AMBHL																							
1998-99	Swift Current	WHL	46	4	4	8	58										6	0	1	1	8				
99-2000	Swift Current	WHL	67	14	15	29	138										12	1	0	1	22				
2000-01	Swift Current	WHL	69	13	17	30	151																		
2001-02	Swift Current	WHL	67	30	41	71	153										12	4	3	7	18				
2002-03	Swift Current	WHL	67	33	36	69	98										3	0	1	1	11				
	Idaho Steelheads	WCHL	4	0	3	3	0										5	0	1	1	6				
2003-04	St. John's	AHL	60	6	11	17	102																		
2004-05	St. John's	AHL	78	7	11	18	137										5	0	1	1	7				
2005-06	**Toronto**	**NHL**	**22**	**0**	**0**	**0**	**18**	**0**	**0**	**0**	**17**	**0.0**	**–10**	**28**	**50.0**	**10:07**									
	Toronto Marlies	AHL	53	12	17	29	104										5	1	2	3	4				
2006-07	**Toronto**	**NHL**	**16**	**0**	**2**	**2**	**20**	**0**	**0**	**0**	**7**	**0.0**	**–5**	**9**	**44.4**	**4:54**									
	Toronto Marlies	AHL	29	8	3	11	35																		
	NHL Totals		**38**	**0**	**2**	**2**	**38**	**0**	**0**	**0**	**24**	**0.0**		**37**	**48.6**	**7:55**									

Signed as a free agent by **Idaho** (WCHL), March 23, 2003. Signed as a free agent by **St. John's** (AHL), September 1, 2003. Signed as a fee agent by **Toronto**, May 27, 2004.

O'NEILL, Jeff

(oh-NEEL, JEHF)

Right wing. Shoots right. 6'1", 195 lbs. Born, Richmond Hill, Ont., February 23, 1976. Hartford's 1st choice, 5th overall, in 1994 Entry Draft.

Season	Club	League	GP	G	A	Pts	PIM	PP	SH	GW	S	%	+/-	TF	F%	Min	GP	G	A	Pts	PIM	PP	SH	GW	Min
1990-91	Richmond Hill	Minor-ON	78	56	134	190																			
1991-92	Thornhill	MTJHL	43	27	*53	80	48																		
1992-93	Guelph Storm	OHL	65	32	47	79	88										5	2	2	4	6				
1993-94	Guelph Storm	OHL	66	45	81	126	95										9	2	11	13	31				
1994-95	Guelph Storm	OHL	57	43	81	124	56										14	8	18	26	34				
1995-96	**Hartford**	**NHL**	**65**	**8**	**19**	**27**	**40**	**1**	**0**	**1**	**65**	**12.3**	**–3**												
1996-97	**Hartford**	**NHL**	**72**	**14**	**16**	**30**	**40**	**2**	**1**	**2**	**101**	**13.9**	**–24**												
	Springfield	AHL	1	0	0	0	0																		
1997-98	**Carolina**	**NHL**	**74**	**19**	**20**	**39**	**67**	**7**	**1**	**4**	**114**	**16.7**	**–8**												
1998-99	**Carolina**	**NHL**	**75**	**16**	**15**	**31**	**66**	**4**	**0**	**2**	**121**	**13.2**	**3**	**941**	**45.6**	**16:44**	**6**	**0**	**1**	**1**	**0**	**0**	**0**	**0**	**19:25**
99-2000	**Carolina**	**NHL**	**80**	**25**	**38**	**63**	**72**	**4**	**0**	**7**	**189**	**13.2**	**–9**	**1337**	**49.5**	**19:20**									
2000-01	**Carolina**	**NHL**	**82**	**41**	**26**	**67**	**106**	**17**	**0**	**5**	**242**	**16.9**	**–18**	**726**	**50.0**	**18:20**	**6**	**1**	**2**	**3**	**10**	**0**	**0**	**1**	**17:33**
2001-02	**Carolina**	**NHL**	**76**	**31**	**33**	**64**	**63**	**11**	**0**	**6**	**272**	**11.4**	**–5**	**831**	**56.7**	**19:44**	**22**	**8**	**5**	**13**	**27**	**3**	**0**	**1**	**19:00**
2002-03	**Carolina**	**NHL**	**82**	**30**	**31**	**61**	**38**	**11**	**0**	**7**	**316**	**9.5**	**–21**	**986**	**54.1**	**19:09**									
2003-04	**Carolina**	**NHL**	**67**	**14**	**20**	**34**	**60**	**7**	**0**	**4**	**207**	**6.8**	**–12**	**660**	**57.6**	**17:29**									
2004-05		DID NOT PLAY																							
2005-06	**Toronto**	**NHL**	**74**	**19**	**19**	**38**	**64**	**14**	**0**	**6**	**169**	**11.2**	**–19**	**45**	**51.1**	**12:39**									
2006-07	**Toronto**	**NHL**	**74**	**20**	**22**	**42**	**54**	**6**	**0**	**3**	**165**	**12.1**	**1**	**249**	**57.8**	**13:43**									
	NHL Totals		**821**	**237**	**259**	**496**	**670**	**84**	**2**	**47**	**1961**	**12.1**		**5775**	**52.0**	**17:13**	**34**	**9**	**8**	**17**	**37**	**3**	**0**	**2**	**18:49**

OHL All-Rookie Team (1993) • OHL Rookie of the Year (1993) • OHL First All-Star Team (1995)

Played in NHL All-Star Game (2003)

Transferred to **Carolina** after **Hartford** franchise relocated, June 25, 1997. Traded to **Toronto** by **Carolina** for Toronto's 4th round choice (later traded to St. Louis - St. Louis selected Reto Berra) in 2006 Entry Draft, July 30, 2005.

ORPIK, Brooks

(OHR-pihk, BRUKS) **PIT.**

Defense. Shoots left. 6'2", 219 lbs. Born, San Francisco, CA, September 26, 1980. Pittsburgh's 1st choice, 18th overall, in 2000 Entry Draft.

Season	Club	League	GP	G	A	Pts	PIM	PP	SH	GW	S	%	+/-	TF	F%	Min	GP	G	A	Pts	PIM	PP	SH	GW	Min
1996-97	Thayer Academy	High-MA	20	4	1	5																			
1997-98	Thayer Academy	High-MA	22	0	7	7																			
1998-99	Boston College	H-East	41	1	10	11	*96																		
99-2000	Boston College	H-East	38	1	9	10	102																		
2000-01	Boston College	H-East	40	0	20	20	*124																		
2001-02	Wilkes-Barre	AHL	78	2	18	20	99																		
2002-03	**Pittsburgh**	**NHL**	**6**	**0**	**0**	**0**	**2**	**0**	**0**	**0**	**2**	**0.0**	**–5**	**0**	**0.0**	**18:19**									
	Wilkes-Barre	AHL	71	4	14	18	105										6	0	0	0	14				
2003-04	**Pittsburgh**	**NHL**	**79**	**1**	**9**	**10**	**127**	**0**	**0**	**0**	**56**	**1.8**	**–36**	**0**	**0.0**	**18:25**									
	Wilkes-Barre	AHL	3	0	0	0	2										24	0	4	4	53				
2005-06	**Pittsburgh**	**NHL**	**64**	**2**	**7**	**9**	**124**	**0**	**0**	**0**	**32**	**6.3**	**–3**	**0**	**0.0**	**18:50**									
2006-07	**Pittsburgh**	**NHL**	**70**	**0**	**6**	**6**	**82**	**0**	**0**	**0**	**59**	**0.0**	**4**	**0**	**0.0**	**16:37**	**5**	**0**	**0**	**0**	**8**	**0**	**0**	**0**	**15:43**
	NHL Totals		**219**	**3**	**22**	**25**	**335**	**0**	**0**	**0**	**149**	**2.0**		**0**	**0.0**	**17:58**	**5**	**0**	**0**	**0**	**8**	**0**	**0**	**0**	**15:43**

ORR, Colton

(OHR, KOHL-tuhn) **NYR**

Right wing. Shoots right. 6'3", 220 lbs. Born, Winnipeg, Man., March 3, 1982.

			Regular Season														Playoffs								
Season	Club	League	GP	G	A	Pts	PIM	PP	SH	GW	S	%	+/-	TF	F%	Min	GP	G	A	Pts	PIM	PP	SH	GW	Min
1998-99	St. Boniface	MJHL	STATISTICS NOT AVAILABLE																						
	Swift Current	WHL	2	0	0	0	0																		
99-2000	Swift Current	WHL	61	3	2	5	130										12	1	0	1	25				
2000-01	Swift Current	WHL	19	0	4	4	67																		
	Kamloops Blazers	WHL	41	8	1	9	179										3	0	0	0	20				
2001-02	Kamloops Blazers	WHL	1	0	0	0	7										2	0	0	0	2				
2002-03	Kamloops Blazers	WHL	3	2	0	2	17																		
	Regina Pats	WHL	37	6	2	8	170										3	0	0	0	19				
	Providence Bruins	AHL	1	0	0	0	7																		
2003-04	**Boston**	**NHL**	**1**	**0**	**0**	**0**	**0**	**0**	**0**	**0**	**0**	**0.0**	**-1**	**0**	**0.0**	**2:13**									
	Providence Bruins	AHL	64	1	4	5	257										2	0	0	0	9				
2004-05	Providence Bruins	AHL	61	1	6	7	279										17	1	0	1	44				
2005-06	**Boston**	**NHL**	**20**	**0**	**0**	**0**	**27**	**0**	**0**	**0**	**1**	**0.0**	**0**	**0**	**0.0**	**1:49**									
	NY Rangers	**NHL**	**15**	**0**	**1**	**1**	**44**	**0**	**0**	**0**	**0**	**0.0**	**1**	**0**	**0.0**	**4:19**	**1**	**0**	**0**	**0**	**2**	**0**	**0**	**0**	**4:17**
2006-07	**NY Rangers**	**NHL**	**53**	**2**	**1**	**3**	**126**	**0**	**0**	**1**	**23**	**8.7**	**-2**	**0**	**0.0**	**5:20**	**4**	**0**	**0**	**0**	**12**	**0**	**0**	**0**	**4:57**
	NHL Totals		**89**	**2**	**2**	**4**	**197**	**0**	**0**	**1**	**24**	**8.3**		**0**	**0.0**	**4:20**	**5**	**0**	**0**	**0**	**14**	**0**	**0**	**0**	**4:49**

Signed as a free agent by **Boston**, September 19, 2001. • Missed majority of 2001-02 season recovering from wrist injury suffered in game vs. Red Deer (WHL), October 20, 2001. Claimed on waivers by **NY Rangers** from **Boston**, November 29, 2005.

ORSZAGH, Vladimir

(OHR-sahg, vla-DIH-meer)

Right wing. Shoots left. 5'11", 195 lbs. Born, Banska Bystrica, Czech., May 24, 1977. NY Islanders' 4th choice, 106th overall, in 1995 Entry Draft.

			Regular Season														Playoffs								
Season	Club	League	GP	G	A	Pts	PIM	PP	SH	GW	S	%	+/-	TF	F%	Min	GP	G	A	Pts	PIM	PP	SH	GW	Min
1993-94	B. Bystrica Jr.	Slovak-Jr.	38	38	27	65																			
1994-95	B. Bystrica	Slovak-2	38	18	12	30																			
1995-96	B. Bystrica	Slovakia	31	9	5	14	22																		
1996-97	Utah Grizzlies	IHL	68	12	15	27	30										3	0	1	1	4				
1997-98	**NY Islanders**	**NHL**	**11**	**0**	**1**	**1**	**2**	**0**	**0**	**0**	**9**	**0.0**	**-3**												
	Utah Grizzlies	IHL	62	13	10	23	60										4	2	0	2	0				
1998-99	**NY Islanders**	**NHL**	**12**	**1**	**0**	**1**	**6**	**0**	**0**	**0**	**4**	**20.0**	**2**	**0**	**0.0**	**6:36**									
	Lowell	AHL	68	18	23	41	57										3	2	2	4	2				
99-2000	**NY Islanders**	**NHL**	**11**	**2**	**1**	**3**	**4**	**0**	**0**	**0**	**16**	**12.5**	**1**	**0**	**0.0**	**11:55**									
	Lowell	AHL	55	8	12	20	22										7	3	3	6	2				
2000-01	Djurgarden	Sweden	50	23	13	36	62										16	*7	3	10	20				
2001-02	**Nashville**	**NHL**	**79**	**15**	**21**	**36**	**56**	**5**	**0**	**3**	**113**	**13.3**	**-15**	**10**	**20.0**	**16:04**									
2002-03	**Nashville**	**NHL**	**78**	**16**	**16**	**32**	**38**	**3**	**0**	**3**	**152**	**10.5**	**-1**	**17**	**29.4**	**17:34**									
2003-04	**Nashville**	**NHL**	**82**	**16**	**21**	**37**	**74**	**2**	**2**	**3**	**124**	**12.9**	**-4**	**39**	**25.6**	**17:00**	**6**	**2**	**0**	**2**	**4**	**0**	**0**	**0**	**16:09**
2004-05	HKm Zvolen	Slovakia	37	16	14	30	50										17	5	2	7	24				
	B. Bystrica	Slovak-2	2	2	0	2	4																		
2005-06	Lulea HF	Sweden	19	8	5	13	42																		
	St. Louis	**NHL**	**16**	**4**	**5**	**9**	**14**	**1**	**0**	**0**	**23**	**17.4**	**-2**	**4**	**25.0**	**16:52**									
2006-07			DID NOT PLAY – INJURED																						
	NHL Totals		**289**	**54**	**65**	**119**	**194**	**11**	**2**	**9**	**441**	**12.2**		**70**	**25.7**	**16:14**	**6**	**2**	**0**	**2**	**4**	**0**	**0**	**0**	**16:08**

Signed as a free agent by **Nashville**, May 30, 2001. Signed as a free agent by **Zvolen** (Slovakia), October 6, 2004. Claimed on waivers by **St. Louis** from **Nashville**, December 30, 2005. • Missed entire 2006-07 season recovering from knee surgery.

ORTMEYER, Jed

(OHRT-migh-uhr, JEHD) **NSH.**

Center. Shoots right. 6', 197 lbs. Born, Omaha, NE, September 3, 1978.

			Regular Season														Playoffs								
Season	Club	League	GP	G	A	Pts	PIM	PP	SH	GW	S	%	+/-	TF	F%	Min	GP	G	A	Pts	PIM	PP	SH	GW	Min
1997-98	Omaha Lancers	USHL	54	23	25	48	52										14	3	4	7	31				
1998-99	Omaha Lancers	USHL	52	23	36	59	81										12	5	6	11	16				
99-2000	U. of Michigan	CCHA	41	8	16	24	40																		
2000-01	U. of Michigan	CCHA	27	10	11	21	52																		
2001-02	U. of Michigan	CCHA	41	15	23	38	40																		
2002-03	U. of Michigan	CCHA	36	18	16	34	48																		
2003-04	**NY Rangers**	**NHL**	**58**	**2**	**4**	**6**	**16**	**0**	**0**	**0**	**48**	**4.2**	**-10**	**16**	**31.3**	**9:52**									
	Hartford	AHL	13	2	8	10	4										16	5	2	7	6				
2004-05	Hartford	AHL	61	7	20	27	63										6	0	1	1	4				
2005-06	**NY Rangers**	**NHL**	**78**	**5**	**2**	**7**	**38**	**0**	**0**	**1**	**90**	**5.6**	**2**	**21**	**23.8**	**11:06**	**4**	**1**	**0**	**1**	**4**	**0**	**0**	**0**	**11:40**
2006-07	**NY Rangers**	**NHL**	**41**	**2**	**9**	**11**	**22**	**0**	**1**	**0**	**67**	**3.0**	**7**	**8**	**12.5**	**12:35**	**9**	**0**	**0**	**0**	**2**	**0**	**0**	**0**	**9:37**
	Hartford	AHL	8	1	3	4	6																		
	NHL Totals		**177**	**9**	**15**	**24**	**76**	**0**	**1**	**1**	**205**	**4.4**		**45**	**24.4**	**11:02**	**13**	**1**	**0**	**1**	**6**	**0**	**0**	**0**	**10:15**

Signed as a free agent by **NY Rangers**, May 10, 2003. Signed as a free agent by **Nashville**, July 2, 2007.

O'SULLIVAN, Patrick

(oh-SUHL-ih-van, PAT-rihk) **L.A.**

Center. Shoots left. 5'11", 190 lbs. Born, Winston Salem, NC, February 1, 1985. Minnesota's 2nd choice, 56th overall, in 2003 Entry Draft.

			Regular Season														Playoffs								
Season	Club	League	GP	G	A	Pts	PIM	PP	SH	GW	S	%	+/-	TF	F%	Min	GP	G	A	Pts	PIM	PP	SH	GW	Min
99-2000	Strathroy Rockets	OHA-B	45	6	13	19	53																		
2000-01	USNTDP	U-17	8	8	10	18	12																		
	USNTDP	NAHL	56	22	35	57	57																		
2001-02	Mississauga	OHL	68	34	58	92	61																		
	USNTDP	USHL	1	1	0	1	2																		
2002-03	Mississauga	OHL	56	40	41	81	57										5	2	9	11	18				
2003-04	Mississauga	OHL	53	43	39	82	32										24	12	11	23	16				
2004-05	Mississauga	OHL	57	31	59	90	63										5	0	4	4	6				
2005-06	Houston Aeros	AHL	78	47	46	93	64										8	5	5	10	4				
2006-07	**Los Angeles**	**NHL**	**44**	**5**	**14**	**19**	**14**	**2**	**0**	**1**	**92**	**5.4**	**-6**	**127**	**46.5**	**14:04**									
	Manchester	AHL	41	18	21	39	12										16	8	9	17	10				
	NHL Totals		**44**	**5**	**14**	**19**	**14**	**2**	**0**	**1**	**92**	**5.4**		**127**	**46.5**	**14:04**									

Canadian Major Junior Rookie of the Year (2002) • AHL All-Rookie Team (2006) • Dudley "Red" Garrett Memorial Trophy (Top Rookie - AHL) (2006)

Traded to **Los Angeles** by **Minnesota** with Edmonton's 1st round choice (previously acquired, Los Angeles selected Trevor Lewis) in 2006 Entry Draft for Pavol Demitra, June 24, 2006.

OTT, Steve

(AWT, STEEV) **DAL.**

Center. Shoots left. 6', 195 lbs. Born, Summerside, P.E.I., August 19, 1982. Dallas' 1st choice, 25th overall, in 2000 Entry Draft.

			Regular Season														Playoffs								
Season	Club	League	GP	G	A	Pts	PIM	PP	SH	GW	S	%	+/-	TF	F%	Min	GP	G	A	Pts	PIM	PP	SH	GW	Min
1998-99	Leamington Flyers	OHA-B	48	14	30	44	110																		
99-2000	Windsor Spitfires	OHL	66	23	39	62	131										12	3	5	8	21				
2000-01	Windsor Spitfires	OHL	55	50	37	87	164										9	3	8	11	27				
2001-02	Windsor Spitfires	OHL	53	43	45	88	178										14	6	10	16	49				
2002-03	Utah Grizzlies	AHL	40	9	11	20	98																		
	Dallas	**NHL**	**26**	**3**	**4**	**7**	**31**	**0**	**0**	**0**	**25**	**12.0**	**6**	**4**	**50.0**	**8:46**	**1**	**0**	**0**	**0**	**0**	**0**	**0**	**0**	**6:57**
2003-04	**Dallas**	**NHL**	**73**	**2**	**10**	**12**	**152**	**0**	**0**	**1**	**74**	**2.7**	**-2**	**59**	**49.2**	**10:14**	**4**	**1**	**0**	**1**	**0**	**0**	**0**	**1**	**6:55**
2004-05	Hamilton	AHL	67	18	21	39	279										4	0	0	0	20				
2005-06	**Dallas**	**NHL**	**82**	**5**	**17**	**22**	**178**	**0**	**0**	**1**	**89**	**5.6**	**1**	**535**	**49.2**	**11:54**	**5**	**0**	**1**	**1**	**2**	**0**	**0**	**0**	**7:41**
2006-07	**Dallas**	**NHL**	**19**	**0**	**4**	**4**	**35**	**0**	**0**	**0**	**17**	**0.0**	**-4**	**39**	**59.0**	**9:11**	**6**	**0**	**0**	**0**	**8**	**0**	**0**	**0**	**6:43**
	Iowa Stars	AHL	3	0	0	0	8																		
	NHL Totals		**200**	**10**	**35**	**45**	**396**	**0**	**0**	**2**	**205**	**4.9**		**637**	**49.8**	**10:38**	**16**	**1**	**1**	**2**	**10**	**0**	**0**	**1**	**7:05**

OHL Second All-Star Team (2002)

• Missed majority of 2006-07 season recovering from ankle injury suffered in game vs. Los Angeles, October 28, 2006.

OUELLET, Michel
(oo-LEHT, mee-SHEHL) **T.B.**

Right wing. Shoots right. 6', 203 lbs. Born, Rimouski, Que., March 5, 1982. Pittsburgh's 4th choice, 124th overall, in 2000 Entry Draft.

			Regular Season														Playoffs								
Season	Club	League	GP	G	A	Pts	PIM	PP	SH	GW	S	%	+/-	TF	F%	Min	GP	G	A	Pts	PIM	PP	SH	GW	Min
1997-98	Jonquiere Elites	QAAA	33	20	32	52	52	....	....	....	....	....	....	....	....	....	....	....	....	....	....	....	....	....	....
1998-99	Rimouski Oceanic	QMJHL	28	7	13	20	10	....	....	....	....	....	....	....	....	....	11	0	1	1	6	....	....	....	....
99-2000	Rimouski Oceanic	QMJHL	72	36	53	89	38	....	....	....	....	....	....	....	....	....	14	4	5	9	14	....	....	....	....
2000-01	Rimouski Oceanic	QMJHL	63	42	50	92	50	....	....	....	....	....	....	....	....	....	11	6	7	13	8	....	....	....	....
2001-02	Rimouski Oceanic	QMJHL	61	40	58	98	66	....	....	....	....	....	....	....	....	....	7	3	6	9	4	....	....	....	....
2002-03	Wilkes-Barre	AHL	4	0	2	2	0	....	....	....	....	....	....	....	....	....	....	....	....	....	....	....	....	....	....
	Wheeling Nailers	ECHL	55	20	26	46	40	....	....	....	....	....	....	....	....	....	....	....	....	....	....	....	....	....	....
2003-04	Wilkes-Barre	AHL	79	30	19	49	34	....	....	....	....	....	....	....	....	....	22	2	10	12	6	....	....	....	....
2004-05	Wilkes-Barre	AHL	80	31	32	63	56	....	....	....	....	....	....	....	....	....	11	2	3	5	6	....	....	....	....
2005-06	**Pittsburgh**	**NHL**	**50**	**16**	**16**	**32**	**16**	**11**	**0**	**0**	**87**	**18.4**	**-13**	**16**	**37.5**	**14:02**	....	....	....	....	....	....	....	....	....
	Wilkes-Barre	AHL	19	10	20	30	12	....	....	....	....	....	....	....	....	....	....	....	....	....	....	....	....	....	....
2006-07	**Pittsburgh**	**NHL**	**73**	**19**	**29**	**48**	**30**	**11**	**0**	**2**	**148**	**12.8**	**-3**	**8**	**37.5**	**13:20**	**5**	**0**	**2**	**2**	**6**	**0**	**0**	**0**	**12:54**
	NHL Totals		**123**	**35**	**45**	**80**	**46**	**22**	**0**	**2**	**235**	**14.9**		**24**	**37.5**	**13:37**	**5**	**0**	**2**	**2**	**6**	**0**	**0**	**0**	**12:54**

AHL All-Rookie Team (2004)

Signed as a free agent by **Tampa Bay**, July 1, 2007.

OVECHKIN, Alex
(oh-VEHCH-kihn, AL-ehx) **WSH.**

Left wing. Shoots right. 6'2", 220 lbs. Born, Moscow, USSR, September 17, 1985. Washington's 1st choice, 1st overall, in 2004 Entry Draft.

Season	Club	League	GP	G	A	Pts	PIM	PP	SH	GW	S	%	+/-	TF	F%	Min	GP	G	A	Pts	PIM	PP	SH	GW	Min
2001-02	Dyn'o Moscow 2	Russia-3	19	18	8	26	20	....	....	....	....	....	....	....	....	....	....	....	....	....	....	....	....	....	....
	Dynamo Moscow	Russia	22	2	2	4	4	....	....	....	....	....	....	....	....	....	3	0	0	0	0	....	....	....	....
2002-03	Dynamo Moscow	Russia	40	8	7	15	28	....	....	....	....	....	....	....	....	....	5	0	0	0	2	....	....	....	....
2003-04	Dynamo Moscow	Russia	53	13	11	24	40	....	....	....	....	....	....	....	....	....	3	0	0	0	2	....	....	....	....
2004-05	Dynamo Moscow	Russia	37	13	13	26	32	....	....	....	....	....	....	....	....	....	10	2	4	6	31	....	....	....	....
2005-06	**Washington**	**NHL**	**81**	**52**	**54**	**106**	**52**	**21**	**3**	**5**	**425**	**12.2**	**2**	**16**	**12.5**	**21:37**	....	....	....	....	....	....	....	....	....
	Russia	Olympics	8	5	0	5	8	....	....	....	....	....	....	....	....	....	....	....	....	....	....	....	....	....	....
2006-07	**Washington**	**NHL**	**82**	**46**	**46**	**92**	**52**	**16**	**0**	**8**	**392**	**11.7**	**-19**	**17**	**47.1**	**21:23**	....	....	....	....	....	....	....	....	....
	NHL Totals		**163**	**98**	**100**	**198**	**104**	**37**	**3**	**13**	**817**	**12.0**		**33**	**30.3**	**21:30**	....	....	....	....	....	....	....	....	....

Olympic Tournament All-Star Team (2006) • NHL All-Rookie Team (2006) • NHL First All-Star Team (2006, 2007) • Calder Memorial Trophy (2006)

Played in NHL All-Star Game (2007)

OZOLINSH, Sandis
(OH-zoh-LIHNCH, SAN-dihz)

Defense. Shoots left. 6'3", 220 lbs. Born, Riga, USSR, August 3, 1972. San Jose's 3rd choice, 30th overall, in 1991 Entry Draft.

Season	Club	League	GP	G	A	Pts	PIM	PP	SH	GW	S	%	+/-	TF	F%	Min	GP	G	A	Pts	PIM	PP	SH	GW	Min
1990-91	Dynamo Riga	USSR	44	0	3	3	51	....	....	....	....	....	....	....	....	....	....	....	....	....	....	....	....	....	....
	Riga 2	USSR-3	11	3	....	....	....	....	....	....	....	....	....	....	....	....	....	....	....	....	....	....	....	....	....
1991-92	Rigas Stars	CIS	30	6	0	6	42	....	....	....	....	....	....	....	....	....	....	....	....	....	....	....	....	....	....
	Kansas City	IHL	34	6	9	15	20	....	....	....	....	....	....	....	....	....	15	2	5	7	22	....	....	....	....
1992-93	**San Jose**	**NHL**	**37**	**7**	**16**	**23**	**40**	**2**	**0**	**0**	**83**	**8.4**	**-9**	....	....	....	....	....	....	....	....	....	....	....	....
1993-94	**San Jose**	**NHL**	**81**	**26**	**38**	**64**	**24**	**4**	**0**	**3**	**157**	**16.6**	**16**	....	....	....	**14**	**0**	**10**	**10**	**8**	**0**	**0**	**0**	....
1994-95	**San Jose**	**NHL**	**48**	**9**	**16**	**25**	**30**	**3**	**1**	**2**	**83**	**10.8**	**-6**	....	....	....	**11**	**3**	**2**	**5**	**6**	**1**	**0**	**0**	....
1995-96	San Francisco	IHL	2	1	0	1	0	....	....	....	....	....	....	....	....	....	....	....	....	....	....	....	....	....	....
	San Jose	**NHL**	**7**	**1**	**3**	**4**	**4**	**1**	**0**	**0**	**21**	**4.8**	**2**	....	....	....	....	....	....	....	....	....	....	....	....
	♦ Colorado	**NHL**	**66**	**13**	**37**	**50**	**50**	**7**	**1**	**1**	**145**	**9.0**	**0**	....	....	....	**22**	**5**	**14**	**19**	**16**	**2**	**0**	**1**	....
1996-97	**Colorado**	**NHL**	**80**	**23**	**45**	**68**	**88**	**13**	**0**	**4**	**232**	**9.9**	**4**	....	....	....	**17**	**4**	**13**	**17**	**24**	**2**	**0**	**1**	....
1997-98	**Colorado**	**NHL**	**66**	**13**	**38**	**51**	**65**	**9**	**0**	**2**	**135**	**9.6**	**-12**	....	....	....	**7**	**0**	**7**	**7**	**14**	**0**	**0**	**0**	....
1998-99	**Colorado**	**NHL**	**39**	**7**	**25**	**32**	**22**	**4**	**0**	**3**	**81**	**8.6**	**10**	**0**	**0.0**	**22:06**	**19**	**4**	**8**	**12**	**22**	**3**	**0**	**1**	**22:24**
99-2000	**Colorado**	**NHL**	**82**	**16**	**36**	**52**	**46**	**6**	**0**	**1**	**210**	**7.6**	**17**	**0**	**0.0**	**22:41**	**17**	**5**	**5**	**10**	**20**	**3**	**0**	**1**	**18:35**
2000-01	**Carolina**	**NHL**	**72**	**12**	**32**	**44**	**71**	**4**	**2**	**2**	**145**	**8.3**	**-25**	**0**	**0.0**	**22:12**	**6**	**0**	**2**	**2**	**5**	**0**	**0**	**0**	**19:04**
2001-02	**Carolina**	**NHL**	**46**	**4**	**19**	**23**	**34**	**1**	**0**	**0**	**71**	**5.6**	**-4**	**0**	**0.0**	**19:30**	....	....	....	....	....	....	....	....	....
	Florida	**NHL**	**37**	**10**	**19**	**29**	**24**	**2**	**0**	**1**	**101**	**9.9**	**-3**	**0**	**0.0**	**30:30**	....	....	....	....	....	....	....	....	....
	Latvia	Olympics	1	0	4	4	0	....	....	....	....	....	....	....	....	....	....	....	....	....	....	....	....	....	....
2002-03	**Florida**	**NHL**	**51**	**7**	**19**	**26**	**40**	**5**	**0**	**2**	**83**	**8.4**	**-16**	**0**	**0.0**	**28:23**	....	....	....	....	....	....	....	....	....
	Anaheim	**NHL**	**31**	**5**	**13**	**18**	**16**	**1**	**0**	**1**	**54**	**9.3**	**10**	**0**	**0.0**	**22:08**	**21**	**2**	**6**	**8**	**10**	**0**	**0**	**1**	**23:37**
2003-04	**Anaheim**	**NHL**	**36**	**5**	**11**	**16**	**24**	**1**	**0**	**2**	**58**	**8.6**	**-7**	**0**	**0.0**	**19:57**	....	....	....	....	....	....	....	....	....
2004-05			DID NOT PLAY																						
2005-06	**Anaheim**	**NHL**	**17**	**3**	**3**	**6**	**8**	**0**	**0**	**2**	**17**	**17.6**	**-4**	**0**	**0.0**	**17:45**	....	....	....	....	....	....	....	....	....
	NY Rangers	**NHL**	**19**	**3**	**11**	**14**	**20**	**2**	**0**	**0**	**41**	**7.3**	**2**	**0**	**0.0**	**23:48**	**3**	**0**	**0**	**0**	**6**	**0**	**0**	**0**	**21:27**
	Latvia	Olympics	5	1	3	4	0	....	....	....	....	....	....	....	....	....	....	....	....	....	....	....	....	....	....
2006-07	**NY Rangers**	**NHL**	**21**	**0**	**3**	**3**	**8**	**0**	**0**	**0**	**15**	**0.0**	**-8**	**0**	**0.0**	**18:51**	....	....	....	....	....	....	....	....	....
	NHL Totals		**836**	**164**	**384**	**548**	**614**	**65**	**4**	**26**	**1732**	**9.5**		**0**	**0.0**	**22:57**	**137**	**23**	**67**	**90**	**131**	**11**	**0**	**5**	**21:28**

NHL First All-Star Team (1997)

Played in NHL All-Star Game (1994, 1997, 1998, 2000, 2001, 2002, 2003)

• Missed majority of 1992-93 season recovering from knee injury suffered in game vs. Philadelphia, December 30, 1992. Traded to **Colorado** by **San Jose** for Owen Nolan, October 26, 1995. Traded to **Carolina** by **Colorado** with Columbus' 2nd round choice (previously acquired, Carolina selected Tomas Kurka) in 2000 Entry Draft for Nolan Pratt, Carolina's 1st (Vaclav Nedorost) and 2nd (Jared Aulin) round choices in 2000 Entry Draft and Philadelphia's 2nd round choice (previously acquired, Colorado selected Agris Saviels) in 2000 Entry Draft, June 24, 2000. Traded to **Florida** by **Carolina** with Byron Ritchie for Bret Hedican, Kevyn Adams and Tomas Malec, January 16, 2002. Traded to **Anaheim** by **Florida** with Lance Ward for Pavel Trnka, Matt Cullen and Anaheim's 4th round choice (James Pemberton) in 2003 Entry Draft, January 30, 2003. • Missed majority of 2003-04 season recovering from shoulder injury suffered in game vs. Colorado, December 19, 2003. Traded to **NY Rangers** by **Anaheim** for San Jose's 3rd round choice (previously acquired, Anaheim selected John DeGray) in 2006 Entry Draft, March 9, 2006. • Missed majority of 2006-07 season due to a recurring knee injury.

PAETSCH, Nathan
(PASH, NAY-thuhn) **BUF.**

Defense. Shoots left. 6', 198 lbs. Born, Humboldt, Sask., March 30, 1983. Buffalo's 8th choice, 202nd overall, in 2003 Entry Draft.

Season	Club	League	GP	G	A	Pts	PIM	PP	SH	GW	S	%	+/-	TF	F%	Min	GP	G	A	Pts	PIM	PP	SH	GW	Min
1998-99	Tisdale Trojans	SMHL	74	20	55	75	120	....	....	....	....	....	....	....	....	....	....	....	....	....	....	....	....	....	....
	Moose Jaw	WHL	2	0	0	0	0	....	....	....	....	....	....	....	....	....	....	....	....	....	....	....	....	....	....
99-2000	Moose Jaw	WHL	68	9	35	44	49	....	....	....	....	....	....	....	....	....	4	0	1	1	0	....	....	....	....
2000-01	Moose Jaw	WHL	70	8	54	62	118	....	....	....	....	....	....	....	....	....	4	1	2	3	6	....	....	....	....
2001-02	Moose Jaw	WHL	59	16	36	52	86	....	....	....	....	....	....	....	....	....	12	0	4	4	16	....	....	....	....
2002-03	Moose Jaw	WHL	59	15	39	54	81	....	....	....	....	....	....	....	....	....	13	3	10	13	6	....	....	....	....
2003-04	Rochester	AHL	54	5	5	10	49	....	....	....	....	....	....	....	....	....	16	1	1	2	28	....	....	....	....
2004-05	Rochester	AHL	80	4	19	23	150	....	....	....	....	....	....	....	....	....	9	1	1	2	16	....	....	....	....
2005-06	**Buffalo**	**NHL**	**1**	**0**	**1**	**1**	**0**	**0**	**0**	**0**	**0**	**0.0**	**-1**	**0**	**0.0**	**15:38**	**1**	**0**	**0**	**0**	**0**	**0**	**0**	**0**	**12:06**
	Rochester	AHL	72	11	39	50	90	....	....	....	....	....	....	....	....	....	....	....	....	....	....	....	....	....	....
2006-07	**Buffalo**	**NHL**	**63**	**2**	**22**	**24**	**50**	**0**	**0**	**0**	**62**	**3.2**	**10**	**0**	**0.0**	**15:15**	....	....	....	....	....	....	....	....	....
	NHL Totals		**64**	**2**	**23**	**25**	**50**	**0**	**0**	**0**	**62**	**3.2**		**0**	**0.0**	**15:15**	**1**	**0**	**0**	**0**	**0**	**0**	**0**	**0**	**12:06**

• Re-entered NHL Entry Draft. Originally Washington's 1st choice, 58th overall, in 2001 Entry Draft.

WHL East Second All-Star Team (2003)

PAHLSSON, Samuel
(PAWL-suhn, SAM-ew-l) **ANA.**

Center. Shoots left. 6', 205 lbs. Born, Ornskoldsvik, Sweden, December 17, 1977. Colorado's 10th choice, 176th overall, in 1996 Entry Draft.

Season	Club	League	GP	G	A	Pts	PIM	PP	SH	GW	S	%	+/-	TF	F%	Min	GP	G	A	Pts	PIM	PP	SH	GW	Min
1992-93	Ange IK	Sweden-4	9	0	0	0	0	....	....	....	....	....	....	....	....	....	....	....	....	....	....	....	....	....	....
1993-94	Ange IK	Sweden-4	STATISTICS NOT AVAILABLE					....	....	....	....	....	....	....	....	....	....	....	....	....	....	....	....	....	....
1994-95	MoDo	Sweden	1	0	0	0	0	....	....	....	....	....	....	....	....	....	....	....	....	....	....	....	....	....	....
1995-96	MoDo Jr.	Swe-Jr.	30	10	11	21	26	....	....	....	....	....	....	....	....	....	....	....	....	....	....	....	....	....	....
	MoDo	Sweden	36	1	3	4	8	....	....	....	....	....	....	....	....	....	4	0	0	0	0	....	....	....	....
1996-97	MoDo Jr.	Swe-Jr.	5	2	6	8	2	....	....	....	....	....	....	....	....	....	....	....	....	....	....	....	....	....	....
	MoDo	Sweden	49	8	9	17	83	....	....	....	....	....	....	....	....	....	....	....	....	....	....	....	....	....	....
1997-98	MoDo	Sweden	23	6	11	17	24	....	....	....	....	....	....	....	....	....	9	3	0	3	6	....	....	....	....
1998-99	MoDo	Sweden	50	17	17	34	44	....	....	....	....	....	....	....	....	....	13	3	3	6	10	....	....	....	....
99-2000	MoDo	Sweden	47	16	11	27	67	....	....	....	....	....	....	....	....	....	13	3	3	6	8	....	....	....	....
	MoDo	EuroHL	4	1	0	1	0	....	....	....	....	....	....	....	....	....	3	1	1	2	2	....	....	....	....
2000-01	**Boston**	**NHL**	**17**	**1**	**1**	**2**	**6**	**0**	**0**	**0**	**13**	**7.7**	**-5**	**239**	**40.2**	**14:19**	....	....	....	....	....	....	....	....	....
	Anaheim	**NHL**	**59**	**3**	**4**	**7**	**14**	**1**	**1**	**1**	**46**	**6.5**	**-9**	**867**	**45.1**	**14:14**	....	....	....	....	....	....	....	....	....
2001-02	**Anaheim**	**NHL**	**80**	**6**	**14**	**20**	**26**	**1**	**1**	**0**	**99**	**6.1**	**-16**	**1201**	**49.8**	**16:24**	....	....	....	....	....	....	....	....	....

			Regular Season														Playoffs								
Season	Club	League	GP	G	A	Pts	PIM	PP	SH	GW	S	%	+/-	TF	F%	Min	GP	G	A	Pts	PIM	PP	SH	GW	Min
2002-03	Anaheim	NHL	34	4	11	15	18	0	1	2	28	14.3	10	118	52.5	13:20	21	2	4	6	12	0	0	0	16:41
	Cincinnati	AHL	13	1	7	8	24	....	....	....	....	....	....	....	....	....	....	....	....	....	....	....	....	....	....
2003-04	Anaheim	NHL	82	8	14	22	52	1	0	2	134	6.0	–2	908	55.3	16:51	....	....	....	....	....	....	....	....	....
2004-05	Frolunda	Sweden	48	6	18	24	56	....	....	....	....	....	....	....	....	....	14	4	7	11	24	....	....	....	....
2005-06	Anaheim	NHL	82	11	10	21	34	0	3	1	116	9.5	–1	1517	52.8	16:30	16	2	3	5	18	0	0	2	17:06
	Sweden	Olympics	8	2	2	4	8	....	....	....	....	....	....	....	....	....	....	....	....	....	....	....	....	....	....
2006-07 ♦	Anaheim	NHL	82	8	18	26	42	0	0	1	111	7.2	–4	1523	52.7	17:22	21	3	9	12	20	0	0	2	19:25
	NHL Totals		436	41	72	113	192	3	6	7	547	7.5		6373	51.0	16:04	58	7	16	23	50	0	0	4	17:47

Traded to **Boston** by **Colorado** with Brian Rolston, Martin Grenier and New Jersey's 1st round choice (previously acquired, Boston selected Martin Samuelsson) in 2000 Entry Draft for Raymond Bourque and Dave Andreychuk, March 6, 2000. Traded to **Anaheim** by **Boston** for Patrick Traverse and Andrei Nazarov, November 18, 2000. Signed as a free agent by **Frolunda** (Sweden), September, 2004.

PAILLE, Dan

(PIGH-yay, DAN) **BUF.**

Left wing. Shoots left. 6', 197 lbs. Born, Welland, Ont., April 15, 1984. Buffalo's 2nd choice, 20th overall, in 2002 Entry Draft.

Season	Club	League	GP	G	A	Pts	PIM	PP	SH	GW	S	%	+/-	TF	F%	Min	GP	G	A	Pts	PIM	PP	SH	GW	Min
99-2000	Welland Cougars	OHA-B	42	14	17	31	19	....	....	....	....	....	....	....	....	....	16	16	16	32	....	....	....	....	....
2000-01	Guelph Storm	OHL	64	22	31	53	57	....	....	....	....	....	....	....	....	....	4	2	0	2	2	....	....	....	....
2001-02	Guelph Storm	OHL	62	27	30	57	54	....	....	....	....	....	....	....	....	....	9	5	2	7	9	....	....	....	....
2002-03	Guelph Storm	OHL	54	30	27	57	28	....	....	....	....	....	....	....	....	....	11	8	6	14	6	....	....	....	....
2003-04	Guelph Storm	OHL	59	37	43	80	63	....	....	....	....	....	....	....	....	....	22	9	9	18	14	....	....	....	....
2004-05	Rochester	AHL	79	14	15	29	54	....	....	....	....	....	....	....	....	....	9	2	2	4	6	....	....	....	....
2005-06	Buffalo	NHL	14	1	2	3	2	0	0	0	15	6.7	5	4	25.0	10:24	....	....	....	....	....	....	....	....	....
	Rochester	AHL	45	14	13	27	29	....	....	....	....	....	....	....	....	....	....	....	....	....	....	....	....	....	....
2006-07	Buffalo	NHL	29	3	8	11	18	0	0	0	45	6.7	5	6	33.3	12:47	1	0	0	0	0	0	0	0	4:52
	Rochester	AHL	29	7	14	21	12	....	....	....	....	....	....	....	....	....	....	....	....	....	....	....	....	....	....
	NHL Totals		43	4	10	14	20	0	0	0	60	6.7		10	30.0	12:00	1	0	0	0	0	0	0	0	4:52

PANDOLFO, Jay

(pan-DAWL-foh, JAY) **N.J.**

Left wing. Shoots left. 6'1", 190 lbs. Born, Winchester, MA, December 27, 1974. New Jersey's 2nd choice, 32nd overall, in 1993 Entry Draft.

Season	Club	League	GP	G	A	Pts	PIM	PP	SH	GW	S	%	+/-	TF	F%	Min	GP	G	A	Pts	PIM	PP	SH	GW	Min
1989-90	Burlington	High-MA	23	33	30	63	18	....	....	....	....	....	....	....	....	....	....	....	....	....	....	....	....	....	....
1990-91	Burlington	High-MA	20	19	27	46	10	....	....	....	....	....	....	....	....	....	....	....	....	....	....	....	....	....	....
1991-92	Burlington	High-MA	20	35	34	69	14	....	....	....	....	....	....	....	....	....	....	....	....	....	....	....	....	....	....
1992-93	Boston University	H-East	37	16	22	38	16	....	....	....	....	....	....	....	....	....	....	....	....	....	....	....	....	....	....
1993-94	Boston University	H-East	37	17	25	42	27	....	....	....	....	....	....	....	....	....	....	....	....	....	....	....	....	....	....
1994-95	Boston University	H-East	20	7	13	20	6	....	....	....	....	....	....	....	....	....	....	....	....	....	....	....	....	....	....
1995-96	Boston University	H-East	39	*38	29	67	6	....	....	....	....	....	....	....	....	....	....	....	....	....	....	....	....	....	....
	Albany River Rats	AHL	5	3	1	4	0	....	....	....	....	....	....	....	....	....	3	0	0	0	0	....	....	....	....
1996-97	New Jersey	NHL	46	6	8	14	6	0	0	1	61	9.8	–1	....	....	....	6	0	1	1	0	0	0	0	....
	Albany River Rats	AHL	12	3	9	12	0	....	....	....	....	....	....	....	....	....	....	....	....	....	....	....	....	....	....
1997-98	New Jersey	NHL	23	1	3	4	4	0	0	0	23	4.3	–4	....	....	....	3	0	2	2	0	0	0	0	....
	Albany River Rats	AHL	51	18	19	37	24	....	....	....	....	....	....	....	....	....	....	....	....	....	....	....	....	....	....
1998-99	New Jersey	NHL	70	14	13	27	10	1	1	4	100	14.0	3	10	40.0	15:13	7	1	0	1	0	0	0	0	13:19
99-2000 ♦	New Jersey	NHL	71	7	8	15	4	0	0	0	86	8.1	0	19	47.4	13:25	23	0	5	5	0	0	0	0	15:35
2000-01	New Jersey	NHL	63	4	12	16	16	0	0	0	57	7.0	3	15	53.3	14:05	25	1	4	5	4	0	0	0	12:38
2001-02	New Jersey	NHL	65	4	10	14	15	0	1	0	72	5.6	12	12	41.7	13:59	6	0	0	0	0	0	0	0	16:11
2002-03 ♦	New Jersey	NHL	68	6	11	17	23	0	1	4	92	6.5	12	13	23.1	16:08	24	6	6	12	2	0	0	1	16:34
2003-04	New Jersey	NHL	82	13	13	26	14	1	2	4	140	9.3	5	25	44.0	16:00	5	0	0	0	0	0	0	0	13:41
2004-05	Salzburg	Austria	19	5	7	12	0	....	....	....	....	....	....	....	....	....	....	....	....	....	....	....	....	....	....
2005-06	New Jersey	NHL	82	10	10	20	16	0	0	0	116	8.6	2	13	30.8	18:03	9	1	4	5	0	0	1	1	18:37
2006-07	New Jersey	NHL	82	13	14	27	8	0	1	1	109	11.9	–5	16	6.3	18:37	11	1	0	1	4	0	0	0	19:39
	NHL Totals		652	78	102	180	116	2	6	14	856	9.1		123	36.6	15:50	119	10	22	32	10	0	1	2	15:35

Hockey East First All-Star Team (1996) • Hockey East Player of the Year (1996) • NCAA East First All-American Team (1996)

Signed as a free agent by **Salzburg** (Austria), December 27, 2004.

PANDOLFO, Mike

(pan-DAWL-foh, MIGHK) **N.J.**

Left wing. Shoots left. 6'3", 225 lbs. Born, Winchester, MA, September 15, 1979. Buffalo's 5th choice, 77th overall, in 1998 Entry Draft.

Season	Club	League	GP	G	A	Pts	PIM	PP	SH	GW	S	%	+/-	TF	F%	Min	GP	G	A	Pts	PIM	PP	SH	GW	Min
1996-97	St. Sebastian's	High-MA	32	27	28	55	30	....	....	....	....	....	....	....	....	....	....	....	....	....	....	....	....	....	....
1997-98	St. Sebastian's	High-MA	28	29	23	52	18	....	....	....	....	....	....	....	....	....	....	....	....	....	....	....	....	....	....
1998-99	Boston University	H-East	34	13	4	17	26	....	....	....	....	....	....	....	....	....	....	....	....	....	....	....	....	....	....
99-2000	Boston University	H-East	41	13	10	23	37	....	....	....	....	....	....	....	....	....	....	....	....	....	....	....	....	....	....
2000-01	Boston University	H-East	37	16	13	29	30	....	....	....	....	....	....	....	....	....	....	....	....	....	....	....	....	....	....
2001-02	Boston University	H-East	38	22	18	40	22	....	....	....	....	....	....	....	....	....	....	....	....	....	....	....	....	....	....
2002-03	Syracuse Crunch	AHL	74	9	9	18	31	....	....	....	....	....	....	....	....	....	....	....	....	....	....	....	....	....	....
2003-04	Columbus	NHL	3	0	0	0	0	0	0	0	3	0.0	–2	0	0.0	8:18	....	....	....	....	....	....	....	....	....
	Syracuse Crunch	AHL	77	18	19	37	29	....	....	....	....	....	....	....	....	....	7	1	0	1	2	....	....	....	....
2004-05	Syracuse Crunch	AHL	62	8	8	16	18	....	....	....	....	....	....	....	....	....	....	....	....	....	....	....	....	....	....
2005-06	Binghamton	AHL	1	0	0	0	4	....	....	....	....	....	....	....	....	....	....	....	....	....	....	....	....	....	....
	Reading Royals	ECHL	23	14	11	25	8	....	....	....	....	....	....	....	....	....	....	....	....	....	....	....	....	....	....
2006-07	Lowell Devils	AHL	24	4	5	9	4	....	....	....	....	....	....	....	....	....	....	....	....	....	....	....	....	....	....
	Trenton Titans	ECHL	48	36	31	67	10	....	....	....	....	....	....	....	....	....	1	0	0	0	0	....	....	....	....
	NHL Totals		3	0	0	0	0	0	0	0	3	0.0		0	0.0	8:18	....	....	....	....	....	....	....	....	....

ECHL Second All-Star Team (2007)

Rights traded to **Columbus** by **Buffalo** with Detroit's 1st round choice (previously acquired, later traded to Atlanta – Atlanta selected Jim Slater) in 2002 Entry Draft for New Jersey's 1st round choice (previously acquired, Buffalo selected Dan Paille) in 2002 Entry Draft, June 22, 2002.

PAPINEAU, Justin

(PA-pee-noh, JUHS-tihn) **N.J.**

Center. Shoots left. 5'11", 205 lbs. Born, Ottawa, Ont., January 15, 1980. St. Louis' 3rd choice, 75th overall, in 2000 Entry Draft.

Season	Club	League	GP	G	A	Pts	PIM	PP	SH	GW	S	%	+/-	TF	F%	Min	GP	G	A	Pts	PIM	PP	SH	GW	Min
1995-96	Ott. Jr. Senators	CJHL	52	31	19	50	51	....	....	....	....	....	....	....	....	....	....	....	....	....	....	....	....	....	....
1996-97	Belleville Bulls	OHL	50	10	32	42	32	....	....	....	....	....	....	....	....	....	....	....	....	....	....	....	....	....	....
1997-98	Belleville Bulls	OHL	66	41	53	94	34	....	....	....	....	....	....	....	....	....	10	5	9	14	6	....	....	....	....
1998-99	Belleville Bulls	OHL	68	52	47	99	28	....	....	....	....	....	....	....	....	....	21	*21	*30	*51	20	....	....	....	....
99-2000	Belleville Bulls	OHL	60	40	36	76	52	....	....	....	....	....	....	....	....	....	16	4	12	16	16	....	....	....	....
2000-01	Worcester IceCats	AHL	43	7	22	29	33	....	....	....	....	....	....	....	....	....	11	7	3	10	8	....	....	....	....
2001-02	St. Louis	NHL	1	0	0	0	0	0	0	0	0	0.0	–2	7	42.9	8:40	....	....	....	....	....	....	....	....	....
	Worcester IceCats	AHL	75	*38	38	76	86	....	....	....	....	....	....	....	....	....	3	1	2	3	4	....	....	....	....
2002-03	St. Louis	NHL	11	2	1	3	0	0	0	1	15	13.3	–1	99	44.4	10:59	....	....	....	....	....	....	....	....	....
	Worcester IceCats	AHL	44	21	17	38	42	....	....	....	....	....	....	....	....	....	....	....	....	....	....	....	....	....	....
	NY Islanders	NHL	5	1	2	3	4	0	0	1	8	12.5	1	15	53.3	14:50	1	0	0	0	0	0	0	0	5:12
	Bridgeport	AHL	5	7	1	8	4	....	....	....	....	....	....	....	....	....	7	1	3	4	7	....	....	....	....
2003-04	NY Islanders	NHL	64	8	5	13	8	5	0	2	44	18.2	4	49	38.8	7:42	....	....	....	....	....	....	....	....	....
2004-05	Bridgeport	AHL	59	18	15	33	52	....	....	....	....	....	....	....	....	....	....	....	....	....	....	....	....	....	....
2005-06	Bridgeport	AHL	12	6	6	12	12	....	....	....	....	....	....	....	....	....	....	....	....	....	....	....	....	....	....
2006-07	Lowell Devils	AHL	29	12	17	29	24	....	....	....	....	....	....	....	....	....	5	1	3	4	4	....	....	....	....
	NHL Totals		81	11	8	19	12	5	0	4	67	16.4		170	43.5	8:36	1	0	0	0	0	0	0	0	5:12

• Re-entered NHL Entry Draft. Originally Los Angeles' 2nd choice, 46th overall, in 1998 Entry Draft.

Traded to **NY Islanders** by **St. Louis** with St. Louis' 2nd round choice (Jeremy Colliton) in 2003 Entry Draft for Chris Osgood and NY Islanders' 3rd round choice (Konstantin Barulin) in 2003 Entry Draft, March 11, 2003. Signed as a free agent by **New Jersey**, August 10, 2006. • Spent majority of 2006-07 season as a healthy reserve. Signed as a free agent by **Basel** (Swiss), June 21, 2007.

PARENT, Ryan

(PAIR-ehnt, RIGH-uhn) **PHI.**

Defense. Shoots left. 6'2", 200 lbs. Born, Prince Albert, Sask., March 17, 1987. Nashville's 1st choice, 18th overall, in 2005 Entry Draft.

Season	Club	League	GP	G	A	Pts	PIM	PP	SH	GW	S	%	+/-	TF	F%	Min	GP	G	A	Pts	PIM	PP	SH	GW	Min
2002-03	Waterloo Siskins	OHA-B	41	2	8	10	35	....	....	....	....	....	....	....	....	....	....	....	....	....	....	....	....	....	....
2003-04	Guelph Storm	OHL	58	1	5	6	18	....	....	....	....	....	....	....	....	....	22	0	0	0	2	....	....	....	....
2004-05	Guelph Storm	OHL	66	2	17	19	36	....	....	....	....	....	....	....	....	....	4	0	1	1	4	....	....	....	....
2005-06	Guelph Storm	OHL	60	4	17	21	122	....	....	....	....	....	....	....	....	....	15	1	4	5	24	....	....	....	....
	Milwaukee	AHL	....	....	....	....	....	....	....	....	....	....	....	....	....	....	10	0	0	0	4	....	....	....	....

			Regular Season														Playoffs								
Season	Club	League	GP	G	A	Pts	PIM	PP	SH	GW	S	%	+/-	TF	F%	Min	GP	G	A	Pts	PIM	PP	SH	GW	Min
2006-07	**Philadelphia**	**NHL**	**1**	**0**	**0**	**0**	**0**	**0**	**0**	**0**	**1**	**0.0**	**0**	**0**	**0.0**	**14:10**	....	....	....	....	....	....	....	....	....
	Philadelphia	AHL	6	1	0	1	4	....	....	....	....	....	....	....	....	....	....	....	....	....	....	....	....	....	....
	Guelph Storm	OHL	43	3	7	10	86	....	....	....	....	....	....	....	....	....	4	0	1	1	14	....	....	....	....
	NHL Totals		**1**	**0**	**0**	**0**	**0**	**0**	**0**	**0**	**1**	**0.0**		**0**	**0.0**	**14:10**	....	....	....	....	....	....	....	....	....

OHL Second All-Star Team (2006, 2007)

Traded to **Philadelphia** by **Nashville** with Scottie Upshall and Nashville's 1st (later traded back to Nashville - Nashville selected Jonathon Blum) and 3rd (later traded to Washington - Washington selected Phil Desimone) round choices in 2007 Entry Draft for Peter Forsberg, February 15, 2007.

PARENTEAU, Pierre (pair-ehn-TOH, PEE-air) CHI.

Left wing. Shoots right. 5'11", 194 lbs. Born, Hull, Que., March 24, 1983. Anaheim's 11th choice, 264th overall, in 2001 Entry Draft.

Season	Club	League	GP	G	A	Pts	PIM	PP	SH	GW	S	%	+/-	TF	F%	Min	GP	G	A	Pts	PIM	PP	SH	GW	Min
99-2000	Charles-Lemoyne	QAAA	40	25	40	65	18	....	....	....	....	....	....	....	....	....	16	4	9	13	8	....	....	....	....
2000-01	Moncton Wildcats	QMJHL	45	10	19	29	38	....	....	....	....	....	....	....	....	....	....	....	....	....	....	....	....	....	....
	Chicoutimi	QMJHL	28	10	13	23	14	....	....	....	....	....	....	....	....	....	7	4	7	11	2	....	....	....	....
2001-02	Chicoutimi	QMJHL	68	51	67	118	120	....	....	....	....	....	....	....	....	....	4	3	1	4	10	....	....	....	....
2002-03	Chicoutimi	QMJHL	31	20	35	55	56	....	....	....	....	....	....	....	....	....	....	....	....	....	....	....	....	....	....
	Sherbrooke	QMJHL	28	13	35	48	84	....	....	....	....	....	....	....	....	....	12	8	11	19	6	....	....	....	....
2003-04	Cincinnati	AHL	66	14	16	30	20	....	....	....	....	....	....	....	....	....	7	1	2	3	6	....	....	....	....
2004-05	Cincinnati	AHL	76	17	24	41	58	....	....	....	....	....	....	....	....	....	9	2	0	2	8	....	....	....	....
2005-06	Portland Pirates	AHL	56	22	27	49	42	....	....	....	....	....	....	....	....	....	19	5	17	22	24	....	....	....	....
	Augusta Lynx	ECHL	2	0	1	1	0	....	....	....	....	....	....	....	....	....	....	....	....	....	....	....	....	....	....
2006-07	Portland Pirates	AHL	28	15	13	28	35	....	....	....	....	....	....	....	....	....	....	....	....	....	....	....	....	....	....
	Chicago	**NHL**	**5**	**0**	**1**	**1**	**2**	**0**	**0**	**0**	**7**	**0.0**	**−1**	**2**	**50.0**	**11:05**	....	....	....	....	....	....	....	....	....
	Norfolk Admirals	AHL	40	15	36	51	12	....	....	....	....	....	....	....	....	....	6	2	1	3	2	....	....	....	....
	NHL Totals		**5**	**0**	**1**	**1**	**2**	**0**	**0**	**0**	**7**	**0.0**		**2**	**50.0**	**11:05**	....	....	....	....	....	....	....	....	....

Traded to **Chicago** by **Anaheim** with Bruno St. Jacques for Sebastien Caron, Matt Keith and Chris Durno, December 28, 2006.

PARISE, Zach (pah-REE-say, ZAK) N.J.

Left wing. Shoots left. 5'11", 190 lbs. Born, Minneapolis, MN, July 28, 1984. New Jersey's 1st choice, 17th overall, in 2003 Entry Draft.

Season	Club	League	GP	G	A	Pts	PIM	PP	SH	GW	S	%	+/-	TF	F%	Min	GP	G	A	Pts	PIM	PP	SH	GW	Min
2000-01	Shat.-St. Mary's	High-MN	58	69	93	162	....	....	....	....	....	....	....	....	....	....	....	....	....	....	....	....	....	....	....
2001-02	Shat.-St. Mary's	High-MN	67	77	101	178	58	....	....	....	....	....	....	....	....	....	....	....	....	....	....	....	....	....	....
	USNTDP	U-18	12	7	7	14	6	....	....	....	....	....	....	....	....	....	....	....	....	....	....	....	....	....	....
2002-03	North Dakota	WCHA	39	26	35	61	34	....	....	....	....	....	....	....	....	....	....	....	....	....	....	....	....	....	....
2003-04	North Dakota	WCHA	37	23	32	55	24	....	....	....	....	....	....	....	....	....	....	....	....	....	....	....	....	....	....
2004-05	Albany River Rats	AHL	73	18	40	58	56	....	....	....	....	....	....	....	....	....	....	....	....	....	....	....	....	....	....
2005-06	**New Jersey**	**NHL**	**81**	**14**	**18**	**32**	**28**	**2**	**0**	**5**	**133**	**10.5**	**−1**	**162**	**42.6**	**13:08**	**9**	**1**	**2**	**3**	**2**	**0**	**0**	**0**	**15:03**
2006-07	**New Jersey**	**NHL**	**82**	**31**	**31**	**62**	**30**	**9**	**0**	**7**	**247**	**12.6**	**−3**	**52**	**44.2**	**17:32**	**11**	**7**	**3**	**10**	**8**	**2**	**0**	**1**	**19:08**
	NHL Totals		**163**	**45**	**49**	**94**	**58**	**11**	**0**	**12**	**380**	**11.8**		**214**	**43.0**	**15:21**	**20**	**8**	**5**	**13**	**10**	**2**	**0**	**1**	**17:18**

WCHA All-Rookie Team (2003) • WCHA First All-Star Team (2004) • NCAA West First All-American Team (2004)

PARK, Richard (PAHRK, RIH-chuhrd) NYI

Right wing. Shoots right. 5'11", 190 lbs. Born, Seoul, South Korea, May 27, 1976. Pittsburgh's 2nd choice, 50th overall, in 1994 Entry Draft.

Season	Club	League	GP	G	A	Pts	PIM	PP	SH	GW	S	%	+/-	TF	F%	Min	GP	G	A	Pts	PIM	PP	SH	GW	Min
1991-92	Tor. Young Nats	MTHL	76	49	58	107	91	....	....	....	....	....	....	....	....	....	....	....	....	....	....	....	....	....	....
1992-93	Belleville Bulls	OHL	66	23	38	61	38	....	....	....	....	....	....	....	....	....	5	0	0	0	14	....	....	....	....
1993-94	Belleville Bulls	OHL	59	27	49	76	70	....	....	....	....	....	....	....	....	....	12	3	5	8	18	....	....	....	....
1994-95	Belleville Bulls	OHL	45	28	51	79	35	....	....	....	....	....	....	....	....	....	16	9	18	27	12	....	....	....	....
	Pittsburgh	**NHL**	**1**	**0**	**1**	**1**	**2**	**0**	**0**	**0**	**4**	**0.0**	**1**	....	....	....	**3**	**0**	**0**	**0**	**2**	**0**	**0**	**0**	....
1995-96	Belleville Bulls	OHL	6	7	6	13	2	....	....	....	....	....	....	....	....	....	14	18	12	30	10	....	....	....	....
	Pittsburgh	**NHL**	**56**	**4**	**6**	**10**	**36**	**0**	**1**	**1**	**62**	**6.5**	**3**	....	....	....	**1**	**0**	**0**	**0**	**0**	**0**	**0**	**0**	....
1996-97	**Pittsburgh**	**NHL**	**1**	**0**	**0**	**0**	**0**	**0**	**0**	**0**	**1**	**0.0**	**−1**	....	....	....	....	....	....	....	....	....	....	....	....
	Cleveland	IHL	50	12	15	27	30	....	....	....	....	....	....	....	....	....	....	....	....	....	....	....	....	....	....
	Anaheim	**NHL**	**11**	**1**	**1**	**2**	**10**	**0**	**0**	**0**	**9**	**11.1**	**0**	....	....	....	**11**	**0**	**1**	**1**	**2**	**0**	**0**	**0**	....
1997-98	**Anaheim**	**NHL**	**15**	**0**	**2**	**2**	**8**	**0**	**0**	**0**	**14**	**0.0**	**−3**	....	....	....	....	....	....	....	....	....	....	....	....
	Cincinnati	AHL	56	17	26	43	36	....	....	....	....	....	....	....	....	....	....	....	....	....	....	....	....	....	....
1998-99	**Philadelphia**	**NHL**	**7**	**0**	**0**	**0**	**0**	**0**	**0**	**0**	**5**	**0.0**	**−1**	**15**	**53.3**	**9:21**	....	....	....	....	....	....	....	....	....
	Philadelphia	AHL	75	41	42	83	33	....	....	....	....	....	....	....	....	....	16	9	6	15	4	....	....	....	....
99-2000	Utah Grizzlies	IHL	82	28	32	60	36	....	....	....	....	....	....	....	....	....	5	1	0	1	0	....	....	....	....
2000-01	Cleveland	IHL	75	27	21	48	29	....	....	....	....	....	....	....	....	....	4	0	2	2	4	....	....	....	....
2001-02	**Minnesota**	**NHL**	**63**	**10**	**15**	**25**	**10**	**2**	**1**	**2**	**115**	**8.7**	**−1**	**79**	**41.8**	**16:28**	....	....	....	....	....	....	....	....	....
	Houston Aeros	AHL	13	4	10	14	6	....	....	....	....	....	....	....	....	....	....	....	....	....	....	....	....	....	....
2002-03	**Minnesota**	**NHL**	**81**	**14**	**10**	**24**	**16**	**2**	**2**	**3**	**149**	**9.4**	**−3**	**178**	**48.9**	**16:36**	**18**	**3**	**3**	**6**	**4**	**0**	**0**	**1**	**17:03**
2003-04	**Minnesota**	**NHL**	**73**	**13**	**12**	**25**	**28**	**4**	**0**	**1**	**142**	**9.2**	**0**	**379**	**40.1**	**16:30**	....	....	....	....	....	....	....	....	....
2004-05	Malmo	Sweden	9	1	3	4	4	....	....	....	....	....	....	....	....	....	....	....	....	....	....	....	....	....	....
	Langnau	Swiss	10	3	0	3	8	....	....	....	....	....	....	....	....	....	6	4	1	5	6	....	....	....	....
2005-06	**Vancouver**	**NHL**	**60**	**8**	**10**	**18**	**29**	**0**	**1**	**2**	**97**	**8.2**	**−2**	**26**	**26.9**	**11:00**	....	....	....	....	....	....	....	....	....
2006-07	**NY Islanders**	**NHL**	**82**	**10**	**16**	**26**	**33**	**0**	**2**	**2**	**93**	**10.8**	**4**	**218**	**39.0**	**11:39**	**5**	**0**	**1**	**1**	**2**	**0**	**0**	**0**	**9:16**
	NHL Totals		**450**	**60**	**73**	**133**	**172**	**8**	**7**	**11**	**691**	**8.7**		**895**	**41.6**	**14:24**	**38**	**3**	**5**	**8**	**10**	**0**	**0**	**1**	**15:22**

OHL All-Rookie Team (1993) • AHL Second All-Star Team (1999)

Traded to **Anaheim** by **Pittsburgh** for Roman Oksiuta, March 18, 1997. Signed as a free agent by **Philadelphia**, August 24, 1998. Signed as a free agent by **Utah** (IHL), September 22, 1999. Signed as a free agent by **Minnesota**, June 6, 2000. Signed as a free agent by **Malmo** (Sweden), November 8, 2004. Signed as a free agent by **Langnau** (Swiss), January 4, 2005. Signed as a free agent by **Vancouver**, August 8, 2005. Signed as a free agent by **NY Islanders**, October 2, 2006.

PARKER, Scott (PAR-kuhr, SKAWT) COL.

Right wing. Shoots right. 6'5", 240 lbs. Born, Hanford, CA, January 29, 1978. Colorado's 4th choice, 20th overall, in 1998 Entry Draft.

Season	Club	League	GP	G	A	Pts	PIM	PP	SH	GW	S	%	+/-	TF	F%	Min	GP	G	A	Pts	PIM	PP	SH	GW	Min
1993-94	Alaska Arctic Ice	AAHL	34	8	12	20	86	....	....	....	....	....	....	....	....	....	....	....	....	....	....	....	....	....	....
1994-95	Spokane Braves	KIJHL	43	7	21	28	128	....	....	....	....	....	....	....	....	....	....	....	....	....	....	....	....	....	....
1995-96	Kelowna Rockets	WHL	64	3	4	7	159	....	....	....	....	....	....	....	....	....	6	0	0	0	12	....	....	....	....
1996-97	Kelowna Rockets	WHL	68	18	8	26	*330	....	....	....	....	....	....	....	....	....	6	0	2	2	4	....	....	....	....
1997-98	Kelowna Rockets	WHL	71	30	22	52	243	....	....	....	....	....	....	....	....	....	7	6	0	6	23	....	....	....	....
1998-99	**Colorado**	**NHL**	**27**	**0**	**0**	**0**	**71**	**0**	**0**	**0**	**3**	**0.0**	**−3**	**1**	**0.0**	**1:37**	....	....	....	....	....	....	....	....	....
	Hershey Bears	AHL	32	4	3	7	143	....	....	....	....	....	....	....	....	....	4	0	0	0	6	....	....	....	....
99-2000	Hershey Bears	AHL	68	12	7	19	206	....	....	....	....	....	....	....	....	....	11	1	1	2	56	....	....	....	....
2000-01♦	**Colorado**	**NHL**	**69**	**2**	**3**	**5**	**155**	**0**	**0**	**1**	**35**	**5.7**	**−2**	**2**	**0.0**	**5:42**	**4**	**0**	**0**	**0**	**2**	**0**	**0**	**0**	**2:12**
2001-02	**Colorado**	**NHL**	**63**	**1**	**4**	**5**	**154**	**0**	**0**	**0**	**32**	**3.1**	**0**	**0**	**0.0**	**5:50**	....	....	....	....	....	....	....	....	....
2002-03	**Colorado**	**NHL**	**43**	**1**	**3**	**4**	**82**	**0**	**0**	**0**	**20**	**5.0**	**6**	**0**	**0.0**	**6:15**	**1**	**0**	**0**	**0**	**2**	**0**	**0**	**0**	**1:44**
2003-04	**San Jose**	**NHL**	**50**	**1**	**3**	**4**	**101**	**0**	**0**	**0**	**20**	**5.0**	**0**	**5**	**40.0**	**6:37**	....	....	....	....	....	....	....	....	....
2004-05			DID NOT PLAY																						
2005-06	**San Jose**	**NHL**	**10**	**1**	**0**	**1**	**38**	**0**	**0**	**0**	**6**	**16.7**	**3**	**0**	**0.0**	**5:39**	....	....	....	....	....	....	....	....	....
2006-07	**San Jose**	**NHL**	**11**	**0**	**0**	**0**	**22**	**0**	**0**	**0**	**0**	**0.0**	**0**	**1**	**0.0**	**5:03**	....	....	....	....	....	....	....	....	....
	Colorado	**NHL**	**10**	**1**	**1**	**2**	**6**	**0**	**0**	**0**	**2**	**50.0**	**0**	**1**	**0.0**	**5:35**	....	....	....	....	....	....	....	....	....
	NHL Totals		**283**	**7**	**14**	**21**	**629**	**0**	**0**	**1**	**121**	**5.8**		**10**	**20.0**	**5:33**	**5**	**0**	**0**	**0**	**4**	**0**	**0**	**0**	**2:06**

♦ Re-entered NHL Entry Draft. Originally New Jersey's 6th choice, 63rd overall, in 1996 Entry Draft.

Traded to **San Jose** by **Colorado** for Colorado's 5th round choice (previously acquired, Colorado selected Brad Richardson) in 2003 Entry Draft, June 21, 2003. • Missed majority of 2005-06 season recovering from facial (pre-season) and head (November 21, 2005 at Edmonton) injuries. Traded to **Colorado** by **San Jose** for Colorado's 6th round choice in 2008 Entry Draft, February 27, 2007. • Missed majority of 2006-07 season recovering from back and ankle injuries.

PARRISH, Mark (PAIR-ihsh, MAHRK) MIN.

Right wing. Shoots right. 5'11", 205 lbs. Born, Bloomington, MN, February 2, 1977. Colorado's 3rd choice, 79th overall, in 1996 Entry Draft.

Season	Club	League	GP	G	A	Pts	PIM	PP	SH	GW	S	%	+/-	TF	F%	Min	GP	G	A	Pts	PIM	PP	SH	GW	Min
1994-95	Jefferson Jaguars	High-MN	27	40	20	60	42	....	....	....	....	....	....	....	....	....	....	....	....	....	....	....	....	....	....
1995-96	St. Cloud State	WCHA	39	15	13	28	30	....	....	....	....	....	....	....	....	....	....	....	....	....	....	....	....	....	....
1996-97	St. Cloud State	WCHA	35	*27	15	42	60	....	....	....	....	....	....	....	....	....	....	....	....	....	....	....	....	....	....
1997-98	Seattle	WHL	54	54	38	92	29	....	....	....	....	....	....	....	....	....	5	2	3	5	2	....	....	....	....
	New Haven	AHL	1	1	0	1	2	....	....	....	....	....	....	....	....	....	....	....	....	....	....	....	....	....	....
1998-99	**Florida**	**NHL**	**73**	**24**	**13**	**37**	**25**	**5**	**0**	**5**	**129**	**18.6**	**−6**	**1**	**0.0**	**13:59**	....	....	....	....	....	....	....	....	....
	New Haven	AHL	2	1	0	1	0	....	....	....	....	....	....	....	....	....	....	....	....	....	....	....	....	....	....

			Regular Season														Playoffs								
Season	Club	League	GP	G	A	Pts	PIM	PP	SH	GW	S	%	+/-	TF	F%	Min	GP	G	A	Pts	PIM	PP	SH	GW	Min
99-2000	**Florida**	**NHL**	81	26	18	44	39	6	0	3	152	17.1	1	8	75.0	14:04	4	0	1	1	0	0	0	0	12:37
2000-01	**NY Islanders**	**NHL**	70	17	13	30	28	6	0	3	123	13.8	−27	3	33.3	15:27	....	....	....	....	....	....	....	....	....
2001-02	**NY Islanders**	**NHL**	78	30	30	60	32	9	1	6	162	18.5	10	10	40.0	16:48	7	2	1	3	6	2	0	0	17:27
2002-03	**NY Islanders**	**NHL**	81	23	25	48	28	9	0	5	147	15.6	−11	9	44.4	16:12	5	1	0	1	4	1	0	0	16:02
2003-04	**NY Islanders**	**NHL**	59	24	11	35	18	6	0	6	105	22.9	8	5	20.0	17:20	5	1	2	3	0	0	0	0	20:35
2004-05			DID NOT PLAY																						
2005-06	**NY Islanders**	**NHL**	57	24	17	41	16	13	0	5	102	23.5	−14	12	16.7	19:34	....	....	....	....	....	....	....	....	....
	Los Angeles	**NHL**	19	5	3	8	4	3	0	0	35	14.3	−9	0	0.0	15:29	....	....	....	....	....	....	....	....	....
	United States	Olympics	6	0	0	0	4	....	....	....	....	....	....	....	....	....	....	....	....	....	....	....	....	....	....
2006-07	**Minnesota**	**NHL**	76	19	20	39	18	5	0	4	141	13.5	9	13	30.8	14:20	5	1	0	1	0	0	0	0	15:46
	NHL Totals		**594**	**192**	**150**	**342**	**208**	**62**	**1**	**37**	**1096**	**17.5**		**61**	**36.1**	**15:48**	**26**	**5**	**4**	**9**	**10**	**3**	**0**	**0**	**16:43**

NCAA West Second All-American Team (1997) • WHL West First All-Star Team (1998)

Played in NHL All-Star Game (2002)

Rights traded to **Florida** by **Colorado** with Anaheim's 3rd round choice (previously acquired, Florida selected Lance Ward) in 1998 Entry Draft for Tom Fitzgerald, March 24, 1998. Traded to **NY Islanders** by **Florida** with Oleg Kvasha for Roberto Luongo and Olli Jokinen, June 24, 2000. Traded to **Los Angeles** by **NY Islanders** with Brent Sopel for Denis Grebeshkov and Jeff Tambellini, March 8, 2006. Signed as a free agent by **Minnesota**, July 1, 2006.

PARROS, George

(PAIR-ohs, JOHRJ) **ANA.**

Right wing. Shoots right. 6'5", 232 lbs. Born, Washington, PA, December 29, 1979. Los Angeles' 9th choice, 222nd overall, in 1999 Entry Draft.

Season	Club	League	GP	G	A	Pts	PIM	PP	SH	GW	S	%	+/-	TF	F%	Min	GP	G	A	Pts	PIM	PP	SH	GW	Min
1996-97	Delbarton	High-NJ	14	15	8	23	....	....	....	....	....	....	....	....	....	....	....	....	....	....	....	....	....	....	....
1997-98	Delbarton	High-NJ	15	22	17	39	....	....	....	....	....	....	....	....	....	....	....	....	....	....	....	....	....	....	....
1998-99	Chicago Freeze	NAHL	54	30	20	50	126	....	....	....	....	....	....	....	....	....	....	....	....	....	....	....	....	....	....
99-2000	Princeton	ECAC	27	4	2	6	14	....	....	....	....	....	....	....	....	....	....	....	....	....	....	....	....	....	....
2000-01	Princeton	ECAC	31	7	10	17	38	....	....	....	....	....	....	....	....	....	....	....	....	....	....	....	....	....	....
2001-02	Princeton	ECAC	31	9	13	22	36	....	....	....	....	....	....	....	....	....	....	....	....	....	....	....	....	....	....
2002-03	Princeton	ECAC	22	0	7	7	29	....	....	....	....	....	....	....	....	....	....	....	....	....	....	....	....	....	....
	Manchester	AHL	9	0	1	1	7	....	....	....	....	....	....	....	....	....	....	....	....	....	....	....	....	....	....
2003-04	Manchester	AHL	57	3	6	9	126	....	....	....	....	....	....	....	....	....	5	0	0	0	4	....	....	....	....
2004-05	Manchester	AHL	67	14	8	22	247	....	....	....	....	....	....	....	....	....	6	1	1	2	27	....	....	....	....
	Reading Royals	ECHL	3	0	0	0	9	....	....	....	....	....	....	....	....	....	....	....	....	....	....	....	....	....	....
2005-06	**Los Angeles**	**NHL**	55	2	3	5	138	0	0	0	23	8.7	1	1	0.0	4:56	....	....	....	....	....	....	....	....	....
2006-07	**Colorado**	**NHL**	2	0	0	0	0	0	0	0	1	0.0	−1	0	0.0	3:33	....	....	....	....	....	....	....	....	....
	♦ Anaheim	**NHL**	32	1	0	1	102	0	0	0	18	5.6	−2	0	0.0	5:09	5	0	0	0	10	0	0	0	3:49
	NHL Totals		**89**	**3**	**3**	**6**	**240**	**0**	**0**	**0**	**42**	**7.1**		**1**	**0.0**	**4:59**	**5**	**0**	**0**	**0**	**10**	**0**	**0**	**0**	**3:49**

Claimed on waivers by **Colorado** from **Los Angeles**, October 3, 2006. Traded to **Anaheim** by **Colorado** with Colorado's 3rd round choice (later traded to Tampa Bay - Tampa Bay selected Luca Cunti) in 2007 Entry Draft for Atlanta's 2nd round choice (previously acquired, Colorado selected T.J. Galiardi) in 2007 Entry Draft and Anaheim's 3rd round choice (later traded to San Jose - San Jose selected Tyson Sexsmith) in 2007 Entry Draft, November 13, 2006. • Missed majority of 2006-07 season recovering from a shoulder injury and as a healthy reserve.

PAVELSKI, Joe

(pah-VEHL-skee, JOH) **S.J.**

Center. Shoots left. 5'11", 195 lbs. Born, Plover, WI, July 11, 1984. San Jose's 7th choice, 205th overall, in 2003 Entry Draft.

Season	Club	League	GP	G	A	Pts	PIM	PP	SH	GW	S	%	+/-	TF	F%	Min	GP	G	A	Pts	PIM	PP	SH	GW	Min
2002-03	Waterloo	USHL	60	36	33	69	32	....	....	....	....	....	....	....	....	....	7	5	7	12	8	....	....	....	....
2003-04	Waterloo	USHL	54	21	31	52	58	....	....	....	....	....	....	....	....	....	12	6	6	12	10	....	....	....	....
2004-05	U. of Wisconsin	WCHA	41	16	29	45	26	....	....	....	....	....	....	....	....	....	....	....	....	....	....	....	....	....	....
2005-06	U. of Wisconsin	WCHA	43	23	33	56	34	....	....	....	....	....	....	....	....	....	....	....	....	....	....	....	....	....	....
2006-07	**San Jose**	**NHL**	46	14	14	28	18	5	0	3	111	12.6	4	389	48.6	15:02	6	1	0	1	0	0	0	0	10:27
	Worcester Sharks	AHL	16	8	18	26	8	....	....	....	....	....	....	....	....	....	....	....	....	....	....	....	....	....	....
	NHL Totals		**46**	**14**	**14**	**28**	**18**	**5**	**0**	**3**	**111**	**12.6**		**389**	**48.6**	**15:02**	**6**	**1**	**0**	**1**	**0**	**0**	**0**	**0**	**10:27**

USHL All-Rookie Team (2003) • USHL First All-Star Team (2003) • USHL Rookie of the Year (2003) • WCHA All-Rookie Team (2005) • WCHA Second All-Star Team (2006) • NCAA West Second All-American Team (2006)

PAYER, Serge

(pie-YAY, SAIRZH)

Center. Shoots left. 6', 191 lbs. Born, Rockland, Ont., May 7, 1979.

Season	Club	League	GP	G	A	Pts	PIM	PP	SH	GW	S	%	+/-	TF	F%	Min	GP	G	A	Pts	PIM	PP	SH	GW	Min
1994-95	Cumberland Colts	ODMHA	42	37	46	83	55	....	....	....	....	....	....	....	....	....	....	....	....	....	....	....	....	....	....
1995-96	Kitchener Rangers	OHL	66	8	16	24	18	....	....	....	....	....	....	....	....	....	12	0	2	2	2	....	....	....	....
1996-97	Kitchener Rangers	OHL	63	7	16	23	27	....	....	....	....	....	....	....	....	....	13	1	3	4	2	....	....	....	....
1997-98	Kitchener Rangers	OHL	44	20	21	41	51	....	....	....	....	....	....	....	....	....	6	3	0	3	7	....	....	....	....
1998-99	Kitchener Rangers	OHL	40	18	19	37	22	....	....	....	....	....	....	....	....	....	....	....	....	....	....	....	....	....	....
99-2000	Kitchener Rangers	OHL	44	10	26	36	53	....	....	....	....	....	....	....	....	....	5	0	3	3	6	....	....	....	....
2000-01	**Florida**	**NHL**	43	5	1	6	21	0	1	0	34	14.7	0	97	42.3	7:27	....	....	....	....	....	....	....	....	....
	Louisville Panthers	AHL	32	6	6	12	15	....	....	....	....	....	....	....	....	....	....	....	....	....	....	....	....	....	....
2001-02	Utah Grizzlies	AHL	20	6	2	8	9	....	....	....	....	....	....	....	....	....	....	....	....	....	....	....	....	....	....
2002-03	San Antonio	AHL	78	10	31	41	30	....	....	....	....	....	....	....	....	....	1	0	0	0	2	....	....	....	....
2003-04	**Ottawa**	**NHL**	5	0	1	1	2	0	0	0	2	0.0	1	43	46.5	10:30	....	....	....	....	....	....	....	....	....
	Binghamton	AHL	67	14	20	34	91	....	....	....	....	....	....	....	....	....	2	0	0	0	0	....	....	....	....
2004-05	San Antonio	AHL	3	1	1	2	4	....	....	....	....	....	....	....	....	....	....	....	....	....	....	....	....	....	....
2005-06	**Florida**	**NHL**	71	2	4	6	26	0	0	0	70	2.9	−7	543	47.5	9:53	....	....	....	....	....	....	....	....	....
2006-07	**Ottawa**	**NHL**	5	0	0	0	0	0	0	0	4	0.0	−1	13	61.5	7:01	....	....	....	....	....	....	....	....	....
	Binghamton	AHL	43	6	12	18	31	....	....	....	....	....	....	....	....	....	....	....	....	....	....	....	....	....	....
	NHL Totals		**124**	**7**	**6**	**13**	**49**	**0**	**1**	**0**	**110**	**6.4**		**696**	**47.0**	**8:57**	....	....	....	....	....	....	....	....	....

Signed as a free agent by **Florida**, September 30, 1997. • Missed majority of 2001-02 season recovering from back injury suffered in training camp, September, 2001. Traded to **Ottawa** by **Florida** for Ottawa's 9th round choice (Luke Beaverson) in 2004 Entry Draft, September 10, 2003. Signed as a free agent by **Florida**, July 23, 2004. Signed as a free agent by **Ottawa**, August 2, 2006.

PEAT, Stephen

(PEET, STEE-vehn)

Right wing. Shoots right. 6'3", 230 lbs. Born, Princeton, B.C., March 10, 1980. Anaheim's 2nd choice, 32nd overall, in 1998 Entry Draft.

Season	Club	League	GP	G	A	Pts	PIM	PP	SH	GW	S	%	+/-	TF	F%	Min	GP	G	A	Pts	PIM	PP	SH	GW	Min
1995-96	Langley Thunder	BCJHL	59	5	15	20	112	....	....	....	....	....	....	....	....	....	....	....	....	....	....	....	....	....	....
	Red Deer Rebels	WHL	1	0	0	0	0	....	....	....	....	....	....	....	....	....	....	....	....	....	....	....	....	....	....
1996-97	Red Deer Rebels	WHL	68	3	14	17	161	....	....	....	....	....	....	....	....	....	16	0	2	2	22	....	....	....	....
1997-98	Red Deer Rebels	WHL	63	6	12	18	189	....	....	....	....	....	....	....	....	....	5	0	0	0	8	....	....	....	....
1998-99	Red Deer Rebels	WHL	31	2	6	8	98	....	....	....	....	....	....	....	....	....	....	....	....	....	....	....	....	....	....
	Tri-City	WHL	5	0	0	0	19	....	....	....	....	....	....	....	....	....	....	....	....	....	....	....	....	....	....
99-2000	Tri-City	WHL	12	0	2	2	48	....	....	....	....	....	....	....	....	....	....	....	....	....	....	....	....	....	....
	Calgary Hitmen	WHL	23	0	8	8	100	....	....	....	....	....	....	....	....	....	13	0	1	1	33	....	....	....	....
2000-01	Portland Pirates	AHL	6	0	0	0	16	....	....	....	....	....	....	....	....	....	....	....	....	....	....	....	....	....	....
2001-02	**Washington**	**NHL**	38	2	2	4	85	0	0	0	11	18.2	−1	0	0.0	5:04	....	....	....	....	....	....	....	....	....
	Portland Pirates	AHL	17	2	2	4	57	....	....	....	....	....	....	....	....	....	....	....	....	....	....	....	....	....	....
2002-03	**Washington**	**NHL**	27	1	0	1	57	0	0	0	7	14.3	−3	0	0.0	4:09	....	....	....	....	....	....	....	....	....
	Portland Pirates	AHL	18	0	0	0	52	....	....	....	....	....	....	....	....	....	....	....	....	....	....	....	....	....	....
2003-04	**Washington**	**NHL**	64	5	0	5	90	0	0	0	21	23.8	−10	4	0.0	6:38	....	....	....	....	....	....	....	....	....
2004-05	Danbury Trashers	UHL	7	0	1	1	45	....	....	....	....	....	....	....	....	....	....	....	....	....	....	....	....	....	....
2005-06	**Washington**	**NHL**	1	0	0	0	2	0	0	0	2	0.0	−2	0	0.0	4:47	....	....	....	....	....	....	....	....	....
	Hershey Bears	AHL	5	0	1	1	7	....	....	....	....	....	....	....	....	....	....	....	....	....	....	....	....	....	....
	Lowell	AHL	3	1	1	2	23	....	....	....	....	....	....	....	....	....	....	....	....	....	....	....	....	....	....
2006-07	Albany River Rats	AHL	1	0	0	0	0	....	....	....	....	....	....	....	....	....	....	....	....	....	....	....	....	....	....
	NHL Totals		**130**	**8**	**2**	**10**	**234**	**0**	**0**	**0**	**41**	**19.5**		**4**	**0.0**	**5:38**	....	....	....	....	....	....	....	....	....

• Missed majority of 1999-2000 season recovering from injuries sustained off ice, February 8, 2000. Rights traded to **Washington** by **Anaheim** for Washington's 4th round choice (later traded to Montreal – later traded to Pittsburgh – Pittsburgh selected Michel Ouellet) in 2000 Entry Draft, June 1, 2000. • Missed majority of 2000-01 season recovering from groin injury suffered in training camp, September 29, 2000. Signed as a free agent by **Danbury** (UHL), December 16, 2004. Traded to **Carolina** by **Washington** for Colin Forbes, December 28, 2005. • Missed majority of 2005-06 and 2006-07 seasons recovering from a groin/abdominal injury.

PECA, Michael
(PEH-kuh, MIGH-kuhl)

Center. Shoots right. 5'11", 190 lbs. Born, Toronto, Ont., March 26, 1974. Vancouver's 2nd choice, 40th overall, in 1992 Entry Draft.

			Regular Season															Playoffs								
Season	**Club**	**League**	**GP**	**G**	**A**	**Pts**	**PIM**	**PP**	**SH**	**GW**	**S**	**%**	**+/-**	**TF**	**F%**	**Min**	**GP**	**G**	**A**	**Pts**	**PIM**	**PP**	**SH**	**GW**	**Min**
1989-90	Tor. Red Wings	MTHL	39	42	53	95	40	....	....	....	....	....	....	....	....	....	....	....	....	....	....	....	....	....	....
1990-91	Sudbury Wolves	OHL	62	14	27	41	24	....	....	....	....	....	....	....	....	....	5	1	0	1	7	....	....	....	....
1991-92	Sudbury Wolves	OHL	39	16	34	50	61	....	....	....	....	....	....	....	....	....	....	....	....	....	....	....	....	....	....
	Ottawa 67's	OHL	27	8	17	25	32	....	....	....	....	....	....	....	....	....	11	6	10	16	6	....	....	....	....
1992-93	Ottawa 67's	OHL	55	38	64	102	80	....	....	....	....	....	....	....	....	....	....	....	....	....	....	....	....	....	....
	Hamilton	AHL	9	6	3	9	11	....	....	....	....	....	....	....	....	....	....	....	....	....	....	....	....	....	....
1993-94	Ottawa 67's	OHL	55	50	63	113	101	....	....	....	....	....	....	....	....	....	17	7	22	29	30	....	....	....	....
	Vancouver	**NHL**	**4**	**0**	**0**	**0**	**2**	**0**	**0**	**0**	**5**	**0.0**	**-1**	....	....	....	....	....	....	....	....	....	....	....	....
1994-95	Syracuse Crunch	AHL	35	10	24	34	75	....	....	....	....	....	....	....	....	....	....	....	....	....	....	....	....	....	....
	Vancouver	**NHL**	**33**	**6**	**6**	**12**	**30**	**2**	**0**	**1**	**46**	**13.0**	**-6**	....	....	....	**5**	**0**	**1**	**1**	**8**	**0**	**0**	**0**	....
1995-96	**Buffalo**	**NHL**	**68**	**11**	**20**	**31**	**67**	**4**	**3**	**1**	**109**	**10.1**	**-1**	....	....	....	....	....	....	....	....	....	....	....	....
1996-97	**Buffalo**	**NHL**	**79**	**20**	**29**	**49**	**80**	**5**	**6**	**4**	**137**	**14.6**	**26**	....	....	....	**10**	**0**	**2**	**2**	**8**	**0**	**0**	**0**	....
1997-98	**Buffalo**	**NHL**	**61**	**18**	**22**	**40**	**57**	**6**	**5**	**1**	**132**	**13.6**	**12**	....	....	....	**13**	**3**	**2**	**5**	**8**	**0**	**0**	**1**	....
1998-99	**Buffalo**	**NHL**	**82**	**27**	**29**	**56**	**81**	**10**	**0**	**8**	**199**	**13.6**	**7**	**1855**	**49.4**	**20:44**	**21**	**5**	**8**	**13**	**18**	**2**	**1**	**0**	**22:28**
99-2000	**Buffalo**	**NHL**	**73**	**20**	**21**	**41**	**67**	**2**	**0**	**3**	**144**	**13.9**	**6**	**1604**	**48.6**	**19:57**	**5**	**0**	**1**	**1**	**4**	**0**	**0**	**0**	**18:42**
2000-01			DID NOT PLAY																						
2001-02	**NY Islanders**	**NHL**	**80**	**25**	**35**	**60**	**62**	**3**	**6**	**5**	**168**	**14.9**	**19**	**1804**	**52.4**	**20:14**	**5**	**1**	**0**	**1**	**2**	**0**	**0**	**0**	**16:15**
	Canada	Olympics	6	0	2	2	2	....	....	....	....	....	....	....	....	....	....	....	....	....	....	....	....	....	....
2002-03	**NY Islanders**	**NHL**	**66**	**13**	**29**	**42**	**43**	**4**	**2**	**2**	**117**	**11.1**	**-4**	**1315**	**53.0**	**18:57**	**5**	**0**	**0**	**0**	**4**	**0**	**0**	**0**	**20:10**
2003-04	**NY Islanders**	**NHL**	**76**	**11**	**29**	**40**	**71**	**0**	**1**	**0**	**117**	**9.4**	**17**	**1674**	**53.1**	**19:02**	**5**	**0**	**0**	**0**	**6**	**0**	**0**	**0**	**23:01**
2004-05			DID NOT PLAY																						
2005-06	**Edmonton**	**NHL**	**71**	**9**	**14**	**23**	**56**	**2**	**2**	**1**	**108**	**8.3**	**-4**	**1048**	**54.9**	**16:39**	**24**	**6**	**5**	**11**	**20**	**0**	**1**	**1**	**19:06**
2006-07	**Toronto**	**NHL**	**35**	**4**	**11**	**15**	**60**	**0**	**0**	**2**	**42**	**9.5**	**2**	**615**	**49.9**	**17:25**	....	....	....	....	....	....	....	....	....
	NHL Totals		**728**	**164**	**245**	**409**	**676**	**38**	**25**	**28**	**1324**	**12.4**		**9915**	**51.5**	**19:11**	**93**	**15**	**19**	**34**	**78**	**2**	**2**	**2**	**20:19**

Frank J. Selke Trophy (1997, 2002)

Traded to **Buffalo** by **Vancouver** with Mike Wilson and Vancouver's 1st round choice (Jay McKee) in 1995 Entry Draft for Alexander Mogilny and Buffalo's 5th round choice (Todd Norman) in 1995 Entry Draft, July 8, 1995. • Missed entire 2000-01 season after failing to come to contract terms with **Buffalo**. Rights traded to **NY Islanders** by **Buffalo** for Tim Connolly and Taylor Pyatt, June 24, 2001. Traded to **Edmonton** by **NY Islanders** for Mike York and Edmonton's 4th round choice (later traded to Colorado - Colorado selected Kevin Montgomery) in 2006 Entry Draft, August 3, 2005. Signed as a free agent by **Toronto**, July 18, 2006. • Missed remainder of 2006-07 season recovering from leg injury suffered in game vs. Chicago, December 22, 2006.

PELLEY, Rod
(PEHL-lee, RAWD) **N.J.**

Center. Shoots left. 6', 200 lbs. Born, Kitimat, B.C., September 1, 1984.

Season	**Club**	**League**	**GP**	**G**	**A**	**Pts**	**PIM**	**PP**	**SH**	**GW**	**S**	**%**	**+/-**	**TF**	**F%**	**Min**	**GP**	**G**	**A**	**Pts**	**PIM**	**PP**	**SH**	**GW**	**Min**
2002-03	Ohio State	CCHA	43	8	3	11	26	....	....	....	....	....	....	....	....	....	....	....	....	....	....	....	....	....	....
2003-04	Ohio State	CCHA	42	10	12	22	38	....	....	....	....	....	....	....	....	....	....	....	....	....	....	....	....	....	....
2004-05	Ohio State	CCHA	41	22	19	41	54	....	....	....	....	....	....	....	....	....	....	....	....	....	....	....	....	....	....
2005-06	Ohio State	CCHA	39	7	7	14	42	....	....	....	....	....	....	....	....	....	....	....	....	....	....	....	....	....	....
2006-07	**New Jersey**	**NHL**	**9**	**0**	**0**	**0**	**0**	**0**	**0**	**0**	**8**	**0.0**	**-3**	**98**	**40.8**	**11:00**	....	....	....	....	....	....	....	....	....
	Lowell Devils	AHL	65	17	12	29	35	....	....	....	....	....	....	....	....	....	....	....	....	....	....	....	....	....	....
	NHL Totals		**9**	**0**	**0**	**0**	**0**	**0**	**0**	**0**	**8**	**0.0**		**98**	**40.8**	**11:00**	....	....	....	....	....	....	....	....	....

CCHA Second All-Star Team (2005)

Signed as a free agent by **New Jersey**, July 24, 2006.

PELTONEN, Ville
(PEHL-TOH-nen, VIHL-ee) **FLA.**

Left wing. Shoots left. 5'11", 182 lbs. Born, Vantaa, Finland, May 24, 1973. San Jose's 4th choice, 58th overall, in 1993 Entry Draft.

Season	**Club**	**League**	**GP**	**G**	**A**	**Pts**	**PIM**	**PP**	**SH**	**GW**	**S**	**%**	**+/-**	**TF**	**F%**	**Min**	**GP**	**G**	**A**	**Pts**	**PIM**	**PP**	**SH**	**GW**	**Min**
1989-90	HIFK Helsinki U18	Fin-U18	24	21	24	45	14	....	....	....	....	....	....	....	....	....	....	....	....	....	....	....	....	....	....
1990-91	HIFK Helsinki Jr.	Fin-Jr.	36	21	16	37	16	....	....	....	....	....	....	....	....	....	7	2	3	5	10	....	....	....	....
1991-92	HIFK Helsinki Jr.	Fin-Jr.	37	28	23	51	28	....	....	....	....	....	....	....	....	....	4	0	2	2	0	....	....	....	....
	HIFK Helsinki	Finland	6	0	0	0	0	....	....	....	....	....	....	....	....	....	....	....	....	....	....	....	....	....	....
1992-93	HIFK Helsinki Jr.	Fin-Jr.	2	4	2	6	4	....	....	....	....	....	....	....	....	....	....	....	....	....	....	....	....	....	....
	HIFK Helsinki	Finland	46	13	24	37	16	....	....	....	....	....	....	....	....	....	4	0	2	2	2	....	....	....	....
1993-94	HIFK Helsinki	Finland	43	16	22	38	14	....	....	....	....	....	....	....	....	....	3	0	0	0	2	....	....	....	....
	Finland	Olympics	8	4	3	7	0	....	....	....	....	....	....	....	....	....	....	....	....	....	....	....	....	....	....
1994-95	HIFK Helsinki	Finland	45	20	16	36	16	....	....	....	....	....	....	....	....	....	3	0	0	0	0	....	....	....	....
1995-96	**San Jose**	**NHL**	**31**	**2**	**11**	**13**	**14**	**0**	**0**	**0**	**58**	**3.4**	**-7**	....	....	....	....	....	....	....	....	....	....	....	....
	Kansas City	IHL	29	5	13	18	8	....	....	....	....	....	....	....	....	....	....	....	....	....	....	....	....	....	....
1996-97	**San Jose**	**NHL**	**28**	**2**	**3**	**5**	**0**	**1**	**0**	**0**	**35**	**5.7**	**-8**	....	....	....	....	....	....	....	....	....	....	....	....
	Kentucky	AHL	40	22	30	52	21	....	....	....	....	....	....	....	....	....	....	....	....	....	....	....	....	....	....
1997-98	V.Frolunda	Sweden	45	22	29	51	44	....	....	....	....	....	....	....	....	....	7	4	2	6	0	....	....	....	....
	Finland	Olympics	6	2	1	3	6	....	....	....	....	....	....	....	....	....	....	....	....	....	....	....	....	....	....
1998-99	**Nashville**	**NHL**	**14**	**5**	**5**	**10**	**2**	**1**	**0**	**0**	**31**	**16.1**	**1**	**0**	**0.0**	**15:54**	....	....	....	....	....	....	....	....	....
99-2000	**Nashville**	**NHL**	**79**	**6**	**22**	**28**	**22**	**2**	**0**	**2**	**125**	**4.8**	**-1**	**1**	**100.0**	**14:41**	....	....	....	....	....	....	....	....	....
2000-01	**Nashville**	**NHL**	**23**	**3**	**1**	**4**	**2**	**0**	**0**	**0**	**38**	**7.9**	**-7**	**2**	**0.0**	**11:40**	....	....	....	....	....	....	....	....	....
	Milwaukee	IHL	53	27	33	60	26	....	....	....	....	....	....	....	....	....	5	2	1	3	6	....	....	....	....
2001-02	Jokerit Helsinki	Finland	30	11	18	29	8	....	....	....	....	....	....	....	....	....	....	....	....	....	....	....	....	....	....
2002-03	Jokerit Helsinki	Finland	49	23	19	42	14	....	....	....	....	....	....	....	....	....	10	4	6	10	0	....	....	....	....
2003-04	HC Lugano	Swiss	48	28	44	72	14	....	....	....	....	....	....	....	....	....	16	4	7	11	8	....	....	....	....
2004-05	HC Lugano	Swiss	44	24	33	57	16	....	....	....	....	....	....	....	....	....	5	0	3	3	2	....	....	....	....
2005-06	HC Lugano	Swiss	39	22	25	47	22	....	....	....	....	....	....	....	....	....	17	*12	12	24	8	....	....	....	....
	Finland	Olympics	8	4	5	9	6	....	....	....	....	....	....	....	....	....	....	....	....	....	....	....	....	....	....
2006-07	**Florida**	**NHL**	**72**	**17**	**20**	**37**	**28**	**4**	**0**	**0**	**145**	**11.7**	**7**	**35**	**31.4**	**16:25**	....	....	....	....	....	....	....	....	....
	NHL Totals		**247**	**35**	**62**	**97**	**68**	**8**	**0**	**2**	**432**	**8.1**		**38**	**31.6**	**15:04**	....	....	....	....	....	....	....	....	....

IHL Second All-Star Team (2001)

Traded to **Nashville** by **San Jose** for Nashville's 5th round choice (later traded to Phoenix – Phoenix selected Josh Blackburn) in 1998 Entry Draft, June 26, 1998. • Missed majority of 1998-99 season recovering from shoulder surgery, December 10, 1998. Signed as a free agent by **Jokerit Helsinki** (Finland), April 26, 2001. Signed as a free agent by **Lugano** (Swiss), April 9, 2003. Signed as a free agent by **Florida**, June 15, 2006.

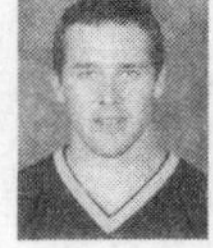

PENNER, Dustin
(PEH-nuhr, DUHS-tihn) **EDM.**

Left wing. Shoots left. 6'4", 245 lbs. Born, Winkler, Man., September 28, 1982.

Season	**Club**	**League**	**GP**	**G**	**A**	**Pts**	**PIM**	**PP**	**SH**	**GW**	**S**	**%**	**+/-**	**TF**	**F%**	**Min**	**GP**	**G**	**A**	**Pts**	**PIM**	**PP**	**SH**	**GW**	**Min**
2001-02	MSU - Bottineau	NJCAA	23	20	12	32	30	....	....	....	....	....	....	....	....	....	....	....	....	....	....	....	....	....	....
2002-03	U. of Maine	H-East	DID NOT PLAY – FRESHMAN																						
2003-04	U. of Maine	H-East	43	11	12	23	52	....	....	....	....	....	....	....	....	....	....	....	....	....	....	....	....	....	....
2004-05	Cincinnati	AHL	77	10	18	28	82	....	....	....	....	....	....	....	....	....	9	2	3	5	13	....	....	....	....
2005-06	**Anaheim**	**NHL**	**19**	**4**	**3**	**7**	**14**	**2**	**0**	**1**	**46**	**8.7**	**3**	**1**	**0.0**	**11:58**	**13**	**3**	**6**	**9**	**12**	**0**	**0**	**0**	**13:16**
	Portland Pirates	AHL	57	39	45	84	68	....	....	....	....	....	....	....	....	....	5	4	3	7	0	....	....	....	....
2006-07♦	**Anaheim**	**NHL**	**82**	**29**	**16**	**45**	**58**	**9**	**0**	**5**	**204**	**14.2**	**-2**	**58**	**46.6**	**13:59**	**21**	**3**	**5**	**8**	**2**	**0**	**0**	**2**	**14:05**
	NHL Totals		**101**	**33**	**19**	**52**	**72**	**11**	**0**	**6**	**250**	**13.2**		**59**	**45.8**	**13:36**	**34**	**6**	**11**	**17**	**14**	**0**	**0**	**2**	**13:46**

NCAA Championship All-Tournament Team (2004) • AHL Second All-Star Team (2006)

Signed as a free agent by **Anaheim**, May 12, 2004. Signed as a free agent by **Edmonton**, August 2, 2007.

PEREZHOGIN, Alexander
(pehr-eh-ZHOI-gihn, al-EHX-AN-duhr)

Left wing. Shoots left. 6', 205 lbs. Born, Ust-Kamenogorsk, USSR, August 10, 1983. Montreal's 2nd choice, 25th overall, in 2001 Entry Draft.

Season	**Club**	**League**	**GP**	**G**	**A**	**Pts**	**PIM**	**PP**	**SH**	**GW**	**S**	**%**	**+/-**	**TF**	**F%**	**Min**	**GP**	**G**	**A**	**Pts**	**PIM**	**PP**	**SH**	**GW**	**Min**
1998-99	Omsk 2	Russia-4	10	3	4	7	0	....	....	....	....	....	....	....	....	....	....	....	....	....	....	....	....	....	....
99-2000	Omsk 2	Russia-3	22	12	11	23	12	....	....	....	....	....	....	....	....	....	....	....	....	....	....	....	....	....	....
	Avangard Omsk	Russia	1	0	0	0	0	....	....	....	....	....	....	....	....	....	....	....	....	....	....	....	....	....	....
2000-01	Omsk 2	Russia-3	41	47	24	71	40	....	....	....	....	....	....	....	....	....	....	....	....	....	....	....	....	....	....
	Avangard Omsk	Russia	....	....	....	....	....	....	....	....	....	....	....	....	....	....	1	0	0	0	0	....	....	....	....
2001-02	Avangard Omsk	Russia	4	1	0	1	4	....	....	....	....	....	....	....	....	....	....	....	....	....	....	....	....	....	....
	Mostovik Kurgan	Russia-2	19	14	10	24	10	....	....	....	....	....	....	....	....	....	....	....	....	....	....	....	....	....	....
2002-03	Avangard Omsk	Russia	48	15	6	21	28	....	....	....	....	....	....	....	....	....	8	0	2	2	4	....	....	....	....
2003-04	Hamilton	AHL	77	23	27	50	52	....	....	....	....	....	....	....	....	....	5	3	3	6	16	....	....	....	....
2004-05	Avangard Omsk	Russia	43	15	18	33	18	....	....	....	....	....	....	....	....	....	11	3	2	5	8	....	....	....	....

			Regular Season														Playoffs								
Season	Club	League	GP	G	A	Pts	PIM	PP	SH	GW	S	%	+/-	TF	F%	Min	GP	G	A	Pts	PIM	PP	SH	GW	Min
2005-06	**Montreal**	**NHL**	**67**	**9**	**10**	**19**	**38**	**3**	**0**	**2**	**109**	**8.3**	**5**	**6**	**33.3**	**10:08**	**6**	**1**	**1**	**2**	**4**	**0**	**0**	**0**	**13:42**
	Hamilton	AHL	11	0	2	2	8	....	....	....	....	....	....	....	....	....	....	....	....	....	....	....	....	....	....
2006-07	**Montreal**	**NHL**	**61**	**6**	**9**	**15**	**48**	**1**	**0**	**1**	**103**	**5.8**	**11**	**7**	**0.0**	**11:51**	....	....	....	....	....	....	....	....	....
	NHL Totals		**128**	**15**	**19**	**34**	**86**	**4**	**0**	**3**	**212**	**7.1**		**13**	**15.4**	**10:57**	**6**	**1**	**1**	**2**	**4**	**0**	**0**	**0**	**13:42**

PERRAULT, Joel

(pair-OH, JOHL) **PHX.**

Center. Shoots right. 6'1", 197 lbs. Born, Montreal, Que., April 6, 1983. Anaheim's 7th choice, 137th overall, in 2001 Entry Draft.

Season	Club	League	GP	G	A	Pts	PIM	PP	SH	GW	S	%	+/-	TF	F%	Min	GP	G	A	Pts	PIM	PP	SH	GW	Min
99-2000	Antoine-Girouard	QAAA	19	4	7	11	6	....	....	....	....	....	....	....	....	....	....	....	....	....	....	....	....	....	....
2000-01	Baie-Comeau	QMJHL	68	10	14	24	46	....	....	....	....	....	....	....	....	....	11	1	1	2	10	....	....	....	....
2001-02	Baie-Comeau	QMJHL	57	18	44	62	96	....	....	....	....	....	....	....	....	....	5	2	0	2	6	....	....	....	....
2002-03	Baie-Comeau	QMJHL	70	51	65	*116	93	....	....	....	....	....	....	....	....	....	12	3	7	10	14	....	....	....	....
2003-04	Cincinnati	AHL	65	14	14	28	38	....	....	....	....	....	....	....	....	....	9	1	1	2	2	....	....	....	....
2004-05	Cincinnati	AHL	51	9	19	28	40	....	....	....	....	....	....	....	....	....	....	....	....	....	....	....	....	....	....
2005-06	Portland Pirates	AHL	25	12	12	24	20	....	....	....	....	....	....	....	....	....	....	....	....	....	....	....	....	....	....
	Phoenix	**NHL**	**5**	**1**	**1**	**2**	**2**	**0**	**0**	**0**	**7**	**14.3**	**0**	**47**	**34.0**	**11:29**	....	....	....	....	....	....	....	....	....
	San Antonio	AHL	12	1	6	7	4	....	....	....	....	....	....	....	....	....	....	....	....	....	....	....	....	....	....
2006-07	**Phoenix**	**NHL**	**15**	**1**	**2**	**3**	**14**	**0**	**0**	**0**	**18**	**9.1**	**−3**	**109**	**82.6**	**11:29**	....	....	....	....	....	....	....	....	....
	St. Louis	**NHL**	**11**	**0**	**0**	**0**	**0**	**0**	**0**	**0**	**13**	**0.0**	**−4**	**20**	**25.0**	**8:19**	....	....	....	....	....	....	....	....	....
	Peoria Rivermen	AHL	2	0	2	2	7	....	....	....	....	....	....	....	....	....	....	....	....	....	....	....	....	....	....
	San Antonio	AHL	21	10	4	14	8	....	....	....	....	....	....	....	....	....	....	....	....	....	....	....	....	....	....
	NHL Totals		**31**	**2**	**3**	**5**	**16**	**0**	**0**	**0**	**38**	**5.3**		**176**	**63.1**	**10:21**	....	....	....	....	....	....	....	....	....

QMJHL First All-Star Team (2003) • Canadian Major Junior First All-Star Team (2003)

Traded to **Phoenix** by **Anaheim** for Sean O'Donnell, March 9, 2006. Claimed on waivers by **St. Louis** from **Phoenix**, October 31, 2006. Claimed on waivers by **Phoenix** from **St. Louis**, December 19, 2006.

PERREAULT, Yanic

(pair-OH, YAH-nihk) **CHI.**

Center. Shoots left. 5'11", 185 lbs. Born, Sherbrooke, Que., April 4, 1971. Toronto's 1st choice, 47th overall, in 1991 Entry Draft.

Season	Club	League	GP	G	A	Pts	PIM	PP	SH	GW	S	%	+/-	TF	F%	Min	GP	G	A	Pts	PIM	PP	SH	GW	Min
1987-88	Montreal L'est	QAAA	42	*70	57	*127	14	....	....	....	....	....	....	....	....	....	8	12	10	22	6	....	....	....	....
1988-89	Trois-Rivieres	QMJHL	70	53	55	108	48	....	....	....	....	....	....	....	....	....	....	....	....	....	....	....	....	....	....
1989-90	Trois-Rivieres	QMJHL	63	51	63	114	75	....	....	....	....	....	....	....	....	....	7	6	5	11	19	....	....	....	....
1990-91	Trois-Rivieres	QMJHL	67	*87	98	*185	103	....	....	....	....	....	....	....	....	....	6	4	7	11	6	....	....	....	....
1991-92	St. John's	AHL	62	38	38	76	19	....	....	....	....	....	....	....	....	....	16	7	8	15	4	....	....	....	....
1992-93	St. John's	AHL	79	49	46	95	56	....	....	....	....	....	....	....	....	....	9	4	5	9	2	....	....	....	....
1993-94	**Toronto**	**NHL**	**13**	**3**	**3**	**6**	**0**	**2**	**0**	**0**	**24**	**12.5**	**1**	....	....	....	....	....	....	....	....	....	....	....	....
	St. John's	AHL	62	45	60	105	38	....	....	....	....	....	....	....	....	....	11	*12	6	18	14	....	....	....	....
1994-95	Phoenix	IHL	68	51	48	99	52	....	....	....	....	....	....	....	....	....	....	....	....	....	....	....	....	....	....
	Los Angeles	**NHL**	**26**	**2**	**5**	**7**	**20**	**0**	**0**	**1**	**43**	**4.7**	**3**	....	....	....	....	....	....	....	....	....	....	....	....
1995-96	**Los Angeles**	**NHL**	**78**	**25**	**24**	**49**	**16**	**8**	**3**	**7**	**175**	**14.3**	**−11**	....	....	....	....	....	....	....	....	....	....	....	....
1996-97	**Los Angeles**	**NHL**	**41**	**11**	**14**	**25**	**20**	**1**	**1**	**0**	**98**	**11.2**	**0**	....	....	....	....	....	....	....	....	....	....	....	....
1997-98	**Los Angeles**	**NHL**	**79**	**28**	**20**	**48**	**32**	**3**	**2**	**3**	**206**	**13.6**	**6**	....	....	....	**4**	**1**	**2**	**3**	**6**	**1**	**0**	**0**	....
1998-99	**Los Angeles**	**NHL**	**64**	**10**	**17**	**27**	**30**	**2**	**2**	**1**	**113**	**8.8**	**−3**	**1024**	**56.5**	**15:24**	....	....	....	....	....	....	....	....	....
	Toronto	**NHL**	**12**	**7**	**8**	**15**	**12**	**2**	**1**	**2**	**28**	**25.0**	**10**	**164**	**62.8**	**13:20**	**17**	**3**	**6**	**9**	**6**	**0**	**0**	**2**	**15:55**
99-2000	**Toronto**	**NHL**	**58**	**18**	**27**	**45**	**22**	**5**	**0**	**4**	**114**	**15.8**	**3**	**987**	**61.8**	**15:18**	**1**	**0**	**1**	**1**	**0**	**0**	**0**	**0**	**12:56**
2000-01	**Toronto**	**NHL**	**76**	**24**	**28**	**52**	**52**	**5**	**0**	**2**	**134**	**17.9**	**0**	**1055**	**62.7**	**14:01**	**11**	**2**	**3**	**5**	**4**	**1**	**0**	**1**	**12:20**
2001-02	**Montreal**	**NHL**	**82**	**27**	**29**	**56**	**40**	**6**	**0**	**7**	**156**	**17.3**	**−3**	**1485**	**61.3**	**16:47**	**11**	**3**	**5**	**8**	**0**	**2**	**0**	**1**	**13:05**
2002-03	**Montreal**	**NHL**	**73**	**24**	**22**	**46**	**30**	**7**	**0**	**4**	**145**	**16.6**	**−11**	**1156**	**62.9**	**16:05**	....	....	....	....	....	....	....	....	....
2003-04	**Montreal**	**NHL**	**69**	**16**	**15**	**31**	**40**	**5**	**0**	**3**	**114**	**14.0**	**−10**	**861**	**65.2**	**13:46**	**9**	**2**	**2**	**4**	**0**	**0**	**0**	**1**	**12:29**
2004-05			DID NOT PLAY																						
2005-06	**Nashville**	**NHL**	**69**	**22**	**35**	**57**	**30**	**10**	**0**	**2**	**145**	**15.2**	**−3**	**899**	**62.2**	**14:57**	**1**	**0**	**0**	**0**	**2**	**0**	**0**	**0**	**10:09**
2006-07	**Phoenix**	**NHL**	**49**	**19**	**14**	**33**	**30**	**7**	**0**	**5**	**101**	**18.8**	**−2**	**666**	**62.6**	**17:35**	....	....	....	....	....	....	....	....	....
	Toronto	**NHL**	**17**	**2**	**3**	**5**	**4**	**0**	**0**	**0**	**24**	**8.3**	**1**	**140**	**63.6**	**9:42**	....	....	....	....	....	....	....	....	....
	NHL Totals		**806**	**238**	**264**	**502**	**378**	**63**	**9**	**41**	**1620**	**14.7**		**8437**	**61.8**	**15:13**	**54**	**11**	**19**	**30**	**18**	**4**	**0**	**5**	**13:43**

QMJHL All-Rookie Team (1989) • QMJHL Offensive Rookie of the Year (1989) • Canadian Major Junior Rookie of the Year (1989) • QMJHL First All-Star Team (1991) • QMJHL MVP (1991)

Played in NHL All-Star Game (2007)

Traded to **Los Angeles** by **Toronto** for Los Angeles' 4th round choice (later traded to Philadelphia – later traded back to Los Angeles – Los Angeles selected Mikael Simons) in 1996 Entry Draft, July 11, 1994. Traded to **Toronto** by **Los Angeles** for Jason Podollan and Toronto's 3rd round choice (Cory Campbell) in 1999 Entry Draft, March 23, 1999. Signed as a free agent by **Montreal**, July 4, 2001. Signed as a free agent by **Nashville**, October 3, 2005. Signed as a free agent by **Phoenix**, October 29, 2006. Traded to **Toronto** by **Phoenix** with Phoenix's 5th round choice in 2008 Entry Draft for Brendan Bell and Toronto's 2nd round choice in 2008 Entry Draft, February 27, 2007. Signed as a free agent by **Chicago**, July 1, 2007.

PERRIN, Eric

(peh-REHN, AIR-ihk) **ATL.**

Center. Shoots left. 5'9", 180 lbs. Born, Laval, Que., November 1, 1975.

Season	Club	League	GP	G	A	Pts	PIM	PP	SH	GW	S	%	+/-	TF	F%	Min	GP	G	A	Pts	PIM	PP	SH	GW	Min
1991-92	Laval-Laurentides	QAAA	42	41	50	91	....	....	....	....	....	....	....	....	....	....	12	7	16	23	....	....	....	....	....
1992-93	Laval College	CEGEP	STATISTICS NOT AVAILABLE																						
1993-94	U. of Vermont	ECAC	32	24	21	45	34	....	....	....	....	....	....	....	....	....	....	....	....	....	....	....	....	....	....
1994-95	U. of Vermont	ECAC	35	28	39	67	38	....	....	....	....	....	....	....	....	....	....	....	....	....	....	....	....	....	....
1995-96	U. of Vermont	ECAC	38	29	56	85	38	....	....	....	....	....	....	....	....	....	....	....	....	....	....	....	....	....	....
1996-97	U. of Vermont	ECAC	36	26	33	59	40	....	....	....	....	....	....	....	....	....	....	....	....	....	....	....	....	....	....
1997-98	Cleveland	IHL	69	12	31	43	34	....	....	....	....	....	....	....	....	....	....	....	....	....	....	....	....	....	....
	Quebec Rafales	IHL	13	2	12	14	4	....	....	....	....	....	....	....	....	....	....	....	....	....	....	....	....	....	....
1998-99	Kansas City	IHL	82	24	37	61	71	....	....	....	....	....	....	....	....	....	3	0	0	0	0	....	....	....	....
99-2000	Kansas City	IHL	21	3	15	18	16	....	....	....	....	....	....	....	....	....	....	....	....	....	....	....	....	....	....
2000-01	Jokerit Helsinki	Finland	6	1	1	2	4	....	....	....	....	....	....	....	....	....	....	....	....	....	....	....	....	....	....
	Assat Pori	Finland	43	15	23	38	70	....	....	....	....	....	....	....	....	....	....	....	....	....	....	....	....	....	....
2001-02	Assat Pori	Finland	45	13	13	26	16	....	....	....	....	....	....	....	....	....	....	....	....	....	....	....	....	....	....
	HPK Hameenlinna	Finland	12	5	10	15	4	....	....	....	....	....	....	....	....	....	8	2	4	6	6	....	....	....	....
2002-03	JYP Jyvaskyla	Finland	56	18	28	46	36	....	....	....	....	....	....	....	....	....	7	4	6	10	8	....	....	....	....
2003-04♦	**Tampa Bay**	**NHL**	**4**	**0**	**0**	**0**	**0**	**0**	**0**	**0**	**3**	**0.0**	**−1**	**30**	**60.0**	**8:32**	**12**	**0**	**1**	**1**	**6**	**0**	**0**	**0**	**5:20**
	Hershey Bears	AHL	71	21	54	75	49	....	....	....	....	....	....	....	....	....	....	....	....	....	....	....	....	....	....
2004-05	Hershey Bears	AHL	80	24	49	73	46	....	....	....	....	....	....	....	....	....	....	....	....	....	....	....	....	....	....
2005-06	SC Bern	Swiss	44	13	25	38	28	....	....	....	....	....	....	....	....	....	6	2	4	6	8	....	....	....	....
2006-07	**Tampa Bay**	**NHL**	**82**	**13**	**23**	**36**	**30**	**2**	**1**	**0**	**151**	**8.6**	**−7**	**407**	**50.9**	**17:00**	**6**	**1**	**1**	**2**	**2**	**0**	**0**	**0**	**12:32**
	NHL Totals		**86**	**13**	**23**	**36**	**30**	**2**	**1**	**0**	**154**	**8.4**		**437**	**51.5**	**16:37**	**18**	**1**	**2**	**3**	**8**	**0**	**0**	**0**	**7:44**

ECAC All-Rookie Team (1994) • ECAC Rookie of the Year (1994) • ECAC First All-Star Team (1995, 1996) • ECAC Player of the Year (1996) • NCAA East First All-American Team (1996) • AHL First All-Star Team (2004)

Signed as a free agent by **Tampa Bay**, June 19, 2003. Signed as a free agent by **Bern** (Swiss), August 22, 2005. Signed as a free agent by **Atlanta**, July 1, 2007.

PERROTT, Nathan

(pair-OH, NAY-thuhn)

Right wing. Shoots right. 6', 225 lbs. Born, Owen Sound, Ont., December 8, 1976. New Jersey's 2nd choice, 44th overall, in 1995 Entry Draft.

Season	Club	League	GP	G	A	Pts	PIM	PP	SH	GW	S	%	+/-	TF	F%	Min	GP	G	A	Pts	PIM	PP	SH	GW	Min
1992-93	Walkerton	OHA-C	25	6	13	19	45	....	....	....	....	....	....	....	....	....	....	....	....	....	....	....	....	....	....
1993-94	St. Mary's Lincolns	OHA-B	41	11	26	37	249	....	....	....	....	....	....	....	....	....	....	....	....	....	....	....	....	....	....
1994-95	Oshawa Generals	OHL	63	18	28	46	233	....	....	....	....	....	....	....	....	....	2	1	1	2	9	....	....	....	....
1995-96	Oshawa Generals	OHL	59	30	32	62	158	....	....	....	....	....	....	....	....	....	5	2	3	5	8	....	....	....	....
	Albany River Rats	AHL	4	0	0	0	12	....	....	....	....	....	....	....	....	....	....	....	....	....	....	....	....	....	....
1996-97	Oshawa Generals	OHL	5	1	0	1	17	....	....	....	....	....	....	....	....	....	....	....	....	....	....	....	....	....	....
	Sault Ste. Marie	OHL	37	18	23	41	120	....	....	....	....	....	....	....	....	....	11	5	5	10	60	....	....	....	....
1997-98	Indianapolis Ice	IHL	31	4	3	7	76	....	....	....	....	....	....	....	....	....	....	....	....	....	....	....	....	....	....
	Jacksonville	ECHL	30	6	8	14	135	....	....	....	....	....	....	....	....	....	....	....	....	....	....	....	....	....	....
1998-99	Indianapolis Ice	IHL	72	14	11	25	307	....	....	....	....	....	....	....	....	....	7	3	1	4	45	....	....	....	....
99-2000	Cleveland	IHL	65	12	9	21	248	....	....	....	....	....	....	....	....	....	9	2	1	3	19	....	....	....	....
2000-01	Norfolk Admirals	AHL	73	11	17	28	268	....	....	....	....	....	....	....	....	....	9	2	0	2	18	....	....	....	....
2001-02	Norfolk Admirals	AHL	2	0	0	0	5	....	....	....	....	....	....	....	....	....	....	....	....	....	....	....	....	....	....
	Nashville	**NHL**	**22**	**1**	**2**	**3**	**74**	**0**	**0**	**1**	**7**	**14.3**	**−1**	**1**	**0.0**	**4:55**	....	....	....	....	....	....	....	....	....
	Milwaukee	AHL	56	6	10	16	190	....	....	....	....	....	....	....	....	....	....	....	....	....	....	....	....	....	....
2002-03	**Nashville**	**NHL**	**1**	**0**	**0**	**0**	**5**	**0**	**0**	**0**	**0**	**0.0**	**0**	**0**	**0.0**	**4:13**	....	....	....	....	....	....	....	....	....
	Milwaukee	AHL	27	1	2	3	106	....	....	....	....	....	....	....	....	....	....	....	....	....	....	....	....	....	....
	St. John's	AHL	36	7	8	15	97	....	....	....	....	....	....	....	....	....	....	....	....	....	....	....	....	....	....

			Regular Season														Playoffs								
Season	Club	League	GP	G	A	Pts	PIM	PP	SH	GW	S	%	+/-	TF	F%	Min	GP	G	A	Pts	PIM	PP	SH	GW	Min
2003-04	**Toronto**	**NHL**	40	1	2	3	116	0	0	0	47	2.1	–1	5	20.0	7:40	....	....	....	....	....	....	....	....	....
2004-05	St. John's	AHL	60	16	12	28	276	....	....	....	....	....	....	....	....	....	2	0	0	0	6	....	....	....	....
2005-06	**Toronto**	**NHL**	3	0	0	0	2	0	0	0	2	0.0	–5	0	0.0	9:07	....	....	....	....	....	....	....	....	....
	Dallas	**NHL**	23	2	1	3	54	0	0	1	17	11.8	2	3	33.3	5:02	....	....	....	....	....	....	....	....	....
2006-07	Toronto Marlies	AHL	4	0	0	0	19	....	....	....	....	....	....	....	....	....	....	....	....	....	....	....	....	....	....
	NHL Totals		89	4	5	9	251	0	0	2	73	5.5		9	22.2	6:19	....	....	....	....	....	....	....	....	....

Signed as a free agent by **Chicago**, August 27, 1997. Traded to **Nashville** by **Chicago** for future considerations, October 9, 2001. Traded to **Toronto** by **Nashville** for Bob Wren, Deceber 31, 2002. • Spent majority of 2003-04 season as a healthy reserve. Traded to **Dallas** by **Toronto** for Dallas' 6th round choice (Leo Komarov) in 2006 Entry Draft, November 6, 2005. Signed as a free agent by **Toronto** (AHL), October 15, 2006. Signed as a free agent by **Bern** (Swiss), February 21, 2007.

PERRY, Corey (PAIR-ee, KOH-ree) ANA.

Right wing. Shoots right. 6'3", 202 lbs. Born, Peterborough, Ont., May 16, 1985. Anaheim's 2nd choice, 28th overall, in 2003 Entry Draft.

Season	Club	League	GP	G	A	Pts	PIM	PP	SH	GW	S	%	+/-	TF	F%	Min	GP	G	A	Pts	PIM	PP	SH	GW	Min
2000-01	Peterborough	Minor-ON	64	69	46	115	20	....	....	....	....	....	....	....	....	....	3	3	0	3	0	....	....	....	....
2001-02	London Knights	OHL	67	28	31	59	56	....	....	....	....	....	....	....	....	....	12	2	3	5	30	....	....	....	....
2002-03	London Knights	OHL	67	25	53	78	145	....	....	....	....	....	....	....	....	....	14	7	16	23	27	....	....	....	....
2003-04	London Knights	OHL	66	40	*73	113	98	....	....	....	....	....	....	....	....	....	15	7	15	22	20	....	....	....	....
	Cincinnati	AHL	....	....	....	....	....	....	....	....	....	....	....	....	....	....	3	1	1	2	4	....	....	....	....
2004-05	London Knights	OHL	60	*47	*83	*130	117	....	....	....	....	....	....	....	....	....	18	11	*27	*38	46	....	....	....	....
2005-06	**Anaheim**	**NHL**	56	13	12	25	50	4	0	2	98	13.3	1	11	27.3	11:34	11	0	3	3	16	0	0	0	9:33
	Portland Pirates	AHL	19	16	18	34	32	....	....	....	....	....	....	....	....	....	1	1	0	1	0	....	....	....	....
2006-07 ♦	**Anaheim**	**NHL**	82	17	27	44	55	4	0	3	194	8.8	12	21	42.9	12:28	21	6	9	15	37	1	0	1	16:30
	NHL Totals		138	30	39	69	105	8	0	5	292	10.3		32	37.5	12:06	32	6	12	18	53	1	0	1	14:06

OHL First All-Star Team (2004, 2005) • Canadian Major Junior First All-Star Team (2005) • Memorial Cup Tournament All-Star Team (2005) • Stafford Smythe Memorial Trophy (Memorial Cup Tournament MVP) (2005)

PETERS, Andrew (PEE-tuhrz, AN-droo) BUF.

Left wing. Shoots left. 6'4", 228 lbs. Born, St. Catharines, Ont., May 5, 1980. Buffalo's 2nd choice, 34th overall, in 1998 Entry Draft.

Season	Club	League	GP	G	A	Pts	PIM	PP	SH	GW	S	%	+/-	TF	F%	Min	GP	G	A	Pts	PIM	PP	SH	GW	Min
1996-97	Georgetown	OPJHL	46	11	16	27	65	....	....	....	....	....	....	....	....	....	....	....	....	....	....	....	....	....	....
1997-98	Oshawa Generals	OHL	60	11	7	18	220	....	....	....	....	....	....	....	....	....	7	2	0	2	19	....	....	....	....
1998-99	Oshawa Generals	OHL	54	14	10	24	137	....	....	....	....	....	....	....	....	....	15	2	7	9	36	....	....	....	....
99-2000	Kitchener Rangers	OHL	42	6	13	19	95	....	....	....	....	....	....	....	....	....	4	0	1	1	14	....	....	....	....
2000-01	Rochester	AHL	49	0	4	4	118	....	....	....	....	....	....	....	....	....	....	....	....	....	....	....	....	....	....
2001-02	Rochester	AHL	67	4	1	5	*388	....	....	....	....	....	....	....	....	....	....	....	....	....	....	....	....	....	....
2002-03	Rochester	AHL	57	3	0	3	223	....	....	....	....	....	....	....	....	....	3	0	0	0	24	....	....	....	....
2003-04	**Buffalo**	**NHL**	42	2	0	2	151	0	0	0	19	10.5	–3	2	0.0	4:10	....	....	....	....	....	....	....	....	....
2004-05	Bodens IK	Sweden-2	22	2	4	6	195	....	....	....	....	....	....	....	....	....	....	....	....	....	....	....	....	....	....
2005-06	**Buffalo**	**NHL**	28	0	0	0	100	0	0	0	6	0.0	–2	2	100.0	3:16	....	....	....	....	....	....	....	....	....
2006-07	**Buffalo**	**NHL**	58	1	1	2	125	0	0	0	19	5.3	–1	0	0.0	3:46	....	....	....	....	....	....	....	....	....
	NHL Totals		128	3	1	4	376	0	0	0	44	6.8		4	50.0	3:48	....	....	....	....	....	....	....	....	....

Signed as a free agent by **Bodens** (Sweden-2), August 20, 2004.

PETERSEN, Toby (PEE-tuhr-suhn, TOH-bee) DAL.

Center. Shoots left. 5'10", 197 lbs. Born, Minneapolis, MN, October 27, 1978. Pittsburgh's 9th choice, 244th overall, in 1998 Entry Draft.

Season	Club	League	GP	G	A	Pts	PIM	PP	SH	GW	S	%	+/-	TF	F%	Min	GP	G	A	Pts	PIM	PP	SH	GW	Min
1995-96	Jefferson Jaguars	High-MN	25	29	30	59	....	....	....	....	....	....	....	....	....	....	....	....	....	....	....	....	....	....	....
1996-97	Colorado College	WCHA	40	17	21	38	18	....	....	....	....	....	....	....	....	....	....	....	....	....	....	....	....	....	....
1997-98	Colorado College	WCHA	40	16	17	33	34	....	....	....	....	....	....	....	....	....	....	....	....	....	....	....	....	....	....
1998-99	Colorado College	WCHA	21	12	12	24	2	....	....	....	....	....	....	....	....	....	....	....	....	....	....	....	....	....	....
99-2000	Colorado College	WCHA	37	14	19	33	8	....	....	....	....	....	....	....	....	....	....	....	....	....	....	....	....	....	....
2000-01	**Pittsburgh**	**NHL**	12	2	6	8	4	0	0	1	25	8.0	3	39	35.9	13:22	....	....	....	....	....	....	....	....	....
	Wilkes-Barre	AHL	73	26	41	67	22	....	....	....	....	....	....	....	....	....	21	7	6	13	4	....	....	....	....
2001-02	**Pittsburgh**	**NHL**	79	8	10	18	4	1	1	0	116	6.9	–15	338	45.6	12:16	....	....	....	....	....	....	....	....	....
2002-03	Wilkes-Barre	AHL	80	31	35	66	24	....	....	....	....	....	....	....	....	....	6	1	3	4	4	....	....	....	....
2003-04	Wilkes-Barre	AHL	62	15	29	44	4	....	....	....	....	....	....	....	....	....	21	2	10	12	12	....	....	....	....
2004-05	Edmonton	AHL	78	14	15	29	21	....	....	....	....	....	....	....	....	....	....	....	....	....	....	....	....	....	....
2005-06	**Edmonton**	**NHL**	....	....	....	....	....	....	....	....	....	....	....	....	....	....	2	1	0	1	0	0	0	0	6:23
	Iowa Stars	AHL	79	26	47	73	48	....	....	....	....	....	....	....	....	....	7	2	4	6	2	....	....	....	....
2006-07	**Edmonton**	**NHL**	64	6	9	15	4	0	2	1	92	6.5	–18	214	48.1	13:40	....	....	....	....	....	....	....	....	....
	Iowa Stars	AHL	7	2	6	8	0	....	....	....	....	....	....	....	....	....	....	....	....	....	....	....	....	....	....
	NHL Totals		155	16	25	41	12	1	3	2	233	6.9		591	45.9	12:56	2	1	0	1	0	0	0	0	6:23

WCHA All-Rookie Team (1997) • AHL All-Rookie Team (2001)

Signed as a free agent by **Edmonton**, July 30, 2004. Signed as a free agent by **Dallas**, July 6, 2007.

PETIOT, Richard (PEH-tee-awt, RIH-chuhrd) L.A.

Defense. Shoots left. 6'2", 190 lbs. Born, Daysland, Alta., August 20, 1982. Los Angeles' 6th choice, 116th overall, in 2001 Entry Draft.

Season	Club	League	GP	G	A	Pts	PIM	PP	SH	GW	S	%	+/-	TF	F%	Min	GP	G	A	Pts	PIM	PP	SH	GW	Min
2000-01	Camrose Kodiaks	AJHL	55	8	16	24	81	....	....	....	....	....	....	....	....	....	8	2	1	3	8	....	....	....	....
2001-02	Colorado College	WCHA	39	4	6	10	35	....	....	....	....	....	....	....	....	....	....	....	....	....	....	....	....	....	....
2002-03	Colorado College	WCHA	38	1	6	7	86	....	....	....	....	....	....	....	....	....	....	....	....	....	....	....	....	....	....
2003-04	Colorado College	WCHA	39	3	5	8	61	....	....	....	....	....	....	....	....	....	....	....	....	....	....	....	....	....	....
2004-05	Colorado College	WCHA	26	3	5	8	42	....	....	....	....	....	....	....	....	....	....	....	....	....	....	....	....	....	....
2005-06	**Los Angeles**	**NHL**	2	0	0	0	2	0	0	0	1	0.0	–2	0	0.0	4:47	....	....	....	....	....	....	....	....	....
	Manchester	AHL	63	4	10	14	52	....	....	....	....	....	....	....	....	....	7	1	0	1	6	....	....	....	....
2006-07	Manchester	AHL	13	1	1	2	25	....	....	....	....	....	....	....	....	....	2	0	0	0	2	....	....	....	....
	NHL Totals		2	0	0	0	2	0	0	0	1	0.0		0	0.0	4:47	....	....	....	....	....	....	....	....	....

AJHL All-Rookie Team (2001) • AJHL South Second All-Star Team (2001)

• Missed majority of 2006-07 season recovering from a knee injury.

PETROVICKY, Ronald (PEHT-roh-vih-kee, RAW-nohld)

Right wing. Shoots right. 5'11", 190 lbs. Born, Zilina, Czech., February 15, 1977. Calgary's 9th choice, 228th overall, in 1996 Entry Draft.

Season	Club	League	GP	G	A	Pts	PIM	PP	SH	GW	S	%	+/-	TF	F%	Min	GP	G	A	Pts	PIM	PP	SH	GW	Min
1993-94	Dukla Trencin Jr.	Slovak-Jr.	36	28	27	55	42	....	....	....	....	....	....	....	....	....	....	....	....	....	....	....	....	....	....
	Dukla Trencin	Slovakia	1	0	0	0	0	....	....	....	....	....	....	....	....	....	....	....	....	....	....	....	....	....	....
1994-95	Tri-City	WHL	39	4	11	15	86	....	....	....	....	....	....	....	....	....	....	....	....	....	....	....	....	....	....
	Prince George	WHL	21	4	6	10	37	....	....	....	....	....	....	....	....	....	....	....	....	....	....	....	....	....	....
1995-96	Prince George	WHL	39	19	21	40	61	....	....	....	....	....	....	....	....	....	....	....	....	....	....	....	....	....	....
1996-97	Prince George	WHL	72	32	37	69	119	....	....	....	....	....	....	....	....	....	15	4	9	13	31	....	....	....	....
1997-98	Regina Pats	WHL	71	64	49	113	168	....	....	....	....	....	....	....	....	....	9	2	4	6	11	....	....	....	....
1998-99	Saint John Flames	AHL	78	12	21	33	114	....	....	....	....	....	....	....	....	....	7	1	2	3	19	....	....	....	....
99-2000	Saint John Flames	AHL	67	23	33	56	131	....	....	....	....	....	....	....	....	....	3	1	1	2	6	....	....	....	....
2000-01	**Calgary**	**NHL**	30	4	5	9	54	1	0	1	30	13.3	0	7	42.9	11:33	....	....	....	....	....	....	....	....	....
2001-02	**Calgary**	**NHL**	77	5	7	12	85	1	0	1	78	6.4	0	28	46.4	11:42	....	....	....	....	....	....	....	....	....
2002-03	**NY Rangers**	**NHL**	66	5	9	14	77	2	1	1	65	7.7	–12	52	42.3	12:25	....	....	....	....	....	....	....	....	....
2003-04	**Atlanta**	**NHL**	78	16	15	31	123	0	0	1	102	15.7	–9	27	40.7	14:16	....	....	....	....	....	....	....	....	....
2004-05	MsHK SKP Zilina	Slovakia	34	10	9	19	34	....	....	....	....	....	....	....	....	....	....	....	....	....	....	....	....	....	....
	Brynas IF Gavle	Sweden	10	0	5	5	27	....	....	....	....	....	....	....	....	....	....	....	....	....	....	....	....	....	....
	Brynas IF Gavle	Sweden-Q	9	0	2	2	0	....	....	....	....	....	....	....	....	....	....	....	....	....	....	....	....	....	....
2005-06	**Atlanta**	**NHL**	60	8	12	20	62	2	0	2	70	11.4	–8	25	52.0	11:53	....	....	....	....	....	....	....	....	....
	Slovakia	Olympics	6	1	0	1	2	....	....	....	....	....	....	....	....	....	....	....	....	....	....	....	....	....	....
2006-07	**Pittsburgh**	**NHL**	31	3	3	6	28	0	0	1	27	11.1	4	4	50.0	8:20	3	0	0	0	2	0	0	0	5:10
	Wilkes-Barre	AHL	4	0	0	0	4	....	....	....	....	....	....	....	....	....	....	....	....	....	....	....	....	....	....
	NHL Totals		342	41	51	92	429	6	1	7	372	11.0		143	44.8	12:08	3	0	0	0	2	0	0	0	5:10

WHL East Second All-Star Team (1998)

• Missed majority of 2000-01 season recovering from wrist injury suffered in game vs. Detroit, October 5, 2000. Claimed by **NY Rangers** from **Calgary** in Waiver Draft, October 4, 2002. Claimed by **Atlanta** from **NY Rangers** in Waiver Draft, October 3, 2003. Signed as a free agent by **Zilina** (Slovakia), September 17, 2004. Signed as a free agent by **Gavle** (Sweden), January 23, 2005. Signed as a free agent by **Pittsburgh**, July 24, 2006. • Missed majority of 2006-07 season recovering from pre-season hip surgery.

PETTINEN, Tomi

(PEH-tih-nehn, TAW-mee)

Defense. Shoots left. 6'3", 220 lbs. Born, Ylojarvi, Finland, June 17, 1977. NY Islanders' 9th choice, 267th overall, in 2000 Entry Draft.

			Regular Season														Playoffs								
Season	Club	League	GP	G	A	Pts	PIM	PP	SH	GW	S	%	+/-	TF	F%	Min	GP	G	A	Pts	PIM	PP	SH	GW	Min
1994-95	Ilves Tampere U18	Fin-U18	31	1	6	7	46	....	....	....	....	....	....	....	....	....	4	0	0	0	2	....	....	....	....
	Ilves Tampere Jr.	Fin-Jr.	1	0	0	0	0	....	....	....	....	....	....	....	....	....	....	....	....	....	....	....	....	....	....
1995-96	Ilves Tampere Jr.	Fin-Jr.	12	1	1	2	18	....	....	....	....	....	....	....	....	....	....	....	....	....	....	....	....	....	....
	KooVee Jr.	Fin-Jr.	21	0	0	0	64	....	....	....	....	....	....	....	....	....	....	....	....	....	....	....	....	....	....
1996-97	Ilves Tampere	Finland	16	1	0	1	12	....	....	....	....	....	....	....	....	....	....	....	....	....	....	....	....	....	....
	Ilves Tampere Jr.	Fin-Jr.	26	3	8	11	44	....	....	....	....	....	....	....	....	....	....	....	....	....	....	....	....	....	....
1997-98	Ilves Tampere Jr.	Fin-Jr.	14	1	4	5	24	....	....	....	....	....	....	....	....	....	....	....	....	....	....	....	....	....	....
	Ilves Tampere	Finland	3	0	0	0	0	....	....	....	....	....	....	....	....	....	....	....	....	....	....	....	....	....	....
	Lukko Rauma	Finland	27	0	2	2	16	....	....	....	....	....	....	....	....	....	....	....	....	....	....	....	....	....	....
	Lukko Rauma Jr.	Fin-Jr.	11	2	6	8	14	....	....	....	....	....	....	....	....	....	....	....	....	....	....	....	....	....	....
1998-99	HIFK Helsinki	Finland	4	0	0	0	2	....	....	....	....	....	....	....	....	....	....	....	....	....	....	....	....	....	....
	Hermes Kokkola	Finland-2	42	8	6	14	76	....	....	....	....	....	....	....	....	....	3	0	0	0	6	....	....	....	....
99-2000	Ilves Tampere	Finland	51	1	6	7	84	....	....	....	....	....	....	....	....	....	3	1	2	3	2	....	....	....	....
2000-01	Ilves Tampere	Finland	56	2	2	4	86	....	....	....	....	....	....	....	....	....	9	0	0	0	4	....	....	....	....
2001-02	Ilves Tampere	Finland	48	5	4	9	51	....	....	....	....	....	....	....	....	....	3	0	0	0	4	....	....	....	....
	Bridgeport	AHL	....	....	....	....	....	....	....	....	....	....	....	....	....	....	9	0	1	1	0	....	....	....	....
2002-03	**NY Islanders**	**NHL**	**2**	**0**	**0**	**0**	**0**	**0**	**0**	**0**	**0**	**0.0**	**1**	**0**	**0.0**	**11:34**	....	....	....	....	....	....	....	....	....
	Bridgeport	AHL	75	1	8	9	56	....	....	....	....	....	....	....	....	....	9	0	0	0	17	....	....	....	....
2003-04	**NY Islanders**	**NHL**	**4**	**0**	**0**	**0**	**2**	**0**	**0**	**0**	**2**	**0.0**	**–2**	**0**	**0.0**	**10:24**	....	....	....	....	....	....	....	....	....
	Bridgeport	AHL	71	1	8	9	37	....	....	....	....	....	....	....	....	....	7	1	0	1	0	....	....	....	....
2004-05	Lukko Rauma	Finland	56	6	14	20	49	....	....	....	....	....	....	....	....	....	9	0	2	2	33	....	....	....	....
2005-06	**NY Islanders**	**NHL**	**18**	**0**	**0**	**0**	**16**	**0**	**0**	**0**	**7**	**0.0**	**–2**	**0**	**0.0**	**14:40**	....	....	....	....	....	....	....	....	....
	Bridgeport	AHL	29	0	6	6	38	....	....	....	....	....	....	....	....	....	7	0	1	1	14	....	....	....	....
2006-07	Frolunda	Sweden	27	0	0	0	14	....	....	....	....	....	....	....	....	....	....	....	....	....	....	....	....	....	....
	NHL Totals		**24**	**0**	**0**	**0**	**18**	**0**	**0**	**0**	**9**	**0.0**		**0**	**0.0**	**13:41**	....	....	....	....	....	....	....	....	....

Signed as a free agent by **Rauma** (Finland), June 7, 2004. Signed as a free agent by **Frolunda** (Sweden), May 5, 2006.

PETTINGER, Matt

(PEH-tihn-juhr, MAT) **WSH.**

Left wing. Shoots left. 6'1", 210 lbs. Born, Edmonton, Alta., October 22, 1980. Washington's 2nd choice, 43rd overall, in 2000 Entry Draft.

Season	Club	League	GP	G	A	Pts	PIM	PP	SH	GW	S	%	+/-	TF	F%	Min	GP	G	A	Pts	PIM	PP	SH	GW	Min
1994-95	Victoria Racquet	BCAHA	55	52	48	100	41	....	....	....	....	....	....	....	....	....	....	....	....	....	....	....	....	....	....
1995-96	Victoria Racquet	BCAHA	60	80	65	145	45	....	....	....	....	....	....	....	....	....	....	....	....	....	....	....	....	....	....
1996-97	Victoria Salsa	BCHL	49	22	14	36	31	....	....	....	....	....	....	....	....	....	....	....	....	....	....	....	....	....	....
1997-98	Victoria Salsa	BCHL	55	22	20	42	56	....	....	....	....	....	....	....	....	....	7	5	1	6	8	....	....	....	....
1998-99	U. of Denver	WCHA	33	6	14	20	44	....	....	....	....	....	....	....	....	....	....	....	....	....	....	....	....	....	....
99-2000	U. of Denver	WCHA	19	2	6	8	49	....	....	....	....	....	....	....	....	....	....	....	....	....	....	....	....	....	....
	Calgary Hitmen	WHL	27	14	6	20	41	....	....	....	....	....	....	....	....	....	11	2	6	8	30	....	....	....	....
2000-01	**Washington**	**NHL**	**10**	**0**	**0**	**0**	**2**	**0**	**0**	**0**	**6**	**0.0**	**–1**	**2**	**50.0**	**7:47**	....	....	....	....	....	....	....	....	....
	Portland Pirates	AHL	64	19	17	36	92	....	....	....	....	....	....	....	....	....	2	0	0	0	4	....	....	....	....
2001-02	**Washington**	**NHL**	**61**	**7**	**3**	**10**	**44**	**1**	**0**	**1**	**73**	**9.6**	**–8**	**5**	**20.0**	**9:39**	....	....	....	....	....	....	....	....	....
	Portland Pirates	AHL	9	3	3	6	24	....	....	....	....	....	....	....	....	....	....	....	....	....	....	....	....	....	....
2002-03	**Washington**	**NHL**	**1**	**0**	**0**	**0**	**0**	**0**	**0**	**0**	**0**	**0.0**	**0**	**1**	**0.0**	**3:30**	....	....	....	....	....	....	....	....	....
	Portland Pirates	AHL	69	14	13	27	72	....	....	....	....	....	....	....	....	....	3	0	2	2	2	....	....	....	....
2003-04	**Washington**	**NHL**	**71**	**7**	**5**	**12**	**37**	**1**	**0**	**1**	**92**	**7.6**	**–9**	**18**	**44.4**	**11:25**	....	....	....	....	....	....	....	....	....
2004-05	Ljubljana	Slovenia	1	0	1	1	0	....	....	....	....	....	....	....	....	....	....	....	....	....	....	....	....	....	....
	Ljubljana	Interliga	7	2	4	6	41	....	....	....	....	....	....	....	....	....	....	....	....	....	....	....	....	....	....
2005-06	**Washington**	**NHL**	**71**	**20**	**18**	**38**	**39**	**4**	**5**	**2**	**134**	**14.9**	**–2**	**39**	**12.8**	**15:29**	....	....	....	....	....	....	....	....	....
2006-07	**Washington**	**NHL**	**64**	**16**	**16**	**32**	**22**	**4**	**3**	**2**	**111**	**14.4**	**–13**	**23**	**30.4**	**16:53**	....	....	....	....	....	....	....	....	....
	NHL Totals		**278**	**50**	**42**	**92**	**144**	**10**	**8**	**6**	**416**	**12.0**		**88**	**25.0**	**13:10**	....	....	....	....	....	....	....	....	....

Left **University of Denver** (WCHA) and signed as a free agent with **Calgary** (WHL), January 10, 2000. Signed as a free agent by **Ljubljana** (Slovenia), December 6, 2004.

PEVERLEY, Rich

(PEH-vuhr-lee, RIHTCH) **NSH.**

Center. Shoots right. 6', 185 lbs. Born, Guelph, Ont,, July 8, 1982.

Season	Club	League	GP	G	A	Pts	PIM	PP	SH	GW	S	%	+/-	TF	F%	Min	GP	G	A	Pts	PIM	PP	SH	GW	Min
2000-01	St. Lawrence	ECAC	29	2	4	6	4	....	....	....	....	....	....	....	....	....	....	....	....	....	....	....	....	....	....
2001-02	St. Lawrence	ECAC	34	10	21	31	18	....	....	....	....	....	....	....	....	....	....	....	....	....	....	....	....	....	....
2002-03	St. Lawrence	ECAC	34	15	23	38	12	....	....	....	....	....	....	....	....	....	....	....	....	....	....	....	....	....	....
2003-04	St. Lawrence	ECAC	41	17	25	42	34	....	....	....	....	....	....	....	....	....	....	....	....	....	....	....	....	....	....
2004-05	Portland Pirates	AHL	1	0	0	0	0	....	....	....	....	....	....	....	....	....	....	....	....	....	....	....	....	....	....
	South Carolina	ECHL	69	30	28	58	72	....	....	....	....	....	....	....	....	....	4	2	2	4	6	....	....	....	....
2005-06	Milwaukee	AHL	65	12	34	46	44	....	....	....	....	....	....	....	....	....	21	2	9	11	18	....	....	....	....
	Reading Royals	ECHL	11	4	11	15	4	....	....	....	....	....	....	....	....	....	....	....	....	....	....	....	....	....	....
2006-07	**Nashville**	**NHL**	**13**	**0**	**1**	**1**	**0**	**0**	**0**	**0**	**9**	**0.0**	**–1**	**45**	**48.9**	**7:31**	....	....	....	....	....	....	....	....	....
	Milwaukee	AHL	66	30	38	68	62	....	....	....	....	....	....	....	....	....	4	1	2	3	8	....	....	....	....
	NHL Totals		**13**	**0**	**1**	**1**	**0**	**0**	**0**	**0**	**9**	**0.0**		**45**	**48.9**	**7:31**	....	....	....	....	....	....	....	....	....

Signed as a free agent by **Nashville**, January 18, 2007.

PHANEUF, Dion

(fah-NOOF, DEE-awn) **CGY.**

Defense. Shoots left. 6'3", 210 lbs. Born, Edmonton, Alta., April 10, 1985. Calgary's 1st choice, 9th overall, in 2003 Entry Draft.

Season	Club	League	GP	G	A	Pts	PIM	PP	SH	GW	S	%	+/-	TF	F%	Min	GP	G	A	Pts	PIM	PP	SH	GW	Min
2000-01	Southgate Lions	AMBHL	35	15	50	65	208	....	....	....	....	....	....	....	....	....	4	3	4	7	15	....	....	....	....
2001-02	Red Deer Rebels	WHL	67	5	12	17	170	....	....	....	....	....	....	....	....	....	21	0	2	2	14	....	....	....	....
2002-03	Red Deer Rebels	WHL	71	16	14	30	185	....	....	....	....	....	....	....	....	....	23	7	7	14	34	....	....	....	....
2003-04	Red Deer Rebels	WHL	62	19	24	43	126	....	....	....	....	....	....	....	....	....	19	2	9	11	30	....	....	....	....
2004-05	Red Deer Rebels	WHL	55	24	32	56	73	....	....	....	....	....	....	....	....	....	7	1	4	5	12	....	....	....	....
2005-06	**Calgary**	**NHL**	**82**	**20**	**29**	**49**	**93**	**16**	**0**	**7**	**242**	**8.3**	**5**	**0**	**0.0**	**21:44**	**7**	**1**	**0**	**1**	**7**	**1**	**0**	**0**	**18:37**
2006-07	**Calgary**	**NHL**	**79**	**17**	**33**	**50**	**98**	**13**	**0**	**4**	**230**	**7.4**	**10**	**0**	**0.0**	**25:40**	**6**	**1**	**0**	**1**	**7**	**1**	**0**	**0**	**26:24**
	NHL Totals		**161**	**37**	**62**	**99**	**191**	**29**	**0**	**11**	**472**	**7.8**		**0**	**0.0**	**23:39**	**13**	**2**	**0**	**2**	**14**	**2**	**0**	**0**	**22:12**

WHL East First All-Star Team (2004, 2005) • WHL Defenseman of the Year (2004, 2005) • Canadian Major Junior First All-Star Team (2004, 2005) • NHL All-Rookie Team (2006)

Played in NHL All-Star Game (2007)

PHILLIPS, Chris

(FIHL-ihps, KRIHS) **OTT.**

Defense. Shoots left. 6'3", 216 lbs. Born, Calgary, Alta., March 9, 1978. Ottawa's 1st choice, 1st overall, in 1996 Entry Draft.

Season	Club	League	GP	G	A	Pts	PIM	PP	SH	GW	S	%	+/-	TF	F%	Min	GP	G	A	Pts	PIM	PP	SH	GW	Min
1993-94	Fort McMurray	AJHL	56	6	16	22	72	....	....	....	....	....	....	....	....	....	10	0	3	3	16	....	....	....	....
1994-95	Fort McMurray	AJHL	48	16	32	48	127	....	....	....	....	....	....	....	....	....	11	4	2	6	10	....	....	....	....
1995-96	Prince Albert	WHL	61	10	30	40	97	....	....	....	....	....	....	....	....	....	18	2	12	14	30	....	....	....	....
1996-97	Prince Albert	WHL	32	3	23	26	58	....	....	....	....	....	....	....	....	....	....	....	....	....	....	....	....	....	....
	Lethbridge	WHL	26	4	18	22	28	....	....	....	....	....	....	....	....	....	19	4	*21	25	20	....	....	....	....
1997-98	**Ottawa**	**NHL**	**72**	**5**	**11**	**16**	**38**	**2**	**0**	**2**	**107**	**4.7**	**2**	....	....	....	**11**	**0**	**2**	**2**	**2**	**0**	**0**	**0**	....
1998-99	**Ottawa**	**NHL**	**34**	**3**	**3**	**6**	**32**	**2**	**0**	**0**	**51**	**5.9**	**–5**	**0**	**0.0**	**18:06**	**3**	**0**	**0**	**0**	**0**	**0**	**0**	**0**	**13:50**
99-2000	**Ottawa**	**NHL**	**65**	**5**	**14**	**19**	**39**	**0**	**0**	**1**	**96**	**5.2**	**12**	**0**	**0.0**	**16:50**	**6**	**0**	**1**	**1**	**4**	**0**	**0**	**0**	**18:17**
2000-01	**Ottawa**	**NHL**	**73**	**2**	**12**	**14**	**31**	**2**	**0**	**0**	**77**	**2.6**	**8**	**1**	**0.0**	**21:28**	**1**	**1**	**0**	**1**	**0**	**0**	**0**	**0**	**20:52**
2001-02	**Ottawa**	**NHL**	**63**	**6**	**16**	**22**	**29**	**1**	**0**	**1**	**103**	**5.8**	**5**	**0**	**0.0**	**19:31**	**12**	**0**	**0**	**0**	**12**	**0**	**0**	**0**	**21:44**
2002-03	**Ottawa**	**NHL**	**78**	**3**	**16**	**19**	**71**	**2**	**0**	**1**	**97**	**3.1**	**7**	**0**	**0.0**	**20:13**	**18**	**2**	**4**	**6**	**12**	**0**	**0**	**1**	**21:36**
2003-04	**Ottawa**	**NHL**	**82**	**7**	**16**	**23**	**46**	**0**	**0**	**1**	**93**	**7.5**	**15**	**1**	**100.0**	**20:50**	**7**	**1**	**0**	**1**	**12**	**1**	**0**	**0**	**20:26**
2004-05	Brynas IF Gavle	Sweden	27	5	3	8	45	....	....	....	....	....	....	....	....	....	....	....	....	....	....	....	....	....	....
	Brynas IF Gavle	Sweden-Q	9	1	2	3	2	....	....	....	....	....	....	....	....	....	....	....	....	....	....	....	....	....	....
2005-06	**Ottawa**	**NHL**	**69**	**1**	**18**	**19**	**90**	**0**	**0**	**0**	**79**	**1.3**	**19**	**0**	**0.0**	**20:52**	**9**	**2**	**0**	**2**	**6**	**0**	**0**	**0**	**21:41**
2006-07	**Ottawa**	**NHL**	**82**	**8**	**18**	**26**	**80**	**0**	**1**	**3**	**94**	**8.5**	**36**	**2**	**0.0**	**22:22**	**20**	**0**	**0**	**0**	**24**	**0**	**0**	**0**	**23:11**
	NHL Totals		**618**	**40**	**124**	**164**	**456**	**9**	**1**	**9**	**797**	**5.0**		**4**	**25.0**	**20:16**	**87**	**6**	**7**	**13**	**72**	**1**	**0**	**1**	**21:22**

WHL Rookie of the Year (1996) • WHL East First All-Star Team (1997) • Canadian Major Junior First All-Star Team (1997) • Memorial Cup Tournament All-Star Team (1997)

• Missed majority of 1998-99 season recovering from ankle injury suffered in game vs. Buffalo, December 30, 1998. Signed as a free agent by **Gavle** (Sweden), November 2, 2004.

PICARD, Alexandre

(pee-KAR, al-ehx-AHN-druh) **PHI.**

Defense. Shoots left. 6'2", 220 lbs. Born, Gatineau, Que., July 5, 1985. Philadelphia's 5th choice, 85th overall, in 2003 Entry Draft.

			Regular Season														Playoffs								
Season	Club	League	GP	G	A	Pts	PIM	PP	SH	GW	S	%	+/-	TF	F%	Min	GP	G	A	Pts	PIM	PP	SH	GW	Min
2000-01	Gatineau	QAAA	42	6	15	21	38										11	0	1	1	8				
2001-02	Halifax	QMJHL	59	2	12	14	28										13	2	3	5	6				
2002-03	Halifax	QMJHL	71	4	30	34	64										25	1	5	6	14				
2003-04	Cape Breton	QMJHL	57	10	26	36	44										5	0	0	0	0				
2004-05	Halifax	QMJHL	68	15	23	38	46										13	1	5	6	14				
	Philadelphia	AHL															2	0	0	0	0				
2005-06	**Philadelphia**	**NHL**	**6**	**0**	**0**	**0**	**4**	**0**	**0**	**0**	**9**	**0.0**	**–2**	**0**	**0.0**	**9:33**									
	Philadelphia	AHL	75	7	26	33	82																		
2006-07	**Philadelphia**	**NHL**	**62**	**3**	**19**	**22**	**17**	**1**	**0**	**0**	**56**	**5.4**	**–19**	**0**	**0.0**	**18:29**									
	Philadelphia	AHL	6	1	2	3	2																		
	NHL Totals		**68**	**3**	**19**	**22**	**21**	**1**	**0**	**0**	**65**	**4.6**		**0**	**0.0**	**17:41**									

QMJHL Second All-Star Team (2005)

PICARD, Alexandre

(pee-KAR, al-ehx-AHN-druh) **CBJ**

Left wing. Shoots left. 6'2", 190 lbs. Born, Les Saules, Que., October 9, 1985. Columbus' 1st choice, 8th overall, in 2004 Entry Draft.

Season	Club	League	GP	G	A	Pts	PIM	PP	SH	GW	S	%	+/-	TF	F%	Min	GP	G	A	Pts	PIM	PP	SH	GW	Min
2000-01	St-Francois	QAAA	5	1	1	2	0																		
2001-02	St-Francois	QAAA	41	21	30	51	48										8	2	7	9	8				
	Sherbrooke	QMJHL	6	0	3	3	0																		
2002-03	Sherbrooke	QMJHL	66	14	15	29	41										12	4	0	4	10				
2003-04	Lewiston	QMJHL	69	39	41	80	88										7	7	4	11	6				
2004-05	Lewiston	QMJHL	65	40	45	85	160										8	5	2	7	18				
2005-06	**Columbus**	**NHL**	**17**	**0**	**0**	**0**	**14**	**0**	**0**	**0**	**10**	**0.0**	**–2**	**3**	**33.3**	**9:09**									
	Syracuse Crunch	AHL	45	15	15	30	54										6	1	0	1	19				
2006-07	**Columbus**	**NHL**	**23**	**0**	**1**	**1**	**6**	**0**	**0**	**0**	**20**	**0.0**	**–3**	**0**	**0.0**	**7:49**									
	Syracuse Crunch	AHL	48	11	18	29	73																		
	NHL Totals		**40**	**0**	**1**	**1**	**20**	**0**	**0**	**0**	**30**	**0.0**		**3**	**33.3**	**8:23**									

QMJHL Second All-Star Team (2004)

PIHLMAN, Tuomas

(PIHL-mahn, TAWH-muhs) **N.J.**

Left wing. Shoots left. 6'2", 215 lbs. Born, Espoo, Finland, November 13, 1982. New Jersey's 3rd choice, 48th overall, in 2001 Entry Draft.

Season	Club	League	GP	G	A	Pts	PIM	PP	SH	GW	S	%	+/-	TF	F%	Min	GP	G	A	Pts	PIM	PP	SH	GW	Min
1997-98	JYP Jyvaskyla U18	Fin-U18	30	2	5	7	18										4	1	3	4	6				
1998-99	JYP Jyvaskyla U18	Fin-U18	35	21	20	41	64										6	1	1	2	12				
99-2000	JYP Jyvaskyla U18	Fin-U18	3	3	0	3	0																		
	JYP Jyvaskyla Jr.	Fin-Jr.	20	4	4	8	54										4	0	0	0	8				
	JYP Jyvaskyla	Finland	17	0	0	0	18																		
2000-01	JYP Jyvaskyla Jr.	Fin-Jr.	1	1	0	1	2										6	2	4	6	4				
	JYP Jyvaskyla	Finland	47	3	6	9	59																		
2001-02	JYP Jyvaskyla Jr.	Fin-Jr.	3	1	1	2	4																		
	JYP Jyvaskyla	Finland	44	9	2	11	95																		
2002-03	JYP Jyvaskyla	Finland	53	19	15	34	58										1	0	0	0	0				
2003-04	**New Jersey**	**NHL**	**2**	**0**	**0**	**0**	**2**	**0**	**0**	**0**	**1**	**0.0**	**0**	**0**	**0.0**	**6:56**									
	Albany River Rats	AHL	73	10	19	29	59																		
2004-05	Albany River Rats	AHL	68	9	13	22	48																		
2005-06	**New Jersey**	**NHL**	**11**	**1**	**1**	**2**	**10**	**0**	**0**	**0**	**14**	**7.1**	**–1**	**22**	**40.9**	**10:04**									
	Albany River Rats	AHL	63	12	15	27	64																		
2006-07	**New Jersey**	**NHL**	**2**	**0**	**0**	**0**	**0**	**0**	**0**	**0**	**0**	**0.0**	**0**	**0**	**0.0**	**6:32**									
	Lowell Devils	AHL	67	8	18	26	34																		
	NHL Totals		**15**	**1**	**1**	**2**	**12**	**0**	**0**	**0**	**15**	**6.7**		**22**	**40.9**	**9:11**									

PILAR, Karel

(PEE-lahr, KAH-rehl) **ATL.**

Defense. Shoots right. 6'3", 210 lbs. Born, Prague, Czech., December 23, 1977. Toronto's 2nd choice, 39th overall, in 2001 Entry Draft.

Season	Club	League	GP	G	A	Pts	PIM	PP	SH	GW	S	%	+/-	TF	F%	Min	GP	G	A	Pts	PIM	PP	SH	GW	Min
99-2000	Litvinov	CzRep	49	2	12	14	61										7	0	0	0	4				
2000-01	Litvinov	CzRep	52	12	26	38	52										4	1	1	2	25				
2001-02	**Toronto**	**NHL**	**23**	**1**	**3**	**4**	**8**	**0**	**0**	**0**	**32**	**3.1**	**3**	**0**	**0.0**	**16:03**	**11**	**0**	**4**	**4**	**12**	**0**	**0**	**0**	**17:47**
	St. John's	AHL	52	10	14	24	26																		
2002-03	**Toronto**	**NHL**	**17**	**3**	**4**	**7**	**12**	**1**	**0**	**1**	**22**	**13.6**	**–7**	**0**	**0.0**	**18:29**									
	St. John's	AHL	7	2	5	7	28																		
2003-04	**Toronto**	**NHL**	**50**	**2**	**17**	**19**	**22**	**1**	**0**	**1**	**74**	**2.7**	**2**	**0**	**0.0**	**18:03**	**1**	**1**	**0**	**1**	**0**	**0**	**0**	**0**	**20:48**
	St. John's	AHL	6	3	4	7	6																		
2004-05	HC Sparta Praha	CzRep	52	13	15	28	70																		
2005-06	HC Sparta Praha	CzRep	6	0	1	1	20										14	3	3	6	45				
2006-07	Toronto Marlies	AHL	10	2	5	7	6																		
	HC Sparta Praha	CzRep															1	0	0	0	2				
	NHL Totals		**90**	**6**	**24**	**30**	**42**	**2**	**0**	**2**	**128**	**4.7**		**0**	**0.0**	**17:38**	**12**	**1**	**4**	**5**	**12**	**0**	**0**	**0**	**18:02**

• Missed remainder of 2002-03 season, the start of 2003-04 season and the majority of the 2005-06 and 2006-07 seasons after being diagnosed with a heart condition, January, 2003. Signed as a free agent by **Sparta** (CzRep), August 9, 2004. Signed as a free agent by **Atlanta**, August 8, 2007.

PIRJETA, Lasse

(PEER-yeh-tuh, LAH-say)

Center. Shoots left. 6'4", 225 lbs. Born, Haukipudas, Finland, April 4, 1974. Columbus' 7th choice, 133rd overall, in 2002 Entry Draft.

Season	Club	League	GP	G	A	Pts	PIM	PP	SH	GW	S	%	+/-	TF	F%	Min	GP	G	A	Pts	PIM	PP	SH	GW	Min
1989-90	Karpat Oulu Jr.	Fin-Jr.	2	0	0	0	0																		
1990-91	Karpat Oulu Jr.	Fin-Jr.	28	6	7	13	12																		
1991-92	Karpat Oulu Jr.	Fin-Jr.	7	1	4	5	8																		
	Tacoma Rockets	WHL	16	5	2	7	4																		
	Karpat Oulu	Finland-2	2	0	0	0	0																		
1992-93	Karpat Oulu Jr.	Fin-Jr.	24	13	19	32	34																		
	Karpat Oulu	Finland-2	20	4	3	7	6																		
1993-94	TPS Turku Jr.	Fin-Jr.	6	2	2	4	2										4	6	2	8	2				
	Kiekko-67 Turku	Finland-2	2	2	1	3	0																		
	TPS Turku	Finland	43	9	9	18	14										11	4	0	4	2				
1994-95	TPS Turku Jr.	Fin-Jr.	1	0	0	0	0																		
	TPS Turku	Finland	49	7	13	20	64										8	0	1	1	29				
1995-96	TPS Turku	Finland	45	13	14	27	34										11	6	3	9	4				
1996-97	V.Frolunda	Sweden	50	14	8	22	36										3	0	1	1	4				
	V.Frolunda	EuroHL	5	2	6	8	4																		
1997-98	Tappara Tampere	Finland	48	24	22	46	20										4	1	1	2	2				
1998-99	Tappara Tampere	Finland	54	22	19	41	32																		
99-2000	HIFK Helsinki	Finland	54	18	25	43	24										9	2	3	5	10				
	HIFK Helsinki	EuroHL	6	1	3	4	6										2	1	1	2	0				
2000-01	HIFK Helsinki	Finland	56	15	18	33	20																		
2001-02	Karpat Oulu	Finland	55	15	26	41	24										4	2	2	4	2				
2002-03	**Columbus**	**NHL**	**51**	**11**	**10**	**21**	**12**	**2**	**0**	**2**	**80**	**13.8**	**–4**	**327**	**43.1**	**11:28**									
2003-04	**Columbus**	**NHL**	**57**	**2**	**8**	**10**	**20**	**0**	**0**	**0**	**78**	**2.6**	**–6**	**465**	**49.5**	**10:46**									
	Syracuse Crunch	AHL	5	1	2	3	2																		
	Pittsburgh	**NHL**	**13**	**6**	**6**	**12**	**0**	**1**	**0**	**1**	**33**	**18.2**	**3**	**187**	**51.9**	**14:22**									
2004-05	HIFK Helsinki	Finland	45	16	20	36	26										5	2	0	2	2				
2005-06	**Pittsburgh**	**NHL**	**25**	**4**	**3**	**7**	**18**	**0**	**0**	**0**	**30**	**13.3**	**4**	**220**	**46.4**	**9:15**									
	Wilkes-Barre	AHL	8	1	4	5	6																		
	Kloten Flyers	Swiss	6	0	2	2	2										9	0	2	2	2				
2006-07	Malmo	Sweden	54	10	16	26	44																		
	Malmo	Sweden-Q	10	2	1	3	6																		
	NHL Totals		**146**	**23**	**27**	**50**	**50**	**3**	**0**	**3**	**221**	**10.4**		**1199**	**47.5**	**11:04**									

Traded to **Pittsburgh** by **Columbus** for Brian Holzinger, March 9, 2004. Signed as a free agent by **HIFK Helsinki** (Finland), September 30, 2004. Assigned to **Kloten** (Swiss) by **Pittsburgh**. January 20, 2006. Signed as a free agent by **Malmo** (Sweden), June 17, 2006.

PISANI, Fernando
(pih-ZAN-ee, FUHR-nan-DOH) **EDM.**

Right wing. Shoots left. 6'1", 205 lbs. Born, Edmonton, Alta., December 27, 1976. Edmonton's 9th choice, 195th overall, in 1996 Entry Draft.

Season	Club	League	GP	G	A	Pts	PIM	PP	SH	GW	S	%	+/-	TF	F%	Min	GP	G	A	Pts	PIM	PP	SH	GW	Min
			Regular Season														Playoffs								
1993-94	St. Albert Saints	AJHL	50	6	21	27	24	....	....	....	....	....	....	....	....	....	....	....	....	....	....	....	....	....	....
1994-95	Bonnyville	AJHL	16	4	34	37	97	....	....	....	....	....	....	....	....	....	....	....	....	....	....	....	....	....	....
	St. Albert Saints	AJHL	40	26	21	47	16	....	....	....	....	....	....	....	....	....	....	....	....	....	....	....	....	....	....
1995-96	St. Albert Saints	AJHL	58	40	63	103	134	....	....	....	....	....	....	....	....	....	18	7	22	29	28	....	....	....	....
1996-97	Providence	H-East	35	12	18	30	36	....	....	....	....	....	....	....	....	....	....	....	....	....	....	....	....	....	....
1997-98	Providence	H-East	36	16	18	34	20	....	....	....	....	....	....	....	....	....	....	....	....	....	....	....	....	....	....
1998-99	Providence	H-East	38	14	37	51	42	....	....	....	....	....	....	....	....	....	....	....	....	....	....	....	....	....	....
99-2000	Providence	H-East	38	14	24	38	56	....	....	....	....	....	....	....	....	....	....	....	....	....	....	....	....	....	....
2000-01	Hamilton	AHL	52	12	13	25	28	....	....	....	....	....	....	....	....	....	....	....	....	....	....	....	....	....	....
2001-02	Hamilton	AHL	79	26	34	60	60	....	....	....	....	....	....	....	....	....	15	4	6	10	4	....	....	....	....
2002-03	**Edmonton**	**NHL**	**35**	**8**	**5**	**13**	**10**	**0**	**1**	**0**	**32**	**25.0**	**9**	**1**	**100.0**	**10:43**	**6**	**1**	**0**	**1**	**2**	**0**	**0**	**0**	**13:48**
	Hamilton	AHL	41	17	15	32	24	....	....	....	....	....	....	....	....	....	....	....	....	....	....	....	....	....	....
2003-04	**Edmonton**	**NHL**	**76**	**16**	**14**	**30**	**46**	**4**	**1**	**1**	**99**	**16.2**	**14**	**10**	**20.0**	**12:46**	....	....	....	....	....	....	....	....	....
2004-05	Langnau	Swiss	7	1	3	4	0	....	....	....	....	....	....	....	....	....	....	....	....	....	....	....	....	....	....
	Asiago	Italy	12	1	5	6	6	....	....	....	....	....	....	....	....	....	9	4	6	10	0	....	....	....	....
2005-06	**Edmonton**	**NHL**	**80**	**18**	**19**	**37**	**42**	**4**	**1**	**2**	**131**	**13.7**	**5**	**35**	**22.9**	**13:51**	**24**	***14**	**4**	**18**	**10**	**3**	**1**	**5**	**17:12**
2006-07	**Edmonton**	**NHL**	**77**	**14**	**14**	**28**	**40**	**2**	**1**	**0**	**142**	**9.9**	**-1**	**20**	**40.0**	**16:54**	....	....	....	....	....	....	....	....	....
	NHL Totals		**268**	**56**	**52**	**108**	**138**	**10**	**4**	**3**	**404**	**13.9**		**66**	**28.8**	**14:01**	**30**	**15**	**4**	**19**	**12**	**3**	**1**	**5**	**16:31**

Signed as a free agent by **Langnau** (Swiss), October 24, 2004. Signed as a free agent by **Asiago** (Italy), December 23, 2004.

PISKULA, Joe
(PIHS-koo-luh, JOH) **L.A.**

Defense. Shoots left. 6'3", 214 lbs. Born, Antigo, WI, July 5, 1984.

Season	Club	League	GP	G	A	Pts	PIM	PP	SH	GW	S	%	+/-	TF	F%	Min	GP	G	A	Pts	PIM	PP	SH	GW	Min
2002-03	Chicago Steel	USHL	13	0	0	0	18	....	....	....	....	....	....	....	....	....	....	....	....	....	....	....	....	....	....
	Des Moines	USHL	32	2	6	8	18	....	....	....	....	....	....	....	....	....	4	0	1	1	4	....	....	....	....
2003-04	Des Moines	USHL	58	2	4	6	68	....	....	....	....	....	....	....	....	....	3	0	1	1	0	....	....	....	....
2004-05	U. of Wisconsin	WCHA	40	0	6	6	24	....	....	....	....	....	....	....	....	....	....	....	....	....	....	....	....	....	....
2005-06	U. of Wisconsin	WCHA	34	2	9	11	22	....	....	....	....	....	....	....	....	....	....	....	....	....	....	....	....	....	....
2006-07	U. of Wisconsin	WCHA	38	1	4	5	34	....	....	....	....	....	....	....	....	....	....	....	....	....	....	....	....	....	....
	Los Angeles	**NHL**	**5**	**0**	**0**	**0**	**6**	**0**	**0**	**0**	**4**	**0.0**	**-3**	**0**	**0.0**	**9:59**	....	....	....	....	....	....	....	....	....
	NHL Totals		**5**	**0**	**0**	**0**	**6**	**0**	**0**	**0**	**4**	**0.0**		**0**	**0.0**	**9:59**	....	....	....	....	....	....	....	....	....

Signed as a free agent by **Los Angeles**, March 21, 2007.

PITKANEN, Joni
(PIHT ka nuhn, YOH-nee) **EDM.**

Defense. Shoots left. 6'3", 210 lbs. Born, Oulu, Finland, September 19, 1983. Philadelphia's 1st choice, 4th overall, in 2002 Entry Draft.

Season	Club	League	GP	G	A	Pts	PIM	PP	SH	GW	S	%	+/-	TF	F%	Min	GP	G	A	Pts	PIM	PP	SH	GW	Min
1998-99	Karpat Oulu U18	Fin-U18	30	1	5	6	12	....	....	....	....	....	....	....	....	....	....	....	....	....	....	....	....	....	....
99-2000	Karpat Oulu U18	Fin-U18	36	12	14	26	26	....	....	....	....	....	....	....	....	....	6	1	4	5	2	....	....	....	....
	Karpat Oulu Jr.	Fin-Jr.	2	0	0	0	0	....	....	....	....	....	....	....	....	....	....	....	....	....	....	....	....	....	....
2000-01	Karpat Oulu Jr.	Fin-Jr.	24	6	11	17	77	....	....	....	....	....	....	....	....	....	....	....	....	....	....	....	....	....	....
	Karpat Oulu	Finland	21	0	0	0	10	....	....	....	....	....	....	....	....	....	2	0	0	0	2	....	....	....	....
2001-02	Karpat Oulu Jr.	Fin-Jr.	....	....	....	....	....	....	....	....	....	....	....	....	....	....	1	0	0	0	0	....	....	....	....
	Karpat Oulu	Finland	49	4	15	19	65	....	....	....	....	....	....	....	....	....	4	0	0	0	12	....	....	....	....
2002-03	Karpat Oulu	Finland	35	5	15	20	38	....	....	....	....	....	....	....	....	....	....	....	....	....	....	....	....	....	....
2003-04	**Philadelphia**	**NHL**	**71**	**8**	**19**	**27**	**44**	**5**	**0**	**2**	**133**	**6.0**	**15**	**0**	**0.0**	**16:35**	**15**	**0**	**3**	**3**	**6**	**0**	**0**	**0**	**12:13**
2004-05	Philadelphia	AHL	76	6	35	41	105	....	....	....	....	....	....	....	....	....	21	3	4	7	16	....	....	....	....
2005-06	**Philadelphia**	**NHL**	**58**	**13**	**33**	**46**	**78**	**5**	**0**	**3**	**118**	**11.0**	**22**	**0**	**0.0**	**23:43**	**6**	**0**	**2**	**2**	**2**	**0**	**0**	**0**	**24:12**
	Finland	Olympics	DID NOT PLAY – INJURED																						
2006-07	**Philadelphia**	**NHL**	**77**	**4**	**39**	**43**	**88**	**1**	**0**	**0**	**137**	**2.9**	**-25**	**0**	**0.0**	**24:33**	....	....	....	....	....	....	....	....	....
	NHL Totals		**206**	**25**	**91**	**116**	**210**	**11**	**0**	**5**	**388**	**6.4**		**0**	**0.0**	**21:34**	**21**	**0**	**5**	**5**	**8**	**0**	**0**	**0**	**15:39**

NHL All-Rookie Team (2004)

Traded to **Edmonton** by **Philadelphia** with Geoff Sanderson and Philadelphia's 3rd round choice in 2009 Entry Draft for Jason Smith and Joffrey Lupul, July 1, 2007.

PLATT, Geoff
(PLAT, JEHF) **CBJ**

Center. Shoots left. 5'9", 175 lbs. Born, Toronto, Ont., July 10, 1985.

Season	Club	League	GP	G	A	Pts	PIM	PP	SH	GW	S	%	+/-	TF	F%	Min	GP	G	A	Pts	PIM	PP	SH	GW	Min
2000-01	St. Mike's B's	OPJHL	6	2	0	2	4	....	....	....	....	....	....	....	....	....	....	....	....	....	....	....	....	....	....
2001-02	North Bay	OHL	63	4	6	10	34	....	....	....	....	....	....	....	....	....	5	0	0	0	6	....	....	....	....
2002-03	Saginaw Spirit	OHL	62	32	22	54	81	....	....	....	....	....	....	....	....	....	....	....	....	....	....	....	....	....	....
2003-04	Saginaw Spirit	OHL	27	7	13	20	49	....	....	....	....	....	....	....	....	....	....	....	....	....	....	....	....	....	....
	Erie Otters	OHL	28	18	11	29	22	....	....	....	....	....	....	....	....	....	9	9	1	10	22	....	....	....	....
2004-05	Erie Otters	OHL	68	45	34	79	84	....	....	....	....	....	....	....	....	....	6	2	3	5	16	....	....	....	....
	Atlantic City	ECHL	2	0	2	2	0	....	....	....	....	....	....	....	....	....	3	0	0	0	0	....	....	....	....
2005-06	**Columbus**	**NHL**	**15**	**0**	**5**	**5**	**16**	**0**	**0**	**0**	**29**	**0.0**	**-4**	**53**	**45.3**	**11:12**	....	....	....	....	....	....	....	....	....
	Syracuse Crunch	AHL	66	31	34	65	58	....	....	....	....	....	....	....	....	....	6	3	0	3	6	....	....	....	....
2006-07	**Columbus**	**NHL**	**26**	**4**	**5**	**9**	**10**	**0**	**0**	**0**	**40**	**10.0**	**1**	**168**	**56.6**	**10:04**	....	....	....	....	....	....	....	....	....
	Syracuse Crunch	AHL	53	28	21	49	59	....	....	....	....	....	....	....	....	....	....	....	....	....	....	....	....	....	....
	NHL Totals		**41**	**4**	**10**	**14**	**26**	**0**	**0**	**0**	**69**	**5.8**		**221**	**53.8**	**10:29**	....	....	....	....	....	....	....	....	....

Signed as a free agent by **Syracuse** (AHL), September 23, 2005. Signed as a free agent by **Columbus**, November 25, 2005.

PLEKANEC, Tomas
(pleh-KA-nyehts, TAW-mahsh) **MTL.**

Left wing. Shoots left. 5'10", 196 lbs. Born, Kladno, Czech., October 31, 1982. Montreal's 4th choice, 71st overall, in 2001 Entry Draft.

Season	Club	League	GP	G	A	Pts	PIM	PP	SH	GW	S	%	+/-	TF	F%	Min	GP	G	A	Pts	PIM	PP	SH	GW	Min
1996-97	Kladno U17	CzR-U17	13	1	3	4	....	....	....	....	....	....	....	....	....	....	....	....	....	....	....	....	....	....	....
1997-98	HC Kladno U17	CzR-U17	45	38	26	64	....	....	....	....	....	....	....	....	....	....	....	....	....	....	....	....	....	....	....
1998-99	HC Kladno Jr.	CzRep-Jr.	53	22	20	42	....	....	....	....	....	....	....	....	....	....	....	....	....	....	....	....	....	....	....
99-2000	HC Kladno Jr.	CzRep-Jr.	43	14	16	30	....	....	....	....	....	....	....	....	....	....	....	....	....	....	....	....	....	....	....
	Kralupy	CzRep-3	6	2	2	4	2	....	....	....	....	....	....	....	....	....	....	....	....	....	....	....	....	....	....
	HC CKD Slany	CzRep-3	3	0	1	1	6	....	....	....	....	....	....	....	....	....	....	....	....	....	....	....	....	....	....
2000-01	Kladno	CzRep	47	9	9	18	24	....	....	....	....	....	....	....	....	....	....	....	....	....	....	....	....	....	....
	HC Kladno Jr.	CzRep-Jr.	9	6	4	10	4	....	....	....	....	....	....	....	....	....	....	....	....	....	....	....	....	....	....
2001-02	Kladno	CzRep	48	7	16	23	28	....	....	....	....	....	....	....	....	....	....	....	....	....	....	....	....	....	....
	BK Mlada Boleslav	CzRep-3	6	6	3	9	14	....	....	....	....	....	....	....	....	....	....	....	....	....	....	....	....	....	....
	Kladno	CzRep-Q	5	0	1	1	0	....	....	....	....	....	....	....	....	....	....	....	....	....	....	....	....	....	....
2002-03	Hamilton	AHL	77	19	27	46	74	....	....	....	....	....	....	....	....	....	13	3	2	5	8	....	....	....	....
2003-04	**Montreal**	**NHL**	**2**	**0**	**0**	**0**	**0**	**0**	**0**	**0**	**0**	**0.0**	**0**	**11**	**45.5**	**9:02**	....	....	....	....	....	....	....	....	....
	Hamilton	AHL	74	23	43	66	90	....	....	....	....	....	....	....	....	....	10	2	5	7	6	....	....	....	....
2004-05	Hamilton	AHL	80	29	35	64	68	....	....	....	....	....	....	....	....	....	4	2	4	6	6	....	....	....	....
2005-06	**Montreal**	**NHL**	**67**	**9**	**20**	**29**	**32**	**1**	**0**	**0**	**99**	**9.1**	**4**	**708**	**50.3**	**13:15**	**6**	**0**	**4**	**4**	**6**	**0**	**0**	**0**	**18:00**
	Hamilton	AHL	2	0	0	0	2	....	....	....	....	....	....	....	....	....	....	....	....	....	....	....	....	....	....
2006-07	**Montreal**	**NHL**	**81**	**20**	**27**	**47**	**36**	**5**	**2**	**1**	**150**	**13.3**	**10**	**1159**	**48.3**	**15:59**	....	....	....	....	....	....	....	....	....
	NHL Totals		**150**	**29**	**47**	**76**	**68**	**6**	**2**	**1**	**249**	**11.6**		**1878**	**49.0**	**14:40**	**6**	**0**	**4**	**4**	**6**	**0**	**0**	**0**	**18:00**

PLIHAL, Tomas
(PLEE-hahl, TAW-mahsh) **S.J.**

Center. Shoots left. 6'1", 190 lbs. Born, Frydlant v Cechach, Czech., March 28, 1983. San Jose's 4th choice, 140th overall, in 2001 Entry Draft.

Season	Club	League	GP	G	A	Pts	PIM	PP	SH	GW	S	%	+/-	TF	F%	Min	GP	G	A	Pts	PIM	PP	SH	GW	Min
99-2000	Liberec U17	CzR-U17	38	22	14	36		....	....	....	....	....	....	....	....	....	....	....	....	....	....	....	....	....	....
	Liberec Jr.	CzRep-Jr.	2	0	0	0	0	....	....	....	....	....	....	....	....	....	....	....	....	....	....	....	....	....	....
2000-01	HC Liberec U17	CzR-U17	18	3	5	8	....	....	....	....	....	....	....	....	....	....	....	....	....	....	....	....	....	....	....
	HC Liberec Jr.	CzRep-Jr.	33	16	12	28	....	....	....	....	....	....	....	....	....	....	....	....	....	....	....	....	....	....	....
2001-02	Kootenay Ice	WHL	72	32	54	86	28	....	....	....	....	....	....	....	....	....	22	4	10	14	14	....	....	....	....
2002-03	Kootenay Ice	WHL	67	35	42	77	113	....	....	....	....	....	....	....	....	....	11	2	4	6	18	....	....	....	....
2003-04	Cleveland Barons	AHL	51	4	12	16	16	....	....	....	....	....	....	....	....	....	6	0	3	3	2	....	....	....	....
2004-05	Cleveland Barons	AHL	62	17	11	28	26	....	....	....	....	....	....	....	....	....	....	....	....	....	....	....	....	....	....
2005-06	Cleveland Barons	AHL	74	11	19	30	53	....	....	....	....	....	....	....	....	....	....	....	....	....	....	....	....	....	....

			Regular Season														Playoffs								
Season	Club	League	GP	G	A	Pts	PIM	PP	SH	GW	S	%	+/-	TF	F%	Min	GP	G	A	Pts	PIM	PP	SH	GW	Min
2006-07	**San Jose**	**NHL**	**3**	**0**	**0**	**0**	**0**	**0**	**0**	**0**	**10**	**0.0**	**0**	**8**	**75.0**	**9:44**									
	Worcester Sharks	AHL	47	6	9	15	28																		
	NHL Totals		**3**	**0**	**0**	**0**	**0**	**0**	**0**	**0**	**10**	**0.0**		**8**	**75.0**	**9:44**									

George Parsons Trophy (Memorial Cup Tournament Most Sportsmanlike Player) (2002)

POCK, Thomas

(PAWK, TAW-muhs) **NYR**

Defense. Shoots left. 6'1", 210 lbs. Born, Klagenfurt, Austria, December 2, 1981.

Season	Club	League	GP	G	A	Pts	PIM	PP	SH	GW	S	%	+/-	TF	F%	Min	GP	G	A	Pts	PIM	PP	SH	GW	Min
1998-99	Klagenfurt Jr.	Austria-Jr.	31	0	0	0	2																		
99-2000	Klagenfurter AC	Austria	15	3	8	11	14																		
	Klagenfurt	Alpenliga	33	4	11	15	48																		
2000-01	Massachusetts	H-East	33	6	6	12	59																		
2001-02	Massachusetts	H-East	23	5	7	12	26																		
	Austria	Nat-Tm	10	1	2	3	4																		
	Austria	Olympics	4	0	0	0	2																		
2002-03	Massachusetts	H-East	37	17	20	37	46																		
2003-04	Massachusetts	H-East	37	16	25	41	48																		
	NY Rangers	**NHL**	**6**	**2**	**2**	**4**	**0**	**0**	**0**	**0**	**8**	**25.0**	**–4**	**0**	**0.0**	**18:38**									
2004-05	Hartford	AHL	50	1	5	6	55										6	0	1	1	8				
	Charlotte	ECHL	3	0	2	2	2																		
2005-06	**NY Rangers**	**NHL**	**8**	**1**	**1**	**2**	**4**	**0**	**0**	**0**	**15**	**6.7**	**–3**	**0**	**0.0**	**15:10**									
	Hartford	AHL	67	15	46	61	99										6	0	3	3	15				
2006-07	**NY Rangers**	**NHL**	**44**	**4**	**4**	**8**	**16**	**0**	**0**	**0**	**76**	**5.3**	**–4**	**0**	**0.0**	**16:14**	**4**	**0**	**3**	**3**	**4**	**0**	**0**	**0**	**13:29**
	Hartford	AHL	4	0	1	1	2																		
	NHL Totals		**58**	**7**	**7**	**14**	**20**	**0**	**0**	**0**	**99**	**7.1**		**0**	**0.0**	**16:20**	**4**	**0**	**3**	**3**	**4**	**0**	**0**	**0**	**13:29**

Hockey East Second All-Star Team (2003) • Hockey East First All-Star Team (2004) • NCAA East First All-American Team (2004) • AHL Second All-Star Team (2006)

Signed as a free agent by **NY Rangers**, March 23, 2004.

POHL, John

(PAWL, JAWN) **TOR.**

Center. Shoots right. 6', 196 lbs. Born, Rochester, MN, June 29, 1979. St. Louis' 8th choice, 255th overall, in 1998 Entry Draft.

Season	Club	League	GP	G	A	Pts	PIM	PP	SH	GW	S	%	+/-	TF	F%	Min	GP	G	A	Pts	PIM	PP	SH	GW	Min
1997-98	Red Wing High	High-MN	28	30	77	107	18																		
	Twin Cities	USHL	10	5	3	8	10																		
1998-99	U. of Minnesota	WCHA	42	7	10	17	18																		
99-2000	U. of Minnesota	WCHA	41	18	41	59	26																		
2000-01	U. of Minnesota	WCHA	38	19	26	45	24																		
2001-02	U. of Minnesota	WCHA	44	27	*52	*79	26																		
2002-03	Worcester IceCats	AHL	58	26	32	58	34										3	0	1	1	6				
2003-04	**St. Louis**	**NHL**	**1**	**0**	**0**	**0**	**0**	**0**	**0**	**0**	**1**	**0.0**	**–2**	**9**	**55.6**	**8:18**									
	Worcester IceCats	AHL	65	16	25	41	65										3	0	1	1	2				
2004-05	Worcester IceCats	AHL	13	3	6	9	2																		
2005-06	**Toronto**	**NHL**	**7**	**3**	**1**	**4**	**4**	**1**	**0**	**0**	**17**	**17.6**	**2**	**41**	**53.7**	**12:47**									
	Toronto Marlies	AHL	60	36	39	75	42										5	1	5	6	10				
2006-07	**Toronto**	**NHL**	**74**	**13**	**16**	**29**	**10**	**3**	**0**	**1**	**105**	**12.4**	**–4**	**553**	**53.4**	**11:21**									
	NHL Totals		**82**	**16**	**17**	**33**	**14**	**4**	**0**	**1**	**123**	**13.0**		**603**	**53.4**	**11:26**									

WCHA Second All-Star Team (2000) • WCHA First All-Star Team (2002) • NCAA Championship All-Tournament Team (2002)

Traded to **Toronto** by **St. Louis** for future considerations, August 24, 2005.

POLAK, Roman

(POH-lahk, ROH-muhn) **ST.L.**

Defense. Shoots right. 6'1", 198 lbs. Born, Ostrava, Czech., April 28, 1986. St. Louis' 6th choice, 180th overall, in 2004 Entry Draft.

Season	Club	League	GP	G	A	Pts	PIM	PP	SH	GW	S	%	+/-	TF	F%	Min	GP	G	A	Pts	PIM	PP	SH	GW	Min
2001-02	HC Ostrava Jr.	CzRep-Jr.	46	4	9	13	84																		
2002-03	HC Ostrava Jr.	CzRep-Jr.	32	3	12	15	34																		
2003-04	HC Vitkovice Jr.	CzRep-Jr.	52	4	8	12	48																		
2004-05	Kootenay Ice	WHL	65	5	18	23	85										9	0	0	0	6				
2005-06	HC Vitkovice Jr.	CzRep-Jr.	1	0	0	0	4																		
	Vitkovice	CzRep	37	0	1	1	16										6	0	0	0	6				
2006-07	**St. Louis**	**NHL**	**19**	**0**	**0**	**0**	**6**	**0**	**0**	**0**	**13**	**0.0**	**–3**	**0**	**0.0**	**13:38**									
	Peoria Rivermen	AHL	53	4	8	12	66																		
	NHL Totals		**19**	**0**	**0**	**0**	**6**	**0**	**0**	**0**	**13**	**0.0**		**0**	**0.0**	**13:38**									

POLAK, Vojtech

(POH-lahk, VOI-tehk) **DAL.**

Left wing. Shoots left. 5'11", 180 lbs. Born, Ostrov nad Ohri, Czech., June 27, 1985. Dallas' 2nd choice, 36th overall, in 2003 Entry Draft.

Season	Club	League	GP	G	A	Pts	PIM	PP	SH	GW	S	%	+/-	TF	F%	Min	GP	G	A	Pts	PIM	PP	SH	GW	Min
99-2000	Karlovy Vary Jr.	CzRep-Jr.	49	17	23	40	48																		
2000-01	Karlovy Vary Jr.	CzRep-Jr.	47	36	33	69	38																		
	Karlovy Vary	CzRep	2	0	0	0	0																		
2001-02	Karlovy Vary Jr.	CzRep-Jr.	37	11	14	25	26																		
	Karlovy Vary	CzRep	9	1	1	2	2																		
2002-03	Karlovy Vary	CzRep	41	7	9	16	51																		
	Karlovy Vary Jr.	CzRep-Jr.	6	3	7	10	18																		
2003-04	HC Sparta Praha	CzRep	1	1	0	1	0																		
	Karlovy Vary	CzRep	44	0	8	8	42																		
	Karlovy Vary Jr.	CzRep-Jr.	5	8	4	12	2																		
2004-05	Jihlava Jr.	CzRep-Jr.	5	4	1	5	6																		
	HC Dukla Jihlava	CzRep	16	1	2	3	12																		
	Karlovy Vary Jr.	CzRep-Jr.	3	5	5	10	6																		
	SK Kadan	CzRep-2	7	1	2	3	39																		
	Karlovy Vary	CzRep	26	1	5	6	4																		
2005-06	**Dallas**	**NHL**	**3**	**0**	**0**	**0**	**0**	**0**	**0**	**0**	**3**	**0.0**	**–1**	**2**	**50.0**	**6:31**									
	Iowa Stars	AHL	60	12	22	34	41										3	0	1	1	0				
2006-07	**Dallas**	**NHL**	**2**	**0**	**0**	**0**	**0**	**0**	**0**	**0**	**2**	**0.0**	**–1**	**0**	**0.0**	**7:43**									
	Iowa Stars	AHL	67	17	28	45	48										7	1	0	1	8				
	NHL Totals		**5**	**0**	**0**	**0**	**0**	**0**	**0**	**0**	**5**	**0.0**		**2**	**50.0**	**7:00**									

POLLOCK, Jame

(PAWL-luhk, JAY-mee) **WSH.**

Defense. Shoots right. 6'1", 210 lbs. Born, Quebec City, Que., June 16, 1979. St. Louis' 4th choice, 106th overall, in 1997 Entry Draft.

Season	Club	League	GP	G	A	Pts	PIM	PP	SH	GW	S	%	+/-	TF	F%	Min	GP	G	A	Pts	PIM	PP	SH	GW	Min
1994-95	Victoria Legion	BCAHA	43	22	56	78	96																		
1995-96	Seattle	WHL	32	0	1	1	15																		
1996-97	Seattle	WHL	66	15	19	34	94										15	3	5	8	16				
1997-98	Seattle	WHL	66	11	36	47	78										5	0	1	1	17				
1998-99	Seattle	WHL	59	10	32	42	78										11	3	4	7	8				
99-2000	Worcester IceCats	AHL	56	12	12	24	50										9	5	3	8	6				
2000-01	Worcester IceCats	AHL	55	15	8	23	36										11	1	7	8	10				
2001-02	Worcester IceCats	AHL	71	23	43	66	89										3	1	0	1	2				
2002-03	Worcester IceCats	AHL	44	5	17	22	50										3	1	0	1	2				
2003-04	**St. Louis**	**NHL**	**9**	**0**	**0**	**0**	**6**	**0**	**0**	**0**	**19**	**0.0**	**–1**	**0**	**0.0**	**15:25**									
	Worcester IceCats	AHL	44	8	24	32	52										7	1	4	5	14				
2004-05	Kloten Flyers	Swiss	26	4	8	12	34																		
	HC Lugano	Swiss															2	0	1	1	8				
2005-06	Nurnberg	Germany	52	8	11	19	130										4	1	0	1	10				
2006-07	Nurnberg	Germany	46	22	32	54	78										13	5	9	14	46				
	NHL Totals		**9**	**0**	**0**	**0**	**6**	**0**	**0**	**0**	**19**	**0.0**		**0**	**0.0**	**15:25**									

Signed as a free agent by **Kloten** (Swiss), April 6, 2004. Signed as a free agent by **Lugano** (Swiss), February 22, 2005. Signed as a free agent by **Washington**, July 5, 2007.

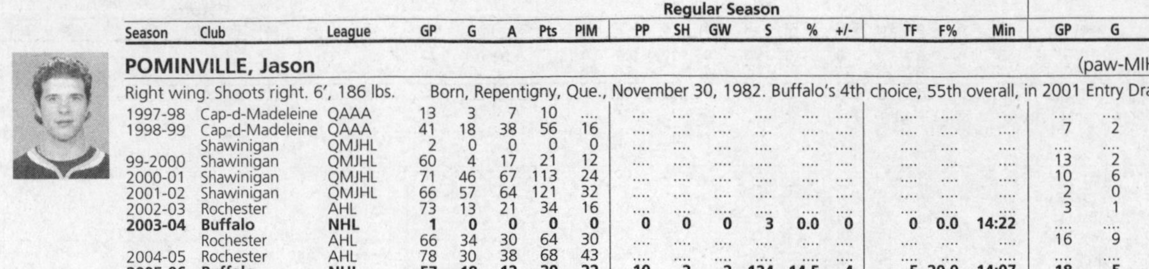

POMINVILLE, Jason

(paw-MIHN-vihl, JAY-suhn) **BUF.**

Right wing. Shoots right. 6', 186 lbs. Born, Repentigny, Que., November 30, 1982. Buffalo's 4th choice, 55th overall, in 2001 Entry Draft.

			Regular Season														Playoffs								
Season	Club	League	GP	G	A	Pts	PIM	PP	SH	GW	S	%	+/-	TF	F%	Min	GP	G	A	Pts	PIM	PP	SH	GW	Min
1997-98	Cap-d-Madeleine	QAAA	13	3	7	10	....																		
1998-99	Cap-d-Madeleine	QAAA	41	18	38	56	16										7	2	7	9	0				
	Shawinigan	QMJHL	2	0	0	0	0																		
99-2000	Shawinigan	QMJHL	60	4	17	21	12										13	2	3	5	0				
2000-01	Shawinigan	QMJHL	71	46	67	113	24										10	6	6	12	0				
2001-02	Shawinigan	QMJHL	66	57	64	121	32										2	0	0	0	0				
2002-03	Rochester	AHL	73	13	21	34	16										3	1	1	2	0				
2003-04	**Buffalo**	**NHL**	**1**	**0**	**0**	**0**	**0**	**0**	**0**	**0**	**3**	**0.0**	**0**	**0**	**0.0**	**14:22**									
	Rochester	AHL	66	34	30	64	30										16	9	10	19	6				
2004-05	Rochester	AHL	78	30	38	68	43																		
2005-06	**Buffalo**	**NHL**	**57**	**18**	**12**	**30**	**22**	**10**	**2**	**2**	**124**	**14.5**	**–4**	**5**	**20.0**	**14:07**	**18**	**5**	**5**	**10**	**8**	**0**	**1**	**1**	**12:11**
	Rochester	AHL	18	19	7	26	11																		
2006-07	**Buffalo**	**NHL**	**82**	**34**	**34**	**68**	**30**	**2**	**2**	**5**	**212**	**16.0**	**25**	**14**	**42.9**	**17:25**	**16**	**4**	**6**	**10**	**0**	**0**	**0**	**0**	**17:54**
	NHL Totals		**140**	**52**	**46**	**98**	**52**	**12**	**4**	**7**	**339**	**15.3**		**19**	**36.8**	**16:03**	**34**	**9**	**11**	**20**	**8**	**0**	**1**	**1**	**14:52**

QMJHL First All-Star Team (2002)

PONIKAROVSKY, Alexei

(poh-nih-kahr-OHV-skee, al-EHX-ay) **TOR.**

Left wing. Shoots left. 6'4", 220 lbs. Born, Kiev, USSR, April 9, 1980. Toronto's 4th choice, 87th overall, in 1998 Entry Draft.

Season	Club	League	GP	G	A	Pts	PIM	PP	SH	GW	S	%	+/-	TF	F%	Min	GP	G	A	Pts	PIM	PP	SH	GW	Min
1996-97	Dyn'o Moscow 2	Russia-3	60	12	15	27	30																		
	Dyn'o Moscow 2	Russia-3	2	0	0	0	2																		
1997-98	Dynamo Moscow	Russia	24	1	2	3	30																		
1998-99	Krylja Sovetov	Russia	13	2	1	3	2																		
	Dynamo Moscow	Russia	....	....	....	....	....										3	0	0	0	2				
99-2000	THK Tver	Russia-2	29	8	14	22	26																		
	Dynamo Moscow	Russia	19	1	0	1	8										1	0	0	0	0				
	Dynamo Moscow	EuroHL	2	0	2	2	0																		
2000-01	**Toronto**	**NHL**	**22**	**1**	**3**	**4**	**14**	**0**	**0**	**0**	**21**	**4.8**	**–1**	**7**	**28.6**	**8:32**									
	St. John's	AHL	49	12	24	36	44										4	0	0	0	4				
2001-02	**Toronto**	**NHL**	**8**	**2**	**0**	**2**	**0**	**0**	**0**	**1**	**8**	**25.0**	**2**	**2**	**50.0**	**8:03**	**10**	**0**	**0**	**0**	**4**	**0**	**0**	**0**	**8:15**
	St. John's	AHL	72	21	27	48	74										5	2	1	3	8				
	Ukraine	Olympics	4	1	1	2	6																		
2002-03	**Toronto**	**NHL**	**13**	**0**	**3**	**3**	**11**	**0**	**0**	**0**	**13**	**0.0**	**4**	**4**	**25.0**	**10:43**									
	St. John's	AHL	63	24	22	46	68																		
2003-04	**Toronto**	**NHL**	**73**	**9**	**19**	**28**	**44**	**1**	**0**	**2**	**110**	**8.2**	**14**	**20**	**30.0**	**11:36**	**13**	**1**	**3**	**4**	**8**	**0**	**0**	**1**	**14:20**
2004-05	Voskresensk	Russia	19	1	5	6	16																		
2005-06	**Toronto**	**NHL**	**81**	**21**	**17**	**38**	**68**	**2**	**4**	**3**	**157**	**13.4**	**15**	**13**	**30.8**	**14:06**									
2006-07	**Toronto**	**NHL**	**71**	**21**	**24**	**45**	**63**	**6**	**0**	**1**	**198**	**10.6**	**8**	**4**	**25.0**	**17:06**									
	NHL Totals		**268**	**54**	**66**	**120**	**200**	**9**	**4**	**7**	**507**	**10.7**		**50**	**30.0**	**13:25**	**23**	**1**	**3**	**4**	**12**	**0**	**0**	**1**	**11:42**

Signed as a free agent by **Voskresensk** (Russia), November 13, 2004.

POPOVIC, Mark

(poh-PUH-vihk, MAHRK) **ATL.**

Defense. Shoots left. 6'1", 210 lbs. Born, Stoney Creek, Ont., October 11, 1982. Anaheim's 2nd choice, 35th overall, in 2001 Entry Draft.

Season	Club	League	GP	G	A	Pts	PIM	PP	SH	GW	S	%	+/-	TF	F%	Min	GP	G	A	Pts	PIM	PP	SH	GW	Min
1997-98	Mississauga	OPJHL	51	10	16	26	32																		
1998-99	St. Michael's	OHL	60	6	26	32	46																		
99-2000	St. Michael's	OHL	68	11	29	40	68																		
2000-01	St. Michael's	OHL	61	7	35	42	54										18	3	5	8	22				
2001-02	St. Michael's	OHL	58	12	29	41	42										15	1	11	12	10				
2002-03	Cincinnati	AHL	73	3	21	24	46																		
2003-04	**Anaheim**	**NHL**	**1**	**0**	**0**	**0**	**0**	**0**	**0**	**0**	**1**	**0.0**	**0**	**0**	**0.0**	**13:48**									
	Cincinnati	AHL	74	4	10	14	63										9	1	2	3	4				
2004-05	Cincinnati	AHL	74	1	17	18	47										11	2	3	5	6				
2005-06	**Atlanta**	**NHL**	**7**	**0**	**0**	**0**	**0**	**0**	**0**	**0**	**6**	**0.0**	**–5**	**0**	**0.0**	**11:04**									
	Chicago Wolves	AHL	73	12	26	38	51																		
2006-07	**Atlanta**	**NHL**	**3**	**0**	**1**	**1**	**0**	**0**	**0**	**0**	**1**	**0.0**	**1**	**0**	**0.0**	**10:15**									
	Chicago Wolves	AHL	65	16	24	40	51										15	3	6	9	4				
	NHL Totals		**11**	**0**	**1**	**1**	**0**	**0**	**0**	**0**	**8**	**0.0**		**0**	**0.0**	**11:05**									

OHL First All-Star Team (2002)

Traded to **Atlanta** by **Anaheim** for Kip Brennan, August 23, 2005.

POTHIER, Brian

(POH-thee-uhr, BRIGH-uhn) **WSH.**

Defense. Shoots right. 6', 198 lbs. Born, New Bedford, MA, April 15, 1977.

Season	Club	League	GP	G	A	Pts	PIM	PP	SH	GW	S	%	+/-	TF	F%	Min	GP	G	A	Pts	PIM	PP	SH	GW	Min
1995-96	NMH School	High-MA	27	11	22	33	36																		
1996-97	RPI Engineers	ECAC	34	1	11	12	42																		
1997-98	RPI Engineers	ECAC	35	2	9	11	28																		
1998-99	RPI Engineers	ECAC	37	5	13	18	36																		
99-2000	RPI Engineers	ECAC	36	9	24	33	44																		
2000-01	**Atlanta**	**NHL**	**3**	**0**	**0**	**0**	**2**	**0**	**0**	**0**	**0**	**0.0**	**4**	**0**	**0.0**	**20:38**									
	Orlando	IHL	76	12	29	41	69										16	3	5	8	11				
2001-02	**Atlanta**	**NHL**	**33**	**3**	**6**	**9**	**22**	**1**	**0**	**1**	**65**	**4.6**	**–19**	**0**	**0.0**	**21:41**									
	Chicago Wolves	AHL	39	6	13	19	30																		
2002-03	**Ottawa**	**NHL**	**14**	**2**	**4**	**6**	**6**	**0**	**0**	**1**	**23**	**8.7**	**11**	**0**	**0.0**	**15:23**	**1**	**0**	**0**	**0**	**2**	**0**	**0**	**0**	**13:11**
	Binghamton	AHL	68	7	40	47	58										8	2	8	10	4				
2003-04	**Ottawa**	**NHL**	**55**	**2**	**6**	**8**	**24**	**1**	**0**	**1**	**78**	**2.6**	**6**	**0**	**0.0**	**16:43**	**7**	**0**	**0**	**0**	**6**	**0**	**0**	**0**	**17:15**
2004-05	Binghamton	AHL	77	12	36	48	64										6	0	1	1	6				
2005-06	**Ottawa**	**NHL**	**77**	**5**	**30**	**35**	**59**	**3**	**0**	**0**	**133**	**3.8**	**29**	**0**	**0.0**	**16:46**	**8**	**2**	**1**	**3**	**2**	**0**	**0**	**0**	**15:02**
2006-07	**Washington**	**NHL**	**72**	**3**	**25**	**28**	**44**	**2**	**0**	**0**	**118**	**2.5**	**–11**	**0**	**0.0**	**23:59**									
	NHL Totals		**254**	**15**	**71**	**86**	**157**	**7**	**0**	**3**	**417**	**3.6**		**0**	**0.0**	**19:25**	**16**	**2**	**1**	**3**	**10**	**0**	**0**	**0**	**15:53**

ECAC Second All-Star Team (2000) • ECAC All-Tournament Team (2000) • NCAA East Second All-American Team (2000) • Ken McKenzie Trophy (U.S. - Born Rookie of the Year – IHL) (2001) • Garry F. Longman Memorial Trophy (Rookie of the Year – IHL) (2001) • AHL Second All-Star Team (2003, 2005)

Signed as a free agent by **Atlanta**, March 27, 2000. Traded to **Ottawa** by **Atlanta** for Shawn McEachern and Ottawa's 6th round choice (Dan Turple) in 2004 Entry Draft, June 29, 2002. Signed as a free agent by **Washington**, July 1, 2006.

POTI, Tom

(POH-tee, TAWM) **WSH.**

Defense. Shoots left. 6'3", 202 lbs. Born, Worcester, MA, March 22, 1977. Edmonton's 4th choice, 59th overall, in 1996 Entry Draft.

Season	Club	League	GP	G	A	Pts	PIM	PP	SH	GW	S	%	+/-	TF	F%	Min	GP	G	A	Pts	PIM	PP	SH	GW	Min
1992-93	St. Peter's Marian	High-MA	55	25	46	71	....																		
1993-94	Cushing	High-MA	30	10	35	45	....																		
1994-95	Cushing	High-MA	36	17	54	71	35																		
	Central-Mass	MBAHL	8	8	10	18	....																		
1995-96	Cushing	High-MA	29	14	59	73	18																		
1996-97	Boston University	H-East	38	4	17	21	54																		
1997-98	Boston University	H-East	38	13	29	42	60																		
1998-99	**Edmonton**	**NHL**	**73**	**5**	**16**	**21**	**42**	**2**	**0**	**3**	**94**	**5.3**	**10**	**0**	**0.0**	**19:33**	**4**	**0**	**1**	**1**	**2**	**0**	**0**	**0**	**28:02**
99-2000	**Edmonton**	**NHL**	**76**	**9**	**26**	**35**	**65**	**2**	**1**	**1**	**125**	**7.2**	**8**	**0**	**0.0**	**24:10**	**5**	**0**	**1**	**1**	**0**	**0**	**0**	**0**	**23:53**
2000-01	**Edmonton**	**NHL**	**81**	**12**	**20**	**32**	**60**	**6**	**0**	**3**	**161**	**7.5**	**–4**	**0**	**0.0**	**22:44**	**6**	**0**	**2**	**2**	**2**	**0**	**0**	**0**	**20:25**
2001-02	**Edmonton**	**NHL**	**55**	**1**	**16**	**17**	**42**	**1**	**0**	**0**	**100**	**1.0**	**–6**	**0**	**0.0**	**24:32**									
	United States	Olympics	6	0	1	1	4																		
	NY Rangers	**NHL**	**11**	**1**	**7**	**8**	**2**	**1**	**0**	**1**	**9**	**11.1**	**–4**	**0**	**0.0**	**21:45**									
2002-03	**NY Rangers**	**NHL**	**80**	**11**	**37**	**48**	**58**	**3**	**0**	**2**	**148**	**7.4**	**–6**	**0**	**0.0**	**24:43**									
2003-04	**NY Rangers**	**NHL**	**67**	**10**	**14**	**24**	**47**	**4**	**0**	**5**	**124**	**8.1**	**–1**	**0**	**0.0**	**22:28**									

Season	Club	League	Regular Season														Playoffs								
			GP	G	A	Pts	PIM	PP	SH	GW	S	%	+/-	TF	F%	Min	GP	G	A	Pts	PIM	PP	SH	GW	Min
2004-05			DID NOT PLAY																						
2005-06	**NY Rangers**	**NHL**	**73**	**3**	**20**	**23**	**70**	**2**	**0**	**2**	**122**	**2.5**	**16**	**4**	**25.0**	**20:46**	**4**	**0**	**0**	**0**	**2**	**0**	**0**	**0**	**19:39**
2006-07	**NY Islanders**	**NHL**	**78**	**6**	**38**	**44**	**74**	**6**	**0**	**1**	**134**	**4.5**	**–1**	**0**	**0.0**	**25:43**	**5**	**0**	**3**	**3**	**6**	**0**	**0**	**0**	**27:34**
	NHL Totals		**594**	**58**	**194**	**252**	**460**	**27**	**1**	**18**	**1017**	**5.7**		**4**	**25.0**	**23:04**	**24**	**0**	**7**	**7**	**12**	**0**	**0**	**0**	**23:46**

NCAA Championship All-Tournament Team (1997) • Hockey East First All-Star Team (1998) • NCAA East First All-American Team (1998) • NHL All-Rookie Team (1999)

Played in NHL All-Star Game (2003)

Traded to **NY Rangers** by **Edmonton** with Rem Murray for Mike York and NY Rangers' 4th round choice (Ivan Koltsov) in 2002 Entry Draft, March 19, 2002. Signed as a free agent by **NY Islanders**, July 8, 2006. Signed as a free agent by **Washington**, July 1, 2007.

POTULNY, Ryan

(poh-TUHL-nee, RIGH-uhn) **PHI.**

Center. Shoots left. 6', 190 lbs. Born, Grand Forks, ND, September 5, 1984. Philadelphia's 6th choice, 87th overall, in 2003 Entry Draft.

Season	Club	League	GP	G	A	Pts	PIM	PP	SH	GW	S	%	+/-	TF	F%	Min	GP	G	A	Pts	PIM	PP	SH	GW	Min
2001-02	Lincoln Stars	USHL	60	23	34	57	65	....	....	....	....	....	....	....	....	....	4	0	1	1	2	....	....	....	....
2002-03	Lincoln Stars	USHL	54	35	*43	*78	18	....	....	....	....	....	....	....	....	....	10	6	*11	*17	8	....	....	....	....
2003-04	U. of Minnesota	WCHA	15	6	8	14	10	....	....	....	....	....	....	....	....	....	....	....	....	....	....	....	....	....	....
2004-05	U. of Minnesota	WCHA	44	24	17	41	20	....	....	....	....	....	....	....	....	....	....	....	....	....	....	....	....	....	....
2005-06	U. of Minnesota	WCHA	41	*38	25	*63	31	....	....	....	....	....	....	....	....	....	....	....	....	....	....	....	....	....	....
	Philadelphia	**NHL**	**2**	**0**	**1**	**1**	**0**	**0**	**0**	**0**	**0**	**0.0**	**1**	**9**	**44.4**	**6:09**	....	....	....	....	....	....	....	....	....
2006-07	**Philadelphia**	**NHL**	**35**	**7**	**5**	**12**	**22**	**0**	**0**	**2**	**56**	**12.5**	**1**	**278**	**43.5**	**11:00**	....	....	....	....	....	....	....	....	....
	Philadelphia	AHL	30	12	14	26	34	....	....	....	....	....	....	....	....	....	....	....	....	....	....	....	....	....	....
	NHL Totals		**37**	**7**	**6**	**13**	**22**	**0**	**0**	**2**	**56**	**12.5**		**287**	**43.6**	**10:44**	....	....	....	....	....	....	....	....	....

USHL First All-Star Team (2003) • USHL Player of the Year (2003) • USA Junior Player of the Year (2003) • WCHA First All-Star Team (2006) • NCAA West First All-American Team (2006)

• Missed majority of 2003-04 season recovering from knee injury suffered in game vs. North Dakota (WCHA), November 7, 2003.

POULIOT, Benoit

(POO-lee-oh, BEHN-wah) **MIN.**

Left wing. Shoots left. 6'3", 199 lbs. Born, Alfred, Ont., September 29, 1986. Minnesota's 1st choice, 4th overall, in 2005 Entry Draft.

Season	Club	League	GP	G	A	Pts	PIM	PP	SH	GW	S	%	+/-	TF	F%	Min	GP	G	A	Pts	PIM	PP	SH	GW	Min
2002-03	Clarence Beavers	OHA-B	38	13	17	30	86	....	....	....	....	....	....	....	....	....	5	0	2	2	8	....	....	....	....
	Hawkesbury	CJHL	1	1	0	1	0	....	....	....	....	....	....	....	....	....	....	....	....	....	....	....	....	....	....
2003-04	Hawkesbury	CJHL	45	21	21	42	85	....	....	....	....	....	....	....	....	....	6	3	7	10	10	....	....	....	....
	Sudbury Wolves	OHL	4	2	2	4	0	....	....	....	....	....	....	....	....	....	4	2	1	3	0	....	....	....	....
2004-05	Sudbury Wolves	OHL	67	29	38	67	102	....	....	....	....	....	....	....	....	....	12	6	8	14	20	....	....	....	....
2005-06	Sudbury Wolves	OHL	51	35	30	65	141	....	....	....	....	....	....	....	....	....	8	8	3	11	16	....	....	....	....
	Houston Aeros	AHL	....	....	....	....	....	....	....	....	....	....	....	....	....	....	2	0	0	0	2	....	....	....	....
2006-07	**Minnesota**	**NHL**	**3**	**0**	**0**	**0**	**0**	**0**	**0**	**0**	**1**	**0.0**	**–1**	**2**	**0.0**	**6:58**	....	....	....	....	....	....	....	....	....
	Houston Aeros	AHL	67	19	17	36	109	....	....	....	....	....	....	....	....	....	....	....	....	....	....	....	....	....	....
	NHL Totals		**3**	**0**	**0**	**0**	**0**	**0**	**0**	**0**	**1**	**0.0**		**2**	**0.0**	**6:58**	....	....	....	....	....	....	....	....	....

OHL First All-Star Team (2005) • OHL Rookie of the Year (2005) • Canadian Major Junior All-Rookie Team (2005) • Canadian Major Junior Rookie of the Year (2005)

POULIOT, Marc-Antoine

(POO-lee-awt, MAHRK-AN-twahn) **EDM.**

Center. Shoots right. 6'1", 195 lbs. Born, Quebec City, Que., May 22, 1985. Edmonton's 1st choice, 22nd overall, in 2003 Entry Draft.

Season	Club	League	GP	G	A	Pts	PIM	PP	SH	GW	S	%	+/-	TF	F%	Min	GP	G	A	Pts	PIM	PP	SH	GW	Min
2000-01	Ste-Foy	QAAA	38	16	39	55	52	....	....	....	....	....	....	....	....	....	16	8	12	20	16	....	....	....	....
2001-02	Rimouski Oceanic	QMJHL	28	9	14	23	32	....	....	....	....	....	....	....	....	....	5	0	0	0	4	....	....	....	....
2002-03	Rimouski Oceanic	QMJHL	65	32	41	73	100	....	....	....	....	....	....	....	....	....	....	....	....	....	....	....	....	....	....
2003-04	Rimouski Oceanic	QMJHL	42	25	33	58	62	....	....	....	....	....	....	....	....	....	9	5	7	12	12	....	....	....	....
2004-05	Rimouski Oceanic	QMJHL	70	45	69	114	83	....	....	....	....	....	....	....	....	....	13	4	15	19	8	....	....	....	....
2005-06	**Edmonton**	**NHL**	**8**	**1**	**0**	**1**	**0**	**0**	**0**	**0**	**5**	**20.0**	**1**	**56**	**55.4**	**8:30**	....	....	....	....	....	....	....	....	....
	Hamilton	AHL	65	15	31	46	63	....	....	....	....	....	....	....	....	....	....	....	....	....	....	....	....	....	....
2006-07	**Edmonton**	**NHL**	**46**	**4**	**7**	**11**	**18**	**0**	**0**	**0**	**73**	**5.5**	**–2**	**353**	**48.7**	**13:03**	....	....	....	....	....	....	....	....	....
	Wilkes-Barre	AHL	33	14	17	31	20	....	....	....	....	....	....	....	....	....	11	5	5	10	4	....	....	....	....
	NHL Totals		**54**	**5**	**7**	**12**	**18**	**0**	**0**	**0**	**78**	**6.4**		**409**	**49.6**	**12:22**	....	....	....	....	....	....	....	....	....

QMJHL First All-Star Team (2005) • George Parsons Trophy (Memorial Cup Tournament Most Sportsmanlike Player) (2005)

PRATT, Nolan

(PRAT, NOH-luhn)

Defense. Shoots left. 6'3", 207 lbs. Born, Fort McMurray, Alta., August 14, 1975. Hartford's 4th choice, 115th overall, in 1993 Entry Draft.

Season	Club	League	GP	G	A	Pts	PIM	PP	SH	GW	S	%	+/-	TF	F%	Min	GP	G	A	Pts	PIM	PP	SH	GW	Min
1991-92	Bonnyville	AJHL	33	3	7	10	57	....	....	....	....	....	....	....	....	....	....	....	....	....	....	....	....	....	....
	Portland	WHL	22	2	9	11	13	....	....	....	....	....	....	....	....	....	6	1	3	4	12	....	....	....	....
1992-93	Portland	WHL	70	4	19	23	97	....	....	....	....	....	....	....	....	....	16	2	7	9	31	....	....	....	....
1993-94	Portland	WHL	72	4	32	36	105	....	....	....	....	....	....	....	....	....	10	1	2	3	14	....	....	....	....
1994-95	Portland	WHL	72	6	37	43	196	....	....	....	....	....	....	....	....	....	9	1	6	7	10	....	....	....	....
1995-96	Springfield	AHL	62	2	6	8	72	....	....	....	....	....	....	....	....	....	2	0	0	0	0	....	....	....	....
	Richmond	ECHL	4	1	0	1	2	....	....	....	....	....	....	....	....	....	....	....	....	....	....	....	....	....	....
1996-97	**Hartford**	**NHL**	**9**	**0**	**2**	**2**	**6**	**0**	**0**	**0**	**4**	**0.0**	**0**	....	....	....	....	....	....	....	....	....	....	....	....
	Springfield	AHL	66	1	18	19	127	....	....	....	....	....	....	....	....	....	17	0	3	3	18	....	....	....	....
1997-98	**Carolina**	**NHL**	**23**	**0**	**2**	**2**	**44**	**0**	**0**	**0**	**11**	**0.0**	**–2**	....	....	....	....	....	....	....	....	....	....	....	....
	New Haven	AHL	54	3	15	18	135	....	....	....	....	....	....	....	....	....	....	....	....	....	....	....	....	....	....
1998-99	**Carolina**	**NHL**	**61**	**1**	**14**	**15**	**95**	**0**	**0**	**1**	**46**	**2.2**	**15**	**0**	**0.0**	**16:45**	**3**	**0**	**0**	**0**	**2**	**0**	**0**	**0**	**19:58**
99-2000	**Carolina**	**NHL**	**64**	**3**	**1**	**4**	**90**	**0**	**0**	**1**	**47**	**6.4**	**–22**	**0**	**0.0**	**19:10**	....	....	....	....	....	....	....	....	....
2000-01	**Colorado**	**NHL**	**46**	**1**	**2**	**3**	**40**	**0**	**0**	**1**	**26**	**3.8**	**2**	**1**	**0.0**	**9:50**	....	....	....	....	....	....	....	....	....
2001-02	**Tampa Bay**	**NHL**	**46**	**0**	**3**	**3**	**51**	**0**	**0**	**0**	**38**	**0.0**	**–4**	**1**	**0.0**	**18:25**	....	....	....	....	....	....	....	....	....
2002-03	**Tampa Bay**	**NHL**	**67**	**1**	**7**	**8**	**35**	**0**	**0**	**0**	**38**	**2.6**	**–6**	**0**	**0.0**	**17:34**	**4**	**0**	**1**	**1**	**0**	**0**	**0**	**0**	**21:01**
2003-04♦	**Tampa Bay**	**NHL**	**58**	**1**	**3**	**4**	**42**	**0**	**0**	**0**	**35**	**2.9**	**11**	**0**	**0.0**	**16:25**	**20**	**0**	**0**	**0**	**8**	**0**	**0**	**0**	**18:06**
2004-05	EV Duisburg	German-2	10	2	2	4	14	....	....	....	....	....	....	....	....	....	12	0	3	3	10	....	....	....	....
2005-06	**Tampa Bay**	**NHL**	**82**	**0**	**9**	**9**	**60**	**0**	**0**	**0**	**26**	**0.0**	**7**	**0**	**0.0**	**17:59**	**5**	**0**	**0**	**0**	**7**	**0**	**0**	**0**	**15:30**
2006-07	**Tampa Bay**	**NHL**	**81**	**1**	**7**	**8**	**44**	**0**	**0**	**0**	**30**	**3.3**	**0**	**1**	**0.0**	**15:47**	**6**	**0**	**0**	**0**	**5**	**0**	**0**	**0**	**14:32**
	NHL Totals		**537**	**8**	**50**	**58**	**507**	**0**	**0**	**3**	**301**	**2.7**		**3**	**0.0**	**16:42**	**38**	**0**	**1**	**1**	**22**	**0**	**0**	**0**	**17:39**

Transferred to **Carolina** after **Hartford** franchise relocated, June 25, 1997. Traded to **Colorado** by **Carolina** with Carolina's 1st (Vaclav Nedorost) and 2nd (Jared Aulin) round choices in 2000 Entry Draft and Philadelphia's 2nd round choice (previously acquired, Colorado selected Agris Saviels) in 2000 Entry Draft for Sandis Ozolinsh and Columbus' 2nd round choice (previously acquired, Carolina selected Tomas Kurka) in 2000 Entry Draft, June 24, 2000. Traded to **Tampa Bay** by **Colorado** for Los Angeles' 6th round choice (previously acquired, Colorado selected Scott Horvath) in 2001 Entry Draft, June 24, 2001. Signed as a free agent by **Duisburg** (German-2), January 15, 2005.

PREISSING, Tom

(PREH-sihng, TAWM) **L.A.**

Defense. Shoots right. 6', 198 lbs. Born, Arlington Heights, IL, December 3, 1978.

Season	Club	League	GP	G	A	Pts	PIM	PP	SH	GW	S	%	+/-	TF	F%	Min	GP	G	A	Pts	PIM	PP	SH	GW	Min
1997-98	Green Bay	USHL	56	8	13	21	30	....	....	....	....	....	....	....	....	....	4	0	2	2	2	....	....	....	....
1998-99	Green Bay	USHL	53	18	37	55	40	....	....	....	....	....	....	....	....	....	6	3	6	9	2	....	....	....	....
99-2000	Colorado College	WCHA	36	4	14	18	20	....	....	....	....	....	....	....	....	....	....	....	....	....	....	....	....	....	....
2000-01	Colorado College	WCHA	33	6	18	24	26	....	....	....	....	....	....	....	....	....	....	....	....	....	....	....	....	....	....
2001-02	Colorado College	WCHA	43	6	26	32	42	....	....	....	....	....	....	....	....	....	....	....	....	....	....	....	....	....	....
2002-03	Colorado College	WCHA	42	23	29	52	16	....	....	....	....	....	....	....	....	....	....	....	....	....	....	....	....	....	....
2003-04	**San Jose**	**NHL**	**69**	**2**	**17**	**19**	**12**	**2**	**0**	**1**	**89**	**2.2**	**8**	**0**	**0.0**	**18:12**	**11**	**0**	**1**	**1**	**0**	**0**	**0**	**0**	**12:49**
2004-05	Krefeld Pinguine	Germany	33	1	6	7	32	....	....	....	....	....	....	....	....	....	....	....	....	....	....	....	....	....	....
2005-06	**San Jose**	**NHL**	**74**	**11**	**32**	**43**	**26**	**2**	**0**	**2**	**131**	**8.4**	**17**	**1**	**0.0**	**20:30**	**11**	**1**	**6**	**7**	**4**	**0**	**0**	**0**	**23:50**
2006-07	**Ottawa**	**NHL**	**80**	**7**	**31**	**38**	**18**	**3**	**0**	**0**	**94**	**7.4**	**40**	**0**	**0.0**	**15:15**	**20**	**2**	**5**	**7**	**10**	**1**	**0**	**1**	**15:02**
	NHL Totals		**223**	**20**	**80**	**100**	**56**	**7**	**0**	**3**	**314**	**6.4**		**1**	**0.0**	**17:54**	**42**	**3**	**12**	**15**	**14**	**1**	**0**	**1**	**16:45**

WCHA First All-Star Team (2003) • NCAA West First All-American Team (2003)

Signed as a free agent by **San Jose**, April 4, 2003. Signed as a free agent by **Krefeld** (Germany), November 15, 2004. Traded to **Chicago** by **San Jose** with Josh Hennessy for Mark Bell, July 9, 2006. Traded to **Ottawa** by **Chicago** with Josh Hennessy, Michal Barinka and Chicago's 2nd round choice in 2008 Entry Draft for Martin Havlat and Bryan Smolinski, July 10, 2006. Signed as a free agent by **Los Angeles**, July 2, 2007.

PRIMEAU, Wayne

(PREE-moh, WAYN) **CGY.**

Center. Shoots left. 6'4", 231 lbs. Born, Scarborough, Ont., June 4, 1976. Buffalo's 1st choice, 17th overall, in 1994 Entry Draft.

			Regular Season														Playoffs								
Season	Club	League	GP	G	A	Pts	PIM	PP	SH	GW	S	%	+/-	TF	F%	Min	GP	G	A	Pts	PIM	PP	SH	GW	Min
1991-92	Whitby Flyers	Minor-ON	63	36	50	86	96																		
1992-93	Owen Sound	OHL	66	10	27	37	108										8	1	4	5	0				
1993-94	Owen Sound	OHL	65	25	50	75	75										9	1	6	7	8				
1994-95	Owen Sound	OHL	66	34	62	96	84										10	4	9	13	15				
	Buffalo	**NHL**	**1**	**1**	**0**	**1**	**0**	**0**	**0**	**1**	**2**	**50.0**	**-2**												
1995-96	Owen Sound	OHL	28	15	29	44	52																		
	Oshawa Generals	OHL	24	12	13	25	33										3	2	3	5	2				
	Buffalo	**NHL**	**2**	**0**	**0**	**0**	**0**	**0**	**0**	**0**	**0**	**0.0**	**0**												
	Rochester	AHL	8	2	3	5	6										17	3	1	4	11				
1996-97	**Buffalo**	**NHL**	**45**	**2**	**4**	**6**	**64**	**1**	**0**	**0**	**25**	**8.0**	**-2**				**9**	**0**	**0**	**0**	**6**	**0**	**0**	**0**	
	Rochester	AHL	24	9	5	14	27										1	0	0	0	0				
1997-98	**Buffalo**	**NHL**	**69**	**6**	**6**	**12**	**87**	**2**	**0**	**1**	**51**	**11.8**	**9**				**14**	**1**	**3**	**4**	**6**	**0**	**0**	**0**	
1998-99	**Buffalo**	**NHL**	**67**	**5**	**8**	**13**	**38**	**2**	**0**	**0**	**55**	**9.1**	**-6**	**529**	**48.6**	**10:19**	**19**	**3**	**4**	**7**	**6**	**1**	**0**	**0**	**13:29**
99-2000	**Buffalo**	**NHL**	**41**	**5**	**7**	**12**	**38**	**2**	**0**	**1**	**40**	**12.5**	**-8**	**430**	**45.6**	**11:03**									
	Tampa Bay	**NHL**	**17**	**2**	**3**	**5**	**25**	**0**	**0**	**0**	**35**	**5.7**	**-4**	**290**	**45.5**	**14:21**									
2000-01	**Tampa Bay**	**NHL**	**47**	**2**	**13**	**15**	**77**	**0**	**0**	**0**	**47**	**4.3**	**-17**	**630**	**52.2**	**14:11**									
	Pittsburgh	**NHL**	**28**	**1**	**6**	**7**	**54**	**0**	**0**	**0**	**30**	**3.3**	**0**	**318**	**51.3**	**12:45**	**18**	**1**	**3**	**4**	**2**	**0**	**0**	**0**	**15:06**
2001-02	**Pittsburgh**	**NHL**	**33**	**3**	**7**	**10**	**18**	**0**	**1**	**0**	**28**	**10.7**	**-1**	**519**	**53.2**	**12:38**									
2002-03	**Pittsburgh**	**NHL**	**70**	**5**	**11**	**16**	**55**	**1**	**0**	**0**	**101**	**5.0**	**-30**	**1240**	**50.4**	**16:17**									
	San Jose	**NHL**	**7**	**1**	**1**	**2**	**0**	**0**	**0**	**0**	**13**	**7.7**	**2**	**98**	**45.9**	**15:59**									
2003-04	**San Jose**	**NHL**	**72**	**9**	**20**	**29**	**90**	**0**	**0**	**1**	**142**	**6.3**	**4**	**867**	**46.6**	**15:28**	**17**	**1**	**2**	**3**	**4**	**0**	**0**	**0**	**15:41**
2004-05			DID NOT PLAY																						
2005-06	**San Jose**	**NHL**	**21**	**5**	**3**	**8**	**17**	**1**	**1**	**1**	**35**	**14.3**	**-6**	**194**	**41.8**	**13:55**									
	Boston	**NHL**	**50**	**6**	**8**	**14**	**40**	**0**	**0**	**0**	**66**	**9.1**	**-10**	**749**	**49.8**	**17:16**									
2006-07	**Boston**	**NHL**	**51**	**7**	**8**	**15**	**75**	**2**	**1**	**1**	**72**	**9.7**	**-15**	**652**	**50.5**	**15:05**									
	Calgary	**NHL**	**27**	**3**	**4**	**7**	**36**	**0**	**1**	**2**	**35**	**8.6**	**-2**	**199**	**46.2**	**10:38**	**6**	**0**	**2**	**2**	**14**	**0**	**0**	**0**	**13:29**
	NHL Totals		**648**	**63**	**109**	**172**	**714**	**9**	**5**	**8**	**777**	**8.1**		**6715**	**49.2**	**13:57**	**83**	**6**	**14**	**20**	**38**	**1**	**0**	**0**	**14:36**

Traded to **Tampa Bay** by **Buffalo** with Cory Sarich, Brian Holzinger and Buffalo's 3rd round choice (Alexander Kharitonov) in 2000 Entry Draft for Chris Gratton and Tampa Bay's 2nd round choice (Derek Roy) in 2001 Entry Draft, March 9, 2000. Traded to **Pittsburgh** by **Tampa Bay** for Matthew Barnaby, February 1, 2001. • Missed majority of 2001-02 season recovering from knee injury suffered in game vs. Buffalo, January 8, 2002. Traded to **San Jose** by **Pittsburgh** for Matt Bradley, March 11, 2003. Traded to **Boston** by **San Jose** with Brad Stuart and Marco Sturm for Joe Thornton, November 30, 2005. Traded to **Calgary** by **Boston** with Brad Stuart for Andrew Ference and Chuck Kobasew, February 10, 2007.

PRINTZ, David

(PRIHNTS, DAY-vihd)

Defense. Shoots left. 6'5", 220 lbs. Born, Stockholm, Sweden, July 24, 1980. Philadelphia's 9th choice, 225th overall, in 2001 Entry Draft.

Season	Club	League	GP	G	A	Pts	PIM	PP	SH	GW	S	%	+/-	TF	F%	Min	GP	G	A	Pts	PIM	PP	SH	GW	Min
1996-97	AIK Solna Jr.	Swe-Jr.	1	0	0	0	0																		
1997-98	AIK Solna Jr.	Swe-Jr.	8	0	0	0	6																		
1998-99	AIK Solna Jr.	Swe-Jr.	23	1	0	1	14																		
99-2000	AIK Solna Jr.	Swe-Jr.	36	8	4	12	53																		
2000-01	Great Falls	AWHL	54	13	23	36	93										13	3	5	8	16				
2001-02	AIK Solna Jr.	Swe-Jr.	8	2	3	5	20																		
	AIK Solna	Sweden	37	3	2	5	59																		
	AIK Solna	Sweden-Q	10	0	0	0	12																		
2002-03	HPK Hameenlinna	Finland	17	1	0	1	10																		
	Ilves Tampere	Finland	25	1	2	3	10																		
2003-04	AIK Solna	Sweden-2	51	2	9	11	60										5	2	0	2	4				
2004-05	Philadelphia	AHL	50	1	5	6	66										1	0	0	0	0				
	Trenton Titans	ECHL	2	0	1	1	0																		
2005-06	**Philadelphia**	**NHL**	**1**	**0**	**0**	**0**	**0**	**0**	**0**	**0**	**0**	**0.0**	**0**	**0**	**0.0**	**5:45**									
	Philadelphia	AHL	80	6	14	20	135																		
2006-07	**Philadelphia**	**NHL**	**12**	**0**	**0**	**0**	**4**	**0**	**0**	**0**	**1**	**0.0**	**-3**	**0**	**0.0**	**6:33**									
	Philadelphia	AHL	62	4	12	16	73																		
	NHL Totals		**13**	**0**	**0**	**0**	**4**	**0**	**0**	**0**	**1**	**0.0**		**0**	**0.0**	**6:29**									

Signed as a free agent by **Djurgarden** (Sweden), June 4, 2007.

PRONGER, Chris

(PRAHN-guhr, KRIHS) **ANA.**

Defense. Shoots left. 6'6", 220 lbs. Born, Dryden, Ont., October 10, 1974. Hartford's 1st choice, 2nd overall, in 1993 Entry Draft.

Season	Club	League	GP	G	A	Pts	PIM	PP	SH	GW	S	%	+/-	TF	F%	Min	GP	G	A	Pts	PIM	PP	SH	GW	Min
1990-91	Stratford Cullitons	OHA-B	48	15	37	52	132																		
1991-92	Peterborough	OHL	63	17	45	62	90										10	1	8	9	28				
1992-93	Peterborough	OHL	61	15	62	77	108										21	15	25	40	51				
1993-94	**Hartford**	**NHL**	**81**	**5**	**25**	**30**	**113**	**2**	**0**	**0**	**174**	**2.9**	**-3**												
1994-95	**Hartford**	**NHL**	**43**	**5**	**9**	**14**	**54**	**3**	**0**	**1**	**94**	**5.3**	**-12**												
1995-96	**St. Louis**	**NHL**	**78**	**7**	**18**	**25**	**110**	**3**	**1**	**1**	**138**	**5.1**	**-18**				**13**	**1**	**5**	**6**	**16**	**0**	**0**	**0**	
1996-97	**St. Louis**	**NHL**	**79**	**11**	**24**	**35**	**143**	**4**	**0**	**0**	**147**	**7.5**	**15**				**6**	**1**	**1**	**2**	**22**	**0**	**0**	**0**	
1997-98	**St. Louis**	**NHL**	**81**	**9**	**27**	**36**	**180**	**1**	**0**	**2**	**145**	**6.2**	**47**				**10**	**1**	**9**	**10**	**26**	**0**	**0**	**0**	
	Canada	Olympics	6	0	0	0	4																		
1998-99	**St. Louis**	**NHL**	**67**	**13**	**33**	**46**	**113**	**8**	**0**	**0**	**172**	**7.6**	**3**	**0**	**0.0**	**30:36**	**13**	**1**	**4**	**5**	**28**	**1**	**0**	**0**	**35:53**
99-2000	**St. Louis**	**NHL**	**79**	**14**	**48**	**62**	**92**	**8**	**0**	**3**	**192**	**7.3**	**52**	**1**	**0.0**	**30:14**	**7**	**3**	**4**	**7**	**32**	**2**	**0**	**2**	**30:14**
2000-01	**St. Louis**	**NHL**	**51**	**8**	**39**	**47**	**75**	**4**	**0**	**0**	**121**	**6.6**	**21**	**0**	**0.0**	**27:45**	**15**	**1**	**7**	**8**	**32**	**0**	**0**	**0**	**33:50**
2001-02	**St. Louis**	**NHL**	**78**	**7**	**40**	**47**	**120**	**4**	**1**	**3**	**204**	**3.4**	**23**	**0**	**0.0**	**29:28**	**9**	**1**	**7**	**8**	**24**	**0**	**0**	**0**	**27:51**
	Canada	Olympics	6	0	1	1	2																		
2002-03	**St. Louis**	**NHL**	**5**	**1**	**3**	**4**	**10**	**0**	**0**	**0**	**11**	**9.1**	**-2**	**1**	**0.0**	**21:39**	**7**	**1**	**3**	**4**	**14**	**0**	**0**	**0**	**24:36**
2003-04	**St. Louis**	**NHL**	**80**	**14**	**40**	**54**	**88**	**7**	**0**	**3**	**203**	**6.9**	**-1**	**2**	**0.0**	**27:28**	**5**	**0**	**1**	**1**	**16**	**0**	**0**	**0**	**27:54**
2004-05			DID NOT PLAY																						
2005-06	**Edmonton**	**NHL**	**80**	**12**	**44**	**56**	**74**	**10**	**0**	**3**	**155**	**7.7**	**2**	**1**	**0.0**	**27:59**	**24**	**5**	**16**	**21**	**26**	**3**	**0**	**0**	**30:57**
	Canada	Olympics	6	1	2	3	16																		
2006-07♦	**Anaheim**	**NHL**	**66**	**13**	**46**	**59**	**69**	**8**	**0**	**2**	**166**	**7.8**	**27**	**4**	**25.0**	**27:06**	**19**	**3**	**12**	**15**	**26**	**1**	**0**	**0**	**30:11**
	NHL Totals		**868**	**119**	**396**	**515**	**1241**	**62**	**2**	**18**	**1922**	**6.2**		**9**	**11.1**	**28:38**	**128**	**18**	**69**	**87**	**262**	**7**	**0**	**2**	**30:57**

OHL All-Rookie Team (1992) • OHL First All-Star Team (1993) • Canadian Major Junior First All-Star Team (1993) • Canadian Major Junior Defenseman of the Year (1993) • NHL All-Rookie Team (1994) • NHL Second All-Star Team (1998, 2004, 2007) • Bud Ice Plus/Minus Award (1998) • NHL First All-Star Team (2000) • Bud Light Plus/Minus Award (2000) • James Norris Memorial Trophy (2000) • Hart Memorial Trophy (2000)

Played in NHL All-Star Game (1999, 2000, 2002, 2004)

Traded to **St. Louis** by **Hartford** for Brendan Shanahan, July 27, 1995. • Missed majority of 2002-03 season recovering from wrist and knee surgery, September 10, 2002. Traded to **Edmonton** by **St. Louis** for Eric Brewer, Doug Lynch and Jeff Woywitka, August 2, 2005. Traded to **Anaheim** by **Edmonton** for Joffrey Lupul, Ladislav Smid, Anaheim's 1st round choice (later traded to Phoenix - Phoenix selected Nick Ross) in 2007 Entry Draft and Anaheim's 1st round choice in 2008 Entry Draft, July 3, 2006.

PROSPAL, Vaclav

(PRAWS-puhl, VAT-slav) **T.B.**

Center. Shoots left. 6'1", 194 lbs. Born, Ceske Budejovice, Czech., February 17, 1975. Philadelphia's 2nd choice, 71st overall, in 1993 Entry Draft.

Season	Club	League	GP	G	A	Pts	PIM	PP	SH	GW	S	%	+/-	TF	F%	Min	GP	G	A	Pts	PIM	PP	SH	GW	Min
1991-92	C. Budejovice Jr.	Czech-Jr.	36	16	16	32	12																		
1992-93	C. Budejovice Jr.	Czech-Jr.	32	26	31	57	24																		
1993-94	Hershey Bears	AHL	55	14	21	35	38										2	0	0	0	2				
1994-95	Hershey Bears	AHL	69	13	32	45	36										2	1	0	1	4				
1995-96	Hershey Bears	AHL	68	15	36	51	59										5	2	4	6	2				
1996-97	**Philadelphia**	**NHL**	**18**	**5**	**10**	**15**	**4**	**0**	**0**	**0**	**35**	**14.3**	**3**				**5**	**1**	**3**	**4**	**4**	**0**	**0**	**0**	
	Philadelphia	AHL	63	32	63	95	70																		
1997-98	**Philadelphia**	**NHL**	**41**	**5**	**13**	**18**	**17**	**4**	**0**	**0**	**60**	**8.3**	**-10**												
	Ottawa	**NHL**	**15**	**1**	**6**	**7**	**4**	**0**	**0**	**0**	**28**	**3.6**	**-1**				**6**	**0**	**0**	**0**	**0**	**0**	**0**	**0**	
1998-99	**Ottawa**	**NHL**	**79**	**10**	**26**	**36**	**58**	**2**	**0**	**3**	**114**	**8.8**	**8**	**997**	**56.2**	**13:03**	**4**	**0**	**0**	**0**	**0**	**0**	**0**	**0**	**12:37**
99-2000	**Ottawa**	**NHL**	**79**	**22**	**33**	**55**	**40**	**5**	**0**	**4**	**204**	**10.8**	**-2**	**1331**	**49.6**	**16:26**	**6**	**0**	**4**	**4**	**4**	**0**	**0**	**0**	**17:40**
2000-01	**Ottawa**	**NHL**	**40**	**1**	**12**	**13**	**12**	**0**	**0**	**0**	**68**	**1.5**	**1**	**501**	**50.1**	**12:57**									
	Florida	**NHL**	**34**	**4**	**12**	**16**	**10**	**0**	**0**	**0**	**68**	**5.9**	**-2**	**487**	**54.6**	**16:36**									
2001-02	**Tampa Bay**	**NHL**	**81**	**18**	**37**	**55**	**38**	**7**	**0**	**2**	**166**	**10.8**	**-11**	**555**	**52.8**	**17:31**									
2002-03	**Tampa Bay**	**NHL**	**80**	**22**	**57**	**79**	**53**	**9**	**0**	**4**	**134**	**16.4**	**9**	**161**	**51.6**	**18:39**	**11**	**4**	**2**	**6**	**8**	**2**	**0**	**0**	**21:15**
2003-04	**Anaheim**	**NHL**	**82**	**19**	**35**	**54**	**54**	**7**	**0**	**4**	**185**	**10.3**	**-9**	**45**	**46.7**	**18:37**									
2004-05	C. Budejovice	CzRep-2	39	28	60	88	82										16	15	15	30	32				

			Regular Season														Playoffs								
Season	Club	League	GP	G	A	Pts	PIM	PP	SH	GW	S	%	+/-	TF	F%	Min	GP	G	A	Pts	PIM	PP	SH	GW	Min
2005-06	**Tampa Bay**	**NHL**	**81**	**25**	**55**	**80**	**50**	**10**	**0**	**3**	**236**	**10.6**	**–3**	**267**	**45.3**	**19:10**	**5**	**0**	**2**	**2**	**0**	**0**	**0**	**0**	**15:56**
	Czech Republic	Olympics	8	4	2	6	2	....	....	....	....	....	....	....	....	....	....	....	....	....	....	....	....	....	....
2006-07	**Tampa Bay**	**NHL**	**82**	**14**	**41**	**55**	**36**	**2**	**0**	**1**	**219**	**6.4**	**–24**	**124**	**52.4**	**19:04**	**6**	**1**	**4**	**5**	**4**	**0**	**0**	**1**	**22:19**
	NHL Totals		**712**	**146**	**337**	**483**	**376**	**47**	**0**	**21**	**1517**	**9.6**		**4468**	**51.9**	**17:11**	**43**	**6**	**15**	**21**	**20**	**2**	**0**	**1**	**18:52**

AHL First All-Star Team (1997)

Traded to **Ottawa** by **Philadelphia** with Pat Falloon and Dallas' 2nd round choice (previously acquired, Ottawa selected Chris Bala) in 1998 Entry Draft for Alexandre Daigle, January 17, 1998. Traded to **Florida** by **Ottawa** for future considerations, January 20, 2001. Traded to **Tampa Bay** by **Florida** for Ryan Johnson and Tampa Bay's 6th round choice (later traded back to Tampa Bay – Tampa Bay selected Doug O'Brien) in 2003 Entry Draft, July 10, 2001. Signed as a free agent by **Anaheim**, July 17, 2003. Traded to **Tampa Bay** by **Anaheim** for Tampa Bay's 2nd round choice (Brendan Mikkelson) in 2005 Entry Draft, August 16, 2004. Signed as a free agent by **Ceske Budejovice** (CzRep-2), September 17, 2004.

PRUCHA, Petr
(PROO-khah, PEE-tuhr) **NYR**

Right wing. Shoots right. 6', 175 lbs. Born, Chrudim, Czech., September 14, 1982. NY Rangers' 8th choice, 240th overall, in 2002 Entry Draft.

Season	Club	League	GP	G	A	Pts	PIM	PP	SH	GW	S	%	+/-	TF	F%	Min	GP	G	A	Pts	PIM	PP	SH	GW	Min
99-2000	HC Chrudim Jr.	CzRep-Jr.	43	35	27	62	62	....	....	....	....	....	....	....	....	....	....	....	....	....	....	....	....	....	....
2000-01	HC Pardubice Jr.	CzRep-Jr.	54	39	22	61	18	....	....	....	....	....	....	....	....	....	....	....	....	....	....	....	....	....	....
2001-02	HC Pardubice Jr.	CzRep-Jr.	28	38	28	66	18	....	....	....	....	....	....	....	....	....	3	2	6	8	0	....	....	....	....
	Sumperk	CzRep-2	8	6	4	10	0	....	....	....	....	....	....	....	....	....	....	....	....	....	....	....	....	....	....
	Sumperk	CzRep-Q	5	5	3	8	0	....	....	....	....	....	....	....	....	....	....	....	....	....	....	....	....	....	....
	Pardubice	CzRep	20	1	1	2	2	....	....	....	....	....	....	....	....	....	5	0	0	0	0	....	....	....	....
2002-03	Pardubice	CzRep	49	7	9	16	12	....	....	....	....	....	....	....	....	....	17	2	6	8	8	....	....	....	....
	HC Pardubice Jr.	CzRep-Jr.	4	5	4	9	25	....	....	....	....	....	....	....	....	....	....	....	....	....	....	....	....	....	....
	Hr. Kralove	CzRep-2	11	3	5	8	35	....	....	....	....	....	....	....	....	....	....	....	....	....	....	....	....	....	....
2003-04	Pardubice	CzRep	48	11	13	24	24	....	....	....	....	....	....	....	....	....	7	4	3	7	2	....	....	....	....
	Hr. Kralove	CzRep-2	3	1	0	1	25	....	....	....	....	....	....	....	....	....	....	....	....	....	....	....	....	....	....
2004-05	Pardubice	CzRep	47	7	10	17	24	....	....	....	....	....	....	....	....	....	16	6	7	13	2	....	....	....	....
2005-06	**NY Rangers**	**NHL**	**68**	**30**	**17**	**47**	**32**	**16**	**0**	**2**	**130**	**23.1**	**3**	**150**	**52.0**	**13:42**	**4**	**1**	**0**	**1**	**0**	**1**	**0**	**0**	**14:13**
	Hartford	AHL	2	2	1	3	0	....	....	....	....	....	....	....	....	....	....	....	....	....	....	....	....	....	....
2006-07	**NY Rangers**	**NHL**	**79**	**22**	**18**	**40**	**30**	**8**	**0**	**2**	**136**	**16.2**	**–7**	**70**	**50.0**	**13:00**	**10**	**0**	**1**	**1**	**4**	**0**	**0**	**0**	**13:35**
	NHL Totals		**147**	**52**	**35**	**87**	**62**	**24**	**0**	**4**	**266**	**19.5**		**220**	**51.4**	**13:19**	**14**	**1**	**1**	**2**	**4**	**1**	**0**	**0**	**13:46**

PRUST, Brandon
(PROOST, BRAN-duhn) **CGY.**

Center/Left wing. Shoots left. 5'11", 195 lbs. Born, London, Ont., March 16, 1984. Calgary's 2nd choice, 70th overall, in 2004 Entry Draft.

Season	Club	League	GP	G	A	Pts	PIM	PP	SH	GW	S	%	+/-	TF	F%	Min	GP	G	A	Pts	PIM	PP	SH	GW	Min
2001-02	London Nationals	OHA-B	52	17	35	52	38	....	....	....	....	....	....	....	....	....	....	....	....	....	....	....	....	....	....
2002-03	London Knights	OHL	65	12	17	29	94	....	....	....	....	....	....	....	....	....	14	2	1	3	21	....	....	....	....
2003-04	London Knights	OHL	64	19	33	52	269	....	....	....	....	....	....	....	....	....	15	7	13	20	33	....	....	....	....
2004-05	London Knights	OHL	48	10	20	30	174	....	....	....	....	....	....	....	....	....	15	3	5	8	*71	....	....	....	....
2005-06	Omaha	AHL	79	12	14	26	294	....	....	....	....	....	....	....	....	....	....	....	....	....	....	....	....	....	....
2006-07	**Calgary**	**NHL**	**10**	**0**	**0**	**0**	**25**	**0**	**0**	**0**	**1**	**0.0**	**1**	**0**	**0.0**	**6:03**	....	....	....	....	....	....	....	....	....
	Omaha	AHL	63	17	10	27	211	....	....	....	....	....	....	....	....	....	6	0	3	3	20	....	....	....	....
	NHL Totals		**10**	**0**	**0**	**0**	**25**	**0**	**0**	**0**	**1**	**0.0**		**0**	**0.0**	**6:03**	....	....	....	....	....	....	....	....	....

PURINTON, Dale
(PUHR-ihn-TUHN, DAYL) **COL.**

Defense. Shoots left. 6'3", 228 lbs. Born, Fort Wayne, IN, October 11, 1976. NY Rangers' 5th choice, 117th overall, in 1995 Entry Draft.

Season	Club	League	GP	G	A	Pts	PIM	PP	SH	GW	S	%	+/-	TF	F%	Min	GP	G	A	Pts	PIM	PP	SH	GW	Min
1992-93	Moose Jaw	SMHL	34	1	16	17	107	....	....	....	....	....	....	....	....	....	....	....	....	....	....	....	....	....	....
	Moose Jaw	WHL	2	0	0	0	2	....	....	....	....	....	....	....	....	....	....	....	....	....	....	....	....	....	....
1993-94	Vernon Vipers	BCJHL	42	1	6	7	194	....	....	....	....	....	....	....	....	....	....	....	....	....	....	....	....	....	....
1994-95	Tacoma Rockets	WHL	65	0	8	8	291	....	....	....	....	....	....	....	....	....	3	0	0	0	13	....	....	....	....
1995-96	Kelowna Rockets	WHL	22	1	4	5	88	....	....	....	....	....	....	....	....	....	....	....	....	....	....	....	....	....	....
	Lethbridge	WHL	37	3	6	9	144	....	....	....	....	....	....	....	....	....	4	1	1	2	25	....	....	....	....
1996-97	Lethbridge	WHL	51	6	26	32	254	....	....	....	....	....	....	....	....	....	18	3	5	8	*88	....	....	....	....
1997-98	Hartford	AHL	17	0	0	0	95	....	....	....	....	....	....	....	....	....	....	....	....	....	....	....	....	....	....
	Charlotte	ECHL	34	3	5	8	186	....	....	....	....	....	....	....	....	....	....	....	....	....	....	....	....	....	....
1998-99	Hartford	AHL	45	1	3	4	306	....	....	....	....	....	....	....	....	....	7	0	2	2	24	....	....	....	....
99-2000	**NY Rangers**	**NHL**	**1**	**0**	**0**	**0**	**7**	**0**	**0**	**0**	**1**	**0.0**	**–1**	**0**	**0.0**	**12:45**	....	....	....	....	....	....	....	....	....
	Hartford	AHL	62	4	4	8	415	....	....	....	....	....	....	....	....	....	23	0	3	3	*87	....	....	....	....
2000-01	**NY Rangers**	**NHL**	**42**	**0**	**2**	**2**	**180**	**0**	**0**	**0**	**13**	**0.0**	**5**	**0**	**0.0**	**9:33**	....	....	....	....	....	....	....	....	....
	Hartford	AHL	11	0	1	1	75	....	....	....	....	....	....	....	....	....	....	....	....	....	....	....	....	....	....
2001-02	**NY Rangers**	**NHL**	**40**	**0**	**4**	**4**	**113**	**0**	**0**	**0**	**11**	**0.0**	**4**	**0**	**0.0**	**7:37**	....	....	....	....	....	....	....	....	....
2002-03	**NY Rangers**	**NHL**	**58**	**3**	**9**	**12**	**161**	**0**	**0**	**0**	**50**	**6.0**	**–2**	**0**	**0.0**	**15:02**	....	....	....	....	....	....	....	....	....
2003-04	**NY Rangers**	**NHL**	**40**	**1**	**1**	**2**	**117**	**0**	**0**	**0**	**31**	**3.2**	**–9**	**0**	**0.0**	**12:47**	....	....	....	....	....	....	....	....	....
2004-05	Victoria	ECHL	25	3	9	12	192	....	....	....	....	....	....	....	....	....	....	....	....	....	....	....	....	....	....
2005-06	Hartford	AHL	25	3	3	6	109	....	....	....	....	....	....	....	....	....	10	0	2	2	45	....	....	....	....
2006-07	Hartford	AHL	55	3	7	10	240	....	....	....	....	....	....	....	....	....	5	0	1	1	29	....	....	....	....
	NHL Totals		**181**	**4**	**16**	**20**	**578**	**0**	**0**	**0**	**106**	**3.8**		**0**	**0.0**	**11:37**	....	....	....	....	....	....	....	....	....

• Spent majority of 2003-04 season as a healthy reserve. Signed as a free agent by **Victoria** (ECHL), December 3, 2004. • Missed majority of 2005-06 season recovering from knee (November 6, 2005 at Springfield - AHL) and finger (January 3, 2006 in practice) injuries. Signed as a free agent by **Colorado**, July 17, 2007.

PUSHKAREV, Konstantin
(puhsh-KAR-ehv, KAWN-stan-tihn) **DAL.**

Right wing. Shoots left. 6', 180 lbs. Born, Ust-Kamenogorsk, USSR, February 12, 1985. Los Angeles' 4th choice, 44th overall, in 2003 Entry Draft.

Season	Club	League	GP	G	A	Pts	PIM	PP	SH	GW	S	%	+/-	TF	F%	Min	GP	G	A	Pts	PIM	PP	SH	GW	Min
2002-03	Ust-Kam'gorsk 2	Russia-3	STATISTICS NOT AVAILABLE																						
	Ust-Kamenogorsk	Russia-2	4	0	0	0	4	....	....	....	....	....	....	....	....	....	....	....	....	....	....	....	....	....	....
2003-04	Avangard Omsk	Russia	5	1	0	1	0	....	....	....	....	....	....	....	....	....	....	....	....	....	....	....	....	....	....
	Omsk 2	Russia-3	34	17	11	28	64	....	....	....	....	....	....	....	....	....	....	....	....	....	....	....	....	....	....
2004-05	Avangard Omsk	Russia	1	0	0	0	0	....	....	....	....	....	....	....	....	....	....	....	....	....	....	....	....	....	....
	Calgary Hitmen	WHL	69	22	30	52	50	....	....	....	....	....	....	....	....	....	12	2	5	7	4	....	....	....	....
2005-06	**Los Angeles**	**NHL**	**1**	**0**	**1**	**1**	**0**	**0**	**0**	**0**	**0**	**0.0**	**0**	**0**	**0.0**	**9:33**	....	....	....	....	....	....	....	....	....
	Manchester	AHL	77	19	19	38	95	....	....	....	....	....	....	....	....	....	7	1	1	2	4	....	....	....	....
2006-07	**Los Angeles**	**NHL**	**16**	**2**	**2**	**4**	**8**	**0**	**0**	**0**	**10**	**20.0**	**–2**	**1**	**0.0**	**9:10**	....	....	....	....	....	....	....	....	....
	Manchester	AHL	35	4	11	15	29	....	....	....	....	....	....	....	....	....	....	....	....	....	....	....	....	....	....
	Iowa Stars	AHL	15	2	5	7	25	....	....	....	....	....	....	....	....	....	12	1	4	5	18	....	....	....	....
	NHL Totals		**17**	**2**	**3**	**5**	**8**	**0**	**0**	**0**	**10**	**20.0**		**1**	**0.0**	**9:12**	....	....	....	....	....	....	....	....	....

Traded to **Dallas** by **Los Angeles** with Mattias Norstrom and Los Angeles' 3rd (Sergei Korostin) and 4th (later traded to Columbus - Columbus selected Maxim Mayorov) round choices in 2007 Entry Draft for Jaroslav Modry, the rights to Johan Fransson, Dallas' 2nd (Oscar Moller) and 3rd (Bryan Cameron) round choices in 2007 Entry Draft and Dallas' 1st round choice in 2008 Entry Draft , February 27, 2007.

PUSHOR, Jamie
(PUH-shohr, JAY-mee)

Defense. Shoots right. 6'3", 218 lbs. Born, Lethbridge, Alta., February 11, 1973. Detroit's 2nd choice, 32nd overall, in 1991 Entry Draft.

Season	Club	League	GP	G	A	Pts	PIM	PP	SH	GW	S	%	+/-	TF	F%	Min	GP	G	A	Pts	PIM	PP	SH	GW	Min
1988-89	Lethbridge	AMHL	37	1	8	9	20	....	....	....	....	....	....	....	....	....	....	....	....	....	....	....	....	....	....
	Lethbridge	WHL	2	0	0	0	0	....	....	....	....	....	....	....	....	....	....	....	....	....	....	....	....	....	....
1989-90	Lethbridge	AMHL	35	6	27	33	92	....	....	....	....	....	....	....	....	....	....	....	....	....	....	....	....	....	....
	Lethbridge	WHL	10	0	2	2	2	....	....	....	....	....	....	....	....	....	16	0	0	0	63	....	....	....	....
1990-91	Lethbridge	WHL	71	1	13	14	202	....	....	....	....	....	....	....	....	....	....	....	....	....	....	....	....	....	....
1991-92	Lethbridge	WHL	49	2	15	17	232	....	....	....	....	....	....	....	....	....	5	0	0	0	33	....	....	....	....
1992-93	Lethbridge	WHL	72	6	22	28	200	....	....	....	....	....	....	....	....	....	4	0	1	1	9	....	....	....	....
1993-94	Adirondack	AHL	73	1	17	18	124	....	....	....	....	....	....	....	....	....	12	0	0	0	22	....	....	....	....
1994-95	Adirondack	AHL	58	2	11	13	129	....	....	....	....	....	....	....	....	....	4	0	1	1	0	....	....	....	....
1995-96	**Detroit**	**NHL**	**5**	**0**	**1**	**1**	**17**	**0**	**0**	**0**	**6**	**0.0**	**2**	....	....	....	....	....	....	....	....	....	....	....	....
	Adirondack	AHL	65	2	16	18	126	....	....	....	....	....	....	....	....	....	3	0	0	0	5	....	....	....	....
1996-97♦	**Detroit**	**NHL**	**75**	**4**	**7**	**11**	**129**	**0**	**0**	**0**	**63**	**6.3**	**1**	....	....	....	**5**	**0**	**1**	**1**	**5**	**0**	**0**	**0**	....
1997-98	**Detroit**	**NHL**	**54**	**2**	**5**	**7**	**71**	**0**	**0**	**0**	**43**	**4.7**	**2**	....	....	....	....	....	....	....	....	....	....	....	....
	Anaheim	**NHL**	**10**	**0**	**2**	**2**	**10**	**0**	**0**	**0**	**8**	**0.0**	**1**	....	....	....	....	....	....	....	....	....	....	....	....
1998-99	**Anaheim**	**NHL**	**70**	**1**	**2**	**3**	**112**	**0**	**0**	**0**	**75**	**1.3**	**–20**	**0**	**0.0**	**19:16**	**4**	**0**	**0**	**0**	**6**	**0**	**0**	**0**	**14:08**
99-2000	**Dallas**	**NHL**	**62**	**0**	**8**	**8**	**53**	**0**	**0**	**0**	**27**	**0.0**	**0**	**0**	**0.0**	**11:36**	**5**	**0**	**0**	**0**	**5**	**0**	**0**	**0**	**10:06**
2000-01	**Columbus**	**NHL**	**75**	**3**	**10**	**13**	**94**	**0**	**1**	**0**	**64**	**4.7**	**7**	**0**	**0.0**	**20:48**	....	....	....	....	....	....	....	....	....
2001-02	**Columbus**	**NHL**	**61**	**0**	**6**	**6**	**54**	**0**	**0**	**0**	**46**	**0.0**	**–10**	**0**	**0.0**	**17:06**	....	....	....	....	....	....	....	....	....
	Pittsburgh	**NHL**	**15**	**0**	**2**	**2**	**30**	**0**	**0**	**0**	**14**	**0.0**	**–3**	**0**	**0.0**	**19:03**	....	....	....	....	....	....	....	....	....
2002-03	**Pittsburgh**	**NHL**	**76**	**3**	**1**	**4**	**76**	**0**	**0**	**0**	**54**	**5.6**	**–28**	**0**	**0.0**	**16:58**	....	....	....	....	....	....	....	....	....

Season	Club	League	Regular Season														Playoffs								
			GP	G	A	Pts	PIM	PP	SH	GW	S	%	+/-	TF	F%	Min	GP	G	A	Pts	PIM	PP	SH	GW	Min
2003-04	Syracuse Crunch	AHL	17	1	4	5	24	....	....	....	....	....	....	....	....	....	....	....	....	....	....	....	....	....	....
	Columbus	**NHL**	**7**	**0**	**0**	**0**	**2**	**0**	**0**	**0**	**6**	**0.0**	**–2**	**0**	**0.0**	**13:12**	....	....	....	....	....	....	....	....	....
	NY Rangers	**NHL**	**7**	**0**	**0**	**0**	**0**	**0**	**0**	**0**	**4**	**0.0**	**–3**	**0**	**0.0**	**13:08**	....	....	....	....	....	....	....	....	....
	Hartford	AHL	14	0	2	2	21	....	....	....	....	....	....	....	....	....	16	1	1	2	18	....	....	....	....
2004-05	Syracuse Crunch	AHL	68	1	9	10	85	....	....	....	....	....	....	....	....	....	....	....	....	....	....	....	....	....	....
2005-06	**Columbus**	**NHL**	**4**	**1**	**2**	**3**	**0**	**0**	**0**	**0**	**2**	**50.0**	**1**	**0**	**0.0**	**18:13**	....	....	....	....	....	....	....	....	....
	Syracuse Crunch	AHL	72	5	17	22	132	....	....	....	....	....	....	....	....	....	6	0	1	1	9	....	....	....	....
2006-07	Syracuse Crunch	AHL	37	2	9	11	63	....	....	....	....	....	....	....	....	....	....	....	....	....	....	....	....	....	....
	NHL Totals		**521**	**14**	**46**	**60**	**648**	**0**	**1**	**0**	**412**	**3.4**		**0**	**0.0**	**17:15**	**14**	**0**	**1**	**1**	**16**	**0**	**0**	**0**	**11:53**

Traded to **Anaheim** by **Detroit** with Detroit's 4th round choice (Viktor Wallin) in 1998 Entry Draft for Dmitri Mironov, March 24, 1998. Claimed by **Atlanta** from **Anaheim** in Expansion Draft, June 25, 1999. Traded to **Dallas** by **Atlanta** for Jason Botterill, July 15, 1999. Claimed by **Columbus** from **Dallas** in Expansion Draft, June 23, 2000. Traded to **Pittsburgh** by **Columbus** for Pittsburgh's 4th round choice (Kevin Jarman) in 2003 Entry Draft, March 15, 2002. Signed as a free agent by **Syracuse** (AHL), November 18, 2003. Signed as a free agent by **Columbus**, December 10, 2003. Traded to **NY Rangers** by **Columbus** for NY Rangers' 8th round choice (Matt Greer) in 2004 Entry Draft, January 23, 2004. Signed as a free agent by **Syracuse** (AHL), August 9, 2004. Traded to **Phoenix** by **Detroit** for Phoenix's 7th round choice (Nick Oslund) in 2006 Entry Draft, March 9, 2006. Signed as a free agent by **Columbus**, July 21, 2006.

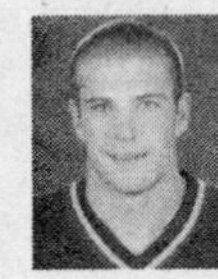

PYATT, Taylor

(PIGH-at, TAY-luhr) **VAN.**

Left wing. Shoots left. 6'4", 220 lbs. Born, Thunder Bay, Ont., August 19, 1981. NY Islanders' 2nd choice, 8th overall, in 1999 Entry Draft.

Season	Club	League	GP	G	A	Pts	PIM	PP	SH	GW	S	%	+/-	TF	F%	Min	GP	G	A	Pts	PIM	PP	SH	GW	Min
1996-97	Thunder Bay	TBAHA	60	52	61	113	72	....	....	....	....	....	....	....	....	....	....	....	....	....	....	....	....	....	....
1997-98	Sudbury Wolves	OHL	58	14	17	31	104	....	....	....	....	....	....	....	....	....	10	3	1	4	8	....	....	....	....
1998-99	Sudbury Wolves	OHL	68	37	38	75	95	....	....	....	....	....	....	....	....	....	4	0	4	4	6	....	....	....	....
99-2000	Sudbury Wolves	OHL	68	40	49	89	98	....	....	....	....	....	....	....	....	....	12	8	7	15	25	....	....	....	....
2000-01	**NY Islanders**	**NHL**	**78**	**4**	**14**	**18**	**39**	**1**	**0**	**2**	**86**	**4.7**	**–17**	**1**	**0.0**	**12:14**	....	....	....	....	....	....	....	....	....
2001-02	**Buffalo**	**NHL**	**48**	**10**	**10**	**20**	**35**	**0**	**0**	**0**	**61**	**16.4**	**4**	**0**	**0.0**	**13:30**	....	....	....	....	....	....	....	....	....
	Rochester	AHL	27	6	4	10	36	....	....	....	....	....	....	....	....	....	....	....	....	....	....	....	....	....	....
2002-03	**Buffalo**	**NHL**	**78**	**14**	**14**	**28**	**38**	**2**	**0**	**0**	**110**	**12.7**	**–8**	**8**	**25.0**	**14:06**	....	....	....	....	....	....	....	....	....
2003-04	**Buffalo**	**NHL**	**63**	**8**	**12**	**20**	**25**	**1**	**2**	**4**	**98**	**8.2**	**–7**	**19**	**26.3**	**15:36**	....	....	....	....	....	....	....	....	....
2004-05	Hammarby	Sweden-2	24	11	9	20	20	....	....	....	....	....	....	....	....	....	....	....	....	....	....	....	....	....	....
2005-06	**Buffalo**	**NHL**	**41**	**6**	**6**	**12**	**33**	**0**	**0**	**1**	**62**	**9.7**	**–1**	**11**	**18.2**	**11:14**	**14**	**0**	**5**	**5**	**10**	**0**	**0**	**0**	**11:08**
2006-07	**Vancouver**	**NHL**	**76**	**23**	**14**	**37**	**42**	**9**	**0**	**4**	**150**	**15.3**	**5**	**4**	**0.0**	**13:58**	**12**	**2**	**4**	**6**	**6**	**0**	**0**	**1**	**18:02**
	NHL Totals		**384**	**65**	**70**	**135**	**212**	**13**	**2**	**11**	**567**	**11.5**		**43**	**20.9**	**13:33**	**26**	**2**	**9**	**11**	**16**	**0**	**0**	**1**	**14:19**

OHL First All-Star Team (2000)

Traded to **Buffalo** by **NY Islanders** with Tim Connolly for Michael Peca, June 24, 2001. Signed as a free agent by **Hammarby** (Sweden-2), November 16, 2004. Rights traded to **Vancouver** by **Buffalo** for Vancouver's 4th round choice (later traded to Calgary - Calgary selected Keith Aulie) in 2007 Entry Draft, July 14, 2006.

QUINCEY, Kyle

(KWIHN-see, KIGHL) **DET.**

Defense. Shoots left. 6'1", 207 lbs. Born, Kitchener, Ont., August 12, 1985. Detroit's 2nd choice, 132nd overall, in 2003 Entry Draft.

Season	Club	League	GP	G	A	Pts	PIM	PP	SH	GW	S	%	+/-	TF	F%	Min	GP	G	A	Pts	PIM	PP	SH	GW	Min
2001-02	Mississauga	OPJHL	27	5	14	19	31	....	....	....	....	....	....	....	....	....	....	....	....	....	....	....	....	....	....
2002-03	London Knights	OHL	66	6	12	18	77	....	....	....	....	....	....	....	....	....	14	3	4	7	11	....	....	....	....
2003-04	London Knights	OHL	3	0	2	2	4	....	....	....	....	....	....	....	....	....	....	....	....	....	....	....	....	....	....
	Mississauga	OHL	61	14	23	37	135	....	....	....	....	....	....	....	....	....	24	3	13	16	32	....	....	....	....
2004-05	Mississauga	OHL	59	15	31	46	111	....	....	....	....	....	....	....	....	....	5	0	3	3	4	....	....	....	....
2005-06	**Detroit**	**NHL**	**1**	**0**	**0**	**0**	**0**	**0**	**0**	**0**	**1**	**0.0**	**0**	**0**	**0.0**	**11:37**	....	....	....	....	....	....	....	....	....
	Grand Rapids	AHL	70	7	26	33	107	....	....	....	....	....	....	....	....	....	16	0	1	1	27	....	....	....	....
2006-07	**Detroit**	**NHL**	**6**	**1**	**0**	**1**	**0**	**0**	**0**	**0**	**7**	**14.3**	**0**	**0**	**0.0**	**11:26**	**13**	**0**	**0**	**0**	**2**	**0**	**0**	**0**	**8:11**
	Grand Rapids	AHL	65	4	18	22	126	....	....	....	....	....	....	....	....	....	2	0	0	0	0	....	....	....	....
	NHL Totals		**7**	**1**	**0**	**1**	**0**	**0**	**0**	**0**	**8**	**12.5**		**0**	**0.0**	**11:27**	**13**	**0**	**0**	**0**	**2**	**0**	**0**	**0**	**8:11**

OHL Second All-Star Team (2005)

QUINT, Deron

(KWIHNT, DAIR-uhn)

Defense. Shoots left. 6'2", 219 lbs. Born, Durham, NH, March 12, 1976. Winnipeg's 1st choice, 30th overall, in 1994 Entry Draft.

Season	Club	League	GP	G	A	Pts	PIM	PP	SH	GW	S	%	+/-	TF	F%	Min	GP	G	A	Pts	PIM	PP	SH	GW	Min
1990-91	Cardigan Mtn.	High-NH	31	67	54	121	....	....	....	....	....	....	....	....	....	....	....	....	....	....	....	....	....	....	....
1991-92	Cardigan Mtn.	High-NH	21	111	58	169	....	....	....	....	....	....	....	....	....	....	....	....	....	....	....	....	....	....	....
1992-93	Tabor	High-MA	28	15	26	41	30	....	....	....	....	....	....	....	....	....	1	0	2	2	0	....	....	....	....
1993-94	Seattle	WHL	63	15	29	44	47	....	....	....	....	....	....	....	....	....	9	4	12	16	8	....	....	....	....
1994-95	Seattle	WHL	65	29	60	89	82	....	....	....	....	....	....	....	....	....	3	1	2	3	6	....	....	....	....
1995-96	**Winnipeg**	**NHL**	**51**	**5**	**13**	**18**	**22**	**2**	**0**	**0**	**97**	**5.2**	**–2**	....	....	....	....	....	....	....	....	....	....	....	....
	Springfield	AHL	11	2	3	5	4	....	....	....	....	....	....	....	....	....	10	2	3	5	6	....	....	....	....
	Seattle	WHL	....	....	....	....	....	....	....	....	....	....	....	....	....	....	5	4	1	5	6	....	....	....	....
1996-97	**Phoenix**	**NHL**	**27**	**3**	**11**	**14**	**4**	**1**	**0**	**0**	**63**	**4.8**	**–4**	....	....	....	**7**	**0**	**2**	**2**	**0**	**0**	**0**	**0**	....
	Springfield	AHL	43	6	18	24	20	....	....	....	....	....	....	....	....	....	12	2	7	9	4	....	....	....	....
1997-98	**Phoenix**	**NHL**	**32**	**4**	**7**	**11**	**16**	**1**	**0**	**1**	**61**	**6.6**	**–6**	....	....	....	....	....	....	....	....	....	....	....	....
	Springfield	AHL	8	1	7	8	10	....	....	....	....	....	....	....	....	....	1	0	0	0	0	....	....	....	....
1998-99	**Phoenix**	**NHL**	**60**	**5**	**8**	**13**	**20**	**2**	**0**	**0**	**94**	**5.3**	**–10**	**0**	**0.0**	**16:12**	....	....	....	....	....	....	....	....	....
99-2000	**Phoenix**	**NHL**	**50**	**3**	**7**	**10**	**22**	**2**	**0**	**1**	**88**	**3.4**	**0**	**0**	**0.0**	**16:39**	....	....	....	....	....	....	....	....	....
	New Jersey	**NHL**	**4**	**1**	**0**	**1**	**2**	**0**	**0**	**0**	**6**	**16.7**	**–2**	**0**	**0.0**	**16:26**	....	....	....	....	....	....	....	....	....
2000-01	**Columbus**	**NHL**	**57**	**7**	**16**	**23**	**16**	**3**	**0**	**0**	**148**	**4.7**	**–19**	**1**	**100.0**	**24:06**	....	....	....	....	....	....	....	....	....
	Syracuse Crunch	AHL	21	5	15	20	30	....	....	....	....	....	....	....	....	....	....	....	....	....	....	....	....	....	....
2001-02	**Columbus**	**NHL**	**75**	**7**	**18**	**25**	**26**	**3**	**0**	**1**	**169**	**4.1**	**–34**	**0**	**0.0**	**22:01**	....	....	....	....	....	....	....	....	....
2002-03	Springfield	AHL	4	1	2	3	4	....	....	....	....	....	....	....	....	....	....	....	....	....	....	....	....	....	....
	Phoenix	**NHL**	**51**	**7**	**10**	**17**	**20**	**2**	**0**	**0**	**85**	**8.2**	**–5**	**0**	**0.0**	**15:51**	....	....	....	....	....	....	....	....	....
2003-04	**Chicago**	**NHL**	**51**	**4**	**7**	**11**	**18**	**2**	**0**	**0**	**72**	**5.6**	**–26**	**0**	**0.0**	**18:08**	....	....	....	....	....	....	....	....	....
2004-05	HC Forst Bolzano	Italy	14	5	11	16	10	....	....	....	....	....	....	....	....	....	9	4	5	9	12	....	....	....	....
2005-06	Kloten Flyers	Swiss	16	5	10	15	6	....	....	....	....	....	....	....	....	....	....	....	....	....	....	....	....	....	....
	Eisbaren Berlin	Germany	31	5	7	12	26	....	....	....	....	....	....	....	....	....	11	4	7	11	6	....	....	....	....
2006-07	**NY Islanders**	**NHL**	**5**	**0**	**0**	**0**	**0**	**0**	**0**	**0**	**2**	**0.0**	**0**	**0**	**0.0**	**10:34**	....	....	....	....	....	....	....	....	....
	Eisbaren Berlin	Germany	52	18	28	46	34	....	....	....	....	....	....	....	....	....	3	1	0	1	12	....	....	....	....
	NHL Totals		**463**	**46**	**97**	**143**	**166**	**16**	**0**	**3**	**885**	**5.2**		**1**	**100.0**	**18:56**	**7**	**0**	**2**	**2**	**0**	**0**	**0**	**0**	....

WHL West First All-Star Team (1995)

Transferred to **Phoenix** after **Winnipeg** franchise relocated, July 1, 1996. Traded to **New Jersey** by **Phoenix** with Phoenix's 3rd round choice (later traded back to Phoenix – Phoenix selected Beat Forster) in 2001 Entry Draft for Lyle Odelein, March 7, 2000. Traded to **Columbus** by **New Jersey** to complete transaction that sent Krzysztof Oliwa to Columbus (June 12, 2000) and Turner Stevenson to New Jersey (June 23, 2000), June 23, 2000. Signed to a PTO (tryout) contract by **Springfield** (AHL), October 16, 2002. Signed as a free agent by **Phoenix**, October 26, 2002. Signed as a free agent by **Chicago**, August 5, 2003. Signed as a free agent by **Bolzano** (Italy), December 20, 2004. Signed as a free agent by **Kloten** (Swiss), May 21, 2005. Signed as a free agent by **Berlin** (Germany), November 11, 2005. Signed as a free agent by **NY Islanders**, March 31, 2007.

RACHUNEK, Karel

(ra-KHOO-nehk, KAH-rehl) **N.J.**

Defense. Shoots right. 6'2", 220 lbs. Born, Gottwaldov/Zlin, Czech., August 27, 1979. Ottawa's 8th choice, 229th overall, in 1997 Entry Draft.

Season	Club	League	GP	G	A	Pts	PIM	PP	SH	GW	S	%	+/-	TF	F%	Min	GP	G	A	Pts	PIM	PP	SH	GW	Min
1995-96	AC ZPS Zlin Jr.	CzRep-Jr.	38	8	11	19	....	....	....	....	....	....	....	....	....	....	....	....	....	....	....	....	....	....	....
1996-97	AC ZPS Zlin Jr.	CzRep-Jr.	27	2	11	13	....	....	....	....	....	....	....	....	....	....	....	....	....	....	....	....	....	....	....
1997-98	Zlin	CzRep	27	1	2	3	16	....	....	....	....	....	....	....	....	....	....	....	....	....	....	....	....	....	....
1998-99	Zlin	CzRep	39	3	9	12	88	....	....	....	....	....	....	....	....	....	6	0	0	0	....	....	....	....	....
99-2000	**Ottawa**	**NHL**	**6**	**0**	**0**	**0**	**2**	**0**	**0**	**0**	**3**	**0.0**	**0**	**0**	**0.0**	**8:03**	....	....	....	....	....	....	....	....	....
	Grand Rapids	IHL	62	6	20	26	64	....	....	....	....	....	....	....	....	....	9	0	5	5	6	....	....	....	....
2000-01	**Ottawa**	**NHL**	**71**	**3**	**30**	**33**	**60**	**3**	**0**	**0**	**77**	**3.9**	**17**	**0**	**0.0**	**20:54**	**3**	**0**	**0**	**0**	**0**	**0**	**0**	**0**	**22:38**
2001-02	**Ottawa**	**NHL**	**51**	**3**	**15**	**18**	**24**	**1**	**0**	**2**	**55**	**5.5**	**7**	**2**	**0.0**	**19:19**	....	....	....	....	....	....	....	....	....
2002-03	Yaroslavl	Russia	9	3	0	3	8	....	....	....	....	....	....	....	....	....	....	....	....	....	....	....	....	....	....
	Ottawa	**NHL**	**58**	**4**	**25**	**29**	**30**	**3**	**0**	**1**	**110**	**3.6**	**23**	**3**	**33.3**	**21:46**	**17**	**1**	**3**	**4**	**14**	**0**	**0**	**0**	**23:14**
	Binghamton	AHL	6	0	2	2	10	....	....	....	....	....	....	....	....	....	....	....	....	....	....	....	....	....	....
2003-04	**Ottawa**	**NHL**	**60**	**1**	**16**	**17**	**29**	**0**	**0**	**0**	**99**	**1.0**	**17**	**0**	**0.0**	**19:43**	....	....	....	....	....	....	....	....	....
	NY Rangers	**NHL**	**12**	**1**	**3**	**4**	**4**	**1**	**0**	**0**	**21**	**4.8**	**–9**	**0**	**0.0**	**19:04**	....	....	....	....	....	....	....	....	....
2004-05	Znojmo	CzRep	21	5	6	11	55	....	....	....	....	....	....	....	....	....	....	....	....	....	....	....	....	....	....
	Yaroslavl	Russia	27	6	8	14	69	....	....	....	....	....	....	....	....	....	9	2	0	2	6	....	....	....	....

			Regular Season														Playoffs								
Season	**Club**	**League**	**GP**	**G**	**A**	**Pts**	**PIM**	**PP**	**SH**	**GW**	**S**	**%**	**+/-**	**TF**	**F%**	**Min**	**GP**	**G**	**A**	**Pts**	**PIM**	**PP**	**SH**	**GW**	**Min**
2005-06	Yaroslavl	Russia	45	11	16	27	73	....	....	....	....	....	....	....	....	....	2	0	0	0	29	....	....	....	....
2006-07	**NY Rangers**	**NHL**	**66**	**6**	**20**	**26**	**38**	**4**	**1**	**1**	**99**	**6.1**	**–9**	**0**	**0.0**	**19:23**	**6**	**0**	**4**	**4**	**2**	**0**	**0**	**0**	**18:22**
	NHL Totals		**324**	**18**	**109**	**127**	**187**	**12**	**1**	**4**	**464**	**3.9**		**5**	**20.0**	**19:58**	**26**	**1**	**7**	**8**	**16**	**0**	**0**	**0**	**22:03**

Traded to **NY Rangers** by **Ottawa** with Alexandre Giroux for Greg De Vries, March 9, 2004. Signed as a free agent by **Znojmo** (CzRep), September 6, 2004. Signed as a free agent by **Yaroslavl** (Russia), November 1, 2004. Signed as a free agent by **New Jersey**, July 3, 2007.

RADIVOJEVIC, Branko

(ra-dih-VOI-uh-vihch, BRAN-koh) **MIN.**

Right wing. Shoots right. 6'2", 210 lbs. Born, Piestany, Czech., November 24, 1980. Colorado's 3rd choice, 93rd overall, in 1999 Entry Draft.

Season	**Club**	**League**	**GP**	**G**	**A**	**Pts**	**PIM**	**PP**	**SH**	**GW**	**S**	**%**	**+/-**	**TF**	**F%**	**Min**	**GP**	**G**	**A**	**Pts**	**PIM**	**PP**	**SH**	**GW**	**Min**
1997-98	Dukla Trencin Jr.	Slovak-Jr.	52	30	31	61	50	....	....	....	....	....	....	....	....	....	....	....	....	....	....	....	....	....	....
	Dukla Trencin	Slovakia	1	0	0	0	2	....	....	....	....	....	....	....	....	....	....	....	....	....	....	....	....	....	....
1998-99	Belleville Bulls	OHL	68	20	38	58	61	....	....	....	....	....	....	....	....	....	21	7	17	24	18	....	....	....	....
99-2000	Belleville Bulls	OHL	59	23	49	72	86	....	....	....	....	....	....	....	....	....	16	5	8	13	32	....	....	....	....
2000-01	Belleville Bulls	OHL	61	34	70	104	77	....	....	....	....	....	....	....	....	....	10	6	10	16	18	....	....	....	....
2001-02	**Phoenix**	**NHL**	**18**	**4**	**2**	**6**	**4**	**0**	**0**	**1**	**19**	**21.1**	**1**	**0**	**0.0**	**9:22**	**1**	**0**	**0**	**0**	**2**	**0**	**0**	**0**	**8:07**
	Springfield	AHL	62	18	21	39	64	....	....	....	....	....	....	....	....	....	....	....	....	....	....	....	....	....	....
2002-03	**Phoenix**	**NHL**	**79**	**12**	**15**	**27**	**63**	**1**	**0**	**3**	**109**	**11.0**	**–2**	**20**	**40.0**	**13:18**	....	....	....	....	....	....	....	....	....
2003-04	**Phoenix**	**NHL**	**53**	**9**	**14**	**23**	**36**	**2**	**1**	**2**	**83**	**10.8**	**–5**	**30**	**30.0**	**16:27**	....	....	....	....	....	....	....	....	....
	Philadelphia	**NHL**	**24**	**1**	**8**	**9**	**36**	**0**	**0**	**0**	**24**	**4.2**	**0**	**11**	**54.6**	**10:28**	**18**	**1**	**1**	**2**	**32**	**0**	**0**	**0**	**9:56**
2004-05	HC Vsetin	CzRep	31	7	11	18	114	....	....	....	....	....	....	....	....	....	....	....	....	....	....	....	....	....	....
	Lulea HF	Sweden	10	6	5	11	8	....	....	....	....	....	....	....	....	....	4	0	0	0	44	....	....	....	....
2005-06	**Philadelphia**	**NHL**	**64**	**8**	**6**	**14**	**44**	**1**	**0**	**1**	**84**	**9.5**	**–6**	**14**	**42.9**	**12:46**	**5**	**1**	**0**	**1**	**0**	**0**	**0**	**0**	**10:34**
2006-07	**Minnesota**	**NHL**	**82**	**11**	**13**	**24**	**21**	**4**	**0**	**3**	**116**	**9.5**	**–9**	**18**	**50.0**	**12:59**	**5**	**0**	**0**	**0**	**2**	**0**	**0**	**0**	**14:14**
	NHL Totals		**320**	**45**	**58**	**103**	**204**	**8**	**1**	**10**	**435**	**10.3**		**93**	**40.9**	**13:12**	**29**	**2**	**1**	**3**	**36**	**0**	**0**	**0**	**10:44**

OHL First All-Star Team (2001)

Signed as a free agent by **Phoenix**, June 19, 2001. Traded to **Philadelphia** by **Phoenix** with Sean Burke and Ben Eager for Mike Comrie, February 9, 2004. Signed as a free agent by **Vsetin** (CzRep), September 17, 2004. Signed as a free agent by **Lulea** (Sweden), January 27, 2005. Signed as a free agent by **Minnesota**, July 6, 2006.

RADULOV, Alexander

(ra-DEW-lahf, al-EHX-AN-duhr) **NSH.**

Right wing. Shoots left. 6'1", 188 lbs. Born, Nizhny Tagil, USSR, July 5, 1986. Nashville's 1st choice, 15th overall, in 2004 Entry Draft.

Season	**Club**	**League**	**GP**	**G**	**A**	**Pts**	**PIM**	**PP**	**SH**	**GW**	**S**	**%**	**+/-**	**TF**	**F%**	**Min**	**GP**	**G**	**A**	**Pts**	**PIM**	**PP**	**SH**	**GW**	**Min**
2002-03	Dyn'o Moscow 2	Russia-3	STATISTICS NOT AVAILABLE																						
2003-04	Dyn'o Moscow 2	Russia-3	STATISTICS NOT AVAILABLE																						
	THK Tver	Russia-2	42	15	16	31	102																		
	Dynamo Moscow	Russia	1	0	0	0	2	....	....	....	....	....	....	....	....	....	....	....	....	....	....	....	....	....	....
2004-05	Quebec Remparts	QMJHL	65	32	43	75	64	....	....	....	....	....	....	....	....	....	13	6	5	11	15	....	....	....	....
2005-06	Quebec Remparts	QMJHL	62	61	*91	*152	101	....	....	....	....	....	....	....	....	....	23	21	*34	*55	30	....	....	....	....
2006-07	**Nashville**	**NHL**	**64**	**18**	**19**	**37**	**26**	**5**	**0**	**4**	**96**	**18.8**	**19**	**0**	**0.0**	**11:38**	**4**	**3**	**1**	**4**	**19**	**0**	**0**	**0**	**13:10**
	Milwaukee	AHL	11	6	12	18	26	....	....	....	....	....	....	....	....	....	....	....	....	....	....	....	....	....	....
	NHL Totals		**64**	**18**	**19**	**37**	**26**	**5**	**0**	**4**	**96**	**18.8**		**0**	**0.0**	**11:38**	**4**	**3**	**1**	**4**	**19**	**0**	**0**	**0**	**13:10**

QMJHL All-Rookie Team (2005) • QMJHL First All-Star Team (2006) • QMJHL Player of the Year (2006) • Canadian Major Junior First All-Star Team (2006) • Canadian Major Junior Player of the Year (2006) • Memorial Cup Tournament All-Star Team (2006) • Stafford Smythe Memorial Trophy (Memorial Cup Tournament MVP) (2006)

RAFALSKI, Brian

(ra-FAWL-skee, BRIGH-uhn) **DET.**

Defense. Shoots right. 5'10", 195 lbs. Born, Dearborn, MI, September 28, 1973.

Season	**Club**	**League**	**GP**	**G**	**A**	**Pts**	**PIM**	**PP**	**SH**	**GW**	**S**	**%**	**+/-**	**TF**	**F%**	**Min**	**GP**	**G**	**A**	**Pts**	**PIM**	**PP**	**SH**	**GW**	**Min**
1990-91	Madison Capitols	USHL	47	12	11	23	28	....	....	....	....	....	....	....	....	....	....	....	....	....	....	....	....	....	....
1991-92	U. of Wisconsin	WCHA	34	3	14	17	34	....	....	....	....	....	....	....	....	....	....	....	....	....	....	....	....	....	....
1992-93	U. of Wisconsin	WCHA	32	0	13	13	10	....	....	....	....	....	....	....	....	....	....	....	....	....	....	....	....	....	....
1993-94	U. of Wisconsin	WCHA	37	6	17	23	26	....	....	....	....	....	....	....	....	....	....	....	....	....	....	....	....	....	....
1994-95	U. of Wisconsin	WCHA	43	11	34	45	48	....	....	....	....	....	....	....	....	....	....	....	....	....	....	....	....	....	....
1995-96	Brynas IF Gavle	Sweden	40	4	14	18	26	....	....	....	....	....	....	....	....	....	9	0	1	1	2	....	....	....	....
1996-97	HPK Hameenlinna	Finland	49	11	24	35	26	....	....	....	....	....	....	....	....	....	10	6	5	11	4	....	....	....	....
1997-98	HIFK Helsinki	Finland	40	13	10	23	20	....	....	....	....	....	....	....	....	....	9	5	6	11	0	....	....	....	....
1998-99	HIFK Helsinki	Finland	53	19	34	53	18	....	....	....	....	....	....	....	....	....	11	5	*9	*14	4	....	....	....	....
	HIFK Helsinki	EuroHL	6	4	6	10	10	....	....	....	....	....	....	....	....	....	4	1	0	1	2	....	....	....	....
99-2000 ♦	**New Jersey**	**NHL**	**75**	**5**	**27**	**32**	**28**	**1**	**0**	**1**	**128**	**3.9**	**21**	**1**	**0.0**	**18:51**	**23**	**2**	**6**	**8**	**8**	**0**	**0**	**1**	**21:25**
2000-01	**New Jersey**	**NHL**	**78**	**9**	**43**	**52**	**26**	**6**	**0**	**1**	**142**	**6.3**	**36**	**2**	**100.0**	**21:41**	**25**	**7**	**11**	**18**	**7**	**1**	**0**	**3**	**22:08**
2001-02	**New Jersey**	**NHL**	**76**	**7**	**40**	**47**	**18**	**2**	**0**	**4**	**125**	**5.6**	**15**	**0**	**0.0**	**22:08**	**6**	**3**	**2**	**5**	**4**	**3**	**0**	**0**	**21:45**
	United States	Olympics	6	1	2	3	2	....	....	....	....	....	....	....	....	....	....	....	....	....	....	....	....	....	....
2002-03 ♦	**New Jersey**	**NHL**	**79**	**3**	**37**	**40**	**14**	**2**	**0**	**0**	**178**	**1.7**	**18**	**1**	**0.0**	**23:09**	**23**	**2**	**9**	**11**	**8**	**2**	**0**	**0**	**25:46**
2003-04	**New Jersey**	**NHL**	**69**	**6**	**30**	**36**	**24**	**2**	**0**	**1**	**130**	**4.6**	**6**	**0**	**0.0**	**22:48**	**5**	**0**	**1**	**1**	**0**	**0**	**0**	**0**	**22:22**
2004-05			DID NOT PLAY																						
2005-06	**New Jersey**	**NHL**	**82**	**6**	**43**	**49**	**36**	**3**	**0**	**2**	**126**	**4.8**	**0**	**1**	**0.0**	**25:32**	**9**	**1**	**8**	**9**	**2**	**1**	**0**	**0**	**27:26**
	United States	Olympics	5	0	2	2	0	....	....	....	....	....	....	....	....	....	....	....	....	....	....	....	....	....	....
2006-07	**New Jersey**	**NHL**	**82**	**8**	**47**	**55**	**34**	**3**	**1**	**4**	**148**	**5.4**	**4**	**0**	**0.0**	**25:29**	**11**	**2**	**6**	**8**	**8**	**2**	**0**	**0**	**22:54**
	NHL Totals		**541**	**44**	**267**	**311**	**180**	**19**	**1**	**13**	**977**	**4.5**		**5**	**40.0**	**22:52**	**102**	**17**	**43**	**60**	**37**	**9**	**0**	**4**	**23:20**

WCHA First All-Star Team (1995) • NCAA West First All-American Team (1995) • NHL All-Rookie Team (2000)

Played in NHL All-Star Game (2004, 2007)

Signed as a free agent by **New Jersey**, June 18, 1999. Signed as a free agent by **Detroit**, July 1, 2007.

RANGER, Paul

(RAIN-juhr, PAWL) **T.B.**

Defense. Shoots left. 6'2", 215 lbs. Born, Whitby, Ont., September 12, 1984. Tampa Bay's 7th choice, 183rd overall, in 2002 Entry Draft.

Season	**Club**	**League**	**GP**	**G**	**A**	**Pts**	**PIM**	**PP**	**SH**	**GW**	**S**	**%**	**+/-**	**TF**	**F%**	**Min**	**GP**	**G**	**A**	**Pts**	**PIM**	**PP**	**SH**	**GW**	**Min**
2000-01	Oshawa Generals	OHL	32	0	1	1	2	....	....	....	....	....	....	....	....	....	....	....	....	....	....	....	....	....	....
2001-02	Oshawa Generals	OHL	62	0	9	9	49	....	....	....	....	....	....	....	....	....	5	0	0	0	4	....	....	....	....
2002-03	Oshawa Generals	OHL	68	10	28	38	70	....	....	....	....	....	....	....	....	....	13	0	3	3	10	....	....	....	....
2003-04	Oshawa Generals	OHL	62	12	31	43	72	....	....	....	....	....	....	....	....	....	7	0	1	1	10	....	....	....	....
2004-05	Springfield	AHL	69	3	8	11	46	....	....	....	....	....	....	....	....	....	....	....	....	....	....	....	....	....	....
2005-06	**Tampa Bay**	**NHL**	**76**	**1**	**17**	**18**	**58**	**0**	**0**	**1**	**73**	**1.4**	**5**	**0**	**0.0**	**17:07**	**5**	**2**	**4**	**6**	**0**	**1**	**0**	**0**	**21:43**
	Springfield	AHL	1	1	2	3	0	....	....	....	....	....	....	....	....	....	....	....	....	....	....	....	....	....	....
2006-07	**Tampa Bay**	**NHL**	**72**	**4**	**24**	**28**	**42**	**0**	**0**	**2**	**90**	**4.4**	**5**	**0**	**0.0**	**20:19**	**6**	**0**	**1**	**1**	**4**	**0**	**0**	**0**	**21:22**
	NHL Totals		**148**	**5**	**41**	**46**	**100**	**0**	**0**	**3**	**163**	**3.1**		**0**	**0.0**	**18:40**	**11**	**2**	**5**	**7**	**4**	**1**	**0**	**0**	**21:31**

RASMUSSEN, Erik

(RAS-moo-suhn, AIR-ihk)

Left wing/Center. Shoots left. 6'1", 215 lbs. Born, Minneapolis, MN, March 28, 1977. Buffalo's 1st choice, 7th overall, in 1996 Entry Draft.

Season	**Club**	**League**	**GP**	**G**	**A**	**Pts**	**PIM**	**PP**	**SH**	**GW**	**S**	**%**	**+/-**	**TF**	**F%**	**Min**	**GP**	**G**	**A**	**Pts**	**PIM**	**PP**	**SH**	**GW**	**Min**
1992-93	St. Louis Park	High-MN	23	16	24	40	50	....	....	....	....	....	....	....	....	....	....	....	....	....	....	....	....	....	....
1993-94	St. Louis Park	High-MN	18	25	18	43	80	....	....	....	....	....	....	....	....	....	....	....	....	....	....	....	....	....	....
1994-95	St. Louis Park	High-MN	23	19	33	52	80	....	....	....	....	....	....	....	....	....	....	....	....	....	....	....	....	....	....
1995-96	U. of Minnesota	WCHA	40	16	32	48	55	....	....	....	....	....	....	....	....	....	....	....	....	....	....	....	....	....	....
1996-97	U. of Minnesota	WCHA	34	15	12	27	*123	....	....	....	....	....	....	....	....	....	....	....	....	....	....	....	....	....	....
1997-98	**Buffalo**	**NHL**	**21**	**2**	**3**	**5**	**14**	**0**	**0**	**0**	**28**	**7.1**	**2**	....	....	....	....	....	....	....	....	....	....	....	....
	Rochester	AHL	53	9	14	23	83	....	....	....	....	....	....	....	....	....	1	0	0	0	5	....	....	....	....
1998-99	**Buffalo**	**NHL**	**42**	**3**	**7**	**10**	**37**	**0**	**0**	**0**	**40**	**7.5**	**6**	**67**	**40.3**	**12:22**	**21**	**2**	**4**	**6**	**18**	**0**	**0**	**1**	**12:51**
	Rochester	AHL	37	12	14	26	47	....	....	....	....	....	....	....	....	....	....	....	....	....	....	....	....	....	....
99-2000	**Buffalo**	**NHL**	**67**	**8**	**6**	**14**	**43**	**0**	**0**	**2**	**76**	**10.5**	**1**	**130**	**44.6**	**11:27**	**3**	**0**	**0**	**0**	**4**	**0**	**0**	**0**	**8:59**
2000-01	**Buffalo**	**NHL**	**82**	**12**	**19**	**31**	**51**	**1**	**0**	**3**	**95**	**12.6**	**0**	**565**	**43.7**	**13:47**	**3**	**0**	**1**	**1**	**0**	**0**	**0**	**0**	**16:26**
2001-02	**Buffalo**	**NHL**	**69**	**8**	**11**	**19**	**34**	**0**	**0**	**2**	**89**	**9.0**	**–1**	**236**	**39.8**	**13:03**	....	....	....	....	....	....	....	....	....
2002-03	**Los Angeles**	**NHL**	**57**	**4**	**12**	**16**	**28**	**0**	**0**	**1**	**75**	**5.3**	**–1**	**278**	**44.6**	**13:39**	....	....	....	....	....	....	....	....	....
2003-04	**New Jersey**	**NHL**	**69**	**7**	**6**	**13**	**41**	**0**	**0**	**0**	**68**	**10.3**	**5**	**423**	**44.4**	**11:34**	**5**	**0**	**2**	**2**	**2**	**0**	**0**	**0**	**14:44**
2004-05			DID NOT PLAY																						
2005-06	**New Jersey**	**NHL**	**67**	**5**	**5**	**10**	**32**	**1**	**0**	**0**	**45**	**11.1**	**–4**	**230**	**37.4**	**7:04**	**9**	**0**	**0**	**0**	**8**	**0**	**0**	**0**	**6:44**
2006-07	**New Jersey**	**NHL**	**71**	**3**	**7**	**10**	**25**	**0**	**0**	**0**	**80**	**3.8**	**–3**	**52**	**48.1**	**9:28**	**11**	**0**	**0**	**0**	**14**	**0**	**0**	**0**	**5:21**
	NHL Totals		**545**	**52**	**76**	**128**	**305**	**2**	**0**	**8**	**596**	**8.7**		**1981**	**42.9**	**11:31**	**52**	**2**	**7**	**9**	**46**	**0**	**0**	**1**	**10:22**

Minnesota High School Player of the Year (1995)

Traded to **Los Angeles** by **Buffalo** for Adam Mair and Los Angeles' 5th round choice (Thomas Morrow) in 2003 Entry Draft, July 24, 2002. Signed as a free agent by **New Jersey**, July 25, 2003.

RATHJE, Mike

(RATH-jee, MIGHK) **PHI.**

Defense. Shoots left. 6'5", 235 lbs. Born, Mannville, Alta., May 11, 1974. San Jose's 1st choice, 3rd overall, in 1992 Entry Draft.

Season	Club	League	GP	G	A	Pts	PIM	PP	SH	GW	S	%	+/-	TF	F%	Min	GP	G	A	Pts	PIM	PP	SH	GW	Min
			Regular Season														Playoffs								
1989-90	Sherwood Park	AMHL	33	6	11	17	30	....	....	....	....	....	....	....	....	....	6	1	1	2	2	....	....	....	....
1990-91	Medicine Hat	WHL	64	1	16	17	28	....	....	....	....	....	....	....	....	....	12	0	4	4	2	....	....	....	....
1991-92	Medicine Hat	WHL	67	11	23	34	99	....	....	....	....	....	....	....	....	....	4	0	1	1	2	....	....	....	....
1992-93	Medicine Hat	WHL	57	12	37	49	103	....	....	....	....	....	....	....	....	....	10	3	3	6	12	....	....	....	....
	Kansas City	IHL	....	....	....	....	....	....	....	....	....	....	....	....	....	....	5	0	0	0	12	....	....	....	....
1993-94	**San Jose**	**NHL**	**47**	**1**	**9**	**10**	**59**	**1**	**0**	**0**	**30**	**3.3**	**-9**	....	....	....	**1**	**0**	**0**	**0**	**0**	**0**	**0**	**0**	....
	Kansas City	IHL	6	0	2	2	0	....	....	....	....	....	....	....	....	....	....	....	....	....	....	....	....	....	....
1994-95	Kansas City	IHL	6	0	1	1	7	....	....	....	....	....	....	....	....	....	....	....	....	....	....	....	....	....	....
	San Jose	**NHL**	**42**	**2**	**7**	**9**	**29**	**0**	**0**	**0**	**38**	**5.3**	**-1**	....	....	....	**11**	**5**	**2**	**7**	**4**	**5**	**0**	**0**	....
1995-96	**San Jose**	**NHL**	**27**	**0**	**7**	**7**	**14**	**0**	**0**	**0**	**26**	**0.0**	**-16**	....	....	....	....	....	....	....	....	....	....	....	....
	Kansas City	IHL	36	6	11	17	34	....	....	....	....	....	....	....	....	....	....	....	....	....	....	....	....	....	....
1996-97	**San Jose**	**NHL**	**31**	**0**	**8**	**8**	**21**	**0**	**0**	**0**	**22**	**0.0**	**-1**	....	....	....	....	....	....	....	....	....	....	....	....
1997-98	**San Jose**	**NHL**	**81**	**3**	**12**	**15**	**59**	**1**	**0**	**0**	**61**	**4.9**	**-4**	....	....	....	**6**	**1**	**0**	**1**	**6**	**1**	**0**	**0**	....
1998-99	**San Jose**	**NHL**	**82**	**5**	**9**	**14**	**36**	**2**	**0**	**1**	**67**	**7.5**	**15**	**0**	**0.0**	**20:07**	**6**	**0**	**0**	**0**	**4**	**0**	**0**	**0**	**22:08**
99-2000	**San Jose**	**NHL**	**66**	**2**	**14**	**16**	**31**	**0**	**0**	**0**	**46**	**4.3**	**-2**	**0**	**0.0**	**22:11**	**12**	**1**	**3**	**4**	**8**	**0**	**0**	**0**	**21:32**
2000-01	**San Jose**	**NHL**	**81**	**0**	**11**	**11**	**48**	**0**	**0**	**0**	**89**	**0.0**	**7**	**0**	**0.0**	**22:20**	**6**	**0**	**1**	**1**	**4**	**0**	**0**	**0**	**24:20**
2001-02	**San Jose**	**NHL**	**52**	**5**	**12**	**17**	**48**	**4**	**0**	**0**	**56**	**8.9**	**23**	**0**	**0.0**	**21:31**	**12**	**1**	**3**	**4**	**6**	**1**	**0**	**0**	**23:29**
2002-03	**San Jose**	**NHL**	**82**	**7**	**22**	**29**	**48**	**3**	**0**	**1**	**147**	**4.8**	**-19**	**1**	**0.0**	**24:07**	....	....	....	....	....	....	....	....	....
2003-04	**San Jose**	**NHL**	**80**	**2**	**17**	**19**	**46**	**0**	**1**	**0**	**105**	**1.9**	**18**	**0**	**0.0**	**23:27**	**17**	**1**	**5**	**6**	**13**	**0**	**0**	**0**	**23:26**
2004-05			DID NOT PLAY																						
2005-06	**Philadelphia**	**NHL**	**79**	**3**	**21**	**24**	**46**	**1**	**1**	**1**	**55**	**5.5**	**22**	**0**	**0.0**	**20:08**	**6**	**0**	**0**	**0**	**6**	**0**	**0**	**0**	**16:27**
2006-07	**Philadelphia**	**NHL**	**18**	**0**	**1**	**1**	**6**	**0**	**0**	**0**	**13**	**0.0**	**-7**	**0**	**0.0**	**20:49**	....	....	....	....	....	....	....	....	....
	NHL Totals		**768**	**30**	**150**	**180**	**491**	**12**	**2**	**3**	**755**	**4.0**		**1**	**0.0**	**21:58**	**77**	**9**	**14**	**23**	**51**	**7**	**0**	**0**	**22:18**

WHL East Second All-Star Team (1992, 1993)

• Missed majority of 1996-97 season recovering from groin injury suffered in game vs. Dallas, November 8, 1996. Signed as a free agent by **Philadelphia**, August 2, 2005. • Missed majority of 2006-07 season recovering from a recurring back injury.

READY, Ryan

(REH-dee, RIGH-uhn)

Left wing. Shoots left. 6'2", 195 lbs. Born, Peterborough, Ont., November 7, 1978. Calgary's 8th choice, 100th overall, in 1997 Entry Draft.

Season	Club	League	GP	G	A	Pts	PIM	PP	SH	GW	S	%	+/-	TF	F%	Min	GP	G	A	Pts	PIM	PP	SH	GW	Min
1994-95	Peterborough	OPJHL	48	20	33	53	65	....	....	....	....	....	....	....	....	....	....	....	....	....	....	....	....	....	....
1995-96	Belleville Bulls	OHL	63	5	13	18	54	....	....	....	....	....	....	....	....	....	10	0	2	2	2	....	....	....	....
1996-97	Belleville Bulls	OHL	66	23	24	47	102	....	....	....	....	....	....	....	....	....	6	1	3	4	4	....	....	....	....
1997-98	Belleville Bulls	OHL	66	33	39	72	80	....	....	....	....	....	....	....	....	....	10	5	2	7	12	....	....	....	....
1998-99	Belleville Bulls	OHL	63	33	59	92	73	....	....	....	....	....	....	....	....	....	21	10	28	38	22	....	....	....	....
99-2000	Syracuse Crunch	AHL	70	4	12	16	59	....	....	....	....	....	....	....	....	....	2	0	0	0	0	....	....	....	....
2000-01	Kansas City	IHL	67	10	15	25	75	....	....	....	....	....	....	....	....	....	....	....	....	....	....	....	....	....	....
2001-02	Manitoba Moose	AHL	72	23	32	55	73	....	....	....	....	....	....	....	....	....	7	5	1	6	4	....	....	....	....
2002-03	Manitoba Moose	AHL	68	24	26	50	52	....	....	....	....	....	....	....	....	....	14	2	5	7	2	....	....	....	....
2003-04	Manitoba Moose	AHL	64	7	18	25	55	....	....	....	....	....	....	....	....	....	....	....	....	....	....	....	....	....	....
	Worcester IceCats	AHL	16	2	5	7	10	....	....	....	....	....	....	....	....	....	10	1	2	3	10	....	....	....	....
2004-05	Philadelphia	AHL	72	7	18	25	104	....	....	....	....	....	....	....	....	....	19	2	11	13	6	....	....	....	....
2005-06	**Philadelphia**	**NHL**	**7**	**0**	**1**	**1**	**0**	**0**	**0**	**0**	**9**	**0.0**	**0**	**2**	**50.0**	**8:08**	....	....	....	....	....	....	....	....	....
	Philadelphia	AHL	40	7	10	17	67	....	....	....	....	....	....	....	....	....	....	....	....	....	....	....	....	....	....
2006-07	Iserlohn Roosters	Germany	47	9	15	24	74	....	....	....	....	....	....	....	....	....	....	....	....	....	....	....	....	....	....
	NHL Totals		**7**	**0**	**1**	**1**	**0**	**0**	**0**	**0**	**9**	**0.0**		**2**	**50.0**	**8:08**	....	....	....	....	....	....	....	....	....

OHL First All-Star Team (1999)

Signed as a free agent by **Vancouver**, June 16, 1999. Traded to **St. Louis** by **Vancouver** for Sergei Varlamov, March 9, 2004. Signed as a free agent by **Philadelphia**, August 23, 2004. Signed as a free agent by **Iserlohn** (Germany), September 15, 2006.

REASONER, Marty

(REE-suh-nuhr, MAHR-tee) **EDM.**

Center. Shoots left. 6'1", 200 lbs. Born, Honeoye Falls, NY, February 26, 1977. St. Louis' 1st choice, 14th overall, in 1996 Entry Draft.

Season	Club	League	GP	G	A	Pts	PIM	PP	SH	GW	S	%	+/-	TF	F%	Min	GP	G	A	Pts	PIM	PP	SH	GW	Min
1993-94	Deerfield	High-MA	22	27	25	52	....	....	....	....	....	....	....	....	....	....	....	....	....	....	....	....	....	....	....
1994-95	Deerfield	High-MA	26	25	32	57	14	....	....	....	....	....	....	....	....	....	....	....	....	....	....	....	....	....	....
1995-96	Boston College	H-East	34	16	29	45	32	....	....	....	....	....	....	....	....	....	....	....	....	....	....	....	....	....	....
1996-97	Boston College	H-East	35	20	24	44	31	....	....	....	....	....	....	....	....	....	....	....	....	....	....	....	....	....	....
1997-98	Boston College	H-East	42	*33	40	*73	56	....	....	....	....	....	....	....	....	....	....	....	....	....	....	....	....	....	....
1998-99	**St. Louis**	**NHL**	**22**	**3**	**7**	**10**	**8**	**1**	**0**	**0**	**33**	**9.1**	**2**	**224**	**53.6**	**13:55**	....	....	....	....	....	....	....	....	....
	Worcester IceCats	AHL	44	17	22	39	24	....	....	....	....	....	....	....	....	....	4	2	1	3	6	....	....	....	....
99-2000	**St. Louis**	**NHL**	**32**	**10**	**14**	**24**	**20**	**3**	**0**	**0**	**51**	**19.6**	**9**	**379**	**49.6**	**15:20**	**7**	**2**	**1**	**3**	**4**	**1**	**0**	**0**	**13:12**
	Worcester IceCats	AHL	44	23	28	51	39	....	....	....	....	....	....	....	....	....	....	....	....	....	....	....	....	....	....
2000-01	**St. Louis**	**NHL**	**41**	**4**	**9**	**13**	**14**	**0**	**0**	**0**	**65**	**6.2**	**-5**	**454**	**53.1**	**14:00**	**10**	**3**	**1**	**4**	**0**	**0**	**0**	**1**	**12:21**
	Worcester IceCats	AHL	34	17	18	35	25	....	....	....	....	....	....	....	....	....	....	....	....	....	....	....	....	....	....
2001-02	**Edmonton**	**NHL**	**52**	**6**	**5**	**11**	**41**	**3**	**0**	**2**	**66**	**9.1**	**0**	**470**	**55.5**	**11:44**	....	....	....	....	....	....	....	....	....
2002-03	**Edmonton**	**NHL**	**70**	**11**	**20**	**31**	**28**	**2**	**2**	**0**	**102**	**10.8**	**19**	**968**	**53.5**	**14:50**	**6**	**1**	**0**	**1**	**2**	**1**	**0**	**0**	**14:22**
	Hamilton	AHL	2	0	2	2	2	....	....	....	....	....	....	....	....	....	....	....	....	....	....	....	....	....	....
2003-04	**Edmonton**	**NHL**	**17**	**2**	**6**	**8**	**10**	**0**	**1**	**0**	**28**	**7.1**	**5**	**321**	**52.7**	**16:30**	....	....	....	....	....	....	....	....	....
2004-05	Salzburg	Austria	11	5	4	9	12	....	....	....	....	....	....	....	....	....	....	....	....	....	....	....	....	....	....
2005-06	**Edmonton**	**NHL**	**58**	**9**	**17**	**26**	**20**	**5**	**0**	**1**	**63**	**14.3**	**-12**	**524**	**52.5**	**12:45**	....	....	....	....	....	....	....	....	....
	Boston	**NHL**	**19**	**2**	**6**	**8**	**8**	**1**	**0**	**0**	**39**	**5.1**	**-2**	**227**	**46.7**	**15:09**	....	....	....	....	....	....	....	....	....
2006-07	**Edmonton**	**NHL**	**72**	**6**	**14**	**20**	**60**	**0**	**0**	**1**	**84**	**7.1**	**-15**	**765**	**54.6**	**13:52**	....	....	....	....	....	....	....	....	....
	NHL Totals		**383**	**53**	**98**	**151**	**209**	**15**	**3**	**4**	**531**	**10.0**		**4332**	**53.0**	**13:54**	**23**	**6**	**2**	**8**	**6**	**2**	**0**	**1**	**13:08**

Hockey East Rookie of the Year (1996) • Hockey East First All-Star Team (1997, 1998) • NCAA East First All-American Team (1998) • NCAA Championship All-Tournament Team (1998)

Traded to **Edmonton** by **St. Louis** with Jochen Hecht and Jan Horacek for Doug Weight and Michel Riesen, July 1, 2001. • Missed majority of 2003-04 season recovering from ankle (November 8, 2003 vs. Toronto) and knee (January 13, 2004 vs. Florida) injuries. Signed as a free agent by **Salzburg** (Austria), January 30, 2005. Traded to **Boston** by **Edmonton** with Yan Stastny and Edmonton's 2nd round choice (Milan Lucic) in 2006 Entry Draft for Sergei Samsonov, March 9, 2006. Signed as a free agent by **Edmonton**, July 4, 2006.

RECCHI, Mark

(REH-kee, MAHRK) **PIT.**

Right wing. Shoots left. 5'10", 195 lbs. Born, Kamloops, B.C., February 1, 1968. Pittsburgh's 4th choice, 67th overall, in 1988 Entry Draft.

Season	Club	League	GP	G	A	Pts	PIM	PP	SH	GW	S	%	+/-	TF	F%	Min	GP	G	A	Pts	PIM	PP	SH	GW	Min
1984-85	Langley Eagles	BCJHL	51	26	39	65	39	....	....	....	....	....	....	....	....	....	....	....	....	....	....	....	....	....	....
	New Westminster	WHL	4	1	0	1	0	....	....	....	....	....	....	....	....	....	....	....	....	....	....	....	....	....	....
1985-86	New Westminster	WHL	72	21	40	61	55	....	....	....	....	....	....	....	....	....	....	....	....	....	....	....	....	....	....
1986-87	Kamloops Chiefs	WHL	40	26	50	76	63	....	....	....	....	....	....	....	....	....	13	3	16	19	17	....	....	....	....
1987-88	Kamloops Chiefs	WHL	62	61	*93	154	75	....	....	....	....	....	....	....	....	....	17	10	*21	*31	18	....	....	....	....
1988-89	**Pittsburgh**	**NHL**	**15**	**1**	**1**	**2**	**0**	**0**	**0**	**0**	**11**	**9.1**	**-2**	....	....	....	....	....	....	....	....	....	....	....	....
	Muskegon	IHL	63	50	49	99	86	....	....	....	....	....	....	....	....	....	14	7	*14	*21	28	....	....	....	....
1989-90	**Pittsburgh**	**NHL**	**74**	**30**	**37**	**67**	**44**	**6**	**2**	**4**	**143**	**21.0**	**6**	....	....	....	....	....	....	....	....	....	....	....	....
	Muskegon	IHL	4	7	4	11	2	....	....	....	....	....	....	....	....	....	....	....	....	....	....	....	....	....	....
1990-91♦	**Pittsburgh**	**NHL**	**78**	**40**	**73**	**113**	**48**	**12**	**0**	**9**	**184**	**21.7**	**0**	....	....	....	**24**	**10**	**24**	**34**	**33**	**5**	**0**	**2**	....
1991-92	**Pittsburgh**	**NHL**	**58**	**33**	**37**	**70**	**78**	**16**	**1**	**4**	**156**	**21.2**	**-16**	....	....	....	....	....	....	....	....	....	....	....	....
	Philadelphia	**NHL**	**22**	**10**	**17**	**27**	**18**	**4**	**0**	**1**	**54**	**18.5**	**-5**	....	....	....	....	....	....	....	....	....	....	....	....
1992-93	**Philadelphia**	**NHL**	**84**	**53**	**70**	**123**	**95**	**15**	**4**	**6**	**274**	**19.3**	**1**	....	....	....	....	....	....	....	....	....	....	....	....
1993-94	**Philadelphia**	**NHL**	**84**	**40**	**67**	**107**	**46**	**11**	**0**	**5**	**217**	**18.4**	**-2**	....	....	....	....	....	....	....	....	....	....	....	....
1994-95	**Philadelphia**	**NHL**	**10**	**2**	**3**	**5**	**12**	**1**	**0**	**2**	**17**	**11.8**	**-6**	....	....	....	....	....	....	....	....	....	....	....	....
	Montreal	**NHL**	**39**	**14**	**29**	**43**	**16**	**8**	**0**	**1**	**104**	**13.5**	**-3**	....	....	....	....	....	....	....	....	....	....	....	....
1995-96	**Montreal**	**NHL**	**82**	**28**	**50**	**78**	**69**	**11**	**2**	**6**	**191**	**14.7**	**20**	....	....	....	**6**	**3**	**3**	**6**	**0**	**3**	**0**	**0**	....
1996-97	**Montreal**	**NHL**	**82**	**34**	**46**	**80**	**58**	**7**	**2**	**3**	**202**	**16.8**	**-1**	....	....	....	**5**	**4**	**2**	**6**	**2**	**0**	**0**	**0**	....
1997-98	**Montreal**	**NHL**	**82**	**32**	**42**	**74**	**51**	**9**	**1**	**6**	**216**	**14.8**	**11**	....	....	....	**10**	**4**	**8**	**12**	**6**	**0**	**0**	**2**	....
	Canada	Olympics	5	0	2	2	0	....	....	....	....	....	....	....	....	....	....	....	....	....	....	....	....	....	....
1998-99	**Montreal**	**NHL**	**61**	**12**	**35**	**47**	**28**	**3**	**0**	**2**	**152**	**7.9**	**-4**	**239**	**44.8**	**20:37**	....	....	....	....	....	....	....	....	....
	Philadelphia	**NHL**	**10**	**4**	**2**	**6**	**6**	**0**	**0**	**0**	**19**	**21.1**	**-3**	**4**	**25.0**	**19:30**	**6**	**0**	**1**	**1**	**2**	**0**	**0**	**0**	**19:35**
99-2000	**Philadelphia**	**NHL**	**82**	**28**	***63**	**91**	**50**	**7**	**1**	**5**	**223**	**12.6**	**20**	**353**	**49.6**	**21:43**	**18**	**6**	**12**	**18**	**6**	**2**	**0**	**1**	**23:10**
2000-01	**Philadelphia**	**NHL**	**69**	**27**	**50**	**77**	**33**	**7**	**1**	**8**	**191**	**14.1**	**15**	**138**	**42.8**	**21:40**	**6**	**2**	**2**	**4**	**2**	**1**	**0**	**1**	**23:01**
2001-02	**Philadelphia**	**NHL**	**80**	**22**	**42**	**64**	**46**	**7**	**2**	**4**	**205**	**10.7**	**5**	**82**	**53.7**	**20:40**	**4**	**0**	**0**	**0**	**2**	**0**	**0**	**0**	**21:10**
2002-03	**Philadelphia**	**NHL**	**79**	**20**	**32**	**52**	**35**	**8**	**1**	**3**	**171**	**11.7**	**0**	**168**	**52.4**	**18:50**	**13**	**7**	**3**	**10**	**2**	**1**	**0**	**1**	**18:00**
2003-04	**Philadelphia**	**NHL**	**82**	**26**	**49**	**75**	**47**	**14**	**1**	**5**	**167**	**15.6**	**18**	**298**	**52.4**	**17:12**	**18**	**4**	**2**	**6**	**4**	**2**	**0**	**0**	**16:46**

			Regular Season														Playoffs								
Season	Club	League	GP	G	A	Pts	PIM	PP	SH	GW	S	%	+/-	TF	F%	Min	GP	G	A	Pts	PIM	PP	SH	GW	Min
2004-05			DID NOT PLAY																						
2005-06	**Pittsburgh**	**NHL**	**63**	**24**	**33**	**57**	**56**	**11**	**0**	**2**	**164**	**14.6**	**−28**	**387**	**48.3**	**21:17**	....	....	....	....	....	....	....	....	....
	♦ Carolina	**NHL**	**20**	**4**	**3**	**7**	**12**	**2**	**0**	**1**	**35**	**11.4**	**−8**	**6**	**33.3**	**17:37**	**25**	**7**	**9**	**16**	**18**	**2**	**0**	**2**	**16:34**
2006-07	**Pittsburgh**	**NHL**	**82**	**24**	**44**	**68**	**62**	**14**	**0**	**3**	**190**	**12.6**	**1**	**26**	**46.2**	**19:42**	**5**	**0**	**4**	**4**	**0**	**0**	**0**	**0**	**19:09**
	NHL Totals		**1338**	**508**	**825**	**1333**	**910**	**173**	**18**	**80**	**3286**	**15.5**		**1701**	**48.9**	**20:03**	**140**	**47**	**70**	**117**	**77**	**16**	**0**	**9**	**18:59**

WHL West First All-Star Team (1988) • IHL Second All-Star Team (1989) • NHL Second All-Star Team (1992)

Played in NHL All-Star Game (1991, 1993, 1994, 1997, 1998, 1999, 2000)

Traded to **Philadelphia** by **Pittsburgh** with Brian Benning and Los Angeles' 1st round choice (previously acquired, Philadelphia selected Jason Bowen) in 1992 Entry Draft for Rick Tocchet, Kjell Samuelsson, Ken Wregget and Philadelphia's 3rd round choice (Dave Roche) in 1993 Entry Draft, February 19, 1992. Traded to **Montreal** by **Philadelphia** with Philadelphia's 3rd round choice (Martin Hohenberger) in 1995 Entry Draft for Eric Desjardins, Gilbert Dionne and John LeClair, February 9, 1995. Traded to **Philadelphia** by **Montreal** for Danius Zubrus, Philadelphia's 2nd round choice (Matt Carkner) in 1999 Entry Draft and NY Islanders' 6th round choice (previously acquired, Montreal selected Scott Selig) in 2000 Entry Draft, March 10, 1999. Signed as a free agent by **Pittsburgh**, July 9, 2004. Traded to **Carolina** by **Pittsburgh** for Niklas Nordgren, Krys Kolanos and Carolina's 2nd round choice (later traded to San Jose - later traded to Philadlphia - Philadelphia selected Kevin Marshall) in 2007 Entry Draft, March 9, 2006. Signed as a free agent by **Pittsburgh**, July 25, 2006.

REDDEN, Wade

(REH-duhn, WAYD) **OTT.**

Defense. Shoots left. 6'2", 208 lbs. Born, Lloydminster, Sask., June 12, 1977. NY Islanders' 1st choice, 2nd overall, in 1995 Entry Draft.

Season	Club	League	GP	G	A	Pts	PIM	PP	SH	GW	S	%	+/-	TF	F%	Min	GP	G	A	Pts	PIM	PP	SH	GW	Min
1992-93	Lloydminster	AJHL	34	4	11	15	64	....	....	....	....	....	....	....	....	....	....	....	....	....	....	....	....	....	....
1993-94	Brandon	WHL	63	4	35	39	98	....	....	....	....	....	....	....	....	....	14	2	4	6	10	....	....	....	....
1994-95	Brandon	WHL	64	14	46	60	83	....	....	....	....	....	....	....	....	....	18	5	10	15	8	....	....	....	....
1995-96	Brandon	WHL	51	9	45	54	55	....	....	....	....	....	....	....	....	....	19	5	10	15	19	....	....	....	....
1996-97	**Ottawa**	**NHL**	**82**	**6**	**24**	**30**	**41**	**2**	**0**	**1**	**102**	**5.9**	**1**	....	....	....	**7**	**1**	**3**	**4**	**2**	**0**	**0**	**0**	....
1997-98	**Ottawa**	**NHL**	**80**	**8**	**14**	**22**	**27**	**3**	**0**	**2**	**103**	**7.8**	**17**	....	....	....	**9**	**0**	**2**	**2**	**2**	**0**	**0**	**0**	....
1998-99	**Ottawa**	**NHL**	**72**	**8**	**21**	**29**	**54**	**3**	**0**	**1**	**127**	**6.3**	**7**	**0**	**0.0**	**23:27**	**4**	**1**	**2**	**3**	**2**	**1**	**0**	**0**	**26:39**
99-2000	**Ottawa**	**NHL**	**81**	**10**	**26**	**36**	**49**	**3**	**0**	**2**	**163**	**6.1**	**−1**	**0**	**0.0**	**23:43**	....	....	....	....	....	....	....	....	....
2000-01	**Ottawa**	**NHL**	**78**	**10**	**37**	**47**	**49**	**4**	**0**	**0**	**159**	**6.3**	**22**	**0**	**0.0**	**25:17**	**4**	**0**	**0**	**0**	**0**	**0**	**0**	**0**	**27:29**
2001-02	**Ottawa**	**NHL**	**79**	**9**	**25**	**34**	**48**	**4**	**1**	**1**	**156**	**5.8**	**22**	**1**	**0.0**	**25:06**	**12**	**3**	**2**	**5**	**6**	**1**	**0**	**1**	**27:56**
2002-03	**Ottawa**	**NHL**	**76**	**10**	**35**	**45**	**70**	**4**	**0**	**3**	**154**	**6.5**	**23**	**0**	**0.0**	**25:24**	**18**	**1**	**8**	**9**	**10**	**0**	**0**	**1**	**25:28**
2003-04	**Ottawa**	**NHL**	**81**	**17**	**26**	**43**	**65**	**12**	**0**	**3**	**175**	**9.7**	**21**	**0**	**0.0**	**24:54**	**7**	**1**	**0**	**1**	**2**	**1**	**0**	**0**	**26:47**
2004-05			DID NOT PLAY																						
2005-06	**Ottawa**	**NHL**	**65**	**10**	**40**	**50**	**63**	**8**	**0**	**4**	**153**	**6.5**	**35**	**1**	**100.0**	**23:28**	**9**	**2**	**8**	**10**	**10**	**2**	**0**	**1**	**25:06**
	Canada	Olympics	6	1	0	1	0																		
2006-07	**Ottawa**	**NHL**	**64**	**7**	**29**	**36**	**50**	**4**	**0**	**3**	**122**	**5.7**	**1**	**0**	**0.0**	**22:54**	**20**	**3**	**7**	**10**	**10**	**3**	**0**	**1**	**23:37**
	NHL Totals		**758**	**95**	**277**	**372**	**516**	**47**	**1**	**20**	**1414**	**6.7**		**2**	**50.0**	**24:20**	**90**	**12**	**32**	**44**	**44**	**8**	**0**	**4**	**25:37**

WHL Rookie of the Year (1994) • WHL East Second All-Star Team (1995) • WHL East First All-Star Team (1996) • Memorial Cup Tournament All-Star Team (1996)

Played in NHL All-Star Game (2002)

Traded to **Ottawa** by **NY Islanders** with Damian Rhodes for Don Beaupre, Martin Straka and Bryan Berard, January 23, 1996.

REGEHR, Richie

(reh-GEER, RIH-chee)

Defense. Shoots right. 6', 190 lbs. Born, Bundung, Indonesia, January 17, 1983.

Season	Club	League	GP	G	A	Pts	PIM	PP	SH	GW	S	%	+/-	TF	F%	Min	GP	G	A	Pts	PIM	PP	SH	GW	Min
99-2000	Kelowna Rockets	WHL	50	6	8	14	22	....	....	....	....	....	....	....	....	....	5	0	1	1	0	....	....	....	....
2000-01	Kelowna Rockets	WHL	71	10	27	37	68	....	....	....	....	....	....	....	....	....	6	0	1	1	4	....	....	....	....
2001-02	Kelowna Rockets	WHL	15	1	9	10	12	....	....	....	....	....	....	....	....	....	....	....	....	....	....	....	....	....	....
	Portland	WHL	37	7	27	34	50	....	....	....	....	....	....	....	....	....	7	2	5	7	8	....	....	....	....
2002-03	Portland	WHL	67	16	45	61	115	....	....	....	....	....	....	....	....	....	7	2	2	4	8	....	....	....	....
2003-04	Portland	WHL	65	9	34	43	88	....	....	....	....	....	....	....	....	....	5	0	1	1	6	....	....	....	....
2004-05	Lowell	AHL	64	9	16	25	60	....	....	....	....	....	....	....	....	....	11	1	6	7	2	....	....	....	....
2005-06	**Calgary**	**NHL**	**14**	**0**	**2**	**2**	**6**	**0**	**0**	**0**	**12**	**0.0**	**0**	**0**	**0.0**	**11:21**	....	....	....	....	....	....	....	....	....
	Omaha	AHL	48	7	23	30	56	....	....	....	....	....	....	....	....	....	....	....	....	....	....	....	....	....	....
2006-07	**Calgary**	**NHL**	**6**	**1**	**1**	**2**	**0**	**1**	**0**	**0**	**4**	**25.0**	**−1**	**0**	**0.0**	**8:44**	....	....	....	....	....	....	....	....	....
	Omaha	AHL	22	5	9	14	37	....	....	....	....	....	....	....	....	....	....	....	....	....	....	....	....	....	....
	NHL Totals		**20**	**1**	**3**	**4**	**6**	**1**	**0**	**0**	**16**	**6.3**		**0**	**0.0**	**10:34**	....	....	....	....	....	....	....	....	....

Signed as a free agent by **Calgary**, July 6, 2004. • Missed majority of 2006-07 season recovering from head injury. Signed as a free agent by **Frankfurt** (Germany), July 16, 2007.

REGEHR, Robyn

(reh-GEER, RAW-bihn) **CGY.**

Defense. Shoots left. 6'3", 225 lbs. Born, Recife, Brazil, April 19, 1980. Colorado's 3rd choice, 19th overall, in 1998 Entry Draft.

Season	Club	League	GP	G	A	Pts	PIM	PP	SH	GW	S	%	+/-	TF	F%	Min	GP	G	A	Pts	PIM	PP	SH	GW	Min
1995-96	Prince Albert	SMHL	59	8	24	32	157	....	....	....	....	....	....	....	....	....	....	....	....	....	....	....	....	....	....
1996-97	Kamloops Blazers	WHL	64	4	19	23	96	....	....	....	....	....	....	....	....	....	5	0	1	1	18	....	....	....	....
1997-98	Kamloops Blazers	WHL	65	4	10	14	120	....	....	....	....	....	....	....	....	....	5	0	3	3	8	....	....	....	....
1998-99	Kamloops Blazers	WHL	54	12	20	32	130	....	....	....	....	....	....	....	....	....	12	1	4	5	21	....	....	....	....
99-2000	**Calgary**	**NHL**	**57**	**5**	**7**	**12**	**46**	**2**	**0**	**0**	**64**	**7.8**	**−2**	**0**	**0.0**	**18:24**	....	....	....	....	....	....	....	....	....
	Saint John Flames	AHL	5	0	0	0	0	....	....	....	....	....	....	....	....	....	....	....	....	....	....	....	....	....	....
2000-01	**Calgary**	**NHL**	**71**	**1**	**3**	**4**	**70**	**0**	**0**	**0**	**62**	**1.6**	**−7**	**1**	**0.0**	**19:43**	....	....	....	....	....	....	....	....	....
2001-02	**Calgary**	**NHL**	**77**	**2**	**6**	**8**	**93**	**0**	**0**	**0**	**82**	**2.4**	**−24**	**0**	**0.0**	**20:54**	....	....	....	....	....	....	....	....	....
2002-03	**Calgary**	**NHL**	**76**	**0**	**12**	**12**	**87**	**0**	**0**	**0**	**109**	**0.0**	**−9**	**1**	**100.0**	**22:45**	....	....	....	....	....	....	....	....	....
2003-04	**Calgary**	**NHL**	**82**	**4**	**14**	**18**	**74**	**2**	**0**	**1**	**106**	**3.8**	**14**	**2**	**50.0**	**22:21**	**26**	**2**	**7**	**9**	**20**	**0**	**0**	**0**	**26:27**
2004-05			DID NOT PLAY																						
2005-06	**Calgary**	**NHL**	**68**	**6**	**20**	**26**	**67**	**5**	**0**	**2**	**89**	**6.7**	**6**	**1**	**100.0**	**23:08**	**7**	**1**	**3**	**4**	**6**	**1**	**0**	**0**	**22:22**
	Canada	Olympics	6	0	1	1	2																		
2006-07	**Calgary**	**NHL**	**78**	**2**	**19**	**21**	**75**	**0**	**0**	**0**	**66**	**3.0**	**27**	**1**	**0.0**	**21:55**	**1**	**0**	**0**	**0**	**0**	**0**	**0**	**0**	**11:15**
	NHL Totals		**509**	**20**	**81**	**101**	**512**	**9**	**0**	**3**	**578**	**3.5**		**6**	**50.0**	**21:25**	**34**	**3**	**10**	**13**	**26**	**1**	**0**	**0**	**25:10**

WHL West First All-Star Team (1999)

Traded to **Calgary** by **Colorado** with Rene Corbet, Wade Belak and Colorado's 2nd round compensatory choice (Jarret Stoll) in 2000 Entry Draft for Theoren Fleury and Chris Dingman, February 28, 1999.

REGIER, Steve

(reh-GEER, STEEV) **NYI**

Left wing. Shoots left. 6'4", 194 lbs. Born, Edmonton, Alta., August 31, 1984. NY Islanders' 5th choice, 148th overall, in 2004 Entry Draft.

Season	Club	League	GP	G	A	Pts	PIM	PP	SH	GW	S	%	+/-	TF	F%	Min	GP	G	A	Pts	PIM	PP	SH	GW	Min
2000-01	Leduc Oil Kings	AMHL	35	22	39	61	135	....	....	....	....	....	....	....	....	....	....	....	....	....	....	....	....	....	....
2001-02	Medicine Hat	WHL	59	1	4	5	31	....	....	....	....	....	....	....	....	....	....	....	....	....	....	....	....	....	....
2002-03	Medicine Hat	WHL	61	11	10	21	114	....	....	....	....	....	....	....	....	....	11	2	2	4	20	....	....	....	....
2003-04	Medicine Hat	WHL	72	25	35	60	111	....	....	....	....	....	....	....	....	....	18	5	11	16	20	....	....	....	....
2004-05	Bridgeport	AHL	75	7	15	22	43	....	....	....	....	....	....	....	....	....	....	....	....	....	....	....	....	....	....
2005-06	**NY Islanders**	**NHL**	**9**	**0**	**0**	**0**	**0**	**0**	**0**	**0**	**4**	**0.0**	**−1**	**0**	**0.0**	**6:02**	....	....	....	....	....	....	....	....	....
	Bridgeport	AHL	73	16	21	37	54	....	....	....	....	....	....	....	....	....	7	0	2	2	6	....	....	....	....
2006-07	**NY Islanders**	**NHL**	**1**	**0**	**0**	**0**	**0**	**0**	**0**	**0**	**0**	**0.0**	**0**	**0**	**0.0**	**4:41**	....	....	....	....	....	....	....	....	....
	Bridgeport	AHL	77	19	27	46	77	....	....	....	....	....	....	....	....	....	....	....	....	....	....	....	....	....	....
	NHL Totals		**10**	**0**	**0**	**0**	**0**	**0**	**0**	**0**	**4**	**0.0**		**0**	**0.0**	**5:54**	....	....	....	....	....	....	....	....	....

REICH, Jeremy

(REECH, JAIR-eh-mee) **BOS.**

Left wing. Shoots left. 6'1", 200 lbs. Born, Craik, Sask., February 11, 1979. Chicago's 3rd choice, 39th overall, in 1997 Entry Draft.

Season	Club	League	GP	G	A	Pts	PIM	PP	SH	GW	S	%	+/-	TF	F%	Min	GP	G	A	Pts	PIM	PP	SH	GW	Min
1993-94	Pilote Butte	SAHA	80	70	65	135	120	....	....	....	....	....	....	....	....	....	....	....	....	....	....	....	....	....	....
1994-95	Sask. Contacts	SMHL	35	13	20	33	81	....	....	....	....	....	....	....	....	....	....	....	....	....	....	....	....	....	....
1995-96	Seattle	WHL	65	11	11	22	88	....	....	....	....	....	....	....	....	....	5	0	1	1	10	....	....	....	....
1996-97	Seattle	WHL	62	19	31	50	134	....	....	....	....	....	....	....	....	....	15	2	5	7	36	....	....	....	....
1997-98	Seattle	WHL	43	24	23	47	121	....	....	....	....	....	....	....	....	....	....	....	....	....	....	....	....	....	....
	Swift Current	WHL	22	8	8	16	47	....	....	....	....	....	....	....	....	....	12	5	6	11	37	....	....	....	....
1998-99	Swift Current	WHL	67	21	28	49	220	....	....	....	....	....	....	....	....	....	6	0	3	3	26	....	....	....	....
99-2000	Swift Current	WHL	72	33	58	91	167	....	....	....	....	....	....	....	....	....	12	2	10	12	19	....	....	....	....
2000-01	Syracuse Crunch	AHL	56	6	9	15	108	....	....	....	....	....	....	....	....	....	5	0	0	0	6	....	....	....	....
2001-02	Syracuse Crunch	AHL	59	9	7	16	178	....	....	....	....	....	....	....	....	....	10	4	0	4	16	....	....	....	....
2002-03	Syracuse Crunch	AHL	78	14	13	27	195	....	....	....	....	....	....	....	....	....	....	....	....	....	....	....	....	....	....
2003-04	**Columbus**	**NHL**	**9**	**0**	**1**	**1**	**20**	**0**	**0**	**0**	**3**	**0.0**	**−3**	**0**	**0.0**	**7:38**	....	....	....	....	....	....	....	....	....
	Syracuse Crunch	AHL	72	14	37	51	150	....	....	....	....	....	....	....	....	....	6	1	1	2	13	....	....	....	....
2004-05	Syracuse Crunch	AHL	50	4	5	9	189	....	....	....	....	....	....	....	....	....	....	....	....	....	....	....	....	....	....
	Houston Aeros	AHL	18	3	4	7	34	....	....	....	....	....	....	....	....	....	5	0	1	1	28	....	....	....	....

Season	Club	League	GP	G	A	Pts	PIM	PP	SH	GW	S	%	+/-	TF	F%	Min	GP	G	A	Pts	PIM	PP	SH	GW	Min
			Regular Season														Playoffs								
2005-06	Providence Bruins	AHL	77	8	15	23	235	....	....	....	....	....	....	....	....	....	6	0	0	0	27	....	....	....	....
2006-07	**Boston**	**NHL**	**32**	**0**	**1**	**1**	**63**	**0**	**0**	**0**	**27**	**0.0**	**–10**	**4**	**25.0**	**8:14**	....	....	....	....	....	....	....	....	....
	Providence Bruins	AHL	46	4	7	11	105	....	....	....	....	....	....	....	....	....	....	....	....	....	....	....	....	....	....
	NHL Totals		**41**	**0**	**2**	**2**	**83**	**0**	**0**	**0**	**30**	**0.0**		**4**	**25.0**	**8:06**	....	....	....	....	....	....	....	....	....

Signed as a free agent by **Columbus**, May 17, 2000. Loaned to **Houston** (AHL) by **Syracuse** (AHL) for the loan of Jason Beckett, March 10, 2005. Signed as a free agent by **Boston**, September 7, 2005.

REID, Brandon

(REED, BRAN-duhn)

Center. Shoots right. 5'8", 185 lbs. Born, Kirkland, Que., March 9, 1981. Vancouver's 5th choice, 208th overall, in 2000 Entry Draft.

Season	Club	League	GP	G	A	Pts	PIM	PP	SH	GW	S	%	+/-	TF	F%	Min	GP	G	A	Pts	PIM	PP	SH	GW	Min
1996-97	Lac St-Louis Lions	QAAA	44	17	34	51	....	....	....	....	....	....	....	....	....	....	7	2	3	5	....	....	....	....	....
1997-98	Halifax	QMJHL	67	13	21	36	6	....	....	....	....	....	....	....	....	....	5	1	0	1	15	....	....	....	....
1998-99	Halifax	QMJHL	70	32	25	57	33	....	....	....	....	....	....	....	....	....	5	2	2	4	0	....	....	....	....
99-2000	Halifax	QMJHL	62	44	80	124	10	....	....	....	....	....	....	....	....	....	10	7	11	18	4	....	....	....	....
2000-01	Val-d'Or Foreurs	QMJHL	57	45	81	126	18	....	....	....	....	....	....	....	....	....	21	13	29	42	14	....	....	....	....
2001-02	Manitoba Moose	AHL	60	18	19	37	6	....	....	....	....	....	....	....	....	....	7	0	3	3	0	....	....	....	....
2002-03	**Vancouver**	**NHL**	**7**	**2**	**3**	**5**	**0**	**0**	**0**	**0**	**15**	**13.3**	**4**	**69**	**55.1**	**9:47**	**9**	**0**	**1**	**1**	**0**	**0**	**0**	**0**	**9:36**
	Manitoba Moose	AHL	73	18	36	54	18	....	....	....	....	....	....	....	....	....	1	1	1	2	0	....	....	....	....
2003-04	**Vancouver**	**NHL**	**3**	**0**	**1**	**1**	**0**	**0**	**0**	**0**	**2**	**0.0**	**1**	**38**	**47.4**	**9:21**	....	....	....	....	....	....	....	....	....
	Manitoba Moose	AHL	73	19	39	58	20	....	....	....	....	....	....	....	....	....	....	....	....	....	....	....	....	....	....
2004-05	Hamburg Freezers	Germany	45	18	29	47	41	....	....	....	....	....	....	....	....	....	6	0	3	3	4	....	....	....	....
2005-06	Rapperswil	Swiss	44	16	18	34	14	....	....	....	....	....	....	....	....	....	12	4	7	11	14	....	....	....	....
2006-07	**Vancouver**	**NHL**	**3**	**0**	**0**	**0**	**0**	**0**	**0**	**0**	**8**	**0.0**	**–1**	**7**	**42.9**	**11:43**	**1**	**0**	**1**	**1**	**0**	**0**	**0**	**0**	**11:06**
	Manitoba Moose	AHL	53	15	17	32	19	....	....	....	....	....	....	....	....	....	10	2	3	5	4	....	....	....	....
	NHL Totals		**13**	**2**	**4**	**6**	**0**	**0**	**0**	**0**	**25**	**8.0**		**114**	**51.8**	**10:08**	**10**	**0**	**2**	**2**	**0**	**0**	**0**	**0**	**9:45**

QMJHL Second All-Star Team (2000) • George Parsons Trophy (Memorial Cup Tournament Most Sportsmanlike Player) (2000, 2001) • QMJHL First All-Star Team (2001) • Canadian Major Junior Sportsman of the Year (2001)

Signed as a free agent by **Hamburg** (Germany), July 7, 2004. Signed as a free agent by **Rapperswil** (Swiss), April 1, 2005. Signed as a free agent by **Dusseldorf** (Germany), May 29, 2007.

REID, Darren

(REED, DAIR-ehn) **PHI.**

Right wing. Shoots right. 6'2", 205 lbs. Born, Lac La Biche, Alta., May 8, 1983. Tampa Bay's 11th choice, 256th overall, in 2002 Entry Draft.

Season	Club	League	GP	G	A	Pts	PIM	PP	SH	GW	S	%	+/-	TF	F%	Min	GP	G	A	Pts	PIM	PP	SH	GW	Min
2000-01	Drayton Valley	AJHL	55	8	18	26	116	....	....	....	....	....	....	....	....	....	....	....	....	....	....	....	....	....	....
2001-02	Drayton Valley	AJHL	31	9	12	21	195	....	....	....	....	....	....	....	....	....	....	....	....	....	....	....	....	....	....
	Medicine Hat	WHL	37	8	9	17	70	....	....	....	....	....	....	....	....	....	....	....	....	....	....	....	....	....	....
2002-03	Medicine Hat	WHL	63	14	30	44	163	....	....	....	....	....	....	....	....	....	11	5	0	5	19	....	....	....	....
2003-04	Medicine Hat	WHL	67	33	48	81	194	....	....	....	....	....	....	....	....	....	20	*13	8	21	31	....	....	....	....
2004-05	Springfield	AHL	56	3	19	22	99	....	....	....	....	....	....	....	....	....	....	....	....	....	....	....	....	....	....
2005-06	**Tampa Bay**	**NHL**	**7**	**0**	**1**	**1**	**0**	**0**	**0**	**0**	**3**	**0.0**	**–2**	**0**	**0.0**	**5:41**	....	....	....	....	....	....	....	....	....
	Springfield	AHL	50	8	9	17	59	....	....	....	....	....	....	....	....	....	....	....	....	....	....	....	....	....	....
2006-07	Springfield	AHL	10	1	0	1	5	....	....	....	....	....	....	....	....	....	....	....	....	....	....	....	....	....	....
	Philadelphia	**NHL**	**14**	**0**	**0**	**0**	**18**	**0**	**0**	**0**	**8**	**0.0**	**–7**	**1**	**100.0**	**8:11**	....	....	....	....	....	....	....	....	....
	Philadelphia	AHL	43	16	14	30	20	....	....	....	....	....	....	....	....	....	....	....	....	....	....	....	....	....	....
	NHL Totals		**21**	**0**	**1**	**1**	**18**	**0**	**0**	**0**	**11**	**0.0**		**1**	**100.0**	**7:21**	....	....	....	....	....	....	....	....	....

Traded to **Philadelphia** by **Tampa Bay** for Daniel Corso, November 9, 2006.

REINPRECHT, Steve

(REIGHN-prehkt, STEEV) **PHX.**

Center. Shoots left. 6', 195 lbs. Born, Edmonton, Alta., May 7, 1976.

Season	Club	League	GP	G	A	Pts	PIM	PP	SH	GW	S	%	+/-	TF	F%	Min	GP	G	A	Pts	PIM	PP	SH	GW	Min
1993-94	Edmonton SSAC	AMHL	71	48	77	125	....	....	....	....	....	....	....	....	....	....	....	....	....	....	....	....	....	....	....
1994-95	St. Albert Saints	AJHL	56	35	44	79	14	....	....	....	....	....	....	....	....	....	....	....	....	....	....	....	....	....	....
1995-96	St. Albert Saints	AJHL	39	24	33	57	16	....	....	....	....	....	....	....	....	....	....	....	....	....	....	....	....	....	....
1996-97	U. of Wisconsin	WCHA	38	11	9	20	12	....	....	....	....	....	....	....	....	....	....	....	....	....	....	....	....	....	....
1997-98	U. of Wisconsin	WCHA	41	19	24	43	18	....	....	....	....	....	....	....	....	....	....	....	....	....	....	....	....	....	....
1998-99	U. of Wisconsin	WCHA	38	16	17	33	14	....	....	....	....	....	....	....	....	....	....	....	....	....	....	....	....	....	....
99-2000	U. of Wisconsin	WCHA	37	26	40	*66	14	....	....	....	....	....	....	....	....	....	....	....	....	....	....	....	....	....	....
	Los Angeles	**NHL**	**1**	**0**	**0**	**0**	**2**	**0**	**0**	**0**	**0**	**0.0**	**0**	**6**	**50.0**	**6:01**	....	....	....	....	....	....	....	....	....
2000-01	**Los Angeles**	**NHL**	**59**	**12**	**17**	**29**	**12**	**3**	**2**	**3**	**72**	**16.7**	**11**	**676**	**41.4**	**12:39**	....	....	....	....	....	....	....	....	....
	♦ Colorado	**NHL**	**21**	**3**	**4**	**7**	**2**	**0**	**0**	**0**	**28**	**10.7**	**–1**	**209**	**51.2**	**15:38**	**22**	**2**	**3**	**5**	**2**	**0**	**0**	**0**	**12:09**
2001-02	**Colorado**	**NHL**	**67**	**19**	**27**	**46**	**18**	**4**	**0**	**3**	**111**	**17.1**	**14**	**413**	**52.1**	**16:32**	**21**	**7**	**5**	**12**	**8**	**0**	**0**	**2**	**16:23**
2002-03	**Colorado**	**NHL**	**77**	**18**	**33**	**51**	**18**	**2**	**1**	**1**	**146**	**12.3**	**–6**	**928**	**46.4**	**17:22**	**7**	**1**	**2**	**3**	**0**	**0**	**0**	**0**	**15:32**
2003-04	**Calgary**	**NHL**	**44**	**7**	**22**	**29**	**4**	**3**	**0**	**1**	**68**	**10.3**	**1**	**120**	**40.0**	**17:05**	....	....	....	....	....	....	....	....	....
2004-05	HC Mulhouse	France	22	20	27	47	6	....	....	....	....	....	....	....	....	....	10	7	6	13	2	....	....	....	....
2005-06	**Calgary**	**NHL**	**52**	**10**	**19**	**29**	**24**	**5**	**0**	**1**	**72**	**13.9**	**10**	**340**	**49.4**	**14:49**	....	....	....	....	....	....	....	....	....
	Phoenix	**NHL**	**28**	**12**	**11**	**23**	**8**	**4**	**1**	**2**	**58**	**20.7**	**1**	**526**	**47.3**	**19:06**	....	....	....	....	....	....	....	....	....
2006-07	**Phoenix**	**NHL**	**49**	**9**	**24**	**33**	**28**	**2**	**0**	**1**	**71**	**12.7**	**–3**	**537**	**52.3**	**15:40**	....	....	....	....	....	....	....	....	....
	NHL Totals		**398**	**90**	**157**	**247**	**116**	**23**	**4**	**12**	**626**	**14.4**		**3755**	**47.5**	**15:57**	**50**	**10**	**10**	**20**	**10**	**0**	**0**	**2**	**14:24**

WCHA Second All-Star Team (1998) • WCHA First All-Star Team (2000) • WCHA Player of the Year (2000) • NCAA West First All-American Team (2000)

Signed as a free agent by **Los Angeles**, March 31, 2000. Traded to **Colorado** by **Los Angeles** with Rob Blake for Adam Deadmarsh, Aaron Miller, a player to be named later (Jared Aulin, March 22, 2001) and Colorado's 1st round choices in 2001 (Dave Steckel) and 2003 (Brian Boyle) Entry Drafts, February 21, 2001. Traded to **Buffalo** by **Colorado** for Keith Ballard, July 3, 2003. Traded to **Calgary** by **Buffalo** with Rhett Warrener for Chris Drury and Steve Begin, July 3, 2003. Signed as a free agent by **Mulhouse** (France), September 28, 2004. Traded to **Phoenix** by **Calgary** with Philippe Sauve for Brian Boucher and Mike Leclerc, February 2, 2006.

REITZ, Erik

(REETZ, AIR-ihk) **MIN.**

Defense. Shoots right. 6'1", 210 lbs. Born, Detroit, MI, July 29, 1982. Minnesota's 5th choice, 170th overall, in 2000 Entry Draft.

Season	Club	League	GP	G	A	Pts	PIM	PP	SH	GW	S	%	+/-	TF	F%	Min	GP	G	A	Pts	PIM	PP	SH	GW	Min
1998-99	Leamington Flyers	OHA-B	50	5	10	15	80	....	....	....	....	....	....	....	....	....	....	....	....	....	....	....	....	....	....
99-2000	Barrie Colts	OHL	63	2	10	12	85	....	....	....	....	....	....	....	....	....	25	0	5	5	44	....	....	....	....
2000-01	Barrie Colts	OHL	68	5	21	26	178	....	....	....	....	....	....	....	....	....	5	1	0	1	21	....	....	....	....
2001-02	Barrie Colts	OHL	61	13	27	40	153	....	....	....	....	....	....	....	....	....	20	4	16	20	40	....	....	....	....
2002-03	Houston Aeros	AHL	62	6	13	19	112	....	....	....	....	....	....	....	....	....	11	0	3	3	31	....	....	....	....
2003-04	Houston Aeros	AHL	69	5	19	24	148	....	....	....	....	....	....	....	....	....	2	0	0	0	0	....	....	....	....
2004-05	Houston Aeros	AHL	38	2	12	14	91	....	....	....	....	....	....	....	....	....	....	....	....	....	....	....	....	....	....
2005-06	**Minnesota**	**NHL**	**5**	**0**	**0**	**0**	**4**	**0**	**0**	**0**	**0**	**0.0**	**–2**	**0**	**0.0**	**13:09**	....	....	....	....	....	....	....	....	....
	Houston Aeros	AHL	72	5	23	28	139	....	....	....	....	....	....	....	....	....	8	0	5	5	20	....	....	....	....
2006-07	**Minnesota**	**NHL**	**1**	**0**	**0**	**0**	**0**	**0**	**0**	**0**	**0**	**0.0**	**1**	**0**	**0.0**	**10:36**	....	....	....	....	....	....	....	....	....
	Houston Aeros	AHL	73	9	25	34	132	....	....	....	....	....	....	....	....	....	....	....	....	....	....	....	....	....	....
	NHL Totals		**6**	**0**	**0**	**0**	**4**	**0**	**0**	**0**	**0**	**0.0**		**0**	**0.0**	**12:44**	....	....	....	....	....	....	....	....	....

Memorial Cup Tournament All-Star Team (2000) • OHL First All-Star Team (2002)

• Missed majority of 2004-05 season recovering from elbow injury suffered in game vs. Milwaukee (AHL), February 5, 2005.

RHEAUME, Pascal

(RAY-awm, pas-KAL)

Center. Shoots left. 6'1", 220 lbs. Born, Quebec City, Que., June 21, 1973.

Season	Club	League	GP	G	A	Pts	PIM	PP	SH	GW	S	%	+/-	TF	F%	Min	GP	G	A	Pts	PIM	PP	SH	GW	Min
1990-91	Ste-Foy	QAAA	37	20	38	58	25	....	....	....	....	....	....	....	....	....	7	7	1	8	6	....	....	....	....
1991-92	Trois-Rivieres	QMJHL	65	17	20	37	84	....	....	....	....	....	....	....	....	....	14	5	4	9	23	....	....	....	....
1992-93	Sherbrooke	QMJHL	65	28	34	62	88	....	....	....	....	....	....	....	....	....	14	6	5	11	31	....	....	....	....
1993-94	Albany River Rats	AHL	55	17	18	35	43	....	....	....	....	....	....	....	....	....	5	0	1	1	0	....	....	....	....
1994-95	Albany River Rats	AHL	78	19	25	44	46	....	....	....	....	....	....	....	....	....	14	3	6	9	19	....	....	....	....
1995-96	Albany River Rats	AHL	68	26	42	68	50	....	....	....	....	....	....	....	....	....	4	1	2	3	2	....	....	....	....
1996-97	**New Jersey**	**NHL**	**2**	**1**	**0**	**1**	**0**	**0**	**0**	**0**	**5**	**20.0**	**1**	....	....	....	....	....	....	....	....	....	....	....	....
	Albany River Rats	AHL	51	22	23	45	40	....	....	....	....	....	....	....	....	....	16	2	8	10	16	....	....	....	....
1997-98	**St. Louis**	**NHL**	**48**	**6**	**9**	**15**	**35**	**1**	**0**	**0**	**45**	**13.3**	**4**	....	....	....	**10**	**1**	**3**	**4**	**8**	**1**	**0**	**0**	....
1998-99	**St. Louis**	**NHL**	**60**	**9**	**18**	**27**	**24**	**2**	**0**	**0**	**85**	**10.6**	**10**	**21**	**71.4**	**13:19**	**5**	**1**	**0**	**1**	**4**	**0**	**0**	**0**	**11:36**
99-2000	**St. Louis**	**NHL**	**7**	**1**	**1**	**2**	**6**	**0**	**0**	**0**	**5**	**20.0**	**–2**	**2**	**0.0**	**10:08**	....	....	....	....	....	....	....	....	....
	Worcester IceCats	AHL	7	1	1	2	4	....	....	....	....	....	....	....	....	....	....	....	....	....	....	....	....	....	....
2000-01	Worcester IceCats	AHL	56	23	35	58	63	....	....	....	....	....	....	....	....	....	11	2	4	6	2	....	....	....	....
	St. Louis	**NHL**	**8**	**2**	**0**	**2**	**5**	**2**	**0**	**0**	**16**	**12.5**	**–1**	**7**	**42.9**	**11:56**	**3**	**0**	**1**	**1**	**0**	**0**	**0**	**0**	**11:30**
2001-02	**Chicago**	**NHL**	**19**	**0**	**2**	**2**	**4**	**0**	**0**	**0**	**19**	**0.0**	**–1**	**165**	**51.5**	**9:22**	....	....	....	....	....	....	....	....	....
	Atlanta	**NHL**	**42**	**11**	**9**	**20**	**25**	**6**	**0**	**2**	**61**	**18.0**	**–3**	**510**	**45.9**	**14:27**	....	....	....	....	....	....	....	....	....

			Regular Season														Playoffs								
Season	Club	League	GP	G	A	Pts	PIM	PP	SH	GW	S	%	+/-	TF	F%	Min	GP	G	A	Pts	PIM	PP	SH	GW	Min
2002-03	**Atlanta**	**NHL**	**56**	**4**	**9**	**13**	**24**	**0**	**2**	**1**	**70**	**5.7**	**-8**	**602**	**46.8**	**12:17**									
	♦ New Jersey	**NHL**	**21**	**4**	**1**	**5**	**8**	**0**	**1**	**1**	**23**	**17.4**	**3**	**248**	**51.6**	**11:50**	**24**	**1**	**2**	**3**	**13**	**0**	**0**	**0**	**13:32**
2003-04	**NY Rangers**	**NHL**	**17**	**0**	**0**	**0**	**5**	**0**	**0**	**0**	**15**	**0.0**	**-3**	**46**	**56.5**	**10:02**									
	Hartford	AHL	3	1	0	1	0																		
	St. Louis	**NHL**	**25**	**1**	**3**	**4**	**4**	**0**	**0**	**0**	**23**	**4.3**	**-3**	**26**	**38.5**	**10:19**	**3**	**0**	**0**	**0**	**2**	**0**	**0**	**0**	**6:55**
2004-05	Albany River Rats	AHL	78	24	25	49	85																		
2005-06	**New Jersey**	**NHL**	**12**	**0**	**0**	**0**	**4**	**0**	**0**	**0**	**11**	**0.0**	**-6**	**81**	**42.0**	**9:15**									
	Albany River Rats	AHL	9	2	0	2	9																		
	Phoenix	**NHL**	**1**	**0**	**0**	**0**	**0**	**0**	**0**	**0**	**0**	**0.0**	**-1**	**3**	**66.7**	**6:10**									
	San Antonio	AHL	47	13	13	26	35																		
2006-07	San Antonio	AHL	79	15	32	47	63																		
	NHL Totals		**318**	**39**	**52**	**91**	**144**	**11**	**3**	**4**	**378**	**10.3**		**1711**	**47.9**	**12:04**	**45**	**3**	**6**	**9**	**27**	**1**	**0**	**0**	**12:31**

Signed as a free agent by **New Jersey**, October 1, 1993. Claimed by **St. Louis** from **New Jersey** in Waiver Draft, September 28, 1997. • Missed majority of 1999-2000 season recovering from shoulder surgery, August, 1999. Signed as a free agent by **Chicago**, July 31, 2001. Claimed on waivers by **Atlanta** from **Chicago**, November 14, 2001. Traded to **New Jersey** by **Atlanta** for future considerations, February 24, 2003. Signed as a free agent by **NY Rangers**, October 22, 2003. Claimed on waivers by **St. Louis** from **NY Rangers**, January 29, 2004. Signed as a free agent by **New Jersey**, August 13, 2004. Traded to **Phoenix** by **New Jersey** with Ray Schultz and Steven Spencer for Brad Ference, November 25, 2005.

RIBEIRO, Mike

(rih-BAIR-roh, MIGHK) **DAL.**

Center. Shoots left. 6', 175 lbs. Born, Montreal, Que., February 10, 1980. Montreal's 2nd choice, 45th overall, in 1998 Entry Draft.

Season	Club	League	GP	G	A	Pts	PIM	PP	SH	GW	S	%	+/-	TF	F%	Min	GP	G	A	Pts	PIM	PP	SH	GW	Min
1996-97	Mtl-Bourassa	QAAA	43	32	57	89	48										16	15	23	38	14				
1997-98	Rouyn-Noranda	QMJHL	67	40	*85	125	55										6	3	1	4	0				
1998-99	Rouyn-Noranda	QMJHL	69	*67	*100	*167	137										11	5	11	16	12				
	Fredericton	AHL															5	0	1	1	2				
99-2000	**Montreal**	**NHL**	**19**	**1**	**1**	**2**	**2**	**1**	**0**	**0**	**18**	**5.6**	**-6**	**95**	**34.7**	**10:40**									
	Quebec Citadelles	AHL	3	0	0	0	2																		
	Rouyn-Noranda	QMJHL	2	1	3	4	0																		
	Quebec Remparts	QMJHL	21	17	28	45	30										11	3	20	23	38				
2000-01	**Montreal**	**NHL**	**2**	**0**	**0**	**0**	**2**	**0**	**0**	**0**	**3**	**0.0**	**0**	**11**	**18.2**	**10:38**									
	Quebec Citadelles	AHL	74	26	40	66	44										9	1	5	6	23				
2001-02	**Montreal**	**NHL**	**43**	**8**	**10**	**18**	**12**	**3**	**0**	**0**	**48**	**16.7**	**-11**	**141**	**44.0**	**13:55**									
	Quebec Citadelles	AHL	23	9	14	23	36										3	0	3	3	0				
2002-03	**Montreal**	**NHL**	**52**	**5**	**12**	**17**	**6**	**2**	**0**	**0**	**57**	**8.8**	**-3**	**358**	**50.3**	**11:07**									
	Hamilton	AHL	3	0	1	1	0																		
2003-04	**Montreal**	**NHL**	**81**	**20**	**45**	**65**	**34**	**7**	**0**	**5**	**103**	**19.4**	**15**	**913**	**44.8**	**17:05**	**11**	**2**	**1**	**3**	**18**	**0**	**0**	**0**	**16:31**
2004-05	Blues Espoo	Finland	17	8	9	17	4																		
2005-06	**Montreal**	**NHL**	**79**	**16**	**35**	**51**	**36**	**8**	**0**	**2**	**130**	**12.3**	**-6**	**843**	**44.7**	**16:35**	**6**	**0**	**2**	**2**	**0**	**0**	**0**	**0**	**18:22**
2006-07	**Dallas**	**NHL**	**81**	**18**	**41**	**59**	**22**	**6**	**0**	**3**	**111**	**16.2**	**3**	**678**	**46.6**	**14:56**	**7**	**0**	**3**	**3**	**4**	**0**	**0**	**0**	**18:28**
	NHL Totals		**357**	**68**	**144**	**212**	**114**	**27**	**0**	**10**	**470**	**14.5**		**3039**	**45.4**	**14:51**	**24**	**2**	**6**	**8**	**22**	**0**	**0**	**0**	**17:33**

QMJHL Second All-Star Team (1998) • QMJHL First All-Star Team (1999) • Canadian Major Junior First All-Star Team (1999)

Signed as a free agent by **Espoo** (Finland), January 17, 2005. Traded to **Dallas** by **Montreal** with Montreal's 6th round choice in 2008 Entry Draft for Janne Niinimaa and Dallas' 5th round choice (Andrew Conboy) in 2007 Entry Draft, September 30, 2006.

RICCI, Mike

(REE-CHEE, MIGHK)

Center. Shoots left. 6', 200 lbs. Born, Scarborough, Ont., October 27, 1971. Philadelphia's 1st choice, 4th overall, in 1990 Entry Draft.

Season	Club	League	GP	G	A	Pts	PIM	PP	SH	GW	S	%	+/-	TF	F%	Min	GP	G	A	Pts	PIM	PP	SH	GW	Min
1986-87	Toronto Marlies	MTHL	38	39	42	81	27																		
1987-88	Peterborough	OHL	41	24	37	61	20										8	5	5	10	4				
1988-89	Peterborough	OHL	60	54	52	106	43										17	19	16	35	18				
1989-90	Peterborough	OHL	60	52	64	116	39										12	5	7	12	26				
1990-91	**Philadelphia**	**NHL**	**68**	**21**	**20**	**41**	**64**	**9**	**0**	**4**	**121**	**17.4**	**-8**												
1991-92	**Philadelphia**	**NHL**	**78**	**20**	**36**	**56**	**93**	**11**	**2**	**0**	**149**	**13.4**	**-10**												
1992-93	**Quebec**	**NHL**	**77**	**27**	**51**	**78**	**123**	**12**	**1**	**10**	**142**	**19.0**	**8**				**6**	**0**	**6**	**6**	**8**	**0**	**0**	**0**	
1993-94	**Quebec**	**NHL**	**83**	**30**	**21**	**51**	**113**	**13**	**3**	**6**	**138**	**21.7**	**-9**												
1994-95	**Quebec**	**NHL**	**48**	**15**	**21**	**36**	**40**	**9**	**0**	**1**	**73**	**20.5**	**5**				**6**	**1**	**3**	**4**	**8**	**0**	**0**	**0**	
1995-96♦	**Colorado**	**NHL**	**62**	**6**	**21**	**27**	**52**	**3**	**0**	**1**	**73**	**8.2**	**1**				**22**	**6**	**11**	**17**	**18**	**3**	**0**	**1**	
1996-97	**Colorado**	**NHL**	**63**	**13**	**19**	**32**	**59**	**5**	**0**	**3**	**74**	**17.6**	**-3**				**17**	**2**	**4**	**6**	**17**	**0**	**0**	**1**	
1997-98	**Colorado**	**NHL**	**6**	**0**	**4**	**4**	**2**	**0**	**0**	**0**	**5**	**0.0**	**0**												
	San Jose	**NHL**	**59**	**9**	**14**	**23**	**30**	**5**	**0**	**2**	**86**	**10.5**	**-4**				**6**	**1**	**3**	**4**	**6**	**0**	**0**	**0**	
1998-99	**San Jose**	**NHL**	**82**	**13**	**26**	**39**	**68**	**2**	**1**	**2**	**98**	**13.3**	**1**	**1465**	**49.6**	**15:23**	**6**	**2**	**3**	**5**	**10**	**1**	**0**	**0**	**16:54**
99-2000	**San Jose**	**NHL**	**82**	**20**	**24**	**44**	**60**	**10**	**0**	**5**	**134**	**14.9**	**14**	**1522**	**50.7**	**16:52**	**12**	**5**	**1**	**6**	**2**	**3**	**0**	**1**	**17:37**
2000-01	**San Jose**	**NHL**	**81**	**22**	**22**	**44**	**60**	**9**	**2**	**4**	**141**	**15.6**	**3**	**1631**	**51.4**	**18:00**	**6**	**0**	**3**	**3**	**0**	**0**	**0**	**0**	**19:44**
2001-02	**San Jose**	**NHL**	**79**	**19**	**34**	**53**	**44**	**5**	**2**	**0**	**115**	**16.5**	**9**	**1501**	**49.0**	**17:04**	**12**	**4**	**6**	**10**	**4**	**0**	**0**	**1**	**19:51**
2002-03	**San Jose**	**NHL**	**75**	**11**	**23**	**34**	**53**	**5**	**1**	**2**	**101**	**10.9**	**-12**	**1152**	**51.6**	**16:31**									
2003-04	**San Jose**	**NHL**	**71**	**7**	**19**	**26**	**40**	**2**	**0**	**0**	**48**	**14.6**	**8**	**1116**	**54.8**	**14:21**	**17**	**2**	**3**	**5**	**4**	**0**	**0**	**0**	**15:31**
2004-05			DID NOT PLAY																						
2005-06	**Phoenix**	**NHL**	**78**	**10**	**6**	**16**	**69**	**5**	**1**	**1**	**50**	**20.0**	**-22**	**1146**	**49.2**	**12:48**									
2006-07	**Phoenix**	**NHL**	**7**	**0**	**1**	**1**	**4**	**0**	**0**	**0**	**4**	**0.0**	**-1**	**50**	**48.0**	**9:54**									
	San Antonio	AHL	2	0	0	0	0																		
	NHL Totals		**1099**	**243**	**362**	**605**	**974**	**105**	**13**	**41**	**1552**	**15.7**		**9583**	**50.8**	**15:49**	**110**	**23**	**43**	**66**	**77**	**7**	**0**	**4**	**17:36**

OHL Second All-Star Team (1989) • OHL First All-Star Team (1990) • OHL MVP (1990) • Canadian Major Junior Player of the Year (1990) • OHL First All-Star Team (1990)

Traded to **Quebec** by **Philadelphia** with Steve Duchesne, Peter Forsberg, Kerry Huffman, Ron Hextall, Philadelphia's 1st round choice (Jocelyn Thibault) in 1993 Entry Draft, $15,000,000 and future considerations (Chris Simon and Philadelphia's 1st round choice (later traded to Toronto – later traded to Washington – Washington selected Nolan Baumgartner) in 1994 Entry Draft, July 21, 1992) for Eric Lindros, June 30, 1992. Transferred to **Colorado** after **Quebec** franchise relocated, June 21, 1995. Traded to **San Jose** by **Colorado** with Colorado's 2nd round choice (later traded to Buffalo – Buffalo selected Jaroslav Kristek) in 1998 Entry Draft for Shean Donovan and San Jose's 1st round choice (Alex Tanguay) in 1998 Entry Draft, November 21, 1997. Signed as a free agent by **Phoenix**, July 9, 2004. • Missed majority of 2006-07 season recovering from recurring neck injury.

RICHARDS, Brad

(RIH-chards, BRAD) **T.B.**

Center. Shoots left. 6', 198 lbs. Born, Murray Harbour, P.E.I., May 2, 1980. Tampa Bay's 2nd choice, 64th overall, in 1998 Entry Draft.

Season	Club	League	GP	G	A	Pts	PIM	PP	SH	GW	S	%	+/-	TF	F%	Min	GP	G	A	Pts	PIM	PP	SH	GW	Min
1996-97	Notre Dame	SJHL	63	39	48	87	73																		
1997-98	Rimouski Oceanic	QMJHL	68	33	82	115	44										19	8	24	32	2				
1998-99	Rimouski Oceanic	QMJHL	59	39	92	131	55										11	9	12	21	6				
99-2000	Rimouski Oceanic	QMJHL	63	*71	*115	*186	69										12	13	*24	*37	16				
2000-01	**Tampa Bay**	**NHL**	**82**	**21**	**41**	**62**	**14**	**7**	**0**	**3**	**179**	**11.7**	**-10**	**955**	**41.4**	**16:54**									
2001-02	**Tampa Bay**	**NHL**	**82**	**20**	**42**	**62**	**13**	**5**	**0**	**0**	**251**	**8.0**	**-18**	**911**	**41.2**	**19:48**									
2002-03	**Tampa Bay**	**NHL**	**80**	**17**	**57**	**74**	**24**	**4**	**0**	**2**	**277**	**6.1**	**3**	**1007**	**47.5**	**19:56**	**11**	**0**	**5**	**5**	**12**	**0**	**0**	**0**	**22:21**
2003-04♦	**Tampa Bay**	**NHL**	**82**	**26**	**53**	**79**	**12**	**5**	**1**	**6**	**244**	**10.7**	**14**	**1167**	**46.7**	**20:26**	**23**	**12**	**14**	***26**	**4**	**7**	**0**	**7**	**23:28**
2004-05	Ak Bars Kazan	Russia	6	2	5	7	16																		
2005-06	**Tampa Bay**	**NHL**	**82**	**23**	**68**	**91**	**32**	**7**	**4**	**0**	**282**	**8.2**	**0**	**1288**	**50.2**	**22:45**	**5**	**3**	**5**	**8**	**6**	**0**	**0**	**0**	**24:11**
	Canada	Olympics	6	2	2	4	6																		
2006-07	**Tampa Bay**	**NHL**	**82**	**25**	**45**	**70**	**23**	**12**	**1**	**3**	**272**	**9.2**	**-19**	**1580**	**51.4**	**24:07**	**6**	**3**	**5**	**8**	**6**	**2**	**0**	**0**	**25:39**
	NHL Totals		**490**	**132**	**306**	**438**	**118**	**40**	**6**	**14**	**1505**	**8.8**		**6908**	**47.1**	**20:40**	**45**	**18**	**29**	**47**	**28**	**9**	**0**	**7**	**23:34**

QMJHL First All-Star Team (2000) • Canadian Major Junior First All-Star Team (2000) • Canadian Major Junior Player of the Year (2000) • Memorial Cup Tournament All-Star Team (2000) • Stafford Smythe Memorial Trophy (Memorial Cup Tournament MVP) (2000) • NHL All-Rookie Team (2001) • Lady Byng Memorial Trophy (2004) • Conn Smythe Trophy (2004)

Signed as a free agent by **Kazan** (Russia), November 8, 2004.

RICHARDS, Mike

(RIH-chards, MIGHK) **PHI.**

Center. Shoots left. 5'11", 195 lbs. Born, Kenora, Ont., February 11, 1985. Philadelphia's 2nd choice, 24th overall, in 2003 Entry Draft.

Season	Club	League	GP	G	A	Pts	PIM	PP	SH	GW	S	%	+/-	TF	F%	Min	GP	G	A	Pts	PIM	PP	SH	GW	Min
2000-01	Kenora Stars	NOHA	85	76	73	149	20																		
2001-02	Kitchener Rangers	OHL	65	20	38	58	52										4	0	1	1	6				
2002-03	Kitchener Rangers	OHL	67	37	50	87	99										21	9	18	27	24				
2003-04	Kitchener Rangers	OHL	58	36	53	89	82										1	0	0	0	0				
2004-05	Kitchener Rangers	OHL	43	22	36	58	75										15	11	17	28	36				
	Philadelphia	AHL															14	7	8	15	28				

			Regular Season														Playoffs								
Season	Club	League	GP	G	A	Pts	PIM	PP	SH	GW	S	%	+/-	TF	F%	Min	GP	G	A	Pts	PIM	PP	SH	GW	Min
2005-06	**Philadelphia**	**NHL**	**79**	**11**	**23**	**34**	**65**	**1**	**3**	**1**	**168**	**6.5**	**6**	**914**	**45.7**	**15:23**	**6**	**0**	**1**	**1**	**0**	**0**	**0**	**0**	**15:41**
2006-07	**Philadelphia**	**NHL**	**59**	**10**	**22**	**32**	**52**	**1**	**4**	**3**	**130**	**7.7**	**–12**	**978**	**47.8**	**17:50**	....	....	....	....	....	....	....	....	....
	NHL Totals		**138**	**21**	**45**	**66**	**117**	**2**	**7**	**4**	**298**	**7.0**		**1892**	**46.8**	**16:26**	**6**	**0**	**1**	**1**	**0**	**0**	**0**	**0**	**15:41**

Memorial Cup Tournament All-Star Team (2003) • OHL Second All-Star Team (2005)

RICHARDSON, Brad

(RIH-chard-suhn, BRAD) **COL.**

Center. Shoots left. 5'11", 185 lbs. Born, Belleville, Ont., February 4, 1985. Colorado's 4th choice, 163rd overall, in 2003 Entry Draft.

Season	Club	League	GP	G	A	Pts	PIM	PP	SH	GW	S	%	+/-	TF	F%	Min	GP	G	A	Pts	PIM	PP	SH	GW	Min
2001-02	Owen Sound	OHL	58	12	21	33	20	....	....	....	....	....	....	....	....	....	....	....	....	....	....	....	....	....	....
2002-03	Owen Sound	OHL	67	27	40	67	54	....	....	....	....	....	....	....	....	....	4	1	1	2	10	....	....	....	....
2003-04	Owen Sound	OHL	15	7	9	16	4	....	....	....	....	....	....	....	....	....	....	....	....	....	....	....	....	....	....
2004-05	Owen Sound	OHL	68	41	56	97	60	....	....	....	....	....	....	....	....	....	8	6	4	10	8	....	....	....	....
2005-06	**Colorado**	**NHL**	**41**	**3**	**10**	**13**	**12**	**1**	**0**	**0**	**51**	**5.9**	**0**	**305**	**41.0**	**10:44**	**9**	**1**	**0**	**1**	**6**	**0**	**0**	**0**	**11:41**
	Lowell	AHL	29	4	13	17	20	....	....	....	....	....	....	....	....	....	....	....	....	....	....	....	....	....	....
2006-07	**Colorado**	**NHL**	**73**	**14**	**8**	**22**	**28**	**0**	**3**	**3**	**129**	**10.9**	**4**	**358**	**40.8**	**13:10**	....	....	....	....	....	....	....	....	....
	Albany River Rats	AHL	3	0	1	1	2	....	....	....	....	....	....	....	....	....	....	....	....	....	....	....	....	....	....
	NHL Totals		**114**	**17**	**18**	**35**	**40**	**1**	**3**	**3**	**180**	**9.4**		**663**	**40.9**	**12:18**	**9**	**1**	**0**	**1**	**6**	**0**	**0**	**0**	**11:41**

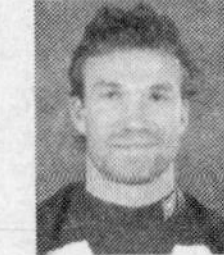

RICHARDSON, Luke

(RIH-chard-suhn, LEWK) **OTT.**

Defense. Shoots left. 6'4", 215 lbs. Born, Ottawa, Ont., March 26, 1969. Toronto's 1st choice, 7th overall, in 1987 Entry Draft.

Season	Club	League	GP	G	A	Pts	PIM	PP	SH	GW	S	%	+/-	TF	F%	Min	GP	G	A	Pts	PIM	PP	SH	GW	Min
1984-85	Ottawa Knights	Minor-ON	35	5	26	31	72	....	....	....	....	....	....	....	....	....	....	....	....	....	....	....	....	....	....
1985-86	Peterborough	OHL	63	6	18	24	57	....	....	....	....	....	....	....	....	....	16	2	1	3	50	....	....	....	....
1986-87	Peterborough	OHL	59	13	32	45	70	....	....	....	....	....	....	....	....	....	12	0	5	5	24	....	....	....	....
1987-88	**Toronto**	**NHL**	**78**	**4**	**6**	**10**	**90**	**0**	**0**	**0**	**49**	**8.2**	**–25**	....	....	....	**2**	**0**	**0**	**0**	**0**	**0**	**0**	**0**	....
1988-89	**Toronto**	**NHL**	**55**	**2**	**7**	**9**	**106**	**0**	**0**	**0**	**59**	**3.4**	**–15**	....	....	....	....	....	....	....	....	....	....	....	....
1989-90	**Toronto**	**NHL**	**67**	**4**	**14**	**18**	**122**	**0**	**0**	**0**	**80**	**5.0**	**–1**	....	....	....	**5**	**0**	**0**	**0**	**22**	**0**	**0**	**0**	....
1990-91	**Toronto**	**NHL**	**78**	**1**	**9**	**10**	**238**	**0**	**0**	**0**	**68**	**1.5**	**–28**	....	....	....	....	....	....	....	....	....	....	....	....
1991-92	**Edmonton**	**NHL**	**75**	**2**	**19**	**21**	**118**	**0**	**0**	**0**	**85**	**2.4**	**–9**	....	....	....	**16**	**0**	**5**	**5**	**45**	**0**	**0**	**0**	....
1992-93	**Edmonton**	**NHL**	**82**	**3**	**10**	**13**	**142**	**0**	**2**	**0**	**78**	**3.8**	**–18**	....	....	....	....	....	....	....	....	....	....	....	....
1993-94	**Edmonton**	**NHL**	**69**	**2**	**6**	**8**	**131**	**0**	**0**	**0**	**92**	**2.2**	**–13**	....	....	....	....	....	....	....	....	....	....	....	....
1994-95	**Edmonton**	**NHL**	**46**	**3**	**10**	**13**	**40**	**1**	**1**	**1**	**51**	**5.9**	**–6**	....	....	....	....	....	....	....	....	....	....	....	....
1995-96	**Edmonton**	**NHL**	**82**	**2**	**9**	**11**	**108**	**0**	**0**	**0**	**61**	**3.3**	**–27**	....	....	....	....	....	....	....	....	....	....	....	....
1996-97	**Edmonton**	**NHL**	**82**	**1**	**11**	**12**	**91**	**0**	**0**	**0**	**67**	**1.5**	**9**	....	....	....	**12**	**0**	**2**	**2**	**14**	**0**	**0**	**0**	....
1997-98	**Philadelphia**	**NHL**	**81**	**2**	**3**	**5**	**139**	**2**	**0**	**0**	**57**	**3.5**	**7**	....	....	....	**5**	**0**	**0**	**0**	**0**	**0**	**0**	**0**	....
1998-99	**Philadelphia**	**NHL**	**78**	**0**	**6**	**6**	**106**	**0**	**0**	**0**	**49**	**0.0**	**–3**	**0**	**0.0**	**16:33**	....	....	....	....	....	....	....	....	....
99-2000	**Philadelphia**	**NHL**	**74**	**2**	**5**	**7**	**140**	**0**	**0**	**1**	**50**	**4.0**	**14**	**0**	**0.0**	**16:11**	**18**	**0**	**1**	**1**	**41**	**0**	**0**	**0**	**21:58**
2000-01	**Philadelphia**	**NHL**	**82**	**2**	**6**	**8**	**131**	**0**	**1**	**0**	**75**	**2.7**	**23**	**1**	**0.0**	**20:42**	**6**	**0**	**0**	**0**	**4**	**0**	**0**	**0**	**24:39**
2001-02	**Philadelphia**	**NHL**	**72**	**1**	**8**	**9**	**102**	**0**	**0**	**0**	**65**	**1.5**	**18**	**0**	**0.0**	**18:17**	**5**	**0**	**0**	**0**	**4**	**0**	**0**	**0**	**19:18**
2002-03	**Columbus**	**NHL**	**82**	**0**	**13**	**13**	**73**	**0**	**0**	**0**	**56**	**0.0**	**–16**	**2**	**50.0**	**23:32**	....	....	....	....	....	....	....	....	....
2003-04	**Columbus**	**NHL**	**64**	**1**	**5**	**6**	**48**	**0**	**0**	**1**	**34**	**2.9**	**–11**	**0**	**0.0**	**20:07**	....	....	....	....	....	....	....	....	....
2004-05			DID NOT PLAY																						
2005-06	**Columbus**	**NHL**	**44**	**1**	**6**	**7**	**30**	**0**	**0**	**0**	**24**	**4.2**	**–18**	**0**	**0.0**	**15:15**	....	....	....	....	....	....	....	....	....
	Toronto	**NHL**	**21**	**0**	**3**	**3**	**41**	**0**	**0**	**0**	**16**	**0.0**	**–1**	**0**	**0.0**	**18:48**	....	....	....	....	....	....	....	....	....
2006-07	**Tampa Bay**	**NHL**	**27**	**0**	**3**	**3**	**16**	**0**	**0**	**0**	**3**	**0.0**	**3**	**0**	**0.0**	**7:07**	....	....	....	....	....	....	....	....	....
	NHL Totals		**1339**	**33**	**159**	**192**	**2012**	**3**	**4**	**3**	**1119**	**2.9**		**3**	**33.3**	**18:20**	**69**	**0**	**8**	**8**	**130**	**0**	**0**	**0**	**22:04**

Traded to **Edmonton** by **Toronto** with Vincent Damphousse, Peter Ing and Scott Thornton for Grant Fuhr, Glenn Anderson and Craig Berube, September 19, 1991. Signed as a free agent by **Philadelphia**, July 23, 1997. Signed as a free agent by **Columbus**, July 4, 2002. Traded to **Toronto** by **Columbus** for Toronto's 5th round choice (Nick Sucharski) in 2006 Entry Draft, March 8, 2006. Signed as a free agent by **Tampa Bay**, July 11, 2006. • Spent majority of 2006-07 season as a healthy reserve. Signed as a free agent by **Ottawa**, August 8, 2007.

RICHMOND, Danny

(RIHCH-muhnd, DA-nee) **CHI.**

Defense. Shoots left. 6', 192 lbs. Born, Chicago, IL, August 1, 1984. Carolina's 2nd choice, 31st overall, in 2003 Entry Draft.

Season	Club	League	GP	G	A	Pts	PIM	PP	SH	GW	S	%	+/-	TF	F%	Min	GP	G	A	Pts	PIM	PP	SH	GW	Min
2000-01	Team Illinois	MWEHL	79	25	40	65		....	....	....	....	....	....	....	....	....	....	....	....	....	....	....	....	....	....
2001-02	Chicago Steel	USHL	56	8	45	53	129	....	....	....	....	....	....	....	....	....	4	0	4	4	20	....	....	....	....
2002-03	U. of Michigan	CCHA	43	3	19	22	48	....	....	....	....	....	....	....	....	....	....	....	....	....	....	....	....	....	....
2003-04	London Knights	OHL	59	13	22	35	92	....	....	....	....	....	....	....	....	....	15	5	6	11	10	....	....	....	....
2004-05	Lowell	AHL	63	4	9	13	139	....	....	....	....	....	....	....	....	....	6	0	2	2	8	....	....	....	....
2005-06	**Carolina**	**NHL**	**10**	**0**	**1**	**1**	**7**	**0**	**0**	**0**	**7**	**0.0**	**–3**	**0**	**0.0**	**9:00**	....	....	....	....	....	....	....	....	....
	Lowell	AHL	32	4	11	15	60	....	....	....	....	....	....	....	....	....	....	....	....	....	....	....	....	....	....
	Chicago	**NHL**	**10**	**0**	**0**	**0**	**18**	**0**	**0**	**0**	**6**	**0.0**	**–3**	**0**	**0.0**	**13:36**	....	....	....	....	....	....	....	....	....
	Norfolk Admirals	AHL	31	4	8	12	42	....	....	....	....	....	....	....	....	....	3	0	1	1	2	....	....	....	....
2006-07	**Chicago**	**NHL**	**22**	**0**	**2**	**2**	**48**	**0**	**0**	**0**	**13**	**0.0**	**–1**	**0**	**0.0**	**12:20**	....	....	....	....	....	....	....	....	....
	Norfolk Admirals	AHL	57	10	24	34	144	....	....	....	....	....	....	....	....	....	6	0	0	0	8	....	....	....	....
	NHL Totals		**42**	**0**	**3**	**3**	**73**	**0**	**0**	**0**	**26**	**0.0**		**0**	**0.0**	**11:50**	....	....	....	....	....	....	....	....	....

USHL All-Rookie Team (2002) • USHL First All-Star Team (2002) • USHL Rookie of the Year (2002) • CCHA All-Rookie Team (2003)

Left **University of Michigan** (CCHA) and signed with **London** (OHL), June 6, 2003. Traded to **Chicago** by **Carolina** with Columbus' 4th round choice (previously acquired, later traded to Toronto - Toronto selected James Reimer) in 2006 Entry Draft for Anton Babchuk and Chicago's 4th round choice (later traded to St. Louis - St. Louis selected Cade Fairchild) in 2007 Entry Draft, January 20, 2006.

RISSMILLER, Patrick

(RIGHZ-mih-luhr, PAT-rihk) **S.J.**

Left wing. Shoots left. 6'4", 215 lbs. Born, Belmont, MA, October 26, 1978.

Season	Club	League	GP	G	A	Pts	PIM	PP	SH	GW	S	%	+/-	TF	F%	Min	GP	G	A	Pts	PIM	PP	SH	GW	Min
1997-98	The Hill School	High-PA	STATISTICS NOT AVAILABLE																						
1998-99	Holy Cross	MAAC	34	13	28	41	23	....	....	....	....	....	....	....	....	....	....	....	....	....	....	....	....	....	....
99-2000	Holy Cross	MAAC	35	10	17	27	22	....	....	....	....	....	....	....	....	....	....	....	....	....	....	....	....	....	....
2000-01	Holy Cross	MAAC	29	14	15	29	40	....	....	....	....	....	....	....	....	....	....	....	....	....	....	....	....	....	....
2001-02	Holy Cross	MAAC	33	16	*30	*46	31	....	....	....	....	....	....	....	....	....	....	....	....	....	....	....	....	....	....
2002-03	Cleveland Barons	AHL	72	14	26	40	24	....	....	....	....	....	....	....	....	....	....	....	....	....	....	....	....	....	....
	Cincinnati	ECHL	2	2	2	4	0	....	....	....	....	....	....	....	....	....	....	....	....	....	....	....	....	....	....
2003-04	**San Jose**	**NHL**	**4**	**0**	**0**	**0**	**0**	**0**	**0**	**0**	**2**	**0.0**	**0**	**26**	**53.9**	**7:07**	....	....	....	....	....	....	....	....	....
	Cleveland Barons	AHL	75	14	31	45	66	....	....	....	....	....	....	....	....	....	9	0	1	1	8	....	....	....	....
2004-05	Cleveland Barons	AHL	69	21	23	44	50	....	....	....	....	....	....	....	....	....	....	....	....	....	....	....	....	....	....
2005-06	**San Jose**	**NHL**	**18**	**3**	**3**	**6**	**8**	**1**	**0**	**1**	**26**	**11.5**	**1**	**3**	**0.0**	**9:22**	**11**	**2**	**1**	**3**	**6**	**0**	**0**	**0**	**8:06**
	Cleveland Barons	AHL	68	15	37	52	30	....	....	....	....	....	....	....	....	....	....	....	....	....	....	....	....	....	....
2006-07	**San Jose**	**NHL**	**79**	**7**	**15**	**22**	**22**	**1**	**0**	**0**	**100**	**7.0**	**1**	**25**	**36.0**	**12:10**	**11**	**1**	**3**	**4**	**0**	**0**	**0**	**1**	**12:40**
	NHL Totals		**101**	**10**	**18**	**28**	**30**	**2**	**0**	**1**	**128**	**7.8**		**54**	**42.6**	**11:28**	**22**	**3**	**4**	**7**	**6**	**0**	**0**	**1**	**10:23**

MAAC All-Rookie Team (1999) • MAAC First All-Star Team (2002) • MAAC Offensive Player of the Year (2002)

Signed as a free agent by **Cleveland** (AHL), September 23, 2002. Signed as a free agent by **San Jose**, June 30, 2003.

RITA, Jani

(REETA, YAH-nee) **PIT.**

Left wing. Shoots left. 6'1", 206 lbs. Born, Helsinki, Finland, July 25, 1981. Edmonton's 1st choice, 13th overall, in 1999 Entry Draft.

Season	Club	League	GP	G	A	Pts	PIM	PP	SH	GW	S	%	+/-	TF	F%	Min	GP	G	A	Pts	PIM	PP	SH	GW	Min
1995-96	Jokerit U18	Fin-U18	5	0	0	0	0	....	....	....	....	....	....	....	....	....	....	....	....	....	....	....	....	....	....
1996-97	Jokerit U18	Fin-U18	27	22	7	29	4	....	....	....	....	....	....	....	....	....	....	....	....	....	....	....	....	....	....
	Jokerit Helsinki Jr.	Fin-Jr.	3	0	0	0	0	....	....	....	....	....	....	....	....	....	....	....	....	....	....	....	....	....	....
1997-98	Jokerit U18	Fin-U18	7	7	4	11	2	....	....	....	....	....	....	....	....	....	....	....	....	....	....	....	....	....	....
	Jokerit Helsinki Jr.	Fin-Jr.	36	15	9	24	2	....	....	....	....	....	....	....	....	....	8	4	1	5	0	....	....	....	....
	Jokerit Helsinki	Finland	....	....	....	....	....	....	....	....	....	....	....	....	....	....	1	0	0	0	0	....	....	....	....
1998-99	Jokerit Helsinki Jr.	Fin-Jr.	20	9	13	22	8	....	....	....	....	....	....	....	....	....	6	1	1	2	8	....	....	....	....
	Jokerit Helsinki	Finland	41	3	2	5	39	....	....	....	....	....	....	....	....	....	....	....	....	....	....	....	....	....	....
	Jokerit Helsinki	EuroHL	3	0	0	0	0	....	....	....	....	....	....	....	....	....	....	....	....	....	....	....	....	....	....
99-2000	Jokerit Helsinki Jr.	Fin-Jr.	1	1	0	1	0	....	....	....	....	....	....	....	....	....	....	....	....	....	....	....	....	....	....
	Jokerit Helsinki	Finland	49	6	3	9	10	....	....	....	....	....	....	....	....	....	11	1	0	1	0	....	....	....	....
2000-01	Jokerit Helsinki Jr.	Fin-Jr.	3	3	2	5	0	....	....	....	....	....	....	....	....	....	....	....	....	....	....	....	....	....	....
	Jokerit Helsinki	Finland	50	5	10	15	18	....	....	....	....	....	....	....	....	....	5	0	0	0	2	....	....	....	....
2001-02	**Edmonton**	**NHL**	**1**	**0**	**0**	**0**	**0**	**0**	**0**	**0**	**0**	**0.0**	**0**	**0**	**0.0**	**6:09**	....	....	....	....	....	....	....	....	....
	Hamilton	AHL	76	25	17	42	32	....	....	....	....	....	....	....	....	....	15	8	4	12	0	....	....	....	....
2002-03	**Edmonton**	**NHL**	**12**	**3**	**1**	**4**	**0**	**0**	**0**	**0**	**18**	**16.7**	**2**	**1**	**0.0**	**9:32**	....	....	....	....	....	....	....	....	....
	Hamilton	AHL	64	21	27	48	18	....	....	....	....	....	....	....	....	....	23	3	4	7	2	....	....	....	....

Season	Club	League	GP	G	A	Pts	PIM	PP	SH	GW	S	%	+/-	TF	F%	Min	GP	G	A	Pts	PIM	PP	SH	GW	Min
			Regular Season														Playoffs								
2003-04	Edmonton	NHL	2	0	0	0	0	0	0	0	1	0.0	0	0	0.0	4:34	....	....	....	....	....	....	....	....	....
	Toronto	AHL	64	17	24	41	18	....	....	....	....	....	....	....	....	....	1	1	0	1	0	....	....	....	....
2004-05	HPK Hameenlinna	Finland	56	21	18	39	12	....	....	....	....	....	....	....	....	....	10	7	4	11	4	....	....	....	....
2005-06	Edmonton	NHL	21	3	0	3	6	0	0	0	13	23.1	0	2	0.0	6:46	....	....	....	....	....	....	....	....	....
	Pittsburgh	NHL	30	3	4	7	4	0	0	0	36	8.3	–6	104	45.2	10:06	....	....	....	....	....	....	....	....	....
2006-07	Jokerit Helsinki	Finland	56	*32	20	52	28	....	....	....	....	....	....	....	....	....	10	6	1	7	2	....	....	....	....
	NHL Totals		66	9	5	14	10	0	0	0	68	13.2		107	43.9	8:42	....	....	....	....	....	....	....	....	....

Signed as a free agent by **Hameenlinna** (Finland), August 17, 2004. Traded to **Pittsburgh** by **Edmonton** with Cory Cross for Dick Tarnstrom, January 26, 2006.

RITCHIE, Byron

(RIHT-chee, BIGH-rohn) **VAN.**

Center. Shoots left. 5'10", 190 lbs. Born, Burnaby, B.C., April 24, 1977. Hartford's 6th choice, 165th overall, in 1995 Entry Draft.

Season	Club	League	GP	G	A	Pts	PIM	PP	SH	GW	S	%	+/-	TF	F%	Min	GP	G	A	Pts	PIM	PP	SH	GW	Min
1992-93	North Delta	BCAHA	60	102	151	253	147	....	....	....	....	....	....	....	....	....	....	....	....	....	....	....	....	....	....
1993-94	Lethbridge	WHL	44	4	11	15	44	....	....	....	....	....	....	....	....	....	6	0	0	0	14	....	....	....	....
1994-95	Lethbridge	WHL	58	22	28	50	132	....	....	....	....	....	....	....	....	....	....	....	....	....	....	....	....	....	....
1995-96	Lethbridge	WHL	66	55	51	106	163	....	....	....	....	....	....	....	....	....	4	0	2	2	4	....	....	....	....
	Springfield	AHL	6	2	1	3	4	....	....	....	....	....	....	....	....	....	8	0	3	3	0	....	....	....	....
1996-97	Lethbridge	WHL	63	50	76	126	115	....	....	....	....	....	....	....	....	....	18	*16	12	*28	28	....	....	....	....
1997-98	New Haven	AHL	65	13	18	31	97	....	....	....	....	....	....	....	....	....	....	....	....	....	....	....	....	....	....
1998-99	Carolina	NHL	3	0	0	0	0	0	0	0	0	0.0	0	5	20.0	3:25	....	....	....	....	....	....	....	....	....
	New Haven	AHL	66	24	33	57	139	....	....	....	....	....	....	....	....	....	....	....	....	....	....	....	....	....	....
99-2000	Carolina	NHL	26	0	2	2	17	0	0	0	13	0.0	–10	155	49.7	7:24	....	....	....	....	....	....	....	....	....
	Cincinnati	IHL	34	8	13	21	81	....	....	....	....	....	....	....	....	....	10	1	6	7	32	....	....	....	....
2000-01	Cincinnati	IHL	77	31	35	66	166	....	....	....	....	....	....	....	....	....	5	3	2	5	10	....	....	....	....
2001-02	Carolina	NHL	4	0	0	0	2	0	0	0	5	0.0	0	9	44.4	11:30	....	....	....	....	....	....	....	....	....
	Lowell	AHL	43	25	30	55	38	....	....	....	....	....	....	....	....	....	....	....	....	....	....	....	....	....	....
	Florida	NHL	31	5	6	11	34	2	0	0	55	9.1	–2	324	50.9	12:26	....	....	....	....	....	....	....	....	....
2002-03	Florida	NHL	30	0	3	3	19	0	0	0	29	0.0	–4	251	48.2	9:18	....	....	....	....	....	....	....	....	....
	San Antonio	AHL	26	3	14	17	68	....	....	....	....	....	....	....	....	....	3	1	0	1	0	....	....	....	....
2003-04	Florida	NHL	50	5	6	11	84	0	0	2	65	7.7	–10	168	48.8	13:54	....	....	....	....	....	....	....	....	....
2004-05	Rogle	Sweden-2	30	17	16	33	111	....	....	....	....	....	....	....	....	....	2	0	0	0	4	....	....	....	....
2005-06	Calgary	NHL	45	4	2	6	69	0	0	0	34	11.8	–2	313	52.4	9:52	7	0	0	0	0	0	0	0	9:15
2006-07	Calgary	NHL	64	8	6	14	68	0	1	0	46	17.4	3	282	50.0	9:46	1	0	0	0	10	0	0	0	4:41
	NHL Totals		253	22	25	47	293	2	1	2	247	8.9		1507	50.1	10:35	8	0	0	0	10	0	0	0	8:41

WHL East Second All-Star Team (1996, 1997) • Memorial Cup Tournament All-Star Team (1997)

Rights transferred to **Carolina** after **Hartford** franchise relocated, June 25, 1997. Traded to **Florida** by **Carolina** with Sandis Ozolinsh for Bret Hedican, Kevyn Adams and Tomas Malec, January 16, 2002. Signed as a free agent by **Calgary**, July 2, 2004. Signed as a free agent by **Rogle** (Sweden-2) September 25, 2004. Signed as a free agent by **Vancouver**, July 3, 2007.

RIVERS, Jamie

(RIH-vuhrs, JAY-mee) **MTL.**

Defense. Shoots left. 6'1", 206 lbs. Born, Ottawa, Ont., March 16, 1975. St. Louis' 2nd choice, 63rd overall, in 1993 Entry Draft.

Season	Club	League	GP	G	A	Pts	PIM	PP	SH	GW	S	%	+/-	TF	F%	Min	GP	G	A	Pts	PIM	PP	SH	GW	Min
1989-90	Ottawa South	ODMHA	50	26	46	72	46	....	....	....	....	....	....	....	....	....	....	....	....	....	....	....	....	....	....
1990-91	Ott. Jr. Senators	CJHL	55	4	30	34	74	....	....	....	....	....	....	....	....	....	....	....	....	....	....	....	....	....	....
1991-92	Sudbury Wolves	OHL	55	3	13	16	20	....	....	....	....	....	....	....	....	....	8	0	0	0	0	....	....	....	....
1992-93	Sudbury Wolves	OHL	62	12	43	55	20	....	....	....	....	....	....	....	....	....	14	7	19	26	4	....	....	....	....
1993-94	Sudbury Wolves	OHL	65	32	*89	121	58	....	....	....	....	....	....	....	....	....	10	1	9	10	14	....	....	....	....
1994-95	Sudbury Wolves	OHL	46	9	56	65	30	....	....	....	....	....	....	....	....	....	18	7	26	33	22	....	....	....	....
1995-96	St. Louis	NHL	3	0	0	0	2	0	0	0	5	0.0	–1	....	....	....	....	....	....	....	....	....	....	....	....
	Worcester IceCats	AHL	75	7	45	52	130	....	....	....	....	....	....	....	....	....	4	0	1	1	4	....	....	....	....
1996-97	St. Louis	NHL	15	2	5	7	6	1	0	0	9	22.2	–4	....	....	....	....	....	....	....	....	....	....	....	....
	Worcester IceCats	AHL	63	8	35	43	83	....	....	....	....	....	....	....	....	....	5	1	2	3	14	....	....	....	....
1997-98	St. Louis	NHL	59	2	4	6	36	1	0	1	53	3.8	5	....	....	....	....	....	....	....	....	....	....	....	....
1998-99	St. Louis	NHL	76	2	5	7	47	1	0	0	78	2.6	–3	0	0.0	14:10	9	1	1	2	2	1	0	1	6:29
99-2000	NY Islanders	NHL	75	1	16	17	84	1	0	0	95	1.1	–4	0	0.0	19:39	....	....	....	....	....	....	....	....	....
2000-01	Ottawa	NHL	45	2	4	6	44	0	0	0	41	4.9	6	0	0.0	14:01	1	0	0	0	4	0	0	0	12:45
	Grand Rapids	IHL	2	0	0	0	2	....	....	....	....	....	....	....	....	....	....	....	....	....	....	....	....	....	....
2001-02	Ottawa	NHL	2	0	0	0	4	0	0	0	3	0.0	–3	0	0.0	11:37	....	....	....	....	....	....	....	....	....
	Boston	NHL	64	4	2	6	45	1	0	1	48	8.3	6	39	33.3	8:27	3	0	0	0	0	0	0	0	4:57
2002-03	Florida	NHL	1	0	0	0	2	0	0	0	2	0.0	–2	0	0.0	18:27	....	....	....	....	....	....	....	....	....
	San Antonio	AHL	50	6	19	25	68	....	....	....	....	....	....	....	....	....	3	0	1	1	10	....	....	....	....
2003-04	Detroit	NHL	50	3	4	7	41	0	0	0	31	9.7	9	1	0.0	10:14	2	0	0	0	2	0	0	0	5:40
	Grand Rapids	AHL	2	0	0	0	4	....	....	....	....	....	....	....	....	....	....	....	....	....	....	....	....	....	....
2004-05	Hershey Bears	AHL	50	7	13	20	46	....	....	....	....	....	....	....	....	....	....	....	....	....	....	....	....	....	....
2005-06	Detroit	NHL	15	0	1	1	12	0	0	0	4	0.0	0	0	0.0	8:51	....	....	....	....	....	....	....	....	....
	Phoenix	NHL	18	0	5	5	26	0	0	0	32	0.0	2	0	0.0	20:06	....	....	....	....	....	....	....	....	....
2006-07	St. Louis	NHL	31	1	3	4	36	1	0	0	17	5.9	–7	0	0.0	14:11	....	....	....	....	....	....	....	....	....
	Peoria Rivermen	AHL	30	4	19	23	24	....	....	....	....	....	....	....	....	....	....	....	....	....	....	....	....	....	....
	NHL Totals		454	17	49	66	385	6	0	2	418	4.1		40	32.5	13:49	15	1	1	2	8	1	0	1	6:29

OHL First All-Star Team (1994) • Canadian Major Junior Second All-Star Team (1994) • OHL Second All-Star Team (1995) • AHL Second All-Star Team (1997)

Claimed by **NY Islanders** from **St. Louis** in Waiver Draft, September 27, 1999. Signed as a free agent by **Ottawa**, November 30, 2000. Claimed on waivers by **Boston** from **Ottawa**, October 13, 2001. Signed as a free agent by **San Antonio** (AHL), November 2, 2002. Signed as a free agent by **Florida**, December 16, 2002. Signed as a free agent by **Detroit**, July 29, 2003. Signed as a free agent by **Hershey** (AHL), November 3, 2004. Traded to **Phoenix** by **Detroit** for Phoenix's 7th round choice (Nick Oslund) in 2006 Entry Draft, March 9, 2006. • Spent majority of 2005-06 season as a healthy reserve. Signed as a free agent by **St. Louis**, August 18, 2006. Signed as a free agent by **Montreal**, July 5, 2007.

RIVET, Craig

(rih-VAY, KRAYG) **S.J.**

Defense. Shoots right. 6'2", 210 lbs. Born, North Bay, Ont., September 13, 1974. Montreal's 4th choice, 68th overall, in 1992 Entry Draft.

Season	Club	League	GP	G	A	Pts	PIM	PP	SH	GW	S	%	+/-	TF	F%	Min	GP	G	A	Pts	PIM	PP	SH	GW	Min
1990-91	Barrie Colts	OHA-B	42	9	17	26	55	....	....	....	....	....	....	....	....	....	....	....	....	....	....	....	....	....	....
1991-92	Kingston	OHL	66	5	21	26	97	....	....	....	....	....	....	....	....	....	....	....	....	....	....	....	....	....	....
1992-93	Kingston	OHL	64	19	55	74	117	....	....	....	....	....	....	....	....	....	16	5	7	12	39	....	....	....	....
1993-94	Kingston	OHL	61	12	52	64	100	....	....	....	....	....	....	....	....	....	6	0	3	3	6	....	....	....	....
	Fredericton	AHL	4	0	2	2	2	....	....	....	....	....	....	....	....	....	....	....	....	....	....	....	....	....	....
1994-95	Fredericton	AHL	78	5	27	32	126	....	....	....	....	....	....	....	....	....	12	0	4	4	17	....	....	....	....
	Montreal	NHL	5	0	1	1	5	0	0	0	2	0.0	2	....	....	....	....	....	....	....	....	....	....	....	....
1995-96	Montreal	NHL	19	1	4	5	54	0	0	0	9	11.1	4	....	....	....	....	....	....	....	....	....	....	....	....
	Fredericton	AHL	49	5	18	23	189	....	....	....	....	....	....	....	....	....	6	0	0	0	12	....	....	....	....
1996-97	Montreal	NHL	35	0	4	4	54	0	0	0	24	0.0	7	....	....	....	5	0	1	1	14	0	0	0	....
	Fredericton	AHL	23	3	12	15	99	....	....	....	....	....	....	....	....	....	....	....	....	....	....	....	....	....	....
1997-98	Montreal	NHL	61	0	2	2	93	0	0	0	26	0.0	–3	....	....	....	5	0	0	0	2	0	0	0	....
1998-99	Montreal	NHL	66	2	8	10	66	0	0	0	39	5.1	–3	0	0.0	14:20	....	....	....	....	....	....	....	....	....
99-2000	Montreal	NHL	61	3	14	17	76	0	0	1	71	4.2	11	0	0.0	19:03	....	....	....	....	....	....	....	....	....
2000-01	Montreal	NHL	26	1	2	3	36	0	0	0	22	4.5	–8	0	0.0	19:04	....	....	....	....	....	....	....	....	....
2001-02	Montreal	NHL	82	8	17	25	76	0	0	0	90	8.9	1	1	0.0	19:00	12	0	3	3	4	0	0	0	21:26
2002-03	Montreal	NHL	82	7	15	22	71	3	0	2	118	5.9	1	0	0.0	22:00	....	....	....	....	....	....	....	....	....
2003-04	Montreal	NHL	80	4	8	12	98	2	0	1	96	4.2	–1	0	0.0	19:28	11	1	4	5	2	1	0	0	24:07
2004-05	TPS Turku	Finland	18	3	1	4	28	....	....	....	....	....	....	....	....	....	6	0	0	0	39	....	....	....	....
2005-06	Montreal	NHL	82	7	27	34	109	5	0	1	122	5.7	–5	2	0.0	22:27	6	0	2	2	2	0	0	0	24:09
2006-07	Montreal	NHL	54	6	10	16	57	2	0	0	58	10.3	–7	0	0.0	21:04	....	....	....	....	....	....	....	....	....
	San Jose	NHL	17	1	7	8	12	0	0	0	31	3.2	8	0	0.0	23:31	11	2	3	5	18	1	0	0	25:18
	NHL Totals		670	40	119	159	807	12	0	5	708	5.6		3	0.0	19:49	50	3	13	16	42	2	0	0	23:39

• Missed majority of 2000-01 season recovering from shoulder injury suffered in game vs. Vancouver, October 30, 2000. Signed as a free agent by **Turku** (Finland), January 11, 2005. Traded to **San Jose** by **Montreal** with Montreal's 5th round choice in 2008 Entry Draft for Josh Gorges and San Jose's 1st round choice (Max Pacioretty) in 2007 Entry Draft, February 25, 2007.

ROACH, Andy

(ROHCH, AN-dee)

Defense. Shoots right. 5'11", 181 lbs. Born, Mattawan, MI, August 22, 1973.

			Regular Season														Playoffs								
Season	Club	League	GP	G	A	Pts	PIM	PP	SH	GW	S	%	+/-	TF	F%	Min	GP	G	A	Pts	PIM	PP	SH	GW	Min
1991-92	Waterloo	USHL	45	12	16	28	6	....	....	....	....	....	....	....	....	....	....	....	....	....	....	....	....	....	....
1992-93	Waterloo	USHL	42	13	17	30	22	....	....	....	....	....	....	....	....	....	....	....	....	....	....	....	....	....	....
1993-94	Ferris State	CCHA	32	4	15	19	18	....	....	....	....	....	....	....	....	....	....	....	....	....	....	....	....	....	....
1994-95	Ferris State	CCHA	36	11	19	30	26	....	....	....	....	....	....	....	....	....	....	....	....	....	....	....	....	....	....
1995-96	Ferris State	CCHA	33	15	19	34	44	....	....	....	....	....	....	....	....	....	....	....	....	....	....	....	....	....	....
1996-97	Ferris State	CCHA	37	12	34	46	18	....	....	....	....	....	....	....	....	....	....	....	....	....	....	....	....	....	....
1997-98	San Antonio	IHL	67	8	16	24	30	....	....	....	....	....	....	....	....	....	....	....	....	....	....	....	....	....	....
1998-99	Long Beach	IHL	41	5	21	26	34	....	....	....	....	....	....	....	....	....	....	....	....	....	....	....	....	....	....
	Utah Grizzlies	IHL	44	7	10	17	18	....	....	....	....	....	....	....	....	....	....	....	....	....	....	....	....	....	....
99-2000	Krefeld Pinguine	Germany	55	19	22	41	40	....	....	....	....	....	....	....	....	....	4	0	0	0	2	....	....	....	....
2000-01	Adler Mannheim	Germany	59	7	13	20	32	....	....	....	....	....	....	....	....	....	12	2	2	4	6	....	....	....	....
2001-02	Adler Mannheim	Germany	60	9	21	30	16	....	....	....	....	....	....	....	....	....	12	1	5	6	8	....	....	....	....
2002-03	Adler Mannheim	Germany	49	18	16	34	16	....	....	....	....	....	....	....	....	....	8	4	5	9	4	....	....	....	....
2003-04	Adler Mannheim	Germany	46	11	21	32	26	....	....	....	....	....	....	....	....	....	6	2	0	2	6	....	....	....	....
2004-05	Lausanne HC	Swiss	14	4	5	9	20	....	....	....	....	....	....	....	....	....	10	4	3	7	12	....	....	....	....
	Lausanne HC	Swiss-Q	7	2	3	5	2	....	....	....	....	....	....	....	....	....	....	....	....	....	....	....	....	....	....
2005-06	**St. Louis**	**NHL**	**5**	**1**	**2**	**3**	**10**	**1**	**0**	**0**	**2**	**50.0**	**0**	**0**	**0.0**	**14:20**	....	....	....	....	....	....	....	....	....
	Peoria Rivermen	AHL	10	2	3	5	6	....	....	....	....	....	....	....	....	....	....	....	....	....	....	....	....	....	....
	ZSC Lions Zurich	Swiss	14	4	7	11	16	....	....	....	....	....	....	....	....	....	10	1	5	6	10	....	....	....	....
2006-07	Eisbaren Berlin	Germany	48	13	28	41	74	....	....	....	....	....	....	....	....	....	3	0	0	0	0	....	....	....	....
	NHL Totals		**5**	**1**	**2**	**3**	**10**	**1**	**0**	**0**	**2**	**50.0**		**0**	**0.0**	**14:20**	....	....	....	....	....	....	....	....	....

Signed as a free agent by **St. Louis**, June 30, 2004. Signed as a free agent by **Lausanne** (Swiss), November 18, 2004. Assigned to **Zurich** (Swiss) by **St. Louis**, December 20, 2005. Signed as a free agent by **Berlin** (Germany), July 21, 2006.

ROBERTS, Gary

(RAW-buhrts, GAIR-ree) **PIT.**

Left wing. Shoots left. 6'2", 209 lbs. Born, North York, Ont., May 23, 1966. Calgary's 1st choice, 12th overall, in 1984 Entry Draft.

			Regular Season														Playoffs								
Season	Club	League	GP	G	A	Pts	PIM	PP	SH	GW	S	%	+/-	TF	F%	Min	GP	G	A	Pts	PIM	PP	SH	GW	Min
1980-81	Hamilton Kilty B's	OHA-B	3	0	1	1	0	....	....	....	....	....	....	....	....	....	....	....	....	....	....	....	....	....	....
1981-82	Whitby	Minor-ON	44	55	31	86	133	....	....	....	....	....	....	....	....	....	....	....	....	....	....	....	....	....	....
1982-83	Ottawa 67's	OHL	53	12	8	20	83	....	....	....	....	....	....	....	....	....	5	1	0	1	19	....	....	....	....
1983-84	Ottawa 67's	OHL	48	27	30	57	144	....	....	....	....	....	....	....	....	....	13	10	7	17	62	....	....	....	....
1984-85	Ottawa 67's	OHL	59	44	62	106	186	....	....	....	....	....	....	....	....	....	5	2	8	10	10	....	....	....	....
	Moncton	AHL	7	4	2	6	7	....	....	....	....	....	....	....	....	....	....	....	....	....	....	....	....	....	....
1985-86	Ottawa 67's	OHL	24	26	25	51	83	....	....	....	....	....	....	....	....	....	....	....	....	....	....	....	....	....	....
	Guelph Platers	OHL	23	18	15	33	65	....	....	....	....	....	....	....	....	....	20	18	13	31	43	....	....	....	....
1986-87	**Calgary**	**NHL**	**32**	**5**	**10**	**15**	**85**	**0**	**0**	**0**	**38**	**13.2**	**6**	....	....	....	**2**	**0**	**0**	**0**	**4**	**0**	**0**	**0**	....
	Moncton	AHL	38	20	18	38	72	....	....	....	....	....	....	....	....	....	....	....	....	....	....	....	....	....	....
1987-88	**Calgary**	**NHL**	**74**	**13**	**15**	**28**	**282**	**0**	**0**	**1**	**118**	**11.0**	**24**	....	....	....	**9**	**2**	**3**	**5**	**29**	**0**	**0**	**0**	....
1988-89 ♦	**Calgary**	**NHL**	**71**	**22**	**16**	**38**	**250**	**0**	**1**	**2**	**123**	**17.9**	**32**	....	....	....	**22**	**5**	**7**	**12**	**57**	**0**	**0**	**0**	....
1989-90	**Calgary**	**NHL**	**78**	**39**	**33**	**72**	**222**	**5**	**0**	**5**	**175**	**22.3**	**31**	....	....	....	**6**	**2**	**5**	**7**	**41**	**0**	**0**	**0**	....
1990-91	**Calgary**	**NHL**	**80**	**22**	**31**	**53**	**252**	**0**	**0**	**3**	**132**	**16.7**	**15**	....	....	....	**7**	**1**	**3**	**4**	**18**	**0**	**0**	**0**	....
1991-92	**Calgary**	**NHL**	**76**	**53**	**37**	**90**	**207**	**15**	**0**	**2**	**196**	**27.0**	**32**	....	....	....	....	....	....	....	....	....	....	....	....
1992-93	**Calgary**	**NHL**	**58**	**38**	**41**	**79**	**172**	**8**	**3**	**4**	**166**	**22.9**	**32**	....	....	....	**5**	**1**	**6**	**7**	**43**	**1**	**0**	**0**	....
1993-94	**Calgary**	**NHL**	**73**	**41**	**43**	**84**	**145**	**12**	**3**	**5**	**202**	**20.3**	**37**	....	....	....	**7**	**2**	**6**	**8**	**24**	**1**	**0**	**1**	....
1994-95	**Calgary**	**NHL**	**8**	**2**	**2**	**4**	**43**	**2**	**0**	**0**	**20**	**10.0**	**1**	....	....	....	....	....	....	....	....	....	....	....	....
1995-96	**Calgary**	**NHL**	**35**	**22**	**20**	**42**	**78**	**9**	**0**	**5**	**84**	**26.2**	**15**	....	....	....	....	....	....	....	....	....	....	....	....
1996-97	**Calgary**	**NHL**	DID NOT PLAY – INJURED																						
1997-98	**Carolina**	**NHL**	**61**	**20**	**29**	**49**	**103**	**4**	**0**	**2**	**106**	**18.9**	**3**	....	....	....	....	....	....	....	....	....	....	....	....
1998-99	**Carolina**	**NHL**	**77**	**14**	**28**	**42**	**178**	**1**	**1**	**4**	**138**	**10.1**	**2**	**15**	**46.7**	**19:36**	**6**	**1**	**1**	**2**	**8**	**0**	**0**	**0**	**21:01**
99-2000	**Carolina**	**NHL**	**69**	**23**	**30**	**53**	**62**	**12**	**0**	**1**	**150**	**15.3**	**–10**	**7**	**28.6**	**18:31**	....	....	....	....	....	....	....	....	....
2000-01	**Toronto**	**NHL**	**82**	**29**	**24**	**53**	**109**	**8**	**2**	**3**	**138**	**21.0**	**16**	**13**	**46.2**	**17:08**	**11**	**2**	**9**	**11**	**0**	**0**	**0**	**0**	**19:49**
2001-02	**Toronto**	**NHL**	**69**	**21**	**27**	**48**	**63**	**6**	**2**	**2**	**122**	**17.2**	**–4**	**6**	**33.3**	**17:23**	**19**	**7**	**12**	**19**	**56**	**3**	**0**	**1**	**19:28**
2002-03	**Toronto**	**NHL**	**14**	**5**	**3**	**8**	**10**	**3**	**0**	**0**	**22**	**22.7**	**–2**	**4**	**50.0**	**15:35**	**7**	**1**	**1**	**2**	**8**	**0**	**0**	**0**	**21:04**
2003-04	**Toronto**	**NHL**	**72**	**28**	**20**	**48**	**84**	**11**	**1**	**7**	**124**	**22.6**	**9**	**12**	**33.3**	**17:33**	**13**	**4**	**4**	**8**	**10**	**2**	**0**	**1**	**17:45**
2004-05			DID NOT PLAY																						
2005-06	**Florida**	**NHL**	**58**	**14**	**26**	**40**	**51**	**4**	**0**	**1**	**122**	**11.5**	**4**	**19**	**31.6**	**16:45**	....	....	....	....	....	....	....	....	....
2006-07	**Florida**	**NHL**	**50**	**13**	**16**	**29**	**71**	**2**	**0**	**3**	**94**	**13.8**	**5**	**28**	**60.7**	**17:05**	....	....	....	....	....	....	....	....	....
	Pittsburgh	**NHL**	**19**	**7**	**6**	**13**	**26**	**4**	**0**	**1**	**31**	**22.6**	**–5**	**3**	**66.7**	**15:47**	**5**	**2**	**2**	**4**	**2**	**1**	**0**	**0**	**17:07**
	NHL Totals		**1156**	**431**	**457**	**888**	**2493**	**106**	**13**	**51**	**2301**	**18.7**		**107**	**44.9**	**17:39**	**119**	**30**	**59**	**89**	**300**	**8**	**0**	**3**	**19:18**

OHL Second All-Star Team (1985, 1986) • Bill Masterton Memorial Trophy (1996)

Played in NHL All-Star Game (1992, 1993, 2004)

• Missed remainder of 1994-95 season and majority of 1995-96 season recovering from neck injury suffered in game vs. Toronto, February 4, 1995. • Missed remainder of 1995-96 season and entire 1996-97 season recovering from neck injury suffered in game vs. Vancouver, April 3, 1996. Traded to **Carolina** by **Calgary** with Trevor Kidd for Andrew Cassels and Jean-Sebastien Giguere, August 25, 1997. Signed as a free agent by **Toronto**, July 4, 2000. • Missed majority of 2002-03 season recovering from off-season shoulder surgery, August 13, 2002. Signed as a free agent by **Florida**, August 1, 2005. Traded to **Pittsburgh** by **Florida** for Noah Welch, February 27, 2007.

ROBIDAS, Stephane

(ROH-bih-dah, STEH-fan) **DAL.**

Defense. Shoots right. 5'11", 189 lbs. Born, Sherbrooke, Que., March 3, 1977. Montreal's 7th choice, 164th overall, in 1995 Entry Draft.

			Regular Season														Playoffs								
Season	Club	League	GP	G	A	Pts	PIM	PP	SH	GW	S	%	+/-	TF	F%	Min	GP	G	A	Pts	PIM	PP	SH	GW	Min
1992-93	Magog	QAAA	41	3	12	15	16	....	....	....	....	....	....	....	....	....	5	1	1	2	2	....	....	....	....
1993-94	Shawinigan	QMJHL	67	3	18	21	33	....	....	....	....	....	....	....	....	....	1	0	0	0	0	....	....	....	....
1994-95	Shawinigan	QMJHL	71	13	56	69	44	....	....	....	....	....	....	....	....	....	15	7	12	19	4	....	....	....	....
1995-96	Shawinigan	QMJHL	67	23	56	79	53	....	....	....	....	....	....	....	....	....	6	1	5	6	10	....	....	....	....
1996-97	Shawinigan	QMJHL	67	24	51	75	59	....	....	....	....	....	....	....	....	....	7	4	6	10	14	....	....	....	....
1997-98	Fredericton	AHL	79	10	21	31	50	....	....	....	....	....	....	....	....	....	4	0	2	2	0	....	....	....	....
1998-99	Fredericton	AHL	79	8	33	41	59	....	....	....	....	....	....	....	....	....	15	1	5	6	10	....	....	....	....
99-2000	**Montreal**	**NHL**	**1**	**0**	**0**	**0**	**0**	**0**	**0**	**0**	**0**	**0.0**	**0**	**0**	**0.0**	**15:54**	....	....	....	....	....	....	....	....	....
	Quebec Citadelles	AHL	76	14	31	45	36	....	....	....	....	....	....	....	....	....	3	0	1	1	0	....	....	....	....
2000-01	**Montreal**	**NHL**	**65**	**6**	**6**	**12**	**14**	**1**	**0**	**0**	**77**	**7.8**	**0**	**1**	**100.0**	**20:44**	....	....	....	....	....	....	....	....	....
2001-02	**Montreal**	**NHL**	**56**	**1**	**10**	**11**	**14**	**1**	**0**	**0**	**68**	**1.5**	**–25**	**3**	**33.3**	**18:58**	**2**	**0**	**0**	**0**	**4**	**0**	**0**	**0**	**13:07**
2002-03	**Dallas**	**NHL**	**76**	**3**	**7**	**10**	**35**	**0**	**0**	**1**	**47**	**6.4**	**15**	**1**	**100.0**	**12:54**	**12**	**0**	**1**	**1**	**20**	**0**	**0**	**0**	**13:54**
2003-04	**Dallas**	**NHL**	**14**	**1**	**0**	**1**	**8**	**1**	**0**	**0**	**8**	**12.5**	**–2**	**1**	**100.0**	**12:57**	....	....	....	....	....	....	....	....	....
	Chicago	**NHL**	**45**	**2**	**10**	**12**	**33**	**0**	**1**	**1**	**55**	**3.6**	**6**	**0**	**0.0**	**20:56**	....	....	....	....	....	....	....	....	....
2004-05	Frankfurt Lions	Germany	51	15	32	47	64	....	....	....	....	....	....	....	....	....	6	1	2	3	6	....	....	....	....
2005-06	**Dallas**	**NHL**	**75**	**5**	**15**	**20**	**67**	**1**	**1**	**0**	**95**	**5.3**	**15**	**0**	**0.0**	**16:59**	**5**	**0**	**2**	**2**	**4**	**0**	**0**	**0**	**16:42**
2006-07	**Dallas**	**NHL**	**75**	**0**	**17**	**17**	**86**	**0**	**0**	**0**	**106**	**0.0**	**–1**	**0**	**0.0**	**18:04**	**7**	**0**	**1**	**1**	**2**	**0**	**0**	**0**	**19:02**
	NHL Totals		**407**	**18**	**65**	**83**	**257**	**4**	**2**	**2**	**456**	**3.9**		**6**	**66.7**	**17:35**	**26**	**0**	**4**	**4**	**30**	**0**	**0**	**0**	**15:45**

QMJHL First All-Star Team (1996, 1997)

Claimed by **Atlanta** from **Montreal** in Waiver Draft, October 4, 2002. Traded to **Dallas** by **Atlanta** for future considerations, October 4, 2002. Traded to **Chicago** by **Dallas** with Dallas' 2nd round choice (Jakub Sindel) in 2004 Entry Draft for Jon Klemm and NY Rangers' 4th round choice (previously acquired, Dallas selected Fredrik Naslund) in 2004 Entry Draft, November 17, 2003. Signed as a free agent by **Frankfurt** (Germany), September 17, 2004. Signed as a free agent by **Dallas**, August 6, 2005.

ROBINSON, Nathan

(RAW-bihn-suhn, NAY-thuhn) **BOS.**

Center. Shoots left. 5'9", 181 lbs. Born, Scarborough, Ont., December 31, 1981.

			Regular Season														Playoffs								
Season	Club	League	GP	G	A	Pts	PIM	PP	SH	GW	S	%	+/-	TF	F%	Min	GP	G	A	Pts	PIM	PP	SH	GW	Min
1998-99	Belleville Bulls	OHL	50	11	8	19	23	....	....	....	....	....	....	....	....	....	21	4	4	8	14	....	....	....	....
99-2000	Belleville Bulls	OHL	61	19	18	37	45	....	....	....	....	....	....	....	....	....	15	3	4	7	10	....	....	....	....
2000-01	Belleville Bulls	OHL	66	32	37	69	57	....	....	....	....	....	....	....	....	....	10	6	10	16	7	....	....	....	....
2001-02	Belleville Bulls	OHL	67	47	63	*110	74	....	....	....	....	....	....	....	....	....	11	8	6	14	10	....	....	....	....
2002-03	Toledo Storm	ECHL	9	5	9	14	29	....	....	....	....	....	....	....	....	....	....	....	....	....	....	....	....	....	....
	Grand Rapids	AHL	53	3	14	17	24	....	....	....	....	....	....	....	....	....	8	0	3	3	0	....	....	....	....
2003-04	**Detroit**	**NHL**	**5**	**0**	**0**	**0**	**2**	**0**	**0**	**0**	**5**	**0.0**	**–1**	**0**	**0.0**	**6:01**	....	....	....	....	....	....	....	....	....
	Grand Rapids	AHL	69	24	26	50	41	....	....	....	....	....	....	....	....	....	3	0	0	0	2	....	....	....	....
2004-05	Grand Rapids	AHL	50	8	16	24	10	....	....	....	....	....	....	....	....	....	....	....	....	....	....	....	....	....	....
	Syracuse Crunch	AHL	19	6	14	20	18	....	....	....	....	....	....	....	....	....	....	....	....	....	....	....	....	....	....

			Regular Season														Playoffs								
Season	Club	League	GP	G	A	Pts	PIM	PP	SH	GW	S	%	+/-	TF	F%	Min	GP	G	A	Pts	PIM	PP	SH	GW	Min
2005-06	**Boston**	**NHL**	**2**	**0**	**0**	**0**	**0**	**0**	**0**	**0**	**1**	**0.0**	**0**	**0**	**0.0**	**3:32**	....	....	....	....	....	....	....	....	....
	Providence Bruins	AHL	70	29	31	60	55	....	....	....	....	....	....	....	....	....	6	4	5	9	2	....	....	....	....
2006-07	Adler Mannheim	Germany	50	15	29	44	34	....	....	....	....	....	....	....	....	....	11	4	7	11	26	....	....	....	....
	NHL Totals		**7**	**0**	**0**	**0**	**2**	**0**	**0**	**0**	**6**	**0.0**		**0**	**0.0**	**5:18**	....	....	....	....	....	....	....	....	....

OHL First All-Star Team (2002) • Canadian Major Junior First All-Star Team (2002)

Signed as a free agent by **Detroit**, October 12, 2002. Loaned to **Syracuse** (AHL) by **Grand Rapids** (AHL) for loan of Jeff Panzer, March 11, 2005. Signed as a free agent by **Boston**, August 15, 2005.

ROBITAILLE, Louis

(ROH-buh-tigh, LOO-ee)

Left wing. Shoots left. 6’1”, 192 lbs. Born, Montreal, Que., March 16, 1982.

Season	Club	League	GP	G	A	Pts	PIM	PP	SH	GW	S	%	+/-	TF	F%	Min	GP	G	A	Pts	PIM	PP	SH	GW	Min
99-2000	Montreal Rocket	QMJHL	71	3	21	24	266	....	....	....	....	....	....	....	....	....	5	1	1	2	18	....	....	....	....
2000-01	Montreal Rocket	QMJHL	69	2	10	12	269	....	....	....	....	....	....	....	....	....	....	....	....	....	....	....	....	....	....
2001-02	Montreal Rocket	QMJHL	71	3	28	31	294	....	....	....	....	....	....	....	....	....	7	3	0	3	241	....	....	....	....
2002-03	Montreal Rocket	QMJHL	60	7	23	30	191	....	....	....	....	....	....	....	....	....	7	0	10	10	12	....	....	....	....
2003-04	Portland Pirates	AHL	58	1	5	6	103	....	....	....	....	....	....	....	....	....	5	1	0	1	17	....	....	....	....
	Quad City	UHL	2	0	1	1	10	....	....	....	....	....	....	....	....	....	....	....	....	....	....	....	....	....	....
2004-05	Portland Pirates	AHL	59	2	3	5	186	....	....	....	....	....	....	....	....	....	....	....	....	....	....	....	....	....	....
2005-06	**Washington**	**NHL**	**2**	**0**	**0**	**0**	**5**	**0**	**0**	**0**	**0**	**0.0**	**–1**	**0**	**0.0**	**4:42**	....	....	....	....	....	....	....	....	....
	Hershey Bears	AHL	65	7	12	19	334	....	....	....	....	....	....	....	....	....	21	0	2	2	64	....	....	....	....
2006-07	Hershey Bears	AHL	67	6	8	14	254	....	....	....	....	....	....	....	....	....	13	0	1	1	30	....	....	....	....
	NHL Totals		**2**	**0**	**0**	**0**	**5**	**0**	**0**	**0**	**0**	**0.0**		**0**	**0.0**	**4:42**	....	....	....	....	....	....	....	....	....

Signed as a free agent by **Washington**, August 24, 2004.

ROBITAILLE, Randy

(ROH-buh-tigh, RAN-dee)

Center. Shoots left. 5’11”, 200 lbs. Born, Ottawa, Ont., October 12, 1975.

Season	Club	League	GP	G	A	Pts	PIM	PP	SH	GW	S	%	+/-	TF	F%	Min	GP	G	A	Pts	PIM	PP	SH	GW	Min
1993-94	Ott. Jr. Senators	CJHL	57	33	55	88	31	....	....	....	....	....	....	....	....	....	....	....	....	....	....	....	....	....	....
1994-95	Ott. Jr. Senators	CJHL	54	48	77	*125	111	....	....	....	....	....	....	....	....	....	....	....	....	....	....	....	....	....	....
1995-96	Miami U.	CCHA	36	14	31	45	26	....	....	....	....	....	....	....	....	....	....	....	....	....	....	....	....	....	....
1996-97	Miami U.	CCHA	39	27	34	61	44	....	....	....	....	....	....	....	....	....	....	....	....	....	....	....	....	....	....
	Boston	**NHL**	**1**	**0**	**0**	**0**	**0**	**0**	**0**	**0**	**0**	**0.0**	**0**	....	....	....	....	....	....	....	....	....	....	....	....
1997-98	**Boston**	**NHL**	**4**	**0**	**0**	**0**	**0**	**0**	**0**	**0**	**5**	**0.0**	**–2**	....	....	....	....	....	....	....	....	....	....	....	....
	Providence Bruins	AHL	48	15	29	44	16	....	....	....	....	....	....	....	....	....	....	....	....	....	....	....	....	....	....
1998-99	**Boston**	**NHL**	**4**	**0**	**2**	**2**	**0**	**0**	**0**	**0**	**5**	**0.0**	**–1**	**24**	**25.0**	**10:11**	**1**	**0**	**0**	**0**	**0**	**0**	**0**	**0**	**7:14**
	Providence Bruins	AHL	74	28	*74	102	34	....	....	....	....	....	....	....	....	....	19	6	*14	20	20	....	....	....	....
99-2000	**Nashville**	**NHL**	**69**	**11**	**14**	**25**	**10**	**2**	**0**	**1**	**113**	**9.7**	**–13**	**528**	**51.5**	**12:52**	....	....	....	....	....	....	....	....	....
2000-01	**Nashville**	**NHL**	**62**	**9**	**17**	**26**	**12**	**5**	**0**	**0**	**121**	**7.4**	**–11**	**481**	**48.4**	**14:10**	....	....	....	....	....	....	....	....	....
	Milwaukee	IHL	19	10	23	33	4	....	....	....	....	....	....	....	....	....	....	....	....	....	....	....	....	....	....
2001-02	**Los Angeles**	**NHL**	**18**	**4**	**3**	**7**	**17**	**2**	**0**	**0**	**30**	**13.3**	**–9**	**60**	**65.0**	**12:54**	....	....	....	....	....	....	....	....	....
	Manchester	AHL	6	7	3	10	0	....	....	....	....	....	....	....	....	....	....	....	....	....	....	....	....	....	....
	Pittsburgh	**NHL**	**40**	**10**	**20**	**30**	**16**	**3**	**0**	**1**	**91**	**11.0**	**–14**	**599**	**51.4**	**18:08**	....	....	....	....	....	....	....	....	....
2002-03	**Pittsburgh**	**NHL**	**41**	**5**	**12**	**17**	**8**	**1**	**0**	**2**	**61**	**8.2**	**5**	**429**	**55.9**	**13:58**	....	....	....	....	....	....	....	....	....
	NY Islanders	**NHL**	**10**	**1**	**2**	**3**	**2**	**1**	**0**	**0**	**8**	**12.5**	**0**	**68**	**48.5**	**12:28**	**5**	**1**	**1**	**2**	**0**	**1**	**0**	**0**	**13:03**
2003-04	**Atlanta**	**NHL**	**69**	**11**	**26**	**37**	**20**	**5**	**0**	**2**	**121**	**9.1**	**–12**	**1069**	**50.2**	**15:51**	....	....	....	....	....	....	....	....	....
2004-05	ZSC Lions Zurich	Swiss	36	22	*45	*67	56	....	....	....	....	....	....	....	....	....	15	2	16	18	10	....	....	....	....
2005-06	**Minnesota**	**NHL**	**67**	**12**	**28**	**40**	**54**	**7**	**0**	**2**	**112**	**10.7**	**–5**	**381**	**51.4**	**14:44**	....	....	....	....	....	....	....	....	....
2006-07	**Philadelphia**	**NHL**	**28**	**5**	**12**	**17**	**22**	**2**	**0**	**0**	**46**	**10.9**	**–4**	**280**	**53.6**	**14:34**	....	....	....	....	....	....	....	....	....
	NY Islanders	**NHL**	**50**	**6**	**17**	**23**	**22**	**1**	**0**	**1**	**74**	**8.1**	**–2**	**519**	**53.2**	**13:54**	**5**	**0**	**2**	**2**	**8**	**0**	**0**	**0**	**14:12**
	NHL Totals		**463**	**74**	**153**	**227**	**183**	**29**	**0**	**9**	**787**	**9.4**		**4438**	**51.6**	**14:31**	**11**	**1**	**3**	**4**	**8**	**1**	**0**	**0**	**13:02**

CCHA First All-Star Team (1997) • NCAA West First All-American Team (1997) • AHL First All-Star Team (1999) • Les Cunningham Award (MVP – AHL) (1999)

Signed as a free agent by **Boston**, March 27, 1997. Traded to **Atlanta** by **Boston** for Peter Ferraro, June 25, 1999. Traded to **Nashville** by **Atlanta** for Denny Lambert, August 16, 1999. Signed as a free agent by **Los Angeles**, July 6, 2001. Claimed on waivers by **Pittsburgh** from **Los Angeles**, January 4, 2002. Traded to **NY Islanders** by **Pittsburgh** for Philadelphia’s 5th round choice (previously acquired, Pittsburgh selected Evgeni Isakov) in 2003 Entry Draft, March 9, 2003. Signed as a free agent by **Atlanta**, August 12, 2003. Signed as a free agent by **Zurich** (Swiss), April 26, 2004. Signed as a free agent by **Nashville**, August 19, 2005. Claimed on waivers by **Minnesota** from **Nashville**, October 4, 2005. Signed as a free agent by **Philadelphia**, July 4, 2006. Traded to **NY Islanders** by **Philadelphia** with Philadelphia’s 5th round choice in 2008 Entry Draft for Mike York, December 20, 2006.

ROCHE, Travis

(ROHSH, TRA-vihs) **PHX.**

Defense. Shoots right. 6’1”, 200 lbs. Born, Grand Cache, Alta., June 17, 1978.

Season	Club	League	GP	G	A	Pts	PIM	PP	SH	GW	S	%	+/-	TF	F%	Min	GP	G	A	Pts	PIM	PP	SH	GW	Min
1996-97	Trail	BCHL	49	17	40	57	159	....	....	....	....	....	....	....	....	....	....	....	....	....	....	....	....	....	....
1997-98	Trail	BCHL	38	11	31	42	104	....	....	....	....	....	....	....	....	....	11	0	8	8	21	....	....	....	....
1998-99	North Dakota	WCHA	DID NOT PLAY – FRESHMAN																						
99-2000	North Dakota	WCHA	42	6	22	28	60	....	....	....	....	....	....	....	....	....	....	....	....	....	....	....	....	....	....
2000-01	North Dakota	WCHA	42	11	38	49	42	....	....	....	....	....	....	....	....	....	....	....	....	....	....	....	....	....	....
	Minnesota	**NHL**	**1**	**0**	**0**	**0**	**0**	**0**	**0**	**0**	**0**	**0.0**	**0**	**0**	**0.0**	**15:22**	....	....	....	....	....	....	....	....	....
2001-02	**Minnesota**	**NHL**	**4**	**0**	**0**	**0**	**2**	**0**	**0**	**0**	**1**	**0.0**	**–1**	**0**	**0.0**	**12:30**	....	....	....	....	....	....	....	....	....
	Houston Aeros	AHL	60	13	21	34	107	....	....	....	....	....	....	....	....	....	12	2	3	5	6	....	....	....	....
2002-03	Houston Aeros	AHL	65	14	34	48	42	....	....	....	....	....	....	....	....	....	23	3	5	8	26	....	....	....	....
2003-04	**Minnesota**	**NHL**	**5**	**0**	**1**	**1**	**0**	**0**	**0**	**0**	**5**	**0.0**	**–3**	**0**	**0.0**	**16:07**	....	....	....	....	....	....	....	....	....
	Houston Aeros	AHL	60	8	30	38	18	....	....	....	....	....	....	....	....	....	2	0	0	0	2	....	....	....	....
2004-05	Chicago Wolves	AHL	73	12	38	50	59	....	....	....	....	....	....	....	....	....	18	1	6	7	18	....	....	....	....
2005-06	Chicago Wolves	AHL	59	8	31	39	73	....	....	....	....	....	....	....	....	....	....	....	....	....	....	....	....	....	....
2006-07	**Phoenix**	**NHL**	**50**	**6**	**13**	**19**	**22**	**2**	**0**	**1**	**32**	**18.8**	**2**	**0**	**0.0**	**17:01**	....	....	....	....	....	....	....	....	....
	San Antonio	AHL	17	1	8	9	16	....	....	....	....	....	....	....	....	....	....	....	....	....	....	....	....	....	....
	NHL Totals		**60**	**6**	**14**	**20**	**24**	**2**	**0**	**1**	**38**	**15.8**		**0**	**0.0**	**16:37**	....	....	....	....	....	....	....	....	....

BCHL Second All-Star Team (1997) • BCHL Rookie of the Year Award (1997) • BCHL Playoff MVP Award (1997) • BCHL First All-Star Team (1998) • BCHL Best Defenseman Award (1998) • WCHA All-Rookie Team (2000) • WCHA First All-Star Team (2001) • NCAA West First All-American Team (2001) • NCAA Championship All-Tournament Team (2001) • Yanick Dupre Memorial Award (Outstanding Humanitarian Contribution - AHL) (2002) • AHL First All-Star Team (2005)

Signed as a free agent by **Minnesota**, April 8, 2001. Signed as a free agent by **Atlanta**, July 14, 2004. Signed as a free agent by **Phoenix**, July 20, 2006.

ROENICK, Jeremy

(ROH-nihk, JAIR-eh-mee)

Center. Shoots right. 6’1”, 196 lbs. Born, Boston, MA, January 17, 1970. Chicago’s 1st choice, 8th overall, in 1988 Entry Draft.

Season	Club	League	GP	G	A	Pts	PIM	PP	SH	GW	S	%	+/-	TF	F%	Min	GP	G	A	Pts	PIM	PP	SH	GW	Min
1986-87	Thayer Academy	High-MA	24	31	34	65	....	....	....	....	....	....	....	....	....	....	....	....	....	....	....	....	....	....	....
1987-88	Thayer Academy	High-MA	24	34	50	84	....	....	....	....	....	....	....	....	....	....	....	....	....	....	....	....	....	....	....
1988-89	Hull Olympiques	QMJHL	28	34	36	70	14	....	....	....	....	....	....	....	....	....	....	....	....	....	....	....	....	....	....
	Chicago	**NHL**	**20**	**9**	**9**	**18**	**4**	**2**	**0**	**0**	**52**	**17.3**	**4**	....	....	....	**10**	**1**	**3**	**4**	**7**	**1**	**0**	**1**	....
1989-90	**Chicago**	**NHL**	**78**	**26**	**40**	**66**	**54**	**6**	**0**	**4**	**173**	**15.0**	**2**	....	....	....	**20**	**11**	**7**	**18**	**8**	**4**	**0**	**1**	....
1990-91	**Chicago**	**NHL**	**79**	**41**	**53**	**94**	**80**	**15**	**4**	**10**	**194**	**21.1**	**38**	....	....	....	**6**	**3**	**5**	**8**	**4**	**1**	**0**	**1**	....
1991-92	**Chicago**	**NHL**	**80**	**53**	**50**	**103**	**98**	**22**	**3**	**13**	**234**	**22.6**	**23**	....	....	....	**18**	**12**	**10**	**22**	**12**	**4**	**0**	**3**	....
1992-93	**Chicago**	**NHL**	**84**	**50**	**57**	**107**	**86**	**22**	**3**	**3**	**255**	**19.6**	**15**	....	....	....	**4**	**1**	**2**	**3**	**2**	**0**	**0**	**0**	....
1993-94	**Chicago**	**NHL**	**84**	**46**	**61**	**107**	**125**	**24**	**5**	**5**	**281**	**16.4**	**21**	....	....	....	**6**	**1**	**6**	**7**	**2**	**0**	**0**	**1**	....
1994-95	Kolner Haie	Germany	3	3	1	4	2	....	....	....	....	....	....	....	....	....	....	....	....	....	....	....	....	....	....
	Chicago	**NHL**	**33**	**10**	**24**	**34**	**14**	**5**	**0**	**1**	**93**	**10.8**	**5**	....	....	....	**8**	**1**	**2**	**3**	**16**	**0**	**0**	**0**	....
1995-96	**Chicago**	**NHL**	**66**	**32**	**35**	**67**	**109**	**12**	**4**	**2**	**171**	**18.7**	**9**	....	....	....	**10**	**5**	**7**	**12**	**2**	**1**	**0**	**1**	....
1996-97	**Phoenix**	**NHL**	**72**	**29**	**40**	**69**	**115**	**10**	**3**	**7**	**228**	**12.7**	**–7**	....	....	....	**6**	**2**	**4**	**6**	**4**	**0**	**0**	**0**	....
1997-98	**Phoenix**	**NHL**	**79**	**24**	**32**	**56**	**103**	**6**	**1**	**3**	**182**	**13.2**	**5**	....	....	....	**6**	**5**	**3**	**8**	**4**	**2**	**2**	**2**	....
	United States	Olympics	4	0	1	1	6	....	....	....	....	....	....	....	....	....	....	....	....	....	....	....	....	....	....
1998-99	**Phoenix**	**NHL**	**78**	**24**	**48**	**72**	**130**	**4**	**0**	**3**	**203**	**11.8**	**7**	**956**	**47.6**	**20:10**	**1**	**0**	**0**	**0**	**0**	**0**	**0**	**0**	**26:55**
99-2000	**Phoenix**	**NHL**	**75**	**34**	**44**	**78**	**102**	**6**	**3**	**12**	**192**	**17.7**	**11**	**925**	**50.1**	**20:51**	**5**	**2**	**2**	**4**	**10**	**1**	**0**	**0**	**19:46**
2000-01	**Phoenix**	**NHL**	**80**	**30**	**46**	**76**	**114**	**13**	**0**	**7**	**192**	**15.6**	**–1**	**888**	**49.1**	**21:00**	....	....	....	....	....	....	....	....	....
2001-02	**Philadelphia**	**NHL**	**75**	**21**	**46**	**67**	**74**	**5**	**0**	**3**	**167**	**12.6**	**32**	**1329**	**49.1**	**18:14**	**5**	**0**	**0**	**0**	**14**	**0**	**0**	**0**	**18:41**
	United States	Olympics	6	1	4	5	2	....	....	....	....	....	....	....	....	....	....	....	....	....	....	....	....	....	....
2002-03	**Philadelphia**	**NHL**	**79**	**27**	**32**	**59**	**75**	**8**	**1**	**6**	**197**	**13.7**	**20**	**1088**	**53.0**	**18:48**	**13**	**3**	**5**	**8**	**8**	**0**	**0**	**1**	**21:07**
2003-04	**Philadelphia**	**NHL**	**62**	**19**	**28**	**47**	**62**	**10**	**1**	**1**	**128**	**14.8**	**1**	**846**	**51.5**	**17:37**	**18**	**4**	**9**	**13**	**8**	**2**	**0**	**1**	**18:05**

Season	Club	League	Regular Season														Playoffs								
			GP	G	A	Pts	PIM	PP	SH	GW	S	%	+/-	TF	F%	Min	GP	G	A	Pts	PIM	PP	SH	GW	Min
2004-05			DID NOT PLAY																						
2005-06	**Los Angeles**	**NHL**	**58**	**9**	**13**	**22**	**36**	**2**	**0**	**1**	**111**	**8.1**	**–5**	**536**	**49.4**	**17:22**	....	....	....	....	....	....	....	....	....
2006-07	**Phoenix**	**NHL**	**70**	**11**	**17**	**28**	**32**	**4**	**0**	**1**	**89**	**12.4**	**–18**	**595**	**51.4**	**13:54**	....	....	....	....	....	....	....	....	....
	NHL Totals		**1252**	**495**	**675**	**1170**	**1413**	**176**	**28**	**82**	**3142**	**15.8**		**7163**	**50.1**	**18:37**	**136**	**51**	**65**	**116**	**101**	**16**	**2**	**12**	**19:30**

QMJHL Second All-Star Team (1989)

Played in NHL All-Star Game (1991, 1992, 1993, 1994, 1999, 2000, 2002, 2003, 2004)

Traded to **Phoenix** by **Chicago** for Alex Zhamnov, Craig Mills and Phoenix's 1st round choice (Ty Jones) in 1997 Entry Draft, August 16, 1996. Signed as a free agent by **Philadelphia**, July 2, 2001. Traded to **Los Angeles** by **Philadelphia** with Nashville's 3rd round choice (previously acquired, Los Angeles selected Bud Holloway) in 2006 Entry Draft for future considerations, August 4, 2005. Signed as a free agent by **Phoenix**, July 4, 2006.

ROLSTON, Brian

(ROHL-stuhn, BRIGH-uhn) **MIN.**

Center/Right wing. Shoots left. 6'2", 211 lbs. Born, Flint, MI, February 21, 1973. New Jersey's 2nd choice, 11th overall, in 1991 Entry Draft.

Season	Club	League	GP	G	A	Pts	PIM	PP	SH	GW	S	%	+/-	TF	F%	Min	GP	G	A	Pts	PIM	PP	SH	GW	Min
1989-90	Det. Compuware	NAHL	40	36	37	73	57	....	....	....	....	....	....	....	....	....	....	....	....	....	....	....	....	....	....
1990-91	Det. Compuware	NAHL	36	49	46	95	14	....	....	....	....	....	....	....	....	....	....	....	....	....	....	....	....	....	....
1991-92	Lake Superior	CCHA	37	14	23	37	14	....	....	....	....	....	....	....	....	....	....	....	....	....	....	....	....	....	....
1992-93	Lake Superior	CCHA	39	33	31	64	20	....	....	....	....	....	....	....	....	....	....	....	....	....	....	....	....	....	....
1993-94	United States	Nat-Tm	41	20	28	48	36	....	....	....	....	....	....	....	....	....	....	....	....	....	....	....	....	....	....
	United States	Olympics	8	7	0	7	8	....	....	....	....	....	....	....	....	....	....	....	....	....	....	....	....	....	....
	Albany River Rats	AHL	17	5	5	10	8	....	....	....	....	....	....	....	....	....	5	1	2	3	0	....	....	....	....
1994-95	Albany River Rats	AHL	18	9	11	20	10	....	....	....	....	....	....	....	....	....	....	....	....	....	....	....	....	....	....
	♦ New Jersey	**NHL**	**40**	**7**	**11**	**18**	**17**	**2**	**0**	**3**	**92**	**7.6**	**5**	....	....	....	**6**	**2**	**1**	**3**	**4**	**1**	**0**	**0**	....
1995-96	**New Jersey**	**NHL**	**58**	**13**	**11**	**24**	**8**	**3**	**1**	**4**	**139**	**9.4**	**9**	....	....	....	....	....	....	....	....	....	....	....	....
1996-97	**New Jersey**	**NHL**	**81**	**18**	**27**	**45**	**20**	**2**	**2**	**3**	**237**	**7.6**	**6**	....	....	....	**10**	**4**	**1**	**5**	**6**	**1**	**2**	**0**	....
1997-98	**New Jersey**	**NHL**	**76**	**16**	**14**	**30**	**16**	**0**	**2**	**1**	**185**	**8.6**	**7**	....	....	....	**6**	**1**	**0**	**1**	**2**	**0**	**1**	**0**	....
1998-99	**New Jersey**	**NHL**	**82**	**24**	**33**	**57**	**14**	**5**	**5**	**3**	**210**	**11.4**	**11**	**51**	**45.1**	**18:49**	**7**	**1**	**0**	**1**	**2**	**0**	**1**	**0**	**17:36**
99-2000	**New Jersey**	**NHL**	**11**	**3**	**1**	**4**	**0**	**1**	**0**	**2**	**33**	**9.1**	**–2**	**37**	**37.8**	**19:09**	....	....	....	....	....	....	....	....	....
	Colorado	**NHL**	**50**	**8**	**10**	**18**	**12**	**1**	**0**	**3**	**107**	**7.5**	**–6**	**65**	**41.5**	**16:18**	....	....	....	....	....	....	....	....	....
	Boston	**NHL**	**16**	**5**	**4**	**9**	**6**	**3**	**0**	**1**	**66**	**7.6**	**–4**	**265**	**41.1**	**22:13**	....	....	....	....	....	....	....	....	....
2000-01	**Boston**	**NHL**	**77**	**19**	**39**	**58**	**28**	**5**	**0**	**4**	**286**	**6.6**	**6**	**666**	**45.7**	**19:19**	....	....	....	....	....	....	....	....	....
2001-02	**Boston**	**NHL**	**82**	**31**	**31**	**62**	**30**	**6**	**9**	**7**	**331**	**9.4**	**11**	**1289**	**46.6**	**20:24**	**6**	**4**	**1**	**5**	**0**	**1**	**1**	**0**	**20:37**
	United States	Olympics	6	0	3	3	0	....	....	....	....	....	....	....	....	....	....	....	....	....	....	....	....	....	....
2002-03	**Boston**	**NHL**	**81**	**27**	**32**	**59**	**32**	**6**	**5**	**5**	**281**	**9.6**	**1**	**1148**	**47.6**	**20:28**	**5**	**0**	**2**	**2**	**0**	**0**	**0**	**0**	**18:39**
2003-04	**Boston**	**NHL**	**82**	**19**	**29**	**48**	**40**	**3**	**2**	**3**	**257**	**7.4**	**9**	**1205**	**50.7**	**19:38**	**7**	**1**	**0**	**1**	**8**	**0**	**0**	**0**	**16:33**
2004-05			DID NOT PLAY																						
2005-06	**Minnesota**	**NHL**	**82**	**34**	**45**	**79**	**50**	**15**	**5**	**7**	**293**	**11.6**	**14**	**403**	**46.4**	**20:21**	....	....	....	....	....	....	....	....	....
	United States	Olympics	6	3	1	4	4	....	....	....	....	....	....	....	....	....	....	....	....	....	....	....	....	....	....
2006-07	**Minnesota**	**NHL**	**78**	**31**	**33**	**64**	**46**	**13**	**1**	**6**	**305**	**10.2**	**6**	**295**	**45.4**	**21:16**	**5**	**1**	**1**	**2**	**4**	**0**	**0**	**0**	**20:25**
	NHL Totals		**896**	**255**	**320**	**575**	**319**	**65**	**32**	**52**	**2822**	**9.0**		**5424**	**47.1**	**19:47**	**52**	**14**	**6**	**20**	**26**	**3**	**5**	**0**	**18:36**

NCAA Championship All-Tournament Team (1992, 1993) • CCHA First All-Star Team (1993) • NCAA West Second All-American Team (1993)

Played in NHL All-Star Game (2007)

Traded to **Colorado** by **New Jersey** with New Jersey's 1st round choice (later traded to Boston – Boston selected Martin Samuelsson) in 2000 Entry Draft for Claude Lemieux and Colorado's 1st (David Hale) and 2nd (Matt DeMarchi) round choices in 2000 Entry Draft, November 3, 1999. Traded to **Boston** by **Colorado** with Martin Grenier, Samuel Pahlsson and New Jersey's 1st round choice (previously acquired, Boston selected Martin Samuelsson) in 2000 Entry Draft for Raymond Bourque and Dave Andreychuk, March 6, 2000. Signed as a free agent by **Minnesota**, July 8, 2004.

ROME, Aaron

(ROHM, AIR-ruhn) **ANA.**

Defense. Shoots left. 6'1", 230 lbs. Born, Nesbitt, Man., September 27, 1983. Los Angeles' 4th choice, 104th overall, in 2002 Entry Draft.

Season	Club	League	GP	G	A	Pts	PIM	PP	SH	GW	S	%	+/-	TF	F%	Min	GP	G	A	Pts	PIM	PP	SH	GW	Min
1998-99	Sask. Contacts	SMHL	STATISTICS NOT AVAILABLE																						
	Saskatoon Blades	WHL	1	0	0	0	0	....	....	....	....	....	....	....	....	....	....	....	....	....	....	....	....	....	....
99-2000	Saskatoon Blades	WHL	47	0	6	6	22	....	....	....	....	....	....	....	....	....	1	0	0	0	0	....	....	....	....
2000-01	Saskatoon Blades	WHL	3	0	0	0	2	....	....	....	....	....	....	....	....	....	....	....	....	....	....	....	....	....	....
	Kootenay Ice	WHL	53	2	8	10	43	....	....	....	....	....	....	....	....	....	11	1	3	4	6	....	....	....	....
2001-02	Kootenay Ice	WHL	33	4	13	17	55	....	....	....	....	....	....	....	....	....	....	....	....	....	....	....	....	....	....
	Swift Current	WHL	37	3	11	14	113	....	....	....	....	....	....	....	....	....	10	1	4	5	23	....	....	....	....
2002-03	Swift Current	WHL	61	12	44	56	201	....	....	....	....	....	....	....	....	....	4	1	0	1	20	....	....	....	....
2003-04	Swift Current	WHL	41	7	26	33	122	....	....	....	....	....	....	....	....	....	....	....	....	....	....	....	....	....	....
	Moose Jaw	WHL	28	3	16	19	88	....	....	....	....	....	....	....	....	....	8	0	6	6	17	....	....	....	....
2004-05	Cincinnati	AHL	75	2	14	16	130	....	....	....	....	....	....	....	....	....	12	3	3	6	33	....	....	....	....
2005-06	Portland Pirates	AHL	64	5	19	24	87	....	....	....	....	....	....	....	....	....	18	1	4	5	33	....	....	....	....
2006-07	**♦ Anaheim**	**NHL**	**1**	**0**	**0**	**0**	**0**	**0**	**0**	**0**	**1**	**0.0**	**–1**	**0**	**0.0**	**14:31**	**1**	**0**	**0**	**0**	**0**	**0**	**0**	**0**	**11:01**
	Portland Pirates	AHL	76	8	17	25	139	....	....	....	....	....	....	....	....	....	....	....	....	....	....	....	....	....	....
	NHL Totals		**1**	**0**	**0**	**0**	**0**	**0**	**0**	**0**	**1**	**0.0**		**0**	**0.0**	**14:31**	**1**	**0**	**0**	**0**	**0**	**0**	**0**	**0**	**11:01**

WHL East Second All-Star Team (2004)

Signed as a free agent by **Anaheim**, June 7, 2004.

ROURKE, Allan

(RAWRK, AL-lan) **EDM.**

Defense. Shoots left. 6'2", 215 lbs. Born, Mississauga, Ont., March 6, 1980. Toronto's 6th choice, 154th overall, in 1998 Entry Draft.

Season	Club	League	GP	G	A	Pts	PIM	PP	SH	GW	S	%	+/-	TF	F%	Min	GP	G	A	Pts	PIM	PP	SH	GW	Min
1995-96	Mississauga Reps	MTHL	38	15	25	40	173	....	....	....	....	....	....	....	....	....	....	....	....	....	....	....	....	....	....
1996-97	Kitchener Rangers	OHL	25	1	1	2	12	....	....	....	....	....	....	....	....	....	6	0	0	0	0	....	....	....	....
1997-98	Kitchener Rangers	OHL	48	5	17	22	59	....	....	....	....	....	....	....	....	....	6	1	1	2	6	....	....	....	....
1998-99	Kitchener Rangers	OHL	66	11	28	39	79	....	....	....	....	....	....	....	....	....	1	0	0	0	2	....	....	....	....
99-2000	Kitchener Rangers	OHL	67	31	43	74	57	....	....	....	....	....	....	....	....	....	5	0	6	6	13	....	....	....	....
2000-01	St. John's	AHL	64	9	19	28	36	....	....	....	....	....	....	....	....	....	....	....	....	....	....	....	....	....	....
2001-02	St. John's	AHL	62	2	9	11	48	....	....	....	....	....	....	....	....	....	10	0	2	2	6	....	....	....	....
2002-03	St. John's	AHL	65	12	19	31	49	....	....	....	....	....	....	....	....	....	....	....	....	....	....	....	....	....	....
2003-04	**Carolina**	**NHL**	**25**	**1**	**2**	**3**	**22**	**0**	**0**	**0**	**24**	**4.2**	**4**	**0**	**0.0**	**12:28**	....	....	....	....	....	....	....	....	....
	Lowell	AHL	45	5	9	14	45	....	....	....	....	....	....	....	....	....	....	....	....	....	....	....	....	....	....
2004-05	Lowell	AHL	60	7	9	16	75	....	....	....	....	....	....	....	....	....	11	1	2	3	40	....	....	....	....
2005-06	**NY Islanders**	**NHL**	**6**	**0**	**1**	**1**	**0**	**0**	**0**	**0**	**2**	**0.0**	**1**	**1**	**0.0**	**17:15**	....	....	....	....	....	....	....	....	....
	Bridgeport	AHL	58	9	21	30	42	....	....	....	....	....	....	....	....	....	1	1	0	1	0	....	....	....	....
2006-07	**NY Islanders**	**NHL**	**11**	**0**	**1**	**1**	**4**	**0**	**0**	**0**	**1**	**0.0**	**0**	**0**	**0.0**	**10:40**	....	....	....	....	....	....	....	....	....
	Bridgeport	AHL	60	5	15	20	60	....	....	....	....	....	....	....	....	....	....	....	....	....	....	....	....	....	....
	NHL Totals		**42**	**1**	**4**	**5**	**26**	**0**	**0**	**0**	**27**	**3.7**		**1**	**0.0**	**12:41**	....	....	....	....	....	....	....	....	....

OHL Second All-Star Team (2000)

Traded to **Carolina** by **Toronto** for Harold Druken, May 29, 2003. Signed as a free agent by **NY Islanders**, August 12, 2005. Traded to **Edmonton** by **NY Islanders** with NY Islanders' 3rd round choice in 2008 Entry Draft for Edmonton's 2nd round choice in 2008 Entry Draft, July 5, 2007.

ROY, Andre

(WAH, AWN-dray) **T.B.**

Right wing. Shoots left. 6'4", 225 lbs. Born, Port Chester, NY, February 8, 1975. Boston's 5th choice, 151st overall, in 1994 Entry Draft.

Season	Club	League	GP	G	A	Pts	PIM	PP	SH	GW	S	%	+/-	TF	F%	Min	GP	G	A	Pts	PIM	PP	SH	GW	Min
1992-93	Nord Selects	QAHA	STATISTICS NOT AVAILABLE																						
1993-94	Goulbourn Royals	OHA-C	9	9	13	22	98	....	....	....	....	....	....	....	....	....	....	....	....	....	....	....	....	....	....
	Beauport	QMJHL	33	6	7	13	125	....	....	....	....	....	....	....	....	....	....	....	....	....	....	....	....	....	....
	Chicoutimi	QMJHL	32	4	14	18	152	....	....	....	....	....	....	....	....	....	25	3	6	9	94	....	....	....	....
1994-95	Chicoutimi	QMJHL	20	15	8	23	90	....	....	....	....	....	....	....	....	....	....	....	....	....	....	....	....	....	....
	Drummondville	QMJHL	34	18	13	31	233	....	....	....	....	....	....	....	....	....	4	2	0	2	34	....	....	....	....
1995-96	**Boston**	**NHL**	**3**	**0**	**0**	**0**	**0**	**0**	**0**	**0**	**0**	**0.0**	**0**	....	....	....	....	....	....	....	....	....	....	....	....
	Providence Bruins	AHL	58	7	8	15	167	....	....	....	....	....	....	....	....	....	1	0	0	0	10	....	....	....	....
1996-97	**Boston**	**NHL**	**10**	**0**	**2**	**2**	**12**	**0**	**0**	**0**	**12**	**0.0**	**–5**	....	....	....	....	....	....	....	....	....	....	....	....
	Providence Bruins	AHL	50	17	11	28	234	....	....	....	....	....	....	....	....	....	....	....	....	....	....	....	....	....	....
1997-98	Providence Bruins	AHL	36	3	11	14	154	....	....	....	....	....	....	....	....	....	....	....	....	....	....	....	....	....	....
	Charlotte	ECHL	27	10	8	18	132	....	....	....	....	....	....	....	....	....	7	2	3	5	34	....	....	....	....
1998-99	Fort Wayne	IHL	65	15	6	21	*395	....	....	....	....	....	....	....	....	....	2	0	0	0	11	....	....	....	....
99-2000	**Ottawa**	**NHL**	**73**	**4**	**3**	**7**	**145**	**0**	**0**	**1**	**39**	**10.3**	**3**	**3**	**33.3**	**6:29**	**5**	**0**	**0**	**0**	**2**	**0**	**0**	**0**	**5:54**
2000-01	**Ottawa**	**NHL**	**64**	**3**	**5**	**8**	**169**	**0**	**0**	**0**	**33**	**9.1**	**1**	**2**	**50.0**	**4:36**	**2**	**0**	**0**	**0**	**16**	**0**	**0**	**0**	**4:16**
2001-02	**Ottawa**	**NHL**	**56**	**6**	**8**	**14**	**148**	**0**	**0**	**0**	**60**	**10.0**	**3**	**1**	**100.0**	**8:23**	....	....	....	....	....	....	....	....	....
	Tampa Bay	**NHL**	**9**	**1**	**1**	**2**	**63**	**0**	**0**	**0**	**6**	**16.7**	**–5**	**0**	**0.0**	**8:58**	....	....	....	....	....	....	....	....	....

Season	Club	League	GP	G	A	Pts	PIM	PP	SH	GW	S	%	+/-	TF	F%	Min	GP	G	A	Pts	PIM	PP	SH	GW	Min
			Regular Season														Playoffs								
2002-03	**Tampa Bay**	**NHL**	**62**	**10**	**7**	**17**	**119**	**0**	**0**	**2**	**85**	**11.8**	**0**	**7**	**57.1**	**10:46**	**5**	**0**	**1**	**1**	**2**	**0**	**0**	**0**	**12:31**
2003-04 ♦	**Tampa Bay**	**NHL**	**33**	**1**	**1**	**2**	**78**	**0**	**0**	**0**	**24**	**4.2**	**–5**	**2**	**50.0**	**7:52**	**21**	**1**	**2**	**3**	**61**	**0**	**0**	**1**	**6:11**
2004-05			DID NOT PLAY																						
2005-06	**Pittsburgh**	**NHL**	**42**	**2**	**1**	**3**	**116**	**0**	**0**	**1**	**11**	**18.2**	**–3**	**1**	**100.0**	**5:03**	....	....	....	....	....	....	....	....	....
2006-07	**Pittsburgh**	**NHL**	**5**	**0**	**0**	**0**	**12**	**0**	**0**	**0**	**1**	**0.0**	**–1**	**1**	**0.0**	**3:12**	....	....	....	....	....	....	....	....	....
	Tampa Bay	**NHL**	**51**	**1**	**2**	**3**	**116**	**0**	**0**	**0**	**14**	**7.1**	**–3**	**2**	**0.0**	**4:35**	**6**	**0**	**0**	**0**	**17**	**0**	**0**	**0**	**2:31**
	NHL Totals		**408**	**28**	**30**	**58**	**978**	**0**	**0**	**4**	**285**	**9.8**		**19**	**47.4**	**6:51**	**39**	**1**	**3**	**4**	**98**	**0**	**0**	**1**	**6:18**

Signed as a free agent by **Ottawa**, April 28, 1999. Traded to **Tampa Bay** by **Ottawa** with Ottawa's 6th round choice (Paul Ranger) in 2002 Entry Draft for Juha Ylonen, March 15, 2002. • Spent majority of 2003-04 season as a healthy reserve. Signed as a free agent by **Pittsburgh**, August 4, 2005. Claimed on waivers by **Tampa Bay** from **Pittsburgh**, December 2, 2006.

ROY, Derek (ROI, DAIR-ihk) BUF.

Center. Shoots left. 5'9", 186 lbs. Born, Ottawa, Ont., May 4, 1983. Buffalo's 2nd choice, 32nd overall, in 2001 Entry Draft.

Season	Club	League	GP	G	A	Pts	PIM	PP	SH	GW	S	%	+/-	TF	F%	Min	GP	G	A	Pts	PIM	PP	SH	GW	Min
1998-99	Ontario East	Minor-ON	34	61	31	92	42	....	....	....	....	....	....	....	....	....	....	....	....	....	....	....	....	....	....
99-2000	Kitchener Rangers	OHL	66	34	53	87	44	....	....	....	....	....	....	....	....	....	5	4	1	5	6	....	....	....	....
2000-01	Kitchener Rangers	OHL	65	42	39	81	114	....	....	....	....	....	....	....	....	....	....	....	....	....	....	....	....	....	....
2001-02	Kitchener Rangers	OHL	62	43	46	89	92	....	....	....	....	....	....	....	....	....	4	1	2	3	2	....	....	....	....
2002-03	Kitchener Rangers	OHL	49	28	50	78	73	....	....	....	....	....	....	....	....	....	21	9	*23	32	14	....	....	....	....
2003-04	**Buffalo**	**NHL**	**49**	**9**	**10**	**19**	**12**	**1**	**0**	**4**	**71**	**12.7**	**–8**	**715**	**47.4**	**15:19**	....	....	....	....	....	....	....	....	....
	Rochester	AHL	26	10	16	26	20	....	....	....	....	....	....	....	....	....	16	6	8	14	18	....	....	....	....
2004-05	Rochester	AHL	67	16	45	61	60	....	....	....	....	....	....	....	....	....	9	6	5	11	6	....	....	....	....
2005-06	**Buffalo**	**NHL**	**70**	**18**	**28**	**46**	**57**	**5**	**1**	**1**	**151**	**11.9**	**1**	**807**	**48.0**	**17:02**	**18**	**5**	**10**	**15**	**16**	**1**	**1**	**0**	**17:03**
	Rochester	AHL	8	7	13	20	10	....	....	....	....	....	....	....	....	....	....	....	....	....	....	....	....	....	....
2006-07	**Buffalo**	**NHL**	**75**	**21**	**42**	**63**	**60**	**6**	**1**	**3**	**130**	**16.2**	**37**	**1129**	**48.5**	**18:28**	**16**	**2**	**5**	**7**	**14**	**0**	**0**	**0**	**18:03**
	NHL Totals		**194**	**48**	**80**	**128**	**129**	**12**	**2**	**8**	**352**	**13.6**		**2651**	**48.1**	**17:09**	**34**	**7**	**15**	**22**	**30**	**1**	**1**	**0**	**17:31**

OHL All-Rookie Team (2000) • OHL Rookie of the Year (2000) • CHL All-Rookie Team (2000) • CHL Plus/Minus Award (2000) • CHL Most Sportsmanlike Player (2000) • Memorial Cup Tournament All-Star Team (2003) • Stafford Smythe Memorial Trophy (Memorial Cup Tournament MVP) (2003)

ROY, Mathieu (WAH, MA-tyew) EDM.

Defense. Shoots right. 6'2", 214 lbs. Born, St-Georges, Que., August 10, 1983. Edmonton's 10th choice, 215th overall, in 2003 Entry Draft.

Season	Club	League	GP	G	A	Pts	PIM	PP	SH	GW	S	%	+/-	TF	F%	Min	GP	G	A	Pts	PIM	PP	SH	GW	Min
1998-99	Levis	QAAA	11	4	1	5	16	....	....	....	....	....	....	....	....	....	....	....	....	....	....	....	....	....	....
99-2000	Levis	QAAA	24	3	4	7	88	....	....	....	....	....	....	....	....	....	6	1	1	2	22	....	....	....	....
	Val-d'Or Foreurs	QMJHL	48	1	4	5	66	....	....	....	....	....	....	....	....	....	....	....	....	....	....	....	....	....	....
2000-01	Val-d'Or Foreurs	QMJHL	30	0	7	7	60	....	....	....	....	....	....	....	....	....	17	0	0	0	4	....	....	....	....
2001-02	Val-d'Or Foreurs	QMJHL	53	7	26	33	103	....	....	....	....	....	....	....	....	....	7	0	2	2	19	....	....	....	....
2002-03	Val-d'Or Foreurs	QMJHL	52	11	21	32	164	....	....	....	....	....	....	....	....	....	7	1	0	1	8	....	....	....	....
2003-04	Toronto	AHL	30	0	2	2	46	....	....	....	....	....	....	....	....	....	....	....	....	....	....	....	....	....	....
	Columbus	ECHL	10	1	2	3	13	....	....	....	....	....	....	....	....	....	....	....	....	....	....	....	....	....	....
2004-05	Edmonton	AHL	51	3	22	25	68	....	....	....	....	....	....	....	....	....	....	....	....	....	....	....	....	....	....
2005-06	**Edmonton**	**NHL**	**1**	**0**	**0**	**0**	**0**	**0**	**0**	**0**	**0**	**0.0**	**–1**	**0**	**0.0**	**13:00**	....	....	....	....	....	....	....	....	....
	Hamilton	AHL	50	3	16	19	82	....	....	....	....	....	....	....	....	....	....	....	....	....	....	....	....	....	....
2006-07	**Edmonton**	**NHL**	**16**	**2**	**0**	**2**	**30**	**0**	**0**	**0**	**18**	**11.1**	**–7**	**0**	**0.0**	**14:06**	....	....	....	....	....	....	....	....	....
	Hamilton	AHL	31	6	12	18	40	....	....	....	....	....	....	....	....	....	....	....	....	....	....	....	....	....	....
	NHL Totals		**17**	**2**	**0**	**2**	**30**	**0**	**0**	**0**	**18**	**11.1**		**0**	**0.0**	**14:03**	....	....	....	....	....	....	....	....	....

ROZSIVAL, Michal (roh-ZIH-vahl, MEE-khahl) NYR

Defense. Shoots right. 6'2", 210 lbs. Born, Vlasim, Czech., September 3, 1978. Pittsburgh's 5th choice, 105th overall, in 1996 Entry Draft.

Season	Club	League	GP	G	A	Pts	PIM	PP	SH	GW	S	%	+/-	TF	F%	Min	GP	G	A	Pts	PIM	PP	SH	GW	Min
1994-95	Jihlava Jr.	CzRep-Jr.	31	8	13	21	....	....	....	....	....	....	....	....	....	....	....	....	....	....	....	....	....	....	....
1995-96	HC Dukla Jihlava	CzRep	36	3	4	7	....	....	....	....	....	....	....	....	....	....	....	....	....	....	....	....	....	....	....
1996-97	Swift Current	WHL	63	8	31	39	80	....	....	....	....	....	....	....	....	....	10	0	6	6	15	....	....	....	....
1997-98	Swift Current	WHL	71	14	55	69	122	....	....	....	....	....	....	....	....	....	12	0	5	5	33	....	....	....	....
1998-99	Syracuse Crunch	AHL	49	3	22	25	72	....	....	....	....	....	....	....	....	....	....	....	....	....	....	....	....	....	....
99-2000	**Pittsburgh**	**NHL**	**75**	**4**	**17**	**21**	**48**	**1**	**0**	**1**	**73**	**5.5**	**11**	**1**	**0.0**	**19:01**	**2**	**0**	**0**	**0**	**4**	**0**	**0**	**0**	**30:56**
2000-01	**Pittsburgh**	**NHL**	**30**	**1**	**4**	**5**	**26**	**0**	**0**	**0**	**17**	**5.9**	**3**	**1**	**100.0**	**17:06**	....	....	....	....	....	....	....	....	....
	Wilkes-Barre	AHL	29	8	8	16	32	....	....	....	....	....	....	....	....	....	21	3	*19	22	23	....	....	....	....
2001-02	**Pittsburgh**	**NHL**	**79**	**9**	**20**	**29**	**47**	**4**	**0**	**4**	**89**	**10.1**	**–6**	**0**	**0.0**	**20:01**	....	....	....	....	....	....	....	....	....
2002-03	**Pittsburgh**	**NHL**	**53**	**4**	**6**	**10**	**40**	**1**	**0**	**0**	**61**	**6.6**	**–5**	**0**	**0.0**	**20:25**	....	....	....	....	....	....	....	....	....
2003-04	Wilkes-Barre	AHL	1	0	0	0	2	....	....	....	....	....	....	....	....	....	....	....	....	....	....	....	....	....	....
2004-05	HC Ocelari Trinec	CzRep	35	1	10	11	40	....	....	....	....	....	....	....	....	....	....	....	....	....	....	....	....	....	....
	Pardubice	CzRep	16	1	3	4	30	....	....	....	....	....	....	....	....	....	16	1	2	3	34	....	....	....	....
2005-06	**NY Rangers**	**NHL**	**82**	**5**	**25**	**30**	**90**	**3**	**0**	**3**	**115**	**4.3**	**35**	**1**	**0.0**	**22:27**	**4**	**0**	**1**	**1**	**8**	**0**	**0**	**0**	**24:31**
2006-07	**NY Rangers**	**NHL**	**80**	**10**	**30**	**40**	**52**	**7**	**0**	**3**	**104**	**9.6**	**10**	**3**	**0.0**	**23:46**	**10**	**3**	**4**	**7**	**10**	**2**	**0**	**1**	**24:45**
	NHL Totals		**399**	**33**	**102**	**135**	**303**	**16**	**0**	**11**	**459**	**7.2**		**6**	**16.7**	**20:55**	**16**	**3**	**5**	**8**	**22**	**2**	**0**	**1**	**25:28**

WHL East First All-Star Team (1998)

• Missed majority of 2003-04 season recovering from knee injury suffered in training camp, September 18, 2003. Signed as a free agent by **Trinec** (CzRep), September 17, 2004. Signed as a free agent by **Pardubice** (CzRep), January, 2005. Signed as a free agent by **NY Rangers**, August 29, 2005.

RUCCHIN, Steve (ROO-chihn, STEEV) ATL.

Center. Shoots left. 6'2", 215 lbs. Born, Thunder Bay, Ont., July 4, 1971. Anaheim's 1st choice, 2nd overall, in 1994 Supplemental Draft.

Season	Club	League	GP	G	A	Pts	PIM	PP	SH	GW	S	%	+/-	TF	F%	Min	GP	G	A	Pts	PIM	PP	SH	GW	Min
1989-90	Banting	High-ON	STATISTICS NOT AVAILABLE																						
	Thamesford	OHA-D	2	1	2	3	0	....	....	....	....	....	....	....	....	....	....	....	....	....	....	....	....	....	....
1990-91	Western Ontario	OUAA	34	13	16	29	14	....	....	....	....	....	....	....	....	....	....	....	....	....	....	....	....	....	....
1991-92	Western Ontario	OUAA	37	28	34	62	36	....	....	....	....	....	....	....	....	....	....	....	....	....	....	....	....	....	....
1992-93	Western Ontario	OUAA	34	22	26	48	16	....	....	....	....	....	....	....	....	....	....	....	....	....	....	....	....	....	....
1993-94	Western Ontario	OUAA	35	30	23	53	30	....	....	....	....	....	....	....	....	....	....	....	....	....	....	....	....	....	....
1994-95	San Diego Gulls	IHL	41	11	15	26	14	....	....	....	....	....	....	....	....	....	....	....	....	....	....	....	....	....	....
	Anaheim	**NHL**	**43**	**6**	**11**	**17**	**23**	**0**	**0**	**1**	**59**	**10.2**	**7**	....	....	....	....	....	....	....	....	....	....	....	....
1995-96	**Anaheim**	**NHL**	**64**	**19**	**25**	**44**	**12**	**8**	**1**	**4**	**113**	**16.8**	**3**	....	....	....	....	....	....	....	....	....	....	....	....
1996-97	**Anaheim**	**NHL**	**79**	**19**	**48**	**67**	**24**	**6**	**1**	**2**	**153**	**12.4**	**26**	....	....	....	**8**	**1**	**2**	**3**	**10**	**0**	**0**	**0**	....
1997-98	**Anaheim**	**NHL**	**72**	**17**	**36**	**53**	**13**	**8**	**1**	**3**	**131**	**13.0**	**8**	....	....	....	....	....	....	....	....	....	....	....	....
1998-99	**Anaheim**	**NHL**	**69**	**23**	**39**	**62**	**22**	**5**	**1**	**5**	**145**	**15.9**	**11**	**1845**	**52.3**	**22:33**	**4**	**0**	**3**	**3**	**0**	**0**	**0**	**0**	**21:55**
99-2000	**Anaheim**	**NHL**	**71**	**19**	**38**	**57**	**16**	**10**	**0**	**2**	**131**	**14.5**	**9**	**1996**	**53.4**	**22:12**	....	....	....	....	....	....	....	....	....
2000-01	**Anaheim**	**NHL**	**16**	**3**	**5**	**8**	**0**	**2**	**0**	**0**	**19**	**15.8**	**–5**	**289**	**51.6**	**18:47**	....	....	....	....	....	....	....	....	....
2001-02	**Anaheim**	**NHL**	**38**	**7**	**16**	**23**	**6**	**4**	**0**	**1**	**57**	**12.3**	**–3**	**808**	**52.2**	**19:17**	....	....	....	....	....	....	....	....	....
2002-03	**Anaheim**	**NHL**	**82**	**20**	**38**	**58**	**12**	**6**	**1**	**4**	**194**	**10.3**	**–14**	**1613**	**54.2**	**21:05**	**21**	**7**	**3**	**10**	**2**	**1**	**0**	**2**	**23:35**
2003-04	**Anaheim**	**NHL**	**82**	**20**	**23**	**43**	**12**	**9**	**1**	**1**	**148**	**13.5**	**–14**	**1446**	**53.6**	**19:46**	....	....	....	....	....	....	....	....	....
2004-05			DID NOT PLAY																						
2005-06	**NY Rangers**	**NHL**	**72**	**13**	**23**	**36**	**10**	**4**	**1**	**0**	**111**	**11.7**	**6**	**1038**	**47.7**	**16:00**	**4**	**1**	**0**	**1**	**0**	**1**	**0**	**0**	**13:50**
2006-07	**Atlanta**	**NHL**	**47**	**5**	**16**	**21**	**14**	**1**	**0**	**1**	**56**	**8.9**	**–4**	**864**	**51.6**	**18:20**	....	....	....	....	....	....	....	....	....
	NHL Totals		**735**	**171**	**318**	**489**	**164**	**63**	**7**	**24**	**1317**	**13.0**		**9899**	**52.4**	**19:59**	**37**	**9**	**8**	**17**	**12**	**2**	**0**	**2**	**22:00**

• Missed majority of 2000-01 season recovering from jaw injury suffered in game vs. Colorado, November 15, 2000. • Missed majority of 2001-02 season recovering from leg injury suffered in game vs. San Jose, November 16, 2001. Traded to **NY Rangers** by **Anaheim** for Trevor Gillies and NY Rangers' 4th round choice (later traded back to NY Rangers) - later traded to Washington - Washington selected Brett Bruneteau) in 2007 Entry Draft, August 23, 2005. Signed as a free agent by **Atlanta**, July 3, 2006.

RUCINSKY, Martin (roo-CHIHN-skee, MAHR-tihn) ST.L.

Left wing. Shoots left. 6'1", 207 lbs. Born, Most, Czech., March 11, 1971. Edmonton's 2nd choice, 20th overall, in 1991 Entry Draft.

Season	Club	League	GP	G	A	Pts	PIM	PP	SH	GW	S	%	+/-	TF	F%	Min	GP	G	A	Pts	PIM	PP	SH	GW	Min
1988-89	CHZ Litvinov	Czech	3	1	0	1	2	....	....	....	....	....	....	....	....	....	....	....	....	....	....	....	....	....	....
1989-90	CHZ Litvinov	Czech	39	12	6	18		....	....	....	....	....	....	....	....	....	8	5	3	8		....	....	....	....
1990-91	HC CHZ Litvinov	Czech	56	24	20	44	69	....	....	....	....	....	....	....	....	....	....	....	....	....	....	....	....	....	....
1991-92	**Edmonton**	**NHL**	**2**	**0**	**0**	**0**	**0**	**0**	**0**	**0**	**1**	**0.0**	**–3**	....	....	....	....	....	....	....	....	....	....	....	....
	Cape Breton	AHL	35	11	12	23	34	....	....	....	....	....	....	....	....	....	....	....	....	....	....	....	....	....	....
	Quebec	**NHL**	**4**	**1**	**1**	**2**	**2**	**0**	**0**	**0**	**4**	**25.0**	**1**	....	....	....	....	....	....	....	....	....	....	....	....
	Halifax Citadels	AHL	7	1	1	2	6	....	....	....	....	....	....	....	....	....	....	....	....	....	....	....	....	....	....
1992-93	**Quebec**	**NHL**	**77**	**18**	**30**	**48**	**51**	**4**	**0**	**1**	**133**	**13.5**	**16**	....	....	....	**6**	**1**	**1**	**2**	**4**	**1**	**0**	**0**	....
1993-94	**Quebec**	**NHL**	**60**	**9**	**23**	**32**	**58**	**4**	**0**	**1**	**96**	**9.4**	**4**	....	....	....	....	....	....	....	....	....	....	....	....

			Regular Season														Playoffs								
Season	Club	League	GP	G	A	Pts	PIM	PP	SH	GW	S	%	+/-	TF	F%	Min	GP	G	A	Pts	PIM	PP	SH	GW	Min
1994-95	Litvinov	CzRep	13	12	10	22	54	....	....	....	....	....	....	....	....	....	....	....	....	....	....	....	....	....	....
	Quebec	**NHL**	**20**	**3**	**6**	**9**	**14**	**0**	**0**	**0**	**32**	**9.4**	**5**	....	....	....	....	....	....	....	....	....	....	....	....
1995-96	HC Petra Vsetin	CzRep	1	1	1	2	0	....	....	....	....	....	....	....	....	....	....	....	....	....	....	....	....	....	....
	Colorado	**NHL**	**22**	**4**	**11**	**15**	**14**	**0**	**0**	**1**	**39**	**10.3**	**10**	....	....	....	....	....	....	....	....	....	....	....	....
	Montreal	**NHL**	**56**	**25**	**35**	**60**	**54**	**9**	**2**	**3**	**142**	**17.6**	**8**	....	....	....	....	....	....	....	....	....	....	....	....
1996-97	**Montreal**	**NHL**	**70**	**28**	**27**	**55**	**62**	**6**	**3**	**3**	**172**	**16.3**	**1**	....	....	....	**5**	**0**	**0**	**0**	**4**	**0**	**0**	**0**	....
1997-98	**Montreal**	**NHL**	**78**	**21**	**32**	**53**	**84**	**5**	**3**	**3**	**192**	**10.9**	**13**	....	....	....	**10**	**3**	**0**	**3**	**4**	**1**	**0**	**0**	....
	Czech Republic	Olympics	6	3	1	4	4	....	....	....	....	....	....	....	....	....	....	....	....	....	....	....	....	....	....
1998-99	Litvinov	CzRep	3	2	2	4	0	....	....	....	....	....	....	....	....	....	....	....	....	....	....	....	....	....	....
	Montreal	**NHL**	**73**	**17**	**17**	**34**	**50**	**5**	**0**	**1**	**180**	**9.4**	**–25**	**12**	**50.0**	**18:12**	....	....	....	....	....	....	....	....	....
99-2000	**Montreal**	**NHL**	**80**	**25**	**24**	**49**	**70**	**7**	**1**	**4**	**242**	**10.3**	**1**	**31**	**54.8**	**18:54**	....	....	....	....	....	....	....	....	....
2000-01	**Montreal**	**NHL**	**57**	**16**	**22**	**38**	**66**	**5**	**1**	**4**	**141**	**11.3**	**–5**	**5**	**40.0**	**19:11**	....	....	....	....	....	....	....	....	....
2001-02	**Montreal**	**NHL**	**18**	**2**	**6**	**8**	**12**	**1**	**0**	**0**	**41**	**4.9**	**–1**	**5**	**80.0**	**16:15**	....	....	....	....	....	....	....	....	....
	Dallas	**NHL**	**42**	**6**	**11**	**17**	**24**	**2**	**0**	**1**	**63**	**9.5**	**3**	**7**	**57.1**	**14:33**	....	....	....	....	....	....	....	....	....
	Czech Republic	Olympics	4	0	3	3	2	....	....	....	....	....	....	....	....	....	....	....	....	....	....	....	....	....	....
	NY Rangers	**NHL**	**15**	**3**	**10**	**13**	**6**	**0**	**0**	**1**	**24**	**12.5**	**6**	**3**	**33.3**	**16:39**	....	....	....	....	....	....	....	....	....
2002-03	Litvinov	CzRep	2	1	0	1	2	....	....	....	....	....	....	....	....	....	....	....	....	....	....	....	....	....	....
	St. Louis	**NHL**	**61**	**16**	**14**	**30**	**38**	**4**	**4**	**3**	**135**	**11.9**	**–1**	**19**	**57.9**	**16:55**	**7**	**4**	**2**	**6**	**4**	**0**	**0**	**0**	**16:52**
2003-04	**NY Rangers**	**NHL**	**69**	**13**	**29**	**42**	**62**	**0**	**1**	**2**	**161**	**8.1**	**13**	**14**	**14.3**	**18:51**	....	....	....	....	....	....	....	....	....
	Vancouver	**NHL**	**13**	**1**	**2**	**3**	**10**	**0**	**0**	**0**	**45**	**2.2**	**2**	**2**	**0.0**	**19:03**	**7**	**1**	**1**	**2**	**6**	**1**	**0**	**0**	**17:02**
2004-05	Litvinov	CzRep	38	15	26	41	87	....	....	....	....	....	....	....	....	....	....	....	....	....	....	....	....	....	....
2005-06	**NY Rangers**	**NHL**	**52**	**16**	**39**	**55**	**56**	**4**	**0**	**4**	**152**	**10.5**	**10**	**44**	**34.1**	**18:25**	**2**	**0**	**1**	**1**	**2**	**0**	**0**	**0**	**13:29**
	Czech Republic	Olympics	8	1	3	4	0	....	....	....	....	....	....	....	....	....	....	....	....	....	....	....	....	....	....
2006-07	**St. Louis**	**NHL**	**52**	**12**	**21**	**33**	**48**	**4**	**0**	**3**	**96**	**12.5**	**–3**	**14**	**21.4**	**16:43**	....	....	....	....	....	....	....	....	....
	NHL Totals		**921**	**236**	**360**	**596**	**781**	**60**	**15**	**35**	**2091**	**11.3**		**156**	**41.7**	**17:51**	**37**	**9**	**5**	**14**	**24**	**3**	**0**	**0**	**16:31**

Played in NHL All-Star Game (2000)

Traded to **Quebec** by **Edmonton** for Ron Tugnutt and Brad Zavisha, March 10, 1992. Transferred to **Colorado** after **Quebec** franchise relocated, June 21, 1995. Traded to **Montreal** by **Colorado** with Andrei Kovalenko and Jocelyn Thibault for Patrick Roy and Mike Keane, December 6, 1995. Traded to **Dallas** by **Montreal** with Benoit Brunet for Donald Audette and Shaun Van Allen, November 21, 2001. Traded to **NY Rangers** by **Dallas** with Roman Lyashenko for Manny Malhotra and Barrett Heisten, March 12, 2002. Signed as a free agent by **St. Louis**, October 30, 2002. Signed as a free agent by **NY Rangers**, August 28, 2003. Traded to **Vancouver** by **NY Rangers** for R.J. Umberger and Martin Grenier, March 9, 2004. Signed as a free agent by **Litvinov** (CzRep), August 20, 2004. Signed as a free agent by **NY Rangers**, August 3, 2005. Signed as a free agent by **St. Louis**, August 2, 2006.

RUPP, Mike

(RUHP, MIGHK) **N.J.**

Center. Shoots left. 6'5", 230 lbs. Born, Cleveland, OH, January 13, 1980. New Jersey's 7th choice, 76th overall, in 2000 Entry Draft.

Season	Club	League	GP	G	A	Pts	PIM	PP	SH	GW	S	%	+/-	TF	F%	Min	GP	G	A	Pts	PIM	PP	SH	GW	Min
1996-97	St. Edward's	High-OH	20	26	24	50	....	....	....	....	....	....	....	....	....	....	....	....	....	....	....	....	....	....	....
1997-98	Windsor Spitfires	OHL	38	9	8	17	60	....	....	....	....	....	....	....	....	....	....	....	....	....	....	....	....	....	....
	Erie Otters	OHL	26	7	3	10	57	....	....	....	....	....	....	....	....	....	7	3	1	4	6	....	....	....	....
1998-99	Erie Otters	OHL	63	22	25	47	102	....	....	....	....	....	....	....	....	....	5	0	2	2	25	....	....	....	....
99-2000	Erie Otters	OHL	58	32	21	53	134	....	....	....	....	....	....	....	....	....	13	5	5	10	22	....	....	....	....
2000-01	Albany River Rats	AHL	71	10	10	20	63	....	....	....	....	....	....	....	....	....	....	....	....	....	....	....	....	....	....
2001-02	Albany River Rats	AHL	78	13	17	30	90	....	....	....	....	....	....	....	....	....	....	....	....	....	....	....	....	....	....
2002-03 ♦	**New Jersey**	**NHL**	**26**	**5**	**3**	**8**	**21**	**2**	**0**	**3**	**34**	**14.7**	**0**	**150**	**44.7**	**11:39**	**4**	**1**	**3**	**4**	**0**	**0**	**0**	**1**	**11:28**
	Albany River Rats	AHL	47	8	11	19	74	....	....	....	....	....	....	....	....	....	....	....	....	....	....	....	....	....	....
2003-04	**New Jersey**	**NHL**	**51**	**6**	**5**	**11**	**41**	**1**	**0**	**1**	**64**	**9.4**	**–1**	**386**	**47.9**	**10:38**	....	....	....	....	....	....	....	....	....
	Phoenix	**NHL**	**6**	**0**	**1**	**1**	**6**	**0**	**0**	**0**	**12**	**0.0**	**–3**	**94**	**57.5**	**16:59**	....	....	....	....	....	....	....	....	....
2004-05	Danbury Trashers	UHL	14	5	5	10	30	....	....	....	....	....	....	....	....	....	11	3	4	7	38	....	....	....	....
2005-06	**Phoenix**	**NHL**	**1**	**0**	**0**	**0**	**0**	**0**	**0**	**0**	**1**	**0.0**	**0**	**1**	**0.0**	**6:30**	....	....	....	....	....	....	....	....	....
	Columbus	**NHL**	**39**	**4**	**2**	**6**	**58**	**0**	**0**	**0**	**38**	**10.5**	**–3**	**264**	**48.1**	**9:04**	....	....	....	....	....	....	....	....	....
	Syracuse Crunch	AHL	3	1	2	3	12	....	....	....	....	....	....	....	....	....	....	....	....	....	....	....	....	....	....
2006-07	**New Jersey**	**NHL**	**76**	**6**	**3**	**9**	**92**	**0**	**0**	**1**	**60**	**10.0**	**–10**	**33**	**45.5**	**6:27**	**9**	**0**	**1**	**1**	**7**	**0**	**0**	**0**	**2:46**
	NHL Totals		**199**	**21**	**14**	**35**	**218**	**3**	**0**	**5**	**209**	**10.0**		**928**	**48.3**	**9:02**	**13**	**1**	**4**	**5**	**7**	**0**	**0**	**1**	**5:27**

• Re-entered NHL Entry Draft. Originally NY Islanders' 1st choice, 9th overall, in 1998 Entry Draft.

Traded to **Phoenix** by **New Jersey** with New Jersey's 2nd round choice (later traded to Edmonton – Edmonton selected Geoff Paukovich) in 2004 Entry Draft for Jan Hrdina, March 5, 2004. Signed as a free agent by **Danbury** (UHL), February 10, 2005. Traded to **Columbus** by **Phoenix** with Cale Hulse and Jason Chimera for Geoff Sanderson and Tim Jackman, October 8, 2005. Signed as a free agent by **New Jersey**, July 10, 2006.

RUUTU, Jarkko

(ROO-too, YAHR-koh) **PIT.**

Right wing. Shoots left. 6', 200 lbs. Born, Vantaa, Finland, August 23, 1975. Vancouver's 3rd choice, 68th overall, in 1998 Entry Draft.

Season	Club	League	GP	G	A	Pts	PIM	PP	SH	GW	S	%	+/-	TF	F%	Min	GP	G	A	Pts	PIM	PP	SH	GW	Min
1991-92	HIFK Helsinki Jr.	Fin-Jr.	1	0	0	0	0	....	....	....	....	....	....	....	....	....	....	....	....	....	....	....	....	....	....
1992-93	HIFK Helsinki U18	Fin-U18	33	26	21	47	53	....	....	....	....	....	....	....	....	....	....	....	....	....	....	....	....	....	....
	HIFK Helsinki Jr.	Fin-Jr.	1	0	0	0	0	....	....	....	....	....	....	....	....	....	....	....	....	....	....	....	....	....	....
1993-94	HIFK Helsinki Jr.	Fin-Jr.	19	9	12	21	44	....	....	....	....	....	....	....	....	....	....	....	....	....	....	....	....	....	....
1994-95	HIFK Helsinki Jr.	Fin-Jr.	35	26	22	48	117	....	....	....	....	....	....	....	....	....	....	....	....	....	....	....	....	....	....
1995-96	Michigan Tech	WCHA	39	12	10	22	96	....	....	....	....	....	....	....	....	....	....	....	....	....	....	....	....	....	....
1996-97	HIFK Helsinki	Finland	48	11	10	21	155	....	....	....	....	....	....	....	....	....	....	....	....	....	....	....	....	....	....
1997-98	HIFK Helsinki	Finland	37	10	10	20	166	....	....	....	....	....	....	....	....	....	9	7	4	11	10	....	....	....	....
1998-99	HIFK Helsinki	Finland	25	10	4	14	136	....	....	....	....	....	....	....	....	....	9	0	2	2	43	....	....	....	....
	HIFK Helsinki	EuroHL	5	1	2	3	8	....	....	....	....	....	....	....	....	....	....	....	....	....	....	....	....	....	....
99-2000	**Vancouver**	**NHL**	**8**	**0**	**1**	**1**	**6**	**0**	**0**	**0**	**4**	**0.0**	**–1**	**0**	**0.0**	**8:47**	....	....	....	....	....	....	....	....	....
	Syracuse Crunch	AHL	65	26	32	58	164	....	....	....	....	....	....	....	....	....	4	3	1	4	8	....	....	....	....
2000-01	**Vancouver**	**NHL**	**21**	**3**	**3**	**6**	**32**	**0**	**1**	**0**	**23**	**13.0**	**1**	**0**	**0.0**	**10:39**	**4**	**0**	**1**	**1**	**8**	**0**	**0**	**0**	**10:18**
	Kansas City	IHL	46	11	18	29	111	....	....	....	....	....	....	....	....	....	....	....	....	....	....	....	....	....	....
2001-02	**Vancouver**	**NHL**	**49**	**2**	**7**	**9**	**74**	**0**	**0**	**0**	**37**	**5.4**	**–1**	**5**	**0.0**	**10:11**	**1**	**0**	**0**	**0**	**0**	**0**	**0**	**0**	**8:53**
	Finland	Olympics	4	0	0	0	4	....	....	....	....	....	....	....	....	....	....	....	....	....	....	....	....	....	....
2002-03	**Vancouver**	**NHL**	**36**	**2**	**2**	**4**	**66**	**0**	**0**	**1**	**36**	**5.6**	**–7**	**6**	**16.7**	**8:58**	**13**	**0**	**2**	**2**	**14**	**0**	**0**	**0**	**11:59**
2003-04	**Vancouver**	**NHL**	**71**	**6**	**8**	**14**	**133**	**1**	**0**	**0**	**70**	**8.6**	**–13**	**20**	**30.0**	**11:29**	**6**	**1**	**0**	**1**	**10**	**0**	**0**	**0**	**9:13**
2004-05	HIFK Helsinki	Finland	50	10	18	28	215	....	....	....	....	....	....	....	....	....	3	0	0	0	41	....	....	....	....
2005-06	**Vancouver**	**NHL**	**82**	**10**	**7**	**17**	**142**	**2**	**0**	**2**	**85**	**11.8**	**1**	**11**	**0.0**	**11:42**	....	....	....	....	....	....	....	....	....
	Finland	Olympics	8	0	0	0	31	....	....	....	....	....	....	....	....	....	....	....	....	....	....	....	....	....	....
2006-07	**Pittsburgh**	**NHL**	**81**	**7**	**9**	**16**	**125**	**0**	**0**	**2**	**63**	**11.1**	**0**	**3**	**100.0**	**9:20**	**5**	**0**	**0**	**0**	**10**	**0**	**0**	**0**	**6:38**
	NHL Totals		**348**	**30**	**37**	**67**	**578**	**3**	**1**	**5**	**318**	**9.4**		**45**	**22.2**	**10:29**	**29**	**1**	**3**	**4**	**42**	**0**	**0**	**0**	**10:09**

• Spent majority of 2002-03 season as a healthy reserve. Signed as a free agent by **HIFK Helsinki** (Finland), September 23, 2004. Signed as a free agent by **Pittsburgh**, July 4, 2006.

RUUTU, Tuomo

(ROO-too, TOO-oh-moh) **CHI.**

Center/Left wing. Shoots left. 6', 200 lbs. Born, Vantaa, Finland, February 16, 1983. Chicago's 1st choice, 9th overall, in 2001 Entry Draft.

Season	Club	League	GP	G	A	Pts	PIM	PP	SH	GW	S	%	+/-	TF	F%	Min	GP	G	A	Pts	PIM	PP	SH	GW	Min
1998-99	HIFK Helsinki U18	Fin-U18	25	9	11	20	88	....	....	....	....	....	....	....	....	....	2	1	1	2	2	....	....	....	....
99-2000	HIFK Helsinki U18	Fin-U18	5	0	3	3	12	....	....	....	....	....	....	....	....	....	3	1	2	3	2	....	....	....	....
	HIFK Helsinki Jr.	Fin-Jr.	35	11	16	27	32	....	....	....	....	....	....	....	....	....	3	0	1	1	4	....	....	....	....
	HIFK Helsinki	Finland	1	0	0	0	2	....	....	....	....	....	....	....	....	....	....	....	....	....	....	....	....	....	....
2000-01	Jokerit Helsinki Jr.	Fin-Jr.	2	1	0	1	0	....	....	....	....	....	....	....	....	....	....	....	....	....	....	....	....	....	....
	Jokerit Helsinki	Finland	47	11	11	22	94	....	....	....	....	....	....	....	....	....	5	0	0	0	4	....	....	....	....
2001-02	Jokerit Helsinki	Finland	51	7	16	23	69	....	....	....	....	....	....	....	....	....	10	0	6	6	29	....	....	....	....
2002-03	HIFK Helsinki	Finland	30	12	15	27	24	....	....	....	....	....	....	....	....	....	....	....	....	....	....	....	....	....	....
2003-04	**Chicago**	**NHL**	**82**	**23**	**21**	**44**	**58**	**10**	**0**	**3**	**174**	**13.2**	**–31**	**317**	**46.4**	**16:24**	....	....	....	....	....	....	....	....	....
2004-05			DID NOT PLAY																						
2005-06	**Chicago**	**NHL**	**15**	**2**	**3**	**5**	**31**	**1**	**0**	**0**	**30**	**6.7**	**–7**	**90**	**46.7**	**14:43**	....	....	....	....	....	....	....	....	....
2006-07	**Chicago**	**NHL**	**71**	**17**	**21**	**38**	**95**	**1**	**0**	**1**	**115**	**14.8**	**4**	**347**	**42.7**	**17:21**	....	....	....	....	....	....	....	....	....
	NHL Totals		**168**	**42**	**45**	**87**	**184**	**12**	**0**	**4**	**319**	**13.2**		**754**	**44.7**	**16:39**	....	....	....	....	....	....	....	....	....

• Missed majority of 2005-06 season recovering from back (October 15, 2005 at San Jose) and ankle (January 8, 2006 vs. Nashville) injuries.

RUZICKA, Stefan
(roo-ZHEECH-kuh, STEH-fan) **PHI.**

Right wing. Shoots right. 6', 205 lbs. Born, Nitra, Czech., February 17, 1985. Philadelphia's 4th choice, 81st overall, in 2003 Entry Draft.

			Regular Season														Playoffs								
Season	Club	League	GP	G	A	Pts	PIM	PP	SH	GW	S	%	+/-	TF	F%	Min	GP	G	A	Pts	PIM	PP	SH	GW	Min
2000-01	Nitra Jr.	Slovak-Jr.	38	30	15	45	....	....	....	....	....	....	....	....	....	....	....	....	....	....	....	....	....	....	....
2001-02	HKM Nitra Jr.	Slovak-Jr.	29	27	25	52	....	....	....	....	....	....	....	....	....	....	....	....	....	....	....	....	....	....	....
	HKM Nitra	Slovakia	19	0	5	5	29	....	....	....	....	....	....	....	....	....	....	....	....	....	....	....	....	....	....
2002-03	HKM Nitra Jr.	Slovak-Jr.	30	18	22	40	64	....	....	....	....	....	....	....	....	....	....	....	....	....	....	....	....	....	....
	HKM Nitra	Slovak-2	17	5	7	12	4	....	....	....	....	....	....	....	....	....	....	....	....	....	....	....	....	....	....
2003-04	Owen Sound	OHL	62	34	38	72	63	....	....	....	....	....	....	....	....	....	7	1	6	7	8	....	....	....	....
	Philadelphia	AHL	2	0	0	0	0	....	....	....	....	....	....	....	....	....	3	1	0	1	2	....	....	....	....
2004-05	Owen Sound	OHL	62	37	33	70	61	....	....	....	....	....	....	....	....	....	8	3	3	6	14	....	....	....	....
2005-06	**Philadelphia**	**NHL**	**1**	**0**	**0**	**0**	**2**	**0**	**0**	**0**	**1**	**0.0**	**0**	**1**	**0.0**	**4:48**	....	....	....	....	....	....	....	....	....
	Philadelphia	AHL	73	16	32	48	88	....	....	....	....	....	....	....	....	....	....	....	....	....	....	....	....	....	....
2006-07	**Philadelphia**	**NHL**	**40**	**3**	**10**	**13**	**18**	**1**	**0**	**0**	**75**	**4.0**	**-6**	**3**	**0.0**	**12:44**	....	....	....	....	....	....	....	....	....
	Philadelphia	AHL	32	16	11	27	29	....	....	....	....	....	....	....	....	....	....	....	....	....	....	....	....	....	....
	NHL Totals		**41**	**3**	**10**	**13**	**20**	**1**	**0**	**0**	**76**	**3.9**		**4**	**0.0**	**12:32**	....	....	....	....	....	....	....	....	....

OHL All-Rookie Team (2004) • OHL Second All-Star Team (2004)

RYAN, Matt
(RIGH-uhn, MAT)

Center. Shoots right. 5'11", 185 lbs. Born, Sharon, Ont., November 12, 1983.

			Regular Season														Playoffs								
Season	Club	League	GP	G	A	Pts	PIM	PP	SH	GW	S	%	+/-	TF	F%	Min	GP	G	A	Pts	PIM	PP	SH	GW	Min
2001-02	Niagara University	CHA	32	7	12	19	32	....	....	....	....	....	....	....	....	....	....	....	....	....	....	....	....	....	....
2002-03	Niagara University	CHA	9	6	2	8	14	....	....	....	....	....	....	....	....	....	....	....	....	....	....	....	....	....	....
	Guelph Storm	OHL	48	14	11	25	34	....	....	....	....	....	....	....	....	....	11	2	7	9	0	....	....	....	....
2003-04	Guelph Storm	OHL	68	42	35	77	63	....	....	....	....	....	....	....	....	....	22	8	11	19	24	....	....	....	....
2004-05	Manchester	AHL	77	9	15	24	59	....	....	....	....	....	....	....	....	....	6	0	1	1	4	....	....	....	....
2005-06	**Los Angeles**	**NHL**	**12**	**0**	**1**	**1**	**2**	**0**	**0**	**0**	**8**	**0.0**	**-4**	**64**	**45.3**	**6:07**	....	....	....	....	....	....	....	....	....
	Manchester	AHL	68	12	12	24	79	....	....	....	....	....	....	....	....	....	7	1	1	2	8	....	....	....	....
2006-07	Manchester	AHL	56	8	16	24	50	....	....	....	....	....	....	....	....	....	16	3	5	8	13	....	....	....	....
	NHL Totals		**12**	**0**	**1**	**1**	**2**	**0**	**0**	**0**	**8**	**0.0**		**64**	**45.3**	**6:07**	....	....	....	....	....	....	....	....	....

Signed as a free agent by **Los Angeles**, August 2, 2004.

RYAN, Michael
(RIGH-uhn, MIGH-kuhl) **BUF.**

Center. Shoots left. 6'1", 186 lbs. Born, Boston, MA, May 16, 1980. Dallas' 1st choice, 32nd overall, in 1999 Entry Draft.

			Regular Season														Playoffs								
Season	Club	League	GP	G	A	Pts	PIM	PP	SH	GW	S	%	+/-	TF	F%	Min	GP	G	A	Pts	PIM	PP	SH	GW	Min
1997-98	Bos. College High	High-MA	23	22	14	36	28	....	....	....	....	....	....	....	....	....	....	....	....	....	....	....	....	....	....
1998-99	Bos. College High	High-MA	21	20	24	44	22	....	....	....	....	....	....	....	....	....	....	....	....	....	....	....	....	....	....
99-2000	Northeastern	H-East	32	4	9	13	47	....	....	....	....	....	....	....	....	....	....	....	....	....	....	....	....	....	....
2000-01	Northeastern	H-East	33	17	12	29	52	....	....	....	....	....	....	....	....	....	....	....	....	....	....	....	....	....	....
2001-02	Northeastern	H-East	36	24	15	39	54	....	....	....	....	....	....	....	....	....	....	....	....	....	....	....	....	....	....
2002-03	Northeastern	H-East	34	18	14	32	30	....	....	....	....	....	....	....	....	....	....	....	....	....	....	....	....	....	....
2003-04	Rochester	AHL	45	3	9	12	31	....	....	....	....	....	....	....	....	....	....	....	....	....	....	....	....	....	....
2004-05	Rochester	AHL	59	11	11	22	20	....	....	....	....	....	....	....	....	....	5	0	1	1	4	....	....	....	....
2005-06	Rochester	AHL	56	15	22	37	70	....	....	....	....	....	....	....	....	....	....	....	....	....	....	....	....	....	....
2006-07	**Buffalo**	**NHL**	**19**	**3**	**2**	**5**	**2**	**0**	**1**	**0**	**34**	**8.8**	**-8**	**2**	**0.0**	**13:40**	....	....	....	....	....	....	....	....	....
	Rochester	AHL	50	28	23	51	68	....	....	....	....	....	....	....	....	....	6	4	0	4	4	....	....	....	....
	NHL Totals		**19**	**3**	**2**	**5**	**2**	**0**	**1**	**0**	**34**	**8.8**		**2**	**0.0**	**13:40**	....	....	....	....	....	....	....	....	....

Traded to **Buffalo** by **Dallas** with Dallas's 2nd round choice (Branislav Fabry) in 2003 Entry Draft for Stu Barnes, March 10, 2003.

RYAN, Prestin
(RIGH-uhn, PREH-stuhn) **CHI.**

Defense. Shoots left. 6', 190 lbs. Born, Arcola, Sask., June 29, 1980.

			Regular Season														Playoffs								
Season	Club	League	GP	G	A	Pts	PIM	PP	SH	GW	S	%	+/-	TF	F%	Min	GP	G	A	Pts	PIM	PP	SH	GW	Min
2000-01	U. of Maine	H-East	DID NOT PLAY – FRESHMAN																						
2001-02	U. of Maine	H-East	39	6	9	15	*91	....	....	....	....	....	....	....	....	....	....	....	....	....	....	....	....	....	....
2002-03	U. of Maine	H-East	37	1	8	9	*120	....	....	....	....	....	....	....	....	....	....	....	....	....	....	....	....	....	....
2003-04	U. of Maine	H-East	43	4	18	22	*148	....	....	....	....	....	....	....	....	....	....	....	....	....	....	....	....	....	....
	Syracuse Crunch	AHL	....	....	....	....	....	....	....	....	....	....	....	....	....	....	3	0	0	0	2	....	....	....	....
2004-05	Syracuse Crunch	AHL	59	3	6	9	161	....	....	....	....	....	....	....	....	....	....	....	....	....	....	....	....	....	....
2005-06	**Vancouver**	**NHL**	**1**	**0**	**0**	**0**	**2**	**0**	**0**	**0**	**0**	**0.0**	**-1**	**0**	**0.0**	**7:30**	....	....	....	....	....	....	....	....	....
	Manitoba Moose	AHL	64	11	12	23	63	....	....	....	....	....	....	....	....	....	13	1	1	2	25	....	....	....	....
2006-07	Manitoba Moose	AHL	58	5	16	21	125	....	....	....	....	....	....	....	....	....	13	2	3	5	33	....	....	....	....
	NHL Totals		**1**	**0**	**0**	**0**	**2**	**0**	**0**	**0**	**0**	**0.0**		**0**	**0.0**	**7:30**	....	....	....	....	....	....	....	....	....

Hockey East Second All-Star Team (2004) • NCAA East Second All-American Team (2004) • NCAA Championship All-Tournament Team (2004)

Signed as a free agent by **Columbus**, April 12, 2004. Signed as a free agent by **Vancouver**, August 18, 2005. Signed as a free agent by **Chicago**, July 27, 2007.

RYCROFT, Mark
(RIGH-krawft, MAHRK) **COL.**

Right wing. Shoots right. 6', 192 lbs. Born, Penticton, B.C., July 12, 1978.

			Regular Season														Playoffs								
Season	Club	League	GP	G	A	Pts	PIM	PP	SH	GW	S	%	+/-	TF	F%	Min	GP	G	A	Pts	PIM	PP	SH	GW	Min
1993-94	Penticton Ice	BCAHA	60	47	65	112	100	....	....	....	....	....	....	....	....	....	....	....	....	....	....	....	....	....	....
1994-95	Penticton Ice	BCAHA	43	33	43	76	90	....	....	....	....	....	....	....	....	....	....	....	....	....	....	....	....	....	....
1995-96	Nanaimo Clippers	BCHL	60	17	28	45	28	....	....	....	....	....	....	....	....	....	....	....	....	....	....	....	....	....	....
1996-97	Nanaimo Clippers	BCHL	58	32	35	67	79	....	....	....	....	....	....	....	....	....	....	....	....	....	....	....	....	....	....
1997-98	U. of Denver	WCHA	35	15	17	32	28	....	....	....	....	....	....	....	....	....	....	....	....	....	....	....	....	....	....
1998-99	U. of Denver	WCHA	41	19	18	37	36	....	....	....	....	....	....	....	....	....	....	....	....	....	....	....	....	....	....
99-2000	U. of Denver	WCHA	41	17	17	34	87	....	....	....	....	....	....	....	....	....	....	....	....	....	....	....	....	....	....
2000-01	Worcester IceCats	AHL	71	24	26	50	68	....	....	....	....	....	....	....	....	....	11	2	5	7	4	....	....	....	....
2001-02	**St. Louis**	**NHL**	**9**	**0**	**3**	**3**	**4**	**0**	**0**	**0**	**14**	**0.0**	**0**	**1**	**0.0**	**9:50**	....	....	....	....	....	....	....	....	....
	Worcester IceCats	AHL	66	12	19	31	68	....	....	....	....	....	....	....	....	....	3	0	1	1	0	....	....	....	....
2002-03	Worcester IceCats	AHL	45	8	18	26	35	....	....	....	....	....	....	....	....	....	1	0	0	0	0	....	....	....	....
2003-04	**St. Louis**	**NHL**	**71**	**9**	**12**	**21**	**32**	**0**	**0**	**0**	**110**	**8.2**	**2**	**11**	**63.6**	**14:23**	**3**	**0**	**0**	**0**	**2**	**0**	**0**	**0**	**9:41**
2004-05	HC Briancon	France	13	8	8	16	18	....	....	....	....	....	....	....	....	....	4	2	1	3	0	....	....	....	....
2005-06	**St. Louis**	**NHL**	**80**	**6**	**4**	**10**	**46**	**0**	**1**	**2**	**77**	**7.8**	**-14**	**23**	**34.8**	**10:27**	....	....	....	....	....	....	....	....	....
2006-07	**Colorado**	**NHL**	**66**	**6**	**6**	**12**	**31**	**0**	**0**	**2**	**74**	**8.1**	**3**	**36**	**50.0**	**9:25**	....	....	....	....	....	....	....	....	....
	NHL Totals		**226**	**21**	**25**	**46**	**113**	**0**	**1**	**4**	**275**	**7.6**		**71**	**46.5**	**11:22**	**3**	**0**	**0**	**0**	**2**	**0**	**0**	**0**	**9:41**

WCHA All-Rookie Team (1998)

Signed as a free agent by **St. Louis**, May 15, 2000. Signed as a free agent by **Briancon** (France), November 9, 2004. Signed as a free agent by **Colorado**, July 12, 2006.

RYDER, Michael
(RIGH-duhr, MIGH-kuhl) **MTL.**

Right wing. Shoots right. 6', 192 lbs. Born, Bonavista, Nfld., March 31, 1980. Montreal's 9th choice, 216th overall, in 1998 Entry Draft.

			Regular Season														Playoffs								
Season	Club	League	GP	G	A	Pts	PIM	PP	SH	GW	S	%	+/-	TF	F%	Min	GP	G	A	Pts	PIM	PP	SH	GW	Min
1996-97	Bonavista Saints	NFAHA	23	31	17	48	....	....	....	....	....	....	....	....	....	....	....	....	....	....	....	....	....	....	....
1997-98	Hull Olympiques	QMJHL	69	34	28	62	41	....	....	....	....	....	....	....	....	....	10	4	2	6	4	....	....	....	....
1998-99	Hull Olympiques	QMJHL	69	44	43	87	65	....	....	....	....	....	....	....	....	....	23	*20	16	36	39	....	....	....	....
99-2000	Hull Olympiques	QMJHL	63	50	58	108	50	....	....	....	....	....	....	....	....	....	15	11	17	28	28	....	....	....	....
2000-01	Tallahassee	ECHL	5	4	5	9	6	....	....	....	....	....	....	....	....	....	....	....	....	....	....	....	....	....	....
	Quebec Citadelles	AHL	61	6	9	15	14	....	....	....	....	....	....	....	....	....	....	....	....	....	....	....	....	....	....
2001-02	Mississippi	ECHL	20	14	13	27	2	....	....	....	....	....	....	....	....	....	....	....	....	....	....	....	....	....	....
	Quebec Citadelles	AHL	50	11	17	28	9	....	....	....	....	....	....	....	....	....	3	0	1	1	2	....	....	....	....
2002-03	Hamilton	AHL	69	34	33	67	43	....	....	....	....	....	....	....	....	....	23	11	6	17	8	....	....	....	....
2003-04	**Montreal**	**NHL**	**81**	**25**	**38**	**63**	**26**	**10**	**0**	**4**	**215**	**11.6**	**10**	**25**	**24.0**	**16:00**	**11**	**1**	**2**	**3**	**4**	**0**	**0**	**0**	**16:52**
2004-05	Leksands IF	Sweden-2	42	34	27	61	32	....	....	....	....	....	....	....	....	....	....	....	....	....	....	....	....	....	....
2005-06	**Montreal**	**NHL**	**81**	**30**	**25**	**55**	**40**	**18**	**0**	**6**	**243**	**12.3**	**-5**	**17**	**52.9**	**16:10**	**6**	**2**	**3**	**5**	**0**	**1**	**0**	**1**	**16:09**
2006-07	**Montreal**	**NHL**	**82**	**30**	**28**	**58**	**60**	**17**	**2**	**3**	**221**	**13.6**	**-25**	**28**	**42.9**	**16:17**	....	....	....	....	....	....	....	....	....
	NHL Totals		**244**	**85**	**91**	**176**	**126**	**45**	**2**	**13**	**679**	**12.5**		**70**	**38.6**	**16:09**	**17**	**3**	**5**	**8**	**4**	**1**	**0**	**1**	**16:37**

NHL All-Rookie Team (2004)

Signed as a free agent by **Leksands** (Sweden-2), September 19, 2004.

RYPIEN, Rick

(RIH-pihn, RIHK) **VAN.**

Center. Shoots right. 5'11", 181 lbs. Born, Coleman, Alta, May 16, 1984.

Season	Club	League	GP	G	A	Pts	PIM	PP	SH	GW	S	%	+/-	TF	F%	Min	GP	G	A	Pts	PIM	PP	SH	GW	Min
			Regular Season														**Playoffs**								
2001-02	Crowsnest Pass	AJHL	57	12	10	22	143	....	....	....	....	....	....	....	....	....	....	....	....	....	....	....	....	....	....
	Regina Pats	WHL	1	0	0	0	0	....	....	....	....	....	....	....	....	....	....	....	....	....	....	....	....	....	....
2002-03	Regina Pats	WHL	50	6	12	18	159	....	....	....	....	....	....	....	....	....	5	1	1	2	21	....	....	....	....
2003-04	Regina Pats	WHL	65	19	26	45	186	....	....	....	....	....	....	....	....	....	4	0	1	1	18	....	....	....	....
2004-05	Regina Pats	WHL	63	22	29	51	148	....	....	....	....	....	....	....	....	....	....	....	....	....	....	....	....	....	....
	Manitoba Moose	AHL	8	1	1	2	5	....	....	....	....	....	....	....	....	....	14	0	0	0	35	....	....	....	....
2005-06	**Vancouver**	**NHL**	**5**	**1**	**0**	**1**	**4**	**0**	**0**	**0**	**6**	**16.7**	**1**	**22**	**36.4**	**6:19**	....	....	....	....	....	....	....	....	....
	Manitoba Moose	AHL	49	9	6	15	122	....	....	....	....	....	....	....	....	....	13	1	1	2	22	....	....	....	....
2006-07	**Vancouver**	**NHL**	**2**	**0**	**0**	**0**	**5**	**0**	**0**	**0**	**0**	**0.0**	**0**	**6**	**66.7**	**4:46**	....	....	....	....	....	....	....	....	....
	Manitoba Moose	AHL	14	3	3	6	35	....	....	....	....	....	....	....	....	....	....	....	....	....	....	....	....	....	....
	NHL Totals		**7**	**1**	**0**	**1**	**9**	**0**	**0**	**0**	**6**	**16.7**		**28**	**42.9**	**5:53**	....	....	....	....	....	....	....	....	....

Signed to an ATO (tryout) contract by **Manitoba** (AHL), March 22, 2005. Signed as a free agent by **Vancouver**, November 9, 2005. • Missed majority of 2006-07 season recovering from recurring groin injury.

RYZNAR, Jason

(RIHZ-nuhr, JAY-suhn) **N.J.**

Left wing. Shoots left. 6'4", 205 lbs. Born, Anchorage, AK, February 19, 1983. New Jersey's 3rd choice, 64th overall, in 2002 Entry Draft.

Season	Club	League	GP	G	A	Pts	PIM	PP	SH	GW	S	%	+/-	TF	F%	Min	GP	G	A	Pts	PIM	PP	SH	GW	Min
99-2000	USNTDP	NAHL	52	5	10	15	22	....	....	....	....	....	....	....	....	....	3	1	1	2	4	....	....	....	....
2000-01	USNTDP	U-18	42	11	14	25	71	....	....	....	....	....	....	....	....	....	....	....	....	....	....	....	....	....	....
	USNTDP	USHL	24	4	3	7	31	....	....	....	....	....	....	....	....	....	....	....	....	....	....	....	....	....	....
2001-02	U. of Michigan	CCHA	40	9	7	16	22	....	....	....	....	....	....	....	....	....	....	....	....	....	....	....	....	....	....
2002-03	U. of Michigan	CCHA	34	7	9	16	24	....	....	....	....	....	....	....	....	....	....	....	....	....	....	....	....	....	....
2003-04	U. of Michigan	CCHA	36	6	11	17	28	....	....	....	....	....	....	....	....	....	....	....	....	....	....	....	....	....	....
2004-05	U. of Michigan	CCHA	36	6	17	23	46	....	....	....	....	....	....	....	....	....	....	....	....	....	....	....	....	....	....
2005-06	**New Jersey**	**NHL**	**8**	**0**	**0**	**0**	**2**	**0**	**0**	**0**	**1**	**0.0**	**–1**	**0**	**0.0**	**5:19**	....	....	....	....	....	....	....	....	....
	Albany River Rats	AHL	59	7	18	25	52	....	....	....	....	....	....	....	....	....	....	....	....	....	....	....	....	....	....
2006-07	Lowell Devils	AHL	55	5	5	10	25	....	....	....	....	....	....	....	....	....	....	....	....	....	....	....	....	....	....
	NHL Totals		**8**	**0**	**0**	**0**	**2**	**0**	**0**	**0**	**1**	**0.0**		**0**	**0.0**	**5:19**	....	....	....	....	....	....	....	....	....

SAFRONOV, Kirill

(sah-FRAW-nawf, kih-RIHL) **NSH.**

Defense. Shoots left. 6'2", 215 lbs. Born, Leningrad, USSR, February 26, 1981. Phoenix's 2nd choice, 19th overall, in 1999 Entry Draft.

Season	Club	League	GP	G	A	Pts	PIM	PP	SH	GW	S	%	+/-	TF	F%	Min	GP	G	A	Pts	PIM	PP	SH	GW	Min
1996-97	St. Petersburg 2	Russia-3	9	0	0	0	6	....	....	....	....	....	....	....	....	....	....	....	....	....	....	....	....	....	....
	St. Petersburg	Russia	1	0	0	0	0	....	....	....	....	....	....	....	....	....	....	....	....	....	....	....	....	....	....
1997-98	St. Petersburg 2	Russia-3	34	4	3	7	36	....	....	....	....	....	....	....	....	....	....	....	....	....	....	....	....	....	....
	St. Petersburg	Russia	9	0	1	1	4	....	....	....	....	....	....	....	....	....	1	0	0	0	0	....	....	....	....
1998-99	St. Petersburg 2	Russia-4	4	2	1	3	2	....	....	....	....	....	....	....	....	....	....	....	....	....	....	....	....	....	....
	St. Petersburg	Russia	45	1	3	4	32	....	....	....	....	....	....	....	....	....	....	....	....	....	....	....	....	....	....
99-2000	Quebec Remparts	QMJHL	55	11	32	43	95	....	....	....	....	....	....	....	....	....	11	2	4	6	14	....	....	....	....
2000-01	Springfield	AHL	65	5	13	18	77	....	....	....	....	....	....	....	....	....	....	....	....	....	....	....	....	....	....
2001-02	**Phoenix**	**NHL**	**1**	**0**	**0**	**0**	**0**	**0**	**0**	**0**	**0**	**0.0**	**–2**	**0**	**0.0**	**6:08**	....	....	....	....	....	....	....	....	....
	Springfield	AHL	68	3	19	22	26	....	....	....	....	....	....	....	....	....	....	....	....	....	....	....	....	....	....
	Atlanta	**NHL**	**2**	**0**	**0**	**0**	**2**	**0**	**0**	**0**	**2**	**0.0**	**–3**	**0**	**0.0**	**21:11**	....	....	....	....	....	....	....	....	....
	Chicago Wolves	AHL	8	0	2	2	2	....	....	....	....	....	....	....	....	....	25	2	6	8	8	....	....	....	....
2002-03	**Atlanta**	**NHL**	**32**	**2**	**2**	**4**	**14**	**0**	**0**	**0**	**21**	**9.5**	**–10**	**1**	**0.0**	**15:02**	....	....	....	....	....	....	....	....	....
	Chicago Wolves	AHL	44	4	15	19	29	....	....	....	....	....	....	....	....	....	9	1	2	3	4	....	....	....	....
2003-04	Chicago Wolves	AHL	21	1	4	5	8	....	....	....	....	....	....	....	....	....	....	....	....	....	....	....	....	....	....
	Milwaukee	AHL	59	4	16	20	41	....	....	....	....	....	....	....	....	....	21	0	6	6	20	....	....	....	....
2004-05	Yaroslavl	Russia	19	0	1	1	49	....	....	....	....	....	....	....	....	....	....	....	....	....	....	....	....	....	....
	Voskresensk	Russia	35	5	8	13	34	....	....	....	....	....	....	....	....	....	....	....	....	....	....	....	....	....	....
2005-06	St. Petersburg	Russia	46	1	13	14	38	....	....	....	....	....	....	....	....	....	2	0	0	0	0	....	....	....	....
2006-07	St. Petersburg	Russia	46	2	2	4	68	....	....	....	....	....	....	....	....	....	3	0	0	0	2	....	....	....	....
	NHL Totals		**35**	**2**	**2**	**4**	**16**	**0**	**0**	**0**	**23**	**8.7**		**1**	**0.0**	**15:08**	....	....	....	....	....	....	....	....	....

Traded to **Atlanta** by **Phoenix** with the rights to Ruslan Zainullin and Phoenix's 5th round choice (Patrick Dwyer) in 2002 Entry Draft for Darcy Hordichuk and Atlanta's 4th (Lance Monych) and 5th (John Zeiler) round choices in 2002 Entry Draft, March 19, 2002. Traded to **Nashville** by **Atlanta** with Simon Gamache for Ben Simon and Tomas Kloucek, December 2, 2003. Signed as a free agent by **Yaroslavl** (Russia), June 13, 2004. Signed as a free agent by **Voskresensk** (Russia), December, 2004. Signed as a free agent by **St. Petersburg** (Russia), July 22, 2005.

ST. JACQUES, Bruno

(SAINT ZHAWK, BROO-noh) **CHI.**

Defense. Shoots left. 6'2", 216 lbs. Born, Montreal, Que., August 22, 1980. Philadelphia's 12th choice, 253rd overall, in 1998 Entry Draft.

Season	Club	League	GP	G	A	Pts	PIM	PP	SH	GW	S	%	+/-	TF	F%	Min	GP	G	A	Pts	PIM	PP	SH	GW	Min
1996-97	Mtl-Bourassa	QAAA	40	5	8	13	....	....	....	....	....	....	....	....	....	....	16	0	7	7	....	....	....	....	....
1997-98	Baie-Comeau	QMJHL	63	1	11	12	140	....	....	....	....	....	....	....	....	....	....	....	....	....	....	....	....	....	....
1998-99	Baie-Comeau	QMJHL	49	8	13	21	85	....	....	....	....	....	....	....	....	....	....	....	....	....	....	....	....	....	....
99-2000	Baie-Comeau	QMJHL	60	8	28	36	120	....	....	....	....	....	....	....	....	....	6	0	2	2	10	....	....	....	....
	Philadelphia	AHL	3	0	1	1	0	....	....	....	....	....	....	....	....	....	1	0	0	0	0	....	....	....	....
2000-01	Philadelphia	AHL	45	1	16	17	83	....	....	....	....	....	....	....	....	....	10	1	0	1	16	....	....	....	....
2001-02	**Philadelphia**	**NHL**	**7**	**0**	**0**	**0**	**2**	**0**	**0**	**0**	**4**	**0.0**	**4**	**0**	**0.0**	**13:51**	....	....	....	....	....	....	....	....	....
	Philadelphia	AHL	55	3	11	14	59	....	....	....	....	....	....	....	....	....	4	0	0	0	0	....	....	....	....
2002-03	**Philadelphia**	**NHL**	**6**	**0**	**0**	**0**	**2**	**0**	**0**	**0**	**5**	**0.0**	**–1**	**0**	**0.0**	**14:35**	....	....	....	....	....	....	....	....	....
	Philadelphia	AHL	30	0	7	7	46	....	....	....	....	....	....	....	....	....	....	....	....	....	....	....	....	....	....
	Carolina	**NHL**	**18**	**2**	**5**	**7**	**12**	**0**	**0**	**0**	**14**	**14.3**	**–3**	**0**	**0.0**	**18:15**	....	....	....	....	....	....	....	....	....
	Lowell	AHL	8	1	1	2	8	....	....	....	....	....	....	....	....	....	....	....	....	....	....	....	....	....	....
2003-04	**Carolina**	**NHL**	**35**	**0**	**2**	**2**	**31**	**0**	**0**	**0**	**16**	**0.0**	**–7**	**0**	**0.0**	**11:50**	....	....	....	....	....	....	....	....	....
	Lowell	AHL	6	0	0	0	8	....	....	....	....	....	....	....	....	....	....	....	....	....	....	....	....	....	....
2004-05	Lowell	AHL	68	2	12	14	60	....	....	....	....	....	....	....	....	....	11	1	4	5	4	....	....	....	....
2005-06	**Anaheim**	**NHL**	**1**	**1**	**0**	**1**	**0**	**0**	**0**	**0**	**2**	**50.0**	**1**	**0**	**0.0**	**13:53**	....	....	....	....	....	....	....	....	....
	Portland Pirates	AHL	60	6	19	25	55	....	....	....	....	....	....	....	....	....	14	3	4	7	18	....	....	....	....
2006-07	Portland Pirates	AHL	25	1	8	9	26	....	....	....	....	....	....	....	....	....	....	....	....	....	....	....	....	....	....
	Norfolk Admirals	AHL	37	4	8	12	33	....	....	....	....	....	....	....	....	....	6	0	2	2	10	....	....	....	....
	NHL Totals		**67**	**3**	**7**	**10**	**47**	**0**	**0**	**0**	**41**	**7.3**		**0**	**0.0**	**14:03**	....	....	....	....	....	....	....	....	....

Traded to **Carolina** by **Philadelphia** with Pavel Brendl for Sami Kapanen and Ryan Bast, February 7, 2003. • Missed majority of 2003-04 season recovering from abdominal injury suffered in game vs. Philadelphia, November 28, 2003. Traded to **Anaheim** by **Carolina** for Craig Adams, October 3, 2005. Traded to **Chicago** by **Anaheim** with Pierre Parenteau for Sebastien Caron, Matt Keith and Chris Durno, December 28, 2006.

ST. LOUIS, Martin

(SAINT loo-EE, mahr-TEHN) **T.B.**

Right wing. Shoots left. 5'9", 185 lbs. Born, Laval, Que., June 18, 1975.

Season	Club	League	GP	G	A	Pts	PIM	PP	SH	GW	S	%	+/-	TF	F%	Min	GP	G	A	Pts	PIM	PP	SH	GW	Min
1991-92	Laval-Laurentides	QAAA	42	29	*74	*103	38	....	....	....	....	....	....	....	....	....	12	7	15	22	16	....	....	....	....
1992-93	Hawkesbury	CJHL	31	37	50	87	70	....	....	....	....	....	....	....	....	....	....	....	....	....	....	....	....	....	....
1993-94	U. of Vermont	ECAC	33	15	36	51	24	....	....	....	....	....	....	....	....	....	....	....	....	....	....	....	....	....	....
1994-95	U. of Vermont	ECAC	35	23	48	71	36	....	....	....	....	....	....	....	....	....	....	....	....	....	....	....	....	....	....
1995-96	U. of Vermont	ECAC	35	29	56	85	38	....	....	....	....	....	....	....	....	....	....	....	....	....	....	....	....	....	....
1996-97	U. of Vermont	ECAC	36	24	*36	60	65	....	....	....	....	....	....	....	....	....	....	....	....	....	....	....	....	....	....
1997-98	Cleveland	IHL	56	16	34	50	24	....	....	....	....	....	....	....	....	....	....	....	....	....	....	....	....	....	....
	Saint John Flames	AHL	25	15	11	26	20	....	....	....	....	....	....	....	....	....	20	5	15	20	16	....	....	....	....
1998-99	**Calgary**	**NHL**	**13**	**1**	**1**	**2**	**10**	**0**	**0**	**0**	**14**	**7.1**	**–2**	**0**	**0.0**	**8:15**	....	....	....	....	....	....	....	....	....
	Saint John Flames	AHL	53	28	34	62	30	....	....	....	....	....	....	....	....	....	7	4	4	8	2	....	....	....	....
99-2000	**Calgary**	**NHL**	**56**	**3**	**15**	**18**	**22**	**0**	**0**	**1**	**73**	**4.1**	**–5**	**3**	**0.0**	**14:41**	....	....	....	....	....	....	....	....	....
	Saint John Flames	AHL	17	15	11	26	14	....	....	....	....	....	....	....	....	....	....	....	....	....	....	....	....	....	....
2000-01	**Tampa Bay**	**NHL**	**78**	**18**	**22**	**40**	**12**	**3**	**3**	**4**	**141**	**12.8**	**–4**	**48**	**41.7**	**15:14**	....	....	....	....	....	....	....	....	....
2001-02	**Tampa Bay**	**NHL**	**53**	**16**	**19**	**35**	**20**	**6**	**1**	**2**	**105**	**15.2**	**4**	**33**	**39.4**	**18:41**	....	....	....	....	....	....	....	....	....
2002-03	**Tampa Bay**	**NHL**	**82**	**33**	**37**	**70**	**32**	**12**	**3**	**5**	**201**	**16.4**	**10**	**37**	**37.8**	**19:43**	**11**	**7**	**5**	**12**	**0**	**1**	**2**	**3**	**22:21**
2003-04♦	**Tampa Bay**	**NHL**	**82**	**38**	***56**	***94**	**24**	**8**	**8**	**7**	**212**	**17.9**	**35**	**24**	**33.3**	**20:35**	**23**	**9**	***15**	**24**	**14**	**3**	**1**	**3**	**22:52**
2004-05	Lausanne HC	Swiss	23	9	16	25	16	....	....	....	....	....	....	....	....	....	....	....	....	....	....	....	....	....	....

			Regular Season														Playoffs								
Season	Club	League	GP	G	A	Pts	PIM	PP	SH	GW	S	%	+/-	TF	F%	Min	GP	G	A	Pts	PIM	PP	SH	GW	Min
2005-06	**Tampa Bay**	**NHL**	**80**	**31**	**30**	**61**	**38**	**9**	**3**	**7**	**221**	**14.0**	**–3**	**13**	**23.1**	**20:59**	**5**	**4**	**0**	**4**	**2**	**1**	**0**	**1**	**22:53**
	Canada	Olympics	6	2	1	3	0	....	....	....	....	....	....	....	....	....	....	....	....	....	....	....	....	....	....
2006-07	**Tampa Bay**	**NHL**	**82**	**43**	**59**	**102**	**28**	**14**	**5**	**7**	**273**	**15.8**	**7**	**20**	**35.0**	**24:09**	**6**	**3**	**5**	**8**	**8**	**1**	**0**	**0**	**28:07**
	NHL Totals		**526**	**183**	**239**	**422**	**186**	**52**	**23**	**33**	**1240**	**14.8**		**178**	**36.5**	**19:09**	**45**	**23**	**25**	**48**	**24**	**6**	**3**	**7**	**23:27**

ECAC First All-Star Team (1995, 1996, 1997) • ECAC Player of the Year (1995) • NCAA East First All-American Team (1995, 1996, 1997) • NCAA Championship All-Tournament Team (1996) • NHL First All-Star Team (2004) • Art Ross Trophy (2004) • Lester B. Pearson Award (2004) • Hart Memorial Trophy (2004) • NHL Second All-Star Team (2007)

Played in NHL All-Star Game (2003, 2004, 2007)

Signed as a free agent by **Calgary**, February 19, 1998. Signed as a free agent by **Tampa Bay**, July 31, 2000. Signed as a free agent by **Lausanne** (Swiss), November 4, 2004.

ST. PIERRE, Martin

(SAINT PEE-aihr, mahr-TEHN) **CHI.**

Center. Shoots left. 5'9", 185 lbs. Born, Ottawa, Ont., August 11, 1983.

Season	Club	League	GP	G	A	Pts	PIM	PP	SH	GW	S	%	+/-	TF	F%	Min	GP	G	A	Pts	PIM	PP	SH	GW	Min
2000-01	Guelph Storm	OHL	68	20	49	69	40	....	....	....	....	....	....	....	....	....	4	0	0	0	4	....	....	....	....
2001-02	Guelph Storm	OHL	66	32	53	85	68	....	....	....	....	....	....	....	....	....	9	3	9	12	12	....	....	....	....
2002-03	Guelph Storm	OHL	55	11	45	56	74	....	....	....	....	....	....	....	....	....	11	5	11	16	4	....	....	....	....
2003-04	Guelph Storm	OHL	68	45	65	110	95	....	....	....	....	....	....	....	....	....	22	8	*27	*35	20	....	....	....	....
2004-05	Greenville	ECHL	45	14	39	53	55	....	....	....	....	....	....	....	....	....	7	2	5	7	6	....	....	....	....
	Edmonton	AHL	18	4	3	7	8	....	....	....	....	....	....	....	....	....	....	....	....	....	....	....	....	....	....
2005-06	**Chicago**	**NHL**	**2**	**0**	**0**	**0**	**0**	**0**	**0**	**0**	**1**	**0.0**	**–1**	**15**	**33.3**	**12:02**	....	....	....	....	....	....	....	....	....
	Norfolk Admirals	AHL	77	23	50	73	98	....	....	....	....	....	....	....	....	....	4	0	3	3	2	....	....	....	....
2006-07	**Chicago**	**NHL**	**14**	**1**	**3**	**4**	**8**	**1**	**0**	**0**	**13**	**7.7**	**–3**	**129**	**48.1**	**12:29**	....	....	....	....	....	....	....	....	....
	Norfolk Admirals	AHL	65	27	72	99	100	....	....	....	....	....	....	....	....	....	6	0	1	1	6	....	....	....	....
	NHL Totals		**16**	**1**	**3**	**4**	**8**	**1**	**0**	**0**	**14**	**7.1**		**144**	**46.5**	**12:26**	....	....	....	....	....	....	....	....	....

AHL All-Rookie Team (2006) • AHL First All-Star Team (2007)

Signed as a free agent by **Chicago**, November 3, 2005. Signed as a free agent by **Mytischi** (Russia), June 22, 2007.

SAKIC, Joe

(SAK-ihk, JOH) **COL.**

Center. Shoots left. 5'11", 195 lbs. Born, Burnaby, B.C., July 7, 1969. Quebec's 2nd choice, 15th overall, in 1987 Entry Draft.

Season	Club	League	GP	G	A	Pts	PIM	PP	SH	GW	S	%	+/-	TF	F%	Min	GP	G	A	Pts	PIM	PP	SH	GW	Min
1985-86	Burnaby	BCAHA	80	83	73	156	96	....	....	....	....	....	....	....	....	....	....	....	....	....	....	....	....	....	....
	Lethbridge	WHL	3	0	0	0	0	....	....	....	....	....	....	....	....	....	....	....	....	....	....	....	....	....	....
1986-87	Swift Current	WHL	72	60	73	133	31	....	....	....	....	....	....	....	....	....	4	0	1	1	0	....	....	....	....
1987-88	Swift Current	WHL	64	*78	82	*160	64	....	....	....	....	....	....	....	....	....	10	11	13	24	12	....	....	....	....
1988-89	**Quebec**	**NHL**	**70**	**23**	**39**	**62**	**24**	**10**	**0**	**2**	**148**	**15.5**	**–36**	....	....	....	....	....	....	....	....	....	....	....	....
1989-90	**Quebec**	**NHL**	**80**	**39**	**63**	**102**	**27**	**8**	**1**	**2**	**234**	**16.7**	**–40**	....	....	....	....	....	....	....	....	....	....	....	....
1990-91	**Quebec**	**NHL**	**80**	**48**	**61**	**109**	**24**	**12**	**3**	**7**	**245**	**19.6**	**–26**	....	....	....	....	....	....	....	....	....	....	....	....
1991-92	**Quebec**	**NHL**	**69**	**29**	**65**	**94**	**20**	**6**	**3**	**1**	**217**	**13.4**	**5**	....	....	....	....	....	....	....	....	....	....	....	....
1992-93	**Quebec**	**NHL**	**78**	**48**	**57**	**105**	**40**	**20**	**2**	**4**	**264**	**18.2**	**–3**	....	....	....	**6**	**3**	**3**	**6**	**2**	**1**	**0**	**0**	....
1993-94	**Quebec**	**NHL**	**84**	**28**	**64**	**92**	**18**	**10**	**1**	**9**	**279**	**10.0**	**–8**	....	....	....	....	....	....	....	....	....	....	....	....
1994-95	**Quebec**	**NHL**	**47**	**19**	**43**	**62**	**30**	**3**	**2**	**5**	**157**	**12.1**	**7**	....	....	....	**6**	**4**	**1**	**5**	**0**	**1**	**1**	**1**	....
1995-96♦	**Colorado**	**NHL**	**82**	**51**	**69**	**120**	**44**	**17**	**6**	**7**	**339**	**15.0**	**14**	....	....	....	**22**	***18**	**16**	***34**	**14**	**6**	**0**	**6**	....
1996-97	**Colorado**	**NHL**	**65**	**22**	**52**	**74**	**34**	**10**	**2**	**5**	**261**	**8.4**	**–10**	....	....	....	**17**	**8**	***17**	**25**	**14**	**3**	**0**	**0**	....
1997-98	**Colorado**	**NHL**	**64**	**27**	**36**	**63**	**50**	**12**	**1**	**2**	**254**	**10.6**	**0**	....	....	....	**6**	**2**	**3**	**5**	**6**	**0**	**1**	**2**	....
	Canada	Olympics	4	1	2	3	4	....	....	....	....	....	....	....	....	....	....	....	....	....	....	....	....	....	....
1998-99	**Colorado**	**NHL**	**73**	**41**	**55**	**96**	**29**	**12**	**5**	**6**	**255**	**16.1**	**23**	**1723**	**51.4**	**25:35**	**19**	**6**	**13**	**19**	**8**	**1**	**1**	**1**	**25:01**
99-2000	**Colorado**	**NHL**	**60**	**28**	**53**	**81**	**28**	**5**	**1**	**5**	**242**	**11.6**	**30**	**1392**	**53.8**	**23:16**	**17**	**2**	**7**	**9**	**8**	**2**	**0**	**0**	**23:50**
2000-01♦	**Colorado**	**NHL**	**82**	**54**	**64**	**118**	**30**	**19**	**3**	**12**	**332**	**16.3**	**45**	**2292**	**53.0**	**23:01**	**21**	***13**	**13**	***26**	**6**	**5**	**0**	**3**	**21:33**
2001-02	**Colorado**	**NHL**	**82**	**26**	**53**	**79**	**18**	**9**	**1**	**4**	**260**	**10.0**	**12**	**2148**	**52.2**	**22:01**	**21**	**9**	**10**	**19**	**4**	**4**	**0**	**1**	**22:44**
	Canada	Olympics	6	4	3	7	0	....	....	....	....	....	....	....	....	....	....	....	....	....	....	....	....	....	....
2002-03	**Colorado**	**NHL**	**58**	**26**	**32**	**58**	**24**	**8**	**0**	**1**	**190**	**13.7**	**4**	**1359**	**50.8**	**21:12**	**7**	**6**	**3**	**9**	**2**	**2**	**0**	**1**	**22:29**
2003-04	**Colorado**	**NHL**	**81**	**33**	**54**	**87**	**42**	**13**	**1**	**3**	**253**	**13.0**	**11**	**1705**	**52.6**	**20:16**	**11**	**7**	**5**	**12**	**8**	**1**	**1**	**2**	**21:15**
2004-05			DID NOT PLAY																						
2005-06	**Colorado**	**NHL**	**82**	**32**	**55**	**87**	**60**	**10**	**0**	**6**	**263**	**12.2**	**10**	**1669**	**52.5**	**19:55**	**9**	**4**	**5**	**9**	**6**	**1**	**0**	**1**	**21:38**
	Canada	Olympics	6	1	2	3	0	....	....	....	....	....	....	....	....	....	....	....	....	....	....	....	....	....	....
2006-07	**Colorado**	**NHL**	**82**	**36**	**64**	**100**	**46**	**16**	**0**	**4**	**258**	**14.0**	**2**	**1368**	**53.1**	**20:11**	....	....	....	....	....	....	....	....	....
	NHL Totals		**1319**	**610**	**979**	**1589**	**588**	**200**	**32**	**85**	**4451**	**13.7**		**13656**	**52.4**	**21:52**	**162**	**82**	**96**	**178**	**78**	**27**	**4**	**18**	**22:49**

WHL East Second All-Star Team (1987) • WHL East Rookie of the Year (1987) • WHL East Player of the Year (1987) • WHL East First All-Star Team (1988) • WHL Player of the Year (1988) • Canadian Major Junior Player of the Year (1988) • Conn Smythe Trophy (1996) • NHL First All-Star Team (2001, 2002, 2004) • Bud Light Plus/Minus Award (2001) (tied with Patrik Elias) • Lady Byng Memorial Trophy (2001) • Lester B. Pearson Award (2001) • Hart Memorial Trophy (2001) • Olympic Tournament MVP (2002)

Played in NHL All-Star Game (1990, 1991, 1992, 1993, 1994, 1996, 1998, 2000, 2001, 2002, 2004, 2007)

Transferred to **Colorado** after **Quebec** franchise relocated, June 21, 1995.

SALEI, Ruslan

(sah-LAY, roos-LAHN) **FLA.**

Defense. Shoots left. 6'1", 212 lbs. Born, Minsk, USSR, November 2, 1974. Anaheim's 1st choice, 9th overall, in 1996 Entry Draft.

Season	Club	League	GP	G	A	Pts	PIM	PP	SH	GW	S	%	+/-	TF	F%	Min	GP	G	A	Pts	PIM	PP	SH	GW	Min
1992-93	Dynamo Moscow	CIS	9	1	0	1	10	....	....	....	....	....	....	....	....	....	....	....	....	....	....	....	....	....	....
1993-94	Tivali Minsk	CIS	39	2	3	5	50	....	....	....	....	....	....	....	....	....	....	....	....	....	....	....	....	....	....
1994-95	Tivali Minsk	CIS	51	4	2	6	44	....	....	....	....	....	....	....	....	....	....	....	....	....	....	....	....	....	....
1995-96	Las Vegas	IHL	76	7	23	30	123	....	....	....	....	....	....	....	....	....	15	3	7	10	18	....	....	....	....
1996-97	**Anaheim**	**NHL**	**30**	**0**	**1**	**1**	**37**	**0**	**0**	**0**	**14**	**0.0**	**–8**	....	....	....	....	....	....	....	....	....	....	....	....
	Baltimore Bandits	AHL	12	1	4	5	12	....	....	....	....	....	....	....	....	....	....	....	....	....	....	....	....	....	....
	Las Vegas	IHL	8	0	2	2	24	....	....	....	....	....	....	....	....	....	3	2	1	3	6	....	....	....	....
1997-98	**Anaheim**	**NHL**	**66**	**5**	**10**	**15**	**70**	**1**	**0**	**0**	**104**	**4.8**	**7**	....	....	....	....	....	....	....	....	....	....	....	....
	Cincinnati	AHL	6	3	6	9	14	....	....	....	....	....	....	....	....	....	....	....	....	....	....	....	....	....	....
	Belarus	Olympics	7	1	0	1	4	....	....	....	....	....	....	....	....	....	....	....	....	....	....	....	....	....	....
1998-99	**Anaheim**	**NHL**	**74**	**2**	**14**	**16**	**65**	**1**	**0**	**0**	**123**	**1.6**	**1**	**0**	**0.0**	**22:03**	**3**	**0**	**0**	**0**	**4**	**0**	**0**	**0**	**15:40**
99-2000	**Anaheim**	**NHL**	**71**	**5**	**5**	**10**	**94**	**1**	**0**	**0**	**116**	**4.3**	**3**	**0**	**0.0**	**20:21**	....	....	....	....	....	....	....	....	....
2000-01	**Anaheim**	**NHL**	**50**	**1**	**5**	**6**	**70**	**0**	**0**	**0**	**73**	**1.4**	**–14**	**0**	**0.0**	**20:40**	....	....	....	....	....	....	....	....	....
2001-02	**Anaheim**	**NHL**	**82**	**4**	**7**	**11**	**97**	**0**	**0**	**1**	**96**	**4.2**	**–10**	**0**	**0.0**	**21:25**	....	....	....	....	....	....	....	....	....
	Belarus	Olympics	6	2	1	3	4	....	....	....	....	....	....	....	....	....	....	....	....	....	....	....	....	....	....
2002-03	**Anaheim**	**NHL**	**61**	**4**	**8**	**12**	**78**	**0**	**0**	**0**	**93**	**4.3**	**2**	**0**	**0.0**	**21:53**	**21**	**2**	**3**	**5**	**26**	**0**	**0**	**1**	**26:05**
2003-04	**Anaheim**	**NHL**	**82**	**4**	**11**	**15**	**110**	**0**	**1**	**2**	**145**	**2.8**	**–1**	**0**	**0.0**	**23:42**	....	....	....	....	....	....	....	....	....
2004-05	Ak Bars Kazan	Russia	35	8	12	20	36	....	....	....	....	....	....	....	....	....	4	0	0	0	2	....	....	....	....
2005-06	**Anaheim**	**NHL**	**78**	**1**	**18**	**19**	**114**	**0**	**0**	**0**	**108**	**0.9**	**17**	**2**	**100.0**	**22:31**	**16**	**3**	**2**	**5**	**18**	**0**	**0**	**1**	**22:08**
2006-07	**Florida**	**NHL**	**82**	**6**	**26**	**32**	**102**	**2**	**0**	**0**	**148**	**4.1**	**–13**	**0**	**0.0**	**23:20**	....	....	....	....	....	....	....	....	....
	NHL Totals		**676**	**32**	**105**	**137**	**837**	**5**	**1**	**3**	**1020**	**3.1**		**2**	**100.0**	**22:06**	**40**	**5**	**5**	**10**	**48**	**0**	**0**	**2**	**23:44**

Signed as a free agent by **Kazan** (Russia), October 20, 2004. Signed as a free agent by **Florida**, July 2, 2006.

SALMELAINEN, Tony

(sal-meh-LIGH-nehn, TOH-nee)

Left wing. Shoots right. 5'9", 185 lbs. Born, Espoo, Finland, August 8, 1981. Edmonton's 3rd choice, 41st overall, in 1999 Entry Draft.

Season	Club	League	GP	G	A	Pts	PIM	PP	SH	GW	S	%	+/-	TF	F%	Min	GP	G	A	Pts	PIM	PP	SH	GW	Min
1996-97	K-Espoo U18	Fin-U18	30	8	5	13	38	....	....	....	....	....	....	....	....	....	....	....	....	....	....	....	....	....	....
1997-98	K-Espoo U18	Fin-U18	5	2	2	4	10	....	....	....	....	....	....	....	....	....	....	....	....	....	....	....	....	....	....
	HIFK Helsinki U18	Fin-U18	28	23	16	39	30	....	....	....	....	....	....	....	....	....	....	....	....	....	....	....	....	....	....
	HIFK Helsinki Jr.	Fin-Jr.	5	0	0	0	0	....	....	....	....	....	....	....	....	....	....	....	....	....	....	....	....	....	....
1998-99	HIFK Helsinki U18	Fin-U18	6	5	4	9	16	....	....	....	....	....	....	....	....	....	2	1	2	3	12	....	....	....	....
	HIFK Helsinki Jr.	Fin-Jr.	31	23	18	41	55	....	....	....	....	....	....	....	....	....	....	....	....	....	....	....	....	....	....
99-2000	HIFK Helsinki Jr.	Fin-Jr.	1	0	1	1	0	....	....	....	....	....	....	....	....	....	....	....	....	....	....	....	....	....	....
	HIFK Helsinki	Finland	1	1	0	1	0	....	....	....	....	....	....	....	....	....	....	....	....	....	....	....	....	....	....
	HIFK Helsinki	EuroHL	1	0	0	0	0	....	....	....	....	....	....	....	....	....	....	....	....	....	....	....	....	....	....
2000-01	HIFK Helsinki Jr.	Fin-Jr.	3	3	3	6	0	....	....	....	....	....	....	....	....	....	....	....	....	....	....	....	....	....	....
	HIFK Helsinki	Finland	19	1	0	1	6	....	....	....	....	....	....	....	....	....	....	....	....	....	....	....	....	....	....
	Ilves Tampere Jr.	Fin-Jr.	3	1	2	3	2	....	....	....	....	....	....	....	....	....	....	....	....	....	....	....	....	....	....
	Ilves Tampere	Finland	26	3	10	13	4	....	....	....	....	....	....	....	....	....	3	0	0	0	0	....	....	....	....
2001-02	Ilves Tampere Jr.	Fin-Jr.	2	6	0	6	0	....	....	....	....	....	....	....	....	....	....	....	....	....	....	....	....	....	....
	Ilves Tampere	Finland	49	10	9	19	32	....	....	....	....	....	....	....	....	....	3	0	0	0	2	....	....	....	....
2002-03	Hamilton	AHL	67	14	19	33	14	....	....	....	....	....	....	....	....	....	17	6	8	14	0	....	....	....	....
2003-04	**Edmonton**	**NHL**	**13**	**0**	**1**	**1**	**4**	**0**	**0**	**0**	**17**	**0.0**	**–1**	**0**	**0.0**	**9:39**	....	....	....	....	....	....	....	....	....
	Toronto	AHL	58	19	25	44	27	....	....	....	....	....	....	....	....	....	3	0	1	1	0	....	....	....	....

			Regular Season													Playoffs								
Season	Club	League	GP	G	A	Pts	PIM	PP	SH	GW	S	%	+/-	TF	F%	Min	GP	G	A	Pts	PIM	PP	SH	GW	Min
2004-05	Edmonton	AHL	76	22	24	46	26	....	....	....	....	....	....	....	....	....	....	....	....	....	....	....	....	....	....
2005-06	HIFK Helsinki	Finland	53	*27	28	*55	63	....	....	....	....	....	....	....	....	....	12	4	2	6	36	....	....	....	....
2006-07	**Chicago**	**NHL**	**57**	**6**	**11**	**17**	**26**	**0**	**0**	**1**	**54**	**11.1**	**–3**	**1**	**0.0**	**9:52**	....	....	....	....	....	....	....	....	....
	NHL Totals		**70**	**6**	**12**	**18**	**30**	**0**	**0**	**1**	**71**	**8.5**		**1**	**0.0**	**9:50**	....	....	....	....	....	....	....	....	....

Traded to **Chicago** by **Edmonton** for Jaroslav Spacek, January 26, 2006. Traded to **Montreal** by **Chicago** with Jassen Cullimore for Sergei Samsonov, June 16, 2007.

SALO, Sami

(SA-loh, SA-mee) **VAN.**

Defense. Shoots right. 6'3", 215 lbs. Born, Turku, Finland, September 2, 1974. Ottawa's 7th choice, 239th overall, in 1996 Entry Draft.

Season	Club	League	GP	G	A	Pts	PIM	PP	SH	GW	S	%	+/-	TF	F%	Min	GP	G	A	Pts	PIM	PP	SH	GW	Min
1991-92	Kiekko-67 Jr.	Fin-Jr.	23	4	5	9	26	....	....	....	....	....	....	....	....	....	....	....	....	....	....	....	....	....	....
1992-93	Kiekko-67 Jr.	Fin-Jr.	21	9	4	13	4	....	....	....	....	....	....	....	....	....	....	....	....	....	....	....	....	....	....
1993-94	TPS Turku Jr.	Fin-Jr.	36	7	13	20	16	....	....	....	....	....	....	....	....	....	7	0	1	1	10	....	....	....	....
1994-95	TPS Turku Jr.	Fin-Jr.	14	1	3	4	6	....	....	....	....	....	....	....	....	....	....	....	....	....	....	....	....	....	....
	Kiekko-67 Turku	Finland-2	19	4	2	6	4	....	....	....	....	....	....	....	....	....	....	....	....	....	....	....	....	....	....
	TPS Turku	Finland	7	1	2	3	6	....	....	....	....	....	....	....	....	....	1	0	0	0	0	....	....	....	....
1995-96	TPS Turku	Finland	47	7	14	21	32	....	....	....	....	....	....	....	....	....	11	1	3	4	8	....	....	....	....
1996-97	TPS Turku	Finland	48	9	6	15	10	....	....	....	....	....	....	....	....	....	10	2	3	5	4	....	....	....	....
	TPS Turku	EuroHL	6	0	2	2	6	....	....	....	....	....	....	....	....	....	2	0	0	0	2	....	....	....	....
1997-98	Jokerit Helsinki	Finland	35	3	5	8	24	....	....	....	....	....	....	....	....	....	8	0	1	1	2	....	....	....	....
	Jokerit Helsinki	EuroHL	6	1	1	2	2	....	....	....	....	....	....	....	....	....	....	....	....	....	....	....	....	....	....
1998-99	**Ottawa**	**NHL**	**61**	**7**	**12**	**19**	**24**	**2**	**0**	**1**	**106**	**6.6**	**20**	**0**	**0.0**	**19:42**	**4**	**0**	**0**	**0**	**0**	**0**	**0**	**0**	**21:32**
	Detroit Vipers	IHL	5	0	2	2	0	....	....	....	....	....	....	....	....	....	....	....	....	....	....	....	....	....	....
99-2000	**Ottawa**	**NHL**	**37**	**6**	**8**	**14**	**2**	**3**	**0**	**1**	**85**	**7.1**	**6**	**0**	**0.0**	**20:18**	**6**	**1**	**1**	**2**	**0**	**1**	**0**	**0**	**24:11**
2000-01	**Ottawa**	**NHL**	**31**	**2**	**16**	**18**	**10**	**1**	**0**	**0**	**61**	**3.3**	**9**	**0**	**0.0**	**19:44**	**4**	**0**	**0**	**0**	**0**	**0**	**0**	**0**	**22:30**
2001-02	**Ottawa**	**NHL**	**66**	**4**	**14**	**18**	**14**	**1**	**1**	**2**	**122**	**3.3**	**1**	**0**	**0.0**	**19:52**	**12**	**2**	**1**	**3**	**4**	**0**	**0**	**0**	**20:23**
	Finland	Olympics	4	0	0	0	0	....	....	....	....	....	....	....	....	....	....	....	....	....	....	....	....	....	....
2002-03	**Vancouver**	**NHL**	**79**	**9**	**21**	**30**	**10**	**4**	**0**	**1**	**126**	**7.1**	**9**	**0**	**0.0**	**20:08**	**12**	**1**	**3**	**4**	**0**	**0**	**0**	**0**	**20:52**
2003-04	**Vancouver**	**NHL**	**74**	**7**	**19**	**26**	**22**	**5**	**0**	**2**	**143**	**4.9**	**8**	**1**	**100.0**	**22:14**	**7**	**1**	**2**	**3**	**2**	**1**	**0**	**0**	**22:59**
2004-05	Frolunda	Sweden	41	6	8	14	18	....	....	....	....	....	....	....	....	....	14	1	6	7	2	....	....	....	....
2005-06	**Vancouver**	**NHL**	**59**	**10**	**23**	**33**	**38**	**9**	**0**	**2**	**140**	**7.1**	**9**	**0**	**0.0**	**24:30**	....	....	....	....	....	....	....	....	....
	Finland	Olympics	6	1	3	4	0	....	....	....	....	....	....	....	....	....	....	....	....	....	....	....	....	....	....
2006-07	**Vancouver**	**NHL**	**67**	**14**	**23**	**37**	**26**	**5**	**0**	**6**	**143**	**9.8**	**21**	**0**	**0.0**	**21:27**	**10**	**0**	**1**	**1**	**4**	**0**	**0**	**0**	**25:53**
	NHL Totals		**474**	**59**	**136**	**195**	**146**	**30**	**1**	**15**	**926**	**6.4**		**1**	**100.0**	**21:05**	**55**	**5**	**8**	**13**	**10**	**2**	**0**	**0**	**22:28**

NHL All-Rookie Team (1999)

• Missed majority of 1999-2000 season recovering from wrist injury suffered in game vs. Philadelphia, November 28, 1999. • Missed majority of 2000-01 season recovering from shoulder injury suffered in game vs. Atlanta, December 14, 2000. Traded to **Vancouver** by **Ottawa** for Peter Schaefer, September 21, 2002. Signed as a free agent by **Frolunda** (Sweden), September 24, 2004.

SALVADOR, Bryce

(SAL-vuh-dohr, BRIGHS) **ST.L.**

Defense. Shoots left. 6'2", 222 lbs. Born, Brandon, Man., February 11, 1976. Tampa Bay's 6th choice, 138th overall, in 1994 Entry Draft.

Season	Club	League	GP	G	A	Pts	PIM	PP	SH	GW	S	%	+/-	TF	F%	Min	GP	G	A	Pts	PIM	PP	SH	GW	Min
1991-92	Brandon	MAHA	52	6	23	29	38	....	....	....	....	....	....	....	....	....	....	....	....	....	....	....	....	....	....
1992-93	Lethbridge	WHL	64	1	4	5	29	....	....	....	....	....	....	....	....	....	4	0	0	0	0	....	....	....	....
1993-94	Lethbridge	WHL	61	4	14	18	36	....	....	....	....	....	....	....	....	....	9	0	1	1	2	....	....	....	....
1994-95	Lethbridge	WHL	67	1	9	10	88	....	....	....	....	....	....	....	....	....	....	....	....	....	....	....	....	....	....
1995-96	Lethbridge	WHL	56	4	12	16	75	....	....	....	....	....	....	....	....	....	3	0	1	1	2	....	....	....	....
1996-97	Lethbridge	WHL	63	8	32	40	81	....	....	....	....	....	....	....	....	....	19	0	7	7	14	....	....	....	....
1997-98	Worcester IceCats	AHL	46	2	8	10	74	....	....	....	....	....	....	....	....	....	11	0	1	1	45	....	....	....	....
1998-99	Worcester IceCats	AHL	69	5	13	18	129	....	....	....	....	....	....	....	....	....	4	0	1	1	2	....	....	....	....
99-2000	Worcester IceCats	AHL	55	0	13	13	53	....	....	....	....	....	....	....	....	....	9	0	1	1	2	....	....	....	....
2000-01	**St. Louis**	**NHL**	**75**	**2**	**8**	**10**	**69**	**0**	**0**	**1**	**60**	**3.3**	**–4**	**1**	**0.0**	**16:38**	**14**	**2**	**0**	**2**	**18**	**0**	**0**	**1**	**14:41**
2001-02	**St. Louis**	**NHL**	**66**	**5**	**7**	**12**	**78**	**1**	**0**	**2**	**37**	**13.5**	**3**	**0**	**0.0**	**16:55**	**10**	**0**	**1**	**1**	**4**	**0**	**0**	**0**	**12:34**
2002-03	**St. Louis**	**NHL**	**71**	**2**	**8**	**10**	**95**	**1**	**0**	**0**	**73**	**2.7**	**7**	**0**	**0.0**	**18:57**	**7**	**0**	**0**	**0**	**2**	**0**	**0**	**0**	**17:17**
2003-04	**St. Louis**	**NHL**	**69**	**3**	**5**	**8**	**47**	**0**	**0**	**1**	**60**	**5.0**	**–4**	**0**	**0.0**	**17:29**	**5**	**0**	**0**	**0**	**2**	**0**	**0**	**0**	**14:31**
	Worcester IceCats	AHL	2	0	1	1	0	....	....	....	....	....	....	....	....	....	....	....	....	....	....	....	....	....	....
2004-05	Missouri	UHL	7	0	0	0	16	....	....	....	....	....	....	....	....	....	3	0	0	0	0	....	....	....	....
2005-06	**St. Louis**	**NHL**	**46**	**1**	**4**	**5**	**26**	**0**	**0**	**0**	**23**	**4.3**	**–24**	**1**	**0.0**	**19:48**	....	....	....	....	....	....	....	....	....
2006-07	**St. Louis**	**NHL**	**64**	**2**	**5**	**7**	**55**	**0**	**0**	**0**	**40**	**5.0**	**–5**	**0**	**0.0**	**19:44**	....	....	....	....	....	....	....	....	....
	NHL Totals		**391**	**15**	**37**	**52**	**370**	**2**	**0**	**4**	**293**	**5.1**		**2**	**0.0**	**18:08**	**36**	**2**	**1**	**3**	**26**	**0**	**0**	**1**	**14:35**

Signed as a free agent by **St. Louis**, December 16, 1996. Signed as a free agent by **Missouri** (UHL), March 11, 2005.

SAMSONOV, Sergei

(sam-SAWN-nahf, SAIR-gay) **CHI.**

Left wing. Shoots right. 5'8", 188 lbs. Born, Moscow, USSR, October 27, 1978. Boston's 2nd choice, 8th overall, in 1997 Entry Draft.

Season	Club	League	GP	G	A	Pts	PIM	PP	SH	GW	S	%	+/-	TF	F%	Min	GP	G	A	Pts	PIM	PP	SH	GW	Min
1994-95	CSKA Moscow 2	CIS-2	50	110	72	182	....	....	....	....	....	....	....	....	....	....	....	....	....	....	....	....	....	....	....
	CSKA Moscow	CIS	13	2	2	4	14	....	....	....	....	....	....	....	....	....	2	0	0	0	0	....	....	....	....
1995-96	CSKA Moscow	CIS	51	21	17	38	12	....	....	....	....	....	....	....	....	....	3	1	1	2	4	....	....	....	....
1996-97	Detroit Vipers	IHL	73	29	35	64	18	....	....	....	....	....	....	....	....	....	19	8	4	12	12	....	....	....	....
1997-98	**Boston**	**NHL**	**81**	**22**	**25**	**47**	**8**	**7**	**0**	**3**	**159**	**13.8**	**9**	....	....	....	**6**	**2**	**5**	**7**	**0**	**0**	**0**	**1**	....
1998-99	**Boston**	**NHL**	**79**	**25**	**26**	**51**	**18**	**6**	**0**	**8**	**160**	**15.6**	**–6**	**0**	**0.0**	**16:23**	**11**	**3**	**1**	**4**	**0**	**0**	**0**	**0**	**16:11**
99-2000	**Boston**	**NHL**	**77**	**19**	**26**	**45**	**4**	**6**	**0**	**3**	**145**	**13.1**	**–6**	**3**	**0.0**	**16:32**	....	....	....	....	....	....	....	....	....
2000-01	**Boston**	**NHL**	**82**	**29**	**46**	**75**	**18**	**3**	**0**	**3**	**215**	**13.5**	**6**	**14**	**42.9**	**19:23**	....	....	....	....	....	....	....	....	....
2001-02	**Boston**	**NHL**	**74**	**29**	**41**	**70**	**27**	**3**	**0**	**4**	**192**	**15.1**	**21**	**1**	**0.0**	**18:47**	**6**	**2**	**2**	**4**	**0**	**0**	**0**	**0**	**17:41**
	Russia	Olympics	6	1	2	3	4	....	....	....	....	....	....	....	....	....	....	....	....	....	....	....	....	....	....
2002-03	**Boston**	**NHL**	**8**	**5**	**6**	**11**	**2**	**1**	**0**	**3**	**23**	**21.7**	**8**	**0**	**0.0**	**20:20**	**5**	**0**	**2**	**2**	**0**	**0**	**0**	**0**	**17:07**
2003-04	**Boston**	**NHL**	**58**	**17**	**23**	**40**	**4**	**3**	**0**	**5**	**132**	**12.9**	**12**	**4**	**25.0**	**17:27**	**7**	**2**	**5**	**7**	**0**	**0**	**0**	**0**	**17:18**
2004-05	Dynamo Moscow	Russia	3	1	0	1	0	....	....	....	....	....	....	....	....	....	3	1	2	3	0	....	....	....	....
2005-06	**Boston**	**NHL**	**55**	**18**	**19**	**37**	**22**	**6**	**0**	**1**	**107**	**16.8**	**–3**	**1**	**100.0**	**16:53**	....	....	....	....	....	....	....	....	....
	Edmonton	**NHL**	**19**	**5**	**11**	**16**	**6**	**4**	**0**	**0**	**36**	**13.9**	**0**	**2**	**0.0**	**15:26**	**24**	**4**	**11**	**15**	**14**	**1**	**0**	**0**	**14:30**
2006-07	**Montreal**	**NHL**	**63**	**9**	**17**	**26**	**10**	**0**	**0**	**0**	**114**	**7.9**	**–4**	**14**	**14.3**	**13:59**	....	....	....	....	....	....	....	....	....
	NHL Totals		**596**	**178**	**240**	**418**	**119**	**39**	**0**	**30**	**1283**	**13.9**		**39**	**25.6**	**17:08**	**59**	**13**	**26**	**39**	**14**	**1**	**0**	**1**	**15:50**

Garry F. Longman Memorial Trophy (Rookie of the Year – IHL) (1997) • NHL All-Rookie Team (1998) • Calder Memorial Trophy (1998)

Played in NHL All-Star Game (2001)

• Missed majority of 2002-03 season recovering from wrist injury suffered in game vs. Columbus, October 18, 2002. Signed as a free agent by **Dynamo Moscow** (Russia), February 2, 2005. Traded to **Edmonton** by **Boston** for Marty Reasoner, Yan Stastny and Edmonton's 2nd round choice (Milan Lucic) in 2006 Entry Draft, March 9, 2006. Signed as a free agent by **Montreal**, July 12, 2006. Traded to **Chicago** by **Montreal** for Jassen Cullimore and Tony Salmelainen, June 16, 2007.

SAMUELSSON, Martin

(SAM-yuhl-suhn, MAHR-tihn) **BOS.**

Right wing. Shoots left. 6'2", 210 lbs. Born, Upplands-Vasby, Sweden, January 25, 1982. Boston's 2nd choice, 27th overall, in 2000 Entry Draft.

Season	Club	League	GP	G	A	Pts	PIM	PP	SH	GW	S	%	+/-	TF	F%	Min	GP	G	A	Pts	PIM	PP	SH	GW	Min
1996-97	Hammarby Jr.	Swe-Jr.	6	1	1	2	0	....	....	....	....	....	....	....	....	....	....	....	....	....	....	....	....	....	....
1997-98	Hammarby Jr.	Swe-Jr.	20	13	12	25	....	....	....	....	....	....	....	....	....	....	....	....	....	....	....	....	....	....	....
	Hammarby	Sweden-2	2	0	0	0	0	....	....	....	....	....	....	....	....	....	....	....	....	....	....	....	....	....	....
1998-99	Malmo Jr.	Swe-Jr.	31	18	13	31	10	....	....	....	....	....	....	....	....	....	....	....	....	....	....	....	....	....	....
99-2000	MoDo U18	Swe-U18	6	3	0	3	4	....	....	....	....	....	....	....	....	....	....	....	....	....	....	....	....	....	....
	Malmo Jr.	Swe-Jr.	19	9	8	17	18	....	....	....	....	....	....	....	....	....	2	1	0	1	2	....	....	....	....
2000-01	Hammarby	Sweden-2	24	13	4	17	8	....	....	....	....	....	....	....	....	....	5	0	0	0	2	....	....	....	....
	Hammarby Jr.	Swe-Jr.	1	0	1	1	0	....	....	....	....	....	....	....	....	....	....	....	....	....	....	....	....	....	....
2001-02	Hammarby Jr.	Swe-Jr.	2	5	2	7	2	....	....	....	....	....	....	....	....	....	....	....	....	....	....	....	....	....	....
	Hammarby	Sweden-2	44	13	10	23	45	....	....	....	....	....	....	....	....	....	2	0	0	0	2	....	....	....	....
2002-03	**Boston**	**NHL**	**8**	**0**	**1**	**1**	**2**	**0**	**0**	**0**	**3**	**0.0**	**–1**	**0**	**0.0**	**11:42**	....	....	....	....	....	....	....	....	....
	Providence Bruins	AHL	64	24	15	39	34	....	....	....	....	....	....	....	....	....	4	0	0	0	0	....	....	....	....
2003-04	**Boston**	**NHL**	**6**	**0**	**0**	**0**	**0**	**0**	**0**	**0**	**7**	**0.0**	**–1**	**1**	**0.0**	**5:38**	....	....	....	....	....	....	....	....	....
	Providence Bruins	AHL	56	1	9	10	15	....	....	....	....	....	....	....	....	....	1	0	0	0	0	....	....	....	....
2004-05	Providence Bruins	AHL	64	7	10	17	35	....	....	....	....	....	....	....	....	....	10	1	0	1	6	....	....	....	....
2005-06	Linkopings HC	Sweden	44	3	4	7	45	....	....	....	....	....	....	....	....	....	8	0	0	0	29	....	....	....	....
2006-07	Linkopings HC	Sweden	33	4	2	6	14	....	....	....	....	....	....	....	....	....	15	0	1	1	8	....	....	....	....
	NHL Totals		**14**	**0**	**1**	**1**	**2**	**0**	**0**	**0**	**10**	**0.0**		**1**	**0.0**	**9:06**	....	....	....	....	....	....	....	....	....

SAMUELSSON, Mikael
(SAM-yuhl-suhn, MIH-kigh-ehl) **DET.**

Right wing. Shoots left. 6'2", 210 lbs. Born, Mariefred, Sweden, December 23, 1976. San Jose's 7th choice, 145th overall, in 1998 Entry Draft.

			Regular Season														Playoffs								
Season	Club	League	GP	G	A	Pts	PIM	PP	SH	GW	S	%	+/-	TF	F%	Min	GP	G	A	Pts	PIM	PP	SH	GW	Min
1994-95	Sodertalje SK Jr.	Swe-Jr.	30	8	6	14	12																		
1995-96	Sodertalje SK Jr.	Swe-Jr.	22	13	12	25	20																		
	Sodertalje SK	Sweden-2	18	5	1	6	0										4	0	0	0	0				
1996-97	Sodertalje SK Jr.	Swe-Jr.	2	2	1	3																			
	Sodertalje SK	Sweden	29	3	2	5	10										10	0	0	0	4				
1997-98	Nykoping	Sweden-2	10	5	1	6	14																		
	Sodertalje SK	Sweden	41	11	9	20	66																		
1998-99	Sodertalje SK	Sweden-2	18	13	10	23	26										10	2	2	4	12				
	V.Frolunda	Sweden	27	0	5	5	10																		
99-2000	Brynas IF Gavle	Sweden	40	4	3	7	76										11	7	2	9	6				
	Brynas IF Gavle	EuroHL	4	0	2	2	4																		
2000-01	**San Jose**	**NHL**	**4**	**0**	**0**	**0**	**0**	**0**	**0**	**0**	**3**	**0.0**	**0**	**0**	**0.0**	**4:41**									
	Kentucky	AHL	66	32	46	78	58										3	1	0	1	0				
2001-02	**NY Rangers**	**NHL**	**67**	**6**	**10**	**16**	**23**	**1**	**2**	**1**	**94**	**6.4**	**10**	**5**	**40.0**	**11:52**									
	Hartford	AHL	8	3	6	9	12																		
2002-03	**NY Rangers**	**NHL**	**58**	**8**	**14**	**22**	**32**	**1**	**1**	**2**	**118**	**6.8**	**0**	**35**	**42.9**	**15:32**									
	Pittsburgh	**NHL**	**22**	**2**	**0**	**2**	**8**	**1**	**0**	**0**	**36**	**5.6**	**–21**	**8**	**75.0**	**14:04**									
2003-04	**Florida**	**NHL**	**37**	**3**	**6**	**9**	**35**	**0**	**0**	**1**	**50**	**6.0**	**0**	**28**	**28.6**	**12:15**									
2004-05	Geneve	Swiss	12	2	4	6	14																		
	Sodertalje SK	Sweden	29	7	13	20	45										10	3	3	6	24				
2005-06	**Detroit**	**NHL**	**71**	**23**	**22**	**45**	**42**	**7**	**0**	**3**	**187**	**12.3**	**27**	**11**	**27.3**	**13:31**	**6**	**0**	**1**	**1**	**6**	**0**	**0**	**0**	**15:33**
	Rapperswil	Swiss	1	0	0	0	0																		
	Sweden	Olympics	8	1	3	4	2																		
2006-07	**Detroit**	**NHL**	**53**	**14**	**20**	**34**	**28**	**6**	**0**	**2**	**189**	**7.4**	**1**	**3**	**66.7**	**15:09**	**18**	**3**	**8**	**11**	**14**	**1**	**0**	**1**	**15:27**
	NHL Totals		**312**	**56**	**72**	**128**	**168**	**16**	**3**	**9**	**677**	**8.3**		**90**	**40.0**	**13:35**	**24**	**3**	**9**	**12**	**20**	**1**	**0**	**1**	**15:28**

Traded to **NY Rangers** by **San Jose** with Christian Gosselin for Adam Graves and future considerations, June 24, 2001. Traded to **Pittsburgh** by **NY Rangers** with Joel Bouchard, Richard Lintner and Rico Fata for Mike Wilson, Alex Kovalev, Janne Laukkanen and Dan LaCouture, February 10, 2003. Traded to **Florida** by **Pittsburgh** with Pittsburgh's 1st round choice (Nathan Horton) and 2nd round compensatory choice (Stefan Meyer) in 2003 Entry Draft for Florida's 1st (Marc-Andre Fleury) and 3rd (Daniel Carcillo) round choices in 2003 Entry Draft, June 21, 2003. • Missed majority of 2003-04 season recovering from jaw (November 21, 2003 vs. Washington) and hand (January 21, 2004 vs. Columbus) injuries. Signed as a free agent by **Geneve** (Swiss), September 8, 2004. Signed as a free agent by **Sodertalje** (Sweden), October 26, 2004. Signed as a free agent by **Detroit**, September 17, 2005.

SANDERSON, Geoff
(SAN-duhr-sohn, JEHF) **EDM.**

Left wing. Shoots left. 6', 190 lbs. Born, Hay River, N.W.T., February 1, 1972. Hartford's 2nd choice, 36th overall, in 1990 Entry Draft.

			Regular Season														Playoffs								
Season	Club	League	GP	G	A	Pts	PIM	PP	SH	GW	S	%	+/-	TF	F%	Min	GP	G	A	Pts	PIM	PP	SH	GW	Min
1987-88	St. Albert Royals	AMHL	45	65	55	120	175																		
1988-89	Swift Current	WHL	58	17	11	28	16										12	3	5	8	6				
1989-90	Swift Current	WHL	70	32	62	94	56										4	1	4	5	8				
1990-91	Swift Current	WHL	70	62	50	112	57										3	1	2	3	4				
	Hartford	**NHL**	**2**	**1**	**0**	**1**	**0**	**0**	**0**	**0**	**2**	**50.0**	**–2**				**3**	**0**	**0**	**0**	**0**	**0**	**0**	**0**	
	Springfield	AHL															1	0	0	0	2				
1991-92	**Hartford**	**NHL**	**64**	**13**	**18**	**31**	**18**	**2**	**0**	**1**	**98**	**13.3**	**5**				**7**	**1**	**0**	**1**	**2**	**0**	**0**	**0**	
1992-93	**Hartford**	**NHL**	**82**	**46**	**43**	**89**	**28**	**21**	**2**	**4**	**271**	**17.0**	**–21**												
1993-94	**Hartford**	**NHL**	**82**	**41**	**26**	**67**	**42**	**15**	**1**	**6**	**266**	**15.4**	**–13**												
1994-95	HPK Hameenlinna	Finland	12	6	4	10	24																		
	Hartford	**NHL**	**46**	**18**	**14**	**32**	**24**	**4**	**0**	**4**	**170**	**10.6**	**–10**												
1995-96	**Hartford**	**NHL**	**81**	**34**	**31**	**65**	**40**	**6**	**0**	**7**	**314**	**10.8**	**0**												
1996-97	**Hartford**	**NHL**	**82**	**36**	**31**	**67**	**29**	**12**	**1**	**4**	**297**	**12.1**	**–9**												
1997-98	**Carolina**	**NHL**	**40**	**7**	**10**	**17**	**14**	**2**	**0**	**0**	**96**	**7.3**	**–4**												
	Vancouver	**NHL**	**9**	**0**	**3**	**3**	**4**	**0**	**0**	**0**	**29**	**0.0**	**–1**												
	Buffalo	**NHL**	**26**	**4**	**5**	**9**	**20**	**0**	**0**	**2**	**72**	**5.6**	**6**				**14**	**3**	**1**	**4**	**4**	**1**	**0**	**1**	
1998-99	**Buffalo**	**NHL**	**75**	**12**	**18**	**30**	**22**	**1**	**0**	**1**	**155**	**7.7**	**8**	**4**	**50.0**	**12:55**	**19**	**4**	**6**	**10**	**14**	**0**	**0**	**1**	**13:52**
99-2000	**Buffalo**	**NHL**	**67**	**13**	**13**	**26**	**22**	**4**	**0**	**3**	**136**	**9.6**	**4**	**3**	**100.0**	**12:54**	**5**	**0**	**2**	**2**	**8**	**0**	**0**	**0**	**12:16**
2000-01	**Columbus**	**NHL**	**68**	**30**	**26**	**56**	**46**	**9**	**0**	**7**	**199**	**15.1**	**4**	**726**	**49.0**	**16:37**									
2001-02	**Columbus**	**NHL**	**42**	**11**	**5**	**16**	**12**	**5**	**0**	**2**	**112**	**9.8**	**–15**	**322**	**42.9**	**16:50**									
2002-03	**Columbus**	**NHL**	**82**	**34**	**33**	**67**	**34**	**15**	**2**	**2**	**286**	**11.9**	**–4**	**96**	**41.7**	**18:44**									
2003-04	**Columbus**	**NHL**	**67**	**13**	**16**	**29**	**34**	**5**	**0**	**1**	**191**	**6.8**	**–9**	**102**	**47.1**	**16:20**									
	Vancouver	**NHL**	**13**	**3**	**4**	**7**	**4**	**1**	**0**	**1**	**36**	**8.3**	**–1**	**14**	**21.4**	**14:46**	**7**	**1**	**1**	**2**	**4**	**0**	**0**	**0**	**12:54**
2004-05	Geneve	Swiss	9	4	1	5	29																		
2005-06	**Columbus**	**NHL**	**2**	**0**	**0**	**0**	**0**	**0**	**0**	**0**	**7**	**0.0**	**–1**	**1**	**0.0**	**10:54**									
	Phoenix	**NHL**	**75**	**25**	**21**	**46**	**58**	**11**	**1**	**1**	**152**	**16.4**	**–14**	**359**	**51.0**	**13:47**									
2006-07	**Philadelphia**	**NHL**	**58**	**11**	**18**	**29**	**44**	**3**	**0**	**2**	**143**	**7.7**	**–16**	**163**	**41.7**	**13:59**									
	NHL Totals		**1063**	**352**	**335**	**687**	**495**	**116**	**7**	**48**	**3032**	**11.6**		**1790**	**47.0**	**15:14**	**55**	**9**	**10**	**19**	**32**	**1**	**0**	**2**	**13:23**

Played in NHL All-Star Game (1994, 1997)

Transferred to **Carolina** after **Hartford** franchise relocated, June 25, 1997. Traded to **Vancouver** by **Carolina** with Sean Burke and Enrico Ciccone for Kirk McLean and Martin Gelinas, January 3, 1998. Traded to **Buffalo** by **Vancouver** for Brad May and Buffalo's 3rd round choice (later traded to Tampa Bay – Tampa Bay selected Jimmie Olvestad) in 1999 Entry Draft, February 4, 1998. Claimed by **Columbus** from **Buffalo** in Expansion Draft, June 23, 2000. Traded to **Vancouver** by **Columbus** for Vancouver's 3rd round choice (Daniel Lacosta) in 2004 Entry Draft, March 9, 2004. Claimed on waivers by **Columbus** from **Vancouver**, June 28, 2004. Signed as a free agent by **Geneve** (Swiss), January 5, 2005. Traded to **Phoenix** by **Columbus** with Tim Jackman for Cale Hulse, Mike Rupp and Jason Chimera, October 8, 2005. Signed as a free agent by **Philadelphia**, July 19, 2006. Traded to **Edmonton** by **Philadelphia** with Joni Pitkanen and Philadelphia's 3rd round choice in 2009 Entry Draft for Jason Smith and Joffrey Lupul, July 1, 2007.

SANTALA, Tommi
(SAHN-tah-luh, TAW-mee)

Center. Shoots right. 6'3", 210 lbs. Born, Helsinki, Finland, June 27, 1979. Atlanta's 10th choice, 245th overall, in 1999 Entry Draft.

			Regular Season														Playoffs								
Season	Club	League	GP	G	A	Pts	PIM	PP	SH	GW	S	%	+/-	TF	F%	Min	GP	G	A	Pts	PIM	PP	SH	GW	Min
1995-96	Jokerit U18	Fin-U18	25	8	4	12	12										6	1	2	3	4				
1996-97	Jokerit U18	Fin-U18	30	13	19	32	64																		
	Jokerit Helsinki Jr.	Fin-Jr.	20	0	2	2	10										5	0	0	0	0				
1997-98	Jokerit Helsinki Jr.	Fin-Jr.	36	10	28	38	48										8	0	1	1	4				
1998-99	Jokerit Helsinki Jr.	Fin-Jr.	30	20	24	44	20										8	1	3	4	22				
	Jokerit Helsinki	Finland	30	0	0	0	14										3	0	0	0	0				
	Jokerit Helsinki	EuroHL	1	0	2	2	0										1	0	0	0	0				
99-2000	Jokerit Helsinki Jr.	Fin-Jr.	5	6	4	10	4																		
	Jokerit Helsinki	Finland	14	0	1	1	2																		
	HPK Jr.	Fin-Jr.	6	7	3	10	4																		
	HPK Hameenlinna	Finland	38	8	19	27	63										8	3	4	7	10				
2000-01	HPK Hameenlinna	Finland	56	16	24	40	90																		
2001-02	HPK Hameenlinna	Finland	17	6	16	22	14																		
2002-03	HPK Hameenlinna	Finland	50	13	38	51	92										13	6	6	12	18				
2003-04	**Atlanta**	**NHL**	**33**	**1**	**2**	**3**	**22**	**0**	**0**	**1**	**23**	**4.3**	**–7**	**252**	**51.2**	**10:08**									
	Chicago Wolves	AHL	50	15	22	37	34										10	1	6	7	31				
2004-05	Chicago Wolves	AHL	67	8	40	48	83										18	5	6	11	42				
2005-06	Jokerit Helsinki	Finland	43	9	23	32	80																		
2006-07	**Vancouver**	**NHL**	**30**	**1**	**5**	**6**	**24**	**0**	**0**	**0**	**20**	**5.0**	**0**	**139**	**56.8**	**7:22**	**1**	**0**	**0**	**0**	**0**	**0**	**0**	**0**	**2:16**
	Manitoba Moose	AHL	6	0	3	3	8																		
	NHL Totals		**63**	**2**	**7**	**9**	**46**	**0**	**0**	**1**	**43**	**4.7**		**391**	**53.2**	**8:49**	**1**	**0**	**0**	**0**	**0**	**0**	**0**	**0**	**2:16**

Assigned to **Jokerit Helsinki** (Finland) by **Atlanta**. October 5, 2005. Traded to **Vancouver** by **Atlanta** with Atlanta's 5th round choice (Charles-Antoine Messier) in 2007 Entry Draft for Atlanta's 4th round choice (previously acquired, Atlanta selected Niklas Lucenius) in 2007 Entry Draft, June 14, 2006. • Missed majority of 2006-07 season recovering from a knee injury.

SAPRYKIN, Oleg
(sah-PRIH-kihn, OH-lehg)

Left wing. Shoots left. 6'1", 190 lbs. Born, Moscow, USSR, February 12, 1981. Calgary's 1st choice, 11th overall, in 1999 Entry Draft.

			Regular Season														Playoffs								
Season	Club	League	GP	G	A	Pts	PIM	PP	SH	GW	S	%	+/-	TF	F%	Min	GP	G	A	Pts	PIM	PP	SH	GW	Min
1997-98	HK CSKA Moscow	Russia-Q	15	0	3	3	6																		
	HK CSKA Moscow	Russia	20	0	2	2	8																		
1998-99	Seattle	WHL	66	47	46	93	107										11	5	11	16	36				
99-2000	**Calgary**	**NHL**	**4**	**0**	**1**	**1**	**2**	**0**	**0**	**0**	**2**	**0.0**	**–4**	**0**	**0.0**	**12:35**									
	Seattle	WHL	48	30	36	66	91										6	3	3	6	37				
2000-01	**Calgary**	**NHL**	**59**	**9**	**14**	**23**	**43**	**2**	**0**	**0**	**95**	**9.5**	**4**	**2**	**50.0**	**12:10**									
2001-02	**Calgary**	**NHL**	**3**	**0**	**0**	**0**	**0**	**0**	**0**	**0**	**9**	**0.0**	**–2**	**0**	**0.0**	**13:25**									
	Saint John Flames	AHL	52	5	19	24	53																		

			Regular Season														Playoffs								
Season	Club	League	GP	G	A	Pts	PIM	PP	SH	GW	S	%	+/-	TF	F%	Min	GP	G	A	Pts	PIM	PP	SH	GW	Min
2002-03	Calgary	NHL	52	8	15	23	46	1	0	1	116	6.9	5	1	0.0	11:53	....	....	....						
	Saint John Flames	AHL	21	12	9	21	22	....	....	....	....	....	....	....	....	....	....	....	....	....	....	....	....	....	....
2003-04	Calgary	NHL	69	12	17	29	41	4	0	0	151	7.9	1	13	23.1	13:48	26	3	3	6	14	1	0	1	14:01
2004-05	CSKA Moscow	Russia	40	15	8	23	105	....	....	....	....	....	....	....	....	....	....	....	....	....	....	....	....	....	....
2005-06	Phoenix	NHL	67	11	14	25	50	3	0	1	126	8.7	–16	18	38.9	13:42	....	....	....	....	....	....	....	....	....
2006-07	Phoenix	NHL	59	14	20	34	54	2	0	2	135	10.4	8	16	12.5	13:29	....	....	....	....	....	....	....	....	....
	Ottawa	NHL	12	1	1	2	4	0	0	0	15	6.7	–3	2	100.0	7:25	15	1	1	2	4	0	0	1	7:31
	NHL Totals		325	55	82	137	240	12	0	4	649	8.5		52	28.8	12:52	41	4	4	8	18	1	0	2	11:38

WHL West Second All-Star Team (1999, 2000)

Traded to **Phoenix** by **Calgary** with Denis Gauthier for Daymond Langkow, August 26, 2004. Signed as a free agent by **CSKA Moscow** (Russia), September 25, 2004. Traded to **Ottawa** by **Phoenix** with Phoenix's 7th round choice (Torrie Jung) in 2007 Entry Draft for Ottawa's 2nd round choice in 2008 Entry Draft, February 27, 2007. Signed as a free agent by **CSKA Moscow** (Russia), July 30, 2007.

SARICH, Cory
(SAHR-ihch, KOH-ree) **CGY.**

Defense. Shoots right. 6'3", 210 lbs. Born, Saskatoon, Sask., August 16, 1978. Buffalo's 2nd choice, 27th overall, in 1996 Entry Draft.

Season	Club	League	GP	G	A	Pts	PIM	PP	SH	GW	S	%	+/-	TF	F%	Min	GP	G	A	Pts	PIM	PP	SH	GW	Min
1994-95	Sask. Contacts	SMHL	31	5	22	27	99	....	....	....	....	....	....	....	....	....	....	....	....	....	....	....	....	....	....
	Saskatoon Blades	WHL	6	0	0	0	4	....	....	....	....	....	....	....	....	....	3	0	1	1	0	....	....	....	....
1995-96	Saskatoon Blades	WHL	59	5	18	23	54	....	....	....	....	....	....	....	....	....	3	0	0	0	4	....	....	....	....
1996-97	Saskatoon Blades	WHL	58	6	27	33	158	....	....	....	....	....	....	....	....	....	....	....	....	....	....	....	....	....	....
1997-98	Saskatoon Blades	WHL	33	5	24	29	90	....	....	....	....	....	....	....	....	....	....	....	....	....	....	....	....	....	....
	Seattle	WHL	13	3	16	19	47	....	....	....	....	....	....	....	....	....	....	....	....	....	....	....	....	....	....
1998-99	Buffalo	NHL	4	0	0	0	0	0	0	0	2	0.0	3	0	0.0	13:11	....	....	....	....	....	....	....	....	....
	Rochester	AHL	77	3	26	29	82	....	....	....	....	....	....	....	....	....	20	2	4	6	14	....	....	....	....
99-2000	Buffalo	NHL	42	0	4	4	35	0	0	0	49	0.0	2	0	0.0	17:42	....	....	....	....	....	....	....	....	....
	Rochester	AHL	15	0	6	6	44	....	....	....	....	....	....	....	....	....	....	....	....	....	....	....	....	....	....
	Tampa Bay	NHL	17	0	2	2	42	0	0	0	20	0.0	–8	0	0.0	20:42	....	....	....	....	....	....	....	....	....
2000-01	Tampa Bay	NHL	73	1	8	9	106	0	0	1	66	1.5	–25	3	0.0	18:44	....	....	....	....	....	....	....	....	....
	Detroit Vipers	IHL	3	0	2	2	2	....	....	....	....	....	....	....	....	....	....	....	....	....	....	....	....	....	....
2001-02	Springfield	AHL	2	0	0	0	0	....	....	....	....	....	....	....	....	....	....	....	....	....	....	....	....	....	....
	Tampa Bay	NHL	72	0	11	11	105	0	0	0	55	0.0	–4	2	50.0	16:06	....	....	....	....	....	....	....	....	....
2002-03	Tampa Bay	NHL	82	5	9	14	63	0	0	2	79	6.3	–3	3	0.0	19:36	11	0	2	2	6	0	0	0	21:18
2003-04♦	Tampa Bay	NHL	82	3	16	19	89	0	1	1	93	3.2	5	1	0.0	18:31	23	0	2	2	25	0	0	0	19:11
2004-05			DID NOT PLAY																						
2005-06	Tampa Bay	NHL	82	1	14	15	79	0	0	0	88	1.1	–2	0	0.0	18:34	5	0	1	1	4	0	0	0	15:46
2006-07	Tampa Bay	NHL	82	0	15	15	70	0	0	0	64	0.0	–6	1	0.0	18:07	6	0	0	0	2	0	0	0	16:37
	NHL Totals		536	10	79	89	589	0	1	4	516	1.9		10	10.0	18:18	45	0	5	5	37	0	0	0	18:59

WHL West Second All-Star Team (1998) • AHL All-Rookie Team (1999)

Traded to **Tampa Bay** by **Buffalo** with Wayne Primeau, Brian Holzinger and Buffalo's 3rd round choice (Alexander Kharitonov) in 2000 Entry Draft for Chris Gratton and Tampa Bay's 2nd round choice (Derek Roy) in 2001 Entry Draft, March 9, 2000. Signed as a free agent by **Calgary**, July 1, 2007.

SATAN, Miroslav
(shuh-TAN, MEER-oh-slav) **NYI**

Left wing. Shoots left. 6'3", 191 lbs. Born, Topolcany, Czech., October 22, 1974. Edmonton's 6th choice, 111th overall, in 1993 Entry Draft.

Season	Club	League	GP	G	A	Pts	PIM	PP	SH	GW	S	%	+/-	TF	F%	Min	GP	G	A	Pts	PIM	PP	SH	GW	Min
1991-92	Topolcany Jr.	Czech-Jr.	31	30	22	52	....	....	....	....	....	....	....	....	....	....	....	....	....	....	....	....	....	....	....
	VTJ Topolcany	Czech-2	9	2	1	3	6	....	....	....	....	....	....	....	....	....	....	....	....	....	....	....	....	....	....
1992-93	Dukla Trencin	Czech	38	11	6	17	....	....	....	....	....	....	....	....	....	....	....	....	....	....	....	....	....	....	....
1993-94	Dukla Trencin	Slovakia	30	32	16	48	16	....	....	....	....	....	....	....	....	....	....	....	....	....	....	....	....	....	....
	Slovakia	Olympics	8	*9	0	9	0	....	....	....	....	....	....	....	....	....	....	....	....	....	....	....	....	....	....
1994-95	Cape Breton	AHL	25	24	16	40	15	....	....	....	....	....	....	....	....	....	....	....	....	....	....	....	....	....	....
	Detroit Vipers	IHL	8	1	3	4	4	....	....	....	....	....	....	....	....	....	....	....	....	....	....	....	....	....	....
	San Diego Gulls	IHL	6	0	2	2	6	....	....	....	....	....	....	....	....	....	....	....	....	....	....	....	....	....	....
1995-96	Edmonton	NHL	62	18	17	35	22	6	0	4	113	15.9	0	....	....	....	....	....	....	....	....	....	....	....	....
1996-97	Edmonton	NHL	64	17	11	28	22	5	0	2	90	18.9	–4	....	....	....	....	....	....	....	....	....	....	....	....
	Buffalo	NHL	12	8	2	10	4	2	0	1	29	27.6	1	....	....	....	7	0	0	0	0	0	0	0	....
1997-98	Buffalo	NHL	79	22	24	46	34	9	0	4	139	15.8	2	....	....	....	14	5	4	9	4	4	0	1	....
1998-99	Buffalo	NHL	81	40	26	66	44	13	3	6	208	19.2	24	9	55.6	20:49	12	3	5	8	2	1	0	1	21:18
99-2000	Dukla Trencin	Slovakia	3	2	8	10	2	....	....	....	....	....	....	....	....	....	....	....	....	....	....	....	....	....	....
	Buffalo	NHL	81	33	34	67	32	5	3	5	265	12.5	16	7	14.3	20:35	5	3	2	5	0	0	0	0	19:52
2000-01	Buffalo	NHL	82	29	33	62	36	8	2	4	206	14.1	5	11	36.4	19:56	13	3	10	13	8	1	0	0	21:18
2001-02	Buffalo	NHL	82	37	36	73	33	15	5	5	267	13.9	14	4	50.0	21:10	....	....	....	....	....	....	....	....	....
	Slovakia	Olympics	2	0	1	1	0	....	....	....	....	....	....	....	....	....	....	....	....	....	....	....	....	....	....
2002-03	Buffalo	NHL	79	26	49	75	20	11	1	3	240	10.8	–3	10	20.0	21:23	....	....	....	....	....	....	....	....	....
2003-04	Bratislava	Slovakia	7	6	4	10	41	....	....	....	....	....	....	....	....	....	....	....	....	....	....	....	....	....	....
	Buffalo	NHL	82	29	28	57	30	11	1	5	206	14.1	–15	9	22.2	20:02	....	....	....	....	....	....	....	....	....
2004-05	Bratislava	Slovakia	18	11	9	20	14	....	....	....	....	....	....	....	....	....	18	*15	7	*22	16	....	....	....	....
2005-06	NY Islanders	NHL	82	35	31	66	54	17	0	2	253	13.8	–8	342	53.2	19:10	....	....	....	....	....	....	....	....	....
	Slovakia	Olympics	6	0	2	2	2	....	....	....	....	....	....	....	....	....	....	....	....	....	....	....	....	....	....
2006-07	NY Islanders	NHL	81	27	32	59	46	7	1	2	216	12.5	–12	164	55.5	18:35	5	1	2	3	0	0	0	0	15:15
	NHL Totals		867	321	323	644	377	109	16	43	2232	14.4		556	52.0	20:12	56	15	23	38	14	6	0	2	20:14

Played in NHL All-Star Game (2000, 2003)

Traded to **Buffalo** by **Edmonton** for Barrie Moore and Craig Millar, March 18, 1997. Signed as a free agent by **Bratislava** (Slovakia), December 29, 2004. Signed as a free agent by **NY Islanders**, August 3, 2005.

SAUER, Kurt
(SAW-uhr, KUHRT) **COL.**

Defense. Shoots left. 6'4", 220 lbs. Born, St. Cloud, MN, January 16, 1981. Colorado's 5th choice, 88th overall, in 2000 Entry Draft.

Season	Club	League	GP	G	A	Pts	PIM	PP	SH	GW	S	%	+/-	TF	F%	Min	GP	G	A	Pts	PIM	PP	SH	GW	Min
1998-99	North Iowa	USHL	52	1	4	5	67	....	....	....	....	....	....	....	....	....	....	....	....	....	....	....	....	....	....
99-2000	Spokane Chiefs	WHL	71	3	12	15	48	....	....	....	....	....	....	....	....	....	15	2	1	3	8	....	....	....	....
2000-01	Spokane Chiefs	WHL	48	5	10	15	85	....	....	....	....	....	....	....	....	....	3	1	0	1	2	....	....	....	....
2001-02	Spokane Chiefs	WHL	61	4	20	24	73	....	....	....	....	....	....	....	....	....	11	0	3	3	12	....	....	....	....
2002-03	Anaheim	NHL	80	1	2	3	74	0	0	0	50	2.0	–23	0	0.0	18:33	21	1	1	2	6	0	1	1	20:45
2003-04	Anaheim	NHL	55	1	4	5	32	0	0	0	32	3.1	–8	0	0.0	16:54	....	....	....	....	....	....	....	....	....
	Colorado	NHL	14	0	1	1	19	0	0	0	12	0.0	–3	0	0.0	15:04	3	0	0	0	0	0	0	0	11:56
2004-05			DID NOT PLAY																						
2005-06	Colorado	NHL	37	1	4	5	24	0	0	0	19	5.3	5	0	0.0	12:48	9	0	0	0	4	0	0	0	8:39
	Lowell	AHL	4	0	0	0	0	....	....	....	....	....	....	....	....	....	....	....	....	....	....	....	....	....	....
2006-07	Colorado	NHL	48	0	6	6	24	0	0	0	29	0.0	–3	0	0.0	18:20	....	....	....	....	....	....	....	....	....
	NHL Totals		234	3	17	20	173	0	0	0	142	2.1		0	0.0	17:00	33	1	1	2	10	0	1	1	16:39

WHL West First All-Star Team (2002)

Signed as a free agent by **Anaheim**, July 6, 2002. Traded to **Colorado** by **Anaheim** with Anaheim's 4th round choice (Raymond Macias) in 2005 Entry Draft for Martin Skoula, February 21, 2004.

SAVARD, Marc
(sa-VAHR, MAHRK) **BOS.**

Center. Shoots left. 5'10", 196 lbs. Born, Ottawa, Ont., July 17, 1977. NY Rangers' 3rd choice, 91st overall, in 1995 Entry Draft.

Season	Club	League	GP	G	A	Pts	PIM	PP	SH	GW	S	%	+/-	TF	F%	Min	GP	G	A	Pts	PIM	PP	SH	GW	Min
1992-93	Metcalfe Jets	OHA-B	36	*44	55	*99	38	....	....	....	....	....	....	....	....	....	....	....	....	....	....	....	....	....	....
1993-94	Oshawa Generals	OHL	61	18	39	57	20	....	....	....	....	....	....	....	....	....	5	4	3	7	8	....	....	....	....
1994-95	Oshawa Generals	OHL	66	43	96	*139	78	....	....	....	....	....	....	....	....	....	7	5	6	11	8	....	....	....	....
1995-96	Oshawa Generals	OHL	48	28	59	87	77	....	....	....	....	....	....	....	....	....	5	4	5	9	6	....	....	....	....
1996-97	Oshawa Generals	OHL	64	43	*87	*130	94	....	....	....	....	....	....	....	....	....	18	13	*24	*37	20	....	....	....	....
1997-98	NY Rangers	NHL	28	1	5	6	4	0	0	0	32	3.1	–4	....	....	....	....	....	....	....	....	....	....	....	....
	Hartford	AHL	58	21	53	74	66	....	....	....	....	....	....	....	....	....	15	8	19	27	24	....	....	....	....
1998-99	NY Rangers	NHL	70	9	36	45	38	4	0	1	116	7.8	–7	956	48.4	14:35	....	....	....	....	....	....	....	....	....
	Hartford	AHL	9	3	10	13	16	....	....	....	....	....	....	....	....	....	7	1	12	13	16	....	....	....	....
99-2000	Calgary	NHL	78	22	31	53	56	4	0	3	184	12.0	–2	1021	49.6	16:36	....	....	....	....	....	....	....	....	....
2000-01	Calgary	NHL	77	23	42	65	46	10	1	5	197	11.7	–12	1050	53.1	19:13	....	....	....	....	....	....	....	....	....
2001-02	Calgary	NHL	56	14	19	33	48	7	0	3	140	10.0	–18	577	54.8	17:20	....	....	....	....	....	....	....	....	....
2002-03	Calgary	NHL	10	1	2	3	8	0	0	0	21	4.8	–3	89	52.8	14:41	....	....	....	....	....	....	....	....	....
	Atlanta	NHL	57	16	31	47	77	6	0	4	127	12.6	–11	1247	50.9	19:50	....	....	....	....	....	....	....	....	....
2003-04	Atlanta	NHL	45	19	33	52	85	6	1	3	133	14.3	–8	1083	49.9	22:19	....	....	....	....	....	....	....	....	....

			Regular Season														Playoffs								
Season	Club	League	GP	G	A	Pts	PIM	PP	SH	GW	S	%	+/-	TF	F%	Min	GP	G	A	Pts	PIM	PP	SH	GW	Min
2004-05	HC Thurgau	Swiss-2	13	9	19	28	10	....	....	....	....	....	....	....	....	....	....	....	....	....	....	....	....	....	....
	SC Bern	Swiss	5	1	2	3	0	....	....	....	....	....	....	....	....	....	....	....	....	....	....	....	....	....	....
2005-06	**Atlanta**	**NHL**	82	28	69	97	100	14	1	4	212	13.2	7	1529	51.6	20:30	....	....	....	....	....	....	....	....	....
2006-07	**Boston**	**NHL**	82	22	74	96	96	10	1	3	221	10.0	–19	1420	50.1	20:13	....	....	....	....	....	....	....	....	....
	NHL Totals		585	155	342	497	558	61	4	26	1383	11.2		8972	50.9	18:39	....	....	....	....	....	....	....	....	....

OHL Second All-Star Team (1995)

Traded to **Calgary** by **NY Rangers** with NY Rangers 1st round choice (Oleg Saprykin) in 1999 Entry Draft for the rights to Jan Hlavac and Calgary's 1st (Jamie Lundmark) and 3rd (later traded back to Calgary – Calgary selected Craig Andersson) round choices in 1999 Entry Draft, June 26, 1999. Traded to **Atlanta** by **Calgary** for Ruslan Zainullin, November 15, 2002. Signed as a free agent by **Thurgau** (Swiss-2), October 11, 2004. Signed as a free agent by **Bern** (Swiss), November 23, 2004. Signed as a free agent by **Boston**, July 1, 2006.

SCATCHARD, Dave

(SKAT-chuhrd, DAYV)

Center. Shoots right. 6'3", 220 lbs. Born, Hinton, Alta., February 20, 1976. Vancouver's 3rd choice, 42nd overall, in 1994 Entry Draft.

Season	Club	League	GP	G	A	Pts	PIM	PP	SH	GW	S	%	+/-	TF	F%	Min	GP	G	A	Pts	PIM	PP	SH	GW	Min
1991-92	Salmon Arm	BCAHA	65	98	100	198	167	....	....	....	....	....	....	....	....	....	....	....	....	....	....	....	....	....	....
1992-93	Kimberley	RMJHL	51	20	23	43	61	....	....	....	....	....	....	....	....	....	....	....	....	....	....	....	....	....	....
1993-94	Portland	WHL	47	9	11	20	46	....	....	....	....	....	....	....	....	....	10	2	1	3	4	....	....	....	....
1994-95	Portland	WHL	71	20	30	50	148	....	....	....	....	....	....	....	....	....	8	0	3	3	21	....	....	....	....
1995-96	Portland	WHL	59	19	28	47	146	....	....	....	....	....	....	....	....	....	7	1	8	9	14	....	....	....	....
	Syracuse Crunch	AHL	1	0	0	0	0	....	....	....	....	....	....	....	....	....	15	2	5	7	29	....	....	....	....
1996-97	Syracuse Crunch	AHL	26	8	7	15	65	....	....	....	....	....	....	....	....	....	....	....	....	....	....	....	....	....	....
1997-98	**Vancouver**	**NHL**	76	13	11	24	165	0	0	1	85	15.3	–4	....	....	....	....	....	....	....	....	....	....	....	....
1998-99	**Vancouver**	**NHL**	82	13	13	26	140	0	2	2	130	10.0	–12	1007	56.3	13:46	....	....	....	....	....	....	....	....	....
99-2000	**Vancouver**	**NHL**	21	0	4	4	24	0	0	0	25	0.0	–3	190	59.5	10:12	....	....	....	....	....	....	....	....	....
	NY Islanders	**NHL**	44	12	14	26	93	0	1	1	103	11.7	0	710	55.8	13:42	....	....	....	....	....	....	....	....	....
2000-01	**NY Islanders**	**NHL**	81	21	24	45	114	4	0	5	176	11.9	–9	1322	55.1	16:50	....	....	....	....	....	....	....	....	....
2001-02	**NY Islanders**	**NHL**	80	12	15	27	111	3	1	4	117	10.3	–4	788	53.8	12:31	7	1	1	2	22	0	0	0	12:38
2002-03	**NY Islanders**	**NHL**	81	27	18	45	108	5	0	2	165	16.4	9	1147	52.7	14:30	5	1	0	1	6	0	0	1	15:58
2003-04	**NY Islanders**	**NHL**	61	9	16	25	78	1	1	1	111	8.1	12	1052	52.7	16:13	5	0	1	1	6	0	0	0	16:18
2004-05			DID NOT PLAY																						
2005-06	**Boston**	**NHL**	16	4	6	10	28	1	0	0	40	10.0	–2	272	54.8	16:56	....	....	....	....	....	....	....	....	....
	Phoenix	**NHL**	47	11	12	23	84	4	0	3	81	13.6	–11	594	53.2	14:44	....	....	....	....	....	....	....	....	....
2006-07	**Phoenix**	**NHL**	46	3	5	8	72	0	0	1	77	3.9	–18	385	52.5	13:31	....	....	....	....	....	....	....	....	....
	NHL Totals		635	125	138	263	1017	18	5	20	1110	11.3		7467	54.3	14:25	17	2	2	4	34	0	0	1	14:41

Traded to **NY Islanders** by **Vancouver** with Kevin Weekes and Bill Muckalt for Felix Potvin, NY Islanders' 2nd round compensatory choice (later traded to New Jersey – New Jersey selected Teemu Laine) in 2000 Entry Draft and NY Islanders' 3rd round choice (Thatcher Bell) in 2000 Entry Draft, December 19, 1999. Signed as a free agent by **Boston**, August 2, 2005. Traded to **Phoenix** by **Boston** for David Tanabe, November 18, 2005.

SCHAEFER, Peter

(SHAY-fuhr, PEE-tuhr) **BOS.**

Left wing. Shoots left. 5'11", 195 lbs. Born, Yellow Grass, Sask., July 12, 1977. Vancouver's 3rd choice, 66th overall, in 1995 Entry Draft.

Season	Club	League	GP	G	A	Pts	PIM	PP	SH	GW	S	%	+/-	TF	F%	Min	GP	G	A	Pts	PIM	PP	SH	GW	Min
1993-94	Yorkton Mallers	SMHL	32	27	14	41	133	....	....	....	....	....	....	....	....	....	....	....	....	....	....	....	....	....	....
	Brandon	WHL	2	1	0	1	0	....	....	....	....	....	....	....	....	....	....	....	....	....	....	....	....	....	....
1994-95	Brandon	WHL	68	27	32	59	34	....	....	....	....	....	....	....	....	....	18	5	3	8	18	....	....	....	....
1995-96	Brandon	WHL	69	47	61	108	53	....	....	....	....	....	....	....	....	....	19	10	13	23	5	....	....	....	....
1996-97	Brandon	WHL	61	49	74	123	85	....	....	....	....	....	....	....	....	....	6	1	4	5	4	....	....	....	....
	Syracuse Crunch	AHL	5	0	3	3	0	....	....	....	....	....	....	....	....	....	3	1	3	4	14	....	....	....	....
1997-98	Syracuse Crunch	AHL	73	19	44	63	41	....	....	....	....	....	....	....	....	....	5	2	1	3	2	....	....	....	....
1998-99	**Vancouver**	**NHL**	25	4	4	8	8	1	0	1	24	16.7	–1	6	0.0	13:21	....	....	....	....	....	....	....	....	....
	Syracuse Crunch	AHL	41	10	19	29	66	....	....	....	....	....	....	....	....	....	....	....	....	....	....	....	....	....	....
99-2000	**Vancouver**	**NHL**	71	16	15	31	20	2	2	4	101	15.8	0	21	19.1	15:28	....	....	....	....	....	....	....	....	....
	Syracuse Crunch	AHL	2	0	0	0	2	....	....	....	....	....	....	....	....	....	....	....	....	....	....	....	....	....	....
2000-01	**Vancouver**	**NHL**	82	16	20	36	22	3	4	2	163	9.8	4	25	32.0	16:18	3	0	0	0	0	0	0	0	13:08
2001-02	TPS Turku	Finland	33	16	15	31	93	....	....	....	....	....	....	....	....	....	8	1	2	3	2	....	....	....	....
2002-03	**Ottawa**	**NHL**	75	6	17	23	32	0	0	1	93	6.5	11	44	20.5	14:59	16	2	3	5	6	0	1	0	11:51
2003-04	**Ottawa**	**NHL**	81	15	24	39	26	2	2	3	112	13.4	22	39	23.1	15:36	7	0	2	2	4	0	0	0	14:25
2004-05	HC Forst Bolzano	Italy	15	11	14	25	10	....	....	....	....	....	....	....	....	....	10	1	7	8	12	....	....	....	....
2005-06	**Ottawa**	**NHL**	82	20	30	50	40	4	4	2	137	14.6	16	27	37.0	15:49	10	2	5	7	14	0	0	0	16:39
2006-07	**Ottawa**	**NHL**	77	12	34	46	32	5	0	2	132	9.1	7	7	28.6	16:44	20	1	5	6	10	0	0	0	14:32
	NHL Totals		493	89	144	233	180	17	12	15	762	11.7		169	24.9	15:42	56	5	15	20	34	0	1	0	14:03

WHL East First All-Star Team (1996, 1997) • WHL Player of the Year (1997) • Canadian Major Junior First All-Star Team (1997)

Signed as a free agent by **Turku** (Finland), October 18, 2001. Traded to **Ottawa** by **Vancouver** for Sami Salo, September 21, 2002. Signed as a free agent by **Bolzano** (Italy), November 30, 2004. Traded to **Boston** by **Ottawa** for Shean Donovan, July 17, 2007.

SCHNEIDER, Mathieu

(SHNIGH-duhr, MA-thew) **ANA.**

Defense. Shoots left. 5'11", 191 lbs. Born, New York, NY, June 12, 1969. Montreal's 4th choice, 44th overall, in 1987 Entry Draft.

Season	Club	League	GP	G	A	Pts	PIM	PP	SH	GW	S	%	+/-	TF	F%	Min	GP	G	A	Pts	PIM	PP	SH	GW	Min
1985-86	Mount St. Charles	High-RI	19	3	27	30	....	....	....	....	....	....	....	....	....	....	....	....	....	....	....	....	....	....	....
1986-87	Cornwall Royals	OHL	63	7	29	36	75	....	....	....	....	....	....	....	....	....	5	0	0	0	22	....	....	....	....
1987-88	Cornwall Royals	OHL	48	21	40	61	83	....	....	....	....	....	....	....	....	....	11	2	6	8	14	....	....	....	....
	Montreal	**NHL**	4	0	0	0	2	0	0	0	2	0.0	–1	....	....	....	....	....	....	....	....	....	....	....	....
	Sherbrooke	AHL	....	....	....	....	....	....	....	....	....	....	....	....	....	....	3	0	3	3	12	....	....	....	....
1988-89	Cornwall Royals	OHL	59	16	57	73	96	....	....	....	....	....	....	....	....	....	18	7	20	27	30	....	....	....	....
1989-90	**Montreal**	**NHL**	44	7	14	21	25	5	0	1	84	8.3	2	....	....	....	9	1	3	4	31	1	0	0	....
	Sherbrooke	AHL	28	6	13	19	20	....	....	....	....	....	....	....	....	....	....	....	....	....	....	....	....	....	....
1990-91	**Montreal**	**NHL**	69	10	20	30	63	5	0	3	164	6.1	7	....	....	....	13	2	7	9	18	1	0	0	....
1991-92	**Montreal**	**NHL**	78	8	24	32	72	2	0	1	194	4.1	10	....	....	....	10	1	4	5	6	1	0	0	....
1992-93 ♦	**Montreal**	**NHL**	60	13	31	44	91	3	0	2	169	7.7	8	....	....	....	11	1	2	3	16	0	0	0	....
1993-94	**Montreal**	**NHL**	75	20	32	52	62	11	0	4	193	10.4	15	....	....	....	1	0	0	0	0	0	0	0	....
1994-95	**Montreal**	**NHL**	30	5	15	20	49	2	0	0	82	6.1	–3	....	....	....	....	....	....	....	....	....	....	....	....
	NY Islanders	**NHL**	13	3	6	9	30	1	0	2	36	8.3	–5	....	....	....	....	....	....	....	....	....	....	....	....
1995-96	**NY Islanders**	**NHL**	65	11	36	47	93	7	0	1	155	7.1	–18	....	....	....	....	....	....	....	....	....	....	....	....
	Toronto	**NHL**	13	2	5	7	10	0	0	0	36	5.6	–2	....	....	....	6	0	4	4	8	0	0	0	....
1996-97	**Toronto**	**NHL**	26	5	7	12	20	1	0	1	63	7.9	3	....	....	....	....	....	....	....	....	....	....	....	....
1997-98	**Toronto**	**NHL**	76	11	26	37	44	4	1	1	181	6.1	–12	....	....	....	....	....	....	....	....	....	....	....	....
	United States	Olympics	4	0	0	0	6	....	....	....	....	....	....	....	....	....	....	....	....	....	....	....	....	....	....
1998-99	**NY Rangers**	**NHL**	75	10	24	34	71	5	0	2	159	6.3	–19	0	0.0	24:35	....	....	....	....	....	....	....	....	....
99-2000	**NY Rangers**	**NHL**	80	10	20	30	78	3	0	1	228	4.4	–6	0	0.0	22:31	....	....	....	....	....	....	....	....	....
2000-01	**Los Angeles**	**NHL**	73	16	35	51	56	7	1	2	183	8.7	0	0	0.0	23:04	13	0	9	9	10	0	0	0	25:51
2001-02	**Los Angeles**	**NHL**	55	7	23	30	68	4	0	0	123	5.7	3	0	0.0	22:25	7	0	1	1	18	0	0	0	22:52
2002-03	**Los Angeles**	**NHL**	65	14	29	43	57	10	0	1	162	8.6	0	0	0.0	22:20	....	....	....	....	....	....	....	....	....
	Detroit	**NHL**	13	2	5	7	16	1	0	0	37	5.4	2	0	0.0	22:42	4	0	0	0	6	0	0	0	28:16
2003-04	**Detroit**	**NHL**	78	14	32	46	56	4	1	4	165	8.5	22	4	0.0	24:29	12	1	2	3	8	1	0	1	26:30
2004-05			DID NOT PLAY																						
2005-06	**Detroit**	**NHL**	72	21	38	59	86	11	0	4	188	11.2	33	4	25.0	24:31	6	1	7	8	6	0	0	0	26:44
	United States	Olympics	6	1	2	3	16	....	....	....	....	....	....	....	....	....	....	....	....	....	....	....	....	....	....
2006-07	**Detroit**	**NHL**	68	11	41	52	66	2	1	2	184	6.0	12	0	0.0	23:35	11	2	4	6	16	1	0	1	23:35
	NHL Totals		1132	200	463	663	1115	88	4	32	2788	7.2		8	12.5	23:28	103	9	43	52	143	5	0	2	25:25

OHL First All-Star Team (1988, 1989)

Played in NHL All-Star Game (1996, 2003)

Traded to **NY Islanders** by **Montreal** with Kirk Muller and Craig Darby for Pierre Turgeon and Vladimir Malakhov, April 5, 1995. Traded to **Toronto** by **NY Islanders** with Wendel Clark and D.J. Smith for Darby Hendrickson, Sean Haggerty, Kenny Jonsson and Toronto's 1st round choice (Roberto Luongo) in 1997 Entry Draft, March 13, 1996. • Missed majority of 1996-97 season recovering from groin injury suffered in game vs. St. Louis, December 27, 1996. Rights traded to **NY Rangers** by **Toronto** for Alexander Karpovtsev and NY Rangers' 4th round choice (Mirko Murovic) in 1999 Entry Draft, October 14, 1998. Claimed by **Columbus** from **NY Rangers** in Expansion Draft, June 23, 2000. Signed as a free agent by **Los Angeles**, August 14, 2000. Traded to **Detroit** by **Los Angeles** for Sean Avery, Maxim Kuznetsov, Detroit's 1st round choice (Jeff Tambellini) in 2003 Entry Draft and Detroit's 2nd round choice (later traded to Boston – Boston selected Martins Karsums) in 2004 Entry Draft, March 11, 2003. Signed as a free agent by **Anaheim**, July 1, 2007.

SCHREMP, Rob (SHREHMP, RAWB) EDM.

Center. Shoots left. 5'11", 200 lbs. Born, Syracuse, NY, July 1, 1986. Edmonton's 2nd choice, 25th overall, in 2004 Entry Draft.

Season	Club	League	GP	G	A	Pts	PIM	PP	SH	GW	S	%	+/-	TF	F%	Min	Playoffs GP	G	A	Pts	PIM	PP	SH	GW	Min
2000-01	Syracuse	OPJHL	49	32	46	78	....	....	....	....	....	....	....	....	....	....	....	....	....	....	....	....	....	....	....
2001-02	Syracuse	OPJHL	47	41	47	88	93	....	....	....	....	....	....	....	....	....	1	1	2	3	0	....	....	....	....
2002-03	Mississauga	OHL	65	26	48	74	25	....	....	....	....	....	....	....	....	....	2	1	0	1	0	....	....	....	....
2003-04	USNTDP	U-18	2	0	0	0	8	....	....	....	....	....	....	....	....	....	....	....	....	....	....	....	....	....	....
	Mississauga	OHL	3	2	4	6	0	....	....	....	....	....	....	....	....	....	....	....	....	....	....	....	....	....	....
	London Knights	OHL	60	28	41	69	18	....	....	....	....	....	....	....	....	....	15	7	6	13	2	....	....	....	....
2004-05	London Knights	OHL	62	41	49	90	54	....	....	....	....	....	....	....	....	....	18	13	16	29	16	....	....	....	....
2005-06	London Knights	OHL	57	*57	*88	*145	74	....	....	....	....	....	....	....	....	....	19	10	*37	*47	35	....	....	....	....
2006-07	**Edmonton**	**NHL**	**1**	**0**	**0**	**0**	**0**	**0**	**0**	**0**	**2**	**0.0**	**0**	**12**	**50.0**	**13:50**	....	....	....	....	....	....	....	....	....
	Wilkes-Barre	AHL	69	17	36	53	36	....	....	....	....	....	....	....	....	....	....	....	....	....	....	....	....	....	....
	NHL Totals		**1**	**0**	**0**	**0**	**0**	**0**	**0**	**0**	**2**	**0.0**		**12**	**50.0**	**13:50**	....	....	....	....	....	....	....	....	....

OHL All-Rookie Team (2003) • OHL Rookie of the Year (2003) • OHL First All-Star Team (2006)

SCHUBERT, Christoph (SHOO-buhrt, KRIHS-tawf) OTT.

Defense. Shoots left. 6'3", 237 lbs. Born, Munich, West Germany, February 5, 1982. Ottawa's 5th choice, 127th overall, in 2001 Entry Draft.

Season	Club	League	GP	G	A	Pts	PIM	PP	SH	GW	S	%	+/-	TF	F%	Min	Playoffs GP	G	A	Pts	PIM	PP	SH	GW	Min
1998-99	EV Landshut Jr.	Ger-Jr.	28	15	20	35	77	....	....	....	....	....	....	....	....	....	....	....	....	....	....	....	....	....	....
99-2000	EV Landshut Jr.	Ger-Jr.	11	14	11	25	51	....	....	....	....	....	....	....	....	....	....	....	....	....	....	....	....	....	....
	EV Landshut	German-3	55	7	5	12	68	....	....	....	....	....	....	....	....	....	....	....	....	....	....	....	....	....	....
2000-01	Munchen Barons	Germany	55	6	3	9	80	....	....	....	....	....	....	....	....	....	10	0	2	2	27	....	....	....	....
2001-02	Munchen Barons	Germany	50	5	11	16	125	....	....	....	....	....	....	....	....	....	9	3	4	7	32	....	....	....	....
2002-03	Binghamton	AHL	70	2	8	10	102	....	....	....	....	....	....	....	....	....	8	0	1	1	2	....	....	....	....
2003-04	Binghamton	AHL	70	2	10	12	69	....	....	....	....	....	....	....	....	....	1	0	0	0	0	....	....	....	....
2004-05	Binghamton	AHL	76	10	22	32	110	....	....	....	....	....	....	....	....	....	6	2	2	4	20	....	....	....	....
2005-06	**Ottawa**	**NHL**	**56**	**4**	**6**	**10**	**48**	**0**	**1**	**0**	**72**	**5.6**	**4**	**5**	**0.0**	**11:06**	**7**	**0**	**1**	**1**	**4**	**0**	**0**	**0**	**7:53**
	Germany	Olympics	5	0	1	1	2	....	....	....	....	....	....	....	....	....	....	....	....	....	....	....	....	....	....
2006-07	**Ottawa**	**NHL**	**80**	**8**	**17**	**25**	**56**	**1**	**0**	**1**	**97**	**8.2**	**30**	**1**	**0.0**	**11:13**	**20**	**0**	**1**	**1**	**22**	**0**	**0**	**0**	**9:10**
	NHL Totals		**136**	**12**	**23**	**35**	**104**	**1**	**1**	**1**	**169**	**7.1**		**6**	**0.0**	**11:10**	**27**	**0**	**2**	**2**	**26**	**0**	**0**	**0**	**8:50**

SCHULTZ, Jeff (SHUHLTZ, JEHF) WSH.

Defense. Shoots left. 6'6", 224 lbs. Born, Calgary, Alta., February 25, 1986. Washington's 2nd choice, 27th overall, in 2004 Entry Draft.

Season	Club	League	GP	G	A	Pts	PIM	PP	SH	GW	S	%	+/-	TF	F%	Min	Playoffs GP	G	A	Pts	PIM	PP	SH	GW	Min
2000-01	Calgary Hawks	CBHL	27	7	8	15	20	....	....	....	....	....	....	....	....	....	....	....	....	....	....	....	....	....	....
2001-02	Calgary Rangers	CBHL	27	5	18	23	42	....	....	....	....	....	....	....	....	....	....	....	....	....	....	....	....	....	....
2002-03	Calgary Hitmen	WHL	50	2	1	3	4	....	....	....	....	....	....	....	....	....	4	0	0	0	0	....	....	....	....
2003-04	Calgary Hitmen	WHL	72	11	24	35	33	....	....	....	....	....	....	....	....	....	7	1	1	2	0	....	....	....	....
2004-05	Calgary Hitmen	WHL	72	2	27	29	31	....	....	....	....	....	....	....	....	....	12	2	1	3	6	....	....	....	....
2005-06	Calgary Hitmen	WHL	68	7	33	40	36	....	....	....	....	....	....	....	....	....	13	4	6	10	6	....	....	....	....
	Hershey Bears	AHL	....	....	....	....	....	....	....	....	....	....	....	....	....	....	7	1	3	4	4	....	....	....	....
2006-07	**Washington**	**NHL**	**38**	**0**	**3**	**3**	**16**	**0**	**0**	**0**	**22**	**0.0**	**5**	**0**	**0.0**	**18:13**	....	....	....	....	....	....	....	....	....
	Hershey Bears	AHL	44	2	10	12	39	....	....	....	....	....	....	....	....	....	19	0	1	1	18	....	....	....	....
	NHL Totals		**38**	**0**	**3**	**3**	**16**	**0**	**0**	**0**	**22**	**0.0**		**0**	**0.0**	**18:13**	....	....	....	....	....	....	....	....	....

WHL East Second All-Star Team (2006)

SCHULTZ, Jesse (SHUHLTZ, JEH-see) ATL.

Right wing. Shoots right. 6'1", 195 lbs. Born, Strasbourg, Sask., September 28, 1982.

Season	Club	League	GP	G	A	Pts	PIM	PP	SH	GW	S	%	+/-	TF	F%	Min	Playoffs GP	G	A	Pts	PIM	PP	SH	GW	Min
99-2000	Tri-City	WHL	62	10	6	16	34	....	....	....	....	....	....	....	....	....	4	1	1	2	2	....	....	....	....
2000-01	Tri-City	WHL	30	5	8	13	16	....	....	....	....	....	....	....	....	....	....	....	....	....	....	....	....	....	....
	Prince Albert	WHL	35	14	18	32	14	....	....	....	....	....	....	....	....	....	....	....	....	....	....	....	....	....	....
2001-02	Prince Albert	WHL	45	18	24	42	16	....	....	....	....	....	....	....	....	....	....	....	....	....	....	....	....	....	....
	Kelowna Rockets	WHL	28	10	12	22	14	....	....	....	....	....	....	....	....	....	....	....	....	....	....	....	....	....	....
2002-03	Kelowna Rockets	WHL	72	53	51	104	47	....	....	....	....	....	....	....	....	....	19	*12	16	*28	21	....	....	....	....
2003-04	Manitoba Moose	AHL	2	0	1	1	0	....	....	....	....	....	....	....	....	....	....	....	....	....	....	....	....	....	....
	Columbia Inferno	ECHL	52	27	21	48	72	....	....	....	....	....	....	....	....	....	4	1	2	3	2	....	....	....	....
2004-05	Manitoba Moose	AHL	70	9	15	24	33	....	....	....	....	....	....	....	....	....	14	3	2	5	2	....	....	....	....
2005-06	Manitoba Moose	AHL	80	37	30	67	63	....	....	....	....	....	....	....	....	....	13	5	7	12	10	....	....	....	....
2006-07	**Vancouver**	**NHL**	**2**	**0**	**0**	**0**	**0**	**0**	**0**	**0**	**6**	**0.0**	**0**	**0**	**0.0**	**10:09**	....	....	....	....	....	....	....	....	....
	Manitoba Moose	AHL	67	18	21	39	35	....	....	....	....	....	....	....	....	....	7	0	0	0	2	....	....	....	....
	NHL Totals		**2**	**0**	**0**	**0**	**0**	**0**	**0**	**0**	**6**	**0.0**		**0**	**0.0**	**10:09**	....	....	....	....	....	....	....	....	....

WHL West First All-Star Team (2003)

Signed as a free agent by **Vancouver**, July 31, 2003. Traded to **Atlanta** by **Vancouver** for Jim Sharrow, June 23, 2007.

SCHULTZ, Nick (SHUHLTZ, NIHK) MIN.

Defense. Shoots left. 6'1", 201 lbs. Born, Strasbourg, Sask., August 25, 1982. Minnesota's 2nd choice, 33rd overall, in 2000 Entry Draft.

Season	Club	League	GP	G	A	Pts	PIM	PP	SH	GW	S	%	+/-	TF	F%	Min	Playoffs GP	G	A	Pts	PIM	PP	SH	GW	Min
1997-98	Yorkton Mallers	SMHL	59	10	30	40	74	....	....	....	....	....	....	....	....	....	....	....	....	....	....	....	....	....	....
1998-99	Prince Albert	WHL	58	5	18	23	37	....	....	....	....	....	....	....	....	....	14	0	7	7	0	....	....	....	....
99-2000	Prince Albert	WHL	72	11	33	44	38	....	....	....	....	....	....	....	....	....	6	0	3	3	2	....	....	....	....
2000-01	Prince Albert	WHL	59	17	30	47	120	....	....	....	....	....	....	....	....	....	....	....	....	....	....	....	....	....	....
	Cleveland	IHL	4	1	1	2	2	....	....	....	....	....	....	....	....	....	3	0	1	1	0	....	....	....	....
2001-02	**Minnesota**	**NHL**	**52**	**4**	**6**	**10**	**14**	**1**	**0**	**1**	**47**	**8.5**	**0**	**0**	**0.0**	**16:08**	....	....	....	....	....	....	....	....	....
	Houston Aeros	AHL	....	....	....	....	....	....	....	....	....	....	....	....	....	....	14	1	5	6	2	....	....	....	....
2002-03	**Minnesota**	**NHL**	**75**	**3**	**7**	**10**	**23**	**0**	**0**	**1**	**70**	**4.3**	**11**	**0**	**0.0**	**18:28**	**18**	**0**	**1**	**1**	**10**	**0**	**0**	**0**	**19:39**
2003-04	**Minnesota**	**NHL**	**79**	**6**	**10**	**16**	**16**	**1**	**0**	**0**	**72**	**8.3**	**12**	**0**	**0.0**	**20:19**	....	....	....	....	....	....	....	....	....
2004-05	Kassel Huskies	Germany	46	7	15	22	26	....	....	....	....	....	....	....	....	....	7	0	4	4	6	....	....	....	....
2005-06	**Minnesota**	**NHL**	**79**	**2**	**12**	**14**	**43**	**0**	**0**	**0**	**45**	**4.4**	**2**	**0**	**0.0**	**17:58**	....	....	....	....	....	....	....	....	....
2006-07	**Minnesota**	**NHL**	**82**	**2**	**10**	**12**	**42**	**0**	**0**	**1**	**69**	**2.9**	**0**	**0**	**0.0**	**20:13**	**5**	**0**	**1**	**1**	**0**	**0**	**0**	**0**	**18:06**
	NHL Totals		**367**	**17**	**45**	**62**	**138**	**2**	**0**	**3**	**303**	**5.6**		**0**	**0.0**	**18:49**	**23**	**0**	**2**	**2**	**10**	**0**	**0**	**0**	**19:18**

Signed as a free agent by **Kassel** (Germany), September 24, 2004.

SCUDERI, Rob (SKUD-uh-ree, RAWB) PIT.

Defense. Shoots left. 6', 213 lbs. Born, Syosset, NY, December 30, 1978. Pittsburgh's 5th choice, 134th overall, in 1998 Entry Draft.

Season	Club	League	GP	G	A	Pts	PIM	PP	SH	GW	S	%	+/-	TF	F%	Min	Playoffs GP	G	A	Pts	PIM	PP	SH	GW	Min
1995-96	NY Apple Core	MtJHL	76	18	60	78	....	....	....	....	....	....	....	....	....	....	....	....	....	....	....	....	....	....	....
1996-97	NY Apple Core	MtJHL	82	42	70	112	64	....	....	....	....	....	....	....	....	....	....	....	....	....	....	....	....	....	....
1997-98	Boston College	H-East	42	0	24	24	12	....	....	....	....	....	....	....	....	....	....	....	....	....	....	....	....	....	....
1998-99	Boston College	H-East	41	2	8	10	20	....	....	....	....	....	....	....	....	....	....	....	....	....	....	....	....	....	....
99-2000	Boston College	H-East	42	1	12	13	22	....	....	....	....	....	....	....	....	....	....	....	....	....	....	....	....	....	....
2000-01	Boston College	H-East	43	4	19	23	42	....	....	....	....	....	....	....	....	....	....	....	....	....	....	....	....	....	....
2001-02	Wilkes-Barre	AHL	75	1	22	23	66	....	....	....	....	....	....	....	....	....	....	....	....	....	....	....	....	....	....
2002-03	Wilkes-Barre	AHL	74	4	17	21	44	....	....	....	....	....	....	....	....	....	6	0	1	1	4	....	....	....	....
2003-04	**Pittsburgh**	**NHL**	**13**	**1**	**2**	**3**	**4**	**0**	**0**	**0**	**4**	**25.0**	**2**	**0**	**0.0**	**20:06**	....	....	....	....	....	....	....	....	....
	Wilkes-Barre	AHL	64	1	15	16	54	....	....	....	....	....	....	....	....	....	24	0	3	3	14	....	....	....	....
2004-05	Wilkes-Barre	AHL	79	2	18	20	34	....	....	....	....	....	....	....	....	....	11	2	1	3	2	....	....	....	....
2005-06	**Pittsburgh**	**NHL**	**57**	**0**	**4**	**4**	**36**	**0**	**0**	**0**	**28**	**0.0**	**–18**	**0**	**0.0**	**20:15**	....	....	....	....	....	....	....	....	....
	Wilkes-Barre	AHL	13	0	8	8	8	....	....	....	....	....	....	....	....	....	....	....	....	....	....	....	....	....	....
2006-07	**Pittsburgh**	**NHL**	**78**	**1**	**10**	**11**	**28**	**0**	**0**	**0**	**31**	**3.2**	**3**	**0**	**0.0**	**18:49**	**5**	**0**	**0**	**0**	**2**	**0**	**0**	**0**	**17:14**
	NHL Totals		**148**	**2**	**16**	**18**	**68**	**0**	**0**	**0**	**63**	**3.2**		**0**	**0.0**	**19:29**	**5**	**0**	**0**	**0**	**2**	**0**	**0**	**0**	**17:14**

NCAA Championship All-Tournament Team (2001)

SEABROOK, Brent

(SEE-bruk, BREHNT) **CHI.**

Defense. Shoots right. 6'3", 220 lbs. Born, Richmond, B.C., April 20, 1985. Chicago's 1st choice, 14th overall, in 2003 Entry Draft.

			Regular Season														Playoffs								
Season	Club	League	GP	G	A	Pts	PIM	PP	SH	GW	S	%	+/-	TF	F%	Min	GP	G	A	Pts	PIM	PP	SH	GW	Min
2000-01	Delta Ice Hawks	PIJHL	54	16	26	42	55	....	....	....	....	....	....	....	....	....	....	....	....	....	....	....	....	....	....
	Lethbridge	WHL	4	0	0	0	0	....	....	....	....	....	....	....	....	....	....	....	....	....	....	....	....	....	....
2001-02	Lethbridge	WHL	67	6	33	39	70	....	....	....	....	....	....	....	....	....	4	1	1	2	2	....	....	....	....
2002-03	Lethbridge	WHL	69	9	33	42	113	....	....	....	....	....	....	....	....	....	....	....	....	....	....	....	....	....	....
2003-04	Lethbridge	WHL	61	12	29	41	107	....	....	....	....	....	....	....	....	....	....	....	....	....	....	....	....	....	....
2004-05	Lethbridge	WHL	63	12	42	54	107	....	....	....	....	....	....	....	....	....	5	1	2	3	10	....	....	....	....
	Norfolk Admirals	AHL	3	0	0	0	2	....	....	....	....	....	....	....	....	....	6	0	1	1	6	....	....	....	....
2005-06	**Chicago**	**NHL**	**69**	**5**	**27**	**32**	**60**	**1**	**0**	**2**	**114**	**4.4**	**5**	**0**	**0.0**	**20:02**	....	....	....	....	....	....	....	....	....
2006-07	**Chicago**	**NHL**	**81**	**4**	**20**	**24**	**104**	**0**	**0**	**0**	**144**	**2.8**	**-6**	**2**	**50.0**	**20:46**	....	....	....	....	....	....	....	....	....
	NHL Totals		**150**	**9**	**47**	**56**	**164**	**1**	**0**	**2**	**258**	**3.5**		**2**	**50.0**	**20:26**	....	....	....	....	....	....	....	....	....

WHL East Second All-Star Team (2005)

SEDIN, Daniel

(suh-DEEN, DAN-yehl) **VAN.**

Left wing. Shoots left. 6'1", 185 lbs. Born, Ornskoldsvik, Sweden, September 26, 1980. Vancouver's 1st choice, 2nd overall, in 1999 Entry Draft.

			Regular Season														Playoffs								
Season	Club	League	GP	G	A	Pts	PIM	PP	SH	GW	S	%	+/-	TF	F%	Min	GP	G	A	Pts	PIM	PP	SH	GW	Min
1997-98	Malmo Jr.	Swe-Jr.	4	3	3	6	4	....	....	....	....	....	....	....	....	....	....	....	....	....	....	....	....	....	....
	MoDo Jr.	Swe-Jr.	26	26	14	40	....	....	....	....	....	....	....	....	....	....	....	....	....	....	....	....	....	....	....
	MoDo	Sweden	45	4	8	12	26	....	....	....	....	....	....	....	....	....	9	0	0	0	2	....	....	....	....
1998-99	MoDo	Sweden	50	21	21	42	20	....	....	....	....	....	....	....	....	....	13	4	8	12	14	....	....	....	....
99-2000	MoDo	Sweden	50	19	26	45	28	....	....	....	....	....	....	....	....	....	13	*8	6	14	18	....	....	....	....
	MoDo	EuroHL	4	3	3	6	0	....	....	....	....	....	....	....	....	....	2	0	0	0	0	....	....	....	....
2000-01	**Vancouver**	**NHL**	**75**	**20**	**14**	**34**	**24**	**10**	**0**	**3**	**127**	**15.7**	**-3**	**10**	**60.0**	**13:00**	**4**	**1**	**2**	**3**	**0**	**0**	**0**	**0**	**16:15**
2001-02	**Vancouver**	**NHL**	**79**	**9**	**23**	**32**	**32**	**4**	**0**	**2**	**117**	**7.7**	**1**	**18**	**33.3**	**12:22**	**6**	**0**	**1**	**1**	**0**	**0**	**0**	**0**	**10:44**
2002-03	**Vancouver**	**NHL**	**79**	**14**	**17**	**31**	**34**	**4**	**0**	**2**	**134**	**10.4**	**8**	**24**	**45.8**	**12:26**	**14**	**1**	**5**	**6**	**8**	**1**	**0**	**1**	**12:23**
2003-04	**Vancouver**	**NHL**	**82**	**18**	**36**	**54**	**18**	**1**	**0**	**3**	**153**	**11.8**	**18**	**71**	**47.9**	**13:33**	**7**	**1**	**2**	**3**	**0**	**1**	**0**	**0**	**16:03**
2004-05	MODO	Sweden	49	13	20	33	40	....	....	....	....	....	....	....	....	....	6	0	3	3	6	....	....	....	....
2005-06	**Vancouver**	**NHL**	**82**	**22**	**49**	**71**	**34**	**11**	**0**	**4**	**204**	**10.8**	**7**	**49**	**42.9**	**16:40**	....	....	....	....	....	....	....	....	....
	Sweden	Olympics	8	1	3	4	2	....	....	....	....	....	....	....	....	....	....	....	....	....	....	....	....	....	....
2006-07	**Vancouver**	**NHL**	**81**	**36**	**48**	**84**	**36**	**16**	**0**	**8**	**236**	**15.3**	**19**	**44**	**22.7**	**18:04**	**12**	**2**	**3**	**5**	**4**	**0**	**0**	**0**	**21:31**
	NHL Totals		**478**	**119**	**187**	**306**	**178**	**46**	**0**	**22**	**971**	**12.3**		**216**	**40.7**	**14:23**	**43**	**5**	**13**	**18**	**12**	**2**	**0**	**1**	**15:40**

Signed as a free agent by **MODO** (Sweden), September 18, 2004.

SEDIN, Henrik

(suh-DEEN, HEHN-rihk) **VAN.**

Center. Shoots left. 6'2", 190 lbs. Born, Ornskoldsvik, Sweden, September 26, 1980. Vancouver's 2nd choice, 3rd overall, in 1999 Entry Draft.

			Regular Season														Playoffs								
Season	Club	League	GP	G	A	Pts	PIM	PP	SH	GW	S	%	+/-	TF	F%	Min	GP	G	A	Pts	PIM	PP	SH	GW	Min
1997-98	MoDo Jr.	Swe-Jr.	26	14	22	36	....	....	....	....	....	....	....	....	....	....	....	....	....	....	....	....	....	....	....
	Malmo Jr.	Swe-Jr.	8	4	7	11	6	....	....	....	....	....	....	....	....	....	....	....	....	....	....	....	....	....	....
	MoDo	Sweden	39	1	4	5	8	....	....	....	....	....	....	....	....	....	7	0	0	0	0	....	....	....	....
1998-99	MoDo	Sweden	49	12	22	34	32	....	....	....	....	....	....	....	....	....	13	2	8	10	6	....	....	....	....
99-2000	MoDo	Sweden	50	9	38	47	22	....	....	....	....	....	....	....	....	....	13	5	9	14	2	....	....	....	....
2000-01	**Vancouver**	**NHL**	**82**	**9**	**20**	**29**	**38**	**2**	**0**	**1**	**98**	**9.2**	**-2**	**1020**	**44.1**	**13:31**	**4**	**0**	**4**	**4**	**0**	**0**	**0**	**0**	**16:31**
2001-02	**Vancouver**	**NHL**	**82**	**16**	**20**	**36**	**36**	**3**	**0**	**1**	**78**	**20.5**	**9**	**785**	**47.4**	**12:48**	**6**	**3**	**0**	**3**	**0**	**0**	**0**	**1**	**11:55**
2002-03	**Vancouver**	**NHL**	**78**	**8**	**31**	**39**	**38**	**4**	**1**	**1**	**81**	**9.9**	**9**	**995**	**48.2**	**13:58**	**14**	**3**	**2**	**5**	**8**	**1**	**0**	**0**	**13:01**
2003-04	**Vancouver**	**NHL**	**76**	**11**	**31**	**42**	**32**	**2**	**0**	**2**	**99**	**11.1**	**23**	**961**	**50.0**	**14:02**	**7**	**2**	**2**	**4**	**2**	**2**	**0**	**0**	**16:02**
2004-05	MODO	Sweden	44	14	22	36	50	....	....	....	....	....	....	....	....	....	6	1	3	4	6	....	....	....	....
2005-06	**Vancouver**	**NHL**	**82**	**18**	**57**	**75**	**56**	**5**	**1**	**0**	**113**	**15.9**	**11**	**1238**	**50.7**	**16:54**	....	....	....	....	....	....	....	....	....
	Sweden	Olympics	8	3	1	4	2	....	....	....	....	....	....	....	....	....	....	....	....	....	....	....	....	....	....
2006-07	**Vancouver**	**NHL**	**82**	**10**	**71**	**81**	**66**	**1**	**0**	**2**	**134**	**7.5**	**19**	**1220**	**52.5**	**18:26**	**12**	**2**	**2**	**4**	**14**	**1**	**0**	**1**	**22:12**
	NHL Totals		**482**	**72**	**230**	**302**	**266**	**17**	**2**	**7**	**603**	**11.9**		**6219**	**49.1**	**14:58**	**43**	**10**	**10**	**20**	**24**	**4**	**0**	**2**	**16:15**

Signed as a free agent by **MODO** (Sweden), September 18, 2004.

SEIDENBERG, Dennis

(SIGH-dehn-buhrg, DEH-nihs) **CAR.**

Defense. Shoots left. 6'1", 210 lbs. Born, Schwenningen, West Germany, July 18, 1981. Philadelphia's 6th choice, 172nd overall, in 2001 Entry Draft.

			Regular Season														Playoffs								
Season	Club	League	GP	G	A	Pts	PIM	PP	SH	GW	S	%	+/-	TF	F%	Min	GP	G	A	Pts	PIM	PP	SH	GW	Min
99-2000	Mannheim Jr.	Ger-Jr.	52	12	28	40	28	....	....	....	....	....	....	....	....	....	....	....	....	....	....	....	....	....	....
	Adler Mannheim	Germany	3	0	0	0	0	....	....	....	....	....	....	....	....	....	....	....	....	....	....	....	....	....	....
2000-01	Mannheim Jr.	Ger-Jr.	9	3	8	11	20	....	....	....	....	....	....	....	....	....	....	....	....	....	....	....	....	....	....
	Adler Mannheim	Germany	55	2	5	7	6	....	....	....	....	....	....	....	....	....	12	0	1	1	10	....	....	....	....
2001-02	Adler Mannheim	Germany	55	7	13	20	56	....	....	....	....	....	....	....	....	....	8	0	0	0	2	....	....	....	....
2002-03	**Philadelphia**	**NHL**	**58**	**4**	**9**	**13**	**20**	**1**	**0**	**0**	**123**	**3.3**	**8**	**1**	**0.0**	**16:50**	....	....	....	....	....	....	....	....	....
	Philadelphia	AHL	19	5	6	11	17	....	....	....	....	....	....	....	....	....	....	....	....	....	....	....	....	....	....
2003-04	**Philadelphia**	**NHL**	**5**	**0**	**0**	**0**	**2**	**0**	**0**	**0**	**14**	**0.0**	**-4**	**0**	**0.0**	**17:20**	**3**	**0**	**0**	**0**	**0**	**0**	**0**	**0**	**7:36**
	Philadelphia	AHL	33	7	12	19	31	....	....	....	....	....	....	....	....	....	9	2	2	4	4	....	....	....	....
2004-05	Philadelphia	AHL	79	13	28	41	47	....	....	....	....	....	....	....	....	....	18	2	8	10	19	....	....	....	....
2005-06	**Philadelphia**	**NHL**	**29**	**2**	**5**	**7**	**4**	**1**	**0**	**0**	**34**	**5.9**	**-4**	**1**	**0.0**	**14:22**	....	....	....	....	....	....	....	....	....
	Phoenix	**NHL**	**34**	**1**	**10**	**11**	**14**	**1**	**0**	**0**	**49**	**2.0**	**-9**	**0**	**0.0**	**19:13**	....	....	....	....	....	....	....	....	....
	Germany	Olympics	5	0	0	0	6	....	....	....	....	....	....	....	....	....	....	....	....	....	....	....	....	....	....
2006-07	**Phoenix**	**NHL**	**32**	**1**	**1**	**2**	**16**	**0**	**0**	**0**	**36**	**2.8**	**-4**	**0**	**0.0**	**14:43**	....	....	....	....	....	....	....	....	....
	Carolina	**NHL**	**20**	**1**	**5**	**6**	**2**	**0**	**0**	**0**	**47**	**2.1**	**-12**	**0**	**0.0**	**18:29**	....	....	....	....	....	....	....	....	....
	NHL Totals		**178**	**9**	**30**	**39**	**58**	**3**	**0**	**0**	**303**	**3.0**		**2**	**0.0**	**16:42**	**3**	**0**	**0**	**0**	**0**	**0**	**0**	**0**	**7:36**

• Missed majority of 2003-04 season recovering from leg injury suffered in game vs. Edmonton, January 10, 2004. Traded to **Phoenix** by **Philadelphia** with Phoenix's 4th round choice (Joonas Lehtivuori) in 2006 Entry Draft for Petr Nedved and Philadelphia's 4th round choice (later traded to NY Islanders - NY Islanders selected Tomas Marcinko) in 2006 Entry Draft, January 20, 2006. Traded to **Carolina** by **Phoenix** for Kevyn Adams, January 8, 2007.

SEJNA, Peter

(SHAY-nah, PEE-tuhr)

Left wing. Shoots left. 5'11", 198 lbs. Born, Liptovsky Mikulas, Czech., October 5, 1979.

			Regular Season														Playoffs								
Season	Club	League	GP	G	A	Pts	PIM	PP	SH	GW	S	%	+/-	TF	F%	Min	GP	G	A	Pts	PIM	PP	SH	GW	Min
1995-96	L. Mikulas U18	Svk-U18	44	40	23	63	20	....	....	....	....	....	....	....	....	....	....	....	....	....	....	....	....	....	....
1996-97	L. Mikulas U18	Svk-U18	40	32	19	51	6	....	....	....	....	....	....	....	....	....	....	....	....	....	....	....	....	....	....
	L. Mikulas	Slovakia	29	3	5	8	2	....	....	....	....	....	....	....	....	....	....	....	....	....	....	....	....	....	....
	L. Mikulas Jr.	Slovak-Jr.	17	14	10	24	8	....	....	....	....	....	....	....	....	....	....	....	....	....	....	....	....	....	....
1997-98	L. Mikulas	Slovakia	34	5	6	11	6	....	....	....	....	....	....	....	....	....	....	....	....	....	....	....	....	....	....
1998-99	Des Moines	USHL	52	40	23	63	26	....	....	....	....	....	....	....	....	....	14	11	6	17	8	....	....	....	....
99-2000	Des Moines	USHL	58	41	53	94	36	....	....	....	....	....	....	....	....	....	9	4	5	9	4	....	....	....	....
2000-01	Colorado College	WCHA	41	29	29	58	10	....	....	....	....	....	....	....	....	....	....	....	....	....	....	....	....	....	....
2001-02	Colorado College	WCHA	43	26	24	50	16	....	....	....	....	....	....	....	....	....	....	....	....	....	....	....	....	....	....
2002-03	Colorado College	WCHA	42	*36	46	*82	12	....	....	....	....	....	....	....	....	....	....	....	....	....	....	....	....	....	....
	St. Louis	**NHL**	**1**	**1**	**0**	**1**	**0**	**1**	**0**	**0**	**3**	**33.3**	**0**	**0**	**0.0**	**15:22**	....	....	....	....	....	....	....	....	....
2003-04	**St. Louis**	**NHL**	**20**	**2**	**2**	**4**	**4**	**2**	**0**	**0**	**36**	**5.6**	**-9**	**7**	**42.9**	**14:58**	....	....	....	....	....	....	....	....	....
	Worcester IceCats	AHL	59	12	29	41	13	....	....	....	....	....	....	....	....	....	10	3	3	6	10	....	....	....	....
2004-05	Worcester IceCats	AHL	64	17	21	38	24	....	....	....	....	....	....	....	....	....	....	....	....	....	....	....	....	....	....
2005-06	**St. Louis**	**NHL**	**6**	**1**	**1**	**2**	**4**	**0**	**0**	**0**	**9**	**11.1**	**1**	**1**	**0.0**	**11:43**	....	....	....	....	....	....	....	....	....
	Peoria Rivermen	AHL	44	19	31	50	18	....	....	....	....	....	....	....	....	....	4	3	0	3	2	....	....	....	....
2006-07	**St. Louis**	**NHL**	**22**	**3**	**1**	**4**	**4**	**0**	**0**	**0**	**34**	**8.8**	**2**	**4**	**75.0**	**10:00**	....	....	....	....	....	....	....	....	....
	Peoria Rivermen	AHL	39	12	24	36	12	....	....	....	....	....	....	....	....	....	....	....	....	....	....	....	....	....	....
	NHL Totals		**49**	**7**	**4**	**11**	**12**	**3**	**0**	**0**	**82**	**8.5**		**12**	**50.0**	**12:21**	....	....	....	....	....	....	....	....	....

WCHA Rookie of the Year (2001) • WCHA First All-Star Team (2003) • WCHA Player of the Year (2003) • NCAA West First All-American Team (2003) • Hobey Baker Memorial Award (Top U.S. Collegiate Player) (2003)

Signed as a free agent by **St. Louis**, April 6, 2003.

SEKERA, Andrej
(SEH-kuhr-ah, AWN-dray) **BUF.**

Defense. Shoots left. 6', 201 lbs. Born, Bojnice, Czech., June 8, 1986. Buffalo's 3rd choice, 71st overall, in 2004 Entry Draft.

			Regular Season														Playoffs								
Season	Club	League	GP	G	A	Pts	PIM	PP	SH	GW	S	%	+/-	TF	F%	Min	GP	G	A	Pts	PIM	PP	SH	GW	Min
2001-02	Dukla Trencin Jr.	Slovak-Jr.	52	5	10	15	10																		
2002-03	Dukla Trencin Jr.	Slovak-Jr.	48	9	15	24	20																		
2003-04	Dukla Trencin Jr.	Slovak-Jr.	42	5	12	17	40										2	0	1	1	4				
	Dukla Trencin	Slovakia	3	0	0	0	2																		
	Dukla Trencin U18	Svk-U18	5	0	0	0	0																		
2004-05	Owen Sound	OHL	51	7	21	28	18										6	0	4	4	4				
2005-06	Owen Sound	OHL	51	21	34	55	54										11	5	8	13	9				
2006-07	**Buffalo**	**NHL**	**2**	**0**	**0**	**0**	**2**	**0**	**0**	**0**	**0**	**0.0**	**1**	**0**	**0.0**	**7:31**									
	Rochester	AHL	54	3	16	19	28																		
	NHL Totals		**2**	**0**	**0**	**0**	**2**	**0**	**0**	**0**	**0**	**0.0**		**0**	**0.0**	**7:31**									

OHL All-Rookie Team (2005) • OHL First All-Star Team (2006)

SELANNE, Teemu
(seh-LAHN-ay, TEE-moo)

Right wing. Shoots right. 6', 204 lbs. Born, Helsinki, Finland, July 3, 1970. Winnipeg's 1st choice, 10th overall, in 1988 Entry Draft.

			Regular Season														Playoffs								
Season	Club	League	GP	G	A	Pts	PIM	PP	SH	GW	S	%	+/-	TF	F%	Min	GP	G	A	Pts	PIM	PP	SH	GW	Min
1986-87	Jokerit U18	Fin-U18															7	10	3	13	2				
	Jokerit Helsinki Jr.	Fin-Jr.	33	10	12	22	8																		
1987-88	Jokerit Helsinki Jr.	Fin-Jr.	33	43	23	66	18										5	4	3	7	2				
	Jokerit Helsinki	Finland-2	5	1	1	2	0																		
1988-89	PvUK Lahti Jr.	Fin-Jr.	3	3	1	4	2																		
	Jokerit Helsinki Jr.	Fin-Jr.	3	8	8	16	4																		
	Jokerit Helsinki	Finland-2	35	36	33	69	14										5	7	3	10	4				
1989-90	Jokerit Helsinki	Finland	11	4	8	12	0																		
1990-91	Jokerit Helsinki Jr.	Fin-Jr.	4	3	2	5	10																		
	Jokerit Helsinki	Finland	42	33	25	58	12																		
1991-92	Jokerit Helsinki	Finland	44	39	23	62	20										10	10	7	17	18				
	Finland	Olympics	8	7	4	11	6																		
1992-93	**Winnipeg**	**NHL**	**84**	***76**	**56**	**132**	**45**	**24**	**0**	**7**	**387**	**19.6**	**8**				**6**	**4**	**2**	**6**	**2**	**2**	**0**	**2**	
1993-94	**Winnipeg**	**NHL**	**51**	**25**	**29**	**54**	**22**	**11**	**0**	**2**	**191**	**13.1**	**–23**												
1994-95	Jokerit Helsinki	Finland	20	7	12	19	6																		
	Winnipeg	**NHL**	**45**	**22**	**26**	**48**	**2**	**8**	**2**	**1**	**167**	**13.2**	**1**												
1995-96	**Winnipeg**	**NHL**	**51**	**24**	**48**	**72**	**18**	**6**	**1**	**4**	**163**	**14.7**	**3**												
	Anaheim	**NHL**	**28**	**16**	**20**	**36**	**4**	**3**	**0**	**1**	**104**	**15.4**	**2**												
1996-97	**Anaheim**	**NHL**	**78**	**51**	**58**	**109**	**34**	**11**	**1**	**8**	**273**	**18.7**	**28**				**11**	**7**	**3**	**10**	**4**	**3**	**0**	**1**	
1997-98	**Anaheim**	**NHL**	**73**	***52**	**34**	**86**	**30**	**10**	**1**	**10**	**268**	**19.4**	**12**												
	Finland	Olympics	5	4	6	10	8																		
1998-99	**Anaheim**	**NHL**	**75**	***47**	**60**	**107**	**30**	**25**	**0**	**7**	**281**	**16.7**	**18**	**5**	**20.0**	**22:47**	**4**	**2**	**2**	**4**	**2**	**1**	**0**	**0**	**22:23**
99-2000	**Anaheim**	**NHL**	**79**	**33**	**52**	**85**	**12**	**8**	**0**	**6**	**236**	**14.0**	**6**	**13**	**23.1**	**22:44**									
2000-01	**Anaheim**	**NHL**	**61**	**26**	**33**	**59**	**36**	**10**	**0**	**5**	**202**	**12.9**	**–8**	**4**	**50.0**	**21:51**									
	San Jose	**NHL**	**12**	**7**	**6**	**13**	**0**	**2**	**0**	**2**	**31**	**22.6**	**1**	**4**	**75.0**	**18:14**	**6**	**0**	**2**	**2**	**2**	**0**	**0**	**0**	**17:13**
2001-02	**San Jose**	**NHL**	**82**	**29**	**25**	**54**	**40**	**9**	**1**	**8**	**202**	**14.4**	**–11**	**12**	**25.0**	**16:58**	**12**	**5**	**3**	**8**	**2**	**2**	**0**	**1**	**16:51**
	Finland	Olympics	4	3	0	3	2																		
2002-03	**San Jose**	**NHL**	**82**	**28**	**36**	**64**	**30**	**7**	**0**	**5**	**253**	**11.1**	**–6**	**107**	**42.1**	**19:14**									
2003-04	**Colorado**	**NHL**	**78**	**16**	**16**	**32**	**32**	**6**	**1**	**4**	**182**	**8.8**	**2**	**80**	**43.8**	**16:10**	**10**	**0**	**3**	**3**	**2**	**0**	**0**	**0**	**12:53**
2004-05			DID NOT PLAY																						
2005-06	**Anaheim**	**NHL**	**80**	**40**	**50**	**90**	**44**	**18**	**0**	**5**	**267**	**15.0**	**28**	**209**	**41.6**	**17:48**	**16**	**6**	**8**	**14**	**6**	**1**	**0**	**2**	**17:56**
	Finland	Olympics	8	6	5	11	4																		
2006-07 ♦	**Anaheim**	**NHL**	**82**	**48**	**46**	**94**	**82**	**25**	**0**	**10**	**257**	**18.7**	**26**	**351**	**50.7**	**17:42**	**21**	**5**	**10**	**15**	**10**	**0**	**0**	**2**	**19:08**
	NHL Totals		**1041**	**540**	**595**	**1135**	**461**	**183**	**7**	**85**	**3464**	**15.6**		**785**	**45.5**	**19:16**	**86**	**29**	**33**	**62**	**30**	**9**	**0**	**8**	**17:34**

NHL All-Rookie Team (1993) • NHL First All-Star Team (1993, 1997) • Calder Memorial Trophy (1993) • NHL Second All-Star Team (1998, 1999) • Maurice "Rocket" Richard Trophy (1999)

Played in NHL All-Star Game (1993, 1994, 1996, 1997, 1998, 1999, 2000, 2002, 2003, 2007) • Olympic Tournament All-Star Team (2006) • Best Forward at Olympics (2006) • Bill Masterton Memorial Trophy (2006)

• Missed majority of 1989-90 season recovering from leg injury suffered in game vs. HIFK Helsinki (Finland), October 19, 1989. Traded to **Anaheim** by **Winnipeg** with Marc Chouinard and Winnipeg's 4th round choice (later traded to Toronto – later traded to Montreal – Montreal selected Kim Staal) in 1996 Entry Draft for Chad Kilger, Oleg Tverdovsky and Anaheim's 3rd round choice (Per-Anton Lundstrom) in 1996 Entry Draft, February 7, 1996. Traded to **San Jose** by **Anaheim** for Jeff Friesen, Steve Shields and San Jose's 2nd round choice (later traded to Dallas – Dallas selected Vojtech Polak) in 2003 Entry Draft, March 5, 2001. Signed as a free agent by **Colorado**, July 3, 2003. Signed as a free agent by **Anaheim**, August 22, 2005.

SEMENOV, Alexei
(seh-MEH-nahv, al-EHX-ay) **S.J.**

Defense. Shoots left. 6'6", 235 lbs. Born, Murmansk, USSR, April 10, 1981. Edmonton's 2nd choice, 36th overall, in 1999 Entry Draft.

			Regular Season														Playoffs								
Season	Club	League	GP	G	A	Pts	PIM	PP	SH	GW	S	%	+/-	TF	F%	Min	GP	G	A	Pts	PIM	PP	SH	GW	Min
1997-98	Krylja Sovetov 2	Russia-3	52	1	2	3	48																		
1998-99	St. Petersburg 2	Russia-4	19	0	1	1	20																		
	Sudbury Wolves	OHL	28	0	3	3	28										2	0	0	0	4				
99-2000	Sudbury Wolves	OHL	65	9	35	44	135										12	1	3	4	23				
	Hamilton	AHL															3	0	0	0	0				
2000-01	Sudbury Wolves	OHL	65	21	42	63	106										12	4	13	17	17				
2001-02	Hamilton	AHL	78	5	11	16	67																		
2002-03	**Edmonton**	**NHL**	**46**	**1**	**6**	**7**	**58**	**0**	**0**	**0**	**33**	**3.0**	**–7**	**0**	**0.0**	**19:41**	**6**	**0**	**0**	**0**	**0**	**0**	**0**	**0**	**13:05**
	Hamilton	AHL	37	4	3	7	45																		
2003-04	**Edmonton**	**NHL**	**46**	**2**	**3**	**5**	**32**	**1**	**0**	**0**	**36**	**5.6**	**8**	**0**	**0.0**	**17:16**									
2004-05	St. Petersburg	Russia	50	0	8	8	26																		
2005-06	Yaroslavl	Russia	2	0	1	1	2																		
	Edmonton	**NHL**	**11**	**1**	**1**	**2**	**17**	**0**	**0**	**0**	**3**	**33.3**	**–3**	**0**	**0.0**	**10:49**									
	Florida	**NHL**	**16**	**1**	**1**	**2**	**21**	**1**	**0**	**0**	**13**	**7.7**	**–1**	**0**	**0.0**	**12:33**									
	Rochester	AHL	3	0	0	0	7																		
2006-07	**Florida**	**NHL**	**23**	**0**	**5**	**5**	**28**	**0**	**0**	**0**	**23**	**0.0**	**9**	**1**	**0.0**	**12:22**									
	Rochester	AHL	4	0	0	0	6																		
	Ufa	Russia	20	1	2	3	32																		
	NHL Totals		**142**	**5**	**16**	**21**	**156**	**2**	**0**	**0**	**108**	**4.6**		**1**	**0.0**	**16:14**	**6**	**0**	**0**	**0**	**0**	**0**	**0**	**0**	**13:05**

OHL First All-Star Team (2001)

Signed as a free agent by **St. Petersburg** (Russia), July 30, 2004. Traded to **Florida** by **Edmonton** for Florida's 5th round choice (Bryan Pitton) in 2006 Entry Draft, November 19, 2005. Signed as a free agent by **San Jose**, July 27, 2007.

SEMIN, Alexander
(SEH-min, al-EHX-AN-duhr) **WSH.**

Left wing. Shoots left. 6'2", 200 lbs. Born, Krasnoyarsk, USSR, March 3, 1984. Washington's 2nd choice, 13th overall, in 2002 Entry Draft.

			Regular Season														Playoffs								
Season	Club	League	GP	G	A	Pts	PIM	PP	SH	GW	S	%	+/-	TF	F%	Min	GP	G	A	Pts	PIM	PP	SH	GW	Min
2001-02	Chelyabinsk	Russia-2	46	13	8	21	52										2	2	0	2	0				
2002-03	Lada Togliatti	Russia	47	10	7	17	36										10	*5	3	8	10				
2003-04	**Washington**	**NHL**	**52**	**10**	**12**	**22**	**36**	**4**	**0**	**2**	**92**	**10.9**	**–2**	**6**	**50.0**	**12:37**									
	Portland Pirates	AHL	4	3	1	4	6										7	4	7	11	19				
2004-05	Lada Togliatti	Russia	50	19	11	30	56										10	1	1	2	0				
2005-06	Lada Togliatti	Russia	16	5	4	9	52																		
	Mytischi	Russia	26	3	7	10	24										8	3	2	5	6				
2006-07	**Washington**	**NHL**	**77**	**38**	**35**	**73**	**90**	**17**	**0**	**6**	**243**	**15.6**	**–7**	**44**	**27.3**	**18:24**									
	NHL Totals		**129**	**48**	**47**	**95**	**126**	**21**	**0**	**8**	**335**	**14.3**		**50**	**30.0**	**16:04**									

Signed as a free agent by **Togliatti** (Russia), September 25, 2004. • Suspended by **Washington** for failing to report to **Portland** (AHL), September 28, 2004. Signed as a free agent by **Mytischi** (Russia), November 22, 2005.

SEVERSON, Cam

(SEH-vuhr-SUHN, KAM)

Left wing. Shoots left. 6'1", 215 lbs. Born, Canora, Sask., January 15, 1978. San Jose's 6th choice, 192nd overall, in 1997 Entry Draft.

			Regular Season														Playoffs								
Season	Club	League	GP	G	A	Pts	PIM	PP	SH	GW	S	%	+/-	TF	F%	Min	GP	G	A	Pts	PIM	PP	SH	GW	Min
1996-97	Lethbridge	WHL	45	12	13	25	169																		
	Prince Albert	WHL	16	5	13	18	54										4	4	0	4	8				
1997-98	Prince Albert	WHL	41	23	25	48	129																		
	Spokane Chiefs	WHL	23	9	11	20	88										18	11	4	15	51				
1998-99	Spokane Chiefs	WHL	46	16	17	33	190																		
	Oklahoma City	CHL	5	6	3	9	4										10	4	0	4	26				
99-2000	Louisiana	ECHL	7	0	2	2	22																		
	Peoria Rivermen	ECHL	56	19	8	27	138										18	3	4	7	41				
2000-01	Portland Pirates	AHL	8	0	0	0	11																		
	Quad City	UHL	46	22	26	48	129																		
	Cincinnati	AHL	20	4	7	11	60										3	1	1	2	0				
2001-02	Hartford	AHL	65	11	10	21	116										5	0	0	0	7				
2002-03	**Anaheim**	**NHL**	**2**	**0**	**0**	**0**	**8**	**0**	**0**	**0**	**1**	**0.0**	**0**	**0**	**0.0**	**6:44**	**1**	**0**	**0**	**0**	**0**	**0**	**0**	**0**	**2:24**
	Cincinnati	AHL	71	12	9	21	156																		
2003-04	**Anaheim**	**NHL**	**31**	**3**	**0**	**3**	**50**	**1**	**0**	**0**	**24**	**12.5**	**–3**	**3**	**66.7**	**7:21**									
	Cincinnati	AHL	38	7	7	14	145																		
2004-05	Milwaukee	AHL	63	6	8	14	255										4	0	0	0	12				
2005-06	Omaha	AHL	54	13	7	20	146																		
	Columbus	**NHL**	**4**	**0**	**0**	**0**	**5**	**0**	**0**	**0**	**2**	**0.0**	**0**	**1**	**0.0**	**3:06**									
	Syracuse Crunch	AHL	12	4	3	7	28										3	0	0	0	21				
2006-07	Straubing Tigers	Germany	45	14	8	22	76																		
	NHL Totals		**37**	**3**	**0**	**3**	**63**	**1**	**0**	**0**	**27**	**11.1**		**4**	**50.0**	**6:51**	**1**	**0**	**0**	**0**	**0**	**0**	**0**	**0**	**2:24**

Signed as a free agent by **Hartford** (AHL), September 24, 2001. Signed as a free agent by **Anaheim**, August 22, 2002. Signed as a free agent by **Nashville**, July 22, 2004. Signed as a free agent by **Calgary**, August 11, 2005. Traded to **Columbus** by **Calgary** for Cale Hulse, February 28, 2006. Signed as a free agent by **Straubing** (Germany), July 29, 2006.

SHANAHAN, Brendan

(SHA-na-HAN, BREHN-duhn) **NYR**

Left wing. Shoots right. 6'3", 220 lbs. Born, Mimico, Ont., January 23, 1969. New Jersey's 1st choice, 2nd overall, in 1987 Entry Draft.

Season	Club	League	GP	G	A	Pts	PIM	PP	SH	GW	S	%	+/-	TF	F%	Min	GP	G	A	Pts	PIM	PP	SH	GW	Min
1984-85	Mississauga Reps	MTHL	36	20	21	41	26																		
	Dixie Beehives	OJHL	1	0	0	0	0																		
1985-86	London Knights	OHL	59	28	34	62	70										5	5	5	10	5				
1986-87	London Knights	OHL	56	39	53	92	92																		
1987-88	**New Jersey**	**NHL**	**65**	**7**	**19**	**26**	**131**	**2**	**0**	**2**	**72**	**9.7**	**–20**				**12**	**2**	**1**	**3**	**44**	**1**	**0**	**0**	
1988-89	**New Jersey**	**NHL**	**68**	**22**	**28**	**50**	**115**	**9**	**0**	**0**	**152**	**14.5**	**2**												
1989-90	**New Jersey**	**NHL**	**73**	**30**	**42**	**72**	**137**	**8**	**0**	**5**	**196**	**15.3**	**15**				**6**	**3**	**3**	**6**	**20**	**1**	**0**	**1**	
1990-91	**New Jersey**	**NHL**	**75**	**29**	**37**	**66**	**141**	**7**	**0**	**2**	**195**	**14.9**	**4**				**7**	**3**	**5**	**8**	**12**	**2**	**0**	**0**	
1991-92	**St. Louis**	**NHL**	**80**	**33**	**36**	**69**	**171**	**13**	**0**	**2**	**215**	**15.3**	**–3**				**6**	**2**	**3**	**5**	**14**	**1**	**0**	**0**	
1992-93	**St. Louis**	**NHL**	**71**	**51**	**43**	**94**	**174**	**18**	**0**	**8**	**232**	**22.0**	**10**				**11**	**4**	**3**	**7**	**18**	**2**	**0**	**0**	
1993-94	**St. Louis**	**NHL**	**81**	**52**	**50**	**102**	**211**	**15**	**7**	**8**	**397**	**13.1**	**–9**				**4**	**2**	**5**	**7**	**4**	**0**	**0**	**0**	
1994-95	Dusseldorfer EG	Germany	3	5	3	8	4																		
	St. Louis	**NHL**	**45**	**20**	**21**	**41**	**136**	**6**	**2**	**6**	**153**	**13.1**	**7**				**5**	**4**	**5**	**9**	**14**	**1**	**0**	**1**	
1995-96	**Hartford**	**NHL**	**74**	**44**	**34**	**78**	**125**	**17**	**2**	**6**	**280**	**15.7**	**2**												
1996-97	**Hartford**	**NHL**	**2**	**1**	**0**	**1**	**0**	**0**	**1**	**0**	**13**	**7.7**	**1**												
	♦ Detroit	**NHL**	**79**	**46**	**41**	**87**	**131**	**20**	**2**	**7**	**323**	**14.2**	**31**				**20**	**9**	**8**	**17**	**43**	**2**	**0**	**2**	
1997-98	**♦ Detroit**	**NHL**	**75**	**28**	**29**	**57**	**154**	**15**	**1**	**9**	**266**	**10.5**	**6**				**20**	**5**	**4**	**9**	**22**	**3**	**0**	**2**	
	Canada	Olympics	6	2	0	2	0																		
1998-99	**Detroit**	**NHL**	**81**	**31**	**27**	**58**	**123**	**5**	**0**	**5**	**288**	**10.8**	**2**	**18**	**44.4**	**17:31**	**10**	**3**	**7**	**10**	**6**	**1**	**0**	**1**	**18:31**
99-2000	**Detroit**	**NHL**	**78**	**41**	**37**	**78**	**105**	**13**	**1**	**9**	**283**	**14.5**	**24**	**24**	**50.0**	**18:35**	**9**	**3**	**2**	**5**	**10**	**0**	**0**	**0**	**17:36**
2000-01	**Detroit**	**NHL**	**81**	**31**	**45**	**76**	**81**	**15**	**1**	**7**	**278**	**11.2**	**9**	**115**	**43.5**	**18:22**	**2**	**2**	**2**	**4**	**0**	**0**	**0**	**1**	**21:02**
2001-02	**♦ Detroit**	**NHL**	**80**	**37**	**38**	**75**	**118**	**12**	**3**	**7**	**277**	**13.4**	**23**	**70**	**47.1**	**18:55**	**23**	**8**	**11**	**19**	**20**	**1**	**0**	**2**	**19:06**
	Canada	Olympics	6	0	1	1	0																		
2002-03	**Detroit**	**NHL**	**78**	**30**	**38**	**68**	**103**	**13**	**0**	**6**	**260**	**11.5**	**5**	**28**	**60.7**	**18:38**	**4**	**1**	**1**	**2**	**4**	**1**	**0**	**0**	**22:03**
2003-04	**Detroit**	**NHL**	**82**	**25**	**28**	**53**	**117**	**8**	**0**	**7**	**280**	**8.9**	**15**	**32**	**46.9**	**18:05**	**12**	**1**	**5**	**6**	**20**	**0**	**1**	**0**	**16:49**
2004-05			DID NOT PLAY																						
2005-06	**Detroit**	**NHL**	**82**	**40**	**41**	**81**	**105**	**14**	**0**	**6**	**289**	**13.8**	**29**	**26**	**50.0**	**16:35**	**6**	**1**	**1**	**2**	**6**	**0**	**0**	**0**	**18:54**
2006-07	**NY Rangers**	**NHL**	**67**	**29**	**33**	**62**	**47**	**14**	**3**	**3**	**295**	**9.8**	**2**	**281**	**48.0**	**19:49**	**10**	**5**	**2**	**7**	**12**	**3**	**0**	**2**	**19:00**
	NHL Totals		**1417**	**627**	**667**	**1294**	**2425**	**224**	**23**	**105**	**4744**	**13.2**		**594**	**47.6**	**18:16**	**167**	**58**	**68**	**126**	**269**	**19**	**1**	**12**	**18:40**

NHL First All-Star Team (1994, 2000) • NHL Second All-Star Team (2002) • King Clancy Memorial Trophy (2003)

Played in NHL All-Star Game (1994, 1996, 1997, 1998, 1999, 2000, 2002, 2007)

Signed as a free agent by **St. Louis**, July 25, 1991. Traded to **Hartford** by **St. Louis** for Chris Pronger, July 27, 1995. Traded to **Detroit** by **Hartford** with Brian Glynn for Paul Coffey, Keith Primeau and Detroit's 1st round choice (Nikos Tselios) in 1997 Entry Draft, October 9, 1996. Signed as a free agent by **NY Rangers**, July 9, 2006.

SHANNON, Ryan

(SHA-nuhn, RIGH-uhn) **VAN.**

Center. Shoots right. 5'9", 173 lbs. Born, Darien, CT, March 2, 1983.

Season	Club	League	GP	G	A	Pts	PIM	PP	SH	GW	S	%	+/-	TF	F%	Min	GP	G	A	Pts	PIM	PP	SH	GW	Min
2001-02	Boston College	H-East	38	8	17	25	12																		
2002-03	Boston College	H-East	36	14	24	38	4																		
2003-04	Boston College	H-East	42	15	27	42	22																		
2004-05	Boston College	H-East	38	14	31	45	22																		
	Cincinnati	AHL	4	1	0	1	2																		
2005-06	Portland Pirates	AHL	71	27	59	86	44										19	11	11	22	8				
2006-07	**♦ Anaheim**	**NHL**	**53**	**2**	**9**	**11**	**10**	**0**	**0**	**0**	**77**	**2.6**	**–2**	**25**	**52.0**	**10:39**	**11**	**0**	**0**	**0**	**6**	**0**	**0**	**0**	**4:04**
	Portland Pirates	AHL	14	2	7	9	12																		
	NHL Totals		**53**	**2**	**9**	**11**	**10**	**0**	**0**	**0**	**77**	**2.6**		**25**	**52.0**	**10:39**	**11**	**0**	**0**	**0**	**6**	**0**	**0**	**0**	**4:04**

Hockey East First All-Star Team (2004) • NCAA East Second All-American Team (2004) • AHL All-Rookie Team (2006)

Signed as a free agent by **Anaheim**, November 28, 2005. Traded to **Vancouver** by **Anaheim** for Jason King and future considerations, June 23, 2007.

SHARP, Patrick

(SHAHRP, PAT-rihk) **CHI.**

Center. Shoots right. 6'1", 197 lbs. Born, Thunder Bay, Ont., December 27, 1981. Philadelphia's 2nd choice, 95th overall, in 2001 Entry Draft.

Season	Club	League	GP	G	A	Pts	PIM	PP	SH	GW	S	%	+/-	TF	F%	Min	GP	G	A	Pts	PIM	PP	SH	GW	Min
1998-99	Thunder Bay	USHL	55	19	24	43	48										3	1	1	2	0				
99-2000	Thunder Bay	USHL	56	20	35	55	41																		
2000-01	U. of Vermont	ECAC	34	12	15	27	36																		
2001-02	U. of Vermont	ECAC	31	13	13	26	50																		
2002-03	**Philadelphia**	**NHL**	**3**	**0**	**0**	**0**	**2**	**0**	**0**	**0**	**3**	**0.0**	**0**	**7**	**42.9**	**5:59**									
	Philadelphia	AHL	53	14	19	33	39																		
2003-04	**Philadelphia**	**NHL**	**41**	**5**	**2**	**7**	**55**	**0**	**0**	**1**	**44**	**11.4**	**–3**	**272**	**46.7**	**9:56**	**12**	**1**	**0**	**1**	**2**	**0**	**0**	**0**	**6:12**
	Philadelphia	AHL	35	15	14	29	45										1	2	0	2	0				
2004-05	Philadelphia	AHL	75	23	29	52	80										21	8	13	*21	20				
2005-06	**Philadelphia**	**NHL**	**22**	**5**	**3**	**8**	**10**	**1**	**0**	**3**	**33**	**15.2**	**4**	**38**	**52.6**	**7:43**									
	Chicago	**NHL**	**50**	**9**	**14**	**23**	**36**	**0**	**1**	**2**	**111**	**8.1**	**1**	**664**	**48.0**	**16:19**									
2006-07	**Chicago**	**NHL**	**80**	**20**	**15**	**35**	**74**	**5**	**3**	**1**	**160**	**12.5**	**–15**	**1008**	**46.5**	**17:04**									
	NHL Totals		**196**	**39**	**34**	**73**	**177**	**6**	**4**	**7**	**351**	**11.1**		**1989**	**47.2**	**14:10**	**12**	**1**	**0**	**1**	**2**	**0**	**0**	**0**	**6:12**

Traded to **Chicago** by **Philadelphia** with Eric Meloche for Matt Ellison and Chicago's 3rd round choice (later traded to Montreal - Montreal selected Ryan White) in 2006 Entry Draft, December 5, 2005.

SHELLEY, Jody

(SHEH-lee, JOH-dee) **CBJ**

Left wing. Shoots left. 6'4", 230 lbs. Born, Thompson, Man., February 7, 1976.

Season	Club	League	GP	G	A	Pts	PIM	PP	SH	GW	S	%	+/-	TF	F%	Min	GP	G	A	Pts	PIM	PP	SH	GW	Min
1994-95	Halifax	QMJHL	72	10	12	22	194										7	0	1	1	12				
1995-96	Halifax	QMJHL	50	13	19	32	319										6	0	2	2	36				
1996-97	Halifax	QMJHL	58	25	19	44	*448										17	6	6	12	*123				
1997-98	Dalhousie	AUAA	19	6	11	17	145																		
	Saint John Flames	AHL	18	1	1	2	50																		
1998-99	Saint John Flames	AHL	8	0	0	0	46																		
	Johnstown Chiefs	ECHL	52	12	17	29	325																		

			Regular Season														Playoffs								
Season	Club	League	GP	G	A	Pts	PIM	PP	SH	GW	S	%	+/-	TF	F%	Min	GP	G	A	Pts	PIM	PP	SH	GW	Min
99-2000	Johnstown Chiefs	ECHL	36	9	17	26	256	....	....	....	....	....	....	....	....	....	....	....	....	....	....	....	....	....	....
	Saint John Flames	AHL	22	1	4	5	93	....	....	....	....	....	....	....	....	....	3	0	0	0	2	....	....	....	....
2000-01	Syracuse Crunch	AHL	69	1	7	8	*357	....	....	....	....	....	....	....	....	....	5	0	0	0	21	....	....	....	....
	Columbus	**NHL**	**1**	**0**	**0**	**0**	**10**	**0**	**0**	**0**	**0**	**0.0**	**0**	**0**	**0.0**	**1:33**	....	....	....	....	....	....	....	....	....
2001-02	**Columbus**	**NHL**	**52**	**3**	**3**	**6**	**206**	**0**	**0**	**0**	**35**	**8.6**	**1**	**0**	**0.0**	**6:32**	....	....	....	....	....	....	....	....	....
	Syracuse Crunch	AHL	22	3	5	8	165	....	....	....	....	....	....	....	....	....	....	....	....	....	....	....	....	....	....
2002-03	**Columbus**	**NHL**	**68**	**1**	**4**	**5**	***249**	**0**	**0**	**0**	**39**	**2.6**	**−5**	**1**	**0.0**	**6:08**	....	....	....	....	....	....	....	....	....
2003-04	**Columbus**	**NHL**	**76**	**3**	**3**	**6**	**228**	**1**	**0**	**0**	**62**	**4.8**	**−10**	**3**	**0.0**	**7:14**	....	....	....	....	....	....	....	....	....
2004-05	JYP Jyvaskyla	Finland	11	0	1	1	20	....	....	....	....	....	....	....	....	....	3	0	0	0	25	....	....	....	....
2005-06	**Columbus**	**NHL**	**80**	**3**	**7**	**10**	**163**	**0**	**0**	**1**	**39**	**7.7**	**−4**	**7**	**14.3**	**5:58**	....	....	....	....	....	....	....	....	....
2006-07	**Columbus**	**NHL**	**72**	**1**	**1**	**2**	**125**	**0**	**0**	**0**	**32**	**3.1**	**−6**	**2**	**0.0**	**4:52**	....	....	....	....	....	....	....	....	....
	NHL Totals		**349**	**11**	**18**	**29**	**981**	**1**	**0**	**1**	**207**	**5.3**		**13**	**7.7**	**6:07**	....	....	....	....	....	....	....	....	....

Signed as a free agent by **Calgary**, September 1, 1998. Signed as a free agent by **Syracuse** (AHL), September 15, 2000. Signed as a free agent by **Columbus**, January 31, 2001. Signed as a free agent by **Jyvaskyla** (Finland), January 17, 2005.

SHISHKANOV, Timofei
(shihsh-KAHN-ahv, tee-moh-FAY) **ST.L.**

Left wing. Shoots right. 6'1", 209 lbs. Born, Moscow, USSR, June 10, 1983. Nashville's 2nd choice, 33rd overall, in 2001 Entry Draft.

Season	Club	League	GP	G	A	Pts	PIM	PP	SH	GW	S	%	+/-	TF	F%	Min	GP	G	A	Pts	PIM	PP	SH	GW	Min
99-2000	Spartak 2	Russia-3	14	6	5	11	10	....	....	....	....	....	....	....	....	....	....	....	....	....	....	....	....	....	....
	Spartak Moscow	Russia-2	14	1	0	1	2	....	....	....	....	....	....	....	....	....	....	....	....	....	....	....	....	....	....
2000-01	Spartak 2	Russia-3	STATISTICS NOT AVAILABLE																						
2001-02	HK CSKA Moscow	Russia-2	23	7	6	13	8	....	....	....	....	....	....	....	....	....	....	....	....	....	....	....	....	....	....
	Spartak Moscow	Russia	12	0	0	0	2	....	....	....	....	....	....	....	....	....	....	....	....	....	....	....	....	....	....
	HK CSKA 2	Russia-3	13	7	9	16	14	....	....	....	....	....	....	....	....	....	....	....	....	....	....	....	....	....	....
2002-03	Quebec Remparts	QMJHL	51	36	46	82	60	....	....	....	....	....	....	....	....	....	11	5	12	17	14	....	....	....	....
2003-04	**Nashville**	**NHL**	**2**	**0**	**0**	**0**	**0**	**0**	**0**	**0**	**0**	**0.0**	**−1**	**0**	**0.0**	**6:32**	....	....	....	....	....	....	....	....	....
	Milwaukee	AHL	63	23	20	43	46	....	....	....	....	....	....	....	....	....	22	2	6	8	17	....	....	....	....
2004-05	Milwaukee	AHL	70	20	15	35	31	....	....	....	....	....	....	....	....	....	6	1	0	1	2	....	....	....	....
2005-06	Milwaukee	AHL	46	14	15	29	34	....	....	....	....	....	....	....	....	....	....	....	....	....	....	....	....	....	....
	St. Louis	**NHL**	**22**	**3**	**2**	**5**	**6**	**0**	**0**	**0**	**26**	**11.5**	**−1**	**2**	**0.0**	**8:28**	....	....	....	....	....	....	....	....	....
	Peoria Rivermen	AHL	12	3	2	5	8	....	....	....	....	....	....	....	....	....	2	1	0	1	0	....	....	....	....
2006-07	Vityaz Chekhov	Russia	38	9	5	14	63	....	....	....	....	....	....	....	....	....	3	0	0	0	2	....	....	....	....
	NHL Totals		**24**	**3**	**2**	**5**	**6**	**0**	**0**	**0**	**26**	**11.5**		**2**	**0.0**	**8:18**	....	....	....	....	....	....	....	....	....

QMJHL First All-Star Team (2003) • AHL All-Rookie Team (2004)
Traded to **St. Louis** by **Nashville** for Mike Sillinger, January 30, 2006. Signed as a free agent by **Chekhov** (Russia), August 30, 2006.

SHVIDKI, Denis
(SHVIHD-kee, DEH-nihs) **FLA.**

Right wing. Shoots left. 6'2", 210 lbs. Born, Kharkov, USSR, November 21, 1980. Florida's 1st choice, 12th overall, in 1999 Entry Draft.

Season	Club	League	GP	G	A	Pts	PIM	PP	SH	GW	S	%	+/-	TF	F%	Min	GP	G	A	Pts	PIM	PP	SH	GW	Min
1996-97	Yaroslavl 2	Russia-3	35	21	12	33	32	....	....	....	....	....	....	....	....	....	....	....	....	....	....	....	....	....	....
	Yaroslavl	Russia	17	3	2	5	6	....	....	....	....	....	....	....	....	....	....	....	....	....	....	....	....	....	....
1997-98	Yaroslavl 2	Russia-2	32	20	13	33	20	....	....	....	....	....	....	....	....	....	....	....	....	....	....	....	....	....	....
	Yaroslavl	Russia	15	1	1	2	2	....	....	....	....	....	....	....	....	....	....	....	....	....	....	....	....	....	....
1998-99	Barrie Colts	OHL	61	35	59	94	8	....	....	....	....	....	....	....	....	....	12	7	9	16	2	....	....	....	....
99-2000	Barrie Colts	OHL	61	41	65	106	55	....	....	....	....	....	....	....	....	....	9	3	1	4	2	....	....	....	....
2000-01	**Florida**	**NHL**	**43**	**6**	**10**	**16**	**16**	**0**	**0**	**1**	**28**	**21.4**	**6**	**4**	**50.0**	**10:21**	....	....	....	....	....	....	....	....	....
	Louisville Panthers	AHL	34	15	11	26	20	....	....	....	....	....	....	....	....	....	....	....	....	....	....	....	....	....	....
2001-02	**Florida**	**NHL**	**8**	**1**	**2**	**3**	**2**	**0**	**0**	**0**	**11**	**9.1**	**−4**	**1**	**0.0**	**11:57**	....	....	....	....	....	....	....	....	....
	Utah Grizzlies	AHL	8	2	4	6	2	....	....	....	....	....	....	....	....	....	....	....	....	....	....	....	....	....	....
2002-03	**Florida**	**NHL**	**23**	**4**	**2**	**6**	**12**	**2**	**0**	**1**	**29**	**13.8**	**−7**	**5**	**60.0**	**14:14**	....	....	....	....	....	....	....	....	....
	San Antonio	AHL	54	8	18	26	28	....	....	....	....	....	....	....	....	....	....	....	....	....	....	....	....	....	....
2003-04	**Florida**	**NHL**	**2**	**0**	**0**	**0**	**0**	**0**	**0**	**0**	**4**	**0.0**	**0**	**0**	**0.0**	**14:05**	....	....	....	....	....	....	....	....	....
	San Antonio	AHL	77	15	39	54	30	....	....	....	....	....	....	....	....	....	....	....	....	....	....	....	....	....	....
2004-05	Yaroslavl	Russia	52	7	11	18	24	....	....	....	....	....	....	....	....	....	4	0	0	0	8	....	....	....	....
2005-06	Sibir Novosibirsk	Russia	25	1	5	6	6	....	....	....	....	....	....	....	....	....	2	0	1	1	0	....	....	....	....
2006-07	Amur Khabarovsk	Russia	32	6	5	11	32	....	....	....	....	....	....	....	....	....	....	....	....	....	....	....	....	....	....
	NHL Totals		**76**	**11**	**14**	**25**	**30**	**2**	**0**	**2**	**72**	**15.3**		**10**	**50.0**	**11:47**	....	....	....	....	....	....	....	....	....

OHL All-Rookie Team (1999) • OHL Second All-Star Team (1999)
• Missed majority of 2001-02 season recovering from head injury suffered in game vs. Philadelphia, October 4, 2001. Signed as a free agent by **Novosibirsk** (Russia). November 22, 2005.

SIGALET, Jonathan
(SIH-ga-leht, JAWN-ah-thuhn) **BOS.**

Defense. Shoots left. 6'1", 185 lbs. Born, Vancouver, B.C., February 12, 1986. Boston's 4th choice, 100th overall, in 2005 Entry Draft.

Season	Club	League	GP	G	A	Pts	PIM	PP	SH	GW	S	%	+/-	TF	F%	Min	GP	G	A	Pts	PIM	PP	SH	GW	Min
2002-03	Salmon Arm	BCHL	52	13	39	52	34	....	....	....	....	....	....	....	....	....	....	....	....	....	....	....	....	....	....
2003-04	Bowling Green	CCHA	37	3	12	15	26	....	....	....	....	....	....	....	....	....	....	....	....	....	....	....	....	....	....
2004-05	Bowling Green	CCHA	35	3	13	16	36	....	....	....	....	....	....	....	....	....	....	....	....	....	....	....	....	....	....
2005-06	Providence Bruins	AHL	75	9	27	36	59	....	....	....	....	....	....	....	....	....	6	2	1	3	9	....	....	....	....
2006-07	**Boston**	**NHL**	**1**	**0**	**0**	**0**	**4**	**0**	**0**	**0**	**1**	**0.0**	**−2**	**0**	**0.0**	**14:41**	....	....	....	....	....	....	....	....	....
	Providence Bruins	AHL	50	9	13	22	37	....	....	....	....	....	....	....	....	....	....	....	....	....	....	....	....	....	....
	NHL Totals		**1**	**0**	**0**	**0**	**4**	**0**	**0**	**0**	**1**	**0.0**		**0**	**0.0**	**14:41**	....	....	....	....	....	....	....	....	....

SILLINGER, Mike
(SIHL-ihn-juhr, MIGHK) **NYI**

Center. Shoots right. 5'11", 198 lbs. Born, Regina, Sask., June 29, 1971. Detroit's 1st choice, 11th overall, in 1989 Entry Draft.

Season	Club	League	GP	G	A	Pts	PIM	PP	SH	GW	S	%	+/-	TF	F%	Min	GP	G	A	Pts	PIM	PP	SH	GW	Min
1986-87	Regina Kings	SMHL	31	83	51	134	....	....	....	....	....	....	....	....	....	....	....	....	....	....	....	....	....	....	....
1987-88	Regina Pats	WHL	67	18	25	43	17	....	....	....	....	....	....	....	....	....	4	2	2	4	0	....	....	....	....
1988-89	Regina Pats	WHL	72	53	78	131	52	....	....	....	....	....	....	....	....	....	....	....	....	....	....	....	....	....	....
1989-90	Regina Pats	WHL	70	57	72	129	41	....	....	....	....	....	....	....	....	....	11	12	10	22	2	....	....	....	....
	Adirondack	AHL	....	....	....	....	....	....	....	....	....	....	....	....	....	....	1	0	0	0	0	....	....	....	....
1990-91	Regina Pats	WHL	57	50	66	116	42	....	....	....	....	....	....	....	....	....	8	6	9	15	4	....	....	....	....
	Detroit	**NHL**	**3**	**0**	**1**	**1**	**0**	**0**	**0**	**0**	**6**	**0.0**	**−2**	....	....	....	**3**	**0**	**1**	**1**	**0**	**0**	**0**	**0**	....
1991-92	Adirondack	AHL	64	25	41	66	26	....	....	....	....	....	....	....	....	....	15	9	*19	*28	12	....	....	....	....
	Detroit	**NHL**	....	....	....	....	....	....	....	....	....	....	....	....	....	....	**8**	**2**	**2**	**4**	**2**	**0**	**0**	**0**	....
1992-93	**Detroit**	**NHL**	**51**	**4**	**17**	**21**	**16**	**0**	**0**	**0**	**47**	**8.5**	**0**	....	....	....	....	....	....	....	....	....	....	....	....
	Adirondack	AHL	15	10	20	30	31	....	....	....	....	....	....	....	....	....	11	5	13	18	10	....	....	....	....
1993-94	**Detroit**	**NHL**	**62**	**8**	**21**	**29**	**10**	**0**	**1**	**1**	**91**	**8.8**	**2**	....	....	....	....	....	....	....	....	....	....	....	....
1994-95	CE Wien	Austria	13	13	14	27	10	....	....	....	....	....	....	....	....	....	....	....	....	....	....	....	....	....	....
	Anaheim	**NHL**	**15**	**2**	**5**	**7**	**6**	**2**	**0**	**0**	**28**	**7.1**	**1**	....	....	....	....	....	....	....	....	....	....	....	....
	Detroit	**NHL**	**13**	**2**	**6**	**8**	**2**	**0**	**0**	**0**	**11**	**18.2**	**3**	....	....	....	....	....	....	....	....	....	....	....	....
1995-96	**Anaheim**	**NHL**	**62**	**13**	**21**	**34**	**32**	**7**	**0**	**2**	**143**	**9.1**	**−20**	....	....	....	....	....	....	....	....	....	....	....	....
	Vancouver	**NHL**	**12**	**1**	**3**	**4**	**6**	**0**	**1**	**0**	**16**	**6.3**	**2**	....	....	....	**6**	**0**	**0**	**0**	**2**	**0**	**0**	**0**	....
1996-97	**Vancouver**	**NHL**	**78**	**17**	**20**	**37**	**25**	**3**	**3**	**2**	**112**	**15.2**	**−3**	....	....	....	....	....	....	....	....	....	....	....	....
1997-98	**Vancouver**	**NHL**	**48**	**10**	**9**	**19**	**34**	**1**	**2**	**1**	**56**	**17.9**	**−14**	....	....	....	....	....	....	....	....	....	....	....	....
	Philadelphia	**NHL**	**27**	**11**	**11**	**22**	**16**	**1**	**2**	**0**	**40**	**27.5**	**3**	....	....	....	**3**	**1**	**0**	**1**	**0**	**0**	**0**	**0**	....
1998-99	**Philadelphia**	**NHL**	**25**	**0**	**3**	**3**	**8**	**0**	**0**	**0**	**23**	**0.0**	**−9**	**229**	**62.9**	**10:42**	....	....	....	....	....	....	....	....	....
	Tampa Bay	**NHL**	**54**	**8**	**2**	**10**	**28**	**0**	**2**	**0**	**69**	**11.6**	**−20**	**320**	**57.8**	**13:57**	....	....	....	....	....	....	....	....	....
99-2000	**Tampa Bay**	**NHL**	**67**	**19**	**25**	**44**	**86**	**6**	**3**	**1**	**126**	**15.1**	**−29**	**493**	**56.0**	**19:42**	....	....	....	....	....	....	....	....	....
	Florida	**NHL**	**13**	**4**	**4**	**8**	**16**	**2**	**0**	**1**	**20**	**20.0**	**−1**	**248**	**61.3**	**19:33**	**4**	**2**	**1**	**3**	**2**	**0**	**0**	**0**	**20:24**
2000-01	**Florida**	**NHL**	**55**	**13**	**21**	**34**	**44**	**1**	**0**	**2**	**100**	**13.0**	**−12**	**1028**	**59.7**	**18:52**	....	....	....	....	....	....	....	....	....
	Ottawa	**NHL**	**13**	**3**	**4**	**7**	**4**	**0**	**0**	**0**	**19**	**15.8**	**1**	**215**	**63.3**	**14:31**	**4**	**0**	**0**	**0**	**2**	**0**	**0**	**0**	**13:40**
2001-02	**Columbus**	**NHL**	**80**	**20**	**23**	**43**	**54**	**8**	**0**	**5**	**150**	**13.3**	**−35**	**2024**	**57.0**	**20:51**	....	....	....	....	....	....	....	....	....
2002-03	**Columbus**	**NHL**	**75**	**18**	**25**	**43**	**52**	**9**	**3**	**3**	**128**	**14.1**	**−21**	**1490**	**56.5**	**19:08**	....	....	....	....	....	....	....	....	....
2003-04	**Phoenix**	**NHL**	**60**	**8**	**6**	**14**	**54**	**0**	**1**	**0**	**66**	**12.1**	**−14**	**771**	**56.3**	**15:22**	....	....	....	....	....	....	....	....	....
	St. Louis	**NHL**	**16**	**5**	**5**	**10**	**14**	**0**	**1**	**0**	**40**	**12.5**	**4**	**351**	**57.8**	**20:08**	**5**	**3**	**1**	**4**	**6**	**0**	**1**	**0**	**22:17**

Season	Club	League	GP	G	A	Pts	PIM	PP	SH	GW	S	%	+/-	TF	F%	Min	GP	G	A	Pts	PIM	PP	SH	GW	Min
			Regular Season														Playoffs								
2004-05			DID NOT PLAY																						
2005-06	**St. Louis**	**NHL**	**48**	**22**	**19**	**41**	**49**	**11**	**1**	**1**	**131**	**16.8**	**–17**	**797**	**55.3**	**19:41**									
	Nashville	**NHL**	**31**	**10**	**12**	**22**	**14**	**3**	**0**	**1**	**80**	**12.5**	**0**	**542**	**56.6**	**18:34**	**5**	**2**	**1**	**3**	**12**	**1**	**0**	**0**	**17:09**
2006-07	**NY Islanders**	**NHL**	**82**	**26**	**33**	**59**	**46**	**11**	**2**	**3**	**152**	**17.1**	**5**	**1708**	**58.8**	**19:19**	**5**	**1**	**1**	**2**	**2**	**1**	**0**	**0**	**20:49**
	NHL Totals		**990**	**224**	**296**	**520**	**616**	**65**	**22**	**23**	**1654**	**13.5**		**10216**	**57.7**	**18:13**	**43**	**11**	**7**	**18**	**28**	**2**	**1**	**0**	**19:01**

WHL East Second All-Star Team (1990) • WHL East First All-Star Team (1991)

Traded to **Anaheim** by **Detroit** with Jason York for Stu Grimson, Mark Ferner and Anaheim's 6th round choice (Magnus Nilsson) in 1996 Entry Draft, April 4, 1995. Traded to **Vancouver** by **Anaheim** for Roman Oksiuta, March 15, 1996. Traded to **Philadelphia** by **Vancouver** for Philadelphia's 5th round choice (later traded back to Philadelphia – Philadelphia selected Garrett Prosofsky) in 1998 Entry Draft, February 5, 1998. Traded to **Tampa Bay** by **Philadelphia** with Chris Gratton for Mikael Renberg and Daymond Langkow, December 12, 1998. Traded to **Florida** by **Tampa Bay** for Ryan Johnson and Dwayne Hay, March 14, 2000. Traded to **Ottawa** by **Florida** for future considerations, March 13, 2001. Signed as a free agent by **Columbus**, July 7, 2001. Traded to **Dallas** by **Columbus** with Columbus' 2nd round choice (Johan Fransson) in 2004 Entry Draft for Darryl Sydor, July 22, 2003. Traded to **Phoenix** by **Dallas** with future considerations for Teppo Numminen, July 22, 2003. Traded to **St. Louis** by **Phoenix** for Brent Johnson, March 4, 2004. Traded to **Nashville** by **St. Louis** for Timofei Shishkanov, January 30, 2006. Signed as a free agent by **NY Islanders**, July 2, 2006.

SIM, Jon

(SIHM, JAWN) **NYI**

Left wing. Shoots left. 5'10", 195 lbs. Born, New Glasgow, N.S., September 29, 1977. Dallas' 2nd choice, 70th overall, in 1996 Entry Draft.

Season	Club	League	GP	G	A	Pts	PIM	PP	SH	GW	S	%	+/-	TF	F%	Min	GP	G	A	Pts	PIM	PP	SH	GW	Min
1994-95	Laval Titan	QMJHL	9	0	1	1	6																		
	Sarnia Sting	OHL	25	9	12	21	19										4	3	2	5	2				
1995-96	Sarnia Sting	OHL	63	56	46	102	130										10	8	7	15	26				
1996-97	Sarnia Sting	OHL	64	*56	39	95	109										12	9	5	14	32				
1997-98	Sarnia Sting	OHL	59	44	50	94	95										5	1	4	5	14				
1998-99 ♦	**Dallas**	**NHL**	**7**	**1**	**0**	**1**	**12**	**0**	**0**	**0**	**8**	**12.5**	**1**	**6**	**50.0**	**11:26**	**4**	**0**	**0**	**0**	**0**	**0**	**0**	**0**	**6:27**
	Michigan	IHL	68	24	27	51	91										5	3	1	4	18				
99-2000	**Dallas**	**NHL**	**25**	**5**	**3**	**8**	**10**	**2**	**0**	**1**	**44**	**11.4**	**4**	**4**	**75.0**	**10:51**	**7**	**1**	**0**	**1**	**6**	**0**	**0**	**0**	**11:11**
	Michigan	IHL	35	14	16	30	65																		
2000-01	**Dallas**	**NHL**	**15**	**0**	**3**	**3**	**6**	**0**	**0**	**0**	**18**	**0.0**	**–2**	**1**	**100.0**	**8:47**									
	Utah Grizzlies	IHL	39	16	13	29	44																		
2001-02	**Dallas**	**NHL**	**26**	**3**	**0**	**3**	**10**	**1**	**0**	**0**	**43**	**7.0**	**–3**	**3**	**0.0**	**9:30**									
	Utah Grizzlies	AHL	31	21	6	27	63																		
2002-03	**Dallas**	**NHL**	**4**	**0**	**0**	**0**	**0**	**0**	**0**	**0**	**7**	**0.0**	**–1**	**2**	**50.0**	**9:10**									
	Utah Grizzlies	AHL	42	16	31	47	85																		
	Nashville	**NHL**	**4**	**1**	**0**	**1**	**0**	**0**	**0**	**0**	**3**	**33.3**	**0**	**14**	**35.7**	**9:18**									
	Los Angeles	**NHL**	**14**	**0**	**2**	**2**	**19**	**0**	**0**	**0**	**29**	**0.0**	**–3**	**3**	**33.3**	**12:05**									
2003-04	**Los Angeles**	**NHL**	**48**	**6**	**7**	**13**	**27**	**0**	**0**	**1**	**73**	**8.2**	**0**	**19**	**31.6**	**10:01**									
	Pittsburgh	**NHL**	**15**	**2**	**3**	**5**	**6**	**0**	**0**	**1**	**27**	**7.4**	**–4**	**0**	**0.0**	**13:39**									
2004-05	Utah Grizzlies	AHL	10	2	2	4	12																		
	Philadelphia	AHL	63	35	26	61	66										21	*10	7	17	44				
2005-06	**Philadelphia**	**NHL**	**39**	**7**	**7**	**14**	**28**	**4**	**0**	**2**	**80**	**8.8**	**–6**	**1**	**0.0**	**10:59**									
	Florida	**NHL**	**33**	**10**	**8**	**18**	**26**	**4**	**0**	**3**	**92**	**10.9**	**–1**	**0**	**0.0**	**12:28**									
2006-07	**Atlanta**	**NHL**	**77**	**17**	**12**	**29**	**60**	**2**	**0**	**1**	**141**	**12.1**	**–1**	**9**	**22.2**	**11:45**	**4**	**0**	**0**	**0**	**0**	**0**	**0**	**0**	**5:29**
	NHL Totals		**307**	**52**	**45**	**97**	**204**	**13**	**0**	**9**	**565**	**9.2**		**62**	**35.5**	**11:05**	**15**	**1**	**0**	**1**	**6**	**0**	**0**	**0**	**8:24**

OHL Second All-Star Team (1998)

Traded to **Nashville** by **Dallas** for Bubba Berenzweig and future considerations, February 17, 2003. Claimed on waivers by **Los Angeles** from **Nashville**, March 8, 2003. Claimed on waivers by **Pittsburgh** from **Los Angeles**, March 4, 2004. Signed as a free agent by **Phoenix**, September 2, 2004. Loaned to **Philadelphia** (AHL) by **Phoenix** (Utah - AHL) for the loan of Peter White, November 14, 2004. Signed as a free agent by **Philadelphia**, August 2, 2005. Traded to **Florida** by **Philadelphia** for Florida's 6th round choice (Patrick Maroon) in 2007 Entry Draft, January 23, 2006. Signed as a free agent by **Atlanta**, July 14, 2006. Signed as a free agent by **NY Islanders**, July 1, 2007.

SIMON, Ben

(SIGH-mohn, BEHN)

Left wing. Shoots left. 6', 195 lbs. Born, Shaker Heights, OH, June 14, 1978. Chicago's 5th choice, 110th overall, in 1997 Entry Draft.

Season	Club	League	GP	G	A	Pts	PIM	PP	SH	GW	S	%	+/-	TF	F%	Min	GP	G	A	Pts	PIM	PP	SH	GW	Min
1992-93	Shaker Heights	High-OH	25	15	21	36																			
1993-94	Shaker Heights	High-OH	24	45	41	86																			
1994-95	Shaker Heights	High-OH	25	61	68	129																			
1995-96	Cleveland Barons	NAHL	45	38	33	71											5	7	13	20					
1996-97	U. of Notre Dame	CCHA	30	4	15	19	79																		
1997-98	U. of Notre Dame	CCHA	37	9	28	37	91																		
1998-99	U. of Notre Dame	CCHA	37	18	24	42	65																		
99-2000	U. of Notre Dame	CCHA	40	13	19	32	53																		
2000-01	Orlando	IHL	77	8	12	20	47										16	6	5	11	20				
2001-02	**Atlanta**	**NHL**	**6**	**0**	**0**	**0**	**6**	**0**	**0**	**0**	**7**	**0.0**	**1**	**32**	**40.6**	**9:20**									
	Chicago Wolves	AHL	74	11	23	34	56										25	2	3	5	24				
2002-03	**Atlanta**	**NHL**	**10**	**0**	**1**	**1**	**9**	**0**	**0**	**0**	**7**	**0.0**	**0**	**54**	**31.5**	**9:25**									
	Chicago Wolves	AHL	69	15	17	32	78										9	0	0	0	6				
2003-04	Milwaukee	AHL	18	1	3	4	6																		
	Atlanta	**NHL**	**52**	**3**	**0**	**3**	**28**	**0**	**0**	**0**	**30**	**10.0**	**–10**	**203**	**33.0**	**6:05**									
2004-05	Chicago Wolves	AHL	53	11	10	21	58										18	1	5	6	44				
2005-06	**Columbus**	**NHL**	**13**	**0**	**0**	**0**	**4**	**0**	**0**	**0**	**7**	**0.0**	**–4**	**53**	**24.5**	**5:38**									
	Syracuse Crunch	AHL	66	13	24	37	88										3	0	1	1	2				
2006-07	Syracuse Crunch	AHL	56	9	12	21	77																		
	Grand Rapids	AHL	21	4	5	9	28										7	0	0	0	9				
	NHL Totals		**81**	**3**	**1**	**4**	**47**	**0**	**0**	**0**	**51**	**5.9**		**342**	**32.2**	**6:40**									

CCHA Second All-Star Team (1999)

Rights traded to **Atlanta** by **Chicago** for Atlanta's 9th round choice (Peter Flache) in 2000 Entry Draft, June 25, 2000. Signed as a free agent by **Nashville**, July 14, 2003. Traded to **Atlanta** by **Nashville** with Tomas Kloucek for Simon Gamache and Kirill Safronov, December 2, 2003. Signed as a free agent by **Columbus**, August 11, 2005.

SIMON, Chris

(SIGH-mohn, KRIHS) **NYI**

Left wing. Shoots left. 6'4", 235 lbs. Born, Wawa, Ont., January 30, 1972. Philadelphia's 2nd choice, 25th overall, in 1990 Entry Draft.

Season	Club	League	GP	G	A	Pts	PIM	PP	SH	GW	S	%	+/-	TF	F%	Min	GP	G	A	Pts	PIM	PP	SH	GW	Min
1986-87	Wawa Flyers	NOHA	36	12	20	32	108																		
1987-88	Soo Thunderbirds	NOHA	55	42	36	78	172																		
1988-89	Ottawa 67's	OHL	36	4	2	6	31																		
1989-90	Ottawa 67's	OHL	57	36	38	74	146										3	2	1	3	4				
1990-91	Ottawa 67's	OHL	20	16	6	22	69										17	5	9	14	59				
1991-92	Ottawa 67's	OHL	2	1	1	2	24																		
	Sault Ste. Marie	OHL	31	19	25	44	143										11	5	8	13	49				
1992-93	**Quebec**	**NHL**	**16**	**1**	**1**	**2**	**67**	**0**	**0**	**1**	**15**	**6.7**	**–2**				**5**	**0**	**0**	**0**	**26**	**0**	**0**	**0**	
	Halifax Citadels	AHL	36	12	6	18	131																		
1993-94	**Quebec**	**NHL**	**37**	**4**	**4**	**8**	**132**	**0**	**0**	**1**	**39**	**10.3**	**–2**												
1994-95	**Quebec**	**NHL**	**29**	**3**	**9**	**12**	**106**	**0**	**0**	**0**	**33**	**9.1**	**14**				**6**	**1**	**1**	**2**	**19**	**0**	**0**	**1**	
1995-96 ♦	**Colorado**	**NHL**	**64**	**16**	**18**	**34**	**250**	**4**	**0**	**1**	**105**	**15.2**	**10**				**12**	**1**	**2**	**3**	**11**	**0**	**0**	**0**	
1996-97	**Washington**	**NHL**	**42**	**9**	**13**	**22**	**165**	**3**	**0**	**1**	**89**	**10.1**	**–1**												
1997-98	**Washington**	**NHL**	**28**	**7**	**10**	**17**	**38**	**4**	**0**	**1**	**71**	**9.9**	**–1**				**18**	**1**	**0**	**1**	**26**	**0**	**0**	**0**	
1998-99	**Washington**	**NHL**	**23**	**3**	**7**	**10**	**48**	**0**	**0**	**0**	**29**	**10.3**	**–4**	**2**	**50.0**	**12:08**									
99-2000	**Washington**	**NHL**	**75**	**29**	**20**	**49**	**146**	**7**	**0**	**5**	**201**	**14.4**	**11**	**7**	**28.6**	**15:32**	**4**	**2**	**0**	**2**	**24**	**0**	**0**	**0**	**18:07**
2000-01	**Washington**	**NHL**	**60**	**10**	**10**	**20**	**109**	**4**	**0**	**2**	**123**	**8.1**	**–12**	**3**	**33.3**	**14:34**	**6**	**0**	**1**	**1**	**4**	**0**	**0**	**0**	**9:55**
2001-02	**Washington**	**NHL**	**82**	**14**	**17**	**31**	**137**	**1**	**0**	**1**	**121**	**11.6**	**–8**	**7**	**28.6**	**12:11**									
2002-03	**Washington**	**NHL**	**10**	**0**	**2**	**2**	**23**	**0**	**0**	**0**	**16**	**0.0**	**–3**	**0**	**0.0**	**8:53**									
	Chicago	**NHL**	**61**	**12**	**6**	**18**	**125**	**2**	**0**	**2**	**72**	**16.7**	**–4**	**5**	**20.0**	**11:06**									
2003-04	**NY Rangers**	**NHL**	**65**	**14**	**9**	**23**	**225**	**3**	**0**	**0**	**116**	**12.1**	**14**	**3**	**0.0**	**11:56**									
	Calgary	**NHL**	**13**	**3**	**2**	**5**	**25**	**1**	**0**	**0**	**31**	**9.7**	**1**	**2**	**100.0**	**16:38**	**16**	**5**	**2**	**7**	***74**	**4**	**0**	**1**	**15:06**
2004-05			DID NOT PLAY																						
2005-06	**Calgary**	**NHL**	**72**	**8**	**14**	**22**	**94**	**2**	**0**	**3**	**76**	**10.5**	**0**	**17**	**47.1**	**10:26**	**6**	**0**	**1**	**1**	**7**	**0**	**0**	**0**	**10:12**
2006-07	**NY Islanders**	**NHL**	**67**	**10**	**17**	**27**	**75**	**2**	**0**	**0**	**82**	**12.2**	**17**	**44**	**47.7**	**11:00**									
	NHL Totals		**744**	**143**	**159**	**302**	**1765**	**33**	**0**	**18**	**1219**	**11.7**		**90**	**42.2**	**12:26**	**73**	**10**	**7**	**17**	**191**	**4**	**0**	**2**	**13:35**

• Missed majority of 1990-91 season recovering from shoulder surgery, October, 1990. Traded to **Quebec** by **Philadelphia** with Philadelphia's 1st round choice (later traded to Toronto – later traded to Washington – Washington selected Nolan Baumgartner) in 1994 Entry Draft to complete transaction that sent Eric Lindros to Philadelphia (June 30, 1992), July 21, 1992. Transferred to **Colorado** after **Quebec** franchise relocated, June 21, 1995. Traded to **Washington** by **Colorado** with Curtis Leschyshyn for Keith Jones and Washington's 1st (Scott Parker) and 4th (later traded back to Washington – Washington selected Krys Barch) round choices in 1998 Entry Drarft, November 2, 1996. Traded to **Chicago** by **Washington** with Andrei Nikolishin for Michael Nylander, Chicago's 3rd round choice (Stephen Werner) in 2003 Entry Draft and future considerations, November 1, 2002. Signed as a free agent by **NY Rangers**, July 25, 2003. Traded to **Calgary** by **NY Rangers** with NY Rangers' 7th round choice (Matt Schneider) in 2004 Entry Draft for Jamie McLennan, Blair Betts and Greg Moore, March 6, 2004. Signed as a free agent by **NY Islanders**, July 11, 2006.

SIMPSON, Todd

(SIHMP-suhn, TAWD)

Defense. Shoots left. 6'3", 218 lbs. Born, North Vancouver, B.C., May 28, 1973.

			Regular Season														Playoffs								
Season	Club	League	GP	G	A	Pts	PIM	PP	SH	GW	S	%	+/-	TF	F%	Min	GP	G	A	Pts	PIM	PP	SH	GW	Min
1991-92	Brown U.	ECAC	18	1	4	5	38	....	....	....	....	....	....	....	....	....	....	....	....	....	....	....	....	....	....
1992-93	Tri-City	WHL	69	5	18	23	196	....	....	....	....	....	....	....	....	....	4	0	0	0	13	....	....	....	....
1993-94	Tri-City	WHL	12	2	3	5	32	....	....	....	....	....	....	....	....	....	....	....	....	....	....	....	....	....	....
	Saskatoon Blades	WHL	51	7	19	26	175	....	....	....	....	....	....	....	....	....	16	1	5	6	42	....	....	....	....
1994-95	Saint John Flames	AHL	80	3	10	13	321	....	....	....	....	....	....	....	....	....	5	0	0	0	4	....	....	....	....
1995-96	**Calgary**	**NHL**	**6**	**0**	**0**	**0**	**32**	**0**	**0**	**0**	**3**	**0.0**	**0**	....	....	....	....	....	....	....	....	....	....	....	....
	Saint John Flames	AHL	66	4	13	17	277	....	....	....	....	....	....	....	....	....	16	2	3	5	32	....	....	....	....
1996-97	**Calgary**	**NHL**	**82**	**1**	**13**	**14**	**208**	**0**	**0**	**0**	**85**	**1.2**	**–14**	....	....	....	....	....	....	....	....	....	....	....	....
1997-98	**Calgary**	**NHL**	**53**	**1**	**5**	**6**	**109**	**0**	**0**	**1**	**51**	**2.0**	**–10**	....	....	....	....	....	....	....	....	....	....	....	....
1998-99	**Calgary**	**NHL**	**73**	**2**	**8**	**10**	**151**	**0**	**0**	**0**	**52**	**3.8**	**18**	**1**	**100.0**	**17:19**	....	....	....	....	....	....	....	....	....
99-2000	**Florida**	**NHL**	**82**	**1**	**6**	**7**	**202**	**0**	**0**	**0**	**50**	**2.0**	**5**	**0**	**0.0**	**16:35**	**4**	**0**	**0**	**0**	**4**	**0**	**0**	**0**	**15:24**
2000-01	**Florida**	**NHL**	**25**	**1**	**3**	**4**	**74**	**0**	**0**	**1**	**26**	**3.8**	**0**	**0**	**0.0**	**16:29**	....	....	....	....	....	....	....	....	....
	Phoenix	**NHL**	**13**	**0**	**1**	**1**	**12**	**0**	**0**	**0**	**9**	**0.0**	**–4**	**0**	**0.0**	**13:56**	....	....	....	....	....	....	....	....	....
2001-02	**Phoenix**	**NHL**	**67**	**2**	**13**	**15**	**152**	**0**	**0**	**0**	**51**	**3.9**	**20**	**0**	**0.0**	**17:20**	**5**	**0**	**2**	**2**	**6**	**0**	**0**	**0**	**18:30**
2002-03	**Phoenix**	**NHL**	**66**	**2**	**7**	**9**	**135**	**0**	**0**	**0**	**67**	**3.0**	**7**	**0**	**0.0**	**16:59**	....	....	....	....	....	....	....	....	....
2003-04	**Anaheim**	**NHL**	**46**	**4**	**3**	**7**	**105**	**0**	**0**	**0**	**42**	**9.5**	**–6**	**0**	**0.0**	**14:18**	....	....	....	....	....	....	....	....	....
	Ottawa	**NHL**	**16**	**0**	**1**	**1**	**47**	**0**	**0**	**0**	**10**	**0.0**	**–1**	**1**	**0.0**	**14:21**	....	....	....	....	....	....	....	....	....
2004-05	Herning Blue Fox	Denmark	7	2	3	5	35	....	....	....	....	....	....	....	....	....	16	3	5	8	82	....	....	....	....
2005-06	**Chicago**	**NHL**	**45**	**0**	**3**	**3**	**116**	**0**	**0**	**0**	**25**	**0.0**	**–2**	**2**	**0.0**	**13:05**	....	....	....	....	....	....	....	....	....
	Montreal	**NHL**	**6**	**0**	**0**	**0**	**14**	**0**	**0**	**0**	**6**	**0.0**	**0**	**0**	**0.0**	**15:59**	....	....	....	....	....	....	....	....	....
2006-07	Hannover Scorp.	Germany	45	1	9	10	174	....	....	....	....	....	....	....	....	....	6	0	0	0	49	....	....	....	....
	NHL Totals		**580**	**14**	**63**	**77**	**1357**	**0**	**0**	**2**	**477**	**2.9**		**4**	**25.0**	**16:06**	**9**	**0**	**2**	**2**	**10**	**0**	**0**	**0**	**17:07**

Signed as free agent by **Calgary**, July 6, 1994. Traded to **Florida** by **Calgary** for Bill Lindsay, September 30, 1999. • Missed majority of 2000-01 season recovering from head injury suffered in game vs. NY Islanders, December 6, 2000. Traded to **Phoenix** by **Florida** for Phoenix's 2nd round choice (later traded to New Jersey – New Jersey selected Tuomas Pihlman) in 2001 Entry Draft, March 13, 2001. Claimed by **Anaheim** from **Phoenix** in Waiver Draft, October 3, 2003. Traded to **Ottawa** by **Anaheim** for Petr Schastlivy, February 4, 2004. Signed as a free agent by **Herning** (Denmark), December 16, 2004. Signed as a free agent by **Chicago**, August 23, 2005. Traded to **Montreal** by **Chicago** for Montreal's 6th round choice (Chris Auger) in 2006 Entry Draft, March 9, 2006.

SIVEK, Michal

(sih-VIHK, MEE-khahl) **PIT.**

Center. Shoots left. 6'3", 213 lbs. Born, Nachod, Czech., January 21, 1981. Washington's 2nd choice, 29th overall, in 1999 Entry Draft.

			Regular Season														Playoffs								
Season	Club	League	GP	G	A	Pts	PIM	PP	SH	GW	S	%	+/-	TF	F%	Min	GP	G	A	Pts	PIM	PP	SH	GW	Min
1997-98	Sparta Jr.	CzRep-Jr.	31	13	8	21	....	....	....	....	....	....	....	....	....	....	....	....	....	....	....	....	....	....	....
	HC Sparta Praha	CzRep	25	1	1	2	10	....	....	....	....	....	....	....	....	....	5	1	0	1	0	....	....	....	....
1998-99	HC Sparta Praha	CzRep	1	1	0	1	....	....	....	....	....	....	....	....	....	....	....	....	....	....	....	....	....	....	....
	Kladno	CzRep	34	3	8	11	24	....	....	....	....	....	....	....	....	....	....	....	....	....	....	....	....	....	....
99-2000	Prince Albert	WHL	53	23	37	60	65	....	....	....	....	....	....	....	....	....	6	1	4	5	10	....	....	....	....
2000-01	HC Sparta Praha	CzRep	32	6	7	13	28	....	....	....	....	....	....	....	....	....	13	4	2	6	8	....	....	....	....
2001-02	Wilkes-Barre	AHL	25	4	8	12	30	....	....	....	....	....	....	....	....	....	....	....	....	....	....	....	....	....	....
	HC Sparta Praha	CzRep	17	5	3	8	20	....	....	....	....	....	....	....	....	....	12	0	1	1	10	....	....	....	....
2002-03	**Pittsburgh**	**NHL**	**38**	**3**	**3**	**6**	**14**	**1**	**0**	**0**	**45**	**6.7**	**–5**	**32**	**43.8**	**13:05**	....	....	....	....	....	....	....	....	....
	Wilkes-Barre	AHL	40	10	17	27	33	....	....	....	....	....	....	....	....	....	6	3	2	5	20	....	....	....	....
2003-04	Wilkes-Barre	AHL	22	4	7	11	6	....	....	....	....	....	....	....	....	....	....	....	....	....	....	....	....	....	....
2004-05	HC Sparta Praha	CzRep	37	1	5	6	48	....	....	....	....	....	....	....	....	....	5	0	0	0	2	....	....	....	....
2005-06	HC Sparta Praha	CzRep	36	10	9	19	30	....	....	....	....	....	....	....	....	....	17	4	1	5	18	....	....	....	....
2006-07	HC Sparta Praha	CzRep	47	10	8	18	76	....	....	....	....	....	....	....	....	....	16	3	3	6	32	....	....	....	....
	NHL Totals		**38**	**3**	**3**	**6**	**14**	**1**	**0**	**0**	**45**	**6.7**		**32**	**43.8**	**13:05**	....	....	....	....	....	....	....	....	....

Traded to **Pittsburgh** by **Washington** with Kris Beech, Ross Lupaschuk and future considerations for Jaromir Jagr and Frantisek Kucera, July 11, 2001. • Missed majority of 2003-04 season recovering from finger injury suffered in game vs. Syracuse (AHL), October 17, 2003. Signed as a free agent by **Sparta Praha** (CzRep), May 19, 2004.

SJOSTROM, Fredrik

(SHAW-strahm, FREHD-rihk) **PHX.**

Right wing. Shoots left. 6'1", 217 lbs. Born, Fargelanda, Sweden, May 6, 1983. Phoenix's 1st choice, 11th overall, in 2001 Entry Draft.

			Regular Season														Playoffs								
Season	Club	League	GP	G	A	Pts	PIM	PP	SH	GW	S	%	+/-	TF	F%	Min	GP	G	A	Pts	PIM	PP	SH	GW	Min
99-2000	MoDo U18	Swe-U18	4	0	2	2	6	....	....	....	....	....	....	....	....	....	....	....	....	....	....	....	....	....	....
	Malmo Jr.	Swe-Jr.	18	4	6	10	8	....	....	....	....	....	....	....	....	....	....	....	....	....	....	....	....	....	....
2000-01	V.Frolunda Jr.	Swe-Jr.	11	3	7	10	12	....	....	....	....	....	....	....	....	....	4	1	2	3	6	....	....	....	....
	V.Frolunda	Sweden	31	3	2	5	6	....	....	....	....	....	....	....	....	....	5	0	0	0	2	....	....	....	....
2001-02	Calgary Hitmen	WHL	58	19	31	50	51	....	....	....	....	....	....	....	....	....	4	1	1	2	8	....	....	....	....
2002-03	Calgary Hitmen	WHL	63	34	43	77	95	....	....	....	....	....	....	....	....	....	5	1	3	4	4	....	....	....	....
	Springfield	AHL	2	1	0	1	0	....	....	....	....	....	....	....	....	....	6	2	0	2	12	....	....	....	....
2003-04	**Phoenix**	**NHL**	**57**	**7**	**6**	**13**	**22**	**0**	**0**	**1**	**73**	**9.6**	**–7**	**7**	**28.6**	**11:35**	....	....	....	....	....	....	....	....	....
	Springfield	AHL	17	0	7	7	8	....	....	....	....	....	....	....	....	....	....	....	....	....	....	....	....	....	....
2004-05	Utah Grizzlies	AHL	80	14	24	38	57	....	....	....	....	....	....	....	....	....	....	....	....	....	....	....	....	....	....
2005-06	**Phoenix**	**NHL**	**75**	**6**	**17**	**23**	**42**	**1**	**0**	**1**	**109**	**5.5**	**1**	**8**	**12.5**	**13:20**	....	....	....	....	....	....	....	....	....
2006-07	**Phoenix**	**NHL**	**78**	**9**	**9**	**18**	**48**	**2**	**0**	**1**	**125**	**7.2**	**–11**	**15**	**13.3**	**14:07**	....	....	....	....	....	....	....	....	....
	NHL Totals		**210**	**22**	**32**	**54**	**112**	**3**	**0**	**3**	**307**	**7.2**		**30**	**16.7**	**13:09**	....	....	....	....	....	....	....	....	....

SKOLNEY, Wade

(SKOHL-nee, WAYD)

Defense. Shoots right. 6', 197 lbs. Born, Wynyard, Sask., June 24, 1981.

			Regular Season														Playoffs								
Season	Club	League	GP	G	A	Pts	PIM	PP	SH	GW	S	%	+/-	TF	F%	Min	GP	G	A	Pts	PIM	PP	SH	GW	Min
1996-97	Niacam Bantams	SBHL	54	33	70	103	193	....	....	....	....	....	....	....	....	....	....	....	....	....	....	....	....	....	....
	Brandon	WHL	1	0	0	0	0	....	....	....	....	....	....	....	....	....	....	....	....	....	....	....	....	....	....
1997-98	Brandon	WHL	42	1	11	12	49	....	....	....	....	....	....	....	....	....	3	0	0	0	0	....	....	....	....
1998-99	Brandon	WHL	39	3	10	13	60	....	....	....	....	....	....	....	....	....	5	0	1	1	16	....	....	....	....
99-2000	Brandon	WHL	13	0	2	2	23	....	....	....	....	....	....	....	....	....	....	....	....	....	....	....	....	....	....
2000-01	Brandon	WHL	28	2	9	11	37	....	....	....	....	....	....	....	....	....	....	....	....	....	....	....	....	....	....
2001-02	Brandon	WHL	50	4	12	16	179	....	....	....	....	....	....	....	....	....	19	2	7	9	56	....	....	....	....
2002-03	Philadelphia	AHL	68	2	7	9	102	....	....	....	....	....	....	....	....	....	....	....	....	....	....	....	....	....	....
2003-04	Philadelphia	AHL	56	1	8	9	106	....	....	....	....	....	....	....	....	....	12	0	0	0	23	....	....	....	....
2004-05	Philadelphia	AHL	35	0	8	8	104	....	....	....	....	....	....	....	....	....	21	0	1	1	43	....	....	....	....
2005-06	**Philadelphia**	**NHL**	**1**	**0**	**0**	**0**	**2**	**0**	**0**	**0**	**0**	**0.0**	**0**	**0**	**0.0**	**6:52**	....	....	....	....	....	....	....	....	....
	Philadelphia	AHL	56	0	5	5	197	....	....	....	....	....	....	....	....	....	....	....	....	....	....	....	....	....	....
2006-07	Wilkes-Barre	AHL	62	1	6	7	216	....	....	....	....	....	....	....	....	....	11	0	2	2	8	....	....	....	....
	NHL Totals		**1**	**0**	**0**	**0**	**2**	**0**	**0**	**0**	**0**	**0.0**		**0**	**0.0**	**6:52**	....	....	....	....	....	....	....	....	....

Signed as a free agent by **Philadelphia**, May 20, 2002. • Missed majority of 2004-05 season recovering from head injury suffered in game on November 19, 2004. Signed as a free agent by **Pittsburgh**, July 21, 2006. Signed as a free agent by **Straubing** (Germany), July 20, 2007.

SKOULA, Martin

(SHKOO-la, MAHR-tihn) **MIN.**

Defense. Shoots left. 6'3", 215 lbs. Born, Litomerice, Czech., October 28, 1979. Colorado's 2nd choice, 17th overall, in 1998 Entry Draft.

			Regular Season														Playoffs								
Season	Club	League	GP	G	A	Pts	PIM	PP	SH	GW	S	%	+/-	TF	F%	Min	GP	G	A	Pts	PIM	PP	SH	GW	Min
1995-96	Litvinov Jr.	CzRep-Jr.	38	0	4	4	....	....	....	....	....	....	....	....	....	....	....	....	....	....	....	....	....	....	....
	Litvinov	CzRep	....	....	....	....	....	....	....	....	....	....	....	....	....	....	1	0	0	0	0	....	....	....	....
1996-97	Litvinov Jr.	CzRep-Jr.	38	2	9	11	....	....	....	....	....	....	....	....	....	....	....	....	....	....	....	....	....	....	....
	Litvinov	CzRep	1	0	0	0	0	....	....	....	....	....	....	....	....	....	....	....	....	....	....	....	....	....	....
1997-98	Barrie Colts	OHL	66	8	36	44	36	....	....	....	....	....	....	....	....	....	6	1	3	4	4	....	....	....	....
1998-99	Barrie Colts	OHL	67	13	46	59	46	....	....	....	....	....	....	....	....	....	12	3	10	13	13	....	....	....	....
	Hershey Bears	AHL	....	....	....	....	....	....	....	....	....	....	....	....	....	....	1	0	0	0	0	....	....	....	....
99-2000	**Colorado**	**NHL**	**80**	**3**	**13**	**16**	**20**	**2**	**0**	**0**	**66**	**4.5**	**5**	**0**	**0.0**	**18:15**	**17**	**0**	**2**	**2**	**4**	**0**	**0**	**0**	**18:45**
2000-01 ♦	**Colorado**	**NHL**	**82**	**8**	**17**	**25**	**38**	**3**	**0**	**2**	**108**	**7.4**	**8**	**1**	**100.0**	**20:41**	**23**	**1**	**4**	**5**	**8**	**0**	**0**	**0**	**11:59**
2001-02	**Colorado**	**NHL**	**82**	**10**	**21**	**31**	**42**	**5**	**0**	**1**	**100**	**10.0**	**–3**	**0**	**0.0**	**22:18**	**21**	**0**	**6**	**6**	**2**	**0**	**0**	**0**	**14:37**
	Czech Republic	Olympics	4	0	0	0	0	....	....	....	....	....	....	....	....	....	....	....	....	....	....	....	....	....	....
2002-03	**Colorado**	**NHL**	**81**	**4**	**21**	**25**	**68**	**2**	**0**	**0**	**93**	**4.3**	**11**	**1**	**100.0**	**18:27**	**7**	**0**	**1**	**1**	**4**	**0**	**0**	**0**	**11:05**
2003-04	**Colorado**	**NHL**	**58**	**2**	**14**	**16**	**30**	**0**	**0**	**0**	**54**	**3.7**	**2**	**0**	**0.0**	**17:21**	....	....	....	....	....	....	....	....	....
	Anaheim	**NHL**	**21**	**2**	**7**	**9**	**2**	**1**	**0**	**0**	**30**	**6.7**	**3**	**1**	**0.0**	**21:14**	....	....	....	....	....	....	....	....	....
2004-05	Litvinov	CzRep	47	4	15	19	101	....	....	....	....	....	....	....	....	....	6	0	0	0	6	....	....	....	....

Season	Club	League	GP	G	A	Pts	PIM	PP	SH	GW	S	%	+/-	TF	F%	Min	GP	G	A	Pts	PIM	PP	SH	GW	Min
			Regular Season														Playoffs								
2005-06	**Dallas**	**NHL**	**61**	**4**	**11**	**15**	**36**	**3**	**0**	**1**	**78**	**5.1**	**6**	**0**	**0.0**	**18:41**	....	....	....	....	....	....	....	....	....
	Minnesota	**NHL**	**17**	**1**	**5**	**6**	**10**	**0**	**0**	**0**	**14**	**7.1**	**0**	**0**	**0.0**	**20:49**	....	....	....	....	....	....	....	....	....
2006-07	**Minnesota**	**NHL**	**81**	**0**	**15**	**15**	**36**	**0**	**0**	**0**	**91**	**0.0**	**9**	**0**	**0.0**	**20:14**	**5**	**0**	**0**	**0**	**4**	**0**	**0**	**0**	**19:02**
	NHL Totals		**563**	**34**	**124**	**158**	**282**	**16**	**0**	**4**	**634**	**5.4**		**3**	**66.7**	**19:39**	**73**	**1**	**13**	**14**	**22**	**0**	**0**	**0**	**14:43**

OHL All-Rookie Team (1998) • OHL Second All-Star Team (1999)

Traded to **Anaheim** by **Colorado** for Kurt Sauer and Anaheim's 4th round choice (Raymond Macias) in 2005 Entry Draft, February 21, 2004. Signed as a free agent by **Litvinov** (CzRep), September 17, 2004. Signed as a free agent by **Dallas**, August 3, 2005. Traded to **Minnesota** by **Dallas** with Shawn Belle for Willie Mitchell and Minnesota's 2nd round choice (Nico Sacchetti) in 2007 Entry Draft, March 8, 2006.

SKRASTINS, Karlis

(SKRAS-tihnz, KAR-lihs) **COL.**

Defense. Shoots left. 6'1", 210 lbs. Born, Riga, USSR, July 9, 1974. Nashville's 8th choice, 230th overall, in 1998 Entry Draft.

Season	Club	League	GP	G	A	Pts	PIM	PP	SH	GW	S	%	+/-	TF	F%	Min	GP	G	A	Pts	PIM	PP	SH	GW	Min
1992-93	Pardaugava Riga	CIS	40	3	5	8	16	....	....	....	....	....	....	....	....	....	2	0	0	0	0	....	....	....	....
1993-94	Pardaugava Riga	CIS	42	7	5	12	18	....	....	....	....	....	....	....	....	....	2	1	0	1	4	....	....	....	....
1994-95	Pardaugava Riga	CIS	52	4	14	18	69	....	....	....	....	....	....	....	....	....	....	....	....	....	....	....	....	....	....
1995-96	TPS Turku	Finland	50	4	11	15	32	....	....	....	....	....	....	....	....	....	11	2	2	4	10	....	....	....	....
1996-97	TPS Turku	Finland	50	2	8	10	20	....	....	....	....	....	....	....	....	....	12	0	4	4	2	....	....	....	....
	TPS Turku	EuroHL	6	0	1	1	4	....	....	....	....	....	....	....	....	....	4	0	0	0	14	....	....	....	....
1997-98	TPS Turku	Finland	48	4	15	19	67	....	....	....	....	....	....	....	....	....	4	0	0	0	0	....	....	....	....
	TPS Turku	EuroHL	6	0	1	1	6	....	....	....	....	....	....	....	....	....	....	....	....	....	....	....	....	....	....
1998-99	**Nashville**	**NHL**	**2**	**0**	**1**	**1**	**0**	**0**	**0**	**0**	**0**	**0.0**	**0**	**0**	**0.0**	**11:47**	....	....	....	....	....	....	....	....	....
	Milwaukee	IHL	75	8	36	44	47	....	....	....	....	....	....	....	....	....	2	0	1	1	2	....	....	....	....
99-2000	**Nashville**	**NHL**	**59**	**5**	**6**	**11**	**20**	**1**	**0**	**2**	**51**	**9.8**	**-7**	**0**	**0.0**	**20:51**	....	....	....	....	....	....	....	....	....
	Milwaukee	IHL	19	3	8	11	10	....	....	....	....	....	....	....	....	....	....	....	....	....	....	....	....	....	....
2000-01	**Nashville**	**NHL**	**82**	**1**	**11**	**12**	**30**	**0**	**0**	**1**	**66**	**1.5**	**-12**	**0**	**0.0**	**19:12**	....	....	....	....	....	....	....	....	....
2001-02	**Nashville**	**NHL**	**82**	**4**	**13**	**17**	**36**	**0**	**0**	**1**	**84**	**4.8**	**-12**	**0**	**0.0**	**20:29**	....	....	....	....	....	....	....	....	....
	Latvia	Olympics	1	0	0	0	0	....	....	....	....	....	....	....	....	....	....	....	....	....	....	....	....	....	....
2002-03	**Nashville**	**NHL**	**82**	**3**	**10**	**13**	**44**	**0**	**1**	**0**	**86**	**3.5**	**-18**	**0**	**0.0**	**20:17**	....	....	....	....	....	....	....	....	....
2003-04	**Colorado**	**NHL**	**82**	**5**	**8**	**13**	**26**	**0**	**1**	**1**	**102**	**4.9**	**18**	**0**	**0.0**	**21:49**	**11**	**0**	**2**	**2**	**2**	**0**	**0**	**0**	**23:07**
2004-05	HK Riga 2000	Latvia	4	0	4	4	0	....	....	....	....	....	....	....	....	....	9	3	10	13	33	....	....	....	....
	HK Riga 2000	BelOpen	34	8	17	25	30	....	....	....	....	....	....	....	....	....	3	0	0	0	25	....	....	....	....
2005-06	**Colorado**	**NHL**	**82**	**3**	**11**	**14**	**65**	**0**	**2**	**0**	**58**	**5.2**	**-7**	**0**	**0.0**	**21:49**	**9**	**0**	**1**	**1**	**10**	**0**	**0**	**0**	**23:24**
	Latvia	Olympics	5	0	1	1	0	....	....	....	....	....	....	....	....	....	....	....	....	....	....	....	....	....	....
2006-07	**Colorado**	**NHL**	**68**	**0**	**11**	**11**	**30**	**0**	**0**	**0**	**65**	**0.0**	**0**	**0**	**0.0**	**21:14**	....	....	....	....	....	....	....	....	....
	NHL Totals		**539**	**21**	**71**	**92**	**251**	**1**	**4**	**5**	**512**	**4.1**		**0**	**0.0**	**20:46**	**20**	**0**	**3**	**3**	**12**	**0**	**0**	**0**	**23:15**

Traded to **Colorado** by **Nashville** for Colorado's 3rd round choice (later traded to Ottawa – Ottawa selected Peter Regin Jensen) in 2004 Entry Draft, June 30, 2003. Signed as a free agent by **Riga** (Latvia), September 25, 2004.

SLANEY, John

(SLAY-nee, JAWN)

Defense. Shoots left. 6', 189 lbs. Born, St. John's, Nfld., February 7, 1972. Washington's 1st choice, 9th overall, in 1990 Entry Draft.

Season	Club	League	GP	G	A	Pts	PIM	PP	SH	GW	S	%	+/-	TF	F%	Min	GP	G	A	Pts	PIM	PP	SH	GW	Min
1987-88	St. John's	NFAHA	65	41	69	110	70	....	....	....	....	....	....	....	....	....	....	....	....	....	....	....	....	....	....
1988-89	Cornwall Royals	OHL	66	16	43	59	23	....	....	....	....	....	....	....	....	....	18	8	16	24	10	....	....	....	....
1989-90	Cornwall Royals	OHL	64	38	59	97	68	....	....	....	....	....	....	....	....	....	6	0	8	8	11	....	....	....	....
1990-91	Cornwall Royals	OHL	34	21	25	46	28	....	....	....	....	....	....	....	....	....	....	....	....	....	....	....	....	....	....
1991-92	Cornwall Royals	OHL	34	19	41	60	43	....	....	....	....	....	....	....	....	....	6	3	8	11	0	....	....	....	....
	Baltimore	AHL	6	2	4	6	0	....	....	....	....	....	....	....	....	....	....	....	....	....	....	....	....	....	....
1992-93	Baltimore	AHL	79	20	46	66	60	....	....	....	....	....	....	....	....	....	7	0	7	7	8	....	....	....	....
1993-94	**Washington**	**NHL**	**47**	**7**	**9**	**16**	**27**	**3**	**0**	**1**	**70**	**10.0**	**3**	....	....	....	**11**	**1**	**1**	**2**	**2**	**1**	**0**	**0**	....
	Portland Pirates	AHL	29	14	13	27	17	....	....	....	....	....	....	....	....	....	....	....	....	....	....	....	....	....	....
1994-95	**Washington**	**NHL**	**16**	**0**	**3**	**3**	**6**	**0**	**0**	**0**	**21**	**0.0**	**-3**	....	....	....	....	....	....	....	....	....	....	....	....
	Portland Pirates	AHL	8	3	10	13	4	....	....	....	....	....	....	....	....	....	7	1	3	4	4	....	....	....	....
1995-96	**Colorado**	**NHL**	**7**	**0**	**3**	**3**	**4**	**0**	**0**	**0**	**12**	**0.0**	**2**	....	....	....	....	....	....	....	....	....	....	....	....
	Cornwall Aces	AHL	5	0	4	4	2	....	....	....	....	....	....	....	....	....	....	....	....	....	....	....	....	....	....
	Los Angeles	**NHL**	**31**	**6**	**11**	**17**	**10**	**3**	**1**	**0**	**63**	**9.5**	**5**	....	....	....	....	....	....	....	....	....	....	....	....
1996-97	**Los Angeles**	**NHL**	**32**	**3**	**11**	**14**	**4**	**1**	**0**	**1**	**60**	**5.0**	**-10**	....	....	....	....	....	....	....	....	....	....	....	....
	Phoenix	IHL	35	9	25	34	8	....	....	....	....	....	....	....	....	....	....	....	....	....	....	....	....	....	....
1997-98	**Phoenix**	**NHL**	**55**	**3**	**14**	**17**	**24**	**1**	**0**	**1**	**74**	**4.1**	**-3**	....	....	....	....	....	....	....	....	....	....	....	....
	Las Vegas	IHL	5	2	2	4	10	....	....	....	....	....	....	....	....	....	....	....	....	....	....	....	....	....	....
1998-99	**Nashville**	**NHL**	**46**	**2**	**12**	**14**	**14**	**0**	**0**	**1**	**84**	**2.4**	**-12**	**0**	**0.0**	**20:39**	....	....	....	....	....	....	....	....	....
	Milwaukee	IHL	7	0	1	1	0	....	....	....	....	....	....	....	....	....	....	....	....	....	....	....	....	....	....
99-2000	**Pittsburgh**	**NHL**	**29**	**1**	**4**	**5**	**10**	**1**	**0**	**0**	**27**	**3.7**	**-10**	**35**	**40.0**	**12:13**	**2**	**1**	**0**	**1**	**2**	**1**	**0**	**0**	**5:43**
	Wilkes-Barre	AHL	49	30	30	60	25	....	....	....	....	....	....	....	....	....	....	....	....	....	....	....	....	....	....
2000-01	Wilkes-Barre	AHL	40	12	38	50	4	....	....	....	....	....	....	....	....	....	....	....	....	....	....	....	....	....	....
	Philadelphia	AHL	25	6	11	17	10	....	....	....	....	....	....	....	....	....	10	2	6	8	6	....	....	....	....
2001-02	**Philadelphia**	**NHL**	**1**	**0**	**0**	**0**	**0**	**0**	**0**	**0**	**1**	**0.0**	**2**	**0**	**0.0**	**23:33**	**1**	**0**	**0**	**0**	**0**	**0**	**0**	**0**	**11:20**
	Philadelphia	AHL	64	20	39	59	26	....	....	....	....	....	....	....	....	....	5	2	1	3	0	....	....	....	....
2002-03	Philadelphia	AHL	55	9	33	42	36	....	....	....	....	....	....	....	....	....	....	....	....	....	....	....	....	....	....
2003-04	**Philadelphia**	**NHL**	**4**	**0**	**2**	**2**	**0**	**0**	**0**	**0**	**0**	**0.0**	**0**	**0**	**0.0**	**13:38**	....	....	....	....	....	....	....	....	....
	Philadelphia	AHL	59	19	29	48	31	....	....	....	....	....	....	....	....	....	12	3	4	7	6	....	....	....	....
2004-05	Philadelphia	AHL	78	14	30	44	39	....	....	....	....	....	....	....	....	....	21	3	7	10	12	....	....	....	....
2005-06	Philadelphia	AHL	79	8	42	50	60	....	....	....	....	....	....	....	....	....	....	....	....	....	....	....	....	....	....
2006-07	Philadelphia	AHL	55	9	24	33	26	....	....	....	....	....	....	....	....	....	....	....	....	....	....	....	....	....	....
	NHL Totals		**268**	**22**	**69**	**91**	**99**	**9**	**1**	**4**	**412**	**5.3**		**35**	**40.0**	**17:17**	**14**	**2**	**1**	**3**	**4**	**2**	**0**	**0**	**7:35**

OHL First All-Star Team (1990) • Canadian Major Junior Defenseman of the Year (1990) • OHL Second All-Star Team (1991) • AHL First All-Star Team (2001, 2002) • Eddie Shore Award (Outstanding Defenseman – AHL) (2001, 2002) • AHL Second All-Star Team (2004)

Traded to **Colorado** by **Washington** for Philadelphia's 3rd round choice (previously acquired, Washington selected Shawn McNeil) in 1996 Entry Draft, July 12, 1995. Traded to **Los Angeles** by **Colorado** for Winnipeg's 6th round choice (previously acquired, Colorado selected Brian Willsie) in 1996 Entry Draft, December 28, 1995. Signed as a free agent by **Phoenix**, August 19, 1997. Claimed by **Nashville** from **Phoenix** in Expansion Draft, June 26, 1998. Signed as a free agent by **Pittsburgh**, September 30, 1999. Traded to **Philadelphia** by **Pittsburgh** for Kevin Stevens, January 14, 2001.

SLATER, Jim

(SLAY-tuhr, JIHM) **ATL.**

Center. Shoots left. 6', 190 lbs. Born, Petoskey, MI, December 9, 1982. Atlanta's 2nd choice, 30th overall, in 2002 Entry Draft.

Season	Club	League	GP	G	A	Pts	PIM	PP	SH	GW	S	%	+/-	TF	F%	Min	GP	G	A	Pts	PIM	PP	SH	GW	Min
1998-99	USNTDP	U-18	3	0	1	1	0	....	....	....	....	....	....	....	....	....	....	....	....	....	....	....	....	....	....
	Cleveland Barons	NAHL	50	13	20	33	58	....	....	....	....	....	....	....	....	....	2	0	0	0	2	....	....	....	....
99-2000	Cleveland Barons	NAHL	56	35	50	85	129	....	....	....	....	....	....	....	....	....	3	1	3	4	4	....	....	....	....
2000-01	Cleveland Barons	NAHL	48	27	37	64	122	....	....	....	....	....	....	....	....	....	6	6	6	12	6	....	....	....	....
2001-02	Michigan State	CCHA	37	11	21	32	50	....	....	....	....	....	....	....	....	....	....	....	....	....	....	....	....	....	....
2002-03	Michigan State	CCHA	37	18	26	44	26	....	....	....	....	....	....	....	....	....	....	....	....	....	....	....	....	....	....
2003-04	Michigan State	CCHA	42	19	29	*48	38	....	....	....	....	....	....	....	....	....	....	....	....	....	....	....	....	....	....
2004-05	Michigan State	CCHA	41	16	32	48	30	....	....	....	....	....	....	....	....	....	....	....	....	....	....	....	....	....	....
2005-06	**Atlanta**	**NHL**	**71**	**10**	**10**	**20**	**46**	**1**	**0**	**0**	**108**	**9.3**	**1**	**287**	**56.5**	**10:06**	....	....	....	....	....	....	....	....	....
	Chicago Wolves	AHL	4	0	2	2	2	....	....	....	....	....	....	....	....	....	....	....	....	....	....	....	....	....	....
2006-07	**Atlanta**	**NHL**	**74**	**5**	**14**	**19**	**62**	**0**	**0**	**2**	**90**	**5.6**	**8**	**373**	**54.4**	**10:14**	**4**	**0**	**0**	**0**	**2**	**0**	**0**	**0**	**5:10**
	NHL Totals		**145**	**15**	**24**	**39**	**108**	**1**	**0**	**2**	**198**	**7.6**		**660**	**55.3**	**10:10**	**4**	**0**	**0**	**0**	**2**	**0**	**0**	**0**	**5:10**

CCHA All-Rookie Team (2002) • CCHA First All-Star Team (2003, 2004) • NCAA West Second All-American Team (2004)

SLEGR, Jiri

(SLAY-guhr, YIH-ree)

Defense. Shoots left. 6'1", 210 lbs. Born, Jihlava, Czech., May 30, 1971. Vancouver's 3rd choice, 23rd overall, in 1990 Entry Draft.

Season	Club	League	GP	G	A	Pts	PIM	PP	SH	GW	S	%	+/-	TF	F%	Min	GP	G	A	Pts	PIM	PP	SH	GW	Min
1987-88	CHZ Litvinov	Czech	4	1	1	2	0	....	....	....	....	....	....	....	....	....	....	....	....	....	....	....	....	....	....
1988-89	CHZ Litvinov	Czech	8	0	0	0	4	....	....	....	....	....	....	....	....	....	....	....	....	....	....	....	....	....	....
1989-90	CHZ Litvinov	Czech	51	4	15	19	....	....	....	....	....	....	....	....	....	....	....	....	....	....	....	....	....	....	....
1990-91	HC CHZ Litvinov	Czech	47	11	36	47	26	....	....	....	....	....	....	....	....	....	....	....	....	....	....	....	....	....	....
1991-92	Litvinov	Czech	42	9	23	32	38	....	....	....	....	....	....	....	....	....	....	....	....	....	....	....	....	....	....
	Czechoslovakia	Olympics	8	1	1	2	14	....	....	....	....	....	....	....	....	....	....	....	....	....	....	....	....	....	....
1992-93	**Vancouver**	**NHL**	**41**	**4**	**22**	**26**	**109**	**2**	**0**	**0**	**89**	**4.5**	**16**	....	....	....	**5**	**0**	**3**	**3**	**4**	**0**	**0**	**0**	....
	Hamilton	AHL	21	4	14	18	42	....	....	....	....	....	....	....	....	....	....	....	....	....	....	....	....	....	....
1993-94	**Vancouver**	**NHL**	**78**	**5**	**33**	**38**	**86**	**1**	**0**	**0**	**160**	**3.1**	**0**	....	....	....	....	....	....	....	....	....	....	....	....

								Regular Season									Playoffs								
Season	Club	League	GP	G	A	Pts	PIM	PP	SH	GW	S	%	+/-	TF	F%	Min	GP	G	A	Pts	PIM	PP	SH	GW	Min
1994-95	Litvinov	CzRep	11	3	10	13	80																		
	Vancouver	NHL	19	1	5	6	32	0	0	1	42	2.4	0												
	Edmonton	NHL	12	1	5	6	14	1	0	0	27	3.7	–5												
1995-96	Edmonton	NHL	57	4	13	17	74	0	1	1	91	4.4	–1												
	Cape Breton	AHL	4	1	2	3	4																		
1996-97	Litvinov	CzRep	1	0	0	0	0																		
	Sodertalje SK	Sweden	30	4	14	18	62										10	4	2	6	32				
1997-98	Pittsburgh	NHL	73	5	12	17	109	1	1	0	131	3.8	10				6	0	4	4	2	0	0	0	
	Czech Republic	Olympics	6	1	0	1	8																		
1998-99	Pittsburgh	NHL	63	3	20	23	86	1	0	0	91	3.3	13	2	0.0	18:42	13	1	3	4	12	0	0	1	19:50
99-2000	Pittsburgh	NHL	74	11	20	31	82	0	0	2	144	7.6	20	3	66.7	21:22	10	2	3	5	19	0	0	1	20:02
2000-01	Pittsburgh	NHL	42	5	10	15	60	0	1	1	67	7.5	–9	0	0.0	17:37									
	Atlanta	NHL	33	3	16	19	36	2	0	0	78	3.8	–1	1	0.0	21:34									
2001-02	Atlanta	NHL	38	3	5	8	51	1	0	0	56	5.4	–21	0	0.0	21:21									
	◆ Detroit	NHL	8	0	1	1	8	0	0	0	11	0.0	1	0	0.0	19:16	1	0	0	0	2	0	0	0	17:11
2002-03	Litvinov	CzRep	10	2	3	5	14																		
	Avangard Omsk	Russia	6	1	2	3	8										9	0	3	3	*45				
2003-04	Vancouver	NHL	16	2	5	7	8	1	1	1	15	13.3	6	0	0.0	12:16									
	Boston	NHL	36	4	15	19	27	0	0	1	83	4.8	5	0	0.0	20:03	7	1	1	2	0	0	0	0	18:08
2004-05	Litvinov	CzRep	46	6	23	29	135										6	1	2	3	30				
2005-06	Boston	NHL	32	5	11	16	56	4	0	0	59	8.5	–2	0	0.0	16:22									
2006-07	Litvinov	CzRep	41	8	8	16	134																		
	NHL Totals		622	56	193	249	838	14	4	7	1144	4.9		6	33.3	19:21	42	4	14	18	39	0	0	2	19:26

Czechoslovakian First All-Star Team (1991)

Traded to **Edmonton** by **Vancouver** for Roman Oksiuta, April 7, 1995. Traded to **Pittsburgh** by **Edmonton** for Pittsburgh's 3rd round choice (later traded to New Jersey – New Jersey selected Brian Gionta) in 1998 Entry Draft, August 12, 1997. Traded to **Atlanta** by **Pittsburgh** for San Jose's 3rd round choice (previously acquired, later traded to Columbus – Columbus selected Aaron Johnson) in 2001 Entry Draft, January 14, 2001. Traded to **Detroit** by **Atlanta** for Yuri Butsayev and Detroit's 3rd round choice (later traded to Columbus – Columbus selected Jeff Genovy) in 2002 Entry Draft, March 19, 2002. Signed as a free agent by **Vancouver**, September 4, 2003. Traded to **Boston** by **Vancouver** for future considerations, January 17, 2004. Signed as a free agent by **Litvinov** (CzRep), August 20, 2004. • Missed remainder of 2005-06 season recovering from back surgery (January, 2006). Signed as a free agent by **Litvinov** (CzRep), July 31, 2006.

SMID, Ladislav

(SHMIHD, LA-dih-slahv) **EDM.**

Defense. Shoots left. 6'3", 204 lbs. Born, Frydlant V Cechach, Czech., February 1, 1986. Anaheim's 1st choice, 9th overall, in 2004 Entry Draft.

Season	Club	League	GP	G	A	Pts	PIM	PP	SH	GW	S	%	+/-	TF	F%	Min	GP	G	A	Pts	PIM	PP	SH	GW	Min
2001-02	HC Liberec Jr.	CzRep-Jr.	43	6	10	16	87																		
2002-03	HC Liberec Jr.	CzRep-Jr.	32	1	14	15	12										8	2	1	3	31				
	Liberec	CzRep	4	0	0	0	0																		
2003-04	HC Liberec Jr.	CzRep-Jr.	14	4	10	14	38										2	1	0	1	6				
	Beroun	CzRep-2															3	1	1	2	4				
	Liberec	CzRep	45	1	1	2	51																		
2004-05	HC Liberec Jr.	CzRep-Jr.	3	0	1	1	4																		
	Liberec	CzRep	39	1	3	4	14										12	0	0	0	6				
2005-06	Portland Pirates	AHL	71	3	25	28	48										16	0	1	1	16				
2006-07	Edmonton	NHL	77	3	7	10	37	0	0	0	53	5.7	–16	0	0.0	19:14									
	NHL Totals		77	3	7	10	37	0	0	0	53	5.7		0	0.0	19:14									

Traded to **Edmonton** by **Anaheim** with Joffrey Lupul, Anaheim's 1st round choice (later traded to Phoenix - Phoenix selected Nick Ross) in 2007 Entry Draft and Anaheim's 1st round choice in 2008 Entry Draf for Chris Pronger, July 3, 2006.

SMIRNOV, Alexei

(smihr-NAHV, al-EHX-ay)

Left wing. Shoots left. 6'3", 211 lbs. Born, Tver, USSR, January 28, 1982. Anaheim's 1st choice, 12th overall, in 2000 Entry Draft.

Season	Club	League	GP	G	A	Pts	PIM	PP	SH	GW	S	%	+/-	TF	F%	Min	GP	G	A	Pts	PIM	PP	SH	GW	Min
1997-98	Dyn'o Moscow 2	Russia-2	11	1	1	2	4																		
1998-99	Dyn'o Moscow 2	Russia-3	27	9	3	12	24																		
99-2000	Dyn'o Moscow 2	Russia-3	12	5	3	8	34																		
	THK Tver	Russia-2	35	3	5	8	24																		
	Dynamo Moscow	Russia	1	0	0	0	0																		
2000-01	Dynamo Moscow	Russia	29	2	0	2	16																		
2001-02	CSKA Moscow 2	Russia-3	2	1	0	1	0																		
	CSKA Moscow	Russia	51	5	11	16	42																		
2002-03	Anaheim	NHL	44	3	2	5	18	0	0	1	46	6.5	–1	6	16.7	8:50	4	0	0	0	2	0	0	0	4:22
	Cincinnati	AHL	19	7	3	10	12																		
2003-04	Anaheim	NHL	8	0	1	1	2	0	0	0	8	0.0	0	3	0.0	7:17									
	Cincinnati	AHL	51	9	10	19	34										2	0	0	0	2				
2004-05	Cincinnati	AHL	65	9	9	18	53										4	0	0	0	0				
2005-06	Avangard Omsk	Russia	27	1	2	3	18										10	1	1	2	18				
2006-07	Long Beach	ECHL	38	12	19	31	44																		
	NHL Totals		52	3	3	6	20	0	0	1	54	5.6		9	11.1	8:36	4	0	0	0	2	0	0	0	4:22

Signed as a free agent by **Omsk** (Russia). August 12, 2005.

SMITH, Brandon

(SMIHTH, BRAN-duhn)

Defense. Shoots left. 6'1", 209 lbs. Born, Hazelton, B.C., February 25, 1973.

Season	Club	League	GP	G	A	Pts	PIM	PP	SH	GW	S	%	+/-	TF	F%	Min	GP	G	A	Pts	PIM	PP	SH	GW	Min
1989-90	Portland	WHL	59	2	17	19	16																		
1990-91	Portland	WHL	17	8	5	13	8																		
1991-92	Portland	WHL	70	12	32	44	63																		
1992-93	Portland	WHL	72	20	54	74	38										16	4	9	13	6				
1993-94	Portland	WHL	72	19	63	82	47										10	2	10	12	8				
1994-95	Dayton Bombers	ECHL	60	16	49	65	57										4	2	3	5	0				
	Minnesota Moose	IHL	1	0	0	0	0																		
	Adirondack	AHL	14	1	2	3	7										3	0	0	0	2				
1995-96	Adirondack	AHL	48	4	13	17	22										3	0	1	1	2				
1996-97	Adirondack	AHL	80	8	26	34	30										4	0	0	0	0				
1997-98	Adirondack	AHL	64	9	27	36	26										1	0	1	1	0				
1998-99	Boston	NHL	5	0	0	0	0	0	0	0	2	0.0	2	0	0.0	9:38									
	Providence Bruins	AHL	72	16	46	62	32										19	1	9	10	12				
99-2000	Boston	NHL	22	2	4	6	10	0	0	0	24	8.3	–4	0	0.0	19:29									
	Providence Bruins	AHL	55	8	30	38	20										14	1	11	12	2				
2000-01	Boston	NHL	3	1	0	1	0	1	0	0	2	50.0	–1	0	0.0	6:46									
	Providence Bruins	AHL	63	11	28	39	30										17	0	5	5	6				
2001-02	Cleveland Barons	AHL	59	6	29	35	26																		
2002-03	NY Islanders	NHL	3	0	0	0	0	0	0	0	1	0.0	–2	0	0.0	9:59									
	Bridgeport	AHL	63	9	32	41	37										9	1	3	4	5				
2003-04	Bridgeport	AHL	74	5	23	28	39										7	1	3	4	9				
2004-05	Rochester	AHL	67	4	14	18	32										8	1	1	2	4				
2005-06	Rochester	AHL	39	3	11	14	39																		
2006-07	Rochester	AHL	71	9	36	45	54										5	0	2	2	2				
	NHL Totals		33	3	4	7	10	1	0	0	29	10.3		0	0.0	15:58									

WHL West Second All-Star Team (1993, 1994) • ECHL First All-Star Team (1995) • ECHL Defenseman of the Year (1995) • AHL First All-Star Team (1999)

Signed as a free agent by **Detroit**, July 22, 1997. Signed as a free agent by **Boston**, August 5, 1998. Signed as a free agent by **San Jose**, July 23, 2001. Signed as a free agent by **NY Islanders**, August 3, 2002. Signed as a free agent by **Rochester** (AHL), September 10, 2004. Signed as a free agent by **Berlin** (Germany), July 31, 2007.

SMITH, Dan

(SMIHTH, DAN) **CBJ**

Defense. Shoots left. 6'2", 200 lbs. Born, Fernie, B.C., October 19, 1976. Colorado's 7th choice, 181st overall, in 1995 Entry Draft.

Season	Club	League	GP	G	A	Pts	PIM	PP	SH	GW	S	%	+/-	TF	F%	Min	GP	G	A	Pts	PIM	PP	SH	GW	Min
1994-95	U.B.C.	CWUAA	28	1	3	4	26																		
1995-96	Tri-City	WHL	58	1	21	22	70										11	1	3	4	14				
1996-97	Tri-City	WHL	72	5	19	24	174																		
	Hershey Bears	AHL	8	0	1	1	6										15	0	1	1	25				
1997-98	Hershey Bears	AHL	50	1	2	3	71										6	0	0	0	4				
1998-99	Colorado	NHL	12	0	0	0	9	0	0	0	6	0.0	5	0	0.0	12:14									
	Hershey Bears	AHL	54	5	7	12	72										5	0	1	1	0				

			Regular Season														Playoffs								
Season	Club	League	GP	G	A	Pts	PIM	PP	SH	GW	S	%	+/-	TF	F%	Min	GP	G	A	Pts	PIM	PP	SH	GW	Min
99-2000	**Colorado**	**NHL**	3	0	0	0	0	0	0	0	0	0.0	2	0	0.0	11:03	....	....	....	....	....	....	....	....	....
	Hershey Bears	AHL	49	7	15	22	56	....	....	....	....	....	....	....	....	....	....	....	....	....	....	....	....	....	....
2000-01	Hershey Bears	AHL	58	2	12	14	34	....	....	....	....	....	....	....	....	....	12	0	1	1	4	....	....	....	....
2001-02	Colorado	WCHL	12	0	2	2	16	....	....	....	....	....	....	....	....	....	....	....	....	....	....	....	....	....	....
	Lukko Rauma	Finland	32	1	2	3	18	....	....	....	....	....	....	....	....	....	....	....	....	....	....	....	....	....	....
2002-03	Springfield	AHL	69	1	14	15	53	....	....	....	....	....	....	....	....	....	6	0	2	2	0	....	....	....	....
2003-04	Toronto	AHL	66	4	9	13	41	....	....	....	....	....	....	....	....	....	....	....	....	....	....	....	....	....	....
2004-05	Edmonton	AHL	72	5	10	15	72	....	....	....	....	....	....	....	....	....	....	....	....	....	....	....	....	....	....
2005-06	**Edmonton**	**NHL**	7	0	0	0	7	0	0	0	1	0.0	1	0	0.0	11:21	....	....	....	....	....	....	....	....	....
	Hamilton	AHL	69	0	15	15	61	....	....	....	....	....	....	....	....	....	....	....	....	....	....	....	....	....	....
2006-07	Grand Rapids	AHL	80	1	10	11	97	....	....	....	....	....	....	....	....	....	7	0	1	1	8	....	....	....	....
	NHL Totals		22	0	0	0	16	0	0	0	7	0.0		0	0.0	11:47	....	....	....	....	....	....	....	....	....

Signed as a free agent by **Colorado** (WCHL), October 26, 2001. Signed as a free agent by **Rauma** (Finland) after receiving release from Colorado (WCHL), November 21, 2001. Signed as a free agent by **Edmonton**, August 21, 2003. Signed as a free agent by **Detroit**, July 13, 2006. Signed as a free agent by **Columbus**, July 11, 2007.

SMITH, Jason

(SMIHTH, JAY-suhn) **PHI.**

Defense. Shoots right. 6'3", 215 lbs. Born, Calgary, Alta., November 2, 1973. New Jersey's 1st choice, 18th overall, in 1992 Entry Draft.

Season	Club	League	GP	G	A	Pts	PIM	PP	SH	GW	S	%	+/-	TF	F%	Min	GP	G	A	Pts	PIM	PP	SH	GW	Min
1990-91	Calgary Canucks	AJHL	45	3	15	18	69	....	....	....	....	....	....	....	....	....	....	....	....	....	....	....	....	....	....
	Regina Pats	WHL	2	0	0	0	7	....	....	....	....	....	....	....	....	....	4	0	0	0	2	....	....	....	....
1991-92	Regina Pats	WHL	62	9	29	38	138	....	....	....	....	....	....	....	....	....	....	....	....	....	....	....	....	....	....
1992-93	Regina Pats	WHL	64	14	52	66	175	....	....	....	....	....	....	....	....	....	13	4	8	12	39	....	....	....	....
	Utica Devils	AHL	....	....	....	....	....	....	....	....	....	....	....	....	....	....	1	0	0	0	2	....	....	....	....
1993-94	**New Jersey**	**NHL**	41	0	5	5	43	0	0	0	47	0.0	7	....	....	....	6	0	0	0	7	0	0	0	....
	Albany River Rats	AHL	20	6	3	9	31	....	....	....	....	....	....	....	....	....	....	....	....	....	....	....	....	....	....
1994-95	Albany River Rats	AHL	7	0	2	2	15	....	....	....	....	....	....	....	....	....	11	2	2	4	19	....	....	....	....
	New Jersey	**NHL**	2	0	0	0	0	0	0	0	5	0.0	−3	....	....	....	....	....	....	....	....	....	....	....	....
1995-96	**New Jersey**	**NHL**	64	2	1	3	86	0	0	0	52	3.8	5	....	....	....	....	....	....	....	....	....	....	....	....
1996-97	**New Jersey**	**NHL**	57	1	2	3	38	0	0	0	48	2.1	−8	....	....	....	....	....	....	....	....	....	....	....	....
	Toronto	**NHL**	21	0	5	5	16	0	0	0	26	0.0	−4	....	....	....	....	....	....	....	....	....	....	....	....
1997-98	**Toronto**	**NHL**	81	3	13	16	100	0	0	0	97	3.1	−5	....	....	....	....	....	....	....	....	....	....	....	....
1998-99	**Toronto**	**NHL**	60	2	11	13	40	0	0	0	53	3.8	−9	0	0.0	17:31	....	....	....	....	....	....	....	....	....
	Edmonton	**NHL**	12	1	1	2	11	0	0	0	15	6.7	0	0	0.0	20:26	4	0	1	1	4	0	0	0	26:29
99-2000	**Edmonton**	**NHL**	80	3	11	14	60	0	0	1	96	3.1	16	1	100.0	21:15	5	0	1	1	4	0	0	0	21:56
2000-01	**Edmonton**	**NHL**	82	5	15	20	120	1	1	0	140	3.6	14	1	0.0	21:40	6	0	2	2	6	0	0	0	25:27
2001-02	**Edmonton**	**NHL**	74	5	13	18	103	0	1	1	85	5.9	14	0	0.0	21:00	....	....	....	....	....	....	....	....	....
2002-03	**Edmonton**	**NHL**	68	4	8	12	64	0	0	1	93	4.3	5	0	0.0	21:46	6	0	0	0	19	0	0	0	21:17
2003-04	**Edmonton**	**NHL**	68	7	12	19	98	0	1	1	84	8.3	13	2	50.0	21:22	....	....	....	....	....	....	....	....	....
2004-05				DID NOT PLAY																					
2005-06	**Edmonton**	**NHL**	76	4	13	17	84	0	0	0	79	5.1	1	0	0.0	19:39	24	1	4	5	16	0	0	1	22:29
2006-07	**Edmonton**	**NHL**	82	2	9	11	103	0	0	1	61	3.3	−13	1	0.0	21:08	....	....	....	....	....	....	....	....	....
	NHL Totals		868	39	119	158	966	1	3	5	981	4.0		5	20.0	20:44	51	1	8	9	56	0	0	1	23:01

WHL East First All-Star Team (1993) • Canadian Major Junior First All-Star Team (1993)

• Missed majority of 1994-95 season recovering from knee injury suffered in practice, November 5, 1994. Traded to **Toronto** by **New Jersey** with Steve Sullivan and the rights to Alyn McCauley for Doug Gilmour, Dave Ellett and New Jersey's 4th round choice (previously acquired, New Jersey selected Andre Lakos) in 1999 Entry Draft, February 25, 1997. Traded to **Edmonton** by **Toronto** for Edmonton's 4th round choice (Jonathon Zion) in 1999 Entry Draft and Edmonton's 2nd round choice (Kris Vernarsky) in 2000 Entry Draft, March 23, 1999. Traded to **Philadelphia** by **Edmonton** with Joffrey Lupul for Joni Pitkanen, Geoff Sanderson and Philadelphia's 3rd round choice in 2009 Entry Draft, July 1, 2007.

SMITH, Mark

(SMIHTH, MAHRK)

Center. Shoots left. 5'10", 215 lbs. Born, Edmonton, Alta., October 24, 1977. San Jose's 7th choice, 219th overall, in 1997 Entry Draft.

Season	Club	League	GP	G	A	Pts	PIM	PP	SH	GW	S	%	+/-	TF	F%	Min	GP	G	A	Pts	PIM	PP	SH	GW	Min
1993-94	Nipawin Hawks	SJHL	62	14	12	26	44	....	....	....	....	....	....	....	....	....	....	....	....	....	....	....	....	....	....
1994-95	Lethbridge	WHL	49	3	4	7	25	....	....	....	....	....	....	....	....	....	....	....	....	....	....	....	....	....	....
1995-96	Lethbridge	WHL	71	11	24	35	59	....	....	....	....	....	....	....	....	....	4	2	0	2	2	....	....	....	....
1996-97	Lethbridge	WHL	62	19	38	57	125	....	....	....	....	....	....	....	....	....	19	7	13	20	51	....	....	....	....
1997-98	Lethbridge	WHL	70	42	67	109	206	....	....	....	....	....	....	....	....	....	3	0	2	2	18	....	....	....	....
	Kentucky	AHL	2	0	0	0	0	....	....	....	....	....	....	....	....	....	....	....	....	....	....	....	....	....	....
1998-99	Kentucky	AHL	78	18	21	39	101	....	....	....	....	....	....	....	....	....	12	2	7	9	16	....	....	....	....
99-2000	Kentucky	AHL	79	21	45	66	153	....	....	....	....	....	....	....	....	....	9	0	5	5	22	....	....	....	....
2000-01	Kentucky	AHL	6	2	6	8	23	....	....	....	....	....	....	....	....	....	....	....	....	....	....	....	....	....	....
	San Jose	**NHL**	42	2	2	4	51	0	0	0	39	5.1	2	308	52.9	8:48	....	....	....	....	....	....	....	....	....
2001-02	**San Jose**	**NHL**	49	3	3	6	72	0	0	1	40	7.5	−1	368	54.1	8:03	....	....	....	....	....	....	....	....	....
2002-03	**San Jose**	**NHL**	75	4	11	15	64	0	0	0	68	5.9	1	632	57.0	9:21	....	....	....	....	....	....	....	....	....
2003-04	**San Jose**	**NHL**	36	1	3	4	72	0	0	0	31	3.2	−5	207	50.2	8:22	10	1	0	1	11	0	0	1	7:44
2004-05	Victoria	ECHL	20	6	9	15	41	....	....	....	....	....	....	....	....	....	....	....	....	....	....	....	....	....	....
2005-06	**San Jose**	**NHL**	80	9	15	24	97	2	1	1	100	9.0	3	514	52.0	12:03	11	3	0	3	6	1	0	0	13:21
2006-07	**San Jose**	**NHL**	41	3	10	13	42	2	0	0	38	7.9	−4	79	59.5	10:25	3	0	0	0	4	0	0	0	8:28
	NHL Totals		323	22	44	66	398	4	1	2	316	7.0		2108	54.1	9:46	24	4	0	4	21	1	0	1	10:24

WHL East Second All-Star Team (1998)

• Spent majority of 2003-04 season as a healthy reserve. Signed as a free agent by **Victoria** (ECHL), January 21, 2005.

SMITH, Nathan

(SMIHTH, NAY-thun) **PIT.**

Center. Shoots left. 6'2", 206 lbs. Born, Edmonton, Alta., February 9, 1982. Vancouver's 1st choice, 23rd overall, in 2000 Entry Draft.

Season	Club	League	GP	G	A	Pts	PIM	PP	SH	GW	S	%	+/-	TF	F%	Min	GP	G	A	Pts	PIM	PP	SH	GW	Min
1997-98	Sherwood Park	AMHL	35	15	13	28	24	....	....	....	....	....	....	....	....	....	....	....	....	....	....	....	....	....	....
1998-99	Swift Current	WHL	47	5	8	13	26	....	....	....	....	....	....	....	....	....	....	....	....	....	....	....	....	....	....
99-2000	Swift Current	WHL	70	21	28	49	72	....	....	....	....	....	....	....	....	....	12	1	6	7	4	....	....	....	....
2000-01	Swift Current	WHL	67	28	62	90	78	....	....	....	....	....	....	....	....	....	19	4	3	7	20	....	....	....	....
2001-02	Swift Current	WHL	47	22	38	60	52	....	....	....	....	....	....	....	....	....	12	3	6	9	18	....	....	....	....
2002-03	Manitoba Moose	AHL	53	9	8	17	30	....	....	....	....	....	....	....	....	....	14	1	3	4	25	....	....	....	....
2003-04	**Vancouver**	**NHL**	2	0	0	0	0	0	0	0	1	0.0	−1	12	33.3	5:16	....	....	....	....	....	....	....	....	....
	Manitoba Moose	AHL	76	4	16	20	71	....	....	....	....	....	....	....	....	....	....	....	....	....	....	....	....	....	....
2004-05	Manitoba Moose	AHL	72	7	9	16	67	....	....	....	....	....	....	....	....	....	14	2	4	6	20	....	....	....	....
2005-06	**Vancouver**	**NHL**	1	0	0	0	0	0	0	0	2	0.0	0	9	33.3	10:52	....	....	....	....	....	....	....	....	....
	Manitoba Moose	AHL	20	5	4	9	57	....	....	....	....	....	....	....	....	....	....	....	....	....	....	....	....	....	....
2006-07	**Vancouver**	**NHL**	1	0	0	0	0	0	0	0	0	0.0	0	9	66.7	8:45	4	0	0	0	0	0	0	0	6:57
	Manitoba Moose	AHL	72	19	21	40	76	....	....	....	....	....	....	....	....	....	6	0	1	1	12	....	....	....	....
	NHL Totals		4	0	0	0	0	0	0	0	3	0.0		30	43.3	7:32	4	0	0	0	0	0	0	0	6:57

• Missed remainder of 2005-06 season recovering from knee injury suffered in game vs. Cleveland (AHL), November 27, 2005. Signed as a free agent by **Pittsburgh**, July 12, 2007.

SMITH, Wyatt

(SMIHTH, WIGH-uht)

Center. Shoots left. 5'11", 200 lbs. Born, Thief River Falls, MN, February 13, 1977. Phoenix's 6th choice, 233rd overall, in 1997 Entry Draft.

Season	Club	League	GP	G	A	Pts	PIM	PP	SH	GW	S	%	+/-	TF	F%	Min	GP	G	A	Pts	PIM	PP	SH	GW	Min
1994-95	Warroad Warriors	High-MN	28	29	31	60	28	....	....	....	....	....	....	....	....	....	....	....	....	....	....	....	....	....	....
1995-96	U. of Minnesota	WCHA	32	4	5	9	32	....	....	....	....	....	....	....	....	....	....	....	....	....	....	....	....	....	....
1996-97	U. of Minnesota	WCHA	38	16	14	30	44	....	....	....	....	....	....	....	....	....	....	....	....	....	....	....	....	....	....
1997-98	U. of Minnesota	WCHA	39	24	23	47	62	....	....	....	....	....	....	....	....	....	....	....	....	....	....	....	....	....	....
1998-99	U. of Minnesota	WCHA	43	23	20	43	37	....	....	....	....	....	....	....	....	....	....	....	....	....	....	....	....	....	....
99-2000	**Phoenix**	**NHL**	2	0	0	0	0	0	0	0	0	0.0	−2	20	30.0	11:39	....	....	....	....	....	....	....	....	....
	Springfield	AHL	60	14	26	40	26	....	....	....	....	....	....	....	....	....	5	2	3	5	13	....	....	....	....
2000-01	**Phoenix**	**NHL**	42	3	7	10	13	0	1	0	40	7.5	7	335	40.9	12:20	....	....	....	....	....	....	....	....	....
	Springfield	AHL	18	5	7	12	11	....	....	....	....	....	....	....	....	....	....	....	....	....	....	....	....	....	....
2001-02	**Phoenix**	**NHL**	10	0	0	0	0	0	0	0	4	0.0	−5	81	48.2	10:36	....	....	....	....	....	....	....	....	....
	Springfield	AHL	69	23	32	55	69	....	....	....	....	....	....	....	....	....	....	....	....	....	....	....	....	....	....
2002-03	**Nashville**	**NHL**	11	1	0	1	0	0	0	0	8	12.5	−1	123	49.6	11:56	....	....	....	....	....	....	....	....	....
	Milwaukee	AHL	56	24	27	51	89	....	....	....	....	....	....	....	....	....	4	1	0	1	2	....	....	....	....
2003-04	**Nashville**	**NHL**	18	3	1	4	2	0	1	0	21	14.3	2	193	57.0	10:22	....	....	....	....	....	....	....	....	....
	Milwaukee	AHL	40	9	7	16	40	....	....	....	....	....	....	....	....	....	22	5	7	12	25	....	....	....	....
2004-05	Milwaukee	AHL	69	19	28	47	89	....	....	....	....	....	....	....	....	....	7	1	4	5	10	....	....	....	....

			Regular Season														Playoffs								
Season	Club	League	GP	G	A	Pts	PIM	PP	SH	GW	S	%	+/-	TF	F%	Min	GP	G	A	Pts	PIM	PP	SH	GW	Min
2005-06	NY Islanders	NHL	42	0	8	8	26	0	0	0	37	0.0	-7	384	48.4	11:14	....	....	....	....	....	....	....	....	....
	Bridgeport	AHL	39	13	16	29	40	....	....	....	....	....	....	....	....	....	....	....	....	....	....	....	....	....	....
2006-07	Minnesota	NHL	61	3	3	6	16	1	0	0	44	6.8	-8	508	43.5	9:31	4	0	0	0	0	0	0	0	11:02
	Houston Aeros	AHL	12	4	3	7	12	....	....	....	....	....	....	....	....	....	....	....	....	....	....	....	....	....	....
	NHL Totals		186	10	19	29	57	1	2	0	154	6.5		1644	46.2	10:51	4	0	0	0	0	0	0	0	11:02

Signed as a free agent by **Nashville**, July 15, 2002. Signed as a free agent by **NY Islanders**, August 10, 2005. Signed as a free agent by **Minnesota**, July 19, 2006.

SMITHSON, Jerred

(SMIHTH-suhn, JEHR-rehd) **NSH.**

Center. Shoots right. 6'3", 194 lbs. Born, Vernon, B.C., February 4, 1979.

Season	Club	League	GP	G	A	Pts	PIM	PP	SH	GW	S	%	+/-	TF	F%	Min	GP	G	A	Pts	PIM	PP	SH	GW	Min
1994-95	Vernon	BCAHA	64	39	46	85	120	....	....	....	....	....	....	....	....	....	....	....	....	....	....	....	....	....	....
1995-96	Calgary Hitmen	WHL	60	4	2	6	16	....	....	....	....	....	....	....	....	....	....	....	....	....	....	....	....	....	....
1996-97	Calgary Hitmen	WHL	65	3	6	9	49	....	....	....	....	....	....	....	....	....	....	....	....	....	....	....	....	....	....
1997-98	Calgary Hitmen	WHL	65	12	9	21	65	....	....	....	....	....	....	....	....	....	18	0	2	2	25	....	....	....	....
1998-99	Calgary Hitmen	WHL	63	14	22	36	108	....	....	....	....	....	....	....	....	....	21	3	7	10	17	....	....	....	....
99-2000	Calgary Hitmen	WHL	66	14	25	39	111	....	....	....	....	....	....	....	....	....	10	1	1	2	16	....	....	....	....
2000-01	Lowell	AHL	24	1	1	2	10	....	....	....	....	....	....	....	....	....	4	0	0	0	2	....	....	....	....
	Trenton Titans	ECHL	3	0	1	1	2	....	....	....	....	....	....	....	....	....	....	....	....	....	....	....	....	....	....
2001-02	Manchester	AHL	78	5	13	18	45	....	....	....	....	....	....	....	....	....	5	0	1	1	4	....	....	....	....
2002-03	Los Angeles	NHL	22	0	2	2	21	0	0	0	9	0.0	-5	175	48.0	8:50	....	....	....	....	....	....	....	....	....
	Manchester	AHL	38	4	21	25	60	....	....	....	....	....	....	....	....	....	3	0	0	0	4	....	....	....	....
2003-04	Los Angeles	NHL	8	0	1	1	4	0	0	0	2	0.0	0	86	64.0	10:39	....	....	....	....	....	....	....	....	....
	Manchester	AHL	66	7	13	20	51	....	....	....	....	....	....	....	....	....	6	0	1	1	10	....	....	....	....
2004-05	Milwaukee	AHL	80	11	11	22	92	....	....	....	....	....	....	....	....	....	5	0	0	0	4	....	....	....	....
2005-06	Nashville	NHL	66	5	9	14	54	0	0	1	50	10.0	9	613	54.3	11:50	3	0	0	0	4	0	0	0	9:26
	Milwaukee	AHL	8	0	0	0	12	....	....	....	....	....	....	....	....	....	....	....	....	....	....	....	....	....	....
2006-07	Nashville	NHL	64	5	7	12	42	1	1	2	47	10.6	-8	420	56.4	11:03	5	0	0	0	17	0	0	0	11:30
	NHL Totals		160	10	19	29	121	1	1	3	108	9.3		1294	54.8	11:03	8	0	0	0	21	0	0	0	10:44

Signed as a free agent by **Los Angeles**, February 18, 2000. Signed as a free agent by **Nashville**, July 22, 2004.

SMOLINSKI, Bryan

(smoh-LIHN-skee, BRIGH-uhn) **MTL.**

Center. Shoots right. 6'1", 215 lbs. Born, Toledo, OH, December 27, 1971. Boston's 1st choice, 21st overall, in 1990 Entry Draft.

Season	Club	League	GP	G	A	Pts	PIM	PP	SH	GW	S	%	+/-	TF	F%	Min	GP	G	A	Pts	PIM	PP	SH	GW	Min
1987-88	Det. Caesars	MNHL	80	43	77	120	....	....	....	....	....	....	....	....	....	....	....	....	....	....	....	....	....	....	....
1988-89	Stratford Cullitons	OHA-B	46	32	62	94	132	....	....	....	....	....	....	....	....	....	....	....	....	....	....	....	....	....	....
1989-90	Michigan State	CCHA	35	9	13	22	34	....	....	....	....	....	....	....	....	....	....	....	....	....	....	....	....	....	....
1990-91	Michigan State	CCHA	35	9	12	21	24	....	....	....	....	....	....	....	....	....	....	....	....	....	....	....	....	....	....
1991-92	Michigan State	CCHA	41	28	33	61	55	....	....	....	....	....	....	....	....	....	....	....	....	....	....	....	....	....	....
1992-93	Michigan State	CCHA	40	31	37	*68	93	....	....	....	....	....	....	....	....	....	....	....	....	....	....	....	....	....	....
	Boston	NHL	9	1	3	4	0	0	0	0	10	10.0	3	....	....	....	4	1	0	1	2	0	0	0	....
1993-94	Boston	NHL	83	31	20	51	82	4	3	5	179	17.3	4	....	....	....	13	5	4	9	4	2	0	0	....
1994-95	Boston	NHL	44	18	13	31	31	6	0	5	121	14.9	-3	....	....	....	5	0	1	1	4	0	0	0	....
1995-96	Pittsburgh	NHL	81	24	40	64	69	8	2	1	229	10.5	6	....	....	....	18	5	4	9	10	0	0	1	....
1996-97	Detroit Vipers	IHL	6	5	7	12	10	....	....	....	....	....	....	....	....	....	....	....	....	....	....	....	....	....	....
	NY Islanders	NHL	64	28	28	56	25	9	0	1	183	15.3	9	....	....	....	....	....	....	....	....	....	....	....	....
1997-98	NY Islanders	NHL	81	13	30	43	34	3	0	4	203	6.4	-16	....	....	....	....	....	....	....	....	....	....	....	....
1998-99	NY Islanders	NHL	82	16	24	40	49	7	0	3	223	7.2	-7	1011	48.3	19:19	....	....	....	....	....	....	....	....	....
99-2000	Los Angeles	NHL	79	20	36	56	48	2	0	0	160	12.5	2	1545	50.9	18:35	4	0	0	0	2	0	0	0	18:22
2000-01	Los Angeles	NHL	78	27	32	59	40	5	3	5	183	14.8	10	952	48.7	18:32	13	1	5	6	14	0	0	0	20:35
2001-02	Los Angeles	NHL	80	13	25	38	56	4	1	0	187	7.0	7	1316	45.7	19:23	7	2	0	2	2	1	0	0	18:15
2002-03	Los Angeles	NHL	58	18	20	38	18	6	1	8	150	12.0	-1	831	46.3	19:02	....	....	....	....	....	....	....	....	....
	Ottawa	NHL	10	3	5	8	2	0	0	0	26	11.5	1	127	46.5	15:42	18	2	7	9	6	0	0	0	15:21
2003-04	Ottawa	NHL	80	19	27	46	49	4	0	3	182	10.4	22	880	44.7	16:39	7	1	1	2	4	0	0	0	16:04
2004-05	Motor City	UHL	21	9	23	32	18	....	....	....	....	....	....	....	....	....	....	....	....	....	....	....	....	....	....
2005-06	Ottawa	NHL	81	17	31	48	46	4	0	5	178	9.6	8	1039	49.8	14:48	10	3	3	6	2	1	0	0	12:34
2006-07	Chicago	NHL	62	14	23	37	29	4	3	3	122	11.5	10	911	51.0	18:36	....	....	....	....	....	....	....	....	....
	Vancouver	NHL	20	4	3	7	8	2	1	0	41	9.8	-3	301	48.5	16:06	12	2	2	4	8	0	0	0	18:39
	NHL Totals		992	266	360	626	586	68	14	43	2377	11.2		8913	48.3	17:58	111	22	27	49	58	4	0	1	17:00

CCHA First All-Star Team (1993) • NCAA West First All-American Team (1993)

Traded to **Pittsburgh** by **Boston** with Glen Murray and Boston's 3rd round choice (Boyd Kane) in 1996 Entry Draft for Kevin Stevens and Shawn McEachern, August 2, 1995. Traded to **NY Islanders** by **Pittsburgh** for Darius Kasparaitis and Andreas Johansson, November 17, 1996. Traded to **Los Angeles** by **NY Islanders** with Ziggy Palffy, Marcel Cousineau and New Jersey's 4th round choice (previously acquired, Los Angeles selected Daniel Johansson) in 1999 Entry Draft for Olli Jokinen, Josh Green, Mathieu Biron and Los Angeles' 1st round choice (Taylor Pyatt) in 1999 Entry Draft, June 20, 1999. Traded to **Ottawa** by **Los Angeles** for the rights to Tim Gleason, March 11, 2003. Signed as a free agent by **Motor City** (UHL), February 11, 2005. Traded to **Chicago** by **Ottawa** with Martin Havlat for Tom Preissing, Josh Hennessy, Michal Barinka and Chicago's 2nd round choice in 2008 Entry Draft, July 10, 2006. Traded to **Vancouver** by **Chicago** for Vancouver's 2nd round choice (Akim Aliu) in 2007 Entry Draft, February 26, 2007. Signed as a free agent by **Montreal**, July 2, 2007.

SMYTH, Ryan

(SMIHTH, RIGH-uhn) **COL.**

Left wing. Shoots left. 6'1", 190 lbs. Born, Banff, Alta., February 21, 1976. Edmonton's 2nd choice, 6th overall, in 1994 Entry Draft.

Season	Club	League	GP	G	A	Pts	PIM	PP	SH	GW	S	%	+/-	TF	F%	Min	GP	G	A	Pts	PIM	PP	SH	GW	Min
1990-91	Banff Blazers	ABHL	25	100	50	150	....	....	....	....	....	....	....	....	....	....	....	....	....	....	....	....	....	....	....
	Lethbridge	AMHL	34	8	21	29	....	....	....	....	....	....	....	....	....	....	....	....	....	....	....	....	....	....	....
1991-92	Caronport	SMHL	35	55	61	116	98	....	....	....	....	....	....	....	....	....	....	....	....	....	....	....	....	....	....
	Moose Jaw	WHL	2	0	0	0	0	....	....	....	....	....	....	....	....	....	....	....	....	....	....	....	....	....	....
1992-93	Moose Jaw	WHL	64	19	14	33	59	....	....	....	....	....	....	....	....	....	....	....	....	....	....	....	....	....	....
1993-94	Moose Jaw	WHL	72	50	55	105	88	....	....	....	....	....	....	....	....	....	....	....	....	....	....	....	....	....	....
1994-95	Moose Jaw	WHL	50	41	45	86	66	....	....	....	....	....	....	....	....	....	10	6	9	15	22	....	....	....	....
	Edmonton	NHL	3	0	0	0	0	0	0	0	2	0.0	-1	....	....	....	....	....	....	....	....	....	....	....	....
1995-96	Edmonton	NHL	48	2	9	11	28	1	0	0	65	3.1	-10	....	....	....	....	....	....	....	....	....	....	....	....
	Cape Breton	AHL	9	6	5	11	4	....	....	....	....	....	....	....	....	....	....	....	....	....	....	....	....	....	....
1996-97	Edmonton	NHL	82	39	22	61	76	20	0	4	265	14.7	-7	....	....	....	12	5	5	10	12	1	0	2	....
1997-98	Edmonton	NHL	65	20	13	33	44	10	0	2	205	9.8	-24	....	....	....	12	1	3	4	16	1	0	0	....
1998-99	Edmonton	NHL	71	13	18	31	62	6	0	2	161	8.1	0	5	20.0	14:26	3	3	0	3	0	2	0	0	24:35
99-2000	Edmonton	NHL	82	28	26	54	58	11	0	4	238	11.8	-2	24	54.2	19:12	5	1	0	1	6	0	1	0	19:18
2000-01	Edmonton	NHL	82	31	39	70	58	11	0	6	245	12.7	10	17	35.3	19:58	6	3	4	7	4	0	0	0	24:46
2001-02	Edmonton	NHL	61	15	35	50	48	7	1	5	150	10.0	7	12	41.7	19:27	....	....	....	....	....	....	....	....	....
	Canada	Olympics	6	0	1	1	0	....	....	....	....	....	....	....	....	....	....	....	....	....	....	....	....	....	....
2002-03	Edmonton	NHL	66	27	34	61	67	10	0	3	199	13.6	5	42	42.9	19:21	6	2	0	2	16	0	1	0	17:39
2003-04	Edmonton	NHL	82	23	36	59	70	8	2	6	245	9.4	11	484	47.1	19:39	....	....	....	....	....	....	....	....	....
2004-05			DID NOT PLAY																						
2005-06	Edmonton	NHL	75	36	30	66	58	19	2	3	230	15.7	-5	159	47.8	20:13	24	7	9	16	22	4	0	1	21:27
	Canada	Olympics	6	0	1	1	4	....	....	....	....	....	....	....	....	....	....	....	....	....	....	....	....	....	....
2006-07	Edmonton	NHL	53	31	22	53	38	14	1	5	161	19.3	2	63	47.6	20:09	....	....	....	....	....	....	....	....	....
	NY Islanders	NHL	18	5	10	15	14	1	0	0	49	10.2	0	9	22.2	22:26	5	1	3	4	4	0	0	0	22:42
	NHL Totals		788	270	294	564	621	118	6	40	2215	12.2		815	46.5	19:09	73	23	24	47	80	8	2	3	21:30

WHL East Second All-Star Team (1995)

Played in NHL All-Star Game (2007)

Traded to **NY Islanders** by **Edmonton** for Ryan O'Marra, Robert Nilsson and NY Islanders' 1st round choice (Alex Plante) in 2007 Entry Draft, February 27, 2007. Signed as a free agent by **Colorado**, July 1, 2007.

SONNENBERG, Martin

(SOHN-nehn-BUHRG, MAHR-tihn)

Left wing. Shoots left. 6', 197 lbs. Born, Wetaskiwin, Alta., January 23, 1978.

Season	Club	League	GP	G	A	Pts	PIM	PP	SH	GW	S	%	+/-	TF	F%	Min	GP	G	A	Pts	PIM	PP	SH	GW	Min
1994-95	Leduc Oil Barons	AMHL	35	20	40	68	34	....	....	....	....	....	....	....	....	....	....	....	....	....	....	....	....	....	....
1995-96	Saskatoon Blades	WHL	58	8	7	15	24	....	....	....	....	....	....	....	....	....	3	0	0	0	2	....	....	....	....
1996-97	Saskatoon Blades	WHL	72	38	26	64	79	....	....	....	....	....	....	....	....	....	....	....	....	....	....	....	....	....	....
1997-98	Saskatoon Blades	WHL	72	40	52	92	87	....	....	....	....	....	....	....	....	....	6	1	3	4	9	....	....	....	....
1998-99	Pittsburgh	NHL	44	1	1	2	19	0	0	0	12	8.3	-2	2	0.0	4:00	7	0	0	0	0	0	0	0	3:03
	Syracuse Crunch	AHL	36	15	9	24	31	....	....	....	....	....	....	....	....	....	....	....	....	....	....	....	....	....	....
99-2000	Pittsburgh	NHL	14	1	2	3	0	1	0	0	19	5.3	0	7	28.6	7:26	....	....	....	....	....	....	....	....	....
	Wilkes-Barre	AHL	62	20	33	53	109	....	....	....	....	....	....	....	....	....	....	....	....	....	....	....	....	....	....

			Regular Season														Playoffs								
Season	Club	League	GP	G	A	Pts	PIM	PP	SH	GW	S	%	+/-	TF	F%	Min	GP	G	A	Pts	PIM	PP	SH	GW	Min
2000-01	Wilkes-Barre	AHL	73	14	18	32	89										21	4	3	7	6				
2001-02	Wilkes-Barre	AHL	78	20	30	50	127																		
2002-03	Saint John Flames	AHL	54	11	10	21	63																		
2003-04	**Calgary**	**NHL**	**5**	**0**	**0**	**0**	**2**	**0**	**0**	**0**	**7**	**0.0**	**–2**	**5**	**80.0**	**8:51**									
	Lowell	AHL	48	20	22	42	46																		
2004-05	Utah Grizzlies	AHL	65	13	13	26	94																		
2005-06	San Antonio	AHL	41	10	7	17	34																		
	Hartford	AHL	29	4	10	14	16										13	3	3	6	8				
2006-07	KalPa Kuopio	Finland	56	19	17	36	76																		
	KalPa Kuopio	Finland-Q															4	6	4	10	2				
	NHL Totals		**63**	**2**	**3**	**5**	**21**	**1**	**0**	**0**	**38**	**5.3**		**14**	**42.9**	**5:09**	**7**	**0**	**0**	**0**	**0**	**0**	**0**	**0**	**3:03**

Signed as a free agent by **Pittsburgh**, October 9, 1998. Signed as a free agent by **Calgary**, July 9, 2002. Signed as a free agent by **Phoenix**, September 2, 2004. Traded to **NY Rangers** by **Phoenix** for Jeff Taffe, January 24, 2006. Signed as a free agent by **Kuopio** (Finland), July 18, 2006.

SOPEL, Brent

(SOH-puhl, BREHNT)

Defense. Shoots right. 6'1", 205 lbs. Born, Calgary, Alta., January 7, 1977. Vancouver's 6th choice, 144th overall, in 1995 Entry Draft.

			Regular Season														Playoffs								
Season	Club	League	GP	G	A	Pts	PIM	PP	SH	GW	S	%	+/-	TF	F%	Min	GP	G	A	Pts	PIM	PP	SH	GW	Min
1992-93	Sask. Legion	SMHL	36	7	17	24	95																		
1993-94	Saskatoon Blazers	SMHL	34	9	30	39	180																		
	Saskatoon Blades	WHL	11	2	2	4	2																		
1994-95	Saskatoon Blades	WHL	22	1	10	11	31																		
	Swift Current	WHL	41	4	19	23	50										3	0	3	3	0				
1995-96	Swift Current	WHL	71	13	48	61	87										6	1	2	3	4				
	Syracuse Crunch	AHL	1	0	0	0	0																		
1996-97	Swift Current	WHL	62	15	41	56	109										10	5	11	16	32				
	Syracuse Crunch	AHL	2	0	0	0	0										3	0	0	0	0				
1997-98	Syracuse Crunch	AHL	76	10	33	43	70										5	0	7	7	12				
1998-99	**Vancouver**	**NHL**	**5**	**1**	**0**	**1**	**4**	**1**	**0**	**0**	**5**	**20.0**	**–1**	**0**	**0.0**	**11:58**									
	Syracuse Crunch	AHL	53	10	21	31	59																		
99-2000	**Vancouver**	**NHL**	**18**	**2**	**4**	**6**	**12**	**0**	**0**	**1**	**11**	**18.2**	**9**	**0**	**0.0**	**10:31**									
	Syracuse Crunch	AHL	50	6	25	31	67										4	0	2	2	8				
2000-01	**Vancouver**	**NHL**	**52**	**4**	**10**	**14**	**10**	**0**	**0**	**1**	**57**	**7.0**	**4**	**0**	**0.0**	**16:01**	**4**	**0**	**0**	**0**	**2**	**0**	**0**	**0**	**19:05**
	Kansas City	IHL	4	0	1	1	0																		
2001-02	**Vancouver**	**NHL**	**66**	**8**	**17**	**25**	**44**	**1**	**0**	**3**	**116**	**6.9**	**21**	**0**	**0.0**	**19:01**	**6**	**0**	**2**	**2**	**2**	**0**	**0**	**0**	**24:45**
2002-03	**Vancouver**	**NHL**	**81**	**7**	**30**	**37**	**23**	**6**	**0**	**1**	**167**	**4.2**	**–15**	**0**	**0.0**	**21:42**	**14**	**2**	**6**	**8**	**4**	**1**	**0**	**1**	**22:33**
2003-04	**Vancouver**	**NHL**	**80**	**10**	**32**	**42**	**36**	**6**	**0**	**2**	**173**	**5.8**	**11**	**0**	**0.0**	**21:56**	**7**	**0**	**1**	**1**	**0**	**0**	**0**	**0**	**23:55**
2004-05		DID NOT PLAY																							
2005-06	**NY Islanders**	**NHL**	**57**	**2**	**25**	**27**	**64**	**2**	**0**	**0**	**121**	**1.7**	**–9**	**0**	**0.0**	**23:35**									
	Los Angeles	**NHL**	**11**	**0**	**1**	**1**	**6**	**0**	**0**	**0**	**12**	**0.0**	**–4**	**0**	**0.0**	**22:02**									
2006-07	**Los Angeles**	**NHL**	**44**	**4**	**19**	**23**	**14**	**2**	**0**	**2**	**104**	**3.8**	**2**	**3**	**33.3**	**21:06**									
	Vancouver	**NHL**	**20**	**1**	**4**	**5**	**10**	**0**	**0**	**0**	**27**	**3.7**	**0**	**0**	**0.0**	**18:25**	**11**	**0**	**0**	**0**	**2**	**0**	**0**	**0**	**19:44**
	NHL Totals		**434**	**39**	**142**	**181**	**223**	**18**	**0**	**10**	**793**	**4.9**		**3**	**33.3**	**20:07**	**42**	**2**	**9**	**11**	**10**	**1**	**0**	**1**	**22:02**

Traded to **NY Islanders** by **Vancouver** for NY Islanders' 2nd round choice (later traded to Anaheim - Anaheim selected Bryce Swan) in 2006 Entry Draft, August 3, 2005. Traded to **Los Angeles** by **NY Islanders** with Mark Parrish for Denis Grebeshkov and Jeff Tambellini, March 8, 2006. Traded to **Vancouver** by **Los Angeles** for Anaheim's 2nd round choice (previously acquired, Los Angeles selected Wayne Simmonds) in 2007 Entry Draft and and Vancouver's 4th round choice in 2008 Entry Draft, February 26, 2006.

SOURAY, Sheldon

(SOO-ray, SHEHL-duhn) **EDM.**

Defense. Shoots left. 6'4", 227 lbs. Born, Elk Point, Alta., July 13, 1976. New Jersey's 3rd choice, 71st overall, in 1994 Entry Draft.

			Regular Season														Playoffs								
Season	Club	League	GP	G	A	Pts	PIM	PP	SH	GW	S	%	+/-	TF	F%	Min	GP	G	A	Pts	PIM	PP	SH	GW	Min
1990-91	Bonnyville Sabres	AAHA	30	15	20	35	100																		
1991-92	Quesnel	BCAHA	20	5	15	20	200																		
	Alberta Cycle	AMHL	11	0	5	5	67																		
1992-93	Ft. Saskatchewan	AJHL	35	0	12	12	125																		
	Tri-City	WHL	2	0	0	0	0																		
1993-94	Tri-City	WHL	42	3	6	9	122																		
1994-95	Tri-City	WHL	40	2	24	26	140																		
	Prince George	WHL	11	2	3	5	23																		
	Albany River Rats	AHL	7	0	2	2	8																		
1995-96	Prince George	WHL	32	9	18	27	91																		
	Kelowna Rockets	WHL	27	7	20	27	94										6	0	5	5	2				
	Albany River Rats	AHL	6	0	2	2	12										4	0	1	1	4				
1996-97	Albany River Rats	AHL	70	2	11	13	160										16	2	3	5	47				
1997-98	**New Jersey**	**NHL**	**60**	**3**	**7**	**10**	**85**	**0**	**0**	**1**	**74**	**4.1**	**18**				**3**	**0**	**1**	**1**	**2**	**0**	**0**	**0**	
	Albany River Rats	AHL	6	0	0	0	8																		
1998-99	**New Jersey**	**NHL**	**70**	**1**	**7**	**8**	**110**	**0**	**0**	**0**	**101**	**1.0**	**5**	**0**	**0.0**	**14:56**	**2**	**0**	**1**	**1**	**0**	**0**	**0**	**0**	**12:57**
99-2000	**New Jersey**	**NHL**	**52**	**0**	**8**	**8**	**70**	**0**	**0**	**0**	**74**	**0.0**	**–6**	**0**	**0.0**	**17:12**									
	Montreal	**NHL**	**19**	**3**	**0**	**3**	**44**	**0**	**0**	**0**	**39**	**7.7**	**7**	**0**	**0.0**	**19:18**									
2000-01	**Montreal**	**NHL**	**52**	**3**	**8**	**11**	**95**	**0**	**0**	**2**	**103**	**2.9**	**–11**	**0**	**0.0**	**20:36**									
2001-02	**Montreal**	**NHL**	**34**	**3**	**5**	**8**	**62**	**1**	**0**	**0**	**56**	**5.4**	**–5**	**1**	**100.0**	**18:11**	**12**	**0**	**1**	**1**	**16**	**0**	**0**	**0**	**19:01**
2002-03	**Montreal**	**NHL**	DID NOT PLAY – INJURED																						
2003-04	**Montreal**	**NHL**	**63**	**15**	**20**	**35**	**104**	**6**	**1**	**3**	**186**	**8.1**	**4**	**0**	**0.0**	**23:26**	**11**	**0**	**2**	**2**	**39**	**0**	**0**	**0**	**23:55**
2004-05	Farjestad	Sweden	39	9	8	17	117										15	1	6	7	77				
2005-06	**Montreal**	**NHL**	**75**	**12**	**27**	**39**	**116**	**7**	**1**	**0**	**202**	**5.9**	**–11**	**0**	**0.0**	**22:15**	**6**	**3**	**2**	**5**	**8**	**2**	**0**	**0**	**18:47**
2006-07	**Montreal**	**NHL**	**81**	**26**	**38**	**64**	**135**	**19**	**1**	**6**	**224**	**11.6**	**–28**	**2**	**100.0**	**23:11**									
	NHL Totals		**506**	**66**	**120**	**186**	**821**	**33**	**3**	**12**	**1059**	**6.2**		**3**	**100.0**	**20:13**	**34**	**3**	**7**	**10**	**65**	**2**	**0**	**0**	**20:19**

WHL West Second All-Star Team (1996)

Played in NHL All-Star Game (2004, 2007)

Traded to **Montreal** by **New Jersey** with Josh DeWolf and New Jersey's 2nd round choice (later traded to Washington – later traded to Tampa Bay – Tampa Bay selected Andreas Holmqvist) in 2001 Entry Draft for Vladimir Malakhov, March 1, 2000. • Missed remainder of 2001-02 season and entire 2002-03 season recovering from wrist injury suffered in game vs. Tampa Bay, November 17, 2001. Signed as a free agent by **Farjestad** (Sweden), September 22, 2004. Signed as a free agent by **Edmonton**, July 12, 2007.

SPACEK, Jaroslav

(SPAH-chehk, YAHR-roh-slav) **BUF.**

Defense. Shoots left. 5'11", 204 lbs. Born, Rokycany, Czech., February 11, 1974. Florida's 5th choice, 117th overall, in 1998 Entry Draft.

			Regular Season														Playoffs								
Season	Club	League	GP	G	A	Pts	PIM	PP	SH	GW	S	%	+/-	TF	F%	Min	GP	G	A	Pts	PIM	PP	SH	GW	Min
1992-93	HC Skoda Plzen	Czech	16	1	3	4																			
1993-94	HC Skoda Plzen	CzRep	34	2	6	8																			
1994-95	Plzen	CzRep	38	4	8	12	14										3	1	0	1	2				
1995-96	HC ZKZ Plzen	CzRep	40	3	10	13	42										3	0	1	1	4				
1996-97	HC ZKZ Plzen	CzRep	52	9	29	38	44																		
1997-98	Farjestad	Sweden	45	10	16	26	63										12	2	5	7	14				
	Farjestad	EuroHL	6	2	3	5	2																		
1998-99	**Florida**	**NHL**	**63**	**3**	**12**	**15**	**28**	**2**	**1**	**0**	**92**	**3.3**	**15**	**1**	**100.0**	**19:27**									
	New Haven	AHL	14	4	8	12	15																		
99-2000	**Florida**	**NHL**	**82**	**10**	**26**	**36**	**53**	**4**	**0**	**1**	**111**	**9.0**	**7**	**1**	**0.0**	**22:40**	**4**	**0**	**0**	**0**	**0**	**0**	**0**	**0**	**20:29**
2000-01	**Florida**	**NHL**	**12**	**2**	**1**	**3**	**8**	**1**	**0**	**0**	**21**	**9.5**	**–4**	**0**	**0.0**	**19:12**									
	Chicago	**NHL**	**50**	**5**	**18**	**23**	**20**	**2**	**0**	**1**	**85**	**5.9**	**7**	**0**	**0.0**	**21:31**									
2001-02	**Chicago**	**NHL**	**60**	**3**	**10**	**13**	**29**	**0**	**0**	**1**	**64**	**4.7**	**5**	**0**	**0.0**	**16:25**									
	Czech Republic	Olympics	4	0	0	0	0																		
	Columbus	**NHL**	**14**	**2**	**3**	**5**	**24**	**1**	**1**	**1**	**29**	**6.9**	**–9**	**0**	**0.0**	**23:35**									
2002-03	**Columbus**	**NHL**	**81**	**9**	**36**	**45**	**70**	**5**	**0**	**1**	**166**	**5.4**	**–23**	**0**	**0.0**	**24:47**									
2003-04	**Columbus**	**NHL**	**58**	**5**	**17**	**22**	**45**	**2**	**1**	**2**	**108**	**4.6**	**–13**	**0**	**0.0**	**23:26**									
2004-05	Plzen	CzRep	30	3	8	11	26																		
	HC Slavia Praha	CzRep	17	4	9	13	29										7	0	2	2	8				
2005-06	**Chicago**	**NHL**	**45**	**7**	**17**	**24**	**72**	**1**	**0**	**0**	**80**	**8.8**	**8**	**0**	**0.0**	**23:00**									
	Edmonton	**NHL**	**31**	**5**	**14**	**19**	**24**	**3**	**0**	**0**	**70**	**7.1**	**3**	**0**	**0.0**	**24:37**	**24**	**3**	**11**	**14**	**24**	**2**	**0**	**0**	**25:53**
2006-07	**Buffalo**	**NHL**	**65**	**5**	**16**	**21**	**62**	**1**	**0**	**2**	**78**	**6.4**	**20**	**0**	**0.0**	**19:09**	**16**	**0**	**0**	**0**	**10**	**0**	**0**	**0**	**14:39**
	NHL Totals		**561**	**56**	**170**	**226**	**435**	**22**	**3**	**9**	**904**	**6.2**		**2**	**50.0**	**21:36**	**44**	**3**	**11**	**14**	**34**	**2**	**0**	**0**	**21:18**

Traded to **Chicago** by **Florida** for Anders Eriksson, November 6, 2000. Traded to **Columbus** by **Chicago** with Chicago's 2nd round choice (Dan Fritsche) in 2003 Entry Draft for Lyle Odelein, March 19, 2002. Signed as a free agent by **Plzen** (CzRep), September 17, 2004. Signed as a free agent by **Slavia Praha** (CzRep), January 4, 2005. Signed as a free agent by **Chicago**, August 3, 2005. Traded to **Edmonton** by **Chicago** for Tony Salmelainen, January 26, 2006. Signed as a free agent by **Buffalo**, July 5, 2006.

SPEZZA, Jason

(SPEHT-zuh, JAY-suhn) **OTT.**

Center. Shoots right. 6'3", 213 lbs. Born, Mississauga, Ont., June 13, 1983. Ottawa's 1st choice, 2nd overall, in 2001 Entry Draft.

Season	Club	League	Regular Season GP	G	A	Pts	PIM	PP	SH	GW	S	%	+/-	TF	F%	Min	Playoffs GP	G	A	Pts	PIM	PP	SH	GW	Min
1997-98	Toronto Marlies	MTHL	54	53	61	114	42	....	....	....	....	....	....	....	....	....	....	....	....	....	....	....	....	....	....
1998-99	Brampton	OHL	67	22	49	71	18	....	....	....	....	....	....	....	....	....	....	....	....	....	....	....	....	....	....
99-2000	Mississauga	OHL	52	24	37	61	33	....	....	....	....	....	....	....	....	....	....	....	....	....	....	....	....	....	....
2000-01	Mississauga	OHL	15	7	23	30	11	....	....	....	....	....	....	....	....	....	....	....	....	....	....	....	....	....	....
	Windsor Spitfires	OHL	41	36	50	86	32	....	....	....	....	....	....	....	....	....	9	4	5	9	10	....	....	....	....
2001-02	Windsor Spitfires	OHL	27	19	26	45	16	....	....	....	....	....	....	....	....	....	....	....	....	....	....	....	....	....	....
	Belleville Bulls	OHL	26	23	37	60	26	....	....	....	....	....	....	....	....	....	11	5	6	11	18	....	....	....	....
	Grand Rapids	AHL	....	....	....	....	....	....	....	....	....	....	....	....	....	....	3	1	0	1	2	....	....	....	....
2002-03	**Ottawa**	**NHL**	**33**	**7**	**14**	**21**	**8**	**3**	**0**	**0**	**65**	**10.8**	**–3**	**330**	**45.8**	**12:40**	**3**	**1**	**1**	**2**	**0**	**1**	**0**	**0**	**11:34**
	Binghamton	AHL	43	22	32	54	71	....	....	....	....	....	....	....	....	....	2	1	2	3	4	....	....	....	....
2003-04	**Ottawa**	**NHL**	**78**	**22**	**33**	**55**	**71**	**5**	**0**	**3**	**142**	**15.5**	**22**	**956**	**47.7**	**14:38**	**3**	**0**	**0**	**0**	**2**	**0**	**0**	**0**	**9:44**
2004-05	Binghamton	AHL	80	32	*85	*117	50	....	....	....	....	....	....	....	....	....	6	1	3	4	6	....	....	....	....
2005-06	**Ottawa**	**NHL**	**68**	**19**	**71**	**90**	**33**	**7**	**0**	**5**	**156**	**12.2**	**23**	**1220**	**52.6**	**19:00**	**10**	**5**	**9**	**14**	**2**	**3**	**0**	**1**	**17:59**
2006-07	**Ottawa**	**NHL**	**67**	**34**	**53**	**87**	**45**	**13**	**1**	**5**	**162**	**21.0**	**19**	**1261**	**53.0**	**19:17**	**20**	**7**	***15**	***22**	**10**	**3**	**0**	**0**	**20:58**
	NHL Totals		**246**	**82**	**171**	**253**	**157**	**28**	**1**	**13**	**525**	**15.6**		**3767**	**50.9**	**16:51**	**36**	**13**	**25**	**38**	**14**	**7**	**0**	**1**	**18:25**

OHL All-Rookie Team (1999) • AHL All-Rookie Team (2003) • AHL First All-Star Team (2005) • John P. Sollenberger Trophy (Top Scorer - AHL) (2005) • Les Cunningham Award (MVP – AHL) (2005)

SPILLER, Matthew

(SPIHL-uhr, MA-thew) **NYI**

Defense. Shoots left. 6'5", 233 lbs. Born, Daysland, Alta., February 7, 1983. Phoenix's 2nd choice, 31st overall, in 2001 Entry Draft.

Season	Club	League	Regular Season GP	G	A	Pts	PIM	PP	SH	GW	S	%	+/-	TF	F%	Min	Playoffs GP	G	A	Pts	PIM	PP	SH	GW	Min
1998-99	East Central Chill	AMBHL	36	8	19	27	140	....	....	....	....	....	....	....	....	....	....	....	....	....	....	....	....	....	....
99-2000	Seattle	WHL	60	1	10	11	108	....	....	....	....	....	....	....	....	....	7	0	0	0	25	....	....	....	....
2000-01	Seattle	WHL	71	4	7	11	174	....	....	....	....	....	....	....	....	....	....	....	....	....	....	....	....	....	....
2001-02	Seattle	WHL	72	8	23	31	168	....	....	....	....	....	....	....	....	....	1	0	0	0	4	....	....	....	....
2002-03	Seattle	WHL	68	11	24	35	198	....	....	....	....	....	....	....	....	....	15	2	7	9	36	....	....	....	....
2003-04	**Phoenix**	**NHL**	**51**	**0**	**0**	**0**	**54**	**0**	**0**	**0**	**22**	**0.0**	**–11**	**0**	**0.0**	**10:42**	....	....	....	....	....	....	....	....	....
	Springfield	AHL	21	1	2	3	32	....	....	....	....	....	....	....	....	....	....	....	....	....	....	....	....	....	....
2004-05	Utah Grizzlies	AHL	79	4	7	11	160	....	....	....	....	....	....	....	....	....	....	....	....	....	....	....	....	....	....
2005-06	**Phoenix**	**NHL**	**8**	**0**	**1**	**1**	**13**	**0**	**0**	**0**	**3**	**0.0**	**–1**	**0**	**0.0**	**10:30**	....	....	....	....	....	....	....	....	....
	San Antonio	AHL	69	2	7	9	167	....	....	....	....	....	....	....	....	....	....	....	....	....	....	....	....	....	....
2006-07	San Antonio	AHL	80	1	7	8	187	....	....	....	....	....	....	....	....	....	....	....	....	....	....	....	....	....	....
	NHL Totals		**59**	**0**	**1**	**1**	**67**	**0**	**0**	**0**	**25**	**0.0**		**0**	**0.0**	**10:40**	....	....	....	....	....	....	....	....	....

Signed as a free agent by **NY Islanders**, July 3, 2007.

SPRUKTS, Janis

(SPRUKTS, YAN-ish) **FLA.**

Center. Shoots left. 6'3", 235 lbs. Born, Riga, USSR, January 31, 1982. Florida's 7th choice, 234th overall, in 2000 Entry Draft.

Season	Club	League	Regular Season GP	G	A	Pts	PIM	PP	SH	GW	S	%	+/-	TF	F%	Min	Playoffs GP	G	A	Pts	PIM	PP	SH	GW	Min
99-2000	Lukko Rauma Jr.	Fin-Jr.	26	2	5	7	6	....	....	....	....	....	....	....	....	....	3	0	0	0	0	....	....	....	....
	HC Essamika Jr.	EEHL-2	2	4	4	8	0	....	....	....	....	....	....	....	....	....	....	....	....	....	....	....	....	....	....
2000-01	Lukko Rauma Jr.	Fin-Jr.	36	15	22	37	24	....	....	....	....	....	....	....	....	....	3	0	0	0	0	....	....	....	....
	Lukko Rauma	Finland	9	0	0	0	2	....	....	....	....	....	....	....	....	....	....	....	....	....	....	....	....	....	....
2001-02	Acadie-Bathurst	QMJHL	63	35	44	79	46	....	....	....	....	....	....	....	....	....	16	14	8	22	12	....	....	....	....
2002-03	Sport Vaasa	Finland-2	21	5	6	11	8	....	....	....	....	....	....	....	....	....	....	....	....	....	....	....	....	....	....
	Acadie-Bathurst	QMJHL	30	9	29	38	12	....	....	....	....	....	....	....	....	....	11	3	5	8	0	....	....	....	....
2003-04	ASK Ogre	Latvia	5	2	4	6	0	....	....	....	....	....	....	....	....	....	....	....	....	....	....	....	....	....	....
	Odense IK	Denmark	2	0	1	1	2	....	....	....	....	....	....	....	....	....	....	....	....	....	....	....	....	....	....
2004-05	HK Riga 2000	BelOpen	21	7	9	16	10	....	....	....	....	....	....	....	....	....	3	0	0	0	2	....	....	....	....
	HK Riga 2000	Latvia	3	2	3	5	0	....	....	....	....	....	....	....	....	....	9	3	4	7	2	....	....	....	....
2005-06	HPK Hameenlinna	Finland	35	18	10	28	14	....	....	....	....	....	....	....	....	....	13	3	4	7	14	....	....	....	....
2006-07	**Florida**	**NHL**	**13**	**1**	**2**	**3**	**2**	**0**	**0**	**0**	**10**	**10.0**	**1**	**61**	**44.3**	**6:19**	....	....	....	....	....	....	....	....	....
	Rochester	AHL	58	18	41	59	60	....	....	....	....	....	....	....	....	....	6	1	3	4	4	....	....	....	....
	NHL Totals		**13**	**1**	**2**	**3**	**2**	**0**	**0**	**0**	**10**	**10.0**		**61**	**44.3**	**6:19**	....	....	....	....	....	....	....	....	....

• Released by **Vaasa** (Finland-2) and returned to **Acadie-Bathurst** (QMJHL), January 3, 2003.

STAAL, Eric

(STAHL, AIR-ihk) **CAR.**

Center. Shoots left. 6'4", 205 lbs. Born, Thunder Bay, Ont., October 29, 1984. Carolina's 1st choice, 2nd overall, in 2003 Entry Draft.

Season	Club	League	Regular Season GP	G	A	Pts	PIM	PP	SH	GW	S	%	+/-	TF	F%	Min	Playoffs GP	G	A	Pts	PIM	PP	SH	GW	Min
99-2000	Thunder Bay	Exhib.	7	4	8	12	0	....	....	....	....	....	....	....	....	....	....	....	....	....	....	....	....	....	....
2000-01	Peterborough	OHL	63	19	30	49	23	....	....	....	....	....	....	....	....	....	7	2	5	7	4	....	....	....	....
2001-02	Peterborough	OHL	56	23	39	62	40	....	....	....	....	....	....	....	....	....	6	3	6	9	10	....	....	....	....
2002-03	Peterborough	OHL	66	39	59	98	36	....	....	....	....	....	....	....	....	....	7	9	5	14	6	....	....	....	....
2003-04	**Carolina**	**NHL**	**81**	**11**	**20**	**31**	**40**	**2**	**1**	**3**	**164**	**6.7**	**–6**	**669**	**43.1**	**16:40**	....	....	....	....	....	....	....	....	....
2004-05	Lowell	AHL	77	26	51	77	88	....	....	....	....	....	....	....	....	....	11	2	8	10	12	....	....	....	....
2005-06 ♦	**Carolina**	**NHL**	**82**	**45**	**55**	**100**	**81**	**19**	**4**	**4**	**279**	**16.1**	**–8**	**1309**	**42.6**	**19:39**	**25**	**9**	***19**	***28**	**8**	**7**	**0**	**1**	**19:48**
2006-07	**Carolina**	**NHL**	**82**	**30**	**40**	**70**	**68**	**12**	**1**	**1**	**288**	**10.4**	**–6**	**1238**	**45.2**	**20:08**	....	....	....	....	....	....	....	....	....
	NHL Totals		**245**	**86**	**115**	**201**	**189**	**33**	**6**	**8**	**731**	**11.8**		**3216**	**43.7**	**18:49**	**25**	**9**	**19**	**28**	**8**	**7**	**0**	**1**	**19:48**

OHL Second All-Star Team (2003) • Canadian Major Junior First All-Star Team (2003) • NHL Second All-Star Team (2006)

Played in NHL All-Star Game (2007)

STAAL, Jordan

(STAHL, JOHR-dahn) **PIT.**

Center. Shoots left. 6'4", 220 lbs. Born, Thunder Bay, Ont., September 10, 1988. Pittsburgh's 1st choice, 2nd overall, in 2006 Entry Draft.

Season	Club	League	Regular Season GP	G	A	Pts	PIM	PP	SH	GW	S	%	+/-	TF	F%	Min	Playoffs GP	G	A	Pts	PIM	PP	SH	GW	Min
2004-05	Peterborough	OHL	66	9	19	28	29	....	....	....	....	....	....	....	....	....	14	5	5	10	16	....	....	....	....
2005-06	Peterborough	OHL	68	28	40	68	69	....	....	....	....	....	....	....	....	....	19	10	6	16	16	....	....	....	....
2006-07	**Pittsburgh**	**NHL**	**81**	**29**	**13**	**42**	**24**	**4**	**7**	**4**	**131**	**22.1**	**16**	**383**	**37.1**	**14:56**	**5**	**3**	**0**	**3**	**2**	**0**	**0**	**0**	**16:00**
	NHL Totals		**81**	**29**	**13**	**42**	**24**	**4**	**7**	**4**	**131**	**22.1**		**383**	**37.1**	**14:56**	**5**	**3**	**0**	**3**	**2**	**0**	**0**	**0**	**16:00**

NHL All-Rookie Team (2007)

STAFFORD, Drew

(STA-fuhrd, DROO) **BUF.**

Right wing. Shoots right. 6'2", 213 lbs. Born, Milwaukee, WI, October 30, 1985. Buffalo's 1st choice, 13th overall, in 2004 Entry Draft.

Season	Club	League	Regular Season GP	G	A	Pts	PIM	PP	SH	GW	S	%	+/-	TF	F%	Min	Playoffs GP	G	A	Pts	PIM	PP	SH	GW	Min
2001-02	Shat.-St. Mary's	High-MN	45	35	53	88	30	....	....	....	....	....	....	....	....	....	....	....	....	....	....	....	....	....	....
2002-03	Shat.-St. Mary's	High-MN	65	49	67	116	....	....	....	....	....	....	....	....	....	....	....	....	....	....	....	....	....	....	....
2003-04	North Dakota	WCHA	36	11	21	32	30	....	....	....	....	....	....	....	....	....	....	....	....	....	....	....	....	....	....
2004-05	North Dakota	WCHA	42	13	25	38	34	....	....	....	....	....	....	....	....	....	....	....	....	....	....	....	....	....	....
2005-06	North Dakota	WCHA	42	24	24	48	63	....	....	....	....	....	....	....	....	....	....	....	....	....	....	....	....	....	....
2006-07	**Buffalo**	**NHL**	**41**	**13**	**14**	**27**	**33**	**3**	**0**	**3**	**67**	**19.4**	**5**	**13**	**46.2**	**13:08**	**10**	**2**	**2**	**4**	**4**	**0**	**0**	**0**	**11:52**
	Rochester	AHL	34	22	22	44	30	....	....	....	....	....	....	....	....	....	....	....	....	....	....	....	....	....	....
	NHL Totals		**41**	**13**	**14**	**27**	**33**	**3**	**0**	**3**	**67**	**19.4**		**13**	**46.2**	**13:08**	**10**	**2**	**2**	**4**	**4**	**0**	**0**	**0**	**11:52**

STAIOS, Steve

(STAY-ohs, STEEV) **EDM.**

Defense. Shoots right. 6'1", 200 lbs. Born, Hamilton, Ont., July 28, 1973. St. Louis' 1st choice, 27th overall, in 1991 Entry Draft.

Season	Club	League	Regular Season GP	G	A	Pts	PIM	PP	SH	GW	S	%	+/-	TF	F%	Min	Playoffs GP	G	A	Pts	PIM	PP	SH	GW	Min
1988-89	Hamilton Huskies	Minor-ON	58	13	39	52	78	....	....	....	....	....	....	....	....	....	....	....	....	....	....	....	....	....	....
1989-90	Hamilton Kilty B's	OHA B	40	9	27	36	66	....	....	....	....	....	....	....	....	....	....	....	....	....	....	....	....	....	....
1990-91	Niagara Falls	OHL	66	17	29	46	115	....	....	....	....	....	....	....	....	....	12	2	3	5	10	....	....	....	....
1991-92	Niagara Falls	OHL	65	11	42	53	122	....	....	....	....	....	....	....	....	....	17	7	8	15	27	....	....	....	....
1992-93	Niagara Falls	OHL	12	4	14	18	30	....	....	....	....	....	....	....	....	....	....	....	....	....	....	....	....	....	....
	Sudbury Wolves	OHL	53	13	44	57	67	....	....	....	....	....	....	....	....	....	11	5	6	11	22	....	....	....	....
1993-94	Peoria Rivermen	IHL	38	3	9	12	42	....	....	....	....	....	....	....	....	....	....	....	....	....	....	....	....	....	....
1994-95	Peoria Rivermen	IHL	60	3	13	16	64	....	....	....	....	....	....	....	....	....	6	0	0	0	10	....	....	....	....
1995-96	Peoria Rivermen	IHL	6	0	1	1	14	....	....	....	....	....	....	....	....	....	....	....	....	....	....	....	....	....	....
	Worcester IceCats	AHL	57	1	11	12	114	....	....	....	....	....	....	....	....	....	....	....	....	....	....	....	....	....	....
	Boston	**NHL**	**12**	**0**	**0**	**0**	**4**	**0**	**0**	**0**	**4**	**0.0**	**–5**	....	....	....	**3**	**0**	**0**	**0**	**0**	**0**	**0**	**0**	....
	Providence Bruins	AHL	7	1	4	5	8	....	....	....	....	....	....	....	....	....	....	....	....	....	....	....	....	....	....

			Regular Season														Playoffs								
Season	Club	League	GP	G	A	Pts	PIM	PP	SH	GW	S	%	+/-	TF	F%	Min	GP	G	A	Pts	PIM	PP	SH	GW	Min
1996-97	Boston	NHL	54	3	8	11	71	0	0	0	56	5.4	-26	....	....	....	....	....	....	....	....	....	....	....	....
	Vancouver	NHL	9	0	6	6	20	0	0	0	10	0.0	2	....	....	....	....	....	....	....	....	....	....	....	....
1997-98	Vancouver	NHL	77	3	4	7	134	0	0	1	45	6.7	-3	....	....	....	....	....	....	....	....	....	....	....	....
1998-99	Vancouver	NHL	57	0	2	2	54	0	0	0	33	0.0	-12	4	25.0	6:53	....	....	....	....	....	....	....	....	....
99-2000	Atlanta	NHL	27	2	3	5	66	0	0	0	38	5.3	-5	2	50.0	13:01	....	....	....	....	....	....	....	....	....
2000-01	Atlanta	NHL	70	9	13	22	137	4	0	0	156	5.8	-23	1	0.0	21:45	....	....	....	....	....	....	....	....	....
2001-02	Edmonton	NHL	73	5	5	10	108	0	0	1	101	5.0	10	0	0.0	18:05	....	....	....	....	....	....	....	....	....
2002-03	Edmonton	NHL	76	5	21	26	96	1	3	0	126	4.0	13	1	0.0	22:17	6	0	0	0	4	0	0	0	23:27
2003-04	Edmonton	NHL	82	6	22	28	86	1	0	1	153	3.9	17	0	0.0	23:03	....	....	....	....	....	....	....	....	....
2004-05	Lulea HF	Sweden	7	2	1	3	12	....	....	....	....	....	....	....	....	....	....	....	....	....	....	....	....	....	....
2005-06	Edmonton	NHL	82	8	20	28	84	1	0	1	140	5.7	10	0	0.0	20:53	24	1	5	6	28	1	0	0	21:31
2006-07	Edmonton	NHL	58	2	15	17	97	0	0	0	71	2.8	-5	0	0.0	21:23	....	....	....	....	....	....	....	....	....
	NHL Totals		677	43	119	162	957	7	3	4	933	4.6		8	25.0	19:17	33	1	5	6	32	1	0	0	21:54

Traded to **Boston** by **St. Louis** with Kevin Sawyer for Steve Leach, March 8, 1996. Claimed on waivers by **Vancouver** from **Boston**, March 18, 1997. Claimed by **Atlanta** from **Vancouver** in Expansion Draft, June 25, 1999. • Missed majority of 1999-2000 season recovering from knee injury suffered in game vs. Colorado, October 23, 1999. Traded to **New Jersey** by **Atlanta** for New Jersey's 9th round choice (Simon Gamache) in 2000 Entry Draft, June 12, 2000. Traded to **Atlanta** by **New Jersey** for future considerations, July 10, 2000. Signed as a free agent by **Edmonton**, July 12, 2001. Signed as a free agent by **Lulea** (Sweden), January 28, 2005.

STAJAN, Matt

(STAY-juhn, MAHT) **TOR.**

Center. Shoots left. 6'1", 200 lbs. Born, Mississauga, Ont., December 19, 1983. Toronto's 2nd choice, 57th overall, in 2002 Entry Draft.

Season	Club	League	GP	G	A	Pts	PIM	PP	SH	GW	S	%	+/-	TF	F%	Min	GP	G	A	Pts	PIM	PP	SH	GW	Min
99-2000	Miss. Senators	GTHL	STATISTICS NOT AVAILABLE																						
2000-01	Belleville Bulls	OHL	57	9	18	27	27	....	....	....	....	....	....	....	....	....	7	1	6	7	5	....	....	....	....
2001-02	Belleville Bulls	OHL	68	33	52	85	50	....	....	....	....	....	....	....	....	....	11	3	8	11	14	....	....	....	....
2002-03	Belleville Bulls	OHL	57	34	60	94	75	....	....	....	....	....	....	....	....	....	7	5	8	13	16	....	....	....	....
	St. John's	AHL	1	0	1	1	0	....	....	....	....	....	....	....	....	....	....	....	....	....	....	....	....	....	....
	Toronto	NHL	1	1	0	1	0	0	0	0	1	100.0	1	12	33.3	11:00	....	....	....	....	....	....	....	....	....
2003-04	Toronto	NHL	69	14	13	27	22	0	0	0	63	22.2	7	450	38.9	11:00	3	0	0	0	2	0	0	0	11:13
2004-05	St. John's	AHL	80	23	43	66	43	....	....	....	....	....	....	....	....	....	5	2	2	4	6	....	....	....	....
2005-06	Toronto	NHL	80	15	12	27	50	3	4	5	83	18.1	5	373	44.5	11:38	....	....	....	....	....	....	....	....	....
2006-07	Toronto	NHL	82	10	29	39	44	1	1	1	132	7.6	3	985	46.1	16:09	....	....	....	....	....	....	....	....	....
	NHL Totals		232	40	54	94	116	4	5	6	279	14.3		1820	43.9	13:02	3	0	0	0	2	0	0	0	11:13

• Scored a goal in his first NHL game (April 5, 2003 vs. Ottawa).

STASTNY, Paul

(STAS-nee, PAWL) **COL.**

Center. Shoots left. 6', 205 lbs. Born, Quebec City, Que., December 27, 1985. Colorado's 2nd choice, 44th overall, in 2005 Entry Draft.

Season	Club	League	GP	G	A	Pts	PIM	PP	SH	GW	S	%	+/-	TF	F%	Min	GP	G	A	Pts	PIM	PP	SH	GW	Min
2003-04	River City Lancers	USHL	56	30	*47	77	46	....	....	....	....	....	....	....	....	....	3	1	2	3	0	....	....	....	....
2004-05	U. of Denver	WCHA	42	17	28	45	30	....	....	....	....	....	....	....	....	....	....	....	....	....	....	....	....	....	....
2005-06	U. of Denver	WCHA	39	19	34	53	79	....	....	....	....	....	....	....	....	....	....	....	....	....	....	....	....	....	....
2006-07	Colorado	NHL	82	28	50	78	42	11	0	6	185	15.1	4	1226	48.5	18:10	....	....	....	....	....	....	....	....	....
	NHL Totals		82	28	50	78	42	11	0	6	185	15.1		1226	48.5	18:10	....	....	....	....	....	....	....	....	....

WCHA All-Rookie Team (2005) • WCHA Rookie of the Year (2005) • NCAA Championship All-Tournament Team (2005) • WCHA First All-Star Team (2006) • NCAA West Second All-American Team (2006) • NHL All-Rookie Team (2007)

STASTNY, Yan

(STAS-nee, YAHN) **ST.L.**

Center. Shoots left. 5'11", 175 lbs. Born, Quebec City, Que., September 30, 1982. Boston's 6th choice, 259th overall, in 2002 Entry Draft.

Season	Club	League	GP	G	A	Pts	PIM	PP	SH	GW	S	%	+/-	TF	F%	Min	GP	G	A	Pts	PIM	PP	SH	GW	Min
99-2000	St. Louis Sting	NAHL	45	12	23	35	77	....	....	....	....	....	....	....	....	....	....	....	....	....	....	....	....	....	....
2000-01	St. Louis Jr. Blues	CSJHL	6	0	2	2	23	....	....	....	....	....	....	....	....	....	....	....	....	....	....	....	....	....	....
	Omaha Lancers	USHL	44	17	14	31	101	....	....	....	....	....	....	....	....	....	11	6	6	12	12	....	....	....	....
2001-02	U. of Notre Dame	CCHA	33	6	11	17	38	....	....	....	....	....	....	....	....	....	....	....	....	....	....	....	....	....	....
2002-03	U. of Notre Dame	CCHA	39	14	9	23	44	....	....	....	....	....	....	....	....	....	....	....	....	....	....	....	....	....	....
2003-04	Nurnberg	Germany	44	9	20	29	83	....	....	....	....	....	....	....	....	....	6	0	1	1	6	....	....	....	....
2004-05	Nurnberg	Germany	51	24	30	54	60	....	....	....	....	....	....	....	....	....	6	2	1	3	8	....	....	....	....
2005-06	Edmonton	NHL	3	0	0	0	0	0	0	0	1	0.0	-2	17	41.2	6:53	....	....	....	....	....	....	....	....	....
	Iowa Stars	AHL	51	14	17	31	42	....	....	....	....	....	....	....	....	....	....	....	....	....	....	....	....	....	....
	Boston	NHL	17	1	3	4	10	0	0	0	13	7.7	-2	122	42.6	10:16	....	....	....	....	....	....	....	....	....
	Providence Bruins	AHL	....	....	....	....	....	....	....	....	....	....	....	....	....	....	6	0	5	5	12	....	....	....	....
2006-07	Boston	NHL	21	0	2	2	19	0	0	0	7	0.0	-3	51	45.1	7:28	....	....	....	....	....	....	....	....	....
	Providence Bruins	AHL	11	3	9	12	12	....	....	....	....	....	....	....	....	....	....	....	....	....	....	....	....	....	....
	Peoria Rivermen	AHL	39	11	17	28	35	....	....	....	....	....	....	....	....	....	....	....	....	....	....	....	....	....	....
	NHL Totals		41	1	5	6	29	0	0	0	21	4.8		190	43.2	8:35	....	....	....	....	....	....	....	....	....

Signed as a free agent by **Nurnberg** (Germany), September 18, 2003. Traded to **Edmonton** by **Boston** for Boston's 4th round choice (previously acquired, later traded to San Jose - San Jose selected James Delory) in 2006 Entry Draft, August 30, 2005. Traded to **Boston** by **Edmonton** with Marty Reasoner and Edmonton's 2nd round choice (Milan Lucic) in 2006 Entry Draft for Sergei Samsonov, March 9, 2006. Traded to **St. Louis** by **Boston** for St. Louis' 5th round choice (Denis Reul) in 2007 Entry Draft, January 16, 2006.

STECKEL, David

(STEH-kuhl, DAY-vihd) **WSH.**

Center. Shoots left. 6'5", 222 lbs. Born, Westbend, WI, March 15, 1982. Los Angeles' 2nd choice, 30th overall, in 2001 Entry Draft.

Season	Club	League	GP	G	A	Pts	PIM	PP	SH	GW	S	%	+/-	TF	F%	Min	GP	G	A	Pts	PIM	PP	SH	GW	Min
1998-99	USNTDP	USHL	2	0	0	0	2	....	....	....	....	....	....	....	....	....	....	....	....	....	....	....	....	....	....
	USNTDP	NAHL	51	3	14	17	18	....	....	....	....	....	....	....	....	....	....	....	....	....	....	....	....	....	....
99-2000	USNTDP	U-18	6	2	5	7	14	....	....	....	....	....	....	....	....	....	....	....	....	....	....	....	....	....	....
	USNTDP	USHL	52	13	13	26	94	....	....	....	....	....	....	....	....	....	....	....	....	....	....	....	....	....	....
2000-01	Ohio State	CCHA	33	17	18	35	80	....	....	....	....	....	....	....	....	....	....	....	....	....	....	....	....	....	....
2001-02	Ohio State	CCHA	36	6	16	22	75	....	....	....	....	....	....	....	....	....	....	....	....	....	....	....	....	....	....
2002-03	Ohio State	CCHA	36	10	8	18	50	....	....	....	....	....	....	....	....	....	....	....	....	....	....	....	....	....	....
2003-04	Ohio State	CCHA	41	17	13	30	44	....	....	....	....	....	....	....	....	....	....	....	....	....	....	....	....	....	....
2004-05	Manchester	AHL	63	10	7	17	26	....	....	....	....	....	....	....	....	....	6	1	1	2	4	....	....	....	....
2005-06	Washington	NHL	7	0	0	0	0	0	0	0	6	0.0	1	48	35.4	7:39	....	....	....	....	....	....	....	....	....
	Hershey Bears	AHL	74	14	20	34	58	....	....	....	....	....	....	....	....	....	21	10	5	15	20	....	....	....	....
2006-07	Washington	NHL	5	0	0	0	2	0	0	0	4	0.0	-2	43	65.1	12:26	....	....	....	....	....	....	....	....	....
	Hershey Bears	AHL	71	30	31	61	46	....	....	....	....	....	....	....	....	....	19	6	9	15	16	....	....	....	....
	NHL Totals		12	0	0	0	2	0	0	0	10	0.0		91	49.5	9:39	....	....	....	....	....	....	....	....	....

CCHA All-Rookie Team (2001)

Signed as a free agent by **Washington**, August 25, 2005.

STEEN, Alex

(STEEN, AL-ehx) **TOR.**

Center. Shoots left. 6'1", 205 lbs. Born, Winnipeg, Man., March 1, 1984. Toronto's 1st choice, 24th overall, in 2002 Entry Draft.

Season	Club	League	GP	G	A	Pts	PIM	PP	SH	GW	S	%	+/-	TF	F%	Min	GP	G	A	Pts	PIM	PP	SH	GW	Min
99-2000	V.Frolunda Jr.	Swe-Jr.	8	5	7	12	0	....	....	....	....	....	....	....	....	....	....	....	....	....	....	....	....	....	....
	V.Frolunda U18	Swe-U18	14	3	5	8	16	....	....	....	....	....	....	....	....	....	....	....	....	....	....	....	....	....	....
2000-01	V.Frolunda Jr.	Swe-Jr.	23	11	12	23	15	....	....	....	....	....	....	....	....	....	3	1	0	1	2	....	....	....	....
	V.Frolunda U18	Swe-U18	6	3	3	6	9	....	....	....	....	....	....	....	....	....	....	....	....	....	....	....	....	....	....
2001-02	V.Frolunda Jr.	Swe-Jr.	23	21	17	38	47	....	....	....	....	....	....	....	....	....	2	1	1	2	2	....	....	....	....
	V.Frolunda	Sweden	26	0	3	3	14	....	....	....	....	....	....	....	....	....	10	1	2	3	0	....	....	....	....
2002-03	V.Frolunda	Sweden	45	5	10	15	18	....	....	....	....	....	....	....	....	....	16	2	3	5	4	....	....	....	....
	V.Frolunda Jr.	Swe-Jr.	2	0	2	2	0	....	....	....	....	....	....	....	....	....	....	....	....	....	....	....	....	....	....
2003-04	V.Frolunda	Sweden	48	10	14	24	50	....	....	....	....	....	....	....	....	....	10	4	6	10	14	....	....	....	....
2004-05	MODO	Sweden	50	9	8	17	26	....	....	....	....	....	....	....	....	....	6	1	0	1	4	....	....	....	....
2005-06	Toronto	NHL	75	18	27	45	42	9	1	3	176	10.2	-9	29	24.1	17:37	....	....	....	....	....	....	....	....	....
2006-07	Toronto	NHL	82	15	20	35	26	4	0	5	192	7.8	5	44	34.1	15:42	....	....	....	....	....	....	....	....	....
	NHL Totals		157	33	47	80	68	13	1	8	368	9.0		73	30.1	16:37	....	....	....	....	....	....	....	....	....

STEFAN, Patrik

(SHTEH-fan, PAT-rihk)

Center. Shoots left. 6'2", 210 lbs. Born, Pribram, Czech., September 16, 1980. Atlanta's 1st choice, 1st overall, in 1999 Entry Draft.

			Regular Season														Playoffs								
Season	Club	League	GP	G	A	Pts	PIM	PP	SH	GW	S	%	+/-	TF	F%	Min	GP	G	A	Pts	PIM	PP	SH	GW	Min
1996-97	HC Sparta Praha	CzRep	5	0	1	1	2	....	....	....	....	....	....	....	....	....	7	1	0	1	0	....	....	....	....
1997-98	HC Sparta Praha	CzRep	27	2	6	8	16	....	....	....	....	....	....	....	....	....	....	....	....	....	....	....	....	....	....
	Long Beach	IHL	25	5	10	15	10	....	....	....	....	....	....	....	....	....	10	1	1	2	2	....	....	....	....
1998-99	Long Beach	IHL	33	11	24	35	26	....	....	....	....	....	....	....	....	....	....	....	....	....	....	....	....	....	....
99-2000	**Atlanta**	**NHL**	**72**	**5**	**20**	**25**	**30**	**1**	**0**	**0**	**117**	**4.3**	**–20**	**988**	**41.4**	**14:49**	....	....	....	....	....	....	....	....	....
2000-01	**Atlanta**	**NHL**	**66**	**10**	**21**	**31**	**22**	**0**	**0**	**1**	**93**	**10.8**	**–3**	**834**	**42.9**	**14:07**	....	....	....	....	....	....	....	....	....
2001-02	**Atlanta**	**NHL**	**59**	**7**	**16**	**23**	**22**	**0**	**1**	**0**	**67**	**10.4**	**–4**	**628**	**41.9**	**15:58**	....	....	....	....	....	....	....	....	....
	Chicago Wolves	AHL	5	3	0	3	0	....	....	....	....	....	....	....	....	....	....	....	....	....	....	....	....	....	....
2002-03	**Atlanta**	**NHL**	**71**	**13**	**21**	**34**	**12**	**3**	**0**	**2**	**96**	**13.5**	**–10**	**1125**	**45.7**	**16:50**	....	....	....	....	....	....	....	....	....
2003-04	**Atlanta**	**NHL**	**82**	**14**	**26**	**40**	**26**	**3**	**2**	**2**	**110**	**12.7**	**–7**	**1446**	**45.6**	**16:29**	....	....	....	....	....	....	....	....	....
2004-05	Ilves Tampere	Finland	37	13	28	41	47	....	....	....	....	....	....	....	....	....	7	1	6	7	4	....	....	....	....
2005-06	**Atlanta**	**NHL**	**64**	**10**	**14**	**24**	**36**	**2**	**0**	**3**	**81**	**12.3**	**3**	**820**	**46.3**	**13:50**	....	....	....	....	....	....	....	....	....
2006-07	**Dallas**	**NHL**	**41**	**5**	**6**	**11**	**10**	**0**	**1**	**1**	**41**	**12.2**	**5**	**218**	**48.2**	**12:13**	....	....	....	....	....	....	....	....	....
	NHL Totals		**455**	**64**	**124**	**188**	**158**	**9**	**4**	**9**	**605**	**10.6**		**6059**	**44.4**	**15:06**	....	....	....	....	....	....	....	....	....

Signed as a free agent by **Ilves Tampere** (Finland), October 23, 2004. Traded to **Dallas** by **Atlanta** with Jaroslav Modry for Niko Kapanen and Dallas' 7th round choice (Will O'Neill) in 2006 Entry Draft, June 24, 2006.

STEMPNIAK, Lee

(STEHMP-nee-ak, LEE) **ST.L.**

Right wing. Shoots right. 6', 190 lbs. Born, Buffalo, NY, February 4, 1983. St. Louis' 7th choice, 148th overall, in 2003 Entry Draft.

Season	Club	League	GP	G	A	Pts	PIM	PP	SH	GW	S	%	+/-	TF	F%	Min	GP	G	A	Pts	PIM	PP	SH	GW	Min
2000-01	Buffalo Lightning	OPJHL	48	34	51	86	36	....	....	....	....	....	....	....	....	....	....	....	....	....	....	....	....	....	....
2001-02	Dartmouth	ECAC	32	12	9	21	8	....	....	....	....	....	....	....	....	....	....	....	....	....	....	....	....	....	....
2002-03	Dartmouth	ECAC	34	21	28	49	32	....	....	....	....	....	....	....	....	....	....	....	....	....	....	....	....	....	....
2003-04	Dartmouth	ECAC	34	16	22	38	42	....	....	....	....	....	....	....	....	....	....	....	....	....	....	....	....	....	....
2004-05	Dartmouth	ECACHL	35	14	*29	43	34	....	....	....	....	....	....	....	....	....	....	....	....	....	....	....	....	....	....
2005-06	**St. Louis**	**NHL**	**57**	**14**	**13**	**27**	**22**	**5**	**0**	**2**	**100**	**14.0**	**–10**	**7**	**42.9**	**14:22**	....	....	....	....	....	....	....	....	....
	Peoria Rivermen	AHL	26	8	7	15	32	....	....	....	....	....	....	....	....	....	3	0	3	3	2	....	....	....	....
2006-07	**St. Louis**	**NHL**	**82**	**27**	**25**	**52**	**33**	**8**	**0**	**4**	**166**	**16.3**	**–2**	**7**	**14.3**	**14:43**	....	....	....	....	....	....	....	....	....
	NHL Totals		**139**	**41**	**38**	**79**	**55**	**13**	**0**	**6**	**266**	**15.4**		**14**	**28.6**	**14:34**	....	....	....	....	....	....	....	....	....

ECAC All-Rookie Team (2002) • ECAC First All-Star Team (2004, 2005) • NCAA East First All-American Team (2004) • NCAA East Second All-American Team (2005)

STEPHENSON, Shay

(STEE-vehn-suhn, SHAY)

Left wing. Shoots left. 6'4", 200 lbs. Born, Outlook, Sask., September 13, 1983. Carolina's 7th choice, 198th overall, in 2003 Entry Draft.

Season	Club	League	GP	G	A	Pts	PIM	PP	SH	GW	S	%	+/-	TF	F%	Min	GP	G	A	Pts	PIM	PP	SH	GW	Min
99-2000	Notre Dame	SMHL	42	23	7	30	46	....	....	....	....	....	....	....	....	....	....	....	....	....	....	....	....	....	....
2000-01	Red Deer Rebels	WHL	44	1	4	5	30	....	....	....	....	....	....	....	....	....	22	0	0	0	15	....	....	....	....
2001-02	Red Deer Rebels	WHL	59	9	10	19	55	....	....	....	....	....	....	....	....	....	23	0	3	3	14	....	....	....	....
2002-03	Red Deer Rebels	WHL	67	17	15	32	84	....	....	....	....	....	....	....	....	....	23	6	5	11	33	....	....	....	....
2003-04	Red Deer Rebels	WHL	60	11	19	30	34	....	....	....	....	....	....	....	....	....	19	5	7	12	16	....	....	....	....
2004-05	Sundsvall	Sweden-2	30	11	9	20	66	....	....	....	....	....	....	....	....	....	....	....	....	....	....	....	....	....	....
2005-06	Manchester	AHL	6	0	0	0	4	....	....	....	....	....	....	....	....	....	....	....	....	....	....	....	....	....	....
	Reading Royals	ECHL	62	19	22	41	42	....	....	....	....	....	....	....	....	....	4	0	2	2	8	....	....	....	....
2006-07	**Los Angeles**	**NHL**	**2**	**0**	**0**	**0**	**0**	**0**	**0**	**0**	**0**	**0.0**	**0**	**12**	**25.0**	**7:19**	....	....	....	....	....	....	....	....	....
	Manchester	AHL	55	11	10	21	67	....	....	....	....	....	....	....	....	....	5	1	0	1	4	....	....	....	....
	NHL Totals		**2**	**0**	**0**	**0**	**0**	**0**	**0**	**0**	**0**	**0.0**		**12**	**25.0**	**7:19**	....	....	....	....	....	....	....	....	....

• Re-entered NHL Entry Draft. Originally Edmonton's 11th choice, 278th overall, in 2001 Entry Draft.
Signed as a free agent by **Sundsvall** (Sweden-2), August 25, 2004. Signed as a free agent by **Los Angeles**, August 17, 2005. Signed as a free agent by **Milano** (Italy), August 12, 2007.

STEVENSON, Grant

(STEE-vehn-suhn, GRANT) **CGY.**

Center. Shoots right. 5'11", 170 lbs. Born, Spruce Grove, Alta., October 15, 1981.

Season	Club	League	GP	G	A	Pts	PIM	PP	SH	GW	S	%	+/-	TF	F%	Min	GP	G	A	Pts	PIM	PP	SH	GW	Min
1998-99	Spruce Grove	RAMHL	26	15	32	47	90	....	....	....	....	....	....	....	....	....	8	10	10	20	30	....	....	....	....
99-2000	Bonnyville	AJHL	63	20	38	58	....	....	....	....	....	....	....	....	....	....	....	....	....	....	....	....	....	....	....
2000-01	Grand Prairie	AJHL	53	24	49	73	62	....	....	....	....	....	....	....	....	....	15	7	2	9	38	....	....	....	....
2001-02	Minnesota State	WCHA	38	8	8	16	36	....	....	....	....	....	....	....	....	....	....	....	....	....	....	....	....	....	....
2002-03	Minnesota State	WCHA	38	27	36	63	38	....	....	....	....	....	....	....	....	....	....	....	....	....	....	....	....	....	....
2003-04	Cleveland Barons	AHL	71	13	26	39	45	....	....	....	....	....	....	....	....	....	9	0	7	7	6	....	....	....	....
2004-05	Cleveland Barons	AHL	77	14	25	39	70	....	....	....	....	....	....	....	....	....	....	....	....	....	....	....	....	....	....
	Johnstown Chiefs	ECHL	2	1	0	1	2	....	....	....	....	....	....	....	....	....	....	....	....	....	....	....	....	....	....
2005-06	**San Jose**	**NHL**	**47**	**10**	**12**	**22**	**14**	**5**	**0**	**2**	**67**	**14.9**	**–7**	**6**	**33.3**	**11:57**	**5**	**0**	**0**	**0**	**4**	**0**	**0**	**0**	**6:59**
	Cleveland Barons	AHL	17	8	8	16	8	....	....	....	....	....	....	....	....	....	....	....	....	....	....	....	....	....	....
2006-07	Worcester Sharks	AHL	59	14	25	39	30	....	....	....	....	....	....	....	....	....	6	2	0	2	2	....	....	....	....
	NHL Totals		**47**	**10**	**12**	**22**	**14**	**5**	**0**	**2**	**67**	**14.9**		**6**	**33.3**	**11:57**	**5**	**0**	**0**	**0**	**4**	**0**	**0**	**0**	**6:59**

WCHA First All-Star Team (2003) • NCAA West Second All-American Team (2003)
Signed as a free agent by **San Jose**, April 18, 2003. Signed as a free agent by **Calgary**, July 4, 2007.

STEWART, Anthony

(STEW-ahrt, AN-thu-nee) **FLA.**

Center. Shoots right. 6'2", 239 lbs. Born, LaSalle, Que., January 5, 1985. Florida's 2nd choice, 25th overall, in 2003 Entry Draft.

Season	Club	League	GP	G	A	Pts	PIM	PP	SH	GW	S	%	+/-	TF	F%	Min	GP	G	A	Pts	PIM	PP	SH	GW	Min
2000-01	North York	MTHL	34	30	70	100	....	....	....	....	....	....	....	....	....	....	....	....	....	....	....	....	....	....	....
	St. Mike's B's	OPJHL	5	0	2	2	0	....	....	....	....	....	....	....	....	....	....	....	....	....	....	....	....	....	....
2001-02	Kingston	OHL	65	19	24	43	12	....	....	....	....	....	....	....	....	....	1	0	0	0	0	....	....	....	....
2002-03	Kingston	OHL	68	32	38	70	47	....	....	....	....	....	....	....	....	....	....	....	....	....	....	....	....	....	....
2003-04	Kingston	OHL	53	35	23	58	76	....	....	....	....	....	....	....	....	....	5	3	4	7	7	....	....	....	....
2004-05	Kingston	OHL	62	32	35	67	70	....	....	....	....	....	....	....	....	....	....	....	....	....	....	....	....	....	....
	San Antonio	AHL	10	1	2	3	14	....	....	....	....	....	....	....	....	....	....	....	....	....	....	....	....	....	....
2005-06	**Florida**	**NHL**	**10**	**2**	**1**	**3**	**2**	**1**	**0**	**0**	**16**	**12.5**	**2**	**1**	**0.0**	**7:13**	....	....	....	....	....	....	....	....	....
	Rochester	AHL	4	2	3	5	0	....	....	....	....	....	....	....	....	....	....	....	....	....	....	....	....	....	....
2006-07	**Florida**	**NHL**	**10**	**0**	**1**	**1**	**2**	**0**	**0**	**0**	**8**	**0.0**	**1**	**0**	**0.0**	**6:51**	....	....	....	....	....	....	....	....	....
	Rochester	AHL	62	13	14	27	64	....	....	....	....	....	....	....	....	....	6	2	0	2	2	....	....	....	....
	NHL Totals		**20**	**2**	**2**	**4**	**4**	**1**	**0**	**0**	**24**	**8.3**		**1**	**0.0**	**7:02**	....	....	....	....	....	....	....	....	....

• Missed remainder of 2005-06 season recovering from wrist injury suffered in game vs. Carolina, November 11, 2005.

STEWART, Karl

(STEW-ahrt, KAHRL) **T.B.**

Left wing. Shoots left. 5'11", 185 lbs. Born, Aurora, Ont., June 30, 1983.

Season	Club	League	GP	G	A	Pts	PIM	PP	SH	GW	S	%	+/-	TF	F%	Min	GP	G	A	Pts	PIM	PP	SH	GW	Min
99-2000	Thornhill Rattlers	OPJHL	49	15	19	34	61	....	....	....	....	....	....	....	....	....	....	....	....	....	....	....	....	....	....
2000-01	Plymouth Whalers	OHL	68	9	14	23	87	....	....	....	....	....	....	....	....	....	19	3	4	7	14	....	....	....	....
2001-02	Plymouth Whalers	OHL	65	20	23	43	104	....	....	....	....	....	....	....	....	....	6	0	2	2	21	....	....	....	....
2002-03	Plymouth Whalers	OHL	68	35	50	85	120	....	....	....	....	....	....	....	....	....	17	7	10	17	31	....	....	....	....
2003-04	**Atlanta**	**NHL**	**5**	**0**	**1**	**1**	**4**	**0**	**0**	**0**	**2**	**0.0**	**0**	**10**	**10.0**	**4:27**	....	....	....	....	....	....	....	....	....
	Chicago Wolves	AHL	72	10	32	42	186	....	....	....	....	....	....	....	....	....	10	2	3	5	29	....	....	....	....
2004-05	Chicago Wolves	AHL	77	16	8	24	226	....	....	....	....	....	....	....	....	....	12	4	2	6	32	....	....	....	....
2005-06	**Atlanta**	**NHL**	**8**	**0**	**0**	**0**	**15**	**0**	**0**	**0**	**6**	**0.0**	**–3**	**3**	**100.0**	**5:40**	....	....	....	....	....	....	....	....	....
	Chicago Wolves	AHL	71	22	18	40	184	....	....	....	....	....	....	....	....	....	....	....	....	....	....	....	....	....	....
2006-07	**Pittsburgh**	**NHL**	**3**	**0**	**0**	**0**	**2**	**0**	**0**	**0**	**0**	**0.0**	**–1**	**1**	**100.0**	**3:23**	....	....	....	....	....	....	....	....	....
	Chicago	**NHL**	**37**	**2**	**3**	**5**	**43**	**0**	**1**	**0**	**19**	**10.5**	**–2**	**2**	**50.0**	**9:22**	....	....	....	....	....	....	....	....	....
	Tampa Bay	**NHL**	**7**	**0**	**0**	**0**	**2**	**0**	**0**	**0**	**2**	**0.0**	**–2**	**0**	**0.0**	**7:10**	....	....	....	....	....	....	....	....	....
	NHL Totals		**60**	**2**	**4**	**6**	**66**	**0**	**1**	**0**	**29**	**6.9**		**16**	**37.5**	**7:55**	....	....	....	....	....	....	....	....	....

Signed as a free agent by **Atlanta**, September 28, 2001. Traded to **Anaheim** by **Atlanta** with Atlanta's 2nd round choice (later traded to Colorado - Colorado selected T.J. Galiardi) in 2007 Entry Draft and future considerations for Vitaly Vishnevski, August 17, 2006. Claimed on waivers by **Pittsburgh** from **Anaheim**, September 27, 2006. Claimed on waivers by **Chicago** from **Pittsburgh**, October 26, 2006. Traded to **Tampa Bay** by **Chicago** with Florida's 6th round choice (previously acquired) in 2008 Entry Draft for Nikita Alexeev, February 27, 2007.

STILLMAN, Cory

(STIHL-mahn, KOHR-ee) **CAR.**

Left wing. Shoots left. 6', 200 lbs. Born, Peterborough, Ont., December 20, 1973. Calgary's 1st choice, 6th overall, in 1992 Entry Draft.

			Regular Season														Playoffs								
Season	Club	League	GP	G	A	Pts	PIM	PP	SH	GW	S	%	+/-	TF	F%	Min	GP	G	A	Pts	PIM	PP	SH	GW	Min
1989-90	Peterborough	OHA-B	41	30	*54	84	76	....	....	....	....	....	....	....	....	....	....	....	....	....	....	....	....	....	....
1990-91	Windsor Spitfires	OHL	64	31	70	101	31	....	....	....	....	....	....	....	....	....	11	3	6	9	8	....	....	....	....
1991-92	Windsor Spitfires	OHL	53	29	61	90	59	....	....	....	....	....	....	....	....	....	7	2	4	6	8	....	....	....	....
1992-93	Peterborough	OHL	61	25	55	80	55	....	....	....	....	....	....	....	....	....	18	3	8	11	18	....	....	....	....
1993-94	Saint John Flames	AHL	79	35	48	83	52	....	....	....	....	....	....	....	....	....	7	2	4	6	16	....	....	....	....
1994-95	Saint John Flames	AHL	63	28	53	81	70	....	....	....	....	....	....	....	....	....	5	0	2	2	2	....	....	....	....
	Calgary	**NHL**	**10**	**0**	**2**	**2**	**2**	**0**	**0**	**0**	**7**	**0.0**	**1**	....	....	....	....	....	....	....	....	....	....	....	....
1995-96	**Calgary**	**NHL**	**74**	**16**	**19**	**35**	**41**	**4**	**1**	**3**	**132**	**12.1**	**–5**	....	....	....	**2**	**1**	**1**	**2**	**0**	**0**	**0**	**0**	....
1996-97	**Calgary**	**NHL**	**58**	**6**	**20**	**26**	**14**	**2**	**0**	**0**	**112**	**5.4**	**–6**	....	....	....	....	....	....	....	....	....	....	....	....
1997-98	**Calgary**	**NHL**	**72**	**27**	**22**	**49**	**40**	**9**	**4**	**1**	**178**	**15.2**	**–9**	....	....	....	....	....	....	....	....	....	....	....	....
1998-99	**Calgary**	**NHL**	**76**	**27**	**30**	**57**	**38**	**9**	**3**	**5**	**175**	**15.4**	**7**	**535**	**46.5**	**16:19**	....	....	....	....	....	....	....	....	....
99-2000	**Calgary**	**NHL**	**37**	**12**	**9**	**21**	**12**	**6**	**0**	**3**	**59**	**20.3**	**–9**	**283**	**54.4**	**17:45**	....	....	....	....	....	....	....	....	....
2000-01	**Calgary**	**NHL**	**66**	**21**	**24**	**45**	**45**	**7**	**0**	**4**	**148**	**14.2**	**–6**	**346**	**43.9**	**18:50**	....	....	....	....	....	....	....	....	....
	St. Louis	**NHL**	**12**	**3**	**4**	**7**	**6**	**3**	**0**	**0**	**26**	**11.5**	**–2**	**36**	**61.1**	**18:37**	**15**	**3**	**5**	**8**	**8**	**1**	**0**	**1**	**14:58**
2001-02	**St. Louis**	**NHL**	**80**	**23**	**22**	**45**	**36**	**6**	**0**	**4**	**140**	**16.4**	**8**	**196**	**46.4**	**15:03**	**9**	**0**	**2**	**2**	**2**	**0**	**0**	**0**	**12:46**
2002-03	**St. Louis**	**NHL**	**79**	**24**	**43**	**67**	**56**	**6**	**0**	**4**	**157**	**15.3**	**12**	**266**	**41.7**	**18:20**	**6**	**2**	**2**	**4**	**2**	**2**	**0**	**1**	**18:05**
2003-04♦	**Tampa Bay**	**NHL**	**81**	**25**	**55**	**80**	**36**	**11**	**1**	**6**	**178**	**14.0**	**18**	**38**	**31.6**	**19:32**	**21**	**2**	**5**	**7**	**15**	**0**	**1**	**0**	**17:22**
2004-05			DID NOT PLAY																						
2005-06♦	**Carolina**	**NHL**	**72**	**21**	**55**	**76**	**32**	**10**	**0**	**3**	**177**	**11.9**	**–9**	**11**	**27.3**	**18:40**	**25**	**9**	**17**	**26**	**14**	**4**	**0**	**3**	**18:42**
2006-07	**Carolina**	**NHL**	**43**	**5**	**22**	**27**	**24**	**1**	**0**	**0**	**85**	**5.9**	**–8**	**7**	**28.6**	**17:25**	....	....	....	....	....	....	....	....	....
	NHL Totals		**760**	**210**	**327**	**537**	**382**	**74**	**9**	**33**	**1574**	**13.3**		**1718**	**46.3**	**17:45**	**78**	**17**	**32**	**49**	**41**	**7**	**1**	**5**	**16:51**

OHL Rookie of the Year (1991)

• Missed majority of 1999-2000 season recovering from shoulder injury suffered in game vs. Philadelphia, December 27, 1999. Traded to **St. Louis by Calgary** for Craig Conroy and St. Louis' 7th round choice (David Moss) in 2001 Entry Draft, March 13, 2001. Traded to **Tampa Bay** by **St. Louis** for Tampa Bay's 2nd round choice (David Backes) in 2003 Entry Draft, June 21, 2003. Signed as a free agent by **Carolina**, August 2, 2005.

STOLL, Jarret

(STOHL, JEHR-eht) **EDM.**

Center. Shoots right. 6'1", 201 lbs. Born, Melville, Sask., June 25, 1982. Edmonton's 3rd choice, 36th overall, in 2002 Entry Draft.

Season	Club	League	GP	G	A	Pts	PIM	PP	SH	GW	S	%	+/-	TF	F%	Min	GP	G	A	Pts	PIM	PP	SH	GW	Min
1997-98	Saskatoon Blazers	SMHL	44	45	44	*89	78	....	....	....	....	....	....	....	....	....	....	....	....	....	....	....	....	....	....
	Edmonton Ice	WHL	8	2	3	5	4	....	....	....	....	....	....	....	....	....	....	....	....	....	....	....	....	....	....
1998-99	Kootenay Ice	WHL	57	13	21	34	38	....	....	....	....	....	....	....	....	....	4	0	0	0	2	....	....	....	....
99-2000	Kootenay Ice	WHL	71	37	38	75	64	....	....	....	....	....	....	....	....	....	20	7	9	16	24	....	....	....	....
2000-01	Kootenay Ice	WHL	62	40	66	106	105	....	....	....	....	....	....	....	....	....	11	5	9	14	22	....	....	....	....
2001-02	Kootenay Ice	WHL	47	32	34	66	64	....	....	....	....	....	....	....	....	....	22	6	14	20	35	....	....	....	....
2002-03	**Edmonton**	**NHL**	**4**	**0**	**1**	**1**	**0**	**0**	**0**	**0**	**5**	**0.0**	**–3**	**30**	**63.3**	**7:44**	....	....	....	....	....	....	....	....	....
	Hamilton	AHL	76	21	33	54	86	....	....	....	....	....	....	....	....	....	23	5	8	13	25	....	....	....	....
2003-04	**Edmonton**	**NHL**	**68**	**10**	**11**	**21**	**42**	**1**	**1**	**2**	**107**	**9.3**	**8**	**1019**	**54.1**	**13:54**	....	....	....	....	....	....	....	....	....
2004-05	Edmonton	AHL	66	21	17	38	92	....	....	....	....	....	....	....	....	....	....	....	....	....	....	....	....	....	....
2005-06	**Edmonton**	**NHL**	**82**	**22**	**46**	**68**	**74**	**11**	**1**	**4**	**243**	**9.1**	**4**	**1348**	**56.8**	**18:23**	**24**	**4**	**6**	**10**	**24**	**2**	**0**	**1**	**17:06**
2006-07	**Edmonton**	**NHL**	**51**	**13**	**26**	**39**	**48**	**6**	**1**	**2**	**115**	**11.3**	**2**	**901**	**55.6**	**18:12**	....	....	....	....	....	....	....	....	....
	NHL Totals		**205**	**45**	**84**	**129**	**164**	**18**	**3**	**8**	**470**	**9.6**		**3298**	**55.7**	**16:38**	**24**	**4**	**6**	**10**	**24**	**2**	**0**	**1**	**17:06**

• Re-entered NHL Entry Draft. Originally Calgary's 3rd choice, 46th overall, in 2000 Entry Draft.

WHL East First All-Star Team (2001) • Canadian Major Junior First All-Star Team (2001) • WHL West First All-Star Team (2002)

STORTINI, Zachery

(stohr-TEE-nee, ZA-kuh-ree) **EDM.**

Right wing. Shoots right. 6'3", 228 lbs. Born, Elliot Lake, Ont., September 11, 1985. Edmonton's 5th choice, 94th overall, in 2003 Entry Draft.

Season	Club	League	GP	G	A	Pts	PIM	PP	SH	GW	S	%	+/-	TF	F%	Min	GP	G	A	Pts	PIM	PP	SH	GW	Min
2000-01	Newmarket	OPJHL	34	3	10	13	68	....	....	....	....	....	....	....	....	....	....	....	....	....	....	....	....	....	....
2001-02	Sudbury Wolves	OHL	65	8	6	14	187	....	....	....	....	....	....	....	....	....	5	1	0	1	24	....	....	....	....
2002-03	Sudbury Wolves	OHL	62	13	16	29	222	....	....	....	....	....	....	....	....	....	....	....	....	....	....	....	....	....	....
2003-04	Sudbury Wolves	OHL	62	21	16	37	151	....	....	....	....	....	....	....	....	....	7	1	1	2	14	....	....	....	....
	Toronto	AHL	2	0	0	0	7	....	....	....	....	....	....	....	....	....	3	0	0	0	4	....	....	....	....
2004-05	Sudbury Wolves	OHL	58	13	27	40	186	....	....	....	....	....	....	....	....	....	12	2	5	7	27	....	....	....	....
2005-06	Iowa Stars	AHL	27	2	1	3	108	....	....	....	....	....	....	....	....	....	....	....	....	....	....	....	....	....	....
	Milwaukee	AHL	37	0	7	7	153	....	....	....	....	....	....	....	....	....	....	....	....	....	....	....	....	....	....
2006-07	**Edmonton**	**NHL**	**29**	**1**	**0**	**1**	**105**	**0**	**0**	**0**	**17**	**5.9**	**–7**	**3**	**100.0**	**7:09**	....	....	....	....	....	....	....	....	....
	Hamilton	AHL	47	9	6	15	195	....	....	....	....	....	....	....	....	....	22	3	0	3	*56	....	....	....	....
	NHL Totals		**29**	**1**	**0**	**1**	**105**	**0**	**0**	**0**	**17**	**5.9**		**3**	**100.0**	**7:09**	....	....	....	....	....	....	....	....	....

STRAKA, Martin

(STRAH-kuh, MAHR-tihn) **NYR**

Center. Shoots left. 5'9", 180 lbs. Born, Plzen, Czech., September 3, 1972. Pittsburgh's 1st choice, 19th overall, in 1992 Entry Draft.

Season	Club	League	GP	G	A	Pts	PIM	PP	SH	GW	S	%	+/-	TF	F%	Min	GP	G	A	Pts	PIM	PP	SH	GW	Min
1989-90	Skoda Plzen	Czech	1	0	3	3	....	....	....	....	....	....	....	....	....	....	....	....	....	....	....	....	....	....	....
1990-91	HC Skoda Plzen	Czech	47	7	24	31	6	....	....	....	....	....	....	....	....	....	....	....	....	....	....	....	....	....	....
1991-92	HC Skoda Plzen	Czech	50	27	28	55	20	....	....	....	....	....	....	....	....	....	....	....	....	....	....	....	....	....	....
1992-93	**Pittsburgh**	**NHL**	**42**	**3**	**13**	**16**	**29**	**0**	**0**	**1**	**28**	**10.7**	**2**	....	....	....	**11**	**2**	**1**	**3**	**2**	**0**	**0**	**0**	....
	Cleveland	IHL	4	4	3	7	0	....	....	....	....	....	....	....	....	....	....	....	....	....	....	....	....	....	....
1993-94	**Pittsburgh**	**NHL**	**84**	**30**	**34**	**64**	**24**	**2**	**0**	**6**	**130**	**23.1**	**24**	....	....	....	**6**	**1**	**0**	**1**	**2**	**0**	**0**	**0**	....
1994-95	Plzen	CzRep	19	10	11	21	18	....	....	....	....	....	....	....	....	....	....	....	....	....	....	....	....	....	....
	Pittsburgh	**NHL**	**31**	**4**	**12**	**16**	**16**	**0**	**0**	**0**	**36**	**11.1**	**0**	....	....	....	....	....	....	....	....	....	....	....	....
	Ottawa	**NHL**	**6**	**1**	**1**	**2**	**0**	**0**	**0**	**0**	**13**	**7.7**	**–1**	....	....	....	....	....	....	....	....	....	....	....	....
1995-96	**Ottawa**	**NHL**	**43**	**9**	**16**	**25**	**29**	**5**	**0**	**1**	**63**	**14.3**	**–14**	....	....	....	....	....	....	....	....	....	....	....	....
	NY Islanders	**NHL**	**22**	**2**	**10**	**12**	**6**	**0**	**0**	**0**	**18**	**11.1**	**–6**	....	....	....	....	....	....	....	....	....	....	....	....
	Florida	**NHL**	**12**	**2**	**4**	**6**	**6**	**1**	**0**	**0**	**17**	**11.8**	**1**	....	....	....	**13**	**2**	**2**	**4**	**2**	**0**	**0**	**0**	....
1996-97	**Florida**	**NHL**	**55**	**7**	**22**	**29**	**12**	**2**	**0**	**1**	**94**	**7.4**	**9**	....	....	....	**4**	**0**	**0**	**0**	**0**	**0**	**0**	**0**	....
1997-98	**Pittsburgh**	**NHL**	**75**	**19**	**23**	**42**	**28**	**4**	**3**	**4**	**117**	**16.2**	**–1**	....	....	....	**6**	**2**	**0**	**2**	**2**	**0**	**1**	**0**	....
	Czech Republic	Olympics	6	1	2	3	0	....	....	....	....	....	....	....	....	....	....	....	....	....	....	....	....	....	....
1998-99	**Pittsburgh**	**NHL**	**80**	**35**	**48**	**83**	**26**	**5**	**4**	**4**	**177**	**19.8**	**12**	**845**	**43.6**	**23:35**	**13**	**6**	**9**	**15**	**6**	**1**	**0**	**0**	**25:00**
99-2000	**Pittsburgh**	**NHL**	**71**	**20**	**39**	**59**	**26**	**3**	**1**	**2**	**146**	**13.7**	**24**	**651**	**42.9**	**23:58**	**11**	**3**	**9**	**12**	**10**	**1**	**0**	**0**	**24:27**
2000-01	**Pittsburgh**	**NHL**	**82**	**27**	**68**	**95**	**38**	**7**	**1**	**4**	**185**	**14.6**	**19**	**331**	**43.2**	**23:01**	**18**	**5**	**8**	**13**	**8**	**3**	**0**	**2**	**21:24**
2001-02	**Pittsburgh**	**NHL**	**13**	**5**	**4**	**9**	**0**	**1**	**0**	**1**	**33**	**15.2**	**3**	**5**	**60.0**	**18:00**	....	....	....	....	....	....	....	....	....
2002-03	**Pittsburgh**	**NHL**	**60**	**18**	**28**	**46**	**12**	**7**	**0**	**4**	**136**	**13.2**	**–18**	**115**	**45.2**	**20:37**	....	....	....	....	....	....	....	....	....
2003-04	**Pittsburgh**	**NHL**	**22**	**4**	**8**	**12**	**16**	**1**	**0**	**0**	**34**	**11.8**	**–16**	**121**	**38.8**	**21:32**	....	....	....	....	....	....	....	....	....
	Los Angeles	**NHL**	**32**	**6**	**8**	**14**	**4**	**1**	**1**	**0**	**34**	**17.6**	**–9**	**66**	**48.5**	**16:47**	....	....	....	....	....	....	....	....	....
2004-05	Plzen	CzRep	45	16	18	34	76	....	....	....	....	....	....	....	....	....	....	....	....	....	....	....	....	....	....
2005-06	**NY Rangers**	**NHL**	**82**	**22**	**54**	**76**	**42**	**4**	**0**	**4**	**171**	**12.9**	**17**	**237**	**39.7**	**19:09**	**4**	**0**	**0**	**0**	**2**	**0**	**0**	**0**	**20:30**
	Czech Republic	Olympics	8	2	6	8	6	....	....	....	....	....	....	....	....	....	....	....	....	....	....	....	....	....	....
2006-07	**NY Rangers**	**NHL**	**77**	**29**	**41**	**70**	**24**	**8**	**0**	**6**	**165**	**17.6**	**16**	**213**	**40.4**	**19:57**	**10**	**2**	**8**	**10**	**2**	**1**	**0**	**0**	**19:48**
	NHL Totals		**889**	**243**	**433**	**676**	**338**	**51**	**10**	**38**	**1597**	**15.2**		**2584**	**42.7**	**21:19**	**96**	**23**	**37**	**60**	**36**	**6**	**1**	**2**	**22:29**

Czechoslovakian First All-Star Team (1992)

Played in NHL All-Star Game (1999)

Traded to **Ottawa** by **Pittsburgh** for Troy Murray and Norm Maciver, April 7, 1995. Traded to **NY Islanders** by **Ottawa** with Don Beaupre and Bryan Berard for Damian Rhodes and Wade Redden, January 23, 1996. Claimed on waivers by **Florida** from **NY Islanders**, March 15, 1996. Signed as a free agent by **Pittsburgh**, August 6, 1997. • Missed majority of 2001-02 season recovering from leg injury suffered in game vs. Florida, October 28, 2001. Traded to **Los Angeles** by **Pittsburgh** for Martin Strbak and Sergei Anshakov, November 30, 2003. Signed as a free agent by **Plzen** (CzRep), September 17, 2004. Signed as a free agent by **NY Rangers**, August 2, 2005.

STREIT, Mark

(STREET, MAHRK) **MTL.**

Defense. Shoots left. 6', 196 lbs. Born, Englisberg, Switz., December 11, 1977. Montreal's 8th choice, 262nd overall, in 2004 Entry Draft.

Season	Club	League	GP	G	A	Pts	PIM	PP	SH	GW	S	%	+/-	TF	F%	Min	GP	G	A	Pts	PIM	PP	SH	GW	Min
1995-96	Fribourg	Swiss	34	2	2	4	6	....	....	....	....	....	....	....	....	....	4	0	0	0	2	....	....	....	....
1996-97	HC Davos	Swiss	46	2	9	11	18	....	....	....	....	....	....	....	....	....	6	0	0	0	0	....	....	....	....
1997-98	HC Ambri-Piotta	Swiss	2	0	0	0	0	....	....	....	....	....	....	....	....	....	....	....	....	....	....	....	....	....	....
	HC Davos	Swiss	38	4	10	14	14	....	....	....	....	....	....	....	....	....	18	1	5	6	20	....	....	....	....
1998-99	HC Davos	Swiss	44	7	18	25	42	....	....	....	....	....	....	....	....	....	6	3	3	6	8	....	....	....	....

			Regular Season														Playoffs								
Season	Club	League	GP	G	A	Pts	PIM	PP	SH	GW	S	%	+/-	TF	F%	Min	GP	G	A	Pts	PIM	PP	SH	GW	Min
99-2000	Springfield	AHL	43	3	12	15	18	....	....	....	....	....	....	....	....	....	5	0	0	0	2	....	....	....	....
	Utah Grizzlies	IHL	1	0	1	1	2	....	....	....	....	....	....	....	....	....	....	....	....	....	....	....	....	....	....
	Tallahassee	ECHL	14	0	5	5	16	....	....	....	....	....	....	....	....	....	....	....	....	....	....	....	....	....	....
2000-01	ZSC Lions Zurich	Swiss	44	5	11	16	48	....	....	....	....	....	....	....	....	....	16	2	5	7	37	....	....	....	....
2001-02	ZSC Lions Zurich	Swiss	28	6	17	23	36	....	....	....	....	....	....	....	....	....	16	0	6	6	14	....	....	....	....
	Switzerland	Olympics	4	1	1	2	0	....	....	....	....	....	....	....	....	....	....	....	....	....	....	....	....	....	....
2002-03	ZSC Lions Zurich	Swiss	37	4	19	23	62	....	....	....	....	....	....	....	....	....	12	1	7	8	2	....	....	....	....
2003-04	ZSC Lions Zurich	Swiss	48	12	24	36	78	....	....	....	....	....	....	....	....	....	13	5	2	7	14	....	....	....	....
2004-05	ZSC Lions Zurich	Swiss	44	14	29	43	46	....	....	....	....	....	....	....	....	....	15	4	11	15	20	....	....	....	....
2005-06	**Montreal**	**NHL**	**48**	**2**	**9**	**11**	**28**	**2**	**0**	**0**	**52**	**3.8**	**-6**	**1**	**0.0**	**14:36**	**1**	**0**	**0**	**0**	**0**	**0**	**0**	**0**	**3:29**
	Switzerland	Olympics	6	2	1	3	6	....	....	....	....	....	....	....	....	....	....	....	....	....	....	....	....	....	....
2006-07	**Montreal**	**NHL**	**76**	**10**	**26**	**36**	**14**	**2**	**1**	**1**	**102**	**9.8**	**-5**	**12**	**33.3**	**14:01**	....	....	....	....	....	....	....	....	....
	NHL Totals		**124**	**12**	**35**	**47**	**42**	**4**	**1**	**1**	**154**	**7.8**		**13**	**30.8**	**14:14**	**1**	**0**	**0**	**0**	**0**	**0**	**0**	**0**	**3:29**

STRUDWICK, Jason

(STRUHD-wihk, JAY-suhn) **NYR**

Defense. Shoots left. 6'4", 225 lbs. Born, Edmonton, Alta., July 17, 1975. NY Islanders' 3rd choice, 63rd overall, in 1994 Entry Draft.

Season	Club	League	GP	G	A	Pts	PIM	PP	SH	GW	S	%	+/-	TF	F%	Min	GP	G	A	Pts	PIM	PP	SH	GW	Min
1991-92	Edmonton Legion	AMHL	35	3	8	11	67	....	....	....	....	....	....	....	....	....	....	....	....	....	....	....	....	....	....
1992-93	Edmonton Pats	AMHL	33	8	20	28	135	....	....	....	....	....	....	....	....	....	....	....	....	....	....	....	....	....	....
1993-94	Kamloops Blazers	WHL	61	6	8	14	118	....	....	....	....	....	....	....	....	....	19	0	4	4	24	....	....	....	....
1994-95	Kamloops Blazers	WHL	72	3	11	14	183	....	....	....	....	....	....	....	....	....	21	1	1	2	39	....	....	....	....
1995-96	**NY Islanders**	**NHL**	**1**	**0**	**0**	**0**	**7**	**0**	**0**	**0**	**0**	**0.0**	**0**	....	....	....	....	....	....	....	....	....	....	....	....
	Worcester IceCats	AHL	60	2	7	9	119	....	....	....	....	....	....	....	....	....	4	0	1	1	0	....	....	....	....
1996-97	Kentucky	AHL	80	1	9	10	198	....	....	....	....	....	....	....	....	....	4	0	0	0	0	....	....	....	....
1997-98	**NY Islanders**	**NHL**	**17**	**0**	**1**	**1**	**36**	**0**	**0**	**0**	**3**	**0.0**	**1**	....	....	....	....	....	....	....	....	....	....	....	....
	Kentucky	AHL	39	3	1	4	87	....	....	....	....	....	....	....	....	....	....	....	....	....	....	....	....	....	....
	Vancouver	**NHL**	**11**	**0**	**1**	**1**	**29**	**0**	**0**	**0**	**5**	**0.0**	**-3**	....	....	....	....	....	....	....	....	....	....	....	....
	Syracuse Crunch	AHL	....	....	....	....	....	....	....	....	....	....	....	....	....	....	3	0	0	0	6	....	....	....	....
1998-99	**Vancouver**	**NHL**	**65**	**0**	**3**	**3**	**114**	**0**	**0**	**0**	**25**	**0.0**	**-19**	**0**	**0.0**	**12:49**	....	....	....	....	....	....	....	....	....
99-2000	**Vancouver**	**NHL**	**63**	**1**	**3**	**4**	**64**	**0**	**0**	**0**	**18**	**5.6**	**-13**	**0**	**0.0**	**15:12**	....	....	....	....	....	....	....	....	....
2000-01	**Vancouver**	**NHL**	**60**	**1**	**4**	**5**	**64**	**0**	**0**	**1**	**21**	**4.8**	**16**	**0**	**0.0**	**9:59**	**2**	**0**	**0**	**0**	**0**	**0**	**0**	**0**	**2:15**
2001-02	**Vancouver**	**NHL**	**44**	**2**	**4**	**6**	**96**	**0**	**0**	**0**	**13**	**15.4**	**4**	**0**	**0.0**	**9:45**	....	....	....	....	....	....	....	....	....
2002-03	**Chicago**	**NHL**	**48**	**2**	**3**	**5**	**87**	**0**	**0**	**0**	**19**	**10.5**	**-4**	**3**	**0.0**	**8:32**	....	....	....	....	....	....	....	....	....
2003-04	**Chicago**	**NHL**	**54**	**1**	**3**	**4**	**73**	**0**	**0**	**0**	**32**	**3.1**	**-16**	**1**	**0.0**	**14:55**	....	....	....	....	....	....	....	....	....
2004-05	Ferencvaros	Hungary	6	1	2	3	8	....	....	....	....	....	....	....	....	....	....	....	....	....	....	....	....	....	....
2005-06	**NY Rangers**	**NHL**	**65**	**3**	**4**	**7**	**66**	**0**	**0**	**0**	**31**	**9.7**	**-10**	**3**	**33.3**	**15:31**	**3**	**0**	**0**	**0**	**0**	**0**	**0**	**0**	**13:35**
2006-07	**NY Rangers**	**NHL**	**8**	**0**	**0**	**0**	**2**	**0**	**0**	**0**	**3**	**0.0**	**0**	**0**	**0.0**	**13:40**	....	....	....	....	....	....	....	....	....
	HC Lugano	Swiss	34	2	3	5	28	....	....	....	....	....	....	....	....	....	6	0	0	0	4	....	....	....	....
	NHL Totals		**436**	**10**	**26**	**36**	**638**	**0**	**0**	**1**	**170**	**5.9**		**7**	**14.3**	**12:39**	**5**	**0**	**0**	**0**	**0**	**0**	**0**	**0**	**9:03**

Traded to **Vancouver** by **NY Islanders** for Gino Odjick, March 23, 1998. Signed as a free agent by **Chicago**, July 15, 2002. Signed as a free agent by **NY Rangers**, July 20, 2004. Signed as a free agent by **Ferencvaros** (Hungary), January 17, 2005.

STUART, Brad

(STEW-ahrt, BRAD) **L.A.**

Defense. Shoots left. 6'2", 213 lbs. Born, Rocky Mountain House, Alta., November 6, 1979. San Jose's 1st choice, 3rd overall, in 1998 Entry Draft.

Season	Club	League	GP	G	A	Pts	PIM	PP	SH	GW	S	%	+/-	TF	F%	Min	GP	G	A	Pts	PIM	PP	SH	GW	Min
1995-96	Red Deer	AMHL	35	12	25	37	83	....	....	....	....	....	....	....	....	....	....	....	....	....	....	....	....	....	....
	Regina Pats	WHL	3	0	0	0	0	....	....	....	....	....	....	....	....	....	....	....	....	....	....	....	....	....	....
1996-97	Regina Pats	WHL	57	7	36	43	58	....	....	....	....	....	....	....	....	....	5	0	4	4	14	....	....	....	....
1997-98	Regina Pats	WHL	72	20	45	65	82	....	....	....	....	....	....	....	....	....	9	3	4	7	10	....	....	....	....
1998-99	Regina Pats	WHL	29	10	19	29	43	....	....	....	....	....	....	....	....	....	....	....	....	....	....	....	....	....	....
	Calgary Hitmen	WHL	30	11	22	33	26	....	....	....	....	....	....	....	....	....	21	8	15	23	59	....	....	....	....
99-2000	**San Jose**	**NHL**	**82**	**10**	**26**	**36**	**32**	**5**	**1**	**3**	**133**	**7.5**	**3**	**0**	**0.0**	**20:24**	**12**	**1**	**0**	**1**	**6**	**1**	**0**	**0**	**16:30**
2000-01	**San Jose**	**NHL**	**77**	**5**	**18**	**23**	**56**	**1**	**0**	**2**	**119**	**4.2**	**10**	**0**	**0.0**	**20:06**	**5**	**1**	**0**	**1**	**0**	**0**	**0**	**0**	**20:19**
2001-02	**San Jose**	**NHL**	**82**	**6**	**23**	**29**	**39**	**2**	**0**	**2**	**96**	**6.3**	**13**	**0**	**0.0**	**21:41**	**12**	**0**	**3**	**3**	**8**	**0**	**0**	**0**	**19:42**
2002-03	**San Jose**	**NHL**	**36**	**4**	**10**	**14**	**46**	**2**	**0**	**1**	**63**	**6.3**	**-6**	**0**	**0.0**	**20:53**	....	....	....	....	....	....	....	....	....
2003-04	**San Jose**	**NHL**	**77**	**9**	**30**	**39**	**34**	**5**	**0**	**0**	**129**	**7.0**	**9**	**0**	**0.0**	**22:09**	**17**	**1**	**5**	**6**	**13**	**0**	**0**	**0**	**23:23**
2004-05			DID NOT PLAY																						
2005-06	**San Jose**	**NHL**	**23**	**2**	**10**	**12**	**14**	**1**	**0**	**0**	**41**	**4.9**	**-2**	**0**	**0.0**	**23:15**	....	....	....	....	....	....	....	....	....
	Boston	**NHL**	**55**	**10**	**21**	**31**	**38**	**6**	**0**	**2**	**122**	**8.2**	**-6**	**0**	**0.0**	**25:40**	....	....	....	....	....	....	....	....	....
2006-07	**Boston**	**NHL**	**48**	**7**	**10**	**17**	**26**	**1**	**0**	**2**	**74**	**9.5**	**-22**	**0**	**0.0**	**22:55**	....	....	....	....	....	....	....	....	....
	Calgary	**NHL**	**27**	**0**	**5**	**5**	**18**	**0**	**0**	**0**	**35**	**0.0**	**12**	**0**	**0.0**	**22:48**	**6**	**0**	**1**	**1**	**6**	**0**	**0**	**0**	**25:16**
	NHL Totals		**507**	**53**	**153**	**206**	**303**	**23**	**1**	**12**	**812**	**6.5**		**0**	**0.0**	**21:56**	**52**	**3**	**9**	**12**	**33**	**1**	**0**	**0**	**20:52**

WHL East Second All-Star Team (1998) • WHL East First All-Star Team (1999) • Canadian Major Junior First All-Star Team (1999) • Canadian Major Junior Defenseman of the Year (1999) • NHL All-Rookie Team (2000)

• Missed majority of 2002-03 season recovering from ankle (January 4, 2003 vs. Los Angeles) and head (February 21, 2003 vs. Columbus) injuries. Traded to **Boston** by **San Jose** with Marco Sturm and Wayne Primeau for Joe Thornton, November 30, 2005. Traded to **Calgary** by **Boston** with Wayne Primeau for Andrew Ference and Chuck Kobasew, February 10, 2007. Signed as a free agent by **Los Angeles**, July 3, 2007.

STUART, Mark

(STEW-ahrt, MAHRK) **BOS.**

Defense. Shoots left. 6'1", 219 lbs. Born, Rochester, MN, April 27, 1984. Boston's 1st choice, 21st overall, in 2003 Entry Draft.

Season	Club	League	GP	G	A	Pts	PIM	PP	SH	GW	S	%	+/-	TF	F%	Min	GP	G	A	Pts	PIM	PP	SH	GW	Min
99-2000	Roch. Lourdes	High-MN	28	19	22	41	....	....	....	....	....	....	....	....	....	....	....	....	....	....	....	....	....	....	....
2000-01	USNTDP	U-17	12	1	5	6	6	....	....	....	....	....	....	....	....	....	....	....	....	....	....	....	....	....	....
	USNTDP	NAHL	52	2	11	13	114	....	....	....	....	....	....	....	....	....	....	....	....	....	....	....	....	....	....
2001-02	USNTDP	U-18	40	9	9	18	....	....	....	....	....	....	....	....	....	....	....	....	....	....	....	....	....	....	....
	USNTDP	USHL	12	0	1	1	25	....	....	....	....	....	....	....	....	....	....	....	....	....	....	....	....	....	....
	USNTDP	NAHL	9	0	1	1	18	....	....	....	....	....	....	....	....	....	....	....	....	....	....	....	....	....	....
2002-03	Colorado College	WCHA	38	3	17	20	81	....	....	....	....	....	....	....	....	....	....	....	....	....	....	....	....	....	....
2003-04	Colorado College	WCHA	37	4	11	15	100	....	....	....	....	....	....	....	....	....	....	....	....	....	....	....	....	....	....
2004-05	Colorado College	WCHA	43	5	14	19	94	....	....	....	....	....	....	....	....	....	....	....	....	....	....	....	....	....	....
2005-06	**Boston**	**NHL**	**17**	**1**	**1**	**2**	**10**	**0**	**0**	**0**	**9**	**11.1**	**-1**	**0**	**0.0**	**17:46**	....	....	....	....	....	....	....	....	....
	Providence Bruins	AHL	60	4	3	7	76	....	....	....	....	....	....	....	....	....	6	0	0	0	25	....	....	....	....
2006-07	**Boston**	**NHL**	**15**	**0**	**1**	**1**	**14**	**0**	**0**	**0**	**4**	**0.0**	**7**	**0**	**0.0**	**10:23**	....	....	....	....	....	....	....	....	....
	Providence Bruins	AHL	49	4	16	20	62	....	....	....	....	....	....	....	....	....	3	0	1	1	9	....	....	....	....
	NHL Totals		**32**	**1**	**2**	**3**	**24**	**0**	**0**	**0**	**13**	**7.7**		**0**	**0.0**	**14:19**	....	....	....	....	....	....	....	....	....

WCHA All-Rookie Team (2003) • WCHA Second All-Star Team (2005) • NCAA West First All-American Team (2005)

STUART, Mike

(STEW-ahrt, MIGHK)

Defense. Shoots right. 6', 200 lbs. Born, Rochester, MN, August 31, 1980. Nashville's 6th choice, 137th overall, in 2000 Entry Draft.

Season	Club	League	GP	G	A	Pts	PIM	PP	SH	GW	S	%	+/-	TF	F%	Min	GP	G	A	Pts	PIM	PP	SH	GW	Min
1996-97	Rochester	USHL	46	4	9	13	22	....	....	....	....	....	....	....	....	....	....	....	....	....	....	....	....	....	....
1997-98	Rochester	USHL	50	4	15	19	40	....	....	....	....	....	....	....	....	....	....	....	....	....	....	....	....	....	....
1998-99	Colorado College	WCHA	40	2	12	14	44	....	....	....	....	....	....	....	....	....	....	....	....	....	....	....	....	....	....
99-2000	Colorado College	WCHA	32	2	5	7	26	....	....	....	....	....	....	....	....	....	....	....	....	....	....	....	....	....	....
2000-01	Colorado College	WCHA	33	1	13	14	36	....	....	....	....	....	....	....	....	....	....	....	....	....	....	....	....	....	....
2001-02	Colorado College	WCHA	35	3	9	12	46	....	....	....	....	....	....	....	....	....	....	....	....	....	....	....	....	....	....
2002-03	Peoria Rivermen	ECHL	19	2	7	9	12	....	....	....	....	....	....	....	....	....	....	....	....	....	....	....	....	....	....
	Worcester IceCats	AHL	41	1	5	6	19	....	....	....	....	....	....	....	....	....	3	0	0	0	2	....	....	....	....
2003-04	**St. Louis**	**NHL**	**2**	**0**	**0**	**0**	**0**	**0**	**0**	**0**	**0**	**0.0**	**0**	**0**	**0.0**	**9:31**	....	....	....	....	....	....	....	....	....
	Worcester IceCats	AHL	30	0	4	4	20	....	....	....	....	....	....	....	....	....	....	....	....	....	....	....	....	....	....
2004-05	Worcester IceCats	AHL	70	1	10	11	26	....	....	....	....	....	....	....	....	....	....	....	....	....	....	....	....	....	....
2005-06	**St. Louis**	**NHL**	**1**	**0**	**0**	**0**	**0**	**0**	**0**	**0**	**1**	**0.0**	**0**	**0**	**0.0**	**12:59**	....	....	....	....	....	....	....	....	....
	Peoria Rivermen	AHL	56	0	13	13	30	....	....	....	....	....	....	....	....	....	4	0	2	2	0	....	....	....	....
2006-07	Peoria Rivermen	AHL	63	0	9	9	56	....	....	....	....	....	....	....	....	....	....	....	....	....	....	....	....	....	....
	NHL Totals		**3**	**0**	**0**	**0**	**0**	**0**	**0**	**0**	**1**	**0.0**		**0**	**0.0**	**10:40**	....	....	....	....	....	....	....	....	....

USHL All-Rookie Team (1997)

Signed as a free agent by **St. Louis**, October 7, 2002. • Missed majority of 2003-04 season recovering from groin injury suffered in game vs. Hartford (AHL), January 28, 2004.

STUMPEL, Jozef

(STUM-puhl, JOH-zehf) **FLA.**

Center. Shoots right. 6'3", 222 lbs. Born, Nitra, Czech., July 20, 1972. Boston's 2nd choice, 40th overall, in 1991 Entry Draft.

			Regular Season														Playoffs								
Season	Club	League	GP	G	A	Pts	PIM	PP	SH	GW	S	%	+/-	TF	F%	Min	GP	G	A	Pts	PIM	PP	SH	GW	Min
1989-90	Plastika Nitra	Czech-2	38	12	11	23	....	....	....	....	....	....	....	....	....	....	....	....	....	....	....	....	....	....	....
1990-91	AC Nitra	Czech	49	23	22	45	14	....	....	....	....	....	....	....	....	....	....	....	....	....	....	....	....	....	....
1991-92	Kolner EC	Germany	33	19	18	37	35	....	....	....	....	....	....	....	....	....	4	1	1	2	0	....	....	....	....
	Boston	**NHL**	**4**	**1**	**0**	**1**	**0**	**0**	**0**	**0**	**3**	**33.3**	**1**	....	....	....	....	....	....	....	....	....	....	....	....
1992-93	**Boston**	**NHL**	**13**	**1**	**3**	**4**	**4**	**0**	**0**	**0**	**8**	**12.5**	**–3**	....	....	....	....	....	....	....	....	....	....	....	....
	Providence Bruins	AHL	56	31	61	92	26	....	....	....	....	....	....	....	....	....	6	4	4	8	0	....	....	....	....
1993-94	**Boston**	**NHL**	**59**	**8**	**15**	**23**	**14**	**0**	**0**	**1**	**62**	**12.9**	**4**	....	....	....	**13**	**1**	**7**	**8**	**4**	**0**	**0**	**0**	....
	Providence Bruins	AHL	17	5	12	17	4	....	....	....	....	....	....	....	....	....	....	....	....	....	....	....	....	....	....
1994-95	Kolner Haie	Germany	25	16	23	39	18	....	....	....	....	....	....	....	....	....	....	....	....	....	....	....	....	....	....
	Boston	**NHL**	**44**	**5**	**13**	**18**	**8**	**1**	**0**	**2**	**46**	**10.9**	**4**	....	....	....	**5**	**0**	**0**	**0**	**0**	**0**	**0**	**0**	....
1995-96	**Boston**	**NHL**	**76**	**18**	**36**	**54**	**14**	**5**	**0**	**2**	**158**	**11.4**	**–8**	....	....	....	**5**	**1**	**2**	**3**	**0**	**0**	**0**	**0**	....
1996-97	**Boston**	**NHL**	**78**	**21**	**55**	**76**	**14**	**6**	**0**	**1**	**168**	**12.5**	**–22**	....	....	....	....	....	....	....	....	....	....	....	....
1997-98	**Los Angeles**	**NHL**	**77**	**21**	**58**	**79**	**53**	**4**	**0**	**2**	**162**	**13.0**	**17**	....	....	....	**4**	**1**	**2**	**3**	**2**	**0**	**0**	**0**	....
1998-99	**Los Angeles**	**NHL**	**64**	**13**	**21**	**34**	**10**	**1**	**0**	**1**	**131**	**9.9**	**–18**	**1484**	**54.0**	**19:44**	....	....	....	....	....	....	....	....	....
99-2000	**Los Angeles**	**NHL**	**57**	**17**	**41**	**58**	**10**	**3**	**0**	**7**	**126**	**13.5**	**23**	**1088**	**50.6**	**19:16**	**4**	**0**	**4**	**4**	**8**	**0**	**0**	**0**	**21:06**
2000-01	Bratislava	Slovakia	9	2	4	6	16	....	....	....	....	....	....	....	....	....	....	....	....	....	....	....	....	....	....
	Los Angeles	**NHL**	**63**	**16**	**39**	**55**	**14**	**9**	**0**	**6**	**95**	**16.8**	**20**	**1278**	**52.7**	**19:35**	**13**	**3**	**5**	**8**	**10**	**2**	**0**	**1**	**21:56**
2001-02	**Los Angeles**	**NHL**	**9**	**1**	**3**	**4**	**4**	**0**	**0**	**0**	**7**	**14.3**	**1**	**164**	**48.2**	**20:06**	....	....	....	....	....	....	....	....	....
	Boston	**NHL**	**72**	**7**	**47**	**54**	**14**	**1**	**0**	**3**	**93**	**7.5**	**21**	**1346**	**49.7**	**18:36**	**6**	**0**	**2**	**2**	**0**	**0**	**0**	**0**	**16:43**
	Slovakia	Olympics	2	2	1	3	0	....	....	....	....	....	....	....	....	....	....	....	....	....	....	....	....	....	....
2002-03	**Boston**	**NHL**	**78**	**14**	**37**	**51**	**12**	**4**	**0**	**2**	**110**	**12.7**	**0**	**1601**	**54.7**	**18:27**	**5**	**0**	**2**	**2**	**0**	**0**	**0**	**0**	**17:31**
2003-04	**Los Angeles**	**NHL**	**64**	**8**	**29**	**37**	**16**	**4**	**0**	**0**	**78**	**10.3**	**5**	**1105**	**49.3**	**18:46**	....	....	....	....	....	....	....	....	....
2004-05	HC Slavia Praha	CzRep	52	13	26	39	41	....	....	....	....	....	....	....	....	....	7	4	2	6	10	....	....	....	....
2005-06	**Florida**	**NHL**	**74**	**15**	**37**	**52**	**26**	**3**	**1**	**1**	**115**	**13.0**	**11**	**916**	**49.1**	**17:47**	....	....	....	....	....	....	....	....	....
	Slovakia	Olympics	3	0	0	0	0	....	....	....	....	....	....	....	....	....	....	....	....	....	....	....	....	....	....
2006-07	**Florida**	**NHL**	**73**	**23**	**34**	**57**	**22**	**9**	**2**	**4**	**131**	**17.6**	**2**	**986**	**50.5**	**19:07**	....	....	....	....	....	....	....	....	....
	NHL Totals		**905**	**189**	**468**	**657**	**235**	**50**	**3**	**32**	**1493**	**12.7**		**9968**	**51.6**	**18:54**	**55**	**6**	**24**	**30**	**24**	**2**	**0**	**1**	**19:55**

Traded to **Los Angeles** by **Boston** with Sandy Moger and Boston's 4th round choice (later traded to New Jersey – New Jersey selected Pierre Dagenais) in 1998 Entry Draft for Dmitri Kristich and Byron Dafoe, August 29, 1997. Traded to **Boston** by **Los Angeles** with Glen Murray for Jason Allison and Mikko Eloranta, October 24, 2001. Traded to **Los Angeles** by **Boston** with Boston's 7th round choice (later traded to Nashville – Nashville selected Miroslav Hanuljak) in 2003 Entry Draft for Philadelphia's 4th round choice (previously acquired, Boston selected Patrick Valcak) in 2003 Entry Draft and Detroit's 2nd round choice (previously acquired, Boston selected Martins Karsums) in 2004 Entry Draft, June 22, 2003. Signed as a free agent by **Slavia Praha** (CzRep), August 28, 2004. Signed as a free agent by **Florida**, August 17, 2005.

STURM, Marco

(STURHM, MAHR-koh) **BOS.**

Left wing. Shoots left. 6', 198 lbs. Born, Dingolfing, West Germany, September 8, 1978. San Jose's 2nd choice, 21st overall, in 1996 Entry Draft.

			Regular Season														Playoffs								
Season	Club	League	GP	G	A	Pts	PIM	PP	SH	GW	S	%	+/-	TF	F%	Min	GP	G	A	Pts	PIM	PP	SH	GW	Min
1995-96	EV Landshut	Germany	47	12	20	32	50	....	....	....	....	....	....	....	....	....	11	1	3	4	18	....	....	....	....
1996-97	EV Landshut	Germany	46	16	27	43	40	....	....	....	....	....	....	....	....	....	7	1	4	5	6	....	....	....	....
1997-98	**San Jose**	**NHL**	**74**	**10**	**20**	**30**	**40**	**2**	**0**	**3**	**118**	**8.5**	**–2**	....	....	....	**2**	**0**	**0**	**0**	**0**	**0**	**0**	**0**	....
	Germany	Olympics	2	0	0	0	0	....	....	....	....	....	....	....	....	....	....	....	....	....	....	....	....	....	....
1998-99	**San Jose**	**NHL**	**78**	**16**	**22**	**38**	**52**	**3**	**2**	**3**	**140**	**11.4**	**7**	**576**	**45.0**	**15:23**	**6**	**2**	**2**	**4**	**4**	**0**	**0**	**1**	**14:16**
99-2000	**San Jose**	**NHL**	**74**	**12**	**15**	**27**	**22**	**2**	**4**	**3**	**120**	**10.0**	**4**	**183**	**45.4**	**14:07**	**12**	**1**	**3**	**4**	**6**	**0**	**0**	**0**	**13:00**
2000-01	**San Jose**	**NHL**	**81**	**14**	**18**	**32**	**28**	**2**	**3**	**5**	**153**	**9.2**	**9**	**517**	**40.2**	**16:06**	**6**	**0**	**2**	**2**	**0**	**0**	**0**	**0**	**18:18**
2001-02	**San Jose**	**NHL**	**77**	**21**	**20**	**41**	**32**	**4**	**3**	**5**	**174**	**12.1**	**23**	**105**	**47.6**	**15:39**	**12**	**3**	**2**	**5**	**2**	**0**	**0**	**0**	**15:33**
	Germany	Olympics	5	0	1	1	0	....	....	....	....	....	....	....	....	....	....	....	....	....	....	....	....	....	....
2002-03	**San Jose**	**NHL**	**82**	**28**	**20**	**48**	**16**	**6**	**0**	**2**	**208**	**13.5**	**9**	**83**	**48.2**	**16:31**	....	....	....	....	....	....	....	....	....
2003-04	**San Jose**	**NHL**	**64**	**21**	**20**	**41**	**36**	**10**	**2**	**6**	**158**	**13.3**	**0**	**7**	**42.9**	**16:25**	....	....	....	....	....	....	....	....	....
2004-05	ERC Ingolstadt	Germany	45	22	16	38	56	....	....	....	....	....	....	....	....	....	11	3	4	7	12	....	....	....	....
2005-06	**San Jose**	**NHL**	**23**	**6**	**10**	**16**	**16**	**3**	**0**	**0**	**48**	**12.5**	**–8**	**9**	**44.4**	**17:28**	....	....	....	....	....	....	....	....	....
	Boston	**NHL**	**51**	**23**	**20**	**43**	**32**	**5**	**0**	**6**	**132**	**17.4**	**14**	**3**	**33.3**	**18:44**	....	....	....	....	....	....	....	....	....
2006-07	**Boston**	**NHL**	**76**	**27**	**17**	**44**	**46**	**10**	**2**	**1**	**224**	**12.1**	**–24**	**13**	**61.5**	**18:36**	....	....	....	....	....	....	....	....	....
	NHL Totals		**680**	**178**	**182**	**360**	**320**	**47**	**16**	**34**	**1475**	**12.1**		**1496**	**43.9**	**16:23**	**38**	**6**	**9**	**15**	**12**	**0**	**0**	**1**	**14:56**

Played in NHL All-Star Game (1999)

Signed as a free agent by **Ingolstadt** (Germany), August 8, 2004. Traded to **Boston** by **San Jose** with Brad Stuart and Wayne Primeau for Joe Thornton, November 30, 2005.

SUCHY, Radoslav

(soo-KHEE, RAD-oh-slav)

Defense. Shoots left. 6'2", 204 lbs. Born, Kezmarok, Czech., April 7, 1976.

			Regular Season														Playoffs								
Season	Club	League	GP	G	A	Pts	PIM	PP	SH	GW	S	%	+/-	TF	F%	Min	GP	G	A	Pts	PIM	PP	SH	GW	Min
1993-94	SKP PS Poprad Jr.	Slovak-Jr.	30	11	12	23	16	....	....	....	....	....	....	....	....	....	....	....	....	....	....	....	....	....	....
	SKP PS Poprad	Slovakia	3	0	0	0	0	....	....	....	....	....	....	....	....	....	....	....	....	....	....	....	....	....	....
1994-95	Sherbrooke	QMJHL	69	12	32	44	30	....	....	....	....	....	....	....	....	....	7	0	3	3	2	....	....	....	....
1995-96	Sherbrooke	QMJHL	68	15	53	68	68	....	....	....	....	....	....	....	....	....	7	0	3	3	2	....	....	....	....
1996-97	Sherbrooke	QMJHL	32	6	34	40	14	....	....	....	....	....	....	....	....	....	....	....	....	....	....	....	....	....	....
	Chicoutimi	QMJHL	28	5	24	29	26	....	....	....	....	....	....	....	....	....	19	6	15	21	12	....	....	....	....
1997-98	Las Vegas	IHL	26	1	4	5	10	....	....	....	....	....	....	....	....	....	....	....	....	....	....	....	....	....	....
	Springfield	AHL	41	6	15	21	16	....	....	....	....	....	....	....	....	....	4	0	1	1	2	....	....	....	....
1998-99	Springfield	AHL	69	4	32	36	10	....	....	....	....	....	....	....	....	....	3	0	1	1	0	....	....	....	....
99-2000	**Phoenix**	**NHL**	**60**	**0**	**6**	**6**	**16**	**0**	**0**	**0**	**36**	**0.0**	**2**	**0**	**0.0**	**15:09**	**5**	**0**	**1**	**1**	**0**	**0**	**0**	**0**	**16:18**
	Springfield	AHL	2	0	1	1	0	....	....	....	....	....	....	....	....	....	....	....	....	....	....	....	....	....	....
2000-01	**Phoenix**	**NHL**	**72**	**0**	**10**	**10**	**22**	**0**	**0**	**0**	**33**	**0.0**	**1**	**0**	**0.0**	**17:09**	....	....	....	....	....	....	....	....	....
2001-02	**Phoenix**	**NHL**	**81**	**4**	**13**	**17**	**10**	**1**	**0**	**0**	**49**	**8.2**	**25**	**1**	**100.0**	**18:05**	**5**	**1**	**0**	**1**	**0**	**0**	**0**	**0**	**20:35**
2002-03	**Phoenix**	**NHL**	**77**	**1**	**8**	**9**	**18**	**1**	**0**	**0**	**48**	**2.1**	**2**	**1**	**0.0**	**16:26**	....	....	....	....	....	....	....	....	....
2003-04	**Phoenix**	**NHL**	**82**	**7**	**14**	**21**	**8**	**2**	**0**	**2**	**82**	**8.5**	**1**	**1**	**100.0**	**19:40**	....	....	....	....	....	....	....	....	....
2004-05	HK SKP Poprad	Slovakia	34	5	10	15	24	....	....	....	....	....	....	....	....	....	5	0	0	0	2	....	....	....	....
2005-06	**Columbus**	**NHL**	**79**	**1**	**7**	**8**	**30**	**0**	**0**	**0**	**33**	**3.0**	**–8**	**0**	**0.0**	**19:55**	....	....	....	....	....	....	....	....	....
	Slovakia	Olympics	6	1	1	2	0	....	....	....	....	....	....	....	....	....	....	....	....	....	....	....	....	....	....
2006-07	ZSC Lions Zurich	Swiss	44	4	10	14	38	....	....	....	....	....	....	....	....	....	7	0	0	0	12	....	....	....	....
	NHL Totals		**451**	**13**	**58**	**71**	**104**	**4**	**0**	**2**	**281**	**4.6**		**3**	**66.7**	**17:52**	**10**	**1**	**1**	**2**	**0**	**0**	**0**	**0**	**18:27**

QMJHL All-Rookie Team (1995) • QMJHL Second All-Star Team (1997) • George Parsons Trophy (Memorial Cup Tournament Most Sportsmanlike Player) (1997)

Signed as a free agent by **Phoenix**, September 26, 1997. Traded to **Columbus** by **Phoenix** with Phoenix's 6th round choice (Derek Reinhart) in 2005 Entry Draft for Columbus' 4th round choice (later traded to Philadelphia - Philadelphia selected Jeremy Duchesne) in 2005 Entry Draft, July 6, 2004. Signed as a free agent by **Poprad** (Slovakia), October 4, 2004. Signed as a free agent by **Zurich** (Swiss), August 18, 2006.

SUGLOBOV, Alexander

(suh-GLOH-bahf, al-EHX-AN-duhr)

Right wing. Shoots left. 6', 200 lbs. Born, Elektrostal, USSR, January 15, 1982. New Jersey's 3rd choice, 56th overall, in 2000 Entry Draft.

			Regular Season														Playoffs								
Season	Club	League	GP	G	A	Pts	PIM	PP	SH	GW	S	%	+/-	TF	F%	Min	GP	G	A	Pts	PIM	PP	SH	GW	Min
1998-99	Spartak 2	Russia-4	1	0	0	0	0	....	....	....	....	....	....	....	....	....	....	....	....	....	....	....	....	....	....
	Spartak Moscow	Russia	1	0	0	0	0	....	....	....	....	....	....	....	....	....	....	....	....	....	....	....	....	....	....
99-2000	Yaroslavl 2	Russia-3	38	23	10	33	....	....	....	....	....	....	....	....	....	....	....	....	....	....	....	....	....	....	....
2000-01	St. Petersburg	Russia	8	1	0	1	6	....	....	....	....	....	....	....	....	....	....	....	....	....	....	....	....	....	....
	Ufa	Russia	6	0	0	0	4	....	....	....	....	....	....	....	....	....	....	....	....	....	....	....	....	....	....
	Yaroslavl	Russia	4	0	0	0	2	....	....	....	....	....	....	....	....	....	11	1	2	3	6	....	....	....	....
2001-02	Yaroslavl 2	Russia-3	6	5	2	7	20	....	....	....	....	....	....	....	....	....	....	....	....	....	....	....	....	....	....
	Yaroslavl	Russia	25	4	2	6	26	....	....	....	....	....	....	....	....	....	5	1	1	2	18	....	....	....	....
2002-03	Nizhnekamsk	Russia	6	0	0	0	4	....	....	....	....	....	....	....	....	....	....	....	....	....	....	....	....	....	....
	Yaroslavl	Russia	17	4	2	6	12	....	....	....	....	....	....	....	....	....	5	1	0	1	2	....	....	....	....
2003-04	**New Jersey**	**NHL**	**1**	**0**	**0**	**0**	**0**	**0**	**0**	**0**	**2**	**0.0**	**0**	**0**	**0.0**	**8:18**	....	....	....	....	....	....	....	....	....
	Albany River Rats	AHL	35	11	11	22	54	....	....	....	....	....	....	....	....	....	....	....	....	....	....	....	....	....	....
2004-05	Albany River Rats	AHL	72	25	21	46	77	....	....	....	....	....	....	....	....	....	....	....	....	....	....	....	....	....	....
2005-06	**New Jersey**	**NHL**	**1**	**1**	**0**	**1**	**0**	**1**	**0**	**0**	**2**	**50.0**	**–2**	**0**	**0.0**	**12:55**	....	....	....	....	....	....	....	....	....
	Albany River Rats	AHL	51	25	23	48	52	....	....	....	....	....	....	....	....	....	....	....	....	....	....	....	....	....	....
	Toronto	**NHL**	**2**	**0**	**0**	**0**	**0**	**0**	**0**	**0**	**3**	**0.0**	**–1**	**0**	**0.0**	**11:31**	....	....	....	....	....	....	....	....	....
	Toronto Marlies	AHL	15	8	2	10	21	....	....	....	....	....	....	....	....	....	5	5	2	7	2	....	....	....	....

			Regular Season														Playoffs								
Season	Club	League	GP	G	A	Pts	PIM	PP	SH	GW	S	%	+/-	TF	F%	Min	GP	G	A	Pts	PIM	PP	SH	GW	Min
2006-07	Toronto	NHL	14	0	0	0	4	0	0	0	17	0.0	–6	0	0.0	7:25	....	....	....	....	....	....	....	....	....
	Toronto Marlies	AHL	32	3	10	13	16	....	....	....	....	....	....	....	....	....	....	....	....	....	....	....	....	....	....
	NHL Totals		18	1	0	1	4	1	0	0	24	4.2		0	0.0	8:14									

• Missed majority of 2003 04 season recovering from wrist injury suffered in game vs. Edmonton, January 5, 2004. Traded to **Toronto** by **New Jersey** for Ken Klee, March 8, 2006. Signed as a free agent by **St. Petersburg** (Russia), May 21, 2007.

SULLIVAN, Steve (SUHL-ih-vuhn, STEEV) NSH.

Right wing. Shoots right. 5'8", 165 lbs. Born, Timmins, Ont., July 6, 1974. New Jersey's 10th choice, 233rd overall, in 1994 Entry Draft.

Season	Club	League	GP	G	A	Pts	PIM	PP	SH	GW	S	%	+/-	TF	F%	Min	GP	G	A	Pts	PIM	PP	SH	GW	Min
1991-92	Timmins	NOJHA	47	66	55	121	141	....	....	....	....	....	....	....	....	....	....	....	....	....	....	....	....	....	....
1992-93	Sault Ste. Marie	OHL	62	36	27	63	44	....	....	....	....	....	....	....	....	....	16	3	8	11	18	....	....	....	....
1993-94	Sault Ste. Marie	OHL	63	51	62	113	82	....	....	....	....	....	....	....	....	....	14	9	16	25	22	....	....	....	....
1994-95	Albany River Rats	AHL	75	31	50	81	124	....	....	....	....	....	....	....	....	....	14	4	7	11	10	....	....	....	....
1995-96	New Jersey	NHL	16	5	4	9	8	2	0	1	23	21.7	3	....	....	....	....	....	....	....	....	....	....	....	....
	Albany River Rats	AHL	53	33	42	75	127	....	....	....	....	....	....	....	....	....	4	3	0	3	6	....	....	....	....
1996-97	New Jersey	NHL	33	8	14	22	14	2	0	2	63	12.7	9	....	....	....	....	....	....	....	....	....	....	....	....
	Albany River Rats	AHL	15	8	7	15	16	....	....	....	....	....	....	....	....	....	....	....	....	....	....	....	....	....	....
	Toronto	NHL	21	5	11	16	23	1	0	1	45	11.1	5	....	....	....	....	....	....	....	....	....	....	....	....
1997-98	Toronto	NHL	63	10	18	28	40	1	0	1	112	8.9	–8	....	....	....	....	....	....	....	....	....	....	....	....
1998-99	Toronto	NHL	63	20	20	40	28	4	0	5	110	18.2	12	685	44.4	14:12	13	3	3	6	14	2	0	0	16:20
99-2000	Toronto	NHL	7	0	1	1	4	0	0	0	11	0.0	–1	47	48.9	11:52	....	....	....	....	....	....	....	....	....
	Chicago	NHL	73	22	42	64	52	2	1	6	169	13.0	20	692	48.0	18:05	....	....	....	....	....	....	....	....	....
2000-01	Chicago	NHL	81	34	41	75	54	6	8	3	204	16.7	3	649	42.4	20:32	....	....	....	....	....	....	....	....	....
2001-02	Chicago	NHL	78	21	39	60	67	3	0	8	155	13.5	23	758	48.9	19:10	5	1	0	1	2	0	0	0	18:04
2002-03	Chicago	NHL	82	26	35	61	42	4	2	3	190	13.7	15	382	46.1	19:15	....	....	....	....	....	....	....	....	....
2003-04	Chicago	NHL	56	15	28	43	36	4	2	4	140	10.7	–7	103	44.7	21:19	....	....	....	....	....	....	....	....	....
	Nashville	NHL	24	9	21	30	12	7	0	0	78	11.5	8	124	43.6	20:02	6	1	1	2	6	0	0	1	18:58
2004-05			DID NOT PLAY																						
2005-06	Nashville	NHL	69	31	37	68	50	13	4	5	192	16.1	2	42	52.4	19:06	5	0	2	2	0	0	0	0	17:02
2006-07	Nashville	NHL	57	22	38	60	20	6	3	4	122	18.0	16	39	38.5	19:25	....	....	....	....	....	....	....	....	....
	NHL Totals		723	228	349	577	450	55	20	43	1614	14.1		3521	46.0	18:52	29	5	6	11	22	2	0	1	17:18

AHL First All-Star Team (1996)

Traded to **Toronto** by **New Jersey** with Jason Smith and the rights to Alyn McCauley for Doug Gilmour, Dave Ellett and New Jersey's 3rd round choice (previously acquired, New Jersey selected Andre Lakos) in 1999 Entry Draft, February 25, 1997. Claimed on waivers by **Chicago** from **Toronto**, October 23, 1999. Traded to **Nashville** by **Chicago** for Nashville's 2nd round choices in 2004 (Ryan Garlock) and 2005 (Michael Blunden) Entry Drafts, February 16, 2004.

SUNDIN, Mats (suhn-DEEN, MATS) TOR.

Center. Shoots right. 6'5", 231 lbs. Born, Bromma, Sweden, February 13, 1971. Quebec's 1st choice, 1st overall, in 1989 Entry Draft.

Season	Club	League	GP	G	A	Pts	PIM	PP	SH	GW	S	%	+/-	TF	F%	Min	GP	G	A	Pts	PIM	PP	SH	GW	Min
1988-89	Nacka HK	Sweden-2	25	10	8	18	18	....	....	....	....	....	....	....	....	....	....	....	....	....	....	....	....	....	....
1989-90	Djurgarden	Sweden	34	10	8	18	16	....	....	....	....	....	....	....	....	....	8	7	0	7	4	....	....	....	....
1990-91	Quebec	NHL	80	23	36	59	58	4	0	0	155	14.8	–24	....	....	....	....	....	....	....	....	....	....	....	....
1991-92	Quebec	NHL	80	33	43	76	103	8	2	2	231	14.3	–19	....	....	....	....	....	....	....	....	....	....	....	....
1992-93	Quebec	NHL	80	47	67	114	96	13	4	9	215	21.9	21	....	....	....	6	3	1	4	6	1	0	0	....
1993-94	Quebec	NHL	84	32	53	85	60	6	2	4	226	14.2	1	....	....	....	....	....	....	....	....	....	....	....	....
1994-95	Djurgarden	Sweden	12	7	2	9	14	....	....	....	....	....	....	....	....	....	....	....	....	....	....	....	....	....	....
	Toronto	NHL	47	23	24	47	14	9	0	4	173	13.3	–5	....	....	....	7	5	4	9	4	2	0	1	....
1995-96	Toronto	NHL	76	33	50	83	46	7	6	7	301	11.0	8	....	....	....	6	3	1	4	4	2	0	1	....
1996-97	Toronto	NHL	82	41	53	94	59	7	4	8	281	14.6	6	....	....	....	....	....	....	....	....	....	....	....	....
1997-98	Toronto	NHL	82	33	41	74	49	9	1	5	219	15.1	–3	....	....	....	....	....	....	....	....	....	....	....	....
	Sweden	Olympics	4	3	0	3	4	....	....	....	....	....	....	....	....	....	....	....	....	....	....	....	....	....	....
1998-99	Toronto	NHL	82	31	52	83	58	4	0	6	209	14.8	22	1993	57.3	20:41	17	8	8	16	16	3	0	2	22:46
99-2000	Toronto	NHL	73	32	41	73	46	10	2	7	184	17.4	16	1619	50.8	20:11	12	3	5	8	10	0	0	1	21:27
2000-01	Toronto	NHL	82	28	46	74	76	9	0	6	226	12.4	15	1870	56.6	19:21	11	6	7	13	14	2	1	1	20:12
2001-02	Toronto	NHL	82	41	39	80	94	10	2	9	262	15.6	6	1812	57.5	19:20	8	2	5	7	4	0	0	0	20:07
	Sweden	Olympics	4	5	4	*9	10	....	....	....	....	....	....	....	....	....	....	....	....	....	....	....	....	....	....
2002-03	Toronto	NHL	75	37	35	72	58	16	3	8	223	16.6	1	1774	56.1	20:15	7	1	3	4	6	1	0	0	24:17
2003-04	Toronto	NHL	81	31	44	75	52	11	1	10	226	13.7	11	1705	53.0	19:52	9	4	5	9	8	0	0	1	18:24
2004-05			DID NOT PLAY																						
2005-06	Toronto	NHL	70	31	47	78	58	16	2	2	220	14.1	7	1557	54.0	19:59	....	....	....	....	....	....	....	....	....
	Sweden	Olympics	8	3	5	8	4	....	....	....	....	....	....	....	....	....	....	....	....	....	....	....	....	....	....
2006-07	Toronto	NHL	75	27	49	76	62	6	1	3	321	8.4	–2	1790	55.2	20:28	....	....	....	....	....	....	....	....	....
	NHL Totals		1231	523	720	1243	989	145	30	90	3672	14.2		14120	55.2	20:00	83	35	39	74	72	11	1	7	21:18

NHL Second All-Star Team (2002, 2004)

Played in NHL All-Star Game (1996, 1997, 1998, 1999, 2000, 2001, 2002, 2004)

Traded to **Toronto** by **Quebec** with Garth Butcher, Todd Warriner and Philadelphia's 1st round choice (previously acquired, later traded to Washington – Washington selected Nolan Baumgartner) in 1994 Entry Draft for Wendel Clark, Sylvain Lefebvre, Landon Wilson and Toronto's 1st round choice (Jeffrey Kealty) in 1994 Entry Draft, June 28, 1994.

SUNDSTROM, Niklas (SUHND-struhm, NIHK-luhs)

Right wing. Shoots left. 6', 191 lbs. Born, Ornskoldsvik, Sweden, June 6, 1975. NY Rangers' 1st choice, 8th overall, in 1993 Entry Draft.

Season	Club	League	GP	G	A	Pts	PIM	PP	SH	GW	S	%	+/-	TF	F%	Min	GP	G	A	Pts	PIM	PP	SH	GW	Min
1991-92	MoDo	Sweden	9	1	3	4	0	....	....	....	....	....	....	....	....	....	....	....	....	....	....	....	....	....	....
1992-93	MoDo Jr.	Swe-Jr.	2	3	1	4	0	....	....	....	....	....	....	....	....	....	....	....	....	....	....	....	....	....	....
	MoDo	Sweden	40	7	11	18	18	....	....	....	....	....	....	....	....	....	3	0	0	0	0	....	....	....	....
1993-94	MoDo Jr.	Swe-Jr.	3	3	4	7	2	....	....	....	....	....	....	....	....	....	....	....	....	....	....	....	....	....	....
	MoDo	Sweden	37	7	12	19	28	....	....	....	....	....	....	....	....	....	11	4	3	7	2	....	....	....	....
1994-95	MoDo	Sweden	33	8	13	21	30	....	....	....	....	....	....	....	....	....	....	....	....	....	....	....	....	....	....
1995-96	NY Rangers	NHL	82	9	12	21	14	1	1	2	90	10.0	2	....	....	....	11	4	3	7	4	1	0	0	....
1996-97	NY Rangers	NHL	82	24	28	52	20	5	1	4	132	18.2	23	....	....	....	9	0	5	5	2	0	0	0	....
1997-98	NY Rangers	NHL	70	19	28	47	24	4	0	1	115	16.5	0	....	....	....	....	....	....	....	....	....	....	....	....
	Sweden	Olympics	4	1	1	2	2	....	....	....	....	....	....	....	....	....	....	....	....	....	....	....	....	....	....
1998-99	NY Rangers	NHL	81	13	30	43	20	1	2	3	89	14.6	–2	376	40.4	19:11	....	....	....	....	....	....	....	....	....
99-2000	San Jose	NHL	79	12	25	37	22	2	1	2	90	13.3	9	10	50.0	15:10	12	0	2	2	2	0	0	0	15:09
2000-01	San Jose	NHL	82	10	39	49	28	4	1	0	100	10.0	10	26	30.8	16:44	6	0	3	3	2	0	0	0	16:40
2001-02	San Jose	NHL	73	9	30	39	50	0	1	0	74	12.2	7	9	33.3	15:57	12	1	6	7	6	0	0	0	16:25
	Sweden	Olympics	4	1	3	4	0	....	....	....	....	....	....	....	....	....	....	....	....	....	....	....	....	....	....
2002-03	San Jose	NHL	47	2	10	12	22	0	0	0	36	5.6	–4	1	0.0	14:09	....	....	....	....	....	....	....	....	....
	Montreal	NHL	33	5	9	14	8	0	0	1	35	14.3	3	10	40.0	14:26	....	....	....	....	....	....	....	....	....
2003-04	Montreal	NHL	66	8	12	20	18	0	0	2	67	11.9	3	20	15.0	14:17	4	1	0	1	2	0	0	0	13:10
2004-05	Milano Vipers	Italy	33	9	27	36	40	....	....	....	....	....	....	....	....	....	15	4	14	18	20	....	....	....	....
2005-06	Montreal	NHL	55	6	9	15	30	0	0	2	54	11.1	–6	11	18.2	14:02	5	0	3	3	4	0	0	0	9:29
2006-07	MODO	Sweden	47	9	36	45	116	....	....	....	....	....	....	....	....	....	20	5	8	13	26	....	....	....	....
	NHL Totals		750	117	232	349	256	17	7	17	882	13.3		463	38.2	15:47	59	6	22	28	22	1	0	0	14:51

Traded to **Tampa Bay** by **NY Rangers** with Dan Cloutier and NY Rangers' 1st (Nikita Alexeev) and 3rd (later traded to San Jose – later traded to Chicago – Chicago selected Igor Radulov) round choices in 2000 Entry Draft for Chicago's 1st round choice (previously acquired, NY Rangers selected Pavel Brendl) in 1999 Entry Draft, June 26, 1999. Traded to **San Jose** by **Tampa Bay** with NY Rangers' 3rd round choice (previously acquired, later traded to Chicago – Chicago selected Igor Radulov) in 2000 Entry Draft for Bill Houlder, Andrei Zyuzin, Shawn Burr and Steve Guolla, August 4, 1999. Traded to **Montreal** by **San Jose** with San Jose's 3rd round choice (later traded to Los Angeles – Los Angeles selected Paul Baier) in 2004 Entry Draft for Jeff Hackett, January 23, 2003. Signed as a free agent by **Milano** (Italy), October 1, 2004.

SUROVY, Tomas (suh-ROH-vee, TAW-mahsh) PHX.

Center. Shoots left. 6'1", 205 lbs. Born, Banska Bystrica, Czech., September 24, 1981. Pittsburgh's 5th choice, 120th overall, in 2001 Entry Draft.

Season	Club	League	GP	G	A	Pts	PIM	PP	SH	GW	S	%	+/-	TF	F%	Min	GP	G	A	Pts	PIM	PP	SH	GW	Min
99-2000	B. Bystrica	Slovak-2	39	25	29	54	4	....	....	....	....	....	....	....	....	....	....	....	....	....	....	....	....	....	....
2000-01	HC SKP Poprad	Slovakia	53	22	28	50	30	....	....	....	....	....	....	....	....	....	6	2	1	3	14	....	....	....	....
2001-02	Wilkes-Barre	AHL	65	23	10	33	37	....	....	....	....	....	....	....	....	....	....	....	....	....	....	....	....	....	....
2002-03	Pittsburgh	NHL	26	4	7	11	10	1	0	2	47	8.5	0	2	50.0	14:19	....	....	....	....	....	....	....	....	....
	Wilkes-Barre	AHL	39	19	20	39	18	....	....	....	....	....	....	....	....	....	6	2	3	5	2	....	....	....	....
2003-04	Pittsburgh	NHL	47	11	12	23	16	3	0	1	112	9.8	–8	4	25.0	12:28	....	....	....	....	....	....	....	....	....
	Wilkes-Barre	AHL	30	14	15	29	14	....	....	....	....	....	....	....	....	....	24	6	10	16	8	....	....	....	....
2004-05	Wilkes-Barre	AHL	80	17	32	49	43	....	....	....	....	....	....	....	....	....	11	2	6	8	9	....	....	....	....

			Regular Season														Playoffs								
Season	Club	League	GP	G	A	Pts	PIM	PP	SH	GW	S	%	+/-	TF	F%	Min	GP	G	A	Pts	PIM	PP	SH	GW	Min
2005-06	Pittsburgh	NHL	53	12	13	25	45	3	0	1	107	11.2	–13	11	36.4	13:35	....	....	....	....	....	....	....	....	....
	Wilkes-Barre	AHL	25	16	12	28	26	....	....	....	....	....	....	....	....	....	....	....	....	....	....	....	....	....	....
	Slovakia	Olympics	6	0	1	1	2	....	....	....	....	....	....	....	....	....	....	....	....	....	....	....	....	....	....
2006-07	Lulea HF	Sweden	55	23	32	55	38	....	....	....	....	....	....	....	....	....	4	1	1	2	29	....	....	....	....
	NHL Totals		126	27	32	59	71	7	0	4	266	10.2		17	35.3	13:19	....	....	....	....	....	....	....	....	....

Signed as a free agent by **Lulea** (Sweden), August 16, 2006. Signed as a free agent by **Phoenix**, July 13, 2007.

SUTER, Ryan

(SOO-tuhr, RIGH-uhn) **NSH.**

Defense. Shoots left. 6'1", 196 lbs. Born, Madison, WI, January 21, 1985. Nashville's 1st choice, 7th overall, in 2003 Entry Draft.

Season	Club	League	GP	G	A	Pts	PIM	PP	SH	GW	S	%	+/-	TF	F%	Min	GP	G	A	Pts	PIM	PP	SH	GW	Min
2000-01	Culver Academy	High-IN	26	13	32	45	....	....	....	....	....	....	....	....	....	....	....	....	....	....	....	....	....	....	....
2001-02	USNTDP	U-17	8	2	11	13	21	....	....	....	....	....	....	....	....	....	....	....	....	....	....	....	....	....	....
	USNTDP	U-18	27	4	10	14	6	....	....	....	....	....	....	....	....	....	....	....	....	....	....	....	....	....	....
	USNTDP	NAHL	35	2	10	12	75	....	....	....	....	....	....	....	....	....	....	....	....	....	....	....	....	....	....
2002-03	USNTDP	U-18	42	7	17	24	124	....	....	....	....	....	....	....	....	....	....	....	....	....	....	....	....	....	....
	USNTDP	NAHL	9	2	5	7	12	....	....	....	....	....	....	....	....	....	....	....	....	....	....	....	....	....	....
2003-04	U. of Wisconsin	WCHA	39	3	16	19	93	....	....	....	....	....	....	....	....	....	....	....	....	....	....	....	....	....	....
2004-05	Milwaukee	AHL	63	7	16	23	70	....	....	....	....	....	....	....	....	....	7	1	5	6	16	....	....	....	....
2005-06	**Nashville**	**NHL**	**71**	**1**	**15**	**16**	**66**	0	0	0	84	1.2	7	0	0.0	17:21	....	....	....	....	....	....	....	....	....
2006-07	**Nashville**	**NHL**	**82**	**8**	**16**	**24**	**54**	1	0	0	87	9.2	10	0	0.0	20:09	5	1	0	1	8	0	0	0	23:19
	NHL Totals		**153**	**9**	**31**	**40**	**120**	1	0	0	171	5.3		0	0.0	18:51	5	1	0	1	8	0	0	0	23:19

WCHA All-Rookie Team (2004)

SUTHERBY, Brian

(SUH-thur-bee, BRIGH-uhn) **WSH.**

Center. Shoots left. 6'3", 215 lbs. Born, Edmonton, Alta., March 1, 1982. Washington's 1st choice, 26th overall, in 2000 Entry Draft.

Season	Club	League	GP	G	A	Pts	PIM	PP	SH	GW	S	%	+/-	TF	F%	Min	GP	G	A	Pts	PIM	PP	SH	GW	Min
1997-98	CAC Cement	AMHL	36	36	23	59	60	....	....	....	....	....	....	....	....	....	....	....	....	....	....	....	....	....	....
1998-99	Moose Jaw	WHL	66	9	12	21	47	....	....	....	....	....	....	....	....	....	11	0	1	1	0	....	....	....	....
99-2000	Moose Jaw	WHL	47	18	17	35	102	....	....	....	....	....	....	....	....	....	4	1	1	2	12	....	....	....	....
2000-01	Moose Jaw	WHL	59	34	43	77	138	....	....	....	....	....	....	....	....	....	4	2	1	3	10	....	....	....	....
2001-02	**Washington**	**NHL**	**7**	**0**	**0**	**0**	**2**	0	0	0	3	0.0	–3	39	35.9	7:17	....	....	....	....	....	....	....	....	....
	Moose Jaw	WHL	36	18	27	45	75	....	....	....	....	....	....	....	....	....	12	7	5	12	33	....	....	....	....
2002-03	**Washington**	**NHL**	**72**	**2**	**9**	**11**	**93**	0	0	0	38	5.3	7	288	43.8	9:44	5	0	0	0	10	0	0	0	4:10
	Portland Pirates	AHL	5	0	5	5	11	....	....	....	....	....	....	....	....	....	....	....	....	....	....	....	....	....	....
2003-04	**Washington**	**NHL**	**30**	**2**	**0**	**2**	**28**	0	0	0	24	8.3	–5	116	41.4	10:15	....	....	....	....	....	....	....	....	....
	Portland Pirates	AHL	6	2	4	6	16	....	....	....	....	....	....	....	....	....	....	....	....	....	....	....	....	....	....
2004-05	Portland Pirates	AHL	53	10	19	29	115	....	....	....	....	....	....	....	....	....	....	....	....	....	....	....	....	....	....
2005-06	**Washington**	**NHL**	**76**	**14**	**16**	**30**	**73**	0	2	0	85	16.5	–17	904	48.7	13:44	....	....	....	....	....	....	....	....	....
2006-07	**Washington**	**NHL**	**69**	**7**	**10**	**17**	**78**	1	0	0	87	8.0	–9	762	50.1	13:41	....	....	....	....	....	....	....	....	....
	NHL Totals		**254**	**25**	**35**	**60**	**274**	1	2	0	237	10.5		2109	47.9	12:00	5	0	0	0	10	0	0	0	4:10

• Missed majority of 2003-04 season recovering from groin injury suffered in game vs. St. Louis, October 18, 2003.

SUTTON, Andy

(SUH-tuhn, AN-dee) **NYI**

Defense. Shoots left. 6'6", 245 lbs. Born, Kingston, Ont., March 10, 1975.

Season	Club	League	GP	G	A	Pts	PIM	PP	SH	GW	S	%	+/-	TF	F%	Min	GP	G	A	Pts	PIM	PP	SH	GW	Min
1991-92	Gananoque	OHA-B	36	11	9	20	....	....	....	....	....	....	....	....	....	....	14	9	21	30	....	....	....	....	....
1992-93	Gananoque	OHA-B	38	14	9	23	....	....	....	....	....	....	....	....	....	....	12	16	13	29	....	....	....	....	....
1993-94	St. Mike's B's	MTJHL	48	17	23	40	161	....	....	....	....	....	....	....	....	....	3	0	0	0	20	....	....	....	....
1994-95	Michigan Tech	WCHA	19	2	1	3	42	....	....	....	....	....	....	....	....	....	....	....	....	....	....	....	....	....	....
1995-96	Michigan Tech	WCHA	33	2	2	4	58	....	....	....	....	....	....	....	....	....	....	....	....	....	....	....	....	....	....
1996-97	Michigan Tech	WCHA	32	2	7	9	73	....	....	....	....	....	....	....	....	....	....	....	....	....	....	....	....	....	....
1997-98	Michigan Tech	WCHA	38	16	24	40	97	....	....	....	....	....	....	....	....	....	....	....	....	....	....	....	....	....	....
	Kentucky	AHL	7	0	0	0	33	....	....	....	....	....	....	....	....	....	....	....	....	....	....	....	....	....	....
1998-99	**San Jose**	**NHL**	**31**	**0**	**3**	**3**	**65**	0	0	0	24	0.0	–4	0	0.0	12:58	....	....	....	....	....	....	....	....	....
	Kentucky	AHL	21	5	10	15	53	....	....	....	....	....	....	....	....	....	5	0	0	0	23	....	....	....	....
99-2000	**San Jose**	**NHL**	**40**	**1**	**1**	**2**	**80**	0	0	0	29	3.4	–5	0	0.0	12:57	....	....	....	....	....	....	....	....	....
	Kentucky	AHL	3	0	1	1	0	....	....	....	....	....	....	....	....	....	....	....	....	....	....	....	....	....	....
2000-01	**Minnesota**	**NHL**	**69**	**3**	**4**	**7**	**131**	2	0	0	64	4.7	–11	3	33.3	12:55	....	....	....	....	....	....	....	....	....
2001-02	**Minnesota**	**NHL**	**19**	**2**	**4**	**6**	**35**	1	0	0	21	9.5	–4	2	0.0	10:57	....	....	....	....	....	....	....	....	....
	Atlanta	**NHL**	**24**	**0**	**4**	**4**	**46**	0	0	0	20	0.0	0	2	0.0	15:25	....	....	....	....	....	....	....	....	....
2002-03	**Atlanta**	**NHL**	**53**	**3**	**18**	**21**	**114**	1	1	0	65	4.6	–8	3	33.3	18:00	....	....	....	....	....	....	....	....	....
2003-04	**Atlanta**	**NHL**	**65**	**8**	**13**	**21**	**94**	7	1	1	102	7.8	0	1	0.0	23:21	....	....	....	....	....	....	....	....	....
2004-05	GCK Lions Zurich	Swiss-2	18	8	18	26	58	....	....	....	....	....	....	....	....	....	6	2	4	6	16	....	....	....	....
	ZSC Lions Zurich	Swiss	8	2	2	4	32	....	....	....	....	....	....	....	....	....	1	0	1	1	2	....	....	....	....
2005-06	**Atlanta**	**NHL**	**76**	**8**	**17**	**25**	**144**	2	1	3	86	9.3	13	1	0.0	21:05	....	....	....	....	....	....	....	....	....
2006-07	**Atlanta**	**NHL**	**55**	**2**	**14**	**16**	**76**	0	1	0	51	3.9	6	0	0.0	19:28	4	0	0	0	10	0	0	0	17:34
	NHL Totals		**432**	**27**	**78**	**105**	**785**	13	4	4	462	5.8		10	20.0	17:26	4	0	0	0	10	0	0	0	17:34

WCHA Second All-Star Team (1998)

Signed as a free agent by **San Jose**, March 20, 1998. Traded to **Minnesota** by **San Jose** with San Jose's 7th round choice (Peter Bartos) in 2000 Entry Draft and 3rd round choice (later traded to Atlanta – later traded to Pittsburgh – later traded to Columbus – Columbus selected Aaron Johnson) in 2001 Entry Draft for Minnesota's 8th round choice (later traded to Calgary – Calgary selected Joe Campbell) in 2001 Entry Draft and future considerations, June 12, 2000. Traded to **Atlanta** by **Minnesota** for Hnat Domenichelli, January 22, 2002. Signed as a free agent by **GCK Zurich** (Swiss-2), September 24, 2004. Loaned to **ZSC Zurich** (Swiss) by **GCK Zurich** (Swiss-2), February 22, 2005. Signed as a free agent by **NY Islanders**, August 10, 2007.

SVATOS, Marek

(SVA-tohs, MAIR-ehk) **COL.**

Right wing. Shoots right. 5'10", 185 lbs. Born, Kosice, Czech., June 17, 1982. Colorado's 10th choice, 227th overall, in 2001 Entry Draft.

Season	Club	League	GP	G	A	Pts	PIM	PP	SH	GW	S	%	+/-	TF	F%	Min	GP	G	A	Pts	PIM	PP	SH	GW	Min
99-2000	HC VSZ Kosice Jr.	Slovak-Jr.	39	43	30	73	28	....	....	....	....	....	....	....	....	....	....	....	....	....	....	....	....	....	....
	HC VSZ Kosice	Slovakia	19	2	2	4	0	....	....	....	....	....	....	....	....	....	....	....	....	....	....	....	....	....	....
2000-01	Kootenay Ice	WHL	39	23	18	41	47	....	....	....	....	....	....	....	....	....	11	7	2	9	26	....	....	....	....
2001-02	Kootenay Ice	WHL	53	38	39	77	58	....	....	....	....	....	....	....	....	....	21	12	6	18	40	....	....	....	....
2002-03	Hershey Bears	AHL	30	9	4	13	10	....	....	....	....	....	....	....	....	....	....	....	....	....	....	....	....	....	....
2003-04	**Colorado**	**NHL**	**4**	**2**	**0**	**2**	**0**	1	0	1	6	33.3	1	0	0.0	10:18	11	1	5	6	2	0	0	1	12:29
2004-05	Hershey Bears	AHL	72	18	28	46	69	....	....	....	....	....	....	....	....	....	....	....	....	....	....	....	....	....	....
2005-06	**Colorado**	**NHL**	**61**	**32**	**18**	**50**	**60**	12	0	9	165	19.4	0	5	20.0	13:45	....	....	....	....	....	....	....	....	....
	Slovakia	Olympics	6	0	0	0	0	....	....	....	....	....	....	....	....	....	....	....	....	....	....	....	....	....	....
2006-07	**Colorado**	**NHL**	**66**	**15**	**15**	**30**	**46**	8	0	2	179	8.4	1	1	100.0	12:30	....	....	....	....	....	....	....	....	....
	NHL Totals		**131**	**49**	**33**	**82**	**106**	21	0	12	350	14.0		6	33.3	13:01	11	1	5	6	2	0	0	1	12:29

WHL West Second All-Star Team (2002)

• Missed majority of 2002-03 season recovering from shoulder injury that required surgery, January 28, 2003. • Missed majority of 2003-04 season recovering from shoulder injury suffered in game vs. St. Louis, October 12, 2003.

SVITOV, Alexander

(SVEE-tawf, al-EHX-AN-duhr) **CBJ**

Center. Shoots left. 6'3", 228 lbs. Born, Omsk, USSR, November 3, 1982. Tampa Bay's 1st choice, 3rd overall, in 2001 Entry Draft.

Season	Club	League	GP	G	A	Pts	PIM	PP	SH	GW	S	%	+/-	TF	F%	Min	GP	G	A	Pts	PIM	PP	SH	GW	Min
1997-98	Novokuznetsk 2	Russia-3	4	0	0	0	0	....	....	....	....	....	....	....	....	....	....	....	....	....	....	....	....	....	....
1998-99	Omsk 2	Russia-4	27	15	8	23	20	....	....	....	....	....	....	....	....	....	....	....	....	....	....	....	....	....	....
	Avangard Omsk	Russia	....	....	....	....	....	....	....	....	....	....	....	....	....	....	1	0	0	0	0	....	....	....	....
99-2000	Omsk 2	Russia-3	14	13	9	22	62	....	....	....	....	....	....	....	....	....	....	....	....	....	....	....	....	....	....
	Avangard Omsk	Russia	18	3	3	6	45	....	....	....	....	....	....	....	....	....	6	1	0	1	16	....	....	....	....
2000-01	Avangard Omsk	Russia	39	8	6	14	115	....	....	....	....	....	....	....	....	....	14	2	1	3	34	....	....	....	....
2001-02	CSKA Moscow 2	Russia-3	2	1	0	1	2	....	....	....	....	....	....	....	....	....	....	....	....	....	....	....	....	....	....
	Avangard Omsk	Russia	2	0	1	1	2	....	....	....	....	....	....	....	....	....	....	....	....	....	....	....	....	....	....
2002-03	**Tampa Bay**	**NHL**	**63**	**4**	**4**	**8**	**58**	1	0	0	69	5.8	–4	395	42.8	8:50	7	0	0	0	6	0	0	0	7:19
	Springfield	AHL	11	4	5	9	17	....	....	....	....	....	....	....	....	....	....	....	....	....	....	....	....	....	....
2003-04	**Tampa Bay**	**NHL**	**11**	**0**	**3**	**3**	**4**	0	0	0	16	0.0	0	79	58.2	9:18	....	....	....	....	....	....	....	....	....
	Hamilton	AHL	30	9	9	18	79	....	....	....	....	....	....	....	....	....	....	....	....	....	....	....	....	....	....
	Columbus	**NHL**	**29**	**2**	**6**	**8**	**16**	0	0	0	36	5.6	–8	293	43.0	12:39	....	....	....	....	....	....	....	....	....
2004-05	Syracuse Crunch	AHL	69	19	23	42	200	....	....	....	....	....	....	....	....	....	....	....	....	....	....	....	....	....	....

			Regular Season														Playoffs								
Season	Club	League	GP	G	A	Pts	PIM	PP	SH	GW	S	%	+/-	TF	F%	Min	GP	G	A	Pts	PIM	PP	SH	GW	Min
2005-06	Avangard Omsk	Russia	32	3	6	9	142	....	....	....	....	....	....	....	....	....	13	4	1	5	10	....	....	....	....
2006-07	**Columbus**	**NHL**	76	7	11	18	145	1	0	2	83	8.4	–10	928	50.9	13:47	....	....	....	....	....	....	....	....	....
	NHL Totals		179	13	24	37	223	2	0	2	204	6.4		1695	48.0	11:35	7	0	0	0	6	0	0	0	7:19

Traded to **Columbus** by **Tampa Bay** with Tampa Bay's 3rd round choice (later traded to Calgary – Calgary selected Dustin Boyd) in 2004 Entry Draft for Darryl Sydor and Columbus' 4th round choice (Mike Lundin) in 2004 Entry Draft, January 27, 2004.

SVOBODA, Jaroslav

(svah-BOH-duh, YAHR-roh-slav)

Left wing. Shoots left. 6'2", 190 lbs. Born, Cervenka, Czech., June 1, 1980. Carolina's 8th choice, 208th overall, in 1998 Entry Draft.

Season	Club	League	GP	G	A	Pts	PIM	PP	SH	GW	S	%	+/-	TF	F%	Min	GP	G	A	Pts	PIM	PP	SH	GW	Min
1995-96	HC Olomouc Jr.	CzRep-Jr.	40	13	15	28	....	....	....	....	....	....	....	....	....	....	....	....	....	....	....	....	....	....	....
1996-97	HC Olomouc Jr.	CzRep-Jr.	39	19	14	33	....	....	....	....	....	....	....	....	....	....	....	....	....	....	....	....	....	....	....
1997-98	HC Olomouc Jr.	CzRep-Jr.	36	14	21	35	....	....	....	....	....	....	....	....	....	....	....	....	....	....	....	....	....	....	....
	HC Olomouc	CzRep-2	13	0	1	1	....	....	....	....	....	....	....	....	....	....	....	....	....	....	....	....	....	....	....
1998-99	Kootenay Ice	WHL	54	26	33	59	46	....	....	....	....	....	....	....	....	....	7	2	2	4	11	....	....	....	....
99-2000	Kootenay Ice	WHL	56	23	43	66	97	....	....	....	....	....	....	....	....	....	21	*15	13	*28	51	....	....	....	....
2000-01	Cincinnati	IHL	52	4	10	14	25	....	....	....	....	....	....	....	....	....	....	....	....	....	....	....	....	....	....
2001-02	**Carolina**	**NHL**	10	2	2	4	2	0	0	0	12	16.7	0	1	0.0	9:23	23	1	4	5	28	1	0	1	14:45
	Lowell	AHL	66	12	16	28	58	....	....	....	....	....	....	....	....	....	....	....	....	....	....	....	....	....	....
2002-03	**Carolina**	**NHL**	48	3	11	14	32	1	0	0	63	4.8	–5	25	40.0	14:33	....	....	....	....	....	....	....	....	....
	Lowell	AHL	9	1	1	2	10	....	....	....	....	....	....	....	....	....	....	....	....	....	....	....	....	....	....
2003-04	**Carolina**	**NHL**	33	3	1	4	6	0	0	1	27	11.1	3	18	33.3	9:08	....	....	....	....	....	....	....	....	....
	Lowell	AHL	9	2	2	4	4	....	....	....	....	....	....	....	....	....	....	....	....	....	....	....	....	....	....
2004-05	HC Olomouc	CzRep-2	18	7	6	13	67	....	....	....	....	....	....	....	....	....	....	....	....	....	....	....	....	....	....
	HC Ocelari Trinec	CzRep	9	0	2	2	14	....	....	....	....	....	....	....	....	....	....	....	....	....	....	....	....	....	....
2005-06	**Dallas**	**NHL**	43	4	3	7	22	0	0	2	33	12.1	–3	3	100.0	7:04	2	0	0	0	2	0	0	0	6:36
2006-07	Znojmo	CzRep	51	10	0	10	160	....	....	....	....	....	....	....	....	....	9	1	1	2	56	....	....	....	....
	NHL Totals		134	12	17	29	62	1	0	3	135	8.9		47	40.4	10:26	25	1	4	5	30	1	0	1	14:06

Traded to **Dallas** by **Carolina** for Dallas' 4th round choice (Jakub Vojta) in 2005 Entry Draft, June 29, 2004. Signed as a free agent by **Olomouc** (CzRep-2), September 27, 2004. Signed as a free agent by **Trinec** (CzRep), January 6, 2005. Signed as a free agent by **Znojmo** (CzRep), September 6, 2006.

SYDOR, Darryl

(sih-DOHR, DAIR-uhl) **PIT.**

Defense. Shoots left. 6'1", 211 lbs. Born, Edmonton, Alta., May 13, 1972. Los Angeles' 1st choice, 7th overall, in 1990 Entry Draft.

Season	Club	League	GP	G	A	Pts	PIM	PP	SH	GW	S	%	+/-	TF	F%	Min	GP	G	A	Pts	PIM	PP	SH	GW	Min
1985-86	Genstar Cement	AAHA	34	20	17	37	60	....	....	....	....	....	....	....	....	....	....	....	....	....	....	....	....	....	....
1986-87	Genstar Cement	AAHA	36	15	20	35	60	....	....	....	....	....	....	....	....	....	....	....	....	....	....	....	....	....	....
1987-88	Edmonton Mets	AJHL	38	10	11	21	54	....	....	....	....	....	....	....	....	....	....	....	....	....	....	....	....	....	....
1988-89	Kamloops Blazers	WHL	65	12	14	26	86	....	....	....	....	....	....	....	....	....	15	1	4	5	19	....	....	....	....
1989-90	Kamloops Blazers	WHL	67	29	66	95	129	....	....	....	....	....	....	....	....	....	17	2	9	11	28	....	....	....	....
1990-91	Kamloops Blazers	WHL	66	27	78	105	88	....	....	....	....	....	....	....	....	....	12	3	*22	25	10	....	....	....	....
1991-92	Kamloops Blazers	WHL	29	9	39	48	33	....	....	....	....	....	....	....	....	....	17	3	15	18	18	....	....	....	....
	Los Angeles	**NHL**	18	1	5	6	22	0	0	0	18	5.6	–3	....	....	....	....	....	....	....	....	....	....	....	....
1992-93	**Los Angeles**	**NHL**	80	6	23	29	63	0	0	1	112	5.4	–2	....	....	....	24	3	8	11	16	2	0	0	....
1993-94	**Los Angeles**	**NHL**	84	8	27	35	94	1	0	0	146	5.5	–9	....	....	....	....	....	....	....	....	....	....	....	....
1994-95	**Los Angeles**	**NHL**	48	4	19	23	36	3	0	0	96	4.2	–2	....	....	....	....	....	....	....	....	....	....	....	....
1995-96	**Los Angeles**	**NHL**	58	1	11	12	34	1	0	0	84	1.2	–11	....	....	....	....	....	....	....	....	....	....	....	....
	Dallas	**NHL**	26	2	6	8	41	1	0	0	33	6.1	–1	....	....	....	....	....	....	....	....	....	....	....	....
1996-97	**Dallas**	**NHL**	82	8	40	48	51	2	0	2	142	5.6	37	....	....	....	7	0	2	2	0	0	0	0	....
1997-98	**Dallas**	**NHL**	79	11	35	46	51	4	1	1	166	6.6	17	....	....	....	17	0	5	5	14	0	0	0	....
1998-99 ♦	**Dallas**	**NHL**	74	14	34	48	50	9	0	2	163	8.6	–1	1	100.0	21:16	23	3	9	12	16	1	0	1	22:20
99-2000	**Dallas**	**NHL**	74	8	26	34	32	5	0	1	132	6.1	6	1	0.0	23:09	23	1	6	7	6	0	0	0	20:48
2000-01	**Dallas**	**NHL**	81	10	37	47	34	8	0	1	140	7.1	5	1	0.0	21:25	10	1	3	4	0	1	0	0	22:42
2001-02	**Dallas**	**NHL**	78	4	29	33	50	2	0	0	183	2.2	3	0	0.0	21:07	....	....	....	....	....	....	....	....	....
2002-03	**Dallas**	**NHL**	81	5	31	36	40	2	0	1	132	3.8	22	0	0.0	18:19	12	0	6	6	6	0	0	0	19:14
2003-04	**Columbus**	**NHL**	49	2	13	15	26	1	0	0	80	2.5	–19	1	0.0	21:54	....	....	....	....	....	....	....	....	....
	♦ **Tampa Bay**	**NHL**	31	1	6	7	6	0	0	0	42	2.4	3	0	0.0	19:06	23	0	6	6	9	0	0	0	21:50
2004-05			DID NOT PLAY																						
2005-06	**Tampa Bay**	**NHL**	80	4	19	23	30	1	0	0	64	6.3	–18	1	0.0	19:06	5	0	1	1	0	0	0	0	17:54
2006-07	**Dallas**	**NHL**	74	5	16	21	36	2	0	1	75	6.7	–4	0	0.0	20:09	7	1	1	2	4	0	0	0	23:19
	NHL Totals		1097	94	377	471	696	42	1	10	1808	5.2		5	20.0	20:38	151	9	47	56	71	4	0	1	21:24

WHL West First All-Star Team (1990, 1991, 1992)

Played in NHL All-Star Game (1998, 1999)

Traded to **Dallas** by **Los Angeles** with Los Angeles' 5th round choice (Ryan Christie) in 1996 Entry Draft for Shane Churla and Doug Zmolek, February 17, 1996. Traded to **Columbus** by **Dallas** for Mike Sillinger and Columbus' 2nd round choice (Johan Fransson) in 2004 Entry Draft, July 22, 2003. Traded to **Tampa Bay** by **Columbus** with Columbus' 4th round choice (Mike Lundin) in 2004 Entry Draft for Alexander Svitov and Tampa Bay's 3rd round choice (later traded to Calgary – Calgary selected Dustin Boyd) in 2004 Entry Draft, January 27, 2004. Traded to **Dallas** by **Tampa Bay** for Dallas' 4th round choice in 2008 Entry Draft, July 2, 2006. Signed as a free agent by **Pittsburgh**, July 2, 2007.

SYKORA, Petr

(sih-KOH-ra, PEE-tuhr)

Center. Shoots right. 6'3", 206 lbs. Born, Pardubice, Czech., December 21, 1978. Detroit's 2nd choice, 76th overall, in 1997 Entry Draft.

Season	Club	League	GP	G	A	Pts	PIM	PP	SH	GW	S	%	+/-	TF	F%	Min	GP	G	A	Pts	PIM	PP	SH	GW	Min
1994-95	HC Pardubice Jr.	CzRep-Jr.	38	35	33	68	....	....	....	....	....	....	....	....	....	....	....	....	....	....	....	....	....	....	....
1995-96	HC Pardubice Jr.	CzRep-Jr.	16	26	17	43	....	....	....	....	....	....	....	....	....	....	....	....	....	....	....	....	....	....	....
1996-97	HC Pardubice Jr.	CzRep-Jr.	12	14	4	18	....	....	....	....	....	....	....	....	....	....	....	....	....	....	....	....	....	....	....
	Pardubice	CzRep	29	1	3	4	4	....	....	....	....	....	....	....	....	....	....	....	....	....	....	....	....	....	....
1997-98	Pardubice	CzRep	39	4	5	9	8	....	....	....	....	....	....	....	....	....	3	0	0	0	....	....	....	....	....
1998-99	**Nashville**	**NHL**	2	0	0	0	0	0	0	0	2	0.0	–1	11	45.5	8:19	....	....	....	....	....	....	....	....	....
	Milwaukee	IHL	73	14	15	29	50	....	....	....	....	....	....	....	....	....	2	1	1	2	0	....	....	....	....
99-2000	Milwaukee	IHL	3	0	1	1	2	....	....	....	....	....	....	....	....	....	....	....	....	....	....	....	....	....	....
	Pardubice	CzRep	36	7	13	20	49	....	....	....	....	....	....	....	....	....	3	0	0	0	2	....	....	....	....
2000-01	Pardubice	CzRep	47	26	18	44	42	....	....	....	....	....	....	....	....	....	7	5	3	8	6	....	....	....	....
2001-02	Pardubice	CzRep	32	18	8	26	72	....	....	....	....	....	....	....	....	....	6	1	2	3	26	....	....	....	....
2002-03	Pardubice	CzRep	45	18	18	36	86	....	....	....	....	....	....	....	....	....	19	7	7	14	39	....	....	....	....
2003-04	Pardubice	CzRep	48	23	23	46	20	....	....	....	....	....	....	....	....	....	7	1	0	1	6	....	....	....	....
2004-05	Pardubice	CzRep	43	25	10	35	28	....	....	....	....	....	....	....	....	....	16	3	2	5	33	....	....	....	....
2005-06	**Washington**	**NHL**	10	2	2	4	6	0	0	0	9	22.2	0	2	50.0	10:41	....	....	....	....	....	....	....	....	....
	Pardubice	CzRep	28	11	14	25	46	....	....	....	....	....	....	....	....	....	....	....	....	....	....	....	....	....	....
2006-07	Pardubice	CzRep	50	*37	16	53	76	....	....	....	....	....	....	....	....	....	18	*12	6	*18	22	....	....	....	....
	NHL Totals		12	2	2	4	6	0	0	0	11	18.2		13	46.2	10:17	....	....	....	....	....	....	....	....	....

Traded to **Nashville** by **Detroit** with Detroit's 3rd round choice (later traded to Edmonton – Edmonton selected Mike Comrie) and 4th round compensatory choice (Alexander Krevsun) in 1999 Entry Draft for Doug Brown, July 14, 1998. Traded to **Washington** by **Nashville** for Washington's 3rd round choice (Paul Brown) in 2003 Entry Draft, June 22, 2002.

SYKORA, Petr

(sih-KOH-ra, PEE-tuhr) **PIT.**

Right wing. Shoots left. 6', 190 lbs. Born, Plzen, Czech., November 19, 1976. New Jersey's 1st choice, 18th overall, in 1995 Entry Draft.

Season	Club	League	GP	G	A	Pts	PIM	PP	SH	GW	S	%	+/-	TF	F%	Min	GP	G	A	Pts	PIM	PP	SH	GW	Min
1991-92	Plzen Jr.	Czech-Jr.	30	50	50	100	....	....	....	....	....	....	....	....	....	....	....	....	....	....	....	....	....	....	....
1992-93	HC Skoda Plzen	Czech	19	12	5	17	....	....	....	....	....	....	....	....	....	....	....	....	....	....	....	....	....	....	....
1993-94	HC Skoda Plzen	CzRep	37	10	16	26	....	....	....	....	....	....	....	....	....	....	4	0	1	1	....	....	....	....	....
	Cleveland	IHL	13	4	5	9	8	....	....	....	....	....	....	....	....	....	....	....	....	....	....	....	....	....	....
1994-95	Detroit Vipers	IHL	29	12	17	29	16	....	....	....	....	....	....	....	....	....	....	....	....	....	....	....	....	....	....
1995-96	**New Jersey**	**NHL**	63	18	24	42	32	8	0	3	128	14.1	7	....	....	....	....	....	....	....	....	....	....	....	....
	Albany River Rats	AHL	5	4	1	5	0	....	....	....	....	....	....	....	....	....	....	....	....	....	....	....	....	....	....
1996-97	**New Jersey**	**NHL**	19	1	2	3	4	0	0	0	26	3.8	–8	....	....	....	2	0	0	0	2	0	0	0	....
	Albany River Rats	AHL	43	20	25	45	48	....	....	....	....	....	....	....	....	....	4	1	4	5	2	....	....	....	....
1997-98	**New Jersey**	**NHL**	58	16	20	36	22	3	1	4	130	12.3	0	....	....	....	2	0	0	0	0	0	0	0	....
	Albany River Rats	AHL	2	4	1	5	0	....	....	....	....	....	....	....	....	....	....	....	....	....	....	....	....	....	....
1998-99	**New Jersey**	**NHL**	80	29	43	72	22	15	0	7	222	13.1	16	33	33.3	16:14	7	3	3	6	4	0	0	1	18:11
99-2000 ♦	**New Jersey**	**NHL**	79	25	43	68	26	5	1	4	222	11.3	24	47	61.7	17:06	23	9	8	17	10	1	0	3	15:20
2000-01	**New Jersey**	**NHL**	73	35	46	81	32	9	2	3	249	14.1	36	15	33.3	17:44	25	10	12	22	12	2	2	2	18:40
2001-02	**New Jersey**	**NHL**	73	21	27	48	44	4	0	4	194	10.8	12	1	0.0	17:51	4	0	1	1	0	0	0	0	17:57
	Czech Republic	Olympics	4	1	0	1	0	....	....	....	....	....	....	....	....	....	....	....	....	....	....	....	....	....	....
2002-03	**Anaheim**	**NHL**	82	34	25	59	24	15	1	5	299	11.4	–7	23	39.1	18:29	21	4	9	13	12	1	0	2	18:39

			Regular Season														Playoffs								
Season	Club	League	GP	G	A	Pts	PIM	PP	SH	GW	S	%	+/-	TF	F%	Min	GP	G	A	Pts	PIM	PP	SH	GW	Min
2003-04	**Anaheim**	**NHL**	**81**	**23**	**29**	**52**	**34**	**6**	**0**	**2**	**277**	**8.3**	**–9**	**9**	**22.2**	**17:57**									
2004-05	Magnitogorsk	Russia	45	18	13	31	46										5	2	3	5	8				
2005-06	**Anaheim**	**NHL**	**34**	**7**	**13**	**20**	**28**	**1**	**0**	**0**	**118**	**5.9**	**1**	**5**	**40.0**	**17:11**									
	NY Rangers	**NHL**	**40**	**16**	**15**	**31**	**22**	**7**	**0**	**0**	**112**	**14.3**	**5**	**69**	**37.7**	**15:11**	**4**	**0**	**0**	**0**	**0**	**0**	**0**	**0**	**17:45**
2006-07	**Edmonton**	**NHL**	**82**	**22**	**31**	**53**	**40**	**6**	**0**	**6**	**206**	**10.7**	**–20**	**462**	**48.1**	**16:40**									
	NHL Totals		**764**	**247**	**318**	**565**	**330**	**79**	**5**	**38**	**2183**	**11.3**		**664**	**45.8**	**17:16**	**88**	**26**	**33**	**59**	**40**	**4**	**2**	**8**	**17:38**

NHL All-Rookie Team (1996)

Traded to **Anaheim** by **New Jersey** with Mike Commodore, Jean-Francois Damphousse and Igor Pohanka for Jeff Friesen, Oleg Tverdovsky and Maxim Balmochnykh, July 6, 2002. Signed as a free agent by **Magnitogorsk** (Russia), August 12, 2004. Traded to **NY Rangers** by **Anaheim** with NY Rangers' 4th round choice (previously acquired, later traded to Washington - Washington selected Brett Bruneteau) in 2007 Entry Draft for Maxim Kondratiev, January 8, 2006. Signed as a free agent by **Edmonton**, August 11, 2006. Signed as a free agent by **Pittsburgh**, July 2, 2007.

SYVRET, Danny

(SIHV-reht, DA-nee) **EDM.**

Defense. Shoots left. 5'11", 203 lbs. Born, Millgrove, Ont., June 13, 1985. Edmonton's 3rd choice, 81st overall, in 2005 Entry Draft.

Season	Club	League	GP	G	A	Pts	PIM	PP	SH	GW	S	%	+/-	TF	F%	Min	GP	G	A	Pts	PIM	PP	SH	GW	Min
2001-02	Cambridge	OHA-B	43	6	41	47	23																		
	London Knights	OHL	1	0	0	0	0																		
2002-03	London Knights	OHL	68	8	14	22	31										14	1	6	7	11				
2003-04	London Knights	OHL	68	3	28	31	32										15	1	6	7	4				
2004-05	London Knights	OHL	62	23	46	69	33										18	5	15	20	4				
2005-06	**Edmonton**	**NHL**	**10**	**0**	**0**	**0**	**6**	**0**	**0**	**0**	**8**	**0.0**	**–1**	**0**	**0.0**	**12:19**									
	Hamilton	AHL	62	0	21	21	38																		
2006-07	**Edmonton**	**NHL**	**16**	**0**	**1**	**1**	**6**	**0**	**0**	**0**	**15**	**0.0**	**–10**	**0**	**0.0**	**18:28**									
	Grand Rapids	AHL	57	4	16	20	16																		
	NHL Totals		**26**	**0**	**1**	**1**	**12**	**0**	**0**	**0**	**23**	**0.0**		**0**	**0.0**	**16:06**									

OHL First All-Star Team (2005) • Canadian Major Junior Defenseman of the Year (2005) • Canadian Major Junior First All-Star Team (2005) • Memorial Cup Tournament All-Star Team (2005)

TAFFE, Jeff

(TAYF, JEHF) **PIT.**

Center. Shoots left. 6'3", 207 lbs. Born, Hastings, MN, February 19, 1981. St. Louis' 1st choice, 30th overall, in 2000 Entry Draft.

Season	Club	League	GP	G	A	Pts	PIM	PP	SH	GW	S	%	+/-	TF	F%	Min	GP	G	A	Pts	PIM	PP	SH	GW	Min
1996-97	Hastings Huskies	High-MN	25	21	37	58																			
1997-98	Hastings Huskies	High-MN	28	37	29	66																			
1998-99	Hastings Huskies	High-MN	28	39	51	90																			
	Rochester	USHL	17	12	9	21	26																		
99-2000	U. of Minnesota	WCHA	39	10	10	20	22																		
2000-01	U. of Minnesota	WCHA	38	12	23	35	56																		
2001-02	U. of Minnesota	WCHA	43	34	24	58	86																		
2002-03	**Phoenix**	**NHL**	**20**	**3**	**1**	**4**	**4**	**1**	**0**	**1**	**18**	**16.7**	**–4**	**113**	**29.2**	**11:34**									
	Springfield	AHL	57	23	26	49	44										5	0	3	3	8				
2003-04	**Phoenix**	**NHL**	**59**	**8**	**10**	**18**	**20**	**5**	**0**	**0**	**67**	**11.9**	**–8**	**219**	**43.4**	**11:02**									
	Springfield	AHL	15	10	6	16	19																		
2004-05	Utah Grizzlies	AHL	27	9	10	19	35																		
2005-06	**NY Rangers**	**NHL**	**2**	**0**	**0**	**0**	**0**	**0**	**0**	**0**	**1**	**0.0**	**0**	**0**	**0.0**	**3:49**									
	Hartford	AHL	36	6	16	22	34																		
	Phoenix	**NHL**	**2**	**0**	**0**	**0**	**0**	**0**	**0**	**0**	**2**	**0.0**	**0**	**1**	**100.0**	**9:06**									
	San Antonio	AHL	33	5	6	11	29																		
2006-07	**Phoenix**	**NHL**	**17**	**4**	**2**	**6**	**2**	**1**	**0**	**0**	**34**	**11.8**	**–7**	**64**	**39.1**	**14:12**									
	San Antonio	AHL	59	20	20	40	22																		
	NHL Totals		**100**	**15**	**13**	**28**	**26**	**7**	**0**	**1**	**122**	**12.3**		**397**	**38.8**	**11:29**									

Rights traded to **Phoenix** by **St. Louis** with Michal Handzus, Ladislav Nagy and St. Louis' 1st round choice (Ben Eager) in 2002 Entry Draft for Keith Tkachuk, March 13, 2001. Traded to **NY Rangers** by **Phoenix** for Jamie Lundmark, October 18 2005. Traded to **Phoenix** by **NY Rangers** for Martin Sonnenberg, January 24, 2006. Signed as a free agent by **Pittsburgh**, July 13, 2007.

TALBOT, Maxime

(TAL-buht, max-EEM) **PIT.**

Center. Shoots left. 5'11", 190 lbs. Born, Lemoyne, Que., February 11, 1984. Pittsburgh's 9th choice, 234th overall, in 2002 Entry Draft.

Season	Club	League	GP	G	A	Pts	PIM	PP	SH	GW	S	%	+/-	TF	F%	Min	GP	G	A	Pts	PIM	PP	SH	GW	Min
99-2000	Antoine-Girouard	QAAA	42	19	21	40	32										7	3	6	9	0				
2000-01	Rouyn-Noranda	QMJHL	40	9	15	24	78																		
	Hull Olympiques	QMJHL	24	6	7	13	60										5	1	0	1	2				
2001-02	Hull Olympiques	QMJHL	65	24	36	60	174										12	4	6	10	51				
2002-03	Hull Olympiques	QMJHL	69	46	58	104	130										20	14	*30	*44	33				
2003-04	Gatineau	QMJHL	51	25	73	98	41										15	*11	*16	*27	0				
2004-05	Wilkes-Barre	AHL	75	7	12	19	62										11	0	1	1	22				
2005-06	**Pittsburgh**	**NHL**	**48**	**5**	**3**	**8**	**59**	**0**	**2**	**1**	**45**	**11.1**	**–12**	**473**	**42.9**	**10:58**									
	Wilkes-Barre	AHL	42	12	20	32	80										11	3	6	9	16				
2006-07	**Pittsburgh**	**NHL**	**75**	**13**	**11**	**24**	**53**	**0**	**4**	**4**	**88**	**14.8**	**–2**	**903**	**44.4**	**13:54**	**5**	**0**	**1**	**1**	**7**	**0**	**0**	**0**	**15:51**
	Wilkes-Barre	AHL	5	4	0	4	2																		
	NHL Totals		**123**	**18**	**14**	**32**	**112**	**0**	**6**	**5**	**133**	**13.5**		**1376**	**43.9**	**12:45**	**5**	**0**	**1**	**1**	**7**	**0**	**0**	**0**	**15:51**

QMJHL Second All-Star Team (2003, 2004)

TALLACKSON, Barry

(TAL-ak-suhn, BAIR-ee) **N.J.**

Right wing. Shoots right. 6'5", 210 lbs. Born, Grafton, ND, April 14, 1983. New Jersey's 2nd choice, 53rd overall, in 2002 Entry Draft.

Season	Club	League	GP	G	A	Pts	PIM	PP	SH	GW	S	%	+/-	TF	F%	Min	GP	G	A	Pts	PIM	PP	SH	GW	Min
99-2000	USNTDP	NAHL	53	14	6	20	90										3	1	0	1	8				
2000-01	USNTDP	U-18	40	16	17	33	45																		
	USNTDP	USHL	23	7	7	14	32																		
2001-02	U. of Minnesota	WCHA	44	13	10	23	44																		
2002-03	U. of Minnesota	WCHA	32	9	14	23	18																		
2003-04	U. of Minnesota	WCHA	44	10	15	25	46																		
2004-05	U. of Minnesota	WCHA	36	11	8	19	54																		
	Albany River Rats	AHL	4	1	1	2	0																		
2005-06	**New Jersey**	**NHL**	**10**	**1**	**1**	**2**	**2**	**0**	**0**	**0**	**11**	**9.1**	**–2**	**2**	**0.0**	**8:04**									
	Albany River Rats	AHL	60	14	23	37	62																		
2006-07	**New Jersey**	**NHL**	**3**	**0**	**0**	**0**	**0**	**0**	**0**	**0**	**3**	**0.0**	**–1**	**0**	**0.0**	**12:06**									
	Lowell Devils	AHL	58	10	24	34	33																		
	NHL Totals		**13**	**1**	**1**	**2**	**2**	**0**	**0**	**0**	**14**	**7.1**		**2**	**0.0**	**9:00**									

TALLINDER, Henrik

(tah-LIHN-duhr, HEHN-rihk) **BUF.**

Defense. Shoots left. 6'3", 214 lbs. Born, Stockholm, Sweden, January 10, 1979. Buffalo's 2nd choice, 48th overall, in 1997 Entry Draft.

Season	Club	League	GP	G	A	Pts	PIM	PP	SH	GW	S	%	+/-	TF	F%	Min	GP	G	A	Pts	PIM	PP	SH	GW	Min
1996-97	AIK Solna Jr.	Swe-Jr.	40	4	13	17	55																		
	AIK Solna	Sweden	1	0	0	0	0																		
1997-98	AIK Solna	Sweden	34	0	0	0	26																		
1998-99	AIK Solna	Sweden	36	0	0	0	30																		
99-2000	AIK Solna	Sweden	50	0	2	2	59																		
2000-01	TPS Turku	Finland	56	5	9	14	62										10	2	1	3	8				
2001-02	**Buffalo**	**NHL**	**2**	**0**	**0**	**0**	**0**	**0**	**0**	**0**	**4**	**0.0**	**–1**	**0**	**0.0**	**18:10**									
	Rochester	AHL	73	6	14	20	26										2	0	0	0	0				
2002-03	**Buffalo**	**NHL**	**46**	**3**	**10**	**13**	**28**	**1**	**0**	**0**	**37**	**8.1**	**–3**	**0**	**0.0**	**19:53**									
2003-04	**Buffalo**	**NHL**	**72**	**1**	**9**	**10**	**26**	**0**	**0**	**0**	**63**	**1.6**	**5**	**1**	**0.0**	**18:23**									
2004-05	Linkopings HC	Sweden	44	6	10	16	63																		
	SC Bern	Swiss															10	1	1	2	4				
2005-06	**Buffalo**	**NHL**	**82**	**6**	**15**	**21**	**74**	**0**	**1**	**1**	**79**	**7.6**	**10**	**0**	**0.0**	**20:21**	**14**	**2**	**6**	**8**	**16**	**0**	**0**	**0**	**22:16**
2006-07	**Buffalo**	**NHL**	**47**	**4**	**10**	**14**	**34**	**0**	**0**	**0**	**34**	**11.8**	**19**	**1**	**0.0**	**21:07**	**16**	**0**	**2**	**2**	**10**	**0**	**0**	**0**	**23:40**
	NHL Totals		**249**	**14**	**44**	**58**	**162**	**1**	**1**	**1**	**217**	**6.5**		**2**	**0.0**	**19:49**	**30**	**2**	**8**	**10**	**26**	**0**	**0**	**0**	**23:01**

Signed as a free agent by **Linkopings** (Sweden), September 9, 2004. Signed as a free agent by **Bern** (Swiss), February 22, 2005.

TAMBELLINI, Jeff

(tam-buh-LEE-nee, JEHF) **NYI**

Left wing. Shoots left. 5'11", 186 lbs. Born, Calgary, Alta., April 13, 1984. Los Angeles' 3rd choice, 27th overall, in 2003 Entry Draft.

			Regular Season														Playoffs								
Season	Club	League	GP	G	A	Pts	PIM	PP	SH	GW	S	%	+/-	TF	F%	Min	GP	G	A	Pts	PIM	PP	SH	GW	Min
99-2000	Port Coquitlam	PIJHL	41	30	34	64	....	....	....	....	....	....	....	....	....	....	....	....	....	....	....	....	....	....	....
2000-01	Chilliwack Chiefs	BCHL	54	21	30	51	13	....	....	....	....	....	....	....	....	....	....	....	....	....	....	....	....	....	....
2001-02	Chilliwack Chiefs	BCHL	34	46	71	117	23	....	....	....	....	....	....	....	....	....	29	27	27	54	....	....	....	....	....
2002-03	U. of Michigan	CCHA	43	26	19	45	24	....	....	....	....	....	....	....	....	....	....	....	....	....	....	....	....	....	....
2003-04	U. of Michigan	CCHA	39	15	12	27	18	....	....	....	....	....	....	....	....	....	....	....	....	....	....	....	....	....	....
2004-05	U. of Michigan	CCHA	42	*24	33	*57	32	....	....	....	....	....	....	....	....	....	....	....	....	....	....	....	....	....	....
2005-06	**Los Angeles**	**NHL**	4	0	0	0	2	0	0	0	6	0.0	–1	1	0.0	9:23	....	....	....	....	....	....	....	....	....
	Manchester	AHL	56	25	31	56	26	....	....	....	....	....	....	....	....	....	....	....	....	....	....	....	....	....	....
	NY Islanders	**NHL**	21	1	3	4	8	0	0	0	11	9.1	2	3	33.3	9:54	....	....	....	....	....	....	....	....	....
	Bridgeport	AHL	....	....	....	....	....	....	....	....	....	....	....	....	....	....	7	1	2	3	2	....	....	....	....
2006-07	**NY Islanders**	**NHL**	23	2	7	9	6	0	0	0	20	10.0	6	1	0.0	7:14	....	....	....	....	....	....	....	....	....
	Bridgeport	AHL	50	30	29	59	46	....	....	....	....	....	....	....	....	....	....	....	....	....	....	....	....	....	....
	NHL Totals		48	3	10	13	16	0	0	0	37	8.1		5	20.0	8:35	....	....	....	....	....	....	....	....	....

CCHA All-Rookie Team (2003) • CCHA Second All-Star Team (2003) • CCHA Rookie of the Year (2003) • CCHA First All-Star Team (2005) • NCAA West Second All-American Team (2005)

Traded to **NY Islanders** by **Los Angeles** with Denis Grebeshkov for Mark Parrish and Brent Sopel, March 8, 2006.

TANABE, David

(tuh-NA-bee, DAY-vihd)

Defense. Shoots right. 6'1", 212 lbs. Born, White Bear Lake, MN, July 19, 1980. Carolina's 1st choice, 16th overall, in 1999 Entry Draft.

Season	Club	League	GP	G	A	Pts	PIM	PP	SH	GW	S	%	+/-	TF	F%	Min	GP	G	A	Pts	PIM	PP	SH	GW	Min
1996-97	Hill-Murray	High-MN	28	12	14	26	....	....	....	....	....	....	....	....	....	....	....	....	....	....	....	....	....	....	....
1997-98	USNTDP	U-18	33	4	15	19	48	....	....	....	....	....	....	....	....	....	....	....	....	....	....	....	....	....	....
	USNTDP	USHL	21	1	3	4	18	....	....	....	....	....	....	....	....	....	....	....	....	....	....	....	....	....	....
	USNTDP	NAHL	12	1	2	3	10	....	....	....	....	....	....	....	....	....	7	2	1	3	20	....	....	....	....
1998-99	U. of Wisconsin	WCHA	35	10	12	22	44	....	....	....	....	....	....	....	....	....	....	....	....	....	....	....	....	....	....
99-2000	**Carolina**	**NHL**	31	4	0	4	14	3	0	0	28	14.3	–4	0	0.0	12:53	....	....	....	....	....	....	....	....	....
	Cincinnati	IHL	32	0	13	13	14	....	....	....	....	....	....	....	....	....	11	1	4	5	6	....	....	....	....
2000-01	**Carolina**	**NHL**	74	7	22	29	42	5	0	1	130	5.4	–9	0	0.0	17:55	6	2	0	2	12	2	0	0	20:47
2001-02	**Carolina**	**NHL**	78	1	15	16	35	0	0	0	113	0.9	–13	0	0.0	18:27	1	0	1	1	0	0	0	0	7:31
2002-03	**Carolina**	**NHL**	68	3	10	13	24	2	0	0	104	2.9	–27	0	0.0	18:12	....	....	....	....	....	....	....	....	....
2003-04	**Phoenix**	**NHL**	45	5	7	12	22	2	0	2	88	5.7	4	0	0.0	23:02	....	....	....	....	....	....	....	....	....
2004-05	Rapperswil	Swiss	8	4	5	9	4	....	....	....	....	....	....	....	....	....	....	....	....	....	....	....	....	....	....
	Kloten Flyers	Swiss	20	3	7	10	18	....	....	....	....	....	....	....	....	....	5	1	4	5	8	....	....	....	....
2005-06	**Phoenix**	**NHL**	21	0	4	4	8	0	0	0	21	0.0	–5	0	0.0	21:08	....	....	....	....	....	....	....	....	....
	Boston	**NHL**	54	4	12	16	48	0	0	1	82	4.9	0	0	0.0	20:08	....	....	....	....	....	....	....	....	....
2006-07	**Carolina**	**NHL**	60	5	12	17	44	2	0	0	83	6.0	5	0	0.0	17:48	....	....	....	....	....	....	....	....	....
	NHL Totals		431	29	82	111	237	14	0	4	649	4.5		0	0.0	18:39	7	2	1	3	12	2	0	0	18:53

WCHA All-Rookie Team (1999)

Traded to **Phoenix** by **Carolina** with Igor Knyazev for Danny Markov and Edmonton's 3rd round choice (previously acquired, later traded to NY Rangers - NY Rangers selected Billy Ryan) in 2004 Entry Draft, June 21, 2003. Signed as a free agent by **Rapperswil** (Swiss), October 21, 2004. Signed as a free agent by **Kloten** (Swiss), November 29, 2004. Traded to **Boston** by **Phoenix** for Dave Scatchard, November 18, 2005. Signed as a free agent by **Carolina**, August 29, 2006.

TANGUAY, Alex

(TAN-guay, AL-ehx) **CGY.**

Left wing. Shoots left. 6'1", 191 lbs. Born, Ste-Justine, Que., November 21, 1979. Colorado's 1st choice, 12th overall, in 1998 Entry Draft.

Season	Club	League	GP	G	A	Pts	PIM	PP	SH	GW	S	%	+/-	TF	F%	Min	GP	G	A	Pts	PIM	PP	SH	GW	Min
1994-95	Cap-d-Madeleine	QAAA	1	0	1	1	0	....	....	....	....	....	....	....	....	....	....	....	....	....	....	....	....	....	....
1995-96	Cap-d-Madeleine	QAAA	44	29	34	63	64	....	....	....	....	....	....	....	....	....	5	2	4	6	14	....	....	....	....
1996-97	Halifax	QMJHL	70	27	41	68	60	....	....	....	....	....	....	....	....	....	12	5	8	13	8	....	....	....	....
1997-98	Halifax	QMJHL	51	47	38	85	32	....	....	....	....	....	....	....	....	....	5	7	6	13	4	....	....	....	....
1998-99	Halifax	QMJHL	31	27	34	61	30	....	....	....	....	....	....	....	....	....	5	1	2	3	2	....	....	....	....
	Hershey Bears	AHL	5	1	2	3	2	....	....	....	....	....	....	....	....	....	5	0	2	2	0	....	....	....	....
99-2000	**Colorado**	**NHL**	76	17	34	51	22	5	0	3	74	23.0	6	11	45.5	15:38	17	2	1	3	2	1	0	1	10:49
2000-01 ♦	**Colorado**	**NHL**	82	27	50	77	37	7	1	3	135	20.0	35	30	43.3	17:51	23	6	15	21	8	1	0	2	19:18
2001-02	**Colorado**	**NHL**	70	13	35	48	36	7	0	2	90	14.4	8	37	40.5	18:20	19	5	8	13	0	3	0	0	17:25
2002-03	**Colorado**	**NHL**	82	26	41	67	36	3	0	5	142	18.3	34	123	39.0	17:48	7	1	2	3	4	0	0	1	19:06
2003-04	**Colorado**	**NHL**	69	25	54	79	42	7	0	5	117	21.4	30	71	40.9	18:21	8	2	2	4	2	1	0	1	15:46
2004-05	HC Lugano	Swiss	6	3	3	6	4	....	....	....	....	....	....	....	....	....	....	....	....	....	....	....	....	....	....
2005-06	**Colorado**	**NHL**	71	29	49	78	46	8	0	4	125	23.2	8	20	30.0	18:22	9	2	4	6	12	0	0	1	18:20
2006-07	**Calgary**	**NHL**	81	22	59	81	44	5	0	0	107	20.6	12	24	25.0	17:40	6	1	3	4	8	1	0	0	17:56
	NHL Totals		531	159	322	481	263	42	1	22	790	20.1		316	38.6	17:42	89	19	35	54	36	7	0	6	16:45

QMJHL All-Rookie Team (1997)

Played in NHL All-Star Game (2004)

Signed as a free agent by **Lugano** (Swiss), October 7, 2004. Traded to **Calgary** by **Colorado** for Jordan Leopold, Calgary's 2nd round choice (Codey Burki) in 2006 Entry Draft and Calgary's 2nd round choice (Trevor Cann) in 2007 Entry Draft, June 24, 2006.

TAPPER, Brad

(TA-puhr, BRAD)

Right wing. Shoots right. 6', 185 lbs. Born, Scarborough, Ont., April 28, 1978.

Season	Club	League	GP	G	A	Pts	PIM	PP	SH	GW	S	%	+/-	TF	F%	Min	GP	G	A	Pts	PIM	PP	SH	GW	Min
1996-97	Wexford Raiders	MTJHL	50	42	70	112	169	....	....	....	....	....	....	....	....	....	....	....	....	....	....	....	....	....	....
1997-98	RPI Engineers	ECAC	34	14	11	25	62	....	....	....	....	....	....	....	....	....	....	....	....	....	....	....	....	....	....
1998-99	RPI Engineers	ECAC	35	20	20	40	60	....	....	....	....	....	....	....	....	....	....	....	....	....	....	....	....	....	....
99-2000	RPI Engineers	ECAC	37	*31	20	51	81	....	....	....	....	....	....	....	....	....	....	....	....	....	....	....	....	....	....
2000-01	**Atlanta**	**NHL**	16	2	3	5	6	0	0	0	21	9.5	1	0	0.0	12:44	....	....	....	....	....	....	....	....	....
	Orlando	IHL	45	7	9	16	39	....	....	....	....	....	....	....	....	....	2	0	0	0	2	....	....	....	....
2001-02	**Atlanta**	**NHL**	20	2	4	6	43	0	0	0	34	5.9	–3	3	66.7	13:21	....	....	....	....	....	....	....	....	....
	Chicago Wolves	AHL	50	14	12	26	62	....	....	....	....	....	....	....	....	....	19	3	4	7	42	....	....	....	....
2002-03	**Atlanta**	**NHL**	35	10	4	14	23	1	0	3	68	14.7	2	4	25.0	13:03	....	....	....	....	....	....	....	....	....
	Chicago Wolves	AHL	28	9	14	23	42	....	....	....	....	....	....	....	....	....	9	1	3	4	10	....	....	....	....
2003-04	Chicago Wolves	AHL	20	1	8	9	26	....	....	....	....	....	....	....	....	....	....	....	....	....	....	....	....	....	....
	Binghamton	AHL	29	9	12	21	26	....	....	....	....	....	....	....	....	....	....	....	....	....	....	....	....	....	....
2004-05	Nurnberg	Germany	50	26	23	49	101	....	....	....	....	....	....	....	....	....	6	0	2	2	18	....	....	....	....
2005-06	Hannover	Germany	46	9	21	30	165	....	....	....	....	....	....	....	....	....	8	2	4	6	*64	....	....	....	....
2006-07	Philadelphia	AHL	5	3	1	4	4	....	....	....	....	....	....	....	....	....	....	....	....	....	....	....	....	....	....
	Hannover Scorp.	Germany	25	6	17	23	38	....	....	....	....	....	....	....	....	....	6	2	2	4	18	....	....	....	....
	NHL Totals		71	14	11	25	72	1	0	3	123	11.4		7	42.9	13:04	....	....	....	....	....	....	....	....	....

ECAC First All-Star Team (2000) • NCAA East Second All-American Team (2000)

Signed as a free agent by **Atlanta**, April 11, 2000. Traded to **Ottawa** by **Atlanta** for Daniel Corso, January 6, 2004. Signed as a free agent by **Nurnberg** (Germany), July 22, 2004. Signed as a free agent by **Philadelphia**, June 26, 2006. Signed as a free agent by **Iserlohn** (Germany), July 3, 2007.

TARNASKY, Nick

(tahr-NAS-kee, NIHK) **T.B.**

Center. Shoots left. 6'2", 233 lbs. Born, Rocky Mtn. House, Alta., November 25, 1984. Tampa Bay's 11th choice, 287th overall, in 2003 Entry Draft.

Season	Club	League	GP	G	A	Pts	PIM	PP	SH	GW	S	%	+/-	TF	F%	Min	GP	G	A	Pts	PIM	PP	SH	GW	Min
99-2000	Leduc Oil Kings	AMBHL	36	21	11	32	59	....	....	....	....	....	....	....	....	....	....	....	....	....	....	....	....	....	....
2000-01	Leduc Oil Kings	AMHL	35	39	29	68	95	....	....	....	....	....	....	....	....	....	....	....	....	....	....	....	....	....	....
2001-02	Drayton Valley	AJHL	20	7	4	11	10	....	....	....	....	....	....	....	....	....	....	....	....	....	....	....	....	....	....
	Vancouver Giants	WHL	10	1	0	1	5	....	....	....	....	....	....	....	....	....	....	....	....	....	....	....	....	....	....
2002-03	Kelowna Rockets	WHL	39	4	12	16	39	....	....	....	....	....	....	....	....	....	....	....	....	....	....	....	....	....	....
	Lethbridge	WHL	30	5	8	13	45	....	....	....	....	....	....	....	....	....	....	....	....	....	....	....	....	....	....
2003-04	Lethbridge	WHL	71	26	23	49	108	....	....	....	....	....	....	....	....	....	....	....	....	....	....	....	....	....	....
2004-05	Springfield	AHL	80	7	10	17	176	....	....	....	....	....	....	....	....	....	....	....	....	....	....	....	....	....	....
2005-06	**Tampa Bay**	**NHL**	12	0	1	1	4	0	0	0	9	0.0	–3	15	40.0	4:40	....	....	....	....	....	....	....	....	....
	Springfield	AHL	68	14	9	23	100	....	....	....	....	....	....	....	....	....	....	....	....	....	....	....	....	....	....
2006-07	**Tampa Bay**	**NHL**	77	5	4	9	80	0	0	1	41	12.2	–6	13	30.8	6:30	6	0	0	0	10	0	0	0	6:13
	NHL Totals		89	5	5	10	84	0	0	1	50	10.0		28	35.7	6:15	6	0	0	0	10	0	0	0	6:13

TARNSTROM, Dick

(TAHRN-struhm, DIHK) **EDM.**

Defense. Shoots left. 6'1", 205 lbs. Born, Sundbyberg, Sweden, January 20, 1975. NY Islanders' 12th choice, 272nd overall, in 1994 Entry Draft.

Season	Club	League	GP	G	A	Pts	PIM	PP	SH	GW	S	%	+/-	TF	F%	Min	GP	G	A	Pts	PIM	PP	SH	GW	Min
			Regular Season														Playoffs								
1992-93	AIK Solna	Sweden	3	0	0	0	0																		
1993-94	AIK Solna	Sweden-2	33	1	4	5																			
1994-95	AIK Solna	Sweden	37	8	4	12	26																		
1995-96	AIK Solna	Sweden	40	0	5	5	32																		
1996-97	AIK Solna	Sweden	49	5	3	8	38										7	0	1	1	6				
1997-98	AIK Solna	Sweden	45	2	12	14	30																		
1998-99	AIK Solna	Sweden	47	9	14	23	36																		
99-2000	AIK Solna	Sweden	42	7	15	22	20																		
2000-01	AIK Solna	Sweden	50	10	18	28	28										5	0	0	0	8				
2001-02	**NY Islanders**	**NHL**	**62**	**3**	**16**	**19**	**38**	**0**	**0**	**0**	**59**	**5.1**	**-12**	**0**	**0.0**	**17:39**	**5**	**0**	**0**	**0**	**2**	**0**	**0**	**0**	**7:13**
	Bridgeport	AHL	9	0	2	2	2																		
2002-03	**Pittsburgh**	**NHL**	**61**	**7**	**34**	**41**	**50**	**3**	**0**	**0**	**115**	**6.1**	**-11**	**0**	**0.0**	**23:54**									
2003-04	**Pittsburgh**	**NHL**	**80**	**16**	**36**	**52**	**38**	**12**	**0**	**0**	**158**	**10.1**	**-37**	**0**	**0.0**	**24:03**									
2004-05	Sodertalje SK	Sweden	50	7	18	25	46										9	1	0	1	6				
2005-06	**Pittsburgh**	**NHL**	**33**	**5**	**5**	**10**	**52**	**4**	**0**	**0**	**40**	**12.5**	**-10**	**1**	**100.0**	**16:54**									
	Edmonton	**NHL**	**22**	**1**	**3**	**4**	**24**	**0**	**0**	**0**	**20**	**5.0**	**-5**	**0**	**0.0**	**16:58**	**12**	**0**	**2**	**2**	**10**	**0**	**0**	**0**	**14:00**
2006-07	HC Lugano	Swiss	44	3	26	29	90										5	1	6	7	8				
	NHL Totals		**258**	**32**	**94**	**126**	**202**	**19**	**0**	**0**	**392**	**8.2**		**1**	**100.0**	**20:57**	**17**	**0**	**2**	**2**	**12**	**0**	**0**	**0**	**12:00**

Claimed on waivers by **Pittsburgh** from **NY Islanders**, August 6, 2002. Signed as a free agent by **Sodertalje** (Sweden), August 9, 2004. Traded to **Edmonton** by **Pittsburgh** for Jani Rita and Cory Cross, January 26, 2006. Signed as a free agent by **Lugano** (Swiss), August 16, 2006. Signed as a free agent by **Edmonton**, July 1, 2007.

TATICEK, Petr

(TA-tih-chehk, PEE-tuhr)

Center. Shoots left. 6'3", 195 lbs. Born, Rakovnik, Czech., September 22, 1983. Florida's 2nd choice, 9th overall, in 2002 Entry Draft.

Season	Club	League	GP	G	A	Pts	PIM	PP	SH	GW	S	%	+/-	TF	F%	Min	GP	G	A	Pts	PIM	PP	SH	GW	Min
1998-99	HC Kladno U17	CzR-U17	42	24	17	41																			
99-2000	HC Kladno Jr.	CzRep-Jr.	48	11	16	27	26																		
	Kladno	CzRep	4	0	0	0	4																		
2000-01	HC Kladno Jr.	CzRep-Jr.	30	7	12	19	54																		
	Kladno	CzRep	3	0	0	0	0																		
2001-02	Sault Ste. Marie	OHL	60	21	42	63	32										6	3	3	6	4				
2002-03	Sault Ste. Marie	OHL	54	12	45	57	44										4	1	0	1	0				
2003-04	San Antonio	AHL	63	4	15	19	6																		
2004-05	San Antonio	AHL	67	7	15	22	21																		
	Laredo Bucks	CHL	4	2	5	7	0																		
2005-06	**Florida**	**NHL**	**3**	**0**	**0**	**0**	**0**	**0**	**0**	**0**	**3**	**0.0**	**0**	**9**	**33.3**	**5:51**									
	Houston Aeros	AHL	44	9	21	30	10																		
	Wilkes-Barre	AHL	17	4	4	8	7										1	0	0	0	2				
2006-07	Hershey Bears	AHL	1	1	0	1	2																		
	HC Rabat Kladno	CzRep	10	0	2	2	6																		
	HC Davos	Swiss	15	4	1	5	8										17	3	4	7	10				
	NHL Totals		**3**	**0**	**0**	**0**	**0**	**0**	**0**	**0**	**3**	**0.0**		**9**	**33.3**	**5:51**									

Traded to **Pittsbugh** by **Florida** for Ric Jackman, March 9, 2006. Signed as a free agent by **Washington**, August 9, 2006.

TAYLOR, Tim

(TAY-luhr, TIHM) **T.B.**

Center. Shoots left. 6'1", 190 lbs. Born, Stratford, Ont., February 6, 1969. Washington's 2nd choice, 36th overall, in 1988 Entry Draft.

Season	Club	League	GP	G	A	Pts	PIM	PP	SH	GW	S	%	+/-	TF	F%	Min	GP	G	A	Pts	PIM	PP	SH	GW	Min
1985-86	Stratford Cullitons	OHA-B	1	0	0	0	0																		
1986-87	Stratford Cullitons	OHA-B	31	25	26	51	51																		
	London Knights	OHL	34	7	9	16	11																		
1987-88	London Knights	OHL	64	46	50	96	66										12	9	9	18	26				
1988-89	London Knights	OHL	61	34	80	114	93										21	*21	25	*46	58				
1989-90	Baltimore	AHL	79	31	36	67	124										9	2	2	4	13				
1990-91	Baltimore	AHL	79	25	42	67	75										5	0	1	1	4				
1991-92	Baltimore	AHL	65	9	18	27	131																		
1992-93	Baltimore	AHL	41	15	16	31	49																		
	Hamilton	AHL	36	15	22	37	37																		
1993-94	**Detroit**	**NHL**	**1**	**1**	**0**	**1**	**0**	**0**	**0**	**0**	**4**	**25.0**	**-1**												
	Adirondack	AHL	79	36	*81	*117	86										12	2	10	12	12				
1994-95	**Detroit**	**NHL**	**22**	**0**	**4**	**4**	**16**	**0**	**0**	**0**	**21**	**0.0**	**3**				**6**	**0**	**1**	**1**	**12**	**0**	**0**	**0**	
1995-96	**Detroit**	**NHL**	**72**	**11**	**14**	**25**	**39**	**1**	**1**	**4**	**81**	**13.6**	**11**				**18**	**0**	**4**	**4**	**4**	**0**	**0**	**0**	
1996-97♦	**Detroit**	**NHL**	**44**	**3**	**4**	**7**	**52**	**0**	**1**	**0**	**44**	**6.8**	**-6**				**2**	**0**	**0**	**0**	**0**	**0**	**0**	**0**	
1997-98	**Boston**	**NHL**	**79**	**20**	**11**	**31**	**57**	**1**	**3**	**0**	**127**	**15.7**	**-16**				**6**	**0**	**0**	**0**	**10**	**0**	**0**	**0**	
1998-99	**Boston**	**NHL**	**49**	**4**	**7**	**11**	**55**	**0**	**0**	**1**	**76**	**5.3**	**-10**	**834**	**58.3**	**15:56**	**12**	**0**	**3**	**3**	**8**	**0**	**0**	**0**	**15:09**
99-2000	**NY Rangers**	**NHL**	**76**	**9**	**11**	**20**	**72**	**0**	**0**	**2**	**79**	**11.4**	**-4**	**1276**	**58.9**	**14:09**									
2000-01	**NY Rangers**	**NHL**	**38**	**2**	**5**	**7**	**16**	**0**	**0**	**1**	**34**	**5.9**	**-6**	**292**	**59.3**	**8:57**									
2001-02	**Tampa Bay**	**NHL**	**48**	**4**	**4**	**8**	**25**	**0**	**1**	**0**	**50**	**8.0**	**-2**	**559**	**54.6**	**13:29**									
2002-03	**Tampa Bay**	**NHL**	**82**	**4**	**8**	**12**	**38**	**0**	**0**	**1**	**95**	**4.2**	**-13**	**961**	**57.9**	**13:43**	**11**	**0**	**1**	**1**	**6**	**0**	**0**	**0**	**13:54**
2003-04♦	**Tampa Bay**	**NHL**	**82**	**7**	**15**	**22**	**25**	**0**	**0**	**1**	**95**	**7.4**	**-5**	**666**	**59.6**	**12:54**	**23**	**2**	**3**	**5**	**31**	**0**	**0**	**0**	**14:17**
2004-05			DID NOT PLAY																						
2005-06	**Tampa Bay**	**NHL**	**82**	**7**	**6**	**13**	**22**	**0**	**0**	**0**	**109**	**6.4**	**-12**	**1013**	**52.1**	**12:27**	**5**	**0**	**0**	**0**	**2**	**0**	**0**	**0**	**11:05**
2006-07	**Tampa Bay**	**NHL**	**71**	**1**	**5**	**6**	**16**	**0**	**0**	**1**	**59**	**1.7**	**-5**	**400**	**56.3**	**7:55**	**6**	**0**	**0**	**0**	**0**	**0**	**0**	**0**	**12:02**
	NHL Totals		**746**	**73**	**94**	**167**	**433**	**2**	**6**	**11**	**874**	**8.4**		**6001**	**57.0**	**12:31**	**89**	**2**	**12**	**14**	**73**	**0**	**0**	**0**	**13:53**

AHL First All-Star Team (1994) • John B. Sollenberger Trophy (Leading Scorer – AHL) (1994)

Traded to **Vancouver** by **Washington** for Eric Murano, January 29, 1993. Signed as a free agent by **Detroit**, July 28, 1993. Claimed by **Boston** from **Detroit** in Waiver Draft, September 28, 1997. Signed as a free agent by **NY Rangers**, July 30, 1999. • Missed majority of 2000-01 season recovering from abdominal injury suffered in game vs. Phoenix, January 4, 2001. Traded to **Tampa Bay** by **NY Rangers** for Kyle Freadrich and Nils Ekman, June 30, 2001.

TENKRAT, Petr

(TEHN-krat, PEE-tuhr)

Right wing. Shoots right. 6', 183 lbs. Born, Kladno, Czech., May 31, 1977. Anaheim's 6th choice, 230th overall, in 1999 Entry Draft.

Season	Club	League	GP	G	A	Pts	PIM	PP	SH	GW	S	%	+/-	TF	F%	Min	GP	G	A	Pts	PIM	PP	SH	GW	Min
1994-95	HC Kladno	CzRep	1	0	0	0	0																		
1995-96	HC Poldi Kladno	CzRep	20	0	4	4	4										3	0	1	1	0				
1996-97	HC Poldi Kladno	CzRep	43	5	9	14	6										3	0	1	1	0				
1997-98	Kladno	CzRep	52	9	10	19	24																		
1998-99	Kladno	CzRep	50	21	14	35	32																		
99-2000	HPK Hameenlinna	Finland	32	20	9	29	31																		
	Ilves Tampere	Finland	22	15	5	20	44										3	1	1	2	14				
2000-01	**Anaheim**	**NHL**	**46**	**5**	**9**	**14**	**16**	**0**	**0**	**2**	**79**	**6.3**	**-11**	**0**	**0.0**	**12:48**									
	Cincinnati	AHL	25	9	9	18	24										4	3	2	5	0				
2001-02	**Anaheim**	**NHL**	**9**	**0**	**0**	**0**	**6**	**0**	**0**	**0**	**13**	**0.0**	**-6**	**1**	**0.0**	**11:47**									
	Cincinnati	AHL	3	2	3	5	2																		
	Nashville	**NHL**	**58**	**8**	**16**	**24**	**28**	**0**	**1**	**2**	**82**	**9.8**	**-4**	**7**	**28.6**	**12:00**									
	Milwaukee	AHL	4	0	0	0	2																		
2002-03	Karpat Oulu	Finland	51	21	19	40	60										14	4	2	6	6				
2003-04	Voskresensk	Russia	19	0	2	2	18																		
	Karpat Oulu	Finland	35	22	15	37	30										15	3	7	10	*45				
2004-05	Karpat Oulu	Finland	53	18	20	38	46										12	*7	4	11	6				
2005-06	Karpat Oulu	Finland	36	10	21	31	22										11	*6	3	9	18				
2006-07	**Boston**	**NHL**	**64**	**9**	**5**	**14**	**34**	**2**	**0**	**1**	**82**	**11.0**	**-16**	**15**	**33.3**	**12:31**									
	Providence Bruins	AHL	7	2	7	9	6																		
	NHL Totals		**177**	**22**	**30**	**52**	**84**	**2**	**1**	**5**	**256**	**8.6**		**23**	**30.4**	**12:23**									

Traded to **Nashville** by **Anaheim** for Patrick Kjellberg, November 1, 2001. Claimed by **Florida** from **Nashville** in Waiver Draft, October 4, 2002. Traded to **Columbus** by **Florida** for Mathieu Biron, October 4, 2002. Signed as a free agent by **Oulu** (Finland), May 15, 2002. Claimed by **Toronto** from **Columbus** in Waiver Draft, October 3, 2003. Traded to **Boston** by **Toronto** for Boston's 7th round choice (later traded to Phoenix - Phoenix selected Chris Frank) in 2006 Entry Draft, June 15, 2006. Signed as a free agent by **Timra** (Sweden), June 18, 2007.

TENUTE, Joey
(teh-NOOT, JOH-ee) **PHX.**

Center. Shoots left. 5'9", 188 lbs. Born, Hamilton, Ont., April 2, 1983. New Jersey's 6th choice, 261st overall, in 2003 Entry Draft.

Season	Club	League	Regular Season GP	G	A	Pts	PIM	PP	SH	GW	S	%	+/-	TF	F%	Min	Playoffs GP	G	A	Pts	PIM	PP	SH	GW	Min
99-2000	Georgetown	OPJHL	47	27	43	70	34	....	....	....	....	....	....	....	....	....	....	....	....	....	....	....	....	....	....
2000-01	Barrie Colts	OHL	61	13	18	31	38	....	....	....	....	....	....	....	....	....	5	1	1	2	10	....	....	....	....
2001-02	Barrie Colts	OHL	66	19	31	50	76	....	....	....	....	....	....	....	....	....	20	7	7	14	28	....	....	....	....
2002-03	Sarnia Sting	OHL	68	41	71	112	75	....	....	....	....	....	....	....	....	....	3	1	2	3	0	....	....	....	....
2003-04	Sarnia Sting	OHL	58	22	56	78	70	....	....	....	....	....	....	....	....	....	3	2	2	4	17	....	....	....	....
2004-05	South Carolina	ECHL	68	34	41	75	102	....	....	....	....	....	....	....	....	....	4	2	1	3	0	....	....	....	....
2005-06	**Washington**	**NHL**	**1**	**0**	**0**	**0**	**0**	**0**	**0**	**0**	**1**	**0.0**	**0**	**4**	**25.0**	**7:21**	....	....	....	....	....	....	....	....	....
	Hershey Bears	AHL	61	20	30	50	60	....	....	....	....	....	....	....	....	....	19	2	3	5	12	....	....	....	....
2006-07	Hershey Bears	AHL	68	28	39	67	58	....	....	....	....	....	....	....	....	....	9	4	1	5	8	....	....	....	....
	NHL Totals		**1**	**0**	**0**	**0**	**0**	**0**	**0**	**0**	**1**	**0.0**		**4**	**25.0**	**7:21**	....	....	....	....	....	....	....	....	....

ECHL All-Rookie Team (2005) • ECHL Second All-Star Team (2005) • ECHL Rookie of the Year (2005)

Signed as a free agent by **Washington**, November 21, 2005. Signed as a free agent by **Phoenix**, July 9, 2007.

TETARENKO, Joey
(teh-tar-EHN-koh, JOH-ee)

Right wing. Shoots right. 6'2", 215 lbs. Born, Prince Albert, Sask., March 3, 1978. Florida's 4th choice, 82nd overall, in 1996 Entry Draft.

Season	Club	League	GP	G	A	Pts	PIM	PP	SH	GW	S	%	+/-	TF	F%	Min	GP	G	A	Pts	PIM	PP	SH	GW	Min
1993-94	North Battleford	SMHL	36	6	13	19	75	....	....	....	....	....	....	....	....	....	....	....	....	....	....	....	....	....	....
1994-95	Portland	WHL	59	0	1	1	134	....	....	....	....	....	....	....	....	....	9	0	0	0	8	....	....	....	....
1995-96	Portland	WHL	71	4	11	15	190	....	....	....	....	....	....	....	....	....	7	0	1	1	17	....	....	....	....
1996-97	Portland	WHL	68	8	18	26	182	....	....	....	....	....	....	....	....	....	2	0	0	0	2	....	....	....	....
1997-98	Portland	WHL	49	2	12	14	148	....	....	....	....	....	....	....	....	....	16	0	2	2	30	....	....	....	....
1998-99	New Haven	AHL	65	4	10	14	154	....	....	....	....	....	....	....	....	....	....	....	....	....	....	....	....	....	....
99-2000	Louisville Panthers	AHL	57	3	11	14	136	....	....	....	....	....	....	....	....	....	4	0	0	0	2	....	....	....	....
2000-01	**Florida**	**NHL**	**29**	**3**	**1**	**4**	**44**	**0**	**0**	**0**	**21**	**14.3**	**−1**	**0**	**0.0**	**6:12**	....	....	....	....	....	....	....	....	....
	Louisville Panthers	AHL	29	1	4	5	74	....	....	....	....	....	....	....	....	....	....	....	....	....	....	....	....	....	....
2001-02	**Florida**	**NHL**	**38**	**1**	**0**	**1**	**123**	**0**	**0**	**0**	**10**	**10.0**	**−5**	**0**	**0.0**	**5:08**	....	....	....	....	....	....	....	....	....
2002-03	San Antonio	AHL	50	4	12	16	123	....	....	....	....	....	....	....	....	....	....	....	....	....	....	....	....	....	....
	Florida	**NHL**	**2**	**0**	**0**	**0**	**4**	**0**	**0**	**0**	**2**	**0.0**	**−1**	**0**	**0.0**	**6:19**	....	....	....	....	....	....	....	....	....
	Binghamton	AHL	14	2	2	4	33	....	....	....	....	....	....	....	....	....	14	0	0	0	36	....	....	....	....
	Ottawa	**NHL**	**2**	**0**	**0**	**0**	**5**	**0**	**0**	**0**	**1**	**0.0**	**0**	**0**	**0.0**	**6:29**	....	....	....	....	....	....	....	....	....
2003-04	**Carolina**	**NHL**	**2**	**0**	**0**	**0**	**0**	**0**	**0**	**0**	**0**	**0.0**	**0**	**1**	**0.0**	**3:31**	....	....	....	....	....	....	....	....	....
	Lowell	AHL	57	1	6	7	167	....	....	....	....	....	....	....	....	....	....	....	....	....	....	....	....	....	....
2004-05	Houston Aeros	AHL	15	0	1	1	49	....	....	....	....	....	....	....	....	....	....	....	....	....	....	....	....	....	....
2005-06	Houston Aeros	AHL	40	1	1	2	125	....	....	....	....	....	....	....	....	....	8	1	0	1	13	....	....	....	....
2006-07	Houston Aeros	AHL	39	2	4	6	94	....	....	....	....	....	....	....	....	....	....	....	....	....	....	....	....	....	....
	NHL Totals		**73**	**4**	**1**	**5**	**176**	**0**	**0**	**0**	**34**	**11.8**		**1**	**0.0**	**5:35**	....	....	....	....	....	....	....	....	....

• Missed majority of 2001-02 season recovering from jaw injury suffered in game vs. NY Rangers, November 3, 2001. Traded to **Ottawa** by **Florida** for Simon Lajeunesse, March 4, 2003. Signed as a free agent by **Carolina**, July 2, 2003. Signed as a free agent by **Houston** (AHL), February 19, 2005.

THOMAS, Bill
(TAW-mas, BIHL) **PHX.**

Right wing. Shoots right. 6'1", 191 lbs. Born, Pittsburgh, PA, June 20, 1983.

Season	Club	League	GP	G	A	Pts	PIM	PP	SH	GW	S	%	+/-	TF	F%	Min	GP	G	A	Pts	PIM	PP	SH	GW	Min
2002-03	Tri-City Storm	USHL	60	29	21	50	20	....	....	....	....	....	....	....	....	....	3	0	3	3	4	....	....	....	....
2003-04	Tri-City Storm	USHL	60	31	38	69	30	....	....	....	....	....	....	....	....	....	11	*9	7	*16	4	....	....	....	....
2004-05	Nebraska-Omaha	CCHA	39	19	26	45	12	....	....	....	....	....	....	....	....	....	....	....	....	....	....	....	....	....	....
2005-06	Nebraska-Omaha	CCHA	41	*27	23	50	43	....	....	....	....	....	....	....	....	....	....	....	....	....	....	....	....	....	....
	Phoenix	**NHL**	**9**	**1**	**2**	**3**	**8**	**1**	**0**	**0**	**15**	**6.7**	**−2**	**2**	**50.0**	**13:30**	....	....	....	....	....	....	....	....	....
2006-07	**Phoenix**	**NHL**	**24**	**8**	**6**	**14**	**2**	**4**	**0**	**1**	**60**	**13.3**	**−6**	**0**	**0.0**	**13:29**	....	....	....	....	....	....	....	....	....
	San Antonio	AHL	47	13	20	33	20	....	....	....	....	....	....	....	....	....	....	....	....	....	....	....	....	....	....
	NHL Totals		**33**	**9**	**8**	**17**	**10**	**5**	**0**	**1**	**75**	**12.0**		**2**	**50.0**	**13:29**	....	....	....	....	....	....	....	....	....

CCHA All-Rookie Team (2005) • CCHA Rookie of the Year (2005) • CCHA Second All-Star Team (2005) • CCHA First All-Star Team (2006)

Signed as a free agent by **Phoenix**, March 27, 2006.

THOMPSON, Nate
(TAWM-suhn, NAYT) **BOS.**

Center. Shoots left. 6', 206 lbs. Born, Anchorage, AK, October 5, 1984. Boston's 8th choice, 183rd overall, in 2003 Entry Draft.

Season	Club	League	GP	G	A	Pts	PIM	PP	SH	GW	S	%	+/-	TF	F%	Min	GP	G	A	Pts	PIM	PP	SH	GW	Min
2001-02	Seattle	WHL	69	13	26	39	42	....	....	....	....	....	....	....	....	....	11	1	3	4	13	....	....	....	....
2002-03	Seattle	WHL	61	10	24	34	48	....	....	....	....	....	....	....	....	....	15	5	4	9	6	....	....	....	....
2003-04	Seattle	WHL	65	13	23	36	24	....	....	....	....	....	....	....	....	....	....	....	....	....	....	....	....	....	....
2004-05	Seattle	WHL	58	19	15	34	39	....	....	....	....	....	....	....	....	....	12	1	2	3	2	....	....	....	....
	Providence Bruins	AHL	....	....	....	....	....	....	....	....	....	....	....	....	....	....	11	0	1	1	6	....	....	....	....
2005-06	Providence Bruins	AHL	74	8	10	18	58	....	....	....	....	....	....	....	....	....	3	0	0	0	10	....	....	....	....
2006-07	**Boston**	**NHL**	**4**	**0**	**0**	**0**	**0**	**0**	**0**	**0**	**5**	**0.0**	**0**	**10**	**40.0**	**4:46**	....	....	....	....	....	....	....	....	....
	Providence Bruins	AHL	67	8	15	23	74	....	....	....	....	....	....	....	....	....	13	0	2	2	9	....	....	....	....
	NHL Totals		**4**	**0**	**0**	**0**	**0**	**0**	**0**	**0**	**5**	**0.0**		**10**	**40.0**	**4:46**	....	....	....	....	....	....	....	....	....

THOMPSON, Rocky
(TAWM-suhn, RAW-kee)

Defense. Shoots right. 6'2", 205 lbs. Born, Calgary, Alta., August 8, 1977. Calgary's 3rd choice, 72nd overall, in 1995 Entry Draft.

Season	Club	League	GP	G	A	Pts	PIM	PP	SH	GW	S	%	+/-	TF	F%	Min	GP	G	A	Pts	PIM	PP	SH	GW	Min
1992-93	Spruce Grove	AMHL	65	13	50	63	295	....	....	....	....	....	....	....	....	....	....	....	....	....	....	....	....	....	....
1993-94	Medicine Hat	WHL	68	1	4	5	166	....	....	....	....	....	....	....	....	....	3	0	0	0	2	....	....	....	....
1994-95	Medicine Hat	WHL	63	1	6	7	220	....	....	....	....	....	....	....	....	....	5	0	0	0	17	....	....	....	....
1995-96	Medicine Hat	WHL	71	9	20	29	260	....	....	....	....	....	....	....	....	....	5	2	3	5	26	....	....	....	....
	Saint John Flames	AHL	4	0	0	0	33	....	....	....	....	....	....	....	....	....	....	....	....	....	....	....	....	....	....
1996-97	Medicine Hat	WHL	47	6	9	15	170	....	....	....	....	....	....	....	....	....	....	....	....	....	....	....	....	....	....
	Swift Current	WHL	22	3	5	8	90	....	....	....	....	....	....	....	....	....	10	1	2	3	22	....	....	....	....
1997-98	**Calgary**	**NHL**	**12**	**0**	**0**	**0**	**61**	**0**	**0**	**0**	**3**	**0.0**	**0**	....	....	....	....	....	....	....	....	....	....	....	....
	Saint John Flames	AHL	51	3	0	3	187	....	....	....	....	....	....	....	....	....	18	1	1	2	47	....	....	....	....
1998-99	**Calgary**	**NHL**	**3**	**0**	**0**	**0**	**25**	**0**	**0**	**0**	**0**	**0.0**	**0**	**0**	**0.0**	**2:01**	....	....	....	....	....	....	....	....	....
	Saint John Flames	AHL	27	2	2	4	108	....	....	....	....	....	....	....	....	....	....	....	....	....	....	....	....	....	....
99-2000	Saint John Flames	AHL	53	2	8	10	125	....	....	....	....	....	....	....	....	....	....	....	....	....	....	....	....	....	....
	Louisville Panthers	AHL	3	0	1	1	54	....	....	....	....	....	....	....	....	....	4	0	0	0	4	....	....	....	....
2000-01	**Florida**	**NHL**	**4**	**0**	**0**	**0**	**19**	**0**	**0**	**0**	**0**	**0.0**	**0**	**0**	**0.0**	**1:28**	....	....	....	....	....	....	....	....	....
	Louisville Panthers	AHL	55	3	5	8	193	....	....	....	....	....	....	....	....	....	....	....	....	....	....	....	....	....	....
2001-02	**Florida**	**NHL**	**6**	**0**	**0**	**0**	**12**	**0**	**0**	**0**	**1**	**0.0**	**0**	**1**	**0.0**	**4:03**	....	....	....	....	....	....	....	....	....
	Hershey Bears	AHL	42	0	3	3	143	....	....	....	....	....	....	....	....	....	8	1	0	1	19	....	....	....	....
2002-03	San Antonio	AHL	79	1	11	12	275	....	....	....	....	....	....	....	....	....	3	0	0	0	4	....	....	....	....
2003-04	Toronto	AHL	69	1	8	9	196	....	....	....	....	....	....	....	....	....	3	1	1	2	0	....	....	....	....
2004-05	Edmonton	AHL	69	3	3	6	231	....	....	....	....	....	....	....	....	....	....	....	....	....	....	....	....	....	....
2005-06	Peoria Rivermen	AHL	59	1	4	5	247	....	....	....	....	....	....	....	....	....	3	0	0	0	19	....	....	....	....
2006-07	Peoria Rivermen	AHL	55	1	7	8	127	....	....	....	....	....	....	....	....	....	....	....	....	....	....	....	....	....	....
	NHL Totals		**25**	**0**	**0**	**0**	**117**	**0**	**0**	**0**	**4**	**0.0**		**1**	**0.0**	**2:47**	....	....	....	....	....	....	....	....	....

Traded to **Florida** by **Calgary** for Filip Kuba, March 16, 2000. Signed as a free agent by **Edmonton**, July 20, 2003.

THORBURN, Chris
(THOHR buhrn, KRIHS) **ATL.**

Center. Shoots right. 6'3", 220 lbs. Born, Sault Ste. Marie, Ont., June 3, 1983. Buffalo's 3rd choice, 50th overall, in 2001 Entry Draft.

Season	Club	League	GP	G	A	Pts	PIM	PP	SH	GW	S	%	+/-	TF	F%	Min	GP	G	A	Pts	PIM	PP	SH	GW	Min
1998-99	Elliot Lake Vikings	NOJHA	40	21	12	33	28	....	....	....	....	....	....	....	....	....	....	....	....	....	....	....	....	....	....
99-2000	North Bay	OHL	56	12	8	20	33	....	....	....	....	....	....	....	....	....	6	0	2	2	0	....	....	....	....
2000-01	North Bay	OHL	66	22	32	54	64	....	....	....	....	....	....	....	....	....	4	0	1	1	9	....	....	....	....
2001-02	North Bay	OHL	67	15	43	58	112	....	....	....	....	....	....	....	....	....	5	1	2	3	8	....	....	....	....
2002-03	Saginaw Spirit	OHL	37	19	19	38	68	....	....	....	....	....	....	....	....	....	....	....	....	....	....	....	....	....	....
	Plymouth Whalers	OHL	27	11	22	33	56	....	....	....	....	....	....	....	....	....	18	11	9	20	10	....	....	....	....
2003-04	Rochester	AHL	58	6	16	22	77	....	....	....	....	....	....	....	....	....	16	3	2	5	18	....	....	....	....
2004-05	Rochester	AHL	73	12	17	29	185	....	....	....	....	....	....	....	....	....	4	0	1	1	2	....	....	....	....

			Regular Season														Playoffs								
Season	Club	League	GP	G	A	Pts	PIM	PP	SH	GW	S	%	+/-	TF	F%	Min	GP	G	A	Pts	PIM	PP	SH	GW	Min
2005-06	Buffalo	NHL	2	0	1	1	7	0	0	0	1	0.0	–1	1	0.0	6:52	....	....	....	....	....	....	....	....	....
	Rochester	AHL	77	23	27	50	134	....	....	....	....	....	....	....	....	....	....	....	....	....	....	....	....	....	....
2006-07	Pittsburgh	NHL	39	3	2	5	69	0	0	1	40	7.5	1	8	25.0	7:54	....	....	....	....	....	....	....	....	....
	Wilkes-Barre	AHL	3	0	1	1	2	....	....	....	....	....	....	....	....	....	....	....	....	....	....	....	....	....	....
	NHL Totals		41	3	3	6	76	0	0	1	41	7.3		9	22.2	7:51	....	....	....	....	....	....	....	....	....

Claimed on waivers by **Pittsburgh** from **Buffalo**, October 3, 2006. Traded to **Atlanta** by **Pittsburgh** for NY Rangers' 3rd round choice (previously acquired, Pittsburgh selected Robert Bortuzzo) in 2007 Entry Draft, June 22, 2007.

THORESEN, Patrick

(THOR-eh-sehn, PAT-rihk) **EDM.**

Center. Shoots left. 5'11", 188 lbs. Born, Oslo, Norway, November 8, 1987.

Season	Club	League	GP	G	A	Pts	PIM	PP	SH	GW	S	%	+/-	TF	F%	Min	GP	G	A	Pts	PIM	PP	SH	GW	Min
99-2000	Storhamar	Norway	25	1	8	9	4	....	....	....	....	....	....	....	....	....	....	....	....	....	....	....	....	....	....
2000-01	Storhamar	Norway	40	18	27	45	24	....	....	....	....	....	....	....	....	....	....	....	....	....	....	....	....	....	....
2001-02	Moncton Wildcats	QMJHL	60	30	43	73	50	....	....	....	....	....	....	....	....	....	....	....	....	....	....	....	....	....	....
2002-03	Baie-Comeau	QMJHL	71	33	*75	108	57	....	....	....	....	....	....	....	....	....	12	2	8	10	8	....	....	....	....
2003-04	Morrums GoIS IK	Sweden-2	38	19	22	41	40	....	....	....	....	....	....	....	....	....	....	....	....	....	....	....	....	....	....
	Djurgarden	Sweden	3	0	0	0	2	....	....	....	....	....	....	....	....	....	....	....	....	....	....	....	....	....	....
2004-05	Djurgarden	Sweden	30	10	7	17	33	....	....	....	....	....	....	....	....	....	12	2	2	4	29	....	....	....	....
2005-06	Djurgarden	Sweden	50	17	19	36	44	....	....	....	....	....	....	....	....	....	....	....	....	....	....	....	....	....	....
	Salzburg	Austria	....	....	....	....	....	....	....	....	....	....	....	....	....	....	9	4	7	11	12	....	....	....	....
2006-07	Edmonton	NHL	68	4	12	16	52	0	1	2	73	5.5	–1	82	51.2	11:25	....	....	....	....	....	....	....	....	....
	Wilkes-Barre	AHL	5	1	5	6	4	....	....	....	....	....	....	....	....	....	....	....	....	....	....	....	....	....	....
	NHL Totals		68	4	12	16	52	0	1	2	73	5.5		82	51.2	11:25	....	....	....	....	....	....	....	....	....

Signed as a free agent by **Edmonton**, June 12, 2006.

THORNTON, Joe

(THOHRN-tuhn, JOH) **S.J.**

Center. Shoots left. 6'4", 235 lbs. Born, London, Ont., July 2, 1979. Boston's 1st choice, 1st overall, in 1997 Entry Draft.

Season	Club	League	GP	G	A	Pts	PIM	PP	SH	GW	S	%	+/-	TF	F%	Min	GP	G	A	Pts	PIM	PP	SH	GW	Min
1993-94	Elgin-Middlesex	Minor-ON	67	*83	*85	*168	45	....	....	....	....	....	....	....	....	....	....	....	....	....	....	....	....	....	....
	St. Thomas Stars	OHA-B	6	2	6	8	2	....	....	....	....	....	....	....	....	....	....	....	....	....	....	....	....	....	....
1994-95	St. Thomas Stars	OHA-B	50	40	64	104	53	....	....	....	....	....	....	....	....	....	....	....	....	....	....	....	....	....	....
1995-96	Sault Ste. Marie	OHL	66	30	46	76	53	....	....	....	....	....	....	....	....	....	4	1	1	2	11	....	....	....	....
1996-97	Sault Ste. Marie	OHL	59	41	81	122	123	....	....	....	....	....	....	....	....	....	11	11	8	19	24	....	....	....	....
1997-98	Boston	NHL	55	3	4	7	19	0	0	1	33	9.1	–6	....	....	....	6	0	0	0	9	0	0	0	....
1998-99	Boston	NHL	81	16	25	41	69	7	0	1	128	12.5	3	1073	48.7	15:21	11	3	6	9	4	2	0	2	19:52
99-2000	Boston	NHL	81	23	37	60	82	5	0	3	171	13.5	–5	1861	49.5	21:18	....	....	....	....	....	....	....	....	....
2000-01	Boston	NHL	72	37	34	71	107	19	1	5	181	20.4	–4	1651	52.1	21:45	....	....	....	....	....	....	....	....	....
2001-02	Boston	NHL	66	22	46	68	127	6	0	5	152	14.5	7	1341	49.1	19:59	6	2	4	6	10	0	0	0	21:09
2002-03	Boston	NHL	77	36	65	101	109	12	2	4	196	18.4	12	1766	49.5	22:33	5	1	2	3	4	1	0	0	20:13
2003-04	Boston	NHL	77	23	50	73	98	4	0	6	187	12.3	18	1671	56.3	21:38	7	0	0	0	14	0	0	0	21:30
2004-05	HC Davos	Swiss	40	10	44	54	80	....	....	....	....	....	....	....	....	....	14	4	*20	*24	29	....	....	....	....
2005-06	Boston	NHL	23	9	*24	*33	6	3	0	2	60	15.0	0	511	52.3	21:33	....	....	....	....	....	....	....	....	....
	San Jose	NHL	58	20	*72	*92	55	8	0	4	135	14.8	31	1287	50.9	21:15	11	2	7	9	12	1	0	1	25:09
	Canada	Olympics	6	1	2	3	0	....	....	....	....	....	....	....	....	....	....	....	....	....	....	....	....	....	....
2006-07	San Jose	NHL	82	22	*92	114	44	10	0	5	213	10.3	24	1522	51.1	20:19	11	1	10	11	10	0	0	0	22:00
	NHL Totals		672	211	449	660	716	74	3	36	1456	14.5		12683	51.1	20:30	57	9	29	38	63	4	0	3	21:52

OHL All-Rookie Team (1996) • OHL Rookie of the Year (1996) • Canadian Major Junior Rookie of the Year (1996) • OHL Second All-Star Team (1997) • NHL Second All-Star Team (2003) • NHL First All-Star Team (2006) • Art Ross Trophy (2006) • Hart Memorial Trophy (2006)

Played in NHL All-Star Game (2002, 2003, 2004, 2007)

Signed as a free agent by **Davos** (Swiss), July 8, 2004. Traded to **San Jose** by **Boston** for Brad Stuart, Marco Sturm and Wayne Primeau, November 30, 2005.

THORNTON, Scott

(THOHRN-tuhn, SKAWT) **L.A.**

Left wing. Shoots left. 6'3", 220 lbs. Born, London, Ont., January 9, 1971. Toronto's 1st choice, 3rd overall, in 1989 Entry Draft.

Season	Club	League	GP	G	A	Pts	PIM	PP	SH	GW	S	%	+/-	TF	F%	Min	GP	G	A	Pts	PIM	PP	SH	GW	Min
1986-87	London	OHA-B	31	10	7	17	10	....	....	....	....	....	....	....	....	....	....	....	....	....	....	....	....	....	....
1987-88	Belleville Bulls	OHL	62	11	19	30	54	....	....	....	....	....	....	....	....	....	6	0	1	1	2	....	....	....	....
1988-89	Belleville Bulls	OHL	59	28	34	62	103	....	....	....	....	....	....	....	....	....	5	1	1	2	6	....	....	....	....
1989-90	Belleville Bulls	OHL	47	21	28	49	91	....	....	....	....	....	....	....	....	....	11	2	10	12	15	....	....	....	....
1990-91	Belleville Bulls	OHL	3	2	1	3	2	....	....	....	....	....	....	....	....	....	6	0	7	7	14	....	....	....	....
	Toronto	NHL	33	1	3	4	30	0	0	0	31	3.2	–15	....	....	....	....	....	....	....	....	....	....	....	....
	Newmarket Saints	AHL	5	1	0	1	4	....	....	....	....	....	....	....	....	....	....	....	....	....	....	....	....	....	....
1991-92	Edmonton	NHL	15	0	1	1	43	0	0	0	11	0.0	–6	....	....	....	1	0	0	0	0	0	0	0	....
	Cape Breton	AHL	49	9	14	23	40	....	....	....	....	....	....	....	....	....	5	1	0	1	8	....	....	....	....
1992-93	Edmonton	NHL	9	0	1	1	0	0	0	0	7	0.0	–4	....	....	....	....	....	....	....	....	....	....	....	....
	Cape Breton	AHL	58	23	27	50	102	....	....	....	....	....	....	....	....	....	16	1	2	3	35	....	....	....	....
1993-94	Edmonton	NHL	61	4	7	11	104	0	0	0	65	6.2	–15	....	....	....	....	....	....	....	....	....	....	....	....
	Cape Breton	AHL	2	1	1	2	31	....	....	....	....	....	....	....	....	....	....	....	....	....	....	....	....	....	....
1994-95	Edmonton	NHL	47	10	12	22	89	0	1	1	69	14.5	–4	....	....	....	....	....	....	....	....	....	....	....	....
1995-96	Edmonton	NHL	77	9	9	18	149	0	2	3	95	9.5	–25	....	....	....	....	....	....	....	....	....	....	....	....
1996-97	Montreal	NHL	73	10	10	20	128	1	1	1	110	9.1	–19	....	....	....	5	1	0	1	2	0	0	0	....
1997-98	Montreal	NHL	67	6	9	15	158	1	0	1	51	11.8	0	....	....	....	9	0	2	2	10	0	0	0	....
1998-99	Montreal	NHL	47	7	4	11	87	1	0	1	56	12.5	–2	466	52.8	12:24	....	....	....	....	....	....	....	....	....
99-2000	Montreal	NHL	35	2	3	5	70	0	0	1	36	5.6	–7	253	51.8	12:40	....	....	....	....	....	....	....	....	....
	Dallas	NHL	30	6	3	9	38	1	0	0	47	12.8	–5	14	14.3	13:03	23	2	7	9	28	0	0	1	14:11
2000-01	San Jose	NHL	73	19	17	36	114	4	0	1	159	11.9	4	29	41.4	13:54	6	3	0	3	8	0	0	1	15:50
2001-02	San Jose	NHL	77	26	16	42	116	6	0	5	144	18.1	11	18	61.1	13:31	12	3	3	6	6	0	0	0	15:52
2002-03	San Jose	NHL	41	9	12	21	41	4	0	1	64	14.1	–7	6	50.0	13:53	....	....	....	....	....	....	....	....	....
2003-04	San Jose	NHL	80	13	14	27	84	1	0	1	127	10.2	–6	27	40.7	13:57	12	2	2	4	22	0	0	0	12:31
2004-05	Sodertalje SK	Sweden	12	2	5	7	10	....	....	....	....	....	....	....	....	....	10	0	3	3	27	....	....	....	....
2005-06	San Jose	NHL	71	10	11	21	84	1	0	2	122	8.2	–8	28	35.7	13:19	11	2	0	2	6	0	0	0	11:18
2006-07	Los Angeles	NHL	58	7	6	13	85	0	1	0	65	10.8	–15	145	57.9	12:24	....	....	....	....	....	....	....	....	....
	NHL Totals		894	139	138	277	1420	20	5	18	1259	11.0		986	51.7	13:19	79	13	14	27	82	0	0	2	13:51

Traded to **Edmonton** by **Toronto** with Vincent Damphousse, Peter Ing and Luke Richardson for Grant Fuhr, Glenn Anderson and Craig Berube, September 19, 1991. Traded to **Montreal** by **Edmonton** for Andrei Kovalenko, September 6, 1996. Traded to **Dallas** by **Montreal** for Juha Lind, January 22, 2000. Signed as a free agent by **San Jose**, July 1, 2000. • Missed majority of 2002-03 season recovering from shoulder (October 7, 2002 in training camp) and head (February 21, 2003 vs. Columbus) injuries. Signed as a free agent by **Sodertalje** (Sweden), January 13, 2005. Signed as a free agent by **Los Angeles**, July 1, 2006.

THORNTON, Shawn

(THOHRN-tohn, SHAWN) **BOS.**

Right wing. Shoots right. 6'1", 209 lbs. Born, Oshawa, Ont., July 23, 1977. Toronto's 6th choice, 190th overall, in 1997 Entry Draft.

Season	Club	League	GP	G	A	Pts	PIM	PP	SH	GW	S	%	+/-	TF	F%	Min	GP	G	A	Pts	PIM	PP	SH	GW	Min
1995-96	Peterborough	OHL	63	4	10	14	192	....	....	....	....	....	....	....	....	....	24	3	0	3	25	....	....	....	....
1996-97	Peterborough	OHL	61	19	10	29	204	....	....	....	....	....	....	....	....	....	11	2	4	6	20	....	....	....	....
1997-98	St. John's	AHL	59	0	3	3	225	....	....	....	....	....	....	....	....	....	....	....	....	....	....	....	....	....	....
1998-99	St. John's	AHL	78	8	11	19	354	....	....	....	....	....	....	....	....	....	5	0	0	0	9	....	....	....	....
99-2000	St. John's	AHL	60	4	12	16	316	....	....	....	....	....	....	....	....	....	....	....	....	....	....	....	....	....	....
2000-01	St. John's	AHL	79	5	12	17	320	....	....	....	....	....	....	....	....	....	3	1	2	3	2	....	....	....	....
2001-02	Norfolk Admirals	AHL	70	8	14	22	281	....	....	....	....	....	....	....	....	....	4	0	0	0	4	....	....	....	....
2002-03	Chicago	NHL	13	1	1	2	31	0	0	0	15	6.7	–4	3	66.7	8:30	....	....	....	....	....	....	....	....	....
	Norfolk Admirals	AHL	50	11	2	13	213	....	....	....	....	....	....	....	....	....	9	0	2	2	28	....	....	....	....
2003-04	Chicago	NHL	8	1	0	1	23	0	0	0	14	7.1	2	19	42.1	11:14	....	....	....	....	....	....	....	....	....
	Norfolk Admirals	AHL	64	6	11	17	259	....	....	....	....	....	....	....	....	....	8	1	1	2	6	....	....	....	....
2004-05	Norfolk Admirals	AHL	71	5	9	14	253	....	....	....	....	....	....	....	....	....	6	0	0	0	8	....	....	....	....
2005-06	Chicago	NHL	10	0	0	0	16	0	0	0	16	0.0	–5	17	58.8	7:18	....	....	....	....	....	....	....	....	....
	Norfolk Admirals	AHL	59	10	22	32	192	....	....	....	....	....	....	....	....	....	4	0	0	0	35	....	....	....	....
2006-07 ♦	Anaheim	NHL	48	2	7	9	88	0	0	0	60	3.3	3	8	25.0	8:26	15	0	0	0	19	0	0	0	3:58
	Portland Pirates	AHL	15	4	4	8	55	....	....	....	....	....	....	....	....	....	....	....	....	....	....	....	....	....	....
	NHL Totals		79	4	8	12	158	0	0	0	105	3.8		47	46.8	8:35	15	0	0	0	19	0	0	0	3:58

Traded to **Chicago** by **Toronto** for Marty Wilford, September 30, 2001. Signed as a free agent by **Anaheim**, July 14, 2006. Signed as a free agent by **Boston**, July 1, 2007.

			Regular Season														Playoffs								
Season	Club	League	GP	G	A	Pts	PIM	PP	SH	GW	S	%	+/-	TF	F%	Min	GP	G	A	Pts	PIM	PP	SH	GW	Min

TIMONEN, Jussi
(TEEM-oh-nehn, YEW-see) **PHI.**

Defense. Shoots left. 6', 200 lbs. Born, Kuopio, Finland, June 29, 1983. Philadelphia's 3rd choice, 146th overall, in 2001 Entry Draft.

Season	Club	League	GP	G	A	Pts	PIM	PP	SH	GW	S	%	+/-	TF	F%	Min	GP	G	A	Pts	PIM	PP	SH	GW	Min
99-2000	KalPa Kuopio U18	Fin-U18	14	3	2	5	10																		
	KalPa Kuopio Jr.	Fin-Jr.	19	1	0	1	6										4	0	0	0	4				
2000-01	KalPa Kuopio U18	Fin-U18	4	1	4	5	10																		
	KalPa Kuopio Jr.	Fin-Jr.	38	6	7	13	22																		
	KalPa Kuopio	Finland-3	7	0	1	1	2										2	1	0	1	0				
2001-02	KalPa Kuopio Jr.	Fin-Jr.	10	1	1	2	10																		
	KalPa Kuopio	Finland-2	41	3	8	11	10										8	0	2	2	0				
2002-03	TPS Turku Jr.	Fin-Jr.	2	0	0	0	0																		
	TuTo Turku	Finland-2	3	0	0	0	0																		
	TPS Turku	Finland	39	1	0	1	10										7	0	2	2	4				
2003-04	TPS Turku	Finland	20	0	0	0	4																		
	Jukurit Mikkeli	Finland-2	25	7	9	16	10										13	0	4	4	0				
2004-05	SaiPa	Finland	54	1	5	6	53																		
2005-06	SaiPa	Finland	52	0	7	7	30										8	1	0	1	27				
2006-07	**Philadelphia**	**NHL**	**14**	**0**	**4**	**4**	**6**	**0**	**0**	**0**	**8**	**0.0**	**-10**	**0**	**0.0**	**14:11**									
	Philadelphia	AHL	46	2	15	17	18																		
	NHL Totals		**14**	**0**	**4**	**4**	**6**	**0**	**0**	**0**	**8**	**0.0**		**0**	**0.0**	**14:11**									

TIMONEN, Kimmo
(TEEM-oh-nehn, KEE-moh) **PHI.**

Defense. Shoots left. 5'10", 194 lbs. Born, Kuopio, Finland, March 18, 1975. Los Angeles' 11th choice, 250th overall, in 1993 Entry Draft.

Season	Club	League	GP	G	A	Pts	PIM	PP	SH	GW	S	%	+/-	TF	F%	Min	GP	G	A	Pts	PIM	PP	SH	GW	Min
1990-91	KalPa Kuopio Jr.	Fin-Jr.	4	0	1	1	2																		
1991-92	KalPa Kuopio Jr.	Fin-Jr.	32	7	10	17	4																		
	KalPa Kuopio	Finland	5	0	0	0	0																		
1992-93	KalPa Kuopio U18	Fin-U18	3	0	5	5	0																		
	KalPa Kuopio Jr.	Fin-Jr.	16	9	15	24	10																		
	KalPa Kuopio	Finland	33	0	2	2	4																		
1993-94	KalPa Kuopio Jr.	Fin-Jr.	5	4	7	11	0																		
	KalPa Kuopio	Finland	46	6	7	13	55																		
1994-95	TPS Turku Jr.	Fin-Jr.	1	0	0	0	0																		
	TPS Turku	Finland	45	3	4	7	10										13	0	1	1	6				
1995-96	TPS Turku	Finland	48	3	21	24	22										9	1	2	3	12				
1996-97	TPS Turku	Finland	50	10	14	24	18										12	2	7	9	6				
	TPS Turku	EuroHL	6	1	0	1	27										4	0	1	1	0				
1997-98	HIFK Helsinki	Finland	45	10	15	25	24										9	3	4	7	8				
	Finland	Olympics	6	0	1	1	2																		
1998-99	**Nashville**	**NHL**	**50**	**4**	**8**	**12**	**30**	**1**	**0**	**0**	**75**	**5.3**	**-4**	**0**	**0.0**	**19:04**									
	Milwaukee	IHL	29	2	13	15	22																		
99-2000	**Nashville**	**NHL**	**51**	**8**	**25**	**33**	**26**	**2**	**1**	**2**	**97**	**8.2**	**-5**	**0**	**0.0**	**21:06**									
2000-01	**Nashville**	**NHL**	**82**	**12**	**13**	**25**	**50**	**6**	**0**	**3**	**151**	**7.9**	**-6**	**2**	**50.0**	**23:11**									
2001-02	**Nashville**	**NHL**	**82**	**13**	**29**	**42**	**28**	**9**	**0**	**1**	**154**	**8.4**	**2**	**0**	**0.0**	**24:12**									
	Finland	Olympics	4	0	1	1	2																		
2002-03	**Nashville**	**NHL**	**72**	**6**	**34**	**40**	**46**	**4**	**0**	**0**	**144**	**4.2**	**-3**	**0**	**0.0**	**22:25**									
2003-04	**Nashville**	**NHL**	**77**	**12**	**32**	**44**	**52**	**8**	**0**	**1**	**180**	**6.7**	**-7**	**1**	**0.0**	**23:52**	**6**	**0**	**0**	**0**	**10**	**0**	**0**	**0**	**24:16**
2004-05	HC Lugano	Swiss	3	0	1	1	0																		
	Brynas IF Gavle	Sweden	10	5	3	8	8																		
	KalPa Kuopio	Finland-2	12	4	13	17	6										8	3	7	10	4				
2005-06	**Nashville**	**NHL**	**79**	**11**	**39**	**50**	**74**	**8**	**0**	**1**	**156**	**7.1**	**-3**	**5**	**80.0**	**22:26**	**5**	**1**	**3**	**4**	**4**	**0**	**1**	**0**	**24:42**
	Finland	Olympics	8	1	4	5	2																		
2006-07	**Nashville**	**NHL**	**80**	**13**	**42**	**55**	**42**	**8**	**0**	**2**	**121**	**10.7**	**20**	**1**	**0.0**	**21:51**	**5**	**0**	**2**	**2**	**4**	**0**	**0**	**0**	**24:33**
	NHL Totals		**573**	**79**	**222**	**301**	**348**	**46**	**1**	**10**	**1078**	**7.3**		**9**	**55.6**	**22:29**	**16**	**1**	**5**	**6**	**18**	**0**	**1**	**0**	**24:29**

Olympic Tournament All-Star Team (2006)

Played in NHL All-Star Game (2004, 2007)

Traded to **Nashville** by **Los Angeles** with Jan Vopat for future considerations, June 26, 1998. Signed as a free agent by **Lugano** (Swiss), October 31, 2004. Signed as a free agent by **Gavle** (Sweden), November 8, 2004. Signed as a free agent by **Kuopio** (Finland-2), January 3, 2005. Traded to **Philadelphia** by **Nashville** with Scott Hartnell for Nashville's 1st round choice (previously acquired, Nashville selected Jonathon Blum) in 2007 Entry Draft, June 18, 2007.

TJARNQVIST, Daniel
(T'YAHRN-kvihst, DAN-yehl)

Defense. Shoots left. 6'2", 200 lbs. Born, Umea, Sweden, October 14, 1976. Florida's 5th choice, 88th overall, in 1995 Entry Draft.

Season	Club	League	GP	G	A	Pts	PIM	PP	SH	GW	S	%	+/-	TF	F%	Min	GP	G	A	Pts	PIM	PP	SH	GW	Min
1992-93	Rogle Jr.	Swe-Jr.	7	1	0	1	0																		
1993-94	Rogle U18	Swe-U18	STATISTICS NOT AVAILABLE																						
1994-95	Rogle	Sweden	18	0	1	1	2																		
	Rogle	Sweden-Q	15	2	3	5	0																		
1995-96	Rogle	Sweden	22	1	7	8	6																		
1996-97	Jokerit Helsinki	Finland	44	3	8	11	4										9	0	3	3	4				
	Jokerit Helsinki	EuroHL	6	1	1	2	2																		
1997-98	Djurgarden	Sweden	40	5	9	14	12										15	1	1	2	2				
1998-99	Djurgarden	Sweden	40	4	3	7	16										4	0	0	0	2				
99-2000	Djurgarden	Sweden	42	3	16	19	8										5	0	0	0	2				
2000-01	Djurgarden	Sweden	45	9	17	26	26										16	6	5	11	2				
2001-02	**Atlanta**	**NHL**	**75**	**2**	**16**	**18**	**14**	**1**	**0**	**0**	**68**	**2.9**	**-22**	**4**	**25.0**	**21:32**									
2002-03	**Atlanta**	**NHL**	**75**	**3**	**12**	**15**	**26**	**1**	**0**	**0**	**65**	**4.6**	**-20**	**3**	**66.7**	**21:53**									
2003-04	**Atlanta**	**NHL**	**68**	**5**	**15**	**20**	**20**	**0**	**2**	**1**	**65**	**7.7**	**-4**	**4**	**25.0**	**22:17**									
2004-05	Djurgarden	Sweden	49	12	12	24	30										12	2	5	7	10				
2005-06	**Minnesota**	**NHL**	**60**	**3**	**15**	**18**	**32**	**3**	**0**	**1**	**54**	**5.6**	**-11**	**0**	**0.0**	**19:46**									
	Sweden	Olympics	8	2	1	3	4																		
2006-07	**Edmonton**	**NHL**	**37**	**3**	**12**	**15**	**30**	**2**	**0**	**0**	**33**	**9.1**	**3**	**0**	**0.0**	**22:42**									
	NHL Totals		**315**	**16**	**70**	**86**	**122**	**7**	**2**	**2**	**285**	**5.6**		**11**	**36.4**	**21:35**									

Traded to **Atlanta** by **Florida** with Gord Murphy, Herbert Vasiljevs and Ottawa's 6th round choice (previously acquired, later traded to Dallas – Dallas selected Justin Cox) in 1999 Entry Draft for Trevor Kidd, June 25, 1999. Signed as a free agent by **Djurgarden** (Sweden), September 16, 2004. Signed as a free agent by **Minnesota**, August 15, 2005. Signed as a free agent by **Edmonton**, July 6, 2006. • Missed majority of 2006-07 season recovering from recurring groin injury.

TJARNQVIST, Mathias
(T'YAHRN-kvihst, MAT-ee-uhs) **PHX.**

Right wing. Shoots left. 6'1", 183 lbs. Born, Umea, Sweden, April 15, 1979. Dallas' 3rd choice, 96th overall, in 1999 Entry Draft.

Season	Club	League	GP	G	A	Pts	PIM	PP	SH	GW	S	%	+/-	TF	F%	Min	GP	G	A	Pts	PIM	PP	SH	GW	Min
1995-96	Rogle Jr.	Swe-Jr.	4	2	0	2	0																		
1996-97	Rogle Jr.	Swe-Jr.	18	5	8	13																			
	Rogle	Sweden-2	15	1	4	5	4																		
1997-98	Rogle	Sweden-2	31	12	11	23	30										4	2	0	2	6				
1998-99	Rogle	Sweden-2	34	18	16	34	44										5	4	1	5	4				
99-2000	Djurgarden	Sweden	50	12	12	24	20										13	3	2	5	16				
2000-01	Djurgarden	Sweden	47	11	8	19	53										16	1	2	3	6				
2001-02	Djurgarden	Sweden	6	0	1	1	4										2	0	0	0	2				
2002-03	Djurgarden	Sweden	38	11	13	24	30										9	4	1	5	12				
2003-04	**Dallas**	**NHL**	**18**	**1**	**1**	**2**	**2**	**0**	**0**	**1**	**11**	**9.1**	**-6**	**4**	**25.0**	**9:43**									
	Utah Grizzlies	AHL	60	15	13	28	51																		
2004-05	HV 71 Jonkoping	Sweden	46	8	9	17	18																		
2005-06	**Dallas**	**NHL**	**33**	**2**	**4**	**6**	**18**	**0**	**0**	**0**	**36**	**5.6**	**4**	**4**	**75.0**	**8:10**									
	Iowa Stars	AHL	34	17	12	29	28										1	0	0	0	0				
2006-07	**Dallas**	**NHL**	**18**	**1**	**3**	**4**	**4**	**0**	**0**	**0**	**13**	**7.7**	**-3**	**7**	**42.9**	**9:15**									
	Iowa Stars	AHL	2	1	1	2	0																		
	Phoenix	**NHL**	**26**	**5**	**4**	**9**	**2**	**0**	**1**	**0**	**31**	**16.1**	**-2**	**11**	**54.6**	**14:50**									
	NHL Totals		**95**	**9**	**12**	**21**	**26**	**0**	**1**	**1**	**91**	**9.9**		**26**	**50.0**	**10:29**									

Signed as a free agent by **Jonkoping** (Sweden), August 30, 2004. Traded to **Phoenix** by **Dallas** with Dallas' 1st round choice (later traded to Edmonton - Edmonton selected Riley Nash) in 2007 Entry Draft for Ladislav Nagy, February 12, 2007.

TKACHUK, Keith

(kuh-CHUK, KEETH) **ST.L.**

Left wing. Shoots left. 6'2", 225 lbs. Born, Melrose, MA, March 28, 1972. Winnipeg's 1st choice, 19th overall, in 1990 Entry Draft.

			Regular Season														Playoffs								
Season	Club	League	GP	G	A	Pts	PIM	PP	SH	GW	S	%	+/-	TF	F%	Min	GP	G	A	Pts	PIM	PP	SH	GW	Min
1988-89	Malden Cath.	High-MA	21	30	16	46	....	....	....	....	....	....	....	....	....	....	....	....	....	....	....	....	....	....	....
1989-90	Malden Cath.	High-MA	6	12	14	26	....	....	....	....	....	....	....	....	....	....	....	....	....	....	....	....	....	....	....
1990-91	Boston University	H-East	36	17	23	40	70	....	....	....	....	....	....	....	....	....	....	....	....	....	....	....	....	....	....
1991-92	United States	Nat-Tm	45	10	10	20	141	....	....	....	....	....	....	....	....	....	....	....	....	....	....	....	....	....	....
	United States	Olympics	8	1	1	2	12	....	....	....	....	....	....	....	....	....	....	....	....	....	....	....	....	....	....
	Winnipeg	**NHL**	**17**	**3**	**5**	**8**	**28**	**2**	**0**	**0**	**22**	**13.6**	**0**	....	....	....	**7**	**3**	**0**	**3**	**30**	**0**	**0**	**0**	....
1992-93	**Winnipeg**	**NHL**	**83**	**28**	**23**	**51**	**201**	**12**	**0**	**2**	**199**	**14.1**	**–13**	....	....	....	**6**	**4**	**0**	**4**	**14**	**1**	**0**	**0**	....
1993-94	**Winnipeg**	**NHL**	**84**	**41**	**40**	**81**	**255**	**22**	**3**	**3**	**218**	**18.8**	**–12**	....	....	....	....	....	....	....	....	....	....	....	....
1994-95	**Winnipeg**	**NHL**	**48**	**22**	**29**	**51**	**152**	**7**	**2**	**2**	**129**	**17.1**	**–4**	....	....	....	....	....	....	....	....	....	....	....	....
1995-96	**Winnipeg**	**NHL**	**76**	**50**	**48**	**98**	**156**	**20**	**2**	**6**	**249**	**20.1**	**11**	....	....	....	**6**	**1**	**2**	**3**	**22**	**0**	**0**	**0**	....
1996-97	**Phoenix**	**NHL**	**81**	***52**	**34**	**86**	**228**	**9**	**2**	**7**	**296**	**17.6**	**–1**	....	....	....	**7**	**6**	**0**	**6**	**7**	**2**	**0**	**0**	....
1997-98	**Phoenix**	**NHL**	**69**	**40**	**26**	**66**	**147**	**11**	**0**	**8**	**232**	**17.2**	**9**	....	....	....	**6**	**3**	**3**	**6**	**10**	**0**	**0**	**0**	....
	United States	Olympics	4	0	2	2	6	....	....	....	....	....	....	....	....	....	....	....	....	....	....	....	....	....	....
1998-99	**Phoenix**	**NHL**	**68**	**36**	**32**	**68**	**151**	**11**	**2**	**7**	**258**	**14.0**	**22**	**770**	**47.7**	**20:59**	**7**	**1**	**3**	**4**	**13**	**1**	**0**	**0**	**25:09**
99-2000	**Phoenix**	**NHL**	**50**	**22**	**21**	**43**	**82**	**5**	**1**	**1**	**183**	**12.0**	**7**	**500**	**50.4**	**19:21**	**5**	**1**	**1**	**2**	**4**	**1**	**0**	**0**	**18:46**
2000-01	**Phoenix**	**NHL**	**64**	**29**	**42**	**71**	**108**	**15**	**0**	**4**	**230**	**12.6**	**6**	**646**	**51.9**	**20:11**	....	....	....	....	....	....	....	....	....
	St. Louis	**NHL**	**12**	**6**	**2**	**8**	**14**	**2**	**0**	**1**	**41**	**14.6**	**–3**	**87**	**54.0**	**19:39**	**15**	**2**	**7**	**9**	**20**	**2**	**0**	**1**	**19:17**
2001-02	**St. Louis**	**NHL**	**73**	**38**	**37**	**75**	**117**	**13**	**0**	**7**	**244**	**15.6**	**21**	**88**	**43.2**	**19:38**	**10**	**5**	**5**	**10**	**18**	**1**	**0**	**0**	**19:24**
	United States	Olympics	5	2	0	2	2	....	....	....	....	....	....	....	....	....	....	....	....	....	....	....	....	....	....
2002-03	**St. Louis**	**NHL**	**56**	**31**	**24**	**55**	**139**	**14**	**0**	**5**	**185**	**16.8**	**1**	**346**	**55.8**	**19:16**	**7**	**1**	**3**	**4**	**14**	**0**	**0**	**0**	**19:22**
2003-04	**St. Louis**	**NHL**	**75**	**33**	**38**	**71**	**83**	**18**	**0**	**8**	**233**	**14.2**	**8**	**410**	**49.5**	**19:39**	**5**	**0**	**2**	**2**	**10**	**0**	**0**	**0**	**19:18**
2004-05			DID NOT PLAY																						
2005-06	**St. Louis**	**NHL**	**41**	**15**	**21**	**36**	**46**	**10**	**0**	**1**	**133**	**11.3**	**–15**	**250**	**50.4**	**19:27**	....	....	....	....	....	....	....	....	....
	United States	Olympics	6	0	0	0	8	....	....	....	....	....	....	....	....	....	....	....	....	....	....	....	....	....	....
2006-07	**St. Louis**	**NHL**	**61**	**20**	**23**	**43**	**92**	**8**	**0**	**1**	**160**	**12.5**	**3**	**678**	**49.4**	**17:26**	....	....	....	....	....	....	....	....	....
	Atlanta	**NHL**	**18**	**7**	**8**	**15**	**34**	**2**	**0**	**3**	**36**	**19.4**	**8**	**348**	**52.9**	**17:41**	**4**	**1**	**2**	**3**	**12**	**0**	**0**	**0**	**16:33**
	NHL Totals		**976**	**473**	**453**	**926**	**2033**	**181**	**12**	**66**	**3048**	**15.5**		**4123**	**50.4**	**19:28**	**85**	**28**	**28**	**56**	**174**	**8**	**0**	**1**	**19:50**

NHL Second All-Star Team (1995, 1998)

Played in NHL All-Star Game (1997, 1998, 1999, 2004)

Transferred to **Phoenix** after **Winnipeg** franchise relocated, July 1, 1996. Traded to **St. Louis** by **Phoenix** for Michal Handzus, Ladislav Nagy, the rights to Jeff Taffe and St. Louis' 1st round choice (Ben Eager) in 2002 Entry Draft, March 13, 2001. Traded to **Atlanta** by **St. Louis** for Glen Metropolit, Atlanta's 1st (later traded to Calgary - Calgary selected Mikael Backlund) and 3rd (Brett Sonne) round choices in 2007 Entry Draft, and Atlanta's 1st (later traded back to Atlanta) and 2nd round choices in 2008 Entry Draft, February 25, 2007. Traded to **St. Louis** by **Atlanta** with future considerations for Atlanta's 1st round choice (previously acquired) in 2008 Entry Draft, June 26, 2007.

TOLLEFSEN, Ole-Kristian

(TOHL-uhf-suhn, OH-lay-KRIHS-tyahn) **CBJ**

Defense. Shoots left. 6'2", 211 lbs. Born, Oslo, Norway, March 29, 1984. Columbus' 3rd choice, 65th overall, in 2002 Entry Draft.

Season	Club	League	GP	G	A	Pts	PIM	PP	SH	GW	S	%	+/-	TF	F%	Min	GP	G	A	Pts	PIM	PP	SH	GW	Min
2000-01	Lillehammer IK	Norway	4	0	0	0	2	....	....	....	....	....	....	....	....	....	....	....	....	....	....	....	....	....	....
2001-02	Lillehammer IK	Norway	37	1	5	6	63	....	....	....	....	....	....	....	....	....	6	1	1	2	10	....	....	....	....
	Lillehammer IK	Nor-Jr.	....	....	....	....	....	....	....	....	....	....	....	....	....	....	1	0	2	2	4	....	....	....	....
2002-03	Brandon	WHL	43	6	14	20	73	....	....	....	....	....	....	....	....	....	17	0	2	2	38	....	....	....	....
2003-04	Brandon	WHL	53	3	27	30	94	....	....	....	....	....	....	....	....	....	11	0	4	4	15	....	....	....	....
2004-05	Syracuse Crunch	AHL	64	0	3	3	115	....	....	....	....	....	....	....	....	....	....	....	....	....	....	....	....	....	....
	Dayton Bombers	ECHL	2	0	0	0	0	....	....	....	....	....	....	....	....	....	....	....	....	....	....	....	....	....	....
2005-06	**Columbus**	**NHL**	**5**	**0**	**0**	**0**	**2**	**0**	**0**	**0**	**3**	**0.0**	**–2**	**0**	**0.0**	**16:18**	....	....	....	....	....	....	....	....	....
	Syracuse Crunch	AHL	58	2	16	18	155	....	....	....	....	....	....	....	....	....	1	0	0	0	6	....	....	....	....
2006-07	**Columbus**	**NHL**	**70**	**2**	**3**	**5**	**123**	**1**	**0**	**0**	**39**	**5.1**	**2**	**0**	**0.0**	**14:14**	....	....	....	....	....	....	....	....	....
	NHL Totals		**75**	**2**	**3**	**5**	**125**	**1**	**0**	**0**	**42**	**4.8**		**0**	**0.0**	**14:22**	....	....	....	....	....	....	....	....	....

TOOTOO, Jordin

(TOO-TOO, JOHR-dahn) **NSH.**

Right wing. Shoots right. 5'9", 194 lbs. Born, Churchill, Man., February 2, 1983. Nashville's 6th choice, 98th overall, in 2001 Entry Draft.

Season	Club	League	GP	G	A	Pts	PIM	PP	SH	GW	S	%	+/-	TF	F%	Min	GP	G	A	Pts	PIM	PP	SH	GW	Min
1997-98	Spruce Grove	AMBHL	STATISTICS NOT AVAILABLE																						
1998-99	OCN Blizzard	MJHL	47	16	21	37	251	....	....	....	....	....	....	....	....	....	....	....	....	....	....	....	....	....	....
99-2000	Brandon	WHL	45	6	10	16	214	....	....	....	....	....	....	....	....	....	....	....	....	....	....	....	....	....	....
2000-01	Brandon	WHL	60	20	28	48	172	....	....	....	....	....	....	....	....	....	6	2	4	6	18	....	....	....	....
2001-02	Brandon	WHL	64	32	39	71	272	....	....	....	....	....	....	....	....	....	16	4	3	7	*58	....	....	....	....
2002-03	Brandon	WHL	51	35	39	74	216	....	....	....	....	....	....	....	....	....	17	6	3	9	49	....	....	....	....
2003-04	**Nashville**	**NHL**	**70**	**4**	**4**	**8**	**137**	**2**	**0**	**0**	**92**	**4.3**	**–6**	**18**	**55.6**	**8:29**	**5**	**0**	**0**	**0**	**4**	**0**	**0**	**0**	**5:09**
2004-05	Milwaukee	AHL	59	10	12	22	266	....	....	....	....	....	....	....	....	....	6	0	0	0	41	....	....	....	....
2005-06	**Nashville**	**NHL**	**34**	**4**	**6**	**10**	**55**	**0**	**0**	**0**	**61**	**6.6**	**9**	**17**	**70.6**	**9:15**	**3**	**0**	**0**	**0**	**0**	**0**	**0**	**0**	**4:04**
	Milwaukee	AHL	41	13	14	27	133	....	....	....	....	....	....	....	....	....	15	9	2	11	35	....	....	....	....
2006-07	**Nashville**	**NHL**	**65**	**3**	**6**	**9**	**116**	**0**	**0**	**0**	**77**	**3.9**	**–11**	**12**	**33.3**	**8:24**	**4**	**0**	**1**	**1**	**21**	**0**	**0**	**0**	**9:32**
	NHL Totals		**169**	**11**	**16**	**27**	**308**	**2**	**0**	**0**	**230**	**4.8**		**47**	**55.3**	**8:37**	**12**	**0**	**1**	**1**	**25**	**0**	**0**	**0**	**6:21**

WHL East First All-Star Team (2003)

TORRES, Raffi

(TOHR-ehz, RA-fee) **EDM.**

Left wing. Shoots left. 6', 216 lbs. Born, Toronto, Ont., October 8, 1981. NY Islanders' 2nd choice, 5th overall, in 2000 Entry Draft.

Season	Club	League	GP	G	A	Pts	PIM	PP	SH	GW	S	%	+/-	TF	F%	Min	GP	G	A	Pts	PIM	PP	SH	GW	Min
1997-98	Thornhill Rattlers	MTJHL	46	17	16	33	90	....	....	....	....	....	....	....	....	....	....	....	....	....	....	....	....	....	....
1998-99	Brampton	OHL	62	35	27	62	32	....	....	....	....	....	....	....	....	....	....	....	....	....	....	....	....	....	....
99-2000	Brampton	OHL	68	43	48	91	40	....	....	....	....	....	....	....	....	....	6	5	2	7	23	....	....	....	....
2000-01	Brampton	OHL	55	33	37	70	76	....	....	....	....	....	....	....	....	....	8	7	4	11	19	....	....	....	....
2001-02	**NY Islanders**	**NHL**	**14**	**0**	**1**	**1**	**6**	**0**	**0**	**0**	**9**	**0.0**	**2**	**0**	**0.0**	**7:35**	....	....	....	....	....	....	....	....	....
	Bridgeport	AHL	59	20	10	30	45	....	....	....	....	....	....	....	....	....	20	8	9	17	26	....	....	....	....
2002-03	**NY Islanders**	**NHL**	**17**	**0**	**5**	**5**	**10**	**0**	**0**	**0**	**12**	**0.0**	**0**	**4**	**25.0**	**7:40**	....	....	....	....	....	....	....	....	....
	Bridgeport	AHL	49	17	15	32	54	....	....	....	....	....	....	....	....	....	....	....	....	....	....	....	....	....	....
	Hamilton	AHL	11	1	7	8	14	....	....	....	....	....	....	....	....	....	23	6	1	7	29	....	....	....	....
2003-04	**Edmonton**	**NHL**	**80**	**20**	**14**	**34**	**65**	**5**	**0**	**3**	**136**	**14.7**	**12**	**21**	**28.6**	**12:38**	....	....	....	....	....	....	....	....	....
2004-05	Edmonton	AHL	67	21	25	46	165	....	....	....	....	....	....	....	....	....	....	....	....	....	....	....	....	....	....
2005-06	**Edmonton**	**NHL**	**82**	**27**	**14**	**41**	**50**	**6**	**0**	**3**	**164**	**16.5**	**4**	**60**	**41.7**	**13:24**	**22**	**4**	**7**	**11**	**16**	**1**	**0**	**1**	**13:15**
2006-07	**Edmonton**	**NHL**	**82**	**15**	**19**	**34**	**88**	**1**	**0**	**0**	**154**	**9.7**	**–7**	**50**	**44.0**	**14:19**	....	....	....	....	....	....	....	....	....
	NHL Totals		**275**	**62**	**53**	**115**	**219**	**12**	**0**	**6**	**475**	**13.1**		**135**	**40.0**	**12:48**	**22**	**4**	**7**	**11**	**16**	**1**	**0**	**1**	**13:15**

OHL All-Rookie Team (1999) • OHL Second All-Star Team (2000, 2001)

Traded to **Edmonton** by **NY Islanders** with Brad Isbister for Janne Niinimaa and Washington's 2nd round choice (previously acquired, NY Islanders selected Evgeni Tunik) in 2003 Entry Draft, March 11, 2003.

TRAVERSE, Patrick

(tra-VAIRZ, PAT-rihk)

Defense. Shoots left. 6'4", 207 lbs. Born, Montreal, Que., March 14, 1974. Ottawa's 3rd choice, 50th overall, in 1992 Entry Draft.

Season	Club	League	GP	G	A	Pts	PIM	PP	SH	GW	S	%	+/-	TF	F%	Min	GP	G	A	Pts	PIM	PP	SH	GW	Min
1990-91	Mtl-Bourassa	QAAA	42	4	19	23	10	....	....	....	....	....	....	....	....	....	5	0	3	3	2	....	....	....	....
1991-92	Shawinigan	QMJHL	59	3	11	14	12	....	....	....	....	....	....	....	....	....	10	0	0	0	4	....	....	....	....
1992-93	Shawinigan	QMJHL	53	5	24	29	24	....	....	....	....	....	....	....	....	....	....	....	....	....	....	....	....	....	....
	St-Jean Lynx	QMJHL	15	1	6	7	0	....	....	....	....	....	....	....	....	....	4	0	1	1	2	....	....	....	....
	New Haven	AHL	2	0	0	0	2	....	....	....	....	....	....	....	....	....	....	....	....	....	....	....	....	....	....
1993-94	St-Jean Lynx	QMJHL	66	15	37	52	30	....	....	....	....	....	....	....	....	....	5	0	4	4	4	....	....	....	....
	P.E.I. Senators	AHL	3	0	1	1	2	....	....	....	....	....	....	....	....	....	....	....	....	....	....	....	....	....	....
1994-95	P.E.I. Senators	AHL	70	5	13	18	19	....	....	....	....	....	....	....	....	....	7	0	2	2	0	....	....	....	....
1995-96	**Ottawa**	**NHL**	**5**	**0**	**0**	**0**	**2**	**0**	**0**	**0**	**2**	**0.0**	**–1**	....	....	....	....	....	....	....	....	....	....	....	....
	P.E.I. Senators	AHL	55	4	21	25	32	....	....	....	....	....	....	....	....	....	5	1	2	3	2	....	....	....	....
1996-97	Worcester IceCats	AHL	24	0	4	4	23	....	....	....	....	....	....	....	....	....	....	....	....	....	....	....	....	....	....
	Grand Rapids	IHL	10	2	1	3	10	....	....	....	....	....	....	....	....	....	2	0	1	1	2	....	....	....	....
1997-98	Hershey Bears	AHL	71	14	15	29	67	....	....	....	....	....	....	....	....	....	7	1	3	4	4	....	....	....	....
1998-99	**Ottawa**	**NHL**	**46**	**1**	**9**	**10**	**22**	**0**	**0**	**0**	**35**	**2.9**	**12**	**0**	**0.0**	**14:56**	....	....	....	....	....	....	....	....	....
99-2000	**Ottawa**	**NHL**	**66**	**6**	**17**	**23**	**21**	**1**	**0**	**0**	**73**	**8.2**	**17**	**0**	**0.0**	**18:43**	**6**	**0**	**0**	**0**	**2**	**0**	**0**	**0**	**17:50**

			Regular Season														Playoffs								
Season	Club	League	GP	G	A	Pts	PIM	PP	SH	GW	S	%	+/-	TF	F%	Min	GP	G	A	Pts	PIM	PP	SH	GW	Min
2000-01	**Anaheim**	**NHL**	**15**	**1**	**0**	**1**	**6**	**0**	**0**	**0**	**7**	**14.3**	**-6**	**0**	**0.0**	**17:19**	....	....	....	....	....	....	....	....	....
	Boston	**NHL**	**37**	**2**	**6**	**8**	**14**	**1**	**0**	**1**	**39**	**5.1**	**4**	**0**	**0.0**	**16:38**	....	....	....	....	....	....	....	....	....
	Montreal	**NHL**	**19**	**2**	**3**	**5**	**10**	**0**	**0**	**0**	**16**	**12.5**	**-8**	**0**	**0.0**	**21:36**	....	....	....	....	....	....	....	....	....
2001-02	**Montreal**	**NHL**	**25**	**2**	**3**	**5**	**14**	**2**	**0**	**0**	**24**	**8.3**	**-7**	**0**	**0.0**	**18:14**	....	....	....	....	....	....	....	....	....
	Quebec Citadelles	AHL	4	0	2	2	4	....	....	....	....	....	....	....	....	....	....	....	....	....	....	....	....	....	....
2002-03	**Montreal**	**NHL**	**65**	**0**	**13**	**13**	**24**	**0**	**0**	**0**	**63**	**0.0**	**-9**	**0**	**0.0**	**20:12**	....	....	....	....	....	....	....	....	....
2003-04	Hamilton	AHL	80	5	21	26	31	....	....	....	....	....	....	....	....	....	10	1	2	3	0	....	....	....	....
2004-05	Houston Aeros	AHL	72	6	9	15	28	....	....	....	....	....	....	....	....	....	5	0	0	0	2	....	....	....	....
2005-06	**Dallas**	**NHL**	**1**	**0**	**0**	**0**	**0**	**0**	**0**	**0**	**1**	**0.0**	**0**	**0**	**0.0**	**11:27**	....	....	....	....	....	....	....	....	....
	Iowa Stars	AHL	40	3	21	24	16	....	....	....	....	....	....	....	....	....	7	1	2	3	2	....	....	....	....
2006-07	Hamilton	AHL	26	1	4	5	10	....	....	....	....	....	....	....	....	....	....	....	....	....	....	....	....	....	....
	Worcester Sharks	AHL	54	5	17	22	14	....	....	....	....	....	....	....	....	....	6	0	2	2	2	....	....	....	....
	NHL Totals		**279**	**14**	**51**	**65**	**113**	**4**	**0**	**1**	**260**	**5.4**		**0**	**0.0**	**18:12**	**6**	**0**	**0**	**0**	**2**	**0**	**0**	**0**	**17:50**

Traded to **Anaheim** by **Ottawa** for Joel Kwiatkowski, June 12, 2000. Traded to **Boston** by **Anaheim** with Andrei Nazarov for Samuel Pahlsson, November 18, 2000. Traded to **Montreal** by **Boston** for Eric Weinrich, February 21, 2001. • Missed majority of 2001-02 season recovering from knee (November 3, 2001 vs. Calgary) and head (January 10, 2002 vs. NY Islanders) injuries. Signed as a free agent by **Dallas**, September 9, 2004. Signed as a free agent by **San Jose**, July 10, 2006. Claimed on waivers by **Montreal** from **San Jose**, September 28, 2006. Traded to **San Jose** by **Montreal** for Mathieu Biron, December 15, 2006.

TREMBLAY, Yannick

(TRAHM-blay, YA-nihk)

Defense. Shoots right. 6'2", 200 lbs. Born, Pointe-aux-Trembles, Que., November 15, 1975. Toronto's 4th choice, 145th overall, in 1995 Entry Draft.

Season	Club	League	GP	G	A	Pts	PIM	PP	SH	GW	S	%	+/-	TF	F%	Min	GP	G	A	Pts	PIM	PP	SH	GW	Min
1991-92	Mtl-Bourassa	QAAA	35	2	5	7	55	....	....	....	....	....	....	....	....	....	8	0	4	4	2	....	....	....	....
1992-93	Mtl-Bourassa	CEGEP	21	2	5	7	10	....	....	....	....	....	....	....	....	....	3	0	0	0	2	....	....	....	....
1993-94	St. Thomas U.	AUAA	25	2	3	5	10	....	....	....	....	....	....	....	....	....	....	....	....	....	....	....	....	....	....
1994-95	Beauport	QMJHL	70	10	32	42	22	....	....	....	....	....	....	....	....	....	17	6	8	14	6	....	....	....	....
1995-96	Beauport	QMJHL	61	12	33	45	42	....	....	....	....	....	....	....	....	....	20	3	16	19	18	....	....	....	....
	St. John's	AHL	3	0	1	1	0	....	....	....	....	....	....	....	....	....	....	....	....	....	....	....	....	....	....
1996-97	**Toronto**	**NHL**	**5**	**0**	**0**	**0**	**0**	**0**	**0**	**0**	**2**	**0.0**	**-4**	....	....	....	....	....	....	....	....	....	....	....	....
	St. John's	AHL	67	7	25	32	34	....	....	....	....	....	....	....	....	....	11	2	9	11	0	....	....	....	....
1997-98	**Toronto**	**NHL**	**38**	**2**	**4**	**6**	**6**	**1**	**0**	**0**	**45**	**4.4**	**-6**	....	....	....	....	....	....	....	....	....	....	....	....
	St. John's	AHL	17	3	7	10	4	....	....	....	....	....	....	....	....	....	4	0	1	1	5	....	....	....	....
1998-99	**Toronto**	**NHL**	**35**	**2**	**7**	**9**	**16**	**0**	**0**	**0**	**37**	**5.4**	**0**	**0**	**0.0**	**17:39**	....	....	....	....	....	....	....	....	....
99-2000	**Atlanta**	**NHL**	**75**	**10**	**21**	**31**	**22**	**4**	**1**	**2**	**139**	**7.2**	**-42**	**3**	**0.0**	**19:27**	....	....	....	....	....	....	....	....	....
2000-01	**Atlanta**	**NHL**	**46**	**4**	**8**	**12**	**30**	**1**	**0**	**1**	**102**	**3.9**	**-6**	**1**	**100.0**	**20:27**	....	....	....	....	....	....	....	....	....
2001-02	**Atlanta**	**NHL**	**66**	**9**	**15**	**24**	**47**	**1**	**0**	**1**	**115**	**7.8**	**-15**	**0**	**0.0**	**21:50**	....	....	....	....	....	....	....	....	....
2002-03	**Atlanta**	**NHL**	**75**	**8**	**22**	**30**	**32**	**5**	**0**	**1**	**151**	**5.3**	**-27**	**1**	**0.0**	**21:45**	....	....	....	....	....	....	....	....	....
2003-04	**Atlanta**	**NHL**	**38**	**2**	**8**	**10**	**13**	**1**	**0**	**1**	**47**	**4.3**	**-13**	**2**	**50.0**	**21:36**	....	....	....	....	....	....	....	....	....
2004-05	Sherbrooke	QNAHL	36	26	25	51	40	....	....	....	....	....	....	....	....	....	....	....	....	....	....	....	....	....	....
	Adler Mannheim	Germany	14	1	4	5	16	....	....	....	....	....	....	....	....	....	14	2	6	8	6	....	....	....	....
2005-06	Adler Mannheim	Germany	46	11	17	28	44	....	....	....	....	....	....	....	....	....	....	....	....	....	....	....	....	....	....
2006-07	**Vancouver**	**NHL**	**12**	**1**	**2**	**3**	**12**	**1**	**0**	**0**	**30**	**3.3**	**-6**	**0**	**0.0**	**12:44**	....	....	....	....	....	....	....	....	....
	Manitoba Moose	AHL	45	12	21	33	40	....	....	....	....	....	....	....	....	....	12	3	7	10	11	....	....	....	....
	NHL Totals		**390**	**38**	**87**	**125**	**178**	**14**	**1**	**6**	**668**	**5.7**		**7**	**28.6**	**20:21**	....	....	....	....	....	....	....	....	....

Claimed by **Atlanta** from **Toronto** in Expansion Draft, June 25, 1999. • Missed majority of 2003-04 season recovering from foot (November 15, 2003 vs. Philadelphia) and hip (January 30, 2004 vs. Toronto) injuries. Signed as a free agent by **Sherbrooke** (QNAHL), November 16, 2004. Signed as a free agent by **Mannheim** (Germany), January 13, 2005. Signed as a free agent by **Vancouver**, July 28, 2006. Signed as a free agent by **Lugano** (Swiss), July 18, 2007.

TRUDEL, Jean-Guy

(TROO-dehl, zhawn-gee) **ST.L.**

Left wing. Shoots left. 5'11", 202 lbs. Born, Sudbury, Ont., October 18, 1975.

Season	Club	League	GP	G	A	Pts	PIM	PP	SH	GW	S	%	+/-	TF	F%	Min	GP	G	A	Pts	PIM	PP	SH	GW	Min
1991-92	Beauport	QMJHL	35	5	7	12	20	....	....	....	....	....	....	....	....	....	....	....	....	....	....	....	....	....	....
1992-93	Beauport	QMJHL	56	1	4	5	20	....	....	....	....	....	....	....	....	....	....	....	....	....	....	....	....	....	....
	Verdun	QMJHL	10	1	0	1	0	....	....	....	....	....	....	....	....	....	2	0	0	0	5	....	....	....	....
1993-94			DID NOT PLAY																						
1994-95	Hull Olympiques	QMJHL	54	29	42	71	76	....	....	....	....	....	....	....	....	....	19	4	13	17	25	....	....	....	....
1995-96	Hull Olympiques	QMJHL	70	50	71	121	96	....	....	....	....	....	....	....	....	....	17	11	18	29	8	....	....	....	....
1996-97	Quad City	ColHL	5	8	7	15	4	....	....	....	....	....	....	....	....	....	....	....	....	....	....	....	....	....	....
	Chicago Wolves	IHL	6	1	2	3	2	....	....	....	....	....	....	....	....	....	....	....	....	....	....	....	....	....	....
	San Antonio	IHL	12	1	5	6	4	....	....	....	....	....	....	....	....	....	....	....	....	....	....	....	....	....	....
	Peoria Rivermen	ECHL	37	25	29	54	47	....	....	....	....	....	....	....	....	....	9	9	10	19	22	....	....	....	....
1997-98	Peoria Rivermen	ECHL	62	39	74	113	147	....	....	....	....	....	....	....	....	....	3	0	0	0	2	....	....	....	....
1998-99	Kansas City	IHL	76	24	25	49	66	....	....	....	....	....	....	....	....	....	3	1	0	1	0	....	....	....	....
99-2000	**Phoenix**	**NHL**	**1**	**0**	**0**	**0**	**0**	**0**	**0**	**0**	**0**	**0.0**	**-1**	**0**	**0.0**	**4:33**	....	....	....	....	....	....	....	....	....
	Springfield	AHL	72	34	39	73	80	....	....	....	....	....	....	....	....	....	3	0	1	1	4	....	....	....	....
2000-01	Springfield	AHL	80	34	65	99	89	....	....	....	....	....	....	....	....	....	....	....	....	....	....	....	....	....	....
2001-02	**Phoenix**	**NHL**	**3**	**0**	**0**	**0**	**2**	**0**	**0**	**0**	**1**	**0.0**	**0**	**0**	**0.0**	**8:42**	....	....	....	....	....	....	....	....	....
	Springfield	AHL	76	22	48	70	83	....	....	....	....	....	....	....	....	....	....	....	....	....	....	....	....	....	....
2002-03	**Minnesota**	**NHL**	**1**	**0**	**0**	**0**	**2**	**0**	**0**	**0**	**0**	**0.0**	**0**	**0**	**0.0**	**5:37**	....	....	....	....	....	....	....	....	....
	Houston Aeros	AHL	79	31	54	85	85	....	....	....	....	....	....	....	....	....	23	7	9	16	22	....	....	....	....
2003-04	HC Ambri-Piotta	Swiss	47	29	39	68	64	....	....	....	....	....	....	....	....	....	7	4	4	8	14	....	....	....	....
2004-05	HC Ambri-Piotta	Swiss	42	23	35	58	105	....	....	....	....	....	....	....	....	....	....	....	....	....	....	....	....	....	....
2005-06	HC Ambri-Piotta	Swiss	44	24	35	59	50	....	....	....	....	....	....	....	....	....	7	4	4	8	12	....	....	....	....
2006-07	HC Ambri-Piotta	Swiss	44	27	26	53	38	....	....	....	....	....	....	....	....	....	7	5	4	9	12	....	....	....	....
	NHL Totals		**5**	**0**	**0**	**0**	**4**	**0**	**0**	**0**	**1**	**0.0**		**0**	**0.0**	**7:15**	....	....	....	....	....	....	....	....	....

QMJHL Second All-Star Team (1996) • ECHL First All-Star Team (1998) • AHL Second All-Star Team (2000, 2002) • AHL First All-Star Team (2001, 2003)

• Sat out 1993-94 season to regain eligibility for U.S. College scholarship. Signed as a free agent by **Phoenix**, July 17, 1999. Signed as a free agent by **Minnesota**, July 16, 2002. Signed as a free agent by **Ambri-Piotta** (Swiss), April 3, 2003. Signed as a free agent by **St. Louis**, June 19, 2007.

TUCKER, Darcy

(TUH-kuhr, DAHR-see) **TOR.**

Right wing. Shoots left. 5'10", 178 lbs. Born, Castor, Alta., March 15, 1975. Montreal's 8th choice, 151st overall, in 1993 Entry Draft.

Season	Club	League	GP	G	A	Pts	PIM	PP	SH	GW	S	%	+/-	TF	F%	Min	GP	G	A	Pts	PIM	PP	SH	GW	Min
1990-91	Red Deer	AMHL	47	70	90	160	48	....	....	....	....	....	....	....	....	....	....	....	....	....	....	....	....	....	....
1991-92	Kamloops Blazers	WHL	26	3	10	13	32	....	....	....	....	....	....	....	....	....	9	0	1	1	16	....	....	....	....
1992-93	Kamloops Blazers	WHL	67	31	58	89	155	....	....	....	....	....	....	....	....	....	13	7	6	13	34	....	....	....	....
1993-94	Kamloops Blazers	WHL	66	52	88	140	143	....	....	....	....	....	....	....	....	....	19	9	*18	*27	43	....	....	....	....
1994-95	Kamloops Blazers	WHL	64	64	73	137	94	....	....	....	....	....	....	....	....	....	21	*16	15	*31	19	....	....	....	....
1995-96	**Montreal**	**NHL**	**3**	**0**	**0**	**0**	**0**	**0**	**0**	**0**	**1**	**0.0**	**-1**	....	....	....	....	....	....	....	....	....	....	....	....
	Fredericton	AHL	74	29	64	93	174	....	....	....	....	....	....	....	....	....	7	7	3	10	14	....	....	....	....
1996-97	**Montreal**	**NHL**	**73**	**7**	**13**	**20**	**110**	**1**	**0**	**3**	**62**	**11.3**	**-5**	....	....	....	**4**	**0**	**0**	**0**	**0**	**0**	**0**	**0**	....
1997-98	**Montreal**	**NHL**	**39**	**1**	**5**	**6**	**57**	**0**	**0**	**0**	**19**	**5.3**	**-6**	....	....	....	....	....	....	....	....	....	....	....	....
	Tampa Bay	**NHL**	**35**	**6**	**8**	**14**	**89**	**1**	**1**	**0**	**44**	**13.6**	**-8**	....	....	....	....	....	....	....	....	....	....	....	....
1998-99	**Tampa Bay**	**NHL**	**82**	**21**	**22**	**43**	**176**	**8**	**2**	**3**	**178**	**11.8**	**-34**	**1470**	**45.6**	**19:24**	....	....	....	....	....	....	....	....	....
99-2000	**Tampa Bay**	**NHL**	**50**	**14**	**20**	**34**	**108**	**1**	**0**	**2**	**98**	**14.3**	**-15**	**152**	**48.7**	**19:58**	....	....	....	....	....	....	....	....	....
	Toronto	**NHL**	**27**	**7**	**10**	**17**	**55**	**0**	**2**	**3**	**40**	**17.5**	**3**	**11**	**54.6**	**16:41**	**12**	**4**	**2**	**6**	**15**	**1**	**0**	**2**	**17:23**
2000-01	**Toronto**	**NHL**	**82**	**16**	**21**	**37**	**141**	**2**	**0**	**4**	**122**	**13.1**	**6**	**413**	**47.0**	**16:09**	**11**	**0**	**2**	**2**	**6**	**0**	**0**	**0**	**13:59**
2001-02	**Toronto**	**NHL**	**77**	**24**	**35**	**59**	**92**	**7**	**0**	**5**	**124**	**19.4**	**24**	**138**	**43.5**	**16:59**	**17**	**4**	**4**	**8**	**38**	**1**	**0**	**1**	**16:50**
2002-03	**Toronto**	**NHL**	**77**	**10**	**26**	**36**	**119**	**4**	**1**	**2**	**108**	**9.3**	**-7**	**68**	**45.6**	**15:21**	**6**	**0**	**3**	**3**	**6**	**0**	**0**	**0**	**21:07**
2003-04	**Toronto**	**NHL**	**64**	**21**	**11**	**32**	**68**	**8**	**1**	**2**	**146**	**14.4**	**4**	**136**	**50.7**	**17:50**	**12**	**2**	**0**	**2**	**14**	**1**	**0**	**0**	**13:54**
2004-05			DID NOT PLAY																						
2005-06	**Toronto**	**NHL**	**74**	**28**	**33**	**61**	**100**	**18**	**0**	**4**	**189**	**14.8**	**-12**	**29**	**58.6**	**17:38**	....	....	....	....	....	....	....	....	....
2006-07	**Toronto**	**NHL**	**56**	**24**	**19**	**43**	**81**	**15**	**0**	**6**	**143**	**16.8**	**-11**	**15**	**40.0**	**17:47**	....	....	....	....	....	....	....	....	....
	NHL Totals		**739**	**179**	**223**	**402**	**1196**	**65**	**7**	**34**	**1274**	**14.1**		**2432**	**46.3**	**17:29**	**62**	**10**	**11**	**21**	**79**	**3**	**0**	**3**	**16:15**

WHL West First All-Star Team (1994, 1995) • Canadian Major Junior First All-Star Team (1994) • Memorial Cup Tournament All-Star Team (1994, 1995) • Stafford Smythe Memorial Trophy (Memorial Cup Tournament MVP) (1994) • Dudley "Red" Garrett Memorial Award (Rookie of the Year – AHL) (1996)

Traded to **Tampa Bay** by **Montreal** with Stephane Richer and David Wilkie for Patrick Poulin, Mick Vukota and Igor Ulanov, January 15, 1998. Traded to **Toronto** by **Tampa Bay** with Tampa Bay's 4th round choice (Miguel Delisle) in 2000 Entry Draft for Mike Johnson, Marek Posmyk and Toronto's 5th (Pavel Sedov) and 6th (Aaron Gionet) round choices in 2000 Entry Draft, February 9, 2000.

TUKONEN, Lauri
(too-KOH-nehn, LOW-ree) **L.A.**

Right wing. Shoots right. 6'2", 200 lbs. Born, Hyvinkaa, Finland, September 1, 1986. Los Angeles' 1st choice, 11th overall, in 2004 Entry Draft.

Season	Club	League	GP	G	A	Pts	PIM	PP	SH	GW	S	%	+/-	TF	F%	Min	GP	G	A	Pts	PIM	PP	SH	GW	Min
								Regular Season									Playoffs								
2001-02	Ahmat Jr.	Fin-Jr.	2	4	0	4	2	....	....	....	....	....	....	....	....	....	....	....	....	....	....	....	....	....	....
	HC Sunne	Sweden-3	2	4	0	4	2	....	....	....	....	....	....	....	....	....	....	....	....	....	....	....	....	....	....
	Ahmat Hyvinkaa	Finland-2	24	7	4	11	6	....	....	....	....	....	....	....	....	....	....	....	....	....	....	....	....	....	....
2002-03	Ahmat Jr.	Fin-Jr.	4	3	1	4	2	....	....	....	....	....	....	....	....	....	....	....	....	....	....	....	....	....	....
	Ahmat Hyvinkaa	Finland-2	12	2	2	4	2	....	....	....	....	....	....	....	....	....	....	....	....	....	....	....	....	....	....
	Blues Espoo Jr.	Fin-Jr.	17	6	6	12	18	....	....	....	....	....	....	....	....	....	5	0	0	0	10	....	....	....	....
2003-04	Suomi U20	Finland-2	6	0	0	0	6	....	....	....	....	....	....	....	....	....	....	....	....	....	....	....	....	....	....
	Blues Espoo Jr.	Fin-Jr.	14	14	9	23	4	....	....	....	....	....	....	....	....	....	....	....	....	....	....	....	....	....	....
	Blues Espoo	Finland	35	3	3	6	16	....	....	....	....	....	....	....	....	....	7	0	0	0	0	....	....	....	....
2004-05	Blues Espoo Jr.	Fin-Jr.	2	0	0	0	2	....	....	....	....	....	....	....	....	....	....	....	....	....	....	....	....	....	....
	Blues Espoo	Finland	43	5	5	10	10	....	....	....	....	....	....	....	....	....	....	....	....	....	....	....	....	....	....
2005-06	Manchester	AHL	62	14	22	36	20	....	....	....	....	....	....	....	....	....	....	....	....	....	....	....	....	....	....
2006-07	**Los Angeles**	**NHL**	**4**	**0**	**0**	**0**	**0**	**0**	**0**	**0**	**1**	**0.0**	**-2**	**0**	**0.0**	**6:33**	....	....	....	....	....	....	....	....	....
	Manchester	AHL	61	13	19	32	30	....	....	....	....	....	....	....	....	....	6	0	3	3	0	....	....	....	....
	NHL Totals		**4**	**0**	**0**	**0**	**0**	**0**	**0**	**0**	**1**	**0.0**		**0**	**0.0**	**6:33**	....	....	....	....	....	....	....	....	....

TURGEON, Pierre
(TUHR-zhawn, PEE-air)

Center. Shoots left. 6'1", 199 lbs. Born, Rouyn, Que., August 28, 1969. Buffalo's 1st choice, 1st overall, in 1987 Entry Draft.

Season	Club	League	GP	G	A	Pts	PIM	PP	SH	GW	S	%	+/-	TF	F%	Min	GP	G	A	Pts	PIM	PP	SH	GW	Min
1984-85	Mtl-Bourassa	QAAA	41	49	52	101	26	....	....	....	....	....	....	....	....	....	5	3	8	11	2	....	....	....	....
1985-86	Granby Bisons	QMJHL	69	47	67	114	31	....	....	....	....	....	....	....	....	....	....	....	....	....	....	....	....	....	....
1986-87	Granby Bisons	QMJHL	58	69	85	154	8	....	....	....	....	....	....	....	....	....	7	9	6	15	15	....	....	....	....
1987-88	**Buffalo**	**NHL**	**76**	**14**	**28**	**42**	**34**	**8**	**0**	**3**	**101**	**13.9**	**-8**	....	....	....	**6**	**4**	**3**	**7**	**4**	**3**	**0**	**0**	....
1988-89	**Buffalo**	**NHL**	**80**	**34**	**54**	**88**	**26**	**19**	**0**	**5**	**182**	**18.7**	**-2**	....	....	....	**5**	**3**	**5**	**8**	**2**	**1**	**0**	**0**	....
1989-90	**Buffalo**	**NHL**	**80**	**40**	**66**	**106**	**29**	**17**	**1**	**10**	**193**	**20.7**	**10**	....	....	....	**6**	**2**	**4**	**6**	**2**	**0**	**0**	**1**	....
1990-91	**Buffalo**	**NHL**	**78**	**32**	**47**	**79**	**26**	**13**	**2**	**3**	**174**	**18.4**	**14**	....	....	....	**6**	**3**	**1**	**4**	**6**	**1**	**0**	**0**	....
1991-92	**Buffalo**	**NHL**	**8**	**2**	**6**	**8**	**4**	**0**	**0**	**0**	**14**	**14.3**	**-1**	....	....	....	....	....	....	....	....	....	....	....	....
	NY Islanders	**NHL**	**69**	**38**	**49**	**87**	**16**	**13**	**0**	**6**	**193**	**19.7**	**8**	....	....	....	....	....	....	....	....	....	....	....	....
1992-93	**NY Islanders**	**NHL**	**83**	**58**	**74**	**132**	**26**	**24**	**0**	**10**	**301**	**19.3**	**-1**	....	....	....	**11**	**6**	**7**	**13**	**0**	**0**	**0**	**0**	....
1993-94	**NY Islanders**	**NHL**	**69**	**38**	**56**	**94**	**18**	**10**	**4**	**6**	**254**	**15.0**	**14**	....	....	....	**4**	**0**	**1**	**1**	**0**	**0**	**0**	**0**	....
1994-95	**NY Islanders**	**NHL**	**34**	**13**	**14**	**27**	**10**	**3**	**2**	**2**	**93**	**14.0**	**-12**	....	....	....	....	....	....	....	....	....	....	....	....
	Montreal	**NHL**	**15**	**11**	**9**	**20**	**4**	**2**	**0**	**2**	**67**	**16.4**	**12**	....	....	....	....	....	....	....	....	....	....	....	....
1995-96	**Montreal**	**NHL**	**80**	**38**	**58**	**96**	**44**	**17**	**1**	**6**	**297**	**12.8**	**19**	....	....	....	**6**	**2**	**4**	**6**	**2**	**0**	**0**	**0**	....
1996-97	**Montreal**	**NHL**	**9**	**1**	**10**	**11**	**2**	**0**	**0**	**0**	**22**	**4.5**	**4**	....	....	....	....	....	....	....	....	....	....	....	....
	St. Louis	**NHL**	**69**	**25**	**49**	**74**	**12**	**5**	**0**	**7**	**194**	**12.9**	**4**	....	....	....	**5**	**1**	**1**	**2**	**2**	**1**	**0**	**0**	....
1997-98	**St. Louis**	**NHL**	**60**	**22**	**46**	**68**	**24**	**6**	**0**	**4**	**140**	**15.7**	**13**	....	....	....	**10**	**4**	**4**	**8**	**2**	**2**	**0**	**0**	....
1998-99	**St. Louis**	**NHL**	**67**	**31**	**34**	**65**	**36**	**10**	**0**	**5**	**193**	**16.1**	**4**	**1285**	**50.0**	**19:07**	**13**	**4**	**9**	**13**	**6**	**0**	**0**	**2**	**19:35**
99-2000	**St. Louis**	**NHL**	**52**	**26**	**40**	**66**	**8**	**8**	**0**	**3**	**139**	**18.7**	**30**	**1016**	**53.2**	**19:13**	**7**	**0**	**7**	**7**	**0**	**0**	**0**	**0**	**19:45**
2000-01	**St. Louis**	**NHL**	**79**	**30**	**52**	**82**	**37**	**11**	**0**	**6**	**171**	**17.5**	**14**	**1569**	**49.7**	**18:50**	**15**	**5**	**10**	**15**	**2**	**1**	**0**	**0**	**19:07**
2001-02	**Dallas**	**NHL**	**66**	**15**	**32**	**47**	**16**	**7**	**0**	**1**	**121**	**12.4**	**-4**	**822**	**48.4**	**16:31**	....	....	....	....	....	....	....	....	....
2002-03	**Dallas**	**NHL**	**65**	**12**	**30**	**42**	**18**	**3**	**0**	**5**	**76**	**15.8**	**4**	**290**	**53.8**	**14:38**	**5**	**0**	**1**	**1**	**0**	**0**	**0**	**0**	**12:21**
2003-04	**Dallas**	**NHL**	**76**	**15**	**25**	**40**	**20**	**6**	**0**	**1**	**104**	**14.4**	**17**	**578**	**49.3**	**14:13**	**5**	**1**	**3**	**4**	**2**	**0**	**0**	**0**	**15:53**
2004-05		DID NOT PLAY																							
2005-06	**Colorado**	**NHL**	**62**	**16**	**30**	**46**	**32**	**7**	**0**	**1**	**94**	**17.0**	**1**	**580**	**48.6**	**12:47**	**5**	**0**	**2**	**2**	**6**	**0**	**0**	**0**	**11:40**
2006-07	**Colorado**	**NHL**	**17**	**4**	**3**	**7**	**10**	**1**	**0**	**0**	**31**	**12.9**	**-1**	**54**	**37.0**	**10:10**	....	....	....	....	....	....	....	....	....
	NHL Totals		**1294**	**515**	**812**	**1327**	**452**	**190**	**10**	**86**	**3154**	**16.3**		**6194**	**50.1**	**16:14**	**109**	**35**	**62**	**97**	**36**	**9**	**0**	**3**	**17:35**

QMJHL Offensive Rookie of the Year) (1986) • Lady Byng Memorial Trophy (1993)

Played in NHL All-Star Game (1990, 1993, 1994, 1996)

Traded to **NY Islanders** by **Buffalo** with Uwe Krupp, Benoit Hogue and Dave McLlwain for Pat LaFontaine, Randy Hillier, Randy Wood and NY Islanders' 4th round choice (Dean Melanson) in 1992 Entry Draft, October 25, 1991. Traded to **Montreal** by **NY Islanders** with Vladimir Malakhov for Kirk Muller, Mathieu Schneider and Craig Darby, April 5, 1995. Traded to **St. Louis** by **Montreal** with Rory Fitzpatrick and Craig Conroy for Murray Baron, Shayne Corson and St. Louis' 5th round choice (Gennady Razin) in 1997 Entry Draft, October 29, 1996. Signed as a free agent by **Dallas**, July 1, 2001. Signed as a free agent by **Colorado**, August 3, 2005. • Missed majority of 2006-07 season recovering from shoulder and calf injuries.

TVERDOVSKY, Oleg
(tvehr-DOHV-skee, OH-lehg) **L.A.**

Defense. Shoots left. 6'1", 211 lbs. Born, Donetsk, USSR, May 18, 1976. Anaheim's 1st choice, 2nd overall, in 1994 Entry Draft.

Season	Club	League	GP	G	A	Pts	PIM	PP	SH	GW	S	%	+/-	TF	F%	Min	GP	G	A	Pts	PIM	PP	SH	GW	Min
1992-93	Krylja Sovetov	CIS	21	0	1	1	6	....	....	....	....	....	....	....	....	....	6	0	0	0	0	....	....	....	....
1993-94	Krylja Sovetov	CIS	46	4	10	14	22	....	....	....	....	....	....	....	....	....	3	1	0	1	2	....	....	....	....
1994-95	Brandon	WHL	7	1	4	5	4	....	....	....	....	....	....	....	....	....	....	....	....	....	....	....	....	....	....
	Anaheim	**NHL**	**36**	**3**	**9**	**12**	**14**	**1**	**1**	**0**	**26**	**11.5**	**-6**	....	....	....	....	....	....	....	....	....	....	....	....
1995-96	**Anaheim**	**NHL**	**51**	**7**	**15**	**22**	**35**	**2**	**0**	**0**	**84**	**8.3**	**0**	....	....	....	....	....	....	....	....	....	....	....	....
	Winnipeg	**NHL**	**31**	**0**	**8**	**8**	**6**	**0**	**0**	**0**	**35**	**0.0**	**-7**	....	....	....	**6**	**0**	**1**	**1**	**0**	**0**	**0**	**0**	....
1996-97	**Phoenix**	**NHL**	**82**	**10**	**45**	**55**	**30**	**3**	**1**	**2**	**144**	**6.9**	**-5**	....	....	....	**7**	**0**	**1**	**1**	**0**	**0**	**0**	**0**	....
1997-98	Hamilton	AHL	9	8	6	14	2	....	....	....	....	....	....	....	....	....	....	....	....	....	....	....	....	....	....
	Phoenix	**NHL**	**46**	**7**	**12**	**19**	**12**	**4**	**0**	**1**	**83**	**8.4**	**1**	....	....	....	**6**	**0**	**7**	**7**	**0**	**0**	**0**	**0**	....
1998-99	**Phoenix**	**NHL**	**82**	**7**	**18**	**25**	**32**	**2**	**0**	**2**	**117**	**6.0**	**11**	**1**	**0.0**	**20:48**	**6**	**0**	**2**	**2**	**6**	**0**	**0**	**0**	**17:43**
99-2000	**Anaheim**	**NHL**	**82**	**15**	**36**	**51**	**30**	**5**	**0**	**5**	**153**	**9.8**	**5**	**1**	**0.0**	**22:46**	....	....	....	....	....	....	....	....	....
2000-01	**Anaheim**	**NHL**	**82**	**14**	**39**	**53**	**32**	**8**	**0**	**3**	**188**	**7.4**	**-11**	**0**	**0.0**	**24:25**	....	....	....	....	....	....	....	....	....
2001-02	**Anaheim**	**NHL**	**73**	**6**	**26**	**32**	**31**	**2**	**0**	**1**	**147**	**4.1**	**0**	**0**	**0.0**	**22:50**	....	....	....	....	....	....	....	....	....
	Russia	Olympics	6	1	1	2	0	....	....	....	....	....	....	....	....	....	....	....	....	....	....	....	....	....	....
2002-03♦	**New Jersey**	**NHL**	**50**	**5**	**8**	**13**	**22**	**2**	**0**	**1**	**76**	**6.6**	**2**	**0**	**0.0**	**16:48**	**15**	**0**	**3**	**3**	**0**	**0**	**0**	**0**	**15:06**
2003-04	Avangard Omsk	Russia	57	16	17	33	58	....	....	....	....	....	....	....	....	....	11	0	2	2	2	....	....	....	....
2004-05	Avangard Omsk	Russia	48	5	15	20	65	....	....	....	....	....	....	....	....	....	11	0	3	3	*35	....	....	....	....
2005-06♦	**Carolina**	**NHL**	**72**	**3**	**20**	**23**	**37**	**0**	**0**	**0**	**91**	**3.3**	**-1**	**0**	**0.0**	**16:36**	**5**	**0**	**0**	**0**	**0**	**0**	**0**	**0**	**5:16**
2006-07	**Los Angeles**	**NHL**	**26**	**0**	**4**	**4**	**10**	**0**	**0**	**0**	**26**	**0.0**	**-10**	**0**	**0.0**	**11:50**	....	....	....	....	....	....	....	....	....
	Manchester	AHL	14	5	8	13	2	....	....	....	....	....	....	....	....	....	14	2	9	11	14	....	....	....	....
	NHL Totals		**713**	**77**	**240**	**317**	**291**	**29**	**2**	**15**	**1170**	**6.6**		**2**	**0.0**	**20:31**	**45**	**0**	**14**	**14**	**6**	**0**	**0**	**0**	**13:49**

Played in NHL All-Star Game (1997)

Traded to **Winnipeg** by **Anaheim** with Chad Kilger and Anaheim's 3rd round choice (Per-Anton Lundstrom) in 1996 Entry Draft for Teemu Selanne, Marc Chouinard and Winnipeg's 4th round choice (later traded to Toronto – later traded to Montreal – Montreal selected Kim Staal) in 1996 Entry Draft, February 7, 1996. Transferred to **Phoenix** after **Winnipeg** franchise relocated, July 1, 1996. Traded to **Anaheim** by **Phoenix** for Travis Green and Anaheim's 1st round choice (Scott Kelman) in 1999 Entry Draft, June 26, 1999. Traded to **New Jersey** by **Anaheim** with Jeff Friesen and Maxim Balmochnykh for Petr Sykora, Mike Commodore, Jean-Francois Damphousse and Igor Pohanka, July 6, 2002. Signed as a free agent by **Omsk** (Russia), August 29, 2003. Signed as a free agent by **Carolina**, August 4, 2005. Traded to **Los Angeles** by **Carolina** with Jack Johnson for Eric Belanger and Tim Gleason, September 29, 2006.

TYUTIN, Fedor
(T'YOO-tihn, feh-DUHR) **NYR**

Defense. Shoots left. 6'3", 210 lbs. Born, Izhevsk, USSR, July 19, 1983. NY Rangers' 2nd choice, 40th overall, in 2001 Entry Draft.

Season	Club	League	GP	G	A	Pts	PIM	PP	SH	GW	S	%	+/-	TF	F%	Min	GP	G	A	Pts	PIM	PP	SH	GW	Min
1998-99	Magnitogorsk 2	Russia-4	7	0	1	1	2	....	....	....	....	....	....	....	....	....	....	....	....	....	....	....	....	....	....
99-2000	Izhstal Izhevsk 2	Russia-3	38	11	8	19	68	....	....	....	....	....	....	....	....	....	....	....	....	....	....	....	....	....	....
	Izhstal Izhevsk	Russia-2	10	0	1	1	12	....	....	....	....	....	....	....	....	....	....	....	....	....	....	....	....	....	....
2000-01	St. Petersburg	Russia	34	2	4	6	20	....	....	....	....	....	....	....	....	....	....	....	....	....	....	....	....	....	....
2001-02	Guelph Storm	OHL	53	19	40	59	54	....	....	....	....	....	....	....	....	....	9	2	8	10	8	....	....	....	....
2002-03	St. Petersburg	Russia	10	1	1	2	16	....	....	....	....	....	....	....	....	....	....	....	....	....	....	....	....	....	....
	Ak Bars Kazan	Russia	10	0	0	0	8	....	....	....	....	....	....	....	....	....	5	0	0	0	4	....	....	....	....
2003-04	**NY Rangers**	**NHL**	**25**	**2**	**5**	**7**	**14**	**0**	**1**	**0**	**33**	**6.1**	**-4**	**1**	**0.0**	**20:08**	....	....	....	....	....	....	....	....	....
	Hartford	AHL	43	5	9	14	50	....	....	....	....	....	....	....	....	....	16	0	5	5	18	....	....	....	....
2004-05	Hartford	AHL	13	2	1	3	10	....	....	....	....	....	....	....	....	....	....	....	....	....	....	....	....	....	....
	St. Petersburg	Russia	35	5	3	8	24	....	....	....	....	....	....	....	....	....	....	....	....	....	....	....	....	....	....
2005-06	**NY Rangers**	**NHL**	**77**	**6**	**19**	**25**	**58**	**4**	**0**	**2**	**102**	**5.9**	**1**	**1**	**0.0**	**20:33**	**4**	**0**	**1**	**1**	**0**	**0**	**0**	**0**	**17:50**
	Russia	Olympics	8	0	1	1	4	....	....	....	....	....	....	....	....	....	....	....	....	....	....	....	....	....	....
2006-07	**NY Rangers**	**NHL**	**66**	**2**	**12**	**14**	**44**	**1**	**1**	**0**	**75**	**2.7**	**-8**	**1**	**0.0**	**20:02**	**10**	**0**	**5**	**5**	**8**	**0**	**0**	**0**	**19:30**
	NHL Totals		**168**	**10**	**36**	**46**	**116**	**5**	**2**	**2**	**210**	**4.8**		**3**	**0.0**	**20:17**	**14**	**0**	**6**	**6**	**8**	**0**	**0**	**0**	**19:01**

Signed as a free agent by **St. Petersburg** (Russia), November 11, 2004.

UMBERGER, R.J.

(UHM-buhr-guhr, AHR-JAY) **PHI.**

Center. Shoots left. 6'2", 210 lbs. Born, Pittsburgh, PA, May 3, 1982. Vancouver's 1st choice, 16th overall, in 2001 Entry Draft.

			Regular Season														Playoffs								
Season	Club	League	GP	G	A	Pts	PIM	PP	SH	GW	S	%	+/-	TF	F%	Min	GP	G	A	Pts	PIM	PP	SH	GW	Min
1997-98	Plum Mustangs	High-PA	26	*60	*56	*116	....	....	....	....	....	....	....	....	....	....	....	....	....	....	....	....	....	....	....
1998-99	USNTDP	USHL	5	2	2	4	0	....	....	....	....	....	....	....	....	....	....	....	....	....	....	....	....	....	....
	USNTDP	NAHL	50	21	21	42	32	....	....	....	....	....	....	....	....	....	....	....	....	....	....	....	....	....	....
99-2000	USNTDP	U-18	6	1	0	1	2	....	....	....	....	....	....	....	....	....	....	....	....	....	....	....	....	....	....
	USNTDP	USHL	57	33	35	68	20	....	....	....	....	....	....	....	....	....	....	....	....	....	....	....	....	....	....
2000-01	Ohio State	CCHA	32	14	23	37	18	....	....	....	....	....	....	....	....	....	....	....	....	....	....	....	....	....	....
2001-02	Ohio State	CCHA	37	18	21	39	31	....	....	....	....	....	....	....	....	....	....	....	....	....	....	....	....	....	....
2002-03	Ohio State	CCHA	43	26	27	53	16	....	....	....	....	....	....	....	....	....	....	....	....	....	....	....	....	....	....
2003-04			DID NOT PLAY																						
2004-05	Philadelphia	AHL	80	21	44	65	36	....	....	....	....	....	....	....	....	....	21	3	7	10	12	....	....	....	....
2005-06	**Philadelphia**	**NHL**	**73**	**20**	**18**	**38**	**18**	**5**	**0**	**2**	**138**	**14.5**	**9**	**163**	**50.3**	**13:14**	**5**	**1**	**0**	**1**	**2**	**0**	**0**	**0**	**11:15**
	Philadelphia	AHL	8	3	7	10	8	....	....	....	....	....	....	....	....	....	....	....	....	....	....	....	....	....	....
2006-07	**Philadelphia**	**NHL**	**81**	**16**	**12**	**28**	**41**	**2**	**2**	**1**	**134**	**11.9**	**–32**	**535**	**44.5**	**14:32**	....	....	....	....	....	....	....	....	....
	NHL Totals		**154**	**36**	**30**	**66**	**59**	**7**	**2**	**3**	**272**	**13.2**		**698**	**45.8**	**13:55**	**5**	**1**	**0**	**1**	**2**	**0**	**0**	**0**	**11:15**

CCHA All-Rookie Team (2001) • CCHA Rookie of the Year (2001) • CCHA First All-Star Team (2003) • NCAA West Second All-American Team (2003)

• Missed entire 2003-04 season due to a contract dispute. Traded to **NY Rangers** by **Vancouver** with Martin Grenier for Martin Rucinsky, March 9, 2004. Signed as a free agent by **Philadelphia**, June 16, 2004.

UPSHALL, Scottie

(UHP-shuhl, SKAW-tee) **PHI.**

Left wing. Shoots left. 6', 197 lbs. Born, Fort McMurray, Alta., October 7, 1983. Nashville's 1st choice, 6th overall, in 2002 Entry Draft.

			Regular Season														Playoffs								
Season	Club	League	GP	G	A	Pts	PIM	PP	SH	GW	S	%	+/-	TF	F%	Min	GP	G	A	Pts	PIM	PP	SH	GW	Min
1998-99	Fort McMurray	AMHL	28	62	40	102	100	....	....	....	....	....	....	....	....	....	....	....	....	....	....	....	....	....	....
99-2000	Fort McMurray	AJHL	52	26	26	52	65	....	....	....	....	....	....	....	....	....	....	....	....	....	....	....	....	....	....
2000-01	Kamloops Blazers	WHL	70	42	45	87	111	....	....	....	....	....	....	....	....	....	4	0	2	2	10	....	....	....	....
2001-02	Kamloops Blazers	WHL	61	32	51	83	139	....	....	....	....	....	....	....	....	....	4	1	2	3	21	....	....	....	....
2002-03	**Nashville**	**NHL**	**8**	**1**	**0**	**1**	**0**	**0**	**0**	**0**	**6**	**16.7**	**2**	**2**	**0.0**	**8:42**	....	....	....	....	....	....	....	....	....
	Kamloops Blazers	WHL	42	25	31	56	111	....	....	....	....	....	....	....	....	....	6	0	2	2	34	....	....	....	....
	Milwaukee	AHL	2	1	0	1	2	....	....	....	....	....	....	....	....	....	6	0	0	0	2	....	....	....	....
2003-04	**Nashville**	**NHL**	**7**	**0**	**1**	**1**	**0**	**0**	**0**	**0**	**6**	**0.0**	**–2**	**8**	**37.5**	**9:11**	....	....	....	....	....	....	....	....	....
	Milwaukee	AHL	31	13	11	24	42	....	....	....	....	....	....	....	....	....	8	3	0	3	4	....	....	....	....
2004-05	Milwaukee	AHL	62	19	27	46	108	....	....	....	....	....	....	....	....	....	5	2	2	4	8	....	....	....	....
2005-06	**Nashville**	**NHL**	**48**	**8**	**16**	**24**	**34**	**1**	**0**	**2**	**72**	**11.1**	**14**	**11**	**45.5**	**10:26**	**2**	**0**	**0**	**0**	**0**	**0**	**0**	**0**	**11:57**
	Milwaukee	AHL	23	17	16	33	44	....	....	....	....	....	....	....	....	....	14	6	10	16	20	....	....	....	....
2006-07	**Nashville**	**NHL**	**14**	**2**	**1**	**3**	**18**	**0**	**0**	**2**	**27**	**7.4**	**–1**	**0**	**0.0**	**10:28**	....	....	....	....	....	....	....	....	....
	Milwaukee	AHL	5	0	1	1	6	....	....	....	....	....	....	....	....	....	....	....	....	....	....	....	....	....	....
	Philadelphia	**NHL**	**18**	**6**	**7**	**13**	**8**	**1**	**1**	**2**	**60**	**10.0**	**4**	**18**	**44.4**	**18:05**	....	....	....	....	....	....	....	....	....
	NHL Totals		**95**	**17**	**25**	**42**	**60**	**2**	**1**	**6**	**171**	**9.9**		**39**	**41.0**	**11:39**	**2**	**0**	**0**	**0**	**0**	**0**	**0**	**0**	**11:57**

WHL All-Rookie Team (2001) • WHL Rookie of the Year (2001) • CHL All-Rookie Team (2001) • Canadian Major Junior Rookie of the Year (2001) • WHL West Second All-Star Team (2002)

• Missed majority of 2003-04 season recovering from knee injury suffered in game vs. Phoenix, December 22, 2003. Traded to **Philadelphia** by **Nashville** with Ryan Parent and Nashville's 1st (later traded back to Nashville - Nashville selected Jonathon Blum) and 3rd (later traded to Washington - Washington selected Phil Desimone) round choices in 2007 Entry Draft for Peter Forsberg, February 15, 2007.

VAANANEN, Ossi

(VAN-ih-nehn, AW-see)

Defense. Shoots left. 6'4", 215 lbs. Born, Vantaa, Finland, August 18, 1980. Phoenix's 2nd choice, 43rd overall, in 1998 Entry Draft.

			Regular Season														Playoffs								
Season	Club	League	GP	G	A	Pts	PIM	PP	SH	GW	S	%	+/-	TF	F%	Min	GP	G	A	Pts	PIM	PP	SH	GW	Min
1995-96	Jokerit U18	Fin-U18	8	0	0	0	2	....	....	....	....	....	....	....	....	....	2	0	0	0	0	....	....	....	....
1996-97	Jokerit U18	Fin-U18	18	1	2	3	43	....	....	....	....	....	....	....	....	....	....	....	....	....	....	....	....	....	....
	Jokerit Helsinki Jr.	Fin-Jr.	1	0	0	0	0	....	....	....	....	....	....	....	....	....	....	....	....	....	....	....	....	....	....
1997-98	Jokerit U18	Fin-U18	7	3	3	6	8	....	....	....	....	....	....	....	....	....	....	....	....	....	....	....	....	....	....
	Jokerit Helsinki Jr.	Fin-Jr.	31	0	6	6	24	....	....	....	....	....	....	....	....	....	7	0	2	2	16	....	....	....	....
1998-99	Jokerit Helsinki Jr.	Fin-Jr.	12	1	6	7	16	....	....	....	....	....	....	....	....	....	6	1	0	1	12	....	....	....	....
	Jokerit Helsinki	Finland	48	0	1	1	42	....	....	....	....	....	....	....	....	....	3	0	1	1	2	....	....	....	....
	Jokerit Helsinki	EuroHL	5	0	0	0	2	....	....	....	....	....	....	....	....	....	1	0	1	1	2	....	....	....	....
99-2000	Jokerit Helsinki	Finland	49	1	6	7	46	....	....	....	....	....	....	....	....	....	11	1	1	2	2	....	....	....	....
2000-01	**Phoenix**	**NHL**	**81**	**4**	**12**	**16**	**90**	**0**	**0**	**2**	**69**	**5.8**	**9**	**0**	**0.0**	**19:09**	....	....	....	....	....	....	....	....	....
2001-02	**Phoenix**	**NHL**	**76**	**2**	**12**	**14**	**74**	**0**	**1**	**0**	**41**	**4.9**	**6**	**0**	**0.0**	**20:13**	**5**	**0**	**0**	**0**	**6**	**0**	**0**	**0**	**20:33**
	Finland	Olympics	2	0	1	1	0	....	....	....	....	....	....	....	....	....	....	....	....	....	....	....	....	....	....
2002-03	**Phoenix**	**NHL**	**67**	**2**	**7**	**9**	**82**	**0**	**0**	**0**	**49**	**4.1**	**1**	**0**	**0.0**	**19:15**	....	....	....	....	....	....	....	....	....
2003-04	**Phoenix**	**NHL**	**67**	**2**	**4**	**6**	**87**	**0**	**0**	**1**	**39**	**5.1**	**–10**	**0**	**0.0**	**19:21**	....	....	....	....	....	....	....	....	....
	Colorado	**NHL**	**12**	**0**	**0**	**0**	**2**	**0**	**0**	**0**	**6**	**0.0**	**–4**	**0**	**0.0**	**18:36**	**11**	**0**	**1**	**1**	**18**	**0**	**0**	**0**	**22:06**
2004-05	Jokerit Helsinki	Finland	28	2	2	4	30	....	....	....	....	....	....	....	....	....	12	0	0	0	26	....	....	....	....
2005-06	**Colorado**	**NHL**	**53**	**0**	**4**	**4**	**56**	**0**	**0**	**0**	**34**	**0.0**	**10**	**1**	**0.0**	**13:34**	**1**	**0**	**0**	**0**	**0**	**0**	**0**	**0**	**13:58**
2006-07	**Colorado**	**NHL**	**74**	**2**	**6**	**8**	**69**	**0**	**0**	**1**	**32**	**6.3**	**6**	**0**	**0.0**	**14:20**	....	....	....	....	....	....	....	....	....
	NHL Totals		**430**	**12**	**45**	**57**	**460**	**0**	**1**	**4**	**270**	**4.4**		**1**	**0.0**	**17:51**	**17**	**0**	**1**	**1**	**24**	**0**	**0**	**0**	**21:10**

Traded to **Colorado** by **Phoenix** with Chris Gratton and Phoenix's 2nd round choice (Paul Stastny) in 2005 Entry Draft for Derek Morris and Keith Ballard, March 9, 2004. Signed as a free agent by **Jokerit Helsinki** (Finland), December 1, 2004.

VANDENBUSSCHE, Ryan

(van-dehn-BUHSH, RIGH-uhn)

Right wing. Shoots right. 6', 200 lbs. Born, Simcoe, Ont., February 28, 1973. Toronto's 9th choice, 173rd overall, in 1992 Entry Draft.

			Regular Season														Playoffs								
Season	Club	League	GP	G	A	Pts	PIM	PP	SH	GW	S	%	+/-	TF	F%	Min	GP	G	A	Pts	PIM	PP	SH	GW	Min
1988-89	Delhi Flames	OHA-D	3	1	1	2	2	....	....	....	....	....	....	....	....	....	....	....	....	....	....	....	....	....	....
1989-90	Norwich	OHA-C	21	12	10	22	146	....	....	....	....	....	....	....	....	....	....	....	....	....	....	....	....	....	....
	Tillsonburg Titans	OHA-B	24	0	5	5	113	....	....	....	....	....	....	....	....	....	....	....	....	....	....	....	....	....	....
1990-91	Massena	CJHL	10	2	3	5	46	....	....	....	....	....	....	....	....	....	....	....	....	....	....	....	....	....	....
	Cornwall Royals	OHL	49	3	8	11	139	....	....	....	....	....	....	....	....	....	....	....	....	....	....	....	....	....	....
1991-92	Cornwall Royals	OHL	61	13	15	28	232	....	....	....	....	....	....	....	....	....	6	0	2	2	9	....	....	....	....
1992-93	Newmarket	OHL	30	15	12	27	161	....	....	....	....	....	....	....	....	....	....	....	....	....	....	....	....	....	....
	Guelph Storm	OHL	29	3	14	17	99	....	....	....	....	....	....	....	....	....	5	1	3	4	13	....	....	....	....
	St. John's	AHL	1	0	0	0	0	....	....	....	....	....	....	....	....	....	....	....	....	....	....	....	....	....	....
1993-94	St. John's	AHL	44	4	10	14	124	....	....	....	....	....	....	....	....	....	....	....	....	....	....	....	....	....	....
	Springfield	AHL	9	1	2	3	29	....	....	....	....	....	....	....	....	....	5	0	0	0	16	....	....	....	....
1994-95	St. John's	AHL	53	2	13	15	239	....	....	....	....	....	....	....	....	....	3	0	0	0	17	....	....	....	....
1995-96	Binghamton	AHL	68	3	17	20	240	....	....	....	....	....	....	....	....	....	4	0	0	0	9	....	....	....	....
1996-97	**NY Rangers**	**NHL**	**11**	**1**	**0**	**1**	**30**	**0**	**0**	**0**	**4**	**25.0**	**–2**	....	....	....	....	....	....	....	....	....	....	....	....
	Binghamton	AHL	38	8	11	19	133	....	....	....	....	....	....	....	....	....	....	....	....	....	....	....	....	....	....
1997-98	**NY Rangers**	**NHL**	**16**	**1**	**0**	**1**	**38**	**0**	**0**	**0**	**2**	**50.0**	**–2**	....	....	....	....	....	....	....	....	....	....	....	....
	Hartford	AHL	15	2	0	2	45	....	....	....	....	....	....	....	....	....	....	....	....	....	....	....	....	....	....
	Chicago	**NHL**	**4**	**0**	**1**	**1**	**5**	**0**	**0**	**0**	**0**	**0.0**	**0**	....	....	....	....	....	....	....	....	....	....	....	....
	Indianapolis Ice	IHL	3	1	1	2	4	....	....	....	....	....	....	....	....	....	....	....	....	....	....	....	....	....	....
1998-99	**Chicago**	**NHL**	**6**	**0**	**0**	**0**	**17**	**0**	**0**	**0**	**3**	**0.0**	**0**	**0**	**0.0**	**9:29**	....	....	....	....	....	....	....	....	....
	Indianapolis Ice	IHL	34	3	10	13	130	....	....	....	....	....	....	....	....	....	....	....	....	....	....	....	....	....	....
	Portland Pirates	AHL	37	4	1	5	119	....	....	....	....	....	....	....	....	....	....	....	....	....	....	....	....	....	....
99-2000	**Chicago**	**NHL**	**52**	**0**	**1**	**1**	**143**	**0**	**0**	**0**	**19**	**0.0**	**–3**	**3**	**0.0**	**5:37**	....	....	....	....	....	....	....	....	....
2000-01	**Chicago**	**NHL**	**64**	**2**	**5**	**7**	**146**	**0**	**0**	**0**	**24**	**8.3**	**–8**	**2**	**0.0**	**7:46**	....	....	....	....	....	....	....	....	....
2001-02	**Chicago**	**NHL**	**50**	**1**	**2**	**3**	**103**	**0**	**0**	**0**	**22**	**4.5**	**–10**	**2**	**50.0**	**6:19**	**1**	**0**	**0**	**0**	**0**	**0**	**0**	**0**	**7:20**
2002-03	**Chicago**	**NHL**	**22**	**0**	**0**	**0**	**58**	**0**	**0**	**0**	**7**	**0.0**	**0**	**1**	**100.0**	**6:30**	....	....	....	....	....	....	....	....	....
	Norfolk Admirals	AHL	4	0	1	1	5	....	....	....	....	....	....	....	....	....	....	....	....	....	....	....	....	....	....
2003-04	**Chicago**	**NHL**	**65**	**4**	**1**	**5**	**120**	**2**	**0**	**0**	**25**	**16.0**	**–10**	**0**	**0.0**	**6:16**	....	....	....	....	....	....	....	....	....
2004-05	Wilkes-Barre	AHL	23	4	7	11	67	....	....	....	....	....	....	....	....	....	11	2	2	4	11	....	....	....	....
2005-06	**Pittsburgh**	**NHL**	**20**	**1**	**0**	**1**	**42**	**0**	**0**	**0**	**5**	**20.0**	**0**	**0**	**0.0**	**4:20**	....	....	....	....	....	....	....	....	....
2006-07	Jokerit Helsinki	Finland	15	0	0	0	39	....	....	....	....	....	....	....	....	....	....	....	....	....	....	....	....	....	....
	New Mexico	CHL	9	0	3	3	29	....	....	....	....	....	....	....	....	....	....	....	....	....	....	....	....	....	....
	NHL Totals		**310**	**10**	**10**	**20**	**702**	**2**	**0**	**0**	**111**	**9.0**		**8**	**25.0**	**6:27**	**1**	**0**	**0**	**0**	**0**	**0**	**0**	**0**	**7:20**

Signed as a free agent by **NY Rangers**, August 22, 1995. Traded to **Chicago** by **NY Rangers** for Ryan Risidore, March 24, 1998. • Missed majority of 2002-03 season recovering from hand injury suffered in game vs. Detroit, January 5, 2003. Signed as a free agent by **Pittsburgh**, July 12, 2004. Signed as a free agent by **Wilkes-Barre** (AHL), February 17, 2005. Signed as a free agent by **Jokerit Helsinki**(Finland), September 26, 2006. Signed as a free agent by **New Mexico**(CHL), November 5, 2006.

VANDERMEER, Jim

(VAN-duhr-meer, JIHM) **CHI.**

Defense. Shoots left. 6'1", 208 lbs. Born, Caroline, Alta., February 21, 1980.

Season	Club	League	Regular Season GP	G	A	Pts	PIM	PP	SH	GW	S	%	+/-	TF	F%	Min	Playoffs GP	G	A	Pts	PIM	PP	SH	GW	Min
1997-98	Red Deer	AMHL	26	4	8	12	51	....	....	....	....	....	....	....	....	....	....	....	....	....	....	....	....	....	....
	Red Deer Rebels	WHL	35	0	3	3	55	....	....	....	....	....	....	....	....	....	2	0	0	0	0	....	....	....	....
1998-99	Red Deer Rebels	WHL	70	5	23	28	258	....	....	....	....	....	....	....	....	....	9	0	1	1	24	....	....	....	....
99-2000	Red Deer Rebels	WHL	71	8	30	38	221	....	....	....	....	....	....	....	....	....	4	0	1	1	16	....	....	....	....
2000-01	Red Deer Rebels	WHL	72	21	44	65	180	....	....	....	....	....	....	....	....	....	22	3	13	16	43	....	....	....	....
2001-02	Philadelphia	AHL	74	1	13	14	88	....	....	....	....	....	....	....	....	....	5	0	2	2	14	....	....	....	....
2002-03	Philadelphia	AHL	48	4	8	12	122	....	....	....	....	....	....	....	....	....	....	....	....	....	....	....	....	....	....
	Philadelphia	**NHL**	**24**	**2**	**1**	**3**	**27**	**0**	**0**	**0**	**22**	**9.1**	**9**	**0**	**0.0**	**13:42**	**8**	**0**	**1**	**1**	**9**	**0**	**0**	**0**	**12:42**
2003-04	**Philadelphia**	**NHL**	**23**	**3**	**2**	**5**	**25**	**0**	**0**	**1**	**24**	**12.5**	**–5**	**0**	**0.0**	**15:47**	....	....	....	....	....	....	....	....	....
	Philadelphia	AHL	26	1	6	7	120	....	....	....	....	....	....	....	....	....	....	....	....	....	....	....	....	....	....
	Chicago	**NHL**	**23**	**2**	**10**	**12**	**58**	**1**	**1**	**0**	**37**	**5.4**	**–6**	**1**	**100.0**	**22:03**	....	....	....	....	....	....	....	....	....
2004-05	Norfolk Admirals	AHL	52	3	10	13	164	....	....	....	....	....	....	....	....	....	....	....	....	....	....	....	....	....	....
2005-06	**Chicago**	**NHL**	**76**	**6**	**18**	**24**	**116**	**2**	**0**	**1**	**93**	**6.5**	**–2**	**1**	**100.0**	**21:47**	....	....	....	....	....	....	....	....	....
2006-07	**Chicago**	**NHL**	**46**	**1**	**6**	**7**	**53**	**0**	**0**	**0**	**50**	**2.0**	**–3**	**0**	**0.0**	**17:50**	....	....	....	....	....	....	....	....	....
	NHL Totals		**192**	**14**	**37**	**51**	**279**	**3**	**1**	**2**	**226**	**6.2**		**2**	**100.0**	**19:08**	**8**	**0**	**1**	**1**	**9**	**0**	**0**	**0**	**12:42**

WHL East First All-Star Team (2001) • Canadian Major Junior Humanitarian Player of the Year (2001)

Signed as a free agent by **Philadelphia**, December 21, 2000. Traded to **Chicago** by **Philadelphia** with the rights to Colin Fraser and Los Angeles' 2nd round choice (previously acquired, Chicago selected Bryan Bickell) in 2004 Entry Draft for Alex Zhamnov and Washington's 4th round choice (previously acquired, Philadelphia selected R.J. Anderson) in 2004 Entry Draft, February 19, 2004.

VANEK, Thomas

(VAH-NEHK, TAW-muhs) **BUF.**

Left wing. Shoots right. 6'2", 203 lbs. Born, Vienna, Austria, January 19, 1984. Buffalo's 1st choice, 5th overall, in 2003 Entry Draft.

Season	Club	League	GP	G	A	Pts	PIM	PP	SH	GW	S	%	+/-	TF	F%	Min	GP	G	A	Pts	PIM	PP	SH	GW	Min
99-2000	Sioux Falls	USHL	35	15	18	33	12	....	....	....	....	....	....	....	....	....	3	0	1	1	0	....	....	....	....
2000-01	Sioux Falls	USHL	20	19	10	29	15	....	....	....	....	....	....	....	....	....	8	5	4	9	2	....	....	....	....
2001-02	Sioux Falls	USHL	53	46	45	91	54	....	....	....	....	....	....	....	....	....	3	0	0	0	9	....	....	....	....
2002-03	U. of Minnesota	WCHA	45	31	31	62	60	....	....	....	....	....	....	....	....	....	....	....	....	....	....	....	....	....	....
2003-04	U. of Minnesota	WCHA	38	26	25	51	72	....	....	....	....	....	....	....	....	....	....	....	....	....	....	....	....	....	....
2004-05	Rochester	AHL	74	42	26	68	62	....	....	....	....	....	....	....	....	....	5	2	3	5	10	....	....	....	....
2005-06	**Buffalo**	**NHL**	**81**	**25**	**23**	**48**	**72**	**11**	**0**	**4**	**204**	**12.3**	**–11**	**23**	**21.7**	**14:44**	**10**	**2**	**0**	**2**	**6**	**2**	**0**	**0**	**10:45**
2006-07	**Buffalo**	**NHL**	**82**	**43**	**41**	**84**	**40**	**15**	**0**	**5**	**237**	**18.1**	**47**	**39**	**28.2**	**16:47**	**16**	**6**	**4**	**10**	**10**	**1**	**0**	**2**	**16:27**
	NHL Totals		**163**	**68**	**64**	**132**	**112**	**26**	**0**	**9**	**441**	**15.4**		**62**	**25.8**	**15:46**	**26**	**8**	**4**	**12**	**16**	**3**	**0**	**2**	**14:15**

USHL First All-Star Team (2002) • USHL MVP (2002) • WCHA All-Rookie Team (2003) • WCHA Second All-Star Team (2003, 2004) • WCHA Rookie of the Year (2003) • NCAA Championship All-Tournament Team (2003) • NCAA Championship Tournament MVP (2003) • NCAA West Second All-American Team (2004) • AHL All-Rookie Team (2005) • NHL Second All-Star Team (2007)

VAN RYN, Mike

(VAN RIHN, MIGHK) **FLA.**

Defense. Shoots right. 6'1", 198 lbs. Born, London, Ont., May 14, 1979. New Jersey's 1st choice, 26th overall, in 1998 Entry Draft.

Season	Club	League	GP	G	A	Pts	PIM	PP	SH	GW	S	%	+/-	TF	F%	Min	GP	G	A	Pts	PIM	PP	SH	GW	Min
1995-96	London Nationals	OHA-B	44	9	14	23	24	....	....	....	....	....	....	....	....	....	....	....	....	....	....	....	....	....	....
1996-97	London Nationals	OHA-B	46	14	31	45	32	....	....	....	....	....	....	....	....	....	....	....	....	....	....	....	....	....	....
1997-98	U. of Michigan	CCHA	38	4	14	18	44	....	....	....	....	....	....	....	....	....	....	....	....	....	....	....	....	....	....
1998-99	U. of Michigan	CCHA	37	10	13	23	52	....	....	....	....	....	....	....	....	....	....	....	....	....	....	....	....	....	....
99-2000	Sarnia Sting	OHL	61	6	35	41	34	....	....	....	....	....	....	....	....	....	7	0	5	5	4	....	....	....	....
2000-01	**St. Louis**	**NHL**	**1**	**0**	**0**	**0**	**0**	**0**	**0**	**0**	**1**	**0.0**	**–2**	**0**	**0.0**	**13:43**	....	....	....	....	....	....	....	....	....
	Worcester IceCats	AHL	37	3	10	13	12	....	....	....	....	....	....	....	....	....	7	1	1	2	2	....	....	....	....
2001-02	**St. Louis**	**NHL**	**48**	**2**	**8**	**10**	**18**	**0**	**0**	**1**	**52**	**3.8**	**10**	**0**	**0.0**	**16:23**	**9**	**0**	**0**	**0**	**0**	**0**	**0**	**0**	**16:04**
	Worcester IceCats	AHL	24	2	7	9	17	....	....	....	....	....	....	....	....	....	....	....	....	....	....	....	....	....	....
2002-03	**St. Louis**	**NHL**	**20**	**0**	**3**	**3**	**8**	**0**	**0**	**0**	**21**	**0.0**	**3**	**0**	**0.0**	**15:04**	....	....	....	....	....	....	....	....	....
	Worcester IceCats	AHL	33	2	8	10	16	....	....	....	....	....	....	....	....	....	....	....	....	....	....	....	....	....	....
	San Antonio	AHL	11	0	3	3	20	....	....	....	....	....	....	....	....	....	3	0	0	0	0	....	....	....	....
2003-04	**Florida**	**NHL**	**79**	**13**	**24**	**37**	**52**	**6**	**1**	**0**	**136**	**9.6**	**–16**	**3**	**33.3**	**24:26**	....	....	....	....	....	....	....	....	....
2004-05			DID NOT PLAY																						
2005-06	**Florida**	**NHL**	**80**	**8**	**29**	**37**	**90**	**3**	**0**	**2**	**154**	**5.2**	**15**	**0**	**0.0**	**22:36**	....	....	....	....	....	....	....	....	....
2006-07	**Florida**	**NHL**	**78**	**4**	**25**	**29**	**64**	**1**	**0**	**0**	**121**	**3.3**	**–5**	**1**	**0.0**	**21:08**	....	....	....	....	....	....	....	....	....
	NHL Totals		**306**	**27**	**89**	**116**	**232**	**10**	**1**	**3**	**485**	**5.6**		**4**	**25.0**	**21:12**	**9**	**0**	**0**	**0**	**0**	**0**	**0**	**0**	**16:04**

OJHL-B First All-Star Team (1997)

Signed as a free agent by **St. Louis**, June 30, 2000. • Missed majority of 2000-01 season recovering from shoulder injury suffered in game vs. Phoenix, October 5, 2000. Traded to **Florida** by **St. Louis** for Valeri Bure and Florida's 5th round choice (Nikita Nikitin) in 2004 Entry Draft, March 11, 2003.

VARADA, Vaclav

(vuh-RA-da, VAT-slav)

Right wing. Shoots left. 6', 208 lbs. Born, Vsetin, Czech., April 26, 1976. San Jose's 4th choice, 89th overall, in 1994 Entry Draft.

Season	Club	League	GP	G	A	Pts	PIM	PP	SH	GW	S	%	+/-	TF	F%	Min	GP	G	A	Pts	PIM	PP	SH	GW	Min
1993-94	HC Vitkovice	CzRep	24	6	7	13	....	....	....	....	....	....	....	....	....	....	5	1	1	2	....	....	....	....	....
1994-95	Tacoma Rockets	WHL	68	50	38	88	108	....	....	....	....	....	....	....	....	....	4	4	3	7	11	....	....	....	....
1995-96	Kelowna Rockets	WHL	59	39	46	85	100	....	....	....	....	....	....	....	....	....	6	3	3	6	16	....	....	....	....
	Buffalo	**NHL**	**1**	**0**	**0**	**0**	**0**	**0**	**0**	**0**	**2**	**0.0**	**0**	....	....	....	....	....	....	....	....	....	....	....	....
	Rochester	AHL	5	3	0	3	4	....	....	....	....	....	....	....	....	....	....	....	....	....	....	....	....	....	....
1996-97	**Buffalo**	**NHL**	**5**	**0**	**0**	**0**	**2**	**0**	**0**	**0**	**2**	**0.0**	**0**	....	....	....	....	....	....	....	....	....	....	....	....
	Rochester	AHL	53	23	25	48	81	....	....	....	....	....	....	....	....	....	10	1	6	7	27	....	....	....	....
1997-98	**Buffalo**	**NHL**	**27**	**5**	**6**	**11**	**15**	**0**	**0**	**1**	**27**	**18.5**	**0**	....	....	....	**15**	**3**	**4**	**7**	**18**	**0**	**0**	**0**	....
	Rochester	AHL	45	30	26	56	74	....	....	....	....	....	....	....	....	....	....	....	....	....	....	....	....	....	....
1998-99	**Buffalo**	**NHL**	**72**	**7**	**24**	**31**	**61**	**1**	**0**	**1**	**123**	**5.7**	**11**	**1**	**0.0**	**14:30**	**21**	**5**	**4**	**9**	**14**	**1**	**0**	**0**	**16:31**
99-2000	HC Vitkovice	CzRep	5	2	3	5	12	....	....	....	....	....	....	....	....	....	....	....	....	....	....	....	....	....	....
	Buffalo	**NHL**	**76**	**10**	**27**	**37**	**62**	**0**	**0**	**0**	**140**	**7.1**	**12**	**1**	**0.0**	**14:58**	**5**	**0**	**0**	**0**	**8**	**0**	**0**	**0**	**14:19**
2000-01	**Buffalo**	**NHL**	**75**	**10**	**21**	**31**	**81**	**2**	**0**	**2**	**112**	**8.9**	**–2**	**2**	**0.0**	**15:57**	**13**	**0**	**4**	**4**	**8**	**0**	**0**	**0**	**18:08**
2001-02	**Buffalo**	**NHL**	**76**	**7**	**16**	**23**	**82**	**1**	**0**	**1**	**138**	**5.1**	**–7**	**3**	**0.0**	**16:33**	....	....	....	....	....	....	....	....	....
2002-03	**Buffalo**	**NHL**	**44**	**7**	**4**	**11**	**23**	**1**	**0**	**0**	**64**	**10.9**	**–2**	**13**	**53.9**	**16:07**	....	....	....	....	....	....	....	....	....
	Ottawa	**NHL**	**11**	**2**	**6**	**8**	**8**	**1**	**0**	**0**	**17**	**11.8**	**3**	**8**	**0.0**	**14:57**	**18**	**2**	**4**	**6**	**18**	**0**	**0**	**0**	**13:57**
2003-04	**Ottawa**	**NHL**	**30**	**5**	**5**	**10**	**26**	**0**	**0**	**1**	**47**	**10.6**	**2**	**14**	**35.7**	**14:21**	**7**	**1**	**1**	**2**	**4**	**0**	**0**	**0**	**12:03**
2004-05	Vitkovice	CzRep	44	8	19	27	83	....	....	....	....	....	....	....	....	....	11	3	3	6	37	....	....	....	....
2005-06	**Ottawa**	**NHL**	**76**	**5**	**16**	**21**	**50**	**1**	**0**	**0**	**114**	**4.4**	**2**	**16**	**25.0**	**9:42**	**8**	**0**	**2**	**2**	**12**	**0**	**0**	**0**	**6:04**
2006-07	HC Davos	Swiss	25	6	4	10	26	....	....	....	....	....	....	....	....	....	....	....	....	....	....	....	....	....	....
	NHL Totals		**493**	**58**	**125**	**183**	**410**	**7**	**0**	**6**	**786**	**7.4**		**58**	**27.6**	**14:31**	**87**	**11**	**19**	**30**	**82**	**1**	**0**	**0**	**14:25**

Traded to **Buffalo** by **San Jose** with Martin Spahnel and Philadelphia's 1st (previously acquired, later traded to Phoenix – Phoenix selected Daniel Briere) and 4th (previously acquired, Buffalo selected Mike Martone) round choices in 1996 Entry Draft for Doug Bodger, November 16, 1995. Traded to **Ottawa** by **Buffalo** with Buffalo's 5th round choice (Tim Cook) in 2003 Entry Draft for Jakub Klepis, February 25, 2003. • Missed majority of 2003-04 season recovering from knee injury suffered in game vs. Boston, December 13, 2003. Signed as a free agent by **Vitkovice** (CzRep), September 17, 2004. Signed as a free agent by **Davos** (Swiss), August 10, 2006.

VASICEK, Josef

(VAS-ih-chehk, YOH-zehf)

Center. Shoots left. 6'5", 214 lbs. Born, Havlickuv Brod, Czech., September 12, 1980. Carolina's 4th choice, 91st overall, in 1998 Entry Draft.

Season	Club	League	GP	G	A	Pts	PIM	PP	SH	GW	S	%	+/-	TF	F%	Min	GP	G	A	Pts	PIM	PP	SH	GW	Min
1995-96	Havl. Brod U17	CzR-U17	36	25	25	50	....	....	....	....	....	....	....	....	....	....	....	....	....	....	....	....	....	....	....
1996-97	Slavia U17	CzR-U17	37	20	40	60	....	....	....	....	....	....	....	....	....	....	....	....	....	....	....	....	....	....	....
1997-98	Slavia Jr.	CzRep-Jr.	34	13	20	33	....	....	....	....	....	....	....	....	....	....	....	....	....	....	....	....	....	....	....
1998-99	Sault Ste. Marie	OHL	66	21	35	56	30	....	....	....	....	....	....	....	....	....	5	3	0	3	10	....	....	....	....
99-2000	Sault Ste. Marie	OHL	54	26	46	72	49	....	....	....	....	....	....	....	....	....	17	5	15	20	8	....	....	....	....
2000-01	**Carolina**	**NHL**	**76**	**8**	**13**	**21**	**53**	**1**	**0**	**0**	**103**	**7.8**	**–8**	**786**	**46.6**	**11:49**	**6**	**2**	**0**	**2**	**0**	**0**	**0**	**0**	**13:56**
	Cincinnati	IHL	....	....	....	....	....	....	....	....	....	....	....	....	....	....	3	0	0	0	0	....	....	....	....
2001-02	**Carolina**	**NHL**	**78**	**14**	**17**	**31**	**53**	**3**	**0**	**3**	**117**	**12.0**	**–7**	**878**	**48.3**	**14:11**	**23**	**3**	**2**	**5**	**12**	**0**	**0**	**1**	**14:50**
2002-03	**Carolina**	**NHL**	**57**	**10**	**10**	**20**	**33**	**4**	**0**	**1**	**87**	**11.5**	**–19**	**652**	**49.5**	**15:57**	....	....	....	....	....	....	....	....	....
2003-04	**Carolina**	**NHL**	**82**	**19**	**26**	**45**	**60**	**6**	**0**	**5**	**161**	**11.8**	**–3**	**262**	**48.9**	**17:06**	....	....	....	....	....	....	....	....	....
2004-05	HC Slavia Praha	CzRep	52	20	23	43	42	....	....	....	....	....	....	....	....	....	7	1	6	7	10	....	....	....	....
2005-06 ♦	**Carolina**	**NHL**	**23**	**4**	**5**	**9**	**8**	**0**	**0**	**0**	**41**	**9.8**	**3**	**46**	**60.9**	**15:23**	**8**	**0**	**0**	**0**	**2**	**0**	**0**	**0**	**10:04**

Season	Club	League	GP	G	A	Pts	PIM	PP	SH	GW	S	%	+/-	TF	F%	Min	GP	G	A	Pts	PIM	PP	SH	GW	Min
			Regular Season														Playoffs								
2006-07	**Nashville**	**NHL**	**38**	**4**	**9**	**13**	**29**	**0**	**0**	**0**	**47**	**8.5**	**1**	**307**	**49.8**	**13:11**	....	....	....	....	....	....	....	....	....
	Carolina	**NHL**	**25**	**2**	**7**	**9**	**22**	**0**	**0**	**0**	**30**	**6.7**	**–6**	**292**	**51.4**	**13:42**	....	....	....	....	....	....	....	....	....
	NHL Totals		**379**	**61**	**87**	**148**	**258**	**14**	**0**	**9**	**586**	**10.4**		**3223**	**48.8**	**14:33**	**37**	**5**	**2**	**7**	**14**	**0**	**0**	**1**	**13:39**

Signed as a free agent by **Slavia Praha** (CzRep), September 17, 2004. • Missed majority of 2005-06 season recovering from knee injury sufferd in game at Florida, November 11, 2005. Traded to **Nashville** by **Carolina** for Scott Walker, July 18, 2006. Traded to **Carolina** by **Nashville** for Eric Belanger, February 9, 2007.

VEILLEUX, Stephane — (VAY-oo, STEH-fan) — MIN.

Left wing. Shoots left. 6'1", 193 lbs. Born, Beauceville, Que., November 16, 1981. Minnesota's 4th choice, 93rd overall, in 2001 Entry Draft.

Season	Club	League	GP	G	A	Pts	PIM	PP	SH	GW	S	%	+/-	TF	F%	Min	GP	G	A	Pts	PIM	PP	SH	GW	Min
1997-98	Beauce-Amiante	QAAA	21	20	17	37	....	....	....	....	....	....	....	....	....	....	....	....	....	....	....	....	....	....	....
	Levis-Lauzon	QAAA	14	3	5	8	....	....	....	....	....	....	....	....	....	....	1	0	0	0	0	....	....	....	....
1998-99	Victoriaville Tigres	QMJHL	65	6	13	19	35	....	....	....	....	....	....	....	....	....	6	1	3	4	2	....	....	....	....
99-2000	Victoriaville Tigres	QMJHL	22	1	4	5	17	....	....	....	....	....	....	....	....	....	....	....	....	....	....	....	....	....	....
	Val-d'Or Foreurs	QMJHL	50	14	28	42	100	....	....	....	....	....	....	....	....	....	....	....	....	....	....	....	....	....	....
2000-01	Val-d'Or Foreurs	QMJHL	68	48	67	115	90	....	....	....	....	....	....	....	....	....	21	15	18	33	42	....	....	....	....
2001-02	Houston Aeros	AHL	77	13	22	35	113	....	....	....	....	....	....	....	....	....	14	2	4	6	20	....	....	....	....
2002-03	**Minnesota**	**NHL**	**38**	**3**	**2**	**5**	**23**	**1**	**0**	**0**	**52**	**5.8**	**–6**	**13**	**7.7**	**12:08**	....	....	....	....	....	....	....	....	....
	Houston Aeros	AHL	29	8	4	12	43	....	....	....	....	....	....	....	....	....	23	7	11	18	12	....	....	....	....
2003-04	**Minnesota**	**NHL**	**19**	**2**	**8**	**10**	**20**	**1**	**1**	**1**	**37**	**5.4**	**0**	**10**	**40.0**	**14:20**	....	....	....	....	....	....	....	....	....
	Houston Aeros	AHL	64	13	25	38	66	....	....	....	....	....	....	....	....	....	2	1	1	2	2	....	....	....	....
2004-05	Houston Aeros	AHL	59	15	24	39	35	....	....	....	....	....	....	....	....	....	....	....	....	....	....	....	....	....	....
2005-06	**Minnesota**	**NHL**	**71**	**7**	**9**	**16**	**63**	**0**	**0**	**1**	**87**	**8.0**	**–13**	**33**	**33.3**	**12:58**	....	....	....	....	....	....	....	....	....
2006-07	**Minnesota**	**NHL**	**75**	**7**	**11**	**18**	**47**	**0**	**0**	**1**	**84**	**8.3**	**3**	**32**	**21.9**	**12:17**	**5**	**0**	**0**	**0**	**4**	**0**	**0**	**0**	**12:40**
	NHL Totals		**203**	**19**	**30**	**49**	**153**	**2**	**1**	**3**	**260**	**7.3**		**88**	**26.1**	**12:41**	**5**	**0**	**0**	**0**	**4**	**0**	**0**	**0**	**12:40**

VERMETTE, Antoine — (vuhr-MEHT, AN-twuhn) — OTT.

Center. Shoots left. 6', 199 lbs. Born, St-Agapit, Que., July 20, 1982. Ottawa's 3rd choice, 55th overall, in 2000 Entry Draft.

Season	Club	League	GP	G	A	Pts	PIM	PP	SH	GW	S	%	+/-	TF	F%	Min	GP	G	A	Pts	PIM	PP	SH	GW	Min
1997-98	Quebec Select	QAHA	19	11	20	31	36	....	....	....	....	....	....	....	....	....	....	....	....	....	....	....	....	....	....
	Levis-Lauzon	QAAA	8	1	1	2	4	....	....	....	....	....	....	....	....	....	1	0	0	0	0	....	....	....	....
1998-99	Quebec Remparts	QMJHL	57	9	17	26	32	....	....	....	....	....	....	....	....	....	13	0	0	0	2	....	....	....	....
99-2000	Victoriaville Tigres	QMJHL	71	30	41	71	87	....	....	....	....	....	....	....	....	....	6	0	1	1	6	....	....	....	....
2000-01	Victoriaville Tigres	QMJHL	71	57	62	119	102	....	....	....	....	....	....	....	....	....	9	4	6	10	14	....	....	....	....
2001-02	Victoriaville Tigres	QMJHL	4	0	2	2	6	....	....	....	....	....	....	....	....	....	22	10	16	26	10	....	....	....	....
2002-03	Binghamton	AHL	80	34	28	62	57	....	....	....	....	....	....	....	....	....	14	2	9	11	10	....	....	....	....
2003-04	**Ottawa**	**NHL**	**57**	**7**	**7**	**14**	**16**	**0**	**1**	**0**	**63**	**11.1**	**5**	**100**	**44.0**	**11:59**	**4**	**0**	**1**	**1**	**4**	**0**	**0**	**0**	**11:35**
	Binghamton	AHL	3	0	0	0	6	....	....	....	....	....	....	....	....	....	....	....	....	....	....	....	....	....	....
2004-05	Binghamton	AHL	78	28	45	73	36	....	....	....	....	....	....	....	....	....	6	1	4	5	10	....	....	....	....
2005-06	**Ottawa**	**NHL**	**82**	**21**	**12**	**33**	**44**	**1**	**6**	**4**	**123**	**17.1**	**17**	**537**	**57.9**	**12:35**	**10**	**2**	**0**	**2**	**4**	**0**	**0**	**1**	**15:00**
2006-07	**Ottawa**	**NHL**	**77**	**19**	**20**	**39**	**52**	**2**	**3**	**2**	**151**	**12.6**	**–2**	**834**	**53.0**	**15:42**	**20**	**2**	**3**	**5**	**6**	**0**	**0**	**0**	**16:20**
	NHL Totals		**216**	**47**	**39**	**86**	**112**	**3**	**10**	**6**	**337**	**13.9**		**1471**	**54.2**	**13:32**	**34**	**4**	**4**	**8**	**14**	**0**	**0**	**1**	**15:23**

AHL All-Rookie Team (2003)
• Missed majority of 2001-02 season recovering from neck injury suffered at Team Canada Jr. Selection Camp, June 3, 2001.

VEROT, Darcy — (vuhr-AWT, DAHR-see)

Left wing. Shoots left. 6', 199 lbs. Born, Radville, Sask., July 13, 1976.

Season	Club	League	GP	G	A	Pts	PIM	PP	SH	GW	S	%	+/-	TF	F%	Min	GP	G	A	Pts	PIM	PP	SH	GW	Min
1994-95	Weyburn	SJHL	57	8	18	26	240	....	....	....	....	....	....	....	....	....	16	5	2	7	50	....	....	....	....
1995-96	Weyburn	SJHL	64	15	30	45	191	....	....	....	....	....	....	....	....	....	3	1	0	1	20	....	....	....	....
1996-97	Weyburn	SJHL	61	26	51	77	218	....	....	....	....	....	....	....	....	....	13	3	8	11	24	....	....	....	....
1997-98	Lake Charles	WPHL	68	11	26	37	269	....	....	....	....	....	....	....	....	....	4	0	1	1	25	....	....	....	....
1998-99	Lake Charles	WPHL	68	17	23	40	236	....	....	....	....	....	....	....	....	....	9	2	4	6	53	....	....	....	....
99-2000	Wheeling Nailers	ECHL	44	7	12	19	240	....	....	....	....	....	....	....	....	....	....	....	....	....	....	....	....	....	....
	Wilkes-Barre	AHL	23	5	5	10	96	....	....	....	....	....	....	....	....	....	....	....	....	....	....	....	....	....	....
2000-01	Wilkes-Barre	AHL	78	10	15	25	347	....	....	....	....	....	....	....	....	....	21	2	3	5	40	....	....	....	....
2001-02	Wilkes-Barre	AHL	71	6	10	16	387	....	....	....	....	....	....	....	....	....	....	....	....	....	....	....	....	....	....
2002-03	Saint John Flames	AHL	73	5	11	16	299	....	....	....	....	....	....	....	....	....	....	....	....	....	....	....	....	....	....
2003-04	**Washington**	**NHL**	**37**	**0**	**2**	**2**	**135**	**0**	**0**	**0**	**11**	**0.0**	**–6**	**183**	**48.6**	**8:48**	....	....	....	....	....	....	....	....	....
	Portland Pirates	AHL	28	3	5	8	89	....	....	....	....	....	....	....	....	....	....	....	....	....	....	....	....	....	....
2004-05	Portland Pirates	AHL	36	0	1	1	189	....	....	....	....	....	....	....	....	....	....	....	....	....	....	....	....	....	....
2005-06	Syracuse Crunch	AHL	20	1	3	4	64	....	....	....	....	....	....	....	....	....	....	....	....	....	....	....	....	....	....
2006-07	Syracuse Crunch	AHL	68	9	14	23	227	....	....	....	....	....	....	....	....	....	....	....	....	....	....	....	....	....	....
	NHL Totals		**37**	**0**	**2**	**2**	**135**	**0**	**0**	**0**	**11**	**0.0**		**183**	**48.6**	**8:48**									

Signed as a free agent by **Wilkes-Barre** (AHL), February 25, 2000. Signed as a free agent by **Pittsburgh**, July 28, 2000. Signed as a free agent by **Calgary**, July 9, 2002. Signed as a free agent by **Washingon**, September 5, 2003. Signed as a free agent by **Columbus**, December 30, 2005. Signed as a free agent by **Chekhov** (Russia), June 27, 2007.

VIGIER, J.P. — (vih-ZHAY, JAY-pee)

Right wing. Shoots right. 6', 200 lbs. Born, Notre Dame de Lourdes, Man., September 11, 1976.

Season	Club	League	GP	G	A	Pts	PIM	PP	SH	GW	S	%	+/-	TF	F%	Min	GP	G	A	Pts	PIM	PP	SH	GW	Min
1995-96	Portage Terriers	MJHL	56	32	49	81	....	....	....	....	....	....	....	....	....	....	....	....	....	....	....	....	....	....	....
1996-97	Northern Mich.	WCHA	36	10	14	24	54	....	....	....	....	....	....	....	....	....	....	....	....	....	....	....	....	....	....
1997-98	Northern Mich.	CCHA	36	12	15	27	60	....	....	....	....	....	....	....	....	....	....	....	....	....	....	....	....	....	....
1998-99	Northern Mich.	CCHA	42	21	18	39	80	....	....	....	....	....	....	....	....	....	....	....	....	....	....	....	....	....	....
99-2000	Northern Mich.	CCHA	39	18	17	35	72	....	....	....	....	....	....	....	....	....	....	....	....	....	....	....	....	....	....
	Orlando	IHL	3	1	0	1	0	....	....	....	....	....	....	....	....	....	....	....	....	....	....	....	....	....	....
2000-01	**Atlanta**	**NHL**	**2**	**0**	**0**	**0**	**0**	**0**	**0**	**0**	**1**	**0.0**	**–2**	**1**	**100.0**	**9:56**	....	....	....	....	....	....	....	....	....
	Orlando	IHL	78	23	17	40	66	....	....	....	....	....	....	....	....	....	16	6	6	12	14	....	....	....	....
2001-02	**Atlanta**	**NHL**	**15**	**4**	**1**	**5**	**4**	**0**	**0**	**0**	**18**	**22.2**	**–5**	**3**	**66.7**	**13:13**	....	....	....	....	....	....	....	....	....
	Chicago Wolves	AHL	62	25	16	41	26	....	....	....	....	....	....	....	....	....	21	7	7	14	20	....	....	....	....
2002-03	**Atlanta**	**NHL**	**13**	**0**	**0**	**0**	**4**	**0**	**0**	**0**	**21**	**0.0**	**–13**	**1**	**0.0**	**14:07**	....	....	....	....	....	....	....	....	....
	Chicago Wolves	AHL	63	29	27	56	54	....	....	....	....	....	....	....	....	....	9	3	1	4	4	....	....	....	....
2003-04	**Atlanta**	**NHL**	**70**	**10**	**8**	**18**	**22**	**2**	**2**	**3**	**110**	**9.1**	**–18**	**53**	**47.2**	**14:36**	....	....	....	....	....	....	....	....	....
2004-05	Chicago Wolves	AHL	76	29	41	70	56	....	....	....	....	....	....	....	....	....	18	5	6	11	19	....	....	....	....
2005-06	**Atlanta**	**NHL**	**41**	**4**	**6**	**10**	**40**	**1**	**1**	**0**	**53**	**7.5**	**–4**	**70**	**24.3**	**14:21**	....	....	....	....	....	....	....	....	....
2006-07	**Atlanta**	**NHL**	**72**	**5**	**8**	**13**	**27**	**1**	**0**	**0**	**83**	**6.0**	**0**	**32**	**31.3**	**11:00**	....	....	....	....	....	....	....	....	....
	NHL Totals		**213**	**23**	**23**	**46**	**97**	**3**	**3**	**3**	**286**	**8.0**		**160**	**34.4**	**13:10**	....	....	....	....	....	....	....	....	....

CCHA Second All-Star Team (1999) • CCHA All-Tournament Team (1999) • AHL Second All-Star Team (2005)
Signed as a free agent by **Atlanta**, April 20, 2000. Signed as a free agent by **Geneve-Servette** (Swiss), August 3, 2007.

VISHNEVSKI, Vitaly — (vihsh-NEHV-skee, vih-TAL-ee) — N.J.

Defense. Shoots left. 6'2", 215 lbs. Born, Kharkov, USSR, March 18, 1980. Anaheim's 1st choice, 5th overall, in 1998 Entry Draft.

Season	Club	League	GP	G	A	Pts	PIM	PP	SH	GW	S	%	+/-	TF	F%	Min	GP	G	A	Pts	PIM	PP	SH	GW	Min
1995-96	Yaroslavl 2	CIS-2	40	4	4	8	20	....	....	....	....	....	....	....	....	....	....	....	....	....	....	....	....	....	....
1996-97	Yaroslavl 2	Russia-3	45	0	2	2	30	....	....	....	....	....	....	....	....	....	....	....	....	....	....	....	....	....	....
1997-98	Yaroslavl 2	Russia-2	47	8	9	17	164	....	....	....	....	....	....	....	....	....	....	....	....	....	....	....	....	....	....
1998-99	Yaroslavl	Russia	34	3	4	7	38	....	....	....	....	....	....	....	....	....	10	0	0	0	4	....	....	....	....
99-2000	**Anaheim**	**NHL**	**31**	**1**	**1**	**2**	**26**	**1**	**0**	**0**	**17**	**5.9**	**0**	**0**	**0.0**	**16:38**	....	....	....	....	....	....	....	....	....
	Cincinnati	AHL	35	1	3	4	45	....	....	....	....	....	....	....	....	....	....	....	....	....	....	....	....	....	....
2000-01	**Anaheim**	**NHL**	**76**	**1**	**10**	**11**	**99**	**0**	**0**	**0**	**49**	**2.0**	**–1**	**0**	**0.0**	**19:14**	....	....	....	....	....	....	....	....	....
2001-02	**Anaheim**	**NHL**	**74**	**0**	**3**	**3**	**60**	**0**	**0**	**0**	**54**	**0.0**	**–10**	**0**	**0.0**	**17:36**	....	....	....	....	....	....	....	....	....
2002-03	**Anaheim**	**NHL**	**80**	**2**	**6**	**8**	**76**	**0**	**1**	**0**	**65**	**3.1**	**–8**	**0**	**0.0**	**14:10**	**21**	**0**	**1**	**1**	**6**	**0**	**0**	**0**	**10:02**
2003-04	**Anaheim**	**NHL**	**73**	**6**	**10**	**16**	**51**	**0**	**0**	**0**	**86**	**7.0**	**0**	**0**	**0.0**	**17:10**	....	....	....	....	....	....	....	....	....
2004-05	Voskresensk	Russia	51	7	17	24	92	....	....	....	....	....	....	....	....	....	....	....	....	....	....	....	....	....	....
2005-06	**Anaheim**	**NHL**	**82**	**1**	**7**	**8**	**91**	**0**	**0**	**0**	**90**	**1.1**	**8**	**1**	**100.0**	**16:26**	**16**	**0**	**4**	**4**	**10**	**0**	**0**	**0**	**13:41**
	Russia	Olympics	8	0	1	1	4	....	....	....	....	....	....	....	....	....	....	....	....	....	....	....	....	....	....

			Regular Season														Playoffs								
Season	Club	League	GP	G	A	Pts	PIM	PP	SH	GW	S	%	+/-	TF	F%	Min	GP	G	A	Pts	PIM	PP	SH	GW	Min
2006-07	**Atlanta**	**NHL**	**52**	**3**	**9**	**12**	**31**	**0**	**0**	**0**	**41**	**7.3**	**–5**	**0**	**0.0**	**19:18**	....	....	....	....	....	....	....	....	....
	Nashville	**NHL**	**15**	**0**	**1**	**1**	**10**	**0**	**0**	**0**	**6**	**0.0**	**1**	**0**	**0.0**	**10:02**	....	....	....	....	....	....	....	....	....
	NHL Totals		**483**	**14**	**47**	**61**	**444**	**1**	**1**	**0**	**408**	**3.4**		**1**	**100.0**	**16:54**	**37**	**0**	**5**	**5**	**16**	**0**	**0**	**0**	**11:36**

Signed as a free agent by **Voskresensk** (Russia), August 25, 2004. Traded to **Atlanta** by **Anaheim** for Karl Stewart, Atlanta's 2nd round choice (later traded to Colorado - Colorado selected T.J. Galiardi) in 2007 Entry Draft and future considerations, August 17, 2006. Traded to **Nashville** by **Atlanta** for Eric Belanger, February 10, 2007. Signed as a free agent by **New Jersey**, July 10, 2007.

VISNOVSKY, Lubomir

(vihsh-NAWV-skee, LOO-boh-mihr) **L.A.**

Defense. Shoots left. 5'10", 188 lbs. Born, Topolcany, Czech., August 11, 1976. Los Angeles' 4th choice, 118th overall, in 2000 Entry Draft.

Season	Club	League	GP	G	A	Pts	PIM	PP	SH	GW	S	%	+/-	TF	F%	Min	GP	G	A	Pts	PIM	PP	SH	GW	Min
1994-95	Bratislava	Slovakia	36	11	12	23	10	....	....	....	....	....	....	....	....	....	9	1	3	4	2	....	....	....	....
1995-96	Bratislava	Slovakia	35	8	6	14	22	....	....	....	....	....	....	....	....	....	13	1	5	6	2	....	....	....	....
1996-97	Bratislava	Slovakia	44	11	12	23	....	....	....	....	....	....	....	....	....	....	2	0	1	1	....	....	....	....	....
	Bratislava	EuroHL	6	3	1	4	2	....	....	....	....	....	....	....	....	....	2	0	0	0	6	....	....	....	....
1997-98	Bratislava	Slovakia	36	7	9	16	16	....	....	....	....	....	....	....	....	....	11	2	4	6	8	....	....	....	....
	Bratislava	EuroHL	6	1	0	1	4	....	....	....	....	....	....	....	....	....	....	....	....	....	....	....	....	....	....
	Slovakia	Olympics	3	0	0	0	2	....	....	....	....	....	....	....	....	....	....	....	....	....	....	....	....	....	....
1998-99	Bratislava	Slovakia	40	9	10	19	31	....	....	....	....	....	....	....	....	....	10	5	5	10	0	....	....	....	....
	Bratislava	EuroHL	6	0	3	3	4	....	....	....	....	....	....	....	....	....	....	....	....	....	....	....	....	....	....
99-2000	Bratislava	Slovakia	52	21	24	45	38	....	....	....	....	....	....	....	....	....	8	5	3	8	16	....	....	....	....
2000-01	**Los Angeles**	**NHL**	**81**	**7**	**32**	**39**	**36**	**3**	**0**	**3**	**105**	**6.7**	**16**	**0**	**0.0**	**16:58**	**8**	**0**	**0**	**0**	**0**	**0**	**0**	**0**	**13:57**
2001-02	**Los Angeles**	**NHL**	**72**	**4**	**17**	**21**	**14**	**1**	**0**	**2**	**95**	**4.2**	**–5**	**0**	**0.0**	**16:15**	**4**	**0**	**1**	**1**	**0**	**0**	**0**	**0**	**8:22**
	Slovakia	Olympics	3	1	2	3	0	....	....	....	....	....	....	....	....	....	....	....	....	....	....	....	....	....	....
2002-03	**Los Angeles**	**NHL**	**57**	**8**	**16**	**24**	**28**	**1**	**0**	**1**	**85**	**9.4**	**2**	**0**	**0.0**	**19:20**	....	....	....	....	....	....	....	....	....
2003-04	**Los Angeles**	**NHL**	**58**	**8**	**21**	**29**	**26**	**5**	**0**	**0**	**114**	**7.0**	**8**	**0**	**0.0**	**24:02**	....	....	....	....	....	....	....	....	....
2004-05	Bratislava	Slovakia	43	13	25	38	40	....	....	....	....	....	....	....	....	....	14	2	10	12	10	....	....	....	....
2005-06	**Los Angeles**	**NHL**	**80**	**17**	**50**	**67**	**50**	**10**	**0**	**3**	**152**	**11.2**	**7**	**1**	**100.0**	**23:16**	....	....	....	....	....	....	....	....	....
	Slovakia	Olympics	6	1	1	2	0	....	....	....	....	....	....	....	....	....	....	....	....	....	....	....	....	....	....
2006-07	**Los Angeles**	**NHL**	**69**	**18**	**40**	**58**	**26**	**8**	**0**	**0**	**159**	**11.3**	**1**	**6**	**33.3**	**24:27**	....	....	....	....	....	....	....	....	....
	NHL Totals		**417**	**62**	**176**	**238**	**180**	**28**	**0**	**9**	**710**	**8.7**		**7**	**42.9**	**20:36**	**12**	**0**	**1**	**1**	**0**	**0**	**0**	**0**	**12:05**

NHL All-Rookie Team (2001)
Played in NHL All-Star Game (2007)
Signed as a free agent by **Bratislava** (Slovakia), September 27, 2004.

VLASIC, Marc-Edouard

(vih-LASH-ihc, MAHRK-EHD-wahrd) **S.J.**

Defense. Shoots left. 6'1", 195 lbs. Born, Montreal, Que., March 30, 1987. San Jose's 2nd choice, 35th overall, in 2005 Entry Draft.

Season	Club	League	GP	G	A	Pts	PIM	PP	SH	GW	S	%	+/-	TF	F%	Min	GP	G	A	Pts	PIM	PP	SH	GW	Min
2003-04	Quebec Remparts	QMJHL	41	1	9	10	4	....	....	....	....	....	....	....	....	....	5	0	1	1	0	....	....	....	....
2004-05	Quebec Remparts	QMJHL	70	5	25	30	33	....	....	....	....	....	....	....	....	....	13	2	7	9	2	....	....	....	....
2005-06	Quebec Remparts	QMJHL	66	16	57	73	57	....	....	....	....	....	....	....	....	....	23	5	24	29	10	....	....	....	....
2006-07	**San Jose**	**NHL**	**81**	**3**	**23**	**26**	**18**	**2**	**0**	**0**	**66**	**4.5**	**13**	**0**	**0.0**	**22:12**	**11**	**0**	**1**	**1**	**2**	**0**	**0**	**0**	**22:52**
	NHL Totals		**81**	**3**	**23**	**26**	**18**	**2**	**0**	**0**	**66**	**4.5**		**0**	**0.0**	**22:12**	**11**	**0**	**1**	**1**	**2**	**0**	**0**	**0**	**22:52**

NHL All-Rookie Team (2007)

VOLCHENKOV, Anton

(vohl-chen-KAHF, AN-tawn) **OTT.**

Defense. Shoots left. 6'1", 226 lbs. Born, Moscow, USSR, February 25, 1982. Ottawa's 1st choice, 21st overall, in 2000 Entry Draft.

Season	Club	League	GP	G	A	Pts	PIM	PP	SH	GW	S	%	+/-	TF	F%	Min	GP	G	A	Pts	PIM	PP	SH	GW	Min
99-2000	HK Moscow 2	Russia-3	6	0	1	1	10	....	....	....	....	....	....	....	....	....	....	....	....	....	....	....	....	....	....
	HK Moscow	Russia-2	30	2	9	11	36	....	....	....	....	....	....	....	....	....	....	....	....	....	....	....	....	....	....
2000-01	Krylja Sovetov	Russia-2	34	3	4	7	56	....	....	....	....	....	....	....	....	....	....	....	....	....	....	....	....	....	....
2001-02	Krylja Sovetov 2	Russia-3	1	0	0	0	0	....	....	....	....	....	....	....	....	....	....	....	....	....	....	....	....	....	....
	Krylja Sovetov	Russia	47	4	16	20	50	....	....	....	....	....	....	....	....	....	3	0	0	0	29	....	....	....	....
2002-03	**Ottawa**	**NHL**	**57**	**3**	**13**	**16**	**40**	**0**	**0**	**0**	**75**	**4.0**	**–4**	**0**	**0.0**	**15:30**	**17**	**1**	**1**	**2**	**4**	**0**	**0**	**1**	**13:31**
2003-04	**Ottawa**	**NHL**	**19**	**1**	**2**	**3**	**8**	**0**	**0**	**0**	**15**	**6.7**	**1**	**0**	**0.0**	**13:04**	**5**	**0**	**0**	**0**	**6**	**0**	**0**	**0**	**11:52**
2004-05	Binghamton	AHL	69	10	35	45	62	....	....	....	....	....	....	....	....	....	6	0	3	3	0	....	....	....	....
2005-06	**Ottawa**	**NHL**	**75**	**4**	**13**	**17**	**53**	**0**	**0**	**0**	**82**	**4.9**	**21**	**0**	**0.0**	**18:03**	**9**	**0**	**4**	**4**	**8**	**0**	**0**	**0**	**13:53**
	Russia	Olympics	8	0	0	0	2	....	....	....	....	....	....	....	....	....	....	....	....	....	....	....	....	....	....
2006-07	**Ottawa**	**NHL**	**78**	**1**	**18**	**19**	**67**	**0**	**0**	**0**	**85**	**1.2**	**37**	**0**	**0.0**	**21:17**	**20**	**2**	**4**	**6**	**24**	**0**	**0**	**1**	**23:19**
	NHL Totals		**229**	**9**	**46**	**55**	**168**	**0**	**0**	**0**	**257**	**3.5**		**0**	**0.0**	**18:06**	**51**	**3**	**9**	**12**	**42**	**0**	**0**	**2**	**17:16**

• Missed majority of 2003-04 season recovering from shoulder injury suffered in game vs. Boston, December 8, 2003.

VOROBIEV, Pavel

(voh-roh-BEE-ehf, PAH-vehl) **CHI.**

Right wing. Shoots right. 6', 195 lbs. Born, Karaganda, USSR, May 5, 1982. Chicago's 2nd choice, 11th overall, in 2000 Entry Draft.

Season	Club	League	GP	G	A	Pts	PIM	PP	SH	GW	S	%	+/-	TF	F%	Min	GP	G	A	Pts	PIM	PP	SH	GW	Min
1996-97	Molot Perm 2	Russia-3	2	0	0	0	0	....	....	....	....	....	....	....	....	....	....	....	....	....	....	....	....	....	....
1997-98	Yaroslavl 2	Russia-2	16	2	0	2	6	....	....	....	....	....	....	....	....	....	....	....	....	....	....	....	....	....	....
1998-99	Yaroslavl 2	Russia-3	17	0	1	1	0	....	....	....	....	....	....	....	....	....	....	....	....	....	....	....	....	....	....
99-2000	Yaroslavl 2	Russia-3	40	19	15	34	20	....	....	....	....	....	....	....	....	....	....	....	....	....	....	....	....	....	....
	Yaroslavl	Russia	8	2	0	2	4	....	....	....	....	....	....	....	....	....	10	2	2	4	0	....	....	....	....
2000-01	Yaroslavl	Russia	36	8	8	16	28	....	....	....	....	....	....	....	....	....	10	4	1	5	8	....	....	....	....
2001-02	Yaroslavl	Russia	9	3	2	5	6	....	....	....	....	....	....	....	....	....	7	0	0	0	4	....	....	....	....
2002-03	Yaroslavl	Russia	44	10	18	28	10	....	....	....	....	....	....	....	....	....	7	0	1	1	2	....	....	....	....
2003-04	**Chicago**	**NHL**	**18**	**1**	**3**	**4**	**4**	**1**	**0**	**1**	**20**	**5.0**	**1**	**0**	**0.0**	**12:48**	....	....	....	....	....	....	....	....	....
	Norfolk Admirals	AHL	57	13	16	29	8	....	....	....	....	....	....	....	....	....	4	0	0	0	0	....	....	....	....
2004-05	Norfolk Admirals	AHL	79	19	25	44	48	....	....	....	....	....	....	....	....	....	6	2	1	3	4	....	....	....	....
2005-06	**Chicago**	**NHL**	**39**	**9**	**12**	**21**	**34**	**2**	**0**	**0**	**87**	**10.3**	**–2**	**8**	**37.5**	**14:18**	....	....	....	....	....	....	....	....	....
	Norfolk Admirals	AHL	32	9	16	25	23	....	....	....	....	....	....	....	....	....	4	1	2	3	0	....	....	....	....
2006-07	Mytischi	Russia	41	8	11	19	24	....	....	....	....	....	....	....	....	....	9	0	2	2	4	....	....	....	....
	NHL Totals		**57**	**10**	**15**	**25**	**38**	**3**	**0**	**1**	**107**	**9.3**		**8**	**37.5**	**13:50**	....	....	....	....	....	....	....	....	....

VRBATA, Radim

(vuhr-BA-tuh, RA-dihm) **PHX.**

Right wing. Shoots right. 6'1", 190 lbs. Born, Mlada Boleslav, Czech., June 13, 1981. Colorado's 10th choice, 212th overall, in 1999 Entry Draft.

Season	Club	League	GP	G	A	Pts	PIM	PP	SH	GW	S	%	+/-	TF	F%	Min	GP	G	A	Pts	PIM	PP	SH	GW	Min
1997-98	Ml. Boleslav Jr.	CzRep-Jr.	35	42	31	73	4	....	....	....	....	....	....	....	....	....	....	....	....	....	....	....	....	....	....
1998-99	Hull Olympiques	QMJHL	54	22	38	60	16	....	....	....	....	....	....	....	....	....	23	6	13	19	6	....	....	....	....
99-2000	Hull Olympiques	QMJHL	58	29	45	74	26	....	....	....	....	....	....	....	....	....	15	3	9	12	8	....	....	....	....
2000-01	Shawinigan	QMJHL	55	56	64	120	67	....	....	....	....	....	....	....	....	....	10	4	7	11	4	....	....	....	....
	Hershey Bears	AHL	....	....	....	....	....	....	....	....	....	....	....	....	....	....	1	0	1	1	2	....	....	....	....
2001-02	**Colorado**	**NHL**	**52**	**18**	**12**	**30**	**14**	**6**	**0**	**3**	**112**	**16.1**	**7**	**8**	**37.5**	**14:32**	**9**	**0**	**0**	**0**	**0**	**0**	**0**	**0**	**13:05**
	Hershey Bears	AHL	20	8	14	22	8	....	....	....	....	....	....	....	....	....	....	....	....	....	....	....	....	....	....
2002-03	**Colorado**	**NHL**	**66**	**11**	**19**	**30**	**16**	**3**	**0**	**4**	**171**	**6.4**	**0**	**14**	**50.0**	**13:55**	....	....	....	....	....	....	....	....	....
	Carolina	**NHL**	**10**	**5**	**0**	**5**	**2**	**3**	**0**	**0**	**44**	**11.4**	**–7**	**15**	**46.7**	**19:00**	....	....	....	....	....	....	....	....	....
2003-04	**Carolina**	**NHL**	**80**	**12**	**13**	**25**	**24**	**4**	**0**	**2**	**195**	**6.2**	**–10**	**21**	**38.1**	**13:42**	....	....	....	....	....	....	....	....	....
2004-05	Liberec	CzRep	45	18	21	39	91	....	....	....	....	....	....	....	....	....	12	3	2	5	0	....	....	....	....
2005-06	**Carolina**	**NHL**	**16**	**2**	**3**	**5**	**6**	**1**	**0**	**0**	**38**	**5.3**	**0**	**3**	**33.3**	**12:37**	....	....	....	....	....	....	....	....	....
	Chicago	**NHL**	**45**	**13**	**21**	**34**	**16**	**5**	**0**	**0**	**147**	**8.8**	**4**	**6**	**50.0**	**15:43**	....	....	....	....	....	....	....	....	....
2006-07	**Chicago**	**NHL**	**77**	**14**	**27**	**41**	**26**	**5**	**0**	**2**	**215**	**6.5**	**–4**	**12**	**33.3**	**16:53**	....	....	....	....	....	....	....	....	....
	NHL Totals		**346**	**75**	**95**	**170**	**104**	**27**	**0**	**11**	**922**	**8.1**		**79**	**41.8**	**14:56**	**9**	**0**	**0**	**0**	**0**	**0**	**0**	**0**	**13:05**

QMJHL First All-Star Team (2001)

Traded to **Carolina** by **Colorado** for Bates Battaglia, March 11, 2003. Signed as a free agent by **Liberec** (CzRep), September 4, 2004. Traded to **Chicago** by **Carolina** for Chicago's 4th round choice (later traded to St. Louis - St. Louis selected Cade Fairchild) in 2007 Entry Draft, December 29, 2005. Traded to **Phoenix** by **Chicago** for Kevyn Adams, August 11, 2007.

VYBORNY, David
(vih-BOHR-nee, DAY-vihd) **CBJ**

Right wing. Shoots left. 5'10", 189 lbs. Born, Jihlava, Czech., January 22, 1975. Edmonton's 3rd choice, 33rd overall, in 1993 Entry Draft.

Season	Club	League	GP	G	A	Pts	PIM	PP	SH	GW	S	%	+/-	TF	F%	Min	Playoffs GP	G	A	Pts	PIM	PP	SH	GW	Min
1991-92	HC Sparta Praha	Czech	32	6	9	15	2																		
1992-93	HC Sparta Praha	Czech	52	20	24	44																			
1993-94	HC Sparta Praha	CzRep	44	15	20	35	0										6	4	7	11	0				
1994-95	Cape Breton	AHL	76	23	38	61	30																		
1995-96	HC Sparta Praha	CzRep	40	12	18	30											12	6	5	11					
1996-97	HC Sparta Praha	CzRep	47	20	29	49	14										10	7	7	14	6				
1997-98	MoDo	Sweden	45	16	21	37	34										9	0	2	2	2				
1998-99	HC Sparta Praha	CzRep	52	24	*46	*70	22										8	1	3	4					
99-2000	HC Sparta Praha	CzRep	50	25	38	63	30										9	3	*8	*11	4				
2000-01	**Columbus**	**NHL**	**79**	**13**	**19**	**32**	**22**	**5**	**0**	**1**	**125**	**10.4**	**–9**	**36**	**44.4**	**15:25**									
2001-02	**Columbus**	**NHL**	**75**	**13**	**18**	**31**	**6**	**6**	**0**	**2**	**103**	**12.6**	**–14**	**25**	**44.0**	**15:27**									
2002-03	**Columbus**	**NHL**	**79**	**20**	**26**	**46**	**16**	**4**	**1**	**4**	**125**	**16.0**	**12**	**46**	**32.6**	**16:20**									
2003-04	**Columbus**	**NHL**	**82**	**22**	**31**	**53**	**40**	**8**	**4**	**2**	**158**	**13.9**	**–26**	**97**	**21.7**	**20:23**									
2004-05	HC Sparta Praha	CzRep	51	12	34	46	10										5	2	5	7	4				
2005-06	**Columbus**	**NHL**	**80**	**22**	**43**	**65**	**50**	**5**	**2**	**6**	**145**	**15.2**	**–9**	**292**	**30.1**	**20:41**									
	Czech Republic	Olympics	8	1	3	4	0																		
2006-07	**Columbus**	**NHL**	**82**	**16**	**48**	**64**	**60**	**6**	**0**	**2**	**158**	**10.1**	**6**	**269**	**37.9**	**20:20**									
	NHL Totals		**477**	**106**	**185**	**291**	**194**	**34**	**7**	**17**	**814**	**13.0**		**765**	**33.1**	**18:10**									

Signed as a free agent by **Columbus**, June 8, 2000. Signed as a free agent by **Sparta Praha** (CzRep), August 9, 2004.

WALKER, Matt
(WAH-kuhr, MAT) **ST.L.**

Defense. Shoots right. 6'3", 229 lbs. Born, Beaverlodge, Alta., April 7, 1980. St. Louis' 3rd choice, 83rd overall, in 1998 Entry Draft.

Season	Club	League	GP	G	A	Pts	PIM	PP	SH	GW	S	%	+/-	TF	F%	Min	Playoffs GP	G	A	Pts	PIM	PP	SH	GW	Min
1996-97	Grand Prairie	AAHA	68	22	62	74	186																		
1997-98	Portland	WHL	64	2	13	15	124										16	0	0	0	21				
1998-99	Portland	WHL	64	1	10	11	151										4	0	1	1	6				
99-2000	Portland	WHL	38	2	7	9	97																		
	Kootenay Ice	WHL	31	4	19	23	53										21	5	13	18	24				
2000-01	Peoria Rivermen	ECHL	8	1	0	1	70																		
	Worcester IceCats	AHL	61	4	8	12	131										11	0	0	0	6				
2001-02	Worcester IceCats	AHL	49	2	11	13	164										3	0	0	0	8				
2002-03	**St. Louis**	**NHL**	**16**	**0**	**1**	**1**	**38**	**0**	**0**	**0**	**13**	**0.0**	**0**	**1**	**100.0**	**11:09**									
	Worcester IceCats	AHL	40	1	8	9	58																		
2003-04	**St. Louis**	**NHL**	**14**	**0**	**1**	**1**	**25**	**0**	**0**	**0**	**8**	**0.0**	**0**	**0**	**0.0**	**11:23**	**4**	**0**	**0**	**0**	**0**	**0**	**0**	**0**	**9:43**
	Worcester IceCats	AHL	4	0	1	1	7																		
2004-05	Worcester IceCats	AHL	20	2	4	6	44																		
2005-06	**St. Louis**	**NHL**	**54**	**0**	**2**	**2**	**79**	**0**	**0**	**0**	**59**	**0.0**	**–7**	**0**	**0.0**	**14:15**									
2006-07	**St. Louis**	**NHL**	**48**	**0**	**5**	**5**	**72**	**0**	**0**	**0**	**34**	**0.0**	**7**	**0**	**0.0**	**15:15**									
	Peoria Rivermen	AHL	2	0	1	1	0																		
	NHL Totals		**132**	**0**	**9**	**9**	**214**	**0**	**0**	**0**	**114**	**0.0**		**1**	**100.0**	**13:56**	**4**	**0**	**0**	**0**	**0**	**0**	**0**	**0**	**9:43**

• Missed majority of 2003-04 season recovering from groin injury suffered in training camp, September 23, 2003.

WALKER, Scott
(WAH-kuhr, SKAWT) **CAR.**

Right wing. Shoots right. 5'10", 196 lbs. Born, Cambridge, Ont., July 19, 1973. Vancouver's 4th choice, 124th overall, in 1993 Entry Draft.

Season	Club	League	GP	G	A	Pts	PIM	PP	SH	GW	S	%	+/-	TF	F%	Min	Playoffs GP	G	A	Pts	PIM	PP	SH	GW	Min
1989-90	Kitchener	OHA-B	6	0	5	5	4																		
	Cambridge	OHA-B	27	7	22	29	87																		
1990-91	Cambridge	OHA-B	45	10	27	37	241																		
1991-92	Owen Sound	OHL	53	7	31	38	128										5	0	7	7	8				
1992-93	Owen Sound	OHL	57	23	68	91	110										8	1	5	6	16				
1993-94	Hamilton	AHL	77	10	29	39	272										4	0	1	1	25				
1994-95	Syracuse Crunch	AHL	74	14	38	52	334																		
	Vancouver	**NHL**	**11**	**0**	**1**	**1**	**33**	**0**	**0**	**0**	**8**	**0.0**	**0**												
1995-96	**Vancouver**	**NHL**	**63**	**4**	**8**	**12**	**137**	**0**	**1**	**1**	**45**	**8.9**	**–7**												
	Syracuse Crunch	AHL	15	3	12	15	52										16	9	8	17	39				
1996-97	**Vancouver**	**NHL**	**64**	**3**	**15**	**18**	**132**	**0**	**0**	**0**	**55**	**5.5**	**2**												
1997-98	**Vancouver**	**NHL**	**59**	**3**	**10**	**13**	**164**	**0**	**1**	**1**	**40**	**7.5**	**–8**												
1998-99	**Nashville**	**NHL**	**71**	**15**	**25**	**40**	**103**	**0**	**1**	**2**	**96**	**15.6**	**0**	**265**	**48.3**	**16:21**									
99-2000	**Nashville**	**NHL**	**69**	**7**	**21**	**28**	**90**	**0**	**1**	**0**	**98**	**7.1**	**–16**	**30**	**36.7**	**15:49**									
2000-01	**Nashville**	**NHL**	**74**	**25**	**29**	**54**	**66**	**9**	**3**	**1**	**159**	**15.7**	**–2**	**541**	**51.4**	**19:17**									
2001-02	**Nashville**	**NHL**	**28**	**4**	**5**	**9**	**18**	**1**	**0**	**0**	**46**	**8.7**	**–13**	**149**	**38.9**	**18:38**									
2002-03	**Nashville**	**NHL**	**60**	**15**	**18**	**33**	**58**	**7**	**0**	**5**	**124**	**12.1**	**2**	**336**	**49.1**	**19:50**									
2003-04	**Nashville**	**NHL**	**75**	**25**	**42**	**67**	**94**	**9**	**3**	**3**	**157**	**15.9**	**4**	**367**	**41.4**	**20:03**	**6**	**0**	**1**	**1**	**6**	**0**	**0**	**0**	**20:10**
2004-05	Cambridge	OHA-Sr.	5	2	6	8	4																		
	Dundas	OHA-Sr.	3	3	2	5	8																		
2005-06	**Nashville**	**NHL**	**33**	**5**	**11**	**16**	**36**	**1**	**0**	**0**	**57**	**8.8**	**2**	**87**	**44.8**	**17:23**	**5**	**0**	**0**	**0**	**6**	**0**	**0**	**0**	**16:01**
2006-07	**Carolina**	**NHL**	**81**	**21**	**30**	**51**	**45**	**6**	**0**	**6**	**183**	**11.5**	**–10**	**95**	**42.1**	**16:10**									
	NHL Totals		**688**	**127**	**215**	**342**	**976**	**33**	**10**	**19**	**1068**	**11.9**		**1870**	**46.6**	**17:53**	**11**	**0**	**1**	**1**	**12**	**0**	**0**	**0**	**18:16**

OHL Second All-Star Team (1993)

Claimed by **Nashville** from **Vancouver** in Expansion Draft, June 26, 1998. Signed as a free agent by **Cambridge** (OHA-Sr.), October 21, 2004. Signed as a free agent by **Dundas** (OHA-Sr.), February 10, 2005. • Missed majority of 2005-06 season recovering from sports hernia (October, 2005) and wrist (February 6, 2006 at Dallas) injuries. Traded to **Carolina** by **Nashville** for Josef Vasicek, July 18, 2006.

WALLIN, Niclas
(WAHL-ihn, NIHK-luhs) **CAR.**

Defense. Shoots left. 6'3", 220 lbs. Born, Boden, Sweden, February 20, 1975. Carolina's 3rd choice, 97th overall, in 2000 Entry Draft.

Season	Club	League	GP	G	A	Pts	PIM	PP	SH	GW	S	%	+/-	TF	F%	Min	Playoffs GP	G	A	Pts	PIM	PP	SH	GW	Min
1994-95	Bodens IK	Swe-Jr.	30	2	13	15	125																		
	Bodens IK	Sweden-2	13	0	0	0	0										2	0	0	0	0				
1995-96	Bodens IK	Swe-Jr.	2	2	2	4	0																		
	Bodens IK	Sweden-2	30	2	7	9	26										2	0	1	1	2				
1996-97	Brynas IF Gavle	Sweden	47	1	1	2	14																		
1997-98	Brynas IF Gavle	Sweden	44	2	3	5	57										3	0	1	1	4				
1998-99	Brynas IF Gavle	Sweden	46	2	4	6	52										14	0	1	1	8				
99-2000	Brynas IF Gavle	Sweden	48	7	9	16	73										11	2	1	3	14				
	Brynas IF Gavle	EuroHL	5	1	1	2	10																		
2000-01	**Carolina**	**NHL**	**37**	**2**	**3**	**5**	**21**	**0**	**0**	**0**	**19**	**10.5**	**–11**	**0**	**0.0**	**14:57**	**3**	**0**	**0**	**0**	**2**	**0**	**0**	**0**	**19:10**
	Cincinnati	IHL	8	1	2	3	4										3	0	0	0	2				
2001-02	**Carolina**	**NHL**	**52**	**1**	**2**	**3**	**36**	**0**	**0**	**0**	**33**	**3.0**	**1**	**0**	**0.0**	**12:12**	**23**	**2**	**1**	**3**	**12**	**0**	**0**	**2**	**15:26**
2002-03	**Carolina**	**NHL**	**77**	**2**	**8**	**10**	**71**	**0**	**0**	**2**	**69**	**2.9**	**–19**	**0**	**0.0**	**16:12**									
2003-04	**Carolina**	**NHL**	**57**	**3**	**7**	**10**	**51**	**0**	**0**	**0**	**74**	**4.1**	**–8**	**0**	**0.0**	**18:40**									
2004-05	Lulea HF	Sweden	39	6	7	13	89										3	0	1	1	6				
2005-06♦	**Carolina**	**NHL**	**50**	**4**	**4**	**8**	**42**	**0**	**0**	**0**	**44**	**9.1**	**2**	**0**	**0.0**	**16:50**	**25**	**1**	**4**	**5**	**14**	**0**	**0**	**1**	**16:39**
2006-07	**Carolina**	**NHL**	**67**	**2**	**8**	**10**	**48**	**0**	**0**	**0**	**76**	**2.6**	**–2**	**0**	**0.0**	**18:33**									
	NHL Totals		**340**	**14**	**32**	**46**	**269**	**0**	**0**	**2**	**315**	**4.4**		**0**	**0.0**	**16:25**	**51**	**3**	**5**	**8**	**28**	**0**	**0**	**3**	**16:15**

Signed as a free agent by **Lulea** (Sweden), September 19, 2004.

WALLIN, Rickard
(WAHL-ihn, RIH-kahrd)

Center. Shoots left. 6'2", 185 lbs. Born, Stockholm, Sweden, April 19, 1980. Phoenix's 8th choice, 160th overall, in 1998 Entry Draft.

Season	Club	League	GP	G	A	Pts	PIM	PP	SH	GW	S	%	+/-	TF	F%	Min	Playoffs GP	G	A	Pts	PIM	PP	SH	GW	Min
1996-97	Vasteras IK Jr.	Swe-Jr.	26	3	3	6																			
1997-98	Farjestad Jr.	Swe-Jr.	29	20	30	50	32										2	1	1	2	2				
1998-99	Farjestad Jr.	Swe-Jr.	21	11	15	26	30																		
	Farjestad	Sweden	5	0	0	0	0																		
99-2000	IF Troja-Ljungby	Sweden-2	46	15	22	37	54																		
2000-01	Farjestad	Sweden	47	9	22	31	24										16	11	3	14	4				
2001-02	Farjestad	Sweden	50	12	31	43	56										10	4	9	13	8				

Season	Club	League	GP	G	A	Pts	PIM	PP	SH	GW	S	%	+/-	TF	F%	Min	Playoffs GP	G	A	Pts	PIM	PP	SH	GW	Min
2002-03	Minnesota	NHL	4	1	0	1	0	0	0	1	1	100.0	1	28	53.6	7:44									
	Houston Aeros	AHL	52	13	22	35	70										23	4	11	15	22				
2003-04	Minnesota	NHL	15	5	4	9	14	3	0	1	16	31.3	1	189	45.5	14:20									
	Houston Aeros	AHL	47	14	18	32	36										2	0	0	0	2				
2004-05	Houston Aeros	AHL	79	12	31	43	61										5	1	0	1	29				
2005-06	Farjestad	Sweden	50	11	19	30	82										18	6	3	9	28				
2006-07	HC Lugano	Swiss	44	14	35	49	87										6	3	3	6	16				
	NHL Totals		19	6	4	10	14	3	0	2	17	35.3		217	46.5	12:56									

Rights traded to **Minnesota** by **Phoenix** for Joe Juneau, June 23, 2000. Reassigned to **Farjestad** (Sweden) by **Minnesota**, September 22, 2005. Signed as a free agent by **Lugano** (Swiss), July 23, 2006.

WALSER, Derrick

(WAHL-zuhr, DAIR-ihk) **TOR.**

Defense. Shoots left. 5'10", 190 lbs. Born, New Glasgow, N.S., May 12, 1978.

Season	Club	League	GP	G	A	Pts	PIM	PP	SH	GW	S	%	+/-	TF	F%	Min	Playoffs GP	G	A	Pts	PIM	PP	SH	GW	Min
1994-95	Beauport	QMJHL	48	4	18	22	34										12	2	5	7	2				
1995-96	Beauport	QMJHL	69	9	31	40	56										20	2	11	13	16				
1996-97	Beauport	QMJHL	37	13	25	38	26																		
	Rimouski Oceanic	QMJHL	31	15	30	45	44										4	2	2	4	6				
1997-98	Rimouski Oceanic	QMJHL	70	41	69	110	135										18	10	*26	36	49				
1998-99	Saint John Flames	AHL	40	3	7	10	24																		
	Johnstown Chiefs	ECHL	24	8	12	20	29																		
99-2000	Saint John Flames	AHL	14	2	3	5	10																		
	Johnstown Chiefs	ECHL	54	17	26	43	104										7	3	3	6	8				
2000-01	Saint John Flames	AHL	76	19	36	55	36										19	7	9	16	14				
2001-02	Columbus	NHL	2	1	0	1	0	0	0	0	2	50.0	−2	0	0.0	16:18									
	Syracuse Crunch	AHL	73	23	38	61	70										10	1	5	6	12				
2002-03	Columbus	NHL	53	4	13	17	34	3	0	2	86	4.7	−9	1	100.0	14:52									
	Syracuse Crunch	AHL	28	7	14	21	30																		
2003-04	Columbus	NHL	27	1	8	9	22	1	0	0	35	2.9	−6	0	0.0	18:23									
	Syracuse Crunch	AHL	48	10	26	36	82										3	1	1	2	4				
2004-05	Eisbaren Berlin	Germany	50	9	14	23	143										12	4	4	8	20				
2005-06	Eisbaren Berlin	Germany	48	19	24	43	120										11	6	1	7	20				
2006-07	Albany River Rats	AHL	6	0	1	1	4																		
	Columbus	NHL	9	2	0	2	0	2	0	0	10	20.0	−1	0	0.0	12:14									
	Syracuse Crunch	AHL	49	9	27	36	59																		
	NHL Totals		91	8	21	29	56	6	0	2	133	6.0		1	100.0	15:41									

QMJHL First All-Star Team (1997, 1998) • Emile Bouchard Trophy (Top Defenseman – QMJHL) (1998) • Canadian Major Junior First All-Star Team (1998) • Canadian Major Junior Defenseman of the Year (1998)

Signed as a free agent by **Calgary**, October 16, 1998. Signed as a free agent by **Columbus**, September 17, 2001. Signed as a free agent by **Berlin** (Germany), May 13, 2004. Rights traded to **Carolina** by **Columbus** with Columbus' 4th round choice (later traded to Toronto - Toronto selected James Reimer) in 2006 Entry Draft for Carolina's 4th round choice (Jared Boll) in 2005 Entry Draft, July 30, 2005. Traded to **Columbus** by **Carolina** for Mark Flood, November 29, 2006. Signed as a free agent by **Berlin** (Germany), July 4, 2007. Signed a free agent by **Toronto**, July 18, 2007.

WALTER, Ben

(WAHL-tuhr, BEHN) **BOS.**

Center. Shoots left. 6'1", 195 lbs. Born, Beaconsfield, Que., May 11, 1984. Boston's 5th choice, 160th overall, in 2004 Entry Draft.

Season	Club	League	GP	G	A	Pts	PIM	PP	SH	GW	S	%	+/-	TF	F%	Min	Playoffs GP	G	A	Pts	PIM	PP	SH	GW	Min
2000-01	Langley Hornets	BCHL	50	8	22	30	19																		
2001-02	Langley Hornets	BCHL	50	29	47	76	29																		
2002-03	U. Mass-Lowell	H-East	35	5	12	17	12																		
2003-04	U. Mass-Lowell	H-East	36	18	16	34	18																		
2004-05	U. Mass-Lowell	H-East	36	*26	13	39	28																		
2005-06	Boston	NHL	6	0	0	0	4	0	0	0	6	0.0	2	32	53.1	11:49									
	Providence Bruins	AHL	62	16	25	41	33										3	2	0	2	2				
2006-07	Boston	NHL	4	0	0	0	0	0	0	0	0	0.0	0	24	41.7	6:11									
	Providence Bruins	AHL	73	24	43	67	58										13	4	4	8	6				
	NHL Totals		10	0	0	0	4	0	0	0	6	0.0		56	48.2	9:34									

Hockey East Second All-Star Team (2005)

WALZ, Wes

(WAHLZ, WEHS) **MIN.**

Center. Shoots right. 5'10", 189 lbs. Born, Calgary, Alta., May 15, 1970. Boston's 3rd choice, 57th overall, in 1989 Entry Draft.

Season	Club	League	GP	G	A	Pts	PIM	PP	SH	GW	S	%	+/-	TF	F%	Min	Playoffs GP	G	A	Pts	PIM	PP	SH	GW	Min
1987-88	Cgy. North Stars	AMHL	35	47	52	99	72																		
	Prince Albert	WHL	1	1	1	2	0																		
1988-89	Lethbridge	WHL	63	29	75	104	32										8	1	5	6	6				
1989-90	Lethbridge	WHL	56	54	86	140	69										19	13	*24	*37	33				
	Boston	NHL	2	1	1	2	0	1	0	0	1	100.0	−1												
1990-91	Boston	NHL	56	8	8	16	32	1	0	1	57	14.0	−14				2	0	0	0	0	0	0	0	
	Maine Mariners	AHL	20	8	12	20	19										2	0	0	0	21				
1991-92	Boston	NHL	15	0	3	3	12	0	0	0	17	0.0	−3												
	Maine Mariners	AHL	21	13	11	24	38																		
	Philadelphia	NHL	2	1	0	1	0	0	0	1	2	50.0	1												
	Hershey Bears	AHL	41	13	28	41	37										6	1	2	3	0				
1992-93	Hershey Bears	AHL	78	35	45	80	106																		
1993-94	Calgary	NHL	53	11	27	38	16	1	0	0	79	13.9	20				6	3	0	3	2	0	0	0	
	Saint John Flames	AHL	15	6	6	12	14																		
1994-95	Calgary	NHL	39	6	12	18	11	4	0	1	73	8.2	7				1	0	0	0	0	0	0	0	
1995-96	Detroit	NHL	2	0	0	0	0	0	0	0	2	0.0	0												
	Adirondack	AHL	38	20	35	55	58																		
1996-97	EV Zug	Swiss	41	24	22	46	67										9	5	1	6	39				
1997-98	EV Zug	Swiss	38	18	34	52	32										20	*16	*12	*28	18				
	EV Zug	EuroHL	5	1	3	4	10																		
1998-99	EV Zug	Swiss	42	22	27	49	75										10	3	9	12	2				
	EV Zug	EuroHL	6	7	5	12	4										2	0	0	0	12				
99-2000	Long Beach	IHL	6	4	3	7	8																		
	HC Lugano	Swiss	13	7	11	18	14										5	3	4	7	4				
2000-01	Minnesota	NHL	82	18	12	30	37	0	7	3	152	11.8	−8	1533	47.2	16:45									
2001-02	Minnesota	NHL	64	10	20	30	43	0	2	5	97	10.3	0	1231	44.8	16:42									
2002-03	Minnesota	NHL	80	13	19	32	63	0	0	4	115	11.3	11	1505	50.4	15:56	18	7	6	13	14	0	2	2	17:24
2003-04	Minnesota	NHL	57	12	13	25	32	0	3	2	70	17.1	5	909	46.3	16:18									
2004-05			DID NOT PLAY																						
2005-06	Minnesota	NHL	82	19	18	37	61	1	1	0	127	15.0	7	1119	46.9	15:54									
2006-07	Minnesota	NHL	62	9	15	24	30	0	1	1	77	11.7	3	786	47.2	14:53	5	0	1	1	4	0	0	0	11:50
	NHL Totals		596	108	148	256	337	8	14	18	869	12.4		7083	47.3	16:06	32	10	7	17	20	0	2	2	16:12

WHL Rookie of the Year (1989) • WHL East First All-Star Team (1990)

Traded to **Philadelphia** by **Boston** with Garry Galley and Boston's 3rd round choice (Milos Holan) in 1993 Entry Draft for Gord Murphy, Brian Dobbin, Philadelphia's 3rd round choice (Sergei Zholtok) in 1992 Entry Draft and Philadelphia's 4th round choice (Charles Paquette) in 1993 Entry Draft, January 2, 1992. Signed as a free agent by **Calgary**, August 26, 1993. Signed as a free agent by **Detroit**, September 6, 1995. Signed as a free agent by **Long Beach** (IHL), October 12, 1999. Signed as a free agent by **Minnesota**, June 28, 2000.

WANVIG, Kyle

(WEHN-vihg, KIGHL) **T.B.**

Right wing. Shoots right. 6'2", 210 lbs. Born, Calgary, Alta., January 29, 1981. Minnesota's 2nd choice, 36th overall, in 2001 Entry Draft.

Season	Club	League	GP	G	A	Pts	PIM	PP	SH	GW	S	%	+/-	TF	F%	Min	Playoffs GP	G	A	Pts	PIM	PP	SH	GW	Min
1996-97	Calgary Blazers	AMHL	26	31	48	79	85																		
1997-98	Edmonton Ice	WHL	62	17	12	29	69																		
1998-99	Kootenay Ice	WHL	71	12	20	32	119										7	1	3	4	18				
99-2000	Kootenay Ice	WHL	6	2	2	4	12																		
	Red Deer Rebels	WHL	58	21	18	39	123										4	1	0	1	4				
2000-01	Red Deer Rebels	WHL	69	55	46	101	202										22	10	12	22	47				
2001-02	Houston Aeros	AHL	34	6	7	13	43										9	0	1	1	23				
2002-03	Houston Aeros	AHL	57	13	16	29	137										21	6	4	10	27				
	Minnesota	NHL	7	1	0	1	13	0	0	0	5	20.0	0	1	100.0	9:14									
2003-04	Minnesota	NHL	6	0	1	1	10	0	0	0	16	0.0	−2	4	75.0	13:48									
	Houston Aeros	AHL	72	25	16	41	147										2	0	1	1	0				

Season	Club	League	GP	G	A	Pts	PIM	PP	SH	GW	S	%	+/-	TF	F%	Min	GP	G	A	Pts	PIM	PP	SH	GW	Min
			Regular Season														Playoffs								
2004-05	Houston Aeros	AHL	76	13	17	30	158	....	....	....	....	....	....	....	....	....	5	1	2	3	8	....	....	....	....
2005-06	Minnesota	NHL	51	4	8	12	64	1	0	0	55	7.3	-8	26	46.2	10:39	....	....	....	....	....	....	....	....	....
2006-07	Chicago Wolves	AHL	26	10	11	21	61	....	....	....	....	....	....	....	....	....	....	....	....	....	....	....	....	....	....
	Tampa Bay	NHL	4	0	0	0	0	0	0	0	0	0.0	0	0	0.0	5:12	....	....	....	....	....	....	....	....	....
	Springfield	AHL	23	11	7	18	40	....	....	....	....	....	....	....	....	....	....	....	....	....	....	....	....	....	....
	NHL Totals		68	5	9	14	87	1	0	0	76	6.6		31	51.6	10:28	....	....	....	....	....	....	....	....	....

• Re-entered NHL Entry Draft. Originally Boston's 3rd choice, 89th overall, in 1999 Entry Draft.

WHL East Second All-Star Team (2001) • Memorial Cup Tournament All-Star Team (2001) • Stafford Smythe Memorial Trophy (Memorial Cup Tournament MVP) (2001)

• Missed majority of 2001-02 season recovering from ankle injury suffered in game vs. Grand Rapids (AHL), December 30, 2001. Signed as a free agent by **Atlanta**, July 18, 2006. Traded to **Tampa Bay** by **Atlanta** with Stephen Baby for Andy Delmore and Andre Deveaux, February 1, 2007.

WARD, Aaron

(WOHRD, AIR-ruhn) **BOS.**

Defense. Shoots right. 6'2", 215 lbs. Born, Windsor, Ont., January 17, 1973. Winnipeg's 1st choice, 5th overall, in 1991 Entry Draft.

Season	Club	League	GP	G	A	Pts	PIM	PP	SH	GW	S	%	+/-	TF	F%	Min	GP	G	A	Pts	PIM	PP	SH	GW	Min
1988-89	Nepean Raiders	CJHL	54	1	14	15	40	....	....	....	....	....	....	....	....	....	....	....	....	....	....	....	....	....	....
1989-90	Nepean Raiders	CJHL	52	6	33	39	85	....	....	....	....	....	....	....	....	....	....	....	....	....	....	....	....	....	....
1990-91	U. of Michigan	CCHA	46	8	11	19	126	....	....	....	....	....	....	....	....	....	....	....	....	....	....	....	....	....	....
1991-92	U. of Michigan	CCHA	42	7	12	19	64	....	....	....	....	....	....	....	....	....	....	....	....	....	....	....	....	....	....
1992-93	U. of Michigan	CCHA	30	5	8	13	73	....	....	....	....	....	....	....	....	....	....	....	....	....	....	....	....	....	....
1993-94	Detroit	NHL	5	1	0	1	4	0	0	0	3	33.3	2	....	....	....	....	....	....	....	....	....	....	....	....
	Adirondack	AHL	58	4	12	16	87	....	....	....	....	....	....	....	....	....	9	2	6	8	6	....	....	....	....
1994-95	Adirondack	AHL	76	11	24	35	87	....	....	....	....	....	....	....	....	....	4	0	1	1	0	....	....	....	....
	Detroit	NHL	1	0	1	1	2	0	0	0	0	0.0	1	....	....	....	....	....	....	....	....	....	....	....	....
1995-96	Adirondack	AHL	74	5	10	15	133	....	....	....	....	....	....	....	....	....	3	0	0	0	6	....	....	....	....
1996-97♦	Detroit	NHL	49	2	5	7	52	0	0	0	40	5.0	-9	....	....	....	19	0	0	0	17	0	0	0	....
1997-98♦	Detroit	NHL	52	5	5	10	47	0	0	1	47	10.6	-1	....	....	....	....	....	....	....	....	....	....	....	....
1998-99	Detroit	NHL	60	3	8	11	52	0	0	0	46	6.5	-5	0	0.0	13:55	8	0	1	1	8	0	0	0	10:15
99-2000	Detroit	NHL	36	1	3	4	24	0	0	0	25	4.0	-4	0	0.0	12:36	3	0	0	0	0	0	0	0	7:36
2000-01	Detroit	NHL	73	4	5	9	57	0	0	1	48	8.3	-4	0	0.0	17:00	....	....	....	....	....	....	....	....	....
2001-02	Carolina	NHL	79	3	11	14	74	0	0	2	69	4.3	0	1	100.0	19:40	23	1	1	2	22	0	0	0	21:12
2002-03	Carolina	NHL	77	3	6	9	90	0	0	1	66	4.5	-23	0	0.0	18:43	....	....	....	....	....	....	....	....	....
2003-04	Carolina	NHL	49	3	5	8	37	2	0	0	51	5.9	1	0	0.0	17:52	....	....	....	....	....	....	....	....	....
2004-05	ERC Ingolstadt	Germany	8	0	3	3	16	....	....	....	....	....	....	....	....	....	11	1	1	2	16	....	....	....	....
2005-06♦	Carolina	NHL	71	6	19	25	62	0	0	1	60	10.0	2	1	0.0	19:07	25	2	3	5	18	0	0	0	21:42
2006-07	NY Rangers	NHL	60	3	10	13	57	0	0	0	45	6.7	-3	0	0.0	19:42	....	....	....	....	....	....	....	....	....
	Boston	NHL	20	1	2	3	18	0	0	0	17	5.9	-8	0	0.0	21:36	....	....	....	....	....	....	....	....	....
	NHL Totals		632	35	80	115	576	2	0	6	517	6.8		2	50.0	17:51	78	3	5	8	65	0	0	0	19:14

Traded to **Detroit** by **Winnipeg** with Toronto's 4th round choice (previously acquired, Detroit selected John Jakopin) in 1993 Entry Draft for Paul Ysebaert and future considerations (Alan Kerr, June 18, 1993), June 11, 1993. • Missed majority of 1999-2000 season recovering from shoulder injury suffered in game vs. Vancouver, January 19, 2000. Traded to **Carolina** by **Detroit** for Carolina's 2nd round choice (Jiri Hudler) in 2002 Entry Draft, July 9, 2001. Signed as a free agent by **Ingolstadt** (Germany), February 15, 2005. Signed as a free agent by **NY Rangers**, July 3, 2006. Traded to **Boston** by **NY Rangers** for Paul Mara, February 27, 2007.

WARD, Jason

(WOHRD, JAY-suhn) **T.B.**

Right wing. Shoots right. 6'2", 205 lbs. Born, Chapleau, Ont., January 16, 1979. Montreal's 1st choice, 11th overall, in 1997 Entry Draft.

Season	Club	League	GP	G	A	Pts	PIM	PP	SH	GW	S	%	+/-	TF	F%	Min	GP	G	A	Pts	PIM	PP	SH	GW	Min
1994-95	Oshawa	OHA-B	47	30	31	61	75	....	....	....	....	....	....	....	....	....	....	....	....	....	....	....	....	....	....
1995-96	Niagara Falls	OHL	64	15	35	50	139	....	....	....	....	....	....	....	....	....	10	6	4	10	23	....	....	....	....
1996-97	Erie Otters	OHL	58	25	39	64	137	....	....	....	....	....	....	....	....	....	5	1	2	3	2	....	....	....	....
1997-98	Erie Otters	OHL	21	7	9	16	42	....	....	....	....	....	....	....	....	....	....	....	....	....	....	....	....	....	....
	Windsor Spitfires	OHL	26	19	27	46	34	....	....	....	....	....	....	....	....	....	....	....	....	....	....	....	....	....	....
	Fredericton	AHL	7	1	0	1	2	....	....	....	....	....	....	....	....	....	1	0	0	0	2	....	....	....	....
1998-99	Windsor Spitfires	OHL	12	8	11	19	25	....	....	....	....	....	....	....	....	....	....	....	....	....	....	....	....	....	....
	Plymouth Whalers	OHL	23	14	13	27	28	....	....	....	....	....	....	....	....	....	11	6	8	14	12	....	....	....	....
	Fredericton	AHL	....	....	....	....	....	....	....	....	....	....	....	....	....	....	10	4	2	6	22	....	....	....	....
99-2000	Montreal	NHL	32	2	1	3	10	1	0	0	24	8.3	-1	86	44.2	9:10	....	....	....	....	....	....	....	....	....
	Quebec Citadelles	AHL	40	14	12	26	30	....	....	....	....	....	....	....	....	....	3	2	1	3	4	....	....	....	....
2000-01	Montreal	NHL	12	0	0	0	12	0	0	0	4	0.0	3	2	50.0	8:16	....	....	....	....	....	....	....	....	....
	Quebec Citadelles	AHL	23	7	12	19	69	....	....	....	....	....	....	....	....	....	....	....	....	....	....	....	....	....	....
2001-02	Quebec Citadelles	AHL	78	24	33	57	128	....	....	....	....	....	....	....	....	....	3	0	0	0	2	....	....	....	....
2002-03	Montreal	NHL	8	3	2	5	0	0	0	0	10	30.0	3	6	50.0	11:17	....	....	....	....	....	....	....	....	....
	Hamilton	AHL	69	31	41	72	78	....	....	....	....	....	....	....	....	....	23	*12	9	*21	20	....	....	....•	....
2003-04	Montreal	NHL	53	5	7	12	21	2	0	1	56	8.9	3	98	41.8	12:39	5	0	2	2	2	0	0	0	15:39
	Hamilton	AHL	2	0	3	3	17	....	....	....	....	....	....	....	....	....	....	....	....	....	....	....	....	....	....
2004-05	Hamilton	AHL	77	20	34	54	66	....	....	....	....	....	....	....	....	....	4	2	1	3	2	....	....	....	....
2005-06	NY Rangers	NHL	81	10	18	28	44	0	2	1	125	8.0	-4	153	47.7	13:12	1	0	0	0	2	0	0	0	2:39
2006-07	NY Rangers	NHL	46	4	6	10	26	0	1	1	68	5.9	-3	191	41.9	12:19	....	....	....	....	....	....	....	....	....
	Los Angeles	NHL	7	0	1	1	4	0	0	0	2	0.0	-1	7	14.3	4:51	....	....	....	....	....	....	....	....	....
	Tampa Bay	NHL	17	4	4	8	10	0	0	0	38	10.5	-11	16	37.5	16:38	6	0	1	1	6	0	0	0	20:03
	NHL Totals		256	28	39	67	127	3	3	3	327	8.6		559	43.5	12:08	12	0	3	3	10	0	0	0	16:46

AHL First All-Star Team (2003) • Les Cunningham Award (MVP – AHL) (2003)

• Missed majority of 2000-01 season recovering from knee injury suffered in game vs. Carolina, January 16, 2001. Signed as a free agent by **Hamilton** (AHL), October 19, 2004. Signed as a free agent by **NY Rangers**, August 4, 2005. Traded to **Los Angeles** by **NY Rangers** with Jan Marek, Marc-Andre Cliche and future considerations for Sean Avery, John Seymour and future considerations, February 5, 2007. Traded to **Tampa Bay** by **Los Angeles** for Tampa Bay's 5th round choice (Joshua Turnbull) in 2007 Entry Draft, February 27, 2007.

WARD, Joel

(WOHRD, JOHL) **MIN.**

Right wing. Shoots right. 6'2", 205 lbs. Born, Toronto, Ont., December 2, 1980.

Season	Club	League	GP	G	A	Pts	PIM	PP	SH	GW	S	%	+/-	TF	F%	Min	GP	G	A	Pts	PIM	PP	SH	GW	Min
1997-98	Owen Sound	OHL	47	8	4	12	14	....	....	....	....	....	....	....	....	....	11	1	1	2	5	....	....	....	....
1998-99	Owen Sound	OHL	58	19	16	35	23	....	....	....	....	....	....	....	....	....	16	2	4	6	0	....	....	....	....
99-2000	Owen Sound	OHL	63	23	20	43	51	....	....	....	....	....	....	....	....	....	....	....	....	....	....	....	....	....	....
2000-01	Owen Sound	OHL	67	26	36	62	45	....	....	....	....	....	....	....	....	....	5	2	4	6	4	....	....	....	....
	Long Beach	WCHL	....	....	....	....	....	....	....	....	....	....	....	....	....	....	8	0	0	0	0	....	....	....	....
2001-02	U. of P.E.I.	CIS	22	13	14	27	16	....	....	....	....	....	....	....	....	....	....	....	....	....	....	....	....	....	....
2002-03	U. of P.E.I.	CIS	19	11	15	26	24	....	....	....	....	....	....	....	....	....	....	....	....	....	....	....	....	....	....
2003-04	U. of P.E.I.	CIS	27	14	24	38	42	....	....	....	....	....	....	....	....	....	....	....	....	....	....	....	....	....	....
2004-05	U. of P.E.I.	CIS	28	16	28	44	42	....	....	....	....	....	....	....	....	....	....	....	....	....	....	....	....	....	....
2005-06	Houston Aeros	AHL	66	8	14	22	34	....	....	....	....	....	....	....	....	....	8	4	2	6	4	....	....	....	....
2006-07	Minnesota	NHL	11	0	1	1	0	0	0	0	12	0.0	0	1	0.0	7:42	....	....	....	....	....	....	....	....	....
	Houston Aeros	AHL	64	9	14	23	45	....	....	....	....	....	....	....	....	....	....	....	....	....	....	....	....	....	....
	NHL Totals		11	0	1	1	0	0	0	0	12	0.0		1	0.0	7:42	....	....	....	....	....	....	....	....	....

Signed as a free agent by **Houston** (AHL), December 4, 2005. Signed as a free agent by **Minnesota**, September 27, 2006.

WARD, Lance

(WOHRD, LANTS)

Defense. Shoots left. 6'3", 210 lbs. Born, Lloydminster, Alta., June 2, 1978. Florida's 3rd choice, 63rd overall, in 1998 Entry Draft.

Season	Club	League	GP	G	A	Pts	PIM	PP	SH	GW	S	%	+/-	TF	F%	Min	GP	G	A	Pts	PIM	PP	SH	GW	Min
1993-94	Lloydminster	AAHA	20	8	12	20	68	....	....	....	....	....	....	....	....	....	....	....	....	....	....	....	....	....	....
1994-95	Red Deer Rebels	WHL	28	0	0	0	57	....	....	....	....	....	....	....	....	....	....	....	....	....	....	....	....	....	....
1995-96	Red Deer Rebels	WHL	72	4	13	17	127	....	....	....	....	....	....	....	....	....	10	0	4	4	10	....	....	....	....
1996-97	Red Deer Rebels	WHL	70	5	34	39	229	....	....	....	....	....	....	....	....	....	16	0	3	3	36	....	....	....	....
1997-98	Red Deer Rebels	WHL	71	8	25	33	233	....	....	....	....	....	....	....	....	....	5	0	0	0	16	....	....	....	....
1998-99	Miami Matadors	ECHL	6	1	0	1	12	....	....	....	....	....	....	....	....	....	....	....	....	....	....	....	....	....	....
	Fort Wayne	IHL	13	0	2	2	28	....	....	....	....	....	....	....	....	....	....	....	....	....	....	....	....	....	....
	New Haven	AHL	43	2	5	7	51	....	....	....	....	....	....	....	....	....	....	....	....	....	....	....	....	....	....
99-2000	Louisville Panthers	AHL	80	4	16	20	190	....	....	....	....	....	....	....	....	....	4	0	0	0	6	....	....	....	....
2000-01	Florida	NHL	30	0	2	2	45	0	0	0	17	0.0	-3	0	0.0	15:50	....	....	....	....	....	....	....	....	....
	Louisville Panthers	AHL	35	3	2	5	78	....	....	....	....	....	....	....	....	....	....	....	....	....	....	....	....	....	....
2001-02	Florida	NHL	68	1	4	5	131	0	0	0	39	2.6	-20	1	0.0	14:31	....	....	....	....	....	....	....	....	....
2002-03	Florida	NHL	36	3	1	4	78	0	0	1	34	8.8	-4	0	0.0	9:07	....	....	....	....	....	....	....	....	....
	Anaheim	NHL	29	0	1	1	43	0	0	0	18	0.0	-2	0	0.0	7:08	....	....	....	....	....	....	....	....	....

			Regular Season														Playoffs								
Season	Club	League	GP	G	A	Pts	PIM	PP	SH	GW	S	%	+/-	TF	F%	Min	GP	G	A	Pts	PIM	PP	SH	GW	Min
2003-04	Anaheim	NHL	46	0	4	4	94	0	0	0	26	0.0	–1	0	0.0	8:41									
	Cincinnati	AHL	5	0	1	1	6																		
2004-05			DID NOT PLAY																						
2005-06	Binghamton	AHL	80	3	20	23	278																		
2006-07	HV 71 Jonkoping	Sweden	50	6	4	10	*273										14	0	0	0	47				
	NHL Totals		209	4	12	16	391	0	0	1	134	3.0		1	0.0	11:28									

• Re-entered NHL Entry Draft. Originally New Jersey's 1st choice, 10th overall, in 1996 Entry Draft.

Traded to **Anaheim** by **Florida** with Sandis Ozolinsh for Pavel Trnka, Matt Cullen and Anaheim's 4th round choice (James Pemberton) in 2003 Entry Draft, January 30, 2003. Signed as a free agent by **Ottawa**, August 26, 2005. Signed as a free agent by **Jonkoping** (Sweden), June 5, 2006.

WARRENER, Rhett

(WAHR-ihn-uhr, REHT) **CGY.**

Defense. Shoots right. 6'1", 208 lbs. Born, Shaunavon, Sask., January 27, 1976. Florida's 2nd choice, 27th overall, in 1994 Entry Draft.

Season	Club	League	GP	G	A	Pts	PIM	PP	SH	GW	S	%	+/-	TF	F%	Min	GP	G	A	Pts	PIM	PP	SH	GW	Min
1991-92	Saskatoon Blazers	SMHL	33	6	5	11	71																		
	Saskatoon Blades	WHL	2	0	0	0	0																		
1992-93	Saskatoon Blades	WHL	68	2	17	19	100										9	0	0	0	14				
1993-94	Saskatoon Blades	WHL	61	7	19	26	131										16	0	5	5	33				
1994-95	Saskatoon Blades	WHL	66	13	26	39	137										10	0	3	3	6				
1995-96	Florida	NHL	28	0	3	3	46	0	0	0	19	0.0	4				21	0	1	1	0	0	0	0	
	Carolina Panthers	AHL	9	0	0	0	4																		
1996-97	Florida	NHL	62	4	9	13	88	1	0	1	58	6.9	20				5	0	0	0	0	0	0	0	
1997-98	Florida	NHL	79	0	4	4	99	0	0	0	66	0.0	–16												
1998-99	Florida	NHL	48	0	7	7	64	0	0	0	33	0.0	–1	0	0.0	19:01									
	Buffalo	NHL	13	1	0	1	20	0	0	0	11	9.1	3	0	0.0	18:13	20	1	3	4	32	0	0	0	22:08
99-2000	Buffalo	NHL	61	0	3	3	89	0	0	0	68	0.0	18	0	0.0	19:51	5	0	0	0	2	0	0	0	21:42
2000-01	Buffalo	NHL	77	3	16	19	78	0	0	2	103	2.9	10	0	0.0	20:24	13	0	2	2	4	0	0	0	22:37
2001-02	Buffalo	NHL	65	5	5	10	113	0	0	1	66	7.6	15	0	0.0	19:39									
2002-03	Buffalo	NHL	50	0	9	9	63	0	0	0	47	0.0	1	0	0.0	18:14									
2003-04	Calgary	NHL	77	3	14	17	97	0	1	1	82	3.7	8	1	0.0	19:52	24	0	1	1	6	0	0	0	24:06
2004-05			DID NOT PLAY																						
2005-06	Calgary	NHL	61	3	3	6	54	0	1	0	40	7.5	7	0	0.0	19:12	7	0	0	0	14	0	0	0	19:56
2006-07	Calgary	NHL	62	4	6	10	67	1	1	1	31	12.9	6	0	0.0	17:08	6	0	0	0	10	0	0	0	21:15
	NHL Totals		683	23	79	102	878	2	3	6	624	3.7		1	0.0	19:14	101	1	7	8	68	0	0	0	22:32

Traded to **Buffalo** by **Florida** with Florida's 5th round choice (Ryan Miller) in 1999 Entry Draft for Mike Wilson, March 23, 1999. Traded to **Calgary** by **Buffalo** with Steve Reinprecht for Chris Drury and Steve Begin, July 3, 2003.

WEAVER, Mike

(WEE-vuhr, MIGHK) **PIT.**

Defense. Shoots right. 5'9", 182 lbs. Born, Bramalea, Ont., May 2, 1978.

Season	Club	League	GP	G	A	Pts	PIM	PP	SH	GW	S	%	+/-	TF	F%	Min	GP	G	A	Pts	PIM	PP	SH	GW	Min
1995-96	Bramalea Blues	OPJHL	48	10	39	49	103																		
1996-97	Michigan State	CCHA	39	0	7	7	46																		
1997-98	Michigan State	CCHA	44	4	22	26	68																		
1998-99	Michigan State	CCHA	42	1	6	7	54																		
99-2000	Michigan State	CCHA	26	0	7	7	20																		
2000-01	Orlando	IHL	68	0	8	8	34										16	0	2	2	8				
2001-02	Atlanta	NHL	16	0	1	1	10	0	0	0	9	0.0	0	0	0.0	13:54									
	Chicago Wolves	AHL	58	2	8	10	67										25	1	3	4	21				
2002-03	Atlanta	NHL	40	0	5	5	20	0	0	0	21	0.0	–5	0	0.0	18:38									
	Chicago Wolves	AHL	33	2	2	4	32										9	0	3	3	4				
2003-04	Atlanta	NHL	1	0	0	0	0	0	0	0	0	0.0	–1	0	0.0	8:28									
	Chicago Wolves	AHL	78	3	14	17	89										9	2	2	4	20				
2004-05	Manchester	AHL	79	1	22	23	61										6	0	1	1	0				
2005-06	Los Angeles	NHL	53	0	9	9	14	0	0	0	21	0.0	–3	0	0.0	15:03									
2006-07	Los Angeles	NHL	39	3	6	9	16	1	0	1	22	13.6	–4	3	66.7	15:20									
	Manchester	AHL	7	1	3	4	2																		
	NHL Totals		149	3	21	24	60	1	0	1	73	4.1		3	66.7	15:55									

OPJHL Defenseman of the Year (1996) • CCHA All-Tournament Team (1997) • CCHA First All-Star Team (1999, 2000) • CCHA Best Defensive Defenseman Award (1999, 2000) • NCAA West Second All-American Team (1999, 2000)

Signed as a free agent by **Atlanta**, June 15, 2000. Signed as a free agent by **Los Angeles**, July 16, 2004. Signed as a free agent by **Pittsburgh**, August 8, 2007.

WEBER, Shea

(WEH-buhr, SHAY) **NSH.**

Defense. Shoots right. 6'3", 213 lbs. Born, Sicamous, B.C., August 14, 1985. Nashville's 4th choice, 49th overall, in 2003 Entry Draft.

Season	Club	League	GP	G	A	Pts	PIM	PP	SH	GW	S	%	+/-	TF	F%	Min	GP	G	A	Pts	PIM	PP	SH	GW	Min
2001-02	Sicamous Eagles	KIJHL	47	9	33	42	87																		
	Kelowna Rockets	WHL	5	0	0	0	0																		
2002-03	Kelowna Rockets	WHL	70	2	16	18	167										19	1	4	5	26				
2003-04	Kelowna Rockets	WHL	60	12	20	32	126										17	3	14	17	16				
2004-05	Kelowna Rockets	WHL	55	12	29	41	95										18	9	8	17	25				
2005-06	Nashville	NHL	28	2	8	10	42	2	0	1	46	4.3	8	0	0.0	17:00	4	2	0	2	8	1	0	0	14:12
	Milwaukee	AHL	46	12	15	27	49										14	6	5	11	16				
2006-07	Nashville	NHL	79	17	23	40	60	6	0	2	152	11.2	13	0	0.0	19:23	5	0	3	3	2	0	0	0	21:41
	NHL Totals		107	19	31	50	102	8	0	3	198	9.6		0	0.0	18:46	9	2	3	5	10	1	0	0	18:22

WHL West Second All-Star Team (2004) • Memorial Cup Tournament All-Star Team (2004) • WHL West First All-Star Team (2005)

WEIGHT, Doug

(WAYT, DUHG) **ST.L.**

Center. Shoots left. 5'11", 201 lbs. Born, Warren, MI, January 21, 1971. NY Rangers' 2nd choice, 34th overall, in 1990 Entry Draft.

Season	Club	League	GP	G	A	Pts	PIM	PP	SH	GW	S	%	+/-	TF	F%	Min	GP	G	A	Pts	PIM	PP	SH	GW	Min
1988-89	Bloomfield Jets	NAHL	34	26	53	79	105																		
1989-90	Lake Superior	CCHA	46	21	48	69	44																		
1990-91	Lake Superior	CCHA	42	29	46	75	86																		
	NY Rangers	NHL															1	0	0	0	0	0	0	0	
1991-92	NY Rangers	NHL	53	8	22	30	23	0	0	2	72	11.1	–3				7	2	2	4	0	1	0	0	
	Binghamton	AHL	9	3	14	17	2										4	1	4	5	6				
1992-93	NY Rangers	NHL	65	15	25	40	55	3	0	1	90	16.7	4												
	Edmonton	NHL	13	2	6	8	10	0	0	0	35	5.7	–2												
1993-94	Edmonton	NHL	84	24	50	74	47	4	1	1	188	12.8	–22												
1994-95	Rosenheim	Germany	8	2	3	5	18																		
	Edmonton	NHL	48	7	33	40	69	1	0	1	104	6.7	–17												
1995-96	Edmonton	NHL	82	25	79	104	95	9	0	2	204	12.3	–19												
1996-97	Edmonton	NHL	80	21	61	82	80	4	0	2	235	8.9	1				12	3	8	11	8	0	0	0	
1997-98	Edmonton	NHL	79	26	44	70	69	9	0	4	205	12.7	1				12	2	7	9	14	2	0	1	
	United States	Olympics	4	0	2	2	2																		
1998-99	Edmonton	NHL	43	6	31	37	12	1	0	0	79	7.6	–8	853	49.5	19:51	4	1	1	2	15	0	0	0	14:43
99-2000	Edmonton	NHL	77	21	51	72	54	3	1	4	167	12.6	6	1588	50.4	20:35	5	3	2	5	4	2	0	1	21:05
2000-01	Edmonton	NHL	82	25	65	90	91	8	0	3	188	13.3	12	1514	51.3	22:08	6	1	5	6	17	0	0	0	22:45
2001-02	St. Louis	NHL	61	15	34	49	40	3	0	1	131	11.5	20	1123	49.2	19:48	10	1	1	2	4	1	0	1	16:26
	United States	Olympics	6	0	3	3	4																		
2002-03	St. Louis	NHL	70	15	52	67	52	7	0	3	182	8.2	–6	1048	50.4	20:23	7	5	8	13	2	5	0	1	22:26
2003-04	St. Louis	NHL	75	14	51	65	37	6	0	5	198	7.1	–3	1115	50.4	20:25	5	2	1	3	6	1	1	0	19:24
2004-05	Frankfurt Lions	Germany	7	6	9	15	26										11	2	10	12	8				

			Regular Season														Playoffs								
Season	Club	League	GP	G	A	Pts	PIM	PP	SH	GW	S	%	+/-	TF	F%	Min	GP	G	A	Pts	PIM	PP	SH	GW	Min
2005-06	St. Louis	NHL	47	11	33	44	50	7	0	1	123	8.9	–11	638	49.8	22:17	....	....	....	....	....	....	....	....	....
	♦ Carolina	NHL	23	4	9	13	25	2	0	0	52	7.7	–6	256	46.1	17:35	23	3	13	16	20	2	0	0	15:27
	United States	Olympics	6	0	3	3	4	....	....	....	....	....	....	....	....	....	....	....	....	....	....	....	....	....	....
2006-07	St. Louis	NHL	82	16	43	59	56	5	0	3	123	13.0	10	1025	47.7	18:17	....	....	....	....	....	....	....	....	....
	NHL Totals		1064	255	689	944	865	72	2	33	2376	10.7		9160	49.8	20:18	92	23	48	71	90	14	1	4	17:54

CCHA First All-Star Team (1991) • NCAA West Second All-American Team (1991)

Played in NHL All-Star Game (1996, 1998, 2001, 2003)

Traded to **Edmonton** by **NY Rangers** for Esa Tikkanen, March 17, 1993. Traded to **St. Louis** by **Edmonton** with Michel Riesen for Marty Reasoner, Jochen Hecht and Jan Horacek, July 1, 2001. Signed as a free agent by **Frankfurt** (Germany), February 11, 2005. Traded to **Carolina** by **St. Louis** with Erkki Rajamaki for Jesse Boulerice, Mike Zigomanis, the rights to Magnus Kahnberg, Carolina's 1st round choice (later traded to New Jersey - New Jersey selected Matthew Corrente) in 2006 Entry Draft, Toronto's 4th round choice (previously acquired, St. Louis selected Reto Berra) in 2006 Entry Draft and Chicago's 4th round choice (previously acquired, St. Louis selected Cade Fairchild) in 2007 Entry Draft, January 30, 2006. Signed as a free agent by **St. Louis**, July 2, 2006.

WEINHANDL, Mattias

(WIGHN-han-duhl, mat-TEE-uhs)

Right wing. Shoots right. 6', 183 lbs. Born, Ljungby, Sweden, June 1, 1980. NY Islanders' 5th choice, 78th overall, in 1999 Entry Draft.

Season	Club	League	GP	G	A	Pts	PIM	PP	SH	GW	S	%	+/-	TF	F%	Min	GP	G	A	Pts	PIM	PP	SH	GW	Min
1995-96	Troja Jr.	Swe-Jr.	28	38	40	78	....	....	....	....	....	....	....	....	....	....	....	....	....	....	....	....	....	....	....
1996-97	Troja Jr.	Swe-Jr.	48	61	69	130	46	....	....	....	....	....	....	....	....	....	....	....	....	....	....	....	....	....	....
1997-98	IF Troja-Ljungby	Sweden-2	28	3	2	5	2	....	....	....	....	....	....	....	....	....	5	0	0	0	2	....	....	....	....
1998-99	IF Troja-Ljungby	Sweden-2	38	20	20	40	30	....	....	....	....	....	....	....	....	....	5	4	3	7	4	....	....	....	....
99-2000	Malmo Jr.	Swe-Jr.	1	2	2	4	2	....	....	....	....	....	....	....	....	....	....	....	....	....	....	....	....	....	....
	MoDo	Sweden	32	15	9	24	6	....	....	....	....	....	....	....	....	....	13	5	3	8	8	....	....	....	....
2000-01	MoDo	Sweden	48	16	16	32	14	....	....	....	....	....	....	....	....	....	6	1	3	4	6	....	....	....	....
2001-02	MODO	Sweden	50	18	16	34	10	....	....	....	....	....	....	....	....	....	14	4	*11	*15	4	....	....	....	....
2002-03	NY Islanders	NHL	47	6	17	23	10	1	0	0	66	9.1	2	5	60.0	13:52	....	....	....	....	....	....	....	....	....
	Bridgeport	AHL	23	9	12	21	14	....	....	....	....	....	....	....	....	....	....	....	....	....	....	....	....	....	....
2003-04	NY Islanders	NHL	55	8	12	20	26	4	0	2	49	16.3	9	6	33.3	12:20	5	0	0	0	2	0	0	0	13:07
	Bridgeport	AHL	10	3	6	9	10	....	....	....	....	....	....	....	....	....	....	....	....	....	....	....	....	....	....
2004-05	MODO	Sweden	50	*26	20	46	18	....	....	....	....	....	....	....	....	....	6	0	0	0	4	....	....	....	....
2005-06	NY Islanders	NHL	53	2	4	6	14	0	0	0	40	5.0	–4	10	40.0	7:36	....	....	....	....	....	....	....	....	....
	Minnesota	NHL	15	2	3	5	10	0	0	0	17	11.8	0	11	27.3	14:43	....	....	....	....	....	....	....	....	....
2006-07	Minnesota	NHL	12	1	1	2	10	0	0	0	3	33.3	–2	1	0.0	6:28	....	....	....	....	....	....	....	....	....
	Houston Aeros	AHL	48	18	27	45	20	....	....	....	....	....	....	....	....	....	....	....	....	....	....	....	....	....	....
	NHL Totals		182	19	37	56	70	5	0	2	175	10.9		33	36.4	11:10	5	0	0	0	2	0	0	0	13:07

Signed as a free agent by **MODO** (Sweden), September 18, 2004. Claimed on waivers by **Minnesota** from **NY Islanders**, March 4, 2006.

WEISS, Stephen

(WIGHS, STEE-vehn) **FLA.**

Center. Shoots left. 5'11", 185 lbs. Born, Toronto, Ont., April 3, 1983. Florida's 1st choice, 4th overall, in 2001 Entry Draft.

Season	Club	League	GP	G	A	Pts	PIM	PP	SH	GW	S	%	+/-	TF	F%	Min	GP	G	A	Pts	PIM	PP	SH	GW	Min
1997-98	Tor. Young Nats	MTHL	48	51	58	109	....	....	....	....	....	....	....	....	....	....	....	....	....	....	....	....	....	....	....
1998-99	North York	OPJHL	35	15	22	37	10	....	....	....	....	....	....	....	....	....	....	....	....	....	....	....	....	....	....
99-2000	Plymouth Whalers	OHL	64	24	42	66	35	....	....	....	....	....	....	....	....	....	23	8	18	26	18	....	....	....	....
2000-01	Plymouth Whalers	OHL	62	40	47	87	45	....	....	....	....	....	....	....	....	....	18	7	16	23	10	....	....	....	....
2001-02	Florida	NHL	7	1	1	2	0	1	0	0	15	6.7	0	107	52.3	16:14	....	....	....	....	....	....	....	....	....
	Plymouth Whalers	OHL	46	25	45	70	69	....	....	....	....	....	....	....	....	....	6	2	7	9	13	....	....	....	....
2002-03	Florida	NHL	77	6	15	21	17	0	0	2	87	6.9	–13	1065	46.3	14:17	....	....	....	....	....	....	....	....	....
2003-04	Florida	NHL	50	12	17	29	10	3	0	2	82	14.6	–10	799	44.9	17:42	....	....	....	....	....	....	....	....	....
	San Antonio	AHL	10	6	3	9	14	....	....	....	....	....	....	....	....	....	....	....	....	....	....	....	....	....	....
2004-05	San Antonio	AHL	62	15	23	38	38	....	....	....	....	....	....	....	....	....	....	....	....	....	....	....	....	....	....
	Chicago Wolves	AHL	18	7	9	16	12	....	....	....	....	....	....	....	....	....	18	2	7	9	17	....	....	....	....
2005-06	Florida	NHL	41	9	12	21	22	5	0	1	74	12.2	–2	514	49.6	15:15	....	....	....	....	....	....	....	....	....
2006-07	Florida	NHL	74	20	28	48	28	10	0	1	176	11.4	–1	1182	45.9	17:07	....	....	....	....	....	....	....	....	....
	NHL Totals		249	48	73	121	77	19	0	6	434	11.1		3667	46.5	16:02	....	....	....	....	....	....	....	....	....

OHL All-Rookie Team (2000)

Loaned to **Chicago** (AHL) by **San Antonio** (AHL) for cash, March 8, 2005.

WELCH, Noah

(WEHLCH, NOH-uh) **FLA.**

Defense. Shoots left. 6'4", 218 lbs. Born, Brighton, MA, August 26, 1982. Pittsburgh's 2nd choice, 54th overall, in 2001 Entry Draft.

Season	Club	League	GP	G	A	Pts	PIM	PP	SH	GW	S	%	+/-	TF	F%	Min	GP	G	A	Pts	PIM	PP	SH	GW	Min
99-2000	St. Sebastian's	High-MA	26	4	11	15	35	....	....	....	....	....	....	....	....	....	....	....	....	....	....	....	....	....	....
	Eastern-Mass	MBAHL	4	0	3	3	6	....	....	....	....	....	....	....	....	....	....	....	....	....	....	....	....	....	....
2000-01	St. Sebastian's	High-MA	30	11	20	31	37	....	....	....	....	....	....	....	....	....	....	....	....	....	....	....	....	....	....
2001-02	Harvard Crimson	ECAC	27	5	6	11	56	....	....	....	....	....	....	....	....	....	....	....	....	....	....	....	....	....	....
2002-03	Harvard Crimson	ECAC	34	6	22	28	70	....	....	....	....	....	....	....	....	....	....	....	....	....	....	....	....	....	....
2003-04	Harvard Crimson	ECAC	34	6	13	19	58	....	....	....	....	....	....	....	....	....	....	....	....	....	....	....	....	....	....
2004-05	Harvard Crimson	ECACHL	34	6	12	18	*86	....	....	....	....	....	....	....	....	....	....	....	....	....	....	....	....	....	....
2005-06	Pittsburgh	NHL	5	1	3	4	2	0	0	0	5	20.0	0	0	0.0	17:24	....	....	....	....	....	....	....	....	....
	Wilkes-Barre	AHL	77	9	20	29	99	....	....	....	....	....	....	....	....	....	11	1	0	1	18	....	....	....	....
2006-07	Pittsburgh	NHL	22	1	1	2	22	0	0	0	14	7.1	1	0	0.0	13:34	....	....	....	....	....	....	....	....	....
	Wilkes-Barre	AHL	27	5	16	21	24	....	....	....	....	....	....	....	....	....	....	....	....	....	....	....	....	....	....
	Florida	NHL	2	1	0	1	2	0	0	0	4	25.0	3	0	0.0	18:08	....	....	....	....	....	....	....	....	....
	Rochester	AHL	11	2	4	6	21	....	....	....	....	....	....	....	....	....	6	0	2	2	12	....	....	....	....
	NHL Totals		29	3	4	7	26	0	0	0	23	13.0		0	0.0	14:33	....	....	....	....	....	....	....	....	....

ECAC All-Rookie Team (2002) • ECAC Second All-Star Team (2002, 2003) • NCAA East Second All-American Team (2003) • ECAC First All-Star Team (2005) • NCAA East First All-American Team (2005)

Traded to **Florida** by **Pittsburgh** for Gary Roberts, February 27, 2007.

WELLWOOD, Kyle

(WEHL-wud, KIGHL) **TOR.**

Center. Shoots right. 5'10", 180 lbs. Born, Windsor, Ont., May 16, 1983. Toronto's 6th choice, 134th overall, in 2001 Entry Draft.

Season	Club	League	GP	G	A	Pts	PIM	PP	SH	GW	S	%	+/-	TF	F%	Min	GP	G	A	Pts	PIM	PP	SH	GW	Min
1998-99	Tecumseh	OHA-B	51	22	41	63	12	....	....	....	....	....	....	....	....	....	....	....	....	....	....	....	....	....	....
99-2000	Belleville Bulls	OHL	65	14	37	51	14	....	....	....	....	....	....	....	....	....	16	3	7	10	6	....	....	....	....
2000-01	Belleville Bulls	OHL	68	35	*83	*118	24	....	....	....	....	....	....	....	....	....	10	3	16	19	4	....	....	....	....
2001-02	Belleville Bulls	OHL	28	16	24	40	4	....	....	....	....	....	....	....	....	....	....	....	....	....	....	....	....	....	....
	Windsor Spitfires	OHL	26	14	21	35	0	....	....	....	....	....	....	....	....	....	16	12	12	24	0	....	....	....	....
2002-03	Windsor Spitfires	OHL	57	41	59	100	0	....	....	....	....	....	....	....	....	....	7	5	9	14	0	....	....	....	....
2003-04	Toronto	NHL	1	0	0	0	0	0	0	0	1	0.0	–1	13	30.8	7:56	....	....	....	....	....	....	....	....	....
	St. John's	AHL	76	20	35	55	6	....	....	....	....	....	....	....	....	....	....	....	....	....	....	....	....	....	....
2004-05	St. John's	AHL	80	38	49	87	20	....	....	....	....	....	....	....	....	....	5	2	2	4	2	....	....	....	....
2005-06	Toronto	NHL	81	11	34	45	14	3	0	0	117	9.4	0	593	56.3	12:47	....	....	....	....	....	....	....	....	....
2006-07	Toronto	NHL	48	12	30	42	0	7	0	2	99	12.1	3	291	56.4	16:38	....	....	....	....	....	....	....	....	....
	NHL Totals		130	23	64	87	14	10	0	2	217	10.6		897	56.0	14:10	....	....	....	....	....	....	....	....	....

OHL First All-Star Team (2001) • Canadian Major Junior Sportsman of the Year (2003)

WESLEY, Glen

(WEH-slee, GLEHN) **CAR.**

Defense. Shoots left. 6'1", 207 lbs. Born, Red Deer, Alta., October 2, 1968. Boston's 1st choice, 3rd overall, in 1987 Entry Draft.

Season	Club	League	GP	G	A	Pts	PIM	PP	SH	GW	S	%	+/-	TF	F%	Min	GP	G	A	Pts	PIM	PP	SH	GW	Min
1983-84	Red Deer Rustlers	AJHL	57	9	20	29	40	....	....	....	....	....	....	....	....	....	....	....	....	....	....	....	....	....	....
	Portland	WHL	3	1	2	3	0	....	....	....	....	....	....	....	....	....	....	....	....	....	....	....	....	....	....
1984-85	Portland	WHL	67	16	52	68	76	....	....	....	....	....	....	....	....	....	6	1	6	7	8	....	....	....	....
1985-86	Portland	WHL	69	16	75	91	96	....	....	....	....	....	....	....	....	....	15	3	11	14	29	....	....	....	....
1986-87	Portland	WHL	63	16	46	62	72	....	....	....	....	....	....	....	....	....	20	8	18	26	27	....	....	....	....
1987-88	Boston	NHL	79	7	30	37	69	1	2	0	158	4.4	21	....	....	....	23	6	8	14	22	4	1	0	....
1988-89	Boston	NHL	77	19	35	54	61	8	1	1	181	10.5	23	....	....	....	10	0	2	2	4	0	0	0	....
1989-90	Boston	NHL	78	9	27	36	48	5	0	4	166	5.4	6	....	....	....	21	2	6	8	36	0	0	1	....
1990-91	Boston	NHL	80	11	32	43	78	5	1	1	199	5.5	0	....	....	....	19	2	9	11	19	2	0	0	....
1991-92	Boston	NHL	78	9	37	46	54	4	0	1	211	4.3	–9	....	....	....	15	2	4	6	16	0	0	0	....
1992-93	Boston	NHL	64	8	25	33	47	4	1	0	183	4.4	–2	....	....	....	4	0	0	0	0	0	0	0	....
1993-94	Boston	NHL	81	14	44	58	64	6	1	1	265	5.3	1	....	....	....	13	3	3	6	12	1	0	0	....
1994-95	Hartford	NHL	48	2	14	16	50	1	0	1	125	1.6	–6	....	....	....	....	....	....	....	....	....	....	....	....

			Regular Season														Playoffs								
Season	Club	League	GP	G	A	Pts	PIM	PP	SH	GW	S	%	+/-	TF	F%	Min	GP	G	A	Pts	PIM	PP	SH	GW	Min
1995-96	**Hartford**	**NHL**	**68**	**8**	**16**	**24**	**88**	**6**	**0**	**1**	**129**	**6.2**	**–9**	....	....	....	....	....	....	....	....	....	....	....	....
1996-97	**Hartford**	**NHL**	**68**	**6**	**26**	**32**	**40**	**3**	**1**	**0**	**126**	**4.8**	**0**	....	....	....	....	....	....	....	....	....	....	....	....
1997-98	**Carolina**	**NHL**	**82**	**6**	**19**	**25**	**36**	**1**	**0**	**1**	**121**	**5.0**	**7**	....	....	....	....	....	....	....	....	....	....	....	....
1998-99	**Carolina**	**NHL**	**74**	**7**	**17**	**24**	**44**	**0**	**0**	**2**	**112**	**6.3**	**14**	**1**	**0.0**	**22:31**	**6**	**0**	**0**	**0**	**2**	**0**	**0**	**0**	**28:21**
99-2000	**Carolina**	**NHL**	**78**	**7**	**15**	**22**	**38**	**1**	**0**	**0**	**99**	**7.1**	**–4**	**0**	**0.0**	**21:32**	....	....	....	....	....	....	....	....	....
2000-01	**Carolina**	**NHL**	**71**	**5**	**16**	**21**	**42**	**3**	**0**	**0**	**92**	**5.4**	**–2**	**0**	**0.0**	**22:21**	**6**	**0**	**0**	**0**	**0**	**0**	**0**	**0**	**22:07**
2001-02	**Carolina**	**NHL**	**77**	**5**	**13**	**18**	**56**	**1**	**0**	**0**	**88**	**5.7**	**–8**	**0**	**0.0**	**20:13**	**22**	**0**	**2**	**2**	**12**	**0**	**0**	**0**	**21:04**
2002-03	**Carolina**	**NHL**	**63**	**1**	**7**	**8**	**40**	**1**	**0**	**0**	**72**	**1.4**	**–5**	**0**	**0.0**	**21:24**	....	....	....	....	....	....	....	....	....
	Toronto	**NHL**	**7**	**0**	**3**	**3**	**4**	**0**	**0**	**0**	**5**	**0.0**	**3**	**0**	**0.0**	**20:41**	**5**	**0**	**1**	**1**	**2**	**0**	**0**	**0**	**27:39**
2003-04	**Carolina**	**NHL**	**74**	**0**	**6**	**6**	**32**	**0**	**0**	**0**	**82**	**0.0**	**18**	**0**	**0.0**	**21:22**	....	....	....	....	....	....	....	....	....
2004-05			DID NOT PLAY																						
2005-06♦	**Carolina**	**NHL**	**64**	**2**	**8**	**10**	**46**	**0**	**0**	**0**	**28**	**7.1**	**10**	**0**	**0.0**	**15:28**	**25**	**0**	**2**	**2**	**16**	**0**	**0**	**0**	**16:10**
2006-07	**Carolina**	**NHL**	**68**	**1**	**12**	**13**	**56**	**0**	**1**	**1**	**51**	**2.0**	**11**	**0**	**0.0**	**15:35**	....	....	....	....	....	....	....	....	....
	NHL Totals		**1379**	**127**	**402**	**529**	**993**	**50**	**8**	**14**	**2493**	**5.1**		**1**	**0.0**	**20:10**	**169**	**15**	**37**	**52**	**141**	**7**	**1**	**1**	**20:27**

WHL West First All-Star Team (1986, 1987) • NHL All-Rookie Team (1988)

Played in NHL All-Star Game (1989)

Traded to **Hartford** by **Boston** for Hartford's 1st round choices in 1995 (Kyle McLaren), 1996 (Johnathan Aitken) and 1997 (Sergei Samsonov) Entry Drafts, August 26, 1994. Transferred to **Carolina** after **Hartford** franchise relocated, June 25, 1997. Traded to **Toronto** by **Carolina** for Toronto's 2nd round choice (later traded to Columbus – Columbus selected Kyle Wharton) in 2004 Entry Draft, March 9, 2003. Signed as a free agent by **Carolina**, July 8, 2003.

WESTCOTT, Duvie

(WEST-koht, DOO-vee) **CBJ**

Defense. Shoots right. 5'11", 197 lbs. Born, Winnipeg, Man., October 30, 1977.

Season	Club	League	GP	G	A	Pts	PIM	PP	SH	GW	S	%	+/-	TF	F%	Min	GP	G	A	Pts	PIM	PP	SH	GW	Min
1996-97	Winnipeg South	MJHL	52	12	47	59	....	....	....	....	....	....	....	....	....	....	....	....	....	....	....	....	....	....	....
1997-98	Alaska Anchorage	WCHA	25	3	5	8	43	....	....	....	....	....	....	....	....	....	....	....	....	....	....	....	....	....	....
	Omaha Lancers	USHL	12	3	3	6	31	....	....	....	....	....	....	....	....	....	14	0	8	8	84	....	....	....	....
1998-99	St. Cloud State	WCHA	DID NOT PLAY – TRANSFERRED COLLEGES																						
99-2000	St. Cloud State	WCHA	36	1	18	19	67	....	....	....	....	....	....	....	....	....	....	....	....	....	....	....	....	....	....
2000-01	St. Cloud State	WCHA	38	10	24	34	116	....	....	....	....	....	....	....	....	....	....	....	....	....	....	....	....	....	....
2001-02	**Columbus**	**NHL**	**4**	**0**	**0**	**0**	**2**	**0**	**0**	**0**	**3**	**0.0**	**–2**	**0**	**0.0**	**15:08**	....	....	....	....	....	....	....	....	....
	Syracuse Crunch	AHL	68	4	29	33	99	....	....	....	....	....	....	....	....	....	10	0	1	1	12	....	....	....	....
2002-03	**Columbus**	**NHL**	**39**	**0**	**7**	**7**	**77**	**0**	**0**	**0**	**27**	**0.0**	**–3**	**0**	**0.0**	**18:41**	....	....	....	....	....	....	....	....	....
	Syracuse Crunch	AHL	22	1	10	11	54	....	....	....	....	....	....	....	....	....	....	....	....	....	....	....	....	....	....
2003-04	**Columbus**	**NHL**	**34**	**0**	**7**	**7**	**39**	**0**	**0**	**0**	**43**	**0.0**	**–15**	**0**	**0.0**	**21:11**	....	....	....	....	....	....	....	....	....
2004-05	JYP Jyvaskyla	Finland	46	11	7	18	106	....	....	....	....	....	....	....	....	....	1	2	0	2	25	....	....	....	....
2005-06	**Columbus**	**NHL**	**78**	**6**	**22**	**28**	**133**	**1**	**1**	**0**	**113**	**5.3**	**1**	**0**	**0.0**	**22:34**	....	....	....	....	....	....	....	....	....
2006-07	**Columbus**	**NHL**	**23**	**4**	**6**	**10**	**18**	**2**	**0**	**1**	**34**	**11.8**	**–13**	**0**	**0.0**	**22:09**	....	....	....	....	....	....	....	....	....
	NHL Totals		**178**	**10**	**42**	**52**	**269**	**3**	**1**	**1**	**220**	**4.5**		**0**	**0.0**	**21:14**	....	....	....	....	....	....	....	....	....

WCHA Second All-Star Team (2001)

Signed as a free agent by **Columbus**, May 10, 2001. • Missed majority of 2003-04 season recovering from ankle (October 13, 2003 vs. Vancouver) and hand (January 31, 2004 vs. Minnesota) injuries. Signed as a free agent by **Jyvaskyla** (Finland), September 30, 2004. • Missed majority of 2006-07 season recovering from finger (November 3, 2006 vs. Calgary) and head (January 6, 2007 vs. San Jose) injuries.

WESTRUM, Erik

(WEHST-ruhm, AIR-ihk)

Center. Shoots left. 6', 204 lbs. Born, Minneapolis, MN, July 26, 1979. Phoenix's 9th choice, 187th overall, in 1998 Entry Draft.

Season	Club	League	GP	G	A	Pts	PIM	PP	SH	GW	S	%	+/-	TF	F%	Min	GP	G	A	Pts	PIM	PP	SH	GW	Min
1995/97	Apple Valley	High-MN	78	56	84	140	....	....	....	....	....	....	....	....	....	....	....	....	....	....	....	....	....	....	....
1997-98	U. of Minnesota	WCHA	39	6	12	18	43	....	....	....	....	....	....	....	....	....	....	....	....	....	....	....	....	....	....
1998-99	U. of Minnesota	WCHA	41	10	26	36	81	....	....	....	....	....	....	....	....	....	....	....	....	....	....	....	....	....	....
99-2000	U. of Minnesota	WCHA	39	27	26	53	99	....	....	....	....	....	....	....	....	....	....	....	....	....	....	....	....	....	....
2000-01	U. of Minnesota	WCHA	42	26	35	61	84	....	....	....	....	....	....	....	....	....	....	....	....	....	....	....	....	....	....
2001-02	Springfield	AHL	73	13	29	42	116	....	....	....	....	....	....	....	....	....	....	....	....	....	....	....	....	....	....
2002-03	Springfield	AHL	70	10	22	32	65	....	....	....	....	....	....	....	....	....	6	0	4	4	6	....	....	....	....
2003-04	**Phoenix**	**NHL**	**15**	**1**	**1**	**2**	**20**	**0**	**0**	**0**	**29**	**3.4**	**–3**	**106**	**39.6**	**16:00**	....	....	....	....	....	....	....	....	....
	Springfield	AHL	56	14	18	32	91	....	....	....	....	....	....	....	....	....	....	....	....	....	....	....	....	....	....
2004-05	Utah Grizzlies	AHL	80	18	15	33	117	....	....	....	....	....	....	....	....	....	....	....	....	....	....	....	....	....	....
2005-06	**Minnesota**	**NHL**	**10**	**0**	**1**	**1**	**2**	**0**	**0**	**0**	**16**	**0.0**	**–1**	**68**	**38.2**	**10:48**	....	....	....	....	....	....	....	....	....
	Houston Aeros	AHL	71	34	64	98	138	....	....	....	....	....	....	....	....	....	8	1	7	8	20	....	....	....	....
2006-07	**Toronto**	**NHL**	**2**	**0**	**0**	**0**	**0**	**0**	**0**	**0**	**0**	**0.0**	**0**	**5**	**40.0**	**3:31**	....	....	....	....	....	....	....	....	....
	Toronto Marlies	AHL	70	23	34	57	135	....	....	....	....	....	....	....	....	....	....	....	....	....	....	....	....	....	....
	NHL Totals		**27**	**1**	**2**	**3**	**22**	**0**	**0**	**0**	**45**	**2.2**		**179**	**39.1**	**13:09**	....	....	....	....	....	....	....	....	....

WCHA Second All-Star Team (2001) • AHL First All-Star Team (2006)

• Statistics for **Apple Valley** (High-MN) are career totals for 1995-1997 seasons. Traded to **Minnesota** by **Phoenix** with Dustin Wood for Zbynek Michalek, August 26, 2005. Signed as a free agent by **Toronto**, July 13, 2006.

WHITE, Colin

(WIGHT, KAW-lihn) **N.J.**

Defense. Shoots left. 6'4", 215 lbs. Born, New Glasgow, N.S., December 12, 1977. New Jersey's 5th choice, 49th overall, in 1996 Entry Draft.

Season	Club	League	GP	G	A	Pts	PIM	PP	SH	GW	S	%	+/-	TF	F%	Min	GP	G	A	Pts	PIM	PP	SH	GW	Min
1994-95	Laval Titan	QMJHL	7	0	1	1	32	....	....	....	....	....	....	....	....	....	....	....	....	....	....	....	....	....	....
	Hull Olympiques	QMJHL	5	0	1	1	4	....	....	....	....	....	....	....	....	....	12	0	0	0	23	....	....	....	....
1995-96	Hull Olympiques	QMJHL	62	2	8	10	303	....	....	....	....	....	....	....	....	....	18	0	4	4	42	....	....	....	....
1996-97	Hull Olympiques	QMJHL	63	3	12	15	297	....	....	....	....	....	....	....	....	....	14	3	12	15	65	....	....	....	....
1997-98	Albany River Rats	AHL	76	3	13	16	235	....	....	....	....	....	....	....	....	....	13	0	0	0	55	....	....	....	....
1998-99	Albany River Rats	AHL	77	2	12	14	265	....	....	....	....	....	....	....	....	....	5	0	1	1	8	....	....	....	....
99-2000♦	**New Jersey**	**NHL**	**21**	**2**	**1**	**3**	**40**	**0**	**0**	**1**	**29**	**6.9**	**3**	**0**	**0.0**	**14:45**	**23**	**1**	**5**	**6**	**18**	**0**	**0**	**1**	**14:25**
	Albany River Rats	AHL	52	5	21	26	176	....	....	....	....	....	....	....	....	....	....	....	....	....	....	....	....	....	....
2000-01	**New Jersey**	**NHL**	**82**	**1**	**19**	**20**	**155**	**0**	**0**	**1**	**114**	**0.9**	**32**	**0**	**0.0**	**19:06**	**25**	**0**	**3**	**3**	**42**	**0**	**0**	**0**	**16:45**
2001-02	**New Jersey**	**NHL**	**73**	**2**	**3**	**5**	**133**	**0**	**0**	**0**	**81**	**2.5**	**6**	**0**	**0.0**	**20:06**	**6**	**0**	**0**	**0**	**2**	**0**	**0**	**0**	**21:50**
2002-03♦	**New Jersey**	**NHL**	**72**	**5**	**8**	**13**	**98**	**0**	**0**	**1**	**81**	**6.2**	**19**	**0**	**0.0**	**19:41**	**24**	**0**	**5**	**5**	**29**	**0**	**0**	**0**	**22:02**
2003-04	**New Jersey**	**NHL**	**75**	**2**	**11**	**13**	**96**	**0**	**0**	**0**	**61**	**3.3**	**10**	**0**	**0.0**	**21:02**	**5**	**0**	**0**	**0**	**4**	**0**	**0**	**0**	**19:40**
2004-05			DID NOT PLAY																						
2005-06	**New Jersey**	**NHL**	**73**	**3**	**14**	**17**	**91**	**1**	**0**	**1**	**60**	**5.0**	**–2**	**0**	**0.0**	**21:48**	**4**	**0**	**0**	**0**	**4**	**0**	**0**	**0**	**17:39**
2006-07	**New Jersey**	**NHL**	**69**	**0**	**8**	**8**	**69**	**0**	**0**	**0**	**47**	**0.0**	**–8**	**0**	**0.0**	**22:28**	**7**	**0**	**0**	**0**	**6**	**0**	**0**	**0**	**21:16**
	NHL Totals		**465**	**15**	**64**	**79**	**682**	**1**	**0**	**4**	**473**	**3.2**		**0**	**0.0**	**20:23**	**94**	**1**	**13**	**14**	**105**	**0**	**0**	**1**	**18:23**

QMJHL All-Rookie Team (1996) • NHL All-Rookie Team (2001)

WHITE, Ian

(WIGHT, EE-uhn) **TOR.**

Defense. Shoots right. 5'10", 185 lbs. Born, Steinbach, Man., June 4, 1984. Toronto's 6th choice, 191st overall, in 2002 Entry Draft.

Season	Club	League	GP	G	A	Pts	PIM	PP	SH	GW	S	%	+/-	TF	F%	Min	GP	G	A	Pts	PIM	PP	SH	GW	Min
99-2000	Eastman Selects	MAHA	32	29	33	62	36	....	....	....	....	....	....	....	....	....	....	....	....	....	....	....	....	....	....
2000-01	Swift Current	WHL	69	12	31	43	24	....	....	....	....	....	....	....	....	....	....	....	....	....	....	....	....	....	....
2001-02	Swift Current	WHL	70	32	47	79	40	....	....	....	....	....	....	....	....	....	12	4	5	9	12	....	....	....	....
2002-03	Swift Current	WHL	64	24	44	68	44	....	....	....	....	....	....	....	....	....	4	0	4	4	0	....	....	....	....
2003-04	Swift Current	WHL	43	9	23	32	32	....	....	....	....	....	....	....	....	....	5	1	3	4	8	....	....	....	....
	St. John's	AHL	8	0	4	4	2	....	....	....	....	....	....	....	....	....	....	....	....	....	....	....	....	....	....
2004-05	St. John's	AHL	78	4	22	26	54	....	....	....	....	....	....	....	....	....	5	0	2	2	2	....	....	....	....
2005-06	**Toronto**	**NHL**	**12**	**1**	**5**	**6**	**10**	**0**	**0**	**0**	**21**	**4.8**	**2**	**0**	**0.0**	**19:07**	....	....	....	....	....	....	....	....	....
	Toronto Marlies	AHL	59	7	30	37	42	....	....	....	....	....	....	....	....	....	5	1	4	5	4	....	....	....	....
2006-07	**Toronto**	**NHL**	**76**	**3**	**23**	**26**	**40**	**1**	**0**	**1**	**138**	**2.2**	**8**	**0**	**0.0**	**18:32**	....	....	....	....	....	....	....	....	....
	NHL Totals		**88**	**4**	**28**	**32**	**50**	**1**	**0**	**1**	**159**	**2.5**		**0**	**0.0**	**18:37**	....	....	....	....	....	....	....	....	....

WHL East Second All-Star Team (2002) • WHL East First All-Star Team (2003)

WHITE, Todd

(WIGHT, TAWD) **ATL.**

Center. Shoots left. 5'10", 195 lbs. Born, Kanata, Ont., May 21, 1975.

			Regular Season														Playoffs								
Season	Club	League	GP	G	A	Pts	PIM	PP	SH	GW	S	%	+/-	TF	F%	Min	GP	G	A	Pts	PIM	PP	SH	GW	Min
1990-91	Powassan	NOJHA	38	34	38	72	118	....	....	....	....	....	....	....	....	....	....	....	....	....	....	....	....	....	....
1991-92	Kanata Valley	CJHL	55	39	49	88	30	....	....	....	....	....	....	....	....	....	....	....	....	....	....	....	....	....	....
1992-93	Kanata Valley	CJHL	49	51	87	138	46	....	....	....	....	....	....	....	....	....	....	....	....	....	....	....	....	....	....
1993-94	Clarkson Knights	ECAC	33	10	12	22	28	....	....	....	....	....	....	....	....	....	....	....	....	....	....	....	....	....	....
1994-95	Clarkson Knights	ECAC	34	13	16	29	44	....	....	....	....	....	....	....	....	....	....	....	....	....	....	....	....	....	....
1995-96	Clarkson Knights	ECAC	38	29	43	72	36	....	....	....	....	....	....	....	....	....	....	....	....	....	....	....	....	....	....
1996-97	Clarkson Knights	ECAC	37	*38	*36	*74	22	....	....	....	....	....	....	....	....	....	....	....	....	....	....	....	....	....	....
1997-98	**Chicago**	**NHL**	7	1	0	1	2	0	0	0	3	33.3	0	....	....	....	....	....	....	....	....	....	....	....	....
	Indianapolis Ice	IHL	65	46	36	82	28	....	....	....	....	....	....	....	....	....	5	2	3	5	4	....	....	....	....
1998-99	**Chicago**	**NHL**	35	5	8	13	20	2	0	0	43	11.6	–1	452	46.0	13:39	....	....	....	....	....	....	....	....	....
	Chicago Wolves	IHL	25	11	13	24	8	....	....	....	....	....	....	....	....	....	10	1	4	5	8	....	....	....	....
99-2000	**Chicago**	**NHL**	1	0	0	0	0	0	0	0	0	0.0	0	9	55.6	13:02	....	....	....	....	....	....	....	....	....
	Cleveland	IHL	42	21	30	51	32	....	....	....	....	....	....	....	....	....	....	....	....	....	....	....	....	....	....
	Philadelphia	**NHL**	3	1	0	1	0	0	0	0	4	25.0	–1	25	40.0	10:29	....	....	....	....	....	....	....	....	....
	Philadelphia	AHL	32	19	24	43	12	....	....	....	....	....	....	....	....	....	5	2	1	3	8	....	....	....	....
2000-01	**Ottawa**	**NHL**	16	4	1	5	4	0	0	0	12	33.3	5	133	57.1	8:33	2	0	0	0	0	0	0	0	7:29
	Grand Rapids	IHL	64	22	32	54	20	....	....	....	....	....	....	....	....	....	10	4	4	8	10	....	....	....	....
2001-02	**Ottawa**	**NHL**	81	20	30	50	24	4	0	1	147	13.6	12	1508	50.5	18:22	12	2	2	4	6	0	0	0	18:57
2002-03	**Ottawa**	**NHL**	80	25	35	60	28	8	1	5	144	17.4	19	1396	50.5	17:58	18	5	1	6	6	1	1	2	16:59
2003-04	**Ottawa**	**NHL**	53	9	20	29	22	1	1	2	98	9.2	12	879	52.0	17:32	7	1	0	1	4	0	0	0	18:04
2004-05	Sodertalje SK	Sweden	1	0	1	1	4	....	....	....	....	....	....	....	....	....	....	....	....	....	....	....	....	....	....
2005-06	**Minnesota**	**NHL**	61	19	21	40	18	5	0	0	109	17.4	–1	886	49.1	17:12	....	....	....	....	....	....	....	....	....
2006-07	**Minnesota**	**NHL**	77	13	31	44	24	6	1	1	162	8.0	8	1051	49.2	17:13	4	0	0	0	0	0	0	0	14:18
	NHL Totals		**414**	**97**	**146**	**243**	**142**	**26**	**3**	**9**	**722**	**13.4**		**6339**	**50.1**	**16:55**	**43**	**8**	**3**	**11**	**16**	**1**	**1**	**2**	**17:01**

ECAC Second All-Star Team (1996) • NCAA East Second All-American Team (1996) • ECAC First All-Star Team (1997) • ECAC Player of the Year (1997) • NCAA East First All-American Team (1997) • Garry F. Longman Memorial Trophy (Rookie of the Year – IHL) (1998)

Signed as a free agent by **Chicago**, August 27, 1997. Traded to **Philadelphia** by **Chicago** for future considerations, January 26, 2000. Signed as a free agent by **Ottawa**, July 12, 2000. Signed as a free agent by **Sodertalje** (Sweden), December 21, 2004. Traded to **Minnesota** by **Ottawa** for Colorado's 4th round choice (previously acquired, Ottawa selected Cody Bass) in 2005 Entry Draft, July 30, 2005. Signed as a free agent by **Atlanta**, July 1, 2007.

WHITFIELD, Trent

(WHIHT-feeld, TREHNT) **ST.L.**

Center. Shoots left. 5'11", 209 lbs. Born, Estevan, Sask., June 17, 1977. Boston's 5th choice, 100th overall, in 1996 Entry Draft.

			Regular Season														Playoffs								
Season	Club	League	GP	G	A	Pts	PIM	PP	SH	GW	S	%	+/-	TF	F%	Min	GP	G	A	Pts	PIM	PP	SH	GW	Min
1993-94	Saskatoon Blazers	SMHL	36	26	22	48	42	....	....	....	....	....	....	....	....	....	....	....	....	....	....	....	....	....	....
	Spokane Chiefs	WHL	5	1	1	2	0	....	....	....	....	....	....	....	....	....	....	....	....	....	....	....	....	....	....
1994-95	Spokane Chiefs	WHL	48	8	17	25	26	....	....	....	....	....	....	....	....	....	11	7	6	13	5	....	....	....	....
1995-96	Spokane Chiefs	WHL	72	33	51	84	75	....	....	....	....	....	....	....	....	....	18	8	10	18	10	....	....	....	....
1996-97	Spokane Chiefs	WHL	58	34	42	76	74	....	....	....	....	....	....	....	....	....	9	5	7	12	10	....	....	....	....
1997-98	Spokane Chiefs	WHL	65	38	44	82	97	....	....	....	....	....	....	....	....	....	18	9	10	19	15	....	....	....	....
1998-99	Portland Pirates	AHL	50	10	8	18	20	....	....	....	....	....	....	....	....	....	....	....	....	....	....	....	....	....	....
	Hampton Roads	ECHL	19	13	12	25	12	....	....	....	....	....	....	....	....	....	4	2	0	2	14	....	....	....	....
99-2000	Portland Pirates	AHL	79	18	35	53	52	....	....	....	....	....	....	....	....	....	3	1	1	2	2	....	....	....	....
	Washington	**NHL**	....	....	....	....	....	....	....	....	....	....	....	....	....	....	3	0	0	0	0	0	0	0	5:47
2000-01	**Washington**	**NHL**	61	2	4	6	35	0	0	0	47	4.3	3	520	51.9	9:39	5	0	0	0	2	0	0	0	7:07
	Portland Pirates	AHL	19	9	11	20	27	....	....	....	....	....	....	....	....	....	....	....	....	....	....	....	....	....	....
2001-02	**Washington**	**NHL**	24	0	1	1	28	0	0	0	15	0.0	–3	189	54.0	7:06	....	....	....	....	....	....	....	....	....
	Portland Pirates	AHL	10	4	4	8	8	....	....	....	....	....	....	....	....	....	....	....	....	....	....	....	....	....	....
	NY Rangers	**NHL**	1	0	0	0	0	0	0	0	0	0.0	1	18	50.0	12:44	....	....	....	....	....	....	....	....	....
	Portland Pirates	AHL	24	10	16	26	16	....	....	....	....	....	....	....	....	....	....	....	....	....	....	....	....	....	....
2002-03	**Washington**	**NHL**	14	1	1	2	6	0	0	1	4	25.0	1	124	57.3	8:30	6	0	0	0	10	0	0	0	11:01
	Portland Pirates	AHL	64	27	34	61	42	....	....	....	....	....	....	....	....	....	....	....	....	....	....	....	....	....	....
2003-04	**Washington**	**NHL**	44	6	5	11	14	0	1	2	38	15.8	–2	598	55.4	12:48	....	....	....	....	....	....	....	....	....
	Portland Pirates	AHL	24	8	7	15	22	....	....	....	....	....	....	....	....	....	....	....	....	....	....	....	....	....	....
2004-05	Portland Pirates	AHL	67	17	38	55	75	....	....	....	....	....	....	....	....	....	....	....	....	....	....	....	....	....	....
2005-06	**St. Louis**	**NHL**	30	2	5	7	14	1	0	0	41	4.9	–3	330	54.6	11:56	....	....	....	....	....	....	....	....	....
	Peoria Rivermen	AHL	41	19	34	53	18	....	....	....	....	....	....	....	....	....	....	....	....	....	....	....	....	....	....
2006-07	Peoria Rivermen	AHL	79	33	45	78	70	....	....	....	....	....	....	....	....	....	....	....	....	....	....	....	....	....	....
	NHL Totals		**174**	**11**	**16**	**27**	**97**	**1**	**1**	**3**	**145**	**7.6**		**1779**	**54.1**	**10:25**	**14**	**0**	**0**	**0**	**12**	**0**	**0**	**0**	**8:30**

WHL West First All-Star Team (1997) • WHL West Second All-Star Team (1998)

Signed as a free agent by **Washington**, September 1, 1998. Claimed on waivers by **NY Rangers** from **Washington**, January 16, 2002. Claimed on waivers by **Washington** from **NY Rangers**, February 1, 2002. Signed as a free agent by **St. Louis**, August 2, 2005.

WHITNEY, Ray

(WHIHT-nee, RAY) **CAR.**

Left wing. Shoots right. 5'10", 180 lbs. Born, Fort Saskatchewan, Alta., May 8, 1972. San Jose's 2nd choice, 23rd overall, in 1991 Entry Draft.

			Regular Season														Playoffs								
Season	Club	League	GP	G	A	Pts	PIM	PP	SH	GW	S	%	+/-	TF	F%	Min	GP	G	A	Pts	PIM	PP	SH	GW	Min
1987-88	Ft. Saskatchewan	AMHL	71	80	155	235	119	....	....	....	....	....	....	....	....	....	....	....	....	....	....	....	....	....	....
1988-89	Spokane Chiefs	WHL	71	17	33	50	16	....	....	....	....	....	....	....	....	....	....	....	....	....	....	....	....	....	....
1989-90	Spokane Chiefs	WHL	71	57	56	113	50	....	....	....	....	....	....	....	....	....	6	3	4	7	6	....	....	....	....
1990-91	Spokane Chiefs	WHL	72	67	118	*185	36	....	....	....	....	....	....	....	....	....	15	13	18	*31	12	....	....	....	....
1991-92	Kolner EC	Germany	10	3	6	9	4	....	....	....	....	....	....	....	....	....	....	....	....	....	....	....	....	....	....
	Canada	Nat-Tm	5	1	0	1	6	....	....	....	....	....	....	....	....	....	....	....	....	....	....	....	....	....	....
	San Jose	**NHL**	2	0	3	3	0	0	0	0	4	0.0	–1	....	....	....	....	....	....	....	....	....	....	....	....
	San Diego Gulls	IHL	63	36	54	90	12	....	....	....	....	....	....	....	....	....	4	0	0	0	0	....	....	....	....
1992-93	**San Jose**	**NHL**	26	4	6	10	4	1	0	0	24	16.7	–14	....	....	....	....	....	....	....	....	....	....	....	....
	Kansas City	IHL	46	20	33	53	14	....	....	....	....	....	....	....	....	....	12	5	7	12	2	....	....	....	....
1993-94	**San Jose**	**NHL**	61	14	26	40	14	1	0	0	82	17.1	2	....	....	....	14	0	4	4	8	0	0	0	....
1994-95	**San Jose**	**NHL**	39	13	12	25	14	4	0	1	67	19.4	–7	....	....	....	11	4	4	8	2	0	0	1	....
1995-96	**San Jose**	**NHL**	60	17	24	41	16	4	2	2	106	16.0	–23	....	....	....	....	....	....	....	....	....	....	....	....
1996-97	**San Jose**	**NHL**	12	0	2	2	4	0	0	0	24	0.0	–6	....	....	....	....	....	....	....	....	....	....	....	....
	Kentucky	AHL	9	1	7	8	2	....	....	....	....	....	....	....	....	....	....	....	....	....	....	....	....	....	....
	Utah Grizzlies	IHL	43	13	35	48	34	....	....	....	....	....	....	....	....	....	7	3	1	4	6	....	....	....	....
1997-98	**Edmonton**	**NHL**	9	1	3	4	0	0	0	0	19	5.3	–1	....	....	....	....	....	....	....	....	....	....	....	....
	Florida	**NHL**	68	32	29	61	28	12	0	2	156	20.5	10	....	....	....	....	....	....	....	....	....	....	....	....
1998-99	**Florida**	**NHL**	81	26	38	64	18	7	0	6	193	13.5	–3	144	43.8	18:20	....	....	....	....	....	....	....	....	....
99-2000	**Florida**	**NHL**	81	29	42	71	35	5	0	3	198	14.6	16	198	49.0	18:41	4	1	0	1	4	0	0	0	18:13
2000-01	**Florida**	**NHL**	43	10	21	31	28	5	0	0	117	8.5	–16	38	39.5	17:41	....	....	....	....	....	....	....	....	....
	Columbus	**NHL**	3	0	3	3	2	0	0	0	3	0.0	–1	19	36.8	20:17	....	....	....	....	....	....	....	....	....
2001-02	**Columbus**	**NHL**	67	21	40	61	12	6	0	3	210	10.0	–22	21	47.6	20:13	....	....	....	....	....	....	....	....	....
2002-03	**Columbus**	**NHL**	81	24	52	76	22	8	2	2	235	10.2	–26	29	44.8	21:00	....	....	....	....	....	....	....	....	....
2003-04	**Detroit**	**NHL**	67	14	29	43	22	3	1	4	119	11.8	7	18	38.9	16:24	12	1	3	4	4	0	0	1	11:56
2004-05			DID NOT PLAY																						
2005-06 ♦	**Carolina**	**NHL**	63	17	38	55	42	12	0	2	147	11.6	0	13	38.5	17:11	24	9	6	15	14	5	0	1	14:07
2006-07	**Carolina**	**NHL**	81	32	51	83	46	6	0	6	215	14.9	–5	7	28.6	18:42	....	....	....	....	....	....	....	....	....
	NHL Totals		**844**	**254**	**419**	**673**	**307**	**74**	**5**	**31**	**1919**	**13.2**		**487**	**45.0**	**18:39**	**65**	**15**	**17**	**32**	**32**	**5**	**0**	**3**	**13:52**

WHL West First All-Star Team (1991) • WHL Player of the Year (1991) • Memorial Cup Tournament All-Star Team (1991) • George Parsons Trophy (Memorial Cup Tournament Most Sportsmanlike Player) (1991)

Played in NHL All-Star Game (2000, 2003)

Signed as a free agent by **Edmonton**, October 1, 1997. Claimed on waivers by **Florida** from **Edmonton**, November 6, 1997. Traded to **Columbus** by **Florida** with future considerations for Kevyn Adams and Columbus's 4th round choice (Michael Woodford) in 2001 Entry Draft, March 13, 2001. Signed as a free agent by **Detroit**, July 30, 2003. Signed as a free agent by **Carolina**, August 7, 2005.

			Regular Season														Playoffs								
Season	Club	League	GP	G	A	Pts	PIM	PP	SH	GW	S	%	+/-	TF	F%	Min	GP	G	A	Pts	PIM	PP	SH	GW	Min

WHITNEY, Ryan (WHIHT-nee, RIGH-uhn) **PIT.**

Defense. Shoots left. 6'4", 219 lbs. Born, Boston, MA, February 19, 1983. Pittsburgh's 1st choice, 5th overall, in 2002 Entry Draft.

Season	Club	League	GP	G	A	Pts	PIM	PP	SH	GW	S	%	+/-	TF	F%	Min	GP	G	A	Pts	PIM	PP	SH	GW	Min
99-2000	Thayer Academy	High-MA	22	5	33	38	....	....	....	....	....	....	....	....	....	....	....	....	....	....	....	....	....	....	....
2000-01	USNTDP	U-18	40	7	23	30	64	....	....	....	....	....	....	....	....	....	....	....	....	....	....	....	....	....	....
	USNTDP	USHL	20	2	8	10	22	....	....	....	....	....	....	....	....	....	....	....	....	....	....	....	....	....	....
2001-02	Boston University	H-East	35	4	17	21	46	....	....	....	....	....	....	....	....	....	....	....	....	....	....	....	....	....	....
2002-03	Boston University	H-East	34	3	10	13	48	....	....	....	....	....	....	....	....	....	....	....	....	....	....	....	....	....	....
2003-04	Boston University	H-East	38	9	16	25	56	....	....	....	....	....	....	....	....	....	....	....	....	....	....	....	....	....	....
	Wilkes-Barre	AHL	....	....	....	....	....	....	....	....	....	....	....	....	....	....	20	1	9	10	6	....	....	....	....
2004-05	Wilkes-Barre	AHL	80	6	35	41	101	....	....	....	....	....	....	....	....	....	11	2	7	9	12	....	....	....	....
2005-06	**Pittsburgh**	**NHL**	**68**	**6**	**32**	**38**	**85**	**2**	**0**	**1**	**113**	**5.3**	**–7**	**1**	**0.0**	**23:50**	....	....	....	....	....	....	....	....	....
	Wilkes-Barre	AHL	9	5	9	14	6	....	....	....	....	....	....	....	....	....	11	1	4	5	8	....	....	....	....
2006-07	**Pittsburgh**	**NHL**	**81**	**14**	**45**	**59**	**77**	**9**	**0**	**2**	**129**	**10.9**	**9**	**5**	**20.0**	**23:56**	**5**	**1**	**1**	**2**	**6**	**1**	**0**	**0**	**22:51**
	NHL Totals		**149**	**20**	**77**	**97**	**162**	**11**	**0**	**3**	**242**	**8.3**		**6**	**16.7**	**23:53**	**5**	**1**	**1**	**2**	**6**	**1**	**0**	**0**	**22:51**

Hockey East All-Rookie Team (2002)

WIDEMAN, Dennis (WIGHD-muhn, DEH-nihs) **BOS.**

Defense. Shoots right. 6', 208 lbs. Born, Kitchener, Ont., March 20, 1983. Buffalo's 9th choice, 241st overall, in 2002 Entry Draft.

Season	Club	League	GP	G	A	Pts	PIM	PP	SH	GW	S	%	+/-	TF	F%	Min	GP	G	A	Pts	PIM	PP	SH	GW	Min
1998-99	Elmira	OHA-B	47	18	30	48	142	....	....	....	....	....	....	....	....	....	....	....	....	....	....	....	....	....	....
99-2000	Sudbury Wolves	OHL	63	10	26	36	64	....	....	....	....	....	....	....	....	....	12	1	2	3	22	....	....	....	....
2000-01	Sudbury Wolves	OHL	25	7	11	18	37	....	....	....	....	....	....	....	....	....	....	....	....	....	....	....	....	....	....
	London Knights	OHL	24	8	8	16	38	....	....	....	....	....	....	....	....	....	5	0	4	4	6	....	....	....	....
2001-02	London Knights	OHL	65	27	42	69	141	....	....	....	....	....	....	....	....	....	12	4	9	13	26	....	....	....	....
2002-03	London Knights	OHL	55	20	27	47	83	....	....	....	....	....	....	....	....	....	14	6	6	12	10	....	....	....	....
2003-04	London Knights	OHL	60	24	41	65	85	....	....	....	....	....	....	....	....	....	15	7	10	17	17	....	....	....	....
2004-05	Worcester IceCats	AHL	79	13	30	43	65	....	....	....	....	....	....	....	....	....	....	....	....	....	....	....	....	....	....
2005-06	**St. Louis**	**NHL**	**67**	**8**	**16**	**24**	**83**	**5**	**1**	**1**	**150**	**5.3**	**–31**	**1**	**0.0**	**21:41**	....	....	....	....	....	....	....	....	....
	Peoria Rivermen	AHL	12	2	4	6	31	....	....	....	....	....	....	....	....	....	....	....	....	....	....	....	....	....	....
2006-07	**St. Louis**	**NHL**	**55**	**5**	**17**	**22**	**44**	**4**	**0**	**1**	**94**	**5.3**	**–7**	**0**	**0.0**	**20:12**	....	....	....	....	....	....	....	....	....
	Boston	**NHL**	**20**	**1**	**2**	**3**	**27**	**0**	**0**	**0**	**28**	**3.6**	**–3**	**1**	**0.0**	**17:20**	....	....	....	....	....	....	....	....	....
	NHL Totals		**142**	**14**	**35**	**49**	**154**	**9**	**1**	**2**	**272**	**5.1**		**2**	**0.0**	**20:30**	....	....	....	....	....	....	....	....	....

OHL First All-Star Team (2004)

Signed as a free agent by **St. Louis**, June 30, 2004. Traded to **Boston** by **St. Louis** for Brad Boyes, February 27, 2007.

WILLIAMS, Jason (WIHL-yuhms, JAY-suhn) **CHI.**

Center. Shoots right. 5'11", 194 lbs. Born, London, Ont., August 11, 1980.

Season	Club	League	GP	G	A	Pts	PIM	PP	SH	GW	S	%	+/-	TF	F%	Min	GP	G	A	Pts	PIM	PP	SH	GW	Min
1995-96	Mount Brydges	OHA-D	36	31	28	59	18	....	....	....	....	....	....	....	....	....	....	....	....	....	....	....	....	....	....
1996-97	Peterborough	OHL	60	4	8	12	8	....	....	....	....	....	....	....	....	....	10	1	0	1	2	....	....	....	....
1997-98	Peterborough	OHL	55	8	27	35	31	....	....	....	....	....	....	....	....	....	4	0	1	1	2	....	....	....	....
1998-99	Peterborough	OHL	68	26	48	74	42	....	....	....	....	....	....	....	....	....	5	1	2	3	2	....	....	....	....
99-2000	Peterborough	OHL	66	36	37	75	64	....	....	....	....	....	....	....	....	....	5	2	1	3	2	....	....	....	....
2000-01	**Detroit**	**NHL**	**5**	**0**	**3**	**3**	**2**	**0**	**0**	**0**	**7**	**0.0**	**1**	**56**	**39.3**	**12:24**	**2**	**0**	**0**	**0**	**0**	**0**	**0**	**0**	**11:45**
	Cincinnati	AHL	76	24	45	69	48	....	....	....	....	....	....	....	....	....	1	0	0	0	2	....	....	....	....
2001-02 ♦	**Detroit**	**NHL**	**25**	**8**	**2**	**10**	**4**	**4**	**0**	**0**	**32**	**25.0**	**2**	**208**	**47.6**	**10:50**	**9**	**0**	**0**	**0**	**2**	**0**	**0**	**0**	**6:12**
	Cincinnati	AHL	52	23	27	50	27	....	....	....	....	....	....	....	....	....	3	0	1	1	6	....	....	....	....
2002-03	**Detroit**	**NHL**	**16**	**3**	**3**	**6**	**2**	**1**	**0**	**0**	**20**	**15.0**	**3**	**78**	**51.3**	**10:43**	....	....	....	....	....	....	....	....	....
	Grand Rapids	AHL	45	23	22	45	18	....	....	....	....	....	....	....	....	....	15	1	7	8	16	....	....	....	....
2003-04	**Detroit**	**NHL**	**49**	**6**	**7**	**13**	**15**	**0**	**0**	**0**	**44**	**13.6**	**1**	**315**	**49.2**	**9:27**	**3**	**0**	**0**	**0**	**2**	**0**	**0**	**0**	**6:11**
2004-05	Assat Pori	Finland	43	26	17	43	52	....	....	....	....	....	....	....	....	....	2	1	1	2	4	....	....	....	....
2005-06	**Detroit**	**NHL**	**80**	**21**	**37**	**58**	**26**	**6**	**0**	**4**	**177**	**11.9**	**4**	**29**	**55.2**	**14:55**	**6**	**1**	**1**	**2**	**6**	**0**	**0**	**0**	**18:10**
2006-07	**Detroit**	**NHL**	**58**	**11**	**15**	**26**	**24**	**3**	**0**	**2**	**111**	**9.9**	**7**	**11**	**45.5**	**14:26**	....	....	....	....	....	....	....	....	....
	Chicago	**NHL**	**20**	**4**	**2**	**6**	**20**	**2**	**1**	**0**	**38**	**10.5**	**–6**	**193**	**42.5**	**18:17**	....	....	....	....	....	....	....	....	....
	NHL Totals		**253**	**53**	**69**	**122**	**93**	**16**	**1**	**6**	**429**	**12.4**		**890**	**47.1**	**13:18**	**20**	**1**	**1**	**2**	**10**	**0**	**0**	**0**	**10:20**

Signed as a free agent by **Detroit**, September 18, 2000. Signed as a free agent by **Pori** (Finland), October 18, 2004. Traded to **Chicago** by **Detroit** for Kyle Calder, February 26, 2007.

WILLIAMS, Jeremy (WIHL-yuhms, JAIR-eh-mee) **TOR.**

Center. Shoots right. 5'11", 188 lbs. Born, Regina, Sask., January 26, 1984. Toronto's 5th choice, 220th overall, in 2003 Entry Draft.

Season	Club	League	GP	G	A	Pts	PIM	PP	SH	GW	S	%	+/-	TF	F%	Min	GP	G	A	Pts	PIM	PP	SH	GW	Min
2001-02	Swift Current	SMMHL	24	18	23	41	64	....	....	....	....	....	....	....	....	....	....	....	....	....	....	....	....	....	....
	Swift Current	WHL	32	6	7	13	30	....	....	....	....	....	....	....	....	....	12	1	0	1	4	....	....	....	....
2002-03	Swift Current	WHL	72	41	52	93	117	....	....	....	....	....	....	....	....	....	4	1	0	1	6	....	....	....	....
2003-04	St. John's	AHL	4	0	2	2	0	....	....	....	....	....	....	....	....	....	....	....	....	....	....	....	....	....	....
	Swift Current	WHL	68	*52	49	101	82	....	....	....	....	....	....	....	....	....	5	2	1	3	12	....	....	....	....
2004-05	St. John's	AHL	75	16	20	36	24	....	....	....	....	....	....	....	....	....	5	0	0	0	0	....	....	....	....
2005-06	**Toronto**	**NHL**	**1**	**1**	**0**	**1**	**0**	**0**	**0**	**0**	**1**	**100.0**	**0**	**0**	**0.0**	**9:31**	....	....	....	....	....	....	....	....	....
	Toronto Marlies	AHL	55	23	33	56	62	....	....	....	....	....	....	....	....	....	5	1	0	1	6	....	....	....	....
2006-07	**Toronto**	**NHL**	**1**	**1**	**0**	**1**	**0**	**0**	**0**	**0**	**3**	**33.3**	**1**	**1**	**0.0**	**7:18**	....	....	....	....	....	....	....	....	....
	Toronto Marlies	AHL	23	6	9	15	27	....	....	....	....	....	....	....	....	....	....	....	....	....	....	....	....	....	....
	NHL Totals		**2**	**2**	**0**	**2**	**0**	**0**	**0**	**0**	**4**	**50.0**		**1**	**0.0**	**8:25**	....	....	....	....	....	....	....	....	....

WHL East First All-Star Team (2004) • Canadian Major Junior First All-Star Team (2004)

• Only player in NHL history to play in just two games and score a goal in both.

WILLIAMS, Justin (WIHL-yuhms, JUHS-tihn) **CAR.**

Right wing. Shoots right. 6'1", 195 lbs. Born, Cobourg, Ont., October 4, 1981. Philadelphia's 1st choice, 28th overall, in 2000 Entry Draft.

Season	Club	League	GP	G	A	Pts	PIM	PP	SH	GW	S	%	+/-	TF	F%	Min	GP	G	A	Pts	PIM	PP	SH	GW	Min
1997-98	Colborne Colts	OHA-C	36	32	35	67	26	....	....	....	....	....	....	....	....	....	....	....	....	....	....	....	....	....	....
	Cobourg Cougars	OPJHL	17	0	3	3	5	....	....	....	....	....	....	....	....	....	....	....	....	....	....	....	....	....	....
1998-99	Plymouth Whalers	OHL	47	4	8	12	28	....	....	....	....	....	....	....	....	....	7	1	2	3	0	....	....	....	....
99-2000	Plymouth Whalers	OHL	68	37	46	83	46	....	....	....	....	....	....	....	....	....	23	*14	16	*30	10	....	....	....	....
2000-01	**Philadelphia**	**NHL**	**63**	**12**	**13**	**25**	**22**	**0**	**0**	**0**	**99**	**12.1**	**6**	**13**	**53.9**	**12:31**	....	....	....	....	....	....	....	....	....
2001-02	**Philadelphia**	**NHL**	**75**	**17**	**23**	**40**	**32**	**0**	**0**	**1**	**162**	**10.5**	**11**	**16**	**25.0**	**14:27**	**5**	**0**	**0**	**0**	**4**	**0**	**0**	**0**	**16:42**
2002-03	**Philadelphia**	**NHL**	**41**	**8**	**16**	**24**	**22**	**0**	**0**	**2**	**105**	**7.6**	**15**	**16**	**50.0**	**15:57**	**12**	**1**	**5**	**6**	**8**	**0**	**0**	**1**	**14:11**
2003-04	**Philadelphia**	**NHL**	**47**	**6**	**20**	**26**	**32**	**3**	**0**	**1**	**107**	**5.6**	**10**	**38**	**31.6**	**15:30**	....	....	....	....	....	....	....	....	....
	Carolina	**NHL**	**32**	**5**	**13**	**18**	**32**	**1**	**0**	**0**	**96**	**5.2**	**2**	**25**	**36.0**	**18:52**	....	....	....	....	....	....	....	....	....
2004-05	Lulea HF	Sweden	49	14	18	32	61	....	....	....	....	....	....	....	....	....	4	0	1	1	29	....	....	....	....
2005-06 ♦	**Carolina**	**NHL**	**82**	**31**	**45**	**76**	**60**	**8**	**4**	**4**	**255**	**12.2**	**1**	**17**	**29.4**	**21:08**	**25**	**7**	**11**	**18**	**34**	**0**	**1**	**1**	**21:36**
2006-07	**Carolina**	**NHL**	**82**	**33**	**34**	**67**	**73**	**12**	**2**	**8**	**258**	**12.8**	**–11**	**24**	**37.5**	**20:51**	....	....	....	....	....	....	....	....	....
	NHL Totals		**422**	**112**	**164**	**276**	**273**	**24**	**6**	**16**	**1082**	**10.4**		**149**	**36.2**	**17:18**	**42**	**8**	**16**	**24**	**46**	**0**	**1**	**2**	**18:54**

Played in NHL All-Star Game (2007)

• Missed majority of 2002-03 season recovering from shoulder (November 15, 2002 vs. Carolina) and knee (January 18, 2003 vs. Tampa Bay) injuries. Traded to **Carolina** by **Philadelphia** for Danny Markov, January 20, 2004. Signed as a free agent by **Lulea** (Sweden), September 21, 2004.

WILLIS, Shane (WIH-lihs, SHAYN) **NSH.**

Right wing. Shoots right. 6'1", 195 lbs. Born, Edmonton, Alta., June 13, 1977. Carolina's 4th choice, 88th overall, in 1997 Entry Draft.

Season	Club	League	GP	G	A	Pts	PIM	PP	SH	GW	S	%	+/-	TF	F%	Min	GP	G	A	Pts	PIM	PP	SH	GW	Min
1992-93	Red Deer	ABHL	36	32	18	50	88	....	....	....	....	....	....	....	....	....	....	....	....	....	....	....	....	....	....
1993-94	Red Deer Royals	AMHL	34	40	26	66	103	....	....	....	....	....	....	....	....	....	....	....	....	....	....	....	....	....	....
1994-95	Prince Albert	WHL	65	24	19	43	38	....	....	....	....	....	....	....	....	....	13	3	4	7	6	....	....	....	....
1995-96	Prince Albert	WHL	69	41	40	81	47	....	....	....	....	....	....	....	....	....	18	11	10	21	18	....	....	....	....
1996-97	Prince Albert	WHL	41	34	22	56	63	....	....	....	....	....	....	....	....	....	....	....	....	....	....	....	....	....	....
	Lethbridge	WHL	26	22	17	39	24	....	....	....	....	....	....	....	....	....	19	13	11	24	20	....	....	....	....
1997-98	Lethbridge	WHL	64	58	54	112	73	....	....	....	....	....	....	....	....	....	4	2	3	5	6	....	....	....	....
	New Haven	AHL	1	0	1	1	2	....	....	....	....	....	....	....	....	....	....	....	....	....	....	....	....	....	....
1998-99	**Carolina**	**NHL**	**7**	**0**	**0**	**0**	**0**	**0**	**0**	**0**	**1**	**0.0**	**–2**	**0**	**0.0**	**2:14**	....	....	....	....	....	....	....	....	....
	New Haven	AHL	73	31	50	81	49	....	....	....	....	....	....	....	....	....	....	....	....	....	....	....	....	....	....

			Regular Season														Playoffs								
Season	Club	League	GP	G	A	Pts	PIM	PP	SH	GW	S	%	+/-	TF	F%	Min	GP	G	A	Pts	PIM	PP	SH	GW	Min
99-2000	Carolina	NHL	2	0	0	0	0	0	0	0	1	0.0	–1	0	0.0	5:50	....	....	....	....	....	....	....	....	....
	Cincinnati	IHL	80	35	25	60	64	....	....	....	....	....	....	....	....	....	11	5	3	8	8	....	....	....	....
2000-01	Carolina	NHL	73	20	24	44	45	9	0	6	172	11.6	–6	10	20.0	15:58	2	0	0	0	0	0	0	0	12:56
2001-02	Carolina	NHL	59	7	10	17	24	2	0	0	126	5.6	–8	10	50.0	13:00	....	....	....	....	....	....	....	....	....
	Tampa Bay	NHL	21	4	3	7	6	0	0	0	29	13.8	0	12	8.3	11:18	....	....	....	....	....	....	....	....	....
2002-03	Springfield	AHL	56	16	16	32	26	....	....	....	....	....	....	....	....	....	6	4	2	6	4	....	....	....	....
2003-04	Tampa Bay	NHL	12	0	6	6	2	0	0	0	27	0.0	1	2	0.0	13:50	....	....	....	....	....	....	....	....	....
	Hershey Bears	AHL	55	27	21	48	71	....	....	....	....	....	....	....	....	....	....	....	....	....	....	....	....	....	....
2004-05	Springfield	AHL	58	18	16	34	29	....	....	....	....	....	....	....	....	....	....	....	....	....	....	....	....	....	....
2005-06	HC Davos	Swiss	32	5	15	20	53	....	....	....	....	....	....	....	....	....	....	....	....	....	....	....	....	....	....
	Linkopings HC	Sweden	6	0	1	1	4	....	....	....	....	....	....	....	....	....	13	6	5	11	10	....	....	....	....
2006-07	Albany River Rats	AHL	43	20	23	43	23	....	....	....	....	....	....	....	....	....	5	3	1	4	0	....	....	....	....
	NHL Totals		174	31	43	74	77	11	0	6	356	8.7		34	23.5	13:35	2	0	0	0	0	0	0	0	12:56

• Re-entered NHL Entry Draft. Originally Tampa Bay's 3rd choice, 56th overall, in 1995 Entry Draft.

WHL East First All-Star Team (1997, 1998) • AHL All-Rookie Team (1999) • AHL First All-Star Team (1999) • Dudley "Red" Garrett Memorial Award (Rookie of the Year – AHL) (1999) • NHL All-Rookie Team (2001)

Traded to **Tampa Bay** by **Carolina** with Chris Dingman for Kevin Weekes, March 5, 2002. Signed as a free agent by **Davos** (Swiss). August 23, 2005. Signed as a free agent by **Carolina**, July 18, 2006. Signed as a free agent by **Nashville**, July 5, 2007.

WILLSIE, Brian

(WIHL-see, BRIGH-uhn) **L.A.**

Right wing. Shoots right. 6'1", 202 lbs. Born, London, Ont., March 16, 1978. Colorado's 7th choice, 146th overall, in 1996 Entry Draft.

Season	Club	League	GP	G	A	Pts	PIM	PP	SH	GW	S	%	+/-	TF	F%	Min	GP	G	A	Pts	PIM	PP	SH	GW	Min
1993-94	Belmont Bombers	OHA-D	13	9	5	14	14	....	....	....	....	....	....	....	....	....	....	....	....	....	....	....	....	....	....
1994-95	St. Thomas Stars	OHA-B	45	35	47	82	47	....	....	....	....	....	....	....	....	....	....	....	....	....	....	....	....	....	....
1995-96	Guelph Storm	OHL	65	13	21	34	18	....	....	....	....	....	....	....	....	....	16	4	2	6	6	....	....	....	....
1996-97	Guelph Storm	OHL	64	37	31	68	37	....	....	....	....	....	....	....	....	....	18	15	4	19	10	....	....	....	....
1997-98	Guelph Storm	OHL	57	45	31	76	41	....	....	....	....	....	....	....	....	....	12	9	5	14	18	....	....	....	....
1998-99	Hershey Bears	AHL	72	19	10	29	28	....	....	....	....	....	....	....	....	....	3	1	0	1	0	....	....	....	....
99-2000	Colorado	NHL	1	0	0	0	0	0	0	0	1	0.0	0	0	0.0	8:16	....	....	....	....	....	....	....	....	....
	Hershey Bears	AHL	78	20	39	59	44	....	....	....	....	....	....	....	....	....	12	2	6	8	8	....	....	....	....
2000-01	Hershey Bears	AHL	48	18	23	41	20	....	....	....	....	....	....	....	....	....	12	7	2	9	14	....	....	....	....
2001-02	Colorado	NHL	56	7	7	14	14	2	0	1	66	10.6	4	8	12.5	11:24	4	0	1	1	2	0	0	0	11:54
2002-03	Colorado	NHL	12	0	1	1	15	0	0	0	12	0.0	0	7	14.3	9:36	6	1	0	1	2	0	0	1	10:48
	Hershey Bears	AHL	59	29	28	57	49	....	....	....	....	....	....	....	....	....	....	....	....	....	....	....	....	....	....
2003-04	Washington	NHL	49	10	5	15	18	1	1	1	85	11.8	–7	46	34.8	12:42	....	....	....	....	....	....	....	....	....
2004-05	Ljubljana	Interliga	12	7	6	13	34	....	....	....	....	....	....	....	....	....	....	....	....	....	....	....	....	....	....
	Ljubljana	Slovenia	2	0	3	3	4	....	....	....	....	....	....	....	....	....	....	....	....	....	....	....	....	....	....
	Portland Pirates	AHL	53	23	17	40	47	....	....	....	....	....	....	....	....	....	....	....	....	....	....	....	....	....	....
2005-06	Washington	NHL	82	19	22	41	77	8	1	2	185	10.3	–19	52	51.9	16:40	....	....	....	....	....	....	....	....	....
2006-07	Los Angeles	NHL	81	11	10	21	49	2	0	1	131	8.4	–20	201	45.3	13:23	....	....	....	....	....	....	....	....	....
	NHL Totals		281	47	45	92	173	13	2	5	480	9.8		314	43.3	13:39	10	1	1	2	4	0	0	1	11:14

OHL First All-Star Team (1998)

Claimed by **Washington** from **Colorado** in Waiver Draft, October 3, 2003. Signed as a free agent by **Ljubljana** (Slovenia), October 8, 2004. Signed as a free agent by **Portland** (AHL), December 15, 2004. Signed as a free agent by **Los Angeles**, July 4, 2006.

WILM, Clarke

(WIHLM, KLAHRK)

Center. Shoots left. 6', 202 lbs. Born, Central Butte, Sask., October 24, 1976. Calgary's 5th choice, 150th overall, in 1995 Entry Draft.

Season	Club	League	GP	G	A	Pts	PIM	PP	SH	GW	S	%	+/-	TF	F%	Min	GP	G	A	Pts	PIM	PP	SH	GW	Min
1991-92	Saskatoon Blazers	SMHL	36	18	28	46	16	....	....	....	....	....	....	....	....	....	....	....	....	....	....	....	....	....	....
	Saskatoon Blades	WHL	....	....	....	....	....	....	....	....	....	....	....	....	....	....	1	0	0	0	0	....	....	....	....
1992-93	Saskatoon Blades	WHL	69	14	19	33	71	....	....	....	....	....	....	....	....	....	9	4	2	6	13	....	....	....	....
1993-94	Saskatoon Blades	WHL	70	18	32	50	181	....	....	....	....	....	....	....	....	....	16	0	9	9	19	....	....	....	....
1994-95	Saskatoon Blades	WHL	71	20	39	59	179	....	....	....	....	....	....	....	....	....	10	6	1	7	21	....	....	....	....
1995-96	Saskatoon Blades	WHL	72	49	61	110	83	....	....	....	....	....	....	....	....	....	4	1	1	2	4	....	....	....	....
1996-97	Saint John Flames	AHL	62	9	19	28	107	....	....	....	....	....	....	....	....	....	5	2	0	2	15	....	....	....	....
1997-98	Saint John Flames	AHL	68	13	26	39	112	....	....	....	....	....	....	....	....	....	21	5	9	14	8	....	....	....	....
1998-99	Calgary	NHL	78	10	8	18	53	2	2	0	94	10.6	11	609	40.9	11:32	....	....	....	....	....	....	....	....	....
99-2000	Calgary	NHL	78	10	12	22	67	1	3	0	81	12.3	–6	872	44.4	12:38	....	....	....	....	....	....	....	....	....
2000-01	Calgary	NHL	81	7	8	15	69	2	0	0	85	8.2	–11	992	51.9	14:11	....	....	....	....	....	....	....	....	....
2001-02	Calgary	NHL	66	4	14	18	61	0	1	0	83	4.8	–1	995	51.1	15:00	....	....	....	....	....	....	....	....	....
2002-03	Nashville	NHL	82	5	11	16	36	0	0	0	108	4.6	–11	339	50.4	11:58	....	....	....	....	....	....	....	....	....
2003-04	Toronto	NHL	10	0	0	0	7	0	0	0	10	0.0	0	43	46.5	11:45	5	0	1	1	2	0	0	0	12:45
	St. John's	AHL	47	16	17	33	97	....	....	....	....	....	....	....	....	....	....	....	....	....	....	....	....	....	....
2004-05	St. John's	AHL	69	11	16	27	145	....	....	....	....	....	....	....	....	....	5	2	2	4	8	....	....	....	....
2005-06	Toronto	NHL	60	1	7	8	43	0	0	0	50	2.0	–15	694	52.3	11:47	....	....	....	....	....	....	....	....	....
2006-07	Jokerit Helsinki	Finland	40	13	14	27	38	....	....	....	....	....	....	....	....	....	10	2	8	10	14	....	....	....	....
	NHL Totals		455	37	60	97	336	5	6	0	511	7.2		4544	48.7	12:49	5	0	1	1	2	0	0	0	12:45

Signed as a free agent by **Nashville**, July 11, 2002. Signed as a free agent by **Toronto**, October 28, 2003. Signed as a free agent by **Jokerit Helsinki** (Finland), October 26, 2006.

WINCHESTER, Brad

(WIHN-chehst-uhr, BRAD) **DAL.**

Center/left wing. Shoots left. 6'5", 230 lbs. Born, Madison, WI, March 1, 1981. Edmonton's 2nd choice, 35th overall, in 2000 Entry Draft.

Season	Club	League	GP	G	A	Pts	PIM	PP	SH	GW	S	%	+/-	TF	F%	Min	GP	G	A	Pts	PIM	PP	SH	GW	Min
1997-98	USNTDP	U-17	24	8	5	13	64	....	....	....	....	....	....	....	....	....	....	....	....	....	....	....	....	....	....
	USNTDP	USHL	5	2	1	3	6	....	....	....	....	....	....	....	....	....	....	....	....	....	....	....	....	....	....
	USNTDP	NAHL	40	11	17	28	84	....	....	....	....	....	....	....	....	....	5	1	0	1	8	....	....	....	....
1998-99	USNTDP	U-18	6	0	3	3	6	....	....	....	....	....	....	....	....	....	....	....	....	....	....	....	....	....	....
	USNTDP	USHL	48	14	23	37	103	....	....	....	....	....	....	....	....	....	....	....	....	....	....	....	....	....	....
99-2000	U. of Wisconsin	WCHA	33	9	9	18	48	....	....	....	....	....	....	....	....	....	....	....	....	....	....	....	....	....	....
2000-01	U. of Wisconsin	WCHA	41	7	9	16	71	....	....	....	....	....	....	....	....	....	....	....	....	....	....	....	....	....	....
2001-02	U. of Wisconsin	WCHA	38	14	20	34	38	....	....	....	....	....	....	....	....	....	....	....	....	....	....	....	....	....	....
2002-03	U. of Wisconsin	WCHA	38	10	6	16	58	....	....	....	....	....	....	....	....	....	....	....	....	....	....	....	....	....	....
2003-04	Toronto	AHL	65	13	6	19	85	....	....	....	....	....	....	....	....	....	3	0	0	0	2	....	....	....	....
2004-05	Edmonton	AHL	76	22	18	40	143	....	....	....	....	....	....	....	....	....	....	....	....	....	....	....	....	....	....
2005-06	Edmonton	NHL	19	0	1	1	21	0	0	0	19	0.0	–2	2	100.0	6:05	10	1	2	3	4	0	0	1	9:14
	Hamilton	AHL	40	26	14	40	118	....	....	....	....	....	....	....	....	....	....	....	....	....	....	....	....	....	....
2006-07	Edmonton	NHL	59	4	5	9	86	0	0	0	66	6.1	–10	3	33.3	8:04	....	....	....	....	....	....	....	....	....
	NHL Totals		78	4	6	10	107	0	0	0	85	4.7		5	60.0	7:35	10	1	2	3	4	0	0	1	9:14

Signed as a free agent by **Dallas**, July 6, 2007.

WISEMAN, Chad

(WIGHZ-man, CHAD)

Left wing. Shoots left. 6', 205 lbs. Born, Burlington, Ont., March 25, 1981. San Jose's 8th choice, 246th overall, in 2000 Entry Draft.

Season	Club	League	GP	G	A	Pts	PIM	PP	SH	GW	S	%	+/-	TF	F%	Min	GP	G	A	Pts	PIM	PP	SH	GW	Min
1997-98	Burlington	OPJHL	50	28	36	64	31	....	....	....	....	....	....	....	....	....	....	....	....	....	....	....	....	....	....
1998-99	Mississauga	OHL	64	11	25	36	29	....	....	....	....	....	....	....	....	....	....	....	....	....	....	....	....	....	....
99-2000	Mississauga	OHL	68	23	45	68	53	....	....	....	....	....	....	....	....	....	....	....	....	....	....	....	....	....	....
2000-01	Mississauga	OHL	30	15	29	44	22	....	....	....	....	....	....	....	....	....	....	....	....	....	....	....	....	....	....
	Plymouth Whalers	OHL	32	11	16	27	12	....	....	....	....	....	....	....	....	....	19	12	8	20	22	....	....	....	....
2001-02	Cleveland Barons	AHL	76	21	29	50	61	....	....	....	....	....	....	....	....	....	....	....	....	....	....	....	....	....	....
2002-03	San Jose	NHL	4	0	0	0	4	0	0	0	1	0.0	–2	0	0.0	9:19	....	....	....	....	....	....	....	....	....
	Cleveland Barons	AHL	77	17	35	52	44	....	....	....	....	....	....	....	....	....	....	....	....	....	....	....	....	....	....
2003-04	NY Rangers	NHL	4	1	0	1	0	0	0	0	3	33.3	–1	0	0.0	8:49	....	....	....	....	....	....	....	....	....
	Hartford	AHL	62	25	27	52	45	....	....	....	....	....	....	....	....	....	15	5	6	11	12	....	....	....	....
2004-05	Hartford	AHL	60	17	16	33	74	....	....	....	....	....	....	....	....	....	6	1	1	2	6	....	....	....	....
2005-06	NY Rangers	NHL	1	0	1	1	4	0	0	0	1	0.0	2	0	0.0	8:47	1	0	0	0	2	0	0	0	6:00
	Hartford	AHL	69	19	35	54	65	....	....	....	....	....	....	....	....	....	11	3	6	9	22	....	....	....	....
2006-07	Hershey Bears	AHL	48	15	20	35	80	....	....	....	....	....	....	....	....	....	16	2	6	8	16	....	....	....	....
	NHL Totals		9	1	1	2	8	0	0	0	5	20.0		0	0.0	9:02	1	0	0	0	2	0	0	0	6:00

Traded to **NY Rangers** by **San Jose** for Nils Ekman, August 12, 2003. Signed as a free agent by **Washington**, July 14, 2006. Signed as a free agent by **Wolfsburg** (Germany), July 9, 2007.

WISNIEWSKI, James

(wihs-NEHV-skee, JAYMS) **CHI.**

Defense. Shoots right. 6', 207 lbs. Born, Canton, MI, February 21, 1984. Chicago's 5th choice, 156th overall, in 2002 Entry Draft.

Season	Club	League	GP	G	A	Pts	PIM	PP	SH	GW	S	%	+/-	TF	F%	Min	Playoffs GP	G	A	Pts	PIM	PP	SH	GW	Min
99-2000	Det. Compuware	NAHL	50	5	11	16	67	....	....	....	....	....	....	....	....	....	5	0	3	3	4	....	....	....	....
2000-01	Plymouth Whalers	OHL	53	6	23	29	72	....	....	....	....	....	....	....	....	....	19	3	10	13	34	....	....	....	....
2001-02	Plymouth Whalers	OHL	62	11	25	36	100	....	....	....	....	....	....	....	....	....	6	1	2	3	6	....	....	....	....
2002-03	Plymouth Whalers	OHL	52	18	34	52	60	....	....	....	....	....	....	....	....	....	18	2	10	12	14	....	....	....	....
2003-04	Plymouth Whalers	OHL	50	17	53	70	63	....	....	....	....	....	....	....	....	....	9	3	7	10	8	....	....	....	....
2004-05	Norfolk Admirals	AHL	66	7	18	25	110	....	....	....	....	....	....	....	....	....	5	1	3	4	2	....	....	....	....
2005-06	**Chicago**	**NHL**	**19**	**2**	**5**	**7**	**36**	**0**	**0**	**0**	**25**	**8.0**	**0**	**1**	**0.0**	**15:52**	....	....	....	....	....	....	....	....	....
	Norfolk Admirals	AHL	61	7	28	35	67	....	....	....	....	....	....	....	....	....	4	1	2	3	6	....	....	....	....
2006-07	**Chicago**	**NHL**	**50**	**2**	**8**	**10**	**39**	**0**	**0**	**0**	**55**	**3.6**	**3**	**1**	**0.0**	**19:00**	....	....	....	....	....	....	....	....	....
	Norfolk Admirals	AHL	10	0	6	6	8	....	....	....	....	....	....	....	....	....	....	....	....	....	....	....	....	....	....
	NHL Totals		**69**	**4**	**13**	**17**	**75**	**0**	**0**	**0**	**80**	**5.0**		**2**	**0.0**	**18:08**	....	....	....	....	....	....	....	....	....

OHL First All-Star Team (2004) • OHL Defenseman of the Year (2004) • Canadian Major Junior First All-Star Team (2004) • Canadian Major Junior Defenseman of the Year (2004)

WITT, Brendan

(WIHT, BREHN-duhn) **NYI**

Defense. Shoots left. 6'2", 223 lbs. Born, Humboldt, Sask., February 20, 1975. Washington's 1st choice, 11th overall, in 1993 Entry Draft.

Season	Club	League	GP	G	A	Pts	PIM	PP	SH	GW	S	%	+/-	TF	F%	Min	Playoffs GP	G	A	Pts	PIM	PP	SH	GW	Min
1990-91	Saskatoon Blazers	SMHL	31	5	13	18	42	....	....	....	....	....	....	....	....	....	....	....	....	....	....	....	....	....	....
	Seattle	WHL	....	....	....	....	....	....	....	....	....	....	....	....	....	....	1	0	0	0	0	....	....	....	....
1991-92	Seattle	WHL	67	3	9	12	212	....	....	....	....	....	....	....	....	....	15	1	1	2	84	....	....	....	....
1992-93	Seattle	WHL	70	2	26	28	239	....	....	....	....	....	....	....	....	....	5	1	2	3	30	....	....	....	....
1993-94	Seattle	WHL	56	8	31	39	235	....	....	....	....	....	....	....	....	....	9	3	8	11	23	....	....	....	....
1994-95			DID NOT PLAY																						
1995-96	**Washington**	**NHL**	**48**	**2**	**3**	**5**	**85**	**0**	**0**	**1**	**44**	**4.5**	**–4**	....	....	....	....	....	....	....	....	....	....	....	....
1996-97	**Washington**	**NHL**	**44**	**3**	**2**	**5**	**88**	**0**	**0**	**0**	**41**	**7.3**	**–20**	....	....	....	....	....	....	....	....	....	....	....	....
	Portland Pirates	AHL	30	2	4	6	56	....	....	....	....	....	....	....	....	....	5	1	0	1	30	....	....	....	....
1997-98	**Washington**	**NHL**	**64**	**1**	**7**	**8**	**112**	**0**	**0**	**0**	**68**	**1.5**	**–11**	....	....	....	**16**	**1**	**0**	**1**	**14**	**0**	**0**	**0**	....
1998-99	**Washington**	**NHL**	**54**	**2**	**5**	**7**	**87**	**0**	**0**	**0**	**51**	**3.9**	**–6**	**0**	**0.0**	**15:50**	....	....	....	....	....	....	....	....	....
99-2000	**Washington**	**NHL**	**77**	**1**	**7**	**8**	**114**	**0**	**0**	**0**	**64**	**1.6**	**5**	**2**	**50.0**	**20:56**	**3**	**0**	**0**	**0**	**0**	**0**	**0**	**0**	**20:52**
2000-01	**Washington**	**NHL**	**72**	**3**	**3**	**6**	**101**	**0**	**0**	**0**	**87**	**3.4**	**2**	**1**	**100.0**	**20:41**	**6**	**2**	**0**	**2**	**12**	**1**	**0**	**0**	**20:50**
2001-02	**Washington**	**NHL**	**68**	**3**	**7**	**10**	**78**	**0**	**0**	**0**	**81**	**3.7**	**–1**	**1**	**100.0**	**20:03**	....	....	....	....	....	....	....	....	....
2002-03	**Washington**	**NHL**	**69**	**2**	**9**	**11**	**106**	**0**	**0**	**0**	**80**	**2.5**	**12**	**0**	**0.0**	**20:55**	**6**	**1**	**0**	**1**	**0**	**0**	**0**	**0**	**23:33**
2003-04	**Washington**	**NHL**	**72**	**2**	**10**	**12**	**123**	**0**	**0**	**0**	**91**	**2.2**	**–22**	**3**	**66.7**	**22:48**	....	....	....	....	....	....	....	....	....
2004-05	Bracknell Bees	Britain-2	3	1	4	5	0	....	....	....	....	....	....	....	....	....	....	....	....	....	....	....	....	....	....
2005-06	**Washington**	**NHL**	**58**	**1**	**10**	**11**	**141**	**0**	**0**	**0**	**62**	**1.6**	**–5**	**0**	**0.0**	**21:41**	....	....	....	....	....	....	....	....	....
	Nashville	**NHL**	**17**	**0**	**3**	**3**	**68**	**0**	**0**	**0**	**13**	**0.0**	**5**	**0**	**0.0**	**17:29**	**5**	**0**	**0**	**0**	**12**	**0**	**0**	**0**	**17:07**
2006-07	**NY Islanders**	**NHL**	**81**	**1**	**13**	**14**	**131**	**0**	**0**	**0**	**75**	**1.3**	**14**	**0**	**0.0**	**21:39**	**5**	**0**	**1**	**1**	**6**	**0**	**0**	**0**	**20:06**
	NHL Totals		**724**	**21**	**79**	**100**	**1234**	**0**	**0**	**1**	**757**	**2.8**		**7**	**71.4**	**20:37**	**41**	**4**	**1**	**5**	**44**	**1**	**0**	**0**	**20:36**

WHL West First All-Star Team (1993, 1994) • Canadian Major Junior First All-Star Team (1994)

• Missed entire 1994-95 season after failing to come to contract terms with **Washington**. Signed as a free agent by **Bracknell** (Britain-2), December 21, 2004. Traded to **Nashville** by **Washington** for Kris Beech and Nashville's 1st round choice (Simeon Varlamov) in 2006 Entry Draft, March 9, 2006. Signed as a free agent by **NY Islanders**, July 3, 2006.

WOLSKI, Wojtek

(WOHL-skee, VOI-tehk) **COL.**

Left wing. Shoots left. 6'3", 200 lbs. Born, Zabrze, Poland, February 24, 1986. Colorado's 1st choice, 21st overall, in 2004 Entry Draft.

Season	Club	League	GP	G	A	Pts	PIM	PP	SH	GW	S	%	+/-	TF	F%	Min	Playoffs GP	G	A	Pts	PIM	PP	SH	GW	Min
2001-02	St. Mike's B's	OPJHL	33	16	33	49	40	....	....	....	....	....	....	....	....	....	....	....	....	....	....	....	....	....	....
2002-03	Brampton	OHL	64	25	32	57	26	....	....	....	....	....	....	....	....	....	11	5	0	5	6	....	....	....	....
2003-04	Brampton	OHL	66	29	41	70	30	....	....	....	....	....	....	....	....	....	12	5	3	8	8	....	....	....	....
2004-05	Brampton	OHL	67	29	44	73	41	....	....	....	....	....	....	....	....	....	6	2	5	7	6	....	....	....	....
2005-06	**Colorado**	**NHL**	**9**	**2**	**4**	**6**	**4**	**2**	**0**	**0**	**9**	**22.2**	**–5**	**4**	**0.0**	**9:44**	**8**	**1**	**3**	**4**	**2**	**0**	**0**	**0**	**12:06**
	Brampton	OHL	56	47	81	128	46	....	....	....	....	....	....	....	....	....	11	7	11	18	4	....	....	....	....
2006-07	**Colorado**	**NHL**	**76**	**22**	**28**	**50**	**14**	**7**	**0**	**2**	**165**	**13.3**	**2**	**3**	**100.0**	**15:31**	....	....	....	....	....	....	....	....	....
	NHL Totals		**85**	**24**	**32**	**56**	**18**	**9**	**0**	**2**	**174**	**13.8**		**7**	**42.9**	**14:54**	**8**	**1**	**3**	**4**	**2**	**0**	**0**	**0**	**12:06**

OHL First All-Star Team (2004) • OHL Second All-Star Team (2006)

WOOLLEY, Jason

(WU-lee, JAY-suhn)

Defense. Shoots left. 6', 203 lbs. Born, Toronto, Ont., July 27, 1969. Washington's 4th choice, 61st overall, in 1989 Entry Draft.

Season	Club	League	GP	G	A	Pts	PIM	PP	SH	GW	S	%	+/-	TF	F%	Min	Playoffs GP	G	A	Pts	PIM	PP	SH	GW	Min
1986-87	St. Mike's B's	OHA-B	35	13	22	35	40	....	....	....	....	....	....	....	....	....	....	....	....	....	....	....	....	....	....
1987-88	St. Mike's B's	OHA-B	31	19	37	56	22	....	....	....	....	....	....	....	....	....	....	....	....	....	....	....	....	....	....
1988-89	Michigan State	CCHA	47	12	25	37	26	....	....	....	....	....	....	....	....	....	....	....	....	....	....	....	....	....	....
1989-90	Michigan State	CCHA	45	10	38	48	26	....	....	....	....	....	....	....	....	....	....	....	....	....	....	....	....	....	....
1990-91	Michigan State	CCHA	40	15	44	59	24	....	....	....	....	....	....	....	....	....	....	....	....	....	....	....	....	....	....
1991-92	Canada	Nat-Tm	60	14	30	44	36	....	....	....	....	....	....	....	....	....	....	....	....	....	....	....	....	....	....
	Canada	Olympics	8	0	5	5	4	....	....	....	....	....	....	....	....	....	....	....	....	....	....	....	....	....	....
	Washington	**NHL**	**1**	**0**	**0**	**0**	**0**	**0**	**0**	**0**	**2**	**0.0**	**1**	....	....	....	....	....	....	....	....	....	....	....	....
	Baltimore	AHL	15	1	10	11	6	....	....	....	....	....	....	....	....	....	....	....	....	....	....	....	....	....	....
1992-93	**Washington**	**NHL**	**26**	**0**	**2**	**2**	**10**	**0**	**0**	**0**	**11**	**0.0**	**3**	....	....	....	....	....	....	....	....	....	....	....	....
	Baltimore	AHL	29	14	27	41	22	....	....	....	....	....	....	....	....	....	1	0	2	2	0	....	....	....	....
1993-94	**Washington**	**NHL**	**10**	**1**	**2**	**3**	**4**	**0**	**0**	**0**	**15**	**6.7**	**2**	....	....	....	**4**	**1**	**0**	**1**	**4**	**0**	**0**	**1**	....
	Portland Pirates	AHL	41	12	29	41	14	....	....	....	....	....	....	....	....	....	9	2	2	4	4	....	....	....	....
1994-95	Detroit Vipers	IHL	48	8	28	36	38	....	....	....	....	....	....	....	....	....	....	....	....	....	....	....	....	....	....
	Florida	**NHL**	**34**	**4**	**9**	**13**	**18**	**1**	**0**	**0**	**76**	**5.3**	**–1**	....	....	....	....	....	....	....	....	....	....	....	....
1995-96	**Florida**	**NHL**	**52**	**6**	**28**	**34**	**32**	**3**	**0**	**0**	**98**	**6.1**	**–9**	....	....	....	**13**	**2**	**6**	**8**	**14**	**1**	**0**	**1**	....
1996-97	**Florida**	**NHL**	**3**	**0**	**0**	**0**	**2**	**0**	**0**	**0**	**7**	**0.0**	**1**	....	....	....	....	....	....	....	....	....	....	....	....
	Pittsburgh	**NHL**	**57**	**6**	**30**	**36**	**28**	**2**	**0**	**1**	**79**	**7.6**	**3**	....	....	....	**5**	**0**	**3**	**3**	**0**	**0**	**0**	**0**	....
1997-98	**Buffalo**	**NHL**	**71**	**9**	**26**	**35**	**35**	**3**	**0**	**2**	**129**	**7.0**	**8**	....	....	....	**15**	**2**	**9**	**11**	**12**	**1**	**0**	**1**	....
1998-99	**Buffalo**	**NHL**	**80**	**10**	**33**	**43**	**62**	**4**	**0**	**2**	**154**	**6.5**	**16**	**0**	**0.0**	**18:43**	**21**	**4**	**11**	**15**	**10**	**2**	**0**	**1**	**17:54**
99-2000	**Buffalo**	**NHL**	**74**	**8**	**25**	**33**	**52**	**2**	**0**	**2**	**113**	**7.1**	**14**	**0**	**0.0**	**17:51**	**5**	**0**	**2**	**2**	**2**	**0**	**0**	**0**	**18:06**
2000-01	**Buffalo**	**NHL**	**67**	**5**	**18**	**23**	**46**	**4**	**0**	**3**	**92**	**5.4**	**0**	**0**	**0.0**	**17:22**	**8**	**1**	**5**	**6**	**2**	**0**	**0**	**1**	**18:30**
2001-02	**Buffalo**	**NHL**	**59**	**8**	**20**	**28**	**34**	**6**	**0**	**2**	**90**	**8.9**	**–6**	**0**	**0.0**	**17:11**	....	....	....	....	....	....	....	....	....
2002-03	**Buffalo**	**NHL**	**14**	**0**	**3**	**3**	**29**	**0**	**0**	**0**	**29**	**0.0**	**–1**	**0**	**0.0**	**15:59**	....	....	....	....	....	....	....	....	....
	Detroit	**NHL**	**62**	**6**	**17**	**23**	**22**	**1**	**0**	**2**	**52**	**11.5**	**12**	**0**	**0.0**	**16:59**	**4**	**1**	**0**	**1**	**0**	**0**	**0**	**0**	**15:25**
2003-04	**Detroit**	**NHL**	**55**	**4**	**15**	**19**	**28**	**0**	**0**	**1**	**60**	**6.7**	**19**	**2**	**50.0**	**15:42**	**4**	**0**	**0**	**0**	**0**	**0**	**0**	**0**	**17:00**
2004-05	Flint Generals	UHL	9	4	2	6	4	....	....	....	....	....	....	....	....	....	....	....	....	....	....	....	....	....	....
2005-06	**Detroit**	**NHL**	**53**	**1**	**18**	**19**	**28**	**0**	**0**	**0**	**43**	**2.3**	**3**	**1**	**0.0**	**11:54**	....	....	....	....	....	....	....	....	....
2006-07	Malmo	Sweden	31	1	5	6	46	....	....	....	....	....	....	....	....	....	....	....	....	....	....	....	....	....	....
	Malmo	Sweden-Q	7	0	0	0	0	....	....	....	....	....	....	....	....	....	....	....	....	....	....	....	....	....	....
	NHL Totals		**718**	**68**	**246**	**314**	**430**	**26**	**0**	**15**	**1050**	**6.5**		**3**	**33.3**	**16:44**	**79**	**11**	**36**	**47**	**44**	**4**	**0**	**5**	**17:43**

CCHA First All-Star Team (1991) • NCAA West First All-American Team (1991)

Signed as a free agent by **Florida**, February 15, 1995. Traded to **Pittsburgh** by **Florida** with Stu Barnes for Chris Wells, November 19, 1996. Traded to **Buffalo** by **Pittsburgh** for Buffalo's 5th round choice (Robert Scuderi) in 1998 Entry Draft, September 24, 1997. Traded to **Detroit** by **Buffalo** for future considerations, November 16, 2002. Signed as a free agent by **Flint** (UHL), February 18, 2005.

WOTTON, Mark

(WAH-tuhn, MAHRK)

Defense. Shoots left. 6'1", 195 lbs. Born, Foxwarren, Man., November 16, 1973. Vancouver's 11th choice, 237th overall, in 1992 Entry Draft.

Season	Club	League	GP	G	A	Pts	PIM	PP	SH	GW	S	%	+/-	TF	F%	Min	Playoffs GP	G	A	Pts	PIM	PP	SH	GW	Min
1988-89	Foxwarren Blades	MAHA	60	10	30	40	70	....	....	....	....	....	....	....	....	....	....	....	....	....	....	....	....	....	....
1989-90	Saskatoon Blades	WHL	51	2	3	5	31	....	....	....	....	....	....	....	....	....	7	1	1	2	15	....	....	....	....
1990-91	Saskatoon Blades	WHL	45	4	11	15	37	....	....	....	....	....	....	....	....	....	....	....	....	....	....	....	....	....	....
1991-92	Saskatoon Blades	WHL	64	11	25	36	62	....	....	....	....	....	....	....	....	....	21	2	6	8	22	....	....	....	....
1992-93	Saskatoon Blades	WHL	71	15	51	66	90	....	....	....	....	....	....	....	....	....	9	6	5	11	18	....	....	....	....
1993-94	Saskatoon Blades	WHL	65	12	34	46	108	....	....	....	....	....	....	....	....	....	16	3	12	15	32	....	....	....	....
1994-95	Syracuse Crunch	AHL	75	12	29	41	50	....	....	....	....	....	....	....	....	....	....	....	....	....	....	....	....	....	....
	Vancouver	**NHL**	**1**	**0**	**0**	**0**	**0**	**0**	**0**	**0**	**2**	**0.0**	**1**	....	....	....	**5**	**0**	**0**	**0**	**4**	**0**	**0**	**0**	....
1995-96	Syracuse Crunch	AHL	80	10	35	45	96	....	....	....	....	....	....	....	....	....	15	1	12	13	20	....	....	....	....
1996-97	**Vancouver**	**NHL**	**36**	**3**	**6**	**9**	**19**	**0**	**1**	**0**	**41**	**7.3**	**8**	....	....	....	....	....	....	....	....	....	....	....	....
	Syracuse Crunch	AHL	27	2	8	10	25	....	....	....	....	....	....	....	....	....	2	0	0	0	4	....	....	....	....

			Regular Season														Playoffs								
Season	Club	League	GP	G	A	Pts	PIM	PP	SH	GW	S	%	+/-	TF	F%	Min	GP	G	A	Pts	PIM	PP	SH	GW	Min
1997-98	**Vancouver**	**NHL**	**5**	**0**	**0**	**0**	**6**	**0**	**0**	**0**	**3**	**0.0**	**–2**	....	....	....	....	....	....	....	....	....	....	....	....
	Syracuse Crunch	AHL	56	12	21	33	80	....	....	....	....	....	....	....	....	....	5	0	0	0	12	....	....	....	....
1998-99	Syracuse Crunch	AHL	72	4	31	35	74	....	....	....	....	....	....	....	....	....	....	....	....	....	....	....	....	....	....
99-2000	Michigan	IHL	70	3	7	10	72	....	....	....	....	....	....	....	....	....	....	....	....	....	....	....	....	....	....
2000-01	**Dallas**	**NHL**	**1**	**0**	**0**	**0**	**0**	**0**	**0**	**0**	**0**	**0.0**	**0**	**0**	**0.0**	**13:45**	....	....	....	....	....	....	....	....	....
	Utah Grizzlies	IHL	63	2	2	4	64	....	....	....	....	....	....	....	....	....	....	....	....	....	....	....	....	....	....
2001-02	Utah Grizzlies	AHL	57	9	18	27	68	....	....	....	....	....	....	....	....	....	4	0	1	1	6	....	....	....	....
2002-03	Utah Grizzlies	AHL	69	8	26	34	68	....	....	....	....	....	....	....	....	....	2	0	0	0	2	....	....	....	....
2003-04	Utah Grizzlies	AHL	23	1	3	4	25	....	....	....	....	....	....	....	....	....	....	....	....	....	....	....	....	....	....
2004-05	St. Petersburg	Russia	50	3	4	7	36	....	....	....	....	....	....	....	....	....	....	....	....	....	....	....	....	....	....
2005-06	Hershey Bears	AHL	69	7	19	26	58	....	....	....	....	....	....	....	....	....	14	0	4	4	6	....	....	....	....
2006-07	Bridgeport	AHL	78	9	24	33	56	....	....	....	....	....	....	....	....	....	....	....	....	....	....	....	....	....	....
	NHL Totals		**43**	**3**	**6**	**9**	**25**	**0**	**1**	**0**	**46**	**6.5**		**0**	**0.0**	**13:45**	**5**	**0**	**0**	**0**	**4**	**0**	**0**	**0**	....

WHL East Second All-Star Team (1994)

Signed as a free agent by **Dallas**, July 9, 1999. • Missed majority of 2003-04 season recovering from knee injury suffered in game vs. Cincinnati (AHL), December 6, 2003. Signed as a free agent by **St. Petersburg** (Russia), July 9, 2004. Signed as a free agent by **Washington**, August 17, 2005. Signed as a free agent by **NY Islanders**, July 27, 2006.

WOYWITKA, Jeff

(WOI-wiht-ka, JEHF) **ST.L.**

Defense. Shoots left. 6'2", 209 lbs. Born, Vermilion, Alta., September 1, 1983. Philadelphia's 1st choice, 27th overall, in 2001 Entry Draft.

Season	Club	League	GP	G	A	Pts	PIM	PP	SH	GW	S	%	+/-	TF	F%	Min	GP	G	A	Pts	PIM	PP	SH	GW	Min
1998-99	Wainwright	AAHA	26	7	15	22	60	....	....	....	....	....	....	....	....	....	....	....	....	....	....	....	....	....	....
99-2000	Red Deer Rebels	WHL	67	4	12	16	40	....	....	....	....	....	....	....	....	....	4	0	3	3	2	....	....	....	....
2000-01	Red Deer Rebels	WHL	72	7	28	35	113	....	....	....	....	....	....	....	....	....	22	2	8	10	25	....	....	....	....
2001-02	Red Deer Rebels	WHL	72	14	23	37	109	....	....	....	....	....	....	....	....	....	23	2	10	12	22	....	....	....	....
2002-03	Red Deer Rebels	WHL	57	16	36	52	65	....	....	....	....	....	....	....	....	....	23	1	9	10	25	....	....	....	....
2003-04	Philadelphia	AHL	29	0	6	6	51	....	....	....	....	....	....	....	....	....	....	....	....	....	....	....	....	....	....
	Toronto	AHL	53	4	18	22	41	....	....	....	....	....	....	....	....	....	3	0	0	0	2	....	....	....	....
2004-05	Edmonton	AHL	80	6	20	26	84	....	....	....	....	....	....	....	....	....	....	....	....	....	....	....	....	....	....
2005-06	**St. Louis**	**NHL**	**26**	**0**	**2**	**2**	**25**	**0**	**0**	**0**	**23**	**0.0**	**–12**	**0**	**0.0**	**10:38**	....	....	....	....	....	....	....	....	....
	Peoria Rivermen	AHL	53	1	14	15	58	....	....	....	....	....	....	....	....	....	4	0	0	0	4	....	....	....	....
2006-07	**St. Louis**	**NHL**	**34**	**1**	**6**	**7**	**12**	**0**	**0**	**0**	**28**	**3.6**	**4**	**0**	**0.0**	**14:45**	....	....	....	....	....	....	....	....	....
	Peoria Rivermen	AHL	41	0	18	18	20	....	....	....	....	....	....	....	....	....	....	....	....	....	....	....	....	....	....
	NHL Totals		**60**	**1**	**8**	**9**	**37**	**0**	**0**	**0**	**51**	**2.0**		**0**	**0.0**	**12:58**	....	....	....	....	....	....	....	....	....

WHL East Second All-Star Team (2002) • WHL East First All-Star Team (2003)

Traded to **Edmonton** by **Philadelphia** with Philadelphia's 1st round choice (Rob Schremp) in 2004 Entry Draft and Philadelphia's 3rd round choice (Danny Syvret) in 2005 Entry Draft for Mike Comrie, December 16, 2003. Traded to **St. Louis** by **Edmonton** with Eric Brewer and Doug Lynch for Chris Pronger, August 2, 2005.

WOZNIEWSKI, Andy

(wuhz-NYOO-skee, AN-dee) **TOR.**

Defense. Shoots left. 6'5", 225 lbs. Born, Buffalo Grove, IL, May 25, 1980.

Season	Club	League	GP	G	A	Pts	PIM	PP	SH	GW	S	%	+/-	TF	F%	Min	GP	G	A	Pts	PIM	PP	SH	GW	Min
99-2000	U. Mass-Lowell	H-East	17	1	1	2	8	....	....	....	....	....	....	....	....	....	....	....	....	....	....	....	....	....	....
2000-01	Texas Tornado	NAHL	54	10	34	44	98	....	....	....	....	....	....	....	....	....	8	2	7	9	12	....	....	....	....
2001-02	U. of Wisconsin	WCHA	39	3	13	16	54	....	....	....	....	....	....	....	....	....	....	....	....	....	....	....	....	....	....
2002-03	U. of Wisconsin	WCHA	33	1	7	8	47	....	....	....	....	....	....	....	....	....	....	....	....	....	....	....	....	....	....
2003-04	U. of Wisconsin	WCHA	43	6	8	14	*104	....	....	....	....	....	....	....	....	....	....	....	....	....	....	....	....	....	....
	St. John's	AHL	3	0	1	1	0	....	....	....	....	....	....	....	....	....	....	....	....	....	....	....	....	....	....
2004-05	St. John's	AHL	28	1	4	5	20	....	....	....	....	....	....	....	....	....	....	....	....	....	....	....	....	....	....
2005-06	**Toronto**	**NHL**	**13**	**0**	**1**	**1**	**13**	**0**	**0**	**0**	**6**	**0.0**	**–8**	**0**	**0.0**	**17:55**	....	....	....	....	....	....	....	....	....
	Toronto Marlies	AHL	31	4	11	15	42	....	....	....	....	....	....	....	....	....	....	....	....	....	....	....	....	....	....
2006-07	**Toronto**	**NHL**	**15**	**0**	**2**	**2**	**14**	**0**	**0**	**0**	**10**	**0.0**	**–1**	**0**	**0.0**	**13:55**	....	....	....	....	....	....	....	....	....
	Toronto Marlies	AHL	5	0	3	3	8	....	....	....	....	....	....	....	....	....	....	....	....	....	....	....	....	....	....
	NHL Totals		**28**	**0**	**3**	**3**	**27**	**0**	**0**	**0**	**16**	**0.0**		**0**	**0.0**	**15:47**	....	....	....	....	....	....	....	....	....

Signed as a free agent by **Toronto**, May 27, 2004. • Missed majority of 2006-07 season recovering from a shoulder injury.

YAKUBOV, Mikhail

(yuh-KOO-bahf, mih-kigh-EHL) **FLA.**

Center. Shoots left. 6'3", 202 lbs. Born, Barnaul, USSR, February 16, 1982. Chicago's 1st choice, 10th overall, in 2000 Entry Draft.

Season	Club	League	GP	G	A	Pts	PIM	PP	SH	GW	S	%	+/-	TF	F%	Min	GP	G	A	Pts	PIM	PP	SH	GW	Min
1997-98	Lada Togliatti 2	Russia-3	7	0	0	0	0	....	....	....	....	....	....	....	....	....	....	....	....	....	....	....	....	....	....
1998-99	Lada Togliatti 2	Russia-4	38	11	4	15	32	....	....	....	....	....	....	....	....	....	....	....	....	....	....	....	....	....	....
99-2000	Lada Togliatti 2	Russia-3	26	12	19	31	14	....	....	....	....	....	....	....	....	....	....	....	....	....	....	....	....	....	....
2000-01	Lada Togliatti	Russia	25	0	0	0	4	....	....	....	....	....	....	....	....	....	4	0	0	0	0	....	....	....	....
2001-02	Red Deer Rebels	WHL	71	32	57	89	54	....	....	....	....	....	....	....	....	....	23	14	9	23	28	....	....	....	....
2002-03	Norfolk Admirals	AHL	62	6	5	11	36	....	....	....	....	....	....	....	....	....	9	0	0	0	8	....	....	....	....
2003-04	**Chicago**	**NHL**	**30**	**1**	**7**	**8**	**8**	**0**	**0**	**0**	**32**	**3.1**	**–12**	**337**	**45.7**	**13:44**	....	....	....	....	....	....	....	....	....
	Norfolk Admirals	AHL	51	9	18	27	22	....	....	....	....	....	....	....	....	....	8	0	3	3	2	....	....	....	....
2004-05	Norfolk Admirals	AHL	59	12	15	27	43	....	....	....	....	....	....	....	....	....	3	0	0	0	0	....	....	....	....
2005-06	Spartak Moscow	Russia	29	5	6	11	38	....	....	....	....	....	....	....	....	....	....	....	....	....	....	....	....	....	....
	Chicago	**NHL**	**10**	**1**	**2**	**3**	**8**	**0**	**0**	**1**	**11**	**9.1**	**0**	**90**	**38.9**	**12:00**	....	....	....	....	....	....	....	....	....
	Norfolk Admirals	AHL	8	1	3	4	8	....	....	....	....	....	....	....	....	....	....	....	....	....	....	....	....	....	....
	Florida	**NHL**	**13**	**0**	**1**	**1**	**4**	**0**	**0**	**0**	**16**	**0.0**	**–1**	**69**	**37.7**	**7:50**	....	....	....	....	....	....	....	....	....
2006-07	Cherepovets	Russia	52	6	16	22	111	....	....	....	....	....	....	....	....	....	5	1	1	2	4	....	....	....	....
	NHL Totals		**53**	**2**	**10**	**12**	**20**	**0**	**0**	**1**	**59**	**3.4**		**496**	**43.3**	**11:58**	....	....	....	....	....	....	....	....	....

WHL East Second All-Star Team (2002)

Claimed on waivers by **Florida** from **Chicago**, January 29, 2006.

YANDLE, Keith

(Yan-duhl, KEETH) **PHX.**

Defense. Shoots left. 6'2", 195 lbs. Born, Boston, MA, September 9, 1986. Phoenix's 3rd choice, 105th overall, in 2005 Entry Draft.

Season	Club	League	GP	G	A	Pts	PIM	PP	SH	GW	S	%	+/-	TF	F%	Min	GP	G	A	Pts	PIM	PP	SH	GW	Min
2004-05	Cushing	High-MA	34	14	40	54	52	....	....	....	....	....	....	....	....	....	....	....	....	....	....	....	....	....	....
2005-06	Moncton Wildcats	QMJHL	66	25	59	84	109	....	....	....	....	....	....	....	....	....	21	6	14	20	36	....	....	....	....
2006-07	**Phoenix**	**NHL**	**7**	**0**	**2**	**2**	**8**	**0**	**0**	**0**	**10**	**0.0**	**0**	**0**	**0.0**	**20:10**	....	....	....	....	....	....	....	....	....
	San Antonio	AHL	69	6	27	33	97	....	....	....	....	....	....	....	....	....	....	....	....	....	....	....	....	....	....
	NHL Totals		**7**	**0**	**2**	**2**	**8**	**0**	**0**	**0**	**10**	**0.0**		**0**	**0.0**	**20:10**	....	....	....	....	....	....	....	....	....

QMJHL First All-Star Team (2006) • Canadian Major Junior Defenseman of the Year (2006)

YASHIN, Alexei

(YAH-shin, al-EHX-ay)

Center. Shoots right. 6'3", 225 lbs. Born, Sverdlovsk, USSR, November 5, 1973. Ottawa's 1st choice, 2nd overall, in 1992 Entry Draft.

Season	Club	League	GP	G	A	Pts	PIM	PP	SH	GW	S	%	+/-	TF	F%	Min	GP	G	A	Pts	PIM	PP	SH	GW	Min
1989-90	Luch Sverdlovsk	USSR-2	STATISTICS NOT AVAILABLE																						
1990-91	Sverdlovsk	USSR	26	2	1	3	10	....	....	....	....	....	....	....	....	....	....	....	....	....	....	....	....	....	....
	Sverdlovsk	USSR-Q	12	1	1	2	12	....	....	....	....	....	....	....	....	....	....	....	....	....	....	....	....	....	....
1991-92	Dynamo Moscow	CIS	35	7	5	12	19	....	....	....	....	....	....	....	....	....	....	....	....	....	....	....	....	....	....
	Dyn'o Moscow 2	CIS-3	6	6	2	8	8	....	....	....	....	....	....	....	....	....	....	....	....	....	....	....	....	....	....
1992-93	Dynamo Moscow	CIS	27	10	12	22	18	....	....	....	....	....	....	....	....	....	10	7	3	10	18	....	....	....	....
1993-94	**Ottawa**	**NHL**	**83**	**30**	**49**	**79**	**22**	**11**	**2**	**3**	**232**	**12.9**	**–49**	....	....	....	....	....	....	....	....	....	....	....	....
1994-95	Las Vegas	IHL	24	15	20	35	32	....	....	....	....	....	....	....	....	....	....	....	....	....	....	....	....	....	....
	Ottawa	**NHL**	**47**	**21**	**23**	**44**	**20**	**11**	**0**	**1**	**154**	**13.6**	**–20**	....	....	....	....	....	....	....	....	....	....	....	....
1995-96	CSKA Moscow	CIS	4	2	2	4	4	....	....	....	....	....	....	....	....	....	....	....	....	....	....	....	....	....	....
	Ottawa	**NHL**	**46**	**15**	**24**	**39**	**28**	**8**	**0**	**1**	**143**	**10.5**	**–15**	....	....	....	....	....	....	....	....	....	....	....	....
1996-97	**Ottawa**	**NHL**	**82**	**35**	**40**	**75**	**44**	**10**	**0**	**5**	**291**	**12.0**	**–7**	....	....	....	**7**	**1**	**5**	**6**	**2**	**1**	**0**	**0**	....
1997-98	**Ottawa**	**NHL**	**82**	**33**	**39**	**72**	**24**	**5**	**0**	**6**	**291**	**11.3**	**6**	....	....	....	**11**	**5**	**3**	**8**	**8**	**3**	**0**	**2**	....
	Russia	Olympics	6	3	3	6	0	....	....	....	....	....	....	....	....	....	....	....	....	....	....	....	....	....	....
1998-99	**Ottawa**	**NHL**	**82**	**44**	**50**	**94**	**54**	**19**	**0**	**5**	**337**	**13.1**	**16**	**1428**	**41.9**	**22:05**	**4**	**0**	**0**	**0**	**10**	**0**	**0**	**0**	**26:06**
99-2000	**Ottawa**	**NHL**	DID NOT PLAY – SUSPENDED																						
2000-01	**Ottawa**	**NHL**	**82**	**40**	**48**	**88**	**30**	**13**	**2**	**10**	**263**	**15.2**	**10**	**1414**	**43.1**	**20:24**	**4**	**0**	**1**	**1**	**0**	**0**	**0**	**0**	**24:54**
2001-02	**NY Islanders**	**NHL**	**78**	**32**	**43**	**75**	**25**	**15**	**0**	**5**	**239**	**13.4**	**–3**	**828**	**46.7**	**20:37**	**7**	**3**	**4**	**7**	**2**	**1**	**0**	**0**	**21:54**
	Russia	Olympics	6	1	1	2	0	....	....	....	....	....	....	....	....	....	....	....	....	....	....	....	....	....	....
2002-03	**NY Islanders**	**NHL**	**81**	**26**	**39**	**65**	**32**	**14**	**0**	**7**	**274**	**9.5**	**–12**	**1074**	**47.2**	**18:32**	**5**	**2**	**2**	**4**	**2**	**0**	**0**	**0**	**21:06**
2003-04	**NY Islanders**	**NHL**	**47**	**15**	**19**	**34**	**10**	**3**	**0**	**1**	**148**	**10.1**	**–1**	**603**	**42.8**	**17:19**	**5**	**0**	**1**	**1**	**0**	**0**	**0**	**0**	**15:33**

Season	Club	League	GP	G	A	Pts	PIM	PP	SH	GW	S	%	+/-	TF	F%	Min	GP	G	A	Pts	PIM	PP	SH	GW	Min
			Regular Season														Playoffs								
2004-05	Yaroslavl	Russia	10	3	3	6	14	....	....	....	....	....	....	....	....	....	9	3	7	10	10	....	....	....	....
2005-06	**NY Islanders**	**NHL**	**82**	**28**	**38**	**66**	**68**	**10**	**0**	**2**	**253**	**11.1**	**−14**	**1116**	**50.2**	**18:30**	....	....	....	....	....	....	....	....	....
	Russia	Olympics	8	1	3	4	4	....	....	....	....	....	....	....	....	....	....	....	....	....	....	....	....	....	....
2006-07	**NY Islanders**	**NHL**	**58**	**18**	**32**	**50**	**44**	**5**	**0**	**3**	**203**	**8.9**	**6**	**527**	**45.9**	**17:04**	**5**	**0**	**0**	**0**	**0**	**0**	**0**	**0**	**11:45**
	NHL Totals		**850**	**337**	**444**	**781**	**401**	**124**	**4**	**49**	**2828**	**11.9**		**6990**	**45.2**	**19:26**	**48**	**11**	**16**	**27**	**24**	**5**	**0**	**2**	**19:59**

NHL Second All-Star Team (1999)

Played in NHL All-Star Game (1994, 1999, 2002)

• Suspended for entire 1999-2000 season by **Ottawa** for refusing to report to team, November 9, 1999. Traded to **NY Islanders** by **Ottawa** for Bill Muckalt, Zdeno Chara and NY Islanders' 1st round choice (Jason Spezza) in 2001 Entry Draft, June 23, 2001. Signed as a free agent by **Yaroslavl** (Russia), February 14, 2005. Signed as a free agent by **Yaroslavl** (Russia), July 20, 2007.

YELLE, Stephane (YEHL, STEH-fan) CGY.

Center. Shoots left. 6'2", 186 lbs. Born, Ottawa, Ont., May 9, 1974. New Jersey's 9th choice, 186th overall, in 1992 Entry Draft.

Season	Club	League	GP	G	A	Pts	PIM	PP	SH	GW	S	%	+/-	TF	F%	Min	GP	G	A	Pts	PIM	PP	SH	GW	Min
1990-91	Cumberland	OHA-B	33	20	30	50	16	....	....	....	....	....	....	....	....	....	....	....	....	....	....	....	....	....	....
1991-92	Oshawa Generals	OHL	55	12	14	26	20	....	....	....	....	....	....	....	....	....	7	2	0	2	2	....	....	....	....
1992-93	Oshawa Generals	OHL	66	24	50	74	20	....	....	....	....	....	....	....	....	....	10	2	4	6	4	....	....	....	....
1993-94	Oshawa Generals	OHL	66	35	69	104	22	....	....	....	....	....	....	....	....	....	5	1	7	8	2	....	....	....	....
1994-95	Cornwall Aces	AHL	40	18	15	33	22	....	....	....	....	....	....	....	....	....	13	7	7	14	8	....	....	....	....
1995-96♦	**Colorado**	**NHL**	**71**	**13**	**14**	**27**	**30**	**0**	**2**	**1**	**93**	**14.0**	**15**	....	....	....	**22**	**1**	**4**	**5**	**8**	**0**	**1**	**0**	....
1996-97	**Colorado**	**NHL**	**79**	**9**	**17**	**26**	**38**	**0**	**1**	**1**	**89**	**10.1**	**1**	....	....	....	**12**	**1**	**6**	**7**	**2**	**0**	**0**	**0**	....
1997-98	**Colorado**	**NHL**	**81**	**7**	**15**	**22**	**48**	**0**	**1**	**0**	**93**	**7.5**	**−10**	....	....	....	**7**	**1**	**0**	**1**	**12**	**0**	**0**	**0**	....
1998-99	**Colorado**	**NHL**	**72**	**8**	**7**	**15**	**40**	**1**	**0**	**0**	**99**	**8.1**	**−8**	**1201**	**51.2**	**15:15**	**10**	**0**	**1**	**1**	**6**	**0**	**0**	**0**	**15:13**
99-2000	**Colorado**	**NHL**	**79**	**8**	**14**	**22**	**28**	**0**	**1**	**1**	**90**	**8.9**	**9**	**1294**	**52.2**	**15:51**	**17**	**1**	**2**	**3**	**4**	**0**	**0**	**0**	**15:38**
2000-01♦	**Colorado**	**NHL**	**50**	**4**	**10**	**14**	**20**	**0**	**1**	**0**	**54**	**7.4**	**−3**	**736**	**56.4**	**14:28**	**23**	**1**	**2**	**3**	**8**	**0**	**0**	**1**	**13:52**
2001-02	**Colorado**	**NHL**	**73**	**5**	**12**	**17**	**48**	**0**	**1**	**1**	**71**	**7.0**	**1**	**1036**	**51.8**	**14:02**	**20**	**0**	**2**	**2**	**14**	**0**	**0**	**0**	**13:26**
2002-03	**Calgary**	**NHL**	**82**	**10**	**15**	**25**	**50**	**3**	**0**	**3**	**121**	**8.3**	**−10**	**1494**	**53.4**	**18:06**	....	....	....	....	....	....	....	....	....
2003-04	**Calgary**	**NHL**	**53**	**4**	**13**	**17**	**24**	**1**	**0**	**0**	**76**	**5.3**	**1**	**996**	**56.6**	**15:48**	**23**	**3**	**3**	**6**	**16**	**0**	**1**	**1**	**17:04**
2004-05			DID NOT PLAY																						
2005-06	**Calgary**	**NHL**	**74**	**4**	**14**	**18**	**48**	**1**	**1**	**1**	**93**	**4.3**	**10**	**1072**	**55.4**	**14:27**	**7**	**1**	**0**	**1**	**8**	**0**	**0**	**0**	**15:28**
2006-07	**Calgary**	**NHL**	**56**	**10**	**14**	**24**	**32**	**1**	**1**	**1**	**55**	**18.2**	**5**	**808**	**50.4**	**14:37**	**6**	**0**	**0**	**0**	**2**	**0**	**0**	**0**	**15:13**
	NHL Totals		**770**	**82**	**145**	**227**	**406**	**7**	**9**	**9**	**934**	**8.8**		**8637**	**53.3**	**15:25**	**147**	**9**	**20**	**29**	**80**	**0**	**2**	**2**	**15:04**

Traded to **Quebec** by **New Jersey** with New Jersey's 11th round choice (Steven Low) in 1994 Entry Draft for Quebec's 11th round choice (Mike Hanson) in 1994 Entry Draft, June 1, 1994. Transferred to **Colorado** after **Quebec** franchise relocated, June 21, 1995. Traded to **Calgary** by **Colorado** with Chris Drury for Derek Morris, Jeff Shantz and Dean McAmmond, October 1, 2002.

YONKMAN, Nolan (YAWNK-man, NOH-luhn) NSH.

Defense. Shoots right. 6'6", 245 lbs. Born, Punnichy, Sask., April 1, 1981. Washington's 5th choice, 37th overall, in 1999 Entry Draft.

Season	Club	League	GP	G	A	Pts	PIM	PP	SH	GW	S	%	+/-	TF	F%	Min	GP	G	A	Pts	PIM	PP	SH	GW	Min
1996-97	Naicam Vikings	SAHA	64	15	23	38	36	....	....	....	....	....	....	....	....	....	....	....	....	....	....	....	....	....	....
	Kelowna Rockets	WHL	4	0	0	0	0	....	....	....	....	....	....	....	....	....	....	....	....	....	....	....	....	....	....
1997-98	Kelowna Rockets	WHL	65	0	2	2	36	....	....	....	....	....	....	....	....	....	7	0	0	0	2	....	....	....	....
1998-99	Kelowna Rockets	WHL	61	1	6	7	129	....	....	....	....	....	....	....	....	....	6	0	0	0	6	....	....	....	....
99-2000	Kelowna Rockets	WHL	71	5	7	12	153	....	....	....	....	....	....	....	....	....	5	0	0	0	8	....	....	....	....
2000-01	Kelowna Rockets	WHL	7	0	1	1	19	....	....	....	....	....	....	....	....	....	....	....	....	....	....	....	....	....	....
	Brandon	WHL	51	6	10	16	94	....	....	....	....	....	....	....	....	....	6	0	1	1	12	....	....	....	....
2001-02	**Washington**	**NHL**	**11**	**1**	**0**	**1**	**4**	**0**	**0**	**0**	**7**	**14.3**	**3**	**0**	**0.0**	**12:44**	....	....	....	....	....	....	....	....	....
	Portland Pirates	AHL	59	4	3	7	116	....	....	....	....	....	....	....	....	....	....	....	....	....	....	....	....	....	....
2002-03	Portland Pirates	AHL	24	1	4	5	40	....	....	....	....	....	....	....	....	....	3	0	1	1	2	....	....	....	....
2003-04	**Washington**	**NHL**	**1**	**0**	**0**	**0**	**0**	**0**	**0**	**0**	**0**	**0.0**	**0**	**0**	**0.0**	**5:00**	....	....	....	....	....	....	....	....	....
	Portland Pirates	AHL	4	0	0	0	11	....	....	....	....	....	....	....	....	....	....	....	....	....	....	....	....	....	....
2004-05	Portland Pirates	AHL	32	0	3	3	68	....	....	....	....	....	....	....	....	....	....	....	....	....	....	....	....	....	....
2005-06	**Washington**	**NHL**	**38**	**0**	**7**	**7**	**86**	**0**	**0**	**0**	**14**	**0.0**	**1**	**0**	**0.0**	**8:13**	....	....	....	....	....	....	....	....	....
	Hershey Bears	AHL	6	0	0	0	15	....	....	....	....	....	....	....	....	....	....	....	....	....	....	....	....	....	....
2006-07	Milwaukee	AHL	77	3	10	13	113	....	....	....	....	....	....	....	....	....	4	0	0	0	2	....	....	....	....
	NHL Totals		**50**	**1**	**7**	**8**	**90**	**0**	**0**	**0**	**21**	**4.8**		**0**	**0.0**	**9:09**	....	....	....	....	....	....	....	....	....

• Missed majority of 2002-03 season recovering from abdominal injury suffered in training camp, September 25, 2002. • Missed majority of 2003-04 and 2004-05 seasons recovering from knee injury suffered in game vs. Worcester (AHL), October 23, 2003. Signed as a free agent by **Nashville**, July 17, 2006.

YORK, Jason (YOHRK, JAY-suhn)

Defense. Shoots right. 6'1", 208 lbs. Born, Nepean, Ont., May 20, 1970. Detroit's 6th choice, 129th overall, in 1990 Entry Draft.

Season	Club	League	GP	G	A	Pts	PIM	PP	SH	GW	S	%	+/-	TF	F%	Min	GP	G	A	Pts	PIM	PP	SH	GW	Min
1986-87	Smiths Falls Bears	CJHL	46	6	13	19	86	....	....	....	....	....	....	....	....	....	....	....	....	....	....	....	....	....	....
1987-88	Hamilton	OHL	58	4	9	13	110	....	....	....	....	....	....	....	....	....	....	....	....	....	....	....	....	....	....
1988-89	Windsor Spitfires	OHL	65	19	44	63	105	....	....	....	....	....	....	....	....	....	....	....	....	....	....	....	....	....	....
1989-90	Windsor Spitfires	OHL	39	9	30	39	38	....	....	....	....	....	....	....	....	....	....	....	....	....	....	....	....	....	....
	Kitchener Rangers	OHL	25	11	25	36	17	....	....	....	....	....	....	....	....	....	17	3	19	22	10	....	....	....	....
1990-91	Windsor Spitfires	OHL	66	13	80	93	40	....	....	....	....	....	....	....	....	....	11	3	10	13	12	....	....	....	....
1991-92	Adirondack	AHL	49	4	20	24	32	....	....	....	....	....	....	....	....	....	5	0	1	1	0	....	....	....	....
1992-93	**Detroit**	**NHL**	**2**	**0**	**0**	**0**	**0**	**0**	**0**	**0**	**1**	**0.0**	**0**	....	....	....	....	....	....	....	....	....	....	....	....
	Adirondack	AHL	77	15	40	55	86	....	....	....	....	....	....	....	....	....	11	0	3	3	18	....	....	....	....
1993-94	**Detroit**	**NHL**	**7**	**1**	**2**	**3**	**2**	**0**	**0**	**0**	**9**	**11.1**	**0**	....	....	....	....	....	....	....	....	....	....	....	....
	Adirondack	AHL	74	10	56	66	98	....	....	....	....	....	....	....	....	....	12	3	11	14	22	....	....	....	....
1994-95	**Detroit**	**NHL**	**10**	**1**	**2**	**3**	**2**	**0**	**0**	**0**	**6**	**16.7**	**0**	....	....	....	....	....	....	....	....	....	....	....	....
	Adirondack	AHL	5	1	3	4	4	....	....	....	....	....	....	....	....	....	....	....	....	....	....	....	....	....	....
	Anaheim	**NHL**	**15**	**0**	**8**	**8**	**12**	**0**	**0**	**0**	**22**	**0.0**	**4**	....	....	....	....	....	....	....	....	....	....	....	....
1995-96	**Anaheim**	**NHL**	**79**	**3**	**21**	**24**	**88**	**0**	**0**	**0**	**106**	**2.8**	**−7**	....	....	....	....	....	....	....	....	....	....	....	....
1996-97	**Ottawa**	**NHL**	**75**	**4**	**17**	**21**	**67**	**1**	**0**	**0**	**121**	**3.3**	**−8**	....	....	....	**7**	**0**	**0**	**0**	**4**	**0**	**0**	**0**	....
1997-98	**Ottawa**	**NHL**	**73**	**3**	**13**	**16**	**62**	**0**	**0**	**0**	**109**	**2.8**	**8**	....	....	....	**7**	**1**	**1**	**2**	**7**	**1**	**0**	**0**	....
1998-99	**Ottawa**	**NHL**	**79**	**4**	**31**	**35**	**48**	**2**	**0**	**0**	**177**	**2.3**	**17**	**2**	**0.0**	**23:49**	**4**	**1**	**1**	**2**	**4**	**0**	**0**	**0**	**24:59**
99-2000	**Ottawa**	**NHL**	**79**	**8**	**22**	**30**	**60**	**1**	**0**	**1**	**159**	**5.0**	**−3**	**0**	**0.0**	**23:20**	**6**	**0**	**2**	**2**	**2**	**0**	**0**	**0**	**25:30**
2000-01	**Ottawa**	**NHL**	**74**	**6**	**16**	**22**	**72**	**3**	**0**	**2**	**133**	**4.5**	**7**	**0**	**0.0**	**23:49**	**4**	**0**	**0**	**0**	**4**	**0**	**0**	**0**	**20:58**
2001-02	**Anaheim**	**NHL**	**74**	**5**	**20**	**25**	**60**	**3**	**0**	**2**	**104**	**4.8**	**−11**	**0**	**0.0**	**19:19**	....	....	....	....	....	....	....	....	....
2002-03	Cincinnati	AHL	4	3	2	5	8	....	....	....	....	....	....	....	....	....	....	....	....	....	....	....	....	....	....
	Nashville	**NHL**	**74**	**4**	**15**	**19**	**52**	**2**	**0**	**0**	**107**	**3.7**	**13**	**0**	**0.0**	**19:57**	....	....	....	....	....	....	....	....	....
2003-04	**Nashville**	**NHL**	**67**	**2**	**13**	**15**	**64**	**0**	**0**	**1**	**80**	**2.5**	**−4**	**1**	**0.0**	**21:17**	**6**	**0**	**3**	**3**	**4**	**0**	**0**	**0**	**21:27**
2004-05			DID NOT PLAY																						
2005-06	HC Lugano	Swiss	34	3	18	21	122	....	....	....	....	....	....	....	....	....	16	1	3	4	8	....	....	....	....
2006-07	**Boston**	**NHL**	**49**	**1**	**7**	**8**	**32**	**0**	**0**	**0**	**27**	**3.7**	**−14**	**0**	**0.0**	**13:04**	....	....	....	....	....	....	....	....	....
	NHL Totals		**757**	**42**	**187**	**229**	**621**	**12**	**0**	**6**	**1161**	**3.6**		**3**	**0.0**	**21:05**	**34**	**2**	**7**	**9**	**25**	**1**	**0**	**0**	**23:16**

AHL First All-Star Team (1994)

Traded to **Anaheim** by **Detroit** with Mike Sillinger for Stu Grimson, Mark Ferner and Anaheim's 6th round choice (Magnus Nilsson) in 1996 Entry Draft, April 4, 1995. Traded to **Ottawa** by **Anaheim** with Shaun Van Allen for Ted Drury and the rights to Marc Moro, October 1, 1996. Signed as a free agent by **Anaheim**, July 3, 2001. Traded to **Nashville** by **Anaheim** for future considerations, October 23, 2002. Signed as a free agent by **Lugano** (Swiss), September 19, 2005. Signed as a free agent by **Boston**, July 21, 2006.

YORK, Mike (YOHRK, MIGHK) PHX.

Left wing. Shoots right. 5'10", 185 lbs. Born, Waterford, MI, January 3, 1978. NY Rangers' 7th choice, 136th overall, in 1997 Entry Draft.

Season	Club	League	GP	G	A	Pts	PIM	PP	SH	GW	S	%	+/-	TF	F%	Min	GP	G	A	Pts	PIM	PP	SH	GW	Min
1992-93	Michigan	MNHL	50	45	50	95	....	....	....	....	....	....	....	....	....	....	....	....	....	....	....	....	....	....	....
1993-94	Det. Compuware	MNHL	85	136	140	276	....	....	....	....	....	....	....	....	....	....	....	....	....	....	....	....	....	....	....
1994-95	Thornhill Islanders	MTJHL	49	39	54	*93	44	....	....	....	....	....	....	....	....	....	11	7	6	13	0	....	....	....	....
1995-96	Michigan State	CCHA	39	12	27	39	20	....	....	....	....	....	....	....	....	....	....	....	....	....	....	....	....	....	....
1996-97	Michigan State	CCHA	37	18	29	47	42	....	....	....	....	....	....	....	....	....	....	....	....	....	....	....	....	....	....
1997-98	Michigan State	CCHA	40	27	34	61	38	....	....	....	....	....	....	....	....	....	....	....	....	....	....	....	....	....	....
1998-99	Michigan State	CCHA	42	22	32	*54	41	....	....	....	....	....	....	....	....	....	....	....	....	....	....	....	....	....	....
	Hartford	AHL	3	2	2	4	0	....	....	....	....	....	....	....	....	....	6	3	1	4	0	....	....	....	....
99-2000	**NY Rangers**	**NHL**	**82**	**26**	**24**	**50**	**18**	**8**	**0**	**4**	**177**	**14.7**	**−17**	**1131**	**48.1**	**1:35**	....	....	....	....	....	....	....	....	....
2000-01	**NY Rangers**	**NHL**	**79**	**14**	**17**	**31**	**20**	**3**	**2**	**4**	**171**	**8.2**	**1**	**1098**	**46.9**	**17:45**	....	....	....	....	....	....	....	....	....
2001-02	**NY Rangers**	**NHL**	**69**	**18**	**39**	**57**	**16**	**2**	**0**	**5**	**188**	**9.6**	**8**	**267**	**43.1**	**20:24**	....	....	....	....	....	....	....	....	....
	United States	Olympics	6	0	1	1	0	....	....	....	....	....	....	....	....	....	....	....	....	....	....	....	....	....	....
	Edmonton	**NHL**	**12**	**2**	**2**	**4**	**0**	**1**	**0**	**1**	**30**	**6.7**	**−1**	**100**	**56.0**	**16:35**	....	....	....	....	....	....	....	....	....
2002-03	**Edmonton**	**NHL**	**71**	**22**	**29**	**51**	**10**	**7**	**2**	**4**	**177**	**12.4**	**−8**	**390**	**43.9**	**19:04**	**6**	**0**	**2**	**2**	**2**	**0**	**0**	**0**	**14:20**

Season	Club	League	GP	G	A	Pts	PIM	PP	SH	GW	S	%	+/-	TF	F%	Min	GP	G	A	Pts	PIM	PP	SH	GW	Min
			Regular Season														Playoffs								
2003-04	**Edmonton**	**NHL**	**61**	**16**	**26**	**42**	**15**	**1**	**2**	**0**	**144**	**11.1**	**18**	**656**	**45.9**	**19:17**	....	....	....	....	....	....	....	....	....
2004-05	Iserlohn Roosters	Germany	52	16	46	62	77	....	....	....	....	....	....	....	....	....	....	....	....	....	....	....	....	....	....
2005-06	**NY Islanders**	**NHL**	**75**	**13**	**39**	**52**	**30**	**4**	**1**	**2**	**146**	**8.9**	**–9**	**1289**	**46.1**	**19:55**	....	....	....	....	....	....	....	....	....
2006-07	**NY Islanders**	**NHL**	**32**	**6**	**7**	**13**	**14**	**2**	**0**	**1**	**46**	**13.0**	**–9**	**432**	**45.6**	**14:47**	....	....	....	....	....	....	....	....	....
	Philadelphia	**NHL**	**34**	**4**	**4**	**8**	**8**	**0**	**0**	**1**	**41**	**9.8**	**–9**	**272**	**47.8**	**10:22**	....	....	....	....	....	....	....	....	....
	NHL Totals		**515**	**121**	**187**	**308**	**131**	**28**	**7**	**22**	**1120**	**10.8**		**5635**	**46.5**	**15:31**	**6**	**0**	**2**	**2**	**2**	**0**	**0**	**0**	**14:20**

CCHA Second All-Star Team (1998) • NCAA West First All-American Team (1998, 1999) • CCHA First All-Star Team (1999) • CCHA Player of the Year (1999) • NHL All-Rookie Team (2000)

Played in NHL All-Star Game (2002)

Traded to **Edmonton** by **NY Rangers** with NY Rangers' 4th round choice (Ivan Koltsov) in 2002 Entry Draft for Tom Poti and Rem Murray, March 19, 2002. Signed as a free agent by **Iserlohn** (Germany), February 25, 2005. Traded to **NY Islanders** by **Edmonton** with Edmonton's 4th round choice (later traded to Colorado - Colorado selected Kevin Montgomery) in 2006 Entry Draft for Michael Peca, August 3, 2005. Traded to **Philadelphia** by **NY Islanders** for Randy Robitaille and Philadelphia's 5th round choice in 2008 Entry Draft, December 20, 2006. Signed as a free agent by **Phoenix**, July 9, 2007.

YOUNG, Bryan (YUHNG, BRIGH-uhn) EDM.

Defense. Shoots left. 6'1", 191 lbs. Born, Kitchener, Ont., August 6, 1986. Edmonton's 6th choice, 146th overall, in 2004 Entry Draft.

Season	Club	League	GP	G	A	Pts	PIM	PP	SH	GW	S	%	+/-	TF	F%	Min	GP	G	A	Pts	PIM	PP	SH	GW	Min
2002-03	Lindsay Muskies	OPJHL	47	1	9	10	56	....	....	....	....	....	....	....	....	....	....	....	....	....	....	....	....	....	....
	Peterborough	OHL	2	0	0	0	0	....	....	....	....	....	....	....	....	....	....	....	....	....	....	....	....	....	....
2003-04	Peterborough	OHL	60	0	8	8	63	....	....	....	....	....	....	....	....	....	....	....	....	....	....	....	....	....	....
2004-05	Peterborough	OHL	60	1	11	12	44	....	....	....	....	....	....	....	....	....	14	0	1	1	10	....	....	....	....
2005-06	Peterborough	OHL	64	0	10	10	113	....	....	....	....	....	....	....	....	....	19	0	0	0	37	....	....	....	....
2006-07	**Edmonton**	**NHL**	**15**	**0**	**0**	**0**	**10**	**0**	**0**	**0**	**2**	**0.0**	**–8**	**0**	**0.0**	**10:06**	....	....	....	....	....	....	....	....	....
	Milwaukee	AHL	22	0	0	0	6	....	....	....	....	....	....	....	....	....	....	....	....	....	....	....	....	....	....
	Stockton Thunder	ECHL	17	0	4	4	24	....	....	....	....	....	....	....	....	....	....	....	....	....	....	....	....	....	....
	Wilkes-Barre	AHL	10	0	1	1	2	....	....	....	....	....	....	....	....	....	4	0	1	1	2	....	....	....	....
	NHL Totals		**15**	**0**	**0**	**0**	**10**	**0**	**0**	**0**	**2**	**0.0**		**0**	**0.0**	**10:06**	....	....	....	....	....	....	....	....	....

ZAJAC, Travis (ZAY-jak, TRA-vihs) N.J.

Center. Shoots right. 6'2", 200 lbs. Born, Winnipeg, Man., May 13, 1985. New Jersey's 1st choice, 20th overall, in 2004 Entry Draft.

Season	Club	League	GP	G	A	Pts	PIM	PP	SH	GW	S	%	+/-	TF	F%	Min	GP	G	A	Pts	PIM	PP	SH	GW	Min
2002-03	Salmon Arm	BCHL	59	16	36	52	27	....	....	....	....	....	....	....	....	....	11	2	4	6	6	....	....	....	....
2003-04	Salmon Arm	BCHL	59	43	69	112	110	....	....	....	....	....	....	....	....	....	14	10	13	23	10	....	....	....	....
2004-05	North Dakota	WCHA	45	20	19	39	16	....	....	....	....	....	....	....	....	....	....	....	....	....	....	....	....	....	....
2005-06	North Dakota	WCHA	46	18	29	47	20	....	....	....	....	....	....	....	....	....	....	....	....	....	....	....	....	....	....
	Albany River Rats	AHL	2	0	1	1	2	....	....	....	....	....	....	....	....	....	....	....	....	....	....	....	....	....	....
2006-07	**New Jersey**	**NHL**	**80**	**17**	**25**	**42**	**16**	**6**	**0**	**2**	**134**	**12.7**	**1**	**904**	**46.9**	**16:03**	**11**	**1**	**4**	**5**	**4**	**0**	**0**	**0**	**16:22**
	NHL Totals		**80**	**17**	**25**	**42**	**16**	**6**	**0**	**2**	**134**	**12.7**		**904**	**46.9**	**16:03**	**11**	**1**	**4**	**5**	**4**	**0**	**0**	**0**	**16:22**

WCHA All-Rookie Team (2005) • NCAA Championship All-Tournament Team (2005)

ZANON, Greg (ZA-nuhn, GREHG) NSH.

Defense. Shoots left. 5'11", 211 lbs. Born, Burnaby, B.C., June 5, 1980. Ottawa's 6th choice, 156th overall, in 2000 Entry Draft.

Season	Club	League	GP	G	A	Pts	PIM	PP	SH	GW	S	%	+/-	TF	F%	Min	GP	G	A	Pts	PIM	PP	SH	GW	Min
1995-96	Burnaby Beavers	BCAHA	49	16	27	43	142	....	....	....	....	....	....	....	....	....	....	....	....	....	....	....	....	....	....
1996-97	Victoria Salsa	BCHL	53	4	13	17	124	....	....	....	....	....	....	....	....	....	....	....	....	....	....	....	....	....	....
1997-98	Victoria Salsa	BCHL	59	11	21	32	108	....	....	....	....	....	....	....	....	....	7	0	2	2	10	....	....	....	....
1998-99	South Surrey	BCHL	59	17	54	71	154	....	....	....	....	....	....	....	....	....	....	....	....	....	....	....	....	....	....
99-2000	Nebraska-Omaha	CCHA	42	3	26	29	56	....	....	....	....	....	....	....	....	....	....	....	....	....	....	....	....	....	....
2000-01	Nebraska-Omaha	CCHA	39	12	16	28	64	....	....	....	....	....	....	....	....	....	....	....	....	....	....	....	....	....	....
2001-02	Nebraska-Omaha	CCHA	41	9	16	25	54	....	....	....	....	....	....	....	....	....	....	....	....	....	....	....	....	....	....
2002-03	Nebraska-Omaha	CCHA	32	6	19	25	44	....	....	....	....	....	....	....	....	....	....	....	....	....	....	....	....	....	....
2003-04	Milwaukee	AHL	62	4	12	16	59	....	....	....	....	....	....	....	....	....	22	2	6	8	31	....	....	....	....
2004-05	Milwaukee	AHL	80	2	17	19	59	....	....	....	....	....	....	....	....	....	7	0	1	1	10	....	....	....	....
2005-06	**Nashville**	**NHL**	**4**	**0**	**2**	**2**	**6**	**0**	**0**	**0**	**3**	**0.0**	**0**	**0**	**0.0**	**17:19**	....	....	....	....	....	....	....	....	....
	Milwaukee	AHL	71	8	27	35	55	....	....	....	....	....	....	....	....	....	21	1	7	8	24	....	....	....	....
2006-07	**Nashville**	**NHL**	**66**	**3**	**5**	**8**	**32**	**0**	**0**	**0**	**43**	**7.0**	**16**	**0**	**0.0**	**17:20**	**5**	**0**	**2**	**2**	**2**	**0**	**0**	**0**	**20:44**
	Milwaukee	AHL	2	0	2	2	0	....	....	....	....	....	....	....	....	....	....	....	....	....	....	....	....	....	....
	NHL Totals		**70**	**3**	**7**	**10**	**38**	**0**	**0**	**0**	**46**	**6.5**		**0**	**0.0**	**17:20**	**5**	**0**	**2**	**2**	**2**	**0**	**0**	**0**	**20:44**

CCHA First All-Star Team (2001) • NCAA West Second All-American Team (2001, 2002) • CCHA Second All-Star Team (2002)

Signed as a free agent by **Nashville**, July 9, 2004.

ZEDNIK, Richard (ZEHD-nihk, RIH-chuhrd) FLA.

Right wing. Shoots left. 6', 200 lbs. Born, Banska Bystrica, Czech., January 6, 1976. Washington's 10th choice, 249th overall, in 1994 Entry Draft.

Season	Club	League	GP	G	A	Pts	PIM	PP	SH	GW	S	%	+/-	TF	F%	Min	GP	G	A	Pts	PIM	PP	SH	GW	Min
1993-94	B. Bystrica	Slovak-2	25	3	6	9	....	....	....	....	....	....	....	....	....	....	....	....	....	....	....	....	....	....	....
1994-95	Portland	WHL	65	35	51	86	89	....	....	....	....	....	....	....	....	....	9	5	5	10	20	....	....	....	....
1995-96	Portland	WHL	61	44	37	81	154	....	....	....	....	....	....	....	....	....	7	8	4	12	23	....	....	....	....
	Washington	**NHL**	**1**	**0**	**0**	**0**	**0**	**0**	**0**	**0**	**0**	**0.0**	**0**	....	....	....	....	....	....	....	....	....	....	....	....
	Portland Pirates	AHL	1	1	1	2	0	....	....	....	....	....	....	....	....	....	21	4	5	9	26	....	....	....	....
1996-97	**Washington**	**NHL**	**11**	**2**	**1**	**3**	**4**	**1**	**0**	**0**	**21**	**9.5**	**–5**	....	....	....	....	....	....	....	....	....	....	....	....
	Portland Pirates	AHL	56	15	20	35	70	....	....	....	....	....	....	....	....	....	5	1	0	1	6	....	....	....	....
1997-98	**Washington**	**NHL**	**65**	**17**	**9**	**26**	**28**	**2**	**0**	**2**	**148**	**11.5**	**–2**	....	....	....	**17**	**7**	**3**	**10**	**16**	**2**	**0**	**0**	....
1998-99	**Washington**	**NHL**	**49**	**9**	**8**	**17**	**50**	**1**	**0**	**2**	**115**	**7.8**	**–6**	**2**	**0.0**	**15:08**	....	....	....	....	....	....	....	....	....
99-2000	**Washington**	**NHL**	**69**	**19**	**16**	**35**	**54**	**1**	**0**	**2**	**179**	**10.6**	**6**	**1**	**100.0**	**15:34**	**5**	**0**	**0**	**0**	**5**	**0**	**0**	**0**	**16:57**
2000-01	**Washington**	**NHL**	**62**	**16**	**19**	**35**	**61**	**4**	**0**	**3**	**155**	**10.3**	**–2**	**1**	**0.0**	**15:32**	....	....	....	....	....	....	....	....	....
	Montreal	**NHL**	**12**	**3**	**6**	**9**	**10**	**1**	**0**	**0**	**23**	**13.0**	**–2**	**0**	**0.0**	**18:29**	....	....	....	....	....	....	....	....	....
2001-02	**Montreal**	**NHL**	**82**	**22**	**22**	**44**	**59**	**4**	**0**	**3**	**249**	**8.8**	**–3**	**10**	**30.0**	**17:39**	**4**	**4**	**4**	**8**	**6**	**2**	**0**	**0**	**21:19**
2002-03	**Montreal**	**NHL**	**80**	**31**	**19**	**50**	**79**	**9**	**0**	**2**	**250**	**12.4**	**4**	**10**	**30.0**	**18:25**	....	....	....	....	....	....	....	....	....
2003-04	**Montreal**	**NHL**	**81**	**26**	**24**	**50**	**63**	**7**	**0**	**9**	**218**	**11.9**	**5**	**6**	**50.0**	**17:30**	**11**	**3**	**3**	**6**	**2**	**0**	**0**	**1**	**18:52**
2004-05	HKm Zvolen	Slovakia	36	15	19	34	56	....	....	....	....	....	....	....	....	....	17	9	10	19	12	....	....	....	....
2005-06	**Montreal**	**NHL**	**67**	**16**	**14**	**30**	**48**	**6**	**0**	**4**	**161**	**9.9**	**–2**	**6**	**16.7**	**15:46**	**6**	**2**	**0**	**2**	**4**	**1**	**0**	**0**	**15:13**
	Slovakia	Olympics	6	1	0	1	12	....	....	....	....	....	....	....	....	....	....	....	....	....	....	....	....	....	....
2006-07	**Washington**	**NHL**	**32**	**6**	**12**	**18**	**16**	**1**	**0**	**1**	**68**	**8.8**	**–4**	**3**	**33.3**	**15:42**	....	....	....	....	....	....	....	....	....
	NY Islanders	**NHL**	**10**	**1**	**2**	**3**	**2**	**0**	**0**	**0**	**15**	**6.7**	**–2**	**1**	**0.0**	**12:51**	**5**	**0**	**0**	**0**	**8**	**0**	**0**	**0**	**10:45**
	NHL Totals		**621**	**168**	**152**	**320**	**474**	**37**	**0**	**28**	**1602**	**10.5**		**40**	**30.0**	**16:36**	**48**	**16**	**10**	**26**	**41**	**5**	**0**	**1**	**16:51**

WHL West Second All-Star Team (1996)

Traded to **Montreal** by **Washington** with Jan Bulis and Washington's 1st round choice (Alexander Perezhogin) in 2001 Entry Draft for Trevor Linden, Dainius Zubrus and New Jersey's 2nd round choice (previously acquired, later traded to Tampa Bay – Tampa Bay selected Andreas Holmqvist) in 2001 Entry Draft, March 13, 2001. Signed as a free agent by **Zvolen** (Slovakia), October 7, 2004. Traded to **Washington** by **Montreal** for Wahington's 3rd round choice (Olivier Fortier) in 2007 Entry Draft, July 12, 2006. Traded to **NY Islanders** by **Washington** for NY Islanders' 2nd round choice (Theo Ruth) in 2007 Entry Draft, February 26, 2007. Signed as a free agent by **Florida**, July 1, 2007.

ZEILER, John (ZIGH-luhr, JAWN) L.A.

Right wing. Shoots right. 6', 193 lbs. Born, Jefferson Hills, PA, November 21, 1982. Phoenix's 7th choice, 132nd overall, in 2002 Entry Draft.

Season	Club	League	GP	G	A	Pts	PIM	PP	SH	GW	S	%	+/-	TF	F%	Min	GP	G	A	Pts	PIM	PP	SH	GW	Min
99-2000	Pittsburgh	PAHA	27	17	15	32	94	....	....	....	....	....	....	....	....	....	....	....	....	....	....	....	....	....	....
2000-01	Sioux City	USHL	56	8	20	28	45	....	....	....	....	....	....	....	....	....	2	0	0	0	26	....	....	....	....
2001-02	Sioux City	USHL	60	23	27	50	116	....	....	....	....	....	....	....	....	....	12	2	3	5	25	....	....	....	....
2002-03	St. Lawrence	ECAC	37	10	17	27	28	....	....	....	....	....	....	....	....	....	....	....	....	....	....	....	....	....	....
2003-04	St. Lawrence	ECAC	41	8	*28	36	42	....	....	....	....	....	....	....	....	....	....	....	....	....	....	....	....	....	....
2004-05	St. Lawrence	ECACHL	38	9	23	32	42	....	....	....	....	....	....	....	....	....	....	....	....	....	....	....	....	....	....
2005-06	St. Lawrence	ECACHL	28	13	15	28	28	....	....	....	....	....	....	....	....	....	....	....	....	....	....	....	....	....	....
	San Antonio	AHL	8	0	1	1	10	....	....	....	....	....	....	....	....	....	....	....	....	....	....	....	....	....	....
	Lubbock	CHL	4	2	0	2	16	....	....	....	....	....	....	....	....	....	....	....	....	....	....	....	....	....	....
2006-07	Manchester	AHL	56	12	16	28	70	....	....	....	....	....	....	....	....	....	16	3	2	5	14	....	....	....	....
	Los Angeles	**NHL**	**23**	**1**	**2**	**3**	**22**	**0**	**0**	**0**	**12**	**8.3**	**–2**	**22**	**40.9**	**8:36**	....	....	....	....	....	....	....	....	....
	NHL Totals		**23**	**1**	**2**	**3**	**22**	**0**	**0**	**0**	**12**	**8.3**		**22**	**40.9**	**8:36**	....	....	....	....	....	....	....	....	....

ECAC All-Rookie Team (2003)

Signed as a free agent by **San Antonio** (AHL), March 18, 2006. Signed as a free agent by **Los Angeles**, February 17, 2007.

			Regular Season														Playoffs								
Season	Club	League	GP	G	A	Pts	PIM	PP	SH	GW	S	%	+/-	TF	F%	Min	GP	G	A	Pts	PIM	PP	SH	GW	Min

ZETTERBERG, Henrik

(ZEH-tuhr-buhrg, HEHN-rihk) **DET.**

Left wing. Shoots left. 5'11", 195 lbs. Born, Njurunda, Sweden, October 9, 1980. Detroit's 4th choice, 210th overall, in 1999 Entry Draft.

Season	Club	League	GP	G	A	Pts	PIM	PP	SH	GW	S	%	+/-	TF	F%	Min	GP	G	A	Pts	PIM	PP	SH	GW	Min
1997-98	Timra IK Jr.	Swe-Jr.	18	9	5	14	4	....	....	....	....	....	....	....	....	....	....	....	....	....	....	....	....	....	....
	Timra IK	Sweden-2	16	1	2	3	4	....	....	....	....	....	....	....	....	....	4	0	1	1	0	....	....	....	....
1998-99	Timra IK	Sweden-2	37	15	13	28	2	....	....	....	....	....	....	....	....	....	4	2	1	3	2	....	....	....	....
99-2000	Timra IK	Sweden-2	32	20	14	34	20	....	....	....	....	....	....	....	....	....	10	10	4	14	4	....	....	....	....
2000-01	Timra IK	Sweden	47	15	31	46	24	....	....	....	....	....	....	....	....	....	....	....	....	....	....	....	....	....	....
2001-02	Timra IK	Sweden	48	10	22	32	20	....	....	....	....	....	....	....	....	....	....	....	....	....	....	....	....	....	....
	Sweden	Olympics	4	0	1	1	0	....	....	....	....	....	....	....	....	....	....	....	....	....	....	....	....	....	....
2002-03	**Detroit**	**NHL**	**79**	**22**	**22**	**44**	**8**	**5**	**1**	**4**	**135**	**16.3**	**6**	**401**	**46.1**	**16:19**	**4**	**1**	**0**	**1**	**0**	**0**	**0**	**0**	**18:19**
2003-04	**Detroit**	**NHL**	**61**	**15**	**28**	**43**	**14**	**7**	**1**	**2**	**137**	**10.9**	**15**	**627**	**45.6**	**18:15**	**12**	**2**	**2**	**4**	**4**	**0**	**0**	**0**	**17:17**
2004-05	Timra IK	Sweden	50	19	31	*50	24	....	....	....	....	....	....	....	....	....	7	6	2	8	2	....	....	....	....
2005-06	**Detroit**	**NHL**	**77**	**39**	**46**	**85**	**30**	**17**	**1**	**9**	**270**	**14.4**	**29**	**583**	**50.3**	**18:57**	**6**	**6**	**0**	**6**	**2**	**4**	**0**	**0**	**21:43**
	Sweden	Olympics	8	3	3	6	0	....	....	....	....	....	....	....	....	....	....	....	....	....	....	....	....	....	....
2006-07	**Detroit**	**NHL**	**63**	**33**	**35**	**68**	**36**	**11**	**1**	**10**	**224**	**14.7**	**26**	**888**	**52.5**	**20:50**	**18**	**6**	**8**	**14**	**12**	**3**	**0**	**1**	**22:45**
	NHL Totals		**280**	**109**	**131**	**240**	**88**	**40**	**4**	**25**	**766**	**14.2**		**2499**	**49.2**	**18:29**	**40**	**15**	**10**	**25**	**18**	**7**	**0**	**1**	**20:30**

Swedish Elite League Rookie of the Year (2001) • NHL All-Rookie Team (2003)
Played in NHL All-Star Game (2007)
Signed as a free agent by **Timra** (Sweden), September 20, 2004.

ZHERDEV, Nikolai

(ZHAIR-dehv, NIH-koh-ligh) **CBJ**

Wing. Shoots right. 6'2", 197 lbs. Born, Kiev, USSR, November 5, 1984. Columbus' 1st choice, 4th overall, in 2003 Entry Draft.

Season	Club	League	GP	G	A	Pts	PIM	PP	SH	GW	S	%	+/-	TF	F%	Min	GP	G	A	Pts	PIM	PP	SH	GW	Min
99-2000	Elektrostal 2	Russia-3	21	10	7	17	26	....	....	....	....	....	....	....	....	....	7	0	0	0	0	....	....	....	....
2000-01	Elektrostal	Russia-2	18	5	8	13	12	....	....	....	....	....	....	....	....	....	....	....	....	....	....	....	....	....	....
	Russia	Exhib.	17	10	11	21	17	....	....	....	....	....	....	....	....	....	....	....	....	....	....	....	....	....	....
2001-02	Elektrostal	Russia-2	53	13	15	28	62	....	....	....	....	....	....	....	....	....	....	....	....	....	....	....	....	....	....
	Elektrostal 2	Russia-3	1	1	0	1	4	....	....	....	....	....	....	....	....	....	....	....	....	....	....	....	....	....	....
2002-03	CSKA Moscow	Russia	44	12	12	24	34	....	....	....	....	....	....	....	....	....	....	....	....	....	....	....	....	....	....
2003-04	CSKA Moscow	Russia	20	2	2	4	14	....	....	....	....	....	....	....	....	....	....	....	....	....	....	....	....	....	....
	Columbus	**NHL**	**57**	**13**	**21**	**34**	**54**	**5**	**0**	**1**	**137**	**9.5**	**–11**	**9**	**11.1**	**16:11**	....	....	....	....	....	....	....	....	....
2004-05	CSKA Moscow	Russia	51	19	21	40	62	....	....	....	....	....	....	....	....	....	....	....	....	....	....	....	....	....	....
2005-06	**Columbus**	**NHL**	**73**	**27**	**27**	**54**	**50**	**10**	**0**	**0**	**194**	**13.9**	**–13**	**20**	**10.0**	**17:36**	....	....	....	....	....	....	....	....	....
	Syracuse Crunch	AHL	2	1	0	1	0	....	....	....	....	....	....	....	....	....	....	....	....	....	....	....	....	....	....
2006-07	Mytischi	Russia	8	2	4	6	10	....	....	....	....	....	....	....	....	....	....	....	....	....	....	....	....	....	....
	Columbus	**NHL**	**71**	**10**	**22**	**32**	**26**	**3**	**0**	**2**	**164**	**6.1**	**–19**	**17**	**23.5**	**16:13**	....	....	....	....	....	....	....	....	....
	NHL Totals		**201**	**50**	**70**	**120**	**130**	**18**	**0**	**3**	**495**	**10.1**		**46**	**15.2**	**16:42**	....	....	....	....	....	....	....	....	....

Signed as a free agent by **CSKA Moscow** (Russia), July 27, 2004. Signed as a free agent by **Mystichi** (Russia), July 20, 2006.

ZHITNIK, Alexei

(ZHIHT-nihk, al-EHX-ay) **ATL.**

Defense. Shoots left. 5'11", 215 lbs. Born, Kiev, USSR, October 10, 1972. Los Angeles' 3rd choice, 81st overall, in 1991 Entry Draft.

Season	Club	League	GP	G	A	Pts	PIM	PP	SH	GW	S	%	+/-	TF	F%	Min	GP	G	A	Pts	PIM	PP	SH	GW	Min
1989-90	Sokol Kiev	USSR	31	3	4	7	16	....	....	....	....	....	....	....	....	....	....	....	....	....	....	....	....	....	....
1990-91	Sokol Kiev	USSR	46	1	4	5	46	....	....	....	....	....	....	....	....	....	....	....	....	....	....	....	....	....	....
	ShVSM Kiev	USSR-3	1	0	....	....	....	....	....	....	....	....	....	....	....	....	....	....	....	....	....	....	....	....	....
1991-92	CSKA Moscow	CIS	44	2	7	9	52	....	....	....	....	....	....	....	....	....	....	....	....	....	....	....	....	....	....
	Russia	Olympics	8	1	0	1	0	....	....	....	....	....	....	....	....	....	....	....	....	....	....	....	....	....	....
1992-93	**Los Angeles**	**NHL**	**78**	**12**	**36**	**48**	**80**	**5**	**0**	**2**	**136**	**8.8**	**–3**	....	....	....	**24**	**3**	**9**	**12**	**26**	**2**	**0**	**1**	....
1993-94	**Los Angeles**	**NHL**	**81**	**12**	**40**	**52**	**101**	**11**	**0**	**1**	**227**	**5.3**	**–11**	....	....	....	....	....	....	....	....	....	....	....	....
1994-95	**Los Angeles**	**NHL**	**11**	**2**	**5**	**7**	**27**	**2**	**0**	**0**	**33**	**6.1**	**–3**	....	....	....	....	....	....	....	....	....	....	....	....
	Buffalo	**NHL**	**21**	**2**	**5**	**7**	**34**	**1**	**0**	**0**	**33**	**6.1**	**–3**	....	....	....	**5**	**0**	**1**	**1**	**14**	**0**	**0**	**0**	....
1995-96	**Buffalo**	**NHL**	**80**	**6**	**30**	**36**	**58**	**5**	**0**	**0**	**193**	**3.1**	**–25**	....	....	....	....	....	....	....	....	....	....	....	....
1996-97	**Buffalo**	**NHL**	**80**	**7**	**28**	**35**	**95**	**3**	**1**	**0**	**170**	**4.1**	**10**	....	....	....	**12**	**1**	**0**	**1**	**16**	**0**	**0**	**0**	....
1997-98	**Buffalo**	**NHL**	**78**	**15**	**30**	**45**	**102**	**2**	**3**	**3**	**191**	**7.9**	**19**	....	....	....	**15**	**0**	**3**	**3**	**36**	**0**	**0**	**0**	....
	Russia	Olympics	6	0	2	2	2	....	....	....	....	....	....	....	....	....	....	....	....	....	....	....	....	....	....
1998-99	**Buffalo**	**NHL**	**81**	**7**	**26**	**33**	**96**	**3**	**1**	**2**	**185**	**3.8**	**–6**	**0**	**0.0**	**25:39**	**21**	**4**	**11**	**15**	***52**	**4**	**0**	**2**	**27:07**
99-2000	**Buffalo**	**NHL**	**74**	**2**	**11**	**13**	**95**	**1**	**0**	**0**	**139**	**1.4**	**–6**	**0**	**0.0**	**24:48**	**4**	**0**	**0**	**0**	**8**	**0**	**0**	**0**	**25:50**
2000-01	**Buffalo**	**NHL**	**78**	**8**	**29**	**37**	**75**	**5**	**0**	**1**	**149**	**5.4**	**–3**	**0**	**0.0**	**24:15**	**13**	**1**	**6**	**7**	**12**	**0**	**0**	**0**	**25:38**
2001-02	**Buffalo**	**NHL**	**82**	**1**	**33**	**34**	**80**	**1**	**0**	**0**	**150**	**0.7**	**–1**	**0**	**0.0**	**25:36**	....	....	....	....	....	....	....	....	....
2002-03	**Buffalo**	**NHL**	**70**	**3**	**18**	**21**	**85**	**0**	**0**	**1**	**138**	**2.2**	**–5**	**1**	**0.0**	**26:33**	....	....	....	....	....	....	....	....	....
2003-04	**Buffalo**	**NHL**	**68**	**4**	**24**	**28**	**102**	**2**	**0**	**0**	**134**	**3.0**	**–13**	**0**	**0.0**	**25:01**	....	....	....	....	....	....	....	....	....
2004-05	Ak Bars Kazan	Russia	23	1	8	9	30	....	....	....	....	....	....	....	....	....	4	0	0	0	2	....	....	....	....
2005-06	**NY Islanders**	**NHL**	**59**	**5**	**24**	**29**	**88**	**3**	**0**	**0**	**99**	**5.1**	**4**	**0**	**0.0**	**24:30**	....	....	....	....	....	....	....	....	....
2006-07	**NY Islanders**	**NHL**	**30**	**2**	**9**	**11**	**40**	**0**	**0**	**1**	**49**	**4.1**	**13**	**1**	**100.0**	**21:37**	....	....	....	....	....	....	....	....	....
	Philadelphia	**NHL**	**31**	**3**	**10**	**13**	**38**	**1**	**0**	**0**	**61**	**4.9**	**–16**	**1**	**0.0**	**25:30**	....	....	....	....	....	....	....	....	....
	Atlanta	**NHL**	**18**	**2**	**12**	**14**	**14**	**2**	**0**	**1**	**22**	**9.1**	**4**	**0**	**0.0**	**25:49**	**4**	**0**	**0**	**0**	**4**	**0**	**0**	**0**	**25:21**
	NHL Totals		**1020**	**93**	**370**	**463**	**1210**	**47**	**5**	**12**	**2109**	**4.4**		**3**	**33.3**	**25:04**	**98**	**9**	**30**	**39**	**168**	**6**	**0**	**3**	**26:22**

Played in NHL All-Star Game (1999, 2002)
Traded to **Buffalo** by **Los Angeles** with Robb Stauber, Charlie Huddy and Los Angeles' 5th round choice (Marian Menhart) in 1995 Entry Draft for Philippe Boucher, Denis Tsygurov and Grant Fuhr, February 14, 1995. Signed as a free agent by **Kazan** (Russia), December 6, 2004. Signed as a free agent by **NY Islanders**, August 2, 2005. Traded to **Philadelphia** by **NY Islanders** for Freddy Meyer and Philadelphia's 3rd round choice (Mark Katic) in 2007 Entry Draft, December 16, 2006. Traded to **Atlanta** by **Philadelphia** for Braydon Coburn, February 24, 2007.

ZIDLICKY, Marek

(zihd-LIH-kee, MAIR-ehk) **NSH.**

Defense. Shoots right. 5'11", 190 lbs. Born, Most, Czech., February 3, 1977. NY Rangers' 6th choice, 176th overall, in 2001 Entry Draft.

Season	Club	League	GP	G	A	Pts	PIM	PP	SH	GW	S	%	+/-	TF	F%	Min	GP	G	A	Pts	PIM	PP	SH	GW	Min
1994-95	HC Kladno	CzRep	30	2	2	4	38	....	....	....	....	....	....	....	....	....	11	1	1	2	10	....	....	....	....
1995-96	HC Poldi Kladno	CzRep	37	4	5	9	74	....	....	....	....	....	....	....	....	....	7	1	1	2	8	....	....	....	....
1996-97	HC Poldi Kladno	CzRep	49	5	16	21	60	....	....	....	....	....	....	....	....	....	2	0	0	0	0	....	....	....	....
1997-98	Kladno	CzRep	51	2	13	15	121	....	....	....	....	....	....	....	....	....	....	....	....	....	....	....	....	....	....
1998-99	Kladno	CzRep	50	10	12	22	94	....	....	....	....	....	....	....	....	....	....	....	....	....	....	....	....	....	....
99-2000	HIFK Helsinki	Finland	47	4	16	20	66	....	....	....	....	....	....	....	....	....	9	3	2	5	24	....	....	....	....
	HIFK Helsinki	EuroHL	4	2	2	4	10	....	....	....	....	....	....	....	....	....	1	0	0	0	0	....	....	....	....
2000-01	HIFK Helsinki	Finland	51	12	25	37	146	....	....	....	....	....	....	....	....	....	5	0	1	1	6	....	....	....	....
2001-02	HIFK Helsinki	Finland	56	11	29	40	107	....	....	....	....	....	....	....	....	....	....	....	....	....	....	....	....	....	....
2002-03	HIFK Helsinki	Finland	54	10	37	47	79	....	....	....	....	....	....	....	....	....	4	0	0	0	4	....	....	....	....
2003-04	**Nashville**	**NHL**	**82**	**14**	**39**	**53**	**82**	**9**	**0**	**4**	**143**	**9.8**	**–16**	**0**	**0.0**	**20:02**	**1**	**0**	**0**	**0**	**0**	**0**	**0**	**0**	**2:16**
2004-05	HIFK Helsinki	Finland	49	11	20	31	91	....	....	....	....	....	....	....	....	....	5	0	3	3	14	....	....	....	....
2005-06	**Nashville**	**NHL**	**67**	**12**	**37**	**49**	**82**	**10**	**0**	**1**	**113**	**10.6**	**8**	**0**	**0.0**	**20:04**	**2**	**0**	**1**	**1**	**2**	**0**	**0**	**0**	**15:19**
	Czech Republic	Olympics	7	4	1	5	16	....	....	....	....	....	....	....	....	....	....	....	....	....	....	....	....	....	....
2006-07	**Nashville**	**NHL**	**79**	**4**	**26**	**30**	**72**	**2**	**0**	**1**	**114**	**3.5**	**8**	**0**	**0.0**	**19:43**	**5**	**0**	**2**	**2**	**4**	**0**	**0**	**0**	**19:19**
	NHL Totals		**228**	**30**	**102**	**132**	**236**	**21**	**0**	**6**	**370**	**8.1**		**0**	**0.0**	**19:56**	**8**	**0**	**3**	**3**	**6**	**0**	**0**	**0**	**16:11**

Traded to **Nashville** by **NY Rangers** with Rem Murray and Tomas Kloucek for Mike Dunham, December 12, 2002. Signed as a free agent by **HIFK Helsinki** (Finland), September 17, 2004.

ZIGOMANIS, Mike

(zih-goh-MAN-ihs, MIGHK) **PHX.**

Center. Shoots right. 6'1", 200 lbs. Born, North York, Ont., January 17, 1981. Carolina's 2nd choice, 46th overall, in 2001 Entry Draft.

Season	Club	League	GP	G	A	Pts	PIM	PP	SH	GW	S	%	+/-	TF	F%	Min	GP	G	A	Pts	PIM	PP	SH	GW	Min
1996-97	Wexford Raiders	MTHL	40	37	48	85	23	....	....	....	....	....	....	....	....	....	....	....	....	....	....	....	....	....	....
	Wexford Raiders	MTJHL	8	2	5	7	2	....	....	....	....	....	....	....	....	....	....	....	....	....	....	....	....	....	....
1997-98	Kingston	OHL	62	23	51	74	30	....	....	....	....	....	....	....	....	....	12	1	6	7	2	....	....	....	....
1998-99	Kingston	OHL	67	29	56	85	36	....	....	....	....	....	....	....	....	....	5	1	7	8	2	....	....	....	....
99-2000	Kingston	OHL	59	40	54	94	49	....	....	....	....	....	....	....	....	....	5	0	4	4	0	....	....	....	....
2000-01	Kingston	OHL	52	40	37	77	44	....	....	....	....	....	....	....	....	....	....	....	....	....	....	....	....	....	....
2001-02	Lowell	AHL	79	18	30	48	24	....	....	....	....	....	....	....	....	....	5	1	1	2	2	....	....	....	....
2002-03	**Carolina**	**NHL**	**19**	**2**	**1**	**3**	**0**	**1**	**1**	**0**	**19**	**10.5**	**–4**	**147**	**59.2**	**9:43**	....	....	....	....	....	....	....	....	....
	Lowell	AHL	38	13	18	31	19	....	....	....	....	....	....	....	....	....	....	....	....	....	....	....	....	....	....
2003-04	**Carolina**	**NHL**	**17**	**0**	**3**	**3**	**2**	**0**	**0**	**0**	**13**	**0.0**	**–1**	**108**	**53.7**	**8:37**	....	....	....	....	....	....	....	....	....
	Lowell	AHL	61	17	35	52	56	....	....	....	....	....	....	....	....	....	....	....	....	....	....	....	....	....	....
2004-05	Lowell	AHL	76	29	31	60	71	....	....	....	....	....	....	....	....	....	11	4	7	11	8	....	....	....	....

Season	Club	League	GP	G	A	Pts	PIM	PP	SH	GW	S	%	+/-	TF	F%	Min	GP	G	A	Pts	PIM	PP	SH	GW	Min
			Regular Season														Playoffs								
2005-06	**Carolina**	**NHL**	**21**	**1**	**0**	**1**	**4**	**0**	**0**	**0**	**16**	**6.3**	**1**	**72**	**50.0**	**9:25**	....	....	....	....	....	....	....	....	....
	Lowell	AHL	11	6	7	13	19	....	....	....	....	....	....	....	....	....	....	....	....	....	....	....	....	....	....
	St. Louis	**NHL**	**2**	**0**	**0**	**0**	**0**	**0**	**0**	**0**	**1**	**0.0**	**0**	**1**	**100.0**	**7:39**	....	....	....	....	....	....	....	....	....
	Peoria Rivermen	AHL	28	10	18	28	16	....	....	....	....	....	....	....	....	....	4	2	4	6	6	....	....	....	....
2006-07	**Phoenix**	**NHL**	**75**	**14**	**9**	**23**	**46**	**2**	**1**	**0**	**142**	**9.9**	**–8**	**1010**	**56.2**	**14:53**	....	....	....	....	....	....	....	....	....
	NHL Totals		**134**	**17**	**13**	**30**	**52**	**3**	**2**	**0**	**191**	**8.9**		**1338**	**56.1**	**12:23**	....	....	....	....	....	....	....	....	....

• Re-entered NHL Entry Draft. Originally Buffalo's 4th choice, 64th overall, in 1999 Entry Draft.

Traded to **St. Louis** by **Carolina** with Jesse Boulerice, the rights to Magnus Kahnberg, Carolina's 1st round choice (later traded to New Jersey - New Jersey selected Matthew Corrente) in 2006 Entry Draft, Toronto's 4th round choice (previously acquired, St. Louis selected Reto Berra) in 2006 Entry Draft and Chicago's 4th round choice (previously acquired, St. Louis selected Cade Fairchild) in 2007 Entry Draft for Doug Weight and Erkki Rajamaki, January 30, 2006. Signed as a free agent by **Phoenix**, July 21, 2006.

ZINGER, Dwayne

(ZIHN-guhr, DWAYN)

Defense. Shoots left. 6'4", 216 lbs. Born, Coronation, Alta., July 5, 1976.

Season	Club	League	GP	G	A	Pts	PIM	PP	SH	GW	S	%	+/-	TF	F%	Min	GP	G	A	Pts	PIM	PP	SH	GW	Min
1995-96	Melville	SJHL	64	7	17	24	....	....	....	....	....	....	....	....	....	....	....	....	....	....	....	....	....	....	....
1996-97	Alaska	CCHA	32	1	5	6	45	....	....	....	....	....	....	....	....	....	....	....	....	....	....	....	....	....	....
1997-98	Alaska	CCHA	32	1	3	4	91	....	....	....	....	....	....	....	....	....	....	....	....	....	....	....	....	....	....
1998-99	Alaska	CCHA	33	4	14	18	42	....	....	....	....	....	....	....	....	....	....	....	....	....	....	....	....	....	....
99-2000	Alaska	CCHA	34	10	4	14	34	....	....	....	....	....	....	....	....	....	....	....	....	....	....	....	....	....	....
	Cincinnati	AHL	13	0	2	2	33	....	....	....	....	....	....	....	....	....	....	....	....	....	....	....	....	....	....
2000-01	Cincinnati	AHL	68	6	9	15	120	....	....	....	....	....	....	....	....	....	4	1	1	2	2	....	....	....	....
2001-02	Cincinnati	AHL	67	6	13	19	156	....	....	....	....	....	....	....	....	....	3	0	1	1	2	....	....	....	....
2002-03	Portland Pirates	AHL	65	1	7	8	67	....	....	....	....	....	....	....	....	....	3	0	0	0	2	....	....	....	....
2003-04	**Washington**	**NHL**	**7**	**0**	**1**	**1**	**9**	**0**	**0**	**0**	**0**	**0.0**	**2**	**0**	**0.0**	**5:24**	....	....	....	....	....	....	....	....	....
	Portland Pirates	AHL	68	6	10	16	49	....	....	....	....	....	....	....	....	....	7	0	0	0	16	....	....	....	....
2004-05	Portland Pirates	AHL	58	0	4	4	118	....	....	....	....	....	....	....	....	....	....	....	....	....	....	....	....	....	....
2005-06	Hershey Bears	AHL	30	0	0	0	74	....	....	....	....	....	....	....	....	....	....	....	....	....	....	....	....	....	....
	San Antonio	AHL	35	1	2	3	68	....	....	....	....	....	....	....	....	....	....	....	....	....	....	....	....	....	....
2006-07	Providence Bruins	AHL	78	3	15	18	100	....	....	....	....	....	....	....	....	....	12	1	1	2	13	....	....	....	....
	NHL Totals		**7**	**0**	**1**	**1**	**9**	**0**	**0**	**0**	**0**	**0.0**		**0**	**0.0**	**5:24**	....	....	....	....	....	....	....	....	....

SJHL First All-Star Team (1996)

Signed as a free agent by **Detroit**, March 13, 2000. Signed as a free agent by **Washington**, July 9, 2002. Traded to **Phoenix** by **Washington** for Doug Doull, February 3, 2006.

ZINOVJEV, Sergei

(zih-NOH-vee-ehv, SAIR-gay) **BOS.**

Center/Left wing. Shoots left. 5'10", 185 lbs. Born, Novokuznetsk, USSR, March 4, 1980. Boston's 6th choice, 73rd overall, in 2000 Entry Draft.

Season	Club	League	GP	G	A	Pts	PIM	PP	SH	GW	S	%	+/-	TF	F%	Min	GP	G	A	Pts	PIM	PP	SH	GW	Min
1995-96	Novokuznetsk 2	CIS-2	10	1	0	1	2	....	....	....	....	....	....	....	....	....	....	....	....	....	....	....	....	....	....
1996-97	Novokuznetsk 2	Russia-3	29	2	1	3	8	....	....	....	....	....	....	....	....	....	....	....	....	....	....	....	....	....	....
1997-98	Novokuznetsk 2	Russia-3	40	7	7	14	36	....	....	....	....	....	....	....	....	....	....	....	....	....	....	....	....	....	....
	Novokuznetsk 2	Russia-3	2	1	0	1	0	....	....	....	....	....	....	....	....	....	....	....	....	....	....	....	....	....	....
1998-99	Novokuznetsk 2	Russia-4	4	0	1	1	8	....	....	....	....	....	....	....	....	....	....	....	....	....	....	....	....	....	....
	Magnitogorsk	Russia	31	2	4	6	14	....	....	....	....	....	....	....	....	....	3	0	0	0	0	....	....	....	....
99-2000	Magnitogorsk	Russia	28	0	2	2	16	....	....	....	....	....	....	....	....	....	....	....	....	....	....	....	....	....	....
2000-01	Yaroslavl	Russia	27	2	10	12	36	....	....	....	....	....	....	....	....	....	....	....	....	....	....	....	....	....	....
	Ufa	Russia	8	4	5	9	6	....	....	....	....	....	....	....	....	....	....	....	....	....	....	....	....	....	....
2001-02	Spartak Moscow	Russia	51	12	18	30	43	....	....	....	....	....	....	....	....	....	....	....	....	....	....	....	....	....	....
2002-03	Ak Bars Kazan	Russia	47	14	17	31	50	....	....	....	....	....	....	....	....	....	5	1	1	2	6	....	....	....	....
2003-04	**Boston**	**NHL**	**10**	**0**	**1**	**1**	**2**	**0**	**0**	**0**	**8**	**0.0**	**1**	**72**	**41.7**	**9:48**	....	....	....	....	....	....	....	....	....
	Providence Bruins	AHL	4	1	2	3	0	....	....	....	....	....	....	....	....	....	....	....	....	....	....	....	....	....	....
	Ak Bars Kazan	Russia	27	5	9	14	75	....	....	....	....	....	....	....	....	....	8	0	1	1	12	....	....	....	....
2004-05	Ak Bars Kazan	Russia	54	17	21	38	82	....	....	....	....	....	....	....	....	....	4	1	0	1	12	....	....	....	....
2005-06	Ak Bars Kazan	Russia	43	15	20	35	58	....	....	....	....	....	....	....	....	....	13	9	8	17	26	....	....	....	....
2006-07	Ak Bars Kazan	Russia	41	19	35	54	103	....	....	....	....	....	....	....	....	....	16	7	10	*17	20	....	....	....	....
	NHL Totals		**10**	**0**	**1**	**1**	**2**	**0**	**0**	**0**	**8**	**0.0**		**72**	**41.7**	**9:48**	....	....	....	....	....	....	....	....	....

Signed as a free agent by **Kazan** (Russia), December 9, 2003.

ZIZKA, Tomas

(ZHIHZH-kuh, TAW-mahsh) **L.A.**

Defense. Shoots left. 6'1", 198 lbs. Born, Sternberk, Czech., October 10, 1979. Los Angeles' 6th choice, 163rd overall, in 1998 Entry Draft.

Season	Club	League	GP	G	A	Pts	PIM	PP	SH	GW	S	%	+/-	TF	F%	Min	GP	G	A	Pts	PIM	PP	SH	GW	Min
1994-95	AC ZPS Zlin Jr.	CzRep-Jr.	39	1	10	11	....	....	....	....	....	....	....	....	....	....	....	....	....	....	....	....	....	....	....
1995-96	AC ZPS Zlin Jr.	CzRep-Jr.	47	2	8	10	....	....	....	....	....	....	....	....	....	....	....	....	....	....	....	....	....	....	....
1996-97	AC ZPS Zlin Jr.	CzRep-Jr.	14	1	0	1	....	....	....	....	....	....	....	....	....	....	....	....	....	....	....	....	....	....	....
1997-98	HC ZPS Zlin Jr.	CzRep-Jr.	11	3	4	7	....	....	....	....	....	....	....	....	....	....	....	....	....	....	....	....	....	....	....
	Zlin	CzRep	33	0	3	3	2	....	....	....	....	....	....	....	....	....	....	....	....	....	....	....	....	....	....
1998-99	Zlin	CzRep	44	3	7	10	14	....	....	....	....	....	....	....	....	....	11	1	2	3	....	....	....	....	....
99-2000	Zlin	CzRep	46	4	6	10	30	....	....	....	....	....	....	....	....	....	4	1	0	1	4	....	....	....	....
2000-01	Zlin	CzRep	43	2	11	13	16	....	....	....	....	....	....	....	....	....	6	0	0	0	6	....	....	....	....
2001-02	Manchester	AHL	58	4	17	21	22	....	....	....	....	....	....	....	....	....	4	1	0	1	14	....	....	....	....
2002-03	**Los Angeles**	**NHL**	**10**	**0**	**3**	**3**	**4**	**0**	**0**	**0**	**12**	**0.0**	**–4**	**0**	**0.0**	**15:24**	....	....	....	....	....	....	....	....	....
	Manchester	AHL	61	13	30	43	50	....	....	....	....	....	....	....	....	....	3	0	2	2	2	....	....	....	....
2003-04	**Los Angeles**	**NHL**	**15**	**2**	**3**	**5**	**12**	**1**	**0**	**0**	**24**	**8.3**	**–4**	**0**	**0.0**	**16:54**	....	....	....	....	....	....	....	....	....
	Manchester	AHL	58	4	24	28	31	....	....	....	....	....	....	....	....	....	5	0	3	3	10	....	....	....	....
2004-05	Spartak Moscow	Russia	23	0	3	3	32	....	....	....	....	....	....	....	....	....	....	....	....	....	....	....	....	....	....
	HC Slavia Praha	CzRep	26	2	4	6	26	....	....	....	....	....	....	....	....	....	2	0	0	0	2	....	....	....	....
2005-06	HC Slavia Praha	CzRep	52	6	9	15	48	....	....	....	....	....	....	....	....	....	14	1	2	3	31	....	....	....	....
2006-07	HC Slavia Praha	CzRep	38	4	5	9	54	....	....	....	....	....	....	....	....	....	6	1	2	3	10	....	....	....	....
	NHL Totals		**25**	**2**	**6**	**8**	**16**	**1**	**0**	**0**	**36**	**5.6**		**0**	**0.0**	**16:18**	....	....	....	....	....	....	....	....	....

Signed as a free agent by **Spartak Moscow** (Russia), August 31, 2004. Signed as a free agent by **Slavia Praha** (CzRep), November, 2004.

ZUBOV, Sergei

(ZOO-bahf, SAIR-gay) **DAL.**

Defense. Shoots right. 6'1", 200 lbs. Born, Moscow, USSR, July 22, 1970. NY Rangers' 6th choice, 85th overall, in 1990 Entry Draft.

Season	Club	League	GP	G	A	Pts	PIM	PP	SH	GW	S	%	+/-	TF	F%	Min	GP	G	A	Pts	PIM	PP	SH	GW	Min
1988-89	CSKA Moscow	USSR	29	1	4	5	10	....	....	....	....	....	....	....	....	....	....	....	....	....	....	....	....	....	....
1989-90	CSKA Moscow	USSR	48	6	2	8	16	....	....	....	....	....	....	....	....	....	....	....	....	....	....	....	....	....	....
1990-91	CSKA Moscow	USSR	41	6	5	11	12	....	....	....	....	....	....	....	....	....	....	....	....	....	....	....	....	....	....
	CSKA Moscow	Super-S	7	0	1	1	0	....	....	....	....	....	....	....	....	....	....	....	....	....	....	....	....	....	....
1991-92	CSKA Moscow	CIS	44	4	7	11	8	....	....	....	....	....	....	....	....	....	....	....	....	....	....	....	....	....	....
	Russia	Olympics	8	0	1	1	0	....	....	....	....	....	....	....	....	....	....	....	....	....	....	....	....	....	....
1992-93	CSKA Moscow	CIS	1	0	1	1	0	....	....	....	....	....	....	....	....	....	....	....	....	....	....	....	....	....	....
	NY Rangers	**NHL**	**49**	**8**	**23**	**31**	**4**	**3**	**0**	**0**	**93**	**8.6**	**–1**	....	....	....	....	....	....	....	....	....	....	....	....
	Binghamton	AHL	30	7	29	36	14	....	....	....	....	....	....	....	....	....	11	5	5	10	2	....	....	....	....
1993-94♦	**NY Rangers**	**NHL**	**78**	**12**	**77**	**89**	**39**	**9**	**0**	**1**	**222**	**5.4**	**20**	....	....	....	**22**	**5**	**14**	**19**	**0**	**2**	**0**	**0**	....
	Binghamton	AHL	2	1	2	3	0	....	....	....	....	....	....	....	....	....	....	....	....	....	....	....	....	....	....
1994-95	**NY Rangers**	**NHL**	**38**	**10**	**26**	**36**	**18**	**6**	**0**	**0**	**116**	**8.6**	**–2**	....	....	....	**10**	**3**	**8**	**11**	**2**	**1**	**0**	**0**	....
1995-96	**Pittsburgh**	**NHL**	**64**	**11**	**55**	**66**	**22**	**3**	**2**	**1**	**141**	**7.8**	**28**	....	....	....	**18**	**1**	**14**	**15**	**26**	**1**	**0**	**0**	....
1996-97	**Dallas**	**NHL**	**78**	**13**	**30**	**43**	**24**	**1**	**0**	**3**	**133**	**9.8**	**19**	....	....	....	**7**	**0**	**3**	**3**	**2**	**0**	**0**	**0**	....
1997-98	**Dallas**	**NHL**	**73**	**10**	**47**	**57**	**16**	**5**	**1**	**2**	**148**	**6.8**	**16**	....	....	....	**17**	**4**	**5**	**9**	**2**	**3**	**0**	**1**	....
1998-99♦	**Dallas**	**NHL**	**81**	**10**	**41**	**51**	**20**	**5**	**0**	**3**	**155**	**6.5**	**9**	**0**	**0.0**	**24:14**	**23**	**1**	**12**	**13**	**4**	**0**	**0**	**0**	**30:16**
99-2000	**Dallas**	**NHL**	**77**	**9**	**33**	**42**	**18**	**3**	**1**	**3**	**179**	**5.0**	**–2**	**0**	**0.0**	**28:50**	**18**	**2**	**7**	**9**	**6**	**1**	**1**	**0**	**26:28**
2000-01	**Dallas**	**NHL**	**79**	**10**	**41**	**51**	**24**	**6**	**0**	**1**	**173**	**5.8**	**22**	**0**	**0.0**	**26:37**	**10**	**1**	**5**	**6**	**4**	**0**	**0**	**0**	**30:37**
2001-02	**Dallas**	**NHL**	**80**	**12**	**32**	**44**	**22**	**8**	**0**	**2**	**198**	**6.1**	**–4**	**0**	**0.0**	**26:46**	....	....	....	....	....	....	....	....	....
2002-03	**Dallas**	**NHL**	**82**	**11**	**44**	**55**	**26**	**8**	**0**	**2**	**158**	**7.0**	**21**	**0**	**0.0**	**25:50**	**12**	**4**	**10**	**14**	**4**	**2**	**0**	**0**	**30:45**
2003-04	**Dallas**	**NHL**	**77**	**7**	**35**	**42**	**20**	**4**	**1**	**1**	**154**	**4.5**	**0**	**0**	**0.0**	**25:50**	**5**	**1**	**1**	**2**	**0**	**1**	**0**	**0**	**28:01**

			Regular Season														Playoffs								
Season	**Club**	**League**	**GP**	**G**	**A**	**Pts**	**PIM**	**PP**	**SH**	**GW**	**S**	**%**	**+/-**	**TF**	**F%**	**Min**	**GP**	**G**	**A**	**Pts**	**PIM**	**PP**	**SH**	**GW**	**Min**
2004-05				DID NOT PLAY																					
2005-06	**Dallas**	**NHL**	**78**	**13**	**58**	**71**	**46**	**9**	**0**	**0**	**141**	**9.2**	**20**	**0**	**0.0**	**26:27**	**5**	**1**	**5**	**6**	**6**	**1**	**0**	**0**	**29:42**
2006-07	**Dallas**	**NHL**	**78**	**12**	**42**	**54**	**26**	**9**	**0**	**3**	**156**	**7.7**	**0**	**1**	**100.0**	**25:57**	**6**	**0**	**4**	**4**	**2**	**0**	**0**	**0**	**30:51**
	NHL Totals		**1012**	**148**	**584**	**732**	**325**	**79**	**5**	**22**	**2167**	**6.8**		**1**	**100.0**	**26:18**	**153**	**23**	**88**	**111**	**58**	**12**	**1**	**1**	**29:23**

NHL Second All-Star Team (2006)

Played in NHL All-Star Game (1998, 1999, 2000)

Traded to **Pittsburgh** by **NY Rangers** with Petr Nedved for Luc Robitaille and Ulf Samuelsson, August 31, 1995. Traded to **Dallas** by **Pittsburgh** for Kevin Hatcher, June 22, 1996.

ZUBRUS, Dainius

(ZOO-bruhs, DAYN-ihs) **N.J.**

Center. Shoots left. 6'5", 225 lbs. Born, Elektrenai, USSR, June 16, 1978. Philadelphia's 1st choice, 15th overall, in 1996 Entry Draft.

Season	Club	League	GP	G	A	Pts	PIM	PP	SH	GW	S	%	+/-	TF	F%	Min	GP	G	A	Pts	PIM	PP	SH	GW	Min
1995-96	Pembroke	CJHL	28	19	13	32	73	....	....	....	....	....	....	....	....	....	....	....	....	....	....	....	....	....	....
	Caledon	MTJHL	7	3	7	10	2	....	....	....	....	....	....	....	....	....	17	11	12	23	4	....	....	....	....
1996-97	**Philadelphia**	**NHL**	**68**	**8**	**13**	**21**	**22**	**1**	**0**	**2**	**71**	**11.3**	**3**	....	....	....	**19**	**5**	**4**	**9**	**12**	**1**	**0**	**1**	....
1997-98	**Philadelphia**	**NHL**	**69**	**8**	**25**	**33**	**42**	**1**	**0**	**5**	**101**	**7.9**	**29**	....	....	....	**5**	**0**	**1**	**1**	**2**	**0**	**0**	**0**	....
1998-99	**Philadelphia**	**NHL**	**63**	**3**	**5**	**8**	**25**	**0**	**1**	**0**	**49**	**6.1**	**–5**	**29**	**51.7**	**11:00**	....	....	....	....	....	....	....	....	....
	Montreal	**NHL**	**17**	**3**	**5**	**8**	**4**	**0**	**0**	**1**	**31**	**9.7**	**–3**	**2**	**50.0**	**16:53**	....	....	....	....	....	....	....	....	....
99-2000	**Montreal**	**NHL**	**73**	**14**	**28**	**42**	**54**	**3**	**0**	**1**	**139**	**10.1**	**–1**	**212**	**39.2**	**17:37**	....	....	....	....	....	....	....	....	....
2000-01	**Montreal**	**NHL**	**49**	**12**	**12**	**24**	**30**	**3**	**0**	**0**	**70**	**17.1**	**–7**	**190**	**41.1**	**18:30**	....	....	....	....	....	....	....	....	....
	Washington	**NHL**	**12**	**1**	**1**	**2**	**7**	**1**	**0**	**0**	**13**	**7.7**	**–4**	**0**	**0.0**	**13:05**	**6**	**0**	**0**	**0**	**2**	**0**	**0**	**0**	**17:24**
2001-02	**Washington**	**NHL**	**71**	**17**	**26**	**43**	**38**	**4**	**0**	**3**	**138**	**12.3**	**5**	**131**	**37.4**	**18:52**	....	....	....	....	....	....	....	....	....
2002-03	**Washington**	**NHL**	**63**	**13**	**22**	**35**	**43**	**2**	**0**	**0**	**104**	**12.5**	**15**	**565**	**50.3**	**16:26**	**6**	**2**	**2**	**4**	**4**	**1**	**0**	**0**	**21:30**
2003-04	**Washington**	**NHL**	**54**	**12**	**15**	**27**	**38**	**6**	**1**	**2**	**115**	**10.4**	**–16**	**916**	**48.0**	**19:32**	....	....	....	....	....	....	....	....	....
2004-05	Lada Togliatti	Russia	42	8	11	19	85	....	....	....	....	....	....	....	....	....	10	3	1	4	22	....	....	....	....
2005-06	**Washington**	**NHL**	**71**	**23**	**34**	**57**	**84**	**13**	**0**	**5**	**181**	**12.7**	**3**	**1118**	**50.3**	**20:22**	....	....	....	....	....	....	....	....	....
2006-07	**Washington**	**NHL**	**60**	**20**	**32**	**52**	**50**	**9**	**0**	**4**	**127**	**15.7**	**–16**	**1096**	**49.7**	**19:51**	....	....	....	....	....	....	....	....	....
	Buffalo	**NHL**	**19**	**4**	**4**	**8**	**12**	**1**	**0**	**0**	**31**	**12.9**	**–3**	**69**	**39.1**	**18:22**	**15**	**0**	**8**	**8**	**8**	**0**	**0**	**0**	**18:38**
	NHL Totals		**689**	**138**	**222**	**360**	**449**	**44**	**2**	**23**	**1170**	**11.8**		**4328**	**48.2**	**17:39**	**51**	**7**	**15**	**22**	**28**	**2**	**0**	**1**	**19:00**

Traded to **Montreal** by **Philadelphia** with Philadelphia's 2nd round choice (Matt Carkner) in 1999 Entry Draft and NY Islanders' 6th round choice (previously acquired, Montreal selected Scott Selig) in 2000 Entry Draft for Mark Recchi, March 10, 1999. Traded to **Washington** by **Montreal** with Trevor Linden and New Jersey's 2nd round choice (previously acquired, later traded to Tampa Bay – Tampa Bay selected Andreas Holmqvist) in 2001 Entry Draft for Richard Zednik, Jan Bulis and Washington's 1st round choice (Alexander Perezhogin) in 2001 Entry Draft, March 13, 2001. Signed as a free agent by **Togliatti** (Russia), July 1, 2004. Traded to **Buffalo** by **Washington** with Timo Helbling for Jiri Novotny and Buffalo's 1st round choice (later traded to San Jose - San Jose selected Nicholas Petrecki) in 2007 Entry Draft, February 27, 2007. Signed as a free agent by **New Jersey**, July 3, 2007.

ZYUZIN, Andrei

(ZYOO-zin, AWN-dray) **CHI.**

Defense. Shoots left. 6'1", 208 lbs. Born, Ufa, USSR, January 21, 1978. San Jose's 1st choice, 2nd overall, in 1996 Entry Draft.

Season	Club	League	GP	G	A	Pts	PIM	PP	SH	GW	S	%	+/-	TF	F%	Min	GP	G	A	Pts	PIM	PP	SH	GW	Min
1994-95	Ufa	CIS	30	3	0	3	16	....	....	....	....	....	....	....	....	....	....	....	....	....	....	....	....	....	....
1995-96	Ufa	CIS	41	6	3	9	24	....	....	....	....	....	....	....	....	....	....	....	....	....	....	....	....	....	....
1996-97	Ufa	Russia	32	7	10	17	28	....	....	....	....	....	....	....	....	....	7	1	1	2	4	....	....	....	....
1997-98	**San Jose**	**NHL**	**56**	**6**	**7**	**13**	**66**	**2**	**0**	**2**	**72**	**8.3**	**8**	....	....	....	**6**	**1**	**0**	**1**	**14**	**0**	**0**	**1**	....
	Kentucky	AHL	17	4	5	9	28	....	....	....	....	....	....	....	....	....	....	....	....	....	....	....	....	....	....
1998-99	**San Jose**	**NHL**	**25**	**3**	**1**	**4**	**38**	**2**	**0**	**0**	**44**	**6.8**	**5**	**0**	**0.0**	**15:56**	....	....	....	....	....	....	....	....	....
	Kentucky	AHL	23	2	12	14	42	....	....	....	....	....	....	....	....	....	....	....	....	....	....	....	....	....	....
99-2000	**Tampa Bay**	**NHL**	**34**	**2**	**9**	**11**	**33**	**0**	**0**	**0**	**47**	**4.3**	**–11**	**0**	**0.0**	**20:28**	....	....	....	....	....	....	....	....	....
2000-01	**Tampa Bay**	**NHL**	**64**	**4**	**16**	**20**	**76**	**2**	**1**	**1**	**92**	**4.3**	**–8**	**0**	**0.0**	**18:39**	....	....	....	....	....	....	....	....	....
	Detroit Vipers	IHL	2	0	1	1	0	....	....	....	....	....	....	....	....	....	....	....	....	....	....	....	....	....	....
2001-02	**Tampa Bay**	**NHL**	**9**	**0**	**2**	**2**	**6**	**0**	**0**	**0**	**14**	**0.0**	**–6**	**0**	**0.0**	**19:41**	....	....	....	....	....	....	....	....	....
	New Jersey	**NHL**	**38**	**1**	**2**	**3**	**25**	**1**	**0**	**0**	**47**	**2.1**	**1**	**0**	**0.0**	**15:04**	....	....	....	....	....	....	....	....	....
	Albany River Rats	AHL	3	0	1	1	2	....	....	....	....	....	....	....	....	....	....	....	....	....	....	....	....	....	....
2002-03	**New Jersey**	**NHL**	**1**	**0**	**1**	**1**	**2**	**0**	**0**	**0**	**0**	**0.0**	**–1**	**0**	**0.0**	**20:03**	....	....	....	....	....	....	....	....	....
	Minnesota	**NHL**	**66**	**4**	**12**	**16**	**34**	**2**	**0**	**0**	**113**	**3.5**	**–7**	**4**	**25.0**	**21:38**	**18**	**0**	**1**	**1**	**14**	**0**	**0**	**0**	**23:07**
2003-04	**Minnesota**	**NHL**	**65**	**8**	**13**	**21**	**48**	**4**	**0**	**1**	**104**	**7.7**	**4**	**0**	**0.0**	**20:22**	....	....	....	....	....	....	....	....	....
2004-05	Ufa	Russia	14	2	1	3	6	....	....	....	....	....	....	....	....	....	....	....	....	....	....	....	....	....	....
	Cherepovets	Russia	10	2	1	3	8	....	....	....	....	....	....	....	....	....	....	....	....	....	....	....	....	....	....
2005-06	**Minnesota**	**NHL**	**57**	**7**	**11**	**18**	**50**	**4**	**0**	**1**	**80**	**8.8**	**–12**	**2**	**50.0**	**18:53**	....	....	....	....	....	....	....	....	....
2006-07	**Calgary**	**NHL**	**49**	**1**	**5**	**6**	**30**	**0**	**0**	**0**	**36**	**2.8**	**–2**	**0**	**0.0**	**13:49**	**5**	**1**	**0**	**1**	**2**	**0**	**1**	**0**	**15:51**
	NHL Totals		**464**	**36**	**79**	**115**	**408**	**17**	**1**	**5**	**649**	**5.5**		**6**	**33.3**	**18:32**	**29**	**2**	**1**	**3**	**30**	**0**	**1**	**1**	**21:32**

• Suspended for remainder of 1998-99 season by **San Jose** for leaving team without permission, April 1, 1999. Traded to **Tampa Bay** by **San Jose** with Bill Houlder, Shawn Burr and Steve Guolla for Niklas Sundstrom and NY Rangers' 3rd round choice (previously acquired, later traded to Chicago – Chicago selected Igor Radulov) in 2000 Entry Draft, August 4, 1999. • Missed majority of 1999-2000 season recovering from shoulder injury suffered in game vs. NY Islanders, January 13, 2000. Traded to **New Jersey** by **Tampa Bay** for Josef Boumedienne, Sascha Goc and the rights to Anton But, November 9, 2001. Claimed on waivers by **Minnesota** from **New Jersey**, November 2, 2002. Signed as a free agent by **Ufa** (Russia), September 25, 2004. Signed as a free agent by **Cherepovets** (Russia), December 20, 2004. Signed as a free agent by **Calgary**, July 1, 2006. Traded to **Chicago** by **Calgary** with Steve Marr for Adrian Aucoin and Chicago's 7th round choice (C. J. Severyn) in 2007 Entry Draft, June 22, 2007.

NHL Goaltenders

David Aebischer

Craig Anderson

Jean-Sebastien Aubin

Alex Auld

Jason Bacashihua

Niklas Backstrom

Ed Belfour

Martin Biron

Brian Boucher

Martin Brodeur

Ilya Bryzgalov

Barry Brust

Peter Budaj

Sean Burke

Sebastian Caron

Scott Clemmensen

Dan Cloutier

Gerald Coleman

Ty Conklin

Yann Danis

Marc Denis

Rick DiPietro

Wade Dubielewicz

Mike Dunham

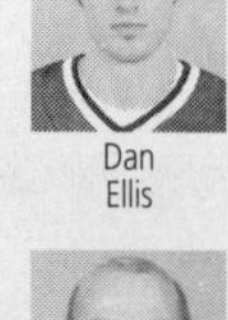
Dan Ellis

Ray Emery

Robert Esche

Manny Fernandez

Brian Finley

Wade Flaherty

Marc-Andre Fleury

Yutaka Fukufuji

Michael Garnett

Mathieu Garon

Martin Gerber

Jean-Sebastien Giguere

John Grahame

Jaroslav Halak

Josh Harding

Dominik Hasek

Johan Hedberg

Johan Holmqvist

James Howard

Cristobal Huet

Brent Johnson

Curtis Joseph

Nikolai Khabibulin

Miikka Kiprusoff

Vitaly Kolesnik

Olaf Kolzig

Jason Labarbera

Patrick Lalime

Pascal Leclaire

Manny Legace

Kari Lehtonen

Michael Leighton

David LeNeveu

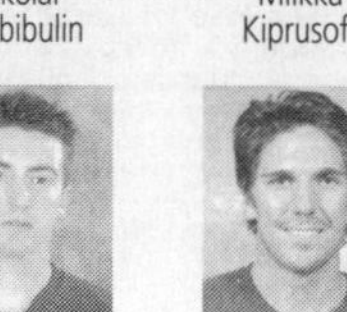
Henrik Lundqvist

Roberto Luongo

Joey MacDonald

Jussi Markkanen

Chris Mason

Jamie McLennan

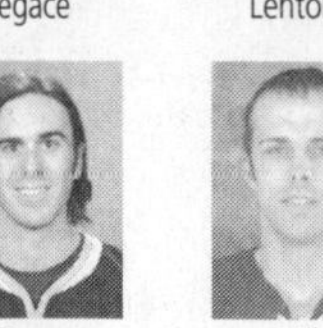

Ryan Miller

Mike Morrison

Evgeni Nabokov

Antero Niittymaki

Mika Noronen

Fredrik Norrena

Chris Osgood

Jean-Marc Pelletier

Karri Ramo

Andrew Raycroft

Dwayne Roloson

Dany Sabourin

Curtis Sanford

Philippe Sauve

Nolan Schaefer

Rastislav Stana

Mikael Tellqvist

Jose Theodore

Jocelyn Thibault

Tim Thomas

Hannu Toivonen

Vesa Toskala

Marty Turco

Tomas Vokoun

Michael Wall

Cam Ward

Kevin Weekes

2007-08 Goaltender Register

Note: The 2007-08 Goaltender Register lists all active NHL goaltenders, every goaltender drafted in the 2007 Entry Draft, goaltenders on NHL Reserve Lists and other goaltenders.

Trades and roster changes are current as of August 14, 2007.

To calculate a goaltender's goals-against per game average **(Avg)**, divide goals against **(GA)** by minutes played **(Mins)** and multiply this result by **60**.

Abbreviations: GP – games played; **W** – wins; **L** – losses; **T** – ties; **GA** – goals against; **SO** – shutouts; **Avg** – goals-against per game average.
♦ – member of Stanley Cup-winning team.

NHL Player Register begins on page 343.

Prospect Register begins on page 271.

League Abbreviations are listed on page 654.

AEBISCHER, David (A-bih-shuhr, DAY-vihd) PHX.

Goaltender. Catches left. 6'1", 185 lbs. Born, Fribourg, Switz., February 7, 1978.
(Colorado's 7th choice, 161st overall, in 1997 Entry Draft).

			Regular Season								Playoffs						
Season	**Club**	**League**	**GP**	**W**	**L**	**O/T**	**Mins**	**GA**	**SO**	**Avg**	**GP**	**W**	**L**	**Mins**	**GA**	**SO**	**Avg**
1996-97	Fribourg	Swiss	10	....	....	....	577	34	0	3.54	3	1	2	184	13	0	4.24
1997-98	Chesapeake	ECHL	17	5	7	2	930	52	0	3.35	....	....	....	....	....	....	....
	Wheeling Nailers	ECHL	10	5	3	1	564	30	1	3.19	....	....	....	....	....	....	....
	Hershey Bears	AHL	2	0	0	1	79	5	0	3.76	....	....	....	....	....	....	....
	Fribourg	Swiss	1	1	0	0	60	1	0	1.00	4	....	....	240	17	....	4.25
1998-99	Hershey Bears	AHL	38	17	10	5	1932	79	2	2.45	3	1	2	152	6	0	2.37
99-2000	Hershey Bears	AHL	58	29	23	2	3259	180	1	3.31	14	7	6	788	40	2	3.05
2000-01 ♦	**Colorado**	**NHL**	**26**	**12**	**7**	**3**	**1393**	**52**	**3**	**2.24**	**1**	**0**	**0**	**1**	**0**	**0**	**0.00**
2001-02	**Colorado**	**NHL**	**21**	**13**	**6**	**0**	**1184**	**37**	**2**	**1.88**	**1**	**0**	**0**	**34**	**1**	**0**	**1.76**
	Switzerland	Olympics	2	1	0	0	81	6	0	4.43	....	....	....	....	....	....	....
2002-03	**Colorado**	**NHL**	**22**	**7**	**12**	**0**	**1235**	**50**	**1**	**2.43**	....	....	....	....	....	....	....
2003-04	**Colorado**	**NHL**	**62**	**32**	**19**	**9**	**3703**	**129**	**4**	**2.09**	**11**	**6**	**5**	**662**	**23**	**1**	**2.08**
2004-05	HC Lugano	Swiss	18	12	2	3	1019	41	0	2.41	4	1	3	240	10	0	2.50
	EHC Chur	Swiss-2	....	....	....	....	....	....	....	....	2	....	....	130	4	0	1.84
2005-06	**Colorado**	**NHL**	**43**	**25**	**14**	**2**	**2477**	**123**	**3**	**2.98**	....	....	....	....	....	....	....
	Switzerland	Olympics	4	....	....	....	200	7	0	2.10	....	....	....	....	....	....	....
	Montreal	**NHL**	**7**	**4**	**3**	**0**	**418**	**26**	**0**	**3.73**	....	....	....	....	....	....	....
2006-07	**Montreal**	**NHL**	**32**	**13**	**12**	**3**	**1760**	**93**	**0**	**3.17**	....	....	....	....	....	....	....
	NHL Totals		**213**	**106**	**73**	**17**	**12170**	**510**	**13**	**2.51**	**13**	**6**	**5**	**697**	**24**	**1**	**2.07**

Signed as a free agent by **Lugano** (Swiss), September 17, 2004. Traded to **Montreal** by **Colorado** for Jose Theodore, March 8, 2006. Signed as a free agent by **Phoenix**, July 19, 2007.

AKERLUND, Magnus (AK-uhr-luhnd, MAG-nuhs) CAR.

Goaltender. Catches right. 6'1", 183 lbs. Born, Osby, Sweden, April 25, 1986.
(Carolina's 5th choice, 137th overall, in 2004 Entry Draft).

			Regular Season								Playoffs						
Season	**Club**	**League**	**GP**	**W**	**L**	**O/T**	**Mins**	**GA**	**SO**	**Avg**	**GP**	**W**	**L**	**Mins**	**GA**	**SO**	**Avg**
2002-03	HV 71 Jr.	Swe-Jr.	18	....	....	....	861	44	1	3.07	2	....	....	80	6	0	4.50
2003-04	HV 71 Jr.	Swe-Jr.	26	....	....	....	1556	85	1	3.28	2	....	....	119	10	0	5.04
2004-05	HV 71 Jr.	Swe-Jr.	19	....	....	....	1096	48	1	2.63	....	....	....	....	....	....	....
	HV 71 Jonkoping	Sweden	3	....	....	....	185	9	0	2.92	....	....	....	....	....	....	....
	Skovde IK	Sweden-2	22	....	....	....	1290	55	1	2.56	....	....	....	....	....	....	....
2005-06	HV 71 Jr.	Swe-Jr.	4	....	....	....	214	17	0	4.76	....	....	....	....	....	....	....
	Nykoping	Sweden-2	21	....	....	....	1236	67	0	3.25	....	....	....	....	....	....	....
2006-07	Skovde IK	Sweden-3	38	....	....	....	2293	91	6	2.38	....	....	....	....	....	....	....
	HV 71 Jonkoping	Sweden	1	....	....	....	65	1	0	0.92	....	....	....	....	....	....	....

ANDERSON, Craig (AN-duhr-suhn, KRAYG) FLA.

Goaltender. Catches left. 6'2", 180 lbs. Born, Park Ridge, IL, May 21, 1981.
(Chicago's 4th choice, 73rd overall, in 2001 Entry Draft).

			Regular Season								Playoffs						
Season	**Club**	**League**	**GP**	**W**	**L**	**O/T**	**Mins**	**GA**	**SO**	**Avg**	**GP**	**W**	**L**	**Mins**	**GA**	**SO**	**Avg**
1997-98	Chicago Jets	MEHL	50	....	....	....	2991	143	2	2.86	....	....	....	....	....	....	....
1998-99	Chicago Freeze	NAHL	14	11	3	0	840	40	0	2.56	....	....	....	....	....	....	....
	Guelph Storm	OHL	21	12	5	1	1006	52	1	3.10	3	0	2	114	9	0	4.74
99-2000	Guelph Storm	OHL	38	12	17	2	1955	117	0	3.59	3	0	1	110	5	0	2.73
2000-01	Guelph Storm	OHL	59	30	19	9	3555	156	3	2.63	4	0	4	240	17	0	4.25
2001-02	Norfolk Admirals	AHL	28	9	13	4	1568	77	2	2.95	1	0	1	21	1	0	2.83
2002-03	**Chicago**	**NHL**	**6**	**0**	**3**	**2**	**270**	**18**	**0**	**4.00**	....	....	....	....	....	....	....
	Norfolk Admirals	AHL	32	15	11	5	1795	58	4	1.94	5	2	3	345	15	0	2.61
2003-04	**Chicago**	**NHL**	**21**	**6**	**14**	**0**	**1205**	**57**	**1**	**2.84**	....	....	....	....	....	....	....
	Norfolk Admirals	AHL	37	17	20	0	2108	74	3	2.11	5	2	3	327	10	0	1.84
2004-05	Norfolk Admirals	AHL	15	9	4	1	886	27	2	1.83	6	2	4	356	14	0	2.36
2005-06	**Chicago**	**NHL**	**29**	**6**	**12**	**4**	**1554**	**86**	**1**	**3.32**	....	....	....	....	....	....	....
2006-07	**Florida**	**NHL**	**5**	**1**	**1**	**1**	**217**	**8**	**0**	**2.21**	....	....	....	....	....	....	....
	Rochester	AHL	34	23	10	1	2060	88	1	2.56	6	2	4	376	18	0	2.87
	NHL Totals		**61**	**13**	**30**	**7**	**3246**	**169**	**2**	**3.12**	....	....	....	....	....	....	....

• Re-entered NHL Entry Draft. Originally Calgary's 3rd choice, 77th overall, in 1999 Entry Draft.

OHL First All-Star Team (2001)

Claimed on waivers by **Boston** from **Chicago**, January 19, 2006. Claimed on waivers by **St. Louis** from **Boston**, January 31, 2006. Claimed on waivers by **Chicago** from **St. Louis**, February 3, 2006. Signed as a free agent by **Togliatti** (Russia), May 25, 2006. Traded to **Florida** by **Chicago** for Florida's 6th round choice in 2008 Entry Draft, June 24, 2006.

AUBIN, Jean-Sebastien (oh-BEHN, ZHAWN-suh-BAS-tee-yeh)

Goaltender. Catches right. 5'11", 180 lbs. Born, Montreal, Que., July 19, 1977.
(Pittsburgh's 2nd choice, 76th overall, in 1995 Entry Draft).

			Regular Season								Playoffs						
Season	**Club**	**League**	**GP**	**W**	**L**	**O/T**	**Mins**	**GA**	**SO**	**Avg**	**GP**	**W**	**L**	**Mins**	**GA**	**SO**	**Avg**
1993-94	Montreal-Bourassa	QAAA	27	14	13	0	1524	96	1	3.74	4	1	3	222	19	0	5.14
1994-95	Sherbrooke	QMJHL	27	13	10	1	1287	73	1	3.40	3	1	2	185	11	0	3.57
1995-96	Sherbrooke	QMJHL	40	18	14	2	2140	127	0	3.57	4	1	3	238	23	0	5.55
1996-97	Sherbrooke	QMJHL	4	3	1	0	249	8	0	1.93	1	0	1	60	4	0	4.00
	Moncton Wildcats	QMJHL	22	9	12	0	1252	67	1	3.21	....	....	....	....	....	....	....
	Laval Titan	QMJHL	11	2	6	1	532	41	0	4.62	....	....	....	....	....	....	....
1997-98	Syracuse Crunch	AHL	8	2	4	1	380	26	0	4.10	....	....	....	....	....	....	....
	Dayton Bombers	ECHL	21	15	2	2	1177	59	1	3.01	3	1	1	142	4	0	1.69
1998-99	**Pittsburgh**	**NHL**	**17**	**4**	**3**	**6**	**756**	**28**	**2**	**2.22**	....	....	....	....	....	....	....
	Kansas City Blades	IHL	13	5	7	1	751	41	0	3.28	....	....	....	....	....	....	....
99-2000	**Pittsburgh**	**NHL**	**51**	**23**	**21**	**3**	**2789**	**120**	**2**	**2.58**	....	....	....	....	....	....	....
	Wilkes-Barre	AHL	11	2	8	0	538	39	0	4.35	....	....	....	....	....	....	....
2000-01	**Pittsburgh**	**NHL**	**36**	**20**	**14**	**1**	**2050**	**107**	**0**	**3.13**	**1**	**0**	**0**	**1**	**0**	**0**	**0.00**
2001-02	**Pittsburgh**	**NHL**	**21**	**3**	**12**	**1**	**1094**	**65**	**0**	**3.56**	....	....	....	....	....	....	....
2002-03	**Pittsburgh**	**NHL**	**21**	**6**	**13**	**0**	**1132**	**59**	**1**	**3.13**	....	....	....	....	....	....	....
	Wilkes-Barre	AHL	16	8	6	1	919	29	3	1.89	6	3	3	356	12	0	2.02
2003-04	**Pittsburgh**	**NHL**	**22**	**7**	**9**	**0**	**1067**	**53**	**1**	**2.98**	....	....	....	....	....	....	....
	Wilkes-Barre	AHL	13	4	5	2	670	31	0	2.78	....	....	....	....	....	....	....
2004-05	St. John's	AHL	23	12	9	0	1336	64	3	2.87	1	0	0	47	1	0	1.27
2005-06	**Toronto**	**NHL**	**11**	**9**	**0**	**2**	**677**	**25**	**1**	**2.22**	....	....	....	....	....	....	....
	Toronto Marlies	AHL	46	19	18	2	2491	126	2	3.03	5	1	4	359	17	0	2.84
2006-07	**Toronto**	**NHL**	**20**	**3**	**5**	**2**	**804**	**46**	**0**	**3.43**	....	....	....	....	....	....	....
	NHL Totals		**199**	**75**	**77**	**15**	**10369**	**503**	**7**	**2.91**	**1**	**0**	**0**	**1**	**0**	**0**	**0.00**

Signed to a PTO (tryout) contract by **St. John's** (AHL), November 13, 2004. Signed as a free agent by **Toronto**, August 18, 2005.

AULD, Alex (AWLD, AL-ehx) PHX.

Goaltender. Catches left. 6'4", 200 lbs. Born, Cold Lake, Alta., January 7, 1981.
(Florida's 2nd choice, 40th overall, in 1999 Entry Draft).

			Regular Season								Playoffs						
Season	**Club**	**League**	**GP**	**W**	**L**	**O/T**	**Mins**	**GA**	**SO**	**Avg**	**GP**	**W**	**L**	**Mins**	**GA**	**SO**	**Avg**
1996-97	Thunder Bay Kings	TBMHL	35	....	....	....	2100	46	10	1.35	....	....	....	....	....	....	....
1997-98	Sturgeon Falls Lynx	NOJHA	11	4	6	0	611	46	0	4.52	....	....	....	....	....	....	....
	North Bay	OHL	6	0	4	0	206	17	0	4.95	....	....	....	....	....	....	....
1998-99	North Bay	OHL	37	9	20	1	1894	106	1	3.36	3	0	3	170	10	0	3.53
99-2000	North Bay	OHL	55	21	26	6	3047	167	2	3.29	6	2	4	374	12	0	*1.93
2000-01	North Bay	OHL	40	22	11	5	2319	98	1	2.54	4	0	4	240	15	0	3.75
2001-02	**Vancouver**	**NHL**	**1**	**1**	**0**	**0**	**60**	**2**	**0**	**2.00**	....	....	....	....	....	....	....
	Columbia Inferno	ECHL	6	3	1	2	375	12	0	1.92	....	....	....	....	....	....	....
	Manitoba Moose	AHL	21	11	9	0	1104	65	1	3.53	1	0	0	20	0	0	0.00
2002-03	**Vancouver**	**NHL**	**7**	**3**	**3**	**0**	**382**	**10**	**1**	**1.57**	**1**	**0**	**0**	**20**	**1**	**0**	**3.00**
	Manitoba Moose	AHL	37	15	19	3	2209	97	3	2.64	....	....	....	....	....	....	....
2003-04	**Vancouver**	**NHL**	**6**	**2**	**2**	**2**	**349**	**12**	**0**	**2.06**	**3**	**1**	**2**	**222**	**9**	**0**	**2.43**
	Manitoba Moose	AHL	40	18	16	4	2329	99	4	2.55	....	....	....	....	....	....	....
2004-05	Manitoba Moose	AHL	50	25	18	4	2764	118	2	2.56	3	0	2	128	7	0	3.29
2005-06	**Vancouver**	**NHL**	**67**	**33**	**26**	**6**	**3859**	**189**	**0**	**2.94**	....	....	....	....	....	....	....
2006-07	**Florida**	**NHL**	**27**	**7**	**13**	**5**	**1471**	**82**	**1**	**3.34**	....	....	....	....	....	....	....
	NHL Totals		**108**	**46**	**44**	**13**	**6121**	**295**	**2**	**2.89**	**4**	**1**	**2**	**242**	**10**	**0**	**2.48**

Rights traded to **Vancouver** by **Florida** for Vancouver's 2nd round compensatory choice (later traded to New Jersey – New Jersey selected Tuomas Pihlman) in 2001 Entry Draft and Vancouver's 3rd round choice (later traded to Atlanta – later traded to Buffalo – Buffalo selected John Adams) in 2002 Entry Draft, May 31, 2001. Traded to **Florida** by **Vancouver** with Todd Bertuzzi and Bryan Allen for Roberto Luongo, Lukas Krajicek and Florida's 6th round choice (Sergei Shirokov) in 2006 Entry Draft, June 23, 2006. Signed as a free agent by **Phoenix**, August 13, 2007.

BACASHIHUA, Jason (buh-KAH-shoo-wuh, JAY-suhn) ST.L.

Goaltender. Catches left. 5'11", 177 lbs. Born, Garden City, MI, September 20, 1982.
(Dallas' 1st choice, 26th overall, in 2001 Entry Draft).

			Regular Season								Playoffs						
Season	**Club**	**League**	**GP**	**W**	**L**	**O/T**	**Mins**	**GA**	**SO**	**Avg**	**GP**	**W**	**L**	**Mins**	**GA**	**SO**	**Avg**
99-2000	Chicago Freeze	NAHL	41	20	19	2	2432	118	2	2.91	2	0	2	103	12	0	6.97
2000-01	Chicago Freeze	NAHL	39	24	14	0	2246	121	1	3.23	3	1	2	190	12	0	3.79
2001-02	Plymouth Whalers	OHL	46	26	12	7	2688	105	*5	2.34	6	2	4	360	15	0	2.50
	Utah Grizzlies	AHL	1	0	1	0	61	3	0	2.97	....	....	....	....	....	....	....
2002-03	Utah Grizzlies	AHL	39	18	18	2	2245	118	3	3.15	1	0	1	59	2	0	2.05
2003-04	Utah Grizzlies	AHL	39	13	19	5	2234	99	3	2.66	....	....	....	....	....	....	....
2004-05	Worcester IceCats	AHL	35	18	13	1	1909	80	2	2.51	....	....	....	....	....	....	....
2005-06	**St. Louis**	**NHL**	**19**	**4**	**10**	**1**	**966**	**52**	**0**	**3.23**	....	....	....	....	....	....	....
	Peoria Rivermen	AHL	15	9	4	0	820	36	2	2.63	....	....	....	....	....	....	....

Season	Club	League	GP	W	L	O/T	Mins	GA	SO	Avg	GP	W	L	Mins	GA	SO	Avg
2006-07	**St. Louis**	**NHL**	**19**	**3**	**7**	**3**	**894**	**47**	**0**	**3.15**	....	....	....	....	....	....	....
	Peoria Rivermen	AHL	20	5	10	4	1139	55	1	2.90	....	....	....	....	....	....	....
	NHL Totals		**38**	**7**	**17**	**4**	**1860**	**99**	**0**	**3.19**	....	....	....	....	....	....	....

Traded to **St. Louis** by **Dallas** for the rights to Shawn Belle, June 25, 2004.

BACHMAN, Richard (BAWK-mahn, RIH-chuhrd) DAL.

Goaltender. Catches left. 5'11", 160 lbs. Born, Salt Lake City, UT, July 25, 1987.
(Dallas' 3rd choice, 120th overall, in 2006 Entry Draft).

			Regular Season								Playoffs						
Season	**Club**	**League**	**GP**	**W**	**L**	**O/T**	**Mins**	**GA**	**SO**	**Avg**	**GP**	**W**	**L**	**Mins**	**GA**	**SO**	**Avg**
2004-05	Cushing	High-MA	28	....	....	....	1498	53	3	1.89	....	....	....	....	....	....	....
	Boston Jr. Bruins	EmJHL	25	....	....	....	....	....	....	....	....	....	....	....	....	....	....
2005-06	Cushing	High-MA	30	....	....	....	1598	60	4	2.25	....	....	....	....	....	....	....
	Boston Jr. Bruins	EmJHL	....	31	1	2	....	....	....	1.69	....	....	....	....	....	....	....
2006-07	Chicago Steel	USHL	7	2	5	0	359	29	0	4.85	....	....	....	....	....	....	....
	Cedar Rapids	USHL	26	14	10	2	1565	78	4	2.99	6	4	1	329	7	*2	*1.28

BACKSTROM, Niklas (BAK-struhm, NIHK-luhs) MIN.

Goaltender. Catches left. 6'2", 196 lbs. Born, Helsinki, Finland, February 14, 1982.

			Regular Season								Playoffs						
Season	**Club**	**League**	**GP**	**W**	**L**	**O/T**	**Mins**	**GA**	**SO**	**Avg**	**GP**	**W**	**L**	**Mins**	**GA**	**SO**	**Avg**
1994-95	HIFK Helsinki U18	Fin-U18					STATISTICS NOT AVAILABLE										
1995-96	HIFK Helsinki U18	Fin-U18	12	....	....	....	699	44	....	3.77	4	....	....	203	9	....	2.66
1996-97	HIFK Helsinki Jr.	Fin-Jr.	21	....	....	....	1243	57	....	2.75	....	....	....	....	....	....	....
	PiTa Helsinki	Finland-2	8	....	....	....	390	24	....	3.69	....	....	....	....	....	....	....
	HIFK Helsinki	Finland	2	0	0	0	30	3	0	5.85	....	....	....	....	....	....	....
1997-98	HIFK Helsinki Jr.	Fin-Jr.	14	7	7	0	847	42	....	2.98	....	....	....	....	....	....	....
	Hermes Kokkola	Finland-2	9	4	3	1	468	23	1	2.95	....	....	....	....	....	....	....
1998-99	HIFK Helsinki	Finland	16	9	5	1	923	26	1	*1.69	....	....	....	....	....	....	....
	HIFK Helsinki Jr.	Fin-Jr.	15	7	7	1	898	45	1	3.01	....	....	....	....	....	....	....
99-2000	HIFK Helsinki	Finland	4	0	4	0	155	17	0	6.58	....	....	....	....	....	....	....
	FPS Forssa	Finland-2	22	13	8	1	1320	50	1	2.27	3	1	2	178	8	0	2.69
2000-01	SaiPa	Finland	49	22	24	3	2826	120	2	2.55	....	....	....	....	....	....	....
2001-02	AIK Solna	Sweden	40	....	....	....	2186	111	1	3.05	....	....	....	....	....	....	....
	AIK Solna	Sweden-Q	9	....	....	....	543	20	0	2.21	....	....	....	....	....	....	....
2002-03	Karpat Oulu	Finland	36	16	8	9	2136	77	4	2.16	*15	7	8	*990	33	1	2.00
2003-04	Karpat Oulu	Finland	43	24	8	0	2572	87	7	2.03	*15	*9	6	*927	36	1	2.33
2004-05	Karpat Oulu	Finland	47	27	10	10	2819	102	7	2.17	*12	*10	2	720	15	*3	*1.25
2005-06	Karpat Oulu	Finland	51	*32	9	10	3077	86	*10	*1.68	4	3	1	195	6	0	1.84
2006-07	**Minnesota**	**NHL**	**41**	**23**	**8**	**6**	**2227**	**73**	**5**	***1.97**	**5**	**1**	**4**	**297**	**11**	**0**	**2.22**
	NHL Totals		**41**	**23**	**8**	**6**	**2227**	**73**	**5**	**1.97**	**5**	**1**	**4**	**297**	**11**	**0**	**2.22**

William M. Jennings Trophy (2007) (shared with Manny Fernandez) • MBNA Roger Crozier Saving Grace Award (2007)

Signed as a free agent by **Minnesota**, June 1, 2006.

BARULIN, Konstantin (bah-ROO-lihn, KAWN-stan-tihn) ST.L.

Goaltender. Catches left. 6', 180 lbs. Born, Karaganda, USSR, September 4, 1984.
(St. Louis' 3rd choice, 84th overall, in 2003 Entry Draft).

			Regular Season								Playoffs						
Season	**Club**	**League**	**GP**	**W**	**L**	**O/T**	**Mins**	**GA**	**SO**	**Avg**	**GP**	**W**	**L**	**Mins**	**GA**	**SO**	**Avg**
2001-02	Gazovik Tyumen	Russia-2	4	....	....	....	190	15	0	4.73	....	....	....	....	....	....	....
2002-03	Gazovik Tyumen	Russia-2	41	....	....	....	2361	67	5	1.70	....	....	....	....	....	....	....
2003-04	Gazovik Tyumen	Russia-2	11	....	....	....	663	24	....	2.17	....	....	....	....	....	....	....
	SKA St. Petersburg	Russia	1	....	....	....	1	0	0	0.00	....	....	....	....	....	....	....
	St. Petersburg 2	Russia-3	11	....	....	....	668	24	1	2.15	....	....	....	....	....	....	....
2004-05	Gazovik Tyumen	Russia-2	30	....	....	....	1773	59	6	2.00	3	....	....	136	9	0	3.97
2005-06	Spartak Moscow	Russia	36	....	....	....	2102	75	2	2.14	2	....	....	104	4	0	2.30
2006-07	Mytischi	Russia	26	....	....	....	1249	45	1	2.16	1	....	....	48	3	0	3.76

BEAUCHEMIN, Rejean (boh-sheh-MEH, ray-JAWN) PHI.

Goaltender. Catches left. 6'1", 202 lbs. Born, Winnipeg, Man., May 3, 1985.
(Philadelphia's 10th choice, 191st overall, in 2003 Entry Draft).

			Regular Season								Playoffs						
Season	**Club**	**League**	**GP**	**W**	**L**	**O/T**	**Mins**	**GA**	**SO**	**Avg**	**GP**	**W**	**L**	**Mins**	**GA**	**SO**	**Avg**
2001-02	Winnipeg Warriors	MMMHL	29	6	8	4	1026	54	0	3.15	4	3	1	240	12	0	3.00
2002-03	Prince Albert	WHL	34	12	15	1	1618	86	1	3.19	....	....	....	....	....	....	....
2003-04	Prince Albert	WHL	62	30	21	6	3540	137	6	2.32	6	2	4	360	14	0	2.33
2004-05	Prince Albert	WHL	54	21	24	4	3052	133	5	2.61	17	11	6	1062	38	2	2.15
2005-06	Philadelphia	AHL	15	3	8	1	824	37	0	2.70	....	....	....	....	....	....	....
	Trenton Titans	ECHL	32	9	18	4	1856	92	0	2.97	2	0	2	125	6	0	2.89
2006-07	Philadelphia	AHL	7	2	5	0	295	23	1	4.68	....	....	....	....	....	....	....
	Bakersfield	ECHL	9	5	2	2	562	29	0	3.10	9	4	4	480	22	1	2.75

WHL East Second All-Star Team (2004)

BECKFORD-TSEU, Chris (BEHK-fuhrd-TSEW, KRIHS)

Goaltender. Catches left. 6'2", 201 lbs. Born, Toronto, Ont., June 22, 1984.
(St. Louis' 8th choice, 159th overall, in 2003 Entry Draft).

			Regular Season								Playoffs						
Season	**Club**	**League**	**GP**	**W**	**L**	**O/T**	**Mins**	**GA**	**SO**	**Avg**	**GP**	**W**	**L**	**Mins**	**GA**	**SO**	**Avg**
2000-01	St. Mike's B's	OPJHL	25	9	15	1	1506	119	1	4.75	4	1	3	240	10	0	2.50
2001-02	Oshawa	OPJHL					STATISTICS NOT AVAILABLE										
	Guelph Storm	OHL	5	2	0	0	207	16	0	4.64	....	....	....	....	....	....	....
	Oshawa Generals	OHL	7	2	3	0	341	19	0	3.34	5	1	4	310	16	0	3.10
2002-03	Oshawa Generals	OHL	54	25	26	2	2978	157	4	3.16	13	6	7	727	48	1	3.96
2003-04	Oshawa Generals	OHL	9	1	5	2	495	28	0	3.39	....	....	....	....	....	....	....
	Kingston	OHL	40	16	19	2	2226	121	3	3.26	5	1	4	303	18	0	3.56
2004-05	Worcester IceCats	AHL	1	0	0	0	29	0	0	0.00	....	....	....	....	....	....	....
	Peoria Rivermen	ECHL	29	11	12	3	1594	72	1	2.71	....	....	....	....	....	....	....
2005-06	Peoria Rivermen	AHL	16	7	5	1	737	38	0	3.10	4	0	4	238	15	0	3.78
	Alaska Aces	ECHL	19	16	1	2	1152	36	2	1.87	12	8	4	795	27	*3	*2.04
2006-07	Peoria Rivermen	AHL	29	12	11	4	1654	75	1	2.72	....	....	....	....	....	....	....
	Alaska Aces	ECHL	7	7	0	0	426	9	2	1.27	....	....	....	....	....	....	....

BEECH, Kevin (BEECH, KEH-vihn)

Goaltender. Catches left. 6'4", 183 lbs. Born, London, Ont., September 23, 1986.
(Tampa Bay's 8th choice, 165th overall, in 2005 Entry Draft).

			Regular Season								Playoffs						
Season	**Club**	**League**	**GP**	**W**	**L**	**O/T**	**Mins**	**GA**	**SO**	**Avg**	**GP**	**W**	**L**	**Mins**	**GA**	**SO**	**Avg**
2003-04	Sudbury Wolves	OHL	16	3	9	0	811	48	0	3.55	1	1	0	56	0	0	0.00
2004-05	Sudbury Wolves	OHL	21	9	9	2	1132	50	2	2.65	6	2	1	276	12	0	2.61
2005-06	Sudbury Wolves	OHL	63	33	25	5	3690	181	0	2.94	10	4	5	612	28	*2	2.75
2006-07	Sudbury Wolves	OHL	36	15	14	5	1968	102	1	3.11	....	....	....	....	....	....	....
	Erie Otters	OHL	23	4	15	1	1186	104	0	5.26	....	....	....	....	....	....	....
	Springfield Falcons	AHL	6	0	3	0	211	11	0	3.13	....	....	....	....	....	....	....

BELFOUR, Ed (BEHL-fohr, EHD)

Goaltender. Catches left. 5'11", 202 lbs. Born, Carman, Man., April 21, 1965.

			Regular Season								Playoffs						
Season	**Club**	**League**	**GP**	**W**	**L**	**O/T**	**Mins**	**GA**	**SO**	**Avg**	**GP**	**W**	**L**	**Mins**	**GA**	**SO**	**Avg**
1983-84	Winkler Flyers	MJHL	14	....	....	....	818	68	0	4.99	....	....	....	....	....	....	....
1984-85	Winkler Flyers	MJHL	34	....	....	....	1973	145	1	4.41	7	3	4	528	41	0	4.66
1985-86	Winkler Flyers	MJHL	33	....	....	....	1943	124	1	3.83	....	....	....	....	....	....	....
1986-87	North Dakota	WCHA	34	29	4	0	2049	81	3	2.37	....	....	....	....	....	....	....
1987-88	Saginaw Hawks	IHL	61	32	25	0	*3446	183	3	3.19	9	4	5	561	33	0	3.53
1988-89	**Chicago**	**NHL**	**23**	**4**	**12**	**3**	**1148**	**74**	**0**	**3.87**	....	....	....	....	....	....	....
	Saginaw Hawks	IHL	29	12	10	0	1760	92	0	3.14	5	2	3	298	14	0	2.82
1989-90	Canada	Nat-Tm	33	13	12	6	1808	93	0	3.09	....	....	....	....	....	....	....
	Chicago	**NHL**	....	....	....	....	....	....	....	....	**9**	**4**	**2**	**409**	**17**	**0**	**2.49**
1990-91	**Chicago**	**NHL**	***74**	***43**	**19**	**7**	***4127**	**170**	**4**	***2.47**	**6**	**2**	**4**	**295**	**20**	**0**	**4.07**
1991-92	**Chicago**	**NHL**	**52**	**21**	**18**	**10**	**2928**	**132**	***5**	**2.70**	**18**	**12**	**4**	**949**	**39**	**1**	***2.47**
1992-93	**Chicago**	**NHL**	***71**	**41**	**18**	**11**	***4106**	**177**	***7**	**2.59**	**4**	**0**	**4**	**249**	**13**	**0**	**3.13**
1993-94	**Chicago**	**NHL**	**70**	**37**	**24**	**6**	**3998**	**178**	***7**	**2.67**	**6**	**2**	**4**	**360**	**15**	**0**	**2.50**
1994-95	**Chicago**	**NHL**	**42**	**22**	**15**	**3**	**2450**	**93**	***5**	**2.28**	**16**	**9**	**7**	**1014**	**37**	**1**	**2.19**
1995-96	**Chicago**	**NHL**	**50**	**22**	**17**	**10**	**2956**	**135**	**1**	**2.74**	**9**	**6**	**3**	**666**	**23**	**1**	***2.07**
1996-97	**Chicago**	**NHL**	**33**	**11**	**15**	**6**	**1966**	**88**	**1**	**2.69**	....	....	....	....	....	....	....
	San Jose	**NHL**	**13**	**3**	**9**	**0**	**757**	**43**	**1**	**3.41**	....	....	....	....	....	....	....
1997-98	**Dallas**	**NHL**	**61**	**37**	**12**	**10**	**3581**	**112**	**9**	***1.88**	**17**	**10**	**7**	**1039**	**31**	**1**	***1.79**
1998-99 ◆	**Dallas**	**NHL**	**61**	**35**	**15**	**9**	**3536**	**117**	**5**	**1.99**	***23**	***16**	**7**	***1544**	**43**	***3**	***1.67**
99-2000	**Dallas**	**NHL**	**62**	**32**	**21**	**7**	**3620**	**127**	**4**	**2.10**	***23**	**14**	**9**	**1443**	**45**	***4**	**1.87**
2000-01	**Dallas**	**NHL**	**63**	**35**	**20**	**7**	**3687**	**144**	**8**	**2.34**	**10**	**4**	**6**	**671**	**25**	**0**	**2.24**
2001-02	**Dallas**	**NHL**	**60**	**21**	**27**	**11**	**3467**	**153**	**1**	**2.65**	....	....	....	....	....	....	....
	Canada	Olympics					DID NOT PLAY – SPARE GOALTENDER										
2002-03	**Toronto**	**NHL**	**62**	**37**	**20**	**5**	**3738**	**141**	**7**	**2.26**	**7**	**3**	**4**	**532**	**24**	**0**	**2.71**
2003-04	**Toronto**	**NHL**	**59**	**34**	**19**	**6**	**3444**	**122**	**10**	**2.13**	**13**	**6**	**7**	**774**	**27**	**3**	**2.09**
2004-05							DID NOT PLAY										
2005-06	**Toronto**	**NHL**	**49**	**22**	**22**	**4**	**2897**	**159**	**0**	**3.29**	....	....	....	....	....	....	....
2006-07	**Florida**	**NHL**	**58**	**27**	**17**	**10**	**3289**	**152**	**1**	**2.77**	....	....	....	....	....	....	....
	NHL Totals		**963**	**484**	**320**	**125**	**55695**	**2317**	**76**	**2.50**	**161**	**88**	**68**	**9945**	**359**	**14**	**2.17**

WCHA First All-Star Team (1987) • NCAA Championship All-Tournament Team (1987) • IHL First All-Star Team (1988) • Garry F. Longman Memorial Trophy (Rookie of the Year – IHL) (1988) (co-winner - John Cullen) • NHL All-Rookie Team (1991) • NHL First All-Star Team (1991, 1993) • Trico Goaltender Award (1991) • Calder Memorial Trophy (1991) • William M. Jennings Trophy (1991, 1993, 1995) • Vezina Trophy (1991, 1993) • NHL Second All-Star Team (1995) • William M. Jennings Trophy (1999) (shared with Roman Turek) • MBNA Roger Crozier Saving Grace Award (2000)

Played in NHL All-Star Game (1992, 1993, 1996, 1998, 1999)

Signed as a free agent by **Chicago**, September 25, 1987. Traded to **San Jose** by **Chicago** for Chris Terreri, Ulf Dahlen and Michal Sykora, January 25, 1997. Signed as a free agent by **Dallas**, July 2, 1997. Traded to **Nashville** by **Dallas** with Cameron Mann for David Gosselin and Nashville's 5th round choice (Eero Kilpelainen) in 2003 Entry Draft, June 29, 2002. Signed as a free agent by **Toronto**, July 2, 2002. Signed as a free agent by **Florida**, July 25, 2006.

BENNETT, Brett (BEHN-neht, BREHT) PHX.

Goaltender. Catches left. 6'1", 185 lbs. Born, Buffalo, NY, March 8, 1988.
(Phoenix's 4th choice, 130th overall, in 2006 Entry Draft).

			Regular Season								Playoffs						
Season	**Club**	**League**	**GP**	**W**	**L**	**O/T**	**Mins**	**GA**	**SO**	**Avg**	**GP**	**W**	**L**	**Mins**	**GA**	**SO**	**Avg**
2003-04	Det. Honeybaked	MWEHL	31	....	....	....	....	....	....	....	....	....	....	....	....	....	....
2004-05	USNTDP	U-17	14	10	6	1	930	41	0	2.65	....	....	....	....	....	....	....
	USNTDP	NAHL	23	10	7	1	1217	56	1	2.76	10	7	3	598	20	3	2.01
2005-06	USNTDP	U-18	12	7	2	0	593	24	0	2.43	....	....	....	....	....	....	....
	USNTDP	NAHL	5	3	0	0	238	5	0	1.26	....	....	....	....	....	....	....
2006-07	Boston University	H-East	1	1	0	0	60	1	0	1.00	....	....	....	....	....	....	....

BERKHOEL, Adam (BUHRK-uhl, A-duhm) DET.

Goaltender. Catches left. 5'11", 185 lbs. Born, St. Paul, MN, May 16, 1981.
(Chicago's 12th choice, 240th overall, in 2000 Entry Draft).

			Regular Season								Playoffs						
Season	**Club**	**League**	**GP**	**W**	**L**	**O/T**	**Mins**	**GA**	**SO**	**Avg**	**GP**	**W**	**L**	**Mins**	**GA**	**SO**	**Avg**
99-2000	Twin Cities	USHL	49	25	15	7	2848	129	0	2.72	13	7	6	797	43	0	3.24
2000-01	U. of Denver	WCHA	15	7	6	1	745	38	1	3.06	....	....	....	....	....	....	....
2001-02	U. of Denver	WCHA	18	12	4	1	1026	40	1	2.34	....	....	....	....	....	....	....
2002-03	U. of Denver	WCHA	26	12	6	4	1436	55	3	*2.30	....	....	....	....	....	....	....
2003-04	U. of Denver	WCHA	39	24	11	4	2225	91	*7	2.45	....	....	....	....	....	....	....
2004-05	Chicago Wolves	AHL	1	0	1	0	59	4	0	4.04	....	....	....	....	....	....	....
	Gwinnett	ECHL	24	9	10	5	1458	59	2	2.43	7	4	1	353	9	0	*1.53
2005-06	**Atlanta**	**NHL**	**9**	**2**	**4**	**1**	**473**	**30**	**0**	**3.81**	....	....	....	....	....	....	....
	Chicago Wolves	AHL	11	3	6	0	526	32	0	3.65	....	....	....	....	....	....	....
	Gwinnett	ECHL	15	10	4	1	902	41	1	2.73	9	6	3	551	30	0	3.27
2006-07	Rochester	AHL	6	2	3	0	316	17	0	3.22	....	....	....	....	....	....	....
	Dayton Bombers	ECHL	43	23	17	3	2584	105	5	2.44	*22	12	10	1385	59	*3	2.56
	NHL Totals		**9**	**2**	**4**	**1**	**473**	**30**	**0**	**3.81**	....	....	....	....	....	....	....

USHL All-Rookie Team (2000) • USHL Second All-Star Team (2000) • NCAA Championship All-Tournament Team (2004) • NCAA Championship Tournament MVP (2004) • ECHL First All-Star Team (2007)

Traded to **Atlanta** by **Chicago** for Atlanta's 7th round choice (Adam Hobson) in 2005 Entry Draft, June 27, 2004. Signed as a free agent by **Detroit**, July 3, 2007.

BERNIER, Jonathan (BAIRN-yay, JAWN-ah-thuhn) L.A.

Goaltender. Catches left. 5'11", 177 lbs. Born, Laval, Que., August 7, 1988.
(Los Angeles' 1st choice, 11th overall, in 2006 Entry Draft).

			Regular Season								Playoffs						
Season	**Club**	**League**	**GP**	**W**	**L**	**O/T**	**Mins**	**GA**	**SO**	**Avg**	**GP**	**W**	**L**	**Mins**	**GA**	**SO**	**Avg**
2004-05	Lewiston	QMJHL	23	7	12	3	1353	67	0	2.97	1	0	0	20	0	0	0.00
2005-06	Lewiston	QMJHL	54	27	26	0	3241	146	2	2.70	6	2	4	359	17	1	2.84
2006-07	Lewiston	QMJHL	37	26	10	....	2186	94	2	2.58	17	*16	1	1025	40	1	2.34

QMJHL Second All-Star Team (2007)

BERRA, Reto (BAIR-ruh, REH-toh) ST.L.

Goaltender. Catches left. 6'4", 189 lbs. Born, Bulach, Switz., January 3, 1987.
(St. Louis' 6th choice, 106th overall, in 2006 Entry Draft).

			Regular Season								Playoffs						
Season	**Club**	**League**	**GP**	**W**	**L**	**O/T**	**Mins**	**GA**	**SO**	**Avg**	**GP**	**W**	**L**	**Mins**	**GA**	**SO**	**Avg**
2004-05	GCK Zurich Jr.	Swiss-Jr.	22	....	....	....	....	....	....	....	....	....	....	....	....	....	....
	GCK Lions Zurich	Swiss-2	3	....	....	....	180	12	0	4.00	....	....	....	....	....	....	....
	EHC Dubendorf	Swiss-3					STATISTICS NOT AVAILABLE										
2005-06	GCK Zurich Jr.	Swiss-Jr.	23	....	....	....	....	....	....	....	....	....	....	....	....	....	....
	GCK Lions Zurich	Swiss-2	15	....	....	....	835	51	1	3.56	....	....	....	....	....	....	....
	ZSC Lions Zurich	Swiss	2	0	1	0	90	6	0	3.99	....	....	....	....	....	....	....
2006-07	Switzerland U20	Swiss-2	3	0	3	0	179	13	0	4.69	....	....	....	....	....	....	....
	GCK Lions Zurich	Swiss-2	6	4	2	0	359	18	0	3.01	....	....	....	....	....	....	....
	ZSC Lions Zurich	Swiss	2	1	0	0	78	4	0	3.08	4	0	3	188	9	0	2.87

BIRON, Martin (BEE-rawn, MAHR-tihn) PHI.

Goaltender. Catches left. 6'3", 163 lbs. Born, Lac-St-Charles, Que., August 15, 1977.
(Buffalo's 2nd choice, 16th overall, in 1995 Entry Draft).

			Regular Season								Playoffs						
Season	Club	League	GP	W	L	O/T	Mins	GA	SO	Avg	GP	W	L	Mins	GA	SO	Avg
1993-94	Trois-Rivieres	QAAA	23	14	8	1	1412	80	1	3.40	2	1	1	112	7	0	3.73
1994-95	Beauport Harfangs	QMJHL	56	29	16	9	3193	132	3	*2.48	16	8	7	900	37	*4	2.47
1995-96	Beauport Harfangs	QMJHL	55	29	17	7	3201	152	1	2.85	*19	*12	7	1134	64	0	3.39
	Buffalo	**NHL**	**3**	**0**	**2**	**0**	**119**	**10**	**0**	**5.04**	....	....	....	....	....	....	....
1996-97	Beauport Harfangs	QMJHL	18	6	9	1	928	61	1	3.94	....	....	....	....	....	....	....
	Hull Olympiques	QMJHL	16	11	4	1	974	43	2	2.65	6	3	1	325	19	0	3.51
1997-98	South Carolina	ECHL	2	0	1	1	86	3	0	2.09	....	....	....	....	....	....	....
	Rochester	AHL	41	14	18	6	2312	113	*5	2.93	4	1	3	239	16	0	4.01
1998-99	**Buffalo**	**NHL**	**6**	**1**	**2**	**1**	**281**	**10**	**0**	**2.14**	....	....	....	....	....	....	....
	Rochester	AHL	52	36	13	3	3129	108	*6	*2.07	*20	12	8	1167	42	1	*2.16
99-2000	**Buffalo**	**NHL**	**41**	**19**	**18**	**2**	**2229**	**90**	**5**	**2.42**	....	....	....	....	....	....	....
	Rochester	AHL	6	6	0	0	344	12	1	2.09	....	....	....	....	....	....	....
2000-01	**Buffalo**	**NHL**	**18**	**7**	**7**	**1**	**918**	**39**	**2**	**2.55**	....	....	....	....	....	....	....
	Rochester	AHL	4	3	1	0	239	4	1	1.00	....	....	....	....	....	....	....
2001-02	**Buffalo**	**NHL**	**72**	**31**	**28**	**10**	**4085**	**151**	**4**	**2.22**	....	....	....	....	....	....	....
2002-03	**Buffalo**	**NHL**	**54**	**17**	**28**	**6**	**3170**	**135**	**4**	**2.56**	....	....	....	....	....	....	....
2003-04	**Buffalo**	**NHL**	**52**	**26**	**18**	**5**	**2972**	**125**	**2**	**2.52**	....	....	....	....	....	....	....
2004-05							DID NOT PLAY										
2005-06	**Buffalo**	**NHL**	**35**	**21**	**8**	**3**	**1934**	**93**	**1**	**2.89**	....	....	....	....	....	....	....
2006-07	**Buffalo**	**NHL**	**19**	**12**	**4**	**1**	**1066**	**54**	**0**	**3.04**	....	....	....	....	....	....	....
	Philadelphia	**NHL**	**16**	**6**	**8**	**2**	**935**	**47**	**0**	**3.02**	....	....	....	....	....	....	....
	NHL Totals		**316**	**140**	**123**	**31**	**17709**	**754**	**18**	**2.55**	....	....	....	....	....	....	....

QMJHL All-Rookie Team (1995) • Canadian Major Junior First All-Star Team (1995) • Canadian Major Junior Goaltender of the Year (1995) • AHL First All-Star Team (1999) • Harry "Hap" Holmes Memorial Award (fewest goals against – AHL) (1999) (shared with Tom Draper) • Aldege "Baz" Bastien Memorial Award (Outstanding Goaltender – AHL) (1999)

Traded to **Philadelphia** by **Buffalo** for Philadelphia's 2nd round choice (T.J. Brennan) in 2007 Entry Draft, February 27, 2007.

BISHOP, Ben (BIH-shuhp, BEHN) ST.L.

Goaltender. Catches left. 6'5", 205 lbs. Born, Denver, CO, November 21, 1986.
(St. Louis' 3rd choice, 85th overall, in 2005 Entry Draft).

			Regular Season								Playoffs						
Season	Club	League	GP	W	L	O/T	Mins	GA	SO	Avg	GP	W	L	Mins	GA	SO	Avg
2003-04	St.L. AAA Blues	MAHL	11	8	1	2	660	19	1	1.73	....	....	....	....	....	....	....
	St.L. AAA Blues	Exhib.	26	15	7	4	1480	62	3	2.51	....	....	....	....	....	....	....
2004-05	Texas Tornado	NAHL	45	*35	8	0	2577	83	5	1.93	*11	*9	2	*660	30	0	2.73
2005-06	University of Maine	H-East	31	21	8	2	1788	68	0	2.28	....	....	....	....	....	....	....
2006-07	University of Maine	H-East	34	21	9	2	1907	68	3	2.14	....	....	....	....	....	....	....

Hockey East All-Rookie Team (2006)

BJURLING, Bjorn (b-YUHR-lihng, b-YOHRN) EDM.

Goaltender. Catches left. 6', 205 lbs. Born, Stockholm, Sweden, August 21, 1979.
(Edmonton's 10th choice, 274th overall, in 2004 Entry Draft).

			Regular Season								Playoffs						
Season	Club	League	GP	W	L	O/T	Mins	GA	SO	Avg	GP	W	L	Mins	GA	SO	Avg
2000-01	Bodens IK	Sweden-2	32	....	....	....	1914	80	0	2.51	6	....	....	398	16	1	2.41
2001-02	Bodens IK	Sweden-2	43	....	....	....	2568	128	2	2.99	9	....	....	508	36	0	4.25
2002-03	Bodens IK	Sweden-2	3	....	....	....	179	7	1	2.35	....	....	....	....	....	....	....
	Djurgarden	Sweden	15	....	....	....	571	21	2	2.21	....	....	....	....	....	....	....
2003-04	Djurgarden	Sweden	45	....	....	....	2601	100	4	2.31	2	....	....	100	15	0	9.00
2004-05	Djurgarden	Sweden	24	....	....	....	1441	61	1	2.54	....	....	....	....	....	....	....
2005-06	Salzburg	Austria	23	....	....	....	1367	78	1	3.42	....	....	....	....	....	....	....
	Geneve	Swiss	7	2	2	2	430	24	1	3.35	....	....	....	....	....	....	....
2006-07	Valerengen IF Oslo	Norway	35	....	....	....	2027	69	5	2.04	15	....	....	907	32	1	2.11

BOUCHER, Brian (BOO-shay, BRIGH-uhn) PHI.

Goaltender. Catches left. 6'2", 198 lbs. Born, Woonsocket, RI, January 2, 1977.
(Philadelphia's 1st choice, 22nd overall, in 1995 Entry Draft).

			Regular Season								Playoffs						
Season	Club	League	GP	W	L	O/T	Mins	GA	SO	Avg	GP	W	L	Mins	GA	SO	Avg
1993-94	Mount St. Charles	High-RI	15	*14	0	1	*504	*8	*9	*0.57	4	*4	0	*180	*6	*1	*1.20
1994-95	Wexford Raiders	MTJHL	8	....	....	....	425	23	0	3.25	....	....	....	....	....	....	....
	Tri-City Americans	WHL	35	17	11	2	1969	108	1	3.29	13	6	5	795	50	0	3.77
1995-96	Tri-City Americans	WHL	55	33	19	2	3183	181	1	3.41	11	6	5	653	37	*2	3.40
1996-97	Tri-City Americans	WHL	41	10	24	6	2458	149	1	3.64	....	....	....	....	....	....	....
1997-98	Philadelphia	AHL	34	16	12	3	1901	101	0	3.19	2	0	0	30	1	0	1.95
1998-99	Philadelphia	AHL	36	20	8	5	2061	89	2	2.59	16	9	7	947	45	0	2.85
99-2000	**Philadelphia**	**NHL**	**35**	**20**	**10**	**3**	**2038**	**65**	**4**	***1.91**	**18**	**11**	**7**	**1183**	**40**	**1**	**2.03**
	Philadelphia	AHL	1	0	0	1	65	3	0	2.77	....	....	....	....	....	....	....
2000-01	**Philadelphia**	**NHL**	**27**	**8**	**12**	**5**	**1470**	**80**	**1**	**3.27**	**1**	**0**	**0**	**37**	**3**	**0**	**4.86**
2001-02	**Philadelphia**	**NHL**	**41**	**18**	**16**	**4**	**2295**	**92**	**2**	**2.41**	**2**	**0**	**1**	**88**	**2**	**0**	**1.36**
2002-03	**Phoenix**	**NHL**	**45**	**15**	**20**	**8**	**2544**	**128**	**0**	**3.02**	....	....	....	....	....	....	....
2003-04	**Phoenix**	**NHL**	**40**	**10**	**19**	**10**	**2364**	**108**	**5**	**2.74**	....	....	....	....	....	....	....
2004-05	HV 71 Jonkoping	Sweden	4	....	....	....	235	13	0	3.32	....	....	....	....	....	....	....
2005-06	**Phoenix**	**NHL**	**11**	**3**	**6**	**0**	**512**	**33**	**0**	**3.87**	....	....	....	....	....	....	....
	San Antonio	AHL	6	2	3	0	345	8	0	1.39	....	....	....	....	....	....	....
	Calgary	**NHL**	**3**	**1**	**2**	**0**	**182**	**15**	**0**	**4.95**	....	....	....	....	....	....	....
2006-07	**Chicago**	**NHL**	**15**	**1**	**10**	**3**	**827**	**45**	**1**	**3.26**	....	....	....	....	....	....	....
	Columbus	**NHL**	**3**	**1**	**1**	**0**	**142**	**9**	**0**	**3.80**	....	....	....	....	....	....	....
	NHL Totals		**220**	**77**	**96**	**33**	**12374**	**575**	**13**	**2.79**	**21**	**11**	**8**	**1308**	**45**	**1**	**2.06**

WHL West Second All-Star Team (1996) • WHL West First All-Star Team (1997) • WHL Goaltender of the Year (1997) • NHL All-Rookie Team (2000)

Traded to **Phoenix** by **Philadelphia** with Nashville's 3rd round choice (previously acquired, Phoenix selected Joe Callahan) in 2002 Entry Draft for Michal Handzus and Robert Esche, June 12, 2002. Signed as a free agent by **Jonkoping** (Sweden), October 20, 2004. Traded to **Calgary** by **Phoenix** with Mike Leclerc for Steve Reinprecht and Philippe Sauve, February 2, 2006. Signed as a free agent by **Chicago**, September 24, 2006. Claimed on waivers by **Columbus** from **Chicago**, February 27, 2007. Signed as a free agent by **Philadelphia** (AHL), July 23, 2007.

BOUTIN, Jonathan (boo-TEHN, JAWN-ah-thuhn) T.B.

Goaltender. Catches left. 6'1", 200 lbs. Born, Granby, Que., March 28, 1985.
(Tampa Bay's 3rd choice, 96th overall, in 2003 Entry Draft).

			Regular Season								Playoffs						
Season	Club	League	GP	W	L	O/T	Mins	GA	SO	Avg	GP	W	L	Mins	GA	SO	Avg
2001-02	Fort Saskatchewan	AJHL					STATISTICS NOT AVAILABLE										
	Halifax	QMJHL	11	4	1	1	459	18	0	2.35	2	0	0	15	0	0	0.00
2002-03	Halifax	QMJHL	47	22	11	2	2190	106	4	2.90	1	0	0	27	0	0	0.00
2003-04	PEI Rocket	QMJHL	30	13	12	2	1612	80	1	2.98	11	6	5	672	23	0	2.06
2004-05	PEI Rocket	QMJHL	32	15	14	2	1814	98	1	3.24	....	....	....	....	....	....	....
	Quebec Remparts	QMJHL	10	4	5	0	534	30	0	3.37	10	5	4	558	30	*1	3.22
2005-06	Springfield Falcons	AHL	22	8	12	2	1266	67	1	3.18	....	....	....	....	....	....	....
	Johnstown Chiefs	ECHL	19	8	9	2	1145	56	2	2.93	3	1	2	170	10	0	3.53
2006-07	Springfield Falcons	AHL	37	9	17	1	1660	91	1	3.29	....	....	....	....	....	....	....
	Johnstown Chiefs	ECHL	2	0	2	0	117	6	0	3.07	....	....	....	....	....	....	....

BRATHWAITE, Fred (BRAYTH-wayt, FREHD) ATL.

Goaltender. Catches left. 5'7", 185 lbs. Born, Ottawa, Ont., November 24, 1972.

			Regular Season								Playoffs						
Season	Club	League	GP	W	L	O/T	Mins	GA	SO	Avg	GP	W	L	Mins	GA	SO	Avg
1988-89	Smiths Falls Bears	CJHL	38	16	18	1	2130	187	0	5.27	....	....	....	....	....	....	....
1989-90	Orillia Terriers	OJHL-B	15	....	....	....	782	47	0	3.61	....	....	....	....	....	....	....
	Oshawa Generals	OHL	20	11	2	1	886	43	1	2.91	10	4	2	451	22	0	*2.93
1990-91	Oshawa Generals	OHL	39	25	6	3	1986	112	1	3.38	13	*9	2	677	43	0	3.81
1991-92	Oshawa Generals	OHL	24	12	7	2	1248	81	0	3.89	....	....	....	....	....	....	....
	London Knights	OHL	23	15	6	2	1325	61	*4	2.76	10	5	5	615	36	0	3.51
1992-93	Detroit	OHL	37	23	10	4	2192	134	0	3.67	15	9	6	858	48	1	3.36
1993-94	**Edmonton**	**NHL**	**19**	**3**	**10**	**3**	**982**	**58**	**0**	**3.54**	....	....	....	....	....	....	....
	Cape Breton Oilers	AHL	2	1	1	0	119	6	0	3.04	....	....	....	....	....	....	....
1994-95	**Edmonton**	**NHL**	**14**	**2**	**5**	**1**	**601**	**40**	**0**	**3.99**	....	....	....	....	....	....	....
1995-96	**Edmonton**	**NHL**	**7**	**0**	**2**	**0**	**293**	**12**	**0**	**2.46**	....	....	....	....	....	....	....
	Cape Breton Oilers	AHL	31	12	16	0	1699	110	1	3.88	....	....	....	....	....	....	....
1996-97	Manitoba Moose	IHL	58	22	22	5	2945	167	1	3.40	....	....	....	....	....	....	....
1997-98	Manitoba Moose	IHL	51	23	18	4	2736	138	1	3.03	2	0	1	72	4	0	3.30
1998-99	Canada	Nat-Tm	24	6	8	3	989	47	2	2.85	....	....	....	....	....	....	....
	Calgary	**NHL**	**28**	**11**	**9**	**7**	**1663**	**68**	**1**	**2.45**	....	....	....	....	....	....	....
99-2000	**Calgary**	**NHL**	**61**	**25**	**25**	**7**	**3448**	**158**	**5**	**2.75**	....	....	....	....	....	....	....
	Saint John Flames	AHL	2	2	0	0	120	4	0	2.00	....	....	....	....	....	....	....
2000-01	**Calgary**	**NHL**	**49**	**15**	**17**	**10**	**2742**	**106**	**5**	**2.32**	....	....	....	....	....	....	....
2001-02	**St. Louis**	**NHL**	**25**	**9**	**11**	**4**	**1446**	**54**	**2**	**2.24**	**1**	**0**	**0**	**1**	**0**	**0**	**0.00**
2002-03	**St. Louis**	**NHL**	**30**	**12**	**9**	**4**	**1615**	**74**	**2**	**2.75**	....	....	....	....	....	....	....
2003-04	**Columbus**	**NHL**	**21**	**4**	**11**	**1**	**1050**	**59**	**0**	**3.37**	....	....	....	....	....	....	....
	Syracuse Crunch	AHL	3	0	2	1	188	7	1	2.23	....	....	....	....	....	....	....
2004-05	Ak Bars Kazan	Russia	34	....	....	....	1958	61	9	1.87	2	....	....	128	2	1	0.94
2005-06	Ak Bars Kazan	Russia	32	....	....	....	1866	66	6	2.12	11	....	....	623	16	1	*1.54
2006-07	Chicago Wolves	AHL	40	22	13	5	2410	110	2	2.74	5	1	3	260	7	1	1.62
	NHL Totals		**254**	**81**	**99**	**37**	**13840**	**629**	**15**	**2.73**	**1**	**0**	**0**	**1**	**0**	**0**	**0.00**

• Scored a goal while with Detroit (OHL), April 20, 1993. Signed as a free agent by **Edmonton**, October 6, 1993. • Scored a goal while with Manitoba (IHL), November 9, 1996. Signed as a free agent by **Calgary**, January 6, 1999. Traded to **St. Louis** by **Calgary** with Daniel Tkaczuk, Sergei Varlamov and Calgary's 9th round choice (Grant Jacobsen) in 2001 Entry Draft for Roman Turek and St. Louis' 4th round choice (Yegor Shastin) in 2001 Entry Draft, June 23, 2001. • Played 6 seconds of playoff game vs. Detroit, May 4, 2002. Signed as a free agent by **Columbus**, June 2, 2003. Signed as a free agent by **Kazan** (Russia), June 19, 2004. Signed as a free agent by **Atlanta**, July 4, 2006.

BRODEUR, Martin (broh-DUHR, MAHR-tihn) N.J.

Goaltender. Catches left. 6'2", 215 lbs. Born, Montreal, Que., May 6, 1972.
(New Jersey's 1st choice, 20th overall, in 1990 Entry Draft).

			Regular Season								Playoffs						
Season	Club	League	GP	W	L	O/T	Mins	GA	SO	Avg	GP	W	L	Mins	GA	SO	Avg
1988-89	Montreal-Bourassa	QAAA	27	13	12	1	1580	98	0	3.72	3	0	3	210	14	0	3.99
1989-90	St-Hyacinthe Laser	QMJHL	42	23	13	2	2333	156	0	4.01	12	5	7	678	46	0	4.07
1990-91	St-Hyacinthe Laser	QMJHL	52	22	24	4	2946	162	2	3.30	4	0	4	232	16	0	4.14
1991-92	St-Hyacinthe Laser	QMJHL	48	27	16	4	2846	161	2	3.39	5	2	3	317	14	0	2.65
	New Jersey	**NHL**	**4**	**2**	**1**	**0**	**179**	**10**	**0**	**3.35**	**1**	**0**	**1**	**32**	**3**	**0**	**5.63**
1992-93	Utica Devils	AHL	32	14	13	5	1952	131	0	4.03	4	1	3	258	18	0	4.19
1993-94	**New Jersey**	**NHL**	**47**	**27**	**11**	**8**	**2625**	**105**	**3**	**2.40**	**17**	**8**	**9**	**1171**	**38**	**1**	**1.95**
1994-95 ♦	**New Jersey**	**NHL**	**40**	**19**	**11**	**6**	**2184**	**89**	**3**	**2.45**	***20**	***16**	**4**	***1222**	**34**	***3**	***1.67**
1995-96	**New Jersey**	**NHL**	**77**	**34**	**30**	**12**	***4433**	**173**	**6**	**2.34**	....	....	....	....	....	....	....
1996-97	**New Jersey**	**NHL**	**67**	**37**	**14**	**13**	**3838**	**120**	***10**	***1.88**	**10**	**5**	**5**	**659**	**19**	**2**	***1.73**
1997-98	**New Jersey**	**NHL**	**70**	***43**	**17**	**8**	**4128**	**130**	**10**	**1.89**	**6**	**2**	**4**	**366**	**12**	**0**	**1.97**
1998-99	**New Jersey**	**NHL**	***70**	***39**	**21**	**10**	***4239**	**162**	**4**	**2.29**	**7**	**3**	**4**	**425**	**20**	**0**	**2.82**
99-2000 ♦	**New Jersey**	**NHL**	**72**	***43**	**20**	**8**	**4312**	**161**	**6**	**2.24**	***23**	***16**	**7**	***1450**	**39**	**2**	***1.61**
2000-01	**New Jersey**	**NHL**	**72**	***42**	**17**	**11**	**4297**	**166**	**9**	**2.32**	***25**	**15**	**10**	***1505**	**52**	***4**	**2.07**
2001-02	**New Jersey**	**NHL**	***73**	**38**	**26**	**9**	***4347**	**156**	**4**	**2.15**	**6**	**2**	**4**	**381**	**9**	**1**	**1.42**
	Canada	Olympics	5	*4	0	1	300	9	0	*1.80	....	....	....	....	....	....	....
2002-03 ♦	**New Jersey**	**NHL**	**73**	***41**	**23**	**9**	**4374**	**147**	***9**	**2.02**	***24**	***16**	**8**	***1491**	**41**	***7**	**1.65**
2003-04	**New Jersey**	**NHL**	***75**	***38**	**26**	**11**	***4555**	**154**	***11**	**2.03**	**5**	**1**	**4**	**298**	**13**	**0**	**2.62**
2004-05							DID NOT PLAY										
2005-06	**New Jersey**	**NHL**	**73**	***43**	**23**	**7**	**4365**	**187**	**5**	**2.57**	**9**	**5**	**4**	**533**	**20**	**1**	**2.25**
	Canada	Olympics	4	2	2	0	239	8	0	2.01	....	....	....	....	....	....	....
2006-07	**New Jersey**	**NHL**	***78**	***48**	**23**	**7**	***4697**	**171**	***12**	**2.18**	**11**	**5**	**6**	**688**	**28**	**1**	**2.44**
	NHL Totals		**891**	**494**	**263**	**119**	**52573**	**1931**	**92**	**2.20**	**164**	**94**	**70**	**10221**	**328**	**22**	**1.93**

QMJHL All-Rookie Team (1990) • QMJHL Second All-Star Team (1992) • NHL All-Rookie Team (1994) • Calder Memorial Trophy (1994) • NHL Second All-Star Team (1997, 1998, 2006) • William M. Jennings Trophy (1997) (shared with Mike Dunham) • William M. Jennings Trophy (1998, 2004) • NHL First All-Star Team (2003, 2004, 2007) • William M. Jennings Trophy (2003) (tied with Roman Cechmanek/Robert Esche) • Vezina Trophy (2003, 2004, 2007)

Played in NHL All-Star Game (1996, 1997, 1998, 1999, 2000, 2001, 2003, 2004, 2007)

• Scored a goal in playoffs vs. Montreal, April 17, 1997.

BRODEUR, Mike (broh-DUHR, MIGHK) CHI.

Goaltender. Catches left. 6'2", 171 lbs. Born, Calgary, Alta., March 30, 1983.
(Chicago's 7th choice, 211th overall, in 2003 Entry Draft).

			Regular Season								Playoffs						
Season	Club	League	GP	W	L	O/T	Mins	GA	SO	Avg	GP	W	L	Mins	GA	SO	Avg
2000-01	Cgy. AAA Flames	AMHL	21	11	8	3	1231	54	1	2.63	10	6	4	620	31	0	3.00
2001-02	Camrose Kodiaks	AJHL	24	13	9	1	1299	65	1	2.91	....	....	....	....	....	....	....
2002-03	Camrose Kodiaks	AJHL	48	28	16	2	2570	113	2	2.64	21	16	5	1378	48	4	2.09
2003-04	Moose Jaw	WHL	41	23	12	5	2385	84	5	2.11	10	6	4	624	18	1	*1.73
2004-05	Norfolk Admirals	AHL	1	0	1	0	39	4	0	6.17	....	....	....	....	....	....	....
	Greenville Grrrowl	ECHL	35	19	15	1	2081	93	2	2.68	5	2	3	302	10	1	1.98
2005-06	Greenville Grrrowl	ECHL	24	14	8	2	1466	63	1	2.58	....	....	....	....	....	....	....
2006-07	Norfolk Admirals	AHL	10	4	3	0	495	28	0	3.39	1	0	0	8	2	0	14.17
	Augusta Lynx	ECHL	2	2	0	0	120	4	1	2.00	....	....	....	....	....	....	....
	Toledo Storm	ECHL	5	3	2	0	300	10	2	2.00	....	....	....	....	....	....	....

BROWN, David (BROWN, DAY-vihd) PIT.

Goaltender. Catches left. 6', 185 lbs. Born, Stoney Creek, Ont., February 11, 1985.
(Pittsburgh's 11th choice, 228th overall, in 2004 Entry Draft).

			Regular Season								Playoffs						
Season	Club	League	GP	W	L	O/T	Mins	GA	SO	Avg	GP	W	L	Mins	GA	SO	Avg
2002-03	Hamilton Kilty B's	OPJHL	35	....	....	....	....	....	....	3.11	....	....	....	....	....	....	....
2003-04	U. of Notre Dame	CCHA	26	14	7	3	1445	56	5	2.32	....	....	....	....	....	....	....
2004-05	U. of Notre Dame	CCHA	15	2	10	1	767	55	0	4.30	....	....	....	....	....	....	....
2005-06	U. of Notre Dame	CCHA	31	9	15	4	1724	71	0	2.47	....	....	....	....	....	....	....
2006-07	U. of Notre Dame	CCHA	39	*30	6	3	2390	63	*6	*1.58	....	....	....	....	....	....	....

CCHA First All-Star Team (2007) • CCHA Player of the Year (2007) • NCAA West First All-American Team (2007)

BROWN, Mike (BROWN, MIGHK) BOS.

Goaltender. Catches left. 6', 203 lbs. Born, Syracuse, NY, March 4, 1985.
(Boston's 7th choice, 153rd overall, in 2003 Entry Draft).

			Regular Season								Playoffs						
Season	Club	League	GP	W	L	O/T	Mins	GA	SO	Avg	GP	W	L	Mins	GA	SO	Avg
2001-02	Baldwinsville Bees	High-NY	7	....	....	....	420	8	4	0.86	5	3	2	300	6	1	1.20

2002-03	Saginaw Spirit	OHL	39	8	23	3	2186	134	0	3.68	....	....	....	....	....	....	....
2003-04	Saginaw Spirit	OHL	51	14	32	3	2886	156	4	3.24	....	....	....	....	....	....	....
2004-05	Saginaw Spirit	OHL	26	7	17	1	1482	91	0	3.68	....	....	....	....	....	....	....
	Owen Sound	OHL	33	17	11	4	1956	81	3	2.48	8	4	4	485	19	*2	2.35
2005-06	Providence Bruins	AHL	2	0	0	0	42	2	0	2.87	....	....	....	....	....	....	....
	South Carolina	ECHL	3	0	1	2	188	15	0	4.79	....	....	....	....	....	....	....
	Dayton Bombers	ECHL	18	4	12	2	1050	64	0	3.66	....	....	....	....	....	....	....
2006-07	Providence Bruins	AHL	1	0	0	0	20	0	0	0.00	....	....	....	....	....	....	....
	Long Beach	ECHL	43	15	21	2	2283	124	1	3.26	....	....	....	....	....	....	....

BRUST, Barry (BRUHST, BAIR-ree)

Goaltender. Catches left. 6'2", 210 lbs. Born, Swan River, Man., August 8, 1983.
(Minnesota's 4th choice, 73rd overall, in 2002 Entry Draft).

			Regular Season								Playoffs						
Season	Club	League	GP	W	L	O/T	Mins	GA	SO	Avg	GP	W	L	Mins	GA	SO	Avg
99-2000	Swan Valley	MJHL	19	10	9	0	1140	67	0	3.50	....	....	....	....	....	....	....
2000-01	Spokane Chiefs	WHL	16	4	6	1	777	42	0	3.24	....	....	....	....	....	....	....
2001-02	Spokane Chiefs	WHL	60	28	21	10	3540	152	1	2.58	11	6	5	677	23	0	2.04
2002-03	Spokane Chiefs	WHL	*59	22	31	4	*3385	194	0	3.44	11	4	7	722	37	0	3.07
2003-04	Spokane Chiefs	WHL	27	10	13	2	1505	75	0	2.99	....	....	....	....	....	....	....
	Calgary Hitmen	WHL	25	12	8	3	1448	54	2	2.24	7	3	4	457	15	2	1.97
2004-05	Reading Royals	ECHL	42	27	9	4	2413	79	4	1.96	8	4	4	481	14	2	1.74
2005-06	Manchester	AHL	35	19	14	1	1971	89	2	2.71	5	2	2	279	17	1	3.66
	Reading Royals	ECHL	6	3	3	0	361	18	0	3.00	....	....	....	....	....	....	....
2006-07	**Los Angeles**	**NHL**	**11**	**2**	**4**	**1**	**486**	**30**	**0**	**3.70**	....	....	....	....	....	....	....
	Manchester	AHL	18	9	7	0	951	38	2	2.40	5	2	1	199	6	0	1.81
	NHL Totals		**11**	**2**	**4**	**1**	**486**	**30**	**0**	**3.70**	....	....	....	....	....	....	....

WHL West First All-Star Team (2002)

Signed as a free agent by **Los Angeles**, June 10, 2004.

BRYZGALOV, Ilya (breez-GAH-lahf, IHL-yah) ANA.

Goaltender. Catches left. 6'3", 208 lbs. Born, Togliatti, USSR, June 22, 1980.
(Anaheim's 2nd choice, 44th overall, in 2000 Entry Draft).

			Regular Season								Playoffs						
Season	Club	League	GP	W	L	O/T	Mins	GA	SO	Avg	GP	W	L	Mins	GA	SO	Avg
1996-97	Lada Togliatti 2	Russia-3	5	....	....	....	....	....	....	....	....	....	....	....	....	....	....
1997-98	Lada Togliatti 2	Russia-3	8	....	....	....	....	28	....	....	....	....	....	....	....	....	....
1998-99	Lada Togliatti 2	Russia-4	20	....	....	....	....	43	....	....	....	....	....	....	....	....	....
99-2000	Spartak Moscow	Russia-2	10	....	....	....	500	21	....	2.52	....	....	....	....	....	....	....
	Lada Togliatti 2	Russia-3	2	....	....	....	....	5	....	....	....	....	....	....	....	....	....
	Lada Togliatti	Russia	14	....	....	....	796	18	3	1.36	7	....	....	407	10	1	1.47
2000-01	Lada Togliatti	Russia	34	....	....	....	1992	61	8	1.84	5	....	....	249	8	0	1.93
2001-02	**Anaheim**	**NHL**	**1**	**0**	**0**	**0**	**32**	**1**	**0**	**1.88**	....	....	....	....	....	....	....
	Cincinnati	AHL	45	20	16	4	2399	99	4	2.48	....	....	....	....	....	....	....
	Russia	Olympics	DID NOT PLAY – SPARE GOALTENDER														
2002-03	Cincinnati	AHL	54	12	26	9	3020	142	1	2.82	....	....	....	....	....	....	....
2003-04	**Anaheim**	**NHL**	**1**	**1**	**0**	**0**	**60**	**2**	**0**	**2.00**	....	....	....	....	....	....	....
	Cincinnati	AHL	*64	27	25	10	*3748	145	6	2.32	9	5	4	536	27	1	3.02
2004-05	Cincinnati	AHL	36	17	13	1	2007	87	4	2.60	7	3	3	314	13	0	2.48
2005-06	**Anaheim**	**NHL**	**31**	**13**	**12**	**1**	**1575**	**66**	**1**	**2.51**	**11**	**6**	**4**	**659**	**16**	***3**	***1.46**
	Russia	Olympics	1	0	1	0	60	5	0	5.00	....	....	....	....	....	....	....
2006-07 ♦	**Anaheim**	**NHL**	**27**	**10**	**8**	**6**	**1509**	**62**	**1**	**2.47**	**5**	**3**	**1**	**267**	**10**	**0**	**2.25**
	NHL Totals		**60**	**24**	**20**	**7**	**3176**	**131**	**2**	**2.47**	**16**	**9**	**5**	**926**	**26**	**3**	**1.68**

BUDAJ, Peter (BOO-digh, PEE-tuhr) COL.

Goaltender. Catches left. 6'1", 200 lbs. Born, Banska Bystrica, Czech., September 18, 1982.
(Colorado's 1st choice, 63rd overall, in 2001 Entry Draft).

			Regular Season								Playoffs						
Season	Club	League	GP	W	L	O/T	Mins	GA	SO	Avg	GP	W	L	Mins	GA	SO	Avg
99-2000	St. Michael's	OHL	34	6	18	1	1676	112	1	4.01	....	....	....	....	....	....	....
2000-01	St. Michael's	OHL	37	17	12	3	1996	95	3	2.86	11	6	4	621	26	1	2.51
2001-02	St. Michael's	OHL	42	26	9	5	2329	89	2	*2.29	12	5	6	620	34	*1	3.29
2002-03	Hershey Bears	AHL	28	10	10	2	1467	65	2	2.66	1	0	0	6	2	0	20.81
2003-04	Hershey Bears	AHL	46	17	20	6	2574	120	3	2.80	....	....	....	....	....	....	....
2004-05	Hershey Bears	AHL	59	29	25	2	3356	148	5	2.65	....	....	....	....	....	....	....
2005-06	**Colorado**	**NHL**	**34**	**14**	**10**	**6**	**1803**	**86**	**2**	**2.86**	....	....	....	....	....	....	....
	Slovakia	Olympics	3	2	1	0	179	6	0	2.01	....	....	....	....	....	....	....
2006-07	**Colorado**	**NHL**	**57**	**31**	**16**	**6**	**3199**	**143**	**3**	**2.68**	....	....	....	....	....	....	....
	NHL Totals		**91**	**45**	**26**	**12**	**5002**	**229**	**5**	**2.75**	....	....	....	....	....	....	....

OHL Second All-Star Team (2002)

BURKE, Sean (BUHRK, SHAWN)

Goaltender. Catches left. 6'4", 211 lbs. Born, Windsor, Ont., January 29, 1967.
(New Jersey's 2nd choice, 24th overall, in 1985 Entry Draft).

			Regular Season								Playoffs						
Season	Club	League	GP	W	L	O/T	Mins	GA	SO	Avg	GP	W	L	Mins	GA	SO	Avg
1983-84	St. Mike's B's	MTJHL	25	....	....	....	1482	120	0	4.86	....	....	....	....	....	....	....
1984-85	Toronto Marlboros	OHL	49	25	21	3	2987	211	0	4.24	5	1	3	266	25	0	5.64
1985-86	Toronto Marlboros	OHL	47	16	27	3	2840	233	0	4.92	4	0	4	238	24	0	6.05
1986-87	Canada	Nat-Tm	42	27	13	2	2550	130	0	3.05	....	....	....	....	....	....	....
1987-88	Canada	Nat-Tm	37	19	9	2	1962	92	1	2.81	....	....	....	....	....	....	....
	Canada	Olympics	4	1	2	1	238	12	0	3.02	....	....	....	....	....	....	....
	New Jersey	**NHL**	**13**	**10**	**1**	**0**	**689**	**35**	**1**	**3.05**	**17**	**9**	**8**	**1001**	**57**	***1**	**3.42**
1988-89	**New Jersey**	**NHL**	**62**	**22**	**31**	**9**	**3590**	**230**	**3**	**3.84**	....	....	....	....	....	....	....
1989-90	**New Jersey**	**NHL**	**52**	**22**	**22**	**6**	**2914**	**175**	**0**	**3.60**	**2**	**0**	**2**	**125**	**8**	**0**	**3.84**
1990-91	**New Jersey**	**NHL**	**35**	**8**	**12**	**8**	**1870**	**112**	**0**	**3.59**	....	....	....	....	....	....	....
1991-92	Canada	Nat-Tm	31	18	6	4	1721	75	1	2.61	....	....	....	....	....	....	....
	Canada	Olympics	7	5	2	0	429	17	0	2.37	....	....	....	....	....	....	....
	San Diego Gulls	IHL	7	4	2	1	424	17	0	2.41	3	0	3	160	13	0	4.88
1992-93	**Hartford**	**NHL**	**50**	**16**	**27**	**3**	**2656**	**184**	**0**	**4.16**	....	....	....	....	....	....	....
1993-94	**Hartford**	**NHL**	**47**	**17**	**24**	**5**	**2750**	**137**	**2**	**2.99**	....	....	....	....	....	....	....
1994-95	**Hartford**	**NHL**	**42**	**17**	**19**	**4**	**2418**	**108**	**0**	**2.68**	....	....	....	....	....	....	....
1995-96	**Hartford**	**NHL**	**66**	**28**	**28**	**6**	**3669**	**190**	**4**	**3.11**	....	....	....	....	....	....	....
1996-97	**Hartford**	**NHL**	**51**	**22**	**22**	**6**	**2985**	**134**	**4**	**2.69**	....	....	....	....	....	....	....
1997-98	**Carolina**	**NHL**	**25**	**7**	**11**	**5**	**1415**	**66**	**1**	**2.80**	....	....	....	....	....	....	....
	Vancouver	**NHL**	**16**	**2**	**9**	**4**	**838**	**49**	**0**	**3.51**	....	....	....	....	....	....	....
	Philadelphia	**NHL**	**11**	**7**	**3**	**0**	**632**	**27**	**1**	**2.56**	**5**	**1**	**4**	**283**	**17**	**0**	**3.60**
1998-99	**Florida**	**NHL**	**59**	**21**	**24**	**14**	**3402**	**151**	**3**	**2.66**	....	....	....	....	....	....	....
99-2000	**Florida**	**NHL**	**7**	**2**	**5**	**0**	**418**	**18**	**0**	**2.58**	....	....	....	....	....	....	....
	Phoenix	**NHL**	**35**	**17**	**14**	**3**	**2074**	**88**	**3**	**2.55**	**5**	**1**	**4**	**296**	**16**	**0**	**3.24**
2000-01	**Phoenix**	**NHL**	**62**	**25**	**22**	**13**	**3644**	**138**	**4**	**2.27**	....	....	....	....	....	....	....
2001-02	**Phoenix**	**NHL**	**60**	**33**	**21**	**6**	**3587**	**137**	**5**	**2.29**	**5**	**1**	**4**	**297**	**13**	**0**	**2.63**
2002-03	**Phoenix**	**NHL**	**22**	**12**	**6**	**2**	**1248**	**44**	**2**	**2.12**	....	....	....	....	....	....	....
2003-04	**Phoenix**	**NHL**	**32**	**10**	**15**	**5**	**1795**	**84**	**1**	**2.81**	....	....	....	....	....	....	....
	Philadelphia	**NHL**	**15**	**6**	**5**	**2**	**825**	**35**	**1**	**2.55**	**1**	**0**	**0**	**40**	**1**	**0**	**1.50**
2004-05			DID NOT PLAY														
2005-06	**Tampa Bay**	**NHL**	**35**	**14**	**10**	**4**	**1713**	**80**	**2**	**2.80**	**3**	**0**	**1**	**109**	**7**	**0**	**3.85**
2006-07	Springfield Falcons	AHL	7	2	5	0	345	26	0	4.52	....	....	....	....	....	....	....
	Los Angeles	**NHL**	**23**	**6**	**10**	**5**	**1310**	**68**	**1**	**3.11**	....	....	....	....	....	....	....
	NHL Totals		**820**	**324**	**341**	**110**	**46442**	**2290**	**38**	**2.96**	**38**	**12**	**23**	**2151**	**119**	**1**	**3.32**

Played in NHL All-Star Game (1989, 2001, 2002)

Traded to **Hartford** by **New Jersey** with Eric Weinrich for Bobby Holik and Hartford's 2nd round choice (Jay Pandolfo) in 1993 Entry Draft, August 28, 1992. Transferred to **Carolina** after **Hartford** franchise relocated, June 25, 1997. Traded to **Vancouver** by **Carolina** with Geoff Sanderson and Enrico Ciccone for Kirk McLean and Martin Gelinas, January 3, 1998. Traded to **Philadelphia** by **Vancouver** for Garth Snow, March 4, 1998. Signed as a free agent by **Florida**, September 12, 1998. Traded to **Phoenix** by **Florida** with Florida's 5th round choice (Nate Kiser) in 2000 Entry Draft for Mikhail Shtalenkov and Phoenix's 4th round choice (Chris Eade) in 2000 Entry Draft, November 18, 1999. Traded to **Philadelphia** by **Phoenix** with Branko Radivojevic and Ben Eager for Mike Comrie, February 9, 2004. Signed as a free agent by **Tampa Bay**, August 9, 2005. Claimed on waivers by **Los Angeles** from **Tampa Bay**, January 18, 2007.

CANN, Trevor (KAN, TREH-vuhr) COL.

Goaltender. Catches left. 5'11", 199 lbs. Born, Oakville, Ont., March 30, 1989.
(Colorado's 3rd choice, 49th overall, in 2007 Entry Draft).

			Regular Season								Playoffs						
Season	Club	League	GP	W	L	O/T	Mins	GA	SO	Avg	GP	W	L	Mins	GA	SO	Avg
2005-06	Peterborough	OHL	20	16	2	0	1176	52	1	2.65	1	0	0	35	3	0	5.14
2006-07	Peterborough	OHL	*62	23	32	5	3565	219	0	3.69	....	....	....	....	....	....	....

CARON, Sebastien (KAIR-aw, suh-BAS-tee-yeh)

Goaltender. Catches left. 6'1", 170 lbs. Born, Amqui, Que., June 25, 1980.
(Pittsburgh's 4th choice, 86th overall, in 1999 Entry Draft).

			Regular Season								Playoffs						
Season	Club	League	GP	W	L	O/T	Mins	GA	SO	Avg	GP	W	L	Mins	GA	SO	Avg
1997-98	TGV Pentagone	QAHA	17	....	....	....	762	48	1	2.84	....	....	....	....	....	....	....
1998-99	Rimouski Oceanic	QMJHL	30	13	10	3	1570	85	0	3.25	2	1	0	68	0	0	0.00
99-2000	Rimouski Oceanic	QMJHL	54	*38	11	3	3040	179	1	3.53	14	*12	2	828	50	0	3.62
2000-01	Wilkes-Barre	AHL	30	12	14	3	1746	103	4	3.54	....	....	....	....	....	....	....
2001-02	Wilkes-Barre	AHL	46	14	22	8	2671	139	1	3.12	....	....	....	....	....	....	....
2002-03	**Pittsburgh**	**NHL**	**24**	**7**	**14**	**2**	**1408**	**62**	**2**	**2.64**	....	....	....	....	....	....	....
	Wilkes-Barre	AHL	27	12	14	1	1561	81	1	3.11	....	....	....	....	....	....	....
2003-04	**Pittsburgh**	**NHL**	**40**	**9**	**24**	**5**	**2213**	**138**	**1**	**3.74**	....	....	....	....	....	....	....
	Wilkes-Barre	AHL	14	7	3	4	811	26	2	1.92	7	3	4	395	23	0	3.50
2004-05	Saguenay Fjord	QNAHL	STATISTICS NOT AVAILABLE														
2005-06	**Pittsburgh**	**NHL**	**26**	**8**	**9**	**5**	**1312**	**87**	**1**	**3.98**	....	....	....	....	....	....	....
	Wilkes-Barre	AHL	6	3	3	0	357	7	2	1.18	....	....	....	....	....	....	....
2006-07	**Chicago**	**NHL**	**1**	**1**	**0**	**0**	**60**	**1**	**0**	**1.00**	....	....	....	....	....	....	....
	Norfolk Admirals	AHL	9	4	4	0	506	34	0	4.03	....	....	....	....	....	....	....
	Anaheim	**NHL**	**1**	**0**	**0**	**0**	**28**	**1**	**0**	**2.14**	....	....	....	....	....	....	....
	Portland Pirates	AHL	17	7	6	4	1025	40	0	2.34	....	....	....	....	....	....	....
	NHL Totals		**92**	**25**	**47**	**12**	**5021**	**289**	**4**	**3.45**	....	....	....	....	....	....	....

Memorial Cup Tournament All-Star Team (2000) • Hap Emms Memorial Trophy (Memorial Cup Tournament Top Goaltender) (2000) • NHL All-Rookie Team (2003)

Signed as a free agent by **Saguenay** (QNAHL), September 21, 2004. Signed as a free agent by **Chicago**, August 8, 2006. Traded to **Anaheim** by **Chicago** with Matt Keith and Chris Durno for Pierre Parenteau and Bruno St. Jacques, December 28, 2006. Signed as a free agent by **Fribourg** (Swiss), June 21, 2007.

CARUSO, David (kah-ROO-soh, DAY-vihd) N.J.

Goaltender. Catches left. 6'1", 215 lbs. Born, Roswell, GA, June 18, 1982.

			Regular Season								Playoffs						
Season	Club	League	GP	W	L	O/T	Mins	GA	SO	Avg	GP	W	L	Mins	GA	SO	Avg
2002-03	Ohio State	CCHA	8	5	2	0	460	12	2	1.56	....	....	....	....	....	....	....
2003-04	Ohio State	CCHA	14	9	3	0	762	25	2	*1.97	....	....	....	....	....	....	....
2004-05	Ohio State	CCHA	38	25	9	4	2272	81	2	2.14	....	....	....	....	....	....	....
2005-06	Ohio State	CCHA	36	13	18	5	2146	77	*5	2.15	....	....	....	....	....	....	....
2006-07	Chicago Wolves	AHL	1	1	0	0	36	4	0	6.75	....	....	....	....	....	....	....
	Gwinnett	ECHL	38	23	11	4	2297	120	1	3.13	3	1	2	200	9	0	2.71

Signed as a free agent by **Atlanta**, July 6, 2006. Signed as a free agent by **New Jersey**, August 10, 2007.

CASSIVI, Frederic (KASS-ih-vee, FREHD-uhr-ihk) WSH.

Goaltender. Catches left. 6'4", 220 lbs. Born, Sorel, Que., June 12, 1975.
(Ottawa's 7th choice, 210th overall, in 1994 Entry Draft).

			Regular Season								Playoffs						
Season	Club	League	GP	W	L	O/T	Mins	GA	SO	Avg	GP	W	L	Mins	GA	SO	Avg
1991-92	Abitibi Forestiers	QAAA	22	5	17	0	1320	106	0	4.84	3	1	2	180	15	0	5.06
1992-93			STATISTICS NOT AVAILABLE														
1993-94	St-Hyacinthe Laser	QMJHL	35	15	13	3	1751	127	1	4.35	....	....	....	....	....	....	....
1994-95	Halifax	QMJHL	24	9	12	1	1362	105	0	4.63	....	....	....	....	....	....	....
	St-Jean Lynx	QMJHL	19	12	6	0	1021	55	1	3.23	5	2	3	258	18	0	4.19
1995-96	Thunder Bay	ColHL	12	6	4	2	715	51	0	4.28	....	....	....	....	....	....	....
	P.E.I. Senators	AHL	41	20	14	3	2347	128	1	3.27	5	2	3	317	24	0	4.54
1996-97	Syracuse Crunch	AHL	55	23	22	8	3069	164	2	3.21	1	0	1	60	3	0	3.01
1997-98	Worcester IceCats	AHL	45	20	22	2	2593	140	1	3.24	6	3	3	326	18	0	3.31
1998-99	Cincinnati	IHL	44	21	17	2	2418	123	1	3.05	3	1	2	139	6	0	2.59
99-2000	Hershey Bears	AHL	31	14	9	3	1554	78	1	3.01	2	0	1	63	5	0	4.75
2000-01	Hershey Bears	AHL	49	17	24	3	2620	124	2	2.84	9	7	2	564	14	1	*1.49
2001-02	Hershey Bears	AHL	21	6	10	4	1201	50	0	2.50	....	....	....	....	....	....	....
	Atlanta	**NHL**	**6**	**2**	**3**	**0**	**307**	**17**	**0**	**3.32**	....	....	....	....	....	....	....
	Chicago Wolves	AHL	12	6	2	1	625	26	0	2.50	5	2	2	264	11	0	2.50
2002-03	**Atlanta**	**NHL**	**2**	**1**	**1**	**0**	**123**	**11**	**0**	**5.37**	....	....	....	....	....	....	....
	Chicago Wolves	AHL	21	10	8	1	1171	62	0	3.18	2	0	2	90	3	0	2.00
2003-04	Chicago Wolves	AHL	34	15	12	5	1911	82	1	2.57	....	....	....	....	....	....	....
2004-05	Cincinnati	AHL	46	25	18	2	2549	88	*10	2.07	8	2	4	444	21	0	2.84
2005-06	**Washington**	**NHL**	**1**	**0**	**1**	**0**	**59**	**4**	**0**	**4.07**	....	....	....	....	....	....	....
	Hershey Bears	AHL	*61	*34	19	6	*3538	153	3	2.59	*21	*16	5	*1316	46	*4	2.10
2006-07	**Washington**	**NHL**	**4**	**0**	**1**	**1**	**139**	**6**	**0**	**2.59**	....	....	....	....	....	....	....
	Hershey Bears	AHL	39	22	10	5	2286	90	3	2.36	19	13	6	1169	51	1	2.62
	NHL Totals		**13**	**3**	**6**	**1**	**628**	**38**	**0**	**3.63**	....	....	....	....	....	....	....

Jack A. Butterfield Trophy (Playoff MVP - AHL) (2006)

Signed as a free agent by **Colorado**, August 17, 1999. Traded to **Atlanta** by **Colorado** for Brett Clark, January 24, 2002. Signed as a free agent by **Cincinnati** (AHL), September 28, 2004. Signed as a free agent by **Washington**, August 11, 2005.

CHEVERIE, Marc (she-VEH-ree, MAHRK) FLA.

Goaltender. Catches left. 6'3", 183 lbs. Born, Cole Harbour, N.S., February 22, 1987.
(Florida's 6th choice, 193rd overall, in 2006 Entry Draft).

			Regular Season								Playoffs						
Season	Club	League	GP	W	L	O/T	Mins	GA	SO	Avg	GP	W	L	Mins	GA	SO	Avg
2003-04	Dartmouth	NSMHL	....	19	4	2	1521	76	1	2.99	....	....	....	....	....	....	....
2004-05	Notre Dame	SMHL	25	....	....	....	....	....	....	2.25	....	....	....	....	....	....	....
2005-06	Nanaimo Clippers	BCHL	46	23	9	0	2032	86	4	2.54	....	....	....	....	....	....	....
2006-07	Nanaimo Clippers	BCHL	34	21	9	2	2015	104	3	3.10	....	....	....	....	....	....	....

CLEMMENSEN, Scott (KLEH-mehn-sehn, SKAWT) TOR.

Goaltender. Catches left. 6'3", 205 lbs. Born, Des Moines, IA, July 23, 1977.
(New Jersey's 7th choice, 215th overall, in 1997 Entry Draft).

			Regular Season								Playoffs						
Season	**Club**	**League**	**GP**	**W**	**L**	**O/T**	**Mins**	**GA**	**SO**	**Avg**	**GP**	**W**	**L**	**Mins**	**GA**	**SO**	**Avg**
1995-96	Dubuque	USHL	20	10	7	1	1082	62	0	3.44	....	....	....	....	....	....	....
1996-97	Des Moines	USHL	36	22	9	2	2042	111	1	3.26	4	1	2	200	9	1	2.70
1997-98	Boston College	H-East	37	24	9	4	2205	102	*4	2.78	....	....	....	....	....	....	....
1998-99	Boston College	H-East	*42	26	12	4	*2507	120	1	2.87	....	....	....	....	....	....	....
99-2000	Boston College	H-East	29	19	7	0	1610	59	*5	2.20	....	....	....	....	....	....	....
2000-01	Boston College	H-East	*39	*30	7	2	*2312	82	3	2.13	....	....	....	....	....	....	....
2001-02	**New Jersey**	**NHL**	**2**	**0**	**0**	**0**	**20**	**1**	**0**	**3.00**	....	....	....	....	....	....	....
	Albany River Rats	AHL	29	5	19	4	1677	92	0	3.29	....	....	....	....	....	....	....
2002-03	Albany River Rats	AHL	47	12	24	8	2694	119	1	2.65	....	....	....	....	....	....	....
2003-04	**New Jersey**	**NHL**	**4**	**3**	**1**	**0**	**238**	**4**	**2**	**1.01**	....	....	....	....	....	....	....
	Albany River Rats	AHL	22	5	12	4	1309	67	0	3.07	....	....	....	....	....	....	....
2004-05	Albany River Rats	AHL	46	13	25	5	2645	124	2	2.81	....	....	....	....	....	....	....
2005-06	**New Jersey**	**NHL**	**13**	**3**	**4**	**2**	**627**	**35**	**0**	**3.35**	**1**	**0**	**0**	**7**	**0**	**0**	**0.00**
	Albany River Rats	AHL	1	0	1	0	59	5	0	5.05	....	....	....	....	....	....	....
2006-07	**New Jersey**	**NHL**	**6**	**1**	**1**	**2**	**305**	**16**	**0**	**3.15**	....	....	....	....	....	....	....
	Lowell Devils	AHL	1	1	0	0	60	0	1	0.00	....	....	....	....	....	....	....
	NHL Totals		**25**	**7**	**6**	**4**	**1190**	**56**	**2**	**2.82**	**1**	**0**	**0**	**7**	**0**	**0**	**0.00**

NCAA Championship All-Tournament Team (2001)

Signed as a free agent by **Toronto**, July 6, 2007.

CLOUTIER, Dan (KLOO-tyay, DAN) L.A.

Goaltender. Catches left. 6'1", 195 lbs. Born, Mont-Laurier, Que., April 22, 1976.
(NY Rangers' 1st choice, 26th overall, in 1994 Entry Draft).

			Regular Season								Playoffs						
Season	**Club**	**League**	**GP**	**W**	**L**	**O/T**	**Mins**	**GA**	**SO**	**Avg**	**GP**	**W**	**L**	**Mins**	**GA**	**SO**	**Avg**
1991-92	St. Thomas Stars	OJHL-B	14	....	....	....	823	80	0	5.83	....	....	....	....	....	....	....
1992-93	Timmins	NOJHA	5	4	0	0	255	10	0	2.35	....	....	....	....	....	....	....
	Sault Ste. Marie	OHL	12	4	6	0	572	44	0	4.62	4	1	2	231	12	0	3.12
1993-94	Sault Ste. Marie	OHL	55	28	14	6	2934	174	*2	3.56	14	*10	4	833	52	0	3.75
1994-95	Sault Ste. Marie	OHL	45	15	26	2	2518	185	1	4.41	....	....	....	....	....	....	....
1995-96	Sault Ste. Marie	OHL	13	9	3	0	641	43	0	4.02	....	....	....	....	....	....	....
	Guelph Storm	OHL	17	12	2	2	1004	35	2	2.09	16	11	5	993	52	*2	3.14
1996-97	Binghamton	AHL	60	23	28	8	3367	199	3	3.55	4	1	3	236	13	0	3.31
1997-98	**NY Rangers**	**NHL**	**12**	**4**	**5**	**1**	**551**	**23**	**0**	**2.50**	....	....	....	....	....	....	....
	Hartford Wolf Pack	AHL	24	12	8	3	1417	62	0	2.63	8	5	3	478	24	0	3.01
1998-99	**NY Rangers**	**NHL**	**22**	**6**	**8**	**3**	**1097**	**49**	**0**	**2.68**	....	....	....	....	....	....	....
99-2000	**Tampa Bay**	**NHL**	**52**	**9**	**30**	**3**	**2492**	**145**	**0**	**3.49**	....	....	....	....	....	....	....
2000-01	**Tampa Bay**	**NHL**	**24**	**3**	**13**	**3**	**1005**	**59**	**1**	**3.52**	....	....	....	....	....	....	....
	Detroit Vipers	IHL	1	0	1	0	59	3	0	3.05	....	....	....	....	....	....	....
	Vancouver	**NHL**	**16**	**4**	**6**	**5**	**914**	**37**	**0**	**2.43**	**2**	**0**	**2**	**117**	**9**	**0**	**4.62**
2001-02	**Vancouver**	**NHL**	**62**	**31**	**22**	**5**	**3502**	**142**	**7**	**2.43**	**6**	**2**	**3**	**273**	**16**	**0**	**3.52**
2002-03	**Vancouver**	**NHL**	**57**	**33**	**16**	**7**	**3376**	**136**	**2**	**2.42**	**14**	**7**	**7**	**833**	**45**	**0**	**3.24**
2003-04	**Vancouver**	**NHL**	**60**	**33**	**21**	**6**	**3539**	**134**	**5**	**2.27**	**3**	**1**	**1**	**138**	**5**	**0**	**2.17**
2004-05	Klagenfurter AC	Austria	13	7	0	5	772	25	1	1.94	10	6	4	590	27	1	2.75
2005-06	**Vancouver**	**NHL**	**13**	**8**	**3**	**1**	**681**	**36**	**0**	**3.17**	....	....	....	....	....	....	....
2006-07	**Los Angeles**	**NHL**	**24**	**6**	**14**	**2**	**1281**	**85**	**0**	**3.98**	....	....	....	....	....	....	....
	NHL Totals		**342**	**137**	**138**	**36**	**18438**	**846**	**15**	**2.75**	**25**	**10**	**13**	**1361**	**75**	**0**	**3.31**

OHL Second All-Star Team (1996) • AHL All-Rookie Team (1997)

Traded to **Tampa Bay** by **NY Rangers** with Niklas Sundstrom and NY Rangers' 1st (Nikita Alexeev) and 3rd (later traded to San Jose – later traded to Chicago – Chicago selected Igor Radulov) round choices in 2000 Entry Draft for Chicago's 1st round choice (previously acquired, NY Rangers selected Pavel Brendl) in 1999 Entry Draft, June 26, 1999. Traded to **Vancouver** by **Tampa Bay** for Adrian Aucoin and Vancouver's 2nd round choice (Alexander Polushin) in 2001 Entry Draft, February 7, 2001. Signed as a free agent by **Klagenfurter** (Austria), January 20, 2005. Traded to **Los Angeles** by **Vancouver** for Los Angeles' 2nd round choice (Taylor Ellington) in 2007 Entry Draft and Los Angeles' 3rd round choice in 2009 Entry Draft, July 5, 2006.

COLEMAN, Gerald (KOHL-man, JAIR-uhld) ANA.

Goaltender. Catches left. 6'4", 214 lbs. Born, Romeoville, IL, April 3, 1985.
(Tampa Bay's 5th choice, 224th overall, in 2003 Entry Draft).

			Regular Season								Playoffs						
Season	**Club**	**League**	**GP**	**W**	**L**	**O/T**	**Mins**	**GA**	**SO**	**Avg**	**GP**	**W**	**L**	**Mins**	**GA**	**SO**	**Avg**
99-2000	Chicago	MEHL	26	....	....	....	1560	65	0	2.50	....	....	....	....	....	....	....
2000-01	USNTDP	U-17	9	3	0	4	527	26	0	2.96	....	....	....	....	....	....	....
	USNTDP	NAHL	36	8	23	1	1859	132	0	4.26	....	....	....	....	....	....	....
2001-02	USNTDP	U-18	13	8	1	3	667	38	1	3.42	....	....	....	....	....	....	....
	USNTDP	USHL	2	1	1	0	76	4	0	3.15	....	....	....	....	....	....	....
	USNTDP	NAHL	22	5	14	2	1263	75	0	3.56	....	....	....	....	....	....	....
2002-03	London Knights	OHL	26	6	9	3	1074	59	1	3.30	....	....	....	....	....	....	....
2003-04	London Knights	OHL	33	24	8	0	1852	68	*5	2.20	8	5	2	442	19	1	2.58
2004-05	London Knights	OHL	38	*32	2	2	2224	63	*8	*1.70	8	7	1	455	13	0	*1.71
2005-06	**Tampa Bay**	**NHL**	**2**	**0**	**0**	**1**	**43**	**2**	**0**	**2.79**	....	....	....	....	....	....	....
	Springfield Falcons	AHL	43	14	21	3	2413	156	2	3.88	....	....	....	....	....	....	....
2006-07	Springfield Falcons	AHL	3	2	1	0	179	6	0	2.01	....	....	....	....	....	....	....
	Johnstown Chiefs	ECHL	17	7	9	0	914	52	0	3.41	....	....	....	....	....	....	....
	Portland Pirates	AHL	11	4	5	0	603	29	0	2.89	....	....	....	....	....	....	....
	NHL Totals		**2**	**0**	**0**	**1**	**43**	**2**	**0**	**2.79**	....	....	....	....	....	....	....

Traded to **Anaheim** by **Tampa Bay** with Tampa Bay's 1st round choice (later traded to Minnesota - Minnesota selected Colton Gillies) in 2007 Entry Draft for Shane O'Brien and Colorado's 3rd round choice (previously acquired, Tampa Bay selected Luca Cunti) in 2007 Entry Draft, February 24, 2007.

CONKLIN, Ty (KAWN-klihn, TIGH) PIT.

Goaltender. Catches left. 6', 184 lbs. Born, Anchorage, AK, March 30, 1976.

			Regular Season								Playoffs						
Season	**Club**	**League**	**GP**	**W**	**L**	**O/T**	**Mins**	**GA**	**SO**	**Avg**	**GP**	**W**	**L**	**Mins**	**GA**	**SO**	**Avg**
1995-96	Green Bay	USHL	30	....	....	....	1727	82	1	2.85	....	....	....	....	....	....	....
1996-97	Alaska Anchorage	WCHA	DID NOT PLAY – FRESHMAN														
	Green Bay	USHL	30	19	7	1	1609	86	1	3.21	17	8	9	980	56	1	3.43
1997-98	New Hampshire	H-East	DID NOT PLAY – TRANSFERRED COLLEGES														
1998-99	New Hampshire	H-East	22	18	3	1	1338	41	0	*1.84	....	....	....	....	....	....	....
99-2000	New Hampshire	H-East	*37	*22	8	6	*2194	91	2	2.49	....	....	....	....	....	....	....
2000-01	New Hampshire	H-East	34	17	12	5	2048	70	*5	*2.05	....	....	....	....	....	....	....
2001-02	**Edmonton**	**NHL**	**4**	**2**	**0**	**0**	**148**	**4**	**0**	**1.62**	....	....	....	....	....	....	....
	Hamilton Bulldogs	AHL	37	13	12	8	2043	89	1	2.61	7	4	2	416	18	0	2.60
2002-03	Hamilton Bulldogs	AHL	38	19	13	3	2140	91	4	2.55	17	9	6	1024	38	1	2.23
2003-04	**Edmonton**	**NHL**	**38**	**17**	**14**	**4**	**2086**	**84**	**1**	**2.42**	....	....	....	....	....	....	....
2004-05	Wolfsburg	Germany	11	....	....	....	623	31	0	2.99	7	....	....	414	11	2	1.59
2005-06	**Edmonton**	**NHL**	**18**	**8**	**5**	**1**	**922**	**43**	**1**	**2.80**	**1**	**0**	**1**	**6**	**1**	**0**	**10.00**
	Hamilton Bulldogs	AHL	3	1	2	0	152	8	0	3.17	....	....	....	....	....	....	....
	Hartford Wolf Pack	AHL	2	1	0	1	130	5	0	2.31	....	....	....	....	....	....	....
2006-07	**Columbus**	**NHL**	**11**	**2**	**3**	**2**	**491**	**27**	**0**	**3.30**	....	....	....	....	....	....	....
	Syracuse Crunch	AHL	19	3	12	3	1085	60	0	3.32	....	....	....	....	....	....	....
	Buffalo	**NHL**	**5**	**1**	**2**	**0**	**227**	**13**	**0**	**3.44**	....	....	....	....	....	....	....
	NHL Totals		**76**	**30**	**24**	**7**	**3874**	**171**	**2**	**2.65**	**1**	**0**	**1**	**6**	**1**	**0**	**10.00**

USHL Second All-Star Team (1996) • Hockey East All-Rookie Team (1999) • Hockey East Second All-Star Team (1999) • Hockey East First All-Star Team (2000, 2001) • Hockey East Player of the Year (2000) (co-winner - Mike Mottau) • NCAA East Second All-American Team (2000) • NCAA East First All-American Team (2001)

• Left **Alaska-Anchorage** (WCHA) and returned to **Green Bay** (USHL), November 14, 1996. Signed as a free agent by **Edmonton**, April 18, 2001. Signed as a free agent by **Wolfsburg** (Germany), January 25, 2005. Loaned to **Hartford** (AHL) by **Edmonton**, March 8, 2006. Signed as a free agent by **Columbus**, July 6, 2006. Traded to **Buffalo** by **Columbus** for Buffalo's 5th round choice (later traded to Dallas - Dallas selected Michael Neal) in 2007 Entry Draft, February 27, 2007. Signed as a free agent by **Pittsburgh**, July 19, 2007.

CRAWFORD, Corey (KRAW-fohrd, KOH-ree) CHI.

Goaltender. Catches left. 6'2", 183 lbs. Born, Montreal, Que., December 31, 1984.
(Chicago's 2nd choice, 52nd overall, in 2003 Entry Draft).

			Regular Season								Playoffs						
Season	**Club**	**League**	**GP**	**W**	**L**	**O/T**	**Mins**	**GA**	**SO**	**Avg**	**GP**	**W**	**L**	**Mins**	**GA**	**SO**	**Avg**
2000-01	Gatineau Intrepide	QAAA	21	17	3	1	1260	40	2	1.92	....	....	....	....	....	....	....
2001-02	Moncton Wildcats	QMJHL	38	9	20	3	1863	116	1	3.74	....	....	....	....	....	....	....
2002-03	Moncton Wildcats	QMJHL	50	24	17	6	2855	130	2	2.73	6	2	3	303	20	0	3.97
2003-04	Moncton Wildcats	QMJHL	54	*35	15	3	3019	132	2	2.62	*20	*13	6	*1170	42	0	2.15
2004-05	Moncton Wildcats	QMJHL	51	28	16	6	2942	121	*6	2.47	12	6	6	725	33	*1	2.73
2005-06	**Chicago**	**NHL**	**2**	**0**	**0**	**1**	**86**	**5**	**0**	**3.49**	....	....	....	....	....	....	....
	Norfolk Admirals	AHL	48	22	23	1	2734	134	1	2.94	1	0	0	17	1	0	3.49
2006-07	Norfolk Admirals	AHL	60	38	20	2	3467	164	1	2.84	6	2	4	363	20	0	3.31
	NHL Totals		**2**	**0**	**0**	**1**	**86**	**5**	**0**	**3.49**	....	....	....	....	....	....	....

QMJHL Second All-Star Team (2004, 2005)

CURRY, John (KUH-ree, JAWN) PIT.

Goaltender. Catches left. 5'11", 185 lbs. Born, Shorewood, MN, February 27, 1984.

			Regular Season								Playoffs						
Season	**Club**	**League**	**GP**	**W**	**L**	**O/T**	**Mins**	**GA**	**SO**	**Avg**	**GP**	**W**	**L**	**Mins**	**GA**	**SO**	**Avg**
2003-04	Boston University	H-East	1	0	0	0	5	0	0	0.00	....	....	....	....	....	....	....
2004-05	Boston University	H-East	33	18	11	3	1950	64	3	1.97	....	....	....	....	....	....	....
2005-06	Boston University	H-East	37	24	8	4	2166	81	3	2.24	....	....	....	....	....	....	....
2006-07	Boston University	H-East	36	17	10	8	2154	72	7	2.01	....	....	....	....	....	....	....

NCAA East Second All-American Team (2006) • NCAA East First All-American Team (2007)

Signed as a free agent by **Pittsburgh**, July 13, 2007.

DAIGNEAULT, Maxime (DAYN-yoh, max-EEM)

Goaltender. Catches left. 6'3", 202 lbs. Born, St-Jacques-le-Mineur, Que., January 23, 1984.
(Washington's 4th choice, 59th overall, in 2002 Entry Draft).

			Regular Season								Playoffs						
Season	**Club**	**League**	**GP**	**W**	**L**	**O/T**	**Mins**	**GA**	**SO**	**Avg**	**GP**	**W**	**L**	**Mins**	**GA**	**SO**	**Avg**
99-2000	Magog	QAAA	19	12	3	3	1108	53	3	2.87	18	12	5	945	42	1	2.67
2000-01	Val-d'Or Foreurs	QMJHL	28	14	8	1	1386	82	0	3.55	10	8	1	504	21	0	2.50
2001-02	Val-d'Or Foreurs	QMJHL	61	25	27	5	3270	184	3	3.38	7	3	4	431	23	0	3.20
2002-03	Val-d'Or Foreurs	QMJHL	48	23	18	3	2694	138	2	3.07	8	4	3	487	23	1	2.83
2003-04	Val-d'Or Foreurs	QMJHL	57	23	22	9	3250	158	2	2.92	7	3	4	416	16	0	2.31
2004-05	Portland Pirates	AHL	11	3	2	1	474	23	0	2.91	....	....	....	....	....	....	....
	South Carolina	ECHL	21	11	6	1	1172	59	1	3.02	....	....	....	....	....	....	....
2005-06	Hershey Bears	AHL	3	0	1	2	190	7	0	2.21	....	....	....	....	....	....	....
	South Carolina	ECHL	38	16	12	9	2172	117	1	3.23	....	....	....	....	....	....	....
2006-07	Hershey Bears	AHL	33	23	6	0	1815	80	3	2.64	....	....	....	....	....	....	....

Memorial Cup Tournament All-Star Team (2002) • Hap Emms Memorial Trophy (Memorial Cup Tournement Top Goaltender) (2002)

DAKERS, Taylor (DAK-uhrs, TAY-luhr) S.J.

Goaltender. Catches left. 6'1", 175 lbs. Born, Richmond, B.C., September 14, 1986.
(San Jose's 4th choice, 140th overall, in 2005 Entry Draft).

			Regular Season								Playoffs						
Season	**Club**	**League**	**GP**	**W**	**L**	**O/T**	**Mins**	**GA**	**SO**	**Avg**	**GP**	**W**	**L**	**Mins**	**GA**	**SO**	**Avg**
2002-03	Columbia Valley	KIJHL	37	....	....	....	2077	93	4	2.68	....	....	....	....	....	....	....
2003-04	Kootenay Ice	WHL	19	6	10	0	856	48	1	3.36	....	....	....	....	....	....	....
2004-05	Kootenay Ice	WHL	23	13	7	2	1303	44	4	2.03	....	....	....	....	....	....	....
2005-06	Kootenay Ice	WHL	47	30	15	1	2671	94	8	2.11	6	2	4	378	23	0	3.65
2006-07	Kootenay Ice	WHL	48	33	10	4	2831	102	5	2.16	7	3	4	429	18	1	2.52

WHL East Second All-Star Team (2007)

DANIELS, Ryan (DAN-yehlz, RIGH-uhn) OTT.

Goaltender. Catches left. 6'1", 205 lbs. Born, Scarborough, Ont., June 22, 1988.
(Ottawa's 5th choice, 151st overall, in 2006 Entry Draft).

			Regular Season								Playoffs						
Season	**Club**	**League**	**GP**	**W**	**L**	**O/T**	**Mins**	**GA**	**SO**	**Avg**	**GP**	**W**	**L**	**Mins**	**GA**	**SO**	**Avg**
2003-04	Ajax/Pickering	Minor-ON	STATISTICS NOT AVAILABLE														
	Pickering Panthers	OPJHL	1	0	1	0	60	3	0	3.00	....	....	....	....	....	....	....
2004-05	Pickering Panthers	OPJHL	36	17	10	2	1790	95	2	3.18	6	2	4	372	26	0	4.19
	Saginaw Spirit	OHL	7	0	4	0	280	19	0	4.07	....	....	....	....	....	....	....
2005-06	Saginaw Spirit	OHL	26	16	10	0	1511	104	0	4.13	1	0	1	59	4	0	4.07
2006-07	Saginaw Spirit	OHL	60	38	18	3	3553	174	2	2.94	4	1	3	239	13	0	3.26

DANIS, Yann (DA-nihs, YAN) MTL.

Goaltender. Catches left. 6', 182 lbs. Born, Lafontaine, Que., June 21, 1981.

			Regular Season								Playoffs						
Season	**Club**	**League**	**GP**	**W**	**L**	**O/T**	**Mins**	**GA**	**SO**	**Avg**	**GP**	**W**	**L**	**Mins**	**GA**	**SO**	**Avg**
99-2000	St-Jerome	QJHL	STATISTICS NOT AVAILABLE														
	Cornwall Colts	CJHL	26	....	....	....	1367	71	0	3.12	....	....	....	....	....	....	....
2000-01	Brown U.	ECAC	12	2	8	1	667	40	0	3.60	....	....	....	....	....	....	....
2001-02	Brown U.	ECAC	24	11	10	2	1451	45	3	1.86	....	....	....	....	....	....	....
2002-03	Brown U.	ECAC	*34	15	14	5	*2074	80	5	2.31	....	....	....	....	....	....	....
2003-04	Brown U.	ECAC	30	15	11	4	1821	55	*5	*1.81	....	....	....	....	....	....	....
	Hamilton Bulldogs	AHL	2	2	0	0	120	3	1	1.50	1	0	0	12	0	0	0.00
2004-05	Hamilton Bulldogs	AHL	53	28	17	6	3075	120	5	2.34	4	0	4	237	13	0	3.29
2005-06	**Montreal**	**NHL**	**6**	**3**	**2**	**0**	**312**	**14**	**1**	**2.69**	....	....	....	....	....	....	....
	Hamilton Bulldogs	AHL	39	17	17	3	2242	111	0	2.97	....	....	....	....	....	....	....
2006-07	Hamilton Bulldogs	AHL	44	23	14	5	2540	119	1	2.81	1	1	0	54	1	0	1.12
	NHL Totals		**6**	**3**	**2**	**0**	**312**	**14**	**1**	**2.69**	....	....	....	....	....	....	....

ECAC Second All-Star Team (2002, 2003) • ECAC First All-Star Team (2004) • ECAC Goaltender of the Year (2004) • ECAC Player of the Year (2004) • NCAA East First All-American Team (2004)

Signed as a free agent by **Montreal**, March 19, 2004.

DARLING, Scott (DAHR-lihng, SKAWT) PHX.

Goaltender. Catches left. 6'6", 190 lbs. Born, Lemont, IL, December 22, 1988.
(Phoenix's 7th choice, 153rd overall, in 2007 Entry Draft).

			Regular Season								Playoffs						
Season	Club	League	GP	W	L	O/T	Mins	GA	SO	Avg	GP	W	L	Mins	GA	SO	Avg
2005-06	Chicago	MWEHL	2	0	2	0	120	10	0	5.00	....	....	....	....	....	....	....
	North Iowa	NAHL	8	2	4	0	405	28	0	4.15	....	....	....	....	....	....	....
2006-07	Capital District	EJHL	22	9	9	3	1243	70	1	3.38	....	....	....	....	....	....	....
	North Iowa	NAHL	1	0	0	0	15	3	0	12.00	....	....	....	....	....	....	....

• Signed Letter of Intent to attend **University of Maine** (H-East) in fall of 2008.

DEKANICH, Mark (deh-KAN-ihch, MAHRK) NSH.

Goaltender. Catches left. 6'2", 193 lbs. Born, N. Vancouver, B.C., May 10, 1986.
(Nashville's 3rd choice, 146th overall, in 2006 Entry Draft).

			Regular Season								Playoffs						
Season	Club	League	GP	W	L	O/T	Mins	GA	SO	Avg	GP	W	L	Mins	GA	SO	Avg
2003-04	Coquitlam Express	BCHL	30	13	15	1	1647	89	2	3.24	....	....	....	....	....	....	....
2004-05	Colgate	ECACHL	5	1	1	0	162	5	0	1.85	....	....	....	....	....	....	....
2005-06	Colgate	ECACHL	36	18	11	6	2126	81	4	2.29	....	....	....	....	....	....	....
2006-07	Colgate	ECACHL	36	15	17	4	2136	83	1	2.33	....	....	....	....	....	....	....

ECACHL First All-Star Team (2006) • ECACHL Second All-Star Team (2007)

DENIS, Marc (deh-NEE, MAHRK) T.B.

Goaltender. Catches left. 6'1", 193 lbs. Born, Montreal, Que., August 1, 1977.
(Colorado's 1st choice, 25th overall, in 1995 Entry Draft).

			Regular Season								Playoffs						
Season	Club	League	GP	W	L	O/T	Mins	GA	SO	Avg	GP	W	L	Mins	GA	SO	Avg
1992-93	Montreal-Bourassa	QAAA	26	....	....	....	1559	74	5	2.87	....	....	....	....	....	....	....
1993-94	Trois-Rivieres	QAAA	36	10	22	3	2093	158	0	4.53	4	1	3	249	20	0	4.83
1994-95	Chicoutimi	QMJHL	32	17	9	1	1688	98	0	3.48	6	4	2	372	19	1	3.06
1995-96	Chicoutimi	QMJHL	51	23	21	4	2951	157	2	3.19	16	8	8	957	69	0	4.33
1996-97	Chicoutimi	QMJHL	41	22	15	2	2323	104	4	*2.69	*21	*11	10	*1229	70	*1	3.42
	Colorado	**NHL**	**1**	**0**	**1**	**0**	**60**	**3**	**0**	**3.00**	....	....	....	....	....	....	....
	Hershey Bears	AHL	....	....	....	....	....	....	....	....	4	1	0	56	1	0	1.08
1997-98	Hershey Bears	AHL	47	17	23	4	2588	125	1	2.90	6	3	3	346	15	0	2.59
1998-99	**Colorado**	**NHL**	**4**	**1**	**1**	**1**	**217**	**9**	**0**	**2.49**	....	....	....	....	....	....	....
	Hershey Bears	AHL	52	20	23	5	2908	137	4	2.83	3	1	1	143	7	0	2.93
99-2000	**Colorado**	**NHL**	**23**	**9**	**8**	**3**	**1203**	**51**	**3**	**2.54**	....	....	....	....	....	....	....
2000-01	**Columbus**	**NHL**	**32**	**6**	**20**	**4**	**1830**	**99**	**0**	**3.25**	....	....	....	....	....	....	....
2001-02	**Columbus**	**NHL**	**42**	**9**	**24**	**5**	**2335**	**121**	**1**	**3.11**	....	....	....	....	....	....	....
2002-03	**Columbus**	**NHL**	***77**	**27**	**41**	**8**	***4511**	**232**	**5**	**3.09**	....	....	....	....	....	....	....
2003-04	**Columbus**	**NHL**	**66**	**21**	**36**	**7**	**3796**	**162**	**5**	**2.56**	....	....	....	....	....	....	....
2004-05							DID NOT PLAY										
2005-06	**Columbus**	**NHL**	**49**	**21**	**25**	**1**	**2786**	**151**	**1**	**3.25**	....	....	....	....	....	....	....
2006-07	**Tampa Bay**	**NHL**	**44**	**17**	**18**	**2**	**2353**	**125**	**1**	**3.19**	....	....	....	....	....	....	....
	NHL Totals		**338**	**111**	**174**	**31**	**19091**	**953**	**16**	**3.00**	....	....	....	....	....	....	....

QMJHL First All-Star Team (1997) • Canadian Major Junior First All-Star Team (1997) • Canadian Major Junior Goaltender of the Year (1997)

Traded to **Columbus** by **Colorado** for Columbus' 2nd round choice (later traded to Carolina – Carolina selected Tomas Kurka) in 2000 Entry Draft, June 7, 2000. Traded to **Tampa Bay** by **Columbus** for Fredrik Modin and Fredrik Norrena, June 30, 2006.

DENNIS, Adam (DEH-nihs, A-duhm) BUF.

Goaltender. Catches left. 5'11", 185 lbs. Born, Toronto, Ont., February 8, 1985.
(Buffalo's 6th choice, 182nd overall, in 2005 Entry Draft).

			Regular Season								Playoffs						
Season	Club	League	GP	W	L	O/T	Mins	GA	SO	Avg	GP	W	L	Mins	GA	SO	Avg
2002-03	Guelph Storm	OHL	18	6	7	1	846	45	0	3.19	....	....	....	....	....	....	....
2003-04	Guelph Storm	OHL	46	*33	10	2	2662	111	3	2.50	20	*15	5	1205	40	1	*1.99
2004-05	Guelph Storm	OHL	23	5	11	6	1372	57	3	2.49	....	....	....	....	....	....	....
	London Knights	OHL	16	12	4	0	920	23	3	1.50	11	9	1	629	22	*2	2.10
2005-06	London Knights	OHL	57	*44	9	4	*3444	162	1	2.82	18	12	5	1090	59	0	3.25
2006-07	Rochester	AHL	35	18	17	0	2068	115	1	3.34	....	....	....	....	....	....	....

OHL First All-Star Team (2005, 2006) • Memorial Cup Tournament All-Star Team (2005) • Hap Emms Memorial Trophy (Memorial Cup Tournament Top Goaltender) (2005)

DiPIETRO, Rick (dee-pee-EHT-roh, RIHK) NYI

Goaltender. Catches right. 6'1", 210 lbs. Born, Winthrop, MA, September 19, 1981.
(NY Islanders' 1st choice, 1st overall, in 2000 Entry Draft).

			Regular Season								Playoffs						
Season	Club	League	GP	W	L	O/T	Mins	GA	SO	Avg	GP	W	L	Mins	GA	SO	Avg
1997-98	USNTDP	U-17	10	6	4	0	800	31	0	2.33	....	....	....	....	....	....	....
	USNTDP	USHL	3	0	2	0	117	8	0	4.09	....	....	....	....	....	....	....
	USNTDP	NAHL	30	13	12	0	1602	85	1	3.18	3	2	1	179	7	1	2.35
1998-99	USNTDP	U-18	16	9	5	1	1027	46	....	2.69	....	....	....	....	....	....	....
	USNTDP	USHL	30	22	6	1	1733	67	3	2.32	....	....	....	....	....	....	....
99-2000	Boston University	H-East	29	18	5	5	1790	73	2	2.45	....	....	....	....	....	....	....
2000-01	**NY Islanders**	**NHL**	**20**	**3**	**15**	**1**	**1083**	**63**	**0**	**3.49**	....	....	....	....	....	....	....
	Chicago Wolves	IHL	14	4	5	2	778	44	0	3.39	....	....	....	....	....	....	....
2001-02	Bridgeport	AHL	59	*30	22	7	3472	134	4	2.32	20	12	8	*1270	45	*3	2.13
2002-03	**NY Islanders**	**NHL**	**10**	**2**	**5**	**2**	**585**	**29**	**0**	**2.97**	**1**	**0**	**0**	**15**	**0**	**0**	**0.00**
	Bridgeport	AHL	34	16	10	8	2044	73	3	2.14	5	2	3	299	10	1	2.01
2003-04	**NY Islanders**	**NHL**	**50**	**23**	**18**	**5**	**2844**	**112**	**5**	**2.36**	**5**	**1**	**4**	**303**	**11**	**1**	**2.18**
	Bridgeport	AHL	2	0	2	0	119	3	0	1.51	....	....	....	....	....	....	....
2004-05							DID NOT PLAY										
2005-06	**NY Islanders**	**NHL**	**63**	**30**	**24**	**5**	**3572**	**180**	**1**	**3.02**	....	....	....	....	....	....	....
	United States	Olympics	4	1	3	0	237	9	0	2.28	....	....	....	....	....	....	....
2006-07	**NY Islanders**	**NHL**	**62**	**32**	**19**	**9**	**3627**	**156**	**5**	**2.58**	**4**	**1**	**3**	**236**	**13**	**0**	**3.31**
	NHL Totals		**205**	**90**	**81**	**22**	**11711**	**540**	**11**	**2.77**	**10**	**2**	**7**	**554**	**24**	**1**	**2.60**

Hockey East Second All-Star Team (2000) • Hockey East Rookie of the Year (2000)

DIVIS, Reinhard (DIH-vihs, RIGHN-hard)

Goaltender. Catches left. 6', 200 lbs. Born, Vienna, Austria, July 4, 1975.
(St. Louis' 8th choice, 261st overall, in 2000 Entry Draft).

			Regular Season								Playoffs						
Season	Club	League	GP	W	L	O/T	Mins	GA	SO	Avg	GP	W	L	Mins	GA	SO	Avg
1995-96	VEU Feldkirch	Austria	37	....	....	....	2200	85	0	2.32	....	....	....	....	....	....	....
1996-97	VEU Feldkirch	Alpenliga	45	....	....	....	2738	105	0	2.30	....	....	....	....	....	....	....
	VEU Feldkirch	Austria	....	....	....	....	....	....	....	....	11	....	....	620	27	0	2.61
1997-98	VEU Feldkirch	Alpenliga	13	....	....	....	779	22	0	1.69	....	....	....	....	....	....	....
	VEU Feldkirch	Austria	27	....	....	....	1620	55	0	2.07	....	....	....	....	....	....	....
1998-99	VEU Feldkirch	Austria	15	....	....	....	900	58	0	3.86	....	....	....	....	....	....	....
99-2000	Leksands IF	Sweden	48	....	....	....	2839	160	3	3.38	....	....	....	....	....	....	....
2000-01	Leksands IF	Sweden	41	....	....	....	2451	141	3	3.45	....	....	....	....	....	....	....
2001-02	**St. Louis**	**NHL**	**1**	**0**	**0**	**0**	**25**	**0**	**0**	**0.00**	....	....	....	....	....	....	....
	Worcester IceCats	AHL	55	28	20	5	3173	137	3	2.59	3	1	2	205	8	0	2.34
	Austria	Olympics	4	1	1	2	238	12	0	3.02	....	....	....	....	....	....	....
2002-03	**St. Louis**	**NHL**	**2**	**2**	**0**	**0**	**83**	**1**	**0**	**0.72**	....	....	....	....	....	....	....
	Worcester IceCats	AHL	9	6	1	0	453	17	0	2.25	....	....	....	....	....	....	....
2003-04	**St. Louis**	**NHL**	**13**	**4**	**4**	**2**	**629**	**29**	**0**	**2.77**	**1**	**0**	**0**	**18**	**0**	**0**	**0.00**
	Worcester IceCats	AHL	31	12	10	8	1709	63	3	2.21	....	....	....	....	....	....	....
2004-05	EC Villacher SV	Austria	26	10	10	4	1482	61	2	2.47	3	0	3	169	12	0	4.26
2005-06	**St. Louis**	**NHL**	**12**	**0**	**5**	**1**	**475**	**37**	**0**	**4.67**	....	....	....	....	....	....	....
	Peoria Rivermen	AHL	31	16	10	2	1646	76	2	2.77	....	....	....	....	....	....	....
2006-07	Salzburg	Austria	36	....	....	....	2179	96	2	2.64	....	....	....	....	....	....	....
	NHL Totals		**28**	**6**	**9**	**3**	**1212**	**67**	**0**	**3.32**	**1**	**0**	**0**	**18**	**0**	**0**	**0.00**

Signed as a free agent by **Villacher** (Austria), October 24, 2004.

DOYLE, Frank (DOIL, FRANK) N.J.

Goaltender. Catches left. 6'1", 185 lbs. Born, Guelph, Ont., September 8, 1980.

			Regular Season								Playoffs						
Season	Club	League	GP	W	L	O/T	Mins	GA	SO	Avg	GP	W	L	Mins	GA	SO	Avg
2000-01	Cambridge	OHA-B	32	....	....	....	....	....	4	2.94	....	....	....	....	....	....	....
2001-02	University of Maine	H-East					DID NOT PLAY – FRESHMAN										
2002-03	University of Maine	H-East	21	10	4	5	1180	42	2	*2.14	....	....	....	....	....	....	....
2003-04	University of Maine	H-East	23	19	4	0	1325	40	5	1.81	....	....	....	....	....	....	....
2004-05	Utah Grizzlies	AHL	1	0	1	0	20	3	0	9.00	....	....	....	....	....	....	....
	Idaho Steelheads	ECHL	52	*32	13	4	2938	106	4	2.16	3	1	2	169	12	0	4.26
2005-06	Albany River Rats	AHL	58	21	33	3	3413	176	1	3.09	....	....	....	....	....	....	....
2006-07	Lowell Devils	AHL	49	20	24	4	2907	124	1	2.56	....	....	....	....	....	....	....

Signed as a free agent by **New Jersey**, August 12, 2005.

DROUIN-DESLAURIERS, Jeff (droo-EHN-duh-LAW-ree-yay, JEHF) EDM.

Goaltender. Catches right. 6'4", 189 lbs. Born, St-Jean-Richelieu, Que., May 15, 1984.
(Edmonton's 2nd choice, 31st overall, in 2002 Entry Draft).

			Regular Season								Playoffs						
Season	Club	League	GP	W	L	O/T	Mins	GA	SO	Avg	GP	W	L	Mins	GA	SO	Avg
2000-01	Gatineau Intrepide	QAAA	22	10	9	2	1194	61	2	3.07	2	1	0	125	6	0	2.89
2001-02	Chicoutimi	QMJHL	51	28	20	1	2909	170	1	3.51	4	0	3	197	20	0	6.11
2002-03	Chicoutimi	QMJHL	54	18	24	1	2582	164	0	3.81	4	0	4	240	15	0	9.00
2003-04	Chicoutimi	QMJHL	50	21	20	6	2701	129	1	2.87	18	10	8	956	50	1	3.14
2004-05	Edmonton	AHL	22	6	13	2	1258	62	0	2.96	....	....	....	....	....	....	....
	Greenville Grrrowl	ECHL	11	7	3	1	673	26	1	2.32	....	....	....	....	....	....	....
2005-06	Hamilton Bulldogs	AHL	13	4	7	0	666	35	0	3.15	....	....	....	....	....	....	....
	Greenville Grrrowl	ECHL	6	2	4	0	335	17	0	3.05	....	....	....	....	....	....	....
2006-07	Wilkes-Barre	AHL	40	22	12	3	2231	92	4	2.47	....	....	....	....	....	....	....

QMJHL All-Rookie Team (2002)

DUBIELEWICZ, Wade (DOO-bih-wihtz, WAYD) NYI

Goaltender. Catches left. 5'10", 185 lbs. Born, Invermere, B.C., January 30, 1978.

			Regular Season								Playoffs						
Season	Club	League	GP	W	L	O/T	Mins	GA	SO	Avg	GP	W	L	Mins	GA	SO	Avg
1997-98	Trail Smoke Eaters	BCHL	41	....	....	....	2225	118	0	3.18	....	....	....	....	....	....	....
1998-99	Trail Smoke Eaters	BCHL					STATISTICS NOT AVAILABLE										
	Chilliwack Chiefs	BCHL	14	10	4	0	834	....	0	....	....	....	....	....	....	....	....
99-2000	U. of Denver	WCHA	13	3	5	1	596	27	1	2.72	....	....	....	....	....	....	....
2000-01	U. of Denver	WCHA	29	12	9	3	1542	59	2	2.30	....	....	....	....	....	....	....
2001-02	U. of Denver	WCHA	24	20	4	0	1431	41	2	*1.72	....	....	....	....	....	....	....
2002-03	U. of Denver	WCHA	19	9	8	2	1060	43	3	2.43	....	....	....	....	....	....	....
2003-04	**NY Islanders**	**NHL**	**2**	**1**	**0**	**1**	**105**	**3**	**0**	**1.71**	....	....	....	....	....	....	....
	Bridgeport	AHL	33	20	8	5	1959	45	9	*1.38	3	2	1	181	11	0	3.64
2004-05	Bridgeport	AHL	43	18	23	1	2539	113	1	2.67	....	....	....	....	....	....	....
2005-06	**NY Islanders**	**NHL**	**7**	**2**	**3**	**0**	**310**	**15**	**0**	**2.90**	....	....	....	....	....	....	....
	Bridgeport	AHL	46	20	21	2	2575	134	3	3.12	7	3	4	435	16	0	2.21
2006-07	**NY Islanders**	**NHL**	**8**	**4**	**1**	**0**	**379**	**13**	**0**	**2.06**	**1**	**0**	**1**	**59**	**4**	**0**	**4.07**
	Bridgeport	AHL	40	22	12	5	2405	108	2	2.69	....	....	....	....	....	....	....
	NHL Totals		**17**	**7**	**4**	**1**	**794**	**31**	**0**	**2.34**	**1**	**0**	**1**	**59**	**4**	**0**	**4.07**

WCHA Second All-Star Team (2001, 2003) • WCHA First All-Star Team (2002) • AHL All-Rookie Team (2004) • AHL Second All-Star Team (2004) • Dudley "Red" Garrett Memorial Award (Rookie of the Year - AHL) (2004) • Harry "Hap" Holmes Memorial Award (fewest goals against - AHL) (2004) (shared with Dieter Kochan)

Signed as a free agent by **NY Islanders**, May 25, 2003.

DUBNYK, Devan (DUHN-nihk, DEH-vuhn) EDM.

Goaltender. Catches left. 6'6", 194 lbs. Born, Regina, Sask., May 4, 1986.
(Edmonton's 1st choice, 14th overall, in 2004 Entry Draft).

			Regular Season								Playoffs						
Season	Club	League	GP	W	L	O/T	Mins	GA	SO	Avg	GP	W	L	Mins	GA	SO	Avg
2000-01	Calgary Bruins	CBHL	14	....	....	....	815	39	2	3.10	....	....	....	....	....	....	....
2001-02	Titaanit Kotka Jr.	Fin-Jr.	5	5	0	0	300	7	....	1.40	....	....	....	....	....	....	....
	Calgary Bruins	CBHL	18	7	9	2	1105	68	1	3.69	....	....	....	....	....	....	....
	Kamloops Blazers	WHL	3	1	1	0	143	13	0	5.45	....	....	....	....	....	....	....
2002-03	Kamloops Blazers	WHL	26	12	8	1	1279	68	2	3.19	....	....	....	....	....	....	....
2003-04	Kamloops Blazers	WHL	44	20	18	5	2533	106	6	2.51	4	1	3	245	12	0	2.94
2004-05	Kamloops Blazers	WHL	*65	23	34	7	3699	166	6	2.69	6	2	4	363	22	0	3.64
2005-06	Kamloops Blazers	WHL	54	27	26	1	3207	136	1	2.54	....	....	....	....	....	....	....
2006-07	Wilkes-Barre	AHL	4	2	1	0	204	10	0	2.94	....	....	....	....	....	....	....
	Stockton Thunder	ECHL	43	24	11	7	2529	108	2	2.56	6	2	4	395	18	0	2.73

Canadian Major Junior Scholastic Player of the Year (2004)

DUCHESNE, Jeremy (DOO-shayn, JAIR-eh-mee) PHI.

Goaltender. Catches left. 6', 218 lbs. Born, Silver Spring, MD, October 17, 1986.
(Philadelphia's 3rd choice, 119th overall, in 2005 Entry Draft).

			Regular Season								Playoffs						
Season	Club	League	GP	W	L	O/T	Mins	GA	SO	Avg	GP	W	L	Mins	GA	SO	Avg
2002-03	St-Francois Blizzard	QAAA	26	7	11	5	1341	75	0	3.35	....	....	....	....	....	....	....
2003-04	Victoriaville Tigres	QMJHL	17	3	8	1	870	60	0	4.14	....	....	....	....	....	....	....
2004-05	Victoriaville Tigres	QMJHL	15	2	9	0	711	41	2	*3.46	....	....	....	....	....	....	....
	Halifax	QMJHL	18	12	0	2	921	23	3	*1.50	12	8	4	723	33	*1	2.74
2005-06	Halifax	QMJHL	55	25	29	0	3175	185	4	3.50	11	5	6	626	34	1	3.26
2006-07	Halifax	QMJHL	28	12	15	....	1580	97	1	3.68	....	....	....	....	....	....	....
	Val-d'Or Foreurs	QMJHL	24	13	10	....	1356	66	1	2.92	*18	11	7	*1157	56	0	2.90

DUNHAM, Mike (DUHN-uhm, MIGHK)

Goaltender. Catches left. 6'3", 200 lbs. Born, Johnson City, NY, June 1, 1972.
(New Jersey's 4th choice, 53rd overall, in 1990 Entry Draft).

			Regular Season								Playoffs						
Season	Club	League	GP	W	L	O/T	Mins	GA	SO	Avg	GP	W	L	Mins	GA	SO	Avg
1987-88	Canterbury	High-CT	29	....	....	....	1740	69	4	2.38	....	....	....	....	....	....	....
1988-89	Canterbury	High-CT	25	....	....	....	1500	63	2	2.52	....	....	....	....	....	....	....
1989-90	Canterbury	High-CT	32	....	....	....	1558	68	3	1.96	....	....	....	....	....	....	....
1990-91	University of Maine	H-East	23	14	5	2	1275	63	0	*2.96	....	....	....	....	....	....	....
1991-92	University of Maine	H-East	7	6	0	0	382	14	1	2.20	....	....	....	....	....	....	....
	United States	Nat-Tm	3	0	1	1	157	10	0	3.82	....	....	....	....	....	....	....
1992-93	University of Maine	H-East	25	*21	1	1	1429	63	0	2.65	....	....	....	....	....	....	....
1993-94	United States	Nat-Tm	33	22	9	2	1983	125	2	3.78	....	....	....	....	....	....	....
	United States	Olympics	3	0	1	2	180	15	0	5.00	....	....	....	....	....	....	....
	Albany River Rats	AHL	5	2	2	1	304	26	0	5.12	....	....	....	....	....	....	....

Season	Club	League	GP	W	L	O/T	Mins	GA	SO	Avg	GP	W	L	Mins	GA	SO	Avg
1994-95	Albany River Rats	AHL	35	20	7	8	2120	99	1	2.80	7	6	1	419	20	1	2.86
1995-96	Albany River Rats	AHL	44	30	10	2	2592	109	1	2.52	3	1	2	182	5	1	1.65
1996-97	**New Jersey**	**NHL**	**26**	**8**	**7**	**1**	**1013**	**43**	**2**	**2.55**	....	....	....	....	....	....	....
	Albany River Rats	AHL	3	1	1	1	184	12	0	3.91	....	....	....	....	....	....	....
1997-98	**New Jersey**	**NHL**	**15**	**5**	**5**	**3**	**773**	**29**	**1**	**2.25**	....	....	....	....	....	....	....
1998-99	**Nashville**	**NHL**	**44**	**16**	**23**	**3**	**2472**	**127**	**1**	**3.08**	....	....	....	....	....	....	....
99-2000	**Nashville**	**NHL**	**52**	**19**	**27**	**6**	**3077**	**146**	**0**	**2.85**	....	....	....	....	....	....	....
	Milwaukee	IHL	1	1	0	0	60	1	0	1.00	....	....	....	....	....	....	....
2000-01	**Nashville**	**NHL**	**48**	**21**	**21**	**4**	**2810**	**107**	**4**	**2.28**	....	....	....	....	....	....	....
2001-02	**Nashville**	**NHL**	**58**	**23**	**24**	**9**	**3316**	**144**	**3**	**2.61**	....	....	....	....	....	....	....
	United States	Olympics	1	1	0	0	60	0	*1	0.00	....	....	....	....	....	....	....
2002-03	**Nashville**	**NHL**	**15**	**2**	**9**	**2**	**819**	**43**	**0**	**3.15**	....	....	....	....	....	....	....
	NY Rangers	**NHL**	**43**	**19**	**17**	**5**	**2467**	**94**	**5**	**2.29**	....	....	....	....	....	....	....
2003-04	**NY Rangers**	**NHL**	**57**	**16**	**30**	**6**	**3148**	**159**	**2**	**3.03**	....	....	....	....	....	....	....
2004-05	Skelleftea AIK HK	Sweden-2	13	....	....	....	726	36	4	2.97	....	....	....	....	....	....	....
2005-06	**Atlanta**	**NHL**	**17**	**8**	**5**	**2**	**779**	**36**	**1**	**2.77**	....	....	....	....	....	....	....
	Gwinnett	ECHL	2	2	0	0	120	5	0	2.50	....	....	....	....	....	....	....
2006-07	**NY Islanders**	**NHL**	**19**	**4**	**10**	**3**	**979**	**61**	**0**	**3.74**	....	....	....	....	....	....	....
	NHL Totals		**394**	**141**	**178**	**44**	**21653**	**989**	**19**	**2.74**	....	....	....	....	....	....	....

Hockey East First All-Star Team (1993) • NCAA East First All-American Team (1993) • Harry "Hap" Holmes Memorial Award (fewest goals against – AHL) (1995) (shared with Corey Schwab) • Jack A. Butterfield Trophy (Playoff MVP – AHL) (1995) (co-winner - Corey Schwab) • AHL Second All-Star Team (1996) • William M. Jennings Trophy (1997) (shared with Martin Brodeur)

Claimed by **Nashville** from **New Jersey** in Expansion Draft, June 26, 1998. Traded to **NY Rangers** by **Nashville** for Rem Murray, Tomas Kloucek and Marek Zidlicky, December 12, 2002. Signed as a free agent by **Skelleftea** (Sweden-2), January 31, 2005. Signed as a free agent by **Atlanta**, September 2, 2005. Signed as a free agent by **NY Islanders**, September 29, 2006.

DUNN, Dan (DUHN, DAN) WSH.

Goaltender. Catches left. 6'5", 200 lbs. Born, Oshawa, Ont., June 20, 1988.
(Washington's 7th choice, 154th overall, in 2007 Entry Draft).

			Regular Season								Playoffs						
Season	Club	League	GP	W	L	O/T	Mins	GA	SO	Avg	GP	W	L	Mins	GA	SO	Avg
2005-06	Oshawa	OPJHL	10	2	4	2	494	29	1	3.52	....	....	....	....	....	....	....
	Cobourg Cougars	OPJHL	6	0	5	0	277	33	0	7.14	....	....	....	....	....	....	....
2006-07	Wellington Dukes	OPJHL	27	19	4	2	1546	50	2	1.94	....	....	....	....	....	....	....

• Signed Letter of Intent to attend **St. Cloud State** (WCHA) in fall of 2007.

DUPONT, Michael (DOO-pawnt, MIGH-kuhl) PHI.

Goaltender. Catches left. 6', 178 lbs. Born, Bienne, Switz., December 20, 1987.
(Philadelphia's 9th choice, 175th overall, in 2006 Entry Draft).

			Regular Season								Playoffs						
Season	Club	League	GP	W	L	O/T	Mins	GA	SO	Avg	GP	W	L	Mins	GA	SO	Avg
2004-05	Baie-Comeau	QMJHL	45	14	19	3	2226	132	2	3.56	6	2	3	305	18	0	3.54
2005-06	Baie-Comeau	QMJHL	48	19	24	0	2428	149	2	3.68	4	0	4	240	17	0	4.25
2006-07	Baie-Comeau	QMJHL	59	*31	23	....	3231	198	1	3.68	11	5	6	678	35	0	3.10

EHELECHNER, Patrick (eh-heh-LEHCH-nuhr, PAT-rihk) PIT.

Goaltender. Catches left. 6'2", 169 lbs. Born, Rosenheim, West Germany, September 23, 1984.
(San Jose's 5th choice, 139th overall, in 2003 Entry Draft).

			Regular Season								Playoffs						
Season	Club	League	GP	W	L	O/T	Mins	GA	SO	Avg	GP	W	L	Mins	GA	SO	Avg
2000-01	Jung. Mannheim	German-4	40	....	....	....	2423	171	2	4.23	....	....	....	....	....	....	....
2001-02	EV Landshut	German-3	2	....	....	....	130	6	0	2.77	....	....	....	....	....	....	....
	Hannover	Germany	8	....	....	....	475	24	0	3.03	....	....	....	....	....	....	....
2002-03	ESC Wedemark	German-4	STATISTICS NOT AVAILABLE														
	Hannover	Germany	4	....	....	....	162	16	0	5.90	....	....	....	....	....	....	....
2003-04	Sudbury Wolves	OHL	56	22	26	6	3089	148	3	2.87	7	2	4	390	14	2	2.15
2004-05	Sudbury Wolves	OHL	51	23	21	4	2997	128	3	2.56	10	4	5	497	29	0	3.50
2005-06	Adler Mannheim	Germany	1	....	....	....	59	5	0	5.02	....	....	....	....	....	....	....
	Fuchse Duisburg	Germany	26	....	....	....	1243	75	2	3.62	....	....	....	....	....	....	....
2006-07	Fuchse Duisburg	Germany	6	....	....	....	244	28	0	6.89	....	....	....	....	....	....	....

OHL Second All-Star Team (2004)

Signed as a free agent by **Mannheim** (Germany), April 25, 2005. Traded to **Pittsburgh** by **San Jose** with Nils Ekman for Carolina's 2nd round choice (previously acquired, later traded to Philadelphia - Philadelphia selected Kevin Marshall) in 2007 Entry Draft, July 20, 2006.

EIDSNESS, Bradley (IGHD-nehz, BRAD-lee) BUF.

Goaltender. Catches left. 5'11", 190 lbs. Born, Chestermere, Alta., June 2, 1989.
(Buffalo's 4th choice, 139th overall, in 2007 Entry Draft).

			Regular Season								Playoffs						
Season	Club	League	GP	W	L	O/T	Mins	GA	SO	Avg	GP	W	L	Mins	GA	SO	Avg
2005-06	Okotoks Oilers	AJHL	4	3	1	0	238	4	2	1.01	....	....	....	....	....	....	....
	Strathmore	AMHL	18	12	4	2	1046	45	....	2.58	8	5	3	512	14	....	1.64
2006-07	Okotoks Oilers	AJHL	48	24	18	2	2658	127	4	2.87	....	....	....	....	....	....	....

ELLIOTT, Brian (EHL-lee-awt, BRIGH-uhn) OTT.

Goaltender. Catches left. 6'3", 186 lbs. Born, Newmarket, Ont., April 9, 1985.
(Ottawa's 9th choice, 291st overall, in 2003 Entry Draft).

			Regular Season								Playoffs						
Season	Club	League	GP	W	L	O/T	Mins	GA	SO	Avg	GP	W	L	Mins	GA	SO	Avg
2002-03	Ajax Axemen	OPJHL	39	....	....	....	2097	135	0	3.86	....	....	....	....	....	....	....
2003-04	U. of Wisconsin	WCHA	6	3	3	0	336	12	0	2.14	....	....	....	....	....	....	....
2004-05	U. of Wisconsin	WCHA	9	6	2	1	467	9	3	1.16	....	....	....	....	....	....	....
2005-06	U. of Wisconsin	WCHA	35	*27	5	3	2128	55	*8	*1.55	....	....	....	....	....	....	....
2006-07	U. of Wisconsin	WCHA	36	15	17	2	2053	72	*5	2.10	....	....	....	....	....	....	....
	Binghamton	AHL	8	3	4	0	425	30	0	4.24	....	....	....	....	....	....	....

WCHA Second All-Star Team (2006, 2007) • NCAA West First All-American Team (2006) • NCAA Championship All-Tournament Team (2006)

ELLIS, Dan (EHL-ihs, DAN) NSH.

Goaltender. Catches left. 6', 185 lbs. Born, Orangeville, Ont., June 19, 1980.
(Dallas' 2nd choice, 60th overall, in 2000 Entry Draft).

			Regular Season								Playoffs						
Season	Club	League	GP	W	L	O/T	Mins	GA	SO	Avg	GP	W	L	Mins	GA	SO	Avg
1998-99	Newmarket	OPJHL	28	24	3	1	1670	63	3	2.25	....	....	....	....	....	....	....
99-2000	Omaha Lancers	USHL	55	*34	16	4	*3274	123	*11	*2.25	4	1	3	238	10	0	2.52
2000-01	Nebraska-Omaha	CCHA	40	21	14	3	2285	95	2	2.49	....	....	....	....	....	....	....
2001-02	Nebraska-Omaha	CCHA	40	20	15	4	2405	97	3	2.42	....	....	....	....	....	....	....
2002-03	Nebraska-Omaha	CCHA	39	11	21	5	2211	117	3	3.18	....	....	....	....	....	....	....
2003-04	**Dallas**	**NHL**	**1**	**1**	**0**	**0**	**60**	**3**	**0**	**3.00**	....	....	....	....	....	....	....
	Utah Grizzlies	AHL	20	5	14	0	1130	55	2	2.92	....	....	....	....	....	....	....
	Idaho Steelheads	ECHL	23	13	8	1	1334	57	2	2.56	*16	*13	3	*966	30	*3	*1.86
2004-05	Hamilton Bulldogs	AHL	31	10	19	0	1774	82	1	2.77	....	....	....	....	....	....	....
2005-06	Iowa Stars	AHL	34	16	13	1	1857	86	2	2.78	....	....	....	....	....	....	....
2006-07	Iowa Stars	AHL	55	30	21	1	3194	148	4	2.78	12	6	6	679	35	0	3.09
	NHL Totals		**1**	**1**	**0**	**0**	**60**	**3**	**0**	**3.00**	....	....	....	....	....	....	....

USHL First All-Star Team (2000) • USHL Goaltender of the Year (2000) • USHL Player of the Year (2000) • CCHA Second All-Star Team (2002) • ECHL Playoff MVP (2004)

Signed as a free agent by **Nashville**, July 5, 2007.

ELLIS, Julien (EHL-ihs, JEW-lee-ehn) VAN.

Goaltender. Catches left. 6', 199 lbs. Born, Sorel, Que., January 27, 1986.
(Vancouver's 5th choice, 189th overall, in 2004 Entry Draft).

			Regular Season								Playoffs						
Season	Club	League	GP	W	L	O/T	Mins	GA	SO	Avg	GP	W	L	Mins	GA	SO	Avg
2001-02	Antoine-Girouard	QAAA	22	16	2	1	1227	55	2	2.69	....	....	....	....	....	....	....
2002-03	Antoine-Girouard	QAAA	16	11	4	1	966	29	4	1.80	....	....	....	....	....	....	....
	Shawinigan	QMJHL	7	2	3	0	365	21	0	3.45	....	....	....	....	....	....	....
2003-04	Shawinigan	QMJHL	*59	32	18	2	*3287	156	1	2.85	10	3	6	569	33	0	3.48
2004-05	Shawinigan	QMJHL	*59	27	21	11	*3480	140	4	2.41	4	0	3	175	10	0	3.43
2005-06	Shawinigan	QMJHL	48	27	19	0	2680	154	3	3.45	7	4	3	412	18	*2	2.62
2006-07	Manitoba Moose	AHL	8	1	7	0	463	26	0	3.37	....	....	....	....	....	....	....
	Victoria	ECHL	37	21	14	2	2190	117	1	3.21	4	1	3	213	15	0	4.23

QMJHL All-Rookie Team (2004) • QMJHL First All-Star Team (2005)

EMERY, Ray (EH-muhr-ee, RAY) OTT.

Goaltender. Catches left. 6'2", 202 lbs. Born, Cayuga, Ont., September 28, 1982.
(Ottawa's 4th choice, 99th overall, in 2001 Entry Draft).

			Regular Season								Playoffs						
Season	Club	League	GP	W	L	O/T	Mins	GA	SO	Avg	GP	W	L	Mins	GA	SO	Avg
1998-99	Dunnville Terriers	OJHL-C	22	3	19	0	1320	140	0	6.37	....	....	....	....	....	....	....
99-2000	Welland Cougars	OHA-B	23	13	10	1	1323	62	1	2.68	....	....	....	....	....	....	....
	Sault Ste. Marie	OHL	16	9	3	0	716	36	1	3.02	15	8	7	883	33	*3	2.24
2000-01	Sault Ste. Marie	OHL	52	18	29	2	2938	174	1	3.55	....	....	....	....	....	....	....
2001-02	Sault Ste. Marie	OHL	*59	*33	17	9	*3477	158	4	2.73	6	2	4	360	19	*1	3.17
2002-03	**Ottawa**	**NHL**	**3**	**1**	**0**	**0**	**85**	**2**	**0**	**1.41**	....	....	....	....	....	....	....
	Binghamton	AHL	50	27	17	6	2924	118	*7	2.42	14	8	6	848	40	*2	2.83
2003-04	**Ottawa**	**NHL**	**3**	**2**	**0**	**0**	**126**	**5**	**0**	**2.38**	....	....	....	....	....	....	....
	Binghamton	AHL	53	21	23	7	3109	128	3	2.47	2	0	2	120	6	0	3.01
2004-05	Binghamton	AHL	51	28	18	5	2993	132	0	2.65	6	2	4	409	14	0	2.05
2005-06	**Ottawa**	**NHL**	**39**	**23**	**11**	**4**	**2168**	**102**	**3**	**2.82**	**10**	**5**	**5**	**604**	**29**	**0**	**2.88**
2006-07	**Ottawa**	**NHL**	**58**	**33**	**16**	**6**	**3351**	**138**	**5**	**2.47**	***20**	***13**	**7**	***1249**	**47**	***3**	**2.26**
	NHL Totals		**103**	**59**	**27**	**10**	**5730**	**247**	**8**	**2.59**	**30**	**18**	**12**	**1853**	**76**	**3**	**2.46**

OHL First All-Star Team (2002) • Canadian Major Junior First All-Star Team (2002) • Canadian Major Junior Goaltender of the Year (2002) • AHL All-Rookie Team (2003)

ENGREN, Atte (EHN-grehn, AH-tay) NSH.

Goaltender. Catches left. 6', 188 lbs. Born, Rauma, Finland, February 19, 1988.
(Nashville's 9th choice, 204th overall, in 2007 Entry Draft).

			Regular Season								Playoffs						
Season	Club	League	GP	W	L	O/T	Mins	GA	SO	Avg	GP	W	L	Mins	GA	SO	Avg
2004-05	Lukko Rauma U18	Fin-U18	10	....	....	....	603	22	0	2.19	....	....	....	....	....	....	....
2005-06	Lukko Rauma U18	Fin-U18	16	....	....	....	966	44	0	2.73	....	....	....	....	....	....	....
	Lukko Rauma Jr.	Fin-Jr.	11	....	....	....	637	30	0	2.83	9	....	....	509	27	0	3.18
2006-07	Lukko Rauma Jr.	Fin-Jr.	38	....	....	....	2277	115	1	3.03	....	....	....	....	....	....	....
	Suomi U20	Finland-2	2	....	....	....	100	7	0	4.20	....	....	....	....	....	....	....

ENO, Nick (EE-noh, NIHK) BUF.

Goaltender. Catches left. 6'3", 190 lbs. Born, Howell, MI, February 12, 1989.
(Buffalo's 7th choice, 187th overall, in 2007 Entry Draft).

			Regular Season								Playoffs						
Season	Club	League	GP	W	L	O/T	Mins	GA	SO	Avg	GP	W	L	Mins	GA	SO	Avg
2005-06	Howell	High-MI	25	....	....	....	1020	52	5	2.29	....	....	....	....	....	....	....
2006-07	Green Mountain	EJHL	25	9	14	2	1398	84	1	3.60	....	....	....	....	....	....	....

ENROTH, Jhonas (EHN-rawth, YOH-nuhs) BUF.

Goaltender. Catches left. 5'10", 174 lbs. Born, Stockholm, Sweden, June 25, 1988.
(Buffalo's 2nd choice, 46th overall, in 2006 Entry Draft).

			Regular Season								Playoffs						
Season	Club	League	GP	W	L	O/T	Mins	GA	SO	Avg	GP	W	L	Mins	GA	SO	Avg
2003-04	Huddinge IK U18	Swe-U18	6	....	....	....	324	15	0	2.77	....	....	....	....	....	....	....
2004-05	Huddinge IK Jr.	Swe-Jr.	19	....	....	....	1144	49	3	2.57	3	....	....	186	6	1	1.93
	Huddinge IK U18	Swe-U18	2	....	....	....	125	5	0	2.40	....	....	....	....	....	....	....
	Huddinge IK	Sweden-2	2	....	....	....	51	6	0	6.95	....	....	....	....	....	....	....
2005-06	Sodertalje SK Jr.	Swe-Jr.	39	....	....	....	2378	86	1	2.17	4	....	....	243	9	0	2.22
	Sodertalje SK U18	Swe-U18	2	....	....	....	120	5	0	2.50	....	....	....	....	....	....	....
2006-07	Sodertalje SK Jr.	Swe-Jr.	3	....	....	....	180	4	0	1.33	....	....	....	....	....	....	....
	Sodertalje SK	Sweden-2	33	....	....	....	1938	57	3	1.76	....	....	....	....	....	....	....

ERSBERG, Erik (AIRZ-buhrg, AIR-ihk) L.A.

Goaltender. Catches left. 5'11", 182 lbs. Born, Sala, Sweden, March 8, 1982.

			Regular Season								Playoffs						
Season	Club	League	GP	W	L	O/T	Mins	GA	SO	Avg	GP	W	L	Mins	GA	SO	Avg
99-2000	Vasteras IK U18	Swe-U18	1	....	....	....	60	2	0	2.00	2	....	....	119	10	0	5.02
	Vasteras IK Jr.	Swe-Jr.	16	....	....	....	885	36	0	2.44	....	....	....	....	....	....	....
2000-01	Vasteras	Sweden-4	33	....	....	....	....	....	....	1.48	....	....	....	....	....	....	....
2001-02	Vasteras Jr.	Swe-Jr.	....	....	....	....	....	....	....	....	2	....	....	118	11	0	5.61
	Vasteras	Sweden-3	37	....	....	....	....	....	....	....	....	....	....	....	....	....	....
2002-03	Vasteras	Sweden-2	32	....	....	....	1920	91	1	2.84	....	....	....	....	....	....	....
2003-04	Vasteras	Sweden-2	32	....	....	....	1850	79	3	2.56	....	....	....	....	....	....	....
2004-05	Vasteras	Sweden-2	37	....	....	....	2189	76	3	2.08	5	....	....	308	8	2	1.56
2005-06	VIK Vasteras HK	Sweden-2	2	....	....	....	118	4	0	2.02	....	....	....	....	....	....	....
	HV 71 Jonkoping	Sweden	10	....	....	....	602	18	2	1.79	2	....	....	79	4	0	3.05
	HV 71 Jr.	Swe-Jr.	1	....	....	....	60	1	0	1.00	....	....	....	....	....	....	....
2006-07	HV 71 Jonkoping	Sweden	41	....	....	....	2455	98	4	2.39	14	....	....	834	39	0	2.81

Signed as a free agent by **Los Angeles**, May 31, 2007.

ESCHE, Robert (EHSH, RAW-buhrt)

Goaltender. Catches left. 6'1", 210 lbs. Born, Whitesboro, NY, January 22, 1978.
(Phoenix's 5th choice, 139th overall, in 1996 Entry Draft).

			Regular Season								Playoffs						
Season	Club	League	GP	W	L	O/T	Mins	GA	SO	Avg	GP	W	L	Mins	GA	SO	Avg
1994-95	Gloucester	CJHL	20	10	6	0	1034	70	0	4.06	....	....	....	....	....	....	....
1995-96	Detroit Jr. Whalers	OHL	23	13	6	0	1219	76	1	3.74	3	0	2	105	4	0	2.29
1996-97	Detroit Jr. Whalers	OHL	58	24	28	2	3241	206	2	3.81	5	1	4	317	19	0	3.60
1997-98	Plymouth Whalers	OHL	48	29	13	4	2810	135	3	2.88	15	8	7	869	45	0	3.11
1998-99	**Phoenix**	**NHL**	**3**	**0**	**1**	**0**	**130**	**7**	**0**	**3.23**	....	....	....	....	....	....	....
	Springfield Falcons	AHL	55	24	20	6	2957	138	1	2.80	1	0	1	60	4	0	4.02
99-2000	**Phoenix**	**NHL**	**8**	**2**	**5**	**0**	**408**	**23**	**0**	**3.38**	....	....	....	....	....	....	....
	Houston Aeros	IHL	7	4	2	1	419	16	2	2.29	....	....	....	....	....	....	....
	Springfield Falcons	AHL	21	9	9	2	1207	61	2	3.03	3	1	2	180	12	0	4.01
2000-01	**Phoenix**	**NHL**	**25**	**10**	**8**	**4**	**1350**	**68**	**2**	**3.02**	....	....	....	....	....	....	....

2001-02	Phoenix	NHL	22	6	10	2	1145	52	1	2.72	....	....	....	....	....	....	....
	Springfield Falcons	AHL	1	1	0	0	60	0	1	0.00	....	....	....	....	....	....	....
2002-03	Philadelphia	NHL	30	12	9	3	1638	60	2	2.20	1	0	0	30	1	0	2.00
2003-04	Philadelphia	NHL	40	21	11	7	2322	79	3	2.04	18	11	7	1061	41	1	2.32
2004-05							DID NOT PLAY										
2005-06	Philadelphia	NHL	40	22	11	5	2286	113	1	2.97	6	2	4	314	22	0	4.20
	United States	Olympics	1	0	1	0	59	5	0	5.10	....	....	....	....	....	....	....
2006-07	Philadelphia	NHL	18	5	9	1	860	62	1	4.33	....	....	....	....	....	....	....
	NHL Totals		186	78	64	22	10139	464	10	2.75	25	13	11	1405	64	1	2.73

OHL Second All-Star Team (1998) • AHL All-Rookie Team (1999) • William M. Jennings Trophy (2003) (shared with Roman Cechmanek) (tied with Martin Brodeur)

Traded to **Philadelphia** by **Phoenix** with Michal Handzus for Brian Boucher and Nashville's 3rd round choice (previously acquired, Phoenix selected Joe Callahan) in 2002 Entry Draft, June 12, 2002.

FALLON, Joseph (FA-lohn, JOH-sehf) CHI.

Goaltender. Catches left. 6'3", 203 lbs. Born, Bemidji, MN, February 1, 1985.
(Chicago's 9th choice, 167th overall, in 2005 Entry Draft).

			Regular Season								Playoffs						
Season	Club	League	GP	W	L	O/T	Mins	GA	SO	Avg	GP	W	L	Mins	GA	SO	Avg
2001-02	Rochester	USHL	27	7	16	1	1484	93	0	3.76	....	....	....	....	....	....	....
2002-03	Cedar Rapids	USHL	42	20	15	6	2495	108	2	2.60	7	3	4	426	21	0	2.96
2003-04	Cedar Rapids	USHL	42	25	13	2	2370	108	4	2.73	4	1	3	237	9	0	2.28
2004-05	U. of Vermont	ECACHL	32	17	10	4	1932	63	5	1.96	....	....	....	....	....	....	....
2005-06	U. of Vermont	H-East	33	14	14	5	1931	65	6	2.02	....	....	....	....	....	....	....
2006-07	U. of Vermont	H-East	34	17	14	3	1997	62	6	1.86	....	....	....	....	....	....	....

ECACHL All-Rookie Team (2005) • ECACHL Rookie of the Year (2005)

FERNANDEZ, Manny (fuhr-NAN-dehz, MAN-ee) BOS.

Goaltender. Catches left. 6', 207 lbs. Born, Etobicoke, Ont., August 27, 1974.
(Quebec's 4th choice, 52nd overall, in 1992 Entry Draft).

			Regular Season								Playoffs						
Season	Club	League	GP	W	L	O/T	Mins	GA	SO	Avg	GP	W	L	Mins	GA	SO	Avg
1990-91	Lac St-Louis Lions	QAAA	20	13	5	0	1176	69	*3	3.52	3	2	1	181	12	0	3.98
1991-92	Laval Titan	QMJHL	31	14	13	2	1593	99	1	3.73	9	3	5	468	39	0	5.00
1992-93	Laval Titan	QMJHL	43	26	14	2	2347	141	1	3.60	13	*12	1	818	42	0	3.08
1993-94	Laval Titan	QMJHL	51	29	14	1	2776	143	*5	3.09	19	14	5	1116	49	*1	*2.63
1994-95	Kalamazoo Wings	IHL	46	21	10	9	2470	115	2	2.79	14	10	2	753	34	1	2.71
	Dallas	NHL	1	0	1	0	59	3	0	3.05	....	....	....	....	....	....	....
1995-96	Dallas	NHL	5	0	1	1	249	19	0	4.58	....	....	....	....	....	....	....
	Michigan K-Wings	IHL	47	22	15	9	2664	133	*4	3.00	6	5	1	372	14	0	*2.26
1996-97	Michigan K-Wings	IHL	48	20	24	2	2720	142	2	3.13	4	1	3	277	15	0	3.25
1997-98	Dallas	NHL	2	1	0	0	69	2	0	1.74	1	0	0	2	0	0	0.00
	Michigan K-Wings	IHL	55	27	17	5	3022	139	5	2.76	2	0	2	88	7	0	4.73
1998-99	Dallas	NHL	1	0	1	0	60	2	0	2.00	....	....	....	....	....	....	....
	Houston Aeros	IHL	50	34	6	9	2949	116	2	2.36	*19	*11	8	*1126	49	1	2.61
99-2000	Dallas	NHL	24	11	8	3	1353	48	1	2.13	1	0	0	17	1	0	3.53
2000-01	Minnesota	NHL	42	19	17	4	2461	92	4	2.24	....	....	....	....	....	....	....
2001-02	Minnesota	NHL	44	12	24	5	2463	125	1	3.05	....	....	....	....	....	....	....
2002-03	Minnesota	NHL	35	19	13	2	1979	74	2	2.24	9	3	4	552	18	0	1.96
2003-04	Minnesota	NHL	37	11	14	9	2166	90	2	2.49	....	....	....	....	....	....	....
2004-05	Lulea HF	Sweden	19	....	....	....	1083	50	2	2.77	3	....	....	159	13	0	4.90
2005-06	Minnesota	NHL	58	30	18	7	3411	130	1	2.29	....	....	....	....	....	....	....
2006-07	Minnesota	NHL	44	22	16	1	2422	103	2	2.55	....	....	....	....	....	....	....
	NHL Totals		293	125	113	32	16692	688	13	2.47	11	3	4	571	19	0	2.00

QMJHL First All-Star Team (1994) • QMJHL MVP (1994) • IHL Second All-Star Team (1995) • William M. Jennings Trophy (2007) (shared with Niklas Backstrom)

Rights traded to **Dallas** by **Quebec** for Tommy Sjodin and Dallas' 3rd round choice (Chris Drury) in 1994 Entry Draft, February 13, 1994. Traded to **Minnesota** by **Dallas** with Brad Lukowich for Minnesota's 3rd round choice (Joel Lundqvist) in 2000 Entry Draft and Minnesota's 4th round choice (later traded back to Minnesota – later traded to Los Angeles – Los Angeles selected Aaron Rome) in 2002 Entry Draft, June 12, 2000. Signed as a free agent by **Lulea** (Sweden), December 18, 2004. Traded to **Boston** by **Minnesota** for Petr Kalus and Boston's 4th round choice in 2009 Entry Draft, July 1, 2007.

FINLEY, Brian (FIHN-lee, BRIGH-uhn)

Goaltender. Catches right. 6'3", 205 lbs. Born, Sault Ste. Marie, Ont., July 13, 1981.
(Nashville's 1st choice, 6th overall, in 1999 Entry Draft).

			Regular Season								Playoffs						
Season	Club	League	GP	W	L	O/T	Mins	GA	SO	Avg	GP	W	L	Mins	GA	SO	Avg
1996-97	Soo Carlucci's	NOHA	45	....	....	....	1943	109	3	2.38	....	....	....	....	....	....	....
1997-98	Barrie Colts	OHL	41	23	14	1	2154	105	3	2.92	5	1	3	260	13	0	3.00
1998-99	Barrie Colts	OHL	52	*36	10	4	3063	136	3	2.66	5	4	1	323	15	0	2.79
99-2000	Barrie Colts	OHL	47	24	12	6	2540	130	2	3.07	*23	14	8	1353	58	1	2.57
2000-01	Barrie Colts	OHL	16	5	8	0	818	42	0	3.08	....	....	....	....	....	....	....
	Brampton Battalion	OHL	11	7	3	1	631	31	0	2.95	9	5	4	503	26	1	3.10
2001-02							DID NOT PLAY – INJURED										
2002-03	Nashville	NHL	1	0	0	0	47	3	0	3.83	....	....	....	....	....	....	....
	Milwaukee	AHL	22	7	11	2	1207	59	2	2.93	....	....	....	....	....	....	....
	Toledo Storm	ECHL	7	4	2	0	305	12	0	2.36	1	0	1	60	4	0	4.00
2003-04	Milwaukee	AHL	43	23	15	4	2561	100	2	2.34	1	0	1	59	2	0	2.05
2004-05	Milwaukee	AHL	64	36	22	4	3642	139	7	2.29	7	3	4	458	20	1	2.62
2005-06	Nashville	NHL	1	0	1	0	60	7	0	7.00	....	....	....	....	....	....	....
	Milwaukee	AHL	32	18	7	2	1708	77	4	2.70	8	3	2	415	20	0	2.89
2006-07	Boston	NHL	2	0	1	0	59	3	0	3.05	....	....	....	....	....	....	....
	Providence Bruins	AHL	10	6	3	0	576	29	1	3.02	....	....	....	....	....	....	....
	NHL Totals		4	0	2	0	166	13	0	4.70	....	....	....	....	....	....	....

OHL All-Rookie Team (1998) • OHL First All-Star Team (1999) • OHL Playoff MVP (2000)

• Missed entire 2001-02 season recovering from groin injury suffered during 2000-01 season and re-injured in training camp, October 3, 2001. Signed as a free agent by **Boston**, July 17, 2006.

FISHER, Glenn (FIH-shuhr, GLEHN) EDM.

Goaltender. Catches left. 6'1", 160 lbs. Born, Edmonton, Alta., April 25, 1983.
(Edmonton's 9th choice, 148th overall, in 2002 Entry Draft).

			Regular Season								Playoffs						
Season	Club	League	GP	W	L	O/T	Mins	GA	SO	Avg	GP	W	L	Mins	GA	SO	Avg
99-2000	Edm. Maple Leafs	AMBHL	16	9	5	2	944	62	0	3.94	....	....	....	....	....	....	....
2000-01	Edm. Maple Leafs	AMHL	19	6	9	3	1116	77	0	4.14	....	....	....	....	....	....	....
2001-02	Fort Saskatchewan	AJHL	47	14	26	2	2649	196	2	4.44	3	0	3	180	14	0	4.67
2002-03	Fort Saskatchewan	AJHL	51	17	27	6	2885	202	0	4.20	....	....	....	....	....	....	....
2003-04	U. of Denver	WCHA	9	3	1	1	436	26	0	3.58	....	....	....	....	....	....	....
2004-05	U. of Denver	WCHA	22	14	5	1	1247	59	0	2.84	....	....	....	....	....	....	....
2005-06	U. of Denver	WCHA	21	9	7	2	1102	50	1	2.72	....	....	....	....	....	....	....
2006-07	U. of Denver	WCHA	24	13	9	2	1394	54	3	2.32	....	....	....	....	....	....	....

FLAHERTY, Wade (FLAY-uhr-tee, WAYD) CHI.

Goaltender. Catches left. 6', 171 lbs. Born, Terrace, B.C., January 11, 1968.
(Buffalo's 10th choice, 181st overall, in 1988 Entry Draft).

			Regular Season								Playoffs						
Season	Club	League	GP	W	L	O/T	Mins	GA	SO	Avg	GP	W	L	Mins	GA	SO	Avg
1984-85	Kelowna Wings	WHL	1	0	0	0	55	5	0	5.45	....	....	....	....	....	....	....
1985-86	Seattle	WHL	9	1	3	0	271	36	0	7.97	....	....	....	....	....	....	....
	Spokane Chiefs	WHL	5	0	3	0	161	21	0	7.83	....	....	....	....	....	....	....
1986-87	Nanaimo Clippers	BCJHL	15	....	....	....	830	53	0	3.83	....	....	....	....	....	....	....
	Victoria Cougars	WHL	3	0	2	0	127	16	0	7.56	....	....	....	....	....	....	....
1987-88	Victoria Cougars	WHL	36	20	15	0	2052	135	0	3.95	5	2	3	300	18	0	3.60
1988-89	Victoria Cougars	WHL	42	21	19	0	2408	180	4	4.49	....	....	....	....	....	....	....
1989-90	Greensboro	ECHL	27	12	10	0	1308	96	0	4.40	....	....	....	....	....	....	....
1990-91	Kansas City Blades	IHL	*56	16	31	4	2990	224	0	4.49	....	....	....	....	....	....	....
1991-92	San Jose	NHL	3	0	3	0	178	13	0	4.38	....	....	....	....	....	....	....
	Kansas City Blades	IHL	43	26	14	3	2603	140	1	3.23	1	0	0	1	0	0	0.00
1992-93	San Jose	NHL	1	0	1	0	60	5	0	5.00	....	....	....	....	....	....	....
	Kansas City Blades	IHL	*61	*34	19	7	*3642	195	2	3.21	*12	6	6	733	34	*1	2.78
1993-94	Kansas City Blades	IHL	*60	32	19	9	*3564	202	0	3.40	....	....	....	....	....	....	....
1994-95	San Jose	NHL	18	5	6	1	852	44	1	3.10	7	2	3	377	31	0	4.93
1995-96	San Jose	NHL	24	3	12	1	1137	92	0	4.85	....	....	....	....	....	....	....
1996-97	San Jose	NHL	7	2	4	0	359	31	0	5.18	....	....	....	....	....	....	....
	Kentucky	AHL	19	8	6	2	1032	54	1	3.14	3	1	2	200	11	0	3.30
1997-98	NY Islanders	NHL	16	4	4	3	694	23	3	1.99	....	....	....	....	....	....	....
	Utah Grizzlies	IHL	24	16	5	3	1341	40	3	1.79	....	....	....	....	....	....	....
1998-99	NY Islanders	NHL	20	5	11	2	1048	53	0	3.03	....	....	....	....	....	....	....
	Lowell	AHL	5	1	3	1	305	16	0	3.15	....	....	....	....	....	....	....
99-2000	NY Islanders	NHL	4	0	1	1	182	7	0	2.31	....	....	....	....	....	....	....
2000-01	NY Islanders	NHL	20	6	10	0	1017	56	1	3.30	....	....	....	....	....	....	....
	Tampa Bay	NHL	2	0	2	0	118	8	0	4.07	....	....	....	....	....	....	....
2001-02	Florida	NHL	4	2	1	1	245	12	0	2.94	....	....	....	....	....	....	....
	Utah Grizzlies	AHL	45	22	13	5	2351	92	2	2.35	5	2	3	312	11	0	2.12
2002-03	Nashville	NHL	1	0	1	0	51	4	0	4.71	....	....	....	....	....	....	....
	San Antonio	AHL	30	11	13	5	1791	86	1	2.88	....	....	....	....	....	....	....
2003-04	Milwaukee	AHL	36	21	12	3	2146	78	3	2.18	*21	*16	5	*1371	44	1	1.93
2004-05	Manitoba Moose	AHL	36	19	10	3	2010	78	4	2.33	12	8	4	720	29	2	2.42
2005-06	Manitoba Moose	AHL	49	26	17	4	2822	113	*6	2.40	12	7	5	675	23	0	*2.04
2006-07	Manitoba Moose	AHL	32	17	9	2	1735	70	2	2.42	3	2	1	166	5	0	1.81
	NHL Totals		120	27	56	9	5941	348	5	3.51	7	2	3	377	31	0	4.93

WHL West Second All-Star Team (1988) • ECHL Playoff MVP (1990) • James Norris Memorial Trophy (fewest goals against – IHL) (1992) (shared with Arturs Irbe) • IHL Second All-Star Team (1993, 1994) • Jack A. Butterfield Trophy (Playoff MVP - AHL) (2004) • AHL Second All-Star Team (2006)

Signed as a free agent by **San Jose**, September 3, 1991. Signed as a free agent by **NY Islanders**, July 22, 1997. Traded to **Tampa Bay** by **NY Islanders** for future considerations, February 16, 2001. Signed as a free agent by **Florida**, August 2, 2001. Traded to **Nashville** by **Florida** for Pascal Trepanier, March 9, 2003. Signed as a free agent by **Vancouver**, July 7, 2004. Signed as a free agent by **Chicago**, July 27, 2007.

FLEURY, Marc-Andre (fluh-REE, MAHRK-AWN-dray) PIT.

Goaltender. Catches left. 6'2", 180 lbs. Born, Sorel, Que., November 28, 1984.
(Pittsburgh's 1st choice, 1st overall, in 2003 Entry Draft).

			Regular Season								Playoffs						
Season	Club	League	GP	W	L	O/T	Mins	GA	SO	Avg	GP	W	L	Mins	GA	SO	Avg
99-2000	Charles-Lemoyne	QAAA	15	4	9	0	780	36	1	2.77	....	....	....	....	....	....	....
2000-01	Cape Breton	QMJHL	35	12	13	2	1705	115	0	4.05	2	0	1	32	4	0	7.50
2001-02	Cape Breton	QMJHL	55	26	14	8	3043	141	2	2.78	16	9	7	1003	55	0	3.29
2002-03	Cape Breton	QMJHL	51	17	24	6	2889	162	2	3.36	4	0	4	228	17	0	4.47
2003-04	Pittsburgh	NHL	21	4	14	2	1154	70	1	3.64	....	....	....	....	....	....	....
	Cape Breton	QMJHL	10	8	1	1	606	20	0	1.98	4	1	3	251	13	0	3.10
	Wilkes-Barre	AHL	....	....	....	....	....	....	....	....	2	0	1	92	6	0	3.90
2004-05	Wilkes-Barre	AHL	54	26	19	4	3029	127	5	2.52	4	0	2	151	11	0	4.36
2005-06	Pittsburgh	NHL	50	13	27	6	2809	152	1	3.25	....	....	....	....	....	....	....
	Wilkes-Barre	AHL	12	10	2	0	727	19	0	1.57	5	2	3	311	18	0	3.48
2006-07	Pittsburgh	NHL	67	40	16	9	3905	184	5	2.83	5	1	4	287	18	0	3.76
	NHL Totals		138	57	57	17	7868	406	7	3.10	5	1	4	287	18	0	3.76

QMJHL Second All-Star Team (2003)

Returned to **Cape Breton** (QMJHL) by **Pittsburgh**, January 29, 2004.

FOSTER, Brian (FAW-stuhr, BRIGH-uhn) FLA.

Goaltender. Catches left. 6'1", 155 lbs. Born, Pembroke, NH, February 4, 1987.
(Florida's 6th choice, 161st overall, in 2005 Entry Draft).

			Regular Season								Playoffs						
Season	Club	League	GP	W	L	O/T	Mins	GA	SO	Avg	GP	W	L	Mins	GA	SO	Avg
2003-04	N.H. Jr. Monarchs	EJHL					STATISTICS NOT AVAILABLE										
2004-05	N.H. Jr. Monarchs	EJHL	41	30	6	4	2339	....	3	2.51	....	....	....	....	....	....	....
2005-06	Des Moines	USHL	26	12	9	3	1516	71	0	2.81	1	0	0	12	0	0	0.00
2006-07	New Hampshire	H-East	7	2	2	0	298	11	2	2.21	....	....	....	....	....	....	....

FRAZEE, Jeff (FRAY-zee, JEHF) N.J.

Goaltender. Catches left. 6', 185 lbs. Born, Edina, MN, May 13, 1987.
(New Jersey's 2nd choice, 38th overall, in 2005 Entry Draft).

			Regular Season								Playoffs						
Season	Club	League	GP	W	L	O/T	Mins	GA	SO	Avg	GP	W	L	Mins	GA	SO	Avg
2001-02	Holy Angels	High-MN	6	6	0	0	....	....	....	....	....	....	....	....	....	....	....
2002-03	Holy Angels	High-MN	16	14	1	1	....	....	....	....	....	....	....	....	....	....	....
2003-04	USNTDP	U-17	16	9	3	0	781	31	....	2.38	....	....	....	....	....	....	....
	USNTDP	NAHL	25	14	8	3	1463	71	3	2.91	....	....	....	....	....	....	....
2004-05	USNTDP	U-18	24	....	....	....	1309	59	3	2.71	....	....	....	....	....	....	....
	USNTDP	NAHL	9	8	1	0	500	18	1	2.16	....	....	....	....	....	....	....
2005-06	U. of Minnesota	WCHA	12	6	3	2	660	26	2	2.36	....	....	....	....	....	....	....
2006-07	U. of Minnesota	WCHA	20	14	3	1	1148	45	1	2.35	....	....	....	....	....	....	....

FUKUFUJI, Yutaka (foo-koo-FOO-jee, yoo-TA-ka)

Goaltender. Catches left. 6'1", 180 lbs. Born, Tokyo, Japan, September 17, 1982.
(Los Angeles' 9th choice, 238th overall, in 2004 Entry Draft).

			Regular Season								Playoffs						
Season	Club	League	GP	W	L	O/T	Mins	GA	SO	Avg	GP	W	L	Mins	GA	SO	Avg
2003-04	Kokudo Toyko	AsianHL	7	....	....	....	420	13	....	1.86	....	....	....	....	....	....	....
	Kokudo Toyko	Japan	7	....	....	....	430	12	....	1.67	....	....	....	....	....	....	....
2004-05	Bakersfield	ECHL	44	27	9	5	2517	104	3	2.48	....	....	....	....	....	....	....
2005-06	Manchester	AHL	2	1	1	0	120	6	0	3.00	....	....	....	....	....	....	....
	Reading Royals	ECHL	29	15	9	4	1691	82	1	2.91	4	1	2	196	11	0	3.36
2006-07	Los Angeles	NHL	4	0	3	0	96	7	0	4.38	....	....	....	....	....	....	....
	Manchester	AHL	5	3	1	0	261	4	1	0.92	1	0	0	0	0	0	0.00
	Reading Royals	ECHL	28	13	10	0	1522	75	1	2.96	....	....	....	....	....	....	....
	NHL Totals		4	0	3	0	96	7	0	4.38	....	....	....	....	....	....	....

GAIDUCHENKO, Sergei (gay-doo-CHEHN-koh, SAIR-gay) FLA.

Goaltender. Catches left. 6'5", 222 lbs. Born, Kiev, USSR, June 6, 1989.
(Florida's 8th choice, 202nd overall, in 2007 Entry Draft).

Season	Club	League	Regular Season GP	W	L	O/T	Mins	GA	SO	Avg	Playoffs GP	W	L	Mins	GA	SO	Avg
2006-07	Yaroslavl 2	Russia-3	23				1180	57	3	2.90							

GARNETT, Michael (gahr-NEHT, MIGH-kuhl)

Goaltender. Catches left. 6'1", 205 lbs. Born, Saskatoon, Sask., November 25, 1982.
(Atlanta's 2nd choice, 80th overall, in 2001 Entry Draft).

Season	Club	League	Regular Season GP	W	L	O/T	Mins	GA	SO	Avg	Playoffs GP	W	L	Mins	GA	SO	Avg
1997-98	Sask. Contacts	SMHL	3	1	1	0	82	8	0	5.85							
1998-99	Sask. Contacts	SMHL	STATISTICS NOT AVAILABLE														
99-2000	Kindersley Klippers	SJHL	36				2067	140	1	3.57							
	Red Deer Rebels	WHL	1	0	0	0	14	0	0	0.00	1	0	1	65	2	0	1.85
2000-01	Red Deer Rebels	WHL	21	14	5	1	1133	39	3	2.07							
	Saskatoon Blades	WHL	28	7	17	2	1501	83	1	3.32							
2001-02	Saskatoon Blades	WHL	*67	27	34	4	*3738	205	2	3.29	7	3	4	450	15	0	2.00
2002-03	Chicago Wolves	AHL	2	0	1	0	33	2	0	3.64							
	Greenville Grrrowl	ECHL	38	16	15	3	2092	119	0	3.41	3	1	2	178	13	0	4.38
2003-04	Chicago Wolves	AHL	13	7	3	2	731	32	0	2.63							
	Gwinnett	ECHL	33	21	10	2	1936	69	4	2.14	12	7	5	770	34	0	2.65
2004-05	Chicago Wolves	AHL	24	11	9	0	1321	63	1	2.86	2	2	0	119	3	0	1.51
2005-06	**Atlanta**	**NHL**	**24**	**10**	**7**	**4**	**1271**	**73**	**2**	**3.45**							
	Chicago Wolves	AHL	35	15	12	4	1892	106	1	3.36							
2006-07	Chicago Wolves	AHL	42	23	15	1	2380	120	2	3.03	11	8	3	675	28	1	2.49
	NHL Totals		**24**	**10**	**7**	**4**	**1271**	**73**	**2**	**3.45**							

Signed as a free agent by **Neftekhimik** (Russia), July 13, 2007.

GARON, Mathieu (gah-ROHN, MA-tyew) EDM.

Goaltender. Catches right. 6'2", 192 lbs. Born, Chandler, Que., January 9, 1978.
(Montreal's 2nd choice, 44th overall, in 1996 Entry Draft).

Season	Club	League	Regular Season GP	W	L	O/T	Mins	GA	SO	Avg	Playoffs GP	W	L	Mins	GA	SO	Avg
1993-94	Jonquiere Elites	QAAA	17	0	13	0	834	88	0	6.33							
1994-95	Jonquiere Elites	QAAA	27	13	13	1	1554	94	0	3.63	9	6	2	467	26	0	3.34
1995-96	Victoriaville Tigres	QMJHL	51	18	27	0	2709	189	1	4.19	12	7	4	676	38	1	3.39
1996-97	Victoriaville Tigres	QMJHL	53	29	18	3	3032	150	*6	2.97	6	2	4	330	23	0	4.18
1997-98	Victoriaville Tigres	QMJHL	47	27	18	2	2802	125	5	2.68	6	2	4	345	22	0	3.82
1998-99	Fredericton	AHL	40	14	22	2	2222	114	3	3.08	6	1	1	208	12	0	3.47
99-2000	Quebec Citadelles	AHL	53	17	28	3	2884	149	2	3.10	1	0	0	20	3	0	8.82
2000-01	**Montreal**	**NHL**	**11**	**4**	**5**	**1**	**589**	**24**	**2**	**2.44**							
	Quebec Citadelles	AHL	31	16	13	1	1768	86	1	2.92	8	4	4	459	22	1	2.88
2001-02	**Montreal**	**NHL**	**5**	**1**	**4**	**0**	**261**	**19**	**0**	**4.37**							
	Quebec Citadelles	AHL	50	21	15	12	2988	136	2	2.73	3	0	3	198	12	0	3.63
2002-03	**Montreal**	**NHL**	**8**	**3**	**5**	**0**	**482**	**16**	**2**	**1.99**							
	Hamilton Bulldogs	AHL	20	15	2	2	1150	34	4	1.77							
2003-04	**Montreal**	**NHL**	**19**	**8**	**6**	**2**	**1003**	**38**	**0**	**2.27**	**1**	**0**	**0**	**12**	**0**	**0**	**0.00**
2004-05	Manchester	AHL	52	32	14	4	2969	105	8	2.12	6	2	4	285	17	0	3.58
2005-06	**Los Angeles**	**NHL**	**63**	**31**	**26**	**3**	**3446**	**185**	**4**	**3.22**							
2006-07	**Los Angeles**	**NHL**	**32**	**13**	**10**	**6**	**1779**	**79**	**2**	**2.66**							
	NHL Totals		**138**	**60**	**56**	**12**	**7560**	**361**	**10**	**2.87**	**1**	**0**	**0**	**12**	**0**	**0**	**0.00**

QMJHL All-Rookie Team (1996) • QMJHL Defensive Rookie of the Year (1996) • QMJHL First All-Star Team (1998) • Canadian Major Junior First All-Star Team (1998) • Canadian Major Junior Goaltender of the Year (1998)

Traded to **Los Angeles** by **Montreal** with San Jose's 3rd round choice (previously acquired, Los Angeles selected Paul Baier) in 2004 Entry Draft for Radek Bonk and Cristobal Huet, June 26, 2004. Signed as a free agent by **Edmonton**, July 3, 2007.

GERBER, Martin (GUHR-buhr, MAHR-tihn) OTT.

Goaltender. Catches left. 5'11", 201 lbs. Born, Burgdorf, Switz., September 3, 1974.
(Anaheim's 10th choice, 232nd overall, in 2001 Entry Draft).

Season	Club	League	Regular Season GP	W	L	O/T	Mins	GA	SO	Avg	Playoffs GP	W	L	Mins	GA	SO	Avg
1996-97	SC Langnau	Swiss-2	38				2286	121	0	3.18	8			488	29	0	3.57
1997-98	SC Langnau	Swiss-2	40				2430	141	2	3.48	16			961	42	0	2.62
1998-99	SC Langnau	Swiss	42				2521	203	1	4.83	11			664	50	0	4.52
99-2000	SC Langnau	Swiss	44				2652	161	3	3.64	6			360	13	*2	*2.17
2000-01	SCL Tigers Langnau	Swiss	*44				2671	114	3	2.56	5			319	7	1	1.32
2001-02	Farjestad	Sweden	44				2664	87	*4	*1.96	*10			*657	18	*2	*1.64
	Switzerland	Olympics	3	1	1	1	158	4	0	1.52							
2002-03	**Anaheim**	**NHL**	**22**	**6**	**11**	**3**	**1203**	**39**	**1**	**1.95**	**2**	**0**	**0**	**20**	**1**	**0**	**3.00**
	Cincinnati	AHL	1	1	0	0	60	2	0	2.00							
2003-04	**Anaheim**	**NHL**	**32**	**11**	**12**	**4**	**1698**	**64**	**2**	**2.26**							
2004-05	SCL Tigers Langnau	Swiss	20	6	10	4	1220	59	0	2.90							
	Farjestad	Sweden	30	20	6	4	1827	58	4	1.90	*15	9	6	*900	36	1	2.40
2005-06♦	**Carolina**	**NHL**	**60**	**38**	**14**	**6**	**3493**	**162**	**3**	**2.78**	**6**	**1**	**1**	**221**	**13**	**1**	**3.53**
	Switzerland	Olympics	3				160	11	1	4.13							
2006-07	**Ottawa**	**NHL**	**29**	**15**	**9**	**3**	**1599**	**74**	**1**	**2.78**							
	NHL Totals		**143**	**70**	**46**	**16**	**7993**	**339**	**7**	**2.54**	**8**	**1**	**1**	**241**	**14**	**1**	**3.49**

• Scored a goal in playoffs vs. Martigny (Swiss-2), February 27, 1997. Traded to **Carolina** by **Anaheim** for Tomas Malec and Carolina's 3rd round choice (Kyle Klubertanz) in 2004 Entry Draft, June 18, 2004. Signed as a free agent by **Langnau** (Swiss), September 17, 2004. Signed as a free agent by **Farjestad** (Sweden), November 7, 2004. Signed as a free agent by **Ottawa**, July 1, 2006.

GIGUERE, Jean-Sebastien (zhih-GAIR, ZHAWN-suh-BAS-tee-yeh) ANA.

Goaltender. Catches left. 6'1", 200 lbs. Born, Montreal, Que., May 16, 1977.
(Hartford's 1st choice, 13th overall, in 1995 Entry Draft).

Season	Club	League	Regular Season GP	W	L	O/T	Mins	GA	SO	Avg	Playoffs GP	W	L	Mins	GA	SO	Avg
1992-93	Laval-Laurentides	QAAA	25	12	11	2	1498	76	0	3.02	11	6	5	654	38	0	3.49
1993-94	Verdun	QMJHL	25	13	5	2	1234	66	1	3.21							
1994-95	Halifax	QMJHL	47	14	27	5	2755	181	2	3.94	7	3	4	417	17	1	*2.45
1995-96	Halifax	QMJHL	55	26	23	2	3230	185	1	3.44	6	1	5	354	24	0	4.07
1996-97	**Hartford**	**NHL**	**8**	**1**	**4**	**0**	**394**	**24**	**0**	**3.65**							
	Halifax	QMJHL	50	28	19	3	3014	170	2	3.38	16	9	7	954	58	0	3.65
1997-98	Saint John Flames	AHL	31	16	10	3	1758	72	2	2.46	10	5	3	536	27	0	3.02
1998-99	**Calgary**	**NHL**	**15**	**6**	**7**	**1**	**860**	**46**	**0**	**3.21**							
	Saint John Flames	AHL	39	18	16	3	2145	123	3	3.44	7	3	2	304	21	0	4.14
99-2000	**Calgary**	**NHL**	**7**	**1**	**3**	**1**	**330**	**15**	**0**	**2.73**							
	Saint John Flames	AHL	41	17	17	3	2243	114	0	3.05	3	0	3	178	9	0	3.03
2000-01	**Anaheim**	**NHL**	**34**	**11**	**17**	**5**	**2031**	**87**	**4**	**2.57**							
	Cincinnati	AHL	23	12	7	2	1306	53	0	2.43							
2001-02	**Anaheim**	**NHL**	**53**	**20**	**25**	**6**	**3127**	**111**	**4**	**2.13**							
2002-03	**Anaheim**	**NHL**	**65**	**34**	**22**	**6**	**3775**	**145**	**8**	**2.30**	**21**	**15**	**6**	**1407**	**38**	**5**	***1.62**
2003-04	**Anaheim**	**NHL**	**55**	**17**	**31**	**6**	**3210**	**140**	**3**	**2.62**							
2004-05	Hamburg Freezers	Germany	6				301	12	0	2.39	2			100	7	0	4.20
2005-06	**Anaheim**	**NHL**	**60**	**30**	**15**	**11**	**3381**	**150**	**2**	**2.66**	**6**	**3**	**3**	**318**	**18**	**0**	**3.40**
2006-07♦	**Anaheim**	**NHL**	**56**	**36**	**10**	**8**	**3245**	**122**	**4**	**2.26**	**18**	***13**	**4**	**1067**	**35**	**1**	**1.97**
	NHL Totals		**353**	**156**	**134**	**44**	**20353**	**840**	**25**	**2.48**	**45**	**31**	**13**	**2792**	**91**	**6**	**1.96**

QMJHL Second All-Star Team (1997) • AHL All-Rookie Team (1998) • Harry "Hap" Holmes Memorial Award (fewest goals against – AHL) (1998) (shared with Tyler Moss) • Conn Smythe Trophy (2003)

Transferred to **Carolina** after **Hartford** franchise relocated, June 25, 1997. Traded to **Calgary** by **Carolina** with Andrew Cassels for Gary Roberts and Trevor Kidd, August 25, 1997. Traded to **Anaheim** by **Calgary** for Anaheim's 2nd round choice (later traded to Washington – Washington selected Matt Pettinger) in 2000 Entry Draft, June 10, 2000. Signed as a free agent by **Hamburg** (Germany), January 31, 2005.

GISTEDT, Joel (GIHZ-tehd, JOHL) PHX.

Goaltender. Catches left. 5'11", 176 lbs. Born, Uddevalla, Sweden, December 7, 1987.
(Phoenix's 4th choice, 36th overall, in 2007 Entry Draft).

Season	Club	League	Regular Season GP	W	L	O/T	Mins	GA	SO	Avg	Playoffs GP	W	L	Mins	GA	SO	Avg
2003-04	V.Frolunda U18	Swe-U18	21				1258	49	1	2.34	7			422	11	2	1.57
2004-05	Frolunda U18	Swe-U18	2				120	6	0	3.00	6			366	14	1	2.30
	Frolunda Jr.	Swe-Jr.	8				485	14	0	1.73							
2005-06	Frolunda Jr.	Swe-Jr.	32				1926	76	5	2.37	7			434	18	0	2.49
	Frolunda	Sweden	3				181	5	1	1.66							
2006-07	Frolunda Jr.	Swe-Jr.	2				120	3	1	1.50	8			484	15	0	1.86
	Frolunda	Sweden	35				2050	88	2	2.58							

GLASS, Jeff (GLAS, JEHF) OTT.

Goaltender. Catches left. 6'2", 201 lbs. Born, Calgary, Alta., November 19, 1985.
(Ottawa's 5th choice, 89th overall, in 2004 Entry Draft).

Season	Club	League	Regular Season GP	W	L	O/T	Mins	GA	SO	Avg	Playoffs GP	W	L	Mins	GA	SO	Avg
2001-02	Crowsnest Pass	AJHL	34				1802	126	0	4.20							
2002-03	Kootenay Ice	WHL	35	15	16	3	1884	77	4	2.45	9	4	5	643	23	0	2.15
2003-04	Kootenay Ice	WHL	57	26	20	6	3263	128	5	2.35	4	0	4	239	14	0	3.51
2004-05	Kootenay Ice	WHL	51	34	11	5	3061	90	8	1.76	16	10	6	1027	39	0	2.28
2005-06	Binghamton	AHL	6	1	4	0	312	20	0	3.85							
	Charlotte Checkers	ECHL	39	19	15	4	2221	119	2	3.22	3	1	2	178	11	0	3.71
2006-07	Binghamton	AHL	43	9	24	2	2174	149	1	4.11							

WHL West First All-Star Team (2005) • WHL Goaltender of the Year (2005) • Canadian Major Junior First All-Star Team (2005) • Canadian Major Junior Goaltender of the Year (2005)

GOEHRING, Karl (GAIR-ihng, KAHRL)

Goaltender. Catches left. 5'8", 160 lbs. Born, Apple Valley, MN, August 23, 1978.

Season	Club	League	Regular Season GP	W	L	O/T	Mins	GA	SO	Avg	Playoffs GP	W	L	Mins	GA	SO	Avg
1996-97	Fargo-Moorhead	USHL	32	13	18	1	1909	79	*4	*2.48	5	2	3	251	15	1	3.58
1997-98	North Dakota	WCHA	27	23	3	1	1504	57	1	*2.27							
1998-99	North Dakota	WCHA	31	22	5	2	1774	71	3	2.40							
99-2000	North Dakota	WCHA	30	19	6	4	1747	55	*8	*1.89							
2000-01	North Dakota	WCHA	30	16	6	6	1662	66	*3	2.38							
2001-02	Syracuse Crunch	AHL	15	5	6	3	891	37	1	2.49							
	Dayton Bombers	ECHL	23	11	9	3	1393	52	2	2.24	*14	9	5	*866	35	1	2.43
2002-03	Syracuse Crunch	AHL	49	18	21	4	2608	116	4	2.67							
2003-04	Syracuse Crunch	AHL	38	17	14	6	2234	97	1	2.60	5	2	2	295	16	0	3.26
2004-05	Syracuse Crunch	AHL	49	23	22	0	2788	128	3	2.75							
2005-06	Jokerit Helsinki	Finland	19	5	10	3	1076	57	2	3.18							
	San Antonio	AHL	23	4	16	1	1250	65	1	3.12							
2006-07	Milwaukee	AHL	44	22	15	4	2524	113	1	2.69							

WCHA First All-Star Team (1998, 2000) • WCHA Rookie of the Year (1998) • NCAA West First All-American Team (1998, 2000) • WCHA Second All-Star Team (1999)

Signed as a free agent by **Columbus**, May 7, 2001. Signed as a free agent by **Jokerit Helsinki** (Finland), September 16, 2005. Signed as a free agent by **Nashville**, July 17, 2006.

GRAHAME, John (GRAY-uhm, JAWN) CAR.

Goaltender. Catches left. 6'3", 220 lbs. Born, Denver, CO, August 31, 1975.
(Boston's 7th choice, 229th overall, in 1994 Entry Draft).

Season	Club	League	Regular Season GP	W	L	O/T	Mins	GA	SO	Avg	Playoffs GP	W	L	Mins	GA	SO	Avg
1993-94	Sioux City	USHL	20				1200	73	0	3.70							
1994-95	Lake Superior State	CCHA	28	16	7	3	1616	75	2	2.79							
1995-96	Lake Superior State	CCHA	29	21	4	2	1558	66	2	2.54							
1996-97	Lake Superior State	CCHA	37	19	13	4	2197	134	3	3.66							
1997-98	Providence Bruins	AHL	55	15	31	4	3053	164	3	3.22							
1998-99	Providence Bruins	AHL	48	*37	9	1	2771	134	3	2.90	19	*15	4	*1209	48	1	2.38
99-2000	**Boston**	**NHL**	**24**	**7**	**10**	**5**	**1344**	**55**	**2**	**2.46**							
	Providence Bruins	AHL	27	11	13	2	1528	86	1	3.38	13	10	3	839	35	0	2.50
2000-01	**Boston**	**NHL**	**10**	**3**	**4**	**0**	**471**	**28**	**0**	**3.57**							
	Providence Bruins	AHL	16	4	7	3	893	47	0	3.16	17	8	9	1043	46	2	2.65
2001-02	**Boston**	**NHL**	**19**	**8**	**7**	**2**	**1079**	**52**	**1**	**2.89**							
2002-03	**Boston**	**NHL**	**23**	**11**	**9**	**2**	**1352**	**61**	**1**	**2.71**							
	Tampa Bay	**NHL**	**17**	**6**	**5**	**4**	**914**	**34**	**2**	**2.23**	**1**	**0**	**1**	**111**	**2**	**0**	**1.08**
2003-04♦	**Tampa Bay**	**NHL**	**29**	**18**	**9**	**1**	**1688**	**58**	**1**	**2.06**	**1**	**0**	**0**	**34**	**2**	**0**	**3.53**
2004-05			DID NOT PLAY														
2005-06	**Tampa Bay**	**NHL**	**57**	**29**	**22**	**1**	**3152**	**161**	**5**	**3.06**	**4**	**1**	**3**	**188**	**15**	**0**	**4.79**
	United States	Olympics	1	0	0	1	60	3	0	3.00							
2006-07	**Carolina**	**NHL**	**28**	**10**	**13**	**2**	**1515**	**72**	**0**	**2.85**							
	NHL Totals		**207**	**92**	**79**	**17**	**11515**	**521**	**12**	**2.71**	**6**	**1**	**4**	**333**	**19**	**0**	**3.42**

Traded to **Tampa Bay** by **Boston** for Tampa Bay's 4th round choice (later traded to San Jose – San Jose selected Jason Churchill) in 2004 Entry Draft, January 13, 2003. Signed as a free agent by **Carolina**, July 1, 2006.

GREISS, Thomas (GRIGHS, TAW-muhs) S.J.

Goaltender. Catches left. 6'1", 200 lbs. Born, Straubing, West Germany, January 29, 1986.
(San Jose's 2nd choice, 94th overall, in 2004 Entry Draft).

Season	Club	League	Regular Season GP	W	L	O/T	Mins	GA	SO	Avg	Playoffs GP	W	L	Mins	GA	SO	Avg
2001-02	EV Fussen Jr.	Ger-Jr.	STATISTICS NOT AVAILABLE														
2002-03	Koln Jr.	Ger-Jr.	25				1613	58	0	2.16	3	1	2	180	8	1	2.67
2003-04	Koln Jr.	Ger-Jr.	24				1286	56		2.61							
	Kolner Haie	Germany	1				20	4	0	12.00							
2004-05	Kolner Haie	Germany	8				459	16	0	2.09							
	Regensburg	German-2	1				60	2	0	2.00	2			56	2	0	2.14
2005-06	Kolner Haie	Germany	27				1560	64	1	2.46	9			533	27	*1	3.04
	Germany	Olympics	1	0	1	0	60	5	0	5.00							
2006-07	Worcester Sharks	AHL	43	26	15	2	2555	111	0	2.61	3	0	3	172	12	0	4.18
	Fresno Falcons	ECHL	3	1	2	0	180	7	0	2.34							

GRUMET-MORRIS, Dov (groo-MAY-MAW-rihs, DAWV) NSH.

Goaltender. Catches left. 6'2", 190 lbs. Born, Evanston, IL, February 28, 1982.
(Philadelphia's 4th choice, 161st overall, in 2002 Entry Draft).

			Regular Season								Playoffs						
Season	**Club**	**League**	**GP**	**W**	**L**	**O/T**	**Mins**	**GA**	**SO**	**Avg**	**GP**	**W**	**L**	**Mins**	**GA**	**SO**	**Avg**
2000-01	Danville Wings	NAHL	27	19	5	2	1547	57	3	2.21	5	2	2	300	17	0	3.40
2001-02	Harvard Crimson	ECAC	21	10	8	1	1226	58	1	2.84	....	....	....	....	....	....	....
2002-03	Harvard Crimson	ECAC	29	18	9	2	1741	69	1	2.38	....	....	....	....	....	....	....
2003-04	Harvard Crimson	ECAC	33	16	14	3	1933	76	3	2.36	....	....	....	....	....	....	....
2004-05	Harvard Crimson	ECACHL	31	19	9	3	1911	52	6	1.63	....	....	....	....	....	....	....
2005-06	Laredo Bucks	CHL	25	18	5	2	1477	50	3	*2.03	10	*8	2	644	21	*1	1.96
	San Antonio	AHL	1	0	1	0	60	7	0	7.04	....	....	....	....	....	....	....
2006-07	Portland Pirates	AHL	11	1	6	3	594	30	1	3.03	....	....	....	....	....	....	....
	Cincinnati	ECHL	22	11	8	3	1341	62	0	2.78	....	....	....	....	....	....	....
	Hamilton Bulldogs	AHL	2	1	0	1	125	2	1	0.96	....	....	....	....	....	....	....
	Manitoba Moose	AHL	4	2	1	1	245	5	2	1.23	....	....	....	....	....	....	....

ECAC Second All-Star Team (2005) • NCAA East Second All-American Team (2005)

Signed as a free agent by **Nashville**, July 2, 2007.

GUARD, Kelly (G'YEW-uhrd, KEHL-lee)

Goaltender. Catches left. 6', 190 lbs. Born, Prince Albert, Sask., June 10, 1983.

			Regular Season								Playoffs						
Season	**Club**	**League**	**GP**	**W**	**L**	**O/T**	**Mins**	**GA**	**SO**	**Avg**	**GP**	**W**	**L**	**Mins**	**GA**	**SO**	**Avg**
99-2000	Prince Albert	SMHL					STATISTICS NOT AVAILABLE										
2000-01	Prince Albert	SMHL	25	....	....	....	1488	81	0	3.27	....	....	....	....	....	....	....
	La Ronge	SJHL					STATISTICS NOT AVAILABLE										
2001-02	Kindersley Klippers	SJHL	45	29	11	4	2628	130	1	2.97	19	12	6	1145	60	1	3.14
2002-03	Kelowna Rockets	WHL	53	39	10	3	3018	97	*6	*1.93	19	*16	3	1233	36	*4	*1.75
2003-04	Kelowna Rockets	WHL	62	*44	14	4	3652	95	*13	*1.56	17	11	6	1042	31	1	1.79
2004-05	Charlotte Checkers	ECHL	26	12	11	2	1453	74	0	3.06	2	0	0	40	1	0	1.52
2005-06	Binghamton	AHL	51	25	20	1	2709	139	5	3.08	....	....	....	....	....	....	....
2006-07	Binghamton	AHL	42	11	24	3	2230	127	2	3.42	....	....	....	....	....	....	....

WHL West First All-Star Team (2003, 2004) • Memorial Cup Tournament All-Star Team (2004) • Hap Emms Memorial Trophy (Memorial Cup Tournament Top Goaltender) (2004) • Stafford Smythe Memorial Trophy (Memorial Cup Tournament MVP) (2004)

Signed as a free agent by **Ottawa**, May 11, 2004.

GUSTAFSON, Derek (GUHST-ahf-suhn, DAIR-ihk)

Goaltender. Catches left. 5'11", 210 lbs. Born, Gresham, OR, June 21, 1979.

			Regular Season								Playoffs						
Season	**Club**	**League**	**GP**	**W**	**L**	**O/T**	**Mins**	**GA**	**SO**	**Avg**	**GP**	**W**	**L**	**Mins**	**GA**	**SO**	**Avg**
1995-96	Seattle Ironmen	BCAHA	16	....	....	....	913	46	0	3.02	....	....	....	....	....	....	....
1996-97	Vernon Vipers	BCHL	23	....	....	....	1241	70	0	3.38	....	....	....	....	....	....	....
1997-98	Vernon Vipers	BCHL	42	27	13	2	2270	144	1	3.81	6	2	1	257	13	0	3.04
1998-99	Vernon Vipers	BCHL	42	39	3	0	2505	94	3	2.25	....	....	....	....	....	....	....
99-2000	St. Lawrence	ECAC	24	17	4	2	1475	51	2	2.07	....	....	....	....	....	....	....
2000-01	**Minnesota**	**NHL**	**4**	**1**	**3**	**0**	**239**	**10**	**0**	**2.51**	....	....	....	....	....	....	....
	Cleveland	IHL	24	14	7	1	1293	59	2	2.74	2	0	1	53	5	0	5.64
	Jackson Bandits	ECHL	7	4	3	0	404	15	1	2.23	....	....	....	....	....	....	....
2001-02	**Minnesota**	**NHL**	**1**	**0**	**0**	**0**	**26**	**0**	**0**	**0.00**	....	....	....	....	....	....	....
	Houston Aeros	AHL	38	14	13	6	2016	92	4	2.74	2	0	0	25	1	0	2.37
2002-03	Houston Aeros	AHL	41	23	14	2	2301	108	2	2.82	....	....	....	....	....	....	....
	Louisiana	ECHL	2	1	1	0	118	8	0	4.07	....	....	....	....	....	....	....
2003-04	Louisiana	ECHL	43	28	14	0	2499	87	*5	2.09	8	4	4	560	19	1	2.03
2004-05	Adirondack	UHL	57	32	18	6	3290	155	4	2.83	3	0	3	222	9	0	2.43
2005-06	Providence Bruins	AHL	10	5	3	2	578	22	1	2.28	4	2	2	211	17	0	4.83
	Adirondack	UHL	34	22	7	4	1979	97	1	2.94	....	....	....	....	....	....	....
2006-07	Alaska Aces	ECHL	43	29	11	3	2536	100	5	2.37	15	9	6	890	35	2	2.36
	NHL Totals		**5**	**1**	**3**	**0**	**265**	**10**	**0**	**2.26**	....	....	....	....	....	....	....

ECAC Second All-Star Team (2000) • ECAC Rookie of the Year (2000) • ECHL Second All-Star Team (2004)

Signed as a free agent by **Minnesota**, June 9, 2000. Signed as a free agent by **Louisiana** (ECHL), October 1, 2003. Signed as a free agent by **Adirondack** (UHL) , July 23, 2004. Signed as a free agent by **Providence** (AHL) , Mar. 24, 2006.

HALAK, Jaroslav (HAH-lak, YAHR-roh-slav) MTL.

Goaltender. Catches left. 5'11", 180 lbs. Born, Bratislava, Czech., May 13, 1985.
(Montreal's 11th choice, 271st overall, in 2003 Entry Draft).

			Regular Season								Playoffs						
Season	**Club**	**League**	**GP**	**W**	**L**	**O/T**	**Mins**	**GA**	**SO**	**Avg**	**GP**	**W**	**L**	**Mins**	**GA**	**SO**	**Avg**
2001-02	Bratislava Jr.	Slovak-Jr.	22	....	....	....	1257	41	0	1.96	6	6	0	353	7	2	1.19
2002-03	Bratislava Jr.	Slovak-Jr.	20	13	3	3	1200	41	1	2.02	....	....	....	....	....	....	....
2003-04	Bratislava Jr.	Slovak-Jr.	29	....	....	....	1694	51	....	1.81	....	....	....	....	....	....	....
	HK 91 Senica	Slovak-2	21	....	....	....	1240	54	....	2.61	....	....	....	....	....	....	....
	Bratislava	Slovakia	12	....	....	....	650	18	0	1.66	1			45	6	0	8.00
2004-05	Lewiston	QMJHL	47	24	17	4	2697	125	4	2.78	8	4	4	460	27	0	3.52
2005-06	Hamilton Bulldogs	AHL	13	7	6	0	786	30	3	2.29	....	....	....	....	....	....	....
	Long Beach	ECHL	20	11	4	2	1026	35	2	2.05	4	2	2	252	13	0	3.10
2006-07	**Montreal**	**NHL**	**16**	**10**	**6**	**0**	**912**	**44**	**2**	**2.89**	....	....	....	....	....	....	....
	Hamilton Bulldogs	AHL	28	16	11	0	1618	54	6	*2.00	....	....	....	....	....	....	....
	NHL Totals		**16**	**10**	**6**	**0**	**912**	**44**	**2**	**2.89**	....	....	....	....	....	....	....

AHL All-Rookie Team (2007)

HARDING, Josh (HAHR-dihng, JAWSH) MIN.

Goaltender. Catches right. 6'1", 193 lbs. Born, Regina, Sask., June 18, 1984.
(Minnesota's 2nd choice, 38th overall, in 2002 Entry Draft).

			Regular Season								Playoffs						
Season	**Club**	**League**	**GP**	**W**	**L**	**O/T**	**Mins**	**GA**	**SO**	**Avg**	**GP**	**W**	**L**	**Mins**	**GA**	**SO**	**Avg**
2000-01	Reg. Pat Cdns.	SMHL	36	17	13	0	2106	96	2	2.75	3	1	2	170	11	0	3.88
2001-02	Regina Pats	WHL	42	27	13	1	2389	95	*4	2.39	6	2	4	325	16	0	2.95
2002-03	Regina Pats	WHL	57	18	24	13	*3385	155	3	2.75	5	1	4	321	13	0	2.43
2003-04	Regina Pats	WHL	28	12	14	2	1665	67	2	2.41	....	....	....	....	....	....	....
	Brandon	WHL	27	13	11	3	1612	65	5	2.42	11	5	6	660	36	0	3.27
2004-05	Houston Aeros	AHL	42	21	16	3	2388	80	4	2.01	2	0	2	119	8	0	4.03
2005-06	**Minnesota**	**NHL**	**3**	**2**	**1**	**0**	**185**	**8**	**1**	**2.59**	....	....	....	....	....	....	....
	Houston Aeros	AHL	38	29	8	0	2215	99	2	2.68	8	4	4	476	30	0	3.79
2006-07	**Minnesota**	**NHL**	**7**	**3**	**2**	**1**	**361**	**7**	**1**	**1.16**	....	....	....	....	....	....	....
	Houston Aeros	AHL	38	17	16	4	2270	94	1	2.48	....	....	....	....	....	....	....
	NHL Totals		**10**	**5**	**3**	**1**	**546**	**15**	**2**	**1.65**	....	....	....	....	....	....	....

WHL East Second All-Star Team (2002) • WHL East First All-Star Team (2003) • WHL Goaltender of the Year (2003) • WHL Player of the Year (2003)

HASEK, Dominik (HAH-shihk, DOHM-ihn-ihk) DET.

Goaltender. Catches left. 6'1", 166 lbs. Born, Pardubice, Czech., January 29, 1965.
(Chicago's 11th choice, 207th overall, in 1983 Entry Draft).

			Regular Season								Playoffs						
Season	**Club**	**League**	**GP**	**W**	**L**	**O/T**	**Mins**	**GA**	**SO**	**Avg**	**GP**	**W**	**L**	**Mins**	**GA**	**SO**	**Avg**
1981-82	Tesla Pardubice	Czech	12	....	....	....	661	34	....	3.09	....	....	....	....	....	....	....
1982-83	Tesla Pardubice	Czech	42	....	....	....	2358	105	....	2.67	....	....	....	....	....	....	....
1983-84	Tesla Pardubice	Czech	40	....	....	....	2304	108	....	2.81	....	....	....	....	....	....	....
1984-85	Tesla Pardubice	Czech	42	....	....	....	2419	131	....	3.25	....	....	....	....	....	....	....
1985-86	Tesla Pardubice	Czech	45	....	....	....	2689	138	....	3.08	....	....	....	....	....	....	....
1986-87	Tesla Pardubice	Czech	43	....	....	....	2515	103	....	2.46	....	....	....	....	....	....	....
1987-88	Tesla Pardubice	Czech	31	....	....	....	1862	93	....	3.00	....	....	....	....	....	....	....
	Czechoslovakia	Olympics	5	3	2	0	217	18	1	4.98	....	....	....	....	....	....	....
1988-89	Tesla Pardubice	Czech	42	....	....	....	2507	114	....	2.73	....	....	....	....	....	....	....
1989-90	Dukla Jihlava	Czech	40	....	....	....	2251	80	....	2.13	....	....	....	....	....	....	....
1990-91	**Chicago**	**NHL**	**5**	**3**	**0**	**1**	**195**	**8**	**0**	**2.46**	**3**	**0**	**0**	**69**	**3**	**0**	**2.61**
	Indianapolis Ice	IHL	33	20	11	1	1903	80	*5	*2.52	1	1	0	60	3	0	3.00
1991-92	**Chicago**	**NHL**	**20**	**10**	**4**	**1**	**1014**	**44**	**1**	**2.60**	**3**	**0**	**2**	**158**	**8**	**0**	**3.04**
	Indianapolis Ice	IHL	20	7	10	3	1162	69	1	3.56	....	....	....	....	....	....	....
1992-93	**Buffalo**	**NHL**	**28**	**11**	**10**	**4**	**1429**	**75**	**0**	**3.15**	**1**	**1**	**0**	**45**	**1**	**0**	**1.33**
1993-94	**Buffalo**	**NHL**	**58**	**30**	**20**	**6**	**3358**	**109**	***7**	***1.95**	**7**	**3**	**4**	**484**	**13**	**2**	***1.61**
1994-95	HC Pardubice	CzRep	2	1	0	1	124	6	0	2.90	....	....	....	....	....	....	....
	Buffalo	**NHL**	**41**	**19**	**14**	**7**	**2416**	**85**	***5**	***2.11**	**5**	**1**	**4**	**309**	**18**	**0**	**3.50**
1995-96	**Buffalo**	**NHL**	**59**	**22**	**30**	**6**	**3417**	**161**	**2**	**2.83**	....	....	....	....	....	....	....
1996-97	**Buffalo**	**NHL**	**67**	**37**	**20**	**10**	**4037**	**153**	**5**	**2.27**	**3**	**1**	**1**	**153**	**5**	**0**	**1.96**
1997-98	**Buffalo**	**NHL**	***72**	**33**	**23**	**13**	***4220**	**147**	***13**	**2.09**	**15**	**10**	**5**	**948**	**32**	**1**	**2.03**
	Czech Republic	Olympics	6	*5	1	0	*369	6	*2	*0.97	....	....	....	....	....	....	....
1998-99	**Buffalo**	**NHL**	**64**	**30**	**18**	**14**	**3817**	**119**	**9**	**1.87**	**19**	**13**	**6**	**1217**	**36**	**2**	**1.77**
99-2000	**Buffalo**	**NHL**	**35**	**15**	**11**	**6**	**2066**	**76**	**3**	**2.21**	**5**	**1**	**4**	**301**	**12**	**0**	**2.39**
2000-01	**Buffalo**	**NHL**	**67**	**37**	**24**	**4**	**3904**	**137**	***11**	**2.11**	**13**	**7**	**6**	**833**	**29**	**1**	**2.09**
2001-02 ♦	**Detroit**	**NHL**	**65**	***41**	**15**	**8**	**3872**	**140**	**5**	**2.17**	***23**	***16**	**7**	***1455**	**45**	***6**	**1.86**
	Czech Republic	Olympics	4	1	2	1	239	8	0	2.01	....	....	....	....	....	....	....
2002-03							OUT OF HOCKEY – RETIRED										
2003-04	**Detroit**	**NHL**	**14**	**8**	**3**	**2**	**817**	**30**	**2**	**2.20**	....	....	....	....	....	....	....
2004-05							DID NOT PLAY										
2005-06	**Ottawa**	**NHL**	**43**	**28**	**10**	**4**	**2584**	**90**	**5**	**2.09**	....	....	....	....	....	....	....
	Czech Republic	Olympics	1	0	0	0	9	0	0	0.00	....	....	....	....	....	....	....
2006-07	**Detroit**	**NHL**	**56**	**38**	**11**	**6**	**3341**	**114**	**8**	**2.05**	**18**	**10**	**8**	**1140**	**34**	**2**	**1.79**
	NHL Totals		**694**	**362**	**213**	**92**	**40487**	**1488**	**76**	**2.21**	**115**	**63**	**47**	**7112**	**236**	**14**	**1.99**

Czechoslovakian Goaltender of the Year (1986, 1987, 1988, 1989, 1990) • Czechoslovakian Player of the Year (1987, 1989, 1990) • Czechoslovakian First All-Star Team (1988, 1989, 1990) • IHL First All-Star Team (1991) • NHL All-Rookie Team (1992) • NHL First All-Star Team (1994, 1995, 1997, 1998, 1999, 2001) • William M. Jennings Trophy (1994) (shared with Grant Fuhr) • Vezina Trophy (1994, 1995, 1997, 1998, 1999, 2001) • Lester B. Pearson Award (1997, 1998) • Hart Memorial Trophy (1997, 1998) • William M. Jennings Trophy (2001)

Played in NHL All-Star Game (1996, 1997, 1998, 1999, 2001, 2002)

Traded to **Buffalo** by **Chicago** for Stephane Beauregard and Buffalo's 4th round choice (Eric Daze) in 1993 Entry Draft, August 7, 1992. Traded to **Detroit** by **Buffalo** for Vyacheslav Kozlov, Detroit's 1st round choice (later traded to Columbus – later traded to Atlanta – Atlanta selected Jim Slater) in 2002 Entry Draft, July 1, 2001. • Officially announced retirement, June 25, 2002. • **Detroit** picked up the option on his contract, July 1, 2003. • Missed majority of 2003-04 season recovering from groin injury suffered in game vs. St. Louis, October 29, 2003. Signed as a free agent by **Ottawa**, July 6, 2004. Signed as a free agent by **Detroit**, July 31, 2006.

HAUSER, Adam (HOW-suhr, A-duhm)

Goaltender. Catches left. 6'2", 195 lbs. Born, Bovey, MN, May 27, 1980.
(Edmonton's 4th choice, 81st overall, in 1999 Entry Draft).

			Regular Season								Playoffs						
Season	**Club**	**League**	**GP**	**W**	**L**	**O/T**	**Mins**	**GA**	**SO**	**Avg**	**GP**	**W**	**L**	**Mins**	**GA**	**SO**	**Avg**
1996-97	Greenway Raiders	High-MN	25	....	....	....	1496	63	0	2.54	....	....	....	....	....	....	....
1997-98	USNTDP	U-18	19	9	5	4	1138	44	1	2.32	....	....	....	....	....	....	....
	USNTDP	USHL	13	5	4	3	668	39	1	3.50	....	....	....	....	....	....	....
	USNTDP	NAHL	5	4	1	0	304	11	1	2.17	1	1	0	60	0	1	0.00
1998-99	U. of Minnesota	WCHA	*40	14	18	8	*2350	136	3	3.47	....	....	....	....	....	....	....
99-2000	U. of Minnesota	WCHA	36	20	14	2	2114	104	1	2.95	....	....	....	....	....	....	....
2000-01	U. of Minnesota	WCHA	40	*26	12	2	2366	101	*3	2.56	....	....	....	....	....	....	....
2001-02	U. of Minnesota	WCHA	35	*23	6	4	2003	80	1	2.40	....	....	....	....	....	....	....
2002-03	Providence Bruins	AHL	1	0	0	1	64	3	0	2.80	....	....	....	....	....	....	....
	Jackson Bandits	ECHL	34	20	9	4	2021	83	*5	2.46	....	....	....	....	....	....	....
2003-04	Manchester	AHL	43	20	15	7	2536	82	7	1.94	4	2	2	286	9	2	1.89
	Reading Royals	ECHL	4	3	0	1	245	7	1	1.71	....	....	....	....	....	....	....
2004-05	Manchester	AHL	32	19	11	0	1867	60	5	1.93	2	0	0	70	2	0	1.71
2005-06	**Los Angeles**	**NHL**	**1**	**0**	**0**	**0**	**51**	**6**	**0**	**7.06**	....	....	....	....	....	....	....
	Manchester	AHL	45	22	17	2	2600	111	3	2.56	3	1	2	177	9	0	3.05
2006-07	Kolner Haie	Germany	40	....	....	....	2427	95	4	2.35	9	....	....	554	29	1	3.14
	NHL Totals		**1**	**0**	**0**	**0**	**51**	**6**	**0**	**7.06**	....	....	....	....	....	....	....

NCAA Championship All-Tournament Team (2002) • ECHL All-Rookie Team (2003)

Signed as a free agent by **Manchester** (AHL), August 19, 2003. Signed as a free agent by **Los Angeles**, July 8, 2004. Signed as a free agent by **Kolner** (Germany), July 9, 2006.

HEDBERG, Johan (HEHD-buhrg, YOH-han) ATL.

Goaltender. Catches left. 6', 185 lbs. Born, Leksand, Sweden, May 5, 1973.
(Philadelphia's 8th choice, 218th overall, in 1994 Entry Draft).

			Regular Season								Playoffs						
Season	**Club**	**League**	**GP**	**W**	**L**	**O/T**	**Mins**	**GA**	**SO**	**Avg**	**GP**	**W**	**L**	**Mins**	**GA**	**SO**	**Avg**
1992-93	Leksands IF	Sweden	10	....	....	....	600	24	....	2.40	....	....	....	....	....	....	....
1993-94	Leksands IF	Sweden	17	....	....	....	1020	48	....	2.82	....	....	....	....	....	....	....
1994-95	Leksands IF	Sweden	17	....	....	....	986	58	....	3.53	....	....	....	....	....	....	....
1995-96	Leksands IF	Sweden	34	....	....	....	2013	95	....	2.83	4	....	....	240	13	....	3.25
1996-97	Leksands IF	Sweden	38	....	....	....	2260	95	3	2.52	8	....	....	581	18	1	1.86
1997-98	Detroit Vipers	IHL	16	7	2	2	726	32	1	2.64	....	....	....	....	....	....	....
	Baton Rouge	ECHL	2	1	1	0	100	7	0	4.20	....	....	....	....	....	....	....
	Manitoba Moose	IHL	14	8	4	1	745	32	1	2.58	2	0	2	105	6	0	3.40
	Sweden	Olympics					DID NOT PLAY – SPARE GOALTENDER										
1998-99	Leksands IF	Sweden	*48	....	....	....	*2940	140	0	2.86	4	....	....	255	15	0	3.53
99-2000	Kentucky	AHL	33	18	9	5	1973	88	3	2.68	5	3	2	311	10	1	1.93
2000-01	Manitoba Moose	IHL	46	23	13	7	2697	115	1	2.56	....	....	....	....	....	....	....
	Pittsburgh	**NHL**	**9**	**7**	**1**	**1**	**545**	**24**	**0**	**2.64**	**18**	**9**	**9**	**1123**	**43**	**2**	**2.30**
2001-02	**Pittsburgh**	**NHL**	**66**	**25**	**34**	**7**	**3877**	**178**	**6**	**2.75**	....	....	....	....	....	....	....
	Sweden	Olympics	1	1	0	0	60	1	0	1.00	....	....	....	....	....	....	....
2002-03	**Pittsburgh**	**NHL**	**41**	**14**	**22**	**4**	**2410**	**126**	**1**	**3.14**	....	....	....	....	....	....	....
2003-04	**Vancouver**	**NHL**	**21**	**8**	**6**	**2**	**1098**	**46**	**3**	**2.51**	**2**	**1**	**1**	**98**	**4**	**0**	**2.45**
	Manitoba Moose	AHL	2	0	2	0	125	9	0	4.32	....	....	....	....	....	....	....
2004-05	Leksands IF	Sweden-2	21	....	....	....	1274	45	1	2.12	....	....	....	....	....	....	....
2005-06	**Dallas**	**NHL**	**19**	**12**	**4**	**1**	**1079**	**48**	**0**	**2.67**	....	....	....	....	....	....	....
2006-07	**Atlanta**	**NHL**	**21**	**9**	**4**	**2**	**1057**	**51**	**0**	**2.89**	**2**	**0**	**2**	**117**	**5**	**0**	**2.56**
	NHL Totals		**177**	**75**	**71**	**17**	**10066**	**473**	**10**	**2.82**	**22**	**10**	**12**	**1338**	**52**	**2**	**2.33**

Rights traded to **San Jose** by **Philadelphia** for San Jose's 7th round choice (Pavel Kasparik) in 1999 Entry Draft, August 6, 1998. Traded to **Pittsburgh** by **San Jose** with Bobby Dollas for Jeff Norton, March 12, 2001. Traded to **Vancouver** by **Pittsburgh** for Vancouver's 2nd round choice (Alex Goligoski) in 2004 Entry Draft, August 25, 2003. Signed as a free agent by **Leksands** (Sweden-2), August 1, 2004. Signed as a free agent by **Dallas**, August 5, 2005. Signed as a free agent by **Atlanta**, July 1, 2006.

HELENIUS, Riku (heh-lehn-NEE-uhs, REE-koo) T.B.

Goaltender. Catches left. 6'3", 202 lbs. Born, Palkane, Finland, March 1, 1988.
(Tampa Bay's 1st choice, 15th overall, in 2006 Entry Draft).

			Regular Season								Playoffs						
Season	Club	League	GP	W	L	O/T	Mins	GA	SO	Avg	GP	W	L	Mins	GA	SO	Avg
2004-05	Ilves Tampere U18	Fin-U18	16	....	....	....	903	30	3	1.99	5	....	....	295	15	0	3.05
	Ilves Tampere Jr.	Fin-Jr.	2	....	....	....	86	4	0	2.77	....	....	....	....	....	....	....
2005-06	Suomi U20	Finland-2	1	....	....	....	60	3	0	3.00	....	....	....	....	....	....	....
	Ilves Tampere U18	Fin-U18	2	....	....	....	120	2	0	1.00	5	....	....	300	13	0	2.60
	Ilves Tampere Jr.	Fin-Jr.	26	....	....	....	1565	70	4	2.68	2	....	....	135	7	0	3.11
2006-07	Ilves Tampere Jr.	Fin-Jr.	2	2	0	0	120	4	0	2.00	....	....	....	....	....	....	....

HILLER, Jonas ANA.

Goaltender. Catches right. 6'2", 181 lbs. Born, Felben Wellhausen, Switz., February 12, 1982.

			Regular Season								Playoffs						
Season	Club	League	GP	W	L	O/T	Mins	GA	SO	Avg	GP	W	L	Mins	GA	SO	Avg
2000-01	HC Davos	Swiss	1	0	0	0	9	0	0	0.00	....	....	....	....	....	....	....
2001-02	HC Davos	Swiss					DID NOT PLAY										
2002-03	HC Davos	Swiss					DID NOT PLAY										
2003-04	Chaux-de-Fonds	Swiss-2	1	0	1	0	60	4	0	4.00	....	....	....	....	....	....	....
	Lausanne HC	Swiss	21	....	....	....	1161	64	1	3.31	....	....	....	....	....	....	....
	Lausanne HC	Swiss-Q	....	....	....	....	....	....	....	....	4	4	0	251	7	0	1.67
2004-05	HC Davos	Swiss	43	26	12	4	2519	95	8	2.26	15	12	3	932	34	0	2.19
2005-06	HC Davos	Swiss	44	23	16	5	2676	110	3	2.47	15	9	6	900	45	1	3.00
2006-07	HC Davos	Swiss	44	28	16	0	2656	115	3	2.60	19	12	7	1138	39	3	2.05

Signed as a free agent by **Anaheim**, May 25, 2007.

HNILICKA, Milan (huh-LEETCH-kuh, MEE-lan)

Goaltender. Catches left. 6'1", 190 lbs. Born, Pardubice, Czech., June 25, 1973.
(NY Islanders' 4th choice, 70th overall, in 1991 Entry Draft).

			Regular Season								Playoffs						
Season	Club	League	GP	W	L	O/T	Mins	GA	SO	Avg	GP	W	L	Mins	GA	SO	Avg
1989-90	Poldi Kladno	Czech	24	....	....	....	1113	70	....	3.77	....	....	....	....	....	....	....
1990-91	Poldi Kladno	Czech	40	....	....	....	2122	98	0	2.80	....	....	....	....	....	....	....
1991-92	Poldi Kladno	Czech	38	....	....	....	2066	128	0	3.73	....	....	....	....	....	....	....
1992-93	Swift Current	WHL	*65	*46	12	2	3679	206	2	3.36	*17	*12	5	*1017	54	*2	3.19
1993-94	Salt Lake	IHL	8	5	1	0	378	25	0	3.97	....	....	....	....	....	....	....
	Richmond	ECHL	43	18	16	5	2299	155	4	4.05	....	....	....	....	....	....	....
1994-95	Denver Grizzlies	IHL	15	9	4	1	798	47	1	3.53	....	....	....	....	....	....	....
1995-96	HC Poldi Kladno	CzRep	33	....	....	....	1959	93	1	2.84	8	....	....	493	24	....	2.92
1996-97	HC Poldi Kladno	CzRep	48	....	....	....	2736	120	*4	2.63	3	....	....	151	14	0	5.56
1997-98	HC Sparta Praha	CzRep	49	....	....	....	2847	99	....	2.09	11	....	....	632	31	....	3.00
1998-99	HC Sparta Praha	CzRep	*50	....	....	....	*2877	109	....	2.27	8	....	....	507	13	....	*1.54
99-2000	**NY Rangers**	**NHL**	**2**	**0**	**1**	**0**	**86**	**5**	**0**	**3.49**	....	....	....	....	....	....	....
	Hartford Wolf Pack	AHL	36	22	11	0	1979	71	5	*2.15	3	0	1	99	6	0	3.64
2000-01	**Atlanta**	**NHL**	**36**	**12**	**19**	**2**	**1879**	**105**	**2**	**3.35**	....	....	....	....	....	....	....
2001-02	**Atlanta**	**NHL**	**60**	**13**	**33**	**10**	**3367**	**179**	**3**	**3.19**	....	....	....	....	....	....	....
2002-03	**Atlanta**	**NHL**	**21**	**4**	**13**	**1**	**1097**	**65**	**0**	**3.56**	....	....	....	....	....	....	....
	Chicago Wolves	AHL	15	11	2	1	838	33	1	2.36	....	....	....	....	....	....	....
2003-04	**Los Angeles**	**NHL**	**2**	**0**	**1**	**0**	**80**	**5**	**0**	**3.75**	....	....	....	....	....	....	....
	Manchester	AHL	20	8	10	0	1022	44	1	2.58	2	0	2	127	5	0	2.37
2004-05	Liberec	CzRep	46	....	....	....	2740	106	5	2.32	12	....	....	702	32	0	2.74
2005-06	Liberec	CzRep	45	....	....	....	2644	75	*6	*1.70	4	....	....	158	10	0	3.80
	Czech Republic	Olympics	3	....	....	....	128	6	0	2.82	....	....	....	....	....	....	....
2006-07	Liberec	CzRep	40	....	....	....	2370	73	4	1.85	12	....	....	716	34	0	2.85
	NHL Totals		**121**	**29**	**67**	**13**	**6509**	**359**	**5**	**3.31**	....	....	....	....	....	....	....

Harry "Hap" Holmes Memorial Award (fewest goals against – AHL) (2000) (shared with Jean-Francois Labbe)

Signed as a free agent by **NY Rangers**, July 15, 1999. Signed as a free agent by **Atlanta**, July 28, 2000. Traded to **Los Angeles** by **Atlanta** for future considerations, September 15, 2003. • Missed majority of 2003-04 season recovering from finger injury suffered in game vs. Phoenix, December 31, 2003. Signed as a free agent by **Liberec** (CzRep), May 18, 2004.

HOLMQVIST, Johan (HOHLM-kvihst, YOH-han) T.B.

Goaltender. Catches left. 6'3", 195 lbs. Born, Tolfta, Sweden, May 24, 1978.
(NY Rangers' 9th choice, 175th overall, in 1997 Entry Draft).

			Regular Season								Playoffs						
Season	Club	League	GP	W	L	O/T	Mins	GA	SO	Avg	GP	W	L	Mins	GA	SO	Avg
1996-97	Brynas IF Gavle	Sweden	2	0	0	0	80	4	0	3.00	....	....	....	....	....	....	....
1997-98	Brynas IF Gavle	Sweden	33	....	....	....	1897	82	....	2.59	3	0	3	180	14	....	4.67
1998-99	Brynas IF Gavle	Sweden	41	....	....	....	2383	111	4	2.79	*14	9	5	*855	34	0	2.39
99-2000	Brynas IF Gavle	Sweden	41	....	....	....	2402	104	4	2.60	11	....	....	671	30	1	2.68
2000-01	**NY Rangers**	**NHL**	**2**	**0**	**2**	**0**	**119**	**10**	**0**	**5.04**	....	....	....	....	....	....	....
	Hartford Wolf Pack	AHL	43	19	14	4	2305	111	2	2.89	5	2	3	314	13	0	2.48
2001-02	**NY Rangers**	**NHL**	**1**	**0**	**0**	**0**	**9**	**0**	**0**	**0.00**	....	....	....	....	....	....	....
	Hartford Wolf Pack	AHL	48	26	12	6	2734	140	1	3.07	4	1	2	163	12	0	4.41
2002-03	**NY Rangers**	**NHL**	**1**	**0**	**1**	**0**	**39**	**2**	**0**	**3.08**	....	....	....	....	....	....	....
	Hartford Wolf Pack	AHL	35	14	13	5	1904	84	2	2.65	....	....	....	....	....	....	....
	Charlotte Checkers	ECHL	1	1	0	0	60	2	0	2.00	....	....	....	....	....	....	....
	Houston Aeros	AHL	8	5	3	0	479	23	1	2.88	*23	*15	8	*1499	50	1	2.00
2003-04	Houston Aeros	AHL	59	23	27	7	3467	148	4	2.56	....	....	....	....	....	....	....
2004-05	Brynas IF Gavle	Sweden	42	....	....	....	2445	138	1	3.39	....	....	....	....	....	....	....
2005-06	Brynas IF Gavle	Sweden	26	....	....	....	1539	50	3	*1.95	4	....	....	194	13	0	4.02
2006-07	**Tampa Bay**	**NHL**	**48**	**27**	**15**	**3**	**2548**	**121**	**1**	**2.85**	**6**	**2**	**4**	**370**	**18**	**0**	**2.92**
	NHL Totals		**52**	**27**	**18**	**3**	**2715**	**133**	**1**	**2.94**	**6**	**2**	**4**	**370**	**18**	**0**	**2.92**

Jack A. Butterfield Trophy (Playoff MVP – AHL) (2003)

Traded to **Minnesota** by **NY Rangers** for Lawrence Nycholat, March 11, 2003. Signed as a free agent by **Gavle** (Sweden), July 29, 2004. Signed as a free agent by **Tampa Bay**, June 1, 2006.

HOLT, Chris (HOHLT, KRIHS) NYR

Goaltender. Catches left. 6'3", 221 lbs. Born, Vancouver, B.C., June 5, 1985.
(NY Rangers' 8th choice, 180th overall, in 2003 Entry Draft).

			Regular Season								Playoffs						
Season	Club	League	GP	W	L	O/T	Mins	GA	SO	Avg	GP	W	L	Mins	GA	SO	Avg
2001-02	Billings Bulls	AWHL	24	13	7	1	1184	59	2	2.99	....	....	....	....	....	....	....
2002-03	USNTDP	U-18	27	7	12	2	1519	81	1	3.20	....	....	....	....	....	....	....
	USNTDP	NAHL	5	2	3	0	255	14	0	3.30	....	....	....	....	....	....	....
2003-04	Nebraska-Omaha	CCHA	27	5	17	2	1499	81	0	3.24	....	....	....	....	....	....	....
2004-05	Nebraska-Omaha	CCHA	37	19	14	4	2190	106	1	2.90	....	....	....	....	....	....	....
2005-06	**NY Rangers**	**NHL**	**1**	**0**	**0**	**0**	**10**	**0**	**0**	**0.00**	....	....	....	....	....	....	....
	Hartford Wolf Pack	AHL	9	3	2	1	459	31	0	4.06	8	4	4	487	24	0	2.96
	Charlotte Checkers	ECHL	23	7	11	1	1229	84	0	4.10	....	....	....	....	....	....	....
2006-07	Hartford Wolf Pack	AHL	6	2	1	0	240	8	0	2.00	1	1	0	26	1	0	2.28
	Charlotte Checkers	ECHL	45	24	18	2	2650	139	1	3.15	4	2	2	223	11	0	2.97
	NHL Totals		**1**	**0**	**0**	**0**	**10**	**0**	**0**	**0.00**	....	....	....	....	....	....	....

HOULE, Martin (HOOL, MAHR-tihn) PHI.

Goaltender. Catches left. 5'11", 185 lbs. Born, Montreal, Que., February 12, 1985.
(Philadelphia's 8th choice, 232nd overall, in 2004 Entry Draft).

			Regular Season								Playoffs						
Season	Club	League	GP	W	L	O/T	Mins	GA	SO	Avg	GP	W	L	Mins	GA	SO	Avg
2001-02	Antoine-Girouard	QAAA	23	17	4	2	1309	45	1	2.06	....	....	....	....	....	....	....
	Cape Breton	QMJHL	1	1	0	0	38	0	0	0.00	....	....	....	....	....	....	....
2002-03	Cape Breton	QMJHL	30	4	18	3	1450	98	0	4.06	1	0	0	11	0	0	0.00
2003-04	Cape Breton	QMJHL	51	34	15	1	2951	114	3	2.32	1	0	1	59	4	0	4.10
2004-05	Cape Breton	QMJHL	56	26	18	5	3108	130	*6	2.51	4	1	3	246	10	0	*2.44
2005-06	Philadelphia	AHL	40	18	18	1	2153	91	2	2.54	....	....	....	....	....	....	....
	Trenton Titans	ECHL	7	4	3	0	429	15	1	2.10	....	....	....	....	....	....	....
2006-07	**Philadelphia**	**NHL**	**1**	**0**	**0**	**0**	**2**	**1**	**0**	**30.00**	....	....	....	....	....	....	....
	Philadelphia	AHL	37	12	17	2	1879	104	0	3.32	....	....	....	....	....	....	....
	NHL Totals		**1**	**0**	**0**	**0**	**2**	**1**	**0**	**30.00**	....	....	....	....	....	....	....

QMJHL First All-Star Team (2004)

HOVINEN, Niko (HOH-vih-nehn, NEE-KOH) MIN.

Goaltender. Catches left. 6'6", 208 lbs. Born, Helsinki, Finland, March 16, 1988.
(Minnesota's 5th choice, 132nd overall, in 2006 Entry Draft).

			Regular Season								Playoffs						
Season	Club	League	GP	W	L	O/T	Mins	GA	SO	Avg	GP	W	L	Mins	GA	SO	Avg
2004-05	Jokerit U18	Fin-U18	20	....	....	....	1166	38	3	1.95	4	....	....	246	9	1	2.20
	Jokerit Helsinki Jr.	Fin-Jr.	4	....	....	....	242	13	0	3.21	....	....	....	....	....	....	....
2005-06	Jokerit Helsinki Jr.	Fin-Jr.	26	....	....	....	1480	77	0	3.12	....	....	....	....	....	....	....
	Jokerit U18	Fin-U18	11	....	....	....	637	34	1	3.20	4	....	....	232	14	1	3.62
	Suomi U20	Finland-2	1	....	....	....	60	4	0	4.00	....	....	....	....	....	....	....
2006-07	Jokerit Helsinki Jr.	Fin-Jr.	27	13	10	0	1641	74	1	2.71	5	2	3	303	12	1	2.38
	Suomi U20	Finland-2	6	1	2	0	329	18	0	3.28	....	....	....	....	....	....	....
	Jokerit Helsinki	Finland	1	0	1	0	60	4	0	4.00	....	....	....	....	....	....	....

HOWARD, James (HOW-uhrd, JAYMZ) DET.

Goaltender. Catches left. 6', 218 lbs. Born, Syracuse, NY, March 26, 1984.
(Detroit's 1st choice, 64th overall, in 2003 Entry Draft).

			Regular Season								Playoffs						
Season	Club	League	GP	W	L	O/T	Mins	GA	SO	Avg	GP	W	L	Mins	GA	SO	Avg
2001-02	USNTDP	U-18	19	15	4	1	1170	37	4	1.90	....	....	....	....	....	....	....
	USNTDP	USHL	8	4	3	0	425	14	0	1.98	....	....	....	....	....	....	....
	USNTDP	NAHL	8	3	4	0	381	25	0	3.93	....	....	....	....	....	....	....
2002-03	University of Maine	H-East	21	14	6	0	1151	47	3	2.45	....	....	....	....	....	....	....
2003-04	University of Maine	H-East	23	14	4	3	1364	27	*6	*1.19	....	....	....	....	....	....	....
2004-05	University of Maine	H-East	*39	*19	13	7	*2310	74	*6	1.92	....	....	....	....	....	....	....
2005-06	**Detroit**	**NHL**	**4**	**1**	**2**	**0**	**201**	**10**	**0**	**2.99**	....	....	....	....	....	....	....
	Grand Rapids	AHL	38	27	6	2	2140	92	2	2.58	13	5	7	763	44	0	3.46
2006-07	Grand Rapids	AHL	49	21	21	3	2776	125	6	2.70	7	3	4	434	14	0	1.93
	NHL Totals		**4**	**1**	**2**	**0**	**201**	**10**	**0**	**2.99**	....	....	....	....	....	....	....

Hockey East All-Rookie Team (2003) • Hockey East Rookie of the Year (2003) • Hockey East First All-Star Team (2004) • NCAA East Second All-American Team (2004) • AHL All-Rookie Team (2006)

HUET, Cristobal (hew-AY, KRIHS-toh-bahl) MTL.

Goaltender. Catches left. 6', 204 lbs. Born, St. Martin d'Heres, France, September 3, 1975.
(Los Angeles' 9th choice, 214th overall, in 2001 Entry Draft).

			Regular Season								Playoffs						
Season	Club	League	GP	W	L	O/T	Mins	GA	SO	Avg	GP	W	L	Mins	GA	SO	Avg
1997-98	CSG Grenoble	France					STATISTICS NOT AVAILABLE										
	France	Olympics	2	1	1	0	120	5	0	2.50	....	....	....	....	....	....	....
1998-99	HC Lugano	Swiss	21	....	....	....	1275	58	1	2.73	10	....	....	628	18	1	*1.72
99-2000	HC Lugano	Swiss	31	....	....	....	1886	50	*8	*1.59	13	....	....	783	29	0	2.22
2000-01	HC Lugano	Swiss	39	....	....	....	2365	77	*6	*1.95	*18	....	....	*1141	39	2	2.05
2001-02	HC Lugano	Swiss	39	....	....	....	2313	107	*4	2.78	1	0	1	60	3	0	3.00
	France	Olympics	3	0	2	1	179	10	0	3.36	....	....	....	....	....	....	....
2002-03	**Los Angeles**	**NHL**	**12**	**4**	**4**	**1**	**541**	**21**	**1**	**2.33**	....	....	....	....	....	....	....
	Manchester	AHL	30	16	8	5	1784	68	1	2.29	1	0	1	30	4	0	8.08
2003-04	**Los Angeles**	**NHL**	**41**	**10**	**16**	**10**	**2199**	**89**	**3**	**2.43**	....	....	....	....	....	....	....
2004-05	Adler Mannheim	Germany	36	....	....	....	2001	93	1	2.79	*14	....	....	*850	40	2	2.82
2005-06	**Montreal**	**NHL**	**36**	**18**	**11**	**4**	**2103**	**77**	**7**	**2.20**	**6**	**2**	**4**	**386**	**15**	**0**	**2.33**
	Hamilton Bulldogs	AHL	4	0	4	0	237	15	0	3.79	....	....	....	....	....	....	....
2006-07	**Montreal**	**NHL**	**42**	**19**	**16**	**3**	**2286**	**107**	**2**	**2.81**	....	....	....	....	....	....	....
	NHL Totals		**131**	**51**	**47**	**18**	**7129**	**294**	**13**	**2.47**	**6**	**2**	**4**	**386**	**15**	**0**	**2.33**

Played in NHL All-Star Game (2007)

Traded to **Montreal** by **Los Angeles** with Radek Bonk for Mathieu Garon and San Jose's 3rd round choice (previously acquired, Los Angeles selected Paul Baier) in 2004 Entry Draft, June 26, 2004. Signed as a free agent by **Mannheim** (Germany), September 14, 2004.

IRVING, Leland (UHR-vihng, LEE-land) CGY.

Goaltender. Catches left. 6', 176 lbs. Born, Barrhead, Alta., April 11, 1988.
(Calgary's 1st choice, 26th overall, in 2006 Entry Draft).

			Regular Season								Playoffs						
Season	Club	League	GP	W	L	O/T	Mins	GA	SO	Avg	GP	W	L	Mins	GA	SO	Avg
2004-05	Everett Silvertips	WHL	23	9	8	1	1132	34	2	1.80	....	....	....	....	....	....	....
2005-06	Everett Silvertips	WHL	*67	37	22	4	*3791	121	4	1.92	12	8	3	747	21	3	1.69
2006-07	Everett Silvertips	WHL	48	34	9	3	2802	87	*11	1.86	12	6	5	639	30	0	2.82

WHL West Second All-Star Team (2006, 2007)

JOHNSON, Brent (JAWN-suhn, BREHNT) WSH.

Goaltender. Catches left. 6'3", 199 lbs. Born, Farmington, MI, March 12, 1977.
(Colorado's 5th choice, 129th overall, in 1995 Entry Draft).

			Regular Season								Playoffs						
Season	Club	League	GP	W	L	O/T	Mins	GA	SO	Avg	GP	W	L	Mins	GA	SO	Avg
1993-94	Det. Compuware	NAHL	18	....	....	....	1024	49	1	3.52	....	....	....	....	....	....	....
1994-95	Owen Sound	OHL	18	3	9	1	904	75	0	4.98	....	....	....	....	....	....	....
1995-96	Owen Sound	OHL	58	24	28	1	3211	243	1	4.54	6	2	4	371	29	0	4.69
1996-97	Owen Sound	OHL	50	20	28	1	2798	201	1	4.31	4	0	4	253	24	0	5.69
1997-98	Worcester IceCats	AHL	42	14	15	7	2240	119	0	3.19	6	3	2	332	19	0	3.43
1998-99	**St. Louis**	**NHL**	**6**	**3**	**2**	**0**	**286**	**10**	**0**	**2.10**	....	....	....	....	....	....	....
	Worcester IceCats	AHL	49	22	22	4	2925	146	2	2.99	4	1	3	238	12	0	3.02
99-2000	Worcester IceCats	AHL	58	24	27	5	3319	161	3	2.91	9	4	5	561	23	1	2.46
2000-01	**St. Louis**	**NHL**	**31**	**19**	**9**	**2**	**1744**	**63**	**4**	**2.17**	**2**	**0**	**1**	**62**	**2**	**0**	**1.94**
2001-02	**St. Louis**	**NHL**	**58**	**34**	**20**	**4**	**3491**	**127**	**5**	**2.18**	**10**	**5**	**5**	**590**	**18**	**3**	**1.83**
2002-03	**St. Louis**	**NHL**	**38**	**16**	**13**	**5**	**2042**	**84**	**2**	**2.47**	....	....	....	....	....	....	....
	Worcester IceCats	AHL	2	0	1	1	125	8	0	3.84	....	....	....	....	....	....	....
2003-04	**St. Louis**	**NHL**	**10**	**4**	**3**	**1**	**493**	**20**	**1**	**2.43**	....	....	....	....	....	....	....
	Worcester IceCats	AHL	8	2	2	2	365	14	0	2.30	....	....	....	....	....	....	....
	Phoenix	**NHL**	**8**	**1**	**6**	**1**	**486**	**21**	**0**	**2.59**	....	....	....	....	....	....	....
2004-05							DID NOT PLAY										
2005-06	**Washington**	**NHL**	**26**	**9**	**12**	**1**	**1413**	**81**	**1**	**3.44**	....	....	....	....	....	....	....

Season	Club	League	GP	W	L	O/T	Mins	GA	SO	Avg	GP	W	L	Mins	GA	SO	Avg
2006-07	**Washington**	**NHL**	**30**	**6**	**15**	**7**	**1644**	**99**	**0**	**3.61**	....	....	....	....	....	....	....
	NHL Totals		**207**	**92**	**80**	**21**	**11599**	**505**	**13**	**2.61**	**12**	**5**	**6**	**652**	**20**	**3**	**1.84**

Traded to **St. Louis** by **Colorado** for San Jose's 3rd round choice (previously acquired, Colorado selected Rick Berry) in 1997 Entry Draft, May 30, 1997. Traded to **Phoenix** by **St. Louis** for Mike Sillinger, March 4, 2004. Signed as a free agent by **Vancouver**, September 1, 2005. Claimed on waivers by **Washington** from **Vancouver**, October 4, 2005.

JOHNSON, Chad (JAWN-suhn, CHAD) PIT.

Goaltender. Catches left. 6'2", 175 lbs. Born, Calgary, Alta., June 10, 1986.
(Pittsburgh's 4th choice, 125th overall, in 2006 Entry Draft).

					Regular Season									Playoffs			
Season	Club	League	GP	W	L	O/T	Mins	GA	SO	Avg	GP	W	L	Mins	GA	SO	Avg
2002-03	Calgary Buffaloes	AMHL	....	8	8	2	1145	62	....	3.25	1	0	1	60	3	0	3.00
2003-04	Brooks Bandits	AJHL	31	6	20	3	1782	117	0	3.94	....	....	....	....	....	....	....
2004-05	Brooks Bandits	AJHL	43	25	16	2	2505	109	2	2.61	119	4	5	493	....	....	....
2005-06	Alaska	CCHA	18	6	7	4	985	42	0	2.56	....	....	....	....	....	....	....
2006-07	Alaska	CCHA	19	5	6	2	1002	52	1	3.11	....	....	....	....	....	....	....

JOSEPH, Curtis (JOH-sehf, KUHR-tihs)

Goaltender. Catches left. 5'11", 190 lbs. Born, Keswick, Ont., April 29, 1967.

					Regular Season									Playoffs			
Season	Club	League	GP	W	L	O/T	Mins	GA	SO	Avg	GP	W	L	Mins	GA	SO	Avg
1984-85	King City Dukes	OHA-B	18	....	....	....	947	76	0	4.82	....	....	....	....	....	....	....
	Newmarket Flyers	OPJHL	2	1	1	0	120	16	0	8.00	....	....	....	....	....	....	....
1985-86	Richmond Hill	OPJHL	33	12	18	0	1716	156	1	5.45	....	....	....	....	....	....	....
1986-87	Richmond Hill	OPJHL	30	14	7	6	1764	128	1	4.35	....	....	....	....	....	....	....
1987-88	Notre Dame	SJHL	36	25	4	7	2174	94	1	2.59	....	....	....	....	....	....	....
1988-89	U. of Wisconsin	WCHA	38	21	11	5	2267	94	1	2.49	....	....	....	....	....	....	....
1989-90	Peoria Rivermen	IHL	23	10	8	2	1241	80	0	3.87	....	....	....	....	....	....	....
	St. Louis	**NHL**	**15**	**9**	**5**	**1**	**852**	**48**	**0**	**3.38**	**6**	**4**	**1**	**327**	**18**	**0**	**3.30**
1990-91	**St. Louis**	**NHL**	**30**	**16**	**10**	**2**	**1710**	**89**	**0**	**3.12**	....	....	....	....	....	....	....
1991-92	**St. Louis**	**NHL**	**60**	**27**	**20**	**10**	**3494**	**175**	**2**	**3.01**	**6**	**2**	**4**	**379**	**23**	**0**	**3.64**
1992-93	**St. Louis**	**NHL**	**68**	**29**	**28**	**9**	**3890**	**196**	**1**	**3.02**	**11**	**7**	**4**	**715**	**27**	***2**	**2.27**
1993-94	**St. Louis**	**NHL**	**71**	**36**	**23**	**11**	**4127**	**213**	**1**	**3.10**	**4**	**0**	**4**	**246**	**15**	**0**	**3.66**
1994-95	**St. Louis**	**NHL**	**36**	**20**	**10**	**1**	**1914**	**89**	**1**	**2.79**	**7**	**3**	**3**	**392**	**24**	**0**	**3.67**
1995-96	Las Vegas Thunder	IHL	15	12	2	1	874	29	1	1.99	....	....	....	....	....	....	....
	Edmonton	**NHL**	**34**	**15**	**16**	**2**	**1936**	**111**	**0**	**3.44**	....	....	....	....	....	....	....
1996-97	**Edmonton**	**NHL**	**72**	**32**	**29**	**9**	**4100**	**200**	**6**	**2.93**	**12**	**5**	**7**	**767**	**36**	**2**	**2.82**
1997-98	**Edmonton**	**NHL**	**71**	**29**	**31**	**9**	**4132**	**181**	**8**	**2.63**	**12**	**5**	**7**	**716**	**23**	**3**	**1.93**
1998-99	**Toronto**	**NHL**	**67**	**35**	**24**	**7**	**4001**	**171**	**3**	**2.56**	**17**	**9**	**8**	**1011**	**41**	**1**	**2.43**
99-2000	**Toronto**	**NHL**	**63**	**36**	**20**	**7**	**3801**	**158**	**4**	**2.49**	**12**	**6**	**6**	**729**	**25**	**1**	**2.06**
2000-01	**Toronto**	**NHL**	**68**	**33**	**27**	**8**	**4100**	**163**	**6**	**2.39**	**11**	**7**	**4**	**685**	**24**	**3**	**2.10**
2001-02	**Toronto**	**NHL**	**51**	**29**	**17**	**5**	**3065**	**114**	**4**	**2.23**	**20**	**10**	**10**	**1253**	**48**	**3**	**2.30**
	Canada	Olympics	1	0	1	0	60	5	0	5.00	....	....	....	....	....	....	....
2002-03	**Detroit**	**NHL**	**61**	**34**	**19**	**6**	**3566**	**148**	**5**	**2.49**	**4**	**0**	**4**	**289**	**10**	**0**	**2.08**
2003-04	**Detroit**	**NHL**	**31**	**16**	**10**	**3**	**1708**	**68**	**2**	**2.39**	**9**	**4**	**4**	**518**	**12**	**1**	***1.39**
	Grand Rapids	AHL	1	1	0	0	60	1	0	1.00	....	....	....	....	....	....	....
2004-05							DID NOT PLAY										
2005-06	**Phoenix**	**NHL**	**60**	**32**	**21**	**3**	**3424**	**166**	**4**	**2.91**	....	....	....	....	....	....	....
2006-07	**Phoenix**	**NHL**	**55**	**18**	**31**	**2**	**2993**	**159**	**4**	**3.19**	....	....	....	....	....	....	....
	NHL Totals		**913**	**446**	**341**	**95**	**52813**	**2449**	**51**	**2.78**	**131**	**62**	**66**	**8027**	**326**	**16**	**2.44**

WCHA First All-Star Team (1989) • WCHA Freshman of the Year (1989) • WCHA Most Valuable Player (1989) • NCAA West Second All-American Team (1989) • King Clancy Memorial Trophy (2000)

Played in NHL All-Star Game (1994, 2000)

Signed as a free agent by **St. Louis**, June 16, 1989. Traded to **Edmonton** by **St. Louis** with the rights to Mike Grier for St. Louis' 1st round choices (previously acquired) in 1996 (Marty Reasoner) and 1997 (later traded to Los Angeles – Los Angeles selected Matt Zultek) Entry Drafts, August 4, 1995. Signed as a free agent by **Toronto**, July 15, 1998. Traded to **Calgary** by **Toronto** for Calgary's 3rd round choice (later traded to Minnesota – Minnesota selected Danny Irmen) in 2003 Entry Draft and future considerations, June 30, 2002. Signed as a free agent by **Detroit**, July 2, 2002. Signed as a free agent by **Phoenix**, August 17, 2005.

JUNG, Torrie (YUHNG, TOHR-ee) T.B.

Goaltender. Catches left. 6'2", 170 lbs. Born, Nanaimo, B.C., January 21, 1989.
(Tampa Bay's 7th choice, 183rd overall, in 2007 Entry Draft).

					Regular Season									Playoffs			
Season	Club	League	GP	W	L	O/T	Mins	GA	SO	Avg	GP	W	L	Mins	GA	SO	Avg
2004-05	Saanich Braves	VIJHL	17	....	....	....	1002	58	0	3.47	....	....	....	....	....	....	....
	Nanaimo Clippers	BCHL	1	0	0	0	2	0	0	0.00	....	....	....	....	....	....	....
2005-06	Cowichan Valley	BCHL	18	5	11	0	1051	69	0	3.94	1	0	1	44	5	0	6.82
2006-07	Kelowna Rockets	WHL	33	8	15	7	1874	108	1	3.46	....	....	....	....	....	....	....

KANGAS, Alex (KANG-uhs, AL-ehx) ATL.

Goaltender. Catches left. 6'1", 175 lbs. Born, Rochester, NY, May 28, 1987.
(Atlanta's 4th choice, 135th overall, in 2006 Entry Draft).

					Regular Season									Playoffs			
Season	Club	League	GP	W	L	O/T	Mins	GA	SO	Avg	GP	W	L	Mins	GA	SO	Avg
2001-02	Rochester Century	High-MN	3	3	0	0	....	3	2	1.00	....	....	....	....	....	....	....
2002-03	Rochester Century	High-MN	27	17	9	0	....	50	6	1.76	....	....	....	....	....	....	....
2003-04	Rochester Century	High-MN	28	15	12	1	....	59	3	2.08	....	....	....	....	....	....	....
2004-05	Rochester Century	High-MN	30	23	4	3	....	55	7	1.86	....	....	....	....	....	....	....
2005-06	Sioux Falls	USHL	29	20	6	3	1733	62	3	2.15	6	4	2	359	17	0	2.84
2006-07	Indiana Ice	USHL	46	19	19	5	2467	136	1	3.31	7	6	1	434	18	0	2.49

USHL All-Rookie Team (2006)

• Signed Letter of Intent to attend **University of Minnesota** (WCHA) in fall of 2007.

KEETLEY, Matt (KEET-lee, MAT) CGY.

Goaltender. Catches right. 6'1", 187 lbs. Born, Medicine Hat, Alta., April 27, 1986.
(Calgary's 6th choice, 158th overall, in 2005 Entry Draft).

					Regular Season									Playoffs			
Season	Club	League	GP	W	L	O/T	Mins	GA	SO	Avg	GP	W	L	Mins	GA	SO	Avg
2003-04	Medicine Hat	AMHL	....	7	4	2	813	48	....	3.54	....	....	....	....	....	....	....
	Medicine Hat	WHL	3	0	1	0	72	5	0	4.17	2	0	0	15	1	0	4.00
2004-05	Medicine Hat	WHL	32	21	5	3	1846	51	6	*1.66	3	1	0	103	8	0	4.66
2005-06	Medicine Hat	WHL	62	*42	13	6	3741	130	6	2.09	13	9	2	864	30	0	2.08
2006-07	Medicine Hat	WHL	55	*42	11	1	3258	119	6	2.19	*23	*16	7	*1407	51	*4	2.18

WHL East Second All-Star Team (2006) • WHL East First All-Star Team (2007) • Memorial Cup Tournament All-Star Team (2007) • Hap Emms Memorial Trophy (Memorial Cup Tournament Top Goaltender) (2007)

KESERICH, Ian (kuh-SAIR-ihch, EE-an) COL.

Goaltender. Catches left. 6'2", 190 lbs. Born, Cleveland, OH, January 6, 1986.
(Colorado's 6th choice, 215th overall, in 2004 Entry Draft).

					Regular Season									Playoffs			
Season	Club	League	GP	W	L	O/T	Mins	GA	SO	Avg	GP	W	L	Mins	GA	SO	Avg
2003-04	Cleveland Barons	NAHL					STATISTICS NOT AVAILABLE										
2004-05	Ohio State	CCHA	6	2	2	0	272	11	0	2.42	....	....	....	....	....	....	....
2005-06	Ohio State	CCHA	4	2	1	0	203	9	0	2.66	....	....	....	....	....	....	....
2006-07	Tri-City Storm	USHL	47	26	13	5	2546	111	3	2.62	8	2	4	404	21	0	3.12

KHABIBULIN, Nikolai (khah-bee-BOO-lihn, NIH-koh-ligh) CHI.

Goaltender. Catches left. 6'1", 208 lbs. Born, Sverdlovsk, USSR, January 13, 1973.
(Winnipeg's 8th choice, 204th overall, in 1992 Entry Draft).

					Regular Season									Playoffs			
Season	Club	League	GP	W	L	O/T	Mins	GA	SO	Avg	GP	W	L	Mins	GA	SO	Avg
1988-89	Sverdlovsk	USSR	1	....	....	....	3	0	0	0.00	....	....	....	....	....	....	....
1989-90	Luch Sverdlovsk	USSR-2					STATISTICS NOT AVAILABLE										
1990-91	Nizhny Tagil	USSR-3	10	....	....	....	....	....	....	....	....	....	....	....	....	....	....
	Sverdlovsk	USSR-Q	2	....	....	....	....	7	....	....	....	....	....	....	....	....	....
1991-92	CSKA Moscow 2	CIS-3	11	....	....	....	....	....	....	....	....	....	....	....	....	....	....
	CSKA Moscow	CIS	2	....	....	....	34	2	0	3.53	....	....	....	....	....	....	....
	Russia	Olympics					DID NOT PLAY – SPARE GOALTENDER										
1992-93	CSKA Moscow	CIS	13	....	....	....	491	27	....	3.29	....	....	....	....	....	....	....
	Serov	CIS-2	18	....	....	....	....	....	....	....	....	....	....	....	....	....	....
1993-94	CSKA Moscow	CIS	46	....	....	....	2625	116	....	2.65	....	....	....	....	....	....	....
	Russian Penguins	IHL	12	2	7	2	639	47	0	4.41	....	....	....	....	....	....	....
1994-95	Springfield Indians	AHL	23	9	9	3	1240	80	0	3.87	....	....	....	....	....	....	....
	Winnipeg	**NHL**	**26**	**8**	**9**	**4**	**1339**	**76**	**0**	**3.41**	....	....	....	....	....	....	....
1995-96	**Winnipeg**	**NHL**	**53**	**26**	**20**	**3**	**2914**	**152**	**2**	**3.13**	**6**	**2**	**4**	**359**	**19**	**0**	**3.18**
1996-97	**Phoenix**	**NHL**	**72**	**30**	**33**	**6**	**4091**	**193**	**7**	**2.83**	**7**	**3**	**4**	**426**	**15**	**1**	**2.11**
1997-98	**Phoenix**	**NHL**	**70**	**30**	**28**	**10**	**4026**	**184**	**4**	**2.74**	**4**	**2**	**1**	**185**	**13**	**0**	**4.22**
1998-99	**Phoenix**	**NHL**	**63**	**32**	**23**	**7**	**3657**	**130**	**8**	**2.13**	**7**	**3**	**4**	**449**	**18**	**0**	**2.41**
99-2000	Long Beach	IHL	33	21	11	1	1936	59	5	*1.83	5	2	3	321	15	0	2.81
2000-01	**Tampa Bay**	**NHL**	**2**	**1**	**1**	**0**	**123**	**6**	**0**	**2.93**	....	....	....	....	....	....	....
2001 02	**Tampa Bay**	**NHL**	**70**	**24**	**32**	**10**	**3896**	**153**	**7**	**2.36**	....	....	....	....	....	....	....
	Russia	Olympics	6	3	2	1	*359	14	*1	2.34	....	....	....	....	....	....	....
	Russia	Olympics	6	....	....	....	359	14	1	2.34	....	....	....	....	....	....	....
2002-03	**Tampa Bay**	**NHL**	**65**	**30**	**22**	**11**	**3787**	**156**	**4**	**2.47**	**10**	**5**	**5**	**644**	**26**	**0**	**2.42**
2003-04 ♦	**Tampa Bay**	**NHL**	**55**	**28**	**19**	**7**	**3274**	**127**	**3**	**2.33**	**23**	***16**	**7**	**1401**	**40**	***5**	**1.71**
2004-05	Ak Bars Kazan	Russia	24	....	....	....	1457	40	5	1.65	2	....	....	118	6	0	3.04
2005-06	**Chicago**	**NHL**	**50**	**17**	**26**	**6**	**2815**	**157**	**0**	**3.35**	....	....	....	....	....	....	....
	Russia	Olympics					DID NOT PLAY – INJURED										
2006-07	**Chicago**	**NHL**	**60**	**25**	**26**	**5**	**3425**	**163**	**1**	**2.86**	....	....	....	....	....	....	....
	NHL Totals		**586**	**251**	**239**	**69**	**33347**	**1497**	**36**	**2.69**	**57**	**31**	**25**	**3464**	**131**	**6**	**2.27**

James Gatschene Memorial Trophy (MVP – IHL) (2000) (co-winner - Frederic Chabot)

Played in NHL All-Star Game (1998, 1999, 2002, 2003)

Transferred to **Phoenix** after **Winnipeg** franchise relocated, July 1, 1996. • Missed entire 1999-2000 NHL season and majority of 2000-01 season after failing to come to contract terms with **Phoenix**. Signed as a free agent by **Long Beach** (IHL) with **Phoenix** retaining NHL rights, January 14, 2000. Traded to **Tampa Bay** by **Phoenix** with Stan Neckar for Mike Johnson, Paul Mara, Ruslan Zainullin and NY Islanders' 2nd round choice (previously acquired, Phoenix selected Matthew Spiller) in 2001 Entry Draft, March 5, 2001. Signed as a free agent by **Kazan** (Russia), November 8, 2004. Signed as a free agent by **Chicago**, August 5, 2005.

KHUDOBIN, Anton (khuh-DAW-bihn, AN-tawn) MIN.

Goaltender. Catches left. 5'11", 208 lbs. Born, Ust-Kamenogorsk, USSR, May 7, 1986.
(Minnesota's 11th choice, 206th overall, in 2004 Entry Draft).

					Regular Season									Playoffs			
Season	Club	League	GP	W	L	O/T	Mins	GA	SO	Avg	GP	W	L	Mins	GA	SO	Avg
2003-04	Magnitogorsk 2	Russia-3	38	....	....	....	....	80	....	....	....	....	....	....	....	....	....
2004-05	Magnitogorsk	Russia	4	....	....	....	133	0	1	0.00	....	....	....	....	....	....	....
	Magnitogorsk 2	Russia-3	27	....	....	....	....	52	....	....	....	....	....	....	....	....	....
2005-06	Saskatoon Blades	WHL	44	23	13	3	2362	114	4	2.90	10	4	3	685	32	0	2.80
2006-07	Magnitogorsk	Russia	16	....	....	....	618	28	0	2.72	3	....	....	26	1	0	2.30

KIPRUSOFF, Miikka (KIHP-roo-sawf, MEE-kah) CGY.

Goaltender. Catches left. 6'1", 186 lbs. Born, Turku, Finland, October 26, 1976.
(San Jose's 5th choice, 116th overall, in 1995 Entry Draft).

					Regular Season									Playoffs			
Season	Club	League	GP	W	L	O/T	Mins	GA	SO	Avg	GP	W	L	Mins	GA	SO	Avg
1993-94	TPS Turku Jr.	Fin-Jr.	35	20	9	5	2101	100	0	2.85	6	3	3	369	26	0	4.23
1994-95	TPS Turku Jr.	Fin-Jr.	31	13	14	4	1896	92	2	2.91	....	....	....	....	....	....	....
	Kiekko-67 Turku	Finland-2	1	0	1	0	60	6	0	6.00	....	....	....	....	....	....	....
	TPS Turku	Finland	4	3	1	0	240	12	0	3.00	2	2	0	120	7	0	3.50
1995-96	TPS Turku Jr.	Fin-Jr.	3	1	2	0	180	9	0	3.00	....	....	....	....	....	....	....
	Kiekko-67 Turku	Finland-2	5	5	0	0	300	7	1	1.40	....	....	....	....	....	....	....
	TPS Turku	Finland	12	5	3	1	550	38	0	4.14	3	0	1	113	4	0	2.12
1996-97	AIK Solna	Sweden	42	....	....	....	2440	93	3	2.29	7	....	....	420	22	0	3.14
1997-98	AIK Solna	Sweden	43	....	....	....	2517	111	1	2.65	....	....	....	....	....	....	....
	AIK Solna	Sweden-Q	9	....	....	....	540	15	2	1.67	....	....	....	....	....	....	....
1998-99	TPS Turku	Finland	39	26	6	6	2259	70	4	1.86	10	9	1	580	15	3	1.55
99-2000	Kentucky	AHL	47	23	19	4	2759	114	3	2.48	5	1	3	239	13	0	3.27
2000-01	**San Jose**	**NHL**	**5**	**2**	**1**	**0**	**154**	**5**	**0**	**1.95**	**3**	**1**	**1**	**149**	**5**	**0**	**2.01**
	Kentucky	AHL	36	19	9	6	2038	76	2	2.24	....	....	....	....	....	....	....
2001-02	**San Jose**	**NHL**	**20**	**7**	**6**	**3**	**1037**	**43**	**2**	**2.49**	**1**	**0**	**0**	**8**	**0**	**0**	**0.00**
	Cleveland Barons	AHL	4	4	0	0	242	7	0	1.73	....	....	....	....	....	....	....
2002-03	**San Jose**	**NHL**	**22**	**5**	**14**	**0**	**1199**	**65**	**1**	**3.25**	....	....	....	....	....	....	....
2003-04	**Calgary**	**NHL**	**38**	**24**	**10**	**4**	**2301**	**65**	**4**	***1.69**	***26**	**15**	**11**	***1655**	**51**	***5**	**1.85**
2004-05	Timra IK	Sweden	46	....	....	....	2719	97	5	2.14	6	....	....	356	13	0	2.19
2005-06	**Calgary**	**NHL**	**74**	**42**	**20**	**11**	***4380**	**151**	***10**	***2.07**	**7**	**3**	**4**	**428**	**16**	**0**	**2.24**
	Finland	Olympics					DID NOT PLAY – INJURED										
2006-07	**Calgary**	**NHL**	**74**	**40**	**24**	**9**	**4419**	**181**	**7**	**2.46**	**6**	**2**	**4**	**384**	**18**	**0**	**2.81**
	NHL Totals		**233**	**120**	**75**	**27**	**13490**	**510**	**24**	**2.27**	**43**	**21**	**20**	**2624**	**90**	**5**	**2.06**

NHL First All-Star Team (2006) • Vezina Trophy (2006)

Played in NHL All-Star Game (2007)

Traded to **Calgary** by **San Jose** for Calgary's 2nd round choice (Marc-Edouard Vlasic) in 2005 Entry Draft, November 16, 2003. Signed as a free agent by **Timra** (Sweden), September 20, 2004.

KOLESNIK, Vitaly (koh-LEHZ-nihk, vih-TAL-ee) COL.

Goaltender. Catches left. 6'2", 198 lbs. Born, Ust-Kamenogorsk, USSR, August 20, 1979.

					Regular Season									Playoffs			
Season	Club	League	GP	W	L	O/T	Mins	GA	SO	Avg	GP	W	L	Mins	GA	SO	Avg
1997-98	Ust-Kam'gorsk 2	Russia-3	5	....	....	....	....	8	....	....	....	....	....	....	....	....	....
1998-99	Ust-Kam'gorsk 2	Russia-4	16	....	....	....	....	42	....	....	....	....	....	....	....	....	....
	Ust-Kamenogorsk	Russia-3	2	....	....	....	....	9	....	....	....	....	....	....	....	....	....
99-2000	Ust-Kamenogorsk	Russia-3	14	....	....	....	....	15	....	....	....	....	....	....	....	....	....
2000-01	Ust-Kamenogorsk	Russia-3					STATISTICS NOT AVAILABLE										
2001-02	Ust-Kamenogorsk	Russia-2	4	....	....	....	....	7	....	....	....	....	....	....	....	....	....
2002-03	Ust-Kamenogorsk	Russia-2	25	....	....	....	1308	46	2	2.11	....	....	....	....	....	....	....
2003-04	Ust-Kamenogorsk	Russia-2	35	....	....	....	1899	53	9	1.67	....	....	....	....	....	....	....
	Ust-Kamenogorsk	Kazakh.	15	....	....	....	....	15	....	....	....	....	....	....	....	....	....
2004-05	Ust-Kamenogorsk	Russia-2	42	....	....	....	2329	65	8	1.67	....	....	....	....	....	....	....
	Ust-Kamenogorsk	Kazakh.	20	....	....	....	22	....	....	....	....	....	....	....	....	....	....
2005-06	**Colorado**	**NHL**	**8**	**3**	**3**	**0**	**370**	**20**	**0**	**3.24**	....	....	....	....	....	....	....
	Lowell	AHL	29	15	13	0	1717	80	3	2.80	....	....	....	....	....	....	....
	Kazakhstan	Olympics	2	0	2	0	120	6	0	3.00	....	....	....	....	....	....	....

Season	Club	League	GP	W	L	O/T	Mins	GA	SO	Avg	GP	W	L	Mins	GA	SO	Avg
2006-07	Mytischi	Russia	38				2006	82	4	2.45	9			503	16	*3	1.91
	NHL Totals		**8**	**3**	**3**	**0**	**370**	**20**	**0**	**3.24**							

Signed as a free agent by **Colorado**, August 16, 2005. Signed as a free agent by **Mytischi** (Russia), July 6, 2006.

KOLZIG, Olaf (KOHL-zihg, OH-lahf) WSH.

Goaltender. Catches left. 6'3", 221 lbs. Born, Johannesburg, South Africa, April 6, 1970.
(Washington's 1st choice, 19th overall, in 1989 Entry Draft).

			Regular Season								Playoffs						
Season	Club	League	GP	W	L	O/T	Mins	GA	SO	Avg	GP	W	L	Mins	GA	SO	Avg
1986-87	Abbotsford Pilots	BCAHA	17	5	9	0	857	81	0	5.67							
1987-88	New Westminster	WHL	15	6	5	0	650	48	1	4.43	3	0	3	149	11	0	4.43
1988-89	Tri-City Americans	WHL	30	16	10	2	1671	97	1	*3.48							
1989-90	**Washington**	**NHL**	**2**	**0**	**2**	**0**	**120**	**12**	**0**	**6.00**							
	Tri-City Americans	WHL	48	21	18	3	2504	187	1	4.48	6	4	0	318	27	0	5.09
1990-91	Baltimore Skipjacks	AHL	26	10	12	1	1367	72	0	3.16							
	Hampton Roads	ECHL	21	11	9	1	1248	71	2	3.41	3	1	2	180	14	0	4.66
1991-92	Baltimore Skipjacks	AHL	28	5	17	2	1503	105	1	4.19							
	Hampton Roads	ECHL	14	11	3	0	847	41	0	2.90							
1992-93	**Washington**	**NHL**	**1**	**0**	**0**	**0**	**20**	**2**	**0**	**6.00**							
	Rochester	AHL	49	25	16	4	2737	168	0	3.68	*17	9	8	*1040	61	0	3.52
1993-94	**Washington**	**NHL**	**7**	**0**	**3**	**0**	**224**	**20**	**0**	**5.36**							
	Portland Pirates	AHL	29	16	8	5	1725	88	3	3.06	17	*12	5	1035	44	0	*2.55
1994-95	**Washington**	**NHL**	**14**	**2**	**8**	**2**	**724**	**30**	**0**	**2.49**	**2**	**1**	**0**	**44**	**1**	**0**	**1.36**
	Portland Pirates	AHL	2	1	0	1	125	3	0	1.44							
1995-96	**Washington**	**NHL**	**18**	**4**	**8**	**2**	**897**	**46**	**0**	**3.08**	**5**	**2**	**3**	**341**	**11**	**0**	***1.94**
	Portland Pirates	AHL	5	5	0	0	300	7	1	1.40							
1996-97	**Washington**	**NHL**	**29**	**8**	**15**	**4**	**1645**	**71**	**2**	**2.59**							
1997-98	**Washington**	**NHL**	**64**	**33**	**18**	**10**	**3788**	**139**	**5**	**2.20**	**21**	**12**	**9**	**1351**	**44**	***4**	**1.95**
	Germany	Olympics	2	2	0	0	120	2	1	1.00							
1998-99	**Washington**	**NHL**	**64**	**26**	**31**	**3**	**3586**	**154**	**4**	**2.58**							
99-2000	**Washington**	**NHL**	**73**	**41**	**20**	**11**	***4371**	**163**	**5**	**2.24**	**5**	**1**	**4**	**284**	**16**	**0**	**3.38**
2000-01	**Washington**	**NHL**	**72**	**37**	**26**	**8**	**4279**	**177**	**5**	**2.48**	**6**	**2**	**4**	**375**	**14**	**1**	**2.24**
2001-02	**Washington**	**NHL**	**71**	**31**	**29**	**8**	**4131**	**192**	**6**	**2.79**							
2002-03	**Washington**	**NHL**	**66**	**33**	**25**	**6**	**3894**	**156**	**4**	**2.40**	**6**	**2**	**4**	**404**	**14**	**1**	**2.08**
2003-04	**Washington**	**NHL**	**63**	**19**	**35**	**9**	**3738**	**180**	**2**	**2.89**							
2004-05	Eisbaren Berlin	Germany	8				452	19	2	2.52							
2005-06	**Washington**	**NHL**	**59**	**20**	**28**	**11**	**3506**	**206**	**0**	**3.53**							
	Germany	Olympics	3	0	1	2	179	8	0	2.68							
2006-07	**Washington**	**NHL**	**54**	**22**	**24**	**6**	**3184**	**159**	**1**	**3.00**							
	NHL Totals		**657**	**276**	**272**	**80**	**38107**	**1707**	**34**	**2.69**	**45**	**20**	**24**	**2799**	**100**	**6**	**2.14**

WHL West Second All-Star Team (1989) • Harry "Hap" Holmes Memorial Award (fewest goals against – AHL) (1994) (shared with Byron Dafoe) • Jack A. Butterfield Trophy (Playoff MVP – AHL) (1994) • NHL First All-Star Team (2000) • Vezina Trophy (2000) • King Clancy Memorial Trophy (2006)

Played in NHL All-Star Game (1998, 2000)

• Scored a goal while with Tri-City (WHL), November 29, 1989. Signed as a free agent by **Berlin** (Germany), February 2, 2005.

KOOPMANS, Logan (KOOP-manz, LOH-guhn) DET.

Goaltender. Catches left. 6'2", 182 lbs. Born, Cranbrook, B.C., May 18, 1984.
(Detroit's 5th choice, 166th overall, in 2002 Entry Draft).

			Regular Season								Playoffs						
Season	Club	League	GP	W	L	O/T	Mins	GA	SO	Avg	GP	W	L	Mins	GA	SO	Avg
99-2000	Lethbridge	WHL	5	1	3	0	282	19	0	4.04							
2000-01	Columbia Valley	KIJHL	37				2140	144	1	3.90							
2001-02	Lethbridge	WHL	37	20	12	2	2057	97	3	2.83	4	0	4	237	14	0	3.54
2002-03	Lethbridge	WHL	34	9	17	0	1628	131	1	4.83							
2003-04	Lethbridge	WHL	62	27	25	8	3565	155	5	2.61							
2004-05	Toledo Storm	ECHL	25	12	10	1	1299	61	2	2.82							
2005-06	Grand Rapids	AHL	1	0	1	0	40	5	0	7.54							
	Toledo Storm	ECHL	12	7	2	2	677	33	1	2.93	7	2	5	434	28	0	3.87
2006-07	Toledo Storm	ECHL	26	17	7	1	1463	69	2	2.83	2	0	2	118	9	0	4.57

KOPRIVA, Miroslav (koh-PREE-vuh, MEER-oh-slav) MIN.

Goaltender. Catches left. 6'4", 206 lbs. Born, Kladno, Czech., December 5, 1983.
(Minnesota's 5th choice, 187th overall, in 2003 Entry Draft).

			Regular Season								Playoffs						
Season	Club	League	GP	W	L	O/T	Mins	GA	SO	Avg	GP	W	L	Mins	GA	SO	Avg
99-2000	HC Kladno Jr.	CzRep-Jr.	46				2510	121	4	2.89	4			249	13	0	3.13
2000-01	HC Kladno Jr.	CzRep-Jr.	26				1478	65	2	2.64							
2001-02	HC Kladno Jr.	CzRep-Jr.	41				2367	124	6	3.14							
2002-03	HC Kladno Jr.	CzRep-Jr.	42				2464	80	5	1.95	11			661	16	2	1.45
2003-04	HC Kladno Jr.	CzRep-Jr.	4				240	10	1	2.50							
	Beroun	CzRep-2	31				1837	58	3	1.89							
	HC Rabat Kladno	CzRep	13				687	46	2	4.02							
2004-05	HC Rabat Kladno	CzRep	10				426	19	1	2.68							
	Beroun	CzRep-2	31				1841	59	4	1.92	1			58	2	0	2.07
2005-06	Houston Aeros	AHL	12	6	4	1	649	38	0	3.52							
	Austin Ice Bats	CHL	15	12	3	0	900	35	1	2.33							
2006-07	Houston Aeros	AHL	13	3	6	1	677	42	0	3.72							
	Texas Wildcatters	ECHL	19	9	1	2	910	46	1	3.03							

KOSHECHKIN, Vasily (KOH-shech-kihn, va-SEE-lee) T.B.

Goaltender. Catches left. 6'6", 210 lbs. Born, Togliatti, USSR, March 27, 1983.
(Tampa Bay's 9th choice, 233rd overall, in 2002 Entry Draft).

			Regular Season								Playoffs						
Season	Club	League	GP	W	L	O/T	Mins	GA	SO	Avg	GP	W	L	Mins	GA	SO	Avg
1998-99	Lada Togliatti 2	Russia-4	8					8									
99-2000	Lada Togliatti 2	Russia-3	18					20									
2000-01	Lada Togliatti 2	Russia-3					STATISTICS NOT AVAILABLE										
2001-02	Lada Togliatti 2	Russia-3					STATISTICS NOT AVAILABLE										
2002-03	Lada Togliatti 2	Russia-3					STATISTICS NOT AVAILABLE										
	Kirovo-Chepetsk	Russia-2	10				613	14	3	1.37							
	Almetjevsk	Russia-2	14				675	29	1	2.58							
2003-04	Lada Togliatti 2	Russia-3	13					19	1		3						
	Lada Togliatti	Russia	8				247	10	0	2.43	1			40	3	0	4.50
2004-05	Lada Togliatti	Russia	4				121	5	0	2.47							
	Lada Togliatti	Russia	4				121	5	0	2.47							
2005-06	Lada Togliatti	Russia	41				2375	63	9	1.59	8			474	20	1	2.53
2006-07	Lada Togliatti	Russia	42				2430	82	5	2.02	3			179	13	0	4.35

KOVAR, Jakub (KOH-vahr, YA-kuhb) PHI.

Goaltender. Catches left. 6', 193 lbs. Born, Pisek, Czech., July 19, 1988.
(Philadelphia's 7th choice, 109th overall, in 2006 Entry Draft).

			Regular Season								Playoffs						
Season	Club	League	GP	W	L	O/T	Mins	GA	SO	Avg	GP	W	L	Mins	GA	SO	Avg
2004-05	IHC Pisek U17	CzR-U17	40				2298	137	4	3.58							
2005-06	C. Budejovice Jr.	CzRep-Jr.	19				1048	39	2	2.23	5			304	8	0	1.58
2006-07	C. Budejovice Jr.	CzRep-Jr.	38				2231	77	3	2.07	3			160	16	0	6.00

KRAHN, Brent (KRAWN, BREHNT) CGY.

Goaltender. Catches left. 6'5", 220 lbs. Born, Winnipeg, Man., April 2, 1982.
(Calgary's 1st choice, 9th overall, in 2000 Entry Draft).

			Regular Season								Playoffs						
Season	Club	League	GP	W	L	O/T	Mins	GA	SO	Avg	GP	W	L	Mins	GA	SO	Avg
1997-98	Pembina Valley	MMMHL	22	20	0	1	1265	40	3	1.90	2	2	0	120	2	1	1.00
1998-99	Pembina Valley	MMMHL	13	10	3	0	770	30	2	2.34							
99-2000	Calgary Hitmen	WHL	39	33	6	0	2315	92	4	2.38	5	2	2	266	13	0	2.93
2000-01	Calgary Hitmen	WHL	37	22	10	3	2087	104	1	2.99							
2001-02	Calgary Hitmen	WHL	18	8	6	2	1033	61	0	3.54	2	1	1	119	6	0	3.03
2002-03	Calgary Hitmen	WHL	23	11	10	2	1343	72	2	3.22							
	Seattle	WHL	5	5	0	0	302	9	2	1.79	15	9	6	960	38	2	2.38
2003-04	San Antonio	AHL	14	3	7	1	715	41	0	3.44							
	Lowell	AHL	7	2	3	0	344	15	0	2.62							
	Las Vegas	ECHL	14	7	5	2	828	36	0	2.61							
2004-05	Lowell	AHL	35	20	11	2	1998	83	6	2.49	1	0	0	1	0	0	0.00
2005-06	Omaha	AHL	57	26	20	9	3241	135	3	2.50							
2006-07	Omaha	AHL	28	14	12	0	1564	63	2	2.42	1	0	1	59	3	0	3.06

• Missed majority of 2001-02 season recovering from knee surgery, June, 2001.

LABARBERA, Jason (lah-BAR-buhr-uh, JAY-suhn) L.A.

Goaltender. Catches left. 6'3", 230 lbs. Born, Burnaby, B.C., January 18, 1980.
(NY Rangers' 3rd choice, 66th overall, in 1998 Entry Draft).

			Regular Season								Playoffs						
Season	Club	League	GP	W	L	O/T	Mins	GA	SO	Avg	GP	W	L	Mins	GA	SO	Avg
1995-96	Prince George	BCAHA	31				1860	83	0	2.68							
1996-97	Tri-City Americans	WHL	2	1	0	0	63	4	0	3.81							
	Portland	WHL	9	5	1	1	443	18	0	2.44							
1997-98	Portland	WHL	23	18	4	0	1305	72	1	3.31							
1998-99	Portland	WHL	51	18	23	9	2991	170	4	3.41	4	0	4	252	19	0	4.52
99-2000	Portland	WHL	34	8	24	2	2005	123	1	3.68							
	Spokane Chiefs	WHL	21	12	6	2	1146	50	0	2.62	9	6	1	435	18	1	2.48
2000-01	**NY Rangers**	**NHL**	**1**	**0**	**0**	**0**	**10**	**0**	**0**	**0.00**							
	Hartford Wolf Pack	AHL	4	1	1	0	156	12	0	4.61							
	Charlotte Checkers	ECHL	35	18	10	7	2100	112	1	3.20	2	1	1	143	5	0	2.09
2001-02	Charlotte Checkers	ECHL	13	9	3	1	744	29	0	2.34	4	2	2	212	12	0	3.39
	Hartford Wolf Pack	AHL	20	7	11	1	1058	55	0	3.12							
2002-03	Hartford Wolf Pack	AHL	46	18	17	6	2452	105	2	2.57	2	0	2	117	6	0	3.07
2003-04	**NY Rangers**	**NHL**	**4**	**1**	**2**	**0**	**198**	**16**	**0**	**4.85**							
	Hartford Wolf Pack	AHL	59	34	9	9	3393	90	*13	1.59	16	11	5	1043	30	*3	*1.73
2004-05	Hartford Wolf Pack	AHL	53	31	16	2	2937	90	6	1.84	4	1	3	238	9	0	2.27
2005-06	**Los Angeles**	**NHL**	**29**	**11**	**9**	**2**	**1433**	**69**	**1**	**2.89**							
	Manchester	AHL	3	1	1	1	185	10	0	3.25							
2006-07	Manchester	AHL	*62	*39	20	1	*3619	133	*7	2.21	13	6	7	824	38	1	2.77
	NHL Totals		**34**	**12**	**11**	**2**	**1641**	**85**	**1**	**3.11**							

AHL First All-Star Team (2004, 2007) • Aldege "Baz" Bastien Memorial Award (Outstanding Goaltender - AHL) (2004, 2007) • Les Cunningham Award (MVP - AHL) (2004) • Harry "Hap" Holmes Memorial Trophy (fewest goals against - AHL) (shared with Steve Valiquette) (2005) • Harry "Hap" Holmes Memorial Trophy (fewest goals against - AHL) (2007)

Signed as a free agent by **Los Angeles**, August 2, 2005.

LACASSE, Loic (luh-KAS, LOIK) MTL.

Goaltender. Catches left. 6'3", 178 lbs. Born, Granby, Que., April 23, 1986.
(Montreal's 5th choice, 181st overall, in 2004 Entry Draft).

			Regular Season								Playoffs						
Season	Club	League	GP	W	L	O/T	Mins	GA	SO	Avg	GP	W	L	Mins	GA	SO	Avg
2002-03	Antoine-Girouard	QAAA	24	22	1	1	1453	50	1	2.07							
2003-04	Baie-Comeau	QMJHL	41	9	15	4	1758	117	0	3.99	4	0	4	172	16	0	5.57
2004-05	Baie-Comeau	QMJHL	39	10	22	2	2001	138	1	4.14	2	0	1	54	2	0	2.21
2005-06	Baie-Comeau	QMJHL	27	10	12	0	1394	94	1	4.05							
	Drummondville	QMJHL	6	2	3	0	272	18	0	3.97	5	3	2	280	13	0	2.78
2006-07	Oshawa Generals	OHL	33	16	12	5	1964	129	3	3.94	9	3	5	523	43	0	4.93

LACOSTA, Dan (luh-KAWS-tah, DAN) CBJ

Goaltender. Catches left. 6'2", 186 lbs. Born, Labrador City, Nfld., March 28, 1986.
(Columbus' 4th choice, 93rd overall, in 2004 Entry Draft).

			Regular Season								Playoffs						
Season	Club	League	GP	W	L	O/T	Mins	GA	SO	Avg	GP	W	L	Mins	GA	SO	Avg
2001-02	Wellington Dukes	OPJHL	24	19	2	3	1377	44	2	*1.92							
2002-03	Owen Sound	OHL	28	8	10	3	1321	82	0	3.72							
2003-04	Owen Sound	OHL	37	17	10	1	1810	82	4	2.72							
2004-05	Owen Sound	OHL	25	15	7	2	1423	70	0	2.95							
	Barrie Colts	OHL	21	10	5	2	1054	48	1	2.73	5	1	2	215	11	0	3.07
2005-06	Barrie Colts	OHL	*59	36	17	4	3340	142	6	2.55	11	5	2	654	34	0	3.12
2006-07	Syracuse Crunch	AHL	19	5	7	1	852	40	3	2.82							
	Dayton Bombers	ECHL	10	3	5	1	556	32	0	3.45							

LAFLEUR, Antoine (lah-FLEWR, AN-twuhn) NYR

Goaltender. Catches left. 6'4", 186 lbs. Born, Gatineau, Que., December 12, 1988.
(NY Rangers' 2nd choice, 48th overall, in 2007 Entry Draft).

			Regular Season								Playoffs						
Season	Club	League	GP	W	L	O/T	Mins	GA	SO	Avg	GP	W	L	Mins	GA	SO	Avg
2005-06	PEI Rocket	QMJHL	18	2	7	0	710	56	0	4.73	2	0	0	9	0	0	0.00
2006-07	PEI Rocket	QMJHL	49	27	19		2708	134	3	2.97	7	3	4	430	30	0	4.19

LALANDE, Kevin (lah-LAWND, KEH-vihn) CGY.

Goaltender. Catches left. 6', 182 lbs. Born, Kingston, Ont., February 19, 1987.
(Calgary's 5th choice, 128th overall, in 2005 Entry Draft).

			Regular Season								Playoffs						
Season	Club	League	GP	W	L	O/T	Mins	GA	SO	Avg	GP	W	L	Mins	GA	SO	Avg
2003-04	Hawkesbury	CJHL	35				2010	105	3	3.13	6			286	19	0	3.99
	Belleville Bulls	OHL	3	1	2	0	133	15	0	6.77							
2004-05	Belleville Bulls	OHL	30	15	11	3	1797	79	1	2.64	2	0	2	120	8	0	4.00
2005-06	Belleville Bulls	OHL	50	24	17	5	2789	143	3	3.08							
2006-07	Belleville Bulls	OHL	48	27	17	3	2772	139	3	3.01	15	10	1	989	42	*1	2.55

LALIME, Patrick (lah-LEEM, PAT-rihk) CHI.

Goaltender. Catches left. 6'3", 189 lbs. Born, St-Bonaventure, Que., July 7, 1974.
(Pittsburgh's 6th choice, 156th overall, in 1993 Entry Draft).

			Regular Season								Playoffs						
Season	Club	League	GP	W	L	O/T	Mins	GA	SO	Avg	GP	W	L	Mins	GA	SO	Avg
1990-91	Abitibi Foresters	QAAA	26	9	17	0	1595	151	0	5.81							
1991-92	Shawinigan	QMJHL	6				272	25	0	5.50							
1992-93	Shawinigan	QMJHL	44	10	24	4	2467	192	0	4.67							
1993-94	Shawinigan	QMJHL	48	22	20	0	2733	192	1	4.22	5	1	3	223	25	0	6.73
1994-95	Hampton Roads	ECHL	26	15	7	3	1470	82	2	3.35							
	Cleveland	IHL	23	7	10	4	1230	91	0	4.44							
1995-96	Cleveland	IHL	41	20	12	7	2314	149	0	3.86							
1996-97	**Pittsburgh**	**NHL**	**39**	**21**	**12**	**2**	**2058**	**101**	**3**	**2.94**							
	Cleveland	IHL	14	6	6	2	834	45	1	3.24							

Season	Club	League	GP	W	L	O/T	Mins	GA	SO	Avg	GP	W	L	Mins	GA	SO	Avg
1997-98	Grand Rapids	IHL	31	10	10	9	1749	76	2	2.61	1	0	1	77	4	0	3.11
1998-99	Kansas City Blades	IHL	*66	*39	20	4	*3789	190	2	3.01	3	1	2	179	6	1	2.01
99-2000	**Ottawa**	**NHL**	**38**	**19**	**14**	**3**	**2038**	**79**	**3**	**2.33**	....	....	....	....	....	....	....
2000-01	**Ottawa**	**NHL**	**60**	**36**	**19**	**5**	**3607**	**141**	**7**	**2.35**	**4**	**0**	**4**	**251**	**10**	**0**	**2.39**
2001-02	**Ottawa**	**NHL**	**61**	**27**	**24**	**8**	**3583**	**148**	**7**	**2.48**	**12**	**7**	**5**	**778**	**18**	**4**	***1.39**
2002-03	**Ottawa**	**NHL**	**67**	**39**	**20**	**7**	**3943**	**142**	**8**	**2.16**	**18**	**11**	**7**	**1122**	**34**	**1**	**1.82**
2003-04	**Ottawa**	**NHL**	**57**	**25**	**23**	**7**	**3324**	**127**	**5**	**2.29**	**7**	**3**	**4**	**398**	**13**	**0**	**1.96**
2004-05							DID NOT PLAY										
2005-06	**St. Louis**	**NHL**	**31**	**4**	**18**	**8**	**1699**	**103**	**0**	**3.64**	....	....	....	....	....	....	....
	Peoria Rivermen	AHL	14	6	6	1	798	38	1	2.86	....	....	....	....	....	....	....
2006-07	**Chicago**	**NHL**	**12**	**4**	**6**	**1**	**645**	**33**	**1**	**3.07**	....	....	....	....	....	....	....
	Norfolk Admirals	AHL	4	3	1	0	241	10	0	2.49	....	....	....	....	....	....	....
	NHL Totals		**365**	**175**	**136**	**41**	**20897**	**874**	**34**	**2.51**	**41**	**21**	**20**	**2549**	**75**	**5**	**1.77**

NHL All-Rookie Team (1997) • IHL First All-Star Team (1999)

Played in NHL All-Star Game (2003)

Rights traded to **Anaheim** by **Pittsburgh** for Sean Pronger, March 24, 1998. Traded to **Ottawa** by **Anaheim** for Ted Donato and the rights to Antti-Jussi Niemi, June 18, 1999. Traded to **St. Louis** by **Ottawa** for St. Louis' 4th round choice (Ilja Zubov) in 2005 Entry Draft, June 27, 2004. Signed as a free agent by **Chicago**, July 1, 2006.

LAMOTHE, Marc
(luh-MAWTH, MAHRK)

Goaltender. Catches left. 6'2", 210 lbs. Born, New Liskeard, Ont., February 27, 1974.
(Montreal's 6th choice, 92nd overall, in 1992 Entry Draft).

			Regular Season								Playoffs						
Season	Club	League	GP	W	L	O/T	Mins	GA	SO	Avg	GP	W	L	Mins	GA	SO	Avg
1990-91	Ott. Jr. Senators	CJHL	25	13	7	0	1220	82	1	4.03	....	....	....	....	....	....	....
1991-92	Kingston	OHL	42	10	25	2	2378	189	1	4.77	....	....	....	....	....	....	....
1992-93	Kingston	OHL	45	23	12	6	2489	162	1	3.91	15	8	5	753	48	1	3.82
1993-94	Kingston	OHL	48	23	20	5	2828	177	*2	3.76	6	2	2	224	12	0	3.21
1994-95	Fredericton	AHL	9	2	5	0	428	32	0	4.48	....	....	....	....	....	....	....
	Wheeling	ECHL	13	9	2	1	737	38	0	3.10	....	....	....	....	....	....	....
1995-96	Fredericton	AHL	23	5	9	3	1166	73	1	3.76	3	1	2	161	9	0	3.36
1996-97	Indianapolis Ice	IHL	38	20	14	4	2271	100	1	2.64	1	0	0	20	1	0	3.00
1997-98	Indianapolis Ice	IHL	31	18	10	2	1772	72	3	2.44	4	1	3	177	10	0	3.38
1998-99	Indianapolis Ice	IHL	32	9	16	6	1823	115	1	3.78	6	3	3	338	10	*2	1.78
99-2000	**Chicago**	**NHL**	**2**	**1**	**1**	**0**	**116**	**10**	**0**	**5.17**	....	....	....	....	....	....	....
	Cleveland	IHL	44	19	18	4	2455	112	2	2.74	4	2	2	325	12	0	2.21
2000-01	Syracuse Crunch	AHL	42	17	15	7	2323	112	2	2.89	....	....	....	....	....	....	....
2001-02	Hamilton Bulldogs	AHL	45	22	19	2	2569	102	3	2.38	9	6	3	551	18	0	1.96
2002-03	Grand Rapids	AHL	*60	*33	18	8	*3438	122	6	2.13	15	10	5	945	29	1	1.84
2003-04	**Detroit**	**NHL**	**2**	**1**	**0**	**1**	**125**	**3**	**0**	**1.44**	....	....	....	....	....	....	....
	Grand Rapids	AHL	43	21	16	5	2535	87	4	2.06	4	0	3	200	12	0	3.60
2004-05	Yaroslavl	Russia	55	....	....	....	3357	90	6	1.61	9	....	....	521	21	0	2.42
2005-06	Cherepovets	Russia	42	....	....	....	2378	79	4	1.99	4	....	....	239	9	1	2.26
2006-07	Cherepovets	Russia	42	....	....	....	2384	88	5	2.21	4	....	....	219	6	1	1.64
	NHL Totals		**4**	**2**	**1**	**1**	**241**	**13**	**0**	**3.24**	....	....	....	....	....	....	....

AHL First All-Star Team (2003) • Harry "Hap" Holmes Memorial Award (fewest goals against – AHL) (2003) (shared with Joey MacDonald) • Aldege "Baz" Bastien Memorial Award (Outstanding Goaltender – AHL) (2003)

Signed as a free agent by **Chicago**, September 26, 1996. Signed as a free agent by **Edmonton**, August 16, 2001. Signed as a free agent by **Detroit**, August 5, 2002. Signed as a free agent by **Yaroslavl** (Russia), June 14, 2004. Signed as a free agent by **Cherepovets** (Russia), July 22, 2005.

LARSSON, Daniel
(LAR-suhn, DAN-yehl) **DET.**

Goaltender. Catches left. 6', 170 lbs. Born, Boden, Sweden, February 7, 1986.
(Detroit's 4th choice, 92nd overall, in 2006 Entry Draft).

			Regular Season								Playoffs						
Season	Club	League	GP	W	L	O/T	Mins	GA	SO	Avg	GP	W	L	Mins	GA	SO	Avg
2002-03	Lulea HF U18	Swe-U18	12	....	....	....	731	50	0	4.10	....	....	....	....	....	....	....
2003-04	Lulea HF Jr.	Swe-Jr.	4	....	....	....	239	12	0	3.01	....	....	....	....	....	....	....
	Bodens IK	Sweden-2	1	....	....	....	20	1	0	3.00	....	....	....	....	....	....	....
2004-05	Bodens IK	Sweden-2	28	....	....	....	1514	97	1	3.84	....	....	....	....	....	....	....
2005-06	Hammarby Jr.	Swe-Jr.	9	....	....	....	548	24	1	2.63	....	....	....	....	....	....	....
	Hammarby	Sweden-2	36	....	....	....	2001	90	0	2.70	....	....	....	....	....	....	....
2006-07	Djurgarden	Sweden	24	....	....	....	1259	53	3	2.53	....	....	....	....	....	....	....

LECLAIRE, Pascal
(luh-KLAIR, pas-KAL) **CBJ**

Goaltender. Catches left. 6'2", 200 lbs. Born, Repentigny, Que., November 7, 1982.
(Columbus' 1st choice, 8th overall, in 2001 Entry Draft).

			Regular Season								Playoffs						
Season	Club	League	GP	W	L	O/T	Mins	GA	SO	Avg	GP	W	L	Mins	GA	SO	Avg
1997-98	Cap-d-Madeleine	QAAA	26	6	17	3	1580	127	0	4.90	....	....	....	....	....	....	....
1998-99	Halifax	QMJHL	33	19	11	1	1828	96	2	3.15	1	0	0	17	2	0	7.06
99-2000	Halifax	QMJHL	31	16	8	4	1729	103	1	3.57	5	1	2	198	12	0	3.65
2000-01	Halifax	QMJHL	35	14	16	5	2111	126	1	3.58	2	0	2	109	10	0	5.49
2001-02	Montreal Rocket	QMJHL	45	15	23	4	2513	138	1	3.29	7	3	4	441	15	0	*2.04
2002-03	Syracuse Crunch	AHL	36	8	21	3	1886	112	0	3.56	....	....	....	....	....	....	....
2003-04	**Columbus**	**NHL**	**2**	**0**	**2**	**0**	**119**	**7**	**0**	**3.53**	....	....	....	....	....	....	....
	Syracuse Crunch	AHL	44	21	16	3	2447	125	2	3.06	3	1	2	142	12	0	5.07
2004-05	Syracuse Crunch	AHL	14	5	6	3	845	33	2	2.34	....	....	....	....	....	....	....
2005-06	**Columbus**	**NHL**	**33**	**11**	**15**	**3**	**1804**	**97**	**0**	**3.23**	....	....	....	....	....	....	....
	Syracuse Crunch	AHL	7	3	3	0	340	16	1	2.82	5	2	3	288	11	1	2.29
2006-07	**Columbus**	**NHL**	**24**	**6**	**15**	**2**	**1315**	**65**	**1**	**2.97**	....	....	....	....	....	....	....
	NHL Totals		**59**	**17**	**32**	**5**	**3238**	**169**	**1**	**3.13**	....	....	....	....	....	....	....

LEGACE, Manny
(LEH-gah-see, MAN-ee) **ST.L.**

Goaltender. Catches left. 5'9", 204 lbs. Born, Toronto, Ont., February 4, 1973.
(Hartford's 5th choice, 188th overall, in 1993 Entry Draft).

			Regular Season								Playoffs						
Season	Club	League	GP	W	L	O/T	Mins	GA	SO	Avg	GP	W	L	Mins	GA	SO	Avg
1987-88	Alliston Hornets	OJHL-C	16	7	9	0	960	83	0	5.17	....	....	....	....	....	....	....
1988-89	Vaughan Raiders	MTJHL	23	....	....	....	1303	92	1	4.24	....	....	....	....	....	....	....
1989-90	Vaughan Raiders	MTJHL	21	8	11	1	1180	89	1	4.53	....	....	....	....	....	....	....
	Thornhill	OHA-B	8	3	3	2	480	30	0	3.75	....	....	....	....	....	....	....
1990-91	Niagara Falls	OHL	30	13	11	2	1515	107	0	4.24	4	1	1	119	10	0	5.04
1991-92	Niagara Falls	OHL	43	21	16	3	2384	143	0	3.60	14	8	5	791	56	0	4.25
1992-93	Niagara Falls	OHL	48	22	19	3	2630	171	0	3.90	4	0	4	240	18	0	4.50
1993-94	Canada	Nat-Tm	16	8	6	0	859	36	2	2.51	....	....	....	....	....	....	....
1994-95	Springfield Indians	AHL	39	12	17	6	2169	128	2	3.54	....	....	....	....	....	....	....
1995-96	Springfield Falcons	AHL	37	20	12	4	2196	83	*5	*2.27	4	1	3	220	18	0	4.91
1996-97	Springfield Falcons	AHL	36	17	14	5	2119	107	1	3.03	12	9	3	745	25	*2	2.01
	Richmond	ECHL	3	2	1	0	157	8	0	3.05	....	....	....	....	....	....	....
1997-98	Springfield Falcons	AHL	6	4	2	0	345	16	0	2.78	....	....	....	....	....	....	....
	Las Vegas Thunder	IHL	41	18	16	4	2106	111	1	3.16	4	1	3	237	16	0	4.05
1998-99	**Los Angeles**	**NHL**	**17**	**2**	**9**	**2**	**899**	**39**	**0**	**2.60**	....	....	....	....	....	....	....
	Long Beach	IHL	33	22	8	1	1796	67	2	2.24	6	4	2	338	9	0	*1.60
99-2000	**Detroit**	**NHL**	**4**	**4**	**0**	**0**	**240**	**11**	**0**	**2.75**	....	....	....	....	....	....	....
	Manitoba Moose	IHL	42	17	18	5	2409	104	2	2.59	2	0	2	141	7	0	2.97
2000-01	**Detroit**	**NHL**	**39**	**24**	**5**	**5**	**2136**	**73**	**2**	**2.05**	....	....	....	....	....	....	....
2001-02 ♦	**Detroit**	**NHL**	**20**	**10**	**6**	**2**	**1117**	**45**	**1**	**2.42**	**1**	**0**	**0**	**11**	**1**	**0**	**5.45**
2002-03	**Detroit**	**NHL**	**25**	**14**	**5**	**4**	**1406**	**51**	**0**	**2.18**	....	....	....	....	....	....	....
2003-04	**Detroit**	**NHL**	**41**	**23**	**10**	**5**	**2325**	**82**	**3**	**2.12**	**4**	**2**	**2**	**220**	**8**	**0**	**2.18**
2004-05	Voskresensk	Russia	2	....	....	....	89	10	0	6.73	....	....	....	....	....	....	....
2005-06	**Detroit**	**NHL**	**51**	**37**	**8**	**3**	**2905**	**106**	**7**	**2.19**	**6**	**2**	**4**	**408**	**18**	**0**	**2.65**
	Grand Rapids	AHL	1	1	0	0	60	2	0	2.00	....	....	....	....	....	....	....
2006-07	**St. Louis**	**NHL**	**45**	**23**	**15**	**5**	**2522**	**109**	**5**	**2.59**	....	....	....	....	....	....	....
	NHL Totals		**242**	**137**	**58**	**26**	**13550**	**516**	**18**	**2.28**	**11**	**4**	**6**	**639**	**27**	**0**	**2.54**

OHL First All-Star Team (1993) • AHL First All-Star Team (1996) • Harry "Hap" Holmes Memorial Award (fewest goals against – AHL) (1996) (shared with Scott Langkow) • Aldege "Baz" Bastien Memorial Award (Outstanding Goaltender – AHL) (1996)

Rights transferred to **Carolina** after **Hartford** franchise relocated, June 25, 1997. Traded to **Los Angeles** by **Carolina** for future considerations, July 31, 1998. Signed as a free agent by **Detroit**, August 9, 1999. Claimed on waivers by **Vancouver** from **Detroit**, September 30, 1999. Claimed on waivers by **Detroit** from **Vancouver**, October 13, 1999. Signed as a free agent by **Voskresensk** (Russia), December 20, 2004. Signed as a free agent by **St. Louis**, August 8, 2006.

LEHTONEN, Kari
(LEH-tuh-nehn, KAH-ree) **ATL.**

Goaltender. Catches left. 6'4", 200 lbs. Born, Helsinki, Finland, November 16, 1983.
(Atlanta's 1st choice, 2nd overall, in 2002 Entry Draft).

			Regular Season								Playoffs						
Season	Club	League	GP	W	L	O/T	Mins	GA	SO	Avg	GP	W	L	Mins	GA	SO	Avg
1998-99	Jokerit U18	Fin-U18	2	....	....	....	....	....	....	....	4	2	2	240	7	0	1.75
99-2000	Jokerit Helsinki Jr.	Fin-Jr.	33	21	9	3	1974	86	2	2.61	12	9	3	758	14	4	1.11
2000-01	Jokerit U18	Fin-U18	....	....	....	....	....	....	....	....	6	....	....	....	....	....	....
	Jokerit Helsinki Jr.	Fin-Jr.	31	20	9	1	1799	71	3	2.37	1	0	1	54	4	0	4.44
	Jokerit Helsinki	Finland	4	3	1	0	189	6	0	1.90	....	....	....	....	....	....	....
2001-02	Jokerit Helsinki Jr.	Fin-Jr.	6	5	1	0	360	11	1	1.83	....	....	....	....	....	....	....
	Jokerit Helsinki	Finland	23	13	5	2	1242	37	4	1.79	11	8	2	623	18	3	1.73
2002-03	Jokerit Helsinki	Finland	45	23	14	6	2634	87	5	1.98	10	6	4	626	17	2	1.63
2003-04	**Atlanta**	**NHL**	**4**	**4**	**0**	**0**	**240**	**5**	**1**	**1.25**	....	....	....	....	....	....	....
	Chicago Wolves	AHL	39	20	14	2	2192	88	3	2.41	10	6	4	663	23	1	2.08
2004-05	Chicago Wolves	AHL	57	38	17	2	3378	128	5	2.27	16	10	6	983	28	2	*1.71
2005-06	**Atlanta**	**NHL**	**38**	**20**	**15**	**0**	**2166**	**106**	**2**	**2.94**	....	....	....	....	....	....	....
2006-07	**Atlanta**	**NHL**	**68**	**34**	**24**	**9**	**3934**	**183**	**4**	**2.79**	**2**	**0**	**2**	**118**	**11**	**0**	**5.59**
	NHL Totals		**110**	**58**	**39**	**9**	**6340**	**294**	**7**	**2.78**	**2**	**0**	**2**	**118**	**11**	**0**	**5.59**

AHL Second All-Star Team (2005)

LEIGHTON, Michael
(LAY-tohn, MIGH-kuhl) **CAR.**

Goaltender. Catches left. 6'3", 186 lbs. Born, Petrolia, Ont., May 19, 1981.
(Chicago's 5th choice, 165th overall, in 1999 Entry Draft).

			Regular Season								Playoffs						
Season	Club	League	GP	W	L	O/T	Mins	GA	SO	Avg	GP	W	L	Mins	GA	SO	Avg
1997-98	Petrolia Jets	OHA-B	30	....	....	....	1583	87	2	3.30	....	....	....	....	....	....	....
1998-99	Windsor Spitfires	OHL	28	4	17	2	1389	112	0	4.84	3	0	1	80	10	0	7.50
99-2000	Windsor Spitfires	OHL	42	17	17	2	2272	118	1	3.12	12	5	6	616	32	0	3.12
2000-01	Windsor Spitfires	OHL	54	32	13	5	3035	138	2	2.73	9	4	5	519	27	1	3.12
2001-02	Norfolk Admirals	AHL	52	27	16	8	3114	111	6	2.14	4	1	2	238	8	0	2.02
2002-03	**Chicago**	**NHL**	**8**	**2**	**3**	**2**	**447**	**21**	**1**	**2.82**	....	....	....	....	....	....	....
	Norfolk Admirals	AHL	36	18	13	5	2184	91	4	2.50	4	3	1	240	7	1	1.75
2003-04	**Chicago**	**NHL**	**34**	**6**	**18**	**8**	**1988**	**99**	**2**	**2.99**	....	....	....	....	....	....	....
	Norfolk Admirals	AHL	18	10	7	1	1081	33	1	1.83	4	2	1	212	2	2	0.57
2004-05	Norfolk Admirals	AHL	41	20	16	3	2319	78	7	2.02	....	....	....	....	....	....	....
2005-06	Rochester	AHL	40	15	22	1	2318	124	2	3.21	....	....	....	....	....	....	....
2006-07	Portland Pirates	AHL	16	8	6	1	962	37	2	2.31	....	....	....	....	....	....	....
	Nashville	**NHL**	**1**	**0**	**0**	**0**	**20**	**2**	**0**	**6.00**	....	....	....	....	....	....	....
	Philadelphia	**NHL**	**4**	**2**	**2**	**0**	**195**	**12**	**0**	**3.69**	....	....	....	....	....	....	....
	Philadelphia	AHL	5	2	0	2	270	7	0	1.56	....	....	....	....	....	....	....
	NHL Totals		**47**	**10**	**23**	**10**	**2650**	**134**	**3**	**3.03**	....	....	....	....	....	....	....

AHL All-Rookie Team (2002)

Traded to **Buffalo** by **Chicago** for Milan Bartovic, October 4, 2005. Signed as a free agent by **Anaheim**, July 13, 2006. Claimed on waivers by **Nashville** from **Anaheim**, November 27, 2006. Claimed on waivers by **Philadelphia** from **Nashville**, January 11, 2007. Claimed on waivers by **Montreal** from **Philadelphia**, February 27, 2007. Traded to **Carolina** by **Montreal** for Carolina's 7th round choice (Scott Kishel) in 2007 Entry Draft, June 23, 2007.

LeNEVEU, David
(LEH-neh-voo, DAY-vihd) **PHX.**

Goaltender. Catches left. 6'1", 187 lbs. Born, Fernie, B.C., May 23, 1983.
(Phoenix's 3rd choice, 46th overall, in 2002 Entry Draft).

			Regular Season								Playoffs						
Season	Club	League	GP	W	L	O/T	Mins	GA	SO	Avg	GP	W	L	Mins	GA	SO	Avg
99-2000	Fernie Ghostriders	AWHL	22	15	2	0	1140	48	0	2.49	....	....	....	....	....	....	....
2000-01	Nanaimo Clippers	BCHL	41	....	....	....	2330	127	6	3.29	....	....	....	....	....	....	....
2001-02	Cornell Big Red	ECAC	14	11	2	1	842	21	2	*1.50	....	....	....	....	....	....	....
2002-03	Cornell Big Red	ECAC	32	*28	3	1	1946	39	*9	*1.20	....	....	....	....	....	....	....
2003-04	Springfield Falcons	AHL	38	16	19	3	2217	102	1	2.76	....	....	....	....	....	....	....
2004-05	Utah Grizzlies	AHL	48	11	32	3	2702	132	0	2.93	....	....	....	....	....	....	....
2005-06	**Phoenix**	**NHL**	**15**	**3**	**8**	**2**	**814**	**44**	**0**	**3.24**	....	....	....	....	....	....	....
	San Antonio	AHL	28	10	16	2	1646	80	2	2.92	....	....	....	....	....	....	....
2006-07	**Phoenix**	**NHL**	**6**	**2**	**1**	**0**	**233**	**15**	**0**	**3.86**	....	....	....	....	....	....	....
	San Antonio	AHL	37	13	20	2	2101	104	2	2.97	....	....	....	....	....	....	....
	NHL Totals		**21**	**5**	**9**	**2**	**1047**	**59**	**0**	**3.38**	....	....	....	....	....	....	....

ECAC All-Rookie Team (2002) • ECAC First All-Star Team (2003) • ECAC Goaltender of the Year (2003) • ECAC Player of the Year (2003) (co-winner - Christopher Higgins) • NCAA East First All-American Team (2003)

LEVASSEUR, Jean-Philippe
(leh-VAH-soor, ZHAWN-fihl-EEP) **ANA.**

Goaltender. Catches right. 6'1", 200 lbs. Born, Victoriaville, Que., January 15, 1987.
(Anaheim's 6th choice, 197th overall, in 2005 Entry Draft).

			Regular Season								Playoffs						
Season	Club	League	GP	W	L	O/T	Mins	GA	SO	Avg	GP	W	L	Mins	GA	SO	Avg
2002-03	Magog	QAAA	28	15	10	1	1563	71	3	2.73	....	....	....	....	....	....	....
2003-04	Magog	QAAA	24	12	11	2	1424	86	0	3.62	13	7	5	762	35	0	2.80
	Rouyn-Noranda	QMJHL	3	0	2	1	184	14	0	4.57	....	....	....	....	....	....	....
2004-05	Rouyn-Noranda	QMJHL	29	8	14	3	1393	89	0	3.83	3	0	0	48	3	0	3.76
2005-06	Rouyn-Noranda	QMJHL	58	*35	19	0	3125	178	2	3.42	5	1	4	297	16	0	3.23
2006-07	Rouyn-Noranda	QMJHL	58	*31	21	....	3118	182	1	3.50	15	8	6	852	51	0	3.59

LIV, Stefan
(LIHV, STEH-fan)

Goaltender. Catches left. 6'1", 170 lbs. Born, Gdynia, Poland, December 21, 1980.
(Detroit's 3rd choice, 102nd overall, in 2000 Entry Draft).

			Regular Season								Playoffs						
Season	Club	League	GP	W	L	O/T	Mins	GA	SO	Avg	GP	W	L	Mins	GA	SO	Avg
1997-98	HV 71 Jr.	Swe-Jr.	17	....	....	....	1020	47	....	2.76	....	....	....	....	....	....	....
1998-99	HV 71 Jonkoping	Sweden					DID NOT PLAY – SPARE GOALTENDER										
99-2000	HV 71 Jr.	Swe-Jr.	10	....	....	....	600	17	2	1.70	....	....	....	....	....	....	....
	Tranas AIF	Sweden-2	9	....	....	....	541	20	0	2.17	....	....	....	....	....	....	....
	HV 71 Jonkoping	Sweden	12	....	....	....	716	24	1	2.01	3	....	....	178	12	0	4.04
2000-01	HV 71 Jonkoping	Sweden	*46	....	....	....	*2752	127	4	2.77	....	....	....	....	....	....	....
2001-02	HV 71 Jonkoping	Sweden	38	....	....	....	2184	95	*4	2.61	8	....	....	517	27	0	3.13
2002-03	HV 71 Jonkoping	Sweden	46	....	....	....	2723	124	3	2.73	7	....	....	391	17	1	2.61
2003-04	HV 71 Jonkoping	Sweden	41	....	....	....	2450	91	6	2.23	*18	....	....	*1091	35	*5	1.92
2004-05	HV 71 Jonkoping	Sweden	40	....	....	....	2404	119	2	2.97	....	....	....	....	....	....	....

Season	Club	League	GP	W	L	O/T	Mins	GA	SO	Avg	GP	W	L	Mins	GA	SO	Avg
2005-06	HV 71 Jonkoping	Sweden	40	....	....	....	2407	87	4	2.17	12	....	....	668	38	0	3.41
	Sweden	Olympics	1	1	0	0	60	2	0	2.00	....	....	....	....	....	....	....
2006-07	Grand Rapids	AHL	34	15	15	2	1893	95	2	3.01	....	....	....	....	....	....	....
	Toledo Storm	ECHL	3	1	1	1	184	7	0	2.29	....	....	....	....	....	....	....

LUNDQVIST, Henrik (LUHND-kvihst, HEHN-rihk) NYR

Goaltender. Catches left. 6'1", 195 lbs. Born, Are, Sweden, March 2, 1982.
(NY Rangers' 7th choice, 205th overall, in 2000 Entry Draft).

			Regular Season								Playoffs						
Season	Club	League	GP	W	L	O/T	Mins	GA	SO	Avg	GP	W	L	Mins	GA	SO	Avg
1998-99	V.Frolunda Jr.	Swe-Jr.	35	....	....	....	2100	95	0	2.73	....	....	....	....	....	....	....
99-2000	V.Frolunda Jr.	Swe-Jr.	30	....	....	....	1726	73	0	2.54	5	4	1	300	7	2	1.40
2000-01	V.Frolunda U18	Swe-U18	2	....	....	....	120	5	0	2.50	3	2	1	182	5	0	1.62
	V.Frolunda Jr.	Swe-Jr.	19	....	....	....	1140	50	2	2.64	....	....	....	....	....	....	....
	IF Molndal Hockey	Sweden-2	7	....	....	....	420	29	0	4.22	....	....	....	....	....	....	....
	V.Frolunda	Sweden	4	....	....	....	190	11	0	3.47	....	....	....	....	....	....	....
2001-02	V.Frolunda	Sweden	20	....	....	....	1152	52	2	2.71	8	8	0	489	18	*2	2.21
	V.Frolunda Jr.	Swe-Jr.	1	1	0	0	60	4	0	4.00	....	....	....	....	....	....	....
2002-03	V.Frolunda	Sweden	28	....	....	....	1650	40	*6	*1.45	12	....	....	739	26	*2	2.11
	V.Frolunda Jr.	Swe-Jr.	1	1	0	0	60	4	0	4.00	....	....	....	....	....	....	....
2003-04	V.Frolunda	Sweden	*48	....	....	....	*2897	105	7	2.17	10	....	....	610	20	0	1.97
2004-05	Frolunda	Sweden	44	*33	8	3	2642	79	*6	*1.79	*14	*12	2	854	15	*6	*1.05
2005-06	**NY Rangers**	**NHL**	**53**	**30**	**12**	**9**	**3112**	**116**	**2**	**2.24**	**3**	**0**	**3**	**177**	**13**	**0**	**4.41**
	Sweden	Olympics	6	5	1	0	360	14	0	2.33	....	....	....	....	....	....	....
2006-07	**NY Rangers**	**NHL**	**70**	**37**	**22**	**8**	**4109**	**160**	**5**	**2.34**	**10**	**6**	**4**	**637**	**22**	**1**	**2.07**
	NHL Totals		**123**	**67**	**34**	**17**	**7221**	**276**	**7**	**2.29**	**13**	**6**	**7**	**814**	**35**	**1**	**2.58**

NHL All-Rookie Team (2006)

LUONGO, Roberto (loo-WAHN-goh, roh-BUHR-toh) VAN.

Goaltender. Catches left. 6'3", 205 lbs. Born, Montreal, Que., April 4, 1979.
(NY Islanders' 1st choice, 4th overall, in 1997 Entry Draft).

			Regular Season								Playoffs						
Season	Club	League	GP	W	L	O/T	Mins	GA	SO	Avg	GP	W	L	Mins	GA	SO	Avg
1994-95	Montreal-Bourassa	QAAA	25	10	14	0	94	1465	0	3.85	....	....	....	....	....	....	....
1995-96	Val-d'Or Foreurs	QMJHL	23	6	11	4	1201	74	0	3.70	3	0	1	68	5	0	4.41
1996-97	Val-d'Or Foreurs	QMJHL	60	32	22	2	3305	171	2	3.10	13	8	5	777	44	0	3.40
1997-98	Val-d'Or Foreurs	QMJHL	54	27	20	5	3046	157	*7	3.09	*17	*14	3	*1019	37	*2	*2.18
1998-99	Val-d'Or Foreurs	QMJHL	21	6	10	2	1176	77	1	3.93	....	....	....	....	....	....	....
	Acadie-Bathurst	QMJHL	22	14	7	1	1340	74	0	3.31	*23	*16	6	*1400	64	0	2.74
99-2000	**NY Islanders**	**NHL**	**24**	**7**	**14**	**1**	**1292**	**70**	**1**	**3.25**	....	....	....	....	....	....	....
	Lowell	AHL	26	10	12	4	1517	74	1	2.93	6	3	3	359	18	0	3.01
2000-01	**Florida**	**NHL**	**47**	**12**	**24**	**7**	**2628**	**107**	**5**	**2.44**	....	....	....	....	....	....	....
	Louisville Panthers	AHL	3	1	2	0	178	10	0	3.38	....	....	....	....	....	....	....
2001-02	**Florida**	**NHL**	**58**	**16**	**33**	**4**	**3030**	**140**	**4**	**2.77**	....	....	....	....	....	....	....
2002-03	**Florida**	**NHL**	**65**	**20**	**34**	**7**	**3627**	**164**	**6**	**2.71**	....	....	....	....	....	....	....
2003-04	**Florida**	**NHL**	**72**	**25**	**33**	**14**	**4252**	**172**	**7**	**2.43**	....	....	....	....	....	....	....
2004-05			DID NOT PLAY														
2005-06	**Florida**	**NHL**	***75**	**35**	**30**	**9**	**4305**	**213**	**4**	**2.97**	....	....	....	....	....	....	....
	Canada	Olympics	2	1	1	0	119	3	0	1.51	....	....	....	....	....	....	....
2006-07	**Vancouver**	**NHL**	**76**	**47**	**22**	**6**	**4490**	**171**	**5**	**2.29**	**12**	**5**	**7**	**847**	**25**	**0**	**1.77**
	NHL Totals		**417**	**162**	**190**	**48**	**23624**	**1037**	**32**	**2.63**	**12**	**5**	**7**	**847**	**25**	**0**	**1.77**

NHL Second All-Star Team (2004, 2007)

Played in NHL All-Star Game (2004, 2007)

Traded to **Florida** by **NY Islanders** with Olli Jokinen for Mark Parrish and Oleg Kvasha, June 24, 2000. Traded to **Vancouver** by **Florida** with Lukas Krajicek and Florida's 6th round choice (Sergei Shirokov) in 2006 Entry Draft for Todd Bertuzzi, Bryan Allen and Alex Auld, June 23, 2006.

MacDONALD, Joey (MAK-DAWN-uhld, JOH-ee) NYI

Goaltender. Catches left. 6', 197 lbs. Born, Pictou, N.S., February 7, 1980.

			Regular Season								Playoffs						
Season	Club	League	GP	W	L	O/T	Mins	GA	SO	Avg	GP	W	L	Mins	GA	SO	Avg
1997-98	Halifax	QMJHL	17	3	12	0	815	54	0	3.97	3	1	2	140	15	0	6.43
1998-99	Peterborough	OHL	47	22	15	2	2483	123	3	2.97	3	0	2	145	13	0	5.38
99-2000	Peterborough	OHL	48	20	15	6	2641	125	2	2.84	5	1	4	280	16	1	3.43
2000-01	Peterborough	OHL	57	25	21	7	3284	161	1	2.94	7	3	4	425	18	0	2.54
2001-02	Toledo Storm	ECHL	38	12	15	7	2084	100	1	2.88	....	....	....	....	....	....	....
2002-03	Grand Rapids	AHL	25	14	6	0	1337	49	3	2.20	1	0	0	8	1	0	7.95
2003-04	Grand Rapids	AHL	39	22	12	3	2249	74	6	1.97	1	0	1	40	4	0	6.04
2004-05	Grand Rapids	AHL	*66	34	29	2	*3755	143	5	2.29	....	....	....	....	....	....	....
2005-06	Grand Rapids	AHL	32	17	9	2	1745	91	2	3.13	....	....	....	....	....	....	....
	Toledo Storm	ECHL	1	1	0	0	60	1	0	1.00	....	....	....	....	....	....	....
2006-07	**Detroit**	**NHL**	**8**	**1**	**5**	**1**	**468**	**27**	**0**	**3.46**	....	....	....	....	....	....	....
	Grand Rapids	AHL	2	1	1	0	123	6	0	2.93	....	....	....	....	....	....	....
	Boston	**NHL**	**7**	**2**	**2**	**1**	**358**	**16**	**0**	**2.68**	....	....	....	....	....	....	....
	NHL Totals		**15**	**3**	**7**	**2**	**826**	**43**	**0**	**3.12**	....	....	....	....	....	....	....

Harry "Hap" Holmes Memorial Award (fewest goals against – AHL) (2003) (shared with Marc Lamothe)

Signed as a free agent by **Detroit**, December 21, 2001. Claimed on waivers by **Boston** from **Detroit**, February 24, 2007. Signed as a free agent by **NY Islanders**, July 7, 2007.

MACHESNEY, Daren (muh-KEHS-nee, DAIR-ehn) WSH.

Goaltender. Catches left. 6', 182 lbs. Born, Hamilton, Ont., December 13, 1986.
(Washington's 5th choice, 143rd overall, in 2005 Entry Draft).

			Regular Season								Playoffs						
Season	Club	League	GP	W	L	O/T	Mins	GA	SO	Avg	GP	W	L	Mins	GA	SO	Avg
2003-04	Newmarket	OPJHL	32	....	....	....	1868	82	1	2.63	....	....	....	....	....	....	....
	Brampton Battalion	OHL	5	3	2	0	300	15	0	3.00	....	....	....	....	....	....	....
2004-05	Brampton Battalion	OHL	38	16	13	6	2166	99	1	2.74	5	2	3	331	15	0	2.72
2005-06	Brampton Battalion	OHL	49	28	17	3	2830	143	3	3.03	11	5	5	633	32	0	3.03
2006-07	Hershey Bears	AHL	10	3	3	1	377	20	0	3.18	....	....	....	....	....	....	....
	South Carolina	ECHL	15	5	8	2	836	46	1	3.30	....	....	....	....	....	....	....

OHL All-Rookie Team (2005)

MacINTYRE, Derek (MAK-ihn-tighr, DAIR-ihk) S.J.

Goaltender. Catches left. 6'2", 185 lbs. Born, Elgin, IL, November 1, 1985.
(San Jose's 8th choice, 234th overall, in 2004 Entry Draft).

			Regular Season								Playoffs						
Season	Club	League	GP	W	L	O/T	Mins	GA	SO	Avg	GP	W	L	Mins	GA	SO	Avg
2003-04	Soo Indians	NAHL	39	31	3	2	2200	65	4	*1.77	4	1	1	153	10	0	3.92
2004-05	Ferris State	CCHA	17	5	8	1	883	47	0	3.19	....	....	....	....	....	....	....
2005-06	Ferris State	CCHA	9	3	3	1	464	25	0	3.23	....	....	....	....	....	....	....
2006-07	Ferris State	CCHA	13	7	3	0	682	39	0	3.43	....	....	....	....	....	....	....

MacINTYRE, Drew (MAK-ihn-tighr, DROO) VAN.

Goaltender. Catches left. 6'2", 185 lbs. Born, Charlottetown, PEI, June 24, 1983.
(Detroit's 2nd choice, 121st overall, in 2001 Entry Draft).

			Regular Season								Playoffs						
Season	Club	League	GP	W	L	O/T	Mins	GA	SO	Avg	GP	W	L	Mins	GA	SO	Avg
1998-99	Trenton Sting	OPJHL	20	....	....	....	1173	71	2	3.63	....	....	....	....	....	....	....
99-2000	Sherbrooke	QMJHL	24	10	7	2	1253	67	0	3.21	....	....	....	....	....	....	....
2000-01	Sherbrooke	QMJHL	48	17	22	3	2552	139	4	3.27	4	0	4	238	19	0	4.78
2001-02	Sherbrooke	QMJHL	55	15	34	3	3028	201	1	3.98	....	....	....	....	....	....	....
2002-03	Sherbrooke	QMJHL	*61	31	24	5	*3515	161	2	2.75	12	5	7	767	52	0	4.07
2003-04	Toledo Storm	ECHL	11	6	4	0	574	25	0	2.61	....	....	....	....	....	....	....
2004-05	Grand Rapids	AHL	24	7	8	0	1049	47	1	2.69	....	....	....	....	....	....	....
	Toledo Storm	ECHL	2	0	1	0	87	6	0	4.12	....	....	....	....	....	....	....
2005-06	Grand Rapids	AHL	13	8	4	0	681	33	0	2.91	5	3	1	260	7	0	1.62
	Toledo Storm	ECHL	33	24	7	2	1981	68	2	*2.06	6	5	1	360	12	0	2.00
2006-07	Manitoba Moose	AHL	41	24	12	2	2290	83	3	2.17	11	4	6	633	21	1	1.99

• Missed majority of 2003-04 season recovering from thigh injury suffered in practice, December 27, 2003. Traded to **Vancouver** by **Detroit** for future considerations, September 12, 2006.

MANZATO, Daniel (man-ZA-toh, DAN-yehl) CAR.

Goaltender. Catches left. 6', 178 lbs. Born, Fribourg, Switz., January 17, 1984.
(Carolina's 3rd choice, 160th overall, in 2002 Entry Draft).

			Regular Season								Playoffs						
Season	Club	League	GP	W	L	O/T	Mins	GA	SO	Avg	GP	W	L	Mins	GA	SO	Avg
2000-01	Fribourg Jr.	Swiss-Jr.	36	....	....	....	2160	32	6	0.91	....	....	....	....	....	....	....
2001-02	Victoriaville Tigres	QMJHL	36	20	8	2	1894	102	0	3.23	6	3	0	249	17	0	4.09
2002-03	Victoriaville Tigres	QMJHL	48	23	18	5	2756	155	3	3.37	3	0	3	125	11	0	5.27
2003-04	Victoriaville Tigres	QMJHL	23	7	13	0	1170	78	0	4.00	....	....	....	....	....	....	....
	Kloten Flyers	Swiss	15	....	....	....	912	39	1	2.57	....	....	....	....	....	....	....
2004-05	HC Ambri-Piotta	Swiss	25	....	....	....	1446	65	1	2.70	....	....	....	....	....	....	....
2005-06	EHC Basel	Swiss	41	18	14	9	2449	107	*5	2.62	5	1	4	280	22	0	4.71
2006-07	EHC Basel	Swiss	43	13	30	0	2590	157	1	3.64	13	7	6	795	41	2	3.09

Signed as a free agent by **Kloten** (Swiss), January 5, 2004, following release by **Victoriaville** (QMJHL), January 4, 2004. Signed as a free agent by **Ambri-Piotta** (Swiss), August 5, 2004. Signed as a free agent by **Basel** (Swiss), August, 2005.

MARKKANEN, Jussi (MAHR-kah-nehn, YEW-see)

Goaltender. Catches left. 6', 182 lbs. Born, Imatra, Finland, May 8, 1975.
(Edmonton's 5th choice, 133rd overall, in 2001 Entry Draft).

			Regular Season								Playoffs						
Season	Club	League	GP	W	L	O/T	Mins	GA	SO	Avg	GP	W	L	Mins	GA	SO	Avg
1991-92	SaiPa Jr.	Fin-Jr.	6	3	3	0	360	25	0	4.16	....	....	....	....	....	....	....
1992-93	SaiPa Jr.	Fin-Jr.	7	....	....	....	367	28	0	4.58	....	....	....	....	....	....	....
	SaiPa	Finland-2	16	6	6	2	798	60	0	4.51	....	....	....	....	....	....	....
1993-94	SaiPa Jr.	Fin-Jr.	4	....	....	....	....	....	....	2.26	....	....	....	....	....	....	....
	SaiPa	Finland-2	30	....	....	....	1726	97	....	3.37	....	....	....	....	....	....	....
1994-95	SaiPa	Finland-2	36	....	....	....	2067	95	....	2.76	10	6	4	621	33	0	3.19
1995-96	Tappara Jr.	Fin-Jr.	5	....	....	....	298	21	....	4.23	....	....	....	....	....	....	....
	Tappara Tampere	Finland	23	11	8	2	1239	59	1	2.86	....	....	....	....	....	....	....
1996-97	SaiPa	Finland	41	9	24	7	2340	132	0	3.38	....	....	....	....	....	....	....
1997-98	SaiPa	Finland	48	21	20	5	2870	138	4	2.88	3	0	3	164	11	0	4.02
1998-99	SaiPa	Finland	45	21	19	4	2633	105	4	2.39	7	3	3	366	21	0	3.44
99-2000	SaiPa	Finland	48	14	23	9	2794	150	2	3.24	....	....	....	....	....	....	....
2000-01	Tappara Tampere	Finland	52	30	17	4	3076	107	9	2.09	10	7	3	608	18	1	1.78
2001-02	**Edmonton**	**NHL**	**14**	**6**	**4**	**2**	**784**	**24**	**2**	**1.84**	....	....	....	....	....	....	....
	Hamilton Bulldogs	AHL	4	2	2	0	239	9	0	2.26	....	....	....	....	....	....	....
	Finland	Olympics					DID NOT PLAY										
2002-03	**Edmonton**	**NHL**	**22**	**7**	**8**	**3**	**1180**	**51**	**3**	**2.59**	**1**	**0**	**0**	**14**	**1**	**0**	**4.29**
2003-04	**NY Rangers**	**NHL**	**26**	**8**	**12**	**1**	**1244**	**53**	**2**	**2.56**	....	....	....	....	....	....	....
	Edmonton	**NHL**	**7**	**2**	**2**	**2**	**394**	**12**	**0**	**1.83**	....	....	....	....	....	....	....
2004-05	Lada Togliatti	Russia	54	....	....	....	3157	63	11	1.20	10	....	....	627	15	1	1.44
2005-06	**Edmonton**	**NHL**	**37**	**15**	**12**	**6**	**2016**	**105**	**0**	**3.13**	**6**	**3**	**3**	**360**	**13**	**1**	**2.17**
2006-07	**Edmonton**	**NHL**	**22**	**5**	**9**	**1**	**992**	**52**	**0**	**3.15**	....	....	....	....	....	....	....
	NHL Totals		**128**	**43**	**47**	**15**	**6610**	**297**	**7**	**2.70**	**7**	**3**	**3**	**374**	**14**	**1**	**2.25**

Traded to **NY Rangers** by **Edmonton** with Edmonton's 4th round choice (later traded to Toronto – Toronto selected Roman Kukumberg) for Brian Leetch, June 30, 2003. Traded to **Edmonton** by **NY Rangers** with Petr Nedved for Stephen Valiquette, Dwight Helminen and Edmonton's 2nd round compensatory choice (Dane Byers) in 2004 Entry Draft, March 3, 2004. Signed as a free agent by **Togliatti** (Russia), September 25, 2004.

MARSTERS, Nathan (MAHR-stuhrs, NAY-thuhn)

Goaltender. Catches left. 6'4", 190 lbs. Born, Burlington, Ont., January 28, 1980.
(Los Angeles' 5th choice, 165th overall, in 2000 Entry Draft).

			Regular Season								Playoffs						
Season	Club	League	GP	W	L	O/T	Mins	GA	SO	Avg	GP	W	L	Mins	GA	SO	Avg
1997-98	Bramalea Blues	OPJHL	12	....	....	....	539	25	2	2.78	....	....	....	....	....	....	....
1998-99	Bramalea Blues	OPJHL	29	....	....	....	1711	91	3	3.19	....	....	....	....	....	....	....
99-2000	Bramalea Blues	OPJHL	28	....	....	....	1668	98	2	3.53	....	....	....	....	....	....	....
	Chilliwack Chiefs	BCHL	15	9	6	0	825	63	0	4.58	20	15	5	1187	62	0	3.13
2000-01	RPI Engineers	ECAC	28	14	13	1	1631	64	*4	2.35	....	....	....	....	....	....	....
2001-02	RPI Engineers	ECAC	28	15	9	3	1627	70	1	2.58	....	....	....	....	....	....	....
2002-03	RPI Engineers	ECAC	24	7	15	1	1286	73	0	3.41	....	....	....	....	....	....	....
2003-04	RPI Engineers	ECAC	35	*21	13	1	2094	75	*5	2.15	....	....	....	....	....	....	....
2004-05	Louisiana	ECHL	*54	18	30	4	*3108	182	1	3.51	....	....	....	....	....	....	....
2005-06	Portland Pirates	AHL	37	23	9	2	2050	106	0	3.10	4	1	2	195	9	0	2.77
	Augusta Lynx	ECHL	4	1	1	2	219	14	0	3.83	....	....	....	....	....	....	....
2006-07	Portland Pirates	AHL	5	2	3	0	287	16	0	3.35	....	....	....	....	....	....	....
	Augusta Lynx	ECHL	16	7	6	2	887	58	0	3.92	....	....	....	....	....	....	....
	Laredo Bucks	CHL	8	5	2	0	437	19	0	2.61	....	....	....	....	....	....	....

ECAC Second All-Star Team (2004)

Signed as a free agent by **Anaheim**, November 28, 2005.

MASON, Chris (MAY-sohn, KRIHS) NSH.

Goaltender. Catches left. 6', 195 lbs. Born, Red Deer, Alta., April 20, 1976.
(New Jersey's 7th choice, 122nd overall, in 1995 Entry Draft).

			Regular Season								Playoffs						
Season	Club	League	GP	W	L	O/T	Mins	GA	SO	Avg	GP	W	L	Mins	GA	SO	Avg
1992-93	Red Deer	AMHL	20	....	....	....	1280	76	0	3.35	....	....	....	....	....	....	....
1993-94	Victoria Cougars	WHL	5	1	4	0	237	27	0	6.84	....	....	....	....	....	....	....
1994-95	Prince George	WHL	44	8	30	1	2288	192	1	5.03	....	....	....	....	....	....	....
1995-96	Prince George	WHL	59	16	37	1	3289	236	1	4.31	....	....	....	....	....	....	....
1996-97	Prince George	WHL	50	19	24	4	2851	172	2	3.62	15	9	6	938	44	*1	2.81
1997-98	Cincinnati	AHL	47	13	19	7	2368	136	0	3.45	....	....	....	....	....	....	....
1998-99	**Nashville**	**NHL**	**3**	**0**	**0**	**0**	**69**	**6**	**0**	**5.22**	....	....	....	....	....	....	....
	Milwaukee	IHL	34	15	12	6	1901	92	1	2.90	....	....	....	....	....	....	....
99-2000	Milwaukee	IHL	53	20	21	8	2952	137	2	2.78	3	1	2	252	11	0	2.62
2000-01	**Nashville**	**NHL**	**1**	**0**	**1**	**0**	**59**	**2**	**0**	**2.03**	....	....	....	....	....	....	....
	Milwaukee	IHL	37	17	14	5	2226	87	5	2.35	4	1	3	239	12	0	3.02
2001-02	Milwaukee	AHL	48	17	21	7	2755	116	2	2.53	....	....	....	....	....	....	....
2002-03	San Antonio	AHL	50	25	18	6	2914	122	1	2.51	3	0	3	195	9	0	2.77
2003-04	**Nashville**	**NHL**	**17**	**4**	**4**	**1**	**744**	**27**	**1**	**2.18**	....	....	....	....	....	....	....
	Milwaukee	AHL	1	1	0	0	60	2	0	2.00	....	....	....	....	....	....	....
2004-05	Valerengen IF Oslo	Norway	20	....	....	....	1204	36	1	1.79	11	....	....	657	22	1	2.01
2005-06	**Nashville**	**NHL**	**23**	**12**	**5**	**1**	**1227**	**52**	**2**	**2.54**	**5**	**1**	**4**	**296**	**17**	**0**	**3.45**

Season	Club	League	GP	W	L	O/T	Mins	GA	SO	Avg	GP	W	L	Mins	GA	SO	Avg
2006-07	Nashville	NHL	40	24	11	4	2342	93	5	2.38	....	....	....	....	....	....	....
	NHL Totals		84	40	21	6	4441	180	8	2.43	5	1	4	296	17	0	3.45

Signed as a free agent by **Anaheim**, June 27, 1997. Traded to **Nashville** by **Anaheim** with Marc Moro for Dominic Roussel, October 5, 1998. Signed as a free agent by **Florida**, August 20, 2002. Claimed by **Nashville** from **Florida** in Waiver Draft, October 3, 2003. Signed as a free agent by **Oslo** (Norway), November 30, 2004.

MASON, Steve (MAY-sohn, STEEV) CBJ

Goaltender. Catches right. 6'3", 186 lbs. Born, Oakville, Ont., May 29, 1988.
(Columbus' 2nd choice, 69th overall, in 2006 Entry Draft).

			Regular Season								Playoffs						
Season	Club	League	GP	W	L	O/T	Mins	GA	SO	Avg	GP	W	L	Mins	GA	SO	Avg
2004-05	Grimsby	OJHL-C	19	....	....	....	....	....	4	1.82	....	....	....	....	....	....	....
2005-06	Petrolia Jets	OJHL-B	9	6	3	0	521	....	1	2.53	....	....	....	....	....	....	....
	London Knights	OHL	12	5	3	0	497	22	0	2.66	4	0	0	150	7	0	2.80
2006-07	London Knights	OHL	*62	*45	13	4	*3733	199	2	3.20	16	9	7	931	54	0	3.48

OHL First All-Star Team (2007)

McELHINNEY, Curtis (MAK-IHL-ehn-ee, KUHR-this) CGY.

Goaltender. Catches left. 6'3", 207 lbs. Born, London, Ont., May 23, 1983.
(Calgary's 9th choice, 176th overall, in 2002 Entry Draft).

			Regular Season								Playoffs						
Season	Club	League	GP	W	L	O/T	Mins	GA	SO	Avg	GP	W	L	Mins	GA	SO	Avg
2000-01	Notre Dame	SJHL					STATISTICS NOT AVAILABLE										
2001-02	Colorado College	WCHA	9	6	0	1	441	15	1	2.04	....	....	....	....	....	....	....
2002-03	Colorado College	WCHA	*37	*25	6	5	*2147	85	*4	2.37	....	....	....	....	....	....	....
2003-04	Colorado College	WCHA	19	10	6	1	1015	41	2	2.42	....	....	....	....	....	....	....
2004-05	Colorado College	WCHA	26	*21	4	1	1550	58	2	2.24	....	....	....	....	....	....	....
2005-06	Omaha	AHL	33	9	14	2	1621	68	3	2.52	....	....	....	....	....	....	....
2006-07	Omaha	AHL	57	35	17	1	3181	113	*7	2.13	5	2	3	311	11	0	2.12

WCHA First All-Star Team (2003, 2005) • NCAA West Second All-American Team (2003) • NCAA West First All-American Team (2005) • AHL Second All-Star Team (2007)

McGANN, Pat (muh-GAN, PAT) DAL.

Goaltender. Catches right. 5'11", 160 lbs. Born, Evergreen Park, IL, January 27, 1987.
(Dallas' 7th choice, 223rd overall, in 2005 Entry Draft).

			Regular Season								Playoffs						
Season	Club	League	GP	W	L	O/T	Mins	GA	SO	Avg	GP	W	L	Mins	GA	SO	Avg
2003-04	Chicago Chill	MAHL	31	14	16	1	....	....	....	3.40	....	....	....	....	....	....	....
2004-05	Team Illinois	MWEHL	50	31	18	1	....	91	5	2.21	....	....	....	....	....	....	....
2005-06	Cedar Rapids	USHL	17	5	8	3	998	49	1	2.95	....	....	....	....	....	....	....
2006-07	Cedar Rapids	USHL	6	3	3	0	357	22	0	3.70	....	....	....	....	....	....	....
	Chicago Steel	USHL	17	2	14	1	935	67	0	4.30	....	....	....	....	....	....	....

McKEE, David (muh-KEE, DAY-vihd)

Goaltender. Catches left. 6'1", 180 lbs. Born, Irving, TX, December 5, 1983.

			Regular Season								Playoffs						
Season	Club	League	GP	W	L	O/T	Mins	GA	SO	Avg	GP	W	L	Mins	GA	SO	Avg
2003-04	Cornell Big Red	ECAC	32	16	10	6	1929	59	*5	1.84	....	....	....	....	....	....	....
2004-05	Cornell Big Red	ECACHL	35	*27	5	3	2125	44	*10	*1.24	....	....	....	....	....	....	....
2005-06	Cornell Big Red	ECACHL	35	*22	9	4	2139	74	3	*2.08	....	....	....	....	....	....	....
2006-07	Portland Pirates	AHL	7	5	2	0	379	18	1	2.85	....	....	....	....	....	....	....
	Augusta Lynx	ECHL	52	29	15	2	2811	157	1	3.35	2	0	2	134	5	0	2.23

ECAC All-Rookie Team (2004) • ECAC Rookie of the Year (2004) (co-winner - Brian Ihnacak) • ECACHL First All-Star Team (2005) • ECACHL Player of the Year (2005) • NCAA East First All-American Team (2005)

Signed as a free agent by **Anaheim**, April 1, 2006.

McLENNAN, Jamie (muh-KLEH-nuhn, JAY-mee)

Goaltender. Catches left. 6', 190 lbs. Born, Edmonton, Alta., June 30, 1971.
(NY Islanders' 3rd choice, 48th overall, in 1991 Entry Draft).

			Regular Season								Playoffs						
Season	Club	League	GP	W	L	O/T	Mins	GA	SO	Avg	GP	W	L	Mins	GA	SO	Avg
1987-88	St. Albert Royals	AMHL	21	....	....	....	1224	80	0	3.92	....	....	....	....	....	....	....
1988-89	Spokane Chiefs	WHL	11	....	....	....	578	63	0	6.54	....	....	....	....	....	....	....
	Lethbridge	WHL	7	....	....	....	368	22	0	3.59	....	....	....	....	....	....	....
1989-90	Lethbridge	WHL	34	20	4	2	1690	110	1	3.91	13	6	5	677	44	0	3.90
1990-91	Lethbridge	WHL	56	32	18	4	3230	205	0	3.81	*16	8	8	*970	56	0	3.46
1991-92	Capital District	AHL	18	4	10	2	952	60	1	3.78	....	....	....	....	....	....	....
	Richmond	ECHL	32	16	12	2	1837	114	0	3.72	....	....	....	....	....	....	....
1992-93	Capital District	AHL	38	17	14	6	2171	117	1	3.23	1	0	1	20	5	0	15.00
1993-94	**NY Islanders**	**NHL**	**22**	**8**	**7**	**6**	**1287**	**61**	**0**	**2.84**	**2**	**0**	**1**	**82**	**6**	**0**	**4.39**
	Salt Lake	IHL	24	8	12	2	1320	80	0	3.64	....	....	....	....	....	....	....
1994-95	**NY Islanders**	**NHL**	**21**	**6**	**11**	**2**	**1185**	**67**	**0**	**3.39**	....	....	....	....	....	....	....
	Denver Grizzlies	IHL	4	3	0	1	239	12	0	3.00	11	8	2	640	23	1	*2.15
1995-96	**NY Islanders**	**NHL**	**13**	**3**	**9**	**1**	**636**	**39**	**0**	**3.68**	....	....	....	....	....	....	....
	Utah Grizzlies	IHL	14	9	2	2	728	29	0	2.39	....	....	....	....	....	....	....
	Worcester IceCats	AHL	22	14	7	1	1216	57	0	2.81	2	0	2	119	8	0	4.04
1996-97	Worcester IceCats	AHL	39	18	13	4	2152	100	2	2.79	4	2	2	262	16	0	3.67
1997-98	**St. Louis**	**NHL**	**30**	**16**	**8**	**2**	**1658**	**60**	**2**	**2.17**	**1**	**0**	**0**	**14**	**1**	**0**	**4.29**
1998-99	**St. Louis**	**NHL**	**33**	**13**	**14**	**4**	**1763**	**70**	**3**	**2.38**	**1**	**0**	**1**	**37**	**0**	**0**	**0.00**
99-2000	**St. Louis**	**NHL**	**19**	**9**	**5**	**2**	**1009**	**33**	**2**	**1.96**	....	....	....	....	....	....	....
2000-01	**Minnesota**	**NHL**	**38**	**5**	**23**	**9**	**2230**	**98**	**2**	**2.64**	....	....	....	....	....	....	....
2001-02	Houston Aeros	AHL	51	25	18	4	2852	130	3	2.74	14	8	6	880	31	2	2.11
2002-03	**Calgary**	**NHL**	**22**	**2**	**11**	**4**	**1165**	**58**	**0**	**2.99**	....	....	....	....	....	....	....
2003-04	**Calgary**	**NHL**	**26**	**12**	**9**	**3**	**1446**	**53**	**4**	**2.20**	....	....	....	....	....	....	....
	NY Rangers	**NHL**	**4**	**1**	**3**	**0**	**244**	**12**	**0**	**2.95**	....	....	....	....	....	....	....
2004-05	Guildford Flames	Britain-2	3	2	1	0	185	8	0	2.59	7	4	3	385	13	0	2.02
2005-06	**Florida**	**NHL**	**17**	**2**	**4**	**2**	**678**	**34**	**0**	**3.01**	....	....	....	....	....	....	....
2006-07	**Calgary**	**NHL**	**9**	**3**	**5**	**1**	**533**	**32**	**0**	**3.60**	**1**	**0**	**0**	**0**	**0**	**0**	**0.00**
	NHL Totals		**254**	**80**	**109**	**36**	**13834**	**617**	**13**	**2.68**	**5**	**0**	**2**	**133**	**7**	**0**	**3.16**

WHL East First All-Star Team (1991) • WHL Goaltender of the Year (1991) • Bill Masterton Memorial Trophy (1998)

Signed as a free agent by **St. Louis**, July 15, 1996. Claimed by **Minnesota** from **St. Louis** in Expansion Draft, June 23, 2000. Traded to **Calgary** by **Minnesota** for Calgary's 9th round choice (Mika Hannula) in 2002 Entry Draft, June 22, 2002. Traded to **NY Rangers** by **Calgary** with Blair Betts and Greg Moore for Chris Simon and NY Rangers' 7th round choice (Matt Schneider) in 2004 Entry Draft, March 6, 2004. Signed as a free agent by **Florida**, July 2, 2004. Signed as a free agent by **Guildford** (Britain-2), February 17, 2005. Signed as a free agent by **Calgary**, July 6, 2006.

McVICAR, Rob (muhk-VIH-kuhr, RAWB)

Goaltender. Catches left. 6'4", 201 lbs. Born, Hay River, N.W.T., January 15, 1982.
(Vancouver's 6th choice, 151st overall, in 2002 Entry Draft).

			Regular Season								Playoffs						
Season	Club	League	GP	W	L	O/T	Mins	GA	SO	Avg	GP	W	L	Mins	GA	SO	Avg
1998-99	Brandon Kings	MMMHL	21	....	....	....	1217	69	0	3.40	....	....	....	....	....	....	....
99-2000	Brandon	WHL	14	5	6	0	687	43	0	3.76	....	....	....	....	....	....	....
2000-01	Brandon	WHL	27	12	10	2	1537	76	0	2.97	5	2	3	324	13	1	2.41
2001-02	Brandon	WHL	55	*33	18	2	3276	151	1	2.77	19	11	8	1255	44	1	2.10
2002-03	Brandon	WHL	51	31	14	5	3027	136	2	2.70	13	6	7	737	32	0	2.61
2003-04	Manitoba Moose	AHL	10	4	3	2	514	25	0	2.92	....	....	....	....	....	....	....
	Columbia Inferno	ECHL	19	11	5	2	1088	47	0	2.59	....	....	....	....	....	....	....
2004-05	Manitoba Moose	AHL	1	0	1	0	62	3	0	2.92	....	....	....	....	....	....	....
	Columbia Inferno	ECHL	34	14	14	5	2004	79	3	2.37	....	....	....	....	....	....	....
2005-06	**Vancouver**	**NHL**	**1**	**0**	**0**	**0**	**3**	**0**	**0**	**0.00**	....	....	....	....	....	....	....
	Manitoba Moose	AHL	6	3	3	0	337	17	0	3.03	....	....	....	....	....	....	....
	Victoria	ECHL	33	13	14	2	1741	95	1	3.27	....	....	....	....	....	....	....
2006-07	Utah Grizzlies	ECHL	59	19	28	7	3310	205	1	3.72	....	....	....	....	....	....	....
	NHL Totals		**1**	**0**	**0**	**0**	**3**	**0**	**0**	**0.00**	....	....	....	....	....	....	....

MENSATOR, Lukas (MEHN-suh-tohr, LOO-kahsh) VAN.

Goaltender. Catches left. 5'8", 180 lbs. Born, Sokolov, Czech., August 18, 1984.
(Vancouver's 4th choice, 83rd overall, in 2002 Entry Draft).

			Regular Season								Playoffs						
Season	Club	League	GP	W	L	O/T	Mins	GA	SO	Avg	GP	W	L	Mins	GA	SO	Avg
99-2000	Karlovy Vary U17	CzR-U17	42	....	....	....	2406	160	0	3.99	....	....	....	....	....	....	....
	Karlovy Vary Jr.	CzRep-Jr.	1	1	0	0	60	3	0	3.00	....	....	....	....	....	....	....
2000-01	Karlovy Vary U17	CzR-U17	6	....	....	....	360	15	0	2.50	....	....	....	....	....	....	....
	Karlovy Vary Jr.	CzRep-Jr.	19	....	....	....	1085	60	0	3.32	....	....	....	....	....	....	....
2001-02	Karlovy Vary Jr.	CzRep-Jr.	31	....	....	....	1809	93	0	3.08	9	....	....	459	17	0	2.22
	Banik CHZ Sokolov	CzRep-3	3	....	....	....	180	12	0	4.00	....	....	....	....	....	....	....
2002-03	Ottawa 67's	OHL	42	26	8	5	2395	122	0	3.06	*23	13	8	*1381	63	*2	2.74
2003-04	Ottawa 67's	OHL	50	18	22	7	2924	162	0	3.32	7	3	4	447	23	0	3.09
2004-05	Karlovy Vary	CzRep	13	....	....	....	686	34	1	2.97	....	....	....	....	....	....	....
	IHC Pisek	CzRep-2	14	....	....	....	808	41	1	3.04	....	....	....	....	....	....	....
	BK Mlada Boleslav	CzRep-2	17	....	....	....	991	34	4	2.06	7	....	....	393	17	1	2.60
2005-06	Karlovy Vary	CzRep	36	....	....	....	1981	69	5	2.09	....	....	....	....	....	....	....
	SK Kadan	CzRep-2	1	....	....	....	49	5	0	6.12	....	....	....	....	....	....	....
2006-07	Karlovy Vary	CzRep	22	....	....	....	1166	47	1	2.42	....	....	....	....	....	....	....

Signed as a free agent by **Karlovy Vary** (CzRep), May 17, 2004.

MILLER, Ryan (MIHL-luhr, RIGH-uhn) BUF.

Goaltender. Catches left. 6'2", 172 lbs. Born, East Lansing, MI, July 17, 1980.
(Buffalo's 7th choice, 138th overall, in 1999 Entry Draft).

			Regular Season								Playoffs						
Season	Club	League	GP	W	L	O/T	Mins	GA	SO	Avg	GP	W	L	Mins	GA	SO	Avg
1997-98	Soo Indians	NAHL	37	21	14	0	2113	82	3	2.33	2	0	2	158	7	0	2.66
1998-99	Soo Indians	NAHL	47	31	14	1	2711	104	8	2.30	4	2	2	218	10	1	2.76
99-2000	Michigan State	CCHA	26	16	5	3	1525	39	*8	*1.53	....	....	....	....	....	....	....
2000-01	Michigan State	CCHA	40	*31	5	4	2447	54	*10	*1.32	....	....	....	....	....	....	....
2001-02	Michigan State	CCHA	40	26	9	5	2411	71	*8	*1.77	....	....	....	....	....	....	....
2002-03	**Buffalo**	**NHL**	**15**	**6**	**8**	**1**	**912**	**40**	**1**	**2.63**	....	....	....	....	....	....	....
	Rochester	AHL	47	23	18	5	2817	110	2	2.34	3	1	2	190	13	0	4.11
2003-04	**Buffalo**	**NHL**	**3**	**0**	**3**	**0**	**178**	**15**	**0**	**5.06**	....	....	....	....	....	....	....
	Rochester	AHL	60	27	25	7	3579	132	5	2.21	14	7	7	857	26	2	1.82
2004-05	Rochester	AHL	63	*41	17	4	3741	153	8	2.45	9	5	4	547	24	0	2.63
2005-06	**Buffalo**	**NHL**	**48**	**30**	**14**	**3**	**2862**	**124**	**1**	**2.60**	**18**	**11**	**7**	**1123**	**48**	**1**	**2.56**
	Rochester	AHL	2	1	1	0	120	5	0	2.50	....	....	....	....	....	....	....
2006-07	**Buffalo**	**NHL**	**63**	**40**	**16**	**6**	**3692**	**168**	**2**	**2.73**	**16**	**9**	**7**	**1029**	**38**	**0**	**2.22**
	NHL Totals		**129**	**76**	**41**	**10**	**7644**	**347**	**4**	**2.72**	**34**	**20**	**14**	**2152**	**86**	**1**	**2.40**

CCHA Second All-Star Team (2000) • CCHA First All-Star Team (2001, 2002) • NCAA West First All-American Team (2001, 2002) • CCHA Player of the Year (2001, 2002) • Hobey Baker Memorial Award (Top U.S. Collegiate Player) (2001) • AHL First All-Star Team (2005) • Aldege "Baz" Bastien Memorial Trophy (Top Goaltender - AHL) (2005)

Played in NHL All-Star Game (2007)

MODIG, Mattias (moh-DIHG, MA-tee-uhs) ANA.

Goaltender. Catches left. 6', 171 lbs. Born, Lulea, Sweden, April 1, 1987.
(Anaheim's 7th choice, 121st overall, in 2007 Entry Draft).

			Regular Season								Playoffs						
Season	Club	League	GP	W	L	O/T	Mins	GA	SO	Avg	GP	W	L	Mins	GA	SO	Avg
2002-03	Lulea HF U18	Swe-U18	2	....	....	....	120	4	0	2.00	....	....	....	....	....	....	....
2003-04	Lulea HF U18	Swe-U18	14	....	....	....	854	30	2	2.11	7	....	....	449	14	0	1.87
	Lulea HF Jr.	Swe-Jr.	2	....	....	....	66	2	0	1.81	....	....	....	....	....	....	....
2004-05	Lulea HF U18	Swe-U18	2	....	....	....	120	4	0	2.00	....	....	....	....	....	....	....
	Lulea HF Jr.	Swe-Jr.	14	....	....	....	819	42	2	3.08	5	....	....	306	16	0	3.14
2005-06	Lulea HF Jr.	Swe-Jr.	19	....	....	....	1154	42	1	2.18	3	....	....	175	10	0	3.43
	Lulea HF	Sweden	2	....	....	....	66	3	0	2.74	....	....	....	....	....	....	....
2006-07	Lulea HF Jr.	Swe-Jr.	2	....	....	....	120	7	0	3.50	....	....	....	....	....	....	....
	Lulea HF	Sweden	32	....	....	....	1636	69	1	2.53	1	....	....	20	1	0	3.00

MOLE, Mike NYI

Goaltender. Catches right. 6', 183 lbs. Born, Orleans, Ont., October 12, 1982.

			Regular Season								Playoffs						
Season	Club	League	GP	W	L	O/T	Mins	GA	SO	Avg	GP	W	L	Mins	GA	SO	Avg
99-2000	Mississauga	OHL	37	5	28	0	2007	173	0	5.17	....	....	....	....	....	....	....
2000-01	Mississauga	OHL	45	2	35	4	2435	219	0	5.40	....	....	....	....	....	....	....
2001-02	Mississauga	OHL	23	5	15	2	1342	96	0	4.29	....	....	....	....	....	....	....
	Belleville Bulls	OHL	26	20	4	2	1575	66	2	2.51	11	6	5	685	25	1	2.19
2002-03	Belleville Bulls	OHL	54	25	23	5	3138	153	1	2.93	7	3	4	400	21	0	3.15
	Lowell	AHL	1	0	0	0	20	4	0	12.00	....	....	....	....	....	....	....
2003-04	St. FX University	AUAA	22	16	3	2	1301	54	3	2.49	....	....	....	....	....	....	....
2004-05	St. FX University	AUAA	25	10	11	4	1496	58	3	2.33	....	....	....	....	....	....	....
2005-06	Phoenix	ECHL	48	15	27	3	2617	142	2	3.26	....	....	....	....	....	....	....
	San Diego Gulls	ECHL	9	4	3	2	549	24	0	2.62	....	....	....	....	....	....	....
2006-07	Bridgeport	AHL	15	3	8	0	762	41	0	3.23	....	....	....	....	....	....	....
	Pensacola Ice Pilots	ECHL	39	13	18	3	2189	144	0	3.95	....	....	....	....	....	....	....

Signed as a free agent by **NY Islanders**, July, 2007.

MONTOYA, Al (mawn-TOI-uh, AL) NYR

Goaltender. Catches left. 6'2", 193 lbs. Born, Chicago, IL, February 13, 1985.
(NY Rangers' 1st choice, 6th overall, in 2004 Entry Draft).

			Regular Season								Playoffs						
Season	Club	League	GP	W	L	O/T	Mins	GA	SO	Avg	GP	W	L	Mins	GA	SO	Avg
99-2000	Loyola Academy	High-MN	28	12	13	3	1685	56	1	2.01	....	....	....	....	....	....	....
2000-01	Texas Tornado	NAHL	15	10	3	0	780	38	0	2.92	1	1	0	60	2	0	2.00
	United States	Nat-Tm	2	2	0	0	120	4	0	2.00	....	....	....	....	....	....	....
2001-02	USNTDP	U-17	10	5	5	0	570	24	0	2.53	....	....	....	....	....	....	....
	USNTDP	NAHL	24	6	11	4	1344	79	0	3.53	....	....	....	....	....	....	....
2002-03	U. of Michigan	CCHA	*43	*30	10	3	*2547	99	4	2.33	....	....	....	....	....	....	....
2003-04	U. of Michigan	CCHA	*40	*26	12	2	*2340	87	6	2.23	....	....	....	....	....	....	....
2004-05	U. of Michigan	CCHA	*40	*30	7	3	*2359	99	3	2.52	....	....	....	....	....	....	....
2005-06	Hartford Wolf Pack	AHL	40	23	9	1	2094	91	2	2.61	5	2	1	257	8	1	1.87
	Charlotte Checkers	ECHL	2	1	1	0	123	8	0	3.92	....	....	....	....	....	....	....
2006-07	Hartford Wolf Pack	AHL	48	27	17	0	2556	98	6	2.30	7	3	4	391	20	1	3.07

CCHA All-Rookie Team (2003) • NCAA West Second All-American Team (2004)

MORRISON, Mike (MOHR-ih-suhn, MIGHK)

Goaltender. Catches right. 6'3", 194 lbs. Born, Medford, MA, July 11, 1979.
(Edmonton's 8th choice, 186th overall, in 1998 Entry Draft).

Season	Club	League	GP	W	L	O/T	Mins	GA	SO	Avg	GP	W	L	Mins	GA	SO	Avg
			Regular Season								Playoffs						
1997-98	Exeter	High-NH	27	15	11	2	1632	64	1	2.35	....	....	....	....	....	....	....
1998-99	University of Maine	H-East	11	3	0	1	347	10	1	1.73	....	....	....	....	....	....	....
99-2000	University of Maine	H-East	12	7	2	1	608	27	1	2.67	....	....	....	....	....	....	....
2000-01	University of Maine	H-East	10	2	3	3	490	16	1	1.96	....	....	....	....	....	....	....
2001-02	University of Maine	H-East	30	20	3	4	1645	60	2	2.19	....	....	....	....	....	....	....
2002-03	Columbus	ECHL	38	9	18	6	1948	113	1	3.48	....	....	....	....	....	....	....
2003-04	Toronto	AHL	27	12	8	2	1309	55	3	2.52	....	....	....	....	....	....	....
2004-05	Edmonton	AHL	14	2	5	5	728	21	2	1.73	....	....	....	....	....	....	....
	Greenville Grrrowl	ECHL	26	13	10	2	1576	72	1	2.74	3	1	1	150	9	0	3.61
2005-06	**Edmonton**	**NHL**	**21**	**10**	**4**	**2**	**892**	**42**	**0**	**2.83**	....	....	....	....	....	....	....
	Greenville Grrrowl	ECHL	9	7	2	0	548	20	0	2.19	....	....	....	....	....	....	....
	Ottawa	**NHL**	**4**	**1**	**0**	**1**	**207**	**12**	**0**	**3.48**	....	....	....	....	....	....	....
2006-07	**Phoenix**	**NHL**	**4**	**0**	**3**	**0**	**127**	**13**	**0**	**6.14**	....	....	....	....	....	....	....
	San Antonio	AHL	2	0	1	0	60	11	0	11.01	....	....	....	....	....	....	....
	Phoenix	ECHL	27	9	12	3	1423	80	1	3.37	....	....	....	....	....	....	....
	NHL Totals		**29**	**11**	**7**	**3**	**1226**	**67**	**0**	**3.28**	....	....	....	....	....	....	....

Hockey East First All-Star Team (2002)

Claimed on waivers by **Ottawa** from **Edmonton**, March 9, 2006. Signed as a free agent by **Phoenix**, July 2, 2006.

MRAZEK, Justin (muh-RA-zehk, JUHS-tihn) WSH.

Goaltender. Catches left. 6'3", 185 lbs. Born, Regina, Sask., July 21, 1985.
(Washington's 12th choice, 230th overall, in 2004 Entry Draft).

Season	Club	League	GP	W	L	O/T	Mins	GA	SO	Avg	GP	W	L	Mins	GA	SO	Avg
			Regular Season								Playoffs						
2003-04	Estevan Bruins	SJHL	38	14	16	5	2142	112	0	3.14	....	....	....	....	....	....	....
2004-05	Union College	ECACHL	19	5	12	1	1080	39	1	2.17	....	....	....	....	....	....	....
2005-06	Union College	ECACHL	5	0	1	1	127	12	0	5.69	....	....	....	....	....	....	....
2006-07	Union College	ECACHL	34	13	18	3	1933	97	*3	3.01	....	....	....	....	....	....	....

MUNCE, Ryan (MUNTS, RIGH-uhn) T.B.

Goaltender. Catches left. 6'2", 180 lbs. Born, Mississauga, Ont., April 16, 1985.
(Los Angeles' 5th choice, 82nd overall, in 2003 Entry Draft).

Season	Club	League	GP	W	L	O/T	Mins	GA	SO	Avg	GP	W	L	Mins	GA	SO	Avg
			Regular Season								Playoffs						
2002-03	Sarnia Sting	OHL	27	15	7	0	1410	62	3	2.64	4	1	1	149	8	1	3.22
2003-04	Sarnia Sting	OHL	54	28	21	4	3160	158	2	3.00	5	1	4	298	17	0	3.42
2004-05	Sarnia Sting	OHL	55	12	32	6	3090	163	0	3.17	....	....	....	....	....	....	....
2005-06	Bakersfield	ECHL	55	30	18	5	*3234	150	2	2.78	11	5	5	642	36	0	3.36
2006-07	Reading Royals	ECHL	17	5	6	4	837	46	0	3.30	....	....	....	....	....	....	....
	Johnstown Chiefs	ECHL	14	6	3	1	652	28	0	2.58	1	0	1	59	4	0	4.08

Traded to **Tampa Bay** by **Los Angeles** for Tampa Bay's 4th round choice in 2008 Entry Draft, January 20, 2007.

MUNRO, Adam (muhn-ROH, A-duhm)

Goaltender. Catches left. 6'2", 219 lbs. Born, St. George, Ont., November 12, 1982.
(Chicago's 1st choice, 29th overall, in 2001 Entry Draft).

Season	Club	League	GP	W	L	O/T	Mins	GA	SO	Avg	GP	W	L	Mins	GA	SO	Avg
			Regular Season								Playoffs						
1997-98	Brantford Classics	Minor-ON	15	13	2	0	660	20	*4	*1.36	....	....	....	....	....	....	....
1998-99	Brant County	OJHL-B	10	....	....	....	348	30	0	5.17	....	....	....	....	....	....	....
	Bowmanville	OPJHL	14	....	....	....	816	50	0	3.68	....	....	....	....	....	....	....
	Erie Otters	OHL	1	0	0	0	1	0	0	0.00	....	....	....	....	....	....	....
99-2000	Bowmanville	OPJHL	2	2	0	0	125	5	0	2.40	....	....	....	....	....	....	....
	Erie Otters	OHL	22	8	7	1	948	48	1	3.04	1	0	0	5	1	0	12.00
2000-01	Erie Otters	OHL	41	26	6	6	2283	88	*4	2.31	10	6	2	509	27	1	3.18
2001-02	Erie Otters	OHL	43	24	13	1	2277	128	3	3.37	6	4	2	361	17	0	2.83
2002-03	Erie Otters	OHL	8	2	6	0	426	24	1	3.38	....	....	....	....	....	....	....
	Sault Ste. Marie	OHL	42	20	20	2	2494	160	1	3.85	4	0	4	240	12	0	3.00
2003-04	**Chicago**	**NHL**	**7**	**1**	**5**	**1**	**426**	**26**	**0**	**3.66**	....	....	....	....	....	....	....
	Norfolk Admirals	AHL	12	5	4	1	695	26	0	2.24	....	....	....	....	....	....	....
	Gwinnett	ECHL	6	4	1	1	370	17	0	2.76	1	0	1	60	2	0	2.01
2004-05	Norfolk Admirals	AHL	30	14	10	2	1595	66	4	2.48	....	....	....	....	....	....	....
	Atlantic City	ECHL	5	2	2	1	272	9	0	1.99	....	....	....	....	....	....	....
2005-06	**Chicago**	**NHL**	**10**	**3**	**5**	**2**	**501**	**25**	**1**	**2.99**	....	....	....	....	....	....	....
	Norfolk Admirals	AHL	28	17	8	1	1612	73	1	2.72	4	0	4	239	15	0	3.77
2006-07	Fribourg	Swiss	41	12	28	0	2488	149	0	3.59	....	....	....	....	....	....	....
	NHL Totals		**17**	**4**	**10**	**3**	**927**	**51**	**1**	**3.30**	....	....	....	....	....	....	....

Signed as a free agent by **Fribourg** (Swiss), July 7, 2006. Signed as a free agent by **Syracuse** (AHL), July 23, 2007.

MUNROE, Scott (muhn-ROH, SKAWT) PHI.

Goaltender. Catches left. 6'2", 210 lbs. Born, Moose Jaw, Sask., January 20, 1982.

Season	Club	League	GP	W	L	O/T	Mins	GA	SO	Avg	GP	W	L	Mins	GA	SO	Avg
			Regular Season								Playoffs						
2002-03	AL-Huntsville	CHA	20	11	6	1	1049	49	1	2.80	....	....	....	....	....	....	....
2003-04	AL-Huntsville	CHA	17	5	9	1	891	47	0	3.16	....	....	....	....	....	....	....
2004-05	AL-Huntsville	CHA	31	16	10	4	1805	69	3	2.29	....	....	....	....	....	....	....
2005-06	AL-Huntsville	CHA	31	17	11	2	1813	91	0	3.01	....	....	....	....	....	....	....
	Philadelphia	AHL	2	0	2	0	119	7	0	3.54	....	....	....	....	....	....	....
2006-07	Philadelphia	AHL	40	15	19	2	2298	117	2	3.05	....	....	....	....	....	....	....

CHA All-Rookie Team (2003) • CHA Rookie of the Year (2003)

Signed as a free agent by **Philadelphia** (AHL), March 18, 2006.

NABOKOV, Evgeni (na-BAW-kahv, ehv-GEH-nee) S.J.

Goaltender. Catches left. 6', 200 lbs. Born, Ust-Kamenogorsk, USSR, July 25, 1975.
(San Jose's 9th choice, 219th overall, in 1994 Entry Draft).

Season	Club	League	GP	W	L	O/T	Mins	GA	SO	Avg	GP	W	L	Mins	GA	SO	Avg
			Regular Season								Playoffs						
1991-92	Ust-Kamenogorsk	CIS	1	....	....	....	20	1	0	3.00	....	....	....	....	....	....	....
1992-93	Ust-Kam'gorsk 2	CIS-2	19	....	....	....	....	....	....	....	....	....	....	....	....	....	....
	Ust-Kamenogorsk	CIS	4	....	....	....	109	5	0	2.75	....	....	....	....	....	....	....
1993-94	Ust-Kamenogorsk	CIS	11	....	....	....	539	29	....	3.23	....	....	....	....	....	....	....
1994-95	Dynamo Moscow	CIS	24	....	....	....	1326	40	3	1.81	13	....	....	806	30	2	2.23
1995-96	Dynamo Moscow	CIS	39	....	....	....	2008	67	5	2.00	....	....	....	....	....	....	....
1996-97	Dynamo Moscow	Russia	27	....	....	....	1588	56	2	2.11	4	....	....	255	12	0	2.82
	Dynamo Moscow 2	Russia-3	1	....	....	....	....	2	....	....	....	....	....	....	....	....	....
1997-98	Kentucky	AHL	33	10	21	2	1866	122	0	3.92	1	0	0	23	1	0	2.59
1998-99	Kentucky	AHL	43	26	14	1	2429	106	5	2.62	11	6	5	599	30	*2	3.00
99-2000	**San Jose**	**NHL**	**11**	**2**	**2**	**1**	**414**	**15**	**1**	**2.17**	**1**	**0**	**0**	**20**	**0**	**0**	**0.00**
	Kentucky	AHL	2	1	1	0	120	3	1	1.50	....	....	....	....	....	....	....
	Cleveland	IHL	20	12	4	3	1164	52	0	2.68	....	....	....	....	....	....	....
2000-01	**San Jose**	**NHL**	**66**	**32**	**21**	**7**	**3700**	**135**	**6**	**2.19**	**4**	**1**	**3**	**218**	**10**	**1**	**2.75**
2001-02	**San Jose**	**NHL**	**67**	**37**	**24**	**5**	**3901**	**149**	**7**	**2.29**	**12**	**7**	**5**	**712**	**31**	**0**	**2.61**
2002-03	**San Jose**	**NHL**	**55**	**19**	**28**	**8**	**3227**	**146**	**3**	**2.71**	....	....	....	....	....	....	....
2003-04	**San Jose**	**NHL**	**59**	**31**	**19**	**8**	**3456**	**127**	**9**	**2.20**	**17**	**10**	**7**	**1052**	**30**	**3**	**1.71**
2004-05	Magnitogorsk	Russia	14	....	....	....	808	27	3	2.00	5	....	....	307	13	0	2.53
2005-06	**San Jose**	**NHL**	**45**	**16**	**19**	**7**	**2575**	**133**	**1**	**3.10**	**1**	**0**	**0**	**12**	**1**	**0**	**5.00**
	Russia	Olympics	7	....	....	....	359	8	3	1.34	....	....	....	....	....	....	....
2006-07	**San Jose**	**NHL**	**50**	**25**	**16**	**4**	**2778**	**106**	**7**	**2.29**	**11**	**6**	**5**	**701**	**26**	**1**	**2.23**
	NHL Totals		**353**	**162**	**129**	**40**	**20051**	**811**	**34**	**2.43**	**46**	**24**	**20**	**2715**	**98**	**5**	**2.17**

NHL All-Rookie Team (2001) • Calder Memorial Trophy (2001)

Played in NHL All-Star Game (2001)

• Scored a goal vs. Vancouver, March 10, 2002. Signed as a free agent by **Magnitogorsk** (Russia), December 2, 2004.

NASTIUK, Kevin (NAZ-tee-uhk, KEH-vihn) CAR.

Goaltender. Catches left. 6'1", 180 lbs. Born, Edmonton, Alta., July 20, 1985.
(Carolina's 4th choice, 126th overall, in 2003 Entry Draft).

Season	Club	League	GP	W	L	O/T	Mins	GA	SO	Avg	GP	W	L	Mins	GA	SO	Avg
			Regular Season								Playoffs						
99-2000	Inland Real Estate	EMHA	20	9	6	5	998	59	0	3.25	....	....	....	....	....	....	....
	CAC Cement	AMBHL	1	0	1	0	50	8	0	9.60	....	....	....	....	....	....	....
2000-01	CAC Cement	AMBHL	20	12	7	1	1233	64	0	3.11	1	1	0	60	2	0	2.00
2001-02	Medicine Hat	WHL	19	4	10	0	877	66	0	4.52	....	....	....	....	....	....	....
2002-03	Medicine Hat	WHL	42	15	20	2	2344	172	0	4.40	11	7	4	693	33	0	2.86
2003-04	Medicine Hat	WHL	*68	40	19	8	*4056	187	4	2.77	*20	*16	4	*1182	38	*4	1.93
2004-05	Medicine Hat	WHL	42	23	18	1	2426	88	7	2.18	12	5	7	715	27	0	2.27
2005-06	Lowell	AHL	11	1	7	3	643	37	0	3.45	....	....	....	....	....	....	....
	Florida Everblades	ECHL	20	13	4	2	1190	50	1	2.52	3	1	1	106	7	0	3.96
2006-07	Las Vegas	ECHL	32	16	8	6	1863	79	1	2.54	4	3	1	250	7	1	1.68

WHL Playoff MVP (2004) • WHL East Second All-Star Team (2005)

NEUVIRTH, Michal (NOI-vihrt, MEE-khahl) WSH.

Goaltender. Catches left. 6', 174 lbs. Born, Usti nad Labem, Czech., March 23, 1988.
(Washington's 3rd choice, 34th overall, in 2006 Entry Draft).

Season	Club	League	GP	W	L	O/T	Mins	GA	SO	Avg	GP	W	L	Mins	GA	SO	Avg
			Regular Season								Playoffs						
2003-04	Sparta U17	CzR-U17	55	....	....	....	3137	96	5	1.84	3	....	....	180	13	0	4.33
2004-05	Sparta U17	CzR-U17	20	....	....	....	1178	49	3	2.50	8	....	....	482	17	0	2.12
	Sparta Jr.	CzRep-Jr.	10	....	....	....	501	20	1	2.40	....	....	....	....	....	....	....
2005-06	Sparta Jr.	CzRep-Jr.	42	....	....	....	2516	82	5	1.96	3	....	....	179	9	0	3.02
2006-07	Plymouth Whalers	OHL	41	26	8	4	2223	86	4	2.32	18	14	3	1080	44	0	2.44

OHL Second All-Star Team (2007)

NIITTYMAKI, Antero (nih-tih-MA-kee, AN-tehr-oh) PHI.

Goaltender. Catches left. 6'1", 195 lbs. Born, Turku, Finland, June 18, 1980.
(Philadelphia's 7th choice, 168th overall, in 1998 Entry Draft).

Season	Club	League	GP	W	L	O/T	Mins	GA	SO	Avg	GP	W	L	Mins	GA	SO	Avg
			Regular Season								Playoffs						
1997-98	TPS Turku U18	Fin-U18	12	....	....	....	....	....	....	....	1	1	0	60	1	0	1.00
	TPS Turku Jr.	Fin-Jr.	19	10	8	1	1131	34	....	1.80	4	3	1	220	7	0	1.91
1998-99	TPS Turku Jr.	Fin-Jr.	35	27	8	0	2095	60	3	1.72	6	3	3	362	14	0	2.32
99-2000	TPS Turku Jr.	Fin-Jr.	1	1	0	0	60	1	0	1.00	1	0	1	60	5	0	5.00
	TPS Turku	Finland	32	23	6	3	1899	68	3	2.15	8	6	2	453	13	0	1.72
2000-01	TPS Turku Jr.	Fin-Jr.	....	....	....	....	....	....	....	....	2	1	1	120	4	1	2.00
	TPS Turku	Finland	21	10	5	1	1112	46	2	2.48	....	....	....	....	....	....	....
2001-02	TPS Turku	Finland	27	16	8	1	1498	46	3	1.84	4	2	2	295	11	0	2.24
2002-03	Philadelphia	AHL	40	14	21	2	2283	98	0	2.58	....	....	....	....	....	....	....
2003-04	**Philadelphia**	**NHL**	**3**	**3**	**0**	**0**	**180**	**3**	**0**	**1.00**	....	....	....	....	....	....	....
	Philadelphia	AHL	49	24	13	6	2728	92	7	2.02	12	6	6	796	24	0	1.81
2004-05	Philadelphia	AHL	58	33	21	4	3453	119	6	2.07	*21	*15	5	*1269	37	*3	1.75
2005-06	**Philadelphia**	**NHL**	**46**	**23**	**15**	**6**	**2690**	**133**	**2**	**2.97**	**2**	**0**	**0**	**73**	**5**	**0**	**4.11**
	Finland	Olympics	6	5	1	0	359	8	3	1.34	....	....	....	....	....	....	....
2006-07	**Philadelphia**	**NHL**	**52**	**9**	**29**	**9**	**2943**	**166**	**0**	**3.38**	....	....	....	....	....	....	....
	NHL Totals		**101**	**35**	**44**	**15**	**5813**	**302**	**2**	**3.12**	**2**	**0**	**0**	**73**	**5**	**0**	**4.11**

Jack A. Butterfield Trophy (Playoff MVP – AHL) (2005) • Olympic Tournament All-Star Team (2006) • Olympic Tournament Best Goaltender (2006) • Olympic Tournament MVP (2006)

NORONEN, Mika (NOH-rah-nehn, MEE-kah)

Goaltender. Catches left. 6'2", 200 lbs. Born, Tampere, Finland, June 17, 1979.
(Buffalo's 1st choice, 21st overall, in 1997 Entry Draft).

Season	Club	League	GP	W	L	O/T	Mins	GA	SO	Avg	GP	W	L	Mins	GA	SO	Avg
			Regular Season								Playoffs						
1995-96	Tappara U18	Fin-U18	5	....	....	....	299	13	....	2.61	5	....	....	300	8	....	1.60
	Tappara Jr.	Fin-Jr.	16	....	....	....	962	37	2	2.31	....	....	....	....	....	....	....
1996-97	Tappara Jr.	Fin-Jr.	17	....	....	....	....	....	....	....	....	....	....	....	....	....	....
	Hermes Kokkola	Finland-2	2	....	....	....	91	11	0	7.25	....	....	....	....	....	....	....
	Tappara Tampere	Finland	5	1	3	0	215	17	0	4.73	....	....	....	....	....	....	....
1997-98	Tappara Jr.	Fin-Jr.	6	4	1	1	365	13	....	2.14	4	2	2	262	11	0	2.52
	Tappara Tampere	Finland	31	14	12	3	1703	83	1	2.92	4	1	2	196	12	0	3.67
1998-99	Tappara Tampere	Finland	43	18	20	5	2494	135	2	3.25	....	....	....	....	....	....	....
99-2000	Rochester	AHL	54	*33	13	4	3089	112	*6	2.18	21	13	8	1235	37	*6	*1.80
2000-01	**Buffalo**	**NHL**	**2**	**2**	**0**	**0**	**108**	**5**	**0**	**2.78**	....	....	....	....	....	....	....
	Rochester	AHL	47	26	15	5	2753	100	4	2.18	4	1	3	250	11	0	2.64
2001-02	**Buffalo**	**NHL**	**10**	**4**	**3**	**1**	**518**	**23**	**0**	**2.66**	....	....	....	....	....	....	....
	Rochester	AHL	45	16	17	12	2764	115	3	2.50	1	0	1	59	3	0	3.06
2002-03	**Buffalo**	**NHL**	**16**	**4**	**9**	**3**	**891**	**36**	**1**	**2.42**	....	....	....	....	....	....	....
	Rochester	AHL	19	5	9	5	1169	55	2	2.82	....	....	....	....	....	....	....
2003-04	**Buffalo**	**NHL**	**35**	**11**	**17**	**2**	**1796**	**77**	**2**	**2.57**	....	....	....	....	....	....	....
2004-05	HPK Hameenlinna	Finland	27	14	8	4	1614	54	1	2.01	9	4	4	482	21	1	2.61
2005-06	**Buffalo**	**NHL**	**4**	**1**	**2**	**0**	**169**	**12**	**0**	**4.26**	....	....	....	....	....	....	....
	Rochester	AHL	2	0	2	0	121	6	0	2.99	....	....	....	....	....	....	....
	Vancouver	**NHL**	**4**	**1**	**1**	**0**	**170**	**10**	**0**	**3.53**	....	....	....	....	....	....	....
2006-07	Ak Bars Kazan	Russia	33	....	....	....	1877	66	2	2.11	*16	....	....	*941	35	0	2.23
	NHL Totals		**71**	**23**	**32**	**6**	**3652**	**163**	**3**	**2.68**	....	....	....	....	....	....	....

AHL All-Rookie Team (2000) • AHL Second All-Star Team (2000, 2001) • Dudley "Red" Garrett Memorial Award (Rookie of the Year – AHL) (2000) • Harry "Hap" Holmes Memorial Award (fewest goals against – AHL) (2001) (shared with Tom Askey)

Signed as a free agent by **Hameenlinna** (Finland), November 2, 2004. Traded to **Vancouver** by **Buffalo** for Vancouver's 2nd round choice (Jhonas Enroth) in 2006 Entry Draft, March 9, 2006. Signed as a free agent by **Kazan** (Russia), August 4, 2006.

NORRENA, Fredrik (noh-REH-nah, FREHD-rihk) CBJ

Goaltender. Catches left. 6', 189 lbs. Born, Pietarsaari, Finland, November 29, 1973.
(Tampa Bay's 8th choice, 213th overall, in 2002 Entry Draft).

Season	Club	League	GP	W	L	O/T	Mins	GA	SO	Avg	GP	W	L	Mins	GA	SO	Avg
			Regular Season								Playoffs						
1989-90	UFK Leppalahti	Finland-3	36	....	....	....	....	....	....	....	....	....	....	....	....	....	....
1990-91	UFK Leppalahti	Finland-3	36	....	....	....	....	....	....	....	....	....	....	....	....	....	....
1991-92	UFK Leppalahti	Finland-3	35	....	....	....	....	....	....	....	....	....	....	....	....	....	....

			Regular Season								Playoffs						
1992-93	TPS Turku Jr.	Fin-Jr.	25	15	9	1	1449	74	1	3.06	5	....	....	307	11	1	2.14
	TPS Turku	Finland	2	0	1	0	30	1	0	2.00	....	....	....	....	....	....	....
1993-94	TPS Turku Jr.	Fin-Jr.	2	0	1	0	80	5	0	3.75	1	0	1	58	4	0	4.10
	TPS Turku	Finland	10	3	3	0	387	19	0	2.94	....	....	....	....	....	....	....
	Kiekko-67 Turku	Finland-2	15	7	7	1	884	43	2	2.92	....	....	....	....	....	....	....
1994-95	TPS Turku	Finland	22	14	6	2	1328	60	1	2.71	11	7	4	666	27	1	2.43
	Kiekko-67 Turku	Finland-2	15	....	....	....	828	34	0	2.46	....	....	....	....	....	....	....
1995-96	TPS Turku	Finland	26	14	8	3	1539	68	0	2.65	....	....	....	....	....	....	....
1996-97	Kiekko-67 Turku	Finland-2	12	....	....	....	725	36	0	2.98	....	....	....	....	....	....	....
	AIK Solna	Sweden	5	....	....	....	274	21	1	4.60	....	....	....	....	....	....	....
1997-98	Lukko Rauma	Finland	37	12	19	4	2174	105	0	2.90	....	....	....	....	....	....	....
1998-99	TPS Turku	Finland	20	11	4	1	1010	35	2	2.08	1	0	0	20	2	0	6.00
99-2000	TPS Turku	Finland	21	15	4	0	1175	35	2	1.79	4	3	0	234	10	0	2.56
	TuTo Turku	Finland-2	2	1	1	0	118	7	0	3.54	....	....	....	....	....	....	....
2000-01	TPS Turku	Finland	39	26	10	3	2266	66	6	1.75	10	9	1	603	13	2	1.29
2001-02	TPS Turku	Finland	32	14	11	5	1878	62	2	1.98	4	1	3	256	7	1	1.64
2002-03	V.Frolunda	Sweden	23	....	....	....	1386	56	1	2.42	4	....	....	288	6	1	1.25
2003-04	Linkopings HC	Sweden	40	....	....	....	2414	68	9	1.69	3	....	....	176	6	0	2.05
2004-05	Linkopings HC	Sweden	43	....	....	....	2522	78	5	1.86	6	....	....	383	13	0	2.03
2005-06	Linkopings HC	Sweden	36	....	....	....	2170	78	4	2.16	11	....	....	693	22	2	*1.90
	Finland	Olympics	2	2	0	0	120	0	2	0.00	....	....	....	....	....	....	....
2006-07	**Columbus**	**NHL**	**55**	**24**	**23**	**3**	**2952**	**137**	**3**	**2.78**	....	....	....	....	....	....	....
	NHL Totals		**55**	**24**	**23**	**3**	**2952**	**137**	**3**	**2.78**	....	....	....	....	....	....	....

Traded to **Columbus** by **Tampa Bay** with Fredrik Modin for Marc Denis, June 30, 2006.

OSGOOD, Chris (AWS-gud, KRIHS) DET.

Goaltender. Catches left. 5'10", 176 lbs. Born, Peace River, Alta., November 26, 1972.
(Detroit's 3rd choice, 54th overall, in 1991 Entry Draft).

			Regular Season								Playoffs						
Season	Club	League	GP	W	L	O/T	Mins	GA	SO	Avg	GP	W	L	Mins	GA	SO	Avg
1988-89	Medicine Hat	AMHL	26	....	....	....	1441	88	0	3.66	....	....	....	....	....	....	....
1989-90	Medicine Hat	WHL	57	24	28	2	3094	228	0	4.42	3	0	3	173	17	0	5.91
1990-91	Medicine Hat	WHL	46	23	18	3	2630	173	2	3.95	12	7	5	712	42	0	3.54
1991-92	Medicine Hat	WHL	15	10	3	0	819	44	0	3.22	....	....	....	....	....	....	....
	Brandon	WHL	16	3	10	1	890	60	1	4.04	....	....	....	....	....	....	....
	Seattle	WHL	21	12	7	1	1217	65	1	3.20	15	9	6	904	51	0	3.38
1992-93	Adirondack	AHL	45	19	19	4	2438	159	0	3.91	1	0	1	59	2	0	2.03
1993-94	**Detroit**	**NHL**	**41**	**23**	**8**	**5**	**2206**	**105**	**2**	**2.86**	**6**	**3**	**2**	**307**	**12**	**1**	**2.35**
	Adirondack	AHL	4	3	1	0	239	13	0	3.26	....	....	....	....	....	....	....
1994-95	**Detroit**	**NHL**	**19**	**14**	**5**	**0**	**1087**	**41**	**1**	**2.26**	**2**	**0**	**0**	**68**	**2**	**0**	**1.76**
	Adirondack	AHL	2	1	1	0	120	6	0	3.00	....	....	....	....	....	....	....
1995-96	**Detroit**	**NHL**	**50**	***39**	**6**	**5**	**2933**	**106**	**5**	**2.17**	**15**	**8**	**7**	**936**	**33**	**2**	**2.12**
1996-97♦	**Detroit**	**NHL**	**47**	**23**	**13**	**9**	**2769**	**106**	**6**	**2.30**	**2**	**0**	**0**	**47**	**2**	**0**	**2.55**
1997-98♦	**Detroit**	**NHL**	**64**	**33**	**20**	**11**	**3807**	**140**	**6**	**2.21**	***22**	***16**	**6**	***1361**	**48**	**2**	**2.12**
1998-99	**Detroit**	**NHL**	**63**	**34**	**25**	**4**	**3691**	**149**	**3**	**2.42**	**6**	**4**	**2**	**358**	**14**	**1**	**2.35**
99-2000	**Detroit**	**NHL**	**53**	**30**	**14**	**8**	**3148**	**126**	**6**	**2.40**	**9**	**5**	**4**	**547**	**18**	**2**	**1.97**
2000-01	**Detroit**	**NHL**	**52**	**25**	**19**	**4**	**2834**	**127**	**1**	**2.69**	**6**	**2**	**4**	**365**	**15**	**1**	**2.47**
2001-02	**NY Islanders**	**NHL**	**66**	**32**	**25**	**6**	**3743**	**156**	**4**	**2.50**	**7**	**3**	**4**	**392**	**17**	**0**	**2.60**
2002-03	**NY Islanders**	**NHL**	**37**	**17**	**14**	**4**	**1993**	**97**	**2**	**2.92**	....	....	....	....	....	....	....
	St. Louis	**NHL**	**9**	**4**	**3**	**2**	**532**	**27**	**2**	**3.05**	**7**	**3**	**4**	**417**	**17**	**1**	**2.45**
2003-04	**St. Louis**	**NHL**	**67**	**31**	**25**	**8**	**3861**	**144**	**3**	**2.24**	**5**	**1**	**4**	**287**	**12**	**0**	**2.51**
2004-05							DID NOT PLAY										
2005-06	**Detroit**	**NHL**	**32**	**20**	**6**	**5**	**1846**	**85**	**2**	**2.76**	....	....	....	....	....	....	....
	Grand Rapids	AHL	3	2	1	0	180	10	0	3.34	....	....	....	....	....	....	....
2006-07	**Detroit**	**NHL**	**21**	**11**	**3**	**6**	**1161**	**46**	**0**	**2.38**	....	....	....	....	....	....	....
	NHL Totals		**621**	**336**	**186**	**77**	**35611**	**1455**	**43**	**2.45**	**87**	**45**	**37**	**5085**	**190**	**10**	**2.24**

WHL East Second All-Star Team (1991) • NHL Second All-Star Team (1996) • William M. Jennings Trophy (1996) (shared with Mike Vernon)

Played in NHL All-Star Game (1996, 1997, 1998)

• Scored a goal while with Medicine Hat (WHL), January 3, 1991. • Scored a goal vs. Hartford, March 6, 1996. Claimed by **NY Islanders** from **Detroit** in Waiver Draft, September 28, 2001. Traded to **St. Louis** by **NY Islanders** with NY Islanders' 3rd round choice (Konstantin Barulin) in 2003 Entry Draft for Justin Papineau and St. Louis' 2nd round choice (Jeremy Colliton) in 2003 Entry Draft, March 11, 2003. Signed as a free agent by **Detroit**, August 8, 2005.

PALMER, Joe (PAHL-muhr, JOH) CHI.

Goaltender. Catches left. 6'1", 205 lbs. Born, Yorkville, NY, February 19, 1988.
(Chicago's 6th choice, 96th overall, in 2006 Entry Draft).

			Regular Season								Playoffs						
Season	Club	League	GP	W	L	O/T	Mins	GA	SO	Avg	GP	W	L	Mins	GA	SO	Avg
2003-04	Syracuse Jr. Stars	EmJHL	31	....	....	....	1147	69	1	3.61	6	....	....	368	19	0	3.10
	USNTDP	U-17	1	0	0	0	11	2	0	10.91	....	....	....	....	....	....	....
2004-05	USNTDP	U-17	8	6	1	1	495	22	0	2.67	....	....	....	....	....	....	....
	USNTDP	NAHL	19	10	8	1	1020	56	0	3.29	....	....	....	....	....	....	....
2005-06	USNTDP	U-18	33	16	14	3	1900	99	0	3.13	....	....	....	....	....	....	....
	USNTDP	NAHL	14	13	1	0	776	22	1	1.70	....	....	....	....	....	....	....
2006-07	Ohio State	CCHA	34	15	15	4	1968	97	1	2.96	....	....	....	....	....	....	....

PARISE, Jordan (pah-REE-say, JOHR-dahn) N.J.

Goaltender. Catches left. 5'11", 195 lbs. Born, Faribault, MN, September 19, 1982.

			Regular Season								Playoffs						
Season	Club	League	GP	W	L	O/T	Mins	GA	SO	Avg	GP	W	L	Mins	GA	SO	Avg
2002-03	Waterloo	USHL					STATISTICS NOT AVAILABLE										
2003-04	North Dakota	WCHA	22	14	4	3	1230	42	2	*2.05	....	....	....	....	....	....	....
2004-05	North Dakota	WCHA	27	17	7	3	1575	56	2	*2.13	....	....	....	....	....	....	....
2005-06	North Dakota	WCHA	34	24	9	1	2017	74	6	2.20	....	....	....	....	....	....	....
2006-07	Lowell Devils	AHL	32	17	12	2	1879	84	2	2.68	....	....	....	....	....	....	....

Signed as a free agent by **New Jersey**, July 6, 2006.

PATTERSON, Kent (PA-tuhr-suhn, KEHNT) COL.

Goaltender. Catches left. 6', 184 lbs. Born, St. Louis Park, MI, September 15, 1989.
(Colorado's 6th choice, 113th overall, in 2007 Entry Draft).

			Regular Season								Playoffs						
Season	Club	League	GP	W	L	O/T	Mins	GA	SO	Avg	GP	W	L	Mins	GA	SO	Avg
2004-05	Blake Bears	High-MN	14	9	4	1	673	27	....	2.05	....	....	....	....	....	....	....
2005-06	Blake Bears	High-MN	25	14	8	2	1249	66	....	2.70	....	....	....	....	....	....	....
2006-07	Cedar Rapids	USHL	29	20	5	3	1710	83	2	2.91	1	0	1	41	6	0	8.78

PATZOLD, Dimitri (PATZ-ohld, dih-MEE-tree) S.J.

Goaltender. Catches left. 6', 195 lbs. Born, Ust-Kamenogorsk, USSR, February 3, 1983.
(San Jose's 3rd choice, 107th overall, in 2001 Entry Draft).

			Regular Season								Playoffs						
Season	Club	League	GP	W	L	O/T	Mins	GA	SO	Avg	GP	W	L	Mins	GA	SO	Avg
99-2000	Kolner EC Jr.	Ger-Jr.	38	....	....	....	2131	73	0	2.06	....	....	....	....	....	....	....
	Kolner Haie 2	German-5	16	....	....	....	896	58	0	3.88	....	....	....	....	....	....	....
2000-01	EV Duisburg	German-3	6	....	....	....	360	17	0	2.83	....	....	....	....	....	....	....
	Erding Jets	German-2	24	....	....	....	1378	89	0	3.88	....	....	....	....	....	....	....
2001-02	EV Duisburg	German-2	6	....	....	....	360	17	0	2.83	....	....	....	....	....	....	....
	Kolner Haie	Germany	7	....	....	....	260	16	0	3.69	....	....	....	....	....	....	....
2002-03	Adler Mannheim	Germany	15	....	....	....	817	35	0	2.57	2	....	....	34	2	0	3.53
2003-04	Cleveland Barons	AHL	27	10	15	0	1457	70	3	2.88	....	....	....	....	....	....	....
	Johnstown Chiefs	ECHL	8	7	0	0	443	20	0	2.71	1	0	1	59	2	0	2.02
2004-05	Cleveland Barons	AHL	41	18	16	5	2418	104	1	2.58	....	....	....	....	....	....	....
2005-06	Cleveland Barons	AHL	33	10	21	0	1876	124	0	3.97	....	....	....	....	....	....	....
2006-07	Worcester Sharks	AHL	24	10	8	3	1378	77	0	3.35	4	2	1	256	8	0	1.87
	Fresno Falcons	ECHL	4	2	2	0	239	8	0	2.01	....	....	....	....	....	....	....

PAVELEC, Ondrej (pah-vah-LEK, AWN-dray) ATL.

Goaltender. Catches left. 6'2", 200 lbs. Born, Kladno, Czech., August 31, 1987.
(Atlanta's 2nd choice, 41st overall, in 2005 Entry Draft).

			Regular Season								Playoffs						
Season	Club	League	GP	W	L	O/T	Mins	GA	SO	Avg	GP	W	L	Mins	GA	SO	Avg
2003-04	HC Kladno U17	CzR-U17	38	....	....	....	2079	77	3	2.22	2	....	....	67	7	0	6.27
2004-05	HC Kladno Jr.	CzRep-Jr.	39	....	....	....	2218	85	7	2.30	10	....	....	587	24	1	2.45
	HK LEV Slany	CzRep-3	1	....	....	....	60	4	0	4.00	....	....	....	....	....	....	....
2005-06	Cape Breton	QMJHL	47	27	18	0	2578	108	3	2.51	9	4	5	507	19	0	*2.25
2006-07	Cape Breton	QMJHL	43	28	11	....	2335	98	1	*2.52	16	11	5	970	37	*2	*2.29

QMJHL All-Rookie Team (2006) • QMJHL First All-Star Team (2006, 2007) • QMJHL Defensive Rookie of the Year (2006)

PEARCE, Joe (PEERS-JOH) T.B.

Goaltender. Catches left. 6'5", 215 lbs. Born, Brick, NJ, June 24, 1982.
(Tampa Bay's 3rd choice, 135th overall, in 2002 Entry Draft).

			Regular Season								Playoffs						
Season	Club	League	GP	W	L	O/T	Mins	GA	SO	Avg	GP	W	L	Mins	GA	SO	Avg
2000-01	Bismarck Bobcats	AWHL	17	....	....	....	1020	40	1	2.31	....	....	....	....	....	....	....
2001-02	N.H. Jr. Monarchs	EJHL	32	....	....	....	1885	57	1	1.82	....	....	....	....	....	....	....
2002-03	Chicago Steel	USHL	37	18	12	3	1980	96	1	2.91	....	....	....	....	....	....	....
2003-04	Boston College	H-East	5	2	2	0	270	14	0	3.11	....	....	....	....	....	....	....
2004-05	Boston College	H-East						DID NOT PLAY									
2005-06	Boston College	H-East	3	2	0	1	184	7	0	2.28	....	....	....	....	....	....	....
2006-07	Boston College	H-East	2	0	0	0	13	1	0	4.55	....	....	....	....	....	....	....

PELLETIER, Jean-Marc (PEHL-tyay, ZHAWN-MAHRK)

Goaltender. Catches left. 6'3", 209 lbs. Born, Atlanta, GA, March 4, 1978.
(Philadelphia's 1st choice, 30th overall, in 1997 Entry Draft).

			Regular Season								Playoffs						
Season	Club	League	GP	W	L	O/T	Mins	GA	SO	Avg	GP	W	L	Mins	GA	SO	Avg
1993-94	Richelieu Riverains	QAAA	24	14	8	2	1440	91	0	3.79	2	1	0	104	11	0	6.32
1994-95	Richelieu Riverains	QAAA	21	15	6	0	1260	71	0	3.36	2	1	1	153	11	0	4.32
1995-96	Cornell Big Red	ECAC	5	1	2	0	179	15	0	5.03	....	....	....	....	....	....	....
1996-97	Cornell Big Red	ECAC	11	5	2	3	679	28	1	2.47	....	....	....	....	....	....	....
1997-98	Rimouski Oceanic	QMJHL	34	17	11	3	1913	118	0	3.70	16	11	3	895	51	1	3.42
1998-99	**Philadelphia**	**NHL**	**1**	**0**	**1**	**0**	**60**	**5**	**0**	**5.00**	....	....	....	....	....	....	....
	Philadelphia	AHL	47	25	16	4	2636	122	2	2.78	1	0	0	27	0	0	0.00
99-2000	Philadelphia	AHL	24	14	10	0	1405	58	3	2.48	....	....	....	....	....	....	....
	Cincinnati	IHL	22	14	4	2	1278	52	2	2.44	3	1	1	160	8	1	3.00
2000-01	Cincinnati	IHL	39	18	14	5	2261	119	2	3.16	5	1	4	318	15	0	2.83
2001-02	Lowell	AHL	40	21	12	4	2284	98	2	2.57	5	2	3	298	13	0	2.62
2002-03	Lowell	AHL	17	6	10	0	861	51	1	3.55	....	....	....	....	....	....	....
	Phoenix	**NHL**	**2**	**0**	**2**	**0**	**119**	**6**	**0**	**3.03**	....	....	....	....	....	....	....
	Springfield Falcons	AHL	24	12	7	4	1391	55	2	2.37	6	3	3	368	16	1	2.61
2003-04	**Phoenix**	**NHL**	**4**	**1**	**1**	**0**	**175**	**12**	**0**	**4.11**	....	....	....	....	....	....	....
	Springfield Falcons	AHL	43	10	24	5	2433	109	2	2.69	....	....	....	....	....	....	....
2004-05	Utah Grizzlies	AHL	23	6	12	1	1231	77	0	3.75	....	....	....	....	....	....	....
	Springfield Falcons	AHL	13	2	10	1	715	35	0	2.94	....	....	....	....	....	....	....
2005-06	Rochester	AHL	39	21	15	1	2198	120	0	3.28	....	....	....	....	....	....	....
2006-07	Rochester	AHL	4	4	0	0	244	10	0	2.46	....	....	....	....	....	....	....
	Adler Mannheim	Germany	19	....	....	....	1129	49	0	2.60	11	....	....	674	24	1	*2.14
	NHL Totals		**7**	**1**	**4**	**0**	**354**	**23**	**0**	**3.90**							

Traded to **Carolina** by **Philadelphia** with Rod Brind'Amour and Philadelphia's 2nd round choice (later traded to Colorado – Colorado selected Argis Saviels) in 2000 Entry Draft for Keith Primeau and Carolina's 5th round choice (later traded to NY Islanders – NY Islanders selected Kristofer Ottosson) in 2000 Entry Draft, January 23, 2000. Traded to **Phoenix** by **Carolina** for Patrick DesRochers, December 31, 2002. Signed as a free agent by **Florida**, August 19, 2005.

PENNER, Andrew (PEH-nuhr, AN-droo)

Goaltender. Catches left. 6'2", 205 lbs. Born, Scarborough, Ont., December 21, 1982.

			Regular Season								Playoffs						
Season	Club	League	GP	W	L	O/T	Mins	GA	SO	Avg	GP	W	L	Mins	GA	SO	Avg
1998-99	North York	OPJHL	26	....	....	....	1497	107	0	4.29	....	....	....	....	....	....	....
99-2000	North Bay	OHL	22	3	12	0	1070	79	0	4.43	....	....	....	....	....	....	....
2000-01	North Bay	OHL	32	10	19	1	1787	117	1	3.93	....	....	....	....	....	....	....
2001-02	North Bay	OHL	18	4	8	4	917	52	1	3.40	....	....	....	....	....	....	....
	Guelph Storm	OHL	36	18	12	5	2066	107	0	3.11	9	5	4	546	29	0	3.19
2002-03	Guelph Storm	OHL	51	21	21	7	2975	137	0	2.76	11	5	5	665	34	0	3.07
2003-04	Dayton Bombers	ECHL	50	15	27	2	2764	175	0	3.80	....	....	....	....	....	....	....
2004-05	Syracuse Crunch	AHL	23	8	12	1	1222	55	1	2.70	....	....	....	....	....	....	....
	Dayton Bombers	ECHL	15	6	8	1	893	49	0	3.29	....	....	....	....	....	....	....
2005-06	Syracuse Crunch	AHL	40	20	12	1	2060	112	1	3.26	2	0	1	89	4	0	2.70
	Dayton Bombers	ECHL	3	1	2	0	179	11	0	3.68	....	....	....	....	....	....	....
2006-07	Wilkes-Barre	AHL	28	18	7	1	1610	78	3	2.91	....	....	....	....	....	....	....
	Wheeling Nailers	ECHL	11	5	5	1	566	32	0	3.39	....	....	....	....	....	....	....

Signed as a free agent by **Columbus**, September 17, 2001. Signed as a free agent by **Pittsburgh**, August 18, 2006.

PETERS, Justin (PEE-tuhrz, JUHS-tihn) CAR.

Goaltender. Catches left. 6'1", 209 lbs. Born, Blyth, Ont., August 30, 1986.
(Carolina's 2nd choice, 38th overall, in 2004 Entry Draft).

			Regular Season								Playoffs						
Season	Club	League	GP	W	L	O/T	Mins	GA	SO	Avg	GP	W	L	Mins	GA	SO	Avg
2001-02	Huron-Perth	Minor-ON	17	11	2	4	810	32	1	1.89	13	9	4	285	30	1	2.31
2002-03	St. Michael's	OHL	23	6	10	1	1052	54	0	3.08	7	1	0	126	4	0	1.90
2003-04	St. Michael's	OHL	53	30	16	6	3149	139	4	2.65	18	10	8	1109	37	4	2.00
2004-05	St. Michael's	OHL	58	23	23	5	3150	146	3	2.78	10	4	4	524	25	0	2.86
2005-06	St. Michael's	OHL	20	10	6	3	1174	75	0	3.83	....	....	....	....	....	....	....
	Plymouth Whalers	OHL	35	19	15	1	2073	95	1	2.75	13	6	6	789	42	0	3.19
2006-07	Albany River Rats	AHL	34	10	18	0	1765	96	1	3.26	....	....	....	....	....	....	....
	Florida Everblades	ECHL	1	0	0	1	65	6	0	5.54	....	....	....	....	....	....	....

PHILLIPS, Brad (FIHL-ihps , BRAD) PHI.

Goaltender. Catches left. 6'2", 163 lbs. Born, Allen Park, MI, April 22, 1989.
(Philadelphia's 7th choice, 182nd overall, in 2007 Entry Draft).

			Regular Season								Playoffs						
Season	Club	League	GP	W	L	O/T	Mins	GA	SO	Avg	GP	W	L	Mins	GA	SO	Avg
2004-05	Det. Honeybaked	MWEHL	38	32	3	3	....	50	10	1.32	....	....	....	....	....	....	....
2005-06	USNTDP	U-17	13	8	5	0	610	28	....	2.75	....	....	....	....	....	....	....
	USNTDP	NAHL	21	12	6	3	1261	51	0	2.43	4	1	3	254	12	0	2.83
2006-07	USNTDP	U-18	12	7	1	2	706	29	0	2.46	....	....	....	....	....	....	....
	USNTDP	NAHL	11	8	3	0	660	24	2	2.18	1	0	1	60	3	0	3.00

PIELMEIER, Timo (PEEL-migh-uhr, TEE-moh) S.J.

Goaltender. Catches left. 5'11", 160 lbs. Born, Deggendorf, West Germany, July 7, 1989.
(San Jose's 3rd choice, 83rd overall, in 2007 Entry Draft).

			Regular Season								Playoffs						
Season	Club	League	GP	W	L	O/T	Mins	GA	SO	Avg	GP	W	L	Mins	GA	SO	Avg
2004-05	Mannheimer ERC	German-5	1	....	....	....	....	....	....	8.15	....	....	....	....	....	....	....
	Mannheim Jr.	Ger-Jr.	10	....	....	....	568	33	....	3.49	....	....	....	....	....	....	....
2005-06	Koln Jr.	Ger-Jr.	8	....	....	....	459	52	....	6.79	2	....	....	100	17	....	10.20
2006-07	Koln Jr.	Ger-Jr.	20	....	....	....	1159	77	....	3.99	6	....	....	370	17	....	2.76

PITTON, Bryan (PIH-tuhn, BRIGH-uhn) EDM.

Goaltender. Catches left. 6'2", 168 lbs. Born, Mississauga, Ont., January 26, 1988.
(Edmonton's 3rd choice, 133rd overall, in 2006 Entry Draft).

			Regular Season								Playoffs						
Season	Club	League	GP	W	L	O/T	Mins	GA	SO	Avg	GP	W	L	Mins	GA	SO	Avg
2004-05	Wellington Dukes	OPJHL	....	24	7	3	....	....	2	2.93	....	....	....	....	....	....	....
2005-06	Brampton Battalion	OHL	24	16	4	0	1293	74	0	3.43	2	0	0	45	5	0	6.67
2006-07	Brampton Battalion	OHL	61	26	29	4	3494	208	0	3.57	4	0	2	270	15	0	3.33

PLANTE, Tyler (PLAWNT, TIGH-luhr) FLA.

Goaltender. Catches left. 6'3", 191 lbs. Born, Milwaukee, WI, April 16, 1987.
(Florida's 2nd choice, 32nd overall, in 2005 Entry Draft).

			Regular Season								Playoffs						
Season	Club	League	GP	W	L	O/T	Mins	GA	SO	Avg	GP	W	L	Mins	GA	SO	Avg
2003-04	Brandon	WHL	2	0	0	1	58	2	0	2.07	....	....	....	....	....	....	....
2004-05	Brandon	WHL	48	34	11	2	2833	122	6	2.58	*24	*13	11	*1408	69	0	2.94
2005-06	Brandon	WHL	60	25	24	9	3414	189	2	3.32	6	2	4	360	18	0	3.00
2006-07	Brandon	WHL	54	30	14	9	3215	145	4	2.71	11	6	5	659	37	0	3.37

WHL Rookie of the Year (2005) • Canadian Major Junior All-Rookie Team (2005)

POGGE, Justin (POH-gee, JUHS-tihn) TOR.

Goaltender. Catches left. 6'3", 204 lbs. Born, Ft. McMurray, Alta., April 22, 1986.
(Toronto's 1st choice, 90th overall, in 2004 Entry Draft).

			Regular Season								Playoffs						
Season	Club	League	GP	W	L	O/T	Mins	GA	SO	Avg	GP	W	L	Mins	GA	SO	Avg
2002-03	Summerland Sting	KIJHL	30	....	....	....	1761	91	0	3.13	....	....	....	....	....	....	....
2003-04	Prince George	WHL	44	17	18	2	2271	107	3	2.83	....	....	....	....	....	....	....
2004-05	Prince George	WHL	24	10	9	2	1198	56	4	2.80	....	....	....	....	....	....	....
	Calgary Hitmen	WHL	29	14	12	3	1727	66	2	2.29	12	7	5	742	24	1	1.94
2005-06	Calgary Hitmen	WHL	54	38	10	6	3237	93	*11	*1.72	13	7	5	802	34	2	2.54
2006-07	Toronto Marlies	AHL	48	19	25	2	2812	142	3	3.03	....	....	....	....	....	....	....

WHL East First All-Star Team (2006) • WHL Goaltender of the Year (2006) • WHL Player of the Year (2006) • Canadian Major Junior Goaltender of the Year (2006)

POPPERLE, Tomas (PAW-puhr-lay, TAW-mahsh) CBJ

Goaltender. Catches left. 6'1", 187 lbs. Born, Broumov, Czech., October 10, 1984.
(Columbus' 5th choice, 131st overall, in 2005 Entry Draft).

			Regular Season								Playoffs						
Season	Club	League	GP	W	L	O/T	Mins	GA	SO	Avg	GP	W	L	Mins	GA	SO	Avg
2001-02	Sparta Jr.	CzRep-Jr.	29	....	....	....	1653	65	2	2.36	5	....	....	320	15	0	2.81
2002-03	Sparta Jr.	CzRep-Jr.	28	....	....	....	1500	52	2	2.08	....	....	....	....	....	....	....
2003-04	Sparta Jr.	CzRep-Jr.	30	....	....	....	1778	60	4	2.02	....	....	....	....	....	....	....
	HC Pribram	CzRep-3	2	....	....	....	60	2	0	2.00	....	....	....	....	....	....	....
	Beroun	CzRep-2	5	....	....	....	305	7	0	1.38	2	....	....	120	4	0	2.00
	HC Sparta Praha	CzRep	....	....	....	....	....	....	....	....	1	....	....	11	0	0	0.00
2004-05	Beroun	CzRep-2	16	....	....	....	966	29	1	1.80	2	....	....	120	5	0	2.50
	HC Sparta Praha	CzRep	25	....	....	....	1325	35	4	*1.58	2	....	....	12	4	0	20.00
2005-06	Eisbaren Berlin	Germany	31	....	....	....	1845	67	3	2.18	11	....	....	655	23	1	2.11
2006-07	**Columbus**	**NHL**	**2**	**0**	**0**	**0**	**45**	**1**	**0**	**1.33**	....	....	....	....	....	....	....
	Syracuse Crunch	AHL	49	25	19	4	2833	135	4	2.86	....	....	....	....	....	....	....
	NHL Totals		**2**	**0**	**0**	**0**	**45**	**1**	**0**	**1.33**	....	....	....	....	....	....	....

PRICE, Carey (PRIGHS, KAIR-ee) MTL.

Goaltender. Catches left. 6'3", 212 lbs. Born, Vancouver, B.C., August 16, 1987.
(Montreal's 1st choice, 5th overall, in 2005 Entry Draft).

			Regular Season								Playoffs						
Season	Club	League	GP	W	L	O/T	Mins	GA	SO	Avg	GP	W	L	Mins	GA	SO	Avg
2002-03	Williams Lake	BCAHA	18	....	....	....	1050	48	1	2.70	....	....	....	....	....	....	....
	Tri-City Americans	WHL	1	0	0	0	20	2	0	6.00	....	....	....	....	....	....	....
2003-04	Tri-City Americans	WHL	28	8	9	3	1363	54	1	2.38	8	5	3	470	19	0	2.43
2004-05	Tri-City Americans	WHL	63	24	31	8	3712	145	8	2.34	5	1	4	325	12	0	2.22
2005-06	Tri-City Americans	WHL	55	21	25	6	3072	147	3	2.87	5	1	3	302	12	0	2.38
2006-07	Tri-City Americans	WHL	46	30	13	1	2722	111	3	2.45	6	2	4	348	17	0	2.93
	Hamilton Bulldogs	AHL	2	1	1	0	117	3	0	1.53	*22	*15	6	*1314	45	*2	2.06

WHL West First All-Star Team (2007) • Canadian Major Junior Goaltender of the Year (2007)

PRUSEK, Martin (PREW-sehk, MAHR-tihn)

Goaltender. Catches left. 6'1", 176 lbs. Born, Ostrava, Czech., December 11, 1975.
(Ottawa's 6th choice, 164th overall, in 1999 Entry Draft).

			Regular Season								Playoffs						
Season	Club	League	GP	W	L	O/T	Mins	GA	SO	Avg	GP	W	L	Mins	GA	SO	Avg
1994-95	HC Vitkovice	CzRep	5	....	....	....	232	18	....	4.65	....	....	....	....	....	....	....
1995-96	HC Vitkovice	CzRep	40	....	....	....	2336	113	1	2.90	4	....	....	250	10	1	2.40
1996-97	HC Vitkovice	CzRep	49	....	....	....	2841	109	8	2.30	9	....	....	546	19	1	2.08
1997-98	HC Vitkovice	CzRep	50	....	....	....	2901	129	....	2.67	9	....	....	529	26	....	3.00
1998-99	HC Vitkovice	CzRep	37	....	....	....	1905	85	....	2.68	4	....	....	250	12	....	2.88
99-2000	HC Vitkovice	CzRep	50	....	....	....	2647	132	....	2.99	....	....	....	....	....	....	....
2000-01	HC Vitkovice	CzRep	30	....	....	....	1679	64	....	2.29	9	....	....	460	25	....	3.26
2001-02	**Ottawa**	**NHL**	**1**	**0**	**1**	**0**	**62**	**3**	**0**	**2.90**	....	....	....	....	....	....	....
	Grand Rapids	AHL	33	18	8	5	1903	58	4	*1.83	5	2	3	278	10	0	2.16
2002-03	**Ottawa**	**NHL**	**18**	**12**	**2**	**1**	**935**	**37**	**0**	**2.37**	....	....	....	....	....	....	....
	Binghamton	AHL	4	1	2	1	243	7	1	1.73	....	....	....	....	....	....	....
2003-04	**Ottawa**	**NHL**	**29**	**16**	**6**	**3**	**1528**	**54**	**3**	**2.12**	**1**	**0**	**0**	**40**	**1**	**0**	**1.50**
2004-05	HC Vitkovice Steel	CzRep	14	....	....	....	672	28	0	2.50	....	....	....	....	....	....	....
	Znojmo	CzRep	8	....	....	....	453	18	0	2.38	....	....	....	....	....	....	....
2005-06	**Columbus**	**NHL**	**9**	**3**	**3**	**0**	**373**	**20**	**0**	**3.22**	....	....	....	....	....	....	....
	Syracuse Crunch	AHL	23	12	7	1	1203	60	2	2.99	....	....	....	....	....	....	....
2006-07	SKA St. Petersburg	Russia	22	....	....	....	1161	52	3	2.69	....	....	....	....	....	....	....
	NHL Totals		**57**	**31**	**12**	**4**	**2898**	**114**	**3**	**2.36**	**1**	**0**	**0**	**40**	**1**	**0**	**1.50**

AHL First All-Star Team (2002) • Harry "Hap" Holmes Memorial Award (fewest goals against – AHL) (2002) (shared with Simon Lajeunesse and Mathieu Chouinard) • Aldege "Baz" Bastien Memorial Award (Outstanding Goaltender – AHL) (2002)

Signed as a free agent by **Vitkovice** (CzRep), August 20, 2004. Loaned to **Znojmo** (CzRep) by **Vitkovice** (CzRep), December, 2004. Signed as a free agent by **Columbus**, August 4, 2005.

QUICK, Jonathan (KWIHK, JAWN-ah-thuhn) L.A.

Goaltender. Catches left. 6', 180 lbs. Born, Milford, CT, January 21, 1986.
(Los Angeles' 4th choice, 72nd overall, in 2005 Entry Draft).

			Regular Season								Playoffs						
Season	Club	League	GP	W	L	O/T	Mins	GA	SO	Avg	GP	W	L	Mins	GA	SO	Avg
2002-03	Avon Old Farms	High-CT	13	8	5	0	780	38	0	2.92	....	....	....	....	....	....	....
2003-04	Avon Old Farms	High-CT	21	20	1	0	1260	26	2	1.71	....	....	....	....	....	....	....
2004-05	Avon Old Farms	High-CT	27	25	2	0	1413	1.14	9	1.14	....	....	....	....	....	....	....
2005-06	Massachusetts	H-East	17	4	10	1	905	45	0	2.98	....	....	....	....	....	....	....
2006-07	Massachusetts	H-East	37	19	12	5	2224	80	3	2.16	....	....	....	....	....	....	....

Hockey East Second All-Star Team (2007) • NCAA East Second All-American Team (2007)

RACINE, Jean-Francois (RAY-seen, ZHAWN-fran-SWUH)

Goaltender. Catches left. 6'3", 194 lbs. Born, St-Hyacinthe, Que., April 27, 1982.
(Toronto's 4th choice, 90th overall, in 2000 Entry Draft).

			Regular Season								Playoffs						
Season	Club	League	GP	W	L	O/T	Mins	GA	SO	Avg	GP	W	L	Mins	GA	SO	Avg
1998-99	Magog	QAAA	36	19	12	1	2160	107	3	2.98	11	5	6	656	37	0	3.39
99-2000	Moncton Wildcats	QMJHL	10	3	3	1	410	28	0	4.10	....	....	....	....	....	....	....
	Drummondville	QMJHL	20	14	6	0	1152	63	1	3.28	3	0	0	65	5	0	4.60
2000-01	Drummondville	QMJHL	61	27	26	3	3362	189	4	3.37	5	2	3	303	20	0	3.97
2001-02	Drummondville	QMJHL	65	29	30	3	3640	208	2	3.43	12	5	7	720	42	1	3.50
2002-03	Memphis	CHL	35	22	9	3	2050	94	0	2.75	1	0	1	58	5	0	5.14
2003-04	St. John's	AHL	9	4	5	0	496	24	1	2.90	....	....	....	....	....	....	....
	Memphis	CHL	30	15	10	2	1645	74	2	2.70	....	....	....	....	....	....	....
2004-05	St. John's	AHL	17	10	4	0	893	41	0	2.76	....	....	....	....	....	....	....
	Memphis	CHL	19	9	6	1	951	57	0	3.60	....	....	....	....	....	....	....
2005-06	Toronto Marlies	AHL	36	19	13	2	1882	99	0	3.16	....	....	....	....	....	....	....
2006-07	Toronto Marlies	AHL	30	11	14	3	1642	91	1	3.33	....	....	....	....	....	....	....

RAMO, Karri (RAH-moh, KAH-ree) T.B.

Goaltender. Catches left. 6'2", 192 lbs. Born, Asikkala, Finland, July 1, 1986.
(Tampa Bay's 7th choice, 191st overall, in 2004 Entry Draft).

			Regular Season								Playoffs						
Season	Club	League	GP	W	L	O/T	Mins	GA	SO	Avg	GP	W	L	Mins	GA	SO	Avg
2002-03	K-Reipas U18	Fin-U18	19	12	3	2	1013	47	0	2.78	4	2	2	182	11	0	3.62
2003-04	Pelicans Lahti U18	Fin-U18	3	3	0	0	180	7	0	2.33	5	2	2	268	10	0	2.24
	Pelicans Lahti Jr.	Fin-Jr.	18	5	9	2	960	53	0	3.31	2	2	0	120	1	1	0.50
	Pelicans Lahti	Finland	3	0	2	0	138	10	0	4.34	....	....	....	....	....	....	....
2004-05	Pelicans Lahti Jr.	Fin-Jr.	21	10	5	6	1269	36	6	1.70	4	1	3	206	16	0	4.66
	Pelicans Lahti	Finland	26	4	12	4	1267	84	1	3.98	....	....	....	....	....	....	....
2005-06	Haukat Jarvenpaa	Finland-2	1	....	....	....	60	5	0	5.00	....	....	....	....	....	....	....
	Suomi U20	Finland-2	3	....	....	....	183	12	0	3.93	....	....	....	....	....	....	....
	HPK Hameenlinna	Finland	24	7	8	7	1359	49	2	2.16	3	2	1	204	5	1	1.46
2006-07	**Tampa Bay**	**NHL**	**2**	**0**	**0**	**0**	**70**	**4**	**0**	**3.43**	....	....	....	....	....	....	....
	Springfield Falcons	AHL	45	15	24	1	2432	127	1	3.13	....	....	....	....	....	....	....
	NHL Totals		**2**	**0**	**0**	**0**	**70**	**4**	**0**	**3.43**	....	....	....	....	....	....	....

RASK, Tuukka (RASK, TU-kah) BOS.

Goaltender. Catches left. 6'3", 169 lbs. Born, Savonlinna, Finland, March 10, 1987.
(Toronto's 1st choice, 21st overall, in 2005 Entry Draft).

			Regular Season								Playoffs						
Season	Club	League	GP	W	L	O/T	Mins	GA	SO	Avg	GP	W	L	Mins	GA	SO	Avg
2003-04	Ilves Tampere U18	Fin-U18	9	4	3	2	533	25	0	2.81	....	....	....	....	....	....	....
	Ilves Tampere Jr.	Fin-Jr.	30	12	10	7	1767	65	2	2.21	3	1	2	178	6	0	2.02
2004-05	Ilves Tampere Jr.	Fin-Jr.	26	17	3	4	1517	47	2	1.86	10	9	1	619	9	6	0.87
	Ilves Tampere	Finland	4	0	1	1	201	15	0	4.46	....	....	....	....	....	....	....
2005-06	Ilves Tampere Jr.	Fin-Jr.	1	....	....	....	60	2	0	2.00	....	....	....	....	....	....	....
	Suomi U20	Finland-2	3	....	....	....	179	6	0	2.01	....	....	....	....	....	....	....
	Ilves Tampere	Finland	30	12	8	7	1724	60	2	2.09	3	0	3	180	7	0	2.33
2006-07	Suomi U20	Finland-2	1	0	1	0	58	4	0	4.14	....	....	....	....	....	....	....
	Ilves Tampere	Finland	49	18	18	10	2872	114	3	2.38	7	2	5	397	20	0	3.02

Traded to **Boston** by **Toronto** for Andrew Raycroft, June 24, 2006.

RAYCROFT, Andrew (RAY-krawft, AN-droo) TOR.

Goaltender. Catches left. 6', 185 lbs. Born, Belleville, Ont., May 4, 1980.
(Boston's 4th choice, 135th overall, in 1998 Entry Draft).

			Regular Season								Playoffs						
Season	Club	League	GP	W	L	O/T	Mins	GA	SO	Avg	GP	W	L	Mins	GA	SO	Avg
1996-97	Wellington Dukes	MTJHL	27	....	....	....	1402	92	0	3.94	....	....	....	....	....	....	....
1997-98	Sudbury Wolves	OHL	33	8	16	5	1802	125	0	4.16	2	0	1	89	8	0	5.39
1998-99	Sudbury Wolves	OHL	45	17	22	5	2528	173	1	4.11	3	0	2	96	13	0	8.13
99-2000	Kingston	OHL	*61	33	20	5	3340	191	0	3.43	5	1	4	300	21	0	4.20
2000-01	**Boston**	**NHL**	**15**	**4**	**6**	**0**	**649**	**32**	**0**	**2.96**	....	....	....	....	....	....	....
	Providence Bruins	AHL	26	8	14	4	1459	82	1	3.37	....	....	....	....	....	....	....
2001-02	**Boston**	**NHL**	**1**	**0**	**0**	**1**	**65**	**3**	**0**	**2.77**	....	....	....	....	....	....	....
	Providence Bruins	AHL	56	25	24	6	3317	142	4	2.57	2	0	2	119	5	0	2.52
2002-03	**Boston**	**NHL**	**5**	**2**	**3**	**0**	**300**	**12**	**0**	**2.40**	....	....	....	....	....	....	....
	Providence Bruins	AHL	39	23	10	3	2255	94	1	2.50	4	1	3	264	6	1	*1.36
2003-04	**Boston**	**NHL**	**57**	**29**	**18**	**9**	**3420**	**117**	**3**	**2.05**	**7**	**3**	**4**	**447**	**16**	**1**	**2.15**
2004-05	Tappara Tampere	Finland	11	4	5	2	657	32	1	2.92	3	0	2	104	11	0	6.36
2005-06	**Boston**	**NHL**	**30**	**8**	**19**	**2**	**1619**	**100**	**0**	**3.71**	....	....	....	....	....	....	....
	Providence Bruins	AHL	1	1	0	0	64	3	0	2.80	....	....	....	....	....	....	....
2006-07	**Toronto**	**NHL**	**72**	**37**	**25**	**9**	**4108**	**205**	**2**	**2.99**	....	....	....	....	....	....	....
	NHL Totals		**180**	**80**	**71**	**21**	**10161**	**469**	**5**	**2.77**	**7**	**3**	**4**	**447**	**16**	**1**	**2.15**

OHL First All-Star Team (2000) • Canadian Major Junior First All-Star Team (2000) • Canadian Major Junior Goaltender of the Year (2000) • NHL All-Rookie Team (2004) • Calder Memorial Trophy (2004)

Signed as a free agent by **Tappara Tampere** (Finland), January 17, 2005. Traded to **Toronto** by **Boston** for Tuukka Rask, June 24, 2006.

REGAN, Kevin (REE-guhn, KEH-vihn) BOS.

Goaltender. Catches left. 6'1", 190 lbs. Born, Boston, MA, July 25, 1984.
(Boston's 10th choice, 277th overall, in 2003 Entry Draft).

			Regular Season								Playoffs						
Season	Club	League	GP	W	L	O/T	Mins	GA	SO	Avg	GP	W	L	Mins	GA	SO	Avg
2001-02	St. Sebastian's	High-MA	31	27	4	0	1860	56	0	1.91	....	....	....	....	....	....	....
	USNTDP	U-18	1	0	0	0	12	0	0	0.00	....	....	....	....	....	....	....
	South Boston	USHA	3	3	0	0	158	8	0	2.58	....	....	....	....	....	....	....
2002-03	St. Sebastian's	High-MA	28	....	....	....	1215	47	4	1.81	....	....	....	....	....	....	....
2003-04	Waterloo	USHL	50	*28	19	1	0	111	*6	2.37	*12	*9	3	*735	19	*1	*1.55
2004-05	New Hampshire	H-East	23	15	4	2	1276	50	0	2.35	....	....	....	....	....	....	....
2005-06	New Hampshire	H-East	23	8	8	5	1299	57	3	2.63	....	....	....	....	....	....	....
2006-07	New Hampshire	H-East	35	24	9	2	2066	71	3	2.06	....	....	....	....	....	....	....

Hockey East All-Rookie Team (2005) (co-winners - Cory Schneider and Peter Vetri)

REIMER, James (RIGH-muhr, JAYMZ) TOR.

Goaltender. Catches left. 6'2", 208 lbs. Born, Winnipeg, Man., March 15, 1988.
(Toronto's 3rd choice, 99th overall, in 2006 Entry Draft).

			Regular Season								Playoffs						
Season	Club	League	GP	W	L	O/T	Mins	GA	SO	Avg	GP	W	L	Mins	GA	SO	Avg
2003-04	Interlake Lightning	MMHL	27	6	5	2	863	41	1	2.85	....	....	....	....	....	....	....
2004-05	Interlake Lightning	MMHL	37	19	6	2	1646	58	4	2.11	435	26	0	3.59	....	....	....
2005-06	Red Deer Rebels	WHL	34	7	18	3	1709	80	0	2.81	....	....	....	....	....	....	....
2006-07	Red Deer Rebels	WHL	60	26	23	7	3339	148	3	2.66	7	3	4	417	27	0	3.88

RIDDERWALL, Stefan (RIH-duhr-vahl, STEH-fan) NYI

Goaltender. Catches left. 6'1", 189 lbs. Born, Stockholm, Sweden, March 5, 1988.
(NY Islanders' 12th choice, 173rd overall, in 2006 Entry Draft).

			Regular Season								Playoffs						
Season	Club	League	GP	W	L	O/T	Mins	GA	SO	Avg	GP	W	L	Mins	GA	SO	Avg
2003-04	Huddinge IK U18	Swe-U18	7	....	....	....	345	31	0	5.38	....	....	....	....	....	....	....
2004-05	Djurgarden U18	Swe-U18	3	....	....	....	154	8	0	3.10	4	....	....	234	11	0	2.81
	Djurgarden Jr.	Swe-Jr.	16	....	....	....	972	51	0	3.15	....	....	....	....	....	....	....
2005-06	Djurgarden Jr.	Swe-Jr.	18	....	....	....	1073	43	3	2.40	4	....	....	242	13	1	3.22
	Djurgarden	Sweden	1	....	....	....	4	0	0	0.00	....	....	....	....	....	....	....
2006-07	Djurgarden Jr.	Swe-Jr.	28	....	....	....	1690	50	4	1.78	7	....	....	417	10	1	1.44

RIKSMAN, Juuso ST.L.

Goaltender. Catches left. 6'1", 174 lbs. Born, Helsinki, Finland, April 1, 1977.

			Regular Season								Playoffs						
Season	Club	League	GP	W	L	O/T	Mins	GA	SO	Avg	GP	W	L	Mins	GA	SO	Avg
1994-95	HIFK Helsinki U18	Fin-U18	STATISTICS NOT AVAILABLE														
	HIFK Helsinki Jr.	Fin-Jr.	3	....	....	....	179	17	0	5.70	....	....	....	....	....	....	....
1995-96	HIFK Helsinki Jr.	Fin-Jr.	3	....	....	....	179	11	....	3.69	....	....	....	....	....	....	....
1996-97	HIFK Helsinki Jr.	Fin-Jr.	16	....	....	....	904	51	....	3.39	....	....	....	....	....	....	....
1997-98	HIFK Helsinki Jr.	Fin-Jr.	16	5	8	3	972	55	....	3.39	....	....	....	....	....	....	....
	Hermes Kokkola	Finland-2	4	3	0	0	220	11	0	3.00	3	0	1	75	8	0	6.41
1998-99	Hermes Kokkola	Finland-2	23	7	8	5	1308	66	2	3.03	1	0	1	60	5	0	5.00
99-2000	Team Kiruna IF	Sweden-3	STATISTICS NOT AVAILABLE														
2000-01	Hermes Kokkola	Finland-2	33	18	12	3	1870	91	2	2.92	7	4	3	391	22	0	3.38
2001-02	HIFK Helsinki	Finland	21	8	7	6	1248	52	2	2.50	....	....	....	....	....	....	....
	FPS Forssa	Finland-2	7	....	....	....	....	....	....	3.15	....	....	....	....	....	....	....
	KJT Jarvenpaa	Finland-2	2	....	....	....	....	....	....	5.00	....	....	....	....	....	....	....
2002-03	MODO	Sweden	31	....	....	....	1842	92	3	3.00	2	....	....	119	5	0	2.51
2003-04	MODO	Sweden	45	....	....	....	2607	107	6	2.46	6	....	....	308	17	1	3.31
2004-05	HC Alleghe	Italy	16	....	....	....	957	59	0	3.70	....	....	....	....	....	....	....
	Ilves Tampere	Finland	18	8	6	3	1034	50	1	2.90	....	....	....	....	....	....	....
2005-06	Assat Pori	Finland	52	26	16	9	3103	105	9	2.03	14	8	6	859	38	0	2.65
2006-07	Jokerit Helsinki	Finland	29	18	6	4	1731	65	2	2.25	10	7	3	653	17	1	1.56

Signed as a free agent by **St. Louis**, June 1, 2007.

RINNE, Pekka (RIH-neh, PEH-kuh) NSH.

Goaltender. Catches left. 6'5", 207 lbs. Born, Kempele, Finland, November 3, 1982.
(Nashville's 10th choice, 258th overall, in 2004 Entry Draft).

			Regular Season								Playoffs						
Season	Club	League	GP	W	L	O/T	Mins	GA	SO	Avg	GP	W	L	Mins	GA	SO	Avg
2000-01	Karpat Oulu Jr.	Fin-Jr.	20	9	4	5	1148	63	0	3.29	....	....	....	....	....	....	....
2001-02	Karpat Oulu Jr.	Fin-Jr.	30	19	7	3	1724	61	3	2.12	3	1	2	184	10	1	3.26
2002-03	Karpat Oulu Jr.	Fin-Jr.	25	14	8	3	1479	48	5	1.95	4	1	3	238	7	0	1.76
	Karpat Oulu	Finland	1	0	1	0	60	7	0	7.00	....	....	....	....	....	....	....
2003-04	Karpat Oulu	Finland	14	5	4	4	824	41	0	2.99	2	1	0	22	0	0	0.00
	Hokki Kajaani	Finland-2	8	5	2	1	463	16	2	2.07	....	....	....	....	....	....	....
2004-05	Karpat Oulu	Finland	10	8	0	1	571	16	0	1.68	....	....	....	....	....	....	....
2005-06	**Nashville**	**NHL**	**2**	**1**	**1**	**0**	**63**	**4**	**0**	**3.81**	....	....	....	....	....	....	....
	Milwaukee	AHL	51	30	18	2	2960	139	2	2.82	14	10	4	734	35	3	2.86
2006-07	Milwaukee	AHL	29	15	7	6	1670	65	3	2.34	4	0	4	247	12	0	2.91
	NHL Totals		**2**	**1**	**1**	**0**	**63**	**4**	**0**	**3.81**	....	....	....	....	....	....	....

ROLOSON, Dwayne (ROH-loh-suhn, DWAYN) EDM.

Goaltender. Catches left. 6'1", 178 lbs. Born, Simcoe, Ont., October 12, 1969.

			Regular Season								Playoffs						
Season	Club	League	GP	W	L	O/T	Mins	GA	SO	Avg	GP	W	L	Mins	GA	SO	Avg
1984-85	Simcoe Penguins	OJHL-C	3	....	....	....	100	21	0	12.60	....	....	....	....	....	....	....
1985-86	Simcoe Rams	OJHL-C	1	....	....	....	60	6	0	6.00	....	....	....	....	....	....	....
1986-87	Norwich	OJHL-C	19	....	....	....	1091	55	0	*3.03	....	....	....	....	....	....	....
1987-88	Belleville Bobcats	OJHL-B	21	9	6	1	1070	60	*2	3.36	....	....	....	....	....	....	....
1988-89	Thorold	OJHL-B	27	15	6	4	1490	82	0	3.30	....	....	....	....	....	....	....
1989-90	Thorold	OHA-B	30	18	8	1	1683	108	0	3.85	....	....	....	....	....	....	....
1990-91	U. Mass-Lowell	H-East	15	5	9	0	823	63	0	4.59	....	....	....	....	....	....	....
1991-92	U. Mass-Lowell	H-East	12	3	8	0	660	52	0	4.73	....	....	....	....	....	....	....
1992-93	U. Mass-Lowell	H-East	*39	20	17	2	*2342	150	0	3.84	....	....	....	....	....	....	....
1993-94	U. Mass-Lowell	H-East	*40	*23	10	7	*2305	106	0	2.76	....	....	....	....	....	....	....
1994-95	Saint John Flames	AHL	46	16	21	8	2734	156	1	3.42	5	1	4	298	13	0	2.61
1995-96	Saint John Flames	AHL	67	*33	22	11	4026	190	1	2.83	16	10	6	1027	49	1	2.86
1996-97	**Calgary**	**NHL**	**31**	**9**	**14**	**3**	**1618**	**78**	**1**	**2.89**	....	....	....	....	....	....	....
	Saint John Flames	AHL	8	6	2	0	481	22	1	2.75	....	....	....	....	....	....	....
1997-98	**Calgary**	**NHL**	**39**	**11**	**16**	**8**	**2205**	**110**	**0**	**2.99**	....	....	....	....	....	....	....
	Saint John Flames	AHL	4	3	0	1	245	8	0	1.96	....	....	....	....	....	....	....
1998-99	**Buffalo**	**NHL**	**18**	**6**	**8**	**2**	**911**	**42**	**1**	**2.77**	**4**	**1**	**1**	**139**	**10**	**0**	**4.32**
	Rochester	AHL	2	2	0	0	120	4	0	2.00	....	....	....	....	....	....	....
99-2000	**Buffalo**	**NHL**	**14**	**1**	**7**	**3**	**677**	**32**	**0**	**2.84**	....	....	....	....	....	....	....
2000-01	Worcester IceCats	AHL	52	*32	15	5	*3127	113	*6	*2.17	11	6	5	697	23	1	1.98
2001-02	**Minnesota**	**NHL**	**45**	**14**	**20**	**7**	**2506**	**112**	**5**	**2.68**	....	....	....	....	....	....	....
2002-03	**Minnesota**	**NHL**	**50**	**23**	**16**	**8**	**2945**	**98**	**4**	**2.00**	**11**	**5**	**6**	**579**	**25**	**0**	**2.59**
2003-04	**Minnesota**	**NHL**	**48**	**19**	**18**	**11**	**2847**	**89**	**5**	**1.88**	....	....	....	....	....	....	....
2004-05	Lukko Rauma	Finland	34	20	10	4	2048	70	4	2.05	9	4	5	512	18	2	2.11
2005-06	**Minnesota**	**NHL**	**24**	**6**	**17**	**1**	**1361**	**68**	**1**	**3.00**	....	....	....	....	....	....	....
	Edmonton	**NHL**	**19**	**8**	**7**	**4**	**1163**	**47**	**1**	**2.42**	**18**	**12**	**5**	**1160**	**45**	**1**	**2.33**
2006-07	**Edmonton**	**NHL**	**68**	**27**	**34**	**6**	**3932**	**180**	**4**	**2.75**	....	....	....	....	....	....	....
	NHL Totals		**356**	**124**	**157**	**53**	**20165**	**856**	**22**	**2.55**	**33**	**18**	**12**	**1878**	**80**	**1**	**2.56**

Hockey East First All-Star Team (1994) • Hockey East Player of the Year (1994) • NCAA East First All-American Team (1994) • AHL First All-Star Team (2001) • Aldege "Baz" Bastien Memorial Award (Outstanding Goaltender – AHL) (2001) • MBNA/Mastercard Roger Crozier Saving Grace Award (2004)

Played in NHL All-Star Game (2004)

Signed as a free agent by **Calgary**, July 4, 1994. Signed as a free agent by **Buffalo**, July 15, 1998. Claimed by **Columbus** from **Buffalo** in Expansion Draft, June 23, 2000. Signed as a free agent by **St. Louis**, July 14, 2000. Signed as a free agent by **Minnesota**, July 2, 2001. Signed as a free agent by **Rauma** (Finland), October 18, 2004. Traded to **Edmonton** by **Minnesota** for Edmonton's 1st round choice (later traded to Los Angeles - Los Angeles selected Trevor Lewis) in 2006 Entry Draft and Edmonton's 3rd round chocie (later traded to Atlanta - Atlanta selected Spencer Machacek) in 2007 Entry Draft, March 8, 2006.

ROWAT, Linden (ROH-wat, LIHND-dehn) L.A.

Goaltender. Catches left. 6'1", 177 lbs. Born, Cochrane, Alta., June 27, 1989.
(Los Angeles' 7th choice, 124th overall, in 2007 Entry Draft).

			Regular Season								Playoffs						
Season	Club	League	GP	W	L	O/T	Mins	GA	SO	Avg	GP	W	L	Mins	GA	SO	Avg
2005-06	Regina Pats	WHL	26	8	9	2	1248	65	1	3.13	....	....	....	....	....	....	....
2006-07	Regina Pats	WHL	52	25	18	7	2948	141	4	2.87	10	4	6	624	33	1	3.17

RUDKOWSKY, Cody (ruhd-KOW-skee, KOH-dee)

Goaltender. Catches left. 6'1", 206 lbs. Born, Willingdon, Alta., July 21, 1978.

			Regular Season								Playoffs						
Season	Club	League	GP	W	L	O/T	Mins	GA	SO	Avg	GP	W	L	Mins	GA	SO	Avg
1995-96	Langley Thunder	BCJHL	23	....	....	....	1172	73	1	3.73	....	....	....	....	....	....	....
	Seattle	WHL	2	0	0	0	21	3	0	8.57	....	....	....	....	....	....	....
1996-97	Seattle	WHL	40	19	16	1	2162	124	0	3.44	1	1	0	30	0	0	0.00
1997-98	Seattle	WHL	53	20	22	3	2805	176	1	3.74	5	1	4	278	18	0	3.88
1998-99	Seattle	WHL	64	34	17	10	3665	177	*7	2.90	11	5	6	637	31	1	2.92
99-2000	Worcester IceCats	AHL	28	9	7	6	1405	75	0	3.20	....	....	....	....	....	....	....
	Peoria Rivermen	ECHL	10	6	4	0	599	32	0	3.20	2	1	1	119	6	0	3.02
2000-01	Worcester IceCats	AHL	25	13	8	3	1477	66	3	2.68	....	....	....	....	....	....	....
2001-02	Worcester IceCats	AHL	21	6	10	2	1108	50	1	2.71	....	....	....	....	....	....	....
	Peoria Rivermen	ECHL	12	5	2	4	709	24	3	2.03	2	0	1	78	4	0	3.08
2002-03	**St. Louis**	**NHL**	**1**	**1**	**0**	**0**	**30**	**0**	**0**	**0.00**	....	....	....	....	....	....	....
	Worcester IceCats	AHL	10	1	5	3	577	28	0	2.91	....	....	....	....	....	....	....
	Trenton Titans	ECHL	31	17	9	5	1867	85	2	2.73	3	0	3	178	14	0	4.72
2003-04	Worcester IceCats	AHL	1	0	0	0	49	3	0	3.67	1	0	1	58	2	0	2.07
	Reading Royals	ECHL	46	24	18	4	2728	108	1	2.38	14	8	6	834	28	1	2.02
2004-05	Providence Bruins	AHL	14	4	7	2	731	39	0	3.20	....	....	....	....	....	....	....
	Reading Royals	ECHL	20	8	11	1	1163	42	3	2.17	....	....	....	....	....	....	....
2005-06	Bridgeport	AHL	9	5	2	1	494	17	0	2.06	....	....	....	....	....	....	....
	Reading Royals	ECHL	38	24	11	3	2292	96	2	2.51	1	0	0	5	0	0	0.00
2006-07	Phoenix	ECHL	38	10	22	2	2062	120	1	3.49	4	0	4	249	16	0	3.86
	NHL Totals		**1**	**1**	**0**	**0**	**30**	**0**	**0**	**0.00**	....	....	....	....	....	....	....

WHL West First All-Star Team (1999) • WHL Goaltender of the Year (1999) • WHL Player of the Year (1999) • Canadian Major Junior First All-Star Team (1999) • Canadian Major Junior Goaltender of the Year (1999)

Signed as a free agent by **St. Louis**, March 25, 1999. Signed as a free agent by **Providence** (AHL), December 1, 2004.

SABOURIN, Dany (SA-boo-rihn, DA-nee) PIT.

Goaltender. Catches left. 6'4", 200 lbs. Born, Val-d'Or, Que., September 2, 1980.
(Calgary's 5th choice, 108th overall, in 1998 Entry Draft).

			Regular Season								Playoffs						
Season	Club	League	GP	W	L	O/T	Mins	GA	SO	Avg	GP	W	L	Mins	GA	SO	Avg
1996-97	Amos Forestiers	QAAA	24	6	16	0	1440	107	0	4.48	....	....	....	....	....	....	....
1997-98	Sherbrooke	QMJHL	37	15	15	2	1906	128	1	4.03	....	....	....	....	....	....	....
1998-99	Sherbrooke	QMJHL	30	8	13	2	1477	102	1	4.14	1	0	1	49	2	0	2.45
	Saint John Flames	AHL	....	....	....	....	....	....	....	....	1	0	1	57	4	0	4.19
99-2000	Sherbrooke	QMJHL	55	25	22	5	3067	181	1	3.54	5	1	4	324	18	0	3.33
2000-01	Saint John Flames	AHL	1	1	0	0	40	0	0	0.00	....	....	....	....	....	....	....
	Johnstown Chiefs	ECHL	19	4	9	1	903	56	0	3.72	1	0	0	40	2	0	3.00
2001-02	Johnstown Chiefs	ECHL	27	14	10	1	1539	84	0	3.28	3	0	2	137	5	0	2.18
2002-03	Saint John Flames	AHL	41	15	17	4	2220	100	4	2.70	....	....	....	....	....	....	....
2003-04	**Calgary**	**NHL**	**4**	**0**	**3**	**0**	**169**	**10**	**0**	**3.55**	....	....	....	....	....	....	....
	Lowell	AHL	14	5	7	2	821	39	0	2.85	....	....	....	....	....	....	....
	Las Vegas	ECHL	10	6	3	1	613	24	0	2.35	1	0	1	58	2	0	2.07
2004-05	Wilkes-Barre	AHL	20	8	8	2	1029	38	1	2.22	....	....	....	....	....	....	....
	Wheeling Nailers	ECHL	27	19	6	1	1579	44	5	*1.67	....	....	....	....	....	....	....
2005-06	**Pittsburgh**	**NHL**	**1**	**0**	**1**	**0**	**21**	**4**	**0**	**11.43**	....	....	....	....	....	....	....
	Wilkes-Barre	AHL	49	30	14	4	2943	111	4	*2.26	6	2	4	362	13	1	2.15
2006-07	**Vancouver**	**NHL**	**9**	**2**	**4**	**1**	**480**	**21**	**0**	**2.63**	**2**	**0**	**0**	**14**	**1**	**0**	**4.29**
	Manitoba Moose	AHL	2	1	1	0	119	4	1	2.01	....	....	....	....	....	....	....
	NHL Totals		**14**	**2**	**8**	**1**	**670**	**35**	**0**	**3.13**	**2**	**0**	**0**	**14**	**1**	**0**	**4.29**

AHL First All-Star Team (2006) • Baz Bastien Memorial Trophy (Top Goaltender - AHL) (2006)

Signed as a free agent by **Pittsburgh**, August 10, 2005. Claimed on waivers by **Vancouver** from **Pittsburgh**, October 4, 2006. Signed as a free agent by **Pittsburgh**, July 1, 2007.

SANFORD, Curtis (SAN-fohrd, KUHR-this) VAN.

Goaltender. Catches left. 5'10", 187 lbs. Born, Owen Sound, Ont., October 5, 1979.

			Regular Season								Playoffs						
Season	Club	League	GP	W	L	O/T	Mins	GA	SO	Avg	GP	W	L	Mins	GA	SO	Avg
1994-95	Wiarton Wolves	OJHL-C	18	....	....	....	949	98	0	6.20	....	....	....	....	....	....	....
1995-96	Collingwood	OJHL	21	....	....	....	2128	74	0	3.54	....	....	....	....	....	....	....
1996-97	Owen Sound	OHL	19	4	8	1	847	77	0	5.45	....	....	....	....	....	....	....
	Owen Sound	OJHL-B	6	....	....	....	360	28	0	4.68	....	....	....	....	....	....	....
1997-98	Owen Sound	OHL	30	13	10	2	1542	114	1	4.44	9	4	4	456	30	1	3.95
1998-99	Owen Sound	OHL	56	30	16	5	2998	191	2	3.82	16	9	7	960	58	0	3.63
99-2000	Owen Sound	OHL	53	18	26	6	3124	198	1	3.80	....	....	....	....	....	....	....
	Missouri	UHL	6	3	1	0	237	6	0	1.52	....	....	....	....	....	....	....
2000-01	Worcester IceCats	AHL	5	3	0	1	237	16	0	4.06	....	....	....	....	....	....	....
	Peoria Rivermen	ECHL	27	15	7	4	1511	48	3	*1.91	14	9	4	813	28	*2	2.07
2001-02	Worcester IceCats	AHL	9	5	4	0	537	22	0	2.46	....	....	....	....	....	....	....
	Peoria Rivermen	ECHL	24	13	8	2	1418	58	1	2.45	....	....	....	....	....	....	....
2002-03	**St. Louis**	**NHL**	**8**	**5**	**1**	**0**	**397**	**13**	**1**	**1.96**	....	....	....	....	....	....	....
	Worcester IceCats	AHL	41	18	14	8	2317	93	3	2.41	3	0	3	179	8	0	2.68
2003-04	Worcester IceCats	AHL	43	20	16	3	2367	84	5	2.13	9	4	5	569	24	0	2.53
2004-05	Worcester IceCats	AHL	50	19	25	2	2743	123	2	2.69	....	....	....	....	....	....	....
2005-06	**St. Louis**	**NHL**	**34**	**13**	**13**	**5**	**1830**	**81**	**3**	**2.66**	....	....	....	....	....	....	....
	Peoria Rivermen	AHL	6	4	2	0	358	11	2	1.84	....	....	....	....	....	....	....
2006-07	**St. Louis**	**NHL**	**31**	**8**	**12**	**5**	**1492**	**79**	**0**	**3.18**	....	....	....	....	....	....	....
	Peoria Rivermen	AHL	2	1	1	0	119	5	0	2.52	....	....	....	....	....	....	....
	NHL Totals		**73**	**26**	**26**	**10**	**3719**	**173**	**4**	**2.79**	....	....	....	....	....	....	....

ECHL Second All-Star Team (2001)

Signed as a free agent by **St. Louis**, October 1, 2000. Signed as a free agent by **Vancouver**, July 3, 2007.

SAUER, Billy (SAW-uhr, BIHL-lee) COL.

Goaltender. Catches left. 6'2", 180 lbs. Born, Rochester, NY, January 6, 1988.
(Colorado's 5th choice, 201st overall, in 2006 Entry Draft).

			Regular Season								Playoffs						
Season	Club	League	GP	W	L	O/T	Mins	GA	SO	Avg	GP	W	L	Mins	GA	SO	Avg
2004-05	Chicago Steel	USHL	30	12	12	2	1592	81	2	3.05	....	....	....	....	....	....	....
2005-06	U. of Michigan	CCHA	23	11	6	4	1281	65	1	3.04	....	....	....	....	....	....	....
2006-07	U. of Michigan	CCHA	40	25	14	1	2354	119	1	3.03	....	....	....	....	....	....	....

SAUVE, Philippe (SOH-vay, fihl-EEP)

Goaltender. Catches left. 6', 188 lbs. Born, Buffalo, NY, February 27, 1980.
(Colorado's 6th choice, 38th overall, in 1998 Entry Draft).

			Regular Season								Playoffs						
Season	Club	League	GP	W	L	O/T	Mins	GA	SO	Avg	GP	W	L	Mins	GA	SO	Avg
1995-96	Laval-Laurentides	QAAA	25	9	10	0	1184	87	1	4.11	15	7	8	900	54	0	3.58
1996-97	Rimouski Oceanic	QMJHL	26	11	9	2	1334	84	0	3.78	1	0	0	14	3	0	12.90
1997-98	Rimouski Oceanic	QMJHL	40	23	16	0	2326	131	1	3.38	7	0	5	262	33	0	7.55
1998-99	Rimouski Oceanic	QMJHL	44	16	19	4	2401	155	0	3.87	11	6	4	595	30	*1	3.03
99-2000	Drummondville	QMJHL	28	12	12	2	1526	106	0	4.17							
	Hull Olympiques	QMJHL	17	9	7	1	992	57	0	3.45	12	6	6	735	47	0	3.84
2000-01	Hershey Bears	AHL	42	17	18	1	2182	100	3	2.75	3	0	3	218	10	0	2.75
2001-02	Hershey Bears	AHL	55	25	20	6	3130	111	6	2.13	8	3	5	486	21	0	2.59
2002-03	Hershey Bears	AHL	*60	26	20	12	3394	134	5	2.37	5	2	3	295	14	0	2.85
2003-04	**Colorado**	**NHL**	**17**	**7**	**7**	**3**	**986**	**50**	**0**	**3.04**							
	Hershey Bears	AHL	10	3	7	0	578	25	2	2.59							
2004-05	Mississippi	ECHL	21	13	4	4	1298	56	2	2.59	4	1	3	227	16	0	4.23
2005-06	**Calgary**	**NHL**	**8**	**3**	**3**	**0**	**402**	**22**	**0**	**3.28**							
	Phoenix	**NHL**	**5**	**0**	**4**	**0**	**187**	**17**	**0**	**5.45**							
2006-07	San Antonio	AHL	10	4	5	0	536	34	0	3.80							
	Boston	**NHL**	**2**	**0**	**0**	**0**	**41**	**4**	**0**	**5.85**							
	Providence Bruins	AHL	23	10	11	1	1292	61	1	2.83							
	Hamilton Bulldogs	AHL	6	2	3	0	325	13	1	2.40							
	NHL Totals		**32**	**10**	**14**	**3**	**1616**	**93**	**0**	**3.45**							

Canadian Major Junior Humanitarian Player of the Year (1999)

Signed as a free agent by **Mississippi** (ECHL), January 27, 2005. Traded to **Calgary** by **Colorado** for future considerations, August 9, 2005. Traded to **Phoenix** by **Calgary** with Steve Reinprecht for Brian Boucher and Mike Leclerc, February 2, 2006. Traded to **Boston** by **Phoenix** for Tyler Redenbach, November 14, 2006.

SCHAEFER, Nolan (SHAY-fuhr, NOH-luhn) MIN.

Goaltender. Catches right. 6'2", 200 lbs. Born, Yellow Grass, Sask., January 15, 1980.
(San Jose's 4th choice, 166th overall, in 2000 Entry Draft).

			Regular Season								Playoffs						
Season	Club	League	GP	W	L	O/T	Mins	GA	SO	Avg	GP	W	L	Mins	GA	SO	Avg
1996-97	Yorkton Mallers	SMHL	36	....	....	....	1854	132	0	4.27							
1997-98	Yorkton Mallers	SMHL	5	....	....	....	239	17	0	4.25							
	Nipawin Hawks	SJHL	21	12	4	3	1080	42	*3	*2.33							
1998-99	Nipawin Hawks	SJHL	46	....	....	....	2478	165	0	3.60							
99-2000	Providence College	H-East	14	6	5	1	778	42	0	3.24							
2000-01	Providence College	H-East	25	15	8	2	1529	63	3	2.47							
2001-02	Providence College	H-East	*35	11	18	5	*2062	113	0	3.29							
2002-03	Providence College	H-East	25	13	8	2	1440	71	0	2.96							
2003-04	Cleveland Barons	AHL	27	14	9	3	1592	62	2	2.34	9	4	5	573	24	0	2.51
	Fresno Falcons	ECHL	12	5	5	2	654	34	1	3.12							
2004-05	Cleveland Barons	AHL	43	17	23	1	2418	110	3	2.73							
2005-06	**San Jose**	**NHL**	**7**	**5**	**1**	**0**	**352**	**11**	**1**	**1.88**							
	Cleveland Barons	AHL	36	12	21	2	2058	118	2	3.44							
2006-07	Worcester Sharks	AHL	16	5	8	3	921	43	0	2.80							
	Hershey Bears	AHL	3	0	3	0	162	10	0	3.70							
	Wilkes-Barre	AHL	15	9	5	0	804	30	1	2.24	11	5	6	699	32	0	2.75
	NHL Totals		**7**	**5**	**1**	**0**	**352**	**11**	**1**	**1.88**							

Hockey East Second All-Star Team (2001) • NCAA East Second All-American Team (2001)

Traded to **Pittsburgh** by **San Jose** for Pittsburgh's 7th round choice (Justin Braun) in 2007 Entry Draft, February 27, 2007. Signed as a free agent by **Minnesota**, July 3, 2007.

SCHNEIDER, Cory (SHNIGH-duhr, KOHR-ee) VAN.

Goaltender. Catches left. 6'2", 195 lbs. Born, Marblehead, MA, March 18, 1986.
(Vancouver's 1st choice, 26th overall, in 2004 Entry Draft).

			Regular Season								Playoffs						
Season	Club	League	GP	W	L	O/T	Mins	GA	SO	Avg	GP	W	L	Mins	GA	SO	Avg
2002-03	Andover	High-MA	23	13	7	2	1385	39	3	1.69							
2003-04	Andover	High-MA	24	17	5	2	1336	32	6	1.42							
	USNTDP	U-18	10	9	1	0	559	15	1	1.61							
	USNTDP	NAHL	2	2	0	0	120	6	0	3.00							
2004-05	Boston College	H-East	18	13	1	4	1102	35	1	1.90							
2005-06	Boston College	H-East	*39	*24	13	2	*2362	83	*8	2.11							
2006-07	Boston College	H-East	*42	*29	12	1	*2517	90	6	2.15							

Hockey East All-Rookie Team (2005) (co-winners - Kevin Regan and Peter Vetri) • Hockey East Second All-Star Team (2006) • NCAA East First All-American Team (2006)

SCHWARZ, Marek (SHWAHRTS, MAIR-ehk) ST.L.

Goaltender. Catches right. 6', 180 lbs. Born, Mlada Boleslav, Czech., April 1, 1986.
(St. Louis' 1st choice, 17th overall, in 2004 Entry Draft).

			Regular Season								Playoffs						
Season	Club	League	GP	W	L	O/T	Mins	GA	SO	Avg	GP	W	L	Mins	GA	SO	Avg
2000-01	Ml. Boleslav Jr.	CzRep-Jr.	45	....	....	....	1969	154	0	4.69							
2001-02	Sparta Jr.	CzRep-Jr.	46	....	....	....	2692	86	9	1.92	6	....	....	368	16	0	2.61
2002-03	Sparta Jr.	CzRep-Jr.	34	....	....	....	1778	57	3	1.92	2	....	....	120	5	0	2.50
	HC Sparta Praha	CzRep	1	....	....	....	1	0	0	0.00							
2003-04	Sparta Jr.	CzRep-Jr.	7	....	....	....	352	14	2	2.39							
	Plzen	CzRep	10	....	....	....	603	33	0	3.28							
	HC Sparta Praha	CzRep	8	....	....	....	335	20	0	3.58							
	HC Ocelari Trinec	CzRep	5	....	....	....	280	12	0	2.57							
	BK Mlada Boleslav	CzRep-2	1	....	....	....	63	6	0	5.71							
2004-05	Vancouver Giants	WHL	56	26	24	4	3304	147	2	2.67	6	2	4	378	18	0	2.86
2005-06	Sparta Jr.	CzRep-Jr.	3	....	....	....	178	5	0	1.69							
	HC Sparta Praha	CzRep	15	....	....	....	746	32	1	2.57	1	....	....	1	0	0	0.00
	Beroun	CzRep-2	4	....	....	....	229	17	0	4.45							
2006-07	**St. Louis**	**NHL**	**2**	**0**	**1**	**0**	**60**	**3**	**0**	**3.00**							
	Peoria Rivermen	AHL	34	19	13	0	1912	88	1	2.76							
	NHL Totals		**2**	**0**	**1**	**0**	**60**	**3**	**0**	**3.00**							

SCOTT, Travis (SKAWT, TRA-vihs)

Goaltender. Catches left. 6'2", 185 lbs. Born, Kanata, Ont., September 14, 1975.

			Regular Season								Playoffs						
Season	Club	League	GP	W	L	O/T	Mins	GA	SO	Avg	GP	W	L	Mins	GA	SO	Avg
1991-92	Nepean Raiders	CJHL	19	14	5	0	1065	71	1	4.00							
1992-93	Nepean Raiders	CJHL	36	19	10	2	1968	133	0	4.05							
1993-94	Windsor Spitfires	OHL	45	20	18	0	2312	158	1	4.10	4	0	4	240	16	0	4.00
1994-95	Windsor Spitfires	OHL	48	26	14	3	2644	147	3	3.34	3	0	1	94	6	1	3.83
1995-96	Oshawa Generals	OHL	31	15	9	4	1763	78	3	2.65	5	1	4	315	23	0	4.38
1996-97	Baton Rouge	ECHL	10	5	2	1	501	22	0	2.63							
	Worcester IceCats	AHL	29	14	10	1	1482	75	1	3.04							
1997-98	Baton Rouge	ECHL	36	14	11	6	1949	96	1	2.96							
1998-99	Mississippi	ECHL	44	22	12	5	2337	112	1	2.88	*18	*14	4	*1252	42	3	2.01
99-2000	Lowell	AHL	46	15	23	3	2595	126	3	2.91	1	0	1	60	2	0	2.01
2000-01	**Los Angeles**	**NHL**	**1**	**0**	**0**	**0**	**25**	**3**	**0**	**7.20**							
	Lowell	AHL	34	16	15	1	1977	83	2	2.52	4	1	2	209	7	1	2.01
2001-02	Manchester	AHL	39	21	12	3	2170	83	6	2.30	5	2	3	327	15	0	2.75
2002-03	Manchester	AHL	50	23	19	5	2829	116	4	2.46	3	0	2	148	9	0	3.65
2003-04	San Antonio	AHL	*64	26	31	6	3747	156	4	2.50							
2004-05	San Antonio	AHL	59	18	28	4	3211	126	3	2.35							
2005-06	Magnitogorsk	Russia	43	....	....	....	2563	52	*11	*1.22	11	....	....	683	21	2	1.84
2006-07	Magnitogorsk	Russia	45	....	....	....	2606	70	*9	*1.61	15	....	....	871	28	1	1.93
	NHL Totals		**1**	**0**	**0**	**0**	**25**	**3**	**0**	**7.20**							

ECHL Playoff MVP (1999)

Signed as a free agent by **St. Louis**, December 30, 1996. Signed as a free agent by **Los Angeles**, February 18, 2000. Signed as a free agent by **Florida**, August 12, 2003.

SEXSMITH, Tyson (SEHX-smihth, TIGH-suhn) S.J.

Goaltender. Catches left. 6', 210 lbs. Born, Calgary, Alta., March 19, 1989.
(San Jose's 4th choice, 91st overall, in 2007 Entry Draft).

			Regular Season								Playoffs						
Season	Club	League	GP	W	L	O/T	Mins	GA	SO	Avg	GP	W	L	Mins	GA	SO	Avg
2004-05	Olds Grizzlys	AJHL	STATISTICS NOT AVAILABLE														
	Medicine Hat	WHL	1	0	0	0	5	0	0	0.00							
	Vancouver Giants	WHL	2	1	0	0	80	4	0	3.00							
2005-06	Vancouver Giants	WHL	11	6	3	1	547	21	1	2.30							
2006-07	Vancouver Giants	WHL	51	31	12	8	3047	91	10	*1.79	22	14	7	1339	40	*4	*1.79

SHANTZ, David (SHAWNTS, DAY-vihd) FLA.

Goaltender. Catches left. 6'1", 202 lbs. Born, Burlington, Ont., May 5, 1986.
(Florida's 2nd choice, 37th overall, in 2004 Entry Draft).

			Regular Season								Playoffs						
Season	Club	League	GP	W	L	O/T	Mins	GA	SO	Avg	GP	W	L	Mins	GA	SO	Avg
2002-03	Thorold	OJHL-B	36	30	3	3	2107	63	8	1.79							
2003-04	Mississauga	OHL	43	21	18	3	2483	120	1	2.90	*24	12	12	*1449	49	*5	2.03
2004-05	Mississauga	OHL	27	10	11	3	1524	72	0	2.83	2	0	1	80	2	0	1.50
2005-06	Peterborough	OHL	49	31	14	3	2946	141	2	2.87	*19	*16	3	*1239	54	1	2.62
2006-07	Rochester	AHL	2	1	1	0	120	9	0	4.51							
	Florida Everblades	ECHL	23	13	7	1	1338	66	0	2.96	1	0	0	20	1	0	3.00

OHL All-Rookie Team (2004) • Canadian Major Junior All-Rookie Team (2004)

SIGALET, Jordan (SIH-ga-leht, JOHR-dahn) BOS.

Goaltender. Catches left. 6'1", 180 lbs. Born, New Westminster, B.C., February 19, 1981.
(Boston's 6th choice, 209th overall, in 2001 Entry Draft).

			Regular Season								Playoffs						
Season	Club	League	GP	W	L	O/T	Mins	GA	SO	Avg	GP	W	L	Mins	GA	SO	Avg
99-2000	Victoria Salsa	BCHL	33	....	....	....	1980	108	0	3.28							
2000-01	Victoria Salsa	BCHL	48	23	22	0	2820	142	0	3.03	18	12	5	1060	143	0	2.62
2001-02	Bowling Green	CCHA	13	2	6	2	657	38	0	3.47							
2002-03	Bowling Green	CCHA	20	6	11	2	1208	66	1	3.28							
2003-04	Bowling Green	CCHA	37	10	17	9	2210	101	2	2.74							
2004-05	Bowling Green	CCHA	32	16	12	3	1849	89	1	2.89							
2005-06	**Boston**	**NHL**	**1**	**0**	**0**	**0**	**1**	**0**	**0**	**0.00**							
	Providence Bruins	AHL	37	19	11	2	1955	83	1	2.55	3	0	2	159	10	0	3.77
2006-07	Providence Bruins	AHL	25	15	5	2	1332	53	3	2.39	2	0	0	32	0	0	0.00
	NHL Totals		**1**	**0**	**0**	**0**	**1**	**0**	**0**	**0.00**							

CCHA First All-Star Team (2004) • CCHA Second All-Star Team (2005)

SMITH, Jason (SMIHTH, JAY-suhn) N.J.

Goaltender. Catches left. 6'1", 170 lbs. Born, St-Lambert, Que., July 17, 1985.
(New Jersey's 5th choice, 197th overall, in 2003 Entry Draft).

			Regular Season								Playoffs						
Season	Club	League	GP	W	L	O/T	Mins	GA	SO	Avg	GP	W	L	Mins	GA	SO	Avg
2002-03	Lennoxville	QJHL	29	22	4	1	1622	62	3	2.29	14	11	3	816	34	1	2.52
2003-04	Sacred Heart	AH	5	1	4	0	302	19	0	3.78							
2004-05	Sacred Heart	AH	8	3	5	0	493	31	0	3.77							
2005-06	Sacred Heart	AH	30	18	11	1	1793	67	1	*2.24							
2006-07	Sacred Heart	AH	28	16	9	3	1703	79	1	2.78							

AH First All-Star Team (2007)

SMITH, Jeremy (SMIHTH, JAIR-eh-mee) NSH.

Goaltender. Catches left. 5'11", 161 lbs. Born, Dearborn, MI, April 13, 1989.
(Nashville's 2nd choice, 54th overall, in 2007 Entry Draft).

			Regular Season								Playoffs						
Season	Club	League	GP	W	L	O/T	Mins	GA	SO	Avg	GP	W	L	Mins	GA	SO	Avg
2005-06	Det. Compuware	MWEHL	13	5	6	0	696	31	0	2.67							
	Det. Compuware	Exhib.	3	2	1	0	178	8	0	2.70							
	Plymouth Whalers	OHL	5	0	2	0	111	11	0	5.95							
2006-07	Plymouth Whalers	OHL	34	23	6	1	1901	82	4	2.59	3	2	0	149	8	0	3.22

SMITH, Mike (SMIHTH, MIGHK) DAL.

Goaltender. Catches left. 6'3", 211 lbs. Born, Kingston, Ont., March 22, 1982.
(Dallas' 5th choice, 161st overall, in 2001 Entry Draft).

			Regular Season								Playoffs						
Season	Club	League	GP	W	L	O/T	Mins	GA	SO	Avg	GP	W	L	Mins	GA	SO	Avg
1998-99	Kingston	OPJHL	16	....	....	....	906	53	0	3.51							
99-2000	Kingston	OHL	15	4	5	0	666	42	0	3.78							
2000-01	Kingston	OHL	3	0	0	2	136	8	0	3.53							
	Sudbury Wolves	OHL	43	22	13	7	2571	108	3	2.52	12	7	5	735	26	2	*2.12
2001-02	Sudbury Wolves	OHL	53	19	28	5	3082	157	3	3.06	5	1	4	302	15	0	2.98
2002-03	Lexington	ECHL	27	11	10	4	1553	66	1	2.55	2	0	1	93	8	0	5.14
	Utah Grizzlies	AHL	11	5	5	0	614	33	0	3.23							
2003-04	Utah Grizzlies	AHL	21	8	11	0	1186	56	2	2.83							
2004-05	Houston Aeros	AHL	45	19	17	3	2408	97	5	2.42	3	1	2	181	4	0	1.33
2005-06	Iowa Stars	AHL	50	25	19	6	2998	125	3	2.50	7	3	4	417	19	0	2.74
2006-07	**Dallas**	**NHL**	**23**	**12**	**5**	**2**	**1213**	**45**	**3**	**2.23**							
	NHL Totals		**23**	**12**	**5**	**2**	**1213**	**45**	**3**	**2.23**							

NHL All-Rookie Team (2007)

SPRATT, James (SPRAT, JAYMZ) CGY.

Goaltender. Catches left. 6'1", 185 lbs. Born, Detroit, MI, November 10, 1985.
(Calgary's 9th choice, 213th overall, in 2004 Entry Draft).

			Regular Season								Playoffs						
Season	Club	League	GP	W	L	O/T	Mins	GA	SO	Avg	GP	W	L	Mins	GA	SO	Avg
2002-03	Sioux City	USHL	18	6	6	2	905	49	0	3.25							
2003-04	Sioux City	USHL	34	19	6	5	1922	75	3	2.34	7	4	3	468	19	0	2.44
2004-05	Sioux City	USHL	42	24	11	3	2328	109	2	2.81	*13	*8	5	*752	32	*1	2.55
2005-06	Bowling Green	CCHA	16	4	10	1	923	67	0	4.36							
2006-07	Bowling Green	CCHA	31	6	22	1	1730	105	0	3.64							

STALOCK, Alex (STAY-lahk, AL-ehx) S.J.

Goaltender. Catches left. 5'11", 170 lbs. Born, St. Paul, MN, July 28, 1987.
(San Jose's 3rd choice, 112th overall, in 2005 Entry Draft).

			Regular Season								Playoffs						
Season	Club	League	GP	W	L	O/T	Mins	GA	SO	Avg	GP	W	L	Mins	GA	SO	Avg
2003-04	South St. Paul	High-MN	31	23	7	1	....	....	....	2.20	....	....	....	....	....	....	....
2004-05	Cedar Rapids	USHL	32	19	9	3	1801	82	1	2.73	9	7	2	582	14	*1	*1.44
2005-06	Cedar Rapids	USHL	44	*28	13	3	2641	112	4	2.54	8	3	5	472	25	0	3.18
2006-07	U. Minn-Duluth	WCHA	23	5	14	3	1364	76	1	3.34	....	....	....	....	....	....	....

USHL Playoff MVP (2005) • USHL First All-Star Team (2006) • WCHA All-Rookie Team (2007)

STANA, Rastislav (STAN-ah, RAH-tih-slahv) WSH.

Goaltender. Catches left. 6'2", 184 lbs. Born, Kosice, Czech., January 10, 1980.
(Washington's 8th choice, 193rd overall, in 1998 Entry Draft).

			Regular Season								Playoffs						
Season	Club	League	GP	W	L	O/T	Mins	GA	SO	Avg	GP	W	L	Mins	GA	SO	Avg
1997-98	HC Kosice Jr.	Slovak-Jr.	32	....	....	....	1920	56	2	1.75	....	....	....	....	....	....	....
1998-99	Moose Jaw	WHL	36	21	14	1	2131	123	2	3.46	9	4	5	544	30	0	3.31
99-2000	Moose Jaw	WHL	14	4	9	0	730	48	0	3.95	....	....	....	....	....	....	....
	Calgary Hitmen	WHL	16	13	2	1	971	37	1	2.29	9	7	2	526	21	1	2.40
2000-01	Richmond	ECHL	38	15	16	2	2111	90	1	2.56	3	1	2	178	7	1	2.34
2001-02	Richmond	ECHL	36	20	12	3	2098	95	1	2.72	....	....	....	....	....	....	....
	Portland Pirates	AHL	3	1	2	0	180	11	0	3.66	....	....	....	....	....	....	....
	Slovakia	Olympics	1	1	0	0	60	1	0	1.00	....	....	....	....	....	....	....
2002-03	Portland Pirates	AHL	24	8	11	4	1355	49	2	2.17	1	0	1	59	3	0	3.08
2003-04	**Washington**	**NHL**	**6**	**1**	**2**	**0**	**211**	**11**	**0**	**3.13**	....	....	....	....	....	....	....
	Portland Pirates	AHL	24	14	5	4	1429	40	5	1.68	3	1	2	139	7	0	3.02
2004-05	Sodertalje SK	Sweden	45	....	....	....	2562	116	3	2.72	10	....	....	605	22	1	2.18
2005-06	Sodertalje SK	Sweden	43	....	....	....	2554	129	3	3.03	....	....	....	....	....	....	....
	Sodertalje SK	Sweden-Q	9	....	....	....	548	21	2	2.30	....	....	....	....	....	....	....
2006-07	Malmo	Sweden	29	....	....	....	1636	81	2	2.97	....	....	....	....	....	....	....
	Linkopings HC	Sweden	11	....	....	....	672	21	3	1.88	15	....	....	936	31	0	*1.99
	NHL Totals		**6**	**1**	**2**	**0**	**211**	**11**	**0**	**3.13**	....	....	....	....	....	....	....

STEFANISZIN, Sebastian (steh-fan-IHSH-ihn, suh-BAS-tee-yeh ANA.

Goaltender. Catches left. 6', 190 lbs. Born, Berlin, East Germany, July 22, 1987.
(Anaheim's 6th choice, 98th overall, in 2007 Entry Draft).

			Regular Season								Playoffs						
Season	Club	League	GP	W	L	O/T	Mins	GA	SO	Avg	GP	W	L	Mins	GA	SO	Avg
2002-03	Eisb. Jrs. Berl. Jr.	Ger-Jr.	12	....	....	....	....	....	....	....	....	....	....	....	....	....	....
2003-04	Eisb. Jrs. Berl. Jr.	Ger-Jr.	23	....	....	....	....	....	....	2.87	3	....	....	....	....	....	5.45
2004-05	Eisb. Jrs. Berlin	German-3	4	....	....	....	183	10	1	3.28	....	....	....	....	....	....	....
	Eisb. Jrs. Berl. Jr.	Ger-Jr.	20	....	....	....	1048	55	1	3.15	4	....	....	240	21	0	5.25
2005-06	Eisbaren Berlin	Germany	3	....	....	....	175	11	0	3.77	....	....	....	....	....	....	....
	Eisb. Jrs. Berlin	German-3	16	....	....	....	818	57	0	4.18	....	....	....	....	....	....	....
	Hamburg Freezers	Germany	4	....	....	....	240	8	0	2.00	....	....	....	....	....	....	....
2006-07	Eisbaren Berlin	Germany	2	....	....	....	39	3	0	4.59	....	....	....	....	....	....	....
	Eisb. Jrs. Berlin	German-3	36	....	....	....	2005	130	1	3.89	2	....	....	120	11	0	5.50

STEPHAN, Tobias (STEH-fan, toh-BUY-uhs) DAL.

Goaltender. Catches left. 6'3", 178 lbs. Born, Zurich, Switz., January 21, 1984.
(Dallas' 3rd choice, 34th overall, in 2002 Entry Draft).

			Regular Season								Playoffs						
Season	Club	League	GP	W	L	O/T	Mins	GA	SO	Avg	GP	W	L	Mins	GA	SO	Avg
2000-01	Kloten Flyers Jr.	Swiss-Jr.					STATISTICS NOT AVAILABLE										
2001-02	EHC Chur	Swiss	23	....	....	....	1396	80	0	3.44	10	....	....	604	39	0	3.87
2002-03	Kloten Flyers	Swiss	*44	....	....	....	2670	125	2	2.81	5	....	....	292	20	0	4.11
2003-04	Kloten Flyers	Swiss	26	....	....	....	1547	61	5	2.37	....	....	....	....	....	....	....
2004-05	Kloten Flyers	Swiss	*44	....	....	....	2580	123	4	2.86	5	....	....	301	11	0	2.19
2005-06	Kloten Flyers	Swiss	*44	16	19	8	2663	125	*5	2.82	11	5	6	683	34	0	2.98
2006-07	Iowa Stars	AHL	27	10	15	0	1396	67	1	2.88	2	0	0	52	3	0	3.46

TAYLOR, Daniel (TAY-luhr, DAN-yehl) L.A.

Goaltender. Catches left. 5'11", 179 lbs. Born, Plymouth, England, April 28, 1986.
(Los Angeles' 8th choice, 221st overall, in 2004 Entry Draft).

			Regular Season								Playoffs						
Season	Club	League	GP	W	L	O/T	Mins	GA	SO	Avg	GP	W	L	Mins	GA	SO	Avg
2002-03	Cumberland Grads	CJHL	23	13	3	1	1009	41	1	2.44	6	3	3	432	17	0	2.36
2003-04	Guelph Storm	OHL	26	16	4	3	1462	66	0	2.71	3	1	1	159	9	0	3.40
2004-05	Guelph Storm	OHL	31	13	14	3	1821	80	2	2.64	1	0	1	59	4	0	4.07
2005-06	Kingston	OHL	57	32	15	6	3319	172	3	3.11	....	....	....	....	....	....	....
2006-07	Bakersfield	ECHL	17	7	7	2	969	70	0	4.33	....	....	....	....	....	....	....
	Wheeling Nailers	ECHL	1	0	0	1	62	4	0	3.86	....	....	....	....	....	....	....
	Texas Wildcatters	ECHL	2	0	1	0	74	2	0	1.61	....	....	....	....	....	....	....

TELLQVIST, Mikael (TEHL-kvihst, MIGH-kuhl) PHX.

Goaltender. Catches left. 5'11", 185 lbs. Born, Sundbyberg, Sweden, September 19, 1979.
(Toronto's 3rd choice, 70th overall, in 2000 Entry Draft).

			Regular Season								Playoffs						
Season	Club	League	GP	W	L	O/T	Mins	GA	SO	Avg	GP	W	L	Mins	GA	SO	Avg
1997-98	Djurgarden Jr.	Swe-Jr.	23	....	....	....	1380	55	....	2.39	2	0	2	120	8	0	4.00
1998-99	Djurgarden	Sweden	3	1	2	0	124	8	0	3.87	4	....	....	240	11	0	2.75
	Djurgarden	EuroHL	3	2	1	0	180	8	....	2.33	....	....	....	....	....	....	....
99-2000	Huddinge IK	Sweden-2	11	4	7	0	660	33	....	3.30	....	....	....	....	....	....	....
	Djurgarden	Sweden	30	....	....	....	1909	66	2	*2.07	*13	....	....	*814	21	*3	*1.55
2000-01	Djurgarden	Sweden	43	....	....	....	2622	91	*5	*2.08	*16	....	....	*1006	45	*1	2.68
2001-02	St. John's	AHL	28	8	11	6	1521	79	0	3.12	1	1	0	15	0	0	0.00
	Sweden	Olympics					DID NOT PLAY – SPARE GOALTENDER										
2002-03	**Toronto**	**NHL**	**3**	**1**	**1**	**0**	**86**	**4**	**0**	**2.79**	....	....	....	....	....	....	....
	St. John's	AHL	47	17	25	3	2651	148	1	3.35	....	....	....	....	....	....	....
2003-04	**Toronto**	**NHL**	**11**	**5**	**3**	**2**	**647**	**31**	**0**	**2.87**	....	....	....	....	....	....	....
	St. John's	AHL	23	10	11	1	1343	59	1	2.64	....	....	....	....	....	....	....
2004-05	St. John's	AHL	45	24	16	4	2600	115	0	2.65	5	1	4	253	15	0	3.56
2005-06	**Toronto**	**NHL**	**25**	**10**	**11**	**2**	**1399**	**73**	**2**	**3.13**	....	....	....	....	....	....	....
	Sweden	Olympics	1	0	1	0	60	3	0	3.00	....	....	....	....	....	....	....
2006-07	**Toronto**	**NHL**	**1**	**0**	**1**	**0**	**59**	**2**	**0**	**2.03**	....	....	....	....	....	....	....
	Toronto Marlies	AHL	3	2	1	0	182	12	0	3.95	....	....	....	....	....	....	....
	Phoenix	**NHL**	**30**	**11**	**11**	**3**	**1591**	**90**	**2**	**3.39**	....	....	....	....	....	....	....
	NHL Totals		**70**	**27**	**27**	**7**	**3782**	**200**	**4**	**3.17**	....	....	....	....	....	....	....

Traded to **Phoenix** by **Toronto** for Tyson Nash and Boston's 4th round choice (previously acquired, Toronto selected Matt Frattin) in 2007 Entry Draft, November 28, 2006.

THEODORE, Jose (TEE-uh-dohr, joh-SAY) COL.

Goaltender. Catches right. 5'11", 182 lbs. Born, Laval, Que., September 13, 1976.
(Montreal's 2nd choice, 44th overall, in 1994 Entry Draft).

			Regular Season								Playoffs						
Season	Club	League	GP	W	L	O/T	Mins	GA	SO	Avg	GP	W	L	Mins	GA	SO	Avg
1990-91	Richelieu	QAHA	42	....	....	....	2520	80	0	1.90	....	....	....	....	....	....	....
1991-92	Richelieu Riverains	QAAA	24	9	13	2	1440	96	0	3.99	5	2	3	295	26	0	5.28
1992-93	St-Jean Lynx	QMJHL	34	12	16	2	1776	112	0	3.78	3	0	2	175	11	0	3.77
1993-94	St-Jean Lynx	QMJHL	57	20	29	6	3225	194	0	3.61	5	1	4	296	18	0	3.65
1994-95	Hull Olympiques	QMJHL	*58	*32	22	2	*3348	193	5	3.46	*21	*15	6	*1263	59	*1	2.80
	Fredericton	AHL	....	....	....	....	....	....	....	....	1	0	1	60	3	0	3.00
1995-96	**Montreal**	**NHL**	**1**	**0**	**0**	**0**	**9**	**1**	**0**	**6.67**	....	....	....	....	....	....	....
	Hull Olympiques	QMJHL	48	33	11	2	2807	158	0	3.38	5	2	3	299	20	0	4.01
1996-97	**Montreal**	**NHL**	**16**	**5**	**6**	**2**	**821**	**53**	**0**	**3.87**	**2**	**1**	**1**	**168**	**7**	**0**	**2.50**
	Fredericton	AHL	26	12	12	0	1469	87	0	3.55	....	....	....	....	....	....	....
1997-98	Fredericton	AHL	53	20	23	8	3053	145	2	2.85	4	1	3	237	13	0	3.28
	Montreal	**NHL**	....	....	....	....	....	....	....	....	**3**	**0**	**1**	**120**	**1**	**0**	**0.50**
1998-99	**Montreal**	**NHL**	**18**	**4**	**12**	**0**	**913**	**50**	**1**	**3.29**	....	....	....	....	....	....	....
	Fredericton	AHL	27	12	13	2	1609	77	2	2.87	13	8	5	694	35	1	3.03
99-2000	**Montreal**	**NHL**	**30**	**12**	**13**	**2**	**1655**	**58**	**5**	**2.10**	....	....	....	....	....	....	....
2000-01	**Montreal**	**NHL**	**59**	**20**	**29**	**5**	**3298**	**141**	**2**	**2.57**	....	....	....	....	....	....	....
	Quebec Citadelles	AHL	3	3	0	0	180	9	0	3.00	....	....	....	....	....	....	....
2001-02	**Montreal**	**NHL**	**67**	**30**	**24**	**10**	**3864**	**136**	**7**	**2.11**	**12**	**6**	**6**	**686**	**35**	**0**	**3.06**
2002-03	**Montreal**	**NHL**	**57**	**20**	**31**	**6**	**3419**	**165**	**2**	**2.90**	....	....	....	....	....	....	....
2003-04	**Montreal**	**NHL**	**67**	**33**	**28**	**5**	**3961**	**150**	**6**	**2.27**	**11**	**4**	**7**	**678**	**27**	**1**	**2.39**
2004-05	Djurgarden	Sweden	17	....	....	....	1024	42	0	2.46	12	....	....	728	27	0	2.23
2005-06	**Montreal**	**NHL**	**38**	**17**	**15**	**5**	**2114**	**122**	**0**	**3.46**	....	....	....	....	....	....	....
	Colorado	**NHL**	**5**	**1**	**3**	**1**	**296**	**15**	**0**	**3.04**	**9**	**4**	**5**	**573**	**29**	**0**	**3.04**
2006-07	**Colorado**	**NHL**	**33**	**13**	**15**	**1**	**1748**	**95**	**0**	**3.26**	....	....	....	....	....	....	....
	NHL Totals		**391**	**155**	**176**	**37**	**22098**	**986**	**23**	**2.68**	**37**	**15**	**20**	**2225**	**99**	**1**	**2.67**

QMJHL Second All-Star Team (1995, 1996) • NHL Second All-Star Team (2002) • MBNA Roger Crozier Saving Grace Award (2002) • Vezina Trophy (2002) • Hart Memorial Trophy (2002)

Played in NHL All-Star Game (2002, 2004)

• Scored a goal vs. NY Islanders, January 2, 2001. Signed as a free agent by **Djurgarden** (Sweden), December 20, 2004. Traded to **Colorado** by **Montreal** for David Aebischer, March 8, 2006.

THIBAULT, Jocelyn (TEE-boh, JAW-seh-lihn) BUF.

Goaltender. Catches left. 5'11", 169 lbs. Born, Montreal, Que., January 12, 1975.
(Quebec's 1st choice, 10th overall, in 1993 Entry Draft).

			Regular Season								Playoffs						
Season	Club	League	GP	W	L	O/T	Mins	GA	SO	Avg	GP	W	L	Mins	GA	SO	Avg
1990-91	Laval-Laurentides	QAAA	20	14	5	0	1178	78	1	3.94	5	2	3	300	20	0	4.00
1991-92	Trois-Rivieres	QMJHL	30	14	7	1	1496	77	0	3.09	3	1	1	110	4	0	2.19
1992-93	Sherbrooke	QMJHL	56	34	14	5	3190	159	3	2.99	15	9	6	882	57	0	3.87
1993-94	**Quebec**	**NHL**	**29**	**8**	**13**	**3**	**1504**	**83**	**0**	**3.31**	....	....	....	....	....	....	....
	Cornwall Aces	AHL	4	4	0	0	240	9	1	2.25	....	....	....	....	....	....	....
1994-95	Sherbrooke	QMJHL	13	6	6	1	776	38	1	2.94	....	....	....	....	....	....	....
	Quebec	**NHL**	**18**	**12**	**2**	**2**	**898**	**35**	**1**	**2.34**	**3**	**1**	**2**	**148**	**8**	**0**	**3.24**
1995-96	**Colorado**	**NHL**	**10**	**3**	**4**	**2**	**558**	**28**	**0**	**3.01**	....	....	....	....	....	....	....
	Montreal	**NHL**	**40**	**23**	**13**	**3**	**2334**	**110**	**3**	**2.83**	**6**	**2**	**4**	**311**	**18**	**0**	**3.47**
1996-97	**Montreal**	**NHL**	**61**	**22**	**24**	**11**	**3397**	**164**	**1**	**2.90**	**3**	**0**	**3**	**179**	**13**	**0**	**4.36**
1997-98	**Montreal**	**NHL**	**47**	**19**	**15**	**8**	**2652**	**109**	**2**	**2.47**	**2**	**0**	**0**	**43**	**4**	**0**	**5.58**
1998-99	**Montreal**	**NHL**	**10**	**3**	**4**	**2**	**529**	**23**	**1**	**2.61**	....	....	....	....	....	....	....
	Chicago	**NHL**	**52**	**21**	**26**	**5**	**3014**	**136**	**4**	**2.71**	....	....	....	....	....	....	....
99-2000	**Chicago**	**NHL**	**60**	**25**	**26**	**7**	**3438**	**158**	**3**	**2.76**	....	....	....	....	....	....	....
2000-01	**Chicago**	**NHL**	**66**	**27**	**32**	**7**	**3844**	**180**	**6**	**2.81**	....	....	....	....	....	....	....
2001-02	**Chicago**	**NHL**	**67**	**33**	**23**	**9**	**3838**	**159**	**6**	**2.49**	**3**	**1**	**2**	**159**	**7**	**0**	**2.64**
2002-03	**Chicago**	**NHL**	**62**	**26**	**28**	**7**	**3650**	**144**	**8**	**2.37**	....	....	....	....	....	....	....
2003-04	**Chicago**	**NHL**	**14**	**5**	**7**	**2**	**821**	**39**	**1**	**2.85**	....	....	....	....	....	....	....
2004-05							DID NOT PLAY										
2005-06	**Pittsburgh**	**NHL**	**16**	**1**	**9**	**3**	**807**	**60**	**0**	**4.46**	....	....	....	....	....	....	....
2006-07	**Pittsburgh**	**NHL**	**22**	**7**	**8**	**2**	**1101**	**52**	**1**	**2.83**	**1**	**0**	**0**	**8**	**0**	**0**	**0.00**
	NHL Totals		**574**	**235**	**234**	**73**	**32385**	**1480**	**37**	**2.74**	**18**	**4**	**11**	**848**	**50**	**0**	**3.54**

QMJHL All-Rookie Team (1992) • QMJHL First All-Star Team (1993) • QMJHL MVP (1993) • Canadian Major Junior First All-Star Team (1993) • Canadian Major Junior Goaltender of the Year (1993)

Played in NHL All-Star Game (2003)

Transferred to **Colorado** after **Quebec** franchise relocated, June 21, 1995. Traded to **Montreal** by **Colorado** with Andrei Kovalenko and Martin Rucinsky for Patrick Roy and Mike Keane, December 6, 1995. Traded to **Chicago** by **Montreal** with Dave Manson and Brad Brown for Jeff Hackett, Eric Weinrich, Alain Nasreddine and Tampa Bay's 4th round choice (previously acquired, Montreal selected Chris Dyment) in 1999 Entry Draft, November 16, 1998. • Missed majority of 2003-04 season recovering from hip injury suffered in practice, November 9, 2003. Traded to **Pittsburgh** by **Chicago** for Pittsburgh's 4th round choice (Ben Shutrion) in 2006 Entry Draft, August 10, 2005. Signed as a free agent by **Buffalo**, July 5, 2007.

THOMAS, Tim (TAW-mas, TIHM) BOS.

Goaltender. Catches left. 5'11", 201 lbs. Born, Flint, MI, April 15, 1974.
(Quebec's 11th choice, 217th overall, in 1994 Entry Draft).

			Regular Season								Playoffs						
Season	Club	League	GP	W	L	O/T	Mins	GA	SO	Avg	GP	W	L	Mins	GA	SO	Avg
1992-93	Davison High	High-MI	27	....	....	....	1580	87	....	3.30	....	....	....	....	....	....	....
1993-94	U. of Vermont	ECAC	*33	15	12	6	1864	94	0	3.03	....	....	....	....	....	....	....
1994-95	U. of Vermont	ECAC	34	18	13	2	2010	90	*4	*2.69	....	....	....	....	....	....	....
1995-96	U. of Vermont	ECAC	37	*26	7	4	*2254	88	*3	*2.34	....	....	....	....	....	....	....
1996-97	U. of Vermont	ECAC	36	22	11	3	2158	101	2	2.81	....	....	....	....	....	....	....
1997-98	Birmingham Bulls	ECHL	6	4	1	1	360	13	1	2.17	....	....	....	....	....	....	....
	HIFK Helsinki	Finland	18	13	4	1	1034	28	2	1.62	9	9	0	551	14	3	1.52
	Houston Aeros	IHL	1	0	1	0	59	4	0	4.01	....	....	....	....	....	....	....
1998-99	HIFK Helsinki	Finland	14	8	3	3	833	31	2	2.23	11	7	4	658	25	0	2.28
	Hamilton Bulldogs	AHL	15	6	8	0	837	45	0	3.23	....	....	....	....	....	....	....
99-2000	Detroit Vipers	IHL	36	10	21	3	2020	120	1	3.56	....	....	....	....	....	....	....
2000-01	AIK Solna	Sweden	43	....	....	....	2542	105	3	2.48	5	....	....	299	20	0	4.01
2001-02	Karpat Oulu	Finland	32	15	12	5	1937	79	4	2.44	3	1	2	180	12	0	4.00
2002-03	**Boston**	**NHL**	**4**	**3**	**1**	**0**	**220**	**11**	**0**	**3.00**	....	....	....	....	....	....	....
	Providence Bruins	AHL	35	18	12	5	2049	98	1	2.87	....	....	....	....	....	....	....
2003-04	Providence Bruins	AHL	43	20	16	6	2544	78	9	1.84	2	0	2	84	10	0	7.13
2004-05	Jokerit Helsinki	Finland	54	34	13	7	3266	86	15	1.58	12	8	4	720	22	0	1.83
2005-06	**Boston**	**NHL**	**38**	**12**	**13**	**10**	**2187**	**101**	**1**	**2.77**	....	....	....	....	....	....	....
	Providence Bruins	AHL	26	15	11	0	1515	57	1	2.26	....	....	....	....	....	....	....
2006-07	**Boston**	**NHL**	**66**	**30**	**29**	**4**	**3619**	**189**	**3**	**3.13**	....	....	....	....	....	....	....
	NHL Totals		**108**	**45**	**43**	**14**	**6026**	**301**	**4**	**3.00**	....	....	....	....	....	....	....

ECAC First All-Star Team (1995, 1996) • ECAC Goaltender of the Year (1996) • NCAA East Second All-American Team (1995) • NCAA East First All-American Team (1996)

Signed as a free agent by **Edmonton**, June 4, 1998. Signed as a free agent by **Boston**, August 8, 2002. Signed as a free agent by **Jokerit Helsinki** (Finland), May 17, 2004. Signed as a free agent by **Boston**, September 14, 2005.

THOMPSON, Billy (TAWM-suhn, BIHL-lee)

Goaltender. Catches left. 6'2", 200 lbs. Born, Saskatoon, Sask., September 24, 1982.
(Florida's 7th choice, 136th overall, in 2001 Entry Draft).

			Regular Season								Playoffs						
Season	Club	League	GP	W	L	O/T	Mins	GA	SO	Avg	GP	W	L	Mins	GA	SO	Avg
1997-98	Sask. Contacts	SMHL	23	14	5	3	1336	65	2	2.92	....	....	....	....	....	....	....
1998-99	Lebret Eagles	SJHL					STATISTICS NOT AVAILABLE										
99-2000	Estevan Bruins	SJHL	31	....	....	....	1763	132	1	4.49	5	1	3	328	17	0	3.11
	Prince George	WHL	1	0	1	0	60	5	0	5.00	....	....	....	....	....	....	....

Season	Club	League	GP	W	L	O/T	Mins	GA	SO	Avg	GP	W	L	Mins	GA	SO	Avg
2000-01	Prince George	WHL	57	24	24	3	3185	178	1	3.35	6	2	4	324	22	0	4.07
2001-02	Prince George	WHL	42	20	17	2	2375	108	2	2.73	7	3	4	402	21	0	3.13
2002-03	Prince George	WHL	50	20	26	0	2776	186	0	4.02	5	1	3	239	12	0	3.01
	Binghamton	AHL	1	1	0	0	60	5	0	5.00	....	....	....	....	....	....	....
2003-04	Binghamton	AHL	34	13	14	2	1725	83	2	2.89	....	....	....	....	....	....	....
2004-05	Binghamton	AHL	34	19	8	2	1869	76	1	2.44	....	....	....	....	....	....	....
2005-06	Binghamton	AHL	34	9	17	3	1812	125	0	4.14	....	....	....	....	....	....	....
2006-07	Bridgeport	AHL	33	11	18	1	1690	106	1	3.76	....	....	....	....	....	....	....

WHL West Second All-Star Team (2003)

Traded to **Ottawa** by **Florida** with Greg Watson for Jani Hurme, October 1, 2002. Signed as a free agent by **NY Islanders**, July 25, 2006.

TOIVONEN, Hannu (TOI-voh-nuhn, HA-noo) ST.L.

Goaltender. Catches left. 6'2", 200 lbs. Born, Kalvola, Finland, May 18, 1984.
(Boston's 1st choice, 29th overall, in 2002 Entry Draft).

			Regular Season								Playoffs						
Season	Club	League	GP	W	L	O/T	Mins	GA	SO	Avg	GP	W	L	Mins	GA	SO	Avg
2000-01	HPK U18	Fin-U18	....	....	....	....	....	....	....	....	....	....	....	....	....	....	....
2001-02	HPK U18	Fin-U18	5	4	1	0	277	14	0	3.03	....	....	....	....	....	....	....
	HPK Jr.	Fin-Jr.	31	15	12	4	1877	103	2	3.29	7	3	4	440	31	0	4.23
2002-03	HPK Jr.	Fin-Jr.	6	3	3	0	359	20	0	3.34	....	....	....	....	....	....	....
	HPK Hameenlinna	Finland	24	16	2	4	1432	54	2	2.26	2	1	1	117	3	1	1.53
2003-04	Providence Bruins	AHL	36	15	16	4	2162	83	2	2.30	0	0	0	0	0	0	0.00
2004-05	Providence Bruins	AHL	54	29	18	3	3017	103	7	2.05	17	10	7	1038	42	0	2.43
2005-06	**Boston**	**NHL**	**20**	**9**	**5**	**4**	**1163**	**51**	**1**	**2.63**	....	....	....	....	....	....	....
2006-07	**Boston**	**NHL**	**18**	**3**	**9**	**1**	**894**	**63**	**0**	**4.23**	....	....	....	....	....	....	....
	Providence Bruins	AHL	27	13	13	1	1618	64	2	2.37	13	6	7	742	36	0	2.91
	NHL Totals		**38**	**12**	**14**	**5**	**2057**	**114**	**1**	**3.33**	....	....	....	....	....	....	....

Traded to **St. Louis** by **Boston** for Carl Soderberg, July 23, 2007.

TORDJMAN, Josh (TOHRJ-man, JAWSH) PHX.

Goaltender. Catches left. 6'1", 155 lbs. Born, Montreal, Que., January 11, 1985.

			Regular Season								Playoffs						
Season	Club	League	GP	W	L	O/T	Mins	GA	SO	Avg	GP	W	L	Mins	GA	SO	Avg
2002-03	Valleyfield Braves	QJHL					STATISTICS NOT AVAILABLE										
	Victoriaville Tigres	QMJHL	10	4	3	0	432	24	1	3.33	2	0	1	112	12	0	6.46
2003-04	Victoriaville Tigres	QMJHL	42	10	24	4	2177	143	2	3.94	....	....	....	....	....	....	....
2004-05	Victoriaville Tigres	QMJHL	56	22	28	4	3185	171	5	3.22	7	3	4	435	24	0	3.31
2005-06	Victoriaville Tigres	QMJHL	31	13	17	0	1792	106	2	3.55	....	....	....	....	....	....	....
	Moncton Wildcats	QMJHL	25	18	6	0	1427	55	2	*2.31	21	*15	5	1238	48	*2	2.33
2006-07	San Antonio	AHL	37	15	18	2	2114	91	1	2.58	....	....	....	....	....	....	....
	Phoenix	ECHL	9	4	4	0	480	25	0	3.12	....	....	....	....	....	....	....

QMJHL Second All-Star Team (2006)

Signed as a free agent by **Phoenix**, July 2, 2006.

TOSKALA, Vesa (TAWS-kah-lah, VEH-sa) TOR.

Goaltender. Catches left. 5'10", 195 lbs. Born, Tampere, Finland, May 20, 1977.
(San Jose's 4th choice, 90th overall, in 1995 Entry Draft).

			Regular Season								Playoffs						
Season	Club	League	GP	W	L	O/T	Mins	GA	SO	Avg	GP	W	L	Mins	GA	SO	Avg
1994-95	Ilves Tampere Jr.	Fin-Jr.	17	10	5	1	956	36	2	2.26	7	....	....	393	22	....	3.36
1995-96	Ilves Tampere Jr.	Fin-Jr.	3	3	0	0	180	3	0	1.00	....	....	....	....	....	....	....
	KooVee Tampere	Finland-2	2	1	1	0	119	5	1	2.51	....	....	....	....	....	....	....
	Ilves Tampere	Finland	37	14	14	7	2072	109	1	3.16	2	0	2	78	11	0	8.46
1996-97	Ilves Tampere Jr.	Fin-Jr.	3	....	....	....	184	....	....	2.93	....	....	....	....	....	....	....
	Ilves Tampere	Finland	40	22	12	5	2270	108	0	2.85	8	3	5	479	29	0	3.63
1997-98	Ilves Tampere Jr.	Fin-Jr.	2	2	0	0	120	4	0	2.00	....	....	....	....	....	....	....
	Ilves Tampere	Finland	43	26	13	3	2554	118	1	2.77	9	6	3	519	18	1	2.08
1998-99	Ilves Tampere	Finland	33	21	12	0	1966	70	5	2.14	4	1	3	248	14	0	3.39
99-2000	Farjestad	Sweden	44	....	....	....	2652	118	3	2.67	7	....	....	439	19	0	2.59
2000-01	Kentucky	AHL	44	22	13	5	2466	114	2	2.77	3	0	3	197	8	0	2.43
2001-02	**San Jose**	**NHL**	**1**	**0**	**0**	**0**	**10**	**0**	**0**	**0.00**	....	....	....	....	....	....	....
	Cleveland Barons	AHL	*62	19	33	7	*3574	178	3	2.99	....	....	....	....	....	....	....
2002-03	**San Jose**	**NHL**	**11**	**4**	**3**	**1**	**537**	**21**	**1**	**2.35**	....	....	....	....	....	....	....
	Cleveland Barons	AHL	49	15	30	2	2824	151	1	3.21	....	....	....	....	....	....	....
2003-04	**San Jose**	**NHL**	**28**	**12**	**8**	**4**	**1541**	**53**	**1**	**2.06**	....	....	....	....	....	....	....
2004-05	Ilves Tampere	Finland	3	0	1	2	186	8	0	2.58	6	3	3	357	19	0	3.19
2005-06	**San Jose**	**NHL**	**37**	**23**	**7**	**4**	**2039**	**87**	**2**	**2.56**	**11**	**6**	**5**	**686**	**28**	**1**	**2.45**
	Cleveland Barons	AHL	1	0	0	1	65	0	1	0.00	....	....	....	....	....	....	....
2006-07	**San Jose**	**NHL**	**38**	**26**	**10**	**1**	**2142**	**84**	**4**	**2.35**	....	....	....	....	....	....	....
	NHL Totals		**115**	**65**	**28**	**10**	**6269**	**245**	**8**	**2.34**	**11**	**6**	**5**	**686**	**28**	**1**	**2.45**

Signed as a free agent by **Ilves Tampere** (Finland), January 31, 2005. Traded to **Toronto** by **San Jose** with Mark Bell for Toronto's 1st (later traded to St. Louis - St. Louis selected Lars Eller) and 2nd (later traded to St. Louis - St. Louis selected Aaron Palushaj) round choices in 2007 Entry Draft and Toronto's 4th round choice in 2009 Entry Draft, June 22, 2007.

TURCO, Marty (TUHR-koh, MAHR-tee) DAL.

Goaltender. Catches left. 5'11", 183 lbs. Born, Sault Ste. Marie, Ont., August 13, 1975.
(Dallas' 4th choice, 124th overall, in 1994 Entry Draft).

			Regular Season								Playoffs						
Season	Club	League	GP	W	L	O/T	Mins	GA	SO	Avg	GP	W	L	Mins	GA	SO	Avg
1993-94	Cambridge	OJHL-B	34	19	10	3	1973	114	0	3.47	....	....	....	....	....	....	....
1994-95	U. of Michigan	CCHA	37	*27	7	1	2063	95	1	2.76	....	....	....	....	....	....	....
1995-96	U. of Michigan	CCHA	*42	*34	7	1	*2335	84	*5	*2.16	....	....	....	....	....	....	....
1996-97	U. of Michigan	CCHA	*41	*33	4	4	*2296	87	*4	*2.27	....	....	....	....	....	....	....
1997-98	U. of Michigan	CCHA	*45	*33	10	1	*2640	95	4	2.16	....	....	....	....	....	....	....
1998-99	Michigan K-Wings	IHL	54	24	17	10	3127	136	1	2.61	5	2	3	300	14	0	2.80
99-2000	Michigan K-Wings	IHL	60	23	27	*7	3399	139	*7	2.45	....	....	....	....	....	....	....
2000-01	**Dallas**	**NHL**	**26**	**13**	**6**	**1**	**1266**	**40**	**3**	***1.90**	....	....	....	....	....	....	....
2001-02	**Dallas**	**NHL**	**31**	**15**	**6**	**2**	**1519**	**53**	**2**	**2.09**	....	....	....	....	....	....	....
2002-03	**Dallas**	**NHL**	**55**	**31**	**10**	**10**	**3203**	**92**	**7**	***1.72**	**12**	**6**	**6**	**798**	**25**	**0**	**1.88**
2003-04	**Dallas**	**NHL**	**73**	**37**	**21**	**13**	**4359**	**144**	**9**	**1.98**	**5**	**1**	**4**	**325**	**18**	**0**	**3.32**
2004-05	Djurgarden	Sweden	6	....	....	....	356	12	1	2.02	....	....	....	....	....	....	....
2005-06	**Dallas**	**NHL**	**68**	**41**	**19**	**5**	**3910**	**166**	**3**	**2.55**	**5**	**1**	**4**	**319**	**18**	**0**	**3.39**
	Canada	Olympics					DID NOT PLAY – SPARE GOALTENDER										
2006-07	**Dallas**	**NHL**	**67**	**38**	**20**	**5**	**3764**	**140**	**6**	**2.23**	**7**	**3**	**4**	**509**	**11**	**3**	***1.30**
	NHL Totals		**320**	**175**	**82**	**36**	**18021**	**635**	**30**	**2.11**	**29**	**11**	**18**	**1951**	**72**	**3**	**2.21**

CCHA Rookie of the Year (1995) • NCAA Championship All-Tournament Team (1996, 1998) • CCHA First All-Star Team (1997) • NCAA West First All-American Team (1997) • CCHA Second All-Star Team (1998) • NCAA Championship Tournament MVP (1998) • Garry F. Longman Memorial Trophy (Rookie of the Year – IHL) (1999) • MBNA Roger Crozier Saving Grace Award (2001, 2003) • NHL Second All-Star Team (2003)

Played in NHL All-Star Game (2003, 2004, 2007)

Signed as a free agent by **Djurgarden** (Sweden), November 13, 2004.

TURPLE, Dan (TUHR-puhl, DAN) ATL.

Goaltender. Catches left. 6'6", 210 lbs. Born, Oakville, Ont., January 1, 1985.
(Atlanta's 6th choice, 186th overall, in 2004 Entry Draft).

			Regular Season								Playoffs						
Season	Club	League	GP	W	L	O/T	Mins	GA	SO	Avg	GP	W	L	Mins	GA	SO	Avg
2002-03	Kingston	OHL	12	2	8	0	449	42	0	5.61	....	....	....	....	....	....	....
2003-04	Kingston	OHL	9	4	4	1	534	29	0	3.26	....	....	....	....	....	....	....
	Oshawa Generals	OHL	35	20	7	3	1843	81	2	2.64	7	3	4	443	19	1	2.57
2004-05	Oshawa Generals	OHL	10	4	4	0	469	29	0	3.71	....	....	....	....	....	....	....
	Kitchener Rangers	OHL	40	17	16	5	2335	92	3	2.36	3	0	2	162	9	0	3.33
2005-06	Kitchener Rangers	OHL	57	40	15	2	3306	124	*7	*2.25	5	1	3	326	20	0	3.68
2006-07	Gwinnett	ECHL	34	18	13	3	2052	129	1	3.77	1	0	1	73	5	0	4.11

OHL Second All-Star Team (2006)

UNICE, Josh (EW-nihs, JAWSH) CHI.

Goaltender. Catches left. 5'11", 175 lbs. Born, Toledo, OH, June 24, 1989.
(Chicago's 5th choice, 86th overall, in 2007 Entry Draft).

			Regular Season								Playoffs						
Season	Club	League	GP	W	L	O/T	Mins	GA	SO	Avg	GP	W	L	Mins	GA	SO	Avg
2004-05	Det. Victory Honda	MWEHL	48	21	10	0	....	....	....	2.70	....	....	....	....	....	....	....
2005-06	USNTDP	U-17	6	2	3	1	364	23	....	3.79	....	....	....	....	....	....	....
	USNTDP	NAHL	21	11	7	2	1246	62	0	2.99	8	5	3	490	14	2	1.72
2006-07	USNTDP	U-18	27	15	9	2	1582	83	3	3.15	....	....	....	....	....	....	....
	USNTDP	NAHL	6	5	0	1	369	13	1	2.12	....	....	....	....	....	....	....

VALIQUETTE, Steve (val-ih-KEHT, STEEV) NYR

Goaltender. Catches left. 6'6", 220 lbs. Born, Etobicoke, Ont., August 20, 1977.
(Los Angeles' 8th choice, 190th overall, in 1996 Entry Draft).

			Regular Season								Playoffs						
Season	Club	League	GP	W	L	O/T	Mins	GA	SO	Avg	GP	W	L	Mins	GA	SO	Avg
1993-94	Burlington	OPJHL	30	....	....	....	1663	112	1	4.04	....	....	....	....	....	....	....
1994-95	Rayside-Balfour	NOJHA	2	0	2	0	89	12	0	8.09	....	....	....	....	....	....	....
	Smiths Falls Bears	CJHL	21	10	8	3	1275	75	0	3.53	....	....	....	....	....	....	....
	Sudbury Wolves	OHL	4	2	0	0	138	6	0	2.61	....	....	....	....	....	....	....
1995-96	Sudbury Wolves	OHL	39	13	16	2	1887	123	0	3.91	....	....	....	....	....	....	....
1996-97	Sudbury Wolves	OHL	*61	21	29	7	3311	232	1	4.20	....	....	....	....	....	....	....
	Dayton Bombers	ECHL	3	1	0	0	89	6	0	4.03	2	1	1	118	5	0	2.54
1997-98	Sudbury Wolves	OHL	14	5	7	1	807	50	0	3.72	....	....	....	....	....	....	....
	Erie Otters	OHL	28	16	7	3	1525	65	3	2.56	7	3	4	467	15	1	1.93
1998-99	Lowell	AHL	1	0	1	0	59	3	0	3.05	....	....	....	....	....	....	....
	Hampton Roads	ECHL	31	18	7	3	1713	84	1	2.94	2	0	1	60	7	0	7.00
99-2000	**NY Islanders**	**NHL**	**6**	**2**	**0**	**0**	**193**	**6**	**0**	**1.87**	....	....	....	....	....	....	....
	Lowell	AHL	14	8	5	0	727	36	0	2.97	....	....	....	....	....	....	....
	Providence Bruins	AHL	1	1	0	0	60	3	0	3.00	....	....	....	....	....	....	....
	Trenton Titans	ECHL	12	5	6	1	692	36	1	3.12	....	....	....	....	....	....	....
2000-01	Springfield Falcons	AHL	20	7	10	1	1066	54	0	3.04	....	....	....	....	....	....	....
2001-02	Bridgeport	AHL	20	10	5	1	1071	45	2	2.52	1	0	0	18	1	0	3.30
2002-03	Bridgeport	AHL	34	15	14	3	1962	86	2	2.63	4	3	1	253	9	0	2.13
2003-04	**Edmonton**	**NHL**	**1**	**0**	**0**	**0**	**14**	**2**	**0**	**8.57**	....	....	....	....	....	....	....
	Toronto	AHL	35	14	14	5	2064	89	2	2.59	....	....	....	....	....	....	....
	NY Rangers	**NHL**	**2**	**1**	**1**	**0**	**120**	**6**	**0**	**3.00**	....	....	....	....	....	....	....
	Hartford Wolf Pack	AHL	7	2	4	1	400	15	1	2.25	1	0	0	11	0	0	0.00
2004-05	Hartford Wolf Pack	AHL	35	19	11	1	1900	56	7	*1.77	2	1	1	118	4	0	2.03
2005-06	Yaroslavl	Russia	45	....	....	....	2734	89	4	1.95	8	....	....	458	23	0	3.01
2006-07	**NY Rangers**	**NHL**	**3**	**1**	**2**	**0**	**115**	**6**	**0**	**3.13**	....	....	....	....	....	....	....
	Hartford Wolf Pack	AHL	30	17	12	0	1694	66	2	2.34	....	....	....	....	....	....	....
	NHL Totals		**12**	**4**	**3**	**0**	**442**	**20**	**0**	**2.71**	....	....	....	....	....	....	....

Shared Harry "Hap" Holmes Memorial Trophy (fewest goals against - AHL) with Jason LaBarbera (2005)

Signed as a free agent by **NY Islanders**, August 18, 1998. Signed as a free agent by **Edmonton**, July 20, 2003. Claimed by **Florida** from **Edmonton** in Waiver Draft, October 3, 2003. Claimed on waivers by **Edmonton** from **Florida**, October 9, 2003. Traded to **NY Rangers** by **Edmonton** with Dwight Helminen and Edmonton's 2nd round compensatory choice (Dane Byers) in 2004 Entry Draft for Petr Nedved and Jussi Markkanen, March 3, 2004. Signed as a free agent by **Yaroslavl** (Russia), April 26, 2005. Signed as a free agent by **NY Rangers**, July 1, 2006.

VARLAMOV, Simeon (vahr-LAH-mawv, sih-MEE-awn) WSH.

Goaltender. Catches left. 6'1", 183 lbs. Born, Kuybyshev, USSR, April 27, 1988.
(Washington's 2nd choice, 23rd overall, in 2006 Entry Draft).

			Regular Season								Playoffs						
Season	Club	League	GP	W	L	O/T	Mins	GA	SO	Avg	GP	W	L	Mins	GA	SO	Avg
2004-05	Yaroslavl 2	Russia-3	8	....	....	....	369	15	1	2.43	....	....	....	....	....	....	....
2005-06	Yaroslavl 2	Russia-3	33	....	....	....	1782	60	8	2.02	....	....	....	....	....	....	....
2006-07	Yaroslavl 2	Russia-3	2	....	....	....	120	3	0	1.50	....	....	....	....	....	....	....
	Yaroslavl	Russia	33	....	....	....	1936	70	3	2.17	6	....	....	368	18	0	2.94

VOKOUN, Tomas (voh-KOON, TAW-mas) FLA.

Goaltender. Catches right. 6', 195 lbs. Born, Karlovy Vary, Czech., July 2, 1976.
(Montreal's 11th choice, 226th overall, in 1994 Entry Draft).

			Regular Season								Playoffs						
Season	Club	League	GP	W	L	O/T	Mins	GA	SO	Avg	GP	W	L	Mins	GA	SO	Avg
1993-94	HC Kladno	CzRep	1	0	0	0	20	2	0	6.01	....	....	....	....	....	....	....
1994-95	HC Kladno	CzRep	26	....	....	....	1368	70	....	3.07	5	....	....	240	19	....	4.75
1995-96	Wheeling	ECHL	35	20	10	2	1912	117	0	3.67	7	4	3	436	19	0	2.61
	Fredericton	AHL	....	....	....	....	....	....	....	....	1	0	1	59	4	0	4.09
1996-97	**Montreal**	**NHL**	**1**	**0**	**0**	**0**	**20**	**4**	**0**	**12.00**	....	....	....	....	....	....	....
	Fredericton	AHL	47	12	26	7	2645	154	2	3.49	....	....	....	....	....	....	....
1997-98	Fredericton	AHL	31	13	13	2	1735	90	0	3.11	....	....	....	....	....	....	....
1998-99	**Nashville**	**NHL**	**37**	**12**	**18**	**4**	**1954**	**96**	**1**	**2.95**	....	....	....	....	....	....	....
	Milwaukee	IHL	9	3	2	4	539	22	1	2.45	2	0	2	149	8	0	3.22
99-2000	**Nashville**	**NHL**	**33**	**9**	**20**	**1**	**1879**	**87**	**1**	**2.78**	....	....	....	....	....	....	....
	Milwaukee	IHL	7	5	2	0	364	17	0	2.80	....	....	....	....	....	....	....
2000-01	**Nashville**	**NHL**	**37**	**13**	**17**	**5**	**2088**	**85**	**2**	**2.44**	....	....	....	....	....	....	....
2001-02	**Nashville**	**NHL**	**29**	**5**	**14**	**4**	**1471**	**66**	**2**	**2.69**	....	....	....	....	....	....	....
2002-03	**Nashville**	**NHL**	**69**	**25**	**31**	**11**	**3974**	**146**	**3**	**2.20**	....	....	....	....	....	....	....
2003-04	**Nashville**	**NHL**	**73**	**34**	**29**	**10**	**4221**	**178**	**3**	**2.53**	**6**	**2**	**4**	**356**	**12**	**1**	**2.02**
2004-05	Znojmo	CzRep	27	....	....	....	1599	69	3	2.59	....	....	....	....	....	....	....
	HIFK Helsinki	Finland	19	11	4	4	1149	35	2	1.83	4	0	3	205	12	0	3.51
2005-06	**Nashville**	**NHL**	**61**	**36**	**18**	**7**	**3601**	**160**	**4**	**2.67**	....	....	....	....	....	....	....
	Czech Republic	Olympics	7	3	4	0	342	14	1	2.46	....	....	....	....	....	....	....
2006-07	**Nashville**	**NHL**	**44**	**27**	**12**	**4**	**2601**	**104**	**5**	**2.40**	**5**	**1**	**4**	**324**	**16**	**0**	**2.96**
	NHL Totals		**384**	**161**	**159**	**46**	**21809**	**926**	**21**	**2.55**	**11**	**3**	**8**	**680**	**28**	**1**	**2.47**

Played in NHL All-Star Game (2004)

Claimed by **Nashville** from **Montreal** in Expansion Draft, June 26, 1998. Signed as a free agent by **Znojmo** (CzRep), September 6, 2004. Signed as a free agent by **HIFK Helsinki** (Finland), December 20, 2004. Traded to **Florida** by **Nashville** for Detroit's 2nd round choice (previously acquired, Nashville selected Nick Spaling) in 2007 Entry Draft and Florida's 1st and 2nd round choices in 2008 Entry Draft, June 22, 2007.

WALL, Michael (WAWL, MIGH-kuhl) COL.

Goaltender. Catches left. 6'2", 209 lbs. Born, Telkwa, B.C., July 25, 1985.

			Regular Season								Playoffs						
Season	Club	League	GP	W	L	O/T	Mins	GA	SO	Avg	GP	W	L	Mins	GA	SO	Avg
2001-02	Prince George	WHL	3	0	1	1	107	7	0	3.92	....	....	....	....	....	....	....
2002-03	Prince George	WHL	13	2	5	1	567	40	0	4.23	....	....	....	....	....	....	....
2003-04	Prince George	WHL	1	1	0	0	60	6	0	6.00	....	....	....	....	....	....	....
	Everett Silvertips	WHL	35	11	13	4	1657	59	2	2.14	3	1	0	104	2	0	2.15
2004-05	Everett Silvertips	WHL	56	24	21	8	3191	102	10	1.92	11	4	7	697	25	1	2.15
2005-06	Portland Pirates	AHL	11	5	5	0	603	34	1	3.38	....	....	....	....	....	....	....
	Augusta Lynx	ECHL	21	8	11	1	1103	70	1	3.81	....	....	....	....	....	....	....
2006-07	**Anaheim**	**NHL**	**4**	**2**	**2**	**0**	**202**	**10**	**0**	**2.97**	....	....	....	....	....	....	....
	Portland Pirates	AHL	19	10	6	1	1014	53	0	3.13	....	....	....	....	....	....	....
	Arizona Sundogs	CHL	9	6	3	0	544	20	1	2.20	14	7	7	795	38	2	2.87
	NHL Totals		**4**	**2**	**2**	**0**	**202**	**10**	**0**	**2.97**	....	....	....	....	....	....	....

Signed as a free agent by **Anaheim**, September 29, 2005. Traded to **Colorado** by **Anaheim** for Brad May, February 27, 2007.

WARD, Cam (WOHRD, KAM) CAR.

Goaltender. Catches left. 6'1", 200 lbs. Born, Saskatoon, Sask., February 29, 1984.
(Carolina's 1st choice, 25th overall, in 2002 Entry Draft).

			Regular Season								Playoffs						
Season	Club	League	GP	W	L	O/T	Mins	GA	SO	Avg	GP	W	L	Mins	GA	SO	Avg
1998-99	Sherwood Park	ABHL	24	13	7	4	1403	85	0	3.64	....	....	....	....	....	....	....
99-2000	Sherwood Park	AMHL	20	9	5	1	1194	71	0	3.57	7	4	3	262	22	0	3.57
2000-01	Sherwood Park	AMHL	25	14	6	3	1449	70	0	2.90	....	....	....	....	....	....	....
	Red Deer Rebels	WHL	1	1	0	0	60	0	1	0.00	....	....	....	....	....	....	....
2001-02	Red Deer Rebels	WHL	46	30	11	4	2694	102	1	*2.27	*23	14	9	*1502	53	*2	2.12
2002-03	Red Deer Rebels	WHL	57	*40	13	3	3368	118	5	2.10	*23	14	9	*1407	49	3	2.09
2003-04	Red Deer Rebels	WHL	56	31	16	8	3338	114	4	2.05	19	10	9	1200	37	3	1.85
2004-05	Lowell	AHL	50	27	17	3	2829	94	6	1.99	11	5	6	664	28	2	2.53
2005-06♦	**Carolina**	**NHL**	**28**	**14**	**8**	**2**	**1484**	**91**	**0**	**3.68**	***23**	***15**	**8**	***1320**	**47**	**2**	**2.14**
	Lowell	AHL	2	0	2	0	118	5	0	2.54	....	....	....	....	....	....	....
2006-07	**Carolina**	**NHL**	**60**	**30**	**21**	**6**	**3422**	**167**	**2**	**2.93**	....	....	....	....	....	....	....
	NHL Totals		**88**	**44**	**29**	**8**	**4906**	**258**	**2**	**3.16**	**23**	**15**	**8**	**1320**	**47**	**2**	**2.14**

WHL East First All-Star Team (2002, 2004) • WHL East Second All-Star Team (2003) • WHL Goaltender of the Year (2002, 2004) • WHL Player of the Year (2004) • Canadian Major Junior First All-Star Team (2004) • Canadian Major Junior Goaltender of the Year (2004) • AHL All-Rookie Team (2005) • Conn Smythe Trophy (2006)

WEEKES, Kevin (WEEKS, KEH-vihn) N.J.

Goaltender. Catches left. 6'1", 215 lbs. Born, Toronto, Ont., April 4, 1975.
(Florida's 2nd choice, 41st overall, in 1993 Entry Draft).

			Regular Season								Playoffs						
Season	Club	League	GP	W	L	O/T	Mins	GA	SO	Avg	GP	W	L	Mins	GA	SO	Avg
1990-91	Tor. Red Wings	MTHL					Statistics Not Available										
	St. Mike's B's	MTJHL	1	0	0	0	41	1	0	1.46	....	....	....	....	....	....	....
1991-92	Tor. Red Wings	MTHL	35	....	....	....	1575	68	4	1.94	....	....	....	....	....	....	....
	St. Mike's B's	MTJHL	2	0	1	1	127	11	0	5.20	4	1	2	214	15	1	4.21
1992-93	Owen Sound	OHL	29	9	12	5	1645	143	0	5.22	1	0	0	26	5	0	11.50
1993-94	Owen Sound	OHL	34	13	19	1	1974	158	0	4.80	....	....	....	....	....	....	....
1994-95	Ottawa 67's	OHL	41	13	23	4	2266	153	1	4.05	....	....	....	....	....	....	....
1995-96	Carolina Panthers	AHL	60	24	25	8	3404	229	2	4.04	....	....	....	....	....	....	....
1996-97	Carolina Monarchs	AHL	51	17	28	4	2899	172	1	3.56	....	....	....	....	....	....	....
1997-98	**Florida**	**NHL**	**11**	**0**	**5**	**1**	**485**	**32**	**0**	**3.96**	....	....	....	....	....	....	....
	Fort Wayne	IHL	12	9	2	1	719	34	1	2.84	....	....	....	....	....	....	....
1998-99	Detroit Vipers	IHL	33	19	5	7	1857	64	*4	*2.07	....	....	....	....	....	....	....
	Vancouver	**NHL**	**11**	**0**	**8**	**1**	**532**	**34**	**0**	**3.83**	....	....	....	....	....	....	....
99-2000	**Vancouver**	**NHL**	**20**	**6**	**7**	**4**	**987**	**47**	**1**	**2.86**	....	....	....	....	....	....	....
	NY Islanders	**NHL**	**36**	**10**	**20**	**4**	**2026**	**115**	**1**	**3.41**	....	....	....	....	....	....	....
2000-01	**Tampa Bay**	**NHL**	**61**	**20**	**33**	**3**	**3378**	**177**	**4**	**3.14**	....	....	....	....	....	....	....
2001-02	**Tampa Bay**	**NHL**	**19**	**3**	**9**	**0**	**830**	**40**	**2**	**2.89**	....	....	....	....	....	....	....
	Carolina	**NHL**	**2**	**2**	**0**	**0**	**120**	**3**	**0**	**1.50**	**8**	**3**	**2**	**408**	**11**	**2**	**1.62**
2002-03	**Carolina**	**NHL**	**51**	**14**	**24**	**9**	**2965**	**126**	**5**	**2.55**	....	....	....	....	....	....	....
2003-04	**Carolina**	**NHL**	**66**	**23**	**30**	**11**	**3765**	**146**	**6**	**2.33**	....	....	....	....	....	....	....
2004-05							Did Not Play										
2005-06	**NY Rangers**	**NHL**	**32**	**14**	**14**	**3**	**1850**	**91**	**0**	**2.95**	**1**	**0**	**1**	**60**	**4**	**0**	**4.00**
2006-07	**NY Rangers**	**NHL**	**14**	**4**	**6**	**2**	**761**	**43**	**0**	**3.39**	....	....	....	....	....	....	....
	NHL Totals		**323**	**96**	**156**	**38**	**17699**	**854**	**19**	**2.90**	**9**	**3**	**3**	**468**	**15**	**2**	**1.92**

James Norris Memorial Trophy (fewest goals against – IHL) (1999) (shared with Andrei Trefilov)

Traded to **Vancouver** by **Florida** with Ed Jovanovski, Dave Gagner, Mike Brown and Florida's 1st round choice (Nathan Smith) in 2000 Entry Draft for Pavel Bure, Bret Hedican, Brad Ference and Vancouver's 3rd round choice (Robert Fried) in 2000 Entry Draft, January 17, 1999. Traded to **NY Islanders** by **Vancouver** with Dave Scatchard and Bill Muckalt for Felix Potvin, NY Islanders' 2nd round compensatory choice (later traded to New Jersey – New Jersey selected Teemu Laine) in 2000 Entry Draft and NY Islanders' 3rd round choice (Thatcher Bell) in 2000 Entry Draft, December 19, 1999. Traded to **Tampa Bay** by **NY Islanders** with the rights to Kristian Kudroc and NY Islanders' 2nd round choice (later traded to Phoenix – Phoenix selected Matthew Spiller) in 2001 Entry Draft for Tampa Bay's 1st round choice (Raffi Torres) in 2000 Entry Draft, Calgary's 4th round choice (previously acquired, NY Islanders selected Vladimir Gorbunov) in 2000 Entry Draft and NY Islanders' 7th round choice (previously acquired, NY Islanders selected Ryan Caldwell) in 2000 Entry Draft, June 24, 2000. Traded to **Carolina** by **Tampa Bay** for Shane Willis and Chris Dingman, March 5, 2002. Signed as a free agent by **NY Rangers**, August 26, 2004. Signed as a free agent by **New Jersey**, July 5, 2007.

WEIMAN, Tyler (WIGH-muhn, TIGH-luhr) COL.

Goaltender. Catches left. 5'11", 180 lbs. Born, Saskatoon, Sask., June 5, 1984.
(Colorado's 6th choice, 164th overall, in 2002 Entry Draft).

			Regular Season								Playoffs						
Season	Club	League	GP	W	L	O/T	Mins	GA	SO	Avg	GP	W	L	Mins	GA	SO	Avg
99-2000	Ft. Saskatchewan	AMBHL	21	15	4	2	1239	60	0	2.91	....	....	....	....	....	....	....
2000-01	Tri-City Americans	WHL	44	10	25	4	2464	155	0	3.77	....	....	....	....	....	....	....
2001-02	Tri-City Americans	WHL	47	18	17	5	2492	149	2	3.59	5	1	4	300	14	0	2.80
2002-03	Tri-City Americans	WHL	55	16	34	2	3129	207	1	3.97	....	....	....	....	....	....	....
2003-04	Tri-City Americans	WHL	54	23	21	7	3023	134	1	2.66	5	1	2	234	11	0	2.82
2004-05	Colorado Eagles	CHL	44	*33	6	5	2630	79	*8	*1.80	*13	*8	4	*744	32	1	2.58
2005-06	Lowell	AHL	14	6	6	1	844	36	0	2.56	....	....	....	....	....	....	....
	San Diego Gulls	ECHL	32	14	12	3	1797	84	1	2.81	4	0	4	251	15	0	3.59
2006-07	Albany River Rats	AHL	54	27	22	3	3047	152	2	2.99	5	1	4	294	17	0	3.47

WESLOSKY, Jase (wehs-LAWZ-kee, JAYS) NYI

Goaltender. Catches left. 6'2", 170 lbs. Born, St. Albert, Alta., August 14, 1988.
(NY Islanders' 5th choice, 108th overall, in 2006 Entry Draft).

			Regular Season								Playoffs						
Season	Club	League	GP	W	L	O/T	Mins	GA	SO	Avg	GP	W	L	Mins	GA	SO	Avg
2004-05	St. Albert Blues	EMHA	....	13	3	2	1043	38	....	2.19	....	....	....	....	....	....	....
2005-06	Sherwood Park	AJHL	58	....	....	....	2123	110	2	3.11	....	....	....	....	....	....	....
2006-07	St. Cloud State	WCHA	6	5	1	0	359	16	1	2.67	....	....	....	....	....	....	....

YEATS, Matthew (YAYTS, MA-thew)

Goaltender. Catches left. 5'11", 165 lbs. Born, Montreal, Que., April 6, 1979.
(Los Angeles' 9th choice, 248th overall, in 1998 Entry Draft).

			Regular Season								Playoffs						
Season	Club	League	GP	W	L	O/T	Mins	GA	SO	Avg	GP	W	L	Mins	GA	SO	Avg
1995-96	Lethbridge	WHL	1	0	0	0	20	3	0	9.00	....	....	....	....	....	....	....
1996-97	Olds Grizzlys	AJHL	32	....	....	....	1678	95	1	3.41	....	....	....	....	....	....	....
1997-98	Olds Grizzlys	AJHL	26	12	12	1	1498	96	0	3.85	....	....	....	....	....	....	....
1998-99	University of Maine	H-East					Did Not Play										
99-2000	University of Maine	H-East	32	20	6	4	1821	79	0	2.60	....	....	....	....	....	....	....
2000-01	University of Maine	H-East	33	18	9	4	1897	76	2	2.40	....	....	....	....	....	....	....
2001-02	University of Maine	H-East	20	6	8	3	1048	54	0	3.09	....	....	....	....	....	....	....
2002-03	Philadelphia	AHL	2	1	1	0	90	4	0	2.67	....	....	....	....	....	....	....
	Atlantic City	ECHL	48	23	16	8	2811	141	4	3.01	8	4	1	397	16	1	2.42
2003-04	Portland Pirates	AHL	7	2	1	1	332	12	1	2.17	....	....	....	....	....	....	....
	Washington	**NHL**	**5**	**1**	**3**	**0**	**258**	**13**	**0**	**3.02**	....	....	....	....	....	....	....
2004-05	Reading Royals	ECHL	13	8	2	2	780	31	1	2.38	....	....	....	....	....	....	....
	Idaho Steelheads	ECHL	4	2	1	1	247	9	0	2.19	2	0	1	66	3	0	2.72
2005-06	Idaho Steelheads	ECHL	35	21	7	5	1980	98	1	2.97	5	2	3	289	16	1	3.33
2006-07	Texas Wildcatters	ECHL	60	32	19	7	3342	165	6	2.96	6	2	4	287	16	1	3.35
	NHL Totals		**5**	**1**	**3**	**0**	**258**	**13**	**0**	**3.02**	....	....	....	....	....	....	....

• Ruled ineligible to play 1998-99 season by NCAA due to appearance with **Lethbridge** (WHL) in 1995-96. Signed as a free agent by **Portland** (AHL), November 6, 2003. Signed as a free agent by **Washington**, March 20, 2004. Signed as a free agent by **Reading** (ECHL), December 10, 2004.

YORK, Allen (YOHRK, AL-ihn) CBJ

Goaltender. Catches left. 6'4", 185 lbs. Born, Wetaskiwin, Alta., June 17, 1989.
(Columbus' 6th choice, 158th overall, in 2007 Entry Draft).

			Regular Season								Playoffs						
Season	Club	League	GP	W	L	O/T	Mins	GA	SO	Avg	GP	W	L	Mins	GA	SO	Avg
2006-07	Camrose Kodiaks	AJHL	32	23	4	0	1661	60	2	2.17	22	16	6	1391	46	4	1.98

ZABA, Matt (ZA-buh, MAT) L.A.

Goaltender. Catches left. 6'1", 180 lbs. Born, Yorkton, Sask., July 14, 1983.
(Los Angeles' 8th choice, 231st overall, in 2003 Entry Draft).

			Regular Season								Playoffs						
Season	Club	League	GP	W	L	O/T	Mins	GA	SO	Avg	GP	W	L	Mins	GA	SO	Avg
2000-01	Yorkton Mallers	SMHL	26	13	10	3	1480	79	0	3.20	....	....	....	....	....	....	....
2001-02	Penticton Panthers	BCHL	33	....	....	....	1980	128	0	3.69	....	....	....	....	....	....	....
2002-03	Vernon Vipers	BCHL	44	34	9	0	2012	96	2	2.21	17	14	3	1006	25	3	1.49
2003-04	Colorado College	WCHA	23	10	10	2	1323	50	1	2.27	....	....	....	....	....	....	....
2004-05	Colorado College	WCHA	18	10	5	2	1050	43	2	2.46	....	....	....	....	....	....	....
2005-06	Colorado College	WCHA	36	20	14	2	2068	87	4	2.52	....	....	....	....	....	....	....
2006-07	Colorado College	WCHA	33	15	13	4	1908	76	3	2.39	....	....	....	....	....	....	....

WCHA All-Rookie Team (2004)

ZATKOFF, Jeff (ZAT-kawf, JEHF) L.A.

Goaltender. Catches left. 6'1", 180 lbs. Born, Detroit, MI, June 9, 1987.
(Los Angeles' 4th choice, 74th overall, in 2006 Entry Draft).

			Regular Season								Playoffs						
Season	Club	League	GP	W	L	O/T	Mins	GA	SO	Avg	GP	W	L	Mins	GA	SO	Avg
2004-05	Sioux City	USHL	24	13	6	3	1271	54	1	2.55	2	0	0	68	10	0	8.88
2005-06	Miami U.	CCHA	20	14	5	1	1217	41	3	2.02	....	....	....	....	....	....	....
2006-07	Miami U.	CCHA	26	14	8	3	1542	58	1	2.26	....	....	....	....	....	....	....

Late Additions to Player Register

FREE AGENT SIGNINGS

POTULNY, Grant (Career data panel page 321)
Center. Shoots left. 6'3", 205 lbs. Born, Grand Forks, ND, March 4, 1980.
Signed as a free agent by **Hershey** (AHL), August 16, 2007.

RIDDLE, Troy (Career data panel page 323)
Center. Shoots right. 5'10", 175 lbs. Born, Minneapolis, MN, August 24, 1981.
Signed as a free agent by **Houston** (AHL), August 15, 2007.

ROONEY, Joe
Left wing. Shoots left. 5'10", 170 lbs. Born, Canton, MA., September 15, 1985.

			Regular Season					Playoffs				
Season	Club	League	GP	G	A	Pts	PIM	GP	G	A	Pts	PIM
2003-04	Boston College	H-East	33	4	2	6	10	....	....	....	....	....
2004-05	Boston College	H-East	39	4	16	20	26	....	....	....	....	....
2005-06	Boston College	H-East	40	5	13	18	38	....	....	....	....	....
2006-07	Boston College	H-East	42	16	26	42	32	....	....	....	....	....

Signed as a free agent by **Lowell** (AHL), July 24, 2007.

STEFAN, Patrik (Career data panel page 544)
Center. Shoots left. 6'2", 210 lbs. Born, Pirbram, Czech., September 16, 1980.
Signed as a free agent by **Bern** (Swiss), August 15, 2007.

SVITOV, Alexander (Career data panel page 549)
Center. Shoots left. 6'3", 228 lbs. Born, Omsk, USSR, November 3, 1982.
Signed by **Omsk** (Russia), August 17, 2007.

VANDERMEER, Peter (Career data panel page 336)
Left wing. Shoots left. 6', 210 lbs. Born, Caroline, Alta., October 14, 1975.
Signed as a free agent by **San Antonio** (AHL), August 16, 2006.

VASICEK, Joseph (Career data panel page 561) **NYI**
Center. Shoots left. 6'5", 214 lbs. Born, Havlickuv Brod, Czech., September 12, 1980.
Signed as a free agent by **NY Islanders,** August 15, 2007.

RETIREMENT

RICCI, Mike (Career data panel page 515)
Center. Shoots left. 6', 200 lbs. Born, Scarborough, Ont., October 27, 1971.
Announced retirement August 14, 2007.

COACHING

LOW, Ron
Hired as an Assistant Coach by **Ottawa**, August 15, 2007.

WILSON, Eli
Hired as a Goaltending Coach by **Ottawa**, August 15, 2007.

MINOR-LEAGUE AFFILIATION

COLORADO (Complete list of minor-league affiliations: see page 14)
Announced affiliation with **Johnstown Chiefs** (ECHL), August 16, 2007.

WEIGHT CHANGES

GELINAS, MARTIN (Career data panel page 403) **NSH**
Left wing. Shoots left. 5'11", **202 lbs.** Born, Shawinigan, Que., June 5, 1970.

GRUMET-MORRIS, Dov (Career data panel page 590) **NSH**
Goaltender. Catches left. 6'2", **205 lbs.** Born, Evanston, IL, February 28, 1982.

SETZINGER, Oliver (Career data panel page 327) **NSH**
Center. Shoots left. 6', **189 lbs.** Born, Horn, Austria, July 11, 1983.

SHOOTING SIDE

DIETRICH, Robert (Career data panel page 284) **NSH**
Defense. **Shoots right.** 5'10", 172 lbs. Born, Ordzhonikidze, USSR, July 25, 1986.

OBITUARY

POLLOCK, Sam Honoured Member, Hockey Hall of Fame
General Manager, Montreal Canadiens, 1964-65 to 1977-78
Born, December 25, 1925. **Died, August 15, 2007**

Thommy Abrahamsson

Tommy Albelin

Dave Andreychuk

Jack Arbour

Retired NHL Player Index

Abbreviations: Teams/Cities: – **Ana.** – Anaheim; **Atl.** – Atlanta; **Bos.** – Boston; **Bro.** – Brooklyn; **Buf.** – Buffalo; **Cal.** – California; **Cgy.** – Calgary; **Car.** – Carolina; **Chi.** – Chicago; **Cle.** – Cleveland; **Col.** – Colorado; **CBJ** – Columbus; **Dal.** – Dallas; **Det.** – Detroit; **Edm.** – Edmonton; **Fla.** – Florida; **Ham.** – Hamilton; **Hfd.** – Hartford; **K.C.** – Kansas City; **L.A.** – Los Angeles; **Min.** – Minnesota; **Mtl.** – Montreal; **Mtl.M.** – Montreal Maroons; **Mtl.W.** – Montreal Wanderers; **Nsh.** – Nashville; **N.J.** – New Jersey; **NYA** – NY Americans; **NYI** – NY Islanders; **NYR** – New York Rangers; **Oak.** – Oakland; **Ott.** – Ottawa; **Phi.** – Philadelphia; **Phx.** – Phoenix; **Pit.** – Pittsburgh; **Que.** – Quebec; **St.L.** – St. Louis; **S.J.** – San Jose; **T.B.** – Tampa Bay; **Tor.** – Toronto; **Van.** – Vancouver; **Wpg.** – Winnipeg; **Wsh.** – Washington

A – assists; **G** – goals; **GP** – games played; **PIM** – penalties in minutes; **TP** – total points.
• – deceased. Assists not recorded during 1917-18 season ‡ – Remains active in other leagues.

NHL Seasons – A player or goaltender who does not play in a regular season but who does appear in that year's playoffs is credited with an NHL Season in this Index. Total seasons are rounded off to the nearest full season.

			Regular Schedule					Playoffs							
Name	NHL Teams	NHL Seasons	GP	G	A	TP	PIM	GP	G	A	TP	PIM	NHL Cup Wins	First NHL Season	Last NHL Season
A															
Aalto, Antti	Ana.	4	151	11	17	28	52	4	0	0	0	2	....	1997-98	2000-01
Abbott, Reg	Mtl.	1	3	0	0	0	0	....	....	....	....	....	....	1952-53	1952-53
• Abel, Clarence	NYR, Chi.	8	333	19	18	37	359	38	1	1	2	58	2	1926-27	1933-34
Abel, Gerry	Det.	1	1	0	0	0	0	....	....	....	....	....	....	1966-67	1966-67
• Abel, Sid	Det., Chi.	14	612	189	283	472	376	97	28	30	58	79	3	1938-39	1953-54
Abgrall, Dennis	L.A.	1	13	0	2	2	4	....	....	....	....	....	....	1975-76	1975-76
Abrahamsson, Thommy	Hfd.	1	32	6	11	17	16	....	....	....	....	....	....	1980-81	1980-81
Achtymichuk, Gene	Mtl., Det.	4	32	3	5	8	2	....	....	....	....	....	....	1951-52	1958-59
Acomb, Doug	Tor.	1	2	0	1	1	0	....	....	....	....	....	....	1969-70	1969-70
Acton, Keith	Mtl., Min., Edm., Phi., Wsh., NYI	15	1023	226	358	584	1172	66	12	21	33	88	1	1979-80	1993-94
• Adam, Douglas	NYR	1	4	0	1	1	0	....	....	....	....	....	....	1949-50	1949-50
Adam, Russ	Tor.	1	8	1	2	3	11	....	....	....	....	....	....	1982-83	1982-83
‡ Adams, Bryan	Atl.	2	11	0	1	1	2	....	....	....	....	....	....	1999-00	2000-01
Adams, Greg	Phi., Hfd., Wsh., Edm., Van., Que., Det.	10	545	84	143	227	1173	43	2	11	13	153	....	1980-81	1989-90
Adams, Greg	N.J., Van., Dal., Phx., Fla.	17	1056	355	388	743	326	81	20	22	42	16	....	1984-85	2000-01
• Adams, Jack	Tor., Ott.	7	173	83	32	115	366	10	2	0	2	13	2	1917-18	1926-27
Adams, John	Mtl.	1	42	6	12	18	11	3	0	0	0	0	....	1940-41	1940-41
• Adams, Stew	Chi., Tor.	4	95	9	26	35	60	11	3	3	6	14	....	1929-30	1932-33
Adduono, Rick	Bos., Atl.	2	4	0	0	0	2	....	....	....	....	....	....	1975-76	1979-80
Affleck, Bruce	St.L., Van., NYI	7	280	14	66	80	86	8	0	0	0	0	....	1974-75	1983-84
Agnew, Jim	Van., Hfd.	6	81	0	1	1	257	4	0	0	0	6	....	1986-87	1992-93
Ahern, Fred	Cal., Cle., Col.	4	146	31	30	61	130	2	0	1	1	2	....	1974-75	1977-78
• Ahlin, Rudy	Chi.	1	1	0	0	0	0	....	....	....	....	....	....	1937-38	1937-38
Ahola, Peter	L.A., Pit., S.J., Cgy.	3	123	10	17	27	137	6	0	0	0	2	....	1991-92	1993-94
Ahrens, Chris	Min.	6	52	0	3	3	84	1	0	0	0	0	....	1972-73	1977-78
• Ailsby, Lloyd	NYR	1	3	0	0	0	2	....	....	....	....	....	....	1951-52	1951-52
Aitken, Brad	Pit., Edm.	2	14	1	3	4	25	....	....	....	....	....	....	1987-88	1990-91
‡ Aitken, Johnathan	Bos., Chi.	2	44	0	1	1	70	....	....	....	....	....	....	1999-00	2003-04
Aivazoff, Micah	Det., Edm., NYI	3	92	4	6	10	46	....	....	....	....	....	....	1993-94	1995-96
‡ Alatalo, Mika	Phx.	2	152	17	29	46	58	5	0	0	0	2	....	1999-00	2000-01
Albelin, Tommy	Que., N.J., Cgy.	18	952	44	211	255	417	81	7	15	22	22	2	1987-88	2005-06
• Albright, Clint	NYR	1	59	14	5	19	19	....	....	....	....	....	....	1948-49	1948-49
Aldcorn, Gary	Tor., Det., Bos.	5	226	41	56	97	78	6	1	2	3	4	....	1956-57	1960-61
Aldridge, Keith	Dal.	1	4	0	0	0	0	....	....	....	....	....	....	1999-00	1999-00
Alexander, Claire	Tor., Van.	4	155	18	47	65	36	16	2	4	6	4	....	1974-75	1977-78
• Alexandre, Art	Mtl.	2	11	0	2	2	8	4	0	0	0	0	....	1931-32	1932-33
Allan, Jeff	Cle.	1	4	0	0	0	2	....	....	....	....	....	....	1977-78	1977-78
Allen, Chris	Fla.	2	2	0	0	0	2	....	....	....	....	....	....	1997-98	1998-99
• Allen, George	NYR, Chi., Mtl.	8	339	82	115	197	179	41	9	10	19	32	....	1938-39	1946-47
Allen, Keith	Det.	2	28	0	4	4	8	5	0	0	0	0	1	1953-54	1954-55
Allen, Peter	Pit.	1	8	0	0	0	8	....	....	....	....	....	....	1995-96	1995-96
• Allen, Viv	NYA	1	6	0	1	1	0	....	....	....	....	....	....	1940-41	1940-41
Alley, Steve	Hfd.	2	15	3	3	6	11	3	0	1	1	0	....	1979-80	1980-81
Allison, Dave	Mtl.	1	3	0	0	0	12	....	....	....	....	....	....	1983-84	1983-84
Allison, Jason	Wsh., Bos., L.A., Tor.	12	552	154	331	485	441	25	7	18	25	14	....	1993-94	2005-06
Allison, Mike	NYR, Tor., L.A.	10	499	102	166	268	630	82	9	17	26	135	....	1980-81	1989-90
Allison, Ray	Hfd., Phi.	7	238	64	93	157	223	12	2	3	5	20	....	1979-80	1986-87
• Allum, Bill	NYR	1	1	0	1	1	0	....	....	....	....	....	....	1940-41	1940-41
• Amadio, Dave	Det., L.A.	3	125	5	11	16	163	16	1	2	3	18	....	1957-58	1968-69
Ambroziak, Peter	Buf.	1	12	0	1	1	0	....	....	....	....	....	....	1994-95	1994-95
Amodeo, Mike	Wpg.	1	19	0	0	0	2	....	....	....	....	....	....	1979-80	1979-80
• Anderson, Bill	Bos.	1	....	....	....	....	....	1	0	0	0	0	....	1942-43	1942-43
Anderson, Dale	Det.	1	13	0	0	0	6	2	0	0	0	0	....	1956-57	1956-57
Anderson, Doug	Mtl.	1	....	....	....	....	....	2	0	0	0	0	1	1952-53	1952-53
Anderson, Earl	Det., Bos.	3	109	19	19	38	22	5	0	1	1	0	....	1974-75	1976-77
Anderson, Glenn	Edm., Tor., NYR, St.L.	16	1129	498	601	1099	1120	225	93	121	214	442	6	1980-81	1995-96
Anderson, Jim	L.A.	1	7	1	2	3	2	....	....	....	....	....	....	1967-68	1967-68
Anderson, John	Tor., Que., Hfd.	12	814	282	349	631	263	37	9	18	27	2	....	1977-78	1988-89
Anderson, Murray	Wsh.	1	40	0	1	1	68	....	....	....	....	....	....	1974-75	1974-75
Anderson, Perry	St.L., N.J., S.J.	10	400	50	59	109	1051	36	2	1	3	161	....	1981-82	1991-92
Anderson, Ron	Det., L.A., St.L., Buf.	5	251	28	30	58	146	5	0	0	0	4	....	1967-68	1971-72
Anderson, Ron	Wsh.	1	28	9	7	16	8	....	....	....	....	....	....	1974-75	1974-75
Anderson, Russ	Pit., Hfd., L.A.	9	519	22	99	121	1086	10	0	3	3	28	....	1976-77	1984-85
Anderson, Shawn	Buf., Que., Wsh., Phi.	8	255	11	51	62	117	19	1	1	2	16	....	1986-87	1994-95
• Anderson, Tom	Det., NYA, Bro.	8	319	62	127	189	180	16	2	7	9	8	....	1934-35	1941-42
Andersson, Erik	Cgy.	1	12	2	1	3	8	....	....	....	....	....	....	1997-98	1997-98
Andersson, Kent-Erik	Min., NYR	7	456	72	103	175	78	50	4	11	15	4	....	1977-78	1983-84
Andersson, Mikael	Buf., Hfd., T.B., Phi., NYI	15	761	95	169	264	134	25	2	7	9	10	....	1985-86	1999-00
‡ Andersson, Niklas	Que., NYI, S.J., Nsh., Cgy.	6	164	29	53	82	85	....	....	....	....	....	....	1992-93	2000-01
Andersson, Peter	Wsh., Que.	3	172	10	41	51	81	7	0	2	2	2	....	1983-84	1985-86
Andersson, Peter	NYR, Fla.	2	47	6	13	19	20	....	....	....	....	....	....	1992-93	1993-94
Andrascik, Steve	NYR	1	....	....	....	....	....	1	0	0	0	0	....	1971-72	1971-72
Andrea, Paul	NYR, Pit., Cal., Buf.	4	150	31	49	80	10	....	....	....	....	....	....	1965-66	1970-71
• Andrews, Lloyd	Tor.	4	53	8	5	13	10	2	0	0	0	0	1	1921-22	1924-25
Andreychuk, Dave	Buf., Tor., N.J., Bos., Col., T.B.	23	1639	640	698	1338	1125	162	43	54	97	162	1	1982-83	2005-06
Andrievski, Alexander	Chi.	1	1	0	0	0	0	....	....	....	....	....	....	1992-93	1992-93
Andruff, Ron	Mtl., Col.	5	153	19	36	55	54	2	0	0	0	0	....	1974-75	1978-79
Andrusak, Greg	Pit., Tor.	5	28	0	6	6	16	15	1	0	1	8	....	1993-94	1999-00
Angelstad, Mel	Wsh.	1	2	0	0	0	2	....	....	....	....	....	....	2003-04	2003-04
Angotti, Lou	NYR, Chi., Phi., Pit., St.L.	10	653	103	186	289	228	65	8	8	16	17	....	1964-65	1973-74
Anholt, Darrel	Chi.	1	1	0	0	0	0	....	....	....	....	....	....	1983-84	1983-84
Anslow, Hub	NYR	1	2	0	0	0	0	....	....	....	....	....	....	1947-48	1947-48
Antonovich, Mike	Min., Hfd., N.J.	5	87	10	15	25	37	....	....	....	....	....	....	1975-76	1983-84
Antoski, Shawn	Van., Phi., Pit., Ana.	8	183	3	5	8	599	36	1	3	4	74	....	1990-91	1997-98
• Apps, Syl	Tor.	10	423	201	231	432	56	69	25	29	54	8	3	1936-37	1947-48
Apps, Syl	NYR, Pit., L.A.	10	727	183	423	606	311	23	5	5	10	23	....	1970-71	1979-80
Arbour, Al	Det., Chi., Tor., St.L.	16	626	12	58	70	617	86	1	8	9	92	4	1953-54	1970-71
• Arbour, Amos	Mtl., Ham., Tor.	6	113	52	20	72	77	....	....	....	....	....	....	1918-19	1923-24
• Arbour, Jack	Det., Tor.	2	47	5	1	6	56	....	....	....	....	....	....	1926-27	1928-29
Arbour, John	Bos., Pit., Van., St.L.	5	106	1	9	10	149	5	0	0	0	0	....	1965-66	1971-72
• Arbour, Ty	Pit., Chi.	5	207	28	28	56	112	11	2	0	2	6	....	1926-27	1930-31
Archambault, Michel	Chi.	1	3	0	0	0	0	....	....	....	....	....	....	1976-77	1976-77
Archibald, Dave	Min., NYR, Ott., NYI	8	323	57	67	124	139	5	0	1	1	0	....	1987-88	1996-97
Archibald, Jim	Min.	3	16	1	2	3	45	....	....	....	....	....	....	1984-85	1986-87
Areshenkoff, Ron	Edm.	1	4	0	0	0	0	....	....	....	....	....	....	1979-80	1979-80
Armstrong, Bill	Phi.	1	1	0	1	1	0	....	....	....	....	....	....	1990-91	1990-91
• Armstrong, Bob	Bos.	12	542	13	86	99	671	42	1	7	8	28	....	1950-51	1961-62
‡ Armstrong, Chris	Min., Ana.	2	7	0	1	1	0	....	....	....	....	....	....	2000-01	2003-04
Armstrong, George	Tor.	21	1187	296	417	713	721	110	26	34	60	52	4	1949-50	1970-71
Armstrong, Murray	Tor., NYA, Bro., Det.	8	270	67	121	188	72	30	4	6	10	2	....	1937-38	1945-46

			Regular Schedule					Playoffs							
Name	NHL Teams	NHL Seasons	GP	G	A	TP	PIM	GP	G	A	TP	PIM	NHL Cup Wins	First NHL Season	Last NHL Season
● Armstrong, Norm	Tor.	1	7	1	1	2	2	....	....	....	....	....	....	1962-63	1962-63
Armstrong, Tim	Tor.	1	11	1	0	1	6	....	....	....	....	....	....	1988-89	1988-89
Arnason, Chuck	Mtl., Atl., Pit., K.C., Col., Cle., Min., Wsh.	8	401	109	90	199	122	9	2	4	6	4	....	1971-72	1978-79
Arniel, Scott	Wpg., Buf., Bos.	12	730	149	189	338	599	34	3	3	6	39	....	1981-82	1991-92
Arthur, Fred	Hfd., Phi.	3	80	1	8	9	49	4	0	0	0	2	....	1980-81	1982-83
● Arundel, John	Tor.	1	3	0	0	0	9	....	....	....	....	....	....	1949-50	1949-50
Arvedson, Magnus	Ott., Van.	7	434	100	125	225	241	52	3	8	11	34	....	1997-98	2003-04
● Ashbee, Barry	Bos., Phi.	5	284	15	70	85	291	17	0	4	4	22	1	1965-66	1973-74
● Ashby, Don	Tor., Col., Edm.	6	188	40	56	96	40	12	1	0	1	4	....	1975-76	1980-81
Ashton, Brent	Van., Col., N.J., Min., Que., Det., Wpg., Bos., Cgy.	14	998	284	345	629	635	85	24	25	49	70	....	1979-80	1992-93
Ashworth, Frank	Chi.	1	18	5	4	9	2	....	....	....	....	....	....	1946-47	1946-47
● Asmundson, Oscar	NYR, Det., St.L., NYA, Mtl.	5	111	11	23	34	30	9	0	2	2	4	1	1932-33	1937-38
Astashenko, Kaspars	T.B.	2	23	1	2	3	8	....	....	....	....	....	....	1999-00	2000-01
‡ Astley, Mark	Buf.	3	75	4	19	23	92	2	0	0	0	0	....	1993-94	1995-96
● Atanas, Walt	NYR	1	49	13	8	21	40	....	....	....	....	....	....	1944-45	1944-45
Atcheynum, Blair	Ott., St.L., Nsh., Chi.	5	196	27	33	60	36	23	1	3	4	8	....	1992-93	2000-01
● Atkinson, Steve	Bos., Buf., Wsh.	6	302	60	51	111	104	1	0	0	0	0	....	1968-69	1974-75
Attwell, Bob	Col.	2	22	1	5	6	0	....	....	....	....	....	....	1979-80	1980-81
Attwell, Ron	St.L., NYR	1	22	1	7	8	8	....	....	....	....	....	....	1967-68	1967-68
Aubin, Norm	Tor.	2	69	18	13	31	30	1	0	0	0	0	....	1981-82	1982-83
Aubry, Pierre	Que., Det.	5	202	24	26	50	133	20	1	1	2	32	....	1980-81	1984-85
Aubuchon, Ossie	Bos., NYR	2	50	20	12	32	4	6	1	0	1	0	....	1942-43	1943-44
Audet, Philippe	Det.	1	4	0	0	0	0	....	....	....	....	....	....	1998-99	1998-99
Audette, Donald	Buf., L.A., Atl., Dal., Mtl., Fla.	15	735	260	249	509	584	73	21	27	48	46	....	1989-90	2003-04
● Auge, Les	Col.	1	6	0	3	3	4	....	....	....	....	....	....	1980-81	1980-81
Augusta, Patrik	Tor., Wsh.	2	4	0	0	0	0	....	....	....	....	....	....	1993-94	1998-99
‡ Aulin, Jared	L.A.	1	17	2	2	4	0	....	....	....	....	....	....	2002-03	2002-03
● Aurie, Larry	Det.	12	489	147	129	276	279	24	6	9	15	10	2	1927-28	1938-39
Awrey, Don	Bos., St.L., Mtl., Pit., NYR, Col.	16	979	31	158	189	1065	71	0	18	18	150	2	1963-64	1978-79
● Ayres, Vern	NYA, Mtl.M., St.L., NYR	6	211	6	11	17	350	....	....	....	....	....	....	1930-31	1935-36

B

Name	NHL Teams	NHL Seasons	GP	G	A	TP	PIM	GP	G	A	TP	PIM	NHL Cup Wins	First NHL Season	Last NHL Season
Babando, Pete	Bos., Det., Chi., NYR	6	351	86	73	159	194	17	3	3	6	6	1	1947-48	1952-53
Babcock, Bobby	Wsh.	2	2	0	0	0	2	....	....	....	....	....	....	1990-91	1992-93
Babe, Warren	Min.	3	21	2	5	7	23	2	0	0	0	0	....	1987-88	1990-91
‡ Babenko, Yuri	Col.	1	3	0	0	0	0	....	....	....	....	....	....	2000-01	2000-01
Babin, Mitch	St.L.	1	8	0	0	0	0	....	....	....	....	....	....	1975-76	1975-76
Baby, John	Cle., Min.	2	26	2	8	10	26	....	....	....	....	....	....	1977-78	1978-79
Babych, Dave	Wpg., Hfd., Van., Phi., L.A.	19	1195	142	581	723	970	114	21	41	62	113	....	1980-81	1998-99
Babych, Wayne	St.L., Pit., Que., Hfd.	9	519	192	246	438	498	41	7	9	16	24	....	1978-79	1986-87
Baca, Jergus	Hfd.	2	10	0	2	2	14	....	....	....	....	....	....	1990-91	1991-92
Backman, Mike	NYR	3	18	1	6	7	18	10	2	2	4	2	....	1981-82	1983-84
● Backor, Pete	Tor.	1	36	4	5	9	6	....	....	....	....	....	1	1944-45	1944-45
Backstrom, Ralph	Mtl., L.A., Chi.	17	1032	278	361	639	386	116	27	32	59	68	6	1956-57	1972-73
● Bailey, Ace	Tor.	8	313	111	82	193	472	21	3	4	7	12	1	1926-27	1933-34
● Bailey, Bob	Tor., Det., Chi.	5	150	15	21	36	207	15	0	4	4	22	....	1953-54	1957-58
● Bailey, Garnet	Bos., Det., St.L., Wsh.	10	568	107	171	278	633	15	2	4	6	28	1	1968-69	1977-78
Bailey, Reid	Phi., Tor., Hfd.	4	40	1	3	4	105	16	0	2	2	25	....	1980-81	1983-84
Baillargeon, Joel	Wpg., Que.	3	20	0	2	2	31	....	....	....	....	....	....	1986-87	1988-89
Baird, Ken	Cal.	1	10	0	2	2	15	....	....	....	....	....	....	1971-72	1971-72
Baker, Bill	Mtl., Col., St.L., NYR	3	143	7	25	32	175	6	0	0	0	0	....	1980-81	1982-83
Baker, Jamie	Que., Ott., S.J., Tor.	9	404	71	79	150	271	25	5	4	9	42	....	1989-90	1998-99
Bakovic, Peter	Van.	1	10	2	0	2	48	....	....	....	....	....	....	1987-88	1987-88
‡ Bala, Chris	Ott.	1	6	0	1	1	0	....	....	....	....	....	....	2001-02	2001-02
Balderis, Helmut	Min.	1	26	3	6	9	2	....	....	....	....	....	....	1989-90	1989-90
Baldwin, Doug	Tor., Det., Chi.	3	24	0	1	1	8	....	....	....	....	....	....	1945-46	1947-48
Balfour, Earl	Tor., Chi.	7	288	30	22	52	78	26	0	3	3	4	1	1951-52	1960-61
● Balfour, Murray	Mtl., Chi., Bos.	8	306	67	90	157	393	40	9	10	19	45	1	1956-57	1964-65
Ball, Terry	Phi., Buf.	4	74	7	19	26	26	....	....	....	....	....	....	1967-68	1971-72
Balmochnykh, Maxim	Ana.	1	6	0	1	1	2	....	....	....	....	....	....	1999-00	1999-00
● Balon, Dave	NYR, Mtl., Min., Van.	14	776	192	222	414	607	78	14	21	35	109	2	1959-60	1972-73
Baltimore, Bryon	Edm.	1	2	0	0	0	4	....	....	....	....	....	....	1979-80	1979-80
Baluik, Stan	Bos.	1	7	0	0	0	2	....	....	....	....	....	....	1959-60	1959-60
Bancroft, Steve	Chi., S.J.	2	6	0	1	1	2	....	....	....	....	....	....	1992-93	2001-02
Bandura, Jeff	NYR	1	2	0	1	1	0	....	....	....	....	....	....	1980-81	1980-81
‡ Banham, Frank	Ana., Phx.	4	32	9	2	11	16	....	....	....	....	....	....	1996-97	2002-03
Banks, Darren	Bos.	2	20	2	2	4	73	....	....	....	....	....	....	1992-93	1993-94
‡ Bannister, Drew	T.B., Edm., Ana., NYR	6	164	5	25	30	161	12	0	0	0	30	....	1995-96	2001-02
Barahona, Ralph	Bos.	2	6	2	2	4	0	....	....	....	....	....	....	1990-91	1991-92
● Barbe, Andy	Tor.	1	1	0	0	0	2	....	....	....	....	....	....	1950-51	1950-51
Barber, Bill	Phi.	14	903	420	463	883	623	129	53	55	108	109	2	1972-73	1983-84
Barber, Don	Min., Wpg., Que., S.J.	4	115	25	32	57	64	11	4	4	8	10	....	1988-89	1991-92
● Barilko, Bill	Tor.	5	252	26	36	62	456	47	5	7	12	104	4	1946-47	1950-51
Barkley, Doug	Chi., Det.	6	253	24	80	104	382	30	0	9	9	63	....	1957-58	1965-66
Barlow, Bob	Min.	2	77	16	17	33	10	6	2	2	4	6	....	1969-70	1970-71
Barnes, Blair	L.A.	1	1	0	0	0	0	....	....	....	....	....	....	1982-83	1982-83
Barnes, Norm	Phi., Hfd.	5	156	6	38	44	178	12	0	0	0	8	....	1976-77	1981-82
‡ Barnes, Ryan	Det.	1	2	0	0	0	0	....	....	....	....	....	....	2003-04	2003-04
Baron, Murray	Phi., St.L., Mtl., Phx., Van.	15	988	35	94	129	1309	73	2	8	10	78	....	1989-90	2003-04
Baron, Normand	Mtl., St.L.	2	27	2	0	2	51	3	0	0	0	22	....	1983-84	1985-86
Barr, Dave	Bos., NYR, St.L., Hfd., Det., N.J., Dal.	13	614	128	204	332	520	71	12	10	22	70	....	1981-82	1993-94
Barrault, Doug	Min., Fla.	2	4	0	0	0	2	....	....	....	....	....	....	1992-93	1993-94
Barrett, Fred	Min., L.A.	13	745	25	123	148	671	44	0	2	2	60	....	1970-71	1983-84
Barrett, John	Det., Wsh., Min.	8	488	20	77	97	604	16	2	2	4	50	....	1980-81	1987-88
Barrie, Doug	Pit., Buf., L.A.	3	158	10	42	52	268	....	....	....	....	....	....	1968-69	1971-72
Barrie, Len	Phi., Fla., Pit., L.A.	7	184	19	45	64	290	8	1	0	1	8	....	1989-90	2000-01
Barry, Ed	Bos.	1	19	1	3	4	2	....	....	....	....	....	....	1946-47	1946-47
● Barry, Marty	NYA, Bos., Det., Mtl.	12	509	195	192	387	231	43	15	18	33	34	2	1927-28	1939-40
Barry, Ray	Bos.	1	18	1	2	3	6	....	....	....	....	....	....	1951-52	1951-52
‡ Bartecko, Lubos	St.L., Atl.	5	257	46	65	111	107	12	1	1	2	2	....	1998-99	2002-03
Bartel, Robin	Cgy., Van.	2	41	0	1	1	14	6	0	0	0	16	....	1985-86	1986-87
Bartlett, Jim	Mtl., NYR, Bos.	5	191	34	23	57	273	2	0	0	0	0	....	1954-55	1960-61
● Barton, Cliff	Pit., Phi., NYR	3	85	10	9	19	22	....	....	....	....	....	....	1929-30	1939-40
Bartos, Peter	Min.	1	13	4	2	6	6	....	....	....	....	....	....	2000-01	2000-01
‡ Bashkirov, Andrei	Mtl.	3	30	0	3	3	0	....	....	....	....	....	....	1998-99	2000-01
Bassen, Bob	NYI, Chi., St.L., Que., Dal., Cgy.	15	765	88	144	232	1004	93	9	15	24	134	....	1985-86	1999-00
Bast, Ryan	Phi.	1	2	0	1	1	0	....	....	....	....	....	....	1998-99	1998-99
Bathe, Frank	Det., Phi.	9	224	3	28	31	542	27	1	3	4	42	....	1974-75	1983-84
Bathgate, Andy	NYR, Tor., Det., Pit.	17	1069	349	624	973	624	54	21	14	35	76	1	1952-53	1970-71
Bathgate, Frank	NYR	1	2	0	0	0	2	....	....	....	....	....	....	1952-53	1952-53
● Batters, Jeff	St.L.	2	16	0	0	0	28	....	....	....	....	....	....	1993-94	1994-95
Batyrshin, Ruslan	L.A.	1	2	0	0	0	6	....	....	....	....	....	....	1995-96	1995-96
● Bauer, Bobby	Bos.	9	327	123	137	260	36	48	11	8	19	6	2	1936-37	1951-52
Baumgartner, Ken	L.A., NYI, Tor., Ana., Bos.	12	696	13	41	54	2244	51	1	2	3	106	....	1987-88	1998-99
Baumgartner, Mike	K.C.	1	17	0	0	0	0	....	....	....	....	....	....	1974-75	1974-75
Baun, Bob	Tor., Oak., Det.	17	964	37	187	224	1493	96	3	12	15	171	4	1956-57	1972-73
Bautin, Sergei	Wpg., Det., S.J.	3	132	5	25	30	176	6	0	0	0	2	....	1992-93	1995-96
Bawa, Robin	Wsh., Van., S.J., Ana.	4	61	6	1	7	60	1	0	0	0	0	....	1989-90	1993-94
Baxter, Paul	Que., Pit., Cgy.	8	472	48	121	169	1564	40	0	5	5	162	....	1979-80	1986-87
Beadle, Sandy	Wpg.	1	6	1	0	1	2	....	....	....	....	....	....	1980-81	1980-81
Beaton, Frank	NYR	2	25	1	1	2	43	....	....	....	....	....	....	1978-79	1979-80
● Beattie, Red	Bos., Det., NYA	9	334	62	85	147	137	24	4	2	6	8	....	1930-31	1938-39
Beaudin, Norm	St.L., Min.	2	25	1	2	3	4	....	....	....	....	....	....	1967-68	1970-71
‡ Beaudoin, Eric	Fla.	3	53	3	8	11	41	....	....	....	....	....	....	2001-02	2003-04
Beaudoin, Serge	Atl.	1	3	0	0	0	0	....	....	....	....	....	....	1979-80	1979-80
Beaudoin, Yves	Wsh.	3	11	0	0	0	5	....	....	....	....	....	....	1985-86	1987-88
‡ Beaufait, Mark	S.J.	1	5	1	0	1	0	....	....	....	....	....	....	1992-93	1992-93
Beck, Barry	Col., NYR, L.A.	10	615	104	251	355	1016	51	10	23	33	77	....	1977-78	1989-90
Beckett, Bob	Bos.	4	68	7	6	13	18	....	....	....	....	....	....	1956-57	1963-64
Bedard, James	Chi.	2	22	1	1	2	8	....	....	....	....	....	....	1949-50	1950-51
Beddoes, Clayton	Bos.	2	60	2	8	10	57	....	....	....	....	....	....	1995-96	1996-97

George Armstrong

Doug Baldwin

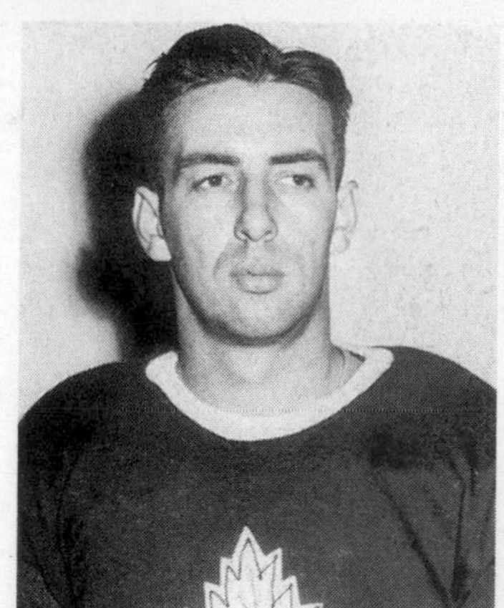

Andy Barbe

John Barrett

John Bednarski

Joe Bell

Bill Bennett

Gary Bergman

Name	NHL Teams	NHL Seasons	Regular Schedule GP	G	A	TP	PIM	Playoffs GP	G	A	TP	PIM	NHL Cup Wins	First NHL Season	Last NHL Season
‡ Bednar, Jaroslav	L.A., Fla.	3	102	10	25	35	30	3	0	0	0	0	....	2001-02	2003-04
Bednarski, John	NYR, Edm.	4	100	2	18	20	114	1	0	0	0	17	....	1974-75	1979-80
Beers, Bob	Bos., T.B., Edm., NYI	8	258	28	79	107	225	21	1	1	2	22	....	1989-90	1996-97
Beers, Eddy	Cgy., St.L.	5	250	94	116	210	256	41	7	10	17	47	....	1981-82	1985-86
• Behling, Dick	Det.	2	5	1	0	1	2	....	....	....	....	....	....	1940-41	1942-43
• Beisler, Frank	NYA	2	2	0	0	0	0	....	....	....	....	....	....	1936-37	1939-40
‡ Bekar, Derek	St.L., L.A., NYI	3	11	0	0	0	6	....	....	....	....	....	....	1999-00	2003-04
Belanger, Alain	Tor.	1	9	0	1	1	6	....	....	....	....	....	....	1977-78	1977-78
‡ Belanger, Francis	Mtl.	1	10	0	0	0	29	....	....	....	....	....	....	2000-01	2000-01
Belanger, Jesse	Mtl., Fla., Van., Edm., NYI	8	246	59	76	135	56	12	0	3	3	2	....	1991-92	2000-01
Belanger, Ken	Tor., NYI, Bos., L.A.	11	248	11	12	23	695	12	1	0	1	16	....	1994-95	2005-06
Belanger, Roger	Pit.	1	44	3	5	8	32	....	....	....	....	....	....	1984-85	1984-85
Belisle, Danny	NYR	1	4	2	0	2	0	....	....	....	....	....	....	1960-61	1960-61
Beliveau, Jean	Mtl.	20	1125	507	712	1219	1029	162	79	97	176	211	10	1950-51	1970-71
• Bell, Billy	Mtl.W., Mtl., Ott.	6	72	4	2	6	14	5	0	0	0	0	1	1917-18	1923-24
Bell, Bruce	Que., St.L., NYR, Edm.	5	209	12	64	76	113	34	3	5	8	41	....	1984-85	1989-90
Bell, Harry	NYR	1	1	0	1	1	0	....	....	....	....	....	....	1946-47	1946-47
Bell, Joe	NYR	2	62	8	9	17	18	....	....	....	....	....	....	1942-43	1946-47
Belland, Neil	Van., Pit.	6	109	13	32	45	54	21	2	9	11	23	....	1981-82	1986-87
‡ Bellefeuille, Blake	CBJ	2	5	0	1	1	0	....	....	....	....	....	....	2001-02	2002-03
• Bellefeuille, Pete	Tor., Det.	4	92	26	4	30	58	....	....	....	....	....	....	1925-26	1929-30
• Bellemer, Andy	Mtl.M.	1	15	0	0	0	0	....	....	....	....	....	....	1932-33	1932-33
Bellows, Brian	Min., Mtl., T.B., Ana., Wsh.	17	1188	485	537	1022	718	143	51	71	122	143	1	1982-83	1998-99
• Bend, Lin	NYR	1	8	3	1	4	2	....	....	....	....	....	....	1942-43	1942-43
‡ Benda, Jan	Wsh.	1	9	0	3	3	6	....	....	....	....	....	....	1997-98	1997-98
Bennett, Adam	Chi., Edm.	3	69	3	8	11	69	....	....	....	....	....	....	1991-92	1993-94
Bennett, Bill	Bos., Hfd.	2	31	4	7	11	65	....	....	....	....	....	....	1978-79	1979-80
Bennett, Curt	St.L., NYR, Atl.	10	580	152	182	334	347	21	1	1	2	57	....	1970-71	1979-80
Bennett, Frank	Det.	1	7	0	1	1	2	....	....	....	....	....	....	1943-44	1943-44
Bennett, Harvey	Pit., Wsh., Phi., Min., St.L.	5	268	44	46	90	347	4	0	0	0	2	....	1974-75	1978-79
• Bennett, Max	Mtl.	1	1	0	0	0	0	....	....	....	....	....	....	1935-36	1935-36
Bennett, Rick	NYR	3	15	1	1	2	13	....	....	....	....	....	....	1989-90	1991-92
Benning, Brian	St.L., L.A., Phi., Edm., Fla.	11	568	63	233	296	963	48	3	20	23	74	....	1984-85	1994-95
Benning, Jim	Tor., Van.	9	605	52	191	243	461	7	1	1	2	2	....	1981-82	1989-90
• Benoit, Joe	Mtl.	5	185	75	69	144	94	11	6	3	9	11	1	1940-41	1946-47
Benson, Bill	NYA, Bro.	2	67	11	25	36	35	....	....	....	....	....	....	1940-41	1941-42
• Benson, Bobby	Bos.	1	8	0	1	1	4	....	....	....	....	....	....	1924-25	1924-25
• Bentley, Doug	Chi., NYR	13	566	219	324	543	217	23	9	8	17	12	....	1939-40	1953-54
• Bentley, Max	Chi., Tor., NYR	12	646	245	299	544	179	51	18	27	45	14	3	1940-41	1953-54
Bentley, Reg	Chi.	1	11	1	2	3	2	....	....	....	....	....	....	1942-43	1942-43
‡ Benysek, Ladislav	Edm., Min.	4	161	3	12	15	74	....	....	....	....	....	....	1997-98	2002-03
Beraldo, Paul	Bos.	2	10	0	0	0	4	....	....	....	....	....	....	1987-88	1988-89
‡ Beranek, Josef	Edm., Phi., Van., Pit.	9	531	118	144	262	398	57	5	8	13	24	....	1991-92	2000-01
Berehowsky, Drake	Tor., Pit., Edm., Nsh., Van., Phx.	13	549	37	112	149	848	22	1	3	4	30	....	1990-91	2003-04
Berenson, Red	Mtl., NYR, St.L., Det.	17	987	261	397	658	305	85	23	14	37	49	1	1961-62	1977-78
Berenzweig, Bubba	Nsh.	4	37	3	7	10	14	....	....	....	....	....	....	1999-00	2002-03
Berezan, Perry	Cgy., Min., S.J.	9	378	61	75	136	279	31	4	7	11	34	....	1984-85	1992-93
Berezin, Sergei	Tor., Phx., Mtl., Chi., Wsh.	7	502	160	126	286	54	52	13	17	30	6	....	1996-97	2002-03
Berg, Bill	NYI, Tor., NYR, Ott.	10	546	55	67	122	488	61	3	4	7	34	....	1988-89	1998-99
• Bergdinon, Fred	Bos.	1	2	0	0	0	0	....	....	....	....	....	....	1925-26	1925-26
Bergen, Todd	Phi.	1	14	11	5	16	4	17	4	9	13	8	....	1984-85	1984-85
Berger, Mike	Min.	2	30	3	1	4	67	....	....	....	....	....	....	1987-88	1988-89
Bergeron, Michel	Det., NYI, Wsh.	5	229	80	58	138	165	....	....	....	....	....	....	1974-75	1978-79
Bergeron, Yves	Pit.	2	3	0	0	0	0	....	....	....	....	....	....	1974-75	1976-77
Bergevin, Marc	Chi., NYI, Hfd., T.B., Det., St.L., Pit., Van.	20	1191	36	145	181	1090	79	3	6	9	50	....	1984-85	2003-04
Bergkvist, Stefan	Pit.	2	7	0	0	0	9	4	0	0	0	2	....	1995-96	1996-97
Bergland, Tim	Wsh., T.B.	5	182	17	26	43	75	26	2	2	4	22	....	1989-90	1993-94
Bergloff, Bob	Min.	1	2	0	0	0	5	....	....	....	....	....	....	1982-83	1982-83
Berglund, Bo	Que., Min., Phi.	3	130	28	39	67	40	9	2	0	2	6	....	1983-84	1985-86
• Bergman, Gary	Det., Min., K.C.	12	838	68	299	367	1249	21	0	5	5	20	....	1964-65	1975-76
Bergman, Thommie	Det.	6	246	21	44	65	243	7	0	2	2	2	....	1972-73	1979-80
Bergqvist, Jonas	Cgy.	1	22	2	5	7	10	....	....	....	....	....	....	1989-90	1989-90
• Berlinquette, Louis	Mtl., Mtl.M., Pit.	8	193	45	33	78	129	11	0	5	5	9	....	1917-18	1925-26
Bernier, Serge	Phi., L.A., Que.	7	302	78	119	197	234	5	1	1	2	0	....	1968-69	1980-81
Berry, Bob	Mtl., L.A.	8	541	159	191	350	344	26	2	6	8	6	....	1968-69	1976-77
Berry, Brad	Wpg., Min., Dal.	8	241	4	28	32	323	13	0	1	1	16	....	1985-86	1993-94
Berry, Doug	Col.	2	121	10	33	43	25	....	....	....	....	....	....	1979-80	1980-81
Berry, Fred	Det.	1	3	0	0	0	0	....	....	....	....	....	....	1976-77	1976-77
Berry, Ken	Edm., Van.	4	55	8	10	18	30	....	....	....	....	....	....	1981-82	1988-89
Bertrand, Eric	N.J., Atl., Mtl.	2	15	0	0	0	4	....	....	....	....	....	....	1999-00	2000-01
Berube, Craig	Phi., Tor., Cgy., Wsh., NYI	17	1054	61	98	159	3149	89	3	1	4	211	....	1986-87	2002-03
• Besler, Phil	Bos., Chi., Det.	2	30	1	4	5	18	....	....	....	....	....	....	1935-36	1938-39
• Bessone, Pete	Det.	1	6	0	1	1	6	....	....	....	....	....	....	1937-38	1937-38
Bethel, John	Wpg.	1	17	0	2	2	4	....	....	....	....	....	....	1979-80	1979-80
Betik, Karel	T.B.	1	3	0	2	2	2	....	....	....	....	....	....	1998-99	1998-99
Bets, Maxim	Ana.	1	3	0	0	0	0	....	....	....	....	....	....	1993-94	1993-94
• Bettio, Sam	Bos.	1	44	9	12	21	32	....	....	....	....	....	....	1949-50	1949-50
Beukeboom, Jeff	Edm., NYR	14	804	30	129	159	1890	99	3	16	19	197	4	1985-86	1998-99
Beverley, Nick	Bos., Pit., NYR, Min., L.A., Col.	11	502	18	94	112	156	7	0	1	1	0	....	1966-67	1979-80
‡ Bezina, Goran	Phx.	1	3	0	0	0	2	....	....	....	....	....	....	2003-04	2003-04
Bialowas, Dwight	Atl., Min.	4	164	11	46	57	46	....	....	....	....	....	....	1973-74	1976-77
Bialowas, Frank	Tor.	1	3	0	0	0	12	....	....	....	....	....	....	1993-94	1993-94
Bianchin, Wayne	Pit., Edm.	7	276	68	41	109	137	3	0	1	1	6	....	1973-74	1979-80
Bicanek, Radim	Ott., Chi., CBJ	7	122	1	11	12	62	7	0	0	0	8	....	1994-95	2001-02
‡ Bicek, Jiri	N.J.	4	62	6	7	13	29	7	0	0	0	0	1	2000-01	2003-04
Bidner, Todd	Wsh.	1	12	2	1	3	7	....	....	....	....	....	....	1981-82	1981-82
Biggs, Don	Min., Phi.	2	12	2	0	2	8	....	....	....	....	....	....	1984-85	1989-90
Bignell, Larry	Pit.	2	20	0	3	3	2	3	0	0	0	2	....	1973-74	1974-75
Bilodeau, Gilles	Que.	1	9	0	1	1	25	....	....	....	....	....	....	1979-80	1979-80
• Bionda, Jack	Tor., Bos.	4	93	3	9	12	113	11	0	1	1	14	....	1955-56	1958-59
‡ Bishai, Mike	Edm.	1	14	0	2	2	19	....	....	....	....	....	....	2003-04	2003-04
Bissett, Tom	Det.	1	5	0	0	0	0	....	....	....	....	....	....	1990-91	1990-91
Bjugstad, Scott	Min., Pit., L.A.	9	317	76	68	144	144	9	0	1	1	2	....	1983-84	1991-92
Black, James	Hfd., Min., Dal., Buf., Chi., Wsh.	11	352	58	57	115	84	13	2	1	3	4	....	1989-90	2000-01
Black, Steve	Det., Chi.	2	113	11	20	31	77	13	0	0	0	13	1	1949-50	1950-51
Blackburn, Bob	NYR, Pit.	3	135	8	12	20	105	6	0	0	0	4	....	1968-69	1970-71
Blackburn, Don	Bos., Phi., NYR, NYI, Min.	6	185	23	44	67	87	12	3	0	3	10	....	1962-63	1972-73
• Blade, Hank	Chi.	2	24	2	3	5	2	....	....	....	....	....	....	1946-47	1947-48
Bladon, Tom	Phi., Pit., Edm., Wpg., Det.	9	610	73	197	270	392	86	8	29	37	70	2	1972-73	1980-81
• Blaine, Garry	Mtl.	1	1	0	0	0	0	....	....	....	....	....	....	1954-55	1954-55
• Blair, Andy	Tor., Chi.	9	402	74	86	160	323	38	6	6	12	32	1	1928-29	1936-37
Blair, Chuck	Tor.	1	1	0	0	0	0	....	....	....	....	....	....	1948-49	1948-49
Blair, Dusty	Tor.	1	2	0	0	0	0	....	....	....	....	....	....	1950-51	1950-51
Blaisdell, Mike	Det., NYR, Pit., Tor.	9	343	70	84	154	166	6	1	2	3	10	....	1980-81	1988-89
Blake, Bob	Bos.	1	12	0	0	0	0	....	....	....	....	....	....	1935-36	1935-36
• Blake, Mickey	Mtl.M., St.L., Tor.	3	10	1	1	2	4	....	....	....	....	....	....	1932-33	1935-36
• Blake, Toe	Mtl.M., Mtl.	14	577	235	292	527	272	58	25	37	62	23	3	1934-35	1947-48
• Blight, Rick	Van., L.A.	7	326	96	125	221	170	5	0	5	5	2	....	1975-76	1982-83
• Blinco, Russ	Mtl.M., Chi.	6	268	59	66	125	24	19	3	3	6	4	1	1933-34	1938-39
Block, Ken	Van.	1	1	0	0	0	0	....	....	....	....	....	....	1970-71	1970-71
Bloemberg, Jeff	NYR	4	43	3	6	9	25	7	0	3	3	5	....	1988-89	1991-92
Blomqvist, Timo	Wsh., N.J.	5	243	4	53	57	293	13	0	0	0	24	....	1981-82	1986-87
Blomsten, Arto	Wpg., L.A.	3	25	0	4	4	8	....	....	....	....	....	....	1993-94	1995-96
Bloom, Mike	Wsh., Det.	3	201	30	47	77	215	....	....	....	....	....	....	1974-75	1976-77
Blouin, Sylvain	NYR, Mtl., Min.	6	115	3	4	7	336	....	....	....	....	....	....	1996-97	2002-03
Blum, John	Edm., Bos., Wsh., Det.	8	250	7	34	41	610	20	0	2	2	27	....	1982-83	1989-90
Bodak, Bob	Cgy., Hfd.	2	4	0	0	0	29	....	....	....	....	....	....	1987-88	1989-90
Boddy, Gregg	Van.	5	273	23	44	67	263	3	0	0	0	0	....	1971-72	1975-76
Bodger, Doug	Pit., Buf., S.J., N.J., L.A., Van.	16	1071	106	422	528	1007	47	6	18	24	25	....	1984-85	1999-00
• Bodnar, Gus	Tor., Chi., Bos.	12	667	142	254	396	207	32	4	3	7	10	2	1943-44	1954-55
Boehm, Ron	Oak.	1	16	2	1	3	10	....	....	....	....	....	....	1967-68	1967-68
• Boesch, Garth	Tor.	4	197	9	28	37	205	34	2	5	7	18	3	1946-47	1949-50
Boh, Rick	Min.	1	8	2	1	3	4	....	....	....	....	....	....	1987-88	1987-88
Bohonos, Lonny	Van., Tor.	4	83	19	16	35	22	9	3	6	9	2	....	1995-96	1998-99

Name	NHL Teams	NHL Seasons	Regular Schedule GP	G	A	TP	PIM	Playoffs GP	G	A	TP	PIM	NHL Cup Wins	First NHL Season	Last NHL Season
Boikov, Alexandre	Nsh.	2	10	0	0	0	15	....	....	....	....	....	....	1999-00	2000-01
● Boileau, Marc	Det.	1	54	5	6	11	8	....	....	....	....	....	....	1961-62	1961-62
‡ Boileau, Patrick	Wsh., Det., Pit.	5	48	5	11	16	26	....	....	....	....	....	....	1996-97	2003-04
● Boileau, Rene	NYA	1	7	0	0	0	0	....	....	....	....	....	....	1925-26	1925-26
Boimistruck, Fred	Tor.	2	83	4	14	18	45	....	....	....	....	....	....	1981-82	1982-83
Boisvert, Serge	Tor., Mtl.	5	46	5	7	12	8	23	3	7	10	4	1	1982-83	1987-88
Boivin, Claude	Phi., Ott.	4	132	12	19	31	364	....	....	....	....	....	....	1991-92	1994-95
Boivin, Leo	Tor., Bos., Det., Pit., Min.	19	1150	72	250	322	1192	54	3	10	13	59	....	1951-52	1969-70
Boland, Mike	Phi.	1	2	0	0	0	0	....	....	....	....	....	....	1974-75	1974-75
Boland, Mike	K.C., Buf.	2	23	1	2	3	29	3	1	0	1	2	....	1974-75	1978-79
Boldirev, Ivan	Bos., Cal., Chi., Atl., Van., Det.	15	1052	361	505	866	507	48	13	20	33	14	....	1970-71	1984-85
Bolduc, Danny	Det., Cgy.	3	102	22	19	41	33	1	0	0	0	0	....	1978-79	1983-84
Bolduc, Michel	Que.	2	10	0	0	0	6	....	....	....	....	....	....	1981-82	1982-83
● Boll, Buzz	Tor., NYA, Bro., Bos.	12	437	133	130	263	148	31	7	3	10	13	....	1932-33	1943-44
Bolonchuk, Larry	Van., Wsh.	4	74	3	9	12	97	....	....	....	....	....	....	1972-73	1977-78
● Bolton, Hugh	Tor.	8	235	10	51	61	221	17	0	5	5	14	1	1949-50	1956-57
Bombardir, Brad	N.J., Min., Nsh.	7	356	8	46	54	127	16	0	1	1	2	1	1997-98	2003-04
Bonar, Dan	L.A.	3	170	25	39	64	208	14	3	4	7	22	....	1980-81	1982-83
Bonin, Brian	Pit., Min.	2	12	0	0	0	0	3	0	0	0	0	....	1998-99	2000-01
Bonin, Marcel	Det., Bos., Mtl.	9	454	97	175	272	336	50	11	14	25	51	4	1952-53	1961-62
‡ Bonni, Ryan	Van.	1	3	0	0	0	0	....	....	....	....	....	....	1999-00	1999-00
Bonsignore, Jason	Edm., T.B.	4	79	3	13	16	34	....	....	....	....	....	....	1994-95	1998-99
‡ Bonvie, Dennis	Edm., Chi., Pit., Bos., Ott., Col.	9	92	1	2	3	311	1	0	0	0	0	....	1994-95	2003-04
Boo, Jim	Min.	1	6	0	0	0	22	....	....	....	....	....	....	1977-78	1977-78
● Boone, Buddy	Bos.	2	34	5	3	8	28	22	2	1	3	25	....	1956-57	1957-58
● Boothman, George	Tor.	2	58	17	19	36	18	5	2	1	3	2	....	1942-43	1943-44
Bordeleau, Christian	Mtl., St.L., Chi.	4	205	38	65	103	82	19	4	7	11	17	1	1968-69	1971-72
Bordeleau, J.P.	Chi.	10	519	97	126	223	143	48	3	6	9	12	....	1969-70	1979-80
Bordeleau, Paulin	Van.	3	183	33	56	89	47	5	2	1	3	0	....	1973-74	1975-76
‡ Bordeleau, Sebastien	Mtl., Nsh., Min., Phx.	7	251	37	61	98	118	5	0	0	0	2	....	1995-96	2001-02
Borotsik, Jack	St.L.	1	1	0	0	0	0	....	....	....	....	....	....	1974-75	1974-75
Borsato, Luciano	Wpg.	5	203	35	55	90	113	7	1	0	1	4	....	1990-91	1994-95
Borschevsky, Nikolai	Tor., Cgy., Dal.	4	162	49	73	122	44	31	4	9	13	4	....	1992-93	1995-96
Boschman, Laurie	Tor., Edm., Wpg., N.J., Ott.	14	1009	229	348	577	2265	57	8	13	21	140	....	1979-80	1992-93
Bossy, Mike	NYI	10	752	573	553	1126	210	129	85	75	160	38	4	1977-78	1986-87
● Bostrom, Helge	Chi.	4	96	3	3	6	58	13	0	0	0	16	....	1929-30	1932-33
Botell, Mark	Phi.	1	32	4	10	14	31	....	....	....	....	....	....	1981-82	1981-82
Bothwell, Tim	NYR, St.L., Hfd.	12	502	28	93	121	382	49	0	3	3	56	....	1978-79	1988-89
Botterill, Jason	Dal., Atl., Cgy., Buf.	6	88	5	9	14	89	....	....	....	....	....	....	1997-98	2003-04
Botting, Cam	Atl.	1	2	0	1	1	0	....	....	....	....	....	....	1975-76	1975-76
Boucha, Henry	Det., Min., K.C., Col.	6	247	53	49	102	157	....	....	....	....	....	....	1971-72	1976-77
Bouchard, Butch	Mtl.	15	785	49	144	193	863	113	11	21	32	121	4	1941-42	1955-56
● Bouchard, Dick	NYR	1	1	0	0	0	0	....	....	....	....	....	....	1954-55	1954-55
● Bouchard, Edmond	Mtl., Ham., NYA, Pit.	8	211	19	21	40	117	....	....	....	....	....	....	1921-22	1928-29
Bouchard, Pierre	Mtl., Wsh.	12	595	24	82	106	433	76	3	10	13	56	5	1970-71	1981-82
● Boucher, Billy	Mtl., Bos., NYA	7	213	93	38	131	409	14	3	0	3	17	1	1921-22	1927-28
● Boucher, Bobby	Mtl.	1	11	1	0	1	0	2	0	0	0	0	1	1923-24	1923-24
● Boucher, Clarence	NYA	2	47	2	2	4	133	....	....	....	....	....	....	1926-27	1927-28
● Boucher, Frank	Ott., NYR	14	557	160	263	423	119	55	16	20	36	12	2	1921-22	1943-44
● Boucher, Georges	Ott., Mtl.M., Chi.	15	449	117	87	204	838	28	5	3	8	88	4	1917-18	1931-32
Boudreau, Bruce	Tor., Chi.	8	141	28	42	70	46	9	2	0	2	0	....	1976-77	1985-86
Boudrias, Andre	Mtl., Min., Chi., St.L., Van.	12	662	151	340	491	216	34	6	10	16	12	....	1963-64	1975-76
Boughner, Barry	Oak., Cal.	2	20	0	0	0	11	....	....	....	....	....	....	1969-70	1970-71
Boughner, Bob	Buf., Nsh., Pit., Cgy., Car., Col.	10	630	15	57	72	1382	65	0	12	12	67	....	1995-96	2005-06
‡ Boumedienne, Josef	N.J., T.B., Wsh.	3	47	4	12	16	36	....	....	....	....	....	....	2001-02	2003-04
Bourbonnais, Dan	Hfd.	2	59	3	25	28	11	....	....	....	....	....	....	1981-82	1983-84
Bourbonnais, Rick	St.L.	3	71	9	15	24	29	4	0	1	1	0	....	1975-76	1977-78
● Bourcier, Conrad	Mtl.	1	6	0	0	0	0	....	....	....	....	....	....	1935-36	1935-36
Bourcier, Jean	Mtl.	1	9	0	1	1	0	....	....	....	....	....	....	1935-36	1935-36
● Bourgeault, Leo	Tor., NYR, Ott., Mtl.	8	307	24	20	44	269	24	1	1	2	18	1	1926-27	1934-35
Bourgeois, Charlie	Cgy., St.L., Hfd.	7	290	16	54	70	788	40	2	3	5	194	....	1981-82	1987-88
Bourne, Bob	NYI, L.A.	14	964	258	324	582	605	139	40	56	96	108	4	1974-75	1987-88
Bourque, Phil	Pit., NYR, Ott.	12	477	88	111	199	516	56	13	12	25	107	2	1983-84	1995-96
Bourque, Raymond	Bos., Col.	22	1612	410	1169	1579	1141	214	41	139	180	171	1	1979-80	2000-01
Boutette, Pat	Tor., Hfd., Pit.	10	756	171	282	453	1354	46	10	14	24	109	....	1975-76	1984-85
Boutilier, Paul	NYI, Bos., Min., NYR, Wpg.	8	288	27	83	110	358	41	1	9	10	45	1	1981-82	1988-89
Bowen, Jason	Phi., Edm.	6	77	2	6	8	109	....	....	....	....	....	....	1992-93	1997-98
Bowler, Bill	CBJ	1	9	0	2	2	8	....	....	....	....	....	....	2000-01	2000-01
Bowman, Kirk	Chi.	3	88	11	17	28	19	7	1	0	1	0	....	1976-77	1978-79
● Bowman, Ralph	Ott., St.L., Det.	7	274	8	17	25	260	22	2	2	4	6	2	1933-34	1939-40
Bownass, Jack	Mtl., NYR	4	80	3	8	11	58	....	....	....	....	....	....	1957-58	1961-62
Bowness, Rick	Atl., Det., St.L., Wpg.	7	173	18	37	55	191	5	0	0	0	2	....	1975-76	1981-82
● Boyd, Bill	NYR, NYA	4	138	15	7	22	72	10	0	0	0	4	1	1926-27	1929-30
● Boyd, Irwin	Bos., Det.	4	96	10	10	20	30	5	0	1	1	4	....	1931-32	1943-44
Boyd, Randy	Pit., Chi., NYI, Van.	8	257	20	67	87	328	13	0	2	2	26	....	1981-82	1988-89
Boyer, Wally	Tor., Chi., Oak., Pit.	7	365	54	105	159	163	15	1	3	4	0	....	1965-66	1971-72
Boyer, Zac	Dal.	2	3	0	0	0	0	2	0	0	0	0	....	1994-95	1995-96
Boyko, Darren	Wpg.	1	1	0	0	0	0	....	....	....	....	....	....	1988-89	1988-89
Bozek, Steve	L.A., Cgy., St.L., Van., S.J.	11	641	164	167	331	309	58	12	11	23	69	....	1981-82	1991-92
Bozon, Philippe	St.L.	4	144	16	25	41	101	19	2	0	2	31	....	1991-92	1994-95
● Brackenborough, John	Bos.	1	7	0	0	0	0	....	....	....	....	....	....	1925-26	1925-26
Brackenbury, Curt	Que., Edm., St.L.	4	141	9	17	26	226	2	0	0	0	0	....	1979 80	1982 83
● Bradley, Bart	Bos.	1	1	0	0	0	0	....	....	....	....	....	....	1949-50	1949-50
Bradley, Brian	Cgy., Van., Tor., T.B.	13	651	182	321	503	528	13	3	7	10	16	....	1985-86	1997-98
Bradley, Lyle	Cal., Cle.	2	6	1	0	1	2	....	....	....	....	....	....	1973-74	1976-77
Brady, Neil	N.J., Ott., Dal.	5	89	9	22	31	95	....	....	....	....	....	....	1989-90	1993-94
Bragnalo, Rick	Wsh.	4	145	15	35	50	46	....	....	....	....	....	....	1975-76	1978-79
‡ Brandner, Christoph	Min.	1	35	4	5	9	8	....	....	....	....	....	....	2003-04	2003-04
● Branigan, Andy	NYA, Bro.	2	27	1	2	3	31	....	....	....	....	....	....	1940-41	1941-42
Brasar, Per-Olov	Min., Van.	5	348	64	142	206	33	13	1	2	3	0	....	1977-78	1981-82
● Brayshaw, Russ	Chi.	1	43	5	9	14	24	....	....	....	....	....	....	1944-45	1944-45
Breault, Francois	L.A.	3	27	2	4	6	42	....	....	....	....	....	....	1990-91	1992-93
Breitenbach, Ken	Buf.	3	68	1	13	14	49	8	0	1	1	4	....	1975-76	1978-79
Bremberg, Fredrik	Edm.	1	8	0	0	0	2	....	....	....	....	....	....	1998-99	1998-99
Brennan, Dan	L.A.	2	8	0	1	1	9	....	....	....	....	....	....	1983-84	1985-86
Brennan, Doug	NYR	3	123	9	7	16	152	16	1	0	1	21	1	1931-32	1933-34
Brennan, Rich	Col., S.J., NYR, L.A., Nsh., Bos.	6	50	2	6	8	33	....	....	....	....	....	....	1996-97	2002-03
● Brennan, Tom	Bos.	2	12	2	2	4	2	....	....	....	....	....	....	1943-44	1944-45
Brenneman, John	Chi., NYR, Tor., Det., Oak.	5	152	21	19	40	46	....	....	....	....	....	1	1964-65	1968-69
● Bretto, Joe	Chi.	1	3	0	0	0	4	....	....	....	....	....	....	1944-45	1944-45
● Brewer, Carl	Tor., Det., St.L.	12	604	25	198	223	1037	72	3	17	20	146	3	1957-58	1979-80
Brickley, Andy	Phi., Pit., N.J., Bos., Wpg.	11	385	82	140	222	81	17	1	4	5	4	....	1982-83	1993-94
● Briden, Archie	Bos., Det., Pit.	2	71	9	5	14	56	....	....	....	....	....	....	1926-27	1929-30
Bridgman, Mel	Phi., Cgy., N.J., Det., Van.	14	977	252	449	701	1625	125	28	39	67	298	....	1975-76	1988-89
● Briere, Michel	Pit.	1	76	12	32	44	20	10	5	3	8	17	....	1969-70	1969-70
‡ Brigley, Travis	Cgy., Col.	3	55	3	6	9	16	....	....	....	....	....	....	1997-98	2003-04
‡ Brimanis, Aris	Phi., NYI, Ana., St.L.	7	113	2	12	14	57	....	....	....	....	....	....	1993-94	2003-04
Brindley, Doug	Tor.	1	3	0	0	0	0	....	....	....	....	....	....	1970-71	1970-71
● Brink, Milt	Chi.	1	5	0	0	0	0	....	....	....	....	....	....	1936-37	1936-37
Brisson, Gerry	Mtl.	1	4	0	2	2	4	....	....	....	....	....	....	1962-63	1962-63
Britz, Greg	Tor., Hfd.	3	8	0	0	0	4	....	....	....	....	....	....	1983-84	1986-87
● Broadbent, Punch	Ott., Mtl.M., NYA	11	303	121	51	172	564	23	4	6	10	60	4	1918-19	1928-29
Brochu, Stephane	NYR	1	1	0	0	0	0	....	....	....	....	....	....	1988-89	1988-89
Broden, Connie	Mtl.	3	6	2	1	3	2	7	0	1	1	0	2	1955-56	1957-58
Brooke, Bob	NYR, Min., N.J.	7	447	69	97	166	520	34	9	9	18	59	....	1983-84	1989-90
Brooks, Gord	St.L., Wsh.	3	70	7	18	25	37	....	....	....	....	....	....	1971-72	1974-75
● Brophy, Bernie	Mtl.M., Det.	3	62	4	4	8	25	2	0	0	0	2	1	1925-26	1929-30
Brossart, Willie	Phi., Tor., Wsh.	6	129	1	14	15	88	1	0	0	0	0	....	1970-71	1975-76
Broten, Aaron	Col., N.J., Min., Que., Tor., Wpg.	12	748	186	329	515	441	34	7	18	25	40	....	1980-81	1991-92
Broten, Neal	Min., Dal., N.J., L.A.	17	1099	289	634	923	569	135	35	63	98	77	1	1980-81	1996-97
Broten, Paul	NYR, Dal., St.L.	7	322	46	55	101	264	38	4	6	10	18	....	1989-90	1995-96
Brousseau, Paul	Col., T.B., Fla.	4	26	1	3	4	29	....	....	....	....	....	....	1995-96	2000-01
● Brown, Adam	Det., Chi., Bos.	10	391	104	113	217	378	26	2	4	6	14	1	1941-42	1951-52
Brown, Arnie	Tor., NYR, Det., NYI, Atl.	12	681	44	141	185	738	22	0	6	6	23	....	1961-62	1973-74
Brown, Cam	Van.	1	1	0	0	0	7	....	....	....	....	....	....	1990-91	1990-91

Andy Blair

Claude Boivin

Leo Boivin

Arnie Brown

Larry Brown

Jerry Butler

Ilja Byakin

Drew Callander

Name	NHL Teams	NHL Seasons	Regular Schedule GP	G	A	TP	PIM	Playoffs GP	G	A	TP	PIM	NHL Cup Wins	First NHL Season	Last NHL Season
• Brown, Connie	Det.	5	73	15	24	39	12	14	2	3	5	0	1	1938-39	1942-43
Brown, Dave	Phi., Edm., S.J.	14	729	45	52	97	1789	80	2	3	5	209	1	1982-83	1995-96
Brown, Doug	N.J., Pit., Det.	15	854	160	214	374	210	109	23	23	46	26	2	1986-87	2000-01
• Brown, Fred	Mtl.M.	1	19	1	0	1	0	9	0	0	0	0	....	1927-28	1927-28
Brown, George	Mtl.	3	79	6	22	28	34	7	0	0	0	2	....	1936-37	1938-39
• Brown, Gerry	Det.	2	23	4	5	9	2	12	2	1	3	4	....	1941-42	1945-46
Brown, Greg	Buf., Pit., Wpg.	4	94	4	14	18	86	6	0	1	1	4	....	1990-91	1994-95
Brown, Harold	NYR	1	13	2	1	3	2	....	....	....	....	....	....	1945-46	1945-46
Brown, Jeff	Que., St.L., Van., Hfd., Car., Tor., Wsh.	13	747	154	430	584	498	87	20	45	65	59	....	1985-86	1997-98
Brown, Jim	L.A.	1	3	0	1	1	5	....	....	....	....	....	....	1982-83	1982-83
Brown, Keith	Chi., Fla.	16	876	68	274	342	916	103	4	32	36	184	....	1979-80	1994-95
Brown, Kevin	L.A., Hfd., Car., Edm.	6	64	7	9	16	28	1	0	0	0	0	....	1994-95	1999-00
Brown, Larry	NYR, Det., Phi., L.A.	9	455	7	53	60	180	35	0	4	4	10	....	1969-70	1977-78
Brown, Mike	Van., Ana., Chi.	3	34	1	2	3	130	....	....	....	....	....	....	2000-01	2005-06
Brown, Rob	Pit., Hfd., Chi., Dal., L.A.	11	543	190	248	438	599	54	12	14	26	45	....	1987-88	1999-00
• Brown, Stan	NYR, Det.	2	48	8	2	10	18	2	0	0	0	0	....	1926-27	1927-28
Brown, Wayne	Bos.	1	....	....	....	....	....	4	0	0	0	2	....	1953-54	1953-54
• Browne, Cecil	Chi.	1	13	2	0	2	4	....	....	....	....	....	....	1927-28	1927-28
Brownschidle, Jack	St.L., Hfd.	9	494	39	162	201	151	26	0	5	5	18	....	1977-78	1985-86
• Brownschidle, Jeff	Hfd.	2	7	0	1	1	2	....	....	....	....	....	....	1981-82	1982-83
Brubaker, Jeff	Hfd., Mtl., Cgy., Tor., Edm., NYR, Det.	8	178	16	9	25	512	2	0	0	0	27	....	1979-80	1988-89
Bruce, David	Van., St.L., S.J.	8	234	48	39	87	338	3	0	0	0	2	....	1985-86	1993-94
• Bruce, Gordie	Bos.	3	28	4	9	13	13	7	2	3	5	4	....	1940-41	1945-46
• Bruce, Morley	Ott.	4	71	8	3	11	27	3	0	0	0	2	2	1917-18	1921-22
‡ Brule, Steve	N.J., Col.	2	2	0	0	0	0	1	0	0	0	0	1	1999-00	2002-03
Brumwell, Murray	Min., N.J.	7	128	12	31	43	70	2	0	0	0	2	....	1980-81	1987-88
Brunet, Benoit	Mtl., Dal., Ott.	13	539	101	161	262	229	54	5	20	25	32	1	1988-89	2001-02
• Bruneteau, Eddie	Det.	7	180	40	42	82	35	31	7	6	13	0	....	1940-41	1948-49
• Bruneteau, Mud	Det.	11	411	139	138	277	80	77	23	14	37	22	3	1935-36	1945-46
• Brydge, Bill	Tor., Det., NYA	9	368	26	52	78	506	2	0	0	0	4	....	1926-27	1935-36
Brydges, Paul	Buf.	1	15	2	2	4	6	....	....	....	....	....	....	1986-87	1986-87
• Brydson, Glenn	Mtl.M., St.L., NYR, Chi.	8	299	56	79	135	203	11	0	0	0	8	....	1930-31	1937-38
• Brydson, Gord	Tor.	1	8	2	0	2	8	....	....	....	....	....	....	1929-30	1929-30
Bubla, Jiri	Van.	5	256	17	101	118	202	6	0	0	0	7	....	1981-82	1985-86
• Buchanan, Al	Tor.	2	4	0	1	1	2	....	....	....	....	....	....	1948-49	1949-50
• Buchanan, Bucky	NYR	1	2	0	0	0	0	....	....	....	....	....	....	1948-49	1948-49
Buchanan, Jeff	Col.	1	6	0	0	0	6	....	....	....	....	....	....	1998-99	1998-99
Buchanan, Mike	Chi.	1	1	0	0	0	0	....	....	....	....	....	....	1951-52	1951-52
Buchanan, Ron	Bos., St.L.	2	5	0	0	0	0	....	....	....	....	....	....	1966-67	1969-70
Buchberger, Kelly	Edm., Atl., L.A., Phx., Pit.	18	1182	105	204	309	2297	97	10	15	25	129	2	1986-87	2003-04
Bucyk, John	Det., Bos.	23	1540	556	813	1369	497	124	41	62	103	42	2	1955-56	1977-78
Bucyk, Randy	Mtl., Cgy.	2	19	4	2	6	8	2	0	0	0	0	....	1985-86	1987-88
• Buhr, Doug	K.C.	1	6	0	2	2	4	....	....	....	....	....	....	1974-75	1974-75
Bukovich, Tony	Det.	2	17	7	3	10	6	6	0	1	1	0	....	1943-44	1944-45
Bullard, Mike	Pit., Cgy., St.L., Phi., Tor.	11	727	329	345	674	703	40	11	18	29	44	....	1980-81	1991-92
• Buller, Hy	Det., NYR	5	188	22	58	80	215	....	....	....	....	....	....	1943-44	1953-54
Bulley, Ted	Chi., Wsh., Pit.	8	414	101	113	214	704	29	5	5	10	24	....	1976-77	1983-84
Burakovsky, Robert	Ott.	1	23	2	3	5	6	....	....	....	....	....	....	1993-94	1993-94
• Burch, Billy	Ham., NYA, Bos., Chi.	11	390	137	61	198	255	2	0	0	0	0	....	1922-23	1932-33
• Burchell, Fred	Mtl.	2	4	0	0	0	2	....	....	....	....	....	....	1950-51	1953-54
Burdon, Glen	K.C.	1	11	0	2	2	0	....	....	....	....	....	....	1974-75	1974-75
Bure, Pavel	Van., Fla., NYR	12	702	437	342	779	484	64	35	35	70	74	....	1991-92	2002-03
Bure, Valeri	Mtl., Cgy., Fla., St.L., Dal.	10	621	174	226	400	221	22	0	7	7	16	....	1994-95	2003-04
Bureau, Marc	Cgy., Min., T.B., Mtl., Phi.	11	567	55	83	138	327	50	5	7	12	46	....	1989-90	1999-00
Burega, Bill	Tor.	1	4	0	1	1	4	....	....	....	....	....	....	1955-56	1955-56
• Burke, Eddie	Bos., NYA	4	106	29	20	49	55	....	....	....	....	....	....	1931-32	1934-35
• Burke, Marty	Mtl., Pit., Ott., Chi.	11	494	19	47	66	560	31	2	4	6	44	2	1927-28	1937-38
• Burmister, Roy	NYA	3	67	4	3	7	2	....	....	....	....	....	....	1929-30	1931-32
‡ Burnett, Garrett	Ana.	1	39	1	2	3	184	....	....	....	....	....	....	2003-04	2003-04
Burnett, Kelly	NYR	1	3	1	0	1	0	....	....	....	....	....	....	1952-53	1952-53
• Burns, Bobby	Chi.	3	20	1	0	1	8	....	....	....	....	....	....	1927-28	1929-30
Burns, Charlie	Det., Bos., Oak., Pit., Min.	11	749	106	198	304	252	31	5	4	9	6	....	1958-59	1972-73
Burns, Gary	NYR	2	11	2	2	4	18	5	0	0	0	2	....	1980-81	1981-82
• Burns, Norm	NYR	1	11	0	4	4	2	....	....	....	....	....	....	1941-42	1941-42
Burns, Robin	Pit., K.C.	5	190	31	38	69	139	....	....	....	....	....	....	1970-71	1975-76
Burr, Shawn	Det., T.B., S.J.	16	878	181	259	440	1069	91	16	19	35	95	....	1984-85	1999-00
Burridge, Randy	Bos., Wsh., L.A., Buf.	13	706	199	251	450	458	107	18	34	52	103	....	1985-86	1997-98
Burrows, Dave	Pit., Tor.	10	724	29	135	164	373	29	1	5	6	25	....	1971-72	1980-81
• Burry, Bert	Ott.	1	4	0	0	0	0	....	....	....	....	....	....	1932-33	1932-33
Burt, Adam	Hfd., Car., Phi., Atl.	13	737	37	115	152	961	21	0	1	1	8	....	1988-89	2000-01
Burton, Cummy	Det.	3	43	0	2	2	21	3	0	0	0	0	....	1955-56	1958-59
Burton, Nelson	Wsh.	2	8	1	0	1	21	....	....	....	....	....	....	1977-78	1978-79
• Bush, Eddie	Det.	2	26	4	6	10	40	11	1	6	7	23	....	1938-39	1941-42
Buskas, Rod	Pit., Van., L.A., Chi.	11	556	19	63	82	1294	18	0	3	3	45	....	1982-83	1992-93
Busniuk, Mike	Phi.	2	143	3	23	26	297	25	2	5	7	34	....	1979-80	1980-81
Busniuk, Ron	Buf.	2	6	0	3	3	13	....	....	....	....	....	....	1972-73	1973-74
• Buswell, Walt	Det., Mtl.	8	368	10	40	50	164	24	2	1	3	10	....	1932-33	1939-40
Butcher, Garth	Van., St.L., Que., Tor.	14	897	48	158	206	2302	50	6	5	11	122	....	1981-82	1994-95
Butler, Dick	Chi.	1	7	2	0	2	0	....	....	....	....	....	....	1947-48	1947-48
Butler, Jerry	NYR, St.L., Tor., Van., Wpg.	11	641	99	120	219	515	48	3	3	6	79	....	1972-73	1982-83
Butsayev, Viacheslav	Phi., S.J., Ana., Fla., Ott., T.B.	6	132	17	26	43	133	....	....	....	....	....	....	1992-93	1999-00
‡ Butsayev, Yuri	Det., Atl.	4	99	10	4	14	28	....	....	....	....	....	....	1999-00	2002-03
Butters, Bill	Min.	2	72	1	4	5	77	....	....	....	....	....	....	1977-78	1978-79
Buttrey, Gord	Chi.	1	10	0	0	0	0	....	....	....	....	....	....	1943-44	1943-44
Buynak, Gord	St.L.	1	4	0	0	0	2	....	....	....	....	....	....	1974-75	1974-75
Buzek, Petr	Dal., Atl., Cgy.	6	157	9	22	31	94	....	....	....	....	....	....	1997-98	2002-03
Byakin, Ilja	Edm., S.J.	2	57	8	25	33	44	....	....	....	....	....	....	1993-94	1994-95
Byce, John	Bos.	3	21	2	3	5	6	8	2	0	2	2	....	1989-90	1991-92
• Byers, Gord	Bos.	1	1	0	1	1	0	....	....	....	....	....	....	1949-50	1949-50
• Byers, Jerry	Min., Atl., NYR	4	43	3	4	7	15	....	....	....	....	....	....	1972-73	1977-78
Byers, Lyndon	Bos., S.J.	10	279	28	43	71	1081	37	2	2	4	96	....	1983-84	1992-93
Byers, Mike	Tor., Phi., L.A., Buf.	4	166	42	34	76	39	4	0	1	1	0	....	1967-68	1971-72
‡ Bykov, Dmitri	Det.	1	71	2	10	12	43	4	0	0	0	0	....	2002-03	2002-03
Bylsma, Dan	L.A., Ana.	9	429	19	43	62	184	16	0	1	1	2	....	1995-96	2003-04
Byram, Shawn	NYI, Chi.	2	5	0	0	0	14	....	....	....	....	....	....	1990-91	1991-92

C

Name	NHL Teams	NHL Seasons	Regular Schedule GP	G	A	TP	PIM	Playoffs GP	G	A	TP	PIM	NHL Cup Wins	First NHL Season	Last NHL Season
• Caffery, Jack	Tor., Bos.	3	57	3	2	5	22	10	1	0	1	4	....	1954-55	1957-58
Caffery, Terry	Chi., Min.	2	14	0	0	0	0	1	0	0	0	0	....	1969-70	1970-71
• Cahan, Larry	Tor., NYR, Oak., L.A.	13	666	38	92	130	700	29	1	1	2	38	....	1954-55	1970-71
• Cahill, Charles	Bos.	2	32	0	1	1	4	....	....	....	....	....	....	1925-26	1926-27
• Cain, Francis	Mtl.M., Tor.	2	61	4	0	4	35	....	....	....	....	....	....	1924-25	1925-26
• Cain, Herb	Mtl.M., Mtl., Bos.	13	570	206	194	400	178	67	16	13	29	13	2	1933-34	1945-46
Cairns, Don	K.C., Col.	2	9	0	1	1	2	....	....	....	....	....	....	1975-76	1976-77
Calder, Eric	Wsh.	2	2	0	0	0	0	....	....	....	....	....	....	1981-82	1982-83
• Calladine, Norm	Bos.	3	63	19	29	48	8	....	....	....	....	....	....	1942-43	1944-45
Callander, Drew	Phi., Van.	4	39	6	2	8	7	....	....	....	....	....	....	1976-77	1979-80
Callander, Jock	Pit., T.B.	5	109	22	29	51	116	22	3	8	11	12	1	1987-88	1992-93
Callighen, Brett	Edm.	3	160	56	89	145	132	14	4	6	10	8	....	1979-80	1981-82
• Callighen, Patsy	NYR	1	36	0	0	0	32	9	0	0	0	0	1	1927-28	1927-28
‡ Caloun, Jan	S.J., CBJ	3	24	8	6	14	2	....	....	....	....	....	....	1995-96	2000-01
Camazzola, James	Chi.	2	3	0	0	0	0	....	....	....	....	....	....	1983-84	1986-87
Camazzola, Tony	Wsh.	1	3	0	0	0	4	....	....	....	....	....	....	1981-82	1981-82
Cameron, Al	Det., Wpg.	6	282	11	44	55	356	7	0	1	1	2	....	1975-76	1980-81
• Cameron, Billy	Mtl., NYA	2	39	0	0	0	2	2	0	0	0	0	1	1923-24	1925-26
Cameron, Craig	Det., St.L., Min., NYI	9	552	87	65	152	196	27	3	1	4	17	....	1966-67	1975-76
Cameron, Dave	Col., N.J.	3	168	25	28	53	238	....	....	....	....	....	....	1981-82	1983-84
• Cameron, Harry	Tor., Ott., Mtl.	6	128	88	51	139	189	11	5	4	9	16	2	1917-18	1922-23
• Cameron, Scotty	NYR	1	35	8	11	19	0	....	....	....	....	....	....	1942-43	1942-43
Campbell, Bryan	L.A., Chi.	5	260	35	71	106	74	22	3	4	7	2	....	1967-68	1971-72
Campbell, Colin	Pit., Col., Edm., Van., Det.	11	636	25	103	128	1292	45	4	10	14	181	....	1974-75	1984-85
• Campbell, Dave	Mtl.	1	2	0	0	0	0	....	....	....	....	....	....	1920-21	1920-21
Campbell, Don	Chi.	1	17	1	3	4	8	....	....	....	....	....	....	1943-44	1943-44
• Campbell, Earl	Ott., NYA	3	76	6	3	9	14	1	0	0	0	6	....	1923-24	1925-26

Name	NHL Teams	NHL Seasons	Regular Schedule GP	G	A	TP	PIM	Playoffs GP	G	A	TP	PIM	NHL Cup Wins	First NHL Season	Last NHL Season
‡ Campbell, Jim	Ana., St.L., Mtl., Chi., Fla., T.B.	9	285	61	75	136	268	14	8	3	11	18	....	1995-96	2005-06
Campbell, Scott	Wpg., St.L.	3	80	4	21	25	243	....	....	....	....	....	....	1979-80	1981-82
Campbell, Wade	Wpg., Bos.	6	213	9	27	36	305	10	0	0	0	20	....	1982-83	1987-88
Campeau, Tod	Mtl.	3	42	5	9	14	16	1	0	0	0	0	....	1943-44	1948-49
Campedelli, Dom	Mtl.	1	2	0	0	0	0	....	....	....	....	....	....	1985-86	1985-86
Capuano, Dave	Pit., Van., T.B., S.J.	4	104	17	38	55	56	6	1	1	2	5	....	1989-90	1993-94
Capuano, Jack	Tor., Van., Bos.	3	6	0	0	0	0	....	....	....	....	....	....	1989-90	1991-92
• Carbol, Leo	Chi.	1	6	0	1	1	4	....	....	....	....	....	....	1942-43	1942-43
Carbonneau, Guy	Mtl., St.L., Dal.	19	1318	260	403	663	820	231	38	55	93	161	3	1980-81	1999-00
Cardin, Claude	St.L.	1	1	0	0	0	0	....	....	....	....	....	....	1967-68	1967-68
Cardwell, Steve	Pit.	3	53	9	11	20	35	4	0	0	0	2	....	1970-71	1972-73
• Carey, George	Que., Ham., Tor.	5	72	21	12	33	20	....	....	....	....	....	....	1919-20	1923-24
Carkner, Terry	NYR, Que., Phi., Det., Fla.	13	858	42	188	230	1588	54	1	9	10	48	....	1986-87	1998-99
Carleton, Wayne	Tor., Bos., Cal.	7	278	55	73	128	172	18	2	4	6	14	1	1965-66	1971-72
Carlin, Brian	L.A.	1	5	1	0	1	0	....	....	....	....	....	....	1971-72	1971-72
Carlson, Jack	Min., St.L.	6	236	30	15	45	417	25	1	2	3	72	....	1978-79	1986-87
Carlson, Kent	Mtl., St.L., Wsh.	5	113	7	11	18	148	8	0	0	0	13	....	1983-84	1988-89
Carlson, Steve	L.A.	1	52	9	12	21	23	4	1	1	2	7	....	1979-80	1979-80
Carlsson, Anders	N.J.	3	104	7	26	33	34	3	1	0	1	2	....	1986-87	1988-89
Carlyle, Randy	Tor., Pit., Wpg.	18	1055	148	499	647	1400	69	9	24	33	120	....	1976-77	1992-93
Carnback, Patrik	Mtl., Ana.	4	154	24	38	62	122	....	....	....	....	....	....	1992-93	1995-96
• Caron, Alain	Oak., Mtl.	2	60	9	13	22	18	....	....	....	....	....	....	1967-68	1968-69
Carpenter, Bob	Wsh., NYR, L.A., Bos., N.J.	19	1178	320	408	728	919	140	21	38	59	136	1	1981-82	1998-99
• Carpenter, Ed	Que., Ham.	2	45	10	5	15	41	....	....	....	....	....	....	1919-20	1920-21
Carr, Gene	St.L., NYR, L.A., Pit., Atl.	8	465	79	136	215	365	35	5	8	13	66	....	1971-72	1978-79
• Carr, Lorne	NYR, NYA, Tor.	13	580	204	222	426	132	53	10	9	19	13	2	1933-34	1945-46
Carr, Red	Tor.	1	5	0	1	1	2	....	....	....	....	....	....	1943-44	1943-44
Carriere, Larry	Buf., Atl., Van., L.A., Tor.	7	367	16	74	90	462	27	0	3	3	42	....	1972-73	1979-80
• Carrigan, Gene	NYR, Det., St.L.	3	37	2	1	3	13	4	0	0	0	0	....	1930-31	1934-35
Carroll, Billy	NYI, Edm., Det.	7	322	30	54	84	113	71	6	12	18	18	4	1980-81	1986-87
• Carroll, George	Mtl.M., Bos.	1	16	0	0	0	11	....	....	....	....	....	....	1924-25	1924-25
Carroll, Greg	Wsh., Det., Hfd.	2	131	20	34	54	44	....	....	....	....	....	....	1978-79	1979-80
Carruthers, Dwight	Det., Phi.	2	2	0	0	0	0	....	....	....	....	....	....	1965-66	1967-68
• Carse, Bill	NYR, Chi.	4	124	28	43	71	38	13	3	2	5	0	....	1938-39	1941-42
• Carse, Bob	Chi., Mtl.	5	167	32	55	87	52	10	0	2	2	2	....	1939-40	1947-48
• Carson, Bill	Tor., Bos.	4	159	54	24	78	156	11	3	0	3	14	1	1926-27	1929-30
• Carson, Frank	Mtl.M., NYA, Det.	7	248	42	48	90	166	27	0	2	2	9	1	1925-26	1933-34
• Carson, Gerry	Mtl., NYR, Mtl.M.	6	261	12	11	23	205	22	0	0	0	12	1	1928-29	1936-37
Carson, Jimmy	L.A., Edm., Det., Van., Hfd.	10	626	275	286	561	254	55	17	15	32	22	....	1986-87	1995-96
Carson, Lindsay	Phi., Hfd.	7	373	66	80	146	524	49	4	10	14	56	....	1981-82	1987-88
Carter, Billy	Mtl., Bos.	3	16	0	0	0	6	....	....	....	....	....	....	1957-58	1961-62
Carter, John	Bos., S.J.	8	244	40	50	90	201	31	7	5	12	51	....	1985-86	1992-93
Carter, Ron	Edm.	1	2	0	0	0	0	....	....	....	....	....	....	1979-80	1979-80
• Carveth, Joe	Det., Bos., Mtl.	11	504	150	189	339	81	69	21	16	37	28	2	1940-41	1950-51
Cashman, Wayne	Bos.	17	1027	277	516	793	1041	145	31	57	88	250	2	1964-65	1982-83
Casselman, Mike	Fla.	1	3	0	0	0	0	....	....	....	....	....	....	1995-96	1995-96
Cassels, Andrew	Mtl., Hfd., Cgy., Van., CBJ, Wsh.	16	1015	204	528	732	410	21	4	7	11	8	....	1989-90	2005-06
Cassidy, Bruce	Chi.	7	36	4	13	17	10	1	0	0	0	0	....	1983-84	1989-90
Cassidy, Tom	Pit.	1	26	3	4	7	15	....	....	....	....	....	....	1977-78	1977-78
Cassolato, Tony	Wsh.	3	23	1	6	7	4	....	....	....	....	....	....	1979-80	1981-82
Caufield, Jay	NYR, Min., Pit.	7	208	5	8	13	759	17	0	0	0	42	2	1986-87	1992-93
Cavallini, Gino	Cgy., St.L., Que.	9	593	114	159	273	507	74	14	19	33	66	....	1984-85	1992-93
Cavallini, Paul	Wsh., St.L., Dal.	10	564	56	177	233	750	69	8	27	35	114	....	1986-87	1995-96
Ceresino, Ray	Tor.	1	12	1	1	2	2	....	....	....	....	....	....	1948-49	1948-49
Cernik, Frantisek	Det.	1	49	5	4	9	13	....	....	....	....	....	....	1984-85	1984-85
Chabot, John	Mtl., Pit., Det.	8	508	84	228	312	85	33	6	20	26	2	....	1983-84	1990-91
• Chad, John	Chi.	3	80	15	22	37	29	10	0	1	1	2	....	1939-40	1945-46
• Chalmers, Chick	NYR	1	1	0	0	0	0	....	....	....	....	....	....	1953-54	1953-54
Chalupa, Milan	Det.	1	14	0	5	5	6	....	....	....	....	....	....	1984-85	1984-85
• Chamberlain, Murph	Tor., Mtl., Bro., Bos.	12	510	100	175	275	769	66	14	17	31	96	2	1937-38	1948-49
Chambers, Shawn	Min., Wsh., T.B., N.J., Dal.	13	625	50	185	235	364	94	7	26	33	72	2	1987-88	1999-00
Champagne, Andre	Tor.	1	2	0	0	0	0	....	....	....	....	....	....	1962-63	1962-63
Chapdelaine, Rene	L.A.	3	32	0	2	2	32	....	....	....	....	....	....	1990-91	1992-93
• Chapman, Art	Bos., NYA	10	438	62	176	238	140	26	1	5	6	9	....	1930-31	1939-40
Chapman, Blair	Pit., St.L.	7	402	106	125	231	158	25	4	6	10	15	....	1976-77	1982-83
Chapman, Brian	Hfd.	1	3	0	0	0	29	....	....	....	....	....	....	1990-91	1990-91
Charbonneau, Jose	Mtl., Van.	4	71	9	13	22	67	11	1	0	1	8	....	1987-88	1994-95
Charbonneau, Stephane	Que.	1	2	0	0	0	0	....	....	....	....	....	....	1991-92	1991-92
Charlebois, Bob	Min.	1	7	1	0	1	0	....	....	....	....	....	....	1967-68	1967-68
Charlesworth, Todd	Pit., NYR	6	93	3	9	12	47	....	....	....	....	....	....	1983-84	1989-90
Charron, Eric	Mtl., T.B., Wsh., Cgy.	8	130	2	7	9	127	6	0	0	0	8	....	1992-93	1999-00
Charron, Guy	Mtl., Det., K.C., Wsh.	12	734	221	309	530	146	....	....	....	....	....	....	1969-70	1980-81
Chartier, Dave	Wpg.	1	1	0	0	0	0	....	....	....	....	....	....	1980-81	1980-81
Chartrand, Brad	L.A.	5	215	25	25	50	122	11	1	1	2	8	....	1999-00	2003-04
Chartraw, Rick	Mtl., L.A., NYR, Edm.	10	420	28	64	92	399	75	7	9	16	80	4	1974-75	1983-84
Chase, Kelly	St.L., Hfd., Tor.	11	458	17	36	53	2017	27	1	1	2	100	....	1989-90	1999-00
Chasse, Denis	St.L., Wsh., Wpg., Ott.	4	132	11	14	25	292	7	1	7	8	23	....	1993-94	1996-97
‡ Chebaturkin, Vladimir	NYI, St.L., Chi.	5	62	2	7	9	52	3	0	0	0	2	....	1997-98	2001-02
Check, Lude	Det., Chi.	2	27	6	2	8	4	....	....	....	....	....	....	1943-44	1944-45
Chernoff, Mike	Min.	1	1	0	0	0	0	....	....	....	....	....	....	1968-69	1968-69
Chernomaz, Rich	Col., N.J., Cgy.	7	51	9	7	16	18	....	....	....	....	....	....	1981-82	1991-92
Cherry, Dick	Bos., Phi.	3	145	12	10	22	45	4	1	0	1	4	....	1956-57	1969-70
Cherry, Don	Bos.	1	....	....	....	....	....	1	0	0	0	0	....	1954-55	1954-55
Chervyakov, Denis	Bos.	1	2	0	0	0	2	....	....	....	....	....	....	1992-93	1992-93
• Chevrefils, Real	Bos., Det.	8	387	104	97	201	185	30	5	4	9	20	....	1951-52	1958-59
• Chiasson, Steve	Det., Cgy., Hfd., Car.	13	751	93	305	398	1107	63	16	19	35	119	....	1986-87	1998-99
Chibirev, Igor	Hfd.	2	45	7	12	19	2	....	....	....	....	....	....	1993-94	1994-95
Chicoine, Dan	Cle., Min.	3	31	1	2	3	12	1	0	0	0	0	....	1977-78	1979-80
Chinnick, Rick	Min.	2	4	0	2	2	0	....	....	....	....	....	....	1973-74	1974-75
Chipperfield, Ron	Edm., Que.	2	83	22	24	46	34	....	....	....	....	....	....	1979-80	1980-81
Chisholm, Art	Bos.	1	3	0	0	0	0	....	....	....	....	....	....	1960-61	1960-61
Chisholm, Colin	Min.	1	1	0	0	0	0	....	....	....	....	....	....	1986-87	1986-87
• Chisholm, Lex	Tor.	2	54	10	8	18	19	3	1	0	1	0	....	1939-40	1940-41
Chorney, Marc	Pit., L.A.	4	210	8	27	35	209	7	0	1	1	2	....	1980-81	1983-84
Chorske, Tom	Mtl., N.J., Ott., NYI, Wsh., Cgy., Pit.	11	596	115	122	237	225	50	5	12	17	10	1	1989-90	1999-00
• Chouinard, Gene	Ott.	1	8	0	0	0	0	....	....	....	....	....	....	1927-28	1927-28
Chouinard, Guy	Atl., Cgy., St.L.	10	578	205	370	575	120	46	9	28	37	12	....	1974-75	1983-84
Christian, Dave	Wpg., Wsh., Bos., St.L., Chi.	15	1009	340	433	773	284	102	32	25	57	27	....	1979-80	1993-94
Christian, Jeff	N.J., Pit., Phx.	5	18	2	2	4	17	....	....	....	....	....	....	1991-92	1997-98
Christie, Mike	Cal., Cle., Col., Van.	7	412	15	101	116	550	2	0	0	0	0	....	1974-75	1980-81
Christie, Ryan	Dal., Cgy.	2	7	0	0	0	0	....	....	....	....	....	....	1999-00	2001-02
Christoff, Steve	Min., Cgy., L.A.	5	248	77	64	141	108	35	16	12	28	25	....	1979-80	1983-84
Chrystal, Bob	NYR	2	132	11	14	25	112	....	....	....	....	....	....	1953-54	1954-55
Church, Brad	Wsh.	1	2	0	0	0	0	....	....	....	....	....	....	1997-98	1997-98
• Church, Jack	Tor., Bro., Bos.	5	130	4	19	23	154	25	1	1	2	18	....	1938-39	1945-46
Churla, Shane	Hfd., Cgy., Min., Dal., L.A., NYR	11	488	26	45	71	2301	78	5	7	12	282	....	1986-87	1996-97
Chychrun, Jeff	Phi., L.A., Pit., Edm.	8	262	3	22	25	744	19	0	2	2	65	1	1986-87	1993-94
Chynoweth, Dean	NYI, Bos.	9	241	4	18	22	667	6	0	0	0	26	....	1988-89	1997-98
Chyzowski, Dave	NYI, Chi.	6	126	15	16	31	144	2	0	0	0	0	....	1989-90	1996-97
Ciavaglia, Peter	Buf.	2	5	0	0	0	0	....	....	....	....	....	....	1991-92	1992-93
Ciccarelli, Dino	Min., Wsh., Det., T.B., Fla.	19	1232	608	592	1200	1425	141	73	45	118	211	....	1980-81	1998-99
Ciccone, Enrico	Min., Wsh., T.B., Chi., Car., Van., Mtl.	9	374	10	18	28	1469	13	1	0	1	48	....	1991-92	2000-01
Cichocki, Chris	Det., N.J.	4	68	11	12	23	27	....	....	....	....	....	....	1985-86	1988-89
‡ Ciernik, Ivan	Ott., Wsh.	5	89	12	14	26	32	2	0	1	1	6	....	1997-98	2003-04
Cierny, Jozef	Edm.	1	1	0	0	0	0	....	....	....	....	....	....	1993-94	1993-94
• Ciesla, Hank	Chi., NYR	4	269	26	51	77	87	6	0	2	2	0	....	1955-56	1958-59
Ciger, Zdeno	N.J., Edm., NYR, T.B.	7	352	94	134	228	101	13	2	6	8	4	....	1990-91	2001-02
Cimellaro, Tony	Ott.	1	2	0	0	0	0	....	....	....	....	....	....	1992-93	1992-93
Cimetta, Rob	Bos., Tor.	4	103	16	16	32	66	1	0	0	0	15	....	1988-89	1991-92
Cirella, Joe	Col., N.J., Que., NYR, Fla., Ott.	15	828	64	211	275	1446	38	0	13	13	98	....	1981-82	1995-96
‡ Cirone, Jason	Wpg.	1	3	0	0	0	2	....	....	....	....	....	....	1991-92	1991-92
Cisar, Marian	Nsh.	3	73	13	17	30	57	....	....	....	....	....	....	1999-00	2001-02
Clackson, Kim	Pit., Que.	2	106	0	8	8	370	8	0	0	0	70	....	1979-80	1980-81
• Clancy, King	Ott., Tor.	16	592	136	147	283	914	55	8	8	16	88	3	1921-22	1936-37
Clancy, Terry	Oak., Tor.	4	93	6	6	12	39	....	....	....	....	....	....	1967-68	1972-73

Tony Camazzola

Bob Carse

Andrew Cassels

Gino Cavallini

Andre Champagne

Lude Check

Gordie Clark

Bill Clement

Name	NHL Teams	NHL Seasons	Regular Schedule GP	G	A	TP	PIM	Playoffs GP	G	A	TP	PIM	NHL Cup Wins	First NHL Season	Last NHL Season
• Clapper, Dit	Bos.	20	833	228	246	474	462	82	13	17	30	50	3	1927-28	1946-47
Clark, Dan	NYR	1	4	0	1	1	6	....	....	....	....	....	....	1978-79	1978-79
Clark, Dean	Edm.	1	1	0	0	0	0	....	....	....	....	....	....	1983-84	1983-84
Clark, Gordie	Bos.	2	8	0	1	1	0	1	0	0	0	0	....	1974-75	1975-76
• Clark, Nobby	Bos.	1	5	0	0	0	0	....	....	....	....	....	....	1927-28	1927-28
Clark, Wendel	Tor., Que., NYI, T.B., Det., Chi.	15	793	330	234	564	1690	95	37	32	69	201	....	1985-86	1999-00
Clarke, Bobby	Phi.	15	1144	358	852	1210	1453	136	42	77	119	152	2	1969-70	1983-84
‡ Clarke, Dale	St.L.	1	3	0	0	0	0	....	....	....	....	....	....	2000-01	2000-01
• Cleghorn, Odie	Mtl., Pit.	10	181	95	34	129	142	12	7	2	9	5	1	1918-19	1927-28
• Cleghorn, Sprague	Ott., Tor., Mtl., Bos.	10	259	83	55	138	538	21	4	3	7	26	2	1918-19	1927-28
Clement, Bill	Phi., Wsh., Atl., Cgy.	11	719	148	208	356	383	50	5	3	8	26	2	1971-72	1981-82
Cline, Bruce	NYR	1	30	2	3	5	10	....	....	....	....	....	....	1956-57	1956-57
Clippingdale, Steve	L.A., Wsh.	2	19	1	2	3	9	1	0	0	0	0	....	1976-77	1979-80
Cloutier, Real	Que., Buf.	6	317	146	198	344	119	25	7	5	12	20	....	1979-80	1984-85
Cloutier, Rejean	Det.	2	5	0	2	2	2	....	....	....	....	....	....	1979-80	1981-82
Cloutier, Roland	Det., Que.	3	34	8	9	17	2	....	....	....	....	....	....	1977-78	1979-80
‡ Cloutier, Sylvain	Chi.	1	7	0	0	0	0	....	....	....	....	....	....	1998-99	1998-99
• Clune, Wally	Mtl.	1	5	0	0	0	6	....	....	....	....	....	....	1955-56	1955-56
Coalter, Gary	Cal., K.C.	2	34	2	4	6	2	....	....	....	....	....	....	1973-74	1974-75
Coates, Steve	Det.	1	5	1	0	1	24	....	....	....	....	....	....	1976-77	1976-77
Cochrane, Glen	Phi., Van., Chi., Edm.	10	411	17	72	89	1556	18	1	1	2	31	....	1978-79	1988-89
Coffey, Paul	Edm., Pit., L.A., Det., Hfd., Phi., Chi., Car., Bos.	21	1409	396	1135	1531	1802	194	59	137	196	264	4	1980-81	2000-01
Coflin, Hugh	Chi.	1	31	0	3	3	33	....	....	....	....	....	....	1950-51	1950-51
Cole, Danton	Wpg., T.B., N.J., NYI, Chi.	7	318	58	60	118	125	1	0	0	0	0	1	1989-90	1995-96
Colley, Tom	Min.	1	1	0	0	0	2	....	....	....	....	....	....	1974-75	1974-75
Collings, Norm	Mtl.	1	1	0	1	1	0	....	....	....	....	....	....	1934-35	1934-35
Collins, Bill	Min., Mtl., Det., St.L., NYR, Phi., Wsh.	11	768	157	154	311	415	18	3	5	8	12	....	1967-68	1977-78
Collins, Gary	Tor.	1	....	....	....	....	....	2	0	0	0	0	....	1958-59	1958-59
Collyard, Bob	St.L.	1	10	1	3	4	4	....	....	....	....	....	....	1973-74	1973-74
• Colman, Michael	S.J.	1	15	0	1	1	32	....	....	....	....	....	....	1991-92	1991-92
• Colville, Mac	NYR	9	353	71	104	175	130	40	9	10	19	14	1	1935-36	1946-47
• Colville, Neil	NYR	12	464	99	166	265	213	46	7	19	26	32	1	1935-36	1948-49
Colwill, Les	NYR	1	69	7	6	13	16	....	....	....	....	....	....	1958-59	1958-59
Comeau, Rey	Mtl., Atl., Col.	9	564	98	141	239	175	9	2	1	3	8	....	1971-72	1979-80
Comrie, Paul	Edm.	1	15	1	2	3	4	....	....	....	....	....	....	1999-00	1999-00
Conacher, Brian	Tor., Det.	5	155	28	28	56	84	12	3	2	5	21	1	1961-62	1971-72
• Conacher, Charlie	Tor., Det., NYA	12	459	225	173	398	523	49	17	18	35	49	1	1929-30	1940-41
Conacher, Jim	Det., Chi., NYR	8	328	85	117	202	91	19	5	2	7	4	....	1945-46	1952-53
• Conacher, Lionel	Pit., NYA, Mtl.M., Chi.	12	498	80	105	185	882	35	2	2	4	34	2	1925-26	1936-37
Conacher, Pat	NYR, Edm., N.J., L.A., Cgy., NYI	13	521	63	76	139	235	66	11	10	21	40	1	1979-80	1995-96
Conacher, Pete	Chi., NYR, Tor.	6	229	47	39	86	57	7	0	0	0	0	....	1951-52	1957-58
• Conacher, Roy	Bos., Det., Chi.	11	490	226	200	426	90	42	15	15	30	14	2	1938-39	1951-52
• Conn, Red	NYA	2	96	9	28	37	22	....	....	....	....	....	....	1933-34	1934-35
Conn, Rob	Chi., Buf.	2	30	2	5	7	20	....	....	....	....	....	....	1991-92	1995-96
• Connelly, Bert	NYR, Chi.	3	87	13	15	28	37	14	1	0	1	0	1	1934-35	1937-38
Connelly, Wayne	Mtl., Bos., Min., Det., St.L., Van.	10	543	133	174	307	156	24	11	7	18	4	....	1960-61	1971-72
Connor, Cam	Mtl., Edm., NYR	5	89	9	22	31	256	20	5	0	5	6	1	1978-79	1982-83
• Connor, Harry	Bos., NYA, Ott.	4	134	16	5	21	149	10	0	0	0	2	....	1927-28	1930-31
• Connors, Bob	NYA, Det.	3	78	17	10	27	110	2	0	0	0	10	....	1926-27	1929-30
Conroy, Al	Phi.	3	114	9	14	23	156	....	....	....	....	....	....	1991-92	1993-94
Contini, Joe	Col., Min.	3	68	17	21	38	34	2	0	0	0	0	....	1977-78	1980-81
Convery, Brandon	Tor., Van., L.A.	4	72	9	19	28	36	5	0	0	0	2	....	1995-96	1998-99
• Convey, Eddie	NYA	3	36	1	1	2	33	....	....	....	....	....	....	1930-31	1932-33
• Cook, Bill	NYR	11	474	229	138	367	386	46	13	11	24	68	2	1926-27	1936-37
• Cook, Bob	Van., Det., NYI, Min.	4	72	13	9	22	22	....	....	....	....	....	....	1970-71	1974-75
• Cook, Bud	Bos., Ott., St.L.	3	50	5	4	9	22	....	....	....	....	....	....	1931-32	1934-35
• Cook, Bun	NYR, Bos.	11	473	158	144	302	444	46	15	3	18	50	2	1926-27	1936-37
• Cook, Lloyd	Bos.	1	4	1	0	1	0	....	....	....	....	....	....	1924-25	1924-25
• Cook, Tom	Chi., Mtl.M.	9	349	77	98	175	184	24	2	4	6	19	1	1929-30	1937-38
• Cooper, Carson	Bos., Mtl., Det.	8	294	110	57	167	111	7	0	0	0	2	....	1924-25	1931-32
Cooper, David	Tor.	3	30	3	7	10	24	....	....	....	....	....	....	1996-97	2000-01
Cooper, Ed	Col.	2	49	8	7	15	46	....	....	....	....	....	....	1980-81	1981-82
• Cooper, Hal	NYR	1	8	0	0	0	2	....	....	....	....	....	....	1944-45	1944-45
• Cooper, Joe	NYR, Chi.	11	420	30	66	96	442	35	3	5	8	58	....	1935-36	1946-47
• Copp, Bobby	Tor.	2	40	3	9	12	26	....	....	....	....	....	....	1942-43	1950-51
• Corbeau, Bert	Mtl., Ham., Tor.	10	258	63	49	112	629	9	2	2	4	38	....	1917-18	1926-27
Corbet, Rene	Que., Col., Cgy., Pit.	8	362	58	74	132	420	53	7	6	13	52	1	1993-94	2000-01
• Corbett, Mike	L.A.	1	....	....	....	....	....	2	0	1	1	2	....	1967-68	1967-68
Corcoran, Norm	Bos., Det., Chi.	4	29	1	3	4	21	4	0	0	0	6	....	1949-50	1955-56
Corkum, Bob	Buf., Ana., Phi., Phx., L.A., N.J., Atl.	12	720	97	103	200	281	62	7	7	14	24	....	1989-90	2001-02
• Cormier, Roger	Mtl.	1	1	0	0	0	0	....	....	....	....	....	....	1925-26	1925-26
Cornforth, Mark	Bos.	1	6	0	0	0	4	....	....	....	....	....	....	1995-96	1995-96
• Corrigan, Chuck	Tor., NYA	2	19	2	2	4	2	....	....	....	....	....	....	1937-38	1940-41
Corrigan, Mike	L.A., Van., Pit.	10	594	152	195	347	698	17	2	3	5	20	....	1967-68	1977-78
Corrinet, Chris	Wsh.	1	8	0	1	1	6	....	....	....	....	....	....	2001-02	2001-02
• Corriveau, Andre	Mtl.	1	3	0	1	1	0	....	....	....	....	....	....	1953-54	1953-54
Corriveau, Yvon	Wsh., Hfd., S.J.	9	280	48	40	88	310	29	5	7	12	50	....	1985-86	1993-94
Corson, Shayne	Mtl., Edm., St.L., Tor., Dal.	19	1156	273	420	693	2357	140	38	49	87	291	....	1985-86	2003-04
Cory, Ross	Wpg.	2	51	2	10	12	41	....	....	....	....	....	....	1979-80	1980-81
Cossette, Jacques	Pit.	3	64	8	6	14	29	3	0	1	1	4	....	1975-76	1978-79
• Costello, Les	Tor.	3	15	2	3	5	11	6	2	2	4	2	1	1947-48	1949-50
Costello, Murray	Chi., Bos., Det.	4	162	13	19	32	54	5	0	0	0	2	....	1953-54	1956-57
Costello, Rich	Tor.	2	12	2	2	4	2	....	....	....	....	....	....	1983-84	1985-86
• Cotch, Charlie	Ham., Tor.	1	12	1	0	1	0	....	....	....	....	....	....	1924-25	1924-25
Cote, Alain	Que.	10	696	103	190	293	383	67	9	15	24	44	....	1979-80	1988-89
Cote, Alain	Bos., Wsh., Mtl., T.B., Que.	9	119	2	18	20	124	11	0	2	2	26	....	1985-86	1993-94
Cote, Patrick	Dal., Nsh., Edm.	6	105	1	2	3	377	....	....	....	....	....	....	1995-96	2000-01
Cote, Ray	Edm.	3	15	0	0	0	4	14	3	2	5	0	....	1982-83	1984-85
Cote, Sylvain	Hfd., Wsh., Tor., Chi., Dal.	19	1171	122	313	435	545	102	11	22	33	62	....	1984-85	2002-03
• Cotton, Baldy	Pit., Tor., NYA	12	503	101	103	204	419	43	4	9	13	46	1	1925-26	1936-37
• Coughlin, Jack	Tor., Que., Mtl., Ham.	3	19	2	0	2	3	....	....	....	....	....	1	1917-18	1920-21
Coulis, Tim	Wsh., Min.	4	47	4	5	9	138	3	1	0	1	2	....	1979-80	1985-86
• Coulson, D'arcy	Phi.	1	28	0	0	0	103	....	....	....	....	....	....	1930-31	1930-31
• Coulter, Art	Chi., NYR	11	465	30	82	112	543	49	4	5	9	61	2	1931-32	1941-42
Coulter, Neal	NYI	3	26	5	5	10	11	....	....	....	....	....	....	1985-86	1987-88
Cournoyer, Yvan	Mtl.	16	968	428	435	863	255	147	64	63	127	47	10	1963-64	1978-79
Courteau, Yves	Cgy., Hfd.	3	22	2	5	7	4	1	0	0	0	0	....	1984-85	1986-87
Courtenay, Ed	S.J.	2	44	7	13	20	10	....	....	....	....	....	....	1991-92	1992-93
Courtnall, Geoff	Bos., Edm., Wsh., St.L., Van.	17	1048	367	432	799	1465	156	39	70	109	262	1	1983-84	1999-00
Courtnall, Russ	Tor., Mtl., Min., Dal., Van., NYR, L.A.	16	1029	297	447	744	557	129	39	44	83	83	....	1983-84	1998-99
‡ Courville, Larry	Van.	3	33	1	2	3	16	....	....	....	....	....	....	1995-96	1997-98
• Coutu, Billy	Mtl., Ham., Bos.	10	244	33	21	54	478	19	1	1	2	39	1	1917-18	1926-27
• Couture, Gerry	Det., Mtl., Chi.	10	385	86	70	156	89	45	9	7	16	4	1	1944-45	1953-54
• Couture, Rosie	Chi., Mtl.	8	309	48	56	104	184	23	1	5	6	15	1	1928-29	1935-36
Couturier, Sylvain	L.A.	3	33	4	5	9	4	....	....	....	....	....	....	1988-89	1991-92
Cowick, Bruce	Phi., Wsh., St.L.	3	70	5	6	11	43	8	0	0	0	9	1	1973-74	1975-76
Cowie, Rob	L.A.	2	78	7	12	19	52	....	....	....	....	....	....	1994-95	1995-96
• Cowley, Bill	St.L., Bos.	13	549	195	353	548	143	64	12	34	46	22	2	1934-35	1946-47
• Cox, Danny	Tor., Ott., Det., NYR	8	319	47	49	96	128	10	0	1	1	6	....	1926-27	1933-34
Coxe, Craig	Van., Cgy., St.L., S.J.	8	235	14	31	45	713	5	1	0	1	18	....	1984-85	1991-92
Craig, Mike	Min., Dal., Tor., S.J.	9	423	71	97	168	550	26	2	2	4	49	....	1990-91	2001-02
Craighead, John	Tor.	1	5	0	0	0	10	....	....	....	....	....	....	1996-97	1996-97
Craigwell, Dale	S.J.	3	98	11	18	29	28	....	....	....	....	....	....	1991-92	1993-94
Crashley, Bart	Det., K.C., L.A.	6	140	7	36	43	50	....	....	....	....	....	....	1965-66	1975-76
Craven, Murray	Det., Phi., Hfd., Van., Chi., S.J.	18	1071	266	493	759	524	118	27	43	70	64	....	1982-83	1999-00
Crawford, Bob	St.L., Hfd., NYR, Wsh.	7	246	71	71	142	72	11	0	1	1	8	....	1979-80	1986-87
Crawford, Bobby	Col., Det.	2	16	1	3	4	6	....	....	....	....	....	....	1980-81	1982-83
• Crawford, Jack	Bos.	13	548	38	140	178	202	66	3	13	16	36	2	1937-38	1949-50
Crawford, Lou	Bos.	2	26	2	1	3	29	1	0	0	0	0	....	1989-90	1991-92
Crawford, Marc	Van.	6	176	19	31	50	229	20	1	2	3	44	....	1981-82	1986-87
• Crawford, Rusty	Ott., Tor.	2	38	10	8	18	117	2	2	1	3	9	1	1917-18	1918-19
Creighton, Adam	Buf., Chi., NYI, T.B., St.L.	14	708	187	216	403	1077	61	11	14	25	137	....	1983-84	1996-97
Creighton, Dave	Bos., Tor., Chi., NYR	12	616	140	174	314	223	51	11	13	24	20	....	1948-49	1959-60
• Creighton, Jimmy	Det.	1	11	1	0	1	2	....	....	....	....	....	....	1930-31	1930-31

Name	NHL Teams	NHL Seasons	Regular Schedule					Playoffs					NHL Cup Wins	First NHL Season	Last NHL Season
			GP	G	A	TP	PIM	GP	G	A	TP	PIM			
Cressman, Dave	Min.	2	85	6	8	14	37	....	....	....	....	....	....	1974-75	1975-76
Cressman, Glen	Mtl.	1	4	0	0	0	2	....	....	....	....	....	....	1956-57	1956-57
Crisp, Terry	Bos., St.L., NYI, Phi.	11	536	67	134	201	135	110	15	28	43	40	2	1965-66	1976-77
Cristofoli, Ed	Mtl.	1	9	0	1	1	4	....	....	....	....	....	....	1989-90	1989-90
● Croghan, Maurice	Mtl.M.	1	16	0	0	0	4	....	....	....	....	....	....	1937-38	1937-38
Crombeen, Mike	Cle., St.L., Hfd.	8	475	55	68	123	218	27	6	2	8	32	....	1977-78	1984-85
Cronin, Shawn	Wsh., Wpg., Phi., S.J.	7	292	3	18	21	877	32	1	0	1	38	....	1988-89	1994-95
● Crossett, Stan	Phi.	1	21	0	0	0	10	....	....	....	....	....	....	1930-31	1930-31
Crossman, Doug	Chi., Phi., L.A., NYI, Hfd., Det., T.B., St.L.	14	914	105	359	464	534	97	12	39	51	105	....	1980-81	1993-94
Croteau, Gary	L.A., Det., Cal., K.C., Col.	12	684	144	175	319	143	11	3	2	5	8	....	1968-69	1979-80
Crowder, Bruce	Bos., Pit.	4	243	47	51	98	156	31	8	4	12	41	....	1981-82	1984-85
Crowder, Keith	Bos., L.A.	10	662	223	271	494	1354	85	14	22	36	218	....	1980-81	1989-90
Crowder, Troy	N.J., Det., L.A., Van.	7	150	9	7	16	433	4	0	0	0	22	....	1987-88	1996-97
Crowe, Phil	L.A., Phi., Ott., Nsh.	6	94	4	5	9	173	3	0	0	0	16	....	1993-94	1999-00
Crowley, Mike	Ana.	3	67	5	15	20	44	....	....	....	....	....	....	1997-98	2000-01
Crowley, Ted	Hfd., Col., NYI	2	34	2	4	6	12	....	....	....	....	....	....	1993-94	1998-99
Crozier, Greg	Pit.	1	1	0	0	0	0	....	....	....	....	....	....	2000-01	2000-01
Crozier, Joe	Tor.	1	5	0	3	3	2	....	....	....	....	....	....	1959-60	1959-60
● Crutchfield, Nels	Mtl.	1	41	5	5	10	20	2	0	1	1	22	....	1934-35	1934-35
Culhane, Jim	Hfd.	1	6	0	1	1	4	....	....	....	....	....	....	1989-90	1989-90
Cullen, Barry	Tor., Det.	5	219	32	52	84	111	6	0	0	0	2	....	1955-56	1959-60
Cullen, Brian	Tor., NYR	7	326	56	100	156	92	19	3	0	3	2	....	1954-55	1960-61
‡ Cullen, David	Phx., Min.	2	19	0	0	0	6	....	....	....	....	....	....	2000-01	2001-02
Cullen, John	Pit., Hfd., Tor., T.B.	11	621	187	363	550	898	53	12	22	34	58	....	1988-89	1998-99
Cullen, Ray	NYR, Det., Min., Van.	6	313	92	123	215	120	20	3	10	13	2	....	1965-66	1970-71
Cummins, Barry	Cal.	1	36	1	2	3	39	....	....	....	....	....	....	1973-74	1973-74
Cummins, Jim	Det., Phi., T.B., Chi., Phx., Mtl., Ana., NYI, Col.	12	511	24	36	60	1538	37	1	2	3	43	....	1991-92	2003-04
Cunneyworth, Randy	Buf., Pit., Wpg., Hfd., Chi., Ott.	16	866	189	225	414	1280	45	7	7	14	61	....	1980-81	1998-99
Cunningham, Bob	NYR	2	4	0	1	1	0	....	....	....	....	....	....	1960-61	1961-62
Cunningham, Jim	Phi.	1	1	0	0	0	4	....	....	....	....	....	....	1977-78	1977-78
● Cunningham, Les	NYA, Chi.	2	60	7	19	26	21	1	0	0	0	0	....	1936-37	1939-40
● Cupolo, Bill	Bos.	1	47	11	13	24	10	7	1	2	3	0	....	1944-45	1944-45
Curran, Brian	Bos., NYI, Tor., Buf., Wsh.	10	381	7	33	40	1461	24	0	1	1	122	....	1983-84	1993-94
Currie, Dan	Edm., L.A.	4	22	2	1	3	4	....	....	....	....	....	....	1990-91	1993-94
Currie, Glen	Wsh., L.A.	8	326	39	79	118	100	12	1	3	4	4	....	1979-80	1987-88
Currie, Hugh	Mtl.	1	1	0	0	0	0	....	....	....	....	....	....	1950-51	1950-51
Currie, Tony	St.L., Van., Hfd.	8	290	92	119	211	83	16	4	12	16	14	....	1977-78	1984-85
● Curry, Floyd	Mtl.	11	601	105	99	204	147	91	23	17	40	38	4	1947-48	1957-58
Curtale, Tony	Cgy.	1	2	0	0	0	0	....	....	....	....	....	....	1980-81	1980-81
Curtis, Paul	Mtl., L.A., St.L.	4	185	3	34	37	161	5	0	0	0	2	....	1969-70	1972-73
Cushenan, Ian	Chi., Mtl., NYR, Det.	5	129	3	11	14	134	....	....	....	....	....	1	1956-57	1963-64
Cusson, Jean	Oak.	1	2	0	0	0	0	....	....	....	....	....	....	1967-68	1967-68
Cyr, Denis	Cgy., Chi., St.L.	6	193	41	43	84	36	4	0	0	0	0	....	1980-81	1985-86
Cyr, Paul	Buf., NYR, Hfd.	9	470	101	140	241	623	24	4	6	10	31	....	1982-83	1991-92

D

Name	NHL Teams	NHL Seasons	GP	G	A	TP	PIM	GP	G	A	TP	PIM	NHL Cup Wins	First NHL Season	Last NHL Season
‡ Dackell, Andreas	Ott., Mtl.	8	613	91	159	250	162	44	5	5	10	10	....	1996-97	2003-04
Dahl, Kevin	Cgy., Phx., Tor., CBJ	8	188	7	22	29	153	16	0	2	2	12	....	1992-93	2000-01
Dahlen, Ulf	NYR, Min., Dal., S.J., Chi., Wsh.	14	966	301	354	655	230	85	15	25	40	12	....	1987-88	2002-03
Dahlin, Kjell	Mtl.	3	166	57	59	116	10	35	6	11	17	6	1	1985-86	1987-88
‡ Dahlman, Toni	Ott.	2	22	1	1	2	0	....	....	....	....	....	....	2001-02	2002-03
Dahlquist, Chris	Pit., Min., Cgy., Ott.	11	532	19	71	90	488	39	4	7	11	30	....	1985-86	1995-96
● Dahlstrom, Cully	Chi.	8	342	88	118	206	58	29	6	8	14	4	1	1937-38	1944-45
Daigle, Alain	Chi.	6	389	56	50	106	122	17	0	1	1	0	....	1974-75	1979-80
Daigneault, J.J.	Van., Phi., Mtl., St.L., Pit., Ana., NYI, Nsh., Phx., Min.	16	899	53	197	250	687	99	5	26	31	100	1	1984-85	2000-01
Dailey, Bob	Van., Phi.	9	561	94	231	325	814	63	12	34	46	105	....	1973-74	1981-82
● Daley, Frank	Det.	1	5	0	0	0	0	2	0	0	0	0	....	1928-29	1928-29
Daley, Pat	Wpg.	2	12	1	0	1	13	....	....	....	....	....	....	1979-80	1980-81
Dalgarno, Brad	NYI	10	321	49	71	120	332	27	2	4	6	37	....	1985-86	1995-96
Dallman, Marty	Tor.	2	6	0	1	1	0	....	....	....	....	....	....	1987-88	1988-89
Dallman, Rod	NYI, Phi.	4	6	1	0	1	26	1	0	1	1	0	....	1987-88	1991-92
● Dame, Bunny	Mtl.	1	34	2	5	7	4	....	....	....	....	....	....	1941-42	1941-42
● Damore, Hank	NYR	1	4	1	0	1	2	....	....	....	....	....	....	1943-44	1943-44
Damphousse, Vincent	Tor., Edm., Mtl., S.J.	18	1378	432	773	1205	1190	140	41	63	104	144	1	1986-87	2003-04
Daneyko, Ken	N.J.	20	1283	36	142	178	2519	175	5	17	22	296	3	1983-84	2002-03
Daniels, Jeff	Pit., Fla., Hfd., Car., Nsh.	12	425	17	26	43	83	41	3	5	8	2	1	1990-91	2002-03
‡ Daniels, Kimbi	Phi.	2	27	1	2	3	4	....	....	....	....	....	....	1990-91	1991-92
Daniels, Scott	Hfd., Phi., N.J.	6	149	8	12	20	667	1	0	0	0	0	....	1992-93	1998-99
Danton, Mike	N.J., St.L.	3	87	9	5	14	182	5	1	0	1	2	....	2000-01	2003-04
Daoust, Dan	Mtl., Tor.	8	522	87	167	254	544	32	7	5	12	83	....	1982-83	1989-90
‡ Darby, Craig	Mtl., NYI, Phi., N.J.	9	196	21	35	56	32	....	....	....	....	....	....	1994-95	2003-04
Dark, Michael	St.L.	2	43	5	6	11	14	....	....	....	....	....	....	1986-87	1987-88
● Darragh, Harold	Pit., Phi., Bos., Tor.	8	308	68	49	117	50	16	1	3	4	4	1	1925-26	1932-33
● Darragh, Jack	Ott.	6	121	66	46	112	113	11	3	0	3	9	3	1917-18	1923-24
David, Richard	Que.	3	31	4	4	8	10	1	0	0	0	0	....	1979-80	1982-83
● Davidson, Bob	Tor.	12	491	94	160	254	398	79	5	17	22	76	2	1934-35	1945-46
● Davidson, Gord	NYR	2	51	3	6	9	8	....	....	....	....	....	....	1942-43	1943-44
‡ Davidson, Matt	CBJ	3	56	5	7	12	28	....	....	....	....	....	....	2000-01	2002-03
‡ Davidsson, Johan	Ana., NYI	2	83	6	9	15	16	1	0	0	0	0	....	1998-99	1999-00
● Davie, Bob	Bos.	3	41	0	1	1	25	....	....	....	....	....	....	1933-34	1935-36
Davies, Buck	NYR	1	....	....	....	....	....	1	0	0	0	0	....	1947-48	1947-48
● Davis, Bob	Det.	1	3	0	0	0	0	....	....	....	....	....	....	1932-33	1932-33
Davis, Kim	Pit., Tor.	4	36	5	7	12	51	4	0	0	0	0	....	1977-78	1980-81
Davis, Lorne	Mtl., Chi., Det., Bos.	6	95	8	12	20	20	18	3	1	4	10	1	1951-52	1959-60
Davis, Mal	Det., Buf.	6	100	31	22	53	34	7	1	0	1	0	....	1978-79	1985-86
● Davison, Murray	Bos.	1	1	0	0	0	0	....	....	....	....	....	....	1965-66	1965-66
Davydov, Evgeny	Wpg., Fla., Ott.	4	155	40	39	79	120	11	2	2	4	2	....	1991-92	1994-95
‡ Daw, Jeff	Col.	1	1	0	1	1	0	....	....	....	....	....	....	2001-02	2001-02
Dawe, Jason	Buf., NYI, Mtl., NYR	8	366	86	90	176	162	22	4	3	7	18	....	1993-94	2001-02
● Dawes, Bob	Tor., Mtl.	4	32	2	7	9	6	10	0	0	0	2	1	1946-47	1950-51
● Day, Hap	Tor., NYA	14	581	86	116	202	601	53	4	7	11	56	1	1924-25	1937-38
Day, Joe	Hfd., NYI	3	72	1	10	11	87	....	....	....	....	....	....	1991-92	1993-94
Daze, Eric	Chi.	11	601	226	172	398	176	37	5	7	12	8	....	1994-95	2005-06
Dea, Billy	NYR, Det., Chi., Pit.	8	397	67	54	121	44	11	2	1	3	6	....	1953-54	1970-71
● Deacon, Don	Det.	3	30	6	4	10	6	2	2	1	3	0	....	1936-37	1939-40
Deadmarsh, Adam	Que., Col., L.A.	10	567	184	189	373	819	105	26	40	66	100	1	1994-95	2003-04
Deadmarsh, Butch	Buf., Atl., K.C.	5	137	12	5	17	155	4	0	0	0	17	....	1970-71	1974-75
Dean, Barry	Col., Phi.	3	165	25	56	81	146	....	....	....	....	....	....	1976-77	1978-79
Dean, Kevin	N.J., Atl., Dal., Chi.	7	331	7	48	55	138	16	2	2	4	2	1	1994-95	2000-01
Debenedet, Nelson	Det., Pit.	2	46	10	4	14	13	....	....	....	....	....	....	1973-74	1974-75
DeBlois, Lucien	NYR, Col., Wpg., Mtl., Que., Tor.	15	993	249	276	525	814	52	7	6	13	38	1	1977-78	1991-92
Debol, Dave	Hfd.	2	92	26	26	52	4	3	0	0	0	0	....	1979-80	1980-81
DeBrusk, Louie	Edm., T.B., Phx., Chi.	11	401	24	17	41	1161	15	2	0	2	10	....	1991-92	2002-03
DeFauw, Brad	Car.	1	9	3	0	3	2	....	....	....	....	....	....	2002-03	2002-03
Defazio, Dean	Pit.	1	22	0	2	2	28	....	....	....	....	....	....	1983-84	1983-84
DeGray, Dale	Cgy., Tor., L.A., Buf.	5	153	18	47	65	195	13	1	3	4	28	....	1985-86	1989-90
● Delisle, Jonathan	Mtl.	1	1	0	0	0	0	....	....	....	....	....	....	1998-99	1998-99
Delisle, Xavier	T.B., Mtl.	2	16	3	2	5	6	....	....	....	....	....	....	1998-99	2000-01
● Delmonte, Armand	Bos.	1	1	0	0	0	0	....	....	....	....	....	....	1945-46	1945-46
Delorme, Gilbert	Mtl., St.L., Que., Det., Pit.	9	541	31	92	123	520	56	1	9	10	56	....	1981-82	1989-90
Delorme, Ron	Col., Van.	9	524	83	83	166	667	25	1	2	3	59	....	1976-77	1984-85
Delory, Val	NYR	1	1	0	0	0	0	....	....	....	....	....	....	1948-49	1948-49
Delparte, Guy	Col.	1	48	1	8	9	18	....	....	....	....	....	....	1976-77	1976-77
Delvecchio, Alex	Det.	24	1549	456	825	1281	383	121	35	69	104	29	3	1950-51	1973-74
● DeMarco, Ab	Chi., Tor., Bos., NYR	7	209	72	93	165	53	11	3	0	3	2	....	1938-39	1946-47
DeMarco, Ab	NYR, St.L., Pit., Van., L.A., Bos.	9	344	44	80	124	75	25	1	2	3	17	....	1969-70	1978-79
● Demers, Tony	Mtl., NYR	6	83	20	22	42	23	2	0	0	0	0	....	1937-38	1943-44
Denis, Jean-Paul	NYR	2	10	0	2	2	2	....	....	....	....	....	....	1946-47	1949-50
Denis, Lulu	Mtl.	2	3	0	1	1	0	....	....	....	....	....	....	1949-50	1950-51
● Denneny, Corb	Tor., Ham., Chi.	9	176	103	42	145	148	6	1	0	1	7	2	1917-18	1927-28

Rusty Crawford

Bruce Crowder

Scott Daniels

Eric Desjardins

Tie Domi

Andre Dore

Jim Drummond

Rick Dudley

Name	NHL Teams	NHL Seasons	Regular Schedule GP	G	A	TP	PIM	Playoffs GP	G	A	TP	PIM	NHL Cup Wins	First NHL Season	Last NHL Season
• Denneny, Cy	Ott., Bos.	12	328	248	85	333	301	25	16	2	18	23	5	1917-18	1928-29
Dennis, Norm	St.L.	4	12	3	0	3	11	5	0	0	0	2	....	1968-69	1971-72
• Denoird, Gerry	Tor.	1	17	0	1	1	0	....	....	....	....	....	....	1922-23	1922-23
DePalma, Larry	Min., S.J., Pit.	7	148	21	20	41	408	3	0	0	0	6	....	1985-86	1993-94
Derlago, Bill	Van., Tor., Bos., Wpg., Que.	9	555	189	227	416	247	13	5	0	5	8	....	1978-79	1986-87
• Desaulniers, Gerard	Mtl.	3	8	0	2	2	4	....	....	....	....	....	....	1950-51	1953-54
Descoteaux, Matthieu	Mtl.	1	5	1	1	2	4	....	....	....	....	....	....	2000-01	2000-01
• Desilets, Joffre	Mtl., Chi.	5	192	37	45	82	57	7	1	0	1	7	....	1935-36	1939-40
Desjardins, Eric	Mtl., Phi.	17	1143	136	439	575	757	168	23	57	80	93	1	1988-89	2005-06
Desjardins, Martin	Mtl.	1	8	0	2	2	2	....	....	....	....	....	....	1989-90	1989-90
• Desjardins, Vic	Chi., NYR	2	87	6	15	21	27	16	0	0	0	0	....	1930-31	1931-32
Deslauriers, Jacques	Mtl.	1	2	0	0	0	0	....	....	....	....	....	....	1955-56	1955-56
Deuling, Jarrett	NYI	2	15	0	1	1	11	....	....	....	....	....	....	1995-96	1996-97
Devine, Kevin	NYI	1	2	0	1	1	8	....	....	....	....	....	....	1982-83	1982-83
• Dewar, Tom	NYR	1	9	0	2	2	4	....	....	....	....	....	....	1943-44	1943-44
• Dewsbury, Al	Det., Chi.	9	347	30	78	108	365	14	1	5	6	16	1	1946-47	1955-56
Deziel, Michel	Buf.	1	....	....	....	....	....	1	0	0	0	0	....	1974-75	1974-75
• Dheere, Marcel	Mtl.	1	11	1	2	3	2	5	0	0	0	6	....	1942-43	1942-43
Diachuk, Edward	Det.	1	12	0	0	0	19	....	....	....	....	....	....	1960-61	1960-61
• Dick, Harry	Chi.	1	12	0	1	1	12	....	....	....	....	....	....	1946-47	1946-47
• Dickens, Ernie	Tor., Chi.	6	278	12	44	56	98	13	0	0	0	4	1	1941-42	1950-51
Dickenson, Herb	NYR	2	48	18	17	35	10	....	....	....	....	....	....	1951-52	1952-53
Diduck, Gerald	NYI, Mtl., Van., Chi., Hfd., Phx., Tor., Dal.	17	932	56	156	212	1612	114	8	16	24	212	....	1984-85	2000-01
Dietrich, Don	Chi., N.J.	2	28	0	7	7	10	....	....	....	....	....	....	1983-84	1985-86
• Dill, Bob	NYR	2	76	15	15	30	135	....	....	....	....	....	....	1943-44	1944-45
• Dillabough, Bob	Det., Bos., Pit., Oak.	9	283	32	54	86	76	17	3	0	3	0	....	1961-62	1969-70
• Dillon, Cecil	NYR, Det.	10	453	167	131	298	105	43	14	9	23	14	1	1930-31	1939-40
Dillon, Gary	Col.	1	13	1	1	2	29	....	....	....	....	....	....	1980-81	1980-81
Dillon, Wayne	NYR, Wpg.	4	229	43	66	109	60	3	0	1	1	0	....	1975-76	1979-80
DiMaio, Rob	NYI, T.B., Phi., Bos., NYR, Car., Dal.	17	894	106	171	277	840	62	7	9	16	40	....	1988-89	2005-06
Dineen, Bill	Det., Chi.	5	323	51	44	95	122	37	1	1	2	18	2	1953-54	1957-58
• Dineen, Gary	Min.	1	4	0	1	1	0	....	....	....	....	....	....	1968-69	1968-69
Dineen, Gord	NYI, Min., Pit., Ott.	13	528	16	90	106	695	40	1	7	8	68	....	1982-83	1994-95
Dineen, Kevin	Hfd., Phi., Car., Ott., CBJ	19	1188	355	405	760	2229	59	23	18	41	127	....	1984-85	2002-03
Dineen, Peter	L.A., Det.	2	13	0	2	2	13	....	....	....	....	....	....	1986-87	1989-90
Dingman, Chris	Cgy., Col., Car., T.B.	8	385	15	19	34	769	52	2	5	7	100	2	1997-98	2005-06
• Dinsmore, Chuck	Mtl.M.	4	100	6	2	8	50	8	1	0	1	2	1	1924-25	1929-30
Dionne, Gilbert	Mtl., Phi., Fla.	6	223	61	79	140	108	39	10	12	22	34	1	1990-91	1995-96
Dionne, Marcel	Det., L.A., NYR	18	1348	731	1040	1771	600	49	21	24	45	17	....	1971-72	1988-89
‡ DiPietro, Paul	Mtl., Tor., L.A.	6	192	31	49	80	96	31	11	10	21	10	1	1991-92	1996-97
Dirk, Robert	St.L., Van., Chi., Ana., Mtl.	9	402	13	29	42	786	39	0	1	1	56	....	1987-88	1995-96
‡ Divisek, Tomas	Phi.	2	5	1	0	1	0	....	....	....	....	....	....	2000-01	2001-02
Djoos, Per	Det., NYR	3	82	2	31	33	58	....	....	....	....	....	....	1990-91	1992-93
Doak, Gary	Det., Bos., Van., NYR	16	789	23	107	130	908	78	2	4	6	121	1	1965-66	1980-81
Dobbin, Brian	Phi., Bos.	5	63	7	8	15	61	2	0	0	0	17	....	1986-87	1991-92
Dobson, Jim	Min., Col., Que.	4	12	0	0	0	6	....	....	....	....	....	....	1979-80	1983-84
• Doherty, Fred	Mtl.	1	1	0	0	0	0	....	....	....	....	....	....	1918-19	1918-19
‡ Doig, Jason	Wpg., Phx., NYR, Wsh.	7	158	6	18	24	285	6	0	1	1	6	....	1995-96	2003-04
Dollas, Bobby	Wpg., Que., Det., Ana., Edm., Pit., Ott., Cgy., S.J.	16	646	42	96	138	467	47	2	1	3	41	....	1983-84	2000-01
‡ Dome, Robert	Pit., Cgy.	3	53	7	7	14	12	....	....	....	....	....	....	1997-98	2002-03
‡ Domenichelli, Hnat	Hfd., Cgy., Atl., Min.	7	267	52	61	113	104	....	....	....	....	....	....	1996-97	2002-03
Domi, Tie	Tor., NYR, Wpg.	16	1020	104	141	245	3515	98	7	12	19	238	....	1989-90	2005-06
Donaldson, Gary	Chi.	1	1	0	0	0	0	....	....	....	....	....	....	1973-74	1973-74
Donatelli, Clark	Min., Bos.	2	35	3	4	7	39	2	0	0	0	0	....	1989-90	1991-92
Donato, Ted	Bos., NYI, Ott., Ana., Dal., St.L., L.A., NYR	13	796	150	197	347	396	58	8	10	18	22	....	1991-92	2003-04
• Donnelly, Babe	Mtl.M.	1	34	0	1	1	14	2	0	0	0	0	....	1926-27	1926-27
Donnelly, Dave	Bos., Chi., Edm.	5	137	15	24	39	150	5	0	0	0	0	....	1983-84	1987-88
Donnelly, Gord	Que., Wpg., Buf., Dal.	12	554	28	41	69	2069	26	0	2	2	61	....	1983-84	1994-95
Donnelly, Mike	NYR, Buf., L.A., Dal., NYI	11	465	114	121	235	255	47	12	12	24	30	....	1986-87	1996-97
‡ Dopita, Jiri	Phi., Edm.	2	73	12	21	33	19	....	....	....	....	....	....	2001-02	2002-03
• Doran, John	NYA, Det., Mtl.	5	98	5	10	15	110	3	0	0	0	0	....	1933-34	1939-40
• Doran, Lloyd	Det.	1	24	3	2	5	10	....	....	....	....	....	....	1946-47	1946-47
• Doraty, Ken	Chi., Tor., Det.	5	103	15	26	41	24	15	7	2	9	2	....	1926-27	1937-38
Dore, Andre	NYR, St.L., Que.	7	257	14	81	95	261	23	1	2	3	32	....	1978-79	1984-85
Dore, Daniel	Que.	2	17	2	3	5	59	....	....	....	....	....	....	1989-90	1990-91
Dorey, Jim	Tor., NYR	4	232	25	74	99	553	11	0	2	2	40	....	1968-69	1971-72
Dorion, Dan	N.J.	2	4	1	1	2	2	....	....	....	....	....	....	1985-86	1987-88
Dornhoefer, Gary	Bos., Phi.	14	787	214	328	542	1291	80	17	19	36	203	2	1963-64	1977-78
Dorohoy, Eddie	Mtl.	1	16	0	0	0	6	....	....	....	....	....	....	1948-49	1948-49
Douglas, Jordy	Hfd., Min., Wpg.	6	268	76	62	138	160	6	0	0	0	4	....	1979-80	1984-85
Douglas, Kent	Tor., Oak., Det.	7	428	33	115	148	631	19	1	3	4	33	3	1962-63	1968-69
• Douglas, Les	Det.	4	52	6	12	18	8	10	3	2	5	2	1	1940-41	1946-47
Doull, Doug	Bos., Wsh.	2	37	0	1	1	151	....	....	....	....	....	....	2003-04	2005-06
Douris, Peter	Wpg., Bos., Ana., Dal.	11	321	54	67	121	80	27	3	5	8	14	....	1985-86	1997-98
• Downie, Dave	Tor.	1	11	0	1	1	2	....	....	....	....	....	....	1932-33	1932-33
Doyon, Mario	Chi., Que.	3	28	3	4	7	16	....	....	....	....	....	....	1988-89	1990-91
• Draper, Bruce	Tor.	1	1	0	0	0	0	....	....	....	....	....	....	1962-63	1962-63
• Drillon, Gordie	Tor., Mtl.	7	311	155	139	294	56	50	26	15	41	10	1	1936-37	1942-43
Driscoll, Peter	Edm.	2	60	3	8	11	97	3	0	0	0	0	....	1979-80	1980-81
Driver, Bruce	N.J., NYR	15	922	96	390	486	670	108	10	40	50	64	1	1983-84	1997-98
Drolet, Rene	Phi., Det.	2	2	0	0	0	0	....	....	....	....	....	....	1971-72	1974-75
‡ Droppa, Ivan	Chi.	2	19	0	1	1	14	....	....	....	....	....	....	1993-94	1995-96
• Drouillard, Clarence	Det.	1	10	0	1	1	0	....	....	....	....	....	....	1937-38	1937-38
Drouin, Jude	Mtl., Min., NYI, Wpg.	12	666	151	305	456	346	72	27	41	68	33	....	1968-69	1980-81
Drouin, P.C.	Bos.	1	3	0	0	0	0	....	....	....	....	....	....	1996-97	1996-97
• Drouin, Polly	Mtl.	7	160	23	50	73	80	5	0	1	1	5	....	1934-35	1940-41
Druce, John	Wsh., Wpg., L.A., Phi.	10	531	113	126	239	347	53	17	6	23	38	....	1988-89	1997-98
Druken, Harold	Van., Car., Tor.	5	146	27	36	63	36	4	0	1	1	0	....	1999-00	2003-04
Drulia, Stan	T.B.	3	126	15	27	42	52	....	....	....	....	....	....	1992-93	2000-01
• Drummond, Jim	NYR	1	2	0	0	0	0	....	....	....	....	....	....	1944-45	1944-45
• Drury, Herb	Pit., Phi.	6	213	24	13	37	203	4	1	1	2	0	....	1925-26	1930-31
‡ Drury, Ted	Cgy., Hfd., Ott., Ana., NYI, CBJ	8	414	41	52	93	367	14	1	0	1	4	....	1993-94	2000-01
‡ Dube, Christian	NYR	2	33	1	1	2	4	3	0	0	0	0	....	1996-97	1998-99
Dube, Gilles	Mtl., Det.	2	12	1	2	3	2	2	0	0	0	0	1	1949-50	1953-54
Dube, Norm	K.C.	2	57	8	10	18	54	....	....	....	....	....	....	1974-75	1975-76
Duberman, Justin	Pit.	1	4	0	0	0	0	....	....	....	....	....	....	1993-94	1993-94
Dubinsky, Steve	Chi., Cgy., Nsh., St.L.	10	375	25	45	70	164	10	1	0	1	14	....	1993-94	2002-03
Duchesne, Gaetan	Wsh., Que., Min., S.J., Fla.	14	1028	179	254	433	617	84	14	13	27	97	....	1981-82	1994-95
Duchesne, Steve	L.A., Phi., Que., St.L., Ott., Det.	16	1113	227	525	752	824	121	16	61	77	96	1	1986-87	2001-02
Dudley, Rick	Buf., Wpg.	6	309	75	99	174	292	25	7	2	9	69	....	1972-73	1980-81
Duerden, Dave	Fla.	1	2	0	0	0	0	....	....	....	....	....	....	1999-00	1999-00
Duff, Dick	Tor., NYR, Mtl., L.A., Buf.	18	1030	283	289	572	743	114	30	49	79	78	6	1954-55	1971-72
Dufour, Luc	Bos., Que., St.L.	3	167	23	21	44	199	18	1	0	1	32	....	1982-83	1984-85
Dufour, Marc	NYR, L.A.	3	14	1	0	1	2	....	....	....	....	....	....	1963-64	1968-69
Dufresne, Donald	Mtl., T.B., L.A., St.L., Edm.	9	268	6	36	42	258	34	1	3	4	47	1	1988-89	1996-97
• Duggan, John	Ott.	1	27	0	0	0	0	2	0	0	0	0	....	1925-26	1925-26
Duggan, Ken	Min.	1	1	0	0	0	0	....	....	....	....	....	....	1987-88	1987-88
Duguay, Ron	NYR, Det., Pit., L.A.	12	864	274	346	620	582	89	31	22	53	118	....	1977-78	1988-89
• Duguid, Lorne	Mtl.M., Det., Bos.	6	135	9	15	24	57	4	1	0	1	6	....	1931-32	1936-37
• Dukowski, Duke	Chi., NYA, NYR	5	200	16	30	46	172	6	0	0	0	6	....	1926-27	1933-34
• Dumart, Woody	Bos.	16	772	211	218	429	99	88	12	15	27	23	2	1935-36	1953-54
Dunbar, Dale	Van., Bos.	2	2	0	0	0	2	....	....	....	....	....	....	1985-86	1988-89
• Duncan, Art	Det., Tor.	5	156	18	16	34	225	5	0	0	0	4	....	1926-27	1930-31
Duncan, Iain	Wpg.	4	127	34	55	89	149	11	0	3	3	6	....	1986-87	1990-91
Duncanson, Craig	L.A., Wpg., NYR	7	38	5	4	9	61	....	....	....	....	....	....	1985-86	1992-93
Dundas, Rocky	Tor.	1	5	0	0	0	14	....	....	....	....	....	....	1989-90	1989-90
• Dunlap, Frank	Tor.	1	15	0	1	1	2	....	....	....	....	....	....	1943-44	1943-44
Dunlop, Blake	Min., Phi., St.L., Det.	11	550	130	274	404	172	40	4	10	14	18	....	1973-74	1983-84
Dunn, Dave	Van., Tor.	3	184	14	41	55	313	10	1	1	2	41	....	1973-74	1975-76
Dunn, Richie	Buf., Cgy., Hfd.	12	483	36	140	176	314	36	3	15	18	24	....	1977-78	1988-89
Dupere, Denis	Tor., Wsh., St.L., K.C., Col.	8	421	80	99	179	66	16	1	0	1	0	....	1970-71	1977-78
Dupont, Andre	NYR, St.L., Phi., Que.	13	800	59	185	244	1986	140	14	18	32	352	2	1970-71	1982-83

				Regular Schedule					Playoffs					NHL	First	Last
	Name	NHL Teams	NHL Seasons	GP	G	A	TP	PIM	GP	G	A	TP	PIM	Cup Wins	NHL Season	NHL Season
	Dupont, Jerome	Chi., Tor.	6	214	7	29	36	468	20	0	2	2	56	....	1981-82	1986-87
	Dupont, Norm	Mtl., Wpg., Hfd.	5	256	55	85	140	52	13	4	2	6	0	....	1979-80	1983-84
•	Dupre, Yanick	Phi.	3	35	2	0	2	16	....	....	....	....	....	....	1991-92	1995-96
•	Durbano, Steve	St.L., Pit., K.C., Col.	6	220	13	60	73	1127	5	0	2	2	8	....	1972-73	1978-79
	Duris, Vitezslav	Tor.	2	89	3	20	23	62	3	0	1	1	2	....	1980-81	1982-83
	Dusablon, Benoit	NYR	1	3	0	0	0	2	....	....	....	....	....	....	2003-04	2003-04
	Dussault, Norm	Mtl.	4	206	31	62	93	47	7	3	1	4	0	....	1947-48	1950-51
•	Dutton, Red	Mtl.M., NYA	10	449	29	67	96	871	18	1	0	1	33	....	1926-27	1935-36
	Dvorak, Miroslav	Phi.	3	193	11	74	85	51	18	0	2	2	6	....	1982-83	1984-85
	Dwyer, Gordie	T.B., NYR, Mtl.	5	108	0	5	5	394	....	....	....	....	....	....	1999-00	2003-04
	Dwyer, Mike	Col., Cgy.	4	31	2	6	8	25	1	1	0	1	0	....	1978-79	1981-82
•	Dyck, Henry	NYR	1	1	0	0	0	0	....	....	....	....	....	....	1943-44	1943-44
•	Dye, Babe	Tor., Ham., Chi., NYA	11	271	201	47	248	221	10	2	0	2	11	1	1919-20	1930-31
	Dykhuis, Karl	Chi., Phi., T.B., Mtl.	12	644	42	91	133	495	62	8	10	18	50	....	1991-92	2003-04
	Dykstra, Steve	Buf., Edm., Pit., Hfd.	5	217	8	32	40	545	1	0	0	0	2	....	1985-86	1989-90
•	Dyte, Jack	Chi.	1	27	1	0	1	31	....	....	....	....	....	....	1943-44	1943-44
	Dziedzic, Joe	Pit., Phx.	3	130	14	14	28	131	21	1	3	4	23	....	1995-96	1998-99

E

	Name	NHL Teams	NHL Seasons	GP	G	A	TP	PIM	GP	G	A	TP	PIM	Cup Wins	First NHL Season	Last NHL Season
	Eagles, Mike	Que., Chi., Wpg., Wsh.	16	853	74	122	196	928	44	2	6	8	34	....	1982-83	1999-00
	Eakin, Bruce	Cgy., Det.	4	13	2	2	4	4	....	....	....	....	....	....	1981-82	1985-86
	Eakins, Dallas	Wpg., Fla., St.L., Phx., NYR, Tor., NYI, Cgy.	10	120	0	9	9	208	5	0	0	0	4	....	1992-93	2001-02
	Eastwood, Mike	Tor., Wpg., Phx., NYR, St.L., Chi., Pit.	13	783	87	149	236	354	97	8	11	19	64	....	1991-92	2003-04
	Eatough, Jeff	Buf.	1	1	0	0	0	0	....	....	....	....	....	....	1981-82	1981-82
	Eaves, Mike	Min., Cgy.	8	324	83	143	226	80	43	7	10	17	14	....	1978-79	1985-86
	Eaves, Murray	Wpg., Det.	8	57	4	13	17	9	4	0	1	1	2	....	1980-81	1989-90
	Ecclestone, Tim	St.L., Det., Tor., Atl.	11	692	126	233	359	344	48	6	11	17	76	....	1967-68	1977-78
	Edberg, Rolf	Wsh.	3	184	45	58	103	24	....	....	....	....	....	....	1978-79	1980-81
•	Eddolls, Frank	Mtl., NYR	8	317	23	43	66	114	31	0	2	2	10	1	1944-45	1951-52
	Edestrand, Darryl	St.L., Phi., Pit., Bos., L.A.	10	455	34	90	124	404	42	3	9	12	57	....	1967-68	1978-79
	Edmundson, Garry	Mtl., Tor.	3	43	4	6	10	49	11	0	1	1	8	....	1951-52	1960-61
	Edur, Tom	Col., Pit.	2	158	17	70	87	67	....	....	....	....	....	....	1976-77	1977-78
	Egan, Pat	NYA, Bro., Det., Bos., NYR	11	554	77	153	230	776	46	9	4	13	48	....	1939-40	1950-51
	Egeland, Allan	T.B.	3	17	0	0	0	16	....	....	....	....	....	....	1995-96	1997-98
	Egers, Jack	NYR, St.L., Wsh.	7	284	64	69	133	154	32	5	6	11	32	....	1969-70	1975-76
•	Ehman, Gerry	Bos., Det., Tor., Oak., Cal.	9	429	96	118	214	100	41	10	10	20	12	1	1957-58	1970-71
	Eisenhut, Neil	Van., Cgy.	2	16	1	3	4	21	....	....	....	....	....	....	1993-94	1994-95
	Eklund, Pelle	Phi., Dal.	9	594	120	335	455	109	66	10	36	46	8	....	1985-86	1993-94
	Eldebrink, Anders	Van., Que.	2	55	3	11	14	29	14	0	0	0	10	....	1981-82	1982-83
‡	Elich, Matt	T.B.	2	16	1	1	2	0	....	....	....	....	....	....	1999-00	2000-01
	Elik, Bo	Det.	1	3	0	0	0	0	....	....	....	....	....	....	1962-63	1962-63
	Elik, Todd	L.A., Min., Edm., S.J., St.L., Bos.	8	448	110	219	329	453	52	15	27	42	48	....	1989-90	1996-97
	Ellett, Dave	Wpg., Tor., N.J., Bos., St.L.	16	1129	153	415	568	985	116	11	46	57	87	....	1984-85	1999-00
•	Elliott, Fred	Ott.	1	43	2	0	2	6	....	....	....	....	....	....	1928-29	1928-29
	Ellis, Ron	Tor.	16	1034	332	308	640	207	70	18	8	26	20	1	1963-64	1980-81
	Elomo, Miika	Wsh.	1	2	0	1	1	2	....	....	....	....	....	....	1999-00	1999-00
	Eloranta, Kari	Cgy., St.L.	5	267	13	103	116	155	26	1	7	8	19	....	1981-82	1986-87
‡	Eloranta, Mikko	Bos., L.A.	4	264	32	44	76	186	7	1	1	2	2	....	1999-00	2002-03
	Elynuik, Pat	Wpg., Wsh., T.B., Ott.	9	506	154	188	342	459	20	6	9	15	25	....	1987-88	1995-96
•	Emberg, Eddie	Mtl.	1	....	....	....	....	....	2	1	0	1	0	....	1944-45	1944-45
	Emerson, Nelson	St.L., Wpg., Hfd., Car., Chi., Ott., Atl., L.A.	12	771	195	293	488	575	40	7	15	22	33	....	1990-91	2001-02
	Emma, David	N.J., Bos., Fla.	5	34	5	6	11	2	....	....	....	....	....	....	1992-93	2000-01
	Emmons, Gary	S.J.	1	3	1	0	1	0	....	....	....	....	....	....	1993-94	1993-94
	Emmons, John	Ott., T.B., Bos.	3	85	2	4	6	64	....	....	....	....	....	....	1999-00	2001-02
•	Emms, Hap	Mtl.M., NYA, Det., Bos.	10	320	36	53	89	311	14	0	0	0	12	....	1926-27	1937-38
	Endean, Craig	Wpg.	1	2	0	1	1	0	....	....	....	....	....	....	1986-87	1986-87
	Engblom, Brian	Mtl., Wsh., L.A., Buf., Cgy.	11	659	29	177	206	599	48	3	9	12	43	3	1976-77	1986-87
	Engele, Jerry	Min.	3	100	2	13	15	162	2	0	1	1	0	....	1975-76	1977-78
	English, John	L.A.	1	3	1	3	4	4	1	0	0	0	0	....	1987-88	1987-88
	Ennis, Jim	Edm.	1	5	1	0	1	10	....	....	....	....	....	....	1987-88	1987-88
	Erickson, Aut	Bos., Chi., Tor., Oak.	7	226	7	24	31	182	7	0	0	0	2	1	1959-60	1969-70
	Erickson, Bryan	Wsh., L.A., Pit., Wpg.	9	351	80	125	205	141	14	3	4	7	7	....	1983-84	1993-94
	Erickson, Grant	Bos., Min.	2	6	1	0	1	0	....	....	....	....	....	....	1968-69	1969-70
	Eriksson, Peter	Edm.	1	20	3	3	6	24	....	....	....	....	....	....	1989-90	1989-90
	Eriksson, Roland	Min., Van.	3	193	48	95	143	26	2	1	0	1	0	....	1976-77	1978-79
	Eriksson, Thomas	Phi.	5	208	22	76	98	107	19	0	3	3	12	....	1980-81	1985-86
	Erixon, Jan	NYR	10	556	57	159	216	167	58	7	7	14	16	....	1983-84	1992-93
	Errey, Bob	Pit., Buf., S.J., Det., Dal., NYR	15	895	170	212	382	1005	99	13	16	29	109	2	1983-84	1997-98
	Esau, Len	Tor., Que., Cgy., Edm.	4	27	0	10	10	24	....	....	....	....	....	....	1991-92	1994-95
	Esposito, Phil	Chi., Bos., NYR	18	1282	717	873	1590	910	130	61	76	137	138	2	1963-64	1980-81
•	Evans, Chris	Tor., Buf., St.L., Det., K.C.	5	241	19	42	61	143	12	1	1	2	8	....	1969-70	1974-75
	Evans, Daryl	L.A., Wsh., Tor.	6	113	22	30	52	25	11	5	8	13	12	....	1981-82	1986-87
	Evans, Doug	St.L., Wpg., Phi.	8	355	48	87	135	502	22	3	4	7	38	....	1985-86	1992-93
•	Evans, Jack	NYR, Chi.	14	752	19	80	99	989	56	2	2	4	97	1	1948-49	1962-63
	Evans, John Paul	Phi.	3	103	14	25	39	34	1	0	0	0	0	....	1978-79	1982-83
	Evans, Kevin	Min., S.J.	2	9	0	1	1	44	....	....	....	....	....	....	1990-91	1991-92
	Evans, Paul	Tor.	2	11	1	1	2	21	2	0	0	0	0	....	1976-77	1977-78
	Evans, Shawn	St.L., NYI	2	9	1	0	1	2	....	....	....	....	....	....	1985-86	1989-90
•	Evans, Stewart	Det., Mtl.M., Mtl.	8	367	28	49	77	425	26	0	0	0	20	1	1930-31	1938-39
	Evason, Dean	Wsh., Hfd., S.J., Dal., Cgy.	13	803	139	233	372	1002	55	9	20	29	132	....	1983-84	1995-96
	Ewen, Todd	St.L., Mtl., Ana., S.J.	11	518	36	40	76	1911	26	0	0	0	87	1	1986-87	1996-97
	Ezinicki, Bill	Tor., Bos., NYR	9	368	79	105	184	713	40	5	8	13	87	3	1944-45	1954-55

F

	Name	NHL Teams	NHL Seasons	GP	G	A	TP	PIM	GP	G	A	TP	PIM	Cup Wins	First NHL Season	Last NHL Season
	Fahey, Trevor	NYR	1	1	0	0	0	0	....	....	....	....	....	....	1964-65	1964-65
	Fairbairn, Bill	NYR, Min., St.L.	11	658	162	261	423	173	54	13	22	35	42	....	1968-69	1978-79
‡	Fairchild, Kelly	Tor., Dal., Col.	4	34	2	3	5	6	....	....	....	....	....	....	1995-96	2001-02
	Falkenberg, Bob	Det.	5	54	1	5	6	26	....	....	....	....	....	....	1966-67	1971-72
	Falloon, Pat	S.J., Phi., Ott., Edm., Pit.	9	575	143	179	322	141	66	11	7	18	16	....	1991-92	1999-00
	Farkas, Jeff	Tor., Atl.	4	11	0	2	2	6	5	1	0	1	0	....	1999-00	2002-03
	Farrant, Walt	Chi.	1	1	0	0	0	0	....	....	....	....	....	....	1943-44	1943-44
	Farrell, Mike	Wsh., Nsh.	3	13	0	0	0	2	....	....	....	....	....	....	2001-02	2003-04
	Farrish, Dave	NYR, Que., Tor.	7	430	17	110	127	440	14	0	2	2	24	....	1976-77	1983-84
	Fashoway, Gordie	Chi.	1	13	3	2	5	14	....	....	....	....	....	....	1950-51	1950-51
‡	Fast, Brad	Car.	1	1	1	0	1	0	....	....	....	....	....	....	2003-04	2003-04
	Faubert, Mario	Pit.	7	231	21	90	111	292	10	2	2	4	6	....	1974-75	1981-82
	Faulkner, Alex	Tor., Det.	3	101	15	17	32	15	12	5	0	5	2	....	1961-62	1963-64
	Fauss, Ted	Tor.	2	28	0	2	2	15	....	....	....	....	....	....	1986-87	1987-88
	Faust, Andre	Phi.	2	47	10	7	17	14	....	....	....	....	....	....	1992-93	1993-94
	Feamster, Dave	Chi.	4	169	13	24	37	154	33	3	5	8	61	....	1981-82	1984-85
	Featherstone, Glen	St.L., Bos., NYR, Hfd., Cgy.	9	384	19	61	80	939	28	0	2	2	103	....	1988-89	1996-97
	Featherstone, Tony	Oak., Cal., Min.	3	130	17	21	38	65	2	0	0	0	0	....	1969-70	1973-74
	Federko, Bernie	St.L., Det.	14	1000	369	761	1130	487	91	35	66	101	83	....	1976-77	1989-90
	Fedotov, Anatoli	Wpg., Ana.	2	4	0	2	2	0	....	....	....	....	....	....	1992-93	1993-94
	Fedyk, Brent	Det., Phi., Dal., NYR	10	470	97	112	209	308	16	3	2	5	12	....	1987-88	1998-99
	Felix, Chris	Wsh.	4	35	1	12	13	10	2	0	1	1	0	....	1987-88	1990-91
	Felsner, Brian	Chi.	1	12	1	3	4	12	....	....	....	....	....	....	1997-98	1997-98
	Felsner, Denny	St.L.	4	18	1	4	5	6	10	2	3	5	2	....	1991-92	1994-95
	Feltrin, Tony	Pit., NYR	4	48	3	3	6	65	....	....	....	....	....	....	1980-81	1985-86
	Fenton, Paul	Hfd., NYR, L.A., Wpg., Tor., Cgy., S.J.	8	411	100	83	183	198	17	4	1	5	27	....	1984-85	1991-92
	Fenyves, David	Buf., Phi.	9	206	3	32	35	119	11	0	0	0	9	....	1982-83	1990-91
	Fergus, Tom	Bos., Tor., Van.	12	726	235	346	581	499	65	21	17	38	48	....	1981-82	1992-93
	Ferguson, Craig	Mtl., Cgy., Fla.	5	27	1	1	2	6	....	....	....	....	....	....	1993-94	1999-00
	Ferguson, George	Tor., Pit., Min.	12	797	160	238	398	431	86	14	23	37	44	....	1972-73	1983-84
•	Ferguson, John	Mtl.	8	500	145	158	303	1214	85	20	18	38	260	5	1963-64	1970-71
	Ferguson, Lorne	Bos., Det., Chi.	8	422	82	80	162	193	31	6	3	9	24	....	1949-50	1958-59
	Ferguson, Norm	Oak., Cal.	4	279	73	66	139	72	10	1	4	5	7	....	1968-69	1971-72
	Ferner, Mark	Buf., Wsh., Ana., Det.	6	91	3	10	13	51	....	....	....	....	....	....	1986-87	1994-95
‡	Ferraro, Chris	NYR, Pit., Edm., NYI, Wsh.	6	74	7	9	16	57	....	....	....	....	....	....	1995-96	2001-02
‡	Ferraro, Peter	NYR, Pit., Bos., Wsh.	6	92	9	15	24	58	2	0	0	0	0	....	1995-96	2001-02

Frank Dunlap

Darryl Edestrand

Shawn Evans

Tom Fitzgerald

Gerry Foley

Val Fonteyne

Harvey Fraser

Dutch Gainor

Name	NHL Teams	NHL Seasons	Regular Schedule GP	G	A	TP	PIM	Playoffs GP	G	A	TP	PIM	NHL Cup Wins	First NHL Season	Last NHL Season
Ferraro, Ray	Hfd., NYI, NYR, L.A., Atl., St.L.	18	1258	408	490	898	1288	68	21	22	43	54	....	1984-85	2001-02
Fetisov, Viacheslav	N.J., Det.	9	546	36	192	228	656	116	2	26	28	147	2	1989-90	1997-98
‡ Fibiger, Jesse	S.J.	1	16	0	0	0	2	....	....	....	....	....	....	2002-03	2002-03
Fidler, Mike	Cle., Min., Hfd., Chi.	7	271	84	97	181	124	....	....	....	....	....	....	1976-77	1982-83
• Field, Wilf	NYA, Bro., Mtl., Chi.	6	219	17	25	42	151	2	0	0	0	2	....	1936-37	1944-45
Fielder, Guyle	Chi., Det., Bos.	4	9	0	0	0	2	6	0	0	0	2	....	1950-51	1957-58
Filimonov, Dmitri	Ott.	1	30	1	4	5	18	....	....	....	....	....	....	1993-94	1993-94
Fillion, Bob	Mtl.	7	327	42	61	103	84	33	7	4	11	10	2	1943-44	1949-50
• Fillion, Marcel	Bos.	1	1	0	0	0	0	....	....	....	....	....	....	1944-45	1944-45
• Filmore, Tommy	Det., NYA, Bos.	4	117	15	12	27	33	....	....	....	....	....	....	1930-31	1933-34
• Finkbeiner, Lloyd	NYA	1	2	0	0	0	0	....	....	....	....	....	....	1940-41	1940-41
Finley, Jeff	NYI, Phi., Wpg., Phx., NYR, St.L.	15	708	13	70	83	457	52	1	6	7	38	....	1987-88	2003-04
Finn, Steven	Que., T.B., L.A.	12	725	34	78	112	1724	23	0	4	4	39	....	1985-86	1996-97
Finney, Sid	Chi.	3	59	10	7	17	4	7	0	2	2	0	....	1951-52	1953-54
• Finnigan, Ed	St.L., Bos.	2	15	1	1	2	2	....	....	....	....	....	....	1934-35	1935-36
• Finnigan, Frank	Ott., Tor., St.L.	14	553	115	88	203	407	38	6	9	15	22	2	1923-24	1936-37
Fiorentino, Peter	NYR	1	1	0	0	0	0	....	....	....	....	....	....	1991-92	1991-92
Fischer, Jiri	Det.	6	305	11	49	60	295	38	4	3	7	55	1	1999-00	2005-06
Fischer, Ron	Buf.	2	18	0	7	7	6	....	....	....	....	....	....	1981-82	1982-83
• Fisher, Alvin	Tor.	1	9	1	0	1	4	....	....	....	....	....	....	1924-25	1924-25
Fisher, Craig	Phi., Wpg., Fla.	4	12	0	0	0	2	....	....	....	....	....	....	1989-90	1996-97
Fisher, Dunc	NYR, Bos., Det.	7	275	45	70	115	104	21	4	4	8	14	....	1947-48	1958-59
• Fisher, Joe	Det.	4	65	8	12	20	13	12	2	1	3	6	1	1939-40	1942-43
Fitchner, Bob	Que.	2	78	12	20	32	59	3	0	0	0	10	....	1979-80	1980-81
Fitzgerald, Rusty	Pit.	2	25	2	2	4	12	5	0	0	0	4	....	1994-95	1995-96
Fitzgerald, Tom	NYI, Fla., Col., Nsh., Chi., Tor., Bos.	17	1097	139	190	329	776	78	7	12	19	90	....	1988-89	2005-06
Fitzpatrick, Ross	Phi.	4	20	5	2	7	0	....	....	....	....	....	....	1982-83	1985-86
Fitzpatrick, Sandy	NYR, Min.	2	22	3	6	9	8	12	0	0	0	0	....	1964-65	1967-68
Flaman, Fern	Bos., Tor.	17	910	34	174	208	1370	63	4	8	12	93	1	1944-45	1960-61
Flatley, Pat	NYI, NYR	14	780	170	340	510	686	70	18	15	33	75	....	1983-84	1996-97
Fleming, Gerry	Mtl.	2	11	0	0	0	42	....	....	....	....	....	....	1993-94	1994-95
Fleming, Reggie	Mtl., Chi., Bos., NYR, Phi., Buf.	12	749	108	132	240	1468	50	3	6	9	106	1	1959-60	1970-71
Flesch, John	Min., Pit., Col.	4	124	18	23	41	117	....	....	....	....	....	....	1974-75	1979-80
Fletcher, Steven	Mtl., Wpg.	2	3	0	0	0	5	1	0	0	0	5	....	1987-88	1988-89
• Flett, Bill	L.A., Phi., Tor., Atl., Edm.	11	689	202	215	417	501	52	7	16	23	42	1	1967-68	1979-80
Fleury, Theoren	Cgy., Col., NYR, Chi.	15	1084	455	633	1088	1840	77	34	45	79	116	1	1988-89	2002-03
Flichel, Todd	Wpg.	3	6	0	1	1	4	....	....	....	....	....	....	1987-88	1989-90
Flockhart, Rob	Van., Min.	5	55	2	5	7	14	1	1	0	1	2	....	1976-77	1980-81
Flockhart, Ron	Phi., Pit., Mtl., St.L., Bos.	9	453	145	183	328	208	19	4	6	10	14	....	1980-81	1988-89
Floyd, Larry	N.J.	2	12	2	3	5	9	....	....	....	....	....	....	1982-83	1983-84
‡ Focht, Dan	Phx., Pit.	3	82	2	6	8	145	1	0	1	1	0	....	2001-02	2003-04
• Fogarty, Bryan	Que., Pit., Mtl.	6	156	22	52	74	119	....	....	....	....	....	....	1989-90	1994-95
• Fogolin, Lee	Det., Chi.	9	427	10	48	58	575	28	0	2	2	30	1	1947-48	1955-56
Fogolin Jr., Lee	Buf., Edm.	13	924	44	195	239	1318	108	5	19	24	173	2	1974-75	1986-87
Folco, Peter	Van.	1	2	0	0	0	0	....	....	....	....	....	....	1973-74	1973-74
Foley, Gerry	Tor., NYR, L.A.	4	142	9	14	23	99	9	0	1	1	2	....	1954-55	1968-69
Foley, Rick	Chi., Phi., Det.	3	67	11	26	37	180	4	0	1	1	4	....	1970-71	1973-74
Foligno, Mike	Det., Buf., Tor., Fla.	15	1018	355	372	727	2049	57	15	17	32	185	....	1979-80	1993-94
Folk, Bill	Det.	2	12	0	0	0	4	....	....	....	....	....	....	1951-52	1952-53
Fontaine, Len	Det.	2	46	8	11	19	10	....	....	....	....	....	....	1972-73	1973-74
Fontas, Jon	Min.	2	2	0	0	0	0	....	....	....	....	....	....	1979-80	1980-81
Fonteyne, Val	Det., NYR, Pit.	13	820	75	154	229	26	59	3	10	13	8	....	1959-60	1971-72
Fontinato, Lou	NYR, Mtl.	9	535	26	78	104	1247	21	0	2	2	42	....	1954-55	1962-63
Forbes, Dave	Bos., Wsh.	6	363	64	64	128	341	45	1	4	5	13	....	1973-74	1978-79
Forbes, Mike	Bos., Edm.	3	50	1	11	12	41	....	....	....	....	....	....	1977-78	1981-82
Forey, Connie	St.L.	1	4	0	0	0	2	....	....	....	....	....	....	1973-74	1973-74
• Forsey, Jack	Tor.	1	19	7	9	16	10	3	0	1	1	0	....	1942-43	1942-43
• Forslund, Gus	Ott.	1	48	4	9	13	2	....	....	....	....	....	....	1932-33	1932-33
Forslund, Tomas	Cgy.	2	44	5	11	16	12	....	....	....	....	....	....	1991-92	1992-93
Forsyth, Alex	Wsh.	1	1	0	0	0	0	....	....	....	....	....	....	1976-77	1976-77
Fortier, Dave	Tor., NYI, Van.	4	205	8	21	29	335	20	0	2	2	33	....	1972-73	1976-77
Fortier, Marc	Que., Ott., L.A.	6	212	42	60	102	135	....	....	....	....	....	....	1987-88	1992-93
‡ Fortin, Jean-Francois	Wsh.	3	71	1	4	5	42	....	....	....	....	....	....	2001-02	2003-04
Fortin, Ray	St.L.	3	92	2	6	8	33	6	0	0	0	8	....	1967-68	1969-70
Foster, Corey	N.J., Phi., Pit., NYI	4	45	5	6	11	24	3	0	0	0	4	....	1988-89	1996-97
Foster, Dwight	Bos., Col., N.J., Det.	10	541	111	163	274	420	35	5	12	17	4	....	1977-78	1986-87
• Foster, Herb	NYR	2	6	1	0	1	5	....	....	....	....	....	....	1940-41	1947-48
• Foster, Yip	NYR, Bos., Det.	4	83	3	2	5	32	....	....	....	....	....	....	1929-30	1934-35
Fotiu, Nick	NYR, Hfd., Cgy., Phi., Edm.	13	646	60	77	137	1362	38	0	4	4	67	....	1976-77	1988-89
• Fowler, Jimmy	Tor.	3	135	18	29	47	39	18	0	3	3	2	....	1936-37	1938-39
Fowler, Tom	Chi.	1	24	0	1	1	18	....	....	....	....	....	....	1946-47	1946-47
Fox, Greg	Atl., Chi., Pit.	8	494	14	92	106	637	44	1	9	10	67	....	1977-78	1984-85
Fox, Jim	L.A.	9	578	186	293	479	143	22	4	8	12	0	....	1980-81	1989-90
• Foyston, Frank	Det.	2	64	17	7	24	32	....	....	....	....	....	....	1926-27	1927-28
Frampton, Bob	Mtl.	1	2	0	0	0	0	3	0	0	0	0	....	1949-50	1949-50
Franceschetti, Lou	Wsh., Tor., Buf.	10	459	59	81	140	747	44	3	2	5	111	....	1981-82	1991-92
Francis, Bobby	Det.	1	14	2	0	2	0	....	....	....	....	....	....	1982-83	1982-83
Francis, Ron	Hfd., Pit., Car., Tor.	23	1731	549	1249	1798	979	171	46	97	143	95	2	1981-82	2003-04
• Fraser, Archie	NYR	1	3	0	1	1	0	....	....	....	....	....	....	1943-44	1943-44
• Fraser, Charles	Ham.	1	1	0	0	0	0	....	....	....	....	....	....	1923-24	1923-24
Fraser, Curt	Van., Chi., Min.	12	704	193	240	433	1306	65	15	18	33	198	....	1978-79	1989-90
• Fraser, Gord	Chi., Det., Mtl., Pit., Phi.	5	144	24	12	36	224	2	1	0	1	6	....	1926-27	1930-31
• Fraser, Harvey	Chi.	1	21	5	4	9	0	....	....	....	....	....	....	1944-45	1944-45
Fraser, Iain	NYI, Que., Dal., Edm., Wpg., S.J.	5	94	23	23	46	31	4	0	0	0	0	....	1992-93	1996-97
Fraser, Scott	Mtl., Edm., NYR	3	72	16	15	31	24	11	1	1	2	0	....	1995-96	1998-99
Frawley, Dan	Chi., Pit.	6	273	37	40	77	674	1	0	0	0	0	....	1983-84	1988-89
Freadrich, Kyle	T.B.	2	23	0	1	1	75	....	....	....	....	....	....	1999-00	2000-01
• Fredrickson, Frank	Det., Bos., Pit.	5	161	39	34	73	206	10	2	3	5	24	....	1926-27	1930-31
Freer, Mark	Phi., Ott., Cgy.	7	124	16	23	39	61	....	....	....	....	....	....	1986-87	1993-94
• Frew, Irv	Mtl.M., St.L., Mtl.	3	96	2	5	7	146	4	0	0	0	6	....	1933-34	1935-36
Friday, Tim	Det.	1	23	0	3	3	6	....	....	....	....	....	....	1985-86	1985-86
Fridgen, Dan	Hfd.	2	13	2	3	5	2	....	....	....	....	....	....	1981-82	1982-83
Friedman, Doug	Edm., Nsh.	2	18	0	1	1	34	....	....	....	....	....	....	1997-98	1998-99
Friest, Ron	Min.	3	64	7	7	14	191	6	1	0	1	7	....	1980-81	1982-83
Frig, Len	Chi., Cal., Cle., St.L.	7	311	13	51	64	479	14	2	1	3	0	....	1972-73	1979-80
Frost, Harry	Bos.	1	4	0	0	0	0	1	0	0	0	0	1	1938-39	1938-39
Frycer, Miroslav	Que., Tor., Det., Edm.	8	415	147	183	330	486	17	3	8	11	16	....	1981-82	1988-89
Fryday, Bob	Mtl.	2	5	1	0	1	0	....	....	....	....	....	....	1949-50	1951-52
Ftorek, Robbie	Det., Que., NYR	8	334	77	150	227	262	19	9	6	15	28	....	1972-73	1984-85
Fullan, Larry	Wsh.	1	4	1	0	1	0	....	....	....	....	....	....	1974-75	1974-75
Fusco, Mark	Hfd.	2	80	3	12	15	42	....	....	....	....	....	....	1983-84	1984-85

G

Name	NHL Teams	NHL Seasons	Regular Schedule GP	G	A	TP	PIM	Playoffs GP	G	A	TP	PIM	NHL Cup Wins	First NHL Season	Last NHL Season
Gadsby, Bill	Chi., NYR, Det.	20	1248	130	438	568	1539	67	4	23	27	92	....	1946-47	1965-66
Gaetz, Link	Min., S.J.	3	65	6	8	14	412	....	....	....	....	....	....	1988-89	1991-92
Gage, Jody	Det., Buf.	6	68	14	15	29	26	....	....	....	....	....	....	1980-81	1991-92
• Gagne, Art	Mtl., Bos., Ott., Det.	6	228	67	33	100	257	11	2	1	3	20	....	1926-27	1931-32
Gagne, Paul	Col., N.J., Tor., NYI	8	390	110	101	211	127	....	....	....	....	....	....	1980-81	1989-90
Gagne, Pierre	Bos.	1	2	0	0	0	0	....	....	....	....	....	....	1959-60	1959-60
Gagner, Dave	NYR, Min., Dal., Tor., Cgy., Fla., Van.	15	946	318	401	719	1018	57	22	26	48	64	....	1984-85	1998-99
Gagnon, Germain	Mtl., NYI, Chi., K.C.	5	259	40	101	141	72	19	2	3	5	2	....	1971-72	1975-76
• Gagnon, Johnny	Mtl., Bos., NYA	10	454	120	141	261	295	32	12	12	24	37	1	1930-31	1939-40
Gagnon, Sean	Phx., Ott.	3	12	0	1	1	34	....	....	....	....	....	....	1997-98	2000-01
Gainey, Bob	Mtl.	16	1160	239	262	501	585	182	25	48	73	151	5	1973-74	1988-89
Gainey, Steve	Dal., Phx.	4	33	0	2	2	34	....	....	....	....	....	....	2000-01	2005-06
• Gainor, Dutch	Bos., NYR, Ott., Mtl.M.	7	246	51	56	107	129	22	2	1	3	14	2	1927-28	1934-35
‡ Galanov, Maxim	NYR, Pit., Atl., T.B.	4	122	8	12	20	44	1	0	0	0	0	....	1997-98	2000-01
Galarneau, Michel	Hfd.	3	78	7	10	17	34	....	....	....	....	....	....	1980-81	1982-83
• Galbraith, Percy	Bos., Ott.	8	347	29	31	60	224	31	4	7	11	24	1	1926-27	1933-34
• Gallagher, John	Mtl.M., Det., NYA	7	205	14	19	33	153	24	2	3	5	27	1	1930-31	1938-39
Gallant, Gerard	Det., T.B.	11	615	211	269	480	1674	58	18	21	39	178	....	1984-85	1994-95
Galley, Garry	L.A., Wsh., Bos., Phi., Buf., NYI	17	1149	125	475	600	1218	89	7	23	30	119	....	1984-85	2000-01
Gallimore, Jamie	Min.	1	2	0	0	0	0	....	....	....	....	....	....	1977-78	1977-78

Name	NHL Teams	NHL Seasons	Regular Schedule GP	G	A	TP	PIM	Playoffs GP	G	A	TP	PIM	NHL Cup Wins	First NHL Season	Last NHL Season
• Gallinger, Don	Bos.	5	222	65	88	153	89	23	5	5	10	19	....	1942-43	1947-48
Gamble, Dick	Mtl., Chi., Tor.	8	195	41	41	82	66	14	1	2	3	4	1	1950-51	1966-67
Gambucci, Gary	Min.	2	51	2	7	9	9	....	....	....	....	....	....	1971-72	1973-74
Ganchar, Perry	St.L., Mtl., Pit.	4	42	3	7	10	36	7	3	1	4	0	....	1983-84	1988-89
Gans, Dave	L.A.	2	6	0	0	0	2	....	....	....	....	....	....	1982-83	1985-86
Gardiner, Bruce	Ott., T.B., CBJ, N.J.	6	312	34	54	88	263	21	1	4	5	8	....	1996-97	2001-02
• Gardiner, Herb	Mtl., Chi.	3	108	10	9	19	52	9	0	1	1	16	....	1926-27	1928-29
Gardner, Bill	Chi., Hfd.	9	380	73	115	188	68	45	3	8	11	17	....	1980-81	1988-89
• Gardner, Cal	NYR, Tor., Chi., Bos.	12	696	154	238	392	517	61	7	10	17	20	2	1945-46	1956-57
Gardner, Dave	Mtl., St.L., Cal., Cle., Phi.	7	350	75	115	190	41	....	....	....	....	....	....	1972-73	1979-80
Gardner, Paul	Col., Tor., Pit., Wsh., Buf.	10	447	201	201	402	207	16	2	6	8	14	....	1976-77	1985-86
Gare, Danny	Buf., Det., Edm.	13	827	354	331	685	1285	64	25	21	46	195	....	1974-75	1986-87
Gariepy, Ray	Bos., Tor.	2	36	1	6	7	43	....	....	....	....	....	....	1953-54	1955-56
• Garland, Scott	Tor., L.A.	3	91	13	24	37	115	7	1	2	3	35	....	1975-76	1978-79
Garner, Rob	Pit.	1	1	0	0	0	0	....	....	....	....	....	....	1982-83	1982-83
Garpenlov, Johan	Det., S.J., Fla., Atl.	10	609	114	197	311	276	44	10	9	19	22	....	1990-91	1999-00
• Garrett, Red	NYR	1	23	1	1	2	18	....	....	....	....	....	....	1942-43	1942-43
Gartner, Mike	Wsh., Min., NYR, Tor., Phx.	19	1432	708	627	1335	1159	122	43	50	93	125	....	1979-80	1997-98
• Gassoff, Bob	St.L.	4	245	11	47	58	866	9	0	1	1	16	....	1973-74	1976-77
Gassoff, Brad	Van.	4	122	19	17	36	163	3	0	0	0	0	....	1975-76	1978-79
Gatzos, Steve	Pit.	4	89	15	20	35	83	1	0	0	0	0	....	1981-82	1984-85
Gaudreau, Rob	S.J., Ott.	4	231	51	54	105	69	14	2	0	2	0	....	1992-93	1995-96
Gaudreault, Armand	Bos.	1	44	15	9	24	27	7	0	2	2	8	....	1944-45	1944-45
• Gaudreault, Leo	Mtl.	3	67	8	4	12	30	....	....	....	....	....	....	1927-28	1932-33
Gaul, Mike	Col., CBJ	2	3	0	0	0	4	....	....	....	....	....	....	1998-99	2000-01
Gaulin, Jean-Marc	Que.	4	26	4	3	7	8	1	0	0	0	0	....	1982-83	1985-86
Gaume, Dallas	Hfd.	1	4	1	1	2	0	....	....	....	....	....	....	1988-89	1988-89
• Gauthier, Art	Mtl.	1	13	0	0	0	0	1	0	0	0	0	....	1926-27	1926-27
Gauthier, Daniel	Chi.	1	5	0	0	0	0	....	....	....	....	....	....	1994-95	1994-95
• Gauthier, Fern	NYR, Mtl., Det.	6	229	46	50	96	35	22	5	1	6	7	....	1943-44	1948-49
Gauthier, Jean	Mtl., Phi., Bos.	10	166	6	29	35	150	14	1	3	4	22	1	1960-61	1969-70
Gauthier, Luc	Mtl.	1	3	0	0	0	2	....	....	....	....	....	....	1990-91	1990-91
Gauvreau, Jocelyn	Mtl.	1	2	0	0	0	0	....	....	....	....	....	....	1983-84	1983-84
Gavin, Stew	Tor., Hfd., Min.	13	768	130	155	285	584	66	14	20	34	75	....	1980-81	1992-93
Geale, Bob	Pit.	1	1	0	0	0	2	....	....	....	....	....	....	1984-85	1984-85
• Gee, George	Chi., Det.	9	551	135	183	318	345	41	6	13	19	32	1	1945-46	1953-54
Geldart, Gary	Min.	1	4	0	0	0	5	....	....	....	....	....	....	1970-71	1970-71
Gendron, Jean-Guy	NYR, Bos., Mtl., Phi.	14	863	182	201	383	701	42	7	4	11	47	....	1955-56	1971-72
Gendron, Martin	Wsh., Chi.	3	30	4	2	6	10	....	....	....	....	....	....	1994-95	1997-98
• Geoffrion, Bernie	Mtl., NYR	16	883	393	429	822	689	132	58	60	118	88	6	1950-51	1967-68
Geoffrion, Danny	Mtl., Wpg.	3	111	20	32	52	99	2	0	0	0	7	....	1979-80	1981-82
• Geran, Gerry	Mtl.W., Bos.	2	37	5	1	6	6	....	....	....	....	....	....	1917-18	1925-26
• Gerard, Eddie	Ott.	6	128	50	48	98	108	11	4	0	4	17	3	1917-18	1922-23
Germain, Eric	L.A.	1	4	0	1	1	13	1	0	0	0	4	....	1987-88	1987-88
Gernander, Ken	NYR	3	12	2	3	5	6	15	0	0	0	0	....	1995-96	2003-04
Getliffe, Ray	Bos., Mtl.	10	393	136	137	273	250	45	9	10	19	30	2	1935-36	1944-45
Giallonardo, Mario	Col.	2	23	0	3	3	6	....	....	....	....	....	....	1979-80	1980-81
Gibbs, Barry	Bos., Min., Atl., St.L., L.A.	13	797	58	224	282	945	36	4	2	6	67	....	1967-68	1979-80
Gibson, Don	Van.	1	14	0	3	3	20	....	....	....	....	....	....	1990-91	1990-91
Gibson, Doug	Bos., Wsh.	3	63	9	19	28	0	1	0	0	0	0	....	1973-74	1977-78
Gibson, John	L.A., Tor., Wpg.	3	48	0	2	2	120	....	....	....	....	....	....	1980-81	1983-84
• Giesebrecht, Gus	Det.	4	135	27	51	78	13	17	2	3	5	0	....	1938-39	1941-42
Giffin, Lee	Pit.	2	27	1	3	4	9	....	....	....	....	....	....	1986-87	1987-88
Gilbert, Ed	K.C., Pit.	3	166	21	31	52	22	....	....	....	....	....	....	1974-75	1976-77
Gilbert, Greg	NYI, Chi., NYR, St.L.	15	837	150	228	378	576	133	17	33	50	162	3	1981-82	1995-96
Gilbert, Jeannot	Bos.	2	9	0	1	1	4	....	....	....	....	....	....	1962-63	1964-65
Gilbert, Rod	NYR	18	1065	406	615	1021	508	79	34	33	67	43	....	1960-61	1977-78
Gilbertson, Stan	Cal., St.L., Wsh., Pit.	6	428	85	89	174	148	3	1	1	2	2	....	1971-72	1976-77
Gilchrist, Brent	Mtl., Edm., Min., Dal., Det., Nsh.	15	792	135	170	305	400	90	17	14	31	48	1	1988-89	2002-03
Giles, Curt	Min., NYR, St.L.	14	895	43	199	242	733	103	6	16	22	118	....	1979-80	1992-93
Gilhen, Randy	Hfd., Wpg., Pit., L.A., NYR, T.B., Fla.	11	457	55	60	115	314	33	3	2	5	26	1	1982-83	1995-96
Gill, Todd	Tor., S.J., St.L., Det., Phx., Col., Chi.	19	1007	82	272	354	1214	103	7	30	37	193	....	1984-85	2002-03
Gillen, Don	Phi., Hfd.	2	35	2	4	6	22	....	....	....	....	....	....	1979-80	1981-82
• Gillie, Farrand	Det.	1	1	0	0	0	0	....	....	....	....	....	....	1928-29	1928-29
Gillies, Clark	NYI, Buf.	14	958	319	378	697	1023	164	47	47	94	287	4	1974-75	1987-88
Gillis, Jere	Van., NYR, Que., Buf., Phi.	9	386	78	95	173	230	19	4	7	11	9	....	1977-78	1986-87
Gillis, Mike	Col., Bos.	6	246	33	43	76	186	27	2	5	7	10	....	1978-79	1983-84
Gillis, Paul	Que., Chi., Hfd.	11	624	88	154	242	1498	42	3	14	17	156	....	1982-83	1992-93
Gilmour, Doug	St.L., Cgy., Tor., N.J., Chi., Buf., Mtl.	20	1474	450	964	1414	1301	182	60	128	188	235	1	1983-84	2002-03
Gingras, Gaston	Mtl., Tor., St.L.	10	476	61	174	235	161	52	6	18	24	20	1	1979-80	1988-89
Girard, Bob	Cal., Cle., Wsh.	5	305	45	69	114	140	....	....	....	....	....	....	1975-76	1979-80
Girard, Jonathan	Bos.	5	150	10	34	44	46	3	0	1	1	2	....	1998-99	2002-03
Girard, Kenny	Tor.	3	7	0	1	1	2	....	....	....	....	....	....	1956-57	1959-60
• Giroux, Art	Mtl., Bos., Det.	3	54	6	4	10	14	2	0	0	0	0	....	1932-33	1935-36
Giroux, Larry	St.L., K.C., Det., Hfd.	7	274	15	74	89	333	5	0	0	0	4	....	1973-74	1979-80
Giroux, Pierre	L.A.	1	6	1	0	1	17	....	....	....	....	....	....	1982-83	1982-83
Gladney, Bob	L.A., Pit.	2	14	1	5	6	4	....	....	....	....	....	....	1982-83	1983-84
Gladu, Jean-Paul	Bos.	1	40	6	14	20	2	7	2	2	4	0	....	1944-45	1944-45
Glennie, Brian	Tor., L.A.	10	572	14	100	114	621	32	0	1	1	66	....	1969-70	1978-79
Glennon, Matt	Bos.	1	3	0	0	0	2	....	....	....	....	....	....	1991-92	1991-92
Gloeckner, Lorry	Det.	1	13	0	2	2	6	....	....	....	....	....	....	1978-79	1978-79
Gloor, Dan	Van.	1	2	0	0	0	0	....	....	....	....	....	....	1973-74	1973-74
• Glover, Fred	Det., Chi.	5	92	13	11	24	62	8	0	0	0	0	1	1948-49	1952-53
Glover, Howie	Chi., Det., NYR, Mtl.	5	144	29	17	46	101	11	1	2	3	2	....	1958-59	1968-69
Glynn, Brian	Cgy., Min., Edm., Ott., Van., Hfd.	10	431	25	79	104	410	57	6	10	16	40	....	1987-88	1996-97
‡ Goc, Sascha	N.J., T.B.	2	22	0	0	0	4	....	....	....	....	....	....	2000-01	2001-02
Godden, Ernie	Tor.	1	5	1	1	2	6	....	....	....	....	....	....	1981-82	1981-82
• Godfrey, Warren	Bos., Det.	16	786	32	125	157	752	52	1	4	5	42	....	1952-53	1967-68
Godin, Eddy	Wsh.	2	27	3	6	9	12	....	....	....	....	....	....	1977-78	1978-79
• Godin, Sam	Ott., Mtl.	3	83	4	3	7	36	....	....	....	....	....	....	1927-28	1933-34
Godynyuk, Alexander	Tor., Cgy., Fla., Hfd.	7	223	10	39	49	224	....	....	....	....	....	....	1990-91	1996-97
Goegan, Pete	Det., NYR, Min.	11	383	19	67	86	365	33	1	3	4	61	....	1957-58	1967-68
Goertz, Dave	Pit.	1	2	0	0	0	2	....	....	....	....	....	....	1987-88	1987-88
• Goldham, Bob	Tor., Chi., Det.	12	650	28	143	171	400	66	3	14	17	53	5	1941-42	1955-56
‡ Goldmann, Erich	Ott.	1	1	0	0	0	0	....	....	....	....	....	....	1999-00	1999-00
• Goldsworthy, Bill	Bos., Min., NYR	14	771	283	258	541	793	40	18	19	37	30	....	1964-65	1977-78
• Goldsworthy, Leroy	NYR, Det., Chi., Mtl., Bos., NYA	10	336	66	57	123	79	24	1	0	1	4	1	1928-29	1938-39
Goldup, Glenn	Mtl., L.A.	9	291	52	67	119	303	16	4	3	7	22	....	1973-74	1981-82
Goldup, Hank	Tor., NYR	6	202	63	80	143	97	26	5	1	6	6	1	1939-40	1945-46
Golubovsky, Yan	Det., Fla.	4	56	1	7	8	32	....	....	....	....	....	....	1997-98	2000-01
Goneau, Daniel	NYR	3	53	12	3	15	14	....	....	....	....	....	....	1996-97	1999-00
• Gooden, Bill	NYR	2	53	9	11	20	15	....	....	....	....	....	....	1942-43	1943-44
Goodenough, Larry	Phi., Van.	6	242	22	77	99	179	22	3	15	18	10	1	1974-75	1979-80
• Goodfellow, Ebbie	Det.	14	557	134	190	324	511	45	8	8	16	65	3	1929-30	1942-43
Gordiouk, Viktor	Buf.	2	26	3	8	11	0	....	....	....	....	....	....	1992-93	1994-95
• Gordon, Fred	Det., Bos.	2	81	8	7	15	68	2	0	0	0	0	....	1926-27	1927-28
Gordon, Jack	NYR	3	36	3	10	13	0	9	1	1	2	7	....	1948-49	1950-51
Gordon, Robb	Van.	1	4	0	0	0	2	....	....	....	....	....	....	1998-99	1998-99
Gorence, Tom	Phi., Edm.	6	303	58	53	111	89	37	9	6	15	47	....	1978-79	1983-84
Goring, Butch	L.A., NYI, Bos.	16	1107	375	513	888	102	134	38	50	88	32	4	1969-70	1984-85
Gorman, Dave	Atl.	1	3	0	0	0	0	....	....	....	....	....	....	1979-80	1979-80
• Gorman, Ed	Ott., Tor.	4	111	14	6	20	108	8	0	0	0	2	1	1924-25	1927-28
Gosselin, Benoit	NYR	1	7	0	0	0	33	....	....	....	....	....	....	1977-78	1977-78
‡ Gosselin, David	Nsh.	2	13	2	1	3	11	....	....	....	....	....	....	1999-00	2001-02
Gosselin, Guy	Wpg.	1	5	0	0	0	6	....	....	....	....	....	....	1987-88	1987-88
Gotaas, Steve	Pit., Min.	3	49	6	9	15	53	3	0	1	1	5	....	1987-88	1990-91
• Gottselig, Johnny	Chi.	16	589	176	195	371	203	43	13	13	26	18	2	1928-29	1944-45
Gould, Bobby	Atl., Cgy., Wsh., Bos.	11	697	145	159	304	572	78	15	13	28	58	....	1979-80	1989-90
Gould, John	Buf., Van., Atl.	9	504	131	138	269	113	14	3	2	5	4	....	1971-72	1979-80
Gould, Larry	Van.	1	2	0	0	0	0	....	....	....	....	....	....	1973-74	1973-74
Goulet, Michel	Que., Chi.	15	1089	548	604	1152	825	92	39	39	78	110	....	1979-80	1993-94
• Goupille, Red	Mtl.	8	222	12	28	40	256	8	2	0	2	6	....	1935-36	1942-43
Govedaris, Chris	Hfd., Tor.	4	45	4	6	10	24	4	0	0	0	2	....	1989-90	1993-94
Goyer, Gerry	Chi.	1	40	1	2	3	4	3	0	0	0	2	....	1967-68	1967-68
Goyette, Phil	Mtl., NYR, St.L., Buf.	16	941	207	467	674	131	94	17	29	46	26	4	1956-57	1971-72

Paul Gardner

Gerry Geran

Kenny Girard

Fred Glover

Bobby Gould

Ted Green

Francois Guay

Al Hangsleben

Name	NHL Teams	NHL Seasons	Regular Schedule GP	G	A	TP	PIM	Playoffs GP	G	A	TP	PIM	NHL Cup Wins	First NHL Season	Last NHL Season
● Graboski, Tony	Mtl.	3	66	6	10	16	24	3	0	0	0	6	....	1940-41	1942-43
● Gracie, Bob	Tor., Bos., NYA, Mtl.M., Mtl., Chi.	9	379	82	109	191	205	33	4	7	11	4	2	1930-31	1938-39
Gradin, Thomas	Van., Bos.	9	677	209	384	593	298	42	17	25	42	20	....	1978-79	1986-87
Graham, Dirk	Min., Chi.	12	772	219	270	489	917	90	17	27	44	92	....	1983-84	1994-95
● Graham, Leth	Ott., Ham.	6	27	3	0	3	0	1	0	0	0	0	1	1920-21	1925-26
Graham, Pat	Pit., Tor.	3	103	11	17	28	136	4	0	0	0	2	....	1981-82	1983-84
Graham, Rod	Bos.	1	14	2	1	3	7	....	....	....	....	....	....	1974-75	1974-75
● Graham, Ted	Chi., Mtl.M., Det., St.L., Bos., NYA	9	346	14	25	39	300	24	3	1	4	30	....	1927-28	1936-37
Granato, Tony	NYR, L.A., S.J.	14	773	248	244	492	1425	79	16	27	43	141	....	1988-89	2000-01
Grant, Danny	Mtl., Min., Det., L.A.	13	736	263	273	536	239	43	10	14	24	19	1	1965-66	1978-79
‡ Gratton, Benoit	Wsh., Cgy., Mtl.	6	58	6	10	16	58	....	....	....	....	....	....	1997-98	2003-04
Gratton, Dan	L.A.	1	7	1	0	1	5	....	....	....	....	....	....	1987-88	1987-88
Gratton, Norm	NYR, Atl., Buf., Min.	5	201	39	44	83	64	6	0	1	1	2	....	1971-72	1975-76
Gravelle, Leo	Mtl., Det.	5	223	44	34	78	42	17	4	1	5	2	....	1946-47	1950-51
Graves, Adam	Det., Edm., NYR, S.J.	16	1152	329	287	616	1224	125	38	27	65	119	2	1987-88	2002-03
Graves, Hilliard	Cal., Atl., Van., Wpg.	9	556	118	163	281	209	2	0	0	0	0	....	1970-71	1979-80
Graves, Steve	Edm.	3	35	5	4	9	10	....	....	....	....	....	....	1983-84	1987-88
● Gray, Alex	NYR, Tor.	2	50	7	0	7	32	13	1	0	1	0	1	1927-28	1928-29
Gray, Terry	Bos., Mtl., L.A., St.L.	6	147	26	28	54	64	35	5	5	10	22	....	1961-62	1970-71
● Green, Red	Ham., NYA, Bos., Det.	6	195	59	26	85	290	1	0	0	0	0	1	1923-24	1928-29
Green, Rick	Wsh., Mtl., Det., NYI	15	845	43	220	263	588	100	3	16	19	73	1	1976-77	1991-92
● Green, Shorty	Ham., NYA	4	103	33	20	53	151	....	....	....	....	....	....	1923-24	1926-27
Green, Ted	Bos.	11	620	48	206	254	1029	31	4	8	12	54	1	1960-61	1971-72
Greenlaw, Jeff	Wsh., Fla.	6	57	3	6	9	108	2	0	0	0	21	....	1986-87	1993-94
Gregg, Randy	Edm., Van.	10	474	41	152	193	333	137	13	38	51	127	5	1981-82	1991-92
Greig, Bruce	Cal.	2	9	0	1	1	46	....	....	....	....	....	....	1973-74	1974-75
‡ Greig, Mark	Hfd., Tor., Cgy., Phi.	9	125	13	27	40	90	5	0	1	1	0	....	1990-91	2002-03
Grenier, Lucien	Mtl., L.A.	4	151	14	14	28	18	2	0	0	0	0	1	1968-69	1971-72
Grenier, Richard	NYI	1	10	1	1	2	2	....	....	....	....	....	....	1972-73	1972-73
Greschner, Ron	NYR	16	982	179	431	610	1226	84	17	32	49	106	....	1974-75	1989-90
Gretzky, Brent	T.B.	2	13	1	3	4	2	....	....	....	....	....	....	1993-94	1994-95
Gretzky, Wayne	Edm., L.A., St.L., NYR	20	1487	894	1963	2857	577	208	122	260	382	66	4	1979-80	1998-99
Grieve, Brent	NYI, Edm., Chi., L.A.	4	97	20	16	36	87	....	....	....	....	....	....	1993-94	1996-97
Grigor, George	Chi.	1	2	1	0	1	0	1	0	0	0	0	....	1943-44	1943-44
Grimson, Stu	Cgy., Chi., Ana., Det., Hfd., Car., L.A., Nsh.	14	729	17	22	39	2113	42	1	1	2	120	....	1988-89	2001-02
Grisdale, John	Tor., Van.	6	250	4	39	43	346	10	0	1	1	15	....	1972-73	1978-79
‡ Groleau, Francois	Mtl.	3	8	0	1	1	6	....	....	....	....	....	....	1995-96	1997-98
‡ Gron, Stanislav	N.J.	1	1	0	0	0	0	....	....	....	....	....	....	2000-01	2000-01
Gronman, Tuomas	Chi., Pit.	2	38	1	3	4	38	1	0	0	0	0	....	1996-97	1997-98
● Gronsdahl, Lloyd	Bos.	1	10	1	2	3	0	....	....	....	....	....	....	1941-42	1941-42
Gronstrand, Jari	Min., NYR, Que., NYI	5	185	8	26	34	135	3	0	0	0	4	....	1986-87	1990-91
‡ Grosek, Michal	Wpg., Buf., Chi., NYR, Bos.	11	526	84	137	221	509	45	9	11	20	77	....	1993-94	2003-04
● Gross, Lloyd	Tor., NYA, Bos., Det.	3	62	11	5	16	20	1	0	0	0	0	....	1926-27	1934-35
● Grosso, Don	Det., Chi., Bos.	9	336	87	117	204	90	48	15	14	29	63	1	1938-39	1946-47
Grosvenor, Len	Ott., NYA, Mtl.	6	149	9	11	20	78	4	0	0	0	2	....	1927-28	1932-33
Groulx, Wayne	Que.	1	1	0	0	0	0	....	....	....	....	....	....	1984-85	1984-85
Gruden, John	Bos., Ott., Wsh.	6	92	1	8	9	46	3	0	1	1	0	....	1993-94	2003-04
Gruen, Danny	Det., Col.	3	49	9	13	22	19	....	....	....	....	....	....	1972-73	1976-77
Gruhl, Scott	L.A., Pit.	3	20	3	3	6	6	....	....	....	....	....	....	1981-82	1987-88
Gryp, Bob	Bos., Wsh.	3	74	11	13	24	33	....	....	....	....	....	....	1973-74	1975-76
Guay, Francois	Buf.	1	1	0	0	0	0	....	....	....	....	....	....	1989-90	1989-90
Guay, Paul	Phi., L.A., Bos., NYI	7	117	11	23	34	92	9	0	1	1	12	....	1983-84	1990-91
Guerard, Daniel	Ott.	1	2	0	0	0	0	....	....	....	....	....	....	1994-95	1994-95
Guerard, Stephane	Que.	2	34	0	0	0	40	....	....	....	....	....	....	1987-88	1989-90
Guevremont, Jocelyn	Van., Buf., NYR	9	571	84	223	307	319	40	4	17	21	18	....	1971-72	1979-80
Guidolin, Aldo	NYR	4	182	9	15	24	117	....	....	....	....	....	....	1952-53	1955-56
Guidolin, Bep	Bos., Det., Chi.	9	519	107	171	278	606	24	5	7	12	35	....	1942-43	1951-52
Guindon, Bobby	Wpg.	1	6	0	1	1	0	....	....	....	....	....	....	1979-80	1979-80
‡ Guolla, Steve	S.J., T.B., Atl., N.J.	6	205	40	46	86	60	....	....	....	....	....	....	1996-97	2002-03
‡ Guren, Miloslav	Mtl.	2	36	1	3	4	16	....	....	....	....	....	....	1998-99	1999-00
Gusarov, Alexei	Que., Col., NYR, St.L.	11	607	39	128	167	313	68	0	14	14	38	1	1990-91	2000-01
Gusev, Sergey	Dal., T.B.	4	89	4	10	14	34	....	....	....	....	....	....	1997-98	2000-01
‡ Gusmanov, Ravil	Wpg.	1	4	0	0	0	0	....	....	....	....	....	....	1995-96	1995-96
Gustafsson, Bengt-Ake	Wsh.	9	629	196	359	555	196	32	9	19	28	16	....	1979-80	1988-89
‡ Gustafsson, Per	Fla., Tor., Ott.	2	89	8	27	35	38	1	0	0	0	0	....	1996-97	1997-98
Gustavsson, Peter	Col.	1	2	0	0	0	0	....	....	....	....	....	....	1981-82	1981-82
Guy, Kevan	Cgy., Van.	6	156	5	20	25	138	5	0	1	1	23	....	1986-87	1991-92

H

Name	NHL Teams	NHL Seasons	Regular Schedule GP	G	A	TP	PIM	Playoffs GP	G	A	TP	PIM	NHL Cup Wins	First NHL Season	Last NHL Season
‡ Haakana, Kari	Edm.	1	13	0	0	0	4	....	....	....	....	....	....	2002-03	2002-03
Haanpaa, Ari	NYI	3	60	6	11	17	37	6	0	0	0	10	....	1985-86	1987-88
Haas, David	Edm., Cgy.	2	7	2	1	3	7	....	....	....	....	....	....	1990-91	1993-94
Habscheid, Marc	Edm., Min., Det., Cgy.	11	345	72	91	163	171	12	1	3	4	13	....	1981-82	1991-92
Hachborn, Len	Phi., L.A.	3	102	20	39	59	29	7	0	3	3	7	....	1983-84	1985-86
Haddon, Lloyd	Det.	1	8	0	0	0	2	1	0	0	0	0	....	1959-60	1959-60
Hadfield, Vic	NYR, Pit.	16	1002	323	389	712	1154	73	27	21	48	117	....	1961-62	1976-77
● Haggarty, Jim	Mtl.	1	5	1	1	2	0	3	2	1	3	0	....	1941-42	1941-42
Haggerty, Sean	Tor., NYI, Nsh.	4	14	1	2	3	4	....	....	....	....	....	....	1995-96	2000-01
● Hagglund, Roger	Que.	1	3	0	0	0	0	....	....	....	....	....	....	1984-85	1984-85
Hagman, Matti	Bos., Edm.	4	237	56	89	145	36	20	5	2	7	6	....	1976-77	1981-82
Haidy, Gord	Det.	1	....	....	....	....	....	1	0	0	0	0	1	1949-50	1949-50
Hajdu, Richard	Buf.	2	5	0	0	0	4	....	....	....	....	....	....	1985-86	1986-87
Hajt, Bill	Buf.	14	854	42	202	244	433	80	2	16	18	70	....	1973-74	1986-87
‡ Hajt, Chris	Edm., Wsh.	2	6	0	0	0	2	....	....	....	....	....	....	2000-01	2003-04
Hakansson, Anders	Min., Pit., L.A.	5	330	52	46	98	141	6	0	0	0	2	....	1981-82	1985-86
● Halderson, Harold	Det., Tor.	1	44	3	2	5	65	....	....	....	....	....	....	1926-27	1926-27
Hale, Larry	Phi.	4	196	5	37	42	90	8	0	0	0	12	....	1968-69	1971-72
Haley, Len	Det.	2	30	2	2	4	14	6	1	3	4	6	....	1959-60	1960-61
Halkidis, Bob	Buf., L.A., Tor., Det., T.B., NYI	11	256	8	32	40	825	20	0	1	1	51	....	1984-85	1995-96
Halko, Steven	Car.	6	155	0	15	15	71	4	0	0	0	2	....	1997-98	2002-03
● Hall, Bob	NYA	1	8	0	0	0	0	....	....	....	....	....	....	1925-26	1925-26
Hall, Del	Cal.	3	9	2	0	2	2	....	....	....	....	....	....	1971-72	1973-74
● Hall, Joe	Mtl.	2	38	15	8	23	189	7	0	1	1	38	....	1917-18	1918-19
Hall, Murray	Chi., Det., Min., Van.	9	164	35	48	83	46	6	0	0	0	0	....	1961-62	1971-72
Hall, Taylor	Van., Bos.	5	41	7	9	16	29	....	....	....	....	....	....	1983-84	1987-88
Hall, Wayne	NYR	1	4	0	0	0	0	....	....	....	....	....	....	1960-61	1960-61
Haller, Kevin	Buf., Mtl., Phi., Hfd., Car., Ana., NYI	13	642	41	97	138	907	64	7	16	23	71	1	1989-90	2001-02
● Halliday, Milt	Ott.	3	67	1	0	1	4	6	0	0	0	0	1	1926-27	1928-29
Hallin, Mats	NYI, Min.	5	152	17	14	31	193	15	1	0	1	13	1	1982-83	1986-87
Halverson, Trevor	Wsh.	1	17	0	4	4	28	....	....	....	....	....	....	1998-99	1998-99
Halward, Doug	Bos., L.A., Van., Det., Edm.	14	653	69	224	293	774	47	7	10	17	113	....	1975-76	1988-89
Hamel, Gilles	Buf., Wpg., L.A.	9	519	127	147	274	276	27	4	5	9	10	....	1980-81	1988-89
● Hamel, Herb	Tor.	1	2	0	0	0	4	....	....	....	....	....	....	1930-31	1930-31
Hamel, Jean	St.L., Det., Que., Mtl.	12	699	26	95	121	766	33	0	2	2	44	....	1972-73	1983-84
● Hamill, Red	Bos., Chi.	12	419	128	94	222	160	24	1	2	3	20	1	1937-38	1950-51
Hamilton, Al	NYR, Buf., Edm.	7	257	10	78	88	258	7	0	0	0	2	....	1965-66	1979-80
Hamilton, Chuck	Mtl., St.L.	2	4	0	2	2	2	....	....	....	....	....	....	1961-62	1972-73
● Hamilton, Jack	Tor.	3	102	28	32	60	20	11	2	1	3	0	....	1942-43	1945-46
Hamilton, Jim	Pit.	8	95	14	18	32	28	6	3	0	3	0	....	1977-78	1984-85
● Hamilton, Reg	Tor., Chi.	12	424	21	87	108	412	64	3	8	11	46	2	1935-36	1946-47
Hammarstrom, Inge	Tor., St.L.	6	427	116	123	239	86	13	2	3	5	4	....	1973-74	1978-79
Hammond, Ken	L.A., Edm., NYR, Tor., Bos., S.J., Van., Ott.	8	193	18	29	47	290	15	0	0	0	24	....	1984-85	1992-93
Hampson, Gord	Cgy.	1	4	0	0	0	5	....	....	....	....	....	....	1982-83	1982-83
Hampson, Ted	Tor., NYR, Det., Oak., Cal., Min.	14	676	108	245	353	94	35	7	10	17	2	....	1959-60	1971-72
Hampton, Rick	Cal., Cle., L.A.	6	337	59	113	172	147	2	0	0	0	0	....	1974-75	1979-80
‡ Hamr, Radek	Ott.	2	11	0	0	0	0	....	....	....	....	....	....	1992-93	1993-94
Hamway, Mark	NYI	3	53	5	13	18	9	1	0	0	0	0	....	1984-85	1986-87
Handy, Ron	NYI, St.L.	2	14	0	3	3	0	....	....	....	....	....	....	1984-85	1987-88
Hangsleben, Al	Hfd., Wsh., L.A.	3	185	21	48	69	396	....	....	....	....	....	....	1979-80	1981-82
Hankinson, Ben	N.J., T.B.	3	43	3	3	6	45	2	1	0	1	4	....	1992-93	1994-95
Hankinson, Casey	Chi., Ana.	3	18	0	1	1	13	....	....	....	....	....	....	2000-01	2003-04

Name	NHL Teams	NHL Seasons	Regular Schedule GP	G	A	TP	PIM	Playoffs GP	G	A	TP	PIM	NHL Cup Wins	First NHL Season	Last NHL Season
● Hanna, John	NYR, Mtl., Phi.	5	198	6	26	32	206	....	....	....	....	....	....	1958-59	1967-68
Hannan, Dave	Pit., Edm., Tor., Buf., Col., Ott.	16	841	114	191	305	942	63	6	7	13	46	2	1981-82	1996-97
● Hannigan, Gord	Tor.	4	161	29	31	60	117	9	2	0	2	8	....	1952-53	1955-56
Hannigan, Pat	Tor., NYR, Phi.	5	182	30	39	69	116	11	1	2	3	11	....	1959-60	1968-69
Hannigan, Ray	Tor.	1	3	0	0	0	2	....	....	....	....	....	....	1948-49	1948-49
Hansen, Richie	NYI, St.L.	4	20	2	8	10	4	....	....	....	....	....	....	1976-77	1981-82
Hansen, Tavis	Wpg., Phx.	5	34	2	1	3	16	2	0	0	0	0	....	1994-95	2000-01
Hanson, Dave	Det., Min.	2	33	1	1	2	65	....	....	....	....	....	....	1978-79	1979-80
● Hanson, Emil	Det.	1	7	0	0	0	6	....	....	....	....	....	....	1932-33	1932-33
Hanson, Keith	Cgy.	1	25	0	2	2	77	....	....	....	....	....	....	1983-84	1983-84
● Hanson, Oscar	Chi.	1	8	0	0	0	0	....	....	....	....	....	....	1937-38	1937-38
Harbaruk, Nick	Pit., St.L.	5	364	45	75	120	273	14	3	1	4	20	....	1969-70	1973-74
Harding, Jeff	Phi.	2	15	0	0	0	47	....	....	....	....	....	....	1988-89	1989-90
Hardy, Joe	Oak., Cal.	2	63	9	14	23	51	4	0	0	0	0	....	1969-70	1970-71
Hardy, Mark	L.A., NYR, Min.	15	915	62	306	368	1293	67	5	16	21	158	....	1979-80	1993-94
Hargreaves, Jim	Van.	2	66	1	7	8	105	....	....	....	....	....	....	1970-71	1972-73
‡ Harkins, Brett	Bos., Fla., CBJ	4	78	6	30	36	22	....	....	....	....	....	....	1994-95	2001-02
Harkins, Todd	Cgy., Hfd.	3	48	3	3	6	78	....	....	....	....	....	....	1991-92	1993-94
Harlock, David	Tor., Wsh., NYI, Atl.	8	212	2	14	16	188	....	....	....	....	....	....	1993-94	2001-02
Harlow, Scott	St.L.	1	1	0	1	1	0	....	....	....	....	....	....	1987-88	1987-88
● Harmon, Glen	Mtl.	9	452	50	96	146	334	53	5	10	15	37	2	1942-43	1950-51
● Harms, John	Chi.	2	44	5	5	10	21	4	3	0	3	2	....	1943-44	1944-45
● Harnott, Walter	Bos.	1	6	0	0	0	2	....	....	....	....	....	....	1933-34	1933-34
Harper, Terry	Mtl., L.A., Det., St.L., Col.	19	1066	35	221	256	1362	112	4	13	17	140	5	1962-63	1980-81
Harrer, Tim	Cgy.	1	3	0	0	0	2	....	....	....	....	....	....	1982-83	1982-83
● Harrington, Hago	Bos., Mtl.	3	72	9	3	12	15	4	1	0	1	2	....	1925-26	1932-33
● Harris, Billy	Tor., Det., Oak., Pit.	13	769	126	219	345	205	62	8	10	18	30	3	1955-56	1968-69
Harris, Billy	NYI, L.A., Tor.	12	897	231	327	558	394	71	19	19	38	48	....	1972-73	1983-84
Harris, Duke	Min., Tor.	1	26	1	4	5	4	....	....	....	....	....	....	1967-68	1967-68
● Harris, Henry	Bos.	1	32	2	4	6	20	....	....	....	....	....	....	1930-31	1930-31
Harris, Hugh	Buf.	1	60	12	26	38	17	3	0	0	0	0	....	1972-73	1972-73
Harris, Ron	Det., Oak., Atl., NYR	11	476	20	91	111	474	28	4	3	7	33	....	1962-63	1975-76
● Harris, Smokey	Bos.	1	6	3	1	4	8	....	....	....	....	....	....	1924-25	1924-25
Harris, Ted	Mtl., Min., Det., St.L., Phi.	12	788	30	168	198	1000	100	1	22	23	230	5	1963-64	1974-75
Harrison, Ed	Bos., NYR	4	194	27	24	51	53	9	1	0	1	2	....	1947-48	1950-51
Harrison, Jim	Bos., Tor., Chi., Edm.	8	324	67	86	153	435	13	1	1	2	43	....	1968-69	1979-80
Hart, Gerry	Det., NYI, Que., St.L.	15	730	29	150	179	1240	78	3	12	15	175	....	1968-69	1982-83
● Hart, Gizzy	Det., Mtl.	3	104	6	8	14	12	8	0	1	1	0	....	1926-27	1932-33
Hartman, Mike	Buf., Wpg., T.B., NYR	9	397	43	35	78	1388	21	0	0	0	106	1	1986-87	1994-95
Hartsburg, Craig	Min.	10	570	98	315	413	818	61	15	27	42	70	....	1979-80	1988-89
Harvey, Buster	Min., Atl., K.C., Det.	7	407	90	118	208	131	14	0	2	2	8	....	1970-71	1976-77
● Harvey, Doug	Mtl., NYR, Det., St.L.	20	1113	88	452	540	1216	137	8	64	72	152	6	1947-48	1968-69
Harvey, Hugh	K.C.	2	18	1	1	2	4	....	....	....	....	....	....	1974-75	1975-76
Harvey, Todd	Dal., NYR, S.J., Edm.	11	671	91	132	223	950	68	3	6	9	52	....	1994-95	2005-06
Hassard, Bob	Tor., Chi.	5	126	9	28	37	22	....	....	....	....	....	1	1949-50	1954-55
Hatcher, Kevin	Wsh., Dal., Pit., NYR, Car.	17	1157	227	450	677	1392	118	22	37	59	252	....	1984-85	2000-01
Hatoum, Ed	Det., Van.	3	47	3	6	9	25	....	....	....	....	....	....	1968-69	1970-71
‡ Hauer, Brett	Edm., Nsh.	3	37	4	4	8	38	....	....	....	....	....	....	1995-96	2001-02
Hawerchuk, Dale	Wpg., Buf., St.L., Phi.	16	1188	518	891	1409	730	97	30	69	99	67	....	1981-82	1996-97
Hawgood, Greg	Bos., Edm., Phi., Fla., Pit., S.J., Van., Dal.	12	474	60	164	224	426	42	2	8	10	37	....	1987-88	2001-02
Hawkins, Todd	Van., Tor.	3	10	0	0	0	15	....	....	....	....	....	....	1988-89	1991-92
Haworth, Alan	Buf., Wsh., Que.	8	524	189	211	400	425	42	12	16	28	28	....	1980-81	1987-88
Haworth, Gord	NYR	1	2	0	1	1	0	....	....	....	....	....	....	1952-53	1952-53
Hawryliw, Neil	NYI	1	1	0	0	0	0	....	....	....	....	....	....	1981-82	1981-82
Hay, Bill	Chi.	8	506	113	273	386	244	67	15	21	36	62	1	1959-60	1966-67
‡ Hay, Dwayne	Wsh., Fla., T.B., Cgy.	4	79	2	4	6	22	....	....	....	....	....	....	1997-98	2000-01
● Hay, George	Chi., Det.	7	239	74	60	134	84	8	2	3	5	2	....	1926-27	1933-34
Hay, Jim	Det.	3	75	1	5	6	22	9	1	0	1	2	1	1952-53	1954-55
Hayek, Peter	Min.	1	1	0	0	0	0	....	....	....	....	....	....	1981-82	1981-82
Hayes, Chris	Bos.	1	....	....	....	....	....	1	0	0	0	0	1	1971-72	1971-72
● Haynes, Paul	Mtl.M., Bos., Mtl.	11	391	61	134	195	164	24	2	8	10	13	....	1930-31	1940-41
Hayward, Rick	L.A.	1	4	0	0	0	5	....	....	....	....	....	....	1990-91	1990-91
Hazlett, Steve	Van.	1	1	0	0	0	0	....	....	....	....	....	....	1979-80	1979-80
Head, Galen	Det.	1	1	0	0	0	0	....	....	....	....	....	....	1967-68	1967-68
● Headley, Fern	Bos., Mtl.	1	30	1	3	4	10	1	0	0	0	0	....	1924-25	1924-25
Healey, Rich	Det.	1	1	0	0	0	2	....	....	....	....	....	....	1960-61	1960-61
Heaphy, Shawn	Cgy.	1	1	0	0	0	0	....	....	....	....	....	....	1992-93	1992-93
Heaslip, Mark	NYR, L.A.	3	117	10	19	29	110	5	0	0	0	2	....	1976-77	1978-79
Heath, Randy	NYR	2	13	2	4	6	15	....	....	....	....	....	....	1984-85	1985-86
Hebenton, Andy	NYR, Bos.	9	630	189	202	391	83	22	6	5	11	8	....	1955-56	1963-64
‡ Hecl, Radoslav	Buf.	1	14	0	0	0	2	....	....	....	....	....	....	2002-03	2002-03
Hedberg, Anders	NYR	7	465	172	225	397	144	58	22	24	46	31	....	1978-79	1984-85
‡ Hedin, Pierre	Tor.	1	3	0	1	1	0	....	....	....	....	....	....	2003-04	2003-04
● Heffernan, Frank	Tor.	1	19	0	1	1	10	....	....	....	....	....	....	1919-20	1919-20
● Heffernan, Gerry	Mtl.	3	83	33	35	68	27	11	3	3	6	8	1	1941-42	1943-44
Heidt, Mike	L.A.	1	6	0	1	1	7	....	....	....	....	....	....	1983-84	1983-84
● Heindl, Bill	Min., NYR	3	18	2	1	3	0	....	....	....	....	....	....	1970-71	1972-73
Heinrich, Lionel	Bos.	1	35	1	1	2	33	....	....	....	....	....	....	1955-56	1955-56
‡ Heins, Shawn	S.J., Pit., Atl.	6	125	4	12	16	154	2	0	0	0	0	....	1998-99	2003-04
Heinze, Steve	Bos., CBJ, Buf., L.A.	12	694	178	158	336	379	69	11	15	26	48	....	1991-92	2002-03
Heiskala, Earl	Phi.	3	127	13	11	24	294	....	....	....	....	....	....	1968-69	1970-71
‡ Heisten, Barrett	NYR	1	10	0	0	0	2	....	....	....	....	....	....	2001-02	2001-02
Helander, Peter	L.A.	1	7	0	1	1	0	....	....	....	....	....	....	1982-83	1982-83
‡ Helenius, Sami	Cgy., T.B., Col., Dal., Chi.	6	155	2	4	6	260	1	0	0	0	0	....	1996-97	2002-03
● Heller, Ott	NYR	15	647	55	176	231	465	61	6	8	14	61	2	1931-32	1945-46
Helman, Harry	Ott.	3	44	1	0	1	7	2	0	0	0	0	1	1922-23	1924-25
‡ Helminen, Raimo	NYR, Min., NYI	3	117	13	46	59	16	2	0	0	0	0	....	1985-86	1988-89
‡ Hemingway, Colin	St.L.	1	3	0	0	0	0	....	....	....	....	....	....	2005-06	2005-06
● Hemmerling, Tony	NYA	2	22	3	3	6	4	....	....	....	....	....	....	1935-36	1936-37
Henderson, Archie	Wsh., Min., Hfd.	3	23	3	1	4	92	....	....	....	....	....	....	1980-81	1982-83
‡ Henderson, Jay	Bos.	4	33	1	3	4	37	....	....	....	....	....	....	1998-99	2001-02
Henderson, Matt	Nsh., Chi.	2	6	0	1	1	2	....	....	....	....	....	....	1998-99	2001-02
Henderson, Murray	Bos.	8	405	24	62	86	305	41	2	3	5	23	....	1944-45	1951-52
Henderson, Paul	Det., Tor., Atl.	13	707	236	241	477	304	56	11	14	25	28	....	1962-63	1979-80
Hendrickson, Darby	Tor., NYI, Van., Min., Col.	11	518	65	64	129	370	25	3	3	6	6	....	1993-94	2003-04
Hendrickson, John	Det.	3	5	0	0	0	4	....	....	....	....	....	....	1957-58	1961-62
Henning, Lorne	NYI	9	544	73	111	184	102	81	7	7	14	8	2	1972-73	1980-81
Henry, Burke	Chi.	2	39	2	6	8	33	....	....	....	....	....	....	2002-03	2003-04
● Henry, Camille	NYR, Chi., St.L.	14	727	279	249	528	88	47	6	12	18	7	....	1953-54	1969-70
Henry, Dale	NYI	6	132	13	26	39	263	14	1	0	1	19	....	1984-85	1989-90
‡ Hentunen, Jukka	Cgy., Nsh.	1	38	4	5	9	4	....	....	....	....	....	....	2001-02	2001-02
Hepple, Alan	N.J.	3	3	0	0	0	7	....	....	....	....	....	....	1983-84	1985-86
Herbers, Ian	Edm., T.B., NYI	2	65	0	5	5	79	....	....	....	....	....	....	1993-94	1999-00
● Herberts, Jimmy	Bos., Tor., Det.	6	206	83	31	114	253	9	3	0	3	10	....	1924-25	1929-30
● Herchenratter, Art	Det.	1	10	1	2	3	2	....	....	....	....	....	....	1940-41	1940-41
Hergerts, Fred	NYA	2	20	2	4	6	2	....	....	....	....	....	....	1934-35	1935-36
● Hergesheimer, Phil	Chi., Bos.	4	125	21	41	62	19	6	0	0	0	2	....	1939-40	1942-43
Hergesheimer, Wally	NYR, Chi.	7	351	114	85	199	106	5	1	0	1	0	....	1951-52	1958-59
● Heron, Red	Tor., Bro., Mtl.	4	106	21	19	40	38	21	2	2	4	6	....	1938-39	1941-42
Heroux, Yves	Que.	1	1	0	0	0	0	....	....	....	....	....	....	1986-87	1986-87
‡ Herperger, Chris	Chi., Ott., Atl.	4	169	18	25	43	75	....	....	....	....	....	....	1999-00	2002-03
Herr, Matt	Wsh., Fla., Bos.	4	58	4	5	9	25	....	....	....	....	....	....	1998-99	2002-03
Herter, Jason	NYI	1	1	0	1	1	0	....	....	....	....	....	....	1995-96	1995-96
Hervey, Matt	Wpg., Bos., T.B.	3	35	0	5	5	97	5	0	0	0	6	....	1988-89	1992-93
Hess, Bob	St.L., Buf., Hfd.	8	329	27	95	122	178	4	1	1	2	2	....	1974-75	1983-84
● Heximer, Obs	NYR, Bos., NYA	3	84	13	7	20	16	5	0	0	0	2	....	1929-30	1934-35
● Hextall, Bryan	NYR	11	449	187	175	362	227	37	8	9	17	19	1	1936-37	1947-48
Hextall, Bryan	NYR, Pit., Atl., Det., Min.	8	549	99	161	260	738	18	0	4	4	59	....	1962-63	1975-76
Hextall, Dennis	NYR, L.A., Cal., Min., Det., Wsh.	13	681	153	350	503	1398	22	3	3	6	45	....	1967-68	1979-80
● Heyliger, Vic	Chi.	2	33	2	3	5	2	....	....	....	....	....	....	1937-38	1943-44
● Hicke, Bill	Mtl., NYR, Oak., Cal., Pit.	14	729	168	234	402	395	42	3	10	13	41	2	1958-59	1971-72
Hicke, Ernie	Cal., Atl., NYI, Min., L.A.	8	520	132	140	272	407	2	1	0	1	0	....	1970-71	1977-78
Hickey, Greg	NYR	1	1	0	0	0	0	....	....	....	....	....	....	1977-78	1977-78
Hickey, Pat	NYR, Col., Tor., Que., St.L.	10	646	192	212	404	351	55	5	11	16	37	....	1975-76	1984-85

Richie Hansen

Tony Hemmerling

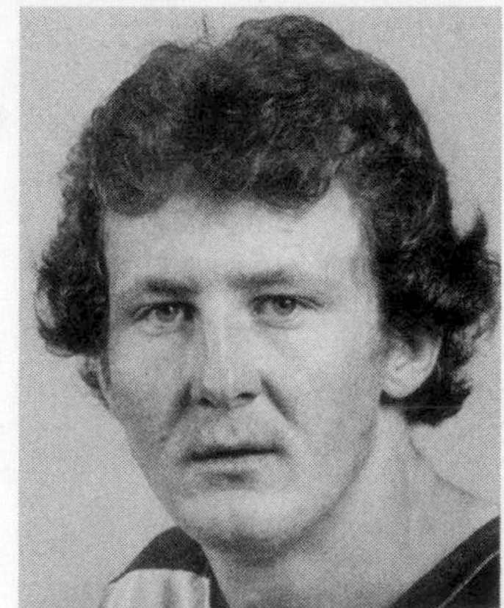
Archie Henderson

Ike Hildebrand

Dutch Hiller

Red Horner

Ed Hospodar

Jim Hrycuik

Name	NHL Teams	NHL Seasons	Regular Schedule GP	G	A	TP	PIM	Playoffs GP	G	A	TP	PIM	NHL Cup Wins	First NHL Season	Last NHL Season
Hicks, Alex	Ana., Pit., S.J., Fla.	5	258	25	54	79	247	15	0	2	2	8	....	1995-96	1999-00
Hicks, Doug	Min., Chi., Edm., Wsh.	9	561	37	131	168	442	18	2	1	3	15	....	1974-75	1982-83
Hicks, Glenn	Det.	2	108	6	12	18	127	....	....	....	....	....	....	1979-80	1980-81
• Hicks, Henry	Mtl.M., Det.	3	96	7	2	9	72	....	....	....	....	....	....	1928-29	1930-31
Hicks, Wayne	Chi., Bos., Mtl., Phi., Pit.	5	115	13	23	36	22	2	0	1	1	2	1	1959-60	1967-68
Hidi, Andre	Wsh.	2	7	2	1	3	9	2	0	0	0	0	....	1983-84	1984-85
Hiemer, Uli	N.J.	3	143	19	54	73	176	....	....	....	....	....	....	1984-85	1986-87
‡ Higgins, Matt	Mtl.	4	57	1	2	3	6	....	....	....	....	....	....	1997-98	2000-01
Higgins, Paul	Tor.	2	25	0	0	0	152	1	0	0	0	0	....	1981-82	1982-83
Higgins, Tim	Chi., N.J., Det.	11	706	154	198	352	719	65	5	8	13	77	....	1978-79	1988-89
• Hildebrand, Ike	NYR, Chi.	2	41	7	11	18	16	....	....	....	....	....	....	1953-54	1954-55
Hill, Al	Phi.	8	221	40	55	95	227	51	8	11	19	43	....	1976-77	1987-88
Hill, Brian	Hfd.	1	19	1	1	2	4	....	....	....	....	....	....	1979-80	1979-80
• Hill, Mel	Bos., Bro., Tor.	9	324	89	109	198	128	43	12	7	19	18	3	1937-38	1945-46
• Hiller, Dutch	NYR, Det., Bos., Mtl.	9	383	91	113	204	163	48	9	8	17	21	2	1937-38	1945-46
Hiller, Jim	L.A., Det., NYR	2	63	8	12	20	116	2	0	0	0	4	....	1992-93	1993-94
Hillier, Randy	Bos., Pit., NYI, Buf.	11	543	16	110	126	906	28	0	2	2	93	1	1981-82	1991-92
Hillman, Floyd	Bos.	1	6	0	0	0	10	....	....	....	....	....	....	1956-57	1956-57
Hillman, Larry	Det., Bos., Tor., Min., Mtl., Phi., L.A., Buf.	19	790	36	196	232	579	74	2	9	11	30	6	1954-55	1972-73
• Hillman, Wayne	Chi., NYR, Min., Phi.	13	691	18	86	104	534	28	0	3	3	19	1	1960-61	1972-73
Hilworth, John	Det.	3	57	1	1	2	89	....	....	....	....	....	....	1977-78	1979-80
• Himes, Normie	NYA	9	402	106	113	219	127	2	0	0	0	0	....	1926-27	1934-35
Hindmarch, Dave	Cgy.	4	99	21	17	38	25	10	0	0	0	6	....	1980-81	1983-84
Hinse, Andre	Tor.	1	4	0	0	0	0	....	....	....	....	....	....	1967-68	1967-68
Hinton, Dan	Chi.	1	14	0	0	0	16	....	....	....	....	....	....	1976-77	1976-77
Hirsch, Tom	Min.	3	31	1	7	8	30	12	0	0	0	6	....	1983-84	1987-88
• Hirschfeld, Bert	Mtl.	2	33	1	4	5	2	5	1	0	1	0	....	1949-50	1950-51
Hislop, Jamie	Que., Cgy.	5	345	75	103	178	86	28	3	2	5	11	....	1979-80	1983-84
• Hitchman, Lionel	Ott., Bos.	12	417	28	34	62	523	35	3	1	4	73	2	1922-23	1933-34
• Hlinka, Ivan	Van.	2	137	42	81	123	28	16	3	10	13	8	....	1981-82	1982-83
Hlushko, Todd	Phi., Cgy., Pit.	6	79	8	13	21	84	3	0	0	0	2	....	1993-94	1998-99
Hocking, Justin	L.A.	1	1	0	0	0	0	....	....	....	....	....	....	1993-94	1993-94
Hodge, Ken	Chi., Bos., NYR	14	881	328	472	800	779	97	34	47	81	120	2	1964-65	1977-78
Hodge Jr., Ken	Min., Bos., T.B.	4	142	39	48	87	32	15	4	6	10	6	....	1988-89	1992-93
Hodgson, Dan	Tor., Van.	4	114	29	45	74	64	....	....	....	....	....	....	1985-86	1988-89
Hodgson, Rick	Hfd.	1	6	0	0	0	6	1	0	0	0	0	....	1979-80	1979-80
Hodgson, Ted	Bos.	1	4	0	0	0	0	....	....	....	....	....	....	1966-67	1966-67
Hoekstra, Cec	Mtl.	1	4	0	0	0	0	....	....	....	....	....	....	1959-60	1959-60
Hoekstra, Ed	Phi.	1	70	15	21	36	6	7	0	1	1	0	....	1967-68	1967-68
Hoene, Phil	L.A.	3	37	2	4	6	22	....	....	....	....	....	....	1972-73	1974-75
Hoffinger, Val	Chi.	2	28	0	1	1	30	....	....	....	....	....	....	1927-28	1928-29
Hoffman, Mike	Hfd.	3	9	1	3	4	2	....	....	....	....	....	....	1982-83	1985-86
Hoffmeyer, Bob	Chi., Phi., N.J.	6	198	14	52	66	325	3	0	1	1	25	....	1977-78	1984-85
Hofford, Jim	Buf., L.A.	3	18	0	0	0	47	....	....	....	....	....	....	1985-86	1988-89
Hogaboam, Bill	Atl., Det., Min.	8	332	80	109	189	100	2	0	0	0	0	....	1972-73	1979-80
Hoganson, Dale	L.A., Mtl., Que.	7	343	13	77	90	186	11	0	3	3	12	....	1969-70	1981-82
‡ Hoglund, Jonas	Cgy., Mtl., Tor.	7	545	117	145	262	112	59	8	11	19	8	....	1996-97	2002-03
Hogue, Benoit	Buf., NYI, Tor., Dal., T.B., Phx., Bos., Wsh.	15	863	222	321	543	877	92	17	16	33	124	1	1987-88	2001-02
Holan, Milos	Phi., Ana.	3	49	5	11	16	42	....	....	....	....	....	....	1993-94	1995-96
Holbrook, Terry	Min.	2	43	3	6	9	4	6	0	0	0	0	....	1972-73	1973-74
‡ Holden, Josh	Van., Car., Tor.	6	60	5	9	14	16	....	....	....	....	....	....	1998-99	2003-04
‡ Holland, Jason	NYI, Buf., L.A.	7	81	4	5	9	36	1	0	0	0	0	....	1996-97	2003-04
Holland, Jerry	NYR	2	37	8	4	12	6	....	....	....	....	....	....	1974-75	1975-76
• Hollett, Flash	Tor., Ott., Bos., Det.	13	562	132	181	313	358	79	8	26	34	38	2	1933-34	1945-46
Hollinger, Terry	St.L.	2	7	0	0	0	2	....	....	....	....	....	....	1993-94	1994-95
• Hollingworth, Gord	Chi., Det.	4	163	4	14	18	201	3	0	0	0	2	....	1954-55	1957-58
Holloway, Bruce	Van.	1	2	0	0	0	0	....	....	....	....	....	....	1984-85	1984-85
• Holmes, Bill	Mtl., NYA	3	52	6	4	10	35	....	....	....	....	....	....	1925-26	1929-30
Holmes, Chuck	Det.	2	23	1	3	4	10	....	....	....	....	....	....	1958-59	1961-62
Holmes, Lou	Chi.	2	59	1	4	5	6	2	0	0	0	2	....	1931-32	1932-33
Holmes, Warren	L.A.	3	45	8	18	26	7	....	....	....	....	....	....	1981-82	1983-84
Holmgren, Paul	Phi., Min.	10	527	144	179	323	1684	82	19	32	51	195	....	1975-76	1984-85
• Holota, John	Det.	2	15	2	0	2	0	....	....	....	....	....	....	1942-43	1945-46
Holst, Greg	NYR	3	11	0	0	0	0	....	....	....	....	....	....	1975-76	1977-78
Holt, Gary	Cal., Cle., St.L.	5	101	13	11	24	133	....	....	....	....	....	....	1973-74	1977-78
Holt, Randy	Chi., Cle., Van., L.A., Cgy., Wsh., Phi.	10	395	4	37	41	1438	21	2	3	5	83	....	1974-75	1983-84
• Holway, Albert	Tor., Mtl.M., Pit.	5	112	7	2	9	48	6	0	0	0	0	1	1923-24	1928-29
Holzinger, Brian	Buf., T.B., Pit., CBJ	10	547	93	145	238	339	52	11	18	29	61	....	1994-95	2003-04
Homenuke, Ron	Van.	1	1	0	0	0	0	....	....	....	....	....	....	1972-73	1972-73
Hoover, Ron	Bos., St.L.	3	18	4	0	4	31	8	0	0	0	18	....	1989-90	1991-92
Hopkins, Dean	L.A., Edm., Que.	6	223	23	51	74	306	18	1	5	6	29	....	1979-80	1988-89
Hopkins, Larry	Tor., Wpg.	4	60	13	16	29	26	6	0	0	0	2	....	1977-78	1982-83
Horacek, Tony	Phi., Chi.	5	154	10	19	29	316	2	1	0	1	2	....	1989-90	1994-95
Horava, Miloslav	NYR	3	80	5	17	22	38	2	0	1	1	0	....	1988-89	1990-91
Horbul, Doug	K.C.	1	4	1	0	1	2	....	....	....	....	....	....	1974-75	1974-75
Hordy, Mike	NYI	2	11	0	0	0	7	....	....	....	....	....	....	1978-79	1979-80
Horeck, Pete	Chi., Det., Bos.	8	426	106	118	224	340	34	6	8	14	43	....	1944-45	1951-52
• Horne, George	Mtl.M., Tor.	3	54	9	3	12	34	4	0	0	0	4	1	1925-26	1928-29
• Horner, Red	Tor.	12	490	42	110	152	1254	71	7	10	17	170	1	1928-29	1939-40
• Hornung, Larry	St.L.	2	48	2	9	11	10	11	0	2	2	2	....	1970-71	1971-72
• Horton, Tim	Tor., NYR, Pit., Buf.	24	1446	115	403	518	1611	126	11	39	50	183	4	1949-50	1973-74
Horvath, Bronco	NYR, Mtl., Bos., Chi., Tor., Min.	9	434	141	185	326	319	36	12	9	21	18	....	1955-56	1967-68
Hospodar, Ed	NYR, Hfd., Phi., Min., Buf.	9	450	17	51	68	1314	44	4	1	5	208	....	1979-80	1987-88
Hostak, Martin	Phi.	2	55	3	11	14	24	....	....	....	....	....	....	1990-91	1991-92
Hotham, Greg	Tor., Pit.	6	230	15	74	89	139	5	0	3	3	6	....	1979-80	1984-85
Houck, Paul	Min.	3	16	1	2	3	2	....	....	....	....	....	....	1985-86	1987-88
Houda, Doug	Det., Hfd., L.A., Buf., NYI, Ana.	15	561	19	63	82	1104	18	0	3	3	21	....	1985-86	2002-03
Houde, Claude	K.C.	2	59	3	6	9	40	....	....	....	....	....	....	1974-75	1975-76
Houde, Eric	Mtl.	3	30	2	3	5	4	....	....	....	....	....	....	1996-97	1998-99
Hough, Mike	Que., Fla., NYI	13	707	100	156	256	675	42	5	5	10	38	....	1986-87	1998-99
Houlder, Bill	Wsh., Buf., Ana., St.L., T.B., S.J., Nsh.	16	846	59	191	250	412	30	5	6	11	14	....	1987-88	2002-03
Houle, Rejean	Mtl.	11	635	161	247	408	395	90	14	34	48	66	5	1969-70	1982-83
Housley, Phil	Buf., Wpg., St.L., Cgy., N.J., Wsh., Chi., Tor.	21	1495	338	894	1232	822	85	13	43	56	36	....	1982-83	2002-03
Houston, Ken	Atl., Cgy., Wsh., L.A.	9	570	161	167	328	624	35	10	9	19	66	....	1975-76	1983-84
Howard, Jack	Tor.	1	2	0	0	0	0	....	....	....	....	....	....	1936-37	1936-37
Howatt, Garry	NYI, Hfd., N.J.	12	720	112	156	268	1836	87	12	14	26	289	2	1972-73	1983-84
Howe, Gordie	Det., Hfd.	26	1767	801	1049	1850	1685	157	68	92	160	220	4	1946-47	1979-80
Howe, Mark	Hfd., Phi., Det.	16	929	197	545	742	455	101	10	51	61	34	....	1979-80	1994-95
Howe, Marty	Hfd., Bos.	6	197	2	29	31	99	15	1	2	3	9	....	1979-80	1984-85
• Howe, Syd	Ott., Phi., Tor., St.L., Det.	17	698	237	291	528	212	70	17	27	44	10	3	1929-30	1945-46
Howe, Vic	NYR	3	33	3	4	7	10	....	....	....	....	....	....	1950-51	1954-55
Howell, Harry	NYR, Oak., Cal., L.A.	21	1411	94	324	418	1298	38	3	3	6	32	....	1952-53	1972-73
• Howell, Ron	NYR	2	4	0	0	0	0	....	....	....	....	....	....	1954-55	1955-56
Howse, Don	L.A.	1	33	2	5	7	6	2	0	0	0	0	....	1979-80	1979-80
Howson, Scott	NYI	2	18	5	3	8	4	....	....	....	....	....	....	1984-85	1985-86
Hoyda, Dave	Phi., Wpg.	4	132	6	17	23	299	12	0	0	0	17	....	1977-78	1980-81
Hrdina, Jiri	Cgy., Pit.	5	250	45	85	130	92	46	2	5	7	24	3	1987-88	1991-92
Hrechkosy, Dave	Cal., St.L.	4	140	42	24	66	41	3	1	0	1	2	....	1973-74	1976-77
Hrkac, Tony	St.L., Que., S.J., Chi., Dal., Edm., NYI, Ana., Atl.	13	758	132	239	371	173	41	7	7	14	12	1	1986-87	2002-03
Hrycuik, Jim	Wsh.	1	21	5	5	10	12	....	....	....	....	....	....	1974-75	1974-75
Hrymnak, Steve	Chi., Det.	2	18	2	1	3	4	2	0	0	0	0	....	1951-52	1952-53
Hrynewich, Tim	Pit.	2	55	6	8	14	82	....	....	....	....	....	....	1982-83	1983-84
Huard, Bill	Bos., Ott., Que., Dal., Edm., L.A.	8	223	16	18	34	594	5	0	0	0	2	....	1992-93	1999-00
Huard, Rolly	Tor.	1	1	1	0	1	0	....	....	....	....	....	....	1930-31	1930-31
Huber, Willie	Det., NYR, Van., Phi.	10	655	104	217	321	950	33	5	5	10	35	....	1978-79	1987-88
Hubick, Greg	Tor., Van.	2	77	6	9	15	10	....	....	....	....	....	....	1975-76	1979-80
Huck, Fran	Mtl., St.L.	3	94	24	30	54	38	11	3	4	7	2	....	1969-70	1972-73
Hucul, Fred	Chi., St.L.	5	164	11	30	41	113	6	1	0	1	10	....	1950-51	1967-68
Huddy, Charlie	Edm., L.A., Buf., St.L.	17	1017	99	354	453	785	183	19	66	85	135	5	1980-81	1996-97
Hudson, Dave	NYI, K.C., Col.	6	409	59	124	183	89	2	1	1	2	0	....	1972-73	1977-78

			Regular Schedule					Playoffs					NHL	First	Last
Name	NHL Teams	NHL Seasons	GP	G	A	TP	PIM	GP	G	A	TP	PIM	Cup Wins	NHL Season	NHL Season
Hudson, Lex	Pit.	1	2	0	0	0	0	2	0	0	0	0	....	1978-79	1978-79
Hudson, Mike	Chi., Edm., NYR, Pit., Tor., St.L., Phx.	9	416	49	87	136	414	49	4	10	14	64	1	1988-89	1996-97
Hudson, Ron	Det.	2	33	5	2	7	2	....	....	....	....	....	....	1937-38	1939-40
Huffman, Kerry	Phi., Que., Ott.	10	401	37	108	145	361	11	0	0	0	2	....	1986-87	1995-96
Huggins, Al	Mtl.M.	1	20	1	1	2	2	....	....	....	....	....	....	1930-31	1930-31
● Hughes, Albert	NYA	2	60	6	8	14	22	....	....	....	....	....	....	1930-31	1931-32
Hughes, Brent	L.A., Phi., St.L., Det., K.C.	8	435	15	117	132	440	22	1	3	4	53	....	1967-68	1974-75
Hughes, Brent	Wpg., Bos., Buf., NYI	8	357	41	39	80	831	29	4	1	5	53	....	1988-89	1996-97
Hughes, Frank	Cal.	1	5	0	0	0	0	....	....	....	....	....	....	1971-72	1971-72
Hughes, Howie	L.A.	3	168	25	32	57	30	14	2	0	2	2	....	1967-68	1969-70
Hughes, Jack	Col.	2	46	2	5	7	104	....	....	....	....	....	....	1980-81	1981-82
● Hughes, James	Det.	1	40	0	1	1	48	....	....	....	....	....	....	1929-30	1929-30
Hughes, John	Van., Edm., NYR	2	70	2	14	16	211	7	0	1	1	16	....	1979-80	1980-81
Hughes, Pat	Mtl., Pit., Edm., Buf., St.L., Hfd.	10	573	130	128	258	646	71	8	25	33	77	3	1977-78	1986-87
Hughes, Ryan	Bos.	1	3	0	0	0	0	....	....	....	....	....	....	1995-96	1995-96
Hulbig, Joe	Edm., Bos.	5	55	4	4	8	16	6	0	1	1	2	....	1996-97	2000-01
Hull, Bobby	Chi., Wpg., Hfd.	16	1063	610	560	1170	640	119	62	67	129	102	1	1957-58	1979-80
Hull, Brett	Cgy., St.L., Dal., Det., Phx.	20	1269	741	650	1391	458	202	103	87	190	73	2	1985-86	2005-06
Hull, Dennis	Chi., Det.	14	959	303	351	654	261	104	33	34	67	30	....	1964-65	1977-78
Hull, Jody	Hfd., NYR, Ott., Fla., T.B., Phi.	16	831	124	137	261	156	69	4	5	9	14	....	1988-89	2003-04
Hulse, Cale	N.J., Cgy., Nsh., Phx., CBJ	10	619	16	79	95	1000	1	0	0	0	0	....	1995-96	2005-06
‡ Huml, Ivan	Bos.	3	49	6	12	18	36	....	....	....	....	....	....	2001-02	2003-04
● Hunt, Fred	NYA, NYR	2	59	15	14	29	6	....	....	....	....	....	....	1940-41	1944-45
Hunter, Dale	Que., Wsh., Col.	19	1407	323	697	1020	3565	186	42	76	118	729	....	1980-81	1998-99
Hunter, Dave	Edm., Pit., Wpg.	10	746	133	190	323	918	105	16	24	40	211	3	1979-80	1988-89
Hunter, Mark	Mtl., St.L., Cgy., Hfd., Wsh.	12	628	213	171	384	1426	79	18	20	38	230	1	1981-82	1992-93
Hunter, Tim	Cgy., Que., Van., S.J.	16	815	62	76	138	3146	132	5	7	12	426	1	1981-82	1996-97
Huras, Larry	NYR	1	2	0	0	0	0	....	....	....	....	....	....	1976-77	1976-77
Hurlburt, Bob	Van.	1	1	0	0	0	2	....	....	....	....	....	....	1974-75	1974-75
Hurlbut, Mike	NYR, Que., Buf.	5	29	1	8	9	20	....	....	....	....	....	....	1992-93	1999-00
Hurley, Paul	Bos.	1	1	0	1	1	0	....	....	....	....	....	....	1968-69	1968-69
Hurst, Ron	Tor.	2	64	9	7	16	70	3	0	2	2	4	....	1955-56	1956-57
Huscroft, Jamie	N.J., Bos., Cgy., T.B., Van., Phx., Wsh.	10	352	5	33	38	1065	21	0	1	1	46	....	1988-89	1999-00
Huska, Ryan	Chi.	1	1	0	0	0	0	....	....	....	....	....	....	1997-98	1997-98
Huston, Ron	Cal.	2	79	15	31	46	8	....	....	....	....	....	....	1973-74	1974-75
Hutchinson, Ron	NYR	1	9	0	0	0	0	....	....	....	....	....	....	1960-61	1960-61
Hutchison, Dave	L.A., Tor., Chi., N.J.	10	584	19	97	116	1550	48	2	12	14	149	....	1974-75	1983-84
● Hutton, Bill	Bos., Ott., Phi.	2	64	3	2	5	8	2	0	0	0	0	....	1929-30	1930-31
● Hyland, Harry	Mtl.W., Ott.	1	17	14	2	16	65	....	....	....	....	....	....	1917-18	1917-18
Hynes, Dave	Bos.	2	22	4	0	4	2	....	....	....	....	....	....	1973-74	1974-75
Hynes, Gord	Bos., Phi.	2	52	3	9	12	22	12	1	2	3	6	....	1991-92	1992-93
‡ Hyvonen, Hannes	S.J., CBJ	2	42	4	5	9	22	....	....	....	....	....	....	2001-02	2002-03
I															
Iafrate, Al	Tor., Wsh., Bos., S.J.	12	799	152	311	463	1301	71	19	16	35	77	....	1984-85	1997-98
Ignatjev, Victor	Pit.	1	11	0	1	1	6	1	0	0	0	2	....	1998-99	1998-99
Ihnacak, Miroslav	Tor., Det.	3	56	8	9	17	39	1	0	0	0	0	....	1985-86	1988-89
Ihnacak, Peter	Tor.	8	417	102	165	267	175	28	4	10	14	25	....	1982-83	1989-90
Imlach, Brent	Tor.	2	3	0	0	0	0	....	....	....	....	....	....	1965-66	1966-67
Ingarfield, Earl	NYR, Pit., Oak., Cal.	13	746	179	226	405	239	21	9	8	17	10	....	1958-59	1970-71
Ingarfield, Earl	Atl., Cgy., Det.	2	39	4	4	8	22	2	0	1	1	0	....	1979-80	1980-81
Inglis, Billy	L.A., Buf.	3	36	1	3	4	4	11	1	2	3	4	....	1967-68	1970-71
● Ingoldsby, Johnny	Tor.	2	29	5	1	6	15	....	....	....	....	....	....	1942-43	1943-44
● Ingram, Frank	Chi.	3	101	24	16	40	69	11	0	1	1	2	....	1929-30	1931-32
● Ingram, John	Bos.	1	1	0	0	0	0	....	....	....	....	....	....	1924-25	1924-25
Ingram, Ron	Chi., Det., NYR	4	114	5	15	20	81	2	0	0	0	0	....	1956-57	1964-65
Intranuovo, Ralph	Edm., Tor.	3	22	2	4	6	4	....	....	....	....	....	....	1994-95	1996-97
● Irvin, Dick	Chi.	3	94	29	23	52	78	2	2	0	2	4	....	1926-27	1928-29
Irvine, Ted	Bos., L.A., NYR, St.L.	11	724	154	177	331	657	83	16	24	40	115	....	1963-64	1976-77
Irwin, Ivan	Mtl., NYR	5	155	2	27	29	214	5	0	0	0	8	....	1952-53	1957-58
● Isaksson, Ulf	L.A.	1	50	7	15	22	10	....	....	....	....	....	....	1982-83	1982-83
Issel, Kim	Edm.	1	4	0	0	0	0	....	....	....	....	....	....	1988-89	1988-89
J															
● Jackson, Art	Tor., Bos., NYA	11	468	123	178	301	144	52	8	12	20	29	2	1934-35	1944-45
● Jackson, Busher	Tor., NYA, Bos.	15	633	241	234	475	437	71	18	12	30	53	1	1929-30	1943-44
Jackson, Dane	Van., Buf., NYI	4	45	12	6	18	58	6	0	0	0	10	....	1993-94	1997-98
Jackson, Don	Min., Edm., NYR	10	311	16	52	68	640	53	4	5	9	147	2	1977-78	1986-87
● Jackson, Harold	Chi., Det.	8	219	17	34	51	208	31	1	2	3	33	2	1936-37	1946-47
Jackson, Jack	Chi.	1	48	2	5	7	38	....	....	....	....	....	....	1946-47	1946-47
Jackson, Jeff	Tor., NYR, Que., Chi.	8	263	38	48	86	313	6	1	1	2	16	....	1984-85	1991-92
Jackson, Jim	Cgy., Buf.	4	112	17	30	47	20	14	3	2	5	6	....	1982-83	1987-88
● Jackson, Lloyd	NYA	1	14	1	1	2	0	....	....	....	....	....	....	1936-37	1936-37
● Jackson, Stan	Tor., Bos., Ott.	5	86	9	6	15	75	....	....	....	....	....	1	1921-22	1926-27
Jackson, Walter	NYA, Bos.	4	84	16	11	27	18	....	....	....	....	....	....	1932-33	1935-36
● Jacobs, Paul	Tor.	1	1	0	0	0	0	....	....	....	....	....	....	1918-19	1918-19
Jacobs, Tim	Cal.	1	46	0	10	10	35	....	....	....	....	....	....	1975-76	1975-76
Jakopin, John	Fla., Pit., S.J.	6	113	1	6	7	145	....	....	....	....	....	....	1997-98	2002-03
Jalo, Risto	Edm.	1	3	0	3	3	0	....	....	....	....	....	....	1985-86	1985-86
Jalonen, Kari	Cgy., Edm.	2	37	9	6	15	4	5	1	0	1	0	....	1982-83	1983-84
James, Gerry	Tor.	5	149	14	26	40	257	15	1	0	1	8	....	1954-55	1959-60
James, Val	Buf., Tor.	2	11	0	0	0	30	....	....	....	....	....	....	1981-82	1986-87
Jamieson, Jim	NYR	1	1	0	1	1	0	....	....	....	....	....	....	1943-44	1943-44
Jankowski, Lou	Det., Chi.	4	127	19	18	37	15	1	0	0	0	0	....	1950-51	1954-55
Janney, Craig	Bos., St.L., S.J., Wpg., Phx., T.B., NYI	12	760	188	563	751	170	120	24	86	110	53	....	1987-88	1998-99
Janssens, Mark	NYR, Min., Hfd., Ana., NYI, Phx., Chi.	14	711	40	73	113	1422	27	5	1	6	33	....	1987-88	2000-01
‡ Jantunen, Marko	Cgy.	1	3	0	0	0	0	....	....	....	....	....	....	1996-97	1996-97
‡ Jardine, Ryan	Fla.	1	8	0	2	2	2	....	....	....	....	....	....	2001-02	2001-02
Jarrett, Doug	Chi., NYR	13	775	38	182	220	631	99	7	16	23	82	....	1964-65	1976-77
Jarrett, Gary	Tor., Det., Oak., Cal.	7	341	72	92	164	131	11	3	1	4	9	....	1960-61	1971-72
Jarry, Pierre	NYR, Tor., Det., Min.	7	344	88	117	205	142	5	0	1	1	0	....	1971-72	1977-78
Jarvenpaa, Hannu	Wpg.	3	114	11	26	37	83	....	....	....	....	....	....	1986-87	1988-89
‡ Jarventie, Martti	Mtl.	1	1	0	0	0	0	....	....	....	....	....	....	2001-02	2001-02
Jarvi, Iiro	Que.	2	116	18	43	61	58	....	....	....	....	....	....	1988-89	1989-90
Jarvis, Doug	Mtl., Wsh., Hfd.	13	964	139	264	403	263	105	14	27	41	42	4	1975-76	1987-88
● Jarvis, James	Pit., Phi., Tor.	3	112	17	15	32	62	....	....	....	....	....	....	1929-30	1936-37
Jarvis, Wes	Wsh., Min., L.A., Tor.	9	237	31	55	86	98	2	0	0	0	2	....	1979-80	1987-88
Javanainen, Arto	Pit.	1	14	4	1	5	2	....	....	....	....	....	....	1984-85	1984-85
Jay, Bob	L.A.	1	3	0	1	1	0	....	....	....	....	....	....	1993-94	1993-94
Jeffrey, Larry	Det., Tor., NYR	8	368	39	62	101	293	38	4	10	14	42	1	1961-62	1968-69
Jelinek, Tomas	Ott.	1	49	7	6	13	52	....	....	....	....	....	....	1992-93	1992-93
Jenkins, Dean	L.A.	1	5	0	0	0	2	....	....	....	....	....	....	1983-84	1983-84
● Jenkins, Roger	Chi., Tor., Mtl., Bos., Mtl.M., NYA	8	325	15	39	54	253	25	1	7	8	12	2	1930-31	1938-39
Jennings, Bill	Det., Bos.	5	108	32	33	65	45	20	4	4	8	6	....	1940-41	1944-45
Jennings, Grant	Wsh., Hfd., Pit., Tor., Buf.	9	389	14	43	57	804	54	2	1	3	68	2	1987-88	1995-96
Jensen, Chris	NYR, Phi.	6	74	9	12	21	27	....	....	....	....	....	....	1985-86	1991-92
Jensen, David	Min.	3	18	0	2	2	11	....	....	....	....	....	....	1983-84	1985-86
Jensen, David	Hfd., Wsh.	4	69	9	13	22	22	11	0	0	0	2	....	1984-85	1987-88
Jensen, Steve	Min., L.A.	7	438	113	107	220	318	12	0	3	3	9	....	1975-76	1981-82
● Jeremiah, Ed	NYA, Bos.	1	15	0	1	1	0	....	....	....	....	....	....	1931-32	1931-32
Jerrard, Paul	Min.	1	5	0	0	0	4	....	....	....	....	....	....	1988-89	1988-89
● Jerwa, Frank	Bos., St.L.	4	81	11	16	27	53	....	....	....	....	....	....	1931-32	1934-35
● Jerwa, Joe	NYR, Bos., NYA	7	234	29	58	87	309	17	2	3	5	16	....	1930-31	1938-39
Jirik, Jaroslav	St.L.	1	3	0	0	0	0	....	....	....	....	....	....	1969-70	1969-70
● Joanette, Rosario	Mtl.	1	2	0	1	1	4	....	....	....	....	....	....	1944-45	1944-45
Jodzio, Rick	Col., Cle.	1	70	2	8	10	71	....	....	....	....	....	....	1977-78	1977-78
Johannesen, Glenn	NYI	1	2	0	0	0	0	....	....	....	....	....	....	1985-86	1985-86
Johannson, John	N.J.	1	5	0	0	0	0	....	....	....	....	....	....	1983-84	1983-84
● Johansen, Bill	Tor.	1	1	0	0	0	0	....	....	....	....	....	....	1949-50	1949-50
Johansen, Trevor	Tor., Col., L.A.	5	286	11	46	57	282	13	0	3	3	21	....	1977-78	1981-82
‡ Johansson, Andreas	NYI, Pit., Ott., T.B., Cgy., NYR, Nsh.	8	377	81	88	169	190	9	0	0	0	0	....	1995-96	2003-04
Johansson, Bjorn	Cle.	2	15	1	1	2	10	....	....	....	....	....	....	1976-77	1977-78

Brett Hull

Ron Ingram

Lloyd Jackson

Roger Jenkins

Greg Johnson

Ed Kachur

Dave Keon

Wayne King

Name	NHL Teams	NHL Seasons	Regular Schedule GP	G	A	TP	PIM	Playoffs GP	G	A	TP	PIM	NHL Cup Wins	First NHL Season	Last NHL Season
Johansson, Calle	Buf., Wsh., Tor.	17	1109	119	416	535	519	105	12	43	55	44	....	1987-88	2003-04
‡ Johansson, Mathias	Cgy., Pit.	1	58	5	10	15	16	....	....	....	....	....	....	2002-03	2002-03
Johansson, Roger	Cgy., Chi.	4	161	9	34	43	163	5	0	1	1	2	....	1989-90	1994-95
Johns, Don	NYR, Mtl., Min.	6	153	2	21	23	76	....	....	....	....	....	....	1960-61	1967-68
Johnson, Allan	Mtl., Det.	4	105	21	28	49	30	11	2	2	4	6	....	1956-57	1962-63
Johnson, Brian	Det.	1	3	0	0	0	5	....	....	....	....	....	....	1983-84	1983-84
• Johnson, Ching	NYR, NYA	12	436	38	48	86	808	61	5	2	7	161	2	1926-27	1937-38
‡ Johnson, Craig	St.L., L.A., Ana., Tor., Wsh.	10	557	75	98	173	260	16	3	2	5	10	....	1994-95	2003-04
• Johnson, Danny	Tor., Van., Det.	3	121	18	19	37	24	....	....	....	....	....	....	1969-70	1971-72
Johnson, Earl	Det.	1	1	0	0	0	0	....	....	....	....	....	....	1953-54	1953-54
Johnson, Greg	Det., Pit., Chi., Nsh.	12	785	145	224	369	345	37	7	6	13	14	....	1993-94	2005-06
Johnson, Jim	NYR, Phi., L.A.	8	302	75	111	186	73	7	0	2	2	2	....	1964-65	1971-72
Johnson, Jim	Pit., Min., Dal., Wsh., Phx.	13	829	29	166	195	1197	51	1	11	12	132	....	1985-86	1997-98
Johnson, Mark	Pit., Min., Hfd., St.L., N.J.	11	669	203	305	508	260	37	16	12	28	10	....	1979-80	1989-90
Johnson, Matt	L.A., Atl., Min.	10	473	23	20	43	1523	16	0	0	0	31	....	1994-95	2003-04
Johnson, Norm	Bos., Chi.	3	61	5	20	25	41	14	4	0	4	6	....	1957-58	1959-60
Johnson, Terry	Que., St.L., Cgy., Tor.	9	285	3	24	27	580	38	0	4	4	118	....	1979-80	1987-88
Johnson, Tom	Mtl., Bos.	17	978	51	213	264	960	111	8	15	23	109	6	1947-48	1964-65
• Johnson, Virgil	Chi.	3	75	1	11	12	27	19	0	3	3	4	1	1937-38	1944-45
Johnston, Bernie	Hfd.	2	57	12	24	36	16	3	0	1	1	0	....	1979-80	1980-81
• Johnston, George	Chi.	4	58	20	12	32	2	....	....	....	....	....	....	1941-42	1946-47
Johnston, Greg	Bos., Tor.	9	187	26	29	55	124	22	2	1	3	12	....	1983-84	1991-92
Johnston, Jay	Wsh.	2	8	0	0	0	13	....	....	....	....	....	....	1980-81	1981-82
Johnston, Joey	Min., Cal., Chi.	6	331	85	106	191	320	....	....	....	....	....	....	1968-69	1975-76
Johnston, Larry	L.A., Det., K.C., Col.	7	320	9	64	73	580	....	....	....	....	....	....	1967-68	1976-77
Johnston, Marshall	Min., Cal.	7	251	14	52	66	58	6	0	0	0	2	....	1967-68	1973-74
Johnston, Randy	NYI	1	4	0	0	0	4	....	....	....	....	....	....	1979-80	1979-80
Johnstone, Eddie	NYR, Det.	10	426	122	136	258	375	55	13	10	23	83	....	1975-76	1986-87
Johnstone, Ross	Tor.	2	42	5	4	9	14	3	0	0	0	0	1	1943-44	1944-45
• Joliat, Aurel	Mtl.	16	655	270	190	460	771	46	9	13	22	66	3	1922-23	1937-38
• Joliat, Rene	Mtl.	1	1	0	0	0	0	....	....	....	....	....	....	1924-25	1924-25
Joly, Greg	Wsh., Det.	9	365	21	76	97	250	5	0	0	0	8	....	1974-75	1982-83
Joly, Yvan	Mtl.	3	2	0	0	0	0	1	0	0	0	0	....	1979-80	1982-83
Jomphe, Jean-Francois	Ana., Phx., Mtl.	4	111	10	29	39	102	....	....	....	....	....	....	1995-96	1998-99
Jonathan, Stan	Bos., Pit.	8	411	91	110	201	751	63	8	4	12	137	....	1975-76	1982-83
Jones, Bob	NYR	1	2	0	0	0	0	....	....	....	....	....	....	1968-69	1968-69
Jones, Brad	Wpg., L.A., Phi.	6	148	25	31	56	122	9	1	1	2	2	....	1986-87	1991-92
Jones, Buck	Det., Tor.	4	50	2	2	4	36	12	0	1	1	18	....	1938-39	1942-43
Jones, Jim	Cal.	1	2	0	0	0	0	....	....	....	....	....	....	1971-72	1971-72
Jones, Jimmy	Tor.	3	148	13	18	31	68	19	1	5	6	11	....	1977-78	1979-80
Jones, Keith	Wsh., Col., Phi.	9	491	117	141	258	765	63	12	12	24	120	....	1992-93	2000-01
Jones, Ron	Bos., Pit., Wsh.	5	54	1	4	5	31	....	....	....	....	....	....	1971-72	1975-76
Jones, Ty	Chi., Fla.	2	14	0	0	0	19	....	....	....	....	....	....	1998-99	2003-04
‡ Jonsson, Hans	Pit.	4	242	10	38	48	92	27	0	1	1	14	....	1999-00	2002-03
‡ Jonsson, Jorgen	NYI, Ana.	1	81	12	19	31	16	....	....	....	....	....	....	1999-00	1999-00
‡ Jonsson, Kenny	Tor., NYI	10	686	63	204	267	298	19	1	3	4	6	....	1994-95	2003-04
Jonsson, Tomas	NYI, Edm.	8	552	85	259	344	482	80	11	26	37	97	2	1981-82	1988-89
Joseph, Chris	Pit., Edm., T.B., Van., Phi., Phx., Atl.	14	510	39	112	151	567	31	3	4	7	24	....	1987-88	2000-01
Joseph, Tony	Wpg.	1	2	1	0	1	0	....	....	....	....	....	....	1988-89	1988-89
Joyal, Eddie	Det., Tor., L.A., Phi.	9	466	128	134	262	103	50	11	8	19	18	....	1962-63	1971-72
Joyce, Bob	Bos., Wsh., Wpg.	6	158	34	49	83	90	46	15	9	24	29	....	1987-88	1992-93
Joyce, Duane	Dal.	1	3	0	0	0	0	....	....	....	....	....	....	1993-94	1993-94
• Juckes, Bing	NYR	2	16	2	1	3	6	....	....	....	....	....	....	1947-48	1949-50
‡ Juhlin, Patrik	Phi.	2	56	7	6	13	23	13	1	0	1	2	....	1994-95	1995-96
Julien, Claude	Que.	2	14	0	1	1	25	....	....	....	....	....	....	1984-85	1985-86
Juneau, Joe	Bos., Wsh., Buf., Ott., Phx., Mtl.	13	828	156	416	572	272	112	25	54	79	69	....	1991-92	2003-04
Junker, Steve	NYI	2	5	0	0	0	0	3	0	1	1	0	....	1992-93	1993-94
Jutila, Timo	Buf.	1	10	1	5	6	13	....	....	....	....	....	....	1984-85	1984-85
Juzda, Bill	NYR, Tor.	9	398	14	54	68	398	42	0	3	3	46	2	1940-41	1951-52

K

Name	NHL Teams	NHL Seasons	Regular Schedule GP	G	A	TP	PIM	Playoffs GP	G	A	TP	PIM	NHL Cup Wins	First NHL Season	Last NHL Season
Kabel, Bob	NYR	2	48	5	13	18	34	....	....	....	....	....	....	1959-60	1960-61
Kachowski, Mark	Pit.	3	64	6	5	11	209	....	....	....	....	....	....	1987-88	1989-90
Kachur, Ed	Chi.	2	96	10	14	24	35	....	....	....	....	....	....	1956-57	1957-58
Kaese, Trent	Buf.	1	1	0	0	0	0	....	....	....	....	....	....	1988-89	1988-89
Kaiser, Vern	Mtl.	1	50	7	5	12	33	2	0	0	0	0	....	1950-51	1950-51
• Kalbfleisch, Walter	Ott., St.L., NYA, Bos.	4	36	0	4	4	32	5	0	0	0	2	....	1933-34	1936-37
• Kaleta, Alex	Chi., NYR	7	387	92	121	213	190	17	1	6	7	2	....	1941-42	1950-51
‡ Kallio, Tomi	Atl., CBJ, Phi.	3	140	24	31	55	48	....	....	....	....	....	....	2000-01	2002-03
Kallur, Anders	NYI	6	383	101	110	211	149	78	12	23	35	32	4	1979-80	1984-85
Kamensky, Valeri	Que., Col., NYR, Dal., N.J.	11	637	200	301	501	383	66	25	35	60	72	1	1991-92	2001-02
Kaminski, Kevin	Min., Que., Wsh.	7	139	3	10	13	528	8	0	0	0	52	....	1988-89	1996-97
• Kaminsky, Max	Ott., Bos., St.L., Mtl.M.	4	130	22	34	56	38	4	0	0	0	0	....	1933-34	1936-37
Kaminsky, Yan	Wpg., NYI	2	26	3	2	5	4	2	0	0	0	4	....	1993-94	1994-95
• Kampman, Bingo	Tor.	5	189	14	30	44	287	47	1	4	5	38	1	1937-38	1941-42
Kane, Francis	Det.	1	2	0	0	0	0	....	....	....	....	....	....	1943-44	1943-44
Kannegiesser, Gord	St.L.	2	23	0	1	1	15	....	....	....	....	....	....	1967-68	1971-72
Kannegiesser, Sheldon	Pit., NYR, L.A., Van.	8	366	14	67	81	292	18	0	2	2	10	....	1970-71	1977-78
Karabin, Ladislav	Pit.	1	9	0	0	0	2	....	....	....	....	....	....	1993-94	1993-94
‡ Karalahti, Jere	L.A., Nsh.	3	149	8	19	27	97	17	0	1	1	20	....	1999-00	2001-02
Karamnov, Vitali	St.L.	3	92	12	20	32	65	2	0	0	0	2	....	1992-93	1994-95
‡ Kariya, Steve	Van.	3	65	9	18	27	32	....	....	....	....	....	....	1999-00	2001-02
Karjalainen, Kyosti	L.A.	1	28	1	8	9	12	3	0	1	1	2	....	1991-92	1991-92
Karlander, Al	Det.	4	212	36	56	92	70	4	0	1	1	0	....	1969-70	1972-73
Karpa, Dave	Que., Ana., Car., NYR	12	557	18	80	98	1374	19	1	1	2	39	....	1991-92	2002-03
Karpov, Valeri	Ana.	3	76	14	15	29	32	....	....	....	....	....	....	1994-95	1996-97
‡ Karpovtsev, Alexander	NYR, Tor., Chi., NYI, Fla.	12	596	34	154	188	430	74	4	14	18	52	1	1993-94	2005-06
Kasatonov, Alexei	N.J., Ana., St.L., Bos.	7	383	38	122	160	326	33	4	7	11	40	....	1989-90	1995-96
Kasper, Steve	Bos., L.A., Phi., T.B.	13	821	177	291	468	554	94	20	28	48	82	....	1980-81	1992-93
Kastelic, Ed	Wsh., Hfd.	7	220	11	10	21	719	8	1	0	1	32	....	1985-86	1991-92
Kaszycki, Mike	NYI, Wsh., Tor.	5	226	42	80	122	108	19	2	6	8	10	....	1977-78	1982-83
• Kea, Ed	Atl., St.L.	10	583	30	145	175	508	32	2	4	6	39	....	1973-74	1982-83
Keane, Mike	Mtl., Col., NYR, Dal., St.L., Van.	16	1161	168	302	470	881	220	34	40	74	135	3	1988-89	2003-04
Kearns, Dennis	Van.	10	677	31	290	321	386	11	1	2	3	8	....	1971-72	1980-81
• Keating, Jack	Det.	2	11	3	0	3	4	....	....	....	....	....	....	1938-39	1939-40
• Keating, John	NYA	2	35	5	5	10	17	....	....	....	....	....	....	1931-32	1932-33
Keating, Mike	NYR	1	1	0	0	0	0	....	....	....	....	....	....	1977-78	1977-78
• Keats, Duke	Bos., Det., Chi.	3	82	30	19	49	113	....	....	....	....	....	....	1926-27	1928-29
Keczmer, Dan	Min., Hfd., Cgy., Dal., Nsh.	10	235	8	38	46	212	12	0	1	1	8	....	1990-91	1999-00
Keefe, Sheldon	T.B.	3	125	12	12	24	78	....	....	....	....	....	....	2000-01	2002-03
• Keeling, Butch	Tor., NYR	12	525	157	63	220	331	47	11	11	22	34	1	1926-27	1937-38
Keenan, Larry	Tor., St.L., Buf., Phi.	6	233	38	64	102	28	46	15	16	31	12	....	1961-62	1971-72
Kehoe, Rick	Tor., Pit.	14	906	371	396	767	120	39	4	17	21	4	....	1971-72	1984-85
Kekalainen, Jarmo	Bos., Ott.	5	55	5	8	13	28	....	....	....	....	....	....	1989-90	1993-94
Kelleher, Chris	Bos.	1	1	0	0	0	0	....	....	....	....	....	....	2001-02	2001-02
Keller, Ralph	NYR	1	3	1	0	1	6	....	....	....	....	....	....	1962-63	1962-63
Kellgren, Christer	Col.	1	5	0	0	0	0	....	....	....	....	....	....	1981-82	1981-82
Kelly, Bob	Phi., Wsh.	12	837	154	208	362	1454	101	9	14	23	172	2	1970-71	1981-82
Kelly, Bob	St.L., Pit., Chi.	6	425	87	109	196	687	23	6	3	9	40	....	1973-74	1978-79
Kelly, Dave	Det.	1	16	2	0	2	4	....	....	....	....	....	....	1976-77	1976-77
Kelly, John Paul	L.A.	7	400	54	70	124	366	18	1	1	2	41	....	1979-80	1985-86
• Kelly, Pep	Tor., Chi., Bro.	8	288	74	53	127	105	38	7	6	13	10	....	1934-35	1941-42
• Kelly, Pete	St.L., Det., NYA, Bro.	7	177	21	38	59	68	19	3	1	4	2	2	1934-35	1941-42
Kelly, Red	Det., Tor.	20	1316	281	542	823	327	164	33	59	92	51	8	1947-48	1966-67
• Kemp, Kevin	Hfd.	1	3	0	0	0	4	....	....	....	....	....	....	1980-81	1980-81
Kemp, Stan	Tor.	1	1	0	0	0	2	....	....	....	....	....	....	1948-49	1948-49
Kenady, Chris	St.L., NYR	2	7	0	2	2	0	....	....	....	....	....	....	1997-98	1999-00
• Kendall, Bill	Chi., Tor.	5	131	16	10	26	28	6	0	0	0	0	1	1933-34	1937-38
Kennedy, Dean	L.A., NYR, Buf., Wpg., Edm.	12	717	26	108	134	1118	36	1	7	8	59	....	1982-83	1994-95
Kennedy, Forbes	Chi., Det., Bos., Phi., Tor.	11	603	70	108	178	988	12	2	4	6	64	....	1956-57	1968-69
Kennedy, Mike	Dal., Tor., NYI	5	145	16	36	52	112	5	0	0	0	9	....	1994-95	1998-99
Kennedy, Sheldon	Det., Cgy., Bos.	8	310	49	58	107	233	24	6	4	10	20	....	1989-90	1996-97
Kennedy, Ted	Tor.	14	696	231	329	560	432	78	29	31	60	32	5	1942-43	1956-57

Name	NHL Teams	NHL Seasons	Regular Schedule GP	G	A	TP	PIM	Playoffs GP	G	A	TP	PIM	NHL Cup Wins	First NHL Season	Last NHL Season
• Kenny, Ernest	NYR, Chi.	2	10	0	0	0	18	....	....	....	....	....	....	1930-31	1934-35
Keon, Dave	Tor., Hfd.	18	1296	396	590	986	117	92	32	36	68	6	4	1960-61	1981-82
Kerch, Alexander	Edm.	1	5	0	0	0	2	....	....	....	....	....	....	1993-94	1993-94
Kerr, Alan	NYI, Det., Wpg.	9	391	72	94	166	826	38	5	4	9	70	....	1984-85	1992-93
Kerr, Reg	Cle., Chi., Edm.	6	263	66	94	160	169	7	1	0	1	7	....	1977-78	1983-84
Kerr, Tim	Phi., NYR, Hfd.	13	655	370	304	674	596	81	40	31	71	58	....	1980-81	1992-93
Kesa, Dan	Van., Dal., Pit., T.B.	4	139	8	22	30	66	13	1	0	1	0	....	1993-94	1999-00
Kessell, Rick	Pit., Cal.	5	135	4	24	28	6	....	....	....	....	....	....	1969-70	1973-74
Ketola, Veli-Pekka	Col.	1	44	9	5	14	4	....	....	....	....	....	....	1981-82	1981-82
Ketter, Kerry	Atl.	1	41	0	2	2	58	....	....	....	....	....	....	1972-73	1972-73
Kharin, Sergei	Wpg.	1	7	2	3	5	2	....	....	....	....	....	....	1990-91	1990-91
‡ Kharitonov, Alexander	T.B., NYI	2	71	7	15	22	12	....	....	....	....	....	....	2000-01	2001-02
Khmylev, Yuri	Buf., St.L.	5	263	64	88	152	133	26	8	6	14	24	....	1992-93	1996-97
Khristich, Dmitri	Wsh., L.A., Bos., Tor.	12	811	259	337	596	422	75	15	25	40	41	....	1990-91	2001-02
Kidd, Ian	Van.	2	20	4	7	11	25	....	....	....	....	....	....	1987-88	1988-89
Kiessling, Udo	Min.	1	1	0	0	0	2	....	....	....	....	....	....	1981-82	1981-82
Kilrea, Brian	Det., L.A.	2	26	3	5	8	12	....	....	....	....	....	....	1957-58	1967-68
• Kilrea, Hec	Ott., Det., Tor.	15	633	167	129	296	438	48	8	7	15	18	3	1925-26	1939-40
• Kilrea, Ken	Det.	5	91	16	23	39	8	15	2	2	4	4	....	1938-39	1943-44
• Kilrea, Wally	Ott., Phi., NYA, Mtl.M., Det.	9	329	35	58	93	87	25	2	4	6	6	2	1929-30	1937-38
Kimble, Darin	Que., St.L., Bos., Chi.	7	311	23	20	43	1082	23	0	0	0	52	....	1988-89	1994-95
Kindrachuk, Orest	Phi., Pit., Wsh.	10	508	118	261	379	648	76	20	20	40	53	2	1972-73	1981-82
King, Derek	NYI, Hfd., Tor., St.L.	14	830	261	351	612	417	47	4	17	21	24	....	1986-87	1999-00
King, Frank	Mtl.	1	10	1	0	1	2	....	....	....	....	....	....	1950-51	1950-51
King, Kris	Det., NYR, Wpg., Phx., Tor., Chi.	14	849	66	85	151	2030	67	8	5	13	142	....	1987-88	2000-01
King, Steven	NYR, Ana.	3	67	17	8	25	75	....	....	....	....	....	....	1992-93	1995-96
King, Wayne	Cal.	3	73	5	18	23	34	....	....	....	....	....	....	1973-74	1975-76
Kinnear, Geordie	Atl.	1	4	0	0	0	13	....	....	....	....	....	....	1999-00	1999-00
Kinsella, Brian	Wsh.	2	10	0	1	1	0	....	....	....	....	....	....	1975-76	1976-77
• Kinsella, Ray	Ott.	1	14	0	0	0	0	....	....	....	....	....	....	1930-31	1930-31
‡ Kiprusoff, Marko	Mtl., NYI	2	51	0	10	10	12	....	....	....	....	....	....	1995-96	2001-02
• Kirk, Bobby	NYR	1	39	4	8	12	14	....	....	....	....	....	....	1937-38	1937-38
Kirkpatrick, Bob	NYR	1	49	12	12	24	6	....	....	....	....	....	....	1942-43	1942-43
Kirton, Mark	Tor., Det., Van.	6	266	57	56	113	121	4	1	2	3	7	....	1979-80	1984-85
Kisio, Kelly	Det., NYR, S.J., Cgy.	13	761	229	429	658	768	39	6	15	21	52	....	1982-83	1994-95
Kitchen, Bill	Mtl., Tor.	4	41	1	4	5	40	3	0	1	1	0	....	1981-82	1984-85
• Kitchen, Hobie	Mtl.M., Det.	2	47	5	4	9	58	....	....	....	....	....	1	1925-26	1926-27
Kitchen, Mike	Col., N.J.	8	474	12	62	74	370	2	0	0	0	2	....	1976-77	1983-84
Kjellberg, Patric	Mtl., Nsh., Ana.	6	394	64	96	160	84	10	0	0	0	0	....	1992-93	2002-03
Klassen, Ralph	Cal., Cle., Col., St.L.	9	497	52	93	145	120	26	4	2	6	12	....	1975-76	1983-84
Klatt, Trent	Min., Dal., Phi., Van., L.A.	13	782	143	200	343	307	74	16	9	25	20	....	1991-92	2003-04
• Klein, Lloyd	Bos., NYA	8	164	30	24	54	68	5	0	0	0	2	1	1928-29	1937-38
Kleinendorst, Scot	NYR, Hfd., Wsh.	8	281	12	46	58	452	26	2	7	9	40	....	1982-83	1989-90
Klima, Petr	Det., Edm., T.B., L.A., Pit.	13	786	313	260	573	671	95	28	24	52	83	1	1985-86	1998-99
‡ Klimovich, Sergei	Chi.	1	1	0	0	0	2	....	....	....	....	....	....	1996-97	1996-97
• Klingbeil, Ike	Chi.	1	5	1	2	3	2	....	....	....	....	....	....	1936-37	1936-37
• Klukay, Joe	Tor., Bos.	11	566	109	127	236	189	71	13	10	23	23	4	1942-43	1955-56
Kluzak, Gord	Bos.	7	299	25	98	123	543	46	6	13	19	129	....	1982-83	1990-91
• Knibbs, Bill	Bos.	1	53	7	10	17	4	....	....	....	....	....	....	1964-65	1964-65
Knipscheer, Fred	Bos., St.L.	3	28	6	3	9	18	16	2	1	3	6	....	1993-94	1995-96
• Knott, Nick	Bro.	1	14	3	1	4	9	....	....	....	....	....	....	1941-42	1941-42
Knox, Paul	Tor.	1	1	0	0	0	0	....	....	....	....	....	....	1954-55	1954-55
Knutsen, Espen	Ana., CBJ	5	207	30	81	111	105	....	....	....	....	....	....	1997-98	2003-04
Kocur, Joe	Det., NYR, Van.	15	820	80	82	162	2519	118	10	12	22	231	3	1984-85	1998-99
‡ Koehler, Greg	Car.	1	1	0	0	0	0	....	....	....	....	....	....	2000-01	2000-01
‡ Kohn, Ladislav	Cgy., Tor., Ana., Atl., Det.	7	186	14	28	42	125	2	0	0	0	5	....	1995-96	2002-03
‡ Koivisto, Tom	St.L.	1	22	2	4	6	10	....	....	....	....	....	....	2002-03	2002-03
‡ Kolarik, Pavel	Bos.	2	23	0	0	0	10	....	....	....	....	....	....	2000-01	2001-02
Kolesar, Mark	Tor.	2	28	2	2	4	14	3	1	0	1	2	....	1995-96	1996-97
Kolstad, Dean	Min., S.J.	3	40	1	7	8	69	....	....	....	....	....	....	1988-89	1992-93
Komadoski, Neil	L.A., St.L.	8	502	16	76	92	632	23	0	2	2	47	....	1972-73	1979-80
Komarniski, Zenith	Van., CBJ	3	21	1	1	2	10	....	....	....	....	....	....	1999-00	2003-04
Konik, George	Pit.	1	52	7	8	15	26	....	....	....	....	....	....	1967-68	1967-68
Konowalchuk, Steve	Wsh., Col.	14	790	171	225	396	703	52	9	12	21	60	....	1991-92	2005-06
Konroyd, Steve	Cgy., NYI, Chi., Hfd., Det., Ott.	15	895	41	195	236	863	97	10	15	25	99	....	1980-81	1994-95
Konstantinov, Vladimir	Det.	6	446	47	128	175	838	82	5	14	19	107	1	1991-92	1996-97
Kontos, Chris	NYR, Pit., L.A., T.B.	8	230	54	69	123	103	20	11	0	11	12	....	1982-83	1992-93
• Kopak, Russ	Bos.	1	24	7	9	16	0	....	....	....	....	....	....	1943-44	1943-44
Korab, Jerry	Chi., Van., Buf., L.A.	15	975	114	341	455	1629	93	8	18	26	201	....	1970-71	1984-85
Kordic, Dan	Phi.	6	197	4	8	12	584	12	1	0	1	22	....	1991-92	1998-99
• Kordic, John	Mtl., Tor., Wsh., Que.	7	244	17	18	35	997	41	4	3	7	131	1	1985-86	1991-92
Korn, Jim	Det., Tor., Buf., N.J., Cgy.	10	597	66	122	188	1801	16	1	2	3	109	....	1979-80	1989-90
Korney, Mike	Det., NYR	4	77	9	10	19	59	....	....	....	....	....	....	1973-74	1978-79
‡ Korolev, Evgeny	NYI	3	42	1	4	5	20	2	0	0	0	0	....	1999-00	2001-02
‡ Korolev, Igor	St.L., Wpg., Phx., Tor., Chi.	12	795	119	227	346	330	41	0	8	8	6	....	1992-93	2003-04
Koroll, Cliff	Chi.	11	814	208	254	462	376	85	19	29	48	67	....	1969-70	1979-80
Kortko, Roger	NYI	2	79	7	17	24	28	10	0	3	3	17	....	1984-85	1985-86
Kostynski, Doug	Bos.	2	15	3	1	4	4	....	....	....	....	....	....	1983-84	1984-85
Kotanen, Dick	NYR	1	1	0	0	0	0	....	....	....	....	....	....	1950-51	1950-51
Kotsopoulos, Chris	NYR, Hfd., Tor., Det.	10	479	44	109	153	827	31	1	3	4	91	....	1980-81	1989-90
‡ Kovalenko, Andrei	Que., Col., Mtl., Edm., Phi., Car., Bos.	9	620	173	206	379	389	33	5	6	11	20	....	1992-93	2000-01
Kowal, Joe	Buf.	2	22	0	5	5	13	2	0	0	0	0	....	1976-77	1977-78
Kozak, Don	L.A., Van.	7	437	96	86	182	480	29	7	2	9	69	....	1972-73	1978-79
Kozak, Les	Tor.	1	12	1	0	1	2	....	....	....	....	....	....	1961-62	1961-62
‡ Kraft, Ryan	S.J.	1	7	0	1	1	0	....	....	....	....	....	....	2002-03	2002-03
• Kraftcheck, Stephen	Bos., NYR, Tor.	4	157	11	18	29	83	6	0	0	0	7	....	1950-51	1958-59
Krake, Skip	Bos., L.A., Buf.	7	249	23	40	63	182	10	1	0	1	17	....	1963-64	1970-71
Kravchuk, Igor	Chi., Edm., St.L., Ott., Cgy., Fla.	12	699	64	210	274	251	51	6	15	21	18	....	1991-92	2002-03
Kravets, Mikhail	S.J.	2	2	0	0	0	0	....	....	....	....	....	....	1991-92	1992-93
Krentz, Dale	Det.	3	30	5	3	8	9	2	0	0	0	0	....	1986-87	1988-89
‡ Krestanovich, Jordan	Col.	2	22	0	2	2	6	....	....	....	....	....	....	2001-02	2003-04
‡ Kristek, Jaroslav	Buf.	1	6	0	0	0	4	....	....	....	....	....	....	2002-03	2002-03
‡ Krivokrasov, Sergei	Chi., Nsh., Cgy., Min., Ana.	10	450	86	109	195	288	21	2	0	2	14	....	1992-93	2001-02
• Krol, Joe	NYR, Bro.	3	26	10	4	14	8	....	....	....	....	....	....	1936-37	1941-42
Kromm, Richard	Cgy., NYI	9	372	70	103	173	138	36	2	6	8	22	....	1983-84	1992-93
Kron, Robert	Van., Hfd., Car., CBJ	12	771	144	194	338	119	16	3	2	5	2	....	1990-91	2001-02
Krook, Kevin	Col.	1	3	0	0	0	2	....	....	....	....	....	....	1978-79	1978-79
‡ Kroupa, Vlastimil	S.J., N.J.	5	105	4	19	23	66	20	1	2	3	25	....	1993-94	1997-98
Krulicki, Jim	NYR, Det.	1	41	0	3	3	6	....	....	....	....	....	....	1970-71	1970-71
Krupp, Uwe	Buf., NYI, Que., Col., Det., Atl.	15	729	69	212	281	660	81	6	23	29	86	1	1986-87	2002-03
Kruppke, Gord	Det.	3	23	0	0	0	32	....	....	....	....	....	....	1990-91	1993-94
Kruse, Paul	Cgy., NYI, Buf., S.J.	11	423	38	33	71	1074	28	5	2	7	36	....	1990-91	2000-01
Krushelnyski, Mike	Bos., Edm., L.A., Tor., Det.	14	897	241	328	569	699	139	29	43	72	106	3	1981-82	1994-95
Krutov, Vladimir	Van.	1	61	11	23	34	20	....	....	....	....	....	....	1989-90	1989-90
Krygier, Todd	Hfd., Wsh., Ana.	9	543	100	143	243	533	48	10	7	17	40	....	1989-90	1997-98
Kryskow, Dave	Chi., Wsh., Det., Atl.	4	231	33	56	89	174	12	2	0	2	4	....	1972-73	1975-76
• Kryzanowski, Ed	Bos., Chi.	5	237	15	22	37	65	18	0	1	1	4	....	1948-49	1952-53
Kucera, Frantisek	Chi., Hfd., Van., Phi., CBJ, Pit., Wsh.	9	465	24	95	119	251	12	0	1	1	0	....	1990-91	2001-02
‡ Kudashov, Alexei	Tor.	1	25	1	0	1	4	....	....	....	....	....	....	1993-94	1993-94
Kudelski, Bob	L.A., Ott., Fla.	9	442	139	102	241	218	22	4	4	8	4	....	1987-88	1995-96
‡ Kudroc, Kristian	T.B., Fla.	3	26	2	2	4	38	....	....	....	....	....	....	2000-01	2003-04
• Kuhn, Gord	NYA	1	12	1	1	2	4	....	....	....	....	....	....	1932-33	1932-33
Kukulowicz, Aggie	NYR	2	4	1	0	1	0	....	....	....	....	....	....	1952-53	1953-54
Kulak, Stu	Van., Edm., NYR, Que., Wpg.	4	90	8	4	12	130	3	0	0	0	2	....	1982-83	1988-89
Kuleshov, Mikhail	Col.	1	3	0	0	0	0	....	....	....	....	....	....	2003-04	2003-04
• Kullman, Arnie	Bos.	2	13	0	1	1	11	....	....	....	....	....	....	1947-48	1949-50
• Kullman, Eddie	NYR	6	343	56	70	126	298	6	1	0	1	2	....	1947-48	1953-54
‡ Kultanen, Jarno	Bos.	3	102	2	11	13	59	....	....	....	....	....	....	2000-01	2002-03
Kumpel, Mark	Que., Det., Wpg.	6	288	38	46	84	113	39	6	4	10	14	....	1984-85	1990-91
• Kuntz, Alan	NYR	2	45	10	12	22	12	6	1	0	1	2	....	1941-42	1945-46
Kuntz, Murray	St.L.	1	7	1	2	3	0	....	....	....	....	....	....	1974-75	1974-75
‡ Kurka, Tomas	Car.	2	17	3	2	5	2	....	....	....	....	....	....	2002-03	2003-04
Kurri, Jari	Edm., L.A., NYR, Ana., Col.	17	1251	601	797	1398	545	200	106	127	233	123	5	1980-81	1997-98
Kurtenbach, Orland	NYR, Bos., Tor., Van.	13	639	119	213	332	628	19	2	4	6	70	....	1960-61	1973-74
Kurtz, Justin	Van.	1	27	3	5	8	14	....	....	....	....	....	....	2001-02	2001-02

Mike Korney

Mike Krushelnyski

Merv Kuryluk

Pete Laframboise

Dave Langevin

Claude Larose

Eric Lavigne

Larry Leach

Name	NHL Teams	NHL Seasons	Regular Schedule					Playoffs					NHL Cup Wins	First NHL Season	Last NHL Season
			GP	G	A	TP	PIM	GP	G	A	TP	PIM			
Kurvers, Tom	Mtl., Buf., N.J., Tor., Van., NYI, Ana.	11	659	93	328	421	350	57	8	22	30	68	1	1984-85	1994-95
Kuryluk, Merv	Chi.	1	....	....	....	....	....	2	0	0	0	0	....	1961-62	1961-62
Kushner, Dale	NYI, Phi.	3	84	10	13	23	215	....	....	....	....	....	....	1989-90	1991-92
‡ Kuznetsov, Maxim	Det., L.A.	4	136	2	8	10	137	....	....	....	....	....	....	2000-01	2003-04
Kuznik, Greg	Car.	1	1	0	0	0	0	....	....	....	....	....	....	2000-01	2000-01
Kuzyk, Ken	Cle.	2	41	5	9	14	8	....	....	....	....	....	....	1976-77	1977-78
Kvartalnov, Dmitri	Bos.	2	112	42	49	91	26	4	0	0	0	0	....	1992-93	1993-94
Kwong, Larry	NYR	1	1	0	0	0	0	....	....	....	....	....	....	1947-48	1947-48
● Kyle, Bill	NYR	2	3	0	3	3	0	....	....	....	....	....	....	1949-50	1950-51
● Kyle, Gus	NYR, Bos.	3	203	6	20	26	362	14	1	2	3	34	....	1949-50	1951-52
Kyllonen, Markku	Wpg.	1	9	0	2	2	2	....	....	....	....	....	....	1988-89	1988-89
Kypreos, Nick	Wsh., Hfd., NYR, Tor.	8	442	46	44	90	1210	34	1	3	4	65	1	1989-90	1996-97
Kyte, Jim	Wpg., Pit., Cgy., Ott., S.J.	13	598	17	49	66	1342	42	0	6	6	94	....	1982-83	1995-96

L

Name	NHL Teams	NHL Seasons	GP	G	A	TP	PIM	GP	G	A	TP	PIM	NHL Cup Wins	First NHL Season	Last NHL Season
Labadie, Mike	NYR	1	3	0	0	0	0	....	....	....	....	....	....	1952-53	1952-53
Labatte, Neil	St.L.	2	26	0	2	2	19	....	....	....	....	....	....	1978-79	1981-82
L'Abbe, Moe	Chi.	1	5	0	1	1	0	....	....	....	....	....	....	1972-73	1972-73
Labelle, Marc	Dal.	1	9	0	0	0	46	....	....	....	....	....	....	1996-97	1996-97
● Labine, Leo	Bos., Det.	11	643	128	193	321	730	60	12	11	23	82	....	1951-52	1961-62
Labossiere, Gord	NYR, L.A., Min.	6	215	44	62	106	75	10	2	3	5	28	....	1963-64	1971-72
Labovitch, Max	NYR	1	5	0	0	0	4	....	....	....	....	....	....	1943-44	1943-44
Labraaten, Dan	Det., Cgy.	4	268	71	73	144	47	8	1	0	1	4	....	1978-79	1981-82
Labre, Yvon	Pit., Wsh.	9	371	14	87	101	788	....	....	....	....	....	....	1970-71	1980-81
Labrie, Guy	Bos., NYR	2	42	4	9	13	16	....	....	....	....	....	....	1943-44	1944-45
Lach, Elmer	Mtl.	14	664	215	408	623	478	76	19	45	64	36	3	1940-41	1953-54
Lachance, Michel	Col.	1	21	0	4	4	22	....	....	....	....	....	....	1978-79	1978-79
‡ Lachance, Scott	NYI, Mtl., Van., CBJ	13	819	31	112	143	567	11	1	2	3	6	....	1991-92	2003-04
Lacombe, Francois	Oak., Buf., Que.	4	78	2	17	19	54	3	1	0	1	0	....	1968-69	1979-80
Lacombe, Normand	Buf., Edm., Phi.	7	319	53	62	115	196	26	5	1	6	49	1	1984-85	1990-91
Lacroix, Andre	Phi., Chi., Hfd.	6	325	79	119	198	44	16	2	5	7	0	....	1967-68	1979-80
Lacroix, Daniel	NYR, Bos., Phi., Edm., NYI	7	188	11	7	18	379	16	0	1	1	26	....	1993-94	1999-00
Lacroix, Eric	Tor., L.A., Col., NYR, Ott.	8	472	67	70	137	361	30	1	5	6	25	....	1993-94	2000-01
Lacroix, Pierre	Que., Hfd.	4	274	24	108	132	197	8	0	2	2	10	....	1979-80	1982-83
Ladouceur, Randy	Det., Hfd., Ana.	14	930	30	126	156	1322	40	5	8	13	59	....	1982-83	1995-96
LaFayette, Nathan	St.L., Van., NYR, L.A.	6	187	17	20	37	103	32	2	7	9	8	....	1993-94	1998-99
‡ Laflamme, Christian	Chi., Edm., Mtl., St.L.	8	324	2	45	47	282	9	0	1	1	6	....	1996-97	2003-04
Lafleur, Guy	Mtl., NYR, Que.	17	1126	560	793	1353	399	128	58	76	134	67	5	1971-72	1990-91
● Lafleur, Roland	Mtl.	1	1	0	0	0	0	....	....	....	....	....	....	1924-25	1924-25
LaFontaine, Pat	NYI, Buf., NYR	15	865	468	545	1013	552	69	26	36	62	36	....	1983-84	1997-98
Laforce, Ernie	Mtl.	1	1	0	0	0	0	....	....	....	....	....	....	1942-43	1942-43
LaForest, Bob	L.A.	1	5	1	0	1	2	....	....	....	....	....	....	1983-84	1983-84
Laforge, Claude	Mtl., Det., Phi.	8	193	24	33	57	82	5	1	2	3	15	....	1957-58	1968-69
Laforge, Marc	Hfd., Edm.	2	14	0	0	0	64	....	....	....	....	....	....	1989-90	1993-94
Laframboise, Pete	Cal., Wsh., Pit.	4	227	33	55	88	70	9	1	0	1	0	....	1971-72	1974-75
Lafrance, Adie	Mtl.	1	3	0	0	0	2	2	0	0	0	0	....	1933-34	1933-34
● Lafrance, Leo	Mtl., Chi.	2	33	2	0	2	6	....	....	....	....	....	....	1926-27	1927-28
Lafreniere, Jason	Que., NYR, T.B.	5	146	34	53	87	22	15	1	5	6	19	....	1986-87	1993-94
Lafreniere, Roger	Det., St.L.	2	13	0	0	0	4	....	....	....	....	....	....	1962-63	1972-73
Lagace, Jean-Guy	Pit., Buf., K.C.	6	197	9	39	48	251	....	....	....	....	....	....	1968-69	1975-76
Laidlaw, Tom	NYR, L.A.	10	705	25	139	164	717	69	4	17	21	78	....	1980-81	1989-90
Laird, Robbie	Min.	1	1	0	0	0	0	....	....	....	....	....	....	1979-80	1979-80
Lajeunesse, Serge	Det., Phi.	5	103	1	4	5	103	....	....	....	....	....	....	1970-71	1974-75
Lakovic, Sasha	Cgy., N.J.	3	37	0	4	4	118	....	....	....	....	....	....	1996-97	1998-99
Lalande, Hec	Chi., Det.	4	151	21	39	60	120	....	....	....	....	....	....	1953-54	1957-58
Lalonde, Bobby	Van., Atl., Bos., Cgy.	11	641	124	210	334	298	16	4	2	6	6	....	1971-72	1981-82
● Lalonde, Newsy	Mtl., NYA	6	99	124	41	165	183	7	15	4	19	32	....	1917-18	1926-27
Lalonde, Ron	Pit., Wsh.	7	397	45	78	123	106	....	....	....	....	....	....	1972-73	1978-79
Lalor, Mike	Mtl., St.L., Wsh., Wpg., S.J., Dal.	12	687	17	88	105	677	92	5	10	15	167	1	1985-86	1996-97
● Lamb, Joe	Mtl.M., Ott., NYA, Bos., Mtl., St.L., Det.	11	443	108	101	209	601	18	1	1	2	51	....	1927-28	1937-38
Lamb, Mark	Cgy., Det., Edm., Ott., Phi., Mtl.	11	403	46	100	146	291	70	7	19	26	51	1	1985-86	1995-96
‡ Lambert, Dan	Que.	2	29	6	9	15	22	....	....	....	....	....	....	1990-91	1991-92
Lambert, Denny	Ana., Ott., Nsh., Atl.	8	487	27	66	93	1391	17	0	1	1	28	....	1994-95	2001-02
Lambert, Lane	Det., NYR, Que.	6	283	58	66	124	521	17	2	4	6	40	....	1983-84	1988-89
Lambert, Yvon	Mtl., Buf.	10	683	206	273	479	340	90	27	22	49	67	4	1972-73	1981-82
Lamby, Dick	St.L.	3	22	0	5	5	22	....	....	....	....	....	....	1978-79	1980-81
● Lamirande, Jean-Paul	NYR, Mtl.	4	49	5	5	10	26	8	0	0	0	4	....	1946-47	1954-55
Lammens, Hank	Ott.	1	27	1	2	3	22	....	....	....	....	....	....	1993-94	1993-94
● Lamoureux, Leo	Mtl.	6	235	19	79	98	175	28	1	6	7	16	2	1941-42	1946-47
Lamoureux, Mitch	Pit., Phi.	3	73	11	9	20	59	....	....	....	....	....	....	1983-84	1987-88
Lampman, Mike	St.L., Van., Wsh.	4	96	17	20	37	34	....	....	....	....	....	....	1972-73	1976-77
Lancien, Jack	NYR	4	63	1	5	6	35	6	0	1	1	2	....	1946-47	1950-51
Landon, Larry	Mtl., Tor.	2	9	0	0	0	2	....	....	....	....	....	....	1983-84	1984-85
‡ Landry, Eric	Cgy., Mtl.	4	68	5	9	14	47	....	....	....	....	....	....	1997-98	2001-02
Lane, Gord	Wsh., NYI	10	539	19	94	113	1228	75	3	14	17	214	4	1975-76	1984-85
● Lane, Myles	NYR, Bos.	3	71	4	1	5	41	11	0	0	0	0	1	1928-29	1933-34
Langdon, Darren	NYR, Car., Van., Mtl., N.J.	11	521	16	23	39	1251	25	1	0	1	20	....	1994-95	2005-06
Langdon, Steve	Bos.	3	7	0	1	1	2	4	0	0	0	0	....	1974-75	1977-78
Langelle, Pete	Tor.	4	136	22	51	73	11	41	5	9	14	4	1	1938-39	1941-42
Langevin, Chris	Buf.	2	22	3	1	4	22	....	....	....	....	....	....	1983-84	1985-86
Langevin, Dave	NYI, Min., L.A.	8	513	12	107	119	530	87	2	17	19	106	4	1979-80	1986-87
Langlais, Alain	Min.	2	25	4	4	8	10	....	....	....	....	....	....	1973-74	1974-75
Langlois, Albert	Mtl., NYR, Det., Bos.	9	497	21	91	112	488	53	1	5	6	50	3	1957-58	1965-66
● Langlois, Charlie	Ham., NYA, Pit., Mtl.	4	151	22	5	27	189	2	0	0	0	0	....	1924-25	1927-28
Langway, Rod	Mtl., Wsh.	15	994	51	278	329	849	104	5	22	27	97	1	1978-79	1992-93
Lank, Jeff	Phi.	1	2	0	0	0	2	....	....	....	....	....	....	1999-00	1999-00
Lanthier, Jean-Marc	Van.	4	105	16	16	32	29	....	....	....	....	....	....	1983-84	1987-88
Lanyon, Ted	Pit.	1	5	0	0	0	4	....	....	....	....	....	....	1967-68	1967-68
Lanz, Rick	Van., Tor., Chi.	10	569	65	221	286	448	28	3	8	11	35	....	1980-81	1991-92
Laperriere, Daniel	St.L., Ott.	4	48	2	5	7	27	....	....	....	....	....	....	1992-93	1995-96
Laperriere, Jacques	Mtl.	12	691	40	242	282	674	88	9	22	31	101	6	1962-63	1973-74
Laplante, Darryl	Det.	3	35	0	6	6	10	....	....	....	....	....	....	1997-98	1999-00
Lapointe, Claude	Que., Col., Cgy., NYI, Phi.	14	879	127	178	305	721	34	4	7	11	44	....	1990-91	2003-04
Lapointe, Guy	Mtl., St.L., Bos.	16	884	171	451	622	893	123	26	44	70	138	6	1968-69	1983-84
● Lapointe, Rick	Det., Phi., St.L., Que., L.A.	11	664	44	176	220	831	46	2	7	9	64	....	1975-76	1985-86
Lappin, Peter	Min., S.J.	2	7	0	0	0	2	....	....	....	....	....	....	1989-90	1991-92
Laprade, Edgar	NYR	10	500	108	172	280	42	18	4	9	13	4	....	1945-46	1954-55
● LaPrairie, Benjamin	Chi.	1	7	0	0	0	0	....	....	....	....	....	....	1936-37	1936-37
Larionov, Igor	Van., S.J., Det., Fla., N.J.	14	921	169	475	644	474	150	30	67	97	60	3	1989-90	2003-04
Lariviere, Garry	Que., Edm.	4	219	6	57	63	167	14	0	5	5	8	....	1979-80	1982-83
Larmer, Jeff	Col., N.J., Chi.	5	158	37	51	88	57	5	1	0	1	2	....	1981-82	1985-86
Larmer, Steve	Chi., NYR	15	1006	441	571	1012	532	140	56	75	131	89	1	1980-81	1994-95
● Larochelle, Wildor	Mtl., Chi.	12	474	92	74	166	211	34	6	4	10	24	2	1925-26	1936-37
Larocque, Denis	L.A.	1	8	0	1	1	18	....	....	....	....	....	....	1987-88	1987-88
‡ Larocque, Mario	T.B.	1	5	0	0	0	16	....	....	....	....	....	....	1998-99	1998-99
● Larose, Bonner	Bos.	1	6	0	0	0	0	....	....	....	....	....	....	1925-26	1925-26
Larose, Claude	Mtl., Min., St.L.	16	943	226	257	483	887	97	14	18	32	143	5	1962-63	1977-78
Larose, Claude	NYR	2	25	4	7	11	2	2	0	0	0	0	....	1979-80	1981-82
Larose, Guy	Wpg., Tor., Cgy., Bos.	6	70	10	9	19	63	4	0	0	0	0	....	1988-89	1994-95
Larouche, Pierre	Pit., Mtl., Hfd., NYR	14	812	395	427	822	237	64	20	34	54	16	2	1974-75	1987-88
Larouche, Steve	Ott., NYR, L.A.	2	26	9	9	18	10	....	....	....	....	....	....	1994-95	1995-96
● Larson, Norm	NYA, Bro., NYR	3	89	25	18	43	12	....	....	....	....	....	....	1940-41	1946-47
Larson, Reed	Det., Bos., Edm., NYI, Min., Buf.	14	904	222	463	685	1391	32	4	7	11	63	....	1976-77	1989-90
Larter, Tyler	Wsh.	1	1	0	0	0	0	....	....	....	....	....	....	1989-90	1989-90
Latal, Jiri	Phi.	3	92	12	36	48	24	....	....	....	....	....	....	1989-90	1991-92
Latos, James	NYR	1	1	0	0	0	0	....	....	....	....	....	....	1988-89	1988-89
Latreille, Phil	NYR	1	4	0	0	0	2	....	....	....	....	....	....	1960-61	1960-61
Latta, David	Que.	4	36	4	8	12	4	....	....	....	....	....	....	1985-86	1990-91
Lauder, Martin	Bos.	1	3	0	0	0	2	....	....	....	....	....	....	1927-28	1927-28
Lauen, Mike	Wpg.	1	4	0	1	1	0	....	....	....	....	....	....	1983-84	1983-84
Lauer, Brad	NYI, Chi., Ott., Pit.	9	323	44	67	111	218	34	7	5	12	24	....	1986-87	1995-96
Laughlin, Craig	Mtl., Wsh., L.A., Tor.	8	549	136	205	341	364	33	6	6	12	20	....	1981-82	1988-89
Laughton, Mike	Oak., Cal.	4	189	39	48	87	101	11	2	4	6	0	....	1967-68	1970-71

Name	NHL Teams	NHL Seasons	Regular Schedule GP	G	A	TP	PIM	Playoffs GP	G	A	TP	PIM	NHL Cup Wins	First NHL Season	Last NHL Season
Laukkanen, Janne	Que., Col., Ott., Pit., T.B.	9	407	22	99	121	335	59	7	9	16	46	....	1994-95	2002-03
Laurence, Don	Atl., St.L.	2	79	15	22	37	14	....	....	....	....	....	....	1978-79	1979-80
Laus, Paul	Fla.	9	530	14	58	72	1702	30	2	7	9	74	....	1993-94	2001-02
LaVallee, Kevin	Cgy., L.A., St.L., Pit.	7	366	110	125	235	85	32	5	8	13	21	....	1980-81	1986-87
LaVarre, Mark	Chi.	3	78	9	16	25	58	1	0	0	0	2	....	1985-86	1987-88
Lavender, Brian	St.L., NYI, Det., Cal.	4	184	16	26	42	174	3	0	0	0	2	....	1971-72	1974-75
Lavigne, Eric	L.A.	1	1	0	0	0	0	....	....	....	....	....	....	1994-95	1994-95
● Laviolette, Jack	Mtl.	1	18	2	1	3	6	2	0	0	0	0	....	1917-18	1917-18
Laviolette, Peter	NYR	1	12	0	0	0	6	....	....	....	....	....	....	1988-89	1988-89
Lavoie, Dominic	St.L., Ott., Bos., L.A.	6	38	5	8	13	32	....	....	....	....	....	....	1988-89	1993-94
Lawless, Paul	Hfd., Phi., Van., Tor.	7	239	49	77	126	54	3	0	2	2	2	....	1982-83	1989-90
Lawrence, Mark	Dal., NYI	6	142	18	26	44	115	....	....	....	....	....	....	1994-95	2000-01
Lawson, Danny	Det., Min., Buf.	5	219	28	29	57	61	16	0	1	1	2	....	1967-68	1971-72
Lawton, Brian	Min., NYR, Hfd., Que., Bos., S.J.	9	483	112	154	266	401	11	1	1	2	12	....	1983-84	1992-93
Laxdal, Derek	Tor., NYI	6	67	12	7	19	88	1	0	2	2	2	....	1984-85	1990-91
● Laycoe, Hal	NYR, Mtl., Bos.	11	531	25	77	102	292	40	2	5	7	39	....	1945-46	1955-56
Lazaro, Jeff	Bos., Ott.	3	102	14	23	37	114	28	3	3	6	32	....	1990-91	1992-93
Leach, Jamie	Pit., Hfd., Fla.	5	81	11	9	20	12	....	....	....	....	....	1	1989-90	1993-94
Leach, Larry	Bos.	3	126	13	29	42	91	7	1	1	2	8	....	1958-59	1961-62
Leach, Reggie	Bos., Cal., Phi., Det.	13	934	381	285	666	387	94	47	22	69	22	1	1970-71	1982-83
Leach, Stephen	Wsh., Bos., St.L., Car., Ott., Phx., Pit.	15	702	130	153	283	978	92	15	11	26	87	....	1985-86	1999-00
Leavins, Jim	Det., NYR	2	41	2	12	14	30	....	....	....	....	....	....	1985-86	1986-87
‡ Lebeau, Patrick	Mtl., Cgy., Fla., Pit.	4	15	3	2	5	6	....	....	....	....	....	....	1990-91	1998-99
Lebeau, Stephan	Mtl., Ana.	7	373	118	159	277	105	30	9	7	16	12	1	1988-89	1994-95
LeBlanc, Fern	Det.	3	34	5	6	11	0	....	....	....	....	....	....	1976-77	1978-79
LeBlanc, J.P.	Chi., Det.	5	153	14	30	44	87	2	0	0	0	0	....	1968-69	1978-79
LeBlanc, John	Van., Edm., Wpg.	7	83	26	13	39	28	1	0	0	0	0	....	1986-87	1994-95
LeBoutillier, Peter	Ana.	2	35	2	1	3	176	....	....	....	....	....	....	1996-97	1997-98
LeBrun, Al	NYR	2	6	0	2	2	4	....	....	....	....	....	....	1960-61	1965-66
Lecaine, Bill	Pit.	1	4	0	0	0	0	....	....	....	....	....	....	1968-69	1968-69
LeClair, Jack	Mtl.	3	160	20	40	60	56	20	6	1	7	6	2	1954-55	1956-57
Leclerc, Mike	Ana., Phx., Cgy.	9	341	64	94	158	288	26	2	9	11	14	....	1996-97	2005-06
Leclerc, Rene	Det.	2	87	10	11	21	105	....	....	....	....	....	....	1968-69	1970-71
Lecuyer, Doug	Chi., Wpg., Pit.	4	126	11	31	42	178	7	4	0	4	15	....	1978-79	1982-83
Ledingham, Walt	Chi., NYI	3	15	0	2	2	4	....	....	....	....	....	....	1972-73	1976-77
● Leduc, Albert	Mtl., Ott., NYR	10	383	57	35	92	614	28	5	6	11	32	2	1925-26	1934-35
LeDuc, Rich	Bos., Que.	4	130	28	38	66	69	5	0	0	0	9	....	1972-73	1980-81
Ledyard, Grant	NYR, L.A., Wsh., Buf., Dal., Van., Bos., Ott., T.B.	18	1028	90	276	366	766	83	6	12	18	96	....	1984-85	2001-02
● Lee, Bobby	Mtl.	1	1	0	0	0	0	....	....	....	....	....	....	1942-43	1942-43
Lee, Edward	Que.	1	2	0	0	0	5	....	....	....	....	....	....	1984-85	1984-85
Lee, Peter	Pit.	6	431	114	131	245	257	19	0	8	8	4	....	1977-78	1982-83
‡ Leeb, Greg	Dal.	1	2	0	0	0	0	....	....	....	....	....	....	2000-01	2000-01
Leeman, Gary	Tor., Cgy., Mtl., Van., St.L.	14	667	199	267	466	531	36	8	16	24	36	1	1982-83	1996-97
Leetch, Brian	NYR, Tor., Bos.	18	1205	247	781	1028	571	95	28	69	97	36	1	1987-88	2005-06
Lefebvre, Patrice	Wsh.	1	3	0	0	0	2	....	....	....	....	....	....	1998-99	1998-99
Lefebvre, Sylvain	Mtl., Tor., Que., Col., NYR	14	945	30	154	184	674	129	4	14	18	101	1	1989-90	2002-03
● Lefley, Bryan	NYI, K.C., Col.	5	228	7	29	36	101	2	0	0	0	0	....	1972-73	1977-78
Lefley, Chuck	Mtl., St.L.	9	407	128	164	292	137	29	5	8	13	10	2	1970-71	1980-81
● Leger, Roger	NYR, Mtl.	5	187	18	53	71	71	20	0	7	7	14	....	1943-44	1949-50
Legge, Barry	Que., Wpg.	3	107	1	11	12	144	....	....	....	....	....	....	1979-80	1981-82
Legge, Randy	NYR	1	12	0	2	2	2	....	....	....	....	....	....	1972-73	1972-73
Lehman, Tommy	Bos., Edm.	3	36	5	5	10	16	....	....	....	....	....	....	1987-88	1989-90
Lehto, Petteri	Pit.	1	6	0	0	0	4	....	....	....	....	....	....	1984-85	1984-85
Lehtonen, Antero	Wsh.	1	65	9	12	21	14	....	....	....	....	....	....	1979-80	1979-80
Lehvonen, Henry	K.C.	1	4	0	0	0	0	....	....	....	....	....	....	1974-75	1974-75
Leier, Edward	Chi.	2	16	2	1	3	2	....	....	....	....	....	....	1949-50	1950-51
Leinonen, Mikko	NYR, Wsh.	4	162	31	78	109	71	20	2	11	13	28	....	1981-82	1984-85
Leiter, Bobby	Bos., Pit., Atl.	10	447	98	126	224	144	8	3	0	3	2	....	1962-63	1975-76
Leiter, Ken	NYI, Min.	5	143	14	36	50	62	15	0	6	6	8	....	1984-85	1989-90
Lemaire, Jacques	Mtl.	12	853	366	469	835	217	145	61	78	139	63	8	1967-68	1978-79
Lemay, Moe	Van., Edm., Bos., Wpg.	8	317	72	94	166	442	28	6	3	9	55	1	1981-82	1988-89
Lemelin, Roger	K.C., Col.	4	36	1	2	3	27	....	....	....	....	....	....	1974-75	1977-78
Lemieux, Alain	St.L., Que., Pit.	6	119	28	44	72	38	19	4	6	10	0	....	1981-82	1986-87
Lemieux, Bob	Oak.	1	19	0	1	1	12	....	....	....	....	....	....	1967-68	1967-68
Lemieux, Claude	Mtl., N.J., Col., Phx., Dal.	20	1197	379	406	785	1756	233	80	78	158	529	4	1983-84	2002-03
Lemieux, Jacques	L.A.	3	19	0	4	4	8	1	0	0	0	0	....	1967-68	1969-70
Lemieux, Jean	Atl., Wsh.	5	204	23	63	86	39	3	1	1	2	0	....	1973-74	1977-78
Lemieux, Jocelyn	St.L., Mtl., Chi., Hfd., N.J., Cgy., Phx.	12	598	80	84	164	740	60	5	10	15	88	....	1986-87	1997-98
Lemieux, Mario	Pit.	18	915	690	1033	1723	834	107	76	96	172	87	2	1984-85	2005-06
● Lemieux, Real	Det., L.A., NYR, Buf.	8	456	51	104	155	262	18	2	4	6	10	....	1966-67	1973-74
Lemieux, Rich	Van., K.C., Atl.	5	274	39	82	121	132	2	0	0	0	0	....	1971-72	1975-76
Lenardon, Tim	N.J., Van.	2	15	2	1	3	4	....	....	....	....	....	....	1986-87	1989-90
● Lepine, Hec	Mtl.	1	33	5	2	7	2	....	....	....	....	....	....	1925-26	1925-26
● Lepine, Pit	Mtl.	13	526	143	98	241	392	41	7	5	12	26	2	1925-26	1937-38
Leroux, Francois	Edm., Ott., Pit., Col.	10	249	3	20	23	577	33	1	3	4	34	....	1988-89	1997-98
Leroux, Gaston	Mtl.	1	2	0	0	0	0	....	....	....	....	....	....	1935-36	1935-36
Leroux, Jean-Yves	Chi.	5	220	16	22	38	146	....	....	....	....	....	....	1996-97	2000-01
Leschyshyn, Curtis	Que., Col., Wsh., Hfd., Car., Min., Ott.	16	1033	47	165	212	669	68	2	6	8	34	1	1988-89	2003-04
● Lesieur, Art	Mtl., Chi.	4	100	4	2	6	50	14	0	0	0	4	1	1928-29	1935-36
Lessard, Rick	Cgy., S.J.	3	15	0	4	4	18	....	....	....	....	....	....	1988-89	1991-92
Lesuk, Bill	Bos., Phi., L.A., Wsh., Wpg.	8	388	44	63	107	368	9	1	0	1	12	1	1968-69	1979-80
● Leswick, Jack	Chi.	1	37	1	7	8	16	....	....	....	....	....	1	1933-34	1933-34
● Leswick, Pete	NYA, Bos.	2	3	1	0	1	0	....	....	....	....	....	....	1936-37	1944-45
● Leswick, Tony	NYR, Det., Chi.	12	740	165	159	324	900	59	13	10	23	91	3	1945-46	1957-58
‡ Letang, Alan	Dal., Cgy., NYI	3	14	0	0	0	2	....	....	....	....	....	....	1999-00	2002-03
● Levandoski, Joe	NYR	1	8	1	1	2	0	....	....	....	....	....	....	1946-47	1946-47
Leveille, Normand	Bos.	2	75	17	25	42	49	....	....	....	....	....	....	1981-82	1982-83
● Leveque, Guy	L.A.	2	17	2	2	4	21	....	....	....	....	....	....	1992-93	1993-94
Lever, Don	Van., Atl., Cgy., Col., N.J., Buf.	15	1020	313	367	680	593	30	7	10	17	26	....	1972-73	1986-87
Levie, Craig	Wpg., Min., St.L., Van.	6	183	22	53	75	177	16	2	3	5	32	....	1981-82	1986-87
Levins, Scott	Wpg., Fla., Ott., Phx.	5	124	13	20	33	316	....	....	....	....	....	....	1992-93	1997-98
● Levinsky, Alex	Tor., NYR, Chi.	9	367	19	49	68	307	37	2	1	3	26	2	1930-31	1938-39
Levo, Tapio	Col., N.J.	2	107	16	53	69	36	....	....	....	....	....	....	1981-82	1982-83
Lewicki, Danny	Tor., NYR, Chi.	9	461	105	135	240	177	28	0	4	4	8	1	1950-51	1958-59
Lewis, Dale	NYR	1	8	0	0	0	0	....	....	....	....	....	....	1975-76	1975-76
Lewis, Dave	NYI, L.A., N.J., Det.	15	1008	36	187	223	953	91	1	20	21	143	....	1973-74	1987-88
● Lewis, Doug	Mtl.	1	3	0	0	0	0	....	....	....	....	....	....	1946-47	1946-47
● Lewis, Herbie	Det.	11	483	148	161	309	248	38	13	10	23	6	2	1928-29	1938-39
Ley, Rick	Tor., Hfd.	6	310	12	72	84	528	14	0	2	2	20	....	1968-69	1980-81
Liba, Igor	NYR, L.A.	1	37	7	18	25	36	2	0	0	0	2	....	1988-89	1988-89
Libby, Jeff	NYI	1	1	0	0	0	0	....	....	....	....	....	....	1997-98	1997-98
Libett, Nick	Det., Pit.	14	982	237	268	505	472	16	6	2	8	2	....	1967-68	1980-81
Licari, Tony	Det.	1	9	0	1	1	0	....	....	....	....	....	....	1946-47	1946-47
Liddington, Bob	Tor.	1	11	0	1	1	2	....	....	....	....	....	....	1970-71	1970-71
Lidster, Doug	Van., NYR, St.L., Dal.	16	897	75	268	343	679	80	6	15	21	64	1	1983-84	1998-99
Lilley, John	Ana.	3	23	3	8	11	13	....	....	....	....	....	....	1993-94	1995-96
Lind, Juha	Dal., Mtl.	3	133	9	13	22	20	15	2	2	4	8	....	1997-98	2000-01
Lindberg, Chris	Cgy., Que.	3	116	17	25	42	47	2	0	1	1	2	....	1991-92	1993-94
Lindbom, Johan	NYR	1	38	1	3	4	28	....	....	....	....	....	....	1997-98	1997-98
Linden, Jamie	Fla.	1	4	0	0	0	17	....	....	....	....	....	....	1994-95	1994-95
Lindgren, Lars	Van., Min.	6	394	25	113	138	325	40	5	6	11	20	....	1978-79	1983-84
Lindgren, Mats	Edm., NYI, Van.	8	387	54	74	128	146	24	1	5	6	10	....	1996-97	2003-04
Lindholm, Mikael	L.A.	1	18	2	2	4	2	....	....	....	....	....	....	1989-90	1989-90
Lindros, Brett	NYI	2	51	2	5	7	147	....	....	....	....	....	....	1994-95	1995-96
‡ Lindsay, Bill	Que., Fla., Cgy., S.J., Mtl., Atl.	13	777	83	141	224	922	42	7	8	15	44	....	1991-92	2003-04
Lindsay, Ted	Det., Chi.	17	1068	379	472	851	1808	133	47	49	96	194	4	1944-45	1964-65
Lindstrom, Willy	Wpg., Edm., Pit.	8	582	161	162	323	200	57	14	18	32	24	2	1979-80	1986-87
Linseman, Ken	Phi., Edm., Bos., Tor.	14	860	256	551	807	1727	113	43	77	120	325	1	1978-79	1991-92
‡ Lintner, Richard	Nsh., NYR, Pit.	3	112	8	12	20	54	....	....	....	....	....	....	1999-00	2002-03
Lipuma, Chris	T.B., S.J.	5	72	0	9	9	146	....	....	....	....	....	....	1992-93	1996-97
● Liscombe, Carl	Det.	9	373	137	140	277	117	59	22	19	41	20	1	1937-38	1945-46
Litzenberger, Ed	Mtl., Chi., Det., Tor.	12	618	178	238	416	283	40	5	13	18	34	4	1952-53	1963-64
Loach, Lonnie	Ott., L.A., Ana.	2	56	10	13	23	29	1	0	0	0	0	....	1992-93	1993-94
● Locas, Jacques	Mtl.	2	59	7	8	15	66	....	....	....	....	....	....	1947-48	1948-49

Brian Leetch

Jacques Lemaire

Normand Leveille

Mark Lofthouse

Claude Loiselle

Don Luce

Bruce MacGregor

Merlin Malinowski

Name	NHL Teams	NHL Seasons	Regular Schedule GP	G	A	TP	PIM	Playoffs GP	G	A	TP	PIM	NHL Cup Wins	First NHL Season	Last NHL Season
Lochead, Bill	Det., Col., NYR	6	330	69	62	131	180	7	3	0	3	6	....	1974-75	1979-80
• Locking, Norm	Chi.	2	48	2	6	8	26	....	....	....	....	....	....	1934-35	1935-36
Loewen, Darcy	Buf., Ott.	5	135	4	8	12	211	....	....	....	....	....	....	1989-90	1993-94
Lofthouse, Mark	Wsh., Det.	6	181	42	38	80	73	....	....	....	....	....	....	1977-78	1982-83
Logan, Dave	Chi., Van.	6	218	5	29	34	470	12	0	0	0	10	....	1975-76	1980-81
Logan, Robert	Buf., L.A.	3	42	10	5	15	0	....	....	....	....	....	....	1986-87	1988-89
Loiselle, Claude	Det., N.J., Que., Tor., NYI	13	616	92	117	209	1149	41	4	11	15	58	....	1981-82	1993-94
• Lomakin, Andrei	Phi., Fla.	4	215	42	62	104	92	....	....	....	....	....	....	1991-92	1994-95
Loney, Brian	Van.	1	12	2	3	5	6	....	....	....	....	....	....	1995-96	1995-96
Loney, Troy	Pit., Ana., NYI, NYR	12	624	87	110	197	1091	67	8	14	22	97	2	1983-84	1994-95
Long, Barry	L.A., Det., Wpg.	5	280	11	68	79	250	5	0	1	1	18	....	1972-73	1981-82
• Long, Stan	Mtl.	1	....	....	....	....	....	3	0	0	0	0	....	1951-52	1951-52
Lonsberry, Ross	Bos., L.A., Phi., Pit.	15	968	256	310	566	806	100	21	25	46	87	2	1966-67	1980-81
Loob, Hakan	Cgy.	6	450	193	236	429	189	73	26	28	54	16	1	1983-84	1988-89
Loob, Peter	Que.	1	8	1	2	3	0	....	....	....	....	....	....	1984-85	1984-85
Lorentz, Jim	Bos., St.L., NYR, Buf.	10	659	161	238	399	208	54	12	10	22	30	1	1968-69	1977-78
Lorimer, Bob	NYI, Col., N.J.	10	529	22	90	112	431	49	3	10	13	83	2	1976-77	1985-86
• Lorrain, Rod	Mtl.	6	179	28	39	67	30	11	0	3	3	0	....	1935-36	1941-42
• Loughlin, Clem	Det., Chi.	3	101	8	6	14	77	....	....	....	....	....	....	1926-27	1928-29
• Loughlin, Wilf	Tor.	1	14	0	0	0	2	....	....	....	....	....	....	1923-24	1923-24
Lovsin, Ken	Wsh.	1	1	0	0	0	0	....	....	....	....	....	....	1990-91	1990-91
Lowdermilk, Dwayne	Wsh.	1	2	0	1	1	2	....	....	....	....	....	....	1980-81	1980-81
Lowe, Darren	Pit.	1	8	1	2	3	0	....	....	....	....	....	....	1983-84	1983-84
Lowe, Kevin	Edm., NYR	19	1254	84	347	431	1498	214	10	48	58	192	6	1979-80	1997-98
Lowe, Odie	NYR	1	4	1	1	2	0	....	....	....	....	....	....	1949-50	1949-50
• Lowe, Ross	Bos., Mtl.	3	77	6	8	14	82	2	0	0	0	0	....	1949-50	1951-52
• Lowrey, Ed	Ott., Ham.	3	27	2	2	4	6	....	....	....	....	....	....	1917-18	1920-21
• Lowrey, Fred	Mtl.M., Pit.	2	53	1	1	2	10	2	0	0	0	6	....	1924-25	1925-26
• Lowrey, Gerry	Tor., Pit., Phi., Chi., Ott.	6	211	48	48	96	148	2	1	0	1	2	....	1927-28	1932-33
Lowry, Dave	Van., St.L., Fla., S.J., Cgy.	19	1084	164	187	351	1191	111	16	20	36	181	....	1985-86	2003-04
Lucas, Danny	Phi.	1	6	1	0	1	0	....	....	....	....	....	....	1978-79	1978-79
Lucas, Dave	Det.	1	1	0	0	0	0	....	....	....	....	....	....	1962-63	1962-63
Luce, Don	NYR, Det., Buf., L.A., Tor.	13	894	225	329	554	364	71	17	22	39	52	....	1969-70	1981-82
Ludvig, Jan	N.J., Buf.	7	314	54	87	141	418	....	....	....	....	....	....	1982-83	1988-89
Ludwig, Craig	Mtl., NYI, Min., Dal.	17	1256	38	184	222	1437	177	4	25	29	244	2	1982-83	1998-99
Ludzik, Steve	Chi., Buf.	9	424	46	93	139	333	44	4	8	12	70	....	1981-82	1989-90
Luhning, Warren	NYI, Dal.	3	29	0	1	1	21	....	....	....	....	....	....	1997-98	1999-00
Lukowich, Bernie	Pit., St.L.	2	79	13	15	28	34	2	0	0	0	0	....	1973-74	1974-75
Lukowich, Morris	Wpg., Bos., L.A.	8	582	199	219	418	584	11	0	2	2	24	....	1979-80	1986-87
Luksa, Charlie	Hfd.	1	8	0	1	1	4	....	....	....	....	....	....	1979-80	1979-80
Lumley, Dave	Mtl., Edm., Hfd.	9	437	98	160	258	680	61	6	8	14	131	2	1978-79	1986-87
Lumme, Jyrki	Mtl., Van., Phx., Dal., Tor.	15	985	114	354	468	620	105	9	35	44	52	....	1988-89	2002-03
Lund, Pentti	Bos., NYR	7	259	44	55	99	40	19	7	5	12	0	....	1946-47	1952-53
Lundberg, Brian	Pit.	1	1	0	0	0	2	....	....	....	....	....	....	1982-83	1982-83
Lunde, Len	Det., Chi., Min., Van.	8	321	39	83	122	75	20	3	2	5	2	....	1958-59	1970-71
Lundholm, Bengt	Wpg.	5	275	48	95	143	72	14	3	4	7	14	....	1981-82	1985-86
Lundrigan, Joe	Tor., Wsh.	2	52	2	8	10	22	....	....	....	....	....	....	1972-73	1974-75
Lundstrom, Tord	Det.	1	11	1	1	2	0	....	....	....	....	....	....	1973-74	1973-74
• Lundy, Pat	Det., Chi.	5	150	37	32	69	31	16	2	2	4	2	....	1945-46	1950-51
‡ Luoma, Mikko	Edm.	1	3	0	1	1	0	....	....	....	....	....	....	2003-04	2003-04
Luongo, Chris	Det., Ott., NYI	5	218	8	23	31	176	....	....	....	....	....	....	1990-91	1995-96
‡ Lupaschuk, Ross	Pit.	1	3	0	0	0	4	....	....	....	....	....	....	2002-03	2002-03
Lupien, Gilles	Mtl., Pit., Hfd.	5	226	5	25	30	416	25	0	0	0	21	2	1977-78	1981-82
• Lupul, Gary	Van.	7	293	70	75	145	243	25	4	7	11	11	....	1979-80	1985-86
• Lyashenko, Roman	Dal., NYR	4	139	14	9	23	55	17	2	1	3	0	....	1999-00	2002-03
Lyle, George	Det., Hfd.	4	99	24	38	62	51	....	....	....	....	....	....	1979-80	1982-83
Lynch, Jack	Pit., Det., Wsh.	7	382	24	106	130	336	....	....	....	....	....	....	1972-73	1978-79
Lynn, Vic	NYR, Det., Mtl., Tor., Bos., Chi.	11	327	49	76	125	274	47	7	10	17	46	3	1942-43	1953-54
Lyon, Steve	Pit.	1	3	0	0	0	2	....	....	....	....	....	....	1976-77	1976-77
• Lyons, Ron	Bos., Phi.	1	36	2	4	6	27	5	0	0	0	0	....	1930-31	1930-31
‡ Lysak, Brett	Car.	1	2	0	0	0	2	....	....	....	....	....	....	2003-04	2003-04
Lysiak, Tom	Atl., Chi.	13	919	292	551	843	567	76	25	38	63	49	....	1973-74	1985-86

M

Name	NHL Teams	NHL Seasons	Regular Schedule GP	G	A	TP	PIM	Playoffs GP	G	A	TP	PIM	NHL Cup Wins	First NHL Season	Last NHL Season
MacAdam, Al	Phi., Cal., Cle., Min., Van.	12	864	240	351	591	509	64	20	24	44	21	1	1973-74	1984-85
MacDermid, Paul	Hfd., Wpg., Wsh., Que.	14	690	116	142	258	1303	43	5	11	16	116	....	1981-82	1994-95
MacDonald, Blair	Edm., Van.	4	219	91	100	191	65	11	0	6	6	2	....	1979-80	1982-83
MacDonald, Brett	Van.	1	1	0	0	0	0	....	....	....	....	....	....	1987-88	1987-88
MacDonald, Doug	Buf.	3	11	1	0	1	2	....	....	....	....	....	....	1992-93	1994-95
MacDonald, Jason	NYR	1	4	0	0	0	19	....	....	....	....	....	....	2003-04	2003-04
MacDonald, Kevin	Ott.	1	1	0	0	0	2	....	....	....	....	....	....	1993-94	1993-94
• MacDonald, Kilby	NYR	4	151	36	34	70	47	15	1	2	3	4	1	1939-40	1944-45
MacDonald, Lowell	Det., L.A., Pit.	13	506	180	210	390	92	30	11	11	22	12	....	1961-62	1977-78
MacDonald, Parker	Tor., NYR, Det., Bos., Min.	14	676	144	179	323	253	75	14	14	28	20	....	1952-53	1968-69
MacDougall, Kim	Min.	1	1	0	0	0	0	....	....	....	....	....	....	1974-75	1974-75
MacEachern, Shane	St.L.	1	1	0	0	0	0	....	....	....	....	....	....	1987-88	1987-88
Macey, Hub	NYR, Mtl.	3	30	6	9	15	0	8	0	0	0	0	....	1941-42	1946-47
MacGregor, Bruce	Det., NYR	14	893	213	257	470	217	107	19	28	47	44	....	1960-61	1973-74
MacGregor, Randy	Hfd.	1	2	1	1	2	2	....	....	....	....	....	....	1981-82	1981-82
MacGuigan, Garth	NYI	2	5	0	1	1	2	....	....	....	....	....	....	1979-80	1983-84
MacInnis, Al	Cgy., St.L.	23	1416	340	934	1274	1511	177	39	121	160	255	1	1981-82	2003-04
MacIntosh, Ian	NYR	1	4	0	0	0	4	....	....	....	....	....	....	1952-53	1952-53
MacIver, Don	Wpg.	1	6	0	0	0	2	....	....	....	....	....	....	1979-80	1979-80
MacIver, Norm	NYR, Hfd., Edm., Ott., Pit., Wpg., Phx.	12	500	55	230	285	350	56	3	11	14	32	....	1986-87	1997-98
MacKasey, Blair	Tor.	1	1	0	0	0	2	....	....	....	....	....	....	1976-77	1976-77
• MacKay, Calum	Det., Mtl.	8	237	50	55	105	214	38	5	13	18	20	1	1946-47	1954-55
MacKay, Dave	Chi.	1	29	3	0	3	26	5	0	1	1	2	....	1940-41	1940-41
• MacKay, Mickey	Chi., Pit., Bos.	4	147	44	19	63	79	11	0	0	0	6	1	1926-27	1929-30
• MacKay, Murdo	Mtl.	4	19	0	3	3	0	15	1	2	3	0	....	1945-46	1948-49
MacKell, Fleming	Tor., Bos.	13	665	149	220	369	562	80	22	41	63	75	2	1947-48	1959-60
• MacKell, Jack	Ott.	2	45	4	2	6	59	2	0	0	0	0	2	1919-20	1920-21
MacKenzie, Barry	Min.	1	6	0	1	1	6	....	....	....	....	....	....	1968-69	1968-69
• MacKenzie, Bill	Chi., Mtl.M., NYR, Mtl.	7	264	15	14	29	145	21	1	1	2	11	1	1932-33	1939-40
Mackey, David	Chi., Min., St.L.	6	126	8	12	20	305	3	0	0	0	2	....	1987-88	1993-94
• Mackey, Reg	NYR	1	34	0	0	0	16	1	0	0	0	0	....	1926-27	1926-27
• Mackie, Howie	Det.	2	20	1	0	1	4	8	0	0	0	0	1	1936-37	1937-38
MacKinnon, Paul	Wsh.	5	147	5	23	28	91	....	....	....	....	....	....	1979-80	1983-84
MacLean, John	N.J., S.J., NYR, Dal.	18	1194	413	429	842	1328	104	35	48	83	152	1	1983-84	2001-02
MacLean, Paul	St.L., Wpg., Det.	11	719	324	349	673	968	53	21	14	35	110	....	1980-81	1990-91
MacLeish, Rick	Phi., Hfd., Pit., Det.	14	846	349	410	759	434	114	54	53	107	38	2	1970-71	1983-84
MacLellan, Brian	L.A., NYR, Min., Cgy., Det.	10	606	172	241	413	551	47	5	9	14	42	1	1982-83	1991-92
MacLeod, Pat	Min., S.J., Dal.	5	53	5	13	18	14	....	....	....	....	....	....	1990-91	1995-96
MacMillan, Billy	Tor., Atl., NYI	7	446	74	77	151	184	53	6	6	12	40	....	1970-71	1976-77
MacMillan, Bob	NYR, St.L., Atl., Cgy., Col., N.J., Chi.	11	753	228	349	577	260	31	8	11	19	16	....	1974-75	1984-85
‡ MacMillan, Jeff	Dal.	1	4	0	0	0	0	....	....	....	....	....	....	2003-04	2003-04
MacMillan, John	Tor., Det.	5	104	5	10	15	32	12	0	1	1	2	2	1960-61	1964-65
MacNeil, Al	Tor., Mtl., Chi., NYR, Pit.	11	524	17	75	92	617	37	0	4	4	67	....	1955-56	1967-68
MacNeil, Bernie	St.L.	1	4	0	0	0	0	....	....	....	....	....	....	1973-74	1973-74
MacNeil, Ian	Phi.	1	2	0	0	0	0	....	....	....	....	....	....	2002-03	2002-03
Macoun, Jamie	Cgy., Tor., Det.	16	1128	76	282	358	1208	159	10	32	42	169	2	1982-83	1998-99
• MacPherson, Bud	Mtl.	7	259	5	33	38	233	29	0	3	3	21	1	1948-49	1956-57
• MacSweyn, Ralph	Phi.	5	47	0	5	5	10	8	0	0	0	6	....	1967-68	1971-72
MacTavish, Craig	Bos., Edm., NYR, Phi., St.L.	17	1093	213	267	480	891	193	20	38	58	218	4	1979-80	1996-97
MacWilliam, Mike	NYI	1	6	0	0	0	14	....	....	....	....	....	....	1995-96	1995-96
Madigan, Connie	St.L.	1	20	0	3	3	25	5	0	0	0	4	....	1972-73	1972-73
Madill, Jeff	N.J.	1	14	4	0	4	46	7	0	2	2	8	....	1990-91	1990-91
Magee, Dean	Min.	1	7	0	0	0	4	....	....	....	....	....	....	1977-78	1977-78
Maggs, Daryl	Chi., Cal., Tor.	3	135	14	19	33	54	4	0	0	0	0	....	1971-72	1979-80
Magnan, Marc	Tor.	1	4	0	1	1	5	....	....	....	....	....	....	1982-83	1982-83
• Magnuson, Keith	Chi.	11	589	14	125	139	1442	68	3	9	12	164	....	1969-70	1979-80
Maguire, Kevin	Tor., Buf., Phi.	6	260	29	30	59	782	11	0	0	0	86	....	1986-87	1991-92
Mahaffy, John	Mtl., NYR	3	37	11	25	36	4	1	0	1	1	0	....	1942-43	1944-45
Mahovlich, Frank	Tor., Det., Mtl.	18	1181	533	570	1103	1056	137	51	67	118	163	6	1956-57	1973-74

Name	NHL Teams	NHL Seasons	Regular Schedule GP	G	A	TP	PIM	Playoffs GP	G	A	TP	PIM	NHL Cup Wins	First NHL Season	Last NHL Season
Mahovlich, Pete	Det., Mtl., Pit.	16	884	288	485	773	916	88	30	42	72	134	4	1965-66	1980-81
Mailhot, Jacques	Que.	1	5	0	0	0	33	....	....	....	....	....	....	1988-89	1988-89
● Mailley, Frank	Mtl.	1	1	0	0	0	0	....	....	....	....	....	....	1942-43	1942-43
Mair, Jim	Phi., NYI, Van.	5	76	4	15	19	49	3	1	2	3	4	....	1970-71	1974-75
● Majeau, Fern	Mtl.	2	56	22	24	46	43	1	0	0	0	0	1	1943-44	1944-45
Major, Bruce	Que.	1	4	0	0	0	0	....	....	....	....	....	....	1990-91	1990-91
Major, Mark	Det.	1	2	0	0	0	5	....	....	....	....	....	....	1996-97	1996-97
Makarov, Sergei	Cgy., S.J., Dal.	7	424	134	250	384	317	34	12	11	23	8	....	1989-90	1996-97
Makela, Mikko	NYI, L.A., Buf., Bos.	7	423	118	147	265	139	18	3	8	11	14	....	1985-86	1994-95
Maki, Chico	Chi.	15	841	143	292	435	345	113	17	36	53	43	1	1960-61	1975-76
● Maki, Wayne	Chi., St.L., Van.	6	246	57	79	136	184	2	1	0	1	2	....	1967-68	1972-73
Makkonen, Kari	Edm.	1	9	2	2	4	0	....	....	....	....	....	....	1979-80	1979-80
Malakhov, Vladimir	NYI, Mtl., N.J., NYR, Phi.	13	712	86	260	346	697	75	8	19	27	64	1	1992-93	2005-06
Maley, David	Mtl., N.J., Edm., S.J., NYI	9	466	43	81	124	1043	46	5	5	10	111	1	1985-86	1993-94
Malgunas, Stewart	Phi., Wpg., Wsh., Cgy.	7	129	1	5	6	144	....	....	....	....	....	....	1993-94	1999-00
Malinowski, Merlin	Col., N.J., Hfd.	5	282	54	111	165	121	....	....	....	....	....	....	1978-79	1982-83
Malkoc, Dean	Van., Bos., NYI	4	116	1	3	4	299	....	....	....	....	....	....	1995-96	1998-99
Mallette, Troy	NYR, Edm., N.J., Ott., Bos., T.B.	9	456	51	68	119	1226	15	2	2	4	99	....	1989-90	1997-98
Malone, Cliff	Mtl.	1	3	0	0	0	0	....	....	....	....	....	....	1951-52	1951-52
Malone, Greg	Pit., Hfd., Que.	11	704	191	310	501	661	20	3	5	8	32	....	1976-77	1986-87
● Malone, Joe	Mtl., Que., Ham.	7	126	143	32	175	57	9	6	2	8	6	1	1917-18	1923-24
Maloney, Dan	Chi., L.A., Det., Tor.	11	737	192	259	451	1489	40	4	7	11	35	....	1970-71	1981-82
Maloney, Dave	NYR, Buf.	11	657	71	246	317	1154	49	7	17	24	91	....	1974-75	1984-85
Maloney, Don	NYR, Hfd., NYI	13	765	214	350	564	815	94	22	35	57	101	....	1978-79	1990-91
Maloney, Phil	Bos., Tor., Chi.	5	158	28	43	71	16	6	0	0	0	0	....	1949-50	1959-60
Maltais, Steve	Wsh., Min., T.B., Det., CBJ	6	120	9	18	27	53	1	0	0	0	0	....	1989-90	2000-01
Maluta, Ray	Bos.	2	25	2	3	5	6	2	0	0	0	0	....	1975-76	1976-77
Manastersky, Tom	Mtl.	1	6	0	0	0	11	....	....	....	....	....	....	1950-51	1950-51
● Mancuso, Gus	Mtl., NYR	4	42	7	9	16	17	....	....	....	....	....	....	1937-38	1942-43
‡ Manderville, Kent	Tor., Edm., Hfd., Car., Phi., Pit.	12	646	37	67	104	348	67	3	3	6	44	....	1991-92	2002-03
Mandich, Dan	Min.	4	111	5	11	16	303	7	0	0	0	2	....	1982-83	1985-86
‡ Maneluk, Mike	Phi., Chi., NYR, CBJ	3	85	11	10	21	57	....	....	....	....	....	....	1998-99	2000-01
Manery, Kris	Cle., Min., Van., Wpg.	4	250	63	64	127	91	....	....	....	....	....	....	1977-78	1980-81
Manery, Randy	Det., Atl., L.A.	10	582	50	206	256	415	13	0	2	2	12	....	1970-71	1979-80
‡ Mann, Cameron	Bos., Nsh.	5	93	14	10	24	40	1	0	0	0	0	....	1997-98	2002-03
Mann, Jack	NYR	2	9	3	4	7	0	....	....	....	....	....	....	1943-44	1944-45
Mann, Jimmy	Wpg., Que., Pit.	8	293	10	20	30	895	22	0	0	0	89	....	1979-80	1987-88
Mann, Ken	Det.	1	1	0	0	0	0	....	....	....	....	....	....	1975-76	1975-76
● Mann, Norm	Tor.	3	31	0	3	3	4	2	0	0	0	0	....	1935-36	1940-41
● Manners, Rennison	Pit., Phi.	2	37	3	2	5	14	....	....	....	....	....	....	1929-30	1930-31
‡ Manning, Paul	CBJ	1	8	0	0	0	2	....	....	....	....	....	....	2002-03	2002-03
Manno, Bob	Van., Tor., Det.	8	371	41	131	172	274	17	2	4	6	12	....	1976-77	1984-85
Manson, Dave	Chi., Edm., Wpg., Phx., Mtl., Dal., Tor.	16	1103	102	288	390	2792	112	7	24	31	343	....	1986-87	2001-02
Manson, Ray	Bos., NYR	2	2	0	1	1	0	....	....	....	....	....	....	1947-48	1948-49
● Mantha, Georges	Mtl.	13	488	89	102	191	148	36	6	2	8	24	2	1928-29	1940-41
Mantha, Moe	Wpg., Pit., Edm., Min., Phi.	12	656	81	289	370	501	17	5	10	15	18	....	1980-81	1991-92
● Mantha, Sylvio	Mtl., Bos.	14	542	63	78	141	671	39	5	5	10	64	3	1923-24	1936-37
● Maracle, Bud	NYR	1	11	1	3	4	4	4	0	0	0	0	....	1930-31	1930-31
Marcetta, Milan	Tor., Min.	3	54	7	15	22	10	17	7	7	14	4	1	1966-67	1968-69
● March, Mush	Chi.	17	759	153	230	383	540	45	12	15	27	41	2	1928-29	1944-45
Marchinko, Brian	Tor., NYI	4	47	2	6	8	0	....	....	....	....	....	....	1970-71	1973-74
Marchment, Bryan	Wpg., Chi., Hfd., Edm., T.B., S.J., Col., Tor., Cgy.	17	926	40	142	182	2307	83	4	3	7	102	....	1988-89	2005-06
Marcinyshyn, Dave	N.J., Que., NYR	3	16	0	1	1	49	....	....	....	....	....	....	1990-91	1992-93
Marcon, Lou	Det.	3	60	0	4	4	42	....	....	....	....	....	....	1958-59	1962-63
Marcotte, Don	Bos.	15	868	230	254	484	317	132	34	27	61	81	2	1965-66	1981-82
‡ Marha, Josef	Col., Ana., Chi.	6	159	21	32	53	32	....	....	....	....	....	....	1995-96	2000-01
Marini, Hector	NYI, N.J.	5	154	27	46	73	246	10	3	6	9	14	2	1978-79	1983-84
Marinucci, Chris	NYI, L.A.	2	13	1	4	5	2	....	....	....	....	....	....	1994-95	1996-97
● Mario, Frank	Bos.	2	53	9	19	28	24	....	....	....	....	....	....	1941-42	1944-45
● Mariucci, John	Chi.	5	223	11	34	45	308	12	0	3	3	26	....	1940-41	1947-48
Mark, Gordon	N.J., Edm.	4	85	3	10	13	187	....	....	....	....	....	....	1986-87	1994-95
Markell, John	Wpg., St.L., Min.	4	55	11	10	21	36	....	....	....	....	....	....	1979-80	1984-85
● Marker, Gus	Det., Mtl.M., Tor., Bro.	10	322	64	69	133	133	46	5	7	12	36	1	1932-33	1941-42
Markham, Ray	NYR	1	14	1	1	2	21	7	1	0	1	24	....	1979-80	1979-80
● Markle, Jack	Tor.	1	8	0	1	1	0	....	....	....	....	....	....	1935-36	1935-36
● Marks, Jack	Mtl.W., Tor., Que.	2	7	0	0	0	4	....	....	....	....	....	1	1917-18	1919-20
Marks, John	Chi.	10	657	112	163	275	330	57	5	9	14	60	....	1972-73	1981-82
Markwart, Nevin	Bos., Cgy.	8	309	41	68	109	794	19	1	0	1	33	....	1983-84	1991-92
Marois, Daniel	Tor., NYI, Bos., Dal.	8	350	117	93	210	419	19	3	3	6	28	....	1987-88	1995-96
Marois, Mario	NYR, Van., Que., Wpg., St.L.	15	955	76	357	433	1746	100	4	34	38	182	....	1977-78	1991-92
● Marotte, Gilles	Bos., Chi., L.A., NYR, St.L.	12	808	56	265	321	919	29	3	3	6	26	....	1965-66	1976-77
Marquess, Mark	Bos.	1	27	5	4	9	6	4	0	0	0	0	....	1946-47	1946-47
Marsh, Brad	Atl., Cgy., Phi., Tor., Det., Ott.	15	1086	23	175	198	1241	97	6	18	24	124	....	1978-79	1992-93
Marsh, Gary	Det., Tor.	2	7	1	3	4	4	....	....	....	....	....	....	1967-68	1968-69
Marsh, Peter	Wpg., Chi.	5	278	48	71	119	224	26	1	5	6	33	....	1979-80	1983-84
Marshall, Bert	Det., Oak., Cal., NYR, NYI	14	868	17	181	198	926	72	4	22	26	99	....	1965-66	1978-79
Marshall, Don	Mtl., NYR, Buf., Tor.	19	1176	265	324	589	127	94	8	15	23	14	5	1951-52	1971-72
Marshall, Jason	St.L., Ana., Wsh., Min., S.J.	12	526	16	51	67	1004	43	2	3	5	55	....	1991-92	2005-06
Marshall, Paul	Pit., Tor., Hfd.	4	95	15	18	33	17	1	0	0	0	0	....	1979-80	1982-83
Marshall, Willie	Tor.	4	33	1	5	6	2	....	....	....	....	....	....	1952-53	1958-59
Marson, Mike	Wsh., L.A.	6	196	24	24	48	233	....	....	....	....	....	....	1974-75	1979-80
● Martin, Clare	Bos., Det., Chi., NYR	6	237	12	28	40	78	27	0	2	2	6	1	1941-42	1951-52
Martin, Craig	Wpg., Fla.	2	21	0	1	1	24	....	....	....	....	....	....	1994-95	1996-97
● Martin, Frank	Bos., Chi.	6	282	11	46	57	122	10	0	2	2	2	....	1952-53	1957-58
Martin, Grant	Van., Wsh.	4	44	0	4	4	55	1	1	0	1	2	....	1983-84	1986-87
Martin, Jack	Tor.	1	1	0	0	0	0	....	....	....	....	....	....	1960-61	1960-61
Martin, Matt	Tor.	4	76	0	5	5	71	....	....	....	....	....	....	1993-94	1996-97
Martin, Pit	Det., Bos., Chi., Van.	17	1101	324	485	809	609	100	27	31	58	56	....	1961-62	1978-79
Martin, Rick	Buf., L.A.	11	685	384	317	701	477	63	24	29	53	74	....	1971-72	1981-82
● Martin, Ron	NYA	2	94	13	16	29	36	....	....	....	....	....	....	1932-33	1933-34
Martin, Terry	Buf., Que., Tor., Edm., Min.	10	479	104	101	205	202	21	4	2	6	26	....	1975-76	1984-85
Martin, Tom	Tor.	1	3	1	0	1	0	....	....	....	....	....	....	1967-68	1967-68
Martin, Tom	Wpg., Hfd., Min.	6	92	12	11	23	249	4	0	0	0	6	....	1984-85	1989-90
● Martineau, Don	Atl., Min., Det.	4	90	6	10	16	63	....	....	....	....	....	....	1973-74	1976-77
Martini, Darcy	Edm.	1	2	0	0	0	0	....	....	....	....	....	....	1993-94	1993-94
Martinson, Steve	Det., Mtl., Min.	4	49	2	1	3	244	1	0	0	0	10	....	1987-88	1991-92
Maruk, Dennis	Cal., Cle., Min., Wsh.	14	888	356	522	878	761	34	14	22	36	26	....	1975-76	1988-89
Masnick, Paul	Mtl., Chi., Tor.	6	232	18	41	59	139	33	4	5	9	27	1	1950-51	1957-58
● Mason, Charley	NYR, NYA, Det., Chi.	4	95	7	18	25	44	4	0	1	1	0	....	1934-35	1938-39
● Massecar, George	NYA	3	100	12	11	23	46	....	....	....	....	....	....	1929-30	1931-32
Masters, Jamie	St.L.	3	33	1	13	14	2	2	0	0	0	0	....	1975-76	1978-79
● Masterton, Bill	Min.	1	38	4	8	12	4	....	....	....	....	....	....	1967-68	1967-68
● Mathers, Frank	Tor.	3	23	1	3	4	4	....	....	....	....	....	....	1948-49	1951-52
Mathiasen, Dwight	Pit.	3	33	1	7	8	18	....	....	....	....	....	....	1985-86	1987-88
Mathieson, Jim	Wsh.	1	2	0	0	0	4	....	....	....	....	....	....	1989-90	1989-90
Mathieu, Marquis	Bos.	3	16	0	2	2	14	....	....	....	....	....	....	1998-99	2000-01
Matte, Christian	Col., Min.	5	25	2	3	5	12	....	....	....	....	....	....	1996-97	2000-01
● Matte, Joe	Tor., Ham., Bos., Mtl.	4	68	17	15	32	54	....	....	....	....	....	....	1919-20	1925-26
● Matte, Joe	Det., Chi.	2	24	0	3	3	8	....	....	....	....	....	....	1929-30	1942-43
Matteau, Stephane	Cgy., Chi., NYR, St.L., S.J., Fla.	13	848	144	172	316	742	109	12	22	34	80	1	1990-91	2002-03
Matteucci, Mike	Min.	2	6	0	0	0	4	....	....	....	....	....	....	2000-01	2001-02
Mattiussi, Dick	Pit., Oak., Cal.	4	200	8	31	39	124	8	0	1	1	6	....	1967-68	1970-71
● Matz, Johnny	Mtl.	1	30	2	3	5	0	1	0	0	0	0	....	1924-25	1924-25
‡ Mauldin, Greg	CBJ	1	6	0	0	0	4	....	....	....	....	....	....	2003-04	2003-04
Maxner, Wayne	Bos.	2	62	8	9	17	48	....	....	....	....	....	....	1964-65	1965-66
Maxwell, Brad	Min., Que., Tor., Van., NYR	10	612	98	270	368	1292	79	12	49	61	178	....	1977-78	1986-87
Maxwell, Bryan	Min., St.L., Wpg., Pit.	8	331	18	77	95	745	15	1	1	2	86	....	1977-78	1984-85
Maxwell, Kevin	Min., Col., N.J.	3	66	6	15	21	61	16	3	4	7	24	....	1980-81	1983-84
Maxwell, Wally	Tor.	1	2	0	0	0	0	....	....	....	....	....	....	1952-53	1952-53
May, Alan	Bos., Edm., Wsh., Dal., Cgy.	8	393	31	45	76	1348	40	1	2	3	80	....	1987-88	1994-95
Mayer, Derek	Ott.	1	17	2	2	4	8	....	....	....	....	....	....	1993-94	1993-94
Mayer, Jim	NYR	1	4	0	0	0	0	....	....	....	....	....	....	1979-80	1979-80
Mayer, Pat	Pit.	1	1	0	0	0	4	....	....	....	....	....	....	1987-88	1987-88
● Mayer, Shep	Tor.	1	12	1	2	3	4	....	....	....	....	....	....	1942-43	1942-43

Bryan Marchment

Hector Marini

John Mariucci

Jason Marshall

Jack McDonald

Shawn McEachern

John McKenzie

Vic Mercredi

Name	NHL Teams	NHL Seasons	Regular Schedule GP	G	A	TP	PIM	Playoffs GP	G	A	TP	PIM	NHL Cup Wins	First NHL Season	Last NHL Season
• Mazur, Eddie	Mtl., Chi.	6	107	8	20	28	120	25	4	5	9	22	1	1950-51	1956-57
Mazur, Jay	Van.	4	47	11	7	18	20	6	0	1	1	8	....	1988-89	1991-92
McAdam, Gary	Buf., Pit., Det., Cgy., Wsh., N.J., Tor.	11	534	96	132	228	243	30	6	5	11	16	....	1975-76	1985-86
• McAdam, Sam	NYR	1	5	0	0	0	0	....	....	....	....	....	....	1930-31	1930-31
‡ McAllister, Chris	Van., Tor., Phi., Col., NYR	7	301	4	17	21	634	9	0	1	1	4	....	1997-98	2003-04
McAlpine, Chris	N.J., St.L., T.B., Atl., Chi., L.A.	8	289	6	24	30	245	28	0	1	1	18	1	1994-95	2002-03
• McAndrew, Hazen	Bro.	1	7	0	1	1	6	....	....	....	....	....	....	1941-42	1941-42
McAneeley, Ted	Cal.	3	158	8	35	43	141	....	....	....	....	....	....	1972-73	1974-75
McAtee, Jud	Det.	3	46	15	13	28	6	14	2	1	3	0	....	1942-43	1944-45
McAtee, Norm	Bos.	1	13	0	1	1	0	....	....	....	....	....	....	1946-47	1946-47
• McAvoy, George	Mtl.	1	....	....	....	....	....	4	0	0	0	0	....	1954-55	1954-55
McBain, Andrew	Wpg., Pit., Van., Ott.	11	608	129	172	301	633	24	5	7	12	39	....	1983-84	1993-94
McBain, Jason	Hfd.	2	9	0	0	0	0	....	....	....	....	....	....	1995-96	1996-97
‡ McBain, Mike	T.B.	2	64	0	7	7	22	....	....	....	....	....	....	1997-98	1998-99
McBean, Wayne	L.A., NYI, Wpg.	6	211	10	39	49	168	2	1	1	2	0	....	1987-88	1993-94
McBride, Cliff	Mtl.M., Tor.	2	2	0	0	0	0	....	....	....	....	....	....	1928-29	1929-30
McBurney, Jim	Chi.	1	1	0	1	1	0	....	....	....	....	....	....	1952-53	1952-53
• McCabe, Stan	Det., Mtl.M.	4	78	9	4	13	49	....	....	....	....	....	....	1929-30	1933-34
• McCaffrey, Bert	Tor., Pit., Mtl.	7	260	43	30	73	202	8	2	1	3	10	1	1924-25	1930-31
McCahill, John	Col.	1	1	0	0	0	0	....	....	....	....	....	....	1977-78	1977-78
• McCaig, Doug	Det., Chi.	7	263	8	21	29	255	7	0	1	1	10	....	1941-42	1950-51
• McCallum, Dunc	NYR, Pit.	5	187	14	35	49	230	10	1	2	3	12	....	1965-66	1970-71
• McCalmon, Eddie	Chi., Phi.	2	39	5	0	5	14	....	....	....	....	....	....	1927-28	1930-31
McCann, Rick	Det.	6	43	1	4	5	6	....	....	....	....	....	....	1967-68	1974-75
McCarthy, Dan	NYR	1	5	4	0	4	4	....	....	....	....	....	....	1980-81	1980-81
McCarthy, Kevin	Phi., Van., Pit.	10	537	67	191	258	527	21	2	3	5	20	....	1977-78	1986-87
McCarthy, Sandy	Cgy., T.B., Phi., Car., NYR, Bos.	11	736	72	76	148	1534	23	0	2	2	61	....	1993-94	2003-04
• McCarthy, Thomas	Que., Ham.	2	35	22	7	29	10	....	....	....	....	....	....	1919-20	1920-21
McCarthy, Tom	Det., Bos.	4	60	8	9	17	8	....	....	....	....	....	....	1956-57	1960-61
McCarthy, Tom	Min., Bos.	9	460	178	221	399	330	68	12	26	38	67	....	1979-80	1987-88
• McCartney, Walt	Mtl.	1	2	0	0	0	0	....	....	....	....	....	....	1932-33	1932-33
McCaskill, Ted	Min.	1	4	0	2	2	0	....	....	....	....	....	....	1967-68	1967-68
McClanahan, Rob	Buf., Hfd., NYR	5	224	38	63	101	126	34	4	12	16	31	....	1979-80	1983-84
McCleary, Trent	Ott., Bos., Mtl.	4	192	8	15	23	134	....	....	....	....	....	....	1995-96	1999-00
McClelland, Kevin	Pit., Edm., Det., Tor., Wpg.	12	588	68	112	180	1672	98	11	18	29	281	4	1981-82	1993-94
McCord, Bob	Bos., Det., Min., St.L.	7	316	10	58	68	262	14	2	5	7	10	....	1963-64	1972-73
• McCord, Dennis	Van.	1	3	0	0	0	6	....	....	....	....	....	....	1973-74	1973-74
McCormack, John	Tor., Mtl., Chi.	8	311	25	49	74	35	22	1	1	2	0	2	1947-48	1954-55
McCosh, Shawn	L.A., NYR	2	9	1	0	1	6	....	....	....	....	....	....	1991-92	1994-95
McCourt, Dale	Det., Buf., Tor.	7	532	194	284	478	124	21	9	7	16	6	....	1977-78	1983-84
McCreary, Bill	NYR, Det., Mtl., St.L.	8	309	53	62	115	108	48	6	16	22	14	....	1953-54	1970-71
McCreary, Bill	Tor.	1	12	1	0	1	4	....	....	....	....	....	....	1980-81	1980-81
• McCreary, Keith	Mtl., Pit., Atl.	10	532	131	112	243	294	16	0	4	4	6	....	1961-62	1974-75
• McCreedy, John	Tor.	2	64	17	12	29	25	21	4	3	7	16	2	1941-42	1944-45
McCrimmon, Brad	Bos., Phi., Cgy., Det., Hfd., Phx.	18	1222	81	322	403	1416	116	11	18	29	176	1	1979-80	1996-97
McCrimmon, Jim	St.L.	1	2	0	0	0	0	....	....	....	....	....	....	1974-75	1974-75
• McCulley, Bob	Mtl.	1	1	0	0	0	0	....	....	....	....	....	....	1934-35	1934-35
• McCurry, Duke	Pit.	4	148	21	11	32	119	4	0	2	2	2	....	1925-26	1928-29
McCutcheon, Brian	Det.	3	37	3	1	4	7	....	....	....	....	....	....	1974-75	1976-77
McCutcheon, Darwin	Tor.	1	1	0	0	0	2	....	....	....	....	....	....	1981-82	1981-82
McDill, Jeff	Chi.	1	1	0	0	0	0	....	....	....	....	....	....	1976-77	1976-77
McDonagh, Bill	NYR	1	4	0	0	0	2	....	....	....	....	....	....	1949-50	1949-50
McDonald, Ab	Mtl., Chi., Bos., Det., Pit., St.L.	15	762	182	248	430	200	84	21	29	50	42	4	1957-58	1971-72
McDonald, Brian	Chi., Buf.	2	12	0	0	0	29	8	0	0	0	2	....	1967-68	1970-71
• McDonald, Bucko	Det., Tor., NYR	11	446	35	88	123	206	50	6	1	7	24	3	1934-35	1944-45
• McDonald, Butch	Det., Chi.	2	66	8	20	28	2	5	0	2	2	10	....	1939-40	1944-45
McDonald, Gerry	Hfd.	2	8	0	0	0	4	....	....	....	....	....	....	1981-82	1983-84
• McDonald, Jack	Mtl.W., Mtl., Que., Tor.	5	69	26	14	40	30	7	1	3	4	3	....	1917-18	1921-22
McDonald, Jack	NYR	1	43	10	9	19	6	....	....	....	....	....	....	1943-44	1943-44
McDonald, Lanny	Tor., Col., Cgy.	16	1111	500	506	1006	899	117	44	40	84	120	1	1973-74	1988-89
McDonald, Robert	NYR	1	1	0	0	0	0	....	....	....	....	....	....	1943-44	1943-44
McDonald, Terry	K.C.	1	8	0	1	1	6	....	....	....	....	....	....	1975-76	1975-76
McDonnell, Joe	Van., Pit.	3	50	2	10	12	34	....	....	....	....	....	....	1981-82	1985-86
• McDonnell, Moylan	Ham.	1	22	1	2	3	2	....	....	....	....	....	....	1920-21	1920-21
McDonough, Al	L.A., Pit., Atl., Det.	5	237	73	88	161	73	8	0	1	1	2	....	1970-71	1977-78
McDonough, Hubie	L.A., NYI, S.J.	5	195	40	26	66	67	5	1	0	1	4	....	1988-89	1992-93
McDougal, Mike	NYR, Hfd.	4	61	8	10	18	43	....	....	....	....	....	....	1978-79	1982-83
McDougall, Bill	Det., Edm., T.B.	3	28	5	5	10	12	1	0	0	0	0	....	1990-91	1993-94
McEachern, Shawn	Pit., L.A., Bos., Ott., Atl.	14	911	256	323	579	506	97	12	25	37	62	1	1991-92	2005-06
McElmury, Jim	Min., K.C., Col.	5	180	14	47	61	49	....	....	....	....	....	....	1972-73	1977-78
McEwen, Mike	NYR, Col., NYI, L.A., Wsh., Det., Hfd.	12	716	108	296	404	460	78	12	36	48	48	3	1976-77	1987-88
• McFadden, Jim	Det., Chi.	8	412	100	126	226	89	49	10	9	19	30	1	1946-47	1953-54
• McFadyen, Don	Chi.	4	179	12	33	45	77	11	2	2	4	5	1	1932-33	1935-36
McFall, Dan	Wpg.	2	9	0	1	1	0	....	....	....	....	....	....	1984-85	1985-86
• McFarlane, Gord	Chi.	1	2	0	0	0	0	....	....	....	....	....	....	1926-27	1926-27
McGeough, Jim	Wsh., Pit.	4	57	7	10	17	32	....	....	....	....	....	....	1981-82	1986-87
• McGibbon, Irv	Mtl.	1	1	0	0	0	2	....	....	....	....	....	....	1942-43	1942-43
McGill, Bob	Tor., Chi., S.J., Det., NYI, Hfd.	13	705	17	55	72	1766	49	0	0	0	88	....	1981-82	1993-94
• McGill, Jack	Mtl.	3	134	27	10	37	71	3	2	0	2	0	....	1934-35	1936-37
• McGill, Jack	Bos.	4	97	23	36	59	42	27	7	4	11	17	....	1941-42	1946-47
McGill, Ryan	Chi., Phi., Edm.	4	151	4	15	19	391	....	....	....	....	....	....	1991-92	1994-95
McGregor, Sandy	NYR	1	2	0	0	0	2	....	....	....	....	....	....	1963-64	1963-64
• McGuire, Mickey	Pit.	2	36	3	0	3	6	....	....	....	....	....	....	1926-27	1927-28
McHugh, Mike	Min., S.J.	4	20	1	0	1	16	....	....	....	....	....	....	1988-89	1991-92
McIlhargey, Jack	Phi., Van., Hfd.	8	393	11	36	47	1102	27	0	3	3	68	....	1974-75	1981-82
• McInenly, Bert	Det., NYA, Ott., Bos.	6	166	19	15	34	144	4	0	0	0	2	....	1930-31	1935-36
McInnis, Marty	NYI, Cgy., Ana., Bos.	12	796	170	250	420	330	22	3	2	5	4	....	1991-92	2002-03
McIntosh, Bruce	Min.	1	2	0	0	0	0	....	....	....	....	....	....	1972-73	1972-73
McIntosh, Paul	Buf.	2	48	0	2	2	66	2	0	0	0	7	....	1974-75	1975-76
• McIntyre, Jack	Bos., Chi., Det.	11	499	109	102	211	173	29	7	6	13	4	....	1949-50	1959-60
McIntyre, John	Tor., L.A., NYR, Van.	6	351	24	54	78	516	44	0	6	6	54	....	1989-90	1994-95
McIntyre, Larry	Tor.	2	41	0	3	3	26	....	....	....	....	....	....	1969-70	1972-73
McKay, Doug	Det.	1	....	....	....	....	....	1	0	0	0	0	1	1949-50	1949-50
McKay, Randy	Det., N.J., Dal., Mtl.	15	932	162	201	363	1731	123	20	23	43	123	2	1988-89	2002-03
McKay, Ray	Chi., Buf., Cal.	6	140	2	16	18	102	....	....	....	....	....	....	1968-69	1973-74
McKay, Scott	Ana.	1	1	0	0	0	0	....	....	....	....	....	....	1993-94	1993-94
McKechnie, Walt	Min., Cal., Bos., Det., Wsh., Cle., Tor., Col.	16	955	214	392	606	469	15	7	5	12	7	....	1967-68	1982-83
McKee, Mike	Que.	1	48	3	12	15	41	....	....	....	....	....	....	1993-94	1993-94
McKegney, Ian	Chi.	1	3	0	0	0	2	....	....	....	....	....	....	1976-77	1976-77
McKegney, Tony	Buf., Que., Min., NYR, St.L., Det., Chi.	13	912	320	319	639	517	79	24	23	47	56	....	1978-79	1990-91
McKendry, Alex	NYI, Cgy.	4	46	3	6	9	21	6	2	2	4	0	1	1977-78	1980-81
McKenna, Sean	Buf., L.A., Tor.	9	414	82	80	162	181	15	1	2	3	2	....	1981-82	1989-90
McKenna, Steve	L.A., Min., Pit., NYR	8	373	18	14	32	824	3	0	1	1	8	....	1996-97	2003-04
McKenney, Don	Bos., NYR, Tor., Det., St.L.	13	798	237	345	582	211	58	18	29	47	10	1	1954-55	1967-68
McKenny, Jim	Tor., Min.	14	604	82	247	329	294	37	7	9	16	10	....	1965-66	1978-79
McKenzie, Brian	Pit.	1	6	1	1	2	4	....	....	....	....	....	....	1971-72	1971-72
McKenzie, Jim	Hfd., Dal., Pit., Wpg., Phx., Ana., Wsh., N.J., Nsh.	15	880	48	52	100	1739	51	0	0	0	38	1	1989-90	2003-04
McKenzie, John	Chi., Det., NYR, Bos.	12	691	206	268	474	917	69	15	32	47	133	2	1958-59	1971-72
McKim, Andrew	Bos., Det.	3	38	1	4	5	6	....	....	....	....	....	....	1992-93	1994-95
• McKinnon, Alex	Ham., NYA, Chi.	5	193	19	11	30	237	....	....	....	....	....	....	1924-25	1928-29
• McKinnon, John	Mtl., Pit., Phi.	6	208	28	11	39	224	2	0	0	0	4	....	1925-26	1930-31
McLaren, Steve	St.L.	1	6	0	0	0	25	....	....	....	....	....	....	2003-04	2003-04
McLean, Don	Wsh.	1	9	0	0	0	6	....	....	....	....	....	....	1975-76	1975-76
• McLean, Fred	Que., Ham.	2	8	0	0	0	2	....	....	....	....	....	....	1919-20	1920-21
• McLean, Jack	Tor.	3	67	14	24	38	76	13	2	2	4	8	1	1942-43	1944-45
• McLean, Jeff	S.J.	1	6	1	0	1	0	....	....	....	....	....	....	1993-94	1993-94
• McLellan, John	Tor.	1	2	0	0	0	0	....	....	....	....	....	....	1951-52	1951-52
McLellan, Scott	Bos.	1	2	0	0	0	0	....	....	....	....	....	....	1982-83	1982-83
McLellan, Todd	NYI	1	5	1	1	2	0	....	....	....	....	....	....	1987-88	1987-88
• McLenahan, Rollie	Det.	1	9	2	1	3	10	2	0	0	0	0	....	1945-46	1945-46
McLeod, Al	Det.	1	26	2	2	4	24	....	....	....	....	....	....	1973-74	1973-74
McLeod, Jackie	NYR	5	106	14	23	37	12	7	0	0	0	0	....	1949-50	1954-55
‡ McLlwain, Dave	Pit., Wpg., Buf., NYI, Tor., Ott.	10	501	100	107	207	292	20	0	2	2	2	....	1987-88	1996-97

Name	NHL Teams	NHL Seasons	Regular Schedule GP	G	A	TP	PIM	Playoffs GP	G	A	TP	PIM	NHL Cup Wins	First NHL Season	Last NHL Season
● McMahon, Mike	Mtl., Bos.	3	57	7	18	25	102	13	1	2	3	30	1	1942-43	1945-46
McMahon, Mike	NYR, Min., Chi., Det., Pit., Buf.	8	224	15	68	83	171	14	3	7	10	4	....	1963-64	1971-72
McManama, Bob	Pit.	3	99	11	25	36	28	8	0	1	1	6	....	1973-74	1975-76
● McManus, Sammy	Mtl.M., Bos.	2	26	0	1	1	8	1	0	0	0	0	1	1934-35	1936-37
‡ McMorrow, Sean	Buf.	1	1	0	0	0	0	....	....	....	....	....	....	2002-03	2002-03
McMurchy, Tom	Chi., Edm.	4	55	8	4	12	65	....	....	....	....	....	....	1983-84	1987-88
McNab, Max	Det.	4	128	16	19	35	24	25	1	0	1	4	1	1947-48	1950-51
McNab, Peter	Buf., Bos., Van., N.J.	14	954	363	450	813	179	107	40	42	82	20	....	1973-74	1986-87
● McNabney, Sid	Mtl.	1	....	....	....	....	....	5	0	1	1	2	....	1950-51	1950-51
● McNamara, Howard	Mtl.	1	10	1	0	1	4	....	....	....	....	....	....	1919-20	1919-20
● McNaughton, George	Que.	1	1	0	0	0	0	....	....	....	....	....	....	1919-20	1919-20
McNeill, Billy	Det.	6	257	21	46	67	142	4	1	1	2	4	....	1956-57	1963-64
‡ McNeill, Grant	Fla.	1	3	0	0	0	5	....	....	....	....	....	....	2003-04	2003-04
McNeill, Mike	Chi., Que.	2	63	5	11	16	18	....	....	....	....	....	....	1990-91	1991-92
McNeill, Stu	Det.	3	10	1	1	2	2	....	....	....	....	....	....	1957-58	1959-60
McPhee, George	NYR, N.J.	7	115	24	25	49	257	29	5	3	8	69	....	1982-83	1988-89
McPhee, Mike	Mtl., Min., Dal.	11	744	200	199	399	661	134	28	27	55	193	1	1983-84	1993-94
McRae, Basil	Que., Tor., Det., Min., T.B., St.L., Chi.	16	576	53	83	136	2457	78	8	4	12	349	....	1981-82	1996-97
McRae, Chris	Tor., Det.	3	21	1	0	1	122	....	....	....	....	....	....	1987-88	1989-90
McRae, Ken	Que., Tor.	7	137	14	21	35	364	6	0	0	0	4	....	1987-88	1993-94
● McReavy, Pat	Bos., Det.	4	55	5	10	15	4	22	3	3	6	9	1	1938-39	1941-42
McReynolds, Brian	Wpg., NYR, L.A.	3	30	1	5	6	8	....	....	....	....	....	....	1989-90	1993-94
McSheffrey, Bryan	Van., Buf.	3	90	13	7	20	44	....	....	....	....	....	....	1972-73	1974-75
McSorley, Marty	Pit., Edm., L.A., NYR, S.J., Bos.	17	961	108	251	359	3381	115	10	19	29	374	2	1983-84	1999-00
McSween, Don	Buf., Ana.	5	47	3	10	13	55	....	....	....	....	....	....	1987-88	1995-96
McTaggart, Jim	Wsh.	2	71	3	10	13	205	....	....	....	....	....	....	1980-81	1981-82
‡ McTavish, Dale	Cgy.	1	9	1	2	3	2	....	....	....	....	....	....	1996-97	1996-97
McTavish, Gord	St.L., Wpg.	2	11	1	3	4	2	....	....	....	....	....	....	1978-79	1979-80
● McVeigh, Charley	Chi., NYA	9	397	84	88	172	138	4	0	0	0	2	....	1926-27	1934-35
● McVicar, Jack	Mtl.M.	2	88	2	4	6	63	6	0	0	0	2	....	1930-31	1931-32
Meagher, Rick	Mtl., Hfd., N.J., St.L.	12	691	144	165	309	383	62	8	7	15	41	....	1979-80	1990-91
Meehan, Gerry	Tor., Phi., Buf., Van., Atl., Wsh.	10	670	180	243	423	111	10	0	1	1	0	....	1968-69	1978-79
Meeke, Brent	Cal., Cle.	5	75	9	22	31	8	....	....	....	....	....	....	1972-73	1976-77
Meeker, Howie	Tor.	8	346	83	102	185	329	42	6	9	15	50	4	1946-47	1953-54
Meeker, Mike	Pit.	1	4	0	0	0	5	....	....	....	....	....	....	1978-79	1978-79
● Meeking, Harry	Tor., Det., Bos.	3	64	18	12	30	66	9	3	0	3	6	....	1917-18	1926-27
Meger, Paul	Mtl.	6	212	39	52	91	118	35	3	8	11	16	1	1949-50	1954-55
Meighan, Ron	Min., Pit.	2	48	3	7	10	18	....	....	....	....	....	....	1981-82	1982-83
Meissner, Barrie	Min.	2	6	0	1	1	4	....	....	....	....	....	....	1967-68	1968-69
● Meissner, Dick	Bos., NYR	5	171	11	15	26	37	....	....	....	....	....	....	1959-60	1964-65
Melametsa, Anssi	Wpg.	1	27	0	3	3	2	....	....	....	....	....	....	1985-86	1985-86
‡ Melanson, Dean	Buf., Wsh.	2	9	0	0	0	8	....	....	....	....	....	....	1994-95	2001-02
Melin, Roger	Min.	2	3	0	0	0	0	....	....	....	....	....	....	1980-81	1981-82
Mellor, Tom	Det.	2	26	2	4	6	25	....	....	....	....	....	....	1973-74	1974-75
● Melnyk, Gerry	Det., Chi., St.L.	6	269	39	77	116	34	53	6	6	12	6	....	1955-56	1967-68
Melnyk, Larry	Bos., Edm., NYR, Van.	10	432	11	63	74	686	66	2	9	11	127	1	1980-81	1989-90
Melrose, Barry	Wpg., Tor., Det.	6	300	10	23	33	728	7	0	2	2	38	....	1979-80	1985-86
Menard, Hillary	Chi.	1	1	0	0	0	0	....	....	....	....	....	....	1953-54	1953-54
Menard, Howie	Det., L.A., Chi., Oak.	4	151	23	42	65	87	19	3	7	10	36	....	1963-64	1969-70
Mercredi, Vic	Atl.	1	2	0	0	0	0	....	....	....	....	....	....	1974-75	1974-75
Meredith, Greg	Cgy.	2	38	6	4	10	8	5	3	1	4	4	....	1980-81	1982-83
Merkosky, Glenn	Hfd., N.J., Det.	5	66	5	12	17	22	....	....	....	....	....	....	1981-82	1989-90
● Meronek, Bill	Mtl.	2	19	5	8	13	0	1	0	0	0	0	....	1939-40	1942-43
Merrick, Wayne	St.L., Cal., Cle., NYI	12	774	191	265	456	303	102	19	30	49	30	4	1972-73	1983-84
● Merrill, Horace	Ott.	2	8	0	0	0	3	....	....	....	....	....	1	1917-18	1919-20
Mertzig, Jan	NYR	1	23	0	2	2	8	....	....	....	....	....	....	1998-99	1998-99
Messier, Eric	Col., Fla.	8	406	25	50	75	146	72	3	5	8	22	1	1996-97	2003-04
Messier, Joby	NYR	3	25	0	4	4	24	....	....	....	....	....	....	1992-93	1994-95
Messier, Mark	Edm., NYR, Van.	25	1756	694	1193	1887	1910	236	109	186	295	244	6	1979-80	2003-04
Messier, Mitch	Min.	4	20	0	2	2	11	....	....	....	....	....	....	1987-88	1990-91
Messier, Paul	Col.	1	9	0	0	0	4	....	....	....	....	....	....	1978-79	1978-79
Metcalfe, Scott	Edm., Buf.	3	19	1	2	3	18	....	....	....	....	....	....	1987-88	1989-90
Metz, Don	Tor.	9	172	20	35	55	42	42	7	8	15	12	5	1938-39	1948-49
● Metz, Nick	Tor.	12	518	131	119	250	149	76	19	20	39	31	4	1934-35	1947-48
● Michaluk, Art	Chi.	1	5	0	0	0	0	....	....	....	....	....	....	1947-48	1947-48
Michaluk, John	Chi.	1	1	0	0	0	0	....	....	....	....	....	....	1950-51	1950-51
Michayluk, Dave	Phi., Pit.	3	14	2	6	8	8	7	1	1	2	0	1	1981-82	1991-92
Micheletti, Joe	St.L., Col.	3	158	11	60	71	114	11	1	11	12	10	....	1979-80	1981-82
Micheletti, Pat	Min.	1	12	2	0	2	8	....	....	....	....	....	....	1987-88	1987-88
● Mickey, Larry	Chi., NYR, Tor., Mtl., L.A., Phi., Buf.	11	292	39	53	92	160	9	1	0	1	10	....	1964-65	1974-75
● Mickoski, Nick	NYR, Chi., Det., Bos.	13	703	158	185	343	319	18	1	6	7	6	....	1947-48	1959-60
Middendorf, Max	Que., Edm.	4	13	2	4	6	6	....	....	....	....	....	....	1986-87	1990-91
Middleton, Rick	NYR, Bos.	14	1005	448	540	988	157	114	45	55	100	19	....	1974-75	1987-88
Miehm, Kevin	St.L.	2	22	1	4	5	8	2	0	1	1	0	....	1992-93	1993-94
Migay, Rudy	Tor.	10	418	59	92	151	293	15	1	0	1	20	....	1949-50	1959-60
‡ Mika, Petr	NYI	1	3	0	0	0	0	....	....	....	....	....	....	1999-00	1999-00
Mikita, Stan	Chi.	22	1394	541	926	1467	1270	155	59	91	150	169	1	1958-59	1979-80
Mikkelson, Bill	L.A., NYI, Wsh.	4	147	4	18	22	105	....	....	....	....	....	....	1971-72	1976-77
Mikol, Jim	Tor., NYR	2	34	1	4	5	8	....	....	....	....	....	....	1962-63	1964-65
Mikulchik, Oleg	Wpg., Ana.	3	37	0	3	3	33	....	....	....	....	....	....	1993-94	1995-96
Milbury, Mike	Bos.	12	754	49	189	238	1552	86	4	24	28	219	....	1975-76	1986-87
● Milks, Hib	Pit., Phi., NYR, Ott.	8	317	87	41	128	179	11	0	0	0	2	....	1925-26	1932-33
Millar, Craig	Edm., Nsh., T.B.	5	114	8	14	22	73	....	....	....	....	....	....	1996-97	2000-01
● Millar, Hugh	Det.	1	4	0	0	0	0	1	0	0	0	0	....	1946-47	1946-47
Millar, Mike	Hfd., Wsh., Bos., Tor.	5	78	18	18	36	12	....	....	....	....	....	....	1986-87	1990-91
Millen, Corey	NYR, L.A., N.J., Dal., Cgy.	8	335	90	119	209	236	47	5	7	12	22	....	1989-90	1996-97
● Miller, Bill	Mtl.M., Mtl.	3	95	7	3	10	16	12	0	0	0	0	1	1934-35	1936-37
Miller, Bob	Bos., Col., L.A.	6	404	75	119	194	220	36	4	7	11	27	....	1977-78	1984-85
Miller, Brad	Buf., Ott., Cgy.	6	82	1	5	6	321	....	....	....	....	....	....	1988-89	1993-94
● Miller, Earl	Chi., Tor.	5	109	19	14	33	124	10	1	0	1	6	1	1927-28	1931-32
Miller, Jack	Chi.	2	17	0	0	0	4	....	....	....	....	....	....	1949-50	1950-51
Miller, Jason	N.J.	3	6	0	0	0	0	....	....	....	....	....	....	1990-91	1992-93
Miller, Jay	Bos., L.A.	7	446	40	44	84	1723	48	2	3	5	243	....	1985-86	1991-92
Miller, Kelly	NYR, Wsh.	15	1057	181	282	463	512	119	20	34	54	65	....	1984-85	1998-99
Miller, Kevin	NYR, Det., Wsh., St.L., S.J., Pit., Chi., NYI, Ott.	13	620	150	185	335	429	61	7	10	17	49	....	1988-89	2003-04
Miller, Kip	Que., Min., S.J., NYI, Chi., Pit., Ana., Wsh.	12	449	74	165	239	105	25	6	11	17	23	....	1990-91	2003-04
Miller, Paul	Col.	1	3	0	3	3	0	....	....	....	....	....	....	1981-82	1981-82
Miller, Perry	Det.	4	217	10	51	61	387	....	....	....	....	....	....	1977-78	1980-81
Miller, Tom	Det., NYI	4	118	16	25	41	34	....	....	....	....	....	....	1970-71	1974-75
Miller, Warren	NYR, Hfd.	4	262	40	50	90	137	6	1	0	1	0	....	1979-80	1982-83
Mills, Craig	Wpg., Chi.	3	31	0	5	5	36	1	0	0	0	0	....	1995-96	1998-99
Miner, John	Edm.	1	14	2	3	5	16	....	....	....	....	....	....	1987-88	1987-88
Minor, Gerry	Van.	5	140	11	21	32	173	12	1	3	4	25	....	1979-80	1983-84
Mironov, Boris	Wpg., Edm., Chi., NYR	11	716	76	231	307	891	25	5	11	16	45	....	1993-94	2003-04
Mironov, Dmitri	Tor., Pit., Ana., Det., Wsh.	11	556	54	206	260	568	75	10	26	36	48	1	1991-92	2001-02
Miszuk, John	Det., Chi., Phi., Min.	6	237	7	39	46	232	19	0	3	3	19	....	1963-64	1969-70
Mitchell, Bill	Det.	1	1	0	0	0	0	....	....	....	....	....	....	1963-64	1963-64
● Mitchell, Herb	Bos.	2	44	6	0	6	36	....	....	....	....	....	....	1924-25	1925-26
Mitchell, Jeff	Dal.	1	7	0	0	0	7	....	....	....	....	....	....	1997-98	1997-98
● Mitchell, Red	Chi.	3	83	4	5	9	67	....	....	....	....	....	....	1941-42	1944-45
Mitchell, Roy	Min.	1	3	0	0	0	0	....	....	....	....	....	....	1992-93	1992-93
● Moe, Bill	NYR	5	261	11	42	53	163	1	0	0	0	0	....	1944-45	1948-49
Moffat, Lyle	Tor., Wpg.	3	97	12	16	28	51	....	....	....	....	....	....	1972-73	1979-80
● Moffat, Ron	Det.	3	37	1	1	2	8	7	0	0	0	0	....	1932-33	1934-35
Moger, Sandy	Bos., L.A.	5	236	41	38	79	212	5	2	2	4	12	....	1994-95	1998-99
Mogilny, Alexander	Buf., Van., N.J., Tor.	16	990	473	559	1032	432	124	39	47	86	58	1	1989-90	2005-06
Moher, Mike	N.J.	1	9	0	1	1	28	....	....	....	....	....	....	1982-83	1982-83
Mohns, Doug	Bos., Chi., Min., Atl., Wsh.	22	1390	248	462	710	1250	94	14	36	50	122	....	1953-54	1974-75
Mohns, Lloyd	NYR	1	1	0	0	0	0	....	....	....	....	....	....	1943-44	1943-44
Mokosak, Carl	Cgy., L.A., Phi., Pit., Bos.	6	83	11	15	26	170	1	0	0	0	0	....	1981-82	1988-89
Mokosak, John	Det.	2	41	0	2	2	96	....	....	....	....	....	....	1988-89	1989-90
Molin, Lars	Van.	3	172	33	65	98	37	19	2	9	11	7	....	1981-82	1983-84

Earl Miller

Kip Miller

Alexander Mogilny

Alex Motter

Joe Mullen

Mike Murphy

Don Nachbaur

Ted Nolan

Name	NHL Teams	NHL Seasons	Regular Schedule GP	G	A	TP	PIM	Playoffs GP	G	A	TP	PIM	NHL Cup Wins	First NHL Season	Last NHL Season
Moller, Mike	Buf., Edm.	7	134	15	28	43	41	3	0	1	1	0	....	1980-81	1986-87
Moller, Randy	Que., NYR, Buf., Fla.	14	815	45	180	225	1692	78	6	16	22	197	....	1981-82	1994-95
Molloy, Mitch	Buf.	1	2	0	0	0	10	....	....	....	....	....	....	1989-90	1989-90
• Molyneaux, Larry	NYR	2	45	0	1	1	20	10	0	0	0	8	....	1937-38	1938-39
Momesso, Sergio	Mtl., St.L., Van., Tor., NYR	13	710	152	193	345	1557	119	18	26	44	311	....	1983-84	1996-97
Monahan, Garry	Mtl., Det., L.A., Tor., Van.	12	748	116	169	285	484	22	3	1	4	13	....	1967-68	1978-79
Monahan, Hartland	Cal., NYR, Wsh., Pit., L.A., St.L.	7	334	61	80	141	163	6	0	0	0	4	....	1973-74	1980-81
• Mondou, Armand	Mtl.	12	386	47	71	118	99	32	3	5	8	12	2	1928-29	1939-40
Mondou, Pierre	Mtl.	9	548	194	262	456	179	69	17	28	45	26	3	1976-77	1984-85
Mongeau, Michel	St.L., T.B.	4	54	6	19	25	10	2	0	1	1	0	....	1989-90	1992-93
Mongrain, Bob	Buf., L.A.	6	81	13	14	27	14	11	1	2	3	2	....	1979-80	1985-86
Monteith, Hank	Det.	3	77	5	12	17	6	4	0	0	0	0	....	1968-69	1970-71
Montgomery, Jim	St.L., Mtl., Phi., S.J., Dal.	6	122	9	25	34	80	8	1	0	1	2	....	1993-94	2002-03
Moore, Barrie	Buf., Edm., Wsh.	3	39	2	6	8	18	....	....	....	....	....	....	1995-96	1999-00
Moore, Dickie	Mtl., Tor., St.L.	14	719	261	347	608	652	135	46	64	110	122	6	1951-52	1967-68
Moore, Steve	Col.	3	69	5	7	12	41	....	....	....	....	....	....	2001-02	2003-04
• Moran, Amby	Mtl., Chi.	2	35	1	1	2	24	....	....	....	....	....	....	1926-27	1927-28
‡ Moravec, David	Buf.	1	1	0	0	0	0	....	....	....	....	....	....	1999-00	1999-00
More, Jay	NYR, Min., S.J., Phx., Chi., Nsh.	10	406	18	54	72	702	31	0	6	6	45	....	1988-89	1998-99
• Morenz, Howie	Mtl., Chi., NYR	14	550	271	201	472	546	39	13	9	22	58	3	1923-24	1936-37
Moretto, Angelo	Cle.	1	5	1	2	3	2	....	....	....	....	....	....	1976-77	1976-77
• Morin, Pete	Mtl.	1	31	10	12	22	7	1	0	0	0	0	....	1941-42	1941-42
• Morin, Stephane	Que., Van.	5	90	16	39	55	52	....	....	....	....	....	....	1989-90	1993-94
Morisset, Dave	Fla.	1	4	0	0	0	5	....	....	....	....	....	....	2001-02	2001-02
Morissette, Dave	Mtl.	2	11	0	0	0	57	....	....	....	....	....	....	1998-99	1999-00
‡ Morozov, Aleksey	Pit.	7	451	84	135	219	98	39	4	5	9	8	....	1997-98	2003-04
• Morris, Bernie	Bos.	1	6	1	0	1	0	....	....	....	....	....	....	1924-25	1924-25
Morris, Jon	N.J., S.J., Bos.	6	103	16	33	49	47	11	1	7	8	25	....	1988-89	1993-94
• Morris, Moe	Tor., NYR	4	135	13	29	42	58	18	4	2	6	16	1	1943-44	1948-49
Morrison, Dave	L.A., Van.	4	39	3	3	6	4	....	....	....	....	....	....	1980-81	1984-85
• Morrison, Don	Det., Chi.	3	112	18	28	46	12	3	0	1	1	0	....	1947-48	1950-51
Morrison, Doug	Bos.	4	23	7	3	10	15	....	....	....	....	....	....	1979-80	1984-85
Morrison, Gary	Phi.	3	43	1	15	16	70	5	0	1	1	2	....	1979-80	1981-82
Morrison, George	St.L.	2	115	17	21	38	13	3	0	0	0	0	....	1970-71	1971-72
Morrison, Jim	Bos., Tor., Det., NYR, Pit.	12	704	40	160	200	542	36	0	12	12	38	....	1951-52	1970-71
• Morrison, John	NYA	1	18	0	0	0	0	....	....	....	....	....	....	1925-26	1925-26
Morrison, Kevin	Col.	1	41	4	11	15	23	....	....	....	....	....	....	1979-80	1979-80
Morrison, Lew	Phi., Atl., Wsh., Pit.	9	564	39	52	91	107	17	0	0	0	2	....	1969-70	1977-78
Morrison, Mark	NYR	2	10	1	1	2	0	....	....	....	....	....	....	1981-82	1983-84
• Morrison, Rod	Det.	1	34	8	7	15	4	3	0	0	0	0	....	1947-48	1947-48
Morrow, Ken	NYI	10	550	17	88	105	309	127	11	22	33	97	4	1979-80	1988-89
Morrow, Scott	Cgy.	1	4	0	0	0	0	....	....	....	....	....	....	1994-95	1994-95
Morton, Dean	Det.	1	1	1	0	1	2	....	....	....	....	....	....	1989-90	1989-90
Mortson, Gus	Tor., Chi., Det.	13	797	46	152	198	1380	54	5	8	13	68	4	1946-47	1958-59
• Mosdell, Ken	Bro., Mtl., Chi.	16	693	141	168	309	475	80	16	13	29	48	4	1941-42	1958-59
• Mosienko, Bill	Chi.	14	711	258	282	540	121	22	10	4	14	15	....	1941-42	1954-55
Mott, Morris	Cal.	3	199	18	32	50	49	....	....	....	....	....	....	1972-73	1974-75
• Motter, Alex	Bos., Det.	8	255	39	64	103	135	41	3	9	12	41	1	1934-35	1942-43
Moxey, Jim	Cal., Cle., L.A.	3	127	22	27	49	59	....	....	....	....	....	....	1974-75	1976-77
Mrozik, Rick	Cgy.	1	2	0	0	0	0	....	....	....	....	....	....	2002-03	2002-03
Muckalt, Bill	Van., NYI, Ott., Min.	5	256	40	57	97	204	5	0	0	0	0	....	1998-99	2002-03
Mulhern, Richard	Atl., L.A., Tor., Wpg.	6	303	27	93	120	217	7	0	3	3	5	....	1975-76	1980-81
Mulhern, Ryan	Wsh.	1	3	0	0	0	0	....	....	....	....	....	....	1997-98	1997-98
Mullen, Brian	Wpg., NYR, S.J., NYI	11	832	260	362	622	414	62	12	18	30	30	....	1982-83	1992-93
Mullen, Joe	St.L., Cgy., Pit., Bos.	17	1062	502	561	1063	241	143	60	46	106	42	3	1979-80	1996-97
Muller, Kirk	N.J., Mtl., NYI, Tor., Fla., Dal.	19	1349	357	602	959	1223	127	33	36	69	153	1	1984-85	2002-03
Muloin, Wayne	Det., Oak., Cal., Min.	3	147	3	21	24	93	11	0	0	0	2	....	1963-64	1970-71
Mulvenna, Glenn	Pit., Phi.	2	2	0	0	0	4	....	....	....	....	....	....	1991-92	1992-93
Mulvey, Grant	Chi., N.J.	10	586	149	135	284	816	42	10	5	15	70	....	1974-75	1983-84
Mulvey, Paul	Wsh., Pit., L.A.	4	225	30	51	81	613	....	....	....	....	....	....	1978-79	1981-82
• Mummery, Harry	Tor., Que., Mtl., Ham.	6	106	33	19	52	226	2	1	1	2	17	....	1917-18	1922-23
Muni, Craig	Tor., Edm., Chi., Buf., Wpg., Pit., Dal.	16	819	28	119	147	775	113	0	17	17	108	3	1981-82	1997-98
• Munro, Dunc	Mtl.M., Mtl.	8	239	28	18	46	172	21	2	2	4	18	1	1924-25	1931-32
• Munro, Gerry	Mtl.M., Tor.	2	34	1	0	1	37	....	....	....	....	....	....	1924-25	1925-26
Murdoch, Bob	Mtl., L.A., Atl., Cgy.	12	757	60	218	278	764	69	4	18	22	92	2	1970-71	1981-82
Murdoch, Bob	Cal., Cle., St.L.	4	260	72	85	157	127	....	....	....	....	....	....	1975-76	1978-79
Murdoch, Don	NYR, Edm., Det.	6	320	121	117	238	155	24	10	8	18	16	....	1976-77	1981-82
• Murdoch, Murray	NYR	11	508	84	108	192	197	55	9	12	21	28	2	1926-27	1936-37
Murphy, Brian	Det.	1	1	0	0	0	0	....	....	....	....	....	....	1974-75	1974-75
Murphy, Gord	Phi., Bos., Fla., Atl.	14	862	85	238	323	668	53	3	16	19	35	....	1988-89	2001-02
Murphy, Joe	Det., Edm., Chi., St.L., S.J., Bos., Wsh.	15	779	233	295	528	810	120	34	43	77	185	1	1986-87	2000-01
Murphy, Larry	L.A., Wsh., Min., Pit., Tor., Det.	21	1615	287	929	1216	1084	215	37	115	152	201	4	1980-81	2000-01
Murphy, Mike	St.L., NYR, L.A.	12	831	238	318	556	514	66	13	23	36	54	....	1971-72	1982-83
Murphy, Rob	Van., Ott., L.A.	7	125	9	12	21	152	4	0	0	0	2	....	1987-88	1993-94
Murphy, Ron	NYR, Chi., Det., Bos.	18	889	205	274	479	460	53	7	8	15	26	1	1952-53	1969-70
Murray, Allan	NYA	7	271	5	9	14	163	14	0	0	0	10	....	1933-34	1939-40
Murray, Bob	Atl., Van.	4	194	6	16	22	98	10	1	1	2	15	....	1973-74	1976-77
Murray, Bob	Chi.	15	1008	132	382	514	873	112	19	37	56	106	....	1975-76	1989-90
Murray, Chris	Mtl., Hfd., Car., Ott., Chi., Dal.	6	242	16	18	34	550	15	1	0	1	12	....	1994-95	1999-00
Murray, Jim	L.A.	1	30	0	2	2	14	....	....	....	....	....	....	1967-68	1967-68
Murray, Ken	Tor., NYI, Det., K.C.	5	106	1	10	11	135	....	....	....	....	....	....	1969-70	1975-76
• Murray, Leo	Mtl.	1	6	0	0	0	2	....	....	....	....	....	....	1932-33	1932-33
Murray, Mike	Phi.	1	1	0	0	0	0	....	....	....	....	....	....	1987-88	1987-88
Murray, Pat	Phi.	2	25	3	1	4	15	....	....	....	....	....	....	1990-91	1991-92
Murray, Randy	Tor.	1	3	0	0	0	2	....	....	....	....	....	....	1969-70	1969-70
Murray, Rob	Wsh., Wpg., Phx.	8	107	4	15	19	111	9	0	0	0	18	....	1989-90	1998-99
Murray, Terry	Cal., Phi., Det., Wsh.	8	302	4	76	80	199	18	2	2	4	10	....	1972-73	1981-82
Murray, Troy	Chi., Wpg., Ott., Pit., Col.	15	915	230	354	584	875	113	17	26	43	145	1	1981-82	1995-96
Murzyn, Dana	Hfd., Cgy., Van.	14	838	52	152	204	1571	82	9	10	19	166	1	1985-86	1998-99
Musil, Frantisek	Min., Cgy., Ott., Edm.	15	797	34	106	140	1241	42	2	4	6	47	....	1986-87	2000-01
Myers, Hap	Buf.	1	13	0	0	0	6	....	....	....	....	....	....	1970-71	1970-71
‡ Myhres, Brantt	T.B., Phi., S.J., Nsh., Wsh., Bos.	7	154	6	2	8	687	....	....	....	....	....	....	1994-95	2002-03
Myles, Vic	NYR	1	45	6	9	15	57	....	....	....	....	....	....	1942-43	1942-43
Myrvold, Anders	Col., Bos., NYI, Det.	4	33	0	5	5	12	....	....	....	....	....	....	1995-96	2003-04

N

Name	NHL Teams	NHL Seasons	Regular Schedule GP	G	A	TP	PIM	Playoffs GP	G	A	TP	PIM	NHL Cup Wins	First NHL Season	Last NHL Season
‡ Nabokov, Dmitri	Chi., NYI	3	55	11	13	24	28	....	....	....	....	....	....	1997-98	1999-00
Nachbaur, Don	Hfd., Edm., Phi.	8	223	23	46	69	465	11	1	1	2	24	....	1980-81	1989-90
Nahrgang, Jim	Det.	3	57	5	12	17	34	....	....	....	....	....	....	1974-75	1976-77
Namestnikov, John	Van., NYI, Nsh.	6	43	0	9	9	24	2	0	0	0	2	....	1993-94	1999-00
Nanne, Lou	Min.	11	635	68	157	225	356	32	4	10	14	8	....	1967-68	1977-78
Nantais, Rich	Min.	3	63	5	4	9	79	....	....	....	....	....	....	1974-75	1976-77
Napier, Mark	Mtl., Min., Edm., Buf.	11	767	235	306	541	157	82	18	24	42	11	2	1978-79	1988-89
Naslund, Mats	Mtl., Bos.	9	651	251	383	634	111	102	35	57	92	33	1	1982-83	1994-95
Nattrass, Ralph	Chi.	4	223	18	38	56	308	....	....	....	....	....	....	1946-47	1949-50
Nattress, Ric	Mtl., St.L., Cgy., Tor., Phi.	11	536	29	135	164	377	67	5	10	15	60	1	1982-83	1992-93
Natyshak, Mike	Que.	1	4	0	0	0	0	....	....	....	....	....	....	1987-88	1987-88
Nazarov, Andrei	S.J., T.B., Cgy., Ana., Bos., Phx., Min.	12	571	53	71	124	1409	9	0	0	0	11	....	1993-94	2005-06
‡ Ndur, Rumun	Buf., NYR, Atl.	4	69	2	3	5	137	....	....	....	....	....	....	1996-97	1999-00
Neaton, Pat	Pit.	1	9	1	1	2	12	....	....	....	....	....	....	1993-94	1993-94
Nechayev, Viktor	L.A.	1	3	1	0	1	0	....	....	....	....	....	....	1982-83	1982-83
Neckar, Stan	Ott., NYR, Phx., T.B., Nsh.	10	510	12	41	53	316	29	0	3	3	8	1	1994-95	2003-04
Nedomansky, Vaclav	Det., NYR, St.L.	6	421	122	156	278	88	7	3	5	8	0	....	1977-78	1982-83
Nedved, Zdenek	Tor.	3	31	4	6	10	14	....	....	....	....	....	....	1994-95	1996-97
Needham, Mike	Pit., Dal.	3	86	9	5	14	16	14	2	0	2	4	1	1991-92	1993-94
Neely, Bob	Tor., Col.	5	283	39	59	98	266	26	5	7	12	15	....	1973-74	1977-78
Neely, Cam	Van., Bos.	13	726	395	299	694	1241	93	57	32	89	168	....	1983-84	1995-96
Neilson, Jim	NYR, Cal., Cle.	16	1023	69	299	368	904	65	1	17	18	61	....	1962-63	1977-78
Nelson, Gordie	Tor.	1	3	0	0	0	11	....	....	....	....	....	....	1969-70	1969-70
‡ Nelson, Jeff	Wsh., Nsh.	3	52	3	8	11	20	3	0	0	0	4	....	1994-95	1998-99
Nelson, Todd	Pit., Wsh.	2	3	1	0	1	2	4	0	0	0	0	....	1991-92	1993-94
Nemchinov, Sergei	NYR, Van., NYI, N.J.	11	761	152	193	345	251	105	11	20	31	24	2	1991-92	2001-02
Nemecek, Jan	L.A.	2	7	1	0	1	4	....	....	....	....	....	....	1998-99	1999-00

			Regular Schedule					Playoffs					NHL	First	Last
Name	NHL Teams	NHL Seasons	GP	G	A	TP	PIM	GP	G	A	TP	PIM	Cup Wins	NHL Season	NHL Season
Nemeth, Steve	NYR	1	12	2	0	2	2	....	....	....	....	....	....	1987-88	1987-88
‡ Nemirovsky, David	Fla.	4	91	16	22	38	42	3	1	0	1	0	....	1995-96	1998-99
Nesterenko, Eric	Tor., Chi.	21	1219	250	324	574	1273	124	13	24	37	127	1	1951-52	1971-72
Nethery, Lance	NYR, Edm.	2	41	11	14	25	14	14	5	3	8	9	....	1980-81	1981-82
Neufeld, Ray	Hfd., Wpg., Bos.	11	595	157	200	357	816	28	8	6	14	55	....	1979-80	1989-90
• Neville, Mike	Tor., NYA	3	65	5	5	10	14	2	0	0	0	0	....	1924-25	1930-31
Nevin, Bob	Tor., NYR, Min., L.A.	18	1128	307	419	726	211	84	16	18	34	24	2	1957-58	1975-76
Newberry, John	Mtl., Hfd.	4	22	0	4	4	6	2	0	0	0	0	....	1982-83	1985-86
Newell, Rick	Det.	2	6	0	0	0	0	....	....	....	....	....	....	1972-73	1973-74
Newman, Dan	NYR, Mtl., Edm.	4	126	17	24	41	63	3	0	0	0	4	....	1976-77	1979-80
• Newman, John	Det.	1	8	1	1	2	0	....	....	....	....	....	....	1930-31	1930-31
Nicholls, Bernie	L.A., NYR, Edm., N.J., Chi., S.J.	18	1127	475	734	1209	1292	118	42	72	114	164	....	1981-82	1998-99
• Nicholson, Al	Bos.	2	19	0	1	1	4	....	....	....	....	....	....	1955-56	1956-57
• Nicholson, Ed	Det.	1	1	0	0	0	0	....	....	....	....	....	....	1947-48	1947-48
• Nicholson, Hickey	Chi.	1	2	1	0	1	0	....	....	....	....	....	....	1937-38	1937-38
Nicholson, Neil	Oak., NYI	4	39	3	1	4	23	2	0	0	0	0	....	1969-70	1977-78
Nicholson, Paul	Wsh.	3	62	4	8	12	18	....	....	....	....	....	....	1974-75	1976-77
Nicolson, Graeme	Bos., Col., NYR	3	52	2	7	9	60	....	....	....	....	....	....	1978-79	1982-83
Nieckar, Barry	Hfd., Cgy., Ana.	4	8	0	0	0	21	....	....	....	....	....	....	1992-93	1997-98
Niekamp, Jim	Det.	2	29	0	2	2	37	....	....	....	....	....	....	1970-71	1971-72
Nielsen, Chris	CBJ	2	52	6	8	14	8	....	....	....	....	....	....	2000-01	2001-02
Nielsen, Jeff	NYR, Ana., Min.	5	252	20	27	47	70	4	0	0	0	2	....	1996-97	2000-01
Nielsen, Kirk	Bos.	1	6	0	0	0	0	....	....	....	....	....	....	1997-98	1997-98
‡ Niemi, Antti-Jussi	Ana.	2	29	1	1	2	22	....	....	....	....	....	....	2000-01	2001-02
Nienhuis, Kraig	Bos.	3	87	20	16	36	39	2	0	0	0	14	....	1985-86	1987-88
• Nighbor, Frank	Ott., Tor.	13	349	139	98	237	249	20	4	9	13	13	4	1917-18	1929-30
Nigro, Frank	Tor.	2	68	8	18	26	39	3	0	0	0	2	....	1982-83	1983-84
‡ Nikolishin, Andrei	Hfd., Wsh., Chi., Col.	10	628	93	187	280	270	43	1	17	18	22	....	1994-95	2003-04
Nikulin, Igor	Ana.	1	....	....	....	....	....	1	0	0	0	0	....	1996-97	1996-97
Nilan, Chris	Mtl., NYR, Bos.	13	688	110	115	225	3043	111	8	9	17	541	1	1979-80	1991-92
Nill, Jim	St.L., Van., Bos., Wpg., Det.	9	524	58	87	145	854	59	10	5	15	203	....	1981-82	1989-90
Nilsson, Kent	Atl., Cgy., Min., Edm.	9	553	264	422	686	116	59	11	41	52	14	1	1979-80	1994-95
Nilsson, Ulf	NYR	4	170	57	112	169	85	25	8	14	22	27	....	1978-79	1982-83
Nistico, Lou	Col.	1	3	0	0	0	0	....	....	....	....	....	....	1977-78	1977-78
• Noble, Reg	Tor., Mtl.M., Det.	16	510	168	106	274	916	18	2	2	4	33	3	1917-18	1932-33
Noel, Claude	Wsh.	1	7	0	0	0	0	....	....	....	....	....	....	1979-80	1979-80
• Nolan, Paddy	Tor.	1	2	0	0	0	0	....	....	....	....	....	....	1921-22	1921-22
Nolan, Ted	Det., Pit.	3	78	6	16	22	105	....	....	....	....	....	....	1981-82	1985-86
Nolet, Simon	Phi., K.C., Pit., Col.	10	562	150	182	332	187	34	6	3	9	8	1	1967-68	1976-77
Noonan, Brian	Chi., NYR, St.L., Van., Phx.	12	629	116	159	275	518	71	17	19	36	77	1	1987-88	1998-99
Nordmark, Robert	St.L., Van.	4	236	13	70	83	254	7	3	2	5	8	....	1987-88	1990-91
‡ Nordstrom, Peter	Bos.	1	2	0	0	0	0	....	....	....	....	....	....	1998-99	1998-99
Noris, Joe	Pit., St.L., Buf.	3	55	2	5	7	22	....	....	....	....	....	....	1971-72	1973-74
‡ Norris, Dwayne	Que., Ana.	3	20	2	4	6	8	....	....	....	....	....	....	1993-94	1995-96
Norrish, Rod	Min.	2	21	3	3	6	2	....	....	....	....	....	....	1973-74	1974-75
• Northcott, Baldy	Mtl.M., Chi.	11	446	133	112	245	273	31	8	5	13	14	1	1928-29	1938-39
Norton, Jeff	NYI, S.J., St.L., Edm., T.B., Fla., Pit., Bos.	15	799	52	332	384	615	65	4	21	25	89	....	1987-88	2001-02
Norwich, Craig	Wpg., St.L., Col.	2	104	17	58	75	60	....	....	....	....	....	....	1979-80	1980-81
Norwood, Lee	Que., Wsh., St.L., Det., N.J., Hfd., Cgy.	12	503	58	153	211	1099	65	6	22	28	171	....	1980-81	1993-94
‡ Novoseltsev, Ivan	Fla., Phx.	5	234	31	44	75	112	....	....	....	....	....	....	1999-00	2003-04
Novy, Milan	Wsh.	1	73	18	30	48	16	2	0	0	0	0	....	1982-83	1982-83
Nowak, Hank	Pit., Det., Bos.	4	180	26	29	55	161	13	1	0	1	8	....	1973-74	1976-77
‡ Nurminen, Kai	L.A., Min.	2	69	17	11	28	24	....	....	....	....	....	....	1996-97	2000-01
Nykoluk, Mike	Tor.	1	32	3	1	4	20	....	....	....	....	....	....	1956-57	1956-57
Nylund, Gary	Tor., Chi., NYI	11	608	32	139	171	1235	24	0	6	6	63	....	1982-83	1992-93
• Nyrop, Bill	Mtl., Min.	4	207	12	51	63	101	35	1	7	8	22	3	1975-76	1981-82
Nystrom, Bob	NYI	14	900	235	278	513	1248	157	39	44	83	236	4	1972-73	1985-86
O															
Oates, Adam	Det., St.L., Bos., Wsh., Phi., Ana., Edm.	19	1337	341	1079	1420	415	163	42	114	156	66	....	1985-86	2003-04
• Oatman, Russell	Det., Mtl.M., NYR	3	120	20	9	29	100	15	1	0	1	18	....	1926-27	1928-29
O'Brien, Dennis	Min., Col., Cle., Bos.	10	592	31	91	122	1017	34	1	2	3	101	....	1970-71	1979-80
O'Brien, Ellard	Bos.	1	2	0	0	0	0	....	....	....	....	....	....	1955-56	1955-56
‡ Obsut, Jaroslav	St.L., Col.	2	7	0	0	0	2	....	....	....	....	....	....	2000-01	2001-02
O'Callahan, Jack	Chi., N.J.	7	389	27	104	131	541	32	4	11	15	41	....	1982-83	1988-89
O'Connell, Mike	Chi., Bos., Det.	13	860	105	334	439	605	82	8	24	32	64	....	1977-78	1989-90
• O'Connor, Buddy	Mtl., NYR	10	509	140	257	397	34	53	15	21	36	6	2	1941-42	1950-51
O'Connor, Myles	N.J., Ana.	4	43	3	4	7	69	....	....	....	....	....	....	1990-91	1993-94
Oddleifson, Chris	Bos., Van.	9	524	95	191	286	464	14	1	6	7	8	....	1972-73	1980-81
Odelein, Lyle	Mtl., N.J., Phx., CBJ, Chi., Dal., Fla., Pit.	16	1056	50	202	252	2316	86	5	13	18	209	1	1989-90	2005-06
Odelein, Selmar	Edm.	3	18	0	2	2	35	....	....	....	....	....	....	1985-86	1988-89
Odgers, Jeff	S.J., Bos., Col., Atl.	12	821	75	70	145	2364	47	2	1	3	73	....	1991-92	2002-03
Odjick, Gino	Van., NYI, Phi., Mtl.	12	605	64	73	137	2567	44	4	1	5	142	....	1990-91	2001-02
O'Donnell, Fred	Bos.	2	115	15	11	26	98	5	0	1	1	5	....	1972-73	1973-74
O'Donoghue, Don	Oak., Cal.	3	125	18	17	35	35	3	0	0	0	0	....	1969-70	1971-72
Odrowski, Gerry	Det., Oak., St.L.	6	309	12	19	31	111	30	0	1	1	16	....	1960-61	1971-72
O'Dwyer, Bill	L.A., Bos.	5	120	9	13	22	108	10	0	0	0	2	....	1983-84	1989-90
O'Flaherty, Gerry	Tor., Van., Atl.	8	438	99	95	194	168	7	2	2	4	6	....	1971-72	1978-79
O'Flaherty, Peanuts	NYA, Bro.	2	21	5	1	6	0	....	....	....	....	....	....	1940-41	1941-42
Ogilvie, Brian	Chi., St.L.	6	90	15	21	36	29	....	....	....	....	....	....	1972-73	1978-79
• O'Grady, George	Mtl.W.	1	4	0	0	0	0	....	....	....	....	....	....	1917-18	1917-18
Ogrodnick, John	Det., Que., NYR	14	928	402	425	827	260	41	18	8	26	6	....	1979-80	1992-93
‡ Ojanen, Janne	N.J.	4	98	21	23	44	28	3	0	2	2	0	....	1988-89	1992-93
Okerlund, Todd	NYI	1	4	0	0	0	2	....	....	....	....	....	....	1987-88	1987-88
Oksiuta, Roman	Edm., Van., Ana., Pit.	4	153	46	41	87	100	10	2	3	5	0	....	1993-94	1996-97
‡ Olausson, Fredrik	Wpg., Edm., Ana., Pit., Det.	16	1022	147	434	581	450	71	6	23	29	28	1	1986-87	2002-03
Olczyk, Ed	Chi., Tor., Wpg., NYR, L.A., Pit.	16	1031	342	452	794	874	57	19	15	34	57	1	1984-85	1999-00
• Oliver, Harry	Bos., NYA	11	463	127	85	212	147	35	10	6	16	24	1	1926-27	1936-37
Oliver, Murray	Det., Bos., Tor., Min.	17	1127	274	454	728	320	35	9	16	25	10	....	1957-58	1974-75
Oliwa, Krzysztof	N.J., CBJ, Pit., NYR, Bos., Cgy.	9	410	17	28	45	1447	32	2	0	2	47	1	1996-97	2005-06
Olmstead, Bert	Chi., Mtl., Tor.	14	848	181	421	602	884	115	16	43	59	101	5	1948-49	1961-62
Olsen, Darryl	Cgy.	1	1	0	0	0	0	....	....	....	....	....	....	1991-92	1991-92
Olson, Dennis	Det.	1	4	0	0	0	0	....	....	....	....	....	....	1957-58	1957-58
Olsson, Christer	St.L., Ott.	2	56	4	12	16	24	3	0	0	0	0	....	1995-96	1996-97
• O'Neil, Jim	Bos., Mtl.	6	156	6	30	36	109	9	1	1	2	13	....	1933-34	1941-42
O'Neil, Paul	Van., Bos.	2	6	0	0	0	0	....	....	....	....	....	....	1973-74	1975-76
• O'Neill, Tom	Tor.	2	66	10	12	22	53	4	0	0	0	6	1	1943-44	1944-45
Orban, Bill	Chi., Min.	3	114	8	15	23	67	3	0	0	0	0	....	1967-68	1969-70
O'Ree, Willie	Bos.	2	45	4	10	14	26	....	....	....	....	....	....	1957-58	1960-61
O'Regan, Tom	Pit.	3	61	5	12	17	10	....	....	....	....	....	....	1983-84	1985-86
O'Reilly, Terry	Bos.	14	891	204	402	606	2095	108	25	42	67	335	....	1971-72	1984-85
Orlando, Gates	Buf.	3	98	18	26	44	51	5	0	4	4	14	....	1984-85	1986-87
• Orlando, Jimmy	Det.	6	199	6	25	31	375	36	0	9	9	105	1	1936-37	1942-43
Orleski, Dave	Mtl.	2	2	0	0	0	0	....	....	....	....	....	....	1980-81	1981-82
Orr, Bobby	Bos., Chi.	12	657	270	645	915	953	74	26	66	92	107	2	1966-67	1978-79
Osborne, Keith	St.L., T.B.	2	16	1	3	4	16	....	....	....	....	....	....	1989-90	1992-93
Osborne, Mark	Det., NYR, Tor., Wpg.	14	919	212	319	531	1152	87	12	16	28	141	....	1981-82	1994-95
Osburn, Randy	Tor., Phi.	2	27	0	2	2	0	....	....	....	....	....	....	1972-73	1974-75
O'Shea, Danny	Min., Chi., St.L.	5	369	64	115	179	265	39	3	7	10	61	....	1968-69	1972-73
O'Shea, Kevin	Buf., St.L.	3	134	13	18	31	85	12	2	1	3	10	....	1970-71	1972-73
Osiecki, Mark	Cgy., Ott., Wpg., Min.	2	93	3	11	14	43	....	....	....	....	....	....	1991-92	1992-93
O'Sullivan, Chris	Cgy., Van., Ana.	5	62	2	17	19	16	....	....	....	....	....	....	1996-97	2002-03
Otevrel, Jaroslav	S.J.	2	16	3	4	7	2	....	....	....	....	....	....	1992-93	1993-94
Otto, Joel	Cgy., Phi.	14	943	195	313	508	1934	122	27	47	74	207	1	1984-85	1997-98
Ouellette, Eddie	Chi.	1	43	3	2	5	11	1	0	0	0	0	....	1935-36	1935-36
Ouellette, Gerry	Bos.	1	34	5	4	9	0	....	....	....	....	....	....	1960-61	1960-61
Owchar, Dennis	Pit., Col.	6	288	30	85	115	200	10	1	1	2	8	....	1974-75	1979-80
• Owen, George	Bos.	5	183	44	33	77	151	21	2	5	7	25	1	1928-29	1932-33

Joe Noris

Lyle Odelein

Bert Olmstead

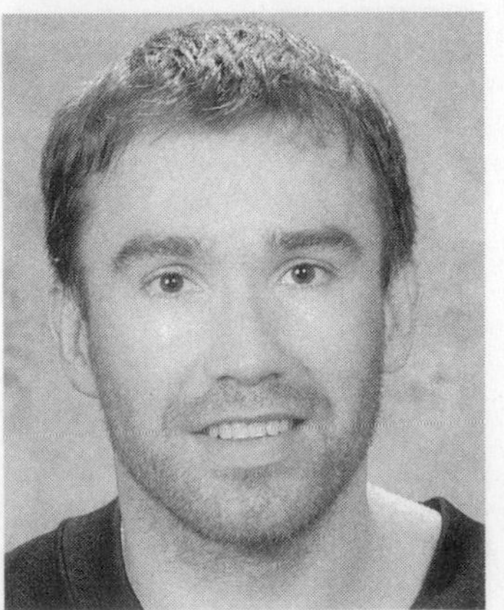
Ziggy Palffy

Brent Peterson

Harry Pidhirny

Bill Plager

Harvie Pocza

Name	NHL Teams	NHL Seasons	Regular Schedule GP	G	A	TP	PIM	Playoffs GP	G	A	TP	PIM	NHL Cup Wins	First NHL Season	Last NHL Season
P															
Pachal, Clayton	Bos., Col.	3	35	2	3	5	95	....	....	....	....	....	....	1976-77	1978-79
Paddock, John	Wsh., Phi., Que.	5	87	8	14	22	86	5	2	0	2	0	....	1975-76	1982-83
Paek, Jim	Pit., L.A., Ott.	5	217	5	29	34	155	27	1	4	5	8	2	1990-91	1994-95
Paiement, Rosaire	Phi., Van.	5	190	48	52	100	343	3	3	0	3	0	....	1967-68	1971-72
Paiement, Wilf	K.C., Col., Tor., Que., NYR, Buf., Pit.	14	946	356	458	814	1757	69	18	17	35	185	....	1974-75	1987-88
• Palangio, Pete	Mtl., Det., Chi.	5	71	13	10	23	28	7	0	0	0	0	1	1926-27	1937-38
• Palazzari, Aldo	Bos., NYR	1	35	8	3	11	4	....	....	....	....	....	....	1943-44	1943-44
Palazzari, Doug	St.L.	4	108	18	20	38	23	2	0	0	0	0	....	1974-75	1978-79
Palffy, Ziggy	NYI, L.A., Pit.	12	684	329	384	713	322	24	9	10	19	8	....	1993-94	2005-06
Palmer, Brad	Min., Bos.	3	168	32	38	70	58	29	9	5	14	16	....	1980-81	1982-83
Palmer, Rob	Chi.	3	16	0	3	3	2	....	....	....	....	....	....	1973-74	1975-76
Palmer, Robert	L.A., N.J.	7	320	9	101	110	115	8	1	2	3	6	....	1977-78	1983-84
• Panagabko, Ed	Bos.	2	29	0	3	3	38	....	....	....	....	....	....	1955-56	1956-57
‡ Pankewicz, Greg	Ott., Cgy.	2	21	0	3	3	22	....	....	....	....	....	....	1993-94	1998-99
‡ Panteleev, Grigori	Bos., NYI	4	54	8	6	14	12	....	....	....	....	....	....	1992-93	1995-96
• Papike, Joe	Chi.	3	20	3	3	6	4	5	0	2	2	0	....	1940-41	1944-45
Pappin, Jim	Tor., Chi., Cal., Cle.	14	767	278	295	573	667	92	33	34	67	101	2	1963-64	1976-77
Paradise, Bob	Min., Atl., Pit., Wsh.	8	368	8	54	62	393	12	0	1	1	19	....	1971-72	1978-79
• Pargeter, George	Mtl.	1	4	0	0	0	0	....	....	....	....	....	....	1946-47	1946-47
Parise, J.P.	Bos., Tor., Min., NYI, Cle.	14	890	238	356	594	706	86	27	31	58	87	....	1965-66	1978-79
Parizeau, Michel	St.L., Phi.	1	58	3	14	17	18	....	....	....	....	....	....	1971-72	1971-72
Park, Brad	NYR, Bos., Det.	17	1113	213	683	896	1429	161	35	90	125	217	....	1968-69	1984-85
Parker, Jeff	Buf., Hfd.	5	141	16	19	35	163	5	0	0	0	26	....	1986-87	1990-91
• Parkes, Ernie	Mtl.M.	1	17	0	0	0	2	....	....	....	....	....	....	1924-25	1924-25
Parks, Greg	NYI	3	23	1	2	3	6	2	0	0	0	0	....	1990-91	1992-93
• Parsons, George	Tor.	3	70	12	13	25	20	7	3	2	5	11	....	1936-37	1938-39
‡ Parssinen, Timo	Ana.	1	17	0	3	3	2	....	....	....	....	....	....	2001-02	2001-02
• Pasek, Dusan	Min.	1	48	4	10	14	30	2	1	0	1	0	....	1988-89	1988-89
Pasin, Dave	Bos., L.A.	2	76	18	19	37	50	3	0	1	1	0	....	1985-86	1988-89
Paslawski, Greg	Mtl., St.L., Wpg., Buf., Que., Phi., Cgy.	11	650	187	185	372	169	60	19	13	32	25	....	1983-84	1993-94
‡ Patera, Pavel	Dal., Min.	2	32	2	7	9	8	....	....	....	....	....	....	1999-00	2000-01
Paterson, Joe	Det., Phi., L.A., NYR	9	291	19	37	56	829	22	3	4	7	77	....	1980-81	1988-89
Paterson, Mark	Hfd.	4	29	3	3	6	33	....	....	....	....	....	....	1982-83	1985-86
Paterson, Rick	Chi.	9	430	50	43	93	136	61	7	10	17	51	....	1978-79	1986-87
Patey, Doug	Wsh.	3	45	4	2	6	8	....	....	....	....	....	....	1976-77	1978-79
Patey, Larry	Cal., St.L., NYR	12	717	153	163	316	631	40	8	10	18	57	....	1973-74	1984-85
Patrick, Craig	Cal., St.L., K.C., Wsh.	8	401	72	91	163	61	2	0	1	1	0	....	1971-72	1978-79
Patrick, Glenn	St.L., Cal., Cle.	4	38	2	3	5	72	....	....	....	....	....	....	1973-74	1976-77
Patrick, James	NYR, Hfd., Cgy., Buf.	21	1280	149	490	639	759	117	6	32	38	86	....	1983-84	2003-04
• Patrick, Lester	NYR	1	1	0	0	0	2	....	....	....	....	....	....	1926-27	1926-27
• Patrick, Lynn	NYR	10	455	145	190	335	240	44	10	6	16	22	1	1934-35	1945-46
• Patrick, Muzz	NYR	5	166	5	26	31	133	25	4	0	4	34	1	1937-38	1945-46
Patrick, Steve	Buf., NYR, Que.	6	250	40	68	108	242	12	0	1	1	12	....	1980-81	1985-86
Patterson, Colin	Cgy., Buf.	10	504	96	109	205	239	85	12	17	29	57	1	1983-84	1992-93
Patterson, Dennis	K.C., Phi.	3	138	6	22	28	67	....	....	....	....	....	....	1974-75	1979-80
Patterson, Ed	Pit.	3	68	3	3	6	56	....	....	....	....	....	....	1993-94	1996-97
• Patterson, George	Tor., Mtl., NYA, Bos., Det., St.L.	9	284	51	27	78	218	3	0	0	0	2	....	1926-27	1934-35
• Paul, Butch	Det.	1	3	0	0	0	0	....	....	....	....	....	....	1964-65	1964-65
‡ Paul, Jeff	Col.	1	2	0	0	0	7	....	....	....	....	....	....	2002-03	2002-03
• Paulhus, Rollie	Mtl.	1	33	0	0	0	0	....	....	....	....	....	....	1925-26	1925-26
Pavelich, Mark	NYR, Min., S.J.	7	355	137	192	329	340	23	7	17	24	14	....	1981-82	1991-92
Pavelich, Marty	Det.	10	634	93	159	252	454	91	13	15	28	74	4	1947-48	1956-57
Pavese, Jim	St.L., NYR, Det., Hfd.	8	328	13	44	57	689	34	0	6	6	81	....	1981-82	1988-89
• Payer, Evariste	Mtl.	1	1	0	0	0	0	....	....	....	....	....	....	1917-18	1917-18
Payne, Davis	Bos.	2	22	0	1	1	14	....	....	....	....	....	....	1995-96	1996-97
Payne, Steve	Min.	10	613	228	238	466	435	71	35	35	70	60	....	1978-79	1987-88
Paynter, Kent	Chi., Wsh., Wpg., Ott.	7	37	1	3	4	69	4	0	0	0	10	....	1987-88	1993-94
Peake, Pat	Wsh.	5	134	28	41	69	105	13	2	2	4	20	....	1993-94	1997-98
• Pearson, Mel	NYR, Pit.	5	38	2	6	8	25	....	....	....	....	....	....	1959-60	1967-68
Pearson, Rob	Tor., Wsh., St.L.	6	269	56	54	110	645	33	4	2	6	94	....	1991-92	1996-97
Pearson, Scott	Tor., Que., Edm., Buf., NYI	10	292	56	42	98	615	10	2	0	2	14	....	1988-89	1999-00
Pedersen, Allen	Bos., Min., Hfd.	8	428	5	36	41	487	64	0	0	0	91	....	1986-87	1993-94
Pederson, Barry	Bos., Van., Pit., Hfd.	12	701	238	416	654	472	34	22	30	52	25	1	1980-81	1991-92
‡ Pederson, Denis	N.J., Van., Phx., Nsh.	8	435	57	71	128	398	27	1	5	6	8	....	1995-96	2002-03
Pederson, Mark	Mtl., Phi., S.J., Det.	5	169	35	50	85	77	2	0	0	0	0	....	1989-90	1993-94
Pederson, Tom	S.J., Tor.	5	240	20	49	69	142	24	1	11	12	10	....	1992-93	1996-97
• Peer, Bert	Det.	1	1	0	0	0	0	....	....	....	....	....	....	1939-40	1939-40
Peirson, Johnny	Bos.	11	545	153	173	326	315	49	10	16	26	26	....	1946-47	1957-58
Pelensky, Perry	Chi.	1	4	0	0	0	5	....	....	....	....	....	....	1983-84	1983-84
Pellerin, Scott	N.J., St.L., Min., Car., Bos., Dal., Phx.	11	536	72	126	198	320	37	1	2	3	26	....	1992-93	2003-04
Pelletier, Roger	Phi.	1	1	0	0	0	0	....	....	....	....	....	....	1967-68	1967-68
Peloffy, Andre	Wsh.	1	9	0	0	0	0	....	....	....	....	....	....	1974-75	1974-75
Peluso, Mike	Chi., Ott., N.J., St.L., Cgy.	9	458	38	52	90	1951	62	3	4	7	107	1	1989-90	1997-98
Peluso, Mike	Chi., Phi.	2	38	4	2	6	19	....	....	....	....	....	....	2001-02	2003-04
Pelyk, Mike	Tor.	9	441	26	88	114	566	40	0	3	3	41	....	1967-68	1977-78
Penney, Chad	Ott.	1	3	0	0	0	2	....	....	....	....	....	....	1993-94	1993-94
Pennington, Cliff	Mtl., Bos.	3	101	17	42	59	6	....	....	....	....	....	....	1960-61	1962-63
Peplinski, Jim	Cgy.	11	711	161	263	424	1467	99	15	31	46	382	1	1980-81	1994-95
Perlini, Fred	Tor.	2	8	2	3	5	0	....	....	....	....	....	....	1981-82	1983-84
Perreault, Fern	NYR	2	3	0	0	0	0	....	....	....	....	....	....	1947-48	1949-50
Perreault, Gilbert	Buf.	17	1191	512	814	1326	500	90	33	70	103	44	....	1970-71	1986-87
Perry, Brian	Oak., Buf.	3	96	16	29	45	24	8	1	1	2	4	....	1968-69	1970-71
Persson, Ricard	N.J., St.L., Ott.	7	229	10	44	54	262	26	1	3	4	59	....	1995-96	2001-02
Persson, Stefan	NYI	9	622	52	317	369	574	102	7	50	57	69	4	1977-78	1985-86
Pesut, George	Cal.	2	92	3	22	25	130	....	....	....	....	....	....	1974-75	1975-76
• Peters, Frank	NYR	1	43	0	0	0	59	4	0	0	0	2	....	1930-31	1930-31
Peters, Garry	Mtl., NYR, Phi., Bos.	8	311	34	34	68	261	9	2	2	4	31	1	1964-65	1971-72
• Peters, Jimmy	Mtl., Bos., Det., Chi.	9	574	125	150	275	186	60	5	9	14	22	3	1945-46	1953-54
Peters, Jimmy	Det., L.A.	9	309	37	36	73	48	11	0	2	2	2	....	1964-65	1974-75
Peters, Steve	Col.	1	2	0	1	1	0	....	....	....	....	....	....	1979-80	1979-80
Peterson, Brent	Det., Buf., Van., Hfd.	11	620	72	141	213	484	31	4	4	8	65	....	1978-79	1988-89
Peterson, Brent	T.B.	3	56	9	1	10	6	....	....	....	....	....	....	1996-97	1998-99
Petit, Michel	Van., NYR, Que., Tor., Cgy., L.A., T.B., Edm., Phi., Phx.	16	827	90	238	328	1839	19	0	2	2	61	....	1982-83	1997-98
Petrenko, Sergei	Buf.	1	14	0	4	4	0	....	....	....	....	....	....	1993-94	1993-94
‡ Petrov, Oleg	Mtl., Nsh.	8	382	72	115	187	101	20	1	6	7	2	....	1992-93	2002-03
‡ Petrovicky, Robert	Hfd., Dal., St.L., T.B., NYI	8	208	27	38	65	118	2	0	0	0	0	....	1992-93	2000-01
Pettersson, Jorgen	St.L., Hfd., Wsh.	6	435	174	192	366	117	44	15	12	27	4	....	1980-81	1985-86
• Pettinger, Eric	Bos., Tor., Ott.	3	98	7	12	19	83	4	1	0	1	8	....	1928-29	1930-31
• Pettinger, Gord	NYR, Det., Bos.	8	292	42	74	116	77	47	4	5	9	11	4	1932-33	1939-40
Phair, Lyle	L.A.	3	48	6	7	13	12	1	0	0	0	0	....	1985-86	1987-88
Phillipoff, Harold	Atl., Chi.	3	141	26	57	83	267	6	0	2	2	9	....	1977-78	1979-80
• Phillips, Bill	Mtl.M.	1	27	1	1	2	6	4	0	0	0	2	....	1929-30	1929-30
• Phillips, Charlie	Mtl.	1	17	0	0	0	6	....	....	....	....	....	....	1942-43	1942-43
• Phillips, Merlyn	Mtl.M., NYA	8	302	52	31	83	232	24	5	1	6	19	1	1925-26	1932-33
Picard, Michel	Hfd., S.J., Ott., St.L., Edm., Phi.	9	166	28	42	70	103	5	0	0	0	2	....	1990-91	2000-01
Picard, Noel	Mtl., St.L., Atl.	7	335	12	63	75	616	50	2	11	13	167	1	1964-65	1972-73
Picard, Robert	Wsh., Tor., Mtl., Wpg., Que., Det.	13	899	104	319	423	1025	36	5	15	20	39	....	1977-78	1989-90
Picard, Roger	St.L.	1	15	2	2	4	21	....	....	....	....	....	....	1967-68	1967-68
Pichette, Dave	Que., St.L., N.J., NYR	7	322	41	140	181	348	28	3	7	10	54	....	1980-81	1987-88
Picketts, Hal	NYA	1	48	3	1	4	32	....	....	....	....	....	....	1933-34	1933-34
Pidhirny, Harry	Bos.	1	2	0	0	0	0	....	....	....	....	....	....	1957-58	1957-58
Pierce, Randy	Col., N.J., Hfd.	8	277	62	76	138	223	2	0	0	0	0	....	1977-78	1984-85
Pike, Alf	NYR	6	234	42	77	119	145	21	4	2	6	12	1	1939-40	1946-47
Pilon, Rich	NYI, NYR, St.L.	14	631	8	69	77	1745	15	0	0	0	50	....	1988-89	2001-02
Pilote, Pierre	Chi., Tor.	14	890	80	418	498	1251	86	8	53	61	102	1	1955-56	1968-69
Pinder, Gerry	Chi., Cal.	3	223	55	69	124	135	17	0	4	4	6	....	1969-70	1971-72
‡ Pirnes, Esa	L.A.	1	57	3	8	11	12	....	....	....	....	....	....	2003-04	2003-04
‡ Piros, Kamil	Atl., Fla.	3	28	4	4	8	10	....	....	....	....	....	....	2001-02	2003-04
Pirus, Alex	Min., Det.	4	159	30	28	58	94	2	0	1	1	2	....	1976-77	1979-80
‡ Pisa, Ales	Edm., NYR	2	53	1	3	4	26	....	....	....	....	....	....	2001-02	2002-03
Pitlick, Lance	Ott., Fla.	8	393	16	33	49	298	24	0	2	2	21	....	1994-95	2001-02

Keith Primeau

Claude Provost

Dan Quinn

Matt Ravlich

Name	NHL Teams	NHL Seasons	Regular Schedule GP	G	A	TP	PIM	Playoffs GP	G	A	TP	PIM	NHL Cup Wins	First NHL Season	Last NHL Season
• Pitre, Didier	Mtl.	6	127	64	34	98	84	9	2	4	6	16	....	1917-18	1922-23
‡ Pittis, Domenic	Pit., Buf., Edm., Nsh.	7	86	5	11	16	71	3	0	0	0	2	....	1996-97	2003-04
‡ Pivko, Libor	Nsh.	1	1	0	0	0	0	....	....	....	....	....	....	2003-04	2003-04
Pivonka, Michal	Wsh.	13	825	181	418	599	478	95	19	36	55	86	....	1986-87	1998-99
• Plager, Barclay	St.L.	10	614	44	187	231	1115	68	3	20	23	182	....	1967-68	1976-77
Plager, Bill	Min., St.L., Atl.	9	263	4	34	38	294	31	0	2	2	26	....	1967-68	1975-76
Plager, Bob	NYR, St.L.	14	644	20	126	146	802	74	2	17	19	195	....	1964-65	1977-78
Plamondon, Gerry	Mtl.	5	74	7	13	20	10	11	5	2	7	2	1	1945-46	1950-51
Plante, Cam	Tor.	1	2	0	0	0	0	....	....	....	....	....	....	1984-85	1984-85
Plante, Dan	NYI	4	159	9	14	23	135	1	1	0	1	2	....	1993-94	1997-98
Plante, Derek	Buf., Dal., Chi., Phi.	8	450	96	152	248	138	41	6	10	16	18	1	1993-94	2000-01
Plante, Pierre	Phi., St.L., Chi., NYR, Que.	9	599	125	172	297	599	33	2	6	8	51	....	1971-72	1979-80
Plantery, Mark	Wpg.	1	25	1	5	6	14	....	....	....	....	....	....	1980-81	1980-81
Plavsic, Adrien	St.L., Van., T.B., Ana.	8	214	16	56	72	161	13	1	7	8	4	....	1989-90	1996-97
• Plaxton, Hugh	Mtl.M.	1	15	1	2	3	4	....	....	....	....	....	....	1932-33	1932-33
Playfair, Jim	Edm., Chi.	3	21	2	4	6	51	....	....	....	....	....	....	1983-84	1988-89
Playfair, Larry	Buf., L.A.	12	688	26	94	120	1812	43	0	6	6	111	....	1978-79	1989-90
Pleau, Larry	Mtl.	3	94	9	15	24	27	4	0	0	0	0	....	1969-70	1971-72
‡ Pletka, Vaclav	Phi.	1	1	0	0	0	0	....	....	....	....	....	....	2001-02	2001-02
• Pletsch, Charles	Ham.	1	1	0	0	0	0	....	....	....	....	....	....	1920-21	1920-21
Plett, Willi	Atl., Cgy., Min., Bos.	13	834	222	215	437	2572	83	24	22	46	466	....	1975-76	1987-88
Plumb, Rob	Det.	2	14	3	2	5	2	....	....	....	....	....	....	1977-78	1978-79
Plumb, Ron	Hfd.	1	26	3	4	7	14	....	....	....	....	....	....	1979-80	1979-80
Poapst, Steve	Wsh., Chi., Pit., St.L.	7	307	8	28	36	173	11	0	0	0	0	....	1995-96	2005-06
Pocza, Harvie	Wsh.	2	3	0	0	0	2	....	....	....	....	....	....	1979-80	1981-82
Poddubny, Walt	Edm., Tor., NYR, Que., N.J.	11	468	184	238	422	454	19	7	2	9	12	....	1981-82	1991-92
Podein, Shjon	Edm., Phi., Col., St.L.	11	699	100	106	206	439	127	14	13	27	132	1	1992-93	2002-03
‡ Podkonicky, Andrej	Fla., Wsh.	2	8	1	0	1	2	....	....	....	....	....	....	2000-01	2003-04
Podloski, Ray	Bos.	1	8	0	1	1	17	....	....	....	....	....	....	1988-89	1988-89
Podollan, Jason	Fla., Tor., L.A., NYI	4	41	1	5	6	19	....	....	....	....	....	....	1996-97	2001-02
Podolsky, Nels	Det.	1	1	0	0	0	0	7	0	0	0	4	....	1948-49	1948-49
Poeschek, Rudy	NYR, Wpg., T.B., St.L.	12	364	6	25	31	817	5	0	0	0	18	....	1987-88	1999-00
• Poeta, Tony	Chi.	1	1	0	0	0	0	....	....	....	....	....	....	1951-52	1951-52
• Poile, Bud	Tor., Chi., Det., NYR, Bos.	7	311	107	122	229	91	23	4	5	9	8	1	1942-43	1949-50
Poile, Don	Det.	2	66	7	9	16	12	4	0	0	0	0	....	1954-55	1957-58
• Poirier, Gordie	Mtl.	1	10	0	0	0	0	....	....	....	....	....	....	1939-40	1939-40
Polanic, Tom	Min.	2	19	0	2	2	53	5	1	1	2	4	....	1969-70	1970-71
• Polich, John	NYR	2	3	0	1	1	0	....	....	....	....	....	....	1939-40	1940-41
Polich, Mike	Mtl., Min.	5	226	24	29	53	57	23	2	1	3	2	1	1976-77	1980-81
Polis, Greg	Pit., St.L., NYR, Wsh.	10	615	174	169	343	391	7	0	2	2	6	....	1970-71	1979-80
Poliziani, Dan	Bos.	1	1	0	0	0	0	3	0	0	0	0	....	1958-59	1958-59
Polonich, Dennis	Det.	8	390	59	82	141	1242	7	1	0	1	19	....	1974-75	1982-83
Pooley, Paul	Wpg.	2	15	0	3	3	0	....	....	....	....	....	....	1984-85	1985-86
Popein, Larry	NYR, Oak.	8	449	80	141	221	162	16	1	4	5	6	....	1954-55	1967-68
Popiel, Poul	Bos., L.A., Det., Van., Edm.	7	224	13	41	54	210	4	1	0	1	4	....	1965-66	1979-80
Popovic, Peter	Mtl., NYR, Pit., Bos.	8	485	10	63	73	291	35	1	4	5	18	....	1993-94	2000-01
• Portland, Jack	Mtl., Bos., Chi.	10	381	15	56	71	323	33	1	3	4	25	1	1933-34	1942-43
Porvari, Jukka	Col., N.J.	2	39	3	9	12	4	....	....	....	....	....	....	1981-82	1982-83
Posa, Victor	Chi.	1	2	0	0	0	2	....	....	....	....	....	....	1985-86	1985-86
Posavad, Mike	St.L.	2	8	0	0	0	0	....	....	....	....	....	....	1985-86	1986-87
Posmyk, Marek	T.B.	2	19	1	2	3	20	....	....	....	....	....	....	1999-00	2000-01
Potomski, Barry	L.A., S.J.	3	68	6	5	11	227	....	....	....	....	....	....	1995-96	1997-98
Potvin, Denis	NYI	15	1060	310	742	1052	1356	185	56	108	164	253	4	1973-74	1987-88
Potvin, Jean	L.A., Phi., NYI, Cle., Min.	11	613	63	224	287	478	39	2	9	11	17	1	1970-71	1980-81
• Potvin, Marc	Det., L.A., Hfd., Bos.	6	121	3	5	8	456	13	0	1	1	50	....	1990-91	1995-96
Poudrier, Daniel	Que.	3	25	1	5	6	10	....	....	....	....	....	....	1985-86	1987-88
Poulin, Daniel	Min.	1	3	1	1	2	2	....	....	....	....	....	....	1981-82	1981-82
Poulin, Dave	Phi., Bos., Wsh.	13	724	205	325	530	482	129	31	42	73	132	....	1982-83	1994-95
Poulin, Patrick	Hfd., Chi., T.B., Mtl.	11	634	101	134	235	299	32	6	2	8	8	....	1991-92	2001-02
Pouzar, Jaroslav	Edm.	4	186	34	48	82	135	29	6	4	10	16	3	1982-83	1986-87
• Powell, Ray	Chi.	1	31	7	15	22	2	....	....	....	....	....	....	1950-51	1950-51
• Powis, Geoff	Chi.	1	2	0	0	0	0	....	....	....	....	....	....	1967-68	1967-68
Powis, Lynn	Chi., K.C.	2	130	19	33	52	25	1	0	0	0	0	....	1973-74	1974-75
Prajsler, Petr	L.A., Bos.	4	46	3	10	13	51	4	0	0	0	0	....	1987-88	1991-92
• Pratt, Babe	NYR, Tor., Bos.	12	517	83	209	292	463	63	12	17	29	90	2	1935-36	1946-47
• Pratt, Jack	Bos.	2	37	2	0	2	42	4	0	0	0	0	....	1930-31	1931-32
Pratt, Kelly	Pit.	1	22	0	6	6	15	....	....	....	....	....	....	1974-75	1974-75
Pratt, Tracy	Oak., Pit., Buf., Van., Col., Tor.	10	580	17	97	114	1026	25	0	1	1	62	....	1967-68	1976-77
Prentice, Dean	NYR, Bos., Det., Pit., Min.	22	1378	391	469	860	484	54	13	17	30	38	....	1952-53	1973-74
• Prentice, Eric	Tor.	1	5	0	0	0	4	....	....	....	....	....	....	1943-44	1943-44
Presley, Wayne	Chi., S.J., Buf., NYR, Tor.	12	684	155	147	302	953	83	26	17	43	142	....	1984-85	1995-96
Preston, Rich	Chi., N.J.	8	580	127	164	291	348	47	4	18	22	56	....	1979-80	1986-87
Preston, Yves	Phi.	2	28	7	3	10	4	....	....	....	....	....	....	1978-79	1980-81
Priakin, Sergei	Cgy.	3	46	3	8	11	2	1	0	0	0	0	....	1988-89	1990-91
Price, Jack	Chi.	3	57	4	6	10	24	4	0	0	0	0	....	1951-52	1953-54
Price, Noel	Tor., NYR, Det., Mtl., Pit., L.A., Atl.	14	499	14	114	128	333	12	0	1	1	8	1	1957-58	1975-76
Price, Pat	NYI, Edm., Pit., Que., NYR, Min.	13	726	43	218	261	1456	74	2	10	12	195	....	1975-76	1987-88
Price, Tom	Cal., Cle., Pit.	5	29	0	2	2	12	....	....	....	....	....	....	1974-75	1978-79
Priestlay, Ken	Buf., Pit.	6	168	27	34	61	63	14	0	0	0	21	1	1986-87	1991-92
• Primeau, Joe	Tor.	9	310	66	177	243	105	38	5	18	23	12	1	1927-28	1935-36
Primeau, Keith	Det., Hfd., Car., Phi.	15	909	266	353	619	1541	128	18	39	57	213	....	1990-91	2005-06
Primeau, Kevin	Van.	1	2	0	0	0	4	....	....	....	....	....	....	1980-81	1980-81
• Pringle, Ellie	NYA	1	6	0	0	0	0	....	....	....	....	....	....	1930-31	1930-31
Probert, Bob	Det., Chi.	16	935	163	221	384	3300	81	16	32	48	274	....	1985-86	2001-02
‡ Prochazka, Martin	Tor., Atl.	2	32	2	5	7	8	....	....	....	....	....	....	1997-98	1999-00
• Prodgers, Goldie	Tor., Ham.	6	111	63	29	92	39	....	....	....	....	....	....	1919-20	1924-25
Prokhorov, Vitali	St.L.	3	83	19	11	30	35	4	0	0	0	0	....	1992-93	1994-95
Prokopec, Mike	Chi.	2	15	0	0	0	11	....	....	....	....	....	....	1995-96	1996-97
Pronger, Sean	Ana., Pit., NYR, L.A., Bos., CBJ, Van.	8	260	23	36	59	159	14	0	2	2	8	....	1995-96	2003-04
Pronovost, Andre	Mtl., Bos., Det., Min.	10	556	94	104	198	408	70	11	11	22	58	4	1956-57	1967-68
Pronovost, Jean	Pit., Atl., Wsh.	14	998	391	383	774	413	35	11	9	20	14	....	1968-69	1981-82
Pronovost, Marcel	Det., Tor.	21	1206	88	257	345	851	134	8	23	31	104	5	1949-50	1969-70
Propp, Brian	Phi., Bos., Min., Hfd.	15	1016	425	579	1004	830	160	64	84	148	151	....	1979-80	1993-94
Proulx, Christian	Mtl.	1	7	1	2	3	20	....	....	....	....	....	....	1993-94	1993-94
• Provost, Claude	Mtl.	15	1005	254	335	589	469	126	25	38	63	86	9	1955-56	1969-70
Prpic, Joel	Bos., Col.	3	18	0	3	3	4	....	....	....	....	....	....	1997-98	2000-01
Pryor, Chris	Min., NYI	6	82	1	4	5	122	....	....	....	....	....	....	1984-85	1989-90
Prystai, Metro	Chi., Det.	11	674	151	179	330	231	43	12	14	26	8	2	1947-48	1957-58
• Pudas, Al	Tor.	1	4	0	0	0	0	....	....	....	....	....	....	1926-27	1926-27
Pulford, Bob	Tor., L.A.	16	1079	281	362	643	792	89	25	26	51	126	4	1956-57	1971-72
Pulkkinen, Dave	NYI	1	2	0	0	0	0	....	....	....	....	....	....	1972-73	1972-73
• Purpur, Fido	St.L., Chi., Det.	5	144	25	35	60	46	16	1	2	3	4	....	1934-35	1944-45
Purves, John	Wsh.	1	7	1	0	1	0	....	....	....	....	....	....	1990-91	1990-91
• Pusie, Jean	Mtl., NYR, Bos.	5	61	1	4	5	28	7	0	0	0	0	1	1930-31	1935-36
Pyatt, Nelson	Det., Wsh., Col.	7	296	71	63	134	69	....	....	....	....	....	....	1973-74	1979-80

Q

Name	NHL Teams	NHL Seasons	Regular Schedule GP	G	A	TP	PIM	Playoffs GP	G	A	TP	PIM	NHL Cup Wins	First NHL Season	Last NHL Season
• Quackenbush, Bill	Det., Bos.	14	774	62	222	284	95	80	2	19	21	8	....	1942-43	1955-56
Quackenbush, Max	Bos., Chi.	2	61	4	7	11	30	6	0	0	0	4	....	1950-51	1951-52
Quenneville, Joel	Tor., Col., N.J., Hfd., Wsh.	13	803	54	136	190	705	32	0	8	8	22	....	1978-79	1990-91
• Quenneville, Leo	NYR	1	25	0	3	3	10	3	0	0	0	0	....	1929-30	1929-30
• Quilty, John	Mtl., Bos.	4	125	36	34	70	81	13	3	5	8	9	....	1940-41	1947-48
Quinn, Dan	Cgy., Pit., Van., St.L., Phi., Min., Ott., L.A.	14	805	266	419	685	533	65	22	26	48	62	....	1983-84	1996-97
Quinn, Pat	Tor., Van., Atl.	9	606	18	113	131	950	11	0	1	1	21	....	1968-69	1976-77
Quinney, Ken	Que.	3	59	7	13	20	23	....	....	....	....	....	....	1986-87	1990-91
Quintal, Stephane	Bos., St.L., Wpg., Mtl., NYR, Chi.	16	1037	63	180	243	1320	52	2	10	12	51	....	1988-89	2003-04
Quintin, Jean-Francois	S.J.	2	22	5	5	10	4	....	....	....	....	....	....	1991-92	1992-93

R

Name	NHL Teams	NHL Seasons	Regular Schedule GP	G	A	TP	PIM	Playoffs GP	G	A	TP	PIM	NHL Cup Wins	First NHL Season	Last NHL Season
Racine, Yves	Det., Phi., Mtl., S.J., Cgy., T.B.	9	508	37	194	231	439	25	5	4	9	37	....	1989-90	1997-98
• Radley, Yip	NYA, Mtl.M.	2	18	0	1	1	13	....	....	....	....	....	....	1930-31	1936-37

Craig Redmond

Leo Reise Jr.

Leo Reise Sr.

Wayne Rivers

			Regular Schedule					Playoffs							
Name	NHL Teams	NHL Seasons	GP	G	A	TP	PIM	GP	G	A	TP	PIM	NHL Cup Wins	First NHL Season	Last NHL Season
‡ Radulov, Igor	Chi.	2	43	9	7	16	22	....	....	....	....	....	....	2002-03	2003-04
Raglan, Herb	St.L., Que., T.B., Ott.	9	343	33	56	89	775	32	3	6	9	50	....	1985-86	1993-94
• Raglan, Rags	Det., Chi.	3	100	4	9	13	52	3	0	0	0	0	....	1950-51	1952-53
Ragnarsson, Marcus	S.J., Phi.	9	632	37	140	177	482	68	2	13	15	60	....	1995-96	2003-04
Raleigh, Don	NYR	10	535	101	219	320	96	18	6	5	11	6	....	1943-44	1955-56
Ralph, Brad	Phx.	1	1	0	0	0	0	....	....	....	....	....	....	2000-01	2000-01
Ramage, Rob	Col., St.L., Cgy., Tor., Min., T.B., Mtl., Phi.	15	1044	139	425	564	2226	84	8	42	50	218	2	1979-80	1993-94
• Ramsay, Beattie	Tor.	1	43	0	2	2	10	....	....	....	....	....	....	1927-28	1927-28
Ramsay, Craig	Buf.	14	1070	252	420	672	201	89	17	31	48	27	....	1971-72	1984-85
Ramsay, Les	Chi.	1	11	2	2	4	2	....	....	....	....	....	....	1944-45	1944-45
Ramsey, Mike	Buf., Pit., Det.	18	1070	79	266	345	1012	115	8	29	37	176	....	1979-80	1996-97
Ramsey, Wayne	Buf.	1	2	0	0	0	0	....	....	....	....	....	....	1977-78	1977-78
• Randall, Ken	Tor., Ham., NYA	10	218	68	50	118	533	6	2	1	3	27	2	1917-18	1926-27
Ranheim, Paul	Cgy., Hfd., Car., Phi., Phx.	15	1013	161	199	360	288	36	3	8	11	6	....	1988-89	2002-03
Ranieri, George	Bos.	1	2	0	0	0	0	....	....	....	....	....	....	1956-57	1956-57
‡ Ratchuk, Peter	Fla.	2	32	1	1	2	10	....	....	....	....	....	....	1998-99	2000-01
Ratelle, Jean	NYR, Bos.	21	1281	491	776	1267	276	123	32	66	98	24	....	1960-61	1980-81
Rathwell, Jake	Bos.	1	1	0	0	0	0	....	....	....	....	....	....	1974-75	1974-75
Ratushny, Dan	Van.	1	1	0	1	1	2	....	....	....	....	....	....	1992-93	1992-93
Rausse, Errol	Wsh.	3	31	7	3	10	0	....	....	....	....	....	....	1979-80	1981-82
Rautakallio, Pekka	Atl., Cgy.	3	235	33	121	154	122	23	2	5	7	8	....	1979-80	1981-82
Ravlich, Matt	Bos., Chi., Det., L.A.	10	410	12	78	90	364	24	1	5	6	16	....	1962-63	1972-73
Ray, Rob	Buf., Ott.	15	900	41	50	91	3207	55	3	2	5	169	....	1989-90	2003-04
• Raymond, Armand	Mtl.	2	22	0	2	2	10	....	....	....	....	....	....	1937-38	1939-40
• Raymond, Paul	Mtl.	4	76	2	3	5	6	5	0	0	0	2	....	1932-33	1938-39
Read, Mel	NYR	1	1	0	0	0	0	....	....	....	....	....	....	1946-47	1946-47
Reardon, Ken	Mtl.	7	341	26	96	122	604	31	2	5	7	62	1	1940-41	1949-50
• Reardon, Terry	Bos., Mtl.	7	193	47	53	100	73	30	8	10	18	12	1	1938-39	1946-47
Reaume, Marc	Tor., Det., Mtl., Van.	9	344	8	43	51	273	21	0	2	2	8	....	1954-55	1970-71
• Reay, Billy	Det., Mtl.	10	479	105	162	267	202	63	13	16	29	43	2	1943-44	1952-53
Redahl, Gord	Bos.	1	18	0	1	1	2	....	....	....	....	....	....	1958-59	1958-59
• Redding, George	Bos.	2	55	3	2	5	23	....	....	....	....	....	....	1924-25	1925-26
Redmond, Craig	L.A., Edm.	5	191	16	68	84	134	3	1	0	1	2	....	1984-85	1988-89
Redmond, Dick	Min., Cal., Chi., St.L., Atl., Bos.	13	771	133	312	445	504	66	9	22	31	27	....	1969-70	1981-82
Redmond, Keith	L.A.	1	12	1	0	1	20	....	....	....	....	....	....	1993-94	1993-94
Redmond, Mickey	Mtl., Det.	9	538	233	195	428	219	16	2	3	5	2	2	1967-68	1975-76
Reeds, Mark	St.L., Hfd.	8	365	45	114	159	135	53	8	9	17	23	....	1981-82	1988-89
Reekie, Joe	Buf., NYI, T.B., Wsh., Chi.	17	902	25	139	164	1326	51	3	4	7	63	....	1985-86	2001-02
• Regan, Bill	NYR, NYA	3	67	3	2	5	67	8	0	0	0	2	....	1929-30	1932-33
Regan, Larry	Bos., Tor.	5	280	41	95	136	71	42	7	14	21	18	....	1956-57	1960-61
Regier, Darcy	Cle., NYI	3	26	0	2	2	35	....	....	....	....	....	....	1977-78	1983-84
• Reibel, Dutch	Det., Chi., Bos.	6	409	84	161	245	75	39	6	14	20	4	2	1953-54	1958-59
‡ Reichel, Robert	Cgy., NYI, Phx., Tor.	11	830	252	378	630	388	70	8	23	31	20	....	1990-91	2003-04
Reichert, Craig	Ana.	1	3	0	0	0	0	....	....	....	....	....	....	1996-97	1996-97
• Reid, Dave	Tor.	3	7	0	0	0	0	....	....	....	....	....	....	1952-53	1955-56
Reid, Dave	Bos., Tor., Dal., Col.	18	961	165	204	369	253	118	9	26	35	34	2	1983-84	2000-01
Reid, Gerry	Det.	1	....	....	....	....	....	2	0	0	0	2	....	1948-49	1948-49
Reid, Gord	NYA	1	1	0	0	0	2	....	....	....	....	....	....	1936-37	1936-37
• Reid, Reg	Tor.	2	39	1	0	1	4	2	0	0	0	0	....	1924-25	1925-26
Reid, Tom	Chi., Min.	11	701	17	113	130	654	42	1	13	14	49	....	1967-68	1977-78
Reierson, Dave	Cgy.	1	2	0	0	0	2	....	....	....	....	....	....	1988-89	1988-89
• Reigle, Ed	Bos.	1	17	0	2	2	25	....	....	....	....	....	....	1950-51	1950-51
Reinhart, Paul	Atl., Cgy., Van.	11	648	133	426	559	277	83	23	54	77	42	....	1979-80	1989-90
• Reinikka, Ollie	NYR	1	16	0	0	0	0	....	....	....	....	....	....	1926-27	1926-27
‡ Reirden, Todd	Edm., St.L., Atl., Phx.	5	183	11	35	46	181	5	0	1	1	0	....	1998-99	2003-04
• Reise, Leo	Ham., NYA, NYR	8	241	43	43	86	187	6	0	0	0	16	....	1920-21	1929-30
Reise, Leo	Chi., Det., NYR	9	494	28	81	109	399	52	8	5	13	68	2	1945-46	1953-54
Renaud, Mark	Hfd., Buf.	5	152	6	50	56	86	....	....	....	....	....	....	1979-80	1983-84
‡ Renberg, Mikael	Phi., T.B., Phx., Tor.	10	661	190	274	464	372	67	16	22	38	42	....	1993-94	2003-04
Reynolds, Bobby	Tor.	1	7	1	1	2	0	....	....	....	....	....	....	1989-90	1989-90
Ribble, Pat	Atl., Chi., Tor., Wsh., Cgy.	8	349	19	60	79	365	8	0	1	1	12	....	1975-76	1982-83
Rice, Steven	NYR, Edm., Hfd., Car.	8	329	64	61	125	275	2	2	1	3	6	....	1990-91	1997-98
Richard, Henri	Mtl.	20	1256	358	688	1046	928	180	49	80	129	181	11	1955-56	1974-75
• Richard, Jacques	Atl., Buf., Que.	10	556	160	187	347	307	35	5	5	10	34	....	1972-73	1982-83
Richard, Jean-Marc	Que.	2	5	2	1	3	2	....	....	....	....	....	....	1987-88	1989-90
• Richard, Maurice	Mtl.	18	978	544	421	965	1285	133	82	44	126	188	8	1942-43	1959-60
‡ Richard, Mike	Wsh.	2	7	0	2	2	0	....	....	....	....	....	....	1987-88	1989-90
Richards, Todd	Hfd.	2	8	0	4	4	4	11	0	3	3	6	....	1990-91	1991-92
Richards, Travis	Dal.	2	3	0	0	0	2	....	....	....	....	....	....	1994-95	1995-96
Richardson, Dave	NYR, Chi., Det.	4	45	3	2	5	27	....	....	....	....	....	....	1963-64	1967-68
Richardson, Glen	Van.	1	24	3	6	9	19	....	....	....	....	....	....	1975-76	1975-76
Richardson, Ken	St.L.	3	49	8	13	21	16	....	....	....	....	....	....	1974-75	1978-79
Richer, Bob	Buf.	1	3	0	0	0	0	....	....	....	....	....	....	1972-73	1972-73
Richer, Stephane	Mtl., N.J., T.B., St.L., Pit.	17	1054	421	398	819	614	134	53	45	98	61	2	1984-85	2001-02
Richer, Stephane	T.B., Bos., Fla.	3	27	1	5	6	20	3	0	0	0	0	....	1992-93	1994-95
Richmond, Steve	NYR, Det., N.J., L.A.	5	159	4	23	27	514	4	0	0	0	12	....	1983-84	1988-89
‡ Richter, Barry	NYR, Bos., NYI, Mtl.	5	151	11	34	45	76	....	....	....	....	....	....	1995-96	2000-01
Richter, Dave	Min., Phi., Van., St.L.	9	365	9	40	49	1030	22	1	0	1	80	....	1981-82	1989-90
Ridley, Mike	NYR, Wsh., Tor., Van.	12	866	292	466	758	424	104	28	50	78	70	....	1985-86	1996-97
‡ Riesen, Michel	Edm.	1	12	0	1	1	4	....	....	....	....	....	....	2000-01	2000-01
Riley, Bill	Wsh., Wpg.	5	139	31	30	61	320	....	....	....	....	....	....	1974-75	1979-80
• Riley, Jack	Det., Mtl., Bos.	4	104	10	22	32	8	4	0	3	3	0	....	1932-33	1935-36
• Riley, Jim	Chi., Det.	1	9	0	2	2	14	....	....	....	....	....	....	1926-27	1926-27
Riopelle, Rip	Mtl.	3	169	27	16	43	73	8	1	1	2	2	....	1947-48	1949-50
Rioux, Gerry	Wpg.	1	8	0	0	0	6	....	....	....	....	....	....	1979-80	1979-80
Rioux, Pierre	Cgy.	1	14	1	2	3	4	....	....	....	....	....	....	1982-83	1982-83
• Ripley, Vic	Chi., Bos., NYR, St.L.	7	278	51	49	100	173	20	4	1	5	10	....	1928-29	1934-35
Risebrough, Doug	Mtl., Cgy.	13	740	185	286	471	1542	124	21	37	58	238	4	1974-75	1986-87
Rissling, Gary	Wsh., Pit.	7	221	23	30	53	1008	5	0	1	1	4	....	1978-79	1984-85
Ritchie, Bob	Phi., Det.	2	29	8	4	12	10	....	....	....	....	....	....	1976-77	1977-78
• Ritchie, Dave	Mtl.W., Ott., Tor., Que., Mtl.	6	58	15	6	21	50	1	0	0	0	0	....	1917-18	1925-26
Ritson, Alex	NYR	1	1	0	0	0	0	....	....	....	....	....	....	1944-45	1944-45
Rittinger, Alan	Bos.	1	19	3	7	10	0	....	....	....	....	....	....	1943-44	1943-44
Rivard, Bob	Pit.	1	27	5	12	17	4	....	....	....	....	....	....	1967-68	1967-68
• Rivers, Gus	Mtl.	3	88	4	5	9	12	16	2	0	2	2	2	1929-30	1931-32
Rivers, Shawn	T.B.	1	4	0	2	2	2	....	....	....	....	....	....	1992-93	1992-93
Rivers, Wayne	Det., Bos., St.L., NYR	7	108	15	30	45	94	....	....	....	....	....	....	1961-62	1968-69
Rizzuto, Garth	Van.	1	37	3	4	7	16	....	....	....	....	....	....	1970-71	1970-71
• Roach, Mickey	Tor., Ham., NYA	8	211	77	34	111	54	....	....	....	....	....	....	1919-20	1926-27
Roberge, Mario	Mtl.	5	112	7	7	14	314	15	0	0	0	24	1	1990-91	1994-95
Roberge, Serge	Que.	1	9	0	0	0	24	....	....	....	....	....	....	1990-91	1990-91
• Robert, Claude	Mtl.	1	23	1	0	1	9	....	....	....	....	....	....	1950-51	1950-51
Robert, Rene	Tor., Pit., Buf., Col.	12	744	284	418	702	597	50	22	19	41	73	....	1970-71	1981-82
Roberto, Phil	Mtl., St.L., Det., K.C., Col., Cle.	8	385	75	106	181	464	31	9	8	17	69	1	1969-70	1976-77
Roberts, David	St.L., Edm., Van.	5	125	20	33	53	85	9	0	0	0	16	....	1993-94	1997-98
Roberts, Doug	Det., Oak., Cal., Bos.	10	419	43	104	147	342	16	2	3	5	46	....	1965-66	1974-75
Roberts, Gordie	Hfd., Min., Phi., St.L., Pit., Bos.	15	1097	61	359	420	1582	153	10	47	57	273	2	1979-80	1993-94
Roberts, Jim	Min.	3	106	17	23	40	33	2	0	0	0	0	....	1976-77	1978-79
Roberts, Jimmy	Mtl., St.L.	15	1006	126	194	320	621	153	20	16	36	160	5	1963-64	1977-78
• Robertson, Fred	Tor., Det.	2	34	1	0	1	35	7	0	0	0	0	1	1931-32	1933-34
Robertson, Geordie	Buf.	1	5	1	2	3	7	....	....	....	....	....	....	1982-83	1982-83
• Robertson, George	Mtl.	2	31	2	5	7	6	....	....	....	....	....	....	1947-48	1948-49
Robertson, Torrie	Wsh., Hfd., Det.	10	442	49	99	148	1751	22	2	1	3	90	....	1980-81	1989-90
Robertsson, Bert	Van., Edm., NYR	4	123	4	10	14	75	5	0	0	0	0	....	1997-98	2000-01
Robidoux, Florent	Chi.	3	52	7	4	11	75	....	....	....	....	....	....	1980-81	1983-84
Robinson, Doug	Chi., NYR, L.A.	7	239	44	67	111	34	11	4	3	7	0	....	1963-64	1970-71
• Robinson, Earl	Mtl.M., Chi., Mtl.	11	417	83	98	181	133	25	5	4	9	0	1	1928-29	1939-40
Robinson, Larry	Mtl., L.A.	20	1384	208	750	958	793	227	28	116	144	211	6	1972-73	1991-92
Robinson, Moe	Mtl.	1	1	0	0	0	0	....	....	....	....	....	....	1979-80	1979-80
Robinson, Rob	St.L.	1	22	0	1	1	8	....	....	....	....	....	....	1991-92	1991-92
Robinson, Scott	Min.	1	1	0	0	0	2	....	....	....	....	....	....	1989-90	1989-90
Robitaille, Luc	L.A., Pit., NYR, Det.	19	1431	668	726	1394	1177	159	58	69	127	174	1	1986-87	2005-06
Robitaille, Mike	NYR, Det., Buf., Van.	8	382	23	105	128	280	13	0	1	1	4	....	1969-70	1976-77
Roche, Dave	Pit., Cgy., NYI	5	171	15	15	30	334	16	2	7	9	26	....	1995-96	2001-02

Name	NHL Teams	NHL Seasons	Regular Schedule GP	G	A	TP	PIM	Playoffs GP	G	A	TP	PIM	NHL Cup Wins	First NHL Season	Last NHL Season
● Roche, Des	Mtl.M., Ott., St.L., Mtl., Det.	4	113	20	18	38	44	....	....	....	....	....	....	1930-31	1934-35
● Roche, Earl	Mtl.M., Bos., Ott., St.L., Det.	4	147	25	27	52	48	2	0	0	0	0	....	1930-31	1934-35
Roche, Ernie	Mtl.	1	4	0	0	0	2	....	....	....	....	....	....	1950-51	1950-51
Rochefort, Dave	Det.	1	1	0	0	0	0	....	....	....	....	....	....	1966-67	1966-67
Rochefort, Leon	NYR, Mtl., Phi., L.A., Det., Atl., Van.	15	617	121	147	268	93	39	4	4	8	16	2	1960-61	1975-76
Rochefort, Normand	Que., NYR, T.B.	13	598	39	119	158	570	69	7	5	12	82	....	1980-81	1993-94
● Rockburn, Harvey	Det., Ott.	3	94	4	2	6	254	....	....	....	....	....	....	1929-30	1932-33
● Rodden, Eddie	Chi., Tor., Bos., NYR	4	97	6	14	20	60	2	0	1	1	0	....	1926-27	1930-31
Rodgers, Marc	Det.	1	21	1	1	2	10	....	....	....	....	....	....	1999-00	1999-00
‡ Roest, Stacy	Det., Min.	5	244	28	48	76	54	3	0	0	0	0	....	1998-99	2002-03
Rogers, John	Min.	2	14	2	4	6	0	....	....	....	....	....	....	1973-74	1974-75
Rogers, Mike	Hfd., NYR, Edm.	7	484	202	317	519	184	17	1	13	14	6	....	1979-80	1985-86
Rohlicek, Jeff	Van.	2	9	0	0	0	8	....	....	....	....	....	....	1987-88	1988-89
Rohlin, Leif	Van.	2	96	8	24	32	40	5	0	0	0	0	....	1995-96	1996-97
Rohloff, Jon	Bos.	3	150	7	25	32	129	10	1	2	3	8	....	1994-95	1996-97
Rohloff, Todd	Wsh., CBJ	2	75	0	6	6	40	....	....	....	....	....	....	2001-02	2003-04
Rolfe, Dale	Bos., L.A., Det., NYR	9	509	25	125	150	556	71	5	24	29	89	....	1959-60	1974-75
Romanchych, Larry	Chi., Atl.	6	298	68	97	165	102	7	2	2	4	4	....	1970-71	1976-77
Romaniuk, Russell	Wpg., Phi.	5	102	13	14	27	63	2	0	0	0	0	....	1991-92	1995-96
Rombough, Doug	Buf., NYI, Min.	4	150	24	27	51	80	....	....	....	....	....	....	1972-73	1975-76
Rominski, Dale	T.B.	1	3	0	1	1	2	....	....	....	....	....	....	1999-00	1999-00
● Romnes, Doc	Chi., Tor., NYA	10	360	68	136	204	42	45	7	18	25	4	2	1930-31	1939-40
Ronan, Ed	Mtl., Wpg., Buf.	6	182	13	23	36	101	27	4	3	7	16	1	1991-92	1996-97
● Ronan, Skene	Ott.	1	11	0	0	0	6	....	....	....	....	....	....	1918-19	1918-19
Ronning, Cliff	St.L., Van., Phx., Nsh., L.A., Min., NYI	18	1137	306	563	869	453	126	29	57	86	72	....	1985-86	2003-04
Ronnqvist, Jonas	Ana.	1	38	0	4	4	14	....	....	....	....	....	....	2000-01	2000-01
Ronson, Len	NYR, Oak.	2	18	2	1	3	10	....	....	....	....	....	....	1960-61	1968-69
Ronty, Paul	Bos., NYR, Mtl.	8	488	101	211	312	103	21	1	7	8	6	....	1947-48	1954-55
Rooney, Steve	Mtl., Wpg., N.J.	5	154	15	13	28	496	25	3	2	5	86	1	1984-85	1988-89
Root, Bill	Mtl., Tor., St.L., Phi.	6	247	11	23	34	180	22	1	2	3	25	....	1982-83	1987-88
‡ Rosa, Pavel	L.A.	4	36	5	13	18	6	....	....	....	....	....	....	1998-99	2003-04
● Ross, Art	Mtl.W.	1	3	1	0	1	12	....	....	....	....	....	....	1917-18	1917-18
Ross, Jim	NYR	2	62	2	11	13	29	....	....	....	....	....	....	1951-52	1952-53
Rossignol, Roly	Det., Mtl.	3	14	3	5	8	6	1	0	0	0	2	....	1943-44	1945-46
Rossiter, Kyle	Fla., Atl.	3	11	0	1	1	9	....	....	....	....	....	....	2001-02	2003-04
Rota, Darcy	Chi., Atl., Van.	11	794	256	239	495	973	60	14	7	21	147	....	1973-74	1983-84
Rota, Randy	Mtl., L.A., K.C., Col.	5	212	38	39	77	60	5	0	1	1	0	....	1972-73	1976-77
● Rothschild, Sam	Mtl.M., Pit., NYA	4	100	8	6	14	25	6	0	0	0	0	1	1924-25	1927-28
● Roulston, Rolly	Det.	3	24	0	6	6	10	....	....	....	....	....	1	1935-36	1937-38
Roulston, Tom	Edm., Pit.	5	195	47	49	96	74	21	2	2	4	2	....	1980-81	1985-86
Roupe, Magnus	Phi.	2	40	3	5	8	42	....	....	....	....	....	....	1987-88	1988-89
Rouse, Bob	Min., Wsh., Tor., Det., S.J.	17	1061	37	181	218	1559	136	7	21	28	198	2	1983-84	1999-00
Rousseau, Bobby	Mtl., Min., NYR	15	942	245	458	703	359	128	27	57	84	69	4	1960-61	1974-75
Rousseau, Guy	Mtl.	2	4	0	1	1	0	....	....	....	....	....	....	1954-55	1956-57
Rousseau, Roland	Mtl.	1	2	0	0	0	0	....	....	....	....	....	....	1952-53	1952-53
Routhier, Jean-Marc	Que.	1	8	0	0	0	9	....	....	....	....	....	....	1989-90	1989-90
● Rowe, Bobby	Bos.	1	4	1	0	1	0	....	....	....	....	....	....	1924-25	1924-25
Rowe, Mike	Pit.	3	11	0	0	0	11	....	....	....	....	....	....	1984-85	1986-87
Rowe, Ron	NYR	1	5	1	0	1	0	....	....	....	....	....	....	1947-48	1947-48
Rowe, Tom	Wsh., Hfd., Det.	7	357	85	100	185	615	3	2	0	2	0	....	1976-77	1982-83
Roy, Jean-Yves	NYR, Ott., Bos.	4	61	12	16	28	26	....	....	....	....	....	....	1994-95	1997-98
Roy, Stephane	Min.	1	12	1	0	1	0	....	....	....	....	....	....	1987-88	1987-88
Royer, Gaetan	T.B.	1	3	0	0	0	2	....	....	....	....	....	....	2001-02	2001-02
Royer, Remi	Chi.	1	18	0	0	0	67	....	....	....	....	....	....	1998-99	1998-99
● Rozzini, Gino	Bos.	1	31	5	10	15	20	6	1	2	3	6	....	1944-45	1944-45
Rucinski, Mike	Chi.	2	1	0	0	0	0	2	0	0	0	0	....	1987-88	1988-89
Rucinski, Mike	Car.	3	26	0	2	2	10	....	....	....	....	....	....	1997-98	2000-01
● Ruelle, Bernie	Det.	1	2	1	0	1	0	....	....	....	....	....	....	1943-44	1943-44
Ruff, Jason	St.L., T.B.	2	14	3	3	6	10	....	....	....	....	....	....	1992-93	1993-94
Ruff, Lindy	Buf., NYR	12	691	105	195	300	1264	52	11	13	24	193	....	1979-80	1990-91
Ruhnke, Kent	Bos.	1	2	0	1	1	0	....	....	....	....	....	....	1975-76	1975-76
Rumble, Darren	Phi., Ott., St.L., T.B.	8	193	10	26	36	216	....	....	....	....	....	1	1990-91	2003-04
Rundqvist, Thomas	Mtl.	1	2	0	1	1	0	....	....	....	....	....	....	1984-85	1984-85
● Runge, Paul	Bos., Mtl.M., Mtl.	7	140	18	22	40	57	7	0	0	0	6	....	1930-31	1937-38
Ruotsalainen, Reijo	NYR, Edm., N.J.	7	446	107	237	344	180	86	15	32	47	44	2	1981-82	1989-90
Rupp, Duane	NYR, Tor., Min., Pit.	10	374	24	93	117	220	10	2	2	4	8	....	1962-63	1972-73
Ruskowski, Terry	Chi., L.A., Pit., Min.	10	630	113	313	426	1354	21	1	6	7	86	....	1979-80	1988-89
Russell, Cam	Chi., Col.	10	396	9	21	30	872	44	0	5	5	16	....	1989-90	1998-99
● Russell, Church	NYR	3	90	20	16	36	12	....	....	....	....	....	....	1945-46	1947-48
Russell, Phil	Chi., Atl., Cgy., N.J., Buf.	15	1016	99	325	424	2038	73	4	22	26	202	....	1972-73	1986-87
Ruuttu, Christian	Buf., Chi., Van.	9	621	134	298	432	714	42	4	9	13	49	....	1986-87	1994-95
Ruzicka, Vladimir	Edm., Bos., Ott.	5	233	82	85	167	129	30	4	14	18	2	....	1989-90	1993-94
Ryan, Terry	Mtl.	3	8	0	0	0	36	....	....	....	....	....	....	1996-97	1998-99
Rychel, Warren	Chi., L.A., Tor., Col., Ana.	9	406	38	39	77	1422	70	8	13	21	121	1	1988-89	1998-99
Rymsha, Andy	Que.	1	6	0	0	0	23	....	....	....	....	....	....	1991-92	1991-92

S

Name	NHL Teams	NHL Seasons	Regular Schedule GP	G	A	TP	PIM	Playoffs GP	G	A	TP	PIM	NHL Cup Wins	First NHL Season	Last NHL Season
Saarinen, Simo	NYR	1	8	0	0	0	0	....	....	....	....	....	....	1984-85	1984-85
Sabol, Shaun	Phi.	1	2	0	0	0	0	....	....	....	....	....	....	1989-90	1989-90
Sabourin, Bob	Tor.	1	1	0	0	0	2	....	....	....	....	....	....	1951-52	1951-52
Sabourin, Gary	St.L., Tor., Cal., Cle.	10	627	169	188	357	397	62	19	11	30	58	....	1967-68	1976-77
Sabourin, Ken	Cgy., Wsh.	4	74	2	8	10	201	12	0	0	0	34	....	1988-89	1991-92
Sacco, David	Tor., Ana.	3	35	5	13	18	22	....	....	....	....	....	....	1993-94	1995-96
Sacco, Joe	Tor., Ana., NYI, Wsh., Phi.	13	738	94	119	213	421	26	2	0	2	8	....	1990-91	2002-03
Sacharuk, Larry	NYR, St.L.	5	151	29	33	62	42	2	1	1	2	2	....	1972-73	1976-77
Saganiuk, Rocky	Tor., Pit.	6	259	57	65	122	201	6	1	0	1	15	....	1978-79	1983-84
Saleski, Don	Phi., Col.	9	543	128	125	253	629	82	13	17	30	131	2	1971-72	1979-80
Salming, Borje	Tor., Det.	17	1148	150	637	787	1344	81	12	37	49	91	....	1973-74	1989-90
‡ Salomonsson, Andreas	N.J., Wsh.	2	71	5	9	14	36	4	0	1	1	0	....	2001-02	2002-03
Salovaara, Barry	Det.	2	90	2	13	15	70	....	....	....	....	....	....	1974-75	1975-76
Salvian, Dave	NYI	1	....	....	....	....	....	1	0	1	1	2	....	1976-77	1976-77
Samis, Phil	Tor.	2	2	0	0	0	0	5	0	1	1	2	1	1947-48	1949-50
Sampson, Gary	Wsh.	4	105	13	22	35	25	12	1	0	1	0	....	1983-84	1986-87
Samuelsson, Kjell	NYR, Phi., Pit., T.B.	14	813	48	138	186	1225	123	4	20	24	178	1	1985-86	1998-99
Samuelsson, Ulf	Hfd., Pit., NYR, Det., Phi.	16	1080	57	275	332	2453	132	7	27	34	272	2	1984-85	1999-00
Sandelin, Scott	Mtl., Phi., Min.	4	25	0	4	4	2	....	....	....	....	....	....	1986-87	1991-92
Sanderson, Derek	Bos., NYR, St.L., Van., Pit.	13	598	202	250	452	911	56	18	12	30	187	2	1965-66	1977-78
Sandford, Ed	Bos., Det., Chi.	9	502	106	145	251	355	42	13	11	24	27	....	1947-48	1955-56
Sandlak, Jim	Van., Hfd.	11	549	110	119	229	821	33	7	10	17	30	....	1985-86	1995-96
● Sands, Charlie	Tor., Bos., Mtl., NYR	12	427	99	109	208	58	34	6	6	12	4	1	1932-33	1943-44
Sandstrom, Tomas	NYR, L.A., Pit., Det., Ana.	15	983	394	462	856	1193	139	32	49	81	183	1	1984-85	1998-99
Sandwith, Terran	Edm.	1	8	0	0	0	6	....	....	....	....	....	....	1997-98	1997-98
Sanipass, Everett	Chi., Que.	5	164	25	34	59	358	5	2	0	2	4	....	1986-87	1990-91
‡ Sarault, Yves	Mtl., Cgy., Col., Ott., Atl., Nsh.	8	106	10	10	20	51	5	0	0	0	2	....	1994-95	2001-02
Sargent, Gary	L.A., Min.	8	402	61	161	222	273	20	5	7	12	8	....	1975-76	1982-83
Sarner, Craig	Bos.	1	7	0	0	0	0	....	....	....	....	....	....	1974-75	1974-75
‡ Sarno, Peter	Edm., CBJ	2	7	1	0	1	2	....	....	....	....	....	....	2003-04	2005-06
Sarrazin, Dick	Phi.	3	100	20	35	55	22	4	0	0	0	0	....	1968-69	1971-72
Sasakamoose, Fred	Chi.	1	11	0	0	0	6	....	....	....	....	....	....	1953-54	1953-54
Sasser, Grant	Pit.	1	3	0	0	0	0	....	....	....	....	....	....	1983-84	1983-84
Sather, Glen	Bos., Pit., NYR, St.L., Mtl., Min.	10	658	80	113	193	724	72	1	5	6	86	....	1966-67	1975-76
Saunders, Bernie	Que.	2	10	0	1	1	8	....	....	....	....	....	....	1979-80	1980-81
Saunders, David	Van.	1	56	7	13	20	10	....	....	....	....	....	....	1987-88	1987-88
● Saunders, Ted	Ott.	1	18	1	3	4	4	....	....	....	....	....	....	1933-34	1933-34
Sauve, Jean-Francois	Buf., Que.	7	290	65	138	203	114	36	9	12	21	10	....	1980-81	1986-87
Savage, Andre	Bos., Phi.	4	66	10	14	24	14	....	....	....	....	....	....	1998-99	2002-03
Savage, Brian	Mtl., Phx., St.L., Phi.	12	674	192	167	359	321	39	3	8	11	12	....	1993-94	2005-06
Savage, Joel	Buf.	1	3	0	1	1	0	....	....	....	....	....	....	1990-91	1990-91
Savage, Reggie	Wsh., Que.	3	34	5	7	12	28	....	....	....	....	....	....	1990-91	1993-94
● Savage, Tony	Bos., Mtl.	1	49	1	5	6	6	2	0	0	0	0	....	1934-35	1934-35
Savard, Andre	Bos., Buf., Que.	12	790	211	271	482	411	85	13	18	31	77	....	1973-74	1984-85
Savard, Denis	Chi., Mtl., T.B.	17	1196	473	865	1338	1336	169	66	109	175	256	1	1980-81	1996-97
Savard, Jean	Chi., Hfd.	3	43	7	12	19	29	....	....	....	....	....	....	1977-78	1979-80

Gordie Roberts

Luc Robitaille

Church Russell

Larry Sacharuk

Brian Savage

Ron Schock

Enio Sclisizzi

Earl Seibert

Name	NHL Teams	NHL Seasons	Regular Schedule GP	G	A	TP	PIM	Playoffs GP	G	A	TP	PIM	NHL Cup Wins	First NHL Season	Last NHL Season
Savard, Serge	Mtl., Wpg.	17	1040	106	333	439	592	130	19	49	68	88	8	1966-67	1982-83
Savoia, Ryan	Pit.	1	3	0	0	0	0	....	....	....	....	....	....	1998-99	1998-99
Sawyer, Kevin	St.L., Bos., Phx., Ana.	6	110	3	3	6	403	....	....	....	....	....	....	1995-96	2002-03
Scamurra, Peter	Wsh.	4	132	8	25	33	59	....	....	....	....	....	....	1975-76	1979-80
Sceviour, Darin	Chi.	1	1	0	0	0	0	....	....	....	....	....	....	1986-87	1986-87
• Schaeffer, Butch	Chi.	1	5	0	0	0	6	....	....	....	....	....	....	1936-37	1936-37
Schamehorn, Kevin	Det., L.A.	3	10	0	0	0	17	....	....	....	....	....	....	1976-77	1980-81
‡ Schastlivy, Petr	Ott., Ana.	5	129	18	22	40	30	1	0	0	0	0	....	1999-00	2003-04
Schella, John	Van.	2	115	2	18	20	224	....	....	....	....	....	....	1970-71	1971-72
Scherza, Chuck	Bos., NYR	2	36	6	6	12	35	....	....	....	....	....	....	1943-44	1944-45
Schinkel, Ken	NYR, Pit.	12	636	127	198	325	163	19	7	2	9	4	....	1959-60	1972-73
‡ Schlegel, Brad	Wsh., Cgy.	3	48	1	8	9	10	7	0	1	1	2	....	1991-92	1993-94
Schliebener, Andy	Van.	3	84	2	11	13	74	6	0	0	0	0	....	1981-82	1984-85
Schmautz, Bobby	Chi., Van., Bos., Edm., Col.	13	764	271	286	557	988	84	28	33	61	92	....	1967-68	1980-81
• Schmautz, Cliff	Buf., Phi.	1	56	13	19	32	33	....	....	....	....	....	....	1970-71	1970-71
‡ Schmidt, Chris	L.A.	1	10	0	2	2	5	....	....	....	....	....	....	2002-03	2002-03
• Schmidt, Clarence	Bos.	1	7	1	0	1	2	....	....	....	....	....	....	1943-44	1943-44
Schmidt, Jackie	Bos.	1	45	6	7	13	6	5	0	0	0	0	....	1942-43	1942-43
Schmidt, Milt	Bos.	16	776	229	346	575	466	86	24	25	49	60	2	1936-37	1954-55
Schmidt, Norm	Pit.	4	125	23	33	56	73	....	....	....	....	....	....	1983-84	1987-88
Schmidt, Otto	Bos.	1	2	0	0	0	0	....	....	....	....	....	....	1943-44	1943-44
‡ Schnabel, Robert	Nsh.	3	22	0	3	3	34	....	....	....	....	....	....	2001-02	2003-04
• Schnarr, Werner	Bos.	2	26	0	0	0	0	....	....	....	....	....	....	1924-25	1925-26
Schneider, Andy	Ott.	1	10	0	0	0	15	....	....	....	....	....	....	1993-94	1993-94
Schock, Danny	Bos., Phi.	2	20	1	2	3	0	1	0	0	0	0	1	1969-70	1970-71
Schock, Ron	Bos., St.L., Pit., Buf.	15	909	166	351	517	260	55	4	16	20	29	....	1963-64	1977-78
Schoenfeld, Jim	Buf., Det., Bos.	13	719	51	204	255	1132	75	3	13	16	151	....	1972-73	1984-85
Schofield, Dwight	Det., Mtl., St.L., Wsh., Pit., Wpg.	7	211	8	22	30	631	9	0	0	0	55	....	1976-77	1987-88
Schreiber, Wally	Min.	2	41	8	10	18	12	....	....	....	....	....	....	1987-88	1988-89
• Schriner, Sweeney	NYA, Tor.	11	484	201	204	405	148	59	18	11	29	54	2	1934-35	1945-46
Schulte, Paxton	Que., Cgy.	2	2	0	0	0	4	....	....	....	....	....	....	1993-94	1996-97
Schultz, Dave	Phi., L.A., Pit., Buf.	9	535	79	121	200	2294	73	8	12	20	412	2	1971-72	1979-80
Schultz, Ray	NYI	6	45	0	4	4	155	2	0	0	0	2	....	1997-98	2002-03
Schurman, Maynard	Hfd.	1	7	0	0	0	0	....	....	....	....	....	....	1979-80	1979-80
Schutt, Rod	Mtl., Pit., Tor.	8	286	77	92	169	177	22	8	6	14	26	....	1977-78	1985-86
Scissons, Scott	NYI	3	2	0	0	0	0	1	0	0	0	0	....	1990-91	1993-94
Sclisizzi, Enio	Det., Chi.	6	81	12	11	23	26	13	0	0	0	6	....	1946-47	1952-53
• Scott, Ganton	Tor., Ham., Mtl.M.	3	57	1	1	2	0	....	....	....	....	....	....	1922-23	1924-25
• Scott, Laurie	NYA, NYR	2	62	6	3	9	28	....	....	....	....	....	....	1926-27	1927-28
Scott, Richard	NYR	2	10	0	0	0	28	....	....	....	....	....	....	2001-02	2003-04
‡ Scoville, Darrel	Cgy., CBJ	3	16	0	1	1	12	....	....	....	....	....	....	1999-00	2003-04
Scremin, Claudio	S.J.	2	17	0	1	1	29	....	....	....	....	....	....	1991-92	1992-93
Scruton, Howard	L.A.	1	4	0	4	4	9	....	....	....	....	....	....	1982-83	1982-83
Seabrooke, Glen	Phi.	3	19	1	6	7	4	....	....	....	....	....	....	1986-87	1988-89
Secord, Al	Bos., Chi., Tor., Phi.	12	766	273	222	495	2093	102	21	34	55	382	....	1978-79	1989-90
Sedlbauer, Ron	Van., Chi., Tor.	7	430	143	86	229	210	19	1	3	4	27	....	1974-75	1980-81
Seftel, Steve	Wsh.	1	4	0	0	0	2	....	....	....	....	....	....	1990-91	1990-91
Seguin, Dan	Min., Van.	2	37	2	6	8	50	....	....	....	....	....	....	1970-71	1973-74
Seguin, Steve	L.A.	1	5	0	0	0	9	....	....	....	....	....	....	1984-85	1984-85
• Seibert, Earl	NYR, Chi., Det.	15	645	89	187	276	746	66	11	8	19	76	2	1931-32	1945-46
Seiling, Ric	Buf., Det.	10	738	179	208	387	573	62	14	14	28	36	....	1977-78	1986-87
Seiling, Rod	Tor., NYR, Wsh., St.L., Atl.	17	979	62	269	331	601	77	4	8	12	55	....	1962-63	1978-79
Sejba, Jiri	Buf.	1	11	0	2	2	8	....	....	....	....	....	....	1990-91	1990-91
‡ Sekeras, Lubomir	Min., Dal.	4	213	18	53	71	122	15	1	1	2	6	....	2000-01	2003-04
Selby, Brit	Tor., Phi., St.L.	8	350	55	62	117	163	16	1	1	2	8	....	1964-65	1971-72
Self, Steve	Wsh.	1	3	0	0	0	0	....	....	....	....	....	....	1976-77	1976-77
Selivanov, Alex	T.B., Edm., CBJ	7	459	121	114	235	379	13	2	3	5	16	....	1994-95	2000-01
Sellars, Luke	Atl.	1	1	0	0	0	2	....	....	....	....	....	....	2001-02	2001-02
Selmser, Sean	CBJ	1	1	0	0	0	5	....	....	....	....	....	....	2000-01	2000-01
Selwood, Brad	Tor., L.A.	3	163	7	40	47	153	6	0	0	0	4	....	1970-71	1979-80
Semak, Alexander	N.J., T.B., NYI, Van.	6	289	83	91	174	187	8	1	1	2	0	....	1991-92	1996-97
Semchuk, Brandy	L.A.	1	1	0	0	0	2	....	....	....	....	....	....	1992-93	1992-93
Semenko, Dave	Edm., Hfd., Tor.	9	575	65	88	153	1175	73	6	6	12	208	2	1979-80	1987-88
Semenov, Anatoli	Edm., T.B., Van., Ana., Phi., Buf.	8	362	68	126	194	122	49	9	13	22	12	....	1989-90	1996-97
• Senick, George	NYR	1	13	2	3	5	8	....	....	....	....	....	....	1952-53	1952-53
Seppa, Jyrki	Wpg.	1	13	0	2	2	6	....	....	....	....	....	....	1983-84	1983-84
Serafini, Ron	Cal.	1	2	0	0	0	2	....	....	....	....	....	....	1973-74	1973-74
Serowik, Jeff	Tor., Bos., Pit.	4	28	0	6	6	16	....	....	....	....	....	....	1990-91	1999-00
Servinis, George	Min.	1	5	0	0	0	0	....	....	....	....	....	....	1987-88	1987-88
Sevcik, Jaroslav	Que.	1	13	0	2	2	2	....	....	....	....	....	....	1989-90	1989-90
Severyn, Brent	Que., Fla., NYI, Col., Ana., Dal.	7	328	10	30	40	825	8	0	0	0	12	....	1989-90	1998-99
Sevigny, Pierre	Mtl., NYR	4	78	4	5	9	64	3	0	1	1	0	....	1993-94	1997-98
Shack, Eddie	NYR, Tor., Bos., L.A., Buf., Pit.	17	1047	239	226	465	1437	74	6	7	13	151	4	1958-59	1974-75
• Shack, Joe	NYR	2	70	9	27	36	20	....	....	....	....	....	....	1942-43	1944-45
Shafranov, Konstantin	St.L.	1	5	2	1	3	0	....	....	....	....	....	....	1996-97	1996-97
Shakes, Paul	Cal.	1	21	0	4	4	12	....	....	....	....	....	....	1973-74	1973-74
Shaldybin, Yevgeny	Bos.	1	3	1	0	1	0	....	....	....	....	....	....	1996-97	1996-97
Shanahan, Sean	Mtl., Col., Bos.	3	40	1	3	4	47	....	....	....	....	....	....	1975-76	1977-78
Shand, Dave	Atl., Tor., Wsh.	8	421	19	84	103	544	26	1	2	3	83	....	1976-77	1984-85
Shank, Daniel	Det., Hfd.	3	77	13	14	27	175	5	0	0	0	22	....	1989-90	1991-92
Shannon, Chuck	NYA	1	4	0	0	0	2	....	....	....	....	....	....	1939-40	1939-40
Shannon, Darrin	Buf., Wpg., Phx.	10	506	87	163	250	344	45	7	10	17	38	....	1988-89	1997-98
Shannon, Darryl	Tor., Wpg., Buf., Atl., Cgy., Mtl	13	544	28	111	139	523	29	4	7	11	16	....	1988-89	2000-01
• Shannon, Gerry	Ott., St.L., Bos., Mtl.M.	5	180	23	29	52	80	9	0	1	1	2	....	1933-34	1937-38
‡ Shantz, Jeff	Chi., Cgy., Col.	10	642	72	139	211	341	44	5	8	13	24	....	1993-94	2002-03
Sharifijanov, Vadim	N.J., Van.	3	92	16	21	37	50	4	0	0	0	0	....	1996-97	1999-00
Sharples, Jeff	Det.	3	105	14	35	49	70	7	0	3	3	6	....	1986-87	1988-89
Sharpley, Glen	Min., Chi.	6	389	117	161	278	199	27	7	11	18	24	....	1976-77	1981-82
Shaunessy, Scott	Que.	2	7	0	0	0	23	....	....	....	....	....	....	1986-87	1988-89
Shaw, Brad	Hfd., Ott., Wsh., St.L.	11	377	22	137	159	208	23	4	8	12	6	....	1985-86	1998-99
Shaw, David	Que., NYR, Edm., Min., Bos., T.B.	16	769	41	153	194	906	45	3	9	12	81	....	1982-83	1997-98
• Shay, Norm	Bos., Tor.	2	53	5	3	8	34	....	....	....	....	....	....	1924-25	1925-26
• Shea, Pat	Chi.	1	10	1	0	1	0	....	....	....	....	....	....	1931-32	1931-32
‡ Shearer, Rob	Col.	1	2	0	0	0	0	....	....	....	....	....	....	2000-01	2000-01
Shedden, Doug	Pit., Det., Que., Tor.	8	416	139	186	325	176	....	....	....	....	....	....	1981-82	1990-91
Sheehan, Bobby	Mtl., Cal., Chi., Det., NYR, Col., L.A.	9	310	48	63	111	40	25	4	3	7	8	1	1969-70	1981-82
Sheehy, Neil	Cgy., Hfd., Wsh.	9	379	18	47	65	1311	54	0	3	3	241	....	1983-84	1991-92
Sheehy, Tim	Det., Hfd.	2	27	2	1	3	0	....	....	....	....	....	....	1977-78	1979-80
Shelton, Doug	Chi.	1	5	0	1	1	2	....	....	....	....	....	....	1967-68	1967-68
• Sheppard, Frank	Det.	1	8	1	1	2	0	....	....	....	....	....	....	1927-28	1927-28
Sheppard, Gregg	Bos., Pit.	10	657	205	293	498	243	82	32	40	72	31	....	1972-73	1981-82
• Sheppard, Johnny	Det., NYA, Bos., Chi.	8	308	68	58	126	224	10	0	0	0	0	1	1926-27	1933-34
Sheppard, Ray	Buf., NYR, Det., S.J., Fla., Car.	13	817	357	300	657	212	81	30	20	50	21	....	1987-88	1999-00
• Sherf, John	Det.	5	19	0	0	0	8	8	0	1	1	2	1	1935-36	1943-44
• Shero, Fred	NYR	3	145	6	14	20	137	13	0	2	2	8	....	1947-48	1949-50
• Sherritt, Gordon	Det.	1	8	0	0	0	12	....	....	....	....	....	....	1943-44	1943-44
Sherven, Gord	Edm., Min., Hfd.	5	97	13	22	35	33	3	0	0	0	0	....	1983-84	1987-88
Shevalier, Jeff	L.A., T.B.	3	32	5	9	14	8	....	....	....	....	....	....	1994-95	1999-00
• Shewchuk, Jack	Bos.	6	187	9	19	28	160	20	0	1	1	19	1	1938-39	1944-45
Shibicky, Alex	NYR	8	324	110	91	201	161	39	12	12	24	12	1	1935-36	1945-46
• Shields, Al	Ott., Phi., NYA, Mtl.M., Bos.	11	459	42	46	88	637	17	0	1	1	14	1	1927-28	1937-38
Shill, Bill	Bos.	3	79	21	13	34	18	7	1	2	3	2	....	1942-43	1946-47
• Shill, Jack	Tor., Bos., NYA, Chi.	6	160	15	20	35	70	25	1	6	7	23	1	1933-34	1938-39
Shinske, Rick	Cle., St.L.	3	63	5	16	21	10	....	....	....	....	....	....	1976-77	1978-79
Shires, Jim	Det., St.L., Pit.	3	56	3	6	9	32	....	....	....	....	....	....	1970-71	1972-73
• Shmyr, Paul	Chi., Cal., Min., Hfd.	7	343	13	72	85	528	34	3	3	6	44	....	1968-69	1981-82
Shoebottom, Bruce	Bos.	4	35	1	4	5	53	14	1	2	3	77	....	1987-88	1990-91
• Shore, Eddie	Bos., NYA	14	550	105	179	284	1047	55	6	13	19	181	2	1926-27	1939-40
• Shore, Hamby	Ott.	1	18	3	8	11	51	....	....	....	....	....	....	1917-18	1917-18
Short, Steve	L.A., Det.	2	6	0	0	0	2	....	....	....	....	....	....	1977-78	1978-79
Shuchuk, Gary	Det., L.A.	5	142	13	26	39	70	20	2	2	4	12	....	1990-91	1995-96
Shudra, Ron	Edm.	1	10	0	5	5	6	....	....	....	....	....	....	1987-88	1987-88
Shutt, Steve	Mtl., L.A.	13	930	424	393	817	410	99	50	48	98	65	5	1972-73	1984-85
• Siebert, Babe	Mtl.M., NYR, Bos., Mtl.	14	592	140	156	296	982	49	7	5	12	62	2	1925-26	1938-39
‡ Siklenka, Mike	Phi., NYR	2	2	0	0	0	0	....	....	....	....	....	....	2002-03	2003-04

			Regular Schedule					Playoffs							
Name	NHL Teams	NHL Seasons	GP	G	A	TP	PIM	GP	G	A	TP	PIM	NHL Cup Wins	First NHL Season	Last NHL Season
Silk, Dave	NYR, Bos., Det., Wpg.	7	249	54	59	113	271	13	2	4	6	13	....	1979-80	1985-86
Siltala, Mike	Wsh., NYR	3	7	1	0	1	2	....	....	....	....	....	....	1981-82	1987-88
Siltanen, Risto	Edm., Hfd., Que.	8	562	90	265	355	266	32	6	12	18	30	....	1979-80	1986-87
Sim, Trevor	Edm.	1	3	0	1	1	2	....	....	....	....	....	....	1989-90	1989-90
Simard, Martin	Cgy., T.B.	3	44	1	5	6	183	....	....	....	....	....	....	1990-91	1992-93
‡ Simicek, Roman	Pit., Min.	2	63	7	10	17	59	....	....	....	....	....	....	2000-01	2001-02
Simmer, Charlie	Cal., Cle., L.A., Bos., Pit.	14	712	342	369	711	544	24	9	9	18	32	....	1974-75	1987-88
Simmons, Al	Cal., Bos.	3	11	0	1	1	21	1	0	0	0	0	....	1971-72	1975-76
• Simon, Cully	Det., Chi.	3	130	4	11	15	121	14	1	0	1	6	1	1942-43	1944-45
Simon, Jason	NYI, Phx.	2	5	0	0	0	34	....	....	....	....	....	....	1993-94	1996-97
Simon, Thain	Det.	1	3	0	0	0	0	....	....	....	....	....	....	1946-47	1946-47
Simon, Todd	Buf.	1	15	0	1	1	0	5	1	0	1	0	....	1993-94	1993-94
Simonetti, Frank	Bos.	4	115	5	8	13	76	12	0	1	1	8	....	1984-85	1987-88
Simpson, Bobby	Atl., St.L., Pit.	5	175	35	29	64	98	6	0	1	1	2	....	1976-77	1982-83
• Simpson, Cliff	Det.	2	6	0	1	1	0	2	0	0	0	2	....	1946-47	1947-48
Simpson, Craig	Pit., Edm., Buf.	10	634	247	250	497	659	67	36	32	68	56	2	1985-86	1994-95
• Simpson, Joe	NYA	6	228	21	19	40	156	2	0	0	0	0	....	1925-26	1930-31
‡ Simpson, Reid	Phi., Min., N.J., Chi., T.B., St.L., Mtl., Nsh., Pit.	12	301	18	18	36	838	10	0	0	0	31	....	1991-92	2003-04
Sims, Al	Bos., Hfd., L.A.	10	475	49	116	165	286	41	0	2	2	14	....	1973-74	1982-83
Sinclair, Reg	NYR, Det.	3	208	49	43	92	139	3	1	0	1	0	....	1950-51	1952-53
• Singbush, Alex	Mtl.	1	32	0	5	5	15	3	0	0	0	4	....	1940-41	1940-41
Sinisalo, Ilkka	Phi., Min., L.A.	11	582	204	222	426	208	68	21	11	32	6	....	1981-82	1991-92
Siren, Ville	Pit., Min.	5	290	14	68	82	276	7	0	0	0	6	....	1985-86	1989-90
Sirois, Bob	Phi., Wsh.	6	286	92	120	212	42	....	....	....	....	....	....	1974-75	1979-80
Sittler, Darryl	Tor., Phi., Det.	15	1096	484	637	1121	948	76	29	45	74	137	....	1970-71	1984-85
• Sjoberg, Lars-Erik	Wpg.	1	79	7	27	34	48	....	....	....	....	....	....	1979-80	1979-80
‡ Sjodin, Tommy	Min., Dal., Que.	2	106	8	40	48	52	....	....	....	....	....	....	1992-93	1993-94
• Skaare, Bjorn	Det.	1	1	0	0	0	0	....	....	....	....	....	....	1978-79	1978-79
Skalde, Jarrod	N.J., Ana., Cgy., S.J., Chi., Dal., Atl., Phi.	9	115	13	21	34	62	....	....	....	....	....	....	1990-91	2001-02
Skarda, Randy	St.L.	2	26	0	5	5	11	....	....	....	....	....	....	1989-90	1991-92
• Skilton, Raymie	Mtl.W.	1	1	0	0	0	0	....	....	....	....	....	....	1917-18	1917-18
• Skinner, Alf	Tor., Bos., Mtl.M., Pit.	4	71	26	10	36	87	2	0	1	1	9	1	1917-18	1925-26
Skinner, Larry	Col.	4	47	10	12	22	8	2	0	0	0	0	....	1976-77	1979-80
‡ Skopintsev, Andrei	T.B., Atl.	3	40	2	4	6	32	....	....	....	....	....	....	1998-99	2000-01
Skov, Glen	Det., Chi., Mtl.	12	650	106	136	242	413	53	7	7	14	48	3	1949-50	1960-61
‡ Skrbek, Pavel	Pit., Nsh.	3	12	0	0	0	8	....	....	....	....	....	....	1998-99	2001-02
Skriko, Petri	Van., Bos., Wpg., S.J.	9	541	183	222	405	246	28	5	9	14	4	....	1984-85	1992-93
Skrlac, Rob	N.J.	1	8	1	0	1	22	....	....	....	....	....	....	2003-04	2003-04
Skrudland, Brian	Mtl., Cgy., Fla., NYR, Dal.	15	881	124	219	343	1107	164	15	46	61	323	2	1985-86	1999-00
• Sleaver, John	Chi.	2	13	1	0	1	6	....	....	....	....	....	....	1953-54	1956-57
Sleigher, Louis	Que., Bos.	6	194	46	53	99	146	17	1	1	2	64	....	1979-80	1985-86
‡ Sloan, Blake	Dal., CBJ, Cgy.	6	290	11	32	43	162	35	0	2	2	20	1	1998-99	2003-04
Sloan, Tod	Tor., Chi.	13	745	220	262	482	831	47	9	12	21	47	2	1947-48	1960-61
• Slobodian, Peter	NYA	1	41	3	2	5	54	....	....	....	....	....	....	1940-41	1940-41
• Slowinski, Ed	NYR	6	291	58	74	132	63	16	2	6	8	6	....	1947-48	1952-53
Sly, Darryl	Tor., Min., Van.	4	79	1	2	3	20	....	....	....	....	....	....	1965-66	1970-71
Smail, Doug	Wpg., Min., Que., Ott.	13	845	210	249	459	602	42	9	2	11	49	....	1980-81	1992-93
Smart, Alex	Mtl.	1	8	5	2	7	0	....	....	....	....	....	....	1942-43	1942-43
Smedsmo, Dale	Tor.	1	4	0	0	0	0	....	....	....	....	....	....	1972-73	1972-73
Smehlik, Richard	Buf., Atl., N.J.	10	644	49	146	195	415	88	1	14	15	40	1	1992-93	2002-03
• Smillie, Don	Bos.	1	12	2	2	4	4	....	....	....	....	....	....	1933-34	1933-34
• Smith, Alex	Ott., Det., Bos., NYA	11	443	41	50	91	645	19	0	2	2	26	1	1924-25	1934-35
• Smith, Art	Tor., Ott.	4	144	15	10	25	249	4	1	1	2	8	....	1927-28	1930-31
Smith, Barry	Bos., Col.	3	114	7	7	14	10	....	....	....	....	....	....	1975-76	1980-81
Smith, Bobby	Min., Mtl.	15	1077	357	679	1036	917	184	64	96	160	245	1	1978-79	1992-93
Smith, Brad	Van., Atl., Cgy., Det., Tor.	9	222	28	34	62	591	20	3	3	6	49	....	1978-79	1986-87
Smith, Brian	Det.	3	61	2	8	10	12	5	0	0	0	0	....	1957-58	1960-61
• Smith, Brian	L.A., Min.	2	67	10	10	20	33	7	0	0	0	0	....	1967-68	1968-69
• Smith, Carl	Det.	1	7	1	1	2	2	....	....	....	....	....	....	1943-44	1943-44
Smith, Clint	NYR, Chi.	11	483	161	236	397	24	42	10	14	24	2	1	1936-37	1946-47
Smith, D.J.	Tor., Col.	3	45	1	1	2	67	....	....	....	....	....	....	1996-97	2002-03
Smith, Dallas	Bos., NYR	16	890	55	252	307	959	86	3	29	32	128	2	1959-60	1977-78
Smith, Dennis	Wsh., L.A.	2	8	0	0	0	4	....	....	....	....	....	....	1989-90	1990-91
Smith, Derek	Buf., Det.	8	335	78	116	194	60	30	9	14	23	13	....	1975-76	1982-83
Smith, Derrick	Phi., Min., Dal.	10	537	82	92	174	373	82	14	11	25	79	....	1984-85	1993-94
• Smith, Des	Mtl.M., Mtl., Chi., Bos.	5	196	22	25	47	236	25	1	4	5	18	1	1937-38	1941-42
• Smith, Don	Mtl.	1	12	1	0	1	6	....	....	....	....	....	....	1919-20	1919-20
• Smith, Don	NYR	1	11	1	1	2	0	1	0	0	0	0	....	1949-50	1949-50
Smith, Doug	L.A., Buf., Edm., Van., Pit.	9	535	115	138	253	624	18	4	2	6	21	....	1981-82	1989-90
Smith, Floyd	Bos., NYR, Det., Tor., Buf.	13	616	129	178	307	207	48	12	11	23	16	....	1954-55	1971-72
Smith, Geoff	Edm., Fla., NYR	10	462	18	73	91	282	13	0	1	1	8	1	1989-90	1998-99
Smith, Glen	Chi.	1	2	0	0	0	0	....	....	....	....	....	....	1950-51	1950-51
• Smith, Glenn	Tor.	1	9	0	0	0	0	....	....	....	....	....	....	1921-22	1921-22
Smith, Gord	Wsh., Wpg.	6	299	9	30	39	284	....	....	....	....	....	....	1974-75	1979-80
Smith, Greg	Cal., Cle., Min., Det., Wsh.	13	829	56	232	288	1110	63	4	7	11	106	....	1975-76	1987-88
• Smith, Hooley	Ott., Mtl.M., Bos., NYA	17	715	200	225	425	1013	54	11	8	19	109	2	1924-25	1940-41
• Smith, Ken	Bos.	7	331	78	93	171	49	30	8	13	21	6	....	1944-45	1950-51
• Smith, Nakina	Det.	1	10	1	2	3	0	....	....	....	....	....	....	1943-44	1943-44
Smith, Nick	Fla.	1	15	0	0	0	0	....	....	....	....	....	....	2001-02	2001-02
Smith, Randy	Min.	2	3	0	0	0	0	....	....	....	....	....	....	1985-86	1986-87
Smith, Rick	Bos., Cal., St.L., Det., Wsh.	11	687	52	167	219	560	78	3	23	26	73	1	1968-69	1980-81
• Smith, Rodger	Pit., Phi.	6	210	20	4	24	172	4	3	0	3	0	....	1925-26	1930-31
Smith, Ron	NYI	1	11	1	1	2	14	....	....	....	....	....	....	1972-73	1972-73
• Smith, Sid	Tor.	12	601	186	183	369	94	44	17	10	27	2	3	1946-47	1957-58
Smith, Stan	NYR	2	9	2	1	3	0	1	0	0	0	0	1	1939-40	1940-41
Smith, Steve	Phi., Buf.	6	18	0	1	1	15	....	....	....	....	....	....	1981-82	1988-89
Smith, Steve	Edm., Chi., Cgy.	16	804	72	303	375	2139	134	11	41	52	288	3	1984-85	2000-01
Smith, Stu	Mtl.	2	4	2	2	4	2	1	0	0	0	0	....	1940-41	1941-42
Smith, Stu	Hfd.	4	77	2	10	12	95	....	....	....	....	....	....	1979-80	1982-83
• Smith, Tommy	Que.	1	10	0	1	1	11	....	....	....	....	....	....	1919-20	1919-20
Smith, Vern	NYI	1	1	0	0	0	0	....	....	....	....	....	....	1984-85	1984-85
Smith, Wayne	Chi.	1	2	1	1	2	2	1	0	0	0	0	....	1966-67	1966-67
‡ Smrek, Peter	St.L., NYR	2	28	2	4	6	18	....	....	....	....	....	....	2000-01	2001-02
Smrke, John	St.L., Que.	3	103	11	17	28	33	....	....	....	....	....	....	1977-78	1979-80
• Smrke, Stan	Mtl.	2	9	0	3	3	0	....	....	....	....	....	....	1956-57	1957-58
Smyl, Stan	Van.	13	896	262	411	673	1556	41	16	17	33	64	....	1978-79	1990-91
• Smylie, Rod	Tor., Ott.	6	74	4	2	6	12	4	0	0	0	2	1	1920-21	1925-26
‡ Smyth, Brad	Fla., L.A., NYR, Nsh., Ott.	6	88	15	13	28	109	....	....	....	....	....	....	1995-96	2002-03
Smyth, Greg	Phi., Que., Cgy., Fla., Tor., Chi.	10	229	4	16	20	783	12	0	0	0	40	....	1986-87	1996-97
Smyth, Kevin	Hfd.	3	58	6	8	14	31	....	....	....	....	....	....	1993-94	1995-96
Snell, Chris	Tor., L.A.	2	34	2	7	9	24	....	....	....	....	....	....	1993-94	1994-95
Snell, Ron	Pit.	2	7	3	2	5	6	....	....	....	....	....	....	1968-69	1969-70
Snell, Ted	Pit., K.C., Det.	2	104	7	18	25	22	....	....	....	....	....	....	1973-74	1974-75
Snepsts, Harold	Van., Min., Det., St.L.	17	1033	38	195	233	2009	93	1	14	15	231	....	1974-75	1990-91
Snow, Sandy	Det.	1	3	0	0	0	2	....	....	....	....	....	....	1968-69	1968-69
Snuggerud, Dave	Buf., S.J., Phi.	4	265	30	54	84	127	12	1	3	4	6	....	1989-90	1992-93
• Snyder, Dan	Atl.	3	49	11	5	16	64	....	....	....	....	....	....	2000-01	2002-03
Sobchuk, Dennis	Det., Que.	2	35	5	6	11	2	....	....	....	....	....	....	1979-80	1982-83
Sobchuk, Gene	Van.	1	1	0	0	0	0	....	....	....	....	....	....	1973-74	1973-74
Solheim, Ken	Chi., Min., Det., Edm.	5	135	19	20	39	34	3	1	1	2	2	....	1980-81	1985-86
Solinger, Bob	Tor., Det.	5	99	10	11	21	19	....	....	....	....	....	....	1951-52	1959-60
• Somers, Art	Chi., NYR	6	222	33	56	89	189	30	1	5	6	20	1	1929-30	1934-35
‡ Somik, Radovan	Phi.	2	113	12	20	32	27	15	2	2	4	10	....	2002-03	2003-04
Sommer, Roy	Edm.	1	3	1	0	1	7	....	....	....	....	....	....	1980-81	1980-81
Songin, Tom	Bos.	3	43	5	5	10	22	....	....	....	....	....	....	1978-79	1980-81
Sonmor, Glen	NYR	2	28	2	0	2	21	....	....	....	....	....	....	1953-54	1954-55
Sorochan, Lee	Cgy.	2	3	0	0	0	0	....	....	....	....	....	....	1998-99	1999-00
• Sorrell, John	Det., NYA	11	490	127	119	246	100	42	12	15	27	10	2	1930-31	1940-41
Spanhel, Martin	CBJ	2	10	2	0	2	4	....	....	....	....	....	....	2000-01	2001-02
• Sparrow, Emory	Bos.	1	8	0	0	0	4	....	....	....	....	....	....	1924-25	1924-25
Speck, Fred	Det., Van.	3	28	1	2	3	2	....	....	....	....	....	....	1968-69	1971-72
• Speer, Bill	Pit., Bos.	4	130	5	20	25	79	8	1	0	1	4	1	1967-68	1970-71
Speers, Ted	Det.	1	4	1	1	2	0	....	....	....	....	....	....	1985-86	1985-86

Gordon Sherritt

Gord Sherven

Al Shields

Dave Silk

Thain Simon

Bob Sirois

Brad Smith

Derek Smith

Name	NHL Teams	NHL Seasons	Regular Schedule GP	G	A	TP	PIM	Playoffs GP	G	A	TP	PIM	NHL Cup Wins	First NHL Season	Last NHL Season
• Spence, Gordon	Tor.	1	3	0	0	0	0	....	....	....	....	....	....	1925-26	1925-26
• Spencer, Brian	Tor., NYI, Buf., Pit.	10	553	80	143	223	634	37	1	5	6	29	....	1969-70	1978-79
• Spencer, Irv	NYR, Bos., Det.	8	230	12	38	50	127	16	0	0	0	8	....	1959-60	1967-68
• Speyer, Chris	Tor., NYA	3	14	0	0	0	0	....	....	....	....	....	....	1923-24	1933-34
Spring, Corey	T.B.	2	16	1	1	2	12	....	....	....	....	....	....	1997-98	1998-99
Spring, Don	Wpg.	4	259	1	54	55	80	6	0	0	0	10	....	1980-81	1983-84
Spring, Frank	Bos., St.L., Cal., Cle.	5	61	14	20	34	12	....	....	....	....	....	....	1969-70	1976-77
• Spring, Jesse	Ham., Pit., Tor., NYA	6	133	11	4	15	74	2	0	2	2	2	....	1923-24	1929-30
Spruce, Andy	Van., Col.	3	172	31	42	73	111	2	0	2	2	0	....	1976-77	1978-79
Srsen, Tomas	Edm.	1	2	0	0	0	0	....	....	....	....	....	....	1990-91	1990-91
St. Amour, Martin	Ott.	1	1	0	0	0	2	....	....	....	....	....	....	1992-93	1992-93
St. Laurent, Andre	NYI, Det., L.A., Pit.	11	644	129	187	316	749	59	8	12	20	48	....	1973-74	1983-84
St. Laurent, Dollard	Mtl., Chi.	12	652	29	133	162	496	92	2	22	24	87	5	1950-51	1961-62
St. Marseille, Frank	St.L., L.A.	10	707	140	285	425	242	88	20	25	45	18	....	1967-68	1976-77
St. Sauveur, Claude	Atl.	1	79	24	24	48	23	2	0	0	0	0	....	1975-76	1975-76
Stackhouse, Ron	Cal., Det., Pit.	12	889	87	372	459	824	32	5	8	13	38	....	1970-71	1981-82
• Stackhouse, Ted	Tor.	1	13	0	0	0	2	1	0	0	0	0	1	1921-22	1921-22
• Stahan, Butch	Mtl.	1	....	....	....	....	....	3	0	1	1	2	....	1944-45	1944-45
Stajduhar, Nick	Edm.	1	2	0	0	0	4	....	....	....	....	....	....	1995-96	1995-96
Staley, Al	NYR	1	1	0	1	1	0	....	....	....	....	....	....	1948-49	1948-49
Stamler, Lorne	L.A., Tor., Wpg.	4	116	14	11	25	16	....	....	....	....	....	....	1976-77	1979-80
Standing, George	Min.	1	2	0	0	0	0	....	....	....	....	....	....	1967-68	1967-68
Stanfield, Fred	Chi., Bos., Min., Buf.	14	914	211	405	616	134	106	21	35	56	10	2	1964-65	1977-78
Stanfield, Jack	Chi.	1	....	....	....	....	....	1	0	0	0	0	....	1965-66	1965-66
Stanfield, Jim	L.A.	3	7	0	1	1	0	....	....	....	....	....	....	1969-70	1971-72
Stankiewicz, Ed	Det.	2	6	0	0	0	2	....	....	....	....	....	....	1953-54	1955-56
Stankiewicz, Myron	St.L., Phi.	1	35	0	7	7	36	1	0	0	0	0	....	1968-69	1968-69
Stanley, Allan	NYR, Chi., Bos., Tor., Phi.	21	1244	100	333	433	792	109	7	36	43	80	4	1948-49	1968-69
• Stanley, Barney	Chi.	1	1	0	0	0	0	....	....	....	....	....	....	1927-28	1927-28
Stanley, Daryl	Phi., Van.	6	189	8	17	25	408	17	0	0	0	30	....	1983-84	1989-90
Stanowski, Wally	Tor., NYR	10	428	23	88	111	160	60	3	14	17	13	4	1939-40	1950-51
Stanton, Paul	Pit., Bos., NYI	5	295	14	49	63	262	44	2	10	12	66	2	1990-91	1994-95
Stapleton, Brian	Wsh.	1	1	0	0	0	0	....	....	....	....	....	....	1975-76	1975-76
Stapleton, Mike	Chi., Pit., Edm., Wpg., Phx., Atl., NYI, Van.	14	697	71	111	182	342	34	1	0	1	39	....	1986-87	2000-01
Stapleton, Pat	Bos., Chi.	10	635	43	294	337	353	65	10	39	49	38	....	1961-62	1972-73
Starikov, Sergei	N.J.	1	16	0	1	1	8	....	....	....	....	....	....	1989-90	1989-90
• Starr, Harold	Ott., Mtl.M., Mtl., NYR	7	205	6	5	11	186	15	1	0	1	4	....	1929-30	1935-36
• Starr, Wilf	NYA, Det.	4	87	8	6	14	25	7	0	2	2	2	....	1932-33	1935-36
Stasiuk, Vic	Chi., Det., Bos.	14	745	183	254	437	669	69	16	18	34	40	3	1949-50	1962-63
Stastny, Anton	Que.	9	650	252	384	636	150	66	20	32	52	31	....	1980-81	1988-89
Stastny, Marian	Que., Tor.	5	322	121	173	294	110	32	5	17	22	7	....	1981-82	1985-86
Stastny, Peter	Que., N.J., St.L.	15	977	450	789	1239	824	93	33	72	105	123	....	1980-81	1994-95
Staszak, Ray	Det.	1	4	0	1	1	7	....	....	....	....	....	....	1985-86	1985-86
• Steele, Frank	Det.	1	1	0	0	0	0	....	....	....	....	....	....	1930-31	1930-31
Steen, Anders	Wpg.	1	42	5	11	16	22	....	....	....	....	....	....	1980-81	1980-81
Steen, Thomas	Wpg.	14	950	264	553	817	753	56	12	32	44	62	....	1981-82	1994-95
Stefaniw, Morris	Atl.	1	13	1	1	2	2	....	....	....	....	....	....	1972-73	1972-73
Stefanski, Bud	NYR	1	1	0	0	0	0	....	....	....	....	....	....	1977-78	1977-78
Stemkowski, Pete	Tor., Det., NYR, L.A.	15	967	206	349	555	866	83	25	29	54	136	1	1963-64	1977-78
Stenlund, Vern	Cle.	1	4	0	0	0	0	....	....	....	....	....	....	1976-77	1976-77
‡ Stephens, Charlie	Col.	2	8	0	2	2	4	....	....	....	....	....	....	2002-03	2003-04
Stephenson, Bob	Hfd., Tor.	1	18	2	3	5	4	....	....	....	....	....	....	1979-80	1979-80
Stern, Ron	Van., Cgy., S.J.	12	638	75	86	161	2077	43	7	7	14	119	....	1987-88	1999-00
Sterner, Ulf	NYR	1	4	0	0	0	0	....	....	....	....	....	....	1964-65	1964-65
Stevens, John	Phi., Hfd.	5	53	0	10	10	48	....	....	....	....	....	....	1986-87	1993-94
Stevens, Kevin	Pit., Bos., L.A., NYR, Phi.	15	874	329	397	726	1470	103	46	60	106	170	2	1987-88	2001-02
Stevens, Mike	Van., Bos., NYI, Tor.	4	23	1	4	5	29	....	....	....	....	....	....	1984-85	1989-90
• Stevens, Phil	Mtl.W., Mtl., Bos.	3	25	1	0	1	3	....	....	....	....	....	....	1917-18	1925-26
Stevens, Scott	Wsh., St.L., N.J.	22	1635	196	712	908	2785	233	26	92	118	402	3	1982-83	2003-04
‡ Stevenson, Jeremy	Ana., Nsh., Min., Dal.	9	207	19	19	38	451	21	0	5	5	20	....	1995-96	2005-06
Stevenson, Shayne	Bos., T.B.	3	27	0	2	2	35	....	....	....	....	....	....	1990-91	1992-93
Stevenson, Turner	Mtl., N.J., Phi.	13	644	75	115	190	969	67	6	12	18	66	1	1992-93	2005-06
Stewart, Allan	N.J., Bos.	6	64	6	4	10	243	....	....	....	....	....	....	1985-86	1991-92
Stewart, Bill	Buf., St.L., Tor., Min.	8	261	7	64	71	424	13	1	3	4	11	....	1977-78	1985-86
Stewart, Blair	Det., Wsh., Que.	7	229	34	44	78	326	....	....	....	....	....	....	1973-74	1979-80
Stewart, Bob	Bos., Cal., Cle., St.L., Pit.	9	575	27	101	128	809	5	1	1	2	2	....	1971-72	1979-80
Stewart, Cam	Bos., Fla., Min.	6	202	16	23	39	120	13	1	3	4	9	....	1993-94	2000-01
Stewart, Gaye	Tor., Chi., Det., NYR, Mtl.	11	502	185	159	344	274	25	2	9	11	16	2	1941-42	1953-54
• Stewart, Jack	Det., Chi.	12	565	31	84	115	765	80	5	14	19	143	2	1938-39	1951-52
Stewart, John	Pit., Atl., Cal.	5	258	58	60	118	158	4	0	0	0	10	....	1970-71	1974-75
Stewart, John	Que.	1	2	0	0	0	0	....	....	....	....	....	....	1979-80	1979-80
Stewart, Ken	Chi.	1	6	1	1	2	2	....	....	....	....	....	....	1941-42	1941-42
• Stewart, Nels	Mtl.M., Bos., NYA	15	650	324	191	515	953	50	9	12	21	47	1	1925-26	1939-40
Stewart, Paul	Que.	1	21	2	0	2	74	....	....	....	....	....	....	1979-80	1979-80
Stewart, Ralph	Van., NYI	7	252	57	73	130	28	19	4	4	8	2	....	1970-71	1977-78
Stewart, Ron	Tor., Bos., St.L., NYR, Van., NYI	21	1353	276	253	529	560	119	14	21	35	60	3	1952-53	1972-73
Stewart, Ryan	Wpg.	1	3	1	0	1	0	....	....	....	....	....	....	1985-86	1985-86
Stienburg, Trevor	Que.	4	71	8	4	12	161	1	0	0	0	0	....	1985-86	1988-89
Stiles, Tony	Cgy.	1	30	2	7	9	20	....	....	....	....	....	....	1983-84	1983-84
Stock, P.J.	NYR, Mtl., Phi., Bos.	7	235	5	21	26	523	8	1	0	1	19	....	1997-98	2003-04
Stoddard, Jack	NYR	2	80	16	15	31	31	....	....	....	....	....	....	1951-52	1952-53
Stojanov, Alek	Van., Pit.	3	107	2	5	7	222	14	0	0	0	21	....	1994-95	1996-97
Stoltz, Roland	Wsh.	1	14	2	2	4	14	....	....	....	....	....	....	1981-82	1981-82
Stone, Steve	Van.	1	2	0	0	0	0	....	....	....	....	....	....	1973-74	1973-74
Storm, Jim	Hfd., Dal.	3	84	7	15	22	44	....	....	....	....	....	....	1993-94	1995-96
Stothers, Mike	Phi., Tor.	4	30	0	2	2	65	5	0	0	0	11	....	1984-85	1987-88
Stoughton, Blaine	Pit., Tor., Hfd., NYR	8	526	258	191	449	204	8	4	2	6	2	....	1973-74	1983-84
Stoyanovich, Steve	Hfd.	1	23	3	5	8	11	....	....	....	....	....	....	1983-84	1983-84
• Strain, Neil	NYR	1	52	11	13	24	12	....	....	....	....	....	....	1952-53	1952-53
Strate, Gord	Det.	3	61	0	0	0	34	....	....	....	....	....	....	1956-57	1958-59
Stratton, Art	NYR, Det., Chi., Pit., Phi.	4	95	18	33	51	24	5	0	0	0	0	....	1959-60	1967-68
‡ Strbak, Martin	L.A., Pit.	1	49	5	11	16	46	....	....	....	....	....	....	2003-04	2003-04
• Strobel, Art	NYR	1	7	0	0	0	0	....	....	....	....	....	....	1943-44	1943-44
Strong, Ken	Tor.	3	15	2	2	4	6	....	....	....	....	....	....	1982-83	1984-85
Stroshein, Garret	Wsh.	1	3	0	0	0	14	....	....	....	....	....	....	2003-04	2003-04
Struch, David	Cgy.	1	4	0	0	0	4	....	....	....	....	....	....	1993-94	1993-94
Strueby, Todd	Edm.	3	5	0	1	1	2	....	....	....	....	....	....	1981-82	1983-84
• Stuart, Billy	Tor., Bos.	7	195	30	20	50	151	12	1	1	2	6	1	1920-21	1926-27
Stumpf, Bob	St.L., Pit.	1	10	1	1	2	20	....	....	....	....	....	....	1974-75	1974-75
Sturgeon, Peter	Col.	2	6	0	1	1	2	....	....	....	....	....	....	1979-80	1980-81
‡ Stutzel, Mike	Phx.	1	9	0	0	0	0	....	....	....	....	....	....	2003-04	2003-04
Suikkanen, Kai	Buf.	2	2	0	0	0	0	....	....	....	....	....	....	1981-82	1982-83
Sulliman, Doug	NYR, Hfd., N.J., Phi.	11	631	160	168	328	175	16	1	3	4	2	....	1979-80	1989-90
• Sullivan, Barry	Det.	1	1	0	0	0	0	....	....	....	....	....	....	1947-48	1947-48
Sullivan, Bob	Hfd.	1	62	18	19	37	18	....	....	....	....	....	....	1982-83	1982-83
Sullivan, Brian	N.J.	1	2	0	1	1	0	....	....	....	....	....	....	1992-93	1992-93
Sullivan, Frank	Tor., Chi.	4	8	0	0	0	2	....	....	....	....	....	....	1949-50	1955-56
Sullivan, Mike	S.J., Cgy., Bos., Phx.	11	709	54	82	136	203	34	4	8	12	14	....	1991-92	2001-02
Sullivan, Peter	Wpg.	2	126	28	54	82	40	....	....	....	....	....	....	1979-80	1980-81
Sullivan, Red	Bos., Chi., NYR	11	557	107	239	346	441	18	1	2	3	6	....	1949-50	1960-61
Summanen, Raimo	Edm., Van.	5	151	36	40	76	35	10	2	5	7	0	....	1983-84	1987-88
• Summerhill, Bill	Mtl., Bro.	4	72	14	17	31	70	3	0	0	0	2	....	1937-38	1941-42
Sundblad, Niklas	Cgy.	1	2	0	0	0	0	....	....	....	....	....	....	1995-96	1995-96
‡ Sundin, Ronnie	NYR	1	1	0	0	0	0	....	....	....	....	....	....	1997-98	1997-98
Sundstrom, Patrik	Van., N.J.	10	679	219	369	588	349	37	9	17	26	25	....	1982-83	1991-92
Sundstrom, Peter	NYR, Wsh., N.J.	6	338	61	83	144	120	23	3	3	6	8	....	1983-84	1989-90
Suomi, Al	Chi.	1	5	0	0	0	0	....	....	....	....	....	....	1936-37	1936-37
‡ Surma, Damian	Car.	2	2	1	1	2	0	....	....	....	....	....	....	2002-03	2003-04
‡ Sushinsky, Maxim	Min.	1	30	7	4	11	29	....	....	....	....	....	....	2000-01	2000-01
Suter, Gary	Cgy., Chi., S.J.	17	1145	203	641	844	1349	108	17	56	73	120	1	1985-86	2001-02
Sutherland, Bill	Mtl., Phi., Tor., St.L., Det.	6	250	70	58	128	99	14	2	4	6	0	....	1962-63	1971-72
• Sutherland, Max	Bos.	1	2	0	0	0	0	....	....	....	....	....	....	1931-32	1931-32
Sutter, Brent	NYI, Chi.	18	1111	363	466	829	1054	144	30	44	74	164	2	1980-81	1997-98
Sutter, Brian	St.L.	12	779	303	333	636	1786	65	21	21	42	249	....	1976-77	1987-88

Name	NHL Teams	NHL Seasons	Regular Schedule GP	G	A	TP	PIM	Playoffs GP	G	A	TP	PIM	NHL Cup Wins	First NHL Season	Last NHL Season
Sutter, Darryl	Chi.	8	406	161	118	279	288	51	24	19	43	26	....	1979-80	1986-87
Sutter, Duane	NYI, Chi.	11	731	139	203	342	1333	161	26	32	58	405	4	1979-80	1989-90
Sutter, Rich	Pit., Phi., Van., St.L., Chi., T.B., Tor.	13	874	149	166	315	1411	78	13	5	18	133	....	1982-83	1994-95
Sutter, Ron	Phi., St.L., Que., NYI, Bos., S.J., Cgy.	19	1093	205	329	534	1352	104	8	32	40	193	....	1982-83	2000-01
Sutton, Ken	Buf., Edm., St.L., N.J., S.J., NYI	11	388	23	80	103	338	32	3	4	7	29	1	1990-91	2001-02
Suzor, Mark	Phi., Col.	2	64	4	16	20	60	....	....	....	....	....	....	1976-77	1977-78
‡ Svartvadet, Per	Atl.	4	247	17	34	51	58	....	....	....	....	....	....	1999-00	2002-03
Svehla, Robert	Fla., Tor.	9	655	68	267	335	649	38	1	14	15	42	....	1994-95	2002-03
Svejkovsky, Jaroslav	Wsh., T.B.	4	113	23	19	42	56	1	0	0	0	2	....	1996-97	1999-00
Svensson, Leif	Wsh.	2	121	6	40	46	49	....	....	....	....	....	....	1978-79	1979-80
Svensson, Magnus	Fla.	2	46	4	14	18	31	....	....	....	....	....	....	1994-95	1995-96
Svoboda, Petr	Mtl., Buf., Phi., T.B.	17	1028	58	341	399	1605	127	4	45	49	140	1	1984-85	2000-01
Svoboda, Petr	Tor.	1	18	1	2	3	10	....	....	....	....	....	....	2000-01	2000-01
Swain, Garry	Pit.	1	9	1	1	2	0	....	....	....	....	....	....	1968-69	1968-69
‡ Swanson, Brian	Edm., Atl.	4	70	4	13	17	16	....	....	....	....	....	....	2000-01	2003-04
Swarbrick, George	Oak., Pit., Phi.	4	132	17	25	42	173	....	....	....	....	....	....	1967-68	1970-71
• Sweeney, Bill	NYR	1	4	1	0	1	0	....	....	....	....	....	....	1959-60	1959-60
Sweeney, Bob	Bos., Buf., NYI, Cgy.	10	639	125	163	288	799	103	15	18	33	197	....	1986-87	1995-96
Sweeney, Don	Bos., Dal.	16	1115	52	221	273	681	108	9	10	19	81	....	1988-89	2003-04
Sweeney, Tim	Cgy., Bos., Ana., NYR	8	291	55	83	138	123	4	0	0	0	2	....	1990-91	1997-98
Sykes, Bob	Tor.	1	2	0	0	0	0	....	....	....	....	....	....	1974-75	1974-75
Sykes, Phil	L.A., Wpg.	10	456	79	85	164	519	26	0	3	3	29	....	1982-83	1991-92
Sykora, Michal	S.J., Chi., T.B., Phi.	7	267	15	54	69	185	7	0	1	1	0	....	1993-94	2000-01
Sylvester, Dean	Buf., Atl.	3	96	21	16	37	32	4	0	0	0	0	....	1998-99	2000-01
• Szura, Joe	Oak.	2	90	10	15	25	30	7	2	3	5	2	....	1967-68	1968-69

T

Name	NHL Teams	NHL Seasons	Regular Schedule GP	G	A	TP	PIM	Playoffs GP	G	A	TP	PIM	NHL Cup Wins	First NHL Season	Last NHL Season
Taft, John	Det.	1	15	0	2	2	4	....	....	....	....	....	....	1978-79	1978-79
Taglianetti, Peter	Wpg., Min., Pit., T.B.	11	451	18	74	92	1106	53	2	8	10	103	2	1984-85	1994-95
Talafous, Dean	Atl., Min., NYR	8	497	104	154	258	163	21	4	7	11	11	....	1974-75	1981-82
Talakoski, Ron	NYR	2	9	0	1	1	33	....	....	....	....	....	....	1986-87	1987-88
Talbot, Jean-Guy	Mtl., Min., Det., St.L., Buf.	17	1056	43	242	285	1006	150	4	26	30	142	7	1954-55	1970-71
Tallon, Dale	Van., Chi., Pit.	10	642	98	238	336	568	33	2	10	12	45	....	1970-71	1979-80
Tambellini, Steve	NYI, Col., N.J., Cgy., Van.	10	553	160	150	310	105	2	0	1	1	0	1	1978-79	1987-88
Tamer, Chris	Pit., NYR, Atl.	11	644	21	64	85	1183	37	0	8	8	52	....	1993-94	2003-04
Tancill, Chris	Hfd., Det., Dal., S.J.	8	134	17	32	49	54	11	1	1	2	8	....	1990-91	1997-98
Tanguay, Christian	Que.	1	2	0	0	0	0	....	....	....	....	....	....	1981-82	1981-82
Tannahill, Don	Van.	2	111	30	33	63	25	....	....	....	....	....	....	1972-73	1973-74
Tanti, Tony	Chi., Van., Pit., Buf.	11	697	287	273	560	661	30	3	12	15	27	....	1981-82	1991-92
Tardif, Marc	Mtl., Que.	8	517	194	207	401	443	62	13	15	28	75	2	1969-70	1982-83
Tardif, Patrice	St.L., L.A.	2	65	7	11	18	78	....	....	....	....	....	....	1994-95	1995-96
Tatarinov, Mikhail	Wsh., Que., Bos.	4	161	21	48	69	184	....	....	....	....	....	....	1990-91	1993-94
Tatchell, Spence	NYR	1	1	0	0	0	0	....	....	....	....	....	....	1942-43	1942-43
• Taylor, Billy	Tor., Det., Bos., NYR	7	323	87	180	267	120	33	6	18	24	13	1	1939-40	1947-48
• Taylor, Billy	NYR	1	2	0	0	0	0	....	....	....	....	....	....	1964-65	1964-65
• Taylor, Bob	Bos.	1	8	0	0	0	6	....	....	....	....	....	....	1929-30	1929-30
‡ Taylor, Chris	NYI, Bos., Buf.	8	149	11	21	32	48	2	0	0	0	2	....	1994-95	2003-04
Taylor, Dave	L.A.	17	1111	431	638	1069	1589	92	26	33	59	145	....	1977-78	1993-94
Taylor, Harry	Tor., Chi.	3	66	5	10	15	30	1	0	0	0	0	1	1946-47	1951-52
Taylor, Mark	Phi., Pit., Wsh.	5	209	42	68	110	73	6	0	0	0	0	....	1981-82	1985-86
• Taylor, Ralph	Chi., NYR	3	99	4	1	5	169	4	0	0	0	10	....	1927-28	1929-30
Taylor, Ted	NYR, Det., Min., Van.	6	166	23	35	58	181	....	....	....	....	....	....	1964-65	1971-72
Teal, Jeff	Mtl.	1	6	0	1	1	0	....	....	....	....	....	....	1984-85	1984-85
• Teal, Skip	Bos.	1	1	0	0	0	0	....	....	....	....	....	....	1954-55	1954-55
Teal, Vic	NYI	1	1	0	0	0	0	....	....	....	....	....	....	1973-74	1973-74
Tebbutt, Greg	Que., Pit.	2	26	0	3	3	35	....	....	....	....	....	....	1979-80	1983-84
Tepper, Stephen	Chi.	1	1	0	0	0	0	....	....	....	....	....	....	1992-93	1992-93
Terbenche, Paul	Chi., Buf.	5	189	5	26	31	28	12	0	0	0	0	....	1967-68	1973-74
Terrion, Greg	L.A., Tor.	8	561	93	150	243	339	35	2	9	11	41	....	1980-81	1987-88
Terry, Bill	Min.	1	5	0	0	0	0	....	....	....	....	....	....	1987-88	1987-88
• Tertyshny, Dmitri	Phi.	1	62	2	8	10	30	1	0	0	0	0	....	1998-99	1998-99
Tessier, Orval	Mtl., Bos.	3	59	5	7	12	6	....	....	....	....	....	....	1954-55	1960-61
‡ Tezikov, Alexei	Wsh., Van.	3	30	1	1	2	2	....	....	....	....	....	....	1998-99	2001-02
Theberge, Greg	Wsh.	5	153	15	63	78	73	4	0	1	1	0	....	1979-80	1983-84
Thelin, Mats	Bos.	3	163	8	19	27	107	5	0	0	0	6	....	1984-85	1986-87
Thelven, Michael	Bos.	5	207	20	80	100	217	34	4	10	14	34	....	1985-86	1989-90
Therien, Chris	Phi., Dal.	11	764	29	130	159	585	104	4	10	14	68	....	1994-95	2005-06
Therrien, Gaston	Que.	3	22	0	8	8	12	9	0	1	1	4	....	1980-81	1982-83
Thibaudeau, Gilles	Mtl., NYI, Tor.	5	119	25	37	62	40	8	3	3	6	2	....	1986-87	1990-91
Thibeault, Lorrain	Det., Mtl.	2	5	0	2	2	2	....	....	....	....	....	....	1944-45	1945-46
Thiffault, Leo	Min.	1	....	....	....	....	....	5	0	0	0	0	....	1967-68	1967-68
Thomas, Cy	Chi., Tor.	1	14	2	2	4	12	....	....	....	....	....	....	1947-48	1947-48
Thomas, Reg	Que.	1	39	9	7	16	6	....	....	....	....	....	....	1979-80	1979-80
Thomas, Scott	Buf., L.A.	3	63	6	4	10	32	12	1	0	1	4	....	1992-93	2000-01
Thomas, Steve	Tor., Chi., NYI, N.J., Ana., Det.	20	1235	421	512	933	1306	174	54	53	107	187	....	1984-85	2003-04
Thomlinson, Dave	St.L., Bos., L.A.	5	42	1	3	4	50	9	3	1	4	4	....	1989-90	1994-95
Thompson, Brent	L.A., Wpg., Phx.	6	121	1	10	11	352	4	0	0	0	4	....	1991-92	1996-97
• Thompson, Cliff	Bos.	2	13	0	1	1	2	....	....	....	....	....	....	1941-42	1948-49
Thompson, Errol	Tor., Det., Pit.	10	599	208	185	393	184	34	7	5	12	11	....	1970-71	1980-81
• Thompson, Ken	Mtl.W.	1	1	0	0	0	0	....	....	....	....	....	....	1917-18	1917-18
• Thompson, Paul	NYR, Chi.	13	582	153	179	332	336	48	11	11	22	54	3	1926-27	1938-39
• Thoms, Bill	Tor., Chi., Bos.	13	548	135	206	341	154	44	6	10	16	6	....	1932-33	1944-45
• Thomson, Bill	Det.	2	9	2	2	4	0	2	0	0	0	0	....	1938-39	1943-44
Thomson, Floyd	St.L.	8	411	56	97	153	341	10	0	2	2	6	....	1971-72	1979-80
Thomson, Jim	Wsh., Hfd., N.J., L.A., Ott., Ana.	7	115	4	3	7	416	1	0	0	0	0	....	1986-87	1993-94
• Thomson, Jimmy	Tor., Chi.	13	787	19	215	234	920	63	2	13	15	135	4	1945-46	1957-58
• Thomson, Rhys	Mtl., Tor.	2	25	0	2	2	38	....	....	....	....	....	....	1939-40	1942-43
Thornbury, Tom	Pit.	1	14	1	8	9	16	....	....	....	....	....	....	1983-84	1983-84
• Thorsteinson, Joe	NYA	1	4	0	0	0	0	....	....	....	....	....	....	1932-33	1932-33
• Thurier, Fred	NYA, Bro., NYR	3	80	25	27	52	18	....	....	....	....	....	....	1940-41	1944-45
Thurlby, Tom	Oak.	1	20	1	1	2	4	....	....	....	....	....	....	1967-68	1967-68
Thyer, Mario	Min.	1	5	0	0	0	0	1	0	0	0	2	....	1989-90	1989-90
‡ Tibbetts, Billy	Pit., Phi., NYR	3	82	2	8	10	269	....	....	....	....	....	....	2000-01	2002-03
Tichy, Milan	Chi., NYI	3	23	0	5	5	40	....	....	....	....	....	....	1992-93	1995-96
Tidey, Alex	Buf., Edm.	3	9	0	0	0	8	2	0	0	0	0	....	1976-77	1979-80
Tikkanen, Esa	Edm., NYR, St.L., N.J., Van., Fla., Wsh.	15	877	244	386	630	1077	186	72	60	132	275	5	1984-85	1998-99
‡ Tiley, Brad	Phx., Phi.	3	11	0	0	0	0	1	0	0	0	0	....	1997-98	2000-01
Tilley, Tom	St.L.	4	174	4	38	42	89	14	1	3	4	19	....	1988-89	1993-94
‡ Timander, Mattias	Bos., CBJ, NYI, Phi.	8	419	13	57	70	165	23	3	5	8	8	....	1996-97	2003-04
• Timgren, Ray	Tor., Chi.	6	251	14	44	58	70	30	3	9	12	6	2	1948-49	1954-55
Tinordi, Mark	NYR, Min., Dal., Wsh.	12	663	52	148	200	1514	70	7	11	18	165	....	1987-88	1998-99
Tippett, Dave	Hfd., Wsh., Pit., Phi.	12	721	93	169	262	317	62	6	16	22	34	....	1983-84	1993-94
Titanic, Morris	Buf.	2	19	0	0	0	0	....	....	....	....	....	....	1974-75	1975-76
Titov, German	Cgy., Pit., Edm., Ana.	9	624	157	220	377	311	34	11	12	23	18	....	1993-94	2001-02
Tkaczuk, Daniel	Cgy.	1	19	4	7	11	14	....	....	....	....	....	....	2000-01	2000-01
Tkaczuk, Walt	NYR	14	945	227	451	678	556	93	19	32	51	119	....	1967-68	1980-81
Toal, Mike	Edm.	1	3	0	0	0	0	....	....	....	....	....	....	1979-80	1979-80
‡ Tobler, Ryan	T.B.	1	4	0	0	0	5	....	....	....	....	....	....	2001-02	2001-02
Tocchet, Rick	Phi., Pit., L.A., Bos., Wsh., Phx.	18	1144	440	512	952	2972	145	52	60	112	471	1	1984-85	2001-02
Todd, Kevin	N.J., Edm., Chi., L.A., Ana.	9	383	70	133	203	225	12	3	2	5	16	....	1988-89	1997-98
Tomalty, Glenn	Wpg.	1	1	0	0	0	0	....	....	....	....	....	....	1979-80	1979-80
Tomlak, Mike	Hfd.	4	141	15	22	37	103	10	0	1	1	4	....	1989-90	1993-94
Tomlinson, Dave	Tor., Wpg., Fla.	4	42	1	3	4	28	....	....	....	....	....	....	1991-92	1994-95
Tomlinson, Kirk	Min.	1	1	0	0	0	0	....	....	....	....	....	....	1987-88	1987-88
‡ Toms, Jeff	T.B., Wsh., NYI, NYR, Pit., Fla.	8	236	22	33	55	59	1	0	0	0	0	....	1995-96	2002-03
• Tomson, Jack	NYA	3	15	1	1	2	0	2	0	0	0	0	....	1938-39	1940-41
Tonelli, John	NYI, Cgy., L.A., Chi., Que.	14	1028	325	511	836	911	172	40	75	115	200	4	1978-79	1991-92
Tookey, Tim	Wsh., Que., Pit., Phi., L.A.	7	106	22	36	58	71	10	1	3	4	2	....	1980-81	1988-89
Toomey, Sean	Min.	1	1	0	0	0	0	....	....	....	....	....	....	1986-87	1986-87
‡ Toporowski, Shayne	Tor.	1	3	0	0	0	7	....	....	....	....	....	....	1996-97	1996-97
Toppazzini, Jerry	Bos., Chi., Det.	12	783	163	244	407	436	40	13	9	22	13	....	1952-53	1963-64
• Toppazzini, Zellio	Bos., NYR, Chi.	5	123	21	22	43	49	2	0	0	0	0	....	1948-49	1956-57
Torgaev, Pavel	Cgy., T.B.	2	55	6	14	20	20	1	0	0	0	0	....	1995-96	1999-00

Garry Swain

Chris Tamer

Ted Taylor

Bill Thoms

Dave Tomlinson

Jerry Toppazzini

Rene Trudell

Carol Vadnais

Name	NHL Teams	NHL Seasons	Regular Schedule GP	G	A	TP	PIM	Playoffs GP	G	A	TP	PIM	NHL Cup Wins	First NHL Season	Last NHL Season
Torkki, Jari	Chi.	1	4	1	0	1	0	....	....	....	....	....	....	1988-89	1988-89
Tormanen, Antti	Ott.	1	50	7	8	15	28	....	....	....	....	....	....	1995-96	1995-96
● Touhey, Bill	Mtl.M., Ott., Bos.	7	280	65	40	105	107	2	1	0	1	0	....	1927-28	1933-34
● Toupin, Jacques	Chi.	1	8	1	2	3	0	4	0	0	0	0	....	1943-44	1943-44
● Townsend, Art	Chi.	1	5	0	0	0	0	....	....	....	....	....	....	1926-27	1926-27
Townshend, Graeme	Bos., NYI, Ott.	5	45	3	7	10	28	....	....	....	....	....	....	1989-90	1993-94
Trader, Larry	Det., St.L., Mtl.	4	91	5	13	18	74	3	0	0	0	0	....	1982-83	1987-88
● Trainor, Wes	NYR	1	17	1	2	3	6	....	....	....	....	....	....	1948-49	1948-49
● Trapp, Bob	Chi.	2	82	4	4	8	129	2	0	0	0	4	....	1926-27	1927-28
Trapp, Doug	Buf.	1	2	0	0	0	0	....	....	....	....	....	....	1986-87	1986-87
● Traub, Percy	Chi., Det.	3	130	3	3	6	217	4	0	0	0	6	....	1926-27	1928-29
Trebil, Dan	Ana., Pit., St.L.	5	85	4	4	8	32	10	0	1	1	8	....	1996-97	2000-01
Tredway, Brock	L.A.	1	....	....	....	....	....	1	0	0	0	0	....	1981-82	1981-82
Tremblay, Brent	Wsh.	2	10	1	0	1	6	....	....	....	....	....	....	1978-79	1979-80
Tremblay, Gilles	Mtl.	9	509	168	162	330	161	48	9	14	23	4	3	1960-61	1968-69
● Tremblay, J.C.	Mtl.	13	794	57	306	363	204	108	14	51	65	58	5	1959-60	1971-72
● Tremblay, Marcel	Mtl.	1	10	0	2	2	0	....	....	....	....	....	....	1938-39	1938-39
Tremblay, Mario	Mtl.	12	852	258	326	584	1043	101	20	29	49	187	5	1974-75	1985-86
● Tremblay, Nils	Mtl.	2	3	0	1	1	0	2	0	0	0	0	....	1944-45	1945-46
‡ Trepanier, Pascal	Col., Ana., Nsh.	6	229	12	22	34	252	2	0	0	0	0	....	1997-98	2002-03
Trimper, Tim	Chi., Wpg., Min.	6	190	30	36	66	153	2	0	0	0	2	....	1979-80	1984-85
‡ Tripp, John	NYR, L.A.	2	43	2	7	9	35	....	....	....	....	....	....	2002-03	2003-04
‡ Trnka, Pavel	Ana., Fla.	7	411	14	63	77	323	4	0	1	1	2	....	1997-98	2003-04
Trottier, Bryan	NYI, Pit.	18	1279	524	901	1425	912	221	71	113	184	277	6	1975-76	1993-94
● Trottier, Dave	Mtl.M., Det.	11	446	121	113	234	517	31	4	3	7	39	1	1928-29	1938-39
Trottier, Guy	NYR, Tor.	3	115	28	17	45	37	9	1	0	1	16	....	1968-69	1971-72
Trottier, Rocky	N.J.	2	38	6	4	10	2	....	....	....	....	....	....	1983-84	1984-85
● Trudel, Lou	Chi., Mtl.	8	306	49	69	118	122	24	1	3	4	4	2	1933-34	1940-41
● Trudell, Rene	NYR	3	129	24	28	52	72	5	0	0	0	2	....	1945-46	1947-48
‡ Tselios, Nikos	Car.	1	2	0	0	0	6	....	....	....	....	....	....	2001-02	2001-02
‡ Tsulygin, Nikolai	Ana.	1	22	0	1	1	8	....	....	....	....	....	....	1996-97	1996-97
Tsygurov, Denis	Buf., L.A.	3	51	1	5	6	45	....	....	....	....	....	....	1993-94	1995-96
Tsyplakov, Vladimir	L.A., Buf.	6	331	69	101	170	90	18	1	2	3	16	....	1995-96	2000-01
Tucker, John	Buf., Wsh., NYI, T.B.	12	656	177	259	436	285	31	10	18	28	24	....	1983-84	1995-96
● Tudin, Connie	Mtl.	1	4	0	1	1	4	....	....	....	....	....	....	1941-42	1941-42
Tudor, Rob	Van., St.L.	3	28	4	4	8	19	3	0	0	0	0	....	1978-79	1982-83
Tuer, Allan	L.A., Min., Hfd.	4	57	1	1	2	208	....	....	....	....	....	....	1985-86	1989-90
‡ Tuomainen, Marko	Edm., L.A., NYI	4	79	9	9	18	84	1	0	0	0	0	....	1994-95	2001-02
Turcotte, Alfie	Mtl., Wpg., Wsh.	7	112	17	29	46	49	5	0	0	0	0	....	1983-84	1990-91
Turcotte, Darren	NYR, Hfd., Wpg., S.J., St.L., Nsh.	12	635	195	216	411	301	35	6	8	14	12	....	1988-89	1999-00
Turgeon, Sylvain	Hfd., N.J., Mtl., Ott.	12	669	269	226	495	691	36	4	7	11	22	....	1983-84	1994-95
Turlick, Gord	Bos.	1	2	0	0	0	2	....	....	....	....	....	....	1959-60	1959-60
Turnbull, Ian	Tor., L.A., Pit.	10	628	123	317	440	736	55	13	32	45	94	....	1973-74	1982-83
Turnbull, Perry	St.L., Mtl., Wpg.	9	608	188	163	351	1245	34	6	7	13	86	....	1979-80	1987-88
Turnbull, Randy	Cgy.	1	1	0	0	0	2	....	....	....	....	....	....	1981-82	1981-82
Turner, Bob	Mtl., Chi.	8	478	19	51	70	307	68	1	4	5	44	5	1955-56	1962-63
Turner, Brad	NYI	1	3	0	0	0	0	....	....	....	....	....	....	1991-92	1991-92
Turner, Dean	NYR, Col., L.A.	4	35	1	0	1	59	....	....	....	....	....	....	1978-79	1982-83
● Tustin, Norm	NYR	1	18	2	4	6	0	....	....	....	....	....	....	1941-42	1941-42
● Tuten, Aud	Chi.	2	39	4	8	12	48	....	....	....	....	....	....	1941-42	1942-43
Tutt, Brian	Wsh.	1	7	1	0	1	2	....	....	....	....	....	....	1989-90	1989-90
Tuttle, Steve	St.L.	3	144	28	28	56	12	17	1	6	7	2	....	1988-89	1990-91
‡ Tuzzolino, Tony	Ana., NYR, Bos.	3	9	0	0	0	7	....	....	....	....	....	....	1997-98	2001-02
‡ Tvrdon, Roman	Wsh.	1	9	0	1	1	2	....	....	....	....	....	....	2003-04	2003-04
Twist, Tony	St.L., Que.	10	445	10	18	28	1121	18	1	1	2	22	....	1989-90	1998-99
U V															
Ubriaco, Gene	Pit., Oak., Chi.	3	177	39	35	74	50	11	2	0	2	4	....	1967-68	1969-70
‡ Ulanov, Igor	Wpg., Wsh., Chi., T.B., Mtl., Edm., NYR, Fla.	14	739	27	135	162	1151	39	1	4	5	84	....	1991-92	2005-06
Ullman, Norm	Det., Tor.	20	1410	490	739	1229	712	106	30	53	83	67	....	1955-56	1974-75
‡ Ulmer, Jeff	NYR	1	21	3	0	3	8	....	....	....	....	....	....	2000-01	2000-01
‡ Ulmer, Layne	NYR	1	1	0	0	0	0	....	....	....	....	....	....	2003-04	2003-04
Unger, Garry	Tor., Det., St.L., Atl., L.A., Edm.	16	1105	413	391	804	1075	52	12	18	30	105	....	1967-68	1982-83
‡ Ustorf, Stefan	Wsh.	2	54	7	10	17	16	5	0	0	0	0	....	1995-96	1996-97
Vachon, Nick	NYI	1	1	0	0	0	0	....	....	....	....	....	....	1996-97	1996-97
Vadnais, Carol	Mtl., Oak., Cal., Bos., NYR, N.J.	17	1087	169	418	587	1813	106	10	40	50	185	2	1966-67	1982-83
‡ Vaic, Lubomir	Van.	2	9	1	1	2	2	....	....	....	....	....	....	1997-98	1999-00
Vail, Eric	Atl., Cgy., Det.	9	591	216	260	476	281	20	5	6	11	6	....	1973-74	1981-82
● Vail, Sparky	NYR	2	50	4	1	5	18	10	0	0	0	2	....	1928-29	1929-30
Vaive, Rick	Van., Tor., Chi., Buf.	13	876	441	347	788	1445	54	27	16	43	111	....	1979-80	1991-92
Valentine, Chris	Wsh.	3	105	43	52	95	127	2	0	0	0	4	....	1981-82	1983-84
‡ Valicevic, Rob	Nsh., L.A., Ana., Dal.	6	193	28	20	48	61	....	....	....	....	....	....	1998-99	2003-04
Valiquette, Jack	Tor., Col.	7	350	84	134	218	79	23	3	6	9	4	....	1974-75	1980-81
Valk, Garry	Van., Ana., Pit., Tor., Chi.	13	777	100	156	256	747	61	6	7	13	79	....	1990-91	2002-03
Vallis, Lindsay	Mtl.	1	1	0	0	0	0	....	....	....	....	....	....	1993-94	1993-94
Van Allen, Shaun	Edm., Ana., Ott., Dal., Mtl.	13	794	84	185	269	481	61	1	7	8	45	....	1990-91	2003-04
Van Boxmeer, John	Mtl., Col., Buf., Que.	11	588	84	274	358	465	38	5	15	20	37	1	1973-74	1983-84
Van Dorp, Wayne	Edm., Pit., Chi., Que.	6	125	12	12	24	565	27	0	1	1	42	....	1986-87	1991-92
Van Drunen, David	Ott.	1	1	0	0	0	0	....	....	....	....	....	....	1999-00	1999-00
‡ Van Impe, Darren	Ana., Bos., NYR, Fla., NYI, CBJ	9	411	25	90	115	397	33	3	9	12	28	....	1994-95	2002-03
Van Impe, Ed	Chi., Phi., Pit.	11	700	27	126	153	1025	66	1	12	13	131	2	1966-67	1976-77
‡ Varis, Petri	Chi.	1	1	0	0	0	0	....	....	....	....	....	....	1997-98	1997-98
‡ Varlamov, Sergei	Cgy., St.L.	4	63	8	7	15	26	1	0	0	0	2	....	1997-98	2002-03
Varvio, Jarkko	Dal.	2	13	3	4	7	4	....	....	....	....	....	....	1993-94	1994-95
Vasilevski, Alexander	St.L.	2	4	0	0	0	2	....	....	....	....	....	....	1995-96	1996-97
Vasiliev, Alexei	NYR	1	1	0	0	0	2	....	....	....	....	....	....	1999-00	1999-00
‡ Vasiljevs, Herbert	Fla., Atl., Van.	4	51	8	7	15	22	....	....	....	....	....	....	1998-99	2001-02
Vasilyev, Andrei	NYI, Phx.	4	16	2	5	7	6	....	....	....	....	....	....	1994-95	1998-99
Vaske, Dennis	NYI, Bos.	9	235	5	41	46	253	22	0	7	7	16	....	1990-91	1998-99
● Vasko, Moose	Chi., Min.	13	786	34	166	200	719	78	2	7	9	73	1	1956-57	1969-70
Vasko, Rick	Det.	3	31	3	7	10	29	....	....	....	....	....	....	1977-78	1980-81
‡ Vauclair, Julien	Ott.	1	1	0	0	0	2	....	....	....	....	....	....	2003-04	2003-04
Vautour, Yvon	NYI, Col., N.J., Que.	6	204	26	33	59	401	....	....	....	....	....	....	1979-80	1984-85
Vaydik, Greg	Chi.	1	5	0	0	0	0	....	....	....	....	....	....	1976-77	1976-77
Veitch, Darren	Wsh., Det., Tor.	10	511	48	209	257	296	33	4	11	15	33	....	1980-81	1990-91
Velischek, Randy	Min., N.J., Que.	10	509	21	76	97	401	44	2	5	7	32	....	1982-83	1991-92
Vellucci, Mike	Hfd.	1	2	0	0	0	11	....	....	....	....	....	....	1987-88	1987-88
Venasky, Vic	L.A.	7	430	61	101	162	66	21	1	5	6	12	....	1972-73	1978-79
Veneruzzo, Gary	St.L.	2	7	1	1	2	0	9	0	2	2	2	....	1967-68	1971-72
Verbeek, Pat	N.J., Hfd., NYR, Dal., Det.	20	1424	522	541	1063	2905	117	26	36	62	225	1	1982-83	2001-02
Vermette, Mark	Que.	4	67	5	13	18	33	....	....	....	....	....	....	1988-89	1991-92
‡ Vernarsky, Kris	Bos.	2	17	1	0	1	2	....	....	....	....	....	....	2002-03	2003-04
Verret, Claude	Buf.	2	14	2	5	7	2	....	....	....	....	....	....	1983-84	1984-85
Verstraete, Leigh	Tor.	3	8	0	1	1	14	....	....	....	....	....	....	1982-83	1987-88
Ververgaert, Dennis	Van., Phi., Wsh.	8	583	176	216	392	247	8	1	2	3	6	....	1973-74	1980-81
Vesey, Jim	St.L., Bos.	3	15	1	2	3	7	....	....	....	....	....	....	1988-89	1991-92
Veysey, Sid	Van.	1	1	0	0	0	0	....	....	....	....	....	....	1977-78	1977-78
Vial, Dennis	NYR, Det., Ott.	8	242	4	15	19	794	....	....	....	....	....	....	1990-91	1997-98
Vickers, Steve	NYR	10	698	246	340	586	330	68	24	25	49	58	....	1972-73	1981-82
Vigneault, Alain	St.L.	2	42	2	5	7	82	4	0	1	1	26	....	1981-82	1982-83
‡ Viitakoski, Vesa	Cgy.	3	23	2	4	6	8	....	....	....	....	....	....	1993-94	1995-96
Vilgrain, Claude	Van., N.J., Phi.	5	89	21	32	53	78	11	1	1	2	17	....	1987-88	1993-94
Vincelette, Dan	Chi., Que.	6	193	20	22	42	351	12	0	0	0	4	....	1986-87	1991-92
Vipond, Pete	Cal.	1	3	0	0	0	0	....	....	....	....	....	....	1972-73	1972-73
Virta, Hannu	Buf.	5	245	25	101	126	66	17	1	3	4	6	....	1981-82	1985-86
‡ Virta, Tony	Min.	1	8	2	3	5	0	....	....	....	....	....	....	2001-02	2001-02
‡ Virtue, Terry	Bos., NYR	2	5	0	0	0	0	....	....	....	....	....	....	1998-99	1999-00
Visheau, Mark	Wpg., L.A.	2	29	1	3	4	107	....	....	....	....	....	....	1993-94	1998-99
Vitolinsh, Harijs	Wpg.	1	8	0	0	0	4	....	....	....	....	....	....	1993-94	1993-94
Viveiros, Emanuel	Min.	3	29	1	11	12	6	....	....	....	....	....	....	1985-86	1987-88
‡ Vlasak, Tomas	L.A.	1	10	1	3	4	2	....	....	....	....	....	....	2000-01	2000-01
● Vokes, Ed	Chi.	1	5	0	0	0	0	....	....	....	....	....	....	1930-31	1930-31
Volcan, Mickey	Hfd., Cgy.	4	162	8	33	41	146	....	....	....	....	....	....	1980-81	1983-84

Name	NHL Teams	NHL Seasons	Regular Schedule GP	G	A	TP	PIM	Playoffs GP	G	A	TP	PIM	NHL Cup Wins	First NHL Season	Last NHL Season
Volchkov, Alexandre	Wsh.	1	3	0	0	0	0	....	....	....	....	....	....	1999-00	1999-00
Volek, David	NYI	6	396	95	154	249	201	15	5	5	10	2	....	1988-89	1993-94
Volmar, Doug	Det., L.A.	4	62	13	8	21	26	2	1	0	1	0	....	1969-70	1972-73
‡ Von Arx, Reto	Chi.	1	19	3	1	4	4	....	....	....	....	....	....	2000-01	2000-01
Von Stefenelli, Phil	Bos., Ott.	2	33	0	5	5	23	....	....	....	....	....	....	1995-96	1996-97
Vopat, Jan	L.A., Nsh.	5	126	11	20	31	70	2	0	1	1	2	....	1995-96	1999-00
‡ Vopat, Roman	St.L., L.A., Chi., Phi.	4	133	6	14	20	253	....	....	....	....	....	....	1995-96	1998-99
Vorobiev, Vladimir	NYR, Edm.	3	33	9	7	16	14	1	0	0	0	0	....	1996-97	1998-99
• Voss, Carl	Tor., NYR, Det., Ott., St.L., NYA, Mtl.M., Chi.	8	261	34	70	104	50	24	5	3	8	0	1	1926-27	1937-38
‡ Vujtek, Vladimir	Mtl., Edm., T.B., Atl., Pit.	6	110	7	30	37	38	....	....	....	....	....	....	1991-92	2002-03
Vukota, Mick	NYI, T.B., Mtl.	11	574	17	29	46	2071	23	0	0	0	73	....	1987-88	1997-98
Vyazmikin, Igor	Edm.	1	4	1	0	1	0	....	....	....	....	....	....	1990-91	1990-91
‡ Vyshedkevich, Sergei	Atl.	2	30	2	5	7	16	....	....	....	....	....	....	1999-00	2000-01
W															
Waddell, Don	L.A.	1	1	0	0	0	0	....	....	....	....	....	....	1980-81	1980-81
• Waite, Frank	NYR	1	17	1	3	4	4	....	....	....	....	....	....	1930-31	1930-31
Walker, Gord	NYR, L.A.	4	31	3	4	7	23	....	....	....	....	....	....	1986-87	1989-90
Walker, Howard	Wsh., Cgy.	3	83	2	13	15	133	....	....	....	....	....	....	1980-81	1982-83
• Walker, Jack	Det.	2	80	5	8	13	18	....	....	....	....	....	....	1926-27	1927-28
Walker, Kurt	Tor.	3	71	4	5	9	142	16	0	0	0	34	....	1975-76	1977-78
Walker, Russ	L.A.	2	17	1	0	1	41	....	....	....	....	....	....	1976-77	1977-78
Wall, Bob	Det., L.A., St.L.	8	322	30	55	85	155	22	0	3	3	2	....	1964-65	1971-72
Wallin, Jesse	Det.	4	49	0	2	2	34	....	....	....	....	....	....	1999-00	2002-03
Wallin, Peter	NYR	2	52	3	14	17	14	14	2	6	8	6	....	1980-81	1981-82
Walsh, Jim	Buf.	1	4	0	1	1	4	....	....	....	....	....	....	1981-82	1981-82
Walsh, Mike	NYI	2	14	2	0	2	4	....	....	....	....	....	....	1987-88	1988-89
Walter, Ryan	Wsh., Mtl., Van.	15	1003	264	382	646	946	113	16	35	51	62	1	1978-79	1992-93
• Walton, Bobby	Mtl.	1	4	0	0	0	0	....	....	....	....	....	....	1943-44	1943-44
Walton, Mike	Tor., Bos., Van., St.L., Chi.	12	588	201	247	448	357	47	14	10	24	45	2	1965-66	1978-79
Wappel, Gord	Atl., Cgy.	3	20	1	1	2	10	2	0	0	0	4	....	1979-80	1981-82
Ward, Dixon	Van., L.A., Tor., Buf., Bos., NYR	10	537	95	129	224	431	62	14	20	34	46	....	1992-93	2002-03
• Ward, Don	Chi., Bos.	2	34	0	1	1	16	....	....	....	....	....	....	1957-58	1959-60
Ward, Ed	Que., Cgy., Atl., Ana., N.J.	8	278	23	26	49	354	....	....	....	....	....	....	1993-94	2000-01
• Ward, Jimmy	Mtl.M., Mtl.	12	527	147	127	274	455	36	4	4	8	26	1	1927-28	1938-39
Ward, Joe	Col.	1	4	0	0	0	2	....	....	....	....	....	....	1980-81	1980-81
Ward, Ron	Tor., Van.	2	89	2	5	7	6	....	....	....	....	....	....	1969-70	1971-72
Ware, Jeff	Tor., Fla.	3	21	0	1	1	12	....	....	....	....	....	....	1996-97	1998-99
Ware, Michael	Edm.	2	5	0	1	1	15	....	....	....	....	....	....	1988-89	1989-90
• Wares, Eddie	NYR, Det., Chi.	9	321	60	102	162	161	45	5	7	12	34	1	1936-37	1946-47
Warner, Bob	Tor.	2	10	1	1	2	4	4	0	0	0	0	....	1975-76	1976-77
Warner, Jim	Hfd.	1	32	0	3	3	10	....	....	....	....	....	....	1979-80	1979-80
Warriner, Todd	Tor., T.B., Phx., Van., Phi., Nsh.	9	453	65	89	154	249	21	2	1	3	6	....	1994-95	2002-03
Warwick, Bill	NYR	2	14	3	3	6	16	....	....	....	....	....	....	1942-43	1943-44
• Warwick, Grant	NYR, Bos., Mtl.	9	395	147	142	289	220	16	2	4	6	6	....	1941-42	1949-50
Washburn, Steve	Fla., Van., Phi.	6	93	14	15	29	42	1	0	1	1	0	....	1995-96	2000-01
• Wasnie, Nick	Chi., Mtl., NYA, Ott., St.L.	7	248	57	34	91	176	20	6	3	9	20	2	1927-28	1934-35
Watson, Bill	Chi.	4	115	23	36	59	12	6	0	2	2	0	....	1985-86	1988-89
Watson, Bryan	Mtl., Det., Oak., Pit., St.L., Wsh.	16	878	17	135	152	2212	32	2	0	2	70	....	1963-64	1978-79
Watson, Dave	Col.	2	18	0	1	1	10	....	....	....	....	....	....	1979-80	1980-81
• Watson, Harry	Bro., Det., Tor., Chi.	14	809	236	207	443	150	62	16	9	25	27	5	1941-42	1956-57
Watson, Jim	Det., Buf.	8	221	4	19	23	345	....	....	....	....	....	....	1963-64	1971-72
Watson, Jimmy	Phi.	10	613	38	148	186	492	101	5	34	39	89	2	1972-73	1981-82
Watson, Joe	Bos., Phi., Col.	14	835	38	178	216	447	84	3	12	15	82	2	1964-65	1978-79
• Watson, Phil	NYR, Mtl.	13	590	144	265	409	532	54	10	25	35	67	2	1935-36	1947-48
‡ Watt, Mike	Edm., NYI, Nsh., Car.	5	157	15	26	41	41	....	....	....	....	....	....	1997-98	2002-03
Watters, Tim	Wpg., L.A.	14	741	26	151	177	1289	82	1	5	6	115	....	1981-82	1994-95
Watts, Brian	Det.	1	4	0	0	0	0	....	....	....	....	....	....	1975-76	1975-76
Webb, Steve	NYI, Pit.	8	321	5	13	18	532	14	0	0	0	28	....	1996-97	2003-04
• Webster, Aubrey	Phi., Mtl.M.	2	5	0	0	0	0	....	....	....	....	....	....	1930-31	1934-35
• Webster, Don	Tor.	1	27	7	6	13	28	5	0	0	0	12	....	1943-44	1943-44
Webster, John	NYR	1	14	0	0	0	4	....	....	....	....	....	....	1949-50	1949-50
Webster, Tom	Bos., Det., Cal.	5	102	33	42	75	61	1	0	0	0	0	....	1968-69	1979-80
• Weiland, Cooney	Bos., Ott., Det.	11	509	173	160	333	147	45	12	10	22	12	2	1928-29	1938-39
Weinrich, Eric	N.J., Hfd., Chi., Mtl., Bos., Phi., St.L., Van.	17	1157	70	318	388	825	81	6	23	29	67	....	1988-89	2005-06
Weir, Stan	Cal., Tor., Edm., Col., Det.	10	642	139	207	346	183	37	6	5	11	4	....	1972-73	1982-83
Weir, Wally	Que., Hfd., Pit.	6	320	21	45	66	625	23	0	1	1	96	....	1979-80	1984-85
• Wellington, Alex	Que.	1	1	0	0	0	0	....	....	....	....	....	....	1919-20	1919-20
Wells, Chris	Pit., Fla.	5	195	9	20	29	193	3	0	0	0	0	....	1995-96	1999-00
Wells, Jay	L.A., Phi., Buf., NYR, St.L., T.B.	18	1098	47	216	263	2359	114	3	14	17	213	1	1979-80	1996-97
Wensink, John	St.L., Bos., Que., Col., N.J.	8	403	70	68	138	840	43	2	6	8	86	....	1973-74	1982-83
• Wentworth, Cy	Chi., Mtl.M., Mtl.	13	575	39	68	107	355	35	5	6	11	20	1	1927-28	1939-40
Werenka, Brad	Edm., Que., Chi., Pit., Cgy.	7	320	19	61	80	299	19	2	1	3	14	....	1992-93	2000-01
Wesenberg, Brian	Phi.	1	1	0	0	0	5	....	....	....	....	....	....	1998-99	1998-99
Wesley, Blake	Phi., Hfd., Que., Tor.	7	298	18	46	64	486	19	2	2	4	30	....	1979-80	1985-86
Westfall, Ed	Bos., NYI	18	1226	231	394	625	544	95	22	37	59	41	2	1961-62	1978-79
Westlund, Tommy	Car.	4	203	9	13	22	48	25	1	0	1	17	....	1999-00	2002-03
Wharram, Kenny	Chi.	14	766	252	281	533	222	80	16	27	43	38	1	1951-52	1968-69
Wharton, Len	NYR	1	1	0	0	0	0	....	....	....	....	....	....	1944-45	1944-45
Wheeldon, Simon	NYR, Wpg.	3	15	0	2	2	10	....	....	....	....	....	....	1987-88	1990-91
• Wheldon, Don	St.L.	1	2	0	0	0	0	....	....	....	....	....	....	1974-75	1974-75
Whelton, Bill	Wpg.	1	2	0	0	0	0	....	....	....	....	....	....	1980-81	1980-81
Whistle, Rob	NYR, St.L.	2	51	7	5	12	16	4	0	0	0	2	....	1985-86	1987-88
White, Bill	L.A., Chi.	9	604	50	215	265	495	91	7	32	39	76	....	1967-68	1975-76
‡ White, Brian	Col.	1	2	0	0	0	0	....	....	....	....	....	....	1998-99	1998-99
White, Moe	Mtl.	1	4	0	1	1	2	....	....	....	....	....	....	1945-46	1945-46
‡ White, Peter	Edm., Tor., Phi., Chi.	9	220	23	37	60	36	19	0	2	2	0	....	1993-94	2003-04
• White, Sherman	NYR	2	4	0	2	2	0	....	....	....	....	....	....	1946-47	1949-50
• White, Tex	Pit., NYA, Phi.	6	203	33	12	45	141	4	0	0	0	4	....	1925-26	1930-31
White, Tony	Wsh., Min.	5	164	37	28	65	104	....	....	....	....	....	....	1974-75	1979-80
Whitelaw, Bob	Det.	2	32	0	2	2	2	8	0	0	0	0	....	1940-41	1941-42
Whitlock, Bob	Min.	1	1	0	0	0	0	....	....	....	....	....	....	1969-70	1969-70
Whyte, Sean	L.A.	2	21	0	2	2	12	....	....	....	....	....	....	1991-92	1992-93
• Wickenheiser, Doug	Mtl., St.L., Van., NYR, Wsh.	10	556	111	165	276	286	41	4	7	11	18	....	1980-81	1989-90
• Widing, Juha	NYR, L.A., Cle.	8	575	144	226	370	208	8	1	2	3	2	....	1969-70	1976-77
Widmer, Jason	NYI, S.J.	3	7	0	1	1	7	....	....	....	....	....	....	1994-95	1996-97
• Wiebe, Art	Chi.	11	414	14	27	41	201	31	1	3	4	10	1	1932-33	1943-44
Wiemer, Jason	T.B., Cgy., Fla., NYI, Min., N.J.	11	726	90	112	202	1420	19	1	0	1	67	....	1994-95	2005-06
Wiemer, Jim	Buf., NYR, Edm., L.A., Bos.	11	325	29	72	101	378	62	5	8	13	63	....	1982-83	1993-94
• Wilcox, Archie	Mtl.M., Bos., St.L.	6	208	8	14	22	158	12	1	0	1	8	....	1929-30	1934-35
Wilcox, Barry	Van.	2	33	3	2	5	15	....	....	....	....	....	....	1972-73	1974-75
• Wilder, Arch	Det.	1	18	0	2	2	2	....	....	....	....	....	....	1940-41	1940-41
Wiley, Jim	Pit., Van.	5	63	4	10	14	8	....	....	....	....	....	....	1972-73	1976-77
Wilkie, Bob	Det., Phi.	2	18	2	5	7	10	....	....	....	....	....	....	1990-91	1993-94
Wilkie, David	Mtl., T.B., NYR	6	167	10	26	36	165	8	1	2	3	14	....	1994-95	2000-01
Wilkins, Barry	Bos., Van., Pit.	9	418	27	125	152	663	6	0	1	1	4	....	1966-67	1975-76
• Wilkinson, John	Bos.	1	9	0	0	0	6	....	....	....	....	....	....	1943-44	1943-44
Wilkinson, Neil	Min., S.J., Chi., Wpg., Pit.	10	460	16	67	83	813	53	3	6	9	41	....	1989-90	1998-99
Wilks, Brian	L.A.	4	48	4	8	12	27	....	....	....	....	....	....	1984-85	1988-89
Willard, Rod	Tor.	1	1	0	0	0	0	....	....	....	....	....	....	1982-83	1982-83
• Williams, Burr	Det., St.L., Bos.	3	19	0	1	1	28	7	0	0	0	8	....	1933-34	1936-37
Williams, Butch	St.L., Cal.	3	108	14	35	49	131	....	....	....	....	....	....	1973-74	1975-76
Williams, Darryl	L.A.	1	2	0	0	0	10	....	....	....	....	....	....	1992-93	1992-93
Williams, David	S.J., Ana.	4	173	11	53	64	157	....	....	....	....	....	....	1991-92	1994-95
Williams, Fred	Det.	1	44	2	5	7	10	....	....	....	....	....	....	1976-77	1976-77
Williams, Gord	Phi.	2	2	0	0	0	2	....	....	....	....	....	....	1981-82	1982-83
Williams, Sean	Chi.	1	2	0	0	0	4	....	....	....	....	....	....	1991-92	1991-92
Williams, Tiger	Tor., Van., Det., L.A., Hfd.	14	962	241	272	513	3966	83	12	23	35	455	....	1974-75	1987-88
Williams, Tom	NYR, L.A.	8	397	115	138	253	73	29	8	7	15	4	....	1971-72	1978-79
• Williams, Tommy	Bos., Min., Cal., Wsh.	13	663	161	269	430	177	10	2	5	7	2	....	1961-62	1975-76
Willson, Don	Mtl.	2	22	2	7	9	0	3	0	0	0	0	....	1937-38	1938-39

Alain Vigneault

Howard Walker

Eric Weinrich

Bill White

Tiger Williams

Bert Wilson

Steve Yzerman

Alex Zhamnov

			Regular Schedule					Playoffs							
Name	NHL Teams	NHL Seasons	GP	G	A	TP	PIM	GP	G	A	TP	PIM	NHL Cup Wins	First NHL Season	Last NHL Season
Wilson, Behn	Phi., Chi.	9	601	98	260	358	1480	67	12	29	41	190	....	1978-79	1987-88
• Wilson, Bert	NYR, St.L., L.A., Cgy.	8	478	37	44	81	646	21	0	2	2	42	....	1973-74	1980-81
Wilson, Bob	Chi.	1	1	0	0	0	0	....	....	....	....	....	....	1953-54	1953-54
Wilson, Carey	Cgy., Hfd., NYR	10	552	169	258	427	314	52	11	13	24	14	....	1983-84	1992-93
• Wilson, Cully	Tor., Mtl., Ham., Chi.	5	127	59	28	87	243	2	1	0	1	6	....	1919-20	1926-27
Wilson, Doug	Chi., S.J.	16	1024	237	590	827	830	95	19	61	80	88	....	1977-78	1992-93
Wilson, Gord	Bos.	1	....	....	....	....	....	2	0	0	0	0	....	1954-55	1954-55
Wilson, Hub	NYA	1	2	0	0	0	0	....	....	....	....	....	....	1931-32	1931-32
Wilson, Jerry	Mtl.	1	3	0	0	0	2	....	....	....	....	....	....	1956-57	1956-57
Wilson, Johnny	Det., Chi., Tor., NYR	13	688	161	171	332	190	66	14	13	27	11	4	1949-50	1961-62
‡ Wilson, Landon	Col., Bos., Phx., Pit.	9	348	51	60	111	331	13	1	1	2	20	....	1995-96	2003-04
• Wilson, Larry	Det., Chi.	6	152	21	48	69	75	4	0	0	0	0	1	1949-50	1955-56
Wilson, Mike	Buf., Fla., Pit., NYR	8	336	16	41	57	264	29	0	2	2	15	....	1995-96	2002-03
Wilson, Mitch	N.J., Pit.	2	26	2	3	5	104	....	....	....	....	....	....	1984-85	1986-87
Wilson, Murray	Mtl., L.A.	7	386	94	95	189	162	53	5	14	19	32	4	1972-73	1978-79
Wilson, Rick	Mtl., St.L., Det.	4	239	6	26	32	165	3	0	0	0	0	....	1973-74	1976-77
Wilson, Rik	St.L., Cgy., Chi.	6	251	25	65	90	220	22	0	4	4	23	....	1981-82	1987-88
Wilson, Roger	Chi.	1	7	0	2	2	6	....	....	....	....	....	....	1974-75	1974-75
Wilson, Ron	Tor., Min.	7	177	26	67	93	68	20	4	13	17	8	....	1977-78	1987-88
Wilson, Ron	Wpg., St.L., Mtl.	14	832	110	216	326	415	63	10	12	22	64	....	1979-80	1993-94
Wilson, Wally	Bos.	1	53	11	8	19	18	1	0	0	0	0	....	1947-48	1947-48
Wing, Murray	Det.	1	1	0	1	1	0	....	....	....	....	....	....	1973-74	1973-74
Winnes, Chris	Bos., Phi.	4	33	1	6	7	6	1	0	0	0	0	....	1990-91	1993-94
Wiseman, Brian	Tor.	1	3	0	0	0	0	....	....	....	....	....	....	1996-97	1996-97
• Wiseman, Eddie	Det., NYA, Bos.	10	456	115	165	280	136	43	10	10	20	16	1	1932-33	1941-42
Wiste, Jim	Chi., Van.	3	52	1	10	11	8	....	....	....	....	....	....	1968-69	1970-71
Witehall, Johan	NYR, Mtl.	3	54	2	5	7	16	....	....	....	....	....	....	1998-99	2000-01
Witherspoon, Jim	L.A.	1	2	0	0	0	2	....	....	....	....	....	....	1975-76	1975-76
Witiuk, Steve	Chi.	1	33	3	8	11	14	....	....	....	....	....	....	1951-52	1951-52
Woit, Benny	Det., Chi.	7	334	7	26	33	170	41	2	6	8	18	3	1950-51	1956-57
Wojciechowski, Steve	Det.	2	54	19	20	39	17	6	0	1	1	0	....	1944-45	1946-47
Wolanin, Craig	N.J., Que., Col., T.B., Tor.	13	695	40	133	173	894	35	4	6	10	67	1	1985-86	1997-98
Wolf, Bennett	Pit.	3	30	0	1	1	133	....	....	....	....	....	....	1980-81	1982-83
Wong, Mike	Det.	1	22	1	1	2	12	....	....	....	....	....	....	1975-76	1975-76
Wood, Dody	S.J.	5	106	8	10	18	471	....	....	....	....	....	....	1992-93	1997-98
Wood, Randy	NYI, Buf., Tor., Dal.	11	741	175	159	334	603	51	8	9	17	40	....	1986-87	1996-97
Wood, Robert	NYR	1	1	0	0	0	0	....	....	....	....	....	....	1950-51	1950-51
Woodley, Dan	Van.	1	5	2	0	2	17	....	....	....	....	....	....	1987-88	1987-88
Woods, Paul	Det.	7	501	72	124	196	276	7	0	5	5	4	....	1977-78	1983-84
Worrell, Peter	Fla., Col.	7	391	19	27	46	1554	4	1	0	1	8	....	1997-98	2003-04
Wortman, Kevin	Cgy.	1	5	0	0	0	2	....	....	....	....	....	....	1993-94	1993-94
• Woytowich, Bob	Bos., Min., Pit., L.A.	8	503	32	126	158	352	24	1	3	4	20	....	1964-65	1971-72
Wren, Bob	Ana., Tor.	3	5	0	0	0	0	1	0	0	0	0	....	1997-98	2001-02
‡ Wright, Jamie	Dal., Cgy., Phi.	6	124	12	20	32	54	5	0	0	0	0	....	1997-98	2002-03
Wright, John	Van., St.L., K.C.	3	127	16	36	52	67	....	....	....	....	....	....	1972-73	1974-75
Wright, Keith	Phi.	1	1	0	0	0	0	....	....	....	....	....	....	1967-68	1967-68
Wright, Larry	Phi., Cal., Det.	5	106	4	8	12	19	....	....	....	....	....	....	1971-72	1977-78
Wright, Tyler	Edm., Pit., CBJ, Ana.	13	613	79	70	149	854	30	3	2	5	40	....	1992-93	2005-06
• Wycherley, Ralph	NYA, Bro.	2	28	4	7	11	6	....	....	....	....	....	....	1940-41	1941-42
• Wylie, Bill	NYR	1	1	0	0	0	0	....	....	....	....	....	....	1950-51	1950-51
Wylie, Duane	Chi.	2	14	3	3	6	2	....	....	....	....	....	....	1974-75	1976-77
Wyrozub, Randy	Buf.	4	100	8	10	18	10	....	....	....	....	....	....	1970-71	1973-74

Y Z

Name	NHL Teams	NHL Seasons	GP	G	A	TP	PIM	GP	G	A	TP	PIM	NHL Cup Wins	First NHL Season	Last NHL Season
‡ Yablonski, Jeremy	St.L.	1	1	0	0	0	5	....	....	....	....	....	....	2003-04	2003-04
‡ Yachmenev, Vitali	L.A., Nsh.	8	487	83	133	216	88	....	....	....	....	....	....	1995-96	2002-03
• Yackel, Ken	Bos.	1	6	0	0	0	2	2	0	0	0	2	....	1958-59	1958-59
Yake, Terry	Hfd., Ana., Tor., St.L., Wsh.	11	403	77	120	197	220	32	4	4	8	36	....	1988-89	2000-01
Yakushin, Dmitri	Tor.	1	2	0	0	0	2	....	....	....	....	....	....	1999-00	1999-00
Yaremchuk, Gary	Tor.	4	34	1	4	5	28	....	....	....	....	....	....	1981-82	1984-85
Yaremchuk, Ken	Chi., Tor.	6	235	36	56	92	106	31	6	8	14	49	....	1983-84	1988-89
Yates, Ross	Hfd.	1	7	1	1	2	4	....	....	....	....	....	....	1983-84	1983-84
Yawney, Trent	Chi., Cgy., St.L.	12	593	27	102	129	783	60	9	17	26	81	....	1987-88	1998-99
• Yegorov, Alexei	S.J.	2	11	3	3	6	2	....	....	....	....	....	....	1995-96	1996-97
Ylonen, Juha	Phx., T.B., Ott.	6	341	26	76	102	90	15	0	7	7	4	....	1996-97	2001-02
York, Harry	St.L., NYR, Pit., Van.	4	244	29	46	75	99	5	0	0	0	2	....	1996-97	1999-00
• Young, B.J.	Det.	1	1	0	0	0	0	....	....	....	....	....	....	1999-00	1999-00
Young, Brian	Chi.	1	8	0	2	2	6	....	....	....	....	....	....	1980-81	1980-81
Young, C.J.	Cgy., Bos.	1	43	7	7	14	32	....	....	....	....	....	....	1992-93	1992-93
• Young, Doug	Det., Mtl.	10	388	35	45	80	303	28	1	5	6	16	2	1931-32	1940-41
• Young, Howie	Det., Chi., Van.	8	336	12	62	74	851	19	2	4	6	46	....	1960-61	1970-71
Young, Scott	Hfd., Pit., Que., Col., Ana., St.L., Dal.	17	1181	342	415	757	448	141	44	43	87	64	2	1987-88	2005-06
Young, Tim	Min., Wpg., Phi.	10	628	195	341	536	438	36	7	24	31	27	....	1975-76	1984-85
Young, Warren	Min., Pit., Det.	7	236	72	77	149	472	....	....	....	....	....	....	1981-82	1987-88
Younghans, Tom	Min., NYR	6	429	44	41	85	373	24	2	1	3	21	....	1976-77	1981-82
Ysebaert, Paul	N.J., Det., Wpg., Chi., T.B.	11	532	149	187	336	217	30	4	3	7	20	....	1988-89	1998-99
‡ Yushkevich, Dmitry	Phi., Tor., Fla., L.A.	11	786	43	182	225	659	72	4	19	23	52	....	1992-93	2002-03
Yzerman, Steve	Det.	22	1514	692	1063	1755	924	196	70	115	185	84	3	1983-84	2005-06
Zabransky, Libor	St.L.	2	40	1	6	7	50	....	....	....	....	....	....	1996-97	1997-98
Zaharko, Miles	Atl., Chi.	4	129	5	32	37	84	3	0	0	0	0	....	1977-78	1981-82
Zaine, Rod	Pit., Buf.	2	61	10	6	16	25	....	....	....	....	....	....	1970-71	1971-72
Zalapski, Zarley	Pit., Hfd., Cgy., Mtl., Phi.	12	637	99	285	384	684	48	4	23	27	47	....	1987-88	1999-00
‡ Zalesak, Miroslav	S.J.	2	12	1	2	3	0	....	....	....	....	....	....	2002-03	2003-04
Zamuner, Rob	NYR, T.B., Ott., Bos.	13	798	139	172	311	467	34	4	5	9	26	....	1991-92	2003-04
Zanussi, Joe	NYR, Bos., St.L.	3	87	1	13	14	46	4	0	1	1	2	....	1974-75	1976-77
Zanussi, Ron	Min., Tor.	5	299	52	83	135	373	17	0	4	4	17	....	1977-78	1981-82
Zavisha, Brad	Edm.	1	2	0	0	0	0	....	....	....	....	....	....	1993-94	1993-94
Zehr, Jeff	Bos.	1	4	0	0	0	2	....	....	....	....	....	....	1999-00	1999-00
Zeidel, Larry	Det., Chi., Phi.	5	158	3	16	19	198	12	0	1	1	12	1	1951-52	1968-69
Zelepukin, Valeri	N.J., Edm., Phi., Chi.	10	595	117	177	294	527	85	13	13	26	48	1	1991-92	2000-01
Zemlak, Richard	Que., Min., Pit., Cgy.	5	132	2	12	14	587	1	0	0	0	10	....	1986-87	1991-92
• Zeniuk, Ed	Det.	1	2	0	0	0	0	....	....	....	....	....	....	1954-55	1954-55
Zent, Jason	Ott., Phi.	3	27	3	3	6	13	....	....	....	....	....	....	1996-97	1998-99
Zetterstrom, Lars	Van.	1	14	0	1	1	2	....	....	....	....	....	....	1978-79	1978-79
Zettler, Rob	Min., S.J., Phi., Tor., Nsh., Wsh.	14	569	5	65	70	920	14	0	0	0	4	....	1988-89	2001-02
Zezel, Peter	Phi., St.L., Wsh., Tor., Dal., N.J., Van.	15	873	219	389	608	435	131	25	39	64	83	....	1984-85	1998-99
Zhamnov, Alex	Wpg., Chi., Phi., Bos.	13	807	249	470	719	668	35	6	13	19	18	....	1992-93	2005-06
• Zholtok, Sergei	Bos., Ott., Mtl., Edm., Min., Nsh.	10	588	111	147	258	166	45	4	14	18	0	....	1992-93	2003-04
‡ Ziegler, Thomas	T.B.	1	5	0	0	0	0	....	....	....	....	....	....	2000-01	2000-01
Zmolek, Doug	S.J., Dal., L.A., Chi.	8	467	11	53	64	905	14	0	1	1	16	....	1992-93	1999-00
Zoborosky, Marty	Chi.	1	1	0	0	0	2	....	....	....	....	....	....	1944-45	1944-45
Zombo, Rick	Det., St.L., Bos.	12	652	24	130	154	728	60	1	11	12	127	....	1984-85	1995-96
Zuke, Mike	St.L., Hfd.	8	455	86	196	282	220	26	6	6	12	12	....	1978-79	1985-86
• Zunich, Rudy	Det.	1	2	0	0	0	2	....	....	....	....	....	....	1943-44	1943-44

Retired NHL Goaltender Index

Abbreviations: Teams/Cities: – **Ana.** – Anaheim; **Atl.** – Atlanta; **Bos.** – Boston; **Bro.** – Brooklyn; **Buf.** – Buffalo; **Cal.** – California; **Cgy.** – Calgary; **Car.** – Carolina; **Chi.** – Chicago; **Cle.** – Cleveland; **Col.** – Colorado; **CBJ** – Columbus; **Dal.** – Dallas; **Det.** – Detroit; **Edm.** – Edmonton; **Fla.** – Florida; **Ham.** – Hamilton; **Hfd.** – Hartford; **K.C.** – Kansas City; **L.A.** – Los Angeles; **Min.** – Minnesota; **Mtl.** – Montreal; **Mtl.M.** – Montreal Maroons; **Mtl.W.** – Montreal Wanderers; **Nsh.** – Nashville; **N.J.** – New Jersey; **NYA** – NY Americans; **NYI** – NY Islanders; **NYR** – New York Rangers; **Oak.** – Oakland; **Ott.** – Ottawa; **Phi.** – Philadelphia; **Phx.** – Phoenix; **Pit.** – Pittsburgh; **Que.** – Quebec; **St.L.** – St. Louis; **S.J.** – San Jose; **T.B.** – Tampa Bay; **Tor.** – Toronto; **Van.** – Vancouver; **Wpg.** – Winnipeg; **Wsh.** – Washington

Avg. – goals against per 60 minutes played; **GA** – goals agains; **GP** – games played; **Mins** – minutes played; **SO** – shutouts.
• – deceased. § – Forward, defenseman or coach who appeared in goal. For complete career, see Retired Player Index. ‡ – Remains active in other leagues.

NHL Seasons – A player or goaltender who does not play in a regular season but who does appear in that year's playoffs is credited with an NHL Season in this Index. Total seasons are rounded off to the nearest full season.

			Regular Schedule								Playoffs										
Name	NHL Teams	NHL Seasons	GP	W	L	T	Mins	GA	SO	Avg	GP	W	L	T	Mins	GA	SO	Avg	NHL Cup Wins	First NHL Season	Last NHL Season
Abbott, George	Bos.	1	1	0	1	0	60	7	0	7.00	....	....	....	....	....	....	....	....		1943-44	1943-44
Adams, John	Bos., Wsh.	2	22	9	10	1	1180	85	1	4.32	....	....	....	....	....	....	....	....		1972-73	1974-75
Aiken, Don	Mtl.	1	1	0	1	0	34	6	0	10.59	....	....	....	....	....	....	....	....		1957-58	1957-58
• Aitkenhead, Andy	NYR	3	106	47	43	16	6570	257	11	2.35	10	6	2	2	608	15	3	1.48	1	1932-33	1934-35
• Almas, Red	Det., Chi.	3	3	0	2	1	180	13	0	4.33	5	1	3	....	263	13	0	2.97		1946-47	1952-53
• Anderson, Lorne	NYR	1	3	1	2	0	180	18	0	6.00	....	....	....	....	....	....	....	....		1951-52	1951-52
‡ Askey, Tom	Ana.	2	7	0	1	2	273	12	0	2.64	1	0	1	....	30	2	0	4.00		1997-98	1998-99
Astrom, Hardy	NYR, Col.	3	83	17	44	12	4456	278	0	3.74	....	....	....	....	....	....	....	....		1977-78	1980-81
Bach, Ryan	L.A.	1	3	0	3	0	108	8	0	4.44	....	....	....	....	....	....	....	....		1998-99	1998-99
Bailey, Scott	Bos.	2	19	6	6	2	965	55	0	3.42	....	....	....	....	....	....	....	....		1995-96	1996-97
Baker, Steve	NYR	4	57	20	20	11	3081	190	3	3.70	14	7	7	....	826	55	0	4.00		1979-80	1982-83
Bales, Mike	Bos., Ott.	4	23	2	15	1	1120	77	0	4.13	....	....	....	....	....	....	....	....		1992-93	1996-97
Bannerman, Murray	Van., Chi.	8	289	116	125	33	16470	1051	8	3.83	40	20	18	....	2322	165	0	4.26		1977-78	1986-87
Baron, Marco	Bos., L.A., Edm.	6	86	34	38	9	4822	292	1	3.63	1	0	1	....	20	3	0	9.00		1979-80	1984-85
Barrasso, Tom	Buf., Pit., Ott., Car., Tor., St.L.	19	777	369	277	86	44180	2385	38	3.24	119	61	54	....	6953	349	6	3.01	2	1983-84	2002-03
Bassen, Hank	Chi., Det., Pit.	9	156	46	66	31	8759	434	5	2.97	5	1	3	....	274	11	0	2.41		1954-55	1967-68
• Bastien, Baz	Tor.	1	5	0	4	1	300	20	0	4.00	....	....	....	....	....	....	....	....		1945-46	1945-46
• Bauman, Garry	Mtl., Min.	3	35	5	16	6	1719	102	0	3.56	....	....	....	....	....	....	....	....		1966-67	1968-69
Beaupre, Don	Min., Wsh., Ott., Tor.	17	667	268	277	75	37396	2151	17	3.45	72	33	31	....	3943	220	3	3.35		1980-81	1996-97
Beauregard, Stephane	Wpg., Phi.	5	90	19	39	11	4402	268	2	3.65	4	1	3	....	238	12	0	3.03		1989-90	1993-94
Bedard, Jim	Wsh.	2	73	17	40	13	4232	278	1	3.94	....	....	....	....	....	....	....	....		1977-78	1978-79
Behrend, Marc	Wpg.	3	39	12	19	3	1991	160	1	4.82	7	1	3	....	312	19	0	3.65		1983-84	1985-86
Belanger, Yves	St.L., Atl., Bos.	6	78	29	33	6	4134	259	2	3.76	....	....	....	....	....	....	....	....		1974-75	1979-80
Belhumeur, Michel	Phi., Wsh.	3	65	9	36	7	3306	254	0	4.61	1	0	0	....	10	1	0	6.00		1972-73	1975-76
• Bell, Gordie	Tor., NYR	2	8	3	5	0	480	31	0	3.88	2	1	1	....	120	9	0	4.50		1945-46	1955-56
• Benedict, Clint	Ott., Mtl.M.	13	362	190	143	28	22367	863	58	2.32	28	11	12	5	1707	53	9	1.86	4	1917-18	1929-30
Bennett, Harvey	Bos.	1	25	10	12	2	1470	103	0	4.20	....	....	....	....	....	....	....	....		1944-45	1944-45
Bergeron, Jean-Claude	Mtl., T.B., L.A.	6	72	21	33	7	3772	232	1	3.69	....	....	....	....	....	....	....	....		1990-91	1996-97
Bernhardt, Tim	Cgy., Tor.	4	67	17	36	7	3748	267	0	4.27	....	....	....	....	....	....	....	....		1982-83	1986-87
Berthiaume, Daniel	Wpg., Min., L.A., Bos., Ott.	9	215	81	90	21	11662	714	5	3.67	14	5	9	....	807	50	0	3.72		1985-86	1993-94
Bester, Allan	Tor., Det., Dal.	10	219	73	99	17	11773	786	7	4.01	11	2	6	....	508	37	0	4.37		1983-84	1995-96
• Beveridge, Bill	Det., Ott., St.L., Mtl.M., NYR	9	297	87	166	42	18375	879	18	2.87	5	2	3	....	300	11	0	2.20		1929-30	1942-43
• Bibeault, Paul	Mtl., Tor., Bos., Chi.	7	214	81	107	25	12890	785	10	3.65	20	6	14	....	1237	71	2	3.44		1940-41	1946-47
Bierk, Zac	T.B., Min., Phx.	6	47	9	20	5	2135	113	1	3.18	....	....	....	....	....	....	....	....		1997-98	2003-04
Billington, Craig	N.J., Ott., Bos., Col., Wsh.	15	332	110	149	31	17097	1034	9	3.63	8	0	2	....	213	15	0	4.23		1985-86	2002-03
Binette, Andre	Mtl.	1	1	1	0	0	60	4	0	4.00	....	....	....	....	....	....	....	....		1954-55	1954-55
Binkley, Les	Pit.	5	196	58	94	34	11046	575	11	3.12	7	5	2	....	428	15	0	2.10		1967-68	1971-72
• Bittner, Richard	Bos.	1	1	0	0	1	60	3	0	3.00	....	....	....	....	....	....	....	....		1949-50	1949-50
Blackburn, Dan	NYR	2	63	20	32	4	3499	188	1	3.22	....	....	....	....	....	....	....	....		2001-02	2002-03
Blake, Mike	L.A.	3	40	13	15	5	2117	150	0	4.25	....	....	....	....	....	....	....	....		1981-82	1983-84
Blue, John	Bos., Buf.	3	46	16	18	7	2521	126	1	3.00	2	0	1	....	96	5	0	3.13		1992-93	1995-96
Boisvert, Gilles	Det.	1	3	0	3	0	180	9	0	3.00	....	....	....	....	....	....	....	....		1959-60	1959-60
Bouchard, Dan	Atl., Cgy., Que., Wpg.	14	655	286	232	113	37919	2061	27	3.26	43	13	30	....	2549	147	1	3.46		1972-73	1985-86
• Bourque, Claude	Mtl., Det.	2	62	16	38	8	3830	193	4	3.02	3	1	2	....	188	8	1	2.55		1938-39	1939-40
Boutin, Rollie	Wsh.	3	22	7	10	1	1137	75	0	3.96	....	....	....	....	....	....	....	....		1978-79	1980-81
• Bouvrette, Lionel	NYR	1	1	0	1	0	60	6	0	6.00	....	....	....	....	....	....	....	....		1942-43	1942-43
Bower, Johnny	NYR, Tor.	15	552	250	195	90	32016	1340	37	2.51	74	35	34	....	4378	180	5	2.47	4	1953-54	1969-70
§ • Branigan, Andy	NYA	1	1	0	0	0	7	0	0	0.00	....	....	....	....	....	....	....	....		1940-41	1940-41
• Brimsek, Frank	Bos., Chi.	10	514	252	182	80	31210	1404	40	2.70	68	32	36	....	4395	186	2	2.54	2	1938-39	1949-50
Brochu, Martin	Wsh., Van., Pit.	3	9	0	5	0	369	22	0	3.58	....	....	....	....	....	....	....	....		1998-99	2003-04
• Broda, Turk	Tor.	14	629	302	224	101	38167	1609	62	2.53	101	60	39	....	6389	211	13	1.98	5	1936-37	1951-52
Broderick, Ken	Min., Bos.	3	27	11	12	1	1464	74	1	3.03	....	....	....	....	....	....	....	....		1969-70	1974-75
Broderick, Len	Mtl.	1	1	1	0	0	60	2	0	2.00	....	....	....	....	....	....	....	....		1957-58	1957-58
Brodeur, Richard	NYI, Van., Hfd.	9	385	131	175	62	21968	1410	6	3.85	33	13	20	....	2009	111	1	3.32		1979-80	1987-88
Bromley, Gary	Buf., Van.	6	136	54	44	28	7427	425	7	3.43	7	2	5	....	360	25	0	4.17		1973-74	1980-81
• Brooks, Art	Tor.	1	4	2	2	0	220	23	0	6.27	....	....	....	....	....	....	....	....		1917-18	1917-18
Brooks, Ross	Bos.	3	54	37	7	6	3047	134	4	2.64	1	0	0	....	20	3	0	9.00		1972-73	1974-75
• Brophy, Frank	Que.	1	21	3	18	0	1249	148	0	7.11	....	....	....	....	....	....	....	....		1919-20	1919-20
Brown, Andy	Det., Pit.	3	62	22	26	9	3373	213	1	3.79	....	....	....	....	....	....	....	....		1971-72	1973-74
Brown, Ken	Chi.	1	1	0	0	0	18	1	0	3.33	....	....	....	....	....	....	....	....		1970-71	1970-71
Brunetta, Mario	Que.	3	40	12	17	1	1967	128	0	3.90	....	....	....	....	....	....	....	....		1987-88	1989-90
Bullock, Bruce	Van.	3	16	3	9	3	927	74	0	4.79	....	....	....	....	....	....	....	....		1972-73	1976-77
• Buzinski, Steve	NYR	1	9	2	6	1	560	55	0	5.89	....	....	....	....	....	....	....	....		1942-43	1942-43
Caley, Don	St.L.	1	1	0	0	0	30	3	0	6.00	....	....	....	....	....	....	....	....		1967-68	1967-68
Caprice, Frank	Van.	6	102	31	46	11	5589	391	1	4.20	....	....	....	....	....	....	....	....		1982-83	1987-88
Carey, Jim	Wsh., Bos., St.L.	5	172	79	65	16	9668	416	16	2.58	10	2	5	....	455	35	0	4.62		1994-95	1998-99
Caron, Jacques	L.A., St.L., Van.	5	72	24	29	11	3846	211	2	3.29	12	4	7	....	639	34	0	3.19		1967-68	1973-74
Carter, Lyle	Cal.	1	15	4	7	0	721	50	0	4.16	....	....	....	....	....	....	....	....		1971-72	1971-72
Casey, Jon	Min., Bos., St.L.	12	425	170	157	55	23255	1246	16	3.21	66	32	31	....	3743	192	3	3.08		1983-84	1996-97
‡ Cechmanek, Roman	Phi., L.A.	4	212	110	64	28	12085	419	25	2.08	23	9	14	....	1441	56	3	2.33		2000-01	2003-04
‡ Centomo, Sebastien	Tor.	1	1	0	0	0	40	3	0	4.50	....	....	....	....	....	....	....	....		2001-02	2001-02
Chabot, Frederic	Mtl., Phi., L.A.	5	32	4	8	4	1262	62	0	2.95	....	....	....	....	....	....	....	....		1990-91	1998-99
• Chabot, Lorne	NYR, Tor., Mtl., Chi., Mtl.M., NYA	11	411	201	148	62	25307	860	72	2.04	37	13	17	6	2498	64	5	1.54	2	1926-27	1936-37
Chadwick, Ed	Tor., Bos.	6	184	57	92	35	11040	541	14	2.94	....	....	....	....	....	....	....	....		1955-56	1961-62
Champoux, Bob	Det., Cal.	2	17	2	11	3	923	80	0	5.20	1	1	0	....	55	4	0	4.36		1963-64	1973-74
‡ Charpentier, Sebastien	Wsh.	3	26	6	14	1	1350	66	0	2.93	....	....	....	....	....	....	....	....		2001-02	2003-04
Cheevers, Gerry	Tor., Bos.	13	418	230	102	74	24394	1174	26	2.89	88	53	34	....	5396	242	8	2.69	2	1961-62	1979-80
Cheveldae, Tim	Det., Wpg., Bos.	9	340	149	136	37	19172	1116	10	3.49	25	9	15	....	1418	71	2	3.00		1988-89	1996-97
Chevrier, Alain	N.J., Wpg., Chi., Pit., Det.	6	234	91	100	14	12202	845	2	4.16	16	9	7	....	1013	44	0	2.61		1985-86	1990-91
‡ Chiodo, Andy	Pit.	1	8	3	4	1	486	28	0	3.46	....	....	....	....	....	....	....	....		2003-04	2003-04
Chouinard, Mathieu	L.A.	1	1	0	0	0	3	0	0	0.00	....	....	....	....	....	....	....	....		2003-04	2003-04
§ • Clancy, King	Ott., Tor.	2	2	0	0	0	3	1	0	20.00	....	....	....	....	....	....	....	....		1924-25	1931-32
§ • Cleghorn, Odie	Pit.	1	1	1	0	0	60	2	0	2.00	....	....	....	....	....	....	....	....		1925-26	1925-26
§ • Cleghorn, Sprague	Ott., Mtl.	2	2	0	0	0	5	0	0	0.00	....	....	....	....	....	....	....	....		1918-19	1921-22
Clifford, Chris	Chi.	2	2	0	0	0	24	0	0	0.00	....	....	....	....	....	....	....	....		1984-85	1988-89
Cloutier, Jacques	Buf., Chi., Que.	12	255	82	102	24	12826	778	3	3.64	8	1	5	....	413	18	1	2.62		1981-82	1993-94
Colvin, Les	Bos.	1	1	0	1	0	60	4	0	4.00	....	....	....	....	....	....	....	....		1948-49	1948-49
§ • Conacher, Charlie	Tor., Det.	3	4	0	0	0	10	0	0	0.00	....	....	....	....	....	....	....	....		1932-33	1938-39
• Connell, Alec	Ott., Det., NYA, Mtl.M.	12	417	193	156	67	26050	830	81	1.91	21	8	5	8	1309	26	4	1.19	2	1924-25	1936-37
Corsi, Jim	Edm.	1	26	8	14	3	1366	83	0	3.65	....	....	....	....	....	....	....	....		1979-80	1979-80
• Courteau, Maurice	Bos.	1	6	2	4	0	360	33	0	5.50	....	....	....	....	....	....	....	....		1943-44	1943-44
Cousineau, Marcel	Tor., NYI, L.A.	4	26	4	10	1	1047	51	1	2.92	....	....	....	....	....	....	....	....		1996-97	1999-00
Cowley, Wayne	Edm.	1	1	0	1	0	57	3	0	3.16	....	....	....	....	....	....	....	....		1993-94	1993-94
• Cox, Abbie	Mtl.M., NYA, Det., Mtl.	3	5	1	1	2	263	11	0	2.51	....	....	....	....	....	....	....	....		1929-30	1935-36
Craig, Jim	Atl., Bos., Min.	3	30	11	10	7	1588	100	0	3.78	....	....	....	....	....	....	....	....		1979-80	1983-84

Name	NHL Teams	NHL Seasons	Regular Schedule GP	W	L	T	Mins	GA	SO	Avg	Playoffs GP	W	L	T	Mins	GA	SO	Avg	NHL Cup Wins	First NHL Season	Last NHL Season
Crha, Jiri	Tor.	2	69	28	27	11	3942	261	0	3.97	5	0	4	....	186	21	0	6.77		1979-80	1980-81
• Crozier, Roger	Det., Buf., Wsh.	14	518	206	197	70	28567	1446	30	3.04	32	14	16	....	1789	82	1	2.75		1963-64	1976-77
• Cude, Wilf	Phi., Bos., Chi., Mtl., Det.	10	282	100	132	49	17586	798	24	2.72	19	7	11	1	1257	51	1	2.43		1930-31	1940-41
Cutts, Don	Edm.	1	6	1	2	1	269	16	0	3.57	....	....	....	....	....	....	....	....		1979-80	1979-80
• Cyr, Claude	Mtl.	1	1	0	0	0	20	1	0	3.00	....	....	....	....	....	....	....	....		1958-59	1958-59
Dadswell, Doug	Cgy.	2	27	8	8	3	1346	99	0	4.41	....	....	....	....	....	....	....	....		1986-87	1987-88
Dafoe, Byron	Wsh., L.A., Bos., Atl.	12	415	171	170	56	23478	1051	26	2.69	27	10	16	....	1686	65	3	2.31		1992-93	2003-04
D'Alessio, Corrie	Hfd.	1	1	0	0	0	11	0	0	0.00	....	....	....	....	....	....	....	....		1992-93	1992-93
Daley, Joe	Pit., Buf., Det.	4	105	34	44	19	5836	326	3	3.35	....	....	....	....	....	....	....	....		1968-69	1971-72
Damore, Nick	Bos.	1	1	1	0	0	60	3	0	3.00	....	....	....	....	....	....	....	....		1941-42	1941-42
D'Amour, Marc	Cgy., Phi.	2	16	2	4	2	579	32	0	3.32	....	....	....	....	....	....	....	....		1985-86	1988-89
Damphousse, Jean-Fr.	N.J.	1	6	1	3	0	294	12	0	2.45	....	....	....	....	....	....	....	....		2001-02	2001-02
§ • Darragh, Jack	Ott.	1	1	0	0	0	2	0	0	0.00	....	....	....	....	....	....	....	....		1919-20	1919-20
Daskalakis, Cleon	Bos.	3	12	3	4	1	506	41	0	4.86	....	....	....	....	....	....	....	....		1984-85	1986-87
Davidson, John	St.L., NYR	10	301	123	124	39	17109	1004	7	3.52	31	16	14	....	1862	77	1	2.48		1973-74	1982-83
Decourcy, Bob	NYR	1	1	0	1	0	29	6	0	12.41	....	....	....	....	....	....	....	....		1947-48	1947-48
Defelice, Norm	Bos.	1	10	3	5	2	600	30	0	3.00	....	....	....	....	....	....	....	....		1956-57	1956-57
DeJordy, Denis	Chi., L.A., Mtl., Det.	12	316	124	128	51	17798	929	15	3.13	18	6	9	....	946	55	0	3.49	1	1960-61	1973-74
DelGuidice, Matt	Bos.	2	11	2	5	1	434	28	0	3.87	....	....	....	....	....	....	....	....		1990-91	1991-92
DeRouville, Philippe	Pit.	2	3	1	2	0	171	9	0	3.16	....	....	....	....	....	....	....	....		1994-95	1996-97
Desjardins, Gerry	L.A., Chi., NYI, Buf.	10	331	122	153	44	19014	1042	12	3.29	35	15	15	....	1874	108	0	3.46		1968-69	1977-78
DesRochers, Patrick	Phx., Car.	2	11	2	6	1	540	33	0	3.67	....	....	....	....	....	....	....	....		2001-02	2002-03
• Dickie, Bill	Chi.	1	1	1	0	0	60	3	0	3.00	....	....	....	....	....	....	....	....		1941-42	1941-42
Dion, Connie	Det.	2	38	23	11	4	2280	119	1	3.13	5	1	4	....	300	17	0	3.40		1943-44	1944-45
Dion, Michel	Que., Wpg., Pit.	6	227	60	118	32	12695	898	2	4.24	5	2	3	....	304	22	0	4.34		1979-80	1984-85
• Dolson, Dolly	Det.	3	93	35	41	17	5820	192	16	1.98	2	0	2	0	120	7	0	3.50		1928-29	1930-31
Dopson, Rob	Pit.	1	2	0	0	0	45	3	0	4.00	....	....	....	....	....	....	....	....		1993-94	1993-94
Dowie, Bruce	Tor.	1	2	0	1	0	72	4	0	3.33	....	....	....	....	....	....	....	....		1983-84	1983-84
Draper, Tom	Wpg., Buf., NYI	6	53	19	23	5	2807	173	1	3.70	7	3	4	....	433	19	1	2.63		1988-89	1995-96
Dryden, Dave	NYR, Chi., Buf., Edm.	9	203	66	76	31	10424	555	9	3.19	3	0	2	....	133	9	0	4.06		1961-62	1979-80
Dryden, Ken	Mtl.	8	397	258	57	74	23352	870	46	2.24	112	80	32	....	6846	274	10	2.40	6	1970-71	1978-79
Duffus, Parris	Phx.	1	1	0	0	0	29	1	0	2.07	....	....	....	....	....	....	....	....		1996-97	1996-97
Dumas, Michel	Chi.	3	8	2	1	2	362	24	0	3.98	1	0	0	....	19	1	0	3.16		1974-75	1976-77
Dupuis, Bob	Edm.	1	1	0	1	0	60	4	0	4.00	....	....	....	....	....	....	....	....		1979-80	1979-80
• Durnan, Bill	Mtl.	7	383	208	112	62	22945	901	34	2.36	45	27	18	....	2871	99	2	2.07	2	1943-44	1949-50
Dyck, Ed	Van.	3	49	8	28	5	2453	178	1	4.35	....	....	....	....	....	....	....	....		1971-72	1973-74
Edwards, Don	Buf., Cgy., Tor.	10	459	208	155	74	26181	1449	16	3.32	42	16	21	....	2302	132	1	3.44		1976-77	1985-86
Edwards, Gary	St.L., L.A., Cle., Min., Edm., Pit.	13	286	88	125	51	16002	973	10	3.65	11	5	4	....	537	34	0	3.80		1968-69	1981-82
Edwards, Marv	Pit., Tor., Cal.	4	61	15	34	7	3467	218	2	3.77	....	....	....	....	....	....	....	....		1968-69	1973-74
• Edwards, Roy	Det., Pit.	7	236	97	88	38	13109	637	12	2.92	4	0	3	....	206	11	0	3.20		1967-68	1973-74
Eklund, Brian	T.B.	1	1	0	1	0	58	3	0	3.10	....	....	....	....	....	....	....	....		2005-06	2005-06
Eliot, Darren	L.A., Det., Buf.	5	89	25	41	12	4931	377	1	4.59	1	0	0	....	40	7	0	10.50		1984-85	1988-89
Ellacott, Ken	Van.	1	12	2	3	4	555	41	0	4.43	....	....	....	....	....	....	....	....		1982-83	1982-83
Erickson, Chad	N.J.	1	2	1	1	0	120	9	0	4.50	....	....	....	....	....	....	....	....		1991-92	1991-92
Esposito, Tony	Mtl., Chi.	16	886	423	306	151	52585	2563	76	2.92	99	45	53	....	6017	308	6	3.07	1	1968-69	1983-84
Essensa, Bob	Wpg., Det., Edm., Phx., Van., Buf.	12	446	173	176	47	24215	1270	18	3.15	16	4	9	....	864	51	0	3.54		1988-89	2001-02
• Evans, Claude	Mtl., Bos.	2	5	1	2	1	260	16	0	3.69	....	....	....	....	....	....	....	....		1954-55	1957-58
Exelby, Randy	Mtl., Edm.	2	2	0	1	0	63	5	0	4.76	....	....	....	....	....	....	....	....		1988-89	1989-90
Fankhouser, Scott	Atl.	2	23	4	12	2	1180	65	0	3.31	....	....	....	....	....	....	....	....		1999-00	2000-01
Farr, Rocky	Buf.	3	19	2	6	3	722	42	0	3.49	....	....	....	....	....	....	....	....		1972-73	1974-75
Favell, Doug	Phi., Tor., Col.	12	373	123	153	69	20771	1096	18	3.17	21	6	15	....	1270	66	1	3.12		1967-68	1978-79
Fichaud, Eric	NYI, Nsh., Car., Mtl.	6	95	22	47	10	4799	251	2	3.14	....	....	....	....	....	....	....	....		1995-96	2000-01
Fiset, Stephane	Que., Col., L.A., Mtl.	13	390	164	153	44	21785	1114	16	3.07	14	1	7	....	563	37	0	3.94	1	1989-90	2001-02
Fitzpatrick, Mark	L.A., NYI, Fla., T.B., Chi., Car.	12	329	113	136	49	18329	953	8	3.12	9	0	3	....	289	23	0	4.78		1988-89	1999-00
• Forbes, Jake	Tor., Ham., NYA, Phi.	13	210	85	114	11	12922	594	19	2.76	2	0	2	0	120	7	0	3.50		1919-20	1932-33
Ford, Brian	Que., Pit.	2	11	3	7	0	580	61	0	6.31	....	....	....	....	....	....	....	....		1983-84	1984-85
Foster, Norm	Bos., Edm.	2	13	7	4	0	623	34	0	3.27	....	....	....	....	....	....	....	....		1990-91	1991-92
Fountain, Mike	Van., Car., Ott.	4	11	2	6	0	483	28	1	3.48	....	....	....	....	....	....	....	....		1996-97	2000-01
• Fowler, Hec	Bos.	1	7	1	6	0	409	42	0	6.16	....	....	....	....	....	....	....	....		1924-25	1924-25
Francis, Emile	Chi., NYR	6	95	31	52	11	5660	355	1	3.76	....	....	....	....	....	....	....	....		1946-47	1951-52
• Franks, Jimmy	Det., NYR, Bos.	4	42	12	23	7	2520	181	1	4.31	1	0	1	....	30	2	0	4.00		1936-37	1943-44
Frederick, Ray	Chi.	1	5	0	4	1	300	22	0	4.40	....	....	....	....	....	....	....	....		1954-55	1954-55
Friesen, Karl	N.J.	1	4	0	2	1	130	16	0	7.38	....	....	....	....	....	....	....	....		1986-87	1986-87
Froese, Bob	Phi., NYR	8	242	128	72	20	13451	694	13	3.10	18	3	9	....	830	55	0	3.98		1982-83	1989-90
Fuhr, Grant	Edm., Tor., Buf., L.A., St.L., Cgy.	19	868	403	295	114	48945	2756	25	3.38	150	92	50	....	8834	430	6	2.92	5	1981-82	1999-00
‡ Gage, Joaquin	Edm.	3	23	4	12	1	1076	67	0	3.74	....	....	....	....	....	....	....	....		1994-95	2000-01
Gagnon, David	Det.	1	2	0	1	0	35	6	0	10.29	....	....	....	....	....	....	....	....		1990-91	1990-91
• Gamble, Bruce	NYR, Bos., Tor., Phi.	10	327	110	150	46	18442	988	22	3.21	5	0	4	....	206	25	0	7.28	1	1958-59	1971-72
Gamble, Troy	Van.	4	72	22	29	9	3804	229	1	3.61	4	1	3	....	249	16	0	3.86		1986-87	1991-92
• Gardiner, Bert	NYR, Mtl., Chi., Bos.	6	144	49	68	27	8760	554	4	3.79	9	4	5	....	647	20	0	1.85		1935-36	1943-44
• Gardiner, Charlie	Chi.	7	316	112	152	52	19687	664	42	2.02	21	12	6	3	1472	35	5	1.43	1	1927-28	1933-34
• Gardner, George	Det., Van.	5	66	16	30	6	3313	207	0	3.75	....	....	....	....	....	....	....	....		1965-66	1971-72
Garner, Tyrone	Cgy.	1	3	0	2	0	139	12	0	5.18	....	....	....	....	....	....	....	....		1998-99	1998-99
Garrett, John	Hfd., Que., Van.	6	207	68	91	37	11763	837	1	4.27	9	4	3	....	461	33	0	4.30		1979-80	1984-85
Gatherum, Dave	Det.	1	3	2	0	1	180	3	1	1.00	....	....	....	....	....	....	....	....	1	1953-54	1953-54
Gauthier, Paul	Mtl.	1	1	0	0	1	70	2	0	1.71	....	....	....	....	....	....	....	....		1937-38	1937-38
Gauthier, Sean	S.J.	1	1	0	0	0	3	0	0	0.00	....	....	....	....	....	....	....	....		1998-99	1998-99
• Gelineau, Jack	Bos., Chi.	4	143	46	64	33	8580	447	7	3.13	4	1	2	....	260	7	1	1.62		1948-49	1953-54
Giacomin, Ed	NYR, Det.	13	609	289	209	96	35633	1672	54	2.82	65	29	35	....	3838	180	1	2.81		1965-66	1977-78
Gilbert, Gilles	Min., Bos., Det.	14	416	192	143	60	23677	1290	18	3.27	32	17	15	....	1919	97	3	3.03		1969-70	1982-83
Gill, Andre	Bos.	1	5	3	2	0	270	13	1	2.89	....	....	....	....	....	....	....	....		1967-68	1967-68
• Goodman, Paul	Chi.	3	52	23	20	9	3240	117	6	2.17	3	0	3	....	187	10	0	3.21	1	1937-38	1940-41
Gordon, Scott	Que.	2	23	2	16	0	1082	101	0	5.60	....	....	....	....	....	....	....	....		1989-90	1990-91
Gosselin, Mario	Que., L.A., Hfd.	9	241	91	107	14	12857	801	6	3.74	32	16	15	....	1816	99	0	3.27		1983-84	1993-94
Goverde, David	L.A.	3	5	1	4	0	278	29	0	6.26	....	....	....	....	....	....	....	....		1991-92	1993-94
Grahame, Ron	Bos., L.A., Que.	4	114	50	43	15	6472	409	5	3.79	4	2	1	....	202	7	0	2.08		1977-78	1980-81
• Grant, Benny	Tor., NYA, Bos.	6	50	17	26	4	2990	187	4	3.75	....	....	....	....	....	....	....	....		1928-29	1943-44
Grant, Doug	Det., St.L.	7	77	27	34	8	4199	280	2	4.00	....	....	....	....	....	....	....	....		1973-74	1979-80
Gratton, Gilles	St.L., NYR	2	47	13	18	9	2299	154	0	4.02	....	....	....	....	....	....	....	....		1975-76	1976-77
Gray, Gerry	Det., NYI	2	8	1	5	1	440	35	0	4.77	....	....	....	....	....	....	....	....		1970-71	1972-73
Gray, Harrison	Det.	1	1	0	1	0	40	5	0	7.50	....	....	....	....	....	....	....	....		1963-64	1963-64
Greenlay, Mike	Edm.	1	2	0	0	0	20	4	0	12.00	....	....	....	....	....	....	....	....		1989-90	1989-90
Guenette, Steve	Pit., Cgy.	5	35	19	16	0	1958	122	1	3.74	....	....	....	....	....	....	....	....		1986-87	1990-91
Hackett, Jeff	NYI, S.J., Chi., Mtl., Bos., Phi.	15	500	166	244	56	28125	1361	26	2.90	12	3	7	....	610	36	0	3.54		1988-89	2003-04
• Hainsworth, George	Mtl., Tor.	11	465	246	145	74	29087	937	94	1.93	52	22	25	5	3486	112	8	1.93	2	1926-27	1936-37
Hall, Glenn	Det., Chi., St.L.	19	906	407	326	163	53484	2222	84	2.49	115	49	65	....	6899	320	6	2.78	2	1951-52	1970-71
Hamel, Pierre	Tor., Wpg.	4	69	13	41	7	3766	276	0	4.40	....	....	....	....	....	....	....	....		1974-75	1980-81
Hanlon, Glen	Van., St.L., NYR, Det.	15	477	167	202	61	26037	1561	13	3.60	35	11	15	....	1756	92	4	3.14		1977-78	1990-91
Harrison, Paul	Min., Tor., Pit., Buf.	7	109	28	59	9	5806	408	2	4.22	4	0	1	....	157	9	0	3.44		1975-76	1981-82
Hayward, Brian	Wpg., Mtl., Min., S.J.	11	357	143	156	37	20025	1242	8	3.72	37	11	18	....	1803	104	0	3.46		1982-83	1992-93
Head, Don	Bos.	1	38	9	26	3	2280	158	2	4.16	....	....	....	....	....	....	....	....		1961-62	1961-62
Healy, Glenn	L.A., NYI, NYR, Tor.	15	437	166	190	47	24256	1361	13	3.37	37	13	15	....	1930	108	0	3.36	1	1985-86	2000-01
Hebert, Guy	St.L., Ana., NYR	10	491	191	222	56	27889	1307	28	2.81	14	4	7	....	744	33	1	2.66		1991-92	2000-01
• Hebert, Sammy	Tor., Ott.	2	4	2	1	0	200	19	0	5.70	....	....	....	....	....	....	....	....	1	1917-18	1923-24
Heinz, Rick	St.L., Van.	5	49	14	19	5	2356	159	2	4.05	1	0	0	....	8	1	0	7.50		1980-81	1984-85
Henderson, John	Bos.	2	46	15	15	15	2688	113	5	2.52	2	0	2	....	120	8	0	4.00		1954-55	1955-56
• Henry, Gord	Bos.	4	3	1	2	0	180	5	1	1.67	5	0	4	....	283	21	0	4.45		1948-49	1952-53
• Henry, Jim	NYR, Chi., Bos.	9	406	161	173	70	24355	1166	27	2.87	29	11	18	....	1741	81	2	2.79		1941-42	1954-55
Herron, Denis	Pit., K.C., Mtl.	14	462	146	203	76	25608	1579	10	3.70	15	5	10	....	901	50	0	3.33		1972-73	1985-86

Name	NHL Teams	NHL Seasons	GP	W	L	T	Mins	GA	SO	Avg	GP	W	L	T	Mins	GA	SO	Avg	NHL Cup Wins	First NHL Season	Last NHL Season
			Regular Schedule								Playoffs										
Hextall, Ron	Phi., Que., NYI	13	608	296	214	69	34750	1723	23	2.97	93	47	43	....	5456	276	2	3.04		1986-87	1998-99
• Highton, Hec	Chi.	1	24	10	14	0	1440	108	0	4.50	....	....	....	....	....	....	....	....		1943-44	1943-44
§ • Himes, Normie	NYA	2	2	0	1	0	79	3	0	2.28	....	....	....	....	....	....	....	....		1927-28	1928-29
Hirsch, Corey	NYR, Van., Wsh., Dal.	7	108	34	45	14	5775	301	4	3.13	6	2	3	....	338	21	0	3.73		1992-93	2002-03
Hodge, Charlie	Mtl., Oak., Van.	14	358	150	125	61	20573	925	24	2.70	16	7	8	....	804	32	2	2.39	5	1954-55	1970-71
Hodson, Kevin	Det., T.B.	6	71	17	18	10	2910	134	4	2.76	1	0	0	....	1	0	0	0.00	2	1995-96	2002-03
Hoffort, Bruce	Phi.	2	9	4	0	3	368	22	0	3.59	....	....	....	....	....	....	....	....		1989-90	1990-91
Hoganson, Paul	Pit.	1	2	0	1	0	57	7	0	7.37	....	....	....	....	....	....	....	....		1970-71	1970-71
Hogosta, Goran	NYI, Que.	2	22	5	12	3	1208	83	1	4.12	....	....	....	....	....	....	....	....		1977-78	1979-80
Holden, Mark	Mtl., Wpg.	4	8	2	2	1	372	25	0	4.03	....	....	....	....	....	....	....	....		1981-82	1984-85
Holland, Ken	Hfd., Det.	2	4	0	2	1	206	17	0	4.95	....	....	....	....	....	....	....	....		1980-81	1983-84
Holland, Rob	Pit.	2	44	11	22	9	2513	171	1	4.08	....	....	....	....	....	....	....	....		1979-80	1980-81
• Holmes, Hap	Tor., Det.	4	103	39	54	10	6510	264	17	2.43	2	1	1	0	120	7	0	3.50	1	1917-18	1927-28
§ • Horner, Red	Tor.	1	1	0	0	0	1	1	0	60.00	....	....	....	....	....	....	....	....		1931-32	1931-32
Hrivnak, Jim	Wsh., Wpg., St.L.	5	85	34	30	3	4217	262	0	3.73	....	....	....	....	....	....	....	....		1989-90	1993-94
Hrudey, Kelly	NYI, L.A., S.J.	15	677	271	265	88	38084	2174	17	3.43	85	36	46	....	5163	283	0	3.29		1983-84	1997-98
‡ Hurme, Jani	Ott., Fla.	4	76	29	25	11	4041	176	6	2.61	....	....	....	....	....	....	....	....		1999-00	2002-03
Ing, Peter	Tor., Edm., Det.	4	74	20	37	9	3941	266	1	4.05	....	....	....	....	....	....	....	....		1989-90	1993-94
Inness, Gary	Pit., Phi., Wsh.	7	162	58	61	27	8710	494	2	3.40	9	5	4	....	540	24	0	2.67		1973-74	1980-81
‡ Irbe, Arturs	S.J., Dal., Van., Car.	13	568	218	236	79	32066	1513	33	2.83	51	23	27	....	2981	142	1	2.86		1991-92	2003-04
Ireland, Randy	Buf.	1	2	0	0	0	30	3	0	6.00	....	....	....	....	....	....	....	....		1978-79	1978-79
Irons, Robbie	St.L.	1	1	0	0	0	3	0	0	0.00	....	....	....	....	....	....	....	....		1968-69	1968-69
• Ironstone, Joe	Ott., NYA, Tor.	3	2	0	0	1	110	3	1	1.64	....	....	....	....	....	....	....	....		1924-25	1927-28
Jablonski, Pat	St.L., T.B., Mtl., Phx., Car.	8	128	28	62	18	6634	413	1	3.74	4	0	0	....	139	6	0	2.59		1989-90	1997-98
Jackson, Doug	Chi.	1	6	2	3	1	360	42	0	7.00	....	....	....	....	....	....	....	....		1947-48	1947-48
Jackson, Percy	Bos., NYA, NYR	4	7	1	3	1	392	26	0	3.98	....	....	....	....	....	....	....	....		1931-32	1935-36
Jaks, Pauli	L.A.	1	1	0	0	0	40	2	0	3.00	....	....	....	....	....	....	....	....		1994-95	1994-95
Janaszak, Steve	Min., Col.	2	3	0	1	1	160	15	0	5.63	....	....	....	....	....	....	....	....		1979-80	1981-82
Janecyk, Bob	Chi., L.A.	6	110	43	47	13	6250	432	2	4.15	3	0	3	....	184	10	0	3.26		1983-84	1988-89
§ • Jenkins, Roger	NYA	1	1	0	1	0	30	7	0	14.00	....	....	....	....	....	....	....	....		1938-39	1938-39
Jensen, Al	Det., Wsh., L.A.	7	179	95	53	18	9974	557	8	3.35	12	5	5	....	598	32	0	3.21		1980-81	1986-87
Jensen, Darren	Phi.	2	30	15	10	1	1496	95	2	3.81	....	....	....	....	....	....	....	....		1984-85	1985-86
Johnson, Bob	St.L., Pit.	2	24	9	9	1	1059	66	0	3.74	....	....	....	....	....	....	....	....		1972-73	1974-75
Johnston, Eddie	Bos., Tor., St.L., Chi.	16	592	234	257	80	34216	1852	32	3.25	18	7	10	....	1023	57	1	3.34	2	1962-63	1977-78
Junkin, Joe	Bos.	1	1	0	0	0	8	0	0	0.00	....	....	....	....	....	....	....	....		1968-69	1968-69
Kaarela, Jari	Col.	1	5	2	2	0	220	22	0	6.00	....	....	....	....	....	....	....	....		1980-81	1980-81
Kamppuri, Hannu	N.J.	1	13	1	10	1	645	54	0	5.02	....	....	....	....	....	....	....	....		1984-85	1984-85
• Karakas, Mike	Chi., Mtl.	8	336	114	169	53	20614	1002	28	2.92	23	11	12	0	1434	72	3	3.01	1	1935-36	1945-46
Keans, Doug	L.A., Bos.	9	210	96	64	26	11388	666	4	3.51	9	2	6	....	432	34	0	4.72		1979-80	1987-88
• Keenan, Don	Bos.	1	1	0	1	0	60	4	0	4.00	....	....	....	....	....	....	....	....		1958-59	1958-59
• Kerr, Dave	Mtl.M., NYA, NYR	11	427	203	148	75	26639	954	51	2.15	40	18	19	3	2616	76	8	1.74	1	1930-31	1940-41
Kidd, Trevor	Cgy., Car., Fla., Tor.	12	387	140	162	52	21426	1014	19	2.84	10	3	5	....	550	36	1	3.93		1991-92	2003-04
King, Scott	Det.	2	2	0	0	0	61	3	0	2.95	....	....	....	....	....	....	....	....		1990-91	1991-92
Kleisinger, Terry	NYR	1	4	0	2	0	191	14	0	4.40	....	....	....	....	....	....	....	....		1985-86	1985-86
Klymkiw, Julian	NYR	1	1	0	0	0	19	2	0	6.32	....	....	....	....	....	....	....	....		1958-59	1958-59
Knickle, Rick	L.A.	2	14	7	6	0	706	44	0	3.74	....	....	....	....	....	....	....	....		1992-93	1993-94
Kochan, Dieter	T.B., Min.	4	21	1	11	1	849	56	0	3.96	....	....	....	....	....	....	....	....		1999-00	2002-03
Konstantinov, Evgeny	T.B.	2	2	0	0	0	21	1	0	2.86	....	....	....	....	....	....	....	....		2000-01	2002-03
Kuntar, Les	Mtl.	1	6	2	2	0	302	16	0	3.18	....	....	....	....	....	....	....	....		1993-94	1993-94
Kurt, Gary	Cal.	1	16	1	7	5	838	60	0	4.30	....	....	....	....	....	....	....	....		1971-72	1971-72
‡ Labbe, Jean-Francois	NYR, CBJ	3	15	3	6	0	628	36	0	3.44	....	....	....	....	....	....	....	....		1999-00	2002-03
Labrecque, Patrick	Mtl.	1	2	0	1	0	98	7	0	4.29	....	....	....	....	....	....	....	....		1995-96	1995-96
Lacher, Blaine	Bos.	2	47	22	16	4	2636	123	4	2.80	5	1	4	....	283	12	0	2.54		1994-95	1995-96
• Lacroix, Frenchy	Mtl.	2	5	1	4	0	280	16	0	3.43	....	....	....	....	....	....	....	....		1925-26	1926-27
LaFerriere, Rick	Col.	1	1	0	0	0	20	1	0	3.00	....	....	....	....	....	....	....	....		1981-82	1981-82
LaForest, Mark	Det., Phi., Tor., Ott.	6	103	25	54	4	5032	354	2	4.22	2	1	0	....	48	1	0	1.25		1985-86	1993-94
Lajeunesse, Simon	Ott.	1	1	0	0	0	24	0	0	0.00	....	....	....	....	....	....	....	....		2001-02	2001-02
‡ Langkow, Scott	Wpg., Phx., Atl.	4	20	3	12	1	943	68	0	4.33	....	....	....	....	....	....	....	....		1995-96	1999-00
• Larocque, Michel	Mtl., Tor., Phi., St.L.	11	312	160	89	45	17615	978	17	3.33	14	6	6	....	759	37	1	2.92	4	1973-74	1983-84
Larocque, Michel	Chi.	1	3	0	2	0	152	9	0	3.55	....	....	....	....	....	....	....	....		2000-01	2000-01
‡ Lasak, Jan	Nsh.	2	6	0	4	0	267	18	0	4.04	....	....	....	....	....	....	....	....		2001-02	2002-03
Laskowski, Gary	L.A.	2	59	19	27	5	2942	228	0	4.65	....	....	....	....	....	....	....	....		1982-83	1983-84
Laxton, Gord	Pit.	4	17	4	9	0	800	74	0	5.55	....	....	....	....	....	....	....	....		1975-76	1978-79
LeBlanc, Ray	Chi.	1	1	1	0	0	60	1	0	1.00	....	....	....	....	....	....	....	....		1991-92	1991-92
§ • Leduc, Albert	Mtl.	1	1	0	0	0	2	1	0	30.00	....	....	....	....	....	....	....	....		1931-32	1931-32
Legris, Claude	Det.	2	4	0	1	1	91	4	0	2.64	....	....	....	....	....	....	....	....		1980-81	1981-82
• Lehman, Hugh	Chi.	2	48	20	24	4	3047	136	6	2.68	2	0	1	1	120	10	0	5.00		1926-27	1927-28
Lemelin, Reggie	Atl., Cgy., Bos.	15	507	236	162	63	28006	1613	12	3.46	59	23	25	....	3119	186	2	3.58		1978-79	1992-93
Lenarduzzi, Mike	Hfd.	2	4	1	1	1	189	10	0	3.17	....	....	....	....	....	....	....	....		1992-93	1993-94
Lessard, Mario	L.A.	6	240	92	97	39	13529	843	9	3.74	20	6	12	....	1136	83	0	4.38		1978-79	1983-84
Levasseur, Jean-Louis	Min.	1	1	0	1	0	60	7	0	7.00	....	....	....	....	....	....	....	....		1979-80	1979-80
§ • Levinsky, Alex	Tor.	1	1	0	0	0	1	1	0	60.00	....	....	....	....	....	....	....	....		1931-32	1931-32
• Lindbergh, Pelle	Phi.	5	157	87	49	15	9150	503	7	3.30	23	12	10	....	1214	63	3	3.11		1981-82	1985-86
• Lindsay, Bert	Mtl.W., Tor.	2	20	6	14	0	1238	118	0	5.72	....	....	....	....	....	....	....	....		1917-18	1918-19
Little, Neil	Phi.	2	2	0	2	0	93	6	0	3.87	....	....	....	....	....	....	....	....		2001-02	2003-04
Littman, David	Buf., T.B.	3	3	0	2	0	141	14	0	5.96	....	....	....	....	....	....	....	....		1990-91	1992-93
Liut, Mike	St.L., Hfd., Wsh.	13	664	294	271	74	38215	2221	25	3.49	67	29	32	....	3814	215	2	3.38		1979-80	1991-92
Lockett, Ken	Van.	2	55	13	15	8	2348	131	2	3.35	1	0	1	....	60	6	0	6.00		1974-75	1975-76
• Lockhart, Howard	Tor., Que., Ham., Bos.	5	59	16	41	0	3413	287	1	5.05	....	....	....	....	....	....	....	....		1919-20	1924-25
LoPresti, Pete	Min., Edm.	6	175	43	102	20	9858	668	5	4.07	2	0	2	....	77	6	0	4.68		1974-75	1980-81
• LoPresti, Sam	Chi.	2	74	30	38	6	4530	236	4	3.13	8	3	5	....	530	17	1	1.92		1940-41	1941-42
Lorenz, Danny	NYI	3	8	1	5	0	357	25	0	4.20	....	....	....	....	....	....	....	....		1990-91	1992-93
Loustel, Ron	Wpg.	1	1	0	1	0	60	10	0	10.00	....	....	....	....	....	....	....	....		1980-81	1980-81
Low, Ron	Tor., Wsh., Det., Que., Edm., N.J.	11	382	102	203	38	20502	1463	4	4.28	7	1	6	....	452	29	0	3.85		1972-73	1984-85
Lozinski, Larry	Det.	1	30	6	11	7	1459	105	0	4.32	....	....	....	....	....	....	....	....		1980-81	1980-81
• Lumley, Harry	Det., NYR, Chi., Tor., Bos.	16	803	330	329	142	48044	2206	71	2.75	76	29	47	....	4778	198	7	2.49	1	1943-44	1959-60
MacKenzie, Shawn	N.J.	1	4	0	1	0	130	15	0	6.92	....	....	....	....	....	....	....	....		1982-83	1982-83
Madeley, Darrin	Ott.	3	39	4	23	5	1928	140	0	4.36	....	....	....	....	....	....	....	....		1992-93	1994-95
Malarchuk, Clint	Que., Wsh., Buf.	11	338	141	130	45	19030	1100	12	3.47	15	2	9	....	781	56	0	4.30		1981-82	1991-92
Maneluk, George	NYI	1	4	1	1	0	140	15	0	6.43	....	....	....	....	....	....	....	....		1990-91	1990-91
Maniago, Cesare	Tor., Mtl., NYR, Min., Van.	15	568	190	257	97	32569	1773	30	3.27	36	15	21	....	2245	100	3	2.67		1960-61	1977-78
‡ Maracle, Norm	Det., Atl.	5	66	14	33	8	3430	177	1	3.10	2	0	0	....	58	3	0	3.10		1997-98	2001-02
Marois, Jean	Tor., Chi.	2	3	1	2	0	180	15	0	5.00	....	....	....	....	....	....	....	....		1943-44	1953-54
Martin, Seth	St.L.	1	30	8	10	7	1552	67	1	2.59	2	0	0	....	73	5	0	4.11		1967-68	1967-68
Mason, Bob	Wsh., Chi., Que., Van.	8	145	55	65	16	7988	500	1	3.76	5	2	3	....	369	12	1	1.95		1983-84	1990-91
Mattsson, Markus	Wpg., Min., L.A.	4	92	21	46	14	5007	343	6	4.11	....	....	....	....	....	....	....	....		1979-80	1983-84
May, Darrell	St.L.	2	6	1	5	0	364	31	0	5.11	....	....	....	....	....	....	....	....		1985-86	1987-88
Mayer, Gilles	Tor.	4	9	2	6	1	540	24	0	2.67	....	....	....	....	....	....	....	....		1949-50	1955-56
• McAuley, Ken	NYR	2	96	17	64	15	5740	537	1	5.61	....	....	....	....	....	....	....	....		1943-44	1944-45
McCartan, Jack	NYR	2	12	2	7	3	680	42	1	3.71	....	....	....	....	....	....	....	....		1959-60	1960-61
• McCool, Frank	Tor.	2	72	34	31	7	4320	242	4	3.36	13	8	5	....	807	30	4	2.23	1	1944-45	1945-46
McDuffe, Peter	St.L., NYR, K.C., Det.	5	57	11	36	6	3207	218	0	4.08	1	0	1	....	60	7	0	7.00		1971-72	1975-76
McGrattan, Tom	Det.	1	1	0	0	0	8	1	0	7.50	....	....	....	....	....	....	....	....		1947-48	1947-48
McKay, Ross	Hfd.	1	1	0	0	0	35	3	0	5.14	....	....	....	....	....	....	....	....		1990-91	1990-91
McKenzie, Bill	Det., K.C., Col.	6	91	18	49	13	4776	326	2	4.10	....	....	....	....	....	....	....	....		1973-74	1979-80
McKichan, Steve	Van.	1	1	0	0	0	20	2	0	6.00	....	....	....	....	....	....	....	....		1990-91	1990-91
McLachlan, Murray	Tor.	1	2	0	1	0	25	4	0	9.60	....	....	....	....	....	....	....	....		1970-71	1970-71
McLean, Kirk	N.J., Van., Car., Fla., NYR	16	612	245	262	72	35090	1904	22	3.26	68	34	34	....	4189	198	6	2.84		1985-86	2000-01
McLelland, Dave	Van.	1	2	1	1	0	120	10	0	5.00	....	....	....	....	....	....	....	....		1972-73	1972-73
McLeod, Don	Det., Phi.	2	18	3	10	1	879	74	0	5.05	....	....	....	....	....	....	....	....		1970-71	1971-72

Name	NHL Teams	NHL Seasons	Regular Schedule GP	W	L	T	Mins	GA	SO	Avg	Playoffs GP	W	L	T	Mins	GA	SO	Avg	NHL Cup Wins	First NHL Season	Last NHL Season
McLeod, Jim	St.L.	1	16	6	6	4	880	44	0	3.00	....	....	....	....	....	....	....	....		1971-72	1971-72
McNamara, Gerry	Tor.	2	7	2	2	1	323	14	0	2.60	....	....	....	....	....	....	....	....		1960-61	1969-70
• McNeil, Gerry	Mtl.	8	276	119	105	52	16535	649	28	2.36	35	17	18	....	2284	72	5	1.89	3	1947-48	1957-58
McRae, Gord	Tor.	5	71	30	22	10	3799	221	1	3.49	8	2	5	....	454	22	0	2.91		1972-73	1977-78
Melanson, Roland	NYI, Min., L.A., N.J., Mtl.	11	291	129	106	33	16452	995	6	3.63	23	4	9	....	801	59	0	4.42	3	1980-81	1991-92
Meloche, Gilles	Chi., Cal., Cle., Min., Pit.	18	788	270	351	131	45401	2756	20	3.64	45	21	19	....	2464	143	2	3.48		1970-71	1987-88
Micalef, Corrado	Det.	5	113	26	59	15	5794	409	2	4.24	3	0	0	....	49	8	0	9.80		1981-82	1985-86
‡ Michaud, Alfie	Van.	1	2	0	1	0	69	5	0	4.35	....	....	....	....	....	....	....	....		1999-00	1999-00
‡ Michaud, Olivier	Mtl.	1	1	0	0	0	18	0	0	0.00	....	....	....	....	....	....	....	....		2001-02	2001-02
Middlebrook, Lindsay	Wpg., Min., N.J., Edm.	4	37	3	23	6	1845	152	0	4.94	....	....	....	....	....	....	....	....		1979-80	1982-83
• Millar, Al	Bos.	1	6	1	4	1	360	25	0	4.17	....	....	....	....	....	....	....	....		1957-58	1957-58
Millen, Greg	Pit., Hfd., St.L., Que., Chi., Det.	14	604	215	284	89	35377	2281	17	3.87	59	27	29	....	3383	193	0	3.42		1978-79	1991-92
• Miller, Joe	NYA, NYR, Pit., Phi.	4	127	24	87	16	7871	383	16	2.92	3	2	1	0	180	3	1	1.00	1	1927-28	1930-31
Minard, Mike	Edm.	1	1	1	0	0	60	3	0	3.00	....	....	....	....	....	....	....	....		1999-00	1999-00
Mio, Eddie	Edm., NYR, Det.	7	192	64	73	30	10428	705	4	4.06	17	9	7	....	986	63	0	3.83		1979-80	1985-86
• Mitchell, Ivan	Tor.	3	22	10	9	0	1190	88	0	4.44	....	....	....	....	....	....	....	....	1	1919-20	1921-22
Moffat, Mike	Bos.	3	19	7	7	2	979	70	0	4.29	11	6	5	....	663	38	0	3.44		1981-82	1983-84
Moog, Andy	Edm., Bos., Dal., Mtl.	18	713	372	209	88	40151	2097	28	3.13	132	68	57	....	7452	377	4	3.04	3	1980-81	1997-98
• Moore, Alfie	NYA, Chi., Det.	4	21	7	14	0	1290	81	1	3.77	3	1	2	....	180	7	0	2.33	1	1936-37	1939-40
Moore, Robbie	Phi., Wsh.	2	6	3	1	1	257	8	2	1.87	5	3	2	....	268	18	0	4.03		1978-79	1982-83
Morissette, Jean-Guy	Mtl.	1	1	0	1	0	36	4	0	6.67	....	....	....	....	....	....	....	....		1963-64	1963-64
‡ Moss, Tyler	Cgy., Car., Van.	4	30	6	16	1	1496	81	0	3.25	....	....	....	....	....	....	....	....		1997-98	2002-03
• Mowers, Johnny	Det.	4	152	65	61	26	9350	399	15	2.56	32	19	13	....	2000	85	2	2.55	1	1940-41	1946-47
Mrazek, Jerome	Phi.	1	1	0	0	0	6	1	0	10.00	....	....	....	....	....	....	....	....		1975-76	1975-76
§ • Mummery, Harry	Que., Ham.	2	4	2	1	0	192	20	0	6.25	....	....	....	....	....	....	....	....		1919-20	1921-22
§ • Munro, Dunc	Mtl.M.	1	1	0	0	0	2	0	0	0.00	....	....	....	....	....	....	....	....		1924-25	1924-25
• Murphy, Hal	Mtl.	1	1	1	0	0	60	4	0	4.00	....	....	....	....	....	....	....	....		1952-53	1952-53
• Murray, Mickey	Mtl.	1	1	0	1	0	60	4	0	4.00	....	....	....	....	....	....	....	....		1929-30	1929-30
‡ Muzzatti, Jason	Cgy., Hfd., NYR, S.J.	5	62	13	25	10	3014	167	1	3.32	....	....	....	....	....	....	....	....		1993-94	1997-98
Myllys, Jarmo	Min., S.J.	4	39	4	27	1	1846	161	0	5.23	....	....	....	....	....	....	....	....		1988-89	1991-92
Mylnikov, Sergei	Que.	1	10	1	7	2	568	47	0	4.96	....	....	....	....	....	....	....	....		1989-90	1989-90
Myre, Phil	Mtl., Atl., St.L., Phi., Col., Buf.	14	439	149	198	76	25220	1482	14	3.53	12	6	5	....	747	41	1	3.29	1	1969-70	1982-83
‡ Naumenko, Gregg	Ana.	1	2	0	1	0	70	7	0	6.00	....	....	....	....	....	....	....	....		2000-01	2000-01
Newton, Cam	Pit.	2	16	4	7	1	814	51	0	3.76	....	....	....	....	....	....	....	....		1970-71	1972-73
Norris, Jack	Bos., Chi., L.A.	4	58	20	25	4	3119	202	2	3.89	....	....	....	....	....	....	....	....		1964-65	1970-71
Nurminen, Pasi	Atl.	3	125	48	54	12	7059	338	5	2.87	....	....	....	....	....	....	....	....		2001-02	2003-04
Oleschuk, Bill	K.C., Col.	4	55	7	28	10	2835	188	1	3.98	....	....	....	....	....	....	....	....		1975-76	1979-80
• Olesevich, Dan	NYR	1	1	0	0	1	29	2	0	4.14	....	....	....	....	....	....	....	....		1961-62	1961-62
O'Neill, Mike	Wpg., Ana.	4	21	0	9	2	855	61	0	4.28	....	....	....	....	....	....	....	....		1991-92	1996-97
‡ Ouellet, Maxime	Phi., Wsh., Van.	3	12	2	6	2	663	34	1	3.08	....	....	....	....	....	....	....	....		2000-01	2005-06
Ouimet, Ted	St.L.	1	1	0	1	0	60	2	0	2.00	....	....	....	....	....	....	....	....		1968-69	1968-69
Pageau, Paul	L.A.	1	1	0	1	0	60	8	0	8.00	....	....	....	....	....	....	....	....		1980-81	1980-81
• Paille, Marcel	NYR	7	107	32	52	22	6342	362	2	3.42	....	....	....	....	....	....	....	....		1957-58	1964-65
Palmateer, Mike	Tor., Wsh.	8	356	149	138	52	20131	1183	17	3.53	29	12	17	....	1765	89	2	3.03		1976-77	1983-84
Pang, Darren	Chi.	3	81	27	35	7	4252	287	0	4.05	6	1	3	....	250	18	0	4.32		1984-85	1988-89
Parent, Bernie	Bos., Phi., Tor.	13	608	271	198	121	35136	1493	54	2.55	71	38	33	....	4302	174	6	2.43	2	1965-66	1978-79
Parent, Bob	Tor.	2	3	0	2	0	160	15	0	5.63	....	....	....	....	....	....	....	....		1981-82	1982-83
Parent, Rich	St.L., T.B., Pit.	4	32	7	11	5	1561	82	1	3.15	....	....	....	....	....	....	....	....		1997-98	2000-01
Parro, Dave	Wsh.	4	77	21	36	10	4015	274	2	4.09	....	....	....	....	....	....	....	....		1980-81	1983-84
‡ Passmore, Steve	Edm., Chi., L.A.	6	93	23	44	12	5045	235	2	2.79	3	0	2	....	138	6	0	2.61		1998-99	2003-04
§ • Patrick, Lester	NYR	1	....	....	....	....	....	....	....	....	1	1	0	0	46	1	0	1.30	1	1927-28	1927-28
Peeters, Pete	Phi., Bos., Wsh.	13	489	246	155	51	27699	1424	21	3.08	71	35	35	....	4200	232	2	3.31		1978-79	1990-91
Pelletier, Marcel	Chi., NYR	2	8	1	6	0	395	32	0	4.86	....	....	....	....	....	....	....	....		1950-51	1962-63
Penney, Steve	Mtl., Wpg.	5	91	35	38	12	5194	313	1	3.62	27	15	12	....	1604	72	4	2.69		1983-84	1987-88
• Perreault, Bob	Mtl., Det., Bos.	3	31	8	16	7	1827	103	3	3.38	....	....	....	....	....	....	....	....		1955-56	1962-63
Pettie, Jim	Bos.	3	21	9	7	2	1157	71	1	3.68	....	....	....	....	....	....	....	....		1976-77	1978-79
Pietrangelo, Frank	Pit., Hfd.	7	141	46	59	6	7141	490	1	4.12	12	7	5	....	713	34	1	2.86	1	1987-88	1993-94
• Plante, Jacques	Mtl., NYR, St.L., Tor., Bos.	18	837	437	246	145	49533	1964	82	2.38	112	71	36	....	6651	237	14	2.14	6	1952-53	1972-73
• Plasse, Michel	St.L., Mtl., K.C., Pit., Col., Que.	11	299	92	136	54	16760	1058	2	3.79	4	1	2	....	195	9	1	2.77	1	1970-71	1981-82
§ • Plaxton, Hugh	Mtl.M.	1	1	0	1	0	57	5	0	5.26	....	....	....	....	....	....	....	....		1932-33	1932-33
Potvin, Felix	Tor., NYI, Van., L.A., Bos.	13	635	266	260	85	36765	1694	32	2.76	72	35	37	....	4435	195	8	2.64		1991-92	2003-04
Pronovost, Claude	Bos., Mtl.	2	3	1	1	0	120	7	1	3.50	....	....	....	....	....	....	....	....		1955-56	1958-59
Puppa, Daren	Buf., Tor., T.B.	15	429	179	161	54	23819	1204	19	3.03	16	4	9	....	786	51	0	3.89		1985-86	1999-00
Pusey, Chris	Det.	1	1	0	0	0	40	3	0	4.50	....	....	....	....	....	....	....	....		1985-86	1985-86
Racicot, Andre	Mtl.	5	68	26	23	8	3357	196	2	3.50	4	0	1	....	31	4	0	7.74	1	1989-90	1993-94
Racine, Bruce	St.L.	1	11	0	3	0	230	12	0	3.13	1	0	0	....	1	0	0	0.00		1995-96	1995-96
Ram, Jamie	NYR	1	1	0	0	0	27	0	0	0.00	....	....	....	....	....	....	....	....		1995-96	1995-96
Ranford, Bill	Bos., Edm., Wsh., T.B., Det.	15	647	240	279	76	35936	2042	15	3.41	53	28	25	....	3110	159	4	3.07	2	1985-86	1999-00
Raymond, Alain	Wsh.	1	1	0	1	0	40	2	0	3.00	....	....	....	....	....	....	....	....		1987-88	1987-88
• Rayner, Chuck	NYA, Bro., NYR	10	424	138	208	77	25491	1294	25	3.05	18	9	9	....	1135	46	1	2.43		1940-41	1952-53
Reaugh, Daryl	Edm., Hfd.	3	27	8	9	1	1246	72	1	3.47	....	....	....	....	....	....	....	....		1984-85	1990-91
Reddick, Pokey	Wpg., Edm., Fla.	6	132	46	58	16	7162	443	0	3.71	4	0	2	....	168	10	0	3.57	1	1986-87	1993-94
§ • Redding, George	Bos.	1	1	0	0	0	11	1	0	5.45	....	....	....	....	....	....	....	....		1924-25	1924-25
Redquest, Greg	Pit.	1	1	0	0	0	13	3	0	13.85	....	....	....	....	....	....	....	....		1977-78	1977-78
Reece, Dave	Bos.	1	14	7	5	2	777	43	2	3.32	....	....	....	....	....	....	....	....		1975-76	1975-76
Reese, Jeff	Tor., Cgy., Hfd., T.B., N.J.	11	174	53	65	17	8667	529	5	3.66	11	3	5	....	515	35	0	4.08		1987-88	1998-99
Resch, Glenn	NYI, Col., N.J., Phi.	14	571	231	224	82	32279	1761	26	3.27	41	17	17	....	2044	85	2	2.50	1	1973-74	1986-87
• Rheaume, Herb	Mtl.	1	31	10	20	1	1889	92	0	2.92	....	....	....	....	....	....	....	....		1925-26	1925-26
Rhodes, Damian	Tor., Ott., Atl.	10	309	99	140	48	17339	820	12	2.84	13	5	7	....	741	27	0	2.19		1990-91	2001-02
Ricci, Nick	Pit.	4	19	7	12	0	1087	79	0	4.36	....	....	....	....	....	....	....	....		1979-80	1982-83
Richardson, Terry	Det., St.L.	5	20	3	11	0	906	85	0	5.63	....	....	....	....	....	....	....	....		1973-74	1978-79
Richter, Mike	NYR	15	666	301	258	73	38183	1840	24	2.89	76	41	33	....	4514	202	9	2.68	1	1988-89	2002-03
Ridley, Curt	NYR, Van., Tor.	6	104	27	47	16	5498	355	1	3.87	2	0	2	....	120	8	0	4.00		1974-75	1980-81
Riendeau, Vincent	Mtl., St.L., Det., Bos.	8	184	85	65	20	10423	573	5	3.30	25	11	12	....	1277	71	1	3.34		1987-88	1994-95
Riggin, Dennis	Det.	2	18	6	10	2	999	52	1	3.12	....	....	....	....	....	....	....	....		1959-60	1962-63
Riggin, Pat	Atl., Cgy., Wsh., Bos., Pit.	9	350	153	120	52	19872	1135	11	3.43	25	8	13	....	1336	72	0	3.23		1979-80	1987-88
Ring, Bob	Bos.	1	1	0	0	0	33	4	0	7.27	....	....	....	....	....	....	....	....		1965-66	1965-66
Rivard, Fern	Min.	4	55	9	27	11	2865	190	2	3.98	....	....	....	....	....	....	....	....		1968-69	1974-75
• Roach, John Ross	Tor., NYR, Det.	14	492	219	204	68	30444	1246	58	2.46	29	12	14	3	1901	60	7	1.89	1	1921-22	1934-35
• Roberts, Moe	Bos., NYA, Chi.	4	10	3	5	0	501	31	0	3.71	....	....	....	....	....	....	....	....		1925-26	1951-52
• Robertson, Earl	Det., NYA, Bro.	6	190	60	95	34	11820	575	16	2.92	15	7	7	....	995	29	2	1.75	1	1936-37	1941-42
• Rollins, Al	Tor., Chi., NYR	9	430	141	205	83	25723	1192	28	2.78	13	6	7	....	755	30	0	2.38	1	1949-50	1959-60
Romano, Roberto	Pit., Bos.	6	126	46	63	8	7111	471	4	3.97	....	....	....	....	....	....	....	....		1982-83	1993-94
Rosati, Mike	Wsh.	1	1	1	0	0	28	0	0	0.00	....	....	....	....	....	....	....	....		1998-99	1998-99
Roussel, Dominic	Phi., Wpg., Ana., Edm.	8	205	77	70	23	10665	555	7	3.12	1	0	0	....	23	0	0	0.00		1991-92	2000-01
Roy, Patrick	Mtl., Col.	19	1029	551	315	131	60235	2546	66	2.54	247	151	94	....	15209	584	23	2.30	4	1984-85	2002-03
• Rupp, Pat	Det.	1	1	0	1	0	60	4	0	4.00	....	....	....	....	....	....	....	....		1963-64	1963-64
Rutherford, Jim	Det., Pit., Tor., L.A.	13	457	151	227	59	25895	1576	14	3.65	8	2	5	....	440	28	0	3.82		1970-71	1982-83
• Rutledge, Wayne	L.A.	3	82	28	37	9	4325	241	2	3.34	8	2	4	....	378	20	0	3.17		1967-68	1969-70
St. Croix, Rick	Phi., Tor.	8	130	49	54	18	7295	451	2	3.71	11	4	6	....	562	29	1	3.10		1977-78	1984-85
St. Laurent, Sam	N.J., Det.	5	34	7	12	4	1572	92	1	3.51	1	0	0	....	10	1	0	6.00		1985-86	1989-90
‡ Salo, Tommy	NYI, Edm., Col.	10	526	210	225	73	30436	1296	37	2.55	22	5	16	....	1369	58	0	2.54		1994-95	2003-04
§ • Sands, Charlie	Mtl.	1	1	0	0	0	25	5	0	12.00	....	....	....	....	....	....	....	....		1939-40	1939-40
Sands, Mike	Min.	2	6	0	5	0	302	26	0	5.17	....	....	....	....	....	....	....	....		1984-85	1986-87
Sarjeant, Geoff	St.L., S.J.	2	8	1	2	1	291	20	0	4.12	....	....	....	....	....	....	....	....		1994-95	1995-96
Sauve, Bob	Buf., Det., Chi., N.J.	13	420	182	154	54	23711	1377	8	3.48	34	15	16	....	1850	95	4	3.08		1976-77	1988-89
• Sawchuk, Terry	Det., Bos., Tor., L.A., NYR	21	971	447	330	172	57194	2389	103	2.51	106	54	48	....	6290	266	12	2.54	4	1949-50	1969-70
• Schaefer, Joe	NYR	2	2	0	2	0	86	8	0	5.58	....	....	....	....	....	....	....	....		1959-60	1960-61
Schafer, Paxton	Bos.	1	3	0	0	0	77	6	0	4.68	....	....	....	....	....	....	....	....		1996-97	1996-97

			Regular Schedule								Playoffs										
Name	NHL Teams	NHL Seasons	GP	W	L	T	Mins	GA	SO	Avg	GP	W	L	T	Mins	GA	SO	Avg	NHL Cup Wins	First NHL Season	Last NHL Season
Schwab, Corey	N.J., T.B., Van., Tor.	8	147	42	63	13	7476	360	6	2.89	3	0	0	....	40	0	0	0.00	1	1995-96	2003-04
Scott, Ron	NYR, L.A.	5	28	8	13	4	1450	91	0	3.77	1	0	0	....	32	4	0	7.50		1983-84	1989-90
Sevigny, Richard	Mtl., Que.	9	176	80	54	20	9485	507	5	3.21	4	0	3	....	208	13	0	3.75	1	1978-79	1986-87
Sharples, Scott	Cgy.	1	1	0	0	1	65	4	0	3.69	....	....	....	....	....	....	....	....		1991-92	1991-92
§ • Shields, Al	NYA	1	2	0	0	0	41	9	0	13.17	....	....	....	....	....	....	....	....		1931-32	1931-32
Shields, Steve	Buf., S.J., Ana., Bos., Fla., Atl.	10	246	80	104	40	13630	606	10	2.67	25	9	16	....	1445	74	1	3.07		1995-96	2005-06
Shtalenkov, Mikhail	Ana., Edm., Phx., Fla.	7	190	62	82	19	9966	480	8	2.89	4	0	3	....	211	10	0	2.84		1993-94	1999-00
Shulmistra, Richard	N.J., Fla.	2	2	1	1	0	122	3	0	1.48	....	....	....	....	....	....	....	....		1997-98	1999-00
Sidorkiewicz, Peter	Hfd., Ott., N.J.	8	246	79	128	27	13884	832	8	3.60	15	5	10	....	912	55	0	3.62		1987-88	1997-98
Simmons, Don	Bos., Tor., NYR	11	249	101	101	41	14555	701	20	2.89	24	13	11	....	1436	62	3	2.59	3	1956-57	1968-69
Simmons, Gary	Cal., Cle., L.A.	4	107	30	57	15	6162	366	5	3.56	1	0	0	....	20	1	0	3.00		1974-75	1977-78
Skidmore, Paul	St.L.	1	2	1	1	0	120	6	0	3.00	....	....	....	....	....	....	....	....		1981-82	1981-82
Skorodenski, Warren	Chi., Edm.	5	35	12	11	4	1732	100	2	3.46	2	0	0	....	33	6	0	10.91		1981-82	1987-88
Skudra, Peter	Pit., Buf., Bos., Van.	6	146	51	47	20	7162	326	6	2.73	3	0	1	....	116	6	0	3.10		1997-98	2002-03
• Smith, Al	Tor., Pit., Det., Buf., Hfd., Col.	10	233	74	99	36	12752	735	10	3.46	6	1	4	....	317	21	0	3.97		1965-66	1980-81
Smith, Billy	L.A., NYI	18	680	305	233	105	38431	2031	22	3.17	132	88	36	....	7645	348	5	2.73	4	1971-72	1988-89
Smith, Gary	Tor., Oak., Cal., Chi., Van., Min., Wsh., Wpg.	14	532	173	261	74	29619	1675	26	3.39	20	5	13	....	1153	62	1	3.23		1965-66	1979-80
• Smith, Normie	Mtl.M., Det.	8	199	81	83	35	12357	479	17	2.33	12	9	2	0	820	18	3	1.32	2	1931-32	1944-45
Sneddon, Bob	Cal.	1	5	0	2	0	225	21	0	5.60	....	....	....	....	....	....	....	....		1970-71	1970-71
Snow, Garth	Que., Phi., Van., Pit., NYI	12	368	135	147	44	19837	925	16	2.80	20	9	8	....	1040	48	1	2.77		1993-94	2005-06
Soderstrom, Tommy	Phi., NYI	5	156	45	69	19	8189	496	10	3.63	....	....	....	....	....	....	....	....		1992-93	1996-97
Soetaert, Doug	NYR, Wpg., Mtl.	12	284	110	104	42	15583	1030	6	3.97	5	1	2	....	180	14	0	4.67	1	1975-76	1986-87
Soucy, Christian	Chi.	1	1	0	0	0	3	0	0	0.00	....	....	....	....	....	....	....	....		1993-94	1993-94
• Spooner, Red	Pit.	1	1	0	1	0	60	6	0	6.00	....	....	....	....	....	....	....	....		1929-30	1929-30
§ • Spring, Jesse	Ham.	1	1	0	0	0	2	0	0	0.00	....	....	....	....	....	....	....	....		1924-25	1924-25
Staniowski, Ed	St.L., Wpg., Hfd.	10	219	67	104	21	12075	818	2	4.06	8	1	6	....	428	28	0	3.93		1975-76	1984-85
§ • Starr, Harold	Mtl.M.	1	1	0	0	0	3	0	0	0.00	....	....	....	....	....	....	....	....		1931-32	1931-32
Stauber, Robb	L.A., Buf.	4	62	21	23	9	3295	209	1	3.81	4	3	1	....	240	16	0	4.00		1989-90	1994-95
Stefan, Greg	Det.	9	299	115	127	30	16333	1068	5	3.92	30	12	17	....	1681	99	1	3.53		1981-82	1989-90
• Stein, Phil	Tor.	1	1	0	0	1	70	2	0	1.71	....	....	....	....	....	....	....	....		1939-40	1939-40
Stephenson, Wayne	St.L., Phi., Wsh.	10	328	146	103	49	18343	937	14	3.06	26	11	12	....	1522	79	2	3.11	1	1971-72	1980-81
• Stevenson, Doug	NYR, Chi.	3	8	2	6	0	480	39	0	4.88	....	....	....	....	....	....	....	....		1944-45	1945-46
Stewart, Charles	Bos.	3	77	30	41	5	4742	194	10	2.45	....	....	....	....	....	....	....	....		1924-25	1926-27
Stewart, Jim	Bos.	1	1	0	1	0	20	5	0	15.00	....	....	....	....	....	....	....	....		1979-80	1979-80
‡ Storr, Jamie	L.A., Car.	10	219	85	86	23	11512	488	16	2.54	5	0	3	....	182	11	0	3.63		1994-95	2003-04
• Stuart, Herb	Det.	1	3	1	2	0	180	5	0	1.67	....	....	....	....	....	....	....	....		1926-27	1926-27
Sylvestri, Don	Bos.	1	3	0	0	2	102	6	0	3.53	....	....	....	....	....	....	....	....		1984-85	1984-85
Tabaracci, Rick	Pit., Wpg., Wsh., Cgy., T.B., Atl., Col.	11	286	93	125	30	15255	760	15	2.99	17	4	12	....	1025	53	0	3.10		1988-89	1999-00
Takko, Kari	Min., Edm.	6	142	37	71	14	7317	475	1	3.90	4	0	1	....	109	7	0	3.85		1985-86	1990-91
Tallas, Robbie	Bos., Chi.	6	99	28	42	10	5069	246	3	2.91	....	....	....	....	....	....	....	....		1995-96	2000-01
Tanner, John	Que.	3	21	2	11	5	1084	65	1	3.60	....	....	....	....	....	....	....	....		1989-90	1991-92
Tataryn, Dave	NYR	1	2	1	1	0	80	10	0	7.50	....	....	....	....	....	....	....	....		1976-77	1976-77
Taylor, Bobby	Phi., Pit.	5	46	15	17	6	2268	155	0	4.10	....	....	....	....	....	....	....	....	1	1971-72	1975-76
• Teno, Harvey	Det.	1	5	2	3	0	300	15	0	3.00	....	....	....	....	....	....	....	....		1938-39	1938-39
Terreri, Chris	N.J., S.J., Chi., NYI	14	406	151	172	43	22369	1143	9	3.07	29	12	12	....	1523	86	0	3.39	2	1986-87	2000-01
Thomas, Wayne	Mtl., Tor., NYR	9	243	103	93	34	13768	766	10	3.34	15	6	8	....	849	50	1	3.53		1972-73	1980-81
• Thompson, Tiny	Bos., Det.	12	553	284	194	75	34175	1183	81	2.08	44	20	24	0	2974	93	7	1.88	1	1928-29	1939-40
§ Toppazzini, Jerry	Bos.	1	1	0	0	0	1	0	0	0.00	....	....	....	....	....	....	....	....		1960-61	1960-61
Torchia, Mike	Dal.	1	6	3	2	1	327	18	0	3.30	....	....	....	....	....	....	....	....		1994-95	1994-95
Trefilov, Andrei	Cgy., Buf., Chi.	7	54	12	25	4	2663	153	2	3.45	1	0	0	....	5	0	0	0.00		1992-93	1998-99
Tremblay, Vincent	Tor., Pit.	5	58	12	26	8	2785	223	1	4.80	....	....	....	....	....	....	....	....		1979-80	1983-84
Tucker, Ted	Cal.	1	5	1	1	1	177	10	0	3.39	....	....	....	....	....	....	....	....		1973-74	1973-74
Tugnutt, Ron	Que., Edm., Ana., Mtl., Ott., Pit., CBJ, Dal.	16	537	186	239	62	29486	1497	26	3.05	25	9	13	....	1482	56	3	2.27		1987-88	2003-04
‡ Turek, Roman	Dal., St.L., Cgy.	8	328	159	115	43	19095	734	27	2.31	22	12	9	....	1342	50	0	2.24	1	1996-97	2003-04
• Turner, Joe	Det.	1	1	0	0	1	70	3	0	2.57	....	....	....	....	....	....	....	....		1941-42	1941-42
Underhill, Matt	Chi.	1	1	0	1	0	61	4	0	3.93	....	....	....	....	....	....	....	....		2003-04	2003-04
Vachon, Rogie	Mtl., L.A., Det., Bos.	16	795	355	291	127	46298	2310	51	2.99	48	23	23	....	2876	133	2	2.77	3	1966-67	1981-82
Vanbiesbrouck, John	NYR, Fla., Phi., NYI, N.J.	20	882	374	346	119	50475	2503	40	2.98	71	28	38	....	3969	177	5	2.68		1981-82	2001-02
Veisor, Mike	Chi., Hfd., Wpg.	10	139	41	62	26	7806	532	5	4.09	4	0	2	....	180	15	0	5.00		1973-74	1983-84
Vernon, Mike	Cgy., Det., S.J., Fla.	19	781	385	273	92	44449	2206	27	2.98	138	77	56	....	8214	367	6	2.68	2	1982-83	2001-02
• Vezina, Georges	Mtl.	9	190	103	81	5	11592	633	13	3.28	13	10	3	0	780	35	2	2.69	1	1917-18	1925-26
Villemure, Gilles	NYR, Chi.	10	205	100	64	29	11581	542	13	2.81	14	5	5	....	656	32	0	2.93		1963-64	1976-77
‡ Waite, Jimmy	Chi., S.J., Phx.	11	106	28	41	12	5253	293	4	3.35	6	0	3	....	211	14	0	3.98		1988-89	1998-99
Wakaluk, Darcy	Buf., Min., Dal., Phx.	8	191	67	75	21	9756	524	9	3.22	8	4	2	....	364	18	0	2.97		1988-89	1996-97
Wakely, Ernie	Mtl., St.L.	5	113	41	42	17	6244	290	8	2.79	10	2	6	....	509	37	1	4.36		1962-63	1971-72
• Walsh, Flat	Mtl.M., NYA	7	108	48	43	16	6641	256	12	2.31	8	2	4	2	570	16	2	1.68		1926-27	1932-33
Wamsley, Rick	Mtl., St.L., Cgy., Tor.	13	407	204	131	46	23123	1287	12	3.34	27	7	18	....	1397	81	0	3.48	1	1980-81	1992-93
Watt, Jim	St.L.	1	1	0	0	0	20	2	0	6.00	....	....	....	....	....	....	....	....		1973-74	1973-74
Weeks, Steve	NYR, Hfd., Van., NYI, L.A., Ott.	18	290	111	119	33	15879	989	5	3.74	12	3	5	....	486	27	0	3.33		1980-81	1992-93
Wetzel, Carl	Det., Min.	2	7	1	4	1	301	22	0	4.39	....	....	....	....	....	....	....	....		1964-65	1967-68
Whitmore, Kay	Hfd., Van., Bos., Cgy.	9	155	60	64	16	8596	508	4	3.55	4	0	2	....	174	13	0	4.48		1988-89	2001-02
Wilkinson, Derek	T.B.	4	22	3	12	3	933	57	0	3.67	....	....	....	....	....	....	....	....		1995-96	1998-99
Willis, Jordan	Dal.	1	1	0	1	0	19	1	0	3.16	....	....	....	....	....	....	....	....		1995-96	1995-96
Wilson, Dunc	Phi., Van., Tor., NYR, Pit.	10	287	80	150	33	15851	988	8	3.74	....	....	....	....	....	....	....	....		1969-70	1978-79
• Wilson, Lefty	Det., Tor., Bos.	3	3	0	0	1	81	1	0	0.74	....	....	....	....	....	....	....	....		1953-54	1957-58
• Winkler, Hal	NYR, Bos.	2	75	35	26	14	4739	126	21	1.60	10	2	3	5	640	18	2	1.69		1926-27	1927-28
Wolfe, Bernie	Wsh.	4	120	20	61	21	6104	424	1	4.17	....	....	....	....	....	....	....	....		1975-76	1978-79
• Wood, Alex	NYA	1	1	0	1	0	70	3	0	2.57	....	....	....	....	....	....	....	....		1936-37	1936-37
• Worsley, Gump	NYR, Mtl., Min.	21	861	335	352	150	50183	2407	43	2.88	70	40	26	....	4084	189	5	2.78	4	1952-53	1973-74
• Worters, Roy	Pit., NYA, Mtl.	12	484	171	229	83	30175	1143	67	2.27	11	3	6	2	690	24	3	2.09		1925-26	1936-37
Worthy, Chris	Oak., Cal.	3	26	5	10	4	1326	98	0	4.43	....	....	....	....	....	....	....	....		1968-69	1970-71
Wregget, Ken	Tor., Phi., Pit., Cgy., Det.	17	575	225	248	53	31663	1917	9	3.63	56	28	25	....	3341	160	3	2.87	1	1983-84	1999-00
‡ Yeremeyev, Vitali	NYR	1	4	0	4	0	212	16	0	4.53	....	....	....	....	....	....	....	....		2000-01	2000-01
§ • Young, Doug	Det.	1	1	0	0	0	21	1	0	2.86	....	....	....	....	....	....	....	....		1933-34	1933-34
Young, Wendell	Van., Phi., Pit., T.B.	10	187	59	86	12	9410	618	2	3.94	2	0	1	....	99	6	0	3.64	2	1985-86	1994-95
Zanier, Mike	Edm.	1	3	1	1	1	185	12	0	3.89	....	....	....	....	....	....	....	....		1984-85	1984-85

Marco Baron

Don Edwards

Howard Lockhart

Steve Shields

Garth Snow

Rogie Vachon

Retired Players, Goaltenders and Coaches Research Project

Throughout the Retired Players and Retired Goaltenders sections of this book, you will notice many players with a bullet (•) by their names. These players, according to our records, are deceased. The editors recognize that our information on the death dates of NHLers is incomplete. If you have documented information on the passing of any player not marked with a bullet (•) in this edition, we would like to hear from you. We also welcome information on deceased NHL head coaches.

Please e-mail ralph.dda@sympatico.ca or send this information to:

Retired Player Research Project
c/o NHL Publishing
194 Dovercourt Road
Toronto, Ontario
M6J 3C8 Canada
Fax: 416/531-3939

Many thanks to the following contributors in 2006-07:

Tim Bateman, Corey Bryant, Paul R. Carroll, Jr., Bob Duff, Peter Fillman, Ernie Fitzsimmons, Chris Gory, Gary J. Pearce, Martin Schmid, Al Tario, Drew "Whitey" White.

Hockey Fights Cancer is a joint initiative created by the National Hockey League and the National Hockey League Players' Association that honors those in the hockey community who have struggled, or continue to struggle, with the disease.

The goal of Hockey Fights Cancer is to raise money and visibility for local cancer care or research, as well as to support the American Cancer Society and Canadian Cancer Society national organizations. Founded by the NHL and the NHLPA, Hockey Fights Cancer is supported by NHL member clubs, NHL Alumni, the NHL Officials Association, Professional Hockey Trainers and Equipment Managers, corporate marketing partners, broadcast partners and fans throughout North America.

Join the Fight! If you would like to make a contribution to Hockey Fights Cancer, please forward a check made payable to Hockey Fights Cancer to one of the following addresses:

For Canadian Residents:
Hockey Fights Cancer
P.O. Box 1282, Station B
Montreal, Quebec H3B 3K9

For U.S. Residents:
Hockey Fights Cancer
P.O. Box 5037
New York, NY 10185-5037

Please include your name and current address so that your donation can be acknowledged. All donations are tax-deductible.

For more information, log-on to www.hockeyfightscancer.com or call 1-800-540-6500.

Ken Dryden
29 – Montreal

Dale Hawerchuk
10 – Phoenix/Winnipeg

Brett Hull
16 – St. Louis

Mario Lemieux
66 – Pittsburgh

Mark Messier
11 – Edmonton

Luc Robitaille
20 – Los Angeles

Serge Savard
18 – Montreal

Mike Vernon
30 – Calgary

Steve Yzerman
19 – Detroit

A Salute to Nine Superb NHL Players

NINE NHL STARS WERE ACCORDED THE HONOR of having their numbers retired in 2006-07. Two members of this select group, Ken Dryden and Mike Vernon, are goaltenders. Serge Savard, whose banner is being hoisted in a ceremony at Montreal's Bell Centre at left, is the only defenseman just as Brett Hull is the only right wing. Luc Robitaille is the only "pure" left wing as Mark Messier earned All-Star Team selections at both left wing and center in his 25-season NHL career. Centers Dale Hawerchuk, Mario Lemieux and Steve Yzerman complete this magic group of nine.

This group of players won a total of 29 Stanley Cup championships, beginning with Savard's in 1968 and ending in 2002 when Detroit teammates Hull, Robitaille and Yzerman hoisted the trophy.

The six forwards in this group all rank in the NHL's top twenty all-time scorers. Combined, the six scored 3,935 goals. Hull leads the group and is third overall with 745 goals. Messier is second overall in points and leads the group with 1,887 (694G-1,193A). Lemieux's spectacular 199-point season (85G-114A) in 1988-89 is the leading single-season performance.

The group also shares 35 All-Star Team berths, topped by Lemieux's nine. Five have already been inducted into the Hockey Hall of Fame and an identical number were recipients of the Conn Smythe Trophy as the most valuable player in the Stanley Cup playoffs, an award won twice by Lemieux in consecutive seasons.

Free Agent Signing Register, 2007

	PLAYER	SIGNED BY	PREVIOUS ORGANIZATION
July 1	– Scott Hartnell	Philadelphia	Philadelphia
	– Jeff Hamilton	Carolina	Chicago
	– Michel Ouellet	Tampa Bay	Pittsburgh
	– Eric Perrin	Atlanta	Tampa Bay
	– Jason Blake	Toronto	NY Islanders
	– Viktor Kozlov	Washington	NY Islanders
	– Tom Poti	Washington	NY Islanders
	– Scott Hannan	Colorado	San Jose
	– Jon Sim	NY Islanders	Atlanta
	– Chris Drury	NY Rangers	Buffalo
	– Scott Gomez	NY Rangers	New Jersey
	– Radek Dvorak	Florida	St. Louis
	– Richard Zednik	Florida	NY Islanders
	– Brian Rafalski	Detroit	New Jersey
	– Shawn Thornton	Boston	Anaheim
	– Yanic Perreault	Chicago	Toronto
	– Mathieu Schneider	Anaheim	Detroit
	– Cory Sarich	Calgary	Tampa Bay
	– Brett McLean	Florida	Colorado
	– Todd White	Atlanta	Minnesota
	– Barret Jackman	St. Louis	St. Louis
	– Pascal Dupuis	Atlanta	Atlanta
	– Denis Grebeshkov	Edmonton	Edmonton
	– Daniel Briere	Philadelphia	Buffalo
	– Jed Ortmeyer	Nashville	NY Rangers
	– Ryan Smyth	Colorado	NY Islanders
	– Paul Kariya	St. Louis	Nashville
July 2	– Rob Scuderi	Pittsburgh	Pittsburgh
	– Ryan Whitney	Pittsburgh	Pittsburgh
	– Petr Sykora	Pittsburgh	Edmonton
	– Dany Sabourin	Pittsburgh	Vancouver
	– Darryl Sydor	Pittsburgh	Dallas
	– Michael Nylander	Washington	NY Rangers
	– Roman Hamrlik	Montreal	Calgary
	– Todd Bertuzzi	Anaheim	Detroit
	– Ladislav Nagy	Los Angeles	Dallas
	– Kyle Calder	Los Angeles	Detroit
	– Tom Preissing	Los Angeles	Ottawa
	– Michal Handzus	Los Angeles	Chicago
	– Ken Klee	Atlanta	Colorado
	– Robert Lang	Chicago	Detroit
	– Greg de Vries	Nashville	Atlanta
	– Radek Bonk	Nashville	Montreal
	– Bryan Smolinski	Montreal	Vancouver
	– Sheldon Brookbank	Columbus	Nashville
	– Alexander Svitov	Columbus	Columbus
	– Ole-Kristian Tollefsen	Columbus	Columbus
July 3	– Brad Isbister	Vancouver	NY Rangers
	– Byron Ritchie	Vancouver	Calgary
	– Lukas Krajicek	Vancouver	Vancouver
	– Owen Nolan	Calgary	Phoenix
	– Dainius Zubrus	New Jersey	Buffalo
	– Karel Rachunek	New Jersey	NY Rangers
	– Brad May	Anaheim	Anaheim
	– Curtis Sanford	Vancouver	St. Louis
	– Wes Walz	Minnesota	Minnesota
	– Eric Belanger	Minnesota	Atlanta
	– Raffi Torres	Edmonton	Edmonton
	– Brad Stuart	Los Angeles	Calgary
	– Jason LaBarbera	Los Angeles	Los Angeles
	– Brad Lukowich	Tampa Bay	New Jersey
July 4	– Tom Kostopoulos	Montreal	Los Angeles
	– Slava Kozlov	Atlanta	Atlanta
	– Ruslan Fedotenko	NY Islanders	Tampa Bay
	– Matt Greene	Edmonton	Edmonton
	– Teppo Numminen	Buffalo	Buffalo
July 5	– Jiri Hudler	Detroit	Detroit
	– Petr Prucha	NY Rangers	NY Rangers
	– Anders Eriksson	Calgary	Columbus
	– Jan Hejda	Columbus	Columbus
	– Kevin Weekes	New Jersey	NY Rangers
	– Erik Christensen	Pittsburgh	Pittsburgh
	– Maxime Talbot	Pittsburgh	Pittsburgh
	– Marek Svatos	Colorado	Colorado
	– Mathieu Biron	Montreal	Montreal
	– Tomas Plekanec	Montreal	Montreal
	– Jamie Rivers	Montreal	Montreal
	– Bill Guerin	NY Islanders	San Jose
	– Mike Comrie	NY Islanders	Ottawa
	– Pierre-Marc Bouchard	Minnesota	Minnesota
	– Michael Ryan	Buffalo	Buffalo
	– Andrew Peters	Buffalo	Buffalo
	– Jocelyn Thibault	Buffalo	Pittsburgh
July 6	– Dominik Hasek	Detroit	Detroit
	– Shane Hnidy	Anaheim	Atlanta
	– Sean Hill	Minnesota	NY Islanders
	– Bobby Allen	Boston	Boston
	– Scott Clemmensen	Toronto	New Jersey
	– Trevor Byrne	Dallas	Washington
	– Toby Petersen	Dallas	Edmonton
	– Brad Winchester	Dallas	Edmonton
	– Mike Egener	Tampa Bay	Tampa Bay
	– Dan Jancevski	Tampa Bay	Montreal
	– Nolan Yonkman	Nashville	Nashville
	– Dan Ellis	Nashville	Dallas
	– Shane Willis	Nashville	Carolina
July 8	– Joey MacDonald	NY Islanders	Boston
July 9	– Dallas Drake	Detroit	St. Louis
	– Mike York	Phoenix	Philadelphia
	– Aaron Miller	Vancouver	Los Angeles
	– Todd Fedoruk	Dallas	Philadelphia
	– Jeremy Reich	Boston	Boston
	– Josh Gratton	Phoenix	Phoenix
July 10	– Vitaly Vishnevski	New Jersey	Nashville
	– Joe Motzko	Washington	Anaheim
	– Andrew Murray	Columbus	Columbus
	– Joakim Lindstrom	Columbus	Columbus
	– Steven Goertzen	Columbus	Columbus
	– Curtis Glencross	Columbus	Columbus
	– Brendan Shanahan	NY Rangers	NY Rangers
July 11	– Henrik Lundqvist	NY Rangers	NY Rangers
	– Eric Boulton	Atlanta	Atlanta
	– Dennis Wideman	Boston	Boston
	– Josh Harding	Minnesota	Minnesota

DATE	PLAYER	SIGNED BY	PREVIOUS ORGANIZATION
July 12	Dan Smith	Columbus	Detroit
–	Derek MacKenzie	Columbus	Atlanta
–	Colby Armstrong	Pittsburgh	Pittsburgh
–	Aaron Johnson	NY Islanders	Columbus
–	Matthew Spiller	NY Islanders	Phoenix
–	Sheldon Souray	Edmonton	Montreal
–	Joel Lundqvist	Dallas	Dallas
–	Mike Ribeiro	Dallas	Dallas
–	Brandon Segal	Anaheim	Nashville
–	Joe Callahan	Anaheim	Anaheim
–	Jesse Schultz	Atlanta	Atlanta
July 13	Alexandre Giroux	Atlanta	Washington
–	Jeff Taffe	Pittsburgh	Phoenix
–	David LeNeveu	Phoenix	Phoenix
–	Paul Ranger	Tampa Bay	Tampa Bay
July 16	Eric Healey	Colorado	Tampa Bay
–	Matt Hussey	Colorado	Detroit
–	Tyler Weiman	Colorado	Colorado
–	Rob Davison	San Jose	San Jose
–	Chris Campoli	NY Islanders	NY Islanders
–	Kamil Kreps	Florida	Florida
–	Rob Globke	Florida	Florida
–	Joel Ward	Minnesota	Minnesota
–	Aaron Voros	Minnesota	Minnesota
–	Eric Reitz	Nashville	Nashville
–	Matt Foy	Nashville	Nashville
–	Greg Zanon	Nashville	Nashville
–	Kevin Klein	Nashville	Nashville
–	Darcy Hordichuk	Nashville	Nashville
–	Matt Jones	Phoenix	Phoenix
–	Aaron Rome	Anaheim	Anaheim
–	Garnet Exelby	Atlanta	Atlanta
–	Josh Gorges	Montreal	Montreal
July 17	Steve Eminger	Washington	Washington
–	Brian Sutherby	Washington	Washington
–	Kurtis Foster	Minnesota	Minnesota
–	Mark Rycroft	Colorado	Colorado
July 18	Mike Brodeur	Chicago	Chicago
–	Danny Richmond	Chicago	Chicago
–	Jim Vandermeer	Chicago	Chicago
–	Ryan Shannon	Vancouver	Vancouver
–	Brad Norton	San Jose	Detroit
–	Brennan Evans	San Jose	San Jose
–	Mike Iggulden	San Jose	San Jose
–	Tom Cavanagh	San Jose	San Jose
–	Riley Armstrong	San Jose	San Jose
–	Vernon Fiddler	Nashville	Nashville
–	Derek Boogaard	Minnesota	Minnesota
–	Brett Skinner	Anaheim	Anaheim
–	Dan LaCouture	Anaheim	New Jersey
July 19	Ty Conklin	Pittsburgh	Buffalo
–	Jonathan Ferland	Montreal	Montreal
–	David Aebischer	Phoenix	Montreal
–	David Steckel	Washington	Washington
July 20	Tim Brent	Pittsburgh	Pittsburgh
July 23	Chris Simon	NY Islanders	NY Islanders
–	Alain Nasreddine	Pittsburgh	Pittsburgh
–	Nick Schultz	Minnesota	Minnesota
July 24	Christoph Schubert	Ottawa	Ottawa
–	Ray Emery	Ottawa	Ottawa
–	Noah Clarke	New Jersey	Los Angeles
–	Ian Moran	New Jersey	Anaheim
–	Grant Marshall	New Jersey	New Jersey
–	Cam Janssen	New Jersey	New Jersey
July 25	Jim Slater	Atlanta	Atlanta
–	Doug Janik	Tampa Bay	Tampa Bay
–	Brooks Laich	Washington	Washington
–	Lee Stempniak	St. Louis	St. Louis
–	Boyd Kane	Philadelphia	Philadelphia
July 26	Martin Gelinas	Nashville	Florida
July 27	Derek Roy	Buffalo	Buffalo
–	Michael Leighton	Carolina	Carolina
–	Alexei Semenov	San Jose	Florida
–	Jim Fahey	Chicago	New Jersey
–	Prestin Ryan	Chicago	Vancouver
–	Wade Flaherty	Chicago	Vancouver
–	Milan Jurcina	Washington	Washington
July 29	Michael Ryder	Montreal	Montreal
July 30	Antti Miettinen	Dallas	Dallas
July 31	Chris Kelly	Ottawa	Ottawa
–	Nathan Paetsch	Buffalo	Buffalo
–	Marcel Hossa	NY Rangers	NY Rangers
Aug. 1	Sean Avery	NY Rangers	NY Rangers
–	Zach Parise	New Jersey	New Jersey
Aug. 2	Dustin Penner	Edmonton	Anaheim
Aug. 3	Trent Hunter	NY Islanders	NY Islanders
–	Patrice Brisebois	Montreal	Colorado
Aug. 6	Ryan Craig	Tampa Bay	Tampa Bay
–	Steve Montador	Florida	Florida
Aug. 7	Michael Cammalleri	Los Angeles	Los Angeles
–	Arron Asham	New Jersey	NY Islanders
–	Kris Beech	Columbus	Washington
Aug. 8	Mike Weaver	Pittsburgh	Los Angeles
–	Karl Pilar	Atlanta	Toronto
–	Milan Bartovic	Atlanta	Chicago
Aug. 10	Andy Sutton	NY Islanders	Atlanta
Aug. 13	Alex Auld	Phoenix	Florida
–	Dimitri Patzold	San Jose	San Jose
–	Pierre Parenteau	Chicago	Chicago
Aug. 14	Joe DiPenta	Anaheim	Anaheim
Aug. 15	Joseph Vasicek	NY Islanders	Carolina
Aug. 16	Paul Martin	New Jersey	New Jersey

Trade Register, 2006-07

August 2006

17– Anaheim traded D **Vitaly Vishnevski** to Atlanta for LW **Karl Stewart**, Atlanta's 2nd-round choice (later traded to Colorado – Colorado selected W **T. J. Galiardi**) in 2007 and a conditional choice in 2008.

September 2006

12–Detroit traded G **Drew MacIntyre** to Vancouver for future considerations.

29–Los Angeles traded C **Eric Belanger** and D **Tim Gleason** to Carolina for D **Oleg Tverdovsky** and D **Jack Johnson**.

30–Montreal traded C **Mike Ribeiro** and its 6th-round choice in 2008 to Dallas for D **Janne Niinimaa** and its 5th-round choice (LW **Andrew Conboy**) in 2007.

October 2006

1–New Jersey traded D **Vladimir Malakhov** and its 1st-round choice (later traded to St. Louis – St. Louis selected LW **David Perron**) in 2007 to San Jose for LW **Alex Korolyuk** and D **Jim Fahey**.

25–Columbus traded C **Eric Boguniecki** to NY Islanders for D **Ryan Caldwell**.

November 2006

9–Tampa Bay traded RW **Darren Reid** to Philadelphia for C **Daniel Corso**.

13–Anaheim traded LW **Stanislav Chistov** to Boston for Phoenix's 3rd-round choice (C **Maxime Mecenauer**) (previously acquired) in 2007 and future considerations.

13–Colorado traded RW **George Parros** and Colorado's 3rd-round choice (later traded to Tampa Bay – Tampa Bay selected C **Luca Cunti**) in 2007 for Atlanta's 2nd-round choice (W **T. J. Galiardi**) (previously acquired) in 2007 and Anaheim's 3rd-round choice (later traded to San Jose – San Jose selected G **Tyson Sexsmith**) in 2007.

13–Anaheim traded LW **Todd Fedoruk** to Philadelphia for Philadelphia's 4th-round choice (LW **Justin Vaive**) in 2007.

14–Phoenix traded G **Philippe Sauve** to Boston for C **Tyler Redenbach**.

21–Carolina traded LW **Brad Isbister** to NY Rangers for RW **Jakub Petruzalek** and a conditional choice in 2008.

28–Toronto traded G **Mikael Tellqvist** to Phoenix for LW **Tyson Nash** and Boston's 4th-round choice (RW **Matt Frattin**) (previously acquired) in 2007.

29–Carolina traded D **Derrick Walser** to Columbus for D **Mark Flood**.

December 2006

15–Montreal traded D **Patrick Traverse** to San Jose for D **Mathieu Biron**.

16–Philadelphia traded D **Freddy Meyer** and its 3rd-round choice (D **Mark Katic**) to NY Islanders for D **Alexei Zhitnik**.

20–Philadelphia traded C **Randy Robitaille** and its 5th-round choice in 2008 to NY Islanders for C **Mike York**.

28–Chicago traded G **Sebastien Caron**, RW **Matt Keith** and LW **Chris Durno** to Anaheim for C **Pierre Parenteau** and D **Bruno St. Jacques**.

January 2007

3–Phoenix traded LW **Mike Comrie** to Ottawa for C **Alexei Kaigorodov**.

3–Florida traded D **Ric Jackman** to Anaheim for Anaheim's 6th-round choice (D **Corey Syvret**) in 2007.

5–NY Islanders traded C **Matt Koalska** to Ottawa for D **Tomas Malec**.

8–Carolina traded C **Kevyn Adams** to Phoenix for D **Dennis Seidenberg**.

16–Boston traded C **Yan Stastny** to St. Louis for its 5th-round choice (D **Denis Reul**) in 2007.

19–Boston traded D **Wade Brookbank** to Pittsburgh for future considerations.

20–Los Angeles traded G **Ryan Munce** to Tampa Bay for its 4th-round choice in 2008.

24–Anaheim traded RW **Colby Genoway** to Vancouver for D **Joe Rullier**.

26–Columbus traded C **Mark Hartigan**, RW **Joe Motzko** and its 4th-round choice (G **Sebastian Stefaniszin**) in 2007 to Anaheim for C **Zenon Konopka**, C **Curtis Glencross** and its 7th-round choice (RW **Trent Vogelhuber**) in 2007.

26–Anaheim traded LW **Chris Durno** to Nashville for C **Shane Endicott**.

29–Los Angeles traded C **Craig Conroy** to Calgary for C **Jamie Lundmark** and Calgary's 4th-round choice (C/LW **Dwight King**) in 2007 and 2nd-round choice in 2008.

February 2007

1–Atlanta traded RW **Steve Baby** and RW **Kyle Wanvig** to Tampa Bay for D **Andy Delmore** and C **Andre Deveaux**.

1–Boston traded D **Milan Jurcina** to Washington for its 4th-round choice in|2008.

3–Chicago traded RW **Brandon Bochenski** to Boston for RW **Kris Versteeg** and a conditional choice in 2008.

5–NY Rangers traded RW **Jason Ward**, C **Jan Marek**, RW **Marc-Andre Cliche** and a conditional choice in 2008 to Los Angeles for LW **Sean Avery**, LW **John Seymour** and a conditional choice in 2008.

9–Minnesota traded LW **Pascal Dupuis** to NY Rangers for RW **Adam Hall**.

9–Carolina traded C **Eric Belanger** to Nashville for C **Josef Vasicek**.

10–Nashville traded C **Eric Belanger** to Atlanta for D **Vitaly Vishnevski**.

10–Boston traded D **Brad Stuart** and C **Wayne Primeau** to Calgary for D **Andrew Ference** and RW **Chuck Kobasew**.

12–Dallas traded LW **Mathias Tjarnqvist** and its 1st-round choice (later traded to Edmonton – Edmonton selected C **Riley Nash**) in 2007 to Phoenix for LW **Ladislav Nagy**.

15–Philadelphia traded C **Peter Forsberg** to Nashville for LW **Scottie Upshall**, D **Ryan Parent** and Nashville's 1st- (later traded back to Nashville – Nashville selected D **Jonathon Blum**) and 3rd-round choices (later traded to Washington – Washington selected C **Phil Desimone**) in 2007.

18–Edmonton traded D **Marc-Andre Bergeron** and a 3rd-round choice in 2008 to NY Islanders for D **Denis Grebeshkov**.

23–Anaheim traded C **Shane Endicott** to Dallas for future considerations.

23–Columbus traded RW **Anson Carter** to Carolina for a 5th-round choice in 2008.

24–Anaheim traded D **Shane O'Brien** and Colorado's 3rd-round choice (C **Luca Cunti**) (previously acquired) in 2007 to Tampa Bay for G **Gerald Coleman** and Tampa Bay's 1st-round choice (later traded to Minnesota – Minnesota selected C **Colton Gillies**) in 2007.

24–Philadelphia traded D **Alexei Zhitnik** to Atlanta for D **Braydon Coburn**.

25–Montreal traded D **Craig Rivet** and its 5th-round choice in 2008 to San Jose for D **Josh Gorges** and San Jose's 1st-round choice (LW **Max Pacioretty**) in 2007.

25–Atlanta traded C **Glen Metropolit**, its 1st- (later traded to Calgary – Calgary selected C **Mikael Backlund**) and 3rd-round choices (C/LW **Brett Sonne**) in 2007 and 2nd-round choice in 2008 to St. Louis for LW **Keith Tkachuk**.

26–Washington traded LW **Richard Zednik** to NY Islanders for the Islanders' 2nd-round choice (D **Theo Ruth**) in 2007.

26–Ottawa traded D **Andy Hedlund** and its 6th-round choice (C **Justin Taylor**) in 2007 to Washington for D **Lawrence Nycholat**.

26–Los Angeles traded D **Brent Sopel** to Vancouver for 2nd- and 4th-round choices in 2008.

26–Chicago traded C **Bryan Smolinski** to Vancouver for Vancouver's 2nd-round choice (C/RW **Akim Aliu**) in 2007.

26–Chicago traded D **Lasse Kukkonen** and its 3rd-round choice (LW **Garrett Klotz**) in 2007 to Philadelphia for LW **Kyle Calder**.

26–Chicago traded LW **Kyle Calder** to Detroit for C **Jason Williams**.

27–Anaheim traded G **Michael Wall** to Colorado for LW **Brad May**.

27–Anaheim traded D **Joe Rullier** to Tampa Bay for D **Doug O'Brien**.

27–Atlanta traded RW **Alex Bourret** to New York Rangers for LW **Pascal Dupuis** and the Rangers' 3rd-round choice (later traded to Pittsburgh – Pittsburgh selected D **Robert Bortuzzo**) in 2007.

27–Boston traded D **Paul Mara** to New York Rangers for D **Aaron Ward**.

27–Boston traded C **Brad Boyes** to St. Louis for D **Dennis Wideman**.

27–Buffalo traded G **Martin Biron** to Philadelphia for Philadelphia's 2nd-round choice (D **T.J. Brennan**) in 2007.

27–Buffalo traded C **Jiri Novotny** and its 1st-round choice (later traded to San Jose – San Jose selected D **Nicholas Petrecki**) in 2007 to Washington for RW **Dainius Zubrus** and D **Timo Helbling**.

27–Chicago traded LW **Karl Stewart** and Florida's 6th-round choice in 2008 (previously acquired) to Tampa Bay for RW **Nikita Alexeev**.

27–Columbus traded G **Ty Conklin** to Buffalo for Buffalo's 5th-round choice (later traded to Dallas – Dallas selected LW **Michael Neal**) in 2007.

27–Dallas traded D **Jaroslav Modry**, D **Johan Fransson**, its 2nd- (RW **Oscar Moller**) and 3rd-round choices (C/RW **Bryan Cameron**) in 2007 and 1st-round choice in 2008 to Los Angeles for D **Mattias Norstrom**, RW **Konstantin Pushkarev** and Los Angeles' 3rd- (RW **Sergei Korostin**) and 4th-round choices (later traded to Columbus - Columbus selected LW **Maxim Mayorov**) in 2007.

27–Edmonton traded LW **Ryan Smyth** to New York Islanders for C **Ryan O'Marra**, C **Robert Nilsson** and the Islanders' 1st-round choice (D **Alex Plante**) in 2007.

27–Florida traded LW **Gary Roberts** to Pittsburgh for D **Noah Welch**.

27–Florida traded D **Joel Kwiatkowski** to Pittsburgh for Florida's 4th-round choice (C **Matt Rust**) (previously acquired) in 2007.
27–Florida traded RW **Todd Bertuzzi** to Detroit for C **Shawn Matthias**, Detroit's 2nd-round choice (later traded to Nashville – Nashville selected C **Nick Spaling**) and a conditional choice in 2008.
27–Los Angeles traded RW **Jason Ward** to Tampa Bay for Tampa Bay's 5th-round choice (C **Joshua Turnbull**) in 2007.
27–Nashville traded D **Mikko Lehtonen** to Buffalo for Buffalo's 4th-round choice (C **Mark Santorelli**) in 2007.
27–New Jersey traded D **David Hale** and its 5th-round choice (later traded to Buffalo – Buffalo selected C **Jean-Simon Allard**) in 2007 to Calgary for Calgary's 3rd-round choice (RW **Nick Palmieri**) in 2007.
27–Phoenix traded LW **Oleg Saprykin** and its 7th-round choice (G **Torrie Jung**) in 2007 to Ottawa for Ottawa's 2nd-round choice in 2008.
27–Phoenix traded RW **Georges Laraque** to Pittsburgh for LW **Dan Carcillo** and Pittsburgh's 3rd-round choice in 2008.
27–Phoenix traded C **Yanic Perreault** and its 5th-round choice in 2008 to Toronto for D **Brendan Bell** and Toronto's 2nd-round choice in 2008.
27–Pittsburgh traded C **Dominic Moore** to Minnesota for Minnesota's 3rd-round choice (C **Casey Pierro-Zabotel**) in 2007.
27–St. Louis traded RW **Bill Guerin** to San Jose for LW **Ville Nieminen**, LW **Jay Barriball** and New Jersey's 1st-round choice (LW **David Perron**) (previously acquired) in 2007.
27–San Jose traded G **Nolan Schaefer** to Pittsburgh for Pittsburgh's 7th-round choice (D **Justin Braun**) in 2007.
27–San Jose traded RW **Scott Parker** to Colorado for Colorado's 6th-round choice in 2008.
27–Washington traded D **Jamie Heward** to Los Angeles for a conditional choice in 2008.
28–New Jersey traded RW **Aaron Voros** to Minnesota for Minnesota's 7th-round choice in 2008.

May 2007

16–Columbus traded D **Adam McQuaid** to Boston for Boston's 5th-round choice (later traded to Dallas – Dallas selected LW **Jamie Benn**) in 2007.
31–NY Rangers traded C **Ryan Russell** to Montreal for Montreal's 7th-round choice (C **David Skokan**) in 2007.

June 2007

13–Florida traded C **Chris Gratton** to Tampa Bay for Tampa Bay's 2nd-round choice in 2008.
16–Montreal traded LW **Sergei Samsonov** to Chicago for D **Jassen Cullimore** and LW **Tony Salmelainen**.
18–Nashville traded D **Kimmo Timonen** and LW **Scott Hartnell** to Philadelphia for Nashville's 1st-round choice (D **Jonathon Blum**) (previously acquired) in 2007.
22–Calgary traded D **Andrei Zyuzin** and D **Steve Marr** to Chicago for D **Adrian Aucoin** and Chicago's 7th-round choice (LW **C. J. Severyn**) in 2007.
22–San Jose traded G **Vesa Toskala** and C **Mark Bell** to Toronto for Toronto's 1st- (later traded to St. Louis – St. Louis selected C **Lars Eller**) and 2nd-round choices (later traded to St. Louis – St. Louis selected RW **Aaron Palushaj**) in 2007 and a 4th-round choice in 2009.
22 – Nashville traded G **Tomas Vokoun** to Florida for Florida's 1st- and 2nd-round choices in 2008 and Detroit's 2nd-round choice (C **Nick Spaling**) (previously acquired) in 2007.
22–Atlanta traded NY Rangers 3rd-round choice (D **Robert Bortuzzo**) (previously acquired) in 2007 to Pittsburgh for C **Chris Thorburn**.
22–St. Louis traded its 1st-round choice (C **Logan Couture**) in 2007 to San Jose for Toronto's 1st- (C **Lars Eller**) (previously acquired) and 2nd-round choice (RW **Aaron Palushaj**) (previously acquired) in 2007 and San Jose's 3rd-round choice in 2008.
22–Anaheim traded Tampa Bay's 1st-round choice (C **Colton Gillies**) (previously acquired) in 2007 to Minnesota for Minnesota's 1st- (C **Logan MacMillan**) and 2nd-round choices (C **Eric Tangardi**) in 2007.
22–Calgary traded its 1st-round choice (D **Ian Cole**) in 2007 to St. Louis for Atlanta's 1st-round choice (C **Mikael Backlund**) (previously acquired) in 2007 and St. Louis' 3rd-round choice (D **John Negrin**) in 2007.
22–Phoenix traded Dallas' 1st-round choice (C **Riley Nash**) (previously acquired) in 2007 to Edmonton for Anaheim's 1st-round choice (D **Nick Ross**) (previously acquired) in 2007 and Edmonton's 2nd-round choice (later traded to Phoenix – Phoenix selected G **Joel Gistedt**) in 2007.
22–Washington traded Buffalo's 1st-round choice (D **Nicholas Petrecki**) (previously acquired) in 2007 to San Jose for Carolina's 2nd-round choice (later traded to Philadelphia – Philadelphia selected D **Kevin Marshall**) (previously acquired) in 2007 and San Jose's 2nd-round choice in 2008.
23–Chicago traded its 2nd-round choice (D **Tommy Cross**) in 2007 to Boston for Boston's 2nd- (LW **Bill Sweatt**) and 3rd-round choices (C **Maxime Tanguay**) in 2007.
23–Washington traded Carolina's 2nd-round choice (D **Kevin Marshall**) (previously acquired) in 2007 to Philadelphia for Nashville's 3rd-round choice (C **Phil Desimone**) (previously acquired) in 2007 and Philadelphia's 2nd-round choice in 2008.
23–Colorado traded Anaheim's 3rd-round choice (G **Tyler Sexsmith**) (previously acquired) in 2007 to San Jose for San Jose's 4th- (later traded back to San Jose – San Jose selected G **Kent Patterson**) and 5th-round choices (later traded to Calgary – Calgary selected C **Mickey Renaud**) in 2007 and a 6th-round choice in 2008.
23–Dallas traded Los Angeles' 4th-round choice (LW **Maxim Mayorov**) (previously acquired) in 2007 to Columbus for Columbus' 5th-round choice (RW **Austin Smith**) in 2007, Boston's 5th-round choice (LW **Jamie Benn**) (previously acquired) in 2007 and Buffalo's 5th-round choice (LW **Michael Neal**) (previously acquired) in 2007.
23–Washington traded its 4th-round choice (D **Alec Martinez**) in 2007 to Los Angeles for Los Angeles' 6th-round choice (G **Dan Dunn**) in 2007 and 4th-round choice in 2008.
23–Anaheim traded C **Tim Brent** to Pittsburgh for C **Stephen Dixon**.
23–Buffalo traded Vancouver's 4th-round choice (D **Keith Aulie**) (previously acquired) in 2007 to Calgary for Calgary's 5th-round choice (G **Bradley Eidsness**) in 2007 and New Jersey's 5th-round choice (C **Jean-Simon Allard**) (previously acquired) in 2007.
23–Colorado traded San Jose's 5th-round choice (C **Mickey Renaud**) (previously acquired) in 2007 to Calgary for Washington's 6th-round choice (D **Jens Hellgren**) (previously acquired) in 2007 and Calgary's 6th-round choice (later traded to Boston – Boston selected D **Radim Ostrcil**) in 2007.
23–Ottawa traded its 5th-round choice (C/RW **Matt Marshall**) in 2007, Phoenix's 7th-round choice (G **Torrie Jung**) (previously acquired) in 2007 and Ottawa's 7th-round choice (LW **Justin Courtnall**) in 2007 to Tampa Bay for Dallas' 4th-round choice in 2008 (previously acquired).
23–Colorado traded Calgary's 6th-round choice (D **Radim Ostrcil**) (previously acquired) in 2007 to Boston for Boston's 6th-round choice in 2008.
23–Montreal traded G **Michael Leighton** to Carolina for Carolina's 7th-round choice (D **Scott Kishel**) in 2007.
23–Anaheim traded RW **Ryan Shannon** to Vancouver for the rights to LW **Jason King** and a conditional choice in 2009.
23–Atlanta traded D **Jim Sharrow** to Vancouver for RW **Jesse Schultz**.
26–Atlanta traded C **Keith Tkachuk** and a conditional draft choice to St. Louis for Atlanta's 1st-round choice (previously acquired) in 2008.

July 2007

1–Minnesota traded G **Manny Fernandez** to Boston for RW **Petr Kalus** and a 4th-round choice in 2009.
1–Philadelphia traded D **Joni Pitkanen**, LW **Geoff Sanderson** and a 3rd-round choice in 2009 to Edmonton for D **Jason Smith** and RW **Joffrey Lupul**.
17–Ottawa traded LW **Peter Schaefer** to Boston for RW **Shean Donovan**.
17–NY Rangers traded C **Matt Cullen** to Carolina for D **Andrew Hutchinson**, C **Joe Barnes** and a 3rd-round choice in 2008.
23–St. Louis traded C **Carl Soderberg** to Boston for G **Hannu Toivonen**.

August 2007

11–Chicago traded RW **Radim Vrbata** to Phoenix for C **Kevyn Adams**.

Trades and free agent signings after August 14, 2007 are listed on page 605.

League Abbreviations

AAHA............Alberta Amateur Hockey Association
AAHL............Alaska Amateur Hockey League
AASHA...........Alaska All-Stars Hockey Association
ACHA............American Collegiate Hockey Association
ACHL............Atlantic Coast Hockey League
AFHL............American Frontier Hockey League
AH..............Atlantic Hockey
AHL.............American Hockey League
AJHL............Alberta Junior Hockey League
Alpenliga........Alpenliga (Austria, Italy, Slovenia 1994-1999)
AMHA............Alberta Minor Hockey Association
AMBHL...........Alberta Major Bantam Hockey League
AMHL............Alberta Midget AAA Hockey League
AUAA............Atlantic University Athletic Association
AtJHL...........Atlantic Junior Hockey League
AWHL............American West Hockey League
BCAHA...........British Columbia Amateur Hockey Association
BCHL............British Columbia (Junior) Hockey League (also BCJHL)
CABHL...........Central Alberta Bantam Hockey League
Cal-Am..........California Amateur Hockey Association
CBHL............Calgary Bantam Hockey League
CCHA............Central Collegiate Hockey Association
CEGEP...........Quebec College Prep
CHA.............College Hockey America
CHL.............Central Hockey League
CIS.............Commonwealth of Independent States
CIS.............Canadian Interuniversity Sport
CJHL............Central Junior A Hockey League
CMHA............Calgary Minor Hockey Association
ColHL...........Colonial Hockey League
CSHL............Central States Hockey League
CSJHL...........Central States Junior Hockey League
CWUAA...........Canadian Western University Athletic Association
ECAC............Eastern College Athletic Conference
ECACHL..........ECAC Hockey League
ECHL............East Coast Hockey League
EEHL............Eastern European Hockey League
EJHL............Eastern Junior Hockey League
EMHA............Edmonton Minor Hockey Association
EmJHL...........Empire Junior B Hockey League
EuroHL..........European Hockey League
Exhib...........Exhibition Games, Series or Season
GLHL............Great Lakes Hockey League
GNML............Greater North Midget League
GPAC............Great Plains Athletic Conference
GTHL............Greater Toronto Hockey League
H-East..........Hockey East
HJHL............Heritage Junior Hockey League
High-(XX)........High School (state/province)
IEHL............Internationale Eishockey Liga
IHL.............International Hockey League
KIJHL...........Kootenay International Junior B Hockey League
LCJHL...........Little Caesar's Junior Hockey League
MAAC............Metro Atlantic Athletic Conference
MAHA............Manitoba Amateur Hockey Association
MAHL............Mid America Hockey League
MBAHL...........Metropolitan Boston Amateur Hockey League
MBHL............Metropolitan Boston Hockey League
MEHL............Midwest Elite Hockey League
Metro-HL........Metro Hockey League
MIAC............Minnesota Intercollegiate Athletic Conference
Minor-(XX)......Minor/Youth hockey (state/province)
MJHL............Manitoba Junior Hockey League
MJrHL...........Maritime Junior A Hockey League
MMBHL...........Manitoba Major Bantam Hockey League
MMHL............Manitoba Midget AAA Hockey League
MMHL............Michigan Minor Hockey League
MMMHL...........Manitoba Minor Midget Hockey League
MNHL............Michigan National Hockey League
MtJHL...........Metropolitan Junior Hockey League (New York)
MTJHL...........Metropolitan Toronto Junior Hockey League
MTHL............Metro Toronto Hockey League
MWEHL...........Midwest Elite Hockey League
NAHL............North American Hockey League (Tier I Junior)
NAJHL...........North American Junior Hockey League
Nat-Team.........National Team (also Nt.-Team)
NBAHA...........New Brunswick Amateur Hockey Association
NBMHL...........New Brunswick Midget Hockey League
NBPEI...........New Brunswick Prince Edward Island Midget Hockey League
NCAA............National Collegiate Athletic Association
NCHA............Northern Collegiate Hockey Association
NEJHL...........New England Junior Hockey League
NFAHA...........Newfoundland Amateur Hockey Association
NHL.............National Hockey League
NJCAA...........National Junior Collegiate Athletic Association
NOBHL...........Northern Ontario Bantam Hockey League
NOHA............Northern Ontario Hockey Association
NOJHA...........Northern Ontario Junior Hockey Association
NOJHL...........Northern Ontario Junior Hockey League
NSBHL...........Nova Scotia Bantam Hockey League
NSMHL...........Nova Scotia Midget AAA Hockey League
NTHL............Noth Texas Hockey League
NWJHL...........Northwest Junior B Hockey League
NYJHL...........New York Junior Hockey League
OCJHL...........Ontario Central Junior A Hockey League
OHA.............Ontario Hockey Association
OHL.............Ontario Hockey League
OJHL-B..........Ontario Junior B Hockey Leagues
OMJHL...........Ontario Major Junior Hockey League
OPJHL...........Ontario Provincial Junior A Hockey League
OUAA............Ontario Universities Athletic Association
PAHA............Pennsylvania Amateur Hockey Association
PCJHL...........Pacific Coast Junior Hockey League
PEIHA...........Prince Edward Island Hockey Association
PIJHL...........Pacific International Junior Hockey League
QAAA............Quebec Amateur Athletic Association
QAHA............Quebec Amateur Hockey Association
QJHL............Quebec Junior Hockey League
QMJHL...........Quebec Major Junior Hockey League
QNAHL...........(Quebec) North American Hockey League
Q-RHL...........(Quebec) Richelieu Elite Hockey League
QSPHL...........Quebec Semi-Pro Hockey League
RAMHL...........Rural Alberta Midget Hockey League
RMJHL...........Rocky Mountain Junior Hockey League
SAHA............Saskatchewan Amateur Hockey Association
SAMHL...........Southern Alberta Midget Hockey League
SBHL............Saskatchewan Bantam Hockey League
SCAHA...........Southern California Amateur Hockey Association
SIJHL...........Superior International Junior Hockey League
SJHL............Saskatchewan Junior Hockey League
SMBHL...........Saskatchewan Major Bantam Hockey League
SMHL............Saskatchewan Midget AAA Hockey League
SMMHL...........Saskatchewan Minor Midget Hockey League
SPHL............Southern Professional Hockey League
SSJHL...........South Saskatchewan Junior B Hockey League
SSMHL...........South Saskatchewan Minor Hockey League
SunHL...........Sunshine Hockey League
TBAHA...........Thunder Bay Amateur Hockey Association
TBJHL...........Thunder Bay Junior Hockey League
TBMHL...........Thunder Bay Midget Hockey League
U-17............Under 17
U-18............Under 18
UHL.............United Hockey League
UMEHL...........Upper Midwest Elite Hockey League
USAHA...........United States Amateur Hockey Association
USHL............United States (Junior A) Hockey League
VIJHL...........Vancouver Island Junior Hockey League
WCHA............Western Collegiate Hockey Association
WCHL............West Coast Hockey League
WHL.............Western Hockey League
WNYHA...........Western New York Hockey Association
WPHL............Western Professional Hockey League
WSJHL...........Western States Junior Hockey League
WMHA............Winnipeg Minor Hockey Association

Contributors

The NHL Official Guide & Record Book is produced with the help of many. Special thanks to:

Manny Almela, Kerry Banks, Jake Bartlett, Christopher M. Baudo, Danny Berry, John Blum, Bob and Minako Borgen, Brad Boutilier, Scott Brand (USHL), Chris Brennan, Peter Brill, William Callihoe, Craig Campbell, Jack Carnefix (ECHL), Jason Chaimovitch (AHL), Steve Cherwonak (CHL), Andrew Chong, Michael Chraba, Bill Ciraulo, Ken Coleman, John Comerford, Rick Cornacchia, Kyle Cosior, Brian Day, Denny Deveau, Rick Dillabough, Brian Doyle, Derek Eisler, Dan Elvidge, Doug Exner, John Gardiner, Ed Gingher, Wayne Goodman, Clarrie Hale, Ron Hamilton, Keith Hendrickson, Ian Ellis (OHL), Jenna Goreham, Stu Hackel, Hockey Hall of Fame, Christopher Hurley, Peter Jagla, Kim Jacobs, Randy Jacobs, Peter Jagla, Karl Jahnke (QMJHL), Mark Jeanneret, Christy Jeffries, Joey Kenward, Larry Knapp, Chris Kostopoulos, Ed Krajewski (ECACHL), Ginny Krusko, Bruce LaRoque, André Leclerc, Gerry Liscumb Jr., Leo MacDonald, Andy Madden, Al Manderson, Chris Masters, Robert McAfee, Penny McEwen (SJHL), Shawn McKelvie, Katie McNamara, Dean Meglio, Gerry Merkley, Bill Michaels, Bruce Moar, Deb Moffatt, Randy Montrose, Mike Moore, Herb Morell (OHL), Dave Morinville, John Moritsugu, Kelly Murray (ECHL), James Naylor, Linda Naylor, NCAA Conference and School Sports Information Departments, NHL Broadcasters' Association, NHL Central Registry, NHL Officiating, NHL Players' Association, Joseph Nieforth, Stan Nieradka, Brian O'Connor (H-East), Richard Ofner, Jim Olander, Tony Perrotti, Fred Pletsch (CCHA), Phil Pritchard, Pearl Rajwanth, Valentina Riazanova, Rob Rice, James Rioux, David Rourke (AH), Tim Roszell, Warren Rychel, David Sales, Bruce Schlitt, Andre Simard, Ralph Slate, SIHR, Doug Spencer (WCHA), Gail Stevenson, Regan Stocco, David Symmes, Szymon Szemberg (IIHF), George Tahan, Wade Taylor, Lindsay Thierry, Robert Toffoli, Matt Trevor, Wade Trevors, Bill Troy, USA Hockey, U.S. Hockey Hall of Fame, James vanRiemsdyk, Jesse Watts (WHL), Jeff Weiss (CHA), Leonard Weiss, Brian Werger (UHL), Drew White, Paul Wilkinson (OPJHL) Christian Wilson.

Researchers and Historians: contact the Society for International Hockey Research www.sihrhockey.org

Photo Credits

Hockey Hall of Fame: Various collections. Getty Images: Dave Abel, Brian Babineau/SA, Steve Babineau/SA, Brian Bahr, Bruce Bennett, Andrew D. Bernstein, Scott Cunningham, Jonathan Daniel, Nick Didlick, Elsa, Jeff Gross, Noah Graham, Harry How, Dana Kaplan/Sports Imagery, Bruce Kluckhorn, Nick Laham, Mitchell Layton, Phil MacCallum, Andy Marlin, Ronald Martinez, Jim McIsaac, Juan Ocampo, Doug Pensinger, Len Redkoles, John A. Russell, Dave Sandford, Gregory Shamus, Don Smith, Mike Strobe, Rick Stewart, Jeff Vinnick. Additional NHL team photographers: Bruce Buckner, Greg Forwerk, Dave Reginek, André Ringuette/Freestyle Photography, Jamie Sabau, Bill Smith, Gerry Thomas, Rocky Widner, Bill Wippert.

Special thanks to Patti Fallick and Jessica Tomao, NHL Images and Paul Michinard, Getty Images.

THREE STAR SELECTION...

NHL PUBLICATIONS ORDER FORM

2007-08 editions available now | 2008-09 editions available Sept. 2008

Please send...

2007-08		2008-09
☐	copies of the *NHL Guide & Record Book*	☐
☐	copies of the *NHL Yearbook magazine*	☐
☐	copies of the *NHL Rule Book*	☐

PRICES:	CANADA	USA	OVERSEAS
GUIDE & RECORD BOOK	$29.95	$27.95	$24.95 U.S.$
Handling (per copy)	$ 9.00	$15.00	$24.00 U.S.$
6% GST	$ 2.34	—	—
Total (per copy)	**$41.29**	**$42.95**	**$48.95 U.S.$**
Add Extra for air/express	$ 9.00	$12.00	$21.00 U.S.$
YEARBOOK	$ 9.95	$ 9.95	$ 9.95 U.S.$
Handling (per copy)	$ 7.00	$10.00	$14.00 U.S.$
6% GST	$ 1.02	—	—
Total (per copy)	**$17.97**	**$19.95**	**$23.95 U.S.$**
Add Extra for air/express	$ 3.00	$ 4.00	$ 8.00 U.S.$
RULE BOOK	$15.95	$14.95	$14.95 U.S.$
Handling (per copy)	$ 5.00	$ 7.50	$10.00 U.S.$
6% GST	$ 1.26	—	—
Total (per copy)	**$22.21**	**$22.45**	**$24.95 U.S.$**
Add Extra for air/express	$ 2.50	$ 3.00	$6.00 U.S.$

Charge my ☐ Visa ☐ MasterCard/EuroCard ☐ Am Ex

Credit Card Account Number ______ Expiry Date (important) ______

Signature ______

☐ Enclosed is my cheque/check or money order.

Name ______

Address ______

Province/State ______ Postal/Zip Code ______

IN CANADA
Mail completed form to:
NHL Official Guide
194 Dovercourt Rd.
Toronto, Ontario
M6J 3C8

IN USA
Mail completed form to:
NHL Official Guide
194 Dovercourt Rd.
Toronto, Ontario
CANADA M6J 3C8
Remit in U.S. funds

OVERSEAS
Mail completed form to:
NHL Official Guide
194 Dovercourt Rd.
Toronto, Ontario
CANADA M6J 3C8
Money order or credit card only. No cheques please.

DELIVERY: Canada & USA – up to three weeks. Overseas – up to five weeks.

NHL OFFICIAL GUIDE IS PLEASED TO OFFER...

1. THE NHL OFFICIAL GUIDE & RECORD BOOK

The NHL's authoritative information source. 76th year in print. 656 pages. The "Bible of Hockey". Read worldwide. This is the book issued to reporters, broadcasters, scouts and general managers.

2. THE NHL YEARBOOK

208-page, full-color magazine with features on each club. Award winners, All-Stars and special statistics.

3. THE NHL RULE BOOK

New larger format for 2007-08. Coil bound, new diagrams and tables. Combines complete playing rules, with the NHL officiating casebook. Plus rink dimensions and officials' signals.

Free Book List with each order.

SECURE ONLINE ORDERING and many more hockey books available at www.nhlofficialguide.com

3 Ways to Order with your Credit Card : ONLINE, by FAX or by E-MAIL

ONLINE ***www.nhlofficialguide.com***

FAX ***416/531-3939 or***

(OVERSEAS CUSTOMERS: USE INTERNATIONAL DIALING CODE FOR CANADA)

E-MAIL ***dda.nhl@sympatico.ca***

24 HOURS

PLEASE INCLUDE YOUR CARD'S EXPIRY DATE